The

EUROPA WORLD
OF LEARNING

2011

The

EUROPA WORLD OF LEARNING 2011

61st Edition

VOLUME I

INTRODUCTORY ESSAYS
INTERNATIONAL ORGANIZATIONS
AFGHANISTAN–MYANMAR

Routledge
Taylor & Francis Group

LONDON AND NEW YORK

First published 1947
Sixty-first Edition 2010
© **Routledge 2010**

Albert House, 1–4 Singer Street, London, EC2A 4BQ, United Kingdom
(Routledge is an imprint of the Taylor & Francis Group, an Informa business)

ISBN13: 978-1-85743-567-2 (The Set)
ISBN13: 978-1-85743-602-0 (Vol. I)

ISSN 0084-2117

Library of Congress Catalog Card Number 47-30172

Editor: Anthony Gladman

Team Leader: Joan Rita O'Brien
Researchers: Anoushka Gupta, Nafisa Sayed, Sabiya Ashraf, Sonia Joy

Freelance editorial team: Eric Smith, Kristina Wischenkämper

Associate Editor, Directory Research: James Middleton

Editorial Director: Paul Kelly

Typeset in New Century Schoolbook

FSC
Mixed Sources
Product group from well-managed
forests and other controlled sources
Cert no. SGS-COC-003788
www.fsc.org
© 1996 Forest Stewardship Council

Typeset by Data Standards Limited, Frome, Somerset.
Printed and bound in Great Britain by Polestar Wheatons, Exeter

FOREWORD

It gives us great pleasure to introduce the 2011 edition of THE EUROPA WORLD OF LEARNING. First published in 1947, it has since become established as an authoritative reference work on academic institutions all over the world.

THE EUROPA WORLD OF LEARNING is unique in offering information over the entire spectrum of academic activity. Our listings cover not just universities and colleges, but also research institutes, libraries and archives, museums and galleries and learned societies. Regulatory and representative bodies are also covered in a section which also includes details of relevant ministries, accrediting bodies and funding organizations. Each chapter has an introductory survey outlining the country's higher education system. All surveys have been updated for this edition.

Each year we invite entrants to review and update their entries. Entrants may do so online at updates.worldoflearning.com, or by email to wol@informa.com. We are, as ever, grateful to those who help bring our information up to date with their prompt replies. Continuous research on the internet and in the world's press, as well as contact with official sources worldwide, supplements this method of revision.

In addition to the regular updating of our entries, this edition has expanded coverage of institutions in the Balkans and South-Eastern Europe. Chapters covering Albania, Bosnia and Herzegovina, Bulgaria, Croatia, Kosovo, Macedonia, Montenegro, Romania, Serbia and Slovenia all have specially expanded and updated chapters.

THE EUROPA WORLD OF LEARNING also contains a collection of essays on themes pertinent to international higher education. In this edition subjects covered include the role of higher education in national development, focusing in particular on South-Eastern Europe and the reconstruction of the Western Balkans. We have also invited authors whose books will shortly be published by Routledge Education to contribute essays on cross-border education and on international research collaborations. For details of the authors contributing to this edition please see page x.

In the sections on Universities and Colleges, our classification follows the practice of the country concerned. This in no way implies any official evaluation on our part. Readers who are interested in the matter of the equivalence of institutions, degrees or diplomas should correspond directly with the institutions concerned, or with the national or international bodies set up for this purpose. Further information on these can be found in the Regulatory and Representative Bodies section of each chapter under the subheading Accreditation.

An online version of THE EUROPA WORLD OF LEARNING is available at www.worldoflearning.com. The site offers regular updates of content and an unprecedented level of access to institutions of higher education and learning worldwide, and to the people who work within them. Please see page vi for further details.

August 2010

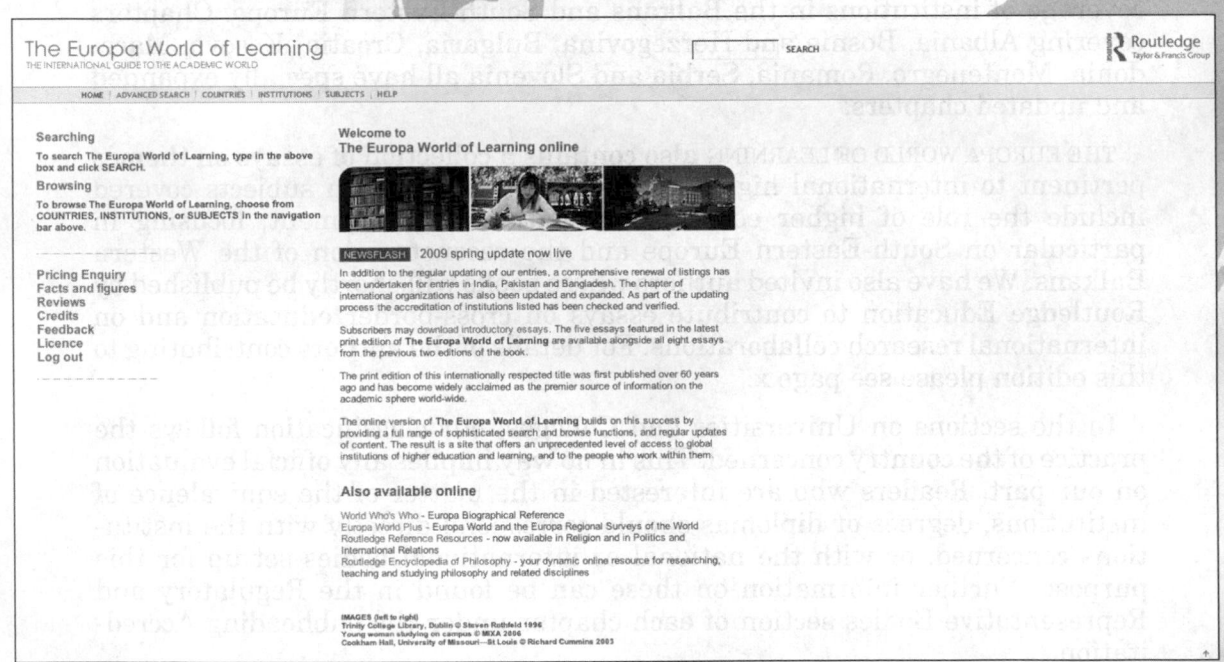

CONTENTS

CONTENTS

● An Index of Institutions is to be found at the end of Volume II

THE CONTRIBUTORS

Prof. Melissa Anderson is Professor of Higher Education and an affiliate faculty member in bioethics at the University of Minnesota. She is principal investigator of a study on integrity in international research collaborations, funded by the U.S. National Institutes of Health. With Nicholas H. Steneck, she edited the Routledge volume, International Research Collaborations: Much to be Gained, Many Ways to Get in Trouble. Her research over the past 20 years has focused on research integrity and misconduct, with particular attention to ways in which research environments influence the behaviour of scientists.

Prof. David W. Chapman is the Birkmaier Professor of Educational Leadership in the Department of Organizational Leadership, Policy and Development at the University of Minnesota. His specialization is in international development assistance. He has worked on development assistance activities in over 45 countries and has authored or edited ten books and over 125 book chapters and journal articles, many of them on issues related to the development of education systems in international settings. His research has examined, among other things, cross-border collaborations in higher education and the role of higher education in national development.

Prof. Robin Sakamoto is a Professor in the Faculty of Foreign Studies of Kyorin University, Japan as well as a lecturer at Tokyo University.

Gareth Williams is Emeritus Professor at the University of London Institute of Education. He founded its Centre for Higher Education Studies in 1985 and its MBA in Higher Education Management (with Michael Shattock) in 2001. An education economist; he has worked mainly on HE policy and finance since publication of Changing Patterns of Finance in Higher Education in 1992. He is a past chairman of the Society for Research in Higher Education. Two recent articles are Higher Education and UK elite formation in the 20th century (with Filippakou) Higher Education 2010; Subject Benchmarking in the United Kingdom in Public Policy for Academic Quality: Analyses of Innovative Policy Instruments, Dill and Beerkens (2010).

Prof. Pavel Zgaga is Full Professor at the University of Ljubljana, Faculty of Education (Slovenia) where he began his academic career in 1978. In 1990–92 and 2001–2004 he was a member of the University Senate; in 2001–2004 he was Dean of the Faculty of Education. He is Director of the Centre for Education Policy Studies, a R&D institute of the University of Ljubljana established in 2000.

In the 1990s, in the period after political changes in Slovenia, he was engaged for several years in Slovenian Government. In 1992–99 he was State Secretary for Higher Education. In 1999–2000 he was Minister of Education and Sports. He was also the head of the working group Education, Training and Youth in the negotiation process for Slovenian accession to the EU (1998–99). On behalf of Slovenia, he signed the Lisbon Recognition Convention (April 1997) and the Bologna Declaration (June 1999). After his return to university he has remained closely connected to the Bologna process. In the period 2002–2003 he was the general rapporteur of the Bologna Follow-up Group (Berlin Report) while in the period June 2004–June 2005 he was a member of the Board of the Bologna Follow-up Group.

His educational background consists of Doctorate in Philosophy in July 1989 and Diploma in Philosophy and Sociology in June 1975, both from University of Ljubljana, Faculty of Arts.

ABBREVIATIONS

AB	Alberta	Corpn	Corporation	HQ	Headquarters
Abog.	Abogado (lawyer)	Corresp.	Correspondent; Corresponding	HRH	His (Her) Royal Highness
Acad.	Academician; Academy	CP	Caixa postal; Case postale;		
ACT	Australian Capital Territory		Casella postale (Post Box)	IA	Iowa
Admin.	Administration; Administrative	Cr	Contador	ID	Idaho
AIDS	acquired immunodeficiency	CRC	Cooperative Research Centre	IL	Illinois
	syndrome	CT	Connecticut	ILO	International Labour
AK	Alaska	Cttee	Committee		Organization
AL	Alabama	cu	cubic	IN	Indiana
Apdo	Apartado (Post Box)			Inc.	Incorporated
approx.	approximately	DC	District of Colombia	incl.	include; includes; including
AR	Arkansas	DE	Delaware	Ind.	Independent
Arq.	Arquitecto (Spanish); Arquiteto	Del.	Delegate; Delegation	Ing.	Ingénieur (Engineer)
	(Portuguese)	Dept	Department	Instn	Institution
Asscn	Association	Deptl	Departmental	Int.	International
Assoc.	Associate	devt	development	Ir	Insinyur (Engineer)
Asst	Assistant	DF	Distrito Federal	irreg.	irregular
Atty	Attorney	Dipl.	Diploma		
Avda	Avenida	Dir	Director	Jl	Jalan (street)
Ave	Avenue	Dist.	District	Jr	Junior
Avv.	Avvocato (Advocate)	Div.	Division	JSC	Joint Stock Company
AZ	Arizona	Divs	Divisions	jt	joint
		Doc.	Docent	jtly	jointly
BA	Bachelor of Arts	Dott.	Dottore		
BC	British Columbia	Dott.ssa	Dottoressa	küç.	küçasi (street)
Bd	Boulevard	Doz.	Dozent (lecturer)	km	kilometre(s)
Bdul	Bulevardul	Dr	Doctor	KS	Kansas
BEng	Bachelor of Engineering	Dr Hab.	Doktor Habilitowany (Assistant	kv.	kvartal (apartment block);
Bld	Boulevard		Professor)		kvartira (apartment)
Bldg	Building	Dr.	Drive	KY	Kentucky
Blv	Boulevard	Dra	Doctora		
Blvd	Boulevard	Drs	Doctorandus (Dutch or	LA	Louisiana
Blvr	Bulevar		Indonesian higher degree)	Lic.	Licenciado
BP	Boîte postale	DVD	digital versatile disc	Licda	Licenciada
Br.	Branch			Lt	Lieutenant
BRGM	Bureau de Recherches	E	East; Eastern	Ltd	Limited
	Géologiques et Minières	e.g.	exempli gratia		
Brig.	Brigadier	Edif.	Edificio (Building)	m	metre(s)
Bro.	Brother	edn	edition	m.	million
Brs	Branches	Eng.	Engineer	MA	Massachusetts; Master of Arts
BSc	Bachelor of Science	EngD	Doctor of Engineering	Mag.	Magister (Masters degree)
Bul.	Bulvar (boulevard)	esp.	especially	Man.	Manager; Managing
bulv.	bulvarỹs (boulevard)	Est.	Established	MB	Manitoba
		etc.	et cetera	MBA	Master of Business
c.	circa (approximately)	EU	European Union		Administration
c/o	care of	Exec.	Executive	MD	Maryland
CA	California			ME	Maine
CAR	Central African Republic	f.	founded	Mem.	Member
Ccl	Council	F.t.e.	Full-time equivalent	Mems	Members
CD-ROM	compact disc read-only memory	FAO	Food and Agriculture	MEng	Master of Engineering
CEA	Commissariat à l'Energie		Organization	Mgr	Monseigneur; Monsignor
	Atomique	Fed.	Federal; Federation	MI	Michigan
CEO	Chief Executive Officer	FL	Florida	Min.	Minister; Ministry
Chair.	Chairman; Chairperson;	fmr	former	misc.	miscellaneous
	Chairwoman	fmrly	formerly	mm	millimetre(s)
CIRAD	Centre de Coopération	Fr	Father	MN	Minnesota
	Internationale en Recherche	ft	feet	MO	Missouri
	Agronomique pour le			MRC	Medical Research Council
	Développement	GA	Georgia	MS	Mississippi
Cmdr	Commander	Gdns	Gardens	MSc	Master of Science
CNR	Consiglio Nazionale delle	Gen.	General	MSS	Manuscripts
	Ricerche	Gov.	Governor	MT	Montana
cnr	corner	Govt	Government		
CNRS	Centre National de la	GPOB	Government Post Office Box	N	North; Northern
	Recherche Scientifique			nám	náměstí (square)
CO	Colorado	HE	His (Her) Excellency; His	NASA	National Aeronautics and
Co	Company; County		Eminence		Space Administration
Col	Colonel	HEI	Higher Education Institution	Nat.	National
Col.	Colonia (District)	HI	Hawaii	NB	New Brunswick
colln	Collection	HIV	human immunodeficiency virus	NC	North Carolina
Comm.	Commission	HM	His (Her) Majesty	ND	North Dakota
Commr	Commissioner	HND	Higher National Diploma	NE	Nebraska; Northeast;
Conf.	Conference	Hon.	Honorary; Honourable		Northeastern

NGO	Non-Governmental Organization	QC	Québec	Treas.	Treasurer
NH	New Hampshire	q.v.	quod vide (to which refer)	TRNC	Turkish Republic of Northern Cyprus
NJ	New Jersey	rd	road	TX	Texas
NL	Newfoundland and Labrador	Rep.	Representative		
NM	New Mexico	retd	retired	u.	utca (street)
NS	Nova Scotia	Rev.	Reverend	UK	United Kingdom
NSW	New South Wales	RI	Rhode Island	ul.	ulica; ulitsa (street)
NT	Northwest Territories	RP	Révérend Père	UN	United Nations
NU	Nunavut Territory	Rr.	Rruga	UNESCO	United Nations Educational, Scientific and Cultural Organization
NV	Nevada	Rt Hon.	Right Honourable		
NW	Northwest; Northwestern	Rt Rev.	Right Reverend		
NY	New York			Univ.	Universidad; Universidade; Università; Universität; Université; Universitas; Universitat; Universitatea; Universiteit; Universitet; Universiteti; Universiti; University; Univerza; Univerzita; Univerzitet; Uniwersytet
NZ	New Zealand	S	South; Southern		
		s/n	sin número (without number)		
obl.	oblast	SA	South Africa(n); South Australia		
Of.	Oficina				
OH	Ohio	SAR	Special Administrative Region		
OK	Oklahoma	SC	South Carolina		
ON	Ontario	SD	South Dakota		
OR	Oregon	SDI	Selective Dissemination of Information	USA	United States of America
Org.	Organization			UT	Utah
		SE	Southeast; Southeastern		
PA	Pennsylvania	Sec.	Secretary		
PE	Prince Edward Island	Sis.	Sister	VA	Virginia
PEN	Poets, Playwrights, Essayists, Editors and Novelists (Club)	SK	Saskatchewan	Vols	Volumes
		Soc.	Society	VT	Vermont
PhD	Doctor of Philosophy	spec.	special	vul.	vulitsa; vulytsa (sreet)
pl.	place; platz; ploshchad (square)	Sq.	Square		
PMB	Private Mail Bag	Sr	Senior	W	West; Western
POB	Post Office Box	St	Saint; Sint; Street	WA	Washington (State); Western Australia
pr.	prospekt (avenue)	Sta	Santa		
Pres.	President	Ste	Sainte	WI	Wisconsin
Prin.	Principal	str.	stradă; strada; Strasse (street)	WV	West Virginia
Prof.	Professor	SW	Southwest; Southwestern	WY	Wyoming
Profa	Professora				
Publ.	Publication	tel.	telephone		
Publs	Publications	TN	Tennessee	YT	Yukon Territory

INTERNATIONAL TELEPHONE CODES

To make international calls to telephone and fax numbers listed in *The Europa World of Learning*, dial the international code of the country from which you are calling, followed by the appropriate country code for the institution you wish to call (listed below), followed by the area code (if applicable) and telephone or fax number listed in the entry.

	Country code	+ or – GMT*		Country code	+ or – GMT*
Afghanistan	93	+4½	Djibouti	253	+3
Albania	355	+1	Dominica	1 767	–4
Algeria	213	+1	Dominican Republic	1 809	–4
Andorra	376	+1	Ecuador	593	–5
Angola	244	+1	Egypt	20	+2
Antigua and Barbuda	1 268	–4	El Salvador	503	–6
Argentina	54	–3	Equatorial Guinea	240	+1
Armenia	374	+4	Eritrea	291	+3
Australia	61	+8 to +10	Estonia	372	+2
Austria	43	+1	Ethiopia	251	+3
Azerbaijan	994	+5	Fiji	679	+12
Bahamas	1 242	–5	Finland	358	+2
Bahrain	973	+3	Åland Islands	358	+2
Bangladesh	880	+6	France	33	+1
Barbados	1 246	–4	French Guiana	594	–3
Belarus	375	+2	French Polynesia	689	–9 to –10
Belgium	32	+1	Guadeloupe	590	–4
Belize	501	–6	Martinique	596	–4
Benin	229	+1	New Caledonia	687	+11
Bhutan	975	+6	Réunion	262	+4
Bolivia	591	–4	Gabon	241	+1
Bosnia and Herzegovina	387	+1	Gambia	220	0
Botswana	267	+2	Georgia	995	+4
Brazil	55	–3 to –4	Germany	49	+1
Brunei	673	+8	Ghana	233	0
Bulgaria	359	+2	Greece	30	+2
Burkina Faso	226	0	Grenada	1 473	–4
Burundi	257	+2	Guatemala	502	–6
Cambodia	855	+7	Guinea	224	0
Cameroon	237	+1	Guinea-Bissau	245	0
Canada	1	–3 to –8	Guyana	592	–4
Cape Verde	238	–1	Haiti	509	–5
Central African Republic	236	+1	Honduras	504	–6
Chad	235	+1	Hungary	36	+1
Chile	56	–4	Iceland	354	0
China, People's Republic	86	+8	India	91	+5½
Hong Kong	852	+8	Indonesia	62	+7 to +9
Macao	853	+8	Iran	98	+3½
China (Taiwan)	886	+8	Iraq	964	+3
Colombia	57	–5	Ireland	353	0
Comoros	269	+3	Israel	972	+2
Congo, Democratic Republic	243	+1	Italy	39	+1
Congo, Republic	242	+1	Jamaica	1 876	–5
Costa Rica	506	–6	Japan	81	+9
Côte d'Ivoire	225	0	Jordan	962	+2
Croatia	385	+1	Kazakhstan	7	+6
Cuba	53	–5	Kenya	254	+3
Cyprus	357	+2	Kiribati	686	+12 to +13
'Turkish Republic of Northern Cyprus'	90 392	+2	Korea, Democratic People's Republic (North Korea)	850	+9
Czech Republic	420	+1	Korea, Republic (South Korea)	82	+9
Denmark	45	+1	Kosovo	381†	+3
Faroe Islands	298	0	Kuwait	965	+3
Greenland	299	–1 to –4			

xiii

	Country code	+ or – GMT*
Kyrgyzstan	996	+5
Laos	856	+7
Latvia	371	+2
Lebanon	961	+2
Lesotho	266	+2
Liberia	231	0
Libya	218	+1
Liechtenstein	423	+1
Lithuania	370	+2
Luxembourg	352	+1
Macedonia, former Yugoslav republic	389	+1
Madagascar	261	+3
Malawi	265	+2
Malaysia	60	+8
Maldives	960	+5
Mali	223	0
Malta	356	+1
Marshall Islands	692	+12
Mauritania	222	0
Mauritius	230	+4
Mexico	52	−6 to −7
Micronesia, Federated States	691	+10 to +11
Moldova	373	+2
Monaco	377	+1
Mongolia	976	+7 to +9
Montenegro	382	+1
Morocco	212	0
Mozambique	258	+2
Myanmar	95	$+6\frac{1}{2}$
Namibia	264	+2
Nauru	674	+12
Nepal	977	$+5\frac{3}{4}$
Netherlands	31	+1
Aruba	297	−4
Netherlands Antilles	599	−4
New Zealand	64	+12
Nicaragua	505	−6
Niger	227	+1
Nigeria	234	+1
Norway	47	+1
Oman	968	+4
Pakistan	92	+5
Palau	680	+9
Palestinian Autonomous Areas	970 or 972	+2
Panama	507	−5
Papua New Guinea	675	+10
Paraguay	595	−4
Peru	51	−5
Philippines	63	+8
Poland	48	+1
Portugal	351	0
Qatar	974	+3
Romania	40	+2
Russian Federation	7	+2 to +12
Rwanda	250	+2
Saint Christopher and Nevis	1 869	−4
Saint Lucia	1 758	−4
Saint Vincent and the Grenadines	1 784	−4
Samoa	685	−11
San Marino	378	+1
São Tomé and Príncipe	239	0
Saudi Arabia	966	+3
Senegal	221	0

	Country code	+ or – GMT*
Serbia	381	+1
Seychelles	248	+4
Sierra Leone	232	0
Singapore	65	+8
Slovakia	421	+1
Slovenia	386	+1
Solomon Islands	677	+11
Somalia	252	+3
South Africa	27	+2
Spain	34	+1
Sri Lanka	94	$+5\frac{1}{2}$
Sudan	249	+2
Suriname	597	−3
Swaziland	268	+2
Sweden	46	+1
Switzerland	41	+1
Syria	963	+2
Tajikistan	992	+5
Tanzania	255	+3
Thailand	66	+7
Timor-Leste	670	+9
Togo	228	0
Tonga	676	+13
Trinidad and Tobago	1 868	−4
Tunisia	216	+1
Turkey	90	+2
Turkmenistan	993	+5
Tuvalu	688	+12
Uganda	256	+3
Ukraine	380	+2
United Arab Emirates	971	+4
United Kingdom	44	0
Northern Ireland	44	0
Bermuda	1 441	−4
Gibraltar	350	+1
Guernsey	44	0
Isle of Man	44	0
Jersey	44	0
United States of America	1	−5 to −10
Guam	1 671	+10
Puerto Rico	1 787	−4
United States Virgin Islands	1 340	−4
Uruguay	598	−3
Uzbekistan	998	+5
Vanuatu	678	+11
Vatican City	39	+1
Venezuela	58	−4
Viet Nam	84	+7
Yemen	967	+3
Zambia	260	+2
Zimbabwe	263	+2

* Time difference in hours + or – Greenwich Mean Time (GMT). The times listed compare the standard (winter) times. Some countries adopt Summer (Daylight Saving) Time — i.e. +1 hour — for part of the year.

† Mobile telephone numbers for Kosovo use either the country code for Monaco (377) or the country code for Slovenia (386).

Note: Telephone and fax numbers using the Inmarsat ocean region code 870 are listed in full. No country or area code is required, but it is necessary to precede the number with the international access code of the country from which the call is made.

PART ONE
Introductory Essays

WILL HIGHER EDUCATION BE THE NEXT BUBBLE TO BURST?

GARETH WILLIAMS

INTRODUCTION

Higher education systems are networks of able, intelligent and creative people with the ability to think critically, so it is not surprising that they interpret what they do in many different ways. Sometimes the narrative is of a disinterested pursuit and dissemination of truth; sometimes it is completing the task of preparing each generation for the society they inherit; sometimes the story is of the maintenance of viable social and political order; and at other times to act as licensed critics of that order. More recently, higher education has come to be seen as investment in human capital, the main source of scientific and technological change. No matter what interpretation we choose to accept, though, there can be no doubt that higher education institutions of the 21st century are global businesses. They are global because their networks cover the whole world, in their student and staff recruitment, their graduate destinations, and their research sponsors; furthermore, their raw material, knowledge, like money, can be flashed across the globe in an instant. They are businesses because the wide spread of university autonomy, financial as well as academic and legal, has resulted in competition for recognition in the global market-place.

Global reach entails global competition; Pakistani graduates compete with those from Brazilian universities for jobs in international companies. Fundamental research from Massachusetts Institute of Technology (MIT) may be used to develop products or processes that can generate income in the growing economy of the People's Republic of China, provided that China has graduates who are able to exploit them. It is not surprising if both the original researchers and those who paid for the research assert their intellectual property rights to ensure that they receive some of the financial benefits that flow from their work anywhere in the world.

Global higher education could, in principle, be closely regulated nationally and internationally. All higher education systems have an element of regulation, from the well-known California master plan that has underpinned the development of higher education in that state since the early 1960s, to the traditionally closely regulated systems of France and Japan. The worldwide interest in the Bologna-inspired qualification frameworks is one example of evolving worldwide coordination arrangements. At the same time, the emergence of mass higher education, and the inevitable diversification that accompanies it, has resulted in a shift towards national systems in which individual higher education institutions have a great deal of financial as well as academic freedom. Almost inevitably, universities have competed for students and research grants and over the past two decades many of them have been very successful in doing so. They have also been encouraged by governments to offer other knowledge-based services and have extended their interests to cover a wide range of knowledge-related 'third mission' activities.

However, business expansion is rarely boundless or continuous. Throughout their long history, universities have grown in fits and starts. While the long-term trend has certainly been upwards, there have been many periods of stagnation. While Clark Kerr's famous aphorism held that the university is one of the very few European institutions to have survived since medieval times, it is much less remarked that many individual higher education institutions have ceased to exist over the period and those that have survived are very different institutions from those of earlier centuries. All are in a continual state of evolution, sometimes painful, as a result of economic, social or political pressures. In brief, markets are not a unique threat and 21st-century universities are likely to have as chequered a history as their predecessors.

A CENTURY OF EXPANSION

Higher education grew massively in most countries throughout the 20th century, though growth was uneven, at different rates in different countries. Like the economy, it grew in fits and starts, sometimes extremely rapidly and sometimes stagnating for several years. Though the timing was not the same in all countries, in general, rapid growth in the 1920s was followed by a decade of stagnation in the 1930s. Growth resumed after the Second World War and accelerated in the 1960s and early 1970s. Then there was a decade and a half of stagnation in the late 1970s and 1980s, followed by more fast growth in the 1990s and the early years of the present century.

Organisation for Economic Co-operation and Development (OECD) figures show that in most of the world's wealthy countries the percentage of the population undertaking higher education has grown by 20% in the present century and the percentage of the adult population with higher education has grown correspondingly (see Tables 1–3). In many developing countries and emerging economies the growth has been even faster. In China, for example, about 10% of school leavers undertook higher education in 1996; now it is about one-quarter of the population.

China has seen an unprecedented expansion in its higher education (HE) sector in the last decade. Total enrolment, for instance, reached 7.3m. in 2006, 3.5 times higher than in 1997. By 2006, total enrolment at China's HE institutions had risen to as high as 25m. with the gross enrolment rate reaching 22% compared with only 3.4% in 1990. (Wu and Zheng, 2008: 1)

This growth continued at least until 2009:

With more than 27m. students, China's current higher education system is the largest in the world. Some 24% of all 18–22 year olds [are] now in a tertiary institution, and hundreds of new universities have been established over the past decade. (Douglass, 2010: 20)

In India, too, there has been massive expansion:

With more than 400 universities and over 20,000 colleges, student enrolment in India crossed 12.9m. in 2007–08, clocking a compounded annual growth rate of 6.2% since 1985–86. (*University World News*, 2009)

Table 1 Percentage of young people aged 20–29 years in education

Average of:	2000	2005	2007
OECD			
Age 20–24	35.3	40.6	41.0
Age 25–29	12.4	14.1	14.0
EU			
Age 20–24	36.5	41.9	42.2
Age 25–29	11.7	13.5	13.6
USA			
Age 20–24	32.5	36.1	35.7
Age 25–29	11.4	11.9	12.4

Source: EAG 2010, Table C3.4a.

Table 2 Entry rates to tertiary education

Average of:	2000	2005	2007
OECD	47	55	56
EU	46	53	55
USA	43	64	65
Australia	59	82	86
Germany	30	36	34
Japan	40	44	46
Netherlands	53	59	60
Poland	65	76	78
Sweden	67	76	73
United Kingdom	47	51	55

Source: EAG 2010, Table A2.5.

Table 3 Percentages of population (aged 25–64 years) with tertiary education

Average of:	2000	2005	2007
OECD	21	26	27
EU	19	24	24
USA	36	39	40
Australia	27	32	34
Germany	23	25	24
Japan	34	40	41
Netherlands	23	30	31
Poland	11	17	19
Sweden	30	30	31
United Kingdom	26	30	32

Source: EAG 2010, Table A1.3a.

The early years of the 21st century were boom years for higher education in most countries. Nearly all the key indicators showed expansion and improvement across the world. Much of the high-level rhetoric is that the growth will continue for some time to come:

Tertiary attainment levels have increased substantially in OECD countries. On average, one-third of 25- to 34-year-olds have concluded tertiary education, up from less than 20% 15 years ago. And if we look at entry rates, they continue to increase, suggesting that the upward trend will continue. (Gurría, 2009)

In emerging economies the growth has been even more spectacular:

In the 1960s, 70s and 80s the higher education agenda in Asia's early developers—Japan, South Korea and Taiwan—was first and foremost to increase the fraction of their populations provided with postsecondary education. Their initial focus was on expanding the number of institutions and their enrolments, and impressive results were achieved. Today, the later and much larger developing nations of Asia—China and India—have an even more ambitious agenda. Both these emerging powers seek to expand the capacity of their systems of higher education, and China has done so dramatically since 1998.[...] China in particular has the will and resources that make it feasible. This aspiration is shared not only by other nations in Asia but also by certain resource-rich nations in the Middle East.

In the Gulf States, hundreds of millions of dollars are being spent to open branches of top US and European universities such as Cornell in Qatar and the Sorbonne in Abu Dhabi.

This past autumn, the new King Abdullah University of Science and Technology opened in Saudi Arabia. Its US$10,000m. endowment exceeds that of all but five American universities.

In India, the Education Ministry recently announced its intention to build 14 new comprehensive universities of 'world-class' stature. (Levin, 2010: 3)

As a minor indicator of the global expansion, the number of institutions included in *The Europa World of Learning* rose from about 8,500 in 1985, to 21,000 in 2000, and to 28,000 in 2010.

'Is it possible that higher education might be the next bubble to burst?' asked Joseph Cronin and Howard Horton in an article in the US *Chronicle of Higher Education* in May 2009. Their concern was with the rapidly rising fees that US private universities charged during the first decade of the century, and they produced evidence to show that these increases were unsustainable. However, there are reasons for wider doubts about whether the unbroken expansion of higher education worldwide can be expected to continue indefinitely, and some indications suggest that even in the shorter term some checks, normal in any business sector, may be anticipated.

ARE THERE NATURAL LIMITS TO GROWTH IN ENROLMENT?

Most OECD countries have now achieved what Martin Trow called mass higher education, and it is being rapidly approached in many other parts of the world. At some stage, everyone who is able or who wishes to take advantage of higher education opportunities will be able to do so. It is not easy to assess the limit. Universities are proving able to adapt to the needs and interests of a wide range of different students, and there is good reason to believe that in rapidly changing societies and economies, lifelong learning will encourage people to undertake higher education episodes throughout most of their lives. However, there is some empirical evidence to suggest that when about one-half of each generation obtains higher education there may be resistance to much more growth in enrolment. For example, according to OECD figures, there has been little growth in enrolment ratios in recent years for some of the early achievers of mass higher education, such as Japan, the Nordic countries and the USA. More generally, the slow-down in growth of participation by young males inspires some questions about the economic benefits to them. In all OECD countries except Japan, the Republic of Korea and Turkey, female participation in higher education now exceeds that of males, often by a considerable margin. This gap has appeared and increased annually over the past two decades; it seems to have occurred as countries approached mass higher education. Do many young men now believe that there are no longer net benefits to be gained from higher education? It is a much under-researched phenomenon.

However, even if there is an ultimate limit on expansion, it is unlikely to show itself in the form of a bursting bubble. Rather, expansion will slow down and the relatively low growth rates in male participation in several OECD countries during the past decade may be a portent of this.

Of more concern is that very high rates of growth result in rapidly increasing numbers of graduates trying to find jobs in economies that are unable to offer them in the short term the kind of employment for which they were hoping. Something like the hog cycle (a cyclical fluctuation in supply and price, typically in the livestock market) caused by lags in production decisions and the resulting output, well known to economists, is one suggested possibility (see Harlow, 1960; Rosen et al., 1994). The basis of the model is straightforward: at a particular point in time potential students observe that the earnings and other rewards of those with particular high-level qualifications are very good. This encourages more of them to seek qualifications in that subject area, but it takes some years for them to obtain the qualification. When they graduate and seek to enter the labour market, they find that many other people have taken the same decision and there is an over-supply of graduates with those skills, so their earnings fall relative to those in other occupations. The number of students electing to study those subjects correspondingly falls and fewer people study that subject, with a corresponding rise in starting salaries a few years later. The cycle then repeats.

Of course, there are many differences between hogs and graduates. The gestation period is much longer, so the cycle is lengthier for graduates. Not all students enter higher education with a job in mind and even those who do embrace a very wide range of skills. It is unlikely that the labour market in all sectors will be flooded at the same time. Furthermore, movements in relative earnings are much more sluggish than meat prices, so cycles are likely to be much less easily identifiable. However, the rapid expansion of higher education in many countries in the late 1920s, and in the 1960s and early 1970s, was followed by a decade or more of stagnant demand and much slower growth in the 1930s and 1980s. There is reason to believe that in both cases this was at least partly due to a perception that the economic value of a degree was less enticing (Freeman, 1975a; Williams, 1985).

More relevant to the 21st century, there are hints that the hugely increased output of graduates in China is finding it difficult to find suitable employment:

Ministry of Education statistics indicate more than 6m. students will graduate in China this year whereas in 2002, the total number comprised only 1.45m.. But the employment rate for graduates last year was less than 70% and the rising number seeking jobs is challenging the government at a time when the current economic crisis will surely exacerbate the problem. It is likely close to 2m. graduates will not find work—many of whom are postgraduates, even doctoral graduates. (Zhou and Lin, 2009: 3)

There are indications of similar problems in Indonesia:

The most recent figures released by the manpower ministry show some 1.15m. unemployed graduates nationwide. The national education ministry's pro-active director-general for higher education Fasli Jalal believes too many graduates emerge without marketable skills. (Jardine, 2009)

However, while over-expansion of higher education in general remains a remote possibility, there are certain features of 21st-century expansion that should give cause for concern. Four in particular need to be watched carefully: rapid growth of private universities; the growth of university expansion across international borders; rapid growth of some subject areas not matched by market demand for their graduates; and concerns about quality.

Private Universities

In an important recent book on global private higher education, Altbach and Levy claimed that:

[...] in the last quarter of the 20th century [...] private higher education has suddenly become the fastest growing segment of higher education worldwide—expanding rapidly in almost all parts of the world. (Altbach and Levy, 2005: 1)

The private higher education sector is expanding most rapidly in Latin America and Asia, with Africa growing slowly but steadily. In countries dominated by public higher enrolments just a decade ago a third or more of their students now attend private institutions. These include several Latin American nations such as Mexico and Chile. Brazil has had a majority of its students in private institutions for a half-century. Indonesia now educates about half its students at private institutions, and Malaysia also has a large private sector. [...] Since the 1990s China has built up a large private sector. (Altbach and Levy, 2005: 3)

Rapid expansion of this sector has continued. Indonesia, for example, now has 2,700 private institutions that call themselves universities. In Russia, where there were effectively no private universities in 1990, there are now about 450 private universities and 650 public institutions. In Poland in 1990 there were 112 higher education institutions, nearly all public, while in 2010 there were the same number of public universities, but they had been supplemented by 195 private institutions.

According to Altbach and Levy:

The financial arrangements of private higher education institutions often lack transparency. The for-profit sector growing in many countries is perhaps easiest to understand since, in many countries these institutions operate as corporate entities. [...] A significant proportion of private higher education initiatives in most countries are at least in part focused on earning money for the owners or operators of the institutions. Specific financial strategies may be hidden from government and the public. Family run private universities in some cases are created as profit-making business operations. While no accurate statistics exist concerning the number or proportion of private higher education institutions that seek to earn a profit for owners, families or management groups, it is likely that a large majority of the newer generation of institutions everywhere fall into these categories. (Altbach and Levy, 2005: 5)

This is what makes much of this growth vulnerable to cyclical ups and downs. Even more than market-driven public sector and non-profit higher education generally, private universities established as commercial enterprises are exposed to the vagaries of the market. The private sector may still be relatively small compared with the great majority of students in public higher education in most countries, but governments in more and more countries are beginning to believe that financially autonomous universities acting like commercial enterprises are less of a burden to public funds. Thus, they are more likely to be in direct competition with private universities and to alter their actions accordingly.

Cross-Border Higher Education

In addition, much of the huge expansion of international education in recent years has been commercially provided. It can take several forms. The longest established is the recruitment of full-cost fee-paying students in universities outside their home country. Whereas 600,000 students went abroad to study for their degrees in 1975, by 2000 the number was 1.8m., in 2005 it reached 2.7m. and in 2007 it was over 3m. (EAG, 2010). In 2007:

International students make up 10% or more of the enrolments in tertiary education in Australia, Austria, New Zealand, Switzerland and the United Kingdom. International students make up more than 20% of enrolments in advanced research programmes in Australia, Belgium, Canada, New Zealand, Switzerland, the United Kingdom and the United States. (EAG, 2010: 309)

International students paying fees boost the resources available, but make the universities vulnerable to political and exchange rate fluctuations, as well as shifts in consumer demand.

There are also longer-term dangers for universities that come to rely on international students as a major source of income. As the OECD figures suggest, much of the flow of international students is from developing countries and emerging economies to universities of wealthier Western countries. However, one of the main reasons why these countries are encouraging study abroad is to build up their own higher education systems. As has been suggested, China is well on the way to self-sufficiency, as is India: two countries that account for a large proportion of the recent upsurge in study in Western universities. Of course, advanced higher education systems do experience many staff and student exchanges, but not on the one-way commercial basis that is typical of most internationalization programmes today. The shift from Western-based to a more globally spread pattern of higher education will not be achieved without considerable stresses and jolts, as has been the case for the manufacturing industry, which moved in a similar direction during the past half century.

Another dimension of internationalization threatens even more turbulence. According to the Observatory on Borderless Higher Education (OBHE), the number of universities across the world establishing branch campuses in other countries is growing rapidly. The number has almost doubled to 162 in 2007–2010 alone, and has jumped eight-fold since 2002. Higher education institutions from 22 countries have now established branch campuses abroad, compared with institutions from 17 countries in 2006. Most of these campuses (111 out of 162) were created by institutions in the Anglophone nations, with the USA continuing to overshadow all others with its 78 offshore bases accounting for 48% of the total (Becker, 2009). In the Arabian Gulf states, hundreds of millions of US dollars are being spent to open branches of US and European universities, some of them leading universities such as Cornell in Qatar and the Sorbonne in Abu Dhabi (Levin, 2010). While a variety of reasons is put forward for these ventures (the words 'cultural imperialism' are used by opponents), there can be little doubt that the primary motivation is commercial.

From the Amsterdam tulip mania in 1624, to the dot-com madness in the late 1990s and the credit crunch of 2008, over-rapid expansion in many commercial ventures has been followed by at least a temporary crash. The OBHE report showed that five international campuses had closed by 2009. It will be surprising if others do not follow.

Subjects of Study

To extend the earlier metaphor of the hog cycle, and rises and falls in demand for higher education through graduate labour market shifts, a closer analogy is with particular subjects of study in higher education. Just as hogs are part of a much broader meat and food production industry, so higher education embraces many kinds of graduates who can be substituted for one another in the labour market to only a limited extent. Much of the press comment in many countries about graduate unemployment turns out on closer inspection to refer to particular areas of graduate employment. This is why it is often possible to read in the same report that the rates of return to higher education remain very good while some graduates are finding it hard to find suitable employment.

In the previously cited study of the Chinese graduate labour market by Zhou and Lin, the authors go on to state that:

> With demands in the job market changing constantly, the tension created by the gap between the supply of graduates and the demand of employers has intensified. Consequently, too many graduates have majored in accounting, Chinese language and literature, law and computer science, whereas jobs in these fields are limited. At the same time, many companies cannot find qualified employees working in specific technical fields. (Zhou and Lin, 2009: 3)

Such subject differences are also shown by differences in graduate earnings by subject of study. A labour force survey in the United Kingdom (UK) in 2002 showed that average earnings of new graduates in engineering were £21,000 per year, while for graduates of humanities subjects the figure was £12,600, some 67% lower (Prospects Net, 2002). In 2005/06 the average starting salaries of engineering graduates were over £23,000, while English literature graduates could expect about £17,000 (HESA, 2007). Another study found that, while the average university leaver could expect to make £160,000 more between the age of 21 and 60 than those who entered the job market with only A-levels, those with degrees in medicine had the highest earnings premium at £340,315, while engineering graduates could expect to make £243,730 more, and those with degrees in geography or history could make £51,549 more (O'Leary and Sloane, 2007).

Quality of Education

There are also more general concerns about the quality of the student experience, shown often by the number of students who fail to complete their course. In the USA, about 30% of higher education enrolees fail to complete their course, but 11% of all students and over 30% of black students were enrolled in colleges or universities in which less than one-third of students graduated (Schneider, 2008). OECD figures show that in both the UK and the USA successful university course completion rates fell considerably between 2000 and 2005 (EAG, 2004; EAG, 2010).

Such indicators do not necessarily foreshadow a bursting bubble, but they do provide warnings that individuals may begin to ask questions about the likely real value to them of embarking on some courses of higher education.

HIGHER EDUCATION AND THE RECESSION

The global financial crisis of 2008/09 and the subsequent recession are having ambiguous implications for higher education. Rising graduate unemployment in some countries where expansion has been particularly rapid has already been discussed. However, graduate unemployment is also linked to the state of the world economy. There is evidence in several countries that new graduates in 2009 and 2010 found it much harder than their predecessors to find suitable first employment because of the general employment situation.

According to the College Employment Research Institute at Michigan State University:

> Hiring levels for college graduates across America are at their lowest level in decades and are not expected to improve in 2010. MSU's 2009 Recruiting Trends Survey [. . .] found that hiring levels plummeted between 35% and 40% in 2009. (*Michigan State University News*, 2010)

There are similar reports from several European countries in relation to first-time employment of graduates. Other evidence, however, shows that unemployment of graduates remains lower than among less skilled workers, so the relative advantages of higher level qualifications remain. Indeed, there are reports from several countries of postgraduate courses benefiting from graduates' belief that the best way of maintaining their positional advantage is to obtain further qualifications. It is likely that the job market for new graduates would need to remain stagnant for several more years before it had a marked effect on overall demand for higher education.

A much more serious danger for higher education institutions is the direct effect of the 2009–10 recession. It has already hit many private and other financially autonomous universities, which receive a significant proportion of their income from donations and investments.

According to a report in *University World News* in December 2009:

> In Asia, Africa, North America, Europe, Britain and down under in Australia and New Zealand, universities have been hit hard as the value of their investments in property and shares and, in many cases, their income from diverse sources crumples.
>
> Komazawa University incurred losses of 15,500m. yen or almost US $170m. in trading high-risk derivatives. Keio University [. . .] accumulated 22,500m. yen ($233m.) in unrealized losses on investments ranging from hedge funds to real estate investment trusts. [. . .] Waseda University, a training ground for Japanese politicians since 1882, expected a 500m. yen ($5.4m.) loss, incurred on investments as of March, to deepen significantly.
>
> In the USA, the University of Texas has reported losing US $1,000m. so far on its investments and endowments in 2008. Elsewhere, Loyola University in Chicago faced losses to its endowment in early October of more than $30m. while Dartmouth University announced it had lost $220m.
>
> In Britain, the first signs that universities were facing grim times came in October when reports that several universities including Cambridge [. . .] were potentially involved in financial crises after being blocked from accessing funds in Icelandic banks amounting to more than £1,160m. (US $1,710m.). Cambridge revealed it had £8.5m. (US $12.6m.) in a subsidiary of the failed Landsbanki and £2.5m. in another, although the funds represented only 3% of the university's total bank deposits. Another 11 universities, including Manchester, the Open University, Glyndwr and Manchester Metropolitan, had deposits in Icelandic banks adding up to £66m.
>
> In Australia [. . .] the nation's oldest and wealthiest universities have seen the value of their properties and investments plummet. The University of Sydney revealed falls in its investments had resulted in cuts to its annual budget of 10% or some A$150m. (US $99m.). (Maslen, 2008)

Such figures from individual universities, however eminent, are not necessarily very significant, but they do demonstrate that higher education globally is operating in a fiercely competitive commercial world and universities cannot expect to escape from the turbulence of the rest of the economy.

Student demand is much more ambiguous. On the one hand it is clear that in some cases families' ability to pay fees has been hit, but there is little evidence of this affecting the demand for higher education as a whole. The relative economic advantages of having higher qualifications remains, though some potential students may be forced to modify their aspirations. In the USA, 'many students who had planned to attend private or out of state public colleges have turned to cheaper in-state options' (Douglass, 2010: 4). A study by Paul Axelrod of universities in Canada during the great depression of the 1930s found that:

[...j]obs, even for university graduates dried up. Many dropped out, and a significant number of those who remained in university faced severe financial challenges. At the University of Saskatchewan in 1934, the administration accepted promissory notes from one-third of its students because they were unable to pay their fees. However, notwithstanding these crises, the universities survived the Depression, diminished but intact. No institutions were closed; indeed enrolments rose by some 10% during the period. History demonstrates that in poor economic times, those able to pay the fees seek to enhance their educational credentials in anticipation of better days ahead. (Axelrod, 2010: 1)

Preliminary evidence suggests that this is happening now. There are many reports of demand for higher education rising as a response to the general unemployment being caused by the recession. In the UK, student applications for university places rose in both 2009 and 2010, while in the USA:

Preliminary evidence [...] is that nationally the number of community college students is up approximately 11.4% in fall 2009 over fall 2008, and that many of these students are nontraditional (over the age of 24) and increasingly enrolled full-time. (Douglass, 2010: 2)

In addition:

According to a February 2010 report by the State Higher Education Officers association (SHEEO), nationally, higher education enrollment in the US grew by 3.4% from 2007–08 to 2008–09 (the beginning stage of the Great Recession), and there are signs of increased access, but with varying stories among the 50 states[...]. (Douglass, 2010: 4)

Enrolment in higher education, like their economies in general, seems to have been relatively little affected in the main Asian countries, with the exception of Japan where, as already noted, a plateau in higher education enrolment seems to have been reached.

According to Moody's (a credit rating and financial forecasting company):

As global recessionary trends persist in many nations, universities are proving to be an appealing investment for government stimulus efforts due to the sector's stabilizing, counter cyclical nature in the short-term, as well as its potential to stimulate long term economic development. (Moody's, 2009: 9)

The Moody's study also shows that in the recessionary years of 1990–92 and 2000–02 growth of higher education enrolment in major OECD countries accelerated.

Nevertheless, higher education institutions in many countries are likely to suffer very severely from the public expenditure reductions made necessary by the Keynesian deficits incurred in 2008–10 to alleviate the worst effects of the financial collapse.

The immediate effect of the financial crisis was to increase public higher education expenditure in many countries as part of the deficit-financing policies to restore economies to growth, though governments seem to have been more concerned to increase spending on university research and research-training than on increasing student participation. However, it is widely believed that as Western economies recover from the recession higher education will be one of the sectors that can expect severe cuts in public expenditure to help reverse the large deficits incurred during the financial crisis. This has already begun in some countries. Many of the states in the USA, which have their own higher education systems and tax-raising capacities, have already seen severe reductions. In the University of California, for example, the state-funded operating budget was reduced by 20% in 2009/10 compared with 2008/09. In the UK, a reduction of 9% in public funds for universities in 2010/11 has been announced, and further reductions were widely expected after the general election in May 2010. Reductions in public funding available for higher education are thought to be imminent in many other OECD countries.

CONCLUDING COMMENT

Higher education is too long-term an investment for individuals and societies, too global and too diverse, and its advocates too articulate, for a catastrophic crash of the whole sector following over-rapid expansion to be at all likely. Families and governments are likely to continue to be willing to make considerable sacrifices to ensure that new generations are able to develop their talents to the best of their ability in the long term. Research is likely to continue to be seen as one of the most powerful drivers of long-term improvements in economic and social welfare. Major universities that have survived for many generations will continue to exist. The sector will continue to expand in emerging economies such as Brazil, China, India and Indonesia. Indeed, one way of interpreting the current turbulence in higher education in the world economy generally is that it is caused by the shifting of the tectonic plates away from Europe and North America, eastwards and southwards.

Yet, there are some booms that are likely to bust in the next few years. One, almost analogous to the sub-prime mortgages that triggered the financial crisis, is the expansion in many countries of institutions that provide qualifications of uncertain value to students whose capacity to benefit from higher education is doubtful. Although the average economic returns to higher education remain good, not all students from all types of higher education benefit. Concerns about quality of some higher education institutions are widespread. Related to this is the explosive growth of commercial private higher education. Such institutions are likely to have similar experiences to other small and medium-sized enterprises: they are exposed to the vagaries of the market and their fortunes will rise and fall. They have had, until 2009, a long run of good years. Those that do find a successful niche in an overcrowded market may find their business captured by financially stronger, newly autonomous public universities supported by public funds. The third bubble waiting to burst is internationalization. It is unrealistic to expect the number of students from India and China, in particular, to continue to grow as these countries expand and strengthen their own universities. Cross-border campuses, which in practice have much in common with commercial private higher education, are particularly vulnerable.

Universities have been under much pressure by governments and international agencies to be more entrepreneurial. Entrepreneurs are rewarded for taking risks, but not all risky ventures are successful.

BIBLIOGRAPHIC REFERENCES

Altbach, P. and Levy, D. C. *Private Higher Education: A Global Revolution*. Rotterdam and Taipeh, Sense Publishers, 2005.

Axelrod, P. 'Universities and the Great Depression: Then and Now?', *Academic matters OCUFA Journal of Higher Education*. Canada, York University, 2010. Available at www.academicmatters.ca/current_issue.article.gk?catalog_item_id=1812&category=featured_articles (accessed 18 May 2010).

Becker, R. *International Branch Campuses: Markets and Strategies*. London, Observatory on Borderless Higher Education, 2009.

Cronin, J. and Horton, H. 'Will Higher Education Be the Next Bubble to Burst?', *Chronicle of Higher Education*, 22 May 2009.

Douglass, J. A. *Higher Education Budgets and the Global Recession: Tracking Varied National Responses and Their Consequences*. Research & Occasional Paper Series: CSHE.4.10, Centre for the Study of Higher Education, University of California, Berkeley, 2010.

EAG. *Education at a Glance 2003*. Paris, OECD, 2004.

Education at a Glance 2009. Paris, OECD, 2010.

Freeman, R. B. 'Legal "Cobwebs". A Recursive Model of the Market for New Lawyers', *The Review of Economics and Statistics*, Vol. 57, No. 2, 1975a.

Freeman, R. B. 'Supply and Salary Adjustments to the Changing Science Manpower Market: Physics, 1948–1973', *The American Economic Review*, Vol. 65, No. 1, 1975b.

Gardner, M. 'GERMANY: Higher Education Spending to Boost Economy', *University World News*, 14 December 2008. Available at www.universityworldnews.com/article.php?story=20081212100423575 (accessed 17 May 2010).

Gurría, A. *The new dynamics of higher education*, address delivered at the UNESCO World Conference on Higher Education in Paris, 5 July 2009. Available at www.oecd.org/document/16/0,3343,en_2649_37455_43264400_1_1_1_1,00.html (accessed 18 May 2010).

Harlow, A. A. 'The Hog Cycle and the Cobweb Theorem', *Journal of Farm Economics* 42 (4), 1960, 842–53.

HESA. *Destinations of Leavers from Higher Education in the United Kingdom for the Academic Year 2005/06*. Cheltenham, UK, Higher Education Statistics Agency, 2007.

Jardine, D. 'Tackling Graduate Unemployment', *University World News*, 8 March 2009. Available at www.universityworldnews.com/article.php?story=20090305191601628 (accessed 17 May 2010).

Levin, R. C. *'The Rise of Asia's Universities'*, lecture delivered to HEPI at The Royal Society, London, UK, 1 February 2010. Available at www.hepi.ac.uk/files/1.Seventh%20Annual%20HEPI%20Lecture%20Richard%20Levin.pdf (accessed 18 May 2010).

Maslen, G. 'GLOBAL: Universities lose billions as recession deepens', *University World News*, 14 December 2008. Available at www.universityworldnews.com/article.php?story=2008121210071413 (accessed 17 May 2010).

Michigan State University News. Recruiting Trends Report 2008–2009. MSU, 2010.

Moody's. 'Global Recession and Universities: Funding strains to keep up with rising demand', *International Public Finance* June 2009. New York, Moodys, 2009. Available at globalhighered.files.wordpress.com/2009/07/s-globrecess-univ-6-09.pdf (accessed 18 May 2010).

O'Leary, N. C. and Sloane, P. J. 'Graduate earnings in the UK', in Gokulsing, K. M. (ed.), *The New Shape of University Education in England: Inter-disciplinary Essays*. Edwin Mellen Press, 2007.

Prospects Net. 'Graduate earnings from the labour force survey (Spring 02)'. Available at www.prospectsnet.com/cms/ShowPage/Home_page/Main_Menu___News_and_information/Graduate_Market_Trends/Graduate_earnings_from_the_labour_force_survey__Spring_02_/p!eXdaLa (accessed 13 May 2010).

Rosen, S., Murphy, K. M., and Scheinkman, J. A. 'Cattle Cycles', *Journal of Political Economy*, 102(1), 1994.

Schneider, M. *The Costs of Failure in American Higher Education*. AEI Outlook Series, 2008.

University World News 'INDIA: Report charts higher education future'. 6 December 2009. Available at www.universityworldnews.com/article.php?story=20091204095943905 (accessed 17 May 2010).

Williams, G. L. 'Graduate Employment and Vocationalism in Higher Education', *European Journal of Education*, 20, 1985, 2–3.

Wu, B. and Zheng, Y. *Expansion of Higher Education in China: Challenges and Implications*. Briefing Series—Issue 36 China Policy Institute, University of Nottingham, 2008.

Zhou, M. and Lin, J. 'Chinese Graduates' Employment: The impact of the financial crisis', in *International Higher Education*, Center for International Higher Education, Boston College, USA, 2009.

THE CHANGING FACE OF CROSS-BORDER HIGHER EDUCATION

DAVID W. CHAPMAN and ROBIN SAKAMOTO

Cross-border collaboration in higher education is big business, and is getting bigger. Colleges and universities in one country generally enter into partnerships with those in other countries to increase revenue, enhance instructional quality, expand curricular offerings, raise institutional prestige, or some combination of these. The opportunities for these collaborations are made increasingly easier by the growing economic and social integration among countries and the widespread availability of inexpensive, high-speed communications, forces that are prominent components of globalization.

Often these collaborations work to the advantage of each partner, but not always. As both the popularity of these collaborations and the range of purposes, activities and mechanisms being pursued through these partnerships have expanded, so too have the complexities. New models of collaboration, the expanding scale of use, changes in government regulations and shifting economic circumstances converge to raise new issues for higher education leaders seeking to reap the benefits of cross-border partnerships.

This paper explores the reasons for the growing popularity of cross-border collaboration in higher education, the major directions in which that collaboration has developed, and the challenges that higher education and government leaders have faced in entering into and sustaining such efforts.

DIMENSIONS AND DIRECTIONS OF COLLABORATION

Cross-border education is already a multi-billion-dollar industry. The international flow of education programmes and related goods and services are a significant component of the export market in many countries. The US $8,500m. in US exports of educational goods and services in 1997 made it the fifth largest service export. By 2006 this had doubled to $14,600m., accounting for 3.6% of total services trade for the USA (Bureau for Economic Analysis, 2007). In the United Kingdom (UK), education exports account for over £9,000m. and in Australia at least A$2,000m. annually, making education products and services a larger export than wheat (Bennell and Pearce, 2002). One important factor fuelling the growth of cross-border collaboration has been the inclusion of higher education in the General Agreement on Trade in Services (GATS). As higher education is treated by the international community as a commodity, it has attracted the attention of new audiences who see education as a new area of international commerce.

The dramatic increase in the scale of cross-border programme delivery is witnessed worldwide, and, in some countries, cross-border education delivery constitutes a significant proportion of their entire international study body. Australia, for example, indicated that one-quarter of its entire international student enrolment is through the offshore programmes (Bannerman et al., 2005).

While cross-border efforts were long dominated by the Western nations, most notably Australia, the UK and the USA, that pattern is changing. More partnerships are developing within regions, and especially in the Asia-Pacific region, where higher education enrolment is escalating. These partnerships provide support for higher education institutions in such areas as quality control, faculty development, and creating research hubs and technology parks through region-wide university networks.

Much of this exchange centres on the delivery of instruction, though even in cross-border partnerships focused on instruction there are significant changes in both the forms of collaboration and the players involved. Increasingly, these cross-border initiatives are moving into non-instructional areas of collaboration, such as research, faculty development and quality assurance. In some respects, increased collaboration in non-instructional areas follows from the growth of collaborative instructional programmes, as those who met in graduate school or early career jobs continue to collaborate when they return to their respective countries. However, motives are broader and may include working across borders to increase access to research funding from multiple sources, hence lessening financial risk (Godfrey, 2008).

WHY DO UNIVERSITIES ESTABLISH CROSS-BORDER EDUCATIONAL PROGRAMMES?

After almost two decades in which most international organizations favoured primary and secondary education, they are giving new attention to higher education as an instrument for socio-economic development (Chapman, 2007; Kot, 2010). Complex economies cannot be managed solely by secondary graduates. As higher education systems expand, many colleges and universities view cross-border collaborative programmes as a strategy for bolstering their quality, improving their image and securing additional resources. Their efforts are made easier by improved transportation options and low-cost communications technologies that often make travel unnecessary. Governments and international organizations have increasingly recognized that without a strong higher education system, it is impossible to decrease the knowledge and technology gap between developed and developing countries.

Some of the frequently mentioned motivations for cross-border education include economic gains, building an international reputation, student and staff advancement, meeting different student needs, increasing access to tertiary education programmes, innovation through new delivery systems and providers, capacity-building in transition economies, and enhancing mutual understanding (Saffu and Mamman, 2000; Sakamoto and Chapman, 2010).

FORMS OF CROSS-BORDER COLLABORATION

A considerable literature distinguishes among types of cross-border collaboration in higher education. Consequently, definitional issues will be addressed only briefly in this paper. Furthermore, 'collaboration' and 'partnership' are used interchangeably (Sakamoto and Chapman, 2010).

Three forms of cross-border collaboration are widely advocated as strategies for improving the quality, relevance and, in some cases, financing of higher education.

First, international *collaboration in the delivery of instruction*, including such mechanisms as student exchange, branch campuses and joint degree programmes, is seen as one way of internationalizing curricula and increasing tuition revenues. Second, cross-border *partnerships in non-instructional activities* include collaboration in, for example, research, faculty development and accreditation. Third, *Cross-national harmonization* of curricula and operating regulations are offered as a means of increasing student mobility and facilitating the cross-national assessment of instructional quality. Each of these forms of collaboration offers benefits, but also poses challenges and risks.

Collaborations Focused on Instruction

While the rationale for cross-border instructional programmes is widely discussed in the higher education literature (Chapman et al., 2010; International Association of Universities, 2005; Knight, 2007), the consensus is that the dominant motive of those *exporting* instructional programmes is revenue generation, while the main motive of those *importing* these programmes tends to be to increase access and build educational capacity (Kot, 2010).

A typology of six categories for student mobility includes: branch campuses, independent institutions, acquisition/mergers, study centre/teaching sites, affiliation/networks, and virtual universities (Knight, 2005). With the exception of networks and virtual universities, these programmes have largely been developed through the physical presence of an institutional programme in an overseas location. Programmes abroad are similar to those offered at the home institution. Financing is clear-cut with tuition paid for credits earned.

As higher education institutions launch new types of joint and dual degree programmes, branch campuses, and franchising agreements, and in some cases construct campuses in foreign settings, college administrators may confront organizational issues well beyond those typically encountered at their home campus, for example differences in legal frameworks that can raise complex issues.

For the most part, unless there is a financial advantage to all parties in the cross-border collaboration, shared commitment and the sustainability of the programme will be at risk. Those risks exacerbate as up-front investments increase, for example when the partnership arrangement involves the construction of facilities, relocation of home-university faculty and on-site oversight of locally contracted instructors. The risk is real, as external circumstances can change in ways that may not be predictable at the time of programme launch. While revenue generation is likely to remain a dominant rationale for the expansion of branch campuses, long-term profits can be an uncertain proposition when regional economies decline or national political alliances shift.

Moving Campuses (Instead of Students) Across Borders

One manifestation of an instructional collaboration is to establish a branch campus. In periods of significant economic development, a country or region may see a rise in its number of branch campuses. Two such examples would be Japan in the 1980s and the current growth of educational cities in the Gulf region (Croom, 2010).

Today, only a handful of branch campuses remain in Japan compared with the over 30 US institutions that were established in the late 1980s to the early 1990s. Problems in maintaining these collaborations ranged from a lack of recognition by the Japanese Government of the degrees obtained, as well as Japanese companies failing to recruit students from these universities as they were seen as being different from traditional, national universities. Perhaps, with time, these problems could have been worked out; however, the economic recession of the 1990s, combined with a sharp population decrease in the 18 year-old cohort, proved to be insurmountable obstacles and most branch campuses chose to leave Japan.

The current hotbed of branch campus activity is in the Gulf region. Education City in Qatar and Dubai International Academic City in the United Arab Emirates (UAE) are not only branch campuses, but a collection of campuses designed into an overarching academic city. Currently, there are six US universities in Education City and 30 post-secondary institutions from around the world in the Dubai International Academic City. There are substantial differences in the philosophy behind the two ventures, ranging from capital investment to long-range vision.

It remains to be seen how successful the collaborations in these educational cities will be as pressures from the current economic crisis as well as the lack of employment opportunities for graduates continue. It is to be hoped that institutions will revisit the lessons learned by branch campus experiences such as those in Japan, to ensure that the opportunities for growth and institutional prestige align with the resources and mission of the educational cities in the Gulf region (Croom, 2010).

Collaboration Focused on Non-instructional Activities

A second and rapidly expanding area of collaboration has been the development of non-instructional partnerships, focused on such things as faculty development, research, technology sharing, joint science and technology initiatives, quality assurance, and delivery of non-academic services (Sakamoto and Chapman, 2010; Altbach, 2004; OECD, 2004). These non-instructional collaborations are generally less well understood than instructional collaborations, particularly as they often involve more complex financial arrangements than do instructional partnerships.

Oman: Cross-Border Collaboration for Quality Assurance

One non-instructional collaboration is illustrated by the Government of Oman's use of cross-border partnerships as a strategy for assuring the quality of private higher education in Oman (Al-Barwani, Ameen and Chapman, 2010).

When the Government of Oman legalized the private provision of higher education in the early 1990s, it lacked its own quality assurance system. To help ensure the quality of the new private colleges and universities, it required each of these institutions to enter into an affiliation with a more established college or university elsewhere in the world, with the intention that these pairings would serve as a quality assurance mechanism. The international partner was to oversee the quality of instructional content and delivery. For the most part this approach worked quite well and was widely judged to have been successful. One consequence, however, was that it led the Omani colleges and universities to adopt a wide variety of curricula and institutional operating procedures, as each took on characteristics of its international (e.g., Jordanian, Indian, US, Egyptian or British) partner.

The Oman experience eventually had an unexpected twist. Over time, concerns emerged among both government leaders and educators about the effectiveness of a few of the international partners in actually ensuring quality. This led the Government, in the mid-2000s, to establish its own national accreditation council, which sought to introduce more consistent standards across all institutions. Resistance emerged when institutional leaders realized that in order to accommodate a common accreditation framework many institutions would have to change their curricula and operating procedures, and in some cases would be subject to increased administrative and financial transparency. Additionally, they feared losing the advantages the affiliation system offered in student recruitment, as they would no longer be able to claim that their graduates would earn a degree issued by a British, French, US or Egyptian university. The resistance emerged not only from institutions involved in weak affiliations wishing to protect their prerogatives, but from institutions involved in strong affiliations that (accurately) thought their existing system was working fine and would be eroded by the anticipated changes. While the Oman case illustrates an initially successful non-instructional cross-border collaboration, those collaborations eventually came into conflict with the Government's own policies (Al-Barwani, Ameen and Chapman, 2010).

One of the main non-instructional areas in which there is substantial cross-border collaboration is research (Vincent-Lancrin, 2010), fuelled in part by the changing pattern of research funding across countries. Rapidly emerging economies, particularly in Asia, are increasingly the producers of scientific research, and governments in a number of these rapidly emerging economies are investing heavily in building research capacity (Chapman, Stolz and Glushko, 2010). Economies that are not members of the Organisation for Economic Co-operation and Development (OECD) are now spending substantially more on research and development (R&D) than in the past, while expenditure in many OECD countries is stagnant or falling (Chapman, Stolz and Glushko, 2010). From 11.7% of the world's R&D expenditure in 1996, non-OECD countries now account for 18.4% (OECD, 2008). For example, in the People's Republic of China, gross expenditure on research and development (GERD) increased by about 19% annually between 2001 and 2006, and reached US $86,800m. in 2006 (OECD, 2008; UNESCO, 2009). Despite the global financial crisis, the Chinese Government's budget for scientific research grew by 25.6% between 2008 and 2009. Similarly, between 2004 and 2005 GERD in South Africa rose by 12%. GERD increased from $9,000m. to $20,000m. in Russia between 1996 and 2006, while India spent $23,700m. in 2004.

One outgrowth of broadening the research enterprise to a wider set of countries is increased cross-border collaboration. Such collaborations are *motivated* by opportunities to tap multiple sources of funding, spread financial risk and sustain friendship patterns among researchers (Chapman, Stolz and Glushko, 2010). In some cases research has moved abroad in response to more favourable government regulatory policies (Senker, Enzing and Reiss, 2008). None the less, one implication of these shifting patterns is that a substantial new cadre of researchers is entering the scene in countries that have less well established research traditions, procedures and systems. This is likely to promote cross-border collaboration, as newer researchers seek collaboration as a way to further develop their own skills.

Harmonization of Higher Education Standards and Procedures

A third mode of cross-national collaboration is represented by international movements being undertaken to harmonize key aspects of higher education systems across countries. The general purpose of these efforts is to introduce more comparability and compatibility in admissions criteria, academic degree standards, graduation standards and quality assurance standards across participating countries (Adelman, 2008a, 2008b).

The best known of the harmonization efforts is the Bologna Process, involving 47 countries across Europe. Initiatives within the Bologna Process introduced increased clarity and transparency regarding length of study and qualifications associated with degree level, credit transfer and quality assurance (Adelman, 2008a, 2008b). One of its goals is to remove obstacles to student and academic mobility across universities in participating countries.

Harmonization of Higher Education Beyond the Bologna Process

While the Bologna Process in Europe is the best known harmonization effort, smaller initiatives are underway in other parts of the world. Since 1999 governments across Latin American and the Caribbean (most notably, Brazil, Mexico and St Christopher) have been working together and with some European governments (Spain and France) to promote comparability in programmes of study, mobility of students and staff, joint degrees and quality assurance.

In Africa, in an initiative led by the Association of African Universities, governments have entered into discussions about an African Higher Education Area aimed at, among other things, the harmonization of higher education policies and regulatory frameworks. A separate higher education harmonization initiative is under way among the West African Economic and Monetary Union (which includes Benin, Burkina Faso, Côte d'Ivoire, Guinea-Bissau, Mali, Niger, Senegal and Togo). Priority areas for this initiative include increasing student and staff mobility across institutions, mutual recognition of degree titles and revision of curricula in common fields of specialization.

Across Asia, multiple organizations have promoted cross-border harmonization efforts, including the Association of Southeast Asian Institutions of Higher Learning (ASAIHL), the ASEAN University Network (AUN), the Asia-Pacific Quality Network (APQN) and the Southeast Asian Ministers of Education Organization's Regional Centre for Higher Education and Development (SEAMEO-RIHED). The common themes that cut across these efforts generally include promoting collaboration around issues of teaching, research, student and staff mobility, and quality assurance (SEAMEO-RIHED, 2008).

Frameworks and Models for Thinking about Cross-Border Collaboration

Researchers have employed a variety of frameworks and models to help understand the pressures that impinge on these types of programmes (Kot, 2010; Sakamoto and Chapman, 2010). Jie (2010) framed her study of cross-border collaboration in terms of *game theory* (Davis, 1970), which concerns how people interact with each other to obtain their individual goals when their interests are interconnected. Child and Faulkner (1998) utilized *transaction cost theory*, which posits that such collaborations are motivated primarily by concern for efficiency. From this perspective, colleges and universities form alliances only if the transaction costs involved are perceived to be lower than those for the other options for achieving similar ends.

Resource dependency theorists, such as Pfeffer and Salancik (1978), propose that organizational survival depends on an organization's ability to acquire and maintain resources. From this perspective, cross-border collaborations emerge when college and university leaders believe they need to reach beyond their immediate environment to achieve their goals (e.g., generating more income or increasing institutional prestige). Cross-border cooperation represents a way to accomplish this. *Strategic positioning theory* posits that alliances are motivated by the desire to shape competition and consolidate an organization's market position (Porter, 1991). Universities enter into collaborations when their leaders believe that doing so will improve their relative market power and competitive positioning, for example by gaining access to a new market (Child and Faulkner, 1998).

Knight (2006, 2007) distinguishes between four types of cross-border education based on what or who moves across-borders: people, programmes, providers and projects/services. Sakamoto and Chapman (2010) offer a *functional model*, which posits that the willingness of higher education institutions to participate in cross-border partnerships is influenced by: a) organizational factors, such as anticipated payoffs balanced against their ability to absorb extra demands such programmes would generate; b) financial viability of the collaboration; c) faculty interest in and incentives for participating; and d) the larger political, legal and regulatory environment in which the collaboration would operate.

Among the common elements across these models is the recognition that collaborative arrangements carry inherent instability (Bannerman et al., 2005; Parkhe, 1993). Each partner is vulnerable to the actions of the others due to the uncertainty of the other partner's future behaviour. The absence of a shared vision, trust, commitment and effective communication among partners is often a key factor contributing to programme erosion and potential termination (Heffernan and Poole, 2004).

ISSUES IN CROSS-BORDER COLLABORATION

This leads us to a consideration of some of the main issues that confront cross-border collaborations. Regardless of the form of cross-border collaboration, there is one common characteristic: all parties believe that they are presumably gaining as much or more than they are giving. However, institutional leaders on each side may not be valuing the same aspects. Indeed, these educators may not fully understand the motivations of their partners or values that underlie partner decisions. Even when both partners believe they are benefiting from the collaboration, their motivations, assessments of activities and outcomes, and the value of said activities and outcomes may differ (Sakamoto and Chapman, 2010). Therefore, it becomes necessary for those considering cross-border collaborations to examine the factors that contribute to successful partnerships and become more aware of the complexity involved.

Where misunderstandings and disagreements tend to emerge during programme implementation centres on standards of student admissions, differences in teaching methods, different approaches to assessing student learning, limited resource support from the parent university and management issues (Jie, 2010). Often these conflicts can be traced to the different perceptions and expectations the partner institutions have for each other and for the collaborative programme. Such disagreements have the potential to undermine trust among partners and their commitment to the programme. As a consequence, well-intentioned administrators and educators involved in cross-border educational programmes often find themselves unprepared, and in unexpected and confronting circumstances (Jie, 2010; Larsen et al., 2005).

New forms of cross-border partnership may necessitate new organizational arrangements and policies as, for example, laws that regulate land rights, quality assurance, awarding of degrees, treatment of human subjects in research studies and intellectual property rights may differ between countries. Differences in partners' views as to what constitutes appropriate faculty responsibilities, work-load and pedagogy can lead to misunderstandings that fuel tension. Institutional policies that have evolved from substantial experience may be deemed curious and irrelevant by international partners who operate from the lens of their own history and experience.

The college administrators of these cross-border programmes may confront organizational issues to which they are unaccustomed at their home campus, including differences in legal frameworks. For instance, a cross-border campus of an institution that operates as a public university in its home country may be legally constituted as a private institution in the partner country (Croom, 2010).

Money is often at the centre of tensions that arise. Financial return is generally not the only motivation in the move of colleges and universities to enter into cross-border partnerships, but it is repeatedly identified as a major factor (Kot, 2010; Olcott, 2009). As cross-border collaborations involve more complex sets of activities that, in turn, involve greater upfront investment in on-site facilities and staffing, financial risks increase and are harder for partners to anticipate and manage.

The initial impetus for participation in cross-border collaboration may indeed come from individual faculty champions, but, as collaborations develop and merge into their own unique identities, the role of the faculty champion may be eclipsed by new levels of interest on the part of university administrators, national governments and international organizations. A related consideration, however, is the need for institutional leaders to be alert in assessing the different opportunities and risks associated with an individual faculty champion's initial efforts at more non-conventional cross-border collaborations.

In their recent volume on cross-border higher education, Chapman and Sakamoto (2010) offer eight cross-cutting observations about the issues posed by the rise of so many new forms of international partnership. They observe that:

1) Cross-impacts emerge from the greater complexity found in the recent forms of cross-border collaboration.

2) The lack of a dominant model for cross-border collaboration results in diversity that is positive in its creativity, but lessons learned may not be generalized across borders.

3) There is less experience upon which to draw for non-instructional-based collaborations and unintended conflict may occur.

4) Operational problems may sometimes be ignored in the need to 'save face' of institutional identity.

5) The role of the faculty champion is moving towards integration within institutional leadership.

6) Governments are becoming more aware of the benefits of cross-border collaboration in promoting larger agendas and thus bottom-up initiatives are now not always the norm.

7) Cross-border collaborations require a long-term approach as there is no quick return on investment.

8) Cross-border collaborations serve as an example of how higher education institutions are addressing social policy beyond the classroom walls.

CONCLUSION

As borders become less relevant in the delivery of higher education, the nature of cross-border partnerships in higher education is changing. Benefits of such collaborations can be significant, but cannot be assumed. Done well, such collaborations provide a significant source of innovative thinking, creative sharing and, possibly, economic return. However, there are also risks. As cross-border collaborations become more institutionalized, require more upfront investment and take on greater complexity, the consequences increase of champions losing interest, disagreement emerging among partner institutions, and regulatory, political and economic changes taking place in the larger environment. None the less, the move towards expanding cross-border partnerships in higher education will continue. Those intent upon pursuing partnerships across borders should be well aware of the changing nature of these collaborations, in order to plan more strategically to be successful over the long term.

BIBLIOGRAPHICAL REFERENCES

Adelman, C. *The Bologna Club: What U.S. Higher Education Can Learn from a Decade of European Reconstruction*. Institute for Higher Education Policy, 2008a.

Learning Accountability from Bologna: A Higher Education Policy Primer, ISSUE BRIEF. Institute for Higher Education Policy, 2008b.

Al-Barwani, T., Ameen, H. and Chapman, D. W. 'Cross-border collaboration for quality assurance in Oman: Contested Terrain', in Chapman, D. W., and Sakamoto, R., *Cross-Border Partnerships in Higher Education: Strategies and Issues*. New York, USA, Routledge, 2010.

Altbach, P. G. 'Higher education crosses borders', *Change*, 36(2), 2004, pp. 18–24.

Bannerman, P., Spiller, J., Yetton, P., and Davis, J. *Strategic alliances in education and training: A literature review*. Canberra, Australia, Department of Education Science and Training (DEST), 2005.

Bennell, P. and Pearce, T. 'The internationalization of higher education: exporting education to developing and transitional economies', *International Journal of Educational Development*, 23, 2, 2002, pp. 215–32.

Bureau for Economic Analysis. *Trade in goods and services*. Washington D.C., 2007, available at www.bea.gov.

Chapman, D. W. 'Higher Education, Part 3', in Ordonez, V., Johanson, R., and Chapman, D. W., *Investing in Education in the Asia-Pacific Region in the Future: A strategic education sector study*. Manila, Philippines, Asian Development Bank, 2007.

Chapman, D. W., Cummings, W. K., and Postiglione, G. A. (eds). *Crossing borders in East Asian Higher Education*. New York, Springer Publishing, 2010.

Chapman, D. W. and Sakamoto, R. 'The Future of cross-border partnerships in higher education', in Chapman, D. W., and Sakamoto, R. (eds), *Cross-border partnerships in higher education: Strategies and issues*. New York, USA, Routledge, 2010.

Chapman, D. W., Stolz, I., and Glushko, H. 'National variations in the organization of scientific research', in Anderson, M. S., and Steneck, N. H. (eds), *International Research Collaborations: Much to be Gained, Many Ways to Get in Trouble*. New York, USA, Routledge, 2010.

Child, J. and Faulkner, D. *Strategies of cooperation: Managing alliances, networks, and joint ventures*. New York, Oxford University Press, 1998.

Croom, P. 'Motivation and aspirations for international branch campuses', in Chapman, D. W., and Sakamoto, R. (eds), *Cross-border collaborations in higher education: Strategies and issues*. New York, USA, Routledge, 2010.

Davis, M. D. *Game Theory: A Nontechnical Introduction*. New York and London, UK, Courier Dover Publications, 1970.

Godfrey, J. 'Oh, Brave World: Finding the right assumptions', paper presented at the Conference on Challenges and Tensions in International Research Collaborations, University of Minnesota, Minneapolis, USA, 22 October 2008.

Heffernan, T. and Poole, D. '"Catch me I'm falling": key factors in the deterioration of offshore education partnerships', *Journal of Higher Education Policy and Management*, 26(1), 2004, pp. 75–90.

International Association of Universities (IAU). *2005 IAU Global Survey Report on the Internationalization of Higher Education: New Directions, New Challenges*. Paris, France, UNESCO, 2005.

Jie, Y. 'Cross-border higher education: An analysis of international inter-organizational collaboration'. Department of Educational Policy and Administration, Minneapolis, University of Minnesota (unpublished paper), 2010.

Knight, J. 'Cross-border Education: An Analytical Framework for Program and Provider Mobility', in Smart, J., and Tierney, W. (eds), *Higher Education: Handbook of Theory and Practice*.

Dordrecht, the Netherlands, Springer Academic Publishers, 2005.

Higher Education Crossing Borders: A Guide to the Implications of GATS for Cross-border Education. Paris, France, Commonwealth of Learning and UNESCO, 2006.

'Cross-border Tertiary Education: An Introduction', in *Cross-border Tertiary Education: A Way Towards Capacity Development*. Paris, France, OECD, World Bank and NUFFIC, 2007, pp. 21–46.

Kot, F. C. 'Factors Associated with Partnership Experiences, Attitudes, and Perceptions in Southern Africa: Case Study of an Anglophone and a Francophone University'. (Unpublished paper) Department of Organizational Leadership, Policy and Development, Minneapolis, USA, University of Minnesota, 2010.

Larsen, K., Momii, K., and Vincent-Lancrin, S. *Cross-border Higher Education: an analysis of current trends, policy strategies and future scenarios*. London, UK, The Observatory on Borderless Higher Education, 2005.

OECD. *Internationalization and Trade of Higher Education— Opportunities and Challenges*. Paris, France, Organisation for Economic Co-operation and Development, 2004.

OECD science, technology and industry outlook. Paris, France, OECD, 2008. Available www.sourceoecd.org/scienceIT/9789264049918 (accessed 18 January 2009).

Olcott, D., Jr. 'Global Connections to Global Partnerships: Navigating the Changing Landscape of Internationalism and Cross-Border Higher Education', *The Journal of Continuing Higher Education*, 57, 2009, pp. 1–9.

Parkhe, A. '"Messy" Research, Methodological Predispositions, and Theory Development in International Joint Ventures', *Academy of Management Review*, 18, 2, 1993, pp. 227–68.

Pfeffer, J. and Salancik, G. R. *The external control of organizations: A resource dependence perspective*. New York, USA, Harper & Row, 1978.

Porter, M. E. 'Towards a Dynamic Theory of Strategy', *Strategic Management Journal*, 12, 1991, pp. 95–117.

Saffu, D. and Mamman, A. 'Contradictions in international tertiary strategic alliances: the case from down under', *International Journal of Public Sector Management*, 16, 6, 2000, pp. 508–18.

Sakamoto, R. and Chapman, D. W. 'Expanding across borders: The growth of cross-border partnerships in higher education', in Chapman, D. W., and Sakamoto, R. (eds), *Cross-border partnerships in higher education: Strategies and issues*. New York, USA, Routledge, 2010.

SEAMEO-RIHED. *Harmonization of Higher Education: Lessons Learned from the Bologna Process*, Lecture Series, Number 1, February 2008.

Senker, J., Enzing, C., and Reiss, T. 'Biotechnology policies and performance in central and eastern Europe', *International Journal of Biotechnology*, 10, 4, 2008, pp. 341–61.

UNESCO. *UNESCO Institute for Statistics database*, 2009. Available stats.uis.unesco.org/unesco/ReportFolders/Report Folders.aspx?IF_ActivePath=P,54&IF_Language=eng (accessed 18 February 2010).

Vincent-Lancrin, S. 'Cross-border Higher Education and the Internationalization of Academic Research', in Chapman, D. W., and Sakamoto, R. (eds). *Cross-Border Partnerships in Higher Education: Strategies and Issues*. New York, USA, Routledge, 2010, pp. 93–114.

INTERNATIONAL RESEARCH COLLABORATIONS
ANTICIPATING CHALLENGES INSTEAD OF BEING SURPRISED

MELISSA S. ANDERSON

Research has always been, in large measure, a global enterprise. The search for new knowledge is undertaken everywhere in the world, and researchers are typically among the best-travelled members of any community. Participation in international networks is a signature activity of top researchers, and most scientists take advantage of education, conferences and exchanges outside their own countries. Indeed, the walls of academic offices are often miniature museums, exhibiting collections of artefacts from far-flung adventures.

At present, there is considerable interest in expanding a particular form of global interaction: international research collaboration, that is, research pursued jointly by scientists whose primary institutional affiliations are in different countries. The emphasis here is not on researchers merely learning from each others' ongoing work, but rather on cross-national teams jointly initiating, pursuing and owning research projects. These ventures range from projects involving two people from different countries, to mid-sized international groups pursuing a line of research, to major ventures involving cooperation among international teams and substantial investment from participating countries (as in the case of the Large Hadron Collider). It is not the size or degree of formality that distinguishes these collaborative projects; it is instead the joint nature of the research process across national boundaries.

Research institutions and funding agencies, like researchers themselves, are increasingly interested in the benefits of international collaboration. Funders' enthusiasm for joint efforts is matched by scientists' eagerness to take advantage of the broader research agendas and opportunities in the international arena. At both levels, however, eagerness to 'go global' often outpaces awareness of the attendant complications. A recent volume on international research collaborations (Anderson and Steneck, 2010) calls attention to a wide variety of challenges embedded in international research. This essay's framework and examples derive largely from that volume.

EXPANSION OF INTERNATIONAL RESEARCH COLLABORATIONS

Authorship is one way of tracking the development of cross-national collaboration. Lists of co-authors from different countries indicate successful, productive collaborations, but, as such, they significantly underestimate the extent of international work, as many collaborations are delayed or unsuccessful in yielding publications, even if they generate useful outcomes of other kinds. Still, trends in international authorship provide evidence of significant growth in cross-national collaboration.

Bruce Alberts (2010), the editor of *Science*, one of the most prestigious international scientific journals, noted recently that over half of the papers published in the journal in 2009 were co-authored by international teams. Data from the US National Science Board (2010) provide relevant trend analysis. Between 1988 and 2007 the percentage of science and engineering articles worldwide that involved international authorship rose from 8% to 22%. The effects of Europe's promotion of international projects are evident in this measure: European international co-authorship rose from 22.4% to 49.9% in the same period. By contrast, the comparable increase in the People's Republic of China was from 22.4% to 24.8%.

Other measures of international collaboration are less reliable. Funding mechanisms that encourage or require international cooperation provide only a partial estimation of collaborative activity. Most research funding is allocated intranationally, and international collaborators often pool funding from their own sources to support their joint research, adding substantially to overall investment in international ventures.

Migration of graduate students and postdoctoral fellows is another rather unsatisfactory measure, as advanced training has always involved significant numbers of international students, and their numbers fluctuate in part on the basis of political conditions in the relevant countries, which may have little to do with changes in research intensiveness. Suffice it to say that participation by trainees in research outside their home countries always accounts for a significant portion of international collaboration.

REASONS FOR INTERNATIONAL COLLABORATION

To some, cross-national research might seem self-evidently valuable or even necessary, as international collaboration becomes the norm in many fields, particularly the sciences. Motivations for international work are not always transparent, however, and sometimes they stem from questionable aims.

Of course, most researchers initiate collaborations because of their desire to work with particular people whose work they have admired or who are pursuing similar lines of inquiry. Specialization of research fields often means that one's closest peers in an area of study are few in number and dispersed around the globe. Connections are made by e-mail or by sharing the stage at a conference symposium. Scientists get in touch through mutual collaborators or service on committees. In any case, researchers inhabit small worlds of research expertise (Clark, 1987) in which they are familiar with most of the other potentially collaborative (or competitive) teams.

The imperatives of specific research problems can also promote international collaboration. The objects of scientific study (e.g., glaciers, malarial swamps, inbred populations) are not evenly distributed around the globe. Research at distant sites increasingly involves participation of local or regional collaborators. Equipment or materials can also prompt collaborative work. At times, incoming researchers need to rely on local access to proper equipment, and in other cases local researchers benefit from equipment manufactured in other countries and brought in by collaborators.

Some ventures require infrastructure far beyond equipment. Major scientific initiatives may require a decade's worth of construction and preparation that no country would be willing or able to fund alone. Worldwide clinical trials are often beyond the scope of any individual nation's capacity to fund and manage. Such 'big-science' projects depend on multinational investment and shared risk. Funding agencies, partly in recognition of these benefits, are now more frequently recommending or insisting upon cross-national components in the work that they support. They thereby provide strong incentives for researchers to find partners outside their home countries.

There are also times when potential collaborators are motivated more by a desire for affiliation with top researchers than by any substantive connection with them. Researchers in the developing world have less ready access to publication outlets, funding and peer networks. Their stature in their own countries and globally can be enhanced by affiliation with well-known researchers in research-intensive nations, who sometimes contribute in only cursory ways. For example, when Hwang Woo-suk of the Republic of Korea (South Korea) was charged with fraudulent research and other offences, his US collaborator, Gerald Shatten, was implicated. Shatten had agreed to serve as senior author on one of the initially most acclaimed but ultimately fraudulent publications, though his actual contribution was limited to revising the manuscript. Hwang was found guilty of embezzlement and ethics violations (Akst, 2009); Shatten was cleared of misconduct but declared guilty of misbehaviour through irresponsibility (Holden,

2006). In another case, Pattium Chiranjeevi, a researcher in India, added dozens of researchers to papers that reported fictitious experiments, in an effort to increase the likelihood of success in publication (Schulz, 2008).

Even less acceptable motives drive some international collaborations. Researchers have been known to focus data-collection efforts in countries that have under-developed or non-existent regulations on the use of human subjects. Doing so can significantly ease the burdens of paperwork and compliance, but it can also put research subjects at risk, without access to mechanisms of redress. One hears stories of researchers who have followed the examples of multi-national corporations and have sited their research where costs will be low, usually because of cheap labour or access to large numbers of subjects whose participation can be bought at a low price. Corruption can be a major deterrent to international collaboration, but some researchers find it easier to work where payments to officials will hasten approvals.

On balance, however, most researchers conduct their international research with integrity and in a spirit of adventure. Scientists get caught up in the excitement of travel, as they become more familiar with other cultures and extend their work's impact to other countries. Collaborations are far easier to manage since the advent of the internet, other electronic networks, inexpensive telephone connections and expanded international air travel. Indeed, young scientists have grown up in a globally connected world. Their experience leads them to be not only open to international research but often dismissive of research that is constrained by national borders.

TRIPPING OVER DIFFERENCES

Driven by the momentum of expanding collaborations and a variety of motivations, many researchers are eager to begin or extend their international work. They may focus on particular objectives in working internationally, or they may have only a general sense of the attractiveness of international projects. They often do not pay much attention to how the international nature of the work will complicate their efforts.

These complications are part of most collaborations, but they come particularly to light when something goes wrong. If improprieties derail a project, the parties often initially blame language differences or cultural misunderstanding. Language is an obvious potential source of miscommunication. Culture represents differences in assumptions, expectations, roles, work styles and so on, which researchers encounter among their international colleagues but often do not fully understand. In blaming either of these factors, researchers seem to suggest that if only all parties could 'be on the same page' in approaching the work to be done, problems in international research would be no worse than those in domestic projects.

The problem with this thinking is that researchers from different countries often *cannot* be on the same page. There are significant differences in national research systems that pose challenges in international collaborations. These differences are largely invisible to or ignored by many researchers who embark on cross-national work, precisely because they are accustomed to taking their own national research systems for granted. This essay and the book on which it draws (Anderson and Steneck, 2010) focus on the influence of these systems on international collaboration, not denying the role that culture plays, but suggesting that vague cultural factors have too often been blamed for problems that may stem from fundamental national differences in the organization, support and conduct of research.

CHALLENGES DUE TO DIFFERENCES IN NATIONAL RESEARCH SYSTEMS

National research systems encompass all the institutions and activities involved in the conduct and support of research. Many differences in national research systems can affect the course of an international collaborative effort. Some differences are quite obvious. If a researcher is accustomed to good facilities and readily available supplies, working with a collaborator who has neither can require considerable adjustment in budgets, schedules, conceptualization of the project

and personal expectations. If a researcher has been working in a country where personal connections and influence are the keys to access in research, it can be quite a challenge to work within an elaborate system of regulation and oversight.

Four dimensions of national research systems are of particular relevance to research collaborations: the organization of the research system (including funding mechanisms), legal and regulatory systems, oversight related to research integrity, and the training of graduate students and postdoctoral fellows. Each is considered here, with illustrations largely from Anderson and Steneck (2010).

Organization of the Research System

Perhaps the most basic systemic feature relevant to research collaborations is how the actual work of research is organized and funded. Institutional structures shape each nation's distinctive research enterprise, including where the work is done (Chapman et al., 2010). In some countries, notably in Central Asia, much of the work is done in research institutes. In others, such as the USA, non-commercial research is done largely in research universities, with a complementary sector of government research facilities in specific locations. In China, the Chinese Academy of Science has laboratories spread across many universities. Emerging pan-European research facilities, such as the European Spallation Source, will play increasingly important roles.

The distribution of research across sectors can be illustrated by research profiles in three Asian contexts (LaRocque, 2007). In Hong Kong 64% of research and development is done in the academic sector, with 33% in the business sector and 3% in the government sector. By contrast, in Japan the academic sector accounts for only 14% of research and development, with business and the government doing 75% and 9%, respectively. Indonesia represents a third distinctive profile, with a mere 5% of research and development in the academic sector and only 14% in the business sector, but 81% in the government sector.

Governments also vary in the extent to which they control research agendas. Some exert a great deal of central control over the direction and scope of research done, to the extent that the priorities of the research system become largely indistinguishable from national priorities. In such cases, national funding usually flows through ministries of science and technology directly to universities, in support of national goals for science. By such means, China has promoted expansive, rapid increases in production of applied research. The USA has taken a more investigator-driven approach to funding and has focused far more attention and investment in basic science. Priorities set by the US Congress and the federal funding agencies do play important roles in shaping research through funding mechanisms, but to a lesser extent than in many other countries. The European Union Framework Programmes have played a role in both altering the organization of research across Europe and in influencing the direction of research by channelling investment to promising areas of inquiry.

Cross-sector collaborative initiatives are supported in some countries and difficult to navigate in others. The US Bayh-Dole Act, for example, has encouraged substantial collaboration between universities and industry by providing mandates and incentives for such cooperation (Bohnhorst et al., 2010). By this Act, the commercial potential of research that is funded by the federal government and conducted at universities must be considered; if such research leads to commercialized products, universities are able to capture some of the revenues through patents and licensing, despite the project's original funding from government sources.

Organizational differences in research systems need to be considered at the local as well as national level. Research systems differ in terms of authority structures, communication networks and decision making. Most scientific research is done in teams, but norms of authority within teams are not universal. In open systems, members of a research group are encouraged and expected to contribute ideas related to the direction of research projects, quite beyond the scope of their assigned work, even if their ideas challenge the project leader. In other systems, project direction is considered the responsibility of the principal investigator, who is not to be openly challenged.

Communication patterns are likewise affected by varying norms. In some contexts, researchers are accustomed to interacting only with those in collaborating groups at the same hierarchical level, while in other national systems it is common for communication to cross hierarchical levels, both within and across teams.

Researchers who are interested in establishing international collaborations may not be aware of organizational and funding differences that can complicate their work. There is no reason to assume that the structural and funding properties of a potential collaborator's institutional home will necessarily impinge on the work to be done, but awareness of organizational differences can help one anticipate problems.

For example, most researchers setting out to initiate an international project do not consider the role of the diplomatic corps. There are times, however, when diplomatic knowledge of a country's institutional structures and research-related norms can deflect problems. Handley (2010) recounts one such situation. A US researcher working in sub-Saharan Africa set out to study the nursing care given by traditional midwives and by nurses in government hospitals. The research team acquired consent from the patients, the institutions involved and the midwives, and they videotaped the caregivers in interaction with patients. When the findings, including the videotaped interactions, were presented at a seminar, it was clear that the care provided by the nurses fell far short of the care given by traditional midwives. The problem was that the seminar was attended by senior government health officials and college administrators. The seminar erupted into a volley of pointed questions and the administrators confiscated the videotapes. Handley's point in providing this illustration is that US diplomats could have provided valuable information concerning the government's wariness about criticism of government officials and traditional versus medical models of care, as well as the role of family members in providing consent to participate in research projects in that country.

In most cross-national collaborations, even those free of sensitive issues, differences in organizational structures lead to complex management protocols. If there is little match or even harmonization between systems for managing budgets, purchasing, payments, materials and oversight, projects can be difficult to administer (Nebeker, 2010). These challenges are particularly pressing when the participating countries have significantly different laws pertaining to research.

Legal and Regulatory Requirements

Countries have different laws and different legal systems, a fact overlooked by many researchers who are eager to collaborate internationally. When working domestically, researchers may have little need to monitor legal requirements or consider the legal implications of their project decisions, largely because they can count on their institutions' staff to handle the legal side of things. In international collaborations, legal staff may themselves be challenged by very different legal requirements and ways of reconciling legal mandates.

Perhaps the most fundamental challenge in the case of mismatched laws is deciding whose laws apply in a given situation. Cross-national research may involve researchers from several nations, all of which may have different requirements. In some cases, contracts can be drawn up at the initiation of a collaboration, specifying whose laws will take precedence in the event of problems (Nebeker, 2010). In the absence of such contracts, legal issues can be a project's greatest headache and the easiest way for researchers to get in trouble.

Bohnhorst et al. (2010) describe a variety of legal challenges relevant to international collaborations. They describe, for example, the difference between European Union and US approaches to intellectual property. The former assumes from the start that intellectual property will be shared by all parties to the collaboration. The USA, through the Bayh-Dole Act, specifies that the parties to a collaboration have a right to intellectual property that they have created, but they are not expected to share that right with others who have not been involved in that creation. Indeed, as Bohnhorst et al. (2010)

note, certain parties to collaboration may simply not be the right people to move a project's output from basic research to commercialization.

Other legal constraints on international collaboration involve the payment of foreign taxes and dealing with passports. Tourist visas are generally easier and quicker to obtain, but collaborators who will be working in another country may not be able to use them; those who try to get by on tourist visas are sometimes detained abroad.

Each country has its own legal requirements, some of which are specific to another nation. Three such requirements in the USA are important worldwide, because of the extent of US participation in international collaborations (including clinical trials) and the serious consequences of violations of these laws. The first derives from US export control law, specifically the International Traffic in Arms Regulations (ITAR), and the Export Administration Regulations (EAR). The first addresses the export of items that have military purposes, and the second covers 'dual use' materials—that is, materials that have both military and non-military uses. Bohnhorst et al. (2010) describe a situation involving these regulations in a collaboration related to climate-change research. The scientists involved wished to transport an instrument to Iceland. The instrument had been used in the USA to map lake beds by sonar. It included, however, an 'inertia motion unit' that was designed to control for the motions of the boat during underwater mapping. This unit had a potential use in missile guidance systems, and it was reclassified from EAR to ITAR, necessitating an ITAR licence before the researchers could take the equipment to Iceland. Such complications can lead to considerable delays, which researchers must accommodate.

A second legal requirement specific to the USA is 'deemed export'. This derives from export control laws that refer to 'items' that may be exported. Under US law such items include information (Bohnhorst et al., 2010), with the consequence that information shared with someone from another country is deemed to have been exported to that country. In combination with restrictions on exports to certain countries, this provision substantially complicates access to information by people from these countries. Consider, for example, the situation of graduate students who work in a laboratory, some of whom are from countries covered by deemed export provisions. These students must not receive information that could have military use, and anyone who provides such information is subject to prosecution. There is, however, a 'Fundamental Research Exclusion' that exempts some basic research from deemed export requirements, but it is extremely important for US researchers and their collaborators to adhere strictly to deemed export rules, which apply even when the US researcher is working in another country.

A third US legal requirement is based on the Foreign Corrupt Practices Act, which addresses corruption, the payment of bribes, and questionable accounting practices. It prohibits any payment of a bribe by a US citizen to a foreign official or to someone who will forward it to a foreign official (Bohnhorst et al., 2010). Corruption has, unfortunately, been a part of the conduct of some collaborative research, as in some countries bureaucratic tangles can essentially stymie a project until a bribe is paid to clear the way. It is important for collaborative agreements with US participation to address the provisions of the Foreign Corrupt Practices Act at the beginning, to be sure that all parties are aware of the law and the consequences of violations.

Integrity Oversight

As legal issues can have serious consequences for international collaborations, so can matters of regulatory oversight. Of particular interest is compliance with policies and regulations that, unlike export control, are specific to research. Included here are policies related to the use of human and animal subjects in research and other policies intended to maintain the integrity of research.

Issues such as research misconduct can be very difficult to deal with in the international context. Boesz and Fischer (2010) present a case that is not, strictly speaking, related to international collaboration, but suggests the kinds of problems that arise when misconduct occurs internationally. A researcher from one country submitted a proposal to a funding agency in another county. The proposal was rejected, in part because of a highly negative review by one particular reviewer. Some time later the researcher was asked to review a proposal. Upon reading it, the researcher discovered that it included part of the text of the original proposal. It was found to have been submitted by the over-critical reviewer. This case of plagiarism was difficult to handle, particularly because it involved grant proposals, which are supposed to remain confidential during the review process. What made it even more difficult, of course, was that the researcher and the reviewer were from different countries.

This case highlights one of the most troubling aspects of international research: there is no body with authority to investigate and adjudicate cases of misconduct internationally (Steneck, 2010). Indeed, there is no shared, global definition of misconduct or approach to investigating it. Researchers who collaborate cross-nationally may find that they need to adhere to different standards than their domestic policies would require, and the project overall must satisfy the strictest provisions of all relevant regulations.

Recent initiatives have addressed the need for harmonization of policies related to research misconduct and oversight. The Global Science Forum of the Organisation for Economic Co-operation and Development (OECD) consulted widely among international officials and experts in the field and, after a workshop in Tokyo in 2007, issued a statement on best practices for ensuring scientific integrity and preventing misconduct (OECD, 2007). The statement identifies core research misconduct as fabrication, falsification and plagiarism, as in the US federal definition of misconduct. It also, however, identifies a range of other types of misconduct, including research practice misconduct (e.g., poor research design, inappropriate treatment of human and animal subjects), data-related misconduct (e.g., inappropriate data management, withholding data), publication-related misconduct (e.g., inappropriate authorship practices, failing to correct errors in the record), personal misconduct (e.g., inadequate mentoring, harassment), and financial/other misconduct (e.g., misuse of research funds, inappropriate peer review) (OECD, 2007). After release of the best-practices statement, a Co-ordinating Committee for Facilitating International Research Misconduct Investigations (2009) was appointed, which issued a final report along with a Practical Guide to investigating allegations in the context of international collaborative research. These efforts and others (Stainthorpe, 2010) may prove influential in moving countries toward harmonized approaches to defining and addressing ethical challenges in research.

Two conferences on research integrity represent another approach to fostering harmonized—if not common—approaches. The First World Conference on Research Integrity, held in Lisbon in 2007 (www.esf.org/index.php?id=4479), was an opportunity for officials, policymakers and researchers to discuss their varying conceptions of research integrity and to suggest ways of handling integrity issues in the cross-national context. The Second World Conference in Singapore during the summer of 2010 (www.wcri2010.org) was to focus on moving toward consensus on some fundamental aspects of integrity, notably in four areas: publication ethics, official responses to misconduct, codes of ethics and instruction in the responsible conduct of research. To the extent that some degree of consensus can be reached in these critical areas, it will support the development of cross-national or even global approaches for handling misbehaviour in research.

In the absence of global mechanisms for integrity oversight, US standards and policies often serve as the framework for ensuring ethical behaviour in research. US influence in this area is bolstered by the large US investment in international research projects and by the highly articulated US system of integrity oversight through the Office of Research Integrity in the Department of Health and Human Services, the Office of the Inspector General of the National Science Foundation, and the Office of Human Research Protections, among others. Capron (2010) argues that US dominance in this area is both

unfortunate and inappropriate, but concludes that until a system of global governance of research ethics is established, the US system will continue to exert undue influence. De Vries et al. (2010) likewise discuss the challenges of reconciling Western conceptions of bioethics and the norms of research with non-Western approaches to ethical dilemmas.

Training of Graduate Students and Postdoctoral Fellows

Most research teams involve young researchers as well as senior investigators. Students and postdoctoral fellows are critical to the success of most research projects, because they are often the ones who collect the data, run the experiments and do the actual analyses under the supervision of the principal investigators. Trainees often participate fully in cross-national research projects as well.

Of course, these young scientists themselves represent an international component, if their training is outside their home countries. They account for a substantial proportion of cross-national scholarly migration, and the work they do with foreign supervisors is perhaps the most common form of international research collaboration. As such, this form of collaboration is subject to all the complications discussed above but also involves problems specific to training.

For example, countries differ in terms of the extent of independent or individual doctoral study (Anderson et al., 2010). In the USA doctoral students typically take courses and most doctoral programmes are run by academic departments with oversight by an institution-level graduate school. By contrast, in some European and Asian countries doctoral study is significantly more individually oriented, with very little coursework, if any, and with supervision largely at the level of the academic adviser (Shaw in Anderson et al., 2010; Jie in Anderson et al., 2010). In Japan, students are trained in the *koza* system, which emphasizes hierarchical structure and harmonious relationships among the members of the research team (Kamata in Anderson et al., 2010).

Young researchers also have differential access to and motivation for internationally collaborative work. Most doctoral students in China are not able to defend their dissertations until they have published in the core journals, and usually the publications must be in nationally or internationally recognized journals (Jie in Anderson et al., 2010). In Brazil also, students are encouraged to submit manuscripts to English-language, internationally recognized journals before completion of their doctoral work (Vasconcelos and Sorenson in Anderson et al., 2010). In Kazakhstan, as in other former members of the USSR (Union of Soviet Socialist Republics), successive waves of educational reform have led to instabilities in graduate education and great interest in partnering with researchers in other countries, despite challenges of access to information and equipment (Kuzhabekova in Anderson et al., 2010). Such challenges are far greater in the Democratic Republic of Congo, where access to information, facilities, technology and researchers with advanced training are all compromised by inadequate institutional infrastructure and political and economic instability (Chiteng Kot in Anderson et al., 2010).

Researchers who themselves have been trained under different systems should be aware that the young investigators on an international project may have different assumptions and expectations about how work and interactions should be conducted. Given the critical contributions that students and postdoctoral fellows make to research projects, it is important for all senior researchers to know how the young investigators have been trained, what they know about regulatory and legal compliance, what kind of supervision they receive, and what they hope to gain professionally from the collaborative experience.

CONCLUSION

International research collaborations will continue to expand as the world becomes more globally connected. Problems that know no national boundaries attract international research teams who find it progressively easier to communicate, travel and co-ordinate their joint activities. They take on the practical challenges of working across different time zones, trying to get materials shipped despite uncertain carriers and customs practices, and dealing with the strains of travel and living abroad. The annoyances that plague any traveller are often magnified under the pressures of trying to complete research projects with collaborators on the other side of the globe. As first-time collaborators figure out how to cope with these practical difficulties, they would do well also to pay attention to the kinds of national differences discussed here.

BIBLIOGRAPHICAL REFERENCES

Akst, J. 'No jail time for Hwang', *The Scientist NewsBlog*, 26 October 2009. Available at www.the-scientist.com/blog/print/56117/ (accessed 3 November 2009).

Alberts, B. 'Editorial: Promoting Scientific Standards', *Science*, Vol. 327, 2010, 12.

Anderson, M. S., Chiteng Kot, F., Jie, Y., Kamata, T., Kuzhabekova, A., Lepkowski, C. C., Shaw, M. A., Sorenson, M. M. and Vasconcelos, S. M. R. 'Differences in National Approaches to Doctoral Education: Implications for International Research Collaborations', in Anderson, M. S., and Steneck, N. H. (eds) *International Research Collaborations: Much to be Gained, Many Ways to Get in Trouble*. New York, Routledge, 2010.

Anderson, M. S., and Steneck, N. H. (eds). *International Research Collaborations: Much to be Gained, Many Ways to Get in Trouble*. New York, Routledge, 2010.

Boesz, C. C. and Fischer, P. L. 'International Cooperation to Ensure Scientific Integrity', in Anderson, M. S., and Steneck, N. H. (eds) *International Research Collaborations: Much to be Gained, Many Ways to Get in Trouble*. New York, Routledge, 2010.

Bohnhorst, M. A., McQuaid, M., Tsantir, S. R. B, Amundson, D. M. and Anderson, M.S. 'Legal and Regulatory Considerations in International Research Collaborations', in Anderson, M. S., and Steneck, N. H. (eds) *International Research Collaborations: Much to be Gained, Many Ways to Get in Trouble*. New York, Routledge, 2010.

Capron, A. M. 'The Governance of Scientific Collaborations: The International Reach of US Law', in Anderson, M. S., and Steneck, N. H. (eds) *International Research Collaborations: Much to be Gained, Many Ways to Get in Trouble*. New York, Routledge, 2010.

Chapman, D. W., Stolz, I. and Glushko, O. 'National Variations in the Organization of Scientific Research', in Anderson, M. S., and Steneck, N. H. (eds) *International Research Collaborations: Much to be Gained, Many Ways to Get in Trouble*. New York, Routledge, 2010.

Clark, B. R. *The Academic Life: Small Worlds, Different Worlds*. Princeton, NJ, Carnegie Foundation for the Advancement of Teaching, 1987.

Co-ordinating Committee for Facilitating International Research Misconduct Investigations. *Final Report*. Organisation for Economic Co-operation and Development (OECD) Global Science Forum, 2009. Available at www.oecd.org/dataoecd/29/4/42713295.pdf (accessed 13 May 2010).

De Vries, R. G., Rott, L. M. and Paruchuri, Y. 'Normative Environments of International Science', in Anderson, M. S., and Steneck, N. H. (eds) *International Research Collaborations: Much to be Gained, Many Ways to Get in Trouble*. New York, Routledge, 2010.

Handley, F. G. 'Considerations Upon Setting Out to Collaborate Internationally', in Anderson, M. S., and Steneck, N. H. (eds) *International Research Collaborations: Much to be Gained, Many Ways to Get in Trouble*. New York, Routledge, 2010.

Holden, C. 'Schatten: Pitt Panel Finds "Misbehavior" but Not Misconduct', *Science*, Vol. 311, 2006, 928.

LaRocque, N. *The Role of Education in Supporting the Development of Science, Technology and Innovation in Developing Member Countries: An Issues Paper*. Manila, Asian Development Bank, 2007.

National Science Board. *Science and Engineering Indicators 2010*. Arlington, VA, National Science Foundation (NSB 10-01), 2010.

Nebeker, C. 'Proactive and Reactive Approaches to Facilitating International Collaborations', in Anderson, M. S., and Steneck, N. H. (eds) *International Research Collaborations: Much to be Gained, Many Ways to Get in Trouble*. New York, Routledge, 2010.

Organisation for Economic Co-operation and Development (OECD) Global Science Forum. *Best Practices for Ensuring Scientific Integrity and Preventing Misconduct*. 2007. Available at www.oecd.org/dataoecd/37/17/40188303.pdf (accessed 13 May 2010).

Schulz, W. G. 'A massive case of fraud: Journal editors are left reeling as publishers move to rid their archives of scientist's falsified research', *Chemical and Engineering News*, Vol. 86, 2008, 37–38.

Stainthorpe, A. C. 'Scientific Integrity in the Context of Pan-European Cooperation', in Anderson, M. S., and Steneck, N. H. (eds) *International Research Collaborations: Much to be Gained, Many Ways to Get in Trouble*. New York, Routledge, 2010.

Steneck, N. H. 'Research Integrity in the Context of Global Cooperation', in Anderson, M. S., and Steneck, N. H. (eds) *International Research Collaborations: Much to be Gained, Many Ways to Get in Trouble*. New York, Routledge, 2010.

THE ROLE OF HIGHER EDUCATION IN NATIONAL DEVELOPMENT

SOUTH-EASTERN EUROPE AND RECONSTRUCTION OF THE WESTERN BALKANS

PAVEL ZGAGA

INTRODUCTION: THE COMPLEXITY OF THE BALKANS

In this essay we focus on a European region that puzzles the uninformed observer with its huge diversity. This is South-Eastern Europe (SEE), also referred to as the Balkan Peninsula or simply the Balkans. The word 'Balkan' comes from Turkish, meaning a mountain chain. It is the name of a 600 km-long mountain range in the central part of the peninsula extending from Serbia across Bulgaria to the Black Sea. In geographical terms, the Balkans ends in the north at the banks of the Danube and Sava rivers and on the slopes of the Alps, while its coasts in the south are lapped by the waves of the Adriatic, Ionian, Aegean and Black Seas. The territories of some countries fit totally within this area (Albania, Bulgaria, Bosnia and Herzegovina, Greece, Kosovo, Macedonia and Montenegro), while others have larger, smaller and symbolic shares (Croatia, Romania, Serbia, Slovenia and Turkey, and a small slice of land around Trieste in Italy), or they only touch its borders (Moldova).

Definitions seem clear in geography textbooks, yet it is not easy to outline the region in cultural and political terms. Mutually comprehensible as well as incomprehensible languages are spoken, various scripts are used in writing and various religions are practised. Aboriginal tribes, the ancient Greeks and Romans, migrating hordes of the mid-first millennium, the Habsburgs and Ottomans, the armies of the First and Second World Wars—all have left their traces in the region.

Indeed, a purely geographic definition does not help much when discussing the region's politics and culture in general, or education in particular. In recent times, particularly during and after the wars of the 1990s, the phrase 'to balkanize' (already coined in local languages before then) was introduced into English. Within the region it became 'politically correct' to break with the Balkans—and to 'Europeanize'. However, the paths taken by, for example, Bulgaria and Serbia at the start of the 1990s were very different: while the former was negotiating to join the European Union (EU), the latter was experiencing North Atlantic Treaty Organization (NATO) bombing. The Balkans entered the third millennium perhaps even more diverse and divided than it was after the Second World War. Due to the negative connotations of 'the Balkans', the term 'South-Eastern Europe' started to be used more frequently. Yet this was deemed inadequate and so an additional name, in broad use today, came into being, again a 'politically correct' way of addressing that part of the region that suffered most and lost most in the transformations of the last two decades. It is the 'Western Balkans': the western part of SEE or the central part of the 'real' Balkans.

The focus here now narrows somewhat and we need a little more context. The Western Balkans is today usually understood to include Albania and the former Yugoslavia, but not Slovenia. With Albania as an exception, the remaining countries of the Western Balkans shared a considerable part of 20th-century political history and the heritage of a common state, Yugoslavia. Its roots only started to grow after the First World War in the Kingdom of Serbs, Croats and Slovenians. Following the Second World War, the Federal Socialist Yugoslavia, as 'neither an Eastern—nor a Western' country, was quite decentralized and after the mid-1960s it was more connected to the West (with 1m. workers abroad), than to the East. Albania to the south-west side of the peninsula was (self-)isolated up until the 1990s. Looking at the Balkans in a broader framework, Bulgaria and Romania belonged to the Soviet bloc, while Moldova was an integral part of the Union of Soviet Socialist Republics (USSR). To the south of the Balkans, Greece was, politically speaking, the frontier to the West.

It is not difficult to realize that such diverse contexts have also influenced the huge diversity seen in the region's higher education systems. The political context makes it easy to understand that after the Second World War Greek higher education took a very different path than that of other countries in the region. However, if these countries are simply put under the common label of 'communism', most of the elements that are important for understanding the transition and reconstruction during the last two decades are lost. Between 1945 and 1990 three different (and occasionally even hostile) political systems were confronted in this region: the countries of the Soviet bloc, the 'non-aligned' Yugoslavia and the 'autarchic' Albania. To discuss the role of higher education in recent social reconstruction it is necessary to set out the background, and therefore we start with a very brief outline of the regional history of higher education.

REGIONAL HIGHER EDUCATION IN AN HISTORICAL CONTEXT

Before 1500 there were no institutions of higher learning in the region. The closest universities were, for example, in Padua (established in 1222), Vienna (1365) and Pécs (1367). The division between the Habsburg Empire and the Ottoman Empire was not only political and economic, it had a deep cultural impact. In the period of the Counter-Reformation, the first colleges were established on the western and north-eastern edges of the region, and it is here that the history of its higher education began.

In the north-east, a Jesuit college was already founded in 1581 in Kolozsvár, Transylvania, today's Cluj in western Romania, but it was later closed. During the Enlightenment period a university was founded in Romania (in 1776), and its heritage and tradition of teaching in the Romanian and Hungarian languages belong today to the well-known Babeş-Bolyai University. Old roots can also be found in the city of Iaşi, on the eastern edges of today's Romania, right at the border with Moldova, where the Princely Academy was founded in 1642. In 1694 a similar institution was founded in Bucharest. The Alexandru Ioan Cuza University of Iaşi was established in 1860 as the first Romanian university, followed by the University of Bucharest in 1864.

To the west, the study of philosophy was provided at a Jesuit college in Ljubljana (in today's Slovenia) from 1595 onwards, and at another in Zagreb (in today's Croatia) after 1662. By 1669 the latter already had been granted the status and privileges of a university. The Jesuit order was dissolved in 1773 and this was the end of the early history of universities in the region. The second half of the 19th century, marked by growing industrialization and rising awareness among the nations of the Austro-Hungarian Empire, promoted the idea of national universities. Today's University of Zagreb dates back to 1874. Calls to establish a university in Ljubljana also appeared at that time, but were only realized after the First World War, in 1919.

In the central part of the region, which belonged to the Ottoman Empire, developments were quite different. Specific forms of higher learning were known here and were quite different from those in the 'Christian' parts of Europe. Thus, a *hanikah*, or higher school of *Sufi* philosophy was established in

Sarajevo in 1531, followed by a *medresa*, or Islamic higher school. The region was outside the direct influence of the Counter-Reformation or Enlightenment, although the cultural and political ideas that had started to spread right across Europe during the Age of Romanticism also found their way here and were embraced, particularly among Serbs. In the revolutionary Serbia that had rebelled against the Ottomans, the Belgrade Higher School (*velika škola*) was founded in 1808 and developed further over the following decades. Another step was taken with the foundation of the Lyceum in Kragujevac in 1838 and its close cooperation with Belgrade schools. The University of Belgrade was officially recognized by a royal charter from 1905. After the First World War, within the Kingdom of Serbs, Croats and Slovenians, the universities of Belgrade, Zagreb and Ljubljana formed a weak but important higher education infrastructure for the new common state.

As we can see, universities started to grow in the central part of the Balkans after the early 19th century—during the wars against the Ottoman regime and for national independence. The oldest university was the Othonian University, founded in 1837, in the early period of the independent, modern Greece (today's University of Athens). In Bulgaria, the St Clement of Ohrid University of Sofia was the first, established in 1888. The Ottoman Empire disappeared in the early 20th century and, between the First and Second World Wars, universities were operating in all new countries of the region, except Albania.

The Second World War erupted in the region in 1941. In Greece it ended with the arrival of the British and US armies, while in eastern parts of the region it involved the arrival of the Red Army. The new division of Europe was reflected in the region's higher education. In Bulgaria and Romania, radical alterations were made to follow the Soviet example: some professors were removed and some newly introduced, 'political' chairs were created, some former departments seceded to form separate institutions, and new ones were established, mainly in 'productive sectors' to strengthen 'the building of socialism'. Traditional academic cooperation with universities abroad was minimized and eastern, rather than Western, influence was reinforced. This was characteristic of the following decades: higher education institutions were a strong factor of the countries' development, but strong measures were always taken to silence any dissonant voices of a critical intelligentsia. However, many students and professors played important roles in the events leading up to and during 1989.

The immediate post-war situation was similar in Yugoslavia, but only to a certain degree. As fascism had been defeated independently of the Red Army, processes ran differently here, particularly after a quarrel with Stalin (Iosif Dzhugashvili) in 1947. At the end of the war, the three pre-war universities, two new universities that were soon established (Sarajevo and Skopje, both in 1949) and a few specialized colleges were involved in the reconstruction. They were institutions of federal units: one university in each of five of the six People's Republics (the University of Montenegro was only established in 1974). Their mission was to train 'highly qualified specialists in the various branches of study, of whom the country stands in need', as we can read in one of the earliest documents written for the international public (Uvalić, 1952: 13).

Yugoslavia had to search for its own identity and its own model—different from the Soviet one. In internal politics this was the so-called 'self-governmental socialism', and in foreign politics it was 'non-aligned movement'. Of course, this also had an effect on the education system. On the one hand, it was decentralized: quite a lot of responsibilities belonged to the Republics. On the other hand, it was much more open to international academic cooperation than the Soviet bloc, in particular after the 'liberal' reforms of 1965. There were also many students from non-aligned countries (Africa and Asia) in this period. Despite periodic repression, universities remained centres of critical thought, social protest and political activism (e.g. the 'Praxis group', student movements in 1968 and later, independent journals, 'alternative' art production, etc.).

During the period of the country's 'socialist self-governmental development', new higher education institutions were growing up. As a first step, almost as a rule, self-standing

(independent) faculties or higher schools were set up, which then associated to form a university. Between the late 1960s and mid-1980s a dozen new universities were established in all six Republics and in both Autonomous Provinces (Vojvodina and Kosovo within Serbia). In half a century higher education had changed its face totally. While in the 10 years of 1930–39 'from all universities in the country, 19,383 students graduated' (and 'of these only 1,288 were engineers'), in 1950 there was already a 'total of 52,480 students enrolled' and in 1960 '9,974 students graduated from Yugoslav universities' (Uvalić, 1952; Crvenkovski, 1962). Upon the disintegration of the federal Yugoslavia in 1990 (with a total population of 21m.), higher education was being provided 'through the existing 19 universities, made up of a total of 220 institutions (faculties and art academies). A total of 341,341 students (of whom 261,161 were regular full-time students) were enrolled in the academic year 1989–90' (Uvalić Trumbić, 1990: 399).

The development of higher education in Albania is a rather more unusual case. During the Ottoman period, use of the Albanian language in schools was totally prohibited and illiteracy remained extremely high far into the 20th century. In 1946 the illiteracy rate was estimated at 85% of the population. Albania became an independent country in 1912, but due to historic circumstances the development of a unified national education system only started after the First World War. Weak attempts at modernization were again stopped by the outbreak of the Second World War. In the post-war period Albania relied on Soviet and Yugoslav support, but had already broken contact with the 'Yugoslavian revisionists' in 1947. The impact of the Soviet model was strong up until 1960 when Albania also severed ties with the Soviets and started to build its own educational model.

The further development of communist Albania—bordering only with Yugoslavia, Greece and Italy across the sea, but not with the Eastern bloc—was autarchic. Nevertheless, education was an important item on the agenda. The weak and interrupted pre-war traditions in higher learning were reinforced by some new institutes established after the war, mainly according to the Soviet model. The state University of Tirana, also the leading higher education institution today, was founded in 1957 as the first Albanian university by combining five existing institutes, of which the oldest one—the Institute of Sciences—was founded in 1947. This remained the only Albanian university up until 1990, although some new institutes or their branches (e.g. in agriculture, teacher training, etc.) were also established during this period. It was crucial for a country that was closed to foreign influences to train its own human resources. It seems that this was quite a paradoxical endeavour. Nevertheless, by the late 1980s illiteracy was practically eliminated, there were already around 40,000 teachers in the country (with a total population of 3.1m.) and the proportion of youngsters continuing with secondary education had increased beyond two-thirds. However, the real growth and expansion of the higher education sector only started after the changes of 1989–90.

HIGHER EDUCATION IN THE WESTERN BALKANS DURING THE TRANSITION PERIOD

With the fall of the Berlin Wall in 1989, the countries of the Soviet bloc lost their 'tutor' and were suddenly free to decide where to go. For all of them, this period was extremely complex, painful and turbulent; however, the transition was mainly perceived as 'internal affairs', as the countries' borders did not change. The only two exceptions were Czechoslovakia, which decided to disintegrate peacefully and consensually into two independent countries, and the former German Democratic Republic (East Germany), which was integrated in the same peaceful way into the *Bundesrepublik*. Whereas a Third World War had been expected with great fear during the previous decades, the story now seemed to have reached a happy end. In the mid-1990s these countries were already associated with the EU and they joined the EU in 2004.

In Albania the political transition also remained within national borders, but it was quite another story. It started with the collapse of the autarchic regime and was followed by chaotic processes and social implosion. At the beginning of the 1990s the country entered an economic and political crisis which escalated into a breakdown of public order and mass vandalism. The education system suffered huge damage; it is reported that one-third of schools were ransacked. Many teachers left their schools in villages and migrated to cities or abroad. Normal life was gradually re-established, however, and over the next few years, supported by important international aid, the country started social reconstruction that included the rebuilding and modernization of its education system.

The rest of the Western Balkans passed the transition period in the worst possible scenario. Seemingly a stable and internationally open country just a few years before (during the Olympic Games in Sarajevo in 1984), Yugoslavia disappeared in fire and smoke. While Checkpoint Charlie in Berlin was made an unrestricted passage, the territories of the former Yugoslavia were divided by impassable new borders. The Berlin Wall did not fall overnight and the disintegration of Yugoslavia was similarly a long process.

Disintegration was deemed likely after Tito's death (1980), but it became more tangible after Slobodan Milošević won power in Serbia (1986). This was a point of no return: Yugoslavia was a train without brakes but it still took quite a lot of time for the final crash to occur. In January 1990 the League of Communists of Yugoslavia broke up; the famous slogan of 'brotherhood and unity' was destroyed by rapidly escalating nationalism. In June 1991 Slovenia and Croatia declared their independence, followed by Macedonia in September. After a '10-day war' in June, Slovenia was out of the Western Balkans, but a real war in Croatia had only just begun. In spring 1992 war also erupted in Bosnia and Herzegovina. The next few years were an enormously malicious period, even when compared with the cruelties of previous wars. International forces involved in the conflicts with great hesitation finally intervened to stop the hostilities. The war in Croatia ended in summer 1995 and in Bosnia and Herzegovina in November, after the NATO air strikes on Bosnian Serb military targets; they were followed by the Dayton Peace Agreement in December 1995.

The wars seemed to have been halted but they were followed by a long and complicated process of political and diplomatic negotiations. The previous federal republics went in very different ways. In the second half of the 1990s, Slovenia was already on its path to the EU. Croatia again established sovereignty over its full territory in 1998. Bosnia and Herzegovina was confronted with an enormous amount of reconstruction work on the economy and civic life on the basis of the Dayton Agreement, which divided the country into cantons, designed mainly along the lines drawn by ethnic cleansing, with a very weak central government. Macedonia seemed to be the only country that achieved its independence without a military conflict, but it was affected by serious political and economic crises. Due to a polemic with Greece, its name is still not internationally recognized. A direct military conflict did not significantly affect Serbia (with Vojvodina and Kosovo now directly subordinated to Belgrade) and Montenegro. They formed the (new) Federal Republic of Yugoslavia in 1992, yet Montenegro proclaimed its independence in 2006, thus putting the final nail in the coffin of Yugoslavia.

However, 1998 was not the end of war in the region. Serbia was in a deep economic and political crisis and social protests were ever louder. Students often went out onto the streets to protest against the autocratic regime and miserable standard of living. Tensions in Kosovo grew into a military conflict and in the summer of 1998 Milošević sent his troops into Kosovo. The recognized scenario was being re-enacted: the international community expressed its concern; the UN first threatened and in the spring of 1999 started air strikes. Serbia withdrew its troops in May 1999 and United Nations Interim Administration Mission in Kosovo (UNMIK) forces entered the province (which declared its independence in 2008, although its full international recognition and status within the international community is still unresolved). Protest and social unrest in Serbia was on the increase. In an extremely volatile situation, elections were held in September 2000 and finally

brought changes to Serbia, strongly supported by students and professors supportive of democracy. After hesitating for a few weeks, Milošević acknowledged defeat. A democratic government was formed by Zoran Đinđić. In April 2001 Milošević was arrested by Serbian police and later extradited to the International Criminal Tribunal for the former Yugoslavia at The Hague, where he died in 2006. Prime Minister Đinđić was not in power for long; he was assassinated in a terrorist attack in March 2003.

Even at this point, weapons did not become silent. Shots were heard throughout almost all of 2001 in Macedonia, which had remained outside the firing zone in previous years. A conflict erupted in part of north-western Macedonia with a strong Albanian minority, on the border with the UN-administered Kosovo. With the Ohrid Agreement in 2001, the rights of the Albanian population (officially over 25%) were improved, including as part of the administration of the country and by making Albanian the second official language, thereby also broadening access to (higher) education.

Tensions and incidents remained a constant of the Western Balkans during this decade but there were no more military conflicts. Countries there started, sooner or later, on economic and social reconstruction. It was clear that damage to education systems was enormous and that education was one of the highest national priorities; however, the circumstances were difficult. Deeply cleaved by wars, often with UN peacekeeping forces in their territories, the countries' reconstruction was impossible without international and, in particular, EU aid and support.

In late 1998 a conference was organized in Graz (Austria) on *European Educational Co-operation for Peace, Stability and Democracy*, which had a huge impact on educational reconstruction in the Western Balkans. This was the beginning of the so-called *Graz Process*. It was disturbed by escalation of the Kosovo crisis, but not stopped. On the contrary, on 10 June 1999 the *Stability Pact for South-East Europe* was adopted in Cologne and reaffirmed the following month in Sarajevo. A detailed action plan was designed and education was included as a priority area in one of the three Working Tables. Thus, the *Graz Process* evolved into the *Enhanced Graz Process* (EGP), encompassing a number of governmental, non-governmental and international organizations. In the following years, it was the main supporter of the region's educational reconstruction, linking up with education trends in other European countries and promoting regional cooperation and networking as instruments for wider participation in international initiatives. Six working groups were established within the EGP Education and Youth Task Force and one of them—coordinated by the European University Association (EUA)—focused on higher education (see Zgaga, 2005: 9–21).

There was an enormous amount of work to do in each individual country of the Western Balkans, now divided into seven new independent countries and the territory of Kosovo with an open status. First of all, there was a need to reconstruct the national systems of higher education. The two former systems of the region—Yugoslav and Albanian—were both obsolete and ruined; in addition, there were political reasons to create a distance from them. The social contexts had changed enormously and were changing in some countries all over again, and the question of how to adapt the education system to the needs of the new society emerging was quite challenging. The two former systems were replaced by many new ones; new legislation and reforms ran in quite different ways in each of them, making them less and less compatible.

RECONSTRUCTION: A FRAGMENTED REGION VS. EUROPEAN INTEGRATION PROCESSES

Alongside launching the *Enhanced Graz Process*, 29 European ministers signed the Bologna Declaration (19 June 1999, see www.bologna2009benelux.org), thus initiating a process aimed at constructing the European Higher Education Area (EHEA) until 2010. Its introductory part stresses that a 'Europe of knowledge' is an irreplaceable factor of social and human growth as it fosters European citizenship, empowers citizens with the necessary competencies for working together, and with an awareness of shared values and belonging to a common social and cultural space. In the third paragraph, the Declaration openly refers to SEE: 'The importance of education and educational cooperation in the development and strengthening of stable, peaceful and democratic societies is universally acknowledged as paramount, the more so in view of the situation in South East Europe.'

Bulgaria, Romania and Slovenia, as EU associated countries, were among the 29 signatory states to the Declaration. Croatia signed the Declaration in 2001 and the remaining five countries signed in 2003. Large parts of the Western Balkans needed serious reconstruction of the whole tertiary education system before entering the Bologna Process and this task was addressed within the framework of the EGP helping with the 'Bologna' agenda. Several common priorities were identified, including the need for new legislation and reform of university governance (the 're-integrated' university); the development of quality assurance mechanisms; the introduction of the European Credit Transfer and Accumulation System (ECTS); curriculum renewal; democratic and ethical standards, recognition of multi-ethnicity, etc. (*Higher Education in Europe*, 2003). In terms of the Bologna Process, these priorities were all part of the public responsibility for higher education, and this was an issue of the utmost concern at the beginning of the post-conflict period in the Western Balkans.

In the former Yugoslavia part of the region, higher education was seriously affected. The horrors of war, forced migration, etc. also hurt students and teachers; the 'brain drain' was enormous. In a number of cases, particularly in Bosnia and Herzegovina, institutions were split along ethnic divisions. Two universities were created sometimes out of a previous single institution, for example the Sarajevo and Mostar University; in Kosovo the University of Prishtina with Albanian as the teaching language and the Serbian University of Priština at a temporary location in Mitrovica. The University of Tirana was also split in 1991, but for quite different reasons. This division had to be taken as a reality, but the key dilemma was how to provide access to the increasing number of young people, and how to maintain the quality of education provision. These were particularly tough questions when we recall that in some places academic activities had stopped for a long period, staff had been displaced and equipment destroyed. Activities were carried on in extreme circumstances: moral resistance was more important than real teaching and learning. For example, in Kosovo Albanians had rejected Milošević's forced education reforms at the beginning of the 1990s and had persisted with a 'parallel education system' in private houses and cellars until the 1999/2000 academic year.

There were high expectations of universities in the newly established nation states. Under circumstances that prevented mobility, new learning opportunities were required in regional centres with no real academic traditions. New faculties were established either from nothing or on the basis of previous branch departments. The tradition of strong 'independent faculties' and a weak university made the mushrooming of new institutions easy. The role of the university in society was reconfirmed in a similar way to in the late 19th and the early 20th centuries: the time for 'the national university' had returned. Rector Rugova explained it in the following way: 'The role and significance of University of Prishtina since its foundation were typical for the roles and significances that universities have played in the western civilized countries, illuminist and liberator from tutelage of the others' (Rugova, 2010).

A process of higher education for the masses started in Yugoslavia just before the period of conflict began. During the 1990s the demand for study places rose enormously everywhere, driven by high unemployment and a general search for opportunities. In 1989 there was a total of 17 universities in the region that we now call the Western Balkans; since then this figure has exponentially expanded. The increase in the number of state universities has been much smaller than in private ones. New state universities have mainly been established on political bases and with very limited budgets, while the new circumstances have made private initiatives in the higher education area almost totally unrestricted.

This trend has been particularly strong in Albania, where around 30 private institutions of various kinds have appeared alongside the old one, as well as 10 new public universities. Kosovo has witnessed similar growth of private institutions—but not public ones. Institutions and their branches have been flourishing across Macedonia, where there are five state universities and twice as many private institutions. The picture is similar in Bosnia and Herzegovina, which has eight state universities and twice as many private institutions. In other countries, the growth of private institutions has been more controlled—not only by national accreditation procedures but by traditional academic leaders. Many of the new institutions could not be classified as proper universities and are instead 'independent faculties' and 'higher schools'. Higher education systems in the region have remained mostly unitary, with the exception of Croatia which differentiates *sveučilišta* (universities, of which it has eight), *veleučilišta* (colleges, of which it has nine) and *visoke škole* (higher schools, of which it has 21). In Serbia there are six, mainly 'old', state universities (excluding the disputed one in Mitrovica, Kosovo) and three times as many private institutions. The Montenegro system is the smallest and consists of one public and one private university.

The growth of private higher education has been predominantly caused by demand and the lack of state support:

'Public higher education institutions depend dominantly on public funding. The regional and local investments to higher education are marginal. Higher education institutions do have a possibility to generate their own income, however the data on the own income is difficult to access. Some estimates suggest that one third of the overall income is generated by the institutions independently.' (Ivošević and Miklavič, 2009: 103)

Fees have been the best way for underfunded public institutions to improve their position. This was a shock for the region, as fees had never been required before; however, called for during the worst period, they were accepted. Usually the government pays fees for a given quota of students, while students outside the quota must pay for themselves. In the fragmented system of 'independent faculties', many teachers also teach at other public or private institutions. This has made the system somewhat opaque, often bringing complaints and the occasional corruption scandal.

The fast-growing higher education sector has raised serious concerns among policy-makers and institutions about reputation. Establishing accreditation procedures has been the most common response, but an evaluation culture also started to develop later, following best practices from EU countries (see EUA, 2004). The more a national system of accreditation was delayed, the more serious the problem: what should be done with the non-recognized institutions that have appeared in the meantime? In addition, in transitional countries accreditation has been often used in clashes between 'old' and 'new' elites for hegemony in the national administration, economy and culture. As mentioned, the wild growth of institutions has also been a result of the tradition of independent faculties—an outcome of an obsolete governance system.

In fact, at Yugoslav universities after the Second World War the council of the university, with the rector as chairman, dealt 'with all general questions concerning the running of all the Faculties', while the faculty councils discussed and took 'decisions on all general questions affecting the ordinary running of the Faculty' (Uvalić, 1952: 4). The radical constitutional and legislative reforms of the mid-1970s (we cannot analyse them here in any depth, so let us only note that they were also some kind of a *divide et impera* approach against the student and academic revolt of 1968; see Zgaga, 2007: 63–82) petrified the concept of independent faculties, which—as legal entities or 'university members'—united to form a university. For various reasons, this concept survived the 1990s and in a modified way it has defined recent developments. In most cases even today, '[u]niversities are a loose confederation of faculties at the best; yet, in fact they do not exist because no important decisions are taken at this level. Even in cases when they are taken individual faculties can behave in a direct contradiction to decisions taken at the level of the university because they are autonomous in relation to the university' (Vukasović, 2005: 402).

This formation can be seen in all former Yugoslavian countries, except Albania. By virtue of this, changes in governance have been slow and have often encountered strong opposition. Slovenia introduced legal provisions for an integrated university in 1993, but it took a lot of time for the system's implementation, including a dispute before the Constitutional Court, which finally decided that faculties were not autonomous, but the university was. It was similar in Croatia, but there a formal decision on autonomous faculties was made, blocking integrative attempts. However, integrative approaches to university governance have not been entirely ruled out and some new practices have appeared, for example some new institutions have a rector claiming an integrative philosophy, supported by academics and external stakeholders. In general, the 'older' universities are more traditional, whereas changes can be expected among the 'younger' ones. The universities in Rijeka (Croatia), Novi Sad (Serbia) and Tuzla (Bosnia and Herzegovina) have often been included in the latter group. Macedonia has also made provision for the functional integration of state universities (2008), although the transformation is expected to be 'a painful process, especially of university-faculty relations' (Pecakovska and Lazarevska, 2009: 46).

The University of Prishtina, in Kosovo, changed significantly during the UN administrative period. On the other side of the border, the SEE University in Tetovo (Macedonia) is a particularly interesting example. Its roots go back to the turbulent start of this decade. Max van der Stoel, Organization for Security and Co-operation in Europe (OSCE) High Commissioner on National Minorities at the time, initiated a project to develop a university that would improve the opportunities for higher education in minority languages. The international community provided funds for a new campus and the Macedonian Government donated the land. The SEE University was opened in November 2001, following the end of the inter-ethnic conflicts that had escalated earlier that year. It is the first private, non-profit university in the region with a modern governance structure, and with Albanian, Macedonian and English teaching languages.

Before the 1990s higher education was perhaps the most 'internationalized' part of social sub-systems in the region. We may refer, for example, to the Inter-University Centre in Dubrovnik (devastated during the war)—the organizer of the 'University Today' international conferences during the 1980s. The higher education sector, therefore, gladly accepted international aid and initiatives for reconstruction. Co-operation within the EGP and the Bologna Process, as well as projects within the TEMPUS programme, were extremely important for overcoming the outcomes of the conflict period and starting reconstruction. In general, 'Europeanization' has been regarded as 'de-Balkanization'.

During the first stage, the big issues were addressed: legislation, finance, quality assurance and governance. Their resolution was assisted through the EGP activities, with important help from the EUA, and later through full membership in the Bologna Process. The implementation of systemic novelties started in around 2005 and brought teaching and learning to the fore. There have been huge discrepancies between the (formally) modernized system and obsolete teaching and learning practices. A lack of human and financial resources, extremely high student to teacher ratios, the heritage of a long period without normally functioning institutions and international isolation have had strong negative impacts.

Several recent surveys in the region have analyzed the impact of system reforms on teaching and learning. In one of them, which focused on teacher education at universities in the region, a problem common to all disciplines and departments was identified: 'The extent of reform of higher education curricula varies from field to field, [...] some institutions have gone further in the reform [...] while in other cases the structure has remained completely the same' (Pantić and Camilleri, 2009: 30).

CONCLUSION: HIGHER EDUCATION IN THE REGION BEYOND 2010

In spring 2010 the Bologna Process crossed the finish line, as defined in 1999. Yet in the Leuven Communiqué (2009) ministers self-critically noted that 'not all the objectives have been completely achieved', and that proper implementation requires 'an increased momentum and commitment beyond 2010'. However, all countries of the EHEA have not been in an equal position in terms of modernizing their higher education systems. The countries of the Western Balkans joined the Process later than other countries, and it should not be a surprise to learn that various criticisms of the Bologna reforms have been often heard there in the last year or two.

These criticisms may be divided into 'conservative' and 'progressive'. The first group recommends boycotting changes, while the latter recommends '[d]istinguish[ing] between the *idea* of the reform with the potentials that it unlocks, from the *reality* of its imperfect implementation with disappointments that it brings' (Gregorić, 2010). 'Progressives' in Croatia propose to draw 'a distinction between the harmonization of higher education in Europe (the Bologna Process) and Bolonja [the phonetic transcription used in colloquial south-Slavonic languages]', which is 'a distortion of the original idea' and 'an example of a failed reform'. Further, Bolonja 'understands the Bologna Process in a way which makes its implementation in Croatia impossible'. Relying on Thomas Kuhn's concept of paradigm change and Paul Feyerabend's interaction of traditions, it is shown 'that "Bologna" is an undesired mixture of our old tradition and the model introduced by the Bologna Declaration' (Kurelić, 2009: 9–10). Siniša Rodin deepens this criticism: 'Implementation of the Bologna reform in Croatia is a failure. In essence, the majority of higher education establishments have extended their original four-year degree programs into five-year ones. At the same time, such extended programs were mechanically split in two parts in order to satisfy the formal requirement of 3+2 or 4+1' (Rodin, 2009: 30). Further on, 'master programs did not develop in direction of diversity and multi-disciplinarity but, as a rule, remained mono-disciplinary and substantively related to the first Bologna cycle' (Rodin, 2009: 26).

Of course, this criticism is far from being limited to Croatia; yet it is a privilege for Croatia to listen to sharp criticism. An experienced 'European connoisseur' of the Balkans' higher education already sensed the danger of purely formal reforms in the whole region several years ago: 'One weakness is the escape into window dressing, such as advertising compliance with the Bologna Process by just cutting and pasting old curricula into the new modes, or by topping old studies with post-graduate programs without sound basics in the graduate programs' (Daxner, 2006: 6). We should note here, however, that these problems are not unknown in certain other European countries. What makes the countries of the Western Balkans more vulnerable at this point is their incomparably different positions. It is extremely difficult to implement ambitious European reforms at an impoverished grass-roots level; it is even more difficult to 'Europeanize' until cooperation on the regional level is revitalized and substantially improved.

Nevertheless, some encouraging steps have been taken in this direction. Let us use as an example the TEMPUS project, Multilingual Internet Step-by-step Maths for All (launched in 2004), which aimed to foster multilingual cooperation in the smaller universities of SEE and to improve basic practical maths skills for students in various study fields. In cooperation with colleagues from Greece and the United Kingdom, the project was carried out at two universities in Macedonia (Bitola and Tetovo). The former is mainly ethnic Macedonian and the latter is mainly ethnic Albanian. The specific value of this project was that it exceeded its direct subject-area aim (i.e. maths learning) and, importantly, contributed to mutual understanding among staff and students from both ethnic groups (see Zgaga, 2008: 42).

The good news is that ambitious projects at a departmental level are growing. The modernization of teaching and learning is really coming to the fore. Often it is connected to implementation of tools and strategies recommended by the Bologna Process, such as the credit system, student workload, learner-centred approaches, etc. For example, at the Sociology Department of the University of Belgrade the four-year 'traditional' study programme was estimated at 319 ECTS points; after a curricular reform this was refreshed and the programme was downgraded to 243 ECTS points, i.e. to the recommended size (see Vukasović, 2005: 402).

However, the grass-roots process of modernization is hindered by ambiguous legislation and a resistant old-fashioned academic culture. Like all European states, countries in the region need 'an increased momentum and commitment beyond 2010'. For this reason, sharp critical analyses might be very important. During the last 10 years a new generation of experts in higher education has also been emerging. They often started as national student representatives in the European Student Union (ESIB/ESU), completing graduate studies abroad before returning home. It is particularly encouraging that they are communicating across national, ethnic or language borders without difficulty.

In general, academics have helped the process by jumping over narrow ethnic fences. In August 2002 rectors from all SEE countries met at the renewed Inter-University Centre in Dubrovnik for the first time since the decade of conflict, to discuss international processes in higher education from a regional point of view. This event was influenced by the Bologna Process, yet it also marked a turning point: the return of regional cooperation to higher education. There are many signs that the will to cooperate across the region (and not solely 'with Europe') is on the increase. Here, a question has been raised: 'is the South Eastern Europe Higher Education Area possible?' (Lacrama, 2007). A regional group from health studies has already responded that 'it is unlikely that a small country can or even should afford an expensive institution with the full spectrum of activities. The result in this situation very often is an institution being too small, understaffed and sub-standard'. Therefore, 'structured regional cooperation may offer the solution' (Burazeri et al., 2005: 98).

Regional cooperation is truly developing. There are also virtual networks that support cooperation, such as the Education Reform Initiative of South-Eastern Europe (ERISEE, see www.erisee.org) and the Coordination of Research Policies with the Western Balkan Countries (INCO-NET, see www.wbc-inco.net). Last, but not least, something else may enhance the momentum. The already quoted connoisseur of the Balkans put it in the following way:

'But there is one thing which I have learned, not least in the Balkans: if there is a place where societies can restart to think themselves, it is in the universities. Many of those who are now on the progressive side, which means on the European side of transition, have been active in student movements, in academic resistance against authoritarian rule, and could learn their future roles within the protective walls of academic freedom. This is one of the strengths of Balkan academia, which some less lucky countries do not share.' (Daxner, 2006: 8)

BIBLIOGRAPHICAL REFERENCES

Burazeri, G., Laaser, U., Bjegovic, V., Georgieva, L., 'Regional collaboration in public health training and research among countries of SEE', *European Journal of Public Health*, Vol. 15, No. 1, 2005, 97–99.

Crvenkovski, K., 'Ability and educational opportunity in present-day Yugoslavia', *International Review of Education*, Vol. 7, No. 4, December 1962.

Daxner, M., 'The Balkans on their way to Europe and to themselves—an agenda for higher education', at EUA Conference 'Strengthening Higher Education and Research in SEE: Priorities for Regional and European Cooperation', Vienna, EUA and University of Vienna, 2–3 March 2006.

EUA, *EUA institutional evaluations of seven Universities of Bosnia and Herzegovina*, Cross-cutting summary report, Brussels, EUA, 2004.

Gregoric, P., 'Achievements and Failures of the Bologna Process to Date', Round Table 'Processing the Bologna Process: Current Losses and Future Gains', Zagreb, University of Zagreb, UNESCO Chair for Governance and Management of Higher Education, 5–6 March 2010, www.unizg.hr/unesco-chair/round-table-march-5-2010/ (accessed 2 April 2010).

Higher Education in Europe, The External Dimension of the Bologna Process: Higher Education in SEE and the EHEA in a Global World, Vol. 28, No. 3, 2003.

Ivošević, V. and Miklavic, K., 'Financing Higher Education: Comparative analysis', in M. Vukasovic (ed.) *Financing Higher Education in SEE: Albania, Croatia, Montenegro, Serbia, Slovenia*, Belgrade, Centre for Education Policy, 2009.

Kurelic, Z., 'How Not to Defend Your Tradition of Higher Education', *Politicka misao / Croatian Political Science Review*, Vol. 46, No. 5, 2009, 9–20.

Lacrama, L. D., Karnyanszky, T. M., 'The South Eastern Europe Higher Education Area: Is it possible?', *Annals. Computer Science Series*, Vol. 5, Fasc. 1, 2007, 129–36.

Pantic, N., Camilleri, A. F. (eds), *Mapping policies and practices for the preparation of teachers for inclusive education in context of social and cultural diversity*, country report for Serbia, Bologna, European Training Foundation, 2009.

Pecakovska, S. and Lazarevska, S., *Long Way to Knowledge Based Society. Macedonian Education in the Light of the EC Education and Training 2010 Work Program Benchmarks and Indicators*, Skopje, Foundation Open Society Macedonia, 2009.

Rodin, S., 'Higher Education Reform in Search of Bologna', *Politicka misao / Croatian Political Science Review*, Vol. 46, No. 5, 2009, 21–38.

Rugova, M. (2010) *Welcome to the University of Prishtina*, 208.116.30.198/?cid=2,5 (accessed 7 June 2010).

Uvalic, R., 'The organization of higher education in Yugoslavia'. Paris, UNESCO, 1952, unesdoc.unesco.org/images/0017/001790/179034eb.pdf (accessed 8 April 2010).

Uvalic Trumbic, S., 'New Trends in Higher Education in Yugoslavia?', *European Journal of Education*, Vol. 25, No. 4, 1990, 399–407.

Vukasovic, M., 'Visoko obrazovanje na putu ka Evropi: cetiri godine kasnije' [Higher Education on the Road to Europe: Four Years Later], in *Visoko obrazovanje na putu ka Evropi: cetiri godine kasnije*, Zbornik radova, Beograd, Alternativna akademska obrazovna mreža, 2005, pp. 400–07.

Zgaga, P., *The Importance of Education in Social Reconstruction: Six years of the Enhanced Graz Process: developments, current status and future prospects of education in South-East Europe*, Ljubljana and Vienna, CEPS, University of Ljubljana and Kultur-Kontakt Austria, 2005, ceps.pef.uni-lj.si/eng.htm (accessed 8 April 2010).

Higher Education in Transition: Reconsiderations on higher education in Europe at the turn of the millennium, Umeå, Umeå University, 2007.

Thematic Review of Tempus Structural Measures: A Survey Report, final report to the DG for Education and Culture of the European Commission, Ljubljana, CEPS, University of Ljubljana, 2008, ceps.pef.uni-lj.si/eng.htm (accessed 8 April 2010).

THE CURRICULUM IN TODAY'S WORLD*

CONFIGURING KNOWLEDGE, IDENTITIES, WORK AND POLITICS

LYN YATES and MADELEINE GRUMET

The collapse of the Cold War and the rise of new forms of war, the digitization of information, globalization of production and the challenges to cultural hegemony produced by migration and the identity politics of the 1970s, have all contributed to the sense that we do not know this world. Yet the *world*, however vague or intuitive, is our horizon: the limit, at any instance, of what is, has been, and what is possible for the figure of our local lives. The world is the object to which the curriculum points as we introduce each generation to the shared histories, practices and possibilities that shape personhood. The school curriculum is the programme nations establish to prepare young people for the world. It points to the world and engages in the formation of personhood. At times of important political change, the curriculum becomes a key site for attention and reworking.

The curriculum's story of the world has always been influenced by politics. Sometimes, especially in proposals to change what is taught as national history, or in the curriculum changes that follow major political events such as the ending of apartheid in South Africa, the political direction of the curriculum is explicit. Often, though, its politics and sources and motives are obscure, indirect. There is the real and reasonable space and time that it takes to make any sense of events, reflected not just in topics, in what is said, but in the ways in which disciplines of human and cultural inquiry develop over time. Then there is the overt concern of schooling with young people's cognitive development, and the sorting and coding that frames the institutional forms in which the curriculum must be offered, and scholarship reformulated into courses of instruction for students along the continuum of K-12 (kindergarten through to year 12, at 16–19 years old) schooling through to university and graduate studies. For each of these cohorts there are deliberative councils that may involve diverse political constituencies to decide not only what enters the curriculum but also how it is taught and how it is to be known.

Curricula that appear not to be directly political may directly bear that origin. For example, we can point to college-level courses instituted in the USA in response to its participation in wars on the European continent. The renowned Western civilization course established in 1919 at Columbia University was derived from its predecessor, a War Aims course initiated in 1918 to introduce prospective soldiers to the European countries and traditions they were about to defend. As the USA readied to fight Germany, it turned from its model of free election of subject choice to the British model of requirements. This Columbia course, bringing together the departments of economics, government, philosophy and history, was paralleled by a multidisciplinary course at Stanford called Problems in Citizenship, as well as one at Dartmouth. We do not know whether the original lectures of these courses acknowledged their national concerns and defensive motives. It is hard to tell whether the suspicion of historian John Higham, reported in Carnochan (1993: 69), that these courses were motivated by the wartime anxiety about the nation's immigrants and their ties to their countries of origin, was operating, although that concern would provide a genealogy for the xenophobia that pervades the Western civilization curriculum, enduring decades after the threat of war in Europe had passed.

Post-11 September 2001, the *New York Times* of Saturday 24 November 2001 records a similar moment, in a report entitled 'Defending Civilization: How Our Universities are Failing America and What Can Be Done About It'. The report

was issued by the American Council of Trustees and Alumni, a conservative group that the *Times* identified as devoted to curbing liberal tendencies in academia. The report proceeds to excoriate US colleges for anti-American bias and to advocate for more courses on US history and Western civilization.

Language studies proliferate as various regions of the world become significant to national interests: as the Japanese economy boomed, so in many of their trading partners did Asian Studies and Japanese language study, and more recently studies of the People's Republic of China and its languages. Today, in the USA, studies of the Middle East, Afghanistan and Pakistan and their languages are becoming more prominent in the curricula of higher education.

By contrast, the curricula of K-12 education, requiring some collective and more extensive consensus, change more slowly. Traditionally, this curriculum looks back: it selects from the nation's history and culture, topics and types of formal learning that are considered to be particularly foundational to that generational formation. In some countries national curricula have been highly prescribed and uniform; elsewhere, as in the USA and Canada, they are determined by states or provinces and by textbook publishers, and by federal funding initiatives and testing formats. At times of important political change the curriculum often becomes a key site for attention and reworking.

As we write, in the USA a new programme for the school curriculum in Texas is under consideration, one that will affect other states due to Texas' large share of the textbook market. If passed, students will learn more about the virtues of free enterprise, biblical values and the Confederacy's cause, and less about slavery and civil rights. Other changes will water down criticism of Senator Joseph McCarthy's anti-Communist witch hunt in the 1950s and portray the UN's funding for international humanitarian relief and environmental initiatives as threats to individual freedom and US sovereignty. In Australia, a country that has not had a strong tradition of 'civics' in its school curriculum, a new national curriculum is being constructed for which developing foundations for 'citizenship' is seen as one of the priorities. The story of what account schooling should be giving young Australians of who they are has been the subject of intense and bitter public debate over the past decade, with different visions of Australian history and identity as a nation central to that debate (Macintyre and Clark, 2003). The priority to be given to celebration of Australia's democratic traditions compared with recognition of ills done to the Aboriginal population, the degree of emphasis to be given to the 'Anzac' tradition (soldiers dying to defend freedom on foreign soil in Europe and Asia in the World Wars), the extent to which the story of Australia is to be linked primarily to the traditions of England and Ireland rather than those of its indigenous population or of the home countries of its large numbers of immigrants from other parts of the world, are all part of those debates. At the same time, economic and political imperatives are cited as justification for a greater turning towards Asia in what is taught: for teaching Asian languages, rather than European ones, as the foreign languages of priority.

In other parts of the world too, political changes produce new agendas for curriculum (Osler and Starkey, 2005). With the formation of the European Union (EU), for example, legal definitions of citizenship and of citizen entitlements, rights and protections have been reworked. In the face of 'temporary' workers and refugees, being a citizen is not coterminous with being a resident of a country. Being a member of the EU confers rights to mount legal challenges, to move and to work that originate from outside national frameworks. In the EU context, curriculum research and curriculum development

*This essay was written as the introduction to the Routledge World Yearbook of Education 2011 (ISBN: 978-0-415-57582-9) and has been adapted for its use here.

projects are now initiated both from within member countries and also as cross-country EU projects.

The world is never still. Nevertheless in the last 50 years we have witnessed profound changes: collapse of colonial powers and their domination; dissolution of the Union of Soviet Socialist Republics (USSR); globalization of production, rapid dissemination of culture and information through communication on the world wide web; the development of international terrorism; all leading to new nations, new alliances, new enemies, new conditions for work and citizenship that influence the curriculum today.

It is interesting to speculate whether these changes in international politics and national specificity have stimulated the imposition of an audit culture on schooling. The rising prominence of comparisons, benchmarking and borrowings between countries, and the impact of agendas and publications of influential meta-national agencies such as the Organisation for Economic Co-operation and Development (OECD) and the World Bank, are evident in many national discussions and policies (Silova and Steiner-Khamsi, 2008; Robertson and Dale, 2009; Rizvi and Lingard, 2010). International comparisons of education achievement have been reported, at least since the 1950s, but in the 1990s and in the current decade, particularly under the aegis of the OECD, they have taken on a much more systemized agenda. Through its publication of league tables of national performance on mathematics, literacy and science in its *PISA* reports (the Programme for International Student Assessment) and in its dissemination of a wide array of education 'indicators' in its *Education at a Glance* reports, the OECD incites national attention, both public and political, to a 'global' perspective on national systems of schooling. This perspective is one where the function of schooling is seen through the lens of economics and where the content of schooling (its curriculum) is visible only in the form of quantitative measures and graphs (Hopmann, Brinek and Retzl, 2009). In its PISA and DeSeCo projects, the OECD promotes a view that what matters is not what is learnt about the world, but what competencies and orientations (such as motivation to be a 'life-long learner') are being produced in learners, as if these are essentially culture-neutral and context-free. The assessment programmes themselves are not tied to what schools have taught in particular countries, but to what problem-solving abilities and 'competencies' are agreed to be the desired outcomes of mathematics, literacy or science.

These influential benchmarking projects, while explicitly outcome-oriented and not claiming to comment on the curriculum, have been a key impetus and source of evidence in many curriculum policy discussions. For one thing, national systems are required to account for and be benchmarked against other national systems, and this challenges former national specificities of curriculum approach and aims, such as the cultural orientation to the curriculum as the formation of the whole person in the European didactics tradition (Hopmann, Brinek and Retzl, 2009). Gaulthier and Le Gouvello (2010) argue that the OECD activities are producing a radical challenge to the French system, one which would replace the construction of the curriculum as a tacit and historical cultural given with new forms of explicit policy-making more attuned to global instrumental agendas. Meanwhile, Karseth and Sivesind begin a recent discussion by considering whether it matters if Norwegian students no longer study one of their great playwrights, Henrik Ibsen. They ask, '[c]an a national culture be described through examples like the dramas of Henrik Ibsen, and will such examples embody values relevant for a global context? Is there a public legitimacy for cultivation of national cultures as an overall purpose of the curriculum, and how is this idea matching ideas of qualifying the students for life?'(Karseth and Sivesind, 2010: 107).

The strong assessment emphasis of the benchmarking activities also casts its own particular orientation to curriculum-making (Grumet, 2006, 2007; Taubman, 2009). As Karseth and Sivesind argue, 'organizations like OECD advocate a new political technology where formalized curriculum-making is ignored or even contested in favour of assessment and accountability systems' (Karseth and Sivesind, 2010: 109).

A different form of meta-national pressure on the curriculum is visited on developing countries through the work of non-governmental organizations (NGOs) such as the World Bank (Silova and Steiner-Khamsi, 2008), or though inter-country commitments such as the Millennium Development Goals of the UN (Yates, 2006). The Millennium Development Goals, for example, include equal education participation for females as for males in all countries. The projects and accounting associated with these goals decline to make specific the curriculum content expected of such education. Like the economic agendas of OECD, the focus here too is on measurable indicators of inputs and outputs as the key agenda for schooling, rather than the substance of what is taught. Nevertheless, in the field of academic curriculum inquiry, these new agreements to have targets for schooling (and other aspects of social and economic life) that apply globally have contributed to some broader discussion about cultural difference, and human rights and capabilities, in relation to the curriculum, across countries as well as within them (Walker and Unterhalter, 2007; Unterhalter, 2009).

In many countries today, curriculum policies and politicians speak of a new, global economically competitive world that the curriculum must address—and against which it must be benchmarked. They speak too of anxieties about citizenship, about alienated youth, about the need for different kinds of skills in the world of the 21st century. Inevitably the curriculum reveals the concerns, anxieties, of the adults who shape it.

So as we write this, we are examining how the curriculum, conceptions of knowledge, conceptions of the rights and responsibilities of citizens, and the school experience of young people engage the great issues of this tumultuous time. Our focus here is not primarily a political science of the curriculum, a story of how power is being exercised, or who is getting to decide between countries or within countries the form and content of the curriculum that has come to be developed. Rather it focuses on the 'what' of curriculum today: what is being put in place in different parts of the world and how curriculum scholars understand this.

'Curriculum' is, of course, an ambiguous term. It encompasses different kinds of focus, including policy statements at the overarching level; curriculum guidelines and frameworks; textbooks; the enacted curriculum of what teachers do and what happens in classrooms; unintended and hidden curriculum relating to school practices and environment; and the issue of what young people themselves receive and perceive as curriculum. Curriculum inquiry may be conceptually tied to what is done in schools; or broadened to refer to other pre- and post-school education institutions; or it may be set free from both of those locations and used to refer to practices outside formal institutions and intentions; or used metaphorically to talk of the curriculum of public spaces, or monuments.

In this essay we have restricted our focus specifically to the curriculum of schooling because it is in schooling that young people undergo a compulsory and institutionalized introduction to the world. The curriculum here is the publicly sanctioned or agreed version of what young people are to learn and who they are to become, additional to, and not reducible to, either their formation in their family setting or the socialization or acculturation of simply being in their culture.

We realize that even in an era of intense nationalism, when the interests and aims of various countries appear discrete and particular, there are always systems of exchange, of identification and differentiation that link apparently distinct national interests to each other. However, in this last decade, as economy and population flows have affected countries and curricula across the world, it is newly interesting to explore the relation of the curriculum to the world from multiple national perspectives.

This essay could have been titled 'The Curriculum in Vulnerable Times'. *Vulnerable* is a term most evidently associated in the USA with the post-11 September 2001 world—signalling a changed awareness of that country's relationship to the world. Of course, many other countries suffer ongoing conflict and directly experience vulnerability, but the post-11 September 2001 period has produced a widespread experience across most countries of sharpened concerns about terrorism, weapons and international relationships. For the curriculum, that raises questions about the story that is told in each place about the nation and its relation to other parts of the world, and about the sense of its citizens, their diversity, religion, values and the relationships it tries to build. Sometimes this story may be told explicitly, through history or civics subjects; sometimes it may be reflected in the arrangements of language policies, or policies on diversity and representation, or in the ways literature is taught.

Vulnerable is also a term that might be associated with other types of uncertainties that are now prominently part of a global rhetoric of concern—in particular the global financial crisis—and issues of environment and climate change (Bowers, 1993). Many countries introduce their new curriculum reports and guidelines of recent times with extensive reference to the new vocational skills that will be needed for both individuals and that nation to flourish in the 21st century. They speak to a sense of economic vulnerability in the future, and address a role for the curriculum to form a new kind of person. Here curriculum serves political purposes in configuring where responsibilities lie for future economic well-being. However, in national settings as diverse as China, Singapore, South Africa and the United Kingdom (UK), we can see the anxieties and interests in renewed attention to configuring how foundations for the new economy should be built, and curriculum scholars have had considerable interest in the ways this task for curriculum intersects other stories of nation, culture and identity.

Vulnerable, or at least 'uncertain', might also be applied to the issue of knowledge itself in these times. Sources of knowledge production are both proliferating (especially via the internet) and also evidently (for education) being steered in new ways by global bodies such as the World Bank and the OECD. While calls for the basics and resurrection of a canon are common in many places, universities themselves are busily re-arranging disciplines and interdisciplinary endeavours to develop new kinds of thinking seen as needed for the big problems of the day. These developments raise new challenges about what selections of knowledge and what forms of knowledge are appropriate and foundational in the school curriculum.

The postmodern critique of knowledge that has characterized much intellectual work of recent decades challenged the generalizations of the academic disciplines, their reliance on rationalism and commitment to Enlightenment ideals of progress. It has been subject to much public criticism for being preoccupied with forms and languages and with the ways these distort and reduce the complexity of experience. In relation to the school curriculum, much of this challenging of traditional subject content came in the first instance not from abstract intellectual theory but from scholars concerned with inequalities and differences between students in school—especially of gender and race—and the problem that only some perspectives in a national culture were given the imprimatur of truth in the school curriculum, while others were marginalized (Grumet, 1988; Yates, 2009). In curriculum studies, though, preoccupations with postmodernism and with the micro-dynamics of classrooms have also distracted curriculum scholars from thinking about what the schools are saying to students about their worlds and about their places in it.

Despite the important changes in the ways we think about the world since the end of the Cold War, the development of global economies, the events of 11 September 2001 and the threat of international terrorism, in many nations the curriculum hides or compensates for these upheavals by turning away from the world to a hypnotic fascination with an audit culture, high-stakes testing and benchmarking (Grumet, 2006, 2007; Taubman, 2009). The international comparative data is ostensibly concerned with competencies and capabilities in such areas as 'problem-solving' or 'communication', but the substance of what identities are being formed and how this enters into how young people in different parts of the world learn to understand others, is left out of these influential political agendas. Recent attempts to return depth to the curriculum call for a new 'disciplinarity', asking the academic disciplines to anchor the curriculum in substance (Muller, 2000). How-

ever, that too does not of itself resolve the substantive selections that are necessarily made, as is apparent from the ongoing debates over the construction of Australia's first national curriculum, and its proposed selections to represent a systematic development in history, or science, or English.

Themes of nation and global change, of values and difference, of politics and who is other, are often overt in those parts of the curriculum that tell the story of history, or civics, or make selections of texts and languages for study. They are found, too, in a second kind of restructuring: how the curriculum today is construing its relationship to the economy, including what it sees as the knowledge and skill foundations of the future, and what is being represented as the work of schools and school students in this configuring. One enduring concern of curriculum scholarship and research has been with inequality, and the different kinds of successes and futures set up in schools for children of different class, race and gender. As the assumed relationship between schooling and the economy takes on new global forms, curriculum scholars study the ways in which old or new forms of inequality are being recreated or are rebuilt in new ways. In South Africa, for example, the post-Apartheid curriculum has been structured to transform a previously segregated one. In the UK the most recent vocational agenda of the curriculum is changing the history of social class-based hierarchies of learning. Equally of interest is the orientation of emerging economies, such as China, to the global and to the potential to be 'modern' in their take-up of science. How does the curriculum address changes in production related to new technologies, dispersed industries and work forces as it projects work futures for young people and adjusts credentials accordingly? The curriculum in China has been reworked to move from a prioritization of political commitment and manual labour in the period of the Cultural Revolution, to its current powerful engagement with the global economy and the knowledge-base of that engagement. Singapore's efforts to develop a strong positioning for the country in a global knowledge-based economy have caused tensions with its equally strong values and citizenship agenda.

Beyond shared rhetoric of forming 'flexible life-long learners', what are countries actually marking out as important in the structures of their schooling? What concept of vocational is at work and does this reflect or not reflect differences between different national economies? How are national qualifications frameworks structuring the relationship between curriculum and the future economy? Notwithstanding ubiquitous references to a new 'knowledge economy', the agendas of contemporary curriculum reform in the UK and elsewhere represent an emptying out of knowledge.

The very questions that this essay poses, 'how do countries around the world configure the curriculum in relation to changes in politics, demographics, economy?', rest on an assumption of nation and, it follows, of curricula constructed by different countries to project and fulfil their national identities. This extends one of the assumptions about the curriculum's function of socialization: the curriculum of public education, certified by the 'state', is expected to prepare children to participate in its customs, laws and culture. Whether globalization is understood to point to transnational processes of production, trade and investment, or to porous national boundaries and increased flow of peoples around the globe, it is understood to have challenged, if not diminished, the clarity of national identities. Furthermore, as conflicts such as the Cold War and the alliances that it shaped have been somewhat resolved, and as international terrorism deploys conflicts that move across alliances and national and religious identities, the specificity of national interests and concerns also appears diluted. Our recognition of these changes may suggest a less fluid past, a time when France was France, and did not have to worry about McDonald's, or when China's economy was not significant to Iran's ambitions. Of course, even before post-structuralism instructed us to be suspicious of simple stories and generalizations, we have recourse to the history of nations which attests to their heterogeneity: dispersed among tribes and clans; saturated with colonial economics and governance; colluding in the alliances and the exchange of arms. We recognize that the nations that provide the locus of their work, their culture, indeed their lives, continue to be contested projects, as do the curricula that represent their aims.

The etymology of *nation* recognizes the instability of this concept. Although derived from *natus* or *nativity* and signifying the place of one's birth, and then associated with a common race or stock, the idea that geography is destiny is a myth that accompanies this term. It is interesting to note this 14th-century usage:

> The term derives from **Latin** *natio* and originally described the colleagues in a **college** or students, above all at the **University of Paris**, who were all born within a *pays*, spoke the same language and expected to be ruled by their own familiar law. In 1383 and 1384, while studying theology at Paris, **Jean Gerson** was twice elected procurator for the French *nation (i.e. the French-born Francophone students at the University). The Paris division of students into nations* was adopted at the **University of Prague**, where from its opening in 1349 the **studium generale** was divided among Bohemian, Bavarian, Saxon and various Polish *nations*.
>
> (www.spiritus-temporis.com/nation/etymology.html, italics in original)

Designating groups of university students as nations and recognizing the necessity for the university to address their diversity suggests the tension that exists between the curriculum and a nation's identity and world view: a tension expressed in current accountability systems, in attempts to grasp and rationalize globalization, in programmes to articulate a nation's history and culture with the diversity of its citizens, in projects to educate students to new ways of working with new technologies. It becomes increasingly clear that the relationship between nation and curriculum is reciprocal: nations construct curricula and curricula construct nations.

BIBLIOGRAPHICAL REFERENCES

Bowers, C. A., *Education, Cultural Myths, and the Ecological Crisis: Toward Deep Changes*. Albany, State University of New York Press, 1993.

Carnochan, W. B., *The Battleground of the Curriculum*. Stanford, CA, Stanford University Press, 1993.

Gaulthier, R.-F. and Le Gouvello, M., 'The French curricular exception and the troubles of education and internationalization: will it be enough to "rearrange the deckchairs"?', *European Journal of Education* 45 (1), 2010: 77–92.

Grumet, M., *Bitter Milk: Women and Teaching*. Amherst, MA, University of Massachusetts Press, 1988.

'Where Does the World Go, When Schooling is about Schooling?', *The Journal of Curriculum Theorizing* 22 (3), 2006: 47–54.

'The Beast in the Matrix', *Curriculum and Teaching Dialogue*, 9 (1 & 2), 2007: 235–46.Hopmann, S., Brinek G. and Retzl, M. (eds), *PISA zufolge PISA. PISA According to PISA.* Wien, LIT-Verlag, 2009.

Karseth, B. and Sivesind, K., 'Conceptualising curriculum knowledge within and beyond the national context', *European Journal of Education* 45 (1), 2010: 107–23.

Macintyre, S. and Clark, A., *The History Wars*. Carlton, Melbourne University Press, 2003.

Muller, J., *Reclaiming knowledge: social theory, curriculum and education policy*. London, RoutledgeFalmer, 2000.

Osler, A. and Starkey, H., *Changing Citizenship: democracy and inclusion in education*. Maidenhead, Open University Press, 2005.

Rizvi, F. and Lingard, B., *Globalizing Education Policy*. London, Routledge, 2010.

Robertson, S. L. and Dale, I. R., 'The World Bank, the IMF and the possibilities of critical education', in M. Apple, W. Au and L. Gandin (eds), *International Handbook of Critical Education*. New York, Routledge, 2009.

Silova, I. and Steiner-Khamsi, G. (eds), *How NGOs React. Globalization and Education Reform in the Caucasus, Central Asia and Mongolia*. Bloomfield, CT, Kumarian Press, 2008.

Taubman, P., *Teaching by Numbers*. New York, Routledge, 2009.

Unterhalter, E., 'Social Justice, development theory and the question of education', in R. Cowen and A. Kazamias (eds), *International Handbook of Comparative Education*. Dordrecht, Springer, 2009.

Walker, M. and Unterhalter, E., 'The Capability Approach: its potential for work in education', in M. Walker and E. Unterhalter (eds), *Amartya Sen's capability approach and social justice in education*. London/New York, Palgrave, 2007.

Yates, L., 'Does curriculum matter? Revisiting women's access and rights to education in the context of UN Millennium Targets', *Theory and Research in Education* 4 (1), 2006: 85–99.

'From curriculum to pedagogy and back again', *Pedagogy, Culture and Society* 17 (1), 2009: 17–28.

PART TWO
International Organizations

INTERNATIONAL ORGANIZATIONS

UNITED NATIONS EDUCATIONAL, SCIENTIFIC AND CULTURAL ORGANIZATION (UNESCO)

7 place de Fontenoy, 75352 Paris 07 SP, France
Telephone: 1-45-68-10-00
Fax: 1-45-67-16-90
E-mail: bpi@unesco.org
Internet: www.unesco.org

Founded UNESCO was established in 1946 'for the purpose of advancing, through the educational, scientific and cultural relations of the peoples of the world, the objectives of international peace and the common welfare of mankind'.

Functions

UNESCO's activities are funded through a budget provided by member states and also through other sources, particularly the UNDP.

International Intellectual Cooperation

UNESCO assists the interchange of experience, knowledge and ideas through a world network of specialists. Apart from the work of its professional staff, UNESCO cooperates regularly with the national associations and international federations of scientists, artists, writers and educators, some of which it helped to establish.

UNESCO convenes conferences and meetings, and coordinates international scientific efforts; it helps to standardize procedures of documentation and provides clearing house services; it offers fellowships; and it publishes a wide range of specialized works, including source books and works of reference.

UNESCO promotes various international agreements, including the Universal Copyright Convention and the World Cultural and Natural Heritage Convention, which member states are invited to accept.

Operational Assistance

UNESCO has established missions that advise governments, particularly in the developing member countries, in the planning of projects; and it appoints experts to assist in carrying them out. The projects are concerned with the teaching of functional literacy to workers in development undertakings; teacher training; establishing of libraries and documentation centres; provision of training for journalists, radio, television and film workers; improvement of scientific and technical education; training of planners in cultural development; and the international exchange of persons and information.

Promotion of Peace

UNESCO organizes various research efforts on racial problems, and is particularly concerned with prevention of discrimination in education, and improving access for women to education. It also promotes studies and research on conflicts and peace, violence and obstacles to disarmament, and the role of

international law and organizations in building peace. It is stressed that human rights, peace and disarmament cannot be dealt with separately, as the observance of human rights is a prerequisite to peace and not vice versa.

Member States

(July 2010)

Afghanistan
Albania
Algeria
Andorra
Angola
Antigua and Barbuda
Argentina
Armenia
Aruba (Associate Member)
Australia
Austria
Azerbaijan
Bahamas
Bahrain
Bangladesh
Barbados
Belarus
Belgium
Belize
Benin
Bhutan
Bolivia
Bosnia and Herzegovina
Botswana
Brazil
British Virgin Islands (Associate Member)
Brunei
Bulgaria
Burkina Faso
Burundi
Cambodia
Cameroon
Canada
Cape Verde
Cayman Islands (Associate Member)
Central African Republic
Chad
Chile
China, People's Republic
Colombia
Comoros
Congo, Democratic Republic
Congo, Republic
Cook Islands
Costa Rica
Côte d'Ivoire
Croatia
Cuba
Cyprus
Czech Republic
Denmark
Djibouti
Dominica
Dominican Republic
Ecuador
Egypt
El Salvador
Equatorial Guinea
Eritrea

Estonia
Ethiopia
Fiji
Finland
France
Gabon
Gambia
Georgia
Germany
Ghana
Greece
Grenada
Guatemala
Guinea
Guinea-Bissau
Guyana
Haiti
Honduras
Hungary
Iceland
India
Indonesia
Iran
Iraq
Ireland
Israel
Italy
Jamaica
Japan
Jordan
Kazakhstan
Kenya
Kiribati
Korea, Democratic People's Republic
Korea, Republic
Kuwait
Kyrgyzstan
Laos
Latvia
Lebanon
Lesotho
Liberia
Libya
Lithuania
Luxembourg
Macao (Associate Member)
Macedonia, former Yugoslav republic
Madagascar
Malawi
Malaysia
Maldives
Mali
Malta
Marshall Islands
Mauritania
Mauritius
Mexico
Micronesia, Federated States
Moldova
Monaco
Mongolia
Montenegro
Morocco
Mozambique
Myanmar
Namibia
Nauru
Nepal
Netherlands
Netherlands Antilles (Associate Member)

31

New Zealand
Nicaragua
Niger
Nigeria
Niue
Norway
Oman
Pakistan
Palau
Panama
Papua New Guinea
Paraguay
Peru
Philippines
Poland
Portugal
Qatar
Romania
Russia
Rwanda
St Christopher and Nevis
St Lucia
St Vincent and the Grenadines
Samoa
San Marino
São Tomé e Príncipe
Saudi Arabia
Senegal
Serbia
Seychelles
Sierra Leone
Slovakia
Slovenia
Solomon Islands
Somalia
South Africa
Spain
Sri Lanka
Sudan
Suriname
Swaziland
Sweden
Switzerland
Syria
Tajikistan
Tanzania
Thailand
Timor-Leste
Togo
Tokelau (Associate Member)
Tonga
Trinidad and Tobago
Tunisia
Turkey
Turkmenistan
Tuvalu
Uganda
Ukraine
United Arab Emirates
United Kingdom
United States of America
Uruguay
Uzbekistan
Vanuatu
Venezuela
Viet Nam
Yemen
Zambia
Zimbabwe

Organization

GENERAL CONFERENCE

The supreme governing body of the Organization. Meets in ordinary session once in two years and is composed of representatives of the member states and associate members.

EXECUTIVE BOARD

Consists of 58 members with a four-year term of office. Prepares the programme to be submitted to the Conference and supervises its execution. Meets twice or three times a year.

SECRETARIAT

Director-General KOÏCHIRO MATSUURA.

The Director-General has an international staff of some 2,500 civil servants. Of the professional staff (specialists in various disciplines and administrators), about two-thirds are on technical assistance missions in member states.

COOPERATING BODIES

In accordance with UNESCO's constitution, national commissions have been set up in most member states. These help to integrate work within the member states and the work of UNESCO.

UNESCO LIAISON OFFICES

UNESCO Liaison Office New York: Suite 900, 2 United Nations Plaza, New York, NY 10017, USA; tel. (212) 963-5995; fax (212) 963-8014; e-mail newyork@unesco.org; Dir HELENE-MARIE GOSSELIN

UNESCO Liaison Office Geneva: Villa 'Les Feuillantines', Palais des Nations, 1211 Geneva, Switzerland; tel. 229173381; fax 229170064; e-mail geneva@unesco.org; Dir INGEBORG BREINES.

UNESCO FIELD OFFICES

(See also under relevant country)

Africa: Bujumbura (Burundi), Yaoundé (Cameroon), Kinshasa (Democratic Republic of Congo), Brazzaville (Republic of Congo), Addis Ababa (Ethiopia), Libreville (Gabon), Accra (Ghana), Nairobi (Kenya), Bamako (Mali), Maputo (Mozambique), Windhoek (Namibia), Abuja (Nigeria), Dakar (Senegal), Dar es Salaam (Tanzania), Harare (Zimbabwe).

Arab States: Cairo (Egypt), Amman (Jordan), Beirut (Lebanon), Rabat (Morocco), Ramallah (Palestinian Authority), Doha (Qatar).

Asia and the Pacific: Kabul (Afghanistan), Dhaka (Bangladesh), Phnom Penh (Cambodia), Beijing (People's Republic of China), New Delhi (India), Jakarta (Indonesia), Tehran (Iran), Almaty (Kazakhstan), Kathmandu (Nepal), Islamabad (Pakistan), Apia (Samoa), Bangkok (Thailand), Tashkent (Uzbekistan), Hanoi (Viet Nam).

Europe and North America: Venice (Italy), Bucharest (Romania), Moscow (Russia).

Latin America and the Caribbean: Santiago (Chile), San José (Costa Rica), Havana (Cuba), Guatemala (Guatemala), Port-au-Prince (Haiti), Kingston (Jamaica), México (Mexico), Lima (Peru), Montevideo (Uruguay).

Activities

EDUCATION

UNESCO has an overall policy of regarding education as a lifelong process. As an example, one implication is the increasing priority given to basic education for all, including early childhood care and development, primary education and adult education. This approach has been the guideline for many of the projects recently planned.

Each year, expert missions are sent to member states on request to advise on all matters concerning education. They also help with programmes for training abroad, and UNESCO provides study fellowships; in these forms of assistance, priority is given to the rural regions of developing member countries. The issues and problems involved in human resources development have been at the forefront of UNESCO's education

programme since the Organization's foundation. Objectives include the eradication of illiteracy, universal primary education, secondary education reform, technical and vocational education, higher education, adult, non-formal and permanent education, population education, and education of women and girls. 1990 was 'International Literacy Year', in the course of which a world conference on 'Education for All' was held in Thailand. In addition to its regular programme budget, UNESCO's extra-budgetary sources include the UN Development Programme (UNDP), the UN Children's Fund (UNICEF), the UN Population Fund (UNFPA) and the World Bank.

NATURAL SCIENCES

UNESCO's activities under the programme 'The Sciences in the Service of Development' aim to support and foster its member states' endeavours in higher education, advanced training and research in the natural sciences as well as in the application of these sciences to development, while at the same time attaching great importance to integrated and transdisciplinary approaches in its programmes. Activities in the natural sciences focus on the advancement, sharing and transfer of scientific and technological knowledge. At the same time, UNESCO continues to enhance human resources development and capacity-building through fellowships, grants, workshops, and seminars, and has produced a number of training tools. At national level, upon request, UNESCO also assists member states in policy-making and planning in the field of science and technology generally, and by organizing training programmes in these fields.

At the international level, UNESCO has over the years set up various forms of intergovernmental cooperation concerned with the environmental sciences and research on natural resources.

The Man and Biosphere Programme (MAB) gives emphasis to the reinforcement of the World Network of Biosphere Reserves, which aims to reconcile the conservation of biodiversity, the quest for social and economic development, and the maintenance of associated cultural values. The MAB also promotes an interdisciplinary approach to solving land-use problems through research and training, covering topics such as arid-land crops, sacred sites, coastal regions, the Sahel-Sahara observatories, and the biology and fertility of tropical soils.

The International Geological Correlation Programme, networking in more than 150 countries, contributes to comparative studies in earth sciences, including the history of the earth and its geological heritage. Geoscientific programmes have resulted in the production of thematic geological maps, postgraduate training, the application of remote sensing and geodata handling, and studies on climate change and industrial pollution. Guidelines and other awareness-building material on disaster prevention, preparedness and mitigation are also prepared.

The International Hydrological Programme deals with the scientific aspects of water resources assessment and management; and the Intergovernmental Oceanographic Commission (*q.v.*) promotes scientific investigation into the nature and resources of the oceans through the concerted action of its member states.

UNESCO provides the secretariat for the World Solar Programme (instituted in 1996) and has been designated lead agency for the Global Renewable Energy Education and Training Programme.

Major disciplinary programmes are promoted in the fields of physics (including support to the Abdus Salam Centre for Theoretical Physics), the chemical sciences, life sciences, including applied microbiology, mathematics, informatics, engineering sciences and new sources of energy.

SOCIAL AND HUMAN SCIENCES

UNESCO promotes teaching and research in the field of social and human sciences and encourages their application to a number of priority issues relating to education, development, urbanization, migration, youth, human rights, democracy and peace. The social sciences constitute a link between the Organization's two main functions: international intellectual cooperation leading to reflection on major problems, and action to solve these problems.

Among the Organization's subjects of research are: the complex relations between demographic changes and socio-cultural transformation on a global scale; the ways in which societies react to global climatic and environmental change; and changes affecting women and families.

UNESCO's programme gives high priority to the problems of young people, who are the first victims of unemployment, economic and social inequalities, and the widening gap between developing and industrialized countries. Under the mobilizing project 'Youth shaping the Future', an International Youth Clearing House and Information Service was to be established in order to increase awareness among public and private decision-makers of the needs, aspirations and potential of young people.

The struggle against all forms of discrimination is a central part of the Organization's programme. It disseminates scientific information aimed at combating racial prejudice, works to improve the status of women and their access to education, and promotes equality between men and women.

CULTURE

In the field of cultural heritage, the programme concentrates on three major lines of action: activities designed to foster the worldwide application of three international conventions aiming at protecting and preserving cultural property and inserting it into the life of contemporary societies; operational activities such as international safeguarding campaigns designed to help member states to conserve and restore monuments and sites; activities designed to improve the quality of museum management, to train specialists, to disseminate information, such as the most up-to-date conservation methods and techniques, and to promote greater public awareness of the value of cultural heritage.

In addition to a new edition of the *History of the Scientific and Cultural Development of Mankind,* work is continuing on histories of Africa, Latin America, the Caribbean and the civilizations of Central Asia, as well as on a six-volume publication on the various aspects of Islamic culture. A 10-year programme for the collection and safeguarding of the non-physical heritage (oral traditions, traditional music, dance, medicine, etc.) was launched in 1988.

With respect to the cultural dimension of development, the programme includes continuing assistance to member states in the preparation and evaluation of cultural development policies, plans and projects and in the training of cultural development personnel. Proclaimed by the UN General Assembly in December 1986, the World Decade for Cultural Development was launched in January 1988 and ended in 1997. The principal objectives of the Decade were: acknowledging the cultural dimension in development; asserting and enhancing cultural identities; broadening participation in cultural life; and promoting international cultural cooperation.

Following the approval by the General Conference of the Recommendation Concerning the Status of the Artist, efforts are being made to encourage its systematic application in the member states. Particular attention is given to the promotion of music, dance, theatre, architecture, fine arts, design, and arts and crafts, as well as the organization of interdisciplinary workshops and other experimental workshops related to the use of new technologies in artistic creation. To contribute to the mutual appreciation of cultures, UNESCO fosters, in the framework of the UNESCO Collection of Representative Works, translation and publication of literary masterpieces, publishes art albums, and produces and disseminates records, cassettes, audiovisual programmes and travelling art exhibitions.

UNESCO's programme for the promotion of books and reading includes activities for the development of book publishing, production and distribution infrastructures as well as for the training of personnel in all the book fields (including editing, layout and design, ad hoc management courses and courses at university level). A major thrust of the programme is aimed at reinforcing the development of reading at all levels of society (and especially that of children) through promotional activities, reading animation programmes, book weeks and book years.

COPYRIGHT

UNESCO's programme in the field of copyright consists of the following types of activities: (i) those aimed at heightening member states' awareness of the role played by copyright as a stimulant to intellectual creativity; (ii) the preparation of international instruments, the implementation of which is assured by the Secretariat (among these instruments should be cited the Universal Copyright Convention, which, guaranteeing the minimal protection of authors, facilitates the circulation of intellectual and cultural materials); (iii) activities intended to ensure the adequacy of traditional laws vis-à-vis the means of reproduction and of successive diffusion made possible by the latest technological revolutions in the field of reprography, satellites, computers, cable television, cassettes and magnetic discs; (iv) the organization of individual or group training courses intended mainly for the nationals of developing countries; (v) activities to promote access to protected works; (vi) publications and a database on legislation for copyright specialists; (vii) production of a video to increase public awareness of the importance of copyright.

COMMUNICATION, INFORMATION AND INFORMATICS

UNESCO's Communication, Information and Informatics Programme is designed to encourage the free flow of ideas and to help reinforce communication, information and informatics capacities in developing countries. Its major innovation is the extension of the 'free flow' principle to all forms of information contributing to the progress of societies, coupled with a comprehensive approach to challenges posed by the converging communication, information and informatics technologies.

Priorities in the area of communication include support for press freedom and the independence and pluralism of the media, reflection on their educational and cultural dimensions, and efforts to reduce violence on the screen. A series of regional seminars on independence and pluralism of the media has resulted in the declarations and plans of action adopted by those fora being implemented in collaboration with professional media organizations. Furthermore, World Press Freedom Day, initiated by UNESCO in commemoration of the Windhoek Declaration, is celebrated every year on 3 May. UNESCO supports the International Freedom of Expression Exchange network, which counts some 260 subscribers committed to protecting press freedom and the safety of journalists. The network of UNESCO Chairs in Communication (ORBICOM), which counts 16 chairs in all regions of the world, provides an enlarged framework for cooperation among media practitioners, researchers and industries. UNESCO also supports the Global Network of Journalism Training and the International Network of Women in the Media. The main operational arm of UNESCO's communication strategy, and a major funding channel, is the International Programme for the Development of Communication (IPDC), which focuses on strengthening news agencies, media training, community media and endogenous audiovisual production in developing countries. Since 1992, IPDC has given priority to projects in favour of independent and pluralist media. The Programme is governed by a Council of 39 member states.

The General Information Programme (PGI) pursues its efforts to promote international cooperation in the fields of libraries, archives and documentation, with emphasis on appropriate policies, in particular for the widest possible access to information in the public domain, and for methodologies and tools for information management. Among recent initiatives is the launching of the UNESCO Network of Associated Libraries (UNAL), which already includes some 300 members. The Memory of the World Programme aims at safeguarding the recorded memory of humanity, with a number of pilot projects under way in different countries. Furthermore, UNESCO organizes international aid campaigns in this field, such as the programme for the restoration of the National and University Library of Bosnia and Herzegovina. PGI's enlarged mandate covers trends and societal impacts of information technologies. The International Congress on Ethical, Legal and Societal Aspects of Digital Information, held for the first time in Monte Carlo, Monaco in March 1997, provided a forum for reflection and debate in this field.

UNESCO also supports the development of computer networking and the training of informatics specialists, through its Intergovernmental Informatics Programme (IIP). UNESCO-sponsored regional informatics networks—RINAF (Africa), RINAS (Arab States), RINSCA and RINSEAP (Asia/Pacific) and RINEE (Eastern Europe)—serve as test grounds for effective networking options, including links to the Internet.

PUBLICATIONS

(Mostly in English, French and Spanish editions; Arabic, Chinese and Russian versions are also available in many cases.)

Atlas of the World's Languages in Danger of Disappearing (online).

Copyright Bulletin (4 a year).

Encyclopedia of Life Support Systems (online).

International Review of Education (4 a year).
International Social Science Journal (4 a year).
Museum International (4 a year).
Nature and Resources (4 a year).
The New Courier (4 a year).
Prospects (quarterly review on education).
UNESCO Sources (12 a year).
UNESCO Statistical Yearbook.
World Communication Report.
World Educational Report (every 2 years).
World Heritage Review (4 a year).
World Information Report.
World Science Report (every 2 years).

INTERNATIONAL BUREAU OF EDUCATION (IBE)

CP 199, 1211 Geneva 20, Switzerland
Telephone: 229177800
Fax: 229177801
E-mail: doc.centre@ibe.unesco.org
Internet: www.ibe.unesco.org
Founded 1925, the IBE became an intergovernmental org. in July 1929 and was incorporated into UNESCO in January 1969 as an int. centre of comparative education.

COUNCIL

The Council of the IBE is composed of representatives of 28 member states designated by the General Conference of UNESCO.
Dir: PIERRE LUISONI (Switzerland).

FUNCTIONS

International Conference on Education (irregular).
International Education Library: 120,000 vols; c. 1,000 journals received regularly; 500,000 research reports on microfiche.

BUDGET

Financed from the budget of UNESCO.

PUBLICATIONS

Educational Innovation and Information (4 a year, newsletter).
Prospects, international comparative education review (quarterly).

INTERNATIONAL INSTITUTE FOR EDUCATIONAL PLANNING (IIEP)

7–9 rue Eugène Delacroix, 75116 Paris, France
Telephone: 1-45-03-77-00
Fax: 1-40-72-83-66
E-mail: information@iiep.unesco.org
Internet: www.unesco.org/iiep
(Regional office: IIEP–Buenos Aires, Aguero 2071, 1425 Buenos Aires, Argentina; tel. (114) 806-9366; fax (114) 806-9458; e-mail webmaster@iipe-buenosaires.org.ar)
Founded 1963 to serve as a world centre for advanced training and research in educa-

tional planning. Its purpose is to help all member states of UNESCO in their social and economic development efforts, by enlarging the fund of knowledge about educational planning and the supply of competent experts in this field.
Legally and administratively a part of UNESCO, the Institute enjoys intellectual autonomy, and its policies and programme are controlled by its own Governing Board, under special statutes voted by the General Conference of UNESCO.
Chair. of Governing Board: Dato' ASIAH BT ABU SAMAH (Malaysia)
Dir: Dr GUDMUND HERNES (Norway)
Publication: A catalogue of publications, listing 440 titles, is available on request

UNITED NATIONS UNIVERSITY (UNU)

53–70, Jingumae 5-chome, Shibuya-ku, Tokyo 150-8925, Japan
Telephone: (3) 3499-2811
Fax: (3) 3499-2828
E-mail: mbox@hq.unu.edu
Internet: www.unu.edu
(Office in Europe: c/o UNESCO, 1 rue Miollis, 75732 Paris Cedex 15, France; tel. 1-45-68-30-08; fax 1-40-65-91-86)
(Office in North America: Room DC2-1462-70, United Nations, New York, NY 10017, USA; tel. (212) 963-6387; fax (212) 371-9454)
The University is an autonomous institution within the UN framework and is sponsored jointly by the UN and UNESCO. It is guaranteed academic freedom by a charter approved by the General Assembly in 1973. Its work began in September 1975. The UNU is governed by a 24-mem. Council who are appointed by the Sec.-Gen. of the UN and the Dir-Gen. of UNESCO to serve for six years. They come from various regions of the world and have diverse academic backgrounds.

The UNU is funded by voluntary contributions from the govts of many countries, bilateral and multilateral development assistance agencies, foundations, and other public and private sources. The UNU receives no funds from the budget of the UN; contributions are made to the UNU Endowment Fund, which yields investment income, and to its operating funds, as well as to specific programmes and projects.

The UNU undertakes problem-oriented, multidisciplinary research on the problems of human survival, development and welfare that are the concern of the UN and its agencies, and works to strengthen research and training capabilities in developing countries. The programme covers the areas of peace and governance, development, environment, and science and technology. Although the UNU has no students or degree courses, it conducts various training activities in association with its programme and provides fellowships for postgraduate scientists and scholars from developing countries.

The research, training and dissemination activities of the UNU are carried out mainly through networks of collaborating institutions and individual scientists and scholars.

These include associated institutions, which are universities and research institutes linked with the University under general agreements of cooperation. The programme is coordinated by the University Centre in Tokyo, Japan, and by research and training centres and programmes that are being established by the UNU to deal with long-term problems and needs. The UNU's research and training centres and programmes include: the UNU World Institute for Development Economics Research in Helsinki, Finland; the UNU Institute for New Technologies in Maastricht, Netherlands; the UNU International Institute for Software Technology in Macao; the UNU Institute for Natural Resources in Africa in Accra, Ghana, with a mineral resources unit in Lusaka, Zambia; the UNU Institute of Advanced Studies in Tokyo, Japan; the UNU Programme for Biotechnology in Latin America and the Caribbean in Caracas, Venezuela; the UNU International Leadership Academy in Amman, Jordan; the UNU International Network on Water, Environment and Health in Ontario, Canada; the UNU Programme on Comparative Regional Integration Studies in Bruges, Belgium; the UNU Food and Nutrition Programme for Human and Social Development, based at Cornell University, USA; the UNU Geothermal Training Programme and UNU fisheries Training Programme, both based in Iceland; and the initiative on Conflict Resolution and Ethnicity, jointly managed by the UNU and the University of Ulster, UK.
Rector: Prof. HANS J. A. VAN GINKEL
Sr Vice-Rector for Environment and Sustainable Development Programme: Prof. ITARU YASUI
Sr Vice-Rector for Peace and Governance Programme: Prof. RAMESH THAKUR

UNIVERSITY FOR PEACE

Apdo postal 138, Ciudad Colón, Costa Rica
Telephone: 2-49-10-72
Fax: 2-49-19-29
E-mail: info@upeace.org
Internet: www.upeace.org
Founded 1980 by the UN but financially independent; conducts academic research on all aspects of peace, including disarmament, conflict resolution and mediation, the relation between peace and development, and the effects on peace of migration and refugees; various international and governmental institutions are collaborating with the University; initiated a programme of extensive reforms and expansion in 1999; World Centre for Research and Training in Conflict Resolution established in Bogotá, Colombia, in 2001.

Library of 8,000 vols

First students were admitted in 1985.

Chancellor: Dr GRAÇA MACHEL (Mozambique)
Rector: JULIA MARTON-LEFÈVRE (France)

Number of teachers: 16
Number of students: 130

Publication: Peace and Conflict Monitor (12 a Year, in English).

INTERNATIONAL COUNCIL OF SCIENTIFIC UNIONS

International Council of Scientific Unions (ICSU)/Conseil International des Unions Scientifiques: 5 rue Auguste Vacquerie, 75116 Paris, France; tel. 1-45-25-03-29; fax 1-42-88-94-31; e-mail secretariat@icsu.org; internet www.icsu.org; f. 1931; succeeded the Int. Research Council (f. 1919), to coordinate int. efforts in the different brs of science and its applications; to initiate the formation of int. asscns or unions deemed to be useful to the progress of science; to enter into relations with the govts of the countries adhering to the Council in order to promote investigations falling within the competence of the Council; adhering orgs represent 103 countries and 27 int. unions; in December 1946 an agreement was signed between UNESCO and ICSU recognizing the latter as the coordinating and representative body of int. scientific unions; Pres. JANE LUBCHENKO; Sec.-Gen. ANA MARIA CETTO (Mexico); Treas. ROGER ELLIOTT (UK).

UNIONS FEDERATED TO THE ICSU

International Astronomical Union/Union Astronomique Internationale: 98 bis blvd Arago, 75014 Paris, France; tel. (1) 43-25-83-58; fax (1) 43-25-26-16; e-mail iau@iap.fr; internet www.iau.org; f. 1919 to facilitate cooperation between astronomers internationally and to advance the study of astronomy in all aspects; 66 affiliated countries, 9,000 individual mems; Pres. RONALD D. EKERS (Australia); Gen. Sec. ODDBJØRN ENGVOLD (Norway); publs *Transactions of the International Astronomical Union Symposia organized by the International Astronomical Union, Highlights of Astronomy* (every 3 years).

International Geographical Union/Union Géographique Internationale: c/o Prof. Ronald F. Abler, 2246 North Pollard St, Arlington, VA 22207-3805, USA; tel. (202) 431-6271; fax (703) 527-3227; e-mail igu@aag.org; internet www.igu-net.org; f. 1922 to encourage the study of problems relating to geography, to promote and coordinate research requiring int. cooperation, and to organize int. congresses and commissions; 83 mem. countries; Pres. Prof. ADALBERTO VALLEGA; Sec.-Gen. and Treas. Prof. RONALD F. ABLER; publ. *Bulletin* (1 a year).

International Mathematical Union: c/o Phillip A. Griffiths, Institute for Advanced Study, Einstein Dr., Princeton, NJ 08540, USA; fax (609) 683-7605; internet www.mathunion.org; f. 1950 to promote int. cooperation in mathematics; to support the Int. Congress of Mathematicians and other int. scientific meetings or conferences; to encourage and support other int. mathematical activities that contribute to the devt of mathematical science—pure, applied, or educational; 52 mem. countries; 2 commissions: Int. Comm. on Mathematical Instruction, Comm. for Devt and Exchange; Jt Int. Comm. on the History of Mathematics, with the Int. Comm. on the History of Mathematics; Pres. JOHN M. BALL (UK); Sec. PHILLIP A. GRIFFITHS (USA).

International Union for Physical and Engineering Sciences in Medicine: c/o Prof. Heikki Terio, Biomedical Eng., MTA C2:44, Karolinska, Univ. Hospital, Huddinge, Stockholm 14186, Sweden; tel. (8) 585-808-52; fax (8) 585-862-90; e-mail heikki.terio@karolinska.se; internet www.iupesm.org; f. 1982; organizes and coordinates the triennial World Congress for Medical Physics and Biomedical Engin-

eering; organizes and/or coordinates int. meetings or conferences for constituent orgs; represents the interests of members in the Int. Council for Science; disseminates, promotes and/or develops standards of practice in the fields of medical physics and biomedical eng. to enhance the quality of health care world-wide; 40,000 mems; Pres. Prof. JOACHIM NAGEL (Germany); Sec.-Gen. Prof. HEIKKI TERIO (Sweden).

International Union for Pure and Applied Biophysics: c/o Institute of Physics, 76 Portland Garching, Germany; tel. (20) 74704937; fax (20) 74704804; e-mail admin.iupap@iop.org; internet www.iupab.org; f. 1961 to organize int. cooperation in biophysics and promote communication between biophysics and allied subjects, to encourage nat. cooperation between biophysical socs, and to contribute to the advancement of biophysical knowledge; 59 affiliated mems, 19 int. commissions, 4 int. assoc. commissions; Pres. Prof. S. USHIODA (Japan); Sec.-Gen. Prof. Dr ROBERT KIRBY HARRIS (UK); publ. *Quarterly Reviews of Biophysics*.

International Union of Biochemistry and Molecular Biology: c/o Prof. Jacques-Henry Weil, Institut de Botanique, 28 rue Goethe, 67083 Strasbourg Cedex, France; tel. 3-90-24-18-32; fax 3-90-24-19-21; e-mail jacques-henry.weil@ibmp-ulp.u-strasbg.fr; internet www.iubmb.org; f. 1955 to encourage the continuance of a series of Int. Congresses and Conferences of Biochemistry and Molecular Biology; to promote int. coordination of research, discussion and publication; to organize permanent cooperation between the socs representing biochemistry and molecular biology in the adherent countries; to contribute to the advancement of biochemistry and molecular biology in all its aspects; mems: 49 adhering bodies, 24 assoc. adhering bodies, 7 assoc. orgs; Pres. Prof. MARY OSBORN (Germany); Sec.-Gen. Prof. JACQUES-HENRY WEIL (France); Treas. Prof. JAN JOEP DE PONT (Netherlands); publs *Biochemistry and Molecular Biology Education* (12 a year), *Biofactors* (4 a year), *Biotechnology and Applied Biochemistry* (6 a year), *IUBMB Life* (12 a year), *Molecular Aspects of Medicine* (6 a year), *Trends in Biochemical Sciences* (12 a year).

International Union of Biological Sciences/Union Internationale des Sciences Biologiques: Bâtiment 442, Université Paris-Sud 11, 91405 Orsay, France; tel. 1-69-15-50-27; fax 1-69-15-79-47; e-mail secretariat@iubs.org; internet www.iubs.org; f. 1919; mems: 41 countries and 83 int. scientific orgs; promotes int. cooperation in biological research and studies; IUBS programmes on biological diversity, integrative biology, bioethics, biological education, ageing, bio-energy, integrative climate change biology; organizes int. congresses on biological sciences; Pres. GIORGIO BERNARDI (Italy); Exec. Dir NATHALIE FOMPROIX (France); publ. *Biology International* (2 a year).

International Union of Crystallography/Union Internationale de Cristallographie: c/o M. H. Dacombe, 2 Abbey Sq., Chester, CH1 2HU, UK; tel. (1244) 345431; fax (1244) 344843; e-mail execsec@iucr.org; internet www.iucr.org; f. 1947 to promote int. cooperation in crystallography; to contribute to the advancement of crystallography in all its aspects, including related topics concerning the non-crystalline states; to facilitate int. standardization of methods, of units, of nomenclature and of symbols used in crystal-

lography; and to form a focus for the relations of crystallography to other sciences; 20 commissions; 40 mem. countries; Pres. Prof. S. LARSEN (Denmark); Gen. Sec. and Treas. Prof. S. LIDIN (Sweden); Exec. Sec. M. H. DACOMBE; publs *Acta Crystallographica* (Sections A and B, 6 a year; Sections C, D, E and F, 12 a year), *Journal of Applied Crystallography* (6 a year), *Journal of Synchrotron Radiation* (6 a year).

International Union of Food Science and Technology: POB 61021, No. 19, 511 Maple Grove Drive, Oakville, ON L6J 6X0, Canada; tel. (905) 815-1926; fax (905) 815-1574; e-mail secretariat@iufost.org; internet www.iufost.org; f. 1970; encourages int. cooperation and exchange of scientific and technical information among scientists, food technologists and specialists of member nations; supporting int. progress in both theoretical and applied areas of food science; advances technology in the processing, manufacturing, preservation, storage and distribution of food products; encourages appropriate education and training in food science and technology; fostering professionalism and professional organization among food scientists and technologists; nat. representatives in 65 mem. countries; Pres. GEOFFREY CAMPBELL-PLATT (UK); Sec.-Gen. and Treas. JUDITH MEECH (Canada); publs *Food Science and Technology* (6 a year), *The International Review of Food Science and Technology* (1 a year), *The World of Food Science* (online, jtly with Institute of Food Technologists), *Trends in Food Science and Technology* (12 a year).

International Union of Geodesy and Geophysics/Union Géodésique et Géophysique Internationale: tel. (721) 6084494; fax (721) 71173; e-mail secretariat@iugg.org; internet www.iugg.org; f. 1919 to promote the study of problems relating to the form and physics of the earth; to initiate, facilitate and coordinate research into those problems of geodesy and geophysics that require int. cooperation; federation of 8 asscns representing Cryospheric Sciences, Geodesy, Geomagnetism and Aeronomy, Hydrological Sciences, Meteorology and Atmospheric Physics, Physical Sciences of the Oceans, Seismology and Physics of the Earth's Interior, and Volcanology and Chemistry of the Earth's Interior, which meet at the Gen. Assemblies of the Union; jt cttees of the various asscns either among themselves or with other unions; organizes scientific meetings and sponsors various permanent services, the object of which is to collect, analyse and publish geophysical data; 65 mem. countries; Pres. TOM BEER (Australia); Vice-Pres. HARSH GUPTA (India); Sec.-Gen. ALIK ISMAIL-ZADEH (Germany); publs *IUGG E-Journal, IUGG Yearbook, Proceedings of Assemblies*.

International Union of Geological Sciences/Union Internationale des Sciences Géologiques: IUGS Secretariat, Geological Survey of Norway, Lade, POB 3006 Lade, 7002 Trondheim, Norway; tel. 73-92-15-00; fax 73-50-22-30; e-mail iugs.secretariat@ngu.no; internet www.iugs.org; f. 1961 from the International Geological Congress; mems from 110 countries; Pres. Prof. ZHANG HONGREN (People's Republic of China); Vice-Presidents Prof. SYLVI HALDORSEN (Norway), Prof. ELDRIDGE M. MOORES (USA); Sec.-Gen. Dr PETER T. BOBROWSKY (Canada); publs *Episodes, International Geoscience Newsmagazine* (4 a Year),

Reviews or annotated bibliographies on geological topics of current interest (irregular).

International Union of Immunological Societies/Union Internationale des Sociétés d'Immunologie: c/o Gerlinde Jahn, Vienna Academy of Postgraduate Medical Education and Research, Alser Str. 4, 1090 Vienna, Austria; tel. (1) 405138318; fax (1) 4078274; e-mail iuis-central-office@medacad .org; internet www.iuisonline.org; f. 1971; mems: 54 nat. and regional socs; Pres. PETER C. DOHERTY (Australia); Sec.-Gen. MOHAMED R. DAHA (The Netherlands); publ. *The Immunologist* (6 a year).

International Union of Microbiological Societies/Union Internationale des Sociétés de Microbiologie: c/o Dr Robert Samson, Head of Applied and Industrial Mycology, Centraalbureau voor Schimmelcultures, Utrecht, 3508 AD, The Netherlands; tel. (30) 2122600; fax (30) 2512097; e-mail samson@cbs.knaw.nl; internet www .iums.org; f. 1930; mems: 90 nat. socs; Pres. KARL-HEINZ SCHLEIFER (Germany); Sec.-Gen. Dr ROBERT SAMSON (Australia); publs *Archives of Virology* (12 a year), *Biological* (4 a year), *International Journal of Food Microbiology* (26 a year), *International Journal of Systematic and Evolutionary Microbiology* (12 a year).

International Union of Nutritional Sciences/Union Internationale des Sciences de la Nutrition: c/o Dr Osman Galal, UCLA School of Public Health, Community Health Sciences, 36-081 CHS, POB 951772, Los Angeles, CA 90095-1772, USA; tel. (310) 206-9639; fax (310) 794-1805; e-mail info@iuns.org; internet www.iuns .org; f. 1946 to study the science of nutrition and its applications; 80 adhering bodies; Pres. Dr RICARDO UAUY (Chile); Sec.-Gen. Dr OSMAN GALAL (USA).

International Union of Pharmacology/Union Internationale de Pharmacologie: c/o Lindsay Hart, Dept of Pharmacology, College of Medicine, University of California, Irvine, CA 92697, USA; tel. (949) 824-1178; fax (949) 824-4855; internet www.iuphar.org; f. 1959 as section of Int. Union of Physiological Sciences, independent 1966; promotes international coordination of research, discussion, symposia, and publication in the field of pharmacology; cooperates with WHO in matters concerning drugs and drug research, and with related int. unions; four-yearly int. congresses; 52 national and 3 regional mem. socs; integral Division of Clinical Pharmacology and sections of Toxicology, Drug Metabolism and Gastro-intestinal Pharmacology, which also arrange int. meetings; Pres. Prof. PAUL M. VANHOUTTE (People's Republic of China); Sec.-Gen. Dr SUE PIPER DUCKLES (USA).

International Union of Physiological Sciences/Union Internationale des Sciences Physiologiques: c/o Susan Orsoni, LGN, Bâtiment CERVI, Hôpital de la Pitié Salpêtrière, 83 blvd de l'Hôpital, 75013 Paris, France; tel. 1-42-17-75-37; fax 1-42-17-75-3; e-mail orsoni@chups.jussieu.fr; internet www.iups.org; f. 1953 for the advancement of physiological sciences, to facilitate the dissemination of knowledge in the field of physiology, to promote the Int. Congresses of Physiology and such other meetings as may be useful for the advancement of physiological sciences; 54 mem. countries; Pres. Prof. AKIMICHI KANEKO (Japan); Sec.-Gen. Prof. OLE PETERSEN (UK); publ. *Physiology* (4 a year).

International Union of Psychological Science/Union Internationale de Psychologie Scientifique: c/o Pierre Ritchie, Ecole de Psychologie, Université d'Ottawa,

145 Jean-Jacques Lussier, CP 450, Succursale A, Ottawa, ON K1N 6N5, Canada; tel. (613) 562-5800 ext. 4827; fax (613) 562-5169; e-mail pritchie@uottawa.ca; internet www .iupsys.org; f. 1951 at the 13th Int. Congress of Psychology; Int. Congress of Psychology held every 4 years; WHO spec. consultative status; mem. of UN Economic and Social Council, Int. Council for Science, Int. Social Science Council; 70 nat. mems; Pres. BRUCE OVERMIER (USA); Sec.-Gen. PIERRE RITCHIE (Canada); publs *International Journal of Psychology* (6 a year), *Psychology Resource CD-ROM* (1 a year).

International Union of Pure and Applied Chemistry/Union internationale de chimie pure et appliquée: POB 13757, Research Triangle Park, NC 27709-3757, USA; tel. (919) 485-8700; fax (919) 485-8706; e-mail secretariat@iupac.org; internet www.iupac.org; f. 1919 to promote cooperation among chemists of the mem. countries; to study topics of int. importance that require regulation, standardization or codification; to cooperate with other int. orgs that deal with topics of a chemical nature; to contribute to the advancement of pure and applied chemistry in all its aspects; 49 mem. countries; Pres. Prof. BRYAN R. HENRY (Canada); Exec. Dir Dr JOHN W. JOST (USA); Sec.-Gen. Prof. DAVID ST C. BLACK (Australia); publs *Chemistry International* (6 a year), *Pure and Applied Chemistry* (12 a year).

International Union of Pure and Applied Physics/Union internationale de physique pure et appliquée: c/o Jackie Beamon-Kiene, American Physical Society, One Physics Ellipse, College Park, MD 20740-3844, USA; tel. (301) 209-3269; fax (301) 209-0865; e-mail beamon@aps.org; internet www.iupap.org; f. 1922 to promote and encourage int. cooperation in physics; 45 countries are affiliated; 19 international commissions; Pres. Y. PETROFF (France); Sec.-Gen. JUDY FRANZ (USA); publ. *IUPAP News Bulletin* (5 or 6 a year).

International Union of the History and Philosophy of Science: c/o Prof. Juan José Saldaña, National University of Mexico, Apdo Postal 21-388, 04000 Mexico, DF, Mexico; tel. (55) 5622-1864; fax (55) 5544-6316; e-mail dhs@servidor.unam.mx; f. 1956; divisions of History of Science and of Logic, Methodology and Philosophy of Science; Sec.-Gen. Prof. JUAN JOSÉ SALDAÑA.

International Union of Theoretical and Applied Mechanics/Union Internationale de Mécanique Théorique et Appliquée: c/o Prof. Dick H. van Campen, Dept of Mechanical Eng., Technische Universiteit Eindhoven, Den Dolech 2, POB 513, 5600 MB Eindhoven, The Netherlands; fax (40) 2461418; e-mail sg@iutam.net; internet www .iutam.net; f. 1946; provides a forum for persons and orgs engaged in scientific work (theoretical or experimental) in mechanics and related sciences; organizes int. meetings for subjects in this field; and engages in other activities to promote the devt of mechanics as a science; the Union is directed by its Gen. Assembly, which is composed of representatives of the orgs affiliated to the Union and of elected mems; 51 mem. countries; Pres. Prof. BEN FREUND (USA); Sec.-Gen. Prof. DICK H. VAN CAMPEN (Netherlands); publs *Proceedings of IUTAM Symposia* (irregular), *Proceedings of IUTAM World Congress* (every 4 years).

International Union of Toxicology: 1821 Michael Faraday Drive, Suite 300, Reston, VA 20190, USA; tel. (703) 438-3103; fax (703) 438-3113; e-mail iutoxhq@iutox.org; internet www.iutox.org; f. 1980; fosters int. scientific

cooperation among toxicologists and promotes global acquisition, dissemination, and use of knowledge in the science of toxicology; ensures continued training and development of toxicologists worldwide; International Congress on Toxicology every 3 years; sponsors Congresses on Toxicology in Developing Countries every 3 years; affiliated to WHO; 47 nat. and regional mems representing approx. 20,000 toxicologists; Pres. Dr KAI SAVOLAINEN (Finland); Sec.-Gen. Dr A. WALLACE HAYES (USA).

International Union of Radio Science/Union Radio-Scientifique Internationale: c/o INTEC, Ghent Univ., Sint-Pietersnieuwstraat 41, 9000 Ghent, Belgium; tel. (9) 264-33-20; fax (9) 264-42-88; e-mail info@ursi .org; internet www.ursi.org; f. 1919; encourages and coordinates research in the field of radio, telecommunication and electronic sciences, and facilitates the establishment of common radio measurement techniques and standards; 44 nat. cttees; Pres. Prof. FRANÇOIS LEFEUVRE (France); Sec.-Gen. Prof. PAUL LAGASSE (Belgium); Exec. Sec. INGE HELEU (Belgium); Admin. Sec. INGE LIEVENS (Belgium); publs *Records of General Assemblies* (every 3 years), *The Radio Science Bulletin* (4 a year).

COMMITTEES

Tasks that fall within the sphere of activities of two or more Unions have been undertaken by the following Scientific or Special Committees set up by the ICSU:

Committee on Capacity Building in Science: c/o Dr Shirley Malcom, AAAS, 1200 New York Ave, Washington, DC 20005, USA; tel. (202) 326-6720; f. 1993; promotes to the public and to policy-makers an understanding and appreciation of the role of science in modern society and provides science education information to primary school teachers worldwide; Chair. Dr SHIRLEY MALCOM.

Committee on Data for Science and Technology: c/o Kathleen Cass, 5 rue Auguste Vacquerie, 75016 Paris, France; tel. (1) 45-25-04-96; fax (1) 42-88-14-66; e-mail codata@dial.oleane.com; internet www.codata.org; f. 1966 by ICSU to improve the quality, reliability and accessibility of scientific data, including quantitative information on the properties and behaviour of matter, and other experimental and observational data; 19 nat. and 15 scientific union mems; Pres. Prof. SHUICHI IWATA (Japan); Exec. Dir KATHLEEN CASS (France); Sec.-Gen. Dr ROBERT CHEN (USA); publs *International Compendium of Numerical Data Projects*, *International Conference Proceedings*.

Committee on Space Research: c/o CNES, 2 pl. Maurice Quentin, 75039 Paris Cedex 01, France; tel. 1-44-76-75-10; fax 1-44-76-74-37; e-mail cospar@cosparhq.cnes.fr; internet cosparhq.cnes.fr; f. 1958 to promote scientific research in space on an int. level, with an emphasis on the exchange of results, information and opinions; promotes the use of space science for the benefit of mankind and for its adoption by developing countries and new space-faring nations; organizes scientific assemblies every 2 years; advises the UN and other int. orgs on space research matters and on the assessment of scientific issues in which space can play a role; prepares scientific and technical standards related to space research; mems: 44 countries and 13 int. scientific unions; Pres. Prof. R.-M. BONNET (France); Exec. Dir Dr J.-L. FELLOUS; Assoc. Dir A. JANOFSKY; publs *Advances in Space Research*, *Space Research Today*.

Scientific Committee on Antarctic Research: SCAR Secretariat, Scott Polar Research Institute, Lensfield Rd, Cambridge,

CB2 1ER, UK; tel. (1223) 336550; fax (1223) 336549; e-mail info@scar.org; internet www .scar.org; f. 1958 by ICSU to continue the promotion of int. cooperation in scientific research in the Antarctic; holds biennial conference; organizes meetings, workshops and symposia; establishes and coordinates int. programmes to address major scientific questions in Antarctica; 31 full mems (nat. acads of science and scientific unions), 9 union mems, 4 assoc. mems; Pres. Prof. MAHLON C. KENNICUTT (USA); Exec. Dir Dr MIKE D. SPARROW; Exec. Officer Dr RENUKA BADHE; publs *SCAR Bulletin* (4 a year), *SCAR Report* (irregular).

Scientific Committee on Oceanic Research: Robinson Hall, College of Earth, Ocean, and Environment, Univ. of Delaware, Newark, DE 19716, USA; tel. (302) 831-7011; fax (302) 831-7012; e-mail secretariat@ scor-int.org; internet www.scor-int.org; f. 1957 to advance int. scientific activity in all brs of oceanic research; c. 20 active working Groups, Cttees and Panels investigate a broad range of oceanographic problems; library of 300 vols; mems: nominated mems by Cttees for Oceanic Research in 38 countries; rep. mems of affiliated orgs; invited mems by the exec. cttee; Pres. Prof. Dr WOLFGANG FENNEL (Germany); Sec. Dr JORMA KUPARINEN (Finland); Exec. Dir Dr EDWARD R. URBAN, Jr (USA); publ. *SCOR Proceedings* (1 a year).

Scientific Committee on Problems of the Environment: 51 blvd de Montmorency, 75016 Paris, France; tel. 1-45-25-04-98; fax 1-42-88-14-66; e-mail secretariat@icsu-scope .org; internet www.icsu-scope.org; f. 1969; interdisciplinary research in the environmental field; mems: 40 Nat. Cttees and 22 International Unions; Pres. Dr JERRY M. MELILLO (USA); Sec.-Gen. Prof. OSVALDO SALA (Argentina); publ. *SCOPE Reports*.

Scientific Committee on Solar-Terrestrial Physics: HAO/NCAR, 3080 Center Green Drive, Boulder, CO 80301, USA; tel. (303) 497-1591; fax (303) 497-1580; e-mail ganglu@ucar.edu; internet www.scostep.ucar .edu; f. 1966 as an Inter-Union Commission by ICSU and became a Scientific Cttee in 1978 to promote and coordinate int. interdisciplinary programmes in solar-terrestrial physics and to work with other ICSU bodies in the coordination of symposia in the field of solar-terrestrial physics; 400 mems; Pres. M. A. GELLER (USA); Scientific Sec. Dr GANG LU (USA).

SERVICES AND INTER-UNION COMMISSIONS

Federation of Astronomical and Geophysical Data Analysis Services: c/o Dr Niels Andersen, Kort and Matrikelstyrelsen, Rentemestervej 8, 2400 Copenhagen NV, Denmark; fax 35-87-50-57; e-mail fags@kms

.dk; internet www.kms.dk/fags/index.html; f. 1956; federates the following Permanent Services: International Earth Rotation Service, Bureau Gravimetrique International, International GPS Service for Geodynamics, International Center for Earth Tides, Permanent Service for Mean Sea Level, International Service of Geomagnetic Indices, Quarterly Bulletin of Solar Activity, International Space Environment Service, World Glacier Monitoring Service, Centre des Données Stellaires, Sunspot Index Data Center; Pres. D. PUGH (UK); Sec. N. ANDERSEN (Denmark).

Scientific Committee on Frequency Allocations for Radio Astronomy and Space Science/Comité scientifique pour l'allocation des fréquences à la radio astronomie et la recherche spatiale: c/o Observatoire de Paris, 5 place Jules Janssen, 92195 Meudon, France; tel. 1-45-07-77-31; fax 1-45-07-77-09; e-mail iucafchair@iucaf .org; internet www.iucaf.org; f. 1960 under auspices of URSI with representatives of URSI, IAU and COSPAR, to study the requirements for frequency bands and radio frequency protection for research in the fields of radio astronomy, earth exploration and space science; and to make their requirements known to the appropriate frequency-allocation authorities; 10 mems; Chair. WIM VAN DRIEL (France).

INTERNATIONAL COUNCIL FOR PHILOSOPHY AND HUMANISTIC STUDIES

International Council for Philosophy and Humanistic Studies (ICPHS)/Conseil International de la Philosophie et des Sciences Humaines: Secretariat Maison de l'UNESCO, 1 rue Miollis, 75732 Paris Cedex 15, France; tel. 1-45-68-48-85; fax 1-40-65-94-80; e-mail cipsh@unesco.org; internet www.unesco.org/cipsh; f. 1949 under the auspices of UNESCO to encourage respect for cultural autonomy by the comparative study of civilization, to contribute towards int. understanding through a better knowledge of man, to develop int. cooperation in philosophy, humanistic and related studies, to encourage the setting up of int. orgs, to promote the dissemination of information in these fields, to sponsor works of learning, etc.; the Council is composed of 13 int. NGOs; these orgs represent 145 countries; in 1951 an agreement was signed between UNESCO and ICPHS recognizing the latter as the coordinating and representative body of orgs in the field of philosophy and humanistic studies; Pres. CHA IN-SUK (Korea); Sec.-Gen. MAURICE AYMARD (France); publs *Bulletin of Information* (every 2 years), *Diogenes* (4 a year).

UNIONS FEDERATED TO THE ICPHS

International Association for the History of Religions/Association Internationale pour l'Histoire des Religions: c/o Prof. Tim Jensen, IFPR, Univ. of Southern Denmark, Campusvej 55, 5230 Odense M, Denmark; tel. 6550-3315; fax 3887-5095; e-mail t.jensen@ifpr.sdu.dk; internet www .iahr.dk; f. 1950 by the 7th Int. Congress for

the Study of the History of Religions to promote the study of the history of religions through the int. collaboration of scholars who research the subject, to organize congresses and to encourage the production of publs; annual spec. or regional conferences, and Quinquennial World Congresses; 37 mem. countries, 5 regional assoc. mems; Pres. Prof. ROSALIND HACKETT (USA); Gen. Sec. Prof. TIM JENSEN (Denmark); publ. *Numen* (4 a year).

International Committee of Historical Sciences/Comité International des Sciences Historiques: c/o Prof. Jean-Claude Robert, Dépt d'Histoire, Université du Québec à Montréal, CP 8888, Succursale Centre ville, Montréal, QC H3C 3P8, Canada; tel. (514) 987-30-00; fax (514) 987-78-13; e-mail cish@uqam.ca; internet www.cish.org; f. 1926; int. congresses since 1900 to work for the advancement of historical sciences by means of int. coordination (every five years); mems in 54 countries; gen. assembly every 2–3 years; Pres. Prof. JOSÉ LUIS PESET (Spain); Sec.-Gen. Prof. JEAN-CLAUDE ROBERT (Canada); publs *Bibliographie Internationale des Sciences Historiques*, *Bulletin d'Information*.

International Committee for the History of Art/Comité international d'histoire de l'art: c/o Philippe Sénéchal, Institut national d'histoire de l'art, 2 rue Vivienne, 75084 Paris, France; tel. 1-47-03-79-25; fax 1-47-03-86-36; internet www.esteticas.unam .mx/ciha; f. 1930 by the 12th Int. Congress on the History of Art for collaboration in the scientific study of the history of art; mems in 31 countries; int. congress every 4 years; int.

colloquium every year; Pres. Prof. STEPHEN BANN (UK); Scientific Sec. PHILIPPE SÉNÉCHAL (France); Treas. and Admin. Sec. Prof. Dr OSKAR BÄTSCHMANN (Switzerland); publ. *Bibliography of the History of Art* (CD-ROM, quarterly).

International Federation for Modern Languages and Literatures/Fédération Internationale des Langues et Littératures Modernes: c/o Anders Pettersson, Umeå Univ., 901 87 Umeå, Sweden; tel. (90) 786-5797; e-mail anders.pettersson@ littvet.umu.se; internet www.fillm.ulg.ac.be; f. 1928 as the Int. Cttee on Modern Literary History; present name and status 1951; aims to establish permanent contact between historians of literature, to develop or perfect facilities for their work and to promote the study of the history of modern literature; 19 mem. asscns, with mems in 92 countries; Pres. Prof. THEO D'HAEN (Belgium); Sec.-Gen. Prof. ANDERS PETTERSSON (Sweden); publ. *Acts of the Triennial Congresses*.

International Federation of Philosophical Societies/Fédération Internationale des Sociétés de Philosophie: c/o Ioanna Kuçuradi, Dept of Philosophy, Hacettepe Univ., Beytepe, 06542 Ankara, Turkey; tel. (312) 2978300; fax (312) 4410297; e-mail ioanna@fisp.org.tr; internet www.fisp.org.tr; f. 1948 under the auspices of UNESCO to encourage int. cooperation in the field of philosophy, and to promote congresses, symposia and publs; 108 mem. socs from 50 countries and 26 int. mem. socs; Pres. IOANNA KUÇURADI (Turkey); Sec.-Gen. PETER KEMP (Denmark); publs under the auspices of

FISP, *Proceedings of the International Congresses of Philosophy*.

International Federation of the Societies of Classical Studies/Fédération Internationale des Associations d'Etudes Classiques: c/o Prof. Paul Schubert, 7 rue des Beaux-Arts, 2000 Neuchâtel, Switzerland; e-mail paul.schubert@unige.ch; internet www.fiecnet.org; f. 1948 under the auspices of UNESCO to encourage research on the ancient civilizations of Greece and Rome; to group the main nat. asscns of this field; to ensure collaboration with relevant int. orgs; affiliated bodies incl. the Int. Soc. for Classical Bibliography, Int. Soc. for Classical Archaeology, Int. Soc. for Byzantine Studies, Int. Asscn for Greek and Latin Epigraphy, Int. Asscn of Papyrologists, Unione internazionale degli Istituti di Archaeologia, Storia e Storia dell'Arte in Roma, Société d'histoire des droits de l'antiquité, Comité int. des Etudes mycéniennes, Asscn int. des Etudes patristiques, etc.; 79 mem. socs in 44 countries; Pres. Prof. HEINRICH VON STADEN (USA); Sec.-Gen. Prof. PAUL SCHUBERT (Switzerland); publ. *L'Année Philologique* (bibliography, 1 a year).

International Musicological Society/ Société Internationale de Musicologie: Nadelstr. 60, 8706 Feldmeilen, Switzerland; tel. (44) 9231022; fax (44) 9231027; e-mail dorothea.baumann@ims-online.ch; internet www.ims-online.ch; f. 1927; promotes musicological research, encourages study in the field and coordinates the work of musicologists worldwide; int. congress every 5 years, intercongressional symposia, int. study groups; 49 mem. countries, 1,000 individual mems; Pres. Prof. Dr TILMAN SEEBASS (Austria); Sec.-Gen. Dr DOROTHEA BAUMANN (Switzerland); Vice-Pres. Prof. Dr MALENA

KUSS; Vice-Pres. Dir CATHERINE MASSIP; publs *Acta Musicologica* (2 a year, online), *Catalogus Musicus* (irregular), *Documenta Musicologica* (irregular), *International Inventory of Musical Sources* (RISM, online and print), *International Repertory of Musical Iconography* (RIDIM, online databases), *International Repertory of Music Literature* (RILM, annual, online), *Répertoire International de la Presse Musicale* (RIPM, online and print).

International Union of Academies/ Union Académique Internationale: Palais des Académies, 1 rue Ducale, 1000 Brussels, Belgium; tel. 550-22-00; fax 550-22-05; e-mail info@uai-iua.org; internet www.uai-iua.org; f. 1919 to promote int. cooperation through collective research in philology, archaeology, history, social sciences and humanities in general; affiliated countries: Argentina, Australia, Austria, Belgium, Bosnia and Herzegovina, Bulgaria, Canada, Chile, China, Costa Rica, Croatia, Czech Republic, Denmark, Egypt, Estonia, Finland, France, Georgia, Germany, Ghana, Greece, Hungary, India, Iran, Ireland, Israel, Italy, Japan, Repub. of Korea, Latvia, Luxembourg, former Yugoslav republic of Macedonia, Madagascar, Mexico, Moldova, Montenegro, Morocco, Netherlands, Norway, Paraguay, Peru, Poland, Portugal, Romania, Russia, Serbia, Slovakia, Slovenia, South Africa, Spain, Sweden, Switzerland, Tunisia, Turkey, Ukraine, UK, USA, Uruguay, Vatican City, Viet Nam; associate members: International Academy of History of Science, African Academy of Languages, World Islamic Academy of Sciences; Pres. MIKLOS MAROTH (Hungary); Vice-Pres. JANUSZ KOZLOWSKI (Poland), LIZ HANNESTAD (Denmark); Admin. Sec. HERVE HASQUIN JEAN-LUC

DE PAEPE (Belgium); publs *Archivum Latinitatis Medii Aevi* (every 2 years), *Compte rendu (de la session annuelle) du Comité* (1 a year), *Novum Glossarium*.

International Union of Anthropological and Ethnological Sciences (IUAES)/ Union Internationale des Sciences Anthropologiques et Ethnologiques: see under ISSC.

International Union of Prehistoric and Protohistoric Sciences/Union Internationale des Sciences Préhistoriques et Protohistoriques: Prof. Luiz Oosterbeek, Instituto Politécnico de Tomar, Av. Dr Cândido Madureira 13, 2300-531 Tomar, Portugal; tel. (249) 34-63-63; fax (249) 34-63-66; e-mail loost@ipt.pt; internet www.uispp.pt.vu; f. 1931 to promote congresses and scientific work in the fields of pre- and protohistory; 120 mem. countries; 40,000 mems; Pres. Prof. IGNACIO SCHMIDT (Brazil); Sec.-Gen. Prof. LUIZ OOSTERBEEK (Portugal); publs *Archaeologia urbium*, *Inventaria archaeologica*, *Proceedings of the XV world Congress, Lisbon*.

Permanent International Committee of Linguists/Comité International Permanent des Linguistes: c/o Prof. P. G. J. van Sterkenburg, IPOB 3023 2301 DA Leiden, The Netherlands; tel. (71) 522-77-37; e-mail cipl.secretary-general@planet.nl; internet www.ciplnet.com; f. 1928 to work for the advancement of linguistics worldwide and to encourage int. cooperation in this field; 33 mem. countries and 2 int. orgs; Pres. Prof. F. KIEFER (Hungary); Sec.-Gen. Prof. P. G. J. VAN STERKENBURG; publ. *Linguistic Bibliography* (1 a year).

INTERNATIONAL SOCIAL SCIENCE COUNCIL

International Social Science Council (ISSC)/Conseil International des Sciences Sociales: Maison de l'UNESCO, 1 rue Miollis, 75732 Paris Cedex 15, France; tel. 1-45-68-48-60; fax 1-45-66-76-03; e-mail issc@unesco.org; internet www.unesco.org/ ngo/issc; f. 1952; advancement of the social sciences worldwide and their application to the major problems of the world and cooperation at an int. level between specialists in the social sciences; Standing Cttees on Int. Human Dimensions of Global Environmental Change Program (IHDP, co-sponsored by ICSU), Comparative Research Programme on Poverty (CROP) and Globalization, Gender and Democratization (GGD), Int. Global Social Change Programme, Research on Ethnic Conflicts and Approaches to Peace (RECAP); 13 mem. assocs, 22 mem. orgs, 18 assoc. mems; Pres. Prof. LOURDES ARIZPE (Mexico); Sec.-Gen. Dr ALI KAZANCIGIL (France); publ. *e-bulletin* (online).

ASSOCIATIONS FEDERATED TO THE ISSC

International Association of Legal Sciences/Association Internationale des Sciences Juridiques: c/o ISSC, UNESCO, 1 rue Miollis, 75015 Paris, France; tel. (1) 45-68-25-58; fax (1) 43-06-87-98; e-mail leker .meir@libertysurf.fr; f. 1950 to promote the

mutual knowledge and understanding of nations and the increase of learning by encouraging worldwide the study of foreign legal systems and the use of the comparative method in legal science; governed by a President and an executive bureau of 10 members known as the International Committee of Comparative Law; national cttees in 46 countries; Pres. Prof. KONSTANTINOS KERAMEUS (Greece); Sec.-Gen. MEIR M. LEKER; Dir of Scientific Research Prof. P. SARCEVIĆ (Croatia).

International Economic Association/ Association Internationale des Sciences Economiques: 23 rue Campagne-Première, 75014 Paris, France; tel. 1-43-27-91-44; fax 1-42-79-92-16; e-mail iea@iea-world.org; internet www.iea-world.org; f. 1949 to promote int. collaboration for the advancement of economic knowledge, to develop personal contacts between economists, and to encourage provision of means for the dissemination of economic knowledge; mem. associations in 57 countries; Pres. JANOS KORNAI (Hungary); Sec.-Gen. JEAN-PAUL FITOUSSI (France).

International Federation of Social Science Organizations/Fédération Internationale des Organisations de Science Sociale: 245/69 Baromtrilokanart Rd, Muang District, 65000 Phitsanulok, Thailand; tel. (55) 244-240; e-mail contact@ifsso .org; internet www.ifsso.org; f. 1979 to suc-

ceed the Conference of Nat. Social Science Councils and Analogous Bodies (f. 1975) to encourage int. cooperation in the social sciences, to advance the devt of the social sciences, especially in the developing world, to advance the exchange of information, ideas and experiences among its mems, to promote a more effective organization of research and teaching and the building of instns in the social sciences; 22 mems; Pres. Prof. Dr CARMENCITA T. AGUILAR (Philippines); Sec.-Gen. Prof. J. BLAHOZ (Czech Republic); publ. *International Directory of Social Science Organizations*.

International Geographical Union/ Union Géographique Internationale: see under ICSU.

International Institute of Administrative Sciences/Institut International des Sciences Administratives: 1 rue Defacqz, Bte 11, 1000 Brussels, Belgium; tel. (2) 536-08-80; fax (2) 537-97-02; e-mail info@iias-iisa .org; internet www.iias-iisa.org; f. 1930 for the comparative examination of admin. experience in mem. countries; research and programmes for improving admin. law and practices and for technical assistance; consultative status with ECOSOC, ILO and UNESCO; int. congresses; considers impact of new technologies on admin., management of multicultural societies, admin. in transitional economies, admin. aspects of political transition, women in public admin., new regulations and new modes of control, implications of globalization and internationalization for nat. and local admin., interaction between NGOs and public admin.; public admin. and the social sectors, innovations in int. admin.; 36 mem. states, 30 nat. sections, 3 int. govt orgs, 38 corporate and individual mems, 6 individuals; Pres. Prof. FRANZ STREHL (Austria); Dir-Gen. ROLET LORETAN (Switzerland); publ. *International Review of Administrative Sciences/Revue internationale des sciences administratives* (4 a year).

International Law Association/Association de Droit International: Charles Clore House, 17 Russell Sq., London, WC1B 5DR, UK; tel. (20) 7323-2978; fax (20) 7323-3580; e-mail info@ila-hq.org; internet www.ila-hq.org; f. 1873 for the study and advancement of int. law, public and private, and the promotion of int. understanding and goodwill; 50 regional brs worldwide; 4,200 mems; 25 int. cttees; Pres. Prof. KARL-HEINZ BOCKSTIEGEL; Chair. Exec. Council Lord SLYNN OF HADLEY (UK); Sec.-Gen. DAVID J. C. WYLD.

International Peace Research Association/Association Internationale de Recherche pour la Paix: c/o Luc Reychler, University of Leuven, Van Evenstraat 2B, Leuven, Belgium; tel. (16) 323241; fax (16) 323088; e-mail luc.reychler@soc.kuleuven.ac.be; internet www.human.mie-u.ac.jp/~peace/about-ipra; f. 1964 to encourage the development of interdisciplinary research into the conditions of peace and the causes of war; mems in 93 countries: 1,050 individuals, 400 corporate, 10 nat. and regional asscns; Sec.-Gen. LUC REYCHLER (Belgium).

International Political Science Association (IPSA)/Association Internationale de Science Politique: 1590 ave Docteur-Penfield, Bureau 331, Montreal, QC H3G 1C5, Canada; tel. (514) 848-8717; fax (514) 848-4095; internet www.ipsa.org; f. 1949; promotes internationally planned research and scholarly collaboration, organizes int. conferences, symposia, triennial world congresses, and provides documentary and reference services; nat. asscns in 50 countries: 97 assoc. mems, 3,100 individual mems; Pres. Dr LOURDES SOLA (Brazil); Sec.-Gen. Prof.

GUY LACHAPELLE (Canada); publs *International Political Science Abstracts* (6 a year), *International Political Science Review* (4 a year).

International Sociological Association/Association Internationale de Sociologie: Facultad CC. Políticas y Sociología, Universidad Complutense, 28223 Madrid, Spain; tel. 91-352-76-50; fax 91-352-49-45; e-mail isa@isa-sociology.org; internet www.isa-sociology.org; f. 1949; promotes sociological research, develops personal contacts among the sociologists of all countries and ensures the exchange of sociological information; 53 research cttees on a wide variety of sociological topics; holds World Congresses every 4 years; 3,500 individual mems, 150 collective mems; Pres. Prof. MICHEL WIEVIORKA (France); Exec. Sec. Dr IZABELA BARLINSKA (Poland); publs *Current Sociology/Sociologie Contemporaine* (4 a year), *e-Bulletin* (3 a year), *International Sociology* (4 a year).

International Studies Association: 324 Social Sciences Bldg, University of Arizona, Tucson, AZ 85721, USA; tel. (520) 621-7715; fax (520) 621-5780; e-mail isa@u.arizona.edu; internet www.isanet.org; f. 1959; promotes research and cooperation into international studies; 3,000 mems in 80 countries; Pres. JACEK KUGLER (USA); Exec. Dir THOMAS J. VOLGY (USA); publs *International Studies Notes, International Studies Quarterly.*

International Union of Anthropological and Ethnological Sciences (IUAES)/Union Internationale des Sciences Anthropologiques et Ethnologiques: c/o Prof. Peter Nas, University of Leiden, Institute of Cultural and Social Studies, POB 9555, 2300 RB Leiden, Netherlands; tel. (71) 5273992; fax (71) 5273619; e-mail nas@fsw.leidenuniv.nl; internet www.leidenuniv.nl/fsw/iuaes; f. 1948 under the auspices of UNESCO to promote research and cooperation among anthropological and ethnological institutions; mems: 20 national, 80 institutional and over 200 individuals worldwide; also federated to ICPHS, ISSC and ICSU; Pres. Prof. LUIS ALBERTO VARGAS (Mexico); Sec.-Gen. Prof. Dr PETER NAS (Netherlands).

International Union of Psychological Science (IUPsyS)/Union International des Sciences Psychologiques: see under ICSU.

International Union for the Scientific Study of Population/Union Internationale pour l'Etude Scientifique de la Population: 3–5 rue Nicolas, 75980, Paris Cedex 20, France; tel. 1-56-06-21-73; fax 1-56-06-22-04; e-mail iussp@iussp.org; internet www.iussp.org; f. 1928, reconstituted 1947, to advance the progress of quantitative and qualitative demography as a science; mems: 1,900 scientists in 124 countries; Pres. JACQUES VALLIN (France); Exec. Dir ERIK KLIJZING (Netherlands); Sec.-Gen. MARY KRITZ (USA); publs *IUSSP papers, Proceedings* (conferences and seminars).

World Association for Public Opinion Research: c/o UNL Gallup Research Center, Univ. of Nebraska, 201 N 13th St, Lincoln, NE 68588-0242, USA; tel. (402) 472-7720; fax (402) 472-7727; e-mail renae@wapor.org; internet www.unl.edu/wapor; f. 1947; to establish and promote contacts between persons in the field of survey research on opinions, attitudes and behaviour of people worldwide, and to advance the use of scientific survey research in nat. and int. affairs; 400 individual mems in over 60 countries; Pres. Dr THOMAS PETERSEN (Germany); Gen. Sec. Prof. Dr ALLAN L. McCUTCHEON (USA); publ. *International Journal for Public Opinion Research* (4 a year).

World Federation for Mental Health/Fédération Mondiale pour la Santé Mentale: POB 16810, Alexandria, VA 22302-0810, USA; tel. (703) 838-7543; fax (703) 519-7648; e-mail info@wfmh.com; internet www.wfmh.org; f. 1948 to promote among all people and nations the highest possible standard of mental health in the broadest biological, medical, educational, and social aspects; to work with ECOSOC, UNESCO, WHO, and other agencies of the UN, to promote mental health; to help other voluntary associations in the improvement of mental health services; 2,600 individual mems, 150 voting orgs, 139 affiliated orgs; Pres. Dr PATT FRANCIOSI (USA); Sec.-Gen. PRESTON GARRISON (USA).

INTERNATIONAL ASSOCIATION OF UNIVERSITIES (IAU)

1 rue Miollis, 75732 Paris Cedex 15, France; tel. 1-45-68-48-00; fax 1-47-34-76-05; e-mail iau@iau-aiu.net; internet www.iau-aiu.net; f. 1950 to provide a centre of cooperation at int. level among univs and similar instns of higher education of all countries; 650 univs and instns of higher education in 150 countries; 12 assoc. mems (int. and nat. univ. orgs)

Organization

GENERAL CONFERENCE

Composed of the full and assoc. mems. Meets every 5 years. Discusses topics of importance for the future of univ. education, determines gen. policy and elects the Pres. and mems of the Admin. Board. Twelfth Gen. Conference was held in São Paulo, Brazil, in 2004.

ADMINISTRATIVE BOARD

Chaired by the Pres. of the IAU, and composed of 20 eminent univ. leaders and scholars and a maximum of 20 deputy mems from all continents. Meets annually, ensures that decisions of the Gen. Conference are implemented and guides the work of the Int. Univs Bureau.

Pres.: JUAN RAMÓN DE LA FUENTE (Former Rector, National Autonomous University of Mexico).

Sec.-Gen. and Exec. Dir EVA EGRON-POLAK

INTERNATIONAL UNIVERSITIES BUREAU (IUB)

The IUB, created in 1949, provides the Permanent Secretariat for the IAU. It is the principal instrument for the execution of the activities of the IAU. Its main tasks include facilitating and promoting the exchange of information, experience and ideas, of students, teachers, researchers and administrators, and of publications and material for teaching and research.

Exec. Dir (Ex-Officio) EVA EGRON-POLAK.

Principal Activities

Information

Under a formal Agreement with UNESCO, the IAU operates a joint IAU/UNESCO Information Centre on Higher Education at its Int. Univs Bureau. The Centre holds 40,000 vols and a large colln of unpublished materials; it has subscriptions to 300 current specialized periodicals and maintains a colln of 4,000 prospectuses of higher education instns, as well as conference reports, occasional papers, CD-ROMs, etc. The Centre was fully computerized in 1989, and all holdings were subsequently catalogued in the Centre's own database (IAUDOC). All references can be found in the int. bibliographical database (HED-BIB), accessible via the IAU website. The database links to nat. and int. information centres and data networks. The IAU acts as the coordinating agency for the World Academic Database (WAD).

Studies, Research and Meetings
The IAU coordinates and carries out studies and research on issues of higher education and higher education policies that are either common to instns and systems worldwide, or where a comparative analysis between different situations and approaches is of particular benefit to higher education instns. Conferences, symposia, colloquia, seminars, round tables and workshops provide an int. forum

for the discussion of topics of common concern to higher education leaders and specialists.

Cooperation
The IAU provides an important clearing-house function to its mems for academic exchange and cooperation. The IAU has adopted the *Kyoto Declaration and Agenda for Sustainable Development 1993*, to promote and support univ. cooperation; the *Durban Declaration on Internationalization 2000* to ensure that higher education instns seize the initiative in the process of internationalization rather than reacting to the forces of globalization and the market; and the *São Paolo Declaration on Information and Communication Technologies (ICTs) 2004*, to act as a platform for information-sharing in regard to the use of ICTs in higher education.

SELECTED PUBLICATIONS

Guide to Higher Education in Africa (irregular).

Higher Education Policy (English; 4 a year).

International Handbook of Universities (English; every 2 years).

Issues in Higher Education (English; 3 or 4 a year).

World Academic Database (WAD)(CD-ROM; English and French; 1 a year).

World Higher Education Database (CD-ROM; English; 1 a year).

World List of Universities and Other Institutions of Higher Education (English and French; every 2 years).

OTHER INTERNATIONAL ORGANIZATIONS

General

Academia Europaea: 4th Fl., 21 Albemarle St, London, W1S 4HS, UK; tel. 7495-3717; e-mail admin@acadeuro.org; internet www.acadeuro.org; f. 1988; a free asscn of individual scholars working in Europe in all disciplines; aims to encourage European activities in scholarship and the undertaking of ind. studies on matters of European importance; holds meetings, symposia, study groups, etc.; 2,300 mems; Pres. Prof. LARS WALLOE (Norway); Exec. Sec. Dr DAVID COATES; publ. *European Review* (4 a year).

Academia Scientiarum et Artium Europaea (European Academy of Sciences and Arts): St Peter-Bezirk 10, 5020 Salzburg, Austria; tel. (662) 84-13-45; fax (662) 84-13-43; e-mail office@european-academy.at; internet www.european-academy.at; f. 1990; promotes an overall view of the sciences and arts on a European level; 1,200 mems; Pres. Prof. Dr FELIX UNGER; Vice-Pres. Prof. Dr NIKOLAUS LOBKOWICZ.

Islamic World Academy of Sciences (IAS): POB 830036, Amman 11183, Jordan; tel. (6) 5522104; fax (6) 5511803; e-mail ias@go.com.jo; internet www.ias-worldwide.org; f. 1986, present name 2005; int., ind., non-political NGO of scientists and technologists, working to promote science, technology and devt in the Islamic and developing worlds; organizes confs and seminars; supervises training workshops; comms research; acts as the scientific adviser to the OIC (Org. of the Islamic Conf.) and developing countries; collaborates with other nat., regional and int. academies of science, UNESCO, COMSTECH; 107 fellows and 13 hon. fellows from 40 countries; Dir-Gen. Dr MONEEF R. ZOU'BI; publs *Islamic Thought and Scientific Creativity* (4 a year), *Medical Journal* (4 a year), *Proceedings* (1 a year).

Agriculture and Veterinary Science

Food and Agriculture Organization of the United Nations/Organisation des Nations Unies pour l'Alimentation et l'Agriculture: Viale delle Terme di Cara-

calla, 00153 Rome, Italy; tel. 06-57051; fax 06-57053152; e-mail fao-hq@fao.org; internet www.fao.org; f. 1945 to raise level of nutrition and living standards, improve production and distribution of food and agricultural products, and improve the conditions of rural populations; the policy and budget are determined by the 192 mem. nations and 1 org. mem. (EU) at the biennial Conf.; the Conference elects a 49-mem. Council, which is served by specialist cttees; there are 3,590 staff mems, two-thirds based at HQ and the rest in offices worldwide; there are 2 main sources of funding: contributions from mem. nations, used for financing the secretariat and Technical Cooperation Programmes; trust funds mainly provided by govts for use in FAO Field Programme; FAO's main activities are concentrated on: improving production in all areas of agriculture, forestry and fisheries; promoting the conservation and management of plant and animal genetic resources; increasing investment in agriculture through irrigation, fertilizer, seed and other rural devt schemes; collecting, analysing and disseminating information needed by govts and int. bodies; making available technical data through the FAO-coordinated AGRIS, CARIS and FAO-STAT computer-based int. information systems; working towards greater world food security by ensuring production of adequate food supplies, maximizing stability in the flow of supplies, and securing access to available supplies for those who need them; and by promoting rural devt schemes; the interpretation and dissemination of information obtained from satellites to predict crop failure is an illustration of FAO's GIEWS and ARTEMIS systems to monitor the world food situation; library: FAO David Lubin Memorial Library (fao.org/library) holds 1m. vols and 7,000 periodicals; Dir-Gen. Dr JACQUES DIOUF (Senegal); publs *Animal Health and Fertilizers, Commodity Review and Outlook, FAO Quarterly Bulletin of Statistics* (4 a year), *Food and Agricultural Legislation* (2 a year), *Forestry and Fisheries, Plant Protection Bulletin, Rural Development* (1 a year), *The State of Food and Agriculture* (1 a year), *State of Food Insecurity in the World, Unasylva* (4 a year), *World Animal Review* (4 a year), *Yearbooks of Trade and Production in Agriculture.*

OTHER ORGANIZATIONS

CAB International (CABI): Nosworthy Way, Wallingford, Oxon, OX10 8DE, UK; tel. (1491) 832111; fax (1491) 833508; e-mail corporate@cabi.org; internet www.cabi.org; f. 1929; global non-profit organization specializing in sustainable solutions for agricultural and environmental problems; CAB International offices in Wallingford (UK), New Delhi (India); CABI Bioscience: centres in Ascot and Egham (UK), Rawalpindi (Pakistan), Delémont (Switzerland); CABI regional centres for Africa (Nairobi, Kenya), Caribbean and Latin America (Curepe, Trinidad), South-East Asia (Serdang, Malaysia), China (Beijing); CABI Publishing: offices in Wallingford (UK) and Cambridge, MA (USA); CABI Trust in Wallingford (UK); CEO TREVOR NICHOLS; publs *Animal Health Research Reviews* (2 a year), *Aquatic Resources, Culture and Development* (4 a year), *British Journal of Nutrition* (12 a year), *Bulletin of Entomological Research* (6 a year), *Chinese Journal of Agricultural Biotechnology* (3 a year), *Equine and Comparative Exercise Physiology* (4 a year), *Forestry Abstracts* (12 a year), *Horticultural Science Abstracts* (12 a year), *International Journal of Tropical Insect Science* (4 a year), *Journal of Helmintology* (4 a year), *Renewable Agriculture and Food Systems* (4 a year), *Rural Development Abstracts* (4 a year), *Leisure, Recreation and Tourism Abstracts* (4 a year), *Pig News and Information* (4 a year), *Plant Breeding Abstracts* (12 a year), *Plant Genetics Resources* (3 a year), *Seed Science Research* (4 a year), *Soils Use and Management* (4 a year), *World Poultry Science* (4 a year).

Commonwealth Forestry Association: The Crib, Dinchope, Craven Arms, Shropshire, SY7 9JJ, UK; tel. (1588) 672868; fax (870) 011-6645; e-mail cfa@cfa-international.org; internet www.cfa-international.org; f. 1921; 1,500 mems; Pres. D. BILL; Chair. J. BALL; publ. *International Forestry Review* (4 a year)

Consultative Group on International Agricultural Research (CGIAR): 1818 H St, NW, MSN G6-601, Washington, DC 20433, USA; tel. (202) 473-8951; fax (202) 473-8110; e-mail cgiar@cgiar.org; internet www.cgiar.org; f. 1971; co-sponsors: World Bank, FAO, IFAD and UNDP; 58 mems incl.

govts, int. orgs and private foundations; Dir FRANCISCO J. B. REIFSCHNEIDER.

Institutions Supported by CGIAR:

Africa Rice Centre (WARDA)/Centre du Riz pour l'Afrique (ADRAO): 01 BP 2031, Cotonou 01, Benin; tel. 35-01-18; fax 35-05-56; e-mail warda@cgiar.org; internet www.warda.cgiar.org; f. 1970; 17 West and Central African mem. states; funds provided through CGIAR and by mem. states, donor nations and orgs, and various foundations; library of 16,442 monographs, 1,523 periodicals; Dir-Gen. Dr KANAYO F. NWANZE; publs *Participatory Rice Improvement and Gender/user Analysis Proceedings* (workshop papers, 1 a year), *Program Report* (1 a year), *Rice Interspecific Hybridization Project Research Highlights* (1 a year), *WARDA Current Contents* (12 a year), *West Africa Rice Research Brief* (in French and English, irregular).

Bioversity International: Via dei Tre Denari 472A, 00057 Maccarese, Rome, Italy; tel. 06-61181; fax 06-61979661; e-mail bioversity@cgiar.org; internet www.cgiar.org; f. 1974 to advance the collection, conservation and use of crop genetic resources worldwide and to encourage research; Dir-Gen. Dr EMILE A. FRISON; publ. *Geneflow*.

Centre for International Forestry Research (CIFOR): POB 6596 JKPWB, Jakarta 10065, Indonesia; Jl. CIFOR, Situ Gede, Sindangbarang, Bogor Barat 16680, Indonesia; tel. (251) 622622; fax (251) 622100; e-mail cifor@cgiar.org; internet www.cifor.cgiar.org; seeks the balanced management of forests and forest lands through collaborative strategic and applied research and related activities; regional offices in Brazil, Cameroon and Zimbabwe; Dir-Gen. DAVID KAIMOWITZ.

International Centre for Agricultural Research in the Dry Areas (ICARDA): POB 5466, Aleppo, Syria; tel. (21) 2213433; fax (21) 2213490; e-mail icarda@cgiar.org; internet www.icarda.cgiar.org; f. 1977; serves the entire developing world for the improvement of lentil, barley and faba bean production; all dry-area developing countries for the improvement of on-farm water-use efficiency, rangeland and small-ruminant production; and West and Central Asia and North Africa for the improvement of bread, durum wheat and chickpea production, and farming systems; promotes sustainable natural-resource management practices; library of 16,129 vols, 958 periodicals; Dir-Gen. Prof. Dr ADEL EL-BELTAGY; publ. *ICARDA Caravan* (2 a year).

International Centre for Tropical Agriculture/Centro Internacional de Agricultura Tropical: Apdo aéreo 6713, Cali, Colombia; tel. (2) 4450000; fax (2) 4450073; internet www.ciat.cgiar.org; f. 1967; research on cultivation of beans, cassava, rice, tropical fruit and fodder, combined with applied social sciences; library of 100,000 records and documents; 1,300 mems; Dir-Gen. JOACHIM VOSS; publ. *Pasturas Tropicales* (3 a year).

International Crops Research Institute for the Semi-Arid Tropics (ICRISAT): Patancheru, Andhra Pradesh 502 324, India; tel. (40) 23296161; fax (40) 23296180; e-mail icrisat@cgnet.com; internet www.icrisat.org; f. 1972 as world centre for genetic improvement of sorghum, millets, pigeonpea, chickpea and groundnut production, and for research on the management of resources in the world's semi-arid tropics; research covers all physical and socio-economic aspects of improving farming systems on un-irrigated land; Dir-Gen. WILLIAM D. DAR (India); publs *International Arachis Newsletter* (1 a year), *International Chickpea and Pigeonpea Newsletter* (1 a year), *International Sorghum and Millet Newsletter* (1 a year), *Research and Information Bulletins, Workshop Proceedings*.

International Food Policy Research Institute: 2033 K St NW, Washington, DC 20006, USA; tel. (202) 862-5600; fax (202) 467-4439; e-mail ifpri@cgiar.org; internet www.ifpri.org; f. 1975 to identify and analyse alternative nat. and int. strategies for improving the food situation of the low-income countries; 6 divs: Environment and Production Technology (EPT), Food Consumption and Nutrition (FCN), Markets, Trade and Institutions (MTI), Int. Service for Nat. Agricultural Research (ISNAR), Devt Strategy and Governance (DSG), Communications and 2020 Vision Initiative; library of 4,200 research reports, 3,000 monographs, 175 periodicals; Dir-Gen. JOACHIM VON BRAUN; publs abstracts, research reports, working papers, etc.

International Institute of Tropical Agriculture: c/o Lambourn (UK) Ltd, Carolyn House, 26 Dingwall Rd, Croydon, CR9 3EE, UK; field office: Oyo Rd, PMB 5320, Ibadan, Oyo State, Nigeria; tel. (2) 241-2626; fax (2) 241-2221; e-mail iita@cgiar.org; internet www.iita.org; f. 1967; projects incl. preserving and enhancing germplasm and agrobiodiversity; developing biological control options; impact, policy and systems analysis; starchy and grain staples in eastern and southern Africa; diverse agricultural systems in the Humid Zone of West and Central Africa; improving and intensifying cereal-legume systems in the moist and dry savannahs of West and Central Africa; library of 76,500 vols and in-house database of 105,500 records; Dir-Gen. PETER HARTMANN.

International Livestock Research Institute: POB 30709, Nairobi 00100, Kenya; tel. (20) 422-3000; fax (20) 422-3001; internet www.ilri.cgiar.orgPOB 5689, Addis Ababa, Ethiopia; tel. (1) 463-215; fax (1) 463-252; f. 1995 as an interdisciplinary research, training and information centre to promote and improve livestock production worldwide; principal research units in Kenya and Ethiopia and field programmes in Ethiopia, Kenya, Niger and Nigeria; library of 37,500 vols, 32,000 microfiches, 1,800 periodicals; Dir-Gen. Dr CARLOS SERÉ; publs *Bulletin, Systems Studies Monographs*, progress and research reports, manuals, bibliographies.

International Maize and Wheat Improvement Centre/Centro Internacional de Mejoramiento de Maíz y Trigo: Apdo 6-641, 06600 México, DF, Mexico; tel. (55) 5804-2004; fax (55) 5804-7558; e-mail cimmyt@cgiar.org; internet www.cimmyt.org; f. 1966; supported by Mexican Min. of Agriculture, various int. agencies, govts and private foundations; aims to help impoverished people in developing countries by improving maize and wheat productivity and promoting environmentally sound farming practices; regional offices in Africa, Asia and South and Central America; Dir-Gen. Dr MASA IWANAGA.

International Potato Centre/Centro Internacional de la Papa: POB 1558, Lima 12, Peru; tel. (1) 349-6017; fax (1) 317-5326; e-mail cip@cgiar.org; internet www.cipotato.org; f. 1971; non-profit instn dedicated to the increased and more sustainable use of potato, sweet potato and other roots and tubers in developing countries, and to the improved management of agricultural resources in mountain areas; regional offices in Lima, Nairobi, Bogor and New Delhi; library of 13,000 vols, 131 online journals, 16,000 reprints, 65,000 references; Dir-Gen. Dr PAMELA K. ANDERSON; publ. *Program Report* (every 2 years).

International Rice Research Institute: DAPO Box 7777, Metro Manila, Philippines; tel. (2) 580-5600; fax (2) 580-5699; e-mail irri@cgiar.org; internet www.irri.org; f. 1960; research on rice and rice-based cropping systems; library of 158,000 vols; Dir-Gen. Dr ROBERT S. ZEIGLER (acting); Deputy Dir-Gen. Dr WILLIAM G. PADOLINA; publs *Facts about Cooperation* (1 a year), *IRRI Hotline* (4 a year), *International Rice Research Notes* (2 a year), *Rice Literature Update* (2 a year), *Rice Today Magazine* (1 a year).

International Water Management Institute (IWMI): POB 2075, Colombo, Sri Lanka; 127 Sunil Mawatha, Pelawatte, Battaramulla, Sri Lanka; tel. (11) 288-0000; fax (11) 278-6854; e-mail iwmi@cgiar.org; internet www.iwmi.cgiar.org; non-profit org. for sustainable management of water and land resources for food, livelihood and nature; national and international partners across Africa and Asia; Dir-Gen. Dr COLIN CHARTRES.

World Agroforestry Centre: United Nations Ave, Gigiri, POB 30677, 00100 Nairobi, Kenya; tel. (20) 7224000; fax (20) 7224001; e-mail icraf@cgiar.org; internet www.worldagroforestry.org; f. 1977; conducts collaborative research on sustainable forestry and its impact on farming, to alleviate poverty and protect the environment; research sites in 23 tropical countries; Dir-Gen. DENNIS PHILIP.

WorldFish Centre: POB 500, GPO 10670 Penang, Malaysia; Jl. Batu Maung, Batu Maung, 11960 Bayan Lepas, Penang, Malaysia; tel. (4) 6261606; fax (4) 6265530; e-mail worldfishcenter@cgiar.org; internet www.worldfishcenter.org; f. 1977; non-profit org. involved in collaborative research in developing countries to promote the sustainable use of living aquatic resources based on environmentally sound management; library of 16,000 books, monographs and reprints, 1,376 periodicals; Dir-Gen. Dr STEPHEN HALL; publ. *NAGA–WorldFish Centre Quarterly*.

Inter-American Institute for Cooperation on Agriculture/Instituto Interamericano de Cooperación para la Agricultura: Apdo 55, 2200 Coronado, San José, Costa Rica; tel. (506) 216-02-22; fax (506) 216-02-33; e-mail iicahq@iica.int; internet www.iica.int; f. 1942; a specialized agency of the inter-American system; aims to encourage, promote and support the efforts of the mem. states to achieve agricultural devt and rural well-being; offices in 29 of its 33 countries; Dir-Gen. CHELSTON W. D. BRATHWAITE (Barbados); publ. *Turrialba* (4 a year).

International Association of Agricultural Economists/Conférence Internationale des Economistes Agricoles: 1211 West 22nd St, Suite 216, Oak Brook, IL 60523-2197, USA; tel. (630) 571-9393; fax (630) 571-9580; e-mail iaae@farmfoundation.org; internet www.iaae-agecon.org; f. 1929 to foster the application of the science of agricultural economics to the improvement of the economic and social conditions of rural communities; to advance knowledge of agricultural processes and the economic organization of agriculture; and to facilitate communication and exchange of information among those concerned with rural welfare worldwide; 1,700 mems in 95 countries; Pres. PRABHU PINGALI (Italy); Sec.-Treas. WALTER J. ARMBRUSTER (USA); publ. *Agricultural Economics: the Journal of the International Association of Agricultural Economists* (incl. Proceedings of Conferences).

International Association of Horticultural Producers/Association Internationale des Producteurs de l'Horticulture: Pasteurlaan 6, POB 280, 2700 AG Zoetermeer, Netherlands; tel. (79) 347-07-07; fax (79) 347-04-05; internet www .aiph.org; f. 1948 to represent through its professional mem. orgs the common interests of commercial horticultural producers by means of frequent meetings, regular publs, press notices, resolutions and addresses to govts and int. authorities; mems: Australia, Austria, Belgium, Canada, China, Colombia, Czech Republic, Denmark, Finland, Luxembourg, Netherlands, Norway, Poland, Spain, Sweden, Switzerland, UK, USA; Pres. Dr DOEKE FABER; Sec.-Gen. SJAAK LANGESLAG.

International Centre for Advanced Mediterranean Agronomic Studies/ Centre International de Hautes Etudes Agronomiques Méditerranéennes: Secretariat 11 rue Newton, 75116 Paris, France; tel. 1-53-23-91-00; fax 1-53-23-91-01; internet www.ciheam.org; f. 1962 to provide a supplementary technical, economic and social education for graduates of the higher schools and faculties of agriculture in Mediterranean countries at a postgraduate level; to examine the int. problems posed by rural devt and regional planning; to develop methods of investigation in ecological topics; to contribute to the devt of int. cooperation among agronomists and economists in Mediterranean countries; scholarships may be granted by the governing body; mems: Albania, Algeria, Egypt, France, Greece, Italy, Lebanon, Malta, Montenegro, Morocco, Portugal, Serbia, Spain, Tunisia, Turkey; Chair. MOUÏN HAMZÉ (Lebanon); Sec.-Gen. BERNARD HERVIEU (France); publ. *Options Méditerranéennes*.

Component Institutes:

Mediterranean Agronomic Institute of Bari: c/o Cosimo Lacirignola, Via Ceglie 9, 70010 Valenzano, Bari, Italy; tel. 080-4606204; fax 080-4606206; internet netserver.iamb.it; courses on irrigation and drainage, soil conservation, pathology of Mediterranean fruit tree species; Dir COSIMO LACIRIGNOLA.

Mediterranean Agronomic Institute of Chania: c/o Alkinoos Nikolaidis, Alsyllio Agrokepiou, POB 85, Chania 73100, Makedonias 1, Alsyllio Agrokepio, Crete, Greece; tel. 28-21035002; fax 28-21035001; e-mail info@maich.gr; internet www.maich.gr; f. 1985; courses on business economics and management; food quality and chemistry of natural products; geoinformation in environmental management; horticultural genetics and biotechnology; sustainable agriculture; Dir ALKINOOS NIKOLAIDIS.

Mediterranean Agronomic Institute of Montpellier: c/o Vincent Dollé, 3191 route de Mende, 34093 Montpellier Cedex 5, France; tel. 4-67-04-60-00; fax 4-67-54-25-27; internet www.iamm.fr; courses on economics and politics of the agricultural sector and food supplies, economics and agricultural policies, rural devt and popularization; Dir VINCENT DOLLÉ.

Mediterranean Agronomic Institute of Zaragoza: c/o Luis Estruelas, Av. Montañana, 1005, 50059 Zaragoza, Spain; tel. (976) 716 000; fax (976) 716 001; e-mail iamz@iamz.ciheam.org; internet www .iamz.ciheam.org; postgraduate courses on animal production, animal nutrition, animal genetics and reproduction, rural development, environment, plant breeding and genetics, agricultural systems, agricultural technologies, agricultural and food products, agro-food marketing, pisciculture, fisheries; Dir LUIS ESTERUELAS

International Commission for Food Industries/Commission internationale des industries agricoles et alimentaires: 42 rue Scheffer, 75116 Paris, France; tel. 1-43-31-30-36; fax 1-43-31-32-02; e-mail ciia@ wanadoo.fr; internet www.ciia-c.com; f. 1934 to develop international cooperation in promoting agricultural and food industries; to organize int. congresses, annual study sessions and advanced training courses for executives and high-level technicians of agricultural and food industries in the scientific, technical, management and economic fields; Sec.-Gen. MICHEL FOUCAULT (France); publs *Industries Alimentaires et Agricoles*, Proceedings of Congresses, Symposia and Seminars.

International Commission of Agricultural Engineering: see under Engineering

International Committee on Veterinary Gross Anatomical Nomenclature (ICV-GAN)/Commission Internationale de la Nomenclature Macroanatomique Vétérinaire: Dept of Veterinary Anatomy, Bischofsholer Damm 15, 30173 Hanover, Germany; tel. (511) 856-7211; fax (511) 856-7683; f. 1957; language of instruction English; 40 mems; Chair. Prof. HELMUT WAIBL (Germany); Sec. Prof. HAGEN GASSE (Germany); publ. *Nomina Anatomica Veterinaria*.

International Congress on Animal Reproduction/Congrès Internationale de Physiologie et Pathologie de la Reproduction Animale: Faculty of Veterinary Science, University of Sydney, NSW 2006, Australia; tel. (2) 9351-3363; fax (2) 9351-3957; e-mail gareth.evans@sydney.edu .au; internet www.vetsci.usyd.edu.au/icar; f. 1948 following the first congress in Milan, Italy; Pres. Prof. HENK BERTSCHINGER (USA); Sec.-Gen. Prof. G. EVANS (Australia); publ. *ICAR Proceedings* (every 4 years).

International Dairy Federation/Fédération Internationale de Laiterie: Diamant Bldg, Blvd Auguste Reyers 80, 1030 Brussels, Belgium; tel. (2) 733-98-88; fax (2) 733-0413; e-mail info@fil-idf.org; internet www.fil-idf.org; f. 1903 to link all dairy asscns in order to encourage the solution of scientific, technical and economic problems affecting the dairy industry; mems: nat. cttees in 35 countries; Pres. RICHARD DOYLE; Dir-Gen. CHRISTIAN ROBERT; publs *Bulletin* (online), *International Standards* (online).

International Federation of Agricultural Producers/Fédération International des Producteurs Agricoles: 60 rue Saint-Lazare, 75009 Paris, France; tel. 1 45-26-05-53; fax 1-48-74-72-12; e-mail ifap@ ifap.org; internet www.ifap.org; f. 1946 to represent, in the int. field, the interests of agricultural producers, by laying the coordinated views of the nat. member orgs before any appropriate int. body; to act as a forum in which leaders of nat. farmers' orgs can meet to exchange information, experiences and ideas, and bring farmers' concerns to the attention of int. meetings of govts and other bodies; 114 nat. farmers' orgs in 82 countries; Pres. JACK WILKINSON (Canada); Sec.-Gen. DAVID KING; publ. *General Conference Reports* (every 2 years).

International Organization for Biological Control of Noxious Animals and Plants (IOBC)/Organisation Internationale de Lutte Biologique Contre les Animaux et les Plantes Nuisibles: c/o Prof. Dr Joop van Lenteren, Laboratory of Entomology, Wageningen University, POB 8031, 6700 EH Wageningen, Netherlands; tel. (317) 482327; fax (317) 484821; e-mail joop.vanlenteren@wur.nl; internet www .unipa.it/iobc; f. 1956 to promote and coordinate research on biological and integrated control of pests and weeds; comprises regional sections based on biogeographical zones; mems: public or private from over 50 countries; Pres. Prof. Dr JACQUES BRODEUR (Canada); Gen. Sec. Prof. Dr JOOP C. VAN LENTEREN (Netherlands); publs *Bulletin*, *Entomophaga* (4 a year).

International Seed Testing Association: Zuerichstr. 50, POB 308, 8303 Bassersdorf, Switzerland; tel. 448386000; fax 448386001; e-mail ista.office@ista.ch; internet www .seedtest.org; f. 1924; promotes uniformity in seed quality evaluation, through research and by organizing triennial congresses, annual ordinary meetings and periodic training courses; produces internationally agreed rules for seed sampling and testing; accredits laboratories; promotes research; provides int. seed analysis certificates and training; disseminates knowledge in seed science and technology; 76 mem. countries, 195 mem. laboratories (114 accredited); Pres. Prof. JOHN HAMPTON (New Zealand); Sec.-Gen. Dr MICHAEL MUSCHICK (Switzerland); publs *ISTA International Rules for Seed Testing* (1 a year), *Seed Science and Technology* (3 a year), *Seed Testing International (ISTA News Bulletin)* (2 a year).

International Society for Horticultural Science/Société Internationale de la Science Horticole: POB 500, 3001 Leuven 1, Belgium; located at: Decroylaan 42 (01.21), 3001 Leuven, Belgium; tel. (16) 22-94-27; fax (16) 22-94-50; e-mail info@ishs.org; internet www.ishs.org; f. 1959 to promote and to encourage research in all branches of horticulture and to facilitate cooperation of scientific activities and knowledge transfer on a global scale by means of its publs, events and scientific structure; 6,500 mems in 150 countries; Pres. Dr NORMAN E. LOONEY (Canada); Exec. Dir JOZEF VAN ASSCHE; publs *Acta Horticulturae* (about 35 a year), *Chronica Horticulturae* (4 a year).

International Society for Tropical Crop Research and Development (ISTCRAD): c/o Prof. N. K. Nayar (Associate Director of Research (Planning)), Kerala Agricultural University, Thrissur 680656, Kerala, India; tel. (487) 370497; fax (487) 370019; e-mail dr@kau.in; f. 1990; provides a forum for interaction among scientists, progressive farmers and entrepreneurs; Dir Dr D. ALEXANDER; publs *News Bulletin* (4 a year), *Scientific Journal* (4 a year).

International Society for Tropical Root Crops (ISTRC): c/o I.S.H.S., Englaan 1, 6703 ET Wageningen, Netherlands; tel. (8370) 21747; fax (8370) 21586; internet www.istrc.org; f. 1964; 300 mems; Pres. Dr S. K. HAHN; Sec. Ir H. H. VAN DER BORG.

International Union of Forest Research Organizations/Union Internationale des Instituts de Recherches Forestières/ Internationaler Verband Forstlicher Forschungsanstalten: Hauptstr. 7, 1140 Vienna–Hadersdorf, Austria; tel. (1) 877-01-51-0; fax (1) 877-01-51-50; e-mail office@iufro .org; internet www.iufro.org; f. 1892 for int. cooperation in the various brs of forestry research and related fields; mems: 700 orgs in 115 countries (15,000 scientists), incl. forestry faculties, experimental stations, research instns, etc.; Pres. Prof. DON K. LEE (Republic of Korea); Exec. Dir Dr PETER

MAYER (Austria); publs *Congress Proceedings*, *IUFRO News* (online, 10 a year), *IUFRO World Series*, scientific papers.

International Union of Soil Science (IUSS)/Association Internationale de la Science du Sol/Internationale Bodenkundliche Gesellschaft: c/o Prof. Stephen Nortcliff, Dept of Soil Science, Univ. of Reading, POB 233, Reading, RG6 6DW, UK; tel. (118) 378-6559; fax (118) 378-6666; e-mail iuss@rdg.ac.uk; internet www.iuss .org; f. 1924 to promote soil science and its applications; federated to ICSU; 45,000 mems in 70 countries; Pres. Prof. R. SWIFT; Sec.-Gen. Prof. STEPHEN NORTCLIFF; publ. *Bulletin* (2 a year).

World Association for Animal Production: Via Tomassetti 3-1/A, 00161 Rome, Italy; tel. 06-44202639; fax 06-86329263; e-mail waap@waap.it; internet www.waap .it; f. 1965; organizes a conference every 5 years; regional discussions; mems: 17 societies (nat. and regional); Pres. ASSEFAW MEDHIN TEWOLDE (Ethiopia); Sec.-Gen. ANDREA ROSATI (Italy); publ. *News Items* (2 a year).

World Veterinary Association/Association Mondiale Vétérinaire: c/o Dr Lars Holsaae, Emdrupvej 28A, 2100 Copenhagen Ø, Denmark; tel. 38-71-01-56; fax 38-71-03-22; internet www.worldvet.org; f. 1863; mem. organizations in 80 countries, 20 assoc. mems; Pres. Dr HERBERT SCHNEIDER (Namibia); Exec. Sec. Dr LARS HOLSAAE (Denmark); publs *Bulletin* (2 a year), *World Veterinary Directory*.

Arts

Asociación de Lingüística y Filología de América Latina/Latin American Association of Linguistics and Philology: c/o Adolfo Elizaincín, Universidad de la República, CP 1410, 11000 Montevideo, Uruguay; e-mail aelizain@gmail.com; internet www .mundoalfal.org; f. 1964; 1,009 mems; Pres. ALBA VALENCIA ESPINOSA (Chile); Sec.-Gen. ADOLFO ELIZAINCÍN (Uruguay); publs *Actas de los Congresos*, *Revista Lingüística*.

Association for Commonwealth Literature and Language Studies: POB 715, Osmania Univ. Post Office, Hyderabad 500 007, India; tel. (40) 27005301; internet www .aclals.org; f. 1965 as an ind. org.; encourages study in Commonwealth literatures and languages, incl. comparative studies between literatures in English and indigenous literatures and languages, new kinds of English and use of mass media; holds triennial conferences and regional meetings; organizes visits and exchanges; collects source material and publishes creative, critical, historical and bibliographical material; 1,600 mems; Chair. MEENAKSHI MUKHERJEE (India); Vice-Chair. HARISH TRIVEDI (India); Vice-Chair. and Sec. C. VIJAYASREE (India); publ. *Bulletin*.

Commonwealth Association of Museums: POB 30192, Chinook Postal Outlet, Calgary, AB T2H 2V9, Canada; tel. (403) 938-3190; fax (403) 938-3190; e-mail irvinel@ fclc.com; internet www.maltwood.uvic.ca/ cam; f. 1974; aims to maintain and strengthen links between mems of the museum profession; encourages and assists mems to obtain additional training and to attend appropriate conferences, seminars; promotes professional excellence; collaborates with nat. and regional museum asscns; runs conferences and workshops, internships, distance-learning programme in basic museum studies; nat., institutional and individual mems in 38 countries; gen. assembly every three years with elections; annual

meeting; 230 mems; Pres. MARTIN SEGGER (Canada); Sec.-Gen. LOIS IRVINE (Canada); publs *Bulletin* (irregular), *Conference and Workshop Proceedings*.

Communauté Africaine de Culture: c/o Présence africaine, 25 bis rue des Ecoles, 75005 Paris, France; tel. (1) 43-54-13-74; fax (1) 43-25-96-67; f. 2005 to create unity and friendship among African scholars for the encouragement of their own cultures; mems from 22 countries; Pres. WOLE SOYINKA; Sec.-Gen. Mme CHRISTIANE DIOP; publ. *Présence Africaine* (4 a year).

Europa Nostra (Our Europe): Lange Voorhout 35, 2514 EC The Hague, The Netherlands; tel. (70) 3024050; fax (70) 3617865; e-mail office@europanostra.org; internet www.europanostra.org; f. 1991 by merger of Europa Nostra and the Int. Castles Institute; pan-European org. for the protection of Europe's architectural and natural heritage, and the promotion of high standards in architecture and in town and country planning; undertakes campaigns, conferences, research, exhibitions and an annual award scheme; language of instruction French; 1,500 mem. orgs and individuals; Pres. HRH THE PRINCE CONSORT OF DENMARK; Exec. Pres. ANDREA SCHULER; Sec.-Gen. SNESKA QUAEDVLIEG-MIHAILOVIC; publs *Awards Review* (1 a year), *Europa Nostra Scientific Bulletin* (1 a year), *European Cultural Heritage Review* (1 a year).

European Cultural Foundation/Fondation Européenne de la Culture: Jan van Goyenkade 5, 1075 HN Amsterdam, Netherlands; tel. (20) 573-38-68; fax (20) 675-22-31; e-mail eurocult@eurocult.org; internet www .eurocult.org; f. 1954 as an ind., non-profit org. to promote cultural cooperation in Europe; an operating foundation that initiates and manages its own projects and programmes and gives grants to other bodies for European-level cultural activities; emphasizes the importance of developing a pluralistic civil soc. in Europe by encouraging the linkage of cultural activity and social responsibility; supports a network of nat. cttees based in 23 European countries; Pres. HRH Princess MARGRIET OF THE NETHERLANDS; Dir GOTTFRIED WAGNER; publ. *Beyond Borders* (3 a year).

European Society of Culture/Società Europea di Cultura/Société Européenne de Culture: Villa Hériot, Giudecca 54 P, 30133 Venice, Italy; tel. 041-5230210; fax 041-5231033; e-mail info@ societaeuropeacultura.it; internet www .societaeuropeacultura.it; f. 1950 to unite artists, poets, scientists, philosophers and others through mutual interests and friendship to safeguard and improve the conditions required for creative activity; and to enhance int. collaboration and peace; 1,500 mems; library of 5,000 vols; Pres. VINCENZO CAPPELLETTI (Italy); Premier Vice-Pres. ARRIGO LEVI (Italy); Int. Gen. Sec. MICHELLE CAMPAGNOLO BOUVIER (Italy); publ. *Comprendre* (irregular).

Fédération Internationale des Ecrivains de Langue Française (FIDELF): 3492 ave Laval, Montreal, QC H2X 3C8, Canada; tel. (515) 849-62-39; f. 1982; 18 mem. asscns; Pres. ALIOUNE BADARA BEYE (Senegal); Sec.-Gen. MAMADOU TRAORÉ DIOP (Senegal).

International Amateur Theatre Association—Organization for Understanding and Education through Theatre: Vene 6, 10123 Tallinn, Estonia; tel. 6418-405; fax 6418-406; e-mail secretariat@aitaiata.org; internet www.aitaiata.org; f. 1952; mems in 70 states; composed of nat. centres; organizes int. conferences, colloquia, seminars, work-

shops, festivals incl. world festival of amateur theatre (every 4 years); Administrator ENE JÜRNA; publ. *Bulletin AITA / IATA*.

International Association for Caribbean Archaeology/Association Internationale d'Archéologie de la Caraïbe/Asociación Internacional de Arqueología del Caribe: BP 4030, Terres Sainvilles Cedex, 97254 Fort-de-France, Martinique; tel. 63-65-51; fax 63-65-51; internet museum-server .archanth.cam.ac.uk/iaca.www/iaca.htm; f. 1962; 59 mems; Pres. Dr JAY HAVISER (Netherlands Antilles); Sec. QUETTA KAYE (UK).

International Association of Applied Linguistics/Association Internationale de Linguistique Appliquée: c/o Prof. Karlfried Knapp, Dept of Applied Linguistics, POB 900221, 99105 Erfurt, Germany; tel. (361) 737-4321; fax (361) 737-4329; e-mail aila@uni-erfurt.de; internet www.aila.info; f. 1964 to promote the application of linguistic theories to the solution of language and language-related problems in society; 8,000 mems; Pres. Prof. SUSAN M. GASS (USA); Sec.-Gen. Prof. KARLFRIED KNAPP (Germany); publs *AILA Book Series* (3 a year), *AILA News* (2 a year), *AILA Review* (1 a year).

International Association of Art: Rosenthaler Str. 11, 10119 Berlin, Germany; tel. (30) 23457666; fax (30) 28099305; e-mail art@igbk.de; internet www.iaa-europe.eu; f. 1954; 81 national cttees; Pres. WERNER SCHAUB.

International Association of Art Critics/Association Internationale des Critiques d'Art: 15 rue Martel, 75010 Paris, France; tel. 1-47-70-17-42; fax 1-47-70-17-81; e-mail office.paris@aica-int.org; internet www.aica-int.org; f. 1949 to promote int. cooperation in the world of plastic arts (painting, sculpture, graphic arts, architecture); consultative status with UNESCO; 3,750 individual mems and 72 National Sections; Pres. HENRY MEYRIC HUGHES (UK); Gen. Sec. RAMON TIO BELLIDO (France); publ. *Annuaire AiCA*.

International Association of Literary Critics/Association Internationale des Critiques Littéraires: 38 rue du Faubourg-St-Jacques, 75014 Paris, France; tel. 1-53-10-12-00; fax 1-53-10-12-12; f. 1969; UNESCO consultative status B; organizes congresses, etc.; Pres. DANIEL LEUVEY; Vice-Pres. SYLVESTRE CLANCIER; publ. *Revue* (1 a year).

International Centre for the Study of the Preservation and Restoration of Cultural Property (ICCROM): Via di San Michele 13, 00153 Rome, Italy; tel. 06-585531; fax 06-58553349; e-mail iccrom@ iccrom.org; internet www.iccrom.org; f. 1959; inter-governmental org.; UNESCO Class A; assembles documentation and disseminates knowledge by way of publications and meetings; coordinates research, organizes training of specialists and short courses; offers technical advice; int. documentation centre; financed by 126 mem. states; library of 100,000 registered references; Dir-Gen. MOUNIR BOUCHENAKI.

International Centre of Films for Children and Young People/Centre International du Film pour l'Enfance et la Jeunesse: Bureau 200, 3774 rue St Denis, Montréal, QC H2W 2M1, Canada; tel. (514) 284-9388; fax (514) 284-0168; e-mail info@ cifej.com; internet www.cifej.com; f. 1955; research centre and clearing-house of information about entertainment films (cinema and television) for children all over the world; 153 mems from 55 countries; Pres. ATHINA RIKAKI (Greece); Sec.-Gen. MONIC

LESSARD (Canada); publ. *CIFEJ Info* (6 a year).

International Committee of Museums and Collections of Arms and Military History (ICOMAM): c/o Dirk Staat, Legermuseum, Korte Geer 1, 2611 CA Delft, Netherlands; tel. (15) 2150500; fax (15) 2150544; e-mail secretary@icomam.icom .museum; internet icomam.icom.museum; f. 1957; officially recoznised Int. Committee of the Int. Ccl of Museums; org. to establish contact between museums and other scientific institutions with collns of arms and armour, military equipment, uniforms, etc., that may be visited by the public; to promote the study of relevant groups of objects; triennial confs; 300 instns in 51 countries; Pres. GUY M. WILSON (UK); Sec. MATHIEU WILLEMSEN (acting) (Netherlands); publs *Glossarium Armourum: Arma Defensiva, Repertory of Museums of Arms and Military History, Triennial Reports.*

International Comparative Literature Association/Association internationale de littérature comparée: c/o Prof. Steven P. Sondrup, Brigham Young Univ., HRCB Provo, UT 84602-4538, USA; e-mail ailc.icla@ gmail.com; internet www.byu.edu/~ida; f. 1954 to promote the devt of the comparative study of literature; 4,000 mems (socs and individuals) in 65 countries; Pres. Prof. MANFRED SCHMELING (Germany); Secs Prof. MARC MAUFORT (Belgium), Prof. STEVEN P. SONDRUP (USA); publs *ICLA Bulletin AILC* (2 a year), *Recherche Littéraire* (2 a year).

International Council for Film, Television and Audiovisual Communication/ Conseil International du Cinéma, de la Télévision et de la Communication audiovisuelle: 1 rue Miollis, Bureau B7.2.23–2.25, 75732 Paris Cedex 15, France; tel. 1-45-68-48-56; e-mail secretariat@ cict-unesco.org; internet www.unesco.org/ iftc; f. 1958 under auspices of UNESCO; seeks to provide a link of information and jt action between member orgs, and to assist them in their int. work in film and television; mems: 36 int. asscns and feds and 12 assocs; Sec.-Gen. LOLA POGGI-GOUJON.

International Council of Graphic Design Associations (ICOGRADA): POB 5, Forest 2, 1190 Brussels, Belgium; tel. (2) 344-58-43; fax (2) 344-71-38; e-mail secretariat@icograda.org; internet www .icograda.org; f. 1963 to raise the standards of graphic design and professional practice and the professional status of graphic designers; to collect and exchange information relating to graphic design; to organize exhibitions and congresses and to issue reports and surveys; 71 assoc. mems in 44 countries; library: slide and book library at Design Museum, London, UK; poster and records archives at University of Reading, UK; Pres. MERVYN KURLANSKY (Denmark); publ. *Board Message* (4 a year).

International Council of Museums (ICOM): Maison de l'UNESCO, 1 rue Miollis, 75732 Paris Cedex 15, France; tel. 1-47-34-05-00; fax 1-43-06-78-62; e-mail secretariat@ icom.museum; internet icom.museum; f. 1946; professional org., open to all mems of the museum profession, established to provide an appropriate org. to advance int. cooperation among museums, and to be the coordinating and representative int. body furthering museum interests; in 115 countries an ICOM Nat. Cttee on int. cooperation among museums has been organized, each as widely representative as possible of museum interests; maintains UNESCO-ICOM Museum Information Centre, a library and information service specializing in the field of museology and museum practice worldwide;

30 int. cttees and 17 int. affiliated asscns on specialized subjects; 28,000 individual and institutional members in 137 countries; Pres. ALISSANDRA CUMMINS (Barbados); Dir-Gen. JULIEN ANFRUNS; publs *ICOM News/Nouvelles de l'ICOM/Noticias del ICOM* (4 a year), *Study Series/Cahier d'Etude* (1 a year).

International Council on Monuments and Sites (ICOMOS)/Conseil International des Monuments et des Sites: 49–51 rue de la Fédération, 75015 Paris, France; tel. 1-45-67-67-70; fax 1-45-66-06-22; e-mail secretariat@icomos.org; internet www .international.icomos.org; f. 1965 to promote the study and preservation of monuments and sites; 7,000 mems, 110 national cttees, 22 int. cttees; library: Documentation Centre on preservation and restoration of monuments and sites: 30,000 vols, 350 periodicals, 25,000 slides; Pres. MICHAEL PETZET (Germany); Sec.-Gen. DINU BUMBARU (Canada); publ. *Icomos Scientific Journal.*

International Federation for Theatre Research/Fédération Internationale pour la Recherche Théâtrale: c/o Prof. David Whitton, DELC, Lancaster Univ., Lancaster, LA1 4YN, UK; internet www .firt-iftr.org; f. 1955 by 21 countries at the Int. Conference on Theatre History, London, UK; int. seminars in theatre history; attached research institute Istituto Internazionale per la Ricerca Teatrale: see Italy chapter; c. 450 mems in approx. 45 countries; Pres. Prof. BRIAN SINGLETON (Ireland); Jt Secs-Gen. Prof. SOPHIE PROUST (France), Prof. DAVID WHITTON (UK); publ. *Theatre Research International* (4 a year).

International Institute for Conservation of Historic and Artistic Works/ Institut International pour la Conservation des Objets d'Art et d'Histoire: 6 Buckingham St, London, WC2N 6BA, UK; tel. (20) 7839-5975; fax (20) 7976-1564; e-mail iic@iiconservation.org; internet www .iiconservation.org; f. 1950; permanent org. for coordinating and improving the knowledge, methods and working standards needed to protect and preserve precious materials of all kinds; publishes information on research into all processes connected with conservation, both scientific and technical, and on the devt of those processes; congress held every 2 years; 2,000 individual mems, 400 institutional mems; Pres. JERRY PODANY; Sec.-Gen. JOSIPHINE KIRBY ATKINSON; Exec. Sec. GRAHAM VOCE; publs *IIC Bulletin* (6 a year), *Studies in Conservation* (4 a year).

International Literary and Artistic Association/Association Littéraire et Artistique Internationale: c/o Kimbrough et Associés, 7 bis rue de Monceau, 75008 Paris, France; tel. 1-53-30-24-24; fax 1-53-30-24-25; internet alai.org; f. 1878 at Congress of Paris, presided over by Victor Hugo; seeks to protect the rights and interests of writers and artists of all lands, through the extension of copyright conventions, etc.; mems: nat. groups in Argentina, Austria, Belgium, Canada, Colombia, Croatia, Denmark, Finland, France, Germany, Greece, Hungary, Ireland, Israel, Italy, Japan, Kazakhstan, Mexico, Netherlands, Norway, Portugal, Russia, Spain, Sweden, Switzerland, UK, Uruguay, USA; Pres. VICTOR NABHAN; Sec.-Gen. YVES GAUBIAC.

International Numismatic Commission/ Commission internationale de numismatique: Cabinet des Médailles, Bibliothèque Nationale de France, 75084 Paris, France; internet www.inc-cin.org; f. 1927 to facilitate cooperation among individuals and instns in the field of numismatics; mems: nat. orgs in 38 countries; Pres. MICHEL AMANDRY

(UK); Sec. Dr CARMEN ARNOLD (USA); publ. *International Numismatic e-News* (irregular).

International PEN (A World Association of Writers): 9–10 Charterhouse Bldgs, Goswell Rd, London, EC1M 7AT, UK; tel. (20) 7253-4308; fax (20) 7253-5711; e-mail intpen@dircon.co.uk; internet www .internationalpen.org.uk; f. 1921 by Mrs Dawson Scott under the presidency of John Galsworthy to promote cooperation between writers all over the world in the interests of literature, freedom of expression and int. goodwill; 138 autonomous centres worldwide; 14,000 mems; Int. Pres. JIRI GRUSA; Int. Sec. TERRY CARLBOM; publ. *PEN International* (in English, French and Spanish, in asscn with UNESCO, 2 a year).

International Pragmatics Association (IPrA): POB 33, 2018 Antwerp 11, Belgium; tel. (3) 265-45-63; fax (3) 230-55-74; e-mail anne.verhaert@uia.ua.ac.be; internet ipra.ua .ac.be; f. 1986; aims to create a framework for the discussion and comparison of results of research in all aspects of language use or functions of language and to disseminate knowledge about pragmatic aspects of language; incorporates a research centre; 1,400 individual mems; Sec.-Gen. JEF VERSCHUEREN; Exec. Sec. ANN VERHAERT; publ. *Pragmatics* (4 a year).

International Robert Musil Society/ Internationale Robert-Musil-Gesellschaft: POB 151150, Univ. des Saarlandes, 66041 Saarbrucken, Germany; tel. (681) 302-3334; fax (681) 302-3034; e-mail info@i-r-m-g.de; internet www.i-r-m-g.de; f. 1974 under the patronage of Bruno Kreisky (Austria), to promote int. cooperation in research and publications on Musil and edns of his writings; 267 mems; organizes colloquia; Pres. Prof. Dr PETER HENNINGER (France); Secs-Gen. Prof. Dr PIERRE BÉHAR (Germany), Prof. Dr ROSMARIE ZELLER (Switzerland); publ. *Musil-Forum* (every 2 years).

International Theatre Institute/Institut International du Théâtre: UNESCO, 1 rue Miollis, 75732 Paris Cedex 15, France; tel. (1) 45-68-48-80; fax (1) 45-68-48-84; e-mail iti@iti-worldwide.org; internet www .iti-worldwide.org/amt; f. 1948 to facilitate cultural exchanges and int. understanding in the domain of the performing arts; conferences, workshops, publs; education and training in performing arts; protection and promotion of cultural diversity; languages of instruction French, English; mems: 102 mem. nations; Pres. RAMENDU MAJUMDAR (Bangladesh); Vice-Pres. ALI MAHDI (Sudan); Vice-Pres. CHRISTINA BABOU-PAGOURELI (Greece); Sec.-Gen. TOBIAS BIANCONE (France); publs *News* (3 a year), *The World of Theatre* (every 2 years), *World Theatre Directory* (online).

International Union of Architects/Union Internationale des Architectes: 51 rue Raynouard, 75016 Paris, France; tel. 1-45-24-36-88; fax 1-45-24-02-78; e-mail uia@ uia-architectes.org; internet www .uia-architectes.org; f. 1948; mems in 106 countries

International Union of Cinema/Union Internationale du Cinéma: c/o Jan P. Essing, Lente 33, 8251 NT Dronten, The Netherlands; tel. (321) 319529; fax (321) 312739; e-mail essing.jan@hetnet.nl; internet www.unica-web.com; f. 1937 to encourage devt of art, techniques and critical judgement among amateurs, to facilitate contacts between nat. asscns, and to promote the exchange of films; mems: nat. feds in 35 countries; library of 500 films and videocassettes; Annual Congress; Sec.-Gen. JAN ESSING; publ. *UNICA News.*

Organization for Museums, Monuments and Sites of Africa/Organisation pour les Musées, les Monuments et les Sites d'Afrique: POB 3343, Accra, Ghana; f. 1975; aims to foster the collection, study and conservation of the natural and cultural heritage of Africa; cooperation between mem. countries through seminars, workshops, conferences, etc., exchange of personnel, developing training facilities, and drawing up legislative and admin. measures; mems from 30 countries; Pres. Dr J. M. ESSOMBA (Cameroon); Dir-Gen. Dr CLAUDE MARTIN (Ghana).

World Academy of Art and Science: see under International—Science.

World Crafts Council: El Comendador 1916, Providencia, 6640064 Santiago, Chile; tel. (2) 3545636; fax (2) 2325811; e-mail wis@wccwis.cl; internet www.wccwis.cl; f. 1964; non-profit org. to maintain the status of crafts as a vital part of cultural life and to promote fellowship among the world's craftsmen; offers help and advice to craftsmen, consults with govts, nat. and int. institutions; mem. bodies in approx 90 countries; Pres. MARÍA CELINA RODRÍGUEZ OLEA (Chile); publ. *World Crafts Council - Asia Pacific* (2 a year).

Bibliography

Association for Health Information and Libraries in Africa: c/o WHO Regional Office for Africa, BP 6, Brazzaville, Republic of Congo; tel. 241-39425; fax 241-39673; internet www.ahila.org; f. 1984, name changed 1989; promotes cooperation among African health information centres and libraries, to enhance health information services and to develop an African *Index Medicus*; Pres. IBRAHIMA BOB; Sec. BACHIR CHAIBOU.

Association of Caribbean University, Research and Institutional Libraries: POB 23317, San Juan, Puerto Rico 00931-3317; tel. (787) 790-8054; fax (787) 763-5685; e-mail acurilsec@yahoo.com; internet acuril.rrp.upr.edu; f. 1969 to facilitate the devt and use of libraries, archives and information services; identification, collection and preservation of information resources in support of intellectual and educational endeavours in the area; 200 mems; Pres. ADELE MERRITT BARNARD (Jamaica); Exec. Dir ONEIDA RIVERA DE ORTIZ (Puerto Rico); publs *ACURILEANA* (online), *Conference Proceedings*.

Commonwealth Library Association: POB 144, Mona, Kingston 7, Jamaica; tel. 927-0083; fax 927-1926; e-mail nkpodo@uwimona.edu.jm; f. 1972 to support and encourage library asscns in the Commonwealth; to create and strengthen professional relationships between librarians; to promote the status and education of librarians and the reciprocal recognition of qualifications; to improve libraries; to initiate research projects designed to promote library provision and to advance technical development of libraries in the Commonwealth; language of instruction English; 52 mems incl. 40 nat. asscns, 130 affiliated mems; Pres. (vacant); publ. *COMLA Bulletin* (3 a year).

European Association for Health Information and Libraries: POB 1393, 3600 BJ Maarssen, Netherlands; fax (346) 550876; e-mail eahil@nic.surfnet.nl; internet www.eahil.net; f. 1987, to bring together and represent health librarians and information officers in Europe; 1,150 mems; Pres. SUZANNE BAKKER (Netherlands); Sec. TONY MCSEÀN (UK); publ. *Journal of EAHIL* (4 a year).

European Theological Libraries/Europäische Bibliotheken für Theologie/Bibliothèques Européennes de Théologie (BETH): 5 Swanston Crescent, Edinburgh, EH10 7BS, UK; tel. (131) 445-1691; e-mail prjhall@aol.com; internet www.beth.be; f. 1961; holds Annual General Assembly; 35 mems (12 ordinary, 13 extraordinary, 10 individuals); Pres. PIERRE BEFFA (Switzerland); Sec. Prof. PENELOPE HALL.

International Association for Mass Communication Research/Association internationale des études et recherches sur l'information: c/o Hamid Mowlana, School of International Service, American University, 4400 Massachusetts Ave NW, Washington, DC 20016, USA; tel. (202) 885-1621; fax (202) 855-2494; e-mail mowlana@american.edu; internet www.humfak.auc.dk/iamcr; f. 1957 to disseminate information on teaching and research in mass media; to encourage research; to provide a forum for the exchange of information; to bring about improvements in communication practice, policy and research; and to encourage the improvement of training for journalism; over 1,000 mems in 63 countries; Pres. HAMID MOWLANA.

International Association of Agricultural Information Specialists/Association Internationale des Spécialistes de l'Information Agricole: POB 63, Lexington, KY 40588-0063, USA; tel. (859) 254-0752; fax (859) 254-8379; e-mail info@iaald.org; internet www.iaald.org; f. 1955, unites agricultural information specialists worldwide, organizes meetings and educational programmes, workshops and annual conferences in various parts of the world, communicates the value of knowledge and information, collaborates with partner orgs; 300 mems, representing 80 countries; Pres. PETER BALLANTYNE; Sec. and Treas. ANTOINETTE P. GREIDER; publ. *Agricultural Information Worldwide* (int. journal for information specialists in agriculture, natural resources and the environment).

International Association of Bibliophiles/Association Internationale de Bibliophilie: c/o Bibliothèque Nationale de France, Réserve des livres rares, Quai François Mauriac, 75706 Paris Cedex 13, France; tel. 1-53-79-54-76; fax 1-53-79-54-60; f. 1963 to form a meeting point for bibliophiles from different countries; int. congresses every 2 years; 500 mems; Pres. T. KIMBALL BROOKER (USA); Sec.-Gen. JEAN-MARC CHATELAIN (France); publ. *Le Bulletin du Bibliophile* (2 a year).

International Association of Law Libraries (IALL)/Association Internationale des Bibliothèques de Droit: ; tel. (1) 8175121; e-mail jaston@lawlibrary.ie; internet www.iall.org; f. 1959 to offer worldwide cooperation in the devt of law libraries and the colln of legal documentation; holds annual conference; 580 mems in 60 countries; Pres. JULES WINTERTON (UK); Sec. JENNEFER ASTON (Ireland); publ. *International Journal of Legal Information* (3 a year).

International Association of Music Libraries, Archives and Documentation Centres (IAML)/Association Internationale des Bibliothèques, Archives et Centres de Documentation Musicaux/Internationale Vereinigung der Musikbibliotheken, Musikarchive und Musikdokumentationszentren: c/o Academy of Music and Drama, University of Gothenburg, Box 210, 405 30 Göteborg, Sweden; tel. (31) 786-40-57; e-mail pia.shekhter@hsm.gu.se; internet www.iaml.info; f. 1951 to facilitate cooperation between music libraries and information centres,

compile music bibliographies, and to promote the professional training of music librarians and documentalists; languages of instruction French, German, English; 1,900 mems in 53 countries, incl. 24 nat. brs; Sec.-Gen. PIA SHEKHTER; publ. *Fontes artis musicae* (4 a year).

International Association of Technological University Libraries (IATUL)/Association Internationale des Bibliothèques d'Universités Polytechniques: c/o Judith Palmer, Radcliffe Science Library, Univ. of Oxford, Parks Rd, Oxford, OX1 3QP, UK; internet www.iatul.org; f. 1955 to promote cooperation between mem. libraries and conduct research on library problems; mems: 200 univ. libraries in 41 countries; Pres. GAYNOR AUSTEN (Australia); Sec. JUDITH PALMER; publs *IATUL News* (4 a year), *IATUL Proceedings* (1 a year).

International Board on Books for Young People (IBBY): Nonnenweg 12, Postfach, 4003 Basel, Switzerland; tel. 612722917; fax 612722757; e-mail ibby@ibby.org; internet www.ibby.org; f. 1953 to support and unify those forces in all countries connected with children's book work; to encourage the production and distribution of good children's books especially in developing countries; to promote scientific investigation into problems of juvenile books; to organize Int. Children's Book Day and a biennial int. congress; to present the Hans Christian Andersen Award every 2 years to a living author and illustrator whose work is an outstanding contribution to children's literature, and the IBBY-Asahi Reading Promotion Award annually to an org. that has made a significant contribution to children's literature; to make a biennial selection of outstanding books to form the IBBY Honour List; Mems: Nat. Sections and individual mems in 68 countries; Pres. PATRICIA ALDANA (Canada); Exec. Dir LIZ PAGE (Switzerland); publ. *Bookbird* (4 a year).

International Committee for Social Science Information and Documentation/Comité International pour l'Information et la Documentation des Sciences Sociales: c/o Clacso, Callao 875 (3° piso), 1023 Buenos Aires, Argentina; e-mail saugy@clacso.edu.ar; f. 1950 to collect and disseminate information on documentation services in social sciences, help improve documentation, advise socs on problems of documentation and to draw up rules likely to improve the presentation of all documents; mems from int. asscns specializing in social sciences or in documentation, and from other specialized fields; Pres. KRISHANA G. TYAGI (India); Sec.-Gen. CATALINA SAUGY (Argentina); publ. *International Bibliography of the Social Sciences* (1 a year, 4 series).

International Council on Archives/Conseil international des archives: 60 rue des Francs-Bourgeois, 75003 Paris, France; tel. 1-40-27-63-06; fax 1-42-72-20-65; e-mail ica@ica.org; internet www.ica.org; f. 1948; 1,690 mems from 195 countries and territories; Pres. IAN WILSON (Canada); Sec.-Gen. DAVID A. LEITCH (France); publs *COMMA International Journal on Archives* (2 a year), *FLASH* (3 a year).

International Federation of Film Archives/Fédération Internationale des Archives du Film: 1 rue Defacqz, 1000 Brussels, Belgium; tel. (2) 538-30-65; fax (2) 534-47-74; e-mail info@fiafnet.org; internet www.fiafnet.org; f. 1938 to encourage the creation of archives worldwide for the collection and conservation of the film heritage of each country; to facilitate cooperation and exchanges between these film archives; to promote public interest in the art of the cinema; to aid research in this field and to compile new documentation; conducts research; publishes manuals, etc.; holds annual congresses; 108 affiliates in 62 countries; Pres. EVA ORBANZ (Germany); Sec.-Gen. MEG LABRUM (Australia).

International Federation of Library Associations and Institutions (IFLA)/ Fédération Internationale des Associations de Bibliothécaires et des Bibliothèques: POB 95312, 2509 CH, The Hague, Netherlands; tel. (70) 314-08-84; fax (70) 383-48-27; e-mail ifla@ifla.org; internet www.ifla.org; f. 1927; to promote int. library cooperation in all fields of library activity, and to provide a representative body in matters of int. interest; 1,700 mems in 150 countries; Pres. ELLEN TISE (SA); Sec.-Gen. JENNEFER NICHOLSON (Netherlands); publs *IFLA Journal* (4 a year), *IFLA Directory* (every 2 years), *IFLA Professional Reports*, *IFLA Publication Series* (6 a year), *International Cataloguing Bibliographic Control* (4 a year).

Associated Centre:

Metropolitan Libraries Section: State Library Queensland, POB 3488, South Brisbane, Qld 4101, Australia; tel. (7) 38429405; fax (7) 38407860; f. 1967 to encourage int. cooperation between large city libraries, in particular the exchange of books, exhibitions, staff and information and participation in the work of the Int. Fed. of Library Asscns; Pres. LIV SAETEREN (Norway); Sec.-Treas. TAY AI CHENG (Singapore)

International Institute for Children's Literature and Reading Research/Institut für Jugendliteratur/Institut International de Littérature pour Enfants et de Recherches sur la Lecture: 1040 Vienna, Mayerhofgasse 6, Austria; tel. (1) 505-03-59; fax (1) 505-03-59-17; e-mail office@jugendliteratur.net; internet www .jugendliteratur.net; f. 1965 as an int. documentation and advisory centre of juvenile literature; promotes int. research; arranges conferences and exhibitions; compiles recommendation lists; mems: individual and group members in 26 countries; Dir Mag. KARIN HALLER (Austria); publ. *1000 und 1 Buch* (4 a year).

International Society for Knowledge Organization (ISKO): c/o Vivien Petras, Institut für Bibliotheks- und Informationswissenschaft, Unter den Linden 6, 10099 Berlin, Germany; tel. (30) 2093-4325; fax (30) 2093-4335; e-mail secr@isko.org; internet www.isko.org; f. 1989 to promote research, devt, and application of all methods for the org. of knowledge; advises on the construction, perfection and application of classification systems, thesauri, terminologies, etc.; organizes int. conference every 2 years; 400 mems; Pres. H. PETER OHLY (Germany); Sec. and Treas. Prof. VIVIEN PETRAS (Germany); publs *Advances in Knowledge Organization*, *Ergon* (Proceedings in English, irregular), *Fortschritte der Wissensorganisation*, *Ergon* (Proceedings in German, irregular), *Knowledge Organization*, *Ergon* (4 a year), *Knowledge Organization in Subject Areas 1994*– (irregular).

International Youth Library/Internationale Jugendbibliothek: Schloss Blutenburg, 81247 Munich, Germany; tel. (89) 891211-0; fax (89) 8117553; e-mail info@ijb .de; internet www.ijb.de; f. 1949; an associated project of UNESCO since 1953 Objects: to encourage int. exchange and cooperation in children's book publishing, research, and promotion of reading; to provide information and advice to students, teachers, publishers, etc.; to organize exhibitions; library: largest collection of int. children's literature in the world: 570,000 vols in over 130 languages; Dir Dr CHRISTIANE RAABE; publs *Das Bücherschloss* (report, 1 a year), *Report* (2 a year), *White Ravens* (selection of int. children's and youth literature, 1 a year).

Ligue des Bibliothèques Européennes de Recherche (LIBER): Koninklijke Bibliotheek, National Library of the Netherlands, POB 90407, 2509 The Hague, The Netherlands; tel. 70-314-01-97; e-mail liber@ kb.nl; internet www.libereurope.eu; f. 1971; 360 mems from more than 40 European countries; represents and promotes the interests of research libraries in Europe, particularly to assist them to create a functional research network across nat. boundaries; Pres. HANS GELEIJNSE; Exec. Dir WOUTER SCHALLIER (The Netherlands); publ. *LIBER Quarterly* (online).

Economics, Political Science and Sociology

International Labour Organization (ILO): 4 route des Morillons, 1211 Geneva 22, Switzerland; tel. (22) 799-61-11; fax (22) 798-86-85; e-mail ilo@ilo.org; internet www .ilo.org; f. 1919, became Specialized Agency of UN in 1946; aims to build a code of int. labour law and practice, is concerned with the safety, health and social security of workers and provides technical expertise where required by member countries; seeks to improve labour conditions, raise living standards and promote productive employment in all countries; library: see under Switzerland; mems: 179 countries; Dir-Gen. JUAN SOMAVIA; publs *Bulletin of Labour Statistics*, *International Labour Documentation*, *International Labour Review*, manuals and reports, *Official Bulletin*, studies, *World of Work*, *Yearbook of Labour Statistics*.

Associated Institutions:

International Institute for Labour Studies: CP 6, 1211 Geneva 22, Switzerland; tel. (22) 799-61-28; fax (22) 799-85-42; e-mail inst@ilo.org; internet www.ilo .org/public/english/bureau/inst; f. 1960 by ILO; aims: to provide a global forum for interaction between business, labour, policy-makers and academics on emerging labour policy issues; to promote research networks on policy implications of changing relationships between labour, business and the State; to develop the research capacities of ministries of labour and employers' and workers' organizations; Dir G. RODGERS.

International Training Centre of the ILO/Centre International de Formation de l'OIT: Viale Maestri del Lavoro 10, 10127 Turin, Italy; tel. 011-693-6111; fax 011-663-8842; e-mail communications@ itcilo.org; internet www.itcilo.org; f. 1964 by International Labour Organization to offer advanced training facilities for managers, trainers and social partners, and technical specialists from ILO mem. states; Exec. Dir FRANÇOIS EYRAUD

OTHER ORGANIZATIONS

African Training and Research Centre in Administration for Development/ Centre Africain de Formation et de Recherche Administratives pour le Développement (CAFRAD): Pavillon International, Blvd Mohammed V, BP 310, 90001 Tangier, Morocco; tel. (661) 30-72-69; fax (539) 32-57-85; e-mail cafrad@cafrad.org; internet www.cafrad.org; f. 1964 by agreement between Morocco and UNESCO; 36 mem. states; training of African senior civil servants; research into admin. problems in Africa, documentation of results, and the provision of a consultation service for govts and orgs in Africa; holds frequent seminars; mems: Algeria, Angola, Benin, Burkina Faso, Burundi, Cameroon, Cape Verde, Central African Republic, Chad, Congo, Côte d'Ivoire, Dem. Rep. of Congo, Djibouti, Equatorial Guinea, Gabon, Gambia, Ghana, Guinea, Guinea-Bissau, Liberia, Libya, Madagascar, Mali, Mauritania, Morocco, Namibia, Niger, Nigeria, São Tomé e Príncipe, Sierra Leone, Somalia, South Africa, Sudan, Togo, Tunisia, Zambia; UNESCO provided assistance 1964– 1970 and UNDP 1971–1983; Pres. S. E. MOHAMED SAÂD EL ALAMI; Dir-Gen. Dr SIMON LELO MAMOSI; publs *African Administrative Studies* (2 a year), *African Public Service Charter*, *Directory of African Consultants in Public Administration*, *Directory of African Training and Research Institutions*, *Proceedings of Pan-African Conference of Ministers of the Civil Service* (every 2 years), *Juelles Verifier et Expedia*, *Studies and Documents (Series)* (irregular).

American Society for Political and Legal Philosophy: c/o The Sec./Treas., Prof. Jacob T. Levy, Political Science, McGill University, 855 Sherbrooke Ave W, Montreal, QC H3A 2T7, Canada; tel. (514) 398-5519; fax (514) 398-1770; e-mail theasplp@ gmail.com; internet www.political-theory .org/asplp.html; f. 1955; 500 mems; Pres. DONALD HOROWITZ; publ. *NOMOS* (Yearbook).

Association of International Accountants: Staithes 3, The Watermark, Metro Riverside, Newcastle upon Tyne, NE11 9SN, UK; tel. (191) 4930277; fax (191) 4930278; e-mail aia@aiaworldwide.com; internet www.aiaworldwide.com; f. 1928; promotes and supports the advancement of the accountancy profession worldwide; offers a professional qualification for accountants and statutory auditors; 18,000 mems and students; Pres. ANDREW LAMB; Chief Exec. PHILIP TURNBULL; publ. *International Accountant* (6 a year).

Association of Social Anthropologists of the Commonwealth: POB 5230, Hove, BN52 9NB, UK; e-mail admin@theasa.org; internet www.theasa.org; f. 1946; 570 mems; Chair. Prof. RICHARD FARDON; Hon. Sec. Dr IRIS JEAN-KLEIN; publs *ASA Annals*, *ASA Essays*, *ASA Methods in Social Anthropology*, *ASA Studies*.

Centre for Democracy and Development/Centre pour la Démocratie et le Développement: Unit 2L Leroy House, 436 Essex Rd, London, N1 3QP, UK; tel. (20) 7359-7775; fax (20) 7359-2221; e-mail cdd@ cdd.org.uk; internet www.cddwestafrica.org; f. 1997; non-profit NGO dedicated to research, information and exchange of ideas on questions of democratic devt and peace-building in West Africa; offers strategic training in promoting democracy and devt; regional offices in Abuja and Lagos, Nigeria; Dir Dr JIBRIN IBRAHIM; publ. *Democracy and Development: Journal of West African Affairs* (2 a year).

Econometric Society: Dept of Economics, NW Univ., 2003 Sheridan Rd, Evanston, IL 60208-2600, USA; tel. (847) 491-3615; fax (847) 491-5427; internet www .econometricsociety.org; f. 1930 to promote studies on the unification of the theoretical-quantitative and the empirical-quantitative approach to economic problems; 6,700 mems; Exec. Vice-Pres. RAFAEL REPULLO (Spain); Gen. Man. CLAIRE SASHI (USA); publ. *Econometrica*.

European Association for Population Studies/Association Européenne pour l'Étude de la Population: POB 11676, 2502 AR The Hague, Netherlands; tel. (70) 3565200; fax (70) 3647187; e-mail contact@eaps.nl; internet www.eaps.nl; f. 1983 to promote the study of population in Europe through cooperation between persons interested or engaged in European demographics; mems: demographers and other population scientists from all European countries; Pres. FRANCOIS HERAN (France); Sec.-Gen. and Treas. FRANCESCO BILLARI (Italy); Exec. Sec. HELGA DE VALK; publ. *European Journal of Population / Revue Européenne de Démographie.*

European Centre for Social Welfare Policy and Research: Berggasse 17, 1090 Vienna, Austria; tel. (1) 3194505-0; fax (1) 3194505-19; e-mail ec@euro.centre.org; internet www.euro.centre.org; non-profit autonomous intergovernmental organization affiliated to the UN; conducts research, and provides training and information, in the fields of welfare and social development; library of 8,000 vols; Exec. Dir Prof. Dr BERND MARIN; publ. *Eurosocial Reports Series* (in English, French and German).

European Economic Association: Università Cattolia del Sacro Cuore, 20123 Milan, Italy; tel. 02-72343050; fax 02-72343051; e-mail eea@unicatt.it; internet www.eeassoc.org; f. 1986 to contribute to the devt and application of economics as a science in Europe; to improve communication and exchange between teachers, researchers and students in economics in different European countries; to develop and sponsor cooperation between teaching instns and research instns in Europe; organizes annual congress; 2,500 mems; Pres. Prof. TIMOTHY BESLEY; Sec. Prof. PIERO TEDESCHI; publ. *Journal of the European Economic Asscn (JEEA)* (6 a year).

European Foundation for Management Development (EFMD): 88 rue Gachard, Boîte 3, 1050 Brussels, Belgium; tel. (2) 629-08-10; fax (2) 629-08-11; e-mail info@efmd.org; internet www.efmd.be; f. 1971; provides forum for worldwide cooperation in management development; European Quality Initiative (EQUAL) project seeks int. cooperation in assessing quality in management education; mem. orgs (business schools, management centres, companies, consultancies) in 41 countries; Pres. GERARD VAN SCHAIK; Dir-Gen. ERIC CORNUEL; publ. *Forum* (3 a year).

Futuribles International: 47 rue de Babylone, 75007 Paris, France; tel. (1) 53-63-37-70; fax (1) 42-22-65-54; internet www.futuribles.com/home.html; f. 1960; aims to act as an early-warning system to identify major trends and challenges of the future; to undertake research on current economic and social issues; to serve as a consulting group for futures studies and strategic planning; major fields of expertise: development strategies, and multi-disciplinary studies on economic, technological, social and cultural changes in industrialized countries; library and documentation centre containing 90,000 vols; Scientific Council: 41 mems in 15 countries; Pres. JACQUES LESOURNE; Dir-Gen. HUGUES DE JOUVENEL (France); publs *Futuribles* (12 a year), *Vigie Info* (4 a year).

Inter-American Statistical Institute/ Instituto Interamericano de Estadística: Rivadavia 733 (PB), C1002AAF Buenos Aires, Argentina; tel. (11) 4344-8474; fax (11) 4344-8475; e-mail efabb@indec.mecon.gov.ar; internet www.indec.mecon.ar/iasi/; f. 1940; fosters statistical devt in the Western Hemisphere; holds seminars and meetings;

282 mems (235 individual, 34 ex-officio, 13 affiliated (institutional); Pres. Dr VÍCTOR M. GUERRERO (Mexico); Technical Sec. Prof. EVELIO O. FABBRONI; publ. *Estadística* (2 a year).

International African Institute (IAI)/ Institut Africain International: School of Oriental and African Studies, Thornhaugh St, Russell Square, London, WC1H 0XG, UK; tel. (20) 7898-4420; fax (20) 7898-4419; e-mail iai@soas.ac.uk; internet www.internationalafricaninstitute.org; f. 1926; encourages the study of African history and society and disseminates the results of research; language of instruction French; Chair. Prof. V. Y. MUDIMBE; Hon. Dir Prof. PHILIP BURNHAM; publs *Africa* (4 a year), *Africa Bibliography* (1 a year).

International Association for South-East European Studies/Association Internationale d'Etudes du Sud-Est Européen (AIESEE): Apt. 18, Nicolae Racota 12–14, 713123 Bucharest, Romania; tel. (21) 2242965; fax (21) 2242964; f. 1963; 23 mem. countries; Pres. Prof. ANDRÉ GUILLOU (France); Sec.-Gen. Prof. RĂZVAN THEODORESCU (Romania); publ. *Bulletin* (1 a year).

International Association for the Study of Insurance Economics/Geneva Association: 53 route de Malagnou, 1208 Geneva, Switzerland; tel. (22) 707-66-00; fax (22) 736-75-36; e-mail secretariat@genevaassociation.org; internet www.genevaassociation.org; f. 1973; non-profit org.; develops research programmes, regular publs and int. meetings; serves as a catalyst for progress in understanding risk and insurance matters; acts as an information creator and disseminator; organizes int. expert networks and manages discussion platforms for insurance execs, specialists, policy-makers, regulators and multilateral orgs; int. insurance 'think tank' for insurance and risk management issues; mems: up to 80 CEOs from the world's insurance companies; Pres. HENRI DE CASTRIES; Sec.-Gen., Man. Dir and Head of Insurance and Finance PATRICK LIEDTKE; Vice Sec.-Gen. and Head of Research Programmes WALTER R. STAHEL; Vice Sec.-Gen. and Head of Progress PROF. MONKIEWICZ; Head of Communications ANTHONY KENNAWAY; publs *The Geneva Papers, The Geneva Papers on Risk and Insurance, The Geneva Risk and Insurance Review.*

International Association of Schools of Social Work (IASSW): c/o Prof. Lynne Healy, Center for International Social Work Studies, University of Connecticut, School of Social Work, 1798 Asylum Ave, West Hartford, CT 06117, USA; tel. (860) 570-9149; fax (860) 570-9139; e-mail iasswsec@comcast.net; internet www.iassw.soton.ac.uk; f. 1928 to provide int. leadership and encourage high standards in social work education; mems: 1,700 schools of social work in 90 countries and 35 nat. associations of schools; Pres. Prof. TASSE ABYE (France); Sec. Prof. LYNNE HEALY (USA).

International Center for Monetary and Banking Studies/Centre International d'Etudes Monétaires et Bancaires: 11A ave de la Paix, 1202 Geneva, Switzerland; tel. 227349548; fax 227333853; internet www.icmb.org; f. 1973; ind., associated with the Graduate Institute of Int. and Devt Studies; scientific study of int. monetary, financial and banking issues; organizes conferences, public lectures; Pres. PHILIPP HILDEBRAND; Dir Prof. CHARLES WYPLOSZ; publ. *Geneva Reports on the World Economy.*

International Centre for Ethnic Studies: 554/6A Peradeniya Rd, Kandy, Sri Lanka; tel. (81) 2232381; fax (81) 2234892; e-mail icesresch@sltnet.lk; internet www.ices.lk; f.

1982 to provide an institutional focus and identity for the study and management of ethnic conflict; encourages cross-national comparative research in ethnic policy studies; library of 6,200 vols, special collections on ethnicity and women's issues; Exec. Dir Prof. MATHIAS DEWATRIPONT (Sri Lanka); publs *Ethnic Studies Report* (2 a year), *Nethra* (social issues, 4 a year).

International Commission for the History of Representative and Parliamentary Institutions/Commission Internationale pour l'Histoire des Assemblées d'Etats: c/o Dept of History, 43 North Bailey, Durham, DH1 3EX, UK; tel. (191) 386-4299; fax (191) 334-1041; e-mail j.m.rogister@dur.ac.uk; f. 1936 to encourage research on the origin and history of representative and parliamentary institutions; mems: individuals in 40 countries; languages of instruction French, English, German; organizes annual conferences, publishes monographs; Pres. Prof. J. ROGISTER (UK); Sec. ESTEVÃO DE REZENDE MARTINS (Brazil); publ. *Parliaments, Estates and Representation* (1 a year).

International Centre of Bantu Civilization/Centre International des Civilisations Bantu: BP 770, Libreville, Gabon; tel. 70-40-96; fax 77-50-90; e-mail ciciba@caramail.com; f. 1983; intergovernmental organization founded by 10 countries containing members of the Bantu peoples: Angola, Central African Republic, Comoros, Democratic Republic of the Congo, Republic of the Congo, Equatorial Guinea, Gabon, Rwanda, São Tomé e Príncipe, Zambia; research and documentation centre for the conservation and promotion of the cultural heritage of the Bantu peoples; activities in all fields of culture, science and education; 50 staff; library of 4,000 vols, and special collection of university theses (microfiche) on 10 member states; Dir-Gen. VATOMENE KUKANDA; publs *CICIBA-Informations* (4 a year), *Muntu* (2 a year).

International Council on Social Welfare/ Conseil International de l'Action Sociale: c/o Netherlands Institute of Care and Welfare, POB 19152, 3501 DD Utrecht, Netherlands; tel. (30) 2306336; fax (30) 2306540; e-mail icsw@icsw.org; internet www.icsw.org; f. 1928 to promote forms of social and economic development that aim to reduce poverty, hardship and vulnerability worldwide, especially in developing countries; 104 mem. orgs worldwide; Pres. SOLVEIG ASKJEM (Norway); Exec. Dir DENYS CORRELL; publ. *Proceedings of International Conferences on Social Welfare* (every 2 years).

International Federation of Business and Professional Women (BPW International)/Federación Internacional de Mujeres de Negocios y Profesionales: POB 568, Horsham, West Sussex, RH13 9ZP, UK; tel. (1403) 739343; fax (1403) 734432; e-mail members@bpw-international.org; internet www.bpwi.org; f. 1930 to promote the interests of business and professional women, and in particular to bring their specialized knowledge and skills to play a more effective part in int. governmental orgs; 250,000 mems; Pres. ANTOINETTE RÜEGG; Exec. Sec. ANN SWAIN.

International Fiscal Association: World Trade Center, Beursplein 37, POB 30215, 3001 DE Rotterdam, Netherlands; tel. (10) 4052990; fax (10) 4055031; e-mail t.gensecr@ifa.nl; internet www.ifa.nl; f. 1938; to study and advance int. and comparative law with regard to public finance and especially int. and comparative fiscal law and the financial and economic aspects of taxation; 11,500 mems in 105 countries, national brs in 60 countries; Pres. M. E. TRON (Mexico); Sec.-Gen. Dr H. A. HOGELS (Netherlands); publs *Cahiers de Droit Fiscal International* (Studies on International Fiscal Law), *Yearbook of the International Fiscal Association*.

International Institute for Ligurian Studies/Istituto Internazionale di Studi Liguri: Via Romana 39, 18012 Bordighera, Italy; tel. (184) 263601; fax (184) 266421; e-mail iisl@istitutostudi.191.it; internet www.iisl.it; f. 1947 to conduct research on ancient monuments and regional traditions in the north-west arc of the Mediterranean; library of 82,000 vols; mems in France, Italy, Spain, Switzerland; Dir Prof. CARLO VARALDO (Italy).

International Institute of Philosophy (IIP)/Institut International de Philosophie: 8 rue Jean-Calvin, 75005 Paris, France; tel. 1-43-36-39-11; fax 1-47-07-77-94; e-mail inst.intern.philo@wanadoo.fr; f. 1937; aims: to clarify fundamental issues of contemporary philosophy in annual meetings, and, by several series of publications, to promote mutual understanding among thinkers of different traditions and cultural backgrounds; a maximum of 115 mems, considered eminent in their field, chosen from all countries and representing different tendencies, are elected; present mems: 107 mems in 46 countries; Pres. TOMÁS CALVO (Spain); Sec.-Gen. P. AUBENQUE (France); publs *Actes des congrès internationaux* (1 a year), *Bibliography of Philosophy* (4 a year), *Philosophical Problems Today*, *Surveys (Chroniques) of Philosophy*.

International Institute of Sociology/Institut International de Sociologie: c/o Prof. Karen S. Cook, Dept of Sociology, Stanford University, Stanford, CA 94305, USA; e-mail iisoc@post.tau.ac.il; internet www.tau.sc.il/~iisoc; f. 1893 to advance the study of sociology; 300 mems in 45 countries; Pres. ELIEZER BEN-RAFAEL (Israel); Gen. Sec. and Treas. Prof. KAREN S. COOK (USA); publ. *Annales de l'Institut International de Sociologie/The Annals of the International Institute of Sociology*.

International Monetary Fund Institute: Washington, DC 20431, USA; tel. (202) 623-6660; fax (202) 623-6490; e-mail insinfo@imf.org; internet www.imf.org/external/np/ins/english/about.htm; f. 1964 to provide specialist training in economic analysis and policy, statistics, public finance, and bank supervision, for officials of mem. countries; courses and seminars in Arabic, English, French and Spanish; library; Dir PATRICK DE FONTENAY; publ. *Courier*.

International Peace Institute: 777 United Nations Plaza, New York, NY 10017-3521, USA; tel. (212) 687-4300; fax (212) 983-8246; e-mail ipi@ipinst.org; internet www.ipinst.org; f. 1970; acts as independent, int. institution, working closely with the UN and other governmental and non-governmental organizations, to promote the prevention and settlement of armed conflicts between and within states, through policy research and development; Pres. TERJE ROD-LARSEN; Vice-Pres. for External Relations WARREN HOGE; Senior Vice-Pres. for Research and Programs Dr EDWARD LUCK; publs *International Peacekeeping* (co-edited by IPI, 4 a year), *IPI Working Papers*.

International Society for Ethnology and Folklore: Meertens Institute, Joan Muyskenweg 25, 1096 CJ Amsterdam, The Netherlands; tel. (20) 4628500; fax (20) 4628555; e-mail sief@meertens.knaw.nl; internet www.siefhome.org; f. 1964, in Athens (Greece); as the successor of an int. scientific org. known as the Comm. Internationale des Arts et Traditions Populaires (CIAP); to establish and maintain collaboration between specialists in folklore and ethnology; major int. congress organized every 3 years (2011 in Lisbon, Portugal); official seat in Amsterdam since 2001; organizes comms, symposia, congresses; attached to American Folklore Soc. (AFS) and European Asscn of Social Anthropologists (EASA): collaboration with UNESCO; 400 mems; Pres. ULLRICH KOCKEL (UK); Exec. Vice-Pres. PETER JAN MARGRY (The Netherlands); Vice-Pres. BIRGITTA SVENSSON (Sweden); publ. *Bulletin d'Informations SIEF* (1 a year).

International Society for the Study of Medieval Philosophy/Société Internationale pour l'Etude de la Philosophie Médiévale: Secretariat: c/o Prof. Dr Maarten Hoenen, Philosophisches Seminar, Platz der Universität 3, 79085 Freiburg im Breisgau, Germany; tel. (761) 203-2440; fax (761) 203-9260; e-mail siepm.membership@philosophie.uni-freiburg.de; internet www.siepm.uni-freiburg.de; f. 1958 to promote the study of medieval thought and the collaboration between individuals and institutions engaged in this field; organizes int. congresses every five years and annual colloquium between congresses; 798 mems in 45 countries; Pres. Prof. Dr JOSEP PUIG MONTADA (Spain); Sec.-Gen. Prof. Dr MAARTEN J. F. M. HOENEN (Germany); publ. *Bulletin de Philosophie Médiévale* (1 a year).

International Society for Third-Sector Research (ISTR): Wyman Park Building (Room 559), 3400 N. Charles St, Baltimore, MD 21218-2608, USA; tel. (410) 516-4678; fax (410) 516-4870; e-mail istr@jhu.edu; internet www.istr.org; f. 1992; encourages research relevant to civil society, non-profit orgs, voluntarism and philanthropy; regional research networks in Africa, Asia, Europe, Latin America and the Caribbean, and Arab-speaking countries; conference every 2 years; 675 mems; Pres. MARK SIDEL (USA); Exec. Dir MARGERY B. DANIELS; publ. *Voluntas* (4 a year).

International Society of Social Defence and Humane Criminal Policy/Société Internationale de Défense Sociale pour une Politique Criminelle Humaniste: c/o Centro nazionale di prevenzione e difesa sociale, Palazzo comunale delle scienze sociali, Piazza Castello 3, 20121 Milan, Italy; tel. (2) 86460714; fax (2) 72008431; e-mail cnpds.ispac@iol.it; internet www.defensesociale.org; f. 1946; non-governmental org. in consultative status with UN Economic and Social Council; the study of crime-related problems in the perspective of a system of reactions, which through prevention and resocialization of deviants, aims to protect the individuals and society at large; 350 mems; Pres. LUIS ARROYO ZAPATERO (Spain); Sec.-Gen. EDMONDO BRUTI LIBERATI (Italy); publ. *Cahiers de défense sociale* (1 a Year, in English, Spanish and French).

Inter-Parliamentary Union/Union Interparlementaire: 5 chemin du Pommier, CP 330, 1218 Le Grand-Saconnex, Geneva, Switzerland; tel. 229194150; fax 229194160; e-mail postbox@mail.ipu.org; internet www.ipu.org; f. 1889 to promote contacts among members of the world's parliaments and unite them in common action for int. peace and cooperation; to promote democracy by strengthening and developing the means of action of representative institutions; studies political, economic, social, juridical, cultural and environmental problems of int. significance, notably through conferences; promotes free and fair elections and provides assistance to representative assemblies; helps to solve cases of violation of parliamentarians' rights; promotes status of women in political life; gathers and disseminates information on parliamentary matters; mems: 155 nat. parliaments; Pres. THEO-BEN GURIRAB (Namibia); Sec.-Gen. ANDERS B. JOHNSSON (Sweden); publs *Chronicle of Parliamentary Elections* (1 a year), *IPU Review: The World of Parliaments* (4 a year), *Panorama of Parliamentary Elections* (1 a year), *World Directory of Parliaments* (1 a year).

Italian–Latin American Institute/Istituto Italo-Latino Americano: Piazza B. Cairoli 3, 00186 Rome, Italy; tel. 06-684921; fax 06-6872834; e-mail info@iila.org; internet www.iila.org; f. 1966 to develop and coordinate research and documentation on the problems, achievements and prospects of mem. countries in cultural, scientific, economic, technical and social fields; organizes meetings and promotes activities representative of the development process of Latin America in its social, economic, cultural and technical-scientific aspects; 21 mem. countries; library: library and documentation centre of 90,000 vols, 4,500 periodicals; Sec.-Gen. PAOLO FAIOLA; publ. *Quaderni IILA* (series *Economia, Scienza, Cooperazione*).

Nordic Institute of Asian Studies/Nordisk Institut for Asienstudier: Leifsgade 33, 2300 Copenhagen S, Denmark; tel. 35-32-95-00; fax 35-32-95-49; e-mail sec@nias.ku.dk; internet www.nias.ku.dk; f. 1967; non-profit org. funded through Nordic Council of Ministers; research and documentation centre for modern Asian studies within humanities and social sciences to promote research and publish books on Asia; library of 28,000 vols and 750 current journals; Chair. Dekan LARS BILLE; Dir Dr GEIR HELGESEN.

Organisation for Economic Co-operation and Development (OECD): 2 rue André-Pascal, 75775 Paris Cedex 16, France; tel. 1-45-24-82-00; fax 1-45-24-85-00; e-mail webmaster@oecd.org; internet www.oecd.org; f. 1961; concerned with the impact of science, technology, education and the changing pattern of employment structures on the balance of economic and social development of its member countries (in Europe, North America and the Pacific area) and with the implications of technological development for the environment as well as with the broader aspects of policy to meet new social objectives; it seeks to coordinate its mems' economic and social policies, and aims at being informative, promotional and catalytic through surveys of the current situation, identification of tentative policies and the establishment of a statistical and methodological base in support of government decision-making; serves as an international clearing-house for exchanges of information and provides a forum where experts and policy-makers can discuss common issues and benefit from mutual cooperation; conducts economic analysis of emerging and transition economies; special programmes include the Programme for Educational Building and the Centre for Educational Research and Innovation (*q.v.*); 30 mem. countries; library: online library of books, periodicals and statistics (www.sourceoecd.org); Sec.-Gen. ANGEL GURRÍA; publs note: certain titles are published in more than one language, *Creditor Reporting System on Aid Activities* (6 a year), *Energy Prices and Taxes* (4 a year), *Financial Market Trends* (3 a year), *Higher Education Management and Policy* (3 a year), *International Trade by Commodity Statistics* (5 a year), *Indicators of Industry and Services* (4 a year), *Journal of Business Cycle Measurement and Analysis* (3 a year), *Main Economic Indicators* (12 a year), *Main Science and Technology Indica-*

tors (2 a year), *Monthly Statistics of International Trade, OECD Papers* (12 a year), *OECD Economic Surveys* (18 a year), *OECD Economic Outlook* (2 a year), *OECD Economic Studies* (2 a year), *OECD Journal of Competition Law and Policy* (4 a year), *OECD Journal of Budgeting* (4 a year), *Oil, Gas, Coal and Electricity—Quarterly Statistics, NEA News* (2 a year), *Nuclear Law Bulletin* (2 a year), *PEB Exchange* (3 a year and online), *Quarterly Labour Force Statistics, Quarterly National Accounts, The DAC Journal* (4 a year), *The OECD Observer* (6 a year).

Pan-African Institute for Development/ Institut Pan-Africain pour le Développement: BP 4056, Douala, Cameroon; tel. 332-28-06; fax 332-28-06; e-mail ipd.sg@ camnet.cm; f. 1964 for the training of African development staff; 2 regional institutes in Cameroon and 1 each in Burkina Faso and Zambia supply support services to development agencies; Sec.-Gen. Dr MBUKI V. MWA- MUFIYA; publs *PAID Report* (2 a year), *Yearly Progress Report*.

Society for International Development/ Société Internationale pour le Développement: Via Panisperna 207, 00184 Rome, Italy; tel. 06-487-2172; fax 06-487-2170; e-mail info@sidint.org; internet www.sidint .org; f. 1957; a global network of individuals and institutions concerned with devt that is participative, pluralistic and sustainable; mobilizes and strengthens civil society groups by building partnerships among them and with other sectors; fosters local initiatives and new forms of social experimentation; 3,000 mems in 125 countries, with 65 local chapters and 55 institutional mems; Pres. JAN PRONK; Sec.-Gen. ROBERTO SAVIO; publ. *Development* (4 a year).

Statistical Institute for Asia and the Pacific: JETRO-IDE Bldg, 3-2-2 Wakaba, Mihama-ku, Chiba-shi, Chiba 261-8787, Japan; tel. (43) 299-9782; fax (43) 299-9780; e-mail staff@unsiap.or.jp; internet www .unsiap.or.jp; f. 1970; subsidiary body of the Economic and Social Comm. for Asia and the Pacific (ESCAP); provides training in official statistics to govt statisticians in the Asia-Pacific region as recommended by resolution 75 (XXIII) of ESCAP; 22 Fellows, (Production and Devt of Official Statistics course), 21 Fellows (ICT course), 24 Fellows (Analysis, Interpretation and Use of Official Statistics course), 7 Fellows (Central Asian Countries course); library of 20,000 vols; Dir DAVAASU- REN CHULTEMJAMTS.

Stockholm International Peace Research Institute (SIPRI): Signalistgatan 9, 169 70 Solna, Sweden; tel. (8) 6559700; fax (8) 6559733; e-mail sipri@sipri.org; internet www.sipri.org; f. 1966 for research into problems of peace and conflict with particular attention to the problems of disarmament and arms control; library of 50,000 vols; Chair. ROLF EKÉUS (Sweden); Dir Dr BATES GILL (USA); publs *SIPRI Fact Sheets and Policy Briefs, SIPRI Insights on Peace and Security, SIPRI policy papers, SIPRI research reports, SIPRI Yearbook.*

UNESCO Institute for Statistics: CP 6128, Succ. Centre-Ville, Montréal, QC H3C 3J7, Canada; tel. (514) 343-6880; fax (514) 343-6882; e-mail information@uis.unesco .org; internet www.uis.unesco.org; f. 1999 to meet the needs of UNESCO member states and the int. community for a wide range of policy-relevant and reliable statistics in the fields of education, science and technology, culture and communication; Dir HENDRIK VAN DER POL.

United Nations Institute for Training and Research (UNITAR)/Institut des

Nations Unies pour la formation et la recherche: Palais des Nations, 1211 Geneva 10, Switzerland; located at: International Environment House, 11–13 chemin des Anémones, 1219 Chatelaine Geneva, Switzerland; tel. 229178455; fax 229178047; internet www.unitar.org; f. 1965 as an autonomous body within the framework of the UN; aims, by training and research, to enhance the effectiveness of the UN in achieving the major objectives of the organization, in particular the maintenance of peace and security and the promotion of economic and social development; conducts seminars for diplomats and others who work in the UN system and carries out training, either at UN headquarters or in the field, which has special relevance for developing countries; conducts research into problems of concern to the UN system; Asst Sec.-Gen. and Exec. Dir MARCEL A. BOISARD (Switzerland); publ. more than 50 titles in English and some in French, Spanish and Russian.

Vienna Institute for International Dialogue and Cooperation/Wiener Institut für Internationalen Dialog und Zusammenarbeit: Moellwaldpl. 5/3, 1040 Vienna, Austria; tel. (1) 713-35-94; fax (1) 713-35-94-73; e-mail office@vidc.org; internet www.vidc.org; f. 1987 as successor to Vienna Institute for Development; aims to disseminate information on problems and achievements of developing countries by all possible means in order to convince the public or industrialized nations of the necessity to increase devt aid and to strengthen int. cooperation; research programmes; organizes cultural exchanges between South and North; engages in anti-racism and anti-discrimination activities in sport at nat. and European levels; Pres. Mag. BARBARA PRAM- MER (Austria); Dir Mag. WALTER POSCH.

World Bank Institute: 1818 H St, NW, Washington, DC 20433, USA; tel. (202) 473- 1000; fax (202) 477-6391; e-mail wbi_infoline@worldbank.org; internet www .worldbank.org/wbi; f. 1955; provides learning programmes and policy advice in the areas of environment and natural resources, economic policy for poverty reduction, governance, regulation, and finance, human development, knowledge networks and outreach; delivers training activities for policy-makers in 149 countries through direct and distance learning; has formal partnerships with 130 academic and training institutions in developed nations and client countries; Vice-Pres. FRANNIE A. LÉAUTIER; publs *Development Outreach* (4 a year), *WBI News* (3 a year).

World Institute for Development Economics Research of the United Nations University (UNU-WIDER): Katajanokan-laituri 6B, 00160 Helsinki, Finland; tel. (9) 6159911; fax (9) 61599333; e-mail wider@ wider.unu.edu; internet www.wider.unu .edu; f. 1984; conducts policy-oriented research into inequality and poverty, global economic development and related issues; Dir Prof. FINN TARP; publ. *WIDER Working Papers.*

World Intellectual Property Organization (WIPO): 34 chemin des Colombettes, 1211 Geneva 20, Switzerland; tel. 223389111; fax 227335428; e-mail wipo .mail@wipo.int; internet www.wipo.int; f. 1970; UN specialized agency; promotes the protection of intellectual property rights worldwide; aims to extend benefits of the int. intellectual property system to all mem. states; main activities are: progressive devt of int. intellectual property law, assisting developing countries and providing services to facilitate the process of obtaining intellectual property rights in multiple countries;

184 mem. states; Dir-Gen. Dr KAMIL IDRIS; publs *Appelations of Origin* (irregular), *International Designs Bulletin* (12 a year), *PCT Newsletter* (12 a year), *WIPO Gazette of International Marks* (52 a year).

World Society for Ekistics: c/o Athens Center of Ekistics, 23 Strat. Syndesmou St, 10673 Athens, Greece; tel. 210-3623216; fax 210-3629337; e-mail ekistics@otenet.gr; internet www.ekistics.org; f. 1965; aims to promote the devt of knowledge and ideas concerning human settlements by research and through publs, conferences, etc.; to encourage the devt and expansion of education in ekistics; to educate public opinion concerning ekistics; to recognize the benefits and necessity of an interdisciplinary approach to the needs of human settlements, and to promote and emphasize such an approach; 200 mems; Pres. Dr MADHAV DEOBHAKTA (India); Sec.-Gen. and Treas. PANAYIS PSOMOPOULOS; publ. conference papers publ. in *Ekistics,* the journal of the Athens Center of Ekistics.

Education

Academic Cooperation Association (ACA): 15 rue d'Egmontstraat, 1000 Brussels, Belgium; tel. (2) 513-22-41; fax (2) 513- 17-76; e-mail info@aca-secretariat.be; internet www.aca-secretariat.be; f. 1993; ind. org. dedicated to the management, analysis and improvement of education and training cooperation within Europe and between Europe and other parts of the world; 23 mems (20 European and 3 non-European), all being major nationally-based orgs responsible for the promotion and funding of education cooperation in their countries; Dir BERND WÄCHTER; publ. *ACA Papers on International Cooperation in Education* (monograph series).

African and Malagasy Council for Higher Education/Conseil Africain et Malgache pour l'Enseignement Supérieur (CAMES): 01 BP 134, Ouagadougou 01, Burkina Faso; tel. 50-36-81-46; fax 50-36-85- 73; e-mail cames@bf.refer.org; internet www .cames.bf.refer.org; f. 1968 to ensure coordination between member states in the fields of higher education and research; mems: governments of Benin, Burkina Faso, Burundi, Cameroon, Central African Republic, Chad, Republic of Congo, Côte d'Ivoire, Gabon, Guinea, Guinea-Bissau, Madagascar, Mali, Niger, Rwanda, Senegal, Togo; Sec.-Gen. Prof. MAMADOU MOUSTAPHA SALL.

Agence Universitaire de la Francophonie: BP 400 Succ. Côte-des-Neiges, Montréal, QC H3S 2S7, Canada; tel. (514) 343-6630; fax (514) 343-2107; internet www.auf.org; f. 1961; aims: documentation, coordination, cooperation, exchange; Pres. CHARLES GOMBE MBALAWA (Republic of the Congo); Rector MICHÈLE GENDREAU-MASSALOUX (France).

Amazonian Universities Association/ Associação de Universidades Amazônicas (UNAMAZ)/Asociación de Universidades Amazónicas: Trav. 3 de Maio 1573, São Braz, 66063-390 Belém, PA, Brazil; tel. and fax (91) 3229-4478; e-mail unamaz@ufpa .br; internet www.ufpa.br/unamaz; f. 1987 to promote cultural, technological and scientific cooperation between universities and research instns in the Amazonian region; 54 mem. univs in Bolivia, Brazil, Colombia, Ecuador, Guyana, Peru, Suriname and Venezuela

Arab Bureau of Education for the Gulf States: POB 94693, Diplomatic Quarters, Riyadh 11614, Saudi Arabia; tel. (1) 4800555; fax (1) 4802839; e-mail abegs@abegs.org;

internet www.abegs.org; f. 1975 to coordinate and integrate the efforts of the mem. states (Bahrain, Kuwait, Oman, Qatar, Saudi Arabia and the United Arab Emirates) in the fields of education, science and culture; aims to unify the educational system for all the mem. states; Gulf Arab States Educational Research Center: see Kuwait chapter; established Arabian Gulf University in Bahrain; Dir-Gen. Dr Saeed Almullais; publ. *Rissalat al-Khaleej al Araby* (Message of the Arab Gulf, 4 a year).

Asian Association of Open Universities: 160 Fuxingmennei St, Beijing, 100031, People's Republic of China; tel. (10) 66490029; fax (10) 66412407; e-mail crtvu.edu.cn; internet www.aaou.net; Pres. Prof. Yaoxue Zhang; Sec.-Gen. Prof. Yawan Li.

Asociación Iberoamericana de Educación Superior a Distancia (AIESAD) (Ibero-American Association for Open University Education): Calle Bravo Murillo 38 (7a Planta), 28015 Madrid, Spain; tel. 91-398-65-49; fax 91-398-65-87; e-mail aiesad@adm.uned.es; internet www.aiesad.org; f. 1980; 13 mem. countries; Pres. Dr Juan A. Gimeno Ullastres; Exec. Sec. Adriana Lozada Hernández.

Associação das Universidades de Língua Portuguesa (AULP) (Association of Portuguese Language Universities): Av. Santos Dumont, 67, 2°, 1050-203 Lisbon, Portugal; tel. (21) 781-63-60; fax (21) 781-63-69; e-mail aulp@aulp.org; internet www.aulp.org; 122 mem. instns in Angola, Brazil, Cape Verde, Guinea-Bissau, Macao, Mozambique, Portugal, São Tomé e Príncipe and Timor-Leste; Pres. João Guerreiro; Sec.-Gen. Cristina Montalvão Sarmento; publ. *Actas dos Encontros*.

Association for Teacher Education in Europe: 60 Rue de la Concorde, 1050 Brussels, Belgium; fax (2) 502-29-03; e-mail ateesecretariat@gmail.com; internet www.atees.org; f. 1976 to establish contacts between institutions for teacher education and those responsible for that education; arranges working groups, annual conference, etc.; undertakes consultancy work for European organizations; Pres. Prof. Dr Giovanni Polliani; Vice-Pres. Justina Erculj; publ. *European Journal of Teacher Education* (3 a year).

Association Internationale de Pédagogie Universitaire: Service Guidance Étude, Bâtiment B33, Université de Liège au Sart Tilman, 4000 Liège, Belgium; tel. (4) 366-20-73; fax (4) 366-29-88; e-mail mdelhaxhe@ulg.ac.be; internet www.ulg.ac.be/aipu; f. 1979; Francophone org. promoting research and development in teaching and higher education; 800 mems; Pres. Jacques Tardif (Canada); Sec.-Gen. Michel Delhaxhe (Belgium); publ. *Res Academica* (2 a year).

Association Montessori Internationale: Koninginneweg 161, 1075 CN Amsterdam, Netherlands; tel. (20) 679-8932; fax (20) 676-7341; e-mail info@montessori-ami.org; internet www.montessori-ami.org; f. 1929 to propagate the ideals and educational methods of Dr Maria Montessori and to spread knowledge on child devt without racial, religious or political prejudice; activities: supervises affiliated training courses for teachers in several countries; sponsors int. congresses and study conferences on Montessori education; creates new training centres and offers affiliation to Montessori societies; Pres. A. Roberfroid; Exec. Dir Lynne Lawrence; publ. *Communications* (2 a year).

Association of African Universities/ Association des Universités Africaines: POB AN5744, Accra-North, Ghana; tel. (21) 774495; fax (21) 774821; e-mail info@aau.org; internet www.aau.org; f. 1967 to collect, classify and disseminate information on higher education and research in Africa; to promote cooperation among African instns in training, research, community services and higher education policy, in curriculum development and in the determination of equivalence in academic degrees; to encourage increased contacts between mems and the int. academic world; to encourage the development and wide use of African languages and support training of univ. teachers and administrators to deal with problems in African education in general; mems: 199 university instns in 45 African countries; Pres. Prof. Is-Haq Olanrewaju Oloyede (Nigeria); Sec.-Gen. Prof. Goolam T. G. Mohamedbhai (Mauritius); publ. *Handbook* (every 2 years).

Association of American International Colleges and Universities: c/o Dr John Bailey, American College of Greece, 6 Gravias St, Aghira Paraskevi, 153 42 Athens, Greece; tel. (210) 600-9800; fax (210) 600-9811; e-mail acg@acg.edu; internet www.acg.edu; f. 1971 to promote cooperation among independent institutions offering int. education in Europe and the Near East; 12 mem. univs and colleges; Pres. Dr John S. Bailey (Greece); Sec. and Treas. Craig Sexson (Greece).

Association of Arab Universities: POB 401, Jubeyha, Amman, Jordan; tel. 5062048; fax 5062051; e-mail secgen@aaru.edu.jo; f. 1964 to consolidate cooperation between Arab universities and institutions of higher education; mems: 213 universities; Sec.-Gen. Prof. Dr Saleh Hashem; publs *Bulletin* (6 a year), *Directory of Arab Universities*, *Directory of Teaching Staff of Arab Universities*, *Proceedings of Seminars*.

Association of Caribbean Universities and Research Institutes (UNICA): c/o Prof. Mervyn C. Alleyne, Department of Liberal Arts, University of the West Indies, St Augustine, Trinidad; f. 1968 to foster contact and collaboration between member universities and institutes; conferences, meetings, seminars, etc.; circulation of information through newsletters, bulletins; facilitates cooperation and the pooling of resources in research; encourages exchanges of staff and students; mems: 50 institutions; Sec.-Gen. Prof. Mervyn C. Alleyne; publ. *Caribbean Educational Bulletin* (4 a year).

Association of Commonwealth Universities (ACU): Woburn House, 20–24 Tavistock Sq., London, WC1H 9HF, UK; tel. (20) 7380-6700; fax (20) 7387-2655; e-mail info@acu.ac.uk; internet www.acu.ac.uk; f. 1913; promotes contact and cooperation in higher education throughout the Commonwealth; provides assistance with staff and student mobility and devt programmes; researches and disseminates information about univs and relevant policy issues; organizes major meetings of Commonwealth univs and their representatives; provides the secretariats for, and administers, various scholarship and fellowship schemes (incl. the Commonwealth Scholarship Commission in the UK, the Marshall Aid Commemoration Commission and the Commonwealth Univs Study Abroad Consortium; also administers the Commonwealth Foundation Medical Electives Bursaries, the ACU Devt Fellowships, the DFID Shared Scholarship Scheme, the T. H. B. Symons Fellowship, and the Canada Memorial Foundation Scholarships); operates various subject specialist networks for higher education staff; provides an appointments, advertising and publicity service; operates a policy research unit; addresses the gender imbalance in higher education leadership through its women's programme; organizes various training workshops; hosts the Observatory on Borderless Higher Education; provides the secretariat for the Staff and Educational Devt Asscn; hosts an Africa Unit; mems: 487 univs; library of 18,500 vols; Sec.-Gen. Dr John Rowett; publs *Commonwealth Universities Yearbook*, *Trends in Academic Recruitment and Retention: a Commonwealth Perspective*, *Who's Who of Executive Heads*, *Vice-Chancellors, Presidents, Principals, Rectors* (every 2½ years).

Association of Southeast Asian Institutions of Higher Learning: c/o Dr Ninnat Olanvoravuth, Jamjuree 1 Bldg, Chulalongkorn Univ., Phayathai Rd, Bangkok 10330, Thailand; tel. (2) 2516966; fax (2) 253-7909; e-mail ninnat.o@chula.ac.th; internet www.seameo.org/asaihl; f. 1956 to promote the economic, cultural and social welfare of the people of Southeast Asia by means of educational cooperation and research programmes; to foster the cultivation of a sense of regional identity and interdependence and to cooperate with other regional and int. orgs; serves as a clearing-house for information, provides opportunities for discussion and recognizes distinctive academic achievements; 170 mem. instns from 19 countries; Sec.-Gen. Dr Ninnat Olanvoravuth; publs *Handbook*, *Seminar Proceedings*.

Association of Universities of Asia and the Pacific (AUAP): c/o Centre for International Affairs, Suranaree University of Technology, 111 University Ave, Muang, Nakhon Ratchasima 30000, Thailand; tel. (44) 224143; fax (44) 224140; e-mail auap@sut.ac.th; internet auap.sut.ac.th; f. 1995; 210 regular mems in 19 countries, 3 assoc. mems in 3 countries; Pres. Dr Carmen Z. Lamagan (Bangladesh); Sec. Prof. Dr Ruben C. Umaly; publ. *Gazette* (4 a year).

Caribbean Network of Educational Innovation for Development (CARNEID): The Towers, 25 Dominica Drive, 3rd Fl., Kingston 5, Jamaica; tel. 427-4771; fax 436-0094; e-mail kingston@unesco.org; internet www.unesco.org/carneid; f. 1981 by UNESCO to advance educational innovation for development through networking among educational institutions and personnel in the Caribbean; publ. *Education Annual*.

Caribbean Regional Council for Adult Education: c/o Azad Hosein, Adult Education Unit, Ministry of Education, 51 Frederick St, Port-of-Spain, Trinidad and Tobago; tel. 625-4091; internet carcae.tripod.com; f. 1978 to promote and facilitate cooperation among national adult education organizations and agencies in non-Spanish-speaking territories of the region; to advocate awareness and recognition of the importance of adult education and to seek funding from governments and other sources; to hold conferences, seminars, training courses, etc.; to advise governments and other bodies on adult education; library of 5,000 vols; Chair. Vilma McClenan (Jamaica); Exec. Sec.-Treas. Azad Hosein.

CEMS—The Global Alliance in Management Education: CEMS Head Office, 1 rue de la Libération, 78350 Jouy-en-Josas, France; tel. 1-39-67-74-57; fax 1-39-67-74-81; e-mail info@cems.org; internet www.cems.org; f. 1988; Masters in int. management, provides education and professional experience for multilingual, multicultural postgraduate students; involves academic and corporate partners in the definition and teaching of curriculum, implementation of a series of joint research projects; mems: 27 European business schools, 8 non-European assoc. members, 53 corporate partners; Chair. Prof. BERNARD RAMANANTSOA (France); Exec. Dir FRANÇOIS COLLIN; publ. *European Business Forum* (4 a year; print and online, in association with PricewaterhouseCoopers).

Conference of Baltic University Rectors (CBUR): Szczecin University, Al. Jedności Narodowej 22A, 70-453 Szczecin, Poland; tel. (91) 434-25-36; fax (91) 434-29-92; e-mail rektorat@univ.szczecin.pl; f. 1990

Congregazione per l'Educazione Cattolica (Congregation for Catholic Education): Palazzo delle Congregazioni, Piazza Pio XII 3, 00193 Rome; tel. (6) 69884167; fax (6) 69884172; e-mail cec@cec.va; internet www .vatican.va/roman_curia/congregations/ ccatheduc; f. 1588; concerned with the direction, temporal admin. and studies of Catholic univs, seminaries, schools and colleges; Prefect Cardinal ZENON GROCHOLEWSKI; Sec. Most Rev. O. P. JEAN-LOUIS BRUGUÈS.

Consejo Superior Universitario Centroamericano (CSUCA) (Higher Council of Central American Universities): Avda Las Américas, 1-03 zona 14, Int. Club Los Arcos, 01014 Guatemala City, Guatemala; tel. 2367-1833; fax 2367-4517; e-mail sg@ listas.csuca.org; internet www.csuca.org; f. 1948; exec. body of the Confederación Universitaria Centroamericana; promotes Central American integration and the strengthening of higher education in the region; 18 mem. univs in Belize, Costa Rica, Dominican Republic, El Salvador, Guatemala, Honduras, Nicaragua, Panama; Sec.-Gen. MSc EFRAÍN MEDINA GUERRA; Exec. Sec. ELVIA CHINCHILLA.

Consorcio-Red de Educación a Distancia (Inter-American Distance Education Consortium): c/o Dr Armando Villarroel, Fischler Graduate School of Education and Human Services, Nova Southeastern University, 1750 NE 167th St, N Miami Beach, FL 33162-8569, USA; tel. (954) 262-8569; e-mail axv4@omnibus.ce.psu.edu; internet www.cde .psu.edu/de/cread/cread.html; f. 1990; networks of individuals and instns in North, Central and South America; Exec. Dir Dr ARMANDO VILLARROEL.

Consortium for North American Higher Education Collaboration (CONAHEC): Univ. of Arizona, POB 210300, Tucson, AZ 85721-0300; Univ. of Arizona, 220 W 6th St, University Services Annex Bldg 300A, Room 108, Tucson, AZ 85701; tel. (520) 621-7761; fax (520) 626-2675; internet www.conahec .org; f. 1994; advises and connects instns wishing to establish or strengthen academic collaborative programmes in the N American region; 122 mem. instns (26 in Canada, 69 in Mexico, 42 in the USA and 8 affiliates outside North America); Pres. DAVID MARSHALL; Exec. Dir FRANCISCO J. MARMOLEJO.

Commonwealth Association of Polytechnics in Africa: c/o Kenya Polytechnic, POB 52428, Nairobi, Kenya; tel. (2) 338232; fax (2) 219689; e-mail polymis@swiftkenya.com; f. 1978 to provide a forum for exchange of professional ideas and practices in technical and business education and training, and to improve the content and methods of polytechnic teaching, to disseminate information through publications and workshops, and to create a data centre and reference library; 135 mem. polytechnics; library of 2,000 vols; Sec.-Gen. WILLIAM RWAMBULLA; publ. *CAPA Journal of Technical Education and Training* (2 a year).

Commonwealth of Learning: 1055 W Hasting St, Suite 1200, Vancouver, BC V6E 2E9, Canada; tel. (604) 775-8200; fax (604) 775-8210; e-mail info@col.org; internet www .col.org; f. 1988 by Commonwealth Heads of Govt to promote cooperation among Commonwealth countries, utilizing distance education techniques, incl. communications technologies, to strengthen mem. countries' capacities in human resources devt; works with ministries of education, schools, colleges, univs and NGOs to increase access to opportunities for learning; mems are the 54 Commonwealth countries; library of 7,800 vols; Pres. and CEO Sir JOHN DANIEL; Vice-Pres. and Programme Dir Prof. ASHA S. KANWAR; Dir of Finance, Admin. and Human Resources DORIS B. MCEACHERN; Dir of Knowledge Management and Information Technology PAUL G. WEST; publs *Connections/EdTech News* (3 a year), *Three-Year Plan*.

Commonwealth Secretariat, Education Department, Social Transformation Programmes Division: Marlborough House, Pall Mall, London, SW1Y 5HX, UK; tel. (20) 7747-6460; fax (20) 7747-6287; e-mail education@commonwealth.int; internet www.thecommonwealth.org; encourages and supports educational consultation and cooperation between Commonwealth countries through conferences, seminars, workshops, meetings of experts, and training courses for educational personnel (with assistance from the Commonwealth Fund for Technical Cooperation); contributes to national educational development through studies of particular problems, handbooks, directories and training manuals, and by providing information on educational subjects; undertakes consultancies for govts on request; triennial conference of Ministers of Education; Dir NANCY SPENCE; publ. *LinkIn* (4 a year).

Coordinación Educativa y Cultural Centroamericana (CECC) (Coordinating Body for Education and Culture in Central America): De la Nunciatura, 100 m al norte, casa N° 8815, Rohmoser, San José, Costa Rica; tel. 232-28-91; fax 231-23-66; e-mail sgcecc@ racsa.co.cr; internet www.sica.int/cecc; f. 1982; promotes and works for integration in the areas of education and culture in Central America; 7 mem. countries (Belize, Costa Rica, El Salvador, Guatemala, Honduras, Nicaragua, Panama), 1 assoc. country (Dominican Republic); Gen. Sec. MARVIN HERRERA ARAYA.

Council for Cultural Cooperation: Council of Europe, 67075 Strasbourg Cedex, France; tel. 3-88-41-20-00; fax 3-88-41-27-88; f. 1962 to draw up and implement the educational and cultural programme of the Council of Europe; mems: 47 states; publs *EUDISED European Educational Research Yearbook*, *European Heritage*.

Danube Rectors' Conference (DRC)/ Donau Rektoren Konferenz: c/o Karolina Bucka, Univ. of Maribor, Int. Relations Office, Slomskov trg 15 2000 Maribor, Slovenia; tel. (2) 235 53 47; fax (2) 235 52 67; e-mail drc@uni-mb.si; internet drc.uni-mb.si; f. 1983 to improve higher education in teaching and research in the region; has established working groups to address the issues of univ. legislation, curricula and the evaluation of teaching and research; 45 higher education instns in 13 countries; Pres. Rector Prof. Dr FERENC HUDECZ (Hungary).

Education International (EI)/Internationale de l'Education (IE): 5 blvd du Roi Albert II, 1210 Brussels, Belgium; tel. (2) 224-0611; fax (2) 224-0606; e-mail headoffice@ei-ie.org; internet www.ei-ie.org; f. 1993 from the merger of the World Confederation of Organizations of the Teaching Profession (WCOTP/CMOPE) and the International Federation of Free Teachers' Unions (IFFTU/SPIE); to advance the cause of organizations of teachers and education employees, promote status, interests and welfare of mems and defend their trade union and professional rights; to promote free, quality, public education for all; to promote peace, democracy, social justice, equality and the application of the Universal Declaration on Human Rights through the development of education and the collective strength of teachers and education employees; World Congress every three years; mems: 305 nat. orgs in 155 countries; Pres. THULAS NXESI (South Africa); Gen. Sec. FRED VAN LEEUWEN (Netherlands); publs *The EI Monthly Monitor* (in English, French and Spanish), *The Education International Quarterly Magazine* (in English, French and Spanish).

ERASMUS (European Community Action Scheme for the Mobility of University Students): 70 rue Montoyer, 1040 Brussels, Belgium; tel. (32) (2) 233-01-11; fax (32) (2) 233-01-50; e-mail eac-info@ec.europa .eu; internet ec.europa.eu/education/ lifelong-learning-programme/doc80_en.htm; f. 1987 by the Council of Ministers of the European Community; aims to encourage greater student and staff mobility throughout the EU and EFTA (European Free Trade Association) countries by means of the creation of a European University Network, the award of 'mobility' grants to students, arrangements for mutual recognition of qualifications and courses, and other supporting measures; publs *ERASMUS and Lingua Action II Directory* (1 a year), *Guidelines for Applicants*.

EuroAsian Universities Association: 119991 Moscow B-106, GSP-1, Moscow State Univ. 'M. V. Lomonosov', Leninskie Gory, Russia; tel. (495) 939-27-69; fax (495) 939-27-69; e-mail eau_msu@rector.msu.ru; internet www.eau.msu.ru; Pres. Acad. VIKTOR SADOVNITCHY.

European Association for International Education: POB 11189, 1001 GD Amsterdam, Netherlands; Herengracht 487, 1017 BT Amsterdam, Netherlands; tel. (20) 3445100; fax (20) 3445119; e-mail eaie@eaie .nl; internet www.eaie.org; f. 1989; non-profit org. with the main aim of stimulating and facilitating the internationalization of higher education in Europe and around the world, and meeting the professional needs of individuals active in int. education; c. 2,000 mems; Pres. BJØRN EINAR AAS (Norway); Dir ALEX OLDE KALTER (Netherlands); publs *Forum*, *Occasional Papers*, *Professional Development Series*.

European Association for the Education of Adults: 27 rue Liedts, 1030 Brussels, Belgium; tel. (2) 513-52-05; fax (2) 513-57-34; e-mail eaea-main@eaea.org; internet www .eaea.org; f. 1953 to encourage cooperation between adult education organizations on questions of methods, materials, and exchange of individuals; arranges study sessions and tours; also has offices in Girona (Spain) and Helsinki (Finland); mems in 30 European countries; Gen. Sec. Dr ELLINOR HAASE.

European Association of Distance Teaching Universities: Postbus 2960, 6401 DL Heerlen, Netherlands; Valkenburgerweg 177, 6419 AT Heerlen, Netherlands; tel. (45) 5762214; fax (45) 5741473; e-mail secretariat@eadtu.nl; internet www.eadtu .nl; f. 1987; aims to promote lifelong, open and flexible learning by means of higher distance education, to support bilateral and multilateral contacts between academic staff, to support cooperation in research, course devt, course transfer and credit transfer, to develop new methods for higher distance education, and to organize common projects in cooperation with European authorities; European Open Univ. Network (f. 1995) acts as exec. arm; mems: 11 mem. univs and 15 mem. asscns from European countries, and 3 assoc. mem. univs from S and N America; Pres. DAVID VINCENT; Sec.-Gen. PIET HENDERIKX (Belgium).

European Association of Institutions in Higher Education (EURASHE): Ravensteingalerij 27/3, 1000 Brussels, Belgium; tel. (2) 211-41-97; fax (2) 211-41-99; e-mail eurashe@eurashe.eu; internet www.eurashe.eu; f. 1990 to promote the interests of professional higher education in the member countries of the EU and in other European countries, in instns that are public or recognized and/or financed by the public authorities of an EU member country or another European country; Pres. LARS LYNGE NIELSEN (Denmark); Sec.-Gen. STEFAN DELPLACE (Belgium).

European Distance and E-Learning Network (EDEN): c/o Budapest Univ. of Technology and Economics, 1111 Budapest, Egry J.u. 1, Hungary; tel. (1) 463-1628; fax (1) 463-1858; e-mail secretariat@eden-online.org; internet www.eden-online.org; f. 1991; to foster devts in flexible, distance and e-learning; 1,078 mems, of which 178 instns, and 900 individuals in the Network of Academics and Professionals; Pres. INGEBORG BØ (Norway); Sec.-Gen. Dr ANDRÁS SZŰCS; publs *Conference Proceedings* (1 a year), *European Journal of Open and Distance Learning* (online).

European Institute of Education and Social Policy: Université Paris IX-Dauphine, 1 place du Maréchal de Lattre de Tassigny, 75775 Paris Cedex 16, France; tel. (1) 44-05-40-01; fax (1) 44-05-40-02; internet www.eiesp.org; f. 1975 by the European Cultural Foundation, the European Commission, the International Council for Educational Development; studies specific issues in education, employment and social policy; policy-oriented and research programmes and seminars undertaken for European governments, int. organizations, universities, or regional and local bodies; Chair. HYWEL CERI JONES; Dir JEAN GORDON; publ. *European Journal of Education* (4 a year, in English).

European University Association/Association Européenne de l'Université: Rue d'Egmont 13, 1000 Brussels Belgium; tel. (2) 230-55-44; fax (2) 230-57-51; e-mail info@eua.be; internet www.eua.be; f. 2001 through merger of Association of European Universities and Confederation of European Union Rectors' Conferences; represents and supports higher education institutions in 46 countries; facilitates partnership in higher education and research within Europe and between Europe and the rest of the world; aims to enhance the contribution of European univs to European integration, principally through the creation of a European Space for Higher Education; approx. 850 individual, collective mems and affiliates in 46 countries; Pres. Prof. JEAN-MARC RAPP (Switzerland); Sec.-Gen. LESLEY WILSON (Belgium); publ. *EUA News* (online).

Fédération Internationale des Professeurs de Français/International Federation of Teachers of French: 1 ave Léon Journault, 92318 Sèvres Cedex, France; tel. 1-46-26-53-16; fax 1-46-26-81-69; internet www.fipf.org; f. 1969 to unite and assist teachers of French as a first or second language worldwide; mems: 180 associations in 140 countries; Pres. JEAN-PIERRE CUQ (France); Vice-Pres. PEIWHA CHI LEE (Taiwan); Vice-Pres. RAYMOND GEVEART (Bel-

gium); Sec.-Gen. MADELINE ROLLE-BOUMLIC (France); publs *Dialogues and Cultures* (1 a year), *Echanges: Lettre FIPF* (4 a year), *Le Français Dans le Monde* (6 a year).

Federation of the Universities of the Islamic World (FUIW)/Fédération des Universités du monde Islamique (FUMI): ISESCO, Ave des F.A.R., Hay Ryad, POB 2275, 10104 Rabat, Morocco; tel. 37-56-60-52; fax 37-56-60-53; e-mail fumi@isesco.org.ma; internet www.fuiw.org; part of Islamic Educational, Scientific and Cultural Organization (*q.v.*); supports univs and higher education instns of comparable level in the Islamic world and encourages cooperation between them; 193 mem. univs; Pres. Dr ABDOLLAH JASSBI; Sec.-Gen. Dr ABDULAZIZ OTHMAN ALTWIJRI.

Institut für den Donauraum und Mitteleuropa (IDM) (Institute for the Danube Region and Central Europe): Hahngasse 6/1/24, 1090 Vienna, Austria; tel. (1) 3197258; fax (1) 3197258-4; e-mail idm@idm.at; internet www.idm.at; f. 1953; extramural research think-tank working in the fields of politics, education, research, culture and business; supports the work of embassies, trade missions, cultural institutes and nat. tourist offices in the countries of the Danube region and Central and S-E Europe; Chair. Dr ERHARD BUSEK; Gen. Sec. Univ. Prof. Dr LEOPOLD MÄRZ; publs *Buchreihe* (book series), *Info Europa* (journal on the enlarged EU, 5 a year), *Studien* (studies on topical issues).

Instituto Internacional para la Educación Superior en América Latina y el Caribe (IESALC) (International Institute for Higher Education in Latin America and the Caribbean): Avda Los Chorros con Calle Acueducto, Edif. Asovincar, Altos de Sebucán, Caracas, Venezuela; tel. (212) 286-10-20; fax (212) 286-03-26; internet www.iesalc.unesco.org.ve; autonomous body operating as part of UNESCO; contributes to the devt of higher education in the region; Dir ANA LÚCIA GAZZOLA.

Inter-American Organization for Higher Education/Organisation Universitaire Interaméricaine: 333 Grande-Allée est, Bureau 230, Québec, QC G1R 2H8, Canada; tel. (418) 650-1515; fax (418) 650-1519; e-mail secretariat@oui-iohe.qc.ca; internet www.oui-iohe.org; f. 1980; inter-university cooperation and exchange; 300 mems; library of 500 vols; Pres. RAÚL ARIAS LOVILLO (Mexico); Exec. Dir PATRICIA GUDIÑO (Canada).

Inter-University Council for East Africa: 3rd Fl., Plot 4, Nile Ave, East African Development Bank Bldg, POB 7110, Kampala, Uganda; tel. (41) 256251; fax (41) 342007; e-mail info@iucea.org; internet www.iucea.org; f. 1984 as Association of Eastern and Southern African Universities; to encourage and develop mutually beneficial collaboration between mem. universities, and between them and nat. govts and other organizations; helps its mems to contribute to meeting nat. and regional development needs, to the resolution of problems in every appropriate sector of activity in the region, and to the development of human resource capacity in the academic arena; Chair. Prof. FREDERICK I. B. KAYANJA (Uganda); Exec. Sec. Prof. CHACHA NYAIGOTTI-CHACHA (Kenya).

International Association for Educational and Vocational Guidance/Association Internationale d'Orientation Scolaire et Professionnelle: IAEVG Administration Centre, 202–119 Ross Ave, Ottawa, Canada; tel. (613) 729-6164; fax (613) 720-3515; e-mail s.hopkins@iaevg.org; internet www.iaevg.org; f. 1951 to contribute

to career devt, vocational guidance practice and promote contact between members across the world; 40,000 mems in 80 countries; Pres. LESTER OAKES (New Zealand); Sec.-Gen. LINDA TAYLOR; publ. *International Journal* (2 a year).

International Association for the Exchange of Students for Technical Experience (IAESTE): IAESTE (UK), British Council, 10 Spring Gardens, London, SW1A 2BN, UK; e-mail iaste@britishcouncil.org; internet www.iaeste.org.uk; f. 1948; arranges technical work experience abroad for science and engineering students; placements in over 80 countries; 62 national committees; Gen. Sec. Dr A. SFEIR.

International Association of Dental Students: c/o FDI World Dental Federation, 13 Chemin du Levant, L'Avant Centre, 01210, Ferney-Voltaire, France; tel. 4-50-40-50-50; fax 4-50-40-55-55; e-mail gsecretary@iads-web.org; internet www.iads-web.org; f. 1951 to promote international contact between dental students, to advance and encourage their interest in the science and art of dentistry, to promote exchanges and int. congresses; mems: 88,000 students globally; Pres. ANDREA VEITOVA (Czech Republic); Sec.-Gen. TAYLAN AKCA (Turkey); publ. *Bulletin* (2 a year).

International Association of University Presidents (IAUP): c/o Siam University, 235 Petkasem Rd, Phasicharoen, Bangkok 10163, Thailand; tel. (2) 868 6885; fax (2) 868 6879; e-mail siam@siam.edu; internet www.iaups.org; f. 1964 to strengthen the quality of education in higher education instns, and to promote global awareness and competence as well as peace and int. understanding through education; c. 600 mems; Pres. BARHAM MADAIN (Chile); Sec.-Gen. HEITOR GURGULINO DE SOUZA (Brazil).

International Baccalaureate Organization (IBO): 15 route des Morillons, 1218 Grand-Saconnex, Geneva, Switzerland; tel. 227917740; fax 227910277; e-mail ibhq@ibo.org; internet www.ibo.org; f. 1968; non-profit foundation encouraging students to be active learners, well-rounded individuals and engaged world citizens; works with 2,815 schools in 128 countries to develop and offer 3 programmes to more than 775,000 students aged 3 to 19 years; Dir-Gen. JEFFREY BEARD; publs *IB World* (3 a year), *Journal of Research in International Education* (3 a year).

International Bureau of Education: see under UNESCO.

International Centre for Agricultural Education (CIEA)/Internationales Studienzentrum für landwirtschaftliches Bildungswesen: Federal Office of Agriculture, 3003 Berne, Switzerland; tel. 313222619; fax 313222634; internet www.ciea.ch; f. 1958; organizes international courses on vocational education and teaching in agriculture every two years; Dir ROLAND STÄHLI.

International Council for Adult Education: 18 de Julio 2095, apt 301, 11200 Montevideo, Uruguay; tel. and fax (2) 409-79-82; e-mail secretariat@icae.org.uy; internet www.icae.org.uy; f. 1973; global network of NGOs promoting adult and lifelong learning; areas of activity: adult literacy, primary healthcare reform, adult education in prison, global citizenship and gender justice, peace education and conflict resolution, globalization, Adult Learners' Week, education and transformative capacity of work spaces; 800 mems in 50 countries; Pres. PAUL BÉLANGER (Canada); publ. *Convergence* (4 a year).

International Council for Open and Distance Education: Lilleakerveien 23, 0283 Oslo, Norway; tel. 22-06-26-30; fax 22-06-26-31; e-mail icde@icde.org; internet www.icde.org; f. 1938 as Int. Council for Correspondence Education, present name 1982; dedicated to furthering the aims and methods of distance education worldwide by promoting and funding research and scholarly publs, encouraging the formation of regional asscns, facilitating communications and information exchange, and organizing conferences and workshops; 7,000 mems in 120 countries; Pres. FRITS PANNEKOEK (Canada); Sec.-Gen. (vacant); publ. *Open Praxis* (electronic, 2 a year).

International Federation of Catholic Universities/Fédération Internationale des Universités Catholiques (FIUC)/ Federación Internacional de Universidades Católicas: c/o Institut Catholique, 21 rue d'Assas, 75270 Paris Cedex 06, France; tel. (1) 44-39-52-26; fax (1) 44-39-52-28; e-mail sgfiuc@bureau.fiuc.org; internet www.fiuc.org; f. 1924, officially recognized by the Holy See in 1949; to ensure a strong bond of mutual assistance among all Catholic univs in the search for truth to help to solve problems of growth and devt, and to cooperate with other int. orgs; 206 mems in 52 countries; Pres. ANTHONY J. CERNERA (USA); Sec.-Gen. Prof. Mgr GUY-RÉAL THIVIERGE (France); publs *Idem Aliter* (12 a year), *Journal / Cahiers / Cuadernos*.

International Federation of University Women/Fédération Internationale des Femmes Diplômées des Universités: 10 rue du Lac, 1207 Geneva, Switzerland; tel. 227312380; fax 227380440; e-mail info@ifuw.org; internet www.ifuw.org; f. 1919 to promote understanding and friendship between univ. women irrespective of race, nationality, religion or political opinions, to encourage int. cooperation, to advance the devt of education, to represent univ. women in int. orgs to encourage the full application of their knowledge and skills to the problems that arise at all levels of public life, and to encourage their participation in the resolution of these problems; consultative status with appropriate inter-governmental orgs; offers fellowships and study grants; undertakes studies dealing with the status of women; affiliates in 75 countries; Pres. LOUISE CROOT (New Zealand); Sec.-Gen. LEIGH BRADFORD RATTEREE (Switzerland).

International Federation of Workers' Education Associations: 227 Royal Exchange, Manchester, M2 7DD, United Kingdom; tel. (161) 819-1200; fax (161) 819-1222; e-mail dave.spooner@ifwea.org; internet www.ifwea.org; f. 1947 to promote cooperation between national non-governmental bodies concerned with adult and workers' education, through clearing-house services, exchange of information, publications, conferences, summer schools, etc.; 105 affiliated orgs; Pres. JOÃO PROENCA (Portugal); Gen. Sec. DAVE SPOONER (United Kingdom); publ. *Workers' Education* (4 a year, in English).

International Institute for Educational Planning: see under UNESCO.

International Phonetic Association (IPA): c/o Dr Katerina Nicolaidis, Dept of Theoretical and Applied Linguistics, School of English, Aristotle Univ. of Thessaloniki, Thessaloniki 54124, Greece; tel. (2310) 997429; fax (2310) 997432; e-mail knicol@enl.auth.gr; internet www.arts.gla.ac.uk/ipa/ipa.html; f. 1886 to promote the scientific study of phonetics and its applications; hosts quadrennial Int. Congress of Phonetic Sciences; offers examinations in phonetics; 550 mems; Pres. Prof. Dr JOHN WELLS (UK); Sec. Asst Prof. Dr KATERINA NICOLAIDIS (Greece); publ. *Journal of the International Phonetic Association* (3 a year).

International Reading Association: 800 Barksdale Rd, POB 8139, Newark, DE 19714-8139, USA; tel. (302) 731-1600; fax (302) 731-1057; e-mail pubinfo@reading.org; internet www.reading.org; f. 1956; sets standards for effective reading instruction; improves the quality of reading instruction through the study of the reading process and teaching techniques; promotes lifetime reading habit and public awareness of global literacy; annual convention, regional conferences, and biennial World Congress; 80,000 mems; library of 6,000 vols; Pres. BARBARA WALKER (USA); Exec. Dir ALAN E. FARSTRUP; publs *Journal of Adolescent and Adult Literature*, *Lectura y Vida* (4 a year), *Reading Research Quarterly*, *The Reading Teacher* (8 a year).

International Schools Association (ISA): c/o Drs Bert Timmermans, Alpenroos 11, 2317 EX Leiden, Netherlands; tel. (715) 210280; fax (715) 727803; internet www.isaschools.org; f. 1951 to coordinate work in International Schools and promote their development; merged in 1968 with the Conference of Internationally-minded Schools (CIS) and now counts in its membership a number of selected national schools; member schools maintain the highest standards and accept pupils of all nationalities, irrespective of sex, race and creed; ISA carries out curriculum research; convenes annual Conferences on problems of curriculum and educational reform; has consultative status with UNESCO, UNICEF, UNHCR, UNEP and ECOSOC; 85 mem. schools worldwide; Chair. CLIVE CARTHEW (Spain); Exec. Dir Drs BERT TIMMERMANS (Netherlands); publ. *Educational Bulletin* (3 a year).

International Society for Business Education/Société Internationale pour l'Enseignement Commercial: 6302 Mineral Point Rd, Ste 100, Madison, WI 53705, USA; tel. (608) 273-8467; e-mail jsutton@matcmadison.edu; internet www.siec-isbe.org; f. 1901 to organize int. courses and congresses on business education; 1,600 mems organized in 19 nat. groups; Pres. MARGARET SARAGINA (USA); Gen. Sec. Dr JUDITH OLSON-SUTTON (USA).

International Society for Education through Art (InSEA)/Société Internationale pour l'Education Artistique: James H. Sanders III, c/o Dept of Art Education, Ohio State University, 128 N Oval Mall, Columbus, OH 43210, USA; e-mail graham.nash@churchie.com.au; internet www.insea.org; f. 1951 to unite art teachers worldwide, to exchange information and coordinate research into art education; non-governmental global organization for the study of art education, international congresses, exhibitions and other activities; c. 1,500 mems; Pres. RITA IRWIN (Canada); Sec. GRAHAM NASH (Australia); publ. *InSEA News* (3 a year).

International Union of Students/Union Internationale des Etudiants: POB 58, 17th November St, 1101 Prague 01, Czech Republic; tel. and fax 271731257; e-mail ius@cfs-fcee.ca; internet www.stud.uni-hannover.de/gruppen/ius; f. 1946 by World Student Congress in Prague; objects: to defend the rights and interests of students, to strive for peace, national independence, academic freedom and democratic education, and to unite the student movement in furtherance of these objectives; activities include conferences, meetings, solidarity campaigns, relief projects, award of scholarships, travel and exchange, sports events, cultural projects, publicity and other activities in the furtherance of the Union's aims; mems: 99 full mem. countries, 25 consultative; Pres. MANISH TEWARI (India); Sec.-Gen. FRAGE SHERIF; publs *Democratization of Education*, various regional and other bulletins (4 a year), *World Student News*.

International Young Christian Workers/ Jeunesse Ouvrière Chrétienne Internationale: 4 Ave Georges Rodenbach, 1030 Brussels, Belgium; tel. (2) 242-18-11; fax (2) 242-48-00; e-mail joci@jociycw.net; internet www.jociycw.net; f. 1925 to train, organize and defend the rights of young workers; develops analysis and action on areas such as informal work, the conditions for young female workers, unemployment, apprenticeships, and temporary and dangerous employment; holds int. councils and training sessions at local, nat. and int. level; mems: nat. orgs in 60 countries; Pres. YOVEL THIRUVALLUVAR; Sec.-Gen. BRIDGET RAUCH.

Islamic Educational, Scientific and Cultural Organization (ISESCO)/Organisation Islamique pour l'Education, les Sciences et la Culture: Ave des F. A. R., Hay Ryad, BP 2275, 10104 Rabat, Morocco; tel. (3) 7-56-60-52; fax (3) 7-56-60-12; internet www.isesco.org.ma; f. 1982 under the aegis of the Islamic Conference Organization to strengthen cooperation between mem. states in the fields of education, culture and science; 51 mems; Islamic Data Bank service (BIDI); Dir-Gen. Dr ABDULAZIZ OTHMAN AL-TWAIJRI; publs *ISESCO Bulletin* (4 a year), *ISESCO Triennial*, *ISESCO Yearbook*, *Islam Today* (2 a year).

Latin American Institute for Educational Communication/Instituto Latinoamericano de la Comunicación Educativa: Calle del Puente 45, Col. Ejidos de Huipulco, Del. Tlalpan, 14380 México, DF, Mexico; tel. (55) 5728-6500 ext. 2100; e-mail contacto@ilce.edu.mx; internet www.ilce.edu.mx; f. 1956; supported by the Mexican Government to provide leadership in educational communication and technical assistance to mems; regional cooperation in research, experimentation, production and distribution of audiovisual materials; produces and broadcasts educational television programmes; offers online educational services; training at the Center for Training and Advanced Studies on Educational Communication (CETEC); operates Center of AV Documentation for Latin America (CEDAL); 13 mem. countries; library of 34,000 vols; Dir-Gen. Lic. DAVID DE LA GARZA LEAL; publ. *Tecnología y Comunicación Educativas* (4 a year).

OECD Centre for Educational Research and Innovation (CERI): 2 rue André Pascal, 75775 Paris Cedex 16, France; tel. 1-45-24-82-00; fax 1-44-30-63-94; e-mail ceri.contact@oecd.org; internet www.oecd.org/edu/ceri; f. 1968; projects include: future thinking in education, university future, evidence-based policy research in education, national reviews on educational research and development, learning sciences and brain research, formative assessment, systemic innovation; vocational education and training; open educational resources, measuring the social outcomes of learning; globalization and linguistic competencies; Head TOM SCHULLER.

Organization of Ibero-American States for Education, Science and Culture/ Organización de Estados Iberoamericanos para la Educación, la Ciencia y la Cultura (OEI): C/ Bravo Murillo 38, 28015 Madrid, Spain; tel. (91) 594-43-82; fax (91) 594-32-86; internet www.oei.es; f. 1949 as

Ibero-American Bureau of Education, name changed 1985; intergovernmental organization for educational, scientific and cultural cooperation within the Ibero-American countries; provides technical assistance to Ibero-American development systems in the above areas; provides information and documentation on the development of education, science and culture; encourages exchanges in these fields; organizes training courses; the General Assembly (at ministerial level) meets every four years; mems: govts of 20 Ibero-American countries; library of 8,000 vols, 500 periodicals; Sec.-Gen. FRANCISCO JOSÉ PIÑÓN.

Organization of the Catholic Universities of Latin America/Organización de Universidades Católicas de América Latina (ODUCAL): c/o Juan Alejandro Tobías, Viamonte 1856, CP 1056, Buenos Aires, Argentina; tel. (11) 4814-9630; fax (11) 4812-4625; internet www.oducal.org; f. 1953; aims to assist the cultural development of Latin America and to promote the activities of Catholic higher education in the region; mems: 34 Catholic univs in Argentina, Brazil, Colombia, Cuba, Ecuador, Mexico, Peru, Puerto Rico, and Venezuela; Pres. JUAN ALEJANDRO TOBIAS; Sec.-Gen. Dr EDUARDO MIRAS.

Pacific Islands Regional Association for Distance Education: c/o Ruby Va'a, University of the South Pacific, (Dir, USP Centre), POB 3014, Apia, Samoa; tel. 20874; fax 23424; e-mail vaa_r@samoa.usp.ac.fj; internet www.col.org/pirade; Pres. RUBY VA'A; Sec. PEPE LUTERU.

Pax Romana: 15 rue du Grand-Bureau, CP 315, 1211 Geneva 24, Switzerland; tel. 228230707; fax 228230708; e-mail miicmica@paxromana.int.ch; internet www.paxromana.org; f. 1921; 2 brs since 1947; student br: *International Movement of Catholic Students* (80 nat. federations); graduate branch: *International Catholic Movement for Intellectual and Cultural Affairs* (60 nat. federations and 5 int. specialized secretariats); Pres. PATRICIO RODE; Sec.-Gen. PAUL ORTEGA; publ. *Convergence* (in English, French and Spanish, 2 a year).

Steering Committee for Higher Education and Research (CDESR): c/o Council of Europe, Higher Education Section, 67075 Strasbourg Cedex, France; tel. 3-88-41-20-00; fax 3-88-41-27-06; e-mail katia.dolgova-dreyer@coe.int; internet www.coe.int/higher-education; f. 1978, under the Council for Cultural Cooperation (CDCC), set up within the Council of Europe by the signatories of the European Cultural Convention, to promote cooperation among European countries in the field of higher education and research; the CDESR is a steering cttee under the Committee of Ministers of the Council of Europe; work programme: univ. policy, academic mobility (especially jt Council of Europe-UNESCO network of information centres on equivalences and mobility and a new jt convention on recognition); main contributor to the Bologna Process aiming to establish a European Higher Education Area by 2010; projects on higher education as a public responsibility, higher education governance, the heritage of European univs, intercultural dialogue; assistance in higher education reform in countries of South-Eastern Europe and newly independent states; 96 delegates (2 per country), who are representatives of higher education instns and senior govt officials from the 48 countries party to the European Cultural Convention; Chair. LUC WEBER (Switzerland); Sec. KATIA DOLGOVA-DREYER.

Southeast Asian Ministers of Education Organization (SEAMEO): Mom Luang Pin Malakul Centenary Bldg, 920 Sukhumvit Rd, Bangkok 10110, Thailand; tel. (2) 3910144; fax (2) 3812587; e-mail secretariat@seameo.org; internet www.seameo.org; f. 1965 to promote cooperation among the Southeast Asian nations through its projects and programmes in education, science and culture; 18 regional centres; mems: Brunei Darussalam, Cambodia, Indonesia, Laos, Malaysia, Myanmar, Philippines, Singapore, Thailand, Timor-Leste, Viet Nam; Associate Member Countries: Australia, Canada, France, Germany, Netherlands, New Zealand, Norway, Spain; 2 affiliate mems: ICDE, Univ. of Tsukuba; library of 2,000 SEAMEO docs; Pres. HE JURIN LAKSANAWISIT (Thailand); Dir Dato' Dr AHAMAD BIN SIPON; publs *SEAMEO Accomplishments Report* (1 a year), *SEAMEO Directory* (1 a year), *SEAMEO Education Agenda* (2 a year).

UNESCO European Centre for Higher Education/Centre Européen pour l'Enseignement Supérieur (CEPES): Str. Stirbei Voda 39, 010102 Bucharest, Romania; tel. (21) 313-08-39; fax (21) 312-35-67; e-mail info@cepes.ro; internet www.cepes.ro; f. 1972; centre for policy development and the promotion of international higher education cooperation in Europe, North America and Israel; Secretariat of Joint UNESCO/Council of Europe European Recognition Convention, and of the ENIC Network of Information Centres on Recognition and Mobility in Europe; library of 6,000 books, 135 periodicals, 3,200 documents; Dir Dr JAN SADLAK; publ. *Higher Education in Europe* (4 a year, in English, online in French and Russian).

UNESCO Institute for Information Technologies in Education: Ul. Kedrova 8, Bldg 3, 117292 Moscow, Russia; tel. (095) 129-29-90; fax (095) 129-12-25; e-mail info@iite.ru; internet www.iite.ru; f. 1997; to develop policy and strategy regarding information and communication technologies (ICTs) in education, to monitor and support use of ICTs in education, to provide training for those working in education, and to assist UNESCO member states in problems relating to ICTs; Chair. Prof. Dr SALEH ABDULRAHMAN AL-ATHEL (Saudi Arabia); Dir VLADIMIR KINELEV.

UNESCO Institute for Lifelong Learning/Institut de l'UNESCO pour l'apprentissage tout au long de la vie/UNESCO-Institut für Lebenslanges Lernen: Feldbrunnenstr. 58, 20148 Hamburg, Germany; tel. (40) 448041-46; fax (40) 4107723; e-mail uil-lib@unesco.org; internet www.unesco.org/uil/documentation; f. 1951; an int. research institute of UNESCO; main concern is the content and quality of education in the framework of lifelong learning, with an emphasis on adult learning, non-formal education and adult literacy; main activities are research, diffusion, promotion, research-based training and documentation; a worldwide network for exchange of information on literacy; a research-oriented training programme; library of 63,000 vols, 180 periodicals; spec. collns: sample learning materials on literacy, post-literacy and continuing education from 120 countries; Dir Dr ADAMA OUANE; publ. *International Review of Education* (6 a year).

UNESCO International Institute for Capacity Building in Africa: POB 2305, Addis Ababa, Ethiopia; tel. (11) 5445284; fax (11) 5514936; e-mail info@unesco-iicba.org; internet www.unesco-iicba.org; f. 1999; the institute's primary responsibility is the development of the capacity of institutions in Africa in the fields of teacher education, curriculum development, educational policy,

planning and management, and distance education; Governing Board of 12 mems, sitting for three years each, selected from UNICEF, UNDP, World Bank, OAU, African Development Bank, Association for the Development of Education in Africa, and from representatives of Africa's geographical and linguistic groups; Officer in Charge Dr JULIEN DABOUE.

UNESCO International Institute for Higher Education in Latin America and the Caribbean/Instituto Internacional de la UNESCO para la Educación en América Latina y el Caribe: Edificio Asovincar, Avda Los Chorros con Calle Acueducto, Altos de Sebucán, Apdo Postal 68.394, Caracas 1062-A, Venezuela; tel. (212) 2861020; fax (212) 2860527; internet www.iesalc.unesco.org.ve; seeks to promote cooperation between member states in the region, and their institutions and establishments of higher education, the improvement of higher education systems, comparisons with and research into higher education in other parts of the world, regional integration, development of nat. and regional systems of evaluation and accreditation, the utilization of new information and communication technologies in higher education, and cooperation with UNESCO and implementation of its programmes; library: Documentation and Information Centre founded in 1979: online public catalogue, 11,325 bibliographies, 2,500 abstracts, 900 digital monographs and occasional papers; Dir CLAUDIO RAMA VITALE.

UNESCO-UNEVOC International Centre for Technical and Vocational Education and Training: UN Campus, Hermann-Ehlers-Str. 10, 53113 Bonn, Germany; tel. (228) 815-0100; fax (228) 815-0199; e-mail info@unevoc.unesco.org; internet www.unevoc.unesco.org; f. 2000; Dir RUPERT MACLEAN (Australia); publ. *UNESCO-UNEVOC Bulletin* (in Arabic, Chinese, English, French, Russian and Spanish, 2 a year).

Union of the Universities of Latin America and the Caribbean/Unión de Universidades de América Latina y el Caribe: Circuito Norponiente del Estadio Olímpico, Ciudad Universitaria, Apdo 70232, Del. Coyoacán, 04510 México, DF, Mexico; tel. (55) 5622-0092; fax (55) 5616-1414; e-mail udual@servidor.unam.mx; internet www.udual.org; f. 1949 to link the Latin American universities and contribute to the cultural and academic integration of the regional nations; organizes General Assemblies and Conferences; permanent statistical work; mems: 167 universities in 21 countries; library of 7,000 vols, 300 serials, records, microforms; Pres. Lic. ROBERTO ANTONIO REYNA TEJADA (Dominican Republic); Sec.-Gen. Lic. RAFAEL CORDERA CAMPOS (Mexico); publs *Boletín UDUAL* (12 a year), *Gaceta UDUAL* (4 a year), *Proceedings of Latin American Universities Conferences, Revista Universidades* (2 a year), *Window* (4 a year).

University of the Arctic: POB 122, 96101 Rovaniemi, Finland; tel. (16) 341341; fax (16) 3414211; internet www.uarctic.org; f. 2001; international cooperating network of 115 'high latitude' universities, colleges and higher education and research institutions; the university's secretariat, the Circumpolar Coordination Office, is hosted by the University of Lapland, Finland; Pres. LARS KULLERUD (Norway); Vice-Pres. OUTI SNELLMAN; Academic programmes: Bachelors of Circumpolar Studies (BCS), Arctic Learning Environment (ALE), Circumpolar Mobility Program (CMP), Northern Research Forum (NRF), UArctic Field School

World Association for Educational Research (WAER)/Asociación Mundial

de Ciencias de la Educación (AMCE)/ Association Mondiale des Sciences de l'Education (AMSE): c/o Yves Lenoir, Faculté d'Éducation, Université de Sherbrooke, 2500 blvd de l'Université, Sherbrooke, QC J1K 2R1, Canada; tel. (819) 821-8000 ext. 61339; fax (819) 829-5343; e-mail amseamcewaer@usherbrooke.ca; internet www.amseamcewaer.usherbrooke .ca; f. 1953, present title adopted 2004; aims: to encourage research in educational sciences by organizing congresses, issuing publs, the exchange of information, etc.; 500 individual mems in 32 countries; Pres. Yves Lenoir; Gen. Sec. Fouad Chafiqi (Morocco); publ. *Recherche en Education autour du Monde* (2 a year).

World Education Fellowship-International (WEF): 54 Fox Lane, Palmers Green, London, N13 4AL, UK; tel. and fax (20) 8245-4561; e-mail generalsecretary@ wef-international.org; internet www .wef-international.org; f. 1921 to promote the exchange and practice of progressive educational ideas worldwide; organizes workshops and one-day conferences; sections and groups in 22 countries; Pres. Christine Wykes; Gen. Sec. Guadalupe G. de Turner; publ. *The New Era in Education* (3 a year).

World Maritime University: POB 500, 201 24 Malmö, Sweden; tel. (40) 356300; fax (40) 128442; e-mail info@wmu.se; internet www .wmu.se; f. 1983 by the Int. Maritime Organization (IMO); offers postgraduate programmes in maritime affairs for students from around the world; language of instruction English; library of 18,000 vols (special collection: IMO depository); 300 students; Pres. Karl Laubstein; publ. *Journal of Maritime Affairs* (2 a year).

World Student Christian Federation (WSCF)/Fédération Universelle des Associations Chrétiennes d'Etudiants: WSCF Inter-Regional Office, 5 route des Morillons, Ecumenical Centre, POB 2100, 1211 Geneva 2, Switzerland; tel. 227916358; fax 227916152; e-mail wscf@wscf.ch; internet www.wscfglobal.org; f. 1895; an ecumenical student, univ. and secondary school org. with participants from all major Christian confessions; consultative status with the UN through ECOSOC and UNESCO; affiliated student Christian movements in 105 countries; languages of instruction French, English, Spanish; Chair. Mesones Horacio (Uruguay); Sec.-Gen. Rev. Michael Wallace (New Zealand); publs *Federation News* (2 a year), *Student World*, *WSCF Journal*.

World Union of Jewish Students: Rechov King George 58, POB 7114, Jerusalem 91070, Israel; 4th Fl., Heichal Shlomo, Rechov King George 58, Jerusalem, Israel; tel. (2) 6213444; fax (2) 6251688; e-mail office@wujs.org.il; internet www.wujs.org.il; f. 1924 to act as a global organization for national Jewish student bodies; organizes educational programmes, leadership training seminars, women's seminars and Project Areivim, a service programme for Diaspora communities; divided into 6 regions; organizes Congress every three years; 51 nat. unions; 700,000 mems; NGO mem. of UNESCO, youth affiliate of World Jewish Congress, mem. org. of World Zionist Organization; Chair. Viktoria Dolburd; Exec. Dir Nir Ortal; publs *Heritage and History* (Jewish student activist yearbook), *WUJS Leads*.

ACCREDITATION AND QUALITY ASSURANCE

Arab Network for Quality Assurance in Higher Education (ANQAHE): POB 533, Maadi, Egypt; 13 Bergas St, Garden City, Cairo, Egypt; tel. (2) 25240113; fax (2)

25240343; e-mail secretariat@anqahe.org; internet english.anqahe.org; f. 2007; aims to create a mechanism between the Arab countries to exchange information about quality assurance, construct new quality assurance orgs, develop standards and disseminate good practice, strengthen liaison between quality assurance bodies in the different countries; works in association with the International Network for Quality Assurance Agencies (q.v.) and the Association of Arab Universities (q.v.); Pres. Dr Nadia Badrawi; Sec.-Gen. Dr Tariq Alsindi.

Asia Pacific Accreditation and Certification Commission (APACC): CPSC, Bldg Blk C, DepEd Complex, Meralco Ave, Pasig City 1600, Metro Manila, Philippines; tel. (2) 633-8413; fax (2) 633-8425; e-mail cpsc@ cpsctech.org; internet www.apacc4hrd.org; f. 2004 to guide Technical and Vocational Education and Training (TVET) instns in equipping themselves with internationally recognized standards and systems; operated by Colombo Plan Staff College for Technician Education (CPSC); 15 mem. countries (Afghanistan, Bangladesh, Bhutan, Fiji, Indonesia, Republic of Korea, Maldives, Mongolia, Myanmar, Nepal, Pakistan, Papua New Guinea, Philippines, Sri Lanka and Thailand); Pres. Prof. Shyamal Majumdar; Jt Coordinator Dr Rajesh Khambayat; Jt Coordinator Dr Theodora Tesoro-Gayondato.

Asia-Pacific Quality Network (APQN): 202 South Shaan Xi Rd, Shanghai, China; tel. (21) 54032285; fax (21) 54670198; e-mail jiangyq@shec.edu.cn; internet www.apqn .org; f. 2003 to enhance the quality of higher education in the region by promoting the devt of the quality assurance agencies and fostering cooperation between them; 64 mems (25 full, 12 intermediate, 6 assoc., 21 institutional) in 24 countries; Pres. Concepcion V. Pijano (Philippines); Sec./Treas. Dr Jiang Yanqiao (China).

Caribbean Area Network for Quality Assurance in Tertiary Education (CANQATE): 6B Oxford Rd, Kingston 5, Jamaica; tel. 929-7299; fax 929-7312; e-mail elondon@ cwjamaica.com; internet www.canqate.org; f. 2002; 63 mems in 10 territories; Pres. Dr Ethley London (Jamaica); Sec. Valda Alleyne (Barbados).

Central and Eastern European Network of Quality Assurance Agencies in Higher Education: 1061 Budapest, Király u. 16, Hungary; tel. (1) 344-0134; fax (1) 344-0313; e-mail rozsnyai@mab.hu; internet www.ceenetwork.hu; f. 2001 as a not-for-profit NGO to share experiences and foster cooperation among member agencies; 21 mem. agencies in Albania, Austria, Bulgaria, Croatia, Czech Republic, Estonia, Germany, Hungary, Latvia, Lithuania, Macedonia, Poland, Romania, Russia, Slovakia, Slovenia; Gen. Sec. Christina Rozsnyai.

Consejo Centroamericano de Acreditación de la Educación Superior (CCA) (Central American Council for Accreditation in Higher Education): 100 m norte y 75 m este de Office Depot, Avda Central, San Pedro, Montes de Oca, San José, Costa Rica; tel. 2202-6133; fax 2224-6903; e-mail cca@ucr.ac.cr; internet www.cca.ucr.ac.cr; f. 2003 to promote the improvement of the quality and the integration of higher education in Central America; Exec. Dir Licda Marianela Aguilar Arce.

European Association for Quality Assurance in Higher Education (ENQA): Unioninkatu 20–22 / Havis Business Center (3rd floor), 00130 Helsinki, Finland; tel. (9) 25225700; fax (9) 25225710; e-mail emmi.helle@enqa.eu; internet www

.enqa.eu; f. 2000; disseminates information, experiences and good practices in the field of quality assurance (QA) in higher education to European QA agencies, public authorities and higher education instns; its activities are financed by the European Commission; 40 full mem. agencies (39 nat., 1 European) in 22 countries; Pres. Bruno Curvale (France); Sec.-Gen. Emmi Helle (Finland).

European Consortium for Accreditation in Higher Education (ECA): NVAO, POB 85498, 2508 CD The Hague, Netherlands; tel. (70) 3122352; fax (70) 3122301; e-mail m .frederiks@nvao.net; internet www .ecaconsortium.net; f. 2003 to achieve the mutual recognition of accreditation decisions among the participants, which will contribute to the recognition of qualifications and the mobility of students in Europe; 13 mem. orgs in 9 countries; Coordinator Mark Frederiks.

International Network for Quality Assurance Agencies in Higher Education (INQAAHE): POB 85498, 2508 CD The Hague, Netherlands; NVAO, Parkstraat 28, 2514 JK The Hague, Netherlands; tel. (70) 3122300; fax (70) 3122301; e-mail inqaahe@ nvao.net; internet www.inqaahe.org; f. 1991; collects and disseminates information on theory and practice in the assessment, improvement and maintenance of quality in higher education; Pres. Dr David Woodhouse (Australia); Sec. Leendert Klaassen (Netherlands); publs *INQAAHE Bulletin* (online, 4 a year), *Quality in Higher Education* (3 a year).

Red Iberoamericana para la Acreditación de la Calidad de la Educación Superior (RIACES) (Iberoamerican Network for Accreditation of Quality in Higher Education): CONEAU, Av. Santa Fe 1385, Piso 4, (C1059ABH), Buenos Aires, Argentina; tel. (11) 4815-1767; fax (11) 4815-0744; e-mail leandroh@coneau.gov.ar; internet www.riaces.net; f. 2003; promotes cooperation and the exchange of information and experiences between Iberoamerican instns concerned with the evaluation and accreditation of quality in higher education; 28 mem. instns in 18 countries; Pres. María José Lemaitre (Chile).

Engineering and Technology

International Union of Technical Associations and Organizations/Union Internationale des Associations et Organismes Techniques (UATI): 1 rue Miollis, 75732 Paris Cedex 15, France; tel. (1) 45-68-48-28; fax (1) 43-06-29-27; e-mail uati@unesco.org; internet www.unesco.org/ uati; f. 1951; activities: working groups and cttees to identify, promote and coordinate actions of mem. asscns in areas of common interest, and to facilitate relations with international bodies, in particular UNESCO, UNIDO and ECOSOC; mems: 25 organizations; Pres. Jacques Rousset (France); Sec.-Gen. Roland Bresson (France); publ. *Convergence* (3 a year).

MEMBER ORGANIZATIONS

International Academy for Production Engineering/Collège International pour la Recherche en Productique: 9 rue Mayran, 75009 Paris, France; tel. 1-45-26-21-80; fax 1-45-26-92-15; e-mail cirp@cirp .net; internet www.cirp.net; f. 1950; aims to promote by scientific research the study of mechanical processing of all solid materials including checks on efficiency and quality of work; 540 mems; Sec.-Gen. Prof. Didier

DUMUR; publs *Annals–Manufacturing Technology* (2 vols, 1 a year), *Dictionaries of Production Engineering*, *Proceedings of Manufacturing Systems Seminars* (1 a year).

International Association for Hydro-Environment Engineering and Research: Paseo Bajo Virgen del Puerto 3, 28005 Madrid, Spain; tel. (91) 335-79-08; fax (91) 335-79-35; e-mail iahr@iahr.org; internet www.iahr.org; f. 1935; 2,300 individual mems, 200 corporate mems; Exec. Dir Dr C. B. GEORGE; publs *Journal of Hydraulic Research* (6 a year), *Journal of HydroEnvironment Research*, *Journal of River Basin Management* (published in partnership with IAHS and INBO, 4 a year), *Newsflash* (12 a year), *Proceedings of World Congresses* (4 a year).

International Commission of Agricultural Engineering/Commission Internationale du Génie Rural (CIGR): c/o Prof. Dr T. Maekawa, University of Tsukuba, Graduate School of Life and Environmental Sciences, 1-1-1 Tennodai, Tsukuba, 305-8572 Ibaraki, Japan; tel. (81) 29-853-6989; fax (81) 29-853-7496; e-mail biopro@sakura.cc.tsukuba.ac.jp; internet www.cigr.org; f. 1930; application of soil and water sciences to agricultural engineering; conservation, irrigation, land improvement and reclamation; rural construction and equipment; agricultural machinery; distribution of electricity in rural areas and its application in the general energy context; scientific organization of agricultural work; food processing; mem. asscns in 30 countries, individual mems in 6 countries; Pres. Prof. LUIS SANTOS (Portugal); Sec.-Gen. Prof. Dr P. SCHULZE LAMMERS (Germany).

International Commission on Glass (ICG): c/o P. Simurkai, Nábrežná 5, 911 01 Bratislava, Trenč, Slovakia; tel. (42) 4601411; fax (42) 4693511; e-mail psimurka@stonline.sk; internet www.icglass.org; f. 1933 in Venice, Italy, to promote the dissemination of information on the art, history, science and technology of glass; mems: nat. socs in 34 countries; Pres. Dr F. NICOLETTI (Italy); Exec. Sec. PETER SIMURKA (Slovakia).

International Commission on Irrigation and Drainage/Commission Internationale des Irrigations et du Drainage: 48 Nyaya Marg, Chanakyapuri, New Delhi 110021, India; tel. (11) 26116837; fax (11) 26115962; e-mail icid@icid.org; internet www.icid.org; f. 1950; to stimulate and promote the devt of the arts, sciences and techniques of engineering, agriculture, economics, ecology and social science in managing water and land resources for irrigation, drainage, flood control and river training applications, incl. research and devt and capacity-building by adopting comprehensive approaches and up-to-date techniques for sustainable agriculture in the world; 65 active mem. countries; 110 Nat. Cttees; Pres. Prof. Dr CHANDRA A. MADRAMOOTOO (Canada); Sec.-Gen. M. GOPALAKRISHNAN (India); Dir VIJAY K. LABHSETWAR; publ. *Irrigation and Drainage- The Journal of the ICID*.

International Commission on Large Dams/Commission Internationale des Grands Barrages: 151 blvd Haussmann, 75008 Paris, France; tel. 1-40-42-68-24; fax 1-40-42-60-71; internet www.icold-cigb.org; f. 1928; mems: national cttees in 80 countries; Pres. C. B. VIOTTI (Brazil); Sec.-Gen. A. BERGERET (France); publs *ICOLD Congress Proceedings and Transactions* (every 3 years), *World Register of Dams*.

International Congress on Fracture (ICF): c/o A. T. Yokobori, Jr, Tohoku University, 1-31-15 Taihoku Aoyama, Sendai, Japan; tel. (22) 795-6894; fax (22) 795-6894; e-mail yokobori@md.mech.tuhoku.ac.jp; internet www.icf11.com; f. 1965; aims to foster research in the mechanics and phenomena of fracture, fatigue, and strength of materials; to promote cooperation among scientists in the field; holds Int. Conference every 4 years; 30 mem. orgs; Founder Pres. Prof. T. YOKOBORI (Japan); Pres. Prof. A. CARPENTER (Italy); Sec.-Gen. A. T. YOKOBORI, JR (Japan); publ. *Proceedings* (every 4 years).

International Dairy Federation: see under Agriculture.

International Federation of Automatic Control (IFAC)/Fédération Internationale de l'Automatique: Schlosspl. 12, 2361 Laxenburg, Austria; tel. (2236) 71447; fax (2236) 72859; e-mail secretariat@ifac-control.org; internet www.ifac-control.org; f. 1957 to promote the science and technology of control in the broadest sense in all systems, e.g. engineering, physical, biological, social and economical, in both theory and application; mems: 49 nat. mem. orgs; Pres. ALBERTO ISIDORI (Italy); Sec. KURT SCHLACHER (Austria); publs *Annual Reviews in Control*, *Automatica* (mainly selected papers of IFAC-sponsored symposia, 12 a year), *Control Engineering Practice* (6 a year), *Engineering Applications of Artificial Intelligence*, *Journal of Process Control*, *Mechatronics*.

International Gas Union/Union Internationale de l'Industrie du Gaz: c/o DONG A/S, POB 550, Agern Allé 24–26, 2970 Hoersholm, Denmark; tel. 45-17-12-00; fax 45-17-19-00; e-mail secr.igu@dong.dk; internet www.igu.org; f. 1931; mem. orgs in 65 countries; Pres. GEORGE H. B. VERBERG; Sec.-Gen. PETER K. STORM.

International Institute of Welding/Institut International de la Soudure: BP 50362, 95942 Roissy CDG Cedex, France; tel. 1-49-90-36-08; fax 1-49-90-36-80; e-mail iiwceo@wanadoo.fr; internet www.iiw-iis.org; f. 1948; mem societies in 46 countries; Pres. CHRIS SMALLBONE (Australia); Chief Exec. DANIEL BEAUFILS (France); publ. *Welding in the World* (6 a year).

International Measurement Confederation (IMEKO)/Confédération Internationale de la Mesure: POB 457, 1371 Budapest, Hungary; tel. 3531-562; fax 3531-562; e-mail imeko.ime@mtesz.hu; internet www.imeko.org; f. 1958; promotes the int. exchange of scientific and technical information relating to devts in measuring techniques, instrument design and manufacture and in the application of instrumentation in scientific research and industry; promotes cooperation among scientists and engineers in the field, and with other int. orgs; organizes congresses, symposia, etc.; 39 mem. orgs, 24 technical cttees; Sec.-Gen. Prof. MLADEN BORSIC; Exec. Sec. KAROLINA HAVRILLA; publs *IMEKO Bulletin* (2 a year), *Measurement* (8 a year).

International Navigation Association/Association Internationale de Navigation: Graaf de Ferraris, 11ème étage, Boîte 3, blvd du Roi Albert II 20, 1000 Brussels, Belgium; tel. (2) 553-71-61; fax (2) 553-71-55; e-mail info@pianc-aipcn.org; internet www.pianc-aipcn.org; f. 1885 to promote inland and ocean navigation by fostering and encouraging progress in the design, construction, improvement, maintenance and operation of inland and maritime waterways, ports, and of coastal areas for the benefit of mankind; 2,002 individual mems, 533 corporate mems; Pres. ERIC VAN DEN EEDE; Sec.-Gen. LOUIS VAN SCHEL; publ. *PIANC Bulletin* (4 a year).

International Union of Laboratories and Experts in Construction Materials, Systems and Structures/Réunion Internationale des Laboratoires d'Essais et Experts des Matériaux, systèmes de constructions et ouvrages (RILEM): 157 rue des Blains, 92220 Bagneux Cedex, France; tel. (331) 45-16-10-20; fax (331) 45-36-63-20; e-mail sg@rilem.org; internet www.rilem.net; f. 1947 to advance scientific knowledge related to construction materials, systems and structures and to encourage the transfer and application of this knowledge worldwide; 1,248 mems; Pres. Dr PETER RICHNER (Switzerland); Sec.-Gen. PASCALE DUCORNET; publ. *Materials and Structures—Matériaux et Constructions* (10 a year).

World Energy Council (WEC)/Conseil Mondial de l'Energie (CME): 5th Fl., Regency House, 1–4 Warwick St, London, W1B 5LT, UK; tel. (20) 7734-5996; fax (20) 7734-5926; e-mail info@worldenergy.org; internet www.worldenergy.org; f. 1924 in London as World Power Conference to consider the potential resources and all means of production, transportation, transformation and utilization of energy in all their aspects, and also to consider energy consumption in its overall relationship to the growth of economic activity; collects and publishes data; holds triennial congress; promotes regional symposia and technical studies; mem. cttees in 96 countries; Chair. ANDRÉ CAILLÉ (Canada); Sec.-Gen. GERALD DOUCET (Canada); publs *Energy Efficiency Policies and Indicators* (every 3 years), *Performance of Generating Plant* (every 3 years), *World Survey of Energy Resources* (every 3 years).

World Foundrymen Organization: National Metalforming Centre, 47 Birmingham Rd, West Bromwich, West Midlands B70 6PY, UK; tel. (121) 601-6976; fax (1544) 340332; e-mail secretary@thewfo.com; internet www.thewfo.com; f. 1927 to promote int. cooperation between member asscns and other orgs; congress every 2 years; mems: 28 nat. technical asscns; Pres. Dr Ing. GOTTHARD WOLF (Germany); Sec.-Gen. Eur. Ing. ANDREW TURNER (UK); publ. *International Foundry Research* (4 a year).

World Road Association/Association Mondiale de la Route: La Grande Arche, Paroi Nord-Niveau 5, 92055 Paris-La Défense Cedex, France; tel. (1) 47-96-81-21; fax (1) 49-00-02-02; e-mail info@piarc.org; internet www.piarc.org; f. 1909 to share information about roads and transport; 1,640 mems; Pres. ANNE-MARIE LECLERC (Canada); Sec.-Gen. JEAN-FRANÇOIS CORTÉ (France); publs *CD-Route* (technical reports, every 2 years), *E-Newsletter* (4 a year), *Reports to International Winter Road Congress* (every 4 years), *Reports to World Road Congress* (every 4 years), *Routes/Roads* (4 a year).

OTHER ORGANIZATIONS

Arab Petroleum Training Institute: POB 6037, Al Tajeyat, Baghdad, Iraq; tel. (1) 5234100; fax (1) 5210526; f. 1979; training of high-level personnel in all aspects of the oil industry; 11 OAPEC mem. states; library of 5,000 vols, bibliographic and non-bibliographic databases; Dir-Gen. Dr TAL'AT NAJEEB HATTAB.

Council of Academies of Engineering and Technological Sciences (CAETS): c/o William C. Salmon, 3601 N Peary St, Arlington, VA 22207, USA; tel. (703) 527-5782; fax (703) 526-0570; e-mail caets@nae.edu; internet www.caets.org; f. 1978 to promote the devt of engineering and technology worldwide and to provide an int. forum for the discussion of technological and engineering issues; encourages int. engineering efforts to promote economic growth and social welfare; 25 nat. mem. acads; Sec. and Treas. WILLIAM C. SALMON (USA).

European Organization for Civil Aviation Equipment (EUROCAE)/Organisation Européenne pour l'Equipement de l'Aviation Civile: 102 rue Etienne Dolet, 92240 Malakoff, France; tel. (1) 40-92-79-30; fax (1) 46-55-62-65; e-mail eurocae@eurocae .net; internet www.eurocae.eu; f. 1963; studies and advises on problems related to the application of equipment to aviation and prepares minimum performance specifications that administrations in Europe may use for approving equipment; 92 mems; Pres. MICHEL LESAGE; Sec. GILBERT AMATO.

European Society for Engineering Education (SEFI)/Société Européenne pour la Formation des Ingénieurs/Europäische Gesellschaft für Ingenieur-Ausbildung: 119 rue de Stassart, 1050 Brussels, Belgium; tel. (2) 502-36-09; fax (2) 502-96-11; e-mail info@sefi.be; internet www.ntb.ch/sefi; f. 1973 to promote the quality of initial and continuing engineering education and to encourage cooperation throughout Europe; provides services and information about engineering education; encourages exchanges between teachers, researchers and students of engineering; Pres. Dr ALFREDO SOEIRO (Portugal); Sec.-Gen. FRANÇOISE CÔME (Belgium); publs *European Journal for Engineering Education* (4 a year), *SEFI News* (4 a year).

ICHCA International Ltd: Suite 2, 85 Western Rd, Romford, Essex, RM1 3LS, UK; tel. (1708) 735295; fax (1708) 735225; e-mail info@ichcainternational.co.uk; internet www.ichcainternational.co.uk; f. 2003 to promote safety and efficiency in the handling and movement of goods; 900 mems from more than 80 countries; Hon. Pres. JOSÉ ARNAIZ BRÁ (Spain); Chair. JAMES HARTUNG (USA); publ. *Cargo World* (1 a year).

International Association for Bridge and Structural Engineering (IABSE)/Association Internationale des Ponts et Charpentes/Internationale Vereinigung für Brückenbau und Hochbau: Secretariat ETH-Zurich, 8093 Zürich, Switzerland; tel. 446332647; fax 446331241; e-mail secretariat@iabse.org; internet www.iabse .org; f. 1929; aims: international cooperation among scientists, engineers, researchers and manufacturers; interchange of knowledge, ideas and the results of research work in the sphere of bridge and structural engineering in general, whether in steel, concrete or another material; 3,900 mems from 100 countries; Pres. JACQUES COMBAULT (France); Exec. Dir UELI BRUNNER; publs *Conference Report* (irregular), *Structural Engineering Document* (1 a year), *Structural Engineering International* (4 a year).

International Association of Public Transport/Union Internationale des Transports Publics (UITP)/Internationaler Verband für Öffentliches Verkehrswesen: 6 rue Ste Marie, 1080 Brussels, Belgium; tel. (2) 673-61-00; fax (2) 660-10-72; e-mail info@uitp.org; internet www.uitp.org; f. 1885 to study all problems related to the operation of public transportation; 3,200 mems; library of 25,000 vols, 200 journals; online library (MOBI +); Pres. ALAIN FLAUSCH; Sec.-Gen. HANS RAT (Netherlands); publ. *Public Transport International* (6 a year, published in English, French, German, Russian, Italian and Spanish).

International Centre for Science and High Technology (ICS): AREA Science Park, Padriciano 99, 34149 Trieste, Italy; tel. 040-9228133; fax 040-9220068; e-mail info@ics.trieste.it; internet www.ics.trieste .it; f. 1988; an int. centre of the United

Nations Industrial Development Organization (UNIDO); promotes technology transfer for the sustainable industrial development of developing countries and operates through 4 scientific core programmes (rational drug design and devt; next-generation biofules and bio-based chemicals; geothermal energy; nanotechnologies); e-learning programme relating to the 4 scientific areas; Man. Dir GIORGIO ROSSO CICOGNA.

International Commission on Illumination (CIE)/Commission Internationale de l'Éclairage: Kegelgasse 27, 1030 Vienna, Austria; tel. (1) 714-31-87-0; fax (1) 714-31-87-18; e-mail ciecb@cie.co.at; internet www .cie.co.at; f. 1900 as Int. Commission on Photometry, reorganized as CIE 1913; objectives: to provide an int. forum for the discussion of all matters relating to science, technology and art in the fields of light and lighting; to develop basic standards and procedures of metrology in the fields of light and lighting; to provide guidance in the application of basic principles and procedures to the devt of int. standards in the fields of light and lighting; to prepare and publish reports and standards; to maintain liaison and technical interaction with relevant int. orgs; 41 Nat. Cttee, 14 supportive mems; Gen. Sec. MARTINA PAUL.

International Council for Research and Innovation in Building and Construction: Postbox 1837, 3014 DB Rotterdam, Netherlands; located at: Kruisplein 25G, 3000 BV Rotterdam, Netherlands; tel. (10) 4110240; fax (10) 4334372; e-mail secretariat@cibworld.nl; internet www .cibworld.nl; f. 1953; facilitates int. cooperation and information exchange between organizations with a research, univ., industry or government background, which collectively are active in all aspects of research and innovation for building and construction; mems: 450 institutes and individuals in 70 countries; Pres. Prof. JOHN MCCARTHY (Australia); Sec.-Gen. Dr WIM BAKENS (Netherlands); publs *CIB Congress and Symposium Proceedings*, *Directory of Building Research and Development Organizations*.

International Council for Scientific and Technical Information (ICSTI)/Conseil International pour l'Information Scientifique et Technique: 51 blvd de Montmorency, 75016 Paris, France; tel. 1-45-25-65-92; fax 1-42-15-12-62; e-mail icsti@icsti.org; internet www.icsti.org; f. 1952 as ICSU Abstracting Board, present name 1984; aims to increase accessibility to and awareness of scientific and technical information, and to foster communication and interaction among participants in the information transfer chain, to take advantage of the progress made independently by each information activity sector; ICSTI is a Scientific Associate of ICSU; 50 nat. and organizational mems in 12 countries; Pres. GÉRARD GIROUD (Germany); Exec. Dir BARRY MAHON (France).

International Council on Large Electric Systems/Conseil International des Grands Réseaux Électriques (CIGRE): 21 rue d'Artois, 75008 Paris, France; tel. 1-53-89-12-90; fax 1-53-89-12-99; e-mail secretary-general@cigre.org; internet www .cigre.org; f. 1921; electrical aspects of electricity generation, sub-stations and transformer stations, high-voltage electrical lines, interconnection of systems and their operation and protection; 6,653 mems in 85 countries; Pres. ANDRÉ MERLIN (France); Sec.-Gen. JEAN KOWAL (France); publs *Electra* (6 a year, bilingual), *Session Papers and Proceedings* (every 2 years), *Symposium Papers (CD)* (irregular).

International Electrotechnical Commission (IEC)/Commission Electrotechnique Internationale: 3 rue de Varembé, POB 131, 1211 Geneva 20, Switzerland; tel. 229190211; fax 229190300; e-mail info@iec .ch; internet www.iec.ch; f. 1906 to promote int. cooperation in the electrotechnical industry; administers int. conformity assessment schemes in the areas of electrical equipment and components testing and certification (IECEE), quality of electronic components, materials and processes (IECQ), and certification of electrical equipment operated in explosive atmospheres (IECEx); prepares and publishes int. standards for all electrical, electronic and related technologies; creator of the 'International System' (SI) of units of measurement; has compiled a multi-language electronic vocabulary with more than 20,000 terms; Pres. JACQUES RÉGIS (Canada); Gen. Sec. AHARON AMIT (Switzerland); publ. *Bulletin* (6 a year).

International Federation for Housing and Planning (IFHP)/Fédération Internationale pour l'Habitation, l'Urbanisme et l'Aménagement des Territoires (FIHUAT)/Internationaler Verband für Wohnungswesen, Städtebau und Raumordnung (IVWSR): Wassenaarseweg 43, 2596 CG The Hague, Netherlands; tel. (70) 324-45-57; fax (70) 328-20-85; e-mail info@ifhp.org; internet www.ifhp.org; f. 1913; global network of professionals from the field of housing and planning; corporate and individual mems; annual congress; Pres. FRANCESC X. VENTURA I TEIXIDOR (Spain); Sec.-Gen. PAUL J. RŸNAARTS (Netherlands); publ. *Latest Developments in the Field of Housing and Planning* (1 a year).

International Federation for Information Processing: Hofstr. 3, 2361 Laxenburg, Austria; tel. (2236) 73616; fax (2236) 736169; e-mail ifip@ifip.org; internet www .ifip.org; f. 1960; aims to promote information science and technology by fostering int. cooperation in this field, stimulating research, development and the application of information processing in science and human activity, furthering the dissemination and exchange of information about the subject, and encouraging education in information processing; 55 mem. organizations in 70 countries; Pres. K. BRUNNSTEIN (Germany); Sec. R. JOHNSON (UK); publs *Computers in Industry, Computers and Security, Information Bulletin*.

International Federation of Automotive Engineering Societies/Fédération Internationale des Sociétés d'Ingénieurs des Techniques de l'Automobile (FISITA): 1 Birdcage Walk, London, SW1H 9JJ, UK; tel. (20) 7973-1275; fax (20) 7973-1285; e-mail info@fisita.com; internet www.fisita.com; f. 1947 to promote the exchange of information between member societies, ensure standardization of techniques and terms, to publish research on technical and managerial problems, and generally to encourage the technical development of mechanical transport; mem. organizations in 36 countries; Pres. DANIEL M. HANCOCK (USA); Exec. Dir IAN DICKIE (UK); publ. *Global Automotive Network* (6 a year).

International Federation of Operational Research Societies (IFORS): c/o Mary Thomas Magrogan, 901 Elkridge Landing Rd, Suite 400, Linthicum, MD 21090, USA; tel. (410) 691-7858; fax (410) 691-6127; e-mail secretary@ifors.org; internet www .ifors.org; f. 1959; aims: the development of operational research as a unified science and its advancement worldwide; 44 nat. socs, 4 kindred socs; Pres. Prof. THOMAS MAGNANTI (USA); Sec. MARY THOMAS MAGROGAN (USA);

publs *International Abstracts* (in Operations Research Bulletin), *International Transactions* (in Operational Research Bulletin).

International Federation of Robotics: IFR Secretariat, c/o Symap, Maison de la Mécanique, 45 rue Louis-Blanc, 92400 Courbevoie, France; tel. 1-47-17-67-07; fax 1-47-17-67-25; e-mail secretariat@ifr.org; internet www.ifr.org; f. 1987; 25 nat. mem. orgs; Chair. PAUL JOHNSTON (Canada); Sec. HERMAN VERBRUGGE (Germany); publs *Industrial Robotics, Service Robotics, World Robotics* (1 a year).

International Federation of Surveyors/ Fédération Internationale des Géomètres/Internationale Vereinigung der Vermessungsingenieure: Kalvebod Brygge 31-33, 1780 Copenhagen V, Denmark; tel. 38-86-10-81; fax 38-86-02-52; e-mail fig@fig.net; internet www.fig.net; f. 1878; 9 technical commissions; 73 nat. mem. assocs; Pres. Prof. Dr-Ing. STIG ENEMARK (Denmark); Admin. Dir MARKKU VILLIKKA (Denmark).

International Information Centre for Terminology (Infoterm): Gymnasiumstrasse 50, 1190 Vienna, Austria; tel. (1) 427758026; fax (1) 587-6990; e-mail infopoint@infoterm.org; internet www .infoterm.info; f. 1971 under UNESCO contract; affiliated to Austrian Standards Institute, associated with DPI and ISONETI; consultative status with ECOSOC; operates the secretariat of ISO/TC 37 'Terminology and Other Language and Content Resources'; library of 5,600 vols, 15,000 vocabulary standards at Cologne Univ. of Applied Sciences; 39 nat. and int. corporate bodies and instns; Dir Dr CHRISTIAN GALINSKI; Dir Mag. ANJA DRAME.

International Institute of Communications: Regent House, 24–25 Nutford Pl., London, W1H 5YN, UK; tel. (20) 7323-7210; fax (20) 7323-9682; e-mail enquiries@iicom .org; internet www.iicom.org; f. 1969 as Int. Broadcast Inst.; worldwide research and education on telecommunications, broadcasting and information technology; hosts seminars and annual conference; mems in 70 countries; library: 15,000 items, 200 periodicals; Pres. ANNE WESSBERG; Dir-Gen. ANDREA MILLWOOD HARGRAVE; publ. *Intermedia* (5 a year).

International Institute of Refrigeration/ Institut International du Froid: 177 blvd Malesherbes, 75017 Paris, France; tel. 1-42-27-32-35; fax 1-47-63-17-98; internet www .iifiir.org; f. 1908; intergovernmental organization; object: the study of all technical, scientific and industrial issues concerning refrigeration systems, cryogenics, air conditioning, heat pumps and their applications; studies are undertaken, under the direction of a Science and Technology Council, by 10 Commissions; organizes congresses and conferences; large library, also computerized abstract database; provides bibliographical searches; mems: 61 countries and private and corporate members; Dir DIDIER COULOMB (France); publs *Bulletin of the IIR* (bibliographical, in French and English), *International Journal of Refrigeration, Proceedings of Conferences.*

International Iron and Steel Institute (IISI)/Institut International du Fer et de l'Acier: 120 rue Col. Bourg, 1140 Brussels, Belgium; tel. (2) 702-89-00; fax (2) 702-88-99; e-mail steel@iisi.be; internet www.worldsteel .org; f. 1967 to promote the interests of the world's steel industries; to undertake research in all aspects of steel industries; to serve as a forum for exchange of knowledge and discussion of problems relating to steel industries; to collect, disseminate and main-

tain statistics and information; to serve as a liaison body between int. and nat. steel orgs; mems in 50 countries; Chair. KU-TAEK LEE (USA); Sec.-Gen. IAN CHRISTMAS; publs *Crude Steel Production Monthly, Iron Production Monthly.*

International Masonry Society: Shermanbury, 6 Church Rd, Whyteleafe, CR3 0AR UK; tel. (20) 8660-3633; fax (20) 8668-6983; e-mail kenneth@fisher5053.fsnet.co .uk; internet www.masonry.org.uk; f. 1986 as British Masonry Soc., changed to International Masonry Soc. 2008; 300 mems; Sec. Dr K. FISHER; publ. *Masonry International* (3 a year).

International Organization for Standardization/Organisation internationale de normalisation: 1 rue de Varembé, CP 56, 1211 Geneva 20, Switzerland; tel. 227490111; fax 227333430; e-mail central@ iso.org; internet www.iso.org; f. 1947 to promote the development of standardization and related activities in the world with a view to facilitating the international exchange of goods and services, and to developing mutual cooperation in the spheres of intellectual, scientific, technological and economic activity; 150 mems; reference library holding full collns of ISO and IEC standards; Pres. HÁKAN MURBY (Sweden); Sec.-Gen. ALAN BRYDEN; publs *ISO Focus* (11 a year), *ISO International Standards, ISO Management Systems* (6 a year).

International Society for Photogrammetry and Remote Sensing (ISPRS)/Société Internationale de Photogrammétrie et de Télédétection: c/o Orhan Eltan, ITU Insaat Fakultesi, 34669 Maslak-, Istanbul, Turkey; tel. (212) 285-3810; fax (212) 285-6587; internet www.isprs.org; f. 1910; research and information on the application of aerial and space photography and remote sensing to exploration and mapping; federated to ICSU; 90 nat. mem. orgs, 11 assoc. mems and 12 regional mem. assocs; Pres. IAN DOWMAN (UK); Sec.-Gen. OHRAN ALTAN (Turkey); publs *Journal of Photogrammetry and Remote Sensing* (4 a year), *International Archives of Photogrammetry and Remote Sensing* (6 a year), *ISPRS Highlights* (4 a year).

International Society for Soil Mechanics and Geotechnical Engineering/Société Internationale de Mécanique des Sols et de la Géotechnique: City Univ., Northampton Sq., London, EC1V 0HB, UK; tel. (20) 7040-8154; fax (20) 7040-8832; e-mail secretariat@issmge.org; internet www.issmge.org; f. 1936; 85 mem. socs, 18,000 individual mems; Pres. Prof. JEAN-LOUIS BRIAUD (USA); Sec.-Gen. Prof. R. NEIL TAYLOR (UK).

International Water Association: Alliance House, 12 Caxton St, London, SW1H 0QS, UK; tel. (20) 7654-5500; fax (20) 7654-5555; e-mail water@iwahq.org.uk; internet www.iwahq.org.uk; f. 1999 by the merger of the International Association on Water Quality and the International Water Supply Association; develops effective and sustainable approaches to global water management; members include academic researchers, research centres, energy utilities, consultants, water industry regulators, industrial water users and water equipment manufacturers; Pres. Dr DAVID GARMAN; Exec. Dir PAUL REITER; publs *Hydrology Research* (5 a year), *Journal of Hydroinformatics* (4 a year), *Journal of Water and Health* (4 a year), *Journal of Water Supply: Research and Technology – AQUA* (8 a year), *Journal of Water and Climate Change* (4 a year), *Water Asset Management International* (4 a year), *Water Intelligence Online*

(12 a year), *Water Practice and Technology* (4 a year), *Water Policy* (6 a year), *Water Research* (20 a year), *Water Science and Technology* (24 a year), *Water Science and Technology: Water Supply* (6 a year), *Water Utility Management International* (4 a year).

Textile Institute: International Headquarters, 1st Fl., St James's Bldgs, Oxford St, Manchester, M1 6FQ, UK; tel. (161) 237-1188; fax (161) 236-1991; e-mail tiihq@ textileinst.org.uk; internet www.texi.org; f. 1910, Royal Charter 1925 and 1955; the international body for those concerned with any aspect of textiles and related industries; promotion of education and training, professional standards and exchange of information within the industry by means of publications, conferences, meetings and information services; 60 national and regional brs; 8,000 mems in 85 countries; library of 1,500 vols, 120 journals; Professional Affairs Dir HELEN YEOWART; Hon. Sec. M. PARKINSON; publs *Journal* (4 a year), *Textiles* (4 a year), *Textile Horizons* (6 a year), *Textile Progress* (4 a year).

Tin Technology Ltd: Unit 3, Curo Park, Frogmore, St Albans, AL2 2DD, UK; tel. (1727) 875544; fax (1727) 871341; e-mail info@tintechnology.com; internet www .tintechnology.biz; f. 1932; aims to maintain and extend the use and effectiveness of tin in modern technology; its work is directed to develop the use of tin and is based on scientific and technical study of the metal, its alloys and compounds, and of industrial processes that use tin or may provide future markets; 200 mems in 35 countries; Man. Dir DAVID BISHOP.

World Wide Web Consortium (W3C): c/o Massachusetts Institute of Technology, Computer Science and Artificial Intelligence Laboratory (CSAIL), 32 Vassar St, Cambridge, MA 02139, USA; tel. (617) 253-2613; fax (617) 258-5999; internet www.w3.org; f. 1994; provides an open forum for discussing the technical evolution of the World Wide Web; develops technical specifications for the Web's infrastructure; 500 mem. orgs worldwide; Chief Operating Officer STEVE BRATT; Dir TIM BERNERS-LEE.

Law

Hague Academy of International Law: Peace Palace, Carnegieplein 2, 2517 KJ The Hague, Netherlands; tel. (70) 3024242; fax (70) 3024153; e-mail hagueacademy@ registration.nl; internet www.hagueacademy .nl; f. 1923 as a centre of higher studies in international law (public and private) and cognate sciences, in order to facilitate a thorough and impartial examination of questions bearing on international juridical relations; Sec.-Gen. Prof. Y. DAUDET.

Associated Centre:

Centre for Studies and Research in International Law and International Relations: The Hague, Netherlands; tel. (70) 3024242; fax (70) 3024153; e-mail hagueacademy@registration.nl; internet www.hagueacademy.nl; f. 1957; postdoctoral 4-week research courses in August and September after courses held by Academy; open only to participants who are highly qualified by intellectual maturity and experience (12 French-speaking, 12 English-speaking); library: use of Peace Palace Library; Head of Secretariat M. CROESE

Hague Conference on Private International Law/Conférence de La Haye de droit international privé: Scheveningseweg 6, 2517 KT The Hague, Netherlands;

tel. (70) 3633303; fax (70) 3604867; e-mail secretariat@hcch.net; internet www.hcch .net; f. 1893 to work for the unification of the rules of private int. law; 68 mems: govts of Albania, Argentina, Australia, Austria, Belarus, Belgium, Bosnia and Herzegovina, Brazil, Bulgaria, Canada, Chile, China, Croatia, Cyprus, Czech Republic, Denmark, Ecuador, Egypt, Estonia, Finland, France, Georgia, Germany, Greece, Hungary, Iceland, Ireland, Israel, Italy, Japan, Jordan, Republic of Korea, Latvia, Lithuania, Luxembourg, former Yugoslav Republic of Macedonia, Malaysia, Malta, Mexico, Monaco, Montenegro, Morocco, Netherlands, New Zealand, Norway, Panama, Paraguay, Peru, Poland, Portugal, Romania, Russia, Serbia, Slovakia, Slovenia, South Africa, Spain, Sri Lanka, Suriname, Sweden, Switzerland, Turkey, Ukraine, UK, USA, Uruguay, Venezuela, and the European Union; Sec.-Gen. J. H. A. VAN LOON; publs *The Judges' Newsletter–International Child Protection* (2 a year), *Proceedings of the Conference's Sessions/ Actes et documents des Sessions de la Conférence.*

Institute of International Law/Institut de Droit International: 24 rue de Morsaint, 1390 Grez-Doiceau, Belgium; tel. 229085720; fax 229086277; e-mail isabelle .gerardi@graduateinstitute.ch; internet www .idi-iil.org; f. 1873 to promote the devt of int. law by endeavouring to formulate general principles in accordance with civilized ethical standards, and by giving assistance to achieve the gradual and progressive codification of int. law; 132 mems and assocs worldwide; Sec.-Gen. Prof. JOE VERHOEVEN; publ. *Tableau général des Résolutions.*

Inter-American Bar Association/Federación Interamericana de Abogados/Federação Interamericana de Advogados/ Fédération Inter-Américaine des Avocats: 1211 Connecticut Ave NW, Ste. 202, Washington, DC 20036, USA; tel. (202) 466-5944; fax (202) 466-5946; e-mail iaba@iaba .org; internet www.iaba.org; f. 1940; mems: 51 bar assocs and individual lawyers in 33 countries; Pres. MERCEDES ARAÚZ DE GRIMALDO; Sec.-Gen. HARRY A. INMAN; publs *Conference Proceedings* (1 a year), *Inter-American Journal of International and Comparative Law* (1 a year).

Intergovernmental Committee of the Universal Copyright Convention: UNESCO, 7 Place de Fontenoy, 75700 Paris, France; tel. 1-45-68-47-11; fax 1-45-68-55-89; internet www.unesco.org/culture/copyright; f. 1952; studies the problems concerning the application and operation of the Universal Copyright Convention; makes preparation for periodic revisions of this Convention; mems: Algeria, Argentina, Austria, Cameroon, China, Croatia, Cuba, France, Greece, Guatemala, India, Israel, Japan, Morocco, Portugal, Russia, Ukraine and USA; Chair. ABDULLAH OUADRHIRI (Morocco); publ. *Copyright Bulletin* (4 a year).

International Association for Penal Law/Association Internationale de Droit Pénal: BP 60118, 33008 Bordeaux Cedex, France; tel. 5-56-06-66-73; fax 1-55-04-92-89; e-mail secretariat@aidp-iapl.org; internet www.penal.org; f. 1924 to promote cooperation between bodies and individuals engaged in the study or practice of criminal law; to study crime, its causes and the means of preventing it, and to advance the theoretical and practical development of int. penal law; 2,000 mems; Pres. Prof. JOSÉ LUIS DE LA CUESTA (Spain); Gen. Sec. Dr H. EPP (Austria); publ. *Revue Internationale de Droit Pénal* (2 a year).

International Association for Philosophy of Law and Social Philosophy (IVR)/ Internationale Vereinigung für Rechts-und Sozialphilosophie: Källerekroken 34, 226 47 Lund, Sweden; tel. (46) 152441; fax (46) 2224444; internet www.cirfid.unibo.it/ ivr; f. 1909 for scientific research in philosophy of law and social philosophy; holds int. congresses every 2 years; 44 nat. sections; 2,300 mems; Pres. (vacant); Sec.-Gen. CHRISTIAN DAHLMAN (Sweden); publ. *Archiv für Rechts- und Sozial-philosophie* (4 a year).

International Association of Democratic Lawyers (IADL)/Association Internationale des Juristes Démocrates: 21 rue Brialmont, 1210 Brussels, Belgium; tel. (2) 223-33-10; fax (2) 223-33-10; e-mail jsharma@del3.vsnl.net.in; internet www .iadllaw.org; f. 1946; aims to facilitate contacts and exchanges of view between lawyers and lawyers' assocs and to foster understanding and goodwill; to work together to achieve the aims of the Charter of the UN; mems in 102 countries; in consultative status with UN Economic and Social Council and UNESCO; Pres. JITENDRA SHARMA (India); Sec.-Gen. BEINUSZ SZMUKLER (Argentina); publ. *Revue Internationale de Droit Contemporain* (2 a year, also published in English and Spanish).

International Association of Lawyers/ Union Internationale des Avocats (UIA): 25 rue du Jour, 75001 Paris, France; tel. 1-44-88-55-66; fax 1-44-88-55-77; e-mail uiacentre@uianet.org; internet www.uianet .org; f. 1927 to promote the independence and freedom of lawyers, and defend their ethical and material interests on an int. level; to contribute to the development of an int. order based on law; mems: 250 organizations, 3,000 individuals; Pres. PAUL NEMO (France); Sec.-Gen. GUY ARENDT (France); publ. *Juriste International.*

International Bar Association: 1 Stephen St, 10th Fl., London, W1T 1AT, UK; tel. (20) 7691-6868; fax (20) 7691-6544; e-mail editor@ int-bar.org; internet www.ibanet.org; f. 1947; mems: 195 nat. bar asscns and law socs and 30,000 individual lawyers from 183 countries; Exec. Dir MARK ELLIS; publs *Business Law International* (3 a year), *International Bar News* (6 a year), *Journal of Energy and Natural Resources Law* (4 a year).

International Bureau of Fiscal Documentation (IBFD): POB 20237, 1000 HE Amsterdam, Netherlands; H. J. E. Wenckebachweg 210, 1096 AS Amsterdam, Netherlands; tel. (20) 554-01-00; fax (20) 622-86-58; e-mail customerservice@ibfd.org; internet www.ibfd.nl; an ind. non-profit foundationf. 1938 to supply information on fiscal law and its application; tax treaties database, European taxation database, and OECD database, on CD-ROM; library of 30,000 vols, 1,000 periodicals; CEO WILLEM FALTER; publs *Bulletin for International Fiscal Documentation* (12 a year), *European Taxation* (12 a year), *International VAT Monitor* (6 a year), *International Transfer Pricing Journal* (6 a year), *Asia–Pacific Tax Bulletin* (12 a year), *Derivatives and Financial Instruments* (6 a year), *Tax News Service* (52 a year).

Attached Academy:

> **IBFD International Tax Academy:** Sarphatistraat 500, 1018 AV Amsterdam, Netherlands; tel. (20) 554-01-60; fax (20) 620-93-97; e-mail ita@ibfd.org; internet www.ibfd.nl; f. 1989 to provide education and training on international and comparative tax law through conferences, courses and traineeships; Head ARCOTIA HATSIDIMITRIS

International Commission of Jurists/ Commission Internationale de Juristes: BP 216, 81A ave de Châtelaine, 1219 Châte-

laine, Geneva, Switzerland; tel. 229793800; fax 229793801; e-mail info@icj.org; internet www.icj.org; f. 1952 to promote and protect human rights, and to strengthen the Rule of Law in all its practical manifestations— institutions, legislation, procedures, etc.— and defend it through the mobilization of world legal opinion in cases of general and systematic violation of, or serious threat to, such principles of justice; library of 2,000 vols; Pres. ARTHUR CHASKALSON (South Africa); Sec.-Gen. NICHOLAS HOWEN (Switzerland); publ. *Attacks on Justice* (online only).

International Confederation of Societies of Authors and Composers/Confédération Internationale des Sociétés d'Auteurs et Compositeurs: 20–26 blvd du Parc, 92200 Neuilly sur Seine, France; tel. 1-55-62-08-50; fax 1-55-62-08-60; e-mail cisac@cisac.org; internet www.cisac.org; f. 1926 to ensure more effective protection of the rights of authors and composers, to improve legislation on literary and artistic rights, and to organize research on problems concerning the rights of authors on the internet; participates in preparatory work for inter-governmental conferences on authors' rights; 203 mem. societies in 104 countries; Pres. CHRISTIAN BRÜHN; Dir-Gen. ERIC BAPTISTE; publ. *CISAC News* (4 a year).

International Development Law Organization: Via di San Sebastianello 16, 00187 Rome, Italy; tel. 06-6979261; fax 06-6781946; e-mail idlo@idlo.int; internet www.idli.org; f. 1983 for mid-career training and technical assistance, primarily for developing and transition country lawyers, legal advisers and judges; Rome-based courses and seminars in English and French address legal topics related to economic development and governance, including negotiation, int. contracting and economic law reform; also designs and organizes in-country training workshops on law-related economic development topics; library in process of formation; Dir-Gen. WILLIAM T. LORIS.

International Federation for European Law/Fédération Internationale pour le Droit Européen (FIDE): Via Nicolò Tartaglia 5, 00197 Rome, Italy; fax 80-80-731; f. 1961 to advance studies on European law among members of the European Community by coordinating activities of member societies and by organizing regular colloquies on topical problems of European law; mems: 17 national associations; Pres. Hon. Mr Justice NIALL FENNELLY; Sec.-Gen. PATRICK McCANN.

International Institute for the Unification of Private Law/Institut International pour l'Unification du Droit Privé (Unidroit): Via Panisperna 28, 00184 Rome, Italy; tel. 06-696211; fax 06-69941394; e-mail info@unidroit.org; internet www.unidroit.org; f. 1926, to prepare for the establishment of uniform legislation, to prepare draft uniform laws and int. conventions for adoption by diplomatic conferences, to prepare drafts of int. agreements on private law, to undertake studies in comparative law, and to organize conferences and publish works on such subjects; meetings of organizations concerned with the unification of law; international congresses on private law; mems: governments of 59 countries; library of 235,000 vols; Pres. Prof. BERARDINO LIBONATI (Italy); Sec.-Gen. Prof. HERBERT KRONKE (Germany); publs *Digest of Legal Activities of International Organizations, Uniform Law Review* (4 a year).

International Institute of Space Law (IISL)/Institut International de Droit de l'Espace: 8–10 rue Mario-Nikis, 75015 Paris, France; tel. (1) 45-67-42-60; fax (1) 42-73-21-20; e-mail secretary@iafastro-iisl.com;

internet www.iafastro-iisl.com; f. 1959 at the XI Congress of the International Astronautical Federation; holds meetings, makes studies on juridical and sociological aspects of astronautics; publishes reports; makes awards; holds an annual Colloquium; mems: 386 individuals elected for life; Pres. Dr N. JASENTULIYANA (USA); Sec. TANJA L. MASSON-ZWAAN (Netherlands); publ. *Proceedings of Colloquia*.

International Juridical Institute/Institut Juridique International: Permanent Office for the Supply of International Legal Information, Spui 186, 2511 BW, The Hague, Netherlands; tel. (70) 346-0974; fax (70) 362-5235; e-mail iji@worldonline.nl; f. 1918 to supply information in connection with any matter of int. interest, not being of a secret nature, respecting int., municipal and foreign law and the application thereof; Chair. Prof. A. V. M. STRUYCKEN; Sec. T. HEUKELS; Dir A. L. G. A. STILLE.

International Maritime Committee/ Comité Maritime International (CMI): Mechelsesteenweg 196, 2018 Antwerp, Belgium; tel. (3) 227-35-26; fax (3) 227-35-28; e-mail admini@cmi-imc.org; internet www .comitemaritime.org; f. 1897 to contribute to the unification of maritime and commercial law, maritime customs, usages and practices; promotes the establishment of national associations of maritime law and cooperates with other int. asscns or organizations having the same object; work includes drafting of conventions on collisions at sea, salvage and assistance at sea, limitation of shipowners' liability, maritime mortgages, etc.; mems: asscns in 51 countries; Pres. JEAN-SERGE ROHART (France); Sec.-Gen. NIGEL FRAWLEY (acting) (Canada); publ. *Year Book*.

World Jurist Association (WJA): 7910 Woodmont Ave, Suite 1440, Bethesda, MD 20814, USA; tel. (202) 466-5428; fax (202) 452-8540; e-mail wja@worldjurist.org; internet www.worldjurist.org; f. 1963 to promote the continued devt of int. law and world order; biennial world conferences, World Law Day, demonstration trials, research programmes and publs have contributed to the growth of law and legal instns by focusing on matters of int. concern; mems: lawyers, jurists and legal scholars in over 150 countries; Pres. VALERIJ O. YEVDOKIMOV (Ukraine); Exec. Vice-Pres. MARGARET M. HENNEBERRY (USA); publs *Law/Technology* (4 a year), *World Jurist* (6 a year).

Affiliated Bodies:

World Association of Center Associates (WACA): 7910 Woodmont Ave, Suite 1440, Bethesda, MD 20814, USA; tel. (202) 466-5428; fax (202) 452-8540; e-mail wja@worldjurist.org; f. 1979 to mobilize interested individuals not in the legal profession to promote the objects of the WJA; Pres. RICK BALTZERSEN (USA).

World Association of Judges (WAJ): 7910 Woodmont Ave, Suite 1440, Bethesda, MD 20814, USA; tel. (202) 466-5428; fax (202) 452-8540; e-mail wja@worldjurist.org; f. 1966 to mobilize judicial leaders on important transnational legal issues and to improve the admin. of justice; over 23 cttees studying int. law; Pres. Prince BOLA AJIBOLA (Nigeria).

World Association of Law Professors (WALP): 7910 Woodmont Ave, Suite 1440, Bethesda, MD 20814, USA; tel. (202) 466-5428; fax (202) 452-8540; e-mail wja@worldjurist.org; f. 1975 to focus the attention of legal scholars and teachers on transnational legal issues, and improve scholarship and education in int. legal matters, incl. training, practice, admin. of justice, human rights, the environment

and coordination of legal systems; Pres. SALVADOR B. LAO (Philippines).

World Association of Lawyers (WAL): 7910 Woodmont Ave, Suite 1440, Bethesda, MD 20814, USA; tel. (202) 466-5428; fax (202) 452-8540; e-mail wja@worldjurist.org; f. 1975 to develop transnational law and improve lawyers' expertise in related areas; over 100 cttees studying the devt of int. law; Pres. JACK STREETER (USA)

Medicine and Public Health

World Health Organization/Organisation Mondiale de la Santé: Ave Appia 20, 1211 Geneva 27, Switzerland; tel. 227912111; fax 227913111; e-mail info@who .int; internet www.who.int; f. 1948; WHO, a specialized agency of the UN, is governed by its mem. states, which decide the organization's priorities and monitor its work; WHO has been given the mandate to help all people—in particular the poor and the vulnerable—to achieve the highest possible level of health; WHO's work includes reducing the global burden of disease by taking action against the main diseases of the world, reducing the risk factors for ill health, increasing the knowledge base on health issues through coordinating and supervising research, setting standards and guidelines, and assisting countries in improving their health systems and making them more equitable; 191 mem. states; library: see entry in Switzerland chapter; Dir-Gen. Dr JONG-WOOK LEE (Republic of Korea); publs *Bulletin* (scientific papers: in English, 12 a year; in French and English, 2 a year), *International Digest of Health Legislation* (online only, 4 a year), *Weekly Epidemiological Record* (51 a year and online), *WHO Drug Information* (4 a year and online), *World Health Report* (1 a year and online).

OTHER ORGANIZATIONS

Council for International Organizations of Medical Sciences (CIOMS)/Conseil des Organisations Internationales des Sciences Médicales: Secretariat c/o WHO, 20 ave Appia, 1211 Geneva 27, Switzerland; tel. (22) 7913406; fax (22) 7910746; e-mail cioms@who.int; internet www.cioms.ch; f. 1949 to facilitate and coordinate the activities of its mems, to act as a coordinating centre between them and the nat. instns, to maintain collaboration with the UN, to promote int. activities in the field of medical sciences, to serve the scientific interests of the int. biomedical community; mems: 66 int. asscns, nat. academic and research ccls in 30 countries; Pres. Prof. MICHEL B. VALLOTTON; Sec.-Gen. Dr GOTTFRIED KREUTZ; publs *International Ethical Guidelines for Biomedical Research Involving Human Subjects*, *International Guidelines for Ethical Review of Epidemiological Studies*, *International Nomenclature of Diseases*, other publications on diverse aspects of drug safety.

INTERNATIONAL MEMBERS OF CIOMS

FDI World Dental Federation/Fédération Dentaire Internationale (FDI): 13 Chemin du Levant, L'Avant Centre, 01210 Ferney-Voltaire, France; tel. 4-50-40-50-50; fax 4-50-40-55-55; e-mail info@fdiworldental .org; internet www.fdiworldental.org; f. 1900; 1m. individual mems, 144 mem. assocs in 134 countries; Pres. Dr BURTON CONROD (Canada); Pres.-Elect Dr ROBERTO VIANNA (Brazil); Treas. Dr TIN CHUN WONG (Hong

Kong); Exec. Dir Dr DAVID C. ALEXANDER (France); publs *International Dental Journal* (6 a year), *Community Dental Health* (4 a year), *Developing Dentistry* (2 a year), *European Journal of Prosthodontics and Restorative Dentistry* (4 a year), *Journal of the International Academy of Periodontology* (4 a year), *Worldental Communiqué* (6 a year).

International Association for the Study of the Liver: c/o Dr Wolfgang H. Caselmann, Bavarian State Ministry of the Environment, Public Health and Consumer Protection, POB 810140, 81901 Munich, Germany; tel. (89) 9214-2141; fax (89) 9214-2384; e-mail secretariat@iaslonline.com; internet www.iaslonline.com; f. 1958 to foster training of experts in hepatology; encourages research on the liver and its diseases and helps to facilitate prevention, recognition and treatment of liver and biliary tract diseases in the int. community; Pres. DING-SHINN CHEN (Taiwan); Sec. and Treas. Dr WOLF-GANG H. CASELMANN (Germany).

International College of Surgeons/Collège International de Chirurgiens: 1516 North Lake Shore Dr., Chicago, IL 60610, USA; tel. (312) 642-3555; fax (312) 787 1624; e-mail info@icsglobal.org; internet www .icsglobal.org; f. 1935 Geneva, inc. Washington 1940; organized as a worldwide instn to advance the art and science of surgery by bringing together surgeons of all nations, irrespective of nationality, creed or colour; through its Surgical Congresses, Research and Scholarship Project and Surgical Teams Project of volunteers to developing countries, an exchange of surgical knowledge is facilitated in the highest interest of patients; also operates the Int. Museum of Surgical Science located at HQ; 7,000 mems; World Pres. Dr FIDEL RUIZ-HEALY; Exec. Dir MAX C. DOWNHAM; publ. *International Surgery* (6 a year).

International Council of Nurses (ICN)/ Conseil International des Infirmières (CII): 3 place Jean-Marteau, 1201 Geneva, Switzerland; tel. 229080100; fax 229080101; e-mail icn@icn.ch; internet www.icn.ch; f. 1899; works to ensure universal quality nursing care, sound health policies worldwide and advancement of nursing knowledge; Council of National Representatives meets every 2 years; congress every 4 years; mems: 125 national nurses' associations; Pres. CHRISTINE HANCOCK; Exec. Dir JUDITH A. OULTON; publ. *International Nursing Review*.

International Diabetes Federation/Fédération Internationale du Diabète: 19 ave Emile De Mot, 1000 Brussels, Belgium; tel. (2) 538-55-11; fax (2) 538-51-14; e-mail info@idf.org; internet www.idf.org; f. 1949; 172 member associations in 134 countries; holds triennial congresses; Pres. PIERRE LEFÈBVRE (Belgium); Exec. Dir LUC HENDRICKX; publs *Diabetes Atlas* (1 a year), *Diabetes Voice* (3 a year), *Triennial Report*.

International Federation of Clinical Neurophysiology/Fédération Internationale de Neurophysiologie Clinique: c/o Venue Vest Conference Services Ltd, Suite 100, 873 Beatty St, Vancouver, BC V6B 2M6, Canada; tel. (604) 681-5226; fax (604) 681-2503; e-mail ifcn@ifcn.info; internet www.ifcn.info; f. 1949 to attain the highest level of knowledge in the field of electro-encephalography and clinical neurophysiology worldwide; 58 mem. orgs (nat. socs); Pres. HIROSHI SHIBASAKI (Japan); Sec. Prof. REINHARD DENGLER (Germany); publs *Clinical Neurophysiology* (12 a year), *EMG and Motor Control* (6 a year), *Evoked Potentials* (6 a year).

International Federation of Oto-Rhino-Laryngological Societies/Fédération

Internationale des Sociétés Oto-rhino-laryngologiques: POB 124, 1135 ZK Edam, Netherlands; fax (299) 373723; e-mail ifos@cest-bien.com; internet www.ifosworld.org; f. 1965; aims: to promote scientific and clinical research into oto-rhino-laryngology; to improve aural health in developing countries; to register educational programmes and promote cooperation; mems from 98 countries and 10 int. socs; Pres. NASSER KOTBY (Egypt); Gen. Sec. JAN J. GROTE (Netherlands).

International Federation of Surgical Colleges/Fédération Internationale des Collèges de Chirurgie: La Panetière, 3 Chemin du Milieu, 1279 Bogis-Bossey, Switzerland;Administration: c/o Royal College of Surgeons in Ireland, 121 St Stephen's Green, Dublin 2, Ireland; tel. (1) 4022707; fax (1) 4022230; e-mail ifsc@rcsi.ie; internet www.ifsc-net.org; f. 1958 in Stockholm, Sweden; objectives: the improvement and maintenance of the standards of surgery worldwide, by establishment and maintenance of cooperation and interchange of medical and surgical information; encouragement of high standards of education, training and research in surgery and its allied sciences; particularly assisting developing countries in surgical advancement; mems: 70 national colleges or societies and 500 associates; Pres. Prof. S. W. A. GUNN (Switzerland); Sec. R. H. S. LANE (UK); publs *Electronic Journal*, *IFSC News* (2 a year).

International Leprosy Association/Association Internationale contre la Lèpre: c/o ALM Way, Greenway, SC 29601, USA; internet www.leprosy-ila.org; f. 1931 to promote int. cooperation in research on and treatment of leprosy; 1,200 mems; Pres. Dr MARCOS VIRMOND (Brazil); Sec. Prof. INDIRA NATH (India); publ. *International Journal of Leprosy and Other Mycobacterial Diseases* (4 a year).

International Paediatric Association/Association Internationale de Pédiatrie: 17 rue du Cendrier, POB 1726, 1211 Geneva 1, Switzerland; tel. 229069152; fax 227322852; e-mail adminoffice@ipa-world .org; internet www.ipa-world.org; f. 1912; holds regional and int. seminars and symposia; organizes int. paediatric congresses every 3 years; 165 mem. socs; Pres. CHOK WAN CHAN (Hong Kong); Exec. Dir JANE G. SCHALLER (USA); publ. *IPA News* (4 a year).

International Rhinologic Society: c/o Prof. David Kennedy, Univ. of Pennsylvania Medical Center, Dept of ORL, 5th Floor, Ravdin Bldg, 3400 Spruce St, Philadelphia, USA; e-mail kennedyd@uphs.upenn.edu; f. 1965; aims to create a central org. with which all nat. and regional socs of rhinology may be affiliated, to organize int. congresses and courses of instruction, and to encourage study, research and scientific advancement in the field of rhinology and related sciences; nat. and regional soc. mems in 31 countries; Pres. Prof. IN YONG PARK (Republic of Korea); Sec.-Treas. Prof. P. A. R. CLEMENT (Belgium); publs *American Journal of Rhinology*, *Journal of Rhinology*.

International Society of Audiology/Société Internationale d'Audiologie: c/o Dr G. Mencher, 121 Anchor Drive, Nova Scotia B3N 3B9 Halifax, Canada; tel. (902) 477-5360; fax (902) 477-5360; e-mail info@isa-audiology.org; internet www .isa-audiology.org; f. 1952 to advance the study of audiology and protect human hearing; 500 individual mems; Pres. Prof. Dr IEDA RUSSO (Brazil); Sec.-Gen. Prof. Dr G. MENCHER; publs *Audinews* (4 a Year), *International Journal of Audiology* (1 a Year).

International Society of Internal Medicine/Société Internationale de Médecine Interne: c/o Prof. Rolf A. Streuli, SRO Hospital, 4901 Langenthal, Switzerland; tel. 629163102; fax 629164155; e-mail r.streuli@sro.ch; internet www.acponline.org/isim; f. 1948 to encourage research and education in internal medicine; sponsors the International Congress of Internal Medicine every other year; 52 national mem. societies; Pres. Prof. THOMAS KJELLSTRÖM (Sweden); Sec.-Gen. Prof. ROLF A. STREULI.

International Society of Physical and Rehabilitation Medicine (ISPRM): Medicongress, Waalpoel 28–34, 9960 Assenede, Belgium; tel. (9) 344-39-59; fax (9) 344-40-10; internet www.isprm.org; Pres. Prof. LINA-MARA BATTISTELLA (Brazil); Exec. Dir WERNER VAN CLEEMPUTTE.

International Union Against Cancer/Union Internationale contre le Cancer: 62 route de Frontenex, 1207 Geneva, Switzerland; tel. 228091811; fax 228091810; e-mail info@uicc.org; internet www.uicc.org; f. 1933; non-governmental org. devoted to promoting on an int. level the campaign against cancer in its research, therapeutic and preventive aspects; mems: 276 organizations in 85 countries; Pres. Dr JOHN SEFFRIN (USA); Exec. Dir ISABEL MORTARA; publs *International Calendar of Meetings on Cancer* (2 a year), *International Journal of Cancer* (30 a year), *UICC News* (4 a year).

Medical Women's International Association (MWIA): 7555 Morley Dr., Burnaby, BC, Canada; tel. (604) 439-8993; fax (604) 439-8994; e-mail secretariat@mwia.net; internet www.mwia.net; f. 1919 to facilitate contacts between medical women and to encourage their cooperation in matters connected with int. health problems; MWIA Congresses and General Assemblies every 3 years; mems: nat. asscns in 48 countries, with 20,000 mems; Pres. Dr ATSUKO HESHIKI (Japan); Sec.-Gen. Dr SHELLEY ROSS (Canada); publs *Congress Report* (every 3 years), *MWIA Update* (3 a year).

World Allergy Organization (WAO): 555 East Wells St, 11th Fl., Milwaukee, WI 53202-3823, USA; tel. (414) 276-1791; fax (414) 276-3349; e-mail info@worldallergy.org; internet www.worldallergy.org; f. 1951 to advance work in the educational, research and practical medical aspects of allergy diseases; 38,000 mems from 58 nat. and regional socs; Pres. Prof. CARLOS E. BAENA-CAGNANI (Argentina); Sec.-Gen. Prof. G. WALTER CANONICA (Italy); publ. *Allergy & Clinical Immunology International* (6 a year).

World Federation for Medical Education: Faculty of Health Sciences, Københavns Universitet, Panum Institute, Blegdamsvej 3, 2200 Copenhagen N, Denmark; tel. 35-32-71-03; fax 35-32-70-70; e-mail wfme@wfme.org; internet www.sund .ku.dk/wfme; f. 1972 to promote and integrate the study and implementation of medical education worldwide; engaged on programme for worldwide reorientation of medical training; non-governmental relations with WHO, UNICEF, UNESCO, UNDP and the World Bank; 6 regional asscns on a global level; Pres. Prof. STEFAN LINDGREN; Exec. Dir ARNOLD BOON.

World Federation of Associations of Paediatric Surgeons: c/o Prof. J. Boix-Ochoa, Apatado de Correos 3, 08490 Tordera, (Barcelona), Spain; internet www.wofaps .org; f. 1974; 60 mem. asscns worldwide; Pres. S. CYWES (South Africa); Sec. and Treas. Prof. J. BOIX-OCHOA.

World Federation of Neurology: c/o Dr Raad Shakir, 12 Chandos St, London, W1G 9DR, UK; tel. (20) 7323-4011; fax (20) 7323-4012; e-mail wfnlondon@aol.com; internet www.wfneurology.org; f. 1957; 96 constituent nat. socs of neurology, representing 24,000 mems; Pres. Dr JOHAN AARLI (Norway); Sec. and Treas.-Gen. Dr RAAD SHAKIR; publs *Journal of the Neurological Sciences*, *World Neurology* (4 a year).

World Gastroenterology Organisation: c/o Bridget Barbieri, WGO Exec. Secretariat Medconnect GmbH, Brünnsteinstr. 10, 81541 Munich, Germany; tel. (89) 41419240; fax (89) 41419245; e-mail info@worldgastroenterology.org; internet www .worldgastroenterology.org; f. 1935; raises awareness of the worldwide prevalence and optimal care of digestive disorders through the provision of high-quality, accessible and independent education and training; workshops, global training centres network, global guidelines, World Digestive Health Day research support, int. digestive cancer alliance; 110 nat. societies and 4 regional asscns; Pres. Prof. RICHARD KOZAREK (USA); Sec.-Gen. Prof. CIHAN YURDAYDIN (Turkey); publ. *World Gastroenterology News* (online).

World Heart Federation: 7 rue des Battoirs, 1211 Geneva, Switzerland; tel. 228070320; fax 228070339; e-mail admin@worldheart.org; internet www.worldheart .org; f. 1978; aims to promote the study, prevention and relief of cardiovascular diseases and strokes through scientific and public education programmes, particularly in low- and middle-income countries; organizes the exchange of materials between its affiliated socs and foundations and with related agencies; world congress every 2 years; 196 mems: 159 nat., 8 continental, 29 assocs; Pres. Dr SHAHRYAR A. SHEIKH (Pakistan); CEO JANET VOÛTE (Switzerland); publs *Nature Clincal Practice Cardiovascular Magazine*, *Prevention and Control* (4 a year).

World Medical Association/Association Médicale Mondiale: 13 chemin du Levant, CIB, Bâtiment A, 01210 Ferney-Voltaire, France; tel. 4-50-40-75-75; fax 4-50-40-59-37; e-mail wma@wma.net; internet www .wma.net; f. 1947 to serve humanity by endeavouring to achieve the highest int. standards in medical education, medical science, medical art and medical ethics, and health care for all people; the unit of membership is the nat. medical asscn; has established relations with UNESCO, WHO and other int. bodies; 6 regions; mems: 95 nat. assocs; Pres. Dr K. DESAI (India); Sec.-Gen. Dr OTMAR KLOIBER (Germany); publ. *World Medical Journal*.

World Psychiatric Association/Association Mondiale de Psychiatrie/Asociación Mundial de Psiquiatría: Geneva Univ. Psychiatric Hospital, 2 chemin du Petit-Bel-Air, 1225 Geneva, Switzerland; tel. 223055737; fax 223055735; e-mail wpasecretariat@wpanet.org; internet www .wpanet.org; f. 1950 at the 1st World Congress of Psychiatry in Paris, France; a not-for-profit charity; aims: to encourage the highest possible standards of clinical practice, to enhance the work of the mem. socs irrespective of their size, to fight stigma and advocate the human right to mental health, to support psychiatrists and other mental health professionals, to disseminate knowledge of the effect of mass violence on mental health, to encourage multi-centre research and enhance standards of training, to promote non-discrimination (parity) in the provision of care of the mentally ill, to organize the World Congress every 3 years and Int. Congresses, and to work with WHO and other governmental agencies to advance public health; 134 mem. socs in 116 countries; Pres. Prof. MARIO MAJ (Italy); Sec.-Gen.

Prof. LEVENT COX (UK); publ. *World Psychiatry* (3 a year).

ASSOCIATE MEMBERS OF CIOMS

American College of Chest Physicians: 3300 Dundee Rd, Northbrook, IL 60062-2348, USA; tel. (847) 498-1400; fax (847) 498-5460; e-mail accp@chestnet.org; internet www.chestnet.org; f. 1935; postgraduate medical education; 15,000 mems; Pres. Dr RICHARD S. IRWIN; Exec. Vice-Pres. and CEO ALVIN LEVER; publ. *Chest* (12 a year).

International Committee of Military Medicine/Comité International de Médecine Militaire: Hôpital Militaire Reine Astrid, 1120 Brussels, Belgium; tel. (2) 264-43-48; fax (2) 264-43-67; e-mail info@cimm-icmm.org; internet cimm-icmm.org; f. 1921 to promote world cooperation on questions of military medicine and to foster its international and humanitarian character; holds congress every two years; 104 countries are represented on the Committee; Pres. Lt Brig.-Gen. S. BIN ABDULLAH, (Malaysia); Sec.-Gen. Dr J. SANABRIA (Belgium); publ. *International Review of the Armed Forces Medical Services* (in English and French, 4 a year).

International Congress on Tropical Medicine and Malaria/Congrès International de Médecine Tropicale et de Paludisme: c/o Dr E. C. Garcia, Institute of Public Health, University of the Philippines, POB EA-460, Manila, Philippines; Congresses are held triennially; Sec.-Gen. Dr E. C. GARCIA.

International Council on Alcohol and Addictions: CP 189, 1001 Lausanne, Switzerland; tel. 213209865; fax 213209817; e-mail secretariat@icaa.ch; internet www.icaa.ch; f. 1907; aims to reduce and prevent the harmful effects of the use of alcohol and other drugs by the study of addiction problems and the development of programmes in this field, the study of concepts and methods of prevention, treatment and rehabilitation, and the dissemination of knowledge in the interests of public health and personal and social well-being; holds Int. Institute annually and Int. Congress every three or four years, symposia, study courses, training courses on substance abuse in developing countries, etc.; mems: 135 organizations, 500 individuals from 85 countries; library: special collection of 6,000 vols on drug dependence, 12,000 pamphlets, reprints, etc., 120 periodicals; Pres. Dr PETER VAMOS; Exec. Dir Dr SHARAFUDDIN MALIK; publ. *ICAA News* (4 a year).

International Federation of Clinical Chemistry and Laboratory Medicine: Via Carlo Farini 81, 20159 Milan, Italy; tel. 02-66809912; fax 02-60781846; e-mail ifcc@ifcc.org; internet www.ifcc.org; f. 1952; mems: 63 national socs (30,000 individuals); Pres. Prof. MATHIAS M. MÜLLER (Austria); Sec. Dr RENZE BAIS (Australia); publ. *Journal* (6 a year).

International Federation of Medical Students' Associations: c/o WMA, BP 63, 01212 Ferney-Voltaire Cedex, France; fax 4-50-40-59-37; e-mail gs@ifmsa.org; internet www.ifmsa.org; f. 1951 to serve medical students worldwide and to promote int. cooperation; organizes professional exchanges in pre-clinical and clinical fields of medicine; holds Gen. Assembly annually; 63 mem. asscns; Pres. ANDREAS RUDKJØBING; Gen. Sec. STEFANIE BÖTTCHER.

International Society of Blood Transfusion/Société Internationale de Transfusion Sanguine: c/o Jan van Goyenkade 11, 1075 HP Amsterdam, Netherlands; tel. (20) 679-3411; fax (20) 673-7306; e-mail isbt@eurocongres.com; internet www.isbt-web.org; f. 1937; mems: 2,080 in 108 countries; Pres. Dr FRANCINE DÉCARY; Sec.-Gen. Dr PAUL F. W. STRENGERS; publs *Transfusion Today*, *Vox Sanguinis*, *World Directory of Blood Transfusion*.

Rehabilitation International—International Society for Rehabilitation of the Disabled/Société Internationale pour la Réadaptation des Handicapés: 25 E 21st St, New York, NY 10010, USA; tel. (212) 420-1500; fax (212) 505-0871; e-mail ri@riglobal.org; internet www.riglobal.org; f. 1922; world congress and regional conferences every 4 years; Pres. ANNE HAWKER; Sec.-Gen. VENUS ILAGAN; publs *International Rehabilitation Review*, *One in Ten*.

OTHER ORGANIZATIONS

African Medical and Research Foundation: Langata Rd, POB 00506-27691, Nairobi, Kenya; tel. (20) 605220; fax (20) 609518; e-mail fundraising@amrefhq.org; internet www.amref.org; f. 1957; independent, non-profit organization working to improve the health of people in Eastern Africa; funds from governmental and non-governmental aid agencies in Africa, Europe and North America, and private donors; official relations with WHO; activities: primary health care, training, teaching aids, health behaviour and education, airborne medicine, flying doctor service, medical radio communication, ground mobile medicine, emergency intervention in famine and other crises, research, consultancies; library of 6,000 vols, 122 periodicals; Chair. Prof. MIRIAM K. WERE (Kenya); Dir-Gen. Dr MICHAEL SMALLEY (Kenya); publs *AMREF News* (4 a year), *AFYA* (4 a year), *COBASHECA* (4 a year), *Defender* (4 a year), *Helper* (4 a year), *HEN* (4 a year).

Asociación Latinoamericana de Análisis y Modificación del Comportamiento (Latin American Association of Analysis and Behavioural Modification): POB 88754, Bogota, Colombia; f. 1974; professional society for psychology in research and teaching on experimental analysis of behaviour; 1,583 mems; Pres. MIGUEL A. ESCOTET; Vice-Pres. CARLOS M. QUIRCE; publs *Alamoc Newsletter* (4 a year), *Learning and Behavior* (2 a year).

Association for Medical Education in Europe: Tay Park House, 484 Perth Rd, Dundee, DD2 1LR, Scotland; tel. (1382) 631953; fax (1382) 631987; e-mail amee@dundee.ac.uk; internet www.amee.org; f. 1972 to promote and integrate the study of medical education in the countries of Europe; mems: asscns for medical education in most European countries, assoc. corporate mems in countries without nat. asscns, and individual mems worldwide; Pres. Prof. MARGARITA BARÓN-MALDONADO (Spain); Gen. Sec. Prof. RONALD M. HARDEN (UK); publ. *Medical Teacher* (8 a year).

Cystic Fibrosis Worldwide: c/o Christine Noke, 210 Park Ave #267, Worcester, MA 10609, USA; tel. (508) 733-6120; e-mail onoke@cfww.org; internet www.cfww.org; f. 2003; promotes access to knowledge and appropriate care to those people living with cystic fibrosis and among medical health professionals and governments worldwide; Pres. MITCH MESSER (Australia); Exec. Dir CHRISTINE NOKE.

European Academy of Anaesthesiology: Waversebaan 319A, 3001 Heverlee, Belgium; tel. and fax (16) 405151; internet eaa.euro-anaesthesiology.org; f. 1978 to improve the standard of training, practice and research in anaesthesiology in Europe; 441 mems (251 full, 190 assoc.); Pres. THOMAS PASCH (Switzerland); Hon. Sec. KLAUS OLK-

KOLA (Finland); publ. *European Journal of Anaesthesiology*.

European Federation of Internal Medicine: c/o Dr C. Davidson, Department of Cardiology, Royal Sussex County Hospital, Eastern Rd, Brighton, BN2 5BE, UK; tel. (1273) 696955; fax (1273) 684554; e-mail chris.davidson@bsuh.nhs.uk; internet www.efim.org; f. 1996; 27 nat. mem. socs; Pres. Prof. J. MERINO (Spain); Sec.-Gen. Dr C. DAVIDSON (UK); publ. *European Journal of Internal Medicine* (4 a year).

European Society of Cardiology: c/o The European Heart House, 2035 Route des Colles, Les Templiers, BP 179, 06903 Sophia Antipolis, France; tel. 4-92-94-76-00; fax 4-92-94-76-01; e-mail webmaster@escardio.org; internet www.escardio.org; f. 1950; aims to bring together societies of cardiology in all European countries, and to provide a forum for working groups on subjects of common interest; 52,000 mems; Pres. Prof. K. FOX (UK); CEO A. J. HOWARD (France); publs *Cardiovascular Nursing* (4 a year), *Cardiovascular Research* (14 a year), *European Journal of Cardiovascular Prevention and Rehabilitation* (24 a year), *European Journal of Echocardiography* (6 a year), *European Journal of Heart Failure* (12 a year), *Europace* (12 a year), *The European Heart Journal* (24 a year, plus 10–18 annual supplements).

Inclusion International: c/o The Rix Centre, University of East London, Docklands Campus, 4–6 University Way, London E16 2RD, UK; tel. (20) 8223-7709; fax (20) 8223-7411; e-mail info@inclusion-international.org; internet www.inclusion-international.org; f. 1960 to promote the interests of the mentally handicapped without regard to nationality, race, religion, age, or degree of handicap; furthers cooperation between national bodies, organizes congresses and symposia; consultative status with UNESCO, UNICEF, WHO, ILO, ECOSOC and the Council of Europe; official relations with IIN, the Comm. of the European Communities and various other orgs; mems: 173 socs in 109 countries; Pres. DIANE RICHLER; Sec.-Gen. THÉRÈSE KEMPENEERS-FOULON; publ. *Proceedings*.

International Academy of Cytology/Academie Internationale de Cytologie/Internationale Akademie für Zytologie/Academia Internacional de Citología: c/o Dr Volker Schneider, Burgunderstr. 1, 79104 Freiburg, Germany; fax (761) 2923802; e-mail centraloffice@cytology-iac.org; internet www.cytology-iac.org; organizes congresses, International Board of Cytopathology examinations; Pres. Dr MATÍAS JIMÉNEZ-AYALA (Spain); Sec.-Gen. Dr VOLKER SCHNEIDER (Germany); publ. *Acta Cytologica—Journal of Clinical Cytology and Cytopathology* (online).

International Agency for Research on Cancer/Centre International de Recherche sur le Cancer: 150 cours Albert-Thomas, 69372 Lyon Cedex 08, France; tel. 4-72-73-84-85; fax 4-72-73-85-75; f. 1965 as an Agency of the World Health Organization; to promote international collaboration in cancer research; 16 mem. countries; library of 8,200 vols, 211 journals; Dir Dr PETER BOYLE; publ. *Report* (every 2 years).

International Agency for the Prevention of Blindness/Organisation mondiale contre la cécité: L. V. Prasad Eye Institute, L. V. Prasad Marg, Banjara Hills, Hyderabad 500034, India; tel. (40) 23545389; fax (40) 23548271; e-mail iapb@lvpei.org; internet www.iapb.org; f. 1975; umbrella org. in official relationship with WHO; promotes the formation of national cttees and programmes on prevention of blindness and the sharing of information; Chair. and Pres. Dr GULLAPALLI N. RAO (India); Sec.-Gen. Dr LOUIS PIZZARELLO (USA); publ. *IAPB News* (2 a year).

International Association for Child and Adolescent Psychiatry and Allied Professions/Association Internationale de Psychiatrie de l'Enfant et de l'Adolescent et de Professions Associées: Dept of Child and Adolescent Psychiatry, Developmental Psychiatry Section, University of Cambridge, Douglas House, 18B Trumpington Rd, Cambridge, CB2 2AH, UK; tel. (1223) 336098; fax (1223) 746122; e-mail ig104@cus.cam.ac.uk; internet www.iacapap.org; f. 1948 to promote the study, treatment, care and prevention of mental disorders and deficiencies of children, adolescents and their families by promoting research and practice through collaboration with allied professions; mems: nat. asscns and individual mems in 39 countries; Pres. Dr HELMUT REMSCHMIDT (Germany); Sec.-Gen. Dr IAN M. GOODYER (UK); publ. *Yearbooks*.

International Association for Humanitarian Medicine (IAHM): 3 chemin du Milieu, 1279 Bogis-Bossey, Switzerland; tel. 227762161; fax 227766417; e-mail swagunn@bluewin.ch; internet www.iahm.org; f. 1984; aims to promote and deliver health care on the principles of humanitarian medicine through the provision of equitable medical, surgical, nursing and rehabilitation care to patients in or from developing countries; brings relief to disaster victims where health aid is lacking; mobilizes hospitals and health specialists in developed countries to receive and treat such patients free of charge; and advocates humanitarian principles in the practice of medicine, on the principle of health as a human right; limited to 100 on invitation; Pres. Prof. S. WILLIAM A. GUNN (Switzerland); Sec. Prof. LEO KLEIN (Czech Republic); publ. *Journal of Humanitarian Medicine* (4 a year).

International Association for Radiation Research: c/o Dr Fiona Stewart, Experimental Therapy, Plesmanlaan 121, 1066 CX Amsterdam, The Netherlands; tel. (20) 5122036; fax (20) 5122050; e-mail f.stewart@nki.nl; internet cbrl.stanford.edu/brown/index.htm; f. 1962 to advance radiation research in the fields of physics, chemistry, biology and medicine; 3,246 mems; quadrennial congress; Pres. Dr MASAO S. SASAKI (Japan); Sec. and Treasurer Dr FIONA A. STEWART (Netherlands); publ. *Proceedings of International Congresses*.

International Association of Agricultural Medicine and Rural Health/Association Internationale de Médecine Agricole et de Santé Rurale: OALI (NIPCH), 33–35 Szabolcs utca, Budapest 1135, Hungary; tel. (1) 450-1768; fax (1) 439-0473; e-mail iaamrhsecr@oali.hu; internet www.iaamrh.org; f. 1961 to study the problems of medicine in agriculture globally and to prevent diseases caused by agricultural production; 500 mems; Pres. Dr ASHOK PATIL (India); Sec.-Gen. Dr ISTVAN SZILARD (acting) (Hungary); publ. *Journal of International Agricultural Medicine and Rural Health* (4 a year).

International Association of Applied Psychology/Association Internationale de Psychologie Appliquée: c/o José M. Prieto, Colegio Oficial de Psicólogos, Cuesta de San Vicente 4, 5°, 28008 Madrid, Spain; tel. 91-3943236; fax 91-3510091; e-mail iaap@psy.ulaval.ea; internet www.iaapsy.org; f. 1920, present title adopted 1955; aims: to establish contacts between those carrying out scientific work on applied psych-

ology, to promote research and the adoption of measures contributing to this work; mems: 2,000 in 80 countries; Pres. MICHAEL FRESE (Germany); Sec.-Gen. JOSÉ M. PRIETO (Spain); publ. *Applied Psychology: An International Review* (4 a year).

International Association of Asthmology/Association Internationale d'Asthmologie (INTERASMA): internet www.interasma.org; f. 1954 to advance medical knowledge of bronchial asthma and allied disorders; c. 1,000 mems in 52 countries; Pres. RONALD DAHL (Denmark); Sec.-Gen. LAWRENCE DUBUSKE (USA); publ. *News Bulletin* (3 a year).

International Association of Environmental Mutagen Societies: 1821 Michael Faraday Dr., Ste 300, Reston, VA 20190-5348, USA; tel. (703) 438-3103; fax (703) 438-3113; e-mail beidemiller@aim-hq.com; internet www.iaems.net; f. 1973 for the stimulation of scientific activity and exchange of information by means of World Conference every 4 years in the field of environmental mutagenesis and genetic toxicology; 11 mem. socs (12,000 individuals); Pres. STEFANO BONASSI; Vice-Pres. Dr MICHELINE KIRSCH-VOLDERS; Vice-Pres. Dr LUCIA RIBEIRO; Exec. Dir Dr BETTY EIDEMILLER (USA); Sec. Dr HESTER VISMER (South Africa).

International Association of Gerontology (IAG): c/o Faculté de Médecine, Institut du Vieillissement, 37 Allées Jules Guesde, Toulouse, 31000, France; tel. 5-61-14-56-39; fax 5-61-14-56-40; e-mail seynes@cict.fr; internet www.iagg.info; f. 1950 to promote research and training in gerontology and geriatrics; 40,000 mems in 70 nat. mem. socs in 65 countries; Pres. Prof. BRUNO VELLAS (France); Sec.-Gen. and Vice-Pres. Prof. ALAIN FRANCO (Canada).

International Association of Hydatidology/Asociación Internacional de Hidatidología: Florida 460, 3° piso, 1005 Buenos Aires, Argentina; tel. (11) 4322-3431 ext. 166; fax (11) 4325-8231; internet iahyd.org; f. 1941; 650 mems in 40 countries; library: specialized library; Pres. ANTÓNIO MENEZES DA SILVA (Portugal); Sec.-Gen. EDUARDO GUARNERA (Argentina); publs *Archivos Internacionales de la Hidatidosis* (every 4 years), *Boletín de Hidatidosis* (4 a year).

International Association of Oral and Maxillofacial Surgeons: 17 West 220 22nd St, Suite 420, Oakbrook Terrace, IL 60181, USA; tel. (630) 833-0945; fax (630) 833-1382; internet www.iaoms.org; f. 1962 to elevate the quality of health care worldwide through the advancement of the art and science of oral and maxillofacial surgery; int. conference every 2 years; promotes collaborative research; educational programmes in developing countries; 3,710 mems; Pres. Dr LARRY NISSEN (USA); Exec. Dir Dr JOHN F. HELFRICK (USA); publ. *International Journal of Oral and Maxillofacial Surgery* (12 a year).

International Brain Research Organization (IBRO): 255 rue Saint Honoré, 75001 Paris, France; tel. 1-46-47-92-92; fax 1-47-46-42-50; e-mail ibro@wanadoo.fr; internet www.ibro.org; f. 1960 to assist all branches of neuroscience; federated to ICSU; 52,000 mems; Pres. Dr A. J. AGUAYO (Canada); Sec.-Gen. JENNIFER LUND (USA); publs *IBRO News* (1 a year), *IBRO Reporter* (online, 12 a year), *Neuroscience* (28 a year).

International Cell Research Organization/Organisation Internationale de Recherche sur la Cellule: c/o UNESCO, SC/BES/LSC, 1 rue Miollis, 75732 Paris Cedex 15, France; tel. 1-45-68-58-18; fax 1-45-68-58-16; e-mail icro@unesco.org; internet www.unesco.org/ngo/icro; f. 1962 to create, encourage and promote cooperation between

scientists of different disciplines worldwide for the advancement of fundamental knowledge of the cell; organizes international training courses and exchange of scientists, etc.; 400 mems; Chair. Prof. Q. S. LIN (China); Exec. Sec. Prof. G. N. COHEN (France).

International Center of Information on Antibiotics: c/o Prof. M. Welsch, Inst. de Pathologie, Université de Liège, Sart-Tilman, 4000 Liège, Belgium; f. 1961 to gather information on antibiotics and strains producing them; to establish contact with discoverers of antibiotics with a view to obtaining samples and filing information; Dir Prof. M. WELSCH; Senior Scientist in Charge Dr L. DELCAMBE.

International Commission on Occupational Health/Commission Internationale de la Santé au Travail: c/o ISPESL, National Institute for Occupational Safety and Prevention, Via Fontana Candida 1, 00040 Monteporzio Catone (Rome), Italy; tel. 06-94181407; fax 06-94181556; e-mail icohsg@iol.it; internet www.icoh.org.sg; f. 1906 to study new findings in the field of occupational health, to publicize the results of study and investigation in occupational health, and to organize meetings on nat. or int. problems in this field; 2,000 mems in 93 countries; recognized by the UN; official languages: English, French; Pres. Prof. JORMA RANTANEN (Finland); Sec.-Gen. Dr SERGIO IAVICOLI (Italy).

International Council of Ophthalmology: c/o Dr Bruce E. Spivey, International Council of Ophthalmology, 945 Green St, #10, San Francisco, CA 94133, USA; fax (415) 409-8403; e-mail info@icoph.org; f. 1857; 75 affiliated national societies; Pres. Dr BRUCE E. SPIVEY.

International Epidemiological Association/Association Internationale d'Epidémiologie: c/o Prof. Ahmed Mandil, IEA Secretary, 38 Ismailiah St, Apt 201, Mostafa Kamel, Alexandria, Egypt; tel. (3) 5467576; fax (3) 5467576; e-mail ieasecretariat@link.net; internet www.ieaweb.org; f. 1954; int. meetings are held every 3 years in different parts of the world and regional meetings are held regularly throughout the world; 1,500 mems in 100 countries; Pres. Prof. NEIL PEARCE; Sec. Prof. AHMED MANDIL; publ. *International Journal of Epidemiology* (6 a year).

International Federation for Medical and Biological Engineering/Fédération Internationale du Génie Médical et Biologique: c/o Prof. Ratko Magjarevic, Faculty of Electrical Engineering and Computing, University of Zagreb, Unska 3, 10000 Zagreb, Croatia; tel. (1) 6129-938; fax (1) 6129-652; e-mail office@ifmbe.org; internet www.ifmbe.org; f. 1959 to promote international cooperation and communication among societies interested in life and engineering sciences; mem. orgs in 47 countries and 2 transnational orgs; Pres. Prof. JOACHIM NAGEL (Germany); Sec.-Gen. Prof. RATKO MAGJAREVIC (Croatia); publs *Medical and Biological Engineering and Computing* (6 a year), *Proceedings of International Conference on Medical and Biological Engineering* (irregular).

International Federation of Anatomists/Fédération Internationale des Associations d'Anatomistes: Dept of Anatomy, Medical College of Ohio, POB 10008, Toledo, OH 43699-0008, USA; tel. (419) 381-4111; f. 1903; mems: 52 national and multinational associations; Pres. Prof. Dr LIBERATO J. A. DIDIO (USA); publs *Directory*, Proceedings of each Federative International Congress of Anatomy (every 4 or 5 years).

International Federation of Gynaecology and Obstetrics/Fédération Internationale de Gynécologie et d'Obstétrique: FIGO House, Suite 3, Waterloo Court, 10 Theed St, London, SE15 6DX, UK; tel. (20) 7928-1166; fax (20) 7928-7099; e-mail figo@figo.org; internet www.figo.org; f. 1954; assists and contributes to research in gynaecology and obstetrics; aims to facilitate the exchange of information and perfect methods of teaching; organizes international congresses; 110 nat. socs; Pres. Dr A. ACOSTA (Paraguay); Sec.-Gen. Prof. S. ARULKUMARAN (UK); publ. *International Journal of Gynecology and Obstetrics* (12 a year).

International Federation of Physical Education/Fédération Internationale d'Education Physique (FIEP): CP 837, 85857-970 Foz do Iguaçu, Paraná, Brazil; tel. (45) 3574-1949; e-mail fiep.brasil@uol.com.br; internet www.fiep.net; f. 1923; aims to develop national and international physical education and sport-for-all; organizes congresses and courses; mems in 116 countries; Pres. (vacant); Gen. Sec. Prof. ALMIR ADOLFO GRUHN (Brazil); publ. *FIEP Bulletin* (in English, French and Spanish; Portuguese edition from Brazil).

International Hospital Federation/Fédération Internationale des Hôpitaux: Immeuble JB Say, 13 chemin du Levant, 01210 Ferney Voltaire, France; tel. 4-50-42-60-00; fax 4-50-42-60-01; e-mail info@ihf-fih.org; internet www.ihf-fih.org; f. 1947; an ind. org. supported by subscribing mems in 100 countries; aims to promote improvements in the planning and management of hospitals and health services through int. conferences, field study courses, training courses, information services, publs and research projects; mems: nat. hospital and health service orgs, governmental and non-governmental, individuals from disciplines and occupations concerned with health services, and professional, commercial and industrial firms working in the health service field; Pres. GÉRARD VINCENT (France); Dir-Gen. IBRAHIM ALABDULHADI (Kuwait); publs *Building Quality in Health*, *Care Journal* (2 a year), *International Hospital Federation Reference Yearbook* (1 a year), *World Hospitals and Health Services* (4 a year).

International Institute on Ageing: 117 St Paul's St, Valletta, VLT 1216, Malta; tel. 21243044; fax 21230248; e-mail info@inia.org.mt; internet www.inia.org.mt; f. 1988 by the UN and Government of Malta; Int. training programmes social gerontology; economic and financial aspects of ageing; health promotion, quality of life and well-being; policy formulation, planning, implementation and monitoring of the Madrid Int. Plan of Action on Ageing; demographic aspects of population ageing, its implications for socio-economic devt policies and plans; 'In-Situ' training programmes in developing countries, research and data colln; technical cooperation (advisory services, project design, planning and implementation of training programmes); library of 800 vols; Dir Prof. JOSEPH TROISI; publ. *BOLD* (4 a year).

International League Against Epilepsy/Ligue Internationale contre l'Epilepsie: 342 N Main St, Hartford, CT 06103, USA; tel. (860) 586-7547; fax (860) 586-7550; e-mail pberry@ilae.org; internet www.ilae.org; f. 1909 to collect and disseminate information concerning epilepsy, to promote treatment of epileptic patients and to foster cooperation with other int. institutions in similar fields; offices in USA; holds scientific congress every 2 years in conjunction with Int. Bureau for Epilepsy; regional congresses every 2 years;

nat. congresses annually by each nat. chapter; 15,000 mems, nat. chapters in 98 countries; Pres. SOLOMON MOSHE; Sec.-Gen. SAMUEL WIEBE; Chief Staff Officer PETER J. BERRY; publs *Epilepsia* (12 a year), *Epilepsies* (French, 4 a year), *Epilepsy & Behavior* (6 a year), *Epilepsy Research* (15 a year), *Epileptic Disorders*, *Seizure* (8 a year).

International Organization Against Trachoma/Organisation Internationale contre le Trachome: c/o Prof. Georges Cornand, La Bergère, Route de Grenoble, 05140 Aspres-sur-Buëch, France; f. 1923 for the research and study of trachomatous conjunctivitis and ophthalmological tropical and sub-tropical diseases; Pres. Prof. GABRIEL COSCAS (France); Sec.-Gen. Prof. GEORGES CORNAND; publ. *Revue Internationale du Trachome* (4 a year).

International Psychoanalytical Association: 'Broomhills', Woodside Lane, London, N12 8UD, UK; tel. (20) 8446-8324; fax (20) 8445-4729; e-mail ipa@ipa.org.uk; internet www.ipa.org.uk; f. 1910; primary accrediting and regulatory body for psychoanalysis; devt of psychoanalysis for benefit of psychoanalytic patients; 12,000 mems in 70 constituent orgs in 33 countries; Pres. CHARLES HANLY; Sec.-Gen. GUNTHER PERDIGAO; publ. *IPA News Magazine* (1 a year).

International Radiation Protection Association: c/o CEPN, 28 rue de la Redoute, 92260 Fontenay-aux-Roses, France; tel. 1-55-52-19-47; fax 1-40-85-19-21; e-mail irpa.exof@irpa.net; internet www.irpa.net; f. 1966 to promote int. contacts and cooperation among those engaged in health physics and radiation protection; to provide for discussion of the scientific and practical aspects of the protection of mankind and his environment from the hazards caused by ionizing and non-ionizing radiation, facilitating the exploitation of radiation and nuclear energy for the benefit of mankind; 37 mem. socs, 16,000 individual mems; Scientific Assoc. of ICSU, official relations with WHO, ILO, IAEA, ICRP; Pres. KEN KASE (USA); Exec. Officer JACQUES LOCHARD (France).

International Scientific Council for Trypanosomiasis Research and Control/Conseil Scientifique International pour la Recherche et la Lutte contre les Trypanosomoses: Secretariat OAU/STRC, Ports Authority Bldg, 26/28 Marina, PMB 2359, Lagos, Nigeria; tel. 2633430; fax 2636093; f. 1949 to review the work on tsetse and trypanosomiasis problems carried out by relevant organizations and workers in laboratories and in the field; to encourage further research and discussion and to promote coordination between research workers and organizations in African countries; to provide opportunity for the discussion of related problems and their resolution; Exec. Sec. Prof. JOHNSON A. EKPERE.

International Society for Clinical Electrophysiology of Vision: c/o Daphne L. McCulloch, ISCEV Secretary-General, Dept of Vision Sciences, Glasgow Caledonian University, Glasgow, G4 0BA, UK; tel. (141) 331-3379; e-mail dlmc@gcal.ac.uk; internet www.iscev.org; f. 1958; 400 mems; Pres. Prof. MICHAEL BACH (Germany); Sec.-Gen. Prof. DAPHNE MCCULLOCH; publ. *Documenta Ophthalmologica* (6 a year).

International Society for the Psychopathology of Expression and Art Therapy/Société Internationale de Psychopathologie de l'Expression et d'Art-Thérapie: c/o M. Sudres, Université Toulouse-Mirail, U.F.R. Psychologie, 5 allée Antonio Machado, 31058 Toulouse, Cedex 9, France; e-mail sipearther@aol.com; internet online-art-therapy.com; f. 1959 to bring

together the various specialists interested in the problems of expression and artistic activities in connection with psychiatric, sociological and psychological research, as well as in the use of methods applied in fields other than that of mental illness; 625 mems; Pres. Prof. L. SCHMITT (France); Sec.-Gen. JEAN-LUC SUDRES (France).

International Society for Vascular Specialists: 900 Cummings Center, 221-U, Beverly, MA 01915, USA; tel. (978) 927-8330; fax (978) 524-8890; internet www.iscvs.vascularweb.org; f. 1950; present name 2003 (comprising members in North and South America, Africa, the Middle East and Australasia); members in Europe and Asia belong to affiliated International Society for Cardiovascular Surgery; promotes the investigation and study of the art, science and therapy of cardiovascular diseases; facilitates the exchange of ideas in the field of vascular diseases through scientific meetings and personal contact between vascular specialists; 2,000 mems; Pres. JAMES MAY; publs *Annals of Vascular Surgery* (6 a year), *Cardiovascular Surgery* (6 a year), *Journal of Vascular Surgery* (12 a year).

International Society of Criminology/Société Internationale de Criminologie: 12 rue Charles Fourier, 75013 Paris, France; tel. (1) 45-88-00-23; fax (1) 45-88-96-40; e-mail crim.sic@wanadoo.fr; internet perso.wanadoo.fr/societe.internationale.de.criminologie/f. 1938 to promote the development of the sciences in their application to crime; library; 800 mems; Pres. LAWRENCE W. SHERMAN (USA); Sec.-Gen. GEORGES PICCA (France); publ. *Annales Internationales de Criminologie*.

International Society of Haematology/Société Internationale d'Hématologie: c/o Dr Emin Kansu, Institute of Oncology, Faculty of Medicine, Haceteppe University, Hacettepe, 06100 Ankara, Turkey; tel. (312) 305-28-66; fax (312) 324-20-09; e-mail ekansu@ada.net.tr; internet www.ish-world.org; f. 1946 to promote and foster the exchange and diffusion of information and ideas relating to blood and blood-forming tissues worldwide; to provide a forum for discussion of haematologic problems on an international scale and to encourage scientific investigation of these problems; to promote the advancement of haematology and its recognition as a branch of the biological sciences; to attempt to standardize on an international scale haematological methods and nomenclature; to promote a better understanding of the scientific basic principles of haematology among practitioners of haematology and physicians in general and to foster better understanding and a greater interest in clinical haematological problems among scientific investigators in the field of haematology; Vice-Pres. of European and African Division GAYLE KENOYER (South Africa), FAYZA HAMMOUDA (Egypt); Sec.-Gen. and Treas. of European and African Division EMIN KANSU (Turkey).

International Society of Hypnosis: c/o Dr Eric Vermetten, Department of Military Psychiatry, Central Military Hospital, University Medical Center Utrecht, Heidelberglaan 100, 3584 CX Utrecht, Netherlands; tel. (30) 2502591; fax (30) 2502282; e-mail admin@ish-web.org; internet www.ish-web.org; f. 1973 as an affiliate of the World Federation of Mental Health; to encourage and improve professional research, cooperative relations among scientific disciplines with regard to the study and application of hypnosis; to bring together persons using hypnosis and set up standards for professional training and adequacy; Pres. Dr ERIC VERMETTEN (Netherlands); Sec. and

Treas. Dr JULIE LINDEN (USA); publ. *International Journal of Clinical and Experimental Hypnosis* (4 a year).

International Society of Lymphology: Dept of Surgery, Rm 4406, 1501 North Campbell Ave, POB 245063, Tucson, AZ 85724-5063, USA; tel. (520) 626-6118; fax (520) 626-0822; e-mail lymph@u.arizona.edu; internet www.u.arizona.edu/~witte/isl.htm; f. 1966 to advance progress in lymphology and related subjects; organizes int. working groups, cooperates with other nat. and int. organizations; int. congresses and postgraduate courses; 400 mems; Pres. M. OHKUMA (Japan); Sec.-Gen. MARLYS WITTE (USA); publs *Lymphology* (4 a Year), *Progress in Lymphology* (every 2 years).

International Society of Neuropathology: c/o Dr Seth Love, Dept of Neuropathology, Institute of Clinical Sciences, Frenchay Hospital, Bristol, BS16 1LE, UK; fax (117) 975-3760; e-mail isn@sethlove.co.uk; internet www.intsocneuropathol.com; f. 1972 to initiate and maintain permanent cooperation between nat. and regional socs of neuropathology, to foster links with other int. orgs in the same field, to initiate int. congresses, symposia, etc.; 2,500 mems; Pres. Dr BERNARDINO GHETTI (USA); Sec.-Gen. Dr SETH LOVE (UK); publ. *Brain Pathology* (4 a year).

International Society of Radiology/Société Internationale de Radiologie: 7910 Woodmont Ave, Suite 400, Bethesda, MD 20814, USA; tel. (301) 657-2652; fax (301) 907-8768; internet www.isradiology.org; f. 1953 to develop and advance medical radiology by giving radiologists in different countries an opportunity of personally submitting their experiences, exchanging and discussing their ideas, and forming personal bonds with their colleagues; 3 permanent Int. Commissions: (*a*) on Radiological Protection (ICRP), (*b*) on Radiation Units and Measurements (ICRU), (*c*) on Radiological Education (ICRE); these Commissions meet during each Congress, held every 2 years or when necessary; Pres. CLAUDE MANELFE (France); Exec. Dir OTHA W. LINTON (USA).

International Society of Surgery (ISS)/ Société Internationale de Chirurgie (SIC): Seltisbergerstr. 16, 4419 Lupsingen, Switzerland; tel. 618159666; fax 618114775; e-mail surgery@iss-sic.ch; internet www .iss-sic.ch; f. 1902; organizes congresses; 3,500 mems; Sec.-Gen. Prof. Dr JEAN-CLAUDE GIVEL; publ. *World Journal of Surgery* (12 a year).

International Union against Sexually Transmitted Infections: c/o Dr Raj Patel, Royal South Hants Hospital, Brintons Terrace, Southampton, SO14 0YG, UK; tel. (23) 8082-5152; fax (23) 8082-5122; internet www .iusti.org; f. 1923; administrative and educational activities, public health, and technical aspects of sexually transmitted diseases, esp. HIV/AIDS; 800 individual, 50 nat. and soc. mems; consultative status with WHO; Pres. Dr FRANK JUDSON (USA); Sec.-Gen. Dr RAJ PATEL (UK).

International Union against Tuberculosis and Lung Disease/Union Internationale contre la Tuberculose et les Maladies Respiratoires: 68 Blvd Saint-Michel, 75006 Paris, France; tel. (1) 44-32-03-60; fax (1) 43-29-90-87; e-mail union@ iuatld.org; internet www.iuatld.org; f. 1920 to coordinate the efforts of anti-tuberculosis associations, to promote programmes and research in tuberculosis control, chest diseases and community health, to cooperate in these respects with the World Health Organization, to promote int. and regional conferences on the above subjects, to collect and disseminate relevant information, to assist in

developing national programmes in cooperation with national associations; mems: associations in 165 countries; 3,000 individual mems; Pres. Prof. ASMA EL SONY (Sudan); Exec. Dir Dr NILS E. BILLO (Switzerland); Sec.-Gen. Dr MOHAMMAD REZA MASJEDI (Iran); publ. *International Journal of Tuberculosis and Lung Disease* (12 a Year, in English).

International Union for Health Promotion and Education/Union Internationale de Promotion de la Santé et d'Education pour la Santé: 42 blvd de la Libération, 93203 St Denis Cedex, France; tel. (1) 48-13-71-20; fax (1) 48-09-17-67; internet www.iuhpe.org; f. 1951; mems: organizations in 21 countries, groups and individuals in 90 countries; Pres. MAURICE MITTELMARK (Norway); Exec. Dir MARIE-CLAUDE LAMARRE (France); publ. *Promotion and Education/International Journal of Health Promotion and Education* (4 a year, in a trilingual edition in English, French and Spanish; special supplement issues throughout the year).

International Vaccine Institute: Kwanak, POB 14, Seoul 151-600, Republic of Korea; tel. (2) 872-2801; fax (2) 872-2803; e-mail iviinfo@ivi.int; internet www.ivi.org; f. 1997; established by the UN Development Programme (UNDP) as an int. centre of research, training and technical assistance for vaccination in the developing world; Chair. Prof. SAMUEL L. KATZ (USA); Dir Dr JOHN D. CLEMENS (Republic of Korea).

Multiple Sclerosis International Federation: Skyline House, 3rd Fl., 200 Union St, London, SE1 0LX, UK; tel. (20) 7620-1911; fax (20) 7620-1922; e-mail info@msif.org; internet www.msif.org; f. 1967 to coordinate and advance the work of nat. multiple sclerosis orgs worldwide, to encourage scientific research in this and related neurological diseases, to collect and disseminate information, and to advise and help in advancing the devt of voluntary nat. multiple sclerosis orgs; Pres. SARAH PHILLIPS (UK); Sec. WEYMAN T. JOHNSON (USA); publs *MSIF Annual Review*, *MS in Focus*.

Organisation Ouest Africaine de la Santé (OOAS)/West African Health Organisation (WAHO): 01 BP 153, Bobo-Dioulasso 01, Burkina Faso; tel. 97-57-75; fax 97-57-72; e-mail wahooas@fasonet.bf; f. 1987 by merger of OCCGE (Organisation de Coordination et de Coopération pour la Lutte contre les Grandes Endémies in Bobo-Dioulaso Burkina Faso) and WAHC (West African Health Community/Communauté Ouest Africaine de la Santé) in Lagos, Nigeria; proactive instrument of regional health integration that enables high-impact and cost-effective interventions; conducts research and trains medical workers; library of 4,072 vols, 21 current serials, 3,196 technical documents; 15 mem. states: Benin, Burkina Faso, Cape Verde, Côte d'Ivoire, Ghana, Guinea, Guinea-Bissau, Liberia, Mali, Niger, Nigeria, Senegal, Sierra Leone, The Gambia, Togo; library of 2,367 vols, 3 current periodicals, 11,010 technical documents; Dir-Gen. Dr PLACIDO M. CARDOSO; publs *Bulletin bibliographique mensuel* (4 a year), *Profil OOAS* (4 a year).

Société de Neurochirurgie de Langue Française (Society of French-Speaking Neurosurgeons): Service de neurochirurgie, Laarbeeklaan 101, 1090 Brussels, Belgium; internet www.snclf.com; f. 1948; 400 mems; Pres. MARC SINDOU; Sec. JEAN D'HAENS; publ. *Neurochirurgie* (6 a year).

Société Internationale de Chirurgie Orthopédique et de Traumatologie/ International Society of Orthopaedic

Surgery and Traumatology: Rue Washington 40-B 9, 1050 Brussels, Belgium; tel. (2) 648-68-23; fax (2) 649-86-01; e-mail hq@sicot.org; internet www.sicot.org; f. 1929 to advance the science and art of orthopaedics and traumatology at an int. level for the enhancement of patient care, to foster and develop teaching, research and education, to facilitate and encourage the interchange of professional experience, and to promote good fellowship among its members; conf. held every year except year of congress, which is held every 3 years; 113 mem. countries, 2,000 individual mems; library of 34 vols of *International Orthopaedics*; Pres. Prof. CODY BUNGER (Denmark); Pres.-Elect Prof. MAURICE HINSENKAMP; Sec.-Gen. Prof. JOCHEN EULERT (Germany); Treas. Prof. PATRICIA FUCS; First Vice-Pres. Dr THAMI BENZAKOUR; Exec. Dir BEATRICE CHAIDRON; publ. *International Orthopaedics* (8 a year).

World Association of Societies of (Anatomic and Clinical) Pathology/Association Mondiale des Sociétés de Pathologie (Anatomique et Clinique): c/o Dept of Clinical Pathology, Koshigaya Hospital, Dokkyo University School of Medicine, 2-1-50 Minamikoshigaya, Koshigaya, Saitama 343, Japan; f. 1947 (formerly International Society of Clinical Pathology) to improve health worldwide by promoting the teaching and practice of all aspects of pathology and laboratory medicine; mems: 50 national associations; Pres. WILLIAM B. ZEILER (USA); Exec. Dir Dr I. SAKURABAYASHI.

World Association of Veterinary Microbiologists, Immunologists and Specialists in Infectious Diseases/Association Mondiale des Vétérinaires Microbiologistes, Immunologistes et Spécialistes des Maladies Infectieuses: Ecole Nationale Vétérinaire d'Alfort, 7 ave du Général de Gaulle, 94704 Maisons-Alfort Cedex, France; tel. 1-43-96-70-21; fax 1-43-96-70-22; f. 1967 to facilitate international contacts in the field of veterinary microbiologists, immunologists and specialists in infectious diseases; Pres. Prof. CH. PILET (France).

World Confederation for Physical Therapy: Kensington Charity Centre, 4th Fl., Charles House, 375 Kensington High St, London, W14 8QH, UK; tel. (20) 7471-6765; fax (20) 7471-6766; e-mail info@wcpt.org; internet www.wcpt.org; f. 1951 to encourage improved standards of physical therapy in education and practice; to promote exchange of information between mem. orgs; to assist the development of informed public opinion regarding physical therapy; to cooperate with appropriate agencies of UN and national and int. organizations; 92 mem. organizations; Pres. SANDRA MERCER MOORE; Sec.-Gen. BRENDA MYERS (UK); publ. *WCPT News* (4 a Year).

World Council of Optometry: 42 Craven St, London WC2N 5NG, UK; fax (207) 839-6800; e-mail enquiries@worldoptometry.org; internet www.worldoptometry.org; f. 1927; aims to coordinate efforts to provide a high standard of ophthalmic optical (optometric) care worldwide; provides a forum for the exchange of ideas between different countries; a large part of its work is concerned with optometric education, and advice upon standards of qualification; involved in getting legislation approvedin relation to optometry worldwide; 85 mem. orgs in 52 countries; Pres. Prof. ROBERT CHAPPELL (UK); Exec. Dir (vacant); publ. *World Optometry*.

World Federation of Neurosurgical Societies/Fédération Mondiale des Sociétés de Neurochirurgie: c/o Janette A. Joseph, 5 rue du Marché, 1260 Nyon, Vaud, Switzerland; tel. 223624303; fax 223624352;

e-mail janjoseph@wfns.ch; internet www
.wfns.org; f. 1955 to facilitate the exchange of
knowledge and to encourage research; 109
mem. societies and affiliated organizations;
Pres. Dr JACQUES BROTCHI; Dir JANETTE A.
JOSEPH (Switzerland).

World Federation of Societies of Anaes-thesiologists (WFSA)/Federación Mundial de Sociedades de Anestesiólogos/Weltverband der Anaesthesisten-Gesellschaften: 21 Portland Place, London,
W1B 1YP, UK; tel. (20) 7631-8880; fax (20)
7631-8882; e-mail wfsahq@
anaesthesiologists.org; internet www
.anaesthesiologists.org; f. 1955 to make available the highest standards of anaesthesia,
pain treatment, trauma management and
resuscitation globally; 122 nat. mem. socs;
Hon. Sec. Dr DAVID WILKINSON (UK); Sec.
Prof. JOHN MOYERS (USA); publs *Update in
Anaesthesia* (2 a year in 5 languages), *World
Anaesthesia* (3 a year in 3 languages).

Music

International Music Council (IMC)/Conseil International de la Musique: c/o
Maison de l'UNESCO, 1 rue Miollis, 75015
Paris, France; tel. 1-45-68-48-50; fax 1-45-68-48-66; e-mail info@imc-cim.org; internet
www.imc-cim.org; f. 1949 under the auspices
of UNESCO to foster the exchange of musicians, music (written and recorded), and
information; to support contemporary composers, traditional music, and young professional musicians; to foster appreciation of
music by the public; promotion of diverse
music; advancement of music rights; 150
mem. orgs; Sec.-Gen. SILJA FISCHER (Paris).

MEMBERS OF IMC

European Festivals Association/Association Européenne des Festivals: Kasteel
Borluut, Kleine Gentstraat 46, 9051 Gent,
Belgium; tel. (9) 241-80-80; fax (9) 241-80-89;
e-mail info@efa-aef.eu; internet www.efa-aef
.eu; f. 1952 to maintain high artistic standards in festivals, widen the field of operation,
organize information and publicity; 87 mem.
festivals in Austria, Belgium, Bosnia and
Herzegovina, Bulgaria, Croatia, Czech
Republic, Denmark, Estonia, Finland,
France, Germany, Greece, Hungary, Iceland,
Ireland, Israel, Italy, Japan, Lebanon,
Lithuania, Luxembourg, former Yugoslav
republic of Macedonia, Mexico, Netherlands,
Norway, Poland, Portugal, Romania, Russia,
Serbia, Slovakia, Slovenia, Spain, Sweden,
Switzerland, Turkey, UK; Sec.-Gen. HUGO DE
GREEF.

**International Council for Traditional
Music/Conseil International de la Musique Traditionelle:** ICTM Secretariat,
School of Music, Australian National University, Bldg 100, Canberra, ACT 0200,
Australia; tel. (2) 612-51449; fax (2) 612-59775; e-mail secretariat@ictmusic.org;
internet www.ictmusic.org; f. 1947 (as International Folk Music Council) to advance the
preservation, study, practice and dissemination of traditional music (including dance)
worldwide; affiliated to UNESCO; 1,600
mems; Pres. Dr ADRIENNE L. KAEPPLER
(USA); Sec.-Gen. Prof. STEPHEN WILD (Australia); publs *Bulletin* (2 a year), *Directory of
Traditional Music* (online for mems), *Yearbook for Traditional Music*.

**International Federation of Musicians/
Fédération Internationale des Musiciens:** 21 bis rue Victor Massé, 75009 Paris,
France; tel. 1-45-26-31-23; fax 1-45-26-31-57;
e-mail office@fim-musicians.org; internet
www.fim-musicians.com; f. 1948 to promote

and protect the interests of musicians in
affiliated unions and to institute protective
measures to safeguard musicians against the
abuse of their performances; promotes the
international exchange of musicians; makes
agreements with other international organizations in the interest of member unions and
of the profession; mems: 70 unions in 65
countries; Pres. JOHN F. SMITH (UK); Gen.
Sec. BENOÎT MACHUEL.

**International Music and Media Centre/
Internationales Musikzentrum und
Medienzentrum:** Stiftgasse 29, 1070
Vienna, Austria; tel. (1) 889-03-15; fax (1)
889-03-15-77; e-mail office@imz.at; internet
www.imz.at; f. 1961 as a non-profit org. for
the promotion and dissemination of opera,
dance, concert and music documentaries
through the audiovisual media (film, television, radio, gramophone); organizes congresses, seminars and screenings on music
in the audiovisual media; organizes competitions to strengthen relations between composers, interpreters and directors, with
particular emphasis on the promotion of the
young generation; mems: 180 broadcasting
orgs and other artistic orgs in 26 countries;
Pres. CHRIS HUNT (UK); Sec.-Gen. FRANZ
PATAY.

International Musicological Society: see
under International Council for Philosophy
and Humanistic Studies.

**International Research Institute for
Media, Communication and Cultural
Development (MEDIACULT):** Anton-von-Webern-Pl. 1, 1030 Vienna, Austria; tel. (1)
71155-8800; fax (1) 71155-8809; e-mail
mediacult@mediacult.mdw.ac.at; internet
www.mdw.ac.at/mediacult; f. 1969; library of
1,200 vols; Pres. Prof. RAYMOND WEBER
(Luxembourg); Dir Dr ANDREW GEBESMAIR;
Sec.-Gen. Dr ALFRED SMUDITS.

**International Society for Contemporary
Music/Société Internationale pour la
Musique Contemporaine:** c/o Muziek Centrum Nederland, Rokin 111, 1012 KN,
Amsterdam, Netherlands; tel. (20) 344-60-60; e-mail info@iscm.org; internet www.iscm
.org; f. 1922 to promote the devt of contemporary music and to organize annual World
Music Days; mem. organizations in 47 countries; Pres. JOHN DAVIS (Australia); Sec. Gen.
ARTHUR VAN DER DRIFT; publ. *World New
Music Magazine* (1 a year).

International Society for Music Education: POB 909, Nedlands WA 6909, Australia; tel. (8) 9386-2654; fax (8) 9386-2658;
e-mail isme@isme.org; internet www.isme
.org; f. 1953 to promote music education as
a part of general education and community
life; organizes int. conferences and seminars;
cooperates with other int. music orgs; acts as
an advisory body to UNESCO; cooperates
with orgs representing other fields of education; 1,650 mems; Pres. HAKAN LUNDSTROM;
Sec.-Gen. JUDY THÖNELL; publs *Conference
and Seminar Proceedings* (every 2 years),
*International Journal of Music Education
(ISME)* (4 a year, No. 1 Research, No. 2
Showcase, No. 3 Practice, No. 4 Research).

Jeunesses Musicales International:
Palais des Beaux-Arts, 10 rue Royale, 1000
Brussels, Belgium; tel. (32) 2-5139774; fax
(32) 2-5144755; e-mail mail@jmi.net; internet
www.jmi.net; f. 1945 to enable young people
to develop through music across all boundaries; runs a World Orchestra and a World
Youth Choir; member organizations in 41
countries; Sec.-Gen. DAG FRANZÉN (acting);
publ. *JMI News* (6 a year).

**World Federation of International
Music Competitions/Fédération Mondiale des Concours Internationaux de
Musique:** 104 rue de Carouge, 1205 Geneva,

Switzerland; tel. 223213620; fax 227811418;
e-mail fmcim@iprolink.ch; internet www
.wfimc.org; f. 1957; coordinates the activities
of members and maintains links between
them, arranges the calendar of competitions,
helps competition-winners to get to know
each other; 118 mem. competitions; Pres.
MARIANNE GRANVIG; Sec.-Gen. RENATE RONNEFELD; publ. *Yearbook.*

OTHER ORGANIZATION

**Répertoire International de Littérature
Musicale (RILM)/International Repertory of Music Literature/Internationales
Repertorium der Musikliteratur:** RILM
International Center, 365 Fifth Avenue, New
York, NY 10016-4309, USA; tel. (212) 817-1990; fax (212) 817-1569; e-mail rilm@gc
.cuny.edu; internet www.rilm.org; f. 1966;
autonomous body sponsored by International
Association of Music Libraries, Archives and
Documentation Centers, and International
Musicological Society; research and gathering of bibliographical references of all significant writings on music, from all nations, for
online, printed and CD-ROM database; 63
mem. national committees; library of 1,200
vols, 500 current music journals; Pres.
BARBARA DOBBS MACKENZIE; publ. *RILM
Abstracts of Music Literature* (1 a year).

Science

**Abdus Salam International Centre for
Theoretical Physics (ICTP):** Strada Costiera 11, 34151 Trieste, Italy; tel. 040-2240111; fax 040-224163; e-mail sci_info@
ictp.it; internet www.ictp.it; f. 1964; administered under a tripartite agreement between
UNESCO, the Int. Atomic Energy Agency,
and the Italian Govt; primary focus on
training and research into high-energy physics and cosmology, condensed matter and
statistical physics, Earth system physics and
mathematics; library of 67,500 vols, 340
journals, 4,000 e-journals, 1,600 electronic
books; Dir FERNANDO QUEVEDO.

**Academy of Sciences for the Developing
World:** c/o Abdus Salam International
Centre for Theoretical Physics, Strada Costiera 11, 34014 Trieste, Italy; located at: ICTP
Enrico Fermi Bldg, 1st Fl., Via Beirut 6,
34014 Trieste, Italy; tel. 040 2240327; fax 040
224559; e-mail info@twas.org; internet www
.twas.org; f. 1983 to give recognition and
support to research carried out by scientists
in developing countries, to facilitate their
contacts and foster research in developing
countries; awards prizes, research grants,
fellowships and associateships to scientists
working and living in developing countries;
844 fellows and assoc. fellows; Pres. JACOB
PALIS (Brazil); Sec.-Gen. DORAIRAJAN BALASU-BRAMANIAN (India); Exec. Dir MOHAMED H. A.
HASSAN (Italy); publ. *TWAS Year Book.*

African Academy of Sciences: POB 24916,
Nairobi, Kenya; tel. (2) 884401; fax (2)
884406; e-mail aas@aasciences.org; f. 1985
to promote and foster the growth of the
scientific community in Africa; activities:
mobilization and strengthening of the African scientific community (includes the Network of African Scientific Institutions,
profiles and data-bank of African scientists
and instns, African Dissertation Internship
Programme, assistance to regional orgs);
research development and public policy; capacity building in science and technology; 162
Fellows; library of 2,000 vols; Pres. Prof.
MOHAMED H. A. HASSAN (Sudan); Exec. Dir
Dr Eng. SHEM ARUNGU-OLENDE (Kenya);
publs *Discovery and Innovation* (4 a Year),
Whydah (4 a Year).

African Association for the Advancement of Science and Technology: c/o Prof. C. Kamala, KNAAS, POB 47288, Nairobi, Kenya; f. 1978; Sec. Prof. C. KAMALA.

African Organization for Cartography and Remote Sensing/Organisation Africaine de Cartographie et Télédétection: BP 102, Hussein Dey, 16040 Algiers, Algeria; tel. (21) 23-17-17; fax (21) 23-33-39; e-mail oact@wissal.dz; internet www.oact.dz; f. 1988 to encourage the development of cartography and of remote sensing by satellite, organize conferences and other meetings, and promote the establishment of training institutions; coordinates four regional training centres, in Burkina Faso, Kenya, Nigeria and Tunisia; 24 mem. countries; Contact MOHAMED SAFAR ZITOUN.

Association for the Taxonomic Study of Tropical African Flora/Association pour l'Etude Taxonomique de la Flore d'Afrique Tropicale: c/o Prof. Dr Sebsebe Demissew, Faculty of Science, Addis Ababa University, POB 3434, Addis Ababa, Ethiopia; tel. (1) 114323; fax (1) 552350; e-mail nat .heb@telecom.net.et; internet www.br.fgov .be/research/meetings/aetfat; f. 1950; language of instruction French; 800 mems from 70 countries; Gen. Sec. Prof. Dr SEBSEBE DEMISSEW; publ. *Bulletin* (1 a Year).

Association of Information and Dissemination Centers: POB 3212, Maple Glen, PA 19002-8212, USA; tel. (215) 654-9129; fax (215) 654-9129; e-mail info@asidic.org; internet www.asidic.org; f. 1968; independent organization with 100 centres representing industry, government and academia in the USA, Canada, Europe, Israel, Japan, India, South Africa and Australia; promotes applied technology of information storage and retrieval, and research and development for more efficient use of databases; Pres. MICHAEL WALKER; Sec. DONALD HAWKINS.

BirdLife International: 1 Wellbrook Court, Girton Rd, Girton, Cambridge, CB3 0NA, UK; tel. (1223) 277318; fax (1223) 277200; e-mail birdlife@birdlife.org; internet www.birdlife.org; f. 1922; determines status of bird species worldwide and compiles data on all endangered species; identifies conservation problems and priorities and runs a programme of related field projects; partners and reps in 90 countries; Chair. PETER SCHEI (Norway); Dir and Chief Exec. Dr MARCO LAMBERTINI (Italy); publs *Bird Conservation International, State of the World's Birds, Threatened Birds of the World, World Birdwatch.*

Charles Darwin Foundation for the Galapagos Isles/Fundación Charles Darwin para las Islas Galápagos: c/o Fernando Espinoza, Casilla 17-01-3891, Quito, Ecuador; located at: Avda 6 de Diciembre N 36-109 y Pasaje California, Quito, Ecuador; tel. 244-803; fax 443-935; internet www .darwinfoundation.org; f. 1959 to organize and maintain the Charles Darwin Research Station in the Galapagos Islands and to advise the Government of Ecuador on scientific research and conservation in the archipelago; Pres. Dr THOMAS H. FRITTS; Exec. Dir Dr FERNANDO ESPINOZA F.; publ. *Noticias de Galápagos* (2 a year).

Circum-Pacific Council for Energy and Mineral Resources: Secretariat, 12201 Sunrise Valley Dr., MS-917A, Reston, VA 20192, USA; tel. (703) 648-5042; fax (703) 648-4227; internet www .circum-pacificcouncil.org; f. 1974; non-profit int. org. of earth scientists and engineers; develops and promotes research and cooperation among industry, govt and academics, for the sustainable use of natural resources in the Pacific region; cooperation of

46 int. geoscience orgs; sponsors conferences, meetings and researchincl. the Circum-Pacific Map Project, and int. training schools; Pres. H. GARY GREENE (USA); Chair. DAVID G. HOWELL (USA); Sec. EDWARD SAADE (USA).

Commonwealth Geographical Bureau: c/o Department of Geography, University of Otago, POB 56, Dunedin, New Zealand; tel. (3) 479-8774; fax (3) 479-9037; e-mail j.a .binns@geography.otago.ac.nz; internet www .commonwealthgeography.org; f. 1968; encourages the development of geographical research and study, particularly in developing Commonwealth countries, through assistance to the profession; regional seminars, assistance for study visits; a board of management represents 5 regions: Asia, Africa, Americas, Australasia and Europe

Commonwealth Science Council: Commonwealth Secretariat, Marlborough House, Pall Mall, London, SW1Y 5HX, UK; tel. (20) 7747-6221; fax (20) 7839-6174; e-mail science@commonwealth.int; f. 1975; an intergovernmental body, the Science and Technology Division of the Commonwealth Secretariat; seeks to increase the capability of Commonwealth countries to apply science and technology for social, economic and environmental development; conducts no inhouse research, but provides support for putting into practice the results of research carried out by others and helps to produce knowledge required to solve developmental problems through research; programmes are: biological and genetic resources, renewable energy, water and mineral resources, advanced technologies; runs a fellowship scheme providing short-term placements at training programmes or research institutes in developing countries; runs a travel-grant scheme to help scientists from member countries attend scientific meetings; 37 mems; Sec. Dr KEN LUM; publs *Commonwealth Scientist* (4 a year), *Report* (4 a year).

Council for International Congresses of Entomology/Comité Permanent des Congrès Internationaux d'Entomologie: c/o Dr James Ridsdill-Smith, CRC for National Plant Security, LPO Box 5012, Bruce, ACT 2617, Australia; tel. (2) 6201-2882; fax (2) 6201-5067; e-mail james .ridsdill-smith@csiro.au; internet www .ice2008.org.za; f. 1910 to act as a link between periodic congresses and to arrange the venue for each congress; the committee is also the entomology section of the International Union of Biological Sciences; Chair. Dr HARI SHARMA (India); Sec. Dr JAMES RIDSDILL-SMITH (Australia).

European Atomic Energy Community (Euratom): 200 rue de la Loi, 1049 Brussels, Belgium; tel. (2) 235-11-11; internet euratom .org; based on a formal treaty signed in Rome, Italy in March 1957, at the same time as the treaty establishing the EEC; aims to integrate the programmes of member states for the peaceful uses of atomic energy; since 1967 combined with the ECSC and EEC

European Centre for Medium-Range Weather Forecasts: Shinfield Park, Reading, Berks., RG2 9AX, United Kingdom; tel. (118) 949-9000; fax (118) 986-9450; e-mail ecmwf-director@ecmwf.int; internet www .ecmwf.int; f. 1975; aims include the development of numerical methods for medium-range weather forecasting, the collection and storage of data and products, providing operational forecasts to the mem. states and cooperating states, and providing advanced training in numerical weather prediction; 18 mem. states; Dir D. MARBOUTY.

European Geosciences Union: Max-Planck-Str. 13, 37191 Katlenburg-Lindau,

Germany; tel. (49) 5556-1440; fax (49) 5556-4709; e-mail egu@copernicus.org; internet www.copernicus.org/egu; f. 2002 by merger of the European Geophysical Society and the European Union of Geosciences; promotes the sciences of the Earth and its environment and of planetary and space sciences, and encourages cooperation between scientists; organizes annual General Assemblies, topical conferences and short courses; Pres. PETER FABIAN; Exec. Sec. Dr ARNE K. RICHTER; publs *Advances in Geosciences, Advances in Radio Science, Annales Geophysicae, Astrophysics and Space Sciences Transactions, Atmospheric Chemistry and Physics, Atmospheric Chemistry and Physics Discussions, Biogeosciences, Geophysical Research Abstracts, Hydrology and Earth System Sciences, Hydrology and Earth System Sciences Discussions, Natural Hazards and Earth System Sciences, Nonlinear Processes in Geophysics, Ocean Science, Ocean Science Discussions, Social Geography.*

European Institute of Environmental Medicine: Odos Kerasundos 2, Athens 162 32, Greece; tel. 210-7628460; fax 210-7628675; e-mail eiem@otonet.gr; f. 1970 to bring together scientists and scholars with cross-sectional background and research interests and to conduct multi-disciplinary educational and research activities studying the interactions between man and his environment (natural and technical); Dir Prof. C. K. KYRILOV.

European Molecular Biology Laboratory: Meyerhofstr. 1, 69117 Heidelberg, Germany; tel. (6221) 3870; fax (6221) 3878306; e-mail info@embl.de; internet www.embl-heidelberg.de; f. 1974; financed by 15 European states and Israel; basic research in molecular biology; outstations in Hinxton, nr Cambridge (European Bioinformatics Institute), Grenoble, Hamburg and Monterotondo (Rome); library of 22,200 vols; Dir-Gen. Prof. FOTIS C. KAFATOS; publs *Handbook of Statistics* (1 a Year), *Research Report* (1 a Year).

European Molecular Biology Organization (EMBO)/Organisation Européenne de Biologie Moléculaire: Postfach 1022.40, 69012 Heidelberg, Germany; located at: Meyerhofstr. 1, 69117 Heidelberg, Germany; tel. (6221) 88910; fax (6221) 8891200; e-mail embo@embo.org; internet www.embo.org; f. 1964 to promote excellence in the molecular life sciences in Europe; awards research fellowships; sponsors scientific meetings; awards installation grants to build scientific capacity in selected countries; provides opportunities for career development to young group leaders in the EMBO Young Investigator Programme; offers fellowships and training for scientists outside Europe; offers scientific advice on European science policy; provides quality reviews of national science programmes, and information and online services for life sciences communities; 1,200 mems; Exec. Dir Prof. FRANK GANNON; publs *EMBO Journal* (24 a year), *EMBO Reports* (12 a year), *Molecular Systems Biology* (online, 26 a year).

European Organization for Nuclear Research (CERN)/Organisation Européenne pour la Recherche Nucléaire: 1211 Geneva 23, Switzerland; tel. 227676111; fax 227676555; e-mail cern.reception@cern.ch; internet www.cern.ch; f. 1954; mems: Austria, Belgium, Czech Republic, Denmark, Finland, France, Germany, Greece, Hungary, Italy, Netherlands, Norway, Poland, Portugal, Slovakia, Spain, Sweden, Switzerland and UK; carries out and coordinates research on fundamental particles; research is undertaken mostly by teams of visiting scientists who remain based at their parent instns; in general, the staff is drawn from mem. states, but scientists from any country may be invited to spend a limited period at CERN; research is carried out with the aid of a proton synchrotron of 28 GeV (the PS), the super proton synchrotron (SPS) of 450 GeV and the 27-km LEP electron-positron collider; Pres. of the Council Prof. ENZO IAROCCI; Dir-Gen. Dr ROBERT AYMAR; publ. *CERN Courier* (12 a year, in English and French).

European Physical Society: 6 rue des Frères Lumière, 68060 Mulhouse Cedex, France; tel. 3-89-32-94-40; fax 3-89-32-94-49; internet www.eps.org; f. 1968; aims to promote the advancement of physics in Europe and neighbouring countries by all suitable means; 41 nat. mem. orgs; 6,500 individual mems; 80 assoc. mems; Sec.-Gen. DAVID LEE; publs *European Journal of Physics* (6 a year), *Europhysics News* (6 a year).

European Science Foundation: 1 quai Lezay-Marnésia, 67080 Strasbourg Cedex, France; tel. 3-88-76-71-00; fax 3-88-37-05-32; f. 1974 to promote research in all branches of fundamental science and the humanities; to advance cooperation in European research; to examine and advise on research and science policy issues; to promote the mobility of research workers and the free flow of information and ideas; to facilitate cooperation in the planning and use of research facilities; to plan and manage collaborative research activities; mems: 76 research-funding agencies from 29 countries; Pres. Dr REINDER VAN DUINEN (Netherlands); CEO BERTIL ANDERSSON; publ. *ESF Communications* (2 a year).

European Southern Observatory/ Organisation Européenne pour des Recherches Astronomiques dans l'Hémisphère Austral: Karl-Schwarzschild-Str. 2, 85748 Garching bei München, Germany; tel. (89) 320060; fax (89) 3202362; internet www.eso.org; f. 1962; aims: astronomical research in the southern hemisphere, construction and operation of an international observatory in Chile (see under Chile), fostering European cooperation in astronomy; mems: govts of Belgium, Denmark, France, Germany, Italy, The Netherlands, Portugal, Sweden, Switzerland; Dir-Gen. Prof. TIM DE ZEEUW; publ. *The Messenger*.

European Space Agency: 8–10 rue Mario Nikis, 75738 Paris Cedex 15, France; tel. 1-53-69-76-54; fax 1-53-69-75-60; e-mail contact@esa.int; internet www.esa.int; f. 1964, name changed 1975, following merger of ELDO and ESRO, to provide for, and to promote collaboration among, European states in space research and technology and their space applications exclusively for peaceful purposes; provides scientific agencies of the mem. countries with the necessary technical facilities for the carrying out of space experiments, ranging from the study of the near terrestrial environment to that of stellar astronomy; also responsible for a European programme of application satellite projects, including telecommunications and meteorology, also for Spacelab and Ariane Launcher; supports the following establishments: European Space Research and Technology Centre (ESTEC), Noordwijk, Netherlands; European Space Operations Centre (ESOC), Darmstadt, Germany; European Space Research Institute (ESRIN), Frascati, Italy; European Astronaut Centre (EAC), Cologne, Germany; mems: Austria, Belgium, Denmark, Finland, France, Germany, Greece, Ireland, Italy, Luxembourg, Netherlands, Norway, Portugal, Spain, Sweden, Switzerland and UK; Canada is linked by a special cooperation agreement; library: library (ESTEC) of 48,000 vols, 1m. microfiche, 42,000 reports and standards; Dir-Gen.

JEAN-JACQUES JORDAIN (France); publs *Bulletin*, *Connect* (2 a year), *Eurocomp* (1 a year), conference proceedings, scientific and technical reports.

Federation of Arab Scientific Research Councils: Alawayh, POB 13027, Baghdad, Iraq; tel. (1) 5372832; fax (1) 8853923; e-mail fasrc@uruklink.net; f. 1976 to strengthen scientific and technological cooperation and coordination between Arab countries; holds conferences, seminars, workshops and training courses; publishes Directory of Arab Scientific Research Institutions; 15 mem. countries; Sec.-Gen. Dr TAHA TAYIH AL-NAIMI; publs *Computer Research*, *Proceedings of Scientific Activities*.

Federation of Asian Scientific Academies and Societies (FASAS): c/o Academy of Sciences Malaysia, 902-4 Jalan Tun Ismail, 50480 Kuala Lumpur, Malaysia; tel. (3) 2694-9898; fax (3) 2694-5858; e-mail nasa@akademisains.gov.my; internet www .fasas.com.my; f. 1984 to promote regional cooperation and national and regional self-reliance in science and technology by organizing meetings, training and research programmes, and encouraging exchange of scientists and information; 16 mems (national scientific academies and societies in Afghanistan, Australia, Bangladesh, People's Republic of China, India, Republic of Korea, Malaysia, Nepal, New Zealand, Pakistan, Philippines, Singapore, Sri Lanka, Thailand; Pres. Prof. LEO TAN (Singapore); Sec. Prof. TING-KUEH SOON (Malaysia).

Foundation for International Scientific Coordination/Fondation 'Pour la Science', Centre international de Synthèse: Acta—UMS 2267 CNRS, 4 rue Lhomond, 75005 Paris, France; tel. 1-55-42-83-13; fax 1-55-42-83-19; e-mail fondation.pourlascience .cis@ens.fr; internet www.ehess.fr/acta/ synthese; f. 1924; Founder HENRI BERR; Co-Dirs MICHAEL BLAY, ÉRIC BRIAN; publs *Revue de Synthèse* (4 a year), *Revue d'Histoire des Sciences* (4 a year), *Semaines de Synthèse*, *L'Evolution de l'Humanité*.

Institute of Mathematical Statistics: POB 22718, Beachwood, OH 44122, USA; tel. (216) 295-2340; fax (216) 295-5661; e-mail ims@imstat.org; internet www.imstat .org; f. 1935; 4,000 mems; Pres. THOMAS G. KURTZ; Exec. Sec. ELYSE GUSTAFSON; publs *Annals of Applied Probability* (4 a year), *Annals of Probability*, *Annals of Statistics* (6 a year), *CBMS Regional Conference Series in Probability and Statistics*, *IMS Bulletin* (6 a year), *IMS Lecture Notes—Monograph Series*, *Statistical Science*.

Intergovernmental Oceanographic Commission (IOC)/Commission Océanographique Intergouvernementale: c/o UNESCO, 1 rue Miollis, 75015 Paris, France; tel. 1-45-68-39-84; fax 1-45-68-58-10; internet ioc.unesco.org; f. 1960 to promote scientific investigation with a view to learning more about the nature and resources of the oceans through the concerted action of its members; mems: 125 governments; Chair. Dr DAVID T. PUGH (UK); Exec. Sec. Dr PATRICIO BERNAL (Chile); publs *IOC Manuals and Guides*, *IOC Technical Series*, *IOC Training Course Reports* (irregular), *IOC Workshop Reports*, *Summary Reports of Sessions*.

International Academy of Astronautics (IAA)/Académie Internationale d'Astronautique: BP 1268-16, 75766 Paris Cedex 16, France; 6 rue Galilée, 75116 Paris, France; tel. 1-47-23-82-15; fax 1-47-23-82-16; internet www.iaanet.org; f. 1960; aims to foster the development of astronautics for peaceful purposes, recognizing individuals who have distinguished themselves in the field, and provides a programme through

which mems can contribute to int. cooperation; liaises with nat. academies of science; developing a multilingual (20 languages) Database; maintains the following cttees: Space Sciences, Int. Space Plans and Policies, Life Sciences, Benefits to Society from Space Activities, Economics of Space Operations, Interstellar Space Exploration, Search for Extraterrestrial Intelligence, Safety and Rescue, Space and Environmental Change, History of Astronautics, Scientific Legal Liaison; mems: 975 in 56 countries; Pres. Prof. E. C. STONE (USA); Vice-Pres Prof. H. CURIEN (France), Prof. K. KASTURIRANGAN (India), Dr Y. N. KOPTEV (Russia), Dr H. MATSUO (Japan); Sec.-Gen. Dr J. M. CONTANT (France); publs *Acta Astronautica* (12 a year), *Proceedings of Symposia*.

International Association for Mathematics and Computers in Simulation/ Association Internationale pour les Mathématiques et Calculateurs en Simulation: c/o Dept of Computer Science, Hill Center, Busch Campus, Rutgers University, New Brunswick, NJ 08903, USA; internet www.research.rutgers.edu/~imacs; f. 1955 to advance the study of general methods for modelling and computer simulation of dynamic systems; Pres. R. VICHNEVETSKY (USA); Sec.-Gen. R. BEAUWENS (Belgium); publs *Applied Numerical Mathematics* (6 a year), *Mathematics and Computers in Simulation*.

International Association for Plant Physiology (IAPP): USDA—URS, Plant Biology Dept, Univeristy of Illinois, 190 ERML, 1201 W. Gregory Drive Urbana, Illinois, USA 61801-3838; e-mail d-ort@life .uiuc.edu; f. 1955 to promote the development of plant physiology at the international level, especially collaboration between developed and developing nations, through international congresses and symposia and by the publication of plant physiology matters and the promotion of cooperation between national and international associations and scientific journals; represents plant physiologists on the IUBS; mems: 40 national societies of plant physiology and related international groups; Pres. Dr DONALD ORT; Sec.-Gen. Dr D. GRAHAM.

International Association for Plant Taxonomy/Association Internationale pour la Taxonomie Végétale: Bureau for Plant Taxonomy and Nomenclature, Institute of Botany, Univ. of Vienna, Rennweg 14, 1030 Vienna, Austria; tel. (1) 427754098; fax (1) 427754099; e-mail office@iapt-taxon.org; internet www.iapt-taxon.org; f. 1950 to promote the development of plant taxonomy and encourage contacts between people and institutes interested in this work; mems: institutes and individuals in 87 countries; Exec. Sec. Dr ALESSANDRA RICCIUTI LAMONEA (Austria); publs *Regnum vegetabile* (irregular), *Taxon* (24 a year).

International Association for the Physical Sciences of the Ocean (IAPSO)/ Association Internationale des Sciences Physiques de l'Océan: POB 820440, Vicksburg, MS 39182-0440, USA; tel. (601) 636-1363; fax (601) 629-9640; internet www .olympus.net/iapso; f. 1919 to promote the study of scientific problems relating to the oceans, chiefly by the aid of mathematics, physics and chemistry; to initiate, facilitate and coordinate research; to provide for discussion, comparison and publication; 81 mem. states; Pres. Prof. SHIRO IMAWAKI (Japan); Sec.-Gen. Dr FRED E. CAMFIELD (USA); publs *Procès-Verbaux* (every 2–4 years), *Publications Scientifiques* (irregular).

International Association for Vegetation Science/Association Internationale pour l'Etude de la Végétation: c/o Dr J. H. J. Schaminée, Alterra, Green World Research, Postbus 47, 6700 AA Wageningen, Netherlands; tel. (317) 477914; fax (317) 424988; e-mail joop.schaminee@wur.nl; internet www.iavs.org; f. 1937; aims for the development of phytosociology; 1,300 mems; Pres. Prof. E. O. Box (USA); Sec. Dr J. H. J. Schaminée; publs *Applied Vegetation Science, Journal of Vegetation Science, Phytocoenologia*.

International Association of Biological Oceanography: Leigh Marine Laboratory, Univ. of Auckland, POB 349, Warkworth, New Zealand; e-mail m.costello@auckland.ac.nz; internet www.iabo.org; f. 1966 to promote the study of the biology of the sea; attached to Int. Union of Biological Sciences; Pres. Dr Annalies Pierrot-Bults (Netherlands); Sec.-Gen. Dr Mark J. Costello (New Zealand).

International Association of Geodesy/Association Internationale de Géodésie: University of Copenhagen, Dept of Geophysics, Juliane Maries Vej 30, 2100 Copenhagen Ø, Denmark; tel. 35-32-06-00; fax 35-36-53-57; e-mail iag@gfy.ku.dk; internet www.gfy.ku.dk/~iag; f. 1922 to promote the study of all scientific problems of geodesy and encourage geodetic research; to promote and coordinate int. cooperation in this field; to publish results; a mem. asscn of IUGG; mems: national cttees in 78 countries; Pres. Prof. G. Beutler; Sec.-Gen. C. C. Tscherning; publs *Journal of Geodesy* (12 a year), *Travaux de l'AIG* (every 4 years).

International Association of Geomagnetism and Aeronomy (IAGA)/Association Internationale de Géomagnétisme et d'Aéronomie: c/o Prof. Mioara Mandea, Université Paris Diderot, Institut de Physique du Globe de Paris Géophysique spatiale et planétaire, Bâtiment Lamarck Case 7011, 5 rue Thomas Mann, 75205. Paris Cedex 13, France; tel. 1-57-27-84-84; fax 1-57-27-84-82; e-mail iaga_sg@gfz-potsdam.de; f. 1919; study of magnetism and aeronomy of the earth and other bodies of the solar system, and of the interplanetary medium and its interaction with these bodies; mems: countries that adhere to the Int. Union of Geodesy and Geophysics are eligible; Pres. Dr Eigil Friis-Christensen (Denmark); Sec.-Gen. Prof. Mioara Mandea (France); publs *IAGA Bulletins* (irregular), *Geomagnetic Data* (1 a year), *IAGA News* (1 a year).

International Association of Hydrological Sciences/Association Internationale des Sciences Hydrologiques: c/o Dr Pierre Hubert, Ecole des Mines de Paris, 35 rue St Honoré, 77305 Fontainebleau, France; tel. 1-64-69-47-40; fax 1-64-69-47-03; e-mail iahs@ensmp.fr; internet www.iahs.info; f. 1922; part of IUGG; aims to promote the study of hydrology, to provide means for discussion, comparison and publication of research findings, and the initiation and coordination of research requiring int. cooperation; organizes general assemblies, symposia, etc.; 84 national cttees; Pres. Prof. Kuniyoshi Takeuchi (Japan); Sec.-Gen. Dr Pierre Hubert (France); publ. *Hydrological Sciences Journal* (6 a year).

International Association of Meteorology and Atmospheric Sciences (IAMAS)/Association Internationale de Météorologie et de Sciences de l'Atmosphère: c/o Dr Hans Volkert, Institut für Physik der Atmosphäre, Deutsches Zentrum für Luft- und Raumfahrt, DLR-Oberpfaffenhofen, 82234 Wessling, Germany; tel. (8153) 28-2570; fax (8153) 28-1841; e-mail hans.volkert@dlr.de; internet www.iamas.org; f. 1919 to organize research symposia and coordinate research in atmospheric science fields; an Association of the International Union of Geodesy and Geophysics; Pres. Prof. Wu, Guoxiong (China); Sec.-Gen. Dr Hans Volkert (Germany); publ. *IAMAP Assembly Proceedings* (every 2 years).

International Association of Sedimentologists: c/o Dr José-Pedro Calvo, Dpto Petrología y Geoquímica, Fac. Ciencias Geológicas, Univ. Complutense, 28040 Madrid, Spain; tel. 91-394-49-05; fax 91-544-25-35; e-mail info@iasnet.org; internet www.iasnet.org; f. 1952; 2,000 mems; Pres. Prof. Finn Surlyk (Denmark); Sec.-Gen. Dr José-Pedro Calvo; publ. *Sedimentology* (6 a year).

International Society of Limnology/Association internationale de Limnologie Théorique et Appliquée: c/o Denise L. Johnson, SIL Business Services Coordinator, Univ. of NC, Chapel Hill, NC 27599-7431, USA; located at: 135 Dauer Dr., ESE, 148 Rosenau Hall, Chapel Hill, NC 27599-7431 USA; tel. (336) 376-9362; fax (336) 376-8825; e-mail denisej@email.unc.edu; internet www.limnology.org; f. 1922; 3,100 mems; Pres. Prof. Dr Brian Moss (UK); Gen. Sec. and Treas. Prof. Dr Morten Søndergaard (Denmark); publs *Mitteilungen, Verhandlungen*.

International Association of Volcanology and Chemistry of the Earth's Interior (IAVCEI)/Association Internationale de Volcanologie et de Chimie de l'Intérieur de la Terre: c/o S. R. McNutt, Alaska Volcano Observatory, Geophysical Institute UAF, POB 757320, Fairbanks, AK 99775, USA; tel. (907) 474-7131; fax (907) 474-5618; e-mail steve@giseis.alaska.edu; internet www.iavcei.org; f. 1919 to promote scientific investigation and discussion on volcanology and in those aspects of petrology and geochemistry relating to the composition of the interior of the Earth; holds scientific general assemblies; sponsors workshops; participates in IUGG general assemblies; 840 individual mems and nat. correspondents; Pres. Prof. Oded Navon (Israel); Sec.-Gen. Prof. Stephen R. McNutt (USA); publs *Bulletin of Volcanology, Catalogue of the Active Volcanoes of the World, Proceedings in Volcanology*.

International Association of Wood Anatomists/Association Internationale des Anatomistes du Bois: c/o Nationaal Herbarium Nederland, Universiteit Leiden Branch, POB 9514, 2300 RA Leiden, Netherlands; fax (71) 527-3511; internet www.kuleuven.ac.be/bio/sys/iawa; f. 1931 for the purpose of study, documentation and exchange of information on the anatomy of wood; 600 mems in 60 countries; Exec. Sec. Dr Regis B. Miller (USA); publ. *IAWA Journal* (4 a year).

International Astronautical Federation (IAF)/Fédération Internationale d'Astronautique: 8–10 rue Mario-Nikis, 75015 Paris, France; located at: 94 bis ave de Suffren, 75015 Paris, France; tel. 1-45-67-42-60; fax 1-42-73-21-20; internet www.iafastro.com; f. 1950 to foster the development of astronautics for peaceful purposes at nat. and int. levels; the IAF created the International Academy of Astronautics (IAA), the International Institute of Space Law (IISL) (for information on these bodies, see elsewhere in this chapter), and cttees on activities and membership; Allan D. Emil Award, finances, publications, liaison with int. organizations and developing nations, education, student activities, SYRE, Solar Sail, astrodynamics, Earth observations, satellite communications, natural disaster reduction, life sciences, microgravity science and processes, space exploration, space power, space propulsion, space transportation, space stations, space systems, and materials and structures; annual student awards; mems: 137 nat. astronautical societies in 45 countries; Pres. James V. Zimmerman (USA); Vice-Pres Mukund Rao (India), Stuart W. Thomson (USA), Yuan Jia-Jun (China), Robert C. Parkinson (UK), Yasunori Matogawa (Japan), Victor Reglero (Spain), Anne-Marie Mainguy (France), Virendra K. Jha (Canada), Anatoly I. Grigoriev (Russia), Klaus Berge (Germany); Exec. Dir Yves Beguin; publ. *Proceedings* (of Annual Congresses).

International Atomic Energy Agency (IAEA): Vienna International Centre, POB 100, 1400 Vienna, Austria; tel. (1) 2600; fax (1) 26007; e-mail official.mail@iaea.org; internet www.iaea.org; f. 1956 by 80 nations; the Board of Govs, consisting of 35 mems designated or elected on a regional basis, carries out the functions of the Agency; aims: the contribution of atomic energy to peace, health and prosperity worldwide; to provide materials, services, equipment and facilities; to foster the exchange of scientific and technical information on peaceful uses of atomic energy; to encourage the exchange and training of scientists and experts in the field of atomic energy; to establish health and safety standards and to prepare a comprehensive set of safety codes and guides covering all aspects of building and operating nuclear power plants; establishes safeguards against the military use of civil nuclear materials or equipment provided through the Agency and applies these safeguards in accordance with the Treaty on the Non-Proliferation of Nuclear Weapons, the Treaty for the Prohibition of Nuclear Weapons in Latin America, the Treaty for a Nuclear-Weapon-Free Zone in Africa, the Treaty for a Nuclear-Weapon-Free Zone in South-East Asia and the Treaty of the South Pacific Nuclear-Free Zone; 146 mem. states; library of 80,000 vols, 708,000 technical reports in microfiche and hardcopy, 3,569 current periodicals, 350 audiovisual items, 1.26m. documents; microcard clearing-house; the Int. Nuclear Information System (INIS) provides worldwide coverage of literature on all aspects of peaceful uses of nuclear energy; the IAEA Energy and Economic Data Bank provides information on the world's energy situation and related economic parameters, based on data obtained from mem. states; Dir-Gen. Dr Mohamed Elbaradei; publs *Atomic Energy Review, INIS Atomindex* (2 a month), *IAEA Bulletin* (2 a year, printed and online, www.iaea.org/publications/magazines/bulletin/bull501), *INIS Database* (www.iaea.org/inisnkm/inis/basis/subscr0.htm), *Meetings on Atomic Energy* (4 a year, online, www.iaea.org/cgi-bin/maeps.page.pl/tableofcontents.htm), *Nuclear Fusion* (12 a year).

International Biometric Society (IBS)/Société Internationale de Biométrie: 1444 I St, NW, Suite 700, Washington, DC 20005, USA; tel. (202) 712-9049; fax (202) 216-9646; e-mail ibs@bostrom.com; internet www.tibs.org; f. 1947; dedicated to the development and application of statistical and mathematical theory and methods in the biosciences; 19 regional organizations and 19 national groups; affiliated to the International Statistical Institute and the World Health Organization, and constitutes the section of Biometry of the International Union of Biological Sciences; mems: 5,200 in more than 70 countries; Pres. Geert Molenberghs (Belgium); Exec. Dir Claire Shanley (USA); publs *Biometrics* (4 a year), *Biometric Bulletin* (4 a year), *Journal of*

Agricultural, Biological and Environmental Statistics (4 a year).

International Bureau of Weights and Measures/Bureau International des Poids et Mesures: Pavillon de Breteuil, 92312 Sèvres Cedex, France; tel. (1) 45-07-70-70; fax (1) 45-34-20-21; internet www .bipm.org; f. 1875 for the preservation of standards of the Int. System of Units (SI) and worldwide unification of the units of measurement; determination of nat. standards; precision measurements in physics; establishment of the int. atomic time-scale; 52 mem. states; Pres. Prof. Dr E. O. GÖBEL (Germany); Sec. Dr R. KAARLS (Netherlands); Dir Prof. A. J. WALLARD; Deputy Dir Prof. Dr M. KÜHNE (Germany); publs *Comptes Rendus des Conférences Générales* (every 4 years), *Metrologia*, *Procès-Verbaux* (1 a year), *Sessions des dix Comités consultatifs auprès du Comité International* (irregular).

International Centre of Insect Physiology and Ecology: POB 30772-00100, Nairobi, Kenya; tel. (20) 861686; fax (20) 860110; internet www.icipe.org; f. 1970 to develop, through research, plant-borne, human and animal disease management and control strategies, and to promote research and the conservation of arthropods; library of 7,500 vols, 3,500 volumes bound periodicals, 200 periodicals; Chair. Prof. PETER ESBJERG (Denmark); Dir-Gen. and CEO Dr HANS R. HERREN; publ. *Insect Science and Its Application*.

International Commission for Optics (ICO)/Commission Internationale d'Optique: c/o Angela M. Guzman, Research Assoc. Prof. Physics, Dept Florida Atlantic Univ. 777 Glades Rd, 33431 Boca Raton, USA; tel. (561) 297-1310; fax (561) 297-2662; e-mail angela.guzman@fau.edu; internet www.ico-optics.org; f. 1948 to contribute on an int. basis to the progress of theoretical and instrumental optics and its application, through conferences, colloquia, summer schools, etc., and to promote int. agreement on nomenclature, specifications, etc.; 51 mem countries, 6 Int. Soc. mems; Pres. Prof. MARÍA L. CALVO (Spain); Sec.-Gen. Prof. ANGELA GUZMAN (USA).

International Commission for the Scientific Exploration of the Mediterranean Sea/Commission Internationale pour l'Exploration Scientifique de la Mer Méditerranée (CIESM): 16 blvd de Suisse, 98000 Monaco; tel. 93-30-38-79; fax 92-16-11-95; e-mail ciesm@ciesm.org; internet www.ciesm.org; f. 1919 for scientific exploration of the Mediterranean Sea, the study of physical and chemical oceanography, marine geosciences, living resources, marine biodiversity, marine biotechnology, coastal environment; 23 mem. states, 2,500 individual mems; Pres. HSH The Prince ALBERT OF MONACO; Dir-Gen. Prof. FRÉDÉRIC BRIAND; Sec.-Gen. Prof. FRANÇOIS DOUMENGE; publ. *Congress Proceedings* (every 3 years).

International Commission on Zoological Nomenclature/Commission Internationale de Nomenclature Zoologique: c/o The Natural History Museum, Cromwell Rd, London, SW7 5BD, UK; tel. (20) 7942-5653; e-mail iczn@nhm.ac.uk; internet www.iczn .org; f. 1895; the Commission, formerly a standing organ of the Int. Zoological Congresses, now reports to the Gen. Assembly of IUBS; the Commission has judicial powers to determine all matters relating to the interpretation of the *International Code of Zoological Nomenclature* and also plenary powers to suspend the operation of the *Code* where strict application would lead to confusion and instability of nomenclature; the Commission is responsible also for maintain-

ing and developing the *Official Lists of Names in Zoology* and the *Official Indexes of Rejected and Invalid Names in Zoology*; Pres. Prof. D. J. BROTHERS (South Africa); Exec. Sec. Dr E. MICHEL (UK); publ. *Bulletin of Zoological Nomenclature*.

International Confederation for Thermal Analysis and Calorimetry (ICTAC): c/o Prof. M. E. Brown, Chemistry Dept, Rhodes University, Grahamstown 6140, South Africa; tel. (46) 6038254; fax (46) 6225109; e-mail m.brown@ru.ac.za; internet www.ictac.org; f. 1968; 600 mems in 40 countries, 5,000 affiliate mems in 20 affiliated regional and national societies and groups; coordinates these groups and supplies information on their scientific activities; supports national regional seminars and symposia; quadrennial int. conference; Pres. Dr JEAN ROUQUEROL (France); Sec. Prof. MICHAEL E. BROWN (South Africa); publ. *News* (2 a year).

International Council for the Exploration of the Sea (ICES)/Conseil International pour l'Exploration de la Mer: H. C. Andersens Blvd 44-46, 1553 Copenhagen V, Denmark; tel. 33-38-67-00; fax 33-93-42-15; e-mail info@ices.dk; internet www.ices .dk; f. 1902 to promote and encourage research and investigations for the study of the sea, particularly those related to its living resources; area of interest: the Atlantic Ocean (primarily the N Atlantic) and its adjacent seas; mems: 20 nat. govts; Pres. MICHAEL M. SINCLAIR (Canada); Gen. Sec. GERD HUBOLD; publs *ICES Cooperative Research Reports*, *ICES Fisheries Statistics*, *ICES Journal of Marine Science*, *ICES Marine Science Symposia*, *ICES Techniques in Marine Environmental Sciences*, *Identification Leaflets for Diseases and Parasites of Fish and Shellfish*, *Identification Leaflets for Plankton*, *ICES Insight*.

International Earth Rotation and Reference Systems Service (IERS): Bundesamt für Kartographie und Geodäsie, Richard-Strauss-Allee 11, 60598 Frankfurt am Main, Germany; tel. (69) 6333273; fax (69) 6333425; internet www.iers.org; f. 1988 to replace Int. Polar Motion Service and the earth-rotation section of the Int. Time Bureau; organized jtly by the IAU and IUGG; responsible for defining and maintaining a conventional terrestrial reference system based on observing stations that use the high-precision techniques of space geodesy; defining and maintaining a conventional celestial reference system based on extragalactic radio sources, and relating it to other celestial reference systems; determining the earth orientation parameters connecting these systems; organizing operational activities for observation and data analysis, collecting and archiving appropriate data and results, and disseminating the results; Dir of Central Bureau Dr BERND RICHTER; publ. *IERS Technical Notes*.

International Federation for Cell Biology/Fédération Internationale de Biologie Cellulaire: c/o Dr Denys Wheatley, Hilton College, MG7, Hilton Pl., Aberdeen, AB24 4FA, UK; tel. (1224) 274173; e-mail pat028@abdn.ac.uk; internet www.ifcbiol .org; f. 1972; sponsors an int. congress every 4 years; Pres. Dr CHENG-WEN WU (China (Taiwan)); Sec.-Gen. Dr DENYS WHEATLEY; publ. *Cell Biology International*.

International Federation of Societies for Microscopy/Fédération Internationale des Sociétés de Microscopie: c/o Prof. C. Barry Carter, Dept of Chemical, Materials and Biomolecular Engineering, 191 Auditorium Rd, Unit 3222, Univ. of Connecticut, Storrs, CT 06269-3222, USA; tel. (860) 486-

4020; fax (860) 486-2959; e-mail cbcarter@ engr.uconn.edu; internet www.ifsm.umn .edu; f. 1955; mems: representative orgs of 39 countries; Pres. Prof. D. COCKAYNE; Sec. Prof. C. B. CARTER.

International Food Information Service: IFIS Publishing, Lane End House, Shinfield, Reading, RG2 9BB, UK; tel. (118) 988-3895; fax (118) 988-5065; e-mail ifis@ifis .org; internet www.ifis.org; f. 1968; governed by CAB International (UK), Institute of Food Technologists (USA), Landbouwpublikaties en Landbouwdocumentatie (Netherlands) and the Bundesministerium für Landwirtschaft Ernährung und Forsten (represented by Deutsche Landwirtschafts-Gesellschaft eV) in Germany, for the promotion of education and research in food science and technology; Gen. Man. J. SELMAN; publs *Food Science Profiles* (12 a year, in print and on diskette), *Food Science and Technology Abstracts* (12 a year, in print, online, CD-ROM), *Viticulture and Enology Abstracts* (4 a year, in print and online).

International Foundation of the High-Altitude Research Stations, Jungfraujoch and Gornergrat/Fondation internationale des stations scientifiques du Jungfraujoch et du Gornergrat: 5 Sidlerstr, 3012 Bern, Switzerland; tel. 316314052; fax 316314405; e-mail louise .wilson@phim.unibe.ch; internet www .ifjungo.ch; f. 1931; Dir Prof. E. FLUECKIGER.

International Genetics Federation: c/o GSA 9560 Rockville Pike, Bethesda, MD 20814-3998, USA; tel. (301) 634-7300; fax (301) 634-7310; e-mail smarts@genetics-gsa .org; internet www.intergenetics.org; f. 1968 to encourage understanding, cooperation and friendship among geneticists worldwide and to plan and support int. congresses of genetics; 37 mem. countries; Exec. Dir Dr SHERRY MARTS (USA).

International Geological Congress/Congrès Géologique International: POB 2694 Solli, 0204 Oslo, Norway; e-mail secretariat@ 33igc.org; internet www.33igc.org; f. 1878 to contribute to the advancement of investigations relating to the study of the Earth and other planets, considered from theoretical and practical points of view; the congress is held every 4 years; Pres. Prof. ARNE BJØRLYKKE; Sec.-Gen. Prof. ANDERS SOLHEIM; publs *Extended Abstracts*, *General Proceedings*.

International Glaciological Society: Scott Polar Research Institute, Lensfield Rd, Cambridge, CB2 1ER, UK; tel. (1223) 355974; fax (1223) 354931; e-mail igsoc@ igsoc.org; internet www.igsoc.org; f. 1936 to encourage interest in and encourage research into the scientific and technical problems of snow and ice in all countries; sponsors int. symposia; 850 mems; Pres. Prof. ERIC BRUN (Switzerland); Sec.-Gen. MAGNÚS MÁR MAGNÚSSON; publs *Annals of Glaciology* (4 a year), *Ice* (news bulletin, 3 a year), *Journal of Glaciology* (6 a year).

International Hydrographic Organization (IHO)/Organisation Hydrographique Internationale: BP 445, 4 quai Antoine 1er, Monte Carlo, 98011 MonacoCedex; tel. 93-10-81-00; fax 93-10-81-40; e-mail info@ihb.mc; internet www.iho.int; f. 1921 to establish a close and permanent association among the hydrographic offices of its mem. states; to coordinate the activities of the national hydrographic offices of mem. states in order to render maritime navigation easier and safer; to obtain uniformity in nautical charts and documents; to encourage the adoption of the best methods of conducting hydrographic surveys and improvement in the theory and practice of hydrography; to encourage surveying in those areas where accurate charts are lacking; to encourage coordination of hydrographic surveys with relevant oceanographic activities and to provide for cooperation between the IHO and international organizations in the fields of maritime safety and oceanography; to extend and facilitate the application of oceanographic knowledge for the benefit of navigators; 80 mem. states; library of 750 vols, 100 periodicals, 26,000 charts published by member states; Pres. Vice-Adm. ALEXANDROS MARATOS (Greece); Dirs Capt. ROBERT WARD (Australia), Capt. HUGO GORZIGLIA (Chile); publ. online publications (see website).

International Institute for Applied Systems Analysis (IIASA): Schlossplatz 1, 2361 Laxenburg, Austria; tel. (2236) 807; fax (2236) 71313; e-mail inf@iiasa.ac.at; internet www.iiasa.ac.at; f. 1972 on the initiative of the USA and the USSR; nongovernmental research organization; concerned with global environmental change, global economic and technological transition, systems methods for the analysis of global change; mems: organizations from 16 countries; Chair. Prof. SIMON LEVIN; Dir Prof. DETLOF VON WINTERFELDT; publ. *Options* (4 a year).

International Institute of Seismology and Earthquake Engineering: Building Research Institute, Ministry of Construction, 1 Tatehara, Tsukuba-shi, Ibaraki Prefecture 305-0802, Japan; tel. (298) 79-0680; fax (298) 64-6777; e-mail iisee@kenken.go.jp; internet iisee.kenken.go.jp; f. 1962 to carry out training and research works on seismology and earthquake engineering for the purpose of fostering these research activities in the developing countries, and undertakes survey, research, guidance and analysis of information on earthquakes and their related matters; 12 mems; Dir TOSHIBUMI FUKUTA; publs *Bulletin of IISEE* (1 a year), *Individual Studies by Participants at the IISEE* (1 a year), *Year Book*.

International Mineralogical Association (IMA): c/o Maryse Ohnenstetter, CNRS-CRPG, 15 rue Notre Dame des Pauvres, BP 20, 54501 Vandoeuvre-lès-Nancy Cedex, France; tel. 3-83-59-42-46; fax 3-83-51-17-98; e-mail mohnen@crpg.cnrs-nancy.fr; internet www.ima-mineralogy.org; f. 1958 to further int. cooperation in the mineralogical sciences; organizes meetings and field excursions; maintains 7 commissions and 5 working groups, which examine and report on certain aspects of mineralogical practice; Commission on New Minerals, Nomenclature and Classification regularly reports on the acceptance of new minerals, and on mineral classification; mems: 38 mineralogical societies or groups in 38 countries; Pres. Prof. TAKAMITSU YAMANAKA (Japan); Sec. MARYSE OHNENSTETTER; publ. *World Directories* (Mineralogists; Mineral Collections).

International Organization of Legal Metrology/Organisation Internationale de Métrologie Légale: 11 rue Turgot, 75009 Paris, France; tel. 1 48-78-12-82; fax 1 42-82-17-27; internet www.oiml.org; f. 1955; documentation and information centre on methods of verifying and checking legal measurements, to study ways of harmonization and to determine the general principles of legal metrology; mems: governments of 59 countries and 54 corresp. mems; Pres. ALAN E. JOHNSTON (acting) (Canada); Dir JEAN-FRANÇOIS MAGAÑA; publs *Bulletin* (4 a year), *International Recommendations and Documents*.

International Ornithological Congress/ Congrès International Ornithologique: c/o Prof. Dr Dominique G. Homberger, Dept of Biological Sciences, 202 Life Sciences Bldg, Louisiana State Univ., Baton Rouge, LA 70803-1715, USA; tel. (225) 578-1747; fax (225) 578-2597; internet www.i-o-c.org; f. 1884; int. congress every 4 years; Pres. Prof. Dr JOHN WINGFIELD (USA); Permanent Sec. Prof. Dr DOMINIQUE G. HOMBERGER.

International Palaeontological Association: Palaeontological Institute, Room 121, Lindley Hall, 1475 Jayhawk Blvd, Univ. of Kansas, Lawrence, KA 66045, USA; tel. (785) 864-3338; fax (785) 864-5276; e-mail rmaddocks@uh.edu; internet ipa.geo.ukans .edu; f. 1933 following the meeting of the Int. Geological Congress; affiliated to the Int. Union of Geological Sciences and the Int. Union of Biological Sciences; meets every 4 years at Int. Geological Congress; mems: nat. orgs, research groups; Pres. RICHARD ALDRIDGE (UK); Sec.-Gen. ROSALIE MADDOCKS (USA); publs *Directory of Palaeontologists of the World*, *IPA Fossil Collections of the World*, *Lethaia*.

International Permafrost Association: c/o Dr Hugues Lantuit Alfred, Wegener Institute for Polar and Marine Research, Telefrafenberg A43, 14473 Potsdam, Germany; tel. (331) 288-2162; fax (331) 288-2188; e-mail contact@ipa-permafrost.org; internet ipa-permafrost.org; f. 1983; promotes cooperation among people, nat. and int. orgs engaged in scientific investigation and engineering work on permafrost; outreach activities incl. coordinating int. networks e.g. Global Terrestrial Network for Permafrost (GTN-P) and International Network of Permafrost Observatories (INPO) and Permafrost Young Researchers Network; working groups; 26 mem. countries; Pres. Prof. HANS-W. HUBBERTEN (Germany); Vice-Pres Prof. HANNE H. CHRISTIANSEN (Norway), Prof. ANTONI G. LEWKOWICZ (Canada); publs *Frozen Ground* (Bulletin, 1 a year), contributes a report twice a year in the journal *Permafrost and Periglacial Processes*.

International Society for Human and Animal Mycology (ISHAM)/Société Internationale de Mycologie Humaine et Animale: c/o Dr Malcolm Richardson, Dept of Bacteriology and Immunology, Haartman Institute, University of Helsinki, Haartmaninkatu 3, POB 21, 00014 Helsinki, Finland; tel. (9) 191-26894; fax (9) 26382; e-mail malcolm.richardson@helsinki.fi; internet www.isham.org; f. 1954 to encourage the practice and study of all aspects of medical and veterinary mycology; 990 mems in 74 countries; Pres. Dr DAVID W. WARNOCK (USA); Gen. Sec. Dr MALCOLM RICHARDSON; publs *ISHAM Mycoses Newsletter* (2 a year), *Medical Mycology* (1 a year, in 6 parts).

International Society for Tropical Ecology: c/o Botany Dept, Banaras Hindu University, Varanasi 5, India; tel. (542) 2368399; fax (542) 2368174; f. 1956 to promote and develop the science of ecology in the tropics in the service of man; to publish a journal to aid ecologists in the tropics in communication of their findings; and to hold symposia from time to time to summarize the state of knowledge in particular of general fields of tropical ecology; mems: 500; Pres. Prof. PETER G. MURPHY; Sec. Prof. J. S. SINGH; publ. *Tropical Ecology* (2 a year).

International Society of Biometeorology: c/o Dr Scott Greene, Department of Geography, University of Oklahoma, Norman, OK 73071, USA; tel. (405) 325-4319; fax (405) 447-8455; e-mail jgreene@ou.edu; internet www.biometeorology.org; f. 1956; aims to unite biometeorologists working in the fields of agricultural, botanical, cosmic, entomological, forestry, human, veterinary, zoological and other branches of biometeorology; 243 individual mems in 44 countries; Pres. Dr IAN BURTON (Canada); Sec.-Gen. Dr SCOTT GREENE; publs *Biometeorology Bulletin* (2 a year), *International Journal of Biometeorology* (4 a year), *Progress in Biometeorology*.

International Society of Cryptozoology: POB 43070, Tucson, AZ 85733, USA; located at: Dept of Zoological Collections, International Wildlife Museum, 4800 W. Gates Pass Rd, Tucson, AZ 85745, USA; tel. (520) 884-8369; fax (520) 884-8369; internet www .internationalsocietyofcryptozoology.org; f. 1982 to serve as focal point for the investigation, analysis, publication, and discussion of all matters related to animals of unexpected form or size, or unexpected occurrence in time or space, and to encourage scientific examination of all evidence related to these matters; 800 mems; Pres. Prof. CHRISTINE M. JANIS (acting) (USA); Sec. J. RICHARD GREENWELL (USA); publ. *Cryptozoology* (1 a year).

International Society of Developmental Biologists: c/o Prof. Ben Scheres, Dept of Molecular Cell Biology, Utrecht University, Padualaan 8, 3584 CH Utrecht, Netherlands; tel. (30) 2533133; fax (30) 2513655; internet www1.elsevier.com/homepage/sah/isdb; f. 1911 as Int. Institute of Embryology; to promote study of developmental biology and to promote int. cooperation among researchers in this field; Developmental Biology Section of the Int. Union of Biological Sciences (*q.v.*); mems: 900 individual, 7 corporate; Pres. Prof. EDWARD M. DE ROBERTIS (USA); Int. Sec. Prof. BEN SCHERES.

International Society of Electrochemistry: crue de Sebeillon 9B, 1004 Lausanne, Switzerland; tel. 526323044; fax 216483975; e-mail info@ise-online.org; internet www .ise-online.org; f. 1949 to promote the advance of electrochemical science and technology and to organize the free exchange of information in basic and applied electrochemistry; 2,200 mems in 67 countries; Sec.-Gen. SHARON ROSCOE (Canada); Pres. Prof. Dr R. HILLMAN (UK); publ. *Electrochimica Acta*.

International Society of Exposure Analysis: c/o JSI Research and Training Institute, 44 Farnsworth St, Boston, MA 02210-1211, USA; tel. (617) 482-9485; fax (617) 482-0617; e-mail iseamail@jsi.com; internet www.iseaweb.org; f. 1989 to foster and advance the science of exposure analysis relating to environmental contaminants, both for human populations and ecosystems; holds annual conferences; 400 mems; Pres. Dr CLIFFORD WEISEL; Sec. Dr NATALIE FREEMAN; publ. *Journal of Exposure Science and Environmental Epidemiology* (6 a year).

International Statistical Institute/Institut International de Statistique: Henri Faasdreef 312, POB 24070, 2490 AB The Hague, Netherlands; tel. (70) 3375737; fax (70) 3860025; e-mail isi@cbs.nl; internet isi .cbs.nl; f. 1885; autonomous soc. devoted to the devt and improvement of statistical methods and their application worldwide; provides a forum for the int. exchange of knowledge between mems, and aims to mobilize mems' expertise to play an effective role in the practical solution of global problems; administers int. statistical education programme, incl. statistical education centre in Kolkata, India, and Indian Statistical Institute; conducts statistical research to undertake operational activities in the field of statistics that help to improve the data used in planning and policy formation, to the benefit of the countries concerned; to advance integration of statistics and promote appropriate use of statistical methods in different socio-cultural settings; 2,020 elected mems, also 11 hon., 145 ex-officio, 65 corporate; Pres. JEF TEUGELS (Belgium); Dir Permanent Office ADA VAN KRIMPEN; publs *Bernoulli Journal* (4 a year), *International Statistical Review/Short Book Reviews* (3 a year).

International Union for Quaternary Research (INQUA): c/o Prof. Peter Coxon, Dept of Geography, Museum Bldg, Trinity College, Dublin 2, Ireland; tel. (1) 896-1213; e-mail pcoxon@tcd.ie; internet www.inqua .tcd.ie; f. 1928 Full Scientific Union Member of ICSU; atmospheric sciences, climate change, geography, geology, ocean science, prehistory, palaeontology, palynology, pedology, stratigraphy; 50 mem. countries; Pres. Exec. Comm. Prof. ALLAN CHIVAS (Australia); Sec.-Gen. Prof. PETER COXON; publs *Proceedings of Congresses, Quaternary International.*

International Union for the Study of Social Insects/Union Internationale pour l'Etude des Insectes Sociaux: c/o Dr M. Brown, Dept of Zoology, Trinity College Dublin, Dublin 2, Ireland; e-mail wolfgang.h.kirchner@ruhr-uni-bochum.de; internet www.iussi.org; f. 1951; mems: 500 individuals from 24 countries; comprises 7 regional and national sections; Pres. WALTER TSCHINKEL; Sec.-Gen. WOLFGANG H. KIRCHNER; publs *Congress Proceedings, Insectes sociaux.*

International Union of Speleology/ Union Internationale de Spéléologie: c/o Institute of Karst Research, Titov trg 2, Postojna, Slovenia; internet www.uis-speleo .org; f. 1965; karstology, speleology; 60 mem. countries; Pres. ANDREW JAMES EAVIS (Great Britain); Sec.-Gen. Dr FADI NADER (Lebanon); publs *Bulletin* (1 or 2 a year), *International Journal of Speleology* (1 a year), *Speleological Abstracts* (1 a year).

IUCN, the International Union for Conservation of Nature/UICN, l'Union internationale pour la conservation de la Nature/La UICN, la Unión Internacional para la Conservacion de la Naturaleza: Rue Mauverney 28, 1196 Gland, Switzerland; tel. 229990000; fax 229990002; e-mail mail@iucn.org; internet www.iucn.org; f. 1948 to influence, encourage and assist socs worldwide to conserve the integrity and diversity of nature and to ensure that any use of natural resources is equitable and ecologically sustainable; biodiversity, climate change, energy, human livelihoods and greening the world economy by supporting scientific research, managing field projects all over the world, and bringing governments, NGOs, the UN and companies together to develop policy, laws and best practice; mems: 1,000 mems (govt agencies, NGOs, affiliate orgs and individual scientists) in 160 countries; Pres. ASHOK KHOSLA (India); Dir-Gen. JULIA MARTON-LEFÈVRE (Switzerland); publs *World Conservation* (in English, French and Spanish), *Red Lists:*

Environmental Policy and Law Papers, Best Policy Guidelines.

NORDITA (Nordic Institute for Theoretical Physics): Roslagstullsbacken 23, 106 91 Stockholm, Sweden; tel. (8) 553-788-81; fax (8) 553-784-04; e-mail info@nordita.org; internet www.nordita.org; f. 1957 as the Nordic Institute for Theoretical Atomic Physics in Copenhagen, Denmark, under the Nordic Council of Ministers, moved to Stockholm, Sweden, in 2007; inter-governmental research institute of Denmark, Finland, Iceland, Norway and Sweden; run jointly by the Royal Institute of Technology (KTH) and Stockholm Univ.; research in astrophysics, condensed matter physics and subatomic physics; Dir LÁRUS THORLACIUS.

OECD Nuclear Energy Agency (NEA)/ Agence de l'OCDE pour l'Energie Nucléaire: Le Seine St-Germain, 12 blvd des Îles, 92130 Issy-les-Moulineaux, France; tel. 1-45-24-10-15; fax 1-45-24-11-10; e-mail nea@nea .fr; internet www.nea.fr; f. 1958, name changed 1972; an intergovernmental org. with the primary objective of assisting its mem. countries to maintain and further develop, through int. cooperation, the scientific, technological and legal bases required for a safe, environmentally friendly and economical use of nuclear energy for peaceful purposes, as input to government decisions on nuclear energy policy and to broader OECD policy analyses in areas such as energy and sustainable devt; non-partisan, unbiased source of information, data and analyses, drawing on int. networks of technical experts; mems: 28 countries; Dir-Gen. LUIS ECHÁVARRI; publs *NEA News* (2 a year), *Nuclear Law Bulletin* (2 a year).

Pacific Science Association/Association Scientifique du Pacifique: Bishop Museum, 1525 Bernice St, Honolulu, HI 96817, USA; tel. (808) 848-4124; fax (808) 847-8252; e-mail psa@pacificscience.org; internet www.pacificscience.org; f. 1920 to cooperate in the study of scientific problems relating to the Pacific region; sponsors congresses and inter-congresses; mems: scientists and scientific institutions interested in the Pacific; Pres. Dr R. GERARD WARD (Australia); Exec. Sec. JOHN BURKE BURNETT; publ. *Information Bulletin.*

Pan-American Institute of Geography and History/Instituto Panamericano de Geografía e Historia: Ex-Arzobispado 29, Col. Observatorio, 11860 México, DF, Mexico; tel. (55) 5277-5888; fax (55) 5271-6172; e-mail secretariageneral@ipgh.org; internet www.ipgh.org; f. 1928; to encourage, coordinate and promote the study of cartography, geophysics, geography, history, anthropology, archaeology and other related scientific studies; mems: countries of the Org. of American States; library of 229,062 vols; Sec.-Gen. MSc SANTIAGO BORRERO (Colombia); publs *Boletín de Antropología Americana* (1 a year), *Revista de Arqueología*

Americana (1 a year), *Revista Cartográfica* (1 a year), *Revista Geofísica, Revista Geográfica* (2 a year), *Revista de Historia de América* (2 a year).

Wetlands International: POB 471, 6700 AL Wageningen, Netherlands; Droevendaalsesteeg 3A, 6708 PB Wageningen, Netherlands; tel. (317) 478854; fax (317) 478850; e-mail post@wetlands.org; internet www .wetlands.org; f. 1954 to sustain and restore wetlands, their resources and biodiversity through worldwide research, information exchange and conservation activities; 58 mem. countries; CEO J. MADGWICK.

World Academy of Art and Science: c/o Dr Walter Truett Anderson, 760 Market St, Suite 315, San Francisco, CA 94102, USA; tel. (415) 915-2449; fax (415) 781-8227; internet www.worldacademy.org; f. 1960; a forum for discussion of the social consequences and policy implications of knowledge; 471 Fellows in 62 countries; Pres. Dr WALTER TRUETT ANDERSON (USA).

World Meteorological Organization/ Organisation Météorologique Mondiale: Secretariat CP 2300, 7 bis ave de la Paix, 1211 Geneva 2, Switzerland; tel. 227308111; fax 227308181; e-mail wmo@wmo.int; internet www.wmo.int; f. 1950; objectives: worldwide cooperation in making and standardizing meteorological, climatological, hydrological and related geophysical observations and their exchange and publication; assists in training, research and technology transfer; furthers the application of meteorology to aviation, shipping, water problems, agriculture, environmental problems (incl. climate and climate change) and to sustainable development; constituent bodies: Congress, Executive Council, 6 regional associations, 8 technical commissions; mems: 181 states and 6 territories maintaining their own meteorological or hydrometeorological services; Pres. Dr A. I. BEDRITSKY (Russia); Sec.-Gen. M. JARRAUD (France); publs *WMO Bulletin* (4 a year), *World Climate News* (4 a year).

World Organisation of Systems and Cybernetics/Organisation Mondiale pour la Systémique et la Cybernétique: c/o Dr Alex Andrew, 95 Finch Rd, Earley, Reading, RG6 7JX, UK; tel. (118) 926-9328; e-mail alexandrew@tiscali.co.uk; internet www.cybsoc.org/wosc; f. 1969 to act as focal point for all socs concerned with cybernetics, systems and allied subjects, to aim for the recognition of cybernetics as a bona fide science and to maintain liaison with other int. bodies; holds int. congresses every 3 years; awards Norbert Wiener Memorial Gold Medal; 41 hon. fellows, nat. orgs in more than 20 countries; Pres. Prof. ROBERT VALLÉE; Dir-Gen. Dr ALEX ANDREW; publ. *Kybernetes* (10 a year, online at www.emeraldinsight.com/k.htm).

PART THREE
Afghanistan–Myanmar

AFGHANISTAN

The Higher Education System

The higher education system in Afghanistan was established with the foundation of Kabul University in 1932. However, during more than 20 years of civil war from 1979 higher education was disrupted by the departure of many teaching staff from Afghanistan. In 1991 there were six institutions of higher education with a total enrolment of 17,000 students. In September 1996 the Islamist Taliban movement gained control of Kabul and issued decrees enforcing their fundamentalist interpretation of Islam, which included banning women from receiving education. In late 2001 a US-led military coalition ousted the Taliban regime following the 11 September terrorist attacks on the USA, which were blamed on the al-Qa'ida organization of Osama bin Laden, a Saudi dissident based in Afghanistan. In March 2002 Kabul University was re-opened for men and women. In 2009 there were 22 universities in operation with some 62,000 students enrolled at the higher education level.

In order to be admitted to higher education students must complete the Baccalauria and pass an entrance examination (Concours). In 2004 The Ministry of Higher Education in cooperation with UNESCO put forward a plan for a four-tier structure of academic institutions: Universities with degree-conferring rights at Bachelors, Masters and Doctoral levels, Technological and Pedagogical Institutes providing the same degrees as universities but within their particular field of specialization, Colleges operating Bachelor degree level programmes and Community Colleges offering courses of up to two years leading to the award of a certificate or diploma. The reform is ongoing. There are also plans to implement a national qualifications framework (NQF) following the Bologna model of three-year Bachelor degree, two-year Masters degree and four-year Doctorate.

In 2009, however, no Afghan universities were in a position to provide teaching at postgraduate level, and no postgraduate degrees were being awarded. In 2006 the USAID-funded Higher Education Project was put into place to rebuild and strengthen the 16 institutions offering four-year teacher education programmes for precisely this reason.

Regulatory and Representative Bodies

GOVERNMENT

Ministry of Culture and Youth Affairs: Mohammad Jan Khan Wat, Kabul; tel. (20) 2101301; fax (20) 2290088; e-mail aziza_ahmadyar@hotmail.com; Minister ABDUL KARIM KHORAM.

Ministry of Education: Mohammad Jan Khan Wat, Kabul; tel. (79) 9332015; e-mail awassay.arian@moe.gov.af; internet www .moe.gov.af; Minister Dr MOHAMMED HANIF ATMAR.

Ministry of Higher Education: Karte Char, Kabul; tel. (20) 2500324; e-mail afmohe@hotmail.com; internet www.mohe .gov.af; Minister Dr MOHAMMAD AZAM DAD-FAR.

NATIONAL BODIES

Afghan Rectors' Conference: c/o Kabul Univ., Kabul; e-mail rida_azimi2004@yahoo .com; Pres. Dr DAUD RAWOSH; Sec.-Gen. RIDA AZIMI.

UNESCO Office Kabul: POB 5, UN Compound, Kabul; tel. (2) 214522; fax (2) 214379; e-mail martin.hadlow@undpafg.org.pk; Dir MARTIN HADLOW.

Learned Societies

GENERAL

Academy of Sciences of Afghanistan: Sher Alikhan St, Char Rahe Sher Poor, Kabul; tel. (20) 2102919; fax (20) 2100268; f. 1979; research in science, technology, humanities and culture; 4 main divs: Centre of Natural Sciences (q.v.), Institute of Social Sciences (q.v.), Institute of Languages and Literature (q.v.), Int. Centre for Pashtu Studies (q.v.); Islamic Studies Centre added 2000; further units incl. Int. Research Centre of Kushan Studies and Archaeology, Publication and Literature Dept, Encyclopedia and Dictionaries Dept; library: Central Library of 5,000 vols, Central Archives; Pres. Dr ABDUL BARI RASHID.

UNESCO Office Kabul: POB 5, UN Compound, Kabul; tel. (2) 214522; fax (2) 214379; e-mail martin.hadlow@undpafg.org.pk; Dir MARTIN HADLOW.

LANGUAGE AND LITERATURE

Goethe-Institut: c/o Embassy of the Federal Republic of Germany, POB 83, Kabul; Wazir Akbar Khan, Shahmahmod St, Kabul; tel. (20) 2105200; fax (20) 2105300; e-mail il@ kabul.goethe.org; internet www.goethe.de/ kabul; promotes cultural exchange with Germany, and contributes to the reconstruction of cultural and educational institutions in Afghanistan; Dir ANNE EBERHARD.

Research Institutes

GENERAL

Afghanistan Research and Evaluation Unit (AREU): Flower St (corner of St 2), Shahr-i-Naw, Kabul; e-mail areu@areu.org .af; internet www.areu.org.af; f. 2002; promotes a culture of research and learning by strengthening analytical capacity in Afghanistan and facilitating reflection and debate; library of 3,000 vols, periodicals, maps, CDs and DVDs; Dir PAUL FISHSTEIN.

Institute of Social Sciences: Kabul; attached to Acad. of Sciences of Afghanistan; philosophy, economics, history, archaeology; Pres. Dr HAKIM HELALI; publs Afghanistan (4 a year in English, French and German), Ariana (4 a year in Pashtu and Dari).

LANGUAGE AND LITERATURE

Institute of Languages and Literature: Kabul; attached to Acad. of Sciences of Afghanistan; linguistics, literature and folklore; study of Pashtu and Dari languages, and Afghanistan dialects; publs Kabul (12 a year, Pashtu), Zayray (48 a year, Pashtu).

International Centre for Pashtu Studies: Kabul; attached to Acad. of Sciences of Afghanistan; research, compilation and translation; publ. Pashtu Quarterly.

MEDICINE

Institute of Public Health: Ansari Wat, Kabul; f. 1962; public health training and research; govt reference laboratory; Dir Dr S. M. SADIQUE; publs Afghan Journal of Public Health (26 a year), books and pamphlets.

NATURAL SCIENCES

General

Centre of Natural Sciences: Kabul; attached to Acad. of Sciences of Afghanistan; institutes of botany, zoology, geology and chemistry, seismology; computer centre, plants museum and botanical garden.

Physical Sciences

Department of Geology and Mineral Survey: Min. of Mines and Industries, Kabul; tel. 25848; f. 1955; research, mapping, prospecting and exploration; library of 8,300 vols; Pres. Dipl. Eng. Haji MOHAMAD NAW-ZADI; publs Journal of Mines and Industries (4 a year), maps and other reference works.

Libraries and Archives

Kabul

Kabul University Library: c/o Min. of Culture and Youth Affairs, Mohammad Jan Khan Wat, Kabul; tel. 42594; f. 1931; 250,000 vols; Dir Prof. ABDUL RASOUL RAHIN.

Library of the National Bank: c/o Min. of Culture and Youth Affairs, Mohammad Jan Khan Wat, Kabul; Bank Millie Afghan, Ibn Sina Wat, Kabul; f. 1941; 5,600 vols; Dir A. AZIZ.

Library of the Press and Information Department: c/o Min. of Culture and Youth Affairs, Mohammad Jan Khan Wat, Kabul; Sanaii Wat, Kabul; f. 1931; 28,000 vols and 800 MSS; Dir MOHAMMED SARWAR RONA.

Ministry of Education Library: c/o Min. of Culture and Youth Affairs, Mohammad Jan Khan Wat, Kabul; f. 1920; 30,000 vols; Chief Officer MOHAMAD QASEM HILAMAN; publ. *Erfan* (12 a year journal in Pashtu and Dari).

Nazo Annah Library: c/o Min. of Culture and Youth Affairs, Mohammad Jan Khan Wat, Kabul; f. 2001 to enable and empower young women through literacy and education; attached to Noor Education Centre; fmrly Women's Welfare Soc. Library; 680 vols.

Public Library: c/o Min. of Culture and Youth Affairs, Mohammad Jan Khan Wat, Kabul; Charaii-i-Malik Asghar, Kabul; f. 1920; attached to Min. of Culture and Youth Affairs; 60,000 vols, 433 MSS, 30 current periodicals; Dir MOHAMAD OMAR SEDDIQUI.

Museums and Art Galleries

Ghazni

Ghazni Museum: c/o Min. of Culture and Youth Affairs, Mohammad Jan Khan Wat, Kabul; Ghazni.

Herat

Herat Museum: c/o Min. of Culture and Youth Affairs, Mohammad Jan Khan Wat, Kabul; Herat.

Kabul

Kabul Museum: c/o Min. of Culture and Youth Affairs, Mohammad Jan Khan Wat, Kabul; tel. 42656; f. 1922; archaeology; Dir ORMA KHAN MASSOUDI.

Kandahar

Kandahar Museum: c/o Min. of of Culture and Youth Affairs, Mohammad Jan Khan Wat, Kabul; Kandahar.

Maimana

Maimana Museum: c/o Min. of Culture and Youth Affairs, Mohammad Jan Khan Wat, Kabul; Maimana.

Mazar-i-Sharif

Mazar-i-Sharif Museum: c/o Min. of Culture and Youth Affairs, Mohammad Jan Khan Wat, Kabul; Mazar-i-Sharif.

Universities

BALKH UNIVERSITY

Mazar-i-Sharif, Balkh
Telephone: 503487
Fax: 503554
Founded 1988
Pres.: Prof. HABIBULLAH
Number of teachers: 83
Number of students: 4,739

Faculties of economics, engineering, journalism, law, literature, medicine and science.

BAYAZID ROSHAN UNIVERSITY OF NANGARHAR

Darunta, Jalalabad, Nangarhar
Founded 1963 from Medical Faculty of Kabul University, reorganized 1978
State control
Language of instruction: Pashtu
Vice-Chancellor: Dr MOHAMMAD TAYAB
Dean: Prof. ABDUL QADIR FAZLI
Number of teachers: 96
Number of students: 3,263

DEANS

Faculty of Medicine: Prof. ASSADULLAH SHINWARI
Faculty of Political Science: MIRWAIS AHMADZAI

There are also faculties of agriculture, education and engineering

HERAT UNIVERSITY

Herat
Internet: heratuniversity.org
Founded 1986
State control
Pres.: Dr MOHAMMAD NAIM ASSAD
Dir of Academic Affairs: MOHAMMAD NASER RAHYAB
Dir of Student Affairs: Dr ABDUL ZAHER O
Librarian: SAID KHALLIL
Library of 2,000 vols
Number of teachers: 210
Number of students: 6,000

Faculties of agriculture, art, computer science, economics, education, engineering, law, literature, medicine, science, theology and Islamic law.

KABUL MEDICAL UNIVERSITY

Kabul
Internet: www.kmu.edu.af
Founded 1932 as Kabul Medical Faculty, initially maintained with collaboration from French and Turkish govts; disrupted under Taliban regime; present name and autonomous univ. status 2005
State control
Dean: Dr OBAIDULLAH OBAID
Library of 20,000 vols
Number of teachers: 213
Number of students: 2,745

Faculties of curative medicine, nursing, paediatrics, stomatology; affiliated teaching hospitals at Aliabad and Maiwand.

KABUL UNIVERSITY

Jamal Mina, Kabul
Telephone: 40341
Internet: www.ku.edu.af
Founded 1932
State control

Academic year: March to January
Language of instruction: Dari
Rector: Prof. MOHAMMAD AKBAR POPAL
Librarian: REYHANA POPALZAI
Library of 200,000 vols
Number of teachers: 450
Number of students: 7,000
Publication: *Natural Science and Social Science* (4 a year)

Faculties of agriculture, economics, engineering, fine arts, history and philosophy, Islamic law, journalism, law, linguistics, pharmacology, psychology, science, social sciences, veterinary science

DEANS

Faculty of Education: Prof. GUL RAHMAN HAKIM
Faculty of Law and Political Science: Prof. IQRAL WASIL
Faculty of Social Sciences: Prof. M. DAUD RAWOSH

ATTACHED RESEARCH CENTRE

National Centre for Policy Research: f. 2003 to promote democracy in Afghanistan; depts of economics, law and political sciences and social science; offers scholarships to Afghani researchers for carrying out postgraduate studies in Germany; financed by Konrad-Adenauer Stiftung (Germany).

KANDAHAR UNIVERSITY

Kandahar
Internet: www.kandaharuniversity.com
Founded 1988
State control
Vice-Pres.: SHAH MAHMUD BARAI
Number of students: 747

UNIVERSITY OF EDUCATION

Kabul
Founded 2002
Number of teachers: 140
Number of students: 1,744

Colleges

Institute of Agriculture: Kabul; f. 1924; veterinary medicine, forestry.

Institute of Arabic and Religious Study: Kabul; Other centres incl. the Najmul-Madares, Nangrahar; the Jamé and Fakhrul Madares, Herat; the Asadia Madrasa, Mazar-i-Sharif; the Takharistan Madrasa, Kunduz; the Zahir Shahi Madrasa, Maimana.

Kabul Art School: Bibi Mahro, near Kabul; music, painting and sculpture courses.

School of Commerce: Kabul; f. 1943; banking, commercial law, economics, business admin., finance.

School of Mechanics: Kabul; for apprentice trainees.

ALBANIA

The Higher Education System

Higher education is offered through universities and higher schools and is governed by legislation enacted in 1999, 2003 and 2007. In 2009 there were nine universities, the oldest of which is the Alexsander Xhuvani University of Elbasan, founded in 1909. The Law on Higher Education of 1999 introduced and guarantees state funding for public higher education. Albania joined the Bologna Process in 2003, and in the same year implemented a new higher education act that introduced a two-tier Bachelors and Masters degree structure. This new system was scheduled to be fully implemented (with the exception of a few subject areas) by the 2006 academic year. The Law on Higher Education of 2007 governs not only the institutions but also the structure, study programmes and cycles, supervision, students' rights and the financial aspects of higher education. Its enactment marked the official start of the implementation of Bologna degrees. As a result, from 2008/09 all Albanian public universities adopted the new curricula of second and third cycles of studies.

In 2006/07 a total of 86,178 students were enrolled at Albania's institutions of higher education.

University Rectors and Higher School Directors and Head-masters belong to the Conference of Rectors, the highest decision-making body in Albania's higher education system. All universities consist of faculties, which are governed by faculty councils, and sometimes of higher schools; the highest decision-making body in a higher school is the school council. Both faculties and higher schools consist of departments, in which the department council is the highest decision-making body.

Admission to higher education is conducted according to quotas and is subject to main and secondary fees. Main admission fees are proposed by the Ministry of Education and Science, following recommendations from the universities and higher schools, and are approved by the Council of Ministers. Secondary fees are levied for specialist education and can equate to a maximum of 10% of the main fees. Admission to public universities and higher schools is based on competitive examinations which are organized by the Ministry of Education and Science on the advice of the Conference of Rectors. Successful students are then admitted subject to the established fees.

Pre-Bologna (until 2007), there were three levels of university qualifications: Diplomë (Diploma), Kandidat í Shkencave (Candidate of Sciences) and Doktor mi Shkencave (Doctor of Sciences). The Diplomë was usually a four-year undergraduate degree, however degrees in engineering, technology and dentistry lasted five years, and courses in medicine lasted six years. The Kandidat íi Shkencave was a first postgraduate degree of two to three years. The Doktor í Shkencave was based on a significant period of research. There was no grading system for this level of study. Qualifications from the three military institutions (the Higher Military Academies in Tirana and Vlora, and the Higher Unified Military School in Tirana) had the same equivalency as civilian qualifications.

Post-Bologna there are six levels of qualification: in the first cycle are the Diplomë Jo-Universitare (Non-University Diploma), which is a higher education award consisting of a study programme of 120 ECTS, in applied subjects, offered at universities and professional colleges (credits can be transferred to a First Level Diploma programme) and the Diplomë e Nivelit te Pare (First Level Diploma), which is a degree awarded after at least three years, of no less than 180 ECTS, and can be issued by universities, academies or professional colleges providing access to second cycle awards. In the second cycle are the Master í Nivelit te Pare (First Level Master), a degree which is an essential requirement for teachers whose first cycle degree is not sufficient, consisting of no less than 60 ECTS, but is not recognized as completion of the second cycle and therefore does not allow access to the third level, and the Diplomë e Nivelit te Dyte (Second Level Diploma), which is a degree awarded after two years' study, involving the attainment of 120 ECTS, allowing entry to the third cycle. In the third cycle are the Master í Nivelit te Dyte (Second Level Master), which is a degree awarded after another one to two years' study and represents the entry requirement to become a university professor, and Doktor í Shekencave (Doctor of Science), which takes three to five years and requires completion of 60 ECTS in the first year (although holders of the Second Level Master are exempt), followed by research and defence of a doctoral thesis.

Quality assessment of universities and higher schools and academic accreditation is carried out by the Accrediting Agency and the Accrediting Council, under the authority of the Council of Ministers.

Regulatory and Representative Bodies

GOVERNMENT

Ministry of Education and Science: Rr. e Durrësit 23, Tiranë; tel. (4) 2226307; fax (4) 2232002; e-mail ministri@mash.gov.al; internet www.mash.gov.al; Minister Prof. Dr MYQEREM TAFAJ.

Ministry of Tourism, Culture, Youth and Sports: Rr. e Kavajës, Tiranë; tel. (4) 222508; e-mail informacion@mtkrs.gov.al; internet www.mtkrs.gov.al; Minister FERDINAND XHAFERAJ.

ACCREDITATION

Agency for Accreditation of Higher Education: Blvd Zhan 'D' Ark, Pallatet e Lanës, no. 2, Shk 2, Ap. 17, Tiranë; tel. (4) 2266302; fax (4) 2266302; e-mail infoaal@gmail.com; internet www.aaal.edu.al; Dir Prof. DHURATA BOZO.

ENIC/NARIC Albania: Drejtoria e Arsimit të Lartë dhe Njohjes së Diplomave, Rr. Durrësit 23, Tiranë; tel. (4) 2227975; fax (4) 2232002; e-mail ecane@mash.gov.al; internet www.mash.gov.al; Specialist EDMOND CANE.

NATIONAL BODIES

Albanian Rectors' Conference: c/o Ministry of Education and Science, Rr. e Durrësit 23, Tiranë.

Department of Higher Education and Recognition of Diplomas: c/o Ministry of Education and Science, Rr. e Durrësit 23, Tiranë; tel. (4) 226307; fax (4) 232002; e-mail amucaj@mash.gov.al; internet www.mash.gov.al; Dir of Higher Education Dr AGIM MUÇAJ.

Learned Societies

GENERAL

Academy of Sciences of Albania: Fan. S. Noli Sq., 35542 Tiranë; tel. (4) 230305; fax (4) 230305; e-mail nnati@akad.edu.al; internet www.akad.edu.al; f. 1972; attached research institutes: see Research Institutes; 28 mems; Pres. GUDAR BEQIRAJ; Scientific Sec. SALVATOR BUSHATI; publs *Albanian Journal of Natural and Technical Sciences* (2 a year), *Art Studies* (2 a year), *Biological Studies* (2 a year), *Folk Culture* (2 a year), *Geographical Studies* (irregular), *Historical Studies* (2 a year), *Ilyria* (2 a year), *Issues of Albanian Folklore* (irregular), *Our Language* (2 a year), *Philological Studies* (2 a year), *Studia Albanica* (2 a year).

Komiteti Shqiptar për Marrëdhënie Kulturore me botën e jashtme (Albanian Committee for Cultural Relations Abroad): Tiranë; Pres. JORGO MELIKA.

LANGUAGE AND LITERATURE

Alliance Française: Rr. e Barrikadave 122, Tiranë; tel. (4) 2274841; fax (4) 2225697; e-mail info@aftirana.org; internet www .aftirana.org; f. 1991; offers courses and examinations in French language and culture; promotes cultural exchange with France; attached teaching centres in Elbasan, Korçë and Shkodra; Dir DRITA HADAJ; Sec. Gen. GENT BEGA; Head of Treasury IRENA CACI.

British Council: Rr. 'Perlat Rexhepi', Pall 197, Ana, Tiranë; tel. (4) 2240856; fax (4) 2240858; e-mail info@britishcouncil.org.al; internet www.britishcouncil.org/albania; offers British literature and examinations in English language and British culture; promotes cultural exchange with the UK; library of 4,000 vols; Dir CLARE SEARS.

Lidhja e Shkrimtarëve dhe e Artistëve të Shqipërisë (Union of Writers and Artists of Albania): Tiranë; f. 1957; 1,750 mems; Pres. DRITËRO AGOLLI; Secs FEIM IBRAHIMI, PETRO KOKUSHTA, NASI LERA; publs *Drita* (journal, weekly), *Les Lettres Albanaises* (4 a year), *Nëntori* (Review, 12 a year).

PEN Centre of Albania: Rr. 'Ded Gjo Luli', Pallati 5, shk. 3/4, Tiranë; Pres. BESNIK MUSTAFAJ.

NATURAL SCIENCES

Physical Sciences

Shoqata e Gjeologëve te Shqipërisë (Geologists' Association of Albania): Blloku 'Vasil Shanto', Tiranë; tel. (4) 2226597; f. 1989; 450 mems; Chair. ALEKSANDËR ÇINA; Sec.-Gen. ILIR ALLIU; publ. *Buletini i Shkencave Gjeologjike.*

Research Institutes

AGRICULTURE, FISHERIES AND VETERINARY SCIENCE

Instituti i Duhanit (Tobacco Institute): Lagja 2, Pallati 51/2, Cërrik; tel. (581) 2800; f. 1956; library of 1,000 vols; Dir BELUL GIXHARI; publ. *Bulletin des sciences de l'agriculture* (4 a year).

Instituti i Kërkimeve Bujqësore Lushnje (Lushnje Institute of Agricultural Research): Lushnje; tel. (65) 224498; f. 1952; focuses on cultivating new varieties of bread and durum wheat, cotton, sunflower and dry bean; library of 8,000 vols; Dir VLADIMIR MALO.

Instituti i Kërkimeve Pyjore dhe Kullotave (Forest and Pasture Research Institute): Rr. Halil Bego 23, Tiranë; tel. (4) 371242; fax (4) 371237; e-mail ikpk@ albaniaonline.net; f. 1992; Dir SPIRO KARADUMI.

Instituti i Kërkimeve të Foragjere (Forage Research Institute): Fushë-Krujë; tel. (4) 233354; f. 1973; Dir VASILLAQ DHIMA.

Instituti i Kërkimeve të Pemëve Frutore dhe Vreshtave (Institute of Fruit Growing and Vineyard Research): Tiranë; tel. (4) 2229704; f. 1984; library of 70 vols; Dir STEFAN GJOKA; publs *Pemëtaria, Bulletini i Shkencave Bujqësore.*

Instituti i Kërkimeve të Zooteknisë (Institute of Animal Husbandry Research): Laprake, Tiranë; tel. (4) 2223135; f. 1955; library of 1,900 vols; Dir MINA SPIRU.

Instituti i Kërkimeve Veterinare (Institute of Veterinary Research): 'Aleksander Moisiu' St 10, Tiranë; tel. (4) 2372912; fax (4) 2372912; f. 1928; Dir Prof. Dr KRISTAQ BERXHOLI; publ. *Veterinaria* (3 a year).

Instituti i Kerkimit te Bimeve te Arave, Stacioni Eksperimental (Experimental Station of the Research Institute for Arable Farming): Rr. Voskopojës, Korçë; fax (824) 3086; e-mail stacionieksperimental@yahoo .com; f. 1953; attached to Min. of Agriculture, Food and Consumer Protection; library of 600 vols; Dir Dr EQREM MEÇOLLARI.

Instituti i Mbrojtjes Bimeve (Institute of Plant Protection Research): Shkozet, Durrës; tel. (52) 22182; fax (52) 22182; e-mail imb@ anep.al.eu.org; f. 1971; library of 2,410 vols; Dir Dr SKENDER VARRAKU.

Qendra e Transferimit te Teknologjive Bujqesore (Agriculture Technologies Transfer Centre (ATTC)): Shkodër; tel. and fax (225) 1200; e-mail qttb_shkoder@yahoo.com; f. 1971 as Institute of Maize and Rice, present name 2006; applied research activity and technology devt; identification, testing, introduction of new methods and materials into agriculture practices; identification, preservation, colln, multiplication of high value authentic genetic resources; preparing of technological package for maize culture and other priority cultures of the region (arboriculture, horticulture, vegetable etc.); production of pre-basic and basic certified seeds and seedlings; activities of technology transfer; laboratory analysis (chemical and biochemical laboratory wide range analysis) of both agriculture and cattle products; 15 mems; library of 4,900 vols; Dir ISMET LLOSHI; publs *Agriculture Science Bulletin* (4 a year), *Albanian Agriculture* (12 a year).

Instituti i Perimeve dhe i Patates (Institute of Vegetables and Potatoes): Rr. Skënder Kosturi, Tiranë; tel. (4) 2228422; f. 1980; library of 6,000 vols; Dir XHEVAT SHIMA; publs *Bulletin of Agricultural Sciences, Bulletin of Vegetables, Bulletin of Vegetables and Potatoes.*

Instituti i Studimeve dhe i Projektimeve të Veprave të Kullimit dhe Ujitjes (Institute of Irrigation and Drainage Studies and Designs): Tiranë; f. 1970; Dir DHIMITËR VOGLI.

Instituti i Studimit të Tokave (Institute of Soil Studies): Tiranë; tel. (4) 2223278; fax (4) 2228367; f. 1971; library of 5,000 vols; Dir ALBERT DUBALI.

Instituti i Ullirit dhe i Agrumeve (Institute of Olives and Citrus Plants): 'Uji i Jtohtë', Vlorë; tel. (33) 23225; fax (33) 23225; f. 1971; library of 500 vols; Dir Dr HAIRI ISMAILI.

Stacioni i Studimeve dhe i Kërkimeve të Peshkimit (Research Station and Fisheries Research): Rr. 'Skenderbeg', L. Teuta, Durrës; tel. (52) 22552; f. 1960; Dir KASTRIOT OSMANI.

ARCHITECTURE AND TOWN PLANNING

Instituti i Monumenteve të Kulturës (Institute of Cultural Monuments): Rr. Aleksandër Moisiu 76, Tiranë; tel. and fax (4) 2340348; e-mail imk@albmail.com; f. 1965; attached to Min. of Tourism, Culture, Youth and Sports; research and restoration of ancient and medieval architecture, cultural bldgs and artistic monuments; library of 9,000 vols; Dir FATJON DAUTI; publ. *Monumentet* (Monuments, 2 a year).

Instituti i Studimeve e Projektimeve Urbanistikë (Institute of Urban Planning and Design): Rr. M. Gjollesha Istn, Tiranë; tel. (4) 2223361; fax (4) 2223361; f. 1991; library of 400 vols; Dir GJERGJ KOTMILO.

ECONOMICS, LAW AND POLITICS

Albanian Institute for International Studies: Rr. Andon Z, Cajupi 20, Tiranë; tel. (4) 2248853; fax (4) 2270337; e-mail aiis@ aiis-albania.org; internet www.aiis-albania .org; non-profit research and policy institute; areas of research incl. issues in Euro–Atlantic integration, democracy, security and transition, regional security and cooperation; Chair. BESNIK MUSTAFAJ; Exec. Dir ALBERT RAKIPI.

Instituti i Studimeve të Marrëdhënieve Ndërkombëtare (Institute of International Relations): Tiranë; tel. (4) 2229521; fax (4) 2232970; f. 1981; Dir SOKRAT PLAKA; publ. *Politika ndërkombëtare* (International Politics, 4 a year).

EDUCATION

Instituti i Studimeve Pedagogjike (Institute of Pedagogical Studies): Rr. Naim Frashëri 37, Tiranë; tel. (4) 2223860; fax (4) 2223860; f. 1970; Dir Prof. BUJAR BASHA; publs *Albanian Language and Literature in School* (2 a year), *Chemistry and Biology in School* (2 a year), *Elementary School* (1 a year), *Foreign Languages in School* (1 a year), *Mathematics and Physics in School* (2 a year), *Nursery School 3–6* (1 a year), *Revista Pedagogjike* (4 a year), *Social Materials in School* (2 a year), *Vocational Schools* (2 a year), *Yllkat* (12 a year).

FINE AND PERFORMING ARTS

Qendra e Studimeve të Artit (Centre for Art Studies): Rr. Don Bosko 60, Tiranë; tel. (4) 2259667; fax (4) 2228274; e-mail qsa@ akad.edu; f. 1984; research in fine arts, music, choreography, theatre, cinema, art and culture instns; attached to Acad. of Sciences of Albania; Dir Prof. JOSIF PAPAGJONI; publ. *Studime për Artin* (Studies for Art, 2 a year).

HISTORY, GEOGRAPHY AND ARCHAEOLOGY

Instituti i Arkeologjisë (Institute of Archaeology): Bulevardi Dëshmorët e Kombit, Sheshi Nënë Tereza, Tiranë; tel. (4) 2271822; fax (4) 2240712; e-mail instark@ albmail.com; f. 1976; attached to Centre of Albanological Studies; performs archaeological research and excavations in Albania; Dir Prof. ILIRIAN GJIPALI; publs *Candavia* (in Albanian, publ. of the Late Antique and Medieval Dept of the Institute of Archaeology), *Iliria* (in Albanian, English and French, 1 a year).

Instituti i Historisë (Institute of History): Rr. Naim Frashëri 7, Tiranë; tel. (4) 2225869; fax (4) 2225869; e-mail ihistorise@ albaniaonline.net; f. 1972; attached to Acad. of Sciences of Albania; study of ancient and modern Albanian history and people; library of 52,000 vols, 10,000 periodicals; Dir Prof. Dr ANA LALAJ; publ. *Studime Historike* (Historical Studies, 4 a year).

Qendra e Kërkimeve Gjeografike (Centre for Geographical Research): Qendri e Studimeve Hidraulike, Sheshi Fan S. Noli, Tiranë; tel. (4) 2227985; fax (4) 2227985; e-mail geography_albania2003@yahooo.com; f. 1986; attached to Acad. of Sciences of Albania; library of 3,200 vols; Dir Prof. Dr ARQILE BERXHOLI; publ. *Studime Gjeografike* (Geographical Studies, 1 a year).

LANGUAGE AND LITERATURE

Instituti i Gjuhësisë dhe i Letërsisë (Institute of Linguistics and Literature): Rr. Naim Frashëri 7, Tiranë; tel. (4) 2235134; fax (4) 2222509; e-mail jbulo@albmail.com; f. 1972; study of Albanian language and literature; attached to Acad. of Sciences of Albania; Dir Prof. Dr JORGO BULO; publs *Gjuha Jonë* (Our Language, 4 a year), *Studime Filologjike* (Philological Studies, 4 a year).

Qendra e Enciklopedisë Shqiptare (Centre for the Albanian Encyclopedical Dictionary): Sheshi Fan S. Noli 7, Tiranë; tel. (4) 2250369; fax (4) 2256777; e-mail encikloped@ yahoo.com; f. 1988 to prepare revised edn of the *Albanian Encyclopedical Dictionary*; sections of social sciences, natural and technical sciences; attached to the Acad. of Sciences of Albania; Dir Prof. Dr EMIL LAFE.

MEDICINE

Instituti i Mjekësisë Popullore (Institute of Folk Medicine): Tiranë; tel. (4) 2223493; f. 1977; Dir Dr GËZIM BOCARI; publ. *Përmbledhje Studimesh* (Collections of Studies, irregular).

Instituti i Shëndetit Publik (Institute of Public Health): Aleksander Moisiu 80, Tiranë; tel. (4) 2374756; fax (4) 2370058; f. 1969 as Research Institute of Hygiene, Epidemiology and Immunobiological Products; present name 1995; Dir Prof. EDUARD KAKARRIQI; publ. *Revista Mjekesore* (Medical Magazine, 6 a year).

NATURAL SCIENCES

Biological Sciences

Instituti i Kërkimeve Biologjike (Institute of Biological Research): Rr. Sami Frasheri 5, Tiranë; tel. (4) 222638; fax (4) 222638; e-mail ikbiol@albmail.com; f. 1978; attached to Acad. of Sciences of Albania; Dir Prof. EFIGJENI KONGJIKA.

Mathematical Sciences

Instituti i Informatikës dhe i Matematikës së Aplikuar (Institute of Informatics and Applied Mathematics): Rr. Lek Dukagjini 3, Tiranë; tel. (4) 2362968; fax (4) 2362122; e-mail inima@inima.al; f. 1971; attached to Acad. of Sciences of Albania; Dir Prof. Dr GUDAR BEQIRAJ.

Physical Sciences

Instituti i Energjetikës (Institute of Energetics): Tiranë; f. 1982; Dir LLAZAR PAPA-JORGJI.

Instituti i Fizikës Bërthamore (Institute of Nuclear Physics): POB 85, Tiranë; tel. (4) 2376341; fax (4) 2362596; e-mail inp@ albaniaonline.net; f. 1970; attached to Acad. of Sciences of Albania; Dir Prof. Dr FATOS YLLI.

Instituti i Hidrometeorologjisë (Institute of Hydrometeorology): Rr. e Durrësit 219, Tiranë; tel. (4) 2223518; fax (4) 2223518; e-mail a.selenica@voila.fr; f. 1962, replaced Hydrometeorological Service f. 1949; attached to Acad. of Sciences of Albania; comprises two divs: Department of Meteorology and Department of Hydrology; Dir Prof. Dr AGIM SELENICA; publ. *Hydrometeorological Reports* (periodic review).

Instituti i Sizmologjise (Institute of Seismology): Tiranë; tel. (4) 2228274; fax (4) 2228274; e-mail sizmo@akad.edu.al; f. 1993; attached to Acad. of Sciences of Albania; Dir Prof. Dr SHYQYRI ALIAJ.

Instituti i Studimeve dhe Projektimeve të Gjeologjisë (Geological Research Institute): Blloku 'Vasil Shanto', Tiranë; tel. (4) 2226597; f. 1962; library of 20,000 vols; Dir ALAUDIN KODRA; publ. *Buletini i Shkencave Gjeologjike* (4 a year).

RELIGION, SOCIOLOGY AND ANTHROPOLOGY

Instituti i Kulturës Popullore (Institute of Folk Culture): Rr. Kont Urani 3, Tiranë; tel. (4) 2222323; fax (4) 2224555; e-mail ikp .alb@icc.al.org; f. 1961, present status 1979; depts of ethnology, ethnomusicology and ethnochoreography, prose and poetry; library of 10,000 vols, 1.5m. verses of poetry; attached to Acad. of Sciences of Albania;

Dir Asst Prof. AFËRDITA ONUZI; publ. *Folk Culture* (2 a year).

TECHNOLOGY

Infraproject Consulting SH.p.K.: Rr. Sami Frasheri, Tiranë; tel. (4) 2225206; fax (4) 2228321; road, railway and waterway engineering; library of 900 vols; Dir Gen. VEHIP GURI.

Instituti i Kerkimeve të Ushqimit (Food Research Institute): Rr. 'Muhamed Gjollesha' 56, Tiranë; tel. (4) 2226770; fax (4) 2226770; e-mail iku@anep.al.eu.org; f. 1961; Dir MAKSIM DELIANA; publ. *Përmbledhje Studimesh* (Collections of Studies, irregular).

Instituti i Studimeve dhe i Projektimeve Gjeologjike të Naftës e të Gazit (Institute for Studies and Design of Oil and Gas Geology): Fier; f. 1965; Dir DRINI MEZINI; publ. *Buletini Nafta dhe Gazi* (2 a year, summaries in English).

Instituti i Studimeve dhe i Projektimeve të Hidrocentraleve (Institute of Hydraulic Studies and Design): Tiranë; f. 1966; Dir EGON GJADRI.

Instituti i Studimeve dhe i Projektimeve të Metalurgjise (Institute for Metallurgical Studies and Designs): Elbasan; tel. (54) 55565; fax (54) 55565; f. 1978; metallurgy of iron, chrome, copper, nickel; library of 6,100 vols; Dir ALFRED MALKJA.

Instituti i Studimeve dhe i Projektimeve të Minierave (Mining Research Institute): Blloku 'Vasil Shanto', Tiranë; tel. (4) 2229445; f. 1983; library of 10,000 vols; Dir ENGJELL HOXHAJ; publ. *Buletini i Shkencave Minerare* (2 a year, summaries in English).

Instituti i Studimeve dhe i Projektimeve të Teknologjisë Kimike (Institute of Chemical Studies and Technological Design): Tiranë; f. 1981; Dir GASTOR AGALLIU.

Instituti i Studimeve dhe i Projektimeve të Teknologjisë Mekanike (Institute of Mechanical Technology Studies and Design): Tiranë; f. 1969; Dir ROBERT LAPERI.

Instituti i Studimeve dhe i Projektimeve Teknologjike të Mineraleve (Institute for Studies and Technology of Minerals): Tiranë; tel. (4) 2225582; f. 1979; mineral-processing research; library of 1,480 vols; Dir JLIR LAKRORI.

Instituti i Studimeve dhe i Projektimeve Teknologjike të Naftës e të Gazit (Institute for Studies and Design of Oil and Gas Technology): Tiranë; f. 1981; Dir PERPARIM HOXHA; publ. *Nafta dhe Gazi* (Oil and Gas, 6 a year).

Instituti i Studimeve dhe i Teknologjisë Ndërtimit (Institute of Building Technology Studies): Rr. 'Muhamet Gjollesha', Tiranë; tel. (4) 227498; fax (4) 2223811; f. 1979; library of 1,500 vols; Dir Ing. MUHANEM DELIU.

Instituti i Studimeve dhe Projektimeve Mekanike (Mechanics Research Institute): Rr. 'Ferit Xajko', Tiranë; tel. (4) 2228543; f. 1970; library of 3,000 vols; Dir NEDIM KAMBO.

Qendra e Kerkimeve Hidraulike (Centre of Hydraulic Research): Rr. Sami Frasheri 5, Tiranë; tel. (4) 2227322; fax (4) 2227322; e-mail qekehid@albmail.com; f. 1957; attached to Acad. of Sciences of Albania; Dir Prof. Dr STAVRI LAMI.

Libraries and Archives

Durrës

Durrës Public Library: Durrës; tel. (52) 22281; f. 1945; 180,462 vols; Dir FLORA DERVISHI.

Elbasan

Elbasan Public Library: Elbasan; f. 1934; 284,000 vols.

Gjirokastër

Gjirokastër Public Library: Gjirokastër; 90,000 vols.

Korçë

Korçë Public Library: Korçë; f. 1938; 139,000 vols.

Shkodër

Shkodër Public Library: Shkodër; tel. (2) 2242307; e-mail biboigjo@yahoo.co.uk; internet www.library-shkodra.com; f. 1931; 260,000 vols from the 15th and 16th centuries printed in Germany, Italy, France, Switzerland; collns incl. MSS, Albans-Balkanology, maps and incunabula; Dir GJOVALIN ÇUNI.

Tiranë

Centre for Scientific and Technical Information and Documentation: Rr. Lek Dukagjini 5, Tiranë; tel. and fax (4) 222491; f. 1981; attached to Min. of Education and Science; Dir HYDAI MYFTIU; publ. *Buletin Analitik Fushor* (Disciplinary Analytical Bulletin, 12 a year).

National Library: Sheshi Skenderbej, Tiranë; tel. (4) 223843; fax (4) 223843; e-mail a_plasari@hotmail.com; internet www.bksh .al; f. 1922; 1m. vols; Dir Dr AUREL PLASARI; publs *National Bibliography of Albanian Books* (4 a year), *National Bibliography of Albanian Periodicals* (12 a year).

Scientific Library: Tiranë; f. 1972; attached to Acad. of Sciences of Albania; Dir NATASHA PANO.

State Archives: Rr. 'Jordan Misja', Tiranë; tel. (4) 227959; fax (4) 227959; e-mail dpa@ albarchive.gov.al; internet www.albarchive .gov.al; document conservation and research; Dir NIKA NEVILA.

Museums and Art Galleries

Berat

District Historical Museum: Berat; tel. (32) 32595; f. 1948; Dir ARBEM JANPAJ.

'Onufri' Iconographic Museum: Lagja Kala, Berat; tel. (32) 32248; e-mail info@ beratmuseum.net; internet www .beratmuseum.net; f. 1986; sited in the town's castle; exhibits incl. icons by the medieval painter Onufri; Dir KASTRIOT DERVISHI.

Ethnographic Museum: Lagja 13, Shtatori, Berat; tel. (32) 32224; e-mail info@ beratmuseum.net; internet www .beratmuseum.net; f. 1979; folk ethnographic culture from Berat and southern Albanian region; Dir KASTRIOT DERVISHI.

Durrës

Archaeological Museum: 1st Quartier, Talantia St, Durrës; tel. (52) 22253; f. 1951; exhibits representing life in ancient Durrës; artefacts from ancient Greek, Roman and medieval periods.

Elbasan

Kristoforidhi, K., House-Museum: Elbasan; birthplace of the patriot and linguist; Dir LIMAN VAROSHI.

Stafa, Q., House-Museum: Elbasan; birthplace of the nat. hero; Dir LIMAN VAROSHI.

Fier

Archaeological Museum: Fier; f. 1958; exhibits incl. archaeological items from the fmr town of Apollonia.

District Historical Museum: Fier; tel. (34) 2583; f. 1948; Dir PETRIT MALUSHI.

Korçë

Mio, V., House-Museum: Korçë; house where the painter worked; contains works of art by Mio.

Museum of Education: L 12, Blvd Shen Gjergji, Korçë; tel. (824) 3022; f. 1887 as the first Albanian school of language, converted to museum 1960; displays the history of the Albanian alphabet and devt of education in Albania.

Museum of the Struggle for National Liberation: Blvd Repuplika, Korçë; tel. (824) 2888; f. 1977; library of 400 vols.

Muzeu Kombetar i Artit Mesjetar (National Museum of Medieval Art): Korçë; tel. (824) 3022; fax (824) 2022; f. 1980; attached to Min. of Culture, Youth and Sports; 7,000 items; colln of icons by Onufri and Onufer Qiprioti and other anonymous artists of 13th and 14th centuries; Dir LORENC GLOZHENI.

Kruja

National Ethnographic Museum: Fortress of Kruja, Kruja; tel. (53) 22225; f. 1989; objects on display depict the Albanian way of living over 300 years; collns incl. ceramics, cotton, silk, wool; various embroideries.

National Museum 'George Kastriot Skenderbeu': Krujë Castle, Kruja; tel. (53) 22225; f. 1982; memorabilia of the nat. hero; items depicting history of 15th-century Albania.

Përmet

Frashëri Brothers Museum: Përmet; birthplace of the brothers Frashëri.

Shkodër

Gurakuqi, Luigi, House-Museum: Shkodër; house where the patriot lived.

Migjeni House-Museum: Shkodër; where the writer Migjeni lived.

Pascha, Vaso, House-Museum: Shkodër; house where the patriot lived.

Tiranë

Albanian National Culture Museum: Tiranë; attached to Institute of Nat. Culture; exhibits incl. agricultural tools of all periods, stock-breeding equipment, interiors and exteriors, household objects, textiles and customs, local crafts and ceramics up to the present day.

Fine Arts Gallery: Blvd Dëshmorët e Kombit, Tiranë; tel. (4) 2233975; fax (4) 2233975; f. 1952; Dir GËZIM QËNDRO.

National Historic Museum: Blvd 'Deshmoret e Kombit', sheshi Skenderbej, Tiranë; tel. (4) 2228389; fax (4) 2228389; f. 1981; displays 4,750 objects in pavilions representing different periods in Albanian history, heraldic emblems of Albanian princes, cathedral columns, icons by Onufri, Illyrian and Greco-Roman artefacts, history of modern Albania; Dir VILSON KURI.

National Museum of Archaeology: Tiranë; tel. (4) 2226541; f. 1948; attached to the Institute of Archaeology of the Acad. of Sciences of Albania; exhibits from prehistoric and historic times up to Middle Ages; responsible for archaeological museums at Durrës, Apollonia and Butrinti; library of 7,200 vols, film and photograph libraries; Curator ILIR GJIPALI; publ. *Illyria* (2 a year).

Natural Science Museum: Tiranë; attached to Univ. of Tiranë; f. 1948; zoology, botany, geology.

Vlorë

District Historical Museum: Vlorë; tel. (63) 2646; f. 1953; archaeology, history of art, history.

Muzeu Etnografik i Vlorës (Ethnographic Museum): Vlorë; tel. (33) 23514.

Muzeu i Pavarësisë (Independence Museum): Vlorë; tel. (33) 2229419; f. 1936; museum bldg was the site of the Ismail Qemali govt and drafting of the declaration of independence; exhibits incl. objects and documents from the Nat. Renaissance period of Albania, rooms where the first Albanian prime min. worked, the meeting room, a camera from 1912; Chief Officer AGRON SKEHU.

Nushi Brothers Museum: Vuno, Vlorë.

Universities

AKADEMIA E ARTEVE TE BUKURA, TIRANË
(Academy of Fine Arts, Tiranë)

Blvd Dëshmorët e Kombit, Sheshi Nen Tereza, Tiranë

Telephone and fax (4) 2225488

Internet: www.artacademy.al

Founded 1966 as Instituti i Lartë i Arteve (Higher Institute of Arts), univ. status 1990

State control

Rector: Prof. PETRIT MALAJ

Deputy Rectors: Assoc. Prof. ARBEN LLOZO, Assoc. Prof. ARTAN PEQUINI

Library Dir: MIRANDA BAKIASI

Library of 50,000 vols

Number of teachers: 386

Number of students: 947

DEANS

Faculty of Fine Arts: Assoc. Prof. SADIK SPAHIJA

Faculty of Music: Prof. SOKOL SHUPO

Faculty of Scenic Arts (Drama): Prof. KASTRIOT ÇAUSHI

AKADEMIA E EDUKIMIT FIZIK DHE SPORTEVE VOJO KUSHI, TIRANË
(Academy of Physical Education and Sports Vojo Kushi, Tiranë)

Rr. Muhamet Gjollesha, Tiranë

Telephone and fax (4) 2226652

E-mail: contact@aefs.edu.al

Internet: www.aefs.edu.al

Founded 1948 as Academy of Teknikumit to Fizkultures, present name 2000

State control

Rector: VEJSEL RIZVANOLLI

Vice-Rector: ARBEN KACURRI

Chancellor: MIRLINDA GALUSHI.

UNIVERSITETI 'ALEKSANDËR MOISIU'

Rr. Currilave 1, Durrës

Telephone: (52) 239162

Fax: (52) 239163

E-mail: info@uamd.edu.al

Internet: www.uamd.edu.al

Founded 2005

State control

Languages of instruction: Albanian, English

Rector: Prof. Dr AGIM KUKELI

Deputy Rectors: Dr MITHAT MEMA, LINDITA MUKLI

Chancellor: ULPIAN HOTI

Head of Int. Relations and Projects Office: BELINA BEDINI

Dir of Library: VENERA ALIAJ

Library of 5,000 vols, foreign scientific periodicals, 26 Albanian periodicals from 1945 to 2003

Number of teachers: 225

Number of students: 4,500

Publication: *Journal of studies on economics and society*

DEANS

Faculty of Economics and Administration: Dr BARDHYL CEKU

Faculty of Education: Dr SOFOKLI GARO

Faculty of Integrated Studies with Practice: Dr VLADIMIR MUKA (acting)

Higher Professional School: VLADIMIR MUKA (Dir)

UNIVERSITETI 'ALEKSANDËR XHUVANI' ELBASAN

Rinia, Elbasan

Telephone: (54) 52782

Fax: (54) 52593

E-mail: info@uniel.edu.al

Internet: www.uniel.edu.al

Founded 1909

State control

Academic year: October to July

Rector: Prof. Dr JANI DODE

Library of 100,000 vols

Number of teachers: 245

Number of students: 11,000

Publications: *Scientific Bulletin* (4 a year), *Studenti* (magazine)

DEANS

Faculty of Economics: Dr ALBERT DELIMETA

Faculty of Human Sciences: Prof. Dr ROLAND GJINI

Faculty of Natural Sciences: Prof. Dr PEÇI NAQELLARI

Faculty of Social Sciences: Prof. Dr VILSON KURI

UNIVERSITETI BUJQËSOR I TIRANËS
(Agricultural University of Tiranë)

Kodër-Kamëz, Tiranë

Telephone: (4) 7200873

Fax: (4) 7200874

E-mail: iroaut@yahoo.com

Internet: www.ubt.edu.al

Founded 1951, as Instituti i Lartë Bujqësor (Higher Agricultural Institute), univ. status 1991

State control

Academic year: October to September

Rector: Prof. Dr FATOS HARIZAJ

Vice-Rector for Education: Prof. Dr BIZENA BIJO

Vice-Rector for Research: Prof. Dr VELESIN PEÇULI

Head of Int. Relations office: Prof. Dr ARBEN VERÇUNI

Head of Research and Scientific Cooperation: Prof. Dr ANILA HODA

Library Dir: ERMIRA TOZAJ

Faculties of agriculture and environment, economy and agribusiness, forest science, biotechnology and food and veterinary medicine

Library of 15,000 vols

Number of teachers: 243

Number of students: 9,581

Publication: *Albanian Review of Agricultural Sciences*

DEANS

Faculty of Agriculture and Environment: Prof. Dr ARDIAN MAÇI
Faculty of Biotechnology and Food: Prof. Dr VLASH MARA
Faculty of Economy and Agribusiness: Prof. Dr BAHRI MUSABELLIU
Faculty of Forestry Sciences: Assoc. Prof. VATH TABAKU
Faculty of Veterinary Medicine: Assoc. Prof. DHIMITËR RAPTI

UNIVERSITETI EQREM ÇABEJ

Rr. Shtatori 18, Gjirokastër
Telephone and fax (84) 63776
E-mail: ugjrektori@albmail.com
Internet: www.uogj.edu.al
Founded 1971
State control
Rector: Prof. Dr GËZIM SALA

DEANS

Faculty of Education and Social Sciences: Prof. Dr ROLAND ZISI
Faculty of Natural Sciences: Assoc. Prof. Dr KRISTAQ KIKINA

UNIVERSITETI FAN S. NOLI

Rr. Gjergj Kastrioti, Korçë
Telephone: (82) 42230
Fax: (82) 42580
E-mail: info@unkorce.edu.al
Internet: www.unkorce.edu.al
Founded 1971 as Higher Agricultural Institute, present name and title 1992
State control
Languages of instruction: Albanian, English
Academic year: October to July
Faculties of agriculture, economy, education, Nursing
Rector: Asst Prof. Dr GJERGJI MERO
Vice-Rector: Assoc. Prof. Dr ALI JASHARI
Chief Admin. Officer: PETRIKA PETRO
Int. Relations Officer: ILO SHANO
Librarian: ANA VELO
Library of 30,000 books
Number of teachers: 94 full-time teachers and 115 part-time teachers
Number of students: 3,080 (incl. part-time and corresp. students)
Publication: Buletin Shkencor (Scientific Bulletin)

DEANS

Faculty of Agriculture: Prof. Dr IRENA KALLÇO
Faculty of Economics: Prof. Dr FREDERIK ÇUÇLLARI
Faculty of Education: Asst Prof. Dr ALEKSANDRA PILURI
Department of Nursing: JETONA MYTEVELIU

PROFESSORS

JASHARI, A., Education
MANOKU, Y., Economics
PENDAVINJI, G., Education
TENEQEXHIU, K., Agriculture
ZEFI, E., Economics

UNIVERSITETI I SHKODRËS 'LUIGJ GURAKUQI'
(University of Shkodra 'Luigj Gurakuqi')

Rektorati, Sheshi 2 Prilli, Shkodër
Telephone and fax (22) 43747

E-mail: iroshkoder@unishk.edu.al
Internet: www.unishk.edu.al
Founded 1991, based on fmr Instituti i Lartë Pedagogjik (Higher Pedagogical Institute), Shkodër (f. 1957)
State control
Languages of instruction: Albanian, French
Academic year: October to July
Chancellor: ROBERT SKENDERIS
Rector: Prof. Dr ARTAN HAXHI
Vice-Rector: Prof. Dr FATMIR VADAHI
Librarian: ALIDA LUKA
Number of teachers: 179 full-time, 368 part-time
Number of students: 9,108 full-time, 2,422 part-time)
Publication: Scientific Bulletin (separate series on Natural Sciences, Social Sciences, Didactics, each 2 a year)

DEANS

Faculty of Economics: Prof. Dr ARJETA TROSHANI
Faculty of Education: Prof. Dr MIT'HAT HOXHA
Faculty of Foreign Languages: Dr RAJMOND KËÇIRA
Faculty of Law: GASPËR KOKAJ
Faculty of Natural Sciences: Prof. Dr ADEM BEKTESHI
Faculty of Social Sciences: Prof. Dr PAULINA HOXHA

UNIVERSITETI I TIRANËS
(University of Tiranë)

Blvr Dëshmorët e Kombit, Sheshi Nen Tereza, POB 183, Tiranë
Telephone: (4) 2228402
Fax: (4) 2223981
E-mail: info@unitir.edu.al
Internet: www.unitir.edu.al
Founded 1957
State control
Academic year: September to June
Rector: Prof. Dr DHORI KULE
Vice-Rector: Prof. Dr ELSA KONE
Sec.: MAKLENA ÇABEJ
Library Dir: ARJANA KITA
Library of 700,000 vols
Number of teachers: 750
Number of students: 27,745
Publications: Buletini i Shkencave Mjekësore (Medicine, 4 a year), Buletini i Shkencave të Natyrës (Natural Sciences, 4 a year), Përmbledhje studimesh (Colln of Studies, 4 a year, with Institute of Geological Research)

DEANS

Faculty of Economics: Dr KADRI XHULALI
Faculty of Foreign Languages: Doc. AVNI XHELILI
Faculty of History and Linguistics: Dr PASKAL MILO
Faculty of Law: ZEF BROZI
Faculty of Mechanics and Electronics: Dr GËZIM KARAPICI
Faculty of Medicine: Doc. KRISTO PANO
Faculty of Natural Science: Prof. Dr LLUKAN PUKA
Faculty of Philosophy and Sociology: Doc. LUAN PIRDENI

UNIVERSITETI POLITEKNIK I TIRANËS
(Polytechnic University of Tirana)

Blvd Dëshmorët e Kombit, Sheshi Nen Tereza, Nr 4, Tiranë
Telephone: (4) 2227996
Fax: (4) 2227914
E-mail: enkjaho@yahoo.com
Internet: www.upt.al
Founded 1951 as Polytechnic Institute, present status 1991
State control
Rector: JORGAQ KACANI
Vice-Rector: AKLI FUNDO
Library of 250,000 vols, 20,000 periodicals
Number of teachers: 470
Number of students: 6,297

DEANS

Faculty of Construction Engineering: ANDREA MALIQARI
Faculty of Electrical Engineering: AIDA SPAHIU
Faculty of Geology and Mining: PERPARIM HOXHA
Faculty of Mechanical Engineering: ANDONAQ LONDO

UNIVERSITETI TEKNOLOGJIK 'ISMAIL QEMAL' VLORË
('Ismail Qemal' Technological University of Vlorë)

Lagija 'Pavaresia', Skele Vlore, Vlorë
Telephone: (63) 24952
Fax: (63) 24952
E-mail: kancelar@univlora.edu.al
Internet: www.univlora.edu.al
Founded 1994 as a Technological University
State control
Rector: EUSTRAT ZHUPA
Chancellor: MIMOZA XHELADINI
Library of 10,100 vols
Number of teachers: 195
Number of students: 15,000

DEANS

Faculty of Economics: Dr ALBERT QARRI
Faculty of Humanities: Dr ENGJELL LICAJ
Faculty of Public Health: Asst Prof. HAJDAR KICAJ
Faculty of Technical Sciences: (vacant)

UNIVERSITY OF NEW YORK TIRANA

Rr. 'Komuna e Parisit' prane Kopshtit Botanik, POB 2301, Tiranë
Telephone: (42) 273056
Fax: (42) 273059
E-mail: admissions@unyt.edu.al
Internet: www.unyt.edu.al
Founded 2002, accredited by Min. of Education and Science 2006
Private control
Rector: Dr DIONYSIOS MENTZENIOTIS
Deputy Rector: KONSTANTINOS GIAKOUMIS
President and Founder: ELIAS FOUTSIS
Faculties of Economics and Business, Mathematics and Natural Sciences, Computer Science and Information Systems, English Language and Literature, Humanities, Social and Political Sciences.

ALGERIA

The Higher Education System

The higher education system in Algeria falls under the authority of the Ministry of Higher Education and Scientific Research. In 2007/08 the number of students receiving higher education was 999,690, and several thousand students also go abroad to study. In addition to the 36 main universities, there are 13 other Centres universitaires and a number of technical colleges.

Students are admitted to higher education on the basis of the Baccalauréat de l'Enseignement Secondaire. The three levels of higher education qualifications are the Diplôme d'études universitaires appliqué (DEUA) or Diplôme d'études supérieures (Licence), Maitrise and Doctorat d'état. The DEUA is awarded after three years of study, whilst the Licence is usually awarded in scientific fields. Engineering, medicine, dentistry and pharmacy degrees and other professional courses last for five years, while the Doctor of Medicine is awarded after seven years. The second degree level (and first postgraduate) is the Maitrise. This is a two-year taught course including a thesis. Finally, following a Maitrise awarded with a grade of at least assez bien, a Doctorat d'état is awarded after three to five years of study.

Students may also undertake technical or vocational training at university level. On completion of basic education, vocational training is offered by Centres de formation professionnelle, and on completion of the three-year course a student is awarded the Certificat d'aptitude professionelle (also called the Certificat de technicien), whilst completion of a four-year course leads to the Brevet de maîtrise.

Instituts de technologie (technological institutes) are educational establishments operated by other ministries or national corporations. Degrees offered include the Diplôme d'études universitaires appliquées (DEUA) (two-and-a-half or three years) and the Diplôme d'ingénieur (five years). These institutes are regulated by the ministry or national corporation responsible, and programmes are not standardized.

Higher education in Algeria is currently undergoing reform. The new system, known as LMD (Licence, Masters, Doctorate) aims to bring Algerian higher education into line with other international education systems, such as the European Bologna model. The first stage, a three-year 180-credit Licence began to be phased in from 2004 and has since been implemented as a pilot project at 10 universities. The second stage, a two-year 120-credit Masters was phased in from 2007/8.

Regulatory and Representative Bodies

GOVERNMENT

Ministry of Culture: Palais de la Culture 'Moufdi Zakaria', Plateau des Annassers, BP 100, Kouba, Algiers; tel. (21) 29-12-28; fax (21) 29-20-89; e-mail info@mcc.gov.dz; Minister KHALIDA TOUMI-MESSAOUDI.

Ministry of Higher Education and Scientific Research: 11 chemin Doudou Mokhtar, Ben Aknoun, Algiers; tel. (21) 91-23-23; e-mail info@mesrs.dz; internet www.mesrs.dz; Minister RACHID HARROUBIA.

Ministry of National Education: 8 rue de Pékin, el-Mouradia, Algiers; tel. (21) 60-67-57; fax (21) 60-57-82; e-mail education@men.dz; internet www.meducation.edu.dz; Minister Prof. BOUBEKEUR BENBOUZID.

Ministry of Training and Vocational Education: Route de Dély-Ibrahim, Ben Aknoun, Algiers; tel. (21) 91-15-28; fax (21) 60-09-36; e-mail abada@mfep.gov.dz; internet www.mfep.gov.dz; Minister Dr EL-HADI KHALDI.

NATIONAL BODY

Commission nationale d'Equivalences (National Commission for Credentials Evaluation): c/o Ministry of Higher Education and Scientific Research, 11 chemin Doudou Mokhtar, Ben Aknoun, Algiers; tel. (21) 91-17-96; fax (21) 91-46-01; e-mail mesrs@ist.cerist.dz; internet www.mesrs.edu.dz/english.

Learned Societies

GENERAL

El-Djazairia el-Mossilia: 1 rue Hamitouche, Algiers; f. 1930; cultural soc., particularly concerned with Arab classical music; 452 mems; Pres. ALI BENMERABET; Sec.-Gen. ABDELHADI MERAOUBI.

HISTORY, GEOGRAPHY AND ARCHAEOLOGY

Société Archéologique du Département de Constantine (Constantine Archaeological Society): Musée Gustave Mercier, Constantine; f. 1852; 250 mems; library of 10,000 vols; Pres. Dr BAGHLI (acting); publ. *Recueil des Notices et Mémoires*.

Société Historique Algérienne (Algerian Historical Society): c/o Faculté des Lettres, Univ. d'Alger, Algiers; f. 1963; 600 mems; publ. *Revue d'Histoire et Civilisation du Maghreb*.

LANGUAGE AND LITERATURE

British Council: British Embassy, 12 rue Slimane Amirate, Hydra, Algiers; tel. (21) 48-09-47; e-mail john.mitchell@britishcouncil.org; offers courses and examinations in English language and British culture and promotes cultural exchange with the UK; Dir JOHN MITCHELL.

Instituto Cervantes: 9 rue Khelifa Boukhalfa, 16000 Algiers; tel. (21) 63-38-02; fax (21) 63-41-36; e-mail cenarg@cervantes.es; internet argel.cervantes.es; f. 1992; offers courses and examinations in Spanish language and culture and promotes cultural exchange with Spain and Spanish-speaking Latin and Central America; Dir FRANCISCO CORRAL SÁNCHEZ-CABEZUDO; Academic Head LUIS ROGER RODRÍGUEZ PANIAGUA; Administrator MARÍA JOSÉ ARTÉS RODRÍGUEZ.

MEDICINE

Union Médicale Algérienne (Algerian Medical Association): POB 8, Aadun St, Algiers; tel. (21) 73-36-00; fax (21) 63-27-77; publ. *Algérie Médicale*.

Research Institutes

GENERAL

Organisme National de la Recherche Scientifique (National Bureau of Scientific Research): Route de Dély Ibrahim, Ben Aknoun, Algiers; main executive body for govt policy; Dir (vacant).

Research Centres:

Centre de Coordination des Etudes et des Recherches sur les Infrastructures, les Equipements du Ministère de l'Enseignement et de la Recherche Scientifique (Centre for the Coordination of Studies and Research on the Infrastructure and Facilities of the Ministry of Education and on Scientific Research): 1 rue Bachir Attar, Algiers; Dir A. GUEDIRI.

Centre de Développement des Energies Renouvelables (CDER) (Renewable Energy Development Centre): BP 62, Route de l'Observatoire, Bouzaréah, Algiers; tel. (21) 90-15-03; fax (21) 90-15-60; e-mail belhamel@cder.dz; internet www.cder.dz; f. 1988 as Centre Nat. d'Etudes et de Recherche en Energie Renouvelable (CRENO); solar energy, wind energy, thermal energy, bio-energy, hydro-energy; CEO BELHAMEL MAIOUF; publ. *Rebue des Energies Renouvelables*.

Centre d'Etudes et de Recherches en Biologie Humaine et Animale (CERBHA) (Study and Research Centre for Human and Animal Biology): BP 9, Université des Sciences et de la Technologie Houari Boumédienne, Algiers; Dir K. BENLATRACHE.

Centre d'Etudes et de Recherche sur le Développement Régional, Annaba (CERDA) (Annaba Study and Research Centre for Regional Development): Université d'Annaba, Annaba; Dir M. AMIRI.

Centre d'Etudes et de Recherche sur le Développement Régional, Oran (CERDO) (Oran Study and Research Centre for Regional Development): Université d'Oran, Es-Senia, Oran; Dir M. TALEB.

Centre d'Information Scientifique et Technique et de Transferts Technologiques (CISTTT) (Centre for Scientific and Technical Information and for Technological Transfer): BP 315, blvd Frantz Fanon, Algiers (Gare); Dir M. TIAR (acting).

Centre National d'Astronomie, d'Astrophysique et de Géophysique (CNAAG) (National Centre of Astronomy, Astrophysics and Geophysics): Observatoire de Bouzaréah, Algiers; Dir H. BEN-HALLOU.

Centre National de Documentation et de Recherche en Pédagogie (CNDRP) (National Documentation and Research Centre for Education): Université d'Alger, 2 rue Didouche Mourad, Algiers; Dir M. D. CHABOU.

Centre National d'Etudes et de Recherches pour l'Aménagement du Territoire (CNERAT) (National Centre for Studies and Research in National and Regional Development): 3 rue Professor Vincent, Telemly, Algiers; Dir MESSAOUD TAIEB.

Centre National de Recherches et d'Application des Géosciences (CRAG) (National Centre for Geoscientific Research and Application): 2 rue Didouche Mourad, Algiers; Dir R. ABDELHALIM.

Centre National de Recherche sur les Zones Arides (CNRZA) (National Centre for Research on Arid Zones): Université d'Alger, 2 rue Didouche Mourad, Algiers; Dir N. BOUNAGA (acting).

Centre National de Traduction et de Terminologie Arabe (CNTTA) (National Centre for Arab Translation and Terminology): 3 blvd Franklin Roosevelt, Algiers; Dir A. MEZIANE.

Centre de Recherches Anthropologiques, Préhistoriques et Ethnographiques (CRAPE) (Centre for Anthropological, Prehistoric and Ethnographical Research): 3 blvd Franklin Roosevelt, Algiers; f. 1957; Dir M. BELKAID.

Centre de Recherches en Architecture et Urbanisme (CRAU) (Centre for Research in Architecture and Town Planning): BP 2, El-Harrach, Algiers; Dir AMEZIANE IKENE.

Centre de Recherches en Economie Appliquées pour le Développement (CREAD) (Centre for Research in Applied Economics for Development): rue Djamal Eddine El-Afghani, El Hamadia-Bouzareah, Algiers; tel. (21) 94-23-67; fax (21) 94-17-16; e-mail cread@wissal.dz; internet www.cread.edu.dz; f. 1985; Dir MOHAMED YACINE FERFERA; publ. *Les Cahiers du CREAD.*

Centre de Recherches Océanographiques et des Pêches (CROP) (Centre for Oceanographic and Fisheries Research): Jetée Nord, Amirauté, Algiers; Dir RACHID SEMROUD.

Centre de Recherches sur les Ressources Biologiques Terrestres (CRBT) (Centre for Research on Biological Resources of the Land): 2 rue Didouche Mourad, Algiers; Dir (vacant).

Centre Universitaire de Recherches, d'Etudes et de Réalisations (CURER) (University Centre for Research, Study and Application): Université de Constantine, 54 rue Larbi Ben M'Hidi, Constantine; agriculture, forestry, energy resources; Dir FELLAH LAZHAR.

AGRICULTURE, FISHERIES AND VETERINARY SCIENCE

Institut National de la Recherche Agronomique (INRAA) (National Institute of Agronomic Research): 2 ave des Frères Ouadak, Belfort, El Harrach, Algiers; tel. (21) 75-63-15; f. 1966; library of 6,500 vols; Dir M. BEKKOUCHE; publ. *Bulletin d'Agronomie Saharienne.*

Institut National de Recherche Forestière (National Institute of Forestry Research): Arboretum de Bainem, Algiers; tel. (21) 79-72-96; fax (21) 78-32-11; f. 1981; library of 4,000 vols; Dir FATEH DAHIEDINE; publ. *Annale de la recherche forestière.*

BIBLIOGRAPHY, LIBRARY SCIENCE AND MUSEOLOGY

Institut de Bibliothéconomie et des Sciences Documentaires (Institute of Library Economics and Documentation): Univ. d'Alger, 2 rue Didouche Mourad, Algiers; tel. (21) 7771088434; fax (21) 93-15-10; e-mail allahoum@yahoo.fr; f. 1975; Dir Prof. RABAH ALLAHOUM.

HISTORY, GEOGRAPHY AND ARCHAEOLOGY

Centre National de Recherches Préhistoriques Anthropologiques et Historiques (National Centre for Prehistorical, Anthropological and Historical Research): 3 rue F. D. Roosevelt, Algiers; tel. and fax (21) 74-79-29; f. 1993; library of 35,000 vols; Dir N. E. SAOUDI; publs *Libyca, Madjallat et Tarikh.*

Institut National de Cartographie (National Institute of Cartography): 123 rue de Tripoli, BP 69, Hussein-Dey, Algiers; f. 1967; under trusteeship of Min. of Defence; Dir NADIR SAADI; publ. maps (100 to 150 a year).

MEDICINE

Institut National d'Hygiène et de Sécurité (National Institute of Hygiene and Safety): Lotissement Meridja, BP 07, 42395 Saoula; f. 1972; research in the fields of hygiene and safety at work; library of 8,000 vols, 110 periodicals, 45,000 microfiches; Dir-Gen. CHÉRIF SOUAMI; publ. *Revue Algérienne de Prévention* (4 a year).

Institut Pasteur d'Algérie (Pasteur Institute in Algeria): rue du Dr Laveran, Algiers; tel. (21) 65-88-60; fax (21) 67-25-03; f. 1910; research and higher studies in microbiology, parasitology and immunology; preparation of vaccines and sera in conjunction with the health services of Algeria; library of 47,000 vols, 500 periodicals; Dir Prof. F. BOULAHBAL; publ. *Archives* (12 a year).

TECHNOLOGY

Commissariat aux Energies Nouvelles (Commission for New Sources of Energy): BP 1017, Algiers Gare; tel. (21) 61-14-18; f. 1983; research and devt in the field of renewable sources of energy, incl. atomic, solar, wind and geothermal energy; incl. centres for energy conversion and for nuclear and solar studies.

Office National de la Recherche Géologique et Minière/Service Géologique de l'Algérie (National Office of Geological and Mining Research): Cité Ib Khaldoun, BP 102, Boumerdès 35000; tel. (24) 81-75-99; fax (24) 81-83-79; e-mail orgm-dg@ogrm.com.dz; internet www.orgm.com.dz; f. 1883; 5 regional divs: East (located in Tebessa), Central (Tizi Ouzou), West (Sidi Bel Abbes), South West (Bechar) and South (Tamanrasset); library of 50,000 vols, periodicals, maps and aerial photographs; Gen. Man. ABDELK-

ADER SEMIANI; publs *Bulletins du Service Géologique d'Algérie* (2 a year), *Mémoires du Service Géologique de l'Algérie* (1 a year).

Libraries and Archives

Algiers

Archives Nationale d'Algérie (National Archives of Algeria): BP 61, Algiers-Gare; tel. (213) 54-21-60; fax (213) 54-16-16; f. 1971; Dir ABDELMADJID CHIKHI.

Bibliothèque de l'Université d'Alger (Library of the University of Algiers): 2 rue Didouche Mourad, Algiers; tel. (21) 64-02-15; fax (21) 61-31-44; f. 1880; 800,000 vols.

Bibliothèque Nationale (National Library): 1 ave Frantz Fanon, Algiers; tel. (21) 63-06-32; f. 1835; 950,000 vols; spec. collns incl. Africa and the Maghreb; Dir MUHAMMAD AÏSSA-MOUSSA; publs *Bibliographie de l'Algérie* (2 a year), *Publications*, several collns in Arabic and French.

Section de Diffusion Scientifique et Technique du Centre Culturel Français d'Alger (Department for the Distribution of Scientific and Technical Information at the French Cultural Centre in Algiers): 7 rue du Médecin Capitaine Hassani Issad, 16000 Algiers; tel. (21) 63-61-83; 25,000 vols, 350 periodicals; Dir MARC SAGAERT.

Constantine

Bibliothèque Municipale (Municipal Library): Hôtel de Ville, Constantine; f. 1895; 25,000 vols.

Museums and Art Galleries

Algiers

Direction du Patrimoine Culturel (Office of Cultural Heritage): Ministère de la Culture et du Tourisme, Kouba, Algiers; f. 1901; gen. admin. of museums, restoration, conservation and archaeological excavations; library of 8,000 vols, 300 periodicals; Dir S. A. BAGHLI; publ. *Bulletin d'Archéologie Algérienne* (1 a year).

Musée National des Antiquités (National Museum of Antiquities): Parc de la Liberté, Algiers; tel. (21) 74-66-86; fax (21) 74-74-71; f. 1897; library of 3,100 vols, 102 periodicals; Dir DRIAS LAKHDAR; publ. *Annales du Musée National des Antiquités.*

Musée National des Beaux Arts d'Alger (National Fine Arts Museum of Algiers): pl. Dar-el-Salem, El-Hamma, Algiers; tel. and fax (21) 66-49-16; f. 1930; library of 17,000 vols, 300 periodicals; Dir DALILA ORFALI; publ. *Revue* (1 a year).

Musée National du Bardo: 3 rue F. D. Roosevelt, Algiers; tel. (21) 74-76-41; fax (21) 74-24-53; f. 1930; prehistory, ethnography; library of 3,000 vols; Dir FATIMA AZZOUG.

Musée National du Djihad: El Madania, Algiers; tel. (21) 65-34-88; f. 1983; contemporary history; publ. *Actes du Musée.*

Constantine

Musée de Cirta: Blvd de la République, Constantine; f. 1853; archaeology, art; library of 20,000 vols; Dir AHMED GUED-DOUDA; publ. *Recueil et Mémoires de la Société Archéologique de Constantine.*

Oran

Musée National Zabana: Blvd Zabana, Oran; tel. (41) 34-37-81; f. 1935; prehistory, Roman and Punic archaeology, ethnography, zoology, geology, botany, sculpture and painting; Dir Dr MALKI NORDINE.

Sétif

Musée National de Sétif: Rue de l'A.L.N., 19000 Sétif; tel. (36) 84-35-36; fax (36) 84-58-13; e-mail mns@elhidhab.cerist.dz; f. 1991; prehistoric, Roman, Byzantine and medieval Islamic antiquities; Curator CHERIF RIACHE.

Skikda

Musée de Skikda: Skikda; Punic and Roman antiquities, modern art.

Tlemcen

Musée de Tlemcen: pl. Khemisti, 13000 Tlemcen; tel. (43) 26-55-06; Islamic art, minerals, botany, Numidian and Roman archaeology.

Universities

UNIVERSITÉ 8 MAI 1945 DE GUELMA

BP 401, Guelma 24000
Telephone: (37) 20-49-80
Fax: (37) 20-72-68
E-mail: martridha@gmail.com
Internet: www.univ-guelma.dz
Founded 2001
State control
Rector: Prof. MOHAMED NEMAMCHA
Number of teachers: 137
Number of students: 6,716
Faculties of Economics and Management, Humanities and Social Sciences, Law, Science and Engineering.

UNIVERSITÉ ABDELHAMID IBN BADIS DE MOSTAGANEM

POB 227, Mostaganem 27000
Telephone: (45) 26-54-55
Fax: (45) 26-54-52
E-mail: webmaster@univ-mosta.dz
Internet: www.univ-mosta.dz
Founded 1978
State control
Rector: Prof. SEDDIKI M'HAMED MOHAMED SALAH EDDINE
Publication: *Annales du Patrimoine* (Arabic and French, 2 a year)
Faculties of arts and letters, law and commerce, physical training and sports, science and engineering, social sciences.

UNIVERSITÉ ABOU BEKR BELKAID DE TLEMCEN

22 rue Abi Ayad Abdelkrim, Faubourg Pasteur, BP 119, 13000 Tlemcen
Telephone: (43) 20-31-89
Fax: (43) 20-41-89
E-mail: webcri@univ-tlemcen.dz
Internet: www.univ-tlemcen.dz
Founded 1974 as Centre Universitaire de Tlemcen
State control (by Min. of Higher Education and Scientific Research)
Languages of instruction: Arabic, French
Academic year: September to July
Rector: ZOUBIR CHAOUCHE-RAMDANE
Vice-Rector for External Relations: SIDI MOHAMMED BOUCHENAK-KHELLADI (Teaching)
Vice-Rector for Planning: FOUAD GHOMARI
Vice-Rector for Teaching: GHAOUTI MEKANCHA
Sec.-Gen.: ABDELDJALIL SARI ALI
Librarian: NOUREDDINE HADJI
Library of 66,000 vols

Number of teachers: 1,130
Number of students: 30,036

PROFESSORS
Medicine:
    ALLAL, M. R., Radiology
    BENKALFAT, F. Z., Cardiology
    BENKALFAT, M., General Surgery
    HADJ ALLAL, F., Otorhinolaryngology
Science:
    BABA AHMED, A., Physical Chemistry
    BENMOUANA, M., Nuclear Engineering
    BENYOUCEF, B., Energy Physics
    BOUAMOUD, M., Atomic Physics
    BOUCHERIF, A., Applied Mathematics
    HADJIAT, M., Mathematics
    TALEB BENDIAB, S. A., Chemistry
Social Sciences and Humanities:
    BELMOKADEM, M., Quantitative Technology
    BENDIABDALLAH, A., Management
    BOUCHENAK KHELLADI, S. M., Management
    DENDOUNI, H., Civil Law
    DERRAGUI, Z., Literature
    KAHLOULA, M., Private Law
    KALFAT, C., Criminology
    SOUTI, M., Finance

DIRECTORS
Institute of Arabic Language and Literature: MOHAMMED ABBAS
Institute of Biology: KEBIR BOUCHERIT
Institute of Civil Engineering: MUSTAPHA DJAFFOUR
Institute of Earth Sciences: MOHAMED EL KHAMIS BAGHLI
Institute of Economics: MOHAMMED ZINE BARKA
Institute of Electronics: FETHI TARIK BENDIMERAD
Institute of Exact Sciences: ABDERRAHIM CHOUKCHOU BRAHAM
Institute of Foreign Languages: ZOUBIR DENDEN
Institute of Forestry: RACHID BOUHRAOUA
Institute of Hydraulics: ZINE EL ABIDINE CHERIF
Institute of Law and Administration: MOHAMMED BENAMAR
Institute of Mechanical Engineering: FETHI METALSI-TANI
Institute of Medical Sciences: FOUZI TALEB
Institute of Popular Culture: OKACHA CHAIF
Institute for the Promotion of the Arabic Language and for Intensive Language Training: BOUMÉDIÈNE BENMOUSSAT

UNIVERSITE AMAR TELIDJI DE LAGHOUAT

Route de Ghardaia, BP 37G, Laghouat 03000
Telephone: (29) 93-59-75
Fax: (29) 93-26-98
E-mail: rectorat@mail.lagh-univ.dz
Internet: www.lagh-univ.dz
Founded 1986 as Ecole Normale Supérieure de l'Enseignement Technique; univ. status 2001
State control
Languages of instruction: Arabic, French
Academic year: October to July
Rector: Dr AZIB MAKHLOUF
Librarian: NOUIOUA HADJIRA
Library of 65,427 vols, 10 periodicals
Number of teachers: 312
Number of students: 9,417 , 41 foreign students
Faculties of Economics and Management, Engineering Science, Law and Humanities.

UNIVERSITÉ BADJI MOKHTAR DE ANNABA

BP 12, 23000 Annaba
Telephone: (38) 87-26-78
Fax: (38) 87-24-36
E-mail: laskri@univ-annaba.org
Internet: www.univ-annaba.org
Founded 1975
State control
Languages of instruction: Arabic, French
Academic year: September to June
Rector: Prof. MOHAMED TAYEB LASKRI
Vice-Rector for External Relations: Prof. L'HADI ATOUI
Vice-Rector for Graduate Studies: Prof. MOHAMED SALAH BOULAKOUD
Vice-Rector for Planning: Prof. MOUSSA OUCHEFOUN
Vice-Rector for Postgraduate Studies and Research: Prof. KADDOUR BOUKHEMIS
Chief Admin. Officer: SAID ARABI
Librarian: N. MANCEUR
Number of teachers: 1,221
Number of students: 37,978
Publications: *Et-Tawassol* (humanities and social sciences, 2 a year), *Synthese* (science and technology, 2 a year)

DEANS
Faculty of Earth Sciences: TAYEB SERRADJ
Faculty of Economics and Management: CHERIF HAMZAOUI
Faculty of Engineering: NASR-EDDINE DEBBACHE
Faculty of Law: DJAMEL ABDELNASSER MANAA
Faculty of Letters, Humanities and Social Sciences: MOHAMED AÏLANE
Faculty of Medicine: ABDESSLEM KAÏDI
Faculty of Science: FAOUZIA REBBANI

UNIVERSITÉ COLONEL AHMED DRAIA D'ADRAR

Rue 11 Décembre 1960, Adrar 01960
Telephone: (49) 96-59-07
Fax: (49) 96-75-71
E-mail: info@univadrar.org
Internet: www.univadrar.org
Founded 2001
State control
Number of teachers: 35
Number of students: 1,030
Faculties of Arts and Humanities, Science and Engineering, Social Sciences and Islamic Studies.

UNIVERSITÉ D'ALGER

2 rue Didouche Mourad, Algiers
Telephone: (21) 64-69-70
E-mail: contact@univ-alger.dz
Internet: www.univ-alger.dz
Founded 1879 (reorganized 1909)
Languages of instruction: Arabic, French
State control
Academic year: September to June
Pres.: Prof. TAHAR HADJAR
Deputy-Pres. for Pedagogy: S. BABA-AMEUR
Deputy-Pres. for Planning: RABAH KHIMA
Deputy-Pres. for Postgraduates and Scientific Research: A. E. R. AZZI
Librarian: ABDELLAH ABDI
Number of teachers: 1,400
Number of students: 32,000

UNIVERSITÉ D'ORAN

BP 1524, El-M'Naouer, Oran 31000
Telephone: (41) 58-19-40
Fax: (41) 41-01-57
E-mail: contact@univ-oran.dz
Internet: www.univ-oran.dz

Founded 1967
State control
Languages of instruction: Arabic, French
Academic year: September to July (2 semesters)
Rector: Prof. LARBI CHAHED
Vice-Rector for Pedagogy and Registration: AHMED BENAYED
Vice-Rector for Planning and Equipment: MOHAMMED DELLIL
Vice-Rector for Postgraduate Studies, Research and External Relations: AHMED AMRANI
Sec.-Gen.: MABROUK IKHLEF
Librarian: S. CHAÏB DRAA
Library of 800,000 vols
Number of teachers: 1,200
Number of students: 45,000
Publications: *Al Bahith Ilqtissady* (2 a year), *Cahiers du Centre de Documentation des Sciences Humaines*, *Cahiers de Géographie de l'Ouest Algérien*, *El Moutarjeem* (1 a year), *Proceedings of the Research Unit in Social and Cultural Anthropology*, *Revue des Langues*, *Social Sciences Review* (1 a year), *University Letters* (4 a year)

DIRECTORS

Faculty of Arabic Language, Foreign Languages and Fine Arts: Prof. CHEIKH BOUGUERBA
Faculty of Economics: Prof. BOULANDUAR BACHIR
Faculty of Geography and Land Management: Prof. MEKAHLI LARBI
Faculty of Humanities and Religious Studies: Prof. BEKRI A. KRIM
Faculty of Law and Admin.: Prof. YELLES CHAOUCH BACHIR
Faculty of Medical Studies: Prof. ZOUBIR FOUATIH
Faculty of Sciences: Prof. ABDELGHANI KRALEFAT
Faculty of Social Sciences: Prof. AHMED LALAOUI
IGLAEIL Institute: Prof. MOHAMED MELIANI
Institute of Natural Sciences: ZITOUNI BOUTIBA

UNIVERSITÉ DE BECHAR

BP 417, Kenadsa-Béchar
Telephone: (49)-81-55-81
Fax: (49)-81-52-44
E-mail: webmaster@univ-bechar.dz
Internet: www.univ-bechar.dz
Founded 1986 as Institut National d'Etude Supérieure; present name 2009
Rector: SLIMANI ABD AL-KADER
Number of teachers: 371
Number of students: 8,461
Faculties of Arts, Human and Social Sciences, Languages, Law and Politics, Science and Technology.

UNIVERSITE DE BEJAIA

Route de Terga Ouzemour, Bejaia 06000
Telephone: (34) 21-43-33
Fax: (34) 21-60-98
E-mail: rectorat@univ-bejaia.dz
Internet: www.univ-bejaia.dz
Founded 1983
State control
Rector: DJOUDI MERABET
Number of students: 3,900

DEANS

Faculty of Arts and Humanities: SALAH DERRADJI
Faculty of Economics and Law: FARID YAICI
Faculty of Natural and Life Sciences: (vacant)

Faculty of Science and Engineering Science: BOUALEM SAIDANI

UNIVERSITÉ DE JIJEL

BP 98, Ouled Aissa, Jijel
Telephone: (34) 50-14-00
Fax: (34) 50-18-65
E-mail: webmaster@univ-jijel.dz
Internet: www.univ-jijel.dz
Founded 1998
State control
Number of teachers: 137
Number of students: 3,757
Faculties of Engineering, Law, Management, Science.

UNIVERSITÉ DE LA FORMATION CONTINUE D'ALGER
(University of Continuous Education)

BP 41, Bois des Cars, Dely Ibrahim, Algiers
Telephone: (21) 91-06-81
Fax: (21) 91-06-82
E-mail: recteur@ufc.dz
Internet: www.ufc.dz
Founded 1990
Rector: ABDELDJEBAR LEMNOUAR
Vice-Rector for Teaching: ABDELKADER NACERI
Vice-Rector for Communication: BRAHIM BOUKRAA
General Secretary: ABDELKARIM SENIANE.

UNIVERSITÉ DE M'SILA

BP 166, Ichebilia, M'sila 28000
Telephone: (35) 55-04-11
Fax: (35) 55-04-04
E-mail: webcell@univ-msila.dz
Internet: www.univ-msila.dz
Founded as Centre Universitaire de M'sila; present status 2001
State control
Rector: Prof. SLIMANE BARHOUMI
Number of teachers: 246
Number of students: 10,355
Faculties of Arts and Social Sciences, Economics, Law, Management and Commercial Sciences, Science and Engineering.

UNIVERSITÉ DE MASCARA

BP 305, Route de Mamounia, Mascara 29000
Telephone: (45) 80-41-69
Fax: (45) 80-41-64
E-mail: cum@univ-mascara.dz
Internet: www.univ-mascara.dz
Faculties of Arts, Commerce and Management, Economics, Languages and Languages of the Social and Human Sciences, Law and Administration, Natural and Life Sciences, Science and Technology.

UNIVERSITÉ DE TÉBESSA

Tébessa 12002
Telephone: (37) 49-00-62
Fax: (37) 49-02-68
E-mail: cutebessa@ist.cerist.dz
Internet: www.univ-tebessa.dz
Rector: Prof. ABDELKRIM GOUASMIA.

UNIVERSITÉ DES SCIENCES ET DE LA TECHNOLOGIE HOUARI BOUMEDIENE

BP 32, El Alia, Bab Ezzouar, Algiers 16111
Telephone: (21) 24-72-83
Fax: (21) 24-79-04
E-mail: benrect@wissal.dz
Internet: www.usthb.dz

Founded 1974
Languages of instruction: Arabic, French
Academic year: September to July
Rector: Prof. BENALI BENZAGHOU
Vice-Rectors: MALEK BOUHADEF, MAHREZ DRIR, MOHAMED SAIDI, DJAMEL EDDINE AKRETCHE
Sec.-Gen.: REDA DJELLID
Librarian: SOUHILA BENRABAH
Number of teachers: 1,509
Number of students: 20,078 undergraduate, 3,098 postgraduate
Publication: *Annales des Sciences et de la Technologie*

DEANS

Faculty of Biological Sciences: FATIMA LARABA-DJEBARI
Faculty of Chemistry: MOHAMED CHATER
Faculty of Civil Engineering: FARID KAOUA
Faculty of Earth Science, Geography and Management Territory: AZIOUZ OUABADI
Faculty of Electronics and Computer Science: ZAIA ALIMAZIGHI
Faculty of Mathematics: KAMEL BOUKHETALA
Faculty of Mechanical Engineering and Chemical Engineering: RACHIDA MAACHI
Faculty of Physics: MOHAMED BENDAOUD

UNIVERSITÉ DES SCIENCES ET DE LA TECHNOLOGIE MOHAMED BOUDIAF D'ORAN

BP 1505, El Mnaouer, Oran
Telephone: (41) 56-03-33
Fax: (41) 56-03-22
E-mail: webmaster@univ-usto.dz
Internet: www.univ-usto.dz
Founded 1975
Languages of instruction: Arabic, French
Academic year: September to July
Rector: Prof. M. BENSAFI
Vice-Rector for Planning and Orientation: MOHAMED TEBBAL
Vice-Rector for Postgraduate Studies, Research and External Relations: BENYOUNES MAZART
Vice-Rector for Teaching and Retraining: MAAMAR BOUDIA
Sec.-Gen.: ELOUADI DORGHAM
Librarian: BACHIR YAKOUBI
Number of teachers: 582
Number of students: 11,491

DEANS

Faculty of Architecture and Civil Engineering: HAMID P. KHELAFI
Faculty of Electrical Engineering: ABDELHAMID MIDOUN
Faculty of Mechanical Engineering: OMAR IMINE
Faculty of Sciences: MOHAMED BENYETTOU

FACULTIES

Faculty of Architecture and Civil Engineering: BP 1505, El M'naouer, Oran; tel. and fax (41) 42-06-82; Depts of Architecture, Civil Engineering, Hydraulics.
Faculty of Electrical Engineering: BP 1505, El M'naouer, Oran; tel. and fax (41) 42-06-81; Depts of Electronics, Electrotechnics.
Faculty of Mechanical Engineering: BP 1505, El M'naouer, Oran; tel. and fax (41) 41-92-69; Depts of Marine Engineering, Mechanical Engineering, Metallurgy.
Faculty of Sciences: BP 1505, El M'naouer, Oran; tel. and fax (41) 42-06-80; Depts of Biology, Computer Sciences, Industrial Chemistry, Languages, Mathematics, Physical Education, Physics.

UNIVERSITE DES SCIENCES ISLAMIQUES EMIR ABDELKADER DE CONSTANTINE

Al Kaddour Bumdus, BP 137, Constantine 25000

Telephone: (31) 92-26-94
Fax: (31) 92-53-71
E-mail: a.boukhalkhal@univ-emir.dz
Internet: www.univ-emir.dz

Founded 1984
State control
Academic year: September to June

Rector: Dr ABDULLAH BOUKHALKHAL

Library of 16,000 vols
Number of teachers: 112
Number of students: 2,476

Faculties of Arts and Humanities, Culture and Sharia, Fundamentals of Islam, Fundamentals of Religion.

UNIVERSITE DJILLALI LIABES DE SIDI BEL ABBÈS

BP 89, Sidi Bel Abbès 22000

Telephone: (48) 54-98-88
Fax: (48) 56-95-46
E-mail: rectorat@univ-sba.dz
Internet: www.uviv-sba.dz

Founded 1978; present status 1989
State control

Rector: ABDEL NACER TOU

Library of 70,000 vols
Number of students: 15,000

DEANS

Faculty of Economics: M. DANI ELKBIR
Faculty of Engineering: A. KHALFI
Faculty of Humanities: N. SEBBAR
Faculty of Law: B. MEKELKEL
Faculty of Medicine: A. DJADEL
Faculty of Science: M. BENYAHYA
Research Centre: F. TEBBOUNE (Dir)

UNIVERSITÉ DR YAHIA FARÈS DE MÉDÉA

Ain d'Heb, Médéa 26000

Telephone: (25) 58-16-87
Fax: (25) 58-28-11
E-mail: cu.medea@gmail.com
Internet: www.cu-medea.dz

Founded 1989

Director: Dr CHAABAIKI MONKEY

Faculties of Arts, Commerce and Management, Economics, Languages, Law, Science and Technology, Social Sciences and Humanities.

UNIVERSITE DU 20 AOÛT 1955 DE SKIKDA

BP 26, Route d'El-Hadaiek, Skikda 21000

Telephone: (38) 70-10-32
Fax: (38) 70-10-04
E-mail: rectorat@univ-skikda.dz
Internet: www.univ-skikda.dz

Founded 2001
State control

Rector: Prof. ALI KOUADRIA

Faculties of Law and Social Sciences, Management and Economics, Science and Engineering.

UNIVERSITÉ FERHAT ABBAS DE SÉTIF

Route de Scipion, 19000 Sétif

Telephone: (36) 72-10-25
Fax: (36) 92-51-27
Internet: www.univ-setif.dz

Founded 1978

State control
Languages of instruction: Arabic, French
Academic year: September to June

Rector: Prof. CHEKIB-ARSLANE BAKI
Vice-Pres. for Det: Dr LARBI MOKRANI
Vice-Pres. for External Relations and Cooperation: BELKACEM NOUICER
Vice-Pres. for Research and Graduate Studies: Prof. MOHAMMED MOSTEFAI
Vice-Pres. for Undergraduate Studies: Prof. NABIL NANCIB
Gen. Sec.: NOUREDDINE BENHENNI
Librarian: CHÉRIF CHIDEKH

Number of teachers: 594
Number of students: 12,700

Publication: *Annales* (4 a year)

DIRECTORS

Institut d'Architecture: TAHAR BELLAL
Institut de Biologie: RACHID GHARZOULI
Institut de Chimie Industrielle: B. DJELLOULI
Institut de Droit: M. KARMED
Institut d'Electronique: S. BERRETILI
Institut d'Electrotechnique: SAAD BELKHIAT
Institut de Génie Civil: M. MIMOUN
Institut d'Informatique: SAMIR AKROUF
Institut des Langues Etrangères: ABDELKRIM ZEGHAD
Institut des Lettres Arabes: BELKACEM NOUICER
Institut de Mathématiques: BOUBEKEUR MEROUANI
Institut de Mécanique: AHMED MANALLAH
Institut de Physique: ABDELAZIZ MANSOURI
Institut des Sciences Economiques: H. SAHRAOUI
Institut des Sciences Médicales: R. TALBI
Institut de Tronc-Commun et Technologie: MABROUK BENKHEDIMALLAH

UNIVERSITÉ HADJI LAKHDAR DE BATNA

5 ave Chahid Boukhlouf, 05000 Batna

Telephone: (33) 81-41-32
Fax: (33) 82-66-77-114
E-mail: recteur@univ-batna.dz
Internet: www.univ-batna.dz

Founded 1977 as Centre Universitaire de Batna

Rector: Prof. MOUSSA ZEREG
Vice-Rector for External Relations: Dr SALAH BOUBECHICHE
Vice-Rector for Planning: Dr HACENE CHAABANE
Vice-Rector for Postgraduate Students and Research: Dr LAMINE MELKEMI
Vice-Rector for Teaching: Dr HACENE SMADI
Sec.-Gen.: ALI LABOUEL

Library of 60,000 vols

Publications: *Revue des Sciences Agronomiques et Forestières* (1 a year), *Revue Sciences Sociales et Humaines* (1 a year), *Revue II IIA* (1 a year)

Faculties of agronomic and veterinary sciences, economics, humanities and social sciences, hydraulic and civil engineering, medicine, science and technology.

UNIVERSITÉ HASSIBA BENBOUALI DE CHLEF

Hay Salam, route nationale 19, Chlef 02000

Telephone: (27) 72-28-77
Fax: (27) 72-28-77
E-mail: info@univ-chlef.dz
Internet: www.univ-chlef.dz

Founded 1983; present status 2001
State control

Rector: A. OUAGUED

Library of 10,220 vols, 127 periodicals
Number of teachers: 275
Number of students: 12,522

Faculties of earth science and agronomy, humanities and social sciences, science and engineering.

UNIVERSITÉ IBN KHALDOUN DE TIARET

BP 78, 14000 Tiaret

Telephone: (46) 42-42-13
Fax: (46) 42-41-47
E-mail: univ-tiaret@mail.univ-tiaret.dz
Internet: www.univ-tiaret.dz

Founded 1980 as Institut National d'Enseignement Supérieur de Tiaret; became Centre Universitaire de Tiaret 1992; present name and status 2001
Languages of instruction: Arabic, French
Academic year: October to July

Rector: Dr NASREDDINE HADJ-ZOUBIR
Vice-Rector of Planning, Orientation and Information: Dr A. BENAMARA
Vice-Rector of Scientific Research, External Relations and Cooperation: Dr M. HASSANE
Vice-Rector of Studies: K. BOUCHENTOUF
Librarian: ABED MAKHLOUFI

Number of teachers: 229
Number of students: 10,493

Depts of Arabic Literature, Biology, Economics, Law, Physics, Technology; institutes of Agronomy, Civil Engineering, Electronic Engineering, Environment, Mechanical Engineering, Veterinary Medicine.

UNIVERSITÉ KASDI MERBAH D'OUARGLA

BP 511, Route de Ghardaïa, Ouargla

Telephone: (29) 71-24-68
Fax: (29) 71-51-61
E-mail: info@ouargla-univ.dz
Internet: www.ouargla-univ.dz

Founded 1987 as Ecole Nationale Supérieure; present status 2001
State control
Academic year: September to June

Dir: MOHAMED EL-KHAMES TIDJANI

Number of teachers: 465
Number of students: 10,118

DEANS

Faculty of Law and Economics: NASREDDINE SEMAR
Faculty of Letters and Languages: SALAH KENNOUR
Faculty of Science and Engineering: BELKHEIR DADA MOUSSA

UNIVERSITÉ LARBI BEN MHIDI D'OUM EL-BOUAGHI

BP 358, Oum El-Bouaghi 04000

Telephone: (32) 42-42-12
Fax: (32) 42-10-36
E-mail: chelfaycal@yahoo.fr
Internet: www.univ-oeb.dz

Founded 1983 as Ecole Normale Supérieure d'Oum El-Bouaghi

Rector: Prof. AHMED BOURAS

Number of teachers: 357
Number of students: 16,243

Institutes of economics and management; exact sciences, foreign languages and literature; law and administration; natural sciences; technology; urban technology management.

UNIVERSITÉ M'HAMED BOUGARA DE BOUMERDÈS

Ave de l'indépendance, Boumerdès 35000

Telephone: (24) 81-69-01
E-mail: rectorat@umbb.dz

Internet: www.umbb.dz
Founded 1981.

Institut Algérien de Pétroléum.
Institut National d'Electricité et d'Electronique.
Institut National de Génie Mécanique.
Institut National des Hydrocarbures.
Institut National des Industries Légères.
Institut National de Productivité et Développement.

UNIVERSITÉ MENTOURI DE CONSTANTINE

Route Ain El Bey, 25017 Constantine
Telephone: (31) 81-88-92
Fax: (31) 81-97-11
Internet: www.umc.edu.dz

Founded 1969
Languages of instruction: Arabic, French

Rector: Prof. ABDELHAMID DJEKOUN
Vice-Rector for Orientation, Planning and
    Information: EMBAREK FERGAG
Vice-Rector for Postgraduate and Scientific
    Research: SALAH EDDINE BOUAOUD
Vice-Rector for Teaching: BELKACEM SLATINA
Sec.-Gen.: FOUDIL BELAOUIRA
Librarian: TEBOURA BENKAID-KESBA

Library of 240,000 vols
Number of teachers: 1,503
Number of students: 27,995

Institutes of Agriculture and Nutrition, Arabic, Architecture and Town Planning, Biology, Chemistry, Civil and Mechanical Engineering, Computer Science, Earth Sciences, Economics, Electronics, Foreign Languages, Industrial Chemistry, Law and Administration, Mathematics, Physical Education, Physics, Psychology, Social Sciences, Sociology, Technology, Veterinary Science; also a Pre-Univ. Centre and Audiovisual Dept.

UNIVERSITÉ MOHAMED KHIDER DE BISKRA

BP 145, Biskra 07000
Telephone: (33) 74-60-61
Fax: (33) 73-07-30
E-mail: webmaster@univ-biksra.dz
Internet: www.univ-biskra.dz
Founded 1998
State control

Rector: Prof. BELKACEM SELATNIA
Vice Rector: BRAHIM MEZERDI

Number of teachers: 800
Number of students: 28,000

Faculties of economics and management, law and political sciences, literature and foreign languages, science, social sciences, technology.

UNIVERSITÉ MOULOUD MAMMERI DE TIZI-OUZOU

BP 17, Oued-Aissi, Tizi-Ouzou
Telephone: (26) 21-53-14
Fax: (26) 21-29-68
E-mail: univ_tizi@mail.ummto.dz
Internet: www.ummto.dz
Founded 1977; present status 2001
State control

Rector: Prof. RABAH KAHLOUCHE
Number of students: 37,600

Faculties of Arts and Humanities, Biology and Agronomy, Construction Engineering, Economics and Management, Electrical and Computer Engineering, Law, Medicine and Science.

UNIVERSITÉ SAAD DAHLAB DE BLIDA

Route de Soumaa, BP 270, Blida 09000
Telephone: (25) 43-38-65
Fax: (25) 43-38-64
E-mail: contact@univ-blida.dz
Internet: www.univ-blida.edu.dz
Founded 1981 as Centre Universitaire de
    Blida

Rector: Prof. ABDELLATIF BABA AHMED
Vice-Rector for Devt: DJAMEL BOUKERCH
Vice-Rector for Communication Relations:
    SALIHA OUKID
Vice-Rector for External Relations: KARIMA
    MENOUERI
Vice-Rector for Graduate Studies: MAHMOUD
    CHERGUI
Vice-Rector for Postgraduate Affairs and
    Scientific Research: MOHAMMED MEGHA-
    TRIA

Number of teachers: 644
Number of students: 45,491

Publication: *Revue de l'Université*

Depts of aeronautics, agronomy, agricultural engineering, architecture, civil engineering, economics, electronics, industrial chemistry, language and literature, law, mathematics, mechanics, medicine, physics, social sciences, veterinary science.

UNIVERSITÉ TAHAR MOULAY DE SAIDA

BP 138, Cité ENNASR, Saida
Telephone: (48) 47-77-29
Fax: (48) 47-11-24
Internet: www.univ-saida.dz.

UNIVERSITÉ ZIANE ACHOUR DE DJELFA

BP 3117 Cudjelfa, Djelfa 17000
Telephone: (27) 90-02-03
Fax: (27) 90-02-01
E-mail: dg_cud@yahoo.fr
Founded 1990

Institutes of Economics, Commerce and Management, Law and Administration, Literature and Languages, Natural and Life Sciences, Science and Technology, Social Sciences and Humanities.

University Centres

CENTRE UNIVERSITAIRE D'EL OUED

POB 789, Central Valley, El Oued 39000
Telephone: (32) 22-30-07
Fax: (32) 22-30-03
E-mail: administration@mail.univ-eloued.dz
Internet: www.univ-eloued.dz
Founded 1995

Dir: Dr IZZ AL-DIN HAFTARI
Number of students: 11,435

Institutes of Arts and Languages, Commerce, Economics and Management, Law and Administration, Science and Technology, Social and Human Sciences.

CENTRE UNIVERSITAIRE D'EL-TARF

BP 73, El-Tarf 36000
Telephone: (38) 60-18-93
Fax: (38) 60-15-28
E-mail: directeur@cuniv-eltaref.edu.dz
Internet: www.cuniv-eltaref.edu.dz
Founded 1992

Number of teachers: 169
Number of students: 3,000

Institutes of Agriculture, Biology, Arab Language and Literature, Social Science and Demography, Veterinary Science.

CENTRE UNIVERSITAIRE DE BORDJ BOU ARRÉRIDJ

Bordj Bou Arréridj
Telephone: (35) 66-65-17
Fax: (35) 66-65-21
E-mail: direction_cubba@wissal.dz
Internet: www.centrebba.africa-web.org
Founded 2001
Number of students: 7,000

Institutes of Computer Science, Electronics, Economics, Management.

CENTRE UNIVERSITAIRE DE BOUIRA

Bouira
Telephone: (26) 93-88-43
Fax: (26) 93-09-24
Dir: Dr AHMED HIDOUCHE

Depts of Arabic Language and Literature, Berber Language and Culture, Economics and Management, Human and Social Sciences, Law.

CENTRE UNIVERSITAIRE DE GHARDAIA

Alnoumrat, Ghardaia 47000
Telephone: (29) 87-01-87
Fax: (29) 87-02-10
Internet: www.cu-ghardaia.edu.dz

Institutes of Humanities and Social Sciences, Natural and Life Sciences, Trade.

CENTRE UNIVERSITAIRE DE KHENCHELA

Route de Constantine, BP 1252, El Houria,
    Khenchela 40004
Telephone: (32) 33-19-66
Fax: (32) 33-19-63
E-mail: cuniv_khenchela@cuniv-khenchela
    .edu.dz
Internet: www.cuniv-khenchela.edu.dz
Founded 2001

Dir: Dr AHMED BAKHOUCHE
Gen. Sec.: YOUCEF HAMADA

Institutes of Commerce and Management, Economics, Human and Social Sciences, Law and Administration, Letters and Languages, Natural and Life Sciences, Science and Technology.

CENTRE UNIVERSITAIRE DE SOUK-AHRAS

Rue Djabar Amor M. Daourouch, Souk-Ahras
    41220
Telephone: (37) 32-62-62
Fax: (37) 32-65-65
Internet: www.cu-soukahras.dz
Founded 2001

Institutes of Law, Science and Engineering.

CENTRE UNIVERSITAIRE KHEMIS MILIANA

Route de Theniet El-Had, Khemis Miliana
    44225
Telephone: (27) 66-42-32
Fax: (27) 66-48-63
E-mail: cukm@cukm.org
Internet: www.cukm.org
Library of 17,968 vols

Institutes of Science and Technology, Natural and Earth Sciences, Economics and Management, Law and Administration.

National Schools and Institutes

ÉCOLE NATIONALE D'ADMINISTRATION

13 chemin Abdelkader Gadouche, Hydra, Algiers
Telephone: (21) 60-13-50
Fax: (21) 60-49-41
E-mail: ena@wissal.dz
Internet: www.ena.dz
Founded 1964
State control
Dir: HOCINE CHERHABIL
Library of 30,000 vols, 600 periodicals
Publication: *Idara* (52 a year)
Provides training for entry into the civil service.

ECOLE NATIONALE D'INFORMATIQUE (ESI)

BP 68M, Oued Smar, El Harrach, Algiers 16309
Telephone: (21) 51-60-77
Fax: (21) 51-61-56
E-mail: de@esi.dz
Internet: www.esi.dz
Founded 2008
Dir: M. HENNI
Training and research in information science.

ECOLE NATIONALE SUPÉRIEURE AGRONOMIQUE (ENSA)

Hacène Badi, El Harrach, Algiers 16200
Telephone: (21) 52-50-84
Fax: (21) 82-27-29
E-mail: ina@ina.dz
Internet: www.ina.dz
Founded 1905
State control
Dir: M. M. ISSOLATT ROZA
Library of 80,000 vols, 120 periodicals
Number of teachers: 165
Number of students: 1,400
Publication: *Annales* (1 a year).

ECOLE NATIONALE SUPÉRIEURE D'HYDRAULIQUE

BP 31, Blida 09000
Telephone: (25) 39-94-47
Fax: (25) 39-94-46
E-mail: miah@ensh.dz
Internet: www.ensh.dz
Founded 1972
State control
Dir: MOHAMED SAÏD BENHAFID
Depts of Continuing Education, Core Courses, Research and Postgraduate Studies, Specialized Subjects, Training and Education.

ECOLE NATIONALE SUPÉRIEURE DES TRAVAUX PUBLICS (ENSTP)

Rue Sidi Garidi, BP 32, Algiers 16051
Telephone: (21) 28-68-38
Fax: (21) 28-14-07
E-mail: entp@wissal.dz
Internet: www.entp.edu.dz
Founded 1966
State control
Publication: *Algérie Équipement*.

ECOLE NATIONALE SUPÉRIEURE POLYTECHNIQUE D'ALGER

10 ave Hassen Badi, BP 182, El-Harrach, Algiers 16200
Telephone: (21) 52-53-01
Fax: (21) 52-29-73
Internet: www.enp.edu.dz
Founded 1925 as Institut Industriel d'Algérie
Dir: Prof. GHANIA NEZZAL
Library of 45,000 vols
Number of teachers: 200
Number of students: 2,000 (1,500 undergraduate, 500 postgraduate)
Depts of Basic Sciences, Chemical Engineering, Civil Engineering, Electrical Engineering, Environmental Engineering, Hydraulics, Industrial Engineering, Languages, Mechanical Engineering, Metallurgy, Mining Engineering.

ECOLE NATIONALE SUPÉRIEURE VÉTÉRINAIRE D'ALGER (ENSV)

BP 161, Hacène Badi, El Harrach, Algiers
Telephone: (21) 52-51-32
Fax: (21) 82-44-81
Internet: www.env.dz
Founded 1970
State control
Dir: Prof. LOUARDI GUEZLANE
Library of 8,000 vols, 40 periodicals
Number of teachers: 60
Number of students: 1,050

ECOLE NORMALE SUPÉRIEURE D'ENSEIGNEMENT TECHNOLOGIQUE

BP 1523, El-M'naouer, Oran 31000
Telephone: (41) 58-20-64
Fax: (41) 58-20-66
E-mail: benziane_baki@yahoo.fr
Internet: www.enset-oran.dz
Founded 1970
Director: BENZIANE BAKI
Library of 34,917 vols
Publication: *COST*
Depts of Chemistry, Civil Engineering, Continuing Education, Electrical Engineering, Mathematics, Mechanical Engineering, Physics.

ECOLE NORMALE SUPÉRIEURE DE CONSTANTINE

Plateau du Mansourah, Constantine
Telephone: (31) 61-21-53
Fax: (31) 63-00-75
Internet: www.ens-constantine.dz
Founded 1984
State control
Publication: *Forum de l'enseignant* (1 a year, in Arabic and French).

ECOLE NORMALE SUPÉRIEURE DE KOUBA

Bachir El Ibrahimi, BP 92, Kouba 16050
E-mail: webmaster@ens-kouba.dz
Internet: www.ens-kouba.dz
Director: Dr ABDELHAMID MERAGHNI
Depts of Chemistry, Computer Science, Education, Mathematics, Music, Natural Sciences, Physics.

ECOLE POLYTECHNIQUE D'ARCHITECTURE ET D'URBANISME

Route de Beaulieu, El Harrache, BP 177, Algiers 16200
Telephone: (21) 52-47-26
Fax: (21) 52-59-54

E-mail: zerouala54@yahoo.com
Internet: www.epau.edu.dz
Founded 1970
Director: Prof. MOHAMED SALAH ZEROUALA
Library of 43,000 vols, 296 periodicals
Number of students: 2,804

INSTITUT NATIONAL DE LA PLANIFICATION ET DE LA STATISTIQUE

11 chemin Doudou Mokhtar, Benaknoun, Algiers
Telephone: (21) 91-21-33
Fax: (21) 91-21-39
E-mail: inps-dz@wissal.dz
Internet: www.inps-alger.dz
Founded 1970
State control
Dir: Dr AHMED ZAKANE
Library of 14,089 vols, 430 periodicals
Number of teachers: 122
Number of students: 1,703
3-Year and 5-year undergraduate courses in planning and statistics, 2-year postgraduate course in economics and applied statistics.

INSTITUT NATIONAL DES SCIENCES DE LA MER ET DE L'AMÉNAGEMENT DU LITTORAL (ISMAL) (National Institute of Marine Sciences and Coastal Management)

Campus Universitaire, BP 19, Bois des Cars Dély Ibrahim, Algiers
E-mail: dg_ismal@ismal.net
Internet: www.ismal.net
Founded 1882
Dir: Prof. RABAH BAKOUR.

Colleges

Conservatoire de Musique et de Déclamation: 2 blvd Ché Guévara, Algiers; f. 1920; library: 6,800 vols; 82 teachers; 2,300 students; Dir-Gen. BACHETARZI MOHIEDDINE; Sec.-Gen. KADDOUR GUECHOUD.

Ecole Supérieure des Beaux-Arts: blvd Krim Belkacem, Parc Zyriab, Algiers 16200; tel. (21) 74-90-09; fax (21) 74-91-14; f. 1881; painting, sculpture, ceramics, design; library: 9,000 vols; 65 teachers; 350 students; Dir NACER EDDINE KASSAB.

Ecole Supérieure de Commerce d'Alger: 1 Rampe Salah Gharbi, Agha, Algiers; tel. (21) 42-32-31; fax (21) 42-37-32; e-mail contact@esc-alger.com; internet www.esc-alger.com; f. 1900; attached to Univ. of Algiers 1966; 4-year first degree courses, 2-year Masters course; 91 teachers; 1,750 students.

Institut Hydrométéorologique de Formation et de Recherches (IHFR): BP 7019, Séddikia, Oran 31025; tel. (41) 42-28-01; fax (41) 42-13-12; e-mail ihfr@djazair-connect.com; internet www.ihfr.net; f. 1970; library: 15,000 vols; 200 students; Dir A. LAGHA.

Institut des Sciences Politiques et de l'Information: 11 chemin Doudou Mokhtar, Ibn-Aknoun, Algiers; tel. (21) 78-15-18; fax (21) 79-66-41; f. 1948 as result of merger between Ecole Supérieure de Journalisme and Institut d'Etudes Politiques; attached to Univ. of Algiers; 100 teachers; 2,000 students; Dir Dr ISMAIL DEBECHE.

ANDORRA

The Higher Education System

University-level education is generally undertaken abroad, although there is one university, the Universitat d'Andorra. The University maintains two centres for vocational training, the School of Nursing and the School of Information Technology and Management, and a School of Virtual Learning for distance education. The Ministry of Culture and Higher Education oversees higher education. In 2005/06 1,066 students were in higher education; 431 students were studying in Andorra, 131 in France and 503 in Spain.

A new baccalaureate examination, which was intended to facilitate direct access for students in the Andorran education system to universities in other European countries, was introduced in 2008.

The Law of Higher Education 12/2008 was passed in June 2008 and a Decree of recognition of foreign qualifications was published in March 2009. With these new regulations, Andorra recognizes levels of qualifications according to the Bologna Process and the Lisbon Convention.

Regulatory and Representative Bodies

GOVERNMENT

Ministry of Culture and Higher Education: Edif. Administratiu, 62–64 C/ Prat de la Creu, AD500 Andorra la Vella; tel. 875634; fax 875637; Minister JULI MINOVES TRIQUELL.

Ministry of Education, Training, Youth and Sports: Edif. el Molí, 21–23 Avda Rocafort, AD600 Sant Julià de Lòria; tel. 743300; fax 743311; Minister ROSER BASTIDA ARENY.

ACCREDITATION

ENIC/NARIC Andorra: Ministra d'Educació, Formació Professional, Joventut i Esports, Edif. el Molí, 4a Planta, 21–23 Avda Rocafort, AD600 Sant Julià de Lòria; tel. 743300; fax 743313; e-mail portal@ govern.ad; internet www.govern.ad; Assessor MERITXELL GALLO YANES.

Learned Societies

GENERAL

Amics de la Cultura (Friends of Culture): Plaça Co-Prínceps 4 bis, Despatx no. 1, AD700 Escaldes-Engordany.

Associació Cultural i Artística Els Esquirols (Els Esquirols Cultural and Arts Association): Sala Parroquial, Plaça de l'Església, AD400 La Massana.

Centre de Trobada de les Cultures Pirenenques (Centre for the Understanding of Pyrenean Culture): Edif. Prada Casadet, C/ Prat de la Creu, AD500 Andorra la Vella; tel. 860768; fax 861998; f. 1983; attached to Comunitat de Treball dels Pirineus; database on the Pyrenees; Dir ELISENDA VIVES BALMAÑA.

Cercle de les Arts i de les Lletres (Arts and Letters Circle): 24 Avda Carlemany, AD700 Escaldes-Engordany; tel. 824815; fax 861050; internet www.cercleartsilletres.com; f. 1968; Pres. JOAN BURGUÉS MARTISELLA.

BIBLIOGRAPHY, LIBRARY SCIENCE AND MUSEOLOGY

International Council of Museums, Andorran National Committee: Patrimoni Cultural d'Andorra, Carretera de Bixessarri s/n Aixovall, AD600 Sant Julià de Lòria; tel. 844141; fax 844343; e-mail icom@ andorra.ad; internet www.icomandorra.ad; f.

1988; 28 mems; Pres. ISABEL DE LA PARTE CANO.

LANGUAGE AND LITERATURE

Alliance Française: Centre Cultural la Llacuna, Mossèn Cinto Verdaguer 4, AD500 Andorra la Vella; tel. 342852; e-mail alianca-af@andorra.ad; internet www .alliance-francaise-andorre.org; offers courses and examinations in French language and culture and promotes cultural exchange with France.

NATURAL SCIENCES

General

Societat Andorrana de Ciències (Andorra Scientific Society): Centre Cultural la Llacuna, C/ M. C. Verdaguer 4, AD500 Andorra la Vella; tel. 829729; fax 852383; e-mail sac@ andorra.ad; internet www.sac.ad; f. 1983; carries out research; organizes talks, conferences and symposiums; 292 mems; Pres. ANGELS MACH; Sec. PERE MUNOZ; Treas. CONXITA NAUDI; publs *Diada Andorrana a la UCE* (1 a year), *El Sac* (12 a year), *Jornades* (1 a year), *Papers de Recerca Històrica* (1 a year), *Recull de Conferències* (1 a year), *Trobades Culturals Pirenenques* (1 a year).

Biological Sciences

Associació per a la Defensa de la Natura (Association for Nature Conservation): Apdo Correus Espanyols 96, AD500 Andorra la Vella; tel. 866086; fax 866586; e-mail adn@ andorra.ad; internet www.adn-andorra.org; f. 1986; disseminates information and organizes courses, conferences, school lectures, awareness campaigns about nature and wildlife in Andorra; 300 mems; Pres. ANGELS CODINA FARRÁS; Sec. JORDI PALAUI PUIGVERT; publ. *Aigüerola*.

Research Institutes

GENERAL

Institut d'Estudis Andorrans (Institute of Andorran Studies): Edif. el Molí, 3r pis, 21– 23 Avda Rocafort, AD600 Sant Julià de Lòria; tel. 742630; fax 843585; e-mail iea@iea.ad; internet www.iea.ad; f. 1976; centres in Barcelona (Spain) and Toulouse (France); Dir JORDI GUILLAMET.

Attached institutes:

Centre de Biodiversitat (Centre for Biodiversity): Edif. el Molí, 3r pis, 21–23 Avda Rocafort, AD600 Sant Julià de Lòria;

tel. 742630; fax 843585; e-mail cbdiea@ andorra.ad; f. 1998; study and monitoring of Andorra's biological diversity; library of 450 vols; Dir MARTA DOMÈNECH FERRÉS; publ. *Hàbitats* (2 a year).

Centre d'Estudis de la Neu i de la Muntanya d'Andorra: Edif. el Molí, 3r pis, 21–23Avda Rocafort, AD600 Sant Julià de Lòria; tel. 742630; fax 843585; e-mail cenma@iea.ad.

Centre de Recerca en Cièncias de la Terra (Centre for Earth Sciences Research): Edif. el Molí, 3r pis, 21–23 Avda Rocafort, AD600 Sant Julià de Lòria; tel. 742630; fax 843585; e-mail crecit@ andorra.ad; internet www.iea.ad/crecit/ index2.html; f. 2001.

Centre de Recerca Sociològica (Centre for Sociological Research): Edif. el Molí, 3r pis, 21–23 Avda Rocafort, AD600 Sant Julià de Lòria; tel. 742630; fax 843585; e-mail cres@iea.ad; internet www.iea.ad/ cres/noticies; f. 2000.

Libraries and Archives

Andorra la Vella

Arxiu Nacional d'Andorra (National Archive of Andorra): Edif. Prada Casadet, C/ Prada Casadet, 8–12, AD500 Andorra la Vella; tel. 802288; fax 868645; e-mail ana .gov@andorra.ad; internet www.arxius.ad; f. 1975; 280,000 documents; Head of Service CINTA VELA PUJAL CARARANTES.

Biblioteca Nacional d'Andorra (National Library of Andorra): Placeta de Saint Esteve, Casa Bauró, AD500 Andorra la Vella; tel. 826445; fax 829445; e-mail bncultura.gov@ andorra.ad; internet www.bibliotecanacional .ad; f. 1974; legal deposit, Andorran standard book number agency (ISBN); 13,000 vols, 120 periodicals; Chief Librarian PILAR BURGUES MONSERRAT.

Biblioteca Publica del Govern (Government Public Library): Edif. Prada Casadet 2, C/ Prat de la Creu, AD500 Andorra la Vella; tel. 828750; fax 829541; e-mail bibliopublica@ andorra.ad; internet www.biblioteques.ad; f. 1930; 5,425 mems; 54,213 vols; Head INÉS DOMINGO SANCHEZ.

Canillo

Biblioteca Comunal de Canillo (Canillo Community Library): Edif. Telecabina, 3er pis, AD100 Canillo; tel. 753623; e-mail bibliocanillo@andorra.ad; internet www .biblioteques.ad/bibliocanillo; f. 1988; 7,643 items; Librarian DOLORS CALVÓ.

Encamp

Biblioteca Comunal d'Encamp (Encamp Community Library): Complex Esportiu i Sociocultural, AD200 Encamp; tel. 832830; fax 832903; e-mail biblioteca@encamp.ad; internet www.biblioteques.ad/biblioencamp; f. 1930; 40,000 vols; Librarian CODINA ALFONS.

Escaldes-Engordany

Biblioteca Comunal d'Escaldes-Engordany (Escaldes-Engordany Community Library): Centre Neuràlgic, Parc de la Mola 6, AD700 Escaldes-Engordany; tel. 890875; internet www.biblioteques.ad/biblioescaldes; f. 1971; 33,500 vols; Librarian ALEXIA CARRERAS SIRES.

La Massana

Biblioteca Comunal de la Massana (La Massana Community Library): Avda St Antoni 2, AD400 La Massana; tel. 838910; fax 736936; e-mail biblioteca@lamassana.ad; internet www.biblioteques.ad/bibliolamassana; f. 1990; 2,484 mems; 15,373 vols, 36 periodicals; Librarian PAINO GABRIELA; Man. Librarian JOSEFA DIÉGUEZ.

Ordino

Biblioteca Comunal d'Ordino (Ordino Community Library): Edif. la Font, 3a pl., AD300 Ordino; tel. 878136; fax 878137; internet www.biblioteques.ad/biblioordino; f. 1995; 11,000 vols.

Sant Julià de Lòria

Biblioteca Communal de Sant Julià de Lòria (Sant Julià de Lòria Community Library): Centre Cultural i de Congressos Lauredià, Plaça de la Germandat, AD600 Sant Julià de Lòria; tel. 744044; fax 744014; e-mail biblioteca@comusantjulia.ad; internet www.biblioteques.ad/bibliostjulia; f. 1993; 15,522 vols.

Museums and Art Galleries

Andorra la Vella

Casa de la Vall: C/ de la Vall, AD500 Andorra la Vella; tel. 829129; fax 869863; f. 1580.

Canillo

Le Sanctuaire de Meritxell (Meritxell Sanctuary): Meritxell, AD100 Canillo; tel. 851253; fax 851253; historical record of the Andorran people's devotion to their patron saint, the Virgin of Meritxell.

Museu de Les Dues Rodes (Museum of Two Wheels): Ctra. General de Canillo s/n, Al Costat de St Joan de Caselles, AD100 Canillo; tel. 853444; fax 853456; e-mail m2r@canillo.ad; internet www.m2r.ad; motorcycles from the early 20th century to the present day.

Encamp

Electricity Museum: Edif. FEDA, Avda de la Bartra s/n, Sortida d'Escaldes en Direcció a Encamp per la CG2, AD200 Encamp; tel. 739111; fax 739110; e-mail museumw@feda.ad.

Museu d'Art Sacre (Sacred Art Museum): Placeta de Santa Eulàlia, AD200 Encamp; tel. 833551; e-mail casacristo@encamp.ad; colln of liturgical objects from the town's churches, exhibits from 14th century to date.

Museu Nacional de l'Automòbil (National Motor Car Museum): Avda Co-Princep Episcopal 64, AD200 Encamp; tel. 839760; fax 832266; f. 1988; cars, motorbikes and bicycles from 1898 to 1950, components, miniature cars in porcelain and iron.

Escaldes-Engordany

Escaldes-Engordany Arts Centre: Avda Carlemany 30, AD700 Escaldes-Engordany; tel. 802255; f. 1934; collns of Josep Viladomat and Andorra Romanesque art.

Museu Viladomat d'Escultura (Municipal Cultural Museum): Avda Parc de la Mola 5, Les Escaldes, AD700 Escaldes-Engordany; tel. 829340; fax 829340; e-mail museuviladomat@andorra.ad; f. 1987; Curator GLORIA PUJOL.

Andorran Model Museum: Avda de Pessebre 16, AD700 Escaldes-Engordany; tel. 861506; models of prominent Andorran monuments and structures.

Museu del Perfum (Perfume Museum): 1era Planta, Avda Carlemany 115, AD700 Escaldes-Engordany; tel. 801926; e-mail museudelperfum@julia.ad; internet www.museudelperfum.ad; history of perfume.

La Massana

Casa Rull de Sispony (Rull House of Sispony): C/ Major, Sispony, AD400 La Massana; tel. 836919; fax 835419; e-mail casarull@andorra.ad; family and heritage.

Farga Rossell (Rossell Forge): Avda del Través s/n, AD400 La Massana; tel. 839760; fax 835857; e-mail fargarosell@andorra.ad; internet www.fargarosell.ad; f. 2002.

Ordino

Badge Museum: Ansalonga la Cortinada, AD300 Ordino; tel. 749000; 108,000 different badges relating to significant historical events.

Museu Casa d'Areny-Plandolit (Areny-Plandolit House Museum): C/ Major s/n, AD300 Ordino; tel. 839760; fax 839660; e-mail casa.areny-plandolit@andorra.ad; internet www.patrimonicultural.ad; f. 1987; typical 17th-century house, with later alterations; furniture, porcelain, costumes.

Museu Postal d'Andorra (Andorra Postal Museum): Borda del Raser, C/ Major, AD300 Ordino; tel. 839760; fax 839660; f. 1986, refounded 1998.

Nicolaï Siadristy's Microminiature Museum: Edif. Coma, AD300 Ordino; tel. 838376.

Centre d'Interpretació de la Natura de les Valls d'Ordino (Ordino Valley Nature Interpretation Centre): AD300 Ordino; tel. 837939; fax 837839; e-mail cinvo@andorra.ad; interprets the cultural landscape (nature and culture) of Ordino.

Sant Jordi Iconography and Christianity Museum: Edif. Maragda, AD300 Ordino; tel. 838338; e-mail azorzano@andornet.ad; Christian and Orthodox icons from the main schools in the Ukraine, Russia, Greece and Bulgaria from the 14th to the 19th centuries; 70 polychrome wood statues of Christ from Spanish schools from the 11th to 19th centuries.

Sant Julià de Lòria

Museu del Tabac (Tobacco Museum): Doctor Palau 17, AD600 Sant Julià de Lòria; tel. 741545; fax 842161; e-mail info@museudeltabac.com; internet www.museudeltabac.com; tools, machines, fittings and aromas used in tobacco factories from the 17th century to date; on site of former Reig tobacco factory (1909 to 1957); Dir MARIA MARTÍ.

University

UNIVERSITAT D'ANDORRA

Plaça de la Germandat 7, AD600 Sant Julià de Lòria

Telephone: 743000
Fax: 743043
E-mail: uda@uda.ad
Internet: www.uda.ad

Founded 1997
Language of instruction: Catalan
Vice-Chancellor: DANIEL BASTIDA OBIOLS

DIRECTORS

School of Information Technology and Management: FLORENCI PLA ALTISENT
School of Nursing: ROSA MARI MANDICÓ ALCOBÉ
Centre of Virtual Learning and Univ. Extension: MONTSERRAT CASALPRIM RAMONET

ANGOLA

The Higher Education System

Higher education was established when Angola was still a Portuguese colony, initially with the foundation in 1958 of institutes for training Catholic priests. In 1962 the Estudos Gerais Universitários de Angola was established in Luanda and became the Universidade de Luanda in 1968; a branch was also set up in Huíla. Following independence in 1975 all non-state institutions were closed, and in 1979 the Universidade de Luanda was renamed Universidade de Angola, which in turn became the Universidade Agostinho Neto in 1985; it remains Angola's only public university. Independent Angola's first private university, the Universidade Católica de Angola, was founded in 1992. Currently there are eight private universities operating. In 2004/05 there were 48,184 students in higher education.

Under legislation passed in 1995 full autonomy was conferred on Universidade Agostinho Neto, and staff were empowered to elect organs and officials. Financing for higher education depends on the status of the university: Universidade Agostinho Neto is heavily reliant on state funding, while the private universities rely on students' fees and donations from individuals and non-governmental organizations.

To attend university students must hold the Habilitação Literárias (secondary school leaving certificate), pass the entrance examinations and complete either a period of state employment or pre-university education.

The first undergraduate qualification is the Bacharel, study for which lasts for four years. Students may continue for a further two years, after which the Licenciado is awarded. The Licenciado may also be awarded on completion of a five-year university course, or a six-year course for medical students. A doctorate requires a further two or three years' research following the award of the Licenciado.

Regulatory Bodies

GOVERNMENT

Ministry of Culture: Av. Comandante Gika, Luanda; tel. 222323979; e-mail mincultura@mincultura.gv.ao; internet www.angola-portal.ao/mincult; Minister BOAVENTURA CARDOSO.

Ministry of Education: Av. Comandante Gika, CP 1281, Luanda; tel. 222320653; fax 222321592; internet www.angola-portal.ao/med; Minister ANTÓNIO BURITY DA SILVA NETO.

Ministry of Science and Technology: Ilha do Cabo, Luanda; tel. 222309794; e-mail dgmk@ebonet.com; Minister JOÃO BAPTISTA NGANDAJINA.

Learned Societies

LANGUAGE AND LITERATURE

Alliance Française: Largo da Sagrada Familia, Traversa Barbosa do Bocage 12, CP 1578, Luanda; tel. and fax 222321993; e-mail afluanda@ebonet.net; offers courses and examinations in French language and culture and promotes cultural exchange with France; attached teaching centres in Benguela, Cabinda and Lubango.

União dos Escritores Angolanos (Association of Angolan Writers): CP 2767-C, Luanda; tel. and fax 222323205; e-mail uea@uea-angola.org; internet www.uea-angola.org; f. 1975; 75 mems; library of 2,000 vols; Sec.-Gen. LUANDINO VIEIRA; publs *Criar* (4 a year), *Lavra & Oficina* (12 a year).

Research Institutes

AGRICULTURE, FISHERIES AND VETERINARY SCIENCE

Centro de Investigação Científica Algodoeira (Cotton Scientific Research Centre): Instituto do Algodão de Angola, Estação Experimental de Onga-Zanga, Catete; fibre technology laboratory, agricultural machinery station, crop irrigation station (Bombagem); library; Dir Eng. Agr. JOAQUIM RODRIGUES PEREIRA.

Instituto de Investigação Agronómica (Agronomic Research Institute): CP 406, Estação Experimental Agrícola da Chianga, Huambo; f. 1962; incorporates agrarian documentation centre; publs *Comunicações*, *Série Divulgação*.

Instituto de Investigação Veterinária (Institute for Veterinary Research): CP 405, Lubango; tel. 222322094; f. 1965; Dir Dr A. M. POMBAL; publ. *Acta Veterinaria-separatas* (1 a year).

NATURAL SCIENCES

Physical Sciences

Direcção Provincial dos Serviços de Geologia e Minas de Angola (Angolan Directorate of Geological and Mining Services): CP 1260-C, Luanda; f. 1914; geology, geological mapping and exploration of mineral deposits; library of 40,000 vols; Dir J. TRIGO MIRA; publs *Boletim*, *Carta Geológica de Angola*, *Memória*.

Libraries and Archives

Luanda

Arquivo Histórico Nacional (National Historical Archive): Rua Pedro Félix Machado 49, Luanda; tel. 222333512; fax 222334410; e-mail ahadg@nexus.ao; f. 1977; 20,000 vols, 3,000 periodicals; Dir ROSA CRUZ E SILVA; publ. *Guias de Informação Documental para o Estudo da História de Angola*.

Biblioteca Municipal (Municipal Library): CP 1227, Luanda; tel. 222392297; fax 222333902; f. 1873; 31,470 vols; Dir CUSTA GANHAR FILIPE.

Biblioteca Nacional de Angola (National Library of Angola): Largo António Jacinto, CP 2915, Luanda; tel. 222326331; fax 222326299; e-mail bibliotecanacional@netangola.com; f. 1969; 84,000 vols; IFLA colln legal deposit, nat. deposit for UNESCO and FAO publs; Dir MARIA JOSÉ F. RAMOS.

Museums and Art Galleries

Luanda

Instituto Nacional do Patrimonio Cultural (National Institute for Cultural Heritage): CP 1267, Luanda; tel. 222332575; e-mail ipc@snet.co.ao; nat. antiquities dept; Dir FRANCISCO XAVIER YAMBO.

Affiliated Museums:

Museu Central das Forças Armadas (Central Museum of the Armed Forces): CP 1267, Luanda; Dir SILVESTRE A. FRANCISCO.

Museu do Dundo (Dundo Museum): CP 14, Chitato, Lunda Norte; ethnography; Dir SONY CAMBOL CIPRIANO.

Museu da Escravatura (Museum of Slavery): CP 1267, Luanda; Dir ANICETE DO AMARAL GOURGEL.

Museu Nacional de Antropologia (National Anthropology Museum): CP 2159, Luanda; tel. 222337024; Dir AMERICO A. CUONONOCA.

Museu Nacional de Arqueologia (National Archaeology Museum): CP 79, Benguela; Dir JOAQUIM PAIS PINTO.

Museu Nacional de História Natural (National Museum of Natural History): CP 1267, Luanda; Dir ANA PAULA DOS SANTOS C. VICTOR.

Museu Regional de Cabinda (Cabinda Regional Museum): CP 283, Cabinda; ethnography; Dir TADEU DOMINGOS.

Museu Regional da Huila (Huila Regional Museum): CP 445, Lubango; ethnography; Dir JOSÉ FERREIRA.

Universities

UNIVERSIDADE AGOSTINHO NETO

CP 815, Avda 4 de Fevereiro 7, 2° andar, Luanda

Telephone: 222330517
Fax: 222330520
E-mail: depinf@diee.fe.uan.ao
Internet: www.uan.ao
Founded 1962
Language of instruction: Portuguese
Academic year: October to June
Rector: JOÃO SEBASTIÃO TETA
Number of teachers: 700
Number of students: 6,800

DEANS
Faculty of Agriculture: Dr AMILCAR MATEUS DE OLIVEIRA SALUMBO

Faculty of Economics: Dr LAURINDA DE JESUS FERNANDES HOYGAARD
Faculty of Engineering: CARLOS ALBERTO ABREU SERENO
Faculty of Law: Dr ADERITO CORREIA
Faculty of Medicine: Dr PAULO ADÃO CAMPOS
Faculty of Sciences: Dr ABILO ALVES FERNANDES

AFFILIATED INSTITUTES

Centro Nacional de Investigação Científica: Avda Revolução de Outubro, Luanda; tel. 222350762; Coordinator Dr NANIZEYI KINDUDI ANDRÉ.

Instituto Superior de Ciências da Educação: Rua Salvador Allende, 12, CP 10609, Luanda; tel. 222394979; fax 222394575; internet www.isced-lda.com; Dean Dr DANIEL MINGAS.

UNIVERSIDADE CATÓLICA DE ANGOLA

Rua N. Sra da Muxima 29, CP 2064, Luanda
Telephone: 222331973
Fax: 222398759
E-mail: info@ucan.edu
Internet: www.ucan.edu
Founded 1992
Controlled by Episcopal Conference of Angola and São Tomé
Academic year: May to December
Chancellor and Rector: Archbishop DAMIÃO FRANKLIN
Vice-Rector: Fr Dr FILOMENO VIEIRA DIAS
Head of Admin.: Fr Dr MANUEL S. GONÇALVES
Head of Library and Documentation: Fr Dr JOSÉ CACHADINHA
Number of teachers: 99
Number of students: 1,800
Faculties of Economics, Informatics, Law, Management.
Publications: *Revista Academica, UCAN Boletim Informativo.*

UNIVERSIDADE JEAN PIAGET DE ANGOLA

Campus Universitário de Viana, Bairro Capalanka, Viana 10365, Brito Godins
Telephone: 222301148
Fax: 222290872
E-mail: info@angola.ipiaget.org
Internet: www.ipiaget.org/campus.asp?id=89
Founded 1998 as a result of collaboration between the Min. for Education and Culture of the Republic of Angola and the Instituto Piaget in Portugal
Courses offered in social sciences and education, science and technology and health.

College

Instituto Médio Industrial de Luanda: Largo de Soweto, CP 2513, Luanda; tel. 222343200; e-mail imil@netangola.com; internet www.netangola.com/imil; f. 1956 as Escola Industrial de Luanda; courses in civil engineering, mechanics, chemistry.

ANTIGUA AND BARBUDA

The Higher Education System

Higher education is provided by an extramural department of the University of the West Indies, which offers several foundation courses leading to higher study at branches elsewhere, and at several other institutes and colleges. Teacher training and technical training are available at the Antigua State College in St John's, which absorbed the Antigua and Barbuda School of Nursing in 2000. There is also an Institute of Technology, a Hotel Training Centre and a private University of Health Sciences.

Admission to tertiary education is usually dependent upon award of the Caribbean Advanced Proficiency Examination (CAPE). Grading in higher education is based on the system used by the University of the West Indies.

Regulatory Bodies

GOVERNMENT

Ministry of Education, Sports and Youth Affairs: Govt Office Complex, Queen Elizabeth Highway, St John's; tel. 462-4959; fax 462-4970; e-mail doristeen.etinoff@ab.gov .ag; Minister Dr JACQUI QUINN-LEANDRO; Sec. EDEN WESTON; Dir of Education JACINTHA PRINGLE.

Ministry of Tourism, Civil Aviation, Culture and the Environment: Govt Office Complex, Bldg 1, Queen Elizabeth Highway, St John's; tel. 462-0480; fax 462-2483; e-mail mblackman@tourism.gov.ag; Minister HAROLD LOVELL; Minister of State with Responsibility for Culture and Independence Celebrations ELESTON ADAMS.

Learned Societies

BIBLIOGRAPHY, LIBRARY SCIENCE AND MUSEOLOGY

Library Association of Antigua and Barbuda: POB 822, St John's; tel. 462-3500; fax 462-1537; f. 1983; 40 mems; Pres. MOLIVAR SPENCER; Sec. TRACY SAMUEL.

LANGUAGE AND LITERATURE

Alliance Française: POB 2086, St John's; tel. 462-3625; offers courses and examinations in French language and culture and promotes cultural exchange with France.

Archives

St John's

Antigua and Barbuda National Archives: Victoria Park, Factory Rd, St John's; tel. 462-4959; fax 462-4970; e-mail archives@ antigua.gov.ag; f. 1982; Dir Dr MARION BLAIR.

Universities

UNIVERSITY OF HEALTH SCIENCES ANTIGUA

Dowhill Campus, Piccadilly, POB 510, St John's

Telephone: 460-1391
Fax: 460-1477
E-mail: admissions@uhsa.edu.ag
Internet: www.uhsa.ag

Founded 1982
Pres.: Dr AKIN OMITOWOJU
Registrar: IVORY TAYLOR
Librarian: (vacant)
Dean, School of Medicine: Dr N. OLOWOPOPO

Library: in process of formation
Number of teachers: 32
Number of students: 203

Schools of Liberal Arts and Sciences, Medicine, Nursing, Veterinary Medicine, Postgraduate Medical Education.

Colleges

Antigua and Barbuda International Institute of Technology (ABIIT): POB 736, St John's; tel. 480-2400; fax 480-2411; e-mail info@abiit.edu.ag; internet www.abiit .edu.ag; f. 2001; Pres. GLADWIN HENRY; Dean of Academics EUSTACE HILL.

Antigua State College: POB 193, Golden Grove, St John's; tel. 462-1434; fax 460-9476; f. 1977 by merger of Leeward Islands Teachers' Training College and Golden Grove Technical College, absorbed Antigua and Barbuda School of Nursing in 2000; hospitality and tourism management, teacher training, technical training.

University of the West Indies School of Continuing Studies (Antigua and Barbuda): POB 142, St John's; tel. 462-1355; fax 462-2968; e-mail university@candw.ag; f. 1949; adult education courses, spec. programmes for women, summer courses for children, occasional seminars and workshops; library: 10,000 vols; 23 part-time tutors; 350 students; Resident Tutor Dr ERMINA OSOBA.

ARGENTINA

The Higher Education System

The Federal Law of Education of 1993 decentralized the education system, with administration devolving to each of the 23 individual provinces and to the Municipality of Buenos Aires. The federal Ministry of Education, Science and Technology is responsible for the provision of university education, while each provincial ministry of education is responsible for education provision at post-secondary, non-university level. Technical education is supervised by the Consejo Nacional de Educación Técnica.

Between 2003 and 2007 a number of laws were passed which defined education as a national priority and laid the foundation for developing a state policy. Among these were: National Education Law (Law No. 26.206, 2007), the Education Finance Act (Law No. 26.075, 2005), the Vocational Technical Education Act (Law No. 26.058, 2005), the National Comprehensive Sex Education (Law No. 26.150, 2006), the Wage Guarantee Act Teacher and 180 days of school (Law No. 25.864, 2003), Law on National Teachers Incentive Fund (Law No. 25.919, 2004) and Law on Protection of the Rights of Children and Adolescents (Act No. 26.061, 2005).

Admission to higher education is dependent upon successful completion of the secondary qualification. There are two levels of higher qualification: first, a Professional Title (Licenciado), study for which lasts for between four and six years depending on the subject; and second the Doctorado, which requires a further two years of study. Vocational and professional post-secondary education and training is available at higher technical schools or institutes of technology, also known as polytechnic institutes, and at higher commercial schools. Courses at these institutions are usually two years in length, and successful students are awarded a title such as Técnico Superior or Técnico Universitario in the area of specialization.

Argentina is a member state of the Mercado Común del Sur (MERCOSUR—Southern Common Market) and as such is a participant in its accreditation programme: El Mecanismo Experimental de Acreditación de Carreras del MERCOSUR. This programme has so far accredited Argentine degrees in agronomy, medicine and engineering.

In 2004 there were 1,805,491 students in higher education, of whom 1,273,156 were enrolled at the 37 universities, 512,002 at general non-university institutions and a further 20,333 at specialized institutions.

Regulatory and Representative Bodies

GOVERNMENT

Ministry of Education: Pizzurno 935, C1020ACA, Buenos Aires; tel. (11) 4129-1000; e-mail info@me.gov.ar; internet www.me.gov.ar; Minister Prof. ALBERTO SILEONI.

ACCREDITATION

Comisión Nacional de Evaluación y Acreditación Universitaria (CONEAU) (National Commission for University Evaluation and Accreditation): Avda Santa Fe 1385, 4°, C1059ABH, Buenos Aires; tel. (11) 4815-1767; fax (11) 4815-0744; e-mail consulta@coneau.gov.ar; internet www.coneau.gov.ar; f. 1996 to foster improvements in univ. education in Argentina; govt agency under Min. of Education; functions according to the Higher Education Act No. 24.521; composed of 12 mems appointed by the Govt for 4 years, the National Interuniversity Council (CIN), the Federal Senate and the Federal Chamber of Deputies nominate 3 mems each, the Council of Rectors of Private Universities (CRUP), the National Academy of Education and the Min. of Education nominate 1 mem. each; evaluates projects submitted by new public and private univs; performs external evaluation of univs; grants accreditation to govt regulated undergraduate programmes; grants accreditation to graduate programmes; conducts evaluation processes for accreditation of private evaluation and accreditation orgs; serves as Secretariat of Red Iberoamericana para la Acreditación de la Calidad de la Educación Superior (RIACES) and plays an active role in the initiatives carried out by the International Network for Quality Assurance Agencies in Higher Education (INQAAHE); contributes to devt of MERCOSUR experimental accreditation mechanism (MEXA); Pres. FRANCISCO JOSÉ MIGUEL TALENTO CUTRÍN; Sec.-Gen. NÉSTOR RAUL PAN.

NATIONAL BODIES

Academia Nacional de Educación (National Academy of Education): Pacheco de Melo 2084, C1126AAF, Buenos Aires; tel. (11) 4806-2818; fax (11) 4806-8817; e-mail info@acaedu.edu.ar; internet www.acaedu.edu.ar; f. 1984 as Argentine Academy of Education; incl. within the nat. academies rule (Decree number 4362/55) by Min. of Education and Justice (ruling no. 107, dated 27 June 1989; ratified by Decree number 1124, dated 26 October 1989); promotes educational creativity and innovation; Pres. HORACIO SANGUINETTI; Vice-Pres MARÍA CELIA AGUDO DE CÓRSICO, PEDRO SIMONCINI; Sec. MARCELO J. VERNENGO.

Consejo Interuniversitario Nacional (CIN) (National Interuniversity Council): Pacheco de Melo 2084, C1126AAF, Buenos Aires; tel. (11) 4806-2269; e-mail info@cin.edu.ar; internet www.cin.edu.ar; f. 1985; proposes and coordinates policy for mem. univs; defines and coordinates academic, research and management programmes of mem. instns; creates regional orgs for interuniv. cooperation; consults on creation or closure of nat. univs; generates and supports self-evaluation and external evaluation policies for mems; promotes compatibility and quality assurance of study programmes; Pres. Ing. OSCAR FEDERICO SPADA.

Consejo de Rectores de las Universidades Privadas (CRUP) (Council of Rectors of Private Universities): Montevideo 1910 PB, C1021AAH, Buenos Aires; tel. (11) 4811-6435; fax (11) 4811-0947; internet www.crup.org.ar; representative and consultative org.; coordinates teaching in private univs in conjunction with Min. of Education and the Provincial Councils of Rectors; fosters collaboration between mem. univs; Pres. Dr HORACIO O'DONNELL; Vice-Pres. Lic. LUIS VELASCO, Mgr Dr ALFREDO ZECCA; Sec. Dr HECTOR SAURET.

Learned Societies

AGRICULTURE, FISHERIES AND VETERINARY SCIENCE

Academia Nacional de Agronomía y Veterinaria (Academy of Agronomy and Veterinary Science): Avda Alvear 1711 (2° piso), 1014 Buenos Aires; tel. (11) 4815-4616; fax (11) 4812-4168; internet www.anav.org.ar; f. 1909; 98 mems; library of 3,000 vols; Pres. Dr C. N. CARLOS O. SCOPPA; Sec.-Gen. Ing. Agr. RODOLFO G. FRANK; publ. Anales (1 a year).

Asociación Argentina de la Ciencia del Suelo (Argentine Association of Soil Science): Pabellón INGEIS, Ciudad Universitaria, 1428 Buenos Aires; tel. (11) 4783-3021; fax (11) 4783-3024; e-mail cosenti@agro.uba.ar; internet www.suelos.org.ar; f. 1958; 800 mems; Pres. GERARDO RUBIO; Sec. PABLO PRYSTUPA; publ. Ciencia del Suelo (2 a year).

Sociedad Rural Argentina (Argentine Agricultural Society): Florida 460, 1005 Buenos Aires; tel. (11) 4322-0468; fax (11) 4325-8231; internet www.sra.org.ar; f. 1866; 10,000 mems; library: see Libraries and Archives; Pres. Dr LUCIANO MIGUENS.

ARCHITECTURE AND TOWN PLANNING

Sociedad Central de Arquitectos (Architects' Association): Montevideo 938, C1019ABT Buenos Aires; tel. (11) 4812-3644; fax (11) 4813-6629; e-mail info@socearq.org; internet www.socearq.org; f. 1886; 8,500 mems; library of 9,200 vols, 90 periodicals; Pres. Arq. DANIEL SILBERFADEN; Sec. Arq. LUIS MARÍA ALBORNOZ; publ. Revista SCA (6 a year).

BIBLIOGRAPHY, LIBRARY SCIENCE AND MUSEOLOGY

Asociación Argentina de Bibliotecas y Centros de Información Científicos y Técnicos (Argentine Association of Scientific and Technical Libraries and Information Centres): Santa Fe 1145, 1059 Buenos Aires; tel. (11) 4393-8406; f. 1937; 84 mems; Pres.

ABILIO BASSETS; Tech. Sec. ERNESTO G. GIETZ; publ. *Union Catalogue of Scientific and Technical Publications.*

Asociación de Bibliotecarios Graduados de la República Argentina (ABGRA) (Association of Argentine Librarians): Tucumán 1424 (8o piso D), C1050AAB Buenos Aires; tel. (11) 4373-0571; fax (11) 4371-5269; e-mail abgra@ciudad.com.ar; internet abgra .sisbi.uba.ar; f. 1953; 1,650 mems; Pres. ANA MARÍA PERUCHENA ZIMMERMANN; Sec.-Gen. ROBERTO JORGE SERVIDIO; publ. *Revista REFERENCIAS* (3 a year).

Comisión Nacional de Museos y de Monumentos y Lugares Históricos (National Commission for Museums and Historic Monuments and Sites): Avda de Mayo 556, 1084 Buenos Aires; tel. (11) 4343-5835; e-mail info@ comisionmonumentos.gov.ar; internet www .monumentosysitios.gov.ar; f. 1938; supervises museums and protects the nat. historical heritage; library; Pres. (vacant); Sec. Arq. JORGE TARTARINI; publ. *Boletín.*

Comisión Nacional Protectora de Bibliotecas Populares (Commission for the Protection of Public Libraries): Ayacucho 1578, 1112 Buenos Aires; tel. (11) 4511-6275; e-mail me@conabip.gov.ar; internet www.conabip.gov.ar; f. 1870; Pres. DANIEL RÍOS; Sec. Prof. ANA T. DOBRA; publ. *Boletín.*

ECONOMICS, LAW AND POLITICS

Academia Nacional de Ciencias Económicas (National Academy of Economic Sciences): Avda Alvear 1790, 1014 Buenos Aires; tel. (11) 4813-2078; fax (11) 4813-2078; f. 1914; 35 mems; library of 13,500 vols; Pres. Dr JOSÉ MARÍA DAGNINO PASTORE; Sec. Dra LUISA MONTUSCHI; publ. *Anales.*

Academia Nacional de Ciencias Morales y Políticas (National Academy of Moral and Political Sciences): Avda Alvear 1711, PB, 1014 Buenos Aires; tel. (11) 4811-2049; e-mail ancmyp@ancmyp.org.ar; internet www.ancmyp.org.ar; f. 1938; 35 mems; library of 13,536 vols; Pres. Dr JORGE A. AJA ESPIL; Sec. CARLOS A. SÁNCHEZ; publ. *Anales.*

Academia Nacional de Derecho y Ciencias Sociales (National Academy of Law and Social Sciences): Avda Alvear 1711 (1°), 1014 Buenos Aires; tel. (11) 4815-6976; internet www.academiadederecho.org.ar; f. 1874; 25 mems; Pres. Dr JULIO CÉSAR OTAEGUI; Secs Dr SANTOS CIFUENTES, Dr HÉCTOR ALEGRÍA; publ. *Anales.*

Academia Nacional de Derecho y Ciencias Sociales (Córdoba) (National Academy of Law and Social Sciences, Córdoba): Artigas 74, 5000 Córdoba; tel. (351) 421-4929; fax (351) 421-4929; e-mail secretaria@ acaderc.org.ar; internet www.acaderc.org.ar; f. 1941; 172 mems; library of 6,578 vols; Pres. Dr LUIS MOISSET DE ESPANÉS; Technical Sec. Dr CHRISTIAN G. SOMMER; publs *Anales, Federalism Journal, History of Law Journal, International Law Journal.*

Colegio de Abogados de la Ciudad de Buenos Aires (Buenos Aires City Bar Association): Montevideo 640, 1019 Buenos Aires; tel. (11) 4371-1110; fax (11) 4375-5442; e-mail info@colabogados.org.ar; internet www.colabogados.org.ar; f. 1913; 1,600 mems; library of 45,000 vols; Pres. ENRIQUE V. DEL CARRIL; Exec. Dir FERNANDO R. FRÁVEGA; publs *Actualidad* (6 a year), *Revista* (2 a year).

FINE AND PERFORMING ARTS

Academia Nacional de Bellas Artes (National Academy of Fine Arts): Sánchez de Bustamante 2663, 2° Piso, 1425 Buenos Aires; tel. (11) 4802-2469; e-mail info@anba .org.ar; internet www.anba.org.ar; f. 1936; 30 mems, 30 foreign corresp. mems; library of 6,000 vols; Pres. JORGE TAVERNA IRIGOYEN; Gen. Sec. OSVALDO SVANASCINI; publs *Anuario, Cuaderno Especial: 'Escenas del Campo Argentino' 1885–1900, Documentos de Arte Argentino, Documentos de Arte Colonial Sudamericano, Monografías de Artistas Argentinos, Serie Estudios de Arte en la Argentina.*

Fondo Nacional de las Artes (National Arts Foundation): Alsina 673, C1087AAI Buenos Aires; tel. (11) 4343-1590; e-mail fnartes@fnartes.gov.ar; internet www .fnartes.gov.ar; f. 1958; promotes and supports the arts; 15 mems; library of 7,000 vols; Pres. Lic. HÉCTOR W. VALLE; publs *Anuario del Teatro Argentino, Bibliografía Argentina de Artes y Letras, Informativo.*

HISTORY, GEOGRAPHY AND ARCHAEOLOGY

Academia Nacional de Geografía (National Academy of Geography): Avda Cabildo 381 (7° piso), C1426AAD Buenos Aires; tel. (11) 4771-3043; fax (11) 4771-3043; e-mail secretaria@an-geografia.org.ar; internet www.an-geografia.org.ar; f. 1956; 32 mems; Pres. Prof. ANTONIO CORNEJO; Sec. HÉCTOR O. J. PENA; publ. *Anales.*

Academia Nacional de la Historia (National Academy of History): Balcarce 139, 1064 Buenos Aires; tel. (11) 4331-5147; fax (11) 4331-4633; e-mail admite@ an-historia.org.ar; internet www.an-historia .org.ar; f. 1893; study of Argentine and American history; 257 mems (34 ordinary, 223 foreign corresp.); Pres. Dr MIGUEL ANGEL DE MARCO; publs *Boletín, Investigaciones y Ensayos.*

Instituto Bonaerense de Numismática y Antigüedades (Buenos Aires Institute of Numismatics and Antiquities): San Martín 336, 1004 Buenos Aires; tel. (11) 449-2659; f. 1872; 107 mems; Pres. HUMBERTO F. BURZIO; publ. *Boletín.*

Junta de Historia Eclesiástica Argentina (Council of Argentine Ecclesiastical History): Reconquista 269, 1003 Buenos Aires; tel. (11) 4343-4397 ext. 309; e-mail info@jhea.org.ar; internet www.jhea.org.ar; f. 1942; 100 mems; Pres. Pbro. Lic. LUIS ALBERTO LAHITOU; Sec. Prof. ANA MARÍA WOITES; publs *Boletín, Revista Archivum* (1 a year).

Sociedad Argentina de Estudios Geográficos (Argentine Society of Geographical Studies): Rodríguez Peña 158 (4° piso Dpto 7), 1020 Buenos Aires; tel. (11) 4373-0588; e-mail informes@gaea.org.ar; internet www .gaea.org.ar; f. 1922; 4,000 mems; library of 12,000 vols; Pres. Dra SUSANA I. CURTO DE CASAS; Sec. Lic. ANALÍA S. CONTE; publs *Anales, Contribuciones Científicas, GAEA Boletín, Geografía de la República Argentina.*

LANGUAGE AND LITERATURE

Academia Argentina de Letras (Argentine Academy of Letters): Sánchez de Bustamante 2663, 1425 Buenos Aires; tel. (11) 4802-3814; fax (11) 4802-8340; internet www .aal.universia.com.ar; f. 1931; 77 mems (24 ordinary, 53 corresp.); Pres. PEDRO LUIS BARCIA; Sec.-Gen. RODOLFO MODERN; publ. *Boletín* (4 a year).

Alliance Française: Avda Córdoba 936–946, 1054 Buenos Aires; tel. (11) 4322-0068; fax (11) 4326-6655; e-mail info@ alianzafrancesa.org.ar; internet www .alianzafrancesa.org.ar; offers courses and examinations in French language and culture and promotes cultural exchange with France; attached teaching offices in Alta Gracia, Azul, Bahia Blanca, Banfield, Baradero, Bell Ville, Bella Vista, Bernal, Bragado, Brandsen, Buenos Aires (Belgrano, Flores and Fortabat), Campana, Campana-Escobar, Chacabuco, Chajari, Chivilcoy, Cinco Saltos, Colon, Comodoro Rivadavia, Concepcion del Uruguay, Córdoba, Coronel-Pringles, Coronel-Suarez, El Trebol, Esperanza, Formosa, Gualeguay, Gualeguaychu, Jesus Maria, Junin, La Plata, Las Varillas, Lincoln, Mar del Plata, Marcos-Juarez, Marcos-Paz, Martinez, Martinez-Olivos, Martinez-San Isidro, Mendoza, Mercedes, Mercedes-Lujan, Neuquén, Neuquén-General Roca, Nogoya, Olavarria, Paraná, Pehuajo, Pergamino, Pigue, Posadas, Quilmes, Rafaela, Reconquista, Resistencia, Rio Cuarto, Rio Gallegos, Rivadavia, Roque Saenz Peña, Rosario, Salta, San Carlos de Bariloche, San Francisco, San Jorge, San Jose, San Juan, San Luis, San Nicolas, San Rafael, San Salvador de Jujuy, Santa Fe, Santa Rosa, Santiago del Estero, Tandil, Trelew, Tres Arroyos, Tucumán, Tuerto, Ushuala, Venado, Vicente Lopez, Vicente Lopez-San Martín, Villa Elisa, Villa Maria, Villa Mercedes and Villaguay; Dir of Operations, Argentina FRANÇOISE COCHAUD.

British Council: Marcelo T. de Alvear 590, C1058AAF Buenos Aires; tel. (11) 4114-8600; fax (11) 4114-8600; e-mail info@ britishcouncil.org.ar; internet www .britishcouncil.org/argentina; offers courses and examinations in English language and British culture and promotes cultural exchange with the UK; Dir HUW JONES.

Goethe-Institut: Avda Corrientes 319, C1043AAD Buenos Aires; tel. (11) 4318-5600; fax (11) 4318-5656; e-mail info@ buenosaires.goethe.org; internet www.goethe .de/buenosaires; offers courses and examinations in German language and culture and promotes cultural exchange with Germany; library of 15,000 vols, 37 periodicals; Dir HARTMUT BECHER.

PEN Club Argentino—Centro Internacional de la Asociación PEN (International PEN Centre): Rivadavia 4060, 1205 Buenos Aires; f. 1930; 100 mems; Pres. MIGUEL A. OLIVERA; publ. *Boletín.*

Sociedad Argentina de Autores y Compositores de Música (SADAIC) (Argentine Society of Authors and Composers): Lavalle 1547, 1048 Buenos Aires; tel. (11) 4379-8600; f. 1936; library of 4,000 vols, 13,000 music scores; Pres. ATILIO STAMPONE; Cultural Dir EUGENIO INCHAUSTI.

Sociedad General de Autores de la Argentina (Argentores) (Argentine Society of Authors): Pacheco de Melo 1820, C1126AAB Buenos Aires; tel. (11) 4811-2582; fax (11) 4811-6954; e-mail info@ argentores.org.ar; internet www.argentores .org.ar; f. 1910; 2,000 mems; library of 60,000 vols; Pres. ISAAC AISEMBERG; Sec. AUGUSTO GIUSTOZZI; publ. *Boletín* (4 a year).

MEDICINE

Academia Argentina de Cirugía (Argentine Academy of Surgery): M. T. de Alvear 2416, 1122 Buenos Aires; tel. (11) 4822-2905; fax (11) 4822-6458; internet www .academiaargentinadecirugia.org; f. 1911; Pres. Dr EDUARDO TRIGO; Gen. Sec. EDUARDO DE SANTIBAÑES.

Academia de Ciencias Médicas de Córdoba: Pueyrredón 59, 2° Piso, 5000 Córdoba; tel. (351) 468-5385; f. 1975; 350 mems; Pres. Dr REMO BERGOGLIO; Sec. Dr JESÚS R. GIRAUDO.

Academia Nacional de Medicina (National Academy of Medicine): Las Heras

3092, 1425ASU Buenos Aires; tel. (11) 4805-6890; fax (11) 4806-6638; e-mail acamedbai@acamedbai.org.ar; internet www.acamedbai.org.ar; f. 1822; medical and scientific instn; 35 mems; library of 50,000 vols; Pres. Acad. Juan M. Ghirlanda; Pres. Acad. Roberto N. Pradier; publ. *Boletín* (2 a year).

Asociación Argentina de Biología y Medicina Nuclear (Argentine Association for Biology and Nuclear Medicine): Luis Sáenz Peña 250, 6° Piso, Of. A, 1110 Buenos Aires; tel. (11) 4382-0583; fax (11) 4382-0583; e-mail aabymn_1@ciudad.com.ar; internet www.aabymn.org.ar; f. 1963; 190 mems; Pres. Dr Arturo J. San Martín; Sec. Dra María del Carmen Alak.

Asociación Argentina de Cirugía (Argentine Association of Surgery): Marcelo T. de Alvear 2415, 1122 Buenos Aires; tel. (11) 4822-2905; fax (11) 4822-6458; e-mail info@aac.org.ar; internet www.aac.org.ar; f. 1930; 4,000 mems; Pres. Dr Eduardo Cassone; Dir Dr Martín Mihura; publs *Anuario*, *Boletín Informativo* (24 a year), *Revista Argentina de Cirugía* (8 a year).

Asociación Argentina de Farmacia y Bioquímica Industrial (Argentine Industrial Biochemistry and Pharmacy Association): Uruguay 469 (2° B), 1015 Buenos Aires; tel. (11) 4373-8900; fax (11) 4372-7389; e-mail info@safybi.org; internet www.safybi.org.ar; f. 1952; 1,100 mems; library of 500 vols; Pres. Dr Federico E. Montes de Oca; Sec. Dra Mirta B. Fariña; publs *Boletín Informativo* (3 a year), *Revista SAFYBI*.

Asociación Argentina de Ortopedia y Traumatología (Argentine Orthopaedic and Traumatology Association): Vicente López 1878, C1128ABC Buenos Aires; tel. (11) 4801-2320; fax (11) 4801-7703; e-mail gerencia@aaot.org.ar; internet www.aaot.org.ar; f. 1936; 2,944 mems; library of 1,460 vols, 67 periodicals; Pres. Dr Gregorio M. Arendar; Sec. Dr Carlos F. Sancineto; publ. *Revista* (4 a year).

Asociación Médica Argentina (Argentine Medical Association): Santa Fe 1171, 1059 Buenos Aires; tel. (11) 4814-2182; fax (11) 4811-3850; e-mail info@ama-med.com; internet www.ama-med.org.ar; f. 1891; 3,520 mems; library of 32,000 vols, 290,000 periodicals; Pres. Dr Elías Hurtado Hoyo; Sec. Miguel A. Galmés; publs *Boletín Informativo* (12 a year), *Revista AMA* (4 a year).

Asociación Odontológica Argentina (Argentine Dental Association): Junín 959, 1113 Buenos Aires; tel. (11) 4961-6141; fax (11) 4961-1110; internet www2.aoa.org.ar; f. 1896; incl. postgraduate school for dentists; 8,000 mems; library of 8,000 vols, 11,300 periodicals; Pres. Dr Eduardo Maiucci; Sec. Juan Carlos Cometti; publ. *Revista*.

Asociación para la Lucha contra la Parálisis Infantil (Association for Combating Infantile Paralysis): San Lorenzo 283 B°, Nueva, Córdoba; tel. (351) 423-2593; fax (351) 422-8183; e-mail alpicordoba@ciudad.com.ar; f. 1943; 30 mems; library of 3,000 vols; Pres. Verónica S. M. de Busto; publ. *Memoria y Balance Anual*.

Federación Argentina de Asociaciones de Anestesia, Analgesia y Reanimación (Argentine Federation of Anaesthesia, Analgesia and Resuscitation Associations): Fragata Sarmiento 541 1er Piso, 1405 Buenos Aires; tel. (11) 4431-2547; fax (11) 4431-2463; internet www.anestesia.org.ar; f. 1970; 1,113 mems; Pres. Dr Saúl Sorotski; Gen. Sec. Dr Daniel Crosara; publs *Revista Argentina de Anestesiología*, *Boletín Informativo*.

Liga Argentina contra la Tuberculosis (Argentine Anti-Tuberculosis League): Uriarte 2477, C1425FNI, Buenos Aires; tel.

(11) 4777-4447; fax (11) 4777-6470; internet www.connmed.com.ar/instituciones/lalac.org.ar; f. 1901; library of 140 series of periodicals; Medical Dir Dr Vicente Donato; publs *Revista Argentina del Tórax*, *La Doble Cruz*.

Sociedad Argentina de Ciencias Neurológicas, Psiquiátricas y Neuroquirúrgicas (Argentine Neurological, Neurosurgical and Psychiatric Society): Santa Fe 1171, 1059 Buenos Aires; tel. (11) 441-1633; f. 1920; 400 mems; library of 35,000 vols; Pres. Prof. Dr Diego Brage; Sec. Prof. Dr Carlos Márquez; publ. *Revista* (12 a year).

Sociedad Argentina de Dermatología (Argentine Society of Dermatology): Avda Callao 852 (2o piso), 1023 Buenos Aires; tel. (11) 4815-4649; fax (11) 4814-4919; e-mail sad@sad.org.ar; internet www.sad.org.ar; f. 1934; 2,100 mems; Pres. Prof. Dr Horacio Cabo; Sec.-Gen. Dra Patricia Troielli; publ. *Dermatología, Argentina* (5 a year).

Sociedad Argentina de Endocrinología y Metabolismo (Argentine Society of Endocrinology and Metabolism): Avda Díaz Vélez 3889, C1200AAF Buenos Aires; tel. and fax (11) 4983-9800; e-mail info@saem.org.ar; internet www.saem.org.ar; f. 1941; 562 mems; Pres. Dr Gerardo Sartorio; Sec. Dr Graciela Stalldecker; publ. *Revista* (4 a year).

Sociedad Argentina de Farmacología y Terapéutica (Argentine Society of Pharmacology and Therapeutics): Santa Fe 1171, 1059 Buenos Aires; tel. (11) 4811-3580; e-mail info@ama-med.com; f. 1929; 100 mems; Pres. Dr Alfredo Vitale; Sec. Dra Cristina Volmer.

Sociedad Argentina de Fisiológia (Argentine Physiological Society): Solís 453, 1078 Buenos Aires; tel. (11) 4378-1151; fax (11) 4381-0323; e-mail safis@safisiol.org.ar; internet www.safisiol.org.ar; f. 1950; 300 mems; library of 600 vols; mem. of IUPS; Pres. Dr Valeria Rettori; Sec. Dr B. Fernandez; publ. *Physiological Mini-Reviews* (12 a year).

Sociedad Argentina de Gastroenterología (Argentine Society of Gastroenterology): Marcelo T. de Alvear 1381 9° Piso, C1058AAU Buenos Aires; tel. (11) 4816-9391; fax (11) 4816-9396; e-mail sage@sage.org.ar; internet www.sage.org.ar; f. 1927; 900 mems; Pres. Dr Roberto Martin Mazure; Gen. Sec. Dra Silvia C. Gutiérrez; publ. *Acta Gastroenterológica Latinoamericana*.

Sociedad Argentina de Gerontología y Geriatría (Argentine Gerontological and Geriatrics Society): San Luis 2538, C1056AAD Buenos Aires; fax (11) 4961-0070; e-mail sagg@connmed.com.ar; internet www.sagg.org.ar; f. 1950; 1,500 mems; Pres. Dr Isidoro Fainstein; Sec. Dr Hugo Alberto Schifis; publs *Revista Argentina de Gerontología y Geriatría* (6 a year), *Vivir en Plenitud* (6 a year).

Sociedad Argentina de Hematología (Argentine Society of Haematology): Julian Alvarez 146, C1414DRD Buenos Aires; tel. (11) 4855-2452; e-mail sah@sah.org.ar; internet www.sah.org.ar; f. 1945; 800 mems; Pres. Dr Jorge H. Riveros; Sec. Dra María Gabriela Flores.

Sociedad Argentina de Investigación Clínica (Argentine Society of Clinical Research): Combatientes de Malvinas 3150, C1427ARO Buenos Aires; tel. (11) 4523-4963; fax (11) 4523-4963; e-mail secretaria@saic.org.ar; internet www.saic.org.ar; f. 1960; 500 mems; Pres. Dra Adriana Seilicovich; Sec. Dr Rodolfo Rey; publ. *Medicina*.

Sociedad Argentina de Oftalmología (Argentine Ophthalmological Society): Viamonte 1465 7°, C1055ABA Buenos Aires; tel. (11) 4373-8826; fax (11) 4373-8828; e-mail info@sao.org.ar; internet www.sao.org.ar; f. 1920; 2,000 mems; Pres. Dr Edgardo Manzitti; Sec. Dr Daniel Weil; publ. *Archivos de Oftalmología de Buenos Aires* (12 a year).

Sociedad Argentina de Patología (Argentine Society of Pathology): Pte. Gral. Perón 2234 1° A, C1040AAJ Buenos Aires; tel. (11) 4951-2152; fax (11) 4951-2152; e-mail infosap@patologia.org.ar; internet www.patologia.org.ar; f. 1933; 220 mems; Pres. Dr Julián Mosto; Gen. Sec. Dra Laura Jufe; publ. *Archivos*.

Sociedad Argentina de Pediatría (Argentine Paediatric Society): Avda Coronel Díaz 1971, C1425DQF Buenos Aires; tel. (11) 4821-8612; e-mail cdsap@sap.org.ar; internet www.sap.org.ar; f. 1911; 7,500 mems; library of 5,000 vols; Pres. Dra Margarita D. Ramonet; Gen. Sec. Dra Angela Gentile; publ. *Archivos Argentinos de Pediatría* (6 a year).

Sociedad de Cirugía de Buenos Aires (Buenos Aires Surgical Society): Santa Fe 1171, 1059 Buenos Aires; tel. (11) 444-0664; Pres. Ivan Goñi Moreno; Sec.-Gen. Guillermo I. Belleville.

Sociedad de Psicología Médica, Psicoanálisis y Medicina Psicosomática (Society of Medical Psychology, Psychoanalysis and Psychosomatic Medicine): Avda Santa Fe 1171, 1059 Buenos Aires; tel. (11) 4814-2182; e-mail amalia.racciatti@gmail.com; internet www.psicoama.com.ar; f. 1939; 80 mems; Pres. Dr Carlos Gibert; Sec. Dra Amalia Racciatti de Messuti.

NATURAL SCIENCES

General

Academia Nacional de Ciencias de Buenos Aires (National Academy of Sciences of Buenos Aires): Avda Alvear 1711 (3° piso), 1014 Buenos Aires; tel. (11) 441-3066; f. 1935; 35 mems; Pres. Dr Julio H. G. Olivera; Sec. Dr Hugo F. Bauzá; publs *Anales*, *Escritos de Filosofía* (4 a year).

Academia Nacional de Ciencias (National Academy of Sciences): CC 36, Avda Vélez Sarsfield 229, 5000 Córdoba; tel. (351) 433-2089; fax (351) 421-6350; e-mail secretaria@acad.uncor.edu; internet www.acad.uncor.edu; f. 1869; 79 mems; library of 12,000 vols, 3,800 periodicals; Pres. Dr Eduardo Humberto Staricco; Sec. Dr Pedro J. Depetris; publs *Actas*, *Boletín*, *Miscelánea*.

Academia Nacional de Ciencias Exactas, Físicas y Naturales (National Academy of Exact, Physical and Natural Sciences): Avda Alvear 1711 (4o), 1014 Buenos Aires; tel. (11) 4811-2998; fax (11) 4811-6951; internet www.ancefn.org.ar; f. 1874; 130 mems (36 full voting, 27 nat. corresp., 61 foreign corresp., 6 hon.); library of 400 collns of periodicals; Pres. Dr Alejandro J. Arvia; Sec.-Gen. Dr Jorge V. Crisci; publ. *Anales* (1 a year).

Asociación Argentina de Ciencias Naturales (Argentine Association of Natural Sciences): Avda Angel Gallardo 470, C1405DJR Buenos Aires; tel. (11) 4982-8370; fax (11) 4982-4494; f. 1912; 450 mems; Pres. Juan Carlos Giacchi; Sec. Dra Cristina Marinone; publ. *Physis* (2 a year).

Asociación Argentina para el Progreso de las Ciencias (Association for the Advancement of Science): Avda Alvear 1711 (4° piso), C1014AAE Buenos Aires; tel. (11) 4811-2998; fax (11) 4811-6951; e-mail secretaria@aargentinapciencias.org; f. 1933; 215 mems (200 ordinary, 15 assoc.); Pres. Dr Eduardo Hernán Charreau; Sec. Dr

AUGUSTO F. GARCÍA; publ. *Ciencia e Investigación*.

Sociedad Científica Argentina (Argentine Scientific Society): Avda Santa Fe 1145, 1059 Buenos Aires; tel. (11) 4816-4745; fax (11) 4816-5406; e-mail sociedad@cientifica.org.ar; internet www.cientifica.org.ar; f. 1872; affiliations in Santa Fe, La Plata, San Juan; 698 mems; library of 39,600 vols; Pres. Dr ARTURO OTAÑO SAHORES; Sec. Lic. ERNESTO CELMAN; publ. *Anales* (1 a year).

Biological Sciences

Asociación Argentina de Micología (Argentine Mycological Society): Suipacha 531, 2000 Rosario; tel. (341) 480-4592; internet www.asam.org.ar; f. 1960; studies in medical and veterinary mycology, and mycotoxins; 150 mems; library; Pres. Dra LAURA RAMOS; Sec. MARISA BIASOLI; publ. *Revista Argentina de Micología* (3 a year).

Asociación Paleontológica Argentina (Argentine Association of Palaeontology): Maipú 645 (1o piso), C1006ACG Buenos Aires; tel. (11) 4326-7463; fax (11) 4326-7463; e-mail secretaria@apaleontologica.org.ar; internet www.apaleontologica.org.ar; f. 1955; 500 mems; Pres. Dr SERGIO F. VIZCAÍNO; Sec. Dra MARÍA DE LAS MERCEDES DI PASQUO; publ. *Ameghiniana* (4 a year).

Sociedad Argentina de Biología (Argentine Biological Society): Vuelta de Obligado 2490, 1428 Buenos Aires; tel. (11) 4783-2869; e-mail biologia@dna.uba.ar; internet proteus.dna.uba.ar/biologia; f. 1920; 140 mems; Pres. Dra ISABEL LÜTHY; Sec. Dr HÉCTOR COIRINI; publ. *Revista* (1 a year).

Sociedad Argentina de Fisiología Vegetal (Argentine Society of Plant Physiology): Departamento de Agronomía, UNS, 8000 Bahía Blanca; tel. (291) 453-1821; fax (291) 459-5127; internet www.safv.uns.edu.ar; f. 1958; 260 mems; Pres. Dra EDITH TALEISNIK; Sec. Dr LUIS F. HERNANDEZ.

Sociedad Entomológica Argentina (SEA) (Argentine Entomological Society): Miguel Lillo 205, 4107 San Miguel de Tucumán; tel. and fax (381) 423-2965; e-mail seatuc@csnat.unt.edu.ar; internet www.sea.secyt.gov.ar; f. 1925; 400 mems; library of 815 vols, 590 periodicals; located in the Museo de la Plata, Buenos Aires, e-mail bibsea@museo.fcnym.unlp.edu.ar; Pres. MERCEDES LIZARRALDE DE GROSSO; Sec. CARMEN REGUILÓN; publs *Publicación Especial de la Sociedad Entomológica Argentina* (irregular), *Revista de la Sociedad Entomológica Argentina* (2 a year).

Mathematical Sciences

Unión Matemática Argentina (Argentine Mathematical Union): Facultad Ciencias Físico Matemáticas y Naturales, Universidad Nacional de San Luis, Ejército de los Andes 950, 5700 San Luis; tel. (2652) 422803; fax (2652) 430224; f. 1936; 600 mems; Pres. Dr FELIPE ZÓ; Sec. Dr HUGO ALVAREZ; publ. *Revista*.

Physical Sciences

Asociación Argentina Amigos de la Astronomía (Argentine Association for the Friends of Astronomy): Avda Patricias Argentinas 550, C1405BWS Buenos Aires; tel. and fax (11) 4863-3366; internet www.amigosdelaastronomia.org; f. 1929; maintains an observatory and museum; 1,000 mems; library of 6,000 vols; Pres. CARLOS E. ANGUEIRA VÁZQUEZ; Sec. LUIS MANTEROLA; publ. *Revista Astronómica* (4 a year).

Asociación Argentina de Astronomía (Argentine Astronomy Association): Observatorio Astronómico, B1900FWA La Plata; tel. (221) 423-6593; fax (221) 423-6591; e-mail

aaacd@fcaglp.fcaglp.unlp.edu.ar; internet www.astronomiaargentina.org.ar; f. 1958; 312 mems; Pres. MARTA GRACIELA ROVIRA; Sec. ROSA BEATRIZ ORELLANA; publ. *Boletín* (1 a year).

Asociación Argentina de Geofísicos y Geodestas (Argentine Association of Geophysicists and Geodesists): c/o Observatorio Astronómico de La Plata, Paseo del Bosque s/n, 1900 La Plata; e-mail jero@aagg.org.ar; internet www.aagg.org.ar; f. 1959; Pres. Dra MARÍA L. ALTINGER; Sec. Dra MARÍA C. POMPOSIELLO; publs *Boletín* (3 a year), *Geoacta* (1 a year).

Asociación Bioquímica Argentina (Argentine Biochemical Association): Venezuela 1823 3er piso, 1096 Buenos Aires; tel. (11) 4381-2907; fax (11) 4384-7415; e-mail info@aba-online.org.ar; internet www.aba-online.org.ar; f. 1934; Pres. Dr ORLANDO GABRIEL CARBALLO; Sec. Dr ALBERTO VILLAGRA.

Asociación Geológica Argentina (Argentine Geological Association): Maipú 645 (1° piso), C1006ACG Buenos Aires; tel. (11) 4325-3104; fax (11) 4325-3104; e-mail raga@geologica.org.ar; internet www.geologica.org.ar; f. 1945; 1,750 mems; Pres. Dr MIGUEL J. F. HALLER; Sec. Lic. VALÉRIE BAUMANN; publ. *Revista* (4 a year).

Asociación Química Argentina (Argentine Chemical Association): Sánchez de Bustamante 1749, 1425 Buenos Aires; tel. (11) 4822-4886; fax (11) 4822-4886; internet www.aqa.org.ar; f. 1912; 1,000 mems; library of 10,000 vols, 500 periodicals; Pres. Dr EDUARDO A. CASTRO; Sec. Dr EDUARDO J. BOTTANI; publs *Anales de la Asociación Química Argentina* (Scientific), *Industria y Química* (Technical).

Centro Argentino de Espeleología (Argentine Centre of Speleological Studies): Avda de Mayo 651 (1o piso), 1428 Buenos Aires; tel. (11) 4331-6798; f. 1970; 60 mems; library of 250 vols; Pres. JULIO GOYÉN AGUADO; Sec. ROBERTO OSCAR BERMEJO; publ. *Las Brujas* (1 a year).

Grupo Argentino del Color (Argentine Colour Group): c/o Secretary of Research, School of Architecture, Buenos Aires Univ., Ciudad Universitaria, Pav. 3 (4o), C1428BFA Buenos Aires; tel. (11) 4789-6289; fax (11) 4702-6009; e-mail gac@fadu.uba.ar; internet www.fadu.uba.ar/sicyt/color/gac.htm; f. 1979; study of colour science; 159 mems; Pres. Dr MARÍA L. DE MATTIELLO; publ. *GAC Revista* (3 a year).

PHILOSOPHY AND PSYCHOLOGY

Sociedad Argentina de Psicología (Buenos Aires Psychological Society): Callao 435 (1o), 1022 Buenos Aires; tel. (11) 4432-3760; f. 1930; Pres. JUAN CUATRECASAS.

RELIGION, SOCIOLOGY AND ANTHROPOLOGY

Asociación Argentina de Estudios Americanos (Argentine Association of American Studies): Maipú 672, 1424 Buenos Aires; tel. (11) 4392-4971.

Sociedad Argentina de Antropología (Argentine Anthropological Society): Moreno 350, 1091 Buenos Aires; e-mail sociedadargentinaantropologia@yahoo.com; internet www.saantropologia.com.ar; f. 1936; 255 mems; Pres. GUSTAVO POLITIS; Sec. VICTORIA COLL MORITÁN; publ. *Relaciones* (1 a year).

Sociedad Argentina de Sociología: Trejo 241, 5000 Córdoba; tel. (351) 44-5901; f. 1950; Pres. Prof. ALFREDO POVIÑA; Sec.-Gen. Prof. ODORICO PIRES PINTO.

TECHNOLOGY

Asociación Argentina del Frío (Argentine Refrigeration Association): Avda Belgrano (3° piso), Oficina K, C1092AAF Buenos Aires; tel. (11) 4343-1560; fax (11) 4343-1560; e-mail aafrio@aafrio.org.ar; internet www.aafrio.org.ar; f. 1932; 178 mems; small library; Pres. Ing. ROBERTO RICARDO AGUILO; Sec. Ing. CARLOS BRIGNONE; publ. *Clima* (12 a year).

Asociación Electrotécnica Argentina (Argentine Electrotechnical Association): Posadas 1659, C1112ADC Buenos Aires; tel. (11) 4804-3454; internet aea.org.ar; f. 1913; 2,000 mems; library of 2,500 vols; Pres. Ing. JULIO H. DI SALVO; Sec. Ing. ABEL J. CRESTA; publ. *Revista Electrotécnica*.

Centro Argentino de Ingenieros (Argentine Centre of Engineering): Cerrito 1250, C1010AAZ Buenos Aires; tel. (11) 4811-4133; fax (11) 4811-4133; e-mail informes@cai.org.ar; internet www.cai.org.ar; f. 1895; 10,231 mems; library of 11,000 vols; Pres. Ing. ROBERTO P. ECHARTE; publ. *Políticas de la Ingeniería*.

Federación Lanera Argentina (Argentine Wool Federation): Avda Paseo Colón 823, C1063ACI Buenos Aires; tel. (11) 4300-7661; fax (11) 4361-6517; f. 1929; concerned with all aspects of wool trade, from breeding to sales; 50 mems; Pres. RICARDO VON GERSTENBERG; Sec. CLAUDIO ULRICH; publ. *Argentine Wool Statistics* (12 a year).

Research Institutes

GENERAL

Instituto Torcuato Di Tella: Miñones 2159/77, 1° Piso, 1428 Buenos Aires; tel. (11) 4783-8630; fax (11) 4783-3061; e-mail salvadororsini@fibertel.com.ar; internet www.itdt.edu; f. 1958; promotes scientific research and artistic creativity on a nat. and int. scale; administers research centres and higher education instns; postgraduate courses in economics, sociology and admin.; library of 85,000 vols; Pres. GREGORIO KLIMOVSKY.

AGRICULTURE, FISHERIES AND VETERINARY SCIENCE

Estación Experimental Agro-Industrial 'Obispo Colombres' ('Obispo Colombres' Agro-Industrial Experimental Research Station): CC 9, Las Talitas, 4101 Tucumán; tel. (381) 452 1000; fax (381) 452 1008; e-mail dt@eeaoc.org.ar; internet www.eeaoc.org.ar; f. 1909 as Agricultural Experiment Station of Tucumán (EEAT); present name since 1978; autonomous unit of the Tucumán provincial govt; research, technological devts. and services for agri-industrial business of North-Western Argentina; library of 8,000 vols, 75,000 periodicals; Pres. and Chair. JUAN JOSÉ BUDEGUER; Technical Dir and CEO Dr LEONARDO DANIEL PLOPER; publs *Avance Agro-Industrial* (4 a year), *Informe Annual EEAOC* (1 a year), *Revista Industrial y Agrícola de Tucumán* (2 a year), *Publicación Especial EEAOC* (irregular).

Instituto Agrario Argentino de Cultura Rural (Argentine Agricultural Institute for Rural Education): Florida 460, 1005 Buenos Aires; tel. (11) 4392-2030; f. 1937; library of 2,000 vols; Dir Dr CORNELIO J. VIERA; Sec. MARÍA LUIS RIVAS; Technical Sec. EURIFUE ALFREDO VIVANA; publs *Reseñas Argentinas*, *Reseñas*, *Comunicados*.

Instituto de Edafología Agrícola (Institute of Agricultural Soil Science): Cerviño 3101, 1425 Buenos Aires; tel. (11) 484-9623; f.

1944; library of 3,200 vols; Dir Ing. Agr. JORGE I. BELLATI; publs *Técnicas Apartados de Artículos Tiradas Internas, Suelos.*

Instituto Nacional de Investigación y Desarrollo Pesquero (National Institute for Fisheries Research and Development): C. C. 175, 7600 Mar del Plata; tel. (223) 486-2586; fax (223) 486-1830; e-mail biblio@inidep.edu.ar; internet www.inidep.edu.ar; f. 1977 from fmr Mar del Plata Marine Biology Institute to perform integral research programmes on fishing grounds, emphasizing the assessment of Argentine fishing resources and sustainable fishing devt; decentralized agency operating under Secretariat of Agriculture, Livestock, Fishing and Food of the Min. of Economy and Production; planning and studies concerning the improvement and devt of catching systems, fishing apparatus and technological processes; devt and colln of growing technologies for raising marine and commercial-interest freshwater organisms, as well as the valorization of fishing crops and marine biodiversity; 300 researchers and assts; library of 4,600 vols, 763 periodicals, 350 theses/dissertations; Dir Lic. OSCAR LASCANO; publs *INIDEP Informe Técnico* (irregular), *Revista de Investigación y Desarrollo Pesquero* (irregular).

Instituto Nacional de Tecnología Agropecuaria (INTA) (National Institute for Agricultural Technology): Rivadavia 1439, 1033 Buenos Aires; tel. (11) 4383-5095; fax (11) 4383-5090; e-mail ctorres@correo.inta.gov.ar; internet www.inta.gov.ar; f. 1956; 42 experimental stations, 13 research institutes; Pres. Ing. Agr. CARLOS CHEPI; Nat. Dir Ing. Agr. ROBERTO BOCHETTO; publs *Idia XXI* (3 a year), *Revista de Investigaciones Agropecuarias* (3 a year).

Main Research Centre:

Centro Nacional de Investigación Agropecuaria (National Centre for Agricultural Research): CC 25, 1712 Castelar, Buenos Aires; tel. (11) 4621-1819; research in all aspects of farming; Dir Dr Vet. HUMBERTO CISALE.

Instituto Nacional de Vitivinicultura (National Vine Growing and Wine Producing Institute): San Martín 430, 5500 Mendoza; tel. (261) 521-6600; internet www.inv.gov.ar/institucional.php?ind=1; f. 1959; library of 20,000 vols, 690 journals; Pres. CPN y Perito Partidor GUILLERMO DANIEL GARCIA; publs *Estadística Vitivinícola* (1 a year), *Exportaciones Argentinas de Productos Vitivinícolas* (1 a year), *Revista Vinifera, Superficie de Vinos por Variedades Implatada en la República Argentina.*

ARCHITECTURE AND TOWN PLANNING

Instituto de Planeamiento Regional y Urbano (IPRU) (Regional and Urban Planning Institute): Calle Posadas 1265 (7°), 1011 Buenos Aires; fax (11) 4815-8673; f. 1952; Dir FERNANDO PASTOR; publs *Cuadernos de IPRU, Plan.*

BIBLIOGRAPHY, LIBRARY SCIENCE AND MUSEOLOGY

Centro de Documentación Bibliotecológica (Centre for Library Science Documentation): Universidad Nacional del Sur, Avda Alem 1253, 8000 Bahía Blanca; tel. (291) 42-8035; fax (291) 455-1447; f. 1962; teaching and research in library science; library of 2,980 vols, 332 periodicals; Chief Librarian MARTA IBARLUCEA DE RUIZ; publs *Bibliografía Bibliotecológica Argentina 1978–81, Documentación Bibliotecológica, Revista de Revistas.*

Instituto de Bibliografía del Ministerio de Educación de la Provincia de Buenos Aires (Bibliographical Institute of the Ministry of Education of the Province of Buenos Aires): Calle 47 No. 510 (6°), 1900 La Plata; tel. (221) 43-5915; Dir MARÍA DEL CARMEN CRESPI DE BUSTOS; publs *Bibliografía Argentina de Historia, Boletín de Información Bibliográfica.*

ECONOMICS, LAW AND POLITICS

Centro de Investigaciones Económicas (Economic Research Centre): Instituto Torcuato Di Tella, Miñones 2159/77, 1° Piso, 1428 Buenos Aires; tel. (11) 4781-5014; fax (11) 4786-2636; e-mail salvadororsini@fibertel.com.ar; internet www.itdt.edu; f. 1960; library of 85,000 vols; Dir ADOLFO CANITROT; publ. *Documentos de Trabajo.*

Instituto de Desarrollo Económico y Social (Institute of Economic and Social Development): Aráoz 2838, 1425 Buenos Aires; tel. (11) 4804-4949; fax (11) 4804-5856; e-mail ides@ides.org.ar; internet www.ides.org.ar; f. 1960; library of 15,000 vols; Pres. MARIANO PLOTKIN; Dir JUAN CARLOS TORRE; publ. *Desarrollo Económico—Revista de Ciencias Sociales* (4 a year).

Instituto Nacional de Estadística y Censos (National Institute of Statistics and Censuses): Avda Julio A. Roca 615, 1067 Buenos Aires; tel. (11) 4349-9200; fax (11) 4349-9601; e-mail ces@indec.mecon.gov.ar; internet www.indec.mecon.gov.ar; f. 1894; library of 30,000 vols; Dir LELIO MARMORA; publs *Anuario Estadístico de la República Argentina* (1 a year), *Comercio Exterior Argentino* (1 a year), *INDEC Informa* (12 a year).

Instituto para el Desarrollo de Empresarial en la Argentina (Institute for Management Development): Moreno 1850, 1094 Buenos Aires; tel. (11) 4372-7667; fax (11) 449-6944; f. 1960; library of 10,000 vols, 50 periodicals; Dir RUBEN D. PUENTEDURA; publ. *IDEA.*

Instituto para la Integración de América Latina y el Caribe (Institute for the Integration of Latin America and the Caribbean): Esmeralda 130 (pisos 16 y 17), C1035ABD Buenos Aires; tel. (11) 4320-1850; fax (11) 4320-1865; e-mail int/inl@iadb.org; internet www.iadb.org/intal; f. 1965 following an agreement between the Inter-American Devt Bank and the govt of Argentina; undertakes research and provides support in all aspects of regional integration and cooperation, incl. infrastructural links among countries, regional devt of border areas, trade liberalization, legal aspects of integration and accession to new agreements; provides technical support for hemispheric integration processes agreed during Summit of the Americas 1994, and to fulfil WTO disciplines; organizes policy-orientated fora for govt officials and other interested parties; library: Documentation Centre of 100,000 documents, 12,000 vols, 400 periodicals; Dir RICARDO CARCIOFI; publs *Caricom Report* (in English, 1 a year), *Informe Andino* (Andean Report, in Spanish and English, 1 a year), *Informe Centroamericano* (Central American Report, in Spanish and English, 1 a year), *Informe Mercosur* (Mercosur Report, 1 a year), *Integración & Comercio* (Integration & Trade, 2 a year).

FINE AND PERFORMING ARTS

Instituto Nacional de Estudios de Teatro (National Institute for the Study of Theatre): Avda Córdoba 1199, 1055 Buenos Aires; tel. and fax (11) 4816-7212; f. 1936; library of 16,000 vols, archives; also nat.

theatre museum; Dir Prof. CRISTINA LASTRA BELGRANO.

HISTORY, GEOGRAPHY AND ARCHAEOLOGY

Departamento de Estudios Históricos Navales (Department of Naval History Studies): Avda Almirante Brown 401, 1155 Buenos Aires; tel. (11) 4362-1248; fax (11) 4362-1130; e-mail estudioshistoricosnavales@yahoo.com.ar; internet www.ara.mil.ar; f. 1957; large number of publs, also paintings and medals; Dir Capt. GUILLERMO ANDRÉS OYARZABAL.

Dirección Nacional del Antártico (National Antarctic Office): Cerrito 1248, C1010AAZ Buenos Aires; tel. (11) 4813-0072; fax (11) 4813-7807; e-mail dna@dna.gov.ar; internet www.dna.gov.ar; f. 1970; scientific colln; maintains Yubany station at King George Island, Antarctica; library of 15,000 vols; Dir Dr MARIANO A. MEMOLLI; publs *Contribuciones Científicas* (irregular), *Revista Antártica, Boletín del SCAR* (3 a year, Spanish edn of SCAR Bulletin).

Attached Institute:

Instituto Antártico Argentino (Argentine Antarctic Institute): Cerrito 1248, C1010AAZ Buenos Aires; tel. and fax (11) 4813-7807; e-mail diriaa@dna.gov.ar; internet www.antartida.gov.ar; f. 1951; Dir Dr SERPIO MAREUSSI.

Instituto Geográfico Militar (Military Geographical Institute): Avda Cabildo 381, 1426 Buenos Aires; tel. (11) 4576-5545; fax (11) 4576-5595; e-mail public@mapas.igm.gov.ar; internet www.igm.gov.ar; f. 1879; topographic survey of Argentina; Dir Coronel FERNANDO MIGUEL GALBÁN; publ. *Revista* (1 a year).

MEDICINE

Administración Nacional de Laboratorios e Institutos de Salud 'Dr Carlos G. Malbran' ('Dr Carlos G. Malbran' National Administration for Laboratories and Institutes of Health): Avda Vélez Sarsfield 563, 1281 Buenos Aires; tel. (11) 4303-1804; fax (11) 4303-1433; e-mail grios@anlis.gov.ar; internet www.anlis.gov.ar; f. 1916; library of 6,500 vols; Dir Dr GUSTAVO RÍOS.

Centro de Investigaciones Neurobiológicas 'Prof. Dr Christfried Jakob' (Christfried Jakob Centre for Neurobiological Research): Avda Amancio Alcorta 1602, 1283 Buenos Aires; tel. and fax (11) 4306-7314; f. 1899; attached to Min. of Public Health and Welfare; neuroscience research; Dir Prof. Dr MARIO-FERNANDO CROCCO; publ. *Folia Neurobiológica Argentina.*

Instituto de Biología y Medicina Experimental (Institute of Biology and Experimental Medicine): Vuelta de Obligado 2490, 1428 Buenos Aires; tel. (11) 4783-2869; fax (11) 4786-2564; e-mail ibyme@dna.uba.ar; internet proteus.dna.uba.ar/ibyme; f. 1944; library of 15,000 vols; Dir Dr EDUARDO H. CHARREAU; publ. *Memoria* (1 a year).

Instituto de Investigaciones Médicas 'Alfredo Lanari' (Alfredo Lanari Institute of Medical Research): Avda Combatientes de Malvinas 3150, C1427ARO Buenos Aires; tel. (11) 4522-1438; e-mail director@lanari.fmed.uba.ar; internet www.lanari.fmed.uba.ar; f. 1957; clinical and basic medical research, teaching; library of 4,185 vols, 6,738 periodicals; Dir Dr DANIEL TOMASONE; publ. *Medicina* (6 a year).

NATURAL SCIENCES

General

Consejo Nacional de Investigaciones Científicas y Técnicas (CONICET) (National Council of Scientific and Technical Research): Avda Rivadavia 1917, 1033 Buenos Aires; tel. (11) 4953-3609; fax (11) 4953-4345; e-mail postmaster@conica.gov.ar; f. 1958; supports 6 regional research centres and 114 research institutes; maintains several scientific services; Pres. ANDRÉS CARRASCO.

Main Research Institutes:

Centro Argentino de Datos Oceanográficos (CEADO) (Argentine Centre of Oceanographic Data): Avda Montes de Oca 2124, 1271 Buenos Aires; tel. (11) 4303-2240; fax (11) 4303-2299; e-mail postmaster@ceado.edu.ar; Dir Capt. ADOLFO GIL VILLANUEVA.

Centro Argentino de Etnología Americana (CAEA) (Argentine Centre for American Ethnology): Avda de Mayo 1437 (1° piso Dpto. A), 1085 Buenos Aires; tel. (11) 4381-1821; e-mail caea@speedy.com.ar; Dir Dr ANATILDE IDOYAGA MOLINA.

Centro Argentino de Primates (CAPRIM) (Argentine Primates Centre): San Cayetano CC 145, 3400 Corrientes; tel. (3783) 42-7790; fax (3783) 42-7790; e-mail ruiz@caprim.edu.ar; Dir Dr JULIO CÉSAR RUIZ.

Centro Austral de Investigaciones Científicas (CADIC) (Southern Centre for Scientific Research): Avda Malvinas Argentinas s/n, CC 92, Ruta Nacional No. 3, Barrio La Misión, Camino Lapataia, 9410 Ushuaia; tel. (2901) 42-2310; fax (2901) 43-0644; e-mail postmaster@cadica.edu.ar; f. 1975; biology, geology, archaeology, anthropology, hydrography, climatology; library of 1,000 vols; Dir Dr EDUARDO B. OLIVERO; publs *Boletín*, *Contribuciones Científicas del CADIC*, *Publicaciones especiales del CADIC*.

Centro de Diagnóstico e Investigaciones Veterinarias Formosa (CEDIVEF) (Formosa Centre of Veterinary Diagnosis and Research): Ruta Nacional No. 11, km 1164, CC 292, 3600 Formosa; fax (3717) 45-1334; Dir Dr CARLOS M. MONZON.

Centro de Ecofisiología Vegetal (CEVEG) (Centre for Plant Ecophysiology): Serrano 669 (pisos 5 y 6), 1414 Buenos Aires; tel. (11) 4856-7110; fax (11) 4856-7110; e-mail postmaster@ceveg.gov.ar; Dir Dr OSVALDO H. CASO.

Centro de Ecología Aplicada del Litoral (CECOAL) (Centre of Coastal Applied Ecology): Ruta Prov. No. 5, Km 2.5, CC 291, 3400 Corrientes; tel. (3783) 45-4418; fax (3783) 45-4421; internet www.cecoal.com.ar; Dir Prof. JUAN JOSÉ NEIFF.

Centro de Estudios e Investigaciones Laborales (CEIL) (Centre of Labour Study and Research): Corrientes 2470 (6o piso, of. 24 y 25), 1046 Buenos Aires; tel. (11) 4952-5273; fax (11) 4952-5273; e-mail postmaster@ceil.edu.ar; f. 1971; Dir Dr JULIO CÉSAR NEFFA; publ. *Boletín-Serie Documentos*.

Centro de Estudios Farmacológicos y Botanicos (CEFYBO) (Centre for Pharmacological Studies and Botany): Serrano 669, 1414 Buenos Aires; tel. (11) 4856-2751; fax (11) 4856-2751; e-mail postmaster@cefybo.edu.ar; f. 1975; Dirs Dra LEONOR STERIN DE BORDA, Dra MARÍA ANTONIETA DEL PERO.

Centro de Estudios Fotosintéticos y Bioquímicos (CEFOBI) (Centre for Studies in Photosynthesis and Biochemistry): Suipacha 531, 2000 Rosario; tel. (341) 437-1955; fax (341) 437-0044; e-mail carlosandreo@cefobi-conicet.gov.ar; f. 1976; Dir Dr CARLOS S. ANDREO.

Centro de Investigación y Desarrollo en Criotecnología de Alimentos (CIDCA) (Research and Development Centre for Food Cryotechnology): Calles 47 y 116, CC 553, 1900 La Plata; tel. (221) 424-9287; fax (221) 425-4853; Dir Dra MARÍA C. AÑON.

Centro de Investigación y Desarrollo en Fermentaciones Industriales (CINDEFI) (Research and Development Centre for Industrial Fermentation): Calles 47 y 115, 1900 La Plata; tel. (221) 483-3794; fax (221) 425-4533; e-mail voget@biol.unlp.edu.ar; Dir Dr RODOLFO J. ERTOLA.

Centro de Investigación y Desarrollo en Ciencias Aplicadas Dr Jorge J. Ronco (CINDECA) (Research and Development Centre for Applied Sciences Dr Jorge J. Ronco): Calle 47 No. 257, CC 59, 1900 La Plata; tel. (221) 421-1353; fax (221) 425-4277; e-mail dir-cindeca@quimica.unlp.edu.ar; internet www.cindeca.org.ar; Dir Prof. Dr LUIS ALBERTO GAMBARO; publs *Applied Catalysis*, *Catalysis Today*, *Journal of Catalysis*, *Journal of Material Chemistry*.

Centro de Investigación y Desarrollo en Tecnología de Pinturas (CIDEPINT) (Research and Development Centre for Paint Technology): Calle 52 a 121 y 122, 1900 La Plata, Buenos Aires; tel. (221) 421-6214; fax (221) 427-1537; e-mail cielsner@isis.unlp.edu.ar; Dir Dr VICENTE J. D. RASCIO.

Centro de Investigación y Estudios Ortopédicos y Traumatológicos (CINEOT) (Research and Study Centre for Orthopaedics and Traumatology): Potosí 4215, 1199 Buenos Aires; tel. (11) 4958-4011; fax (11) 4981-0991; e-mail cineot@impsat1.com.ar; Dir Dr DOMINGO L. MUSCOLO.

Centro de Investigaciones en Antropología Filosófica y Cultural (CIAFIC) (Centre for Research in Philosophical and Cultural Anthropology): Juramento 142, 1609 Boulogne, Buenos Aires; Federico Lacroze 2100, 1426 Buenos Aires; tel. and fax (11) 4776-0913; e-mail postmaster@ciafic.edu.ar; internet www.ciafic.edu.ar; f. 1976; research into education, philosophy, linguistics, epistemology, anthropology; library of 12,000 vols and periodicals; Sec. Mag. CLOTILDE DE LA BARRA; publs *Archivos* (anthropology, 1 a year), *Servicio de Información Bibliográfica Especializada* (2 a year).

Centro de Investigaciones en Recursos Geológicos (CIRGEO) (Centre for Research into Geological Resources): Ramírez de Velasco 847, 1414 Buenos Aires; tel. (11) 4772-9729; fax (11) 4771-3742; e-mail pompo@cirgeo.edu.ar; f. 1976; library of 6,000 vols, 90 periodicals; Dir Dr BERNABÉ J. QUARTINO.

Centro de Investigaciones Endocrinológicas (CEDIE) (Centre of Endocrinological Research): Gallo 1330, 1425 Buenos Aires; tel. (11) 4963-5931; fax (11) 4963-5930; e-mail master@fend.sld.arg; Dir Dr CÉSAR BERGADÁ.

Centro de Investigaciones Opticas (CIOP) (Centre for Optical Research): Camino Parque Centenario e/505 y 506, Gonnet, CC 124, 1900 La Plata, Buenos Aires; tel. (221) 484-0280; fax (221) 453-0189; e-mail postmaster@ciop.edu.ar; Dir Dr MARIO GALLARDO.

Centro de Investigaciónes sobre Regulación de Poblacion de Organismos Nocivos (CIRPON) (Centre for Research into Controlling Harmful Organisms): Pasaje Caseros 1050, 4000 San Miguel de Tucumán; tel. and fax (381) 434-6940; e-mail cirponfml@arnetbiz.com.ar; Dir Dr ALBERTO A. P. FIDALGO; Supervisor Prof. MARIANO ORDANO.

Centro de Referencia para Lactobacilos (CERELA) (Reference Centre for Lactobacillus): Chacabuco 145, 4000 San Miguel de Tucumán; tel. (381) 431-1720; fax (381) 431-1720; e-mail crl@cerela.edu.ar; Dir Dra AÍDA A. P. DE RUIZ HOLGADO.

Centro de Tecnología en Recursos Minerales y Cerámica (CETMIC) (Technology Centre for Mineral and Ceramic Resources): CC 49, 1897 Gonnet, Buenos Aires; Camino Centenario y 506, 1897 Gonnet, Buenos Aires; tel. (221) 484-0247; fax (221) 471-0075; e-mail postmaster@cetmic.edu.ar; Dir Dr ENRIQUE PEREIRA.

Centro Experimental de la Vivienda Económica (CEVE) (Experimental Centre for Low-Cost Housing): Igualdad 3585, Villa Siburu, 5003 Córdoba; tel. (351) 489-4442; fax (351) 489-4442; e-mail postmaster@ceve.org.ar; Dir Arq. HORACIO BERRETTA.

Centro Nacional Patagónico (CNP) (National Patagónia Centre): Blvd Alte. Brown s/n, 9120 Puerto Madryn, Chubut; tel. (2965) 45-1375; fax (2965) 47-2885; e-mail postmaster@cenpat.edu.ar; Dir Dr ADAN E. PUCCI.

Instituto Argentino de Investigaciónes de las Zonas Aridas (IADIZA) (Argentine Institute for Arid Zones Research): Dr Adrián Ruiz Leal s/n, Parque Gral San Martín, 5500 Mendoza; fax (261) 428-7995; e-mail cricyt@planet.losandes.com.ar; f. 1974; Dir Ing. Agr. JUAN CARLOS GUEVARA (acting); publ. *Boletín Informativo*.

Instituto Argentino de Nivologia, Glaciologia y Ciencias Ambientales (IANIGLA) (Argentine Institute for Snow, Ice and Environmental Sciences): Dr Adrián Ruiz Leal s/n, Parque Gral San Martín, CC 131, 5500 Mendoza; tel. (261) 428-7029; fax (261) 428-7029; e-mail cricyt@planet.losandes.com.ar; Dir Dr WOLFGANG VOLKHEIMER.

Instituto Argentino de Oceanografía (IADO) (Argentine Oceanographic Institute): Edificio E3, Complejo de la Carrindanga, Florida 4000, 8000 Bahía Blanca, Buenos Aires; tel. (291) 42-3555; fax (291) 486-1112; e-mail postmaster@criba.edu.ar; f. 1969; Subdirector-in-Charge Dr JOSÉ KOSTADINOFF; publ. *Contribuciones Científicas IADO*.

Instituto Argentino de Radioastronomía (IAR) (Argentine Institute of Radioastronomy): Casilla de Correo 5, 1894 Villa Elisa, Buenos Aires; tel. (221) 482-4903; fax (221) 425-4909; e-mail webmaster@iar.unlp.edu.ar; internet www.iar.unlp.edu.ar; f. 1963; radioastronomy research; electronic equipment devt; library of 10,000 vols, 163 periodicals; Dirs Dr MARCELO ARNAL, Dr GUSTAVO ROMERO; publ. *Boletín Radioastronómico*.

Instituto de Botánica del Nordeste (IBONE) (Northeastern Institute of Botany): Sargento Cabral 2131, CC 209, 3400 Corrientes; tel. (3783) 42-7309; fax (3783) 42-7131; e-mail postmaster@unneib.edu.ar; Dir Ing. ANTONIO KRAPOVICKAS.

Instituto de Desarrollo Tecnológico para la Industria Química (INTEC)

(Technological Development Institute of the Chemical Industry): Güemes 3450, 3000 Santa Fe; tel. (342) 455-9174; fax (342) 455-0944; e-mail director@intec.unl .edu.ar; Dir Dr ALBERTO E. CASSANO (acting).

Instituto de Geocronología y Geología Isotópica (INGEIS) (Institute of Isotope Geochronology and Geology): Pabellón INGEIS, Ciudad Universitaria, 1428 Buenos Aires; tel. (11) 4784-7798; fax (11) 4783-3024; e-mail postmaster@ingeis.uba .ar; Dir Dr ENRIQUE LINARES.

Instituto de Investigación de Productos Naturales, de Análisis y de Síntesis Orgánica (IPNAYS) (Institute for Research, Analysis and Organic Synthesis of Natural Products): Santiago del Estero 2829, 3000 Santa Fe; tel. (342) 455-3958; fax (342) 456-1146; e-mail rmalizia@fiqus .unl.edu.ar; Dir Ing. J. A. RETAMAR.

Instituto de Investigación Médica 'Mercedes y Martín Ferreyra' (INIMEC) (Mercedes and Martín Ferreyra Medical Research Institute): CC 389, 5000 Córdoba; Friuli 2434, Colinas de V. Sarfield, 5016 Córdoba; tel. (351) 468-1465; fax (351) 469-5163; e-mail immf@immf.uncor .edu; internet www.immf.uncor.edu; f. 1946; scientific research and the development of scientific and technical human resources in medical science; Dir Dr ALFREDO CACERESBEAUGE.

Instituto de Investigaciones Bioquímicas (INIBIBB) (Institute for Biochemical Research): Edificio E1, Complejo de la Carrindanga, Florida 4000, 8000 Bahía Blanca, Buenos Aires; tel. (291) 486-1201; fax (291) 486-1200; e-mail rtfjb1@criba.edu.ar; f. 1975; Dir Prof. Dr FRANCISCO JOSÉ BARRANTES.

Instituto de Investigaciónes en Catálisis y Petroquímica (INCAPE) (Catalysis and Petrochemistry Research Institute): Santiago del Estero 2654, 3000 Santa Fe; tel. (342) 453-3858; fax (342) 453-1068; e-mail parera@fiqus.unl.edu.ar; Dir Ing. JOSÉ M. PARERA.

Instituto de Investigaciones Estadísticas (INIE) (Statistical Research Institute): Avda Independencia 1900, CC 209, 4000 San Miguel de Tucumán; tel. (381) 436-4093; fax (381) 436-4105; e-mail postmaster@untiie.edu.ar; Dir Dr RAÚL P. MENTZ.

Instituto de Investigaciones Farmacológicas (ININFA) (Pharmacological Research Institute): Junín 956 (5o), 1113 Buenos Aires; tel. (11) 4961-6784; fax (11) 4963-8593; e-mail ininfa@huemul.ffyb.uba .ar; Dir Dra EDDA ADLER DE GRASCHINSKY.

Instituto de Investigaciones Geohistóricas (IIGHI) (Institute of Geohistorical Research): Avda Castelli 930, CC 438, 3500 Resistencia, Chaco; tel. (3722) 42-7798; fax (3722) 43-9983; e-mail postmaster@iighi .gov.ar; Dir Dr ERNESTO J. A. MAEDER.

Instituto de Limnología Dr Raul A. Ringuelet (ILPLA) (Limnology Institute): CC 712, 1900 La Plata, Buenos Aires; tel. (11) 4275-7799; e-mail acapitul@ilpla.edu.ar; internet www.ilpla .edu.ar; f. 1972; library of 1,160 vols; research in limnology, ecology, biodiversity and fisheries; Dir Dr ALBERTO RODRÍGUEZ CAPÍTULO (acting); publs Aquatec (irregular), Biología Acuática (irregular, online).

Instituto de Matemática (INMABB) (Mathematics Institute): Avda Alem 1253, 8000 Bahía Blanca; tel. (291) 43-3382; fax (291) 455-1447; e-mail inmabb@arcriba .edu.ar; f. 1956; Dir Dra AURORA GERMANI.

Instituto de Mecánica Aplicada (IMA) (Institute of Applied Mechanics): Gorriti 43, 8000 Bahía Blanca; tel. (291) 44-5154; fax (291) 455-1447; e-mail ima@criba.edu .ar; Dir Dr PATRICIO A. A. LAURA.

Instituto de Neurobiología (IDNEU) (Neurobiology Institute): Serrano 669, 1414 Buenos Aires; tel. (11) 4855-7674; fax (11) 4856-7108; e-mail postmaster@ fuacta.sld.ar; Dir Dr JUAN H. TRAMEZZANI.

Instituto Latinoamericano de Investigaciones Comparadas Oriente y Occidente (ILICOO) (Latin American Institute for Comparative East-West Studies): Callao 853, 1023 Buenos Aires; tel. (11) 4811-2270; e-mail postmaster@uscsoc .edu.ar; f. 1973; library of 2,000 vols, 1,500 periodicals; Dir Prof. MARÍA M. TERREN; publ. Oriente—Occidente.

Instituto Multidisciplinario de Biología Celular (IMBICE) (Multidisciplinary Institute of Cellular Biology): Calle 526, e/ 10 y 11, CC 403, 1900 La Plata, Buenos Aires; tel. (221) 421-0112; fax (221) 425-3320; e-mail biblioteca@imbice.org.ar; internet www.imbice.org.ar; Dir Dr ALEJANDRO DANIEL BOLZÁN.

Instituto Rosario de Investigaciónes en Ciencias de la Educación (IRICE) (Rosario Education Research Institute): Blvd 27 de Febrero 210 'bis', 2000 Rosario; tel. (341) 482-1769; fax (341) 482-1772; e-mail irice@ifir.ifir.edu.ar; Dir Dr NÉSTOR DIRECTORIO ROSELLI.

Fundación Miguel Lillo: Miguel Lillo 251, T4000JFE San Miguel de Tucumán; tel. and fax (381) 433-0868; e-mail direccion@lillo.org .ar; internet www.lillo.org.ar; f. 1931; scientific research in natural sciences and history; incl. institutes of botany, geology and zoology; maintains Geobiological Information Centre of NOA, Cultural Centre 'Alberto Rouges', Study Centre 'Juan Dalma', Lillo Museum of Natural Sciences; library of 210,000 vols; Pres. Dr JORGE L. ROUGÉS; Gen. Dir Lic. ANA MARÍA FRÍAS DE FERNÁNDEZ; Dir, Institute of Botany Lic. MARCELA HERNÁNDEZ DE TERÁN; Dir, Institute of Geology Dra. ANA LÍA AHUMADA; Dir, Institute of Zoology Mg. SUSANA G. ARANDA; Dir, Geobiological Information Centre Trad. ROSALINA CORROTO; Dir, Cultural and Study Centres Prof. MARÍA ELENA PERILLI DE COLOMBRES GARMENDIA; Dir, Lillo Museum of Natural Sciences EDUARDO E. RIBOTTA; publs Acta Geologica Lilloana (2 a year), Actas Jornadas la Generación del Centenario (2 a year), Acta Zoologica Lilloana (2 a year), Extensión Científica y Cultural (irregular), Genera et Species Animalium Argentinorum (2 a year), Genera et Species Plantarum Argentinarum (2 a year), Lilloa (botanical, 2 a year), Miscelánea (2 a year), Opera Lilloana (2 a year), Serie Conservación de la Naturaleza (2 a year), Serie Extensión Científica y Cultural (irregular), also Ensayos y Correspondencia by Alberto Rouges, and biographies of C. R. Schreiter, J. G. Sortheix, J. Padilla and J. Heller.

Biological Sciences

Estación Hidrobiológica (Hydrobiology Station): Avda Alte. Brown s/n, esq. calle 520, 7630 Puerto Quequén, Provincia de Buenos Aires; e-mail ehpg@macn.gov.ar; f. 1928; attached to 'B. Rivadavia' Argentine Museum of Natural Sciences; concerned especially with marine hydrobiology; Dir Lic. GUSTAVO CHIARAMONTE; publ. Trabajos de la Estación Hidrobiológica (irregular).

Instituto de Botánica 'C. Spegazzini' (Botanical Institute): Calle 53 No. 477, 1900 La Plata, Buenos Aires; tel. and fax (221) 421-9845; internet www.fcnym.unlp.edu.ar/ institutos/spegazzini/indexibs.html; f. 1930; affiliated to Museo de La Plata; mycological research, biodiversity of saprotrophic and biotrophic fungi; mycological collns from Argentina and all South America; germplasm bank of arbuscular mycorrhizal fungi; Dir Prof. Dr MARTA NOEMI CABELLO.

Instituto de Botánica 'Darwinion' (Darwinian Botanical Institute): Labardén 200, CC 22, B1642HYD San Isidro; tel. 4743-4800; fax 4747-4748; e-mail secretaria@darwin.edu .ar; internet www.darwin.edu.ar; f. 1911; attached to the Academia Nacional de Ciencias Exactas, Físicas y Naturales and the Consejo Nacional de Investigaciones Científicas y Técnicas; fields of research: systematic botany, phytogeography, plant anatomy and cytogenetics, palynology, ethnobotany, archaeobotany; 45 mems; library of 160,000 vols, 2,600 periodicals; Dir Dr FERNANDO O. ZULOAGA; publs Hickenia (irregular), Revista Darwiniana (2 a year).

Instituto Municipal de Botánica, Jardín Botánico 'Carlos Thays' (Municipal Botanical Institute, Carlos Thays Botanical Gardens): Sante Fe 3951, 1425 Buenos Aires; tel. (11) 469-3954; f. 1898; library of 1,000 vols, 7,000 periodicals; Dir ANTONIO AMADO GARCÍA; publs Index Seminum, Revista del Instituto de Botánica.

Instituto Nacional de Limnología (National Institute of Limnology): Ciudad Universitaria, Paraje 'El Pozo', 3000 Santa Fe; tel. (342) 451-1645; fax (342) 451-1648; e-mail secretaria@inali.unl.edu.ar; internet www.santafe-conicet.gov.ar/institut/inali; f. 1962; library of 3,000 vols, 385 periodicals; Dir MSc MERCEDES MARCHESE.

Physical Sciences

Comisión Nacional de Actividades Espaciales (CONAE) (National Commission on Space Activities): Avda Paseo Colón 751, 1063 Buenos Aires; tel. (11) 4331-0074; fax (11) 4331-3446; e-mail insti@conae.gov.ar; internet www.conae.gov.ar; f. 1991; develops Argentina's Nat. Space Programme; Exec. and Technical Dir Dr CONRADO FRANCO VAROTTO.

Comisión Nacional de Energía Atómica (National Atomic Energy Commission): Avda del Libertador 8250, 1429 Buenos Aires; tel. (11) 4704-1201; fax (11) 4704-1154; e-mail comunicacion@cnea.gov.ar; internet www .cnea.gov.ar; f. 1950; govt agency; promotes and undertakes scientific and industrial research and applications of nuclear transmutations and reactions; research centres in Buenos Aires, Constituyentes, Ezeiza and Bariloche; information centre: see Libraries; Pres. Lic. NORMA LUISA BOERO; Gen. Man. Dr CARLOS RUBÉN CALABRESE.

Observatorio Astronómico (Astronomical Observatory): Laprida 854, 5000 Córdoba; tel. (351) 433-1064; fax (351) 433-1063; e-mail library@mail.oac.uncor.edu; internet www.oac.uncor.edu; f. 1871; attached to the Univ. of Córdoba; research and undergraduate and postgraduate teaching; library of 5,000 vols; Dir Prof. Dr LUIS A. MILONE; publs Resultados, Reprints (40 a year).

Observatorio Astronómico (Astronomical Observatory): Paseo del Bosque s/n, 1900 La Plata; tel. (221) 423-6593; fax (221) 423-6591; e-mail academic@fcaglp.fcaglp.unlp.edu.ar; internet www.fcaglp.unlp.edu.ar; f. 1883; library of 25,000 vols, 500 periodicals; Dean Dr JUAN CARLOS MUZZIO.

Servicio Geológico Minero Argentino (Argentine Geological and Mining Service): Avda Julio A. Roca 651, P.B., C1067ABB Buenos Aires; tel. (11) 4349-3200; fax (11) 4349-3198; e-mail veronica@inti.gov.ar; internet www.segemar.gov.ar; f. 1904;

attached to the State Secretariat of Mining of the Min. of Economy and Public Works; Pres. Ing. JORGE OMAR MAYORAL; Admin. Dir RODOLFO JORGE SFORZA; publ. *Estadística Minera de la República Argentina* (1 a year).

Servicio Meteorológico Nacional (National Meteorological Service): 25 de Mayo 658, C1002ABN Buenos Aires; tel. (11) 5167-6767; fax (11) 5167-6709; e-mail smn@smn.gov.ar; internet www.smn.gov.ar; f. 1872; library of 45,000 vols; Dir Dr HÉCTOR CIAPPESONI; publs *Boletín informativo, Boletín climatológico*.

RELIGION, SOCIOLOGY AND ANTHROPOLOGY

Departamento de Estudios Etnográficos y Coloniales (Department of Ethnographical and Colonial Studies): Calle 25 de Mayo 1470, 3000 Santa Fe; tel. (342) 457-3550; fax (342) 457-3550; e-mail etnosfe@ceride.gov.ar; internet www.santafe.gov.ar/cultura/cultura/htm; f. 1940; Dir Arq. LUIS MARIA CALVO; publ. *America* (1 a year).

Instituto Nacional de Antropología y Pensamiento Latinoamericano (National Institute of Anthropology and Latin American Thought): Calle 3 de Febrero 1378, 1426 Buenos Aires; tel. (11) 4784-3371; fax (11) 4784-3371; e-mail postmaster@bibapl.edu.ar; f. 1943; attached to the Secretariat for Culture at the President's Office; library of 15,000 vols, 1,600 periodicals; Dir Dra DIANA BOLANDI DE PERROT; publ. *Cuaderno*.

TECHNOLOGY

Instituto Argentino de Normalización (IRAM) (Argentine Standards Institute): Perú 552/556, C1068AAB Buenos Aires; tel. (11) 4346-0600; fax (11) 4346-0601; e-mail iram4@vianetworks.net.ar; internet www.iram.com.ar; f. 1935; library of 174,300 standards; Dir-Gen. Ing. JOSÉ F. LÓPEZ; publ. *Boletín IRAM* (12 a year).

Instituto de Mecánica Aplicada y Estructuras (Institute of Applied Mechanics and Structures): Riobamba y Berutti, 2000 Rosario; tel. (341) 480-8538; fax (341) 480-8540; e-mail imaesecr@eie.fceia.unr.edu.ar; internet www.fceia.unr.edu.ar/labinfo; f. 1963; attached to Faculty of Exact Sciences, Engineering and Surveying, Universidad Nacional de Rosario; library of 1,000 vols, 3,000 periodicals; Dir Ing. FERNANDO OSCAR MARTÍNEZ.

Instituto Nacional de Tecnología Industrial (INTI) (National Institute of Industrial Technology): Parque Tecnológico Miguelete, Colectora de Avda General Paz 5445 entre Albarellos y Avda de los Constituyentes, Casilla de correo 157, B1650KNA San Martín, Buenos Aires; tel. (11) 4724-6200; e-mail consultas@inti.gob.ar; internet www.inti.gob.ar; f. 1957; library of 32,000 vols, 2,216 periodicals, 105,000 standards; Pres. Ing. LEÓNIDAS J. F. MONTAÑA; publs *Boletín técnico* (irregular), *Dendroenergía* (2 a year), *Noticiteca* (4 a year).

Research Institutes:

Centro de Investigación de Celulosa y Papel (INTI Celulosa y Papel) (Pulp and Paper Research Centre): Avda Gral Paz 5445, 1650 San Martín, Buenos Aires; tel. (11) 4713-4330; fax (11) 4754-4901; e-mail celulosaypapel@inti.gob.ar; internet www.inti.gob.ar/celulosaypapel; f. 1968; technical studies on pulp and paper industry raw materials, production processes, environmental protection, product properties and product devt; Technical Dir Ing. HUGO VÉLEZ.

Centro de Investigación de los Reglamentos Nacionales de Seguridad para Obras Civiles (Centre for Research for National Regulations on Civil Work Safety): Avda de los Immigrantes 1950 (Of. 22 y 24), 1104 Buenos Aires; Dir Ing. MARTA PARMIGIANI.

Centro de Investigación de Tecnologías de Granos (Centre for Research on Technologies for the Industrialization of Grain Production): Avda Alte. Brown e/ Reconquista y Juan Jose Paso, 6500 Nueve de Julio, Buenos Aires; Dir Ing. NICOLÁS APRO.

Centro de Investigación en Tecnologías de Industrialización de Alimentos (Centre for Research on Technologies for the Industrialization of Food Production): Avda Gral Paz e/ Avda de los Constituyentes y Avda Albarellos 40, CC 157, 1650 San Martin, Buenos Aires; Dir Ing. GUILLERMO CAMBIAZZO.

Centro de Investigación y Asistencia Técnica a la Industria (Centre for Research and Technical Assistance to Industry): Avda Mitre y 20 de Junio, CC 548, 8336 Villa Regina, Rio Negro; tel. (2941) 46-2810; Dir Ing. RODOLFO ARDENGHI.

Centro de Investigación y Desarrollo de Carnes (Centre for Meat Research and Development): Avda Gral Paz e/ Avda de los Constituyentes y Avda Albarellos 47, CC 157, 1650 San Martin, Buenos Aires; Dir Ing. NÉLIDA PROLA.

Centro de Investigación y Desarrollo de Electrónica e Informática (Centre for Electronics and Computer Science Research and Development): Avda Gral Paz e/ Avda de los Constituyentes y Avda Albarellos 42, CC 157, 1650 San Martin, Buenos Aires; tel. (220) 4754-4064; fax (220) 4754-5194; Dir Ing. DANIEL LUPI.

Centro de Investigación y Desarrollo de Envases y Embalajes (Centre for Packaging Research and Development): Avda Gral Paz e/ Avda de los Constituyentes y Avda Albarellos 48, CC 157, 1650 San Martin, Buenos Aires; Dir Ing. CARLOS LOMO.

Centro de Investigación y Desarrollo de Ingeniería Ambiental (Centre for Environmental Engineering Research and Development): Paseo Colón 850 (4o), 1063 Buenos Aires; tel. (11) 4345-7541; fax (11) 4331-5362; Dir Ing. LUIS A. DE TULIO.

Centro de Investigación y Desarrollo de la Industria de la Madera y Afines (Centre for the Wood Industry and Related Research and Development): Juana Gorriti 3520, 1708 Hurlingham, Buenos Aires; Dir Ing. GRACIELA RAMIREZ.

Centro de Investigación y Desarrollo del Cuero (Centre for Leather Research and Development): Camino Centenario e/ 505 y 508, CC 6, 1897 Manuel Gonnet, Buenos Aires; tel. 484-1876; fax 484-0244; Dir Ing. ALBERTO SOFÍA.

Centro de Investigación y Desarrollo de Métodos y Técnicas para Pequeñas y Medianas Empresas (Centre for Methods and Techniques Research and Development for Small and Medium-Size Industries): Avda Gral Paz e/ Avda de los Constituyentes y Avda Albarellos 12, CC 157, 1650 San Martin, Buenos Aires; Dir Ing. ROBERTO LÓPEZ.

Centro de Investigación y Desarrollo de Tecnológico de la Industria del Caucho (INTI-Caucho) (Centre for Research and Technological Development of the Rubber Industry): Avda Gral Paz 5445, CPB1650KNA San Martin, Buenos Aires; tel. 4724-6200; fax (11) 4724-6425; e-mail caucho@inti.gob.ar; internet www.inti.gob.ar; f. 1961; physical testing laboratories; chemical laboratory; pilot plants for rubber and latex; adhesive sectors; technical assistance; rubber, latex and adhesives formulations; training courses; 26 mems; Dir Lic. LILIANA REHAK.

Centro de Investigación y Desarrollo de Tecnológico de la Industria de los Plásticos (INTI-Plásticos) (Centre for Research and Technological Development of the Plastics Industry): Avda Gral Paz 5445 e/ Avda de los Constituyentes y Avda Albarellos 16, CC 157, B1650WAB San Martin, Buenos Aires; tel. (11) 4724-6373; fax (11) 4753-5773; e-mail plasticos@inti.gob.ar; internet www.inti.gov.ar/plasticos; f. 1978; research and devt; technology transfer; 45 mems; library of 500 vols; Dir Ing. RICARDO GIMÉNEZ.

Centro de Investigación y Desarrollo en Construcciones (Centre for Construction Research and Development): Avda Gral Paz e/ Avda Albarellos 33/10, CC 157, 1650 San Martin, Buenos Aires; Dir Ing. R. LEONARDO CHECMAREW.

Centro de Investigación y Desarrollo en Física (Centre for Physics Research and Development): Avda Gral Paz e/ Avda de los Constituyentes y Avda Albarellos 3/44, CC 157, 1650 San Martin, Buenos Aires; fax (11) 4713-4140; Dir Lic. GUSTAVO RANGUGNI.

Centro de Investigación y Desarrollo en Mecánica (Centre for Mechanics Research and Development): Avda Gral Paz e/ Avda de los Constituyentes y Avda Albarellos 9/46, CC 157, 1650 San Martin, Buenos Aires; tel. (220) 4752-0818; fax (220) 4754-5301; Dir Ing. MARIO QUINTEIRO.

Centro de Investigación y Desarrollo en Química y Petroquímica (Centre for Chemistry and Petrochemistry Research and Development): Avda Gral Paz e/ Avda de los Constituyentes y Avda Albarellos 38, CC 157, 1650 San Martin, Buenos Aires; Dir Lic. GRACIELA ENRIQUEZ.

Centro de Investigación y Desarrollo para el Uso Racional de la Energía (Centre for Research and Development for the Rational Use of Energy): Avda Gral Paz e/ Avda de los Constituyentes y Avda Albarellos 5, CC 157, 1650 San Martin, Buenos Aires; Dir Ing. MARIO OGARA.

Centro de Investigación y Desarrollo sobre Contaminantes Especiales (Centre for Special Pollutants Research and Development): Avda Gral Paz e/ Avda de los Constituyentes y Avda Albarellos 38, CC 157, 1650 San Martin, Buenos Aires; tel. (220) 4754-4074; fax (220) 4753-5749; Dir Ing. ISABEL FRAGA.

Centro de Investigación y Desarrollo sobre Electrodeposición y Procesos Superficiales (Centre for Electroplating and Superficial Processes Research and Development): Avda Gral Paz e/ Avda de los Constituyentes y Avda Albarellos 46, CC 157, 1650 San Martin, Buenos Aires; Dir Ing. ALICIA NIÑO GÓMEZ.

Centro de Investigación y Desarrollo Textil (Centre for Textile Research and Development): Avda Gral Paz e/ Avda de los Constituyentes y Avda Albarellos 15, CC 157, 1650 San Martin, Buenos Aires; Dir Ing. PATRICIA MARINO.

Libraries and Archives

Bahía Blanca

Asociación Bernardino Rivadavia—Biblioteca Popular (People's Library of the Bernardino Rivadavia Association): Avda Colón 31, 8000 Bahía Blanca; tel. (291) 455-4055; fax (291) 455-9677; e-mail abr@abr.org.ar; internet www.abr.org.ar; f. 1882; funded by its members; 4,500 mems; 158,319 vols, 1,000 periodicals, 1,000 video cassettes and a large archive of newspapers; Pres. Dr NÉSTOR J. CAZZANIGA; Sec. MIGUEL A. LALANNE.

Biblioteca Central de la Universidad Nacional del Sur (Central Library of the National University of the South): Avda Alem 1253, B8000CPB Bahía Blanca; tel. (291) 459-5111; fax (291) 459-5110; e-mail unsbc@uns.edu.ar; internet bc.uns.edu.ar; f. 1948; 164,000 vols, 7,293 periodicals; Chief Librarian LUIS A. HERRERA; publs *Memoria Anual*, *Ultimas Adquisiciones*.

Buenos Aires

Archivo General de la Nación (National Archives): Avda Leandro N. Alem 246, 1003 Buenos Aires; tel. (11) 4331-5531; fax (11) 4334-0065; e-mail archivo@mininterior.gov.ar; internet www.mininterior.gov.ar/agn; f. 1821; Supervisor ENRIQUE TANDETER.

Biblioteca Argentina para Ciegos (Argentine Library for the Blind): Lezica 3909, C1202AAA Buenos Aires; tel. (11) 4981-0137; fax (11) 4981-0137 ext. 15; e-mail bac@bac.org.ar; internet www.bac.org.ar; f. 1924; 14,000 vols in Braille, talking books; Dir FERNANDO GALARRAGA; publs *Burbujas* (in Braille, for children), *Con Fundamento* (in Braille, for young people), *Hacia La Luz* (in Braille, for adults).

Biblioteca Central de la Armada (Central Library of the Navy): Estado Mayor General de la Armada, Calle Comodoro Py 2055 PB of 132, 1107 Buenos Aires; tel. (11) 4317-2000 ext. 2301; e-mail esgnbib@ara.mil.ar; f. 1914; 160,000 vols; 50 brs; Dir ALICIA PEREZ; publ. *Revista de Publicaciones Navales*.

Biblioteca Central de la Universidad del Salvador 'Padre Guillermo Furlong' (Fr Guillermo Furlong Central Library of the University of the Saviour): Tte. Gral. Perón 1818, Subsuelo, C1040AAB Buenos Aires; tel. (11) 4371-0422; e-mail uds-bibl@salvador.edu.ar; f. 1956; 55,000 vols; Dir LILIANA LAURA REGA; publ. *Boletín Bibliográfico*.

Biblioteca de la Sociedad Rural Argentina (Library of Argentine Agricultural Society): Florida 460, 1005 Buenos Aires; tel. (11) 4322-3431; fax (11) 4325-8231; f. 1866; 50,000 items; Dir Dr VÍCTOR LUIS FUNES; publs *Anales de la Sociedad Rural Argentina* (4 a year), *Boletín*, *Memoria* (1 a year).

Biblioteca de Leprología 'Dr Enrique P. Fidanza' (Dr Enrique P. Fidanza Leprosy Library): Federación del Patronato del Enfermo de Lepra de la República Argentina, Beruti 2373/77, 1106 Buenos Aires; tel. (11) 483-1815; f. 1930; 4,000 vols, 35,000 cards in its catalogues; museum of histopathology of skin; publ. *Temas de Leprología*.

Biblioteca del Banco Central de la República Argentina (Library of the Central Bank of the Republic of Argentina): San Martín 216, C1004AAF Buenos Aires; tel. (11) 4348-3772; fax (11) 4348-3771; e-mail biblio@bcra.gov.ar; internet www.bcra.gov.ar; f. 1935; 100,000 vols; Dir MARTA S. GUTIÉRREZ; publs *Boletín Estadístico* (12 a year), *Boletín Monetario y Financiero* (4 a year), *Documentos de Trabajo* (irregular), *Información de Entidades Financieras* (12 a year), *Informe Anual del Presidente al Congreso* (1 a year), *Notas Técnicas* (irregular).

Biblioteca del Bibliotecario 'Dr Augusto Raúl Cortazar' (Library of the Librarian Dr Augusto Raúl Cortazar): México 564, 1097 Buenos Aires; f. 1944; a section of the Escuela Nacional de Bibliotecarios (Instituto Superior de Enseñanza); 2,500 vols; Dir RUBY A. ESCANDE.

Biblioteca del Colegio de Escribanos 'José A. Negri' (José A. Negri Library of the College of Notaries): Callao 1540, 1024 Buenos Aires; tel. and fax (11) 4807-1637; e-mail bibnegri@colegio-escribanos.org.ar; internet www.colegio-escribanos.org.ar; f. 1886; law and social science; 32,500 vols; Librarian ANA MARÍA DANZA; publs *Boletín de Legislación*, *Revista del Notariado*.

Biblioteca del Congreso de la Nación (Library of the National Congress): Hipólito Yrigoyen 1750, C1089AAH Buenos Aires; tel. (11) 4010-3000; e-mail coordinacion@bcnbib.gov.ar; internet www.bcnbib.gov.ar; f. 1859; 2m. vols; Pres. Dr JUAN CARLOS GIOJA; Gen. Coordinating Dir BERNARDINO CABEZAS; publ. *Boletín*.

Biblioteca del Ministerio de Relaciones Exteriores y Culto (Ministry of Foreign Affairs and Religion Library): Arenales 761, 1061 Buenos Aires; tel. (11) 441-1498; 50,000 vols; Dir HORACIO R. PIÑEYRO.

Biblioteca del Museo Nacional de Bellas Artes 'Raquel Edelman' (Raquel Edelman Library of the National Museum of Fine Arts): Avda Libertador 1473, C1425AAA Buenos Aires; tel. (11) 4803-0802; fax (11) 4803-8817 ext. 223; e-mail bibliotecamnba@yahoo.com.ar; f. 1910; visual arts; 150,000 vols.

Biblioteca del Servicio Geológico Minero Argentino (Library of the Argentine Mining Geology Service): Avda Julio A. Roca 651 (9o), 1322 Buenos Aires; tel. (1) 349-3200; fax (1) 349-3198; e-mail mjanit@secind.mecon.gov.ar; internet www.segemar.gov.ar; f. 1904; 150,000 vols, 45,000 pamphlets, 15,000 maps; Dir Lic. MARA JANITENS; publs *Boletines*, *Anales*.

Biblioteca Nacional (National Library): Agüero 2502, C1425EID Buenos Aires; tel. (11) 4808-6000; e-mail bibliotecanacional@bn.gov.ar; internet www.bn.gov.ar; f. 1810; 2m. vols, 46,177 MSS; Dir Dr HORACIO GONZÁLEZ.

Biblioteca Nacional de Aeronáutica (National Aeronautics Library): CC 3389, 1000 Buenos Aires; Paraguay 748, 1057 Buenos Aires; tel. (11) 4312-9038; e-mail binae@ciudad.com.ar; internet www.binae.org.ar; f. 1927; aeronautics, astronautics, aeronautical law; 50,000 vols; Dir Brig. MIGUEL ANGEL AGUILAR; Chief Librarian ANGÉLICA A. LLORCA; publs *Aeroespacio*, *Boletín Bibliográfico* (2 a year).

Biblioteca Nacional de Maestros (National Library for Teachers): Pizzurno 953, 1020 Buenos Aires; tel. (11) 4129-1272; fax (11) 4129-1299; e-mail bnminfo@me.gov.ar; internet www.bnm.me.gov.ar; f. 1870; 150,000 vols; general reference and education; Dir Lic. GRACIELA PERRONE.

Biblioteca Nacional Militar 'Agustín P. Justo' (Agustín P. Justo National Military Library): Avda Santa Fe 750, C1059ABO Buenos Aires; tel. (11) 4311-4560; e-mail biblioteca@circulomilitar.org; f. 1938; 150,000 vols; Dir JESÚS PELLEGRINI.

Biblioteca Tornquist (Tornquist Library): Reconquista 266, Hall San Martín - Planta Baja, C1003ABF Buenos Aires; tel. (11) 4348-3500 ext. 2803; e-mail biblio@bcra.gov.ar; internet www.bcra.gov.ar/index.asp; f. 1916; economics and social sciences; 35,842 vols, 1,155 periodicals; Dir JUAN JOSÉ GALLI.

Centro Argentino de Información Científica y Tecnológica (CAICYT) (Argentine Centre of Scientific and Technological Information): Saavedra 15 (Piso 1), C1083ACA Buenos Aires; tel. (11) 4951-6975; fax (11) 4951-8334; e-mail postmaster@caicyt.edu.ar; internet www.caicyt-conicet.gov.ar; f. 1958; attached to Consejo Nacional de Investigaciones Científicas y Técnicas; Dir MARIO ALBORNOZ.

Centro de Documentación e Información Internacional (International Centre of Documentation and Information): Dirección Nacional General de Cooperación Internacional, Ministerio de Educación, Agüero 2502 (3°), 1425 Buenos Aires; f. 1959; publs by UN, Organization of American States, etc.; 5,000 vols; Dir FRANCISCO PIÑÓN.

Centro de Información de la Comisión Nacional de Energía Atómica (Information Centre of the National Atomic Energy Commission): Biblioteca Eduardo J. Savino, Edificio Tandar - Sector B, Avda General Paz 1499, 1650 San Martín, Buenos Aires; tel. (11) 6772-7946; e-mail referencia@cnea.gov.ar; internet www.cnea.gov.ar/cac/ci/default.htm; f. 1950; 36,700 vols, 450 current periodicals, 450,000 microcards and reports; Dir ALEJANDRA T. CHAVEZ FLORES; publs *Informes CNEA*, *Memoria CNEA*.

Centro de Información y Estadística Industrial (Centre for Industrial Information and Statistics): c/o INTI, Avda Leandro N. Alem 1067 (7o), 1101 Buenos Aires; attached to Instituto Nacional de Tecnología Industrial; Dir Ing. ALFREDO P. GALLIANO.

Dirección General de Bibliotecas Municipales (Public Libraries Administration): Calle Talcahuano 1261, 1014 Buenos Aires; tel. (11) 4811-9027; fax (11) 4811-0867; f. 1928; comprises 25 public municipal libraries in Buenos Aires with an aggregate of 350,000 vols; Dir-Gen. Prof. JOSEFINA DELGADO; publs *Cuadernos de Buenos Aires*, *Guía Cultural de Buenos Aires*.

Sistema de Bibliotecas y de Información, Universidad de Buenos Aires (Library and Information System of the University of Buenos Aires): Azcuénaga 280 (2o), 1029 Buenos Aires; tel. (11) 4951-1366 ext. 500; fax (11) 4952-6557; e-mail postmaster@sisbi.uba.ar; internet www.sisbi.uba.ar; f. 1941; 17 constituent faculty libraries; Gen. Coordinator ELSA ELENA ELIZALDE (acting).

Córdoba

Sistema de Bibliotecas de la Universidad Católica de Córdoba (Library of Córdoba Catholic University): Obispo Trejo 323, 5000 Córdoba; tel. (351) 493-8090; fax (351) 493-8091; e-mail bibdir@uccor.edu.ar; internet www.ucc.edu.ar/biblioteca; f. 1956; 85,000 vols, 3,600 periodicals; Dir Mag. SANDRA GISELA MARTÍN; publs *Diálogos Pedagógicos* (2 a year), *Studia Politicae* (2 a year).

Biblioteca Mayor de la Universidad Nacional de Córdoba (Main Library of Córdoba National University): Calle Obispo Trejo 242 (1° piso), Casilla de Correo 63, 5000 Córdoba; tel. (351) 433-1072; fax (351) 433-1079; e-mail circu@bmayor.unc.edu.ar; internet www.bmayor.unc.edu.ar; f. 1613; 150,000 vols, 3,890 periodicals and pre-1860 newspapers; partial depository for UN publs; Dir Lic. ROSA M. BESTANI.

La Plata

Biblioteca de la Universidad Nacional de La Plata (Library of La Plata National University): Plaza Rocha 137, 1900 La Plata; tel. (221) 423-6607; fax (221) 425-5004; e-mail secretaria@biblio.unlp.edu.ar; internet www.biblio.unlp.edu.ar; f. 1884; 450,000 vols, 5,000 periodicals; spec. collns incl. South American newspapers relating to the Independence movement, South American history and geography and first travels in South America; 60 br. libraries within the univ.; Dir Bibl. NORMA MANGIATERRA; publ. *Informaciones.*

Biblioteca del Ministerio de Gobierno de la Provincia de Buenos Aires (Library of the Buenos Aires Province Ministry of the Interior): Casa de Gobierno, 1900 La Plata; law, politics and economics; 20,000 vols.

Biblioteca y Centro de Documentación del Ministerio de Economía de la Provincia de Buenos Aires (Library and Documentation Centre of the Ministry of the Economy of the Province of Buenos Aires): Calle 8 entre 45 y 46 (piso 1 Of. 25), 1900 La Plata; tel. (221) 429-4400 ext. 4702; 13,800 vols; Dir (vacant); publs *Noticias de Economía* (6 a year), *Cuadernos de Economía* (6 a year).

Mendoza

Biblioteca Central de la Universidad Nacional de Cuyo (Central Library of the National University of Cuyo): Parque Gral San Martín, 5500 Mendoza; tel. (261) 413-5203; e-mail sid@uncu.edu.ar; f. 1939; 120,000 vols; Dir ISABEL BEATRIZ PIÑERO; publs *Boletín Bibliográfico* (irregular), *Cuadernos de la Biblioteca* (irregular).

Biblioteca Pública General San Martín (General San Martín Public Library): Remedios Escalada de San Martín 1843, 5500 Mendoza; tel. (261) 423-1674; f. 1822; 130,000 vols; special collections: local authors, children's books; Dir ANA MARIA GARCIA BUTTINI; publs *BAL* (Biblioteca de Autor Local, 1 a year), *BIL* (Biblioteca Infanto/Juvenil), *Versión II epocá* (1 a year).

Pergamino (Buenos Aires)

Biblioteca Pública Municipal 'Dr Joaquín Menéndez' (Dr Joaquín Menéndez Municipal Public Library): San Martín 838, 2700 Pergamino, Buenos Aires; tel. (2477) 417327; f. 1901; 58,000 vols; Librarian ALICIA D. PARODI.

Resistencia

Centro de Información Bioagropecuaria y Forestal (CIBAGRO) (Bio-Farming and Forestry Information Centre): Dirección de Bibliotecas, Universidad Nacional del Nordeste, Avda Las Heras 727, 3500 Resistencia, Chaco; tel. (3722) 44-3742; fax (3722) 44-3742; e-mail jencinas@bib.unne.edu.ar; f. 1976; 2,500 books, 2,800 pamphlets, 1,000 periodicals; spec. colln: FAO and other int. agricultural orgs; Dir JULIO E. ENCINAS; publs *Agronea*, *Bibliografía Forestal Nacional*, *Bibliografía sobre El Picudo del Algodonero*, *Bibliografía sobre El Quebracho*, *Ciencias Forestales—Bibliografía.*

Forest Information Network for Latin America and the Caribbean (RIFALC): CIBAGRO, Dirección de Bibliotecas, Universidad Nacional del Nordeste, Avda Las Heras 727, 3500 Resistencia, Chaco; tel. and fax (3722) 44-3742; e-mail jencinas@bib.unne .edu.ar; f. 1985; coordinates and integrates at regional level the efforts made by individual networks, and makes accessible in each country all the information available; mems: 19 orgs in 12 countries; Exec. Sec. JULIO E. ENCINAS; publ. *Boletín Informativo.*

Rosario

Biblioteca Argentina 'Dr Juan Alvarez' de la Municipalidad de Rosario (Dr Juan Alvarez Argentine Library of the Municipality of Rosario): Pje Alvarez 1550, 2000 Rosario; tel. (341) 480-2538; fax (341) 480-2561; e-mail biblarg@rosario.gov.ar; f. 1912;

180,000 vols; Dir MARÍA DEL CARMEN D'ANGELO.

Biblioteca Pública 'Estanislao S. Zeballos' (Estanislao S. Zeballos Public Library): Blvd Oroño 1261, 2000 Rosario; tel. (341) 480-2793 ext. 128; fax (341) 480-2797 ext. 110; f. 1915; economics, accountancy, business studies, statistics; 111,000 vols; Dir BEATRIZ LODEZANO; publs *Ciudad y Región* (3 a year), *Revista de la Facultad de Ciencias Económicas y Estadística* (irregular).

San Miguel (Buenos Aires)

Biblioteca de las Facultades de Filosofía y Teología S.I. (Library of the Faculties of Philosophy and Theology): Avda Mitre 3226, 1663 San Miguel, Buenos Aires; tel. (11) 4455-7992; fax (11) 4455-6442; e-mail gerardo@bibusv.edu.ar; f. 1931; central deposit library; 153,000 vols, 700 current periodicals; Librarian Prof. GERARDO LOSADA; publ. *Stromata* (4 a year).

Tucumán

Biblioteca Central de la Universidad Nacional de Tucumán (Central Library of the National University of Tucuman): Lamadrid 817, T4000BEQ San Miguel de Tucumán; tel. (381) 424-7752; fax (381) 424-8025; e-mail bibcen@unt.edu.ar; internet biblio.unt .edu.ar/b_central; f. 1917; 48,000 vols; Dir JUAN RICARDO ACOSTA; publ. *Boletín Bibliográfico.*

Museums and Art Galleries

Buenos Aires

Museo Argentino de Ciencias Naturales 'Bernardino Rivadavia'—Instituto Nacional de Investigación de las Ciencias Naturales (Bernardino Rivadavia Argentine Museum of Natural Sciences—National Research Institute of Natural Sciences): Avda Angel Gallardo 470, C1405DJR Buenos Aires; tel. (11) 4982-0306; fax (11) 4982-5243; e-mail secretaria@macn.gov.ar; internet www.macn.gov.ar; f. 1812; zoology, botany, palaeontology, geology and ecology; library of 500,000 vols; Dir Dr EDGARDO ROMERO; publ. *Revista* (2 or 3 a year).

Museo de Armas de la Nación (National Arms Museum): Maipú 1030, C1059ABO Buenos Aires; tel. (11) 4311-1070; e-mail man@armasdefuego.com.ar; internet www .coleccionables.com.ar/man; f. 1904; library of 1,000 vols; Dir JULIO E. SOLDAINI.

Museo de Arte Español 'Enrique Larreta' (Enrique Larreta Museum of Spanish Art): Juramento 2291 y Obligado 2139, 1428 Buenos Aires; tel. (11) 4784-4040; fax (11) 4783-2640; e-mail museolarreta@infovia.com .ar; f. 1962; 13th- to 18th-century wood carvings, gilt objects and painted panels, paintings of Spanish School from 16th to 20th centuries, tapestries, furniture; library of 9,700 vols; Dir MERCEDES DI PAOLA DE PICOT.

Museo de Arte Hispanoamericano 'Isaac Fernández Blanco' (Isaac Fernández Blanco Museum of Spanish-American Art): Suipacha 1422, 1011 Buenos Aires; tel. (11) 4327-0272; e-mail mifb_prensa@buenosaires .gov.ar; internet www .museofernandezblanco.buenosaires.gov.ar; f. 1947; 16th- to 19th-century Spanish- and Portuguese-American art, silver, furniture; library of 5,000 vols; Dir Lic. JORGE COMETTI.

Museo de Arte Moderno de Buenos Aires (Museum of Modern Art): Ave San Juan 350,

Buenos Aires; tel. (11) 4342-2970; e-mail mambamail@gmail.com; internet www .museodeartemoderno.buenosaires.gov.ar; f. 1956; Latin American paintings, especially Argentine, and contemporary schools; museum closed for construction until October 2010; temporary HQ: Adolfo Alsina 963, 1 piso, Buenos Aires; Dir Prof. LAURA BUCCELLATO.

Museo de Bellas Artes de la Boca (Boca Fine Arts Museum): Pedro de Mendoza 1835, 1169 Buenos Aires; tel. (11) 4301-1080; internet www.buenosaires.gov.ar/areas/ educacion/programas/quinquela; f. 1933; paintings, sculpture, engravings, and maritime museum; Dir Dr GUILLERMO C. DE LA CANAL.

Museo de la Dirección Nacional del Antártico (Museum of the National Antarctic Administration): Angel Gallardo 470, 1405 Buenos Aires; tel. (11) 4812-7327; natural and physical sciences of the Antarctic; Dir Dr RICARDO CAPDEVILA.

Museo de la Policía Federal Argentina (Argentine Federal Police Museum): San Martín 353 (pisos 7 y 8), 1004 Buenos Aires; tel. (11) 4394-6857; f. 1899; Dir JOSÉ A. GUTIÉRREZ.

Museo Etnográfico 'Juan B. Ambrosetti' (Juan B. Ambrosetti Ethnographical Museum): Moreno 350, 1091 Buenos Aires; tel. (11) 4345-8196; fax (11) 4345-8197; e-mail info.museo@filo.uba.ar; internet museoetnografico.filo.uba.ar; f. 1904; attached to the Faculty of Philosophy and Letters of the Univ. of Buenos Aires; ethnography and archaeology of Argentina, the Americas, Africa, Asia and Oceania; library of 80,000 vols; Dir Dr JOSÉ ANTONIO PÉREZ GOLLÁN; publ. *Runa* (1 a year).

Museo Histórico de la Ciudad de Buenos Aires 'Brigadier-General Cornelio de Saavedra' (Brig.-Gen. Cornelio de Saavedra Historical Museum of the City of Buenos Aires): Calle Crisólogo Larralde 6309, 1431 Buenos Aires; tel. (11) 4572-0746; fax (11) 4574-1328; e-mail museosaavedra_direccion @buenosaires.gov.ar; internet www.museos .buenosaires.gov.ar; f. 1921; library of 3,600 vols; Dir Lic. ALBERTO GABRIEL PIÑEIRO.

Museo Histórico Nacional (National History Museum): Defensa 1600, C1143AAD Ciudad Autónoma de Buenos Aires; tel. (11) 4307-1182; fax (11) 4307-3157; e-mail direccion@mhn.gov.ar; internet www.cultura .gov.ar/direcciones/?info=organismo&id=14& idd=5; f. 1889 as City Historical Museum, present status in 1891; library of 15,000 vols, 46,000 artefacts; Dir Dr JOSÉ ANTONIO PÉREZ GOLLÁN; publ. *El Museo Histórico Nacional* (1 a year).

Museo Histórico Sarmiento (Sarmiento History Museum): Juramento 2180, 1428 Buenos Aires; tel. (11) 4782-2989; fax (11) 4782-2354; e-mail info@museosarmiento.gov .ar; internet www.museosarmiento.gov.ar; f. 1938; library of 13,000 vols; Dir Mus. MARTA GERMANI.

Museo Mitre (Mitre Museum): San Martín 336, 1004 Buenos Aires; tel. (11) 4394-7659; fax (11) 4394-8240; internet www .museomitre.gov.ar; f. 1907; preserves the household of Gen. Bartolomé Mitre; antique maps, coins and medals; library of 66,621 vols on American history, geography and ethnology, archive of 80,000 historical documents; Dir Lic. MARÍA GOWLAND.

Museo Nacional de Aeronáutica (National Museum of Aeronautics): Avda Eva Perón 2200, Morón, Buenos Aires; tel. (11) 4697-9769; e-mail mna@uolsinectis.com .ar; internet www.fuerzaaerea.mil.ar/

historia/museo_aeronautico.html; f. 1960; Dir Cmdr SANTOS A. DOMINGUEZ KOCH (RETD).

Museo Nacional de Arte Decorativo (National Museum of Decorative Art): Avda del Libertador 1902, 1425 Buenos Aires; tel. (11) 4801-8248; fax (11) 4802-6606; e-mail museo@mnad.org; internet www.mnad.org; f. 1937; furniture, sculpture, tapestries, European and South American works; library of 2,000 vols; Dir ALBERTO GUILLERMO BELLUCCI.

Museo Nacional de Arte Oriental (National Museum of Oriental Art): Avda del Libertador 1902 (1o), 1425 Buenos Aires; tel. (11) 4801-5988; fax (11) 4801-5988; f. 1966; Asian and African art; library of 1,500 vols, 2,500 periodicals; Dir Lic. MARÍA DEL VALLE GUERRA.

Museo Nacional de Bellas Artes (National Museum of Fine Arts): Avda del Libertador 1473, 1425 Buenos Aires; tel. (11) 4803-0714; fax (11) 4803-4062; f. 1895; Argentine, American and European painting since 19th century, classical painting and sculpture, pre-Columbian art; library of 50,000 vols, 200,000 booklets; Dir Arq. ALBERTO G. BELLUCCI.

Museo Naval de la Nación (National Museum of Naval History): Paseo Victorica 602, Tigre, 1648 Buenos Aires; tel. (11) 4749-0608; e-mail museonaval@hotmail.com; f. 1892; library of 3,000 vols; Dir Capt. HORACIO MOLINA PICO (RETD).

Museo Numismático 'Dr José Evaristo Uriburu' (Dr José Evaristo Uriburu Numismatics Museum): Banco Central de la República Argentina, Calle San Martín 216, 1o, 1004 Buenos Aires; tel. (11) 4348-3882; fax (11) 4348-3699; e-mail museo@bcra.gob.ar; internet www.bcra.gov.ar; f. 1935; attached to Central Bank of Argentina; Dir DANIEL ANTONIO REY.

Museo Social Argentino (Argentine Museum of Sociology): Avda Corrientes 1723, 1042 Buenos Aires; tel. (11) 4375-4601; fax (11) 4375-4600; f. 1911; library of 80,000 vols; Pres. Dr GUILLERMO GARBARINI ISLAS; publs *Foro Economico* (2 a year), *Foro Político* (3 a year).

Córdoba

Museo Botánico (Botanical Museum): Universidad Nacional de Córdoba, CC 495, 5000 Córdoba; tel. (351) 4332104; fax (351) 4332104; e-mail museo@imbiv.unc.edu.ar; f. 1870; conducts research as a unit of Instituto Multidisciplinario de Biología Vegetal (run by CONICET and Universidad Nacional de Córdoba); library of 8,000 vols; Dir Dr ANA M. ANTON; publs *Kurtziana* (1 a year), *Lorentzia* (irregular).

Museo Provincial de Bellas Artes 'Emilio A. Caraffa' (Emilio A. Caraffa Provincial Museum of Fine Arts): Avda Hipólito Yrigoyen 651, 5000 Córdoba; tel. (351) 433-3412; fax (351) 433-3414; f. 1916; Argentine and foreign paintings, sculptures, drawings and engravings; library and archive; Dir Lic. GRACIELA ELIZABETH PALELLA.

Museo Provincial de Ciencias Naturales 'Bartolomé Mitre' (Bartolomé Mitre Provincial Museum of Natural Sciences): Avda Hipólito Yrigoyen 115, 5000 Córdoba; tel. (351) 422-1428; f. 1919; geology, zoology, botany; library of 3,400 vols and periodicals; Dir MARTA CANO DE MARTIN.

Corrientes

Museo Histórico de Corrientes (Corrientes Historical Museum): Calle 9 de Julio 1044, 3400 Corrientes; tel. (4) 75946; e-mail museohistoricoetes@hotmail.com; internet www.culturo.corrientes.gov.ar; f. 1929; history of Corrientes Province; library of 2,000 vols; Dir MIGUEL FERNANDO GONZÁLEZ AZCOAGA; publ. *Boletín de Extensión Cultural* (4 a year).

La Plata

Museo de La Plata (La Plata Museum): Paseo del Bosque s/n, B1900FWA La Plata; tel. (221) 425-7744; e-mail museo@fcnym .unlp.edu.ar; internet www.fcnym.unlp.edu .ar/abamuse.html; f. 1884; anthropology, archaeology, geology, natural history (incl. palaeontological colln of Patagonian mammalia); library of 60,000 vols, 5,000 periodicals; Dir Dra SILVIA AMETRANO; publs *Anales, Notas, Novedades, Obra del Centenario, Obra del Cincuentenario, Revista, Serie Técnica y Didáctica*.

Luján

Complejo Museografico 'Enrique Udaondo' (Enrique Udaondo Museographic Complex): Lezica y Torrezuri 917, 6700 Luján; tel. (2323) 42-0245; internet www .lujan.gov.ar/cultura/centros/museos; f. 1923; comprises 4 museums: Museo Colonial e Histórico (history, archaeology, silver, paintings, furniture), Museo de Transportes (transport), Museo del Automóvil y Pabellón 'Belgrano' y Depósitos (vintage cars); Dir CARLOS A. SCANNAPIECO.

Mendoza

Museo de Ciencias Naturales y Antropológicas 'Juan Cornelio Moyano' (Juan Cornelio Moyano Museum of Anthropology and Natural Sciences): Extremo Sur del Lago, Parque General San Martín, 5500 Mendoza; tel. and fax (261) 428-7666; f. 1911; library of 18,900 vols on American and Argentine history; Asst Dir Prof. CLARA ABAL DE RUSSO; publ. *Boletín* (2 a year).

Paraná

Museo de Ciencias Naturales y Antropológicas 'Prof. Antonio Serrano' (Prof. Antonio Serrano Museum of Anthropology and Natural Sciences): Carlos Gardel 62, E3100FWB Paraná; tel. (343) 420-8894; e-mail biblioserrano@yahoo.com.ar; internet www.museoserrano.com.ar; f. 1917; scientific investigations; papers editions; exhibitions; library of 35,000 vols; Dir Prof. GISELA BAHLER; publs *Catalogos, Memorias*.

Museo Histórico de Entre Rios 'Martiniano Leguizamón' (Martiniano Leguizamón Historical Entre Rios Museum): Laprida y Buenos Aires, 3100 Paraná; tel. (343) 420-7869; internet www.parananews.com.ar/ museos/museo-historico-martiniano-leguizamon.html; f. 1948; library of 27,000 vols; archive; Dir MARIA ANGEL MATHIEU MAYA.

Rosario

Museo Histórico Provincial de Rosario 'Dr Julio Marc' (Rosario Dr Julio Marc Provincial History Museum): Parque Independencia, 2000 Rosario; tel. (341) 472-1457; fax (341) 472-1457; e-mail museomarc@ citynet.net.ar; internet www.santafe.gov.ar/ cultura/museos/historo.htm; f. 1939; library of 33,000 vols; Dir Prof. IRMA B. MONTALVAN.

Museo Municipal de Arte Decorativo 'Firma y Odilo Estevez' (Firma y Odilo Estevez Municipal Decorative Arts Museum): Santa Fe 748, 2000 Rosario; tel. (341) 480-2547; fax (341) 480-2547; e-mail museo@museoestevez.gov.ar; internet www .museoestevez.gov.ar; f. 1968; Curator P. A. SINOPOLI.

Museo Municipal de Bellas Artes 'Juan B. Castagnino' (Juan B. Castagnino Municipal Fine Arts Museum): Avda Pellegrini 2202, 2000 Rosario; tel. (341) 480-2542; fax (341) 480-2543; e-mail comunicacion@ castagninomacro.org; internet www .museocastagnino.org.ar; f. 1937; library of 2,500 vols; Dir Prof. BERNARDO MIGUEL BALLESTEROS.

San Carlos de Bariloche

Museo de la Patagonia 'Dr Francisco P. Moreno' (Dr Francisco P. Moreno Museum of Patagonia): Centro Cívico, 8400 San Carlos de Bariloche, Río Negro; tel. (944) 22309; fax (944) 22309; e-mail museodelapatagonia@ apn.gov.ar; internet www.bariloche.com.ar/ museo; f. 1940; political history of Patagonia, ethnology, natural sciences, archaeology; library of 2,500 vols; Dir Lic. CECILIA GIRGENTI; publs *Antropología, Diversidad Cultural de la Argentina*.

Santa Fé

Museo de Bellas Artes 'Rosa Galisteo de Rodriguez' (Rosa Galisteo de Rodriguez Museum of Fine Arts): 4 de Enero 1510, 3000 Santa Fe; tel. (42) 596142; fax (42) 596142; internet www.digitalmicrofilm.com .ar/rosagalisteo; f. 1922; contemporary Argentine and modern art; library of 4,200 vols; Dir Arq. MARCELO OLMOS.

Museo Histórico Provincial de Santa Fe (Santa Fe Provincial Museum of History): San Martín 1490, S3000FRH Santa Fe; tel. (342) 457-3529; e-mail info@ museohistorico-sfe.gov.ar; internet museohistorico-sfe.gov.ar; f. 1943; Dir Prof. ALICIA TALSKY DE RONCHI.

Museo Provincial de Ciencias Naturales 'Florentino Ameghino' (Florentino Ameghino Provincial Museum of Natural History): 1° Junta 2859, 3000 Santa Fe; tel. (342) 457-3770; fax (342) 457-3730; e-mail ameghino@santafe-conicet.gov.ar; internet www.unl.edu.ar/santafe/museocn.htm; f. 1914; zoology, botany, geology, palaeobiology; library: public library of 50,000 vols; Dir Lic. CARLOS A. VIRASORO.

Santiago del Estero

Museo Provincial de Arqueología 'Wagner' (Wagner Provincial Archaeological Museum): Calle Avellaneda 355, 4200 Santiago del Estero; tel. (385) 4211380; fax (385) 4211380; e-mail museowagnersgo@gmail .com; f. 1917; archaeology of Chaco-Santiagueno and later cultures; Dir ANDRÉS A. CHAZARRETA RUIZ.

Tandil

Museo Municipal de Bellas Artes de Tandil (Tandil Municipal Museum of Fine Arts): Chacabuco 357, 7000 Tandil; tel. (2293) 43-2067; fax (2293) 43-0667; f. 1920; paintings of Classical, Impressionist, Cubist and Modern schools, 20th-century Argentinian art, small statues, furniture, engravings; small library; Dir CRISTIAN SEGURA.

Ushuaia

Museo del Fin del Mundo (The End of the World Museum): Maipú 173, 9410 Ushuaia, Tierra del Fuego; tel. (2901) 42-1863; e-mail museo@tierradelfuego.ml.org; internet www .principiodelmundo.com.ar/museo; f. 1979; history and natural sciences; library of 5,000 vols; Dir OSCAR PABLO ZANOLA; publs *Arqueología de la Isla Grande de Tierra del Fuego, Museo Territorial, Raíces del Fin del Mundo* (3 a year).

Universities

There are three main categories of Universities in Argentina: National (or Federal), which are supported by the Federal Budget; Provincial (or State), supported by the Provincial Budgets; and Private Universities, created and supported entirely by private initiative, but authorized to function by the Ministry of Education.

National Universities

UNIVERSIDAD DE BUENOS AIRES

Calle Viamonte 430/444, C1053ABJ Buenos Aires

Telephone: (11) 4510-1100
Internet: www.uba.ar
Founded 1821
Academic year: March to November

Rector: Dr RUBEN HALLU
Vice-Rector: Dra BEATRIZ GUGLIELMOTTI
Library Dir: Dra SUSANA SOTO

Number of teachers: 21,688
Number of students: 336,947

Library: see under Libraries

Publications: *Encrucijadas* (4 a year), *Oikos* (4 a year)

DEANS

Faculty of Agriculture (Avda San Martín 4453): Ing. Agr. FERNANDO VILELLA
Faculty of Architecture, Design and Town Planning (Ciudad Universitaria, Pabellón 3, Núñez): Arq. BERARDO DUJOVNE
Faculty of Dentistry (M. T. de Alvear 2142): Dr MÁXIMO GIGLIO
Faculty of Economic Sciences (Avda Córdoba 2122): Dr JUAN CARLOS CHERVATIN
Faculty of Engineering (Paseo Colón 850): Ing. CARLOS ALBERTO RAFFO
Faculty of Exact and Natural Sciences (Ciudad Universitaria, Pabellón 2, Núñez): Dr PABLO MIGUEL JACOVKIS
Faculty of Law and Social Sciences (Avda Pte Figueroa Alcorta 2263): Dr ANDRÉS JOSÉ D'ALESSIO
Faculty of Medicine (Paraguay 2155): Dr SALOMÓN SCHÄCHTER
Faculty of Pharmacy and Biochemistry (Junín 954): Dra REGINA WIGDOROVITZ DE WIKINSKI
Faculty of Philosophy and Letters (Puan 470): Dr FRANCISCO RAÚL CARNESE
Faculty of Psychology (Hipólito Irigoyen 3238/46): Lic. RAÚL COUREL
Faculty of Social Sciences (Marcelo T. de Alvear 2230): Dr FORTUNATO MACIMACCI
Faculty of Veterinary Sciences (Chorroarín 280): Med. Vet. ANÍBAL FRANCO

SELECTED AFFILIATED INSTITUTES

Colegio Nacional de Buenos Aires: Bolívar 263, 1066 Buenos Aires; tel. 331-6777; Rector Dr HORACIO SANGUINETTI.

Escuela Superior de Comercio 'Carlos Pellegrini: Marcelo T. de Alvear 1851, 1122 Buenos Aires; tel. (11) 4811-7547; f. 1890; incorporated in the Univ. of Buenos Aires 1912; 6-year course in commercial education; Rector Dr ABRAHAM LEONARDO GAK.

Hospital de Clínicas 'José de San Martín': Avda Córdoba 2351, Buenos Aires; tel. (11) 4508-3888; Dir Dr JORGE ITALA.

Instituto de Investigaciones Médicas 'Alfredo Lanari': see under Research Institutes.

Instituto Modelo de Clínica Médica 'Luis Agote': Avda Córdoba 2351, 11o, Buenos Aires; tel. (1) 961-6001; Exec. Dir Dr FLORENTINO SANGUINETTI.

Instituto de Oncología 'Angel H. Roffo': Avda San Martín 5481, 1417 Buenos Aires; tel. (11) 4580-2800; f. 1966; library of 3,000 vols, 180 periodicals; Dir Dr ALEJO A. L. CARUGATTI.

Instituto de Perfeccionamiento Médico-Quirúrgico 'Prof. Dr José María Jorge': Avda Córdoba 2351, 7o, Buenos Aires; tel. (11) 4961-6001; Exec. Dir Dr FLORENTINO SANGUINETTI.

UNIVERSIDAD NACIONAL DE CATAMARCA

Esquiú 612, 4700 Catamarca
Telephone: (3833) 45-6410
E-mail: privadaunca@arnet.com.ar
Internet: www.unca.edu.ar
Founded 1972
Academic year: February to December

Rector: Ing. FLAVIO SERGIO FAMA
Vice-Rector: Lic. ELINA SIVERA DE BUENADE
Sec.-Gen.: Ing. MARCELO FABIÁN VERA
Librarian: MARÍA EMILIA MARTÍNEZ

Number of teachers: 304
Number of students: 14,067

Publication: *Aportes*

DEANS

Faculty of Agricultural Sciences: Ing. Agr. EDMUNDO JOSÉ A. AGUERO
Faculty of Economics and Administration: CPN DANIEL EDUARDO TOLOZA
Faculty of Exact and Natural Sciences: Ing. Qco. BLANCA STELLA SOSA
Faculty of Health Sciences: Dr JORGE DANIEL BRIZUELA DEL MORAL
Faculty of Humanities: Lic. ROLANDO EDGARDO CORONEL
Faculty of Technology and Applied Sciences: Agrim. FÉLIX RAMÓN DOERING
School of Archaeology: Lic. MÓNICA CATOGGIO DE ACOSTA (Dir)
School of Law: Dra IRMA DEL TRÁNSITO ROMERO NIEVA (Dir)
Fray Mamerto Esquiu Higher School: Prof. HORTENCIA DURANTI DE ALVAREZ (Dir)

UNIVERSIDAD NACIONAL DEL CENTRO DE LA PROVINCIA DE BUENOS AIRES

General Pinto 399, B7000GHG Tandil
Telephone: (2293) 42-2000
Fax: (2293) 42-1608
E-mail: rector@rec.unicen.edu.ar
Internet: www.unicen.edu.ar
Founded 1974
State control
Academic year: February to December

Rector: Cr ROBERTO TASSARA
Vice-Rector: Ing. OMAR LOSARDO
Gen. Sec.: Ing. GILLERMO AMILCAR CORRES
Academic Sec.: Profa MABEL PACHECO
Admin. Sec.: Cr JOSÉ LUIS BIANCHINI
Library Dir: Profa ZULEMA GRANDINETTI DE CAGLIOLO

Number of teachers: 1,585
Number of students: 10,427

Publications: *Alternativas*, *Anuario IEHS*

DEANS

Faculty of Agricultural Sciences: Med. Vet. ARNALDO PISSANI
Faculty of Economics: Cr ROBERTO TASSARA
Faculty of Engineering: Ing. EDUARDO F. IRASSAR
Faculty of Humanities: Lic. ALEJANDRO DILLON
Faculty of Sciences: Dr GERY BIOUL
Faculty of Social Sciences: Lic. CRISTINA BACCIN
Faculty of Theatre: Dr CARLOS CATALANO
Faculty of Veterinary Science: Dr PEDRO STEFFAN

UNIVERSIDAD NACIONAL DEL COMAHUE

Buenos Aires 1400, Q8300BCX Neuquén
Telephone: (299) 449-0300
Fax: (299) 449-0351
E-mail: sprector@uncoma.edu.ar
Internet: www.uncoma.edu.ar
Founded 1972
State control
Academic year: March to March

Rector: Dra ANA MARIA PECHEN DE D'ANGELO
Vice-Rector: Dr TERESA VEGA
Sec.-Gen.: OMAR ANTONIO CALVI
Academic Sec.: Prof. LUIS BERTANI
Admin. Sec.: Lic. OSCAR LUSETTI
Librarian: EUGENIA LUQUE

Number of teachers: 1,700
Number of students: 30,000

DEANS

Faculty of Agricultural Sciences: Ing. Ftal. JORGE LUIS GIRARDIN
Faculty of Economics and Administration: Lic. SUSANA GRACIELA LANDRISCINI
Faculty of Education: Lic. GUILLERMO VILLANUEVA
Faculty of Engineering: Ing. DANIEL BOCCANERA
Faculty of Humanities: Lic. PEDRO BARREIRO
Higher School of Languages: Prof. MARÍA ELENA AGUILAR
Faculty of Law and Social Sciences: Dr JUAN MANUEL SALGADO
Faculty of Tourism: Dra ADRIANA OTERO
Bariloche Regional University Centre: Lic. FEDERICO HORACIO PLANAS
Zona Atlantica Regional University Centre: Ing. Agr. MIGUEL ANGEL SILVA

UNIVERSIDAD NACIONAL DE CÓRDOBA

Calle Raúl Haya de la Torre s/n (2o piso), Pabellón Argentina, Ciudad Universitaria, 5000 Córdoba
Telephone: (351) 433-4081
Fax: (351) 433-4081
Internet: www.uncor.edu
Founded 1613; charter received from Philip III of Spain 1622; fully established by Pope Urban VIII 1634; nationalized 1856
Academic year: February to December

Rector: Ing. JORGE GONZÁLEZ
Vice-Rector: Ing. DANIEL DI GIUSTO
Sec.-Gen.: Ing. GABRIEL TAVELLA
Librarian: Lic. ROSA M. BESTANI

Library: see Libraries and Archives
Number of teachers: 7,753
Number of students: 114,918

Publication: *Revista*

DEANS

Faculty of Agrarian Sciences: Ing. Agr. HECTOR FONTÁN
Faculty of Architecture and Town Planning: Arq. MIGUEL ANGEL ROCA
Faculty of Chemical Sciences: Dr GERARDO FIDELIO
Faculty of Dentistry: Dr NAZARIO KUYUMLIAM
Faculty of Economics: Dr HEBE G. DE ROITTER
Faculty of Exact, Physical and Natural Sciences: Ing. ERNESTO ALVAREZ
Faculty of Languages: Dra CRISTINA ELQUE DE MARTINI
Faculty of Law and Social Sciences: Dra RAMÓN PEDRO YANZI FERREYRA
Faculty of Mathematics, Astronomy and Physics: Dr CRISTIAN URBANO SÁNCHEZ
Faculty of Medicine: Dr PEDRO LEÓN SARACHO CORNET
Faculty of Philosophy and Humanities: Dra SILVIA CAROLINA SCOTTO

Faculty of Psychology: Lic. ANA ALDERETE

DIRECTORS

'Manuel Belgrano' Higher School of Commerce: JOSÉ MARIA ALDAY
Monserrat National College: FRANCISCO BOBONE

UNIVERSIDAD NACIONAL DE CUYO

Centro Universitario, M5502JMA Mendoza
Telephone: (261) 413-5000
Fax: (261) 449-4022
Internet: www.uncu.edu.ar
Founded 1939
State control
Academic year: April to October
Rector: Ing. ARTURO ROBERTO SOMOZA
Vice-Rector: Dr GUSTAVO ANDRÉS KENT
Academic Sec.: ESTELA MARÍA ZALBA DE AGUIRRE
Librarian: Lic. JUAN GUILLERMO MILIA
Library: see Libraries and Archives
Number of teachers: 4,794
Number of students: 31,527
Publication: Boletín Oficial

DEANS

Faculty of Agricultural Sciences: Ing. JORGE TACCHINI
Faculty of Applied Science: Ing. ERNESTO MUÑOZ
Faculty of Arts: Prof. ELIO ORTIZ
Faculty of Dentistry: Dr ONOFRE CIPOLLA
Faculty of Economics: RODOLFO SÍCOLI
Faculty of Engineering: Ing. JUAN MANUEL GOMEZ
Faculty of Law: Dr LUIS ABBIATI
Faculty of Medical Sciences: Dr ISAAC RIVERO
Faculty of Philosophy and Letters: Prof. MIGUEL VERSTRAETE
Faculty of Political and Social Sciences: Lic. CARLOS FINOCHIO
Teacher Training College: MARÍA VICTORIA GOMEZ DE ERICE
Zona Sur: Dis. Ind. ADRIANA RUIZ

ATTACHED INSTITUTE

Centro Regional de Investigaciones Científicas y Tecnológicas (CRICYT): Calle Bajada del Cerro s/n, Parque General San Martín, Casilla de Correo 131, 5500 Mendoza; tel. (261) 428-8314; fax (261) 428-7370; Dir Dr RICARDO PAULINO DEI.

UNIVERSIDAD NACIONAL DE ENTRE RÍOS

Eva Perón 24, 3260 Concepción del Uruguay, Entre Ríos
Telephone: (3442) 42-1500
Fax: (3442) 42-1563
E-mail: webmaster@rect.uner.edu.ar
Internet: www.uner.edu.ar
Founded 1973
State control
Academic year: April to March
Rector: EDUARDO FRANCISCO JOSÉ ASUETA
Vice-Rector: Lic. ELOÍSA DE JONG
Gen. Sec.: HIPOLITO B. FINK
Academic Sec.: Lic. SUSANA ESTHER CELMAN
Library Dir: Prof. JORGE TITO MARTÍNEZ
Number of teachers: 1,219
Number of students: 13,204
Publications: Ciencia, Docencia y Tecnología (3 a year), Guía de Carreras

DEANS

Faculty of Administrative Science: EDUARDO ASUETA
Faculty of Agrarian Sciences: Ing. FRANCISCO RAMÓN ETCHEVERS

Faculty of Bromatology: Lic. SUSANA NOVELLO DE METTLER
Faculty of Economics: JULIO CÉSAR YODICE
Faculty of Education: Prof. MARTHA BENEDETTO DE ALBORNOZ
Faculty of Engineering: Ing. AGUSTÍN CARPIO
Faculty of Health Sciences: Dr JULIO SIMOVICH
Faculty of Nutritional Sciences: Ing. JORGE AMADO GERARD
Faculty of Social Services: A. S. ALICIA MERCEDES GONZÁLEZ ALARCÓN

UNIVERSIDAD NACIONAL DE FORMOSA

Don Bosco 1082, 3600 Formosa
Telephone: (3717) 423-926
Fax: (3717) 423-928
E-mail: adminweb@unf.edu.ar
Internet: www.unf.edu.ar
Founded 1988
State control
Rector: Ing. MARTÍN RENÉ ROMANO
Vice-Rector: Dr ROQUE SILGUERO
Sec.-Gen. (Academic): Lic. OFELIA INÉS FANTÍN
Sec.-Gen. (Science and Technology): Dr CARLOS MONZÓN
Sec. (Management and Devt): LIVIO DANILO PEREIRA (acting)
Sec. (Student Affairs and Univ. Extension): Lic. ARIEL SPEIT
Number of students: 11,937
Library of 12,000 vols

DEANS

Faculty of Economics and Business Administration: Lic. HECTOR CARMELO QUIJANO
Faculty of Health: Dr JOSÉ TRINIDAD ESCOBAR
Faculty of Humanities: Prof. MARÍA DE LA CRUZ COLOMBERA DE CASTAÑEDA
Faculty of Natural Resources: (vacant)

FACULTIES AND DEPARTMENTS

Faculty of Economics and Business Admin. (Campus Universitario, Avda Gobernador Gutnisky 3200, 3600 Formosa; tel. (3717) 451-792; e-mail faen@unf.edu.ar; depts of Accounting, Foreign Trade).
Faculty of Health (Campus Universitario, Avda Gobernador Gutnisky 3200, 3600 Formosa; tel. (3717) 451-836; e-mail adminsalud@unf.edu.ar; depts of Bromatology, Clinical Analysis, Nursing, Nutrition).
Faculty of Humanities (Campus Universitario, Avda Gobernador Gutnisky 3200, 3600 Formosa; tel. (3717) 452-473; e-mail fhumanidades@unf.edu.ar; depts of Biology, Geography, History, Letters, Mathematics, Psychology, Special Education).
Faculty of Natural Resources (Campus Universitario, Avda Gobernador Gutnisky 3200, 3600 Formosa; tel. (3717) 452-241; e-mail frecursosnat@unf.edu.ar; depts of Agribusiness, Civil Engineering, Forestry Engineering, Zootechnical Engineering).

UNIVERSIDAD NACIONAL DE GENERAL SAN MARTÍN

Avda 25 de Mayo y Francia, CP 1650, San Martín, Buenos Aires
Telephone: (11) 4006-1500
Fax: (11) 4006-1511
E-mail: rectorado@unsam.edu.ar
Internet: www.unsam.edu.ar
Founded 1992
State control
Rector: CARLOS RAFAEL RUTA
Vice-Rector: CARLOS GERÓNIMO GIANELLA
Sec.-Gen.: GUILLERMO SCHWEINHEIM
Academic Sec.: JORGE FERNÁNDEZ NIELLO

Admin. Sec.: FRANCISCO HÉCTOR FERNÁNDEZ (acting)
Science and Technology Sec.: ESTEBAN CASSIN
Student Affairs and Univ. Extension Sec.: CARLOS ALMEIDA
Number of students: 7,942
Library of 4,700 vols, 350 periodicals
Publications: Educación en Ciencias, Educación en Ciencias Sociales, Política y Gestión, Revista de la Escuela de Economía y Negocios

DEANS

School of Economics and Business: HORACIO VAL
School of Government and Politics: MARCELO CAVAROZZI
School of Humanities: NORBERTO FERRÉ
School of Science and Technology: DANIEL DI GREGORIO
School of Postgraduate Studies: ALBERTO POCHETTINO
Institute of Biotechnical Research: ALBERTO FRASCH
Institute of Higher Social Studies: ALEJANDRO GRIMSON
Institute of Industrial Quality: JOAQUÍN VALDÉS
Institute of Rehabilitation Sciences and Movement: HUGO RODRÍGUEZ ISARN
Institute for Research and Environment Engineering: ALBERTO POCHETTINO
Dan Beninson Institute of Technology: CARLA NOTARI
Prof. Jorge A. Sabato Institute of Technology: ANA MARÍA MONTI

UNIVERSIDAD NACIONAL DE GENERAL SARMIENTO

Campus Universitario, José M. Gutiérrez entre José L. Suárez y Verdi, 1613 Los Polvorines, Buenos Aires
Telephone: (11) 4469-7500
Fax: (11) 4451-4575
E-mail: info@ungs.edu.ar
Internet: www.ungs.edu.ar
Founded 1993
State control
Academic year: October to April
Rector: Lic. SILVIO ISRAEL FELDMAN
Vice-Rector: Ing. MARCELO OSCAR FERNÁNDEZ
Sec.-Gen.: Lic. ALEJANDRO LUIS LOPEZ ACCOTTO
Sec. (Academic): Prof. ELSA BEATRIZ PEREYRA
Sec. (Administration): DANIELA LETICIA GUARDADO
Sec. (Legal and Technical): Lic. HAYDÉE NÉLIDA UGRIN
Sec. (Research): Lic. CARLOS EDUARDO REBORATTI
Library of 18,000 vols, 121 periodicals
Number of students: 5,547

DIRECTORS

Institute of Human Development: Dr EDUARDO RINESI
Institute of Industry: Ing. NÉSTOR BRUNO BRAIDOT
Institute of Science: Lic. ROSA ELENA BELVEDRESI
Institute of Urban Studies: Lic. MAGDALENA GRACIELA CHIARA

UNIVERSIDAD NACIONAL DE JUJUY

Avda Bolivia 1239, 4600 San Salvador de Jujuy
Telephone: (388) 422-1515
Fax: (388) 422-1507
E-mail: info@unju.edu.ar
Internet: www.unju.edu.ar
Founded 1972
State control

Academic year: March to December

Rector: Dr Ing. ENRIQUE MATEO ARNAU
Vice-Rector: Ing. CARLOS GREGORIO TORRES
Secretary for Academic Affairs: Lic. ANGELICA MERCEDES GARAY DE FUMAGALLI
Secretary for Administrative Affairs: PATRICIA CUELLAR DE COMAS
Secretary for Science and Technology: Dr LILIANA LUPO
Secretary for Student Welfare: MARIO VEGA
Secretary for University Extension: Ing. EDUARDO BERRAFATO
Librarian: MARÍA E. C. DE MARTÍNEZ

Library of 18,000 vols
Number of teachers: 700
Number of students: 12,417

DEANS

Faculty of Agriculture: Dra SUSANA MURUAGA DE L'AGENTIER
Faculty of Economics: CPN LUIS SALVADOR FORTUNI
Faculty of Engineering: Ing. ENRIQUE MATEO ARNAU
Faculty of Humanities and Social Sciences: Lic. MARIO RABEY
School of Mining: Ing. Qco ALBERTO CONSTANTINO ALBESA

ATTACHED RESEARCH INSTITUTES

Institute of Geology and Mining: Avda Bolivia 2355, 4600 San Salvador de Jujuy; tel. (388) 422-1593; fax (388) 422-1594; Dir Dra BEATRIZ COIRA.

Institute of Marine Biology: Avda Bolivia No. 2345/55, 4600 San Salvador de Jujuy; tel. (388) 422-1596; fax (388) 422-1597; Dir Lic. MARTHA G. ARCE DE HAMITY.

UNIVERSIDAD NACIONAL DE LA MATANZA

Florencio Varela 1903, B1754JEC San Justo, Buenos Aires
Telephone: (11) 4480-8900
Fax: (11) 4480-8919
E-mail: webmaster@unlam.edu.ar
Internet: www.unlam.edu.ar
Founded 1990
State control
Academic year: March to December (2 semesters)
Rector: Prof. Lic. DANIEL EDUARDO MARTÍNEZ
Vice-Rector: Dr RENÉ NICOLETTI
Sec.-Gen.: Dr JOSÉ PAQUÉZ
Sec. (Academic): Dr GUSTAVO DUEK
Sec. (Admin.): Cdor. ADRIAN SANCCI
Sec. (Information Technology and Communications): Lic. MARCELO PÉREZ GUNTIN
Sec. (Legal and Technical): Dr CRISTIAN JAVIER CABRAL
Sec. (Management and Planning): Dr JORGE NARVAÉZ
Sec. (Postgraduate Affairs): Dr MARIO ENRIQUE BURKÚN
Sec. (Univ. Public Relations): Lic. ROBERTO LUIS AYUB
Number of students: 19,368

DEANS

Economics: Dr ALBERTO LONGO
Engineering and Technological Research: Ing. ALFREDO VÁZQUEZ
Humanities and Social Sciences: Dr FERNANDO LUJÁN ACOSTA
Law and Political Science: Dr ALEJANDRO FINOCCHIARO

FACULTIES AND DEPARTMENTS

Economics (tel. (11) 4480-8954; e-mail economic@unlam.edu.ar; depts of Accounting, Admin., Int. Trade

Engineering and Technological Research (tel. (11) 4480-8952; e-mail ingenieria@unlam.edu.ar; depts of Computer Engineering, Electronic Engineering, Industrial Engineering

Humanities and Social Sciences (tel. (11) 4480-8900; e-mail sociales@unlam.edu.ar; depts of Labour Relations, Physical Education, Social Communication, Social Work, Public Relations

Law and Political Science (tel. (11) 4480-8995; e-mail derecho@unlm.edu.ar; dept of Law and Political Science

UNIVERSIDAD NACIONAL DE LA PAMPA

Cnel. Gil 353, 6300 Santa Rosa, La Pampa
Telephone: (2954) 451-600
E-mail: info@unlpam.edu.ar
Internet: www.unlpam.edu.ar
Founded 1958
Academic year: April to November
Rector: Lic. SERGIO D. MALUENDRES
General Secretary: JUAN JOSÉ COSTA
Academic Secretary: Lic. LUIS MARÍA MORETE
Librarian: Lic. ATILIO DENOUARD

Number of teachers: 632
Number of students: 9,804

DEANS

Faculty of Agronomy: Ing. Agr. GUILLERMO COVAS
Faculty of Economics: CPN ROBERTO OSCAR VASSIA
Faculty of Exact and Natural Sciences: Profa NORA D. ANDRADA DE GUESALAGA
Faculty of Human Sciences: Prof. JOSÉ RUFINO VILLARREAL
Faculty of Veterinary Science: Dr RAÚL ANTONIO ALVAREZ

UNIVERSIDAD NACIONAL DE LA PATAGONIA AUSTRAL

Lisandro de la Torre 860, 9400 Río Gallegos, Santa Cruz
Telephone: (2966) 442-376
Fax: (2966) 442-376
E-mail: rectorad@unpa.edu.ar
Internet: www.unpa.edu.ar
Founded 1994
State control
Rector: Ing. MARÍA EUGENIA MÁRQUEZ
Vice-Rector: Ing. HUGO SANTOS ROJAS
Sec.-Gen. (Academic): Lic. MARÍA JOSÉ LENO
Sec. (Admin. and Finance): Lic. MARCELO MILJAK
Sec. (Planning): Lic. MARIA VICTORIA HERNANDEZ
Sec. (Science and Technology): Dra SANDRA CASAS
Sec. (Univ. Public Relations): Profa VIRGINIA BARBIERI
Number of students: 6,940

CAMPUS DEANS

Caleta Olivia: DANIEL PANDOLFI
Río Gallegos: Dr ALEJANDRO SÚNICO
Río Turbio: MARCELA VILLA
San Julian: CLAUDIA MALIK DE TCHARA

UNIVERSIDAD NACIONAL DE LA PATAGONIA SAN JUAN BOSCO

Ciudad Universitaria, Km 4, 9005 Comodoro Rivadavia, Chubut
Telephone: (297) 455-7856
E-mail: dzonal@unpata.edu.ar
Internet: www.unp.edu.ar

Founded 1980 by merger of Universidad de la Patagonia San Juan Bosco and Universidad Nacional de la Patagonia
Academic year: February to December
Rector: JORGE MANUEL GIL
Vice-Rector: Ing. ALDO LOPEZ GUIDI
Academic Secretary: Lic. EDUARDO BIBILONI
Librarian: MARIO D'ORTA

Number of teachers: 850
Number of students: 15,952

Library of 40,000 vols

Publication: *Naturalia Patagónica* (4 a year)

DEANS

Faculty of Economics: JORGE STACCO
Faculty of Engineering: Ing. ROBERTO AGUIRRE
Faculty of Humanities and Social Sciences: Lic. DOLORES DEL CASTAÑO
Faculty of Natural Sciences: Lic. OMAR CESARIS

REGIONAL FACULTIES

Esquel: Alvear 1021, 3 piso, 9200 Esquel; tel. (2945) 43729; Dir Lic. ROBERTO VIERA; forestry and economics.

Puerto Madryn: Blvd Almirante Brown 3700, CC 164, 9120 Puerto Madryn; tel. (2965) 45-1024; Dir Dr MIGUEL A. HALLER; marine biology, computer science.

Trelew: Faculty of Economics and Faculty of Humanities and Social Sciences, Fontana 488, 9100 Trelew; tel. (2965) 43-1532; fax (2965) 43-1276Faculty of Engineering and Faculty of Natural Sciences, Belgrano 507, 9100 Trelew; tel. (2965) 43-3305; Dir JUAN PÉREZ AMAT.

Ushuaia: CADIC, 9410 Ushuaia; tel. (2901) 43-0892; Dir Dr ÓSCAR LOBO; tourism, computer science.

UNIVERSIDAD NACIONAL DE LA PLATA

Avda 7 No. 776, 1900 La Plata
Telephone: (221) 423-6804
E-mail: portal@presi.unlp.edu.ar
Internet: www.unlp.edu.ar
Founded 1905
Academic year: March to December
President: Arq. GUSTAVO ADOLFO AZPIAZU
Vice-President: Lic. RAÚL ANIBAL PERDOMO
Gen. Sec.: Arq. FERNANDO ALFREDO TAUBER
Librarian: Dr CARLOS TEJO
Library: see Libraries and Archives
Number of teachers: 6,300
Number of students: 91,135

Publication: *Revista de la Universidad*

DEANS

Faculty of Agriculture: Ing. GUILLERMO MIGUEL HANG
Faculty of Architecture and Town Planning: Arq. JORGE ALBERTO LOMBARDI
Faculty of Astronomy and Geophysics: Prof. CÉSAR AUGUSTO MONDINALLI
Faculty of Dentistry: ALFREDO V. RICCIARDI
Faculty of Economic Sciences: (vacant)
Faculty of Engineering: Ing. LUIS JULIÁN LIMA
Faculty of Exact Sciences: Dr ENRIQUE PEREYRA
Faculty of Fine Arts: Prof. ROBERTO OSCAR ROLLIÉ
Faculty of Humanities and Education: Dr JOSÉ PANETTIERI
Faculty of Juridical and Social Sciences: RICARDO PABLO RECA
Faculty of Medical Sciences: Dr JAIME TRAJTENBERG
Faculty of Natural Sciences: Dr ISIDORO A. SCHALAMUCK

Faculty of Veterinary Sciences: Dr ALBERTO DIBBERN

SELECTED AFFILIATED SCHOOLS AND INSTITUTES

Colegio Nacional 'Rafael Hernández' (National College): Avda 1 y 49, La Plata; Dir Prof. GRACIELA TERESA IBARRA.

Escuela Graduada 'Joaquín V. González' (Graduate School 'Joaquín V. González'): Calle 50 y 119, La Plata; Dir Prof. MARTHA S. BETTI DE MILICHIO.

Escuela Práctica de Agricultura y Ganadería 'María Cruz y Manuel L. Inchausti' (School of Agriculture and Stockbreeding): Estación Valdés, 6660 Veinticinco de Mayo, Pca de Buenos Aires; Dir Dr RICARDO LUIS CABASSI.

Escuela Superior de Periodismo y Comunicación Social (School of Journalism): Avda 44 No. 676, La Plata; Dir Lic. JORGE LUIS BERNETTI.

Instituto de Física de Líquidos y Sistemas Biológicos: Calle 59 No. 789, 1900 La Plata; tel. (221) 44-7545; f. 1981; theoretical and applied research; 9 researchers; library of 582 vols, in process of formation; Dir Dr ANTONIO E. RODRÍGUEZ.

UNIVERSIDAD NACIONAL DE LA RIOJA

Avda Dr Rene Favaloro s/n, 5300 La Rioja
Telephone: (3822) 45-7000
Fax: (3822) 45-7000
E-mail: unlar@unlar.edu.ar
Internet: www.unlar.edu.ar
Founded 1972
State control
Academic year: February to December
Rector: Dr ENRIQUE TELLO ROLDÁN
Vice-Rector: Ing. MANUEL JESÚS MAMANÍ
Administrative Secretary: SANTIAGO ROMERO
Librarian: (vacant)
Library of 23,000 vols
Number of teachers: 1,154
Number of students: 16,519
Publication: *Research Projects* (6 a year)
Faculties of Economics, Engineering, Humanities and Arts, Social Sciences.

UNIVERSIDAD NACIONAL DE LANÚS

29 de Septiembre 3901, 1826 Lanús, Buenos Aires
Telephone: (11) 6322-9200
Fax: (11) 6322-9200
E-mail: info@unla.edu.ar
Internet: www.unla.edu.ar
Founded 1995
State control
Academic year: March to December (two semesters)
Rector: ANA MARÍA JARAMILLO
Vice-Rector and Sec. (Academic): Dr JUAN CARLOS GENEYRO
Sec.-Gen.: JORGE CARTOCIO
Sec. (Admin.): GUILLERMO GROSSKOPF
Sec. (Public Service and Cooperation): Lic. GEORGINA HERNÁNDEZ
Sec. (Research, Science and Technology): Ing. NORBERTO CAMINOA
Librarian: Lic. ELVIRA LOFIEGO
Number of students: 7,079

DIRECTORS

Arts and Humanities: Prof. HECTOR MUZZO-PAPPA
Community Health: Dr DANIEL RODRÍGUEZ
Planning and Public Policy: Dr ALEJANDRO KAWABATA
Production and Labour Development: Dr JORGE MOLINA

UNIVERSIDAD NACIONAL DEL LITORAL

Blvd Pellegrini 2750, S3000ADQ Santa Fe
Telephone: (342) 457-1110
Fax: (342) 457-1110
E-mail: informes@unl.edu.ar
Internet: www.unl.edu.ar
Founded 1919
State control
Academic year: March to December
Rector: Ing. ALBOR CANTARD
Vice-Rector: Dr MARIO T. CADIOTI
Gen.-Sec.: Prof. CLAUDIO LIZÁRRAGA
Academic Sec.: HUGO ERBETTA
Admin. Sec.: Esc. RODOLFO M. R. ACANFORA GRECO
Sec. for International Cooperation: Ing. JULIO C. THEILER
Librarian: MARISA PULIOTTI DE FERRARI
Number of teachers: 2,171
Number of students: 32,924
Publications: *Science and Technology, Society and Culture*

DEANS

Faculty of Agrarian Sciences: Ing. Agr. HUGO ARMANDO ERBETTA
Faculty of Architecture, Design and Town Planning: Arq. JULIO ALEJANDRO TALÍN
Faculty of Biochemistry and Biological Sciences: Bioq. EDUARDO RAMÓN VILLARREAL
Faculty of Chemical Engineering: Ing. PEDRO MÁXIMO MANCINI
Faculty of Economics: FRANCISCA SÁNCHEZ DE DUSSO
Faculty of Education: Prof. LEONOR JUANA CHENA
Faculty of Law and Social Sciences: Dr MARIANO T. CANDIOTI
Faculty of Teacher Training: Prof. LEONOR J. CHENA
Faculty of Veterinary Sciences: Med. Vet. EDUARDO BARONI
Faculty of Water Resources Engineering and Sciences: Ing. CRISTÓBAL VICENTE LOZECO

DIRECTORS

Higher Institute of Music: Prof. MARIANO CABRAL MIGNO
Higher School of Health Services: Dr CARLOS PRONO
Higher School of Industry: Ing. JORGE OSVALDO BASILICO
Institute of Food Technology: Ing. HUGO SÁNCHEZ
Institute of Technological Development for the Chemical Industry (INTEC): Dr ALBERTO ENRIQUE CASSANO
School of Agriculture, Stockbreeding and Farming: Ing. Agr. OSVALDO MARIO HERMANN
University School of Food Analysis: Ing. ALEJANDRO BERNABEU
University School of Food Science: Bioq. LUIS MARÍA NICKISH

UNIVERSIDAD NACIONAL DE LOMAS DE ZAMORA

Ruta Provincial No. 4 Km 2, Llavaloll, Buenos Aires
Telephone: (11) 4282-7818
Fax: (11) 4282-8043
E-mail: unlz@unlz.edu.ar
Internet: www.unlz.edu.ar
Founded 1972
State control
Chancellor: GUIDO DI TELLA
Rector: HORACIO GEGUNDE
Vice-Rectors: DIEGO MOLEA (Admin.), HORACIO DAVID CASABE (Academic)
Sec.-Gen.: LEONARDO CLEMENTE
Chief of Staff: NÉSTOR PAN

Librarian: MARIA LUISA ISHIKAWA
Number of teachers: 3,800
Number of students: 35,000

DEANS

Faculty of Agrarian Science: Ing. FERNANDO RUMIANO
Faculty of Economics: Cdr ALEJANDRO KURUC
Faculty of Engineering: Ing. OSCAR PASCAL
Faculty of Law: Dr ALEJANDRO TULLIO
Faculty of Social Sciences: Lic. GABRIEL MARIOTTO

UNIVERSIDAD NACIONAL DE LUJÁN

Ruta 5 y Avda Constitución, 6700 Luján, Buenos Aires
Telephone: (2323) 42-3171
Fax: (2323) 42-5795
E-mail: informes@unlu.edu.ar
Internet: www.unlu.edu.ar
Founded 1973
Academic year: February to December
Rector: Lic. ANTONIO F. LAPOLLA
Vice-Rector: Dr NORBERTO KRYMKIEWICZ
Registrar: Lic. MARCELO BUSALACCHI
Librarian: Lic. EDUARDO ZEISS
Number of teachers: 1,000
Number of students: 18,803
Publications: *Cuadernos de Economía Política, Cuadernos de Historia Regional*

DEANS

Department of Basic Sciences: Dr JOSÉ AGUIRRE
Department of Education: Prof. HÉCTOR CUCUZZA
Department of Social Sciences: Lic. AMALIA TESTA
Department of Technology: JUAN TREGONING

UNIVERSIDAD NACIONAL DE MAR DEL PLATA

Diagonal J. B. Alberdi 2695, 7600 Mar del Plata, Pca de Buenos Aires
Telephone: (223) 492-1705
Fax: (223) 492-1711
Internet: www.mdp.edu.ar
Founded 1961
State control
Academic year: March to November
Rector: Lic. FRANCISCO MOREA
Vice-Rector: Dr ARMANDO DANIEL ABRUZA
Sec.-Gen. (Planning and Institutional Development): Arq. ARIEL MAGNONI
Acad. Sec.: Lic. MONICA VAN GOOL
Sec.(Economics and Finance): C. P. JORGE HERRADA
Sec. (Extension): Prof. ADRIANA CORTES
Sec. (Technological Development): Lic. OLGA DELLA VEDOVA
Sec. (University Community): Lic. PAULA PAZ
Librarian: Lic. OSCAR FERNÁNDEZ
Number of teachers: 1,600
Number of students: 27,000
Publication: *Revista de Letras* (3 a year)

DEANS

Faculty of Agriculture: Ing. Agr. JOSÉ LUIS BODEGA
Faculty of Architecture and Town Planning: Arq. MANUEL TORRES CANO
Faculty of Economics and Social Sciences: Cont. OTTORINO OSCAR MUCCI
Faculty of Engineering: Ing. MANUEL LORENZO GONZÁLEZ
Faculty of Exact and Natural Sciences: Dr JULIO LUIS DEL RIO
Faculty of Health Sciences and Social Services: Lic. GRISELDA SUSANA VICENS
Faculty of Humanities: Prof. CRISTINA ROSENTHAL

Faculty of Law: Dr LUIS PABLO SLAVIN
Faculty of Psychology: Lic. MARÍA CRISTINA DI DOMÉNICO

DIRECTORS

Centre for Coastal and Quaternary Geology: Lic. DANIEL MARTINEZ
Institute of Biological Research: Dr JORGE JULIAN SANCHEZ
Institute of Science and Materials Technology Research: Dr SUSANA ROSSO

UNIVERSIDAD NACIONAL DE MISIONES

Ruta Nacional No. 12, Km 7½, N3304 Miguel Lanús, Misiones
Telephone: (3752) 48-0916
Fax: (3752) 48-0500
E-mail: info@unam.edu.ar
Internet: www.unam.edu.ar
Founded 1973
State control
Academic year: February to December
Chancellor: Dr ALDO LUIS CABALLERO
Vice-Chancellor: Aldo MA DARÍO MONTINI
Number of teachers: 900
Number of students: 8,800
Publications: Boletín, Revista

DEANS

Faculty of Arts: Prof. ADA SARTORI DE VENCH-ARUTTI
Faculty of Economics: JOSE LUIS LIBUTTI
Faculty of Engineering: Ing. OSCAR EDUARDO PERRONE
Faculty of Forestry: Ing. JUAN CARLOS MULARCZUK KOSARIK
Faculty of Humanities and Social Sciences: Prof. ANA MARÍA CAMBLONG
Faculty of Sciences: Ing. RAUL MARUCCI

UNIVERSIDAD NACIONAL DEL NORDESTE

25 de Mayo 868, 3400 Corrientes
Telephone: (3783) 42-5064
Fax: (3783) 42-54678
E-mail: webmaster@unne.edu.ar
Internet: www.unne.edu.ar
Founded 1957
Academic year: March to December
Rector: Arq. OSCAR VICENTE VALDÉS
Vice-Rector: Dr HUGO ALBERTO DOMITROVIC
Sec.-Gen. for Academic Affairs: Arq. OSCAR V. VALDES
Sec.-Gen. for Admin.: Dr HUGO A. PEIRETTI
Sec.-Gen. for Planning: GABRIEL E. OJEDA
Sec.-Gen. for Science and Technology: Ing. Dr JORGE R. AVANZA
Sec.-Gen. for Social Affairs: Dr SERGIO M. FLINTA
Sec.-Gen. for Univ. Extension: Dr LUCIANO R. FABRIS
Librarian: Prof. ITALO JUAN L. METTINI
Number of teachers: 4,327
Number of students: 54,445
Publications: Cuadernos Serie Agro, Revista de la Facultad de Ciencias Veterinarias, Revista de la Facultad de Derecho, Revista Nordeste, Serie Medicina, Serie Planeamiento

DEANS

Faculty of Agricultural Industries: Ing. MARÍA ALICIA JUDIS
Faculty of Agricultural Sciences: Ing. Agr. LUIS AMADO MROGINSKY
Faculty of Architecture and Town Planning: Arq. HECTOR LUIS CABALLERO
Faculty of Dentistry: Dr VÍCTOR MENDEZ
Faculty of Economics: EDGARDO MARTÍN AYALA

Faculty of Engineering: Ing. MARIO BRUNO NATALINI
Faculty of Humanities: Prof. ANA MARÍA FOSCHIATTI DE DELL'ORTO
Faculty of Law and Social and Political Sciences: Dr JORGE MARIÑO FAGES
Faculty of Medicine: Dr SAMUEL BLUVSTEIN
Faculty of Natural Sciences and Surveying: Lic. MARÍA SILVIA AGUIRRE
Faculty of Veterinary Sciences: Dr ROBERTO A. JACOBO

DIRECTORS

Institute of Administration of Agriculture and Fishing Business: Ing. Agr. ALBERTO DEZA
Institute of Agrotechnology: Ing. CARLOS ENRIQUE TOMEI
Institute of Criminal Sciences: Lic. FRANCISCO CAMACHO
Institute of Economics of Agriculture and Fishing: Ing. Agr. JULIO JORGE ESPERANZA
Institute of Regional Pathology: Dr JORGE O. GORODNER
Industrial Relations, Social Communication and Tourism: Prof. IRMA QUIJANO
Patterns of Foreign Trade: JUAN CARLOS BARBAGALLO

UNIVERSIDAD NACIONAL DE QUILMES

Roque Sáenz Peña 180, 1876 Bernal, Buenos Aires
Telephone: (11) 4365-7100
Fax: (11) 4365-7101
E-mail: info@unq.edu.ar
Internet: www.unq.edu.ar
Founded 1989
State control
Rector: Dr MARIO ERMÁCORA
Vice-Rector: Prof. ROQUE DABAT
Sec. for Academic: Dr MARTÍN BECERRA
Sec. for Admin.: CARMEN CHIARADONNA
Sec. for Communication and Information Technology: Lic. SERGIO NAPOLITANO
Sec. for Legal and Technical: Abog. LORENA LAMPOLIO
Sec. for Postgraduate Affairs: Dr DIEGO GOLOMBEK
Sec. for Research: Dra ANAHÍ BALLENT
Sec. for Univ. Public Relations: Lic. MARCELO GÓMEZ
Librarian: LAURA MANZO
Library of 16,000 vols
Number of students: 11,000
Publications: Prismas. Revista de historía intelectual (intellectual history), Redes (science and technology), Revista de Ciencias Sociales (social sciences)

DIRECTORS

Department of Science and Technology: Dr DANIEL GHIRINGHELLI
Department of Social Sciences: Prof. RODOLFO PASTORE
Centre for Research and Study: Lic. ALBERTO DÍAZ

UNIVERSIDAD NACIONAL DE RÍO CUARTO

Ruta Nacional 36 Km 601, X5804BYA Río Cuarto, Córdoba
Telephone: (358) 467-6200
Fax: (358) 468-0280
E-mail: postmaster@unrc.edu.ar
Internet: www.unrc.edu.ar
Founded 1971
State control
Academic year: February to December
Rector: Ing. OSCAR SPADA
Vice-Rector: Méd. Vet. ANIBA BESSONE
Gen.-Sec.: Méd. Vet. ARMANDO BECERRA

Acad. Sec.: Lic. SILVIA NICOLETTI
Economic Sec.: Lic. JORGE GONZÁLEZ
Extension and Devt Sec.: Lic. RICARDO ROIG
Science and Technology Sec.: Dr ALFREDO BARONIO
Welfare Sec.: Méd. Vet. ENRIQUE BÉRGAMO
Coordinator of Institutional Communication: Arq. LUCÍA FORTUNA
Head of Postgraduate School: Dr Lic. RUBÉN DAVICINO
Librarian: CRISTINA CH. DE FAUDA
Number of teachers: 1,280
Number of students: 20,244
Publications: Contextos de Educación (2 a year), Crónia (2 a year), Fundamentos (2 a year), Interciencia (2 a year), Revista (2 a year), Voces de la Universidad (2 a year)

DEANS

Faculty of Agriculture and Veterinary Science: LUIS ROBERTO ROVERE
Faculty of Economics: Lic. ROBERTO TAFANI
Faculty of Engineering: Ing. PEDRO ENRIQUE DUCANTO
Faculty of Exact, Physical, Chemical and Natural Sciences: Lic. GLADYS B. MORI
Faculty of Humanities: Dr ENRIQUE ARTURO GROTE

UNIVERSIDAD NACIONAL DE ROSARIO

Córdoba 1814, 2000 Rosario
Telephone: (341) 480-2620
E-mail: admin@unr.edu.ar
Internet: www.unr.edu.ar
Founded 1968
State control
Academic year: April to November
Rector: Prof. DARIO MAIORANA
Vice-Rector: Lic. EDUARDO SEMINARA
Head of Administration: Dr CARLOS A. DULONG
Number of teachers: 5,741
Number of students: 75,380

DEANS

Faculty of Agricultural Sciences: Ing. LILIANA MARGARITA
Faculty of Architecture, Planning and Design: Dr HÉCTOR DANTE FLORIANI
Faculty of Biochemistry and Pharmacy: Dra CLAUDIA ELIZABETH BALAGUE
Faculty of Dentistry: Dr HÉCTOR DARÍO MASIA
Faculty of Economic Sciences and Statistics: ALICIA INÉS CASTAGNA
Faculty of Exact Sciences, Engineering and Surveying: Ing. DAVID ESTEBAN ASTEGIANO
Faculty of Humanities and Arts: Prof. DARIO MAIORANA
Faculty of Law: Dr RICARDO ISIDORO
Faculty of Medical Sciences: Dra RAQUEL MADIS CHIARA
Faculty of Political Science and International Relations: Lic. FABIÁN ARIEL BACCIRE
Faculty of Psychology: Dr OVIDE JUAN MENIN
Faculty of Veterinary Sciences: Dr CLAUDIO JUAN GIUDICI

UNIVERSIDAD NACIONAL DE SALTA

Buenos Aires 177, 4400 Salta
Telephone: (387) 425-5440
Fax: (387) 425-5535
E-mail: rectora@unsa.edu.ar
Internet: www.unsa.edu.ar
Founded 1972
Academic year: March to December
Rector: Ing. Agr. STELLA MARIS PÉREZ DE BIANCHI
Vice-Rector: Dr CARLOS CADENA
General Secretary: (vacant)
Academic Secretary: Dr MARÍA CELIA ILVENTO

Administrative Secretary: CPN Sergio Enrique Villalba

Library of 57,633 vols, 42,300 periodicals
Number of teachers: 1,390
Number of students: 22,840

DEANS

Faculty of Economics, Juridical and Social Sciences: CPN Victor Hugo Claros
Faculty of Engineering: Ing. Jorge Félix Almazán
Faculty of Exact Sciences: Ing. Norberto Alejandro Bonini
Faculty of Health Sciences: Lic. Nieve Ubaldina Chavez
Faculty of Humanities: Lic. Flor de Maria del Valle Rionda
Faculty of Natural Sciences: Ing. Guillermo Andres Baudino

ATTACHED INSTITUTE

Consejo de Investigación (Research Council): Pres. Ing. Edgardo Ling Sham.

UNIVERSIDAD NACIONAL DE SAN JUAN

Mitre 396 (E), J5402CWH San Juan

Telephone: (264) 429-5000
E-mail: rector@unsj.edu.ar
Internet: www.unsj.edu.ar

Founded 1973
State control
Academic year: April to March

Rector: Dr Ing. Benjamín Rafael Kuchen
Vice-Rector: Mag. Nelly María Filippa
Admin. and Financial Secretary: Lic. Alejandro Larrea
Librarian: Raúl I. Lozada

Number of teachers: 2,001
Number of students: 21,110

DEANS

Faculty of Architecture, Town Planning and Design: Arq. Romeo Bernabé Platero
Faculty of Engineering: Ing. Roberto Romualdo Gomez Guirado
Faculty of Exact, Physical and Natural Sciences: Ing. Jesús Abelardo Robles
Faculty of Humanities, Philosophy and Arts: Prof. Zulma Lucía Corzo
Faculty of Social Sciences: Lic. Luis Francisco Meritello

UNIVERSIDAD NACIONAL DE SAN LUIS

Ejército de los Andes 950, D5700HHW San Luis

Telephone: (2652) 42-4027
Fax: (2652) 43-0224
Internet: www.unsl.edu.ar

Founded 1974
Academic year: March to December

Rector: Dr José Luis Riccardo
Vice-Rector: Lic. Nelly María Mainero
Librarian: Miguel A. Lucero

Number of teachers: 255
Number of students: 13,893

DEANS

Faculty of Chemistry, Biochemistry and Pharmacy: Dr Roberto Olsina
Faculty of Education: Lic. Nilda E. Picco de Barbeito
Faculty of Engineering and Business Administration (25 de Mayo 374, 5736 Villa Mercedes, San Luis): Ing. Raúl A. Merino
Faculty of Physical, Mathematical and Natural Sciences: Dr Julio C. Benegas

UNIVERSIDAD NACIONAL DE SANTIAGO DEL ESTERO

Avda Belgrano (s) 1912, 4200 Santiago del Estero

Telephone: (385) 450-9500
Fax: (385) 422-2595
E-mail: info@unse.edu.ar
Internet: www.unse.edu.ar

Founded 1973
Academic year: February to December

Rector: Geol. Arnaldo Sergio Tenchini
Vice-Rector: Luis Paradelo
Gen. Sec.: Dra Leonarda Teresa Ross
Librarian: Jorge Lujan Gerez

Library of 20,000 vols
Number of teachers: 848
Number of students: 11,659

Publications: *Cuadernos de la UNSE*, *Revista de Ciencia y Técnica* (1 a year), *Revista 'Quebracho'* (forestry, 1 a year), *Revista 'Unase'* (6 a year)

DEANS

Faculty of Agriculture and Agricultural Industry: Ing. José M. Salgado
Faculty of Forestry: Ing. Victorio Marjot
Faculty of Humanities: Santiago Angel Druetta
Faculty of Science and Technology: Ing. Carlos Alberto Bonetti

UNIVERSIDAD NACIONAL DEL SUR

Avda Colón 80, B8000FTN Bahía Blanca

Telephone: (291) 459-5015
Fax: (291) 459-5016
E-mail: rector@uns.edu.ar
Internet: www.uns.edu.ar

Founded 1956
Academic year: February to December

Rector: Dr Guillermo Héctor Crapiste
Vice-Rector: Dr María del Carmen Vaquero
Gen.-Sec. (Academic): Dra Marcelo Armando Villar
Gen.-Sec. (Culture and University Extension): Lic. Claudia Patricia Legnini
Gen.-Sec. (Institutional Relations and Planning): Dr Osvaldo Enrique Agamennoni
Gen.-Sec. (Scientific and Technological): Dr Alfredo Juan
Gen.-Sec. (Student Affairs): Lic. Claudia Legnini
Gen.-Sec. (Technical-Administrative): Lic. Juan Carlos Schefer
Gen.-Sec. (Univ. Superior Council): Abog. Diego Duprat

Library: see Libraries
Number of teachers: 2,069
Number of students: 22,571

Publications: *Capacitando en Calidad* (3 a year), *Escritos Contables* (2 a year), *Latin American Applied Research* (4 a year), *Reflexiones* (economics), *Revista Diálogos* (4 a year), *Revista Estudios Económicos* (1 a year), *Revista Universitaria de Geografía* (1 a year)

DIRECTORS

Department of Agriculture: Dr Mario Ricardo Sabbatini
Department of Biology, Biochemistry and Pharmacy: Mag. Marta Aveldano
Department of Business Administration: Regina del Carmen Durán
Department of Chemical Engineering: Dr Verónica Bucalá
Department of Chemistry: Dr María Susana Rodriguez
Department of Computing Engineering Sciences: Dr Rafael García
Department of Economics: Mag. Andrea Barbero

Department of Electrical Engineering: Dr Pedro Donate
Department of Engineering: Dr Carlos Rossit
Department of Geography: Lic. Silvia Grippo
Department of Geology: Dr Graciela Raquel Mas
Department of Humanities: Lic. Adriana Claudia Rodriguez
Department of Law: Abog. Andrés Bouzat
Department of Mathematics: Dr Liliana Castro
Department of Physics: Dr Walter Rubén Cravero

ATTACHED RESEARCH INSTITUTES

Centro de Recursos Naturales Renovables de la Zona Semiárida (CERZOS): Altos del Barrio Palihue, 8000 Bahía Blanca; tel. (291) 486-1127; Dir Dr Néstor Curvetto.
Centro Regional de Investigaciones Básicas y Aplicadas Bahía Blanca (CRIBABB): Camino La Carrindanga Km 7, 8000 Bahía Blanca; tel. (291) 486-1666; Dir Ing. Martín Urbicain.
Instituto Argentino de Oceanografía (IADO): Camino La Carrindanga Km 7, 8000 Bahía Blanca; tel. (291) 486-1112; run in conjunction with CONICET; Dir Dra María Cimtia Píccolo.
Instituto de Investigaciones Bioquímicas (INIBIBB): Camino La Carrindanga Km 7, 8000 Bahía Blanca; tel. (291) 486-1201; Dir Dr Francisco José Barrantes.
Instituto de Matemática Bahía Blanca (INMABB): Avda Alem 1253, 8000 Bahía Blanca; tel. (291) 459-5116; Vice-Dir Mag. Aurora Germani.
Planta Piloto de Ingeniería Química (PLAPIQUI): Camino La Carrindanga Km 7, 8000 Bahía Blanca; tel. (291) 486-1700; Dir Dr Enrique Marcelo Vallés.

UNIVERSIDAD NACIONAL DE TRES DE FEBRERO

Avda San Martín 2921, 1678 Caseros, Buenos Aires

Telephone: (11) 4759-9810
Fax: (11) 4759-9810
E-mail: info@untref.edu.ar
Internet: www.untref.edu.ar

Founded 1995
State control
Academic year: March to December

Rector: Lic. Aníbal Y. Jozami
Vice-Rector: Lic. Martín Kaufmann
Sec. (Academic): Ing. Carlos Mundt
Sec. (Research and Cooperation): Dr Félix Peña

Number of students: 4,723

DIRECTORS

Administration and Economics: Dr Martín Gras
Art and Culture: Lic. Fermín Fèvre
Health Sciences and Social Security: Dr Carlos Torres
Mathematics, Statistics and Methodology: Lic. Ernesto Rosa
Social Sciences: Dr César Lorenzano

UNIVERSIDAD NACIONAL DE TUCUMÁN

Ayacucho 491, 4000 San Miguel de Tucumán

Telephone: (381) 424-7762
Fax: (381) 424-8654
E-mail: postmaster@unt.edu.ar
Internet: www.unt.edu.ar

Founded 1914
Language of instruction: Spanish
Academic year: April to December

Rector: JUAN ALBERTO CERISOLA
Vice-Rector: Psic. MARÍA LUISA ROSSI DE HERNÁNDEZ
Gen.-Sec.: JOSÉ HUGO SAAB
Sec. (Academic Affairs): Dra MARTA PESA
Sec. (Admin.): Ing. JUAN CARLOS REIMUNDÍN
Sec. (Planning, Works and Services): MÓNICA INÉS DE LABASTIDA
Sec. (Postgraduate Affairs): Dr SUSANA MAIDANA
Sec. (Science and Technology): Dr DANIEL ENRIQUE CAMPI
Sec. (Student Welfare): Lic. RAMIRO MORENO
Sec. (Univ. Extension): Psic. MANUEL RAÚL ANDUJAR
Dir of International Relations: Dr RAMIRO ALBARRACÍN
Library: see Libraries and Archives
Number of teachers: 3,967
Number of students: 63,291

DEANS

Faculty of Agriculture and Animal Husbandry: Dr CARLOS HUGO BELLONE
Faculty of Architecture and Town Planning: Dr PABLO HOLGADO
Faculty of Biochemistry, Chemistry and Pharmacy: Dr ALICIA BARDÓN
Faculty of Dentistry: Dr GUILLERMO RAIDEN LAZCANO
Faculty of Economics: JUAN ALBERTO CERISOLA
Faculty of Exact Sciences and Technology: Ing. MARIO DONZELLI
Faculty of Fine Arts: Arq. MARCOS FIGUEROA
Faculty of Law and Social Sciences: Prof. PEDRO MARCOS ROUGES
Faculty of Medicine: Dr HORACIO DEZA
Faculty of Natural Sciences and Miguel Lillo Institute: Dr FERNANDO PRADO
Faculty of Philosophy and Letters: Dr ELENA ROJAS
Faculty of Psychology: Prof. MARIA LUISA ROSSI DE HERNANDEZ

UNIVERSIDAD NACIONAL DE VILLA MARÍA

Entre Ríos 1425, 5900 Villa María, Córdoba
Telephone: (353) 453-9100
Fax: (353) 453-9111
E-mail: comunica@unvm.edu.ar
Internet: www.unvm.edu.ar
Founded 1995
State control
Academic year: March to November (2 semesters)
Rector: MARTÍN RODRIGO GILL
Vice-Rector: MARIA CECILIA ANA CONCI
Sec.-Gen.: Abog. GERMÁN CARIGNANO
Sec. (Academic): Dr LUISA MARGARITA SCHWEIZER
Sec. (Finance): PABLO CÉSAR PAGOLA
Sec. (Welfare): Abog. LUIS ALBERTO NEGRETTI
Number of students: 3,000

DIRECTORS

Institute of Basic and Applied Sciences: Cr CARLOS OMAR DOMÍNGUEZ
Institute of Human Sciences: Dr CARLOS DANIEL LASA
Institute of Social Sciences: Lic. DANTE LA ROCCA MARTÍN
Dr Antonino Sobral University Centre: Lic. SILVIA MARÍA PAREDES
University Centre of Mediterranean Studies: Ing. JORGE LUIS FERRERO

UNIVERSIDAD TECNOLÓGICA NACIONAL

Sarmiento 440, C1041AAJ Buenos Aires
Telephone: (11) 5371-5600
Internet: www.utn.edu.ar

Founded 1959
Academic year: April to November
Rector: Ing. HECTOR C. BROTTO
Vice-Rector: Ing. CARLOS E. FANTINI
Academic Sec.: Ing. CIRIO MURAD
Sec. for Finance: Ing. CARLOS RAPP
Sec. for Institutional Relations: Prof. CARLOS RÍOS
Sec. for Student Affairs: Ing. RUBÉN SORO MARTÍNEZ
Sec. for Technological Research: Ing. JORGE FERRANTES
Sec. for University Extension: Ing. DANIEL FERRADAS
Number of teachers: 16,185
Number of students: 70,087
Publication: *Boletín Informativo.*

REGIONAL FACULTIES

Avellaneda: Ing. Marconi 775, 1870 Avellaneda, Buenos Aires; mechanical, electrical and electronic engineering; Dean Ing. HÉCTOR R. GONZÁLEZ.

Bahía Blanca: 11 de Abril 461, 8000 Bahía Blanca, Buenos Aires; construction, electrical and mechanical engineering; Dean Ing. VICENTE EGIDI.

Buenos Aires: Medrano 951, 1179 Buenos Aires; textile, chemical, metallurgical, electronic, construction, electrical and mechanical systems analysis engineering; Dean Arq. LUIS A. DE MARCO.

Concepción del Uruguay: Ing. Pereyra 676, 3260 Concepción del Uruguay, Entre Ríos; electromechanical and construction engineering; Dean Ing. JUAN CARLOS PITER.

Córdoba: Uladíslao Frías s/n, 5000 Córdoba; chemical, metallurgical, mechanical, electronic and electrical engineering; Dean Ing. RUBÉN SORO MARTÍNEZ.

Delta: San Martín 1171, 2804 Campana, Buenos Aires; electrical, mechanical and chemical engineering; Dean Ing. GUSTAVO BAUER.

General Pacheco: Avda Irigoyen 2878, 1617 General Pacheco, Buenos Aires; mechanical engineering; Dean Ing. EUGENIO B. RICCIOLINI.

Haedo: París 532, 1707 Haedo, Buenos Aires; aeronautical engineering, electronics, mechanical engineering; Dean Ing. ELIO BIAGINI.

La Plata: Calle 60 esq. 124, 1900 La Plata, Buenos Aires; chemical, mechanical, electrical and construction engineering; Dean Ing. CARLOS FANTINI.

Mendoza: Rodríguez 273, 5500 Mendoza; construction, electromechanical, chemical, electronic engineering, systems analysis; Dean Ing. JULIO CÉSAR CLETO COBOS.

Paraná: Almafuerte 1033, 3100 Paraná, Entre Ríos; electromechanical and construction engineering; Dean Ing. RAÚL E. ARROYO.

Rafaela: Blvd Roca y Artigas, 2300 Rafaela, Santa Fe; electromechanical and construction engineering; Dean Ing. OSCAR DAVID.

Resistencia: French 414, 3500 Resistencia, Chaco; electromechanical engineering, systems analysis; Dean Ing. SEBASTIÁN VICENTE MARTÍN.

Río Grande: Belgrano 777, 9420 Río Grande, Tierra del Fuego; electronic and industrial engineering; Dean Ing. MARIO FERREIRA.

Rosario: Estanislao Zeballos 1341, 2000 Rosario, Santa Fe; electrical, mechanical, construction, chemical engineering and systems analysis; Dean Ing. DANIEL OSCAR BADÍA.

San Francisco: Avda Gral. Savio 501, 2400 San Francisco, Córdoba; electromechanical engineering, electronics, information technology; Dean Ing. RAÚL C. ALBERTO.

San Nicolás: Colón 332, 2900 San Nicolás, Buenos Aires; electromechanical and metallurgical engineering; Dean Ing. NEORÉN P. FRANCO.

San Rafaél: Comandante Salas 370, 5600 San Rafaél, Mendoza; construction, electromechanical, chemical and civil engineering; Dean Ing. HORACIO P. PESSANO.

Santa Fe: Lavaise 610, 3000 Santa Fe; construction, electrical and mechanical engineering and systems analysis; Dean Ing. RICARDO O. SCHOLTUS.

Tucumán: Rivadavia 1050, 4000 San Miguel de Tucumán; construction, mechanical and civil engineering, information technology; Dean Ing. HUGO E. CELLERINO.

Villa María: Avda Universidad 450, Barrio Bello Horizonte, 5900 Villa María, Córdoba; mechanical and chemical engineering; Dean Ing. CARLOS R. RAPP.

ACADEMIC UNITS

Concordia: Salta 277, 3200 Concordia, Entre Ríos; construction and electromechanical engineering; Dir Ing. JOSÉ BOURREN.

Confluencia: Juan Manuel de Rosas y Juan Soufal, 8318 Plaza Huincul, Neuquén; electronic and chemical engineering; Dir Ing. SUSANA L. TARGHETTA DUR.

La Rioja: Facundo Quiroga y Beccar Varela, 5330 La Rioja; electromechanical engineering; Dir Dr MAURICIO KEJNER.

Rawson: Mitre 764, 9100 Rawson, Chubut; electromechanical and industrial engineering; Dir Ing. ERNESTO A. PASCUALICH.

Reconquista: Freyre 980, 3560 Reconquista, Santa Fe; electromechanical engineering; Dir Ing. OSVALDO DEL VALLE FATALA.

Río Gallegos: Maipú 53, 9400 Río Gallegos, Santa Cruz; electromechanical and industrial engineering; Dir Lic. SERGIO RAÚL RAGGI.

Trenque Lauquen: Villegas y Pereyra Rosas, 6400 Trenque Lauquen, Buenos Aires; electromechanical and construction engineering; Dir Ing. GUILLERMO A. GIL.

Venado Tuerto: Castelli 501, 2600 Venado Tuerto, Santa Fe; electromechanical and construction engineering; Dir Ing. ALFREDO ANÍBAL GUILLAUMET.

Private Universities

UNIVERSIDAD DEL ACONCAGUA

Catamarca 147, 5500 Mendoza
Telephone: (261) 520-1600
Fax: (261) 520-1650
E-mail: informes@uda.edu.ar
Internet: www.uda.edu.ar
Founded 1965
Academic year: April to October
Rector: Prof. Dr OSVALDO S. CABALLERO
Secretary-General: OSCAR DAVID CERUTTI
Librarian: HAYDEE TORRES BOUSOÑO
Number of teachers: 451
Number of students: 4,726

DEANS

Faculty of Economics and Commerce: Dr ROLANDO GALLI REY
Faculty of Phono-audiology: Dr GUSTAVO MAURICIO
Faculty of Psychology: Lic. HUGO LUPIAÑEZ
Faculty of Social Sciences and Administration: Dr JUAN FARRES CAVAGNARO

UNIVERSIDAD ARGENTINA DE LA EMPRESA
(Argentine University of Administration Sciences)

Lima 717, C1073AAO Buenos Aires
Telephone: (11) 4372-5454
E-mail: contactcenter@uade.edu.ar
Internet: www.uade.edu.ar
Founded 1962
Academic year: March to December

Rector: Dr JORGE DEL ÁGUILA
Provost: Lic. ANA MARÍA MASS
Sec. for Student Affairs: ROBERTO PEDRAZA
Librarian: RODOLFO LÖHE

Library of 50,000 vols, 865 periodicals
Number of teachers: 750
Number of students: 15,581
Publication: @ *UADE* (12 a year)

DEANS

School of Communication and Design: Dr OLGA CLAUDIA CORTEZ
School of Economics: Dr RICARDO FELIPE SMURRA
School of Engineering and Exact Sciences: Dr RICARDO OROSCO
School of Legal and Social Sciences: Dr MARIO SERRAFERO

UNIVERSIDAD ARGENTINA 'JOHN F. KENNEDY'

Calle Bartolomé Mitre 1411, 1037 Buenos Aires
Telephone: (11) 4476-4338
Fax: (11) 4476-2271
E-mail: info@kennedy.edu.ar
Internet: www.kennedy.edu.ar
Founded 1961

Rector: Dra MARÍA ELISA HERREN DE DAVID
Vice-Rector: Dr OSCAR ANTONIO CÁMPOLI

Library of 50,000 vols
Number of teachers: 1,800
Number of students: 17,417

UNIVERSIDAD DE BELGRANO

Zabala 1837, 1426 Buenos Aires
Telephone: (11) 4788-5400
Fax: (11) 4576-3912
E-mail: ingresos@ub.edu.ar
Internet: www.ub.edu.ar
Founded 1964
Language of instruction: Spanish
Private control
Academic year: March to November

Rector: Dr AVELINO JOSÉ PORTO
Vice-Rector for Academic Affairs: Prof. BRIGANTE NILDA
Vice-Rector for Institutional Affairs: Prof. ALDO PÉREZ
Vice-Rector for Legal and Technical Admin.: Dr EUSTAQUIO CASTRO
Librarian: MERCEDES PATALANO

Library of 70,043 vols, 2,500 periodicals
Number of teachers: 1,097
Number of students: 10,441
Publications: *Académicos* (12 a year), *Post-cátedra* (4 a year), *UB News* (52 a year)

DEANS

Faculty of Agriculture: Ing. CARLOS MENDEZ ACOSTA
Faculty of Architecture and Urban Planning: Arq. MÓNICA FERNÁNDEZ
Faculty of Distance Learning: Dr CLARA BONFILL
Faculty of Economics: Dr PATRICIA BONATTI
Graduate School of Economics and International Business: Dr CARLOS STEIGER
Faculty of Engineering and Information Technology: Ing. ALBERTO GUERCI

Faculty of Graduate Studies: Dr ANDRÉS FONTANA
Department of Graduate Studies and Continuing Education: Dr CARLOS STEIGER
Faculty of Health Sciences: Dr HERNÁN JAVIER ALDANA MARCOS
Faculty of Humanities: Dr SUSANA SEIDMANN
Faculty of Information Technology: Ing. JOHN R. LESTANI
Faculty of Languages and Foreign Studies: Prof. RAQUEL ALBORNOZ
Faculty of Law and Social Sciences: Dr DINO BELLORIO CLABOT
Faculty of Natural and Exact Sciences: Dr HERNÁN JAVIER ALDANA MARCOS

UNIVERSIDAD CAECE

Avda de Mayo 866, 1084 Buenos Aires
Telephone: (11) 5217-7878 ext 286
Fax: (11) 5217-7887
E-mail: informes@caece.edu.ar
Internet: www.caece.edu.ar
Founded 1967
Private control

Rector: Prof. JORGE E. BOSCH
Gen. Vice-Rector: Prof. HENRI BOSCH
Academic Vice-Rector: ROBERTO P. J. HERNÁNDEZ
Chief Admin. Officer: OLGA VILLAVERDE
Librarian: SUSANA BUONO

Library of 9,000 vols
Number of teachers: 300
Number of students: 2,522
Publication: *Elementos de Matemática.*

PONTIFICIA UNIVERSIDAD CATÓLICA ARGENTINA 'SANTA MARÍA DE LOS BUENOS AIRES'

Alicia Moreau de Justo 1300, C1107AAZ Buenos Aires
Telephone: (11) 4349-0200
Fax: (11) 4349-0246
E-mail: info@uca.com.ar
Internet: www.uca.edu.ar
Founded 1958
Academic year: March to November

Rector: Monseñor Dr ALFREDO HORACIO ZECCA
Vice-Rector: Lic. ERNESTO JOSÉ PARSELIS
Academic Sec.: Dr JORGE NICOLÁS LAFFERRIÈRE
Dir of International Relations: Dr CARLOS EZCURRA

Number of teachers: 3,200
Number of students: 16,800
Publications: *Boletín de Ciencias Económicas* (6 a year), *Colección* (political science, 2 a year), *Letras* (Argentinian and comparative literature, 2 a year), *Prudentia Juris* (2 a year), *Sapientia* (2 a year), *Teología* (2 a year), *Valores* (economics and social ethics, 3 a year)

DEANS

Faculty of Agriculture: Dr CARLOS PACÍFICO
Faculty of Arts and Music: GUILLERMO SCARABINO
Faculty of Canon Law: Lic. VICTOR PINTO
Faculty of Chemistry and Engineering (Mendoza): Lic. LUIS SCOZZINA
Faculty of Economics (Mendoza): Ing. ALFREDO DOMINGO VIOTTI
Faculty of Economic and Social Sciences: Dr LUDOVICO VIDELA
Faculty of Economic Sciences (Rosario): Cr RICARDO PARÍS
Faculty of Health Sciences: Dr CARLOS ALVAREZ
Faculty of Humanities and Education (Mendoza): Prof. ADRIANA MENÉNDEZ DE ZUMER

Faculty of Humanities 'Teresa de Avila' (Paraná): Dr MIGUEL ANGEL NESA
Faculty of Law and Political Sciences: Dr EDUARDO VENTURA
Faculty of Law and Social Sciences (Rosario): Dr GUSTAVO GUILLERMO LO CELSO
Faculty of Philosophy and Letters: Dr HÉCTOR DELBOSCO
Faculty of Physical Sciences, Mathematics and Engineering: Ing. HORACIO CARLOS REGGINI
Faculty of Theology: Dr CARLOS M. GALLI

DIRECTORS

Institute of Bioethics: Dr ALBERTO BOCHATEY
Institute of Social Communication, Journalism and Publicity: Lic. ALICIA PERESON
Institute of Spirituality and Pastoral Action: GUSTAVO LUIS BOQUIN
Institute of University Extension: Dr ALFREDO ZECCA

UNIVERSIDAD CATÓLICA DE CÓRDOBA

Obispo Trejo 323, 5000 Córdoba
Telephone: (351) 421-9000
Fax: (351) 493-8002
E-mail: info@uccor.edu.ar
Internet: www.ucc.edu.ar
Founded 1956
Academic year: February to December

Chancellor: Mgr CARLOS JOSÉ ÑAÑEZ (Archbishop of Córdoba)
Vice-Chancellor: R. P. ALVARO RESTREPO
Rector: Lic. RAFAEL VELASCO
Vice-Rector (Academic): Dr CARLOS F. SCHICKENDANTZ
Vice-Rector (Economy): Dr JORGE O. PÉREZ
Vice-Rector (Univ. Community): DANIELA GARGANTINI
Academic Sec.: Dr JUAN CARLOS BOGGIO
Dir, Library System: Mag. SANDRA GISELA MARTÍN

Library: see Libraries and Archives
Number of teachers: 1,305
Number of students: 7,156

DEANS

Faculty of Agriculture: Dr JUAN CARLOS BOGGIO
Faculty of Architecture: Arq. ESTEBAN TRISTÁN REMIRO BONDONE
Faculty of Chemical Sciences: Bioq. PAULA MARÍA COOKE
Faculty of Economics and Administration: Mag. CARLOS ORLANDO PÉREZ
Faculty of Education: Dr ENRIQUE NÉSTOR BAMBOZZI
Faculty of Engineering: Ing. RAÚL JUAN VACA NARVAJA
Faculty of Law and Social Sciences: Abog. JOSÉ NARCISO REY NORES
Faculty of Medicine: Mag. CARLOS EMILIO GATTI
Faculty of Philosophy and Humanities: Dr CARLOS FEDERICO SCHICKENDANTZ
Faculty of Political Sciences and International Relations: Lic. MARIO GERMÁN RIORDA
Institute of Administrative Sciences: ADOLFO MARTÍN GUSTAVO BERTOA

UNIVERSIDAD CATÓLICA DE CUYO

Avda Ignacio de la Roza 1516, Rivadavia, 5400 San Juan
Telephone: (264) 429-2300
Fax: (264) 429-2310
E-mail: rectorado@uccuyo.edu.ar
Internet: www.uccuyo.edu.ar
Founded 1953

Rector: Dr MARÍA ISABEL LARRAURI
Vice-Rector: Dr ALFONSO OSVALDO MARTÍN

Sec.-Gen. (Academic): Arq. CECILIA TRINCADO DE MURÚA
Dir of Library: EUGENIA CARRASCOSA DE YUNES
Library of 25,000 vols
Number of teachers: 408
Number of students: 3,710
Publications: *La Verdad, Revista Cuadernos*

DEANS

Faculty of Economics and Business: C. P. ALEJANDRO LARGACHA
Faculty of Education: LUCIA GHILARDI DE CARRIZO
Faculty of Food Sciences: CLAUDIO MARCELO LARREA
Faculty of Law and Social Sciences: Dr GILBERTO RIVEROS
Faculty of Medical Sciences: Dr MERCEDES GÓMEZ DE HERRERA
Faculty of Philosophy and Humanities: (vacant)

UNIVERSIDAD CATÓLICA DE LA PLATA

Calle 13 No. 1227, 1900 La Plata
Telephone: (221) 422-7100
Internet: www.ucalp.edu.ar
Founded 1964
Academic year: March to November
Grand Chancellor: Mgr HÉCTOR RUBÉN AGUER
Rector: RAFAEL BREIDE OBEID
Academic Gen.-Sec.: MIGUEL ÁNGEL SARNI
Librarian: GLADYS R. MARDUEL
Number of teachers: 635
Number of students: 3,741
Publication: *Revista*

DEANS

Faculty of Applied Mathematics: Ing. EDUARDO FULCO
Faculty of Architecture: Arq. CARLOS ALBERTO RUOTOLO
Faculty of Economics: Cr MARIO LUIS SZYCHOWSKI
Faculty of Education: Prof. NANCY DI PIERO DE WARR
Faculty of Law: Dr JORGE O. PERRINO
Faculty of Social Sciences: Dr JORGE O. PERRINO
Department of Theology: Pbro Ing. RUBEN A. GARINO (Dir)

UNIVERSIDAD CATÓLICA DE SALTA

Ciudad Universitaria, Campo Castañares, Casilla 18, 4400 Salta
Telephone: (387) 423-3270
E-mail: rectorado@ucasal.net
Internet: www.ucasal.net
Founded 1963
Academic year: March to December
Chancellor: Mgr MARIO ANTONIO CARGNELLO
Rector: Dr ALFREDO GUSTAVO PUIG
Academic Vice-Rector: Prof. GERARDO VIDES ALMONACID
Admin. Vice-Rector: Ing. MANUEL CORNEJO TORINO
Sec.-Gen.: Dr LILIAN CONSTANZA DIEDRICH DE DUBA
Librarian: WARTHA ANSALDI DE VINANTE
Library of 42,000 vols
Number of teachers: 750
Number of students: 19,563

DEANS

Faculty of Architecture and Urban Planning: Arq. JUAN PEDRO COLOMBO SPERONI
Faculty of Economics and Administration: Lic. ROBERTO CADAR

Faculty of Engineering and Informatics: Ing. ERNESTO CLAUDIO MONDADA
Faculty of Law: Dr ARMANDO ISASMENDI
School of Physical Education: Lic. DOLORES MEDINA BOUQUET
School of Social Service: Lic. SONIA ZAMORA
School of Tourism: Lic. CARLOS FRANCISCO SÁNCHEZ

UNIVERSIDAD CATÓLICA DE SANTA FE

Echagüe 7151, S3004JBS Santa Fe
Telephone: (342) 460-3030
Fax: (342) 460-3030
E-mail: postmaster@ucsfre.edu.ar
Internet: www.ucsf.edu.ar
Founded 1957
Academic year: February to December
Grand Chancellor: Mgr EDGARDO GABRIEL STORNI
Rector: Arq. JOSÉ MARÍA PASSEGGI
Vice-Rector for Academic Affairs: Lic. TOMÁS GUTIERREZ
Vice-Rector for Training: Lic. MARCELO MATEO
Sec.-Gen.: Dra MARTA D. V. OLMOS
Library Dir: Dr JUAN CARLOS P. BALLESTEROS
Number of teachers: 480
Number of students: 3,864

DEANS

Faculty of Architecture: Arq. RICARDO MARÍA ROCHETTI
Faculty of Economic Sciences: LUIS ELIO BONINO
Faculty of Education: Dr JUAN CARLOS PABLO BALLESTEROS
Faculty of Engineering, Geoecology and the Environment: Lic. TOMÁS GUTIERREZ
Faculty of Law: Dr RICARDO ANDRÉS VILLA
Faculty of Philosophy: Prof. DANIEL VASCHETTO (acting)
Faculty of Social Communication: Lic. CARLOS TEALDI

UNIVERSIDAD CATÓLICA DE SANTIAGO DEL ESTERO

Avda Alsina y Dalmacio Vélez Sársfield, 4200 Santiago del Estero
Telephone: (385) 421-1777
Fax: (385) 421-1777
E-mail: postmaster@ucse.edu.ar
Internet: www.ucse.edu.ar
Founded 1960
Language of instruction: Spanish
Academic year: April to November
Grand Chancellor: Mgr GERARDO EUSEBIO SUELDO
Rector: Ing. JORGE LUIS FEIJÓO
Admin. Dir: Lic. MARÍA ÉLIDA CERRO DE ÁBALOS
Librarian: Prof. Dr MATIAS ZUZEC
Library of 19,000 vols
Number of teachers: 450
Number of students: 4,000
Publication: *Nuevas Propuestas*

DEANS

Faculty of Applied Mathematics: Ing. OCTAVIO JOSÉ MÉDICI
Faculty of Economics: Lic. VÍCTOR MANUEL FEIJÓO
Faculty of Education: Hna Lic. LILIANA BADALONI
Faculty of Politics, Social Sciences and Law: Abogada MARIA TERESA TENTI DE VOLTA

PROFESSORS

Faculty of Applied Mathematics:
CORONEL, J. C., Introduction to Mathematical Analysis

KORSTANJE, A. P., Operational Research
MARTÍNEZ, E., Systems Evaluation
PASTORINO, M. I., Numerical Methods
TRAJTENBERG, J. O., Introduction to Data Processing
Faculty of Economics:
ALEGRE, J. C., Bankruptcy Law
BRAVO, W., Auditing
CHAYA, H. N., Administration and Personnel
CORONEL, J. C., Budgeting
FERRERO DE AZAR, A. M., Company Law
MARIGLIANO, M., Business Organization
MARTELEUR, R., Introduction to Economics
MORELLINI, P. A., Accounting, Budget Sheet Analysis
OSTENGO, H., Accounting
PASTORINO, M. I., Statistics
TERUEL, R., General Administration
Faculty of Education:
CASTIGLIONE, J. C., Theology
GELID, T., General Sociology and Sociology of Education
MUHN, G., Vocational Orientation
RIERA DE LUCENA, E., Philosophical Anthropology, Basic Epistemology
SGOIFO, M. DEL V., Psychology
Faculty of Politics, Social Sciences and Law:
ALEGRE, J. C., Agricultural and Mining Law
ARGAÑARAZ ORGAZ, C., Administrative Law
ARGUELLO, L. R., Roman Law
ARNEDO, E., Private International Law
AUAD, A., Social Philosophy
BENEVOLE DE GAUNA, T., Legal Consultation
BONACINA, R. A., Introduction to Economics
BRIZUELA, N., General and Social Psychology
BRUNELLO DE ZURITA, A., Civil Law
CASTIGLIONE, J. C., Philosophy of Law
CERRO, F. E., Theory of the State
CHRISTENSEN, E., Finance and Financial Law
HARO DE SURIAN, E., Economic Geography
LEDESMA, A. E., Civil and Penal Procedural Law
NAVARRO, J. V., Penal Law
PAZ, G. M., Civil Law
PAZ, M. J., Commercial Law
RETAMOSA, J. R., History of Ideas and Political Institutions, History of the World, History of Argentina
RIGOURD, C., Public Law
RIMINI, J. C., Commercial Law
SALERA, J. B., Sociology
VICTORIA, M. A., Agricultural and Mining Law
ZURITA DE GONZÁLEZ, M., Civil Law

UNIVERSIDAD DE CONCEPCIÓN DEL URUGUAY

8 de Junio 522, E3260ANJ Concepción del Uruguay, Entre Ríos
Telephone: (3442) 42-5606
Fax: (3442) 42-7721
E-mail: info@ucu.edu.ar
Internet: www.ucu.edu.ar
Founded 1971
Private control
Academic year: February to December
Rector: Dr HÉCTOR CÉSAR SAURET
Vice-Rector: Dra GEORGINA VIERCI
Academic Sec.: CAROLINA THOMPSON
Chief Librarian: Prof. ROSA MURILLO DE ROUSSEAUX
Library of 4,300 vols
Number of teachers: 222
Number of students: 2,580
Publication: *Ucurrencias*

DEANS

Faculty of Agronomy: Ing. CARMEN BLÁZQUEZ
Faculty of Architecture: Arq. CRISTINA BONUS
Faculty of Communication Sciences and Education: Dr LUIS A. CERRUDO
Faculty of Economics: Cr MARCELO GRANILLO
Faculty of Judicial and Social Sciences: Dr FEDERICO LACAVA

UNIVERSIDAD DE LA MARINA MERCANTE
(University of the Merchant Navy)

Avda Rivadavia 2258, C1034ACO Buenos Aires

Telephone: (11) 4953-9000
Fax: (11) 4953-9000
E-mail: info@udemm.edu.ar
Internet: www.udemm.edu.ar

Founded 1974
Private control
Academic year: March to December

Pres.: Ing. GUSTAVO ZOPATTI
Rector: Dr NORBERTO E. FRAGA
Gen.-Sec.: Lic. MIRKO E. MAYER
Admin. Sec.: Dr DANTE STERRANTINO

Number of teachers: 283
Number of students: 2,164

DEANS

Faculty of Administration and Economics: Lic. SILVIA ISABEL GÓMEZ MEANA
Faculty of Engineering: Ing. VICENTE GIMÉNEZ
Faculty of Humanities: Lic. CLAUDIA ETKYN (acting)
Faculty of Law, Social Sciences and Communication: Lic. HECTOR NAREDO

UNIVERSIDAD DE MENDOZA

Avda Boulogne-sur-Mer 683, 5500 Mendoza

Telephone: (261) 420-2017
Fax: (261) 420-1100
E-mail: rectorado@um.edu.ar
Internet: www.um.edu.ar

Founded 1960
Language of instruction: Spanish
Academic year: March to November

Rector: Dr JUAN C. MENGHINI
Vice-Rectors: Dr Ing. SATURNINO LEGUIZAMÓN, Arq. RICARDO PEROTTI
Admin. Officer: ROSA CELESTE

Number of teachers: 785
Number of students: 6,249

Publications: *Idearium, Ideas, Revista*

DEANS

Faculty of Architecture and Town Planning: Arq. RICARDO BEKERMAN
Faculty of Engineering: Dr Ing. SALVADOR NAVARRÍA
Faculty of Health Sciences: Dr JUAN CARLOS BEHLER
Faculty of Law and Social Sciences: Dr EMILIO VÁZQUEZ VIERA

DIRECTORS

Centre of Higher Research: Dr JUAN C. MENGHINI
Department of Evaluation: Arq. CRISTINA INZIRILLO
Department of Scientific Research: Dr Ing. SATURNINO LEGUIZAMÓN
Department of Technology: Ing. DIEGO NAVARRO
Institute of Architectural Technology: Arq. RICARDO BEKERMAN
Institute of Architectural and Urban Culture: Arq. ELIANA BORMIDA
Institute of Design: Dr AURELIO ALVAREZ CAMPI
Institute of Energy: Ing. RUTH GRAVINA

Institute of Environmental, Urban and Regional Research: Arq. RAÚL AMPRIMO
Institute of Informatics: Arq. OSCAR GARCÍA VILA
Institute of Natural Sciences: Prof. RUTH LEITON
Institute of Practical Philosophy: Dr NOLBERTO ESPINOSA
Institute of Private Law: Dra CATALINA A. DERONCHIETTO
Institute of Public Law: (vacant)
Institute of Social Housing: Arq. ALFREDO MÉNDEZ
Institute of Telecommunications: Ing. JORGE MARTÍNEZ
Institute of Virtual Technology: Lic. DANIEL LILLO

UNIVERSIDAD DE MORÓN

Cabildo 134, B1708JPD Morón, Buenos Aires

Telephone: (11) 5627-2000
Fax: (11) 5627-4598
E-mail: postmaster@unimoron.edu.ar
Internet: www.unimoron.edu.ar

Founded 1960
Private control
Academic year: March to December

Rector: Dr HÉCTOR NORBERTO PORTO LEMMA
Sec.-Gen.: Dr JOSÉ MARIA BAÑOS
Sec. (Academic and Research): Dr EDUARDO NÉSTOR COZZA
Sec. (Admin.): Dr JORGE EDUARDO MARCOS
Library Dir: Dr GRACIELA SUSANA PUENTE

Library of 40,000 vols
Number of teachers: 2,000
Number of students: 15,140

Publication: *UM Saber* (24 a year)

DEANS AND DIRECTORS

Faculty of Agronomy and Food Sciences: Ing. Agr. ANTONIO ANGRISANI
Faculty of Architecture, Design, Art and Urban Planning: Arq. OSCAR ANIBAL BORRACHIA
Faculty of Computer Sciences, Communication Sciences and Special Technology: Ing. HUGO RENÉ PADOVANI
Faculty of Economic and Business Sciences: Dr JORGE RAÚL LEMOS
Faculty of Engineering: Dr Ing. EZEQUIEL PALLEJÁ
Faculty of Exact, Chemical and Natural Sciences: Dr AQUILES CARLOS FERRANTI
Faculty of Law, Political and Social Sciences: Dr HÉCTOR NORBERTO PORTO LEMMA
Faculty of Medicine: Dr DOMINGO SANTOS LIOTTA
Faculty of Philosophy, Education and Humanities: Dr ROBERTO MARIO PATERNO
Faculty of Sciences applied to Tourism and Population: Lic. ALEJANDRO GAVRIC
High School of Social Services: Lic. MARÍA CRISTINA DEVITA

UNIVERSIDAD DEL MUSEO SOCIAL ARGENTINO
(University of the Argentine Museum of Sociology)

Avda Corrientes 1723, C1042AAD Buenos Aires

Telephone: (11) 5530-7600
Fax: (11) 5530-7614
E-mail: informes@umsa.edu.ar
Internet: www.umsa.edu.ar

Founded 1912

Rector: Dr GUILLERMO E. GARBARINI ISLAS
Librarian: Lic. GABRIEL MEDINA ERNST
Number of students: 3,591

DEANS

Faculty of Human Recovery Sciences: Lic. ESTELA SALAZAR

Faculty of Information and Opinion Science: Lic. ADRIANA ADAMO
Faculty of Political, Juridical and Economic Sciences: Dr LUIS J. ZABALLA
Faculty of Social Services: Dr GUSTAVO PINARD
School of Economics: ELBA FONT DE MALUGANI
University School of Translation: Lic. ALICIA BERMOLEN
Institute of Political Sciences: Dra MARTA BIAGI
Institute of Professional Training: Lic. MARIA E. PELLANDA

UNIVERSIDAD DEL NORTE SANTO TOMÁS DE AQUINO

9 de Julio 165, T4000IHC San Miguel de Tucumán

Telephone: (381) 430-0698
Fax: (381) 422-4494
E-mail: info@unsta.edu.ar
Internet: www.unsta.edu.ar

Founded 1965
Academic year: March to November

Grand Chancellor: Fr JAVIER POSE
Rector: Dr LUIS RAÚL ALCALDE
Vice-Rector: Ing. RAFAEL ROBERTO CUNSULO
Gen.-Sec.: Ing. JUAN C. MUZZO
Acad. Sec.: Lic. JORGE ABATTE
Dir of the Library: LILIAN GARTNER

Number of teachers: 700
Number of students: 6,282

DEANS

Faculty of Economics and Administration: GUILLERMO JORGE DI LELLA
Faculty of Engineering: (vacant)
Faculty of Humanities: Lic. JUAN JOSE HERRERA
Faculty of Law and Political Sciences: Dra MARIA GILDA PEDICONE DE VALLS
Faculty of Philosophy: Fr JORGE SCAMPINI
Faculty of Psychology and Health Sciences: Dr BERNARDO CARLINO
School of Education: Profa ANA M. BARBADO DE FIORITO (Dir)
Department of Humanistic-Christian Training: Fr JOHN EMERY (Dir)

UNIVERSIDAD NOTARIAL ARGENTINA
(Argentine University for Lawyers)

Avda 51 No. 435, 1900 La Plata

Telephone: (221) 421-9283
Fax: (221) 421-0552
E-mail: uninotlp@universidadnotarial.edu.ar
Internet: www.universidadnotarial.edu.ar

Founded 1964
Academic year: March to November

Chancellor: Not. JORGE F. DUMON
Rector: NÉSTOR O. PÉREZ LOZANO
Vice-Rector: Dr CRISTINA NOEMÍ ARMELLA
General Director: Prof. ALICIA PALAIA
Librarian: Dra DORA C. TÁLICE DE SECO VILLALBA

Number of teachers: 150
Number of students: 2,300

Publication: *Cuadernos Notariales*.

UNIVERSIDAD DEL SALVADOR
(University of the Saviour)

Viamonte 1856, 1056 Buenos Aires

Telephone: (11) 4813-9630
E-mail: uds-secr@salvador.edu.ar
Internet: www.salvador.edu.ar

Founded 1956
Academic year: January to December

Rector: Lic. JUAN ALEJANDRO TOBIAS
Academic Vice-Rector: Lic. JAVIER ALONSO HIDALGO

Vice-Rector (Economics): Dr ENRIQUE A. BETTA
Vice-Rector (Religious Training): Lic. JUAN ALEJANDRO TOBIAS (acting)
Vice-Rector (Research and Devt): Dr FERNANDO LUCERO SCHMIDT
Sec.-Gen.: Prof. PABLO GABRIEL VARELA
Librarian: Lic. LAURA MARTINO
Library: see under Libraries and Archives
Number of teachers: 2,800
Number of students: 16,500
Publications: *Anales*, *Bulletin of Number Theory and Related Topics*, *Signos*

DEANS

Faculty of Administration: Ing. AQUILINO LÓPEZ DIEZ
Faculty of Economics: Dr SERGIO GARCÍA
Faculty of Educational Sciences and Social Communication: Dr GUSTAVO MARTÍNEZ PANDIANJ
Faculty of Law: Dr PRÁXEDES SAGASTA
Faculty of Medicine: Dr ADOLFO LIZARRAGA
Faculty of Philosophy, History and Arts: Dr JUAN CARLOS LUCERO SCHMIDT
Faculty of Psychology and Psychopedagogy: Lic. BERNARDO BÉGUET
Faculty of Science and Technology: Ing. MIGUEL GUERRERO
Faculty of Social Sciences: Lic. EDUARDO SUÁREZ

DIRECTORS

School of Oriental Studies: Prof. LUISA ROSELL
School of Theatre Arts: Prof. ALICE D. DE BEITÍA

National University-Level Institutions

INSTITUTO DE ENSEÑANZA SUPERIOR DEL EJÉRCITO (Institute of Higher Military Education)

Avda Cabildo 65, 1426 Buenos Aires
Telephone: (11) 4576-5648
E-mail: dieseext@iese.edu.ar
Internet: www.iese.edu.ar
Founded 1990
State control
Dir: Dr LUIS EDUARDO PIERRI
Vice-Rector: Col MIGUEL ANGEL PODESTÁ
Sec.-Gen.: Lt-Col Dr VICTORIO CÁNDIDO FONTANA
Sec. (Academic): Col Dr JULIO HORACIO BERGALLO
Sec. (Evaluation): Col Dr HECTOR EDUARDO GALLARDO
Sec. (Univ. Extension): Col Dr ALEJANDRO ALBERTO DIAZ BESSONE
Depts of Distance Learning, Information Technology and Modern Languages.

CONSTITUENT SCHOOLS

Colegio Militar de la Nación: Avda Matienzo y Ruta 201, 1684 El Palomar, Buenos Aires; tel. (11) 4751-8001; fax (11) 4751-0767; e-mail ingresocmn@ejercito.mil .ar; internet www.colegiomilitar.mil.ar; f. 1869.

Escuela Superior de Guerra: Avda Luis María Campos 480, 1426 Buenos Aires; tel. (11) 4576-5689; fax (11) 4576-5692; e-mail esg@iese.edu.ar; internet www .escuelasuperiordeguerra.iese.edu.ar; f. 1900; library of 30,000 vols, 44 periodicals; Dir Col RAÚL ALBERTO APARICIO; publ. *La Revista* (4 a Year).

Escuela Superior Técnica: Avda Cabildo 15, 1426 Buenos Aires, Capital Federal; tel. (11) 4576-5555; fax (11) 4576-5681; e-mail estextuniv@iese.edu.ar; internet www .ingenieriaest.iese.edu.ar; f. 1930; library of 30,000 vols, 100 periodicals; Dir Col JORGE GÓMEZ; publ. *Ingeniería Militar*.

INSTITUTO UNIVERSITARIO AERONÁUTICO

Avda Fuerza Aérea 6500, 5022 Córdoba
Telephone: (351) 568-8800
Fax: (351) 466-1562
E-mail: informes@iua.edu.ar
Internet: www.iua.edu.ar
Founded 1947; integrated into National University System 1971
State control
Language of instruction: Spanish
Academic year: February to December
Rector: Brig. Ing. HÉCTOR EDUARDO RÉ
Vice-Rector (Academic): Cmdr Ing. MIGUEL ANGEL LLABRES
Vice-Rector (Planning): Brig. Ing. ROBERTO ANÍBAL GÓMEZ
Sec.-Gen.: Ing. PEDRO EMILIO MURILLO
Library of 10,000 vols
Associated academic units: Escuela de Aviación Militar; Escuela Superior de Guerra Aérea; Instituto Nacional de Derecho Aeronáutico y Espacial; Escuela de Defensa Electrónica; Liceo Aeronáutico Militar; Escuela de Suboficiales de la Fuerza Aérea; Centro de Instrucción, Perfeccionamiento y Experimentación; Instituto de Formación Ezeiza; Instituto Nacional de Aviación Civil; Unidad de Educación a Distancia en el Exterior; Escuela de Ciencias de la Salud.

DEANS

Faculty of Administration: Brig. Ing. ROBERTO ANÍBAL GÓMEZ
Faculty of Engineering: Brig. Ing. FERNANDO ANÍBAL ÁLVAREZ

INSTITUTO UNIVERSITARIO DE LA POLICÍA FEDERAL ARGENTINA

Rosario 532, 1424 Buenos Aires, Capital Federal
Telephone: (11) 4901-9783
Fax: (11) 4901-9783
E-mail: academica@universidad-policial.edu .ar
Internet: www.universidad-policial.edu.ar
Founded 1974 as Academia Federal de Estudios Policiales; current name and status since 1995
State control
Academic year: March to December (two semesters)
Rector: Dr LUIS MARÍA DESIMONI
Vice-Rector: Lic. CARLOS DANIEL MUSSO
Sec. (Academic): Dr HUGO ALBERTO MÉNDEZ
Sec. (Admin.): Com. Gen. ANGEL JUAN ANTONIO RAMÍREZ
Library of 20,500 vols
Number of students: 3,200
Publication: *Editorial Policial*

DEANS

Faculty of Biomedical Sciences: Dr ENRIQUE LAFRENZ
Faculty of Criminal Sciences: Lic. NORBERTO ANTONIO SANCHEZ
Faculty of Law and Social Sciences: Dr HORACIO TOMAS ARACAMA
Faculty of Security Sciences: Gen. ROBERTO CÉSAR ROSSET

INSTITUTO UNIVERSITARIO DE SEGURIDAD MARÍTIMA

Avda Eduardo Madero 235, 1106 Buenos Aires, Capital Federal
Telephone: (11) 4314-2434
E-mail: arl@arnet.com.ar
Internet: www.prefecturanaval.edu.ar/iupna
Founded 2002
Rector: Prefecto Gen. OSVALDO DANIEL TOURN
Sec. (Academic): Lic. AMALIA INÉS VILLALUSTRE.

INSTITUTO UNIVERSITARIO NACIONAL DEL ARTE

Paraguay 786, 1057 Buenos Aires, Capital Federal
Telephone: (11) 4516-0992
Fax: (11) 4516-0992
Internet: www.iuna.edu.ar
Founded 1996
State control
Rector: Lic. RAÚL OSVALDO MONETA
Sec.-Gen.: Prof. ROBERTO DE ROSE
Publication: *Boletín*.

INSTITUTO UNIVERSITARIO NAVAL

Avda del Libertador 8209, 1429 Buenos Aires, Capital Federal
Telephone: (11) 4704-8200
Fax: (11) 4704-8261
E-mail: administra@inun.edu.ar
Internet: www.inun.edu.ar
Founded 1978 as Instituto Universitario de Estudios Navales y Martimes; current name and status 1991
Controlled by the Armada Argentina (Argentine Navy)
Rector: Ing. JULIO MARCELO PÉREZ
Sec. (Academic): Lic. JULIO E. GROSSO

DIRECTORS

School of Marine Sciences: DANIEL HINDRYCKX
School of Military Naval Studies: CARLOS LUIS MAZZONI
School of Nautical Science: ARMANDO GROSO
School of Navy Officer Studies: EDUARDO OSCAR GUELFO
School of Navy Warfare: PEDRO LUIS DE LA FUENTE

Provincial University

UNIVERSIDAD AUTÓNOMA DE ENTRE RÍOS

Avda Ramírez 1143, 3100 Paraná, Entre Ríos
Telephone: (343) 431-4284
Fax: (343) 420-7880
E-mail: rectorado@uader.edu.ar
Internet: www.uader.edu.ar
Independent control
Rector: Lic. Mag. GRACIELA MINGO DE BEVILACQUA
Sec. for Academic Affairs: Prof. SUSANA RIVAS
Sec. for Extension and Student Welfare: ANÍBAL SATTLER
Sec. for Science and Technology: FRANCISCO CACIK.

Colleges

Escuela Nacional de Bibliotecarios: Agüero 2502, 1425 Buenos Aires; tel. (11) 4808-6095; fax (11) 4863-8805; e-mail escuelabib@red.bibnal.edu.ar; internet www .bibnal.edu.ar/paginas/escuelabib.htm; f.

1956; 15 teachers; Rector Prof. José Edmundo Clemente.

Escuela Nacional de Educación Técnica 'Gral Ing. Enrique Mosconi': Calle Schreiber 892 Cutralco, 8318 Plaza Huincul, Neuquén; tel. (299) 46-3288; f. 1953; specializes in mechanical and petroleum engineering; 600 students; Dir Ing. Armando Paris.

Instituto Tecnológico de Buenos Aires: Avda Eduardo Madero 399, 1106 Buenos Aires; tel. (11) 4314-7778; fax (11) 4314-0270; e-mail postmaster@itba.edu.ar; internet www.itba.edu.ar; f. 1959; private; library: 16,010 books; 350 teachers; 2,010 students; Rector Almirante Dr Enrique E. Molina Pico; publs *Revista del Instituto*

Tecnológico de Buenos Aires, Boletín General, Acontecer.

Schools of Art and Music

Conservatorio Superior de Música 'Manuel de Falla': Gallo 238, 2º piso, Buenos Aires; tel. (11) 4865-9005; f. 1919; 3,000 mems; library: library of 8,000 scores and vols; Dir Augusto B. Rattenbach.

Escuela Nacional de Arte Dramático (National School of Drama): French 3614, 1425 Buenos Aires; tel. (11) 4804-7970; f. 1924; 300 students; library: 4,200 vols; Rector Carlos Albarenga.

Escuela Nacional de Bellas Artes 'Prilidiano Pueyrredón': Las Heras 1749, 1018 Buenos Aires; tel. (11) 442-0657; f. 1878; depts of painting, engraving and sculpture; library: 5,923 vols; 373 students; Dir Domingo Mazzone.

Escuela Nacional de Danzas: Esmeralda 285, 1035 Buenos Aires; tel. (11) 445-5478; Rector Prof. Gladys S. de Mutter.

Escuela Superior de Bellas Artes 'Ernesto de la Cárcova': Tristán Achaval Rodríguez 1701, 1107 Buenos Aires; tel. (11) 4361-5144; f. 1923; painting, sculpture, engraving and décors; museum of tracings; library: 4,500 vols; Rector Prof. Eduardo A. Audivert.

ARMENIA

The Higher Education System

The oldest university in Armenia is the Yerevan State University, which was founded in 1919. Most institutions of higher education were founded while Armenia was a full Union Republic of the Union of Soviet Socialist Republics (USSR). Armenia declared independence from the USSR in 1991. Higher education is overseen by the Ministry of Education and Science, and is governed by the constitution (1995), which states that all citizens have the right to receive an education, and by the Law on Education (1999), which outlines the system's structure. In 2000 the National Assembly approved the State Programme for Education Sector Development 2001–05, which outlined a five-year programme of reforms aimed at rationalizing and modernizing the entire education system. In 2002 the Law on Higher and Postgraduate Professional Education (2002) was passed, outlining the reforms to prepare Armenia for the Bologna process, which it joined in 2005. The Eurasia International University has fully conformed to the requirements of the Bologna Process since 2007.

To enter higher education students must hold the Mijnakarg Yndhanur Krtoutian Attestat (Certificate of Completed Secondary Education) and pass at least one university entrance examination one month after their high school examinations, depending upon their intended area of study. However, as part of higher education reforms, an independent body is to be established to administer university entrance examinations in place of the ministry.

There are three levels of higher education degrees in Armenia, one undergraduate and two postgraduate. The main undergraduate degree is the Bakalavr (Bachelors), which is usually a four-year programme. In line with the reforms of the Bologna process the Government has been introducing the European Credit Transfer System (ECTS) since 2002–2003. The Specialist Diploma, meanwhile, is a Soviet-style degree, which lasts for five years and is offered at professional institutions. From 2007–2008 higher education institutions issued the Diploma Supplement to students graduating from first and second cycle programmes. The first postgraduate degree is the Magistros (Masters), a one- or two-year course, admission to which is by examination. The second and final level of postgraduate education is the Aspirantura (Doctorate), which is split into two stages: the Candidate of Science and the Doctor of Science. The first stage lasts for two years and consists of taught and research components, while the second stage is purely research and necessary only for those who wish to pursue a career in higher education.

The first level of non-university technical and vocational education is Preliminary Professional (Vocational) Education and is open to holders of the Himnakan Yndhanur Krtutyan Attestat (Certificate of Basic Education) or the Certificate of Completed Secondary Education. Courses run for between one and three years. The second level of technical and vocational education is known as Middle Level Professional (Vocational) Education and is open to holders of the Certificate of Completed Secondary Education. The principal aim is to train specialists in fields such as the arts, finance, health, the humanities, pedagogy and technology. Training may last between two and five years. Upon qualification students gain the title Junior Specialist. There are also two levels of teacher training: Junior Specialist for primary and basic school teaching; and Bachelors or Specialist Diploma for secondary school teaching.

The Licensing and Accreditation Service, founded in 2000 as a separate unit under the aegis of the Ministry of Education and Science, is responsible for the licensing and accreditation of all public and private institutions under the terms of the Law on Education (1999). The final decision on the licensing and accreditation of an institution, however, lies with the Minister of Education and Science for approval. In 2008/09 114,400 students were enrolled at one of the 90 higher education institutions (including universities).

Regulatory and Representative Bodies

GOVERNMENT

Ministry of Culture: 0010 Yerevan, Republic Sq. 1, Govt House 3; tel. (10) 52-93-49; fax (10) 52-39-22; e-mail mincult@xter.net; Minister HASMIK POGHOSSIAN.

Ministry of Education and Science: 0010 Yerevan, Main Ave, Govt House 3; tel. (10) 52-66-02; fax (10) 52-73-43; e-mail minister@edu.am; internet www.edu.am; Minister ARMEN ASHOTYAN.

ACCREDITATION

ENIC/NARIC Armenia: Nat. Information Centre for Academic Recognition and Mobility, 0070 Yerevan, Vratsyan 73; tel. and fax (10) 57-84-56; e-mail armenic@cornet.am; internet www.armenic.am; f. 2006; provides information, advice and formal decision on recognition of international qualifications; information centre for recognition and internationalization of education; facilitates int. integration of the nat. education system into worldwide educational services; promotes mobility; supports devt of int. cooperation between educational institutions and other sectors; Exec. Dir Dr GAYANE HARUTYUNYAN; Evaluation Expert HASMIK TALALYAN; Evaluation Expert NAREK KOSYAN; Evaluation Expert RAFIK HAKOBYAN.

Learned Societies

GENERAL

National Academy of Sciences of Armenia: 0019 Yerevan, Marshal Baghramyan Ave 24; tel. (10) 52-70-31; fax (10) 56-92-81; e-mail academy@sci.am; internet www.sci.am; f. 1943; depts of Physical, Mathematical and Technological Sciences, Natural Sciences, Humanities; research institutes attached to depts: see Research Institutes; 119 mems; Pres. F. T. SARGASIAN; Acad.-Sec. and Vice-Pres. V. B. BARKHUDARIAN; publs Astrofizika (Astrophysics), Biologicheskii Zhurnal Armenii (Biological Journal of Armenia), Doklady (Reports), Istoriko-Filologicheskii Zhurnal (Historical and Philological Journal), Izvestiya (Bulletins: Mathematics, Mechanics, Physics, Engineering Sciences, Earth Sciences), Khimicheskii Zhurnal Armenii (Chemical Journal of Armenia), Meditsinskaya Nauka Armenii (Medical Science of Armenia), Neirokhimiya (Neurochemistry), Soobshcheniya Byurakanskoi Observatorii (Reports of the Byurakan Astrophysical Observatory), Vestnik Khirurgii Armenii (Herald of Armenian Surgery), Vestnik Obshchestvennykh Nauk (Herald of Social Sciences).

LANGUAGE AND LITERATURE

Alliance Française: 0010 Yerevan, ul. Aigestan 74; tel. and fax (10) 52-04-01; e-mail alliancefr_arm@hotmail.com; offers courses and examinations in French language and culture and promotes cultural exchange with France.

British Council: 0019 Yerevan, Baghramian Ave 24; tel. (10) 56-99-23; fax (10) 56-99-29; e-mail info@britishcouncil.am; internet www2.britishcouncil.org/armenia.htm; offers courses and examinations in English language and British culture and promotes cultural exchange with the UK; Dir ROGER BUDD.

Research Institutes

GENERAL

Institute of the Arts: 0019 Yerevan, Pr. Marshala Bagramyana 24G; tel. (10) 58-37-02; fax (10) 52-83-18; e-mail instart@sci.am; f. 1958; attached to Nat. Acad. of Sciences of Armenia; depts of Architecture, Fine Arts, Folk Arts, Music, Theatre and Cinema; Dir A. AGHASYAN.

AGRICULTURE, FISHERIES AND VETERINARY SCIENCE

Institute of Hydroponics Problems: 0082 Yerevan, Noragyugh 108; tel. (10) 56-51-62; fax (10) 56-55-90; e-mail hydrop@netsys.am; internet www.sci.am; f. 1947; attached to Nat. Acad. of Sciences of Armenia; devt of basic science and technology for hydroponic cultivation of valuable, rare and endangered medicinal, aromatic and dye-bearing plants, trees and shrubs; 47 mems; library of 9,500 vols; Dir Dr KHACHATUR MAIRAPETYAN; publ. *Communications of IHP* (every 3 years).

Scientific Centre of Agriculture and Plant Protection: 1110 Echmiadzin, Armavir Marz, St Isy le Moulino St 1; tel. (23) 15-34-54; attached to Min. of Agriculture; 143 staff, 6 depts, 11 laboratories; Dir H. HOVSEPIAN.

ECONOMICS, LAW AND POLITICS

Armenian Centre for National and International Studies: 0033 Yerevan, Yerznkian St 75; tel. (10) 52-87-80; fax (10) 52-48-46; e-mail root@acnis.am; internet www.acnis.am; f. 1994 to research issues of public policy, civic education, foreign relations, conflict resolution and the global environment; 25 mems; library of 4,200 vols; Founder and Pres. Dr RAFFI HOVANNISIAN.

Institute of Economics: 0001 Yerevan, ul. Abovyan 15; tel. (10) 58-19-71; fax (10) 56-92-81; e-mail nas_ie@sci.am; f. 1955; attached to Nat. Acad. of Sciences of Armenia; Dir V. E. KHOJABEKYAN.

HISTORY, GEOGRAPHY AND ARCHAEOLOGY

Institute–Museum of Genocide: 0028 Yerevan, Tsitsernakaberd; tel. (10) 39-09-81; e-mail lbars@sci.am; f. 1995; attached to Nat. Acad. of Sciences of Armenia; Dir L. A. BARSEGHYAN.

Institute of Archaeology and Ethnography: 0025 Yerevan, Charents 15; tel. and fax (10) 55-68-96; f. 1959; attached to Nat. Acad. of Sciences of Armenia; library of 15,000 vols; Dir A. A. KALANTARYAN.

Institute of History: 0019 Yerevan, Pr. Marshala Bagramyana 24G; tel. (10) 52-92-63; fax (10) 56-92-81; e-mail history@sci.am; f. 1943; attached to Nat. Acad. of Sciences of Armenia; Dir A. MELKONYAN.

Institute of Oriental Studies: 0019 Yerevan, Pr. Marshala Bagramyana 24G; tel. (10) 58-33-82; e-mail info@orient.sci.am; internet www.orient.sci.am; f. 1971; attached to Nat. Acad. of Sciences of Armenia; history, sociopolitical, int. and regional relations, culture, religion, problems of nat. minorities and ethnic groups of Middle East, Caucasus and Eastern Asia from antiquity to present; 65 mems; library of 60,000 vols; Dir Dr RUBEN A. SAFRASTYAN; Deputy Dir Dr PAVEL A. CHOBANYAN; publs *Near East: History, Politics, Culture, The Countries and Peoples of the Near and Middle East, Turcic and Ottoman Studies.*

Shirak Armenological Study Centre: 3100 Gyumri, Ankakhutyan Sq. 1; tel. (31) 13-31-73; fax (31) 56-92-81; e-mail academy@sci.am; f. 1997; attached to Nat. Acad. of Sciences of Armenia; Dir S. HAYRAPETYAN.

LANGUAGE AND LITERATURE

Abegyan Institute of Literature: 0015 Yerevan, ul. Grikora Lusavoricha 15; tel. (10) 56-32-54; fax (10) 56-32-54; f. 1943; attached to Nat. Acad. of Sciences of Armenia; Dir A. K. EGHIAZARYAN.

Atcharian Institute of Linguistics: 0001 Yerevan, ul. Abovyana 15; tel. (10) 56-53-37; fax (10) 56-92-81; e-mail inslang@sci.am; f. 1943; attached to Nat. Acad. of Sciences of Armenia; Dir G. B. DJAUKYAN.

MEDICINE

Armenian Institute of Spa Treatment and Physiotherapy: 0028 Yerevan, ul. Bratev Orbeli 41; internet www.medlib.am/spa; f. 1930; library of 30,000 vols; Dir Prof. G. AGADJANIAN.

Armenian Research Centre of Maternal and Child Health Care: 0002 Yerevan, Mesrop Mashtots Ave 22; tel. (10) 53-01-72; fax (10) 53-01-92; internet www.armobgyn.com; f. 1931; library of 25,000 vols; Dir Prof. G. OKOYEV.

Centre of Medical Genetics: 0010 Yerevan, Zakyan St 5/1; tel. (10) 54-43-67; fax (10) 56-92-81; e-mail tamsar@sci.am; f. 1999; attached to Nat. Acad. of Sciences of Armenia; Dir Dr T. F. SARGSIAN.

Centre of Traumatology, Orthopaedics, Burns and Radiology: 0047 Yerevan, Marash 9th St; tel. (10) 65-00-40; fax (10) 65-30-40; internet www.ctooir.narod.ru; f. 1945; fmrly Yerevan Scientific Research Institute of Orthopaedics and Traumatology; functioning depts: acute trauma, polytrauma, post-traumatic complications, infection complication, bone pathology, adult orthopaedics, paediatric orthopaedics, morphology, experimental biology; research depts: bone defect reconstruction, joint replacement, vertebral surgery, bone matrix preparation, bone tumour surgery, complex burns treatment; 28 mems; Dir AIVAZYAN VACHAGAN; publ. *Abstracts of Annual Congress of Traumatologists & Orthopaedic Surgeons of Armenia* (1 a year).

Mikaelian Research Institute of Surgery: Yerevan, Hasratyan 9; tel. (10) 28-19-90; fax (10) 28-22-22; e-mail surgery@netsys.am; f. 1974; library of 5,000 vols; Dir H. S. TAMAZIAN.

Research Centre for Epidemiology, Virology and Medical Parasitology: 0009 Yerevan, ul. Gevorga Kochara 21A; tel. (10) 56-21-02; Dir YU. T. ALEKSANYAN.

NATURAL SCIENCES

Biological Sciences

Buniatian, H., Institute of Biochemistry: 0014 Yerevan, ul. Paruyra Sevaga 5/1; tel. (10) 28-18-40; fax (10) 28-19-51; e-mail galoyan@sci.am; f. 1961; attached to Nat. Acad. of Sciences of Armenia; Dir A. A. GALOYAN; publ. *Neurokhimija* (4 a year).

Centre for Ecological–Noosphere Studies: 0025 Yerevan, Abovian 68; tel. (10) 56-93-31; fax (10) 58-02-54; e-mail ecocentr@sci.am; internet www.ecocentre.am; f. 1989; attached to Nat. Acad. of Sciences of Armenia; research area: environment; assessment of natural resources; Dir A. K. SAGHATELYAN.

Institute of Botany: 0063 Yerevan, Avan; tel. (10) 62-17-81; fax (10) 56-92-81; e-mail academy@sci.am; f. 1939; attached to Nat. Acad. of Sciences of Armenia; Dir A. A. CHARCHOGLYAN.

Institute of Microbiology: 2201 Abovian; tel. and fax (222) 2-00-73; e-mail microbio@sci.am; f. 1961; attached to Nat. Acad. of Sciences of Armenia; library of 5,000 vols; Dir L. S. MARKOSYAN.

Institute of Molecular Biology: 0014 Yerevan, Hasratyan 7; tel. (10) 28-16-26; fax (10) 28-61-22; e-mail aboyajyan@sci.am; internet molbiol.sci.am; f. 1966; attached to Nat. Acad. of Sciences of Armenia; Dir Prof. ANNA BOYAJYAN; Deputy Dir ARSEN ARAKELYAN.

Institute of Zoology: 0044 Yerevan, ul. Paruyra Sevaka 7; tel. (10) 28-14-70; fax (10) 28-13-60; e-mail zool@sci.am; f. 1943; attached to Nat. Acad. of Sciences of Armenia; Dir S. H. MOVSESIAN.

Orbeli Institute of Physiology: 375028 Yerevan, Orbeli Bros St 22; tel. and fax (10) 27-38-61; fax (10) 27-22-47; e-mail vsargsyan@neuroscience.am; f. 1943; attached to Nat. Acad. of Sciences of Armenia; library of 4,000 vols; Dir V. V. FANARDJIAN.

Sevan Institute of Hydroecology and Ichthyology: 1510 Sevan, ul. Kirova 186; tel. (10) 56-85-54; fax (10) 56-94-11; e-mail rhovan@sci.am; f. 1923; attached to Nat. Acad. of Sciences of Armenia; Dir R. HOVHANNISYAN.

State Microbial Depository Centre: 2201 Abovian; tel. and fax (222) 2-32-40; e-mail microbio@sci.am; internet www.rcdm.am; f. 1993; attached to Nat. Acad. of Sciences of Armenia; library of 22,000 vols; Dir E. G. AFRIKIAN.

Mathematical Sciences

Institute of Mathematics: 0019 Yerevan, Marshala Bagramyana 24B; tel. (10) 52-47-91; fax (10) 52-48-01; e-mail rafayel@instmath.sci.am; internet math.sci.am; f. 1971; 40 mems; attached to Nat. Acad. of Sciences of Armenia; Dir Prof. Dr BAGRAT T. BATIKYAN; Scientific Sec. Dr RAFAYEL H. BARKHUDARYAN; publs *Armenian Journal of Mathematics* (4 a year), *Journal of Contemporary Mathematical Analysis* (6 a year).

Physical Sciences

Byurakan Astrophysical Observatory: 0213 Byurakan, Ashtarak raion; tel. (10) 24-85-75; fax (10) 56-92-81; e-mail ekhach@bao.sci.am; internet www.sci.am/ac/bao.html; f. 1946; attached to Nat. Acad. of Sciences of Armenia; Dir E. KHACHIKIAN.

Garni Geophysical Observatory: 0019 Yerevan, Pr. Marshal Baghramyana 24A; tel. (10) 52-54-61; fax (10) 56-92-81; e-mail romella.pashayan@geology.am; f. 1982; attached to Nat. Acad. of Sciences of Armenia; Dir L. A. HAKHVERDYAN.

Garni Space Astronomy Institute: 2215 Garni, Kotayk; tel. (10) 64-90-01; fax (10) 56-92-81; f. 1982; attached to Nat. Acad. of Sciences of Armenia; Dir G. A. GURZADYAN.

Institute of Chemical Physics: 0014 Yerevan, ul. Paruyra Sevak 5/2; tel. (10) 28-14-81; fax (10) 29-73-09; e-mail tavadyan@ichph.sci.am; internet www.chph.sci.am; f. 1975; attached to Nat. Acad. of Sciences of Armenia; library of 33,410 vols; Dir Prof. LEVOM TAVADYAN.

Institute of Fine Organic Chemistry: 0014 Yerevan, Pr. Azatutyana 26; tel. (10) 28-83-34; fax (10) 28-83-32; e-mail ifoc@msrc.am; f. 1955; attached to Nat. Acad. of Sciences of Armenia; Dir B. T. GHARIBJANIAN.

Institute of General and Inorganic Chemistry: 0051 Yerevan, ul. Fioletova 11110; tel. (10) 23-07-38; fax (10) 23-12-75; f. 1957; attached to Nat. Acad. of Sciences of Armenia; Dir S. S. KARAKHANIAN.

Institute of Geology: 0019 Yerevan, Pr. Marshala Bagramyana 24A; tel. (10) 52-44-26; fax (10) 56-80-72; e-mail hrshah@sci.am; f. 1935; attached to Nat. Acad. of Sciences of Armenia; Dir R. T. JRBASHIAN.

Institute of Geophysics and Engineering Seismology: 3115 Gjumry, Pr. Leningradyana 5; tel. and fax (312) 3-12-61; e-mail as_iges@shirak.am; f. 1961; attached to Nat. Acad. of Sciences of Armenia; Dir S. M. HOVHANNISYAN.

Institute of Organic Chemistry: 0091 Yerevan, ul. Zakaria Kanakertsy 167A; tel. and fax (10) 28-35-21; f. 1935; attached to Nat. Acad. of Sciences of Armenia; Dir SH. H. BADANYAN.

Research Institute of Radiophysical Measurements: 0014 Yerevan, ul. Komitasa 49/4; tel. (10) 23-49-90; Dir P. M. GERUNI.

Yerevan Physics Institute: 0036 Yerevan, ul. Bratev Alikhanyan 2; tel. (10) 34-15-00; fax (10) 35-00-30; internet www.yerphi.am; f. 1942; particle and nuclear physics; library of 10,000 vols; Dir H. ASATRIAN.

PHILOSOPHY AND PSYCHOLOGY

Institute of Philosophy, Sociology and Law: 375010 Yerevan, ul. Arami 44; tel. (10) 53-05-71; fax (10) 53-10-96; e-mail gevork@sci.am; internet www.sci.am; f. 1969; attached to Nat. Acad. of Sciences of Armenia; library of 6,000 vols; Dir GEVORG POGHOYSAN.

TECHNOLOGY

Institute for Physical Research: 0210 Ashtarak; tel. (10) 28-81-50; fax (10) 56-92-81; f. 1968; attached to Nat. Acad. of Sciences of Armenia; Dir Prof. E. S. VARDANYAN.

Institute of Applied Problems of Physics: 0014 Yerevan, Str. Hr. Nersesian 25; tel. (10) 24-58-96; fax (10) 28-18-65; e-mail amkrtchyan@sci.am; internet www.sci.am/ac/iapp.html; f. 1980; attached to Nat. Acad. of Sciences of Armenia; Dir Dr A. H. MKRTCHYAN.

Institute of Mechanics: 0019 Yerevan, Pr. Marshala Bagramyana 24B; tel. (10) 52-48-90; fax (10) 56-81-89; e-mail mechins@sci.am; f. 1955; attached to Nat. Acad. of Sciences of Armenia; Dir L. A. AGHALOVIAN.

Institute of Problems in Informatics and Automation: 0014 Yerevan, ul. Paruyra Sevaka 1; tel. and fax (10) 28-58-12; e-mail shouk@sci.am; internet ipia.sci.am; f. 1957; attached to Nat. Acad. of Sciences of Armenia; Dir YU. H. SHOUKOURIAN.

Institute of Radiophysics and Electronics: 0210 Ashtarak, ul. Bratev Alikhanyan; tel. (10) 28-78-50; e-mail office@irphe.am; internet www.irphe.am; f. 1960; library of 12,000 vols; attached to Nat. Acad. of Sciences of Armenia; Dir R. M. MARTIROSYAM.

Special Experimental Design Technological Institute: 3101 Gjumry, Sarkisyana 5A; tel. (312) 4-56-63; fax (10) 56-92-81; e-mail academy@sci.am; f. 1976; attached to Nat. Acad. of Sciences of Armenia; Dir R. Y. SARKISSYAN.

Yerevan Automated Control Systems Scientific Research Institute: 0003 Yerevan, ul. A. Akopyana 3; tel. (10) 27-77-79; internet www.yercsi.am; f. 1992; Dir R. ATOIAN.

Yerevan Computer Research and Development Institute: 0033 Yerevan, Hagop Hagopyan 3; tel. (10) 27-77-79; fax (10) 27-68-52; e-mail ghovhan@ycrdi.am; internet www.ycrdi.am; f. 1956; Dir G. T. HOVHANNISIAN.

Yerevan Telecommunications Research Institute: 0015 Yerevan, Dzorapy 26; tel. (10) 56-60-61; fax (10) 56-17-37; e-mail mark@yetri.am; internet www.yetri.am; f. 1978.

Libraries and Archives
Yerevan

Armenian Scientific-Medical Library: Yerevan; tel. (10) 24-96-77; e-mail staff@medlib.am; internet www.medlib.am; attached to Nat. Acad. of Sciences of Armenia; 500,000 vols, theses, serials, microfiche and audiovisual items; Dir A. E. SHIRINIAN.

Fundamental Scientific Library of the National Academy of Sciences of Armenia: 0019 Yerevan, Baghramyana Ave 24D; tel. and fax (10) 52-47-50; e-mail tigran@flib.sci.am; internet www.flib.sci.am; f. 1935; 3m. vols; Dir Dr TIGRAN ZARGARYAN.

Matenadaran Institute of Ancient Armenian Manuscripts: Yerevan, Mashtots Ave 53; tel. (10) 56-25-78; internet www.matenadaran.am; f. 1959; incorporates research institute of Armenian textology and codicology; 17,000 Armenian MSS dating from 5th to 18th centuries, miniature paintings, 100,000 archival documents and works by Greek, Syrian, Persian, Arabic, Latin, Georgian and Ethiopian authors; Dir S. AREVSHATIAN; publ. *Banber Matenadarani*.

National Centre of Innovation and Entrepreneurship: 0051 Yerevan, Komitas 49/3; tel. (10) 23-67-74; fax (10) 23-80-29; e-mail info@innovcentre.am; internet www.innovcentre.am; f. 1961 as Armenian Centre for Scientific and Technical Information, present name 2009; 22m. vols; 87 mems; Dir H. E. MARGARYAN; publ. *Gitutyun ev Tekhnika* (Science and Technology, online).

National Library of Armenia: 0009 Yerevan, Teryan 72; tel. (10) 58-42-59; fax (10) 52-97-11; e-mail nla@arm.r.am; internet www.nla.am; f. 1919; 6.2m. vols; Dir DAVIT SARGSYAN.

Yerevan State University Library: 0049 Yerevan, ul. Mravyana 1,; internet www.ysu.am/~library; 1.5m. vols; Dir V. S. ARSLANIAN.

Museums and Art Galleries
Yerevan

Geological Museum of the Institute of Geology: Yerevan, ul. Aboviana 10; tel. (10) 58-06-63; f. 1937; colln mainly from Armenia; Dir G. B. MEZHLUMYAN.

Armenian State Historical Museum: 0010 Yerevan, Republic Sq. 4; tel. (10) 58-27-61; fax (10) 56-53-22; e-mail museum@xter.net; f. 1919; archaeological, documentary and other evidence charting the history and culture of Armenia from prehistoric times; Dir ANELKA GRIGORIAN.

National Gallery of Armenia: 0010 Yerevan, Arami 1; tel. and fax (10) 58-08-12; e-mail galleryarmenia@yahoo.com; internet www.gallery.am; f. 1921; W European, Armenian, Russian and Oriental art; library of 10,330 vols; Dir FARAON MIRZOYAN.

Yegishe Charents State Museum of Literature and Art: Yerevan, Mashtots St 17; tel. (10) 53-55-94; fax (10) 56-36-61; f. 1921; Armenian literature (since 18th century), theatre, cinema and music; library of 84,526 vols, 862,252 MSS; Dir H. BAKHCHINYAN.

Yerevan Children's Picture Gallery: Yerevan, ul. Aboviana 13; tel. (10) 52-78-93; f. 1970; works of art by children of Armenian and other nationalities; Dir H. IKITIAN.

Universities
ABOVIAN ARMENIAN STATE PEDAGOGICAL UNIVERSITY

0070 Yerevan, Khandyjan 5
Telephone: (10) 52-26-04
Fax: (10) 56-00-82

E-mail: armped@netsys.am
Founded 1922; present status 2000
State control
Academic year: September to July
Rector: MISAK DAVTYAN
Number of teachers: 620
Number of students: 4,200
Publication: *Mankavarzh* (12 a year)

DEANS
Armenian Language and Literature: MARTIN GILAVIAN
Art and Aesthetic Education: ARKADIY SHEKUNTS
Biology and Chemistry: MEZHLUM YERITSIAN
Culture: RUBEN MIRZAKHANIAN
History and Geography: POGHOS SIMONIAN
Industrial Pedagogy: KLEMENT ANANIAN
Mathematics and Physics: ALEXANDER GHUSHCHIAN
Primary Education and Defectology: DIMITRIY NAZARIAN
Psychology and Pedagogics: ROBERT DASHIAN
Public Professions: KAMO MKRYTCHIAN

ARMENIAN–RUSSIAN (SLAVIC) STATE UNIVERSITY

0051 Yerevan, Valutin St 123
Telephone: (10) 55-33-62
E-mail: rectorat@rau.am
Internet: www.rau.am
Founded 1998 by govts of Russia and Armenia
State control
Rector: LEVON MKRTČYAN
Library of 47,000 vols, 2,000 journals
Number of teachers: 156
Number of students: 1,600

DEANS
Faculty of Applied Mathematics and Informatics: Doc. VLADIMIR S. YEGIAZARYAN
Faculty of Economics: ALBERT YE. VARDANYAN
Faculty of Journalism: RAFAEL GR. AIRAPETYAN
Faculty of Law: Prof. Dr ARMEN A. ARUTYUNYAN
Faculty of Politology: Doc. ASHOT P. YENGOYAN
Faculty of Social and Cultural Services and Tourism: NINA I. KEVORKOVA

FRENCH UNIVERSITY OF ARMENIA

0067 Yerevan, Aigestan 8
Telephone: (10) 57-16-04
Fax: (10) 57-84-57
E-mail: ufa@arminco.com
Internet: www.ufa.am
Founded 2000
State control
Rector: PAUL ROUSSET
Sec.-Gen. and Dir of Studies: LUCIE HUCHOT

DEANS
Faculty of Business: NORAYR SAFARIAN
Faculty of Commerce: ARTAK MELKONIAN
Faculty of Law: GRIGOR BADIRIAN

GAVAR STATE UNIVERSITY

1201 Gavar, Azatutian 1
Telephone: (264)25775
Fax: (10) 282075
E-mail: mbadalyan@rambler.ru
Internet: www.gsu.am
Founded 1993
State control; attached to RA Min. of Education and Science
Languages of instruction: Armenian, Russian, English
Academic year: September to June

Rector: RUZANNA HAKOBYAN
Vice-Rectors: VARDAN HAYRAPETYAN, ARSEN APROYAN
Librarian: YELIZAVETA BADALYAN
Library of 31,690 vols: yearly collns of the Materials of GSU Scientific Confs
Number of teachers: 147
Number of students: 2,290

DEANS

Faculty of Economics: SAMVEL AMIRKHANYAN
Faculty of Humanities: HAMLET GHAJOYAN
Faculty of Natural Sciences: MARTIN AVAGIAN
Faculty of Part-Time Education: NELLI KUTUZYAN
Faculty of Philology: VIKTOR KATVALYAN

STATE ENGINEERING UNIVERSITY OF ARMENIA

0009 Yerevan, ul. Teryana 105
Telephone: (10) 52-05-20
Fax: (10) 15-10-68
E-mail: president@seua.am
Internet: www.seua.am
Founded 1933
State control
Rector: Y. L. SARKISSIAN
Library of 667,000 vols
Number of teachers: 1,000
Number of students: 8,000

Faculties of Automation and Instrumentation, Chemical Technology and Environmental Engineering, Cybernetics, Electrical Engineering, Informatics and Computer Systems, Machine Building, Mechanics and Machine Science, Mining and Metallurgy, Power Engineering, Radio Technology and Communications Systems, Transport Systems.

YEREVAN STATE MEDICAL UNIVERSITY, 'MKHITAR HERATSI'

0025 Yerevan, ul. Koryan 2
Telephone and fax (10) 54-72-63
E-mail: info@ysmu.am
Internet: www.ysmu.am
Languages of instruction: Armenian, English, Russian
Founded 1920
State control
Rector: GOHAR P. KYALYAN
Vice Rector for Academic Affairs: VLADIMIR A. SHEKOYAN
Vice-Rector for Int. Relations: YERVAND S. SAHAKYAN
Vice-Rector for Professional Postgraduate and Continuing Medical Education: GEVORG V. YAGHJYAN
Library of 521,751 vols
Number of teachers: 665
Number of students: 3,619 undergraduates, 569 postgraduates
Publications: New Armenian Medical Journal, Apaga Bjishk (Future Doctor), Medicine, Science and Education

Faculties of general medicine, military medicine, pharmacy, stomatology.

YEREVAN STATE UNIVERSITY

0025 Yerevan, Alex Manoogian 1
Telephone: (10) 55-46-29
Fax: (10) 55-46-41

E-mail: rector@ysu.am
Internet: www.ysu.am
Founded 1919
State control
Language of instruction: Armenian
Academic year: September to June
Rector: ARAM H. SIMONYAN
Vice-Rector for Academic Affairs: ALEKSANDR K. GRIGORYAN
Vice-Rector for Administrative-Economic Issues: ARARAT TS. MALKHASYAN
Vice-Rector for Scientific Policy and Int. Cooperation: GEGHAM G. GEVORGYAN
Vice-Rector for Students, Alumni and Public Relations: RUBEN L. MARKOSYAN
Dir of Library: ASHOT S. ALEKSANYAN
Number of teachers: 1,571
Number of students: 13,000

Publications: Proceedings of Yerevan State University, Physical and Mathematical Sciences (3 a year), Scientific Bulletins (geology and geography, biology and chemistry, 3 a year)

DEANS

Faculty of Applied Arts: SPARTAK SARGSYAN
Faculty of Armenian Philology: ARTSRUN AVAGYAN
Faculty of Biology: EMIL GEVORGYAN
Faculty of Chemistry: TARIEL V. GHOCHIKYAN
Faculty of Computer Science and Applied Mathematics: VAHRAM ZH. DUMANYAN
Faculty of Economics: HAYK L. SARGSYAN
Faculty of Geology and Geography: MARAT A. GRIGORYAN
Faculty of History: EDIK G. MINASYAN
Faculty of International Relations: GEGHAM H. PETROSYAN
Faculty of Journalism: NAGHASH N. MARTIROSYAN
Faculty of Law: GAGIK S. GHAZINYAN
Faculty of Mathematics and Mechanics: ARTHUR A. SAHAKYAN
Faculty of Oriental Studies: GURGEN V. MELIKIAN
Faculty of Philosophy, Psychology and Sociology: ALEXANDER S. BAGHDASARYAN
Faculty of Physics: ROLAND M. AVAGYAN
Faculty of Radiophysics: YURI L. VARDANIAN
Faculty of Romanic-Germanic Philology: SAMVEL A. ABRAHAMYAN
Faculty of Russian Philology: PAVEL B. BALAYAN
Faculty of Sociology: ARTHUR E. MKRTCHYAN
Faculty of Theology: ANUSHAVAN BISHOP ZHAMKOCHYAN

YEREVAN STATE UNIVERSITY OF LINGUISTICS, 'V. BRUSOV'

0002 Yerevan, Toumanian 42
Telephone: (10) 53-05-52
Fax: (10) 50-64-29
E-mail: ysifl@edu.am
Internet: www.brusov.am
Founded 1935
State control
Rector: SUREN ZOLYAN
Number of teachers: 440
Number of students: 2,200

Faculties of foreign languages, Romance and Germanic languages, Russian language and literature, social sciences.

Other Higher Educational Institutes

Armenian Agricultural Academy: 0009 Yerevan, ul. Teryana 74; tel. (10) 52-45-41; fax (10) 52-23-61; e-mail agacad@arminco.com; internet www.arminco.com/homepages/usdaes/acad/acad.htm; f. 1994 from merger of Armenian Agricultural Institute (f. 1930) and Yerevan Zootechnical and Veterinary Institute (f. 1928); faculties of Agrarian Studies, Economics, Technology, Zootechnical and Veterinary Studies, Engineering, Advanced Studies; 152 full professors; 419 teachers; 4,322 students; library: 563,389 vols; Rector A. KHACHATRIAN; publs Agronews (52 a year), Agroscience (12 a year), News (52 a year).

Armenian State Institute of Physical Education: 0070 Yerevan, Alex Manoogian 11; tel. (10) 55-24-31; f. 1945; State control; faculties of Education, Sports; Rector VAHRAM ARAKELIAN.

Gyumri M. Nalbandian State Pedagogical Institute: 3126 Gyumri, Paruir Sevak 4; tel. (312) 3-77-32; fax (312) 3-21-99; e-mail postmaster@shirak.am; f. 1935; state control; faculties of Foreign Languages, History and Philology, Natural Sciences and Geography, Pedagogy, Physical Education, Physics and Mathematics; Rector HOURIK HARUTUNIAN.

Vanadzor State Pedagogical Institute: 2000 Vanadzor, Tigran Mets 36; tel. (322) 4-63-87; fax (322) 2-04-68; e-mail mankocol@hragir.aua.am; f. 1969; state control; faculties of Biology, History and Geography, Mathematics and Physics, Philology and Pre-school Education, Psychology; 310 teachers; 1,900 students; Rector RAFIK YEDOVAN; Vice-Rector SHVAITS SAHAKIAN.

Yerevan Institute of Architecture and Construction: 0009 Yerevan, ul. Teryana 105; tel. (10) 58-01-77; fax (10) 56-59-84; internet yeriac.iatp.irex.am; f. 1989; faculties of Architecture, Construction and Urban Economy, Construction, Hydrotechnical Studies, Industrial and Civil Construction, Transport Construction, Technology; 262 teachers; 1,624 students; library: 1.4m. vols; Rector A. G. BEGLARIAN.

Yerevan Komitas State Conservatoire: 0001 Yerevan, Sayat-Nova 1A; tel. (10) 58-11-64; fax (10) 56-35-40; e-mail ysc@edu.am; f. 1920; orchestral, chamber, choral, folk music; library: 130,000 vols; 386 teachers; 1,045 students; Rector Prof. ARMEN SMHATYAN.

Yerevan State Academy of Fine Arts: 0009 Yerevan, Isahakian 36; tel. (10) 56-07-26; fax (10) 54-27-06; e-mail ysifa@edu.am; internet www.iatp.am/yafa; f. 1945; faculties of Art, Decorative Arts, Design; brs in Gjumri and Dilijan; library: 25,000 vols; 98 teachers; 428 students; Rector Prof. ARAM ISABEKIAN.

Yerevan State Institute of Economics: 0025 Yerevan, Nalbandian St 164; tel. (10) 52-17-21; fax (10) 52-88-64; e-mail ysine@ysine.am; internet www.ysine.am; f. 1975; faculties of Economic Planning, Economics and Organization of Labour, Economics of Labour and Sociology, Economics of Trade and Commodities, Finance and Accounting; 326 teachers; 5,600 students; Rector G. KIRAKOSIAN; publ. Economics.

AUSTRALIA

The Higher Education System

In 2009 there were 42 public universities and two private universities, as well as over 100 higher education providers approved by State/Territory to offer specific higher education programmes. In 2008 a total of 1,066,095 students were enrolled in higher education. Under the federal system of government in Australia, the six states and two territories are responsible for providing education services for their own residents. The Australian Constitution, however, empowers the Federal Government to make special-purpose financial grants to the states for education in both government and non-government schools. Responsibility for educational policy rests with the Minister for Education, Science and Training. An education department headed by a Director-General deals with all aspects of education within each state.

The Federal Government is the most important source of funding for universities; in 2003 the Government contributed 41% accounted of funding. Most Australian students contribute to the cost of their courses under the Higher Education Contribution Scheme (HECS), with the amount of the student's contribution depending on the cost of the course and likely future earnings. Financial assistance is available to certain students subject to a means test. In addition, there are a limited number of equity and merit scholarships which exempt students from the HECS charge.

Universities are administered by a Governing Body such as a Council, Senate or Board of Governors, chaired by a Chancellor. A Chief Executive, usually a Vice-Chancellor or President, oversees the day-to-day running of the university and reports to the Governing Body.

In 1990 a Unified National System was established, replacing the previously existing binary system of universities and non-university institutions. The Australian Qualifications Framework (AQF) was introduced in 1995 and implemented by 1999, leading to the development of a comprehensive national framework for post-secondary education and training. The AQF identifies six post-secondary levels of qualification: Diploma, Advanced Diploma, Bachelors degree, Graduate Certificate and Graduate Diploma, Masters degree and Doctoral degree. In May 2009 the Minister for Education announced the creation of a new national regulatory agency, the Tertiary Education Quality and Standards Agency, to come into force in 2012. It was envisaged that its role would be to 'accredit providers, carry out audits, protect the overall quality of the Australian higher education system, encourage best practice and streamline current regulatory arrangements to reduce duplication and provide for national consistency'. It would also decide who qualified for performance funding.

Universities administer their own admissions processes. Admission is usually based on a combination of completion of Year 12, leading to the award of the Senior Secondary Certificate of Education (the name may vary in each state or territory), and entrance test scores. The Diploma and Advanced Diploma, requiring two and three years of study respectively, are sub-degree qualifications that may in certain circumstances allow entry to the second year of a Bachelors degree. The Bachelors degree may be rated either Ordinary/Pass after three years of study or Honours after four years of study. The Graduate Certificate and Graduate Diploma require one or two semesters of full-time study respectively following a Bachelor degree. The Masters degree is awarded after two years of study following an Ordinary/Pass Bachelors or after one year of study following an Honours Bachelors. Finally, the Doctoral degree requires three years of full-time study and research plus submission of a thesis. Other, more recent, Doctoral-level awards include the Professional Doctorate and the Higher Doctorate.

Vocational education and training (VET) is supervised by the Australian National Training Authority, established in 1994. The Australian Recognition Framework approves VET qualifications. VET programmes are offered at upper-secondary schools, Technical and Further Education colleges and State- or Territory-accredited private providers. VET programmes require between one and three years' study depending upon the requirements of the course and the level of qualification sought. The range of VET qualifications is as follows: Certificates I, II, III, IV; Diploma; Advanced Diploma. Teacher training usually requires either a three-year Bachelors degree in the subject to be taught, followed by a one- to two-year (Graduate) Diploma in Education, or the four-year Bachelor of Education.

Regulatory and Representative Bodies

GOVERNMENT

Department of Education, Employment and Workplace Relations: GPOB 9880, Canberra, ACT 2601; 16 Mort St, Canberra, ACT 2601; tel. (2) 6240-8848; internet www.deewr.gov.au; Minister JULIA GILLARD.

Ministerial Council on Education, Employment, Training and Youth Affairs (MCEETYA): POB 202, Carlton South, Vic. 3053; tel. (03) 9639-0588; fax (03) 9639-1790; e-mail enquiries@mceetya.edu.au; internet www.mceetya.edu.au; f. 1993 by merger of the Australian Education Council (AEC), the Council of Ministers of Vocational Education, Employment and Training (MOVEET) and the Youth Ministers Council (YMC); responsible for pre-primary education, primary and secondary education, vocational education and training, higher education, employment and links between employment/labour market programmes and education and training, adult and community education, youth policy pro-grammes and cross-sectoral matters; works in close interaction with the Ministerial Council for Vocational and Technical Education (MCVTE); functions incl. coordination of strategic policy at nat. level, negotiation and devt of nat. agreements on shared objectives and interests (incl. principles for Australian Govt/State relations) in the Council's areas of responsibility, negotiations on scope and format of nat. reporting on areas of responsibility, sharing of information and collaborative use of resources towards agreed objectives and priorities, and coordination of communication with, and collaboration between, related nat. structures; Chair. Dr JANE LOMAX-SMITH.

ACCREDITATION

Australian Qualifications Framework Advisory Board (AQFAB): POB 609, Carlton South, Vic. 3053; Level 3, 15–31 Pelham St, Carlton, Vic. 3053; tel. (3) 9639-1606; fax (3) 9639-1315; e-mail aqfab@aqf.edu.au; internet www.aqf.edu.au; f. 1995 to protect the Australian Qualifications Framework (AQF) qualifications guidelines and to promote and monitor nat. implementation of the AQF; operates as a high-level, cross-sectoral forum; Chair. WARREN GRIMSHAW; Secretariat Exec. Officer Dr JUDY FORSYTH.

Australian Universities Quality Agency: Level 10, 123 Lonsdale St, Melbourne, Vic. 3000; tel. (3) 9664-1000; fax (3) 9639-7377; e-mail admin@auqa.edu.au; internet auqa.edu.au; f. 2000; ind., nat. quality assurance agency responsible for quality audits of higher education instns and accreditation authorities; reports on performance and outcomes and assists in quality enhancement; Exec. Dir Dr DAVID WOODHOUSE.

ENIC/NARIC Australia: AEI-NOOSR, Int. Education Group, Dept of Education, Employment and Workplace Relations, GPOB 1407, Canberra, ACT 2601; tel. (3) 9938-2543; fax (2) 6123-7892; e-mail educational.noosr@deewr.gov.au; internet aei.gov.au/aei/qualificationsrecognition/default.htm; Dir of AEI-NOOSR MARGARET PROCTOR.

NATIONAL BODIES

Adult Learning Australia Quest: GPOB 260, Canberra, ACT 2601; tel. (2) 6274-9500;

fax (2) 9274-9513; e-mail info@ala.asn.au; internet www.ala.asn.au; f. 1961; mem. of ICAE, ASPBAE, ICEA; coordinates and encourages adult and community education at nat. level; publishes educational books; lobbies govts and appropriate depts; holds nat. conferences; 500 mems, also corporate mems; Pres. GREG PEART; Exec. Dir RON ANDERSON; publs *Australian Journal of Adult Learning* (3 a year), *Adult Learning Australia* (4 a year).

Australian Research Council: GPOB 2702, Canberra, ACT 2601; tel. (2) 6284-6605; fax (2) 6284-6601; internet www.arc.gov.au; f. 1965, present name 1988; responsible for the allocation of grants for research in the physical sciences, biological sciences, chemical sciences, earth sciences, applied sciences, social sciences and the humanities by individuals or research teams; and provides advice to relevant Minister on nat. research priorities and the coordination of research policy; 14 mems; Chief Exec. Prof. PETER HØJ.

Centre for Adult Education (CAE): 253 Flinders Lane, Melbourne, Vic. 3000; tel. (3) 9652-0611; fax (3) 9654-6759; e-mail international@cae.edu.au; internet www.cae.edu.au; f. 1947; statutory body engaged in providing adult education and business training in Vic.; funded in part through the Govt of Vic.; library of 50,000 vols; Dir JOHN WILLS; publs *Dialogue* (every 3 years, catalogue of book, film and music titles available for self-directed learning groups), *Program Guide* (5 a year).

Universities Australia: GPOB 1142, Canberra, ACT 2601; tel. (2) 6285-8100; fax (2) 6285-8101; e-mail contact@universitiesaustralia.edu.au; internet www.universitiesaustralia.edu.au; f. 1920 as Australian Vice-Chancellors' Cttee; represents Australian univs; 38 mem univs; Chair. Prof. PETER COALDRAKE; Chief Exec. Dr GLENN WITHERS.

Learned Societies
GENERAL

Academy of the Social Sciences in Australia: GPOB 1956, Canberra, ACT 2601; tel. (2) 6249-1788; fax (2) 6247-4335; e-mail assa.secretariat@anu.edu.au; internet www.assa.edu.au; f. 1971; 447 fellows; Pres. Prof. STUART MACINTYRE; Exec. Dir Dr JOHN BEATON; publs *Dialogue* (3 a year), *Occasional Paper* (irregular).

Australian Academy of the Humanities: GPOB 93, Canberra, ACT 2601; tel. (2) 6125-9860; fax (2) 6248-6287; e-mail enquiries@humanities.org.au; internet www.humanities.org.au; f. 1969; prehistory and archaeology, European languages and cultures, classical studies, history, fine arts, Asian studies, English, linguistics, philosophy, religion and the history of ideas, cultural and communication studies; 500 mems; Pres. Prof. JOSEPH LO BIANCO; Immediate Past Pres. Prof. IAN DONALDSON; Exec. Dir, Secretariat JOHN BYRON; Hon. Sec. Prof. GRAEME CLARKE; Librarian and Archivist Dr JANET H. WILLIAMS; publ. *Humanities Australia*.

AGRICULTURE, FISHERIES AND VETERINARY SCIENCE

Australian Institute of Agricultural Science and Technology: Level 2, 21 Burwood Rd, Hawthorn, Vic. 3122; tel. (3) 9815-3600; fax (3) 9815-3633; internet www.aiast.com.au; f. 1935; 2,500 mems; Pres. CHARLES DREW; Exec. Dir ALLAN JONES; publ. *Agricultural Science* (4 a year).

Australian Veterinary Association: Unit 40, 2A Herbert St, St Leonards, NSW 2065; tel. (2) 9431-5000; fax (2) 9437-9068; e-mail members@ava.com.au; internet www.ava.com.au; f. 1921; professional asscn; 5,000 mems; Pres. KERSTI SEKSEL; Chief Exec. MARGARET CONLEY; publ. *Australian Veterinary Journal* (12 a year).

Dairy Industry Association of Australia Inc.: 84 William St, Melbourne, Vic. 3000; tel. (3) 9760-0422; fax (3) 9642-8144; e-mail kmanser@ozemail.com.au; internet www.diaa.asn.au; f. 1946; divisions in each State; 1,600 mems; Pres. JO DAVEY; Sec. KRISTINE MANSER; publs *Australian Dairy Foods* (6 a year), *The Australian Journal of Dairy Technology* (3 a year).

Primary Industries Ministerial Council: Dept of Agriculture, Fisheries and Forestry, Barton, Canberra, ACT 2600; tel. (2) 6272-5216; fax (2) 6272-4772; internet www.affa.gov.au/docs/operating_environment/armcanz/armcanz.html; f. 2001; mems: Commonwealth, State, Territory and New Zealand ministers responsible for agriculture and rural adjustment; advised by a Standing Committee comprising heads of Commonwealth, State, Territory and New Zealand agencies responsible for agriculture, and representatives from CSIRO and the Bureau of Meteorology; Exec. Dir Dr MAXINE COOPER.

ARCHITECTURE AND TOWN PLANNING

Australian Council of National Trusts: POB 1002, Civic Sq., ACT 2612; tel. (2) 6247-6766; fax (2) 6249-1395; internet www.nationaltrust.org.au; f. 1965; Federal Council of the State and Territory National Trusts established for the conservation of lands and buildings of beauty or of national, historic, scientific, architectural or cultural interest and Aboriginal relics and wildlife; 80,000 mems of the National Trust movement; Chair. SIMON R. MOLESWORTH; Exec. Officer ALAN GRAHAM.

Australian Institute of Quantity Surveyors: National Office, POB 301, Deakin West, ACT 2600; tel. (2) 6282-2222; fax (2) 6285-2427; e-mail contact@aiqs.com.au; internet www.aiqs.com.au; f. 1971; 3,700 mems; Pres. PETER COX; Gen. Man. TERRY SANDERS; publs *Australian Journal of Construction Economics and Building* (2 a year), *The Building Economist* (4 a year).

Planning Institute of Australia: GPOB 1491, Canberra, ACT; tel. (2) 6248-7299; fax (2) 6262-9970; e-mail act@planning.org.au; internet www.planning.org.au; f. 1951; professional asscn for town and regional planners; 3,444 mems; Nat. Pres. MARCUS SPILLER; Pres. CLAIRE MIDDLETON; publs *Australian Planner* (4 a year), *National Office News* (6 a year).

Royal Australian Institute of Architects: 2A Mugga Way, Red Hill, Canberra, ACT 2603; tel. (2) 6208-2100; fax (2) 6208-2106; e-mail act@raia.com.au; internet www.raia.com.au; inc. 1930; 8,500 mems; Nat. Pres. ALEX TZANNES; CEO DAVID PARKEN; ACT Man. SOPHIE CLEMENT; publs *Architecture Australia* (6 a year), occasional newsletters, research papers, seminar and workshop papers, management and law notes.

BIBLIOGRAPHY, LIBRARY SCIENCE AND MUSEOLOGY

Australian Library and Information Association: POB 6335, Kingston, ACT 2604; tel. (2) 6215-8222; fax (2) 6282-2249; internet alia.org.au; f. 1937; 6,000 mems; Pres. ROXANNE MISSINGHAM; Exec. Dir SUE HUTLEY; publs *Australian Academic and Research Libraries* (4 a year), *Australian Library Journal* (4 a year), *inCite* (11 a year).

Bibliographical Society of Australia and New Zealand: c/o Dr Chris Tiffin, Hon. Sec. Research Consultant, School of EMSAH, Univ. of Queensland, Brisbane, Qld 4072; tel. (7) 3369-1783; e-mail c.tiffin@uq.edu.au; internet scriptandprint.blogspot.com; f. 1969 to promote research in bibliography; 200 mems; Pres. JOHN ARNOLD; publs *Broadsheet* (irregular), *Script and Print: Bulletin of the Bibliographical Society of Australia and New Zealand* (4 a year).

Museums Australia: POB 266, Civic Sq., ACT 2608; tel. (2) 6273-2437; fax (2) 6273-2451; e-mail director@museumsaustralia.org.au; internet www.museumsaustralia.org.au; f. 1993 to promote museums and galleries to all levels of govt and the community, and to foster high standards in all aspects of museum operations through nat. advocacy, professional devt, training, research, policy formulation, publs, collaborative facilitation and partnerships; 1,500 mems (instns and individuals); Nat. Pres. DARRYL MCINTYRE; Nat. Dir BERNICE L. MURPHY; Man. LEE SCOTT; publ. *Museums Australia Magazine* (4 a year).

ECONOMICS, LAW AND POLITICS

Australian Bar Association: Bar Association of Queensland, Level 5, Inns of Court, 107 North Quay, Brisbane, Qld 4000; tel. (7) 3236-2477; fax (7) 3236-1180; e-mail president@qldbar.asn.au; internet qldbar.asn.au; f. 1962 to advance the interests of barristers; to maintain and strengthen the position of the Bar, maintaining its independence and the rule of law; to maintain and improve standards of instruction and training of barristers; 3,440 mems; Pres. GLENN MARTIN; Vice-Pres. PETER LYONS; Treas. MARTIN DAUBNEY; Sec. DOUGLAS MURPHY.

Australian Institute of Credit Management: Level 3, 619 Pacific Highway, St Leonards, NSW 2065; tel. (2) 9906-4563; fax (2) 9906-5686; e-mail terry@aicm.com.au; internet www.aicm.com.au; f. 1937 to provide a nat. and professional organization for credit managers and those engaged in the control of credit; 3,000 mems; holds conferences, discussions; maintains educational programmes at CAEs; divs in all states; CEO TERRY COLLINS; Nat. Training Man. DEL CSETI; publ. *Credit Management in Australia* (5 a year).

Australian Institute of International Affairs: 32 Thesiger Court, Deakin, ACT 2600; tel. (2) 6282-2133; fax (2) 6285-2334; e-mail ceo@aiia.asn.au; internet www.aiia.asn.au; f. 1933; 1,600 mems; Pres. CLIVE HILDEBRAND; Exec. Dir MELISSA H. CONLEY TYLER; publs *Australia in World Affairs* (every 5 years), *Australian Journal of International Affairs* (4 a year).

Australian Institute of Management: 181 Fitzroy St, St Kilda, Vic. 3182; tel. (3) 9534-8181; fax (3) 9534-5050; e-mail enquiry@aimvic.com.au; internet www.aim.com.au; f. 1941; professional management asscn; information and training services; divs in all states; 30,000 professional mems, 7,500 corporate mems; library of 20,000 vols; publ. *National Management Today Magazine* (12 a year).

Australian Political Studies Association: Director's Section, RSSS, ANU, Canberra, ACT 0200; tel. (2) 6125-2257; fax (2) 6125-0502; e-mail mary.hapel@anu.edu.au; internet www.auspsa.org.au; f. 1952; sponsors nat. political science projects; int. exchange programmes with similar asscns;

organises an annual conference; workshops; 312 mems; Pres. Prof. ANN CAPLING; Sec. and Treasurer Prof. ROD RHODES; publ. *Australian Journal of Political Science* (4 a year).

Australian Property Institute: 6 Campion St, Deakin, ACT 2600; tel. (2) 6282-2411; fax (2) 6285-2194; internet www.api.org.au; f. 1927; 7,500 mems; Pres. BARRY BRAKEY; Dir GRANT WARNER; publs *Australian & New Zealand Valuation Principles & Standards Manual*, *Australian Property Journal* (4 a year), *Professional Practice* (1 a year), *Valuation Principles and Practices*.

Committee for Economic Development of Australia: Level 5, 136 Exhibition St, Melbourne, Vic. 3000; tel. (3) 9662-3544; fax (3) 9663-7271; e-mail info@ceda.com.au; internet www.ceda.com.au; f. 1960 to facilitate discussion, research and interdisciplinary communication in the interests of the devt of the nat. economy and the future of Australia; holds more than 250 events, seminars and exec. roundtables each year; 1,000 orgs; Chair. IVAN DEVESON; Chief Exec. DAVID BYERS; publs *Australian Chief Executive* (mem. magazine, 4 a year), *Growth Reports* (multi-author long reports on selected research themes), *Information Papers* (single-author short reports on selected themes).

Economic Society of Australia: POB 937, St Ives, NSW 2075; tel. (2) 9402-7635; internet www.ecosoc.org.au; f. 1925; 1,400 mems; brs in each State; Pres. NEVILLE NORMAN; Sec. JEFFREY SHEEN; Treas. ANDREW HUGHES; publs *Economic Papers*, *The Economic Record*.

Institute of Public Affairs: Level 2, 410 Collins St, Melbourne, Vic. 3000; tel. (3) 9600-4744; e-mail ipa@ipa.org.au; internet www.ipa.org.au; f. 1943; non-profit educational org. to study economic and industrial problems and to advance the cause of free enterprise in Australia; supported by 550 companies and 3,500 individuals; Chair. ALAN STOCKDALE; Exec. Dir MIKE NAHAN; publs *Backgrounder* (10 a year), *Current Issues* (5 a year), *IPA Review* (4 a year).

Law Council of Australia: GPO Box 1989, Canberra, ACT 2601; located at: 19 Torrens St, Braddon, ACT 2612; tel. (2) 6246-3788; fax (2) 6248-0639; e-mail mail@lawcouncil.asn.au; internet www.lawcouncil.asn.au; f. 1933; 15 constituent bodies representing 50,000 mems; Sec.-Gen. PETER WEBB; publs *Australian Family Lawyer* (4 a year), *Australian Law Management Journal* (4 a year).

Law Society of New South Wales: 170 Phillip St, Sydney, NSW; tel. (2) 9926-0333; fax (2) 9231-5809; internet www.lawsocnsw .asn.au; f. 1884; 20,000 mems; library of 32,000 vols; Sec. C. CAWLEY; publs *Caveat* (irregular), *Law Society Journal* (11 a year).

Local Government Managers Australia: POB 5175, South Melbourne, Vic. 3205; tel. (3) 9682-9222; fax (3) 9682-8977; e-mail national@lgma.org.au; internet www.lgma .org.au; f. 1936; professional local govt assoc. for gen. managers, chief execs and officers employed in management; 2,500 mems; CEO JOHN RAVLIC; publ. *Local Government Manager* (6 a year).

EDUCATION

Australian College of Educators: 42 Geils Court, Deakin, ACT 2600; tel. (2) 6281-1677; fax (2) 6285-1262; e-mail ace@austcolled.com .au; internet www.auscolled.com.au; f. 1959; an independent professional association of educators from every field of education throughout Australia; encourages professional advancement of its members and the nat. development of education; brs and

regional groups in each state and territory; conducts nat. and state conferences, surveys and studies, etc.; 6,000 mems; CEO CHERYL O'CONNOR; publs *Education Review* (incl. *ACE Perspectives*, 12 a year), chapter newsletters, *Professional Educator* (4 a year).

IDP Education Australia Ltd: GPOB 2006, Canberra, ACT 2601; tel. (2) 6285-8222; fax (2) 6285-3036; e-mail info@idp.com; internet www.idp.com; f. 1969 as the Int. Development Program of Australian Universities and Colleges Ltd, renamed 1994; 37 mem. Australian univs; an independent company owned by the Australian Universities; seeks to promote Australian education and training services overseas; 53 overseas network offices; Chief Exec. L. HYAM; publ. newsletters in Asia-Pacific languages.

Open and Distance Learning Association of Australia Inc.: Teaching and Learning Centre, Univ. of New England, Armidale, NSW 2351; tel. (2) 6773-3628; fax (2) 6773-3510; e-mail odlaa@une.edu.au; internet www.odlaa.org; f. 1974 to advance the practice and study of distance education in Australia; Pres. Dr ROD SIMS; Vice-Pres. SAM MEREDITH; Assoc. Sec. Assoc. Prof. SOM NAIDU; publ. *Distance Education* (3 a year).

FINE AND PERFORMING ARTS

Australia Council for the Arts: 372 Elizabeth St, Surry Hills, NSW 2010; tel. (2) 9215-9000; e-mail mail@australiacouncil.gov.au; internet www.australiacouncil.gov.au; f. 1968; aims to foster the devt of the arts through the programmes of seven funds: Music, Dance, Theatre, Interdisciplinary/New Media Arts, Literature, Visual Arts, Community Partnerships, and one board: Aboriginal and Torres Straits Islander Arts; library of 6,500 vols; Chair. JAMES STRONG; Deputy Chair. JOSEPH GERSH; CEO KATHY KEELE; publ. *Artery* (4 a year).

Musicological Society of Australia: GPOB 2402, Canberra, ACT 2601; e-mail secretary@msa.org.au; internet www.msa .org.au; f. 1963; the advancement of musicology; 290 mems; Pres. HUIB SCHIPPERS; National Sec. BRYDIE-LEIGH BARTLEET; publ. *Musicology Australia* (1 a year).

Royal Art Society of New South Wales: 25–27 Walker St, North Sydney, NSW 2060; tel. (2) 9955-5752; fax (2) 9925-0064; e-mail lavender@cia.com.au; f. 1880; for the promotion of high standards in Australian art; school for painting (beginners to Diploma RAS of NSW); 400 mems; Pres. RON STANNARD; Sec. CHRISTINE FEHER.

Royal Queensland Art Society Inc.: GPOB 1602, Brisbane, Qld 4001; tel. (7) 3831-3455; fax (7) 3831-3452; e-mail rqasi@ oznetcom.com.au; internet www.rqas .ozevents.com; f. 1887; 500 mems; Sec. KAREN KANE.

Royal South Australian Society of Arts: Institute Bldg, Level 1 N Terrace, Adelaide, SA 5000; tel. (8) 8232-0450; fax (8) 8232-0450; f. 1856; 702 mems; Pres. BEVERLY M. BILLS; Hon. Sec. JAMES E. G. RAGGATT; publ. *Kalori* (irregular).

Victorian Artists' Society: 430 Albert St, East Melbourne, Vic. 3002; tel. (3) 9662-1484; fax (3) 9662-2343; e-mail vicartists@vicnet .net.au; internet www.vicnet.net.au/ ~vicartists; f. 1870; 1,000 mems; four galleries and a studio; Pres. JOHN HUNT; Sec. TED DANSEY; publ. *Gallery on Eastern Hill*.

HISTORY, GEOGRAPHY AND ARCHAEOLOGY

Australian and New Zealand Association for Medieval and Early Modern Studies: c/o Dr Lesley O'Brien, School of

Humanities, M208, Univ. of Western Australia, Crawley, WA 6009; e-mail anzamems-membership@arts.uwa.edu.au; internet www.anzamems.arts.uwa.edu.au; f. 1996 by merger of ANZAMRS (Australian and New Zealand Asscn of Medieval and Renaissance Studies) and AHMEME (Australian Historians of Medieval and Early Modern Europe); organizes conferences every 2 years; 200 mems; Pres. CONSTANT MEWS (Monash Univ.); Sec. MEGAN CASSIDY-WELCH (Univ. of Melbourne); publ. *Parergon* (2 a year).

Australian Numismatic Society: POB 366, Brookvale, NSW 2096; tel. (2) 9223-4578; e-mail rodsell@rodsell.com; f. 1913; promotes the study of coins, banknotes and medals with particular reference to Australasia and the Pacific region; monthly meetings in Sydney and Brisbane; 204 mems (incl. overseas); Pres. J. VELTMEYER; Sec. ROD SELL; publs *Report* (2 a year), *NAA Journal* (1 a year).

Geographical Society of New South Wales Inc.: POB 162, Ryde, NSW 1680; tel. (2) 9807-3586; fax (2) 9807-3589; e-mail office@gsnsw.org.au; internet www.gsnsw .org.au; f. 1927; 300 mems; Hon. Sec. E. TARANTO; publ. *Australian Geographer* (3 a year).

Mapping Sciences Institute, Australia: GPO Box 1817, Brisbane, Qld 4000; tel. (7) 3343-7706; fax (7) 3219-2281; e-mail msiau@ gil.com.au; internet www.mappingsciences .org.au; f. 1952; holds biennial conferences; 1,250 mems; Nat. Pres. JOHN MCCORMACK; Hon. Sec. K. H. SMITH; publ. *Cartography* (2 a year).

Royal Australian Historical Society: History House, 133 Macquarie St, Sydney, NSW 2000; tel. (2) 9247-8001; fax (2) 9247-7854; e-mail history@rahs.org.au; internet www .rahs.org.au; f. 1901; 2,000 mems; library of 30,000 items; Man. MARI METZKE; Librarian DONNA NEWTON; publs *Journal* (2 a year), *History Magazine* (4 a year).

Royal Geographical Society of Queensland Inc.: 237 Milton Rd, Milton, Qld 4064; tel. (7) 3368-2066; fax (7) 3367-1011; e-mail admin@rgsq.org.au; internet www.rgsq.org .au; f. 1885; 400 mems; library of 2,500 monographs, 320 periodicals, maps; Pres. KEN GRANGER; Sec. KEITH SMITH.

Royal Historical Society of Queensland: POB 12057, George St, Brisbane, Qld 4003; tel. (7) 3221-4198; fax (7) 3221-4698; e-mail info@queenslandhistory.org.au; internet queenslandhistory.org.au; f. 1913; Welsby library; research; historical documents preserved and filed; photographic colln; social history; museum; 600 mems; Pres. Dr IAN HADWEN; Man. ALLAN R. BELL; publs *Bulletin* (12 a year), *Journal* (4 a year).

Royal Historical Society of Victoria: 239 A'Beckett St, Melbourne, Vic. 3000; tel. (3) 9326-9288; fax (3) 9326-9477; e-mail office@ historyvictoria.org.au; internet www .historyvictoria.org.au; f. 1909; research; collection of historical material; exhibitions; 1,600 mems; library of 8,000 vols, MSS, photographs, paintings and prints; Pres. Prof. WESTON BATE; Exec. Officer Dr ELIZABETH RUSHDEN; publs *Journal* (2 a year), *History News* (12 a year).

Royal Western Australian Historical Society: Stirling House, 49 Broadway, Nedlands, WA 6009; tel. (8) 9386-3841; fax (8) 9386-3309; e-mail histwest@git.com.au; internet www.histwest.org.au; f. 1926; runs museum, research library and bookshop specialising in W Australian history and archival products; 1,000 mems; Pres. BOB NICHOLSON; publs *Early Days* (1 a year), *History West* (12 a year).

Society of Australian Genealogists: Richmond Villa, 120 Kent St, Sydney, NSW 2000; tel. (2) 9247-3953; fax (2) 9241-4872; e-mail info@sag.org.au; internet www.sag.org.au; f. 1932; 7,500 mems; library of 20,000 vols, 1,000 microfilm reels, 1m. names on microfiche, 40,000 photographs, 30,000 MSS; Exec. Officer H. E. GARNSEY; Librarian ANGELA PHIPPEN; publ. *Descent* (4 a year).

LANGUAGE AND LITERATURE

Alliance Française: 66 McCaughey St, Turner, Canberra, ACT 2601; tel. (2) 6247-5027; fax (2) 6257-6696; e-mail administration@afcanberra.com.au; internet www.alliancefrancaise.com.au; offers courses and examinations in French language and culture and promotes cultural exchange with France; attached teaching centres in Adelaide, Albury, Armidale, Atherton, Ballarat, Blue Mountains, Brisbane, Canberra, Darwin, Davenport, Esperance, Eurobodolla, Geelong, Gold Coast, Gosford, Hobart, Illawarra, Launceston, Lismore, Melbourne, Merimbula, Milton/Ulladulla, Newcastle, Perth, Port Macquerie, Rockhampton, Sunshine Coast, Sydney, Toowoomba, Townsville, Wagga Wagga; Dir BRUNO DUPARC.

Australasian and Pacific Society for Eighteenth-Century Studies: c/o Humanities Research Centre, Australian National University, ACT 0200; f. 1970; one of the sponsoring bodies of the David Nichol Smith Seminars; 80 mems; Pres. Prof. IAIN McCALMAN.

Australian Society of Authors Ltd: POB 1566, Strawberry Hills, NSW 2012; tel. (2) 9318-0877; fax (2) 9318-0530; e-mail asa@asauthors.org; internet www.asauthors.org; f. 1963; 3,000 mems; Chair. SUSAN HAYES; publ. *The Australian Author* (3 a year).

British Council: POB 88, Edgecliff, NSW 2027; tel. (2) 9326-2022; fax (2) 9327-4868; e-mail enquiries@britishcouncil.org.au; internet www.britishcouncil.org/au.htm; offers courses and examinations in English language and British culture and promotes cultural exchange with the UK; Dir CHRISTOPHER WADE.

English Association Sydney Inc.: POB 91, Wentworth Bldg, Univ. of Sydney, Sydney, NSW 2006; e-mail r.madelaine@unsw.edu.au; f. 1923; organizes conferences for teachers and study days for students; 70 mems; Pres. Assoc. Prof. RICHARD MADELAINE; Sec. Dr ROB JACKSON; Treas. CERIDWEN LEE; publ. *Southerly* (4 a year).

Fellowship of Australian Writers NSW Inc.: POB 488, Rozelle, NSW 2039; tel. (2) 9810-1307; e-mail honsecretary@fawnsw.org.au; internet www.fawnsw.org.au; f. 1928; 4,000 nat. mems; brs in all states and territories; Pres. TREVAR LANGLANDS; Sec. COLLEEN PARKER; publ. *Writers' Voice* (every 3 months).

Goethe-Institut: 90 Ocean St, Woollahra, Sydney, NSW 2025; tel. (2) 8356-8333; fax (2) 8356-8314; e-mail info@sydney.goethe.org; internet www.goethe.de/sydney; offers courses and examinations in the German language and promotes German culture and cultural exchange with Germany; Dir KLAUS KRISCHOK.

PEN International (Sydney Centre): Faculty of Humanities and Social Sciences, University of Technology, Sydney, NSW 2007; tel. (2) 9514-2738; fax (2) 9514-2778; e-mail sydney@pen.org.au; internet www.pen.org.au; f. 1926; promotes friendship and intellectual co-operation among writers; 160 mems; Pres. NICHOLAS JOSE; publ. *Newsletter* (4 a year).

MEDICINE

Australasian Association of Clinical Biochemists: POB 278, Mt Lawley, WA 6929; tel. (8) 9370-5224; fax (8) 9370-4409; e-mail office@aacb.asn.au; internet www.aacb.asn.au; f. 1961; 1,400 mems; Chair. MARY CONROY; Sec. CONCHITA KUEK; publs *Clinical Biochemist Newsletter* (4 a year), *Clinical Biochemist Reviews* (4 a year).

Australasian Chapter of Sexual Health Medicine: 145 Macquarie St, Sydney, NSW 2000; tel. (2) 9256-9643; fax (2) 9256-9693; e-mail sexualhealthmed@racp.edu.au; internet www.racp.edu.au; f. 1988; aims to further the professional devt of medical practitioners in the discipline of sexual health medicine; 185 mems; Pres. Prof. DARREN RUSSELL; Exec. Officer SUZANNE MARKS.

Australasian College of Dermatologists: POB 2065, Boronia Park, NSW 2111; tel. (2) 8765-0242; fax (2) 9736-1174; e-mail admin@dermcoll.asn.au; internet www.dermcoll.asn.au; f. 1966; 430 mems; undertakes training of dermatologists and scientific research; scientific conferences; provides public education in skin protection; Pres. Dr IAN McCROSSIN; Hon. Sec. Dr CATHY REID; publ. *The Australasian Journal of Dermatology* (3 a year).

Australian Association of Neurologists: Royal Australasian College of Physicians, 145 Macquarie St, Sydney, NSW 2000; tel. (2) 9256-5443; fax (2) 9241-4083; e-mail aansyd@hotkey.net.au; internet www.medeserv.com.au/aan/index.cfm; f. 1950 to bring together clinical neurologists and scientific workers in the field of the nervous system and its diseases by such means as meetings, provision of special facilities and assistance in any publications on these matters; 450 mems; Pres. Prof. GEOFFREY DONNAN; Hon. Sec. Assoc. Prof. RICHARD MACDONNELL; publ. *Clinical and Experimental Neurology* (1 a year).

Australian Dental Association: 75 Lithgow St, POB 520, St Leonards, NSW 2065; tel. (2) 9906-4412; fax (2) 9906-4676; e-mail adainc@ada.org.au; internet www.ada.org.au; f. 1928 to promote the art and science of dentistry and to promote dental health to the public; 9,500 mems; Chief Exec. ROBERT N. BOYD-BOLAND; publs *Australian Dental Journal* (4 a year), *News Bulletin* (12 a year).

Australian Institute of Holistic Medicine: POB 3079, Success, WA 6964; tel. (8) 9417-3553; fax (8) 9417-1881; f. 1946; education and research in the field of natural medicine; Dean of Studies Dr S. JAYAWARDANA.

Australian Medical Association: 42 Macquarie Street, Barton, ACT 2600; tel. (2) 6270-5400; fax (2) 6270-5499; e-mail ama@ama.com.au; internet www.ama.com.au; Sec.-Gen. Dr ROBYN MASON; publs *Australian Medicine, Medical Journal of Australia*.

Australian Physiological Society: c/o Dr David Saint, School of Molecular and Biomedical Science, University of Adelaide, Adelaide, SA 5005; tel. (8) 8303-3931; fax (8) 8303-3356; e-mail david.saint@adelaide.edu.au; internet www.aups.org.au; f. 1960 for the advancement of sciences of physiology; 350 mems; Pres. Prof. DAVID ADAMS; National Sec. Dr DAVID SAINT; publ. *Proceedings* (2 a year).

Australian Physiotherapy Association: Level 1, 1175 Toorak Rd, Camberwell, Vic. 3124; tel. (3) 9092-0888; fax (3) 9092-0899; e-mail national.office@physiotherapy.asn.au; internet www.physiotherapy.asn.au; f. 1905; provides postgraduate courses and professional services; 13,000 mems; Nat. Pres.

PATRICK MAHER; CEO IAN MAYER; publ. *Journal of Physiotherapy* (4 a month).

Australian Society of Clinical Hypnotherapists: POB 471, Eastwood, NSW 2122; tel. and fax (2) 9874-2776; e-mail secretary@asch.com.au; internet www.asch.com.au; f. 1974; to advance knowledge and practice of hypnosis and to maintain the highest ethical standards in its use; 350 mems; Pres. LYNDALL BRIGGS; Sec. EDWARD ZWICKI; publ. *The Australian Journal of Clinical Hypnotherapy and Hypnosis* (2 a year).

Optometrists Association Australia: POB 185, Carlton South, Vic. 3053; tel. (3) 9663-8533; fax (3) 9663-7478; e-mail oaanat@optometrists.asn.au; internet www.optometrists.asn.au; f. 1918; promotes optometry and public education on vision care; 3,600 mems; Pres. ANDREW HARRIS; CEO JOSEPH CHAKMAN; publs *Australian Optometry* (12 a year), *Clinical and Experimental Optometry* (6 a year).

Royal Australasian College of Dental Surgeons: 64 Castlereagh St, Sydney, NSW 2000; tel. (2) 9232-3800; fax (2) 9221-8108; e-mail registrar@racds.org; internet www.racds.org; f. 1965; holds scientific meetings and administers examinations; 1,233 fellows; Pres. NEIL J. PEPPITT; Hon. Sec. STEPHEN C. DAYMOND; publs *Annals* (2 a year), *Lecture Notes in Anatomy* (1 a year), *Lecture Notes in Biochemistry* (1 a year), *Lecture Notes in Histology* (1 a year), *Lecture Notes in Microbiology* (1 a year), *Lecture Notes in Pathology* (1 a year), *Lecture Notes in Physiology* (1 a year), *Sedation Guidelines* (irregular).

Royal Australasian College of Physicians: 145 Macquarie St, Sydney, NSW 2000; tel. (2) 9256-5444; fax (2) 9252-3310; e-mail racp@racp.edu.au; internet www.racp.edu.au; f. 1938; charitable, educational and scientific activities; 7,000 fellows; library of 40,000 vols; History of Medicine library containing Ford Collection of rare Australiana; Pres. Dr JILL SEWELL (Vic.); CEO CRAIG PATTERSON; publs *Internal Medicine Journal* (12 a year), *Journal of Paediatrics and Child Health* (6 a year).

Royal Australasian College of Surgeons: College of Surgeons' Gardens, Melbourne, Vic. 3000; tel. (3) 9249-1200; fax (3) 9249-1219; internet www.surgeons.org; CEO Dr DAVID HILLIS; Pres. Dr ANDREW SUTHERLAND; publ. *Australian and New Zealand Journal of Surgery* (12 a year).

Royal Australian and New Zealand College of Ophthalmologists: 94–98 Chalmers St, Surry Hills, Sydney, NSW 2010; tel. (2) 9690-1001; fax (2) 9690-1321; e-mail ranzco@ranzco.edu; internet www.ranzco.edu; f. 1969 (formerly Ophthalmological Society of Australia); 1,322 mems; CEO ROBERT GUEST; Pres. Dr PETER HENDERSON; Vice-Pres. MICHAEL TREPLIN; Hon. Sec. CRAIG DONALDSON; publ. *Clinical and Experimental Ophthalmology* (6 a year).

The Royal Australian and New Zealand College of Psychiatrists: 309 La Trobe St, Melbourne, Vic. 3000; tel. (3) 9640-0646; fax (3) 9642-5652; e-mail ranzcp@ranzcp.org; internet www.ranzcp.org; f. 1963, present name 1976; 2,429 fellows, 650 trainees; CEO Dr SHARON BROWNIE; publs *Australian and New Zealand Journal of Psychiatry, Australasian Psychiatry*.

Royal Australian and New Zealand College of Radiologists: Level 9, 51 Druitt St, Sydney, NSW 2000; tel. (2) 9268-9777; fax (2) 9268-9799; e-mail ranzcr@ranzcr.edu.au; internet www.ranzcr.edu.au; f. 1935; 2,301 mems; CEO DON SWINBOURNE; publ. *Australasian Radiology*.

Royal College of Nursing, Australia: 1 Napier Close, Deakin West, ACT 2600; tel. (2) 6283-3400; fax (2) 6282-3565; e-mail canberra@rcna.org.au; internet www.rcna .org.au; f. 1949; aims to promote improvement in nursing practice through education and research; grants membership to graduates of approved courses; administers nat. scholarships and research grants; conducts policy and devt programme, distance education programme; 10,000 mems; Pres. STEPHANIE FOX-YOUNG; CEO DEBRA CERASA; publs *Collegian* (4 a year), *Nursing Review* (12 a year), *RCNA News* (12 a year).

Royal College of Pathologists of Australasia: Durham Hall, 207 Albion St, Surry Hills, NSW 2010; tel. (2) 8356-5858; fax (2) 8356-5828; e-mail rcpa@rcpa.edu.au; internet www.rcpa.edu.au; f. 1956; 2,700 mems; Pres. Dr PAUL McKENZIE; CEO Dr DEBRA GRAVES; publ. *Pathology*.

Sydney Medical School Foundation: Edward Ford Bldg A27, University of Sydney, Sydney, NSW 2006; tel. (2) 9351-7315; fax (2) 9036-9182; e-mail smsf@sydney.edu .au; internet www.medicalfoundation.usyd .edu.au; f. 1958 to raise funds for medical research; previously known as the Medical Foundation; supports all areas of medical research within the Faculty of Medicine at the Univ. of Sydney; focuses on the translation of research knowledge to health outcomes through improved treatment options and prevention of disease; funds research; Pres. ROGER CORBETT; Man. SALLY THOMSON.

NATURAL SCIENCES

General

Australian Academy of Science: GPOB 783, Canberra, ACT 2601; tel. (2) 6201-9400; fax (2) 6201-9494; e-mail eb@science.org.au; internet www.science.org.au; f. 1954; ind. non-profit org. for Australia's leading research scientists, elected for their personal contributions to science; recognizes research excellence, advises government, organizes scientific conferences, publishes scientific books and journals; administers int. exchange programmes and promotes science education and public awareness of science and technology; 420 fellows; Pres. Prof. KURT LAMBECK; Chief Exec. SUE MEEK; Sec. for Biological Sciences Prof. GRAHAM FARQUHAR; Sec. for Education and Public Awareness Prof. JULIE CAMPBELL; Sec. for Physical Sciences Dr PETER HALL; Sec. for Science Policy Dr ROBERT WILLAMSON; Foreign Sec. Prof. JENNY GRAVES; Treasurer Prof. MICHAEL DOPITA; publ. *Records*.

Australian and New Zealand Association for the Advancement of Science (ANZAAS): University of Adelaide, Adelaide, SA 5005; tel. (8) 8303-4965; fax (8) 8177-1732; e-mail mail@anzaas.org.au; internet anzaas.org.au; f. 1886; 1,000 mems; divs in NSW, Vic., SA, WA, Tas., ACT and NT, also overseas mems; Sec. ROBERT PERRIN; publ. *ANZAAS Mercury* (4 a year).

Australian Conservation Foundation: Floor 1, 60 Leicester St, Carlton, Vic. 3053; tel. (3) 9345-1111; fax (3) 9345-1166; e-mail acf@acfonline.org.au; internet www.acfonline .org.au; f. 1965; non-profit org. working for an ecologically sustainable society; 60,000 mems and supporters; library of 15,000 vols; Pres. Prof. IAN LOWE; Dir DON HENRY; publs *Bilby Bulletin, Habitat* (6 a year).

Federation of Australian Scientific and Technological Societies: POB 218, Deakin West, Canberra, ACT 2600; tel. (2) 6257-2891; fax (2) 6257-2897; e-mail fasts@anu .edu.au; internet www.fasts.org; f. 1985 to foster close relations between the scientific and technological socs in Australia and to take concerted action for promoting science and technology in Australia; 60 mem. socs; Pres. Prof. CHRIS FELL; Pres.-Elect Prof. SNOW BARLOW; Exec. Dir BRADLEY SMITH; publ. *FASTS Circular* (12 a year).

Royal Society of New South Wales: 6/142 Herring Rd, North Ryde, POB 1525, Macquarie Centre, NSW 2113; tel. (2) 9887-4448; fax (2) 9887-4448; internet www.science.uts .edu.au/rsnsw; f. 1821; collection of monographs and periodicals relating to the history of Australian science, manuscripts of original research results; 305 mems; Pres. K. F. KELLY; Hon. Sec. Prof. Dr P. A. WILLIAMS; publs *Bulletin* (12 a year), *Journal and Proceedings* (2 a year).

Royal Society of Queensland: POB 6021, St Lucia, Qld 4067; e-mail rsocqld@gmail .com; internet qld.royalsoc.org.au; f. 1884; natural and applied sciences; 100 mems; library of 75,000 vols; Pres. CRAIG WALTON; publ. *Proceedings of the Royal Society of Queensland* (1 a year).

Royal Society of South Australia Inc.: c/o South Australian Museum, North Terrace, Adelaide, SA 5000; e-mail roysocsa@gmail .com; internet www.adelaide.edu.au/rssa; f. 1853; natural sciences; 283 mems; Pres. Dr JOHN JENNINGS; Hon. Sec. Dr KIM CRITCHLEY; publs *Regional Natural Histories* (irregular), *Transactions* (1 a year).

Royal Society of Tasmania: GPOB 1166, Hobart, Tas. 7001; tel. (3) 6211-4177; fax (3) 6211-4112; e-mail royal.society@tmag.tas .gov.au; internet rst.org.au; f. 1843; 360 mems; library of 40,000 vols; Pres. Dr PAT QUILTY; Hon. Sec. TONY CULBERG; publ. *Papers and Proceedings* (1 a year).

Royal Society of Victoria: 9 Victoria St, Melbourne, Vic. 3000; tel. (3) 9663-5259; fax (3) 9663-2301; e-mail rsv@sciencevictoria.org .au; internet www.sciencevictoria.org.au; f. 1854; 750 mems; library: large colln of scientific periodicals, incl. *Science* since 1854, *Polar Science* since 1863; Pres. Prof. GRAHAM D. BURROWS; Hon. Sec. Prof. T. FRED SMITH; publ. *Proceedings* (2 a year).

Royal Society of Western Australia: c/o Western Australian Museum, Locked Bag 49, Welshpool DC, WA 6986; tel. (8) 9212-3771; fax (8) 9212-3882; e-mail rswa@museum.wa .gov.au; internet www.ecu.edu.au/pa/rswa; f. 1913; to promote and foster natural and physical science and facilitate interdisciplinary interaction; study of botany, zoology, geology, anthropology, geography, physics and chemistry; 395 mems; Pres. Dr COLIN WALKER; Joint Secs Dr LYNNE MILNE, MARGARET BROCX; publ. *Journal* (4 a year).

Biological Sciences

Australian Society for Fish Biology: WA Marine Research Laboratories, POB 20, North Beach, WA 6020; tel. (8) 9246-8418; e-mail dgaughan@fish.wa.gov.au; internet www.asfb.org.au; f. 1971 to promote the study of fish and fisheries in Australia and provide a communications medium for Australian fish workers; 530 mems; Pres. Dr DAN GAUGHAN; Sec. and Vice-Pres. KIM SMITH; publ. *Newsletter* (2 a year).

Australian Society for Limnology: Museum of Victoria, GPOB 666, Melbourne, Vic. 3001; tel. (3) 8341-7433; fax (3) 8341-7456; e-mail rmarch@museum.vic.gov.au; internet www.asl.org.au; f. 1961; study and management of inland waters, maintenance of biodiversity, restoration of water quality and wise use of aquatic resources; 600 mems, incl. researchers, managers, engineers, teachers and tertiary-level students; Sec. Dr RICHARD MARCHANT; publ. *ASL Newsletter* (4 a year).

Australian Society for Microbiology Inc.: Unit 23, 20 Commercial Rd, Melbourne, Vic. 3004; tel. (3) 9867-8699; fax (3) 9867-8722; f. 1959; 3,200 mems; Pres. Assoc. Prof. JOHN FINLAY-JONES; Sec. Dr J. LANSER; publs *Microbiology Australia* (5 a year), *Recent Advances in Microbiology* (1 a year).

Australian Society for Parasitology: c/o Heather Koch, Secretary, PO Royal Brisbane Hospital, Brisbane, Qld 4029; tel. (2) 6257-9022; fax (2) 6257-9055; e-mail heather .koch@animalhealthalliance.org.au; internet www.parasite.org.au; f. 1964; all aspects of parasitology, including immunology and vaccinology; 450 mems; 34 fellows; Pres. PETER HOLDSWORTH; Sec. HEATHER KOCH; publ. *International Journal for Parasitology* (12 a year).

Ecological Society of Australia Inc.: POB 1564, Canberra, ACT 2601; tel. (8) 8953-7544; fax (8) 8953-7566; e-mail executiveofficer@ecolsoc.org.au; internet www.ecolsoc.org.au; f. 1960 to promote the scientific study of plants and animals in relation to their environment, and publish the results of research; to facilitate the exchange of ideas among ecologists; to promote the application of ecological principles to the devt, utilization and conservation of Australian natural resources; to advise govt and other agencies; to foster the reservation of natural areas for scientific and recreational purposes; 1,564 mems; Pres. C. CATTERALL; Sec. T. SILBERBAUER; Exec. Officers T. HOWARD, L. McMILLAN; publs *Bulletin* (4 a year), *Austral Ecology* (6 a year), *Environmental Management and Restoration* (3 a year).

Entomological Society of New South Wales Inc.: Entomology Dept, The Australian Museum, 6–8 College St, Sydney, NSW 2000; e-mail tanya.james@agric.nsw.gov.au; internet entsocnsw.netfirms.com; f. 1953; 180 mems; Pres. MARTIN HORWOOD; Hon. Sec. TANYA JAMES; publ. *General and Applied Entomology* (1 a year).

Entomological Society of Queensland: POB 537, Indooroopilly, Brisbane, Qld 4072; e-mail esq@uqconnect.net; internet www.esq .org.au/entomologist.html; independent; f. 1923; 300 mems; Pres. Dr P. ALLSOPP; Sec. G. MAYWALD; publs *News Bulletin* (10 a year), *The Australian Entomologist* (3–4 a year).

Field Naturalists Club of Victoria: Locked Bag 3, Post Office, Blackburn, Vic. 3130; tel. (3) 9877-9860; fax (3) 9877-9860; e-mail fncv@vicnet.net.au; internet www .vicnet.net.au/~fncv; f. 1880; study of natural history and conservation of environment; 1,000 mems; Pres. KAREN MUSCAT; publs *The Victorian Naturalist* (6 a year), *Field Nats News* (11 a year).

Malacological Society of Australasia: c/o Dept of Malacology, Australian Museum, 6 College St, Sydney, NSW 2010; tel. (2) 9320-6052; fax (2) 9320-6050; e-mail info@ malsocaus.org; internet www.malsocaus.org; f. 1955; promotes the study of molluscs; 170 mems; Pres. Dr RACHEL PRZESLAWSKI; Treasurer Dr DON COLGAN; publs *Malacological Society of Australasia Newsletter* (3 a year), *Molluscan Research* (3 a year).

Royal Australasian Ornithologists Union & Birds Australia: 415 Riversdale Rd, Hawthorn East, Vic. 3123; tel. (3) 9882-2622; fax (3) 9882-2677; e-mail mail@ birdsaustralia.com.au; internet www .birdsaustralia.com.au; f. 1901; for conservation and scientific study of Australasian birds; extensive library and database; 7,000 mems; CEO JIM DOWNEY; publs *Wingspan, Emu, Stilt* (bulletin of Australasian Wader Studies Group, 2 a year), *Eclectus* (bulletin of Parrot Group, 2 a year), *ASE News* (Seabird

Group newsletter), *ARA News* (Raptor Group newsletter, 2 a year).

Royal Zoological Society of New South Wales: POB 20, Mosman, NSW 2088; tel. (2) 9969-7336; fax (2) 9969-7336; f. 1879; 1,000 mems; Pres. Dr PAT HUTCHINGS; Exec. Officer GILLIAN SIMPSON; publ. *Australian Zoologist* (2 a year).

Royal Zoological Society of South Australia Inc.: Frome Rd, Adelaide, SA 5000; tel. (8) 8267-3255; fax (8) 8239-0637; internet www.zoossa.com.au; f. 1878; maintains public zoo and open-range park; plays an active role in the conservation of endangered species, conservation education and in conservation research; 22,000 mems; library of 4,500 items; books, audiovisual and digital media; CEO Prof. C. WEST.

Wildlife Preservation Society of Australia Inc.: POB 42, Brighton Le Sands, NSW 2216; tel. (2) 9556-1537; fax (2) 9500-0000; e-mail wildlifepreservation@optusnet.com.au; internet www.wpsa.org.au; f. 1909; ind., voluntary, non-profit org., committed to the preservation of Australia's flora and fauna; provides advice to govt agencies and instns regarding environmental and conservation issues; nat. environmental education programmes, political lobbying, advocacy and practical conservation work; 1,000 mems; Nat. Pres. PATRICK W. MEDWAY; Hon. Sec. SUZANNE MEDWAY; publ. *Australian Wildlife Magazine* (4 a year).

Zoological Parks and Gardens Board: POB 74, Parkville, Vic. 3052; tel. (3) 9285-9300; fax (3) 9285-9330; e-mail zpgb@zoo.org.au; internet www.zoo.org.au; f. 1937 as successor to Royal Zoological and Acclimatization Soc. of Victoria (f. 1857); responsible for the management of the Royal Melbourne Zoological Gardens, Healesville Sanctuary and Victoria's Open Range Zoo at Werribee; 9 mems; Chair. TINA MCMECKAN.

Mathematical Sciences

Australian Mathematical Society: Dept of Mathematics, La Trobe University, Bundoora, Vic. 3086; tel. (3) 9479-2597; fax (3) 9479-2466; e-mail secretary@austms.org.au; internet www.austms.org.au; f. 1956; 900 mems; fosters communication among its members, and organizes and supports mathematical conferences in Australasia; makes grants to promote mathematical investigations; awards prizes; raises community awareness about the importance and benefits of mathematics; Pres. Prof. NALINI JOSHI; Sec. Dr PETER STACEY; Treas. Dr ALGY HOWE; publs *ANZIAM Journal* (4 a year), *Bulletin of the Australian Mathematical Society* (6 a year), *Gazette of the Australian Mathematical Society* (5 a year), *Journal of the Australian Mathematical Society* (6 a year).

Statistical Society of Australia, Inc.: POB 5111, Braddon, ACT 2612; tel. (2) 6249-8266; fax (2) 6249-6558; e-mail admin@statsoc.org.au; internet www.statsoc.org.au; f. 1959; 800 mems; Pres. Prof. KAYE BASFORD; Sec. Dr DOUGLAS SHAW; publs *Australian & New Zealand Journal of Statistics* (4 a year), *SSAI Newsletter* (4 a year).

Physical Sciences

Astronomical Society of Australia: c/o School of Physics, Univ. of Sydney, Sydney, NSW 2006; tel. (2) 9351-3184; fax (2) 9351-7726; e-mail john.obyrne@sydney.edu.au; internet asa.astronomy.org.au; f. 1966 as the Org. of Professional Astronomers in Australia; 500 mems; Pres. Prof. WARRICK COUCH; Sec. Dr JOHN O'BYRNE; Sec. Dr. MARC DULDIG; publ. *Publications of the Astronomical Society of Australia* (online, 4 a year).

Astronomical Society of South Australia Inc.: GPOB 199, Adelaide, SA 5001; tel. (8) 8270-3631; e-mail info@assa.org.au; internet www.assa.org.au; f. 1892; 500 mems; library of 400 vols; Pres. DEAN DAVIDSON; Sec. IAN ANDERSON; publ. *The Bulletin* (12 a year).

Astronomical Society of Tasmania Inc.: c/o The Secretary, POB 1654, Hobart, Tas. 7001; tel. (3) 6323-3777; fax (3) 6323-3776; internet www.ast.net.au; f. 1934; 100 mems; Pres. S. W. MATHERS; Sec. LAURIE PRIEST; publs *Annual Ephemeris for Tasmania*, *Bulletin* (6 a year).

Astronomical Society of Victoria Inc.: GPOB 1059, Melbourne, Vic. 3001; tel. (3) 9888-7130; internet www.asv.org.au; f. 1922; 18 sections: Astrophotography, Computing, Comet, Cosmology and Astrophysics, Deep Sky, Demonstrators, Historical, Instrument Making, Lunar and Planetary, Outdoor Lighting Improvement, Meteors, Radio Astronomy, Solar, Variable Stars and Nova Search, Club, Diurnals (day group), Junior (for children aged 17 and under) and New Astronomers' Group; 1,000 mems; library of 3,000 vols; Pres. BARRY ADCOCK; Gen. Sec. ANNE WILLIAMS; publs *Crux Magazine* (6 a year), *Yearbook* (1 a year).

Australasian College of Physical Scientists and Engineers in Medicine: Ste 3.13, 247 Coward St, Mascot, NSW 2020; tel. (2) 9700-8522; fax (2) 9693-5145; e-mail secretary@acpsem.org.au; internet www.acpsem.org.au; f. 1977 to promote the devt of the physical sciences as applied to medicine, to facilitate the exchange of information and ideas among mems and others, to disseminate knowledge relating to physical sciences and their application to medicine; 500 mems; Gen. Man. C. JAMES; Hon. Sec. Dr JOHN R. COLES; publ. *Australasian Physical and Engineering Sciences in Medicine* (4 a year).

Australian Acoustical Society: POB 903, Castlemaine, Vic. 3450; tel. (3) 5470-6381; fax (3) 5470-6381; e-mail watkinsd@castlemaine.net; internet www.acoustics.asn.au; f. 1971; 420 mems; Pres. KEN MIKL; Gen. Sec. D. WATKINS; publ. *Acoustics Australia* (3 a year).

Australian Institute of Physics: 1/21 Vale Street, North Melbourne, Vic. 3051; tel. (3) 9326-6669; fax (3) 9328-2670; internet www.physics.usyd.edu.au/aipaust; f. 1963; 2,500 mems; Pres. Prof. ROBERT ELLMAN; Hon. Sec. Dr IAN BAILEY; publ. *The Physicist* (6 a year).

Geological Society of Australia: Suite 706, 301 George St, Sydney, NSW 2000; tel. (2) 9290-2194; fax (2) 9290-2198; e-mail info@gsa.org.au; internet www.gsa.org.au; f. 1953; 2,300 mems; publs *Australian Journal of Earth Sciences* (8 a year), *Alcheringa* (4 a year).

Royal Australian Chemical Institute: 21 Vale St, North Melbourne, Vic. 3051; tel. (3) 9328-2033; fax (3) 9328-2670; e-mail member@raci.org.au; internet www.raci.org.au; f. 1917, inc. by Royal Charter 1932; it is both the qualifying body for professional chemists and a learned society that aims to promote the science and practice of chemistry in all its branches; 9,500 mems; Pres. DAVID EDMONDS; Hon. Gen. Sec. Dr JANE WEDER; publ. *Chemistry in Australia* (12 a year).

PHILOSOPHY AND PSYCHOLOGY

Australasian Association of Philosophy: POB 1978, Hobart, Tas. 7009; tel. (3) 6294-6319; e-mail elizagoddard@aap.org.au; internet www.aap.org.au; f. 1923; professional org. of academic philosophers in Australia, New Zealand and Singapore; promotes the study of philosophy in Australasia; motes the study of philosophy in Australasia; coordinates professional activities; 400 mems; Chair. Prof. GRAHAM OPPY PRIEST; Exec. Officer ELIZA GODDARD; Sec. Dr TIM OAKLEY; publ. *Australasian Journal of Philosophy* (4 a year).

Australian Psychological Society: POB 38, Flinders Lane, Vic. 8009; 11th Fl., 257 Collins St, Melbourne, Vic. 3000; tel. (3) 8662-3300; fax (3) 9663-6177; e-mail assessments@psychology.org.au; internet www.psychology.org.au; f. 1966; 17,500 mems; Pres. Prof. BOB MONTGOMERY; Exec. Dir Dr LYNDEL LITTLEFIELD; publs *Australian Journal of Psychology* (3 a year), *Australian Psychologist* (3 a year), *In-Psych* (6 a year).

RELIGION, SOCIOLOGY AND ANTHROPOLOGY

The Australian Sociological Association: Institute for Social Research, Swinburne Univ. of Technology, POB 218, Hawthorn, Vic. 3122; tel. (3) 9214-5283; fax (3) 9214-8643; e-mail admin@tasa.org.au; internet www.tasa.org.au; f. 1963; aims to promote devt of sociology in Australia, facilitate sociology teaching and research, and enhance the professional devt of mems; 600 mems; Pres. Prof. MICHAEL GILDING; Vice-Pres. Dr DEB KING; Sec. EILEEN CLARK; Treas. Dr WENDY HILLMAN; publs *Journal of Sociology* (4 a year), *Health Sociology Review* (4 a year).

TECHNOLOGY

Australasian Institute of Mining and Metallurgy: Level 3, 15–31 Pelham St, Carlton, Vic. 3053; tel. (3) 9662-3166; fax (3) 9662-3662; e-mail publications@ausimm.com.au; internet www.ausimm.com.au; f. 1893; incorporated by Royal Charter 1955; 8,500 mems; Pres. IAN GOULD; publ. *The AusIMM Bulletin* (6 a year).

Australian Academy of Technological Sciences and Engineering: Ian McLennan House, 197 Royal Parade, Parkville, Vic. 3052; tel. (3) 9347-0622; fax (3) 9347-8237; e-mail paulaw@atse.org.au; internet www.atse.org.au; f. 1976; promotion of scientific and engineering knowledge for practical purposes; 670 fellows (incl. 8 hon., 9 foreign, 1 Royal); Pres. Dr J. W. ZILLMAN; CEO Dr JOHN DODGSON; publs *Annual Symposia Proceedings*, *ATSE Focus* (4 a year).

Australian Ceramic Society: c/o Dept of Applied Physics, Curtin University of Technology, GPOB U1987, Perth, WA 6845; tel. (8) 9266-7544; fax (8) 9266-2377; e-mail j.low@curtin.edu.au; internet www.austceram.com; f. 1961; to promote ceramic science and technology and its applications for Australian ceramic industry and art; 300 mems; Fed. Pres. Prof. CHRIS BERNDT; Fed. Sec. Assoc. Prof. JIM LOW; publs *Journal of the Australian Ceramic Society* (2 a year), *Newsbulletin of the Australian Ceramic Society* (4 a year).

Australian Institute of Energy: POB 268, Toukley, NSW 2263; tel. and fax (2) 4393-1114; e-mail aie@aie.org.au; internet www.aie.org.au; f. 1978; 1,500 mems; Pres. Dr MALCOLM MESSENGER; Sec. COLIN PAULSON; Treasurer Dr DAVID ALLARDICE; publ. *Energy News* (4 a year).

Australian Institute of Food Science and Technology Inc.: Suite 2, Level 2, 191 Botany Rd, Waterloo, NSW 2017; tel. (612) 8399-3996; fax (612) 8399-3997; e-mail aifst@aifst.asn.au; internet www.aifst.asn.au; f. 1967; nat. asscn for professionals involved in the science and technology of food; Pres. Prof. PAUL BAUMGARTNER; Treasurer Dr JEFF FAIRBROTHER; publ. *Food Australia* (12 a year).

Research Institutes

Australian Institute of Nuclear Science and Engineering: PMB No. 1, Menai, NSW 2234; tel. (2) 9717-3376; fax (2) 9717-9268; e-mail ainse@ansto.gov.au; internet www.ainse.edu.au; f. 1958; consortium of Australian univs and the Univ. of Auckland, New Zealand, in partnership with the Australian Nuclear Science and Technology Org.; aims to assist research and training in nuclear science and engineering and to make the facilities of the Lucas Heights Research Laboratories available to research staff and students from mem. institutions; projects in advanced materials, biomedicine, environmental science, applications of nuclear physics, nuclear technology and engineering; organizes Australian Numerical Simulation and Modelling Services and Australian Radioisotope Services; organizes conferences, awards postgraduate studentships and research grants; 49 mems; Pres. Prof. JOHN WHITE; Vice-Pres. Prof. BRIAN O'CONNOR; Scientific Sec. Dr DENNIS MATHER; publ. *AINSE Conference Books*.

Australian Robotics and Automation Association Inc.: GPO Box 1527, Sydney, NSW 2001; tel. (2) 9959-3239; fax (2) 9959-4632; internet www.araa.asn.au; f. 1981; professional society concerned with robots, their applications and implications, and related automation technologies; Pres. GORDON WYETH; Vice-Pres. JONATHAN ROBERTS; Sec. MATTHEW DUNBABIN; publ. *Newsletter* (4 a year).

Chartered Institute of Logistics and Transport: POB A2333, Sydney South, NSW 1235; tel. (2) 9267-7538; fax (2) 9864-4738; e-mail admin@cilta.com.au; internet www.cilta.com.au; f. 1935; professional soc. concerned with logistics and transport; 30,000 mems worldwide; Chair. MARK BIRKINSHAW; Admin. Man. JESSICA WONG; publ. *Australian Transport Review* (2 a year).

Institution of Engineers, Australia: 11 National Circuit, Barton, ACT 2600; tel. (2) 6270-6555; fax (2) 6273-1488; e-mail memberservices@engineersaustralia.org.au; internet www.engineersaustralia.org.au; f. 1919; incorporates colleges of Biomedical Engineers, Chemical Engineers, Civil Engineers, Electrical Engineers, Environmental Engineers, Information Telecommunications and Electronics Engineers, Mechanical Engineers, and Structural Engineers; 75,000 mems; Chief Exec. PETER TAYLOR; publs *Australian Journal of Civil Engineering*, *Australian Journal of Electrical and Electronics Engineering*, *Australian Journal of Mechanical Engineering*, *Australian Journal of Multidisciplinary Engineering*, *Australian Journal of Water Resources*, *Chemical Engineering in Australia*, *Civil Engineers Australia* (12 a year), *Engineers Australia* (12 a year), *Engineering World* (6 a year), *Transport Engineering in Australia*.

Institution of Surveyors, Australia: 27–29 Napier Close, Deakin, Canberra, ACT 2600; tel. (2) 6282-2282; fax (2) 6282-2576; e-mail info@isaust.org.au; internet www.isaust.org.au; f. 1952; 3,800 mems; CEO JOHN D. CRICKMORE; publs *Geomatics Research Australasia* (2 a year), *The Australian Surveyor* (1 a year), *Trans Tasman Surveyor* (1 a year).

Royal Aeronautical Society, Australian Division: POB 573, Mascot, NSW 2020; tel. (2) 9523-4332; fax (2) 9523-7158; e-mail austdivision@raes.org.au; internet www.raes.org.au; f. 1927; brs in Adalaide, Brisbane, Canberra, Melbourne, Perth, Sydney; Pres. D. FORSYTH; Hon. Sec. R. D. BARKLA; Treasurer R. H. STEVENS; Admin. Officer PETER BROOKS; publ. *Australian Aeronautics* (every 2 years).

GENERAL

Australian Research Council: GPOB 2702, Canberra, ACT 2601; tel. (2) 6287-6600; fax (2) 6287-6601; e-mail info@arc.gov.au; internet www.arc.gov.au; f. 2001; statutory authority within the Australian Govt's Innovation, Industry, Science and Research (IISR) portfolio; its mission is to advance Australia's research excellence to be globally competitive and deliver benefits to the community; provides advice to the Govt on research matters and manages the National Competitive Grants Programme (NCGP), a significant component of Australia's investment in research and devt, supporting high quality fundamental and applied research and research training through national competition across all disciplines, with the exception of clinical medicine and dentistry; Chief Exec. Prof. MARGARET SHEIL; publs *Discovery* (newsletter, 4 a year), *Strategic Plan* (every 2 years).

AGRICULTURE, FISHERIES AND VETERINARY SCIENCE

Department of Infrastructure, Planning and Natural Resources: GPO Box 39, Sydney, NSW 2001; tel. (2) 9228-6111; fax (2) 9228-6455; internet www.dipnr.nsw.gov.au; conservation and management of crown land, rivers and water resources, containment of salinity and acid sulphate soils; Dir-Gen. JENNIFER WESTACOTT.

EDUCATION

Australian Council for Educational Research Ltd: 19 Prospect Hill Rd (Private Bag 55), Camberwell, Vic. 3124; tel. (3) 9277-5555; fax (3) 9277-5500; e-mail sales@acer.edu.au; internet www.acer.edu.au; f. 1930; ind.; educational research and publishing; books for teachers at all levels, students, parents, psychologists, counsellors, administrators, curriculum writers; educational, psychological and personnel tests; CEO Prof. GEOFFREY MASTERS; publs *Australian Education Index* (subscription database), *Australian Journal of Career Development* (3 a year), *Australian Journal of Education* (3 a year), *Australian Thesaurus of Education Descriptors*, *Education Research Theses* (subscription database), *Recent Developments* (2 a year), *Professional Education* (4 a year), *Teacher* (10 a year).

National Centre for Vocational Education Research (NCVER) Ltd: Level 11, 33 King William St, Adelaide, SA 5000; tel. (8) 8230-8400; fax (8) 8212-3436; e-mail ncver@ncver.edu.au; internet www.ncver.edu.au; f. 1981; ind. org. est. by the Fed., State and Territory ministers responsible for vocational and technical education; Australia's principal provider of vocational education and training (VET) research and statistics; responsible for collecting and managing national VET and New Apprenticeship statistics; provides VET research findings from Australian and int. sources through its VOCED research database; library of 40,000 records; 20,000 full-text; Chair. PETER SHERGOLD; Man. Dir Dr TOM KARMEL; publs *Insight* (news and information, 4 a year), *Vocational Education and Training Research Database (VOCED)* (12 a year).

HISTORY, GEOGRAPHY AND ARCHAEOLOGY

Tasmanian Historical Research Association: POB 441, Sandy Bay, Tas. 7006; tel. (3) 6260-2604; internet www.thra.org.au; f. 1951; 400 mems; Pres. and Chair. Dr ALISON ALEXANDER; Sec. ANDREW MCKINLEY; publ. *Papers and Proceedings* (3 a year).

MEDICINE

Australian Radiation Protection and Nuclear Safety Agency (Australian Department of Health and Ageing): 619 Lower Plenty Rd, Yallambie, Vic. 3085; tel. (3) 9433-2211; fax (3) 9432-1835; e-mail arpansa@arpansa.gov.au; internet www.arpansa.gov.au; f. 1929; works to protect the environment and the health and safety of the public from the harmful effects of radiation; library of 10,000 vols; CEO Dr JOHN LOY; publ. *ARPANSA technical reports* (irregular).

Australian Society for Medical Research: 145 Macquarie St, Sydney, NSW 2000; tel. (2) 9256-5450; fax (2) 9252-0294; e-mail asmr@world.net; internet www.asmr.org.au; f. 1961 to provide a forum for discussion of medical research across disciplinary boundaries, and to encourage recent graduates to consider research as a career; holds Nat. Scientific Conference; 1,400 mems; Hon. Sec. Dr BRONWYN KINGWELL; Hon. Treasurer Dr ROHAN BAKER; publ. *Proceedings*.

Baker IDI Heart and Diabetes Institute: POB 6492, St Kilda Rd Central, Melbourne, Vic. 8008; tel. (3) 8532-1111; fax (3) 8532-1100; e-mail genebank@bakeridi.edu.au; internet www.bakeridi.edu.au; f. 1926; basic, clinical and applied research on cardiovascular disease, physiology, pharmacology, endocrinology, molecular and cell biology; affiliated to WHO, Monash Univ., Alfred Hospital incl. the Alfred Baker Medical Unit (f. 1949); library of 15,000 vols; Pres., Bd of Dirs Prof. ROBERT STEWART; Vice-Pres. PAULA DWYER; publ. *Research*.

CSL Ltd: 45 Poplar Rd, Parkville, Vic. 3052; tel. (3) 9389-1911; fax (3) 9389-1434; f. 1916 for research, production and marketing of biologicals; library: Knowledge Library of 8,500 vols; CEO Dr BRIAN McNAMEE.

Institute of Dental Research: Westmead Millenium Institute, POB 412, Westmead, NSW 2145; f. 1946; for research into biological problems relating to dental health; Head Prof. NEIL HUNTER (acting).

Institute of Medical and Veterinary Science: Frome Rd, Adelaide, SA 5000; tel. (8) 8222-3000; fax (8) 8222-3538; f. 1938 for purposes of research into diseases of human beings and animals, and to provide a diagnostic pathology service for the Royal Adelaide Hospital and for the State through 12 regional laboratories; teaching is provided for the Univ. of Adelaide Medical School; Dir BARRIE VERON-ROBERTS.

Kolling Institute of Medical Research: Royal North Shore Hospital, Pacific Highway, St Leonards, NSW 2065; tel. (2) 9926-8486; fax (2) 9926-8484; e-mail kolling@med.usyd.edu.au; internet www.kolling.usyd.edu.au; f. 1930; research in allergic diseases, molecular genetics and growth factors; Exec. Officer CAMILLA SCANLAN; Technical Officer HELEN YU.

Mental Health Research Institute: 155 Oak St, Parkville, Vic. 3052; tel. (3) 9388-1633; fax (3) 9387-5061; internet www.mhri.edu.au; f. 1956; studies aspects of the nature and treatment of psychiatric illnesses with a particular emphasis on a neuroscience approach to Alzheimer's Disease and to the major psychoses, especially schizophrenia; Chair. Prof. SANDRA HACKER; Exec. Dir Prof. COLIN MASTERS.

National Health and Medical Research Council: GPOB 9848, Canberra, ACT 2601; tel. (2) 6289-9184; fax (2) 6289-9197; e-mail exec.sec@nhmrc.gov.au; internet www

.nhmrc.gov.au; f. 1936 to advise on the achievement and maintenance of the highest practicable standards of individual and public health, and to foster research in the interests of improving those standards; CEO Prof. WARWICK ANDERSON; publ. *Triennial Strategic Plan*.

National Vision Research Institute of Australia: 386 Cardigan St, Carlton, Melbourne, Vic. 3053; tel. (3) 9349-7480; fax (3) 9349-7473; e-mail nvri@optometry.unimelb .edu.au; internet www.optometry.unimelb .edu.au/nvri/nvri.htm; f. 1972; basic, applied and clinical research into vision and visual dysfunction; Chair. S. F. KALFF; Dir of Research Prof. P. R. MARTIN.

Queensland Institute of Medical Research: PO Royal Brisbane Hospital, Brisbane, Qld 4029; tel. (7) 3362-0222; fax (7) 3362-0111; e-mail enquiries@qimr.edu.au; internet www.qimr.edu.au; f. 1946; research into medical problems important in the Australian and Asian Pacific region; current areas are tropical medicine, virology, oncology, cell biology, molecular biology, epidemiology, liver disease, melanoma, mental health, indigenous health; State Medical Research Centre (SMRC) to be constructed by 2012; library of 19,100 vols, 3,000 monographs incl. Eugen Hirschfeld colln of German medical texts dating from 1700s. 600 print journals, 500 online journals and ebooks; Chair. of Council JOHN HAY; Dir Prof. MICHAEL F. GOOD.

Walter and Eliza Hall Institute of Medical Research: 1G Royal Parade, Parkville, Vic. 3050; tel. (3) 9345-2555; fax (3) 9347-0852; e-mail information@wehi.edu.au; internet www.wehi.edu.au; f. 1916; research into cellular and molecular immunology, cancer, immunopathology and immunoparasitology, genome science and bioinformatics; 500 staff; library of 20,000 vols; Dir Prof. DOUG HILTON.

NATURAL SCIENCES
General

Commonwealth Scientific and Industrial Research Organisation (CSIRO): Bag 10, Clayton South, Vic. 3169; tel. (3) 9545-2176; fax (3) 9545-2175; e-mail enquiries@csiro.au; internet www.csiro.au; f. 1926; researches all fields of the physical and biological sciences except defence science, nuclear energy and clinical medicine; Sectors: field crops; food processing; forestry, wood and paper industries; horticulture; meat, dairy and aquaculture; wool and textiles; biodiversity; climate and atmosphere; land and water; marine; information technology and telecommunications; built environment; measurement standards; radio astronomy; services; chemicals and plastics; integrated manufactured products; pharmaceuticals and human health; energy; mineral exploration and mining; mineral processing and metal production; petroleum; library: see Libraries and Archives; Chair. CATHERINE LIVINGSTONE; Chief Exec. Dr GEOFF GARRETT; publs *Australian Journal of Agricultural Research* (8 a year), *Australian Systematic Botany* (4 a year), *Australian Journal of Botany* (6 a year), *Australian Journal of Chemistry* (12 a year), *Australian Journal of Experimental Agriculture* (6 a year), *Australian Journal of Invertebrate Taxonomy* (6 a year), *Australian Journal of Marine and Freshwater Research* (6 a year), *Australian Journal of Physics* (6 a year), *Australian Journal of Plant Physiology* (6 a year), *Australian Journal of Reproduction, Fertility and Development* (6 a year), *Australian Journal of Soil Research* (6 a year), *Australian Journal of Wildlife Research* (6 a year),

Australian Journal of Zoology (6 a year), *ECOS* (4 a year), *The Helix* (6 a year).

National Facility Within CSIRO:

CSIRO–Australia Telescope National Facility: POB 76, Epping, NSW 1710; tel. (2) 9372-4100; fax (2) 9372-4310; e-mail atnf-enquiries@csiro.au; internet www .atnf.csiro.au; f. 1988; a radio telescope array consisting of 6 22-m antennas at the Paul Wild Observatory, Narrabri, NSW, a 22-m antenna at Mopra, west of Coonabarabran, NSW, and a 64-m antenna near Parkes, NSW; Dir Prof. BRIAN BOYLE.

Biological Sciences

Australian Institute of Marine Science: PMB 3, Townsville, MC Qld 4810; tel. (7) 4753-4444; fax (7) 4772-5852; e-mail reception@aims.gov.au; internet www.aims .gov.au; f. 1972; to advance knowledge of the sustainable use and protection of the marine environment, through scientific and technological research; 180 mems; library of 10,000 vols, 1,875 periodicals, 1,544 electronic journals, 450 maps, 55 video cassettes; Chair. WAYNE OSBORNE; CEO Dr IAN R. POINER.

Australian National Botanic Gardens: POB 1777, Canberra, ACT 2601; Clunies Ross St, Black Mountain, Canberra; tel. (2) 6250-9450; fax (2) 6250-9599; e-mail anbg-info@anbg.gov.au; internet www.anbg .gov.au; f. 1970, a few plantings date from 1947; grows a colln of Australian native plants (6,500 species); jtly manages with CSIRO the Centre for Plant Biodiversity Research and Australian National Herbarium with about 1.2m. specimens; manages the Australian Plant Image Index, the largest colln of photographs of Australian native plants; 1,500 mems; library of 13,356 vols, 650 serial titles, 5,000 maps; Dir ANNE DUNCAN; Dir, Centre for Plant Biodiversity Research Dr JUDY WEST.

Royal Botanic Gardens Melbourne: Private Bag 2000, S. Yarra, Vic. 3141; tel. (3) 9252-2300; fax (3) 9252-2350; e-mail rbg@rbg .vic.gov.au; internet www.rbg.vic.gov.au; f. 1846; 36-ha (94-acre) garden with more than 10,000 different species and cultivars of Australian and exotic plants; herbarium of 1m. specimens; library of 50,000 vols; also Royal Botanic Gardens, Cranbourne, for growing display and study of native Australian plants; also Australian Research Centre for Urban Ecology; Dir Dr PHILIP MOORS; publ. *Muelleria*.

Royal Botanic Gardens Sydney: Mrs Macquaries Rd, Sydney, NSW 2000; tel. (2) 9231-8111; fax (2) 9251-4403; e-mail botanical.is@rbgsyd.nsw.gov.au; internet www.rbgsyd.nsw.gov.au; f. 1816; 470-ha living plant colln in 3 botanic gardens and herbarium of 1m. specimens; library of 50,000 vols; Mount Tomah Botanic Garden for cool-climate plants; Mount Annan Botanic Garden for native plants; specialization in research on Australian native plants; Exec. Dir TIM ENTWISLE; publs *Cunninghamia, Telopea*.

Therapeutic Goods Administration Laboratories: POB 100, Woden, ACT 2606; tel. (2) 6232-8400; fax (2) 6232-8442; e-mail tga-information-officer@health.gov .au; internet www.tga.gov.au; f. 1958 as National Biological Standards Laboratories to ensure the quality, safety, efficacy and timely availability of therapeutic goods used in or exported from Australia; part of the Therapeutic Goods Administration, Dept of Health and Aged Care; library of 30,000 vols and 5,000 microfiche; Dir Dr R. J. SMITH; publ. *TGA Laboratory Information Bulletin* (1 a year).

Mathematical Sciences

Australian Bureau of Statistics: Locked Bag 10, Belconnen, ACT 2616; tel. (2) 6252-5000; fax (2) 6251-6009; internet www.abs .gov.au; f. 1905; library of 38,000 vols, 9,600 periodicals; Australian Statistician DENNIS TREWIN; publs *Yearbook Australia* (1 a year), and some 400 other titles listed in *Catalogue of ABS Publications*.

Physical Sciences

Australian Nuclear Science and Technology Organisation (ANSTO): Access ANSTO, PMB 1, Menai, NSW 2234; tel. (2) 9717-3111; fax (2) 9717-9274; internet www .ansto.gov.au; f. 1987; Australia's nat. atomic org.; aims to bring the benefits of atomic science and technology to industry, medicine and the community; research and devt programmes focusing on industrial and other applications of atomic science, environmental science, advanced materials, biomedicine and health; operates nat. facilities, provides technical advice and training; library of 40,000 vols, 900,000 fiches; Chief Exec. Dr ADI PATERSON; publ. scientific papers and reports.

Commonwealth Bureau of Meteorology: GPOB 1289K, Melbourne, Vic. 3001; tel. (3) 9669-4000; fax (3) 9669-4699; internet www .bom.gov.au; f. 1908; regional offices in Perth, Adelaide, Brisbane, Sydney, Hobart, Darwin and Melbourne; library of 80,000 vols; Chair. Prof. VICKI SARA; Dir Dr GEOFF LOVE; publs daily weather bulletins and charts, monthly, seasonal and annual rainfall maps and statistical summaries, publs on spec. subjects, climatological reviews, *Australian Meteorological Magazine* (4 a year).

Geological Survey of New South Wales: Dept of Mineral Resources, POB 536, St Leonards, NSW 1590; tel. (2) 9901-8888; fax (2) 9901-8777; e-mail webcoord@minerals .nsw.gov.au; internet www.minerals.nsw.gov .au; f. 1874; advice on geology and mineral resources of NSW, incl. preparation of standard series geological, geophysical and metallogenic maps; research studies in tectonics, palaeontology, petrology and selected mineral commodities; Dir.-Gen. ALAN COUTTS; publs *Bulletins, Geological and Metallogenic Maps* (with notes), *Geological Memoirs, Mineral Industry, Mineral Resources, Palaeontological Memoirs, Records, Quarterly Notes*.

Geological Survey of Victoria: Dept of Primary Industries, POB 500, East Melbourne, Vic. 3002; tel. (3) 9412-5042; fax (3) 9412-5155; e-mail customer.service@dpi.vic .gov.au; internet www.dpi.vic.gov.au; f. 1852; Man. TOM DICKSON; publ. reports, geological maps, bulletins, etc.

Geological Survey of Western Australia: Mineral House, 100 Plain St, East Perth, WA 6004; tel. (8) 9222-3333; fax (8) 9222-3633; e-mail geological.survey@dmp.wa.gov.au; internet www.dmp.wa.gov.au/gswa; Exec. Dir Dr TIM GRIFFIN; publs *Bulletin, Mineral Resources Bulletin*.

Geoscience Australia (GA): GPOB 378, Canberra, ACT 2601; tel. (2) 6249-9111; fax (2) 6249-9999; e-mail reference.library@ga .gov.au; internet www.ga.gov.au; f. 1946 as Bureau of Mineral Resources, Geology and Geophysics (BMR) to develop a comprehensive, scientific understanding of the geology of Australia, its offshore area, and the Australian Antarctic Territory; library of 24,000 vols, 4,000 serials; CEO Dr CHRIS PIGRAM (acting); publ. *Bulletin*.

Mineral Resources Tasmania: POB 56, Rosny Park, Tas. 7018; tel. (3) 6233-8333; fax (3) 6233-8338; e-mail info@mrt.tas.gov.au; internet www.mrt.tas.gov.au; f. 1885; library of 10,000 books, 300 periodicals; Chief Geologist A. V. BROWN; publs *Explanatory Reports*,

Geological Survey Maps, Tasmanian Geological Survey Bulletins, Tasmanian Geological Survey Records.

Mount Stromlo and Siding Spring Observatories: Cotter Rd, Weston Creek, ACT 2611; tel. (2) 6125-0230; fax (2) 6125-0233; e-mail director@mso.anu.edu.au; internet www.mso.anu.edu.au; f. 1924 as Commonwealth Solar Observatory; research in astrophysics, incl. all phases of stellar, galactic and extra-galactic astronomy; transferred to Australian Nat. Univ. 1957; library of 17,000 vols; Dir HARVEY BUTCHER; Sec. PATRICIA THOMSON.

Perth Observatory: 337 Walnut Rd, Bickley, WA 6076; tel. (8) 9293-8255; fax (8) 9293-8138; e-mail perthobs@calm.wa.gov.au; internet www.wa.gov.au/perthobs; f. 1896; astronomy research, education and outreach and information provision; research areas incl. optical astronomy, variable and transient monitoring, photometry, planetary observations, microlens monitoring and minor-body tracking; public star-viewing, guided tours and museum; library of 20,000 vols; Govt Astronomer JAMES BIGGS.

Primary Industries and Resources South Australia: 101 Grenfell St, GPOB 1671, Adelaide, SA 5001; tel. (8) 8463-3000; fax (8) 8204-1880; internet www.pir.sa.gov.au; f. 1892; Geological Survey of S Australia, mining, energy and energy conservation, oil and gas; library of 25,000 vols (spec. colln on early S Australian mining); Chief Exec. JIM HALLION; publs *Geological Survey Bulletin, MESA Journal* (4 a year).

Queensland Department of Natural Resources and Water: GPOB 2454, Brisbane, Qld 4001; 41 George St, Brisbane, Qld 4000; tel. (7) 3224-8790; fax (7) 3224-7571; e-mail library@nrw.qld.gov.au; internet www.nrw.qld.gov.au; f. 1874; climate change, natural resource management, geological mapping, sedimentary basin studies, metallogenic studies, biostratigraphy, geophysics, mineral, petroleum, coal and oil shale resources assessment, extractive industries and environmental management, land use planning, mining safety and technology, energy management, resource economics, computer and information services; library of 8,800 monographs, 27,000 reports, 1,000 serials, records, maps, map commentaries, guidebooks; Dir-Gen. SCOTT SPENCER; publs *DME Reviews, Minerals and Energy Review, Queensland Geology, Queensland Government Mining Journal* (12 a year), *Records.*

Riverview College Observatory: Lane Cove, NSW 2066; tel. (2) 9882-8295; fax (2) 9882-8455; e-mail bwmarsh@riverview.nsw.edu.au; f. 1908; meteorological observations, worldwide standard seismograph network station (1962); Dir R. W. MARSH.

RELIGION, SOCIOLOGY AND ANTHROPOLOGY

Australian Institute of Aboriginal and Torres Strait Islander Studies: GPOB 553, Canberra, ACT 2601; tel. (2) 6246-1111; fax (2) 6261-4285; e-mail corporate@aiatsis.gov.au; internet www.aiatsis.gov.au; f. 1961; statutory body since 1964; provides funds, promotes research and publishes books on all aspects of Aboriginal and Torres Strait Islander studies, traditional and contemporary; library of 11,000 books, 1,220 serial titles, 32,000 book and journal analytics, 2,500 language books, 1,400 rare books, 14,000 pamphlets, 30,000 hours of audio tapes, 9,500 MSS, 650,000 prints and colour slides, 2.5 million feet of film and 5,000 video tapes; Chair. Prof. MICHAEL DODSON; publ. *Australian Aboriginal Studies* (2 a year).

Australian Institute of Archaeology: La Trobe Univ., Vic. 3086; tel. (4) 2159-5966; e-mail director@aiarch.org.au; f. 1946 to investigate discoveries and results that the Institute or any other org. publishes, which relate to the authenticity, historicity, accuracy and inspiration of the Bible; teaching programmes and exhibitions on the ancient Near East and Biblical archaeology; library of 10,000 vols (spec. colln on Palestinian, Egyptian and Mesopotamian archaeology); Dir CHRISTOPHER DAVEY; publ. *Buried History* (1 a year).

Australian Institute of Criminology: GPOB 2994, Canberra, ACT 2601; tel. (2) 6260-9200; fax (2) 6260-9201; e-mail front.desk@aic.gov.au; internet www.aic.gov.au; f. 1973; conducts criminology research, conferences and seminars, provides library and information services, publishes results of research and other materials, and services the Criminology Research Council; library: see Libraries and Archives; Dir Dr ADAM TOMISON; publ. *Trends and Issues in Crime and Criminal Justice* (20 a year).

Elda Vaccari Collection of Multicultural Studies: Library, Victoria Univ. of Technology, POB 14428, Melbourne City Mail Centre, Melbourne, Vic. 8001; tel. (3) 9919-4809; fax (3) 9919-4920; e-mail mark.armstrong-roper@vu.edu.au; internet w2.vu.edu.au/library/specialcollections/vaccari.html; f. 1982; research on immigrant and minority groups in Australia; supported by Vaccari Italian Historical Trust; can be searched online via VU library catalogue at library.vu.edu.au, items prefixed V COLL; library of 4,000 vols; Special Collections Librarian MARK ARMSTRONG-ROPER.

TECHNOLOGY

AMDEL: Level 2, 255 Blackburn Rd, Mount Waverley, Vic. 3149; tel. (3) 8847-0700; fax (3) 8847-0799; internet www.amdel.com; f. 1960; analysis, testing, services in mineral engineering, chemical metallurgy, materials technology, mineralogy and petrology, process control instrument development, petroleum, geoanalysis, chemical analysis; offices and laboratories around Australia and New Zealand and representatives worldwide; 400 staff; Group Gen. Man. RAY DOYLE.

ARRB Group Ltd: 500 Burwood Highway, Vermont South, Vic. 3133; tel. (3) 9881-1555; fax (3) 9887-8104; e-mail info@arrb.com.au; internet www.arrb.com.au; f. 1960; research related to the design, planning, construction, maintenance and use of land transport services; library of 42,000 vols and journals; Man. Dir GERARD WALDRON; Company Sec. SUE ROLLAND; publs *ARRB Briefing, ARRB Research Reports* (irregular), *Australian Transport Index database (ATRI), Proceedings of Biennial Conference, Road and Transport Research* (4 a year), *Special Reports* (irregular), *Transport and Road Update* (12 a year).

Defence Science and Technology Organisation: F2-2-008 Fairbairn Business Park, Canberra, ACT 2600; tel. (2) 6128-6301; fax (2) 6128-6332; e-mail information@dsto.defence.gov.au; internet www.dsto.defence.gov.au; attached to Dept of Defence; Australian Govt's lead agency charged with applying science and technology to protect and defend Australia and its nat. interests; Chief Defence Scientist Dr ROGER LOUGH.

Associated Research Laboratory:

Defence Science and Technology Organisation, Fishermens Bend: 506 Lorimer St, Fishermens Bend, Vic. 3207; f. 1939; incl. divs of Airframes and Engines, Air Operations and Guided Weapons.

Water Research Foundation of Australia: c/o Centre for Resource and Environmental Studies, Australian National Univ., Canberra, ACT 0200; tel. (2) 6125-0651; fax (2) 6125-0757; e-mail office@cres.anu.edu.au; f. 1956; a non-profit research org.; research into the devt, control, use and re-use of Australia's water resources; publ. *Water and the Environment* (6 a year).

Libraries and Archives

Australian Capital Territory

Australian Institute of Criminology, J. V. Barry Library: GPO Box 2944, Canberra, ACT 2601; tel. (2) 6260-9264; fax (2) 6260-9299; e-mail jvbarry@aic.gov.au; internet www.aic.gov.au; f. 1974; material is collected in English in the field of criminology and criminal justice; 30,000 monographs, 800 periodicals; articles and monographs of Australian criminological interest are indexed for CINCH–The Australian Criminology Database, publicly available on the Informit network; main objective is to provide information services to researchers at the Institute; Library Man. JANET SMITH.

Australian National University Library: J. B. Chifley Bldg (15), Canberra, ACT 0200; tel. (2) 6125-2003; fax (2) 6125-6662; e-mail librarian@anu.edu.au; internet anulib.anu.edu.au; f. 1948; 2.3m. vols; Librarian VIC ELLIOTT.

DEEWR Library, Department of Education, Employment and Workplace Relations: C16MTG, GPOB 9880, Canberra, ACT 2601; tel. (2) 6240-8848; fax (2) 6240-8861; e-mail library@deewr.gov.au; f. 1945; 40,000 vols; Library Man. KYM HOLDEN.

High Court of Australia Library: POB 6309, Kingston, ACT 2604; tel. (2) 6270-6922; fax (2) 6273-2110; internet www.hcourt.gov.au/library; f. 1903; private library of the Justices of the Court and barristers appearing before it; 149,000 vols in Canberra; Librarian PETAL KINDER.

IP Australia Library: Discovery House, POB 200, Woden, ACT 2606; tel. (2) 6283-2999; fax (2) 6283-7999; e-mail library@ipaustralia.gov.au; internet www.ipaustralia.gov.au; f. 1904; 14,000 vols, 300 periodicals; Australian and foreign patent specifications from all patent countries, science and technology and industrial property.

National Archives of Australia: POB 7425, Canberra Mail Centre, ACT 2610; tel. (2) 6212-3600; fax (2) 6212-3699; e-mail archives@naa.gov.au; internet www.naa.gov.au; f. 1945; archival authority of the Commonwealth since 1952; responsible for the management of Commonwealth records: survey, storage, preservation, retention or destruction, retrieval and access; provides information to the public on nature and location of Commonwealth records and on agencies and persons responsible for them; collns of documents, maps, plans, films, photographs, records, paintings, models, microforms and electronic records (487,522 shelf m); holdings date from the early 19th century, but most date from Federation (1901), derived from a variety of sources; offices in Canberra, Darwin and all state capitals; Dir-Gen. ROSS GIBBS; publ. *Memento* (4 a year).

National Library of Australia: Parkes Pl., Canberra, ACT 2600; tel. (2) 6262-1111; fax (2) 6257-1703; e-mail www@nla.gov.au; internet www.nla.gov.au; f. 1901; maintains nat. colln of Australian library materials and provides a gateway to nat. and int. sources of information; 2.9m. vols, 41,031 current serial titles, 643,792 maps, 12,895 m of manuscript material, 16,297 oral history recordings, 189,031 music scores, 64,373 pictures and prints, 750,299 photographs, 860,187 aerial photographs, 3,812 electronic media; Dir-Gen. JAN FULLERTON; publs *APAIS* (online only), *Gateways* (electronic only, 6 a year), *NLA News* (electronic and print, monthly).

University of Canberra Library: The Library, University of Canberra, ACT 2601; tel. (2) 6201-2282; fax (2) 6201-5068; e-mail askalibrarian@canberra.edu.au; internet www.canberra.edu.au/library; f. 1968; 480,000 vols; collection includes audiovisual material, access to electronic information services; Librarian ANITA CROTTY.

New South Wales

Charles Sturt University–Division of Library Services: Locked Bag 7003, Bathurst, NSW 2795; tel. (2) 6338-4732; fax (2) 6338-4986; e-mail soakley@csu.edu.au; internet www.csu.edu.au/division/library; f. 1989 by amalgamation of Mitchell College of Advanced Education (f. 1951) and Riverina-Murray Institute of Higher Education (f. 1947); 631,577 vols, 2008 CAUL Statistics non-serial items; libraries at Albury-Wodonga, Bathurst, Wagga Wagga, Orange and Dubbo; Burlington (Ontario, Canada); Exec. Dir, Library Services SHIRLEY OAKLEY.

City of Sydney Library: Customs House Library, Sydney, NSW 2000; tel. (2) 9242-8555; fax (2) 9242-8561; e-mail library@cityofsydney.nsw.gov.au; internet www.cityofsydney.nsw.gov.au; f. 1877; programmes for children and young people, adults, multicultural audiences; local history and user education; Home library and Interlibrary loan services; 8 brs, 2 library links; 500,000 items, incl. books, CDs, DVDs, audio-books, magazines, 100 newspaper titles; spec. collns: Australiana, local govt, Olympic Games, Koori (Aboriginal) material; Library Man. DAVID SHARMAN.

Macquarie University Library: Bldg C7A, Macquarie University, NSW 2109; tel. (2) 9850-7500; fax (2) 9850-9236; e-mail maxine.brodie@library.mq.edu.au; internet www.library.mq.edu.au; f. 1964; will move to a new location in 2011; 1.8m. vols; University Librarian MAXINE BRODIE.

Newcastle Region Public Library: War Memorial Cultural Centre, Laman St, Newcastle, NSW 2300; tel. (2) 4974-5300; fax (2) 4974-5396; e-mail library@ncc.nsw.gov.au; internet www.ncc.nsw.gov.au/library; f. 1948; 406,242 vols; 2,663 periodicals; 121 newspaper titles; special facilities: Information Works, Local Studies, Hunter Photo Bank, Earthquake Database; Lending Services Librarian MICHAEL NEWSOME; publs *Monographs* (irregular), *Newcastle Morning Herald Index* (1861–84, 1 a year).

Parliamentary Library of New South Wales: Parliament House, Sydney, NSW 2000; tel. (2) 9230-2383; fax (2) 9231-1932; e-mail libreq@parliament.nsw.gov.au; internet www.parliament.nsw.gov.au; f. 1840; 200,000 vols; Man. of Reference and Information Services DEBORAH BROWN.

State Library of New South Wales: Macquarie St, Sydney, NSW 2000; tel. (2) 9273-1414; fax (2) 9273-1255; e-mail library@sl.nsw.gov.au; internet www.sl.nsw.gov.au; f. 1826; 5m. items; State legal deposit privileges; special collections: Australiana, historical pictures, maps, MSS, of Australasia and the Pacific; State Librarian and Chief Exec. REGINA A. SUTTON.

State Records Authority of New South Wales: POB 516, Kingswood, NSW 2747; tel. (2) 9673-1788; fax (2) 9833-4518; e-mail srecords@records.nsw.gov.au; internet www.records.nsw.gov.au; f. 1961; 10,000 vols; incl. Univ. Archives and Heritage Centre; records and archives strategy for the NSW Govt and broader public sector; preservation of the State Archives colln; reference services; reading rooms, online access, enquiry and copying services, exhibitions, publs, talks and tours; Dir ALAN VENTRESS.

University of New England Library: Dixson Library, Univ. of New England, Armidale, NSW 2351; tel. (2) 6773-2165; fax (2) 6773-3943; e-mail unilib@une.edu.au; internet www.une.edu.au/library; f. 1954 Univ. College of Univ. of Sydney, 1938-1954; 908,000 vols; agricultural sciences, Australian law, humanities and social sciences, health, medicine, education; special collns: Campbell Howard (Australian plays in manuscript), Gordon Athol Anderson (music), New England, Royal Soc. of New S Wales, Australian League of Rights, Saunders Colln in War and Peace; Univ. Librarian BARBARA PATON.

University of New South Wales Library: Sydney, NSW 2052; tel. (2) 9385-2615; fax (2) 9385-8002; e-mail information@unsw.edu.au; internet info.library.unsw.edu.au; f. 1949; 2.9m. items at Kensington and other centres; University Librarian ANDREW WELLS.

University of Newcastle Library: Callaghan, NSW 2308; tel. (2) 4921-5851; fax (2) 4921-5833; internet www.newcastle.edu.au/services/library; f. 1965; 1.3m. vols; Librarian GREG ANDERSON.

University of Sydney Library: University of Sydney, NSW 2006; tel. (2) 9351-2993; fax (2) 9351-2890; e-mail loanenq@library.usyd.edu.au; internet www.library.usyd.edu.au; f. 1852; network of 18 libraries containing 5.2m. vols, 68,130 electronic journals and 281,600 electronic books; University Librarian JOHN SHIPP.

Northern Territory

Northern Territory Library: Parliament House, POB 42, Darwin, NT 0801; tel. (8) 8999-7177; fax (8) 8999-6927; e-mail ntlinfo.dlghs@nt.gov.au; internet www.ntl.nt.gov.au; f. 1950 as Darwin Public Library; 140,000 books, 4,132 periodicals, 80,000 photographs, 3,000 maps, 2,500 films and video cassettes, 7,000 microforms; incl. the Northern Territory Colln (1 copy of all types of library material dealing with N and Central Australia, and NT in particular); Dir JO McGILL; publ. occasional papers.

Queensland

Queensland Parliamentary Library: Parliamentary Annex, Alice St, Brisbane, Qld 4000; tel. (7) 3406-7219; fax (7) 3210-0172; e-mail library.inquiries@parliament.qld.gov.au; f. 1860; information service to members of State Legislature; statistics, economics, politics, law and education; 120,000 vols; spec. colln: O'Donovan Colln of 19th century literature; audiovisual clippings; Queensland political history; Librarian MARY SEEFRIED; publ. *Queensland Parliamentary Record* (every 3 years).

Queensland University of Technology Library: GPOB 2434, Brisbane, Qld 4001; tel. (7) 3864-1821; fax (7) 3864-2485; e-mail dirlib.pa@qut.edu.au; internet www.library.qut.edu.au; f. 1989; 350,030 vols, 2,815 print and microform periodicals, 91,834 electronic periodicals; Dir JUDY STOKKER.

State Library of Queensland: POB 3488, Brisbane, Qld 4101; tel. (7) 3840-7666; fax (7) 3846-2421; e-mail info@slq.qld.gov.au; internet www.slq.qld.gov.au; f. 1896; State Reference Library, non-lending except for music scores and to libraries, groups and organizations; includes John Oxley Library of Queensland History, James Hardie Library of Australian Fine Arts and Australian Library of Art colln; has library deposit privileges, exhibitions, events; State Librarian LEA GILES-PETERS.

Supreme Court Library: POB 15019, City East, Brisbane, Qld 4002; tel. (7) 3247-4373; fax (7) 3247-9233; e-mail librarian@sclqld.org.au; internet www.sclqld.org.au; f. 1862; 180,000 vols; Librarian ALADIN RAHEMTULA; publs *Qld Legal Indexes*, *Supreme Court History Program Yearbook*.

University of Queensland Library: Qld 4072; tel. (7) 3365-6551; fax (7) 3365-7317; e-mail universitylibrarian@library.uq.edu.au; internet library.uq.edu.au; f. 1911; 2.5m. vols; 10,853 print journals, 47,744 electronic journals, 1,014 networked databases, 370,974 eBooks, 32,645 video cassettes; manuscript, microform and pictorial collns mainly in Australian literature; Librarian KEITH WEBSTER.

South Australia

Flinders University Library: Bedford Park, SA 5042; tel. (8) 8201-2131; fax (8) 8201-2508; e-mail libinfo@flinders.edu.au; internet www.flinders.edu.au/library; f. 1966; 1.5m. vols; Univ. Librarian IAN McBAIN.

State Library of South Australia: North Terrace, GPOB 419, Adelaide, SA 5001; tel. (8) 8207-7200; fax (8) 8207-7247; e-mail info@slsa.sa.gov.au; internet www.slsa.sa.gov.au; f. 1884; State general reference library and legal depository; online services incl. networked CD-ROMs; Bray Reference Colln (400,000 vols, 21,000 serial titles, 6,000 current, 109,000 maps); South Australiana Colln (62,000 vols, 12,000 serial titles, 8,000 current, Archival Collns of 4,500 m); spec. collns incl. Children's Literature Research Colln (55,000 vols), Edwardes Colln of Shipping Photographs (8,000), Arbon-Le Maistre Colln of Shipping Photographs (70,000), Mountford-Sheard Colln of Aboriginal Ethnology, Thomas Hardy Wine Library (1,000 vols), Paul McGuire Maritime Library (3,000 vols), Rare Books Colln (92,000 vols), Royal Geographical Soc. of South Australia Inc. Library, J. D. Somerville Oral History Colln (1,500 cassette tapes), Pictorial Colln (350,000 images), Bradman Colln of Cricketing Memorabilia; supports 138 public libraries (1.5m. vols); Dir ALAN SMITH; publ. *Extra Extra* (2 a year).

University of Adelaide Library: University of Adelaide, Adelaide, SA 5005; tel. (8) 8303-5370; fax (8) 8303-4369; e-mail library@adelaide.edu.au; internet www.adelaide.edu.au/library; f. 1876; 2.1m. items; rare books, spec. collns incl. univ. archives, univ. arts and heritage, univ. press; 2,400,000 vols; University Librarian RAY CHOATE.

University of South Australia Library: Mawson Lakes Blvd, Mawson Lakes, SA 5095; tel. (1300) 137 659; e-mail ocls@unisa.edu.au; internet www.library.unisa.edu.au; libraries located at City East Campus, North Terrace, Adelaide, SA 5000; Mawson Lakes Campus, Mawson Lakes, SA 5095; Magill Campus, Lorne Avenue, Magill, SA 5072; City West Campus, North Terrace, Adelaide, SA 5000; Whyalla Campus, Nicolson Avenue, Whyalla Norrie, SA 5608; f. 1991 (as School of Art 1856); 1m. vols; special collections include Oregon Collection of Theses in Physical Education and Sport, Doris Taylor Collection on Ageing, Gavin Walkley collection on Architectural History; Clearinghouse in Australia for Adult Basic Education and Literacy, Aboriginal and Torres Strait Islander Special Collection, Australian Bureau of Statistics Collection, HOPE Collection; Dir, Library Services HELEN LIVINGSTON.

Tasmania

Community Knowledge Network (State Library of Tasmania): 91 Murray St, Hobart, Tas. 7000; tel. (3) 6233-7511; fax (3) 6231-0927; e-mail state.library@education .tas.gov.au; internet www.statelibrary.tas .gov.au; f. 1850; 913,032 items; state legal deposit privileges; 46 brs, 4 reference and spec. collns; links adult education, state library of Tasmania, online access centres and the Tasmanian archive and heritage office combining learning, information, literacy, library; Dir SIOBHAN GASKELL.

University of Tasmania Library: Private Bag 25, GPO Hobart, Tas. 7001; tel. (3) 6226-2223; fax (3) 6226-2878; internet www.utas .edu.au/library/index.html; f. 1892; 996,832 vols; Sandy Bay Campus libraries: Law, Morris Miller (social sciences and humanities) and Science; Centre for the Arts Library, Hunter St, Hobart; Clinical Library, 43 Collins St, Hobart; Launceston Campus Library, Newnham, Launceston; spec. collns on Quakerism; houses the Royal Soc. of Tasmania Library; Librarian LINDA LUTHER.

Victoria

Commonwealth Scientific and Industrial Research Organisation, Library Network: Bag 10, Clayton South, Vic. 3169; tel. (3) 9518-5940; fax (3) 9518-5959; e-mail thomas.girke@csiro.au; internet www .csiro.au/services/pswn.html; publishes and communicates science information in print, video and multimedia, and electronic databases; disseminates science and research information through CSIRO Library Network, search and inquiry services SEARCH PARTY; archival services for CSIRO research and records; Man. THOMAS GIRKE.

La Trobe University Library: Bundoora, Vic. 3086; tel. (3) 9479-2922; fax (3) 9471-0993; e-mail library@latrobe.edu.au; internet www.lib.latrobe.edu.au; f. 1964; 1.5m. vols; special emphasis on humanities and social sciences, allied health sciences; area studies: Latin America, India, Canada; University Librarian Prof. AINSLIE DEWE.

Monash University Library: Monash University, Vic. 3800; tel. (3) 9905-5054; fax (3) 9905-2610; e-mail libweb@lib.monash.edu .au; internet www.lib.monash.edu.au; f. 1961; 2.9m. vols, 17,800 periodicals; also libraries at Caulfield Campus, Caulfield East, Vic. 3145; Peninsula Campus, Frankston, Vic. 3199; Gippsland Campus, Churchill, Vic. 3842; and Berwick Campus, Berwick, Vic. 3806; Pharmacy College, Royal Parade, Parkville, Vic. 3052; Roodepoort 1725, South Africa; Petaling Jaya, 46150 Selangor, Malaysia; Librarian C. HARBOE-REE.

Public Record Office of Victoria: POB 2100, North Melbourne, Vic. 3051; tel. (3) 9348-5600; fax (3) 9348-5656; e-mail ask .prov@dpc.vic.gov.au; internet www.prov.vic .gov.au; f. 1973; 67,074 linear m of public records; Dir and Keeper of Public Records JUSTINE HEAZLEWOOD; publs Journal (1 a year, online), Profile (4 a year).

State Library of Victoria: 328 Swanston St, Melbourne, Vic. 3000; tel. (3) 8664-7000; fax (3) 9639-4737; e-mail info@slv.vic.gov.au; internet www.slv.vic.gov.au; f. 1854; the oldest publicly funded library in Australia and Victoria's primary gen. reference and research library; legal deposit library responsible for collecting, preserving and making available all published materials and associated material relating to the heritage of the state of Victoria; offers community outreach and learning programmes; works with other library sectors, cultural instns and the education sector to provide access to information and promote Victorian cultural heritage; 2m. vols and periodicals; spec. collns incl. La Trobe Colln (Australiana), art, newspapers, music and performing arts, Anderson Chess Colln, maps, MSS and pictures; digitization of 200,000 items from the Pictures Colln and a broader range of formats incl. text, audio and music are available online; CEO and State Librarian ANNE-MARIE SCHWIRTLICH; publs La Trobe Journal (2 a year), State Library of Victoria News (3 a year).

University of Melbourne Library: Vic. 3010; tel. (3) 8344-9590; fax (3) 8344-9588; internet www.lib.unimelb.edu.au; f. 1855; 3m. vols; spec. collns incl. Australiana, East Asia; responsible for University Archives and Grainger Museum; Librarian HELEN HAYES; publ. Ex Libris (4 a year).

Victorian Parliamentary Library: Parliament of Victoria, Spring St, Melbourne, Vic. 3002; tel. (3) 9651-8640; fax (3) 9650-9775; e-mail info@parliament.vic.gov.au; internet www.parliament.vic.gov.au; f. 1851; reference and research service for MPs and associated staff; statistics, economics, politics, law, government publs; Parliamentary Librarian MARION KING; publ. Victorian Parliamentary Handbook (every 4 years).

Western Australia

Curtin University of Technology Library: POB U1987, Perth, WA 6845; tel. (8) 9266-7205; fax (8) 9266-3213; e-mail i .garner@curtin.edu.au; internet library .curtin.edu.au; f. 1967; 643,994 vols, 65,213 current serial titles; University Librarian IMOGEN GARNER.

State Library of Western Australia: Perth Cultural Centre, Perth, WA 6000; tel. (8) 9427-3111; fax (8) 9427-3256; e-mail info@ slwa.wa.gov.au; internet www.slwa.wa.gov .au; f. 1887; J. S. Battye Library of W Australian History (f. 1887): 138,000 vols, 16,500 serial and newspaper titles, 16,000 microfilm reels, 29,000 cartographic items, 90,000 ephemeral items, 500,000 pictorial images, 6,000 film and video reels, 13,000 oral history hours, 3,100 m of private archives; gen. reference services: 412,000 vols, 6,000 serial and newspaper titles, 49,000 music scores, 15,000 music recordings, 13,000 microfilm reels, 16,000 video and film titles, 23,000 cartographic items; spec. collns of music business genealogy and Australian children's literature; CEO and State Librarian MARGARET ALLEN (acting); Dir of Public Library Services SUSAN FEENEY; Dir, Resource Services ALISON SUTHERLAND; Dir, Strategic and Corporate Services MARK WOODCOCK; publ. Statistical Bulletin for Public Libraries in Western Australia (1 a year).

University of Western Australia Library: 35 Stirling Highway, Crawley, WA 6009; tel. (8) 6488-1777; fax (8) 6488-1012; e-mail uwalibrary@library.uwa.edu.au; internet www.library.uwa.edu.au; f. 1913; 1m. vols; Librarian JOHN ARFIELD.

Museums and Art Galleries

Australian Capital Territory

Australian War Memorial: GPO Box 345, Canberra, ACT 2601; tel. (2) 6243-4211; fax (2) 6243-4325; internet www.awm.gov.au; f. 1917; national war memorial, museum, research centre and art gallery illustrating and recording aspects of all wars in which the Armed Forces of Australia have been engaged; dioramas of historical battles, and a total collection of over 3.5m. items; works of art, relics, documentary and audiovisual records; library: books, serials, pamphlets, photographs, maps, film and sound recordings on military history; repository of operational records of Australian fighting units; Dir Maj.-Gen. STEVE GOWER; publ. Wartime (4 a year).

National Gallery of Australia: POB 1150, Canberra, ACT 2601; tel. (2) 6240-6411; fax (2) 6240-6529; e-mail information@nga.gov .au; internet www.nga.gov.au; f. 1975; the Nat. Colln has 100,000 works of Australian and int. art; Australian colln incl. fine and decorative arts, folk art, commercial art, architecture and design; other collns incl. arts of Asia and South-east Asia, Oceania, Africa and Pre-Columbian America, European art, also prints, drawings, illustrated books since 1800, photography; library of 120,000 monographs, 35,000 auction sales catalogues, 1,200 current serials, 47,000 microfiches, 1m. ephemeral materials; Dir BRIAN P. KENNEDY; publ. Artonview (4 a year).

National Museum of Australia: POB 1901, Canberra, ACT 2601; tel. (2) 6208-5000; fax (2) 6208-5099; e-mail information@ nma.gov.au; internet www.nma.gov.au; f. 1980; Australian history, Aboriginal and Torres Strait Island cultures, social history and environment; library of 35,000 vols; Dir CRADDOCK MORTON (acting).

New South Wales

Art Gallery of New South Wales:; tel. (2) 9225-1700; fax (2) 9221-1701; e-mail artmail@ag.nsw.gov.au; internet www .artgallery.nsw.gov.au; f. 1874; representative collection of Australian art, Aboriginal and Melanesian art; collections of British art since 18th century; European painting and sculpture (since 15th century); Asian art, particularly Chinese and Japanese ceramics and Japanese painting; Australian, British and European prints and drawings, contemporary Australian and foreign art; photography; Pres., Board of Trustees STEVEN LOWY; Dir EDMUND CAPON.

Australian Museum: 6 College St, Sydney, NSW 2010; tel. (2) 9320-6000; fax (2) 9320-6050; e-mail library@austmus.gov.au; internet www.australianmuseum.net.au; f. 1827; natural history, museology, anthropology, palaeontology, mineralogy, biodiversity; library of 100,000 vols; Dir FRANK HOWARTH; publs Records of the Australian Museum (4 a year), Technical Reports of the Australian Museum (irregular).

Australian National Maritime Museum: POB 5131, Sydney, NSW 2001; tel. (2) 9298-3777; fax (2) 9298-3780; internet www.anmm .gov.au; f. 1985, open 1991; illustrates maritime history as exemplified by the colonial navies, the Royal Australian Navy, merchant shipping and trade, whaling and the fishing industry, explorers and cartographers, immigration, the design and use of leisure and sporting craft and int. competition, surfing, surf life saving and the culture of the beach, and the maritime activities of the Aborigines; models, prints and drawings, glass plate negatives, uniforms, relics, full-size vessels; library of 12,000 vols, 750 periodicals; Chair. PETER SINCLAIR; Dir MARY-LOUISE WILLIAMS; publ. Signals (4 a year).

Macleay Museum: Gosper Lane, off Science Rd, Univ. of Sydney, Sydney, NSW 2006; tel. (2) 9351-2274; fax (2) 9351-5646; e-mail macleay.museum@sydney.edu.au; internet www.usyd.edu.au/museums; f. 1888 based on colln begun in 1790; entomology, zoology, ethnology, 19th-century scientific instruments; Australian photographs since 1850s; Dir DAVID ELLIS.

Museum of Applied Arts and Sciences: POB K346, Haymarket, NSW 1238; tel. (2) 9217-0111; fax (2) 9217-0333; e-mail info@ phm.gov.au; internet www .powerhousemuseum.com; f. 1880; comprises Powerhouse Museum (decorative arts, history, science and technology), Sydney Observatory astronomical museum; Dir Dr KEVIN FEWSTER.

Museum of Contemporary Art: POB R1286, Royal Exchange, NSW 1223; located at: Level 5, 140 George St, Sydney, NSW 2000; tel. (2) 9252-4033; fax (2) 9252-4361; e-mail mail@mca.com.au; internet www.mca .com.au; f. 1991; Dir ELIZABETH ANN MAC-GREGOR.

Nicholson Museum: Univ. of Sydney, Sydney, NSW 2006; tel. (2) 9351-2812; fax (2) 9351-7305; e-mail nicholsonmuseum@usyd .edu.au; internet www.usyd.edu.au/ museums/nicholson; f. 1860; colln of Egyptian, Near Eastern, Cypriot, European, Greek and Roman antiquities; Dir DAVID ELLIS; Senior Curator MICHAEL TURNER.

Wilson, J. T., Museum of Human Anatomy: Anderson Stuart Bldg, Dept of Anatomy, Univ. of Sydney, NSW 2006; e-mail hod@anatomy.usyd.edu.au; f. 1886; incl. 1,000 dissected parts and cross-sections of the human body; Curator PETER MILLS.

Northern Territory

Museum and Art Gallery of the Northern Territory: GPOB 4646, Darwin, NT 0801; Conacher St, Bullocky Point, Darwin, NT; tel. (8) 8999-8201; fax (8) 8999-8289; e-mail museum@nt.gov.au; f. 1969; art, history, culture, and natural history of the Northern Territory, particularly Aboriginal visual arts and material culture; South-east Asian and Oceanic art and material culture; maritime archaeology; 5 major permanent galleries; touring gallery; educational facilities for students; library of 10,000 vols, 1,000 serials; Dir ANNA MALGORZEWICZ; publ. *Research Reports* (irregular).

Queensland

Queensland Art Gallery: POB 3686, South Brisbane, Qld 4101; Stanley St, South Brisbane, Qld 4101; tel. (7) 3840-7333; fax (7) 3844-8865; e-mail gallery@qag.qld.gov.au; internet www.qag.qld.gov.au; f. 1895, opened 2nd site, Gallery of Modern Art (GoMA) in 2006, incl. Australian Cinematheque and Children's Art Centre; State colln of Australian and int. paintings, prints, drawings and photographs, sculpture and decorative arts; education and advisory services; holds Asia Pacific Triennial of contemporary art; library of 35,000 books, 500 periodicals, photographs, catalogues, Asia Pacific research colln; Dir TONY ELLWOOD; publ. *Artlines*.

Queensland Herbarium: Brisbane Botanic Gardens Mt Coot-tha, Mt Coot-tha Rd, Toowong, Qld 4066; tel. (7) 3896-9326; fax (7) 3896-9624; internet www.env.qld.gov.au; f. 1874 as Botanic Museum and Herbarium; studies of flora and mapping of vegetation of Queensland, rare and threatened plant species, plant ecology, weeds, poisonous plants and economic botany; 650,000 plant specimens; library of 10,000 vols; Dir G. P. GUYMER; publ. *Austrobaileya* (1 a year).

Queensland Museum: Cultural Centre, South Bank, South Brisbane, Qld 4101; tel. (7) 3840-7555; fax (7) 3846-1918; e-mail inquirycentre@qm.qld.gov.au; internet www .qm.qld.gov.au; f. 1871; zoology, geology, palaeontology, history, anthropology, technology; library of 95,000 vols; Dir Dr IAN

GALLOWAY; publ. *Memoirs of the Queensland Museum.*

South Australia

Art Gallery of South Australia: North Terrace, Adelaide, SA 5000; tel. (8) 8207-7000; fax (8) 8207-7070; e-mail agsa.info@ saugov.sa.gov.au; internet www.artgallery .sa.gov.au; f. 1881, present status 1967; comprehensive colln of Australian works of art, British and European painting, prints, drawings and sculpture 16th century to present; British, European and Asian decorative arts; Indian and Indonesian textiles and Japanese art, early South Australian pictures; education services; library of 35,000 vols; journals, ephemera colln; Dir CHRISTOPHER MENZ.

South Australian Museum: North Terrace, Adelaide, SA 5000; tel. (8) 8207-7500; fax (8) 8207-7430; internet www.samuseum .sa.gov.au; f. 1856; anthropological, geological and zoological material mainly related to S Australia; Australian ethnological colln; education and advisory services; library of 45,000 vols; Dir Dr S. MILLER; publ. *Transactions of the Royal Society of South Australia (incorporating Records of the South Australian Museum).*

Tasmania

Queen Victoria Museum and Art Gallery: POB 403, Launceston, Tas. 7250; tel. (3) 6323-3777; fax (3) 6323-3776; e-mail enquiries@qvmag.tas.gov.au; internet www .qvmag.tas.gov.au; f. 1891; collns comprise pure and applied art, Tasmanian history, Tasmanian and general anthropology, Tasmanian botany, geology, palaeontology and zoology; library of 11,000 vols; Dir PATRICK FILMER-SANKEY; publs *Occasional Paper, Records.*

Tasmanian Museum and Art Gallery: 40 Macquarie St, GPOB 1164, Hobart, Tas. 7001; tel. (3) 6211-4177; fax (3) 6211-4112; e-mail tmagmail@tmag.tas.gov.au; internet www.tmag.tas.gov.au; f. 1852; applied science, art and natural and human history, with emphasis on Tasmania and Australia generally; incl. Tasmanian Herbarium, coin collns, early photography, collns relating to the Aboriginal people of Tasmania; collns also at the West Coast Pioneers' Museum at Zeehan (mining, local history and minerals); and the Australasian Golf Museum at Bothwell (golfing memorabilia); Dir BILL BLEATHMAN; publ. *Research Journal— Kanunnah* (1 a year).

Victoria

Museum Victoria: GPO Box 666E, Melbourne, Vic. 3001; tel. (3) 8341-7777; fax (3) 8341-7778; e-mail webmaster@museum.vic .gov.au; internet www.museum.vic.gov.au; f. 1854; CEO Dr J. PATRICK GREENE.

Constituent Museums:

   Immigration Museum: Old Customs House, 400 Flinders St, Melbourne, Vic. 3000; tel. (3) 9927-2700; fax (3) 9927-2701; e-mail webmaster@museum.vic.gov.au; internet immigration.museum.vic.gov.au; f. 1998.

   Melbourne Museum: Carlton Gardens, Carlton, Vic. 3053; tel. (3) 8341-7777; fax (3) 8341-7768; e-mail webmaster@museum .vic.gov.au; internet melbourne.museum .vic.gov.au; f. 2000; science, technology, Australian society, environment, indigenous cultures and human mind and body; incl. Aboriginal Centre, Children's Museum, living forest gallery, IMAX theatre and Royal Exhibition Building.

   Scienceworks Museum: 2 Booker St, Spotswood, Vic. 3015; tel. (3) 9392-4800;

fax (3) 9391-0100; e-mail webmaster@ museum.vic.gov.au; internet scienceworks .museum.vic.gov.au; f. 1992; science and technology, Melbourne Planetarium, Spotswood Pumping Station.

National Gallery of Victoria: POB 7259, Melbourne, Vic. 8004; tel. (3) 9208-0222; fax (3) 9208-0245; e-mail enquiries@ngv.vic.gov .au; internet www.ngv.vic.gov.au; f. 1861; old masters and depts of prints and drawings, modern European art, Australian art, aboriginal and Oceanic art, decorative art and design, Asian art, antiquities, photography, pre-Columbian art, costume and textiles; library of 45,000 vols, and slides; Dir Dr GERARD VAUGHAN; publs *Art Bulletin of Victoria* (1 a year), *Gallery* (6 a year).

Western Australia

Art Gallery of Western Australia: Perth Cultural Centre, Perth, WA 6000; tel. (8) 9492-6600; fax (8) 9492-6655; e-mail admin@ artgallery.wa.gov.au; internet www .artgallery.wa.gov.au; f. 1895; Aboriginal art, Australian and foreign paintings, sculpture, decorative arts and crafts; free guided tours; public and educational programmes; library of 16,000 vols; Dir STEFANO CARBONI.

Western Australian Museum: 49 Kew St, Welshpool, Perth, WA 6106; tel. (8) 9427-2700; fax (8) 9427-2882; e-mail reception@ museum.wa.gov.au; internet www.museum .wa.gov.au; f. 1891; natural history, archaeology, history, earth sciences, anthropology; library of 20,000 vols, 1,500 journal titles; Dir Dr DAWN CASEY; Exec. Officer and Foundation Dir CATHRIN CASSARCHIS; publs *Records, Records Supplements.*

Universities

UNIVERSITY OF ADELAIDE

Adelaide, SA 5005

Telephone: (8) 8313-4455

Fax: (8) 8313-4401

E-mail: council.secretary@adelaide.edu.au

Internet: www.adelaide.edu.au

Founded 1874

Autonomous institution established by Act of Parliament

Academic year: March to December

Chancellor: JOHN VON DOUSSA

Vice-Chancellor and Pres.: Prof. JAMES McWHA

Deputy Vice-Chancellor and Vice-Pres. for Academic Affairs: Prof. FRED McDOUGALL

Deputy Vice-Chancellor and Vice-Pres. for Research: (vacant)

Vice-Pres. for Services and Resources: PAUL DULDIG

Pro-Vice-Chancellor for Int. Affairs: Prof. JOHN TAPLIN

Univ. Librarian: RAY C. CHOATE

Number of teachers: 929 (full-time)

Number of students: 20,154

Publications: *Adelaide Law Review* (2 a year), *Australian Economic Papers* (2 a year), *Australian Feminist Studies* (2 a year), *Australian Journal of Legal History* (2 a year), *Australian Journal of Social Research* (4 a year), *Australian Women's Studies* (1 a year), *Corporate and Business Law Journal* (2 a year), *Economic Briefings* (3 a year), *The Joseph Fisher Lecture in Commerce* (irregular), *Research Report* (1 a year), *Social Analysis* (2 a year)

EXECUTIVE DEANS

Faculty of Engineering, Computer and Mathematical Sciences: Prof. A. PARKER (acting)

Faculty of Health Sciences: Prof. D. B. FREWIN
Faculty of Humanities and Social Sciences: M. INNES
Faculty of the Professions: F. M. McDOUGALL
Faculty of Sciences: P. D. RATHJEN

PROFESSORS

Faculty of Engineering, Computer and Mathematical Sciences (tel. (8) 8303-4700; fax (8) 8303-4361; e-mail eng.cs.maths@adelaide .edu.au; internet www.adelaide.edu.au/ ecms):

BARTER, C. J., Computer Science
BEGG, S. H., Petroleum Engineering and Management
BEHRBRUCH, P., Petroleum Engineering and Management
BRATVOLD, R. B., Petroleum Engineering and Management
BROOKS, M. J., Computer Science
COLE, P. H., Electrical and Electronic Engineering
COUTTS, R. P., Telecommunications
DANDY, G. D., Civil Engineering
GRAY, D. A., Sensor Signal Processing
HANSEN, C. H., Mechanical Engineering
IRELAND, V., Education Centre for Innovation and Commercialisation
KHURANA, A. K., Petroleum Engineering and Management
KING, K. D., Chemical Engineering
LINTON, V. M., Welded Structures (Cooperative Research Centre)
McLEAN, A. J., Road Accident Research
SARMA, H. K., Petroleum Engineering and Management
WHITE, L. B., Electrical and Electronic Engineering

Faculty of Health Sciences (Medical School North, Frome Rd, Adelaide; tel. (8) 8303-5336; fax (8) 8303-3788; e-mail health .sciences@adelaide.edu.au; internet www .health.adelaide.edu.au):

BARRETT, R. J., Psychiatry
BARTOLD, P. M., Dentistry
BEILBY, J. J., General Practice
BOCHNER, F., Clinical and Experimental Pharmacology
DEKKER, G., Obstetrics and Gynaecology
FREWIN, D. B., Clinical and Experimental Pharmacology
GOLDNEY, R. D., Psychiatry
GOSS, A. N., Dentistry
HENNENBERG, M., Anatomical Sciences
HILLER, J. E., Public Health
HOROWITZ, J. D., Medicine
HOROWITZ, M., Medicine
HOWIE, D. W., Orthopaedics, Trauma
JAMIESON, G. G., Surgery
JONES, N., Surgery
KOTLARSKI, I., Health Sciences Faculty Office
LUDBROOK, G. L., Anaesthesia and Intensive Care
McFARLANE, A. C., Psychiatry
MacLENNAN, A. H., Obstetrics and Gynaecology
MADDERN, G. J., Surgery
MOYES, D. G., Anaesthesia and Intensive Care
NETTELBECK, T. J., Psychology
NORMAN, R. J., Obstetrics and Gynaecology
ROBERTON, D. M., Paediatrics
ROBINSON, J. S., Obstetrics and Gynaecology
RUFFIN, R. E., Medicine
RUNCIMAN, W. B., Anaesthesia and Intensive Care
SAMPSON, W. J., Dentistry
SAWYER, M. G., Paediatrics
SLADE, G. D., Dentistry
SOMOGYI, A. A., Clinical and Experimental Pharmacology
SPENCER, A. J., Dentistry

TAN, H. L., Paediatrics
TAPLIN, J. E., Psychology
THOMPSON, P. D., Medicine
TIERNEY, A. J., Clinical Nursing
TILLEY, W. D., Medicine
TOWNSEND, G. C., Dentistry
VERNON-ROBERTS, B., Pathology
WHITE, J. M., Clinical and Experimental Pharmacology
WORMALD, P. J., Surgery

Faculty of Humanities and Social Sciences (tel. (8) 8303-5345; fax (8) 8303-4382; e-mail humss.office@adelaide.edu.au; internet www .arts.adelaide.edu.au/arts-web):

BODMAN RAE, C., Music
BOUMELHA, P. A., English
BULBECK, C., Social Inquiry
HARVEY, N., Geographical and Environmental Studies
HUGO, G. J., Social Applications of Geographical Information Systems
JAIN, P. C., Asian Studies
MORTENSEN, C. E., Philosophy
MUHLHAUSLER, P., European Studies, General Linguistics
PREST, W. R., History
SHAPCOTT, T. W., English
WILLIAMS, M. A., Geographical and Environmental Studies

Faculty of the Professions (tel. (8) 8303-3986; fax (8) 8303-4416):

ANDERSON, K., Economics
BRADBROOK, A. J., Law
DETMOLD, M. J., Law
FAIRALL, P. A., Law
McDOUGALL, F. M., Graduate School of Business
MARJORIBANKS, K. M., Graduate School of Education
NAFFINE, N. M., Law
PARKER, L. D., Commerce
POMFRET, R. W., Economics
QUESTER, P. G., Commerce
RADFORD, A. D., Architecture, Landscape and Urban Design
SHERIDAN, K., Graduate School of Business
SMOLICZ, J. J., Graduate School of Education
TAYLOR, D. W., Commerce

Faculty of Sciences (tel. (8) 8303-5673; fax (8) 8303-4386; internet www.sciences.adelaide .edu.au):

AUSTIN, A. D., School of Earth and Environmental Sciences
BOWIE, J. H., School of Chemistry and Physics
BRUCE, M. I., School of Chemistry and Physics
BURRELL, C. J., School of Molecular and Biomedical Sciences
COVENTRY, D. R., School of Earth and Environmental Sciences
FINCHER, G. B., School of Agriculture and Wine
GREENHALGH, S. A., School of Earth and Environmental Sciences
HILLIS, R. R., Petroleum Geology and Geophysics (National Centre)
HYND, P. I., School of Agriculture and Wine
KALDI, J. G., Petroleum Geology and Geophysics (National Centre)
LANGRIDGE, P., School of Agriculture and Wine
LINCOLN, S. F., School of Chemistry and Physics
McMILLEN, I. C., School of Molecular and Biomedical Sciences
MILES, T. S., School of Molecular and Biomedical Sciences
MUNCH, J., School of Chemistry and Physics
OWENS, J. A., School of Molecular and Biomedical Sciences

PATON, J. C., School of Molecular and Biomedical Sciences
RANDLES, J. W., School of Agriculture and Wine
RATHJEN, P. D., School of Molecular and Biomedical Sciences
SCHMIDT, O., School of Agriculture and Wine
SEDGLEY, M., School of Agriculture and Wine
SEYMOUR, R. S., School of Earth and Environmental Sciences
SMITH, S. E., School of Earth and Environmental Sciences
TYERMAN, S. D., School of Agriculture and Wine
VINCENT, R. A., School of Chemistry and Physics
WALLACE, J. C., School of Molecular and Biomedical Sciences
WHAN, B., Molecular Plant Breeding (Cooperative Research Centre)

ATTACHED RESEARCH INSTITUTES

Australian Centre for Plant Functional Genomics: Dir Prof. P. LANGRIDGE.

Australian Petroleum Cooperative Research Centre: Dir Dr J. KALDI.

Cooperative Research Centre for Signal and Information Processing: Dir Prof. M. BROOKS.

Cooperative Research Centre for Tissue Growth and Repair: Dir Dr J. BALLARD.

Cooperative Research Centre for Viticulture: Dir Dr J. HARDIE.

Cooperative Research Centre for Weed Management Systems: Dir Assoc. Prof. R. ROUSH.

Cooperative Research Centre for Welded Structure: Dir Prof. V. LINTON.

Key Centre for Social Applications of Geographical Information Systems: Dir Prof. G. HUGO.

Research Data Network Cooperative Research Centre: Dir Dr A. WENDELBORN.

SA Partnership for Advanced Computing: Dir Dr A. G. WILLIAMS.

Special Research Centre for the Subatomic Structure of Matter: Dir Dr A. WILLIAMS.

AFFILIATED RESIDENTIAL COLLEGES

Aquinas College Inc.: North Adelaide; f. 1947; 150 students; Rector Fr M. HEAD.

Kathleen Lumley College Inc.: North Adelaide; f. 1967; 63 students (postgraduate); Master Dr D. L. CLEMENTS.

Lincoln College Inc.: North Adelaide; f. 1951; 240 students; Principal Dr P. GUNN.

Roseworthy College, Inc.: Roseworthy; f. 1991; 250 students; Principal Dr D. TAPLIN.

St Ann's College Inc.: North Adelaide; f. 1939; 154 students; Principal Dr R. BROOKS.

St Mark's College Inc.: North Adelaide; f. 1924; 204 students; Master C. R. ASHWIN.

AUSTRALIAN CATHOLIC UNIVERSITY

POB 968, North Sydney, NSW 2059

Telephone: (2) 9739-2929

Fax: (2) 9739-2905

E-mail: international@acu.edu.au

Internet: www.acu.edu.au

Founded 1991 by amalgamation of Catholic College of Education, Sydney, Institute of Catholic Education, Victoria, McAuley College, Brisbane, and Signadou College, Canberra

Academic year: February to December

Chancellor: Br JULIAN McDONALD

Pro-Chancellor: EDWARD EXELL
Vice-Chancellor: Prof. GREG CRAVEN
Pro-Vice-Chancellor for Academic Affairs:
Prof. GABRIELLE MCMULLEN
Pro-Vice-Chancellor for Quality and Out-
reach: Prof. JOHN O'GORMAN
Pro-Vice-Chancellor for Research and Inter-
national Relations: Prof. GAIL CROSSLEY
(acting)
Exec. Dir., University Services: JOHN
CAMERON

Library of 460,903 vols, 2,296 periodicals,
5,415 online journals
Number of teachers: 514
Number of students: 15,279

Publications: *Interlogue* (2 a year), *Journal of
Religious Education* (4 a year)

DEANS

Arts and Sciences: Dr GAIL CROSSLEY (acting)
Education: Prof. MARIE EMMITT
Health Sciences: Prof. PAULINE NUGENT

AUSTRALIAN NATIONAL UNIVERSITY

Canberra, ACT 0200

Telephone: (2) 6125-5111
Fax: (2) 6125-9062
E-mail: admiss.enq@anu.edu.au
Internet: www.anu.edu.au

Founded 1946 for postgraduate research;
now consists of Institute of Advanced
Studies (postgraduate), the faculties (all
levels)

Academic year: March to December

Chancellor: Prof. P. E. BAUME
Vice-Chancellor: Prof. IAN CHUBB
Deputy Vice-Chancellor and Vice-President:
Prof. LAWRENCE CRAM
Pro-Vice-Chancellor: Prof. ROBIN STANTON
Pro-Vice-Chancellor for Education: Prof. ELI-
ZABETH DEANE
Pro-Vice-Chancellor for Research: Prof.
MANDY THOMAS
Dir of Student and Academic Services:
GILLIAN LUCK
Librarian: VIC ELLIOT
Number of students: 15,416

Library: See under Libraries and Archives

Publication: *ANU Reporter*.

INSTITUTE OF ADVANCED STUDIES

Institute of Advanced Studies: Chair. of
the Institute of Advanced Studies Forum
Prof. G. FARQUHAR (acting); number of academic staff: 727; number of postgraduate
students: 949.

Constituent schools:

**John Curtin School of Medical
Research:** Dir Prof. J. WHITWORTH

PROFESSORS

BOARD, P., Molecular Genetics
DULHUNTY, A., Muscle Research
GAGE, P., Membrane Physiology
YOUNG, I., Cytokine Molecular Biology

**Research School of Astronomy and
Astrophysics:** Dir Prof. PENNY D. SACKETT

PROFESSORS

BESSELL, M., Astronomy
BRIGGS, F. H., Astronomy
DA COSTA, G., Astronomy
DOPITA, M. A., Astronomy
FREEMAN, K. C., Astronomy
NORRIS, J. E., Astronomy
SACKETT, P. D., Astronomy
SCHMIDT, B. P., Astronomy

**Research School of Biological Sci-
ences:** Dir Prof. JONATHAN STONE

PROFESSORS

ANDREWS, T. J., Molecular Genetics
BADGER, M., Photosythetic Functional
Genomics
CLARK-WALKER, D., Molecular Genetics
FARQUHAR, G., Environmental Biology
GIBSON, J., Molecular and Poulation Gen-
etics
GRAVES, J., Comparative Genomics
HARDHAM, A., Phytophthora Laboratory
NOBLE, I., Theoretical Ecology
SRINIVASAN, M., Insect Vision
WILLIAMSON, R., Cell Wall Laboratory

Research School of Chemistry: Dean
Prof. DENIS EVANS

PROFESSORS

BANWELL, M., Organic Chemistry
COLLINS, M., Physical and Theoretical
Chemistry
EASTON, C., Organic Chemistry
EVANS, D., Physical and Theoretical Chem-
istry
HILL, A., Inorganic Chemistry
KRAUSZ, E., Physical and Theoretical
Chemistry
MANDER, L., Organic Chemistry
OTTING, G., Organic Chemistry
RADOM, L., Physical and Theoretical Chem-
istry
WELBERRY, T., Physical and Theoretical
Chemistry
WHITE, J., Physical and Theoretical Chem-
istry
WILD, S., Inorganic Chemistry
WITHERS, R., Inorganic Chemistry

Research School of Earth Sciences: Dir
Prof. MARK HARRISON

PROFESSORS

CHAPPELL, J., Earth Environment
COX, S., Earth Materials
GRIFFITHS, R., Earth Physics
GRUN, R., Earth Environment
JACKSON, I., Earth Materials
KENNETT, B. L. N., Earth Physics
LAMBECK, K., Earth Physics
LISTER, G., Earth Materials
McCULLOCH, M., Earth Environment
O'NEILL, H. ST C., Earth Materials

**Research School of Information Sci-
ences and Engineering:** Dir Prof. JOHN
RICHARDS

PROFESSORS

ANDERSON, B. D. O., Information Engin-
eering
BRENT, R. P., Computer Science
HARTLEY, R., Information Engineering
LLOYD, J., Computer Sciences Laboratory
MOORE, J., Information Engineering

**Research School of Pacific and Asian
Studies:** Dir Prof. J. FOX

PROFESSORS

ANDERSON, A. J., Archaeology and Natural
History
BABBAGE, R.
BALL, D. J., Strategic and Defence Studies
BARMÉ, G. R.
BELLWOOD, P.
CROUCH, H.
DENOON, D. J. N., Pacific and Asian
History
FANE, G.
FOX, J. J., Anthropology
HILL, H.
HOPE, G.
HORNER, D. M.
JHA, R.
JOLLY, M. A.
KERKVLIET, B. J. T., Political and Social
Change
LAL, B.

McCORMACK, G. P., Pacific and Asian
History
McKIBBEN, W., Economics
MARR, D.
MOSKO, M.
NELSON, H. N., Pacific and Asian History
PAWLEY, A. K., Linguistics
RAVENHILL, J.
SPRIGGS, M.
TRYON, D.
WARR, P. G., Agricultural Economics

**Research School of Physical Sciences
and Engineering:** Dir Prof. J. WILLIAMS

PROFESSORS

BATCHELOR, M., Theoretical Physics
BAZHANOV, V., Theoretical Physics
DEWAR, R. L., Plasma Physics and Theor-
etical Physics
DRACOULIS, G. D., Nuclear Physics
ELLIMAN, R. G., Electronic Materials
Engineering
HAMBERGER, S. M., Plasma Research
HYDE, S., Applied Mathematics
JAGADISH, C., Electronic Materials Engin-
eering
LUTHER-DAVIES, B., Laser Physics
MARCELJA, S., Applied Mathematics
MITCHELL, D. J., Optical Sciences Centre
MOORE, J. B., Systems Engineering
SPEAR, R. H., Nuclear Physics
WEIGOLD, E., Atomic and Molecular Phys-
ics
WILLIAMS, J., Electronic Materials Engin-
eering

Research School of Social Sciences:
Dir Prof. F. C. JACKSON

PROFESSORS

BOOTH, A., Economics
BRAITHWAITE, J., Regulatory Institutions
Network
BRENNAN, H. G., Economics and Social and
Political Theory
CANE, P., Law
CHALMERS, D., Philosophy
CHAPMAN, B., Economics
CHARLESWORTH, H., Regulatory Institu-
tions Network
DAVIES, M., Philosophy
DEACON, D., History
DRAHOS, P., Regulatory Institutions Net-
work
DRYZEK, J. S., Political Science
GODFREY-SMITH, P., Philosophy
GOODIN, B., Philosophy
GRABOSKY, P., Regulatory Institutions Net-
work
GREGORY, R. G., Economics
GUNNINGHAM, N., Regulatory Institutions
Network
HAJEK, A., Philosophy
HIGMAN, B., History
HINDESS, B., Political Science
HULL, T., Demography
JACKSON, F. C., Philosophy
JALLAND, P., History
McALLISTER, A., Political Science
McDONALD, P., Demography
McGRATH, A., History
McMILLEN, J., Regulatory Institutions Net-
work
PAGAN, A. R., Economics
RHODES, R., Political Science
RITCHIE, J. D., Australian Dictionary of
Biography
SAWER, M., Political Science
SHEARING, C., Regulatory Institutions Net-
work
SNOOKS, G. D., Economic History
STAPLETON, J., Law
STERELNY, K., Philosophy
WAJCMAN, J., Demography and Sociology
WANNA, J., Political Science

School of Mathematical Sciences:
Dean Prof. A. L. CAREY

PROFESSORS

BATCHELOR, M., Mathematics
BAXTER, R. J., Mathematics
BAZHANOV, V., Mathematics
DALEY, D., Mathematics
GANI, J., Mathematics
HALL, P. J., Statistics
HEATHCOTE, C., Mathematics
HEYDE, C., Mathematics
HUTCHINSON, J., Mathematics
MCINTOSH, A., Mathematics
NEEMAN, A., Mathematics
NEWMAN, M., Mathematics
OSBORNE, M. R., Advanced Computation
ROBINSON, D., Mathematics
TRUDINGER, N., Mathematics
URBAS, J., Mathematics
WELSH, A., Statistics
WICKRAMASINGHE, D., Mathematics
WILSON, S. R., Statistics

THE FACULTIES

The Faculties: Chair. of the Faculties Forum Prof. A. KUMAR (acting); number of academic staff: 586; number of students: 1,836 postgraduate, 8,279 undergraduate

DEANS

Faculty of Arts and Social Sciences: Prof. TONI MAKKAI
Faculty of Asia and the Pacific: Prof. ANDREW MACINTYRE
Faculty of Business and Economics: Prof. K. HOUGHTON
Faculty of Engineering and Computer Science: Prof. CHRIS BAKER
Faculty of Law: Prof. M. D. COPER
Faculty of Medicine and Health Science: Prof. NICK GLASGOW
Faculty of Physical Sciences: Prof. AIDAN BYRNE

PROFESSORS

Faculty of Arts and Social Sciences:

BELLWOOD, P., Archaeology
CAMPBELL, R. J., Philosophy
CURTHOYS, A., History
GREENHALGH, C. M. B., Art History
GRISHIN, S., Art History
GROVES, C., Archaeology
MERLAN, F. C., Anthropology
MILLER, S., Philosophy
PAPADAKIS, E., Social Sciences
SAIKAI, A., Political Sciences
SITSKY, A., Composition
SPRIGGS, M., Archaeology
WARHURST, J. L., Political Science
WIERZBICKA, A. C., Linguistics
WILLIAMS, D., Visual Arts
WRIGHT, I. R., English

Faculty of Asia and the Pacific:

CORBETT, J., Asian Studies
HOOKER, V., Oriental Studies
LOUIE, K., Chinese Studies
MILNER, A. C., Southeast Asian History
WELLS, K., Korean Studies

Faculty of Business and Economics:

CRAIG, R., Commerce
DOWRICK, S., Economics
GREGOR, S., Business Information Management
HATTON, T., Economics
HEATHCOTE, C. R., Mathematical Statistics
MALLER, R., Finance and Applied Statistics
MONROE, G., Business Information Management
NICHOLLS, D. F., Statistics
O'NEILL, T., Applied Statistics
RICHARDSON, M., Economics
SMITH, T., Applied Statistics
TYERS, R., Economics

Faculty of Engineering and Computer Science:

BLAKERS, A., Engineering
CARDEW-HALL, M., Engineering
CUEVAS, A., Engineering
GEDEON, T., Engineering
JAMES, M., Engineering
MCKAY, B., Engineering
QIN, Q., Engineering

Faculty of Law:

CAMPBELL, T. D., Law
COPER, M. D., Law
DAVIS, J. L. R., Law
DISNEY, J. P., Law
GREIG, D. W., Law
GUNNINGHAM, N. A., Law
HAMBLEY, A. D., Law
PEARCE, D. C., Law
SWEENEY, M. D., Law
ZINES, L. R., Law

Faculty of Physical Sciences:

CLARK, I., Biochemistry
COCKBURN, A., Botany and Zoology
COX, S., Structural Geology
DE DECKKER, P., Geology
ELLIS, D., Igneous Petrology
GUNNINGHAM, N., Resources, Environment and Society
KANOWSKI, P. J., Resources, Environment and Society
KIRK, K., Biochemistry
LEVICK, B., Psychology
MCCLELLAND, D., Physics
PASHLEY, R., Colloid Chemistry
RIDE, D., Geology
STANTON, R., Palaeontology
TURNER, J., Psychology

UNIVERSITY CENTRES

Asia-Pacific College of Diplomacy: Dir Prof. W. MALEY.

Asia-Pacific School of Economics and Government (APSEG): Dir Prof. CHONG JU CHOI

APSEG CENTRES

Australia–Japan Research Centre: Exec. Dir Prof. P. DRYSDALE
Australia–South Asia Research Centre: Exec. Dir Prof. R. JHA
Graduate Program in Public Policy: Exec. Dir Prof. G. WITHERS
National Centre for Development Studies: Exec. Dir Prof. R. C. DUNCAN
Centre for Aboriginal Economic Policy Research: Dir Prof. J. C. ALTMAN.
Centre for Advanced Legal Studies in International and Public Law: Dir Prof. H. CHARLESWORTH.
Centre for Arab and Islamic Studies: Dir Prof. AMIN SAIKAL.
Centre for Commercial Law: Dir Prof. STEPHEN BOTTOMLEY.
Centre for Cross-Cultural Research: Dir Prof. H. MORPHY.
Centre for Educational Development and Academic Methods: Dir Dr L. HORT.
Centre for Environmental Law: Dir DON ANTON.
Centre for Mental Health Research: Dir Prof. A. JORM.
Centre for the Public Awareness of Science: Dir SUE STOCKLMAYER.
Centre for Resource and Environmental Studies: Dir Prof. M. HUTCHINSON.
Centre for Sustainable Energy Systems: Dir Prof. ANDREW BLAKERS.
Humanities Research Centre: Dir Prof. I. DONALDSON (acting).

National Centre for Epidemiology and Population Health: Dir Prof. T. MCMICHAEL.

UNIVERSITY OF BALLARAT
POB 663, Ballarat, Vic. 3353
Telephone: (3) 5327-9018
Fax: (3) 5327-9017
E-mail: info@ballarat.edu.au
Internet: www.ballarat.edu.au
Founded 1976 as Ballarat College of Advanced Education; University status acquired 1994
Vice-Chancellor: Prof. DAVID BATTERSBY
Number of students: 22,000 (higher education and Technical and Further Education—TAFE)

DEANS

Arts Academy: Prof. PETER MATTHEWS
School of Behavioural and Social Sciences and Humanities: Assoc. Prof. ROSEMARY GREEN
School of Business: Prof. JULIAN LOWE
School of Business Services—TAFE: RUSSELL BRAY
School of Education: Prof. LAWRIE ANGUS
School of Human Movement and Sport Sciences: Assoc. Prof. LEONIE OTAGO
School of Human Sciences—TAFE: GREG HAINES
School of Information Technology and Mathematical Sciences: Prof. SID MORRIS
School of Manufacturing Services—TAFE: CARLA READING
School of Nursing: Assoc. Prof. HANNELORE BEST
School of Science and Engineering: Prof. MARTIN WESTBROOKE

BOND UNIVERSITY
Qld 4229
Telephone: (7) 5595-1111
Fax: (7) 5595-1140
E-mail: information@bond.edu.au
Internet: www.bond.edu.au
Founded 1987
Private control
Academic year: January to December
Chancellor: HELEN NUGENT
Vice-Chancellor: Prof. ROBERT STABLE
Registrar: ALAN FINCH
Dir of Finance: JOHN LELIEVRE
Dir of Information Services: GRACE SAW
Dir of Marketing and Student Recruitment: ANDREA HARCOURT
Number of teachers: 461
Number of students: 5,370
Publications: *Bond Law Review, Revenue Law Journal*

DEANS

Business, Technology and Sustainable Devt: Prof. G. MARCHANT
Health Sciences and Medicine: Prof. C. DEL MAR
Humanities and Social Sciences: Prof. R. MORTLEY
Law: Prof. L. BOULLE

PROFESSORS

Faculty of Business, Technology and Sustainable Devt:

ARIFF, M., Finance
BERTIN, W., Finance
EARL, G., Sustainable Devt
FISHER, C., Management
GASTON, N., Economics
GORDON, R., Business
ISELIN, E., Accounting
KENT, P., Accounting
MOORES, K., Family Business

MORRISON, I., Information Technology
ROBERTS, E., Hotel, Resort and Tourism Management
SHAW, J. B., Human Resource Management
WILLIAMS, B., Finance

Faculty of Health Sciences and Medicine:
CHESS-WILLIAMS, R., Biomedical Sciences
GASS, G., Exercise and Sports Science
HENLY, D., Biomedical Sciences
QUICK, S., Sport Management
VAN DAAL, A., Forensic Sciences

Faculty of Humanities and Social Sciences:
HICKS, R., Psychology
MOLLOY, B., Film and Television
MORTLEY, R., Philosophy
PEARSON, M., Communication and Media
WEBB, S., Australian Studies
WILSON, P., Criminology

School of Information Technology:
FINNIE, G., Information Systems
KRISHNAN, P., Software Systems

Faculty of Law:
BOULLE, L., Medication, Alternative Dispute Resolution
CARNEY, G., Constitutional and Administrative Law
COLVIN, E., Criminal Law
CORKERY, J., Corporate and Taxation Law
FIELD, D., Criminal Law
FORDER, J., Contract Law, Information Technology and Electric Commerce Law
GERRARD, A., Constitutional Law, Admin. Law, Taxation of Business Entities
HISCOCK, M., Contract Law, Int. Law
LESSING, J., Corporations Law, Partnerships
LUPTON, M., Law and Medicine
MARSHALL, B., Restrictive Trade Practices
ONG, D., Equity, Securities Law
SPENCER, L., Franchise Law
SVANTESSON, D., eCommerce, Private Int. Law
WADE, J., Mediation, Negotiation, Family Law

UNIVERSITY OF CANBERRA

ACT 2601
Telephone: (2) 6201-5111
Fax: (2) 6201-5999
E-mail: international@canberra.edu.au
Internet: www.canberra.edu.au
Founded 1990 from fmr Canberra CAE
Govt control
Academic year: February to December (3 semesters)
Chancellor: Prof. INGRID MOSES
Vice-Chancellor: Prof. STEPHEN PARKER
Pro Vice-Chancellor for Education: Prof. CAROLE KAYROOZ
Pro Vice-Chancellor for Research: Prof. SUE THOMAS
Pro Vice-Chancellor for Quality: Prof. JOHN DEARN
Chief Operating Officer: ANDREW BAILEY
Univ. Librarian: ANITA R. M. CROTTY
Library: see Libraries and Archives
Number of teachers: 497 (full-time)
Number of students: 10,000

DEANS

Faculty of Applied Science: Prof. WILLIAM MAHER
Faculty of Arts and Design: Prof. MONIQUE SKIDMORE
Faculty of Business and Govt: Prof. ATIQUE ISLAM
Faculty of Education: Prof. CATHRYN McCONAGHY
Faculty of Health: Prof. DIANE GIBSON
Faculty of Information Sciences and Engineering: Prof. DHARMENDRA SHARMA

Faculty of Law: Prof. MURRAY RAFF

PROFESSORS

BLOOD, R. W., Professional Communication
BREMNER, C., Architecture
CHO, G., Geoinformatics and the Law
CRAIK, J., Communication
CREAGH, D., Physics
DUNK, A., Accounting
FRITH, S., Architecture
GEORGES, A., Applied Ecology
HALLIGAN, J., Public Administration
HARDING, A.
HAWKINS, S., Health Sciences
HONE, J., Wildlife Management
JONES, G., Freshwater Science
KAYROOZ, C., Education
LEAHY, P.
LENNARD, C., Forensic Studies
MORRISON, P., Nursing
NORRIS, R., Freshwater Ecology
PEGRUM, A., Architecture
PUTNIS, P., Communication
RICHWOOD, D., Psychology
SATHYE, M., Public Administration
SHADDOCK, A., Special Education and Counselling
TAYLOR, P. J., Mathematics Education
TURNER, M., Public Administration
WAGNER, M., Software Engineering
WIDDOWSON, D., International Customs Law and Administration

CQ UNIVERSITY

Bruce Highway, Rockhampton, CQ Mail Centre, Qld 4702
Telephone: (7) 4930-9368
Fax: (7) 4936-1691
E-mail: publicrelations@cqu.edu.au
Internet: www.cqu.edu.au
Founded 1967 as Queensland Institute of Technology (Capricornia); became Capricornia Institute of Advanced Education in 1971; became University College of Central Queensland in 1990 and University of Central Queensland in 1992; became Central Queensland University in 1994; present name 2008
Chancellor: RENNIE FRITSCHY
Vice-Chancellor and Pres.: Prof. JOHN RICKARD
Deputy Vice-Chancellor and Vice-Pres.: Prof. ANGELA DELVES
Deputy Vice Chancellor for Research Scholarship and Industry: Prof. JENNELLE KYD
Exec. Dir for Corporate Services: KEN WINDOW
Exec. Dir for Resources: JOHN NELSON
Dir of Library Services: GRAHAM BLACK
Number of teachers: 321
Number of students: 19,000

DEANS

Faculty of Arts, Business, Informatics, Education: Prof. ELIZABETH TAYLOR
Faculty of Sciences, Engineering and Health: Prof. KEVIN TICKLE
Campuses at Brisbane, Bundaberg, Emerald, Gladstone, Gold Coast, Mackay, Melbourne, Rockhampton and Sydney

CHARLES DARWIN UNIVERSITY

Darwin, NT 0909
Telephone: (8) 8946-6666
Fax: (8) 8927-0612
E-mail: international@cdu.edu.au
Internet: www.cdu.edu.au
Founded 2003 by the merger of Northern Territory University and Centralian College
Federal control
Academic year: February to November

Chancellor: R. RYAN
Vice-Chancellor: Prof. BARNEY GLOVER
Deputy Vice-Chancellor for Research and International: Prof. ROBERT WASSON
Deputy Vice-Chancellor for Teaching and Learning: Prof. C. WEBB
Exec. Dir, Corporate Services: Dr SCOTT SNYDER
Number of academic staff: 500
Number of students: 21,000

DEANS

Education, Health and Science: Prof. G. PEGG
Law, Business and Arts: Prof. GARY DAVIS (acting)

CHARLES STURT UNIVERSITY

Chancellery, The Grange, Panorama Ave, Bathurst, NSW 2795
Telephone: (2) 6338-4000
Fax: (2) 6338-6001
E-mail: inquiry@csu.edu.au
Internet: www.csu.edu.au
Founded 1989 by amalgamation of Mitchell College of Advanced Education (f. 1951) and Riverina-Murray Inst. of Higher Education (f. 1947)
State control
Academic year: January to December
Chancellor: LAWRENCE WILLETT
Vice-Chancellor and Pres.: Prof. IAN GOULTER
Deputy Vice-Chancellor for Academic Affairs: Prof. ROSS CHAMBERS
Deputy Vice Chancellor for Research: Prof. SUE THOMAS
Deputy Vice Chancellor for Admin. Services: Prof. LYN GORMAN
Univ. Sec. and Dir Corporate Affairs: MARK BURDACK
Exec. Dir, Library Services: SHIRLEY OAKLEY
Library of 640,193 vols, 61,573 periodicals
Number of teachers: 672
Number of students: 34,659

DEANS

Faculty of Arts: Prof. ANTHONY CAHALAN
Faculty of Business: Assoc. Prof. KEN DILLON
Faculty of Education: Prof. TONI DOWNES
Faculty of Science: Prof. NICHOLAS KLOMP

PROFESSORS

Faculty of Arts (POB 588, Wagga Wagga, NSW 2678; tel. (2) 6933-2861; fax (2) 6933-2868; internet www.csu.edu.au/faculty/arts):
BRADLEY, B., Psychology
CAMPBELL, T., Centre for Applied Philosophy and Public Ethics
FARRELL, M., Arts
FRYER, D., Social Sciences and Liberal Studies
GREEN, D., Visual and Performing Arts
HAIRE, I., Australian Centre for Christianity and Culture
HUDSON, C., Public and Contextual Theology
KLEINIG, J., Centre for Applied Philosophy and Public Ethics
LUPTON, D., Sociology/Cultural Studies
MAY, L., Social Justice and Applied Ethics
MILLER, S., Philosophy
MILLS, J., Communications
MORAN, C., Humanities and Social Sciences
WECKERT, J., Computing Ethics

Faculty of Business (Panorama Ave, Bathurst, NSW 2795; tel. (2) 6338-4285; fax (2) 6338-4250; internet www.csu.edu.au/faculty/commerce):
BOSSOMAIER, T., Computing Systems
FISH, A., International Business and Human Resource Management
HICKS, J., Economics
JARRATT, D., Marketing

MORRISON, M., Economics and Marketing
OCZKOWSKI, E., Applied Economics
PARTON, K., Strategic Professor– Economics, Agriculture and environmental Science

Faculty of Education (Panorama Ave, Bathurst, NSW 2795; tel. (2) 6338-4444; fax (2) 6338-4182; internet www.csu.edu.au/faculty/educat):

BAIN, A., Education
DALGARNO, B., Information Systems
DOCKETT, S., Early Childhood Education
GREEN, W., Education
HIDER, P., Library and Information Studies
HIGGS, J., Institute of Education for Practice
KEMMIS, S., Education
LOWRIE, T., Education
MARINO, F., Human Movement Studies
MCLEOD, S., Language Acquisition
PERRY, R., Mathematics Education
REID, J., Education
SANTORO, N., Education
SUMSION, J., Early Childhood Education

Faculty of Science (POB 588, Wagga Wagga, NSW 2678; tel. (2) 6933-2864; fax (2) 6933-2868; internet www.csu.edu.au/faculty/science):

ABBOTT, K., Animal and Veterinary Sciences
BALL, P., Rural Pharmacy
BLACKWELL, J., Smart Agricultural Water Technologies
BOWMER, K., Water Policy
BRYANT, R., Dentistry
CHENOWETH, P., Veterinary Reproduction
CHRISTIE, B., Small Animal Medicine
CURTIS, A., Environmental Management
DUFFY, M., Nursing and Midwifery
GURR, G., Applied Ecology
HARDIE, W., Wine Growing Innovation
KEMP, D., Farming Systems
KHAN, S., Hydrology
KLOMP, N., Science
LEMERLE, D., Agricultural Innovation
O'BRIEN, L., Nursing
PARTON, K., Agricultural Economics
PRATLEY, J., Agricultural and Wine Sciences
SANGSTER, N., Pathobiology
SPITHILL, T., Veterinary Parasitology
WANG, L., Clinical Pharmacy/Pharmacology
WILSON, D., Dentistry
WYNN, P., Animal Production

CONSTITUENT CAMPUSES

Albury–Wodonga Campus

POB 789, Albury, NSW 2640
Telephone: (2) 6051-6000
Fax: (2) 6051-6629
E-mail: inquiry@csu.edu.au
Internet: www.csu.edu.au
Founded 1989
Head of Campus: Prof. ALLAN CURTIS

Bathurst Campus

Panorama Ave, Bathurst, NSW 2795
Telephone: (2) 6338-4000
Fax: (2) 6331-9634
E-mail: inquiry@csu.edu.au
Internet: www.csu.edu.au
Founded 1989
Prin.: COLIN SHARP.

Dubbo Campus

Locked Bag 49, Dubbo East, NSW 2830
Telephone: (2) 6884-7209
Fax: (2) 6884-7218
E-mail: inquiry@csu.edu.au
Internet: www.csu.edu.au

Founded 1995
Head of School: BEVERLEY MORIARTY (acting).

Orange Campus

POB 883, Orange, NSW
Telephone: (2) 6365-7555
Fax: (2) 6360-5590
E-mail: inquiry@csu.edu.au
Internet: www.csu.edu.au
Prin.: Prof. KEVIN PARTON.

Wagga Wagga Campus

Locked Bag 588, Wagga Wagga, NSW 2678
Telephone: (2) 6933-2000
Fax: (2) 6933-2639
E-mail: inquiry@csu.edu.au
Internet: www.csu.edu.au
Founded 1989
Head of Campus: ADRIAN LINDNER.

Ontario Campus

860 Harrington Court, Burlington, ON Canada L7N 3N4
Telephone: (5) 333-4955
Fax: (5) 333-6562
E-mail: canada@csu.edu.au
Internet: www.charlessturt.ca
Head of Campus: Prof. ROBERT MEYENN.

CURTIN UNIVERSITY OF TECHNOLOGY

GPO Box U1987, Perth, WA 6845
Telephone: (8) 9266-9266
Fax: (8) 9266-2255
Internet: www.curtin.edu.au
Founded 1967 as Western Australian Inst. of Technology; present name and status 1987
Academic year: February to November (2 semesters)

Chancellor: RICHARD TASTULA (acting)
Vice-Chancellor: Prof. LANCE TWOMEY
Sr Deputy Vice-Chancellor: Prof. LESLEY PARKER
Deputy Vice-Chancellor for Research and Devt: Prof. PAUL ROSSITER
Pro Vice-Chancellor for Academic Services: Prof. JANE DEN HOLLANDER
Pro Vice-Chancellor for International and Enterprise: Prof. JEANETTE HACKETT
Exec. Dean, Curtin Business School: Prof. MICHAEL WOOD
Exec. Dean, Engineering, Science and Computing: PETER LEE
Exec. Dean, Health Sciences: Prof. CHARLES WATSON
Exec. Dean, Humanities: Prof. TOM STANNAGE
Exec. Gen. Man., University Resources: PETER WALTON
University Librarian: VICKI WILLIAMSON
Number of teachers: 1,200
Number of students: 40,374

DEANS

Faculty of Built Environment, Art and Design: L. HEVGOLD
Faculty of Education, Language Studies and Social Work: Dr G. DELLAR
Research and Development (Graduate Studies): Prof. L. RENNIE

ATTACHED INSTITUTES

Australian Telecommunications Research Institute: Dir Prof. S. NORDHAM.
Curtin Sarawak: campus in Malaysia; Dir Prof. K. MCKENNA.
Institute for Research into International Competitiveness: Dir Prof. P. KENYON.

Muresk Institute of Agriculture: Northam, WA 6401; Dir G. HEPWORTH.
National Drug Research Institute: Dir Prof. T. STOCKWELL.
Research Institute for Cultural Heritage: Dir Prof. D. DOLAN.
Western Australian School of Mines: PMB 22, Kalgoorlie, WA 6430; f. 1902, coll. of univ. since 1969; Dir G. LODWICK.

DEAKIN UNIVERSITY

Geelong, Vic. 3217
Telephone: (3) 5227-1100
Fax: (3) 5227-2001
E-mail: dconnect@deakin.edu.au
Internet: www.deakin.edu.au
Founded 1974
Academic year: February to November

Chancellor: R. H. SEARBY
Vice-Chancellor and President: Prof. SALLY WALKER
Deputy Vice-Chancellor for Academic Affairs: Prof. JOHN ROSENBERG
Pro Vice-Chancellor for International Relations: ERIC MEADOWS
Pro Vice-Chancellor for Online Services: Prof. BRIAN CORBITT
Pro Vice-Chancellor for Research: Prof. PHILIP HAMILTON
Pro Vice-Chancellor for Rural and Regional: Prof. ROB WALLIS
Librarian: S. MCKNIGHT
Library of 1,434,864 vols, 15,959 current periodical titles
Number of teachers: 790
Number of students: 34,281

Campuses at Melbourne (Burwood), Geelong, Rusden, Toorak, Warrnambool and Geelong Waterfront

DEANS

Faculty of Arts and Education: Prof. JENNIFER RADBOURNE
Faculty of Business and Law: Prof. GAEL MCDONALD
Faculty of Health, Medicine, Nursing and Behavioural Sciences: Prof. JOHN CATFORD
Faculty of Science and Technology: Prof. BRIAN MCGAW

FACULTIES AND SCHOOLS

Faculty of Arts and Education: 221 Burwood Highway, Burwood, Vic. 3215; tel. (3) 9244-6955; fax (3) 9244-6752; e-mail dean-artsed@deakin.edu.au; Schools of Australian and Int. Studies, Contemporary Arts, Literary and Communication Studies, Social Inquiry.

Faculty of Business and Law: Pigdons Rd, Geelong, Vic. 3217; tel. (3) 5227-1100; fax (3) 5227-2001; e-mail deanbuslaw@deakin.edu.au; internet www.deakin.edu.au/fac_buslaw; Schools of Accounting and Finance, Econ., Law, Management Information Systems; Bowater School of Management and Marketing.

Faculty of Health, Medicine, Nursing and Behavioural Sciences: 221 Burwood Highway, Burwood, Vic. 3217; tel. (3) 9244-6135; fax (3) 9244-6019; e-mail hbs.info@deakin.edu.au; internet www.hbs.deakin.edu.au; Schools of Health Sciences, Nursing, Psychology; Institute of Disability Studies.

Faculty of Science and Technology: 662 Blackburn Rd, Clayton, Vic. 3168; tel. (3) 9244-7100; fax (3) 9244-7134; internet www.deakin.edu.au/fac_st; Schools of Architecture and Building, Biological and Chemical Sciences, Computing and Mathematics, Ecology and Environment, Engineering and Technology.

ATTACHED RESEARCH INSTITUTES

Cell and Organism Bio-engineering: Dir Prof. JULIAN MERCER.

Cellular Metabolism in Health and Disease: Dirs Prof. GREG COLLIER, Prof. MARK HARGREAVES.

Citizenship and Globalization: Dir Dr MICHAEL MUETZELFELDT.

Information Technology for the Information Economy: Dir Prof. GEOFFREY WEBB.

Metals Manufacturing and Performance: Dir Prof. PETER HODGSON.

Palaeoenvironments and Global Change: Dir Prof. NEIL ARCHBOLD.

Quality of Life: Dirs Prof. ROBERT CUMMINS, Dr LIZ ECKERMANN.

Sustainable Environment Management: Dir Prof. GORDON DUFF.

EDITH COWAN UNIVERSITY

Pearson St, Churchlands, WA 6018

Telephone: (8) 9273-8333

Fax: (8) 9387-7095

Internet: www.ecu.edu.au

Founded 1991

State control

Academic year: February to November (2 semesters)

Chancellor: Hon. Justice R. NICHOLSON

Vice-Chancellor: Prof. KERRY O. COX

Deputy Vice-Chancellor for Academic Affairs: Prof. PATRICK GARNETT

Deputy Vice-Chancellor for Research: Prof. JOHN FINLAY-JONES

Deputy Vice-Chancellor for Students, Advancement and International Affairs: Prof. JOHN WOOD

Pro Vice-Chancellor for Equity and Indigenous Affairs: Prof. BRENDA CHEREDNICHENKO

Pro Vice-Chancellor for Teaching and Learning: Prof. RON OLIVER

Pro Vice-Chancellor for Technology and Information Systems: Prof. TONY WATSON

Vice Pres., Resources and Chief Financial Officer: WARREN SNELL

Number of teachers: 772

Number of students: 23,000

Publications: *Digest* (4 a year), *Handbook* (1 a year), *Quest* (4 a year), *Research & Postgraduate Studies* (1 a year)

DEANS

Faculty of Business and Law: Prof. ROBERT HARVEY

Faculty of Computing, Health and Science: ANTHONY WATSON

Faculty of Education and Arts: Prof. BRENDA CHEREDNICHENKO

Faculty of Regional Professional Studies: ROBERT IRVINE

FLINDERS UNIVERSITY

GPOB 2100, Adelaide, SA 5001

Telephone: (8) 8201-3911

Fax: (8) 8201-3757

E-mail: central.records@flinders.edu.au

Internet: www.flinders.edu.au

Founded 1966, merged in 1991 with Sturt Campus of South Australian College of Advanced Education

Academic year: March to November (2 semesters)

Chancellor: Sir STEPHEN GEVLACH

Vice-Chancellor: Prof. MICHAEL N. BARBER

Deputy Vice-Chancellor for Academic: Prof. ANDREW W. PARKIN

Deputy Vice-Chancellor for Int.: Prof. D. FORBES

Deputy Vice-Chancellor for Research: Prof. DAVID DAY

Dir. of Admin.: B. FERGUSSON

Registrar: B. SIMONDSON

Librarian: IAN MCBAIN

Library: see Libraries and Archives

Number of teachers: 625

Number of students: 15,418

Publications: *Australian Bulletin of Labour* (4 a year), *Australian Economic Papers* (with Univ. of Adelaide), *Australian Journal of Political Science*, *Health Sociology Review*

EXECUTIVE DEANS

Education, Humanities, Law and Theology: Prof. F. H. E. TRENT

Health Sciences: Prof. MICHAEL KIDD

Science and Engineering: Prof. WARREN LAWRANCE

Social and Behavioural Sciences: Prof. PHYLLIS THARENOM

PROFESSORS

AYLWARD, P., Medicine

BARRITT, G. T., Medical Biochemistry

BAUM, F., Public Health

BERSTEN, A. A., Medicine

BLESSING, W. W., Medicine

BULL, M., Biological Sciences

BURGOYNE, L., Biological Sciences

BUTCHER, A. R., Communication Disorders

CATCHESIDE, D. E. A., Biological Sciences

CLARE, J. M. R., Nursing

CLARK, D. J., Law

CONDON, J., Psychiatry

COOPER, L. L., Social Administration and Social Work

COSTA, M., Human Physiology

COSTER, D. J., Ophthalmology

CROCKER, A. D., Psychiatry

CROTTY, M., Rehabilitation, Aged and Extended Care

CURROW, D. C., Palliative Care

DEBATS, D. A., American Studies

DODDS, P. G., Mathematics and Statistics

DUNBAR, J., Rural Health

FAIRWEATHER, P. G., Biological Sciences

FORBES, D. K., Geography

FORSYTH, K. D., Paediatrics and Child Health

GIBBINS, I. L., Anatomy and Histology

GOODMAN, A. E., Biology

GORDON, T. P., Immunology, Allergy and Arthritis

HASSAN, R. U., Sociology

HAY, I. M., Geography

HENDERSON, D. W., Medicine

HOLLEDGE, J., Drama

KALUCY, R. S., Psychiatry

KEIRSE, M., Obstetrics and Gynaecology

KNOWLES, G. P., Computer Systems Engineering

KRISHNAN, J., Surgery

LAWRANCE, W., Chemistry

LAWSON, M. J., Education

LEONARD, D., Economics

LINACRE, A., Forensics

LUSZCZ, M. A., Psychology

MCDONALD, J. M., Economics

MACKENZIE, P. I., Clinical Pharmacology

MACKINNON, A., Medicine

MALTBY, R. G., Screen Studies

MARLIN, C. D., Computer Science

MATISONS, J. G., Chemistry, Physics and Earth Sciences

MAVROMARAS, K., Labour Studies

MINERS, J. O., Clinical Pharmacology

MORLEY, A. A., Haematology

OWEN, H., Anaesthesia and Pain Medicine

PARKIN, A., Political and International Studies

PHILLIPS, P., Medicine

PILLER, N. B., Public Health

PRIDEAUX, D. J., Health Professional Education

RICHARDS, E. S., History

RICHARDSON, S., National Institute of Labour Studies

ROACH ANLEU, S. L., Sociology

ROCHE, A. M., National Centre for Education and Training on Addiction

RODDICK, J. F., Computer Science

RUSH, R. A., Human Physiology

RYALL, R. L., Surgery

SAGE, M. R., Medical Imaging

SHERIDAN, S. M., Women's Studies

SIMMONS, C. T., Groundwater

SMITH, M. D., Medicine

STEWART, A. J., Law

STORER, R., Physics

TEUBNER, P. J. O., Physics

TIGGEMANN, M., Psychology

TOMCZAK, M., Earth Sciences

TONKIN, A. M., Medicine

TOOULI, J., Surgery

TRENT, F. H., Education

TULLOCH, G. J., English

WATSON, D., Surgery

WILLOUGHBY, J. O., Medicine

WING, L. M. H., Medicine

WORLEY, P. S., Rural and Remote Health

YOUNG, G. P., Gastroenterology

ZOLA, H., Medicine

GRIFFITH UNIVERSITY

Qld 4111

Telephone: (7) 3735-7111

Fax: (7) 3735-7965

Internet: www.griffith.edu.au

(Griffith Univ. Gold Coast Campus, Parklands Dr., Southport, Qld 4215; tel. (7) 5552-8800; fax (7) 5552-8777)

(Griffith Univ. Logan Campus, University Dr., Meadowbrook, Qld 4131; tel. (7) 3382-7111; fax (7) 3735-7965)

(Griffith Univ. Mount Gravatt Campus, Messines Ridge Rd, Mt Gravatt, Qld 4122; tel. (7) 3735-7111; fax (7) 3735-7965)

(Griffith Univ. Nathan Campus, Kessels Rd, Nathan, Qld 4111; tel. (7) 3735-7111; fax (7) 3735-7965)

(Queensland College of Art, Griffith Univ., 226 Grey St, South Bank, Qld 4101; tel. (7) 3735-3111; fax (7) 3735-3199; f. 1881, became a college of Griffith Univ. 1992)

(Queensland Conservatorium, Griffith Univ., 16 Russell St, South Bank, Qld 4101; tel. (7) 3735-6111; fax (7) 3735-6282; f. 1957, became a college of Griffith Univ. 1991)

Founded 1971

State control

Academic year: February to November

Chancellor: LENEEN FORDE

Vice-Chancellor and Pres.: Prof. I. O'CONNOR

Deputy Vice-Chancellor for Research and Deputy Pres.: Prof. L. JOHNSON

Deputy Vice-Chancellor for Academic Affairs and Deputy Pres.: Prof. J. DEWAR

Pro-Vice-Chancellor for Admin.: COLIN MCANDREW

Pro-Vice-Chancellor for Arts, Education and Law: Prof. M. MCMENIMAN

Pro-Vice-Chancellor for Business: Prof. M. POWELL

Pro-Vice-Chancellor for Community Partnerships: Prof. M. STANDAGE

Pro-Vice-Chancellor for Health: Prof. A. CRIPPS

Pro-Vice-Chancellor for Information Services: JANICE RICKARDS

Pro-Vice-Chancellor for Int. Affairs: C. MADDEN

Pro-Vice-Chancellor for Science, Environment, Engineering and Technology: Prof. N. PANKHURST

Academic Registrar: Dr RICHARD AMOUR

Dir, Queensland College of Art: Prof. P. CLEVELAND
Dir, Queensland Conservatorium: Prof. P. ROENNFELDT
Library of 800,000
Number of teachers: 1,254
Number of students: 36,350
Publication: *Griffith Review* (4 a year)

DEANS

Faculty of Arts: Prof. K. FERRES
Faculty of Education: Prof. C. WYATT-SMITH
Griffith Business School: Prof. W. SHEPHERD (Academic: Prof. L. FULOP (Research: Prof. L. FRAZER (Learning and Teaching)
Griffith Health School: Prof. D. CREEDY (Academic: Prof. K. HALFORD (Research: Assoc. Prof. N. BUYS (Learning and Teaching)
Griffith Law School: Prof. P. BARON
Science, Environment, Engineering and Technology: Assoc. Prof. C. WILD (Academic: G. BUSHELL (Research: D. EDWARDS (Learning and Teaching)
Griffith Graduate Research School: Prof. J. CUMMING

PROFESSORS

AITKEN, L., Nursing
ARTHINGTON, A. H., Environmental Science
AULD, C., Tourism, Leisure, Hotel and Sports Management
BAGNALL, R., Education
BALASUBRAMANIAM, A. B., Engineering
BALFOUR, M., Education
BAMBER, G., Business
BARKER, M., Management
BEACHAM, I., Medical Science
BERNS, S., Law
BORBASI, S., Nursing
BRADDOCK, R., Environmental Sciences
BRAMLEY-MOORE, M., Queensland College of Art
BROWN, L., Environmental Sciences
BROWN, P., Leisure Studies
BUCKLEY, R., Engineering
BUNN, S., Environmental Studies
BURCH, D., Science
BURTON, B., Education
BUSHELL, G., Science
CHABOYER, W., Nursing
CHENOWETH, L., Human Services
CHU, C., Public Health
CLARKE, F., Biomolecular and Physical Sciences
COUCHMAN, P., Management
CREED, P., Psychology
CREEDY, D., Health
CRIPPS, A., Health
CUMMING, J., Education
DALY, K., Criminology and Criminal Justice
DAVIDSON, M. C., Tourism, Leisure, Hotel and Sports Management
DEHNE, F., Information and Communication Technology
DE LEO, D., Suicide Research and Prevention
DEMPSTER, N., Education
DEWAR, J. K., Law
DIMITRIJEV, S., Microelectronic Engineering
DOBSON, J., Science
DRAPER, P., Music
DREW, R., Biomolecular and Physical Sciences
DREW, R., Environmental Studies
DROMEY, R. G., Computing and Information Technology
DYCK, M. J., Business
ELKINS, J., Education
ESTIVILL-CASTRO, V., Information and Communication Technology
FARQHAR, M., International Business and Asian Studies
FERRES, K., Arts
FINNANE, M. J., Arts, Postgraduate Studies
FRAZER, L., Marketing

FULOP, E., Marketing and Management
GAMMON, J., Management
GIDDINGS, J., Law
GLEESON, B., Environmental Planning
GRIFFITHS, L., Medical Science
GUEST, R., Graduate School of Management
GUILDING, C., Tourism, Leisure, Hotel and Sports Management
HALFORD, G., Psychology
HALFORD, W. K., Health and Applied Psychology
HARRISON, H. B., Microelectronic Engineering
HEAD, B., Law
HEADRICK, J., Medical Science
HEALY, P., Science
HOMEL, R. J., Criminology and Criminal Justice
HOPE, G., Science
HUDSON, C. W., Humanities
HUGHES, J., Environmental Sciences
HUNTER, R., Law
HYDE, M. B., Education
ISLAM, Y., International Business and Asian Studies
IVANOVSKI, S., Dentistry and Oral Health
JENKINS, I., Science
JOHNSON, L., Research
JOHNSON, N. W., Dentistry and Oral Health
JOHNSTONE, R., Law
KANE, J., Politics and Public Policy
KEITH, R., International Business and Asian Studies
KITCHING, R. L., Environmental Science
KNIGHT, A. E., Science
KNIGHT, K., International Business and Asian Studies
KWON, O. Y., International Business and Asian Studies
LAM, A. K., Medicine
LEE, S., Environmental Studies
LISNER, P., Microelectronic Engineering
LOO, Y.-C., Engineering
McDONALD, J., Law
MACKAY-SIM, A., Biomolecular and Biomedical Sciences
MACKERRAS, C. P., International Business and Asian Studies
McLURE, R. J., Medicine
McMENIMAN, M., Education
McQUEEN, R. I., Law
McROBBIE, C., Education
McTAINSH, G., Environmental Studies
MAKIN, A., Accounting, Finance and Economics
MERRILEES, W., Marketing and Management
MIA, L., Accounting and Finance
MORAN, A., Arts
MOYLE, W., Nursing
MUIRHEAD, B. D., Education
NESDALE, A. R., Commerce, Management and Applied Psychology
NG, A. C., Accounting
NGUYEN, D. T., Economics
O'CONNOR, I., Economics
O'FAIRCHEALLAIGH, C. S., Politics and Public Policy
O'TOOLE, J., Education
PALIWAL, K., Microelectronic Engineering
PARRY, K., Management
PATEL, B., Biomolecular and Physical Sciences
PEETZ, D., Industrial Relations
PEGG, D. T., Science
POWELL, M. J., Business
QUINN, R. J., Science
RICKARD, C., Nursing
RICKSON, R., Environmental Studies
ROEMFELDT, P. J., Music
SADLER, D. R., Education
SAMPFORD, C. J., Criminology and Criminal Justice
SATTAR, A., Information Technology
SCHULTZ, J., Public Culture
SCHUMAN, A. D., Business
SCUFFHAM, P., Medicine

SEARLE, J., Medicine
SELVANATHAN, A., International Business and Asian Studies
SELVANATHAN, S., Accounting, Finance and Economics
SHEPHERD, W., International Business and Asian Studies
SHORT, S. D., Public Health
SMITH, C., Accounting, Finance and Economics
SPARKS, B., Tourism and Hotel Management
STANDAGE, M., Science and Health
STEVENSON, J. C., Education
STRACHAN, G., Commerce and Business
SUN, C., Computing and Information Technology
TACON, P., Arts
THIEL, D. V., Microelectronic Engineering
TOH, S. H., Multi-faith Centre
TOMLINSON, R., Environmental Engineering
TOPOR, R. W., Computing and Information Technology
TURNBULL, P. G., Arts
VLACIC, L., Microelectronic Engineering
VON ITZTEIN, M., Biomolecular Science
WALLIS, M., Nursing
WANNA, J., Politics and Public Policy
WELLER, P. M., Politics and Public Policy
WISEMAN, H. M., Science
XU, Z., Environmental Studies
YEO, R., Humanities
ZEVENBERGEN, R., Education

ACADEMIC CENTRES AND INSTITUTES

Centre for Applied Linguistics and Languages: tel. (7) 3735-7089; fax (7) 3875-7090; e-mail call@griffith.edu.au; internet www .griffith.edu.au/centre/call; Dir MARGARET CASEY.

Centre for Applied Studies in Deafness: tel. (7) 5552-8619; e-mail m.hyde@griffith .edu.au; internet www.griffith.edu.au/centre/ casd; Dir Prof. MERVYN HYDE.

Centre for Credit and Consumer Law: tel. (7) 3735-4211; fax (7) 3735-5599; e-mail n .howell@griffith.edu.au; internet www .griffith.edu.au/centre/cccl; Dir NICOLA HOWELL.

Centre for Environmental and Population Health: tel. (7) 3735-7458; fax (7) 3735-5318; e-mail c.chu@griffith.edu.au; internet www.griffith.edu.au/centre/ceph; Dir Prof. CORDIA CHU.

Centre for Leadership and Management in Education: tel. (7) 3735-5626; fax (7) 3735-6877; e-mail clme@griffith.edu.au; internet www.griffith.edu.au/centre/clme; Dir (vacant).

Centre for Professional Development: tel. (7) 5552-8452; fax (7) 5552-9076; e-mail b.mclellan@griffith.edu.au; internet www .griffith.edu.au/centre/cpd; Dir Dr M. COOPER.

Griffith Graduate Research School: tel. (7) 3735-5958; e-mail j.cumming@griffith.edu .au; internet www.griffith.edu.au/ggrs; Dir Prof. JOY CUMMING.

Griffith Institute for Higher Education: tel. (7) 3735-5982; fax (7) 3735-5998; e-mail c .birch@griffith.edu.au; internet www.griffith .edu.au/centre/gihe; Dir Prof. KERRI-LEE KRAUSE.

GUMURRII Student Support Centre: tel. (7) 3735-7676; fax (7) 3735-7033; e-mail kerryn.brown@griffith.edu.au; internet www .griffith.edu.au/centre/gumurrii; Dir Prof. B. ROBERTSON.

Institute for Educational Research, Policy and Evaluation: Dir (vacant).

Queensland Centre for Public Health (Griffith Node): tel. (7) 3735-3241; fax (7) 3735-3272; e-mail donald.stewart@griffith

.edu.au; internet www.griffith.edu.au/centre/qcph; Dir Prof. DONALD STEWART.

Unit for Italian Studies: Dir C. KENNEDY.

ATTACHED RESEARCH CENTRES

Applied Cognitive Neuroscience Research Centre: tel. (7) 3735-3456; fax (7) 3735-3388; e-mail acnrc@griffith.edu.au; internet www.griffith.edu.au/school/psy/acnrc; Dir Assoc. Prof. DAVID SHUM.

Australian Centre for Intellectual Property in Agriculture: tel. (7) 3346-7506; fax (7) 3346-7480; e-mail acipa@law.uq.edu.au; internet www.acipa.edu.au; Dir Prof. B. SHERMAN.

Australian Institute for Suicide Research and Prevention: tel. (7) 3735-3382; internet www.griffith.edu.au/school/psy/aisrap; Dir Prof. DIEGO DE LEO.

Centre for Applied Language, Literacy and Communication Studies: tel. (7) 3735-5497; fax (7) 3735-5921; Dir Prof. C. WYATT-SMITH.

Centre for Aquatic Processes and Evolution: tel. (7) 5552-9185; fax (7) 5552-8067; e-mail cpp-capp@griffith.edu.au; internet www.griffith.edu.au/centre/capp; Dir Prof. JOE LEE.

Centre for Forestry and Horticultural Research: tel. (7) 3735-6709; fax (7) 3735-7656; e-mail cfhr@griffith.edu.au; internet www.griffith.edu.au/centre/cfhr; Dir Prof. Z. XU.

Centre for Governance and Public Policy: tel. (7) 3735-7723; fax (7) 3735-7737; e-mail p.weller@griffith.edu.au; internet www.griffith.edu.au/centre/cgpp; Dir Prof. PATRICK WELLER.

Centre for Infrastructure Engineering and Management: tel. (7) 5552 8575; fax (7) 5552 8065; internet www.griffith.edu.au/centre/iem; Dir Prof. SHERIF MOHAMED.

Centre for Innovative Conservation Strategies: tel. (7) 5552 9234; internet www.griffith.edu.au/centre/cics/home.html; Dir Assoc. Prof. JEAN MARC HERO (acting).

Centre for Learning Research: tel. (7) 3735-5724; fax (7) 3735-6868; e-mail h.middleton@griffith.edu.au; internet www.griffith.edu.au/centre/clr; Dir Assoc. Prof. HOWARD MIDDLETON.

Centre for Organisational Governance and Performance Management: tel. (7) 3735-6621; fax (7) 3735-7760; e-mail g.warry@griffith.edu.au; internet www.griffith.edu.au/centre/cogap; Dir Assoc. Prof. NAVA SUBRAMANIAN.

Centre for Public Culture and Ideas: tel. (7) 3735-4131; fax (7) 3735-4132; e-mail j.dragisic@griffith.edu.au; internet www.griffith.edu.au/centre/cpci; Co-Dirs Assoc. Prof. A. HAEBICH, Dr F. PAISLEY.

Centre for Quantum Dynamics: tel. (7) 3735-7279; fax (7) 3735-7773; e-mail h.wiseman@griffith.edu.au; internet www.griffith.edu.au/centre/quantumdynamics; Dir Prof. HOWARD WISEMAN.

Centre for Riverine Landscapes: tel. and fax (7) 3735-7403; e-mail a.arthington@griffith.edu.au; internet www.griffith.edu.au/centre/riverlandscapes; Dir Prof. ANGELA ARTHINGTON.

Centre for Wireless Monitoring and Applications: tel. (7) 3735-7192; fax (7) 3735-5198; e-mail d.thiel@griffith.edu.au; internet www.griffith.edu.au/centre/cwma; Dir Prof. DAVID THIEL.

Centre for Work, Leisure and Community Research: tel. (7) 3735-3714; fax (7) 3735-4298; e-mail h.gray@griffith.edu.au; internet www.griffith.edu.au/centre/wlcr; Dir Prof. ADRIAN WILKINSON (acting).

Eskitis, The Institute for Cell and Molecular Therapies: tel. (7) 3735-6006; fax (7) 3735-7656; e-mail eskitis@griffith.edu.au; internet www.griffith.edu.au/centre/eskitis; Dir Prof. RON QUINN.

Forensic Science Research and Innovation Centre: tel. (7) 3735 5069; fax (7) 3735 7773; e-mail dennis.burns@griffith.edu.au; Dir Assoc. Prof. DENNIS BURNS.

Genomics Research Centre: Dir Prof. L. GRIFFITHS.

Griffith Asia Institute: tel. (7) 3735-7370; fax (7) 3735-3731; e-mail gai@griffith.edu.au; internet www.griffith.edu.au/business/griffith-asia-institute; Dir Prof. MICHAEL WESLEY.

Griffith Centre for Coastal Management: tel. (7) 5552-8506; fax (7) 5552-8067; e-mail r.tomlinson@griffith.edu.au; www.griffith.edu.au/centre/gccm; Dir Prof. RODGER TOMLINSON.

Griffith Psychological Health Research Centre: tel. (7) 3732-8052; fax (7) 3732-8291; e-mail r.tomlinson@griffith.edu.au; internet www.griffith.edu.au/centre/gphrc; Dir Prof. SHARON DAWE.

Heart Foundation Research Centre: tel. (7) 5552-8314; fax (7) 5552-8802; e-mail m.john@griffith.edu.au; internet www.griffith.edu.au/centre/hfrc; Dir Prof. JOHN HEADRICK.

Institute for Ethics, Governance and Law: tel. (7) 3735-6987; fax (7) 3735-6985; e-mail iegl-enquiry@griffith.edu.au; internet www.griffith.edu.au/centre/iegl; Dir Prof. CHARLES SAMPFORD.

Institute for Glycomics: tel. (7) 5552-7025; fax (7) 5552-8098; e-mail m.vonitzstein@griffith.edu.au; internet www.griffith.edu.au/centre/glycomics; Dir Prof. MARK VON ITZSTEIN.

Institute for Integrated and Intelligent Systems: tel. (7) 3735-3757; fax (7) 3735-4066; e-mail n.dunstan@griffith.edu.au; internet iiis.griffith.edu.au; Dir Prof. ABDUL SATTAR.

International Centre for Ecotourism Research: tel. (7) 5552-8677; fax (7) 5552-8895; e-mail r.buckley@griffith.edu.au; internet www.griffith.edu.au/centre/icer; Dir Prof. RALF BUCKLEY.

International Fruit Fly Research Centre: tel. (7) 3735-3696; fax (7) 3735-3697; e-mail d.drew@griffith.edu.au; internet www.griffith.edu.au/centre/icmpff; Dir Prof. RICHARD DREW.

Key Centre for Ethics, Law, Justice and Governance: tel. (7) 3735-6988; fax (7) 3735-6985; e-mail s.stewart@griffith.edu.au; internet www.griffith.edu.au/centre/kceljag; Dir Prof. ROSS HOMEL.

Nanoscale Science and Technology Centre: tel. (7) 3735-7240; fax (7) 3735-7656; e-mail e.gray@griffith.edu.au; internet www.griffith.edu.au/centre/nstc; Dir Assoc. Prof. EVAN GRAY.

Queensland Conservatorium Research Centre: tel. (7) 3735-6335; fax (7) 3735-6262; e-mail qcrc@griffith.edu.au; internet www.griffith.edu.au/centre/qcrc; Dir Assoc. Prof. HUIB SCHIPPERS.

Queensland Microtechnology Facility: tel. (7) 3735-5053; fax (7) 3735-8021; e-mail barry.harrison@griffith.edu.au; internet www.griffith.edu.au/centre/qmf; Dir Prof. H. BARRY HARRISON.

Research Centre for Clinical Practice Innovation: tel. (7) 5552-8931; e-mail cpi-research@griffith.edu.au; internet www.griffith.edu.au/centre/rccpi; Dir Prof. WENDY CHABOYER.

Service Industry Research Centre: tel. (7) 5552-8790; e-mail c.guilding@griffith.edu.au; internet www.griffith.edu.au/centre/sirc; Dir Prof. CHRIS GUILDING.

Socio-Legal Research Centre: tel. (7) 3735-3747; fax (7) 3735-5169; e-mail slrc@griffith.edu.au; internet www.griffith.edu.au/centre/slrc; Dir Prof. R. JOHNSTONE.

Software Quality Institute: tel. (7) 3735-5209; fax (7) 3735-5207; e-mail sqi@cit.gu.edu.au; internet www.sqi.gu.edu.au; Dir Prof. GEOFF DROMEY.

Urban Research Program: tel. (7) 3735-3742; fax (7) 3735-4026; e-mail j.pascoe@griffith.edu.au; internet www.griffith.edu.au/centre/urp; Dir Prof. BRENDAN GLEESON.

JAMES COOK UNIVERSITY

Townsville, Qld 4811

Telephone: Townsville: (7) 4781-4111, Cairns: (7) 4042-1111

Fax: Townsville: (7) 4779-6371, Cairns: (7) 4042-1300

E-mail: vicechancellor@jcu.edu.au

Internet: www.jcu.edu.au

Founded 1970

Academic year: February to November

Chancellor: Lt-Gen. J. GREY
Deputy Chancellor: G. N. WHITMORE
Rector: Prof. SCOT BOWMAN
Vice-Chancellor: Prof. SANDRA HARDING
Deputy Vice-Chancellor: Prof. H. HYLAND
Pro-Vice-Chancellors: B. LILLIS, Prof. R. McTAGGART, Prof. T. N. PALMER, Prof. A. VANN
Registrar: M. KERN
Librarian: J. W. MCKINLAY

Number of teachers: 444 full-time
Number of students: 15,575

Publications: *Academic Calendar, JCU Outlook* (12 a year)

EXECUTIVE DEANS

Faculty of Arts, Education and Social Sciences: Prof. J. D. GREELEY
Faculty of Law, Business and the Creative Arts: Prof. S. SPEEDY
Faculty of Medicine, Health and Molecular Sciences: Prof. I. WRONSKI
Faculty of Science and Engineering: Prof. NED PANKHURST

PROFESSORS

BAXTER, A. G., Biochemistry
BELL, T. H., Earth Sciences
BURNELL, J. N., Biochemistry
CARTER, R. M., Earth Sciences
CLARK, G., Law
COLLINS, B., Tropical Environment
CROZIER, R., Zoology
DAVIS, D. F., Creative Arts
GADEK, P., Tropical Biology
GILBERT, R., Education
GILLIESON, D., Tropical Environment
GLASS, B., Pharmacy
GRAW, S. B., Law
HASSALL, A. J., English
HAVEMANN, P., Law
HAYES, B. A., Nursing
HELMES, E., Psychology
HENDERSON, R. A., Earth Sciences
HERBERT, H. J., Indigenous Australian Studies
HERON, M. L., Physics
HO, Y. H., Medicine
HUGHES, T. P., Marine Biology
KEENE, F. R., Chemistry
KENNEDY, L., Medicine
KINGSFORD, M., Marine Biology
LANKSHEAR, C., Education
LAVERY, B., Information Technology
LAWN, R. J., Tropical Crop Science and CRC for Sustainable Sugar Production

LEAKEY, R., Tropical Biology
LOUGHRAN, J., Engineering
MARSH, H. D., Environmental Science
MILLER, D., Biochemistry and Molecular Biology
NOTT, J., Tropical Environment
OLIVER, N. H. S., Economic Geology
PATTERSON, J. C., Environmental Engineering
PEARCE, P. L., Tourism
PEARSON, R. G., Biological Science
PIERCE, P. F., Australian Literature
PORTER, R., Medicine
PRIDEAUX, B., Business
RANE, A., Medicine
REICHELT, R., CRC Reef Research
SPEARE, R., Public Health and Tropical Medicine
STORK, N. E., CRC Rainforest
SUMMERS, P. M., Tropical Veterinary Science
THORPE, R. M., Social Work
WHITTINGHAM, I., Mathematics and Physics
YELLOWLEES, D., Pharmacy

LA TROBE UNIVERSITY

Bundoora, Vic. 3086
Telephone: (3) 9479-1199
Fax: (3) 9479-3660
E-mail: international@latrobe.edu.au
Internet: www.latrobe.edu.au
Founded 1964
Academic year: March to November
Chancellor: SYLVIA WALTON
Vice-Chancellor: Prof. PAUL JOHNSON
Deputy Vice-Chancellor: Prof. BELINDA PROBERT
Deputy Vice-Chancellor for Research: Prof. TIM BROWN
Pro-Vice-Chancellor for Equity and Access: Prof. K. FERGUSON
Pro-Vice-Chancellor for Information Technology: Prof. E. R. SMITH
Pro-Vice-Chancellor for International Relations: Prof. D. STOCKLEY
University Sec.: D. F. BISHOP
Chief Librarian: AINSLIE DEWE

Number of teachers: 1,253
Number of students: 28,684

DEANS

Education: Prof. LORRAINE LING
Health Sciences: Prof. HAL SWERISSEN
Humanities and Social Sciences: Prof. DAVID DE VAUS
Law and Management: Prof. RAYMOND HARBRIDGE
Science, Technology and Engineering: Prof. D. FINLAY
Albury-Wodonga Campus: LIN CRASE (Dir)
Beechworth Campus: BRIAN MILLAR (Dir)
Bendigo Campus: Prof. ANDREW HARVEY (acting) (Dir)
Mildura Campus: KENT FARRELL (Dir)
Shepparton Campus: ELIZABETH LAVENDER (Dir)

PROFESSORS

AIKHENVALD, A., Research Centre for Linguistics Typology
ALTMAN, D., Politics
ARNASON, J. P., Sociology and Anthropology
BEILHARZ, D. M., Sociology and Anthropology
BERNARD, C., Psychology
BLAKE, B. J., Linguistics
BOLAND, R. C., European Studies
BRANSON, J. E., Education
BROWN, D. F., Accounting and Management
CAHILL, L. W., Electronics Engineering
CAMILLERI, J., Politics
CHANOCK, M., Law and Legal Studies
CROUCH, G., Tourism and Hospitality
DILLON, T. S., Computer Science and Computer Engineering

DIXON, R. M. W., Research Centre for Linguistics Typology
DYSON, P., Physics
ENDACOTT, R., Mental Health
FITZGERALD, J. J., Asian Languages
FOOK, J., Health Sciences
FREADMAN, R. B., English
FROST, A. J., History
GATT-RUTTER, J. A., Italian Studies
GAUNTLETT, E., Hellenic Studies
HANDLEY, C., Human Biosciences
HARBRIDGE, R. J., Management
HOFFMAN, A., Genetics and Human Variation
HOOGENRAAD, N. J., Biochemistry
JEFFREY, R., Politics
KAHN, J., Sociology and Anthropology
KELLEHEAR, S., Public Health
KING, J. E., Economics and Finance
LAKE, M., History
LECKEY, R. C. G., Physics
LEDER, G., Education
LIN, V., Health
LINDQUIST, B. I., Occupational Therapy
LUMLEY, J. M., Mothers' and Children's Health
McDONALD, S. J., Midwifery
McDOWELL, G. H., Agriculture
MILLS, T. M., Mathematics
MOOSA, I. A., Economics and Finance
MORRIS, M. E., Physiotherapy
MURPHY, P., Tourism and Hospitality
MURRAY, T. A., Archaeology
NAY, R. M., Nursing
O'MALLEY, P., Law and Legal Studies
PARISH, R. W., Botany
PEARSON, A., Nursing
PERRY, A. R., Human Communication Science
PITTS, M. K., Health and Sexuality
PORTER, R. S., Business
PRATT, C., Psychological Sciences
RAYMOND, K., Pharmacy
REILLY, S., Human Communication Sciences
ROSENTHAL, D. A., Health Sciences
SALMOND, J. A., History
STEPHENSON, D., Zoology
STREET, A. F., Nursing
SUGIMOTO, Y., Sociology and Anthropology
SULLIVAN, P. A., Education
TAMIS, A., Hellenic Studies
THORNTON, M. R., Law and Legal Studies
TORRANCE, C., Nursing
WALKER, G. R., Law and Legal Studies
WHITE, C. M., Graduate School of Management
WILLIS, E. M., Humanities

MACQUARIE UNIVERSITY

Balaclava Rd, North Ryde, NSW 2109
Telephone: (2) 9850-7111
Fax: (2) 9850-7433
E-mail: mqinfo@mq.edu.au
Internet: www.mq.edu.au
Founded 1964 (opened 1967)
Chancellor: MICHAEL RUEBEN EGAN
Deputy Chancellor: His Hon. Dr J. F. LINCOLN
Vice-Chancellor: Prof. STEVEN SCHWARTZ
Deputy Vice-Chancellor and Chief Operating Officer: Prof. PAUL BOWLER
Deputy Vice-Chancellor for Research: Prof. JIM PIPER
Deputy Vice-Chancellor for Provost: Prof. JUDYTH SACHS
Registrar and Vice-Prin.: B. J. SPENCER
Librarian: MAXINE BRODIE

Number of teachers: 775
Number of students: 32,180

Publications: *Calendar* (1 a year), *Research Report* (1 a year), *Study at Macquarie* (1 a year), *University News* (12 a year)

DEANS

Faculty of Arts: Prof. JOHN SIMMONS
Faculty of Business: Prof. MARK GABBOTT
Faculty of Human Sciences: Prof. JANET GREELEY
Faculty of Science: Prof. STEPHEN THURGATE

DIRECTORS OF INTERDISCIPLINARY CENTRES

Graduate School of the Environment: Prof. PETER NELSON
Graduate School of Management: JOHN HEWSON

PROFESSORS

College of Commerce:
ABELSON, P. W., Economics
CROUCHER, J., Statistics
DAVIS, E., Management
EDDEY, P. H., Accounting, Graduate Accounting and Commerce Centre
HARRISON, G. L., Accounting and Finance
HORNE, J., Economics
HUDSON, M., Statistics
JONG, P. DE, Actuarial Studies
O'DONNELL, R., Economics
QUINN, B., Statistics
THROSBY, C., Economics
WOOD, G., Statistics
YUSUF, F., Business

College of Humanities and Social Sciences:
GIBBS, A. M., English and Cultural Studies
GOOT, M., Politics
HAYWARD, P., Contemporary Music Studies
JEFFERY, M., Law
KANAWATI, N., Ancient History
KANE, D., Chinese
LIEU, S. N., History

College of Science and Technology:
BASSETT, J., Biology
BEATTIE, A.
BERGQUIST, P., Biology
BURNS, A., Linguistics
CANDLIN, C., Linguistics
COLTHEART, M., Psychology
COOPER, D., Biological Sciences
CURSON, P., Health and Chiropractic
DEANE, E., Biology
FAGAN, R., Human Geography
JOSS, J., Biology
MATTHIESSEN, C., Linguistics
MURRAY, D., Linguistics
NEWALL, P., Linguistics
O'REILLY, S., Earth and Planetary Sciences
ORR, B., Chemistry
PITMAN, A., Physical Geography
RAPEE, R., Psychology
SMITH, P., Mathematics
STREET, R., Mathematics
VEAL, D., Biology
WALTER, M., Earth and Planetary Sciences
WENDEROTH, P., Psychology
WESTOBY, M., Biology
WILLIAMS, K., Psychology

UNIVERSITY OF MELBOURNE

Melbourne, Vic. 3010
Telephone: (3) 8344-4000
Fax: (3) 8344-5104
E-mail: vc@unimelb.edu.au
Internet: www.unimelb.edu.au
Founded 1853 (opened 1855)
Autonomous institution established by Act of Parliament (State of Victoria) and financed mainly by Commonwealth Government
Academic year: February to December
Chancellor: ALEX CHERNOV
Deputy Chancellor: IAN RENARD
Vice-Chancellor and Prin.: Prof. GLYN DAVIS
Snr Deputy Vice-Chancellor: (vacant)
Deputy Vice-Chancellor for Research: Prof. PETER RATHJEN

Deputy Vice-Chancellor for Students and Staff: Prof. KWONG LEE DOW
Deputy Vice-Chancellor: Prof. PETER MCPHEE
Asst Vice-Chancellor: Prof. ROBERT RICHARDSON
Snr Vice-Prin.: IAN MARSHMAN
Vice-Prin., Information: LINDA O'BRIEN
Vice-Prin., University Development: ROGER PEACOCK
Vice-Prin. and Academic Registrar: LIN MARTIN
Vice-Prin. and Chief Financial Officer: DAVID PERCIVAL
Vice-Prin. and General Counsel: CHRIS PENMAN
Vice-Prin., Human Resources: LIZ BARÉ
Vice-Prin., Property and Buildings: Dr DOUGLAS DAINES
University Sec.: LENNARD CURRIE
Number of teachers: 2,733
Number of students: 39,873

DEANS

Faculty of Architecture, Building and Planning: Prof. T. KVAN
Faculty of Arts: Prof. MARK CONSIDINE
Faculty of Economics and Commerce: Prof. M. ABERNETHY
Faculty of Education: Prof. FIELD RICKARDS
Faculty of Engineering: Prof. IVEN MAREELS
Faculty of Law: Prof. JAMES C. HATHAWAY
Faculty of Medicine, Dentistry and Health Sciences: Prof. J. ANGUS
Faculty of Music: Prof. CATHERINE FALK
Faculty of Science: Prof. LIZ SONENBERG
Faculty of Veterinary Science: Prof. KEN HINCHCLIFF
Melbourne Business School: Prof. JOHN SEYBOLT
Melbourne School of Land and Environment: Prof. R. ROUSH
School of Graduate Studies: Prof. B. EVANS

PROFESSORS

Faculty of Architecture, Building and Planning (tel. (3) 8344-6429; fax (3) 8344-5532; e-mail apb-info@unimelb.edu.au; internet www.arbld.unimelb.edu.au):

BRAWN, G. W., Architecture
BULL, C., Landscape Architecture
DOVEY, K. G., Architecture and Urban Design
FINCHER, R., Urban Planning
GOAD, P., Architecture, Building and Planning
GREEN, R., Landscape Architecture
HUTSON, A., Architecture
KING, R. J., Environmental Planning
LEWIS, M. B.
ROBINSON, J. R. W., Property and Construction
RODGER, A., Architecture, Building and Planning
YENCKEN, D., Architecture, Building and Planning

Faculty of Arts (tel. (3) 8344-6395; fax (3) 9347-0424; e-mail arts-enquiries@unimelb.edu.au; internet www.arts.unimelb.edu.au):

ANDERSON, J., Fine Arts, Classical Studies and Archaeology
AUSTIN, P. K., Linguistics and Applied Linguistics
BUDIMAN, A., Indonesian
CLARKE, A. F., Equine Studies
COALDRAKE, W. H., Japanese
DURING, S., English
ENRIGHT, N. J., Anthropology, Geography and Environmental Studies
FINLAYSON, B., Anthropology, Geography and Environmental Studies
FREIBERG, A., Criminology
GALLIGAN, B. J., Political Science
GELDER, K., English
GRIMSHAW, P. A., History
HAJEK, J., French and Italian Studies

HOLM, D., Chinese
HOLMES, L. T., Political Science
HOME, R. W., History and Philosophy of Science
HURST, A., School of French
JACKSON, A. C., Social Work
LANGTON, M. L., Australian Indigenous Studies
MCINNES, C. V., Higher Education
MACINTYRE, S. F., History
MCPHEE, P. B., History
MALCOLM, E. L., Irish Studies
NETTELBECK, C., School of Languages
O'BRIEN, A., Creative Arts
PIKE, K., Criminology
PRIEST, P. G., Philosophy
RICKLEFS, M., Melbourne Institute of Asian Languages and Societies
RIDLEY, R., History
SEAR, F. B., Classics and Archaeology
STEELE, P. D., English
WALLACE-CRABBE, C. K., English
WEBBER, M. J., Geography

Faculty of Economics and Commerce (tel. (3) 8344-5328; fax (3) 9347-3986; e-mail commerce-enquiries@unimelb.edu.au; internet www.ecom.unimelb.edu.au):

ABERNETHY, M. A., Accounting and Business Information Systems
BARDSLEY, P., Economics
BORLAND, J., Economics
BROWN, R., Finance
CREEDY, J., Economics
DAVIS, K. T., Finance
DAWKINS, P. J., Melbourne Institute of Applied Economic and Social Research
DICKSON, D., Economics
FREEBAIRN, J. W., Economics
GRIFFITHS, B., Economics
HARDY, C., Management
HOUGHTON, K. A., Accounting
KING, S. P., Economics
KOFMAN, P., Finance
KULIK, C., Management
LEECH, S., Accounting and Business Information Systems
LLOYD, P. J., Economics
MCDONALD, I. M., Economics
MARCHANT, G., Accounting and Business Information Systems
MARTIN, V., Economics
NASSER, S., Accounting and Business Information Systems
NICHOLAS, S., Management
PERKINS, E. J., Economics
SAMSON, D., Management
SHAPIRO, P., Economics
TOURKY, R., Economics
WHEATLEY, S., Finance
WIDING, R. E., Management
WILLIAMS, R. A., Econometrics
WOODEN, M., Melbourne Institute of Applied Economics and Social Research

Faculty of Education (tel. (3) 8344-8628; fax (3) 8344-8529; e-mail enquiries@edfac.unimelb.edu.au; internet www.edfac.unimelb.edu.au):

CALDWELL, B. J., Education (Leadership and Management)
CHRISTIE, F., Language, Literacy and Arts Education
EVANS, G., Learning and Educational Development
GRIFFIN, P. E., Assessment
HILL, P., Education (Leadership and Management)
LAKOMSKI, G., Education
LEE DOW, K., Education
MAGLEN, L. R., Asian Pacific Economics of Education and Training
RABAN-BISBY, B., Early Childhood Studies
RICKARDS, F. W., Education (Learning, Assessment and Special Education)
STACEY, K. C., Science and Mathematics Education

START, B., Learning and Educational Development

Faculty of Engineering (tel. (3) 8344-6703; fax (3) 9349-2182; e-mail eng-info@unimelb.edu.au; internet www.eng.mu.oz.au):

BISHOP, I. D., Geomatics
BOGER, D. V., Chemical Engineering
CHING, M. S., Mechanical and Manufacturing Engineering
EVANS, R. J., Electrical Engineering
FENTON, J. D., Civil and Environmental Engineering
FRASER, C. S., Geomatics
GOOD, M. C., Mechanical and Manufacturing Engineering
HUTCHINSON, G. L., Civil and Environmental Engineering
KOTAGIRI, R., Computer Science and Software Engineering
KRISHNAMURTHY, V., Electrical and Electronic Engineering
MCMAHON, T. A., Environmental Hydrology
MAREELS, I. M. V., Electrical Engineering
MOFFAT, A. M., Computer Science and Software Engineering
MORAN, W., Electronic and Electrical Engineering
STERLING, L. S., Computer Science and Software Engineering
STEVENS, G. W., Chemical Engineering
STUCKLEY, P. J., Computer Science and Software Engineering
TUCKER, R. S., Electrical Engineering
VAN DEVENTER, J., Mineral and Process Engineering
WATSON, H. C., Mechanical and Manufacturing Engineering
WILLIAMSON, I. P., Surveying and Land Information
WOOD, D. G., Engineering
YOUNG, D. M., Engineering Construction Management
ZUCKERMAN, M., Electronic and Electrical Engineering

Institute of Land and Food Resources (tel. (3) 8344-0276; fax (3) 9348-2156; e-mail enquiries@landfood.unimelb.edu.au; internet www.landfood.unimelb.edu.au):

BRITZ, M., Food Science
CHAPMAN, D. F., Pasture Science
COUSENS, R. D., Crop Science
EGAN, A. R., Agriculture (Animal Science)
FALVEY, J. L., Agriculture
FERGUSON, I. S., Forest Science
GODDARD, M., Agriculture
HEMSWORTH, P., Agriculture
HILLIER, A. J., Agriculture
KOLLMORGEN, J. F., Agriculture
MACMILLAN, K. L., Agriculture
RICHARDSON, R. A., Land and Food Resources
ROSS, E. W., Agriculture
VINDEN, P., Forest Industries

Faculty of Law (tel. (3) 8344-6164; fax (3) 9347-2392; e-mail post@law.unimelb.edu.au; internet www.law.unimelb.edu.au):

BRYAN, M., Law
CHRISTIE, A. F., Intellectual Property
COLMAN, P. M., Medical Biology
COWMAN, A. F., Medical Biology
CROMMELIN, B. M. L., Law
MCCORMACK, T. L. H., International Humanitarian Law
MITCHELL, R. J., Law
MORGAN, J. J., Law
RAMSAY, I. M., Commercial Law
RICKETSON, S., Law
SAUNDERS, C. A., Law
SKENE, L., Law
SMITH, M. D. H., Asian Law
TRIGGS, G., Law

Faculty of Medicine, Dentistry and Health Sciences (tel. (3) 8344-5894; fax (3) 9347-7854; e-mail medicine-info@unimelb.edu.au; internet www.medfac.unimelb.edu.au/med):

ADAMS, J. M., Medical Biology
ALCORN, D., Anatomy
ANDERSON, I. P., Public Health
ANDERSON, J. N., Public Health
ANDERSON, V., Psychology
BERK, M., Psychiatry
BERKOVIC, S. F., Medicine
BEST, J. D., Medicine
BHATHAL, P. S., Pathology
BLOCH, S., Psychiatry
BOWES, G., Paediatrics
BREARLEY-MESER, L., Paediatrics
BRENNECKE, S. P., Obstetrics and Gynaecology
BROWN, G. V., Medicine
BYRNE, E., Experimental Neurology
CARLIN, J. B., Public Health
CHAN, S. T. F., Surgery
CHIU, E., Psychiatry
CLEMENT, J. G., Forensic Odontology
CORY, S., Medical Biology
CREAMER, M., Psychiatry
DENNERSTEIN, L., Psychiatry
DOHERTY, P., Microbiology and Immunology
DONNAN, G., Medicine
DOWELL, R. C., Otolaryngology
DUNNING, T., Nursing
FAIRLEY, C. K., Sexual Health
FUNDER, J., Medicine
FURNESS, J. B., Anatomy
GALEA, M. P., Physiotherapy
GAYLER, K. R., Biochemistry and Molecular Biology
GETHING, M. J., Biochemistry and Molecular Biology
GIBSON, R. M., Radiology
GOODWIN, A. W., Anatomy
GRAHAM, H. K., Orthopaedic Surgery
GRAVES, S. E., Orthopaedic Surgery
HARRAP, S. B., Physiology
HARRIS, P. J., Physiology
HARRISON, L. C., Medical Biology
HOPPER, J. L., Public Health
JACKSON, H. J., Psychology
KAYE, A. H., Surgery
LOUIS, W. J., Clinical Pharmacology and Therapeutics
MCCALMAN, J. S., Public Health
MCCLUSKEY, J., Microbiology and Immunology
MCMEEKEN, J., Physiotherapy
MANDERSON, L. H., Women's Health
MASTERS, C. L., Pathology
MESSER, H. H., Restorative Dentistry
MESSER, L. J. B., Child Dental Health
MILLGROM, J., Psychology
MORGAN, T. O., Physiology
MORRISON, W. A., Surgery
MULHOLLAND, E. K., Paediatrics
NELSON, S., Nursing
NICHOLSON, G. C., Medicine
NICOLA, N., Medical Biology
NOLAN, T. M., Public Health
O'BOYLE, M. W., Psychology
OLEKALNS, M., Psychology
PARKER, J. M., Postgraduate Nursing
PATTISON, P. E., Psychology
PERMEZEL, J. M. H., Obstetrics and Gynaecology
PIERCE, R., Medicine
PRIOR, M., Psychology
PROIETTO, J., Medicine
REYNOLDS, E. C., Dental Science
ROBINS-BROWN, R. M., Microbiology and Immunology
SCHWEITZER, I., Psychiatry
SHORTMAN, K. D., Medical Biology and Developmental Immunology
SINGH, B. S., Psychiatry
SMALLWOOD, R. A., Medicine

SPEED, T. P., Medical Biology
STRUGNELL, R. A., Microbiology and Immunology
TAYLOR, H. R., Ophthalmology
TILLER, J. W. G., Psychiatry
TRESS, B. M., Radiology
TRINDER, J. A., Psychology
TYAS, M. J., Dental Science
VADJA, F., Medicine
WARD, T., Psychology
WARK, J. D., Medicine
WATTERS, D. A. K., Surgery
WEARING, A. J., Psychology
WETTENHALL, R. E. H., Biochemistry
WICKS, I. P., Medical Biology
WILLIAMS, D. A., Physiology
YEOMANS, N. D., Medicine
YOUNG, D., General Practice
ZAJAC, J. D., Medicine

Faculty of Music (tel. (3) 8344-5256; fax (3) 8344-5346; e-mail enquiries@music.unimelb.edu.au; internet www.music.unimelb.edu.au):

BEBBINGTON, W. A., Music
BROADSTOCK, B., Music
GRIFFITHS, J. A., Music

Faculty of Science (tel. (3) 8344-6404; fax (3) 8344-5803; e-mail science-queries@unimelb.edu.au; internet www.science.unimelb.edu.au):

BACIC, A., Botany
BAKER, A. J. M., Botany
CAMPBELL, G. D., Zoology
CHAN, D. Y. C., Mathematics
CLARKE, A. E., Botany
COLE, B. L., Optometry
FERGUSON, I. S., Forest Science
GHIGGINO, K. P., Chemistry
GRIESER, F., Chemistry
GUTTMANN, A. J., Mathematics
HYNES, M. J., Genetics
KOTAGIRI, R., Computer Science
KLEIN, A. G., Physics
LADIGES, P. Y., Botany
MCBRIEN, N. A., Optometry
MCKELLAR, B. H. J., Theoretical Physics
MCKENZIE, J. A., Genetics
MILLER, C. F., Mathematics
MORRISON, I., Information Systems
NUGENT, K. A., Physics
PICKETT-HEAPS, J. D., Botany
PLIMER, I. R., Geology
RENFREE, M. B., Zoology
RUBINSTEIN, J. H., Mathematics
SCHIESSER, C., Chemistry
SONENBERG, E. A., Information Systems
STERLING, L. S., Computer Science
TAYLOR, G. N., Physics
THOMPSON, C. J., Mathematics
WEDD, A. G., Chemistry

Faculty of Veterinary Science (tel. (3) 8344-7356; fax (3) 8344-7374; e-mail vet-info@unimelb.edu.au; internet www.vet.unimelb.edu.au):

CAHILL, R. N. P., Veterinary Biology
CAPLE, I. W., Veterinary Medicine
CLARKE, A. F., Equine Studies
SLOCOMBE, R. F., Veterinary Pathology

Melbourne Business School (Leicester St, Carlton, Vic. 3053; tel. (3) 9349-8403; fax (3) 9349-8404; e-mail mbs@unimelb.edu.au; internet www.mbs.unimelb.edu.au):

ALFORD, J. L., Public Sector Management
DAINTY, P., Human Resources Management and Employee Relations
GANS, J. S., Management
GRUNDY, B., Finance
HARPER, I. R., Commerce and Business Administration
KING, S., Economics
LEWIS, G., Strategy
MANN, L., Organizational Behaviour and Decision Making
MISHRA, D., Marketing

OLEKALNS, M., Leadership and Decision Making
RIZZO, P., Finance and Management
SAMSON, D. A., Manufacturing Management
SINCLAIR, A. M. A., Management (Diversity and Change)
SPEED, R., Marketing Management and Advanced Marketing Strategy
WILLIAMS, P. L., Management (Law and Economics)

Victorian College of the Arts (234 St Kilda Rd, Southbank, Vic. 3010; tel. (3) 9685-9300; fax (3) 9682-1841; internet www.vca.unimelb.edu.au):

HULL, A. (Dir)

MONASH UNIVERSITY

Wellington Rd, Clayton, Vic. 3800

Telephone: (3) 9905-4000

Fax: (3) 9905-4007

E-mail: enquiries@adm.monash.edu.au

Internet: www.monash.edu.au

Founded 1958 (opened 1961); merged with Chisholm Institute of Technology and Gippsland Institute of Advanced Education 1990, and with Victorian College of Pharmacy 1992

Academic year: March to November

Chancellor: ALAN FINKEL
Vice-Chancellor: Prof. R. LARKINS
Snr Deputy Vice-Chancellor: Prof. S. PARKER
Deputy Vice-Chancellor for Research: Prof. E. CORNISH
Pro-Vice-Chancellor, Gippsland: Prof. HELEN BARTLETT
Pro-Vice-Chancellor, Monash Malaysia: Prof. ROBIN POLLARD
Pro-Vice-Chancellor, Monash South Africa: Prof. T. B. PRETORIUS
Vice-Pres. for Administration: P. MARSHALL
Vice-Pres. for International Relations: STEPHANIE FAHEY
Dir, Monash Centre, Prato: Prof. LORETTA BALDASSAR
Dir, Monash University Centre, London: Prof. M. EVANS
Librarian: C. HARBOE-REE

Number of teachers: 2,797
Number of students: 55,765

Publications: *Asia-Pacific Journal of Clinical Nutrition* (online), *Eras: School of Historical Studies Online Journal*, *Journal of Australian Taxation* (6 a year), *Journal of Intercultural Studies* (3 a year), *Monash Bioethics Review* (4 a year), *Monash Law Review* (2 a year)

DEANS

Faculty of Art and Design: Prof. J. K. REDMOND
Faculty of Arts: Prof. RAE FRANCES
Faculty of Business and Economics: Prof. STEPHEN KING (acting)
Faculty of Education: Prof. S. WILLIS
Faculty of Engineering: Prof. T. SRIDHAR
Faculty of Information Technology: Prof. R. WEBER
Faculty of Law: Prof. A. FREIBERG
Faculty of Medicine, Nursing and Health Sciences: Prof. STEVE WESSELINGH
Faculty of Science: Prof. R. NORRIS
Victorian College of Pharmacy: Prof. C. B. CHAPMAN

PROFESSORS

Faculty of Art and Design (900 Dandenong Rd, Caulfield East, Vic. 3145; tel. (3) 9903-2707; fax (3) 9903-2845; e-mail enquiries@artdes.monash.edu.au; internet www.artdes.monash.edu.au):

HOFFERT, B. J., Fine Arts
REDMOND, J., Industrial Design

TERSTAPPEN, C., Contemporary Installation and Photography

Faculty of Arts (tel. (3) 9905-2100; fax (3) 9905-2148; e-mail deansec@arts.monash.edu.au; internet www.arts.monash.edu.au):

BENJAMIN, A., Comparative Literature and Cultural Studies
BIGELOW, J. C., Philosophy and Bioethics
BOUMA, G. D., Political and Social Enquiry
BURRIDGE, K., Languages, Cultures and Linguistics
CAINE, B., Historical Studies
COCKLIN, C., Philosophy and Bioethics
DAVISON, G. J., Historical Studies
EDWARDS, I., International Studies
FELIX, U., Languages, Cultures and Linguistics
FITZPATRICK, P., Drama and Theatre Studies
HART, K. J., Comparative Literature and Cultural Studies
JACOBS, J. B., Languages, Cultures and Linguistics
KARTOMI, M. J., Music–Conservatorium
KENT, F. W., Historical Studies
KERSHAW, P. A., Geography and Environmental Science
LE GRAND, H., Philosophy
LIPSIG-MUMME, C., Political and Social Enquiry
LOVE, H. H. R., Literary, Visual and Performance Studies
LYNCH, A., Geography and Environmental Science
MARKUS, A., Jewish Studies
MILNER, A., Comparative Literature and Cultural Studies
MOUER, R., Languages, Cultures and Linguistics
NELSON, B., Languages, Cultures and Linguistics
OPPY, G., Philosophy and Bioethics
PROBYN, C. T., Literary, Visual and Performance Studies
QUARTLY, M., Historical Studies
RUSSELL, L., Australian Indigenous Studies
TAPPER, N., Geography and Environmental Science
VICZIANY, M., Asian Studies
WALTER, J., Political and Social Enquiry

Faculty of Business and Economics (POB 197, Caulfield East, Vic. 3145; tel. (3) 9903-2327; fax (3) 9903-2148; e-mail enquiries.caulfield@buseco.monash.edu.au; internet www.buseco.monash.edu.au):

ARIFF, M., Accounting and Finance
BROOKS, B., Business and Economics
BROOKS, D., Econometrics and Business Statistics
CHENHALL, R. H., Accounting and Finance
CULLEN, R., Business Law and Taxation
DHALIWAL, D., Accounting and Finance
DINGLE, A. E., Economics
DIXON, P. B., Policy Studies
EWING, M., Marketing
FAFF, R., Accounting and Finance
FORSYTH, P. J., Economics
GABBOTT, T. M., Marketing
GODFREY, J. M., Accounting and Finance
HUGHES, O. E., Management
HYNDMAN, R. J., Econometrics and Business Statistics
IN, F., Accounting and Finance
KING, M. L., Business and Economics
LANGFIELD-SMITH, K., Accounting and Finance
MCLAREN, K. R., Econometrics and Business Statistics
MITCHELL, R., Business Law and Taxation
NG, Y., Economics
NYLAND, C., Management
OPPEWAL, H., Marketing
PEARSON, K., Policy Studies
POSKITT, D. S., Econometrics

RAINNIE, A. F., Management
RATNATUNGA, J. T., Accounting and Finance
RICHARDSON, J., Health Programme Evaluation
SARROS, J. C., Management
SILVAPULLE, M., Econometrics and Business Statistics
SKULLY, M. T., Accounting and Finance
SMYTH, R., Economics
SMYTH, R. L., Economics
SOHAL, A., Management
TAM, O. K., MBA Programme
TEICHER, J., Management
VON NESSEN, P., Business Law and Taxation
WEILER, B. V., Management
WILLIS, R. J., MBA Programme
WORTHINGTON, J. S., Marketing
YANG, X., Economics

Faculty of Education (POB 6, Monash University, Clayton, Vic. 3800; tel. (3) 9905-2888; fax (3) 9905-5400; e-mail enquiry@education.monash.edu.au; internet www.education.monash.edu.au):

BURKE, G., Education
FLEER, M., Education
GRONN, P., Education
GUNSTONE, R. F., Education
KENWAY, J., Education
LOUGHRAN, J., Education
MARGINSON, S., Education
SEDDON, T., Education
WILLIS, S. G., Education

Faculty of Engineering (POB 72, Clayton, Vic. 3800; tel. (3) 9905-3404; fax (3) 9905-3409; e-mail enginfo@eng.monash.edu.au; internet www.eng.monash.edu.au):

CURRIE, G., Civil Engineering
DEMIDENKO, S., Electrical and Computer Systems Engineering
EGAN, G. K., Electrical and Computer Systems Engineering
FORSYTH, M., Materials Engineering
HOURIGAN, K., Mechanical Engineering
JARVIS, R. A., Electrical and Computer Systems Engineering
JESSON, D., Materials Engineering
JONES, R., Mechanical Engineering
LEWIS, R. A., Physics
MORGAN, D. L., Electrical and Computer Systems Engineering
MUDDLE, B. C., Materials Engineering
PRINCE, I., Chemical Engineering
PUDLOWSKI, Z. J., UNESCO International Centre for Engineering Education
RHODES, M. J., Chemical Engineering
SHERIDAN, J., Mechanical Engineering
SIMON, G., Materials Engineering
SORIA, J., Mechanical Engineering
SRIDHAR, T., Chemical Engineering
YOUNG, W., Civil Engineering
ZHAO, X.-L., Civil Engineering

Faculty of Information Technology (900 Dandenong Rd, Caulfield East, Vic. 3145; tel. (3) 9903-2433; fax (3) 9903-2745; e-mail admissions@infotech.monash.edu.au; internet www.infotech.monash.edu.au):

ABRAMSON, D., School of Computer Science and Software Engineering
ARNOTT, D. R., School of Information Management and Systems
CROSSLEY, J., School of Computer Science and Software Engineering
DOOLEY, L. S., Gippsland School of Computing and Information Technology
GEORGEFF, M., Dean's Office
GREEN, D., School of Computer Science and Software Engineering
GUPTA, G., Business Systems
KENDALL, E. A., School of Network Computing
MCKEMMISH, S. M., School of Information Management Systems

MARRIOTT, K., School of Computer Science and Software Engineering
SCHAUDER, D., School of Information Management and Systems
SCHMIDT, H. W., School of Computer Science and Software Engineering
SHANKS, G., School of Business Systems
SRINIVASAN, B., School of Computer Science and Software Engineering
WALLACE, M., School of Business Systems
WEBB, G., School of Computer Science and Software Engineering
WEBER, R., Dean

Faculty of Law (POB 12, Monash University, Clayton, Vic. 3800; tel. (3) 9905-9335; fax (3) 9905-5868; e-mail law-general@law.monash.edu.au; internet www.law.monash.edu.au):

BOROS, E., Company Law
FOX, R. G., Criminal Law
FREIBERG, A., Dean
GOLDSWORTHY, J., Legal Philosophy and Constitutional Law
HAMPEL, G., Advocacy Training
HODGE, G., Privatization and Public Accountability
JOSEPH, S., International Human Rights and Constitutional Law
KINLEY, D., Human Rights Law
LEE, H. P., Constitutional and Administrative Law
MCSHERRY, B., Criminal Law, Mental Health Law and Bioethics
PITTARD, M., Industrial Relations and Employment Law
SCHEEPERS, T., International Development Law
WAINCYMER, J., Taxation and International Trade Law
WILLIAMS, C. R., Criminal Law and Evidence

Faculty of Medicine, Nursing and Health Sciences (Bldg 64, Monash University, Clayton, Vic. 3800; tel. (3) 9905-4327; fax (3) 9905-4302; e-mail enquiries@lmed.monash.edu.au; internet www.med.monash.edu.au):

ABRAMSON, M. J., Epidemiology and Preventive Medicine
ADLER, B., Microbiology
ANDERSON, W. P., Physiology/School of Biomedical Sciences
BERTRAM, J., Anatomy and Cell Biology
BROWN, T., Social Work and Human Services
BROWNE, C., Medical and Health Sciences Education
BURROWS, R. F., Obstetrics and Gynaecology
BYRNE, E., Dean
CAMPBELL, D., Health Sciences Research
COLEMAN, G., Psychology
COPPEL, R. L., Microbiology
CORDNER, S. M., Forensic Medicine
CROWE, S., Medicine
DAVIES, J., Microbiology
DAVIS, S. R., Medicine
DE KRETSER, D. M., Reproduction and Development
DOHERTY, R. R., Paediatrics
FRANCIS, K., Nursing
GIBSON, P., Medicine
GODDARD, C. R., Social Work
GODING, J. W., Pathology and Immunology
GOODCHILD, C. S., Anaesthesia
GRIGG, M. J., Surgery
HARDING, R., Physiology
HEALY, D. L., Obstetrics and Gynaecology
HOLDSWORTH, S. R., Medicine
HUMPHREYS, J. S., Rural Health
IRVINE, D., Psychology
JANS, D. A., Biochemistry and Molecular Biology
JENKIN, G., Physiology
JOLLY, B. C., Medical and Health Sciences Education
JUDD, F. K., Psychological Medicine

KOSSMAN, T., Medicine
KRUM, H., Epidemiology and Preventive Medicine
KULKARNI, J., Psychological Medicine
LEWIN, S., Medicine
MCGRATH, B., Medicine
MACKINNON, A., Psychological Medicine
MCNEIL, J. J., Epidemiology and Preventive Medicine
MEADOWS, G., Psychological Medicine
MITCHELL, C., Biochemistry and Molecular Biology
MULLEN, P. E., Psychological Medicine
NAGLEY, P., Biochemistry and Molecular Biology
OAKLEY-BROWN, M., Psychological Medicine
O'CONNOR, D. W., Psychological Medicine
O'CONNOR, M. M., Nursing
OGLOFF, J., Psychological Medicine
O'HEHIR, R. E., Medicine
PITERMAN, L., General Practice
POLGLASE, A., Surgery
PONSFORD, J. L., Psychology
PRIESTLEY, B. G., Epidemiology and Preventive Medicine
PROSKE, U., Physiology
REUTENS, D., Neurosciences
RICHARDS, J., General Practice
ROOD, J., Microbiology
ROSENFELD, J. V., Neurosurgery
SALEM, H. H., Medicine
SCHMIDT, H., Pharmacology
SMITH, J., Surgery
SOLARSH, G., Rural Health
STOELWINDER, J., Epidemiology and Preventive Medicine
STOREY, E., Neurosciences
SUMMERS, R. J., Pharmacology
THOMSON, N. M., Medicine
TOH, B. H., Pathology and Immunology
TONGE, B. J., Psychological Medicine
TROUNSON, A. O., Early Human Development
WHYTE, G., Bendigo Regional Clinical School
WORKMAN, G., Geriatric Medicine
ZIMMET, P., Biochemistry and Molecular Biology

Faculty of Science (POB 19, Clayton, Vic. 3800; tel. (3) 9905-4610; fax (3) 9905-5692; e-mail enquiries@sci.monash.edu.au; internet www.sci.monash.edu.au):

ADELOJU, S. B., Applied Sciences
BARBNIK, R. A., Mathematical Sciences
BOND, A., Chemistry
CALLY, P., Mathematical Sciences
CAS, R. A. F., Geosciences
CLAYTON, M., Biological Sciences
CULL, J. P., Geosciences
DEACON, G. B., Chemistry
HAMILL, J. D., Biological Sciences
HEARN, M., Chemistry
JACKSON, R., Chemistry
JACKSON, W. R., Chemistry
JESSON, D., Physics and Material Engineering
KEAYS, R., Geosciences
KLEBANER, F., Mathematical Sciences
LAKE, P. S., Biological Sciences
LEWIS, R., Physics and Material Engineering
MACFARLANE, D. R., Chemistry
MONAGHAN, J. J., Mathematical Sciences
MURRAY, K. S., Chemistry
NORRIS, R., Dean
REEDER, M., Mathematical Sciences
SIMON, G., Physics and Material Engineering
SMYTH, D. R., Biological Sciences
VICKERS-RICH, P., Geosciences

Victorian College of Pharmacy (381 Royal Parade, Parkville, Vic. 3052; tel. (3) 9903-6000; fax (3) 9903-9581; e-mail info@vcp

.monash.edu.au; internet www.vcp.monash .edu.au):

CHAPMAN, C. B., Immunology
CHARMAN, W. N., Pharmaceutics
DOOLEY, M., Pharmacology
NATION, R. L., Pharmaceutics
POUTON, C. W., Pharmaceutics
REED, B. L., Biopharmaceutics
SCAMMELLS, P. J., Biopharmaceutics
STEWART, P. J., Pharmaceutics

AFFILIATED INSTITUTIONS

Baker Medical Research Institute: Commercial Rd, Melbourne, Vic. 3004; tel. (3) 8532-1111; Dir Prof. G. JENNINGS.

Bureau of Meteorology: 150 Lonsdale St, Melbourne, Vic. 3000; tel. (3) 9669-4915; Dir J. W. ZILLMAN.

MacFarlane Burnet Institute for Medical Research and Public Health Ltd (Burnet Institute): Commercial Rd, Melbourne, Vic. 3004; tel. (3) 9282-2111; Dir Prof. S. WESSELINGH.

Mannix College: Wellington Rd, Monash University, Clayton, Vic. 3800; tel. (3) 9544-8895; Master Rev. K. SAUNDERS.

Mental Health Research Institute of Victoria: Locked Bag No. 11, Parkville, Vic. 3052; tel. (3) 9388-1633; Dir Prof. D. COPOLOV.

Prince Henry's Institute of Medical Research: Monash Medical Centre, Level 4, Block E, 246 Clayton Rd, Clayton, Vic. 3168; tel. (3) 9594-4372; Dir Prof. E. SIMPSON.

MURDOCH UNIVERSITY

South St, Murdoch, WA 6150
Telephone: (8) 9360-6000
Fax: (8) 9360-6847
E-mail: marketing@murdoch.edu.au
Internet: www.murdoch.edu.au
Founded 1973; postgraduate courses began 1974; undergraduate courses began 1975
State control
Academic year: February to November
Chancellor: The Hon. GEOFFREY BOLTON
Pro-Chancellor: Judge KATE O'BRIEN
Vice-Chancellor: Prof. JOHN YOVICH
Pro-Vice-Chancellor for Academic Affairs: Prof. JANETTE THOMAS
Pro-Vice-Chancellor for Regional Development: KATERYNA LONGLEY
Pro-Vice-Chancellor for Research: Prof. ANDRIS STELBOVICS
Pro-Vice-Chancellor for Resource Management: Prof. CRAIG SPENCE (acting)
Pro-Vice-Chancellor for Strategy: GARY MARTIN
Pres., Academic Council: MICHAEL BOROWITZKA
Dir of Library Services: MARGARET JONES
Number of teachers: 455
Number of students: 15,320
Publications: *In Touch* (2 a year), *On Campus* (8 a year), *Research Report* (1 a year), *Synergy* (4 a year)

DEANS

Division of Arts (Information Technology): Assoc. Prof. ARNOLDATHERINE DEPICKERE
Division of Science and Engineering: Exec. Dean Prof. YIANNI ATTIKOUZEL
Division of Social Sciences, Humanities and Education: Exec. Dean Prof. K. LONGLEY
Division of Veterinary and Biomedical Sciences: Exec. Dean Prof. J. YOVICH
School of Education: Prof. DAVID ANDRICH
School of Engineering: Prof. MAURICE ALLEN
School of Health Sciences: Prof. JIM REYNOLDSON (acting)
School of Law: Prof. CHRISTOPHER KENDALL

PROFESSORS

Division of Business, Information Technology and Law (tel. (8) 9360-2414; fax (8) 9360-2994; internet www.murdoch.edu.au/bitl):

FORBES, R., Law
MCLEOD, N. D. B., Law
PENDLETON, M. D., Law
ROBISON, R., Asian and International Politics
SIMMONDS, R., Law
THOMPSON, H. M., Economics

Division of Science (tel. (8) 9360-2161; fax (8) 9360-6304; internet www.science.murdoch .edu.au):

BLOOM, W. R., Mathematics and Statistics
CARNEGIE, P., Biotechnology
DILWORTH, M. J., Biology
GILES, R. G. F., Organic Chemistry
HOBBS, R., Environmental Science
JAMES, I., Mathematics
JENNINGS, P., Physics, Energy Studies
JONES, M. G. K., Plant Sciences
LYONS, T. J., Environmental Science
NICOL, M. J., Mineral Science
POTTER, I. C., Animal Biology
RITCHIE, I. M., Chemistry
WEBB, J. M., Chemistry

Division of Science and Engineering (Rockingham Campus, Dixon Rd, Rockingham, WA; tel. (8) 9360-7100; fax (8) 9360-7104; internet wwweng.murdoch.edu.au):

LEE, P. L., Instrumentation and Control Engineering
ROY, G., Software Engineering

Division of Social Sciences, Humanities and Education (tel. (8) 9360-6045; fax (8) 9360-6367; internet www.sshe.murdoch.edu.au):

ANDRICH, D., Education
BALDOCK, C., Sociology
DE GARIS, B., History
DUREY, M., History
FRODSHAM, J. D., English and Comparative Literature
HILL, B. V., Education
HILL, D., Asian Studies (Head)
INNES, M., Psychology
LOADER, B., Social Enquiry (Head)
MISHRA, V., English and Comparative Literature
NEWMAN, P., Science and Technology Policy
O'TOOLE, L. M., Communication Studies
RUTHROF, H. G., Philosophy

Division of Veterinary and Biomedical Sciences (tel. (8) 9360-2566; fax (8) 9310-7390; internet wwwvet.murdoch.edu.au/home .html):

HAMPSON, D., Microbiology and Immunobiology
SWAN, R. A., Veterinary Clinical Studies
THOMPSON, A., Parasitology
WILCOX, G. E., Virology

UNIVERSITY OF NEW ENGLAND

Armidale, NSW 2351
Telephone: (2) 6773-3333
Fax: (2) 6773-3122
E-mail: admissions@une.edu.au
Internet: www.une.edu.au
Founded 1954; previously New England University College (f. 1938); Armidale College of Advanced Education merged with the University in 1989
Commonwealth govt control
Academic year: February to November (2 semesters)
Chancellor: J. CASSIDY
Deputy Chancellor: J. HARRIS
Vice-Chancellor: Prof. ALAN PETTIGREW
Pro-Vice-Chancellor for Academic: Prof. EVELYN WOODBERRY

Pro-Vice-Chancellor for Research and Development: Prof. R. COOKSEY (acting)
Exec. Dir: G. DENNEHY (Business and Administration)
Sec. to Council: KIM CULL
Librarian: JACK BEDSON (acting)
Library: see under Libraries and Archives
Number of teachers: 484
Number of students: 18,863

Publications: *Australasian Victorian Studies Journal* (1 a year), *Australian Folklore: A Yearly Journal of Folklore Studies*, *Journal of Australian Colonial History* (2 a year), *South Asia* (1 a year), *TalentEd* (3 a year), *The University of New England Law Journal* (2 a year), *Wool Technology and Sheep Breeding* (4 a year)

DEANS

Faculty of Arts and Sciences: Prof. M. SEDGLEY
Faculty of the Professions: Prof. V. MINICHIELLO

PROFESSORS

BINDON, B., CRC for Cattle and Beef Quality
BOULTON, A. J., Environmental Sciences and Natural Resources Management
BRASTED, H. V., Classics, History and Religion
BRUNCKHORST, D., Institute for Rural Futures/UNESCO Centre for Bioregional Resource Management
BYRNE, B. J., Psychology
CARRINGTON, K. L., Social Science
CHOCT, M., Rural Science and Agriculture
COLBRAN, S., Law
COOKSEY, R. W., New England Business School
COTTLE, D., Rural Science and Agriculture
DAVIDSON, I., Human and Environmental Studies
DOLLERY, B. E., Economics
ECKERMAN, A.-K., Professional Development and Leadership
FORD, H. A., Environmental Sciences and Natural Resources Management
FORREST, P. R. H., Social Science
FRANZMANN, M., Classics, History and Religion
GEISER, F., Environmental Sciences and Natural Resources Management
GIBSON, J., Rural Science and Agriculture
GODDARD, C. W., Languages, Cultures and Linguistics
GOSSIP, C. J., Languages, Cultures and Linguistics
GUNTER, M. J., Biological and Molecular Sciences
HORSLEY, G. H. R., Classics, History and Religion
HUTCHINSON, P. J., New England Business School
KAUR, A., Economics
KENT, D. A., Classics, History and Religion
KIERNANDER, A. R. D., English, Communication and Theatre
KINGHORN, B. P., Rural Science and Agriculture
LLOYD, C., Economics
MAGNER, E. S., Law
MEEK, V. L., Professional Development and Leadership
NOBLE, W., Psychology
NOLAN, J. V., Rural Science and Agriculture
PEGG, J. E., Education
ROGERS, L. J., Biological, Biomedical and Molecular Sciences
ROWE, J. B., Rural Science and Agriculture
RUVINSKY, A., Rural Science and Agriculture
SAJEEV, A. S. M., Mathematics, Statistics and Computing Science
SCOTT, J. M., Rural Science and Agriculture
SIMPSON, R. D., Environmental Sciences and Natural Resources Management

TAJI, A., Rural Science and Agriculture
THOMPSON, J. M., Rural Science and Agriculture
TREADGOLD, M. L., Economics
UNSWORTH, L., Education
WALMSLEY, D. J., Human and Environmental Studies
WARE, H. R., Professional Development and Leadership
WATSON, K., Biological, Biomedical and Molecular Sciences

UNIVERSITY OF NEW SOUTH WALES

Sydney, NSW 2052
Telephone: (2) 9385-1000
Fax: (2) 9385-2000
E-mail: studentcentral@unsw.edu.au
Internet: www.unsw.edu.au
Founded 1948
Incorporated by Act of Parliament 1949
Academic year: February to November (2 sessions)

Chancellor: DAVID GONSKI
Vice-Chancellor and Principal: Professor FRED HILMER
Deputy Vice-Chancellor for Academic Affairs: Prof. ROBERT KING
Deputy Vice-Chancellor for Int. Affairs: Prof. JOHN INGLESON
Deputy Vice-Chancellor for Research: Prof. LES FIELD
Pro-Vice-Chancellor for Education: Prof. RICHARD HENRY
Chief Financial Officer: GARRY MCLENNAN
Chief Information Officer: TIM COPE
Principal Librarian: ANDREW WELLS
Number of teachers: 2,300
Number of students: 42,933

DEANS

Faculty of Arts and Social Sciences: Prof. JAMES DONALD
Faculty of the Built Environment: Prof. ALEC TZANNES
Faculty of Commerce and Economics: Prof. JOHN PIGGOTT (acting)
Faculty of Engineering: Prof. GRAHAM DAVIES
Faculty of Law: Prof. DAVID DIXON (acting)
Faculty of Medicine: Prof. PETER SMITH
Faculty of Science: MIKE ARCHER
Australian Graduate School of Management: Prof. ROBERT MCLEAN
College of Fine Arts: Prof. IAN HOWARD
Univ. College, Australian Defence Force Academy: Assoc. Prof. JOHN BAIRD (Rector)

PROFESSORS

Faculty of Arts and Social Sciences:
  ALEXANDER, C., English
  ALEXANDER, P., English
  ASHCROFT, W., English
  BELL, P., History and Philosophy of Science
  BELL, R., History
  BENNETT, B., Humanities
  CAHILL, D., History
  CASS, B., Social Policy
  CHAN, J., Social Science and Policy
  CHANDLER, P., Education
  CONDREN, C., Politics and International Politics
  COOPER, M., Education
  COTTON, J., Humanities
  DANIEL, A., Sociology
  DENNIS, P., Humanities
  DONALD, J., Media, Film and Theatre
  EGGERT, P., Humanities
  GASCOIGNE, J., History
  GREY, J., Humanities
  GROSS, M., Education
  HALL, R., Social Science and Policy
  HUGMAN, R., Social Work
  HUMPHREY, M., Sociology
  JOHNSON, R., History

KATZ, I., Social Policy
KITCHING, G., Politics and International Relations
LYONS, M., History
OLDROYD, D., History and Philosophy of Science
PATTON, P., Philosophy
PEARSON, M., History
SAUNDERS, P., Social Policy
SCHUSTER, J., Media and Communications
SWELLER, J., Education
THAYER, C., Humanities
TYRRELL, I., History
WILLIAMS, M., Politics and International Relations
WOODMAN, S., Humanities

Faculty of the Built Environment:
  CUTHBERT, A., Architecture
  LANG, J., Architecture
  LOOSEMORE, M., Built Environment
  RUAN, X., Architecture
  WEIRICK, J., Landscape Architecture

Faculty of Commerce and Economics:
  ANDERSON, E., Economics
  BALZER, L., Banking and Finance
  BROWN, R., Accounting
  DWYER, L., Accounting
  FELDMAN, D., Banking and Finance
  FIEBIG, D., Economics
  FOSTER, F., Banking and Finance
  FOX, K., Economics
  HILL, R., Economics
  KOHN, R., Economics
  LAYTON, R., Marketing
  MORRISON, P., Marketing
  MOSHIRIAN, F., Banking and Finance
  UNCLES, M., Marketing

Faculty of Engineering:
  ACWORTH, R., Civil Engineering
  ADESINA, A., Chemical Engineering
  ASHBOLT, N., Civil and Environmental Engineering
  BRADFORD, M., Civil and Environmental Engineering
  CARMICHAEL, D., Civil and Environmental Engineering
  CELLER, B., Electrical Engineering
  CHATTOPADHYAY, G., Civil and Environmental Engineering
  COMPTON, P. J., Computer Science
  CROSKY, A., Materials Science and Engineering
  DAVIS, T., Chemical Engineering
  DOCTORS, L., Mechanical Engineering
  DZURAK, A., Electronic Engineering and Telecommunications
  FANE, A., Chemical Engineering
  FELL, R., Civil and Environmental Engineering
  FLEET, G., Chemical Engineering
  FOO, N., Computer Science
  FORSTER, B., Surveying and Spatial Information Systems
  FOSTER, N., Chemical Engineering
  GALVIN, J., Mining Engineering
  GILBERT, R., Civil and Environmental Engineering
  HEBBLEWHITE, B., Mining Engineering
  HEISER, G., Computer Science
  HOUGH, R., Engineering
  JEFFERY, R., Computer Science
  KAEBERNICK, H., Mechanical Engineering
  KELLY, D., Mechanical Engineering
  LEONARDI, E., Mechanical Engineering
  MAROSSZEKY, M., Civil and Environmental Engineering
  MORRISON, G., Mechanical Engineering
  NOWOTNY, J., Materials Science and Engineering
  OSTROVSKI, O., Materials Science and Engineering
  PINCZEWSKI, W., Petroleum Engineering
  RANDALL, R., Mechanical Engineering

RIZOS, C., Surveying and Spatial Information Systems
SAHAJWALLA, V., Materials Science and Engineering
SAMMUT, C., Computer Science
SAVKIN, A., Electrical Engineering
SCHINDHELM, K., Biomedical Engineering
SENEVIRATNE, A., Electrical Engineering
SHARMA, A., Civil and Environmental Engineering
SHAW, J., Computer Science
SKYLLAS-KAZACOS, M., Chemical Engineering
SOLO, V., Electrical Engineering
SORRELL, C., Materials Science and Engineering
TIN LOI, F., Civil and Environmental Engineering
TRIMM, D., Chemical Engineering
TRINDER, J., Surverying and Spatial Information Systems
VALLIAPPAN, S., Civil and Environmental Engineering
WAITE, D., Civil and Environmental Engineering
WENHAM, S., Photovoltaic Engineering
YU, A., Materials Science and Engineering

Faculty of Law:

ARONSON, M., Law
BROWN, D., Law
BYRNES, A., Law
CUNNEEN, C., Law
DISNEY, J., Law
DIXON, D., Law
GREENLEAF, G., Law
KINGSFORD-SMITH, D., Law
KRYGIER, M., Law
REDMOND, P., Law
WILLIAMS, G., Law

Faculty of Medicine:

ANDERSON, D., Medicine
ANDREWS, J., Psychiatry
BARRY, P., Physiology
BENNETT, M., Obstetrics and Gynaecology
BRODATY, H., Psychiatry
CALVERT, G., Medicine
CAMPBELL, T., Medicine
CHESTERMAN, C., Medicine, Pathology
CHISHOLM, D., Medicine, Metabolic Research
CHONG, B., Medicine
COIERA, E., Medical Sciences
COOPER, D., Medicine
CORONEO, M., Ophthalmology
DAY, R., Medicine, Clinical Pharmacology
DEANE, S., Surgery
DICKSON, H., Rehabilitation, Aged and Extended Care
EISENBUCH, I., Medicine
EISMAN, J., Medicine, Bone and Mineral Research
GANDEVIA, S., Medicine
GECZY, C., Pathology
GRAHAM, R., Medicine
HALL, B., Medicine
HARRIS, M., Medicine
HARRISON, G., Anaesthetics
HARVEY, R., Medicine
HENRY, R., Paediatrics
HILLMAN, K., Anaesthetics and Intensive Care
HOGG, P., Pathology
HOLDEN, B. A., Optometry
HOWES, L., Medicine, Physiology
KALDOR, J., Epidemiology
KEARSLEY, J., Surgery
KHACHIGIAN, L., Pathology
KIPPAX, S., HIV Social Research Centre
KRILIS, S., Medicine
KUMAR, R., Pathology
LAWSON, J., Health Services Management
LEE, A., Medical Microbiology
LLOYD, A., Pathology
LORD, R., Surgery
LUMBERS, E., Physiology

MACDONALD, G., Medicine
MCLACHLAN, E., Physiology, Medical Research
MORRIS, D., Surgery
O'ROURKE, M., Medicine
O'SULLIVAN, W., Medical Biochemistry
PARKER, G., Psychiatry
POOLE, M., Surgery
RICHMOND, R., Medicine
ROTEM, A., Medical Education
ROWE, M., Physiology
RUSSELL, P., Medicine
SCHINDHELM, K., Biomedical Engineering
SILOVE, D., Psychiatry
TARANTOLA, D., Medicine
TORDA, T. A., Anaesthetics and Intensive Care
WAKEFIELD, D., Pathology
WHITE, L., Paediatrics
ZWAR, N., Paediatrics
ZWI, A., Paediatrics

Faculty of Science:

ADAMS, M., Biological, Earth and Environmental Science
BALLARD, J., Biotechnology and Biomolecular Science
BISHOP, R., Chemical Sciences
BLACK, D. ST C., Chemical Sciences
BRYANT, R., Psychology
CADOGAN, M., Physics
CAMPBELL, S., Physical, Environmental and Mathematical Sciences
CLARK, R., Physics
COOPER, D., Biological, Earth and Environmental Science
COUCH, W., Physics
COWLING, M., Mathematics
DADDS, M., Psychology
DAIN, S., Optometry
DAWES, W., Biotechnology and Biomolecular Science
DORAN, P., Biotechnology and Biomolecular Science
DUNSMUIR, W., Mathematics
ENGLAND, M., Mathematics
FLAMBAUM, V., Physics
FORGAS, J., Psychology
GAL, M., Physics
GILLAM, B., Psychology
GRAY, P., Biotechnology and Biomolecular Science
HIBBERT, D., Chemical Sciences
HUON, G., Psychology
JACKSON, W., Physical, Environmental and Mathematical Sciences
KEHOE, J., Psychology
KINGSFORD, R., Biological, Earth and Environmental Science
KJELLEBERG, S., Biotechnology and Biomolecular Science
LAMB, R., Chemical Sciences
LESLIE, L., Mathematics
LITTLE, F., Biotechnology and Biomolecular Science
LOVIBOND, P., Psychology
MCCONKEY, K., Psychology
MCLEAN, R., Physical, Environmental and Mathematical Sciences
MCMURTRIE, R., Biological, Earth and Environmental Science
MIDDLETON, J., Mathematics
NEILAN, B., Biotechnology and Biomolecular Science
NEILSON, D., Physics
PASK, C., Physical, Environmental and Mathematical Sciences
ROGERS, C., Mathematics
SAMMUT, R., Physical, Environmental and Mathematical Sciences
SIMMONS, M., Physics
SLOAN, I., Mathematics
STEINBERG, P., Biological, Earth and Environmental Science
STOREY, J., Physics
SUSHKOV, O., Physics

SUTHERLAND, C., Mathematics
SUTHERLAND, P., Mathematics
TAFT, M., Psychology
WAND, M., Mathematics
WARD, C., Biological, Earth and Environmental Science
WEBB, J., Physics
WILKINS, M., Biotechnology and Biomolecular Science
WOLFE, J., Physics

ASSOCIATE COLLEGES

Faculty of the College of Fine Arts: Selwyn St, Paddington, NSW 2021; tel. (2) 9385-0888; f. 1990 following merger of the City Art Institute and the Univ.; Dean and Dir IAN HOWARD.

University College, Australian Defence Force Academy: Northcott Drive, Campbell, ACT 2601; tel. (2) 6268-8111; f. 1981 by agreement between the Commonwealth of Australia and the Univ. of NSW; degree courses started 1986; Rector Prof. ROBERT KING; Exec. Officer T. HODSON.

ASSOCIATED INSTITUTE

Australian Graduate School of Management: Sydney, NSW 2052; tel. (2) 9931-9200; f. 1975; postgraduate MBA and PhD courses, residential courses for execs; 42 faculty mems; library of 25,000 vols; Dir Prof. ROBERT MCLEAN; publ. *Australian Journal of Management*, *AGSM Working Paper Series*.

UNIVERSITY OF NEWCASTLE

University Dr., Callaghan, NSW 2308
Telephone: (2) 4921-5000
Fax: (2) 4985-4200
E-mail: enquirycentre@newcastle.edu.au
Internet: www.newcastle.edu.au
Founded 1965
State control
Academic year: March to November (2 semesters)
Chancellor: Prof. TREVOR WARING
Vice-Chancellor and President: Prof. NICHOLAS SAUNDERS
Deputy Vice-Chancellor for Academic and Global Relations: Prof. KEVIN MCCONKEY
Deputy Vice-Chancellor for Research: MIKE CALFORD
Deputy Vice-Chancellor for University Services: Dr SUE GOULD
Pro-Vice-Chancellor, Central Coast Campus: Dr STEPHEN CRUMP
Library: see under Libraries and Archives
Number of teachers: 800
Number of students: 26,956
Publications: *Cetus* (1 a year), *UniNews*

PRO-VICE-CHANCELLORS

Faculty of Business and Law: Prof. STEPHEN NICHOLAS
Faculty of Education and Arts: Prof. T. LOVAT
Faculty of Engineering and Built Environment: Prof. JOHN CARTER
Faculty of Health: Prof. P. DUNKLEY
Faculty of Science and Information Technology: Prof. B. HOGARTH

PROFESSORS

Faculty of Business and Law (internet www.newcastle.edu.au/faculty/bus-law):

BATES, F., Law
BOYCE, G.
BRAY, M., Employment Studies
BURGESS, K.
CATLEY, B., Management
EASTON, S., Finance
MITCHELL, W., Economics
NICHOLAS, S., International Business Strategy

O'CASS, A., Marketing
WINSEN, J., Commerce
WRIGHT, T., Law

Faculty of Education and Arts (internet www
.newcastle.edu.au/faculty/educ-artsl):

ALBRIGHT, J., Education
ALLEN, M., Sociology and Anthropology
BOURKE, S., Education
CAREY, H., History
CRAIG, H., English
EMELJANOW, V., Drama
EWANS, M., Drama
FOLEY, D.
FOREMAN, P., Education
FUERY, P., Film, Media and Cultural Studies
GORE, J., Curriculum Teaching and Learning
GRAHAM, A., Fine Art
GRAY, M., Social Work
HOLBROOK, A.
LAURA, R., Education
LOVAT, T., Education
MAYNARD, J., Indigenous History
MCDOWELL, J., Theology
PLOTNIKOFF, R.
SCOTT, J.
TARRANT, H., Classics
VELLA, R., Music
WEBB, S.

Faculty of Engineering and Built Environment (internet www.eng.newcastle.edu.au):

BETZ, R., Electrical and Computer Engineering
CARTER, J., Geotechnical Engineering
DLUGOGORSKI, B., Chemical Engineering
EVANS, G., Chemical Engineering
FU, M., Electrical Engineering
GALVIN, K., Chemical Engineering
GOODWIN, G., Electrical Engineering
JAMESON, G., Chemical Engineering
JONES, M., Bulk Solids
KENNEDY, E., Chemical Engineering
KISI, E., Mechanical Engineering
LEHMANN, S., Architecture
MELCHERS, R., Civil Engineering
MIDDLETON, R., Electrical Engineering
MILLER, M., Computer Science and Software Engineering
MOGHTADERI, B., Chemical Engineering
MOHEIMANI, S., Electrical and Computer Engineering
MURCH, G., Materials Engineering
NINNESS, B., Electrical and Computer Engineering
OSTWALD, M., Architecture
ROBERTS, A., Mechanical Engineering
SHENG, D., Civil Engineering
SLOAN, S., Civil Engineering
STEWART, M., Civil Engineering
WALL, T., Fuels and Combustion Engineering

Faculty of Health (internet www.newcastle
.edu.au/faculty/health):

ATTIA, J.
ASHMAN, L., Medical Biochemistry
BAKER, A.
BURNS, G., Medical Biochemistry
BYLES, J.
CALFORD, M., Human Physiology
CALLISTER, R., Anatomy
DAY, T., Anatomy
DEANE, S.
D'ESTE, C., Public Health
DUNKLEY, P., Medical Biochemistry
FAHY, K., Nursing and Midwifery
FORBES, J.
FOSTER, P., Immunology and Microbiology
GARG, M., Pharmacy and Experimental Pharmacology
GLEESON, M., Immunology
HAZELTON, M., Nursing
HENSLEY, M., Medicine
HIGGINS, I., Nursing

JONES, A.
JONES, K., Human Physiology
KEATINGE, D., Paediatrics
KELLY, B., Public Health
LI, S., Pharmacy and Experimental Pharmacology
LUMBERS, E., Pharmacy and Experimental Pharmacology
POND, D., Medical Practice and Population Health
RIVETT, D., Physiotherapy
ROSTAS, J.
RYAN, S., Occupational Therapy
SANSON-FISHER, R., Public Health
SCOTT, R., Medical Genetics
SMITH, D., Occupational Health and Safety
SMITH, R.
ZARDAWI, I.

Faculty of Science and Information Technology (internet www.newcastle.edu.au/faculty/
science-it/):

AITKEN, J., Biological Sciences
BOLAND, N., Mathematics
BORWEIN, J., Mathematics
DASTOOR, P., Physics
ERSKINE, W., Applied Sciences
GROF, C., Biological Sciences
HEATHCOTE, A., Psychology
HOGARTH, B.
JIN, J., Information Technology
KING, B., Physics
LAWRANCE, G., Chemistry
MCCLUSKEY, A., Chemistry
MCGUIRK, P., Geography and Environmental Studies
MENK, F., Physics
O'CONNOR, J., Physics
RAYNER, J., Statistics
RODGER, J., Biological Sciences
ROSE, R., Biological Sciences
STARTUP, M., Psychology
WILLIS, G., Mathematics

NOTRE DAME UNIVERSITY

19 Mouat St, POB 1225, Fremantle, WA 6959
Telephone: (8) 9433-0533
Fax: (8) 9433-0544
E-mail: international@nd.edu.au
Internet: www.nd.edu.au
Founded 1990 by Act of Parliament
Campuses at Broome and Sydney (Broadway and Darlinghurst)
Private control (Archdiocese of Perth)
Language of instruction: English
Academic year: February to December
Vice-Chancellor: Dr CELIA HAMMOND
Deputy Vice-Chancellor, Broome: Prof. SONIA WAGNER
Deputy Vice-Chancellor, Fremantle and Provost (Broome and Fremantle): Prof. MARK MCKENNA
Deputy Vice-Chancellor and Provost, Sydney Campus: Prof. HAYDEN RAMSEY
Exec. Dir for Admissions and Student Services, Fremantle: ROMMIE MASAREI
Exec. Dir for Admissions and Student Services, Sydney: MARK TANNOCK
Exec. Dir for Resources and Development: WAYNE MCGRISKIN
Number of teachers: 170
Number of students: 3,000

DEANS

Broome and Fremantle Campuses:

School of Arts and Sciences: Prof. NEIL DREW
School of Business: Assoc. Prof. SONJA BOGUNOVICH
School of Education: Prof. MICHAEL O'NEILL
School of Health Sciences: Prof. HELEN PARKER
School of Law: Assoc. Prof. JANE POWER

School of Medicine: Prof. GAVIN FROST
School of Nursing: Assoc. Prof. SELMA ALLIEX
School of Philosophy and Theology: Prof. PETER BLACK
School of Science and Technology: Prof. BRIAN COLLINS

Sydney Campus:

School of Arts and Sciences: Prof. GERRY TURCOTTE
School of Business: Prof. JOO-GIM HEANEY
School of Education: Assoc. Prof. MARK TANNOCK
School of Law: Prof. GERARD RYAN
School of Medicine: Prof. JULIE QUINLIVAN
School of Nursing: Prof. MARGOT KEARNS
School of Philosophy and Theology: Prof. HAYDEN RAMSAY

UNIVERSITY OF QUEENSLAND

Qld 4072
St Lucia, Brisbane, Qld 4072
Telephone: (7) 3365-1111
Fax: (7) 3365-1199
E-mail: admissionsenquiries@uq.edu.au
Internet: www.uq.edu.au
Founded 1910
Academic year: January to December (2 semesters, and summer semester)
Chancellor: Hon. Sir LLEWELLYN EDWARDS
Deputy Chancellor: Hon. Justice M. J. WHITE
Vice-Chancellor: Prof. PAUL GREENFIELD
Sr Deputy Vice-Chancellor: Prof. MICHAEL KENIGER
Deputy Vice-Chancellor for Academic Affairs: Prof. DEBORAH TERRY
Deputy Vice-Chancellor for Int. and Devt Affairs: Prof. T. J. GRIGG
Deputy Vice-Chancellor for Research: Prof. D. SIDDLE
Pro-Vice-Chancellor for Ipswich Campus: Prof. A. G. RIX
Pro-Vice-Chancellor for Teaching and Learning: Prof. DEBBIE J. TERRY
Pres. of Academic Board: Prof. M. D. GOULD
Univ. Sec. and Registrar: Prof. D. PORTER
Librarian: K. G. WEBSTER
Library: see Libraries and Archives
Number of teachers: 1,261
Number of students: 38,139
Publication: *University News*

EXECUTIVE DEANS

Faculty of Arts: Prof. R. A. FOTHERINGHAM (acting)
Faculty of Biological and Chemical Sciences: Prof. M. MCMANUS
Faculty of Business, Economics and Law: Prof. TIM BRAILSFORD
Faculty of Engineering, Architecture and Information Technology: Prof. GRAHAM SCHAFFER
Faculty of Health Sciences: Prof. P. M. BROOKS
Faculty of Natural Resources, Agriculture and Veterinary Science: Prof. R. SWIFT
Faculty of Science: Prof. STEPHEN WALKER
Faculty of Social and Behavioural Sciences: Prof. CINDY GALLOIS (acting)

PROFESSORS

Arts (Room E206, Level 2, Forgan Smith Bldg, St Lucia Campus, Qld 4072; tel. (7) 3365-1333; fax (7) 3365-2866; e-mail arts@uq .edu.au; internet www.arts.uq.edu.au):

ALMOND, P. C., History of European Discourses
BRACANIN, P., Music
CRYLE, P. M., History of European Discourses
ELSON, R., History, Philosophy, Religion and Classics

GRIFFITHS, P., History, Philosophy, Religion and Classics
HUNTER, I. R., History of European Discourses
KELLY, V. E., English, Media Studies and Art History
LATTKE, M. S., History, Philosophy, Religion and Classics
MOORHEAD, J. A., History, Philosophy, Religion and Classics
O'REGAN, T., English, Media Studies and Art History
SUSSEX, R. D., Languages and Comparative Cultural Studies
TIFFIN, H. M., English, Media Studies and Art History
TURNER, G., Critical and Cultural Studies
WHITLOCK, G., English, Media Studies and Art History

Biological and Chemical Sciences (Room 313, Level 3, Computer Science Bldg, St Lucia Campus, Qld 4072; tel. (7) 3365-1888; fax (7) 3365-1613; e-mail bacs.enquiries@uq.edu.au; internet bacs.uq.edu.au):

ADAMS, D. J., Biomedical Sciences
BIRCH, R., Integrative Biology
BOWLING, F., Molecular and Microbial Sciences
BROAD, T., Biological and Chemical Sciences
CAMPBELL, G. R., Biomedical Sciences
CAMPBELL, J. H., Bioengineering and Nanotechnology
CRITCHLEY, C., Integrative Biology
DEGNAN, B. M., Integrative Biology
DRENNAN, J., Microscopy and Microanalysis
GRESSHOFF, P. M., Integrative Legume Research
GRIGG, G. C., Integrative Biology
HOEGH-GULDBERG, O., Marine Studies
IRWIN, J. A. G., Integrative Biology, Tropical Plant Protection
JENNINGS, M. P., Molecular and Microbial Sciences
KEY, B., Biomedical Sciences
KITCHING, W., Molecular and Microbial Sciences
MCEWAN, A., Molecular and Microbial Sciences
MCMANUS, M. E., Biological and Chemical Sciences
MINCHIN, R., Biomedical Sciences
NORTON, G. A., Biological Information Technology
O'NEILL, S., Integrative Biology
PETTIGREW, J. D., Vision, Touch and Hearing Research
POSSINGHAM, H., Integrative Biology, Ecology Centre
SMITH, R. W., Molecular and Microbial Sciences
SMITH, S., Molecular and Microbial Sciences
TAYLOR, S. M., Biomedical Sciences
TINDLE, R. W., Clinical Medical Virology Centre
TOTH, I., Molecular and Microbial Sciences
TRAU, M., Bioengineering and Nanotechnology
WENTRUP, C., Molecular and Microbial Sciences
ZALUCKI, M. P., Integrative Biology

Business, Economics and Law (Room 233, Level 2, Colin Clark Bldg, St Lucia Campus, Qld 4072; tel. (7) 3365-7111; fax (7) 3365-4788; e-mail facbel@bel.uq.edu.au; internet www.bel.uq.edu.au):

ALLAN, J. F. P., Law
ASHKANASY, N. M., Business
BALLANTYNE, R. R., Tourism
BRAILSFORD, T., Business
CALLAN, V. J., Business
CAMPBELL, H. F., Economics
CLARKSON, P., Business

COELLI, T., Economics
COOPER, C., Tourism
CORNWELL, T. B., Business
DE LACY, T., Tourism and Leisure Management
DEVEREUX, J., Law
DODGSON, M., Technology and Innovation Management
FINN, F. J., Business, Economics and Law
FOSTER, J., Economics
GRANTHAM, R. B., Law
GRAY, S., Business
KIEL, G. C., Business
LIESCH, P. W., Business
MCCOLL-KENNEDY, J., Business
MCLENNAN, A. M, Economics
MANGAN, J. E., Economics
MENEZES, F. M, Economics
O'KEEFE, T., Business
PURI, K., Law
QUIGGIN, J., Economics
RAO, P., Economics
RATNAPALA, A. S., Law
RICKETT, C., Law
SHERMAN, B. G., Law
TOURKY, R., Economics
WILTSHIRE, K. W., Business
ZHANG, J., Economics
ZIMMER, I., Business, Economics and Law

Engineering, Architecture and Information Technology (Room S204, Level 2, Hawken Engineering Bldg, St Lucia Campus, Qld 4072; tel. (7) 3365-4777; fax (7) 3365-4444; e-mail admin@epsa.uq.edu.au; internet www .epsa.uq.edu.au):

ADAMS, P., Mathematics
ANDRESEN, B., Architecture
BAILES, P. A., Information Technology and Electrical Engineering
BELL, M. J., Geography, Planning and Architecture
BERGMANN, N., Information Technology and Electrical Engineering
BHATIA, S. K., Chemical Engineering
BIALKOWSKI, M. E., Information Technology and Electrical Engineering
BLACKALL, L. L., Advanced Wastewater Management Centre
BOYCE, R. R., Mechanical Engineering
BRACKEN, A. J., Mathematics
BREMHORST, K., Mechanical Engineering
BRERETON, D., Social Responsibility in Mining
BURRAGE, K., Advanced Computational Modelling Centre
CAMERON, I. T., Chemical Engineering
CHARLES, P. M., Civil Engineering
COLLERSON, K. D., Earth Sciences
CROZIER, S., Information Technology and Electrical Engineering
DARVENIZA, M., Information Technology and Electrical Engineering
DO, D. D., Chemical Engineering
DOBSON, A. J., Population Health
DRUMMOND, P. D., Physics
ECCLESTON, J. A., Physical Sciences
FRANZIDIS, J., Mineral Research Centre
GURGENCI, H., Mechanical Engineering
HAYES, I. J., Information Technology and Electrical Engineering
HECKENBERG, N. R., Physics
INDULSKA, J., Information Technology and Electrical Engineering
KELLER, J., Advanced Wastewater Management Centre
KNIGHTS, P. R., Mining and Minerals Process Engineering
LEVER, P. J. A., Mining and Minerals Process Engineering
LINDSAY, P., Information Technology and Electrical Engineering
MCAREE, P. R., Mechanical Engineering
MCLACHLAN, G. J., Mathematics
MEMMOTT, P. C., Geography, Planning and Architecture

MORGAN, R., Mechanical Engineering
NIELSEN, L. K., Chemical Engineering
PAILTHORPE, B., Physical Sciences
PANDOLFI, J. M., Earth Sciences
PHINN, S. R., Geography, Planning and Architecture
POLLETT, P. K., Mathematics
RUBINSZTEIN-DUNLOP, H., Physics
RUDOLPH, V., Chemical Engineering
SAHA, T. K., Information Technology and Electrical Engineering
SANDERSON, P., Information Technology and Electrical Engineering
SCHAFFER, G. B., Materials Engineering
SMART, M. K., Mechanical Engineering
STALKER, R. J., Mechanical Engineering
STROOPER, P. A., Information Technology and Electrical Engineering
WILES, J. H., Information Technology and Electrical Engineering
YUAN, Z., Advanced Water Management
ZHOU, X., Information Technology and Electrical Engineering

Health Sciences (Level 1, Edith Cavell Bldg, Royal Brisbane Hospital, Herston, Qld; tel. (7) 3365-5342; fax (7) 3365-5533; e-mail healthsciences@uq.edu.au; internet www.uq .edu.au/health):

ABERNETHY, A. B., Human Movement Studies
BAKER, P. G., Medical
BATCH, J. A., Paediatrics and Child Health
BELLAMY, N., Population Health; Medicine
BETT, J., Medicine
BICKEL, M., Dentistry
BLACK, B., Surgery
BOYD, A. W., Experimental Haematology
BROOKS, P., Health Sciences
BROWN, W. J., Human Movement Studies
BURGESS, P., Health Systems Division
BUSH, R., Population Health
CAPRA, M. F., Health Sciences
CAPRA, S. M., Health Sciences
CATTS, S., Psychiatry
CHAN, J., Anaesthesiology and Critical Care
CHAPPELL, M. M., Anaesthesiology and Critical Care
CHENERY, H. J., Health Sciences
CLEGHORN, G. J., Medicine
COMAN, W. B., Surgery
CONNELLY, L. B., Medicine
COULTHARD, A., Medical Imaging
CRAWFORD, D. H., Medicine
CRAWFORD, G. S., Anaesthesiology and Critical Care
DASTAGIR, S. M. N., Anaesthesiology and Critical Care
DAVIS, C. A., Anaesthesiology and Critical Care
DING, Y., Anaesthesiology and Critical Care
DOBSON, A. J., Population Health
DOHERTY, B., Anaesthesiology and Critical Care
ELLIS, N. M., Centre for Military and Veterans' Health
FISK, N. R., Clinical Research
FLORIN, T. H., Medicine
GARDINER, R. A., Surgery
GEORGE, S. A., Anaesthesiology and Critical Care
GORDON, R. D., Medicine
GOTLEY, D., Surgery
GOUGH, I. R., Surgery
GRAY, L., Medicine
HEGNEY, D. G., Nursing and Midwifery
HENDY, R., Health Innovation and Solutions
HEWITT, L., Anaesthesiology and Critical Care
HICKSON, L. M. H., Health and Rehabilitation Sciences
HOSKING, J. A., Anaesthesiology and Critical Care

HOY, W. E., Medicine
ISOARDI, J. C., Anaesthesiology and Critical Care
ISOARDI, K., Anaesthesiology and Critical Care
JACKSON, C. L., Medicine
JOHNSON, D. W., Medicine
JULL, G. A., Health and Rehabilitation Sciences
KENARDY, J. A., Medicine
KOUDOS, P., Anaesthesiology and Critical Care
LAKHANI, S., Molecular and Cellular Pathology
LENTZ, A., Anaesthesiology and Critical Care
LOPEZ, A., Population Health
MACDONALD, D., Human Movement Studies
MCINTYRE, H. D., Medicine
MARLEY, J. E., Health Sciences
MARTIN, G., Psychiatry
MARWICK, T., Medicine
MEYERS, I. A., Dentistry
MICHEL, C. A., Anaesthesiology and Critical Care
MONYPENNY, K., Anaesthesiology and Critical Care
MOSER, B., Anaesthesiology and Critical Care
MURDOCH, B. E., Health and Rehabilitation Sciences
NGUI, R. L. C., Population Health
NICHOLLS, K., Anaesthesiology and Critical Care
NIXON, J. W., Paediatrics and Child Health
OCHOLA, J., Anaesthesiology and Critical Care
OWEN, N., Population Health
PANDIE, M. Z., Anaesthesiology and Critical Care
PEARN, J. H., Medicine
PENDER, M. P., Medicine
ROBINSON, L., Health Innovation and Solutions
RYAN, A., Anaesthesiology and Critical Care
SEYMOUR, G. J., Dentistry
SHANNON, C. A., Health Sciences
SHAW, P. N., Pharmacy
SILBURN, P., Surgery
SMITH, M. T., Pharmacy
SOYER, H. P., Medicine
STEWART, D. J., Anaesthesiology and Critical Care
STITZ, R. W., Surgery
STRONG, J., Health and Rehabilitation Sciences
TAYLOR, R. J., Population Health
TETT, S., Pharmacy
TINNING, R. I., Human Movement Studies
TOTH, I., Pharmacy
TUDEHOPE, D. I., Paediatrics and Child Health
TURNER, C. T., Nursing and Midwifery
UNDERWOOD, M., Anaesthesiology and Critical Care
VENKATESH, B., Anaesthesiology and Critical Care
VICENZINO, G. T., Health and Rehabilitation Sciences
WALSH, L. J., Dentistry
WELSH, A., Anaesthesiology and Critical Care
WEST, M. J., Medicine
WHITEFORD, H. A., Health Systems
WILKINSON, D., Medicine
WILLIAMS, G. M., International Health
WILLIAMSON, F., Anaesthesiology and Critical Care
WILLS, C. M., Anaesthesiology and Critical Care
WOOTTON, R., Online Health
WORRALL, L. E., Health and Rehabilitation Sciences

Natural Resources, Agriculture and Veterinary Science (N. W. Britton Admin. Bldg (No. 8101), Gatton Campus, Qld; tel. (7) 5460-1276; fax (7) 5460-1204; e-mail nravs.enquiries@uqg.uq.edu.au; internet www.uq.edu.au/nravs):

ANDERSON, G., Veterinary Science
BASFORD, K. E., Land, Crop and Food Sciences
BOSCH, O. J. H., Natural and Rural Systems Management
BRYDEN, W. L., Animal Studies
BURNS, R. G., Land, Crop and Food Sciences
D'OCCHIO, M., Beef Genetic Technologies
FUKAI, S., Land, Crop and Food Sciences
GIDLEY, M., Nutrition and Food Sciences
HAYNES, R. J., Land, Crop and Food Sciences
HILL, J., Veterinary Science
MCGOWAN, M. R., Veterinary Science
MENZIES, N. W., Land, Crop and Food Sciences
PHILLIPS, C. J., Animal Welfare and Ethics
RAND, J. S., Veterinary Science
ROSS, H., Natural and Rural Systems Management
ROTHWELL, J., Veterinary Science
SWIFT, R. S., Natural Resources, Agriculture and Veterinary Science
WILLIAMS, R. R., Land, Crop and Food Sciences

Social and Behavioural Sciences (Room S423, Level 4, Social Sciences Bldg, St Lucia Campus, Qld 4072; tel. (7) 3365-7487; fax (7) 3346-9136; e-mail sbs@uq.edu.au; internet www.uq.edu.au/sbs):

ALEXANDER, N. M., Australian Centre for Peace and Conflict Studies
ASHMAN, A. F., Education
BALDAUF, R. B. J., Education
BAXTER, J. H., Social Science
BELL, S. R., Political Science and International Studies
BELLAMY, A. J., Political Science and International Studies
BLEIKER, R., Political Science and International Studies
BOREHAM, P., Political Science and International Studies; Social Research
BROMLEY, M. S., Journalism and Communication
GALLOIS, C., Psychology; Social Research in Communication
GILBERT, R. J., Education
GILLIES, R. M., Education
HUMPHREYS, M., Psychology; Human Factors and Applied Cognitive Psychology
KARGER, H., Social Work and Human Services
KENARDY, J. A., Psychology
LAWRENCE, G., Social Science
LEE, C., Psychology
MATTINGLEY, J. B., Psychology
NAJMAN, J. M., Social Science
OEI, T. P. S., Psychology
PETERSON, C. L., Psychology
POWER, C., Education
QUIGGIN, J., Economics
RENSHAW, P. D., Education
SANDERS, M. R., Psychology
SKRBIS, Z., Social Science
SOURDI, T. M., Australian Centre for Peace and Conflict Studies
STIMSON, R. J., Social Research
TRIGGER, D. S., Social Science
VON HIPPEL, W., Psychology
WESTERN, M. C., Social Science
WHITEHOUSE, G. M., Political Science and International Studies
WILSON, J. E., Social Work and Human Services

AFFILIATED RESIDENTIAL COLLEGES

Cromwell College: Principal Rev. Dr H. M. BEGBIE.

Duchesne College: Principal N. KAY.

Emmanuel College: Principal Dr S. GILL.

Gatton Halls of Residence: Principal S. SCOTT.

Grace College: Principal Dr S. FAIREY.

International House: Dir Dr C. TROMANS.

King's College: Master G. EDDY.

St John's College: Warden Rev. Prof. J. MORGAN.

St Leo's College: Rector V. SKELLY.

Union College: Warden P. E. FRASER.

The Women's College: Principal Dr M. G. W. AITKEN.

ATTACHED RESEARCH INSTITUTES; (ALL AT UNIVERSITY OF QUEENSLAND, BRISBANE, UNLESS NOTED OTHERWISE)

Aboriginal Environments Research Centre: Dir Assoc. Prof. P. C. MEMMOTT.

Advanced Computational Modelling Centre: Dir Prof. K. BURRAGE.

Advanced Wastewater Management Centre: Dir Dr J. KELLER.

ARC Centre for Complex Systems: Dir Prof. P. LINDSAY.

ARC Centre of Excellence for Quantum Computer Technology (University of Queensland node): Man. Assoc. Prof. T. C. RALPH.

ARC Centre for Functional Nanomaterials: Dir Prof. G. Q. LU.

Australasian Centre on Ageing: Dir Prof. H. BARTLETT.

Australian Biosecurity Cooperative Research Centre: Emerging Infectious Disease: Dir Dr S. PROWSE.

Australian Centre for Complementary Medicine, Education and Research: Dir Prof. S. P. MYERS.

Australian Centre for Intellectual Property in Agriculture: Dir Prof. B. SHERMAN.

Australian Centre for International and Tropical Health and Nutrition (ACITHN): Dir Prof. H. B. KAY.

Australian Centre for Minerals Extension and Research: Man. R. MCLEAN.

Australian Centre for Peace and Conflict Studies: Dir Prof. K. P. CLEMENTS.

Australian Equine Genetics Research Centre (AEGRC): Dir Prof. A. E. O. TRESIZE.

Australian Institute for Bioengineering and Nanotechnology: Dir PETER GRAY.

Australian Research Council Centre of Excellence for Integrative Legume Research: Dir Prof. P. M. GRESSHOFF.

Australian Research Council Centre of Excellence for Quantum-Atom Optics (Queensland node): Dir Prof. P. D. DRUMMOND.

Australian Research Council Centre of Excellence in Biotechnology and Development (Queensland node): Dir Prof. P. KOOPMAN.

Australian Research Council Key Centre for Human Factors and Applied Cognitive Psychology: Dir Prof. P. SANDERSON.

Australian Studies Centre: Dir Dr D. CARTER.

Behaviour Research and Therapy Centre: Dir Dr P. H. HARNETT.

Brisbane Surface Analysis Facility: Dir Assoc. Prof. I. R. GENTLE.

Burns, Trauma and Critical Care Research Centre: Dir Prof. J. LIPMAN.

Cancer Prevention Research Centre: Dir Prof. N. OWEN.

Catalyst Research Centre for Society and Technology: Dir Prof. D. RADCLIFFE.

Centre for Animal Welfare and Ethics: Dir Prof. C. J. C. PHILLIPS.

Centre for Applied History and Heritage Studies: Dir Dr G. A. C. GINN.

Centre for Bacterial Diversity and Identification: Dir Assoc. Prof. L. I. SLY.

Centre for Biological Information Technology: Dir Prof. G. NORTON.

Centre for Biomolecular Engineering: Dir Prof. A. P. J. MIDDLEBERG.

Centre for Biophotonics and Laser Science: Dir Prof. H. RUBINSZTEIN-DUNLOP.

Centre for Buddhist Studies: Co-Dirs Prof. T. DITRICH, Dr P. PECENKO.

Centre for Burden of Disease and Cost-Effectiveness: Dir Assoc. Prof. T. VOS.

Centre for Business Forensics: Dir Dr L. CHAPPLE.

Centre for Companion Animal Health: Dir Prof. J. RAND.

Centre for Computational Molecular Science: Dir Prof. S. C. SMITH.

Centre for Corporate Valuation: Co-Dirs Prof. A. GRAY, Prof. T. O'KEEFE.

Centre for Critical and Cultural Studies: Dir Prof. G. TURNER.

Centre for Discrete Mathematics and Computing: Dir Assoc. Prof. E. J. BILLINGTON.

Centre for Efficiency and Productivity Analysis: Dir Prof. D. S. P. RAO.

Centre for High Performance Polymers: Dir Assoc. Prof. P. HALLEY.

Centre for History of European Discourses: Dir Prof. P. CRYLE.

Centre for Hypersonics: Dir Prof. R. G. MORGAN.

Centre for Immunology and Cancer Research (CICR): Dir Prof. I. H. FRAZER.

Centre for Integrated Resource Management (CIRM): Exec. Dir Assoc. Prof. J. J. MOTT.

Centre for International Journalism: Dir Dr E. LOUW.

Centre for Magnetic Resonance (CMR): Dir Prof. I. M. BRERETON.

Centre for Marine Studies (CMS): Dir Prof. O. HOEGH-GULDBERG.

Centre for Mathematical Physics: Dir Dr J. R. LINKS.

Centre for Mathematics and Statistics of Complex Systems: an Australian Research Council Centre of Excellence (Queensland node): Dir Prof. P. K. POLLETT.

Centre for Medical Education: Dir Assoc. Prof. R. PETERSON.

Centre for Metals in Biology: Dir Prof. P. V. BERNARDT.

Centre for Microscopy and Microanalysis (CMM): Dir Prof. J. DRENNAN.

Centre for Military and Veterans' Health: Dir Prof. N. ELLIS.

Centre for Mined Land Rehabilitation (CMLR): Dir Dr D. MULLIGAN.

Centre for Nanotechnology and Biomaterials: Dir Prof. M. TRAU.

Centre for Native Floriculture: Dir Prof. D. C. JOYCE.

Centre for Nutrition and Food Sciences: Dir Prof. M. GIDLEY.

Centre for Online Health: Dir Prof. R. WOOTTON.

Centre for Organisational Psychology: Dir Dr R. MARTIN.

Centre for Pesticide Application and Safety: Dir A. J. HEWITT.

Centre for Physical Activity and Sport Education: Man. M. SIMJANOVIC.

Centre for Public, International and Comparative Law: Dir Prof. S. RATNAPALA.

Centre for Remote Sensing and Spatial Information Science: Dir Assoc. Prof. S. R. PHINN.

Centre for Research in Language Processing and Linguistics: Co-Dirs Assoc. Prof. J. WILES, Assoc. Prof. H. CHENERY, Dr J. INGRAM.

Centre for Research in Vascular Biology: Dir Prof. J. H. CAMPBELL.

Centre for Research into Sustainable Urban and Regional Futures (CRSURF): Dir Prof. R. J. STIMSON.

Centre for Research on Group Processes: Dir Dr M. HORNSEY.

Centre for Research on Women, Gender, Culture and Social Change: Dir Assoc. Prof. C. FERRIER.

Centre for Rural and Regional Innovation–Queensland: Dir Assoc. Prof. J. ALLISON.

Centre for Social Research in Communication: Dir Prof. C. GALLOIS.

Centre for Social Responsibility in Mining: Dir Prof. D. BRERETON.

Centre for Statistics: Dir Prof. G. J. MCLACHLAN.

Centre for Sustainable Design: Dir Assoc. Prof. R. HYDE.

Centre for Transport Strategy: Dir Prof. P. M. CHARLES.

Centre for Water Futures: Dir Dr D. A. LOCKINGTON.

Centre for Water in the Minerals Industry: Dir Prof. C. MORAN.

Centre of National Research on Disability and Rehabilitation Medicine (CONROD): Dir Prof. N. BELLAMY.

Children's Nutrition Research Centre: Dir Prof. G. CLEGHORN.

Clinical Medical Virology Centre: Dir Prof. R. TINDLE.

Cognitive Psychophysiology Laboratory: Co-Dirs Prof. G. M. GEFFEN, Prof. L. B. GEFFEN.

Communication Disability in Ageing Research Centre: Co-Dirs Assoc. Prof. L. HICKSON, Prof. L. E. WORRALL.

Cooperative Research Centre for Aboriginal Health: Dir Prof. A. LOPEZ.

Cooperative Research Centre for Australasian Invasive Animals: Dir Prof. W. BRYDEN.

Cooperative Research Centre for Beef Genetic Technologies: Dir Prof. M. D'OCCHIO.

Cooperative Research Centre for Cast Metals Manufacturing (CAST): CEO Prof. D. ST JOHN.

Cooperative Research Centre for Chronic Inflammatory Diseases: CEO Prof. J. HAMILTON.

Cooperative Research Centre for Coal in Sustainable Development: Dir F. VAN SCHAGEN.

Cooperative Research Centre for Coastal Zone, Estuary and Waterway Management: CEO Dr R. FEARON.

Cooperative Research Centre for Contamination Assessment and Remediation of the Environment: Dir Prof. R. SWIFT.

Cooperative Research Centre for Enterprise Distributed Systems Technology: CEO M. GIBSON.

Cooperative Research Centre for Environmental Biotechnology: Exec. Dir Dr D. GARMAN.

Cooperative Research Centre for Interaction Design: Co-Dirs Dr M. BRERETON, Dr M. DOCHERTY.

Cooperative Research Centre for Mining: CEO Prof. M. HOOD.

Cooperative Research Centre for Polymers: Dir Assoc. Prof. P. HALLEY.

Cooperative Research Centre for Rail: CEO Prof. D. ROACH.

Cooperative Research Centre for Sugar Industry Innovation through Biotechnology: Dir Dr P. TWINE.

Cooperative Research Centre for Sustainable Aquaculture of Finfish: Dir Dr P. MONTAGUE.

Cooperative Research Centre for Sustainable Resource Processing: Dir Prof. D. MCKEE.

Cooperative Research Centre for Sustainable Tourism: Dir Prof. T. DE LACY.

Cooperative Research Centre for Tropical Plant Protection: CEO Prof. J. IRWIN.

Cooperative Research Centre for Tropical Rainforest Ecology and Management: Dir Prof. N. STORK.

Cooperative Research Centre for Tropical Savannas Management: Dir Prof. G. DUFF.

Cooperative Research Centre for Water Quality and Treatment: Dir Prof. D. BURSILL.

Earth Systems Science Computational Centre (ESSC): Dir Prof. P. MORA.

The Ecology Centre: Dir Prof. H. PAOSSINGHAM.

Endocrine Hypertension Research Centre: Dir Assoc. Prof. M. STOWASSER.

Environmental Management Unit: Dir Dr D. MCPHEE.

Fred and Eleanor Schonell Special Education Research Centre: Dir Dr C. E. VAN KRAAYENOORD.

Institute for Molecular Bioscience: Dir Prof. B. J. WAINWRIGHT.

International Relations and Asian Politics Research Unit: Dir (vacant).

ISMC Solutions Pty Ltd: Dir (vacant).

Julius Kruttschnitt Mineral Research Centre (JKMRC): Dir Prof. B. J. I. ADAIR.

Marine and Shipping Law Unit: Dir Assoc. Prof. S. DERRINGTON.

Minerals Industry Safety and Health Centre: Dir Prof. J. JOY.

Motor Speech Research Centre: Dir Prof. B. E. MURDOCH.

Nanomaterials Centre (NanoMac): Dir Prof. G. Q. LU.

National Heart Foundation and Prince Charles Hospital Foundation Cardiovascular Research Centre: Dir Prof. M. J. WEST.

National Research Centre for Environmental Toxicology (NRCET): Dir Prof. M. R. MOORE.

Neuroimmunology Research Centre: Dir Prof. M. P. PENDER.

Parker CRC for Integrated Hydrometallurgy Solutions: Dir M. WOFFENDEN.

Particle and Systems Design Centre: Co-Dirs Assoc. Prof. I. T. CAMERON, Prof. J. D. LISTER.

Perinatal Research Centre: Dir Prof. P. B. COLDITZ.

Protein Research Centre: Dir Assoc. Prof. P. A. KROON.

Pyrometallurgy Research Centre: Dir Prof. P. HAYES.

Queensland Alcohol and Drug Research Education Centre: Dir Prof. J. NAJMAN.

Queensland Brain Institute: Dir Prof. P. BARTLETT.

Queensland Centre for Intellectual and Developmental Disability: Dir Assoc. Prof. N. LENNOX.

Queensland Centre for Population Research: Dir Prof. M. BELL.

Queensland Centre for Public Health: UQ Coordinator Dr A. CLAVARINO.

Queensland Liver Transplant Unit: Dir Prof. J. FAWCETT.

Rangelands Australia: Dir Prof. J. TAYLOR.

Renal Research Centre: Dir Prof. D. JOHNSON.

Rotary Centre for International Studies in Peace and Conflict Resolution: Dir Dr M. HANSON.

Social Research Centre: Co-Dirs Prof. P. BOREHAM, Assoc. Prof. M. WESTERN.

Special Research Centre for Functional and Applied Genomics: Deputy Dir Prof. D. HUME.

Sustainable Minerals Institute: Dir Prof. D. MCKEE.

Technology and Innovation Management Centre: Dir Prof. M. DODGSON.

Tropical and Subtropical Weeds Research Unit: Dir Assoc. Prof. S. ADKINS.

University of Queensland Archeological Services Unit: Dir Dr J. M. PRANGNELL.

University of Queensland Blue Care Research and Practice Development Centre: Dir Prof. D. HEGNEY.

Vision, Touch and Hearing Research Centre: Dir Prof. J. D. PETTIGREW.

W. H. Bryan Mining Geology Research Centre: Dir C. G. ALFORD.

QUEENSLAND UNIVERSITY OF TECHNOLOGY

GPOB 2434, Brisbane, Qld 4000

Telephone: (7) 3138-2000
E-mail: qut.information@qut.edu.au
Internet: www.qut.edu.au

Founded 1965; Brisbane CAE merged with the Univ. 1990
State control

Chancellor: Dr C. HIRST
Vice-Chancellor: Prof. P. COALDRAKE
Deputy Vice-Chancellor: Prof. D. GARDINER (acting)
Pro-Vice-Chancellor for Information and Academic Services: T. COCHRANE
Pro-Vice-Chancellor for Research and Advancement: Prof. J. GOUGH (acting)
Exec. Dir, Finance and Resource Planning: STEPHEN PINCUS (acting)
Registrar: Dr C. DICKENSON
Librarian: G. AUSTEN

Library of 672,000 vols
Number of students: 39,359

DEANS
Built Environment and Engineering: Prof. MARTIN BETTS
Business: Prof. PETER LITTLE
Creative Industries: Prof. SUSAN STREET

Education: Prof. WENDY PATTON
Health: Prof. K. J. BOWMAN
Law: Prof. MICHAEL LAVARCH
QUT Carseldine: Prof. RUTH MATCHETT
Science and Technology: Prof. SIMON KAPLAN

PROFESSORS
ABBEY, J., Nursing
ARMSTRONG, H., Design and Built Environment
ARNOLD, N., Advertising, Marketing and Public Relations
ARTHURS, A., Music
BETTS, M., Faculty Office (Built Environment and Engineering)
BOASHASH, B., Electrical and Electronic Systems
BOULTON-LEWIS, G., Learning and Professional Studies
BOWMAN, K., Faculty Office (Health)
BOYCE, G., International Business
BOYD, T., Construction Management and Property
BROMLEY, M., Journalism
CAELLI, W., Data Communications
CARNEY, L., Optometry
CHANG, A., Nursing
CLEMENTS, J., Life Science
COALDRAKE, P., Chancellery
COLLIER, B., Law
COOPER, T., Mathematics, Science and Technology Education
COPE, M., Faculty Office (Law)
CORONES, S., Law Research
COURTNEY, M., Nursing
CRAWFORD, R., Mechanical, Manufacturing and Medical Engineering
CUNNINGHAM, S., Creative Industries Research and Applications Centre
DALE, J., Faculty Office (Science and Technology)
DAWSON, E., Data Communications
DOUGLAS, E., Brisbane Graduate School of Business
DUNCAN, W., Law
EDWARDS, H., Nursing
ENGLISH, L., Mathematics, Science and Technology Education
FERREIRA, L., Civil Engineering
FISHER, D., Law
FITZGERALD, B., Law School
GABLE, G., Information Systems
GARDINER, D., Chancellery
GARDNER, I., Life Science
GEORGE, G., Faculty Office (Science and Technology)
GIBSON, D., Chancellery
GOUGH, J., Research and Advancement
GRIFFIN, M., Faculty Office (Business)
HAMPSON, K., Cooperative Research Centre for Construction
HARDING, S., Faculty Office (Business)
HARTLEY, J., Faculty Office (Creative Industries)
HERINGTON, A., Life Science
HOCKINGS, J., Design and Built Environment
HUDSON, P., Life Science
HURN, A., Economics and Finance
JONES, J., Creative Industries Research and Applications Centre
KABANOFF, B., Management
LANE, W., Law School
LAVERY, P., Creative Industries Faculty Advancement
LAYTON, A., Economics and Finance
LEDWICH, G., Electrical and Electronic Systems
LEHMANN, S., Design and Built Environment
LITTLE, P., Accountancy
McELWAIN, D., Mathematics
McGREGOR-LOWNDES, M., Centre of Philanthropy and Non-profit Studies
McLEAN, V., Faculty Office (Education)
McROBBIE, C., Mathematics, Science and Technology Education

McWILLIAM, E., Cultural and Language Studies in Education
MAEDER, A., Electrical and Electronic Systems
MAHENDRAN, M., Civil Engineering
MATCHETT, R., QUT Carseldine
MATHEW, J., Mechanical, Manufacturing and Medical Engineering
MOODY, M., Electrical and Electronic Systems Engineering
NEWMAN, B., Public Health
OLDENBURG, B., Public Health
PARKER, A., Human Movement Studies
PATTI, C., Advertising, Marketing and Public Relations
PATTON, W., Learning and Professional Studies
PEARCY, M., Mechanical, Manufacturing and Medical Engineering
PETTITT, A., Mathematics
PHAM, B., Information Technology
POPE, J., Physical Sciences
RENFORTH, W., Business
RYAN, N., Management
SARA, V., Life Science
SHEEHAN, M., Psychology and Counselling
SIDWELL, A., Construction Management and Property
SKITMORE, R., Construction Management and Property
SRIDHARAN, S., Electrical and Electronic Systems
TAYLER, C., Early Childhood
THAMBIRATNAM, D., Civil Engineering
TOWERS, S., Creative Industries Faculty Academic Programs
TROCKI, C., Humanities and Human Services
TROUTBECK, R., Civil Engineering
WALDERSEE, R., Business
WILLETT, R., Accountancy
WISSLER, R., Research and Advancement
YOUNG, R., Psychology and Counselling

ROYAL MELBOURNE INSTITUTE OF TECHNOLOGY

GPOB 2476V, Melbourne, Vic. 3001
124 La Trobe St, Melbourne, Vic. 3000

Telephone: (3) 9925-2260
Fax: (3) 9663-5029
E-mail: study@rmit.edu.au
Internet: www.rmit.edu.au

Founded 1887; university status 1992

Campuses in Melbourne, Bundoora and Brunswick; int. campuses in Hanoi and Saigon (Ho Chi Minh City)
Academic year: February to November

Chancellor: Prof. DENNIS GIBSON
Vice-Chancellor and Pres.: Prof. MARGARET GARDINER
Pro-Vice-Chancellor for Business: Prof. GILL PALMER
Pro-Vice-Chancellor for Design and the Social Context: Prof. COLIN FUDGE
Pro-Vice-Chancellor for Finance and Business Services: CAMERON MORONEY
Pro-Vice-Chancellor for International Enterprise and Community Development: Dr MADELEINE REEVE
Pro-Vice-Chancellor for Organisational Capability and Development: COLIN SHARP
Pro-Vice-Chancellor for Research and Innovation: Prof. DAINE ALCORN
Pro-Vice-Chancellor for Science, Engineering and Technology: Prof. PETER COLOE
Pro-Vice-Chancellor for Students: Prof. JOYCE KIRK
Pro-Vice-Chancellor for Teaching and Learning: Prof. GAIL HART
Dir, TAFE: ALLAN BALLAGH
Academic Registrar: MADDY MCMASTER
Library Dir.: CRAIG ANDERSON (acting)

Library of 704,322 vols
Number of students: 70,247

Publications: *Research Highlights* (1 a year), *RMIT Openline* (university news, 5 a year)

DEANS

Faculty of Applied Science: Prof. MALCOLM MCCORMICK
Faculty of Art, Design and Communication: Prof. ROBIN WILLIAMS
Faculty of Business: Prof. MARGARET JACKSON
Faculty of Constructed Environment: Prof. BELINDA PROBERT
Faculty of Education, Language and Community Services: Prof. MARY KALANTZIS
Faculty of Engineering: Prof. ROBERT SNOW
Faculty of Life Sciences: Prof. ALEX RADLOFF

UNIVERSITY OF SOUTH AUSTRALIA

GPOB 2471, Adelaide, SA 5001
Telephone: (8) 8302-6611
Fax: (8) 8302-2466
Internet: www.unisa.edu.au
Founded 1991 by the merger of the South Australian Institute of Technology and three campuses of the South Australian College of Advanced Education; campuses at City East, City West, Magill, Mawson Lakes, Underdale and Whyalla
Autonomous (established by Act of Parliament)
Academic year: January to December
Chancellor: Dr IAN GOULD
Vice-Chancellor and Pres.: Prof. PETER HØJ
Exec. Dir and Vice-Pres. for Finance and Resources: PAUL BEARD
Exec. Dir and Vice-Pres. for Int. and Devt Affairs: Dr ANNA CICCARELLI
Pro-Vice-Chancellor for Access and Learning Support: Prof. PETER LEE
Pro-Vice-Chancellor for the Division of Business and Enterprise: Prof. GERRY GRIFFIN
Pro-Vice-Chancellor for Education, Arts and Social Sciences: Prof. PAL AHLUWALIA
Pro-Vice-Chancellor for the Division of Health Sciences: Prof. ROBYN MCDERMOTT
Pro-Vice-Chancellor for the Division of Information Technology, Engineering and the Environment: Prof. ANDREW PARFITT
Pro-Vice-Chancellor for Organisational Strategy and Change: Prof. HILARY WINCHESTER
Pro-Vice-Chancellor for Research and Innovation: Prof. CAROLINE MCMILLEN
Dir of Student and Academic Services: LUCY SCHULZ
Dir of Library Services: HELEN LIVINGSTON
Library: 1m. vols
Number of teachers: 983
Number of students: 34,391
Publication: *UniSA Researcher* (electronic, 6 a year).

SOUTHERN CROSS UNIVERSITY

POB 157, Lismore, NSW 2480
Campuses at Lismore, Coffs Harbour and Tweed Heads
Telephone: (2) 6620-3000
Fax: (2) 6622-1300
E-mail: webmarketing@scu.edu.au
Internet: www.scu.edu.au
Founded 1993 from Northern Rivers and Coffs Harbour components of the University of New England
Academic year: February to November (2 semesters)
Vice-Chancellor: Prof. PAUL CLARK
Pro-Vice-Chancellors: Prof. B. BAVERSTOCK, Prof. A. C. B. DELVES, Prof. L. Z. KLICH
Exec. Dir and Vice-Pres. for Corporate Services: M. H. MARSHALL
Number of teachers: 350
Number of students: 14,631

Publication: *Research Report* (1 a year)

DEANS

Faculty of Arts and Sciences: JENNY GRAHAM
Faculty of Business and Law: Prof. MICHAEL EVANS

PROFESSORS

ATKINSON, J., Indigenous Australian Peoples
BAVERSTOCK, P., Graduate Research College (and PVC Research)
BRAITHWAITE, R., Tourism and Hospitality Management
DELVES, A., University Enterprise and International Activities (PVC)
GARTSIDE, D. F., Resource Science and Management
GRAHAM, J., Health and Applied Sciences Division (Executive Dean)
HAYDEN, M., Teaching and Learning Unit
HENRY, R. J., Plant Conservation Genetics
JACKSON, J. G., Law and Justice
KLICH, Z., University Academic and Quality Matters (PVC)
KOUZMIN, A., Graduate College of Management
LEIPER, N., Tourism and Hospitality Management
MCCONCHIE, D., Environmental Science and Management
MEREDITH, G., Business Administration
MURUGESAN, S., Multimedia and Information Technology
NECK, P., Business Administration
RICKARD, J., Vice-Chancellor
ROTHWELL, B., Manager, Tweed Gold Coast Campus
SAENGER, P., Environmental Science and Management
SAVERY, L., Business Division (Executive Dean)
SCOTT, D., Commerce and Management
SIMPSON, R., National Marine Science Centre
SPECHT, R., Environmental Science and Management
SPEEDY, G., Teaching and Learning Centre
TAYLOR, B., Nursing and Health Care Practices
THOM, P., Arts Division (Executive Dean)
VANCLAY, J., Environmental Science and Management
WILSON, P., Psychology
YEO, S. M. H., Law and Justice
ZANN, L. P., Environmental Science and Management

UNIVERSITY OF SOUTHERN QUEENSLAND

Toowoomba, Qld 4350
Telephone: (7) 4631-2100
Fax: (7) 4631-2892
E-mail: international@usq.edu.au
Internet: www.usq.edu.au
Founded 1992 (fmrly the University College of Southern Queensland, founded 1991 from the Darling Downs Institute of Advanced Education)
State control
Academic year: January to December
Chancellor: DONALD STEVENS
Vice-Chancellor: Prof. WILLIAM LOVEGROVE
Deputy Vice-Chancellor for Academic and Global Learning: Prof. JAMES TAYLOR
Pro-Vice-Chancellor for Int. Quality: (vacant)
Pro-Vice-Chancellor for Learning and Teaching: Prof. MAURICE FRENCH
Pro-Vice-Chancellor for Planning and Quality: Prof. WILLIAM MACGILLIVRAY
Pro-Vice-Chancellor for Regional Engagement and Social Justice: Prof. FRANK CROWTHER
Pro-Vice-Chancellor for Research: Prof. GRAHAM BAKER

Provost, Wide Bay Campus: Dr KENNETH STOTT
Gen. Man., Univ. Services: STEVE TANZER
Librarian: M. MCPHERSON
Library of 309,000 vols
Number of teachers: 480
Number of students: 26,500

DEANS

Faculty of Arts: Prof. M. FRENCH
Faculty of Business: Assoc. Prof. R. ST HILL
Faculty of Education: Prof. F. CROWTHER
Faculty of Engineering and Surveying: Prof. G. BAKER
Faculty of Sciences: Prof. W. MACGILLIVRAY
School of Transdisciplinary Graduate Studies and Continuing Education: Prof. A. BARNETT

PROFESSORS

BILLINGSLEY, J., Engineering and Surveying
ERWEE, R., Business
FOGARTY, G., Sciences
HEGNEY, D., Sciences
HORSFIELD, B., Arts
MCMILLEN, D., Arts
ROBERTS, A., Sciences
ROSS, D., Engineering and Surveying
SMITH, R., Engineering and Surveying
TERRY, P., Sciences
TRAN-CONG, T., Engineering and Surveying
VAN ERP, G., Engineering and Surveying

UNIVERSITY OF THE SUNSHINE COAST

Locked Bag 4, Maroochydore D.C., Qld 4558
Sippy Downs Dr., Sippy Downs, Qld 4556
Telephone: (7) 5430-1234
Fax: (7) 5430-1111
E-mail: information@usc.edu.au
Internet: www.usc.edu.au
Founded 1996
Academic year: February to December
Vice-Chancellor: Prof. PAUL THOMAS
Deputy Vice-Chancellor: Prof. GREG HILL
Pro-Vice-Chancellor: Prof. ROBERT ELLIOT
Number of teachers: 123 full-time
Number of students: 6,570

DEANS

Faculty of Arts and Social Sciences: Prof. PAM DYER
Faculty of Business: Prof. EVAN J. DOUGLAS
Faculty of Science, Health and Education: Prof. ROD SIMPSON

PROFESSORS

Faculty of Arts and Social Sciences:
ELLIOT, R.
LAMBLE, S.
SCOTT, J.
Faculty of Business:
DOUGLAS, E. J.
HEDE, A.
RALSTON, D.
Faculty of Science, Health and Education:
LOWE, J.
MEYERS, N.
SIMPSON, R.

ATTACHED RESEARCH INSTITUTES

Centre for Healthy Activities, Sport and Exercise (CHASE): Sippy Downs, Qld; tel. (7) 5459-4656; fax (7) 5459-4682; e-mail chase@usc.edu.au; internet www.usc.edu.au/chase; Dir Assoc. Prof. BRENDAN BURKETT.

Centre for Multicultural and Community Development: tel. (7) 5430-1259; fax (7) 5430-2859; e-mail ngopalkr@usc.edu.au; Dir NARAYAN GOPALKRISHNAN.

National Seniors Productive Ageing Centre: POB 1450, Brisbane, Qld 4001; tel.

(7) 3321-7074; fax (7) 3321-9339; e-mail info@ productiveageing.com.au; internet www .productiveageing.com.au; Dir (vacant).

SWINBURNE UNIVERSITY OF TECHNOLOGY

POB 218, Hawthorn, Vic. 3122
Telephone: (3) 9214-8000
Fax: (3) 9818-3648
E-mail: study@swinburne.edu.au
Internet: www.swinburne.edu.au
Founded 1908 as Eastern Suburbs Technical College; present name and status 1992
Academic year: March to November
Chancellor: Dr WILLIAM SCALES
Vice-Chancellor: Prof. IAN YOUNG
Deputy Vice-Chancellor for Research: Prof. ANDREW FLITMAN
Deputy Vice-Chancellor for Academic Affairs: Prof. SHIRLEY LEITCH
Divisional Deputy Vice-Chancellor, Technical and Further Education (TAFE Division): LINDA BROWN
Vice-Pres.: STEPHEN BEALL
Librarian: D. WHITEHEAD
Library of 250,000 vols
Number of teachers: 657 (362 Higher Education, 295 TAFE)
Number of students: 38,000 (incl. 14,118 Higher Education, 23,882 TAFE)
Publication: *Research Report*
Campuses at Hawthorn, Wantirna, Croydon, Healesville, Prahran, Lilydale, Sarawak (Malaysia)

DEANS

Faculty of Business and Enterprise: Prof. MIKE DONNELLY
Faculty of Design: Prof. KEN FREIDMAN (acting)
Faculty of Engineering and Industrial Sciences: Prof. JOHN SEYNON
Faculty of Higher Education, Lilydale: Prof. KAY LIPSON
Faculty of Information and Communication Technologies: LEON STERLING (acting)
Faculty of Life and Social Sciences: Prof. RUSSELL CRAWFORD

UNIVERSITY OF SYDNEY

Sydney, NSW 2006
Telephone: (2) 9351-2222
Fax: (2) 9351-3111
E-mail: infocentre@mail.usyd.edu.au
Internet: www.usyd.edu.au
Founded 1850
Private control
Academic year: February to December
Chancellor: HE Prof. MARIE BASHIR
Deputy Chancellor: ALAN CAMERON
Vice-Chancellor and Principal: Prof. MICHAEL SPENCE
Provost and Deputy Vice-Chancellor: Prof. DON NUTBEAM
Chief Operating Officer and Deputy Vice-Chancellor: BORISLAV (BOB) KOTIC
Deputy Vice-Chancellor for Research: Prof. JILL TREWHELLA
Deputy Vice-Chancellor for International Affairs: Prof. JOHN HEARN
Deputy Vice-Chancellor for Education: Prof. DERRICK ARMSTRONG
Deputy Vice-Chancellor: Prof. ANN BREWER
Pro-Vice-Chancellor for International Affairs: (vacant)
Pro-Vice-Chancellor for Research: Prof. CAROL ARMOUR (acting)
Pro-Vice-Chancellor for Strategic Planning: Prof. SHALOM ISAAC (CHARLIE) BENRIMOJ
Registrar: Dr DERRICK ARMSTRONG
General Counsel: RICHARD FISHER
Univ. Librarian: JOHN SHIPP

Chair. of Academic Bd: Prof. BRUCE SUTTON
Library: see under Libraries and Archives
Number of teachers: 2,714 f.t.e.
Number of students: 46,934 f.t.e.

EXECUTIVE DEANS

Faculties of Arts: Prof. STEPHEN GARTON
Faculties of Health: Prof. BRUCE SUTTON
Faculties of Science: Prof. DAVID DAY

DEANS

Faculty of Agriculture, Food and Natural Resources: Prof. MARK ADAMS
Faculty of Architecture, Design and Planning: Assoc. Prof. WARREN JULIAN
Faculty of Arts: Prof. STEPHEN GARTON
Faculty of Dentistry: Prof. ELI SCHWARTZ
Faculty of Economics and Business: Prof. PETER WOLNIZER
Faculty of Education and Social Work: Prof. DERRICK ARMSTRONG
Faculty of Engineering and Information Technologies: Prof. GREGORY HANCOCK
Faculty of Health Sciences: Prof. GWYNETH LLEWELYN
Faculty of Law: Prof. GILLIAN TRIGGS
Faculty of Medicine: Prof. BRUCE ROBINSON
Faculty of Nursing and Midwifery: Prof. JILL WHITE
Faculty of Pharmacy: Prof. IQBAL RAMZAN
Faculty of Veterinary Science: Assoc. Prof. LEO JEFFCOTT
Sydney College of the Arts: Prof. COLIN RHODES
Sydney Conservatorium of Music: Prof. KIM WALKER

PROFESSORS

Faculty of Agriculture, Food and Natural Resources (tel. (2) 9351-2935; fax (2) 9351-2945; e-mail dean.agriculture@usyd.edu.au):

COPELAND, L., Agriculture
GUEST, D., Horticulture
KENNEDY, I., Agricultural and Environmental Chemistry
McBRATNEY, A., Soil Science
PARK, R., Cereal Rust Research
SHARP, P., Molecular Plant Breeding
SUTTON, B.
TRETHOWAN, R., Plant Breeding

Faculty of Architecture, Design and Planning (tel. (2) 9351-5924; fax (2) 9351-5665; e-mail slalor@arch.usyd.edu.au):

BLAKELY, E., Urban and Regional Planning
GERO, J., Design Science
HENEGHAN, T., Architecture
HYDE, R., Architectural Science
MAHER, M., Design Computing

Faculty of Arts (tel. (2) 9351-2206; fax (2) 9351-2045; e-mail dean@arts.usyd.edu.au):

School of Languages and Cultures:

DUNSTAN, H., Chinese Studies
EBIED, R., Arabic and Islamic Studies
NEWBIGIN, N., Italian Studies
RIEGEL, J., Languages and Cultures
SANKEY, M., French Studies
VICKERS, A., South East Asian Studies
YANG, M., Asian Studies

School of Letters, Art and Media:

BARNES, G., Medieval Literature
BENJAMIN, R., Art History and Aboriginal Art
CLARK, J., Asian Art History
CLUNIES-ROSS, M., English Language and Early English Literature
DIXON, R., Australian Literature
FOLEY, W., Linguistics
GAY, P., English Literature and Drama
MARTIN, J., Linguistics

School of Philosophical and Historical Inquiry:

ALDRICH, R., European History
CSAPO, E., Classics and Ancient History

FLETCHER, R., Theoretical and World Archaeology
GARTON, S., History
GATENS, M., Philosophy
GAUKROGER, S., History of Philosophy and History of Science
IVISON, D., Political Philosophy
MILLER, M., Classical Archaeology
POTTS, D., Middle Eastern Archaeology
PRICE, H., Philosophy
PROBYN, E., Gender and Cultural Studies
REDDING, P., Philosophy
SLUGA, G., International History
WATERHOUSE, R., Australian History
WHITE, S., American History
WILSON, P., Classics

School of Social and Political Sciences:

AUSTIN-BROOS, D., Anthropology
GILL, G., Government and Public Administration
HAGE, G., Anthropology
HUMPHREY, M., Sociology and Social Policy
JACKSON, M., Government and Public Administration
STILWELL, F., Political Economy
TIFFIN, R., Government and International Relations
WEISS, L., Government and International Relations

Faculty of Dentistry (tel. (2) 9351-8334; fax (2) 9211-5912; e-mail dean@dentistry.usyd.edu.au):

BLINKHORN, A., Dentistry
BRYANT, R., Conservative Dentistry
DARENDELILER, M., Orthodontics
KLINEBERG, I., Prosthodontics
MURRAY, G., Dentistry
SWAIN, M., Biomaterials Science

Faculty of Economics and Business (tel. (2) 9351-3084; fax (2) 9351-4433; e-mail dean@econ.usyd.edu.au):

ANDERSON, E., Decision Sciences
ARENI, C., Marketing
ASPROMOURGOUS, A., Economics
BREWER, A., Organizational Logistics
DEAN, G., Accounting
DUPONT, A., International Security
ELLIOTT, S., Information Systems
FRINO, A., Finance
GALLOP, G., Economics
GRANT, D., Organizational Studies
GRAY, S., International Business
GUTHRIE, J., Accounting
HENSHER, D., Management
JOHNSTONE, D., Finance
JONES, S., Accounting
LANSBURY, R., Work and Organizational Studies
McKERN, B., International Business
McLENNAN, A., Economics
O'CONNOR, M., Information Systems
PEARSON, G., Business Law
PITCHFORD, R., Economics
ROBERTS, J., Accounting
SENGUPTA, K., Economics
STOPHER, P., Transport Planning
STYLES, C., Marketing
TIPTON, B., International Business
WALKER, R., Accounting
WOLNIZER, P., Accounting
WOODLAND, A., Econometrics

Faculty of Education and Social Work (tel. (2) 9351-2422; fax (2) 9351-6217; e-mail dean@edfac.usyd.edu.au):

ARMSTRONG, D., Education and Social Work
CONNELL, R., Education and Social Work
FAWCETT, B., Education and Social Work
FREEBODY, P., Education and Social Work
GOODYEAR, P., Education and Social Work
JONES, P., Education and Social Work
MEAGHER, G., Education and Social Work
PALTRIDGE, B., Education and Social Work
REIMANN, P., Education and Social Work
SHERRINGTON, G., History of Education

WELCH, A., Education and Social Work

Faculty of Engineering and Information Technologies (tel. (2) 9351-4739; fax (2) 9351-2111; e-mail engineering@eng.usyd.edu.au):

School of Aerospace, Mechanical and Mechatronic Engineering:

ARMFIELD, S., Aerospace, Mechanical and Mechatronic Engineering
DURRANT-WHYTE, H., Aerospace, Mechanical and Mechatronic Engineering
MAI, Y., Aerospace, Mechanical and Mechatronic Engineering
MASRI, A., Aerospace, Mechanical and Mechatronic Engineering
NEBOT, E., Aerospace, Mechanical and Mechatronic Engineering
TANNER, R., Mechanical Engineering
TONG, L., Aerospace, Mechanical and Mechatronic Engineering
YE, L., Aerospace, Mechanical and Mechatronic Engineering
ZHANG, L., Aerospace, Mechanical and Mechatronic Engineering

School of Chemical and Biomolecular Engineering:

BARTON, G., Chemical and Biomolecular Engineering
COSTER, H., Chemical and Biomolecular Engineering
HAYNES, B., Chemical and Biomolecular Engineering
PETRIE, J., Chemical and Biomolecular Engineering

School of Civil Engineering:

HANCOCK, G., Steel Structures
RASMUSSEN, K., Civil Engineering
SMALL, J., Civil Engineering

School of Electrical and Information Engineering:

AGELIDIS, V., Power Engineering
EADES, P., Software Technology
FENG, D., Electrical and Information Engineering
JOHNSTON, R., Electrical and Information Engineering
MINASIAN, R., Electrical and Information Engineering
PATRICK, J., Language Technologies
VUCETIC, B., Electrical and Information Engineering
YAN, H., Electrical and Information Engineering
ZOMAYA, A., High Performance Computing, Networking and Internetworking

Faculty of Health Sciences (tel. (2) 9351-9161; fax (2) 9351-9412; e-mail fhsuginfo@usyd.edu.au):

BANATI, R., Medical Radiation Sciences
BOHIE, P., Work and Health
BUNDY, A., Occupational Therapy
EINFELD, S., Mental Health
FIATARONE SINGH, M., Exercise and Sport Science
KENDIG, H., Ageing and Health
KENNY, D., Psychology and Music
LLEWELLYN, G., Occupation and Leisure Sciences
MADDEN, R., Classification in Health
MAHER, C., Physiotherapy
MATHEWS, M., Ageing, Health and Disability
ONSLOW, M., Stuttering Research
REFSHAUGE, K., Physiotherapy
VEITCH, C., Community Health
WESTBROOK, J., Health Informatics

Faculty of Law (tel. (2) 9351-0351; fax (2) 9351-0200; e-mail info@law.usyd.edu.au):

ALLARS, M., Law
APPS, P., Public Economics in Law
ASTOR, H., Law
BENNETT, B., Health and Medical Law

BOER, B., Environmental Law
BURNS, L., Taxation Law
BUTT, P., Law
CARNEY, T., Law
CARTER, J., Commercial Law
COOPER, G., Taxation Law
CROCK, M., Public Law
FINDLAY, M., Law
GRAYCAR, R., Law
HILL, J., Law
KINLEY, D., Human Rights Law
MCCALLUM, R., Industrial Law
O'MALLEY, P., Law
PARKINSON, P., Law
SADURSKI, W., Legal Philosophy
STUBBS, J., Criminology
TRIGGS, G., Law
VANN, R., Law

Faculty of Medicine (tel. (2) 9351-6570; fax (2) 9351-3196; e-mail t.rubin@med.usyd.edu.au):

ALLEN, D., Physiology
ALLEN, R., Transplantation Surgery
ANDERSON, C., Stroke Medicine and Clinical Neuroscience
ARMSTRONG, B., Medicine
BANDLER, R., Anatomy and Pain Research
BARTER, P., Medicine
BAUMAN, A., Public Health (Behavioural Epidemiology and Health Promotion)
BAUR, L., Medicine
BAXTER, R., Medicine
BENNETT, M., Physiology
BEREND, N., Respiratory Medicine
BILLSON, F., Clinical Ophthalmology and Eye Health
BISHOP, J., Cancer Medicine
BLACK, J., Medicine
BOKEY, E., Colorectal Surgery
BOOY, R., Medicine
BOYCE, P., Psychological Medicine
BRAITHWAITE, A., Medicine
BRAND-MILLER, J., Medicine
BRITTON, W., Medicine
BURKE, D., Medicine
BYRNE, M., Developmental and Marine Biology
CAMERON, I., Rehabilitation Medicine
CAMPBELL, I., Molecular Biology
CARTER, J., Gynaecological Oncology
CASS, D., Paediatric Surgery
CATERSON, I., Human Nutrition
CELERMAJER, D., Scandrett Cardiology
CHAPMAN, S., Medicine
CHRISTIE, M., Medicine
CHRISTODOULOU, J., Medicine
CHRISTOPHERSON, R., Medicine
CISTULLI, P., Respiratory Medicine
CLARKE, S., Medicine
COATS, A., Medicine
COLAGIURI, S., Metabolic Health
COOK, D., Cellular Physiology
COUSINS, M., Anaesthesia and Pain Management
CRAIG, J., Clinical Epidemiology
CROSSLEY, M., Molecular Genetics
CUMMING, R., Epidemiology and Geriatric Medicine
CUNNINGHAM, A., Medicine
DAMPNEY, R., Cardiovascular Neuroscience
DANDONA, L., International Public Health
DAVIES, M., Medicine
DELBRIDGE, L., Surgery
DOS REMEDIOS, C., Medicine
DREHER, B., Visual Neuroscience
DUNN, S., Psychological Medicine
ELLIOTT, E., Paediatrics and Child Health
FAZEKAS, B., Medicine
FIELD, M., Medicine
FINFER, S., Medicine
FLETCHER, J., Surgery
FRASER, I., Reproductive Medicine
FREEDMAN, S., Cardiology
GAMBLE, J., Vascular Biology
GASKIN, K., Paediatric Nutrition

GEORGE, J., Gastroenterology and Hepatic Medicine
GIBSON, W., Otolaryngology
GILES, W., Medicine
GOTTLIEB, D., Haematology
GÖTZ, J., Molecular Biology
GRAU, G., Vascular Immunology
GUNNING, P., Medicine
GUSS, M., Structural Biology
HABER, P., Medicine
HALL, R., Medicine
HALLIDAY, G., Medicine
HANDELSMAN, D., Reproductive Endocrinology and Andrology
HARPER, C., Neuropathology
HARRIS, D., Medicine
HARRIS, J., Vascular Surgery
HAWKE, S., Medicine
HAZELL, P., Medicine
HEARN, J., Medicine
HICKIE, I., Psychiatry
HORVATH, J., Medicine
HUNT, N., Pathology
HUNYOR, S., Medicine
IRWIG, L., Epidemiology
JEREMY, R., Medicine
JOHNSTON, G., Pharmacology
KAM, C., Anaesthetics
KEECH, A., Medicine, Cardiology and Epidemiology
KEFFORD, R., Medicine
KEMP, A., Paediatric Allergy and Clinical Immunology
KIDD, M., General Practice
KING, N., Medicine
KUCHEL, P., Biochemistry
LAMBERT, T., Psychiatry
LE COUTER, D., Geriatric Medicine
LEEDER, S., Public Health and Community Medicine
LIDDLE, C., Clinical Pharmacology and Hepatology
LINDLEY, R., Geriatric Medicine
LUSBY, R., Surgery
LYLE, D., Rural Health
MCCAUGHAN, G., Gastroenterology and Hepatology
MCINTYRE, P., Medicine
MACINTYRE, R., Medicine
MACMAHON, S., Cardiovascular Medicine and Epidemiology
MCMINN, P., Infectious Diseases
MASON, R., Endocrine Physiology
MAY, J., Surgery
MELLIS, C., Medicine
MINDEL, A., Sexual Health Medicine
MITCHELL, R., Medicine
MITROFANIS, J., Medicine
MORRIS, B., Physiology (Molecular Hypertension)
MORRIS, J., Obstetrics and Gynaecology
MURPHY, C., Histology and Embryology
NANAN, R., Paediatrics
NICHOLSON, G., Medicine
NORTH, K., Paediatrics and Child Health
NORTON, R., Public Health
NUTBEAM, D., Medicine
O'BRIEN, C., Medicine
OUVRIER, R., Paediatric Neurology
PARMENTER, T., Developmental Disability
PEEK, M., Medicine
POLLARD, J., Neurology
POLLOCK, C., Medicine
RASKO, J., Medicine
RASMUSSEN, H., Cardiology
REDDEL, R.
REEVES, P., Microbiology
REICHARDT, J., Molecular Biology (Molecular Medicine)
RICHARDSON, D., Medicine
ROBINSON, B., Medicine (Endocrinology)
ROBINSON, P., Medicine
RUSSELL, P., Medicine
RUSSELL, R., Medical Entomology
RYE, K., Medicine
SALKELD, G., Public Health

SAMBROOK, P., Rheumatology
SEALE, J., Clinical Pharmacology
SEIBEL, M., Endocrinology
SILINK, M., Medicine
SILLENCE, D., Medical Genetics
SIMES, J., Medicine
SIMPSON, J., Biostatistics
SMITH, R., Medicine
SONNABEND, D., Orthopaedic and Traumatic Surgery
SORRELL, T., Clinical Infectious Diseases
STEVENSON, M., Injury Prevention
STOCKER, R., Biochemistry in Vascular Medicine
STONE, J., Retinal and Cerebral Neurobiology
SULLIVAN, C., Medicine
TAM, P., Medicine
TARNOW-MORDI, W., Neonatal Medicine
TATTERSALL, M., Cancer Medicine
THOMPSON, J., Melanoma and Surgical Oncology
TOFLER, G., Preventive Cardiology
TONKIN, M., Hand Surgery
TRENT, R., Medical Molecular Genetics
TREWHELLA, J., Medicine
TRUDINGER, B., Obstetrics and Gynaecology
TRUSCOTT, R., Medicine
USHERWOOD, T., General Practice
VADAS, M., Cancer Medicine and Cell Biology
VAN ASPEREN, P., Paediatric Respiratory Medicine
VAN ZANDWIJK, N., Asbestos Disease
WALL, J., Medicine
WALTER, G., Child and Adolescent Psychiatry
WANG, S., Radiology
WATERHOUSE, P., Medicine
WEBSTER, W., Medicine
WEISS, A., Medicine
WENINGER, W., Dermatology
WILEY, J., Medicine (Haematology)
WILLIAMS, L., Cognitive Neuropsychiatry
YUE, D., Kellion Endocrinology

Faculty of Nursing and Midwifery (tel. (2) 9351-0663; fax (2) 9351-0508; e-mail nursing.enquiries@usyd.edu.au):

LAWLER, J., Nursing
RUDGE, T., Nursing
WHITE, J., Nursing
WHITE, K., Nursing

Faculty of Pharmacy (tel. (2) 9351-2320; fax (2) 9351-4391; e-mail enquiries@pharm.usyd.edu.au):

ARMOUR, C., Pharmacy
BENRIMOJ, S., Pharmacy Practice
BRIEN, J., Clinical Pharmacy
CHAN, H., Pharmaceutics (Advanced Drug Delivery)
MCLACHLAN, A., Pharmacy (Aged Care)
MURRAY, M., Pharmacogenomics (Pharmaceutics)
RAMZAN, I., Pharmaceutics
ROUFOGALIS, B., Pharmaceutical Chemistry
WHITE, L., Pharmacy Management

Faculty of Science (tel. (2) 9351-4123; fax (2) 9351-4124; e-mail dean@science.usyd.edu.au):

School of Biological Sciences:

CHAPMAN, G., Marine Ecology
DICKMAN, C., Terrestrial Ecology
OLDROYD, B., Behavioural Genetics
OVERALL, R., Plant Cell Biology
PARKER, A., Biological Sciences
SHINE, R., Biological Sciences
SIMPSON, S., Biological Sciences
SKURRAY, R., Biology (Genetics)
THOMPSON, M., Zoology
UNDERWOOD, A., Experimental Ecology
WATERHOUSE, P., Biological Sciences

School of Chemistry:

CROSSLEY, M., Chemistry (Organic Chemistry)
HAMBLEY, T., Chemistry
HARROWELL, P., Chemistry
KABLE, S., Chemistry
LAY, P., Chemistry (Inorganic Chemistry)
WARR, G., Chemistry

School of Geosciences:

CLARKE, G., Geosciences
CONNELL, J., Geosciences
HATHERLY, P., Mining Geophysics
HIRSCH, P., Geosciences

School of Mathematics and Statistics:

CANNON, J., Mathematical Statistics
DANCER, E., Pure Mathematics
JOSHI, N., Applied Mathematics
ROBINSON, J., Mathematical Statistics
WEBER, N., Mathematical Statistics

School of Molecular and Microbial Biosciences:

BRAND-MILLER, J., Molecular and Microbial Biosciences
CAMPBELL, I., Molecular Biology
CATERSON, I., Human Nutrition
CHRISTOPHERSON, R., Molecular and Microbial Biosciences
CROSSLEY, M., Molecular and Microbial Biosciences
KUCHEL, P., Molecular and Microbial Biosciences
REEVES, P., Molecular and Microbial Biosciences
WEISS, A., Molecular and Microbial Biosciences

School of Physics:

BALDOCK, C., Medical Physics
BEDDING, T., Astrophysics
CAIRNS, I., Physics
DE STERKE, M., Theoretical Physics
GREEN, A., Physics
HUNSTEAD, R., Astrophysics
LENZEN, M., Astrophysics
MCKENZIE, D., Physics (Material Physics)
MCPHEDRAN, R., Physics (Electromagnetic Physics)
MELROSE, D., Physics
SADLER, E., Physics
VLADIMIROV, S., Physics

School of Psychology:

ANDREWS, S., Psychology
BLASZCZYNSKI, A., Psychology
BUTOW, P., Psychology
MCGREGOR, I., Psychology
TOUYZ, S., Clinical Psychology

Faculty of Veterinary Science (tel. (2) 9351-8783; fax (2) 9351-3056; e-mail vetsci@vetsci.usyd.edu.au):

CANFIELD, P., Veterinary Science
EVANS, G., Veterinary Science
FULKERSON, W., Veterinary Science
HUSBAND, A., Veterinary Science
JEFFCOTT, L., Veterinary Science
MAXWELL, C., Veterinary Science
MORAN, C., Veterinary Science
RAADSMA, H., Veterinary Science
WARD, M., Veterinary Science
WHITTINGTON, R., Veterinary Science

Sydney College of the Arts (tel. (2) 9351-1002; fax (2) 9351-119; e-mail sca@usyd.edu.au):

DUNN, R., Contemporary Visual Art
RHODES, C., Art

Sydney Conservatorium of Music (tel. (2) 9351-1255; fax (2) 9351-1202; e-mail info@greenway.usyd.edu.au):

BOYD, A., Music
CHARTERIS, R., Historical Musicology
MARETT, A., Music
PALLÓ, I., Conducting
WALKER, K., Music

ATTACHED COLLEGES

Sydney College of the Arts: Dir Prof. RON NEWMAN.

Sydney Conservatorium of Music: Principal Prof. S. E. PRETTY.

UNIVERSITY OF TECHNOLOGY, SYDNEY

POB 123, Broadway, Sydney, NSW 2007
Telephone: (2) 9514-2000
Fax: (2) 9514-1551
E-mail: info.office@uts.edu.au
Internet: www.uts.edu.au

Founded 1965 as NSW Institute of Technology; university status 1988
Academic year: March to December
Chancellor: Prof. VICKI SARA
Deputy Chancellor: KENNETH RENNIE
Vice-Chancellor and President: Prof. ROSS MILBOURNE
Deputy Vice-Chancellor and Vice-Pres. for Academic Affairs: Prof. PETER BOOTH
Pro-Vice-Chancellor and Vice-Pres. for Teaching and Learning: Prof. RICHARD. A. JOHNSTONE
Pro-Vice-Chancellor and Vice-Pres. for Research: Prof. SUSAN ROWLEY
Pro-Vice-Chancellor and Vice-Pres. for International Relations: Prof. DAVID GOODMAN
Registrar: Dr JEFF M. FITZGERALD
Librarian: ALEX BYRNE
Library of 626,983 vols, 37,929 e-journals, 3,775 print journals
Number of teachers: 809 (full-time)
Number of students: 32,254
Publications: *CREArTA* (research and education in the arts, 2 a year), *Cultural Studies Review* (published jtly with Univ. of Melbourne; 2 a year), *Form/Work* (irregular), *Literacy and Numeracy Studies* (education and training of adults, 2 a year), *Locality* (3 a year), *Pacific Rim Property Research Journal* (4 a year), *Public History Review* (1 a year), *UTS Law Review* (1 a year), *UTS Writer's Anthology* (1 a year)

DEANS

Faculty of Arts and Social Sciences: Prof. THEO VAN LEEUWEN
Faculty of Business: Prof. ROY GREEN
Faculty of Design, Architecture and Building: Prof. DESLEY LUSCOMBE
Faculty of Education: Prof. SHIRLEY ALEXANDER
Faculty of Engineering and Information Technology: Prof. ARCHIE JOHNSTON
Faculty of Law: Prof. JILL MCKEOUGH
Faculty of Nursing, Midwifery and Health: Prof. JOHN DALY
Faculty of Science: Prof. BRUCE MILTHORPE

UNIVERSITY OF TASMANIA

Hobart campus: POB 252C-52, Hobart, Tas. 7001
Burnie campus: POB 447, Burnie, Tas. 7320
Launceston campus: Locked Bag 1, Launceston, Tas. 7250
Telephone: Hobart campus, (3) 6226-2999; Burnie campus, (3) 6430-4999; Launceston campus, (3) 6324-3999
Fax: Hobart campus, (3) 6226-7871; Burnie campus, (3) 6430-4950; Launceston campus, (3) 6324-3799
E-mail: course.info@utas.edu.au
Internet: www.utas.edu.au

Founded 1991 through merger of the University of Tasmania (f. 1890) and the Tasmanian State Institute of Technology
Academic year: February to October (2 terms)

Chancellor: Dr DAMIAN BUGG
Vice-Chancellor and Principal: Prof. D. LE
 GREW
Deputy Vice-Chancellor: ROD ROBERTS
 YVONNE RUNDLE
Pro-Vice-Chancellor for Research: Prof.
 JOHANNA LAYBOURN-PARRY
Pro-Vice-Chancellor for Teaching and Learn-
 ing: Prof. GAIL HART
Exec. Dir of Finance and Admin.: A. FERRALL
Academic Registrar: C. P. CARSTENS
Librarian: L. L. LUTHER

Library: see under Libraries and Archives
Number of teachers: 800
Number of students: 18,108

Publication: *Law Review*

DEANS

Faculty of Arts: Prof. SUSAN DODDS
Faculty of Commerce: Prof. P. G. H. CARROLL
Faculty of Education: Prof. IAN HAY
Faculty of Health Science: Prof. A. CARMI-
 CHAEL
Faculty of Law: Prof. D. R. C. CHALMERS
Faculty of Science, Engineering and Tech-
 nology: Prof. J. B. REID
Board of Graduate Studies by Research:
 Assoc. Prof. C. J. DENHOLM

PROFESSORS

at Hobart campus:

Faculty of Arts (Private Bag 44, Hobart, Tas.
7001; tel. (3) 6226-1874; fax (3) 6226-7842;
e-mail n.foster@utas.edu.au; internet www
.arts.utas.edu.au):

 BENNETT, M. J., History and Classics
 BLAND, R., Sociology
 FRANKHAM, N. H., Fine Art
 KELLOW, A. J., Government
 KNEHANS, D., Music
 MALPAS, J. E., Philosophy
 PAKULSKI, J., Sociology
 REYNOLDS, H., History and Classics
 WHITE, R., Sociology and Social Work

Faculty of Commerce (Private Bag 84,
Hobart, Tas. 7001; tel. (3) 6226-2160; fax (3)
6226-2170; e-mail course.info@utas.edu.au;
internet www.utas.edu.au/commerce):

 CARROLL, P. G. H., Accounting and Finance
 GODFREY, J., Accounting and Finance
 KEEN, C. D., Information Systems
 RAY, R., Economics

Faculty of Education (Locked Bag 1308,
Launceston, Tas. 7250; tel. (3) 6324-3446;
fax (3) 6324-3303; e-mail secretary@utas.edu
.au; internet www.educ.utas.edu.au):

 ARNOLD, R. M., Empathic Intelligence and
  Pedagogy
 HOGAN, D. J., Sociology of Education
 MULFORD, W. R., Educational Leadership
 WILLIAMSON, J. C., Teaching Studies and
  Teacher Education

Faculty of Health Science (POB 252C-99,
Hobart, Tas. 7001; tel. (3) 6226-4757; fax (3)
6226-4747; e-mail shssec@utas.edu.au;
internet www.healthsci.utas.edu.au):

 CARMICHAEL, A., Paediatrics and Child
  Health
 CLARK, M. G., Biochemistry
 CLEMENT, C., Obstetrics and Gynaecology
 DWYER, T., Population Health
 KIRKBY, K. C., Psychiatry
 MUDGE, P., General Practice
 PETERSON, G., Pharmacy
 STANTON, P. D., Surgery
 VICKERS, J. C., Pathology
 WALTERS, H., Medicine

Faculty of Law (Private Bag 89, Hobart, Tas.
7001; tel. (3) 6226-2066; fax (3) 6226-7623;
e-mail secretary@law.utas.edu.au; internet
www.law.utas.edu.au):

 CHALMERS, D. R. C., Law
 WARNER, C. A., Law

Faculty of Science, Engineering and Technology (Private Bag 50, Hobart, Tas. 7001;
tel. (3) 6226-2125; fax (3) 6226-7809; e-mail
alex.hamiltonsmith@utas.edu.au; internet
www.utas.edu.au/scieng):

 BUDD, W. F., Antarctic and Southern
  Ocean Environment
 BULLEN, F., Engineering
 BUXTON, C. D., Aquaculture and Fisheries
 CANTY, A. J., Chemistry
 CLARK, R. J., Agricultural Science
 CRAWFORD, A., Earth Sciences
 DAVIS, M. R., Civil and Mechanical Engin-
  eering
 FORBES, L., Mathematics
 GRIFFIN, R., Cooperative Research Centre
  for Sustainable Production Forestry
 HADDAD, P. R., Chemistry
 JOHNSON, C., Zoology
 KIRKPATRICK, J. B., Geography and Envir-
  onmental Studies
 LARGE, R. R., Earth Sciences
 MCMEEKIN, T. A., Agricultural Science
 NGUYEN, D. T., Electrical Engineering and
  Computer Science
 REID, J. B., Plant Science
 SALE, A., Computing
 SUMMERS, J. J., Psychology
 VANCLAY, F., Agricultural Science

at Launceston campus:

Faculty of Arts (Private Bag 44, Hobart, Tas.
7001; tel. (3) 6226-1874; fax (3) 6226-7842;
e-mail n.foster@utas.edu.au; internet www
.arts.utas.edu.au):

 BLAND, R., Sociology and Social Work
 HATLEY, B., Asian Languages and Studies
 MCGRATH, V. F., Visual and Performing
  Arts

Faculty of Education (Locked Bag 1308,
Launceston, Tas. 7250; tel. (3) 6324-3446;
fax (3) 6324-3303; e-mail secretary@utas.edu
.au; internet www.educ.utas.edu.au):

 MULFORD, W. R., Educational Leadership
 WILLIAMSON, J. C., Secondary and Post-
  compulsory Education

Faculty of Health Science (Private Bag 99,
Hobart, Tas. 7001; tel. (3) 6226-4757; fax (3)
6226-4747; e-mail shssec@utas.edu.au;
internet www.healthsci.utas.edu.au):

 BALL, M., Biomedical Science
 FARRELL, G., Nursing
 WALKER, J. H., Rural Health

Faculty of Science, Engineering and Technology (Private Bag 50, Hobart, Tas. 7001;
tel. (3) 6226-2125; fax (3) 6226-7809; e-mail
alex.hamiltonsmith@utas.edu.au; internet
www.utas.edu.au/scieng):

 CHOI, Y. J., Computing
 FAY, R., Architecture and Urban Design
 PANKHURST, N. W., Aquaculture

VICTORIA UNIVERSITY

POB 14428, Melbourne, Vic. 8001
Telephone: (3) 9688-4000
Fax: (3) 9689-4069
E-mail: graduate@vu.edu.au
Internet: www.vu.edu.au

Founded 1990

Academic year: March to November

Chancellor: His Honour Mr Justice FRANK
 VINCENT
Pres. and Vice-Chancellor: Prof. ELIZABETH
 HARMAN
Sr Deputy Vice-Chancellor: Prof. JOHN
 MCCALLUM
Deputy Vice-Chancellors: JON HICKMAN, Dr
 ANNE JONES, Prof. LINDA ROSENMAN
Pro Vice-Chancellors: Dr ROB BROWN, Prof.
 PETER CREAMER, BELINDA MCLENNAN, STE-
 PHEN WELLER
Univ. Librarian: (vacant)

Library of 561,341 vols
Number of teachers: 1,635
Number of students: 47,151

Publications: *Beanland Lectures* (1 a year),
 Jipam (journal of inequalities in pure and
 applied mathematics, irregular)

DEANS

Faculty of Arts, Education and Human Devt:
 Prof. MICHAEL HAMEL GREEN
Faculty of Business and Law: Prof. COLIN
 CLARK
Faculty of Health, Engineering and Science:
 Assoc. Prof. MICHELLE TOWSTOLESS (acting)
Faculty of Technical and Trades Innovation:
 CORALIE MORRISSEY
Faculty of Workforce Devt: LOUISE KING
VU College: SUSAN YOUNG

PROFESSORS

ANDERSON, R., Accounting
ANDREWS, N., Law
ARMSTRONG, A., School of Management
ARUP, C., Law
BAKER, H., Nursing
BROCK, D., Psychology
CARLSON, J., Centre for Ageing, Rehabilita-
 tion, Exercise and Sport
CARY, J., Key Research Area of Integrated
 Food Value Chain
CLARK, C., Accounting
DAVIDSON, J., History
DEERY, P., Dept of Asian and Int. Studies
DRAGOMIR, S., Engineering
EADE, R., Arts
FAULKNER, M., Telecommunications
GABB, R., Centre for Educational Devt and
 Support
GEORGE, G., Accounting
GLASBEEK, H., Business and Law
GREWAL, B., Centre for Strategic Economic
 Studies
HOUGHTON, J., Centre for Strategic Economic
 Studies
JAGO, L., Tourism and Hospitality Studies
KALAM, A., Engineering
KING, B., School of Hospitality, Tourism and
 Marketing
LEUNG, C., Computer Science
MCGRATH, M., Information Systems
MCQUEEN, R., Law
MORRIS, A., Human Devt, Health, Engineer-
 ing and Science
PATIENCE, A., Arts
POLONSKY, M., Marketing
PRIESTLY, I., Accounting
PRILLELTENSKY, I., Psychology
ROBERTS, T., School of Human Movement,
 Recreation and Performance
RYAN, M., Education
SEEDSMAN, T., Human Devt, Health, Engin-
 eering and Science
SHEEHAN, P., Centre for Strategic Economic
 Studies
SINCLAIR, J., Arts
THOMAS, I., Centre for Environmental Safety
 and Risk Engineering
THORPE, G., School of the Built Environment
TURNER, L., School of Applied Economics
WILSON, K., Economics
XIE, M., Engineering
ZHANG, Y., Computer Science

UNIVERSITY OF WESTERN AUSTRALIA

35 Stirling Highway, Crawley, WA 6009
Telephone: (8) 6488-6000
Fax: (8) 6488-1380
E-mail: general.enquiries@uwa.edu.au
Internet: www.uwa.edu.au

Founded 1911

Academic year: February to October

Chancellor: Dr M. CHANEY
Pro-Chancellor: Dr P. FLETT

Vice-Chancellor: Prof. A. D. ROBSON
Sr Deputy Vice-Chancellor: Prof. BILL LOUDEN
Deputy Vice-Chancellor for Education: Prof. D. MARKWELL
Deputy Vice-Chancellor for Research and Innovation: Prof. D. McEACHERN
Exec. Dir for Academic Services and Registrar: P. W. CURTIS
Exec. Dir for Finance and Resources: G. McMATH
Librarian: J. ARFIELD
Number of teachers: 1,289
Number of students: 18,650
Publication: *Research Expertise* (1 a year)

DEANS

Faculty of Architecture, Landscape and Visual Arts: D. C. BALL
Faculty of Arts, Humanities and Social Sciences: (vacant)
Faculty of Business: Dr T. HORTON
Faculty of Education: Prof. B. LOUDEN
Faculty of Engineering, Computing and Mathematics: (vacant)
Faculty of Law: Prof. W. J. FORD
Faculty of Life and Physical Sciences: Prof. G. STEWART
Faculty of Medicine, Dentistry and Health Sciences: Prof. I. PUDDEY
Faculty of Natural and Agricultural Sciences: Prof. T. O'DONNELL

PROFESSORS

ABBOTT, L. K., Soil Science and Plant Nutrition
ABBOTT, P. V., Clinical Dentistry
ACKLAND, T. R., Human Movement and Exercise Science
ALMEIDA, O. P., Geriatric Psychiatry
ANDERSON, M., Psychology
ANDRICH, D., Education
ARNOLDA, L. F., Cardiology
ATKINS, C. A., Plant Biology
ATLAS, M. D., Otolaryngology
BADCOCK, D. R., Psychology
BADDELEY, A. J., Mathematics and Statistics
BARLEY, M. E., Earth and Geographical Sciences
BARTLETT, R. H., Law
BASSOM, A., Mathematics and Statistics
BEAZLEY, L. D., Animal Biology
BEILIN, L. J., Medicine
BENNAMOUN, M., Computer Science and Software Engineering
BERNERS-PRICE, S. J., Biological Chemistry
BLAIR, D. G., Physics
BOSWORTH, A. B., Classics and Ancient History
BOSWORTH, R. J. B., History
BOWDLER, S., Archaeology
BRUCE, D. G., Medicine
BUSH, M., Mechanical Engineering
CANTONI, A., Electrical and Electronic Engineering
CASSIDY, M., Offshore Foundation Systems
CAWOOD, P., Tectonic Special Research Centre
CHENG, L., Civil and Resource Engineering
CHISHOLM, J. S., Anatomy and Human Biology
CHRISTIANSEN, F. T., Pathology
CLEMENTS, K. W., Economics
CONSTABLE, I. J., Ophthalmology and Visual Science
CORAM, A. T., Political Science and International Relations
CORDERY, J. L., Management
CROFT, K. D., Medicine
DA SILVA ROSA, R., Financial Studies
DAVIDSON, J. W., Music
DAVIS, T. M. E., Medicine
DAWSON, B. T., Human Movement and Exercise Science
DEEKS, A. J., Civil and Resource Engineering

DELL, J. M., Electrical, Electronic and Computer Engineering
DENCH, A. C., Linguistics
DENTITH, M. C., Geology
DHARMARAJAN, A. M., Anatomy and Human Biology
DYSKIN, A. V., Civil and Resource Engineering
ELLIOTT, B. C., Human Movement and Exercise Science
EMERY, J., General Practice
FAHEY, M., Civil Engineering
FARAONE, L., Electrical and Electronic Engineering
FINN, J. C., Population Health
FORD, W. J., Law
GILES-CORTI, B., Population Health
GILKES, R. J., Soil Science
GRIFFITHS, G., English and Cultural Studies
GROUNDS, M. D., Anatomy and Human Biology
GROVE, J. R., Human Movement and Exercise Science
HALL, J. C., Surgery
HAMMOND, G. R., Psychology
HANDFORD, P. R., Law
HAO, H., Civil and Resource Engineering
HARTMANN, P. E., Biochemistry
HARVEY, A. R., Anatomy and Human Biology
HASKELL, D. J., English
HICKEY, M., Gynaecology
HOLMAN, D., Population Health
HOUGHTON, S. J., Education
HULSE, G. K., Alcohol and Drug Studies
HURLE, B., Oil and Gas Engineering
IMBERGER, J., Water Research
IVEY, G. N., Environmental Systems Engineering
IZAN, H. Y., Financial Studies
JABLENSKY, A. V., Psychiatry
JANCA, A., Psychiatry
JEFFREY, G. P., Medicine
JOHNSON, M. S., Animal Biology
KAKULAS, B. A., Neuropathology
KENNEDY, D. L., Classics and Ancient History
KIRK, T. B., Mechanical Engineering
KIRSNER, P. K., Psychology
KLINKEN, S. P., Clinical Biochemistry
KNUIMAN, M. W., Population Health
LAMBERS, J. T., Plant Biology
LAUTENSCHLAGER, N. T., Geriatric Psychiatry
LEEDMAN, P. J., Cancer Medicine
LEHANE, B. M., Civil and Resource Engineering
LeSOUËF, P. N., Paediatrics
LEVINE, M. P., Philosophy
LEWANDOWSKY, S., Psychology
LIU, Y., Materials Engineering
LONDON, G. L., Architecture
LOUDEN, W. R., Education
LOVALLO, D., Management
McALEER, M., Economics
McCORMICK, P. G., Materials Engineering
McEACHERN, D., Research and Innovation
McGEACHIE, J. K., Anatomy and Human Biology
MacLEOD, C., Psychology
McMENAMIN, P. G., Anatomy and Human Biology
McSHANE, S. L., Management
MADDERN, P. C., History
MARTIN, G. B., Animal Biology
MASTAGLIA, F. L., Neurology
MILLER, K., Mechanical Engineering
MILLER, P. W., Economics
MILLWARD, M. J., Clinical Cancer Care
MILNE, G. J., Computer Science and Software Engineering
MITCHELL, H. W., Physiology
MIZERSKI, R. W., Marketing
MORAHAN, G., Diabetes Research
MORGAN, N. A., Law
MURDOCH, C., Rural and Remote Medicine
NEWNHAM, J. P., Maternal–Foetal Medicine
NIVBRANT, B., Surgery
NOAKES, J. L., Mathematics

NORMAN, P. E., Surgery
NURCOMBE, B., Paediatrics
O'DONOGHUE, T. A., Education
O'DONOVAN, J., Law
OLYNYK, J. K., Gastroenterology
OWENS, R. A., Computer Science
PAECH, M., Anaesthesia
PALMER, L., Population Health
PAN, J., Mechanical Engineering
PANNELL, D. J., Agriculture
PATTIARATCHI, C., Water Research
PAUWELS, A., Linguistics
PLATELL, C. F., Surgery
PLOWMAN, D. H., Management
PORTER, P. H., Int. Relations
POULSEN, D. G., Music
PRAEGER, C. E., Pure Mathematics
PRESCOTT, S. L., Paediatrics
PUDDEY, I., Medicine
PUNCH, K. F., Education
RAKOCZY, P. E., Ophthalmology and Visual Science
RANDOLPH, M. F., Civil Engineering
RASTON, C. L., Chemistry
RAVINE, D., Medical Genetics
REGENAUER-LIEB, K., Earth and Geographical Sciences
RENGEL, Z., Soil Science and Plant Nutrition
RHODES, G., Psychology
RILEY, T. V., Microbiology
ROBERTS, J. D., Animal Biology
ROBERTSON, A., Research Initiatives
ROBERTSON, D., Physiology
ROBINSON, B. W. S., Medicine
ROBSON, A. D., Soil Science and Plant Nutrition
SAMPSON, D. D., Electrical and Electronic Engineering
SAUNDERS, C. M., Surgery
SCHMITT, L. H., Anatomy and Human Biology
SEARES, M., Vice-Chancellery
SHARDA, H., Electrical, Electronic and Computer Engineering
SHELLAM, G. R., Microbiology
SIDDIQUE, K., Agriculture
SIMMER, K., Paediatrics
SINGER, K. P., Surgery
SIVASITHAMPARAM, K., Agriculture
SMETTEM, K. R., Environmental Systems Engineering
SOUTAR, G. N., Management
SPACKMAN, M. A., Chemistry
STACEY, M. C., Vascular Surgery
STACHOWIAK, G. W., Mechanical Engineering
STANLEY, F. J., Paediatrics
STARKSTEIN, S. E., Psychiatry
STEWART, G., Life and Physical Sciences
STEWART, G. A., Microbiology and Immunology
STICK, R., Chemistry
STOCKPORT, G. J., Management
STONE, B. J., Mechanical Engineering
SWEENEY, J. C., Marketing
TAPLIN, J. H. E., Information Management
TAYLOR, W. M., Architecture
TENNANT, M., Oral Biology
TREVELYAN, J. P., Mechanical Engineering
TURKINGTON, D. A., Economics
VENVILLE, G., Education
VRIELINK, A., Biochemistry and Molecular Biology
WADDELL, B. J., Anatomy and Human Biology
WALKER, D. I., Plant Biology
WATTS, G. F., Medicine
WEINSTEIN, P., Population Health
WELLER, R. J., Architecture
WHELAN, J., Biochemistry and Molecular Biology
WHITE, A. H., Chemistry and Crystallography
WHITE, R. S., English and Cultural Studies
WILLIAMS, J. F., Physics
WITHERS, P. C., Animal Biology
WOOD, D. J., Orthopaedics

YEOH, G., Biochemistry and Molecular Biology
ZHENG, M. H., Surgery

UNIVERSITY OF WESTERN SYDNEY

Locked Bag 1797, Penrith, South DC, NSW 1797
Telephone: (2) 9852-5555
Fax: (2) 9852-5556
E-mail: internationalstudy@uws.edu.au
Internet: www.uws.edu.au
Founded 1989
State control
Academic year: March to December
Chancellor: M. JOHN PHILLIPS
Vice-Chancellor: Prof. JANICE REID
Deputy Vice-Chancellor for Academic Services: Prof. ROBERT COOMBES
Deputy Vice-Chancellor for Devt and Int. Affairs: Prof. CHUNG-TONG WU
Academic Registrar: COLIN HAWKINS
Librarian: LIZ CURACH
Library: 1m. vols
Number of teachers: 1,001
Number of students: 32,811

DEANS

College of Arts, Education and Social Sciences: Prof. WAYNE MCKENNA
College of Law and Business: Prof. ROBIN WOELLNER
College of Science, Technology and Environment: Prof. MICK WILSON
College of Social and Health Sciences: Prof. JOHN MCCALLUM

UNIVERSITY OF WOLLONGONG

Northfields Ave, Wollongong, NSW 2522
Telephone: (2) 4221-3555
Fax: (2) 4221-3477
E-mail: askuow@uow.edu.au
Internet: www.uow.edu.au
Founded 1961 as a College of the Univ. of New South Wales; merged with Wollongong Inst. of Education 1982
Public control
Academic year: March to November (2 sessions), and a summer session from December to February
Chancellor: MICHAEL CODD
Deputy Chancellor: SUE CHAPMAN
Vice-Chancellor and Prin.: Prof. GERARD SUTTON
Vice-Prin. for Admin.: CHRIS GRANGE
Vice-Prin. for Overseas Operations: JAMES LANGRIDGE
Deputy Vice-Prin. for Finance and IT: DAMIEN ISRAEL
Deputy Vice-Chancellor for Academic and Int. Affairs: Prof. ROB CASTLE
Deputy Vice-Chancellor for Operations: Prof. JOHN PATTERSON
Pro-Vice-Chancellor for Research: Prof. MARGARET SHEIL
Dean of Studies: YVONNE KERR
Dir of the Dubai Campus: DAVID ROME (acting)
Registrar: Dr DAVID CHRISTIE (acting)
Librarian: FELICITY MCGREGOR
Library of 708,248 vols, 190,191 journals, 7,063 e-books, 510,944 monographs
Number of teachers: 801
Number of students: 23,171
Publications: *Australian Journal of Information Systems, Australian Journal of Natural Resources Law and Policy, Boxkite* (creative arts), *Illawarra Unity* (labour history), *International Journal of Forensic Psychology, Journal of University Teaching and Learning Practice, Rhizome* (2 a year)

DEANS
Faculty of Arts: Prof. JOHN PATTERSON
Faculty of Commerce: Prof. SHIRLEY LEITCH
Faculty of Creative Arts: Prof. AMANDA LAWSON
Faculty of Education: Prof. PAUL CHANDLER
Faculty of Engineering: Prof. CHRIS COOK (acting)
Faculty of Health and Behavioural Sciences: Prof. DON IVERSON
Faculty of Informatics: Prof. JOE CHICHARO
Faculty of Law: Prof. LUKE MCNAMARA
Faculty of Science: Prof. WILL PRICE
Graduate School of Business: Prof. JOHN GLYNN
Graduate School of Medicine: Prof. LIZ FARMER

PROFESSORS
Faculty of Arts:

BEDER, S., Social Sciences, Media and Communication
DODDS, S., English Literatures, Philosophy and Languages
HAGAN, J., Arts
KITLEY, P., Social Sciences, Media and Communication
MARSHALL, D., Social Sciences, Media and Communication
MARTIN, B., Social Sciences, Media and Communication
OMMUNDSEN, W., English Literature, Philosophy and Languages
WOLFERS, E., History and Politics

Faculty of Commerce:

BARRETT, M., Management and Marketing
DAWSON, P., Management and Marketing
DOLNICAR, S., Management and Marketing
GAFFIKIN, M., Accounting and Finance
LEWIS, D., Economics and Information Systems
METWALLY, M., Economics
ROSSITER, J., Management and Marketing
SPEDDING, T., Management and Marketing
VILLE, S., Economics

Faculty of Creative Arts:

LAWSON, J., Arts and Design
MILLER, S., Music and Drama
WOOD CONROY, D., Arts and Design

Faculty of Education:

DINHAM, S., Educational Leadership and Pedagogy
FERRY, B., Education
RUSSELL, T., Education
THOMAS, R., Education

Faculty of Engineering:

ARNDT, G., Mechanical Materials and Mechatronics
ARNOLD, P., Mechanical Materials and Mechatronics
BRINSON, G., Mechanical Materials and Mechatronics
BROWN, H., Coating Technology
CHIU, C., Engineering
CHOWDURY, R., Civil Mining and Environmental Engineering
DIPPENAAR, R., Mechanical Materials and Mechatronics
DOU, S., Mechanical Materials and Mechatronics
DUNNE, D., Mechanical Materials and Mechatronics
INDRARATNA, B., Civil Mining and Environmental Engineering
LEWIS, R., Engineering Physics
LIU, H., ISEM
MCCARTHY, G., Civil Mining and Environmental Engineering
METCALFE, P., Engineering Physics
NORRISH, J., Materials Welding and Joining

PERELOMA, E., Mechanical Materials and Mechatronics
PIGHATEL, G., Engineering Physics
ROBINSON, P., Engineering
ROZENFELD, A., Engineering Physics
SEN, G., Civil Mining and Environmental Engineering
SPINKS, G., Mechanical Materials and Mechatronics
TIEU, A., Mechanical Materials and Mechatronics
VARIN, R. A., Mechanical Materials and Mechatronics
ZHANG, C., Engineering Physics

Faculty of Health and Behavioural Sciences:

BARRY, R., Psychology
BUSHNELL, J., Graduate School of Medicine
CALVERT, D., Health Sciences
CARR, N., Graduate School of Medicine
CROOKES, P., Nursing, Midwifery and Indigenous Health
DEANE, F., Psychology
ELSE, P., Health Sciences
FARMER, E., Graduate School of Medicine
HEAVEN, P., Psychology
HOGG, J., Medicine
HUANG, X., Health Sciences
JONES, S., Centre for Health Initiatives
LILLIOJA, S., Health and Behavioural Sciences
MANOHARAN, A., Medicine
STEELE, J., Health Sciences
TAIT, N., Graduate School of Medicine
TAPSELL, L., Biomedical Sciences
WALSH, K., Nursing, Midwifery and Indigenous Health
YEO, W., Graduate School of Medicine

Faculty of Informatics:

BOUZERDOUM, S., Electrical, Computer and Telecommunications Engineering
BUNDER, M., Mathematics and Applied Statistics
CHAMBERS, R., Mathematics and Applied Statistics
DUTKIEWICZ, E., Electrical, Computer and Telecommunications Engineering
EKLUND, P., Information Systems and Technology
FULCHER, J., Computer Science and Software Engineering
GHOSE, A., Computer Science and Software Engineering
GOSBELL, V., Electrical, Computer and Telecommunications Engineering
GRIFFITHS, D. A., Mathematics and Applied Statistics
HILL, J., Mathematics and Applied Statistics
LANDSTAD, M., Mathematics and Applied Statistics
NAGHDY, F., Electrical, Computer and Telecommunications Engineering
OGUNBONA, P., Information Technology and Computer Science
RAEBURN, I., Mathematics and Applied Statistics
SAFAEI, F., Electrical, Computer and Telecommunications Engineering
SEBERRY, J., Information Technology and Computer Science
SOETANTO, D., Electrical, Computer and Telecommunications Engineering
STEEL, D., Mathematics and Applied Statistics
WAND, M., Mathematics and Applied Statistics
ZHU, S., Mathematics and Applied Statistics

Faculty of Law:

ANTONS, C., Comparative Law
CHAPPELL, D., Centre for Transnational Crime Prevention
CHURCHILL, R., ANCORS

FARRIER, M., Natural Resources Law and Policy

TSAMENYI, M., Centre for Maritime Policy

Faculty of Science:

AYRE, D., Biological Sciences
BRADSTOCK, R., Chemistry
BREMNER, J., Chemistry
BUTTEMER, B., Biological Sciences
CHAPPELL, B., Earth and Environmental Sciences
CHIVAS, A., Geosciences
DIXON, N., Chemistry
GRIFFITH, D., Chemistry
HEAD, L., Earth and Environmental Sciences
HULBERT, T., Biological Sciences
KANE-MAGUIRE, L., Chemistry
MORRISION, J., Earth and Environmental Science
MURRAY-WALLACE, C., Earth and Environmental Science
NANSON, G., Geosciences
NE'EMAN, G., Biological Sciences
OFFICER, D., Intelligent Polymer Research Institute
OLSSEN, M., Biological Sciences
PRICE, W., Chemistry
PYNE, S., Chemistry
WALKER, M., Biological Sciences
WALLACE, G., Intelligent Polymer Research Institute
WILSON, M., Biological Sciences
WOODROFFE, C., Earth and Environmental Sciences

Colleges

Alphacrucis College: POB 125, Chester Hill, NSW 2162; 40 Hector St, Chester Hill, NSW 2162; tel. (2) 9645-9000; fax (2) 9645-9099; e-mail info@alphacrucis.edu.au; internet alphacrucis.edu.au; f. 1948; affiliated to Australian Christian Churches, Assemblies of God and Sydney College of Divinity; campuses in Sydney, Brisbane and Auckland, New Zealand; Pres. Pastor JOHN IULIANO; Prin. Pastor STEPHEN FOGARTY; Acad. Dean Dr JACQUELINE GREY (acting); Dean of Acad. Advancement Dr MARK HUTCHINSON.

Ansto Training: Private Mail Bag 1, Menai, NSW 2234; tel. (2) 9717-9430; fax (2) 9717-9449; internet www.ansto.gov.au; f. 1964; training arm of the University of NSW and the Australian Nuclear Science and Technology Organisation; short courses in use of radioisotopes, radionuclides in medicine, radiation protection and occupational health and safety; Exec. Dir and Chief Exec. Dr IAN SMITH.

Australian Film, Television and Radio School: POB 126, North Ryde, NSW 2113; tel. (2) 9805-6611; fax (2) 9887-1030; f. 1973; library: 20,000 vols; 100 full-time students, 3,000 part-time/short course students; courses: 1- and 2-year courses (postgraduate level), 7-month commercial radio course,

short industry courses; Dir MALCOLM LONG; Library Man. MICHELE BURTON.

Australian Maritime College: POB 986, Launceston, Tas. 7250; tel. (3) 6335-4711; fax (3) 6326-6493; e-mail amcinfo@amc.edu.au; internet www.amc.edu.au; f. 1978; library: 36,800 vols; 75 teachers; 1,300 students; Principal Dr NEIL OTWAY; Asst Registrar ELIZABETH VAGG; Dir of Faculty of Fisheries and Marine Environment Dr PAUL MCSHANE; Dir of Faculty of Maritime Transport and Engineering Dr BARRIE LEWARN; Library Officer MICHELLE STEVENS; publs *AMC News*, *Handbook*.

National Art School: Forbes St, Darlinghurst, NSW 2010; tel. (2) 9339-8744; fax (2) 9339-8740; e-mail nas@det.nsw.edu.au; internet www.nas.edu.au; f. 1843; honours and masters courses offered in ceramics, painting, photography, printmaking, sculpture with painting and art history and art theory; organises a visual arts public programme; 100 teachers; 400 students; Dir BERNARD OLLIS; Deputy Dir GEOFF IRELAND.

National Institute of Dramatic Art: UNSW, Sydney, NSW 2052; tel. (2) 9697-7600; fax (2) 9662-7415; e-mail nida@unsw.edu.au; internet www.nida.edu.au; f. 1958; degree, graduate diploma and advanced diploma courses; library: 28,000 vols, 55 periodicals; 150 full-time students, 5,000 part-time students in Open Program; Dir JOHN R. CLARK.

AUSTRIA

The Higher Education System

Austria's oldest institution is the University of Vienna, established in 1365. Institutes of adult education (Volkshochschulen) are found in all provinces, as are other centres operated by public authorities, church organizations and the Austrian Trade Union Federation. The central controlling and funding body is the Federal Ministry of Education and Research. University-level education is free, and the guiding framework is based on the General Law for University Education (1966) and the University Organization Law (1975). Since 2003 extensive reforms of the higher education system have been enacted. Universities have become quasi-autonomous institutions, independent of state control. A more 'top-down' form of management has been introduced, with university councils responsible for appointing senior managers (Rektorat). Other reforms include the separation of the three medical universities from their parent institutions, the accreditation of private universities and the introduction of competitive hiring practices for recruitment of academic staff. However, reforms have been hampered by the lack of additional funding beyond inflation-level increases.

In 2007 there were 22 universities providing for 209,416 students (excl. private institutions) and 169 tertiary vocational institutions with 28,426 students. Admission to higher education is based on award of the Reifeprüfung (the certificate received upon successful completion of secondary education). In addition, all Austrian citizens over the age of 24 years, and with professional experience, may attend certain university courses in connection with their professional career or trade. However, for certain courses of study offered at Fachhochschulen students may be required to take extra examinations. Students without the Reifeprüfung can gain admission to university study by completing a preparatory course and the Studienberechtigungsprüfung examination. Successful completion of this course gives access to study in the fields in which the examinations were taken.

As one of the original signatories to the Bologna Process, Austria has implemented the two-tier system of undergraduate and graduate Bachelor and Masters level degrees alongside the traditional degrees, with a view to phasing the latter out entirely. However, medical degree programmes and upper-secondary teaching qualifications are exempt from the new system. The following degrees are available: Bakkalaureat, Diplomstudium/Magister, Fachhochschuldiplom and Kurzstudium (all undergraduate); Magisterstudium (Bologna), Aufbaustudium and Doktoratstudium (both postgraduate). The traditional undergraduate degree is the Diplomstudium, leading to the title Magister or Diplom and lasting four to six years. The Bologna equivalent is the Bakkalaureat, lasting three to four years. Students with the Diplom or Magister traditionally proceeded directly to Doctoral studies, which usually lasted between one and three years and required the writing of a thesis and the passing of final examinations, known as Rigorosum. Under the Bologna Process students are now expected to study for up to two years after the Bakkalaureat and earn the Magisterstudium before undertaking doctoral studies.

Non-university higher education is offered in Hochschulen for students, graduates and those who do not have the Reifeprüfung. Fachhochschulen were launched in 1993, entry into which requires the Reifeprüfung. These offer professional training in technology, finance and social affairs which lasts for three to four years and allows admission to doctoral studies. Akademien and Kollegs also offer vocational training.

Regulatory and Representative Bodies

GOVERNMENT

Federal Ministry of Education, Arts and Culture: Minoritenpl. 5, 1014 Vienna; tel. (1) 531-20-00; fax (1) 531-20-30-99; e-mail ministerium@bmukk.gv.at; internet www.bmukk.gv.at; Federal Minister Dr CLAUDIA SCHMIED.

Federal Ministry of Science and Research: Minoritenpl. 5, 1014 Vienna; tel. (1) 531-20-00; fax (1) 531-20-90-99; e-mail infoservice@bmwf.gv.at; internet www.bmwf.gv.at; Federal Min. Dr JOHANNES HAHN.

ACCREDITATION

Austrian Accreditation Council: Palais Harrach, Freyung 3, 1010 Vienna; tel. (1)-53120-5673; fax (1)-53120-815673; e-mail akkreditierungsrat@bmwf.gv.at; internet www.akkreditierungsrat.at; f. 1999; regulates the private instns offering univ. education in Austria; the Council is an ind. body with full decision powers over the accreditation of private univs; half of its members are Austrians, the others being experts from other European countries; this guarantees that int. standards are maintained and that the Council remains ind. of nat. conflicts of interest; Pres. Prof. Dr HANNELORE WECK-HANNEMANN.

ENIC-NARIC Austria: Bundesministerium für Wissenschaft und Forschung, Teinfaltstr. 8, 1014 Vienna; tel. (1) 53120-5920; fax (1) 53120-81-5920; internet www.bmwf.gv.at/naric; f. 1981; assessment and recognition of academic qualifications; counselling services for institutions and persons; Dir Dr HEINZ KASPAROVSKY.

Fachhochschulrat (FHR) (Accreditation Council for Universities of Applied Sciences): Liechtensteinstrasse 22A, 1090 Vienna; tel. (1) 3195034-0; fax (1) 3195034-30; e-mail office@fhr.ac.at; internet www.fhr.ac.at; f. 1993; 16 mems, half of whom are required to have the relevant post-doctoral lecturing qualification (Habilitation), the other half are required to prove that they have worked in the fields relevant for FH degree programmes for several years; ind. body responsible for the external quality assurance (accreditation and evaluation) in the Austrian FH sector; operates under Fachhochschule Studies Act (Federal Law Gazette no. 340/1993 as amended); Pres. Prof. DI Dr LEOPOLD MÄRZ; Man. Dir Dr KURT SOHM.

Österreichische Fachhochschul-Konferenz (Austrian Association of Universities of Applied Sciences): Bösendorferstr. 4/11, 1010 Vienna; tel. (1) 890-6345-20; fax (1) 890-6345-60; e-mail kurt.koleznik@fhk.ac.at; internet www.fhk.ac.at; Pres. WERNER JUNGWIRTH; Sec.-Gen. KURT KOLEZNIK.

NATIONAL BODY

OeAD (Österreichische Austausch-dienst) GmbH (Austrian Agency for International Cooperation in Education and Research): Alserstr. 4/1/3/8, 1090 Vienna; tel. (1) 4277-28101; fax (1) 4277-9281; e-mail office@oead.at; internet www.oead.at; f. 1961; 25 academic delegates; non-profit-making service org. in the field of int. co-operation in education and research; activities cover gen., academic and vocational education with emphasis on academic mobility; CEO Prof. Dr HUBERT DÜRRSTEIN.

Learned Societies

GENERAL

Österreichische Akademie der Wissenschaften (ÖAW) (Austrian Academy of Sciences (AAS)): Dr Ignaz Seipel-Pl. 2, 1010 Vienna; tel. (1) 51581-0; fax (1) 5139541; e-mail webmaster@oeaw.ac.at; internet www.oeaw.ac.at; f. 1847; sections of Mathematics and Natural Sciences (Prof. Dr GEORG STINGL), Humanities and Social Sciences (Prof. Dr HERWIG FRIESINGER (acting)); attached institutes: see Research Institutes; 160 mems, 456 corresp. mems, 16 hon. mems; library: see Libraries and Archives; Gen. Sec. Prof. Dr HERBERT MANG; Pres. Prof. Dr HERWIG FRIESINGER; Sec. Prof. Dr GEORG STINGL; publs *Almanach, Anzeiger math.-nat. Klasse, Anzeiger phil.-hist. Klasse, Denkschriften der Gesamtakademie, Denkschriften math.-nat. Klasse, Denkschriften phil.-hist. Klasse, Monatshefte für Chemie,*

*Sitzungsberichte math.-nat. Klasse Abt. I, II,
Sitzungsberichte phil.-hist. Klasse.*

AGRICULTURE, FISHERIES AND VETERINARY SCIENCE

Österreichische Gesellschaft der Tierärzte (Austrian Society of Veterinary Medicine): Veterinärpl. 1, 1210 Vienna; tel. (1) 25077-1800; fax (1) 71606-900; internet www .oegt.at; f. 1919; 1,200 mems; Pres. Prof. Dr. PETRA WINTER; Sec. Dr MICHAEL WILLMANN; publ. *Wiener Tierärztliche Monatsschrift* (12 a year).

ARCHITECTURE AND TOWN PLANNING

Österreichische Gesellschaft für Raumplanung (Austrian Society for Regional Planning): Wiedner Hauptstr. 8–10, 1040 Vienna; tel. (1) 58801-26633; fax (1) 58801-26699; e-mail oegr@oegr.at; internet www .oegr.at; Pres. Prof. Dr RUDOLF GIFFINGER; publs *FORUM Raumplanung* (2 a year), *Schriftenreihe* (irregular).

Österreichischer Ingenieur- und Architekten-Verein (Austrian Society of Engineers and Architects): Eschenbachgasse 9, 1010 Vienna; tel. (1) 5873536; fax (1) 5873536-5; e-mail office@oiav.at; internet www.oiav.at; f. 1848; 4,000 mems; Pres. Dipl.-Ing. Dr HEINZ BRANDL; Gen. Sec. Dipl.-Ing. PETER REICHEL; publ. *Österreichische Ingenieur- und Architekten-Zeitschrift* (6 a year).

Zentralvereinigung der Architekten Österreichs-ZV (Central Association of Austrian Architects): Salvatorgasse 10, 1010 Vienna; tel. (1) 5334429; e-mail zv@aaf.or.at; internet www.zv-architekten.at; f. 1907; 700 mems; Pres. HANS HOLLEIN.

BIBLIOGRAPHY, LIBRARY SCIENCE AND MUSEOLOGY

Gesellschaft für Landeskunde von Oberösterreich (Upper Austrian Cultural Heritage Association): Haus der Volkskultur, Promenade 33/103-104, 4020 Linz; tel. (732) 770218; fax (732) 770218; e-mail office@ ooelandeskunde.at; internet www .ooelandeskunde.at; f. 1833; offers cultural heritage by publs, referats, excursions; visit of exhibitions and museums; 700 mems; Chair. HR Mag. Dr GERHARD WINKLER; publs *Beiträge zur Landeskunde von Oberösterreich, Jahrbuch, Mitteilungen* (3 a year), *Schriftenreihe.*

Österreichische Gesellschaft für Dokumentation und Information (Austrian Society for Documentation and Information): Lustkandlgasse 4, 1090 Vienna; e-mail office@oegdi.at; internet www.oegdi.at; f. 1951; organizes vocational training for information professionals, workshops, conferences and lectures in the field of information science; 90 mems; Exec. Sec. Dr HERMANN HUEMER.

Vereinigung Österreichischer Bibliothekarinnen und Bibliothekare (Austrian Librarians Association): Fluher str. 4, 6901 Bregenz; tel. (5574) 51144010; fax (5574) 51144095; e-mail voeb@mail.ub .tuwien.ac.at; internet www.univie.ac.at/ voeb; f. 1946; 1,200 mems; Pres. Dr HARALD WEIGEL; publ. *Mitteilungen* (4 a year).

ECONOMICS, LAW AND POLITICS

Nationalökonomische Gesellschaft (Austrian Economics Association): Klagenfurt Univ., c/o Economics Dept, Universitätsstr. 65–67, 9020 Klagenfurt; tel. (463) 2700-4102; fax (463) 2700-4191; internet www.noeg.ac .at; f. 1918; 240 mems; Pres. Prof. REINHARD NECK; Vice-Pres. Prof. GOTTFRIED HABER;

publ. *Empirica* (applied economics and economic policy, 5 a year).

Österreichische Gesellschaft für Aussenpolitik und die Vereinten Nationen (Foreign Policy and United Nations Association of Austria): Hofburg/Stallburg, Reitschulg. 2/2. OG 1010 Vienna; tel. (1) 5354627; fax (1) 5322605; e-mail una .austria@afa.at; internet www.una-austria .org; f. 1945; 700 mems; Pres. Dr WOLFGANG SCHUESSEL; Sec.-Gen. MICHAEL F. PFEIFER.

Österreichische Gesellschaft für Kirchenrecht (Austrian Society for Ecclesiastical Law): c/o Institut für Rechtsphilosophie, Religions- und Kulturrecht Rechtswissenschaftliche, Schenkenstr. 8–10, 4-043b, 1010 Vienna; tel. (1) 427735821; fax (1) 427735899; e-mail harald.baumgartner@ univie.ac.at; internet www.univie.ac.at/ recht-religion/ogk; f. 1949; 200 mems; Pres. hon. Prof. Dr RAOUL KNEUCKER; Vice-Pres. Oberkirchenrat Mag. ROBERT KAUER; Sec. HARALD BAUMGARTNER; publ. *Österreichisches Archiv für Recht und Religion.*

Österreichische Statistische Gesellschaft (Austrian Statistical Society): c/o Statistik Austria, Guglgasse 13, 1110 Vienna; tel. (1) 71128-7269; fax (1) 71128-7445; e-mail osg@statistik.gv.at; internet www.osg.or.at; f. 1951; 600 mems; Pres. Mag. WERNER HOLZER; publ. *Österreichische Zeitschrift für Statistik* (3 or 4 a year).

Wiener Juristische Gesellschaft (Vienna Legal Association): Heinestr. 38, 1020 Vienna; tel. (1) 21300-611; fax (1) 21300-609; e-mail office@wjg.at; internet www.wjg .at; f. 1867; 600 mems; Pres. Prof. Dr WALTER BARFUSS.

EDUCATION

Österreichische Universitätenkonferenz (Universities Austria): Liechtensteinstr. 22, 1090 Vienna; tel. (1) 3105656-0; fax (1) 3105656-22; e-mail office@uniko.ac.at; internet www.uniko.ac.at; f. 1911; 21 mems; Pres. Prof. Dr HANS SÜNKEL; Sec.-Gen. HERIBERT WULZ.

Verband der Akademikerinnen Österreichs (Austrian Association of University Women): Reitschulgasse 2, 1010 Vienna; tel. (1) 5339080; internet www.vaoe.at; f. 1922; promotes scientific and professional advancement of univ. women graduates; 650 mems; Pres. MARIANNE BARGIL; Vice-Pres. Dr HELGA SZABO; publ. *VAÖ-Mitteilungen* (4 a year).

FINE AND PERFORMING ARTS

Bundesdenkmalamt (Federal Office for the Care and Protection of Monuments): Hofburg, Säulenstiege, 1010 Vienna; tel. (1) 53415-0; fax (1) 53415-252; e-mail service@ bda.at; internet www.bda.at; f. 1850; protection and restoration of historical, artistic and cultural monuments; has control of excavations and art export; 200 mems; library of 40,000 vols; Pres. Dr BARBARA NEUBAUER; publs *Corpus der mittelalterlichen Wandmalereien Österreichs, Corpus Vitrearum Medii Aevi Österreich, Dehio Handbuch, Die Kunstdenkmäler Österreichs, Fundberichte aus Österreich, Österreichische-Kunsttopographie, Österreichische Zeitschrift für Kunst und Denkmalpflege, Studien zu Denkmalschutz und Denkmalpflege, Studien zur österreichischen Kunstgeschichte, Wiener Jahrbuch für Kunstgeschichte.*

Gesellschaft der Musikfreunde in Wien (Society of Friends of Music in Vienna): Bösendorferstr. 12, 1010 Vienna; tel. (1) 5058190; fax (1) 5058190-94; e-mail office@ musikverein.at; internet www.musikverein .at; f. 1812; organizes concerts; 11,000 mems; choir of 300 mems; library: see

Libraries; collection of music, MSS, instruments etc.; Pres. Dr DIETRICH KARNER; Exec. and Artistic Dir Dr THOMAS ANGYAN; publ. *Musikfreunde* (8 a year).

Internationale Franz Lehár-Gesellschaft (International Franz Lehár Society): Lothringerstr. 20, 1030 Vienna; tel. (1) 7132761; fax (1) 8873967; e-mail alleslehar@aon.at; internet www .franz-lehar-gesellschaft.com; f. 1949; Gen. Sec. Prof. HARALD SERAFIN.

Johann Strauss-Gesellschaft Wien (Johann Strauss Society of Vienna): Hetzgasse 19/9, 1030 Vienna; tel. and fax (1) 5339194; e-mail johann-strauss-gesellschaft @utanet.at; internet www.johann-strauss-gesellschaft.at; f. 1936; 300 mems; Pres. Prof. PETER WIDHOLZ; Sec.-Gen. Prof. Mag. FRIEDRICH FALTUS; publ. *Wiener Bonbons* (4 a year).

Kunsthistorische Gesellschaft (Art History Society):; tel. (1) 427741410; fax (1) 42779414; e-mail eva-maria.grohs@univie.ac .at; f. 1956; 385 mems; Dir Prof. Dr MICHAEL VIKTER SCHWARE.

Künstlerhaus (Gesellschaft Bildender Künstler Österreichs) (Austrian Artists Association): Karlspl. 5, 1010 Vienna; tel. (1) 5879663; fax (1) 5878736; e-mail office@ k-haus.at; internet www.kuenstlerhaus.at; f. 1861; 460 mems; Pres. Arch. DI MANFRED NEHRER.

Österreichische Gesellschaft für Kommunikationswissenschaft (Austrian Society of Communications): Institut für Kommunikationswissenschaft, Universität Salzburg, Rudolfskai 42, 5020 Salzburg; tel. (662) 80444150; fax (662) 80444190; e-mail oegk@sbg.ac.at; internet www.ogk.at; f. 1976; encourages cooperation between communication researchers and communication practitioners (journalists, mediaworkers); 480 mems; Sec.-Gen. Dr THOMAS STEINMAURER; Dir Dr MICHAEL MANFÉ; publ. *Medien Journal* (4 a year).

Österreichische Gesellschaft für Musik (Austrian Music Society): Hanuschgasse 3, 1010 Vienna; tel. (1) 5123143; fax (1) 5124299; e-mail oegm@music.at; internet www.music.at/oegm; f. 1964; 1,000 mems; library of 1,000 vols mainly on contemporary music, and records; Pres. Dr WALBURGA LITSCHAUER; Vice-Pres. Prof. Dr HARALD GOERTZ; Dir Dr CARMEN OTTNER; publ. *Beiträge* (every 2 years).

Österreichischer Komponistenbund (Association of Austrian Composers): Baumannstr. 8–10, 1031 Vienna; tel. (1) 7147233; fax (1) 7147233; e-mail info@ komponistenbund.at; internet www .komponistenbund.at; f. 1913; 360 mems; Pres. Univ. Prof. KLAUS AGER; Vice-Pres KURT BRUNTHALER, MANFRED SPIES.

Wiener Beethoven Gesellschaft (Vienna Beethoven Society): Heiligenstadt, Probusgasse 6, 1190 Vienna; tel. (1) 3188215; f. 1954; 300 mems; Pres. Prof. ERWIN ORTNER; publ. *Mitteilungsblatt* (4 a year).

Wiener Konzerthausgesellschaft (Vienna Concert Hall Society): Lothringerstr. 20, 1030 Vienna; tel. (1) 24200-333; fax (1) 24200-111; e-mail mail@konzerthaus.at; internet www.konzerthaus.at; f. 1913; 6,700 mems; Pres. Dr THERESA JORDIS; publ. *Konzerthaus Nachrichten* (8 a year).

Wiener Secession (Vienna Secession Association of Visual Artists): Friedrichstr. 12, 1010 Vienna; tel. (1) 5875307; fax (1) 5875307-34; e-mail office@secession.at; internet www.secession.at; f. 1897; promotes exhibitions of contemporary art in its own gallery; 280 mems; Pres. Prof. ANDRAS PALFFY.

HISTORY, GEOGRAPHY AND ARCHAEOLOGY

Geschichtsverein für Kärnten (Historical Association of Carinthia): Museumgasse 2, 9020 Klagenfurt; tel. (463) 53630573; fax (463) 53630550; e-mail geschichtsverein@ landesmuseum-ktn.at; internet www .geschichtsverein-ktn.at; f. 1844; 2,550 mems; Dir Prof. Dr CLAUDIA FRÄSS-EHRFELD; Sec. Prof. Dr GERNOT PICCOTTINI; publs *Archiv für Vaterländische Geschichte und Topographie* (irregular), *Aus Forschung und Kunst* (irregular), *Carinthia I* (1 a year).

Heraldisch-Genealogische Gesellschaft 'Adler' ('Eagle' Heraldry and Genealogy Society): Universitätstr. 6/9B, 1096 Vienna; fax (1) 8775493; e-mail office@adler-wien.at; internet www.adler-wien.at; f. 1870; 700 mems; library of 40,000 vols; Pres. Dr GEORG KUGLER; Sec.-Gen. Dr ANDREAS CORNARO; publs *Jahrbuch*, *Zeitschrift* (4 a year).

Historische Landeskommission für Steiermark (Historical Commission for Styria): Karmeliterpl. 3/II, 8010 Graz; tel. (316) 8773013; fax (316) 8775504; e-mail office@hlkstmk.at; internet www.hlkstmk.at; f. 1892; 30 mems; Pres. Mag. FRANZ VOVES; Sec. Prof. Dr ALFRED ABLEITINGER; publs *Forschungen und Darstellungen zur Geschichte des Steiermärkischen Landtages, Forschungen zur geschichtlichen Landeskunde der Steiermark, Geschichte der Steiermark, Mitteilungsblatt der Korrespondenten der Historischen Landeskommission für Steiermark, Quellen zur geschichtlichen Landeskunde der Steiermark, Veröffentlichungen der Historischen Landeskommission für Steiermark.*

Historischer Verein für Steiermark (Styrian Historical Association): Karmeliterpl. 3, 8010 Graz; tel. and fax (316) 8772366; e-mail histor.verein.stmk@aon.at; internet members.aon.at/histor.verein.stmk; f. 1850; 1,360 mems; Chair. Prof. Dr GERHARD PFERSCHY; Sec. Dr GERNOT OBERSTEINER; publs *Beiträge zur Erforschung Steirischer Geschichtsquellen, Blätter für Heimatkunde, Zeitschrift.*

Kommission für Neuere Geschichte Österreichs (Commission for Modern Austrian History): Fachbereich Geschichte Universität Salzburg, Rudolfskai 42, 5020 Salzburg; tel. (1) 51581-7313; fax (1) 51581-7330; e-mail franz.adlgasser@oeaw.ac.at; f. 1900; research into and publishes about modern Austrian history since the 16th century; 27 mems; Chair. Prof. BRIGITTE MAZOHL; Sec. Dr FRANZ ADLGASSER; publ. *Veröffentlichungen.*

Österreichische Byzantinische Gesellschaft (Austrian Byzantine Society): Postgasse 7–9, 1010 Vienna; tel. (1) 427741001; fax (1) 42779410; internet www .univie.ac.at/byzneo; f. 1946; 145 mems; Pres. Prof. Dr JOHANNES KODER; publ. *Mitteilungen aus der österreichischen Byzantinistik und Neogräzistik* (1 a year).

Österreichische Geographische Gesellschaft (Austrian Geographical Society): Karl Schweighofer-Gasse 3, 1071 Vienna; tel. and fax (1) 5237974; internet www.oegg.info; f. 1856; 1,400 mems; Pres. Dr CHRISTIAN STAUDACHER; Hon. Pres. Dr INGRID KRETSCHMER; library: see Libraries; publ. *Mitteilungen* (1 a year).

Österreichische Gesellschaft für Archäologie (Austrian Archaeological Society): c/o Institut für Alte Geschichte, Altertumskunde und Epigraphik, Universität Wien, Dr Karl Lueger-Ring I, 1010 Vienna; e-mail oega@univie.ac.at; internet www.univie.ac .at/oega; f. 1972; publishes on topics relevant to Austria in archaeology, ancient history

and numismatics; public lectures, excursions; 190 mems; Pres. Doz. Dr PETER SCHERRER; publs *Althistorisch-epigraphische Studien* (irregular), *Austria Antiqua* (irregular), *Römisches Österreich* (1 a year).

Österreichische Gesellschaft für Ur- und Frühgeschichte (Austrian Society for Pre- and Early History): Franz-Klein-Gasse 1, 1190 Vienna; tel. (1) 4277-40473; fax (1) 4277-9404; internet www.oeguf.ac.at; f. 1950; 1,050 mems; Gen. Sec. Mag. ALEXANDRA KRENN-LEEB; publ. *Archäologie Österreichs* (2 a year).

Österreichische Numismatische Gesellschaft (Austrian Numismatic Society): Burgring 5, 1010 Vienna; tel. (1) 52524-4201; fax (1) 52524-4299; e-mail office@oeng.at; internet www.oeng.at; f. 1870; 400 mems; library of 5,000 vols; Pres. Prof. GÜNTHER DEMBSKI; Vice-Pres. DIETMAR SPRANZ; Dir Dr MICHAEL ALRAM; publs *Mitteilungen* (2 a year), *Numismatische Zeitschrift* (irregular).

Österreichische Orient-Gesellschaft (Austrian Orient Society): Dominikanerbastei 6/6, 1010 Vienna; tel. (1) 512893611; fax (1) 512893617; e-mail office@ orient-gesellschaft.at; internet www .orient-gesellschaft.at; f. 1952; Gen.Sec. Dr SIEGFRIED HAAS.

Verband Österreichischer Historiker und Geschichtsvereine (Union of Austrian Historians and Historical Associations): Österreichisches Staatsarchiv Nottendorfergasse 2, 1030 Vienna; tel. (1) 79540-100; fax (1) 79540-109; e-mail lorenz.mikoletzky @ oesta.gv.at; f. 1949; 130 mem. socs; Pres. WILLIBALD ROSNER; Vice-Pres. Prof. Dr LORENZ MIKOLETZKY; Gen. Sec. Dr ERWIN A. SCHMIDL; publ. *Veröffentlichungen des Verbands Österreichischer Historiker und Geschichtsvereine* (every 2 or 3 years).

Verein für Geschichte der Stadt Wien (Association for the History of the City of Vienna): Wiener Stadt- und Landesarchiv, Rathaus, 1082 Vienna; tel. (1) 400084808; fax (1) 400084809; e-mail post@m08.magwien.gv .at; internet www.wien.gv.at/ma08/vgw/; f. 1853; 1,592 mems; Pres. Dr KLARALINDA MA-KIRCHER; Vice-Pres. Dr HELMUT KRETSCHMER; Sec. Dr KARL FISCHER; publs *Studien zur Wiener Geschichte* (1 a year), *Wiener Geschichtsblätter* (4 a year).

LANGUAGE AND LITERATURE

Austria Esperantista Federacio (Austrian Esperanto Society): Postfach 39, 1014 Vienna; tel. (1) 8934196; e-mail aef@ esperanto.at; internet aef.esperanto.at; f. 1935; 500 mems; library of 1,500 vols, 1,000 pamphlets; Pres. Mag. HERBERT MAYER; Vice-Pres. Prof. Dr HANS-MICHAEL MAITZEN; Gen. Sec. RICHARD HABLE; publs *Austria-Esperanto-Revuo, Esperanto-Servo* (4 a year).

British Council: Siebensterngasse 21, 1070 Vienna; tel. (1) 533-2616; fax (1) 533-261665; e-mail office@britishcouncil.at; internet www .britishcouncil.at; f. 1946; offers courses and examinations in English language and British culture and promotes cultural exchange with the UK; library contains large colln of modern British fiction, titles on British studies and English language-learning materials; access to British websites, databases and learning software; Dir WILL TODD.

Eranos Vindobonensis: Institut für Klassische Philologie, Mittel- und Neulatein, Universität Wien, Dr Karl Lueger-Ring 1, 1010 Vienna; tel. (1) 4277-41916; fax (1) 4277-9419; internet www.univie.ac.at/ klassphil/eranos.html; f. 1885; philological soc.; 90 mems; Pres. Prof. Dr F. GREWING; Sec. Dr P. LORENZ.

Gesellschaft für Klassische Philologie in Innsbruck (Classical Philological Society of Innsbruck): Institut für Klassische Philologie, Universität Innsbruck, Innrain 52, Innsbruck; tel. (512) 5074082; fax (512) 5072982; e-mail klassphil@uibk.ac.at; internet www.uibk.ac.at/sci-org/klassphil; f. 1958; 200 mems; Dir Mag. FLORIAN SCHAFFERNATH; Sec. Mag. STEFAN TILG; publ. *Acta philologica Aenipontiana.*

Gesellschaft zur Förderung Slawistischer Studien (Society for Slavic Studies): Teschnergasse 4/17, 1180 Vienna; f. 1983; Dir AAGE HANSEN-LÖVE; publs *Journal* (2 a year), *Wiener Slawistischer Almanach*, monograph series (4 a year).

Instituto Cervantes: Schwarzenbergpl. 2, 1010 Vienna; tel. (1) 5052535; fax (1) 505253518; e-mail cenvie@cervantes.es; internet viena.cervantes.es; f. 1995; offers courses and examinations in Spanish language and culture and promotes cultural exchange with Spain and Spanish-speaking Latin and Central America; library of 27,000 vols, 70 periodicals; Dir CARLOS ORTEGA.

Österreichische Gesellschaft für Literatur (Austrian Literary Society): Herrengasse 5, 1010 Vienna; tel. (1) 5338159; fax (1) 5334067; e-mail office@ogl.at; internet www .ogl.at; f. 1961; Pres. MARIANNE GRUBER.

Wiener Goethe-Verein (Vienna Goethe Association): Stallburggasse 2, 1010 Vienna; internet www.univie.ac.at/goethe-verein; f. 1878; 300 mems; library of 2,000 books; Pres. Prof. Dr HERBERT ZEMAN; publ. *Jahrbuch.*

Wiener Humanistische Gesellschaft: Institut für Klassische Philologie, Mittel- und Neulatein, Univ. Wien, Dr-Karl-Lueger-Ring 1, 1010 Vienna; tel. (1) 4277-41901; fax (1) 4277-9429; e-mail herbert .bannert@univie.ac.at; internet www.univie .ac.at/klassphil; f. 1947; philological soc.; promotes humanities; 600 mems; Jt Pres. Prof. HEINRICH STREMITZER; Jt Pres. Prof. KURT SMOLAK; Sec. Dr MARGIT KAMPTNER; Administrator ANDREA DUCHAC; publ. *Wiener Humanistische Blätter.*

Wiener Sprachgesellschaft (Vienna Language Society): Institut für Sprachwissenschaft, Universität, 1010 Vienna; internet www.univie.ac.at/indogermanistik/ wsg; f. 1947; 150 mems; Pres. Prof. GERHARD BUDIN; Sec.-Gen. Dr H. CH. LUSCHÜTZKY; publ. *Die Sprache* (1 a year).

MEDICINE

Gesellschaft der Ärzte in Wien (Vienna Society of Physicians): Postfach 147, Frankgasse 8, 1090 Vienna; tel. (1) 4054777; fax (1) 4023090; e-mail info@billrothhaus.at; internet www.billrothhaus.at; f. 1837; 2,500 mems; library of 200,000 vols, 25,900 monographs; Pres. Univ. Prof. Dr KARL-HEINZ TRAGL; Secs Univ. Prof. Dr PAUL AIGINGER, Univ. Prof. Dr BEATRIX VOLC-PLATZER; publ. *Wiener Klinische Wochenschrift.*

Gesellschaft der Chirurgen in Wien (Vienna Society of Surgeons): c/o Universitätsklinik für Chirurgie, Klin. Abteilung für Allgemeinchirurgie, Währinger Gürtel 18–20, 1090 Vienna; tel. (1) 404006566; fax (1) 404006566; e-mail chirurgie@billrothhaus.at; internet www.chirurgie-ges.at; f. 1935; 171 mems; Pres. Prof. Dr ADELHEID END; Sec. Prof. Dr BÉLA TELEKY.

Internationale Paracelsus-Gesellschaft: Duerlingerstr. 23, 5020 Salzburg; tel. (662) 826773; e-mail info@paracelsus-ipg.com; internet www.teamforweb.at/kunden/ paracelsus-ipg; f. 1951; 315 mems; 27 mem. asscns; Pres. Prof. Dr HEINZ DOPSCH; Gen. Sec. GERTRAUD WEISS; publs *Parcelsus-Briefe,*

Salzburger Beiträge zur Paracelsusforschung.

Österreichische Gesellschaft für Anästhesiologie, Reanimation und Intensivmedizin (Austrian Society of Anaesthesiology, Resuscitation and Intensive Care Medicine): Höfergasse 13, 1090 Vienna; tel. (1) 4064810; fax (1) 4064811; e-mail office@oegari.at; internet www.oegari .at; f. 1951; 1,300 mems; Pres. Prof. Dr HANS GOMBOTZ; Sec. Prof. Dr C.-G. KRENN; publ. *A + IC News* (4 a year).

Österreichische Gesellschaft für Arbeitsmedizin (Austrian Society for Occupational Health): Kaplanhofstr. 1, 4020 Linz; tel. (732) 781560-0; fax (732) 784594; internet www.gamed.at; f. 1954; 350 mems; Pres. Dr REINHARD JÄGER.

Österreichische Gesellschaft für Chirurgie (Austrian Society for Surgery): Frankgasse 8, POB 80, 1096 Vienna; tel. (1) 4087920; fax (1) 4081328; e-mail chirurgie@ billrothhaus.at; internet www.chirurgie-ges .at; f. 1958; incl. the associated Austrian socs for Traumatology, Orthopaedic, Thoracic and Cardiac Surgery, Vascular Surgery, Neurosurgery, Obesity Surgery, Paediatric Surgery, Plastic, Aesthetic and Reconstructive Surgery, Surgical Oncology, Osteosynthesis, Coloproctology, Hand Surgery, Surgical Research, Maxillo-Facial Surgery, Surgical Endocrinology, Keyhole Surgery, Medical Videography, Surgical Endoscopy, Hernia Surgery, Implantology and Tissue-Integrated Prosthesis, Austrian Section of the Int. Soc. for Digestive Surgery; 4,819 mems; Sec.-Gen. Prof. Dr RUDOLF ROKA; publ. *European Surgery / Acta Chirurgica Austriaca* (6 a year); publ. *Chirurgie* (4 a year).

Österreichische Gesellschaft für Dermatologie und Venereologie (Austrian Dermatological and Venereological Society): c/o Wiener Medizinische Akademie für ärztliche Fortbildung und Forschung, Alser str. 4, 1090 Vienna; tel. (1) 405138320; fax (1) 405138323; internet www.oegdv.at; 876 mems; Pres. Dr H. J. RAUCH; Vice-Pres. Prof. Dr H. PEHAMBERGER.

Österreichische Gesellschaft für Geriatrie und Gerontologie (Austrian Society for Geriatrics and Gerontology): Sozialmedizinisches Zentrum, Apollogasse 19, 1070 Vienna; tel. (1) 521035770; fax (1) 521035779; internet www.geriatrie-online .at; f. 1955; 400 mems; library of 2,000 vols; Pres. Prof. Dr PETER PIETSCHMANN; Vice-Pres. Dr HANNES PLANK; Vice-Pres. Dr MONIKA LECHLEITNER; publs *Aktuelle Gerontologie* (12 a year), *European Journal of Geriatrics*, *Geriatrie Praxis Österreich* (4 a year), *Scriptum Geriatricum* (1 a year).

Österreichische Gesellschaft für Hals-, Nasen-, Ohrenheilkunde Kopf- und Halsschirurgie (Austrian Society of Ear, Nose and Throat Science, Head and Neck Surgery): Ebene 8, Währinger Gürtel 18–20, 1090 Vienna; tel. (1) 40400-3321; fax (1) 40400-3350; e-mail sekretariat@hno.at; internet www.hno.at; f. 1892; 640 mems; Pres. Prof. Dr P. ZOROWKA; Gen. Sec. Prof. Dr KLAUS ALBEGGER; publ. *Zeitschrift.*

Österreichische Gesellschaft für Innere Medizin (Austrian Society for Internal Medicine): Medical University of Graz, University Clinic for Internal Medicine Auenbruggerplatz 15, 8036 Graz; tel. (316) 3856888; fax (316) 3853062; e-mail oegim@ oegim.at; internet www.oegim.at; f. 1886; 400 mems; Pres. Prof. Dr ERNST PILGER; Sec. Prof. Dr MARKUS PECK-RADOSAVLJEVIC; publ. *Wiener Zeitschrift für Innere Medizin.*

Österreichische Gesellschaft für Kinder- und Jugendheilkunde (Austrian Society for Paediatrics): c/o Frau Liesbeth Kautschitsch, LKH Klagenfurt, Abteilung für Kinder- und Jugendheilkunde, St Veiter Str. 47, 9026 Klagenfurt; tel. (463) 538-39403; fax (463) 538-39408; e-mail praesident.oegkj@kabeg.at; internet www .docs4you.at; f. 1962; 805 mems; Pres. Prof. Dr WILHELM KAULFERSCH; Sec. Prim. MARTIN EDLINGER; publs *Monatsschrift Kinderheilkunde* (online), *Pädiatrie und Pädologie* (6 a year).

Österreichische Gesellschaft für Klinische Neurophysiologie (Austrian Clinical Neurophysiological Society): Institut für Neurophysiologie der Universität Wien, Währingerstr. 18–20, 1090 Vienna; internet www.oegkn.at; f. 1954; 250 mems; Pres. Prof Dr CHRISTOPH BAUMGARTNER, Dr MARTIN GRAF; Secs Prof. Dr WOLFGANG SERLES, Dr EUGEN TRINKA; publs *EEG / EMG, Thieme* (4 a year).

Österreichische Gesellschaft für Urologie und Andrologie (Austrian Society for Urology and Andrology): SMZOst-Donauspital, Abteilung f. Urologie und Andrologie, Langobardenstr. 122, 1220 Vienna; tel. (1) 28802-3702; fax (1) 28802-3780; internet www.uro.at; 511 mems; Pres. Prof. Dr WALTER STACKL; Sec. Dr MICHAEL RAUCHENWALD.

Österreichische Gesellschaft zum Studium der Sterilität und Fertilität (Austrian Society for the Study of Sterility and Fertility): Währinger Gürtel 18–20, 1090 Vienna; tel. (1) 404002813; internet www .univie.ac.at/frauenheilkunde/endokrinologie; Pres. Prof. Dr G. TSCHERNE; Sec. Prof. Dr J. C. HUBER.

Österreichische Ophthalmologische Gesellschaft (Austrian Ophthalmological Society): Schlüsselgasse 9, 1080 Vienna; tel. (1) 4028540; fax (1) 4027935; e-mail oeog@ augen.at; internet www.augen.at; f. 1955; 730 mems; library of 2,100 vols; Pres. Prof. Dr SUSANNE BINDER; Sec. Prof. Dr GÜNTHER GRABNER; publ. *Spectrum der Augenheilkunde* (6 a year).

Österreichische Röntgengesellschaft— Gesellschaft für Medizinische Radiologie und Nuklearmedizin (Society for Medical Radiology and Nuclear Medicine): c/o Vienna Medical Academy University Campus, 1 Hof, DION, 2 Stick, Alser Str. 4, 1090 Vienna; tel. (1) 4051-38321; fax (1) 4051-38323; e-mail skonstantinou@medacad.org; internet www.oerg.info; f. 1946; 800 mems; Pres. Prof. Dr DIMITER TSCHOLAKOFF; publ. *ÖRG—Mitteilungen* (4 a year).

Verein für Psychiatrie und Neurologie (Society for Psychiatry and Neurology): Neurologische Universitätsklinik, Währinger Gürtel 18–20, 1090 Vienna; tel. (1) 404003514; f. 1867; Pres. Prof. Dr KENNETH THAU; Secs Prof. Dr GABRIELE SACHS, Dr BERNHARD VOLLER.

Wiener Medizinische Akademie für Ärztliche Fortbildung und Forschung (Vienna Academy of Postgraduate Medical Education and Research): Alser str. 4, 1090 Vienna; tel. (1) 4051383-0; fax (1) 4051383-23; e-mail rk@medacad.org; internet www .medacad.org; f. 1896; Pres. Prof. Dr H. GRÜBER; Exec. Dirs JEROME DEL PICCHIA, ROMANA KÖNIG; Secs Prof. Dr A. TUCHMANN, Prof. Dr C. ZIELINSKI.

NATURAL SCIENCES

General

Naturwissenschaftlicher Verein für Kärnten (Carinthian Association of Natural Sciences): Museumgasse 2, 9021 Klagenfurt; tel. (463) 53630574; fax (463) 53630597; e-mail nwv@landesmuseum-ktn.at; internet www.naturwissenschaft-ktn.at; f. 1848; 1,300 mems; Pres. Dr HELMUT ZWANDER; publ. *Carinthia II* (1 a year, with special issues).

Biological Sciences

Österreichische Mykologische (Pilzkundliche) Gesellschaft (Austrian Mycological Society): Rennweg 14, 1030 Vienna; tel. (1) 4277-54050; fax (1) 4277-9541; e-mail irmgard.greilhuber@univie.ac.at; internet www.myk.univie.ac.at; f. 1919; 320 mems; library of 1,000 vols; mycological herbarium colln, fungal records online database, excursions, lectures, newsletter; Pres. Dkfm A. HAUSKNECHT; Vice-Pres. IRMGARD GREILHUBER; publ. *Österreichische Zeitschrift für Pilzkunde* (1 a year).

Zoologisch-Botanische Gesellschaft in Österreich (Austrian Zoological-Botanical Society): Althanstr. 14, Postfach 207, 1091 Vienna; fax (1) 4277-9542; e-mail wolfgang .punz@univie.ac.at; internet www.univie.ac .at/zoobot; f. 1851; lectures; excursions; library; publs; exchange of publs; nature conservation; botanical illustration courses; library: spec. library for zoology, botany and ecology; 610 mems; Pres. Dr ERICH HÜBL; Sec. Gen. Dr WOLFGANG PUNZ; publs *Abhandlungen* (irregular), *Koleopterologische Rundschau* (1 a year), *Verhandlungen* (1 a year).

Mathematical Sciences

Mathematisch-Physikalische Gesellschaft in Innsbruck (Mathematics and Physics Society of Innsbruck): c/o Manfred P. Leubner, Institut für Astrophysik, Universität Innsbruck, Technikerstr. 25, 6020 Innsbruck; tel. (512) 512-6060; fax (512) 512-2923; e-mail math-phys-ges@uibk.ac.at; internet www.uibk.ac.at/sci-org/ math-phys-ges; f. 1936; 126 mems; Chair. MANFRED P. LEUBNER.

Österreichische Mathematische Gesellschaft (Austrian Mathematical Society): Technische Univ., E104, Wiedner Hauptstr. 8–10, 1040 Vienna; tel. (1) 5880111823; e-mail oemg@oemg.ac.at; internet www.oemg.ac.at; f. 1903; 537 mems; Chair. M. DRMOTA; Sec. F. URBANEK; publs *International Mathematical News* (3 a year), *Monatshefte für Mathematik* (12 a year).

Physical Sciences

Chemisch-Physikalische Gesellschaft in Wien (Vienna Chemical-Physical Society): Strudlhofgasse 4, 1090 Vienna; tel. (1) 427751153; f. 1869; 260 mems; Sec. Prof. Dr GEORG REISCHL; publ. *Bulletin* (2 a year).

Gesellschaft Österreichischer Chemiker (Austrian Chemical Society): Nibelungengasse 11/6, 1010 Vienna; tel. (1) 5874249; fax (1) 5878966; e-mail office@goech.at; internet www.goech.at; f. 1897; educational programme for professional advancement in chemistry; 1,900 mems in attached socs; Pres. Dr HAIO HARMS; Vice-Pres. Prof. Dr WOLFGANG BUCHBERGER; Exec. Dir Dr ERICH LEITNER; publs *Chemiereport.at* (online at: www.chemiereport.at), *Chemistry–A European Journal* (co-author), *Monatshefte für Chemie.*

Österreichische Geologische Gesellschaft (Austrian Geological Society): Geologische Bundesanstalt, Neulinggasse 38, 1030 Vienna; tel. (1) 7125674-0; fax (1) 7125674-56; e-mail oegg@geologie.ac.at; internet www.geol-ges.at; f. 1907; 714 mems; Pres. WOLFGANG NACHTMANN; Vice-Pres. CHRISTIAN SPÖTL; publ. *Austrian Journal of Earth Sciences.*

Österreichische Gesellschaft für Analytische Chemie (Austrian Society for Analytical Chemistry): tel. (1) 427752300;

internet www.asac.at; f. 1948; 400 mems; Pres. Prof. Dr WOLFGANG LINDNER; Sec. Prof. Dr W. BUCHBERGER.

Österreichische Gesellschaft für Erdölwissenschaften (Austrian Society for Petroleum Sciences): c/o Wirtschaftskammer Österreich, Wiedner Hauptstr. 63, Zimmer 4208, 1045 Vienna; tel. (5) 909004891; e-mail oegew@oil-gas.at; internet www.oegew.org; f. 1960; 502 mems; Pres. JOSEF HIEBLINGER; publs *Erdöl Erdgas Kohle*, scientific papers.

Österreichische Gesellschaft für Laboratoriumsmedizin und Klinische Chemie (Austrian Society of Laboratory Medicine and Clinical Chemistry): Tullnertalgasse 72, 1230 Vienna; tel. and fax (1) 8896238; e-mail office@oeglmkc.at; internet www.oeglmkc.at; f. 2004; Pres. Prof. Dr ILSE SCHWARZINGER; Sec. Doz. Dr WOLFGANG HÜBL.

Österreichische Gesellschaft für Meteorologie (Austrian Meteorological Society): Hohe Warte 38, 1190 Vienna; tel. (1) 36026-2201; fax (1) 3602672; internet www.meteorologie.at; f. 1865; 230 mems; Pres. Prof. Dr FRANZ RUBEL; Sec. Dr ERNEST RUDEL; publ. *ÖGM-Bulletin*.

Österreichische Gesellschaft für Molekulare Biowissenschaften und Biotechnologie (Austrian Association for Molecular Life Sciences and Biotechnology): OeGMBT Secretariat, c/o Dept of Applied Genetics and Cell Biology, University of Agricultural Sciences Vienna, Muthgasse 18, 1190 Vienna; e-mail andrea.veitschegger@boku.ac.at; internet www.oegmbt.at; promotion of research and education in biochemistry, molecular biology and cell biology; 900 mems; Pres. HANS GRUNICKE; Vice-Pres. JOSEF GLOESSL; Exec. Dir ANDREA VEITSCHEGGER; publ. *ÖGBM Nachrichten* (4 a year).

Österreichische Physikalische Gesellschaft (Austrian Physical Society): c/o Dr Max E. Lippitsch, Institut für Physik, Karl-Franzens-Universität Graz, Universitätspl. 5, 8010 Graz; tel. (316) 380-5192; fax (316) 380-9816; e-mail office@oepg.at; internet www.oepg.at; f. 1950; 870 mems; Pres. Prof. Dr ERICH GORNIK; Exec. Dir Prof. Dr MAX E. LIPPITSCH; publ. *Mitteilungsblatt der ÖPG*.

Österreichischer Astronomischer Verein (Austrian Astronomical Association): Hasenwartgasse 32, 1230 Vienna; tel. (1) 8893541-0; fax (1) 8893541-11; e-mail astbuero@astronomisches-buero-wien.or.at; internet astronomische-buero-wien.or.at; f. 1924; astronomical phenomenology; organizes lectures and guided tours; 1,500 mems; Pres. Univ. Prof. Dipl.-Ing. Dr ROBERT WEBER; Man. Dir Prof. HERMANN MUCKE; publs *Astronomische Buero: Der Sternenbote* (12 a year), *Der Sternenbote* (12 a year), *Österreichischer Himmelskalender* (1 a year).

PHILOSOPHY AND PSYCHOLOGY

Österreichische Gesellschaft für Parapsychologie und Grenzbereiche der Wissenschaften (Austrian Society for Parapsychology and Frontier Areas of Science): c/o Manfred Kremser, Institute for Social and Cultural Anthropology, Univ. of Vienna, Universitätsstr. 7, 1010 Vienna; tel. (1) 427748507; e-mail office@parapsychologie .ac.at; internet parapsychologie.ac.at; f. 1927; 180 mems; library of 1,200 vols; Pres. Prof. Dr MANFRED KREMSER; Vice-Pres. and Sec.-Gen. Prof. W. PETER MULACZ.

Philosophische Gesellschaft Wien (Philosophical Society of Vienna): Universitätsstr. 7/2/2, 1010 Vienna; tel. (1) 4277-47402; fax (1) 4277-47492; f. 1954; 100 mems; Dir Prof. Dr HANS-DIETER KLEIN.

Sigmund Freud Privatstiftung (Sigmund Freud Foundation): Berggasse 19, 1090 Vienna; tel. (1) 3191596; fax (1) 3170279; e-mail office@freud-museum.at; internet www.freud-museum.at; f. 1968; history and application of psychoanalysis; 1,000 mems; library of 8,000 vols, 15,000 off-prints, 45 journals; archives; Sigmund Freud museum; Chair. Mag. INGE SCHOLZ-STRASSER.

Wiener Psychoanalytische Vereinigung (Vienna Psychoanalytic Society): Salzgries 16/3, 1010 Vienna; tel. (1) 5330767; e-mail office@wpv.at; internet www.wpv.at; f. 1908; 200 mems; Pres. Dr ELISABETH SKALE; Sec. VIOLA SEIBERT.

RELIGION, SOCIOLOGY AND ANTHROPOLOGY

Anthropologische Gesellschaft in Wien (Vienna Anthropological Society): Burgring 7, 1010 Vienna; tel. (1) 52177-569; fax (1) 52177-309; e-mail ag@nhm-wien.ac.at; internet www.nhm-wien.ac.at/ag; f. 1870; 300 mems; Pres. HR. Dr HERBERT KRITSCHER; Sec. HR. Dr ANTON KERN; publs *Anthropologische Forschungen* (irregular), *Mitteilungen der Anthropologischen Gesellschaft in Wien* (1 a year), *Prähistorische Forschungen* (irregular), *Völkerkundliche Veröffentlichungen* (irregular).

Evangelische Akademie Wien (Evangelical Academy in Vienna): Schwarzspanierstr. 13, 1090 Vienna; tel. (1) 4080695; fax (1) 408009533; e-mail akademie@evang.at; internet www.evang.at/akademie; f. 1955; Protestant adult education; documentation on church and society; Dir ROLAND RITTER-WERNECK.

Gesellschaft für die Geschichte des Protestantismus in Österreich (Society for History of Protestantism in Austria): c/o Univ. Prof. Dr Rudolf Leeb, Room 6OG009, Schenkenstr. 8–10, 1010 Vienna; e-mail rudolf.leeb@univie.ac.at; f. 1879; 300 mems; Pres. Prof. Dr RUDOLF LEEB.

Österreichische Gesellschaft für Soziologie (Austrian Sociological Society): Institut für Soziologie der Universität Graz, Universitätsstr. 15/G4, 8010 Graz; tel. (316) 3803544; fax (316) 3809515; e-mail kontakt@oegs.ac.at; internet www.oegs.ac.at; f. 1950; 500 mems; Pres. Prof. Dr CHRISTIAN FLECK; publ. *Österreichische Zeitschrift für Soziologie* (4 a year).

Verein für Landeskunde von Niederösterreich (Association for Regional Studies of Lower Austria): Landhauspl. 1, 3109 St Pölten; tel. (2742) 9005-16255; fax (2742) 9005-16550; e-mail postk2institut@noel.gv .at; internet www.noel.gv.at/bildung/ landeskundliche-forschung/verein-fuer-landeskunde.html; f. 1864; 1,300 mems; Pres. Hofrat Dr ANTON EGGENDORFER; Gen. Sec. Mag. Dr WILLIBALD ROSNER; publs *Forschungen zur Landeskunde von Niederösterreich, Jahrbuch für Landeskunde von Niederösterreich, Unsere Heimat* (4 a year).

Verein für Volkskunde (Society of Ethnography and Popular Culture): Laudongasse 15–19, 1080 Vienna; tel. (1) 4068905; fax (1) 4085342; internet www.volkskundemuseum .at; f. 1894; 900 mems; Pres. Dr KONRAD KÖSTLIN; Sec. Dr MARGOT SCHINDLER; publs *Buchreihe der Österreichischen Zeitschrift für Volkskunde* (irregular), *Documenta Ethnographica* (irregular), *Österreichische Volkskundliche Bibliographie* (every 2–3 years), *Österreichische Zeitschrift für Volkskunde* (4 a year), *Sonderschriften, Volkskunde in Österreich* (12 a year).

Wiener Katholische Akademie (Vienna Catholic Academy): Edith-Stein-Haus, Ebendorferstr. 8/10, 1010 Vienna; tel. and fax (1) 4023917; internet stephanscom.at/edw/ akademie.html; f. 1945; seminars and lectures, symposia, publications; 110 mems; library of 7,000 vols; Protector Erzbischof Cardinal Dr C. SCHÖNBORN; Dir Dr E. MAIER; publ. *Schriften der Wiener Katholischen Akademie*.

TECHNOLOGY

Österreichische Gesellschaft für Artificial Intelligence (Austrian Association for Artificial Intelligence): POB 177, 1014 Vienna; tel. (1) 427763117; e-mail anfrage@ oegai.at; internet www.oegai.at; f. 1981; 150 mems; Pres. ERNST BUCHBERGER; publ. *ÖGAI-Journal* (4 a year).

Österreichische Gesellschaft für Vermessung und Geoinformation (Austrian Society for Surveying and Geoinformation): Schiffamtsgasse 1–3, 1020 Vienna; tel. and fax (1) 2167551; e-mail office@ovg.at; internet www.ovg.at; f. 1973; 600 mems; library of 3,000 vols; Pres. Dipl.-Ing. GERT STEINKELLNER; Sec. Dipl.-Ing. KARL HAUSSTEINER; publ. *Österreichische Zeitschrift für Vermessung und Geoinformation* (4 a year).

Österreichische Studiengesellschaft für Kybernetik (Austrian Society for Cybernetic Studies): Freyung 6/6, 1010 Vienna; tel. (1) 5336112-60; fax (1) 5336112-77; e-mail sec@ofai.at; internet www.ofai.at; f. 1969; 1,238 mems (38 ordinary, 1,200 corresp.); Pres. Prof. Dr ROBERT TRAPPL; publs *Cybernetics and Systems: An International Journal* (8 a year), *Reports* (irregular).

Research Institutes

AGRICULTURE, FISHERIES AND VETERINARY SCIENCE

Bundesamt und Forschungszentrum für Landwirtschaft, Wien (Federal Office and Research Centre for Agriculture, Vienna): Spargelfeldstr. 191, Postfach 400, 1226 Vienna; tel. (1) 73216-0; fax (1) 73216-2100; internet www.bfl.ac.at; f. 1995; library of 100,000 vols; Dir-Gen. Hofrat Dipl.-Ing. A. KÖCHL; publs *Die Bodenkultur* (4 a year), *Pflanzenschutz* (4 a year), *Pflanzenschutzberichte* (2 a year).

Bundesamt und Forschungszentrum für Wald (Federal Office and Research Centre for Forests): Seckendorff-Gudent-Weg 8, 1131 Vienna; tel. (1) 878380; fax (1) 878381250; e-mail direktion@bfw.gv.at; internet bfw.ac.at; f. 1874; library of 48,000 vols; Dir HARALD MAUSER; publ. *BFW-Berichte* (irregular).

Bundesanstalt für Agrarwirtschaft (Federal Institute of Agricultural Economics): Marxergasse 2, 1030 Vienna; tel. (1) 8773651; fax (1) 8773651-7490; e-mail office@awi.bmlfuw.gv.at; internet www.awi .bmlfuw.gv.at; f. 1960; applied research; library of 48,000 vols, 424 periodicals; Dir Dipl.-Ing. Dr HUBERT PFINGSTNER; Librarian HUBERT SCHLIEBER; publs *Agrarpolitische Arbeitsbehelfe* (irregular), *Schriftenreihe der Bundesanstalt* (irregular).

Bundesanstalt für Alpenländische Landwirtschaft, Gumpenstein (Federal Research Institute for Agriculture in Alpine Regions, Gumpenstein): Steiermark, 8952 Irdning; tel. (3682) 22451-0; fax (3682) 22451-21; e-mail office@ raumberg-gumpenstein.at; internet www .gumpenstein.at; f. 1947; library of 21,000 vols; Dir Dr ALBERT SONNLEITNER; publs *BAL-Berichte, BAL-Veröffentlichungen*.

ARCHITECTURE AND TOWN PLANNING

Österreichisches Institut für Raumplanung (Austrian Institute for Regional Studies and Spatial Planning): Franz Josefs Kai 27, 1010 Vienna; tel. (1) 5338747-0; fax (1) 5338747-66; internet www.oir.at; f. 1957; library of 38,000 vols; Dir Mag. PETER SCHNEIDEWIND; publ. *RAUM* (4 a year).

ECONOMICS, LAW AND POLITICS

Bundesanstalt Statistik Österreich/Statistik Austria: Guglgasse 13, 1110 Vienna; tel. (1) 71128-0; fax (1) 71128-7728; e-mail office@statistik.gv.at; internet www.statistik.at; f. 1829; library of 170,000 vols; Dir-Gens Dr KONRAD PESENDORFER (Statistics Div.), Dr. GABRIELA PETROVIC (Commerical Div.); publs *Statistisches Jahrbuch für Österreich* (1 a year), *Statistische Nachrichten* (12 a year).

Dr Karl Kummer Institut für Sozialreform, Sozial- und Wirtschaftspolitik (Institute for Social Reform and Social Politics): Ebendorferstr. 6/4, 1010 Vienna; tel. (1) 4052674; fax (1) 4052674-99; e-mail office@kummer-institut.at; internet www.kummer-institut.at; f. 1953; Exec. Dirs DORIS PALZ, ALEXANDER RAUNER; publ. *Gesellschaft und Politik*.

Institut für Europäische Integrationsforschung (EIF) (Institute for European Integration Research): Strohgasse 45/DG, 1030 Vienna; tel. (1) 51581-7565; fax (1) 51581-7566; e-mail eif@oeaw.ac.at; internet www.eif.oeaw.ac.at; f. 1998; attached to Austrian Acad. of Sciences; Head GERDA FALKNER.

Institut für Höhere Studien (Institute for Advanced Studies): Stumpergasse 56, 1060 Vienna; tel. (1) 59991-0; fax (1) 59991-162; e-mail ihs@ihs.ac.at; internet www.ihs.ac.at; f. 1963; postgraduate training and research in economics and finance, sociology and political science; library of 20,300 vols, 500 current periodicals; Dir Prof. Dr BERNHARD FELDERER; publs *Economics, Sociological and Political Science Series, Empirical Economics* (4 a year), *European Societies* (4 a year), *German Economic Revue* (4 a year).

Österreichische Forschungsstiftung für Internationale Entwicklung (Austrian Research Foundation for International Development): Sensengasse 3, 1090 Vienna; tel. (1) 3174010; fax (1) 3174015; e-mail office@oefse.at; internet www.oefse.at; f. 1967; documentation and information on devt aid, developing countries and int. devt, particularly relating to Austria; library of 60,000 vols, 120 periodicals; Librarian KARIN GRABOVSKY; publs *ÖFSE-Edition* (irregular), *ÖFSE-Forum* (irregular), *Österreichische Entwicklungspolitik. Analysen-Informationen* (1 a year).

Österreichisches Institut für Wirtschaftsforschung (Austrian Institute of Economic Research): Postfach 91, 1103 Vienna; tel. (1) 7982601; fax (1) 7989386; e-mail office@wifo.ac.at; internet www.wifo.ac.at; f. 1927; Dir Prof. Dr KARL AIGINGER; publs *Austrian Economic Quarterly, Empirica* (3 a year, with Austrian Economic Asscn), *Monatsberichte* (12 a year).

Österreichisches Meinungs- und Marktforschungsinstitut (Austrian Public Opinion and Market Research Institute): c/o Karmasin Marktforschung, Österreichisches Gallup Institut, Anastasius-Grün-Gasse 32, 1180 Vienna; tel. (1) 4704724; fax (1) 470472419; e-mail office@gallup.at; internet www.gallup.at; f. 1964; Dirs ROSWITHA HASSLINGER, Prof. FRITZ KARMASIN.

Österreichisches Ost- und Südosteuropa-Institut (Austrian Institute of East and South-East European Studies): Josefsplatz 6, 1010 Vienna; tel. (1) 5121895; fax (1) 512189553; e-mail office@osi.ac.at; internet www.osi.ac.at; f. 1958; library of 43,150 vols, 1,639 periodicals (339 current) and documents; Chair. of Exec. Board Prof. Dr A. SUPPAN; Dir Doz. Dr PETER JORDAN; publ. *Österreichische Osthefte* (4 a year).

Wirtschaftsförderungsinstitut der Wirtschaftskammer Österreich (Institute of Business Promotion of the Austrian Federal Economic Chamber): Wiedner Hauptstr. 63, 1045 Vienna; tel. (1) 476-77; e-mail infocenter@wifiwien.at; internet www.wifi.at; f. 1946; adult education, management and vocational training, public relations for Austrian economy, consulting service, international business skills exchange; Man. Dir Dr MICHAEL LANDERTSHAMMER.

FINE AND PERFORMING ARTS

Abteilung für Inventarisation und Denkmalforschung des Bundesdenkmalamtes (Department of Art Research and Inventory of the Federal Office for the Protection of Monuments): Hofburg, Schweizerhof, Säulenstiege, 1010 Vienna; tel. (1) 53415-121; fax (1) 53415-5120; e-mail denkmalforschung@bda.at; internet www.bda.at; f. 1911; research and documentation on works of art in Austria; library of 22,000 vols; 16 ; Chief Officer Dr ANDREAS LEHNE; publs *Denkmal Heute, Österreichische Zeitschrift für Kunst und Denkmalpflege*.

Gesellschaft für vergleichende Kunstforschung (Society of Comparative Art Research): Universitätscampus AAKH, Spitalgasse 2 (Eingang Garnisongasse 13), 1090 Vienna; tel. (1) 42774142; fax (1) 42779414; e-mail walter.krause@univie.ac.at; f. 1932; 300 mems; Sec.-Gen. Prof. Dr WALTER KRAUSE; publ. *Mitteilungen* (3 a year).

Wiener Gesellschaft für Theaterforschung (Viennese Society for Theatre Research): Hofburg, Batthyanystiege, 1010 Vienna; tel. (1) 427748401; fax (1) 42779484; e-mail otto.schindler@univie.ac.at; f. 1944; Pres. Prof. Dr WOLFGANG GREISENEGGER; Gen. Sec. Dr OTTO G. SCHINDLER; publs *Jahrbuch, Theater in Österreich* (1 a year).

HISTORY, GEOGRAPHY AND ARCHAEOLOGY

Forschungsgesellschaft Wiener Stadtarchäologie (Research Unit for Archaeology in Vienna): Apollogasse 7, 1070 Vienna; tel. (676) 7215105; internet www.archaeologie-wien.at; Chair. Dr ORTOLF HARL; publ. *Onomasticon Provinciarum Europae Latinarum*.

Institut für Demographie (Institute of Demography): Prinz-Eugen-Str. 8, 1040 Vienna; tel. (1) 515817702; fax (1) 515817730; e-mail vid@oeaw.ac.at; internet www.oeaw.ac.at/vid; attached to Austrian Acad. of Sciences; Dir Dr WOLFGANG LUTZ.

Institut für Realienkunde des Mittelalters und der Frühen Neuzeit (Institute for Research into Daily Life and Material Culture in Medieval and Early Modern Times): Körnermarkt 13, 3500 Krems an der Donau; tel. (2732) 84793; fax (2732) 84793-1; e-mail imareal@oeaw.ac.at; internet www.imareal.oeaw.ac.at; f. 1969; attached to Austrian Acad. of Sciences; Dir Dr ELISABETH VAVRA; publs *Forschungen* (every 2 years), *Medium Aevum Quotidianum* (3 or 4 a year), *Veröffentlichungen* (every 2 years).

LANGUAGE AND LITERATURE

Institut für Österreichische Dialekt- und Namenlexika (Institute for Lexicography of Austrian Dialects and Names): Postgasse 7, 1010 Vienna; tel. (1) 51581-3493; fax (1) 51581-3495; e-mail dinamlex@oeaw.ac.at; internet www.oeaw.ac.at/dinamlex; attached to Austrian Acad. of Sciences; Dir INGEBORG GEYER.

MEDICINE

Institut für Biomedizinische Altersforschung (Institute of Biomedical Research on Ageing): Rennweg 10, 6020 Innsbruck; tel. (512) 583919-0; fax (512) 583919-8; e-mail iba@oeaw.ac.at; internet www.iba.oeaw.ac.at; f. 1992; attached to Austrian Acad. of Sciences; Dir BEATRIX GRUBECK-LOEBENSTEIN.

NATURAL SCIENCES

General

Fonds zur Förderung der wissenschaftlichen Forschung (Austrian Science Fund): Haus der Forschung, Sensengasse 1, 1090 Vienna; tel. (1) 5056740; fax (1) 5056739; e-mail office@fwf.ac.at; internet www.fwf.ac.at; f. 1967; all Austrian univs with their faculties, the art schools and the Austrian Academy of Sciences are represented, also delegates of non-univ. research instns and professional asscns; Pres. and Exec. Dir Prof. Dr CHRISTOPH KRATKY.

Institut für Wissenschaft und Kunst (Institute for Science and Art): Berggasse 17, 1090 Vienna; tel. (1) 3174342; fax (1) 3174342; internet www.univie.ac.at/iwk; f. 1946; Gen. Sec. Dr HELGA KASCHL; publ. *Mitteilungen*.

Institut für Wissenschaftstheorie (Institute for the Philosophy of Science):; tel. (662) 909627; e-mail wissenschaftstheorie@sbg.ac.at; f. 1961; philosophy of science, foundations of logic, mathematics and ethics, philosophy of religion; library of 12,000 vols; Dir Prof. Dr PAUL WEINGARTNER; publ. *Forschungsgespräche* (irregular).

Biological Sciences

Biologische Station Neusiedler See (Biological Station Neusiedler See): Amt d. Burgenl. Landesregierung, Abt. 5, 7142 Illmitz; tel. (2175) 2328; fax (2175) 232810; e-mail biol.stat@aon.at; f. 1971; nature conservation, limnology, ornithology, botany; Dir Prof. Dr A. HERZIG; publ. *BFB (Biologisches Forschungsinstitut Burgenland)–Berichte* (irregular).

Institut für Biophysik und Nanosystemforschung (Institute of Biophysics and Nanosystems Research): Schmiedlstr. 6, 8042 Graz; tel. (316) 4120-300; fax (316) 4120-390; e-mail ibn.office@oeaw.ac.at; internet www.ibn.oeaw.ac.at; f. 1847; attached to Austrian Acad. of Sciences; Dir Prof. Dr PETER LAGGNER.

Institut für Botanik der Universität Wien (Institute of Botany of the University of Vienna): Rennweg 14, 1030 Vienna; tel. (1) 4277-54100; fax (1) 4277-9541; e-mail botanik@univie.ac.at; internet www.botanik.univie.ac.at; f. 1754 (Garden) and 1844 (Institute); library of 40,000 vols; Dir Prof. Dr T. F. STUESSY; publs *Neilreichia* (1 a year), *Österreichische Zeitschrift für Pilzkunde* (Austrian Journal of Mycology, 1 a year), *Taxon* (2 a year).

Institut für Limnologie (Institute of Limnology): Herzog Odilo Str. 101, 5310 Mondsee; tel. (6232) 3125; fax (6232) 3578; internet www.oeaw.ac.at/limno; f. 1972; attached to Austrian Acad. of Sciences; Dir Dr THOMAS WEISSE.

Institute of Molecular Biotechnology (IMBA): Dr Bohr-Gasse 3, 1030 Vienna; tel. (1) 79044; fax (1) 79044110; internet www.imba.oeaw.ac.at; attached to Austrian Acad.

of Sciences; Scientific Dir Prof. Dr JOSEF PENNINGER; Admin Dir MICHAEL KREBS.

Physical Sciences

Atominstitut der Österreichischen Universitäten (Atomic Institute of the Austrian Universities): Stadion allee 2, 1020 Vienna; tel. (1) 58801-14111; fax (1) 58801-14199; f. 1958; training of advanced students and basic research; Dir Prof. Dr HELMUT RAUCH.

BMLFUW Abteilung VII/3–Wasserhaushalt (Federal Ministry of Agriculture, Forestry, Environment and Water Management Sub-Dept VII/3–Water Balance): Marxergasse 2, 1030 Vienna; tel. (1) 71100-6942; fax (1) 71100-6851; e-mail wasserhaushalt@bmlfuw.gv.at; internet www.lebensministerium.at; f. 1893; library of 8,000 vols; Head of Division VII/3 Dr Ing. REINHOLD GODINA; publs *Hydrographisches Jahrbuch von Österreich* (1 a year), *Hydrological Atlas of Austria, Mitteilungsblatt des Hydrographischen Dienstes von Österreich* (irregular).

Geologische Bundesanstalt (Geological Survey of Austria): Neulinggasse 38, Postfach 127, 1031 Vienna; tel. (1) 7125674-0; fax (1) 7125674-56; e-mail office@geologie.ac.at; internet www.geologie.ac.at; f. 1849; library of 259,000 vols, 45,000 geological maps, 9,500 aerial photographs, 15,000 archive items, 14,000 microforms; Dir Prof. Dr H. P. SCHÖNLAUB; publs *Abhandlungen, Archiv für Lagerstättenforschung, Berichte, Jahrbuch*, geological maps.

Institut für Astron- und Teilchenphysik, Universität Innsbruck (Institute of Astro- and Particle Physics, University of Innsbruck): Technikerstr. 25, 6020 Innsbruck; tel. (512) 5076031; fax (512) 5072923; e-mail astro@uibk.ac.at; internet astro.uibk.ac.at; f. 1904; library of 4,598 vols; Dir Prof. Dr SABINE SCHINDLER; publ. *Mitteilungen* (irregular).

Institut für Astronomie der Universität Wien (Vienna University Observatory): Türkenschanzstr. 17, 1180 Vienna; tel. (1) 427751801; fax (1) 42779518; internet www.astro.univie.ac.at; f. 1755; library of 117,300 vols; Pres. Prof. GERHARD HENSLER; publ. *Communications in Asteroseismology*.

Associated Body:

Figl Observatorium für Astrophysik (Figl Observatory for Astrophysics): Türkenschanzstr. 17, 1180 Vienna; Mitterschöpfl, Altenmarkt an der Triesting, 2571 Vienna; tel. (1) 427751801; fax (1) 42779518; e-mail admin@astro.univie.ac.at; internet astro.univie.ac.at/foa; f. 1969; astronomical research; lab courses for astronomy programme at Univ of Vienna; public outreach; Head of Science Operations Dr WERNER W. ZEILINGER.

Institut für Hochenergiephysik (Institute of High Energy Physics): Nikolsdorfergasse 18, 1050 Vienna; tel. (1) 5447328; fax (1) 544732854; internet wwwhephy.oeaw.ac.at; attached to Austrian Acad. of Sciences; Dir Prof. Dr WALTER MAJEROTTO.

Institut für Mittelenergiephysik (Institute of Medium Energy Physics): Boltzmanngasse 3, 1090 Vienna; tel. (1) 3108616; fax (1) 3108801; e-mail imep@oeaw.ac.at; internet www.oeaw.ac.at/imep; f. 1910; attached to Austrian Acad. of Sciences; Dir Prof. Dr Mag. PAUL KIENLE.

Institut für Schallforschung (Acoustics Research Institute): Wohllebengasse 12-14 / 1st Fl, 1040 Vienna; tel. (1) 5158-2501; fax (1) 5158-2530; e-mail christiane.herzog@oeaw.ac.at; internet www.kfs.oeaw.ac.at; attached to Austrian Acad. of Sciences; Dir Prof. Dr WERNER A. DEUTSCH.

Institut für Weltraumforschung (Space Research Institute): Schmiedlstr. 6, 8042 Graz; tel. (316) 4120-400; fax (316) 4120-490; e-mail office.iwf@oeaw.ac.at; internet www.iwf.oeaw.ac.at; attached to Austrian Acad. of Sciences; Dir Prof. Dr WOLFGANG BAUMJOHANN.

Kuffner-Sternwarte (Kuffner Observatory): Johann-Staud-Str. 10, 1160 Vienna; tel. (1) 9148130; fax (1) 914813031; e-mail admin@kuffner.ac.at; internet www.kuffner.ac.at; f. 1884; library of 500 vols; Dir PETER HABISON.

Ludwig Boltzmann Institut für Festkörperphysik (Ludwig Boltzmann Institute for Solid State Physics): Operngasse 6, 5. Stock, 1010 Vienna; tel. (1) 5132750; fax (1) 5132310; e-mail office@lbg.ac.at; internet www.lbg.ac.at; f. 1965; research into semiconductors, conducting polymers and high-temperature superconductors; Dir Prof. Dr ALFRED PHILIPP.

Österreichische Geodätische Kommission (Austrian Geodetic Commission): 1030 Vienna, Landstrasser Hauptstr. 55–57; tel. (1) 71100-8213; fax (1) 71100-93-8213; e-mail christoph.twaroch@bmwa.gv.at; internet www.cis.tugraz.at/ivm/oegk; f. 1863; Pres. Prof. Dr FRITZ K. BRUNNER; Sec. Univ. Doz. Dipl.-Ing. Dr CHRISTOPH TWAROCH; publ. *Geodätische Arbeiten Österreichs für die Internationale Erdmessung*.

Sonnenobservatorium Kanzelhöhe der Universität Graz (Kanzelhöhe Solar Observatory of the University of Graz): 9521 Treffen; tel. (4248) 2717; fax (4248) 271715; internet www.solobskh.ac.at; f. 1943; small library; Dir Prof. Dr HEINZ KRENN.

Sternwarte Kremsmünster (Kremsmünster Observatory): 4550 Kremsmünster; tel. (7583) 5275450; fax (7583) 527545; e-mail sternwarte.kremsmuenster@telecom.at; internet members.nextra.at/stewar; f. 1748; library of 25,000 vols; Dir Mag. Dr P. AMAND KRAML; publ. *Naturwissenschaftliche Sammlungen Kremsmünster* (irregular).

Umweltbundesamt (Environment Agency Austria): Spittelauer Lände 5, 1090 Vienna; tel. (1) 31304; fax (1) 31304-5400; e-mail office@umweltbundesamt.at; internet www.umweltbundesamt.at; f. 1985; elaboration of scientific studies and basic data for environmental protection policy in Austria; elaboration of recommendations for decision-makers in politics, business and admin. and devt of strategic perspectives and scenarios for the achievement of environmental policy targets in Austria and Europe; library of 20,000 vols, 300 periodicals; Dir GEORG REBERNIG.

Zentralanstalt für Meteorologie und Geodynamik (Central Institute for Meteorology and Geodynamics): Hohe Warte 38, 1191 Vienna; tel. (1) 36026; fax (1) 3691233; e-mail dion@zamg.ac.at; internet www.zamg.ac.at; f. 1851; provides nat. weather service; acts in all fields of meteorology except aeronautical field; nat. body responsible for geophysics; library of 80,000 vols; Dir Dr ERNEST RUDEL; Sec. HERMI FUERST; publ. *Oesterreichische Beitraege zu Meteorologie und Geophysik* (irregular).

PHILOSOPHY AND PSYCHOLOGY

Institut für Kultur- und Geistesgeschichte Asiens (Institute for the Cultural and Intellectual History of Asia): Prinz-Eugen-Str. 8–10, 1040 Vienna; tel. (1) 51581-6400; fax (1) 51581-6410; e-mail office.ias@oeaw.ac.at; internet ikga.oeaw.ac.at; attached to Austrian Acad. of Sciences; Dir Doz. Dr HELMUT KRASSER.

Konrad-Lorenz-Institut für Vergleichende Verhaltensforschung (Konrad Lorenz Institute of Comparative Behavioural Research): Savoyenstr. 1A, 1160 Vienna; tel. (1) 4515812700; fax (1) 515812800; e-mail initial.name@klivv.oeaw.ac.at; internet www.oeaw.ac.at/klivv; f. 1945; attached to Austrian Acad. of Sciences; Dir Dr DUSTIN PENN.

Psychotechnisches Institut (Psychotechnical Institute): Augasse 9, 2103 Langenzersdorf; tel. (2244) 30996-0; fax (2244) 30996-22; e-mail psychotech@utanet.at; internet www.psychotech.at; f. 1926; training of supervisors of all levels; library of 8,500 vols; Dirs Dr HANS-RICHARD GRÜMM, Dr SUSANNE HACKL-GRÜMM.

RELIGION, SOCIOLOGY AND ANTHROPOLOGY

Institut für Kirchliche Zeitgeschichte (Institute for Contemporary Ecclesiastical History): Mönchsberg 2A, 5020 Salzburg; tel. (662) 842521161; fax (622) 84252118; e-mail kirchliche-zeitgeschichte@ifz.kirchen.net; internet www.kirchen.net/ifz/institute/kirchlzeitgeschichte.htm; f. 1961; library of 8,500 vols; Dir Doz. Dr ALFRED RINNERTHALER; publs *Hirtenbriefe aus Deutschland, Österreich und der Schweiz* (1 a year), *Publikationen des Instituts für Kirchliche Zeitgeschichte*.

Institut für Stadt und Regionalforschung (Institute for Urban and Regional Research): Postgasse 7/4/2, 1010 Vienna; tel. (1) 51581-3520; fax (1) 51581-3533; internet www.oeaw.ac.at/isr; attached to Austrian Acad. of Sciences; Dir Prof. Dr HEINZ FASSMANN.

Mayr-Melnhof Institut für den Christlichen Osten (Mayr-Melnhof Institute of Eastern Christian Studies): Mönchsberg 2A, Salzburg; tel. (662) 842521-141; fax (662) 842521-143; e-mail salzburg@ro-oriente.at; f. 1961; library of 3,000 vols; Dirs Prof. Dr DIETMAR WINKLER, Dr LI TANG, Dr DILIANA ATANASSOVA.

TECHNOLOGY

Austrian Standards Institute (Österreichisches Normungsinstitut): Heinestr. 38, 1020 Vienna; tel. (1) 21300; fax (1) 21300-818; e-mail office@as-institute.at; internet www.as-institute.at; f. 1920; private institute for standardization in all fields; library of 215,000 documents (standards) online, 22,000 Austrian, European, int. standards; Pres. Prof. Dr WALTER BARFUß; Man. Dir Ing. Dr GERHARD HARTMANN; publs *CONNEX* (German, 6 a year), *ON top news* (12 a year).

Erich-Schmid-Institut für Materialwissenschaft (Erich Schmid Institute of Solid Material Sciences): Jahnstr. 12, 8700 Leoben; tel. (3842) 804112; fax (3842) 804116; internet www.oeaw.ac.at/esi; f. 1971; attached to Austrian Acad. of Sciences; Dir Prof. Dr G. DEHM.

Holzforschung Austria (Wood Research Austria): Arsenal, Franz Grillstr. 7, 1030 Vienna; tel. (1) 7982623-0; fax (1) 7982623-50; e-mail hfa@holzforschung.at; internet www.holzforschung.at; f. 1948; research institute of the Austrian Wood Research Society; library of 35,000 vols; Dir Dipl.-Ing. Dr MANFRED BRANDSTÄTTER; publs *Holzforschung und Holzverwertung* (6 a year), *Literature Database of the Austrian Wood Research Society* (2 a month).

Institut für Diskrete Mathematik (Institute of Discrete Mathematics): Fleischmarkt 22, 1010 Vienna; tel. (1) 5129184-91; fax (1) 5129184-92; internet www.ricam.oeaw.ac.at/dismat; f. 1999; attached to Austrian Acad. of Sciences; Dir Prof. Dr HERBERT FLEISCHNER.

Institut für Technikfolgen-Abschätzung (Institute of Technology Assessment): Strohgasse 45/5, 1030 Vienna; tel. (1) 51581-6582; fax (1) 7109883; internet www.oeaw.ac.at/ita; attached to Austrian Acad. of Sciences; Dir Doz. Dr MICHAEL NENTWICH.

Institut für Wasserbau und Hydrometrische Prüfung (Institute for Hydraulic Engineering and Calibration of Hydrometrical Current-Meters): Severingasse 7, 1090 Vienna; tel. (1) 4026802-0; fax (1) 4026802-30; e-mail office.iwb@baw.bmlfuw.gv.at; internet www.iwbhp.at; f. 1913; attached to Federal Agency for Water Management; calculation and implementation of measures concerning the protection and maintenance of waters, as well as flood protection; physical model tests and mathematical models for studies in the field of hydraulic engineering; consulting in hydraulic engineering; devt of ecological bed stabilization methods; 11 mems; library of 5,700 vols, database containing 29,600 articles; Dir Dipl.-Ing. Dr techn. MICHAEL HENGL.

KMU Forschung Austria (Austrian Institute for SME Research): Gusshausstr. 8, 1040 Vienna; tel. (1) 5059761; fax (1) 5034660; e-mail office@kmuforschung.ac.at; internet www.kmuforschung.ac.at; f. 1952 as Österreichisches Institut für Gewerbeforschung; conducts social and economic research with focus on small and medium-sized enterprises; prepares and supplies information and data to facilitate decision-making for businesses and their advisers, for institutions responsible for economic policy and business promotion as well as for universities, colleges of higher education and other research institutions; member of the Austrian Cooperative Research (ACR) and the European Network for Small- and Medium-sized Enterprise Research (ENSR); 1,560 mems; library of 3,200 vols; Pres. Prof. Dr J. HANNS PICHLER; Dir Dr WALTER BORNETT; Dir Mag. PETER VOITHOFER.

Österreichisches Forschungsinstitut für Artificial Intelligence (Austrian Research Institute for Artificial Intelligence): Freyung 6/6, 1010 Vienna; tel. (1) 5336112-60; fax (1) 5336112-77; e-mail sec@ofai.at; internet www.ofai.at; f. 1984; a research institute of the Austrian Soc. for Cybernetic Studies; library of 3,000 vols; Dir Prof. Dr ROBERT TRAPPL; publs *Applied Artificial Intelligence: An International Journal* (10 a year), *Technical Reports* (irregular).

Österreichisches Forschungsinstitut für Technikgeschichte (ÖFiT) am Technischen Museum in Wien (Austrian Research Institute for the History of Technology at the Museum of Technology in Vienna): Mariahilfer Str. 212, 1140 Vienna; tel. (1) 89998-2500; fax (1) 89998-1111; e-mail helmut.lackner@tmw.at; internet www.tmw.at; f. 1931; Pres. Prof. Dr REINHOLD REITH; publ. *Blätter für Technikgeschichte* (1 a year).

Österreichisches Forschungszentrum Seibersdorf GmbH (Austrian Research Centre, Seibersdorf): 2444 Seibersdorf; tel. (50550) 2110; fax (50550) 2131; e-mail seibersdorf@arcs.ac.at; internet www.seibersdorf-research.at; f. 1956; contract research and devt in instrumentation and information technology, process and environmental technologies, engineering, life sciences and systems research; library of 15,500 vols; Dir KONRAD FREYBORN; publ. *OEFSZ Reports*.

Österreichisches Giesserei-Institut (Austrian Foundry Research Institute): Parkstr. 21, 8700 Leoben; tel. (3842) 431010; fax (3842) 431011; e-mail office.ogi@unileoben.ac.at; internet www.ogi.at; f.

1952; library of 2,140 vols; Man. and Tech. Dir Prof. Dr PETER SCHUMACHER; publ. *Giesserei Rundschau* (6 a year).

Österreichisches Textil-Forschungsinstitut (Austrian Textile Research Institute): Spengergasse 20, 1050 Vienna; tel. (1) 5442543-0; fax (1) 5442543-10; e-mail office@oeti.at; internet www.oeti.at; f. 1967; Dir Dipl.-Ing. Dr ERICH ZIPPEL.

Physikalisch-Technische Versuchsanstalt für Wärme- und Schalltechnik am Technologischen Gewerbemuseum (Physical-technical Institute for Research on Heat and Noise Technology at the Technological Industrial Museum): Wexstr. 19–23, 1200 Vienna; tel. (1) 33126411; fax (1) 3305925; Dir Ing. Mag. MATHIAS STANI.

Zentrum für Elektronenmikroskopie Graz (Graz Centre for Electron Microscopy): Steyrergasse 17, 8010 Graz; tel. (316) 8738320; fax (316) 811596; e-mail office@felmi-zfe.at; internet www.felmi-zfe.tugraz .at; f. 1959; library of 2,000 vols; Pres. Prof. Dipl.-Ing. Dr HELMUT LIST; Dir Dipl.-Ing. ULRICH SANTNER.

Libraries and Archives

Admont

Bibliothek der Benediktinerabtei (Library of the Benedictine Abbey): 8911 Admont; tel. (3613) 2312602; fax (3613) 2312359; e-mail tomaschek@stiftadmont.at; internet www.stiftadmont.at; f. 1074; 200,000 vols, 1,400 MSS, 530 incunabula; Librarian Mag. Dr JOHANN TOMASCHEK.

Bregenz

Vorarlberger Landesarchiv (Vorarlberg State Archives): Kirchstr. 28, 6900 Bregenz; tel. (5574) 51145005; fax (5574) 51145095; e-mail landesarchiv@vorarlberg.at; internet www.landesarchiv.at; f. 1898; 25,000 vols; Dir Prof. Dr ALOIS NIEDERSTÄTTER; publ. *Zeitschrift Montfort* (4 a year).

Vorarlberger Landesbibliothek (Vorarlberg State Library): Fluherstr. 4, 6901 Bregenz; tel. (5574) 511-44100; fax (5574) 511-44095; e-mail info.vlb@vorarlberg.at; internet www.vorarlberg.at/vlb; f. 1904; 450,000 vols; Dir Dr HARALD WEIGEL.

Eisenstadt

Burgenländische Landesbibliothek (Burgenland Provincial Library): Europaplatz 1, Landhaus, 7000 Eisenstadt; tel. (2682) 6002356; fax (2682) 6002058; e-mail post.kultur@bgld.gv.at; internet www .burgenland.at; f. 1922; 110,000 vols; Chief Librarian Mag. NORBERT FRANK; publs *Burgenländische Forschungen* (2 or 3 a year), *Burgenländische Heimatblätter* (4 a year), *Burgenländische Landesbibliographie* (1 a year).

Burgenländisches Landesarchiv (Burgenland Provincial Archives): Europapl. 1, 7000 Eisenstadt; tel. (2682) 6002358; fax (2682) 6002058; e-mail post.kultur@bgld.gv .at; f. 1922; Dir Dr JOHANN SEEDOCH; publ. *Burgenländische Heimatblätter* (4 a year).

Graz

Steiermärkische Landesbibliothek (Styrian Federal State Library): Kalchberggasse 2, Graz; tel. (316) 80164600; fax (316) 80164633; e-mail stlbib@stmk.gv.at; f. 1811; 700,000 vols, 2,800 periodicals, 2,300 MSS; Dir Dr CHRISTOPH BINDER; publs *Arbeiten aus der Steiermärkischen Landesbibliothek* (irregular), *Steirische Bibliographie* (irregular), *Steirische Zeitungsdokumentation* (irregular).

Steiermärkisches Landesarchiv (Styrian Provincial Archives): Karmeliterpl. 3, 8010 Graz; tel. (316) 8772361; fax (316) 8772954; e-mail fa1d@stmk.gv.at; internet www .landesarchiv.steiermark.at; f. 1811; 100,000 vols; Dir Prof. Dr JOSEF RIEGLER; publs *Ausstellungsbegleiter* (irregular), *Mitteilungen* (1 a year), *Quellen aus steirischen Archiven* (irregular), *Styriaca* (irregular), *Veröffentlichungen* (irregular).

Universitätsbibliothek der Technischen Universität Graz (Technical University Library): Technikerstr. 4, 8010 Graz; tel. (316) 873-6151; fax (316) 873-6671; e-mail service.bibliothek@tugraz.at; internet www .ub.tugraz.at; f. 1875; 600,000 vols, 1,250 periodicals; Dir EVA BERTHA.

Universitätsbibliothek Graz (University Library, Graz): Universitätspl. 3A, 8010 Graz; tel. (316) 3803102; fax (316) 384987; e-mail ubgraz@uni-graz.at; internet www .uni-graz.at/en/ubwww.htm; f. 1573; 3,600,000 vols, 14,000 electronic journals, 2,203 MSS, 1,150 incunabula; mem. of IFLA, LIBER; Dir Dr WERNER SCHLACHER.

Heiligenkreuz bei Baden

Stiftsarchiv des Zisterzienserstiftes (Cistercian Abbey Archives): 2532 Heiligenkreuz; tel. (2258) 8703; fax (2258) 8703-114; e-mail information@stift-heiligenkreuz.at; internet www.stift-heiligenkreuz.at; archives since foundation of the monastery in 1133; Archivist Dr FR ALCUIN SCHACHENMAYR; publs *Analecta Cisterciensia*, *Sancta Crux*.

Innsbruck

Tiroler Landesarchiv (Tyrolese Provincial Archives): Michael-Gaismair-Str. 1, 6020 Innsbruck; tel. (512) 508-3534; fax (512) 508-3505; e-mail landesarchiv@tirol.gv.at; internet www.tirol.gv.at/landesarchiv; f. 13th century; records from 11th century; Dir Dr RICHARD SCHOBER; publs *Tiroler Erbhöfe* (irregular), *Tiroler Geschichtsquellen* (irregular), *Veröffentlichungen des Tiroler Landesarchivs* (irregular).

Universitätsbibliothek Innsbruck (University Library, Innsbruck): Innrain 50, 6010 Innsbruck; tel. (512) 5072401; fax (512) 5072893; e-mail ub-hb@uibk.ac.at; internet www.uibk.ac.at/ub; f. 1746; 3,200,000 vols, 7,470 current periodicals, 1,100 MSS, 2,000 incunabula; Dir Dr MARTIN WIESER.

Klagenfurt

Kärntner Landesarchiv (Carinthian Provincial Archives): St Ruprechter Str. 7, 9020 Klagenfurt; tel. (463) 56234; fax (463) 56234-20; e-mail post.landesarchiv@ktn.gv.at; internet www.landesarchiv.ktn.gv.at; f. 1904; Dir Dr WILHELM WADL; publ. *Das Kärntner Landesarchiv* (1 a year).

Universitätsbibliothek Klagenfurt (University Library, Klagenfurt): Universitätsstr. 65–67, 9020 Klagenfurt; tel. (463) 2700-9563; fax (463) 2700-9599; e-mail info.bibliothek@ uni-klu.ac.at; internet www.uni-klu.ac.at/ub; f. 1775; 765,000 vols; open to the public; Dir Mag. EDELTRAUD HAAS.

Klosterneuburg

Bibliothek des Augustiner-Chorherrenstiftes (Library of the Augustine Abbey): Stiftspl. 1, 3400 Klosterneuburg; tel. (2243) 411-151; fax (2243) 411-156; e-mail info@ stift-klosterneuburg.at; internet www .stift-klosterneuburg.at; f. 1114; 240,000 vols, 1,250 MSS, 836 incunabula; Dir Dr HEINZ RISTORY.

Leoben

Universitätsbibliothek Leoben (University Library, Leoben): Franz-Josef-Str. 18, 8700 Leoben; tel. (3842) 402-7800; fax (3842)

402-7802; e-mail univbibl@unileoben.ac.at; internet www.unileoben.ac.at/bibliothek; f. 1840; 250,000 vols, 173 current periodicals; Librarians Dr JOHANN DELANOY, Dr CHRISTIAN HASENHÜTTL.

Linz

Bibliothek der Oberösterreichischen Landesmuseen (Library of the Upper Austrian Provincial Museums): Museumstr. 14, 4010 Linz; tel. (732) 774482-41; fax (732) 774482-66; e-mail bibliothek@landesmuseum .at; internet www.landesmuseum.at; f. 1836; 160,000 vols; Chief Librarian WALTRAUD FAISSNER.

Oberösterreichische Landesbibliothek (Federal State Library of Upper Austria): Schillerpl. 2, 4021 Linz; tel. (732) 664071-00; fax (732) 664071-44; e-mail landesbibliothek@ooe.gv.at; internet www .landesbibliothek.at; f. 1774; 400,000 vols; Dirs Dr CHRISTIAN ENICHLMAYR, Dr RUDOLF LINDPOINTNER.

Oberösterreichisches Landesarchiv (Provincial Archives of Upper Austria): Anzengruberstr. 19, 4020 Linz; tel. (732) 772014601; fax (732) 772014619; e-mail landesarchiv@ooe.gv.at; internet www .landesarchiv-ooe.at; f. 1896; Dir Dr GERHART MARCKHGOTT; publs *Beiträge zur Zeitgeschichte Oberösterreichs* (irregular), *Forschungen zur Geschichte Oberösterreichs* (irregular), *Mitteilungen* (irregular), *Quellen zur Geschichte Oberösterreichs* (irregular).

Universitätsbibliothek der Johannes Kepler Universität Linz: Altenberger str. 69, 4040 Linz; tel. (732) 2468 9380; fax (732) 2468 1233; e-mail bibliothek@jku.at; internet www.ubl.jku.at; f. 1965; 1,000,000 vols, 2,500 periodicals; Dir Dr MONIKA SCHENK.

Melk

Bibliothek des Benediktinerklosters Melk in Niederösterreich (Library of the Melk Benedictine Monastery in Lower Austria): 3390 Stift Melk; tel. (2752) 555; fax (2752) 55552; e-mail bibliothek@stiftmelk.at; internet www.stiftmelk.at; f. 1089; 80,000 vols (mostly pre-19th-century), 1,800 codices, 750 incunabula; Librarian GOTTFRIED GLASSNER.

Salzburg

Bibliothek der Benediktiner Erzabtei St Peter (Library of the Benedictine Abbey of St Peter): Postfach 113, 5010 Salzburg; tel. (662) 844576-58; fax (662) 844576-80; e-mail scriptorium@stift-stpeter.at; internet www .stift-stpeter.at; f. 700; 120,000 vols, 1,300 MSS, 923 incunabula; Dir P. PETRUS EDER.

Salzburger Landesarchiv (Salzburg Provincial Archives): Postfach 527, 5010 Salzburg; tel. (662) 80424527; fax (662) 80424661; e-mail landesarchiv@salzburg.gv.at; internet www.salzburg.gv.at/archive.htm; f. 1875; Dir Dr FRITZ KOLLER.

Universitätsbibliothek Salzburg (Salzburg University Library): Hofstallgasse 2–4, 5020 Salzburg; tel. (662) 8044-77550; fax (662) 8044-103; e-mail info.hb@sbg.ac.at; internet www.uni-salzburg.at/bibliothek; f. 1623; 2,000,000 vols, 1,100 MSS, 2,400 incunabula; Dir Mag. Dr URSULA SCHACHL-RABER.

Sankt Florian

Bibliothek des Augustiner-Chorherrenstiftes (Library of the Augustine Canonical Foundation): Stiftstr. 1, 4490 St Florian; tel. (7224) 8902-54; fax (7224) 8902-60; e-mail bibliothek@stift-st-florian.at; internet www .stift-st-florian.at; f. 1071; 150,000 vols, 920 MSS, 800 incunabula; Dir Prof. Dr KARL REHBERGER.

Sankt Pölten

Niederösterreichisches Landesarchiv (Lower Austrian Provincial Archives): Landhauspl. 1, 3100 St Pölten; tel. (2742) 9005-12044; fax (2742) 9005-12052; e-mail post .k2archiv@noel.gv.at; internet www.noel.gv .at/bildung/landesarchiv.htm; 31,000 vols; Dir Mag. Dr WILLIBALD ROSNER; publs *Mitteilungen, NÖLA.*

Niederösterreichische Landesbibliothek (Lower Austrian Provincial Library): Landhauspl. 1, 3109 St Pölten; tel. (2742) 9005-12847; fax (2742) 9005-13860; e-mail post.k3@noel.gv.at; internet www.noe .gv.at/landesbibliothek; f. 1813; 300,000 vols; Dir Dr GEBHARD KOENIG.

Seckau

Bibliothek der Benediktinerabtei (Library of the Benedictine Abbey): 8732 Seckau; f. 1883; 160,000 vols; Dir Dr P. BENNO ROTH.

Vienna

Arbeiterkammer Bibliothek Wien für Sozialwissenschaften (Chamber of Labour Library for Social Sciences): Prinz Eugenstr. 20–22, 1040 Vienna; tel. (1) 501652466; fax (1) 501652229; e-mail bibliothek@akwien.at; internet wien.arbeiterkammer.at/bibliothek; f. 1922; 450,000 vols, 900 periodicals; Dir Dr HERWIG JOBST.

Archiv, Bibliothek und Sammlungen der Gesellschaft der Musikfreunde in Wien (Archives, Library and Collections of the Society of Friends of Music in Vienna): Bösendorferstr. 12, 1010 Vienna; tel. (1) 505868144; fax (1) 505868166; f. 1812; 23,000 vols; 73,000 scores, historical material; Dir Prof. Dr OTTO BIBA.

Archiv der Universität Wien (Archives of the University of Vienna): Postgasse 9, 1010 Vienna; tel. (1) 427717201; fax (1) 42779172; e-mail archiv@univie.ac.at; internet www .univie.ac.at/archiv; f. 1365; records since 13th century; Archivist Dr KURT MÜHLBERGER.

Archiv des Stiftes Schotten (Schotten Abbey Archives): Freyung 6, 1010 Vienna; tel. (1) 53498-0; fax (1) 53498-105; e-mail archiv.bibliothek@schottenstift.at; internet www.schottenstift.at; f. 1155; archives of the Benedictine monastery; Archivist Abbot Dr P. HEINRICH FERENCZY.

Bibliothek der Akademie der Bildenden Künste (Library of the Academy of Fine Arts): Schillerpl. 3, 1010 Vienna; tel. (1) 588162300; fax (1) 588162399; internet www.akbild.ac.at/bib; f. 1773; exhibitions, presentation of new books; 140,000 vols; Dir Doz. Dr BEATRIX BASTL.

Bibliothek der Bundesanstalt Statistik Österreich (Library of Statistics Austria): Guglgasse 13, 1110 Vienna; tel. (1) 71128-7814; fax (1) 71128-7146251; e-mail alois .gerhart@statistik.gv.at; f. 1829; 180,000 vols; Dir Dr ALOIS GEHART.

Bibliothek der Mechitharisten-Congregation: Mechitaristengasse 4, 1070 Vienna; tel. (1) 5236417; fax (1) 5236417111; e-mail vahanhov58@hotmail.com; internet www .mechitaristen.org; f. 1773; literature related to Armenia; 150,000 vols, 3,000 Armenian MSS, all current Armenian newspapers and periodicals; Dir P. VAHAN HOVAGIMIAN; publ. *Handes Amsorya* (1 a year).

Bibliothek und Archiv der Österreichischen Akademie der Wissenschaften (Library and Archive of the Austrian Academy of Sciences): Dr-Ignaz-Seipel-Pl. 2, 1010 Vienna; tel. (1) 515811262; fax (1) 515811256; e-mail bibliothek@oeaw.ac.at; internet www.oeaw.ac.at/biblio; f. 1847; 15

mems; 356,000 vols; Dir Prof. Dr CHRISTINE HARRAUER.

Bibliothek der Österreichischen Geographischen Gesellschaft (Library of the Austrian Geographical Society): Nottendorfer Gasse 2, 1030 Vienna; tel. (1) 5237974; internet arcims.isr.oeaw.ac.at/website/oegg/ oegg.htm; f. 1856; 21,000 vols; Librarian Dr PETER FRITZ.

Bibliothek der Veterinärmedizinischen Universität Wien (Library of Vienna University of Veterinary Medicine): Veterinärpl. 1, 1210 Vienna; tel. (1) 25077-1414; fax (1) 25077-1490; e-mail bibliothekinfo@vu-wien .ac.at; internet www.vu-wien.ac.at/bibl; f. 1767; 201,000 vols; Dir Dr GÜNTER OLENSKY.

Bibliothek der Wirtschaftskammer Wien (Vienna Chamber of Commerce Library): Stubenring 8–10, 1010 Vienna; tel. (1) 51450-1370; fax (1) 51450-1469; e-mail bibliothek@wkw.at; internet bibliothek.wkw .at; f. 1849; 200,000 vols; Dir Dr HERBERT PRIBYL.

Bibliothek des Bundesministeriums für Finanzen (Library of the Ministry of Finance): Himmelpfortgasse 4, 1015 Vienna; tel. (1) 514331247; fax (1) 514331246; internet www.bmf.gv.at; f. 1810; 290,000 vols; Librarian HEINZ RENNER.

Bibliothek des Bundesministeriums für Land- und Forstwirtschaft, Umwelt und Wasserwirtschaft (Library of the Federal Ministry of Agriculture, Forestry, the Environment and Water Management): Stubenring 1, 1012 Vienna; tel. (1) 71100; fax (1) 7103254; e-mail ingrid.saberi@ lebensministerium.at; f. 1868; 127,500 vols; Librarian Mag. INGRID SABERI.

Bibliothek des Bundesministeriums für Soziale Sicherheit, Generationen und Konsumentenschutz (Library of the Federal Ministry for Social Security and Consumer Protection): Stubenring 1, 1010 Vienna; tel. (1) 711006143; fax (1) 718947011-80; e-mail ilga.kubela@bmsg.gv .at; f. 1917; 150,000 vols; Dir ILGA ANNA KUBELA.

Bibliothek des Instituts für Österreichische Geschichtsforschung (Library of the Institute of Austrian Historical Research): Dr Karl Lueger Ring 1, 1010 Vienna; tel. (1) 427727201; fax (1) 42779272; internet www.univie.ac.at/ geschichtsforschung; f. 1854; 75,000 vols; Librarian Dr PAUL HEROLD.

Bibliothek des Österreichischen Patentamtes (Library of the Austrian Patent Office): Dresdner Str. 87, 1200 Vienna; tel. (1) 53424153; fax (1) 53424110; e-mail bibliothek@patentamt.at; internet www .patentamt.at; f. 1899; 26,000,000 vols; Dir Dr INGRID WEIDINGER; publs *Österreichisches Gebrauchsmusterblatt, Österreichischer Markenanzeiger, Österreichischer Musteranzeiger, Österreichisches Patentblatt.*

Bibliothek des Österreichischen Staatsarchivs (Library of the Austrian State Archives): Nottendorfergasse. 2, 1030 Vienna; tel. (1) 79540-113; fax (1) 79540-109; e-mail stabpost@oesta.gv.at; internet www.oesta.gv.at; history, military history; 400,000 vols; Dir Dr GERHARD ARTL.

Büchereien Wien (Municipal Libraries of Vienna): Urban-Loritz-Pl. 2A, 1070 Vienna; tel. (1) 4000-84500; fax (1) 4000-9984510; e-mail post@buechereien.wien.at; internet www.buechereien.wien.at; f. 1945; 1,600,000 vols, 250,000 audio media items; central library and 38 brs; Chief Librarian MARKUS FEIGL.

Bundesstaatliche Paedagogische Bibliothek beim Landesschulrat für Niederösterreich (Library of the Lower Austrian

Education Authority): Rennbahnstr. 29, 3109 St Pöelten; tel. (2742) 2801482; fax (2742) 2801111; e-mail pbn@lsr-noe.gv.at; internet pbn.lsr-noe.gv.at; f. 1923; 160,000 vols, 370 periodicals; Dir Mag. ERNST CHORHERR.

Diözesanarchiv Wien (Vienna Diocesan Archives): Erzbischöfliches Palais, Wollzeile 2, 1010 Vienna; tel. (1) 51552-3239; fax (1) 51552-3240; e-mail daw@edw.or.at; internet stephanscom.at/edw/kulissen/archiv_v.html; f. 1936; history of archdiocese of Vienna and of parishes and convents in Vienna and the eastern part of Lower Austria; 45,000 vols, 800 periodicals, 6,000 documents and files; Dir Dr ANNEMARIE FENZL; Asst Dr JOHANN WEIßENSTEINER.

Fakultätsbibliothek für Rechtswissenschaften (Faculty Library of Legal Studies): Schottenbastei 10–16, 1010 Vienna; tel. (1) 4277-16311; fax (1) 4277-9163; e-mail thomas.luzer@univie.ac.at; internet www.univie.ac.at/fbrecht; f. 1922; 238,000 vols, 1,100 periodicals; Dir Dr THOMAS LUZER.

Österreichische Nationalbibliothek (Austrian National Library): Josefspl. 1, 1015 Vienna; tel. (1) 53410; fax (1) 53410-1280; e-mail onb@onb.ac.at; internet www.onb.ac.at; f. in 14th century; consists of 9 special collns and main library; 7,989,213 books and periodicals, 8,017 incunabula, 465,575 MSS, 17,211 microforms, 275,054 maps, 600 globes, 132,741 vols of printed music, 40,124 audiovisual media, 1,206,278 pictures, 1,013,908 other materials (papyri, exlibris and other collns); Austrian literature archive, portrait colln and picture archive; Int. Esperanto Museum; Dir-Gen. Dr JOHANNA RACHINGER; publs *Ausstellungskataloge* (irregular), *Biblios. Beiträge zu Buch, Bibliothek und Schrift* (2 a year), *Corpus Papyrorum Raineri, Mitteilungen aus der Papyrussammlung* (1 a year), *Nilus* (1 or 2 a year), *Profile. Magazin des Österreichischen Literaturarchivs* (2 or 3 a year), *Sichtungen* (1 a year).

Österreichische Zentralbibliothek für Physik (Austrian Central Library for Physics): Boltzmanngasse 5, 1090 Vienna; tel. (1) 3190011; fax (1) 42779276; internet www.zbp.univie.ac.at; f. 1946; 380,000 vols, 2,890 periodicals, 1,175,000 microfiches; Dir Mag. BRIGITTE KROMP.

Österreichisches Staatsarchiv (Austrian State Archives): Nottendorfer Gasse 2, 1030 Vienna; tel. (1) 79540-0; fax (1) 79540-199; e-mail gdpost@oesta.gv.at; internet www.oesta.gv.at; f. 1945; Domestic, Court and State Archives, Gen. Admin. Archives, Finance and Treasury Archives, War Archives, Archives of the Austrian Republic; Gen. Dir Prof. Dr LORENZ MIKOLETZKY; publ. *Mitteilungen des österreichischen Staatsarchivs*.

Parlamentsbibliothek (Library of Parliament): Dr Karl Renner-Ring 3, 1017 Vienna; tel. (1) 40110-2285; fax (1) 40110-2825; e-mail bibliothek@parlament.gv.at; internet www.parlament.gv.at/bibliothek; f. 1869; 337,700 vols; Dir Dr ELISABETH DIETRICH-SCHULZ.

Universitätsbibliothek und Universitätsarchiv der Universität für Bodenkultur Wien (Library and Archives of the University of Natural Resources and Applied Life Sciences, Vienna): Peter-Jordanstr. 82, 1190 Vienna; tel. (1) 47654-2060; fax (1) 47654-2092; e-mail ub.support@boku.ac.at; internet www.boku.ac.at/bib.html; f. 1872; 530,000 vols, 1,300 periodicals, 13,200 dissertations, 3,500 e-journals; Dir Mag. MARTINA HÖRL.

Universitätsbibliothek der Technischen Universität Wien (Vienna University of Technology Library): Resselgasse 4, 1040 Vienna; tel. (1) 58801-44001; fax (1) 58801-

44099; e-mail info@ub.tuwien.ac.at; internet www.ub.tuwien.ac.at; f. 1815; 1,325,500 vols; Dir Mag. EVA RAMMINGER.

Universitätsbibliothek der Universität für Musik und darstellende Kunst Wien (Library of the Vienna University for Music and Dramatic Art): Lothringerstr. 18, 1030 Vienna; tel. (1) 71155-8101; fax (1) 71155-8199; e-mail infobib@mdw.ac.at; internet www.ub.mdw.ac.at; f. 1909; 225,000 vols, 52,000 audiovisual media items; Bruno Walter Archive; Dir Dr SUSANNE ESCHWÉ.

Universitätsbibliothek der Wirtschaftsuniversität Wien (Library of the Vienna University of Economics and Business Administration): Augasse 2–6, 1090 Vienna; tel. (1) 313364990; fax (1) 31336745; e-mail ubww@wu-wien.ac.at; internet www.wu-wien.ac.at/bib; f. 1898; 800,000 vols; Dir Dr NIKOLAUS BERGER.

Universitätsbibliothek Wien (Vienna University Library): Dr Karl Lueger Ring 1, 1010 Vienna; tel. (1) 427715001; fax (1) 42779150; e-mail direktion@univie.ac.at; internet bibliothek.univie.ac.at; f. 1365; 6,800,000 vols; Dir Hofrätin Mag. MARIA SEISSL.

Wiener Stadt- und Landesarchiv (Municipal and Provincial Archives of Vienna): Rathaus, 1082 Vienna; Vienna 11, Guglgasse 14, Gasometer D; tel. (1) 4000-84808; fax (1) 4000-84809; e-mail post@m08.magwien.gv.at; internet www.magwien.gv.at/ma08; f. 1889; records since 13th century; Dir Prof. Dr FERDINAND OPLL; publ. *Veröffentlichungen*.

Wiener Stadt- und Landesbibliothek (Vienna City and Provincial Library): Rathaus, 1082 Vienna; tel. (1) 400084920; fax (1) 40007219; e-mail post@wienbibliothek.at; internet www.stadtbibliothek.wien.at; f. 1856; 426,000 vols, 220,000 MSS, 65,000 musical items, 16,000 MSS musical items, 150,000 posters; Dir SYLVIA MATTL-WURM.

Zentralarchiv des Deutschen Ordens: Singerstr. 7, 1010 Vienna; tel. (1) 5137014; f. 1852; 11,668 vols; Archivist Dr BERNHARD DEMEL.

Zentralbibliothek im Justizpalast (Central Library of the Palace of Justice): Museumstr. 12, 1016 Vienna; tel. (1) 52152-3351; fax (1) 52152-3677; e-mail bibliothek_ogh@justiz.gv.at; internet www.ogh.gv.at/zentralbibliothek; f. 1829; entrance restricted to qualified lawyers (no students); separate reading rooms, one for judges and public prosecutors and one for all other lawyers; 125 vols, 200 current periodicals; Dir GABRIELE SVIRAK.

Zentrale Verwaltungsbibliothek und Dokumentation für Wirtschaft und Technik (Central Library for Economics and Technology): Bundesministerium für Wirtschaftliche Angelegenheiten I, Stubenring 1, 1011 Vienna; tel. (1) 711005483; fax (1) 711002384; internet www.bmwa.gv.at/bmwa/service/bibliothek/default.htm; f. 1850; 514,000 vols; Dir Dr BRIGITTA KOHLERT-WINDISCH.

Museums and Art Galleries

Bad Deutsch-Altenburg

Archäologisches Museum Carnuntinum (Carnuntinum Archaeological Museum): Badgasse 40–46, 2405 Bad Deutsch-Altenburg; tel. (2165) 62480; fax (2165) 62480-20; f. 1904; Roman archaeology; library of 12,000 vols; Curator Mag. FRANZ HUMER.

Bregenz

Vorarlberger Landesmuseum (Vorarlberg Provincial Museum): Kornmarkt 1, 6900 Bregenz; tel. (5574) 46050; fax (5574) 4605020; e-mail info@vlm.at; internet www.vlm.at; f. 1857; archaeology, art and folklore of the region; closed for renovation until 2013; Dir TOBIAS G. NATTER; publ. *Jahrbuch*.

Eggenburg

Krahuletz Museum: Krahuletzpl., 3730 Eggenburg; tel. (2984) 3400; fax (2984) 34005; e-mail gesellschaft@krahuletzmuseum.at; internet www.krahuletzmuseum.at; colln f. 1866; geology, prehistory, ethnology; Dir Dr JOHANNES M. TUZAR; publ. *Katalogreihe*.

Eisenstadt

Burgenländisches Landesmuseum (Burgenland Provincial Museum): Museumgasse 1–5, 7000 Eisenstadt; tel. (2682) 600-1209; fax (2682) 600-1277; e-mail landesmuseum@bgld.gv.at; internet www.burgenland.at/landesmuseum; f. 1926; archaeology, geology, history of art, natural history, ethnology, numismatics, history of music; library of 31,000 vols; Dir Dr JOSEF TIEFENBACH; publ. *Wissenschaftliche Arbeiten aus dem Burgenland*.

Furth bei Göttweig

Graphische Sammlung und Kunstsammlungen Stift Göttweig (Göttweig Abbey Graphic Art Collection): Stift Göttweig 1, 3511 Furth bei Göttweig; tel. (2732) 85581220; fax (2732) 71848; e-mail graph.kabinett@stiftgoettweig.at; internet www.stiftgoettweig.at; f. 1714; graphic art from the 16th century to the present, music, coins and medals; library of 280,000 vols (history, law, theology, history of art, sciences), 1,110 MSS, 1,120 incunabula, 2,750 archives (1054–1900); Curators Prof. Dr GREGOR MARTIN LECHNER, MICHAEL GRÜNWALD.

Graz

Steiermärkisches Landesmuseum Joanneum (Provincial Museum of Styria): Raubergasse 10, 8010 Graz; tel. (316) 8017-9660; fax (316) 8017-9669; e-mail post@museum-joanneum.at; internet www.museum-joanneum.at; f. 1811; history, natural history, art (exhibits housed on several sites); picture and sound archives; Dir Dr WOLFGANG MUCHITSCH.

Innsbruck

Kaiserliche Hofburg (Imperial Palace): Rennweg 1, 6020 Innsbruck; tel. (512) 587186; fax (512) 587186-13; e-mail hofburg.ibk@burghauptmannschaft.at; internet www.hofburg-innsbruck.at; f. 15th century; built as residence of the Tyrolean provincial rulers under Archduke Sigismund the Rich and extended under Emporer Maximilian I (1459–1519), Maria Theresia (1717–1780) rebuilt the Palace in the late Viennese baroque style; spec. exhibitions throughout the year; Dir WALTRAUD SCHREILECHNER.

Kunsthistorische Museum Sammlungen Schloss Ambras (Museum of Fine Art Collections, Ambras Castle): Schloss-str. 20, Schloss Ambras, 6020 Innsbruck; tel. (1) 52524-4802; fax (1) 52524-4899; e-mail info.ambras@khm.at; internet www.khm.at/ambras; f. 1580; armour, furniture, pictures, sculpture; Curator Dr ALFRED AUER.

Museum im Zeughaus (Zeughaus Museum): Zeughausgasse, 6020 Innsbruck; tel. (512) 59489-311; fax (512) 59489-318; e-mail zeughaus@tiroler-landesmuseum.at; internet www.tiroler-landesmuseum.at; f. 1973; geology, history, technology of the Tyrol; Pres. ANDREAS TRENTINI; Dir WOLF-

GANG MEIGHÖRNER; Curator for Historical Collns Dr CLAUDIA SPORER-HEIS.

Tiroler Landesmuseum Ferdinandeum (Tyrol Provincial Museum): Museumstr. 15, 6020 Innsbruck; tel. (512) 59489-102; fax (512) 59489-109; e-mail sekretariat@tiroler-landesmuseum.at; internet www.tiroler-landesmuseum.at; f. 1823; ancient and early history, art; library of 150,000 vols; Dir ANJA LUTTINGER; publs Ferdinandea (4 a year), Veröffentlichungen des Tiroler Landesmuseums Ferdinandeum (1 a year).

Tiroler Volkskunstmuseum (Tyrol Popular Art Museum): Universitätsstr. 2, 6020 Innsbruck; tel. (512) 584302; fax (512) 584302-70; e-mail volkskunstmuseum@tirol.gv.at; internet www.tiroler-volkskunstmuseum.at; f. 1880; local folk arts and crafts; library of 2,940 vols; Dir Dr HERLINDE MENARDI; Librarian HANSJÖRG BADER.

Klagenfurt

Landesmuseum für Kärnten (Provincial Museum of Carinthia): Museumgasse 2, 9021 Klagenfurt; tel. (50) 53630599; fax (50) 53630540; e-mail info@landesmuseum-ktn.at; internet www.landesmuseum-ktn.at; f. 1844; history, natural history, archaeology, art, folk arts and crafts; library of 120,000 vols; Dir CHRISTIAN WALTL; publs Archiv für Vaterländische Geschichte und Topographie, Carinthia I (archaeology, history, history of art, and folklore), Carinthia II (science), Kärntner Heimatleben.

Landesmuseum Kärnten, Kärntner Botanikzentrum (Carinthian Botanic Centre): Prof.-Dr-Kahler-Pl. 1, 9020 Klagenfurt; tel. (463) 502715-12; e-mail kbz@landesmuseum-ktn.at; internet www.landesmuseum-ktn.at; f. 1862, present location 1958; cultivation of central and southern Alpine flora; school and adult education in botany and nature conservation; collns of orchids, succulents and carnivorous plants, poisonous and medicinal herbs, spices and useful plants, fossils (2,000 specimens); ethnobotanical and carpological collns; herbarium of 150,000 phanerogams and 50,000 cryptogams; garden for the blind; library of 13,000 vols, 16,000 offprints, slide, biographical and bibliographical collns; Head Mag. Dr ROLAND K. EBERWEIN; publs Index Seminum (1 a year), Wulfenia (1 a year).

Krems

WEINSTADT Museum (Museum of the Wine City): Körnermarkt 14, 3500 Krems; tel. (2732) 801-567; fax (2732) 801-576; e-mail museum@krems.gv.at; internet www.weinstadtmuseum.at; f. 1996; located in fmr Dominican monastery; primitive art; Romanesque and Gothic sculptures; Kremser Schmidt's paintings; Dir Dr FRANZ SCHÖNFELLNER.

Linz

Lentos Kunstmuseum Linz: Ernst-Koref-Promenade 1, 4020 Linz; tel. (732) 70703600; fax (732) 70703604; e-mail info@lentos.at; internet www.lentos.at; f. 1947 as Neue Galerie der Stadt Linz; current name 2003; gallery of Contemporary Art with paintings (ranging from Klimt, Schiele and Kokoschka to Arnulf Rainter, Karel Appel and Hermann Nitsch), drawings, prints, posters and sculptures since 19th century; library: library incl. 30,000 catalogues; Dir of Art STELLA ROLLIG; Exec. Dir GERNOT BAROUNIG.

Oberösterreichische Landesmuseen (State Museums for Upper Austria): Museumstr. 14, 4010 Linz; tel. (732) 774482-0; fax (732) 774482-66; internet www.landesmuseum.at; f. 1833; library of 130,000 vols; Dir Mag. Dr PETER ASSMANN;

publs Beiträge zur Naturkunde Oberösterreichs, Denisia, Linzer biologische Beiträge, Neues Museum, Stapfia, Studien zur Kulturgeschichte von Oberösterreich, Vogelkundliche Nachrichten aus Oberösterreich.

Salzburg

Haus der Natur/Museum für Natur und Technik (Natural History Museum): Museumpl. 5, 5020 Salzburg; tel. (662) 842653-0; fax (662) 842653-99; e-mail office@hausdernatur.at; internet www.hausdernatur.at; f. 1924; zoology, botany, anthropology, geology; reptile zoo, aquarium, space hall; Dir Prof. Dr NORBERT WINDING.

Mozarteum: Schwarzstr. 26, 5020 Salzburg; tel. (662) 88940-0; fax (662) 88940-36; e-mail office@mozarteum.at; internet www.mozarteum.at; f. 1914 by 'Internationale Stiftung Mozarteum'; concert rooms, a library of MSS, books and other Mozart memorabilia; Pres. Dr FRIEDRICH GEHMACHER.

Mozarts Wohnhaus: Makartpl. 8, 5020 Salzburg,; tel. (662) 87422740; fax (662) 872924; e-mail archiv@mozarteum.at; internet www.mozarteum.at; multivision 'Mozart and Salzburg'; the world of Mozart 1773–80; instruments from Mozart's time.

Residenzgalerie Salzburg: Residenzpl. 1, 5010 Salzburg; tel. (662) 840451-0; fax (662) 84045116; e-mail residenzgalerie@salzburg.gv.at; internet www.residenzgalerie.at; f. 1923; 16th- to 19th-century European paintings; Dir Dr ROSWITHA JUFFINGER.

Salzburg Museum: Neue Residenz, 5010 Salzburg; tel. (662) 620808-0; fax (662) 620808-720; e-mail office@salzburgmuseum.at; internet www.salzburgmuseum.at; f. 1834; prehistoric and Roman remains, art, coins, musical instruments, costumes, toys; library of 100,000 vols, archives; Dir ERICH MARX.

Schloss Hellbrunn (Hellbrunn Palace): 5020 Salzburg; tel. (662) 820372-0; fax (662) 820372-4931; e-mail info@hellbrunn.at; internet www.hellbrunn.at; f. 1612; furnished 17th-century palace, with water gardens, deer park and open-air theatre; Dir INGRID SONVILLA.

St Pölten

Niederösterreichisches Landesmuseum (Provincial Museum of Lower Austria): Kulturbezirk 5, 3109 St Pölten; tel. (2742) 908090; fax (2742) 908099; e-mail info@landesmuseum.net; internet www.landesmuseum.net; f. 1907; natural history, history of art (since the medieval period); many attached deptl museums are located in Lower Austria, incl. Haydn's birthplace at Rohrau; information centre; Dirs CHRISTIAN BAUER, CORNELIA LAMPRECHTER.

Stillfried/March

Museum für Ur- und Frühgeschichte (Museum for Pre- and Early History): Museumsverein Stillfried, Hauptstr. 23, 2262 Stillfried/March (Niederösterreich); tel. (676) 6113979; e-mail stillfried@aon.at; internet www.museumstillfried.at; f. 1914; local archaeology and palaeontology; Dir Dr WALPURGA ANTL; publ. Museumsnachrichten (3 or 4 a year).

Vienna

Albertina: Albertinapl. 1, 1010 Vienna; tel. (1) 53483-0; fax (1) 53483-430; e-mail info@albertina.at; internet www.albertina.at; f. 1776, fmrly Graphische Sammlung Albertina; prints, drawings, posters; library of 40,000 vols; 500 oil paintings; Dir KLAUS ALBRECHT SCHRÖDER.

Erzbischöfliches Dom- und Diözesanmuseum (Archiepiscopal Cathedral and Diocesan Museum): Stephanspl. 6, 1010 Vienna; tel. (1) 51552-3689; fax (1) 51552-3599; e-mail dommuseum@edw.or.at; internet www.dommuseum.at; f. 1933; ecclesiastical art; Dir BERNHARD BÖHLER.

Gemäldegalerie der Akademie der Bildenden Künste Wien (Vienna Academy of Fine Arts Gallery): Schillerpl. 3, 1010 Vienna; tel. (1) 58816228; fax (1) 5863346; e-mail gemgal@akbild.ac.at; internet www.akademiegalerie.at; f. 1822; paintings since 14th century; Dir Dr RENATE TRNEK.

Heeresgeschichtliches Museum (Military History Museum): III, Arsenal, Vienna; tel. (1) 79561-0; fax (1) 79561-17707; e-mail bmlv.hgm@magnet.at; internet www.hgm.or.at; f. 1891; exhibits dating from Thirty Years War to Second World War; library of 70,000 vols; Dir Dr MANFRIED RAUCHENSTEINER.

Kunsthistorisches Museum (Museum of Fine Arts): Burgring 5, 1010 Vienna; tel. (1) 52524-401; fax (1) 52524503; e-mail info@khm.at; internet www.khm.at; f. 1891 from Hapsburg Imperial collections; paintings, Egyptian and other antiquities, numismatics, armour, historical costume, plastics and handicrafts, musical instruments, secular and ecclesiastical relics of the Holy Roman Empire and the Hapsburg dynasty, state carriages (at Schönbrunn palace); library of 85,000 vols; Gen. Dir Dr WILFRIED SEIPEL.

Kupferstichkabinett der Akademie der Bildenden Künste (Graphic Art Collection of the Academy of Fine Arts): Makartgasse 3, 1010 Vienna; tel. (1) 5813040; fax (1) 5813040-31; e-mail m.knofler@akbild.ac.at; internet www.akbild.at/kuka; f. 1689; drawings, prints, photographs, architecture; library: see Libraries and Archives; Dir Dr MONIKA KNOFLER.

Leopold Museum: Museumspl. 1, 1070 Vienna; tel. (1) 52570-0; fax (1) 52570-1500; e-mail office@leopoldmuseum.org; internet www.leopoldmuseum.org; f. 2001; fmrly private art colln of Rudolf and Elisabeth Leopold; works by Schiele, Klimt, Kokoschka and others; Dir Prof. Dr RUDOLF LEOPOLD.

Medizinhistorische Sammlungen am Josephinum: Währingerstr. 25, 1090 Vienna; tel. (1) 427763404; internet www.meduniwien.ac.at/medizingeschichte/med-histmus_uebersicht.htm; f. 1785 as acad. for military surgeons; 18th-century wax anatomical colln, museum of the 2 Vienna Medical Schools and museum of medical endoscopy; library of 80,000 historical medical books; Head of Medicohistorical Collections Assoc. Prof. Dr MANFRED SKOPEC.

Museum für Völkerkunde (Museum of Ethnology): Neue Hofburg, Ringstrassentrakt, 1010 Vienna; tel. (1) 52524-5052; fax (1) 52524-5199; e-mail info@ethno-museum.ac.at; internet www.ethno-museum.ac.at; f. 1928; ethnology of non-European peoples; 220,000 objects; library of 130,000 vols; Dir Prof. Dr CHRISTIAN FEEST; publs Archiv für Völkerkunde (1 a year), Veröffentlichungen zum Archiv für Völkerkunde.

Museum Moderner Kunst Stiftung Ludwig Wien (Museum of Modern Art Ludwig Foundation Vienna): Museumspl. 1, 1070 Vienna; tel. (1) 52500-0; fax (1) 52500-1300; e-mail info@mumok.at; internet www.mumok.at; f. 1991; modern and contemporary art, incl. American Pop Art and concurrent European movements; library of 25,000 vols; Dir EDELBERT KÖB.

Naturhistorisches Museum (Natural History Museum): I, Burgring 7, 1010 Vienna; tel. (1) 52177-0; fax (1) 5235254; e-mail waswannwo@nhm-wien.ac.at; internet www

.nhm-wien.ac.at; f. 1748; more than 20m. natural objects; ecology, geology, palaeontology, zoology, botany, anthropology, prehistory, speleology; library of 400,000 books; Exec. Dir Prof. Dr CHRISTIAN KÖBERL; Librarian ANDREA KOURGLI; publ. *Annalen*.

Österreichische Galerie Belvedere (Austrian Gallery): Oberes Belvedere, Prinz Eugenstr. 27, 1030 Vienna; tel. (1) 79557-0; fax (1) 79557-121; e-mail public@belvedere .at; internet www.belvedere.at; Austrian painting and sculpture from Middle Ages to present, foreign painting and sculpture since 19th century, spec. colln of sculpture by G. Ambrosi; library of 80,000 vols; Dir Dr AGNES HUSSLEIN-ARCO; publ. *Belvedere*.

Österreichisches Gesellschafts- und Wirtschafts-Museum (Austrian Museum for Economics and Social Affairs): Vogelsanggasse 36, 1050 Vienna; tel. (1) 5452551; fax (1) 5452551-55; e-mail wirtschaftsmuseum@ oegwm.ac.at; internet www.oegwm.ac.at; f. 1925; archives, maps, photographs; public library on 'Austria Yesterday and Today'; Dir Mag. HANS HARTWEGER; publ. *Österreichs Wirtschaft im Überblick* (1 a year; also in English).

Österreichisches Museum für angewandte Kunst (Austrian Museum of Applied Arts): Stubenring 5, 1010 Vienna; tel. (1) 711360; fax (1) 7131026; e-mail office@ mak.at; internet www.mak.at; f. 1864; applied arts from Roman to modern times, incl. furniture and woodwork, textiles and carpets, glass and ceramics, Islamic and East Asian art, metalwork, The Wiener Werkstätte colln and contemporary art; library of 200,000 vols, 300 periodicals, 500,000 prints; Dir PETER NOEVER.

Österreichisches Museum für Volkskunde (Austrian Museum of Folk Life and Folk Art): Laudongasse 15–19, 1080 Vienna; tel. (1) 4068905; fax (1) 4085342; e-mail office@volkskundemuseum.at; internet www .volkskundemuseum.at; f. 1895; incl. nat. furniture colln and other spec. collns (housed on separate sites); Dir Dr MARGOT SCHINDLER; publs *Kataloge* (1–3 issues a year), *Veröffentlichungen* (irregular).

Österreichisches Theatermuseum: Lobkowitzpl. 2, 1010 Vienna; tel. (1) 52524-3460; fax (1) 52524-5399; internet www .theatermuseum.at; f. 1991; library of 80,000 vols; Dir Dr THOMAS TRABITSCH.

Schloss Schönbrunn Kultur- und Betriebsges. m.b.H. (Schönbrunn Palace): Schönbrunn, 1130 Vienna, Schloss; tel. (1) 81113-239; fax (1) 8121106; internet www .schoenbrunn.at; mid 18th-century fmr Imperial summer residence of the Habsburg dynasty; baroque and botanical gardens; zoological garden opened 1752; Dirs Dipl.-Ing. WOLFGANG KIPPES, Dr FRANZ SATTLECKER.

Technisches Museum Wien (Museum of Technology in Vienna): Mariahilferstr. 212, 1140 Vienna; tel. (1) 89998-6000; fax (1) 89998-3333; e-mail museumsbox@tmw.at; internet www.tmw.at; f. 1907; library of 40,000 vols; Dir Mag. PETER DONHAUSER; publ. *Blätter für Technikgeschichte* (1 a year).

Wien Museum: Karlspl., 1040 Vienna; tel. (1) 5058747-0; fax (1) 5058747-7201; e-mail office@wienmuseum.at; internet www .wienmuseum.at; f. 1887; local history from prehistoric times to the present; among many associated museums are premises once occupied by Beethoven, Haydn, Mozart, Schubert and Johann Strauss; Dir Dr WOLFGANG KOS.

Universities

All institutions of higher education have university status.

AKADEMIE DER BILDENDEN KÜNSTE WIEN
(Academy of Fine Arts Vienna)

Schillerpl. 3, 1010 Vienna

Telephone: (1) 588-16-0
Fax: (1) 588-16-1898
E-mail: info@akbild.ac.at
Internet: www.akbild.ac.at

Founded 1692
State control
Academic year: October to June

Rector: Prof. Dr STEPHAN SCHMIDT-WULFFEN
Pro-Rectors: Mag. ANDREAS SPIEGL, Mag. ANNA STEIGER
Librarian: BEATRIX BASTL
Library: see Libraries and Archives
Number of teachers: 190
Number of students: 1,083

PROFESSORS

ALLIEZ, E., Aesthetics and Sociology of Art
BAATZ, W., Conservation and Restoration
BAUER, U. M., Theory, Practice and Transfer of Contemporary Art
BISCHOF, E., Textile Art
DAMISCH, G., Drawing and Graphic Techniques
GIRONCOLI, B., Sculpture
GRAF, F., Expanded Artistic Environment
GRAF, O., Art History
GREEN, R., Conceptual Art
HASPEL, F., Textile Art
KOGLER, P., Computer and Video Art
LAINER, R., Architectural Design
OBHOLZER, W., Abstract Art
PRUSCHA, C., Architectural Design and Habitat, Environment and Conservation
ROSENBLUM, A., Representational Painting and Drawing
SAMSONOW, E., Philosophical and Historical Anthropology of the Arts
SCHLEGEL, E., Photography and Art
SCHMALIX, H., Art in Public Space
SCHREINER, M., Natural Science and Technology in Art
SCHULZ, J., Textile Arts and Crafts, Tapestry
SLOTERDIJK, P., Cultural Philosophy and Media Theory
WAGNER, K., Construction and Technology
WONDER, E., Stage Design
ZENS, H., Education and Science of Art
ZOBERNIG, H., Sculpture

UNIVERSITÄT FÜR ANGEWANDTE KUNST IN WIEN
(University of Applied Arts in Vienna)

Oskar Kokoschkapl. 2, 1010 Vienna

Telephone: (1) 71133-0
Fax: (1) 71133-222
E-mail: pr@uni-ak.ac.at
Internet: www.dieangewandte.at

Founded 1868

Rector: Dr GERALD BAST
Vice-Rectors: Prof. JOSEF KAISER, Prof. WOLF D. PRIX, Prof. BARBARA PUTZ-PLECKO
Chair. of the Academic Senate: Prof. SIGBERT SCHENK
Dean of Studies: Prof. JOSEF KAISER
Univ. Dir: Dr HEINZ ADAMEK
Registrar: SENTA SCHWANDA
Head Librarian: Dr GABRIELE KOLLER
Library of 85,000 vols, 300 periodicals
Number of teachers: 380
Number of students: 1,344
Publications: exhibition catalogues (6–8 a year), *Prospect* (2 a year)

HEADS OF INSTITUTES

Institute of Aesthetics and Cultural Studies/ Art Pedagogy: Prof. JAMES G. SKONE
Institute of Architecture: Prof. WOLF D. PRIX
Institute of Art and Knowledge Transfer: Prof. Dr CHRISTIAN REDER
Institute of Art and Technology: Prof. Dr ALFRED VENDL
Institute of Conservation and Restoration: Prof. Dr GABRIELA KRIST
Institute of Design: Prof. PAOLO PIVA
Institute of Fine and Media Arts: Prof. GABRIELE ROTHEMANN

UNIVERSITÄT FÜR BODENKULTUR WIEN
(University of Natural Resources and Applied Life Sciences, Vienna)

Gregor Mendelstr. 33, 1180 Vienna

Telephone: (1) 47654-0
Fax: (1) 47654-2606
E-mail: bdr@boku.ac.at
Internet: www.boku.ac.at

Founded 1872
State control
Academic year: October to June

Rector: Prof. Dr MARTIN H. GERZABEK
Vice-Rector for Research: Prof. Dr MARTIN H. GERZABEK
Vice-Rector for Studies and Int. Affairs: Prof. Dr ERIKA STAUDACHER
Librarian: Mag. MARTINA HÖRL
Library: see under Libraries and Archives
Number of teachers: 1,000
Number of students: 8,700

Publications: *Blick ins Land* (12 a year), *Die Bodenkultur*, *Ökoenergie* (6 a year), *Zentralblatt für das gesamte Forstwesen* (4 a year)

PROFESSORS

KOSMA, P., Organic Chemistry
LICKA, L., Landscape Architecture
LISCHKA, H., Soil Science
MINSCH, J., Sustainable Economic Devt
ROSENAU, T., Organic Chemistry
SCHNEIDER, W., Surveying, Remote Sensing and Land Information
SCHOPF, A., Forest Entomology, Forest Pathology and Forest Protection
SÖLKNER, J., Livestock Sciences
STINGEDER, G. J., Analytical Chemistry
TREBERSPURG, M., Structural Engineering
TSCHEGG, S., Material Sciences and Process Engineering
WIMMER, R., Wood Science and Technology
WINCKLER, C., Livestock Sciences
WINDISCH, W. M., Animal Food and Nutrition
WU, W., Geotechnical Engineering

ATTACHED RESEARCH CENTRES

Centre for Applied Genetics: internet www.boku.ac.at/zag; Dir Prof. J. GLÖSSL.

Centre for Environmental Studies and Nature Conservation: internet www.boku .ac.at/zun; Dir Prof. W. HOLZNER.

DONAU-UNIVERSITÄT KREMS/ UNIVERSITÄT FÜR WEITERBILDUNG
(Danube University Krems/University of Continuing Education)

Dr-Karl-Dorrek-Str. 30, 3500 Krems

Telephone: (2732) 893-0
Fax: (2732) 893-4000
E-mail: info@donau-uni.ac.at
Internet: www.donau-uni.ac.at

Founded 1994
State control
Languages of instruction: German, English
Academic year: October to June

Rector: Prof. Dr JÜRGEN WILLER

Vice-Rector: Prof. Dr STEFAN NEHRER
Library of 79,312 vols, 24, 698 electronic journals
Number of teachers: 1,590
Number of students: 5,065
Publication: *Upgrade* (4 a year)

PROFESSORS

BAHLI, B., Management and Economics
BAUMGARTNER, P., Interactive Media and Educational Technology
BIFFL, G., Migration, Integration and Security
BRAININ, M., Clinical Medicine and Preventive Medicine
FALKENHAGEN, D., Environmental and Medical Sciences
FILZMAIER, P., Political Communication
FINA, S., European Integration
GARTLEHNER, G., Evidence-based Medicine and Clinical Epidemiology
GENSCH, G., Arts and Management
GRAU, O., Applied Cultural Studies
LEITNER, A., Psychosocial Medicine and Psychotherapy
LEITNER, C., New Public Management and E-Governance
MIKSCH, S., Information and Knowledge Engineering
NEHRER, S., Regenerative Medicine
RISKU, H., Knowledge and Communication Management
STELZEL, M., Interdisciplinary Dentistry and Technology
WAGNER, M., Technology Enhanced Learning and Multimedia
WILLER, J., Interdisciplinary Dentistry and Technology

JOHANNES KEPLER UNIVERSITÄT LINZ
(Johannes Kepler University, Linz)

Altenberger Str. 69, 4040 Linz
Telephone: (732) 2468-3369
Fax: (732) 2468-3365
E-mail: rektor@jku.at
Internet: www.jku.at
Founded as College 1966, present name and status 1975
State control
Languages of instruction: German, English
Academic year: October to June
Rector: Prof. Dr RICHARD HAGELAUER
Vice-Rector for Finance and Resource Management: Dr FRANZ WURM
Vice-Rector for Foreign Affairs: Prof. Dr FRIEDRICH ROITHMAYR
Vice-Rector for Research: Prof. Dr GABRIELE KOTSIS
Vice-Rector for Teaching: Prof. Dr HERBERT KALB
Admin. Dir: Dr JOSEF SCHMIED
Librarian: Dr MONIKA SCHENK
Library: see Libraries and Archives
Number of teachers: 554
Number of students: 12,307
Publication: *UNIVATIONEN—Forschungsmedienservice der Johannes Kepler Universität Linz* (4 a year)

DEANS

Faculty of Engineering and Natural Sciences: Prof. Dipl.-Ing. Dr WOLFGANG BUCHBERGER
Faculty of Law: Prof. Dr HERIBERT FRANZ KÖCK
Faculty of Social Sciences, Economics and Business: Prof. GERHARD WÜHRER

PROFESSORS

Faculty of Engineering and Natural Sciences (Altenberger Str. 69, 4040 Linz; tel. (732) 2468-3220; fax (732) 2468-3225; e-mail tnf-dekanat@jku.at; internet www.tn.jku.at):

AMRHEIN, W., Electrical Drives and Power Electronics
BAUER, G., Semiconductor Physics
BAUER, S., Soft Matter Physics
BÄUERLE, D., Applied Physics
BIERE, A., Formal Models and Verification
BREMER, H., Robotics
BUCHBERGER, W., Analytical Chemistry
CHROUST, G., Systems Engineering and Automation
COOPER, J. B., Functional Analysis
DEL RE, L., Design and Control of Mechatronical Systems
ENGL, H., Industrial Mathematics
FALK, H., Organic Chemistry
FERSCHA, A., Pervasive Computing
GITTLER, P., Fluid Mechanics and Heat Transfer
GRITZNER, G., Chemical Technology of Inorganic Materials
HAGELAUER, R., Integrated Circuits
HOCHREITER, S., Bioinformatics
IRSCHIK, H., Technical Mechanics
JAKOBY, B., Microelectronics
JANTSCH, W., Solid State Physics
JÜTTLER, B., Applied Geometry
KLEMENT, E. P., Fuzzy Logic
KNÖR, G., Inorganic Chemistry
KOTSIS, G., Telecooperation
KROTSCHECK, E., Many Particle Systems
LANGER, U., Computational Mathematics
LARCHER, G., Financial Mathematics
MÖSSENBÖCK, H., System Software
MÜHLBACHER, J., Information Processing and Microprocessor Technology
PAULE, P., Symbolic Computation
PILZ, G., Algebra
POHL, P., Biophysics
SAMHABER, W., Process Engineering
SARICIFTCI, N. S., Physical Chemistry
SCHÄFFLER, F., Semiconductor Physics
SCHEIDL, R., Machine Design and Hydraulic Drives
SCHLACHER, K., Automatic Control and Control Systems Technology
SCHLÖGLMANN, W., Mathematics Education
SCHMIDT, H., Chemical Technology of Organic Materials
SOBCZAK, R., Polymer Science
SPRINGER, A., Communications and Information Engineering
TITULAER, U. M., Condensed Matter Theory
VOLKERT, J., Graphics and Parallel Processing
WAGNER, R., Applied Knowledge Processing
WEIß, P., Stochastics
WIDMER, G., Computational Perception
WINKLER, F., Symbolic Computation
ZAGAR, B., Electrical Measurement Technology
ZEMAN, K., Computer-aided Methods in Mechanical Engineering
ZEPPENFELD, P., Atomic Physics and Surface Science

Faculty of Law (tel. (732) 2468-3201; fax (732) 2468-3205; e-mail re-dekanat@jku.at; internet www.re.jku.at):

ACHATZ, M., Administrative Law and Management
ACHATZ, M., Research Department for Tax Law and Tax Management
APATHY, P., Roman Law
BINDER, B., Administrative Law and Administrative Sciences
BURGSTALLER, A., European and Austrian Civil Procedure Law
DOLINAR, H., Civil Procedure
FLOSZMANN, U., History of Austrian and German Law

FUNK, B.-C., University Law
HAUER, A., Public Law with Special Reference to Austrian Administrative Law
HENGSTSCHLÄGER, J., Constitutional Law and Political Science
JABORNEGG, P., Labour Law and Social Security
KALB, H., Canon Law
KAROLLUS, M., Commercial and Securities Law
KEINERT, H., Commercial and Securities Law
KERSCHNER, F., Civil Law and Environmental Law
KLINGENBERG, G., Roman Law
KÖCK, H., Public International Law and European Law
LEITL, B., Correspondence Course
OBERNDORFER, P., Administrative Law and Administrative Sciences
REISCHAUER, R., Civil Law
RIEDLER, A., Correspondence Course
RUMMEL, P., Civil Law
SPIELBUECHLER, K., Civil Law
WEGSCHEIDER, H., Criminal Law and Procedure
WIDDER, H., Constitutional Law and Political Science
VELTEN, P., Criminal Law and Procedure

Faculty of Social Sciences, Economics and Business (tel. (732) 2468-3211; fax (732) 2468-3215; e-mail sowi-dekanat@jku.at; internet www.sowi.jku.at):

ALTRICHTER, H., Education and Educational Psychology
BACHER, J., Sociology
BATINIC, B., E-learning
BECKER, P., Modern and Contemporary History
BÖHNISCH, W., Business Administration (Management), Human Resources Management
BRUNNER, J., Economics
COCCA, T., Asset Management
DULLECK, U., Economics
DYK, I., Socio-politics
EULER, H. P., Sociology
FELDBAUER-DURSTMÜLLER, B., Business Administration (Accountancy, Auditing, Business Taxation and Controllership)
FRÜHWIRTH-SCHNATTER, S., Applied Statistics and Econometrics
GADENNE, V., Philosophy and Theory of Science
HAUCH, G., Modern and Contemporary History, Gender Studies
KAILER, N., Entrepreneurship and Business Development
LANDESMANN, M., National Economy
MALINSKY, A. H., Environmental Management in Business and Regional Policy
MATZLER, K., Business Administration
MÜLLER, W. G., Applied Statistics
PERNSTEINER, H., Corporate Finance
PILS, M., Data Processing
PÖLL, G., Economics
POMBERGER, G., Software Engineering
ROHATSCHEK, R., Business Administration, Accountancy, Auditing, Business Taxation and Controllership
ROITHMAYR, F., Information Engineering
SANDGRUBER, R., Social and Economic History
SCHAUER, R., Business Administration (Public Administration and Non-Profit Organizations)
SCHNEIDER, F., Economics, Public Economics, Public Choice
SCHREFL, M., Data and Knowledge Engineering
SCHURER, B., Economic and Business Education
SCHUSTER, H., Economics
STARY, C., Communications Engineering
STREHL, F., Business Administration

TUMPEL, M., Business Administration, Accountancy, Auditing, Business Taxation and Controllership
WEIDENHOLZER, J., Social Policy
WINTER-EBMER, R., Economics
WÜHRER, G., Business Administration (Marketing)

KARL-FRANZENS-UNIVERSITÄT GRAZ
(Graz University)

Universitätspl. 3, 8010 Graz
Telephone: (316) 380-0
Fax: (316) 380-9140
E-mail: info@uni-graz.at
Internet: www.uni-graz.at
Founded 1585 legal entity in public law, funded mainly by the Fed. Govt
State control
Academic year: October to September (2 terms)
Rector: Prof. Dr ALFRED GUTSCHELHOFER
Vice-Rectors: Prof. Dr RENATE DWORCZAK, Prof. Dr IRMTRAUD FISCHER, Prof. Dr ROBERTA MAIERHOFER, Prof. Dr MARTIN POLASCHEK
Chief Admin. Officer: Dr MARIA EDLINGER
Librarian: Dr WERNER SCHLACHER
Library: see Libraries and Archives
Number of teachers: 2,563
Number of students: 22,010

DEANS

Faculty of Arts and Humanities: Prof. Dr GERNOT KOCHER
Faculty of Environmental and Regional Sciences and Education: Prof. Dr WERNER LENZ
Faculty of Law: Prof. Dr WILLIBALD POSCH
Faculty of Natural Sciences: Dr GEORG HOINKES
Faculty of Social and Economic Sciences: Prof. Dr WOLF RAUCH
Faculty of Theology: Prof. Dr HANS-FERDINAND ANGEL

PROFESSORS

Faculty of Arts and Humanities (Universitätspl. 3, 8010 Graz; tel. (316) 380-2288; fax (316) 380-9700; e-mail geisteswiss.dekanat@uni-graz.at; internet www.uni-graz.at/en/gewi.htm):

EISMANN, W., Slavic Studies
ERTLER, K.-D., Romance Studies
GOLTSCHNIGG, D., German Studies
GÖPFERICH, S., Translation and Interpreting Studies
HÄRTEL, R., History
HAUG-MORITZ, G., History
HEINEMANN, S., Romance Studies
HELMICH, W., Romance Studies
HIEBEL, H.-H., German Studies
HÖFLECHNER, W., History
HÖLBLING, W., American Studies
HUMMEL, M., Romance Studies
HURCH, B., Linguistics
KASER, K., History
KONRAD, H., History
MAHLER, A., English Studies
MEYER, L., Philosophy
PARNCUTT, R., Music
PIEPER, R., History
PORTMANN, P., German Studies
PRUNC, E., Translation and Interpreting Studies
TOSOVIC, B., Slavic Studies
WALTER, M., Music
WOLF, W., English Studies
ZIEGLER, A., German Studies

Faculty of Environmental and Regional Sciences and Education (Universitätspl. 3 8010 Graz; tel. (316) 380-8020; fax (316) 380-9700;

e-mail urbi.dekan@uni-graz.at; internet www.uni-graz.at/en/brek3www.htm):

HACKL, B., Teacher Training
HOPFNER, J., Education
LENZ, W., Education
SCHEIPL, J., Education
STRASSER, U., Geography and Regional Sciences
SUST, M., Sport Science
ZIMMERMANN, F., Geography and Regional Sciences

Faculty of Law (Universitätsstr. 15/A, 8010 Graz; tel. (316) 380-3260; fax (316) 380-9400; e-mail rewi.dekanat@uni-graz.at; internet www.uni-graz.at/en/enredwww):

BENEDEK, W., International Law and International Relations
KOLLER, P., Legal Philosophy, Sociology and Informatics
MARHOLD, F., Labour Law and Social Security Law
MEDIGOVIC, U., Criminology and Criminal Justice
SCHICK, P., Criminology and Criminal Justice
SCHMALENBACH, K., International Law and International Relations
SCHMÖLZER, G., Criminology and Criminal Justice
SOYER, R., Criminology and Criminal Justice
THÜR, G., Roman Law, Ancient Legal History and Modern Legal History

Faculty of Natural Sciences (Universitätspl. 3 8010 Graz; tel. (316) 380-5000; fax (316) 380-9800; e-mail nawi.dekanat@uni-graz.at; internet www.uni-graz.at/nawi/):

ALBERT, D., Psychology
ALKOFER, R., Physics
ARENDASY, M., Psychology
BAUER, R., Pharmacognosy
BLANZ, P., Botany
CRAILSHEIM, K., Zoology
FISCHER, P., Psychology
FRÖHLICH, K.-U., Molecular Biosciences
GATTRINGER, C., Physics
GRUBER, K., Molecular Biosciences
HAASE, G., Mathematics and Scientific Computing
HANSLMEIER, A., Physics
KALLUS, K. W., Psychology
KAPPEL, F., Mathematics
KIRCHENGAST, G., Physics
KOHLWEIN, S.-D., Molecular Biosciences
KRATKY, C., Molecular Biosciences
KRENN, H., Physics
KUNISCH, K., Mathematics and Scientific Computing
LANG, C., Physics
MADEO, F., Molecular Biosciences
MAYER, B. M., Pharmacology and Toxicology
NETZER, F., Physics
NEUBAUER, A., Psychology
NEUPER, C., Psychology
PAECHTER, M., Psychology
PÖTZ, W., Physics
REIDL, J., Molecular Biosciences
RINDERMANN, H., Psychology
ROITSCH, T., Plant Sciences
RÖMER, H., Zoology
SCHAPPACHER, W., Mathematics and Scientific Computing
SCHIENLE, A., Psychology
SCHULTER, G., Psychology
SPAHN-LANGGUTH, H., Pharmaceutical Sciences
STURMBAUER, CH., Zoology
UHLIG, T., Psychology
ZECHNER, R., Molecular Biosciences
ZIMMER, A., Pharmaceutical Sciences

Faculty of Social and Economic Sciences (Universitätsstr. 15/A 8010 Graz; tel. (316) 380-6813; fax (316) 380-9400; e-mail sowi

.dekanat@uni-graz.at; internet domino .uni-graz.at/dekanat-extern/main.nsf/layout_e):

BAIGENT, N., Public Economics
FISCHER, E., Finance
FOSCHT, T., Marketing
HALLER, M., Sociology
LEOPOLD-WILDBURGER, U., Statistics and Operations Research
ORTLIEB, R., Human Resource Management
RAUCH, W., Information Science and Information Systems
REIMANN, M., Production and Operations Management
WETTERER, A., Sociology

Faculty of Theology (Universitätspl. 3 8010 Graz; tel. (316) 380-3150; fax (316) 380-9300; e-mail theologisches.dekanat@uni-graz.at; internet www-theol.uni-graz.at/cms/ziel/26669/en/):

BECHMANN, U., World Religions
BUCHER, R.-M., Psychology and Pastoral Theology
ESTERBAUER, R., Theology and Philosophy
FISCHER, I., Old Testament Studies
GROEN, B., Liturgics, Church Music and Christian Art
HEIL, C., New Testament Studies
LARCHER, G., Fundamental Theology

UNIVERSITÄT KLAGENFURT
(University of Klagenfurt)

Universitätsstr. 65–67, 9020 Klagenfurt
Telephone: (463) 2700-0
Fax: (463) 2700-9299
E-mail: uni@uni-klu.ac.at
Internet: www.uni-klu.ac.at
Founded 1970
State control
Academic year: October to February,March to June
Rector: Prof. Dr HEINRICH C. MAYR
Vice-Rectors: Prof. Dr PETRA HESSE, Prof. Dr HUBERT LENGAUER, Prof. Dr JUTTA MENSCHIK-BENDELE
Librarian: Dr MANFRED LUBE
Number of teachers: 520
Number of students: 6,959

DEANS

Faculty of Humanities: Prof. Dr ALBERT BERGER
Faculty of Interdisciplinary Research and Education: Prof. Dr ROLAND FISCHER
Faculty of Social Sciences: Prof. Dr HANS-JOACHIM BODENHÖFER
Faculty of Technical Sciences: Prof. Dr MARTIN HINZ

PROFESSORS

Faculty of Humanities (tel. (463) 2700-1002):

ARNOLD, U., Philosophy
ASPETSBERGER, F., German Philology
BAMMÉ, A., Educational Science
BERGER, A., German Philology
BRANDSTETTER, A., German Philology
GSTETTNER, P., Educational Science
HEINTEL, P., Philosophy and Group Dynamics
HÖDL, G., Medieval History and Studies Related to History
HOVORKA, H., Special Educational Theory Relating to Disabilities
JAMES, A., English and American Studies
KARMASIN, M., Communications
KLINGLER, J., Educational Theory
KUNA, F. M., English and American Studies
LARCHER, D., Educational Science
LÖSCHENKOHL, E., Psychology and Developmental Psychology

MAYERTHALER, W., General and Applied Philology
MELEZINEK, A., Teaching Methods
MENSCHIK, J., Educational Science
METER, H., Romance Studies
MORITSCH, A., History of Southern and Eastern Europe
NEUHÄUSER, R., Slavic Studies
NEWEKLOWSKY, G., Slavic Studies
OTTOMEYER, K., Social Psychology
POHL, H.-D., General Philology
POSCH, P., Curriculum Studies
RUMPLER, H., Modern Austrian History
SCHAUSBERGER, N., Modern Austrian History
STROBEL, K., Ancient History and Archaeology
STUHLPFARRER, K., History
VÖLKL, F., Educational Psychology
WANDRUSZKA, U., Romance Studies
ZIMA, P. V., General Comparative Literature

Faculty of Technical Sciences (tel. (463) 2700-5003):

BODENHÖFER, H.-J., Economics of Education
BÖSZÖRMÉNYI, L., Computer Science
DÖRFLER, W., Mathematics
EDER, J., Computer Science
FISCHER, R., Mathematics
FRIEDRICH, G., Computer Science
HELLWAGNER, H., Computer Science
HITZ, M., Computer Science
HORSTER, P., Computer Science
KALSS, S., Law
KALUZA, B., Business Administration
KELLERMANN, P., Sociology of Education
KOFLER, H., Business Administration
KROPFBERGER, D., Business Administration
MAYR, H., Computer Science
MITTERMEIR, R., Computer Science
MÜLLER, W., Mathematics
NADVORNIK, W., Business Administration
NECK, R., Business Administration
PILZ, J., Applied Statistics
POTACS, M., Law
RENDL, F., Mathematics
RIECKMANN, H.-J., Business Administration
RONDO-BROYETTO, P., Business Administration
SAUBERER, M., Geography
SCHNEIDER, D., Business Administration
SCHWARZ, E., Business Administration
SEGER, M., Geography
STETTNER, H., Mathematics

ATTACHED INSTITUTE

Interuniversitäres Institut für Interdisziplinäre Forschung und Fortbildung: Sterneckstr. 15, 9020 Klagenfurt; tel. (463) 2700-754; fax (463) 2700-759; f. 1980; devt of innovative research projects in such fields as man–machine relationship, preventive health policy, in-service teacher training; Dir Prof. Dr ROLAND FISCHER; publ. *Perspektiven für Fernstudien.*

UNIVERSITÄT FÜR KÜNSTLERISCHE UND INDUSTRIELLE GESTALTUNG LINZ
(University of Art and Industrial Design, Linz)

Hauptpl. 8, 4010 Linz
Telephone: (732) 7898-0
Fax: (732) 783508
E-mail: kunstunilinz@ufg.ac.at
Internet: www.ufg.ac.at
Founded 1947, present status 1998
Rector: Prof. Dr REINHARD KANNONIER
Vice-Rectors: Dr MANFRED LECHNER, Dr CHRISTINE WINDSTEIGER, RAINER ZENDRON
Librarian: URSULA GANGLBAUER

Library of 50,000 vols
Number of teachers: 140
Number of students: 985

MEDIZINISCHE UNIVERSITÄT GRAZ

Universitätspl. 3, 8010 Graz
Telephone: (316) 380-0
Fax: (316) 380-9140
E-mail: rektor@meduni-graz.at
Internet: www.meduni-graz.at
Founded 1863 as Medical Faculty of Graz Univ.; univ. status 2002
State control
Language of instruction: German
Rector: Prof. Dr JOSEF SMOLLE
Vice-Rector for Clinical Affairs: Prof. Dr KARLHEINZ TSCHELIESSNIGG
Vice-Rector for Research Management and Int. Cooperation: Dr SABINE HERLITSCHKA
Vice-Rector for Strategy and Innovation: Prof. Dr HELLMUT SAMONIGG
Vice-Rector for Teaching and Studies: Prof. Dr GILBERT REIBNEGGER
Dir of the Organizational Unit for Central Infrastructure: Mag. Dr GERALD WALLAND
Librarian: Dr ULRIKE KORTSCHAK

Number of teachers: 741
Number of students: 4,058

MEDIZINISCHE UNIVERSITÄT INNSBRUCK
(Medical University, Innsbruck)

Christoph-Probst-Pl., Innrain 52, 6020 Innsbruck
Telephone: (512) 507- 0
E-mail: i-master@i-med.ac.at
Internet: www.i-med.ac.at
Founded 2004 from the medical faculty of the Univ. of Innsbruck
State control
Rector: Prof. Dr MANFRED DIERICH
Vice-Rector for Clinical Studies: Prof. Dr ROLAND STAUDINGER
Vice-Rector for Human Resources, Human Resources Devt and Gender Equality: Prof. Dr MARGARETHE HOCHLEITNER
Vice-Rector for Teaching and Studies: Prof. Dr MANFRED DIERICH
Number of students: 3,224

Depts of anatomy, histology, and embryology, of medical statistics, computer sciences and health management, of hygiene, microbiology and social medicine, of medical genetics, molecular and clinical pharmacology and of physiology and medical physics; Innsbruck Biocentre (divs of biological chemistry, cell biology, clinical biochemistry, experimental pathophysiology and immunology, genomics and RNomics, medical biochemistry, molecular biology, molecular pathophysiology, neurobiochemistry); University Medical Centre (depts of anaesthesiology and critical care medicine, dentistry and oral surgery, dermatology and venereology, diagnostic radiology, gynaecology, internal medicine, neurology, neurosurgery, nuclear medicine, medical psychology and psychotherapy, ophthalmology, orthopaedic surgery, otorhinolaryngology, paediatrics, plastic and reconstructive surgery, psychiatry, radiotherapy, surgery, traumatology and sport traumatology and urology; Institute for Addiction Research); Central Laboratory Animal Facilities, Ethics Commission, Gene Discovery Core Facility; Institutes of Legal Medicine, Neuroscience, Pathology and of Pharmacology; School of Public Health.

MEDIZINISCHE UNIVERSITÄT WIEN
(Medical University, Vienna)

Spitalgasse 23, 1090 Vienna
Telephone: (1) 40160-0
Fax: (1) 40160-910000
E-mail: infopoint-meduni@meduniwien.ac.at
Internet: www.meduniwien.ac.at
Founded 2004
Library of 520,000 vols, 2,400 periodicals
Rector: Prof. Dr WOLFGANG SCHÜTZ
Vice-Rector for Academic Affairs: Prof. Dr RUDOLF MALLINGER
Vice-Rector for Clinical Affairs: Prof. CHRISTOPH C. ZIELINSKI
Vice-Rector for Finance: Mag. PETER SOSWINSKI
Vice-Rector for Research and Int. Relations: Prof. HANS-GEORG EICHLER
Number of students: 8,094

MONTANUNIVERSITÄT LEOBEN
(University of Leoben)

Franz-Josef Str. 18, 8700 Leoben
Telephone: (3842) 402-0
Fax: (3842) 402-7702
E-mail: office@unileoben.ac.at
Internet: www.unileoben.ac.at
Founded 1840
Languages of instruction: German, English
Academic year: October to September
Rector: Prof. Dr WOLFHARD WEGSCHEIDER
Vice-Rector for Admin.: Dr MARTHA MÜHLBURGER
Vice-Rector for Finance and Auditing: Prof. Dr HUBERT BIEDERMAN
Librarian: Dr CHRISTIAN HASENHÜTTEL
Library: see Libraries and Archives
Number of students: 2,338
Publications: *BHM- Berg- und Hüttenmannische Monatshefte* (12 a year), *Triple M* (4 a year)

PROFESSORS

BIEDERMANN, H., Economics, Industrial Management and Industrial Engineering
DANZER, R., Ceramics
EBNER, F., Geology and Mineral Resources
EICHLSEDER, W., Mechanical Engineering
ENGELHARDT, C., Industrial Logistics
FISCHER, D., Mechanics
GALLER, R., Subsurface Engineering
HARMUTH, H., Refractory Materials, Ceramics, Glass and Cement
HEINEMANN, Z., Reservoir Engineering
IMRICH, W., Applied Mathematics
JEGLITSCH, F., Physical Metallurgy and Material Testing
KEPPLINGER, W., Industrial Environmental Protection
KESSLER, F., Conveying Technology
KIRSCHENHOFER, P., Mathematics
KNEISSL, A., Metallography
KRIEGER, W., Ferrous Metallurgy
KUCHAR, F., Physics
LANG, R., Plastics
LANGECKER, G., Plastics Technology
LEDERER, K., Chemistry of Plastics
LORBER, K., Decontamination
MAURITSCH, H., Geophysics
MEISEL, T., Gen. and Analytical Chemistry
MILLAHN, K., Applied Geophysics
O'LEARY, P., Automation
PASCHEN, P., Nonferrous Metallurgy
RUTHAMMER, G., Petroleum Engineering
SACHS, H., Applied Geometry
SITTE, W., Physical Chemistry
STEINER, H., Mineral Processing
VORTISCH, W., Applied Sedimentology
WAGNER, H., Mining Engineering
WEISS, G., Electrical Engineering
WOERNDLE, R., Plastics
WOLFBAUER, J., Business Economics

UNIVERSITÄT MOZARTEUM SALZBURG
(University Mozarteum Salzburg)

Schrannengasse 10A, 5020 Salzburg
Telephone: (662) 6198-0
Fax: (662) 6198-3033
E-mail: moz@moz.ac.at
Internet: www.moz.ac.at
Founded 1841
State control
Academic year: October to June

Depts of brass, wind and percussion studies, conducting, composition and music theory, drama, fine arts, art and craft education, keyboard studies, music and dance education, music education (Innsbruck), music education (Salzburg), music theatre, musicology, stage design, string studies, vocal studies

Rector: Prof. REINHART VON GUTZEIT
Vice-Rector for Artistic Projects: Prof. LUKAS HAGEN
Vice-Rector for Business Affairs: Dr BERND LANGE
Vice-Rector for Teaching: Prof. BRIGITTE ENGELHARD
Librarian: Dr MANFRED KAMMERER

Number of teachers: 458
Number of students: 1,361

Publications: *International Summer Academy Mozarteum Brochure* (1 a year), *Uni-Art* (12 a year).

UNIVERSITÄT FÜR MUSIK UND DARSTELLENDE KUNST GRAZ
(University of Music and Dramatic Arts, Graz)

Leonhardstr. 15, POB 208, Palais Meran, 8010 Graz
Telephone: (316) 389-0
Fax: (316) 389-1101
E-mail: info@kug.ac.at
Internet: www.kug.ac.at
Founded 1816, conservatory 1920, academy 1963, present status 1998
State control
Language of instruction: German
Academic year: October to June

Rector: Prof. Mag. Dr GEORG SCHULZ
Vice-Rector for Arts and Research: Prof. Mag. Dr ROBERT HÖLDRICH
Vice-Rector for Quality Management, Human Resource Devt, Gender Mainstreaming: Mag. DORIS CARSTENSEN
Vice-Rector for Study: Prof. EIKE STRAUB
Univ. Dir: Mag. ASTRID WEDENIG
Librarian: ROBERT SCHILLER

Library of 190,000 vols incl. books, journals, sheets, records, tapes and other media
Number of teachers: 257 (f.t.e)
Number of students: 2,269

HEADS OF INSTITUTES

Institute of Aesthetics of Music: Prof. Dr ANDREAS DORSCHEL
Institute of Church Music and Organ: Prof. Dr GUNTHER MICHAEL ROST
Institute of Composition, Music Theory, Music History and Conducting: Prof. PETER REVERS
Institute of Drama: Prof. Dr EVELYN DEUTSCH-SCHREINER
Institute of Early Music and Performance Practice: Prof. Dr EVA MARIA POLLERUS
Institute of Electronic Music and Acoustics: ALOIS SONTACCHI
Institute of Ethnomusicology: Prof. Dr GERD GRUPE
Institute of Jazz: Prof. Dr ANTHONY PARTYKA
Institute of Jazz Research: Prof. Dr FRANZ KERSCHBAUMER
Institute of Opera: BARBARA BEYER

Institute of Music Education: Prof. GERHARD WANKER
Institute of the Oberschützen Campus: Prof. KLAUS ARINGER
Institute of Piano: Prof. EUGEN JAKAB
Institute of Stage Design: Prof. HANS SCHAVERNOCH
Institute of String Instruments: Prof. KERSTIN FELTZ
Institute of Voice, Song and Oratorio: Prof. MARTIN KLIETMANN
Institute of Wind and Percussion Instruments: Prof. THOMAS EIBINGER

UNIVERSITÄT FÜR MUSIK UND DARSTELLENDE KUNST WIEN
(University of Music and Performing Arts, Vienna)

Anton-von-Webern-Pl. 1, 1030 Vienna
Telephone: (1) 71155
Fax: (1) 71155-199
E-mail: rektor@mdw.ac.at
Internet: www.mdw.ac.at
Founded 1812 as Conservatorium der Gesellschaft der Musikfreunde, nationalized 1909
Rector: Prof. Mag. Dr WERNER HASITSCHKA
Vice-Rectors: Prof. Mag. RUDOLF HOFSTÖTTER, Prof. CLAUDIA WALKENSTEINER-PRESCHL, Prof. Dr GREGOR WIDHOLM
Library Dir: Dr SUSANNE ESCHWÉ
Number of teachers: 807
Number of students: 2,333

HEADS OF INSTITUTES

Bruckner Institute (Theory, Aural Training and Conducting): ALOIS GLASSNER
Film Academy: PETER MAYER
Hellmesberger Institute (Stringed Instruments): WOLFGANG AICHINGER
Institute of the Analysis, Theory and History of Music: CORNELIA SZABO-KNOTIK
Institute of Chamber Music and Special Ensembles: AVO KOUYOUMDJIAN
Institute of Composition and Sound Technology: DIETMAR SCHERMANN
Institute of Conducting: THOMAS KREUZBERGER
Institute of Cultural Management: FRANZ-OTTO HOFECKER
Institute of Folk Music Research and Ethnomusicology: GERLINDE HAID
Institute of Keyboard Instruments: HEINZ MEDJIMOREC
Institute of Music and Movement Education and Music Therapy: ANGELIKA HAUSER
Institute of Music Teaching: FRANZ NIERMANN
Institute of Organ, Organ Research and Church Music: ERWIN ORTNER
Institute of Research into Musical Style: HARTMUT KRONES
Institute of the Sociology of Music: IRMGARD BONTINCK
Institute of Song and Musicals: LEOPOLD SPITZER
Institute of Stringed Instruments: STEFAN KROPFITSCH
Institute of Wind and Percussion Instruments: BARBARA GISLER
Ludwig van Beethoven Institute (Keyboard Instruments): URSULA KNEIHS
Max Reinhardt Seminar: HUBERTUS PETROLL
Popular Music: WOLFGANG PUSCHNIG
Salieri Institute (Song): MARIA BAYER
Schubert Institute (Wind and Percussion Instruments): WALTER WRETSCHITSCH
Vienna Institute of Sound: GREGOR WIDHOLM

UNIVERSITÄT SALZBURG
(Salzburg University)

Kapitelgasse 4–6, 5020 Salzburg
Telephone: (662) 8044-0

Fax: (662) 8044214
E-mail: studium@sbg.ac.at
Internet: www.uni-salzburg.at
Founded 1622; closed 1810; College 1810–50, independent faculty of Catholic Theology 1850–1962; reconstituted 1962
State control
Academic year: October to June
Rector: Prof. Dr HEINRICH SCHMIDINGER
Pro-Rectors: Prof. Dr ALBERT DUSCHL, Prof. Dr RUDOLF MOSLER, Prof. Dr SONJA PUNTSCHER-RIEKMANN
Librarian: Dr URSULA SCHACHL-RABER
Library: see under Libraries and Archives
Number of teachers: 750
Number of students: 11,787

DEANS

Faculty of Arts: Prof. Dr GERHARD PETERSMANN
Faculty of Catholic Theology: Prof. Dr HANS-JOACHIM SANDER
Faculty of Law: Prof. Dr KURT SCHMOLLER
Faculty of Natural Science: Prof. Dr URS BAUMANN

PROFESSORS

Faculty of Arts:
BETTEN, A., German
BOTZ, G., History
BRUCHER, G., History of Austrian Art
DALFEN, J., Classical Philology
DOPSCH, H., History
EHMER, J., Modern History
FABRIS, H., Journalism and Communications
FELTEN, F., Classical Archaeology
GOEBL, H., Romance Languages
GRASSL, H., Ancient History
GRÖSSING, S., Sport
HAAS, H., Austrian History
HAIDER, H., Linguistics
HASLINGER, A., German
JALKOTZY, S., Ancient History
KLEIN, H. M., English
KNOCHE, M., Journalism and Communications
KOLMER, L., Medieval History and Historic Auxiliary Sciences
KRONSTEINER, O., Slavic Languages
KRUMM, V., Education
KUON, P., Romance Philology
MAYER, G., Slavic Languages
MESSNER, D., Romance Languages
MORSCHER, E., Philosophy
MÜLLER, E., Physical Education
MÜLLER, U., German
PANAGL, O., Linguistics
PATRY, J. L., Education
PETERSMANN, G., Classical Philology
PIEL, F., Medieval and Modern History of Art
ROSSBACHER, K., German
SCHMOLKE, M., Journalism and Communications
STAGL, J., Sociology
STENZL, J., Music Science
TRUCHLAR, L., English
WEINGARTNER, P., Philosophy
ZAIC, F., English

Faculty of Catholic Theology:
BACHL, G., Dogmatics
BEILNER, W., New Testament Studies
BUCHER, A., Catechism and Religious Education
KÖHLER, W., Christian Philosophy and Psychology
MÖDLHAMMER, J., Ecumenical Theology
NIKOLASCH, F., Liturgy
PAARHAMMER, J., Church Law
PAUS, A., Epistemology and Religious Studies
SCHLEINZER, F., Pastoral Theology
SCHMIDINGER, H., Christian Philosophy

WINKLER, G. B., Church History
WOLBERT, W., Moral Theology

Faculty of Law:

BERKA, W., General Theory of the State, Theory of Administration, Constitutional and Administrative Law
BUSCHMANN, A., German Legal History, German Private and Civil Law
GRILLBERGER, K., Industrial Law
HACKL, K., Roman and Civil Law
HAGEN, J., Sociology of Law
HAMMER, R., Management
HARRER, F., Civil and Commercial Law
KARL, W., International Law
KOJA, F., General Constitutional Law
KOPPENSTEINER, H.-G., Austrian and International Commercial Law
KYRER, A., Economics
MAYER-MALY, TH., German and Austrian Private Law
MIGSCH, E., Civil Law
RAINER, J., Roman and Modern Private Law
SCHÄFFER, H., Public Law
SCHMOLLER, K., Austrian Criminal Law
SCHUMACHER, W., International Commercial Law and Civil Law
SCHWIMANN, M., International Civil Law
STOLZLECHNER, H., Public Law
TRIFFTERER, O., Austrian and International Criminal Law

Faculty of Natural Sciences:

AMTHAUER, G., Geology
BAUMANN, U., Psychology
BENTRUP, F. W., Plant Physiology and Anatomy
BREITENBACH, M., Molecular Genetics
CLAUSEN, H., Systems Analysis
CZIHAK, G., Genetics
FÜRNKRANZ, D., Botany
GERL, P., Mathematics
HERMANN, A., Zoology
NEUBAUER, F., Geology
PERNER, J., Psychology
PFALZGRAF, J., Computer Science
RIEDL, H., Geography
SCHWEIGER, F., Mathematics
STADEL, CH., Geography
STEINHÄUSLER, F., Biophysics
STRACK, H.-B., Biochemistry
WALLBOTT, H., Psychology
WERNER, H., Sciences Education
ZINTERHOF, P., Mathematics

Inter-faculty Institutes:

CROLL, G., Music History of Salzburg
FAUPEL, K., Political Science
GACHOWETZ, H., Organizational Psychology
HAUPTMANN, W., Criminal Psychology
KOPPENSTEINER, H. G., European Law
LAUBER, V., Political Science
MAYER-MALY, TH., Energy Law, Law of Liechtenstein
MIGSCH, E., Private Insurance Law
MORSCHER, E., Philosophy, Technology, Economics
ZINTERHOF, P., Software Technology

TECHNISCHE UNIVERSITÄT GRAZ (Graz University of Technology)

Rechbauerstr. 12, 8010 Graz

Telephone: (316) 873-0
Fax: (316) 873-6009
E-mail: info@tugraz.at
Internet: www.tugraz.at

Founded 1811
Academic year: October to July

Rector: Prof. Dr HANS SÜNKEL
Vice-Rector for Academic Affairs: Prof. Dr HANS MICHAEL MUHR
Vice-Rector for Finances and Personnel: Prof. Dr ULRICH BAUER

Vice-Rector for Infrastructure: Dr HARALD KAINZ
Vice-Rector for Research and Technology: Prof. Dr FRANZ STELZER
Librarian: Dipl.-Ing. EVA BERTHA
Library: see Libraries and Archives
Number of teachers: 569
Number of students: 9,763

DEANS

Faculty of Architecture: Prof. LEONARD HIRSCHBERG
Faculty of Chemistry, Chemical and Process Engineering: Prof. Dr FRANK UHLIG
Faculty of Civil Engineering: Prof. Dr MARTIN FELLENDORF
Faculty of Computer Science: Prof. Dr KLAUS TOCHTERMANN
Faculty of Constructional Engineering: Prof. Dr KLAUS RIESSBERGER
Faculty of Electrical and Information Engineering: Prof. Dr HEINRICH STIGLER
Faculty of Mathematical and Physical Engineering: Prof. Dr ROBERT TICHY
Faculty of Mechanical Engineering and Economics: Prof. Dr REINHARD HABERFELLNER
Faculty of Natural Sciences: Prof. Dr HANS VOGLER

PROFESSORS

ARRIGONI, E., Theoretical Physics
AURENHAMMER, F., Basics of Information Processing
BAUER, U., Industrial Management
BEER, G., Building Statics
BERKES, I., Probability Theory and Statistics
BESENHARD, O. J., Inorganic Chemical Technology
BRASSEUR, G., Electrical Measurement and Measurement Signals Processing
BRENN, G., Fluid Mechanics
BRUNNER, F. K., Geodesy
BURKARD, R., Mathematics
CELIGOJ, CH., Strength of Materials
CERJAK, H., Materials Science and Welding
DOURDOUMAS, N., Automatic Control
EICHLSEDER, H., Combustion Engines
ERNST, W., Experimental Physics
FICKERT, L., Electrical Installations
FRANK, A., Manufacturing Technology
FRANK, I., Interior Design
GAMERITH, H., Building and Design
GESCHEIDT-DEMNER, G., Material Testing
GRAMPP, G., Physical Chemistry
GREINER, R., Timberwork and Elevation
GRIENGL, H., Organic Chemistry
HABERFELLNER, R., Management
HEIGERTH, G., Hydraulic Design and Water Resources Management
HEITMEIR, F., Thermo Turbo-Machinery
HIRSCHBERG, W., Automotive Engineering
HOFMANN-WELLENHOF, B., Theoretical Geodesy
JABERG, H., Hydraulic Turbo-machinery
JÜRGENS, G., Machine Principles
KAHLERT, H., Solid State Physics
KAINZ, H., Hydraulics, Agricultural and Industrial Hydraulic Engineering
KERN, G., Analysis and Applications
KNAPP, G., Analytical Chemistry
KOUDELKA, O., Telecommunications
KUBIN, G., Non-linear Signals Processing
KUPELWIESER, H., Artistic Forms
LEBERL, F., Computer-aided Geometry and Graphics
LECHNER, H., Project Envelopment and Project Management
LEITGEB, N., Hospital Technology
MAASS, W., Information Processing
MACHEROUX, P., Biochemistry
MARR, R. J., Process Engineering
MAURER, H., Information Processing
MEUWISSEN, J. M. C., Building and Town Planning
MORITZ, H., Geodesy

MUHR, H. M., Electrical Power Systems and High Voltage Engineering
NIDETSKY, B., Biotechnology
OSER, J., Materials Handling and Mechanical Engineering Design
PFANNHAUSER, W., Food Chemistry
POSCH, R., Applied Information Processing and Communications Technology
RENTMEISTER, M., Electrical Engineering
RIESSBERGER, K., Railways
RÖSCHEL, O., Geometry
SCHUBERT, W., Rock Mechanics and Tunnelling
SCHWAB, H., Biotechnology
SEMPRICH, S., Soil Mechanics and Foundation Engineering
SPAROWITZ, L., Concrete Construction
STADLER, G., Building
STADLOBER, E., Probability Theory and Statistics
STAUDINGER, G., Instrument Construction and Mechanical Techniques
STELZER, F., Chemical Technology of Organic Materials
STIGLER, H., Electricity Economy and Energy Innovation
SÜNKEL, H., Theoretical Geodesy
TICHY, R., Mathematics
TSCHOM, H., Domestic Architecture
VON DER LINDEN, W., Theoretical Physics
VÖSSNER, S., Mechanical Engineering and Industrial Informatics
WACH, P., Theoretical Methods in Mechanical Engineering and Industrial Informatics
WEISS, R., Computer Engineering
WOESS, W., Mathematics
WOHINZ, J., Industrial Management
WOLFBAUER, O., Chemical and Process Engineering
WÜRSCHUM, R., Materials Science and Physical Methods

ATTACHED INSTITUTES

Institute of Applied Geosciences: Rechbauerstr. 12, 8010 Graz; Dir Prof. Dr MARTIN DIETZEL.

Institute of Architecture and Landscape: Rechbauerstr. 12, 8010 Graz; Dir Prof. DANIELE MARQUES.

Institute of Architecture and Media: Inffeldgasse 10/II, 8010 Graz; Dir Prof. URS LEONHAND HIRSCHBERG.

Institute of Architectural Science and Architectural Design: Rechbauerstr. 12/II, 8010 Graz; Dir Prof. Dr ULLRICH SCHWARZ.

Institute of Architectural Technology: Rechbauerstr. 12/I, 8010 Graz; Dir ROGER RIEWE.

Institute of Architectural Typologies: Lessingstr. 25/IV, 8010 Graz; Dir Prof. HRVOJE NJIRIC.

Institute of Building and Energy: Rechbauerstr. 12, 8010 Graz; Dir Prof. BRIAN CODY.

Institute of Building Construction and Industrial Architecture: Lessingstr. 25/III, 8010 Graz; Dir Prof. Dr HORST GAMERITH.

Institute of Contemporary Art: Inffeldgasse 10/II, 8010 Graz; Dir Prof. HAND KUPELWIESER.

Institute of Construction Management and Economics: Lessingstr. 25/II, 8010 Graz; Dir Prof. HANS LECHNER.

Institute of Domestic Architecture: Rechbauerstr. 12, 8010 Graz; Dir Prof. Dr HANSJÖRG TSCHOM.

Institute of Engineering Geodesy and Measurement Systems: Steyrergasse 30/II, 8010 Graz; Dir Prof. Dr KARL BRUNNER.

Institute of General Mechanics: Technikerstr. 4/II, 8010 Graz; Dir Prof. Dr MARTIN SCHANZ.

Institute of Highway Engineering and Transport Planning: Rechbauerstr. 12/II, 8010 Graz; Dir Prof. Dr WERNER GOBIET.

Institute of History of Art and Cultural Studies: Technikerstr. 4/III, 8010 Graz; Dir Prof. Dr SUSANNE HAUSER.

Institute of Hydraulic Engineering and Water Resources Management: Stremayrgasse 10/II, 8010 Graz; Dir Prof. Dr GÜNTHER HEIGERTH.

Institute of Project Development and Management: Lessingstr. 25/I, 8010 Graz; Dir Prof. Dr ULRICH WALDER.

Institute of Railway Engineering and Transport Economy: Rechbauerstr. 12/II, 8010 Graz; Dir Prof. Dr KLAUS RIEßBERGER.

Institute of Rock Mechanics and Tunnelling: Rechbauerstr. 12, 8010 Graz; Dir Prof. Dr WULF SCHUBERT.

Institute of Soil Mechanics and Foundation Engineering: Rechbauerstr. 12, 8010 Graz; Dir Prof. Dr STEPHAN SEMPRICH.

Institute of Spatial Design: Rechbauerstr. 12/II, 8010 Graz; Dir Prof. IRMGARD FRANK.

Institute of Steel Structures and Shell Structures: Lessingstr. 25/III, 8010 Graz; Dir Prof. Dr RICHARD GREINER.

Institute of Structural Analysis: Lessingstr. 25/II, 8010 Graz; Dir Prof. Dr GERNOT BEER.

Institute of Structural Concrete: Lessingstr. 25, 8010 Graz; Dir Prof. Dr LUTZ SPAROWITZ.

Institute of Structural Design: Technikerstr. 4/IV, 8010 Graz; Dir Prof. Dr LUTZ SPAROWITZ.

Institute of Structural Engineering: Inffeldgasse 24, 8010 Graz; Dir Dr BERNHARD FREYTAG.

Institute of Technology and Testing of Building Materials: Stremayrgasse 11, 8010 Graz; Dir Prof. Dr PETER MAYDL.

Institute of Timber Engineering and Wood Technology: Inffeldgasse 24, 8010 Graz; Dir Prof. Dr GERHARD SCHICKHOFER.

Institute of Urban Water Management and Landscape Water Engineering: Stremayrgasse 10/I, 8010 Graz; Dir Prof. Dr HARALD KAINZ.

Institute of Urbanism: Rechbauerstr. 12, 8010 Graz; Dir Prof. ERNST HUBELI.

TECHNISCHE UNIVERSITÄT WIEN (Vienna University of Technology)

Karlspl. 13, 1040 Vienna

Telephone: (1) 58801-0
Fax: (1) 58801-40199
E-mail: pr@tuwien.ac.at
Internet: www.tuwien.ac.at

Founded 1815
State control
Academic year: October to June (two terms)

Rector: Prof. Dr PETER SKALICKY
Vice-Rector: Prof. Dr GERHARD SCHIMAK
Vice-Rector for Academic Affairs: Prof. Dr ADALBERT PRECHTL
Vice Rector for Finance and Controlling: Dr PAUL JANKOWITSCH
Vice Rector for Infrastructure and Development: Prof. Dr GERHARD SCHIMAK
Vice-Rector for Research: Prof. Dr SABINE SEIDLER
Dir: Mag. EVELINE URBAN
Librarian: Dr PETER KUBALEK

Library: see under Libraries and Archives
Number of teachers: 1,965
Number of students: 18,773

Publication: *ZID-Line*

DEANS

Faculty of Architecture and Planning: Prof. Dr KLAUS SEMSROTH
Faculty of Civil Engineering: Prof. Dr JOSEF EBERHARDSTEINER
Faculty of Electrical Engineering and Information Technology: Prof. Dr EMMERICH BERTAGNOLLI
Faculty of Informatics: Prof. Dr GERALD STEINHARDT
Faculty of Mathematics and Geoinformation: Prof. Dr DIETMAR DORNINGER
Faculty of Mechanical Engineering: Prof. Dr BRUNO GRÖSEL
Faculty of Physics: Prof. Dr GERALD BADUREK
Faculty of Technical Chemistry: Prof. Dr JOHANNES FRÖHLICH

PROFESSORS

Faculty of Architecture and Planning (Karlspl. 13, 1040 Vienna; tel. (1) 58801-25001; fax (1) 58801-25099; e-mail e250@tuwien.ac.at; internet www.rpl-arch.tuwien.ac.at):

ALSOP, W., Building Construction and Building Systems for Architects
BÖKEMANN, D., Town and Country Planning
BRÜLLMANN, K., Residential Building
CERWENKA, P., Transport Systems Planning
DANGSCHAT, J., Urban and Regional Research
FRANCK-OBERASPACH, G., Computer-aided Design and Planning Methods
HIERZEGGER, H., Local Area Planning
JORMAKKA, K. J., Architectural History and Historic Building Survey
JOURDA, F. H., Spatial Design
LESAK, F., Model Construction
MAHDAVI, A., Building Physics and Human Ecology
RICHTER, H., Structural Engineering for Architects
SCHÖNBÄCK, W., Public Finance and Infrastructure Policy
SEMSROTH, K., Urban Design and Planning
STILES, R., Landscape Planning and Garden Architecture
STRAUBE, M., Banking and Securities Law
WEBER, G., History of Art and Cultural Conservation
WEHDORN, M., History of Art, Architectural Conservation, and Industrial Archaeology
WINTER, W., Studies of Structural Design and Timber Construction
WOLFF-PLOTTEGG, M., Building Design and Theory
ZEHETNER, F., Public Law

Faculty of Civil Engineering (Karlspl. 13, 1040 Vienna; tel. (1) 58801-20001; fax (1) 58801-20099; e-mail info@bauwesen.tuwien.ac.at; internet www.bauwesen.tuwien.ac.at):

BRANDL, H., Foundations
BRUNNER, P. H., Waste Management
DREYER, J., Building Material Sciences, Building Physics and Fire Protection
DROBIR, H., Water Plant Construction, Navigable Waterways and Environmental Hydraulics
GUTKNECHT, D., Hydraulics, Hydrology and Water Supply
JODL, H. G., Construction Practice and Methods
KNOFLACHER, H., Traffic Planning and Engineering
KOLBITSCH, A., Building Construction and Industrial Buildings
KOLLEGGER, J., Reinforced Concrete Construction and Massive Construction
KROISS, H., Water Supply, Sewage Purification and Prevention of Water Pollution

LITZKA, J., Road Engineering and Maintenance
MANG, H., Elasticity and Strength
MATSCHE, N., Water Quality and Waste Management
OBERNDORFER, W. J., Construction and Planning
OGRIS, H., Experimental Hydraulics
RAMBERGER, G., Steel Girder Construction
RUBIN, H., Structural Analysis
SCHIMMERL, J., Rational Mechanics
SCHNEIDER, U., Building Materials
TENTSCHERT, E. H., Geology
ZIEGLER, F., Applied Mechanics

Faculty of Electrical Engineering and Information Technology (Gusshausstr. 25–29, 1040 Vienna; tel. (1) 58801-35001; fax (1) 58801-35099; e-mail goppenhe@pop.tuwien.ac.at; internet www.info.tuwien.ac.at/et):

BERTAGNOLLI, E., Solid State Electronics
BONEK, E., High Frequency and Communications Technology
BRAUNER, G., Power Systems
CHABICOVSKY, R., Industrial Electronics and Materials Science
DETTER, H., Precision Engineering
DIETRICH, D., Computer Technology
EIER, R., Data Processing
FALLMANN, W., Industrial Electronics and Materials Science
GORNIK, E., Solid State Electronics
HAAS, H., Fundamentals and Theory of Electrical Engineering
KRAUSZ, F., Photonics
LEEB, W., Communications and Radio-Frequency Engineering
MAGERL, G., Electrical Measurement Technology
MECKLENBRÄUKER, W., Low Frequency Technology
PFUNDNER, P., Industrial Electronics and Materials Science
PRECHTL, A., Theory of Electrical Engineering
RUMMICH, E., Electrical Drives and Machines
RUPP, M., Communications and Radio-Frequency Engineering
SCHMIDT, A., Quantum Electronics and Lasers
SCHRÖDL, M., Electrical Machines and Drives
SELBERHERR, S., Software Technology for Microelectronic Systems
VAN AS, H. R., Communication Networks
VELLEKOOP, M., Industrial Electronics and Materials Science
WEINMANN, A., Electrical Control, Navigation and Power Engineering
WEINRICHTER, J., Communications and Radio-Frequency Engineering
ZACH, F., Electrical Drives and Machines
ZEICHEN, G., Flexible Automation
ZIMMERMANN, H., Electrical Measurements and Circuit Design

Faculty of Informatics (Getreidemarkt 9, 1060 Vienna; tel. (1) 58801-10000; fax (1) 58801-10099; e-mail dek100@mail.zserv.tuwien.ac.at; internet www.cs.tuwien.ac.at):

BREITENEDER, C., Software
BROCKHAUS, M., Information Technology
EITER, T., Information Systems
FLEISSNER, P., Design and Assessment/Social Cybernetics
GOTTLOB, G., Applied Informatics
GRÜNBACHER, H., Computer Engineering (VLSI-Design)
JAZAYERI, M., Information Systems
KAPPEL, G., Software Technology and Interactive Systems
KOPETZ, H., Software Technology
KROPATSCH, W., Design and Manufacturing
KUICH, W., Mathematical Logic and Computer Languages
LEITSCH, A., Computer Languages

MUTZEL, P., Computer Graphics and Algorithms

PURGATHOFER, W., Computer Graphics and Algorithms

SCHILDT, G.-H., Automation Systems

TJOA, A. M., Software Engineering

VIERTL, R., Applied Statistics and Information Science

WAGNER, I., Design and Assessment of Technology

Faculty of Mathematics and Geoinformation (Getreidemarkt 9, 1060 Vienna; tel. (1) 58801-10000; fax (1) 58801-10099; e-mail dekmug@mail.zserv.tuwien.ac.at; internet www.math.tuwien.ac.at):

BARON, G., Geometry

CARSTENSEN, C., Applied and Numerical Mathematics

DIRSCHMID, H., Analysis and Technical Mathematics

DORNINGER, D., Algebra and Computational Mathematics

DUTTER, R., Technical Statistics

EBEL, H., Technical Physics

FRANK, A., Surveying and Geoinformation

GRUBER, P., Mathematical Analysis

HERTLING, J., Applied and Numerical Mathematics

KAHMEN, H., General Geodesy

KAISER, H., Algebra and Computational Mathematics

KELNHOFER, F., Cartography and Reproduction Technology

KUICH, W., Mathematical Logic and Computer Languages

LANGER, H., Applied Analysis

MLITZ, R., Applied and Numerical Mathematics

POTTMANN, A., Geometry

SCHACHERMAYER, W., Statistics and Probability Theory

SCHNABL, R., Analysis and Technical Mathematics

SCHUH, H., Geodesy and Geophysics

STACHEL, H., Geometry

TROCH, I., Analysis and Technical Mathematics

VANA, N., Dosimetry

VIERTL, R., Applied Statistics and Information Science

WERTZ, W., Financial and Actuarial Mathematics

Faculty of Mechanical Engineering (Karlspl. 13, 1040 Vienna; tel. (1) 58801-30001; fax (1) 58801-30099; e-mail mrosen@pop.tuwien.ac.at; internet www.tuwien.ac.at/maschinenbau):

BIBERSCHICK, D., Industrial Engineering, Ergonomics and Business Economics

DEGISCHER, H. P., Materials Science and Testing

GAMER, U., Mechanics

GRÖSEL, B., Handling and Transport Technology and General Design Engineering

HASELBACHER, H., Thermal Turbo-Machinery and Power Plants

JÖRGL, H. P., Machine- and Process-Engineering

KLUWICK, A., Hydrodynamics

KOPACEK, P., Handling Devices and Robotics

LENZ, H. P., Internal Combustion Vehicles

LINZER, W., Theory of Heat

LUGNER, P., Mechanics

MATTHIAS, H. B., Water-powered Machines and Pumps

PATZAK, G., Industrial Engineering, Ergonomics and Business Economics

RAMMERSTORFER, F., Light Engineering, Aeroplane Engineering

RINDER, L., Machine Parts

SCHNEIDER, W., Gas and Thermodynamics

SCHUÖCKER, D., Non-conventional Processing, Forming and Laser Technology

SCHWAIGER, W., Accounting and Controlling

SEIDLER, S., Materials Science and Testing

SPRINGER, H., Machine Dynamics and Measurement

STEPAN, A., Industrial Business Management

TROGER, H., Mechanics

UHLIR, H., Industrial Engineering, Ergonomics and Business Economics

VARGA, T., Welding

WESESLINDTNER, H., Computer Integrated Manufacturing

WOJDA, F., Business Management

ZEMAN, J., Pressure Vessel and Plant Technology

Faculty of Physics (Wiedner Hauptstr. 8–10, 1040 Vienna; tel. (1) 58801-10000; fax (1) 58801-10099; internet www.physik.tuwien.ac.at):

AIGINGER, J., Ionizing Radiation

BADUREK, G., Nuclear Solid State Physics

BALCAR, E., Neutron and Solid State Physics

BENES, E., General Physics

BRÜCKL, E., Geophysics

BURGDÖRFER, J., Theoretical Physics

EBEL, H., Technical Physics

FLECK, M. C., Neutron Physics

KIRCHMAYR, H., Experimental Physics

KRAUS, K., Photogrammetry

KUMMER, W., Theoretical Physics

RAUCH, H., Experimental Nuclear Physics

SCHUH, H., Geodesy and Geophysics

SCHWEDA, M., Theoretical Physics

SKALICKY, P., Applied Physics

WEBER, H. W., Low Temperature Physics

WINTER, H., General Physics

Faculty of Technical Chemistry (Getreidemarkt 9, 1060 Vienna; tel. (1) 58801-10000; fax (1) 58801-10099; e-mail johannes.froehlich@tuwien.ac.at; internet www.chemie.tuwien.ac.at):

FABJAN, C., Technical Electrochemistry and Solid State Chemistry

GRASSERBAUER, M., Analytical Chemistry

GRUBER, H., Chemical Technology of Organic Materials

HAMPEL, W., Biochemical Technology

HOFBAUER, H., Chemical Engineering, Fuel Technology and Environmental Technology

KNÖZINGER, E., Physical Chemistry

KUBEL, F., Mineralogy, Crystallography and Structural Chemistry

MARINI, I., Chemical Engineering, Fuel Technology and Environmental Technology

SCHMID, R., Inorganic Chemistry

SCHUBERT, U., Inorganic Chemistry

SCHWARZ, K., Physical and Theoretical Chemistry

STACHELBERGER, H., Botany, Technical Microscopy and Organic Raw Materials

WEINBERGER, P., Technical Electrochemistry and Solid State Chemistry

WRUSS, W., Chemical Technology of Inorganic Materials

WURST, F., Applied Botany, Technical Microscopy, and Organic Raw Materials Science

---

UNIVERSITÄT WIEN
(Vienna University)

Dr Karl Lueger-Ring 1, 1010 Vienna

Telephone: (1) 4277-0

Fax: (1) 4277-9120

E-mail: public@univie.ac.at

Internet: www.univie.ac.at

Founded 1365

Academic year: October to June

Rector: Prof. Dr GEORG WINCKLER

Vice-Rectors: HEINZ W. ENGL, JOHANN JURENITSCH, ARTHUR METTINGER, CHRISTA SCHNABL

Librarian: MARIA SEISSL

Library: see under Libraries and Archives

Number of teachers: 4,040

Number of students: 70,606

DEANS

Faculty of Business, Economics and Statistics: GEORG PFLUG

Faculty of Catholic Theology: MARTIN JÄGGLE

Faculty of Chemistry: BERNHARD KEPPLER

Faculty of Computer Science: WOLFGANG KLAS

Faculty of Earth Sciences, Geography and Astronomy: HEINZ FAßMANN

Faculty of Historical–Cultural Sciences: MICHAEL VIKTOR SCHWARZ

Faculty of Law: Prof. Dr HEINZ MAYER

Faculty of Life Sciences: HORST SEIDLER

Faculty of Mathematics: HARALD RINDLER

Faculty of Philological–Cultural Sciences: FRANZ RÖMER

Faculty of Philosophy and Educational Sciences: INES MARIA BREINBAUER

Faculty of Physics: CHRISTOPH DELLAGO

Faculty of Protestant Theology: Prof. Dr JAMES ALFRED LOADER

Faculty of Psychology: GERMAIN WEBER

Faculty of Social Sciences: RUDOLF RICHTER

Centre for Sports Sciences and University Sports: NORBERT BACHL

Centre for Translation Studies: NORBERT GREINER

PROFESSORS

Centre for Sports Sciences and University Sports (tel. (1) 4277-59001; fax (1) 4277-9590; e-mail sportwissenschaft@univie.ac.at; internet www.univie.ac.at/sportwissenschaft):

ANKNER, P.

BACHL, N.

BENDA, F.

HACKL-JAGENBREIN, S.

KELLNER, A.

KOLB, M.

MUNZAR, S.

WEIß, O.

Centre for Translation Studies (tel. (1) 4277-58001; fax (1) 4277-9580; e-mail translation@univie.ac.at; internet www.univie.ac.at/transvienna):

BUDIN, G.

FRANK, G.

KASTOVSKY, D.

KLAMBAUER, E.

LEIMEIER, C.

MOLDAU, S.

RESCH, R.

SCHÄTTLE, M.

SNELL-HORNBY, M.

WILDMANN, D.

Faculty of Business, Economics and Statistics (tel. (1) 4277-37030; fax (1) 4277-37045; e-mail dekanat-win@univie.ac.at; internet www.univie.ac.at/wirtschaftswissenschaften):

ALTENBERGER, O., Business Studies

BONZE, I., Economics

CLEMENZ, G., Economics

DIAMANTOPOULOS, A., Business Studies

DOCKNER, E., Business Studies

FINSINGER, J., Business Studies

FITZSIMONS, C. O., Business Languages

HARTL, R., Business Studies

HEIDENBERGER, K., Business Studies

KUNST, R., Computer Science and Business Informatics

LECHNER, E., Commercial Law

MUELLER, D., Economics

NERMUTH, M., Economics

OROSEL, G., Economics

PFEIFFER, T., Business Studies
PFLUG, G., Statistics and Decision Support Systems
PÖTSCHER, B., Statistics and Decision Support Systems
SORGER, G., Economics
TRAXLER, F., Government
VAN DER BELLEN, A., Economics
WAGENER, A., Economics
WAGNER, U., Business Studies
WEILINGER, A., Commercial Law
WINCKLER, G., Economics
WIRL, F., Business Studies
ZECHNER, J., Business Studies

Faculty of Catholic Theology (tel. (1) 4277-3001; fax (1) 4277-9300; internet www.univie.ac.at/ktf):

FEULNER, H.-J., Liturgical Studies
FIGL, J., Study of Religion
GABRIEL, I., Social Ethics
JÄGGLE, M., Religious Education
KÜHSCHELM, R., Ethics and Social Sciences
LANGTHALER, R., Christian Philosophy
MÜLLER, L., Canon Law
PROKSCHI, R., Theology and History of Eastern Churches
REIKERSTORFER, J., Fundamental Theology and Apologetics
SCHLOSSER, M., Theology of Spirituality
STUBENRAUCH, B., Dogmatics
VIRT, G., Moral Theology

Faculty of Chemistry (tel. (1) 4277-51001; fax (1) 4277-9510; e-mail chemie.dekanat@univie.ac.at; internet chemie.univie.ac.at):

BRINKER, U., Organic Chemistry
DICKERT, F., Analytical Chemistry and Food Chemistry
DJINOVIC-CARUGO, K., Biomolecular Structural Chemistry
FRINGELI, U. P., Biophysical Chemistry
IPSER, H., Inorganic Chemistry
KEPPLER, B., Inorganic Chemistry
KONRAT, R., Biomolecular Structural Chemistry
LINDNER, W., Analytical Chemistry and Food Chemistry
LISCHKA, H., Theoretical Chemistry
MULZER, J., Organic Chemistry
SCHMID, W., Organic Chemistry
SCHUSTER, P., Theoretical Chemistry
SONTAG, G., Analytical Chemistry and Food Chemistry
STEINHAUSER, O., Biomolecular Structural Chemistry

Faculty of Computer Science (tel. (1) 4277-39001; fax (1) 4277-9390; internet www.cs.univie.ac.at):

EDER, J., Knowledge and Business Engineering
GROSSMANN, W., Computer Science
HARING, G., Faculty of Computer Science
KARAGIANNIS, D., Knowledge and Business Engineering
KLAS, W., Computer Science
QUIRCHMAYR, G., Distributed and Multimedia Systems
ZIMA, H., Department of Scientific Computing

Faculty of Earth Sciences, Geography and Astronomy (tel. (1) 4277-53001; fax (1) 4277-9530; internet www.univie.ac.at/geowissenschaften):

BREGER, M., Astronomy
FAßMANN, H., Geography and Regional Research
FERGUSON, D. K., Palaeontology
HANTEL, M., Meteorology and Geophysics
HENSLER, G., Astronomy
HOFMANN, T., Environmental Geosciences
KAINZ, W., Geography and Regional Research
RABEDER, G., Palaeontology
RICHTER, W., Lithospheric Sciences

STEINACKER, R., Meteorology and Geophysics
STEINHAUSER, P., Meteorology and Geophysics
TILLMANNS, E., Mineralogy and Crystallography
WEICHHART, P., Geography and Regional Research
WOHLSCHLÄGL, H., Geography and Regional Research

Faculty of Historical–Cultural Sciences (tel. (1) 4277-40001; fax (1) 4277-9400; e-mail guntram.schneider@univie.ac.at; internet www.univie.ac.at/dekanat-hist-kult):

ASH, M., History
BACH, F. T., Art History
BIETAK, M., Egyptology
BOTZ, G., Contemporary History
BRUCKMÜLLER, E., Social and Economic History
BRUNNER, K., History
DIENST, H., History
DOBESCH, G., Ancient History, Papyrology and Epigraphy
DONNERMAIR, C., Social and Economic History
DREKONJA, G., History
EHMER, J., Social and Economic History
FRIESINGER, H., Prehistoric and Medieval Archaeology
HAHN, W., Numismatics and Monetary History
HASELSTEINER, H., East and Southern European History
KAPPELER, A., East and Southern European History
KLIMBURG-SALTER, D., Art History
KODER, J., Byzantine and Modern Greek Studies
KOHLER, A., History
KÖSTLIN, K., European Ethnology
KRESTEN, O., Byzantine and Modern Greek Studies
KRINZINGER, F., Classical Archaeology
LANGE, A., Jewish Studies
LIPPERT, A., Prehistoric and Medieval Archaeology
LORENZ, H., Art History
MALECZEK, W., History
MEYER, M., Classical Archaeology
PALME, B., Ancient History, Papyrology and Epigraphy
PILLINGER, R., Classical Archaeology
ROSENAUER, A., Art History
SACHSE, C., Contemporary History
SAURER, E., History
SCHMALE, W., History
SCHMIDT-COLINET, A., Classical Archaeology
SCHMITT, O., Eastern and Southern European History
SCHWARZ, M., Art History
SIEWERT, P., Institute of Ancient History, Papyrology and Epigraphy
STELZER, W., History
STEMBERGER, G., Jewish Studies
STERN, F., Contemporary History
STIEFEL, D., Social and Economic History
SUPPAN, A., Eastern and Southern European History
THEIS, L., Art History
WERNER, F., Jewish Studies

Faculty of Law (Schottenbastei 10–16, 1010 Vienna; tel. (1) 4277-34001; fax (1) 4277-9340; e-mail dekanat-jur@univie.ac.at; internet www.juridicum.at):

AICHER, J., Commercial Law
BAJONS, E. M., Procedural Law
BENKE, N., Roman Law and Ancient Legal History
BÖHM, P., Civil Procedural Law
BRANDSTETTER, W., Criminal Law and Criminology
BRAUNEDER, W., Austrian and European Legal History

BURGSTALLER, M., Criminal Law and Criminology
DORALT, W., Financial Law
FENYVES, A., Civil Law
FISCHER-CZERMAK, C., Civil Law
FUCHS, H., Criminal Law and Criminology
FUNK, B. CHR., State and Administrative Law
HAFNER, G., International Law and International Relations
HÖPFEL, F., Criminal Law and Criminology
IRO, G., Civil Law
KONECNY, A., Procedural Law
KOPETZKI, C., Commercial and Business Law
KREJCI, H., Commercial Law
LUF, G., Legal Philosophy and Legal Theory
MAYER, H., State and Administrative Law
MAZAL, W., Labour Law and Social Law
MEISSEL, F. S., Roman Law and Antique Legal History
NEUHOLD, H. P., International Law and International Relations
OFNER, H., European, International and Comparative Law
ÖHLINGER, T., State and Administrative Law
PIELER, P. E., Roman Law and History of Ancient Law
POTZ, R., Cultural and Religious Law
RASCHAUER, B., State and Administrative Law
REBHAHN, R., Labour Law and Law of Social Security
RECHBERGER, W., Civil Procedural Law
RIEDL, K., Civil Law
SCHAUER, M., Civil Law
SCHRAMMEL, W., Labour Law and Social Law
SCHREUER, CHR., International Law and International Relations
SIMON, T., Legal and Constitutional History
STELZER, M., State and Administrative Law
TANZER, M., Financial Law
THIENEL, R., State and Administrative Law
VERSCHRÄGEN, B., Comparative Law
WELSER, R., Civil Law
WILHELM, G., Civil Law
WILLVONSEDER, R., Roman Law and Ancient Legal History

Faculty of Mathematics (tel. (1) 4277-56001; fax (1) 4277-9560; e-mail dekanat.mathematik@univie.ac.at; internet www.mat.univie.ac.at):

FRIEDMAN, S.-D., Mathematics
GRÖCHENIG, K.-H., Mathematics
KOTH, M., Mathematics
LOSERT, V., Mathematics
MARKOWICH, P., Mathematics
MITSCH, H., Mathematics
MUTHSAM, H., Mathematics
NEUMAIER, A., Mathematics
RINDLER, H., Mathematics
SCHMIDT, K., Mathematics
SCHWERMER, J., Mathematics
SIGMUND, K., Mathematics

Faculty of Philological–Cultural Sciences (tel. (1) 4277-45001; fax (1) 4277-9450; internet www.univie.ac.at/dekanat-phil-kult):

ALLGAYER-KAUFMANN, R., Musicology
BESTERS-DILGER, J., Slavonic Studies
BIRKHAN, H., German Studies
CAVIC-PODGORNIK, N. A., Slavonic Studies
CYFFER, N., African Studies
DÖNT, E., Classical Philology, Medieval and Neo-Latin Studies
DORMELS, R., East Asian Studies
DRESSLER, W., Linguistics
EBENBAUER, A., German Studies
EICHNER, H., Linguistics
FAISTAUER, R., German Studies

FROSCH, F., Romance Studies
GREISENEGGER, W., Theatre Arts
GRUBER, G., Musicology
HAIDER, H., Theatre Arts
HARRAUER, C., Classical Philology, Medieval and Neo-Latin Studies
HASSAUER, F., Romance Studies
HOLUBOWSKY, E., East Asian Studies
HUBER, W., English and American Studies
HUNGER, H., Near Eastern Studies
HÜTTNER, J., Theatre Arts
KASPER, C., European and Comparative Literature and Language Studies
KASTOVSKY, D., English and American Studies
KÖHBACH, M., Near Eastern Studies
KREMNITZ, G., Romance Studies
KRUMM, H.-J., German Studies
LAAKSO, J., European and Comparative Literature and Language Studies
LINHART, S., East Asian Studies
LIPOLD-STEVENS, I., English and American Studies
LOHLKER, R., Musicology
MARTINO, A., European and Comparative Literature and Language Studies
MEHLMAUER-LARCHER, B., English and American Studies
MENGEL, E., English and American Studies
METZELTIN, M., Romance Studies
MIKLAS, H., Slavonic Studies
NEWEKLOWSKY, G., Slavonic Studies
NEWERKLA, S. M., Slavonic Studies
POLJAKOV, F., Slavonic Studies
PREISENDANZ, K., South Asian, Tibetan and Buddhist Studies
ROHRWASSER, M., German Studies
RÖMER, F., Classical Philology, Medieval and Neo-Latin Studies
ROSSEL, S. H., European and Comparative Literature and Language Studies
RUBIK, M., English and American Studies
SCHENDL, H., English and American Studies
SCHICHO, W., African Studies
SCHJERVE-RINDLER, R., Romance Studies
SCHMIDT-DENGLER, W., German Studies
SEIDLHOFER, B., English and American Studies
SELZ, G., Near Eastern Studies
SMOLAK, K., Classical Philology, Medieval and Neo-Latin Studies
SODEYFI, H., Slavonic Studies
SOOMAN, I., European and Comparative Literature and Language Studies
STEINKELLNER, E., South Asian, Tibetan and Buddhist Studies
VAN UFFELEN, H., European and Comparative Literature and Language Studies
WAGNER, B., Romance Studies
WEIGELIN-SCHWIEDRZIK, S., East Asian Studies
WIESINGER, P., German Studies
WOLDAN, A., Slavonic Studies
WOYTEK, E., Classical Philology, Medieval and Neo-Latin Studies
ZEMAN, H., German Studies

Faculty of Philosophy and Educational Sciences (tel. (1) 4277-46001; fax (1) 4277-9460; internet homehobel.phl.univie.ac.at):
BIEWER, G., Educational Sciences
BREINBAUER, I. M., Educational Sciences
GIAMPIERI-DEUTSCH, P., Philosophy
HÄMMERLE, M., Educational Sciences
HOPMANN, S., Educational Sciences
KAMPITS, P., Philosophy
KLEIN, H.-D., Philosophy
NAGL, H., Philosophy
OESER, E., Philosophy of Science
PIAS, C., Philosophy
POLLMEISTER, K., Educational Sciences
PÖLTNER, G., Philosophy
SWERTZ, C., Educational Sciences
WALLNER, F., Philosophy

Faculty of Physics (tel. (1) 4277-51001; fax (1) 4277-9510; e-mail dekanat.physik@univie.ac.at; internet physics.univie.ac.at):
AICHELBURG, P. C., Theoretical Physics
BARTL, A., Theoretical Physics
DELLAGO, C., Experimental Physics
HAFNER, J., Materials Physics
HORVATH, H., Experimental Physics
KARNTHALER, H.-P., Materials Physics
KUTSCHERA, W., Isotope Research and Nuclear Physics
RUPP, R., Experimental Physics
VOGL, G., Materials Physics
YNGVASON, J., Theoretical Physics
ZEILINGER, A., Experimental Physics

Faculty of Protestant Theology (Rooseveltplatz 10, 1090 Vienna; tel. (1) 4277-32001; fax (1) 4277-9320; internet www.univie.ac.at/etf):
ADAM, G., Religious Education
DANZ, C., Systematic Theology
DEEG, M., Systematic Theology
HEINE, S., Pastoral Theology and Psychology of Religion
KÖRTNER, U., Systematic Theology
LEEB, R., Christian History, Art and Archaeology
LOADER, J., Old Testament and Biblical Archaeology
PRATSCHER, W., New Testament Studies
WISCHMEYER, W., Christian History, Art and Archaeology

Faculty of Psychology (tel. (1) 4277-47001; fax (1) 4277-9470; internet www.univie.ac.at/psychologie):
BAUER, H., Clinical, Biological and Differential Psychology
FORMANN, A., Psychological Basic Research
HERKNER, W., Psychological Basic Research
KIRCHLER, E., Economic Psychology, Educational Psychology and Evaluation
KRYSPIN-EXNER, I., Clinical, Biological and Differential Psychology
KUBINGER, K., Developmental Psychology and Psychological Assessment
LEDER, H., Psychological Basic Research
SPIEL, C., Economic Psychology, Educational Psychology and Evaluation
VORACEK, M., Psychological Basic Research

Faculty of Social Sciences (tel. (1) 4277-49001; fax (1) 4277-9490; internet www.univie.ac.at/sowi):
AMANN, A., Sociology
BAUER, T. A., Communication
DUCHKOWITSCH, W., Communication
FELT, U., Vienna Interdisciplinary Research Unit for the Study of (Techno) Science and Society
GERLICH, P., Government
GINGRICH, A., Social and Cultural Anthropology
GOTTSCHLICH, M., Communication
GOTTWEIS, H., Political Science
GRIMM, J., Communication
KRAMER, H., Political Science
KREISKY, H. E., Political Science
LANGENBUCHER, W., Communication
RICHTER, R., Sociology
ROSENBERGER, S., Political Science
SAUER, B., Political Science
SCHULZ, W., Sociology
SEGERT, D., Political Science
SEIDL, E., Nursing Science
TÁLOS, E., Government
UCAKAR, K., Government
VITOUCH, P., Communication

VETERINÄRMEDIZINISCHE UNIVERSITÄT WIEN
(University of Veterinary Medicine, Vienna)

Veterinärpl. 1, 1210 Vienna
Telephone: (1) 25077-0
Fax: (1) 25077-1090
E-mail: rektor@vu-wien.ac.at
Internet: www.vu-wien.ac.at

Founded 1765
State control
Academic year: October to June
Rector: Dr WOLF-DIETRICH FREIHERR VON FIRCKS
Vice-Rector for Academic Affairs: Prof. Dr WOLFGANG KÜNZEL
Vice-Rector for Animal Hospital: Prof. Dr LASZLO SOLYI
Vice-Rector for Research: Prof. Dr PETER SWETLY
Vice-Rector for Resources: Prof. Dr WOLFGANG KÜNZEL
Admin. Dir: Dr MANFRED KISLING
Library: see Libraries and Archives
Number of teachers: 206
Number of students: 2,140
Publications: *Uni Vet Wien Report* (4 a year), *Wiener Tierärztliche Monatsschrift* (12 a year)

PROFESSORS
ARNOLD, W., Wildlife Biology
AURICH, J. E., Obstetrics, Gynaecology and Andrology
BAMBERG, E., Biochemistry
BAUMGARTNER, W., Internal Medicine and Contagious Diseases of Ruminants and Swine
BÖCK, P., Histology and Embryology
FRANZ, C., Applied Botany
GEMEINER, M., Medical Chemistry
GÜNZBURG, W., Virology
HOFECKER, G., Physiology
KÖNIG, H., Anatomy
MAYRHOFER, E., Radiology
MÜLLER, M., Stock Breeding, Genetics
NIEBAUER, G., Surgery and Ophthalmology
NOHL, H., Pharmacology and Toxicology
ROSENGARTEN, R., Bacteriology, Mycology, Hygiene
SCHMIDT, P., Pathology, Forensic Medicine
SMULDERS, F., Meat Hygiene, Meat Technology, Food Science
STANEK, CH., Orthopaedics in Ungulates
THALHAMMER, J. G., Small Animals and Horses
TROXLER, J., Animal Husbandry, Animal Welfare
WINDISCHBAUER, G., Medical Physics, Biostatistics
ZENTEK, J., Nutrition

WIRTSCHAFTSUNIVERSITÄT WIEN
(Vienna University of Economics and Business Administration)

Augasse 2–6, 1090 Vienna
Telephone: (1) 313 36-0
Fax: (1) 313 36-740
E-mail: presse@wuac.at
Internet: www.wu.ac.at

Founded 1898
State control
Languages of instruction: German, English
Academic year: October to June
Rector: Prof. Dr CHRISTOPH BADELT
Vice-Rector: Prof. Dr EVA EBERHARTINGER
Vice-Rector: Dr MICHAEL HOLOUBEK
Vice-Rector: Prof. Dr KARL SANDNER
Vice-Rector: Prof. Dr BARBARA SPORN
Librarian: Dr NIKOLAUS BERGER
Library: see Libraries and Archives
Number of teachers: 72

Number of students: 24,200

Publication: *Journal für Betriebswirtschaft* (Journal for Business Administration, 6 a year)

PROFESSORS

ABELE, H., Economic Theory and Policy

AFF, J., Economics

ALEXANDER, R. J., English Business Communication

AMBOS, B., International Marketing and Management

BERTL, R., Auditing, Accounting and International Accounting

BOGNER, ST., Department of Corporate Finance

EBERHARTINGER, E., Tax-oriented Business Management

FISCHER, M., Economic and Social Geography

FRANKE, N., Entrepreneurship and Foundation Research

GAREIS, R., Project Management

GRILLER, S., Research Institute for European Affairs

GRÜN, O., Business Organization and Materials Management

HANAPPI-EGGER, E., Gender and Diversity in Organizations

HOLOUBEK, M., Constitutional and Administrative Law

HORNIK, K., Mathematical and Statistical Methods

JAMMERNEGG, W., Industrial Information Processing

JANKO, W., Information Processing and Information Economics

KALSS, S., Business Law

KASPER, H., Management and Management Development

KUBIN, I., International Economics and Development Planning

KUMMER, S., Transportation

LANG, M., International Tax Law

LAURER, H. R., Constitutional and Administrative Law

LIENBACHER, G., Austrian and European Public Law

LUPTÁČIK, M., Economic Theory and Policy

MAUTNER, G., English Business Communication

MAYRHOFER, W., Business and Government Management

MAZANEC, J., Tourism

MEYER, M., Non-profit Management

MOSER, R., International Business

MUGLER, J., Small Business

NEUMANN, G., Business Informatics and New Media

NOWOTNY, C., Commercial Law

NOWOTNY, E., Financial Politics

OBENAUS, W., English Business Communication

OBERMANN, G., Public Finance

PANNY, W., Applied Computer Science

PFEIFFLE, H, Theory of Education

PICHLER, J. H., Economic Theory and Policy

PICHLER, S., Economic Theory and Policy

RAINER, F., Romance Languages

RATHMAYR, R., Slavonic Languages

RIEGLER, C., Integrated Business Accounting

RUNGGALDIER, U., Labour Law, Social Law

SANDNER, K., General Management

SCHEUCH, F., Marketing

SCHLEGELMILCH, B., International Marketing and Management

SCHNEDLITZ, P., Retail Management

SCHNEIDER, U., General Sociology and Economic Sociology

SCHNEIDER, U., Social Policy

SCHUCH, J., International Tax Law

SCHÜLEIN, J. A., General and Economic Sociology

SCHWEIGER, G., Advertising and Market Research

SEICHT, G., Industrial Management

SPECKBACHER, G., Business Management

STEGU, M., Romance Languages

STIASSNY, A., Quantitative Political Economy

STRASSER, H., Experimental Methods of Mathematics and Statistics

TAUDES, A., Industrial Information Processing

VOGEL, G., Technology and Commodity Economics

WALTHER, H., Employment Theory and Policy

WENTGES, P., Business Management

Schools of Applied Science

Fachhochschule IMC Krems: Piaristengasse 1, 3500 Krems; tel. (2732) 802; fax (2732) 802-4; e-mail information@fh-krems .ac.at; internet www.imc-krems.ac.at; f. 1994; courses in corporate governance and e-business management, export-oriented management, health management, medical and pharmaceutical biotechnology and tourism management; library: 4,500 vols, 50 periodicals; 216 teachers; 1,300 students; Dir Prof. Mag. HANS LICHTENWAGNER.

Fachhochschul-Studiengang Bauingenieurwesen-Baumanagement (School of Applied Construction Engineering and Management): Daumegasse 1, 2nd Fl., 1100 Vienna; tel. (1) 6066877-2120; fax (1) 6066877-2129; e-mail bau@fh-campuswien .ac.at; internet www.fachhochschulen.at/fh/ studium/bauingenieurwesen-_baumanagement_147.htm; f. 1996; State control; languages of instruction: German, English; Bachelors and Masters courses in construction engineering and management; Dir Dr DORIS LINK.

Fachhochschul-Studiengang Burgenland (School of Applied Sciences Burgenland): Haydngasse 1, 7000 Burgenland; tel. (5) 9010609-0; fax (5) 9010609-15; e-mail officefh@burgenland.at; internet www .fh-eisenstadt.ac.at; f. 1994; language of instruction: German; Bachelors and Masters courses in economics, environmental and energy management, health studies, information technology and management; 68 teachers; 866 students; Dir Mag. INGRID SCHWAB-MATKOVITS.

Fachhochschul-Studiengang Oberösterreich (School of Applied Sciences of Upper Austria): Franz-Fritsch-Str. 11/3, 4600 Wels; tel. (7242) 44808-0; fax (7242) 44808-77; e-mail info@fh-ooe.at; internet www.fh-ooe .at; f. 1994; language of instruction: German; Bachelors and Masters courses; campuses in Hagenberg (software, information technology and media), Linz (health and social welfare), Steyr (business and management studies) and Wels (engineering and environment and energy studies); Dir KARIN AUSSERSDORFER.

Fachhochschul-Studiengang Salzburg (School of Applied Sciences Salzburg): Schillerstr. 30, 5020 Salzburg; tel. (43) 50-2211-0; e-mail office@fh-sbg.ac.at; internet www .fh-sbg.ac.at; f. 1995; incorporated Holztechnikum Kuchl in 2003; campuses in Kuchl and Urstein; Bachelors and Masters courses in business and technology, media and design and health and welfare; 81 teachers; 1,375 students; Dir ERHARD BOJANOVSKY.

Fachhochschul-Studiengänge bfi Wien (School of Applied Science bfi Vienna): Wohlmutstr. 22, 1020 Vienna; tel. (1) 7201286-0; fax (1) 7201286-19; e-mail info@fh-vie.at; internet www.fh-vie.ac.at; f. 1996, present status 2002; languages of instruction: German, English; courses in banking and finance, European economics and business,

logistics and transport management and project management and information technology; MBAs in Central, South and East Europe Studies and Risk Management; 27 teachers; 1,100 students; Dir HELMUT HOLZINGER.

Fachhochschul-Studiengänge Campus Wien (School of Applied Sciences Vienna Campus): Daumegasse 3, 1100 Vienna; tel. (1) 6066877-100; fax (1) 6066877-109; e-mail office@fh-campuswien.ac.at; internet www .fh-campuswien.ac.at; f. 1999; language of instruction: German; diploma courses in bioengineering, biotechnology, information technology and telecommunications, social work, and technical project and process management; Bachelors courses in construction engineering and management; Masters courses in local management and economics, and social management; Dir Ing. WILHELM BEHENSKY; publ. *Aktuell* (12 a year).

Fachhochschul-Studiengänge Kufstein (School of Applied Sciences Kufstein): Andreas Hofer Str. 7, 6330 Kufstein; tel. (5372) 71819; fax (5372) 71819-104; e-mail info@fh-kufstein.ac.at; internet www .fh-kufstein.ac.at; f. 1997; diploma course in property economics and facility management; Bachelors courses in business information technology, sport, culture and event management, European energy economics, facility management and property economics and international economics and management; Masters courses in crisis and decontamination management; library: 8,500 vols, 90 periodicals; 120 teachers; 2,000 students (1,000 full-time, 1,000 exchange); Dir Mag. NORBERT WITTING.

Fachhochschul-Studiengänge St Pölten (School of Applied Sciences St Pölten): Herzogenburger Str. 68, 3100 St. Pölten; tel. (2742) 313228; fax (2742) 313229; e-mail office@fh-stpoelten.ac.at; internet www .fh-stpoelten.ac.at; f. 1996; language of instruction: German; courses in economics, social sciences and technology; 95 teachers; 1,000 students; Dirs Prof. Ing. Dr JOHANN GÜNTHER, Dipl.-Ing. GERNOT KOHL; publ. *FACTS* (2 a year).

Fachhochschul-Studiengänge Technikum Joanneum (School of Applied Sciences Technikum Joanneum): Alte Poststr. 149, 8020 Graz; tel. (316) 5453-8800; e-mail info@fh-joanneum.at; internet www .fh-joanneum.at; f. 1995; degrees in business and technology, architecture and civil engineering, business, information engineering, mobility, media and design, social services and public health; language of instruction: German; library: 27,000 vols, 600 periodicals; 270 teachers; 1,424 students; Dir Prof. Mag. Dr PETER REININGHAUS.

Fachhochschul-Studiengänge der Wiener Neustadt (School of Applied Sciences Wiener Neustadt): Johannes Gutenberg Str. 3, 2700 Vienna-Neustadt; tel. (2622) 89084-0; fax (2622) 89084-99; e-mail office@fhwn.ac .at; internet www.fhwn.ac.at; f. 1994; languages of instruction: German, English; diploma and Masters courses in business consultancy, business and engineering, information technologies, mechatronics and microsystems engineering, logistics, geographic information technologies, product marketing and project management, management for rural areas and biotechnological processes; 200 teachers; 1,800 students; Dirs Prof. Dr HELMUT DETTER, Prof. Mag. WERNER JUNGWIRTH.

Fachhochschul-Studiengänge WIFI Steiermark (School of Applied Sciences WIFI Styria): Körblergasse 111–113, 8021 Graz; tel. (316) 602-1234; e-mail info@stmk .wifi.at; internet www.stmk.wifi.at; campuses in Graz, Niklasdorf and Unterprem-stätten; courses in business management, business studies, modern languages, information technology, engineering, health and welfare, tourism and gastronomy; Pres. Ing. Mag. PETER HOCHEGGER.

Fachhochschule Technikum Kärnten (School of Applied Science Carinthia): Villa-cher Str. 1, 9800 Spittal; tel. (4762) 90500-0; fax (4762) 90500-1110; e-mail international@fh-kaernten.at; internet www.fh-kaernten.ac.at; f. 1995; courses in civil engineering, electronic engineering, geoinformation, healthcare management, medical information technology, public management, social work, telematics/network engineering; international Masters degree programmes in communication engineering for information technology, geographic information science and operations research, healthcare information technology, integrated systems and circuit design and remote engineering, and spatial decision support systems; Dir Doz. Dipl.-Ing. Dr HERBERT STÖGNER.

Fachhochschule Technikum Wien (School of Applied Science Vienna): Maria-hilfer Str. 37–39, 1060 Vienna; tel. (1) 58839-46; fax (1) 58839-49; e-mail info@technikum-wien.at; internet www.technikum-wien.at; f. 1994; Bachelors programmes in biomedical engineering, business informatics, computer science, electronics and information and communication systems; Masters programmes in biomedical engineering sciences, business informatics, embedded systems, industrial economics, information management and computer security, software development and media informatics, technology and management and telecommunications and internet technologies; diploma engineer courses in

intelligent transport systems, international business engineering, mechatronics/robotics and sports equipment technology; library: 3,000 vols; 400 teachers; 1,500 students; Dir Dr MICHAEL WÜRDINGER.

Fachhochschule Vorarlberg (School of Applied Sciences Vorarlberg): Hochschulstr. 1, 6850 Dornbirn; tel. (5572) 792-0; fax (5572) 792-9500; e-mail info@fhv.at; internet www.tvlbg.ac.at; f. 1994; Bachelors, Masters and diploma programmes in business admin., computer science, mechatronics, media design; diploma programme in social work; other programmes in engineering and business admin.; office for continuing education; library: 35,000 vols, 300 periodicals, 1,500 CDs, 800 DVDs; 86 teachers; 850 students; Dir Prof. Dipl.-Ing. RUDI FEURSTEIN.

Other Colleges

Berg- und Hüttenschule Leoben (Leoben School of Mining and Foundry Engineering): Max-Tendler-Str. 3, 8700 Leoben; tel. (3842) 44888; fax (3842) 44888-3; e-mail schule@htl-leoben.at; internet www.htl-leoben.at; f. 1865; mechanical engineering and metallurgy, industrial engineering, industrial logistics; 27 teachers; 161 students; Dir Prof. HERIBERT RESCH.

Diplomatische Akademie Wien (Diplomatic Academy of Vienna): Favoritenstr. 15A, 1040 Vienna; tel. (1) 5057272; fax (1) 5042265; e-mail info@da-vienna.ac.at; internet www.da-vienna.ac.at; f. 1964; Diploma and Master of Advanced Int. Studies programmes prepare Austrian and foreign graduates for careers in diplomacy, int. business and finance, int. organizations and

public admin.; library: 35,000 vols, 330 news-papers in German, English, French, Spanish, Italian and Russian; 80 students; Dir Dr JIŘÍ GRUSA.

Schools of Art and Music

Kärntner Landeskonservatorium (Carinthian Conservatory of Music): Miessta-lerstr. 8, 9020 Klagenfurt; tel. (463) 511421; fax (463) 511421-40508; e-mail klk@aon.at; internet www.lonse.at; f. 1827; 74 teachers; 920 students; library: 40,000 vols; Dir Mag. ROLAND STREINER.

Konservatorium Wien (Vienna Municipal Conservatory): Johannesgasse 4A, 1010 Vienna; tel. (1) 512-7747; fax (1) 512-7747-7913; e-mail office@konswien.at; internet www.konservatorium-wien.ac.at; f. 1938; affiliated to it are 17 Musikschulen and the Kindersingschule; 806 students; Dirs GOTT-FRIED EISL, RANKO MARKOVIC; Librarian EVA SMEKAL; publ. *Fidelio* (5 a year).

Musikschule der Stadt Innsbruck: Innrain 5, 6010 Innsbruck; tel. (512) 585425-0; fax (512) 585425-5; e-mail musikschule@magibk.at; f. 1818; 70 teachers; 1,800 students; Dir WOLFRAM ROSENBER-GER.

Tiroler Landeskonservatorium (Tirol Conservatory of Music): Paul-Hofhaimer-Gasse 6, 6020 Innsbruck; tel. (512) 508-6850; fax (512) 508-6855; internet www.tirol.gv.at/konservatorium; f. 1818; 75 teachers; 500 students; library: 100,000 vols and musical notes; Dir Dr THOMAS JUEN; Librarian FRANZ BAUER.

AZERBAIJAN

The Higher Education System

The higher education system was established when Azerbaijan was a full Union Republic of the Union of Soviet Socialist Republics (USSR). The main language of instruction is Azerbaijani, but there are also Russian-language schools and some teaching in Georgian and Armenian. From 1992 a Turkic version of the Latin alphabet was used in Azerbaijani-language schools (replacing the Cyrillic script). In June 1999 legislation entitled The Programme of Education Reforms of the Republic of Azerbaijan was passed by presidential decree, affecting reforms at all levels of education. In 2005 Azerbaijan signed up to the Bologna Process, under which all European countries will endeavour to adopt a universal three-tier Bachelors–Masters–Doctorate degree structure. Azerbaijan intends to adopt this system by 2010. In 2008/09 there were 48 state-supported institutions of higher education, including the Azerbaijan State Petroleum Academy which trains engineers for the petroleum industry, and numerous private universities, with 136,587 students in higher education.

The state oversees educational policy, dispenses funding and lays down guidelines for quality assurance. Individual institu-tions are responsible for employing teaching staff and estab-lishing curricula. In 2006 the Ministry of Education established the Standing Commission on Accreditation to act as the main quality assurance body for higher education institutions and secondary specialized institutions. Institutions are subject to inspection every four years. Since 2004/05 entrance examin-ations for state institutions have been organized by a central body, the Talaba Qabulu üzre Dövlat Komissiyasi (TQDK—State Students Admission Commission). An estimated 20% of school-leavers enter higher education through this process.

The three levels of higher education qualifications are Bachelors, Masters and Doctorates. Study for the Bachelors degree lasts for four years, while the Soviet-style Specialist Diploma, which is still offered in some disciplines, lasts for five years. The Masters degree was introduced in 1997/98 and lasts for up to two years. By 2006 Masters degrees had been introduced in 39 higher institutions throughout Azerbaijan, with approximately 10,000 students enrolled. Finally, the Soviet-style Aspirantura and Doctorantura remain the main doctoral degrees, though Bologna Process reforms are being implemented.

Regulatory and Representative Bodies

GOVERNMENT

Ministry of Culture and Tourism: 1000 Baku, Azadlıq meydani 1, House of Govt, 3rd Floor; tel. (12) 493-43-98; fax (12) 493-56-05; e-mail mugam@culture.gov.az; Minister ABULFAZ MURSAL OĞLU KARAYEV.

Ministry of Education: 1008 Baku, Xatai pr. 49; tel. (12) 496-06-47; fax (12) 496-34-83; e-mail office@min.edu.az; internet www.edu.gov.az; Minister MISIR CUMAYIL OĞLU MAR-DANOV.

Talaba Qabulu üzre Dövlat Komissiyasi (TQDK) (State Students Admission Com-mission): Baku, Hasan Aliyev str. 17; tel. (12) 440-30-09; e-mail info@tqdk.gov.az; internet www.tqdk.gov.az; directly subordinate to Pres.; centralized org. for management of student admissions; develops regulations for admission to higher and secondary spec. schools; conducts examinations; prepares and implements organizational, scientific and methodical and planning activities; develops proposals for improvement of higher and secondary spec. education on the basis of systemic analysis of admission campaign results; Chair. ABBASZADE MALEYKA MEHDI.

ACCREDITATION

ENIC/NARIC Azerbaijan: Min. of Educa-tion, 1008 Baku, Khatai Ave 49; tel. (12) 96-34-14; fax (12) 96-34-90; e-mail a_akhundov@yahoo.com; internet www.min.edu.az; Sr Expert AZAD AKHUNDOV.

NATIONAL BODY

Council of University Presidents: 370096 Baku, Mehseti 11; tel. (12) 21-79-27; fax (12) 98-93-79; e-mail contact@khazar.org; internet www.khazar.org; Pres. Prof. HAM-LET ISAXANLI.

Learned Societies

GENERAL

Azerbaijan National Academy of Sci-ences: 1141 Baku, F. Ağayev küç. 9; tel. (12) 441-72-81; fax (12) 441-72-81; e-mail secretary@iit.ab.az; internet www.science.az; f. 1945; depts of Physical, Mathematical and Technical Sciences (Academician-Sec. A. J. HAJIYEV), Chemical Sciences (Academician-Sec. A. A. EFENDIYEV), Earth Sciences (Acad-emician-Sec. A. M. ALIZADEH), Biological Sci-ences (Academician-Sec. M. A. MUSAYEV), Humanities and Social Sciences (Academ-ician-Sec. A. A. AKHUNDOV; attached research institutes: see Research Institutes; Pres. M. K. KERIMOV; Academician-Sec. T. N. SHAKH-TAKHTINSKIY; publs *Proceedings* (in Russian and Azeri, 4 a year), *Transactions* (series: Physical, Mathematical and Technical Sci-ences, Biological Sciences, Historical, Philo-sophical and Judicial, Economics, Literature, Philology and Art, Geological), *Journal of Physics* (in Azeri, Russian and English, 4 a year), *Azerbaijan Journal of Physics* (in Azeri, Russian and English, 4 a year), *Azerbaijan Journal of Chemistry* (in Azeri and Russian, 4 a year), *Processes of Petro-chemistry and Oil Refining Journal* (in Rus-sian and English, 6 a year), *Journal of Turkology* (in Azeri and Russian, 1 a year), *Journal of Problems of Eastern Philosophy* (in Azeri, Arabic, Farsi, Turkish, English, German and French, 2 a year), *Azerbaijan and Azerbaijanists* (in English and Russian, 12 a year), *Applied and Computational Mathematics* (2 a year).

LANGUAGE AND LITERATURE

British Council: 1000 Baku, Vali Mamma-dov küç. 1, Icheri Sheher; tel. (12) 497-20-13; fax (12) 498-92-36; e-mail enquiries@britishcouncil.az; internet www.britishcouncil.org/azerbaijan.htm; office opened 1993; offers courses and examin-ations in English language and British cul-ture and promotes cultural exchange with the UK; Dir MARGARET JACK.

Research Institutes

AGRICULTURE, FISHERIES AND VETERINARY SCIENCE

Agricultural Research Institute: 1016 Baku, U. Hadjibeyov küç. 40; tel. (12) 497-49-31; fax (12) 497-50-45; f. 1950; attached to Min. of Agriculture; Dir A. MUSAYEV.

Institute of Genetic Resources: 1106 Baku, Azadlyg Ave; tel. (12) 462-94-62; fax (12) 449-92-20; e-mail akparov@yahoo.com; f. 2003; attached to Azerbaijan Acad. of Sci-ences; Dir Z. I. AKPAROV; publ. *Transactions* (in Azeri and Russian, irreg.).

Institute of Soil Science and Agrochem-istry: 1073 Baku, M. Arif küç. 5; e-mail soiman@dcacs.ab.az; tel. (12) 438-32-40; f. 1945; attached to Azerbaijan Acad. of Sci-ences; Dir M. P. BABAYEV; publ. *Transactions* (in Azeri and Russian, 1 a year).

Karaev, A. I., Institute of Physiology: 1100 Baku, Sharif-Zade küç. 2; tel. (12) 432-15-20; e-mail inphys@dcacs.ab.az; f. 1968; attached to Azerbaijan Acad. of Sciences; Dir T. M. AQAYEV; publ. *Transactions* (in Azeri and Russian, 1 a year).

Rajably Scientific Research Institute of Horticulture and Sub-Tropical Plants: 4035 Quba, Zardabi; tel. (169) 45-37-17; fax (12) 493-08-84; f. 1926; Dir D. BAYRAMOVA.

ARCHITECTURE AND TOWN PLANNING

Institute of Architecture and Art: 1143 Baku, H. Javid Ave 31; tel. (12) 439-35-39; e-mail ertegin@baku.ab.az; internet www.artandculture.com; f. 1945; attached to Azerbaijan Acad. of Sciences; research in history and theory of architecture; art of Azerbaijan and turkic culture; 105 mems; Dir. Prof. Dr ARTEGIN SALAMZADE; publs *International scientific journal, Problems of art and culture*.

BIBLIOGRAPHY, LIBRARY SCIENCE AND MUSEOLOGY

'Mähämmäd Füzuli' Institute of Manuscripts (IMANAS): 1001 Baku, Istiglaliyyat küç. 8; tel. (12) 492-31-97; fax (12) 492-83-33; e-mail elyazmalarinstitutu@mail.ru; internet www.elyazmalarinstitutu.com; f. 1950; attached to Azerbaijan Nat. Acad. of Sciences; library of 40,000 MSS, documents and vols; Dir Dr MAMMAD ADILOV; publs *Älyazmalar khäzinäsinda* (irregular), *Kechmishimizdän gälän säslär* (irregular), *Orta äsr älyazmalari vä Azärbaycan mädäniyyäti problemläri* (every 2 years).

ECONOMICS, LAW AND POLITICS

Institute of Economics: 1143 Baku, Pr. H. Javid 31; tel. (12) 439-43-98; fax (12) 435-31-12; e-mail economy@eco.ab.az; f. 1958; attached to Azerbaijan Acad. of Sciences; Dir S. M. MURADOV.

Institute of Philosophy and Law: 1143 Baku, Pr. H. Javid 31; tel. (12) 439-37-28; f. 1945; attached to Azerbaijan Acad. of Sciences; Dir A. ABASOV; publ. *Qendershunaslig* (in Azeri and English, 11 a year).

HISTORY, GEOGRAPHY AND ARCHAEOLOGY

Institute of Archaeology and Ethnography: 1143 Baku, Pr. H. Javid 31; tel. (12) 439-36-49; fax (12) 439-39-91; e-mail abbasov@arch.ab.az; attached to Azerbaijan Acad. of Sciences; Dir A. A. ABBASOV.

Institute of Geography: 1143 Baku, Pr. H. Javid 31; tel. (12) 438-29-00; fax (12) 439-35-41; e-mail azgeog@geo.ab.az; f. 1945; attached to Azerbaijan Acad. of Sciences; research into natural resources, industrial and infrastructural problems, desertification, hydrometeorology of the Caspian Sea and its coastal dynamics; 250 mems; library of 53,000 vols; Dir Acad. B. A. BUDAGOV; publ. *Khabarlar* (2 a year).

Institute of History: 1143 Baku, Pr. H. Javid 31; tel. (12) 439-36-15; f. 1940; attached to Azerbaijan Acad. of Sciences; Dep. Dir J. A. BAHRAMOV.

Institute of Oriental Studies: 1143 Baku, Pr. H. Javid 31; tel. (12) 439-23-51; fax (12) 439-23-51; e-mail sharq@lan.ab.az; f. 1958; attached to Azerbaijan Acad. of Sciences; Dir G. B. BAKHSHALIYEVA.

LANGUAGE AND LITERATURE

Nasimi Institute of Linguistics: 1143 Baku, Pr. H. Javid 31; tel. (12) 439-35-71; f. 1932; attached to Azerbaijan Acad. of Sciences; library of 6,000 vols, 50 periodicals; Dir Prof. A. A. AKHUNDOV; publ. *Turkology* (4 a year).

Nizami Institute of Literature: 1143 Baku, 5th Fl., H. Javid 31; tel. (12) 441-74-25; fax (12) 439-56-68; e-mail adib@aas.ab.az; internet www.science.az/en/literature; f. 1932; attached to Azerbaijan Acad. of Sciences; Dir B. A. NABIYEV.

MEDICINE

Azerbaijan Institute of Orthopaedics and Traumatology: 1007 Baku, 32 Abbas Sakhat küç.; tel. (12) 496-62-62.

Azerbaijan Institute of Tuberculosis and Pulmonology: 1001 Baku, 2514 kv., 8 km settlement; tel. (12) 421-22-62.

Azerbaijan Medical Association: 1000 Baku, S. Akhundov küç. 2/1; tel. (12) 31-88-66; fax (12) 31-51-36; e-mail azer.ma@ medmail.com; internet azma.aznet.org; f. 1998; 600 mems; Dir NARIMAN SAFARLI.

Azerbaijan Research Institute of Haematology and Blood Transfusion: 1007

Baku, M. Kaskkay 87; tel. (12) 440-53-18; fax (12) 440-63-34; e-mail hajiev_azad@yahoo .com; f. 1943; Dir AZAD HAJIYEV; publ. *Azerbaijan Medical Journal* (4 a year).

Azerbaijan Research Institute of Ophthalmology: 1065 Baku, 6-ya Kommunisticheskaya küç. 5; tel. (12) 421-22-62.

Research Institute of Gastroenterology: 1110 Baku, Leningradsky pr. 111; tel. (12) 464-45-09; f. 1988; Dir B. A. AGAYEV; publ. *Actual Questions of Gastroenterology* (1 a year).

Research Institute of Medical Rehabilitation and Natural Therapeutic Factors: 1008 Baku, Khatai Ave 3; tel. (12) 466-31-93; fax (12) 466-58-35; f. 1936; Dir Prof. Dr A. V. MUSAYEV.

NATURAL SCIENCES

Biological Sciences

Botanical Garden: 1073 Baku, Patamdartskoe shosse 40; e-mail cbg@lan.ab.az; f. 1934; attached to Azerbaijan Acad. of Sciences; Dir O. V. IBADLI.

Institute of Botany: 1073 Baku, Patamdartskoe shosse 40; tel. (12) 439-32-30; fax (12) 439-33-80; e-mail botanica@baku.ab.az; f. 1936; attached to Azerbaijan Acad. of Sciences; Dir V. H. HAJIYEV.

Institute of Microbiology: 1073 Baku, Patamdart Ave 40; f. 1972; attached to Azerbaijan Acad. of Sciences; Dir M. A. SALMANOV; publ. *Transactions* (in Azeri and Russian, 1 a year).

Institute of Zoology: 1073 Baku, Proezd 1128, kv. 504, A. Abbasov; tel. (12) 439-73-71; fax (12) 439-73-53; e-mail zoology@dcacs.ab .az; f. 1936; attached to Azerbaijan Acad. of Sciences; Dir M. A. MUSAYEV; publ. *Transactions* (in Azeri and Russian, irregular).

Mardakan Arboretum: 1044 Baku; tel. (12) 454-30-12; fax (12) 454-03-74; e-mail dendrary@mail.az; f. 1926; attached to Azerbaijan Acad. of Sciences; Dir T. S. MAMEDOV.

Mathematical Sciences

Institute of Mathematics and Mechanics: 1141 Baku, Agaeva küç. 9; tel. (12) 439-39-24; fax (12) 439-01-02; e-mail frteb@aas.ab .az; attached to Azerbaijan Acad. of Sciences; Dir AKIF GADJIEV; publ. *Proceedings* (in Azeri, Russian and English, 4 a year).

Physical Sciences

Azerbaijan National Aerospace Agency: 1106 Baku, Pr. Azadlyg 159; tel. (12) 462-93-87; fax (12) 462-17-38; e-mail a .shirin-zadeh@box.az; f. 1975; Dir-Gen. Prof. ALCHIN SHIIN-ZADA.

Institute of Chemical Problems: 1143 Baku, Pr. H. Javid 29; tel. (12) 439-29-08; fax (12) 438-77-56; e-mail itpcht@lan.ab.az; f. 1935; attached to Azerbaijan Acad. of Sciences; Dir T. N. SHASKHTAKHTINSKI.

Institute of Geology: 1143 Baku, Pr. H. Javid 29A; tel. (412) 497-52-86; fax (412) 497-52-85; e-mail gia@azdata.net; internet www .gia.az; f. 1938; attached to Azerbaijan Acad. of Sciences; 250 mems; library of 24,000 vols, 70,000 periodicals; Dir A. A. ALI-ZADEH; publs *Proceedings* (1 a year), *Sciences of the Earth* (4 a year).

Institute of Physics: 1143 Baku, Javid Ave, 33; tel. (12) 439-41-51; fax (12) 439-59-61; e-mail director@physics.ab.az; f. 1945; attached to Azerbaijan Nat. Acad. of Sciences; scientific research in the different brs of theoretical and experimental physics; Dir Prof. ARIF GASHIMOV.

Institute of Radiation Problems: 1143 Baku, Pr. H. Javid 31A; tel. (12) 439-33-91; fax (12) 439-83-18; e-mail azerecolab@azerin

.com; f. 1969; attached to Azerbaijan Acad. of Sciences; Dir A. A. GARIBOV.

Şamaxı Astro-Physical Observatory: 5600 Şamaxı, Pos. Mamedalieva; tel. (12) 497-52-68; fax (12) 497-52-68; e-mail shao@ lan.ab.az; f. 1960; attached to Azerbaijan Acad. of Sciences; Dir A. S. GULUYEV; publ. *The Azerbaijan Astronomical Journal* (in Azeri, Russian and English, 4 a year).

TECHNOLOGY

Azerbaijan Energy Research Institute: 1602 Baku, Pr. H. Zardabi 94; tel. (12) 432-80-76; fax (12) 498-13-68; f. 1941; library of 6,000 vols; Dir RAMAZANOV KERIM NAZIR OGLU; publ. *Transactions of the Azerbaijan Energy Research Institute* (1 a year).

Azerbaijan Petroleum Machinery Research and Design Institute (Azinmash): 1029 Baku, 4 Araz küç.; tel. (12) 467-08-88; fax (12) 467-28-88; e-mail office@ azinmash.azeri.com; internet www.azinmash .com; f. 1930; Dir R. DJABBAROV.

Azerbaijan Scientific Gas Research and Projects Institute: 1000 Baku, Yusif Safarov küç. 23; tel. (12) 490-43-59.

Guliyev, A.M., Institute of Additive Chemistry: 1603 Baku, Beyukshorskoe shosse, kv. 2062; tel. (12) 467-65-33; fax (12) 493-33-64; e-mail aki@lan.ab.az; f. 1965; attached to Azerbaijan Acad. of Sciences; lubricant and fuel additives, cutting fluids and erosion inhibitors; library of 9,000 vols; Dir Dr V. M. FARZALIYEV.

Institute of Cybernetics: 1141 Baku, F. Agaeva str. 9; tel. (12) 439-01-51; fax (12) 439-26-33; e-mail cyber@cyber.ab.az; internet www.telmanaliev.az; f. 1965; attached to Azerbaijan Nat. Acad. of Sciences; Dir TELMAN ALIEV; publ. *Transactions of National Academy of Sciences* (2 a year).

Institute of Deep Oil and Gas Deposits: 1143 Baku, Pr. H. Javid 33; tel. (12) 439-21-40; fax (12) 497-58-52; e-mail arif.guliyev@ lan.ab.az; attached to Azerbaijan Acad. of Sciences; Dir A. M. GULIYEV.

Institute of Information Technology: 1141 Baku, F. Agayev; tel. (12) 439-01-67; fax (12) 439-61-21; e-mail secretary@iit.ab .az; f. 2003; attached to Azerbaijan Acad. of Sciences; Dir R. M. ALGULIYEV.

Institute of Polymer Materials: 5004 Sumqayıt, Samed Vargun küç. 124; tel. (12) 497-60-38; fax (164) 42-04-00; e-mail ipoma@ dcacs.ab.az; f. 1966; attached to Azerbaijan Acad. of Sciences; Dir ABASGULU MAMED GULIYEV.

Mamedaliev, Yu. G., Institute of Petrochemical Processes: 1025 Baku, N. Rafiyev 30; tel. (12) 490-24-76; fax (12) 490-35-20; e-mail ipcp@baku-az.net; internet www .science.az/en/oilchemistry; f. 1929; attached to Azerbaijan Acad. of Sciences; Dir M. I. RUSTAMOV; publ. *Process of Petrochemistry and Oil Refining* (in Russian and English, 6 a year).

Oil Research and Design Institute (AzNIPIneft): 1033 Baku, Aga Neimatully küç. 39; tel. (12) 493-64-29.

Research and Design Institute for Oil Engineering: 1000 Baku, Aga Neymatully küç. 39; tel. (12) 466-21-69; fax (12) 467-79-39.

Research Institute of Photoelectronics: 1000 Baku, Block 555, Agaeva küç; tel. (12) 439-13-08; f. 1972; library of 1,095 vols; Dir Prof. S. E. YUNISOGLU.

Libraries and Archives
Baku

Azarbaycan Milli Kitabxanasi (Azerbaijan National Library): 1000 Baku, Khagani küç. 29; tel. (12) 493-40-03; fax (12) 498-08-22; e-mail contact@anl.az; internet www.anl.az; f. 1923, named M. F. Akhundov State Library of Azerbaijan 1939, awarded National Library status 2005; 4,516,845 vols (incl. 352,005 periodicals), 27,490 sound recordings, 52,538 microforms; Dir Dr TAHIROV KARIM MOHAMMAD OĞLU; publs *Azerbaijan in Foreign Press, Information and Bibliographic Indexes, New Literature on Culture, Art and Tourism*.

Azerbaijan Scientific and Technical Library: 1001 Baku, G. Gadzhieva küç. 3; tel. (12) 492-08-07; 9,000,000 vols; Dir G. D. MAMEDOV.

Central Library of the Azerbaijan Academy of Sciences: 1143 Baku, Pr. Narimanova 31; tel. (12) 438-60-17; f. 1925; 2.5m. vols, periodicals and serials; Dir M. M. CASANOVA.

Scientific Library of Baku State University: 1148 Baku, Z. Khalilova küç. 23; tel. (12) 439-06-21; fax (12) 438-33-76; e-mail sara_ibragimova@yahoo.com; f. 1919; 2,458,991 vols; Librarian SARA IBRAGIMOVA; publs *Estestvennikh nauk* (4 a year), *Gumanitarnikh nauk* (4 a year), *Sotsialno-politicheskikh nauk* (4 a year), *Vestnik Bakinskogo Universiteta: Fiziko-Matematicheskikh nauk* (4 a year).

Museums and Art Galleries
Baku

Azerbaijan State Museum of Art: 1001 Baku, Niyazi 9–11; tel. (12) 492-57-89; fax (12) 492-67-69; f. 1920; library of 11,000 vols; Dir A. R. ASRAFILOV.

Baku Museum of Education: 1001 Baku, Niazi küç. 11; tel. (12) 492-04-53; f. 1940; library of 52,000 vols; Dir T. Z. AHMEDZADE.

Huseyn Javid Memorial Flat–Museum: 1000 Baku, Istiglaliyat 8; tel. (12) 492-06-57; f. 1995; attached to Azerbaijan Acad. of Sciences; Dir T. H. JAVID.

Museum of the History of Azerbaijan: 1005 Baku, H. Z. Tagiyev 4; tel. (12) 493-36-48; fax (12) 498-52-11; f. 1920; attached to Azerbaijan Acad. of Sciences; history of the Azerbaijani people since ancient times; Dir N. M. VALIKHANLI.

Nizami Gandjavi State Museum of Azerbaijan Literature: 1001 Baku, Isteglal küç. 53; tel. (12) 492-18-64; f. 1939; history of Azerbaijani literature since ancient times; Dir R. B. HUSEYNOV.

State Museum Palace of Shirvan-Shakh: 1004 Baku, Zamkovski pereulok 76; tel. (12) 492-95-73; fax (12) 492-83-04; e-mail shirvanshah@bakililar.az; internet www.culture.az:8101/museums/shirv/titlerus.htm; f. 1964; historical and architectural museum; Dir SEVDA DADASHEVA.

Stepano-Kert

Stepanakert Museum of the History of Nagornyi-Karabakh: 2600 Xankandi (Stepanakert), Gorkogo küç. 4; history of the Armenian people of Arthakh (Nagornyi Karabakh).

Universities

AZERBAIJAN ARCHITECTURE AND CONSTRUCTION UNIVERSITY/ AZERBAIJAN CIVIL ENGINEERING UNIVERSITY

1073 Baku, A. Sultanova küç. 5
Telephone: (12) 439-05-97
Fax: (12) 498-78-36
Founded 1920
State control
Pres.: G. MAMMADOVA
Number of students: 4,140

Faculties of Architecture, Civil Engineering, Construction, Construction Automation, Construction Technology, Economics, Hydrotechnical Machines, Road Building.

AZERBAIJAN MEDICAL UNIVERSITY

1022 Baku, Bakizkhanova küç. 23
Telephone: (12) 495-35-66
Fax: (12) 495-38-14
E-mail: admin@amu.edu.az
Internet: amu.edu.az
Founded 1930
State control
Rector: A. AMIRASLANOV
Library of 600,000 vols
Number of teachers: 2,000
Number of students: 7,186

Faculties of Dentistry, General Medicine, Paediatrics, Pharmacy, Prophylactic Medicine, Biology.

AZERBAIJAN STATE ECONOMIC UNIVERSITY

1001 Baku, Istiqlaliyyat 6
Telephone: (12) 437-10-86
Fax: (12) 492-59-40
E-mail: aseu@aseu.az
Internet: www.aseu.az
Founded 1929, current name and status 2000
State control
Pres.: ALI ABBASOV
Number of students: 15,190

Faculties of Accountancy, Commerce, Economics, Finance, Management.

AZERBAIJAN STATE PEDAGOGICAL UNIVERSITY 'NASREDDIN TUSI'

1000 Baku, Uzeir Hajibejov 34
Telephone: (12) 493-00-32
Fax: (12) 493-00-32
Founded 1921
State control
Languages of instruction: Azeri, Russian
Pres.: BAHLUL AGAJEV
Number of students: 7,975

Faculties of Azeri Language and Literature, Chemistry and Biology, Drawing and Imitation Arts, Elementary Military Education and Physical Training, Geography, History, Mathematics, Pedagogy and Psychology, Physics.

AZERBAIJAN STATE UNIVERSITY OF CULTURE AND FINE ARTS

1065 Baku, Pr. Insaatchilar 9
Telephone: (12) 439-07-78
Fax: (12) 438-93-48
E-mail: inchmed@azeri.com
Founded 1945
State control
Academic year: September to July
Rector: TEYMURCHIN AFANDIYEV
Vice-Rector: RAFIQ SADIQOV

Library of 115,000 vols
Number of teachers: 190
Number of students: 2,150

DEANS
Faculty of Cultural Studies: ALEKPER MAMMADOV
Faculty of Fine Arts: VEFA ALIYEV
Faculty of Management: BAYRAM HADJIYEV
Faculty of Music: VAMIG MAMMEDALIYEV
Faculty of Painting: DJABBAR HASSANOV
Faculty of Theatre and Cinema: MAMMEDSHAH ATAYEV

AZERBAIJAN STATE UNIVERSITY OF LANGUAGES

1014 Baku, Rashid Bahbudov St 60
Telephone: (12) 421-22-31
E-mail: info@adu.edu.az
Internet: www.adu.edu.az
Founded 1937
State control
Rector: SAMAD SEYIDOV
Number of students: 4,573

Faculties of English, French, German, Philology, Regional Studies and International Relations, Russian, Translation.

AZERBAIJAN TECHNICAL UNIVERSITY

1073 Baku, H. Javid Ave 25
Telephone: (12) 438-33-43
Fax: (12) 438-32-80
E-mail: aztu@aztukm.baku.az
Internet: www.aztu.az
Founded 1950
State control
Languages of instruction: Azeri, Russian
Academic year: September to July
Rector: Dr H. A. MAMEDOV
Vice-Rector for General Affairs: A. A. MIRZALIYEV
Vice-Rector for Int. Relations: Z. M. SULTANZADE
Vice-Rector for Learning and Education: Dr K. G. YAHUDOV
Vice-Rector for Research and Devt: Dr A. N. ALIZADE
Registrar and Chief Admin. Officer: AZIZA B. GASIMLI
Librarian: NARINGUL KHALAFOVA
Library of 600,000 vols
Number of teachers: 695
Number of students: 5,126
Publications: *Research Works* (4 a year), *Ziya* (12 a year)

DEANS
Faculty of Automation and Computing Equipment: Dr R. A. HASANOV
Faculty of Business and Management for the Engineering Industry: Dr I. A. ASLANDAZE
Faculty of Electrical Engineering and Energy: Dr M. M. BASHIROV
Faculty of Machine-Building: Dr N. M. RASULOV
Faculty of Machine Sciences: Dr M. H. GARIBOV
Faculty of Metallurgy: Dr A. I. BABAYEV
Faculty of Radio Engineering and Communications: Dr A. N. HASANOV
Faculty of Technological and Light Industry Machines: A. M. MIRZAYEV
Faculty of Transportation: Dr F. A. HASANOV

PROFESSORS
Faculty of Automation and Computing Technology (tel. (12) 438-94-06):
  ABILOV, C. I., Automation
  ALIYEV, A. B., Higher Mathematics
  ALIZADE, A. N., Applied Mathematics

ASLANOV, G. I., Higher Mathematics
BAYRAMOV, K. T., Computers and Systems
DUNYAMALIEV, M. A., Applied Mathematics
HACHIYEV, M.A., Design and Manufacture of Computers
ISKENDERZADE, Z. A., Applied Physics and Microelectronics
MAMEDOV, H. A., Automation and Control
MELIKOV, A. Z., Automation
NOVRUZBEKHOV, I. G., Applied Mathematics
RZAYEV, T. G., Automation

Faculty of Business and Management for the Engineering Industry (tel. (12) 439-13-96):

ABBASOV, M. A., History
ALIYEV, A. A., Theory of Economics
ALIYEV, A. H., Philosophy and Political Science
ALIYEV, R. Z., Physical Education and Sport
GULIYEV, R. I., Theory of Economics
HUSEYNOV, S. Y., Philosophy and Political Science
ISMAYILOV, R. A., French
JUMSHUDOV, S. Q., Economy and Management of Transportation
NACAFOV, B. I., History
RAMAZANOV, F. F., Philosophy and Political Science
SAMEDZADE, SH. A., Management, Economics and Organization

Faculty of Electrical Engineering and Energy (tel. (12) 439-12-47):

ABDALOV, S. I., Theoretical Electrical Engineering
GURBANOV, M. A., Physics
GURBANOV, T. B., Automation
LAZIMOV, T. M., Automation
NAZIYEV, Y. M., Thermal Engineering and Heating Mechanisms
SHAKHVERDIYEV, A. H., Thermal Engineering and Heating Mechanisms

Faculty of Machine-Building (tel. (12) 439-13-56):

ABBASOV, T. F., Physics
ABBASOV, V. A., Metal-cutting Machines and Tools
EFENDIYEV, SH. M., Physics
GODJAYEV, E. M., Physics
HUSEYNOV, S. O., Hydraulics
MIRZAJANOV, J. B., Machine-building Technology
MOVLAZADE, V. Z., Machine-building Technology
RASULOV, N. M., Machine-building Technology
RUSTAMOV, M. I., Metal-cutting Machines and Tools
SADYKHOV, A. H., Repair Technology of Machines

Faculty of Machine Sciences (tel. (12) 438-94-70):

ABDULLAYEV, A. H., Lift Transport Machines
BAGIROV, SH. M., Mechanical Theory
HUSEYNOV, H. A., Automated Design Systems in Machine-building
KENGERLI, A. M., Mechanical Theory
KHALILOV, A. M., Mechanical Theory
MAMMEDOV, V. A., Mechanical Theory
MUSTAFAYEV, M. R., Mechanical Theory
QAFAROV, A. M., Metrology and Standardization

Faculty of Metallurgy (tel. (12) 438-34-69):

AMIROV, S. T., Construction Materials Technology, Powder Metallurgy and Corrosion
ASKEROV, K. A., Industrial Ecology and Safety
BABAYEV, F. R., Chemistry
EYVAZOV, B. Y., Construction Materials Technology, Powder Metallurgy and Corrosion

HUSEYNOV, R. G., Construction Materials Technology, Powder Metallurgy and Corrosion
MAMEDOV, Z. G., Metallurgy and Science of Metals
MAMMEDOV, A. A., Industrial Ecology and Safety
MAMMEDOV, A. T., Metallurgy and Science of Metals
NOVRUZOV, H. D., Powder Metallurgy and Corrosion
RUSTAMOV, M. A., Chemistry
SHARIFOV, Z. Z., Powder Metallurgy and Science of Metals
SHUKUROV, R. I., Metallurgy and Science of Metals
ZAMANOVA, E. N., Physics

Faculty of Radio-Engineering and Communications (tel. (12) 438-50-13):

EFENDIYEV, C. A., Television and Radio Systems
HASANOV, A. N., Telecommunications
IMAMVERDIYEV, G. M., Electronic Communications
ISMIBEYLI, E. G., Electrodynamics and High Frequency Instruments
KENGERLI, U. S., General Theoretical Radio-Engineering
MAGARRAMOV, V. A., General Theoretical Radio-Engineering
MAMEDOV, F. H., Telecommunications
MAMEDOV, I. R., General Theoretical Radio-Engineering

Faculty of Transportation (tel. (12) 439-12-51):

AHMEDOV, H. M., Road Transport and Road Safety
BAGIROV, S. M., Automation
EFENDIYEV, V. S., Internal Combustion Engine and Refrigeration Machinery
MAKHMUDOV, R. N., Theoretical Mechanics
MIRSALIMOV, V. M., Automechanics of Materials Resistance
NASIBOV, N. E., Theoretical Mechanics
TAGIZADE, A. G., Road Transport and Road Safety

AZERBAIJAN TECHNOLOGICAL UNIVERSITY

2011 Ganca, Aliyev Ave. 103
Telephone: (22) 57-56-29
Fax: (22) 57-29-61
E-mail: info@aztu-ganja.ws
Internet: aztu-ganja.ws
Founded 1970
State control
Rector: Prof. TELMAN GULU MALIKOV
Number of students: 1,713

DEANS

Faculty of Consumer Goods Technology and Examination: Asst Prof. GARAY SURKHAI ABBASOV
Faculty of Economy and Management: Asst Prof. KHALIDA MEHDI AGAYEVA
Faculty of Food Technology and Tourism: Asst Prof. ARZU NAJAF HASANOV
Faculty of Standardization and Technological Machines: Asst Prof. NAMIQ RAZA ASKAROV

BAKU ISLAMIC UNIVERSITY

1000 Baku, Mirza Fatali 7
Telephone: (12) 492-82-23
State control
Pres.: Haj SABIR HASANLI.

BAKU STATE UNIVERSITY

1148 Baku, Academic Zahid Xalilov St 23
Telephone: (12) 430-32-45

Fax: (12) 498-33-76
E-mail: info@bsu.az
Internet: www.bsu.az
Founded 1919
Academic year: September to July
Rector: ABEL MAMMADALI MAHARRAMOV
Pro-Rectors: BAKHRAM MEKHRALI ASKEROV, VUSAT AMIR EFENDIYEV, SHAHVALAD BINNAT KHALILOV, IZZAT ASHRAF RUSTAMOV
Librarian: SARA IBRAGIMOVA

Library: see Libraries and Archives
Number of teachers: 1,380
Number of students: 15,300

Publications: *Estestvennikh nauk* (4 a year), *Gumanitarnikh nauk* (4 a year), *Sotsialno-politicheskikh nauk* (4 a year), *Vestnik Bakinskogo Universiteta: Fiziko–Matematicheskikh nauk* (4 a year)

Depts of applied mathematics, biology, chemistry, commerce, geology and geography, Hebrew studies, int. law and int. relations, journalism, law, library sciences, mathematics, oriental studies, philology, philosophy and psychology, physics, preparatory studies, religion.

GANCA STATE UNIVERSITY

2000 Ganca, Pr. Khatai 187
Telephone: (22) 56-23-12
Fax: (22) 56-19-63
E-mail: admin@ganjasu.com
Internet: www.gsu.az
Founded 1938
State control
Rector: Prof. ELMAN MAMMADOV
Pro-Rectors: ASIF CAVADOV, FAKRADDIN HASANOV, NADIR IBADOV, SALEH SALAHOV

Faculties of Chemistry and Biology, Educational Psychology, Engineering Education, Foreign Languages, History, Mathematics and Computer Science, Philology.

KHAZAR UNIVERSITY

1096 Baku, Mehseti 11
Telephone: (12) 421-79-27
Fax: (12) 498-93-79
E-mail: zamirova@khazar.org
Internet: www.khazar.org
Founded 1991
Private control
Languages of instruction: English, Azeri, Russian
Academic year: September to August
Pres.: Prof. HAMLET ISAXANLI
Vice-Pres.: Prof. MOHAMMAD NOURIYEV
Dir of the Academic Library: (vacant)
Library of 60,000 vols, 87 periodicals
Number of teachers: 70
Number of students: 1,227 (850 undergraduate, 120 postgraduate)
Publications: *Azerbaijani Archaeology* (4 a year), *Journal of Azerbaijani Studies* (4 a year), *Khazar View* (literary and scientific, 24 a year)

DEANS

School of Architecture, Engineering and Applied Science: Prof. RAFIG M. AHMADOV
Faculty of Economics and Management: Prof. MOHAMMAD NOURIYEV
Faculty of Education: ELZA SAMADOVA
Faculty of Humanities and Social Sciences: (vacant)
Faculty of Law: Prof. JABIR KHALILOV
Faculty of Medicine, Dentistry and Public Health: Assoc. Prof. NIGAR BAGHIROVA

LANKARAN STATE UNIVERSITY

4200 Lankaran, Gen. H. Aslanov 50

Telephone: (171) 5-25-88
Fax: (171) 5-27-86
E-mail: office@lsu.edu.az
Internet: www.lsu.edu.az

Founded 1991
State control

Rector: ASAF ISKENDEROV
Number of students: 1,369

Faculties of Economics, Humanities, Natural Sciences, Pedagogy.

NAXÇIVAN STATE UNIVERSITY

7001 Naxçıvan, Mardanov Gardashlari 99

Telephone: (12) 94-99-97
Fax: (12) 95-93-29
E-mail: rector@ndu.edu.az
Internet: www.ndu.edu.az

Founded 1967
State control

Rector: ISSA HABIBBEYLI AKBER
Vice-Rectors: HUSEYN MAMMAD HASHIMLI, VALI ALLAHVERDI HUSEYNOV, MAMMAD HUSEYN RZAYEV

Number of students: 3,261

Other Higher Educational Institutes

Azerbaijan Agricultural Institute: 2000 Ganca, Azizbekova küç. 262; tel. (22) 2-10-64; depts of agrochemistry and soil science, agronomy, fruit and vegetable growing, viticulture; animal husbandry, veterinary science, silkworm breeding; mechanization, electrification, economics and management, accounting; library: 200,000 vols; Rector N. A. SAFAROV.

Azerbaijan State Academy for Physical Training and Sports: 1072 Baku, 98 Fatali Khan Khoyski; tel. (12) 498-47-31; fax (12) 493-86-17; e-mail agacanbox@mail.ru; f. 1930; State control; languages of instruction: Azeri, Russian; faculties of Physical Education, Sports; 3,589 students; Rector AGADJAN ABIYEV.

Azerbaijan State Marine Academy: 1000 Baku, Pr. Azerbaijan 18; tel. (12) 493-09-19;

fax (12) 493-86-17; e-mail agma@azerin.com; f. 1881; State control; languages of instruction: Azeri, Russian; library: 90,000 vols; 55 doctoral staff; 350 students; Pres. SAMBUR HAMDULLAH.

Azerbaijan State Oil Academy: 1010 Baku, Pr. Azadlyg 20; tel. (12) 493-45-57; fax (12) 498-29-41; e-mail ihm@adna.baku .az; internet www.adna.baku.az; f. 1920; faculties of oil and gas exploitation, power engineering, oil mechanical engineering, chemical technology, automation of production, engineering economics; brs in Sumqayıt and Mingaçevir; library: 860,000 vols; 870 teachers; 6,232 students; Rector S. QARAYEV.

Uzeir Hajibeyov Baku Academy of Music: 1014 Baku, Shamsi Badalbeyli 98; tel. (12) 493-22-48; fax (12) 498-13-30; f. 1920; courses: piano, orchestral instruments, folk instruments, singing, choral conducting, composition, musicology; library: 220,000 vols and 25,000 scores; 290 lecturers; 630 students; Rector F. SH. BADALBEYLI.

BAHAMAS

The Higher Education System

The Bahamas is a contributing country to the University of the West Indies (UWI). The UWI Centre for Hotel and Tourism Management is located in Nassau. Other institutions of higher education include the College of the Bahamas (a community college) and Bahamas Law School (part of the UWI). The Ministry of Education is responsible for education and in 2004 it created the Department of Higher Education and Lifelong Learning, which is responsible for tertiary education and quality assurance. To gain admission to degree programmes students must have at least two GCE A-level subjects or equivalent. Available degrees include Associates, Bachelors, Masters and Doctorates. Associate degrees are taken after GCE O-levels and last for two years. Bachelors degrees last for three years, and Masters degrees last for two years after the Bachelors. A Doctorate takes a further two years after the Masters degree. Associate degrees are mostly available at the College of the Bahamas.

In 2002 there were 3,463 students registered at the College of the Bahamas.

Regulatory Body

GOVERNMENT

Ministry of Education: Thompson Blvd, POB N-3913, Nassau; tel. 502-2700; fax 322-8491; e-mail info@moe.gov.bs; internet moe.gov.bs; Minister CARL BETHEL.

Ministry of Youth, Sports and Culture: Nassau; Minister THOMAS DESMOND BANNISTER.

Learned Societies

GENERAL

Bahamas National Trust: POB N-4105, Nassau; tel. 393-1317; fax 393-2548; e-mail bnt@bnt.bs; internet www.bnt.bs; f. 1959; preservation of bldgs, wildlife and areas of beauty or historic interest; manages 21 nat. parks and protected areas; 2,500 mems; Exec. Dir CHRISTOPHER HAMILTON (acting); publ. *Trust Notes* (6 a year).

HISTORY, GEOGRAPHY AND ARCHAEOLOGY

Bahamas Historical Society: POB SS-6833, Nassau-New Providence; tel. 322-4231; e-mail info@bahamashistoricalsociety.com; internet www.bahamashistoricalsociety.com; f. 1959; 400 mems; collection and preservation of material relating to the history of the Bahamas; Pres. STEPHEN B. ARANHA; Corresp. Sec. JOAN CLARKE; publ. *Bahamas Historical Journal* (1 a year).

LANGUAGE AND LITERATURE

Alliance Française: Suite 60, Grosvernor Close, Shirley St, POB CB-13002, Nassau-New Providence; tel. 356-0961; fax 326-5662; internet alliance-bahamas.com; offers courses and examinations in French language and culture and promotes cultural exchange with France.

Libraries and Archives

Freeport

Sir Charles Hayward Public Lending Library: POB F-40040, Freeport, Grand Bahama; f. 1966; 40,000 vols; Librarian ELAINE B. TALMA.

Nassau

College of the Bahamas–Libraries and Instructional Media Services: POB N-4912, Nassau; tel. 302-4552; fax 326-7803; e-mail library@cob.edu.bs; f. 1974; 75,000 vols; spec. collns incl. Bahamiana, Caribbean dissertations; document delivery and interlibrary loans; deposit collns of the UN, WHO and Pan-American Health Organization; Dir WILLAMAE M. JOHNSON; publ. *Library Informer*.

Department of Archives: POB SS-6341, Nassau; tel. 393-2175; fax 393-2855; e-mail archives@batelnet.bs; internet www.bahamasnationalarchives.bs; f. 1971; nat. archival depository; 2,689 linear ft of records; Govt record centre records management; Dir Dr ELAINE TOOTE; publ. *Preservum* (every 2 years).

Nassau Public Library: POB N-3210, Nassau; f. 1837; 80,000 vols; Dir (vacant).

Museum

Nassau

Bahamia Museum: POB N-1510, Nassau.

Colleges

College of the Bahamas: Thompson Blvd, POB N-4912, Nassau; tel. 323-8550; fax 326-7834; internet www.cob.edu.bs; f. 1974; 4-year college; assoc. degrees in arts, natural and social sciences, business, technology, nursing, teaching; Bachelors degrees in banking and finance, management, accounting, nursing, education; continuing education; 160 teachers; 3,463 students; library: 68,000 vols; Pres. Dr LEON HIGGS; publs *At Random* (1 a year), *COBLA Journal* (2 a year), *College Forum* (2 a year).

University of the West Indies (Bahamas Office): POB N-1184, Nassau; tel. 323-6593; fax 328-0622; e-mail matwilliam@hotmail.com; f. 1965; Representative MATTHEW WILLIAM.

BAHRAIN

The Higher Education System

The University of Bahrain was founded in 1986 by Amiri decree as a merger between University College of Arts, Science and Education and Gulf Polytechnic. The other main institutions of higher education are the College of Health Sciences, founded in 1976, the Arabian Gulf University, founded in 1980 as a joint venture between six (now seven) Arab Governments and the Gulf College of Hospitality and Tourism. Some 29,678 students were enrolled in higher education in 2006/07 and in 2009 about 13,000 students were enrolled at the University of Bahrain alone.

In 2009 there were 12 private tertiary education providers registered with the Higher Education Council. These are a combination of institutions which are wholly owned locally, institutions that have international partners, and institutions that are campuses of universities located in other countries.

Admission to higher education is based on a test score of 70% or higher in the Tawjihiya examinations. The main undergraduate qualifications are the Associate and Bachelors degrees, whilst the main postgraduate qualifications are the Masters degree, Doctorate, and Postgraduate Diploma. The undergraduate degrees are based on the US credits system: Associate degrees last for two years and require 60–70 credits, and Bachelors degrees are four years in length and require 130–140 credits. The Masters degree and Postgraduate Diploma are based on the British Masters degree, and last for two to four years, with an equal division between taught classes and research. Finally, the Doctorate, usually PhD, requires three to five years of full-time study and research. All Bahraini students studying abroad are required to have their degrees submitted for recognition by the Commission for the Evaluation of Academic Degrees. A Quality Assurance Authority affiliated to the Higher Education Council has recently been put into place.

Non-university level education is offered at the University of Bahrain in the form of two-year diploma courses in a number subjects. The admissions criteria are the same as those for a full degree course. The College of Health Sciences offers Certificates, Associate degrees, Post-basic diplomas and Bachelors degrees in mostly medical-related subjects. Vocational and technical training is also offered at the Bahrain Training Institute, the Hotel and Catering Training Centre and the Vocational and Training Centre (the latter being run by the Ministry for Labour and Social Affairs).

From the mid-2000s the implantation of branches of foreign universities gathered pace in Bahrain. For example, construction of the Royal College of Surgeons, within Ireland Medical University of Bahrain at Muharraq, was completed in 2008. Plans to establish a Higher Education City were put into place in 2006. The development was scheduled to become operational by 2011. It was to include a full branch of a leading US university, an international research centre and a specialist academy.

In line with Bahrain's Economic Vision – 2030, in 2009 a Quality Assurance Authority (QAA) affiliated to the Higher Education Council was put into place. It had four main monitoring units: the Schools Review Unit, the Vocational Review Unit, the Higher Education Review Unit and the National Examinations Unit. The QAA is one of the key initiatives of the National Education Reform Initiatives, which aim to develop the education system at all levels. The Initiatives also included the establishment of Bahrain Teacher's College and of Bahrain Polytechnic and the creation of a School Improvement Programme. The Higher Education Review Unit does not have the authority to license or accredit university programmes but it does issue institutional quality review reports on degree programmes from private universities.

Regulatory Body

GOVERNMENT

Ministry of Education: POB 43, Manama; tel. 17680105; fax 17687866; e-mail dir .relations@moe.gov.bh; internet www .education.gov.bh; Minister Dr MAJID BIN ALI AN-NO'AIMI.

ACCREDITATION

Quality Assurance Authority: Bahrain; tel. 17583330; e-mail talsindi@batelco.com .bh; f. 2007; affiliated to Higher Education Council; Dir TARIQ ALSINDI.

Learned Societies

ECONOMICS, LAW AND POLITICS

Bahrain Bar Society: POB 5025, Manama; tel. 17720566; fax 17721219; f. 1977; 65 mems; Pres. HASSAN ALI RADHI; publ. *Al Muhami*.

FINE AND PERFORMING ARTS

Bahrain Arts Society: POB 26264, Manama; tel. 17590551; fax 17594211; e-mail info@bahrainartssociety.net; internet www .bahrainartssociety.com; f. 1983; promotes fine arts of Bahrain nationally and internationally; incl. a school of fine arts and art gallery, and the official photography club;

184 mems; library: small library; Pres. ALI AL-MAHMEED.

Bahrain Contemporary Art Association: POB 26232, Manama; tel. 17728046; fax 17723341; e-mail alsaariart@hotmail.com; f. 1970; holds exhibitions; 60 mems; library of 250 vols; Pres. RASHID AL-ORAFI; Dir ABDUL KARIM AL-ORRAYED; Information Officer SAYED HASSAN AL SAARI.

HISTORY, GEOGRAPHY AND ARCHAEOLOGY

Bahrain Historical and Archaeological Society: POB 5087, Manama; tel. 17727895; f. 1953; 143 mems; library: reference library; Pres. Dr ESSA AMIN; Hon. Sec. Dr KHALID KHALIFA; publ. *Dilmun* (2 a year).

LANGUAGE AND LITERATURE

Alliance Française: POB 840, Manama; tel. 17683295; fax 17781137; e-mail info@ afbahrain.com; internet www.afbahrain.com; offers courses and exams in French language and culture and promotes cultural exchange with France.

Bahrain Writers and Literature Association: POB 1010, Manama; tel. 17274866; f. 1969; 40 mems; library of 700 vols; Pres. ALI AL-SHARGAWI; Sec. FAREED RAMADAN.

British Council: AMA Centre, 146, Shaikh Salman Highway, Manama 356, POB 452; tel. 17261555; fax 17252269; e-mail bc

.enquiries@britishcouncil.org.bh; internet www.britishcouncil.org/me-bahrain.htm; office opened 1959; attached teaching centre; offers courses and exams in English language and British culture and promotes cultural exchange with the UK; library of 9,000 vols; Dir AMANDA BURRELL.

MEDICINE

Bahrain Medical Society: POB 26136, Adliya; tel. 17827818; fax 17827814; f. 1972; 350 mems; library of 300 vols; Pres. Dr ALI MOHD MATAR; Gen. Sec. Dr FAISAL A. ALNASIR; publ. *Journal* (4 a year).

RELIGION, SOCIOLOGY AND ANTHROPOLOGY

Bahrain Society of Sociologists: POB 26488, Manama; tel. 17826309; fax 17727485; f. 1979; 65 mems; library of 423 vols; Pres. Dr AHMED AL-SHARYAN; Sec.-Gen. EBRAHIM ALALAWI.

Islamic Association: POB 22484, Manama; tel. 17671788; fax 17676718; e-mail islamyia@islamyia.org; internet www .islamyia.org; f. 1979; teaches the Qur'an, Fiqh, Hadith, Sunnah; distributes zakat and donations; 200 mems; Pres. Dr ABDULATIF MAHMOUD AL-MAHMOUD.

TECHNOLOGY

Bahrain Information Technology Society: POB 26089, Manama; Villa 6, Gate

1334, Rd 3729, Manama 337; tel. 17741770; fax 17919995; e-mail bits@batelco.com.bh; internet www.bits.org.bh; f. 1981; promotes information technology in the kingdom; 260 mems; Pres. ABDULNABI A. KAL AWADH.

Bahrain Society of Engineers: POB 835, Manama; tel. 17727100; fax 17729819; e-mail mohandis@batelco.com.bh; internet www .mohandis.org; f. 1972; 900 mems; Pres. MOHAMED K. ALSAYED; Admin. Man. JAWAD JAFFAR AL-JABAL; publ. *Al-Mohandis* (4 a year).

Research Institute
NATURAL SCIENCES
General

Bahrain Centre for Studies and Research: POB 496, Manama; tel. 17754757; fax 17754678; internet www.bcsr .gov.bh; f. 1981; scientific study and research in economics, politics and strategy, marketing and consumer behaviour, social, educational and tourism studies, int. and inter-civilization studies; library of 6,000 vols, 40 periodicals; Sec.-Gen. Dr HASAN MAHMOOD AL-BASTAKI; publs *Arab Magazine for Food and Nutrition* (2 a year), *Journal of Strategic Research* (irregular).

Libraries and Archives
Isa Town

University of Bahrain Libraries and Information Services: POB 32038, Isa Town; tel. 17838808; fax 17449838; e-mail library@admin.uob.bh; internet libwebserver .uob.edu.bh/assets; f. 1986; 150,000 vols, 700 periodicals; Dir HEDI TALBI.

Manama

Ahmed Al-Farsi Library (College of Health Sciences): POB 12, Manama; tel. 17255555 ext. 5202; fax 17242485; internet www.chs.edu.bh/library; f. 1976; serves Min. of Health staff, also public and reference service; 29,000 vols, 545 periodicals, 375 audiovisual items; Librarian ABBAS AL-KHATEM.

Educational Documentation Library: POB 43, Manama; tel. 17710599; fax 17710376; e-mail edudoc@batelco.com.bh; internet www.education.gov.bh/english/ edu-library; f. 1976; part of Min. of Education; 22,000 vols, 197 periodicals, 300 files of documents; Chief Officer FAIQA SAEED AL-SALEH; publs *Acquisitions List* (12 a year), *Bibliographical Lists* (1 a year), *Educational Index of Arabic Periodicals*, *Educational Index of Foreign Periodicals*, *Educational Indicative Abstracts* (3 a year), *Educational Information Abstracts* (3 a year), *Educational Legislation Index*, *Educational Selective Articles* (6 a year).

Historical Documents Centre: POB 28882, Manama; tel. 17664454; fax 17651050; f. 1978; attached to the Crown Prince's Court; maintains historical documents and MSS on the history of Bahrain and the Gulf; 4,000 vols; Pres. SHAIKH ABDULLAH BIN KHALID AL-KHALIFA; Dir Dr ALI ABA-HUSSAIN; publ. *Al-Watheeka* (2 a year).

Manama Central Library: c/o Ministry of Education, POB 43, Manama; tel. 17231105; fax 17274036; e-mail libman@batelco.com.bh; f. 1946; 171,622 vols, 734 periodicals, 1,475 cassettes; Dir of Public Libraries MANSOOR MOHAMED SARHAN; publ. *Bahrain National Bibliography* (every 4 years).

Museum
Manama

Bahrain National Museum: Ministry of Information, Culture and National Heritage Sector, Museum Directorate, POB 2199, Manama; tel. 17298777; fax 17297871; e-mail musbah@batelco.com.bh; internet www.info.gov.bh/en/culturenationalheritage/ bahrainnationalmuseum; f. 1970; archaeology, ethnography, natural history, art; Dir ABDUL RAHMAN MUSAMAH.

Universities
AHLIA UNIVERSITY

POB 10878, Manama
Telephone: 17298999
Fax: 17290083
E-mail: info@ahlia.edu.bh
Internet: www.ahlia.edu.bh
Private
Founded 2001
Pres.: Prof. ABDULLA Y. AL-HAWAJ
Vice-Pres. for Admin. and Finance: Prof. WAJEEH EL-ALI
Number of students: 1,836
Colleges of arts, science and education; business and finance; engineering; graduate studies and research; information technology; medical and health sciences.

BAHRAIN AMA INTERNATIONAL UNIVERSITY

POB 18041, Salmabad
Telephone: 17787978
Fax: 17879380
E-mail: amaiu@batelco.com.bh
Internet: www.amaiu.edu.bh
Private
Founded 2002
Dir: Dr MARIE REDINA VICTORIA
Registrar: NOLY MANZANO
Librarian: RICHELLE AFINIDAD

DEANS

College of Business Administration: MANOLO ANTO
College of Computer Studies and Engineering: Dr RAMON J. CABIGAO
College of International Studies: Dr ROY TUMANENG

APPLIED SCIENCE UNIVERSITY

POB 5055, Jufair
Telephone: 17728777
Fax: 17728915
E-mail: info@asu.edu.bh
Internet: www.asu.edu.bh
Private
Founded 2004
Pres.: Prof. WAHEEB AHMED AL-KHAJAH.

ARABIAN GULF UNIVERSITY

POB 26671, Manama
Telephone: 17239999
Fax: 17272555
Internet: www.agu.edu.bh
Founded 1980 by the 7 Gulf States
Academic year: September to June
Languages of instruction: Arabic, English
Pres.: Dr KHALID BIN ABDUL-RAHMAN AL OHALY
Dir for Admin. and Financial Affairs: HISHAM ALI AL ANSARI
Head of Personnel Affairs: GHADA ABDULLA AL BOHLASA

Head of Student Affairs: Dr MONA ABDUL AZIZ AL KHALIFA
Registrar: Dr ABDUL HAMEED MARHOON
Librarian: SUAD ALI AL-KHALIFA
Number of teachers: 81
Number of students: 3,623
Publications: *AGU Annual Catalogue, Journal of Scientific Research* (3 a year)

DEANS

College of Applied Sciences: (vacant)
College of Education: Prof. FATHI ABD-EL RAHIM (acting)
College of Medicine and Medical Sciences: Prof. FAZAL KARIM DAR
College of Postgraduate Studies: Prof. WALEED KHALIL ZUBARI

PROFESSORS

AD-DIN, M. N., Microbiology
AKBAR, M. M.
AL-AAQIB, AR-R., Water Engineering, Energy
AL-ABADIN, M. Z., Physiology
AL-DIN, N. A.
AL-KHOLY, U.
AL-ANSARI, M. J.
AL-QAISI, K. A., Botany, Algae
ASH-SHAZALI, H., Paediatrics
BANDARANAYAKE, R. C.
BOTTA, G.
FULEIHAN, F., Internal Medicine
GRANGULY, P. K.
GRANT, N. I.
GREALLY, J.
HAMDY, H.
ISSA, A. A.
KHADER, M. H. A., Organic Chemistry
MATHUR, V., Pharmacology
MATHUR, V. S.
NASSER, A. I., Mechanical Engineering
NAYAR, U.
PRASAD, K.
RAHIM, F. AS-A. A., Education and Psychology
RAKHA, I., General Surgery, Orthopaedics
SACHDEVA, U.
SATIR, A. A.
SKERMAN, J. H.

DELMON UNIVERSITY FOR SCIENCE AND TECHNOLOGY

POB 2469, Manama
Telephone: 17294400
Fax: 17292010
E-mail: info@delmon.bh
Internet: www.delmonuniversity.com
Founded 2004
Private
Pres.: Dr HASSAN M. AL-QUADHI
Vice-Pres. for Academic Affairs: Prof. Dr SAAD Z. DARWISH
Dean of Student Affairs: Dr HISHAM OBAIDA
Faculties of economics and administrative sciences, information technology and computer science, law.

GULF UNIVERSITY

POB 26489, Sanad
Telephone: 17620092
Fax: 17692879
E-mail: info@gulfuniversity.net
Internet: www.gulfuniversity.net
Private
Founded 2001
Pres.: Dr MONA RASHID AL-ZAYANI
Vice-Pres. for Admin. and Finance: MOHANNED AL-ANNI
Colleges of business, management and finance, computer engineering sciences, education, engineering, law.

KINGDOM UNIVERSITY

POB 40434, Manama
Telephone: 17238899
Fax: 17271001
E-mail: info@ku.edu.bh
Internet: www.ku.edu.bh

Founded 2001
Private
Languages of instruction: Arabic, English
Academic year: September to August
Pres.: Dr YOUSEF ABDUL GHAFFAR
Librarian: MOHAMMED AZAHIM SALDEEN
Librarian: HAMDY GHONAIM

Library of 3,250 vols, 20 periodicals
Number of teachers: 35 full time, 15 part
  time, 12 visiting
Number of students: 1,200

Colleges of arts, business and finance, computer and information, engineering, law

DEANS

College of Arts: Dr HANY ALBATAL
College of Business Sciences and Finance: Dr
  WALEED ABDUL AZIZ
College of Computing and Information Technology: Prof. MUSTAFA ABDUL ATHEEM
College of Engineering: Dr SAMI ALI KAMEL
College of Law: Dr MOHAMMED ALHITI

ROYAL COLLEGE OF SURGEONS IN IRELAND MEDICAL UNIVERSITY OF BAHRAIN

POB 15503, Adliya
Telephone: 17351450
Fax: 17330806
E-mail: info@rcsi-mub.com
Internet: www.rcsi-mub.com
State; attached to constituent univ. of Royal
  College of Surgeons, Ireland

Founded 2004

Pres.: Prof. KEVIN O'MALLEY.

ROYAL UNIVERSITY FOR WOMEN

POB 37400, West Riffa
Telephone: 17764444
Fax: 17764445
E-mail: info@ruw.edu.bh
Internet: www.ruw.edu.bh

Founded 2005
Private
Pres.: Prof. MAZIN JUMAH
Librarian: BINDHU NAIR

Library of 10,000 print vols, 21,000 electronic
  vols, 5,000 periodicals, 100,000 art images

DEANS

Faculty of Art, Design and Computing Science: Dr Z. HADDAD
Faculty of Business Studies: Dr Q. ALI
Faculty of Education: (vacant)

UNIVERSITY OF BAHRAIN

POB 32038, Isa Town
Telephone: 17439996
Internet: www.uob.edu.bh

Founded 1986 by merger of Univ. College of
  Arts, Science and Education, and Gulf
  Polytechnic
Autonomous control
Language of instruction: Arabic
Academic year: October to August
Chair. of Bd of Trustees: THE MINISTER OF
  EDUCATION
Pres.: Dr IBRAHIM MOHAMMED JANAHI
Vice-Pres. for Academic Programmes and
  Research: Dr NIZAR AL-BAHARNA
Vice-Pres. for Admin. and Finance: Dr SAMIR
  FAKHRO
Vice-Pres. for Planning and Community Service: Dr GEORGE NAJJAR
Registrar: Dr ISA AL-KHAYAT
Dir of Library and Information Services:
  WARWICK PRICE
Library: see Libraries and Archives
Number of teachers: 320

Number of students: 6,760

DEANS

College of Arts: (vacant)
College of Business: HAMEEDA JASSIM
  ABDULLA ABU HUSSAIN
College of Education: KHALIL YOUSIF SULAIMAN ALKHALILI
College of Engineering: NADER MOHAMMED
  SALEH ALBASTAKI
College of Information Technology: (vacant)
College of Science: HAIFA ALI RASHED AL-MASKATI

Colleges

College of Health Sciences: POB 12, Ministry of Health, Bahrain; tel. 17279664; fax 17251360; e-mail ayousif1@health.gov.bh; internet www.chs.edu.bh; f. 1976; divs of allied health, English, integrated science, nursing; Educational Devt Centre; library: see entry for Ahmed Al-Farsi Library; 111 teachers; Dean Dr SHAWKI ABDULLA AMEEN; Head of Registration and Student Affairs ALI EBRAHIM AL-SAEED; Librarian (Ahmed Al-Farsi Library) ABBAS A. AL-KHATAM.

Gulf College of Hospitality and Tourism: POB 22088, Muharraq; tel. 17320191; fax 17332547; e-mail mancat5@batelco.com.bh; internet www.gulf-college.com; f. 1976; higher nat. diploma and degree courses in hospitality management and travel and tourism; library: 10,000 vols; Dean TONY SPICER; Dir DAVID PATTERSON.

University College of Bahrain: POB 55040, Manama; tel. 17790828; fax 17793858; e-mail ealkhalifa@ucb.edu.bh; internet www.ucb.edu.bh; Private; Pres. Dr KHALID BIN MOHAMMED AL-KHALIFA; Exec. Dir Dr EBRAHIM BIN KHALID AL-KHALIFA; Registrar ISAM AHMED AL-SARAF; Librarian MOUSSA HARB; Schools of business, information technology, media and communication.

BANGLADESH

The Higher Education System

In 2008 there were 26 public and 56 private higher education institutions recognized by the University Grants Commission (UGC). Some 207,577 students were enrolled in universities and 241,336 in technical and vocational institutes. Both public and private universities are governed by the UGC, founded by an Act of Parliament in 1973; private universities are also subject to the Private Universities Act (1992). The Government accounts for 95% of university funding, with the rest coming from students' tuition fees and other compulsory fees. There are four categories of university: General, Special, Open, and Affiliating. The President and/or Prime Minister of Bangladesh acts as the Chancellor of a university and appoints the Vice-Chancellors and the academic and executive heads of the universities. The Syndicate is the university's executive body. Its decisions are ratified by the Senate, a board that also approves the accounts. The Academic Council of a university consists of professors and other teaching representatives. Deans of Faculty are either elected by the faculty or appointed by the Academic Council, depending on the institution in question. Most public universities are modelled on the University of London (United Kingdom), consisting of a central department with affiliated colleges and institutions.

Admission is based on completion of 12 years' general education, receipt of the Higher Secondary Certificate, or equivalent, and success in entrance examinations. The main university degrees are the Bachelors, Masters and Doctor of Philosophy. Bachelors from affiliated colleges of public universities are known as 'Pass' degrees and are three years in length; Bachelors degrees from public universities are known as 'Honours' degrees and last four years. Most private universities have adopted the US-style 'major' and 'minor' subject system with a Grade Point Average grading system. A Masters degree requires two years of further study after a 'Pass' degree, and one year after an 'Honours' degree. The Doctorate requires three years of study and research.

There is a formal system of Islamic education, consisting of a two-year Fazil, roughly equivalent to the Bachelors, and the two-year Kamil, equivalent to the Masters. Students are examined in fields such as Arabic, Hadith, and Tafsir (Koranic interpretation). Technical and vocational education is overseen by the Bangladesh Technical Education Board (BTEB). There are three levels of technician award: SSC, HSC and Diploma. The BTEB also administers a four-year diploma.

There is no formal system of accreditation and quality assurance, and institutions are not legally obliged to seek quality assurance. However, there are legislative plans to establish an Accreditation Council, although as of late 2009 this was still in the planning stage.

Regulatory and Representative Bodies

GOVERNMENT

Ministry of Cultural Affairs: Bangladesh Secretariat, Dhaka 1000; tel. (2) 9570667; fax (2) 7169008; e-mail sas-moca@mailcity.com; internet www.moca.gov.bd; Adviser AYUB QUADRI.

Ministry of Education: Bangladesh Secretariat, Bhaban 6, 17th–18th Floors, Dhaka 1000; tel. (2) 7168711; fax (2) 7167577; e-mail info@moedu.gov.bd; internet www.moedu.gov.bd; Minister NURUL ISLAM NAHID; Sec. SYED ATAUR RAHMAN.

FUNDING

University Grants Commission of Bangladesh: Agargaon, Dhaka 1207; tel. (2) 8112629; fax (2) 8122948; e-mail chairmanugc@yahoo.com; internet www.ugc.gov.bd; f. 1973; supervises, maintains, promotes and co-ordinates univ. education; also responsible for maintaining standard and quality in all the public and private univs in Bangladesh; assesses the needs of the public univs in terms of funding and advises Govt on various issues related to higher education; Chair. Prof. NAZRUL ISLAM; Sec. M. KHALED.

NATIONAL BODIES

Association of Universities of Bangladesh (AUB): House 47, Road 10/A, Dhanmondli R/A, Dhaka 1209; tel. (2) 8126101; fax (2) 8126101; e-mail vc-iu@kushtia.com; coordinates activities of all 17 public univs in Bangladesh and liaises with the Govt and the Univ. Grants Comm. in admin. and financial matters; Chair. MUHAMMAD MUSTAFIZUR RAHMAN; Exec. Sec. S. M. SAIFUDDIN.

Bangaldesh Bureau of Educational Information and Statistics (BANBEIS): 1 Sonargaon Rd, Dhaka 1205; tel. (2) 9665457; e-mail banbeis@bdcom.com; internet www.banbeis.gov.bd; f. 1977; attached to Ministry of Education.

Learned Societies

GENERAL

Society of Arts, Literature and Welfare: Society Park, K. C. Dey Rd, Chittagong; f. 1942; 500 mems; Gen. Sec. NESAR AHMED CHOWDHURY.

UNESCO Office Dhaka: GPOB 57, Dhaka 1207; IDB Bhaban, 16th Floor, E/8-A Rokeya Sharani, Sher-e-Bangla Nagar, Dhaka 1207; tel. (2) 9862073; fax (2) 9871150; e-mail dhaka@unesco.org; internet www.unescodhaka.org; Dir MALAMA MELEISEA.

BIBLIOGRAPHY, LIBRARY SCIENCE AND MUSEOLOGY

Bangladesh Association of Librarians, Information Scientists and Documentalists: CDL, House 67/B, Rd 9/A, Dhanmandi R/A, Dhaka 1209; tel. (2) 8856000; e-mail mmr@northsouth.edu; internet www.balid.org; f. 1986; library professional devt; runs courses in library and information sciences; 550 mems; library of 2,000 vols; Chair. Dr MD. MOSTAFIZUR RAHMAN; Sec.-Gen. Dr MD. HANIF UDDIN; publ. *Informatics* (4 a year).

ECONOMICS, LAW AND POLITICS

Bangladesh Bureau of Statistics: E-27/A, Agargaon, Sher-e-banglanagar, Dhaka 1207; tel. (2) 9118045; fax (2) 9111064; e-mail dg@bbs.gov.bd; internet www.bbs.gov.bd; f. 1971; colln, analysis and publ. of statistics covering all sectors of soc. and the economy; Dir-Gen. A. Y. M. EKRAMUL HOQUE; publs *Child Nutrition Survey* (1 a year), *Foreign Trade Statistics* (1 a year), *Labour Force Survey* (1 a year), *Statistical Bulletin* (12 a year), *Statistical Pocket Book* (1 a year), *Statistical Yearbook* (1 a year), *Yearbook of Agricultural Statistics* (1 a year).

Bangladesh Economic Association: 4/C Eskaton Garden Rd, Dhaka; tel. and fax (2) 9345996; e-mail bea.dhaka@gmail.com; f. 1958; Pres. Dr QAZI KHOLIQUZZAMAN AHMAD; Sec.-Gen. Dr ABUL BARKAT.

LANGUAGE AND LITERATURE

Alliance Française: 26 Mirpur Rd, Dhanmondi, Dhaka 1205; tel. (2) 9675249; fax (2) 8616462; e-mail alliance@afdacca.com; internet www.afdacca.org; offers courses and exams in French language and culture and promotes cultural exchange with France; attached teaching centre in Chittagong; f. 1959; library of 5,600 vols; Pres. M. SADEQ KHAN; Sec. MYRIAM BASSINOT; Treas. M. ARUP KUMAR ROY.

Bangla Academy: Burdwan House 3, Kazi Nazrul Islam Avenue, Ramna, Dhaka 1000; tel. (2) 8619577; fax (2) 8612352; e-mail bacademy@citechco.net; internet www.banglaacademy.org.bd; f. 1972; promotes culture and development of the Bengali language and literature; produces dictionaries, translates scientific and reference works into Bangla; library of 102,000 vols; Pres. Prof. A. NISUZZAMAN; Dir-Gen. Dr ABUL KALAM MANZUR MORSHED; publs *Dhan Shaliker Desh* (juvenile, 12 a year), *Journal* (in English, 2 a year), *Research Journal*, *Science Journal* (in Bangla, 4 a year), *Uttaradhikar* (literary, 12 a year).

British Council: 5 Fuller Rd, POB 161, Dhaka 1000; tel. (2) 8618905; fax (2) 8613375; e-mail dhaka.enquiries@bd.britishcouncil.org; internet www

.britishcouncil.org/bangladesh; teaching centre; offers courses and exams in English language and British culture and promotes cultural exchange with the UK; attached teaching centres in Chittagong and Dhaka; Dir Dr JUNE ROLLINSON.

Goethe-Institut: GPOB 903, Dhaka 1000; House 10, Rd 9 (new), Dhanmondi R/A, Dhaka 1205; tel. (2) 9126525; fax (2) 8110712; e-mail info@dhaka.goethe.org; internet www.goethe.de/dhaka; offers courses and exams in German language and culture and promotes cultural exchange with Germany; library of 4,000 vols, 20 periodicals; Dir Dr TORSTEN OERTEL.

MEDICINE

Bangladesh Medical Association: BMA House, 5/2 Topkhana Rd, Dhaka 1000; tel. (2) 9568714; fax (2) 9566060; e-mail bma@aitlbd .net; internet www.bma.org.bd; f. 1971; 10,000 mems; library of 8,000 vols; Pres. Dr M. A. HADI; Sec.-Gen. Dr A. Z. M. ZAHID HOSSAIN; publ. *Bangladesh Medical Journal* (4 a year).

NATURAL SCIENCES
General

Bangladesh Academy of Sciences: c/o Nat. Science and Technology Museum, Bhaban Agargaon, Dhaka 1207; tel. (2) 9110425; e-mail bas1@bangla.net; internet basbd.org; f. 1973; 59 mems (41 fellows, 9 foreign fellows, 9 expatriate fellows); Pres. Prof. Dr M. SHAMSHER ALI; Vice-Pres Prof. Dr A. K. M. AMINUL HAQUE, Prof. Dr MESBAHUDDIN AHMED; Treas. Prof. Dr SYED HUMAYUN KABIR; Sec. Prof. Dr NAIYYUM CHOUDHURY; publ. *Journal* (2 a year).

Biological Sciences

Zoological Society of Bangladesh: c/o Dept of Zoology, University of Dhaka, Dhaka 1000; tel. (2) 7168321; fax (2) 8615583; e-mail contact@zsbd.org; internet www.zsbd.org; f. 1972; 1,500 mems; Pres. Prof. M. SOHRAB ALI; Gen. Sec. ABDUR RAHMAN; publs *Bangladesh Journal of Zoology* (2 a year), *Bulletin* (irregular), *Proceedings of National Conference* (every 2 years).

RELIGION, SOCIOLOGY AND ANTHROPOLOGY

Asiatic Society of Bangladesh: 5 Old Secretariat Rd (Nimtali), Ramna, Dhaka 1000; tel. (2) 7168940; fax (2) 7168853; e-mail info@asiaticsociety.org.bd; internet www.asiaticsociety.org.bd; f. 1952; study of Man and Nature of Asia; 1,788 mems; library of 10,000 vols, 500 Urdu and Persian MSS; Pres. Prof. SIRAJUL ISLAM; Gen. Sec. Prof. MAHFUZA KHANAM; publs *Journal of the Asiatic Society of Bangladesh — Humanities* (2 a year), *Journal of the Asiatic Society of Bangladesh — Science* (2 a year).

TECHNOLOGY

Institution of Engineers, Bangladesh: Ramna, Dhaka 1000; tel. (2) 9566336; fax (2) 9562447; e-mail ieb@bangla.net; internet www.iebbd.org; f. 1948; 6,000 mems; library of 4,050 vols; Pres. Eng. A. N. H. AKHTAR HOSSAIN; Vice-Pres. for Academic and International Affairs MUHAMMAD MOHSIN ALI; Vice-Pres. for Admin. and Finance MOHAMMAD REAZUL ISLAM; Vice-Pres. for Human Resources Development MUNIR UDDIN AHMED; Hon. Gen. Sec. Eng. KHAN MANJUR MORSHED; publs *Engineering News* (12 a year), *Journal* (4 a year).

Research Institutes
GENERAL

Bangladesh Council of Scientific and Industrial Research: Dr Qudrat-I-Khuda Rd, Dhanmondi, Dhaka 1205; tel. (2) 8620106; fax (2) 8613022; e-mail info@bcsir .gov.bd; internet www.bcsir.gov.bd; f. 1973; library of 15,000 vols, 100 periodicals; Chair. Prof. Dr MD. AKRAM HOSSAIN; publs *Bangladesh Journal of Scientific and Industrial Research*, *Bigganer Joyjattra*, *Purogami Bijnan*, *Science, Technology & Development*, *Scientific & Technological Contributions of BCSIR*.

Attached Research Institutes:

BCSIR Laboratory, Chittagong: Chittagong Cantonment, Chittagong 4220; fax (31) 682505; e-mail ctglab@spnetctg.com; four divisions: chemistry, botany, pharmacology, microbiology; Dir Dr M. MANZUR-I-KHUDA.

BCSIR Laboratory, Dhaka: Dr Qudrat-i-Khuda Rd, Dhanmondi, Dhaka 1205; tel. (2) 8617924; e-mail dhakalab@bcsir.gov.bd; seven divisions: natural products; glass and ceramics; fibres and polymers; leather technology; physical instrumentation; analytical; industrial physics; Dir Dr MIR AMJAD ALI.

BCSIR Laboratory, Rajshahi: Binodpur Bazar, Rajshahi 6206; tel. (721) 750757; fax (721) 750851; four divisions: lac research; fats and oils; fibres; fruit processing and preservation; Dir Dr M. A. KHALEQUE.

Institute of Food Science and Technology, Dhaka: Dr Qudrat-i-Khuda Rd, Dhanmondi, Dhaka 1205; tel. (2) 8621148; e-mail ifst@bcsir.gov.bd; seven divisions: animal food products; biochemistry and applied nutrition; food science and quality control; industrial development; microbiology; plant food products; technology of foodgrains; Dir Dr S. F. RUBBI.

Institute of Fuel Research and Development, Dhaka: Dr Qudrat-i-Khuda Rd, Dhanmondi, Dhaka 1205; tel. (2) 8622908; e-mail ifrd@bcsir.gov.bd; three divisions: biomass and hydrocarbon research; combustion, application and pilot plant; solar energy; Dir Dr M. EUSUF.

Institute of Glass and Ceramic Research and Testing: Dr Qudrat-i-Khuda Rd, Dhanmondi, Dhaka 1205; tel. (2) 9669677; e-mail igcrt@bcsir.gov.bd.

Leather Research Institute: Nayerhat, Savar, Dhaka; tel. (2) 7708754.

Pilot Plant and Process Development Centre: Dr Qudrat-i-Khuda Rd, Dhanmondi, Dhaka 1205; tel. (2) 8622809; e-mail pppdc@bcsir.gov.bd.

AGRICULTURE, FISHERIES AND VETERINARY SCIENCE

Animal Husbandry Research Institute: Comilla; f. 1947; Prin. Scientific Officer SALIL KUMAR DHAR.

Bangladesh Jute Research Institute: Manik Miah Ave, Dhaka 1207; tel. (2) 8121929; fax (2) 9118415; e-mail info@bjri .gov.bd; internet www.bjri.gov.bd; f. 1951; oldest mono-crop research institute; constitutes three main branches, Agricultural, Technological, Marketing and Economic Research on Jute; Dir-Gen. Dr M. FIROZE SHAH SIKDER; Dir of Agriculture M. ASADUZ-ZAMAN; Dir of Technology M. KAMALUDDIN.

BIBLIOGRAPHY, LIBRARY SCIENCE AND MUSEOLOGY

Varendra Research Museum: University of Rajshahi, Aksaya Kumar Maitra Rd, Rajshahi; tel. (721) 752752; f. 1910; under control of University of Rajshahi; museumbased research instn; exhibits from the Indus Valley Civilization, Buddhist and Hindu stone sculptures, Sanskrit, Arabic and Persian scripts and stone inscriptions, indigenous, tribal culture of Rajshahi region; library of 14,000 vols; museum colln; Dir Dr M. SAIFUDDIN CHOWDHURY; publ. *Journal* (1 a year).

ECONOMICS, LAW AND POLITICS

Bangladesh Institute of Development Studies: E-17 Agargaon, Sher-e-Bangla Nagar, POB 3854, Dhaka 1207; tel. (2) 9116959; fax (2) 8113023; e-mail secy10bids@bids.org.bd; internet www.bids .org.bd; f. 1957; divs of agriculture and rural devt, general economic, human resources, industries and physical infrastructures, population studies; 81 mems; library: see Libraries and Archives; Dir-Gen. Dr MUSTAFA KAMAL MUJERI; Chief Librarian MD. ANWARUL ISLAM; publs *Bangladesh Development Studies* (4 a year), *Bangladesh Unnayan Samikhha* (1 a year, in Bengali).

MEDICINE

Centre for Medical Education (CME): National Health Library Bldg, 3rd fl., Mohakhali, Dhaka 1212; tel. (2) 8821809; fax (2) 8822563; e-mail director@cmedhaka.gov.bd; internet www.cmedhaka.gov.bd; f. 1983; conducts research related to health care services, health manpower development and the education of health professionals; library of 2,000 vols, 15,000 journals; Dir Dr S. M. MUSTAFA ANOWER.

ICDDR,B: International Centre for Diarrhoeal Disease Research: GPOB 128, Dhaka 1000; 68 Shahid Tajuddin Ahmed Sharani, Mohakhali, Dhaka 1212; tel. (2) 8860523; fax (2) 8823116; e-mail info@icddrb .org; internet www.icddrb.org; f. 1960; funded by 50 countries and NGOs; library of 40,611 vols, 14,600 documents; Exec. Dir Prof. ALEJANDRO CRAVIOTO; Dir, Clinical Sciences Div. Dr MD. ABDUS SALAM; Dir, Health Systems and Infectious Diseases Div. (vacant); Dir, Laboratory Sciences Div. Dr HUBERT PH. ENDTZ; Dir, Public Health Sciences Div. (vacant); publs *Health and Science Bulletin* (4 a year), *Journal of Health, Population and Nutrition* (4 a year).

Institute of Epidemiology, Disease Control and Research: Mohakhali, Dhaka 1212; tel. (2) 9898796; fax (2) 8821237; e-mail info@iedcr.org; internet www.iedcr .org; f. 1976; depts of biostatistics, epidemiology, medical entomology and vector bionomics, medical social science, microbiology, parasitology, virology, zoonosis; activities incl. disease surveillance, investigation of known and unknown disease outbreaks with rapid response, management of disease outbreak, training and research for the Nat. Influenza Centre of Bangladesh; library of 6,000 vols; Dir Prof. MAHMUDUR RAHMAN.

NATURAL SCIENCES
Physical Sciences

Geological Survey of Bangladesh: 153 Pioneer Rd, Segun Bagicha, Dhaka 1000; tel. (2) 9349502; fax (2) 9339309; e-mail gsb@ dhaka.agni.com; internet www.gsb.gov.bd; f. 1972; govt org. under Ministry of Energy and Mineral Resources; library of 7,000 vols, 97 journals; Dir-Gen. M. NAZRUL ISLAM; publ. *Records* (irregular).

TECHNOLOGY

Bangladesh Atomic Energy Commission: Paramanu Bhaban, E-12/A, Agargaon, Sher-e-Bangla Nagar, Dhaka 1207; tel. (2) 8130469; fax (2) 8130102; e-mail baec@agni.com; internet www.baec.org.bd; f. 1973; library of 25,375 vols, 192 periodicals; Chair. Dr M. A. MANNAN; publ. *Nuclear Science & Applications* (Series A: Biological Sciences, Series B: Physical Sciences).

Attached Institutes:

Atomic Energy Centre: POB 164, Ramna, Dhaka 2; basic and applied research in physics, electronics and chemistry; library of 10,728 vols, 100 periodicals.

Atomic Energy Research Establishment: Ganakbari, Savar, POB 3787, Dhaka; tel. and fax (2) 7701339; fax (2) 7701620; e-mail siu_aere@yahoo.com; internet www.aere.org.bd; f. 1979; library of 10,000 vols of books; consists of 9 separate institutes: Central Engineering Facilities, Institute of Computer Sciences, Institute of Electronics, Institute of Food and Radiation Biology, Institute of Nuclear Science and Technology, Nuclear Mineral Unit, Reactor Operation and Maintenance Unit, Scientific Information Unit, Tissue Banking and Biomaterial Research Unit; Senior Librarian SHAMSUL ISLAM.

Beach and Sand Exploration Centre: Coxbazar.

Radiation Testing and Monitoring Laboratory: Chittagong.

Rooppur Nuclear Plant: Pabna; publ. *AERE Annual technical Report* (1 a year).

Libraries and Archives
Chittagong

Divisional Government Public Library: POB 771, K. C. Dey Rd, Chittagong; tel. (31) 611578; f. 1963; 62,910 vols, 121 periodicals; Senior Librarian A. D. M. ALI AHAMMED.

Dhaka

Bangladesh Central Public Library: 3 Liaquat Ave, Dhaka 1000; tel. (2) 8624713; fax (2) 8610422; internet www.publiclibrary.org.bd; f. 1958; 1.0m. vols, 2,300 periodicals; spec. colln: depository for UNESCO publs; Dir A. F. M. BADIUR RAHMAN.

Bangladesh Institute of Development Studies Library: E-17, Agargaon, Sher-e-Bangla Nagar, Dhaka 1207; tel. (2) 9140755; fax (2) 9143441; internet www.bids-bd.org; f. 1957; 130,000 vols, 600 peridocals; Chief Librarian SHAHANA PARVEEN (acting).

Bangladesh National Scientific and Technical Documentation Centre (BANSDOC): E-14/Y, Agargaon, Sher-e-Bangla Nagar, Dhaka 1207; tel. (2) 8127744; fax (2) 9140066; e-mail bansdoc@bansdoc.gov.bd; internet www.bansdoc.gov.bd; f. 1963; 19,000 vols, 114 nat. periodicals, 350 foreign periodicals; Dir SETARA BANU CHOWDHURY; Chair. YEAFESH OSMAN; publs *Bangladesh Science and Technology Abstracts* (1 a year), *Current Scientific and Technological Research Projects of Bangladesh* (every 2 years), *National Catalogue of Scientific and Technological Periodicals of Bangladesh* (every 2 years), *Report of the Survey of Research and Development Activities in Bangladesh* (every 2 years).

Directorate of Archives and Libraries: 32 Justice S. M. Murshed Sarani, Sher-e-Bangla Nagar (Agargaon), Dhaka 1207; tel. (2) 9129992; fax (2) 9118704; e-mail nabdirector@gmail.com; internet www.nanl.gov.bd; f. 1971; attached to Min. of Cultural Affairs; coordinating centre for archives and libraries at nat. level; 500,000 vols, 105 Bengali periodicals, 10 foreign periodicals, 20 maps, 3,000 microfilms, 60 rolls of microfiche, 235 issues of National Bibliography (1972–1991); Dir M. LATIFUR RAHMAN.

Institutions Under the Control of the Directorate:

National Archives of Bangladesh: Nat. Archives Bldg, Sher-e-Bangla Nagar, Agargaon, Dhaka 1207; f. 1973; 225,000 vols of records and documents, 3,500 books, 58 rolls of microfilm, 10,000 press clippings; Dir M. LATIFUR RAHMAN; publs *Annual Reports 1973–84*, *Bulletin of Dissertations and Theses by Bangladeshi Scholars 1947–73*, *SWARBICA Journal Vol III*.

National Library of Bangladesh: Nat. Library Bldg, Sher-e-Bangla Nagar Agargaon, Dhaka 1207; f. 1968; 1m. books, 2,000 journals; Dir M. LATIFUR RAHMAN; publs *Articles Index*, *Bangladesh National Bibliography*.

University of Dhaka Library: Ramna, Dhaka 1000; tel. (2) 9661900; fax (2) 8615583; e-mail duregstr@bangla.net; f. 1921; 5.5m. vols, 30,000 rare MSS and a large number of tracts (booklets, leaflets, pamphlets, and puthis) in microfilm format; rare books and reports, puthis, Bengali Tracts and private colln of Buchanan on Bengal have been acquired from the British Museum, UK; Librarian Dr MD. SERAJUL ISLAM.

Rajshahi

Rajshahi University Library: Rajshahi; tel. (721) 750666; fax (721) 750064; f. 1953; 250,000 vols, 2,000 journals; Administrator Prof. OBAIDUR RAHMAN PRAMANIK.

Museums and Art Galleries
Dhaka

Ahsan Manzil Museum: Nawab Ahsanulla Rd, Shadarghat, Dhaka; tel. (2) 7391122; fmr home of the Nawab of Dhaka; 23 galleries displaying portraits, furniture and other objects used by the Nawab.

Balda Museum: Dhaka; f. 1927; Bengali art and ancient artifacts; Superintendent MUHAMMAD HANNAN.

Bangabandhu Memorial Museum: House 10 Rd 32, Dhanmondi Residential Area, Dhaka; tel. (2) 8110046; residence of the father of the nation, Bangabandhu Sheikh Mujibur Rahman (1920–75); colln of personal effects and photographs of his lifetime.

Bangladesh National Museum: POB 355, Shahbag, Dhaka 1000; tel. (2) 8619396-99; fax (2) 8615585; e-mail dgmuseum@yahoo.com; internet www.bangladeshmuseum.gov.bd; f. 1913; history and classical art, ethnography and decorative art, natural history, contemporary art and world civilization; conservation, public education; library of 35,816 vols; Chair. Dr M. AZIZUR RAHMAN; Dir-Gen. PROKASH CHANDRA DAS; publ. *Bangladesh Jadughar Samachar* (The journal of Bangladesh National Museum, 4 a year).

Dhaka Zoo: Mirpur-1, Dhaka; tel. (2) 9002954; f. 1964; attached to Min. of Fisheries and Livestock; colln of more than 2,000 native and non-native animals and wildlife; Curator KAZI FAZLUL HAQUE.

Mukti Juddha Museum: 5 Segun Bagicha, Dhaka; tel. (2) 9559091; fax (2) 9559092; e-mail mukti@citechco.net; f. 1996; concerns Bangladesh's Liberation War (1971); ancient Bengali artefacts, and items from the British Raj period and the Pakistani period, photographs of the war and items used by the freedom fighters during the period; Man. Dir AKKU CHOWDHURY.

National Art Gallery: Shilpakala Academy, Segun Bagicha, Dhaka 1000; tel. (2) 9562801; f. 1965; colln of folk art and paintings by Bangladeshi artists.

National Botanical Garden: Mirpur, 16 Km NW of city, Dhaka; tel. (2) 8018092; e-mail info@bforest.gov.bd; internet www.bforest.gov.bd; f. 1961; attached to Min. of Environment and Forests; colln of 50,000 plants, herbs, shrubs and trees on a 200-acre site.

National Science and Technology Museum: Agargaon, Sher-e-Bangla Nagar, Dhaka 1207; tel. (2) 9112084; fax (2) 9114831; e-mail info@nmst.gov.bd; internet www.nmst.gov.bd; f. 1965; attached to Min. of Science, Information and Communication; library of 4,464 vols; Dir SADARUDDIN AHMED; publ. *Nabin Biggani* (4 a year).

Universities
AHSANULLAH UNIVERSITY OF SCIENCE AND TECHNOLOGY

141–142 Love Rd, Tejgaon Industrial Area, Dhaka 1208

Telephone: (2) 9897311
Fax: (2)9860564
E-mail: vc@aust.edu
Internet: www.aust.edu
Private control, sponsored by Dhaka Ahsania Mission
Founded 1995
Chancellor: Pres. of the People's Republic of Bangladesh
Vice-Chancellor: Prof. Dr M. ANWAR HOSSAIN
Registrar: MD. AZIZUL HAQUE (acting)
Librarian: MD. MOSHARRAF HOSSAIN
Number of students: 2,514

DEANS

Faculty of Architecture and Planning: Prof. Dr M. A. MUKTADIR
Faculty of Business and Social Science: Dr SHYMA PADA BISWAS
Faculty of Education: FATEMA KHATUN
Faculty of Engineering: Prof. Dr ABU MD. SHADULLAH

ATTACHED INSTITUTE

Institute of Technical and Vocational Education and Training: ITVET Campus, 20 West Testuri Bazar Rd, Tejgaon, Dhaka 1215; tel. (2) 9130613; f. 1995; offers mid-level programmes in Architecture, Civil Engineering, Electrical Engineering, Electronic Engineering, Computer Technology Engineering and Textile Engineering.

AMERICAN INTERNATIONAL UNIVERSITY BANGLADESH

House 83 Rd 4, Kamal Ataturk Ave, Banani, Dhaka 1213

Telephone: (2) 9890415
Fax: (2) 881233
E-mail: info@aiub.edu
Internet: www.aiub.edu
Founded 1994
Private control
Academic year: January to December
Number of teachers: 100
Number of students: 2,500
Vice-Chancellor: CARMEN Z. LAMAGNA

Pro Vice-Chancellor: Prof. Dr ANWAR HOSSAIN
Number of students: 3,489
Publications: *AIUB Journal of Business and Economics* (2 a year), *AIUB Journal of Science and Engineering* (1 a year)

DEANS

Faculty of Arts and Social Science: Dr CHARLES C. VILLANUEVA
Faculty of Science: Dr A. B. M. SIDDIQUE HOSSAIN

BANGABANDHU SHEIKH MUJIB MEDICAL UNIVERSITY

POB 3048, Dhaka 1000
Telephone: (2) 9661065
Fax: (2) 9661063
E-mail: info@bsmmu.org
Internet: www.bsmmu.org
Founded 1965 as Institute of Postgraduate Medicine and Research; present name and status 1998
Academic year: July to June
Vice-Chancellor: Prof. M. NAZRUL ISLAM
Pro Vice-Chancellors: Prof. MD. CHOUDHURY ALI KAWSER, Prof. MD. KAMAL
Registrar: M. A. GAFUR
Chief Librarian: MD. SHAHADAT HUSSAIN
Colleges and Postgraduate Institutes Inspector: Prof. AKRAM HOSSAIN
Founded 1965
Library of 23,000 vols, 100 periodicals
Number of teachers: 200
Number of students: 704
Publications: *Bangladesh Journal of Neurology* (2 a year), *Bangladesh Journal of Psychiatry* (2 a year), *Journal of the Institute of Postgraduate Medicine and Research* (2 a year)

DEANS

Faculty of Basic Medical Sciences: Prof. M. IQBAL ARSLAN
Faculty of Dentistry: Prof. MOTIUR RAHMAN MOLLA
Faculty of Medicine: Prof. K. M. H. S. SIRAJUL HAQUE
Faculty of Surgery: Prof. MOHAMMAD SAIFUL ISLAM

BANGABANDHU SHEIKH MUJIBUR RAHMAN AGRICULTURAL UNIVERSITY

Salna, Gazipur 1703
Telephone: (2) 9252850
Fax: (2) 9252873
E-mail: bsmrau@sdnbd.org
Founded 1983 as Bangladesh College of Agricultural Sciences; became Institute of Postgraduate Studies in Agriculture 1994; present name 1998
State control
Academic year: November to October
Vice-Chancellor: Prof. Dr M. A. HALIM KHAN
Registrar: MOHAMMAD ABUL KALAM AZAD
Asst Librarian: MOHAMMAD ABDUR ROUF MIAN
Number of teachers: 47
Number of students: 394
Publication: *Annals of Bangladeshi Agriculture* (every 2 years)

DEANS

Faculty of Agriculture: Prof. Dr M. A. HALIM KHAN
Graduate Studies: Prof. Dr ABDUL MANNAN AKANDA

BANGLADESH AGRICULTURAL UNIVERSITY

Mymensingh 2202
Telephone: (91) 66846
Fax: (91) 61580
E-mail: registrar@bau.edu.bd
Internet: www.bau.edu.bd
Founded 1961
Autonomous control
Languages of instruction: English, Bengali
Academic year: July to June (two semesters)
Chancellor: MD. ZILLUR RAHMAN
Vice-Chancellor: Prof. Dr M. A. SATTAR MANDAL
Registrar: MD. NAZIBUR RAHMAN
Public Relations and Publs Dir: DIWAN RASHIDUL HASSAN
Cttee for Advanced Studies and Research Coordinator: Prof. Dr SULTAN UDDIN BHUIYA
Librarian: PRABIR KUMAR MITRA BISWAS
Library of 193,614 vols
Number of teachers: 513
Number of students: 4,767
Publications: *Bangladesh Journal of Agricultural Economics, Bangladesh Journal of Agricultural Engineering, Bangladesh Journal of Agricultural Science, Bangladesh Journal of Animal Science, Bangladesh Journal of Aquaculture, Bangladesh Journal of Crop Science, Bangladesh Journal of Environmental Science* (1 a year), *Bangladesh Journal of Extension Education, Bangladesh Journal of Fisheries* (4 a year), *Bangladesh Journal of Horticulture* (2 a year), *Bangladesh Journal of Plant Pathology, Bangladesh Journal of Seed Science and Technology* (2 a year), *Bangladesh Journal of Training and Development, Bangladesh Veterinary Journal, Journal of Veterinary Medicine, Progressive Agriculture, The Bangladeshi Veterinarian*

DEANS

Faculty of Agricultural Economics and Rural Sociology: Prof. TOFAZZAL HOSSAIN MIAH
Faculty of Agricultural Engineering and Technology: Prof. Dr M. BURHAN-UD-DIN
Faculty of Agriculture: Prof. Dr MOHAMMAD ABDUL KARIM
Faculty of Animal Husbandry: Prof. Dr M. ALI AKBAR
Faculty of Fisheries: Prof. Dr MD. ABDUL WAHAB
Faculty of Veterinary Science: Prof. Dr MD. MOTAHAR HUSSAIN MONDAL

PROFESSORS

Faculty of Agricultural Economics and Rural Sociology:

AKBAR, M., Agribusiness and Marketing
AKTERUZZAMAN, M., Agricultural Economics
ALAM, S., Agribusiness & Marketing
ALI, M., Rural Sociology
BASHAR, M., Agricultural Finance
BEGUM, R., Agricultural Statistics
DEBNATH, S., Agricultural Statistics
HAQUE, M., Agricultural Statistics
HOSSAIN, M., Agricultural Statistics
ISLAM, M., Agricultural Economics
JABBAR, M., Agricultural Finance
JAIM, W., Agricultural Economics
MANDAL, M., Agricultural Economics
MIA, M., Agribusiness and Marketing
MIAH, M., Agricultural Economics
MIAH, T., Agricultural Finance
MODAK, P., Agricultural Statistics
MOLLA, A., Agricultural Economics
QUDDUS, M., Agricultural Statistics
RAHA, S., Agribusiness and Marketing
RAHMAN, K., Agricultural Statistics
RAHMAN, M., Agricultural Economics

RASHID, M., Agricultural Economics
SABUR, S., Agribusiness and Marketing
Faculty of Agricultural Engineering and Technology:

ABEDIN, M., Farm Structure
AHMED, M., Irrigation and Water Management
AKHTARUZZAMAN, M., Farm Power and Machinery
ALAM, M., Farm Power and Machinery
ALI, M., Computer Science and Mathematics
ASHRAF, M., Farm Structure
AWAL, A., Farm Structure
BALA, B., Farm Power and Machinery
BASAK, N., Computer Science and Mathematics
BASUNIA, M., Farm Power and Machinery
HAQUE, M., Farm Power and Machinery
HASSNUZZAMAN, K., Irrigation and Water Management
HOQUE, M., Farm Structure
HOQUE, M., Irrigation and Water Management
HOSSAIN, M., Farm Power and Machinery
HUQ, M., Computer Science and Mathematics
HUSSAIN, M., Farm Power and Machinery
HYE, M., Computer Science and Mathematics
ISLAM, M., Food Technology and Rural Industries
ISLAM, M., Irrigation and Water Management
KHAIR, A., Irrigation and Water Management
KHAN, L., Irrigation and Water Management
MOJID, M., Irrigation and Water Management
RAHMAN, K., Farm Structure
RASHID, M., Farm Structure
SARKER, M., Farm Power and Machinery
SATTAR, M., Farm Power and Machinery
SHAMS-UD-DIN, M., Food Technology and Rural Industries
TALUKDER, M., Irrigation and Water Management
UDDIN, M., Food Technology and Rural Industries
ZIAUDDIN, A., Farm Power and Machinery
Faculty of Agriculture:

AHMAD, M., Entomology
AHMAD, M., Plant Pathology
AHMED, K., Entomology
AHMED, Q., Genetics and Plant Breeding
ALAM, M., Genetics and Plant Breeding
ALI, M., Plant Pathology
ASHRAFUZZAMAN, M., Crop Botany
ASHRAFUZZAMAN, M., Plant Pathology
AWAL, M., Crop Botany
BATEN, M., Environmental Science
BEGUM, M., Agronomy
BHUIYA, M., Agronomy
CHOUDHURY, M., Horticulture
CHOWDHURY, A., Agronomy
CHOWDHURY, B., Biochemistry
CHOWDHURY, M., Agricultural Chemistry
FAKIR, M., Crop Botany
FAROOQUE, A., Horticulture
HAQUE, M., Biotechnology
HAQUE, M., Entomology
HAQUE, M., Ugc Professor
HASHEM, M., Soil Science
HASSAN, L., Genetics and Plant Breeding
HOSSAIN, A., Soil Science
HOSSAIN, I., Plant Pathology
HOSSAIN, M., Agricultural Extension Education
HOSSAIN, M., Agroforestry
HOSSAIN, M., Biochemistry
HOSSAIN, M., Plant Pathology
HOSSAIN, M., Plant Pathology
HUQUE, M., Agricultural Extension Education

ISLAM, K., Entomology
ISLAM, M., Agricultural Extension Education
ISLAM, M., Genetics and Plant Breeding
ISLAM, M., Crop Botany
ISLAM, M., Soil Science
ISLAM, N., Agronomy
JAHAN, M., Entomology
JAHIRUDDIN, M., Soil Science
KARIM, A., Agricultural Extension Education
KARIM, M., Crop Botany
KARIM, S., Agronomy
KASHEM, M., Agricultural Extension Education
KHAN, A., Entomology
KHAN, M., Crop Botany
MATIN, M., Soil Science
MEAH, M., Plant Pathology
MIAH, M., Agricultural Extension Education
MIAN, M., Soil Science
MIAN, M., Soil Science
MONDAL, M., Horticulture
MOSLEHUDDIN, A., Soil Science
NASIRUDDIN, K., Biotechnology
NEWAZ, M., Genetics and Plant Breeding
NEWAZ, M., Biochemistry
PATWARY, M., Genetics and Plant Breeding
PRAMANIK, M., Crop Botany
PRODHAN, A., Crop Botany
QUDDUS, M., Genetics and Plant Breeding
RABBANI, M., Horticulture
RAHIM, M., Horticulture
RAHMAN, G., Agroforestry
RAHMAN, M., Agricultural Chemistry
RAHMAN, M., Agricultural Extension Education
RAHMAN, M., Agronomy
RAHMAN, M., Crop Botany
RAHMAN, M., Horticulture
RAHMAN, M., Soil Science
RASHID, A., Plant Pathology
RASHID, M., Agricultural Extension Education
RASHID, M., Biochemistry
REZA, M., Biochemistry
ROY, P., Biochemistry
SAHA, K., Physics and Chemistry
SALIM, M., Agronomy
SAMAD, M., Agronomy
SARKAR, M., Agronomy
SATTAR, M., Environmental Science
SEAL, H., Physics and Chemistry
SHAHJAHAN, M., Entomology
SHAMSUDDIN, A., Genetics and Plant Breeding
SIDDIQUA, M., Biochemistry
SIDDQUE, M., Horticulture
WAZUDDIN, M., Genetics and Plant Breeding
ZAMAN, M., Agricultural Chemistry

Faculty of Animal Husbandry:

AKBAR, M., Animal Nutrition
AKHTER, S., Animal Science
ALAM, M., Animal Science
ALI, A., Animal Breeding and Genetics
ALI, M., Poultry Science
AMIN, M., Animal Breeding and Genetics
AMIN, M., Animal Science
BHUIYAN, A., Animal Breeding and Genetics
CHOWDHURY, S., Poultry Science
FARUQUE, M., Animal Breeding and Genetics
HASHEM, M., Animal Science
HASSAN, M., Dairy Science
HOSSAIN, M., Animal Science
HOWLIDER, M., Poultry Science
HUSAIN, S., Animal Breeding and Genetics
ISLAM, M., Dairy Science
KHAN, M., Animal Nutrition
KHAN, M., Animal Science
KHAN, M., Dairy Science

KHANDAKER, M., Animal Breeding and Genetics
KHANDAKER, Z., Animal Nutrition
MOKHTARUZZAMAN, M., Dairy Science
WADUD, A., Dairy Science

Faculty of Fisheries:

AHMED, G., Aquaculture
AHMED, N., Fisheries Management
AHMED, Z., Fisheries Management
ALAM, A., Fisheries Technology
ALAM, M., Fisheries Biology and Genetics
ALI, M., Aquaculture
AMIN, M., Aquaculture
CHAKRABORTY, S., Fisheries Technology
CHANDRA, K., Aquaculture
CHOWDHURY, M., Aquaculture
DAS, M., Aquaculture
FARUK, A., Aquaculture
HABIB, M., Aquaculture
HAQ, M., Fisheries Management
HAQUE, A., National Professor
HAQUE, M., Fisheries Management
HAQUE, S., Fisheries Management
HOSEN, M., Aquaculture
HOSSAIN, M., Fisheries Biology and Genetics
HOSSAIN, M., Fisheries Technology
ISLAM, M., Fisheries Technology
KAMAL, M., Fisheries Technology
KHAN, M., Fisheries Biology and Genetics
KHAN, S., Fisheries Management
MANSUR, M., Fisheries Technology
MIAH, M., Aquaculture
MIAH, M., Fisheries Management
MOLLAH, M., Fisheries Biology and Genetics
RAHMAN, M., Fisheries Management
RAHMATULLAH, S., Aquaculture
RASHID, M., Aquaculture
SALAM, M., Aquaculture
SARDER, M., Fisheries Biology and Genetics
UDDIN, M., Fisheries Technology
WAHAB, M., Fisheries Management

Faculty of Veterinary Science:

AHMAD, N., Physiology
AHMED, J., Surgery and Obstetrics
AHMED, M., Anatomy and Histology
ALAM, M., Surgery and Obstetrics
ASADUZZAMAN, M., Anatomy and Histology
AWAL, M., Anatomy and Histology
AWAL, M., Pharmacology
BAKI, M., Pathology
BARI, A., Pathology
BARI, F., Surgery and Obstetrics
BEGUM, M., Parasitology
BHUIYAN, M., Surgery and Obstetrics
CHOWDHURY, E., Pathology
DAS, P., Pathology
HASHIM, M., Surgery and Obstetrics
HOSSAIN, M., Pathology
HOSSAIN, M., Surgery and Obstetrics
ISLAM, M., Microbiology and Hygiene
ISLAM, M., Pathology
KHAN, M., Anatomy and Histology
KHAN, M., Pathology
KHAN, M., Microbiology and Hygiene
MONDAL, M., Parasitology
MOSTOFA, M., Pharmacology
RAHMAN, M., Medicine
RAHMAN, M., Microbiology and Hygiene
RAHMAN, M., Pathology
RAHMAN, M., Physiology
SAMAD, M., Medicine
SEN, M., Medicine
SHAMSUDDIN, M., Surgery and Obstetrics
UDDIN, M., Physiology

DIRECTORS

Agricultural Museum: Prof. Dr M. ABUL KASHEM
Agricultural University Extension Centre: Prof. Dr M. ABDUL MOMEN MIAH
Agricultural University Research System: Prof. Dr M. SHAHID ULLAH TALUKDER

Central Laboratory: Prof. MD. JAHIR UDDIN MIAH
Graduate Training Institute: Prof. M. NAZRUL ISLAM
Seed Pathology Centre: Prof. Dr ISMAIL HOSSAIN
Veterinary Clinic: Prof. Dr FARIDA YEASMIN BARI

CHAIRS

Bureau of Research, Testing and Consultation: Prof. Dr M. BURHAN UDDIN
Bureau of Socio-economic Research and Training: Prof. Dr TOFAZZAL HOSSAIN MIAH

BANGLADESH OPEN UNIVERSITY

Board Bazar, Gazipur 1705
Telephone: (2) 9291112
Fax: (2) 9291130
E-mail: regi@bou.edu.bd
Internet: www.bou.edu.bd
Founded 1992
State control

Chancellor: PRIME MINISTER OF THE PEOPLE'S REPUBLIC OF BANGLADESH
Vice-Chancellor: Prof. Dr R. I. M. AMINUR RASHID
Pro-Vice-Chancellor: Prof. R. I. SHARIF
Registrar: MD. MONZUR-E-KHODA TARAFDAR
Librarian: MUHAMMAD SAADAT ALI

Library of 11,000 vols
Number of teachers: 62
Number of students: 103,000

DEANS

Open School: MD. ALINOOR RAHMAN
School of Agriculture and Rural Development: Dr MD. ABU TALEB
School of Business: Prof. ABDUL AWAL KHAN
School of Education: Prof. MONIRA BEGUM HOSSAIN
School of Science and Technology: Prof. Dr MOFIZ UDDIN AHMED
School of Social Science, Humanities and Languages: Prof. Dr ABUL HOSSAIN AHMED BHUIYAN

REGIONAL RESOURCE CENTRES

Resource Centre, Barishal: Rupatali, Post Jaguar, Barishal; tel. (431) 71322; e-mail rcbrisal@bou.bangla.net.

Resource Centre, Bogra: Bangladesh Open University, Bishwa Rd, Banani, Bogra; tel. (51) 72974; e-mail rrcbogra@bou.bangla.net.

Resource Centre, Chittagong: Bangladesh Open University, C. R. B. Rd (Chittagong Stadium), Cothwali, Chittagong; tel. (31) 619633; e-mail rrcctg@bou.bangla.net.

Resource Centre, Comilla: Bangladesh Open University, Dhaka-Chittagong Trunk Rd, Noapara, Durgapur, Comilla; tel. (81) 77557; e-mail rrccom@bou.bangla.net.

Resource Centre, Dhaka: Government Laboratory, School Rd, Dhanmondi, Dhaka 1205; tel. (2) 8616065; e-mail rrcdhaka@bou.bangla.net.

Resource Centre, Faridpur: Beside Nadigabashana Institute, Harokandi, Barishal Rd, Faridpur; tel. (631) 62081; e-mail rrcfarid@bou.bangla.net.

Resource Centre, Jessore: Jessore Upa-Shahar (Dhaka Rd), Jessore; tel. (421) 73250; e-mail rrcjes@bou.bangla.net.

Resource Centre, Khulna: Rd 5, House 51, Sonadanga Residential Area, Khulna 9000; tel. (41) 731795; e-mail rrckhul@bou.bangla.net.

Resource Centre, Mymensingh: Mashkanda (Dhaka–Mymensingh Highway), Mymensingh; tel. (91) 52408; e-mail rrcmyn@bou.bangla.net.

BANGLADESH

Resource Centre, Rajshahi: Bangladesh Open University, Nohata, Paba, Rajshahi; tel. (721) 761607; e-mail rrcraj@bou.bangla.net.

Resource Centre, Rangpur: Bangladesh Open University, R. K. Rd, Rangpur; tel. (521) 63593; fax (521) 64806; e-mail rrcrnp@bou.bangla.net.

Resource Centre, Sylhet: Bangladesh Open University, Pirijpur, South Surma, Sylhet; tel. (821) 719523; fax (821) 22758; e-mail rrcsyl@bou.bangla.net.

BANGLADESH UNIVERSITY OF ENGINEERING AND TECHNOLOGY

Palassy, Ramna, Dhaka 1000
Telephone: (2) 9665650
Fax: (2) 8613046
E-mail: vc@buet.ac.bd
Internet: www.buet.ac.bd

Founded 1962
State control
Language of instruction: English
Academic year: January to December
Chancellor: PRIME MINISTER OF THE PEOPLE'S REPUBLIC OF BANGLADESH
Vice-Chancellor: Prof. Dr MD. ALEE MURTUZA
Registrar: MOHAMMAD SHAHJAHAN
Librarian: MOHAMMAD ZAHIRUL ISLAM
Library of 132,586 vols
Number of teachers: 501
Number of students: 7,773
Publications: *Bangladesh Journal of Water Resource Research, Chemical Engineering Research Bulletin, Electrical and Electronic Engineering Research Bulletin, Industrial and Production Engineering Research Bulletin, Journal of Energy and Environment, Journal of Mechanical Engineering Research and Development, Protibesh Journal of the Dept of Architecture*

DEANS

Faculty of Architecture and Planning: Prof. KHALEDA RASHID
Faculty of Civil Engineering: Prof. Dr MD. ABDUR ROUF
Faculty of Electrical and Electronic Engineering: Prof. Dr S. SHAHNAWAZ AHMED
Faculty of Engineering: Prof. Dr A. A. M. REZAUL HAQUE
Faculty of Mechanical Engineering: Prof. Dr MD. ABDUR RASHID SARKAR

ATTACHED INSTITUTES

Accident Research Centre: tel. (2) 9669368; fax (2) 8613046; e-mail dirarc@arc.buet.ac.bd; internet www.buet.ac.bd/ari; f. 2002; advancement of safety research in Bangladesh; scientific research and investigation into causes of accidents on roads, railways and waterways; creating awareness on transport safety; Dir Prof. Dr MD. SHAMSUL HOQUE.

Bio-Medical Engineering Centre: tel. (2) 9665636; Dir Prof. Dr M. ABU TAHER ALI.

Centre for Energy Studies: tel. (2) 9665650; fax (2) 8613046; e-mail dirces@buet.ac.bd; internet www.buet.ac.bd/ces; f. 1984; Dir Prof. SHAHIDUL ISLAM KHAN.

Centre for Environmental and Resource Management: tel. (2) 9663693; Dir Prof. Dr MD. DELWAR HOSSAIN.

Directorate of Continuing Education: tel. (2) 9665633; e-mail dirdce@dce.buet.ac.bd; internet www.buet.ac.bd/dce; f. 1995; Dir Prof. Dr MD. ABDUR RASHID SARKAR.

Institute of Appropriate Technology: tel. (2) 9662365; fax (2) 8613026; e-mail iatdir@iat.buet.ac.bd; internet www.buet.ac.bd/iat; Dir Dr MD. KAMAL UDDIN.

Institute of Information and Communication Technology: tel. (2) 9665602; fax (2) 9665602; e-mail lutfulkabir@iict.buet.ac.bd; internet www.buet.ac.bd/iict; f. 2001; Dir Prof. Dr S. M. LUTFUL KABIR.

Institute of Water and Flood Management: tel. (2) 9665601; fax (2) 8613046; e-mail diriwfm@iwfm.buet.ac.bd; internet teacher.buet.ac.bd/diriwfm; f. 1974; Dir Prof. ANISUL HAQUE.

BRAC UNIVERSITY

66 Mohakhali C/A, Dhaka 1212
Telephone: (2) 8824051
Fax: (2) 8810183
E-mail: info@bracu.ac.bd
Internet: www.bracuniversity.net

Founded 2001
Private control, under BRAC non-governmental devt org.
Vice-Chancellor: Prof. JAMILUR REZA CHOUDHURY
Registrar: MAHMOOD HASAN
Librarian: HASINA AFROZ
Number of students: 1,659

DEANS

Faculty of Architecture: Prof. FUAD H. MALLICK
Faculty of Computer Science and Engineering: Prof. SAYEED SALAM
Faculty of Economics and Social Sciences: Dr ANWARUL HOQUE
Faculty of English and Humanities: Prof. FIRDOUS AZIM
Faculty of Mathematics and Natural Sciences: Prof. MOFIZ UDDIN AHMED

ATTACHED SCHOOLS AND INSTITUTES

BRAC Business School: Dir Prof. MOJIB U. AHMED.

BRAC Development Institute: Dir Prof. SYED M. HASHEMI.

Centre for Languages: Dhaka 1212; tel. (2) 8824051; e-mail nsabera@bracu.ac.bd; internet www.bracuniversity.net/cfl; Dir SYEDA SARWAT ABED.

Institute of Educational Development: House 113, Block A, Rd 2, Niketon, Gulshan 1, Dhaka 1212; tel. (2) 8824180; fax (2) 8829157; e-mail bu-ied@brac.net; internet www.bracuniversity.net/i&s/ied; Dir Dr MANZOOR AHMED.

Institute of Governance Studies: 40/6 North Ave, Gulshan-2, Dhaka 1212; tel. (2) 8810306; fax (2) 8832542; e-mail igs-info@bracu.ac.bd; internet www.igs-bracu.ac.bd; Dir MANZOOR HASAN.

James P. Grant School of Public Health: Dhaka 1212; tel. (2) 8824051; fax (2) 8823542; e-mail bsph@bracu.ac.bd; internet sph.bracu.ac.bd; Dir ANWAR ISLAM.

School of Law: Dir Dr SHAHDEEN MALIK.

LEARNING CENTRE

Learning Resource Centre: c/o Ayesha Abed Library, BRAC University, 67 Mohakhali, Dhaka 1212; tel. (2) 8824051; e-mail librarian@bracu.ac.bd; internet library.bracu.ac.bd.

UNIVERSITY OF CHITTAGONG

University Post Office, Chittagong 4331
Telephone: (31) 682042
Fax: (31) 726310
E-mail: vc-cu@spnetctg.com
Internet: www.cu.ac.bd

Founded 1966
Languages of instruction: Bengali, English
Academic year: July to June
Vice-Chancellor: Prof. M. BADIUL ALAM

Pro-Vice-Chancellor: Prof. Dr MOHAMMED SHAMSUDDIN
Registrar: Prof. IDRIS MIYAN
Librarian: SYED MOHAMED ABU TAHER
Library of 201,514 vols
Number of teachers: 643
Number of students: 14,873

DEANS

Faculty of Arts: Prof. Dr MOHAMMED SIRAJUL ISLAM
Faculty of Commerce: Prof. Dr MONJUR MORSHED MAHMUD
Faculty of Law: Dr MORSHED MAHMUD KHAN
Faculty of Medicine: Prof. CHOWDURY B. MAHMUD
Faculty of Science: Prof. Dr ABU SALEH
Faculty of Social Science: Prof. Dr MUINUL ISLAM
Faculty of Veterinary Medicine: Prof. Dr NITISH CHANDRA DEBNATH

PROFESSORS

Faculty of Arts
　Arabic and Islamic Studies:
AHMED, R.
DOZA, H. M. B
HAQUE, A. F. M. A.
KHATIBI, M. A. H.
QUADER, A. K. M. A.
RASHID, M.
　Bengali:
ALAM, M. S.
AMIN, M. N.
AZIM, A.
AZIZ, M. M.
BISWAS, S. N.
CHOWDHURY, A. U. M. Z. H.
DASTIDAR, S. R.
IQBAL, B. M.
ISLAM, A. K. M. N.
MANIRUZZAMAN, M.
QUASEM, M. A.
SHAHJAHAN
ZAMAN, A. L.
　English:
ALAM, M. U.
BARUA, T. J.
BILLA, Q. M.
CHOWDHURY, G. S.
DUTTA, S. K.
ISLAM, M. S.
MOHMOOD, A. B. M. M.
　Fine Arts:
ALI, S. M. A.
AZIM, F.
BANU, N.
ISLAM, M. S.
KARIM, M. M.
KHALED, S. A.
MANSUR, M.
RAHIM, M.
ROY, A.
　History:
CHOWDHURY, M. A.
HOQUE, M.
HOSSAIN, E.
HOSSAIN, H.
KABIR, E.
KHALED, A. M. M. S.
SAYED, A.
SHAH, M.
　Islamic History and Culture:
AHMED, A.
AHMED, S.
ALAM, A. Q. M. S.
BHUIYAN, G. K.
CHOWDHURY, M. T. H.
HUQ, M. I.
SHAFIQ ULLAH, S. M.
YUSUF, A.

Oriental Languages:
BARUA, D. S.
BARUA, R. K.
HALDER, S. R.

Philosophy:
AHMED, R.
ALAM, M. S.
ALI, M. A.
ANWAR, A. J.
CHOWDHURY, M. A.
KHALEQUE, A. S. M. A.
RAHMAN, A. K. M. S.
RAHMAN, A. M. M. W.
RAHMAN, M. B.
RAHMAN, M. L.

Faculty of Commerce
Accounting and Information Systems:
AHMED, S.
BHATTACHARJEE, M. K.
CHOWDHURY, R. K.
DAS, S. R.
DATTA, D. K.
MAHMUD, M. M.
MOHIUDDIN, K. M. G.
NAG, A. B.
PURAHIT, K. K.
RASHID, H.
SALAUDDIN, A.
SHARMA, B. K.

Finance and Banking:
HOQUE, M. J.
LOQMAN, M.
MOQTADIR, A. N. M. A.
NABI, K. A.
RASHID, M. H.

Management:
ALAM, M. F.
ALI, A. F. M. A.
ARIF, M. A. A.
ATHER, S. M.
MAMUN, M. A.
MANNAN, M. A.
SIKDER, Z. H.
TAHER, M. A.

Marketing:
B-HUIYAN, S. M. S. U.
CHOWDHURY, A. J. M.
KARIM, A. N. M. N.
MEHER, M. S.
SHAHIN, S.
SOLAIMAN, M.

Faculty of Law
Law:
ALAM, M. S.

Faculty of Science
Applied Physics and Electronics:
BHUIYAN, M. A. S.
HOSSAIN, A.
KHAN, M. R. H.
SAHA, S. L.

Biochemistry and Molecular Biology:
ALAUDDIN, M.

Botany:
AHMED, M.
ALAMGIR, A. N. M.
BASET, Q. A.
BHADRA, S. K.
CHOWDHURY, A. M.
GAFUR, M. A.
MRIDHA, M. A.
PASHA, M. K.
RAHMAN, M. A.

Chemistry:
AHMED, M. J.
AHMED, M. S. U.
AKHTAR, S.
BEGUM, S. A.
CHOWDHURY, D. A.
CHOWDHURY, M. Z. A.
DEY, B. K.

HABIB ULLAH, M.
HAZARI, S. K. S.
ISLAM, M.
KABIR, A. K. M. S.
NAZIMUDDIN, M.
PALIT, D.
RAHMAN, K. M. M.
ROY, T. G.
SALAM, M. A.
SALEH, M. A.
UDDIN, M. H.

Computer Science:
MOSTAFA, M. N.

Mathematics:
AHMED, M.
AZAD, A. K.
BHATTACHARJEE, N. R.
ISLAM, M. A.
ISLAM, M. N.
MOHIUDDIN, M.
RAHMAN, M. M.

Microbiology:
ANWAR, M. N.
HAKIM, M. A.

Physics:
AHMED, F. K.
AHMED, M.
BANU, H.
BARUA, B. P.
BEGUM, D. A.
DEB, A. K.
ISLAM, M. N.
MIYA, M. M. H.
NABI, S. R.
PAUL, D. P.
ROY, M. K.
SAFIULLAH, M. A.
SAHA, S. K.
SIDDIQA, N.

Soil Science:
OSMAN, K. T.

Statistics:
ISLAM, S. M. S.
PAUL, J. C.
RAHMAN, M. M.
RASUL, M. A.
ROY, M. K.
SHAMSUDDIN, M.
SHIL, R. N.
YAHYA, N. S. M.

Zoology:
AHMED, B.
AHSAN, M. F.
ALAM, M. S.
ASMAT, G. S. M.
AZADI, M. A.
BANU, Q.
BHUIYAN, A. M.
BHUIYAN, M. A.
HAFIZUDDIN, A. K. M.
ISLAM, M. A.
KHAN, M. A. G.
MEAH, M. I.
NASIRUDDIN, M.
ULLAH, G. M. R.

Faculty of Social Science
Anthropology:
CHOWDHURY, A. F. H.

Economics:
ASHRAF, M. A.
AZAD, A. K.
CHOWDHURY, M. A. M.
DEY, H. K.
DUTTA, J. P.
HOQ, M.
HOQUE, M. S.
HOSSAIN, B.
ISLAM, M.
KHAN, I. K.
KHAN, M. S.
MAHBUB, U.

NAG, N. C.
SALEHUDDIN, M.
TAHERA, B. S.

Political Science:
AHMED, A. N. M. M.
AHMED, S. Z.
AKHTER, M. Y.
ALAM, M. B.
CHOWDHURY, M. H.
CHOWDHURY, S. A.
HAKIM, M. A.
HASSAN, M.
HOQUE, M. E.
KABIR, B. M. M.
KHAN, Z. N.
KHANAM, J.
KHANAM, R.
MUSHRAFI, M. E. M.
SHAMSUDDIN, M.

Public Administration:
AHMED, N. U.
AHMED, T.
AMIN, M. R.
BEGUM, A.
ISLAM, M. N.
MASHREQUE, M. S.
NOOR, A.
WAHHAB, M. A.

Sociology:
ALI, A. F. I.
B-HUIYAN, M. A.
CHOWDHURY, A. Q.
CHOWDHURY, H. Z.
CHOWDHURY, I. U.
HUSSAIN, M.
KARIM, M. O.
MAHABUBULLAH, M.
QUDDUS, A. H. G.
SALEHUDDIN, G.
SEN, A.

There are 130 affiliated colleges.

CHITTAGONG UNIVERSITY OF ENGINEERING AND TECHNOLOGY

Chittagong 4349
Telephone: (31) 714946
Fax: (31) 714910
E-mail: registrar@cuet.ac.bd
Internet: www.cuet.ac.bd
Founded 1968 as Engineering College, Chittagong; renamed Bangladesh Institute of Technology, Chittagong 1986; present name and status 2003
State control
Language of instruction: English
Vice-Chancellor: Prof. Dr SHYAMAL KANTI BISWAS
Registrar: M. OHIDUZZAMAN
Librarian: M. ABUL HOSSAIN SHAIKH
Number of students: 1,871

DEANS

Faculty of Electrical and Computer Engineering: Prof. Dr PORITOSH KUMAR SHADHU KHAN
Faculty of Engineering: Prof. Dr M. SAIFUL ISLAM PROFESSOR

ATTACHED INSTITUTES

Bureau of Research, Testing and Consultation.

Centre for Information and Communication Technology: Chair. Prof. Dr PORITOSH KUMAR SHADHU KHAN.

Earthquake Engineering Research Centre: tel. (31) 714948; fax (31) 714910; e-mail eerc@cuet.ac.bd; Coordinator Prof. Dr M. JAHANGIR ALAM.

Institute of Energy Technology: CUET, Chittagong 4349; tel. (31) 714920; e-mail iet@

cuet.ac.bd; internet www.cuet.ac.bd/iet; Dir Prof. Dr MAHMOOD OMAR IMAM.

UNIVERSITY OF DHAKA

Ramna, Dhaka 1000
Telephone: (2) 9661900
Fax: (2) 9661920
E-mail: duregstr@bangla.net
Internet: www.univdhaka.edu
Founded 1921
Independent
Languages of instruction: Bengali, English
Academic year: July to June (three terms)
Chancellor: PRESIDENT OF THE PEOPLE'S REPUBLIC OF BANGLADESH
Vice-Chancellor: Prof. A. A. M. S. AREFIN SIDDIQUE
Pro Vice-Chancellor: Prof. Dr H. RASHID
Treasurer: M. RAHMAN (acting)
Registrar: M. A. HUSSAIN (acting)
Librarian: Dr M. S. ISLAM (acting)
Library: see Libraries and Archives
Number of teachers: 1,492
Number of students: 24,060

Publications: *Dhaka University Studies* (2 a year), *Dhaka Viswa Vidyalaya Bartra* (4 a year), *Dhaka Viswa Vidyalaya Patrika* (3 a year), *Sahitya Patrika* (3 a year)

DEANS

Faculty of Arts: Dr S. AMIN
Faculty of Biological Sciences: Prof. M. ABDUL BASHAR
Faculty of Business Studies: Prof Dr A. ALI KHAN
Faculty of Earth and Environmental Sciences: Prof. Dr S. HUQ-HUSSAIN
Faculty of Education: M. SHAH JAHAN
Faculty of Engineering and Technology: Prof. Dr S. RAFIQ
Faculty of Law: Prof. Dr B. U. KHAN
Faculty of Medicine: Dr A. Z. M. Z. HOSSAIN
Faculty of Pharmacy: Prof. M. A. RASHID
Faculty of Social Sciences: H. RASHID (acting)
Faculty of Science: Dr T. S. A. ISLAM
Faculty of Postgraduate Medical Sciences and Research: Prof. T. AHMED

PROFESSORS

ABEDIN, K. M., Physics
ABRAR, C. R., International Relations
ABULULAYEE, S. K. M., Philosophy
ADBDULLAH, A. S. A., Accounting and Information Systems
ADEEB, K., Nutrition and Food Science
ADITYA, S. K., Applied Physics and Electronics
AFROEZ, D., Psychology
AFTABUDDIN, M., Biochemistry and Molecular Biology
AHAD, S. A., Soil, Water and the Environment
AHMAD, N., Arabic
AHMED, A., Economics
AHMED, A., Political Science
AHMED, A. F., Public Administration
AHMED, A. I. M. U., Sociology
AHMED, A. K. M. U., Economics
AHMED, A. T. A., Zoology
AHMED, A. U., Nutrition and Food Science
AHMED, E., Chemistry
AHMED, E., International Relations
AHMED, F., Applied Physics and Electronics
AHMED, F., Economics
AHMED, I., Business Administration
AHMED, J. U., Finance
AHMED, K. U., Political Science
AHMED, M., Accounting and Information Systems
AHMED, M., Clinical Pharmacy and Pharmacology
AHMED, M., Economics
AHMED, M., Physics

AHMED, M., Public Administration
AHMED, M. F., Finance
AHMED, M. G., Chemistry
AHMED, N., Geography and the Environment
AHMED, S., Anthropology
AHMED, S., Economics
AHMED, S., Economics
AHMED, S., Management Studies
AHMED, S. A., Chemistry
AHMED, S. G., Public Administration
AHMED, S. J., Theatre and Music
AHMED, S. U., History
AHMED, S. U., Management Studies
AHMED, W., Bengali
AHMED, Z., History
AHMED MAJIB, U., Accounting and Information Systems
AHMED MAMATAJ, U., Accounting and Information Systems
AHSAN, A., Management Studies
AHSAN, C. R., Microbiology
AHSAN, M., Pharmaceutical Chemistry
AHSAN, M. A., Education and Research
AHSAN, M. Q., Chemistry
AHSAN, R. M., Geography and the Environment
AKHTER, N., Botany
AKHTER, R., Philosophy
AKHTER, S. H., Geology
AKHTERUZZAMAN, M., Islamic History and Culture
AKKAS, M. A., Management Studies
AKTER, S., Education and Research
ALAM, A. F., Marketing
ALAM, A. M. S., Chemistry
ALAM, B., Physics
ALAM, F., English
ALAM, H. A., Philosophy
ALAM, K. M. U., Geology
ALAM, K. S., Marketing
ALAM, M., Geology
ALAM, M. D., Soil, Water and the Environment
ALAM, M. K., Soil, Water and the Environment
ALAM, M. M., Economics
ALAM, M. M., Geology
ALAM, M. R., Fine Arts
ALAM, S. S., Botany
ALI, A. H. M. M., Fine Arts
ALI, A. K. M. I., Islamic History and Culture
ALI, A. M., Mass Communication and Journalism
ALI, M. A., Education and Research
ALI, M. S., Physics
ALI, M. S., Zoology
ALI, R., Psychology
ALI, S. M. K., Nutrition and Food Science
ALVI, S. A. B., Fine Arts
AMIN, M. R., Islamic Studies
AMIN, S., English
AMIN, S. N., History
AMINUZZAMAN, S. M., Development Studies
ANISUZZAMAN, Philosophy
ANOWAR, A. J., Philosophy
ANOWAR, S. F., Business Administration
ANSARUDDIN, M., Islamic Studies
ARA, R., Philosophy
AREFEEN, H. K. S., Anthropology
ASADUZZAMAN, M., Public Administration
AWAL, A. Z. M. I., History
AZAD, S. A. K., Marketing
AZIM, F., English
AZIZ, A., Botany
BANOO, R., Pharmaceutical Chemistry
BANU, K., Statistics
BANU, N., Zoology
BANU, R., Modern Languages
BANU, S., Mathematics
BANU, S., Psychology
BANU, U. A. B. R. A., Political Science
BAPARY, M. N. A., Political Science
BAQI, A., Islamic Studies
BAQUEE, A. H. M. A., Geography and the Environment
BARI, M. E., Law

BARKAT, M. A., Economics
BARMAN, D. C., Peace and Conflict Studies
BARUA, S., Nutrition and Food Science
BASHAR, M. H., Chemistry
BASHER, A., Zoology
BEGUM, A., Islamic History and Culture
BEGUM, A., Physics
BEGUM, F., Sanskrit and Pali
BEGUM, H. A., Education and Research
BEGUM, H. A., Psychology
BEGUM, H. J., Physics
BEGUM, K., Education and Research
BEGUM, L., Philosophy
BEGUM, M., Botany
BEGUM, N., Economics
BEGUM, N., Islamic History and Culture
BEGUM, R., Botany
BEGUM, R., Clinical Psychology
BEGUM, R., Education and Research
BEGUM, R., Marketing
BEGUM, S., Zoology
BEGUM, S. F., Social Welfare and Research
BEGUM, Z. N. T., Botany
BHATTACHARJEE, D. D., Management Studies
BHATTACHARJEE, H., Marketing
BHOWMIK, D. K., Sanskrit and Pali
BHOWMIK, N. C., Applied Physics and Electronics
BHUIYAN, G. M., Physics
BHUIYAN, M. A. H., Nutrition and Food Science
BHUIYAN, M. M. R., Statistics
BHUIYAN, M. S., Management Studies
BHUIYAN, M. S., Political Science
BHUIYAN, M. Z. H., Marketing
BHUIYAN, S., History
BILLAH, M. M., Statistics
BISWAS, N. C., Sanskrit and Pali
BORHANUDDIN, Geography and the Environment
BSAHAR, M. A., Botany
CHAKMA, N. K., Philosophy
CHOWDHURY, A., Zoology
CHOWDHURY, A. A. M. U., Finance
CHOWDHURY, A. B. M. H., Islamic Studies
CHOWDHURY, A. K. A., Clinical Psychology
CHOWDHURY, A. M., History
CHOWDHURY, A. M. S. U., Applied Chemistry and Chemical Technology
CHOWDHURY, A. R., Law
CHOWDHURY, A. U., Anthropology
CHOWDHURY, B., Bengali
CHOWDHURY, D. K., Accounting and Information Systems
CHOWDHURY, F., Mathematics
CHOWDHURY, G. M., Business Administration
CHOWDHURY, H. U., Political Science
CHOWDHURY, I. G., Business Administration
CHOWDHURY, L. H., Public Administration
CHOWDHURY, M. A., Economics
CHOWDHURY, M. A. I., Marketing
CHOWDHURY, M. A. M., Management Studies
CHOWDHURY, M. H., Social Welfare and Research
CHOWDHURY, M. M., Political Science
CHOWDHURY, M. M. R., Sociology
CHOWDHURY, M. R., Biochemistry and Molecular Biology
CHOWDHURY, M. R., Mathematics
CHOWDHURY, M. S., Physics
CHOWDHURY, M. S., Soil, Water and the Environment
CHOWDHURY, N., Statistics
CHOWDHURY, N., Women's Studies
CHOWDHURY, P. B., Management Studies
CHOWDHURY, Q. A., Sociology
CHOWDHURY, R. R., Accounting and Information Systems
CHOWDHURY, S., Physics
CHOWDHURY, S. Q., Geology
CHOWDHURY, T. A., Chemistry
DAS, A. K., Chemistry
DATTA, B. K., Pharmaceutical Chemistry
ELAHI, S. F., Soil, Water and the Environment

EUSUF, A. Z., Geography and the Environment
FAIZ, B., Soil, Water and the Environment
FAIZ, S. M. A., Soil, Water and the Environment
FAROUK, A. B. M., Pharmaceutical Technology
FERDAUSI, N., Physics
FERDAUSI, R. R., Mathematics
GHOSH, B., Bengali
GHOSH, S. N., Accounting and Information Systems
GOMES, D. J., Microbiology
HADIUZZAM, S., Botany
HAIDER, A. F. M. Y., Physics
HAIDER, A. R. M. A., Islamic Studies
HAKIM, M. A., Accounting and Information Systems
HALDER, A. K., Mathematics
HALIM, M. A., International Relations
HANNAN, F., Sociology
HAQ, M., Fine Arts
HAQ, M., Psychology
HAQ, M. M., Microbiology
HAQ, M. R., International Relations
HAQ, P., Psychology
HAQUE, A. N. M. S., Marketing
HAQUE, I., Sociology
HAQUE, K. B., Management Studies
HAQUE, M., Geology
HAQUE, M. A., Geology
HAQUE, M. E., Biochemistry and Molecular Biology
HAQUE, M. M. N., Education and Research
HAQUE, S. A., Bengali
HAROON, S. M. I., Mass Communication and Journalism
HASAN, C. M., Pharmaceutical Chemistry
HASAN, M. A., Botany
HASAN, M. N., Nutrition and Food Science
HASAN, M. S., Population Sciences
HASAN, P., Islamic History and Culture
HASAN, S. R., Marketing
HASHEM, A., Accounting and Information Systems
HASSAN, S. A., Political Science
HAYE, A. H. M. A., Modern Languages
HOSSAIN, A., Chemistry
HOSSAIN, A., International Relations
HOSSAIN, A., Public Administration
HOSSAIN, A. H. M. M., Islamic Studies
HOSSAIN, A. M. M. M., Nutrition and Food Science
HOSSAIN, B., Marketing
HOSSAIN, K. M., Sociology
HOSSAIN, K. M. A., English
HOSSAIN, M., Bengali
HOSSAIN, M. A., Biochemistry and Molecular Biology
HOSSAIN, M. A., Marketing
HOSSAIN, M. A., Mathematics
HOSSAIN, M. A., Pharmaceutical Chemistry
HOSSAIN, M. F., Political Science
HOSSAIN, M. H., Education and Research
HOSSAIN, M. I., Zoology
HOSSAIN, M. K., Finance
HOSSAIN, M. M., Botany
HOSSAIN, M. M., Mathematics
HOSSAIN, M. N., Arabic
HOSSAIN, M. Q., Geology
HOSSAIN, M. S., Geology
HOSSAIN, M. S., Geology
HOSSAIN, M. S., Physics
HOSSAIN, M. S., Soil, Water and the Environment
HOSSAIN, M. T., Physics
HOSSAIN, M. Z., Business Administration
HOSSAIN, N. M., Microbiology
HOSSAIN, S., English
HOSSAIN, S. A., Bengali
HOSSAIN, S. A., Soil, Water and the Environment
HOSSAIN, S. H., Geography and the Environment
HOSSAIN, S. M., Accounting and Information Systems

HOSSAIN, S. S., Statistical Research and Training
HOWLADER, M. M. A., Zoology
HOWLADER, S. R., Health Economics
HUDA, S. N., Nutrition and Food Science
HUQ, A. K. M. M. S., Political Science
HUQ, A. Q. M. F., Bengali
HUQ, D., Applied Chemistry and Chemical Technology
HUQ, K. M. H., English
HUQ, M. I., Botany
HUQ, R., English
HUQ, S., Soil, Water and the Environment
HUQ, S. A., English
HUQ, S. A., History
HUQ, S. M. F., English
HUQ, S. M. I., Soil, Water and the Environment
HUQ, Z. S. M. M., Geography and the Environment
IBRAHIM, M., Islamic History and Culture
IBRAHIM, M., Physics
ILYAS, K. S. M., Psychology
IMAM, M. B., Geology
IMAM, M. O., Finance
ISLAM, A., Philosophy
ISLAM, A. F. M. M., Business Administration
ISLAM, A. K. M. N., Botany
ISLAM, A. N., Philosophy
ISLAM, K., Nutrition and Food Science
ISLAM, K. M. S., Information Science and Library Management
ISLAM, L. N., Biochemistry and Molecular Biology
ISLAM, M. A., Chemistry
ISLAM, M. A., Marketing
ISLAM, M. A., Mathematics
ISLAM, M. A., Statistics
ISLAM, M. A., Zoology
ISLAM, M. M., History
ISLAM, M. M., Statistics
ISLAM, M. N., Mathematics
ISLAM, M. N., Political Science
ISLAM, M. N., Social Welfare and Research
ISLAM, M. N., Statistics
ISLAM, M. NAZRUL, Sociology
ISLAM, M. NURAL, Sociology
ISLAM, M. S., Applied Physics and Electronics
ISLAM, M. S., Biochemistry and Molecular Biology
ISLAM, M. S., Clinical Pharmacy and Pharmacology
ISLAM, M. S., English
ISLAM, M. S., Management Studies
ISLAM, N., Geography and the Environment
ISLAM, N., Psychology
ISLAM, R., Applied Chemistry and Chemical Technology
ISLAM, S. N., Nutrition and Food Science
ISLAM, T. S. A., Chemistry
ISLAM, Z., Anthropology
JAHAN, K., Nutrition and Food Science
JAHAN, N., Botany
JAHANGIR, M., Modern Languages
JALIL, R., Pharmaceutical Technology
JINNAH, M. A., Public Administration
KABIR, A., Bengali
KABIR, K. A., Physics
KABIR, M. H., Statistical Research and Training
KABIR, Y., Biochemistry and Molecular Biology
KADER, D. A., Modern Languages
KALAM, A., Microbiology
KALIMULLAH, N. A., Public Administration
KAMAL, A. H. A., History
KAMAL, B. A., Bengali
KAMAL, M. M. U., Marketing
KARIM, M. N., Management Studies
KARIM, N., Sociology
KARIM, R., Nutrition and Food Science
KARIM, S. F., Psychology
KARMAKER, J. L., Botany
KARMAKER, S. S., Management Studies
KHAIR, A., Chemistry
KHALEQUE, M. A., Physics

KHALILY, M. A. B., Finance
KHAN, A. A., Geology
KHAN, A. A., Management Studies
KHAN, A. K. M. S. I., Microbiology
KHAN, A. M. M. A. U., Geography and the Environment
KHAN, A. N. M. A. M., Arabic
KHAN, A. T. M. N. R., Bengali
KHAN, A. Z. M. N. A., Botany
KHAN, G. A., Philosophy
KHAN, H., Genetic Engineering and Biotechnology
KHAN, H. R., Zoology
KHAN, M. A. A., Education and Research
KHAN, M. A. H., Fine Arts
KHAN, M. A. H., Soil, Water and the Environment
KHAN, M. A. R., Banking
KHAN, M. A. R., Microbiology
KHAN, M. H., Fine Arts
KHAN, M. H. R., Economics
KHAN, M. H. R., Soil, Water and the Environment
KHAN, M. M., Accounting and Information Systems
KHAN, M. M., Public Administration
KHAN, M. M. I., Sociology
KHAN, M. N. I., Nutrition and Food Science
KHAN, M. S. H., Statistical Research and Training
KHAN, R. U., Bengali
KHAN, S., Public Administration
KHAN, S. A., Mass Communication and Journalism
KHAN, T. H., Soil, Water and the Environment
KHAN, Z. R., Public Administration
KHANAM, B. K., Fine Arts
KHANAM, H., Zoology
KHANAM, M., Psychology
KHANDAKER, M., Botany
KHANDAKER, M., Marketing
KHANDAKER, N., Economics
KHATUN, H., Geography and the Environment
KHATUN, H., Islamic History and Culture
KHATUN, K., Statistical Research and Training
KHATUN, M., Botany
KHATUN, R., Sociology
KHATUN, S., Arabic
KHUDA, B. A., Economics
KIBRIA, R., International Relations
KOWSER, F., Bengali
LATIFA, G. A., Zoology
MABUD, M. A., Arabic
MAHBUB, A. Q. M., Geography and the Environment
MAHMUD, A. H. W. U., Economics
MAHMUD, A. J., Chemistry
MAHMUD, S., Biochemistry and Molecular Biology
MAHMUD, S. H., Psychology
MAHMUDA, S., Bengali
MAHTAB, N., Women's Studies
MAJID, A. K. M. S., Business Administration
MAJUMDER, A. R., Physics
MALEK, M. A., Islamic Studies
MALEK, M. A., Microbiology
MALEK, M. A., Nutrition and Food Science
MALLICK, S. A., Statistics
MAMUM, M. K., History
MAMUN, M. A. A., Chemistry
MAMUN, M. Z., Business Administration
MANNAN, K. A., Mass Communication and Journalism
MANNAN, K. A. I. F. M., Physics
MANNAN, M. A., Management Studies
MANNAN, S. M., Information Science and Library Management
MATIN, A., Botany
MATIN, K. A., Statistical Research and Training
MATIN, M. A., Mathematics
MAWLA, A., Nutrition and Food Science
MAWLA, G., Nutrition and Food Science

MAZUMDAR, M. A. R., Soil, Water and the Environment
MAZUMDER, K. A. B., Persian and Urdu
MAZUMDER, R. K., Applied Physics and Electronics
MAZUMDER, T. I. M. A., Botany
MIAH, M. S., Bengali
MIAH, M. S., Education and Research
MIAH, M. S., Philosophy
MINA, M. S., Finance
MOHIUDDIN, M., Management Studies
MOHSIN, A., International Relations
MOKADDEM, M., Economics
MOLLAH, M. G., Political Science
MOLLAH, M. Y. A., Chemistry
MONDAL, A. C., Mathematics
MONDAL, R., Soil, Water and the Environment
MONSUR, M. H., Geology
MORSHED, A. J. M. H., Finance
MORSHED, M. S., Botany
MOSHIHUZZAMAN, M., Chemistry
MOWLA, S. G., Management Studies
MOYEEN, M. A., Management Studies
MUNSHI, M. S. H., Political Science
MUSA, A. M. M. A., Modern Languages
MUSTAFA, A. I., Applied Chemistry and Chemical Technology
MUTTAQUI, M. I. A., Education and Research
NABI, A. K. M. N., Population Sciences
NABI, M. R., Fine Arts
NAHAR, B., Nutrition and Food Science
NAHAR, L., Nutrition and Food Science
NAHAR, N., Chemistry
NASIRUDDIN, M., Finance
NASREEN, G. A., Mass Communication and Journalism
NAZNEEN, D. R. Z. A., Peace and Conflict Studies
NIZAMI, A. B. M. S. R., Arabic
OSMAN, B., Fine Arts
OSMANY, S. H., History
PAHA, N. A., Chemistry
PARVEEN, K. N., Political Science
PARVEEN, Z., Soil, Water and the Environment
PERVIN, S., Mathematics
QADRI, S. S., Biochemistry and Molecular Biology
QAIS, N., Clinical Pharmacy and Pharmacology
QUADER, M. A., Chemistry
QUASEM, M. A., Philosophy
QUDDUS, M. A., Marketing
QUDDUS, M. A., Mathematics
QUDDUS, M. M. A., Zoology
QUYYUM, M. A., Applied Chemistry and Chemical Technology
RAB, M. A., Geography and the Environment
RABBANI, K. S. E., Physics
RAFIQ, S., Applied Physics and Electronics
RAHIM, K. A., Biochemistry and Molecular Biology
RAHIM, T., Botany
RAHMA, P. K. M. M., Statistical Research and Training
RAHMAN, A., Health Economics
RAHMAN, A., Information Science and Library Management
RAHMAN, A., Modern Languages
RAHMAN, A. H. M. A., Political Science
RAHMAN, A. H. M. H., Finance
RAHMAN, A. H. M. M., Applied Chemistry and Chemical Technology
RAHMAN, A. H. M. M., Soil, Water and the Environment
RAHMAN, A. K. M. M., Information Technology
RAHMAN, A. M. M. H., Modern Languages
RAHMAN, A. S. M. A., Social Welfare and Research
RAHMAN, A. Z. M. A., Accounting and Information Systems
RAHMAN, B. W., Education and Research
RAHMAN, J., Applied Physics and Electronics
RAHMAN, K. M., Nutrition and Food Science

RAHMAN, K. M. M., Statistical Research and Training
RAHMAN, K. R., English
RAHMAN, M., Accounting and Information Systems
RAHMAN, M., Biochemistry and Molecular Biology
RAHMAN, M., Marketing
RAHMAN, M., Public Administration
RAHMAN, M. A., Chemistry
RAHMAN, M. A., Clinical Psychology
RAHMAN, M. A., Law
RAHMAN, M. A., Marketing
RAHMAN, M. A., Mathematics
RAHMAN, M. A., Physics
RAHMAN, M. A., Political Science
RAHMAN, M. F., Arabic
RAHMAN, M. F., Zoology
RAHMAN, M. G., Mass Communication and Journalism
RAHMAN, M. H., Pharmaceutical Technology
RAHMAN, M. H., Sociology
RAHMAN, M. K., Biochemistry and Molecular Biology
RAHMAN, M. K., Soil, Water and the Environment
RAHMAN, M. K., Zoology
RAHMAN, M. L., Computer Science and Engineering
RAHMAN, M. M., Arabic
RAHMAN, M. M., Chemistry
RAHMAN, M. M., Clinical Psychology
RAHMAN, M. M., Marketing
RAHMAN, M. M., Mathematics
RAHMAN, M. M., Microbiology
RAHMAN, M. M., Nutrition and Food Science
RAHMAN, M. M., Philosophy
RAHMAN, M. M., Physics
RAHMAN, M. M., Soil, Water and the Environment
RAHMAN, M. M., Statistics
RAHMAN, M. S., Bengali
RAHMAN, M. S., Education and Research
RAHMAN, M. S., Soil, Water and the Environment
RAHMAN, M. S., Statistics
RAHMAN, M. T., Mathematics
RAHMAN, N., Business Administration
RAHMAN, N., Sociology
RAHMAN, N. N., Pharmaceutical Chemistry
RAHMAN, R., Biochemistry and Molecular Biology
RAHMAN, S. M. L., Bengali
RAHMAN, S. M. M., Banking
RAISUDDIN, A. N. M., Islamic Studies
RASHED, K. B. S., Geography and the Environment
RASHID, A. H. M. H., Philosophy
RASHID, G. H., Soil, Water and the Environment
RASHID, H., Management Studies
RASHID, M. A., Pharmaceutical Chemistry
RASHID, M. H., Accounting and Information Systems
RASHID, M. H., Political Science
RASHID, M. H., Soil, Water and the Environment
RASHID, P., Botany
RASHID, R. I. M. A., Physics
ROY, K. N., English
ROY, P. K., Philosophy
SAHA, M., Applied Chemistry and Chemical Technology
SAHA, M. L., Botany
SAHA, P. K., Education and Research
SAHA, S. K., Accounting and Information Systems
SALAM, S. A., Mass Communication and Journalism
SALAMATULLAH, K., Nutrition and Food Science
SALEH, M. A., Management Studies
SALMA, U., Persian and Urdu
SAMAD, A., Biochemistry and Molecular Biology
SAMAD, M., Social Welfare and Research

SARKER, A. H., Social Welfare and Research
SARKER, A. M., Fine Arts
SARKER, N., Fisheries
SARKER, N. R., Psychology
SARKER, R. H., Botany
SATTER, M. A., Fine Arts
SATTER, M. A., Physics
SEN, K., Statistics
SERAJ, Z. I., Biochemistry and Molecular Biology
SHAFEE, A., Physics
SHAFEE, S., Physics
SHAFI, M., Geology
SHAH, A. K. F. H., Marketing
SHAH, A. S., Fine Arts
SHAHED, S. M., Bengali
SHAHED, S. N., Bengali
SHAHEEN, N., Nutrition and Food Science
SHAHIDULLAH, A. K. M., Political Science
SHAHIDULLAH, K., History
SHAHIDULLAH, S. M., Psychology
SHAHIDUZZAMAN, M., International Relations
SHAMIM, I., Sociology
SHAMSI, S., Botany
SHARIF, M. R. I., Applied Physics and Electronics
SHEIKH, M. D. H., Education and Research
SIDDIQ, A. F. M. A. B., Arabic
SIDDIQ, M. A. B., Arabic
SIDDIQUE, A. A. M. S. A., Mass Communication and Journalism
SIDDIQUE, A. H., Management Studies
SIDDIQUE, S. A., Accounting and Information Systems
SIDDIQUE, T. A., Political Science
SIKDER, S. A., Fine Arts
SUFI, G. B., Zoology
SUKLADAS, J. C., Accounting and Information Systems
SULTANA, A., Mass Communication and Journalism
SULTANA, A., Philosophy
SYED, S., Nutrition and Food Science
TAHER, M. A., Social Welfare and Research
TALUKDER, A. S., Marketing
TASLIM, M. A., Economics
THAKURATA, M. G., International Relations
UDDIN, M. J., Education and Research
ULLAH, A. S. M. O., Geology
ULLAH, S. M., Soil, Water and Environment
WADUD, N., Psychology
WAHID, A. Q. F., Philosophy
YUSUF, H. K. M., Biochemistry and Molecular Biology
ZAFAR, M. A., Bengali
ZAMAN, F., Fine Arts
ZAMAN, N., English
ZAMAN, S. U., Economics

CONSTITUENT AND AFFILIATED COLLEGES

There are 58 constituent colleges and 3 affiliated colleges.

ATTACHED INSTITUTES

Institute of Business Administration: tel. (2) 8617815; fax (2) 8621411; e-mail iba@univdhaka.edu; internet www.iba-du .edu; f. 1966; Dir Prof. M. ZIAULHAQ MAMUN.

Institute of Education and Research: tel. (2) 9661920; fax (2) 8615583; e-mail ier@ udhaka.net; internet www.ierdu.5u.com; f. 1960; Dir Prof. SALMA AKHTER.

Institute of Fine Arts: tel. (2) 9661920; fax (2) 9675219; e-mail ifa@udhaka.net; f. 1948; Dir Prof. ABDUS SHAKOOR SHAH.

Institute of Health Economics: tel. (2) 8620952; fax (2) 8615583; e-mail ihedu@ citechco.net; f. 1998; Dir Prof. AZIZUR RAHMAN.

Institute of Information Technology: tel. (2) 9661920; fax (2) 8615583; e-mail iit@ univdhaka.edu; internet iit.univdhaka.edu; f. 2001; Dir Prof. M. ZULFIQUAR HAFIZ.

Institute of Modern Languages: tel. (2) 8618236; fax (2) 8615583; e-mail hossainanwar@yahoo.com; f. 1964; Dir Dr ANWAR HOSSAIN.

Institute of Nutrition and Food Sciences: tel. (2) 9661900; fax (2) 8615583; e-mail nhassan@bangla.net; f. 1969; Dir Dr NAZMUL HASSAN.

Institute of Social Welfare and Research: tel. (2) 8622860; fax (2) 8615583; e-mail iswr@bttb.net.bd; f. 1973; Dir Dr A. S. M. ATIQUR RAHMAN.

Institute of Statistical Research and Training: tel. (2) 9661920; fax (2) 8615583; e-mail isrt@udhaka.net; internet www.isrt.ac .bd; f. 1964; Dir Dr AZMERI KHAN.

BUREAUX AND RESEARCH CENTRES

Bureau of Business Research.

Bureau of Economic Research.

Bio-Medical Research Centre.

Bose Centre for Advanced Studies and Research in Natural Sciences.

Centre for Advanced Research in Arts and Social Sciences: tel. (2) 8610334; fax (2) 8615583; f. 2005; Dir Prof. Dr A. H. AHMED KAMAL.

Centre for Advanced Research in Physical, Chemical, Biological and Pharmaceutical Sciences: tel. (2) 9661920; fax (2) 8615583; e-mail coe@univdhaka.edu; f. 2003; Dir Prof. SYED SALEHEEN QADRI.

Centre for Advanced Studies and Research in Biological Sciences.

Centre for Advanced Studies in Humanities.

Centre for Advanced Studies in Social Sciences.

Centre for Biotechnology Research: tel. (2) 9661920; fax (2) 8615583; e-mail lailanislam@yahoo.com; f. 2005; Dir Prof. LAILA N. ISLAM.

Centre for Development and Policy Research: f. 1928.

Centre for Disaster Research Training and Management.

Centre for Research in Archives and History.

Delta Study Centre: e-mail dsc@univdhaka .edu; f. 1990; geological studies of Bengal delta region.

Development Centre of Philosophical Research.

Renewable Energy Research Centre: tel. (2) 9661900; fax (2) 8615583; e-mail rerc@ univdhaka.edu; f. 1981; Dir Prof. Dr NEEM CHANDRA BHOWMIK.

Semiconductor Technology Research Centre.

DHAKA UNIVERSITY OF ENGINEERING AND TECHNOLOGY

Gazipur 1700

Telephone: (2) 9204734

Fax: (2) 9204701

E-mail: duet@duet.ac.bd

Internet: www.duet.ac.bd

Founded 1980; present name and status 2003

State control

Language of instruction: English

Vice-Chancellor: Prof. Dr M. SABDER ALI

Registrar: ALIM DAD

Librarian: M. ANISUR RAHMAN

Library of 25,000

Number of students: 1,519

DEANS

Faculty of Civil Engineering: Prof. Dr MOHAMMAD ABDUR RASHID

Faculty of Electrical and Electronic Engineering: Prof. Dr M. SHAHEEN HASAN CHOWDHURY

Faculty of Mechanical Engineering: Dr MOHAMMED ALAUDDIN

HAJEE MOHAMMAD DANESH UNIVERSITY OF SCIENCE AND TECHNOLOGY

Rangpur, Dhaka Highway, Dinajpur 5200

Telephone: (531) 65429

Fax: (531) 61344

E-mail: vcmdstu@dhaka.net

Internet: www.akashghuri.com/hstu/hstu .htm

Founded 1976; present name and status 2002

State control

Vice-Chancellor: Prof. Dr M. AFZAL HOSSAIN

Registrar: Prof. MOHAMED KHALILUR RAHMAN

Librarian: MOHAMED ALAUDDIN KHAN

Number of students: 903

DEANS

Faculty of Agriculture: Prof. M. ABDUL HAMID

Faculty of Agro-Industrial and Food Processing Engineering: Prof. M. RUHUL AMIN

Faculty of Business Studies: Prof. Dr FAHIMA KHANOM

Faculty of Computer Science and Engineering: Prof. M. ROFIQUL ISLAM MAHMUD (acting)

Faculty of Fisheries: Prof. M. ROFIQUL ISLAM MAHMUD (acting)

Faculty of Postgraduate Studies: Prof. M. ABDUL HAMID

INDEPENDENT UNIVERSITY, BANGLADESH

54 Park Rd, Baridhara, Dhaka 1212

Telephone: (2) 9881681

Fax: (2) 8823959

E-mail: info@iub-bd.edu

Internet: www.iub.edu.bd

Founded 1992

Private control

Language of instruction: English

Academic year: August to May

Chancellor: PRES. OF THE PEOPLE'S REPUBLIC OF BANGLADESH

Pro Vice-Chancellor: Prof. OMAR RAHMAN

Vice-Chancellor: Prof. BAZLUL MOBIN CHOWDHURY

Dir of Finance and Accounts: MUHAMMED SAIDUZZAMAN HASSAN

Assoc. Dean for Undergraduate Admissions: YAZMIN Z. MAHMUD

Registrar: Dr TANVIR AHMED KHAN

Librarian: MUHAMMAD HOSSAM HAIDER CHOWDHURY (Assoc. Librarian)

Library of 25,700 vols, 100 journal subscriptions

Number of teachers: 152 , (127 full-time, 25 part-time)

Number of students: 3,128

Publication: *Independent Business Review* (2 a year)

DEANS

School of Business: NADIM JAHANGIR

School of Engineering and Computer Science: MOHAMMED ANWER

School of Environmental Science and Management: HAROUN-ER RASHID

School of Liberal Arts and Science: NAZRUL ISLAM

PROFESSORS

School of Business (internet sb.iub.edu.bd):

KUMAR SEN, D.

MOHAMMAD ABDUR, R.

School of Engineering and Computer Science:

ANWER, M.

KHODADAT KHAN, A. F. M.

NURUZZAMAN, M.

SUFDERUL HUQ, S.

School of Environmental Science and Management (tel. (2) 9884498; internet www.iub .edu.bd/sesm/sesm.html):

HOSSAIN, M. A.

KAMAL, N.

KARIM, Z.

RAHMAN, M. L.

RAHMAN, O.

School of Liberal Arts and Science (tel. (2) 9881917; internet www.iub.edu.bd/slas/slas .html):

ISLAM, N.

INTERNATIONAL UNIVERSITY OF BUSINESS, AGRICULTURE AND TECHNOLOGY

4 Embankment Drive Rd, Sector 10, Uttara Model Town, Dhaka 1230

Telephone: (2) 8963523

Fax: (2) 8922625

E-mail: info@iubat.edu

Internet: www.iubat.edu

Founded 1991

Private control

Language of instruction: English

Academic year: January to December

Chancellor: PRES. OF THE PEOPLE'S REPUBLIC OF BANGLADESH

Vice-Chancellor: Prof. M. ALIMULLAH MIYAN

Pro-Chancellor: Prof. MAHMUDA KHANUM

Registrar: Dr M. A. HANNAN

Librarian: MONOWARA SARWAR

Library of 16,020 vols, 12,080 books, 165 journals, 88 periodicals,

Number of teachers: 170

Number of students: 3,359

Colleges of agricultural sciences, arts and sciences, business administration, engineering and technology, health sciences and medical education, nursing, tourism and hospitality management

DEANS

College of Agricultural Sciences: M. A. HANNAN

College of Arts and Sciences: K. R. KAMAL WADOOD

College of Business Administration: M. ALIMULLAH MIYAN

College of Engineering and Technology: MONIRUL ISLAM

College of Health Sciences and Medical Education: MD. ABDUL WAHED

College of Nursing: KAREN LUND

College of Tourism and Hospitality Management: AMANULLAH

PROFESSORS

ALIMULLAH MIYAN, M.

ALI, F.

AL SIDDIQUE, F.

AMANULLAH, .

DEB, S.

HANNAN, M.

HAQUE, E.

HAQUE, R.

ISLAM, R.

JABBER, M.

KAMAL WADOOD, K.

KARIM, S.

KHANUM, M.

LUND, K.

MANNAN, M.

MIAH, S.

MONIRUL ISLAM, M.

NARAYAN GHOSH, S.

RAHMAN, A.
RAQUIB, A.
RASHIDUZZAMAN, A.
RASUL, T.
SAIFULLAH, A.
SUBHAN, A.

ISLAMIC UNIVERSITY

Shantidanga-Dulalpur, Kushtia
Telephone: (71) 54079
Fax: (71) 54400
E-mail: vciu@kushtia.com
Internet: www.shibiriu.org
Founded 1980
Vice-Chancellor: Prof. FAEZ MAHAMMAD SER-
AJUL HAQUE
Registrar: MD. MOSLEM UDDIN
Librarian: (vacant)
Library of 22,000 vols
Number of teachers: 65
Number of students: 9,284

DEANS

Faculty of Social Sciences: Dr M. MAMUN
Faculty of Theology and Islamic Studies:
Prof. M. A. HAMID (acting)

ISLAMIC UNIVERSITY OF TECHNOLOGY

Board Bazar, Gazipur 1704
Telephone: (2) 9291250
Fax: (2) 9291260
E-mail: vc@iut-dhaka.edu
Internet: www.iutoic-dhaka.edu
Founded 1981 as Islamic Centre for Tech-
nical and Vocational Training and
Research; became Islamic Institute of
Technology 1994; present name 2001
Subsidiary of the Organization of the Islamic
Conference
Academic year: December to September
Vice-Chancellor: Prof. Dr IMTIAZ HOSSAIN
Registrar: MOHAMMAD AHSAN HABIB
Librarian: Dr MIRZA MOHAMMAD REZAUL
ISLAM
Library of 32,000 vols, 17 periodicals
Number of teachers: 103
Number of students: 862
Publications: *Journal of Engineering and
Technology* (2 a year), *News Bulletin* (1 a
year)

PROFESSORS

HOQUE, M. A., Electrical and Electronic
Engineering
ISLAM, K. K., Electrical and Electronic Engin-
eering
IQBAL HUSSAIN, A. K. M., Mechanical Engin-
eering
MOTTALIB, M. A., Computer Science and
Information Technology
RAZZAQ AKHANDA, M. A., Mechanical Engin-
eering
SADRUL ISLAM, A. K. M., Mechanical Engin-
eering
TAPAN, M. S., Training and General Studies
ULLAH, M. S., Electrical and Electronic
Engineering
ZOHRUL KABIR, A. B. M., Mechanical Engin-
eering

JAHANGIRNAGAR UNIVERSITY

Savar, Dhaka 1342
Telephone: (2) 7791045
Fax: (2) 7791052
E-mail: vc@juniv.edu
Internet: www.juniv.edu
Founded 1970
Languages of instruction: Bengali, English
Academic year: July to June (3 terms)

Chancellor: PRES. OF THE REPUBLIC
Vice-Chancellor: Prof. MOHAMMED MUNIRUZ-
ZAMAN
Pro-Vice-Chancellor (Academic): Prof. MD.
ENMUL HUQ KHAN
Pro-Vice-Chancellor (Admin.): Prof. M. IMA-
MUDDIN
Registrar: ABU BAKR SIDDIQUE (acting)
Librarian: Prof. SUBASH CHANDRA DAS
Library of 103,000 vols, 193 periodicals
Number of teachers: 423
Number of students: 8,105

Publications: *Asian Studies, Bangladesh
Geoscience Journal, Bangladesh Journal
of Life Sciences* (Biological and Life Sci-
ences), *Clio* (History), *Copula* (Philosophy),
Harvest (English Studies), *Jahangirnagar
Economic Review, Jahangirnagar Physics
Studies, Jahangirnagar Planning Review,
Jahangirnagar Review* (Arts and Human-
ities), *Jahangirnagar Review* (Social Sci-
ences), *Jahangirnagar University
Chemical Review, Jahangirnagar Univer-
sity Journal of Sciences* (Mathematical and
Physical Sciences), *Journal of Business
Research, Journal of Electronic and Com-
puter Science, Journal of Mathematics and
Mathematical Sciences, Journal of Statis-
tical Studies, Nre Baggan Patrica* (Anthro-
pology), *Pratnatattva* (Archaeology),
Theatre Studies, Vhasa Shahitta Patra
(Bengali Studies), *Vogal Patrica* (Geography)

DEANS

Faculty of Arts and Humanities: Prof. MD.
NASIRUDDIN
Faculty of Biological Sciences: Prof. SHAHA-
BUDDIN KABIR CHOWDHURY (Dir)
Faculty of Mathematical and Physical Sci-
ences: Prof. MAHMOODA GHANI AHMED
Faculty of Social Sciences: Prof. AMIN
MUHAMMAD ALI

ATTACHED INSTITUTES

**Computer Science and Information
Technology Institute:** e-mail citi@juniv
.edu; internet www.juniv.edu/citi.htm; f.
1987; Dir Prof. MAHMOODA GHANI AHMED.
Institute of Remote Sensing: Dir Prof.
MD. SAJED ASHRAF KARIM.
Language Centre: Dir Prof. U. H. M.
SHAMSUN NAHAR.

KHULNA UNIVERSITY

Khulna 9208
Telephone: (41) 721791
Fax: (41) 731244
E-mail: regekuly@bttb.net.bd
Internet: www.ku.ac.bd
Founded 1987
State control
Language of instruction: English
Academic year: July to June
Vice-Chancellor: Prof. Dr M. SAIFUDDIN SHAH
Registrar: MUHAMMAD NAZRUL ISLAM (acting)
Librarian: MOKLESUR RAHMAN (acting)
Library of 30,000 vols
Number of teachers: 154
Number of students: 4,046
Publications: *Business Review* (2 a year),
Khulna University Studies (2 a year)

DEANS

School of Arts, Humanities and Social Sci-
ence: Prof. Dr MOHAMED MAHBUBUR RAH-
MAN
School of Business Administration: Prof. Dr
MOHAMED MAHBUBUR RAHMAN
School of Life Science: Prof. MOHAMED ABDUL
MALIN

School of Science, Engineering and Technology: Prof. Dr MOHAMED RAZAUL KARIM

KHULNA UNIVERSITY OF ENGINEERING AND TECHNOLOGY

Fulbarigate, Khulna 9203
Telephone: (41) 774584
Fax: (41) 774403
E-mail: registrar@kuet.ac.bd
Internet: www.kuet.ac.bd
Founded 1974 as Khulna Engineering Col-
lege; became Bangladesh Institute of Tech-
nology, Khulna 1986; present name and
status 2003
State control
Vice-Chancellor: Prof. Dr M. NAWSHER ALI
MORAL
Registrar: (vacant)
Library of 30,000 vols
Number of teachers: 132
Number of students: 1,887

DEANS

Faculty of Civil Engineering: Prof. Dr
MUHAMMED ALAMGIR
Faculty of Electrical and Electronic Engin-
eering: Prof. Dr BASHUDEB CHANDRA GHOSH
Faculty of Mechanical Engineering: Prof. Dr
M. NAWSHERL ALI MORA

MAWLANA BHASANI UNIVERSITY OF SCIENCE AND TECHNOLOGY

Santosh, Tangail 1902
Telephone: (921) 55399
Fax: (921) 55400
E-mail: registrar@mbstu.ac.bd
Internet: mbstu.ac.bd
Founded 1999
State control
Vice-Chancellor: Prof. Dr M. MONIMUL
HUQUE
Registrar: M. NURUL ISLAM MIA

DEANS

Faculty of Computer Science and Engineer-
ing: Prof. Dr M. MONIMUL HUQUE
Faculty of Life Sciences: Prof. Dr M. MON-
IMUL HUQUE

NATIONAL UNIVERSITY

Board Bazar, Gazipur 1704
Telephone: (2) 9291018
Fax: (2) 8110852
E-mail: vc@nu.edu.bd
Internet: www.nu.edu.bd
Founded 1992
State control
Chancellor: Prime Minister of the People's
Republic of Bangladesh
Vice-Chancellor: Prof. Dr M. MUFAKHARUL
ISLAM
Dean of the School of Undergraduate Stud-
ies: Prof. FAKIR RAFIQUL ALAM
Dean of Graduate Education, Training and
Research: Dr S. M. ABU RAIHAN
Publications: *Jatiya Bishawvidalaya Patrika*
(4 a year), *Journal* (4 a year).

NORTH SOUTH UNIVERSITY

12 Banani Commercial Area, Kemal Ataturk
Ave, Dhaka 1213
Telephone: (2) 9885611
Fax: (2) 8823030
E-mail: registrar@northsouth.edu
Internet: www.northsouth.edu
Founded 1992
Private control
Academic year: January to December (3
semesters)

Number of teachers: 155 (84 full-time, 71 visiting)
Number of students: 6,488
Vice-Chancellor: Dr HAFIZ G. A. SIDDIQI
Registrar: MOHAMMAD ALI
Dep. Librarian: MD. MOSTAFIZUR RAHMAN

DEANS

School of Applied Sciences: Prof. Dr S. A. M. KHAIRUL BASHAR
School of Arts and Social Sciences: Prof. Dr M. ALI RASHID
School of Business: Prof. Dr AMIRUL ISLAM CHOWDHURY

PATUAKHALI UNIVERSITY OF SCIENCE AND TECHNOLOGY

Dumki, Patuakhali 8602
Telephone: (4427) 56011
Fax: (4427) 56009
Internet: www.pstu.ac.bd
Founded 2002
State control
Vice-Chancellor: Prof. Dr SYED SAKHAWAT HUSAIN
Librarian: MOHAMED ANWAR HOSSEIN
Number of students: 578

UNIVERSITY OF RAJSHAHI

Rajshahi 6205
Telephone: (721) 750041
Fax: (721) 750064
E-mail: rajucc@cilechco.net
Internet: www.ru.ac.bd
Founded 1953
Languages of instruction: English, Bengali
Academic year: July to June (3 terms)
Chancellor: PRES. OF THE PEOPLE'S REPUBLIC OF BANGLADESH
Vice-Chancellor: Prof. SAYEEDUR RAHMAN KHAN
Pro-Vice-Chancellor: Prof. MUMNUNUL KERAMAT
Registrar: Prof. MAHAMMAD SHAFI
Librarian: (vacant)
Library: see Libraries and Archives
Number of teachers: 804
Number of students: 26,691
Publications: *Calendar* (every 2 years), *Rajshahi University Studies* (1 a year)

DEANS

Faculty of Agriculture: Prof. M. ABDUL KHALEQUE
Faculty of Arts: Prof. MOHAMMAD SHAFI
Faculty of Business Studies: Prof. M. OMAR ALI
Faculty of Law: Prof. ASMA SIDDIQUA
Faculty of Life and Earth Science: GOLAM KABIR
Faculty of Medicine: Prof. ABU BAKER SIDDIQUE
Faculty of Science: Prof. M. ABUL HASHEM
Faculty of Social Science: Prof. M. SADIQUL ISLAM

PROFESSORS

Faculty of Agriculture:
JOARDER, M. O. I., Genetics and Breeding
KABIR, G., Agronomy and Agricultural Extension
KHALEQUE, M. A., Genetics and Breeding
Faculty of Arts:
ADHIKARY, M. N., Philosophy
AHMED, K. M., Philosophy
AHMED, S., Islamic History and Culture
AHMED, W., History
ALI, A. K. M. Y., Islamic History and Culture

ALI, M. A., English
ALI, M. W., History
ASADULLAH-AL-GHALIB, M., Arabic
BARI, M. A., Islamic History and Culture
CHOWDHURY, N. H., History
FARUK-UZ-ZAMAN, M., History
FAZUL, M. A., Bengali
GHOSE, R. N., Philosophy
HAMID, M. A., Philosophy
HAQUE, A., Philosophy
HAQUE, K. S., Bengali
HAQUE, M. E., English
HARUN-OR-RASHID, M., Bengali
HASSAN, M. A. D., English
HOSSAIN, K. F., Bengali
HOSSAIN, S., History
IBRAHIMI, M. S. A., Arabic
JALIL, M. A., Bengali
JALIL, M. A., Folklore
KHALEQUE, A., Bengali
KHAN, M. A. A., Arabic
MATIN, C. Z., Bengali
MISRA, C. R., History
MOHIUDDIN, A. K. M., English
MONDAL, A. A., Philosophy
NAHAR, S., Islamic History and Culture
QAIYUM, M. N., History
QUASEM, M. A., History
RAHIM, M. A., History
RAHMAN, A. F. M. S., History
RAHMAN, A. K. M. A., Bengali
RAHMAN, M. M., History
RAHMAN, M. M., Islamic History and Culture
RAHMAN, Q., Islamic History and Culture
REHMAN, A. A., English
ROY, K. L., Languages
SALAM, M. A., Arabic
SAMADI, S. S., Bengali
SARKAR, J. N., Philosophy
SARKAR, M. S. A., Philosophy
SHAFI, M., History
SHAFIQULLAH, M., Islamic Studies
SHAHIDULLAH, M., English
SHAHJAHAN, M., Philosophy
SHAMSUDDIN, Philosophy
SHIBLY, A. H., History
TALUKDAR, M. A. H., Philosophy
TAQI, F. M. A. H., Islamic Studies

Faculty of Business Studies:
ADBULLAH-AL-HAROON, M., Accounting
AKAM, M. H. R., Accounting
ALAM, M. S., Accounting
ALI, A. S. M. N., Management
ALI, M. O., Management
ALI, M. S. N., Management
ANJUM, M. N., Management
ANSARI, M. R., Finance and Banking
DEY, M. M., Accounting
HOSSAIN, M. M., Accounting
HOSSAIN, S. Z., Accounting
ISLAM, M. A., Management
ISLAM, M. N., Accounting
MOJID, A. K. M. A., Finance and Banking
PAUL, P., Accounting
PRAMANIK, M. A. R., Accounting
RAHMAN, M. M., Management
SAHA, A. C., Accounting
SAHA, S. K., Marketing

Faculty of Law:
HOSSAIN, M. M.
RAHMAN, M. H.
SIDDIQUE, M. A. B.

Faculty of Life and Earth Science:
AFSARUDDIN, M., Psychology
AHMED, A., Botany
AHMED, M., Geology and Mining
AHMED, M., Psychology
AHMED, R., Geography and Environmental Studies
AHMED, S. S., Geology and Mining
AHMED, S. T., Geology and Mining

ALAM, M. S., Botany
ALAM, M. S., Geography and Environmental Studies
ALI, M. M., Zoology
ALI, M. S., Zoology
AMIN, M. N., Botany
ARA, S., Psychology
BHUIYAN, M. A. S., Zoology
FARUK, T., Psychology
HAQUE, A. B. M. J., Psychology
HAQUE, M. E., Geography and Environmental Studies
HAQUE, M. M., Psychology
HOSSAIN, M. A., Psychology
HOSSAIN, M. A., Zoology
HOSSAIN, M. M., Information and Communication Technology
HOSSAIN, M. MONZUR, Botany
HOSSAIN, M. MOZAHED, Botany
HOSSAIN, N., Botany
HUSSAIN, M. Z., Geography and Environmental Studies
ISLAM, A. K. M. R., Botany
ISLAM, M. A., Geology and Mining
ISLAM, M. B., Geology and Mining
ISLAM, M. S., Zoology
JAHAN, M. S., Zoology
KHALEQUE, M. A., Botany
KHALEQUZZAMAN, M., Zoology
KHAN, J. R., Geography and Environmental Studies
KUNDU, P., Botany
LATIF, M. A., Psychology
MAJUMDER, Q. H., Geology and Mining
MANNAN, M. A., Zoology
NADERUZZAMAN, A. T. M., Botany
NAHAR, S., Botany
PARVEEN, S., Zoology
PAUL, N. K., Botany
RAHMAN, A. S. M. S., Zoology
RAHMAN, M. A., Botany
RAHMAN, M. A., Geography and Environmental Studies
RAHMAN, M. A., Zoology
RAHMAN, M. HABIBUR, Geology and Mining
RAHMAN, M. HAMIDUR, Geology and Mining
RAHMAN, M. S., Botany
RAHMAN, M. S., Zoology
RAHMAN, M. S., Zoology
RAHMAN, S. M., Zoology
RAQUIBUDDIN, M., Geology and Mining
RUMI, S. R. A., Geography and Environmental Studies
SALAM, M. A., Zoology
SHAIKH, M. A. H., Geography and Environmental Studies
TAHA, M. A., Geography and Environmental Studies
WAHAB, M. A., Geography and Environmental Studies
ZAMAN, M., Botany
ZUBERI, M. I., Botany

Faculty of Science:
ABEDIN, S., Statistics
ABSAR, N., Biochemistry
AHMED, M., Mathematics
AHMED, N., Chemistry
AHMED, S. U., Chemistry
ALI, D. M., Mathematics
ALI, M. A., Chemistry
ALI, M. K., Population Science and Human Resource Development
ALI, M. U., Chemistry
ALI, M. Y., Chemistry
ALI, S. M. M., Applied Chemistry and Chemical Technology
ANSARI, M. A., Mathematics
AZAD, M. A. K., Applied Chemistry and Chemical Technology
BAKER, M. A., Applied Chemistry and Chemical Technology
BANU, K., Physics
BASAK, A. K., Physics

BHATTACHARJEE, S., Physics
BHATTACHARJEE, S. K., Mathematics
BHATTACHARJEE, S. K., Statistics
BISWAS, R. K., Applied Chemistry and Chemical Technology
CHAKRAVARTY, P. K., Chemistry
CHOWDHURY, G. M., Physics
DAS, B. K., Chemistry
DEBNATH, R. C., Applied Physics and Electronics
FARUQUI, F. I., Applied Chemistry and Chemical Technology
HAKIM, M. O., Physics
HAQUE, M. E., Chemistry
HAQUE, M. E., Pharmacy
HAQUE, M. E., Physics
HASHEM, M. A., Applied Physics and Electronics
HOSSAIN, M. D., Applied Physics and Electronics
HOSSAIN, M. L., Chemistry
HOWLADER, M. B. H., Chemistry
ISLAM, A. K. M. A., Physics
ISLAM, G. S., Physics
ISLAM, M. A., Chemistry
ISLAM, M. A., Physics
ISLAM, M. F., Applied Chemistry and Chemical Technology
ISLAM, M. N., Chemistry
ISLAM, M. N., Physics
ISLAM, M. S., Applied Chemistry and Chemical Technology
ISLAM, M. S., Chemistry
ISLAM, M. S., Physics
ISLAM, M. W., Mathematics
ISLAM, S. N., Physics
KARMAKER, A. K., Applied Physics and Electronics
KERAMAT, M., Applied Physics and Electronics
KHAN, M. A. R., Chemistry
KHAN, M. K. A., Applied Physics and Electronics
KHAN, M. S. R., Applied Physics and Electronics
LATIF, M. A., Mathematics
MAHATABOALLY, S. Q. G., Physics
MAJUMDER, S., Mathematics
MALLICK, A. K., Mathematics
MIA, M. A. A., Applied Physics and Electronics
MIAH, M. A. B., Statistics
MIAH, M. A. J., Chemistry
MOLLA, M. A. H., Applied Chemistry and Chemical Technology
MONDAL, M. A. S., Physics
MORTUZA, M. G., Physics
MOSTAFA, M. G., Statistics
MOSTOFA, C. H., Applied Chemistry and Chemical Technology
NOOR, A. S. A., Mathematics
NOOR, A. S. A., Population Science and Human Resource Development
PAUL, A. C., Mathematics
PAUL, S. C., Chemistry
RAHMAN, M. A., Applied Chemistry and Chemical Technology
RAHMAN, M. B., Chemistry
RAHMAN, M. L., Chemistry
RAHMAN, M. M., Physics
RAHMAN, M. S., Applied Chemistry and Chemical Technology
RAHMAN, M. Z., Mathematics
RAQIB-UZ-ZAMAN, M., Applied Chemistry and Chemical Technology
RAZZAQUE, M. A., Statistics
SAHA, R. K., Biochemistry
SARKER, M. A. R., Applied Physics and Electronics
SARKER, M. J. A., Physics
SARKER, M. S. A., Mathematics
SATTAR, M. A., Chemistry
SATTAR, M. A., Mathematics
SAYEED, M. A., Applied Chemistry and Chemical Technology
SHAHJAHAN, M., Biochemistry

SOBHAN, M. A., Applied Physics and Electronics
SOBHAN, M. A., Applied Physics and Electronics
TORAFDER, M. T. H., Chemistry

Faculty of Social Science:
AKBAR, M. A., Social Work
ALI, M. M., Economics
BEGUM, H. A., Social Work
BHUIYAN, M. A. Q., Sociology
EUNUS, M., Economics
HABIB, A. H. M. A., Economics
HALIM, M. A., Social Work
HOSSAIN, A. M. M., Economics
HOSSAIN, K. T., Sociology
IMAM, M. H., Sociology
ISLAM, A. S. M. N., Social Work
ISLAM, M. S., Political Science
ISLAM, T. S., Economics
KARIM, A. H. M. Z., Anthropology
KHAN, F. R., Sociology
KHANUM, S. M., Sociology
MIZANUDDIN, M., Sociology
MOAZZEM, M., Economics
MORSHED, G., Political Science
MOSTUFA, S. K., Political Science
NATH, D. K., Economics
NATH, J., Sociology
OBAIDULLAH, A. T. M., Public Administration
QUASEM, M. A., Political Science
QUAYUM, M. A., Economics
RAHMAN, A. H. M. M., Sociology
RAHMAN, M. A., Economics
RAHMAN, M. F., Sociology
RAHMAN, M. M., Political Science
RAHMAN, M. S., Public Administration
RAHMAN, S. M. H., Economics
RAHMAN, S. M. Z., Sociology
SADEQUE, M., Social Work
SAHA, M. S. K., Economics
SARKAR, P. C., Social Work
SIDDIQUI, A. R., Sociology

There are 241 affiliated colleges.

ATTACHED INSTITUTES

Institute of Bangladesh Studies: Rajshahi 6205; tel. (721) 750753; e-mail ibsru@yahoo.com; Dir Prof. M. ABUL BASHAR MIAN.

Institute of Biological Science: Dir Prof. M. WAHIDUL ISLAM.

Institute of Business Administration: Dir Prof. MOHASHIN UL-ISLAM.

Institute of Education and Research: Dir Prof. M. NAZRUL ISLAM.

Institute of Environmental Science: Dir Prof. M. SARWAR ZAHAN.

RAJSHAHI UNIVERSITY OF ENGINEERING AND TECHNOLOGY

Rajshahi Natore Dhaka Rd, Kazla, Rajshahi 6204

Telephone: (721) 6254
Fax: (721) 6254
E-mail: ruetbd@yahoo.com
Internet: www.ruet.ac.bd

Founded 1986 as Engineering College, Rajshahi; present name and status 2003
State control

Vice-Chancellor: Prof. Dr M. FAZLUL BARI
Number of students: 1,763

SHAHJALAL UNIVERSITY OF SCIENCE AND TECHNOLOGY

PO University 3114, Sylhet

Telephone: (821) 713491
Fax: (821) 715257
E-mail: vc@sust.edu
Internet: www.sust.edu

Founded 1987
State control
Languages of instruction: English, Bengali
Academic year: July to June

Chancellor: PRESIDENT OF THE PEOPLE'S REPUBLIC OF BANGLADESH
Vice-Chancellor: Prof. M. AMINUL ISLAM
Registrar: JAMIL AHMED CHOWDHURY
Librarian: MOHAMED ABDUL HAYEE SAMENI (Deputy Librarian)
Library of 41,000 vols
Number of teachers: 307
Number of students: 5,939

Publication: *SUST Studies* (1 a year)

DEANS

School of Agriculture and Mineral Science: Prof. Dr KABIR HUSSAIN (acting)
School of Applied Sciences and Technology: Prof. Dr AKTARUL ISLAM
School of Business Administration: Prof. Dr MD. NAZRUL ISLAM (acting)
School of Life Sciences: Prof. Dr M. HABIBUL AHSAN
School of Medical Science: Prof. Dr REZAUL KARIM
School of Physical Sciences: Prof. Dr SYED SAMSUL ALAM
School of Social Sciences: Prof. Dr TULSHI KUMAR DAS

SHER-E-BANGLA AGRICULTURAL UNIVERSITY

Sher-e-Bangla Nagar, Dhaka 1207

Telephone: (2) 9144270
Fax: (2) 8155800
E-mail: vcsau@dhaka.net
Internet: www.sau.ac.bd

Founded 2001
State control

Vice-Chancellor: Prof. Dr M. SHAH-E-ALAM
Registrar: Prof. Dr A. M. M. SHAMSUZZAMAN (acting)
Librarian: MOHAMED ALI (acting)
Library of 45,700 vols
Number of teachers: 20
Number of students: 1,536

Publications: *Journal of Agricultural Education and Technology, Journal of Agricultural Science and Technology, Journal of Sher-e-Bangla Agricultural University*

DEANS

Faculty of Agribusiness Management: Prof. M. ZAKIR HOSSAIN
Faculty of Agriculture: Prof. Dr M. SERAJUL ISLAM BHUIYAN,

PROFESSORS

ABEDIN, M.
AHMED REZA, Z.
AKHTAR, N.
AKBAR MIA, A.
ALI, M.
ALI, M.
BEGUM, J.
BEGUM, R.
CHANDRA SUTRADHAR, G.
FAZLUL KARIM, M.
HAQUE BEG, M.
HOSSAIN BHUIYAN, M.
HOSSAIN, M.
ISLAM BHUIYAN, M.
JAFAR ULLAH, M.
JALIL, G.
KANTI BISWAS, P.
KUMAR PAUL, A.
MAHTABUDDIN, A.
MANDAL, G.
MANNAN MIAH, M.
NAZRUL ISLAM, M.

NURUL ISLAM, M.
RAHMAN MAZUMDER, M.
RAFIQUEL ISLAM, M.
RAFIQUL ISLAM, M.
RASHID BHUIYAN, M.
RUHUL AMIN, A.
RUHUL AMIN, M.
SADRUL ANAM SARDAR, M.
SAROWAR HOSSAIN, M.
SHADAT ULLA, M.
SHAHJAHAN MIAH, M.
SHAMSUL HOQUE, M.
SHAMSUZZAMAN, A.
UDDIN AHMED, K.
ZAHIDUL HAQUE, M.

Colleges

Bangladesh Agricultural Research Institute: Joydebpur, Gazipur 1701; tel. (2) 9252715; fax (2) 9261415; e-mail dg.bari@bari.gov.bd; internet www.bari.gov.bd; f. 1976; library: 28,092 vols, 150 periodicals; Dir-Gen. Dr M. HARUN-UR-RASHID; Sr Librarian A. B. M. FAZLUR RAHMAN; publ. *Bangladesh Journal of Agricultural Research* (4 a year).

Bangladesh College of Leather Technology: 44–50 Hazaribagh, Dhaka 1209; tel. (2) 8617439; fax (2) 8617439; e-mail bclt47@yahoo.com; internet www.bclt.com.bd; f. 1949; constituent college of The Univ. of Dhaka under the faculty of Engineering and Technology; undergraduate degrees in Leather Technology; 22 teachers; 1,000 students; library: 13,032 vols; Prin. Prof. Dr FAZLUL KARIM.

Bangladesh College of Textile Technology: 92 Shaheed Tajuddin Ahmed Sarani, Tejgaon I/A, Dhaka 1208; tel. (2) 9114260; fax (2) 9124255; internet www.ctet.gov.bd; f. 1950; a constituent college of Dhaka Univ.; degree courses; 27 teachers; library: 8,535 vols; Prin. Prof. M. A. KASHEM.

BARBADOS

The Higher Education System

The main institution of higher education on the island is a branch campus of the University of the West Indies. Non-university post-secondary education is offered by the Samuel Jackson Prescod Polytechnic and Barbados Community College. In 2006/07 there were 11, 405 students enrolled in tertiary education.

Admission to the University is based on satisfactory performance in the Caribbean Advanced Proficiency Examinations. The University offers Associate, Bachelors, Masters and Doctoral degree programmes. The Associate degree lasts for two years, the Bachelors three years, the Masters two years after the Bachelors and the Doctorate two more years after the Masters.

The Samuel Jackman Prescod Polytechnic trade and craft programmes lead to City and Guilds qualifications and Royal Society of Arts qualifications. Two-year Associate degrees are available from the Barbados Community College.

Erdiston Teachers College offers non-graduate teachers a two-year course in primary education, while graduate teachers can pursue further study at the UWI.

A US programme for curriculum reform and the introduction of technology into education, known as Edutech 2000, was scheduled for completion by 2010. A National Accreditation Agency was established in 2004, responsible for the registration of post-secondary and tertiary institutions, and for the accreditation of these institutions and their programmes.

Regulatory Body

GOVERNMENT

Ministry of Education and Human Resources Development: Elsie Payne Complex, Constitution Rd, St Michael; tel. 430-2700; fax 436-2411; e-mail mined1@caribsurf.com; internet www.mes.gov.bb; Min. RONALD D. JONES.

Learned Societies

GENERAL

Caribbean Conservation Association: The Garrison, St Michael; tel. 426-5373; fax 429-8483; e-mail admin@cca.net; internet www.cca.net; f. 1967; ind., non-profit-making; preservation and devt of the environment, and conservation of the cultural heritage in the Caribbean as a whole; 200 mems; small library; Pres. ATHERTON MARTIN; Exec. Dir Dr JOTH SINGH.

BIBLIOGRAPHY, LIBRARY SCIENCE AND MUSEOLOGY

Library Association of Barbados: POB 827E, Bridgetown; f. 1968 to unite qualified librarians, archivists and information specialists, and all other persons engaged or interested in information management and dissemination in Barbados, and to provide opportunities for their meeting together; to promote the active development and maintenance of libraries in Barbados and to foster cooperation between them; to interest the general public in the library services available; 60 mems; Pres. SHIRLEY YEARWOOD; Sec. HAZELYN DEVONISH; publ. *Update* (irregular).

HISTORY, GEOGRAPHY AND ARCHAEOLOGY

Barbados Museum and Historical Society: see Museum.

LANGUAGE AND LITERATURE

Alliance Française: 17 Pine Rd, Belleville, St Michael; tel. 436-4675; e-mail afbb@cariaccess.com; academic year offers courses and exams in French language and culture and promotes cultural exchange with France.

MEDICINE

Barbados Association of Medical Practitioners: BAMP Complex, Spring Garden, St Michael; tel. 429-7569; fax 435-2328; e-mail bamp@sunbeach.net; internet www.bamp.org.bb; f. 1973; 348 mems; Pres. Dr JEROME WALCOTT; Gen. Sec. RANDOLPH CARRINGTON; publ. *BAMP Bulletin* (5 a year).

Barbados Pharmaceutical Society: POB 820E, St Michael; f. 1948, inc. 1961; 155 mems; Pres. DELORES MORRIS; Sec. GEORGE ALLEYNE; publ. *Pharmacy in Progress*.

Research Institute

GENERAL

Bellairs Research Institute: Holetown, St James; tel. 422-2087; fax 422-0692; e-mail bellairs@caribsurf.com; internet www.mcgill.ca/bellairs; f. 1954; affiliated with McGill University, Canada; field courses, workshops, research and teaching in all aspects of tropical environments; library of 200 vols; Dir Dr BRUCE R. DOWNEY.

Libraries and Archives

Bridgetown

Public Library: Coleridge St, Bridgetown; tel. 436-6081; fax 436-1501; f. 1847; an island-wide service is provided from the central library in Bridgetown by means of 7 brs, 6 centres, and a mobile service to 66 primary schools; acts as a nat. repository for legal deposit printed materials; 165,000 vols; spec. Barbadian and West Indian research colln; Dir JUDY BLACKMAN; publ. *National Bibliography of Barbados* (2 a year with annual cumulations).

University of the West Indies Main Library: POB 1334, Bridgetown; tel. 417-4444; fax 417-4460; internet mainlibrary.uwichill.edu.bb/; f. 1963; 155,000 vols, special West Indies collection, OAS, UN, UNESCO and World Bank depository library; Librarian NEL BRETNEY.

St James

Department of Archives: Black Rock, St James; tel. 425-5150; fax 425-5911; e-mail archives@sunbeach.net; f. 1963; part of the Prime Minister's Office; 990 linear m of archives, 2,366 vols and pamphlets, 922 serials, 391 microfilm reels, 2,747 fiches, 220 sound recordings; Chief Archivist DAVID WILLIAMS.

Museum

St Ann's Garrison

Barbados Museum and Historical Society: St Ann's Garrison, St Michael; tel. 427-0201; fax 429-5946; e-mail museum@caribsurf.com; internet www.barbmuse.org.bb; f. 1933; collns illustrating the island's geology, prehistory, history, natural history and marine life; European decorative arts, militaria, furniture; library of 5,000 vols; 1,000 mems; Pres. Dr TREVOR CARMICHAEL; Dir ALISSANDRA CUMMINS; publ. *Journal* (1 a year).

University

THE UNIVERSITY OF THE WEST INDIES, CAVE HILL CAMPUS

POB 64, Bridgetown
Telephone: 417-4000
Fax: 425-1327
E-mail: jacqueline.wade@cavehill.uwi.edu
Internet: www.cavehill.uwi.edu

Founded 1963
Language of instruction: English
Academic year: August to July (2 semesters)
Private control

Chancellor: Sir GEORGE ALLEYNE
Vice-Chancellor: Prof. E. NIGEL HARRIS
Pro-Vice-Chancellor and Principal: Prof. HILARY M. BECKLES
Registrar: JACQUELINE E. WADE
Campus Librarian: KAREN LEQUAY

Library of 185,815 vols, 2,346 serial titles
Number of teachers: 528 (incl. 363 part-time)
Number of students: 8,622

Publications: *Caribbean Journal of Mathematics* (1 a year), *Caribbean Law Bulletin* (2 a year), *Caribbean Law Review* (2 a year), *Journal of Eastern Caribbean Studies* (4 a year)

One of the three campuses of the Univ. of the West Indies, intended to serve Barbados, the Leeward and Windward Islands; see also Jamaica and Trinidad and Tobago; teaching programmes cover humanities, education, law, pure and applied sciences, social sciences and clinical studies in medicine

DEANS

Faculty of Humanities and Education: Prof. HAZEL SIMMONS-MCDONALD
Faculty of Law: Prof. SIMEON MCINTOSH
Faculty of Pure and Applied Sciences: Prof. C. M. SEAN CARRINGTON
Faculty of Social Sciences: Dr GEORGE A. V. BELLE
School of Clinical Medicine and Research: Prof. HENRY FRASER

PROFESSORS

ANDERSON, W., Int. and Environmental Law
ANTOINE, R., Labour Law and Offshore Law
BARRITEAU, E., Gender and Public Policy
BARROW, C., Sociology
BECKLES, H., Economics and Social History
BURGESS, A., Corporate and Commercial Law
CARNEGIE, A., Law
CARRINGTON, S., Plant Biology
CHAUDHURI, P., Computer Science
COBLEY, A., South African and Comparative History
DOWNES, A., Economics
FAIDJOE, A., Public Law
FRASER, H., Medicine and Clinical Pharmacology
HORROCKS, J., Conservation Ecology
HOWARD, M., Economics
HUNTE, W., Ecology and Environmental Sciences
IYARE, S. O., Financial Economics
KACZOROWSKA, A., Public Int. and EU Law
KHAN, J., Devt Admin.
KING, W., Science Education and Curriculum Studies
KODILYNE, G., Property Law
LAVOIE, M., Microbiology

MCDOWELL, S., Theoretical and Computational Chemistry
MCINTOSH, S., Jurisprudence
MCWATT, M., West Indian Literature
MAHON, R., Marine Affairs
MAMINGI, N., Economics
MARSHALL, S., Distance Education
MOSELEY, H., Anaesthesia
MOSELEY, L., Physics
NEWTON, V., Law Librarianship
O'CALLAGHAN, E., West Indian Literature
O'GARRO, L., Plant Pathology
OXENFORD, H., Marine Ecology and Fisheries
PRUSSIA, P., Anatomical Pathology
PUNNETT, B. J., Management Studies
RICHARDSON, A., Educational Psychology
ROBERTS, P., Creole Linguistics
SIMMONS-MCDONALD, H., Applied Linguistics
THOMPSON, A., Caribbean History
TINTO, W., Organic Chemistry
ZBAR, A., Surgery

ATTACHED RESEARCH INSTITUTES

Caribbean Law Institute Centre: POB 64, Bridgetown 11000; tel. 417-4560; fax 424-4138; Exec. Dir Prof. WINSTON ANDERSON (acting).

Cave Hill School of Business: POB 64, Bridgetown 11000; tel. 424-7731; fax 425-1670; e-mail chsb@uwichill.uwi.edu; internet www.uwichsb.org; Dir Dr JEANNINE COMMA.

Centre for Gender and Development Studies: POB 64, Bridgetown 11000; tel. 417-4490; fax 424-3822; e-mail gender@uwichill.edu.bb; internet gender.uwichill.edu .bb; Head Prof. V. EUDINE BARRITEAU.

Shridath Ramphal Centre for International Trade Law, Policy and Services: tel. 417-4533; fax 425-1348; e-mail cis@cavehill.uwi.edu; internet www.cavehill .uwi.edu/tradepolicy; Dir PAMELA COKE-HAMILTON.

Sir Arthur Lewis Institute of Social and Economic Studies (SALISES): tel. 417-4478; fax 424-7291; e-mail salises@uwichill .edu.bb; internet www.cavehill.uwi.edu/ salises; Dir Prof. ANDREW DOWNES.

Tertiary Level Institutions Unit: tel. 415-4506; fax 438-0456; e-mail tliu@uwichill.edu .bb; internet www.cavehill.uwi.edu/tliu; Dir Dr BEVIS F. PETERS.

Colleges

Barbados Community College: 'The Eyrie', Howell's Cross Rd, St Michael; tel. 426-2858; fax 429-5935; e-mail eyrie@bcc.edu .bb; internet www.bcc.edu.bb; f. 1968; commerce, liberal arts, health sciences, fine arts, science, technology, Barbados Language Centre, Hospitality Institute, general and continuing studies, computer studies, physical education; library: 35,000 vols; 449 teachers (149 full-time, 300 part-time); 3,697 students; Prin. NORMA J. I. HOLDER; Registrar SYDNEY O. ARTHUR.

Samuel Jackman Prescod Polytechnic: Wildey, St Michael; tel. 426-1920; fax 426-0843; e-mail info@sjpp.edu.bb; internet www .sjpp.edu.bb; f. 1969 in Bridgetown; merged with Barbados Technical Institute in 1972; div. of Agriculture est. at Eckstein Village and main br. relocated in 1975; relocation to present site 1982; attached to Min. of Education, and Human Resources Devt; divs of building, electrical engineering, mechanical engineering and printing, human ecology, business studies, general studies, agriculture, motor vehicles and welding, distance and continuing education, open and flexible learning centre.

BELARUS

The Higher Education System

Until its independence in 1991 Belarus was part of the Union of Soviet Socialist Republics (USSR), and its education system was based on the Soviet model. Following independence the Government began to introduce greater provision for education in the Belarusian language and more emphasis on Belarusian, rather than Soviet or Russian, history and literature. Higher education is the responsibility of the Ministry of Education, while research is coordinated by the National Academy of Sciences of Belarus. All Belarusians have the right to free higher education. By early 2007 there were 43 state-owned and 12 private higher education institutions, including 29 universities, as well as seven academies, 13 institutes, four higher colleges and two theological seminaries. In 2008/09 420,700 students were enrolled in higher education.

The Ministry of Education administers admission to higher education on the joint basis of the Certificate of General Secondary Education (or equivalent) and competitive university entrance examinations. The main undergraduate degree is the Bachelors, taken in conjunction with the Diploma of Higher Education, lasting four to five years. The first level of postgraduate study is the Magister (Masters), requiring one to two years' study, culminating in research and presentation of a thesis. The final level of postgraduate education includes the Aspirantura, leading to the Kandidat Nauk (Candidate of Sciences), and Doctorantura (Doctorate), leading to the title Doctor of Sciences.

Non-university post-secondary education is provided by technical and vocational schools, sometimes known as technicums. Courses vary in length from one to four years, depending on the level of specialization. There are currently 174 technicums, 26 colleges, 49 intermediate professional education institutions, four higher colleges and eight private secondary specialized establishments.

Reform of the higher education system began in 1993, including the introduction of a standardized syllabus and increased institutional autonomy. In 2001 a number of laws were passed to this effect, culminating in 2007 with On Higher Education, which brought the country in line with the Bologna Process, including adoption of the European Credit Transfer System (ECTS) and recognition of foreign degrees. The law also introduced a department of Quality Control within the Ministry of Education.

Regulatory and Representative Bodies

GOVERNMENT

Ministry of Culture: 220004 Minsk, pr. Pobeditelei 11; tel. (17) 203-75-74; fax (17) 223-90-45; e-mail admin@kultura.by; internet kultura.by; Minister ULADZIMIR F. MATVEICHUK.

Ministry of Education: 220010 Minsk, vul. Savetskaya 9; tel. (17) 227-47-36; fax (17) 200-84-83; e-mail root@minedu.unibel.by; internet www.minedu.unibel.by; Minister ALYAKSANDR M. RADZKOW.

ACCREDITATION

Department of Quality Control in Education of the Ministry of Education: 220037 Minsk, 28 Kozlov St; tel. (17) 237-30-18; fax (17) 231-35-45; e-mail gnikon@rambler.ru; Dir VALERIY STEPANOVICH OVSYANIKOV.

ENIC/NARIC Belarus: Foreign Credentials Assessment Dept (Belarusian ENIC), 220007 Minsk Moskovskaja St 15; tel. (17) 228-13-13; fax (17) 222-83-15; e-mail enicbelarus@nihe .niks.by; Head INA MITSKEVICH.

NATIONAL BODIES

Academy of Postgraduate Education: 220040 Minsk, vul. Nekrasova 20; tel. (17) 285-78-28; fax (17) 285-78-68; e-mail tavgen@ academy.edu.by; internet www.academy.edu .by; f. 1955; attached to Min. of Education; Rector Prof. ALEH TAUHEN.

National Institute for Higher Education: 220001 Minsk, vul. Moskovskaya 15; tel. (17) 224-66-91; fax (17) 222-83-15; e-mail rector@nihe.niks.by; internet www.nihe.niks .by; Rector Prof. Dr MIKHAIL I. DEMCHUK;

Exec. Dir of Belarusian ENIC LUDMILA RUDOVA.

Learned Societies

GENERAL

National Academy of Sciences of Belarus: 220072 Minsk, pr. Nezavisimosti 66; tel. (17) 284-18-01; fax (17) 239-31-63; internet www.ac.by; f. 1929; depts of Biological Sciences (Academician-Sec. I. D. VOLOTOVSKIY, Scientific Sec. V. A. VOINILO), Chemical and Earth Sciences (Academician-Sec. N. P. KRUTKO, Scientific Sec. N. M. LITVINKO), Humanities and Arts (Academician-Sec. P. G. NIKITENKO, Scientific Sec. V. I. LEVKOVICH), Medical Sciences (Academician-Sec. E. D. BELOENKO, Scientific Sec. L. P. MALAEVA), Physical and Technical Sciences (Academician-Sec. S. A. ZHDANOK, Scientific Sec. V. A. GAIKO), and Physics, Mathematics and Information Science (Academician-Sec. S. V. ABLAMEIKO, Scientific Sec. G. A. BUTKIN); 210 mems (94 academicians, 129 corresps, 17 foreign mems, 3 hon. mems); attached research institutes: see Research Institutes; library and archive: see Libraries and Archives; Chair. MIKHAIL V. MYASNIKOVICH (acting); Chief Scientific Sec. NIKOLAI S. KAZAK; publs *Computational Methods in Applied Mathematics* (4 a year), *Doklady* (Reports, 6 a year), *Inzhenerno-Fizicheskii Zhurnal* (Journal of Engineering Physics and Thermophysics, 6 a year), *Litasfera* (Lithosphere, 12 a year), *Materialy, Technologii, Instrumenty* (Materials, Technologies, Tools, 4 a year), *Nonlinear Phenomena in Complex Systems* (4 a year), *Prirodnye Resurcy* (Natural Resources, 4 a year), *Trenie i Iznos* (Friction and Wear, 6 a year), *Vestsi* (Bulletins: Physical-Technical Sciences, Biological Sciences, Biomedical Sciences, Physical-Mathematical Sciences, Humanities, Chemistry, 4 a year), *Zhurnal Priklad-noi Spektroskopii* (Journal of Applied Spectroscopy, 6 a year).

AGRICULTURE, FISHERIES AND VETERINARY SCIENCE

Department of Agricultural Sciences of the National Academy of Sciences of the Republic of Belarus: 220049 Minsk, vul. Nezavisimosti 1; tel. (17) 284-18-12; fax (17) 284-09-95; comprises 16 research institutes and 8 experimental stations; attached to Nat. Acad. of Sciences; 32 mems (13 academicians, 19 corresp. mems); attached research institutes: see Research Institutes; library: see Libraries and Archives; Pres. VLADIMIR G. GUSAKOV; Scientific Sec. SVETLANA A. KASYANCHIK.

HISTORY, GEOGRAPHY AND ARCHAEOLOGY

Department of Humanitarian Sciences and Arts of the National Academy of Sciences of Belarus: 220072 Minsk, pr. Nezavisimosti 66; tel. (17) 284-07-74; fax (17) 239-31-63; internet www.ac.by/organizations/departments/ogum.html; fields of study include: history; historical geography and cartography; comparative historical and structural-typological studies of Belarusian and other languages; Belarusian literature, poetry and folklore; history of philosophy and politics in Belarus; sociolinguistic and psycholinguistic investigation; Acad.-Sec. Acad. PYOTR G. NIKITENKO.

LANGUAGE AND LITERATURE

Goethe-Institut: 220034 Minsk, vul. Frunze 5; tel. (17) 236-34-33; fax (17) 236-73-14; e-mail info@minsk.goethe.org; internet www.goethe.de/minsk; offers courses and exams in German language and culture and promotes cultural exchange with Germany; library of 8,840 vols; Dir BARBARA FRAENKEL-THONET.

MEDICINE

Department of Medical Sciences of the National Academy of Sciences of Belarus: 220072 Minsk, pr. Nezavisimosti 66; tel. and fax (17) 284-07-78; e-mail medicine@presidium.bas-net.by; internet www.ac.by/organizations/departments/omed .html; develops and coordinates research in the fields of: physiology of self-regulation; devt of a theoretical basis for management of compensatory-recombinatory processes; modern ecosystems and their effects on the physiological state and health of humans; and the devt of medical-biological problems connected with the consequences of the Chornobyl (Chernobyl) nuclear accident in 1986; Acad.-Sec. Acad. EVGENIY D. BELOYENKO.

NATURAL SCIENCES

Department of Biological Sciences of the National Academy of Sciences of Belarus: 220072 Minsk, pr. Nezavisimosti 66; tel. (17) 284-03-79; fax (17) 284-28-21; e-mail biology@presidium.bas-net.by; internet www.ac.by/organizations/ departments/obio.html; fields of study include: biodiversity of plants and animals in Belarus; development of methods of protection of flora and fauna; and reproduction and rational use of biological resources in conditions of anthropogenic pressure; Acad.-Sec. Acad. IGOR D. VOLOTOVSKIY.

Department of Chemistry and Earth Sciences of the National Academy of Sciences of Belarus: 220072 Minsk, pr. Nezavisimosti 66; tel. and fax (17) 284-03-71; e-mail chemistry@presidium.bas-net.by; internet www.ac.by/organizations/ departments/ochi.html; develops and coordinates research in the fields of: chemistry of polymers and their application; organic synthesis of substances with valuable properties; chemistry of inorganic materials; physical chemistry; chemistry of proteins, nucleic acids and low-molecular bioregulators; Acad.-Sec. Acad. NIKOLAI P. KRUTKO.

Department of Physical and Engineering Sciences of the National Academy of Sciences of Belarus: 220072 Minsk, pr. Nezavisimosti 66; tel. (17) 284-03-77; fax (17) 284-03-75; e-mail engine@presidium.bas-net .by; internet www.ac.by/organizations/ departments/ochi.html; develops and coordinates research and applied scientific investigations in the fields of: power engineering; conservation of energy and resources; materials and high-energy technologies; and machine building, modelling and diagnostics; Acad.-Sec. Acad. SERGEI A. ZHDANOK.

Department of Physics, Mathematics and Informatics of the National Academy of Sciences of Belarus: 220072 Minsk, pr. Nezavisimosti 66; tel. and fax (17) 284-03-76; e-mail physics@presidium .bas-net.by; internet www.ac.by/ organizations/departments/ochi.html; develops and coordinates research in the fields of: optics, spectroscopy, laser and plasma physics; atomic and molecular analysis and diagnostics; study and control of the natural environment (incl. laser-sensing and airspace spectrometry); development of materials with electrical, magnetic, optical, and physical-mechanical properties; advanced information technologies (incl. fibre optics, design of automated technical systems); image processing (digital cartography, processing of space images), modelling of intelligent processes (incl. voice-recognition and neurocomputing); Acad.-Sec. Prof. SERGEI V. ABLAMEYKO.

Research Institutes

AGRICULTURE, FISHERIES AND VETERINARY SCIENCE

Belarus Research Institute for Potato Cultivation: 223013 Minsk obl., pos. Samokhvalovichi, vul. Kovaleva 2A; tel. (17) 506-61-45; fax (17) 506-70-01; internet mshp .minsk.by/science/kartof; f. 1957; attached to Nat. Acad. of Sciences of Belarus; Dir SERGEI A. BANADYSEV; publ. *Potato Growing* (1 a year).

Belarus Research Institute of Power Engineering for Agro-industrial complex: 220024 Minsk, vul. Stebeneva 20; tel. (17) 275-19-07; fax (17) 275-10-20; e-mail energetika@forenet.by; f. 1994; attached to Acad. of Agricultural Sciences of the Republic of Belarus; Dir Prof. VIKENTIY I. RUSAN; publs *Problems in the Development of Power Engineering and Electrification for Agro-industrial complex, Use of Renewable Energy.*

Belarus Research Institute for Soil Science and Agrochemistry: 220108 Minsk, vul. Kazintsa 62; tel. (17) 277-08-21; fax (17) 277-44-80; e-mail brissa@mail.belpak.by; internet mshp.minsk.by/science/niiagrhru .htm; f. 1931; attached to Acad. of Agricultural Sciences of the Republic of Belarus; Dir Prof. IOSIF M. BOGDEVICH; publs *Soil Investigation and Fertilizer Application* (every 2 years), *Soil Science and Agrochemistry* (1 a year).

Belarus Research and Technological Institute of the Meat and Dairy Industry: 220075 Minsk, Partizansky pr. 72; tel. (17) 244-38-52; fax (17) 244-38-91; attached to Acad. of Agricultural Sciences of the Republic of Belarus; Dir NIKOLAY A. PROKOPEV.

Grodno Zonal Planting Institute: 231510 Grodno raion, Shchuchin, Akademicheskaya 21; tel. (1514) 2-36-90; fax (1514) 2-36-87; e-mail gznii@tut.by; f. 1910; attached to National Acad. of Sciences of Belarus; 87 mems; library of 22,000 vols; Dir VLADIMIR KURILOVICH.

Institute of Agricultural Economics: 220108 Minsk, vul. Kazintsa 103; tel. (17) 277-04-11; fax (17) 278-69-21; e-mail agrecinst@mail.belpak.by; f. 1958; attached to Acad. of Agricultural Sciences of the Republic of Belarus; library of 20,000 vols; Dir Dr VLADIMIR G. GUSAKOV; publ. *Agricultural Economics* (12 a year).

Institute of Agricultural Radiology: 246050 Gomel, vul. Feduninskogo 16; tel. (23) 251-68-21; fax (23) 253-75-60; attached to Acad. of Agricultural Sciences of the Republic of Belarus; Dir SLAVA K. FIRSAKOVA.

Institute of Animal Production: 222160 Minsk obl., Zhodino, vul. Frunze 11; tel. (1775) 3-34-26; fax (1775) 3-52-83; e-mail belniig@tut.by; f. 1949; attached to Nat. Acad. of Sciences of Belarus; library of 68,000 vols; Dir Prof. IVAN P. SHEYKO; publ. *Zootechnic Science of Belarus* (1 a year).

Institute of Arable Farming: 222160 Minsk raion, Zhodino, vul. Timiryazeva 1; tel. (1775) 3-25-68; fax (1775) 3-70-66; e-mail izis@tut.by; internet www.izis.basnet.by; f. 1928 as Institute of Socialist Agriculture; present name 1956; attached to Nat. Acad. of Sciences of the Republic of Belarus; conducts applied and basic research in arable farming, plant growing, selection, genetics and crop protection; creation of highly productive varieties of agricultural crops, working with resource-saving technologies; library of 61,000 vols; Gen. Dir Dr FEDOR IVANOVICH; publ. *Transactions on Arable Farming and Plant Growing* (1 a year).

Institute of Experimental Veterinary Medicine 'S. N. Wysheleski': 223020 Minsk raion, pos. Kuntsevshchina, Vyshelessky 2; tel. and fax (17) 508-81-31; f. 1930; attached to Acad. of Agricultural Sciences of the Republic of Belarus; Dir ALIAKSANDR P. LYSENKA; publ. *Veterinarnaya Nauka-Proisvodstvu* (1 a year).

Institute of Fisheries: 220024 Minsk, vul. Stebeneva 22; tel. (17) 275-36-46; fax (17) 275-36-60; f. 1958; attached to Nat. Acad. of Sciences of Belarus; Dir VICTOR V. KONCHITS; publ. *Belarus Fish Industry Problems* (Russian with summary in English, 1 a year).

Institute of Forestry: 246001 Gomel, Praletarskaya vul. 71; tel. (232) 53-73-73; fax (232) 53-53-89; e-mail forinst@server.by; f. 1930; attached to Nat. Acad. of Sciences of Belarus; Dir Prof. Dr VIKTOR A. IPATEV; publ. *Questions in Forest Sciences* (1 a year).

Institute of Fruit Cultivation: 223013 Minsk raion, pos. Samokhvalovichi, vul. Kovalevea 2; tel. and fax (17) 506-61-40; e-mail belhort@it.org.by; internet mshp .minsk.by/science/niipl.htm; attached to Acad. of Agricultural Sciences of the Republic of Belarus; Dir VYACHESLAV A. SAMUS.

Institute of Land Reclamation and Grass Management: 220040 Minsk, vul. M. Bogdanovicha 153; tel. (17) 232-49-41; fax (17) 232-64-96; e-mail niimel@mail.ru; internet www.niimelio.niks.by; f. 1930; attached to Nat. Acad. of Sciences of Belarus; Dir ANATOLI LIKHATSEVICH; publ. *Reclamation of Overmoistened Land* (2 a year).

RUE 'Scientific and Practical Centre of the National Academy of Sciences of Belarus for Agriculture Mechanization': 220049 Minsk, vul. Knorina 1; tel. and fax (17) 266-02-91; e-mail belagromech@tut.by; f. 1947; attached to Nat. Acad. of Sciences of the Republic of Belarus; devt and implementation of new equipment for crop production and livestock farming, engineering and construction of vegetable storage facilities, creation of technological systems of machinery and equipment for agriculture mechanization; Dir-Gen. VLADIMIR G. SAMOSYUK.

Institute of Plant Protection: 223011 Minsk raion, pos. Priluki, vul. Mira 2; tel. and fax (17) 509-23-39; e-mail entom@izr .belpak.minsk.by; attached to Acad. of Agricultural Sciences of the Republic of Belarus; Dir SERGEY V. SOROKA.

Institute of Vegetable Crops: 220028 Minsk, vul. Mayakovskogo 127A; tel. (17) 221-37-11; e-mail inst@belniio.belpak.minsk .by; internet mshp.minsk.by/science/niiov .htm; attached to Acad. of Agricultural Sciences of the Republic of Belarus; Dir GENNADY I. GANUSH.

ARCHITECTURE AND TOWN PLANNING

Research and Design Institute of Construction Materials 'BelNIIS': 220114 Minsk, Staroborisovsky tr.; tel. (17) 264-10-01; fax (17) 264-87-92; e-mail lmdp@nsys.by; Dir NADEZHDA N. TSYBULKO.

ECONOMICS, LAW AND POLITICS

Economic Research Institute of the Ministry of the Economy: 220086 Minsk, vul. Slavinskogo 1, korp. 1; tel. (17) 264-02-78; fax (17) 264-64-40; e-mail niei@main.gov.by; f. 1962; library of 51,425 vols; Dir STEPAN S. POLONIK.

Institute of Economics: 220072 Minsk, vul. Surganava 1–2, Korpus 2; tel. (17) 284-24-43; fax (17) 284-07-16; e-mail directorship@economics.basnet.by; internet economics.bas-net.by; f. 1931; attached to Nat. Acad. of Sciences of Belarus; Dir Prof. PETR G. NIKITENKO; publ. *Organizatsiya i* *upravleniye* (Organization and Management, in Russian, 4 a year).

Institute for State and Law: 220072 Minsk, vul. Surganava 1, Korpus 2; tel. (17) 284-18-64; fax (17) 284-18-24; e-mail philos@bas-net.by; f. 1999; attached to Nat. Acad. of Sciences of Belarus; Dir Dr VLADIMIR P. IZOTKO.

Research Institute of Criminalistics and Forensic Expertise: 220073 Minsk, Kalvariiskaya vul. 43; tel. and fax (17) 226-72-79; e-mail sudexpertiza@adsl.by; internet www.sudexpertiza.by; f. 1929; attached to Ministry of Justice; library of 10,000 vols; Dir Dr ALEXANDER RUBIS; publ. *Issues of Criminalistics, Criminology and Forensic Expertise* (1 a year).

EDUCATION

National Institute of Education: 220004 Minsk, vul. Korolja 16; tel. (17) 220-59-09; fax (17) 220-56-35; f. 1990; library of 20,000 vols; Dir Dr BORIS KRAIKO; publ. *Adulcatsia i Wychawanne.*

HISTORY, GEOGRAPHY AND ARCHAEOLOGY

Institute of History: 220072 Minsk, vul. Akademicheskaya 1; tel. and fax (17) 284-02-19; f. 1929; attached to Nat. Acad. of Sciences of Belarus; Dir Prof. ALEKSANDR A. KOVALENYA (acting).

LANGUAGE AND LITERATURE

Institute of Linguistics 'Ya. Kolas': 220072 Minsk, vul. Surganava 1, Korpus 2; tel. (17) 268-48-84; fax (17) 284-18-85; e-mail inlinasbel@tut.by; f. 1929; attached to Nat. Acad. of Sciences of Belarus; Dir ALEKSANDR A. LUKASHANETS.

Institute of Literature: 220072 Minsk, pr. Nezavisimosti 66; tel. (17) 268-58-86; e-mail inlit@bas-net.by; f. 1931; attached to Nat. Acad. of Sciences of Belarus; Dir VLADIMIR V. GNILOMEDOV.

MEDICINE

N. N. Alexandrov National Cancer Centre of Belarus: 223040 Minsk, p.o. Lesnoy-2; tel. (17) 269-95-05; fax (17) 265-47-04; e-mail v.chalov@omr.med.by; internet www.omr.med.by; f. 1960 as the N. N. Alexandrov Research Institute of Oncology and Medical Radiology, renamed in March 2008; carries out clinical cancer research; library of 15,000 vols, 55 periodicals; Dir Prof. IOSIF V. ZALUTSKY; publs *Oncology Journal* (4 a year), *Topical Problems in Oncology and Medical Radiology* (1 a year).

Institute of Pulmonology and Phthisiology: 223059 Minsk raion, pos. Novinki; tel. (17) 289-87-95; fax (17) 289-89-50; e-mail niipulm@users.med.by; f. 1923; library of 7,000 vols; Dir VALENTIN V. BORSHCHEVSKIY; publ. *Research Report* (1 a year).

Republican Scientific Practical Centre of Hygiene: 220012 Minsk, Akademicheskaya 8; tel. (17) 284-13-70; fax (17) 284-03-45; e-mail rspch@rspch.by; internet www.rspch.by; f. 1927; library of 11,982 vols; Dir SERGEY SOKOLOV.

Republican Research and Practical Centre for Epidemiology and Microbiology: 220114 Minsk, vul. Filimonova 23; tel. (17) 267-30-50; fax (17) 267-30-93; e-mail belriem@gmail.com; internet www.belriem.org; f. 1924 as Belarusian Pasteur Institute; research to improve surveillance of infectious diseases, study of molecular mechanisms of pathogenicity of main infectious and immune diseases, devt of immuno- and molecular biologic diagnostic preparations against the agents of main infections, elaboration and

implementation into medical practice of up-to-date diagnostic, medical, and vaccine preparations, quality controls of immunobiological products, medical information support in the control of infectious and immune diseases; library of 11,000 vols; Dir Dr ALEXANDER S. PETKEVICH (acting).

Research Institute for Evaluation of the Working Capacity of Disabled People: 220114 Minsk, Staroborisovsky trakt 24; tel. and fax (17) 264-25-08; f. 1974; library of 35,000 vols; Dir Prof. V. B. SMYCHEK.

Research Institute of Neurology, Neurosurgery and Physiotherapy: 220061 Minsk, vul. Filatova 9; tel. (17) 246-40-88.

Research Institute of Traumatology and Orthopaedics: Minsk, vul. Gorkogo 2.

Scientific Practical Centre 'Cardiology': 220036 Minsk, R. Luxemburg St 110; tel. (17) 286-14-66; fax (17) 286-14-66; e-mail info@cardio.by; internet www.cardio.by; f. 1977; cardiology, cardiosurgery; Dir ALEXANDR MROCHEK.

Skin and Venereological Research Institute: Minsk, Prilukskaya vul. 46A.

NATURAL SCIENCES

Biological Sciences

Central Botanical Garden: 220012 Minsk, vul. Surganava 2A; tel. (17) 284-14-84; fax (17) 284-14-83; e-mail cbg@it.org.by; internet hbc.bas-net.by/cbg; f. 1932; attached to Nat. Acad. of Sciences of Belarus; Dir Acad. VLADIMIR N. RESHETNIKOV.

Institute of Biochemistry: 230017 Grodno, bul. Leninskogo Komsomola 50; tel. (15) 233-41-61; fax (15) 233-41-21; e-mail val@biochem.unibel.by; f. 1985; attached to Nat. Acad. of Sciences of Belarus; library of 40,000 vols; Dir Prof. PAVEL S. PRONKO.

Institute of Bio-organic Chemistry: 220141 Minsk, vul. Akad. V. F. Kuprevicha 5; tel. (17) 264-87-61; fax (17) 263-71-32; internet iboch.bas-net.by; f. 1974; attached to Nat. Acad. of Sciences of Belarus; Dir Acad. FYODOR A. LAKHVICH.

Institute of Biophysics and Cell Engineering: 220072 Minsk, vul. Akademicheskaya 27; tel. (17) 284-17-49; fax (17) 284-23-57; e-mail ipb@biobel.bas-net.by; internet biobel.bas-net.by/biophys; f. 1973; attached to Nat. Acad. of Sciences of Belarus; Dir Acad. IGOR D. VOLOTOVSKIY; publ. *Godnev's Lectures: Plant Photobiology and Photosynthesis* (1 a year).

Institute of Experimental Botany 'V. Kuprevich': 220072 Minsk, vul. Akademicheskaya 27; tel. (17) 284-15-64; fax (17) 284-18-53; f. 1931; attached to Nat. Acad. of Sciences of Belarus; Dir Prof. Dr NIKOLAI A. LAMAN.

Institute of Genetics and Cytology: 220072 Minsk, vul. Akademicheskaya 27; tel. (17) 284-18-48; fax (17) 284-19-17; internet biobel.bas-net.by/igc; f. 1965; attached to Nat. Acad. of Sciences of Belarus; Dir ALEKSANDR V. KILCHEVSKIY.

Institute of Microbiology: 220141 Minsk, vul. Akad. V. F. Kuprevicha 2; tel. (17) 202-99-46; fax (17) 264-47-66; internet www.mbio.bas-net.by; f. 1975; attached to Nat. Acad. of Sciences of Belarus; Dir EMILIYA I. KOLOMETS.

Institute for Nature Management: 220114 Minsk, 10 F. Skariny Str.; tel. (17) 267-26-32; fax (17) 267-24-13; e-mail nature@ecology.basnet.by; internet www.ecology.basnet.by; f. 1932; attached to Nat. Acad. of Sciences of Belarus; library of 235,500 vols; nature management, environment protection, geotechnology, geoecology, geography and paleogeography, climatology and hydrogeochemistry; Dir ALEXANDER KARABANOV;

publs *Natural Resources, Nature Management* (2 a year).

Institute of Physiology: 220072 Minsk, vul. Akademichnaya 28; tel. (17) 284-24-61; fax (17) 284-16-30; f. 1953; attached to Nat. Acad. of Sciences of Belarus; basic and applied research in biomedicine; Dir VLADIMIR S. ULASHCHYK.

Institute of Radiobiology: 246007 Gomel, Fedyuninskogo Str. 4; tel. and fax (232) 57-07-06; e-mail irb@mail.gomel.by; internet irb.basnet.by; f. 1987; attached to Nat. Acad. of Sciences of Belarus; monitors and forecasts radioactive contamination level of environment; creates new technologies for prophylaxis of diseases with use of bioactive additives, other medical agents; develops protective measures for overcoming of the long-term radioecological consequences of Chernobyl accident; researches adaptation mechanisms in organism, incl. ionizing radiation; offers postgraduate courses in radiation biology and radioecology; 80 mems; Dir Dr ALIAKSANDR NAVUMAV; Scientific Sec. ALEKSANDER NIKITIN.

Institute of Zoology: 220072 Minsk, vul. Akademichnaya 27; tel. (17) 284-22-75; fax (17) 284-10-36; internet biobel.bas-net.by/zoo; f. 1958; attached to Nat. Acad. of Sciences of Belarus; Dir MIKHAIL E. NIKIFOROV.

Mathematical Sciences

Institute of Mathematics: 220072 Minsk, vul. Surganava 11; tel. (17) 284-17-01; fax (17) 284-22-59; internet im.bas-net.by; f. 1959; attached to Nat. Acad. of Sciences of Belarus; Dir Acad. IVAN V. GAISHUN.

Physical Sciences

Institute of Applied Optics: 212793 Mogilev, vul. Bialynitskaga-Biruli 11; tel. and fax (22) 226-46-49; f. 1970; attached to Nat. Acad. of Sciences of Belarus; Dir V. P. REDKO.

Institute of General and Inorganic Chemistry: 220072 Minsk, vul. Surganava 9; tel. (17) 284-27-23; fax (17) 284-27-03; f. 1959; attached to Nat. Acad. of Sciences of Belarus; Dir NIKOLAI P. KRUTKO.

Institute of Molecular and Atomic Physics: 220072 Minsk, pr. Nezavisimosti 70; tel. (17) 284-16-35; fax (17) 284-00-30; internet imaph.bas-net.by; f. 1992; attached to Nat. Acad. of Sciences of Belarus; Dir Dr SERGEY V. GAPONENKO; publ. *Journal of Applied Spectroscopy.*

Institute of Physical Organic Chemistry: 220072 Minsk, vul. Surganava 13; tel. (17) 284-23-38; fax (17) 284-16-79; e-mail ifoch@ifoch.bas-net.by; internet ifoch.bas-net.by; f. 1929; attached to Nat. Acad. of Sciences of Belarus; Dir Prof. ALEKSANDR V. BILDYUKEVICH (acting).

Institute of Physics 'B. I. Stepanov': 220072 Minsk, pr. Nezavisimosti 68; tel. (17) 284-17-55; fax (17) 284-08-79; internet ifanbel.bas-net.by; f. 1955; attached to Nat. Acad. of Sciences of Belarus; Dir Prof. VLADIMIR V. KABANOV (acting).

Institute of Solid State and Semiconductor Physics: 220072 Minsk, vul. P. Brovki 17; tel. (17) 284-28-14; fax (17) 284-13-13; e-mail ifttpanb@iftt.basnet.minsk.by; f. 1963; attached to Nat. Acad. of Sciences of Belarus; library of 72,000 items; Dir Prof. VALERY M. FEDOSYUK.

PHILOSOPHY AND PSYCHOLOGY

Institute of Philosophy: 220072 Minsk, vul. Surganava 1, korp. 2; tel. (17) 284-18-63; fax (17) 284-29-25; e-mail institute@philosophy.by; internet www.philosophy.by; f. 1931; attached to Nat. Acad. of Sciences of

Belarus; research in the field of theory and methodology of natural scientific and socio-humanitarian cognition, philosophical anthropology, social ecology, ethics and aesthetics; elaboration of innovative strategies of social, spiritual, cultural and scientific progress; study of the actual problems of contemporary socio-political and cultural devt; study and summary of the achievements of the world and nat. philosophical thought; strategic European studies and research in the field of int. humanitarian collaboration; Dir Dr ANATOLY A. LAZAREVICH.

RELIGION, SOCIOLOGY AND ANTHROPOLOGY

Institute of Arts, Ethnography and Folklore: 220072 Minsk, vul. Surganava 1, korp. 2; tel. (17) 239-59-21; f. 1957; attached to Nat. Acad. of Sciences of Belarus; Dir M. P. PILIPENKO.

Institute of Sociology: 220072 Minsk, vul. Surganava 1, korp. 2; tel. (17) 239-48-65; fax (17) 239-59-28; f. 1990; attached to Nat. Acad. of Sciences of Belarus; Dir E. M. BABOSOV.

TECHNOLOGY

Belarus Institute for the Science, Research and Design of Food Products: 220037 Minsk, Kozlova 29; tel. (17) 285-39-70; fax (17) 285-39-71; f. 2000; library of 20,000 vols; Dir ZENON LOVKIS.

Belarusian Institute of System Analysis and Information Support for Scientific and Technical Sphere (BELISA): 220004 Minsk, pr. Pobeditelei 7; tel. (17) 203-14-87; fax (17) 203-35-40; internet www.belisa.org.by; operated by the State Committee on Science and Technologies of Belarus; Dir VALERJY E. KRATENOK.

Engineering Centre 'Plazmoteg': 220141 Minsk, vul. Akad. V. F. Kuprevicha 1, korp. 3; tel. (17) 263-93-41; fax (17) 263-59-20; e-mail pec@bas-net.by; f. 1990; attached to Nat. Acad. of Sciences of Belarus; Dir EDUARD I. TOCHITSKY.

Institute of Applied Physics: 220072 Minsk, vul. Akademicheskaya 16; tel. (17) 284-17-94; fax (17) 284-10-81; internet iaph.bas-net.by; f. 1963; attached to Nat. Acad. of Sciences of Belarus; physics of non-destructive testing; Dir Prof. Dr NIKOLAI P. MIGUN.

Institute of Chemistry of New Materials: 220141 Minsk, vul. Akad. V. F. Kuprevicha 16; tel. and fax (17) 263-19-23; internet www.ichnm.ac.by; f. 1993; attached to Nat. Acad. of Sciences of Belarus; Dir Acad. VLADIMIR E. AGABEKOV.

Institute of Electronics: 220090 Minsk, Logoiskiy trakt 22; tel. (17) 265-34-13; fax (17) 283-91-51; f. 1973; attached to Nat. Acad. of Sciences of Belarus; Dir YURIY V. TROFIMOV.

Institute of Energetics Problems: 220109 Minsk, vul. Akad. Krasina; tel. and fax (17) 246-70-55; f. 1991; attached to Nat. Acad. of Sciences of Belarus; Dir Dr YURIY V. KLIMENKOV.

Institute of Engineering Cybernetics: 220012 Minsk, vul. Surganava 6; tel. (17) 268-51-71; fax (17) 231-84-03; e-mail cic@newman.basnet.minsk.by; f. 1965; attached to Nat. Acad. of Sciences of Belarus; Dir Prof. VYACHESLAV S. TANAYEV.

A. V. Luikov Heat and Mass Transfer Institute: 220072 Minsk, vul. P. Brovki 15; tel. (17) 284-21-36; fax (17) 292-25-13; internet www.itmo.by; f. 1952; attached to Nat. Acad. of Sciences of Belarus; research and devt on problems of heat and mass transfer in capillary-porous bodies, dispersal systems, rheological and non-equilibrium

media, turbulent non-uniform flows, aero-thermo-optical devices and low-temperature generators, laser technologies, hydrogen power engineering, nanomaterials and nano-technologies, plasma and waste treatment, energy and resources saving; Dir Dr ANATOLI M. RUSETSKIY.

Institute of Machine Mechanics and Reliability: 220072 Minsk, vul. Akademicheskaya 12; tel. (17) 210-07-48; fax (17) 284-02-41; f. 1971; attached to Nat. Acad. of Sciences of Belarus; Dir Dr YURIY V. KLIMENKOV.

Institute of Radiation Physical-Chemical Problems: 220109 Minsk, Akad. Krasina 99; tel. (17) 246-77-50; fax (17) 246-73-17; f. 1991; attached to Nat. Acad. of Sciences of Belarus; Dir SERGEY E. CHIGRINOV.

Institute of Radioecological Problems: 220109 Minsk, Sosny; tel. (17) 246-72-53; fax (17) 246-70-17; e-mail irep@sosny.basnet.minsk.by; f. 1991; attached to Nat. Acad. of Sciences of Belarus; Dir G. A. SHAROVAROV.

Institute of Technical Acoustics: 210717 Vitebsk, pr. Lyudnikova 13; tel. (212) 25-41-89; fax (212) 24-39-53; e-mail ita@vitebsk.by; internet www.belpak.vitebsk.by/ita; f. 1995; attached to Nat. Acad. of Sciences of Belarus; library of 43,000 vols; Dir Prof. VASILIY V. RUBANIK.

Institute of Technology of Metals: 212030 Mogilev, vul. Bialynitskaga-Biruli 11; tel. (222) 26-46-43; fax (222) 32-65-93; e-mail inmet@mogilev.unibel.by; internet www.ussr.to/belarus/itm; f. 1992; attached to Nat. Acad. of Sciences of Belarus; Dir Dr EVGENIY MARUKOVICH.

Medical Biotechnological Institute: 220029 Minsk, vul. Varvasheny 17; tel. and fax (17) 234-32-06; internet www.medbiotech.bn.by; f. 1972; 120 mems; Dir VICTOR N. TERECHOV; Dir of Scientific Research K. M. BELIAVSKY.

Metal Polymer Research Institute 'V. A. Belyi': 246050 Gomel, vul. Kirova 32A; tel. (232) 77-52-12; fax (232) 77-52-11; e-mail mpri@mail.ru; internet mpri.org.by; f. 1969; attached to Nat. Acad. of Sciences of Belarus; library of 19,519 vols; Dir Prof. NIKOLAI K. MYSHKIN; publs *Friction and Wear* (6 a year), *Materials, Technologies and Tools* (4 a year).

Non-Traditional Energetics and Energy-Saving Scientific and Engineering Centre: 220109 Minsk, Sosny; tel. (17) 246-76-61; f. 1992; attached to Nat. Acad. of Sciences of Belarus; Dir V. N. YERMASHKEVICH.

Physical-Technical Institute: 220141 Minsk, vul. Akad. V. F. Kuprevicha 10; tel. (17) 264-60-10; fax (17) 263-76-93; e-mail phti@tut.by; internet phti.at.tut.by; f. 1931; attached to Nat. Acad. of Sciences of Belarus; Dir ANATOLIY I. GORDIENKO.

Republican Scientific and Engineering Centre for Environmental Remote Sensing 'Ecomir': 220012 Minsk, vul. Surganava 2; tel. (17) 284-00-49; fax (17) 284-00-47; e-mail ecomir@open.by; internet www.ecomir-eeica.com; f. 1990; attached to Nat. Acad. of Sciences of Belarus; Dir Prof. A. A. KOVALEV.

Scientific-Engineering Republican Unitary Enterprise 'Belavtotraktorostroenie': 220072 Minsk, vul. Akademicheskaya 12; tel. (17) 210-07-49; fax (17) 284-02-41; e-mail bats@ncpmm.bas-net.by; internet www.bats.basnet.by; f. 1993; attached to Nat. Acad. of Sciences of Belarus; Dir Acad. M. S. VYSOTSKY.

Libraries and Archives
Brest
Brest Oblast Library 'M. Gorky': 210601 Brest, bul. Kosmanavtov 48; tel. and fax (162) 22-22-01; e-mail brl@tut.by; internet grl.brest.by; f. 1940; regional centre for 19 central libraries and 818 brs; 740,000 vols; Dir TAMARA P. DANILYUK; publ. *Bibliopanorama* (irregular).

Gomel
Gomel Oblast Universal Library 'V. I. Lenin': 246000 Gomel, pl. Pobedy 2A; tel. (232) 77-36-51; e-mail goub@it.org.by; Dir VALENTINA P. DUBROVA.

Minsk
Belarus Agricultural Library: 220108 Minsk, vul. Kazintsa 86/2; tel. (17) 212-15-61; fax (17) 212-00-66; internet belal.by; f. 1960; attached to Nat. Acad. of Sciences of Belarus; 500,000 vols; Dir VALENTINA YURCHENKO.

Belarus State University Library: 220050 Minsk, pr. Skoriny 4; tel. (17) 220-78-23; fax (17) 226-59-40; e-mail lapo@bsu.by; internet www.library.bsu.by; f. 1921; 2.0m. vols; Dir PETR M. LAPO.

Central Scientific Archive of the National Academy of Sciences of Belarus: 220072 Minsk, pr. Nezavisimosti 66; tel. (17) 284-22-87; fax (17) 284-18-70; f. 1931; Head MARYNA HLEB.

Central Scientific Library of the National Academy of Sciences of Belarus 'Ya. Kolas': 220072 Minsk, vul. Surganava 15; tel. and fax (17) 284-14-28; internet www.csl.bas-net.by; f. 1925; 3.1m. vols; Dir NATALIYA YU. BEREZKINA.

National Library of Belarus: 220114 Minsk, Nezavisimosty Ave 116; tel. (17) 266-37-00; fax (17) 266-37-06; internet nlb.by; f. 1922; 8.9m. vols; Dir Prof. ROMAN MATULSKY; publs *Chernobyl: Bibliographical Index* (2 a year), *New Literature on the Culture and Art of Belarus* (12 a year), *Novyja Knigi* (12 a year), *Social Sciences* (12 a year).

Republican Library for Science and Technology of Belarus: 220004 Minsk, pr. Pobediteley 7; tel. and fax (17) 203-31-38; e-mail rlst@rlst.org.by; internet www.rlst.org.by; f. 1977; 2.0m. vols (excl. patents); Dir RAISA SUKHORUKOVA.

Republican Scientific Medical Library: 220007 Minsk, vul. Fabritsiusa 28; tel. (17) 226-21-52; fax (17) 216-20-43; e-mail rsml@rsml.med.by; internet www.rsml.med.by; f. 1941; 860,000 vols; Dir VLADIMIR N. SOROKO.

Mogilev
Mogilev Oblast Library 'V. I. Lenin': 212030 Mogilev, vul. Krylenko 8; tel. and fax (222) 25-07-58; e-mail adm@mlib.basnet.by; internet www.mlib.basnet.by; f. 1935; Dir ALLA M. VASILENKO; publs *Bibliographic Indices* (irregular), *Bulletin* (irregular).

Vitebsk
Vitebsk Oblast Library 'V. I. Lenin': 210601 Vitebsk, vul. Lenina 8A; tel. (212) 37-45-21; fax (212) 37-30-58; f. 1921; Dir ALEKSANDR SEMKIN.

Museums and Art Galleries
Belovezhskaya Pushcha
'Belovezhskaya Pushcha' National Park Museum: 225063 Brestskaya oblast, Kame-

netzky raion; tel. (1631) 5-63-96; fax (1631) 2-50-56; e-mail box@npbprom.belpak.brest.by; internet www.npbp.cis.by; f. 1960; displays flora and fauna of the Belovezhskaya Pushcha Primeval Forest, and shows work being done to preserve the biological diversity in the primeval forest, particularly with respect to the European Bison; Dir NIKOLAI N. BAMBIZA.

Grodno

Grodno State Historical and Archaeological Museum: 230023 Grodno, Zamkovaya vul. 22; tel. and fax (152) 74-08-33; e-mail grodno_museum@tut.by; f. 1920; museum colln contains 186,000 items; library of 35,000 vols; Dir Dr YURY KITURKA; publ. *Krayaznauchya zapiski* (Journal of Regional Studies, every 2 years).

Minsk

Great Patriotic War Museum: 220030 Minsk, pr. Nezavisimosti 25A; tel. and fax (17) 227-11-66; e-mail museumww2@tut.by; internet nacbibl.org.by/war_museum; f. 1943; Soviet Army and partisans' war history 1941–1945; library of 14,000 vols; Dir GENNADIY I. BARKUN.

National Art Museum of the Republic of Belarus: 220030 Minsk, vul. Lenina 20; tel. and fax (17) 227-56-72; internet www.artmuseum.by; f. 1939; Belarusian art from 11th century to early 20th century; European art from 16th century to early 20th century; Russian art from 18th century to early 20th century; temporary exhibitions; Dir VLADIMIR I. PROKOPTSOV.

National Museum of the History and Culture of Belarus: 220030 Minsk, vul. K. Marksa 12; tel. (17) 328-63-75; fax (17) 227-36-65; e-mail histmuseum@tut.by; f. 1957; history and local natural history; archaeological, ethnographical and coin collections; library of 20,000 vols; Dir SERGEJ VECHER.

Universities

BARANOVICHI STATE UNIVERSITY

225404 Baranovichi, vul. Voikova 21

Telephone: (163) 45-78-60

Fax: (163) 45-78-31

E-mail: barsu@brest.by

Internet: www.barsu.by

Founded 2004

Rector: Prof. VASILIY I. KOCHURKO

Library of 266,109 vols

Number of teachers: 562

Number of students: 8,875

Faculties of engineering, finance and jurisprudence, foreign languages, pedagogy, pre-university training, qualifications improvement and personnel retraining; external faculties of engineering, finance and jurisprudence, pedagogy

DEANS

Faculty of Economy and Law: ELENA IVANOVNA PLATONENKO

Faculty of Education by Correspondence: NATALYA IVANOVNA SHLYAGO

Faculty of Engineering: ALEXANDR VLADIMIROVICH AKULOV

Faculty of Foreign Languages: IRINA VYACHESLAVOVNA PINYUTA

Faculty of Pedagogy: ZOYA NIKOLAYEVNA KOZLOVA

Faculty of Pre-University Training: IGOR VIKTOROVICH DUBEN

Faculty of Persistent Training: MARIYA NIKOLAYEVNA MAKUTA

Institute of Refresher Training and Re-Training: VERA VALERYEVNA KHITRYUK

Lyakhovichi State Agrarian College: VYACHESLAV LUKICH SELMANOVICH (Dir)

BELARUS STATE ECONOMIC UNIVERSITY

220070 Minsk, Partizanski pr. 26

Telephone: (17) 249-40-32

Fax: (17) 249-51-06

E-mail: umoms@bseu.by

Internet: www.bseu.by

Founded 1933

Language of instruction: Russian

Rector: Prof. Dr VLADIMIR SHIMOV

Library: 1.5m. vols

Number of teachers: 1,400

Number of students: 26,000

Publications: *Belarusian Economic Journal*, *Bookkeeping, Accounting and Analysis*

DEANS

Faculty of Accounting and Economics: V. BEREZOVSKY

Faculty of Commerce, Economics and Management: A. YARTSEV

Faculty of Finance and Banking: N. BOGDAN

Faculty of International Business Communication: N. V. POPOK

Faculty of International Economics Relations: G. SHMARLOVSKAYA

Faculty of Law: A. SHKLYAREVSKY

Faculty of Management: V. A. SIMKHOVICH

Faculty of Marketing: V. BORODENYA

Faculty of Pre-University Training: S. KUCHUK

Higher School of Business and Management: S. YU. KRYCHEVSKIY

Higher School of Tourism: N. I. KABUSHKIN

Special Faculty of Psychology and Pedagogy for Teachers of Economics: B. KRAYKO

BELARUS STATE TECHNOLOGICAL UNIVERSITY

220050 Minsk, vul. Sverdlova 13

Telephone: (17) 226-14-32

Fax: (17) 227-62-17

E-mail: root@bstu.unibel.by

Internet: www.bstu.unibel.by

Founded 1930

Rector: IVAN M. ZHARSKIY

Pro-Rector for Academic Affairs: ALEKSANDR S. FEDORENCHIK

Pro-Rector for Administrative Affairs: BORIS V. ALDANOV

Pro-Rector for Economic Affairs: ALEKSANDR I. KUPTSOV

Pro-Rector for Education: GENNADY M. KVESKO

Pro-Rector for Research: PETR A. LYSHCHIK

Library of 1,200,000 vols

Number of teachers: 607

Number of students: 9,103

DEANS

Faculty of Chemical Technology and Engineering: SVETLANA E. OREKHOVA

Faculty of Engineering Economics: MIKHAIL I. BARANOV

Faculty of External Studies: ANDREY R. GORONOVSKIY

Faculty of Forestry: VALERIY K. GVOZDEV

Faculty of Forestry Technology: NIKOLAY P. VYRKO

Faculty of Organic Substance Technology: VALERIY N. FARAFONTOV

Faculty of Publishing and Printing: LEONID M. DAVIDOVICH

Faculty of Qualifications Improvement and Retraining of Specialists: ANDREY I. ROVKACH

BELARUSIAN NATIONAL TECHNICAL UNIVERSITY

220027 Minsk, pr. Nezavisimosti 65

Telephone: (17) 232-74-26

Fax: (17) 232-74-26

E-mail: bntu@bntu.by

Internet: www.bntu.by

Founded 1920

Faculties of architecture, construction, economics and management, instrument-making, mechanics and technology, motor vehicles and tractors, power engineering, road construction, robots and robot systems

Rector: Prof. BORIS M. KHRUSTALEV

Library: 2m. vols

Number of teachers: 2,643

Number of students: 15,000

Publications: *Energetica* (4 a year), *Mir Technologij* (4 a year), *Vestnik BNTU* (4 a year).

BELARUSIAN-RUSSIAN UNIVERSITY

212005 Mogilev, pr. Mira 43

Telephone: (222) 23-61-00

Fax: (222) 22-58-21

E-mail: bru@bru.mogilev.by

Internet: www.bru.mogilev.by

Founded 1961

Rector: IGOR S. SAZONOV

First Pro-Rector: FEDOR G. LOVSHENKO

Pro-Rectors for Academic Affairs: ALEKSANDR A. KATKALO, ALEKSANDR A. ZHOLOBOV

Pro-Rector for Academic, Economic and Int. Affairs: GRIGORIY P. KOSYACHENKO

Library: 1.5 m. vols

Number of teachers: 1,100

Number of students: 6,300

DEANS

Faculty of Automotive and Mechanical Engineering: STANISLAV B. PARTNOV

Faculty of Construction: SERGEY D. GALYUZHIN

Faculty of Economics: NIKOLAY S. ZHELTOK

Faculty of Electrotechnology: ALEKSANDR S. KOVAL

Faculty of Machine Building: VIKTOR A. POPKOVSKY

BELARUSIAN STATE AGRARIAN TECHNICAL UNIVERSITY

220023 Minsk, pr. Nezavisimosti 99

Telephone: (17) 264-47-71

Fax: (17) 264-41-16

E-mail: rektorat@batu.edu.by

Internet: www.batu.edu.by

Founded 1954

Faculties of agroenergy, agromechanics, business and management, humanities and ecology in social work, pre-university training and technical service, qualifications improvement and personnel retraining and vocational guidance

Rector: Prof. NIKOLAY V. KAZAROVETS

Library of 381,968 vols

Number of teachers: 519

Number of students: 8,783

BELARUSIAN STATE PEDAGOGICAL UNIVERSITY 'M. TANK'

220050 Minsk, ul. Sovetskaya 18

Telephone: (17) 226-40-20

Fax: (17) 226-40-24

E-mail: rector@bspu.unibel.by

Internet: www.bspu.unibel.by

Founded 1922

Rector: PETR D. KUKHARCHUK

First Pro-Rector: ALEKSANDR I. ANDARALO

Pro-Rector for Academic Affairs: SERGEY M. BYKADOROV

Pro-Rector for Admin. Affairs: VLADIMIR V. YADLOVSKIY

Pro-Rector for Education and Social Affairs: SVETLANA I. KOPTEVA

Pro-Rector for Information and Analytical Affairs: VALERIY B. TARANCHUK

Pro-Rector for Research: VASILIY V. BUSHCHIK

Librarian: N. P. KOPTEVA

Library: 1.3m. vols
Number of teachers: 1,180
Number of students: 9,000

DEANS

Faculty of Mathematics: PAVEL V. KIKEL

Faculty of National Culture: MIKHAIL M. KRUTALEVICH

Faculty of Natural History: MARAT G. YASO-VEEV

Faculty of Physics: IGOR S. TASHLYKOV

Faculty of Pre-University Training: VIKTOR L. TSYBOVSKIY

Faculty of Primary Education: NIKOLAY I. MITSKEVICH

Faculty of Russian Philology: VASILIY D. STARICHENOK

Faculty of Social Pedagogy and Technology: TATYANA P. MIKHNEVICH

BELARUSIAN STATE UNIVERSITY

220050 Minsk, pr. Nezavisimosti 4

Telephone: (17) 209-52-03
Fax: (17) 226-59-40
E-mail: bsu@bsu.by
Internet: www.bsu.by

Founded 1921

State control

Languages of instruction: Belarusan, Russian

Academic year: September to June

Rector: VASILIY I. STRAZHEV

First Pro-Rector: SERGEY K. RAKHMANOV

Pro-Rectors for Academic Affairs: VLADIMIR L. KLYUNYA, VIKTOR V. SAMOKHVAL

Pro-Rector for Admin. and Finance: VLADIMIR V. ROGOVITSKIY

Pro-Rector for Economic and Commercial Affairs: IGOR V. VOYTOV

Pro-Rector for Education and Social Affairs: VLADIMIR V. SUVOROV

Pro-Rector for Int. Affairs: VLADIMIR A. ASTAPENKO

Library: 2m. vols
Number of teachers: 2,400
Number of students: 16,500

Publications: *Belarusskiy Universitet* (24 a year), *Higher School* (6 a year), *Sociology* (4 a year), *Vestnik BGU* (12 a year)

DEANS

Faculty of Applied Mathematics: P. A. MAN-DRIK

Faculty of Biology: V. V. LYSAK

Faculty of Chemistry: G. A. BRANITSKY

Faculty of Economics: M. M. KOVALEV

Faculty of Geography: I. I. PIROZHNIK

Faculty of History: S. N. KHODZIN

Faculty of International Relations: A. V. SHARAPO

Faculty of Journalism: V. P. VOROBIOV

Faculty of Law: S. A. BALASHENKO

Faculty of Management and Social Technologies: V. G. BULAVKO

Faculty of Mechanics and Mathematics: N. I. YURCHUK

Faculty of Philology: I. S. ROVDO

Faculty of Philosophy and Social Studies: A. I. ZELENKOV

Faculty of Physics: V. M. ANISCHUK

Faculty of Radiophysics and Electronics: S. G. MULIARCHIK

International Graduate School of Business and Management of Technology: V. V. APANASOVICH

BELARUSIAN STATE UNIVERSITY OF INFORMATICS AND RADIOELECTRONICS

220013 Minsk, ul. Brovska 6

Telephone: (17) 293-89-17
Fax: (17) 293-23-33
E-mail: oms@bsuir.by
Internet: www.bsuir.by

Founded 1964

State control

Accredited by Min. of Education of the Republic of Belarus

Languages of instruction: Russian, Belarusian, English

Academic year: September to May

Rector: Prof. MIKHAIL P. BATURA

First Vice-Rector: Dr ANATOLY OSIPOV

Vice-Rector for Admin.: VLADIMIR I. TARASE-VITCH

Vice-Rector for Education: Prof. ALEXANDER A. KHMYL

Vice-Rector for Education: Dr BORIS NIKUL-SHIN

Vice-Rector for Education: Dr HELENA ZHI-VITSKAYA

Vice-Rector for Research and Devt: Prof. ALEXANDER P. KUZNETSOV

Chief Librarian: LUDMILA SIZOVA

Library: 1.5m. vols, 300 periodicals
Number of teachers: 1,000
Number of students: 15,000

Publication: *Doklady Bguir*

DEANS

Faculty of Computer-Aided Design: Dr SER-GEY DICK

Faculty of Computer Systems and Networks: Dr VALERY PRITKOV

Continuous and Distance Education: Dr VASILY BONDARIK

Faculty of Engineering Economics: Dr LUD-MILA KNYAZEVA

Faculty of Extramural Training: Dr ALEXAN-DER V. LOMAKO

Faculty of Information Technologies and Control Systems: Dr ARTUR BUDNIK

Faculty of Military Studies: Col. ALEXANDER DMITRIUK

Faculty of Pre-University Preparation and Occupational Guidance: Dr GALINA F. SMIRNOVA

Faculty of Radioengineering and Electronics: Dr ALEXANDER KOROTKEVICH

Faculty of Telecommunications: Dr OLEG D. TCHERNUKHO

PROFESSORS

ABRAMOV, I., Quantum Mechanics and Statistical Physics

AKSENCHIK, A., Probability Theory

ASAYONOK, I., Psychophysiology

BAKHTIZIN, V., Software Design and Programming Language

BELAYEV, B., Information Protection and Intellectual Property Management

BOBOV, M., Protection of Databases and Software

BORBOTKO, T., Information Protection in Bank Technologies

BORISENKO, V., Nanoelectronics

BRIGIDIN, A., Methods and Devices for Signal Shaping

DASHENKOV, V., Radiotechnical Circuits and Signals

DROBOT, S., Radioelectronics

DVORNIKOV, O., Designing of Integrated Circuits Topology

GAPONENKO, N., Nanophotonics

GASENKOVA, I., Information Protection and Intellectual Property Management

GOLENKOV, V., Mathematical Framework for Artificial Intelligence

GOLIKOV, V., Cryptoprotection of Information in Telecommunications

GULYAKINA, N., General Systems Theory

GURSKY, A., Digital and Microprocessor Units of Gauge Devices

KATKOVSKY, V., Information Protection and Intellectual Property Management

KHATKO, V., General Systems Theory

KIRILLOV, V., Metrological Support

KIRVEL, I., Ecology and Energy Saving, Environmental Economics

KLIUEV, L., Electrical Communication Theory

KOBRINSKY, G., Labour Management

KOLOSOV, S., Algorithmization and Programming

KOMLICHENKO, V., Computer Networks

KONOPELKO, V., Coding Theory

KRIVONOSOVA, T., Programming

KUREYCHIK, K., Computer Architecture

KUZNETSOV, A., Control System Calculation against Random Input

LISTOPAD, N., Transmitter-Receivers, Computer Systems for Data Transfer

LOSIK, G., Cognitive Graphics

LUKIYANETS, S., Automated Control Theory

LYNKOV, L., Information Protection and Intellectual Property Management

MALYKHINA, G., Logics

MUKHA, V., Statistical Methods for Data Processing

MUKHUROV, N., Information Protection and Intellectual Property Management

MURAVYOV, V., Satellite and Radio-Relay Communication Systems

NELAEV, V., Computer-Aided Design Systems in Micro- and Nanoelectronics

NOVIK, E., History of Belarus

PASHUTO, V., Foreign Economic Activities, Labour Management and Rating

PETROV, N., Theory and Methodology of Athletic Training

PRISCHEPA, S., Systems for CAD of Digital Devices

RESHETILOV, A., Electronics and Microcircuitry

SADYKHOV, R., Digital Processing of Signals and Images

SAK, A., Economic Forecasting and Planning

SHILIN, L., Theory of Electrical Circuits

SINITSYN, A., Algorithmization and Programming

SMIRNOV, A., Devices Based on Quantum and Magnetic Effects and Sensors

STOLER, V., Descriptive Geometry and Engineering Graphics

SURIN, V., Engineering Mechanics

TARCHENKO, N., Communication Systems

VILKOTSKY, M., EMC of Radioelectronic Appliances

YARMOLIK, V., Control and Diagnostics of Computer Equipment

YASHIN, K., Novel Production Equipment, Innovative Technologies, Labour Safety

ZABRODSKI, E., Political Science, Human Rights, Ideology of the Belarusian State

BELARUSIAN STATE UNIVERSITY OF PHYSICAL CULTURE

220020 Minsk, pr. Pobediteley 105

Telephone: (17) 250-80-08
Fax: (17) 250-80-08
E-mail: oo@sportedu.by
Internet: www.sportedu.by

Founded 1937

Rector: MIKHAIL E. KOBRINSKY

First Vice-Rector: OLGA A. GUSAROVA

Vice-Rector for Economic Affairs: (vacant)

Vice-Rector for Education: ALEXEY G. GATA-TULLIN

Vice-Rector for Science: TATYANA D. POLIA-
KOVA
Number of teachers: 388
Publication: *The World of Sport* (Scientific
Journal)

DEANS

Faculty of Health Oriented Physical Training
and Tourism: NATALYA M. MASHARSKAYA
Faculty of Pre-University Education: VLADI-
MIR M. LITVINOVICH
Faculty of Sports Games and Combative
Sport: ALEXANDR M. SHAKHLAY
Institute of Tourism: LIUDMILA V. SAKUN
Shachlay Faculty of Mass Sports: ANATOLIY
G. DAVYDOVSKY

BELARUSIAN STATE UNIVERSITY OF TRANSPORT

246653 Gomel, ul. Kirova 34
Telephone: (232) 95-20-96
Founded 1953
Rector: Prof. VENIAMIN I. SENKO
First Pro-Rector and Pro-Rector for Academic
Affairs: Prof. VIKTOR YA. NEGREY
Pro-Rector for Academic Affairs: SERGEY I.
SUKHOPAROV
Pro-Rector for Administrative Affairs:
VALERIY V. BABIY
Pro-Rector for Economics: GALINA M.
BYCHKOVA
Pro-Rector for Education: GALINA M. CHAYAN-
KOVA
Pro-Rector for Research: Prof. KONSTANTIN A.
BOCHKOV
Library of 650,000 vols
Number of teachers: 358
Number of students: 3,390
Publication: *Vestnik BelGUTa: Nauka i
Transport* (4 a year)

DEANS

Faculty of Continuing Education: VLADIMIR
V. PIGUNOV
Faculty of Electrical Engineering: ALEKSANDR
V. GRAPOV
Faculty of Engineering: VIKTOR A. BERBILO
Faculty of Foreign Students: IRINA G. PASHKO
Faculty of Humanities and Economics: YURI
P. LYCH
Faculty of Industrial and Civil Construction:
ANATOLIY G. TASHNIKOV
Faculty of Mechanical Engineering: YURI G.
SAMODUM
Faculty of Military Transportation: Col VLA-
DIMIR V. LEVTRINSKIY
Faculty of Transport Management: NIKOLAY
P. BERLIN
Faculty of Vocational Guidance and Pre-
University Training: OLEG P. GORAEV

BELARUSIAN TRADE AND ECONOMIC UNIVERSITY OF CONSUMER CO-OPERATIVES

246029 Gomel, pr. Oktyabrya 50
Telephone: (232) 78-17-07
Fax: (232) 47-80-68
E-mail: priem@bteu.by
Internet: www.bteu.by
Founded 1964
Rector: Doc. ANNA A. NAUMCHIK
First Pro-Rector: Doc. PAVEL G. PONOMAR-
ENKO
Pro-Rectors for Academic Affairs: Doc. VASI-
LIY V. BOGUSH, Doc. LYUBOMIR M. SKORIK
Pro-Rector for Academic Research: Doc.
LYUDMILA V. MISINKOVA
Pro-Rector for Administration: Dr VASILIY D.
POTAPOV
Pro-Rector for Education and Information
Technology: Dr ALEKSANDR I. KAPSHTYK

Pro-Rector for Scientific Research: Dr GEOR-
GIY S. MITYURICH
Library of 500,000 vols
Number of teachers: 330
Number of students: 8,450

DEANS

Faculty of Accounting and Finance: VALEN-
TINA A. ASTAFEVA
Faculty of Commerce: KLAVDIYA I. LOKTEVA
Faculty of Economics and Management:
TATYANA V. EMELYANOVA
External Faculty of Commerce and Manage-
ment: GALINA S. TURILKINA
External Faculty of Economics and Manage-
ment: ANDREY A. KOLESNIKOV

BREST STATE TECHNICAL UNIVERSITY

224017 Brest, vul. Moskovskaya 267
Telephone: (162) 42-33-93
Fax: (162) 42-21-27
E-mail: canc@bstu.by
Internet: www.bstu.by
Founded 1966
Faculties of civil engineering (civil engineering, production of building elements and
structures, construction of roads and transport facilities, architecture), economics
(accounting, analysis, audit; world economy
and international economic relations; marketing), electronic and mechanical engineering (technology, equipment and automation
of machine-building; automatic data processing systems; computers, systems and networks), extramural studies and preparatory
training, water supply systems and soil
conservation (water supply and sewage disposal systems, soil conservation and water
resources management)
Rector: Prof. Dr P. S. POJTA
Library of 395,000 vols
Number of teachers: 499
Number of students: 6,438

BREST STATE UNIVERSITY 'A. S. PUSHKIN'

224016 Brest, bul. Kosmonavtov 21
Telephone: (162) 23-33-40
Fax: (162) 23-09-96
E-mail: box@brsu.brest.by
Internet: www.brsu.brest.by
Founded 1945
Rector: Prof. Dr MECHISLAV E. CHESNOVSKIY
First Pro-Rector: Prof. KONSTANTIN K. KRA-
SOVSKIY
Pro-Rector for Academic Affairs: Prof. STANI-
SLAV G. RACHEVSKIY
Pro-Rector for Admin. and Managerial
Affairs: SERGEY V. KLIMUK
Pro-Rector for Educational Affairs: Prof. Dr
ANNA N. SENDER
Pro-Rector for Educational and Social
Affairs: Asst Prof. LIUDMILA A. GODUYKO
Pro-Rector for Scientific Affairs and Econom-
ics: Asst Prof. SERGEY A. MARZAN

DEANS

Faculty of Biology: NATALIA M. GOLUB
Faculty of Foreign Languages: SERGEY N.
SIEVIERIN
Faculty of Geography: VLADIMIR I. BOYKO
Faculty of History: NATALYA P. GALIMOVA
Faculty of Law: YELENA N. GRIGOROVICH
Faculty of Mathematics: ALEXANDER Y.
BUDKO
Faculty of Philology: OLGA A. FIELKINA
Faculty of Physical Education: NIKOLAY I.
PRISTUPA
Faculty of Physics: IGOR I. MAKOYED
Faculty of Pre-School Education: LARISA D.
GUSAROVA

Faculty of Pre-University Education: YELENA
I. MIRSKAYA
Faculty of Psychology and Pedagogy: ALEK-
SANDER I. OSTAPUK
Faculty of Social Sciences and Pedagogics:
ANATOLIY N. GIERASIEVICH

GOMEL STATE MEDICAL UNIVERSITY

224016 Gomel, vul. Lante 5
Telephone: (232) 74-41-21
Fax: (232) 74-98-31
E-mail: medinst@mail.gomel.by
Internet: www.medinstitut.gomel.by
Founded 1990
Public control
Languages of instruction: Russian, Belaru-
sian, English
Rector: Prof. ANATOLY N. LYZIKOV
Vice-Rector for Academic Work: Doc. ALEX-
ANDR A. KOZLOVSKY
Vice-Rector for Admin. and Economic Work:
Prof. SERGEY N. GLUSHKOV
Vice-Rector for Education and Ideological
Work: Prof. VICTOR M. UMANETS
Vice-Rector for Medical Work: Prof. VLADIMIR
V. ANICHKIN
Vice-Rector for Scientific Work: Prof. VALERY
P. SITNIKOV
Librarian: SVETLANA M. POLADIEVA
Library of 250,600 vols, 28,400 periodicals
Number of teachers: 490
Number of students: 3,000
Publication: *Problems of Health and Ecology*

DEANS

Faculty of General Medicine: Doc. VYACHE-
SLAV A. PODOLYAKO
Faculty of General Medicine for Overseas
Students: Doc. SVETLANA A. HODULEVA
Faculty of Medical Diagnostics: Doc. ANDREY
L. KALININ
Faculty of Pre-University Education: Doc.
MIHAIL E. ABRAMENKO

PAVEL SUKHOI STATE TECHNICAL UNIVERSITY OF GOMEL

246746 Gomel, pr. Oktyabrya 48
Telephone: (232) 48-16-00
Fax: (232) 47-91-65
E-mail: rector@gstu.gomel.by
Internet: www.gstu.gomel.by
Founded 1981
Academic year: September to August
Rector: SERGEI I. TIMOSHIN
First Vice-Rector: OLEG D. ASENCHIK
Vice-Rector for Construction: VICTOR A.
SOLOMADZE
Vice-Rector for Education and Educative
Work: VIKTOR V. KIRIENKO
Vice-Rector for Education and Instruction:
ALEKSANDER V. SYCHEV
Vice-Rector for Maintenance Admin.: GENNA-
DII I. AVSEIKOV
Vice-Rector for Research: ANDREI A. BOIKA
Library of 546,011 vols
Number of teachers: 397
Number of students: 8,340

DEANS

Faculty of Automation and Information Sys-
tems: GEORGIY I. SELIVESTROV
Faculty of External Studies: PETR V. LYCHEV
Faculty of Humanities and Economics: RAISA
I. GROMYKO
Faculty of Machine Building: ALEKSEY T.
BELSKY
Faculty of Mechanical Engineering and
Technology: IGOR B. ODARCHENKO
Faculty of Power Engineering: MIKHAIL N.
NOVIKOV

Faculty of Pre-University Training: SERGEY A. YURIS

Faculty of Upgrading and Retraining: YURIY N. KOLESNIK

GOMEL STATE UNIVERSITY 'F. SKORINA'

246699 Gomel, Sovetskaya vul. 104

Telephone: (232) 56-31-13

Fax: (232) 57-81-11

E-mail: selkin@gsu.unibel.by

Internet: www.gsu.unibel.by

Founded 1969

State control

Languages of instruction: Russian, Belarusan

Academic year: September to July

Faculties of biology, economics, foreign languages, geology and geography, history, law, mathematics, philology, physical training, physics, psychology and preparatory training; France–Belarus Institute of Management, Institute of Qualification Improvement

Rector: Prof. Dr MIKHAIL V. SELKIN

First Pro-Rector: ALEKSANDR P. KARMAZIN

Library: 1m. vols

Number of teachers: 570

Number of students: 5,843

Publications: *Belarusan Language*, *Problems in Algebra*, *University News* (in Russian, Belarusan and English, 6 a year).

GRODNO STATE AGRARIAN UNIVERSITY

230008 Grodno, vul. Tereshkovoy 28

Telephone: (152) 77-01-68

Fax: (152) 72-13-65

E-mail: ggay@uni-agro.grodno.by

Internet: www.uni.agro-grodno.com

Founded 1951

State control

Rector: VITOLD K. PESTIS

First Pro-Rector: ALEKSANDR A. DUDUK

Pro-Rector for Administrative Affairs: VALERIY N. TRIKUTS

Pro-Rector for Education: FEDOR N. LEONOV

Pro-Rector for Research: ALEKSANDR V. GLAZ

Librarian: NADEZHDA P. KHODOTCHUK

Library of 300,000 vols

Number of teachers: 209

Number of students: 3,842

DEANS

Faculty of Agronomy: FEDOR F. SEDLYAR

Faculty of Economics: IOSIF I. DEGTYAREVICH

Faculty of Plant Protection: GALINA A. ZEZYU-LINA

Faculty of Pre-University Training: REGINA K. YANKELEVICH

Faculty of Qualifications Improvement and Retraining of Agricultural Personnel: OLEG E. MOLYAVKO (Pro-Rector)

Faculty of Veterinary Medicine: MIKHAIL A. KAVRUS

Faculty of Zooengineering: EVGENIY A. DOBRUK

GRODNO STATE MEDICAL UNIVERSITY

230015 Grodno, vul. Gorkogo 80

Telephone: (152) 233-03-65

Fax: (152) 233-53-41

E-mail: mailbox@grsmu.by

Internet: www.grsmu.by

Founded 1958

State control

Rector: PETR V. GARELIK

First Pro-Rector: IGOR G. ZHUK

Pro-Rector for Admin. and Economic Affairs: VLADIMIR P. KUZMICH

Pro-Rector for Commercial Activities and Int. Relations: VIKTOR V. ZINCHUK

Pro-Rector for Information and Pedagogical Affairs: VITALY V. VOROBYOV

Pro-Rector for Medical Affairs: SERGEY M. SMOTRIN

Pro-Rector for Research: SERGEY M. ZIMATKIN

DEANS

Faculty of Foreign Students: IGOR P. BOGDA-NOVICH

Faculty of General Medicine: GENNADIY G. MARMYSH

Faculty of Medical Nurses with Higher Education: EVGENY M. TISCHENKO

Faculty of Medical Psychology: TATYANA M. SHAMOVA

Faculty of Paediatrics: NELLA S. PARAMONOVA

GRODNO STATE UNIVERSITY 'YANKA KUPALA'

230023 Grodno, vul. Ozheshko 22

Telephone: (152) 73-19-00

Fax: (152) 73-19-10

E-mail: mail@grsu.by

Internet: www.grsu.by

Founded 1940

State control

Academic year: September to June

Rector: Prof. Dr hab. CHOODAWAT

First Vice-Rector: Assoc. Prof. IVAN BURLYKA

Vice-Rector for Academic Affairs and Quality Management: Assoc. Dr YURY BEITIUK

Vice-Rector for Admin. and Economic Devt: Assoc. Dr VASIL SIANKO

Vice-Rector for Infrastructure Devt and Resources: Dr YURY HNIAZDOUSKI

Vice-Rector for Research and Innovations: Prof. HENADZ KHATSKEVICH

Vice-Rector for Social Issues: Assoc. Prof. SVIATLANA AHIJAVETS

Library of 716,130 vols

Number of teachers: 1,193

Number of students: 17,343

Publications: *Vestnik GrGU—Economics* (2 a year), *Vestnik GrGU—History, Philosophy, Political Science, Sociology* (3 a year), *Vestnik GrGU—Law* (4 a year), *Vestnik GrGU—Mathematics, Physics, Computer Science, Computer Engineering, Biology* (3 a year), *Vestnik GrGU—Philology, Pedagogics, Psychology* (3 a year)

DEANS

Faculty of Arts: Assoc. Prof. RAISA LEVINA

Faculty of Biology and Ecology: Associ. Prof. Dr hab. VASILI BURDZ

Faculty of Economics and Management: Assoc. Prof. TCHON LI

Faculty of Engineering and Transportation: Assoc. Prof. ULADIMIR BARSUKOU

Faculty of History and Sociology: Assoc. Prof. EDMUND YARMUSIK

Faculty of Humanities: Dr IOSIF I. VELENTO

Faculty of Law: Assoc. Prof. IRYNA BELOVA

Faculty of Mathematics: Dr VALERY K. BOIKO

Faculty of Pedagogy: Prof. VIKTAR TARANTSEI

Faculty of Philology: Assoc. Prof. VALERY VARANOVICH

Faculty of Physical Training: Assoc. Prof. ANDREI I. NAVOICHIK

Faculty of Physics and Engineering: Assoc. Prof. HENADZ HACHKO

Faculty of Psychology: Prof. Dr hab. ULADI-SLAU BARKOU

Faculty of Tourism and Service: Assoc. Prof. IOSIF VELENTA

INTERNATIONAL SAKHAROV ENVIRONMENTAL UNIVERSITY

220009 Minsk, vul. Dolgobrodskaya 23

Telephone: (17) 230-69-98

Fax: (17) 230-68-88

E-mail: rector@iseu.by

Internet: www.iseu.by

Founded 1992

State control

Rector: Prof. SEMYON P. KUNDAS

Library of 150,000 vols

Number of teachers: 105

Number of students: 600

DEANS

Faculty of Advanced Training and Retraining: IVAN I. MATVEENKO

Faculty of Environmental Medicine: Asst Prof. MIKHAIL S. MAROZIK

Faculty of Environmental Monitoring: Prof. NIKOLAY S. LESHENYUK

Faculty of Pre-University Training: Asst Prof. LYUDMILA M. SHEIKO

MINSK STATE LINGUISTIC UNIVERSITY

220034 Minsk, vul. Zakharova 21

Telephone: (17) 284-80-67

Fax: (17) 236-75-04

E-mail: info@mslu.by

Internet: www.mslu.by

Founded 1948

Schools of English, French, German, intercultural communication, retraining and teacher devt, Russian as a foreign language, Spanish, translation and interpreting

Rector: NATALYA P. BARANOVA

Library: 1m. vols and periodicals

Number of teachers: 737

Number of students: 7,659

Publications: *Foreign Languages in the Republic of Belarus* (4 a year), *Methodology of Teaching Foreign Languages* (1 a year), *Studies in Romanic and Germanic Languages* (1 a year), *Vestnik of MSLU: History, Philosophy and Economics* (1 a year), *Vestnik of MSLU: Phylology and Linguistics* (2 a year), *Vestnik of MSLU: Psychology, Didactics and Methods of Foreign Language Teaching* (1 a year).

MOGILEV STATE FOODSTUFFS UNIVERSITY

212027 Mogilev, pr. Shmidta 3

Telephone: (22) 244-03-63

Fax: (22) 244-00-11

E-mail: info@mgup.net

Internet: www.mgup.net

Founded 1973

State control

Rector: Prof. VYACHESLAV SHARSHUNOV

Library of 500,000 vols

Number of teachers: 250

Number of students: 5,530

DEANS

Faculty of Chemical Technology: T. I. PISKUN

Faculty of Economics: NADEZHDA V. ABRAMO-VICH

Faculty of External Studies: A. V. OBOTUROV

Faculty of Mechanical Engineering: VALERIY P. CHIRKIN

Faculty of Pre-University Training: ELENA N. ANDREYCHIKOVA

Faculty of Technology: LIDIYA A. KASYANOVA

MOGILEV STATE UNIVERSITY 'A. A. KULESHOV'

220009 Minsk, vul. Dolgobrodskaya 23

Telephone: (17) 230-69-98

Fax: (17) 230-68-88

E-mail: rector@iseu.by

Internet: msu.mogilev.by

Founded 1913; present name and status 1997
Rector: KONSTANTIN M. BONDARENKO
First Pro-Rector: MIKHAIL I. VISHNEVSKIY
Pro-Rector for Academic Affairs: VLADIMIR I. POPOV
Pro-Rector for Research: NIKOLAY P. BUZUK
Library of 500,000 vols
Number of teachers: 450
Number of students: 7,600

POLOTSK STATE UNIVERSITY

211440 Novopolotsk, vul. Blokhina 29
Telephone: (214) 53-20-12
Fax: (214) 53-42-63
E-mail: post@psu.by
Internet: www.psu.by
Founded 1968
State control
Rector: DMITRIY N. LAZOVSKIY
First Pro-Rector: NATALYA N. BELORUSOVA
Pro-Rector for Academic Affairs: VASILIY V. BULAKH
Pro-Rector for Admin. Affairs: VLADIMIR P. STRIZHAK
Pro-Rector for Education and Social Affairs: VIKENTIY G. TSYGANOK
Pro-Rector for the Environment: VLADIMIR K. LIPSKIY
Pro-Rector for Information Systems: DMITRIY O. GLUKHOV
Pro-Rector for Innovation: NIKOLAY N. POPOK
Pro-Rector for Int. Affairs: SERGEY V. PESHKUN
Pro-Rector for Maintenance and Construction: VILEN S. LEVIN
Pro-Rector for Research: FEDOR I. PANTALEENKO
Library of 427,000 vols
Number of teachers: 500
Number of students: 6,000

VITEBSK STATE ORDER OF PEOPLES' FRIENDSHIP MEDICAL UNIVERSITY

210023 Vitebsk, pr. Frunze 27
Telephone: (212) 21-04-33
Fax: (212) 37-21-07
E-mail: admin@vgmu.vitebsk.by
Internet: www.vgmu.vitebsk.by
Founded 1934
State control
Academic year: September to July
Languages of instruction: Russian, English
Rector: Prof. DEIKALO VALERY PETROVICH
Vice-Rector for Admin. Affairs: SHCHERBINSKAYA NELYA MIHAILOVNA
Vice-Rector for Clinical and Pharmaceutical Affairs: KRISHTOPOV LEONID EGOROVICH
Vice-Rector for Educational Work and Int. Affairs: Prof. Dr KONEVALOVA NATALIA YURIEVNA
Vice-Rector for Pedagogical and Ideological Affairs: SYRODOYEVA OLGA ARKADIEVNA
Dir of Library: BORZENKOVA ELENA IVANOVNA
Library: 1.5m. vols
Number of teachers: 538
Number of students: 6,259
Publications: *Herald* (4 a year), *Immunopathology, Allergology, Infectology* (4 a year), *Maternity and Child Protection* (4 a year), *Pharmacy News* (4 a year), *Surgery News* (4 a year)
VSMU also has a clinic and stomatological polyclinic

DEANS

Faculty for Mastering Skills of Specialists and Collective of Employees Re-training: Prof. RADETSKAYA LYUDMILA YEUGENIEVNA
Faculty of Overseas Students Training: Assoc. Prof. PRISTUPA VADIM VITALIEVICH

Faculty of Pedagogics and Psychology: Prof. KUNTSEVICH ZINAIDA STEPANOVNA
Faculty of Professional Orientation and Preparatory Training: Doc. PASHKOV ALEXANDER ALEXANDROVICH
Medical Faculty: Prof. Dr SEMENOV VALERIY MIHAILOVICH
Pharmaceutical Faculty: Prof. GURINA NATALYA SERGEYEVNA
Stomatological Faculty: Doc. KABANOVA SVETLANA ALEKSEYEVNA

VITEBSK STATE TECHNOLOGICAL UNIVERSITY

210035 Vitebsk, Moskovskiy pr. 72
Telephone: (212) 27-50-26
Fax: (212) 27-74-01
E-mail: vstu@vstu.vitebsk.by
Internet: www.vstu.vitebsk.by
Founded 1959
State control
Rector: Prof. VALERIY S. BASHMETOV
First Pro-Rector: IVAN A. MOSKALEV
Pro-Rector for Admin. Affairs: ALEKSEY N. SHUT
Pro-Rector for Education: ANATOLIY A. BELOV
Pro-Rector for Research: SERGEY M. BASHMETOV
Pro-Rector for Social and Economic Affairs and Construction: BORIS E. RYKLIN
Library of 300,000 vols
Number of teachers: 293
Number of students: 5,500 (incl. 2,500 external)

DEANS

Faculty of Arts and Technology: GALINA V. KAZARNOVSKAYA
Faculty of Civil Engineering and Technology: VITALIY K. SMELKOV
Faculty of Economics: VLADIMIR P. SHARSTNEV
Faculty of External Studies: ANATOLIY M. TIMOFEEV
Faculty of Mechanical Engineering and Technology: VALERIY I. OLSHANSKIY
Faculty of Pre-University Training and Vocational Guidance: ALEKSANDR P. SUVOROV
Faculty of Qualifications Improvement: IGOR M. KONTOROVICH

VITEBSK STATE UNIVERSITY 'P. M. MASHEROV'

210038 Vitebsk, Moskovskiy pr. 33
Telephone: (212) 21-58-66
E-mail: vsu@vsu.by
Internet: www.vsu.by
Founded 1910 as Teacher Training Institute; present name and status 1955
State control
Rector: Prof. ARKADIY V. RUSETSKIY
First Pro-Rector: IOSIF E. ANDRUSHKEVICH
Pro-Rector for Research: GENNADY I. MIKHASYOV
Pro-Rector for Studies: TATYANA G. ALEYNIKOVA
Publications: *departmental publications, My i Chas, Vestnik VGU*

DEANS

Faculty of Belarusian Philology and Culture: VIKTOR I. NESTOROVICH
Faculty of Biology: VITALIY YA. KUZMENKO
Faculty of Graphic Arts: VALENTIN P. KLIMOVICH
Faculty of History: VENIAMIN A. KOSMACH
Faculty of Law: VYACHESLAV I. PUSHKIN
Faculty of Mathematics: NIKOLAY E. BOLSHAKOV
Faculty of Pedagogy: ANATOLIY I. MURASHKIN
Faculty of Philology: LEONID M. VARDOMATSKIY
Faculty of Physics: ILLARION V. GALUZO

Faculty of Social Pedagogy and Psychology: SERGEY A. MOTOROV

Other Institutes of Higher Education

Academy of the Ministry of Internal Affairs: 220771 Minsk, pr. Pobeditelei 6; tel. (17) 284-31-15; fax (17) 288-27-58; e-mail info@amia.unibel.by; internet amia.nsys.by; f. 1958; faculties of distance education, forensic medicine, investigation, military studies, officer training and professional training; Rector VITALIY I. APARASEVICH.

Academy of Public Administration of the President of the Republic of Belarus: 220007 Minsk, vul. Moskovskaya 17; tel. and fax (17) 222-82-05; e-mail rector@pacademy.edu.by; internet www.pacademy.edu.by; f. 1991 as instn of higher and advanced education for the training of public admin. personnel, acquired presidential institution status 1995; 3 constituent institutes: Institute of Civil Service, Institute of Public Admin., Institute of Sr Management Personnel; library: 200,000 vols; Rector PETR KUKHARCHYK; publ. *Issues of Management.*

Belarusian Medical Academy of Postgraduate Education: 220013 Minsk, vul. P. Brovki 3; tel. and fax (17) 232-25-83; e-mail rector@belmapo.edu.by; internet www.belmapo.edu.by; f. 1931; faculties of dentistry, paediatrics, public health and protection, surgery and therapy; attached Laboratory of Scientific Research; 16,000 students; Rector Prof. GENNADIY Y. KHULUP; Librarian ANNA A. KOLBASKO.

Belarus State Academy of Arts: 220012 Minsk, pr. Nezavisimosti 81; tel. (17) 232-15-42; fax (17) 232-20-41; e-mail belam@user.unibel.by; internet belam.by.com; f. 1945; faculties of decorative-applied arts, fine arts and design and theatre; postgraduate courses in theatre art, television, cinema and visual arts, fine and decorative-applied arts and architecture, theory of arts, technical aesthetics and design; library: 83,538 vols; Rector Prof. RICHARD B. SMOLSKIY.

Belarusian State Academy of Music: 220030 Minsk, Internatsionalnaya vul. 30; tel. (17) 227-49-42; fax (17) 206-55-01; e-mail bgam@tut.by; internet www.bgam.edu.by; f. 1932; courses: piano, orchestral and folk instruments, singing, composition, pedagogics, musicology, ethnomusicology, choir and symphony conducting; library: 211,702 vols; 307 teachers; 979 students; Rector M. A. KOZINETS.

Belarus State Agricultural Academy: 213410 Mogilev raion, Gorki, vul. Michurina 5; tel. and fax (2233) 5-14-20; internet www.belagro.org.by; f. 1840; faculties of accounting, agribusiness and law, agroecology, agronomy, animal husbandry, economics, mechanization, land management and hydromelioration; library: 1.0m. vols; 800 teachers; 11,000 students; Rector Prof. ALEKSANDR R. TSYGANOV; publ. collection of research works (1 a year).

Minsk Institute of Management: 220102 Minsk, vul. Lazo 12; tel. (17) 242-97-97; fax (17) 243-67-61; e-mail mik@mikby.com; internet www.miu.by; f. 1991; faculties of accounting and finance, economics and law; Rector Dr NIKOLAY V. SUSHA.

Minsk State Higher Education College of Civil Aviation: 220096 Minsk, vul. Uborevitcha 17; tel. (17) 201-02-81; fax (17) 241-66-32; e-mail aviakollege@ivcavia.com; internet www.avia.by/mgvak_en.shtml; f. 1974; trains specialists in aircraft and engine technical exploitation, lifting and transportation, operation of building and road machinery, technical exploitation of aviation technology (electrical devices and light technical equipment), information technology systems and networks, air traffic control and operation; Head ALEXANDER I. NAUMENKO.

Vitebsk State Academy of Veterinary Medicine: 210026 Vitebsk, vul. 1-ya Dovatora 7/11; tel. (212) 37-20-44; fax (212) 37-02-84; e-mail vet@lib.belpak.vitebsk.by; f. 1924; faculties of correspondence studies, specialist upgrading, veterinary medicine and zooengineering; library: 340,000 vols; 348 teachers; 3,109 students; Rector A. I. YATUSEVICH.

BELGIUM

The Higher Education System

The higher education system in Belgium reflects divisions of language, with separate ministries of education for the Dutch (or Flemish), French (Walloon) and German-speaking communities. This division was enshrined in legislation passed in 1963, under which French was established as the medium of instruction in Wallonia, Flemish in Flanders and German in the East-Cantons (Ostkantone). Brussels, the capital, is officially bilingual (French and Flemish). Both public and private universities are funded through their respective communities, but Roman Catholic institutions are regarded as 'free' and account for about 60% of Belgium's students. In 2007/08 a total of 64,372 students were enrolled in universities. Non-university institutions of higher education provide arts education, technical training and teacher training; in 2007/08 a total of 104,174 students were enrolled in such institutions. A national study fund provides grants where necessary and almost 20% of students receive scholarships.

The requirement for university entrance is the Certificat d'Enseignement Secondaire or Diploma Secundair Onderwijs. Hogescholen (see below) are open to all applicants holding the required certificates or wishing to attend courses as a 'free' student. The latter category of students is only eligible for certificates, not diplomas, after completing part of these studies. Generally, there are no entrance examinations or selective admission systems in use. However, in specific areas like nautical sciences and some art courses (audio-visual arts, music and dance), entrance examinations are compulsory.

The French community controls nine university-level institutions, while the Flemish community controls seven. Courses are divided into a period of general preparation followed by a period of specialization, each lasting two to three years. Belgium began implementing the Bologna Process in the 2004/05 academic year with reforms being carried out by all three communities. The traditional systems were gradually replaced and Bachelors and Masters degrees were fully implemented by 2008/2009. Most universities use ECTS and issue the Diploma Supplement for free The Bachelors replaces a number of different degrees, notably one-cycle programmes of up to three years which resulted in either Gegradueerde (Flemish) or Graduat (Walloon), and two-cycle programmes of four or more years consisting of Candidat and Licencié (Walloon) or Kandidaat and Licentiaat (Flemish). The first part of the two-cycle degree (Candidat/Kandidaat) provided a general education, and lasted two years, whilst the second part (Licencié/Licentiaat) provided more specialized training over two or more years. The Masters is broadly equivalent to the old degrees of complementary education, the Gediplomeerde in de Aanvullende Studiën (Flemish) and Diplômé d'Etudes Complémentaires (Walloon), and degrees of advanced studies, Diplômé d'Etudes Approfondies (Walloon) and Diploma van Grondige Studies (Flemish). The final, and highest, level of academic degree is the Doctorate, which has no time limit but cannot be awarded until at least two years after completion of the second-cycle degree (now Bachelors).

Previously, non-university post-secondary education was provided by Hautes Ecoles (in Wallonia), Hogescholen (in Flanders) and a number of specialist colleges of technology, agriculture, para-medical studies, economics, social studies and teacher training. In Walloon-controlled institutions, courses were divided into eight subject categories, leading either to a Graduat after a 'short' course of three years or a Licencié after a 'long' course of four years. In 2004/2005 this system changed in line with the Bologna model. Hence, these Haute Ecoles now offer professional Bachelor degrees (180 ECTS) and Masters degrees (60 to 120 ECTS) in conjunction with universities. Furthermore, students can progress to a Diplôme de Spécialisation (DS) of 60 ECTS after the professional Bachelor degree; this is particularly relevant for paramedical subjects.

Programmes in the Hogescholen were also divided into 'long/short' courses of one or two cycles, but have now changed to the Bologna system. Hogescholen can offer professional Bachelor degrees (180 ECTS) and Masters degree programmes in association with a university. Professional Bachelor degrees do not provide direct entry to a Masters degree programme; candidates have to complete a bridging programme of about 45 to 90 ECTS.

Technical and vocational training is available either through an employer or an institution and is divided into three categories: apprenticeship contract; industrial apprenticeship contract and part-time work and/or training.

The Joint Accreditation Body of the Netherlands and Flanders (NVAO) works within the framework of the European Consortium for Accreditation to mutually recognize the accreditation decisions of its members.

Regulatory and Representative Bodies

GOVERNMENT

Ministry of Flanders and the Dutch-speaking Community, Department of Work, Education and Training: Hendrik Consciencegebouw, Koning Albert II-laan 15, 1210 Brussels; tel. (2) 553-86-11; fax (2) 553-95-25; internet www.ond.vlaanderen.be; Min. FRANK VANDENBROUCKE.

Ministry of the French-speaking Community, Office for Higher Education, Scientific Research and International Relations: Rue Belliard 9–13, 1040 Brussels; tel. (2) 213-35-11; fax (2) 213-35-23; Min. MARIE-DOMINIQUE SIMONET.

Ministry of the German-speaking Community, Department of Education and Training: Gospertstr. 1, 4700 Eupen; tel. (8) 759-64-81; fax (8) 755-64-75; e-mail unterricht@dgov.be; Min. OLIVER PAASCH.

ACCREDITATION

ENIC/NARIC Belgium (French Community): NARIC of the Belgian French Community, Direction générale de l'enseignement non obligatoire et de la recherche scientifique, Rue A. Lavallée 1, 1080 Brussels; tel. (2) 690-87-03; fax (2) 690-87-60; e-mail infosup@cfwb.be; internet www.enseignement.be/infosup; Dir CHANTAL KAUFMANN.

NARIC Belgium (Flanders): NARIC-Flanders, Ministry of Education and Training, Hendrik Consciencegebouw Toren A 7, Koning Albert II-laan 15, 1210 Brussels; tel. (2) 553-98-19; fax (2) 553-98-45; e-mail naric@vlaanderen.be; Policy Maker ERWIN MALFROY.

REGIONAL AND COMMUNITY BODIES

Conseil des Recteurs des Universités Francophones de Belgique (CReF) (Rectors' Conference of the French-speaking Community of Belgium): 5 rue d'Egmont, 1000 Brussels; tel. (2) 504-93-00; fax (2) 514-93-43; e-mail kokkelkoren@cref.be; internet www.cref.be; f. 1990 by rectors of French-speaking Belgian univs, to address issues of higher education and scientific research; 9 mems; Pres. PHILIPPE VINCKE.

Conseil général des Hautes Ecoles (Regional Council of Hautes Ecoles): 1 rue Adolphe Lavallée, 1080 Brussels; tel. (2) 690-88-45; fax (2) 690-88-46; e-mail jean-pierre.postula@cfwb.be; internet www.enseignement.be; Pres. MICHEL TORDOIR; Sec. JEAN-PIERRE POSTULA.

Conseil Interuniversitaire de la Communauté française de Belgique (CIUF) (Interuniversity Council of the French-speaking Community in Belgium): Rue d'Egmont 5, 1000 Brussels; tel. (2) 504-92-91; fax (2) 502-27-68; e-mail info@ciuf.be; internet www.ciuf.be; f. 2003; represents 9 univs. and univ.-level instns in the French-speaking community; advises on education policy; promotes cooperation between univs and univ.-level instns; Pres. BERNARD RENTIER.

Vlaamse hogescholenraad (VLHORA) (Flemish Council for Non-university Higher Education): Wolvengracht 38/2, 1000 Brussels; tel. (2) 211-41-90; fax (2) 211-41-99; internet www.vlhora.be; f. 1996, awarded statute of public utility institution by decree in 1998; gives advice to the Flemish authorities on all policy aspects regarding college education, scientific project research, social services and the practice of the arts; organizes and stimulates consultation between the institutions on all issues related to the univ. colleges (hogescholen); Sec.-Gen. LUC VAN DE VELDE.

Vlaamse Interuniversitaire Raad (VLIR) (Flemish Interuniversity Council): Ravensteingalerij 27, bus 6, 1000 Brussels; tel. (2) 792-55-00; fax (2) 211-41-99; e-mail administratie@vlir.be; internet www.vlir.be; f. 1976; autonomous body financed by univs; advises on and presents proposals to minister with regard to univ. education; research activities; Sec.-Gen. ROSETTE S' JEGERS.

Learned Societies

GENERAL

Académie Royale des Sciences, des Lettres et des Beaux-Arts de Belgique (Royal Academy of Science, Letters and Fine Arts of Belgium): Palais des Académies, 1 rue Ducale, 1000 Brussels; tel. (2) 550-22-11; fax (2) 550-22-05; e-mail arb@cfwb.be; internet www.arb.cfwb.be; f. 1772; divs of fine arts (Dir LÉON WUIDAR), letters and moral and political sciences (Dir MARC RICHELLE), science (Dir ALBERT GOLDBETER); 400 mems (200 ordinary, 200 assoc.); library of 520,000 vols; Pres. MARC RICHELLE; Permanent Sec. HERVE HASQUIN; Librarian CLAIRE PASCAUD; publs *Bulletin de la Classe des Beaux-Arts* (1 a year), *Bulletin de la Classe des Sciences* (1 a year), *Bulletin de la Classe des Sciences morales et politiques* (1 a year), *Mémoires de l'Académie Royale de Belgique* (5–10 a year), *Nouvelle Biographie Nationale* (every 2 years).

Académie Royale des Sciences d'Outre-Mer/Koninklijke Academie voor Overzeese Wetenschappen (Royal Academy for Overseas Sciences): 1 rue Defacqz, 1000 Brussels; tel. (2) 538-02-11; fax (2) 539-23-53; e-mail kaowarsom@skynet.be; internet www.kaowarsom.be; f. 1928; the promotion of scientific knowledge of overseas areas, especially those with particular devt problems; Permanent Sec. DANIELLE SWINNE; 127 mems (61 assoc. mems; publs *Actes Symposiums/Acta Symposia, Biographie belge d'Outre-Mer/Belgische Overzeese Biografie, Bulletin des Séances/Mededelingen der Zittingen, Mémoires/Verhandelingen, Recueils d'études historiques/Historische bijdragen.*

Koninklijke Vlaamse Academie van België voor Wetenschappen en Kunsten (Royal Flemish Academy of Belgium for Science and the Arts): Paleis der Academiën, Hertogsstraat 1, 1000 Brussels; tel. (2) 550-23-23; fax (2) 550-23-25; e-mail info@kvab.be; internet www.kvab.be; f. 1938; divs of arts (Dir V. NEES), humanities and social sciences (Dir C. STEEL), natural science (Dir J. VANDEKERCKHOVE); 289 mems (90 ordinary, 30 corresp., 19 hon., 150 foreign assoc.); library of 50,000 vols; Pres. M. EYSKENS; Permanent Sec. N. SCHAMP; publs *Academiae Analecta, Collectanea Biblica et Religiosa Antiqua, Collectanea Hellenistica, Collectanea Maritima, Fontes Historiae Artis Neer-*

landicae, Iuris Scripta Historica, Iusti Lipsi Epistolae, Memoirs.

Attached Institute:

Commission Royale d'Histoire/Koninklijke Commissie voor Geschiedenis (Royal Historical Commission): Palais des Académies, 1 rue Ducale, 1000 Brussels; e-mail academie .royaledebelgique@cfwb.be; internet www .kbr.be/crh-kcg; f. 1834; research, analysis and publ. of written sources concerning the history of Belgium; Pres. JEAN-MARIE DUVOSQUEL; Vice-Pres. GUSTAAF JANSSENS; Sec. C. BRUNEEL; Admin. Sec. J.-L. DE PAEPE; publs *Actes des Princes Belges* (irregular), *Bulletin* (4 a year), *Instruments de Travail* (irregular).

AGRICULTURE, FISHERIES AND VETERINARY SCIENCE

Fédération Wallonne de l'Agriculture: Chaussée de Namur 47, 5030 Gembloux; tel. and fax (81) 60-00-60; e-mail fwa@fwa.be; internet www.fwa.be; f. 1930; protects professional interests.

Attached Institute:

Committee of Agricultural Organizations in the EU (Copa): Rue de Trèves 61 1040 Brussels; tel. (2) 287-27-11; fax (2) 287-27-00; e-mail mail@copa-cogeca.eu; internet www.copa-cogeca.eu; f. 1958; 60 mem. orgs; Pres. PADRAIG WALSHE.

ARCHITECTURE AND TOWN PLANNING

Association Royale des Demeures Historiques de Belgique (Royal Association for Historic Buildings): 67 rue de Trèves, 1040 Brussels; tel. (2) 400-77-08; fax (2) 235-20-08; e-mail administration@ demeures-historiques.be; internet www .demeures-historiques.be; f. 1934; Pres. Prince ALEXANDRE DE MERODE; publ. *La Maison d'Hier et d'Aujourd'hui* (4 a year).

Fédération Royale des Sociétés d'Architectes de Belgique: 21 rue Ernest Allard, 1000 Brussels; tel. (2) 512-34-52; fax (2) 502-82-04; e-mail info@fab-arch.be; internet www .fab-arch.be; f. 1905; Sec.-Gen. JAN KETELAER.

Société Centrale d'Architecture de Belgique: Maison des Architectes, 21/4 rue Ernest Allard, 1000 Brussels; tel. (2) 511-34-92; fax (2) 511-16-72; e-mail info@scab.be; internet scab.archiscab.be; f. 1872; promotion of architecture and town planning; 180 mems; library: c. 1,500 vols; Pres. WENLI KAO; Sec. MAURICE HEISTERCAMP; publ. *Bulletin mensuel* (12 a year).

BIBLIOGRAPHY, LIBRARY SCIENCE AND MUSEOLOGY

Archives et Bibliothèques de Belgique: 4 blvd de l'Empereur, 1000 Brussels; tel. (2) 519-53-93; fax (2) 519-56-10; e-mail frankd@ kbr.be; f. 1907; a sub-committee of UNESCO, studies methods of standardization of bibliography; 350 mems; Pres. Dr FRANK DAELEMANS; publs *Archives et Bibliothèques de Belgique, Coll* (1 a year).

Association Professionnelle des Bibliothécaires et Documentalistes: Ave Rêve d'or 30, 7100 La Louvière; tel. (71) 61-43-35; fax (71) 61-16-34; f. 1975; 300 mems; Pres. LAURENCE BOULANGER; Vice-Pres. ALEXANDRE LEMAIRE, ANDRÉ MORUE; publ. *Bloc-Notes* (4 a year).

Service Belge des Echanges Internationaux/Belgische Dienst Internationale Ruil (Belgian International Exchange Service): Keizerslaan, 4 blvd de l'Empereur, 1000 Brussels; tel. (2) 519-53-94; fax (2) 519-54-04; e-mail nathael.istasse@kbr.be; f.

1889; information, documentation, exchange and transmission; Dir Dr NATHAËL ISTASSE; Librarian CHRISTOPHE JOUNIAUX; Librarian NATHALIE GEOFFROIT.

Vereniging van Antwerpse Bibliofielen (Antwerp Bibliophile Society): Museum Plantin-Moretus, Vrijdagmarkt 22, 2000 Antwerp; tel. (3) 221-14-67; fax (3) 221-14-71; e-mail pierre.meulepas@stad.antwerpen .be; internet www.boekgeschiedenis.be; f. 1877 to advance the study of the history of the printed book, particularly in Belgium and the Netherlands; fmrly Maatschappij der Antwerpsche Bibliophilen; 175 mems; Pres. Dr F. DE NAVE; Sec. PIERRE MEULEPAS; publ. *De Gulden Passer* (2 a year).

Vlaamse Museumvereniging (Flemish Museums Association): Plaatsnydersstraat 2, 2000 Antwerp; tel. (3) 216-03-60; fax (3) 257-08-61; e-mail info@museumvereniging .be; internet www.museumvereniging.be; f. 1962 to defend the interests of museums and museum personnel; 650 mems; Pres. S. THOMAS; publs *Museumkatern* (4 a year), *VMV Nieuwsbrief.*

ECONOMICS, LAW AND POLITICS

Société Royale d'Economie Politique de Belgique (Royal Belgian Society of Political Economy): c/o CIFOP, 1B ave Gén. Michel, 6000 Charleroi; tel. (71) 53-29-08; fax (71) 53-29-00; e-mail jf.husson@cifop.be; internet www.cifop.be/srepb2.html; f. 1855; for popularization and progress in political economy; 900 mems; Pres. ETIENNE DE CALLATAY; Sec.-Gen. JEAN-FRANÇOIS HUSSON; publ. *Comptes rendus des travaux* (5 or 6 a year).

Union Royale Belge pour les Pays d'Outre-Mer (UROME): 22 rue de Stassart, 1050 Brussels; internet www.urome.be; f. 1912; 28 mems; Chair. PIERRE ANDRÉ.

Vereniging voor Politieke Wetenschappen (Institute of Political Science): Van Evenstraat 2B, 3000 Leuven; tel. (16) 32-32-54; fax (16) 32-30-88; e-mail res.publica@soc .kuleuven.be; internet www.respublica.be; f. 1958; annual conf. jointly with Dutch Political Science Association; PhD seminars; 700 mems; Pres. Prof. Dr MARC HOOGHE; publs *Belgian Political Yearbook* (Dutch, English, French), *Res Publica* (Dutch, English, French, 4 a year), *Res Publica Library.*

FINE AND PERFORMING ARTS

Association Belge de Photographie et de Cinématographie: 1A rue de Sévigné, Anderlecht, Brussels; tel. (2) 640-51-30; fax (2) 515-76-77; e-mail jacques.guilmin@ hotmail.com; internet abpc066.hautetfort .com; f. 1874; 130 mems; Pres. J. PEETERS; publ. *Informations* (12 a year).

HISTORY, GEOGRAPHY AND ARCHAEOLOGY

Académie Royale d'Archéologie de Belgique/Koninklijke Academie voor Oudheidkunde van België (Royal Academy of Archaeology of Belgium): Palais des Académies, Rue Ducale 1, 1000 Brussels; e-mail info@acad.be; internet www.acad.be; f. 1842; to promote study of the art history of the Southern Low Countries, Liège and Belgium; 100 mems (60 ordinary, 40 corresp.); Pres. Prof. Dr JOOS VANDER AUWERA; Sec. Dr ALAIN JACOBS; publs *Bibliography of the History of the National Art* (online), *Revue Belge d'Archéologie et d'Histoire de l'Art/Belgisch Tijdschrift voor Oudheidkunde en Kunstgeschiedenis* (1 a year).

Association Egyptologique Reine Elisabeth/Egyptologisch Genootschap Kongingin Elisabeth: Parc du Cinquantenaire 10, 1000 Brussels; tel. (2) 741-73-64; fax (2)

733-77-35; e-mail aere.egke@kmkg-mrah.be;
f. 1923 to encourage Egyptological and
papyrological studies; 650 mems; library of
30,000 vols; Pres. Comte D'ARSCHOT; Dirs H.
DE MEULENAERE, A. MARTIN; publs *Bibliographie Papyrologique* (4 a year), *Chronique
d'Egypte* (2 a year).

**Belgische Vereniging voor Aardrijks-
kundige Studies/Société Belge d'Etudes
Géographiques** (Belgian Society for Geographical Studies): W. de Croylaan 42, 3001
Heverlee (Leuven); tel. (16) 32-24-27; fax (16)
32-29-80; f. 1931; Pres. J. CHARLIER; Sec. F.
WITLOX; centralizes and co-ordinates geographical research in Belgium; 150 mems;
publ. *BELGEO* (2 a year).

Institut Archéologique du Luxembourg:
13 rue des Martyrs, 6700 Arlon; tel. (63) 21-
28-49; fax (63) 22-47-65; e-mail info@ial.be;
internet www.ial.be; f. 1847; Luxembourgeois Museum covers prehistoric period,
Belgian-Roman period, Frankish period;
Musée Gaspar displays works by Jean-Marie
Gaspar and local art since the 16th century;
500 mems; library of 25,000 vols; Pres. LOUIS
LEJEUNE; publs *Annales, Bulletin* (4 a year).

Institut Archéologique Liégeois: Grand
Curtius, 13 quai de Maastricht, 4000 Liège;
tel. and fax (4) 232-98-60; f. 1850; studies of
history and archaeology and related sciences
in the Dist. of Liège; language of instruction:
French; 250 mems (200 ordinary, 50 corresp.); Pres. PIERRE GILISSEN; Sec. MAURICE
LORENZI; publ. *Bulletin* (1 a year).

**Institut Géographique National/Natio-
naal Geografisch Instituut:** Abbaye de la
Cambre 13, 1000 Brussels; tel. (2) 629-82-11;
fax (2) 629-82-12; e-mail sales@ngi.be;
internet www.ign.be; f. 1831; land surveying
and cartography; 267 mems; library: 15,000
maps; Dir-Gen. INGRID VANDEN BERGHE; publ.
Catalog (1 a year).

Société Archéologique de Namur: Hôtel
de Croix, 3 rue Saintraint, 5000 Namur; tel.
(81) 22-43-62; fax (81) 22-43-62; f. 1845;
museum and library; 450 mems; Pres. M.
PACCO; Sec. J. JEANNEART; publ. *Annales*.

**Société Belge d'Études Byzantines/Bel-
gisch Genootschap voor Byzantijnse
Studies:** 1 rue Ducale, 1000 Brussels; tel.
(9) 264-40-39; fax (9) 264-41-64; e-mail floris
.bernard@ugent.be; f. 1956; 57 mems; Pres.
Prof. ANNE TIHON; Sec. FLORIS BERNARD; publ.
Byzantion.

Société Royale Belge de Géographie:
Laboratoire de géographie humaine, Campus
de la Plaine ULB, accès 5, blvd du Triomphe,
CP 246, 1050 Brussels; tel. (2) 650-50-72; fax
(2) 650-50-92; e-mail srbg@ulb.ac.be; internet
www.srbg.be; f. 1876; 130 mems; library of
9,500 vols; Pres. Prof. Dr C. VANDERMOTTEN;
Sec.-Gen. Dr B. WAYENS; publ. *Belgeo* (4 a
year).

**Société Royale d'Archéologie de Brux-
elles:** c/o Université Libre de Bruxelles, CP
175, ave Franklin Roosevelt 50, 1050 Brussels; tel. (2) 650-24-86; fax (2) 650-24-50;
internet www.srab.be; f. 1887; sections for
archaeology proper, and the history of art;
other collns in Musées Royaux d'Art et
d'Histoire; library of 20,000 vols; 450 mems;
Pres. P. P. BONENFANTI; Sec.-Gen. A. VANRIE;
Librarian R. LAURENT; publs *Annales, Bulletins*.

**Société Royale de Numismatique de
Belgique:** Bibliothèque Royale de Belgique,
Cabinet des Médailles, 4 blvd de l'Empereur,
1000 Brussels; tel. (2) 639-00-00; fax (2) 466-
86-02; e-mail jm@bvdmc.com; f. 1841; promotion of numismatics through publications
and conferences; 277 mems (50 full, 15 hon.,
112 nat. corresp., 100 foreign corresp.); Pres.
JEAN-LUC DENGIS; Sec. JAN MOENS; publ.

*Revue Belge de Numismatique et de Sigillo-
graphie* (1 a year).

LANGUAGE AND LITERATURE

**Académie Royale de Langue et de Lit-
térature Françaises** (Royal Academy of
French Language and Literature): Palais
des Académies, 1 rue Ducale, 1000 Brussels;
tel. (2) 550-22-72; fax (2) 550-22-75; e-mail
alf@cfwb.be; internet www
.academiedelitterature.be; f. 1920; sections of
literature, philology; 30 Belgian mems; 10
foreign mems; Dir RAYMOND TROUSSON; Permanent Sec. ANDRÉ GOOSSE; publs *Annuaire,
Bulletin, Mémoires*.

Alliance Française: 26 rue de la Loi, 1040
Brussels; tel. (2) 502-46-49; fax (2) 736-47-00;
e-mail accueil@alliancefr.be; internet www
.alliancefr.be; offers courses and exams in
French language and culture and promotes
cultural exchange with France; attached
offices in Antwerp, Condroz-Meuse-Hesbaye,
Hainaut, Kortrijk, Limburg, Verviers and
Gand; library of 5,000 vols; Dir CLAIRE-LISE
DAUTRY.

**Association des Ecrivains Belges de
Langue Française** (Association of Belgian
Writers in the French Language): Maison
Camille Lemonnier-Maison des Ecrivains,
150 chaussée de Wavre, 1050 Brussels; tel.
(2) 512-29-68; internet www.ecrivainsbelges
.be; f. 1902; 500 mems; library of 11,000 vols;
awards prizes for essays, poetry and prose;
Camille Lemonnier museum; Pres. FRANCE
BASTIA; Vice-Pres. MARIE NICOLAÏ, EMILE
KESTEMAN; publ. *Nos Lettres* (10 a year).

British Council: Leopold Plaza, Rue du
Trône 108, 1050 Brussels; tel. (2) 227-08-40;
fax (2) 227-08-49; e-mail enquiries@
britishcouncil.be; internet www
.britishcouncil.be; offers courses and exams
in English language and British culture and
promotes cultural exchange with the UK;
also responsible for Luxembourg; Dir Dr
ROMAN STEPHAN.

Goethe-Institut: 58 Rue Belliard, 1040
Brussels; tel. (2) 230-39-70; fax (2) 230-77-
25; e-mail info@bruessel.goethe.org; internet
www.goethe.de/bruessel; offers courses and
examinations in German language and culture and promotes cultural exchange with
Germany; library of 20,000 vols, 90 periodicals; Dir BERTHOLD FRANKE.

Instituto Cervantes: 64 ave de Tervuren-
laan, 1040 Brussels; tel. (2) 737-01-90; fax (2)
735-44-04; e-mail cenbru@cervantes.es;
internet bruselas.cervantes.es; offers courses
and exams in Spanish language and culture
and promotes cultural exchange with Spain
and Spanish-speaking Latin and Central
America; library of 13,500 vols; Dir JOSÉ
EDUARDO MIRA GONZÁLEZ.

**International PEN Club, French-speak-
ing Branch:** c/o Huguette de Broqueville, 10
ave des Cerfs, 1950 Kraainem; tel. (2) 731-48-
47; fax (2) 731-48-47; e-mail huguette.db@
skynet.be; f. 1922; 540 mems; Pres. HUGU-
ETTE DE BROQUEVILLE; Gen. Sec. ALISON JANE
BELL.

**International PEN Club, PEN-Centre
Belgium:** POB 12, King Albertpark, 2600
Antwerp; e-mail info@penvlaanderen.be;
internet www.penvlaanderen.be; Dutch-
speaking branch; f. 1935; 140 mems; Pres.
GEERT VAN ISTENDAEL; Gen. Sec. PAUL KOECK;
publ. *PEN-Tijdingen* (4 a year).

**Koninklijke Academie voor Neder-
landse Taal- en Letterkunde** (Royal Academy of Dutch Language and Literature):
Koningstraat 18, 9000 Ghent; tel. (9) 265-
93-40; fax (9) 265-93-49; e-mail secretariaat@
kantl.be; internet www.kantl.be; f. 1886; 74
mems (30 ordinary, 5 extraordinary, 14 hon.

mems, 25 foreign hon.); library of 40,000 vols;
Permanent Sec. Prof. Dr WERNER WATER-
SCHOOT; Librarian Lic. MARIJKE DE WIT;
publ. *Verslagen en Mededelingen* (3 a year).

**Société Belge des Auteurs, Composi-
teurs et Editeurs (SABAM):** 75–77 rue
d'Arlon, Brussels 1040; tel. (2) 286-82-11; fax
(2) 230-05-89; e-mail info@sabam.be; internet
www.sabam.be; f. 1922; colln and distribution of copyrights; 25,000 mems; Gen. Dir
JACQUES LION; Man. Dirs CHRISTOPHE DEPR-
ETER, LUC VAN OYCKE WILLY HEYNS, SERGE
VLOEBERGHS, DIRK VAN SOOM, THIERRY DACHE-
LET; publs *Newsletter* (6 a year), *Sabam
Magazine* (4 a year).

**Société de Langue et de Littérature
Wallonnes** (Society for Walloon Language
and Literature): Université de Liège, 7 place
du XX Août, 4000 Liège; tel. (86) 34-44-32;
e-mail sllw.be@skynet.be; internet users
.skynet.be/sllw; f. 1856; 400 mems; library of
20,000 vols (Bibliothèque des Dialectes de
Wallonie, 8 Place des Carmes, 4000 Liège;
tel. (41) 23-19-60 ext. 139); Pres. GUY BELLE-
FLAMME; Sec. V. GEORGE; publs *Dialectes de
Wallonie* (1 a year), *Littérature dialectale
d'aujourd'hui* (1 a year), *Mémoire Wallonne*
(1 a year), *Wallonnes* (4 a year).

**Société d'Etudes Latines de Bruxelles
(LATOMUS) absl** (Brussels Society for
Latin Studies): 6 rue du Palais St Jacques,
7500 Tournai; tel. (69) 21-47-13; fax (69) 21-
47-13; e-mail latomus@belgacom.net;
internet users.belgacom.net/latomus; f.
1937; languages of instruction: English,
French, German, Italian, Latin, Spanish;
750 mems; Pres. C. DEROUX; publs *Collection
Latomus, Review Latomus* (4 a year).

MEDICINE

**Académie Royale de Médecine de Belgi-
que** (Royal Academy of Medicine of Belgium): Palais des Académies, 1 rue Ducale,
1000 Brussels; tel. (2) 550-22-55; fax (2) 550-
22-65; e-mail contact@armb.be; internet
www.armb.be; f. 1841; divs of biological
sciences, human medicine, immunology,
microbiology, parasitology, pharmacy, public
health and forensic medicine, surgery and
obstetrics, veterinary medicine; 332 mems
(80 ordinary, 37 corresp., 12 hon., 127 hon.
foreign, 76 foreign corresp.); Pres. Prof. L.
HUE; Dir J. DUBUCQ; Permanent Sec. Prof. J.
FRÜHLING; publ. *Bulletin et Mémoires* (12 a
year).

Association Belge de Santé Publique
(Belgian Public Health Association): c/o Scientific Institute of Public Health, 14 rue
Juliette Weytsman, 1050 Brussels; tel. (2)
642-57-07; fax (2) 642-54-26; f. 1938; promotes public health research in Belgium; 200
mems; Pres. Prof. Dr G. VAN HAL; publ.
Archives de Santé Publique.

**Association Royale des Sociétés Scienti-
fiques Médicales Belges:** 138A ave Circulaire, 1180 Brussels; tel. (2) 374-51-58; fax (2)
374-96-88; e-mail amb@skynet.be; internet
www.ulb.ac.be/medecine/loce/amb.htm; f.
1945; 4,000 mems; Pres. Dr G. STALPAERT;
Sec.-Gen. Dr P. DOR; publs *Acta Anaesthe-
siologica Belgica, Acta Chirurgica Belgica,
Acta Gastro-Enterologica Belgica, Acta Neurologica Belgica, Acta Orthopedica Belgica,
JBR-BTR* (Belgian Journal of Radiology).

**Koninklijke Academie voor Genees-
kunde van België** (Royal Academy of Medicine of Belgium): Hertogsstraat 1, 1000
Brussels; tel. (2) 550-23-00; fax (2) 550-23-
05; e-mail academiegeneeskunde@
vlaanderen.be; internet www
.academiegeneeskunde.be; f. 1938; divs of
human medicine, pharmacy, veterinary
medicine; 168 mems (73 ordinary, 53 foreign
corresp., 40 hon.); Pres. Prof. Dr GUY DE

BACKER; Sec.-Gen. Prof. Dr BERNARD HIM-PENS; publs *Dissertationes–Series Historica*, *Proceedings*.

Société Belge de Médecine Tropicale/ Belgische Vereniging voor Tropische Geneeskunde: Nationalestraat 155, Antwerp; tel. (3) 247-62-01; fax (3) 237-67-31; e-mail dir@itg.be; f. 1920; 569 mems (24 Belgian and foreign hon., 66 assoc., 85 titular, 394 corresp.); Sec. Prof. Dr B. GRYSEELS; publ. *Tropical Medicine and International Health* (12 a year).

Société Belge d'Ophtalmologie, section francophone (Belgian Society of Ophthalmology, French-speaking section): c/o Marlene Verlaeckt, Kapucijnenvoer 33, 3000 Louvain; tel. (16) 33-23-98; fax (16) 33-26-78; f. 1896; Sec. Prof. J. M. LEMAGNE; publ. *Bulletin* (4 a year).

NATURAL SCIENCES
General

Association pour la Promotion des Publications Scientifiques (APPS): 26 ave de l'Amarante, 1020 Brussels; tel. (2) 268-29-33; fax (2) 268-25-14; f. 1981; 80 mems and 20 assoc. mems; Pres. Dr JEAN BAUDET; publ. *Ingénieur et Industrie* (12 a year).

Société Royale des Sciences de Liège (Royal Society of Sciences of Liège): Institut de Mathématique B37, Université de Liège, 4000 Liège I; tel. (4) 366-38-41; fax (4) 366-95-47; e-mail srsl@guest.ulg.ac.be; internet www.srsl-ulg.net; f. 1835; promotion of biological, chemical, mathematical, mineral and physical sciences; 200 mems; Pres. EMMA-NUELLE JAVAUX; Sec.-Gen. Prof. JACQUES AGHION; publ. *Bulletin* (online, 400 pages a year).

Société Scientifique de Bruxelles: 61 rue de Bruxelles, 5000 Namur; tel. (81) 72-41-36; e-mail anne-martine.baert@fundp.ac.be; f. 1875; 140 mems; Sec.-Gen. GUY DEMORTIER; Admin. ANNE-MARTINE BAERT; publ. *Revue des Questions Scientifiques* (4 a year).

Biological Sciences

Koninklijke Maatschappij voor Dierkunde van Antwerpen (Royal Zoological Society of Antwerp): 26 Koningin Astridplein, 2018 Antwerp; tel. (3) 202-45-40; fax (3) 231-00-18; internet www.kmda.org; f. 1843; zoological and botanical gardens, aquarium, nature reserve, laboratories; educational and cultural services and scientific research; 32,000 mems; library of 34,000 vols; Dir R. VAN EYSENDEYK; publ. *Zoo* (in Dutch, 4 a year).

Société Belge de Biochimie et de Biologie Moléculaire/Belgische Vereniging voor Biochemie en Moleculaire Biologie (SBBBM/BVBMB): 75 ave Hippocrate, UCL-ICP 74.39, 1200 Brussels; tel. (2) 764-74-39; fax (2) 762-68-53; e-mail info@biochemistry.be; internet www.biochemistry.be; f. 1951; 500 mems; Pres. Prof. LODE WYNS; Sec. Prof. FRED R. OPPERDOES.

Société Belge de Biologie Clinique (Belgische Vereniging voor Klinische Biologie): Laboratoriumgeneeskunde, UZ Gasthuisberg, Herestraat 49, 3000 Leuven; tel. (16) 34-79-02; fax (16) 34-79-31; internet www.bvkb-sbbc.org; 110 mems; Sec. A. LEONARD.

Société Royale Belge d'Entomologie (Royal Belgian Entomological Society): 29 rue Vautier, 1000 Brussels; tel. (2) 627-43-21; fax (2) 627-41-32; e-mail srbe@naturalsciences.be; internet www.sciencesnaturelles.be/srbe/page1.htm; f. 1855; 250 mems; library of 23,000 vols; Pres. G. WAUTHY; Sec. P. GROOTAERT; publs *Belgian Journal of Entomology* (2 a year),

Bulletin (2 a year), *Catalogue des Coléoptères de Belgique* (irregular), *Mémoires* (irregular).

Société Royale de Botanique de Belgique: c/o Anne-Laure Jacquemart, Croix-du-Sud 2/14, 1348 Louvain-la-Neuve; tel. (10) 47-34-56; fax (10) 47-34-90; e-mail jacquemart@ecol.ucl.ac.be; internet www.biol.ucl.ac.be/socbota/socbotaun.htm; f. 1862; 250 mems; Pres. P. MEERTS; Sec. A.-L. JACQUEMART; publ. *Belgian Journal of Botany* (2 a year).

Société Royale Zoologique de Belgique/ Koninklijke Belgische Vereniging voor Dierkunde: 50 ave F. D. Roosevelt, 1050 Brussels; tel. (2) 650-22-63; fax (2) 650-22-31; e-mail kbvd@uia.ua.ac.be; internet kbvd-www.uia.ac.be/kbvd; f. 1863; 400 mems; library of 1,500 periodicals; Pres. G. JOSENS; Sec. H. LEIRS; publ. *Belgian Journal of Zoology* (2 a year).

Mathematical Sciences

Belgian Mathematical Society: Dept of Mathematics and Computer Science, Univ. of Antwerp, Middelheimlaan 1, 2020 Antwerp; tel. (3) 265-38-89; fax (3) 265-37-77; e-mail bms@ulb.ac.be; internet bms.ulb.ac.be; f. 1921; promotion of mathematical activities; 240 mems (incl. 60 libraries, with which there is an exchange agreement); library of 200 vols; Secs Prof. JAN VAN CASTEREN, CATHERINE FINET, GUY VAN STEEN; publ. *Bulletin of the Belgian Mathematical Society* (4 or 5 a year).

Conseil Supérieur de Statistique: 44 rue de Louvain, 1000 Brussels; tel. (2) 548-62-11; fax (2) 548-62-62; e-mail philippe.mauroy@economie.fgov.be; f. 1841; 36 mems; Pres. MARTINE VAN WOUWE; Sec. PHILIPPE MAUROY.

Physical Sciences

Geologica Belgica: 13 rue Jenner, 1000 Brussels; tel. (2) 788-76-30; fax (2) 647-73-59; e-mail wdevos@naturalsciences.be; internet www.ulg.ac.be/geolsed/gb; f. 1887; promotes geological knowledge; 250 mems; Pres. Prof. RUDY. SWENNEN; Sec. Dr ERIC GOEMAERE; Librarian and Treasurer Dr WALTER DE VOS; publ. *Geologica Belgica* (2 or 3 a year).

Koninklijk Sterrenkundig Genootschap van Antwerpen/Société Royale d'Astronomie d'Anvers (Royal Astronomical Society of Antwerp): c/o Willy de Kort, Kapelsesteenweg 340, 2930 Brasschaat; tel. (3) 664-28-93; e-mail ksga@pandora.be; f. 1905; dissemination, teaching and aid for the promotion of astronomy; 180 mems; Pres. WILLY DE KORT; Sec. F. DELATIN; publ. *Astronomische Gazet* (6 a year).

Société Astronomique de Liège (Liège Society of Astronomy): Avenue de Cointe 5, B-4000 Liège; tel. (4) 253-35-90; fax (4) 252-74-74; e-mail sal@astro.ulg.ac.be; internet www.astro.ulg.ac.be/~sal/; f. 1938; brings together amateurs of astronomy, and promotes public understanding; 800 mems; library of 500 vols; Pres. A. LAUSBERG; Sec. L. PAUQUAY; publ. *Le Ciel* (12 a year).

Société Géologique de Belgique (Geological Society of Belgium): Unité de documentation, B6 Allée de la Chimie, 4000 Liège; tel. (4) 366-53-56; fax (4) 366-56-36; e-mail a.anceau@ulg.ac.be; f. 1874; 300 mems; Pres. J. VANDER AUWERA; Sec.-Gen. A. ANCEAU; publ. *Geologica Belgica* (2 a year).

Société Royale Belge d'Astronomie, de Météorologie et de Physique du Globe: 3 ave Circulaire, 1180 Brussels; tel. (2) 373-02-53; fax (2) 374-98-22; internet www.srba.be; f. 1894; 800 mems; Pres. M. VANDIEPENDEECK; Sec.-Gen. R. DEJAIFFE; publ. *Ciel et Terre* (6 a year).

Société Royale de Chimie: ULB, CP 160/07, 50 ave F. Roosevelt, 1050 Brussels; tel. (2)

650-52-08; fax (2) 650-51-84; e-mail src@ulb.ac.be; internet www.ulb.ac.be/assoc/src/; f. 1887; 1,000 mems; library at 48 ave Depage, Brussels; Pres. Prof. J. M. FRÈRE; Gen. Sec. Prof. J. C. BRAEKMAN; publ. *Chimie Nouvelle* (4 a year).

PHILOSOPHY AND PSYCHOLOGY

Société Philosophique de Louvain: c/o Institut Supérieur de Philosophie, Place du Cardinal Mercier 14, 1348 Louvain-la-Neuve; tel. (10) 47-47-87; fax (10) 47-82-19; e-mail nathalie.frogneux@uclouvain.be; internet www.isp.ucl.ac.be/associations/socphil.html; f. 1888; 71 mems; Pres. N. FROGNEUX; Sec. H. POURTOIS.

RELIGION, SOCIOLOGY AND ANTHROPOLOGY

Institut Belge des Hautes Etudes Chinoises: c/o Musées Royaux d'Art et d'Histoire, 10 parc du Cinquantenaire, 1000 Brussels; tel. and fax (2) 741-73-55; e-mail inst.chin@kmkg-mrah.be; f. 1929; Sinology and Buddhism; lectures, courses on Chinese art, history, painting and calligraphy; library of 60,000 vols; approx. 300 mems; Dir J.-M. SIMONET; publ. *Mélanges Chinois et Bouddhiques* (every 2 years).

Ruusbroecgenootschap: Prinsstraat 13, 2000 Antwerp; tel. (3) 220-43-69; fax (3) 220-44-20; f. 1925, inc. as Centrum voor Spiritualiteit of Universiteit Antwerpen in 1973; soc. of mainly Flemish Jesuits engaged in spiritual studies of the Low Countries; library of 115,000 vols (incl. 30,000 old and rare books), 500 MSS, 35,000 devotional prints; Dir Prof. Dr THEO CLEMENS; publ. *Ons Geestelijk Erf* (4 a year).

Société des Bollandistes: 24 blvd St Michel, 1040 Brussels; tel. (2) 740-24-21; fax (2) 740-24-24; e-mail info@bollandistes.be; internet www.bollandistes.be; f. 1630; research and publs in critical hagiography; library of 500,000 vols; Dir Dr ROBERT GODDING; publs *Analecta Bollandiana* (critical hagiography, 2 a year), *Subsidia Hagiographica* (irregular), *Tabularium Hagiographicum* (irregular).

Société Royale Belge d'Anthropologie et de Préhistoire: 29 rue Vautier, 1000 Brussels; tel. (2) 627-43-85; fax (2) 627-41-13; f. 1882; Pres. MARTINE VERCAUTEREN; Sec.-Gen. A. HAUZEUR; 130 mems; publs *Anthropologie et Préhistoire* (1 a year), *Hominid Remains* (series).

TECHNOLOGY

Bureau de Normalisation (NBN) (Standards Bureau): 29 ave de la Brabançonne, 1000 Brussels; tel. (2) 738-01-11; fax (2) 733-42-64; e-mail info@nbn.be; internet www.nbn.be; f. 1946; Belgian nat. mem. of the CEN (European Cttee of Standardization) and the ISO (Int. Org. for Standardization); 962 mems; Pres. of Directorate CHRISTOPHE VAN VAERENBERGH; publ. *NBN Revue* (10 a year).

Koninklijke Vlaamse Ingenieursvereniging (Royal Flemish Association of Engineers): KVIV Ingenieurshuis, Desguinlei 214, 2018 Antwerp; tel. (3) 260-08-40; fax (3) 216-06-89; internet www.kviv.be; f. 1928; 10,000 mems; Pres. Ir L. COOREMAN; Sec.-Gen. Ir P. ERAUW; publs *Het Ingenieursblad* (12 a year), *KVIV-Direkt* (12 a year).

Société Belge de Photogrammétrie, de Télédétection et de Cartographie (Belgian Society for Photogrammetry, Remote Sensing and Cartography): C.A.E.-Tour Finances (Bte 38), 50 blvd du Jardin Botanique, 1010 Brussels; tel. (2) 210-35-98; f. 1931; 163 mems; Pres. R. THONNARD; Sec. J. VAN HEMELRIJCK; publ. *Bulletin* (4 a year).

Société Royale Belge des Electriciens: c/o VUB-TW-ETEC, 2 Blvd de la Plaine, 1050 Brussels; tel. (2) 629-28-19; fax (2) 629-36-20; e-mail srbe-kbve@vub.ac.be; internet www .kbve-srbe.be; f. 1884; organizes seminars; 1,600 mems; Sec.-Gen. BRIGITTE SNEYERS; publ. *Revue E Tijdschrift* (4 a year).

Société Royale Belge des Ingénieurs et des Industriels: Hôtel Ravenstein, 3 rue Ravenstein, 1000 Brussels; tel. (2) 511-58-56; fax (2) 514-57-95; internet energie.wallonie .be/energieplus/cogeneration/cdrom/reper-toire/s/15.htm; f. 1885; 2,000 mems; Pres. PIERRE KLEES; publ. *SRBII info* (12 a year).

Research Institutes

AGRICULTURE, FISHERIES AND VETERINARY SCIENCE

Centre de Recherches Agronomiques de Gembloux: 9 rue de Liroux, 5030 Gembloux; tel. (81) 62-65-55; fax (81) 62-65-59; e-mail cra@cra.wallonia.be; internet www.cragx .fgov.be; f. 1872; agricultural research at 8 research depts; Dir R. BISTON; publ. *Rapport d'activité.*

Centrum voor Onderzoek in Diergen-eeskunde en Agrochemie/Centre d'Etude et de Recherches Vétérinaires et Agrochimiques (Veterinary and Agro-chemical Research Centre): Groeselenberg 99, 1180 Brussels; tel. (2) 379-04-00; fax (2) 379-04-01; e-mail info@var.fgov.be; internet www.var.fgov.be; f. 1997; research sites in Brussels, Tervuren and Machelen; Pres. and Dir Dr J. E. PEETERS; publ. *Activiteitsverlag/ Rapport d'activité* (1 a year).

ECONOMICS, LAW AND POLITICS

Centre for European Policy Studies (CEPS): 1 place du Congrès, Brussels 1000; tel. (2) 229-39-11; fax (2) 219-41-51; e-mail info@ceps.eu; internet www.ceps.eu; f. 1983; ind. instn dedicated to producing sound policy research leading to constructive solu-tions to the challenges facing Europe today; CEO KAREL LANNOO; Dir DANIEL GROS; Research Fellow and Head of Communica-tions MARCO INCERTI.

Institut Royal des Relations Internatio-nales: 69 rue de Namur, 1000 Brussels; tel. (2) 223-41-14; fax (2) 223-41-16; e-mail info@ egmontinstitute.be; internet www .egmontinstitute.be; f. 1947; 1,000 mems; research in int. relations, int. economics, int. politics, int. law, European affairs; docu-mentation centre covering EU integration, central Africa, European security and defence policy; archives; library of 1,000 vols; Dir-Gen. MARC TRENTESEAU; publs *Egmont Papers* (irregular), *Studia Diplomat-ica* (4 a year).

FINE AND PERFORMING ARTS

Centre d'Etude de la Peinture du XVe Siècle dans les Pays-Bas Méridionaux et la Principauté de Liège/Studiecentrum voor de 15de-Eeuwse Schilderkunst in de Zuidelijke Nederlanden en het Prins-bisdom Luik (Centre for the Study of 15th Century Painting in the Southern Nether-lands and the Principality of Liège): Royal Institute for Cultural Heritage, Jubelpark 1, 1000 Brussels; tel. (2) 739-68-66; fax (2) 732-01-05; e-mail helene.mund@kikirpa.be; internet xv.kikirpa.be; f. 1950; research into 15th-century Flemish painting; language of instruction: French; 13 mems; library of 6,400 vols; Pres. Dr C. STROO; Dir M. SERCK-DEWAIDE; Scientific Secs H. MUND; publs *Contributions, Corpus de la Peinture des Pays-Bas Méridionaux et de la Principauté de Liège au 15e Siècle, Répertoire.*

MEDICINE

Born-Bunge Research Foundation: Uni-versiteitsplein 1, 2610 Antwerp (Wilrijk); tel. (3) 820-26-02; fax (3) 820-22-48; e-mail jjmneuro@uia.ac.be; internet www.bbf.uia.ac .be/bbf; f. 1963; research in neurological sciences and cardiology; Dir Dr J. J. MARTIN.

Fondation Médicale Reine Elisabeth/ Geneeskundige Stichting Koningin Eli-sabeth (Queen Elisabeth Medical Founda-tion): 3 ave J. J. Crocqlaan, 1020 Brussels; tel. (2) 478-35-56; fax (2) 478-24-13; e-mail fmre.gske@skynet.be; internet www .fmre-gske.be; f. 1926; supports medical research in the field of neurobiology through several Belgian univ. laboratories; Scientific Dir Prof. Dr BARON DE BARSY.

Institut Neurologique Belge: 152 rue de Linthout, 1040 Brussels; tel. (2) 737-85-60; f. 1924; Pres. Comte EDOUARD D'OULTREMONT; publs *Acta Neurologica, Psychiatrica Belgica.*

Institut Pasteur de Bruxelles: 642 rue Engeland, 1180 Brussels; tel. (2) 373-31-11; fax (2) 373-32-82; e-mail lschoofs@pasteur.be; internet www.pasteur.be; f. 1900; scientific biomedical research, analyses; Dir JEAN CON-TENT.

NATURAL SCIENCES

General

Institut Royal des Sciences Naturelles de Belgique/Koninklijk Belgisch Insti-tuut voor Natuurwetenschappen: 29 rue Vautier, 1000 Brussels; tel. (2) 627-42-11; fax (2) 627-41-13; e-mail info@naturalsciences .be; internet www.naturalsciences.be; f. 1846; library: see Libraries; biology, zoology, palaeontology, geology, anthropology; Dir C. PISANI; publs *Bulletin: Biology, Bulletin: Entomology, Bulletin: Palaeontology, Study Documents* (irregular).

Biological Sciences

Jardin botanique national de Belgique/ Nationale Plantentuin van België: Domein van Bouchout, 1860 Meise; tel. (2) 260-09-20; fax (2) 260-09-45; e-mail office@br .fgov.be; internet www.br.fgov.be; f. 1870; botanical taxonomy and geography, espe-cially of African and European plants, includ-ing Cryptogams; gene bank of Phaseolinae; herbarium with over 2,000,000 specimens; library of 200,000 vols; Dir Prof. Dr JAN RAMMELOO; publs *Systematics and Geog-raphy of Plants* (2 a year), *Flore illustrée des champignons d'Afrique Centrale* (1 a year), *Distributiones plantarum africanarum* (irregular), *Dumortiera* (3 a year), *Flore d'Afrique Centrale* (irregular), *Icones myco-logicae* (irregular), *Opera Botanica Belgica* (irregular), *Scripta Botanica Belgica* (irregu-lar).

Mathematical Sciences

Institut National de Statistique: 44 rue de Louvain, 1000 Brussels; tel. (2) 548-62-11; fax (2) 548-63-67; internet statbel.fgov.be; f. 1831; Dir-Gen. CLAUDE CHERUY; publs *Annuaire statistique de la Belgique, Bulletin de Statistique* (12 a year), etc.

Physical Sciences

Centre d'Etude de l'Energie Nucléaire (Studiecentrum voor Kernenergie): Boere-tang 200, 2400 Mol; tel. (14) 33-21-11; fax (14) 31-50-21; internet www.sckcen.be; f. 1952; nuclear research and development, reactor safety, fuel and materials irradiation, characterization and geological disposal of waste, decontamination and dismantling of facilities, radioprotection, nuclear services incl. irradiation in BR2 and post-irradiation examination; Chair. FRANK DECONINCK; Man. Dir CLAUDE TRUFFIN; publ. *Scientific Report* (1 a year).

Institut d'Aéronomie Spatiale de Belgi-que: Ave Circulaire 3, 1180 Brussels; tel. (2) 373-04-13; fax (2) 375-93-36; e-mail bira-iasb_webmaster@aeronomie.be; internet www.aeronomie.be; f. 1964 to undertake research in aeronomy (physics and chemistry of the atmosphere) from information gained from space vehicles; library of 3,000 vols and 150 periodicals; Dir Prof. PAUL C. SIMON; Sec. MARC DELANCKER.

Institut Royal Météorologique de Belgi-que: Ave Circulaire 3, 1180 Brussels; tel. (2) 373-05-08; fax (2) 375-05-28; e-mail irni_info@oma.be; internet www.meteo.be; f. 1913; deps for aerology, aerometry, applied meteorology, climatology, geophysics and numerical calculus; Dir Dr H. MALCORPS; publs *Bulletin Quotidien du temps* (1 a day), *Climatologie, Hydrologie* (1 a year), *Observa-tions climatologiques, Magnétisme terrestre, Marées terrestres à Dourbes, Observations d'ozone* (4 a year), *Observations géophysi-ques, Observations ionosphériques* (12 a year), *Observations synoptiques, Rayonne-ment solaire.*

Observatoire Royal de Belgique/ Koninklijke Sterrenwacht van Belgie: Ave Circulaire 3, 1180 Brussels; tel. (2) 373-02-11; fax (2) 374-98-22; internet www.astro .oma.be/ksb-orb; f. 1826; astrometry, astro-physics, celestial mechanics, earth tides, fundamental astronomy, gravimetry, radio-astronomy, satellite positioning, seismology, solar physics, time service; Dir Prof. P. PÂQUET; publs *Annuaire, Bulletin Astronom-ique, Communications.*

PHILOSOPHY AND PSYCHOLOGY

Centre National de Recherches de Logi-que: Fondation Universitaire, 11 rue d'Egmont, 1000 Brussels; internet www.lofs .ucl.ac.be/cnrl; f. 1951; 32 mems; Pres. J. P. VAN BENDEGEM; Sec. SONIA SMETS; publ. *Logique et Analyse* (4 a year).

RELIGION, SOCIOLOGY AND ANTHROPOLOGY

Centre d'Etudes et de Recherches Ara-bes: Université de Mons, Académie Univer-sitaire Wallonie-Bruxelles (UMONS-ULB), 17 ave Champ de Mars, 7000 Mons; tel. (65) 32-37-36-15; fax (65) 32-39-45-21; e-mail cerm.umh@gmail.com; internet www .strademed.eu; f. 1978; incl. Euro–Mediter-ranean studies section, int. relations section and Arabic language, translation and inter-preting (graduate studies); training and research (FTI and ISL) in translation and interpreting; Arabic, English, French (post-graduate studies and Phd); visiointerpreting (e-learning); audiovisual translation: respeaking, subtitling, audiodescription, dubbing and AT/CAT; 9 mems; library of 2,500 vols; Dir Prof. H. SAFAR.

Institut d'Etudes du Judaïsme (Institute for the study of Judaism): 17 ave Roosevelt, 1050 Brussels; tel. (2) 650-33-48; fax (2) 650-33-47; e-mail iej@ulb.ac.be; internet www.ulb .ac.be/philo/judaism/; f. 1959; studies, publs and documentation on contemporary Juda-ism; library of 8,000 vols; Dir THOMAS GERGELY; publs *Mosaïque* (1 a year), *Nou-velles* (4 a year).

TECHNOLOGY

Institut Meurice (IIF–IMC–ISI): 1 ave Emile Gryzon, Anderlecht, 1070 Brussels; tel. (2) 526-73-00; fax (2) 524-30-82; e-mail cv@meurice.heldb.be; internet www

.heldb-meurice.be; f. 1892; research and training centre for industrial engineers in chemistry and biochemistry; Dir Dr Ir PATRICK DYSSELER.

Institut Scientifique de Service Public: 200 rue du Chéra, 4000 Liège; tel. (4) 229-83-11; fax (4) 252-46-65; e-mail direction@issep .be; internet www.issep.be; f. 1990; applied research, devt and demonstration relating to natural resources, the environment, technical and industrial security, solid fuels, radiocommunications; library of 11,000 vols; Gen. Man. J. JADIN.

Von Karman Institute for Fluid Dynamics: Chaussée de Waterloo 72, 1640 Rhode-St-Genese; tel. (2) 359-96-11; fax (2) 359-96-00; e-mail secretariat@vki.ac.be; internet www.vki.ac.be; f. 1956; multinational postgraduate teaching and research in aerodynamics, supported by the countries of NATO; depts of aeronautics/aerospace, turbomachinery and propulsion, environmental fluid dynamics; library of 2,000 vols, 55,000 reports; Dir Prof. MARIO CARBONARO; publ. *Lecture Series Monographs* (10 to 12 a year).

Libraries and Archives

Antwerp

AMVC—Letterenhuis (AMVC—Literary Centre): Minderbroedersstraat 22, 2000 Antwerp; tel. (3) 222-93-20; fax (3) 222-93-21; e-mail amvc.letterenhuis@stad .antwerpen.be; internet www.letterenhuis .be; f. 1933; archives of Flemish literature, theatre, music, arts and culture; files and MSS can be seen on application; 55,000 files, 2m. letters and MSS, 50,000 posters, 130,000 photographs; Dir LEEN VAN DIJCK.

Bibliotheek Universitaire Instelling Antwerpen: Universiteitsplein 1, 2610 Antwerp; tel. (3) 820-21-41; fax (3) 820-21-59; internet lib.ua.ac.be; f. 1972; 400,000 vols; Dir J. VAN BORM.

FelixArchief/Stadsarchief (City Archives): Oudeleeuwenrui 29, 2000 Antwerp; tel. (3) 338-94-11; fax (3) 338-94-10; e-mail stadsarchief@stad.antwerpen.be; internet www.felixarchief.be; f. 1796; 21 km of documents concerning the admin. of Antwerp since the 13th century; history, genealogy, heraldry, cartography, sigillography; 11,000 specialized vols, 245 periodicals; Archivist INGE SCHOUPS.

Rijksarchief te Antwerpen (Antwerp State Archives): Kruibekesteenweg 39/1, 9120 Beveren; tel. (3) 236-73-00; fax (3) 775-26-46; e-mail rijksarchief.antwerpen@arch .be; internet arch.arch.be/frame_nl_d2.htm; f. 1896; history of the province of Antwerp; documents since 12th century; Dir Dr MICHEL OOSTERBOSCH.

Rubenianum: Kolveniersstraat 20, 2000 Antwerp; tel. (3) 201-15-77; fax (3) 231-93-87; e-mail rubenianum@stad.antwerpen.be; internet www.rubenianum.be; library and documentation centre for the study of 16th –17th century Flemish art, esp. the works of Jordaens, Rubens and Van Dyck; 45,000 vols and exhibition catalogues, books on art, artists and art history, journals, sales catalogues; Curator VÉRONIQUE VAN DE KERCKHOF; Curator MARC VANDENVEN; Subject librarian UTE STAES; publ. *Corpus Rubenianum Ludwig Burchard* (The complete edition of the works of Rubens).

Stadsbibliotheek: Hendrik Conscience-plein 4, 2000 Antwerp; tel. (3) 206-87-10; fax (3) 206-87-75; e-mail sba@antwerpen.be; internet stadsbibliotheek.antwerpen.be; f. 1481, reorganized 1834; Flemish and Dutch literature, history, humanities, local press;

open to the public; 1,000,000 vols; Dir R. RENNENBERG.

Universiteit Antwerpen–Bibliotheek: Stadscampus, Prinsstraat 9, 2000 Antwerp; tel. (3) 220-44-30; fax (3) 220-44-37; e-mail helpdesk@lib.ua.ac.be; internet lib.ua.ac.be; f. 1852; 870,000 vols; Dir TH. BOECKX; Chief Librarian TRUDI NOORDERMEER.

Universiteit Antwerpen—Bibliotheek campus Middelheim/Groenenborge: Middelheimlaan 1, 2020 Antwerp; tel. (3) 265-37-94; fax (3) 265-36-52; e-mail helpdesk@lib.ua.ac.be; internet lib.ua.ac.be; f. 1965; 75,000 vols; (mathematics and computer sciences: campus Middelheimlaan 1, 2020; natural sciences: Groenenborgerlaan 171,2610 Antwerp); Chief Librarian Dr TRUDI NOORDERMEER.

Arlon

Archives de l'Etat à Arlon: Parc des Expositions, 6700 Arlon; tel. (63) 22-06-13; fax (63) 22-42-94; e-mail archives.arlon@arch .be; internet arch.arch.be/arlon.htm; f. 1849; documents concerning the Province of Luxembourg since 12th century; 18 km of shelving; 100,000 vols; Archivist M. TRIGALET, V. PIRLOT; publs guides, inventories, exhibition catalogues, minutes of symposia.

Bruges

Rijksarchief te Brugge: Academiestraat 14, 8000 Bruges; tel. (50) 33-72-88; fax (50) 61-09-18; e-mail rijksarchief.brugge@arch .be; internet arch.arch.be; f. 1796; documents on Western Flanders since 12th century; Archivist Dr MAURICE VANDERMAESEN.

Brussels

Archives de la Ville de Bruxelles: 65 rue des Tanneurs, 1000 Brussels; tel. (2) 279-53-20; fax (2) 279-53-29; e-mail archives@ brucity.be; internet bold.belnet.be/bold/html/ fr/avb.html; historical archives of the city of Brussels; 20,000 reference vols, 100 periodicals; Archivist ANNE VANDENBULCKE.

Archives et Musée du Centre Public d'Action Sociale de Bruxelles: 298A rue Haute, Brussels; tel. (2) 543-60-55; fax (2) 543-61-06; e-mail dguilardian@cpasbru .irisnet.be; f. 1796; archives concerning hospitals and welfare since 12th century; approx. 20,000 archives; 15,000 vols; Archivist D. GUILARDIAN.

Archives Générales du Royaume/Algemeen Rijksarchief—Generalstaatsarchiv: 2–4 rue de Ruysbroeck, 1000 Brussels; tel. (2) 513-76-80; fax (2) 513-76-81; e-mail archives .generales@arch.be; internet arch.arch.be; f. 1815; 50 km documents concerning the Low Countries, Belgium and Brabant since 11th century; execution of legislation on Public Records; 400,000 vols; Gen. Archivist K. VELLE (acting).

Attached Centre:

Centre d'études et de documentation guerre et société contemporaine (CEGES) (Centre for Studies and Documentation on War and Contemporary Society): 29 Square de l'Aviation, 1070 Brussels; tel. (2) 556-92-11; fax (2) 556-92-00; e-mail cegesoma@cegesoma.be; internet www.cegesoma.be; Dir R. VAN DOORSLAER.

Bibliothèque artistique, Académie Royale des Beaux-Arts: 144 rue du Midi, 1000 Brussels; tel. (2) 506-10-35; fax (2) 506-10-38; e-mail bib.aca@brunette.brucity.be; internet www.brunette.brucity.be/bib/bibp1/bibaca/ accueil_ba.html; f. 1886; 18,000 vols, 400 rare books from the 17th and 18th centuries; more than 10,000 books on the applied arts from the 19th century, collns of photographs from the 19th and early 20th centuries (architec-

ture, applied arts, travel); Librarian CHRISTINE FERON.

Bibliothèque Centrale du Ministère de l'Education, de la Recherche et de la Formation (Communauté Française): 44 blvd Leopold II, 1080 Brussels; tel. (2) 413-31-48; fax (2) 413-33-48; e-mail jean-michel .andrin@cfwb.be; f. 1879; contains vols on administration and law, all branches of science and pedagogy, educational books; 400,000 vols, 900 periodicals; open only to teachers and mems of French Dept; Dir J.-M. ANDRIN.

Bibliothèque d'Art, Ecole Nationale Supérieure des Arts Visuels de la Cambre: 21 abbaye de la Cambre, 1000 Brussels; tel. (2) 626-17-86; fax (2) 640-96-93; e-mail bibliotheque@lacambre.be; internet www .lacambre.be; f. 1926; 60,000 vols; Librarian RÉGINE CARPENTIER.

Bibliothèque de l'Institut Royal des Sciences Naturelles de Belgique/Bibliotheek en Documentatiedienst van het Koninklijk Belgisch Instituut voor Natuurwetenschappen (Library and Documentation Service of the Royal Belgian Institute of Natural Sciences): 29 rue Vautier, 1000 Brussels; tel. (2) 627-41-89; fax (2) 627-41-13; e-mail bib@naturalsciences.be; internet www.naturalsciences.be; f. 1846; 750,000 vols, 2,900 periodicals; Dir CAMILLE PISANI; Librarian LAURENT MEESE; publs *Bulletin de l'Institut Royal des Sciences Naturelles de Belgique, Série Biologie, Bulletin de l'Institut Royal des Sciences Naturelles de Belgique, Série Entomologie, Bulletin de l'Institut Royal des Sciences Naturelles de Belgique, Série Sciences de la Terre.*

Bibliothèque des Facultés Universitaires Saint-Louis: 43 blvd du Jardin Botanique, 1000 Brussels; tel. (2) 211-79-09; fax (2) 211-79-97; e-mail lib@fusl.ac.be; internet www4.fusl.ac.be; f. 1858; 260,000 vols; Librarians M.-C. MINGUET, N. PETIT.

Bibliothèque, Documentation, Publications du Ministère de l'Emploi et du Travail: 1 Ernesr Blerotst, 1070 Brussels; fax (2) 233-42-57; e-mail info@employment .belgium.be; internet employment.belgium .be; f. 1896 (since the foundation of the Board of Labour); 80,000 specialized vols, 500 periodicals on social sciences and labour relations; Dir J.-C. CASSIMONS.

Bibliothèque du Parlement: rue de la Loi 13, 1000 Brussels; tel. (2) 549-92-12; e-mail bibliotheque@lachambre.be; f. 1831; 500,000 vols, 1,200 periodicals, collections on microfilms; Librarians ROLAND VAN NIEUWENBORGH, BERNARD VANSTEELANDT.

Bibliothèque Fonds Quetelet (Fonds Quetelet Library): 50 Vooruitgangstraat, 1210 Brussels; tel. (2) 277-55-55; fax (2) 277-55-53; e-mail quetelet@economie.fgov.be; internet quetelet.economie.fgov.be; f. 1841; library of the Federal Public Service Economy, SMEs, Self-Employed and Energy; open to the public; reference and computer-assisted bibliographic services; 1,200,000 vols on statistics, economic and social sciences, agriculture, 8,000 periodicals (of which 2,000 current); Chief Librarian STEFAAN JACOBS; publ. *Aanwinsten=Accroissements* (online at www.economie.fgov.be/informations/quetelet/acquisitions_nl.htm).

Bibliothèque Royale de Belgique/ Koninklijke Bibliotheek van België (The Royal Library of Belgium): 4 blvd de l'Empereur, 1000 Brussels; tel. (2) 519-53-11; fax (2) 519-55-33; e-mail contacts@kbr.be; internet www.kbr.be; f. 1837; national depository library; 5,000,000 vols, 18,000 periodicals, 35,000 MSS, 35,000 rare printed books, 700,000 prints, 140,000 maps, 200,000 coins and medals, 10,000 records; Dir -Gen. PATRICK LEFÈVRE (acting).

Bibliothèques de l'Université Libre de Bruxelles: 50 ave Franklin D. Roosevelt, CP 180, 1050 Brussels; tel. (2) 650-23-70; fax (2) 650-41-86; e-mail bibdir@ulb.ac.be; internet www.bib.ulb.ac.be; f. 1846; 2,000,000 vols including periodicals and theses; Librarian Prof. JEAN-PIERRE DEVROEY.

Central Library of the European Commission: VM18 1/18, rue Van Maerlant 18 1049 Brussels; tel. (2) 295-04-28; fax (2) 295-68-26; internet ec.europa.eu/libraries/doc/index_en.htm; f. 1958; a central library linking a system of specialized library/documentation units; forms part of the EC's Directorate-Gen. for Education and Culture; 500,000 vols and periodicals on European integration and EU policies; also br. library in the Bech bldg in Luxembourg (tel. 4301-33341); Head of Unit ROBERTA PERSICHELLI-SCOLA.

NATO Multimedia Library, Public Diplomacy Division: Room Nb 123, 1110 Brussels; tel. (2) 707-44-14; fax (2) 707-42-49; e-mail library@hq.nato.int; internet www.nato.int/structur/library/library-e.html; f. 1950; serves the int. staff, int. military staff, delegations and PfP countries; subject areas: biography, current affairs, int. law, int. orgs, military science, politics, strategy; 22,000 vols, 200 periodicals; incls. the NATO audiovisual material; Librarian ISABEL FERNANDEZ; publs *Acquisitions List* (12 a year), *Current Affairs Awareness Service* (12 a year), *Thematic Bibliographies* (12 a year).

SIST-DWTI (Scientific and Technical Information Service): 4 blvd de l'Empereur, 1000 Brussels; tel. (2) 519-56-40; fax (2) 519-56-45; e-mail stis@stis.fgov.be; internet www.stis .fgov.be; f. 1964; provides information in the fields of medicine, science and technology; focal point for library, documentation and information networks (nat. and int.); Head of Unit Dr JEAN MOULIN.

Vrije Universiteit Brussel, Universiteitsbibliotheek: Pleinlaan 2, 1050 Brussels; tel. (2) 629-26-09; fax (2) 629-26-93; e-mail info@biblio.vub.ac.be; internet www .vub.ac.be/biblio; f. 1972; 550,000 vols, 360,000 monographs and 160,000 bound periodicals; Head Librarian Dr PATRICK VANOUPLINES.

Gembloux

Bibliothèque de la Faculté Universitaire des Sciences Agronomiques: 2 passage des Déportés, 5030 Gembloux; tel. (81) 62-21-02; fax (81) 61-45-44; e-mail bibliotheque@ fsagx.ac.be; internet www.bib.fsagx.ac.be; f. 1860; 100,000 vols, 1,000 journals; Chief Librarian BERNARD POCHET; publ. *Biotechnologies, Agronomie, Société et Environnement* (4 a year).

Ghent

Leeszaal Faculteit Landbouwkundige en Toegepaste Biologische Wetenschappen (Reading room, Faculty of Agricultural and Applied Biological Sciences): Universiteit, Coupure links 653, 9000 Ghent; 65,000 vols.

Universiteitsbibliotheek Gent: Rozier 9, 9000 Ghent; tel. (9) 264-38-51; fax (9) 264-38-52; e-mail libservice@ugent.be; internet www .lib.ugent.be; f. 1797/1817; 3,000,000 vols, 5,060 MSS; open to the public; Chief Librarian Dr S. VAN PETEGHEM.

Liège

Archives de l'Etat à Liège: 79 rue du Chéra, 4000 Liège; tel. (41) 252-03-93; fax (41) 229-33-50; e-mail archives.liege@arch .be; internet arch.arch.be/frame_fr_d3.htm;

state archives, Belgian fed. scientific and cultural institute; 18 km of public and private records relating to the history of the Liège district since the 9th century; Archivist Dr BRUNO DUMONT.

Bibliothèque 'Chiroux-Croisiers': 8 place des Carmes, 4000 Liège; tel. (41) 23-19-60; fax (41) 23-20-62; e-mail chiroux@liege.be; internet www.bib.chiroux-croisiers.liege.be; f. 1907; general library, MSS, ancient works, maps; 1,300,000 vols, local history, architecture, Walloon dialectology, c. 1,000 periodicals; Dir J. P. ROUGE.

Bibliothèque de l'Institut Archéologique Liégeois: Grand Curtius, 13 quai de Maastricht, 4000 Liège; tel. and fax (4) 232-98-60; e-mail monique.merland@crmsf.be; f. 1850; archaeology, decorative arts; 27,000 vols (mostly periodicals); Librarian MONIQUE MERLAND; publ. *Bulletin de l'Institut Archéologique Liégeois* (1 a year).

Réseau des Bibliothèques de l'Université de Liège: Grande Traverse 12, bât. B37, 4000 Liège (Sart-Tilman); tel. (4) 366-52-90; fax (4) 366-99-22; e-mail bib.direction@ulg.ac .be; internet www.ulg.ac.be/libnet; f. 1817; institutional repository; spec. collns incl. Fonds Québecois (French Canadian literature and society); language of instruction: French; 2,600,000 vols and pamphlets (incl. 12,000 current serials, 6,000 MSS and 500 early printed books); Chief Librarian Dr PAUL THIRION; publ. *Bibliotheca Universitatis Leodiensis*.

Louvain

Universiteitsbibliotheek-K.U. Leuven: Mgr Ladeuzeplein 21, 3000 Leuven; tel. (16) 32-46-60; fax (16) 32-46-16; e-mail centrale .bibliotheek@bib.kuleuven.be; internet www .bib.kuleuven.be; f. 1636; 4,300,000 vols (of which 3m. in faculty and dept libraries), c. 1,000 MSS; Chief Librarian Prof. MEL COLLIER.

Louvain-la-Neuve

Bibliothèques de l'Université Catholique de Louvain: c/o Service central des bibliothèques, 1 pl. de l'Université, 1348 Louvain-la-Neuve; tel. (10) 47-82-99; fax (10) 47-82-98; e-mail sceb@sceb.ucl.ac.be; internet www.bib.ucl.ac.be; 2,000,000 vols, 8,000 current periodicals; Chief Librarian CH.-H. NYNS.

Maredsous

Bibliothèque de l'Abbaye de Saint-Benoît: Abbaye de Maredsous, 5537 Denée; tel. (82) 69-82-11; fax (82) 69-83-21; e-mail biblioteque@maredsous.com; f. 1872; books of learning, especially history and theology; 400,000 vols, 50,000 brochures; Chief Librarian IGNACE BAISE; publ. *Revue Bénédictine*.

Mechelen

Archdiocesan Archives, Mechelen: Varkensstraat 6, 2800 Mechelen; tel. (15) 29-84-22; fax (15) 21-90-94; e-mail archiv@diomb .be; archives of the archdiocese of Mechelen and its predecessors since 12th century; MSS and books; photographs, iconographs, souvenirs; Archivist Drs GERRIT VANDEN BOSCH.

Archief en Stadsbibliotheek: Goswin de Stassartstraat 145, 2800 Mechelen; tel. (15) 20-43-46; fax (15) 21-64-48; e-mail stadsarchief@mechelen.be; f. 1802; archives of the city of Malines (Mechelen) since the 13th century and the library of the Great Ccl of the Netherlands; Archivist WILLY VAN DE VIJVER; publs *Catalogue méthodique de la Bibliothèque de Malines* (1 vol), *Inventaire des Archives de la ville de Malines* (8 vols).

Mons

Archives de l'Etat: 23 place du Parc, 7000 Mons; tel. (65) 35-45-06; e-mail archives .mons@arch.be; internet arch.arch.be/mons .htm; 25,000 vols; archives since 10th century; the bldgs were badly damaged during the war and many records lost; ongoing renovation and additions to archives; archives from the Abbeys and noble families of Hainaut; Dir P.-J. NIEBES.

Bibliothèque de l'Université de Mons: 2 rue Marguerite Bervoets, 7000 Mons; tel. (65) 37-30-55; fax (65) 37-30-68; e-mail bibliotheque.centrale@umons.ac.be; internet www.umons.ac.be; f. 1797; 900,000 vols, 3,622 MSS and incunabula, maps, prints; Dir CATHERINE MASSELUS.

Namur

Archives de l'Etat à Namur: 45 rue d'Arquet, 5000 Namur; tel. (81) 22-34-98; fax (81) 65-41-99; e-mail archives.namur@ arch.be; internet arch.arch.be; f. 1848; documents concerning the County and Province of Namur since the 8th century; Dir EMMANUEL BODART.

Bibliothèque Universitaire Moretus Plantin: 19 rue Grandgagnage, 5000 Namur; tel. (81) 72-46-30; fax (81) 72-46-45; e-mail direction.bump@fundp.ac.be; internet www.bump.fundp.ac.be; f. 1921; history of W Europe, Classical, Roman and German philology, philosophy, law, economics, art, biomedical sciences, life sciences, earth sciences; 800,000 vols; spec. colln: rare books on natural sciences; Dir KATRIEN BERGÉ.

Sint Niklaas Waas

Bibliotheek voor Hedendaagse Dokumentatie (Library on Contemporary Documentation): Parklaan 2, 9100 Sint Niklaas Waas; tel. (3) 776-50-63; e-mail akses@skynet .be; f. 1964; private political, social and economic library; 120,000 vols, 4,000 periodicals, 15,000 maps; spec. collns on governmental research, public admin.; US govt documents depository colln; Librarian JOHN HESS; publs *Bibliographical Series* (irregular), *Bulletin* (12 a year), *Governmental Publications Survey* (1 a year).

Ypres

Stedelijke Openbare Bibliotheek: Weverijstraat 7, 8900 Ypres; tel. (57) 23-94-20; fax (57) 23-94-29; e-mail bibliotheek@ieper.be; internet www.ieper.be; f. 1839; general interest; 120,000 vols, 400 periodicals; Librarian EDDY BARBRY.

Museums and Art Galleries

Antwerp

Etnografisch Museum: Suikerrui 19, 2000 Antwerp; tel. (3) 220-86-00; fax (3) 227-08-71; e-mail etnografisch.museum@stad .antwerpen.be; internet museum.antwerpen .be/etnografisch_museum; f. 1988; arts and crafts of pre-literate and non-European people; library of 12,000 vols; Dir JAN VAN ALPHEN; publ. *Bulletin van de Vrienden van het Etnografisch Museum Antwerpen*.

Koninklijk Museum voor Schone Kunsten (Royal Museum of Fine Arts): Leopold De Waelplaats, 2000 Antwerp; tel. (3) 238-78-09; fax (3) 248-08-10; e-mail info@kmska.be; internet www.kmska.be; f. 1890; collns of Flemish Primitifs, early foreign schools, Rubens, 16th–17th-century Antwerp School, 17th-century Dutch School, works of Belgian artists since 19th century; important works of De Braekeleer, Ensor, Leys, , Magritte,

Permeke, Smits, Wouters; from May 2011 to May 2012 the colln highlights will be kept on display at Museum aan de Stroom (Museum on the Stream) as this musuem will be closed for renovation; library of 50,000 vols; Dir Dr PAUL HUVENNE; publs *Dossiertentoonstelling* (2 a year), *Museumkrant* (4 a year), *Restauratie Schone Kunst* (2 a year).

Middelheimmuseum (Openluchtmuseum voor beeldhouwkunst) (Open-air Museum of Sculpture): Middelheimlaan 61, 2020 Antwerp; tel. (3) 827-15-34; fax (3) 825-28-35; e-mail middelheimmuseum@stad .antwerpen.be; internet www .middelheimmuseum.be; f. 1950; important colln of contemporary sculpture, incl. Cragg, Gargallo, Graham, Kirkeby, Maillol, Manzu, Marini, Moore, Muñoz, Rodin and Zadkine, exhibited in a large park; exhibitions devoted to modern and contemporary sculpture; library of 60,000 vols; Dir MENNO MEEWIS.

Museum Brouwershuis: Adriaan Brouwerstraat 20, 2000 Antwerp; tel. (3) 232-65-11; fax (3) 232-65-11; internet museum .antwerpen.be/brouwershuis; f. 1933 closed until further notice; 16th century installations for water-supply to breweries, ccl chamber; Curator F. DE NAVE.

Museum Mayer van den Bergh: Lange Gasthuisstraat 19, 2000 Antwerp; tel. (3) 232-42-37; fax (3) 231-73-35; e-mail museum .mayervandenbergh@stad.antwerpen.be; internet www.museummayervandenbergh .be; f. 1904; paintings, including Aertsen, Breughel, Bronzino, de Vos, Heda, Metsys, Mostaert, and medieval sculpture, ivories, etc.; Chief Curator HANS NIEUWDORP.

Museum Plantin-Moretus/Prentenkabinet: Vrijdagmarkt 22, 2000 Antwerp; tel. (3) 221-14-50; fax (3) 221-14-71; e-mail museum.plantin.moretus@stad.antwerpen .be; internet www.museumplantinmoretus .be; f. 1876; print room f. 1938; UNESCO World Heritage site; 16th–18th century patrician house with ancient printing office and foundry, engravings on copper and wood; typographical collns, drawings, prints and paintings by Rubens; illuminated MSS; rare books and atlases; library of 30,000 rare books (15th–18th century) and modern reference library on humanism and book history, family and business archives (16th–19th century); spec. collns: Max Horn Legacy, Ensemble Emile Verhaeren; Dir Dr MARIJKE HELLEMANS.

Museum Smidt van Gelder: Lange Nieuwstraat 24, 2000 Antwerp; tel. (3) 239-06-52; fax (3) 230-22-81; e-mail museum .smidtvangelder@stad.antwerpen.be; internet museum.antwerpen.be/smidtvangelder; f. 1950; Chinese and European porcelains, Dutch 17th century paintings, 18th century French furniture; Curator CLARA VANDERHENST.

Museum Vleeshuis (Sound of the City): Vleeshouwersstraat 38, 2000 Antwerp; tel. (3) 292-61-00; fax (3) 292-61-29; e-mail vleeshuis@stad.antwerpen.be; internet museumvleeshuis.be; f. 1913; applied art, archaeology, arms, ceramics, Egyptian, Greek and Roman antiquities, furniture, local history, musical instruments, numismatics, posters, sculpture; library of 15,000 vols; Curator KAREL MOENS.

Nationaal Scheepvaartmuseum (Steen) (National Maritime Museum): Steenplein 1, 2000 Antwerp; tel. (3) 201-93-40; fax (3) 201-93-41; e-mail scheepmus@stad.antwerpen .be; internet museum.antwerpen.be/ scheepvaartmuseum; f. 1952; maritime history, especially concerning Belgium; library of 43,000 vols; Asst Dir R. JALON.

Rubenshuis (Rubens House): Wapper 9–11, 2000 Antwerp; tel. (3) 201-15-55; fax (3) 227-

36-92; e-mail rubenshuis@stad.antwerpen .be; internet www.rubenshuis.be; f. 1946; reconstruction of Rubens' house and studio; original 17th-century portico and pavilion; paintings by P. P. Rubens, his collaborators and pupils; 17th-century furnishings; Curator BEN VAN BENEDEN.

Volkskundemuseum: Gildekamersstraat 2–6, 2000 Antwerp; tel. (3) 220-86-66; fax (3) 220-83-68; internet museum.antwerpen .be/volkskunde; f. 1907; folklore of the Flemish provinces, esp. folk art and craft; library of 18,000 vols; Curator WERNER VAN HOOF.

Bouillon

Musée Ducal 'Les Amis de Vieux Bouillon': Rue du Petit 1–3, 6830 Bouillon; tel. (61) 46-41-89; fax (61) 46-41-99; e-mail courrier@museeducal.be; internet www .museeducal.be; f. 1947; archives, historical manuscripts and documents; archaeology, folklore; exhibition of the history of Godefroy de Bouillon; small library; Curator Mme MICHEL GOURDIN.

Bruges

Arentshuis: Dijver 16, 8000 Bruges; tel. (50) 44-87-11; fax (50) 44-87-78; e-mail musea@ brugge.be; internet www.museabrugge.be; 18th century manor house, contains a colln of lace and a permanent exhibition of works by Frank Brangwyn; additional exhibitions from the Groeningemuseum; Dir Dr MANFRED SELLINK.

Bruggemuseum–Archeologie (Bruges Museum–Archaeology): Mariastr. 36A, 8000 Bruges; tel. (50) 44-87-11; fax (50) 44-87-37; e-mail musea.secretariaat@brugge.be; internet www.museabrugge.be; f. 1997; Curator HUBERT DE WITTE.

Bruggemuseum–Gruuthuse: Dijver 17, 8000 Bruges; tel. (50) 44-87-11; fax (50) 44-87-37; e-mail musea.secretariaat@brugge.be; internet www.brugge.be; f. 1895; one of seven locations of the Bruggemuseum; a municipal collection in the 15th-century Palace of the Lords of Gruuthuse; furniture, sculpture, ceramics, tapestries, metalwork, instruments; Chief Curator HUBERT DE WITTE.

Bruggemuseum—Volkskunde (Municipal Museum of Folklore): Rolweg 40, 8000 Bruges; tel. (50) 44-87-11; fax (50) 44-87-37; e-mail musea@brugge.be; internet www .brugge.be; f. 1973; popular art, 19th century trades and crafts (shoemaker, grocer, cooper, confectioner, chemist, hatter, tailor), domestic interiors, classroom, devotional objects, pipes and tobacco, typical Flemish living room, period tavern *The Black Cat*; Curator HUBERT DE WITTE.

Groeningemuseum (Municipal Art Gallery): Dijver 12, 8000 Bruges; tel. (50) 44-87-11; fax (50) 44-87-78; e-mail musea@ brugge.be; internet www.brugge.be/musea/ fr/groeningefrans.htm; Belgian and Dutch paintings and etchings from late medieval times to present; Art Dir MANFRED SELLINK.

Hospitaalmuseum Sint-Janshospital: St John's Hospital, Mariastraat 38, 8000 Bruges; tel. (50) 44-87-11; fax (50) 44-87-35; e-mail musea@brugge.be; internet www .brugge.be/musea; f. c.1150; paintings by Hans Memling and Jan Provost, furniture and sculpture from 15th–19th century; mediaeval instruments and books; 17th century pharmacy; Chief Curator EVA TAHON.

Museum Onze-Lieve-Vrouw ter Potterie: Potterierei 79, 8000 Bruges; tel. (50) 44-87-11; fax (50) 44-87-78; e-mail musea@brugge .be; internet www.brugge.be/musea/nl/mpotn .htm; f. 1276; old hospital, museum and church; church ornaments, furniture, paintings, sculptures, 17th century tapestries, etc.; Chief Curator Dr MANFRED SELLINK.

Brussels

Koninklijk Museum voor Midden-Afrika/Musée Royal de l'Afrique Centrale: Leuvensesteenweg 13, 3080 Tervuren; tel. (2) 769-52-11; fax (2) 767-02-42; e-mail biblita@africamuseum.be; internet www .africamuseum.be; f. 1897; large collections in the fields of prehistory, ethnography, native arts and crafts; geology, mineralogy, palaeontology; zoology (entomology, ornithology, mammals, reptiles, etc.); history, economics; library of 110,000 vols; 37 scientific staff; Dir G. GRYSEELS; publ. *Annales* (5 publs dealing with botany, geology, zoology, the humanities and economics).

Musée d'Ixelles: 71 rue Jean Van Volsem, Ixelles, 1050 Brussels; tel. (322) 515-64-21; fax (322) 515-64-24; e-mail musee@ixelles.be; internet www.musee-ixelles.be; f. 1892; ancient and modern masters, water-colours, drawings, engravings, sculptures, posters, etc.; works of Belgian and foreign schools; library of 3,000 vols (bibliography); Curator NICOLE D'HUART.

Musée Royal de l'Armée et d'Histoire Militaire: Parc du Cinquantenaire 3, 1000 Brussels; tel. (2) 737-78-11; fax (2) 737-78-02; e-mail infocom@klm-mra.be; internet www .klm-mra.be; f. 1910; colln incl. int. military history from 10th century onwards; arms, uniforms, decorations, paintings, sculpture, maps; library of 450,000 vols and archives; Dir-Gen. DOMINQUE HANSON; publs *Bulletin du MRA* (1 a year), *Bulletin van het KLM* (1 a year).

Musées Royaux d'Art et d'Histoire: Parc du Cinquantenaire 10, 1000 Brussels; tel. (2) 741-72-11; fax (2) 733-77-35; e-mail info@ kmkg-mrah.be; internet www.kmkg-mrah .be; f. 1835; Dir ANNE CAHEN-DELHAYE.

Component Museums:

Musée du Cinquantenaire: 10 parc du Cinquantenaire, 1000 Brussels; tel. (2) 741-72-11; fax (2) 733-77-35; e-mail info@ kmkg-mrah.be; internet www.kmkg-mrah .be; f. 1835; archaeology of Belgium, the Americas, Asia, the Pacific and North Africa, and of ancient Iran and the Near East, Egypt, Greece and Rome; European decorative arts; library of 100,000 vols; Dir ANNE CAHEN-DELHAYE; publ. *Musze* (3 a year).

Musical Instrument Museum: 2 Montagne de la Cour, 1000 Brussels; tel. (2) 545-01-30; fax (2) 545-01-77; e-mail info@ mim.be; internet www.mim.be; f. 1877; musical instruments; Dir MALOU HAINE; Head of Communications JO SANTY.

Pavillon Chinois et Tour Japonaise: 44 ave Van Praet, 1020 Brussels; tel. (2) 268-16-08; fax (2) 268-16-08; e-mail info@ kmkg-mrah.be; internet www.kmkg-mrah .be; f. 1904; Chinese art, porcelain and furniture; Japanese architecture and decorative arts; Dir CHANTAL KOZYREFF.

Pavillon Horta-Lambeaux: Parc du Cinquantenaire, 1000 Brussels; tel. (2) 741-72-11; fax (2) 733-77-35; e-mail info@ kmkg-mrah.be; internet www.kmkg-mrah .be; f. 1899; marble relief of the Human Passions; Dir ANNE CAHEN-DELHAYE.

Porte de Hal/Halleepoort: Blvd du Midi, 1000 Brussels; tel. (2) 534-15-18; e-mail info@kmkg-mrah.be; internet www .kmkg-mrah.be; f. 1835; temporary exhibitions; Dir ELS VAN DER ELST.

Musées Royaux des Beaux-Arts de Belgique: 9 rue du Musée, 1000 Brussels; tel. (2) 508-32-11; fax (2) 508-32-32; e-mail info@ fine-arts-museum.be; internet www .fine-arts-museum.be; f. 1801; Brussels, medieval, Renaissance and modern pictures, drawings and sculpture; library of 164,000 vols; Chief Curator MICHEL DRAGUET; publ. *Bulletin*.

Attached Museums:

Musée Constantin Meunier: 59 rue de l'Abbaye, 1000 Brussels; tel. (2) 508-32-11; fax (2) 508-32-32; e-mail info@fine-arts-museum.be; internet www.fine-arts-museum.be; f. 1978; paintings, drawings and sculptures by Constantin Meunier, the artist's house and studio; Dir MICHEL DRAGUET.

Musée d'Art Ancien: 3 rue de la Régence, 1000 Brussels; tel. (2) 508-32-11; fax (2) 508-32-32; e-mail info@fine-arts-museum .be; internet www.fine-arts-museum.be; f. 1801; 15th–18th-century paintings, drawings and sculpture; Chief Curator MICHEL DRAGUET.

Musée d'Art Moderne: 1–2 Place Royale, 1000 Brussels; tel. (2) 508-32-11; fax (2) 508-32-32; e-mail info@fine-arts-museum .be; internet www.fine-arts-museum.be; f. 1984; paintings since 19th century, drawings and sculpture; Chief Curator MICHEL DRAGUET.

Musée Wiertz: 62 rue Vautier, 1000 Brussels; tel. (2) 508-32-11; fax (2) 508-32-32; e-mail info@fine-arts-museum.be; internet www.fine-arts-museum.be; f. 1868; paintings by Antoine Wiertz; the artist's house and studio; Chief Curator MICHEL DRAGUET.

Museum Erasmus: 31 rue du Chapitre, 1070 Brussels; tel. (2) 521-13-83; fax (2) 527-12-69; e-mail erasmushuis .maisonerasme@skynet.be; f. 1932; documents, paintings, early editions and manuscripts relating to Erasmus and other Humanists of the 16th century; library of 5,000 vols; Curator A. VANAUTGAERDEN.

Ghent

Museum voor Schone Kunsten (Museum for Fine Arts): Ch. de Kerchovelaan 187A, 9000 Ghent; tel. (9) 240-07-00; fax (9) 240-07-90; e-mail museum.msk@gent.be; internet www.mskgent.be; f. 1902; contains ancient and modern paintings, sculpture, tapestries, prints and drawings, icons from the Middle Ages to the first half of the 20th century; library; Dir ROBERT HOOZEE.

Oudheidkundig Museum van de Stad Gent: Godshuizenlaan 2, 9000 Ghent; tel. (9) 225-11-06; fax (9) 233-34-59; e-mail museum.bijloke@gent.be; internet www.gent .be; f. 1833; prehistory, local history, applied arts, furniture, arms, numismatics, collection of Chinese art, tapestries, costumes; Dir JEANNINE BALDEWIJNS.

Stedelijk Museum voor Actuele Kunst (Museum of Contemporary Art): Citadelpark, 9000 Ghent; tel. (9) 240-76-01; fax (9) 221-71-09; e-mail museum.smak@gent.be; internet www.smak.be; f. 1975; drawings, etchings, paintings, sculpture; featured movements incl. arte povera, cobra, conceptualism, minimalism, pop art; library of 40,000 vols, 195 periodicals; Dir PHILIPPE VAN CAUTEREN.

Liège

Collections artistiques de l'Université de Liège: 7 place du 20 août, 4000 Liège; tel. (4) 366-56-07; fax (4) 366-58-54; e-mail wittert@ulg.ac.be; internet www.ulg.ac.be/ wittert; f. 1903; 30,000 prints and drawings, paintings of 15th and 16th century; modern Belgian paintings; 5,483 coins; collection of Zairian art and craft; Curator Dr JEAN-PATRICK DUCHESNE.

Musée d'Art Moderne et d'Art Contemporain: 3 parc de la Boverie, 4020 Liège; tel. (4) 343-04-03; fax (4) 344-19-07; e-mail mamac@skynet.be; internet www.mamac

.org; f. 1981; modern paintings, sculptures and abstracts of the Belgian School, French and foreign masters; Curators FRANCINE DAWANS, FRANÇOISE DUMONT FRANÇOISE SAFIN.

Musée de la Vie Wallonne: Cour des Mineurs, 4000 Liège; tel. (4) 237-90-40; fax (4) 237-90-89; internet www.viewallonne.be; f. 1912; varied collection covering south Belgium in the fields of ethnography, folklore, arts and crafts and history; 450,000 documents; library of 35,000 vols; Man. Dir MARIE-CLAUDE THURION; publ. *Enquêtes* (1 a year).

Musées d'Archéologie et d'Arts Décoratifs de Liège: Institut Archéologique Liégeois, 13 quai de Maastricht, 4000 Liège; tel. (4) 221-94-04; fax (4) 221-94-32; Curator LUC ENGEN.

Attached Museums Include:

Musée Curtius: 13 quai de Maastricht, 4000 Liège; tel. (4) 221-83-83; fax (4) 221-94-80; f. 1909; chief sections: prehistory, Romano-Belgian and Frankish, Liège coins, decorative arts (from the Middle Ages to the 19th century); Annexe: lapidary colln in Palais de Justice; the museum is the HQ of the Archaeological Institute of Liège (*q.v.*).

Musée d'Ansembourg: 114 Féronstrée, 4000 Liège; tel. (4) 221-94-02; f. 1905; collns of 18th-century decorative arts of Liège; reconstituted interiors.

Musée du Verre: 13 quai de Maastricht, 4000 Liège; tel. (4) 221-94-04; fax (4) 221-94-32; f. 1959; all the main centres of production, from the earliest times to present, are represented.

Mariemont

Musée Royal et Domaine de Mariemont: 100 Chaussée de Mariemont, 7140 Morlanwelz, Mariemont; tel. (64) 21-21-93; fax (64) 26-29-24; e-mail info@musee-mariemont.be; internet www.musee-mariemont.be; f. 1920; contains antiquities from Egypt, Greece, Rome, China, Japan; nat. archaeology; Tournai porcelain; bookbindings; library of 100,000 vols; Dirs FRANÇOIS MAIRESSE, MARIE-CÉCILE BRUWIER; publs *Bulletin d'Information* (4 a year), *Les Cahiers de Mariemont* (1 a year).

Mechelen

Stadsmuseum: Hof van Busleyden-Fred. de Merodestraat 65–67, 2800 Mechelen; tel. (15) 29-40-30; fax (15) 29-40-31; e-mail stedelijkemusea@mechelen.be; internet www .mechelen.be/stedelijkemusea; f. 1844; municipal museum; history, art, applied art; Curator HEIDI DE NIJN.

Verviers

Centre Touristique de la Laine et de la Mode (Wool and Fashion Tourist Centre): 30 rue de la Chapelle, 4800 Verviers; tel. (87) 35-57-03; fax (87) 31-20-95; e-mail info@ aqualaine.be; internet www.aqualaine.be; f. 1985; history of wool-making before the industrial revolution of 1800.

Musée d'Archéologie et de Folklore: 42 rue des Raines, 4800 Verviers; tel. (87) 33-16-95; e-mail musees.verviers@skynet.be; internet www.lesmuseesenwallonie.be; f. 1959; history of art, archaeology, folklore, local history; Curator MARIE-PAULE DEBLANC.

Musée des Beaux-Arts et de la Céramique: 17 rue Renier, 4800 Verviers; tel. (87) 33-16-95; e-mail musees.verviers@skynet.be; internet www.lesmuseesenwallonie.be; f. 1884; sculpture, paintings; ceramics of Europe and Asia; MARIE-PAULE LEBLANC; publ. *Guide du Visiteur*.

Universities

UNIVERSITEIT ANTWERPEN
(University of Antwerp)

Prinsstraat 13 2000 Antwerp

Telephone: (3) 265-41-11

Fax: (3) 265-44-20

E-mail: info@ua.ac.be

Internet: www.ua.ac.be

Founded 2003 by merger of Universitaire Centrum Antwerpen, Universitaire Faculteiten Sint-Ignatius Antwerpen and Universitaire Insteling Antwerpen

State control

Languages of instruction: Dutch, English

Academic year: September to July

Library of 1,351,000 vols

Rector: Prof. Dr ALAIN VERSCHOREN

Pres.: Prof. Dr ANDRE VAN POECH

Chair of Education Council: Prof. Dr JOKE DENEKENS

Chair of Research Council: Prof. Dr JEAN PIERRE TIMMERMANS

Chair of Services Council: Prof. Dr JOHAN MEEUSEN

Man.: Prof. Dr BART HEIJNEN

Librarian: TRUDI NOORDERMEER

Number of teachers: 989

Number of students: 13,032

Publications: *Antwerpse Studies over Nederlandse Literatuurgeschiedenis, Bijdragen tot de Geschiedenis, Computer Assisted Language Learning, CSB-Berichten, Economische Didaktiek, Genetic Joyce Studies* (e-journal on the works of James Joyce), *Gezelliana, Kroniek van de Gezellestudie, Het Teken van de Ram, In de Steigers, Miscellanea Neerlandica, OASeS Cahiers and Documenten, Ons Geestelijk Erf, Pragmatics*

DEANS

Faculty of Applied Economics: Prof. Dr KAREL SOUDAN

Faculty of Arts and Philosophy: Prof. Dr BRUNO TRITSMANS

Faculty of Law: Prof. Dr GERT STRAETMANS

Faculty of Medicine: Prof. Dr PAUL VAN DE HEYNING

Faculty of Pharmaceutical, Biomedical and Veterinary Sciences: Prof. Dr FRANS VAN MEIR

Faculty of Political and Social Sciences: Prof. Dr RIA JANVIER

Faculty of Science: Prof. Dr JHERWIG LEIRS

ATTACHED RESEARCH INSTITUTES

Aisthesis: tel. (3) 220-43-04; fax (3) 220-45-46; e-mail luc.vandendries@ua.ac.be; internet www.ua.ac.be/main .aspx?c=*faclw=18390; Dir Prof. Dr LUK VAN DEN DRIES.

Antwerps Innovatie Centrum: Drie Eikenstraat 661, 2650 Edegem; tel. (3) 265-93-04; fax (3) 265-93-78; e-mail luc .lammens@antwerpinnovation.com; internet www.antwerpinnovation.com; Gen. Manager LUC LAMMENS.

Antwerp Institute for Enterprise Computing (AIFEC): Prinsstraat 13, 2000 Antwerpen; e-mail carlos.debacher@ua.ac .be; Dir Prof. Dr CARLOS DE BACHER.

Antwerp University Hospital: Wilrijkstraat 10, 2650 Edegem; tel. (3) 821-30-00; fax (3) 829-05-20; e-mail info@uza.be; internet www.uza.be/uza; Dir JOHNNY VAN DER STRAETEN.

Austrian Centre Antwerp: tel. (3) 265-42-48; fax (3) 265-42-59; e-mail octant@ua.ac.be; internet www.ua.ac.be/octant; Dir Prof. Dr CLEMENS RUTHNER.

Centre for ASEAN Studies: Kipdorp 61, 2000 Antwerpen; tel. (3) 265-50-34; fax (3) 265-50-26; e-mail ludo.cuyvers@ua.ac.be; internet webh01.ua.ac.be/cas; Dir Prof. Dr LUDO CUYVERS.

Centre for European and International Business Education and Research: tel. (3) 265-50-28; fax (3) 265-50-26; e-mail liliane .vanhoof@ua.ac.be; Dir Prof. Dr LILIANE VAN HOOF.

Centre for Grammar, Cognition and Typology: tel. (3) 265-45-50; fax (3) 265-45-46; e-mail johan.vanderauwera@ua.ac.be; internet webhost.ua.ac.be/cgct/id11.htm; Dir Prof. Dr JOHAN VAN DER AUWERA.

Centre for International Management and Development: Lange Sint Annastraat 7 , 2000 Antwerpen; tel. (3) 265-45-25; fax (3) 265-48-53; e-mail filip.debeule@ua.ac.be; internet www.ua.ac.be/cimda; Dir Prof. Dr DANNY VAN DEN BULCKE.

Centre for Mexican Studies: Prinsstraat 9, 2000 Antwerpen; tel. (3) 265-44-42; fax (3) 265-44-20; e-mail ingeborg.jongbloet@ua.ac .be; internet www.ua.ac.be/cms; Dir Prof. Dr JEAN VAN HOUTTE.

Centre for Migration and Intercultural Studies (CeMIS): Lange Nieuwstraat 55, 2000 Antwerpen; tel. (3) 265-59-65; fax (3) 265-59-26; e-mail ina.lodewyckx@ua.ac.be; internet www.ua.ac.be/cemis; Dir Prof. Dr CHRISTIANE TIMMERMAN.

Centre for Philosophical Psychology: tel. (3) 265-43-08; fax (3) 265-44-20; e-mail joachim.leilich@ua.ac.be; internet www.ua.ac .be/main.aspx?c=.philosophyofmind; Dir Prof. Dr JOACHIM LEILICH.

Centre for Proteomics and Mass Spectrometry: Groenenborgerlaan 171, 2020 Antwerpen; tel. (3) 34-96; fax (3) 34-88; e-mail eddy.esmans@ua.ac.be; internet www .ceproma.ua.ac.be/ceproma.html; Lab Dir Prof. Dr YVES GUISEZ.

Centre for Psycholinguistics: tel. (3) 265-42-47; fax (3) 265-42-59; e-mail dominiek .sandra@ua.ac.be; internet www.cpl.ua.ac .be; Dir Prof. Dr DOMINIEK SANDRA.

Centre for Social Policy Herman Deleeck: Sint-Jacobsstraat 2, 2000 Antwerpen; tel. (3) 265-53-74; fax (3) 265-57-90; e-mail ingrid.vanzele@ua.ac.be; internet www.centrum-voorsociaalbelcid.be; Dir Prof. Dr BEA CANTILLON.

Centre for the Economic Study of Innovation and Technology: tel. (3) 265-40-54; fax (3) 265-40-26; e-mail sigrid.suetens@ua .ac.be; internet webh01.ua.ac.be/cesit; Dirs Prof. Dr WIM MEEUSEN, Prof. Dr JEF PLASMANS.

Centre for the Evaluation of Vaccination: Universiteitsplein 1, 2610 Antwerpen-Wilrijk; tel. (3) 265-26-52; fax (3) 265-26-40; e-mail cev@ua.ac.be; internet www.ua.ac .be/cev; Dir Prof. Dr PIERRE VAN DAMME.

Centre for the Study of the Great Lakes Region of Africa: Lange Sint Annastraat 7 , 2000 Antwerpen; tel. (3) 265-56-99; fax (3) 265-57-71; e-mail stefaan.marysse@ua.ac.be; internet www.ua.ac.be/main.aspx?c=.gralac; Dir Prof. Dr STEFAAN MARYSSE.

Centrum Nascholing Onderwijs: Universiteitsplein 1, 2610 Antwerpen-Wilrijk; tel. (3) 265-29-60; fax (3) 265-29-57; e-mail paul .reynders@ua.ac.be; internet www.ua.ac.be/ cno; Dir Prof. Dr PAUL MAHIEU.

Centrum Pieter Gillis: tel. (3) 265-44-77; fax (3) 265-49-38; e-mail nina.vleugels@ua.ac .be; internet www.ua.ac.be/main .aspx?c=pietergil; Dir Prof. Dr GUY VANHEESWIJCK.

Centrum voor Bedrijfsgeschiedenis: tel. (3) 265-42-52; fax (3) 265-45-46; e-mail helma

.desmedt@ua.ac.be; internet www.ua.ac.be/ main.aspx?c=*faclw=3314; Dir Prof. Dr HELMA DE SMEDT.

Centrum voor Begaafdheidsonderzoek: Grote Steenweg 40, 2600 Antwerpen-Berchem; tel. (3) 265-30-88; fax (3) 265-31-86; e-mail info@cbo-antwerpen.be; internet www.ua.ac.be/main.aspx?c=cbo; Dir Dr TESSA KIEBOOM.

Centrum voor Bekkenbodemkunde: Universiteitsplein 1, 2610 Antwerpen-Wilrijk; tel. (3) 265-25-35; fax (3) 265-25-01; e-mail jeanjacques.wyndaele@ua.ac.be; Dir Prof. Dr JEAN-JACQUES WYNDAELE.

Centrum voor Beroepsvervolmaking Rechten: Venusstraat 35, 2000 Antwerpen; tel. (3) 265-54-48; fax (3) 265-59-79; e-mail cbr@ua.ac.be; internet www.ua.ac.be/cbr; Dir PASCALE BUYCK.

Centrum voor Biomedische Beeldvorming: Groenenborgerlaan 171 , 2020 Antwerpen; tel. (3) 32-30; fax (3) 32-33; e-mail annemie.vanderlinden@ua.ac.be; internet www.ua.c.be/biomedischebeeldvorming; Dir Prof. Dr ANNEMIE VAN DER LINDEN.

Centrum voor de Filosofie van de Religie: Koningstraat 8, 2000 Antwerpen; tel. (3) 265-46-60; fax (3) 265-44-20; e-mail luc .braeckmans@ua.ac.be; Dir Prof. Dr LUC BRAECKMANS.

Centrum voor Ethiek: tel. (3) 265-43-07; fax (3) 265-44-20; e-mail johan.taels@ua.ac .be; Dir Prof. Dr JOHAN TAELS.

Centrum voor Filosofie van de Kunst en Literatuur: tel. (3) 265-43-08; fax (3) 265-44-20; e-mail erik.oger@ua.ac.be; Dir Prof. Dr ERIK OGER.

Centrum voor Kankerpreventie: Universiteitsplein 1, 2610 Antwerpen-Wilrijk; tel. (3) 265-26-53; fax (3) 265-26-40; e-mail rsc@ ua.ac.be; internet www.ua.ac.be/main .aspx?c=esoc; Dir Prof. Dr JOOST WEYLER.

Centrum voor Longitudinaal en Levenslooponderzoek: Sint-Jacobsstraat 2, 2000 Antwerpen; tel. (3) 265-55-35; fax (3) 265-57-93; e-mail dimitri.mortelmans@ua.ac.be; internet www.ua.ac.be/cell0; Dir Prof. Dr DIMITRI MORTELMANS.

Centrum voor Metafysica en Cultuur: tel. (3) 265-43-41; fax (3) 265-44-20; e-mail guy.vanheeswijck@ua.ac.be; Dir Prof. Dr GUIDO VANHEESWIJCK.

Centrum voor Nederlandse Taal en Spraak: Universiteitsplein 1, 2610 Antwerpen-Wilrijk; tel. (3) 265-27-66; fax (3) 265-27-62; e-mail walter.daelemans@ua.ac.be; internet www.cnts.ua.ac.be/cnts; Dir Prof. Dr WALTER DAELEMANS.

Centrum voor Rechtssociologie: tel. (3) 265-41-11; fax (3) 265-44-20; e-mail francis .vanloon@ua.ac.be; Dir Prof. Dr FRANCIS VAN LOON.

Centrum voor Roemenië Studies: tel. (3) 265-45-50; fax (3) 265-45-46; e-mail liliane .tasmowski@ua.ac.be; Dir Prof. Dr LILIANE TASMOWSKI.

Centrum voor Stadsgeschiedenis: Prinsstraat 13, 2000 Antwerpen; tel. (3) 265-42-78; fax (3) 265-44-20; e-mail bruno.blonde@ua.ac .be; Dir Prof. Dr BERT DE MUNCH.

Centrum voor Tekstgenetica: tel. (3) 265-42-57; fax (3) 265-45-46; e-mail geert .lernout@ua.ac.be; Dir Prof. Dr GEERT LERNOUT.

Centrum voor Thoracale Oncologie Groep Antwerpen: Universiteitsplein 1, 2610 Antwerpen-Wilrijk; tel. (3) 265-26-39; fax (3) 265-25-01; e-mail paul.germonpre@ua .ac.be; Dir Prof. Dr PAUL GERMONPRÉ.

Centrum voor Zorg: Universiteitsplein 1, 2610 Antwerpen-Wilrijk; tel. (3) 265-23-12;

fax (3) 265-23-12; e-mail bart.geraets@ua.ac .be.

Collaborative Antwerp Psychiatric Research Institute: Universiteitsplein 1, 2610 Antwerpen-Wilrijk; tel. (3) 265-24-01; fax (3) 265-24-14; e-mail bernard.sabbe@ua .ac.be; internet www.ua.ac.be/main.aspx?c= .capri; Dir Prof. Dr BERNARD SABBE.

Department of General Practice: Universiteitsplein 1, 2610 Antwerpen-Wilrijk; tel. (3) 265-25-29; fax (3) 265-25-26; e-mail chris .monteyne@ua.ac.be; internet webh01.ua.ac .be/cha; Dirs Prof. Dr JOKE DENEKENS, Prof. Dr PAUL VAN ROYEN.

Europacentrum Jean Monnet: tel. (3) 265-40-88; fax (3) 265-44-20; e-mail evrard .claessens@ua.ac.be; Dir Prof. Dr EVRARD CLAESSENS.

Expertise Centrum Hoger Onderwijs: Venusstr. 35 2000 Antwerpen; tel. (3) 265-45-08; fax (3) 265-45-01; e-mail echo@ua.ac .be; internet www.ua.ac.be/echo; Dir Prof. Dr PETER VAN PETEGEM.

Institute of Development Policy and Management: Prinstraat 1, 2000 Antwerpen; tel. (3) 265-57-70; fax (3) 265-57-71; e-mail dev@ua.ac.be; internet www.ua.ac.be/ iob; Dir Prof. Dr ROBRECHT RENARC.

Institute of Environment Sustainable Development: Universiteitsplein 1, 2610 Antwerpen-Wilrijk; tel. (3) 265-21-14; fax (3) 265-21-28; e-mail milieu@ua.ac.be; internet www.ua.ac.be/imdo; Dir Prof. Dr AVIEL VERBRUGGEN.

Institute of Jewish Studies: Prinstraat 13, 2000 Antwerpen; tel. (3) 265-52-43; fax (3) 265-52-41; e-mail ijs@ua.ac.be; internet www .ua.ac.be/ijs; Dir Prof. Dr VIVIAN LISKA.

Institute of Molecular Neurosciences: Universiteitsplein 1, 2610 Antwerpen-Wilrijk; tel. (3) 265-10-02; fax (3) 265-10-12; e-mail gisele.smeyers@ua.ac.be; internet www.molgen.ua.ac.be; Dir Prof. Dr CHRISTINE VAN BROECKHOVEN.

Institute of Transport and Maritime Management, Antwerp: Keizerstraat 64, 2000 Antwerpen; tel. (3) 265-51-51; fax (3) 265-51-50; e-mail frank.vanlaeke@ua.ac.be; internet www.ua.ac.be/itmma; Pres. Prof. Dr THEO NOTTEBOOM.

Instituut voor de Geschiedenis van de Geneeskunde en de Natuurwetenschappen: Universiteitsplein 1, 2610 Antwerpen-Wilrijk; tel. (3) 265-25-37; fax (3) 265-21-28; e-mail robrecht.vanhee@ua.ac.be; Dir Prof. Dr ROBRECHT VAN HEE.

Instituut voor de Geschiedenis van de Spiritualiteit in de Nederlanden tot ca. 1750: tel. (3) 265-57-80; fax (3) 265-44-20; e-mail thom.mertens@ua.ac.be; Dir Prof. Dr THOM MERTENS.

Instituut voor de Studie van de Letterkunde in de Nederlanden: tel. (3) 265-42-91; fax (3) 265-44-20; e-mail els.crauwels@ua .ac.be; internet www.ua.ac.be/isln; Dir Prof. Dr PIET COUTTENIER.

Instituut voor Onderwijs- en Informatiewetenschappen: Venusstraat 35, 2000 Antwerpen; tel. and fax (3) 265-45-0; e-mail ioiw@ua.ac.be; internet www.ua.ac.be/ ioiw-ua; Dir Prof. Dr PETER VAN PETEGEM.

Instituut voor Samenwerking tussen Universiteit en Arbeidersbeweging: Venusstraat 23, 2000 Antwerpen; tel. (3) 265-58-86; fax (3) 265-59-77; e-mail els .peeters@ua.ac.be; internet www.ua.ac.be/ isua; Dir Prof. Dr MARC RIGAUX.

International Pragmatics Association: tel. (3) 265-45-63; fax (3) 265-55-74; e-mail ann.verhaert@ua.ac.be; internet ipra.ua.ac .be; Dir Prof. Dr JEF VERSCHUEREN.

Linguapolis: Institute for Language and Communication: Kleine Hauwenberg 12, 2000 Antwerpen; tel. (3) 265-48-03; fax (3) 265-46-37; e-mail info@linguapolis.be; internet www.linguapolis.be; Dir Prof. Dr POL CUVELIER.

Louis Paul Boon Documentatiecentrum: Lange Winkelstraat 40-42, 2000 Antwerp; tel. (3) 265-52-50; fax (3) 265-52-24; e-mail kris.humbeeck@ua.ac.be; internet www .lpbooncentrum.be; Dir Prof. Dr KRIS HUMBEECK.

Micro and Trace Analysis Center: Universiteitsplein 1, 2610 Antwerpen-Wilrijk; tel. (3) 265-23-40; fax (3) 265-23-76; e-mail rene.vangrieken@ua.ac.be; Dir Prof. Dr RENÉ VAN GRIEKEN.

Referentiecentrum voor Biologische Merkers van Geheugenstoornissen: Universiteitsplein 1, 2610 Antwerpen-Wilrijk; tel. (3) 265-26-20; fax (3) 265-26-69; e-mail peter.dedeyn@ua.ac.be; Dir Prof. Dr PETER DE DEYN.

Research Centre on Technology, Energy and Environment: Prinsstraat 13, 2000 Antwerpen; tel. (3) 265-49-00; fax (3) 265-49-01; e-mail aviel.verbruggen@ua.ac.be; internet www.ua.ac.be/stem; Dir Prof. Dr AVIEL VERBRUGGEN.

Research Park Waterfront: Drie Eikenstraat 661, 2650 Edegem; tel. (3) 265-93-00; fax (3) 265-93-09; e-mail chris.deceulaerde@ ubca.be; internet www.waterfront.be; Dir CHRIS DE CEULAERDE.

Steunpunt Buitenlands Beleid: Lange Sint-Annastraat 7, 2000 Antwerpen; tel. (3) 265-56-37; fax (3) 265-57-98; e-mail vsbb@ua .ac.be; internet www.ua.ac.be/vsbbe; Dir ANNICK SCHRAMME.

Steunpunt Gelijkekansenbeleid: Lange Nieuwstraat 55, 2000 Antwerpen; tel. (3) 265-59-43; e-mail steunpuntgeka@ua.ac.be; internet www.ua.ac.be/sgk; Dir NICO STEEGMANS.

Studie Centrum voor Onderneming en Beurs: Middelheimlaan 1, 2020 Antwerpen; tel. (3) 265-35-38; e-mail frans.buelens@ua.ac .be; internet www.scob.be; Dir Prof. Dr LUDO CUYVERS.

Studie- en Documentatiecentrum Hugo Claus: Prinsstraat 13, 2000 Antwerpen; tel. (3) 265-52-49; fax (3) 265-44-20; e-mail georges.wildemeersch@ua.ac.be; internet www.clauscentrum.be/main.aspx?c=claus; Dir Prof. Dr GEORGES WILDEMEERSCH.

Universitair Wetenschappelijk Instituut voor Drugproblemen: tel. (3) 265-40-65; fax (3) 265-44-20; e-mail a.uwid@antwerpen .be; internet www.uwid.be; Dir Prof. Dr BOB VERMERGHT.

University of Antwerp Legal School: Venusstraat 23, 2000 Antwerpen; tel. (3) 265-54-45; fax (3) 265-51-20; e-mail mieke .briels@ua.ac.be; internet www.ua.ac.be/uals; Dir Prof. Dr MAURICE ADAMS.

University of Antwerp Management School: Sint-Jacobsmarkt 9-13, 2000 Antwerpen; tel. (3) 265-49-89; fax (3) 265-47-59; e-mail info@uams.be; internet www .uams.be/en; Dean Prof. Dr PHILIP NAERT (acting).

HOGESCHOOL-UNIVERSITEIT BRUSSEL

Vrijheidslaan 17, 1081 Brussels

Telephone: (2) 210-12-11

E-mail: info@hubrussel.be

Internet: www.hubrussel.be

Founded 1968 as Universitaire Faculteiten Sint-Aloysius; became Katholieke Universiteit Brussel 1991; merged with European University College, VLEKHO and HONIM in 2007

Language of instruction: Dutch; attached to Katholieke Universiteit Leuven

Private control

Academic year: October to July

Rector: Prof. Dr DIRK DE CEULAER

Library of 70,000 vols

Number of teachers: 1,000

Number of students: 9,000

DEANS

Department of Economic Sciences: G. RASPOET

Department of Germanic Philology: L. TEEUWEN

Department of History: E. DEFOORT

Department of Law: F. FLEERACKERS

Department of Philosophy: J. F. LINDEMANS

Department of Social and Political Sciences: J. DELWAIDE

PROFESSORS

ACX, R., Bank and Credit Sciences
BOUSSET, H., Dutch Literature
BRAEKMAN, W. L., English Literature
CARPENTIER, N.
DE BOECK, A.
DE CLERCQ, M., European Literature and Introduction to Modern Literature
DEFOORT, E., Modern French Texts
DEGADT, J., Economic Science and Social Statistics
DE LATHOUWER, L.
DELWAIDE, J.
DE MARTELAERE, P., Philosophic Anthropology
DEPREEUW, E.
DE SCHRYVER, J.
DESMET, J.
DE VIN, D., Dutch Literature
DEWINTER, L.
ELST, M.
FLEERACKERS, F.
FOBLETS, M.-C.
GEERAERTS, R.
GOOSSENS, W., Historic Introduction to Philosophy
GOTZEN, F., Introduction to Law
HEMMERECHTS, L.
HEYSSE, T.
JAKOBS, D.
JANSSENS, J., History of Medieval Dutch Literature
JANSSENS, P., Modern Times
LINDEMANS, J.-F., Traditional Logics
LOOSVELDT, G., Methods and Techniques of Social Sciences
MOONS, T., History of Antiquity
MUYLLE, J., Art and Cultural History
NELDE, P. H., Germanic Linguistics
OOSTERBOSCH, A., Physics
SCHOENMAECKERS, R.
SWYNGEDOUW, M.
TACQ, J., Sociology
VANDEN BROECKE, S.
VAN DEN WIJNGAERT, M., History of Modern Times
VANDEN WYNGAERD, G.
VAN DE WOESTYNE, I.
VANHEMELRYCK, F., History of Modern Times
VAN HOECKE, M., Introduction to Law
VERRETH, H.
VERSTRAELEN, L., Mathematics
VERTONGHEN, R., Accountancy
WINTGENS, L.

UNIVERSITÉ LIBRE DE BRUXELLES
(Free University of Brussels)

50 ave Franklin Roosevelt, 1050 Brussels

Telephone: (2) 650-23-17

Fax: (2) 650-36-30

E-mail: elennertz@admin.ulb.ac.be

Internet: www.ulb.ac.be

Founded 1834; became ind. from the Vrije Univ. Brussel in 1970

Language of instruction: French

Private control

Academic year: September to July

Pres.: JEAN-LOUIS VANHERWEGHEM

Vice-Pres.: FABRIZIO BUCELLA

Rector: PIERRE DE MARET

Sec.: SERGE BODSON

Librarian: Prof. JEAN-PIERRE DEVROEY

Library: see Libraries and Archives

Number of teachers: 1,300

Number of students: 20,000

Publication: *Esprit Libre* (magazine, 12 a year)

DEANS

Faculty of Applied Sciences: Prof. PHILIPPE VINCKE

Faculty of Law: Prof. PAUL-ALAIN FORIERS

Faculty of Medicine: Prof. ELIE COGAN

Faculty of Philosophy and Letters: Prof. JEAN-PIERRE DEVROEY

Faculty of Psychology and Education: Prof. ASSAAD ELIA AZZI

Faculty of Science: Prof. GUY LATOUCHE

Faculty of Social, Political and Economic Sciences: Prof. ANDRÉ FARBER

ASSOCIATED INSTITUTES AND SCHOOLS

Centre de Recherches Industrielles et Agronomiques (CRIA): Pres. JEAN-CLAUDE LEGROS.

Centre d'Etudes Canadiennes (Centre for Canadian Studies): Pres. GINETTE KURGAN-VAN HENTENRYK.

Centre Emile Bernheim: Pres. ANDRÉ FARBER.

Centre Interdisciplinaire D'Etude des Religions et de la Laïcité (CIERL): Dir JEAN-PHILIPPE SCHREIBER.

Département d'Economie Appliquée (Applied Economics Department): 2 ave Paul Héger, 1050 Brussels; Dirs HENRI CAPRON, ROBERT PLASMAN.

Ecole de Commerce Ernest Solvay (Ernest Solvay Business School): Pres. PHILIPPE BILTIAU.

Ecole d'Infirmières annexée à l'Université (Nursing School attached to the University): Campus Erasme, 808 Route de Lennik, 1070 Brussels; Dir GABRIELLE BUSCARLET.

European Centre for Advanced Research in Economics and Statistics (ECARES): Dirs MARC HALLIN, VICTOR GINSBURGH.

Groupe d'Etudes sur l'Ethnicité, le Racisme, les Migrations et l'Exclusion (GERME): Dir ANDREA REA.

Institut de Recherche Interdisciplinaire en Biologie Humaine et Moléculaire (IRIBHM): Dir GILBERT VASSART.

Institut de Sociologie (Institute of Sociology): 44 ave Jeanne, 1050 Brussels; f. 1901; Dir FIROUZEH NAHAVANDI.

Institut Jules Bordet (Jules Bordet Institute): 1 rue Héger-Bordet, 1000 Brussels; tel. (2) 538-28-20; diagnosis and treatment of tumours; Dir JEAN KLASTERSKY.

VRIJE UNIVERSITEIT BRUSSEL
(Free University of Brussels)

Pleinlaan 2, 1050 Brussels

Telephone: (2) 629-21-11

Fax: (2) 629-22-82

E-mail: infovub@vub.ac.be

Internet: www.vub.ac.be

Founded 1834; became independent from the Université Libre de Bruxelles in 1970

Languages of instruction: Dutch, English

Private control

Academic year: October to July

President: R. VAN AERSCHOT

Rector: P. DE KNOP

Vice-Rectors: H. CASMAN, Y. MICHOTTE, L. WYNS

Director-General: J. VAN LEEMPUT

Librarian: P. VANOUPLINES

Number of teachers: 700

Number of students: 10,000

Publications: *Akademos*, *Newsletter* (electronic), *Nieuw Tijdschrift van de VUB*, *VUB-Press*

DEANS

Faculty of Applied Science: JACQUES DE RUYCK

Faculty of Law: VAN LIMBERGHEN

Faculty of Medicine: A. DUPONT

Faculty of Philosophy and Letters: JEAN PAUL VAN BENDEGEM

Faculty of Physical Education and Kinesiology: PETER VAN ROY

Faculty of Psychology and Education: ROLAND PEPERMANS

Faculty of Sciences and Bioengineering: PATRICK DE BAETSELIER

Faculty of Social, Political and Economic Sciences: ROSETTE S'JEGERS

CONSTITUENT COLLEGE

Vesalius College: Pleinlaan 2, 1050 Brussels; tel. (2) 629-28-22; fax (2) 629-36-37; f. 1987 in asscn with Boston Univ.; degree courses in arts, sciences and engineering; language of instruction: English; Dean JEAN-PIERRE DE GRÈVE.

UNIVERSITEIT GENT
(Ghent University)

St-Pietersnieuwstraat 25, 9000 Ghent

Telephone: (9) 264-31-11

Fax: (9) 264-82-93

E-mail: communicatie@ugent.be

Internet: www.ugent.be

Founded 1817

Language of instruction: Dutch

State control

Academic year: October to July

Rector: Prof. PAUL VAN CAUWENBERGE

Vice-Rector: Prof. LUC MOENS

Govt Commr: YANNICK DE CLERCQ

Academic Admin.: Prof. KOEN GOETHALS

Logistic Administrator: DIRK MANGELEER

Sec. of the Board of Govs: KRISTOF DE MOOR

Library: see Libraries and Archives

Number of teachers: 960

Number of students: 32,000

Publication: *Universiteit Gent* (8 a year)

DEANS

Faculty of Arts and Philosophy: FREDDY MORTIER

Faculty of Bioscience Engineering: GUIDO VAN HUYLENBROECK

Faculty of Economics and Business Administration: MARC DE CLERCQ

Faculty of Engineering: LUC TAERWE

Faculty of Law: PIET TAELMAN

Faculty of Medicine and Health Sciences: ERIC MORTIER

Faculty of Pharmaceutical Sciences: JEAN PAUL REMON

Faculty of Political and Social Sciences: RUDDY DOOM

Faculty of Psychology and Educational Sciences: GEERT DESOETE

Faculty of Sciences: HERWIG DEJONGHE

Faculty of Veterinary Sciences: HUBERT DEBRABANDER

PROFESSORS

Faculty of Arts and Philosophy (Blandijnberg 2, 9000 Ghent; tel. (9) 264-39-32; fax (9) 264-41-95):

ART, J., Modern History

BOURGEOIS, J., Archaeology and Ancient History of Europe

COMMERS, M., Philosophy and Moral Sciences

DECREUS, F., Latin and Greek

DETREZ, R., Slavonic and East-European Studies

DEVOS, I., Early Modern History

DEVOS, M., Dutch Linguistics

KABUTA, N., African Languages and Cultures

LAUREYS, G., Nordic Studies

LEMAN, M., Art, Music and Theatre Sciences

MOERLOOSE, E., Languages and Cultures of South and East Asia

PINXTEN, H., Comparative Sciences of Culture

ROEGIEST, E., Language and Communication

SLEMBROUCK, S., English

TANRET, M., Languages and Cultures of the Near East and North Africa

THOEN, E., Medieval History

VERHULST, S., Romance Languages (Other than French)

VERVAECK, B., Dutch Literature

WILLEMS, D., French

WILLEMS, K., German

Faculty of Bioscience Engineering (Coupure Links 653, 9000 Ghent; tel. (9) 264-59-01; fax (9) 264-62-45):

DEVLIEGHERE, F., Food Safety and Food Quality

JANSSEN, C., Applied Ecology and Environmental Biology

OTTOY, J., Applied Mathematics, Biometrics and Process Control

PIETERS, J., Biosystems Engineering

REHEUL, D., Plant Production

SORGELOOS, P., Animal Production

STEURBAUT, W., Crop Protection

VAN MEIRVENNE, M., Soil Management

VAN OOSTVELDT, P., Molecular Biotechnology

VERHÉ, R., Organic Chemistry

VERHEYEN, K., Forest and Water Management

VERLOO, M., Applied Analytical and Physical Chemistry

VERSTRAETE, W., Biochemical and Microbial Technology

VIAENE, J., Agricultural Economics

Faculty of Economics and Business Administration (Hoveniersberg 24, 9000 Ghent; tel. (9) 264-34-61; fax (9) 264-35-92):

DE BEELDE, I., Accountancy and Corporate Finance

DE CLERCQ, M., General Economics

HEENE, A., Management, Innovation and Entrepreneurship

OMEY, E., Social Economics

VANDER VENNET, R., Financial Economics

VANHOUCKE, M., Management Information Science and Operation Management

VAN KENHOVE, P., Marketing

Faculty of Engineering (Jozef Plateaustraat 22, 9000 Ghent; tel. (9) 264-79-50; fax (9) 264-95-99):

BRUNEEL, H., Telecommunications and Information Processing

DE BAETS, P., Mechanical Construction and Production

DEGRIECK, J., Materials Science and Engineering

DE ROUCK, J., Civil Engineering

DE ZUTTER, D., Information Technology

KIEKENS, P., Textiles

LEYS, C., Applied Physics

MARIN, G., Chemical Engineering and Technical Chemistry

MELKEBEEK, J., Electrical Energy, Systems and Automation

SIERENS, R., Flow, Heat and Combustion Mechanics

TAERWE, L., Structural Engineering

VAN CAMPENHOUT, J., Electronics and Information Systems

VAN KEER, R., Mathematical Analysis

VAN LANDEGHEM, H., Industrial Management

VERSCHAFFEL, B., Architecture and Urban Planning

Faculty of Law (Universiteitstraat 4, 9000 Ghent; tel. (9) 264-67-62; fax (9) 264-69-99):

BOCKEN, H., Civil Law

BOUCKAERT, B., Legal Theory and Legal History

ERAUW, J., Procedural Law, Arbitration and Private International Law

HUMBLET, P., Labour Law and Social Security Law

MARESCEAU, M., European Institute

SOMERS, E., International Public Law

VAN ACKER, C., Business Law

VAN CROMBRUGGE, S., Tax Law

VENY, L., Public law

VERMEULEN, G., Penal Law and Criminology

Faculty of Medicine and Health Sciences (Campus Heymans, De Pintelaan 185, 9000 Ghent; tel. (9) 332-41-90; fax (9) 332-49-90):

CAMBIER, D., Physical Therapy and Motor Rehabilitation

DE BACKER, G., Public Health

DE CLERCQ, D., Movement and Sports Sciences

DE HEMPTINNE, B., Surgery

DE MAESENEER, J., General Practice and Primary Health Care

DE PAUW, G., Dentistry

DE VOS, M., Internal Medicine

DE WAGTER, C., Radiotherapy and Nuclear Medicine

KESTELYN, P., Opthalmology

LAMBERT, J., Dermatology

LEFEBVRE, R., Pharmacology

MATTHYS, D., Pediatrics and Medical Genetics

MORTIER, E., Anaesthesiology

PIETTE, M., Forensic Medicine

PLUM, J., Clinical Chemistry, Microbiology and Immunology

TEMMERMAN, M., Uro-Gynaecology

THIERENS, H., Basic Medical Sciences

VAN CAUWENBERGE, P., Oto-Rhino-Laryngology

VANDEKERCKHOVE, J., Biochemistry

VAN HEERINGEN, C., Psychiatry and Medical Psychology

VERDONK, R., Physical Medicine and Orthopaedic Surgery

VERSTRAETE, K., Radiology

Faculty of Pharmaceutical Sciences (Campus Heymans, Harelbekestraat 72, 9000 Ghent; tel. (9) 264-80-40; fax (9) 264-81-94):

NELIS, H., Pharmaceutical Analysis

REMON, J., Pharmaceutics

VAN PETEGHEM, C., Bio-Analysis

Faculty of Political and Social Sciences (Universiteitstraat 8, 9000 Ghent; tel. (9) 264-67-80; fax (9) 264-69-86):

BILTEREYST, D., Communication Studies

BRACKE, P., Sociology

COOLSAET, H., Political Science

WALRAET, A., Third World Studies

Faculty of Psychology and Educational Sciences (Henri Dunantlaan 2, 9000 Ghent; tel. (9) 264-63-41; fax (9) 264-64-98):

BROECKAERT, E., Special Education

CLAES, R., Personnel Management, Work and Organizational Psychology

CROMBEZ, G., Experimental Clinical and Health Psychology
DE BIE, M., Social Welfare Studies
DE CORTE, W., Data-Analysis
HARTSUIKER, R., Experimental Psychology
MERVIELDE, I., Developmental, Personality and Social Psychology
SPOELDERS, M., Pedagogy
VALCKE, M., Educational Studies
VERHAEGHE, P., Psychoanalysis and Clinical Consulting

Faculty of Sciences (K. L. Ledeganckstraat 35, 9000 Ghent; tel. (9) 264-50-42; fax (9) 264-53-40):

CLAUWS, P., Solid State Sciences
DE CLERCK, F., Pure Mathematics and Computer Algebra
DE CLERCQ, P., Organic Chemistry
DE MAEYER, P., Geography
DEPICKER, A., Plant Biotechnology and Genetics
DE VOS, P., Biochemistry and Microbiology
HOSTE, S., Inorganic and Physical Chemistry
HUYSSEUNE, A., Biology
JACOBS, P., Geology and Soil Science
RYCKBOSCH, D., Subatomic and Radiation Physics
SARLET, W., Mathematical Physics and Astronomy
STRIJCKMANS, K., Analytical Chemistry
VANDEN BERGHE, G., Applied Mathematics and Computer Science
VAN DER STRAETEN, D., Physiology
VAN ROY, F., Biomedical Molecular Biology

Faculty of Veterinary Sciences (Salisburylaan 133, 9820 Merelbeke; tel. (9) 264-75-03; fax (9) 264-77-99):

DE BACKER, P., Pharmacology, Toxicology and Biochemistry
DE BRABANDER, H., Veterinary Public Health and Food Safety
DE KRUIF, A., Obstetrics, Reproduction and Herd Health
DEPREZ, P., Internal Medicine and Clinical Biology of Large Animals
DUCHATEAU, L., Physiology and Biometry
GASTHUYS, F., Surgery and Anaesthesiology of Domestic Animals
HAESEBROUCK, F., Pathology, Bacteriology and Poultry Diseases
SIMOENS, P., Morphology
VAN BREE, H., Veterinary Medical Imaging and Small Animal Orthopaedics
VAN HAM, L., Medicine and Clinical Biology of Small Animals
VAN ZEVEREN, A., Animal Nutrition, Genetics, Breeding and Ethology
VERCRUYSSE, J., Virology, Parasitology and Immunology

HASSELT UNIVERSITEIT

Campus Diepenbeek Agoralaan, Gebouw D, 3590 Diepenbeek
Telephone: (11) 26-81-11
Fax: (11) 26-81-99
E-mail: info@uhasselt.be
Internet: www.uhasselt.be

Founded 1971; inc. Economische Hogeschool Limburg in 1991; the Univ. of Limburg (www.tul.edu) was est. in 2001, in partnership with Univ. Maastricht (see chapter on the Netherlands)
State control
Languages of instruction: Dutch, English

Rector: MARIE-PAULE JACOBS
Librarian: Prof. Dr LEO EGGHE

Number of teachers: 380
Number of students: 2,219

Faculties of Applied Economics, Medicine, Sciences.

UNIVERSITÉ DE LIÈGE
(University of Liège)

Place du 20-Août 7, 4000 Liège
Telephone: (4) 366-21-11
Fax: (4) 366-57-00
E-mail: international@ulg.ac.be
Internet: www.ulg.ac.be

Founded 1817
Language of instruction: French
Academic year: October to September

Rector: BERNARD RENTIER
Vice-Rector for Research: ALBERT CORHAY
Vice-Rector for Research: PIERRE WOLPER
Vice-Rector for Evaluation and Quality: FREDDY COIGNOUL
Vice-Rector for Int. Relations: JEAN MARCHAL
Vice-Rector for Gembloux Agro-Bio Tech: ERIC HAUBRUGE
Administrator: FRANÇOIS RONDAY
Gen. Dir for Education and Training: MONIQUE MARCOURT
Library: see under Libraries
Number of teachers: 593
Number of students: 16,073

DEANS

Faculty of Applied Sciences: MICHEL HOGGE
Faculty of Law and Political Science: OLIVIER CAPRASSE
Faculty of Medicine: GUSTAVE MOONEN
Faculty of Philosophy and Letters: JEAN-PIERRE BERTRAND
Faculty of Psychology and Education: SERGE BREDART
Faculty of Science: RUDI CLOOTS
Faculty of Veterinary Medicine: PIERRE LEKEUX
HEC-Management School - ULg: THOMAS FROEHLICHER
Institute for Human and Social Sciences: DIDIER VRANCKEN

PROFESSORS WITH CHAIRS

Faculty of Applied Sciences (Chemin des Chevreuils, 1, B52/3 Sart Tilman, 4000 Liège):

BOIGELOT, B., Computer Science
CESCOTTO, S., Mechanics of Materials
CHARLIER, R., Geomechanics and Engineering Geology
CRINE, M., Chemical Engineering
DASSARGUES, A., Hydrogeology and Environmental Geology
DE MARNEFFE, P.-A., Computer Science
DELHEZ, E., General Mathematics
DESTINE, J., Microelectronics
DUYSINX, P., Land Vehicle Engineering
ESSERS, J. A., Aerodynamics
FLEURY, CL., Aerospatial Structures
GERMAIN, A., Industrial Chemistry
GOLINVAL, J.-C., Vibration and Structure Identification
GRIBOMONT, P., Computer Science and Artificial Intelligence
HOGGE, M., Thermomechanics
JASPART, J.-P., Structural Adequacy of Techno-economic Performance and Operation Requirements
LEDUC, G., Computer Networks
MARCHAL, J., Transport Systems and Shipbuilding
PIRARD, E., Mineral Geo-Resources and Geological Imaging
PIRARD, J. P., Applied Physical Chemistry
PONTHOT, J.-P., Non Linear Digital LTAS-Mechanics
SEPULCHRE, R., Systems and Modelling
VERLY, J., Signal and Image Processing
WEHENKEL, L., Systems and Modelling
WOLPER, P., Computer Science

Faculty of Law and Political Science—J. Constant School of Criminology (7 Blvd du Rectorat, B 31, Sart Tilman, 4000 Liège):

BIQUET, C., Contract and Credit Law
CAPRASSE, O., Commercial Law
DE LEVAL, G., Civil Law
JACOBS, A., Criminal Law and Criminal Law Procedure
LECOCQ, P., Property and Evidentiary Law
LELEU, Y.-H., Family Law and Medical Law
PARENT, X., Tax Law
WAUTELET, P., Private International Law

Faculty of Medicine (Ave de l'hôpital, 1, B 36 Sart Tilman, 4000 Liège):

ADELIN, A., Public Health Science
ANGENOT, L., Pharmacy
ANSSEAU, M., Psychiatry and Medical Psychology
BELAICHE, J., Hepato-gastroenterology
BONIVER, J., Anatomy and Pathological Cytology
BOURS, V., General and Human Genetics
CRIELAARD, J.-M., Physical Skills Evaluation and Conditioning
CROMMEN, J., Drug Analysis
D'ORIO, V., Emergency Medicine
DEFRAIGNE, J.-O., Cardiovascular and Thoracic Surgery
DEFRESNE, M.-P., Histology–Cytology
DE LEVAL, J., Urology
DE MOL, P., Medical Microbiology and Virology
FILLET, G., Haematology
FOIDART, J. M., Gynecology–Obstetrics
GRISAR, T., Human and Pathological Biochemistry and Physiology
HEINEN, E., Human Histology
LIMME, M., Orthodontics and Pedodontics
MALAISE, M., Rhumatology
MEURISSE, M., Abdominal Surgery
MOONEN, G., Normal and Pathological Physiology
PIERARD, L., Cardiology
PIROTTE, B., Pharmaceutical Chemistry
REGINSTER, J.-Y., Epidemiology and Public Health
ROMPEN, E., Bucco-dental Surgery and Periodontics
SCHEEN, A., Diabetology, Nutrition and Metabolic Disorders
SCHOENEN, J., Neuro-anatomy

Faculty of Philosophy and Letters (Place du 20-Août, 7, A1 (Centre Ville), 4000 Liège):

ALLART, D., Art History and Archaeology of Modern Times
BAJOMEE, D., Contemporary French Literature
BALACE, F., Contemporary History
BERTRAND, J.-P., 19th and 20th Century French Literature
CURRERI, L., Italian Language and Literature
DELVILLE, M., Modern English and American Literature
DOR, J., Medieval English Language and Literature
DUCHESNE, J.-P., Art History and Contemporary Archaeology
DUMORTIER, J.-L., Romance Language Teacher Training: French, Spanish, Italian
DURAND, P., Cultural Institutions and Information
GIOVANNANGELI, D., History of Modern and Contemporary Philosophy
GOB, A., Museology
KLINKENBERG, J.-M., Rhetoric and Semiology
KUPPER, J. L., History of the Middle Ages and Historical Geography
LAFFINEUR, R., Art History and Archaeology of Classical Antiquity
OTTE, M., Prehistoric Archaeology
RAXHON, P., Historical Criticism
TUNCA, O., Modern English Philology
VROMANS, J., Modern Dutch Language and Synchronic Linguistics

WINAND, J., Egyptology

Faculty of Psychology and Education (5 Blvd du Rectorat, B 32 Sart Tilman, 4000 Liège):

BECKERS, J., Professional Teacher Training
BORN, M., Psychology of Criminality and Psycho-Social Development
BREDART, S., Cognitive Psychology
HANSENNE, M., Personality and Individual Differences Psychology
LECLERCQ, D., Economy and Rural Development
LEROY, J.-F., Social Psychology of Groups and Organizations
MEULEMANS, T., Neuropsychology
TIRELLI, E., Behavioural Neuroscience and Experimental Psychopharmacology

Faculty of Science (Allée de la Chimie, 5, B6 Sart Tilman, 4000 Liège):

ADELIN, A.
BASTIN, F., Analysis, Functional Analysis, Wavelets
BECKERS, J., Physical Oceanography
BOULVAIN, F., Sedimentary Petrology
BOUQUEGNEAU, J.-M., Oceanology
CLOOTS, R., Structural Inorganic Chemistry
CUGNON, J., Theoretical Physics
DE PAUW, E., Physical Chemistry, Mass Spectrometry
DEMOULIN, V., Algology, Mycology and Experimental Systematics
DOMMES, J., Plant Molecular Biology and Biotechnology
DONNAY, J.-P., Geographic Information Systems and Mapping
FRANSOLET, A. M., Mineralogy
GHOSEZ, P., Theoretical Material Physics
LECOMTE, P., Geometry and Algorithm Theory
LUXEN, A., Synthetic Organic Chemistry
MARTIAL, J., Molecular Biology and Genetic Engineering
MOTTE, P., Functional Genomics and Plant Molecular Imaging
PETIT, F.-F., Geomorphology, Hydrography
RENTIER, B., Basic Virology
SCHOUMAKER-MERENNE, B., Economic Geography
SURDEJ, J., Extragalactic Astrophysics and Space Observation
THOME, J.-P., Animal Ecology and Ecotoxicology
THONART, PH., Microbiology
VANDEWALLE, N., Statistical Physics
VANDEWALLE, P., Functional and Developmental Morphology

Faculty of Veterinary Medicine (20 Blvd du Colonster, B 42 Sart Tilman 4000 Liège):

BALLIGAND, M., Surgery and Surgical Clinical Practice in small animals
CLERCX, C., Small animal Medical Pathology
COIGNOUL, F., Pathological Anatomy and Autopsies
DESMECHT, D., Special Pathology and Autopsies
GEORGES, M., Animal Genomics
GODEAU, J. M., Biochemistry
GUSTIN, P., Pharmacology, Pharmacotherapeutics and Toxicology
LEKEUX, P., Physiology
LEROY, P., Information Science Applied to Animal Husbandry
LOSSON, B., Parasitology and Pathology of Parasitic Diseases
MAINIL, J., Bacteriology and Pathology of Bacterial Diseases
SERTEYN, D., General Anesthesiology and Surgical Pathology in Larger Animals
THIRY, E., Virology, Epidemiology, and Pathology of Viral Diseases
VANDERPLASSCHEN, A., Immunology and Vaccinology

HEC—ULg School of Management (Rue Louvrex, 14, N1, 4000 Liège):

BAIR, J., International Relations
CHOFFRAY, J.-M., Computer Decision Support
CORHAY, A., Accounting and Finance
CORNET, A., Management of Human Resources and Organizations
CRAMA, Y., Operational Research and Production Management
DEFOURNY, J., Social Economy and Economic Systems
FELD, S., Development Economics
JURION, B., Political Economy
PAHUD DE MORTANGES, C., General Marketing
PICHAULT, F., Human Resource Management
SURLEMONT, B., International Management–Entrepreneurship

Institute for Human and Social Sciences (Blvd du Rectorat, 7, B31, Sart Tilman, 4000 Liège):

PONCELET, M., Occupational Psychology
VRANCKEN, D., Sociological Practice

Gembloux Agro-Bio-Tech (Passage des Déportés, 2, 5030 Gembloux):

BAUDOIN, J.-P., Agricultural Science
BOCK, L., Environmental Science and Technology
CLAUSTRIAUX, J.-J., Agricultural Science
DEBOUCHE, C., Environmental Science and Technology
DEROANNE, C., Chemistry and Bio-industries
DESTAIN, M.-F., Environmental Science and Technology
DU JARDIN, P., Agricultural Science
HAUBRUGE, E., Agricultural Science
LEBAILLY, P., Agricultural Science
LEPOIVRE, P., Agricultural Science
PAQUOT, M., Chemistry and Bio-Industries
PORTETELLE, D., Chemistry and Bio-industries
RONDEUX, J., Environmental Science and Technology
THEWIS, A., Agricultural Science
THONART, P., Chemistry and Bio-industries

KATHOLIEKE UNIVERSITEIT LEUVEN
(Catholic University of Leuven)

Naamsestraat 22, 3000 Louvain (Leuven)

Telephone: (16) 32-40-67
Fax: (16) 32-41-96
E-mail: info@kuleuven.be
Internet: www.kuleuven.ac.be

Founded 1425 by Papal Bull; in 1970 the Katholieke Univ. Leuven was officially split into two autonomous univs: the Katholieke Univ. Leuven and the Univ. Catholique de Louvain
Languages of instruction: Dutch, English
Private control
Academic year: October to July

Rector: ANDRE OOSTERLINCK
Vice-Rector for Biomedical Sciences: GUY MANNAERTS
Vice-Rector for Exact Sciences: GUIDO LANGOUCHE
Vice-Rector for Humanities: MARC VERVENNE
Vice-Rector for Kortrijk Campus: PIET VANDEN ABEELE
Librarian: R. DEKEYSER

Library: see Libraries and Archives
Number of students: 28,057

Publication: *Campuskrant* (12 a year)

DEANS

Faculty of Agricultural and Applied Biological Sciences: R. SCHOONHEYDT
Faculty of Arts: W. EVENEPOEL

Faculty of Canon Law: R. TORFS
Faculty of Economics and Applied Economics: F. ABRAHAM
Faculty of Engineering: Y. WILLEMS
Faculty of Law: F. VANISTENDAEL
Faculty of Medicine: J. JANSSENS
Faculty of Pharmaceutical Sciences: P. DE CLERCK
Faculty of Philosophy: A. VAN DE PUTTE
Faculty of Physical Education and Physiotherapy: M. BUEKERS
Faculty of Psychology and Educational Sciences: J. CORVELEYN
Faculty of Science: A. VERBEURE
Faculty of Social Sciences: E. GERARD
Faculty of Theology: M. LAMBERIGTS

UNIVERSITÉ CATHOLIQUE DE LOUVAIN
(Catholic University of Louvain)

Place de l'Université 1, 1348 Louvain-la-Neuve

Telephone: (10) 47-21-11
Fax: (10) 47-38-03
E-mail: info-portail@uclouvain.be
Internet: www.ucl.ac.be

Founded 1425 by Papal Bull; became ind. when the Katholieke Univ. Leuven split into two autonomous univs in 1970
Private control
Language of instruction: French
Academic year: September to May

Rector: M. CROCHET
Vice-Rectors: M. MOLITOR, X. RENDERS
Gen. Administrator: A.-M. KUMPS
Librarian: CH. H. NIJNS

Library: see Libraries and Archives
Number of teachers: 1,260
Number of students: 20,517

Publication: *Bulletin des Amis de Louvain*

DEANS

Faculty of Applied Sciences: J.-D. LEGAT
Faculty of Biological, Agricultural and Environmental Engineering: J. DUFEY
Faculty of Economic, Political and Social Sciences: A. SPINEUX
Faculty of Economic and Social Policy: P. REMAN
Faculty of Law: H. SIMONART
Faculty of Medicine: J.-J. ROMBOUTS
Faculty of Philosophy and Letters: B. COULIE
Faculty of Psychology and Education: G. LORIES
Faculty of Sciences: J. FASTREZ
Faculty of Theology and Canon Law: C. FOCANT
Higher Institute of Philosophy: M. DUPUIS

PRESIDENTS OF INSTITUTES

Higher Institute of Religious Studies: A. HAQUIN
Institute for Developing Countries: J.-PH. PEEMANS
Institute of Family Studies and Sexology: J. SOSSON
Institute of Labour Studies: C. DEMEZ
'Open' Faculty of Economic and Social Politics: G. LIENARD
Oriental Institute: B. COULIE

UNIVERSITÉ DE MONS-HAINAUT
(University of Mons-Hainaut)

20 place du Parc, 7000 Mons

Telephone: (65) 37-31-11
Fax: (65) 37-30-54
E-mail: martine.vanelslande@umh.ac.be
Internet: www.umh.ac.be

Founded 1965
Language of instruction: French
State control
Academic year: October to September

Rector: BERNARD LUX
Vice-Rector: MICHEL HECQ
Administrator: D. VINCE
Librarian: RENÉ PLISNIER
Number of teachers: 250
Number of students: 3,000
Publication: *UMH Dedicace* (4 a year)

DEANS

Faculty of Applied Economics: KARIN COMBLÉ
Faculty of Medicine and Pharmacy: HENRI ALEXANDRE
Faculty of Psychology and Educational Sciences: BERNARD HARMEGNIES
Faculty of Sciences: CATHERINE FINET

PROFESSORS

ALEXANDRE, H., Biology and Embryology
BELAYEW, A., Molecular Biology
BIEMONT, E., Astrophysics and Spectroscopy
BREDAS, J.-L., Chemistry of New Materials
BRIHAYE, Y., Theoretical Physics and Mathematics
BRUYÈRE, V., Theoretical Computer Science
BRUYNINCKX, H., Linguistics and Data Processing
CHERON, G., Electrophysiology
COMBLÉ-DARJA, K., Accountancy and Finance
COUVREUR, P., Applied Statistics
DANG, N. N., Probability and Statistics
DE CONINCK, J., Molecular Modelling
DEFRAITEUR, R., Fiscal System
DEPOVER, C., Moulding Technology
DESMET, H., Social and Community Psychology
DONNAY-RICHELLE, J., Clinical Psychology
DOSIERE, M., Physics and Chemistry of Polymers
DUBOIS, P., Polymeric and Composite Materials
DUFOUR, P., Computer Sciences
DUPONT, P., Methodology and Formation
ESCARMELLE, J.-F., Public Economy
FALMAGNE, P., Biological Chemistry
FINET, C., Mathematical Analysis
FORGES, G., Language Teaching
GILLIS, P., Experimental and Biological Physics
GOCZOL, J., Microeconomics and Marketing
GODAUX, E., Neurosciences
HARMEGNIES, B., Metrology in Psychology and Education
HECQ, M., Analytical and Inorganic Chemistry
HERQUET, P., Physics
ISAAC-VANDEPUTTE, M.-T., Historical Bibliography
JANGOUX, M., Marine Biology
LAUDE, L., Solid State Physics
LEBRUN-CARTON, C., Mathematics
LOWENTHAL, F., Cognitive Sciences
LUX, B., Company Management and Economics
MAGEROTTE, G., Education of the Handicapped
MAHY, B., Economic Analysis
MICHAUX, CH., Logic Mathematics
PAGANO, G., Public Finance and Management
PLATTEN, J., General Chemistry
POURTOIS, J.-P., Psychosociology of Family and School Education
RADOUX, C., Mathematics and Number Theory
RASMONT, P., Zoology
SAUSSEZ, S., Anatomy
SPILLEBOUDT-DETERCK, M., Finance
SPINDEL, P., Mechanics and Gravitation
STANDAERT, S., International Economic Analysis
TEGHEM-LORIS, J., Mathematics and Actuarial Science
THIRY, P., Management Information Science
TOUBEAU, G., Histology
TROESTLER, C., Numerical Analysis
VAN DAELE, A., Psychology of Labour

VAN HAVERBEKE, Y., Organic Chemistry
VANSNICK, J.-C., Quantitative Methods
VERHEVE, D., Chemical Technology
WAUTELET, H., Experimental Photonics
WIJSEN, J., Information Systems Science

ATTACHED INSTITUTES

Centre de Didactique des Sciences: 8 ave Maistriau, 7000 Mons; Dir PHILIPPE HERQUET.

Centre d'Informatique, de l'Audiovisuel et du Multimédia: 6 ave du Champ de Mars, 7000 Mons; Dir CHANTAL POIRET.

Ecole d'Interprètes Internationaux: Ave du Champ de Mars, 7000 Mons; tel. (65) 37-36-09; fax (65) 37-36-22; Dir ALAIN PIETTE.

Institut de Linguistique: 19 place du Parc, 7000 Mons; Dir BERNARD HARMEGNIES.

Institutions with University Status

FACULTÉ POLYTECHNIQUE DE MONS

9 rue de Houdain, 7000 Mons
Telephone: (65) 37-41-11
Fax: (65) 37-42-00
E-mail: recteur@fpms.ac.be
Internet: www.fpms.ac.be
Founded 1837
Academic year: September to June
Pres. of the Board: R. URBAIN
Rector: Prof. S. BOUCHER
Dean: Prof. J. HANTON
Library: see under Libraries
Number of teachers: 70
Number of students: 1,000

Publications: *Bulletin de l'AIMS* (12 a year), *Mons Mines* (4 a year), *PolyTech News* (4 a year)

PROFESSORS

ANCIA, PH., Mining Engineering
BLONDEL, M., Electromagnetism and Telecommunications
BOUCHER, S., Theoretical Mechanics
BOUQUEGNEAU, C., General Physics
BROCHE, C., Electrotechnics
CONTI, C., Theoretical Mechanics
COUSSEMENT, G., Fluid Mechanics, Applied Mechanics
CRAPPE, R., Microelectronics
DE HAAN, A., General Chemistry, Electrochemistry
DE MEYER, M., Applied Chemistry and Biochemistry
DEHOMBREUX, P., Mechanical Engineering
DELHAYE, M., Electrotechnology
DELVOSALLE, C., Chemical and Biochemical Engineering
DUMORTIER, C., Metallurgy
DUPUIS, C., Geology
DURAND, Y., Mechanical Engineering
DUTOIT, T., Signals Processing
FILIPPI, E., Mechanical Engineering
FORTEMPS, P., Mathematics, Operational Research
FRÈRE, M., Thermodynamics
GUERLEMENT, G., Strength of Materials, Stability of Buildings
HANCQ, J., Signal Processing
HANTON, J., Fluid Mechanics, Applied Mechanics
LAMBLIN, D., Strength of Materials, Stability of Buildings
LAMQUIN, M., Electromagnetism and Telecommunications
LIBERT, G., Computer Science
LIÉNARD, PH., Metallurgy

LOBRY, J., Transport and Distribution of High-Voltage Electricity
LYBAERT, P., Heat Transfer
MACQ, D., Electronics
MANNEBACK, P., Computer Science
MEGRET, P., Electromagnetism and Telecommunications
MOINY, F., General Physics
PILATTE, A., Thermodynamics
PIRLOT, M., Mathematics, Operational Research
QUINIF, Y., Geology
REMY, M., Automation
RENGLET, M., Electronics
RENOTTE, CH., Automation
RIQUIER, Y., Metallurgy
SAUCEZ, PH., Mathematics, Operational Research
TEGHEM, J., Mathematics, Operational Research
TRÉCAT, J., Transport and Distribution of High-Voltage Electricity
TSHIBANGU, J. P., Mining Engineering
TUYTTENS, D., Mathematics, Operational Research
VANDER WOUWER, A., Automation
VANKERKEM, M., Business Administration
VERLINDEN, O., Theoretical Mechanics
WILQUIN, H., Architecture

FACULTÉ UNIVERSITAIRE DE THÉOLOGIE PROTESTANTE DE BRUXELLES/UNIVERSITAIRE FACULTEIT VOOR PROTESTANTSE GODGELEERDHEID TE BRUSSEL

40 rue des Bollandistes, 1040 Brussels
Telephone: (2) 735-67-46
Fax: (2) 735-47-31
E-mail: info@protestafac.ac.be
Internet: www.protestafac.ac.be
Founded 1942
Languages of instruction: French, Dutch
Private control (United Protestant Church)
Rector: W. WILLEMS
Chair. of Admin. Board: C. PEETERS
Dean of Dutch-speaking Section: J. WIERSMA
Dean of French-speaking Section: B. HORT
Sec.: A. JOUÉ
Librarian: E. EVRARD
Library of 41,134 vols
Number of teachers: 20
Number of students: 110

Publications: *Analecta Bruxellensia* (1 a year), *Belgische Protestantse Biografieën / Biographies Protestantes Belges* (4 a year), *FACtualité / FACtualiteit* (4 a year), *Programme et Horaire des Cours / Studiegids* (1 a year)

PROFESSORS

Dutch-speaking Section:

DE LANGE, J., Practical Theology
REIJNEN, A. M., Ethics
SMELIK, K., Old Testament Studies, Hebrew
TOMSON, P., New Testament Studies, Greek
WIERSMA, J., Dogmatics, Philosophy
WILLEMS, W., Church History, History of Dogma and 16th-century History

French-speaking Section:

HORT, B., Dogmatics, History of Philosophy and Religious Philosophy
MUTOMBO, F., Old Testament Studies and Hebrew
REIJNEN, A. M., Church History, Ethics
ROUVIÈRE, C., Practical Theology
VAN MOERE, R., New Testament Studies
WILLEMS, W., Church History and Methodology

FACULTÉS UNIVERSITAIRES CATHOLIQUES DE MONS

Chaussée de Binche 151, 7000 Mons
Telephone: (65) 32-32-11
Fax: (65) 31-56-91
E-mail: international@fucam.ac.be
Internet: www.fucam.ac.be
Founded 1896 as Institut Supérieur Commercial et Consulaire; univ. status 1965
Private control
Language of instruction: French
Academic year: October to September
Rector: Prof. CHRISTIAN DELPORTE
Vice-Rector: Prof. MICHEL DELATTRE

Number of teachers: 120
Number of students: 1,400

Courses in economics, management science and political science.

FACULTÉS UNIVERSITAIRES NOTRE-DAME DE LA PAIX

61 rue de Bruxelles, 5000 Namur
Telephone: (81) 72-41-11
Fax: (81) 72-40-03
E-mail: relations_exterieures@fundp.ac.be
Internet: www.fundp.ac.be
Founded 1831
Language of instruction: French
Academic year: September to June
Rector: M. SCHEUER
Vice-Rector: PH. LAMBIN
Sec.: R. LESUISSE
Chief Librarian: J. M. ANDRÉ

Library: see Libraries and Archives
Number of teachers: 210
Number of students: 4,100

DEANS

Faculty of Computer Science: J.-M. JACQUET
Faculty of Economics, Social Sciences and Management: A. DE CROMBRUGGHE
Faculty of Law: B. COLSON
Faculty of Medicine: M. HERIN
Faculty of Philosophy and Letters: X. HERMAND
Faculty of Sciences: R. SPORKEN

PROFESSORS

Faculty of Computer Science (21 rue Grandgagnage, 5000 Namur; tel. (81) 72-49-66; fax (81) 72-49-67; e-mail doyen@info.fundp.ac.be; internet www.info.fundp.ac.be):

BERLEUR, J., Informatics and Sciences, Informatics and Rationality (Epistemological questions), Informatics and Society
BODART, F., Information Systems Design, Decision Support System, User/Machine Interface Engineering
BONAVENTURE, O., Computer Architecture, Computer Networks
FICHEFET, J., Graph Theory, Linear Programming, Numerical Analysis, Operations Research, Multicriteria Decision Aid, Management
HABRA, N., Software Engineering, Software Development
HAINAUT, J. L., Database Technology, Database Design, Database Engineering
JACQUET, J.-M., Programming Methodology, Programming Projects, Artificial Intelligence Techniques, Theory of Programming Languages
LE CHARLIER, B., Programming Methodology, Theory of Programming Languages, Abstract Interpretation
LECLERCQ, J.-P., Scientific Methods and Applications, Graph Theory
LESUISSE, R., Organization Design, Strategic Management and Information Systems, Organization Theory

LOBET-MARIS, C., Organization Theories, Psychological Aspects of Information Systems, Communication
NOIRHOMME-FRAITURE, M., Stochastic Processes, Simulation of Systems, Data Mining and Database Analysis, Performance Models and Evaluation
RAMAEKERS, J., Operating Systems, Performance and Measurement of Computer Systems, Computer System Reliability and Security
SCHOBBENS, P.-Y., Artificial Intelligence Techniques, Automatic Testing and Program Testing, Artificial Intelligence in DSSs, Language Theory

Faculty of Economics, Social Sciences and Management (61 rue de Bruxelles, 5000 Namur; tel. (81) 72-48-55; fax (81) 72-48-40; e-mail veronique.gilson@fundp.ac.be; internet www.fundp.ac.be/eco/eco.html):

BALAND, J.-M., Development Economics
BERTELS, K., Information Management
BODART, F., Management Information Systems
BRACKELAIRE, J. L., Psychology
CHEFFERT, J. M., Micro-economics
COLSON, B., Political Sociology and Comparative History of Institutions
DE COMBBRUGGHE DE PICQUENDAELE, A., International Trade Project Evaluation
DESCHAMPS, R., Macro-economics
GLEJSER, H., Econometrics, International and Interregional Economics
GREGOIRE, P., Corporate Finance and Portfolio Management
HOTTE, L., Industrial Economics, Development Economics
JACQUEMIN, J.-C., International Trade, Methods of Economic Investigation
JACQUES, J.-M., Business Policy, International Strategy
JAUMOTTE, CH., Political Economy, Regional and Sectoral Economic Analysis
LEGRAND, M., Epistemology, Philosophical Anthropology
LESUISSE, R., Computer Science
LOUVEAUX, F., Mathematical Statistics, Mathematical Programming, Operations Research
MANIQUET, F., Micro-economics
MIGNOLET, M., Fiscal Policy and Business Strategies, Macro-economics
NIZET, J., Sociology
PLATTEAU, J.-PH., Economic Development, Institutional Economics
PLATTEN, I., Finance and Financial Modelling
REDING, P., Money and Banking, Monetary Theory and Policy, International Monetary Economics
RIGAUX, N., Sociology
SCHEPENS, G., Operations Management, Management Information Systems
VALOGNES, F., Advanced Mathematics
VAN WYMEERSCH, C., Managerial Finance, Business Forecasting, Accounting
VAN YPERSELE, T., Public Economics, Regional Economics
WALLEMACQ, A., Human Resources Management
WUIDAR, J., Mathematics
WYNANTS, B., Introduction to Sociology
WYNANTS, P., History

Faculty of Law (5 Rempart de la Vierge, 5000 Namur; tel. (81) 72-47-94; fax (81) 72-52-00; e-mail secretariat.droit@fundp.ac.be):

COIPEL, N., Methodology and Legal Sources
COIPEL, M., Commercial Law
DIJON, X., Natural Law
DUPLAT, J.-L., Fiscal Law
FIERENS, J., Legal Methodology and Human Rights
KIGANAHÉ, Criminal Law
POULLET, Y., Roman Law

ROBAYE, R., History of Private Law
THIRY, PH., General Theory of Knowledge and Philosophy
THUNIS, X., Comparative Law and Law of Obligation
VUYE, H., Constitutional Law, Dutch Legal Terminology
WÉRY, P., General Principles of Private Law

Faculty of Medicine (61 rue de Bruxelles, 5000 Namur; tel. (81) 72-43-47; fax (81) 72-43-27; e-mail administration-medecine@fundp.ac.be; internet www.fundp.ac.be/medecine):

BOSLY, A., Immunology
DONCKIER, J., Endocrinology
DULIEU, J., Human Anatomy
FLAMION, B., Physiology, Pharmacology
GOFFINET, A., Special Physiology
HÉRIN, M., Histology, Embryology
JADOT, M., Human Biochemistry, General Biochemistry
LALOUX, P., Physiopathology
MARCHANOL, E., Human Physiology
MERCIER, M., Psychology and Medical Psychology
PIRONT, A., General Physiology
POUMAY, Y., General Histology
TRIGAUX, J. P., Radiological Anatomy
VANDERPAS, J., Epidemiology
ZECH, F., Microbiology

Faculty of Philosophy and Letters (1 rue J. Grafé, 5000 Namur; tel. (81) 72-42-07; fax (81) 72-42-03; e-mail dolores.bouchat@fundp.ac.be; internet www.fundp.ac.be/philo_lettres):

ALLARD, A., Classical Philology
BOSSE, A., German and Comparative Literature
BRACKELAIRE, J.-L., Psychology
BURNEZ, L., Prehistoric Art, Archaeology
DELABASTITA, D., English, General and Comparative Literature
DE RUYT, C., History of Ancient Art, Archaeology
DOYEN, A.-M., Greek Language and Literature
GANTY, E., Modern Philosophy
GIOT, J., French Linguistics
HANTSON, A., English Language, Linguistics
LEGROS, G., Romance Philology, Theory of Literature
LEIJNSE, E., Dutch, General and Comparative Literature
LENOIR, Y., History of Music
MARCHETTI, P., Classical Philology, Antiquity and Latin Authors
MORENO, P., Italian Language
NOËL, R., Medieval History
PETERS, M., German Language, Linguistics
PHILIPPART, G., Medieval History
RIZZERIO, L., Ancient Philosophy
SAUVAGE, P., History of the 19th and 20th Centuries
SELDESLACHTS, H., Latin Language, Greek and Latin Linguistics
VANDEN BEMDEN, Y., History of Post-Classical Art, Archaeology
VAN DEN BERGHE, K., Spanish Language
WEISSHAUPT, J., Dutch Language, Linguistics
WYNANTS, P., History of Belgian Institutions

Faculty of Sciences (61 rue de Bruxelles, 5000 Namur; tel. (81) 72-54-35; fax (81) 72-53-06; e-mail decanat-sciences@fundp.ac.be; internet www.fundp.ac.be/sciences):

ANDRE, J.-M., Quantum Chemistry, Physical Chemistry
BLANQUET, GH., Molecular Infrared Spectroscopy and General Physics
B'NAGY, J., General Chemistry, Spectroscopy

BODART, F., Experimental Physics, Atomic and Nuclear Physics
CALLIER, F., Differential and Integral Calculus, Graph Theory
DE BOLLE, X., Statistics, Biostatistics, Bioinformatics
DELHALLE, J., General Chemistry
DEMORTIER, G., X-ray Physics, General Physics and Nuclear Physics
DEPIEREUX, E., Statistics, Biostatistics, Bioinformatics
DESCY, J.-P., Ecology
DEVOS, P., Endocrinology and Zoology
DUCHENE, J., Philosophy of Science
DURANT, F., Radiocrystallography and General Chemistry
EVRARD, G., Radiocrystallography
GIFFROY, J.-M., Anatomy, Embryology and Ethology of Animals
HALLET, V., Mineralogy, Geology
HARDY, A., Mathematics and Statistics
HENRARD, J., Mathematics, Celestial Mechanics, Astronomy
HEVESI, L., Organic Chemistry
HOUSSIAU, L., Experimental Physics, Thermodynamics
KESTEMONT, P., Ecology
KRIEF, A., Organic Chemistry
LAMBERT, D., Philosophy of Science
LAMBERTS, L., Analytical Chemistry
LAMBIN, P., Analytical Mechanics, Theoretical Physics
LETESSON, J. J., Microbiology, Immunology
LUCAS, A., Theoretical Solid State Physics and Quantum Physics
MAES, A., Mathematics, Differential and Integral Calculus
MASEREEL, B., Pharmaceutical Sciences, Biochemistry and Cytology
MEKHALIF, Z., General Chemistry, Physical Chemistry, Polymers
MESSIAEN, J., General Biology, Vegetal Physiology
MICHA, J.-CL., Ecology
NGUYEN, V. H., Differential and Integral Calculus, Optimization and Applied Mathematics
ORBAN-FERAUGE, F., Geography, Cartography
PAQUAY, R., Animal Physiology
PIREAUX, J.-J., Experimental Physics, Atomic and Molecular Physics
PIRSON, P., Methodology of Chemistry
RAES, M., Biochemistry
RASSON, J.-P., Probabilities
REMACLE, J., Biochemistry
REMON, M., Programming Statistics
ROUSSELET, D., Methodology of Biology
SCHNEIDER, M., Methodology of Mathematics
STOIKEN, R., Physics, Electronics
STRODIOT, J.-J., Optimization
SU, B. L., General Chemistry
THILL, G., Philosophy of Science
THIRAN, J.-P., Numerical Analysis
THIRY, P., Solid State Physics, General Physics
TOINT, PH., Algebra, Numerical Analysis
VAN CUTSEM, P., Biotechnology
VANDENHAUTE, J., Genetics
VERCAUTEREN, D., General Chemistry, Kinetics, Physical Chemistry
VIGNERON, J.-P., Solid State Physics

FACULTÉS UNIVERSITAIRES SAINT-LOUIS

43 blvd du Jardin Botanique, 1000 Brussels
Telephone: (2) 211-78-11
Fax: (2) 211-79-97
E-mail: webmaster@fusl.ac.be
Internet: www.fusl.ac.be
Founded 1858
Language of instruction: French
Academic year: October to May

Rector: J. P. LAMBERT
Vice-Rector: F. OST
Library: see Libraries and Archives
Number of teachers: 82
Number of students: 1,200
Publications: *Revue interdisciplinaire d'Etudes Juridiques* (2 a year), *Revue internationale des droits de l'Antiquité*

DEANS

Faculty of Economic, Social and Political Sciences: M. HUBERT
Faculty of Law: H. DUMONT
Faculty of Philosophy and Letters: J. P. NANDRIN

PROFESSORS

Faculty of Economic, Social and Political Sciences:
BERTRAND, P., Physics
CALLUT, J. P., English Language
CITTA-VANTHEMSCHE, M., Mathematics
D'ASPREMONT LYNDEN, C., Philosophy and Social Sciences
DE KERCHOVE DE DENTERGHEM, A. M., Economics
DEPRINS, D., Statistics
DE RONGE, Y., Accountancy
DE SAINT-GEORGES, P., Social Communication
DE STEXHE, G., Philosophy and Ethics
EVERAERT-DESMEDT, N., Semiology
FRANCK, C., Political Science
GILLARDIN, J., Introduction to Law
GUERRA, F., Accountancy
HARDY, A., Mathematics
HUBERT, M., Sociology
LAMBERT, J. P., Economics
LECLERCQ, N. C., Civil Law
LEPERS, A., Accountancy
LOUTE, E., Mathematics and Computer Science
MARQUET, J., Sociology
MITCHELL, J., Economics
RIGAUX, M.-F., Introduction to Law, Public Law
SERVAIS, P., Economic and Social History
SIMAR, L., Statistics
SOETE, J. L., Contemporary History
SONVEAUX, E., Chemistry
STREYDIO, J. M., Physics
STRODIOT, J. J., Mathematics
TULKENS, H., Political Economy
VAN CAMPENHOUDT, L., Sociology
VAN RILLAER, J., Social and Industrial Psychology
VERHOEVEN, J., International Law
WIBAUT, S., Political Economy
WITTERWULGHE, R., Political Economy
Faculty of Law:
CARTUYVELS, Y., Introduction to Law
DE BROUWER, J. L., Political Science
DE JEMEPPE, B., Dutch Language
DE THEUX, A., Introduction to Law
DEVILLE, A., Sociology
DILLENS, A. M., Philosophy
DUMONT, H., Public Law
GERARD, P., Introduction to Law
HANARD, G., Roman Law
JACOB, R., Private Law
LORIAUX, C., English
MAHIEU, M., Introduction to Law
NANDRIN, J. P., History
OST, F., Introduction to Law
SEGERS, M. J., Psychology
STROWEL, A., Introduction to Law
VAN DE KERCHOVE, M., Introduction to Law
VAN GEHUCHTEN, P. P., Law
WANTHY, X., Political Economy
Faculty of Philosophy and Letters:
BOUSSET, H., Dutch Authors and Literature
BRAIVE, J., History
BRISART, R., Philosophy

CAUCHIES, J. M., History
CHEYNS, A., Greek Philology and Authors
CUPERS, J.-L., English Authors and Literature
DAUCHY, S., History
DE RUYT, C., Ancient History and History of Art
DUCHESNE, J.-P., History of Art
HEIDERSCHEIDT, J., English Phonetics and Grammar
JONGEN, R., German Phonetics and Grammar, Linguistics
LENOBLE-PINSON, M., Modern French Grammar, Philology
LEONARDY, E., German Literature
LOGE, T., French Literature
LONGREE, D., Latin Philology and Authors
MAESCHALCK, M., Philosophy
MARRANT, A., Latin Authors
MATTENS, W., Dutch Grammar and Philology
RENARD, M. C., French Authors, Modern Literatures, Italian and Spanish
TOCK, B. M., History
WILLEMS, M., Medieval French Literature
XHARDEY, D., History of Greek and Latin Literature and Greek Philology

ATTACHED INSTITUTE

Ecole des Sciences Philosophiques et Religieuses: Brussels; f. 1925; Pres. A.-M. DIBLEUR; 10 teachers; 230 students.

GEMBLOUX AGRO-BIO TECH

2 passage des Déportés, 5030 Gembloux
Telephone: (81) 62-21-05
Fax: (81) 62-25-20
E-mail: fsagx@fsagx.ac.be
Internet: www.fsagx.ac.be
Founded 1860, univ. status 1947
Language of instruction: French
State control
Academic year: September to June
Vice-Rector: E. HAUBRUGE
Dean: P. DU JARDIN
Sec.: J. HEBERT
Library: see under Libraries
Number of teachers: 65
Number of students: 1,100
Publication: *BASE* (4 a year)

PROFESSORS

AUBINET, M., Physics
BAUDOIN, J.-P., Phytotechnology of Tropical Zones
BOCK, L., Soil Sciences
BODSON, B., Phytotechnology of Temperate Zones
BODSON, M., General Horticulture
CHARLES, C., Applied Mathematics
CLAUSTRIAUX, J.-J., Statistics and Data Processing
CULOT, M., Microbial Ecology and Wastewater Treatment
DEBOUCHE, C., Fluid Mechanics and Environment
DOUCET, J. L., Tropical Forestry
DEROANNE, C., Food Technology, Organic and Biological Chemistry
DESTAIN, M.-F., Machinery and Construction
DU JARDIN, P., Plant Biology
FELTZ, C., Land Planning
HAUBRUGE, E., General and Applied Zoology
LEBAILLY, J.-P., Economics and Rural Development
LEPOIVRE, P., Phytopathology
LOGNAY, G., Analytical Chemistry
MAHY, G., Ecology
PAQUOT, M., Industrial Biological Chemistry
PAUL, R., Environmental Toxicology
PORTETELLE, D., Animal and Microbial Biology

RONDEUX, J., Forest Management and Economics
SCHIFFERS, B., Phytopharmacy
THEWIS, A., Stockbreeding
THONART, P., Bio-industries
WATHELET, J. P., General and Organic Chemistry

LIMBURGS UNIVERSITAIR CENTRUM

Universitaire Campus, Gebouw D, 3590 Diepenbeek
Telephone: (11) 26-81-11
Fax: (11) 26-81-99
E-mail: luc-rect@luc.ac.be
Internet: www.luc.ac.be
Founded 1971
Private control; state-aided
Academic year: October to July
Chair.: T. KELCHTERMANS
Vice-Chair.: L. GELDERS
Rector: L. DE SCHEPPER
Vice-Rector: M. VAN HAEGENDOREN
Permanent Sec.: W. GOETSTOUWERS
Librarian: L. EGGHE
Number of teachers: 110 (full-time)
Number of students: 2,116

DEANS

Faculty of Applied Economics: G. HEEREN
Faculty of Medicine: E. VAN KERKHOVE
Faculty of Sciences: E. NAUWELAERTS

ATTACHED INSTITUTES
IMOMEC: Dir H. MARTENS.
Science Park Limburg: Dir I. BREESCH.
WTCM: Scientific Consultant H. MARTENS.

University Level Institutions

COLLEGE OF EUROPE

Dijver 11, 8000 Bruges
Telephone: (50) 47-71-11
Fax: (50) 47-71-10
E-mail: info@coleurope.eu
Internet: www.coleurope.eu
Founded 1949; institute of postgraduate European studies
Languages of instruction: English, French
Academic year: September to June
Pres. of Admin. Council: IÑIGO MENDEZ DE VIGO
Rector: Prof. PAUL DEMARET
Librarian: ERIC DE SOUZA
Library of 100,000 vols
Number of teachers: 140
Number of students: 400
Publication: Collegium

DIRECTORS

Department of Administration: D. MAHNCKE
Department of Development of Human Resources: R. PICHT
Department of Economic Studies: J. PELKMANS
EU International Relations and Diplomacy Studies: D. MAHNCKE
European Legal Studies: I. GOVAERE
European Political and Administrative studies: J. MONAR
Programme of European Interdisciplinary Studies: E. LANNON

CAMPUS IN POLAND
College of Europe: ul. Nowoursynowska 84, 02-797 Warsaw 78; tel. (22) 545-94-01; fax (22) 649-13-52; e-mail info.pl@coleurope.eu; Vice-Rector EWA OSNIECKA-TAMECKA.

ÉCOLE DES HAUTES ÉTUDES COMMERCIALES

14 rue Louvrex, 4000 Liège
Telephone: (4) 232-72-11
Fax: (4) 232-72-40
E-mail: info@hec.be
Internet: www.hec.be
Founded 1898
Language of instruction: French
Academic year: September to June
Pres.: YVES NOEL
Dir-Gen.: M. DUBRU
Academic Dir: LOUIS ESCH
Sec.-Gen.: JACQUES DEFER
Librarian: M.A. THOMAS
Library of 12,000 vols
Number of teachers: 217
Number of students: 1,620

ECONOMISCHE HOGESCHOOL SINT-ALOYSIUS

Stormstraat 2, 1000 Brussels
Telephone: (2) 210-12-11
Fax: (2) 217-64-64
E-mail: info@ehsal.be
Internet: www.ehsal.be
Founded 1925
Languages of instruction: Dutch, English
Academic year: September to June
A univ.-level school of economics
Dir: Prof. Dr D. DE CEULAER
Number of teachers: 150
Number of students: 5,000
Publications: Arcade (in Dutch), In4you (information for students, in Dutch and English), International programme brochures (in English)

DEAN
Department of Economics and Management: WALTER PLATTEAU

DIRECTOR
Centre for External Cooperation: INGEBORG VANDENBULCKE

ERASMUSHOGESCHOOL-BRUSSEL

Nijverheidskaai 170, 1070 Brussels
Telephone: (2) 523-37-37
E-mail: info@ehb.be
Internet: www.ehb.be
Founded 1991 by the amalgamation of the Administratieve en Economische Hogeschool (f. 1938) and the School for Translators and Interpreters (f. 1958)
Language of instruction: Dutch, but multilingual for postgraduate studies
Private control
Director-General and Delegate Administrator: H.-J. VERMEYLEN
Assistant Director: J. TERWECOREN
Publications: Medium—Tijdschrift voor Toegepaste Taalwetenschap (3 a year), Tijdschrift voor Bestuurswetenschappen en Publike Recht (12 a year).

FACULTEIT VOOR VERGELIJKENDE GODSDIENSTWETENSCHAPPEN (Faculty for Comparative Study of Religions)

Bist 164, 2610 Antwerp (Wilrijk)
Telephone: (3) 830-51-58
Fax: (3) 825-26-73
E-mail: info@antwerpfvg.org
Internet: www.antwerpfvg.org
Founded by Royal Decree in 1980
Languages of instruction: Dutch, English, French, German

Academic year: October to June
Chair. of Board: JEREMY ROSEN
Rector: CHRISTIAAN J. G VONCK
Deans: LYDIA BONTE, JAN VAN REETH, FRANK STAPPAERTS
Librarians: WU JEN, EDDY VAN LAERHOVEN, HUGO PEERLINCK, CHRISTIAN VANDEKERKHOVE
Library of 35,000 vols
Number of teachers: 44
Number of students: 120
Publication: Acta Comparanda (1 a year)

PROFESSORS
BOCKEN, I., Gnosticism
BRIOT, P., Philosophy
DETHIER, H., Humanism
GERDING, H., Parapsychological Approach in Religion
KAPOOR, S., Sikhism
KERSTEN, H., Bahá'í
KUMAR, V., Indology
MERTENS, H., Christianity
PEEL, K. A., Buddhism
ROSEN, J., Judaism
SHAH, N., Jainism
TAYLOR, FR., American Natives
VAN DEN BROECK, L., Islam
VONCK, CH., Protestantism

HAUTE ÉCOLE DE BRUXELLES

34 rue Joseph Hazard, 1180 Brussels
Telephone: (2) 340-12-95
Fax: (2) 347-52-64
E-mail: heb@heb.be
Internet: www.heb.be
Academic year: September to June
Pres. and Dir: JEAN-MARIE VAN DER MEERSCHEN
Librarians: J. P. GAHIDE, O. GALMA
Library of 45,000 vols
Number of teachers: 189
Number of students: 2,200
Publication: Équivalences (2 a year)

DIRECTORS
Institute of Economics and Technology: MARIANNE COESSENS
Institute of Teacher-Training: LUC BARBAY
Institute of Translating and Interpreting: FRANS DE LAET

HOGER INSTITUUT VOOR ARCHITECTUURWETENSCHAPPEN HENRY VAN DE VELDE (Henry van de Velde Higher Institute for Architectural Sciences)

Mutsaardstraat 31, 2000 Antwerp
Telephone: (3) 205-71-70
Fax: (3) 226-04-11
E-mail: designsciences@ha.be
Internet: www.ontwerpwetenschappen.be
Founded 1663 by Teniers; ind. 1952
Publication: Antwerp Design Sciences Cahiers (ADSC) (every 6 months).

INSTITUT CATHOLIQUE DES HAUTES ÉTUDES COMMERCIALES

2 blvd Brand Whitlock, 1200 Brussels
Telephone: (2) 739-37-11
Fax: (2) 739-38-03
E-mail: communication@ichec.be
Internet: www.ichec.be
Founded 1934
Languages of instruction: Dutch, English, French
Rector: CHRISTIAN OST
Pres.: E. DAVIGNON
Gen.-Sec.: P. FLAHAUT
Librarian: (vacant)

Library of 16,000 vols
Number of teachers: 170
Number of students: 2,000

Publication: *Reflets et Perspectives de la Vie Economique.*

ATTACHED SCHOOL

Ecole Supérieure des Sciences Fiscales: 2 blvd Brand Whitlock, 1150 Brussels; f. 1958; library of 2,000 vols; 28 teachers; 200 students; Pres. Prof. P. DUPRIEZ; Librarian M.-C. SIBILLE-VAN GRIEKEN.

INSTITUT COOREMANS

11 place Anneessens, 1000 Brussels
Telephone: (2) 551-02-10
Fax: (2) 551-02-16
Internet: www.brunette.brucity.be/ferrer/eco
Founded 1911
Academic year: September to June
Language of instruction: French (English in some postgraduate programmes)
Pres.: P. LAMBERT
Dean: L. COOREMANS
Number of teachers: 80
Number of students: 400

Courses at Bachelors and Masters degree level in commerce and administration

Publication: *ECOO* (4 a year).

INSTITUT GRAMME LIÈGE INSTITUT SUPÉRIEUR INDUSTRIEL

28 quai du Condroz, 4030 Angleur (Liège)
Telephone: (4) 340-34-30
Fax: (4) 343-30-28
E-mail: secr.direction@gramme.hemes.be
Internet: www.gramme.be
Founded 1906
Language of instruction: French
Dir: JEAN-PIERRE POSTULA
Librarian: NICOLE GRAVIER
Library of 11,528 vols
Number of teachers: 64
Number of students: 480

Courses in industrial engineering

Publications: *Annuaire, Nouvelles de l'Union Gramme* (4 a year).

INSTITUT SUPÉRIEUR D'ARCHITECTURE DE LA COMMUNAUTÉ FRANÇAISE—LA CAMBRE

19 place Eugène Flagey, 1050 Brussels
Telephone: (2) 640-96-96
Fax: (2) 647-46-55
E-mail: isacf@lacambre-archi.org
Internet: www.lacambre-archi.be
Founded 1926
State control
Language of instruction: French
Director: Prof. J.-L. GENARD
Deputy Director: Dr GUY PILATE
Head of Academic Affairs: (vacant)
Librarian: MARIE-MICHÈLE BOSMANS
Library of 8,000 vols.

INSTITUT SUPÉRIEUR D'ARCHITECTURE INTERCOMMUNAL (ISAI)

Site Victor Horta, CP 248, Blvd du Triomphe, 1050 Brussels
Telephone: (2) 650-50-52
Fax: (2) 650-50-93
E-mail: isahorta@ulb.ac.be
Internet: horta.ulb.ac.be

Founded 1711; associated with Free University of Brussels and schools of architecture at Liège and Mons (ISAI)
Language of instruction: French
Director: GERARD VAN GOOLEN
Library of 30,000 vols
Number of teachers: 60
Number of students: 650

Publication: *I.S.A.Br* (12 a year)

Courses in architecture, restoration and heritage conservation, urban design.

INSTITUUT VOOR TROPISCHE GENEESKUNDE/INSTITUT DE MÉDECINE TROPICALE (Institute of Tropical Medicine)

Nationalestraat 155, 2000 Antwerp
Telephone: (3) 247-66-66
Fax: (3) 216-14-31
E-mail: info@itg.be
Internet: www.itg.be
Founded 1906, Royal Decree 1931
Languages of instruction: French, English
Academic year: September to July
Pres.: C. BERX
Dir: Prof. Dr B. GRYSEELS
Admin. Dir: L. SCHUEREMANS
Librarian: D. SCHOONBAERT
Library of 30,000 books and 15,000 pamphlets
Number of teachers: 30
Number of students: 400

Publication: *Journal of Tropical Medicine and International Health* (12 a year)

PROFESSORS

BERKVENS, D., Animal Health
BOELAERT, M., Public Health Epidemiology
BUSCHER, PH., Serology
BUVE, A., Microbiology
COLEBUNDERS, B., Clinical Services
COOSEMANS, M., Parasitology
CRIEL, B., Public Health
D'ALESSANDRO, U., Parasitology
DE BROUWERE, V., Public Health
DORNY, P., Animal Health
DUJARDIN, J.C., Parasitology
FRANSEN, C., Microbiology
GEYSEN, D., Animal Health
GRYSEELS, B., Medical Helminthology
JACOBS, J., Tropical Laboratory
KEGELS, G., Public Health
KESTENS, L., Immunology
KOLSTEREN, P., Nutrition and Child Health
LAGA, M., Epidemiology, Sexually-transmitted Diseases
UNGER, J. P., Public Health
VAN DAMME, W., Public Health
VANDENBOSSCHE, P., Animal Health
VAN DEN ENDE, J., Tropical Pathology
VAN DER STUYFT, P., Epidemiology, Public Health
VAN GOMPEL, A., Tropical Pathology
VAUHAN, G., Microbiology

ATTACHED INSTITUTE

Leopold II Kliniek: Kronenburgstraat 43, 2000 Antwerp; tropical and travel medicine; treats sexually-transmitted diseases; Dir Dr F. VAN GOMPEL.

LESSIUS HOGESCHOOL

Jozef de Bomstraat 11, 2018 Antwerp
Telephone: (3) 206-04-80
Fax: (3) 206-04-81
E-mail: info@lessius.eu
Internet: www.lessius.eu
Founded 2000 following the merger of Handelshogeschool (f. 1923) and Katholieke Vlaamse Hogeschool (f. 1919)
Language of instruction: Dutch

Academic year: September to July
CEO: PHILIPPE MICHIELS
Vice-Chancellor: Prof. Dr FLORA CARRIJN
Dir of Academic Services: Prof. Dr PAUL PAUWELS
Dir of Admin. Services: GEERT LOOS
Number of teachers: 300
Number of students: 4,500

PROFESSORS

BEHIELS, L., Spanish and Cultural Studies
GILLAERTS, P., Dutch and Text Studies
LAGAE, W., Sports Marketing and Economics
PAUWELS, P., English and Text Linguistics
STEURS, F., English and Terminology Management
VERHEYEN, P., Mathematics

VLERICK LEUVEN GENT MANAGEMENT SCHOOL

Ghent campus: Bellevue 6, 9050 Ghent
Leuven campus: Vlamingenstraat 83, 3000 Leuven Louvain
St Petersburg Campus Birzhevaya Linia 16, 199034 St Petersburg
Telephone: (9) 210-97-11
Fax: (9) 210-97-00
E-mail: info@vlerick.be
Internet: www.vlerick.com
Founded 1953
Academic year: September to July
Associated with Ghent University and Katholieke Universiteit Leuven
Dean: Prof. PHILIPPE HASPESLAGH
Librarian: ISABELLE VANDENBROCRE
Library of 11,000 books and 135 serials
Number of teachers: 70
Number of students: 480 undergraduate students
Number of students: 7,000 executives

PROFESSORS

(The list indicates whether the professor holds a position at either Katholieke Universiteit Leuven or Ghent University)

Accounting and Finance:

BRUGGEMAN, W. (Ghent University)
COLMART, B.
KEULENEER, L. (Katholieke Universiteit Leuven and Ghent University)
MANIGART, S. (Ghent University)
ROODHOOFT, F. (Katholieke Universiteit Leuven)
SALVA, C.
VAN HULLE, C. (Katholieke Universiteit Leuven)
VAN HULLE, H. (Katholieke Universiteit Leuven)
VANTHIENEN, L.
WAUMAUS, K.

Entrepreneurship, Governance and Strategy:

ABRAHAM, F. (Katholieke Universiteit Leuven)
BUYST, E. (Katholieke Universiteit Leuven)
CRIJNS, H. (Ghent University)
DE BONDT, R. (Katholieke Universiteit Leuven)
HASPESLAGH, P. (Ghent University)
HUELEMAN, H.
LOUCHE, C.
SCHOORS, K. (Ghent University)
SLEUWAEGAN, L. (Katholieke Universiteit Leuven)
THIBEAULT, A.
VAN DEN BERGHE, L. (Ghent University)
VERBEKE, L.
VEUWEIRE, K.
VOISEY, C.

Marketing:

DEBRUYNE, M.

MUYLLE, S.
RANGARAJAN, D.
SAELEN, J. P.
VAN OSSEL, G.
WARLOP, L. (Katholieke Universiteit Leuven)
WEYREN, B.
ZEUPMER, ROTH. K.

Operations and Technology Management:
BLINDENBACH, D. F.
BOUTE, R.
CLARYSSE, B. (Ghent University)
DESCHOOLMEESTER, D. (Ghent University)
DIRICKX, Y. (Katholieke Universiteit Leuven)
KNOCKOURT, M. (Ghent University)
VAN DIERDONCK, R.
VANAELST, J.
VANHOUCKE, M.
VANMAELE, H. (Ghent University)
VEREECKE, A. (Ghent University)
VIAENE, S.
YANCHEUSKI, A.

People and Organization:
BUELENS, M. (Ghent University)
BUYENS, D. (Ghent University)
DE VOS, A.
DEWETTINCK, K.
STRENING, B.
TIELEMAN, K.
VAN DEN BROECK, H. (Ghent University)
VANDERHEYDEN, K.
VENTER, D.

Colleges

Ecole Royale Militaire/Koninklijke Militaire School: 30 ave de la Renaissance, 1000 Brussels; tel. (2) 737-60-01; fax (2) 737-60-32; internet www.rma.ac.be; f. 1834; academic education of officers for Army, Navy, Air Force, Medical Service and Gendarmerie; languages of instruction: French, Dutch; 117 teachers; 900 students; library: 100,000 vols; Dir, Academic Studies Col.-Adm JEAN MARSIA; Dir of Support Maj. EDDY DELPORTE; Library Dir RITA LAMOTE.

Horeca en Sportinstituut Wemmel: Zijp 14–16, 1780 Wemmel; tel. (2) 456-01-01; fax (2) 456-51-91; e-mail kta.hsiw.wemmel@rago.be; internet schoolweb.rago.be/kta/wemmel; Dir NORA DE CALUWÉ (acting).

Institut des Hautes Études de Belgique: 44 ave Jeanne, 1050 Brussels; tel. (2)-649-75-39; fax (2)-649-27-82; e-mail iheb@ulb.ac.be;

f. 1894; language of instruction: French; courses in arts and letters, economics, history, mechanics, natural sciences, philosophy, social and political sciences; Pres. S. HUYBERECHTS; Gen. Sec. G. SAMUEL.

Attached School:

Ecole d'Ergologie: 50 ave F. D. Roosevelt, 1050 Brussels; f. 1925; Dir J. HOFMANS.

Institut Libre Marie Haps: 11 rue d'Arlon, 1050 Brussels; tel. (2) 511-92-92; fax (2) 511-98-37; e-mail information@ilmh.be; internet www.ilmh.be; f. 1919; two- and three-year courses for translators and interpreters; three-year courses in psychology and speech therapy, audiology; languages of instruction: Arabic, Chinese, Dutch, English, French, German, Italian, Russian, Spanish, Turkish; library: 17,700 vols; 161 teachers; 1,500 students; Dir C. CAMPOLINI; Sec.-Gen. B. QUOILIN-CLAUDE; Librarian M. VAN LIL; publ. *Le langage et l'homme* (3 a year).

Koninklijke Belgische Marine Academie/Académie Royale de Marine de Belgique: Ed. Arsenstraat 64, 2640 Mortsel; f. 1935; Pres. CHRISTIAN KONINCKX; Sec.-Gen. LIONEL TRICOT; publs *Communications* (1 a year), *Mededelingen*.

Schools of Music, Art and Architecture

Académie Royale des Beaux-Arts de Bruxelles (Brussels Royal Academy of Fine Arts): 144 rue du Midi, 1000 Brussels; tel. (2) 511-04-91; fax (2) 513-27-54; e-mail info@aca-bxl.be; internet www.aca-bxl.be; f. 1711; drawing, engraving, environmental art, illustration, interior design, painting, publicity and visual communication, sculpture, tapestry-textile creation; 80 teachers; 450 students; library: see Libraries and Archives; Dir M. BAUDSON.

Conservatoire Royal de Bruxelles: 30 rue de la Régence, 1000 Brussels; tel. (2) 511-04-27; fax (2) 512-69-79; e-mail administration@conservatoire.be; internet www.conservatoire.be; f. 1832; library: 1,000,000 vols; 250 teachers; 500 students; Dir FRÉDÉRIC DE ROOS; Librarian PAUL PROSPÉ.

Conservatoire Royal de Mons: 7 rue de Nimy, 7000 Mons; tel. (65) 34-73-77; fax (65) 34-99-06; e-mail info@conservatoire-mons.be;

internet www.conservatoire-mons.be; f. 1926; 420 students; library: 30,000 vols; Dir ANDRÉ FOULON.

Conservatoire Royal de Musique de Liège: 14 rue Forgeur, 4000 Liège; tel. (4) 222-03-06; fax (4) 222-03-84; e-mail info@crlg.be; internet www.crlg.be; f. 1826; 80 professors; students taken from 15 years of age; all branches of music and theatre; Dir BERNARD DEKAISE; Admin. Sec. CLAUDETTE VAN HOLSAET; Librarian PHILIPPE GILSON.

Ecole Nationale Supérieure des Arts Visuels de la Cambre: Abbaye de la cambre 21, 1000 Brussels; tel. (2) 648-96-19; fax (2) 640-96-93; e-mail lacambre@lacambre.be; internet www.lacambre.be; f. 1926; library: see Libraries and Archives; 500 students; Dir CAROLINE MIEROP.

Hogeschool Antwerpen, Herman Teirlinck Instituut: Maarschalk Gérardstraat 4, 2000 Antwerp; tel. (3) 231-54-65; fax (3) 232-22-34; e-mail hti@ha.be; internet www.teirlinckinstituut.be; f. 1946; 4-year full-time academic education and professional training in theatre and related performing arts; Dir JOHAN VAN ASSCHE.

Insas (Institut National Supérieur des Arts du Spectacle et Techniques de Diffusion): Rue Thérésienne 8, 1000 Brussels; tel. (2) 511-92-86; fax (2) 511-02-79; e-mail sec@insas.be; internet www.insas.be; f. 1962 for advanced studies in dramatic art, cinema and broadcasting technique, including television; 3- and 4-year courses; Dir J. P. CASIMIR.

Koninklijke Academie voor Schone Kunsten (Royal Academy of Fine Arts): Mutsaardstraat 31, 2000 Antwerp; tel. (3) 213-71-00; fax (3) 213-71-19; e-mail academie@artesis.be; internet www.artesis.be/academie; f. 1663; awards first and Masters degrees; 100 staff; library: 20,000 vols and prints, 250 periodicals; Dir G. GAUDAEN; Scientific Librarian Dr G. PERSOONS.

Koninklijk Vlaams Conservatorium Antwerpen (Royal Flemish Conservatoire Antwerp): Desguinlei 25, 2018 Antwerp; tel. (3) 244-18-00; fax (3) 238-90-17; e-mail secr@ha.be; internet www.conservatorium.be; f. 1898; languages of instruction: Dutch, English, French, German; library: 600,000 vols; 180 teachers; 350 students; Prin. PASCALE DE GROOTE; Admin. Sec. ROGER QUADFLIEG; Librarian JAN DEWILDE.

BHUTAN

The Higher Education System

Traditionally, education in Bhutan was purely monastic; the establishment of the contemporary state education system was the result of the reforming zeal of the third King, Jigme Dorji Wangchuck (r. 1952–72). There are five main linguistic groups in Bhutan; Dzongkha, spoken in western Bhutan, is the official language but English is the medium of school instruction. Tertiary education includes various first degree courses offered by institutes under the supervision of the Royal University of Bhutan (RUB), which was established in 2003. Adult literacy and non-formal education (NFE) programmes began in Bhutan in 1992, with the establishment of 10 pilot NFE centres targeting those who had left school before completing the curriculum and those without a formal education. The programme offered a one-year basic literacy programme together with a nine-month post-literacy course in Dzongkha covering practical issues such as agriculture, health and sanitation. By 2008 there were 747 NFEs with some 13,829 adults enrolled.

Admission to higher education is made on the basis of completion of grade 12 and passing of examinations leading to award of either the Indian School Certifcate or Bhutan Higher Secondary Education Certificate. Bachelors which degrees last for three to four years are offered at the RUB as well as other colleges and non-university institutions. The Masters degree is currently offered on a very limited basis. There are no doctoral programmes in Bhutan.

The Department of Human Resources of the Ministry of Labour and Human Resources was founded in 1999 to supervise technical and vocational education and training. Within the Department, the Department of Occupational Standards (formerly Bhutan Vocational Qualifications Authority) has developed a three-tier Bhutan Vocational Qualifications Framework. The grades of occupational training are Apprenticeship Training Programmes, Special Skills Development Programmes and Village Skills Development Programmes. Constituent colleges of the RUB also offer technical and vocational programmes of education.

Regulatory Bodies

GOVERNMENT

Department of Occupational Standards: Ministry of Labour and Human Resources, POB 1036, Thongsel Lam, Lower Motithang, Thimphu; tel. (2) 333867; fax (2) 326731; e-mail sangaydorjee@hotmail.com; internet www.molhr.gov.bt; f. 2000; improves and monitors the quality of vocational skills acquired by individuals through the Bhutan Vocational Qualifications Framework (BVQF); comprises 3 divs: standards and qualifications, assessment and certification, review and audit; Dir SANGAY DORJEE.

Ministry of Education: POB 112, Thimphu; tel. (2) 325325; fax (2) 325183; e-mail p_thinley@hotmail.com; internet www .education.gov.bt; Min. Lyonpo THINLEY GYAMTSHO.

Ministry of Home and Cultural Affairs: Tashichhodzong, POB 133, Thimphu; tel. (2) 322301; fax (2) 324320; internet www.mohca .gov.bt; Min. (vacant).

Libraries and Archives

Thimphu

National Library of Bhutan: POB 185, Thimphu; tel. (2) 324314; fax (2) 322693; e-mail nlibrary@druknet.net.bt; internet www.library.gov.bt/nlb.htm; f. 1967; 1,600 vols of Tibetan MS and block-print books, 90,000 Tibetan books in other forms; 15,000 foreign (mainly English) books; Eastern branch: Kuenga Rabten, nr Tongsa; Dir MYNAK TULKU (acting); publ. *Rigter* (2 a year).

Thimphu Public Library: POB 295 Thimphu; f. 1980; incl. the Jigme Dorji Wangchuk Library (f. 1978); UN depository library; 6,000 vols; Librarian Mrs TSHEWANG ZAM.

Museum and Art Gallery

Paro

National Museum of Bhutan: Ta Dzong, Paro; tel. (8) 271257; fax (8) 271510; e-mail nmb@druknet.net.bt; f. 1968; housed in seven-storey 17th-century fortress; gallery of paintings (Thankas), images, decorative art, arms, jewellery; copper, bronze, wood and bamboo objects, philately, photographs; natural history of Bhutan; reference library with books on Bhutan, Northern Buddhism, Tibetology, museology and conservation; Dir Dr C. T. DORJI.

University

ROYAL UNIVERSITY OF BHUTAN (RUB)

POB 708, Semtokha, Thimphu
Telephone: (2) 351626
Fax: (2) 351710
E-mail: tshetenwangyel@yahoo.com
Internet: www.rub.edu.bt
Founded 2003
State control
Chancellor: HM JIGME KHESAR NAMGYEL WANGCHUCK
Vice-Chancellor: DASHO ZANGLEY DUKPA
Number of teachers: 354
Number of students: 3,820

10 Mem. instns: College of Natural Resources (located in Lobesa, Thimphu), College of Science and Technology (Rinchhending, Phuntsholing), Institute of Language and Culture Studies (Semtokha, Thimphu), Jigme Namgyel Polytechnic (Dewathang), National Institute of Traditional Medicine (Thimphu), Paro College of Education (Paro), Royal Institute of Health Science (Thimphu), Royal Institute of Management (Semtokha, Thimphu), Samtse College of Education (Samtse), Sherubtse College (Kanglung, Trashigang).

Colleges

National Institute of Education: Samtse; tel. (5) 365273; fax (5) 365363; e-mail dorjee@druknet.net.bt; f. 1968; 3-year BEd course, 2-year certificate course, 1-year postgraduate certificate course in Education, 5-year distance-learning course; academic year August to July; 35 teachers; 273 students; library: 15,000 vols, 20 periodicals; Dir DORJEE TSHERING; Prin. TSHEWANG CHHODEN WANGDI.

Royal Bhutan Polytechnic: Dewathang; tel. (7) 260286; f. 1974; 3-year diploma courses in civil, mechanical and electrical engineering; 2-year certificate courses in surveying and draughtsmanship; library: 2,000 vols; Prin. KEZANG CHADOR.

Royal Institute of Management: POB 416, Semtokha, Thimphu; tel. (2) 351013; fax (2) 351029; internet www.rim.edu.bt; f. 1986; training courses for civil service and private sector at certificate, diploma and postgraduate diploma levels; Dir KARMA TSHERING; library: 13,000 vols, 60 periodicals; 32 teachers; 292 students; publ. *dZinchong Rigphel* (2 a year).

Royal Technical Institute: Kharbandi; tel. (5) 252317; fax (5) 252171; e-mail rti@druknet.net.bt; f. 1965; 3- and 5-year certificate courses for electricians, draughtsmen, mechanics, motor mechanics; 42 teachers; 313 students; Principal SANGAY DORJEE.

Sherubtse Degree College: Kanglung, Trashigang; tel. (4) 535208; fax (4) 535129; e-mail shercol@druknet.bt; internet www .sherubtse.edu.bt; f. 1983; affiliated college of Univ. of Delhi (*q.v.*, see India chapter); 3-year honours degree courses in economics, English, geography, Dzongkha and commerce, and general degree courses in sciences; 2-year pre-univ. course in science; language of instruction: English; 46 teachers; 484 students; library: 22,000 vols; Prin. Dr JAGAR DORJI; Asst Prins LOPON JAMPEL CHOGYEL, LHATO JAMBA, NIDUP DORJI; publ. *Sherub Doenme* (journal, in English, 2 a year).

Ugyen Wangchuck University: in process of formation.

BOLIVIA

The Higher Education System

In 2006 there were a total of 69 legally recognised universities offering degree programmes. They fall into one of five categories: Public autonomous universities and members of the Bolivian University System, Public non-autonomous universities, Public non-autonomous universities and members of the Bolivian University System, Universities under special regime, and Private universities.

There are 16 public universities, 10 of which are members of the Comité Ejecutivo de la Universidad Boliviana (CEUB). Ten of these public universities are classified as public autonomous universities as they are self-financing, free to develop their own programmes and undertake research according to the Act of the Constitution of the Bolivian University System. All 10 public autonomous universities are equal in status and offer degrees and research programmes under their own autonomous Sistema de la Universidad Boliviana (SUB). There are also two public non-autonomous universities: Escuela Militar de Ingeniería (Military School of Engineering) and the Universidad Católica Boliviana (Catholic University of Bolivia). These are state-funded higher education institutions and members of the CEUB. However, they do not have the authority to offer all types of degrees, which are administered by the Bolivian Army and Catholic Church in this case. There are four public universities which do not participate in the SUB, do not have autonomy and are administered directly by the Ministry of Education and Culture. This group of institutions consists of the Universidad Militar de las Fuerzas Armadas (UMFA), the Universidad Pedagógica Nacional (UPN), the Universidad Públicade El Alto (UPEA) and the Universidad de la Policía Boliviana.

In 2006 there were 52 private universities, which have been offering degrees since the mid-1980s. Most private universities are members of the Asociación Nacional de Universidades Privadas (ANUP), founded in 1992, but are under the supervision of the Ministry of Education and Culture.

One university, the Universidad Andina Simón Bolivar (UASB) has special status in Bolivia. UASB is an international university with campuses in Ecuador, Peru, Venezuela, Colombia and Bolivia. It was established by the Andean Parliament in December 2005 and is considered an international centre of excellence in postgraduate training, research and providing services for the transfer of scientific and technological knowledge. The Bolivian campus in Sucre offers postgraduate programmes in subjects such as medicine, administration and management and law.

The Diploma de Bachiller Científico-Humanístico serves as the principle entry requirement for access to higher education. Unlike some other countries in Latin America, there is no national university entrance examination. Some universities have their own admissions policy which may include passing an entrance examination.

Higher education in Bolivia is offered at four levels: the Técnico Universitario Medio (two years), Técnico Universitario Superior (three years), Bachillerato Universitario (four years) and the Licenciatura (5 years). National standards establishing the general requirements for each of these were set following the Tenth National Congress of Universities in May 2003. Since 2006 these have been applied to all undergraduate degrees at public autonomous universities. At postgraduate level there are four types of degrees: specialist degrees in medical disciplines, specialist degrees in non-medical disciplines, Masters and Doctoral studies. On completion students receive an academic not a professional title. In 2006/07 there were some 346,100 students enrolled in further and higher education.

Accreditation of higher education is carried out by the Consejo Nacional Evaluación y Acreditación de la Educación Superior (CONAES). CONAES was established in 2002 as an independent agency responsible for conducting external evaluation of degree programmes in public and private universities. The system of accreditation is mainly programmatic and not compulsory. As a member of MERCOSUR, CONAES has already established an evaluation committee for first level medical degrees so that these qualifications will be automatically recognised throughout all MERCOSUR member states.

Regulatory and Representative Bodies

GOVERNMENT

Ministry of Education and Culture: Casilla 6500, La Paz; tel. (2) 2203576; internet www.minedu.gov.bo; Min. VÍCTOR CÁCERES RODRÍGUEZ.

NATIONAL BODIES

Comité Ejecutivo de la Universidad Boliviana (CEUB) (Executive Committee of the Bolivian University): Av. Arce esq. Pinilla 2606 y Hnos Manchego 2559, La Paz; tel. (2) 2435302; e-mail rrpp@ceub.edu.bo; internet www.ceub.edu.bo; Nat. Exec. Sec. Dr GONZALO TABOADA LÓPEZ.

Secretaría Nacional de Investigación, Ciencia y Tecnología (Secretariat for Research, Science and Technology): Casilla 11253, La Paz; tel. (2) 2434368; fax (2) 2433929; e-mail sicyt@caoba.entelnet.bo; internet www.ceub.edu.bo/ceub/secretarias/sicyt.html; directs and coordinates activities related to research, science and technology in Bolivian univs; Nat. Sec. Ing. RUBEN MEDINACELI ORTIZ.

Learned Societies

GENERAL

Academia Boliviana (Bolivian Academy): Casilla 4145, La Paz; f. 1927; Corresponding Academy of the Real Academia Española in Madrid; 26 mems; Dir Mons. JUAN QUIRÓS; Permanent Sec. CARLOS CASTAÑÓN BARRIENTOS; Pro-Sec. MARIO FRÍAS INFANTE; publ. *Revista*.

UNESCO Office La Paz: Casilla 5112, La Paz; Edificio del B.B.A. Piso 10, Avda Camacho 1413, La Paz; tel. (2) 2204009; fax (2) 2204029; e-mail la-paz@unesco.org; Dir YVES DE LA GOUBLAYE DE MENORVAL.

AGRICULTURE, FISHERIES AND VETERINARY SCIENCE

Sociedad Rural Boliviana (Agricultural Society): Casilla 786, Edif. El Condor piso 10, Of. 1005, La Paz; f. 1934; 30 assoc. mems; Pres. Ing. JOSÉ LUIS ARAMAYO V.; publs *Cotar, El Surco, IFAP News, Universitas*.

ARCHITECTURE AND TOWN PLANNING

Colegio de Arquitectos de Bolivia: Casilla 8779, La Paz; tel. 39-15-68; fax 39-15-68; f. 1940; architecture and town planning; 3,000 mems; library of 5,000 vols; Pres. FROILÁN CAVERO M.; Sec. JUAN C. BARRIENTOS M.; publs *Arquitectura y Ciudad, CDALP Informa, Punku*.

FINE AND PERFORMING ARTS

Círculo de Bellas Artes (Fine Arts Circle): Plaza Teatro, La Paz; f. 1912; Pres. ERNESTO PEÑARANDA.

HISTORY, GEOGRAPHY AND ARCHAEOLOGY

Academia Nacional de la Historia (National Academy of History): Avda Abel Iturralde 205, La Paz; f. 1929; 18 mems; Pres. Dr DAVID ALVESTEGUI; Sec.-Gen. Dr HUMBERTO VÁZQUEZ-MACHICADO.

Sociedad de Estudios Geográficos e Históricos (Geographical and Historical Society): Plaza 24 de Setiembre, Santa Cruz de la Sierra; f. 1903; Pres. Gral. LUCIO AÑEZ; Vice-Pres. Lic. PLÁCIDO MOLINA B.; Sec. AVELINO PEREDO; publ. *Boletín*.

Sociedad Geográfica de La Paz (La Paz Geographical Society): Casilla 1487, Edif. Santa Mónica, 13 Plaza Abaroa, La Paz; f. 1889; depts of prehistory, history, folklore, geography; 580 mems; Pres. Dr GREGORIO LOZA BALSA; publ. *Boletín* (2 a year).

Sociedad Geográfica y de Historia 'Potosí' (Geographical and Historical Society): Casilla 39, Potosí; tel. (62) 2-27-77; fax (62) 2-27-77; f. 1905; 20 mems; library of 4,000 vols; Pres. Prof. ALFREDO TAPIA VARGS; Sec. WALTER ZAVAL; publ. *Boletín*.

Sociedad Geográfica y de Historia 'Sucre': Plaza 25 de Mayo, Sucre; f. 1887; 8 mems; library of 3,000 vols; Dir Dr JOAQUÍN GANTIER V.; publ. *Boletín*.

LANGUAGE AND LITERATURE

Alliance Française: Calle Guachalla 399—esq. Avda 20 de Octubre, Casilla 10220, La Paz; tel. (2) 2425004; fax (2) 2426293; e-mail adminlpz@afbolivia.org; internet www .afbolivia.org; offers courses and exams in French language and culture and promotes cultural exchange with France; attached teaching offices in Cochabamba, Santa Cruz, Tarija and Sucre; Dir MARIE GRANGEON-MAZAT.

Goethe-Institut: Avda Arce 2708, Casilla 2195, La Paz; tel. (2) 2431916; fax (2) 2431998; e-mail info@lapaz.goethe.org; internet www.goethe.de/ins/bo/lap/esindex .htm; offers courses and exams in German language and culture and promotes cultural exchange with Germany; library of 10,000 vols; Dir Dr SIGRID SAVELSBERG.

PEN Club de Bolivia–Centro Internacional de Escritores (International PEN Centre): Calle Goitia 17, Casilla 149, La Paz; f. 1931; 40 Bolivian mems; 7 from other South American countries; Pres. (vacant); Sec. YOLANDA BEDREGAL DE CÓNITZER.

MEDICINE

Ateneo de Medicina de Sucre (Athenaeum of Medicine): Sucre; Pres. Dr AGUSTÍN BENÁVIDES; Vice-Pres. Dr ABERTO MARTÍNEZ; Sec.-Gen. Dr ROMELIO A. SUBIETA.

Sociedad de Pediatría de Cochabamba (Paediatrics Society): Casilla 1429, Cochabamba; f. 1945; 14 mems; Pres. Dr JULIO CORRALES BADANI; Sec. Dr MOISÉS SEJAS.

NATURAL SCIENCES

General

Academia Nacional de Ciencias de Bolivia (Bolivian National Academy of Sciences): Avda 16 de Julio 1732, Paseo El Prado, Casilla de Correos 5829, La Paz; tel. (2) 2363990; fax (2) 2379681; e-mail secretaria@ aciencias.org.bo; internet www.aciencias.org .bo; f. 1960; 42 mems; library of 8,000 vols; Pres. Acad. GONZALO TABOADA LÓPEZ; Gen. Sec. Acad. JOSÉ ANTONIO BALDERRAMA GÓMEZ ORTEGA; Librarian TERESA OCHOA GONZÁLES; publs *Boletín Informativo* (12 a year), *Publicaciones* (irregular), *Revista* (2 a year).

Physical Sciences

Colegio de Géologos de Bolivia: Edif. Sergeomin, calle Federico Zuazo, esq. Reyes Ortiz 1673, Casilla 8941, La Paz; f. 1961 as Sociedad Geológica Boliviana, present name 1996; Pres. Ing. DIONISIO GARZÓN MARTINEZ.

TECHNOLOGY

Asociación de Ingenieros y Geólogos de Yacimientos Petrolíferos Fiscales Bolivianos (AIG—YPFB): Casilla 401, La Paz; f. 1959; 210 mems in 4 brs: La Paz, Camiri, Cochabamba, Santa Cruz; Pres. Ing. JUAN CARRASCO; publ. *Revista Técnica de Yacimientos Petrolíferos Fiscales Bolivianos* (4 a year).

Research Institutes

GENERAL

Institut de Recherche pour le Développement (IRD): CP 9214, La Paz; tel. (2) 784925; fax (2) 782944; e-mail cecilia.ird@ mail.megalink.com; geology, hydrobiology, medical entomology, agronomy, nutrition, hydrology, climatology, social sciences; Dir Dr JEAN-PIERRE CAMOUZE; (see main entry under France).

AGRICULTURE, FISHERIES AND VETERINARY SCIENCE

Sistema Boliviano de Tecnología Agropecuaria (SIBTA): Avda Héctor Ormachea 1000, esq. Calle 12, Piso 3, Obrajes, La Paz; tel. (2) 2786937; fax (2) 2782161; e-mail ucpsa@sibta.gov.bo; f. 1975; 380 mems; library of 47,000 vols, 260 periodicals; Dir Dr GONZALO ROMERO G.

ECONOMICS, LAW AND POLITICS

Instituto Nacional de Estadística (National Institute of Statistics): Calle J. Carrasco 1391, Miraflores, La Paz; tel. (2) 2222333; fax (2) 222693; e-mail ceninf@ine .gov.bo; internet www.ine.gov.bo; f. 1937; nat., economic and social statistics and censuses; library of 10,500 vols, 370 periodicals; Exec. Dir JOSÉ LUIS CARJAVAL B.; publs *Actualidad Estadística* (52 a year), *Actualidad Estadística Departamental* (12 a year), *Anuario Estadística, Encuenta Integrada de Hogares* (1 a year).

HISTORY, GEOGRAPHY AND ARCHAEOLOGY

Instituto Geográfico Militar (Military Institute of Geography): Avda Saavedra 2303, (Estado Mayor), Casilla 7641, La Paz; tel. (2) 2220513; fax (2) 2228329; e-mail igm@ ejercito.mil.bo; internet www.igmbolivia.gov .bo; f. 1936; geodesy, nat. topographical survey; Commandant Col HUGO MÉNDEZ SARAVIA; publ. *Boletín Informativo*.

Instituto Nacional de Arqueología de Bolivia: Calle Tiwanaku 93, Casilla 20319, La Paz; tel. 329624; f. 1975; 26 mems; library of 6,000 vols; Dir CARLOS URQUIZO SOSSA; publ. *Arqueología Boliviana*.

LANGUAGE AND LITERATURE

Instituto Nacional de Estudios Lingüísticos (INEL): Junín 608, Casilla 7846, La Paz; f. 1965; part of *Instituto Nacional de Historia, Literatura y Antropología*; linguistic, social and educational research and teaching; specializations: Quechua and Aymara; library of 1,200 vols; Dir VITALIANO HUANCA TORREZ; publs specialized papers, *Notas y Noticias Lingüísticas* (12 a year), *Yatiñataki.*

MEDICINE

Instituto de Cancerología 'Cupertino Arteaga': Hospital de Clínicas, Plaza de Libertad, Sucre; f. 1947; Dir Dr H. NUNEZ R.

Instituto Médico Sucre (Medical Institute): Calle San Alberto 32, Casilla 82, Sucre; e-mail inmedsuc@yahoo.com; f. 1895; library of 8,000 vols, incl. *Flora Peruviensis* and 16th-century edn of *Aforismos de Hipocrates*, 6,000 pamphlets; research and production of vaccines and sera; Pres. Dr EZEQUIEL L. OSORIO; Sec. Dr JOSÉ AGUIRRE; Librarian Dr GUSTAVO VACA GUZMÁN; publ. *Revista* (4 a year).

Instituto Nacional de Medicina Nuclear (National Institute of Nuclear Medicine): Casilla Postal 5795, La Paz; Calle Mayor Rafael Zubieta 1555, Miraflores, La Paz; tel. (2) 2226116; fax (2) 2112784; e-mail inamen@

caoba.entelnet.bo; f. 1962; Dir Prof. LUIS F. BARRAGÁN M.

NATURAL SCIENCES

Physical Sciences

Observatorio San Calixto: Casilla 12656, La Paz; tel. (2) 2406222; fax (2) 2116723; e-mail oscdrake@entelnet.bo; internet www .observatoriosancalixto.org.bo; f. 1913; meteorology and seismology; library of 11,000 vols; Dir Dr ESTELLA MINAYA.

Servicio Nacional de Geología y Técnico de Minas (SERGEOTECMIN): Federico Zuazo 1673, Casilla 2729, La Paz; tel. (2) 2330766; fax (2) 2391725; e-mail sergeotecmin@sergeomin.gov.bo; internet www.sergeomin.gov.bo; f. 1956 as a nat. dept, reorganized 1965, 1996 and 2004; 136 mems; 10 laboratories; library of 5,124 vols; Exec. Dir ZOILO MONCADA; publs *Boletín Informativo 'Sergeotecmin Informa'* (3 a year), *Boletines Especiales* (technical reports), geological maps.

RELIGION, SOCIOLOGY AND ANTHROPOLOGY

Instituto de Sociología Boliviana (ISBO) (Institute of Sociology): Apdo 215, Sucre; f. 1941; investigates economic, juridical and sociological problems; library of 15,000 vols; Dir TOMÁS LENZ B.; publ. *Revista del Instituto de Sociología Boliviana.*

TECHNOLOGY

Instituto Boliviano de Ciencia y Tecnología Nuclear: Casilla 4821, La Paz; Avda 6 de Agosto 2905, La Paz; tel. (2) 433481; fax (2) 433063; e-mail ibten@datacom-bo.net; f. 1983; Dirs JORGE CHUNGARA CASTRO, FERNANDO BARRIENTOS ZAMORA (acting).

Instituto Boliviano del Petróleo (IBP): Casilla 4722, La Paz; f. 1959 to support and coordinate scientific, technical and economic studies on the oil industry in Bolivia; 50 mems; library of 1,000 technical vols; Pres. Ing. JOSÉ PATIÑO; Gen. Sec. Ing. REYNALDO SALGUEIRO PABÓN; publs *Boletín, Manual de Signos Convencionales.*

Libraries and Archives

Cochabamba

Biblioteca Central Universitaria 'José Antonio Arze' (Universidad Mayor de San Simón): Avda Oquendo esq. Sucre, Casilla 992, Cochabamba; tel. (42) 31733; fax (42) 31691; f. 1930; 30,000 vols; Dir LUIS ALBERTO PONCE; publ. *Boletín Bibliográfico.*

La Paz

Biblioteca Central de la Universidad Mayor de San Andrés: Avda Villazón 1995, La Paz; tel. (2) 359505; internet www .umsa.bo/umsa/app?service=page/ac0300; f. 1930; 121,000 vols; Dir Lic. ALBERTO CRESPO RODAS.

Biblioteca del Instituto Boliviano de Estudio y Acción Social: Avda Arce 2147, La Paz; special collections on social science, Boliviana, education and government documents; 12,000 vols; Dir ELENA PEDDLE.

Biblioteca del Ministerio de Relaciones Exteriores (Library of the Ministry of Foreign Affairs): Plaza Murillo, La Paz; f. 1930; 10,039 vols; private library; Dir Prof. PACÍFICO LUNA QUIJARRO.

Biblioteca Municipal 'Mariscal Andrés de Santa Cruz' (Municipal Library): Zona Central, Plaza del Estudiante, Calle Cañada Strongest esquina México, La Paz; tel. (2) 2378477; fax (2) 2378477; internet saludpublica.bvsp.org.bo/sys/?s2=1; f. 1838; 35,000 vols; Dir YOLOTZIN SALDAÑA.

Biblioteca y Archivo Histórico del Honorable Congreso Nacional (Congress Library): Calle Mercado esquina Ayacucho No. 308, La Paz; tel. (2) 314731; internet www.congreso.gov.bo/5biblioteca; f. 1912; 22,000 vols; Dir VÍCTOR BERNAL SOLARES; Chief Librarian NELLY ARRAYA VASQUEZ; publ. *Reports of Congress*.

Centro Nacional de Documentación Científica y Tecnológica (Bolivian National Scientific and Technological Documentation Centre): Casilla 14538, La Paz; Avda Mariscal Santa Cruz 1175, esquina Calle Ayacucho, La Paz; tel. (2) 359583; fax (2) 359586; e-mail iiicndct@huayna.umsa .edu.bo; internet www.bolivian.com/ industrial/cndct; f. 1967 to provide extensive information service for research and development; attached to Instituto de Investigaciones Industriales, Universidad Mayor de San Andrés; depository library for FAO, WHO and ILO; 9,800 vols; Dir RUBÉN VALLE VERA; publ. *Actualidades* (4 a year).

Potosí

Biblioteca Central Universitaria: Universidad Autónoma 'Tomás Frías', Casilla 54, Avda del Maestro, Potosí; tel. (62) 27313; f. 1942; 43,796 vols, 1,471 periodicals; 1 central library, 8 specialized libraries; Dir JULIA B. DE LÓPEZ; publs *Revista Científica*, *Revista de Ciencias*, *Revista Orientación Pedagógica*.

Biblioteca Municipal 'Ricardo Jaime Freires': Potosí; f. 1920; 30,000 vols; Dir LUIS E. HEREDIA.

Sucre

Biblioteca Central de la Universidad Mayor de San Francisco Xavier: Plaza 25 de Mayo, Apdo 212, Sucre; Dir AGAR PEÑARANDA.

Biblioteca y Archivo Nacional de Bolivia (National Library and Archives): Casilla 338, Sucre; Calle Bolívar, Sucre; tel. (64) 1481; f. 1836; 150,000 vols; Dir GUNNAR MENDOZA.

Museums and Art Galleries

La Paz

Museo 'Casa de Murillo': Calle Apolinar Jaén 790, La Paz; tel. (2) 2280758; f. 1950; folk and colonial art, paintings, furniture, national costume, herb medicine and magic; Dir (vacant).

Museo Costumbrista 'Juan de Vargas': Calle Sucre s/n, esq. Jaén, La Paz; f. 1979; history of La Paz.

Museo de Metales Preciosos Precolombinos: Calle Jaén 777, Casilla 609, La Paz; tel. (2) 2280758; f. 1983; pre-Columbian archaeology (especially gold and silver); Dir JOSÉ DE MESA.

Museo Nacional de Arqueología (National Archaeological Museum): Calle Tihuanaco 93, Casilla oficial, La Paz; tel. (2) 2311621; f. 1846, reinaugurated 1961; archaeological and ethnographical collections; Lake Titicaca district exhibits; Dir JULIO CESAR VELASQUEZ ALQUIZALETH; publ. *Anales*.

Museo Nacional de Arte: Calle Socabaya esq. Calle Comercio, CP 11390, La Paz; tel. (2) 408542; fax (2) 408600; f. 1964; housed in 18th-century baroque palace; colonial art, sculpture and furniture; Bolivian and Latin-American modern art; Dir TERESA VILLEGAS DE ANEIVA.

Potosí

Museo de la Casa Nacional de Moneda (Museum of the National Mint): Calle Ayacucho s/n, Potosí; tel. (2) 6223986; fax (2) 6222777; e-mail cnm@ casanacionaldemoneda.org.bo; internet .casanacionaldemoneda.org.bo; f. 1938; housed in the 'Casa de Moneda', the Royal Mint, founded 1572, now restored, said to be the most outstanding civic monument of the colonial period in South America; colonial art, 18th-century wooden machinery, coins, historical archives, mineralogy, weapons, Indian ethnography, archaeology, modern art; Dir LUIS ALFONSO FERNÁNDEZ; publ. see under Sociedad Geográfica y de Historia 'Potosí'.

Sucre

Casa de la Libertad: Casilla postal 101, Sucre; Plaza 25 de Mayo 11, Sucre; tel. (4) 6454200; fax (4) 6452690; e-mail cdl@ casadelalibertad.org.bo; internet www .casadelalibertad.org.bo; fmrly Casa de la Independencia; historical collection concerned with Independence, including Bolivian Declaration of Independence; library of 4,000 vols, 1,000 maps; publ. *Memorias*.

Museo Charcas: Universidad Boliviana Mayor, Real y Pontificia de San Francisco Xavier, Calle Bolívar 698, Sucre; tel. (4) 6453285; f. 1944; anthropological collection with pre-Inca archaeology: Dir JAIME URIOSTE ARANA; ethnographical and folklore collection: Dir ELIZABETH ROJAS TORO; colonial and modern art section, including Princesa de la Glorieta collection: Dir MANUEL GIMÉNEZ CARRAZANA; publ. *Boletín Antropológico*.

Universities

UNIVERSIDAD AMAZÓNICA DE PANDO

Calle Enrique Cornejo 77, Pando, Cobija
Telephone: (3) 8422411
Fax: (3) 8429710
E-mail: recuap@hotmail.com
Founded 1993
State control
Rector: ADOLFO MEJIDO.

UNIVERSIDAD AUTÓNOMA DEL BENI 'JOSÉ BALLIVIÁN'

Casilla 38, Trinidad, Beni
Telephone: (46) 20744
E-mail: secretariogeneral@uabjb.edu.bo
Internet: www.uabjb.edu.bo
Founded 1967
State control
Rector: M.Sc. GUILLERMO SUÁREZ ZAMBRANO
Vice-Rector: Dr CARMELO APONTE VÉLEZ
Gen. Sec.: Ing. RUBÉN TORRES TAGLE
Librarian: LORGIA S. DE TANAKA
Library of 9,600 vols
Number of teachers: 155
Number of students: 1,039
Publications: *Boletines de los Institutos de Investigaciones*, *Ictícola del Beni*, *Investigaciones Forestales y de Defensa de la Amazonía*, *Socio-económicas*

DEANS

Faculty of Agriculture: Lic. CASTO PLAZA CUENCA
Faculty of Economics: RODOLFO ARTEAGA CÉSPEDES
Faculty of Stockbreeding: Dr PABLO MEMM DORADO

ATTACHED RESEARCH INSTITUTES

Instituto de Investigaciones Forestales y Defensa del Medio Ambiente de la Amazonia: Casilla 12, Riberalta, Beni; tel. 82484; Dir OSCAR LLANQUE.

Instituto de Investigaciones Icticolas del Beni: Casilla 38, Trinidad, Beni; tel. 21705; Dir Dr RENÉ VASQUEZ PÉREZ.

Instituto de Investigaciones Socio-económicas: Casilla 38, Trinidad, Beni; tel. 21566; Dir Lic. CARLOS NAVIA RIBERA.

UNIVERSIDAD AUTÓNOMA 'GABRIEL RENÉ MORENO'

Plaza 24 de Septiembre, Santa Cruz de la Sierra
Telephone: (3) 3365533
Fax: (3) 3342160
E-mail: uagrmrec@bibosi.scz.entelnet.bo
Internet: www.uagrm.edu.bo
Founded 1879
State control
Language of instruction: Spanish
Academic year: February to December
Rector: Abog. REYMI FERREIRA JUSTINIANO
Vice-Rector: Dr JULIO ARGENTINO SALEK MERY
Sec.-Gen.: Dr JOSÉ MIRTENBAUM KNIEVEL
Univ. Dir of Academic Affairs: Ing. JOSÉ FREDDY SÁNCHEZ SÁNCHEZ
Univ. Dir of Admin. and Finance: Lic. WALDO LOPEZ APARICIO
Univ. Dir of Extension: Arq. ROBERT RIVERA CAMACHO
Univ. Dir of Research: Dr ALFREDO MENACHO VACA
Univ. Dir of Social Welfare: Ing. PILAR DÁVALOS SÁNCHEZ
Librarian: Lic. JOSÉ MELCHOR MANSILLA
Library of 40,000 vols
Number of teachers: 1,019
Number of students: 27,600
Publication: *Universidad*

DEANS

Faculty of Agriculture: Ing. ALFREDO PÉREZ ANGULO
Faculty of Economics and Finance: Lic. ALFREDO JALDÍN FARELL
Faculty of Exact Sciences and Technology: Ing. WALTER YABETA SÁNCHEZ
Faculty of Habitat, Integral Design and Art: Arq. CARLOS BARRERO SUAREZ
Faculty of Health Sciences: Lic. NELSON VILLEGAS ROJAS
Faculty of Humanities: Dr EMILIO DURÁN RIVERA
Faculty of Juridical, Political and Social Sciences: Dr OSVALDO ULLOA PEÑA
Faculty of Veterinary Medicine and Zootechnology: Dr SERGIO SANTA CRUZ GIL
Polytechnic Faculty: Ing. LUIZ ALBERTO VACA PINTO
Polytechnic Faculty of Camiri: Ing. ROBERTO SAAVEDRA ARÉVALO

UNIVERSIDAD AUTÓNOMA 'JUAN MISAEL SARACHO'

Avda Victor Paz 149, CP 51, Tarija
Telephone: (66) 43110
Fax: (66) 43403
E-mail: rector@uajms.edu.bo
Internet: www.uajms.edu.bo
Founded 1946
State control
Academic year: March to December
Rector: Lic. EDUARDO CORTEZ BALDIVIEZO
Number of teachers: 611
Number of students: 12,634
Publications: *Astro Información* (12 a year), *Visión Universitaria* (12 a year)

BOSNIA AND HERZEGOVINA

The Higher Education System

Bosnia and Herzegovina emerged in its present form from the conflict that, from 1991, engulfed the republics hitherto constituting Yugoslavia. In accordance with the General Framework Agreement for Peace in Bosnia and Herzegovina, signed in 1995, Bosnia and Herzegovina is a single state, which consists of two political entities: the Federation of Bosnia and Herzegovina, principally comprising the Bosniak (Muslim)- and Croat-majority areas, and Republika Srpska, principally comprising the Serb-majority area. Although there is a central (state) Government of Bosnia and Herzegovina, based in Sarajevo, both constituent entities have their own governments. In the Federation of Bosnia and Herzegovina, higher education is the responsibility of the Ministry of Education and Science, based in Sarajevo, and in the Republika Srpska higher education is overseen by the Ministry of Education and Culture, based in Banja Luka. At present, higher education is centrally funded. Although the cantons are responsible for financing higher education, only three of the eight existing cantons coincide with university centres. There are no adequate resources at cantonal level for the financing of higher education.

In 2006/07 in the Federation of Bosnia and Herzegovina, 77,009 students attended 105 higher education institutions. In 2007 there were eight universities, as well as other university faculties, specialist institutes and Visoke skole (high schools). In August 2003 officials of the Federation, Republika Srpska, the cantonal Governments and the Interim District Government of Brčko signed an agreement to replace the country's three ethnically-based education systems with a single unified system. (However, some local authorities remained resistant to the unification of the education system.) In the same year Bosnia and Herzegovina became a signatory to the Bologna Process. However, despite the immediate preparation of a new law pertaining to the implementation of a two-tier higher education system (as well as ECTS, and the Diploma Supplement), the new Law on Higher Education was only adopted in 2007.

Higher education admission is made on the basis of a Secondary School Leaving Certificate. Higher education has been reorganized and credited according to the ECTS. Although a three-cycle structure has existed for most fields of study in all countries of former Yugoslavia, the new framework clearly corresponds with the Bologna scheme of three cycles of higher education: Bachelor, Masters and Doctoral programmes. There are four university degrees: two at undergraduate level (Diploma Višeg Obrazovanje and Diploma Visokog Obrazovanja) and two at postgraduate level (Magistar and Doktor Nauka). The Diploma Višeg Obrazovanje (Diploma of Higher Education) is a two- to three-year course, resulting in a professional title, but is not a full degree. The Diploma Visokog Obrazovanja (Advanced Diploma of Higher Education) is a full degree course of four to six years leading to a professional title. At postgraduate level the Magistar (Masters) requires two years of research and defence of a thesis, and the Doktor Nauka (Doctor of Science) requires further research and defence of a thesis, but in a non-specified timeframe.

Regulatory and Representative Bodies

GOVERNMENT

Ministry of Culture and Sports: Obala Maka Dizdara 2, 71000 Sarajevo; tel. (33) 254-100; fax (33) 664-381; e-mail kabinet@fmksa.com; internet www.fmks.gov.ba; Min. GAVRILO GRAHOVAC.

Ministry of Education and Science: Stjepana Radića 33, 71000 Mostar; tel. (36) 355-700; fax (36) 355-742; e-mail info@fmon.gov.ba; internet www.fmon.gov.ba; Min. Prof. MELIHA ALIĆ.

ACCREDITATION

ENIC/NARIC Bosnia and Herzegovina: Min. of Civil Affairs, Sektor za obrazovanje/Education Sector (Unit for Collecting ENIC-NARIC Information), Vilsonovo šetalište 10, 71000 Sarajevo; tel. (33) 655-339; fax (33) 713-956; e-mail miljan.popic@mcp.gov.ba; internet www.mcp.gov.ba; Contact MILJAN POPIC.

Learned Societies

GENERAL

Akademija Nauka i Umjetnosti BiH (Academy of Arts and Sciences of Bosnia and Herzegovina): Bistrik 7, 71000 Sarajevo; tel. (33) 206-034; fax (33) 206-033; e-mail akademik@anubih.ba; internet www.anubih.ba; f. 1951 as the Scientific Society, present name and status 1966; attached research institute: see Research Institutes; responsible for the overall devt of science and the arts by organizing scientific research and arts-related events, publishing papers written by its members and associates; 57 mems; library of 50,000 vols; Pres. Dr BOŽIDAR MATIĆ; Vice-Pres. Dr SLOBODAN LOGA; Sec.-Gen. Dr ZIJO PAŠIĆ; publs *Godišnjak* (Annals), *Herbologia*, *Ljetopis* (Yearbook), *Sarajevo Journal of Mathematics* (2 a year).

Hrvatsko Kulturno Društvo Napredak ('Napredak' Croatian Cultural Society): Središnja uprava, Ulica Maršala Tita 56, 71000 Sarajevo; tel. (33) 222-876; fax (33) 663-380; e-mail ured@napredak.com.ba; internet www.napredak.com.ba; f. 1902; Pres. FRANJO TOPIĆ; Sec. Gen. VANJA RAVEN; 20,000 mems; publ. *Stecak* (cultural and social issues, 12 a year).

Srpske Prosvjetno Kulturno Društvo 'Prosvjeta' Sarajevo ('Prosvjeta' Serbian Cultural Society, Sarajevo): Sime Milutinovića-Sarajlije 1, 71000 Sarajevo; tel. (33) 444-230; fax (33) 444-230; e-mail prosvjeta@bih.net.ba; f. 1902; science, art and literature; 140 mems; library of 3,000 vols; Pres. TEODOR ROMANIĆ; Sec. DRAGAN SELEDA; publ. *Bosanska Vila*.

Udruženje Gradjana Bošnjačka Zajednica Kulture Preporod u BiH ('Preporod' Cultural Association of the Bosniak Community of Bosnia and Herzegovina): Branilaca Sarajeva 30, 71000 Sarajevo; tel. (33) 205-553; fax (33) 205-553.

UNESCO Office Sarajevo: Titova 48/4, 71000 Sarajevo; tel. (33) 222-792; fax (33) 222-795; e-mail sarajevo@unesco.org; Dir COLIN KAISER.

AGRICULTURE, FISHERIES AND VETERINARY SCIENCE

Bosnia and Herzegovina Small Animal Veterinary Association: Alipašina St 37, 71000 Sarajevo; tel. (33) 442-303; fax (33) 442-303; e-mail veterins@bih.net.ba; Pres. Dr JOSIP KRASNI.

ARCHITECTURE AND TOWN PLANNING

Društvo Urbanista Bosne i Hercegovine (Society of Town Planning of Bosnia and Herzegovina): Zavod za urbanizam, Aleja bosanskih vladara 6, 75000 Tuzla; tel. (35) 252-038; fax (35) 251-575; f. 1993; 500 ; Pres. ZEHRA MORANKIĆ; publ. *URBO* (1 a year).

BIBLIOGRAPHY, LIBRARY SCIENCE AND MUSEOLOGY

Društvo Arhivskih Radnika Bosne i Hercegovine (Association of Archive Workers of Bosnia and Herzegovina): Franje Ledera 1, 75000 Tuzla; tel. (35) 252-620; fax (35) 252-620; Pres. Dr AZEM KOŽAR; publ. *Glasnik Arhiva i Društva Arhivski Radnika Bosne i Hercegovine* (1 a year).

Društvo Bibliotekara BiH (Librarians' Society of Bosnia and Herzegovina): Zmaja od Bosne 8B, 71000 Sarajevo; tel. (33) 275-325; fax (33) 212-435; f. 1949; 450 mems; Pres. NEVENKA HAJDAROVIĆ; publs *Bibliotekarstvo* (1 a year), *Bilten*.

ECONOMICS, LAW AND POLITICS

Advokatska-Odvjetnicka Komora Federacije Bosne i Hercegovine (Bar Association of the Federation of Bosnia and Herzegovina): Obala Kulina Bana 6, 71000 Sarajevo; tel. (33) 261-090; fax (33) 209-976; internet www.advokomfbih.ba; 830 members, incl. 670 attorneys and 160 law trainees; Pres. AMILA KUNOSIC-FERIZOVIC.

Advokatska Komora Bosne i Hercegovine (Law Society of Bosnia and Herzegovina): Šemaluša 2, 71000 Sarajevo; tel. (33) 471-156; fax (33) 471-156.

Udruženje Sudija i Sudaca u Federacije Bosne i Hercegovine (Association of Judges of the Federation of Bosnia and Herzegovina): Valtera Perića 15, Kancelarija udruženja br. 203, 71000 Sarajevo; tel. (33) 668-035; fax (33) 668-035; e-mail usfbih@bih .net.ba; internet www.usfbih.ba; f. 1996; advocacy and training; 320 mems; Pres. VILDANA HELIĆ; Vice-Pres STJEPAN MIKULIC, GORAN SALIHOVIC; publ. *Mjesečni Časopis*.

Udruženje Sudija i Tužilaca Republike Srpske (Judges' and Prosecutors' Association of Republika Srpska): Kralja Petra 1 Karadjordjevica 12, 78000 Banja Luka; tel. (51) 212-725; fax (51) 212-725; e-mail maja@ inneco.net; f. 1998; 400 mems; Pres. MIRKO DABIĆ; Sec. ŽIVANA BAJIĆ; publs *Glasnik Pravde* (3 a year), *Bulletin* (6 a year).

EDUCATION

Pedagoško Društvo BiH (Pedagogical Society of Bosnia and Herzegovina): Djure Djakovića 4, 71000 Sarajevo.

FINE AND PERFORMING ARTS

Muzička Omladina Sarajeva BiH (Jeunesses Musicales of Sarajevo): Dalmatinska 2/1, 71000 Sarajevo; tel. (33) 665-713; fax (33) 665-713; e-mail muzomlsa@soros.org.ba; internet jm-sa.open.net.ba; f. 1958; organizes concerts and theatre events; 12,000 mems; library of 1,000 vols, record library of 1,000 items; Pres. REŠAD ARNAUTOVIĆ; Sec. SLAVICA ŠPOLJARIĆ.

Udruženje Muzičkih Umjetnika BiH (Association of Musicians of Bosnia and Herzegovina): Sv. Markovicá 1, 71000 Sarajevo.

HISTORY, GEOGRAPHY AND ARCHAEOLOGY

Društvo Istoričara BiH (Historical Society of Bosnia and Herzegovina): Račkog 1, Filozofski fakultet, 71000 Sarajevo.

Geografsko Društvo BiH (Geographical Society of Bosnia and Herzegovina): Prirodnomatematički fakultet, Vojvode Putnika 43A, 71000 Sarajevo; f. 1947; 1,541 mems; Pres. Dr MILOŠ BJELOVITIĆ; Vice-Pres. Dr KREŠIMIR PAPIĆ; publs *Geografski list* (5 a year), *Geografski pregled*, *Nastava geografije* (1 a year).

Geografsko Društvo Republike Srpske (Society of Geographers of Republika Srpska): Bana Lazarevića 1, 78000 Banja Luka; tel. (51) 235-625.

LANGUAGE AND LITERATURE

British Council: Ljubljianska 9, 71000 Sarajevo; tel. (33) 250-220; fax (33) 250-240; e-mail british.council@britishcouncil.ba; internet www.britishcouncil.ba; offers courses and examinations in English language and British culture and promotes cultural exchange with the UK; f. 1996; library of 6,500 vols; Dir MICHAEL MOORE; Deputy Dir GORJANA ŠEVELJ PEĆANAC.

Društvo Pisaca BiH (Association of Writers of Bosnia and Herzegovina): Kranjčevićeva 24, 71000 Sarajevo; tel. (33) 557-940; fax (33) 557-940; e-mail d_pisaca@bih.net.ba; f. 1993; organizes the Int. Festival of Poetry and Sarajevo Poetry days; 165 mems; library of 1,500 vols; Pres. GRADIMIR GOJER; Sec. MUHAMED ČUROVAC; publs *Lica i Život* (4 a year), *Slovo* (12 a year).

Goethe-Institut: Bentbaša 1A, 71000 Sarajevo; tel. (33) 570-000; fax (33) 570-030; e-mail info@sarajevo.goethe.org; internet www.goethe.de/sarajevo; offers courses and examinations in German language and cul-

ture and promotes cultural exchange with Germany; f. 2000, present bldg 2004; Dir Dr PETRA RAYMOND; Deputy Dir Dr NINA WICHMANN.

PEN Centar BiH (PEN Centre of Bosnia and Herzegovina): Vrazova 1, 71000 Sarajevo; tel. (33) 200-155; fax (33) 217-854; e-mail krugpen@bih.net.ba; internet www .penbih.ba; f. 1992; 75 mems; Pres. UGO VLAISAVLJEVIĆ; Exec. Dir. FERIDA DURAKOVIĆ; publ. *Novi Izraz* (4 a year).

MEDICINE

Društvo Ljekara BiH (Physicians' Society of Bosnia and Herzegovina): Zavod za zdravst-venu zaštitu BiH, Maršala Tita 7, 71000 Sarajevo.

Farmaceutsko društvo Republike Srpske (Pharmaceutical Society of Republika Srpske): Ranka Sipke 32, 78000 Banja Luka; tel. (51) 318-699; e-mail farmacia@teol .net; internet www.farmaceutskodrustvo.org; f. 1996; br. offices in Banja Luka, Doboj, Bijeljina, Foca, Sarajevo, Prijedor, Trebinje and Zvornik; training programmes, devt of health education; Pres. RADA AMIDŽIĆ.

Udruga/Udruženje Pedijatara u Bosni i Hercegovini (Paediatric Society in Bosnia and Herzegovina): Sveučilisna klinička bolnica Mostar Klinika za dječje bolest, 88000 Mostar; tel. (36) 343-348; fax (36) 343-348; e-mail tajnica@upubih.org; internet www .upubih.org; f. 2006 as legal successor of the Paediatric Association of Bosnia and Herzegovina in Sarajevo, registered with the Min. of Justice; disease prevention and health care; Pres. ZELJKO RONCEVIC; Vice-Pres AMIRA SKAKA, ZDRAVKO KUZMAN.

Udruženje Farmakologa Federacije Bosne i Hercegovine (Association of Pharmacologists of the Federation of Bosnia and Herzegovina): Čekaluša 90/II, 71000 Sarajevo; tel. (33) 441-813; fax (33) 441-895; e-mail farma@bih.net.ba; f. 1980; 54 mems; library of 5,000 vols; Pres. Prof. Dr NEDŽAD MULABEGOVIĆ; Sec. Asst Prof. SVJETLANA LOGA; publs *Bosnian Journal of Basic Medical Sciences* (6 a year), *Drug Plus* (1 a year).

Udruženje Stomatologa BiH (Dental Association of Bosnia and Herzegovina): School of Dentistry, Bolnička 4A, 71000 Sarajevo; tel. (33) 214-259; fax (33) 214-259; e-mail mganibeg@utic.net.ba; internet www .usfbih.org.ba; f. 1997; 500 mems; Pres. Prof. MAIDA GANIBEGOVIĆ; Vice-Pres. MARINKO TOPIĆ; Gen. Sec. NINA MARKOVIC; publs *Bilten Stomatologia BiH* (in the nat. languages of Bosnia and Herzegovina and in English, 3 a year), *Stomatološki vjesnik* (in the nat. languages of Bosnia and Herzegovina and in English, 2 a year).

NATURAL SCIENCES

General

Društvo Fizičara u BiH (Physical Society in Bosnia and Herzegovina): Zmaja od Bosne 35, zgrada Prirodno-matematički fakultet, 71000 Sarajevo; tel. (33) 653-294; e-mail dfubih@gmail.com; internet www .drustvofizicara.com.ba; organizes competitions, seminars and lectures for the popularization of physics; Pres. RAJFA MUSEMIĆ; Vice-Pres REFIK FAZLIĆ, SLAVICA EREŠ-BRKIĆ, ZALKIDA HADŽIBEGOVIĆ.

Mathematical Sciences

Društvo Matematičara Republike Srpske (Society of Mathematicians of Republika Srpska): Bana Lazarevića 1, 78000 Banja Luka; tel. (51) 268-686.

PHILOSOPHY AND PSYCHOLOGY

Društvo Psihologa BiH (Association of Psychologists of Bosnia and Herzegovina):

Aleja lipa 81, 71000 Sarajevo; tel. (33) 659-184.

Društvo Psihologa Republike Srpske (Association of Psychologists of Republika Srpske): Bana Lazarevića 1, treći sprat, soba 47, 78000 Banja Luka; e-mail dprs@ drustvo-psihologa.rs.ba; internet www .drustvo-psihologa.rs.ba; f. 2003; devt and application of theoretical and applied psychology; organization of professional education; Pres. Dr MILENA PASIC; Vice-Pres. SINISA LAKIC.

Research Institutes

GENERAL

Bošnjački Institut—Fondacija Adila Zulfikarpašića (Bosniak Institute—Adil Zulfikarpašić Foundation): Mula Mustafe Bašeskie 21, 71000 Sarajevo; tel. (33) 279-800; fax (33) 279-777; e-mail bosinst@ bosnjackiinstitut.org; internet www .bosnjackiinstitut.org; f. 1988 in Zurich; 2001 in Sarajevo; researches into the history, literature, art, language and religion of the Bosniaks and other people of Bosnia and Herzegovina and the promotion of their cultural heritage; library: reference library of 80,000 vols, open to the public; Exec. Dir AMINA RIZVANBEGOVIC DZUVIC; Archivist AHMET ZULFIKARPAŠIĆ; Librarians VESNA ČEFO, NARCISA PULJEK-BUBRIĆ.

Centre for Philosophical Research: Bistrik 7, 71000 Sarajevo; tel. (33) 210-902; fax (33) 206-033; e-mail akademija@anubih.ba; internet www.anubih.ba; attached to Acad. of Arts and Sciences of Bosnia and Herzegovina; Dir ARIF TANOVIC; publ. *Dialogue* (4 a year).

Kantonalni Zavod za Zaštitu Kulturno-Historisjkog i Prirodnog Naslijedja Sarajevo (Institute for the Protection of the Cultural, Historical and Natural Heritage of the Canton of Sarajevo): Josipa Štadlera 32, 71000 Sarajevo; tel. (33) 475-020; fax (33) 475-034; e-mail heritsa@bih.net.ba; internet www.spomenici-sa.ba; f. 1965; documentation of monuments; devt projects; surveys and studies; promotes awareness of culture, history and natural heritage; library of 15,000 vols; Dir MUNIB BULJINA; Exec. Dir VALIDA ČELIĆ-CEMERLIĆ.

Orijentalni Institut u Sarajevu (Oriental Institute, Sarajevo): Zmaja od Bosne 8B, 71000 Sarajevo; tel. (33) 225-353; fax (33) 225-353; e-mail ois@bih.net.ba; internet www .ois.unsa.ba; f. 1950; history, philology and culture of the Ottoman Balkans and the Middle East; library of 10,000 vols, 1,200 periodicals; Scientific Advisor and Dir Dr BEHIJA ZLATAR; Pres. of Steering Committee HALIL BJELAK; publ. *Prilozi za orijentalnu filologiju / Revue de philologie orientale* (1 a year).

Zavod za Zaštitu Kulturnog, Historijskog i Prirodnog Naslijedja BiH (Institute for the Protection of the Cultural, Historical and Natural Heritage of Bosnia and Herzegovina): Alekse Šantića 8/III, 71000 Sarajevo; tel. (33) 663-299; fax (33) 663-299; e-mail h_c_bih@bih.net.ba; f. 1947; protection and preservation of monuments; conservation, registering of moveable and non-moveable heritage; colln of documents; raising awareness and evaluation of heritage, projects and studies; Dir DŽIHAD PAŠIĆ; publ. *Naše Starine*.

ARCHITECTURE AND TOWN PLANNING

Centar za Islamsku Arhitektura (Centre for Islamic Architecture): Blvr Mese Selimovića 85, 71000 Sarajevo; tel. (33) 459-780; fax (33) 459-700; e-mail centaria@bih.net.ba;

internet www.rijaset.ba; f. 1995; attached to Rijaset Islamske Zajednice u Bosni i Hercegovini (Islamic Community in Bosnia and Herzegovina); restoration and reconstruction of damaged and destroyed religious sites; Dir KEMAL ŽUKIĆ.

ECONOMICS, LAW AND POLITICS

Ekonomski Institut Sarajevo (Institute of Economics, Sarajevo): Branilaca Sarajevo 47, 71000 Sarajevo; tel. (33) 565-870; fax (33) 565-874; e-mail ekonomski.institut@efsa .unsa.ba; internet www.eis.ba; f. 1961; economic research for improvement of public policy and business consulting services, increasing competitiveness in the business sector; library of 12,400 vols; Dir Dr ANTO DOMAZET.

Ekonomski Institut Tuzla (Tuzla Institute of Economics): Zvonka Cerića 1, 75000 Tuzla; tel. (35) 214-657; fax (35) 214-336; Dir SEAD BABOVIĆ.

Human Rights Centre: Zmaja od Bosne 8, 71000 Sarajevo; tel. (33) 668-251; fax (33) 668-251; e-mail hrc_sa@hrc.unsa.ba; internet www.hrc.unsa.ba; f. 1996; attached to Univ. of Sarajevo; education and training, research and consulting, documentation and information services; Dir SAŠA MADACKI; Librarians AJLA MUHAMEDOVIĆ, AIDA HAJRO, MAJA KALJANAC, NINA KARAĆ.

Institut za istraživanje zločina protiv čovječnosti i međunarodnog prava (Institute for Research of Crimes Against Humanity and International Law): ul. Halida Nazecica 4, 71000 Sarajevo; tel. (33) 561-350; fax (33) 561-351; e-mail info@institut-genocid .ba; internet www.institut-genocid.ba; f. 1992; attached to Univ. of Sarajevo; public scientific institution; provides analysis of crimes against int. law, human rights violations and genocide; Chair., Brd of Management Prof. Dr ISMET DIZDAREVIĆ; Chair., Scientific Council Prof. Dr SMAIL ČEKIĆ.

HISTORY, GEOGRAPHY AND ARCHAEOLOGY

Institut za Istoriju (Institute of History): Alipašina 9, 71000 Sarajevo; tel. (33) 209-364; fax (33) 217-263; e-mail nauka@bih.net .ba; internet www.iis.unsa.ba; f. 1959; public research institute; deals with research work in field of history; library of 3,000 journals, 12,070 monographs, rare periodicals from the pre-war and 1941–45 period; Dir Dr HUSNIJA KAMBEROVIĆ; Pres. Prof. Dr MUSTAFA IMAMOVIC; Sec. ASIDE ŠAHBEGOVIĆ; publ. *Prilozi* (Contributions, 1 a year).

LANGUAGE AND LITERATURE

Institut za Jezik i Književnost (Institute of Language and Literature): Hasana Kikića 12, 71000 Sarajevo; tel. (33) 200-117.

Language Institute: Hasana Kikića 12, 71000 Sarajevo; tel. (33) 200-117; f. 1973; library of 3,200 vols; Dir Dr IBRAHIM ČEDIĆ; publs *Dijalektološki Zbornik* (Dialect Colln, irregular), *Književni jezik* (Literary Language, 4 a year), *Radovi* (Works, 1 a year).

Media Plan Institute: Antuna Branka Šimića 5/2, 71000 Sarajevo; tel. (33) 717-840; fax (33) 717-850; e-mail mediaplan@ mediaplan.ba; internet www.mediaplan.ba; f. 1995; research into and analysis of the media; educational projects, media campaign, adult education; 14 mems; Pres. ZORAN UDOVIČIĆ; Exec. Dir BOJANA ŠUTVIĆ.

NATURAL SCIENCES

Mathematical Sciences

Agencija za Statistiku Bosne i Hercegovine (Agency for Statistics of Bosnia and Herzegovina): Zelenih beretki 26, 71000

Sarajevo; tel. (33) 220-626; fax (33) 220-622; e-mail bhas@bhas.ba; internet www.bhas.ba; f. 1998; dir and two deputies consisting of one Serb, one Croat and one Muslim; documents statistical changes in economic, demographic and social fields, environment and natural resources; Dir ZDENKO MILINOVIĆ; publs *First Release* (12 a year), *Statistical Bulletins* (6–8 a year).

Federalni Zavod za Statistiku (Institute of Statistics of the Federation of Bosnia and Herzegovina): Zeleni beretki 26, 71000 Sarajevo; tel. (33) 664-553; fax (33) 664-553; e-mail fedstat@fzs.ba; internet www.fzs.ba; f. 1997; organizes and conducts statistical research; library of 6,940 vols; Dir DERVIŠ ĐURĐEVIĆ; Sec. SUADA ČUKOJEVIĆ; publs *Federacija BiH u Brojkama* (1 a year), *GDP* (1 a year), *Kanton u Brojkama* (1 a year), *Obrazovanje* (1 a year), *Poljoprivedra* (1 a year), *Pravosudje* (1 a year), *Socjalna Zaštita* (Statistical Bulletin, 1 a year), *Statistički Godisnjak* (1 a year), *Statistički Podaci o Privrednim i Drugim Kretanjima u Federacije BiH* (12 a year), *Statistički Podaci o Privrednim i Drugim Kretanjim o Kantonima* (12 a year), *Zaposlenost i Plaće* (1 a year).

Republički Zavod za Statistiku Republike Srpske (Institute of Statistics of Republika Srpska): Veljka Mlađenovića 12D, 78000 Banja Luka; tel. (51) 450-275; fax (51) 450-279; e-mail stat@rzs.rs.ba; internet www.rzs .rs.ba; f. 1992; attached to Min. of Finance; performs statistical activity for the territory of Republika Srpska; Dir SLAVKO ŠOBOT; publs *Agricultural Statistics Bulletin* (1 a year), *Annual Demographic Review*, *Bulletin of Monthly Statistical Reviews* (12 a year), *Data on Industrial Production* (in Serbian, 1 a year), *Education Statistics Bulletin (Basic and Secondary Education)* (1 a year), *Forestry Statistics Bulletin* (1 a year), *Gender Statistics Bulletin* (1 a year), *Social Welfare Bulletin* (1 a year), *Quarterly Statistical Review*.

Physical Sciences

Federalni Meteorološki Zavod (Federal Hydrometeorological Institute): Bardakčije 12, 71000 Sarajevo; tel. (33) 276-701; fax (33) 276-700; e-mail kontakt@fhmzbih.gov .ba; internet www.fhmzbih.gov.ba; Dir ENES SARAČ.

Geodetski Zavod Bosne i Hercegovine (Geodetic Institute of Bosnia and Herzegovina): Bulevar Meše Selimovića 95, 71000 Sarajevo; tel. (33) 469-357; fax (33) 468-989.

Institute of Meteorology: Hadži Loje 4, 71000 Sarajevo; f. 1891; Dir M. V. VEMIĆ.

Metalurški Institut 'Kemal Kapetanović' (Kemal Kapetanović Metallurgical Institute): Travnička cesta 7, 72000 Zenica; tel. (32) 247-999; fax (32) 247-980; e-mail miz@miz .ba; internet www.miz.ba; f. 1961, fmrly Hasan Brkić; attached to University in Zenica; depts in physical metallurgy, chemistry, heat engineering, welding, metal casting, electrical engineering and automation; conducts research and devt in natural sciences, technological and architectural engineering, technical testing and analysis, education-related activities; Dir Dr MIRSADA ORUČ.

Zavod za Geologiju (Institute of Geology): Ustanička 11, Ilidža 71210 Sarajevo; tel. (33) 621-567; fax (33) 621-567; e-mail zgeolbih@ bih.net.ba; internet www.fzzg.ba; f. 1946 as Geologic Research Institute of the Ministry of Industry and Mining; Asst Dir ALOJZ FILIPOVIĆ.

TECHNOLOGY

Institut za standardizaciju BiH (Institute for Standardization of Bosnia and Herzego-

vina): V. Radomira Putnika 34, 71123 Sarajevo; tel. (57) 310-560; fax (57) 310-575; e-mail stand@bas.gov.ba; internet www.bas .gov.ba; f. 1992 as Institut za standarde, mjeriteljstvo i intelektualno vlasništvo; present 2007; proposes the strategy of standardization in Bosnia and Herzegovina; participates in preparing technical regulations, develops and establishes the information system of standards; organizes and carries out specialist education of personnel in standardization area; adopted more than 12,000 int. and European standards by endorsement method; library of 950 vols; Dir GORAN TESANOVIC (acting); publ. *Glasnik Standardizacije* (4 a year).

Rudarski Institut: Rudarska 72, 75000 Tuzla; tel. (35) 282-406; fax (35) 282-700; e-mail rituzla@bih.net.ba; internet www .rudarski-institut.com.ba; f. 1960; planning and consulting in mining, electrical, mechanical and civil engineering, geology, geoengineering, occupational safety and environmental protection, testing materials and constructions; Dir Dr RASIM PIRIĆ.

Libraries and Archives

Banja Luka

Arhiv Republike Srpske (Archives of Republika Srpska): ul. Svetog Save 1, 78000 Banja Luka; tel. (51) 340-240; fax (51) 340-231; e-mail arhivrs@inecco.net; internet www.arhivrs.org; f. 1953; attached to Min. of Education and Culture; 2,500 m of records from all periods; 12,000 vols, 15,000 photographs; Dir Prof. LJILJANA RADOSEVIC.

Narodna i Univerzitetska Biblioteka Republike Srpske (National and University Library of Republika Srpska): Jevrejska 30, 78000 Banja Luka; tel. (51) 215-894; fax (51) 217-040; e-mail nubrs@urc.bl.ac.yu; internet www.nubrs.rs.ba; f. 1936; organizes continuous educational programmes for librarians; 500,000 vols; Dir RANKO RISOJEVIĆ; Library Sec. LJILJANA BABIĆ; publs *Information Bulletin ISBN/ISMN*, *National Bibliography of Republika Srpska*.

Bihać

Arhiv Unsko-sanskog Kantona Bihać (Una-Sana Canton Archives, Bihać): ul. Bosanskih banova 7, 77000 Bihać; tel. (37) 327-384; fax (37) 327-384; f. 1988; Dir Prof. OSMAN ALTIĆ.

Javna Biblioteka Unsko-sanskog Kantona (Una-Sana Canton Public Library): Trg Slobode 8, 77000 Bihać; tel. (37) 333-372; fax (37) 333-372; f. 1954; Dir REUF MUSTAFIĆ.

Fojnica

Franjevački Samostan Fojnica, Biblioteka (Library of the Franciscan Monastery, Fojnica): 71270 Fojnica; tel. (33) 837-410; fax (33) 837-412; f. 1668; 12,500 vols, 13 incunabula, archives incl. documents in Turkish and Bosnian; Guardian Fra STJEPAN DUVNJAK.

Kraljevska Sutjeska

Franjevački Samostan Kraljeva Sutjeska, Biblioteka (Library of the Franciscan Monastery, Kraljeva Sutjeska): 72244 Kraljeva Sutjeska; tel. (32) 771-700; fax (32) 771-705; e-mail urednistvo@ kraljeva-sutjeska.com; internet www .kraljeva-sutjeska.com; f. 1350; 11,000 vols, 31 incunabula, archives incl. parish registers and MSS in Bosnian Cyrillic and Turkish; Guardian Fra ILIJA BOZIĆ.

Kreševo

Franjevački Samostan Kreševo, Biblioteka (Library of the Franciscan Monastery,

Library of 436,122 vols
Number of teachers: 703
Number of students: 14,420
Publication: *Pula* (2 a year)

DEANS
Faculty of Business: S. V. CHINYOKA
Faculty of Education: Dr G. T. TSAYANG
Faculty of Engineering and Technology: Prof.
A. B. NGOWI
Faculty of Health Sciences: Dr T. T.
MOKOENA
Faculty of Humanities: Prof. K. H. MOAHI
Faculty of Science: Dr M. P. MODISI
Faculty of Social Sciences: Prof. B. TSIE
School of Graduate Studies: Prof. U. SCHMIDT

Colleges

Botswana College of Agricultur
tent Farm, Sebele, Gaborone; PMB
Gaborone; tel. 3650100; fax 3⁹
internet www.bca.bw; f. 1967; ass
instn of Univ. of Botswana; library:
vols, 118 periodicals; 79 teachers; 4
dents; Prin. E. J. KEMSLEY.

Botswana Institute of Administ
and Commerce: POB 10026, Ga
tel. 3956324; fax 3959768; f. 1970;
7,000 vols; 73 teachers; Prin. L. L.
publ. *Newsletter* (4 a year).

Kreševo): 71260 Kreševo; tel. (30) 806-075; f.
1767; 25,000 vols, archive; Guardian Fra
MATO CVIJETKOVIĆ.

Mostar

Arhiv Hercegovine Mostar (Archives of
Herzegovina, Mostar): Trg 1 Maj 17, 88000
Mostar; tel. (36) 551-047; fax (36) 551-047;
e-mail arhiv@cob.net.ba; f. 1954; records
from the 13th century onwards; spec. Oriental colln of 800 MSS and 2,000 documents;
9,000 vols; Dir EDIN ČELEBIĆ; publ. *Hercego-
vina* (1 a year).

Narodna Biblioteka Mostar (Mostar Public Library): Marsala Tita bb., 88000 Mostar;
tel. (36) 551-487; fax (36) 551-487; e-mail
biblioteka@mostar.ba; Dir RASIM PRGUDA.

Mrkonjić Grad

Narodna Biblioteka Mrkonjić Grad
(National Library, Mrkonjić Grad): Svetog
Save 1, 70260 Mrkonjić Grad; tel. (50) 220-
271; e-mail kontakt@junbmg.info; internet
www.junbmg.info; f. 1900 as Serbian Orthodox Church-Nikolajević Glee Club, present
bldg 1973; activities incl. literary evenings,
book promotions, professional and scientific
lectures, exhibitions, round tables and workshops; 20,000 books; Dir BILJANA ĆELIĆ.

Sarajevo

Arhiv Bosne i Hercegovine (Archive of
Bosnia and Herzegovina): Reisa Džemalu-
dina Čauševića 6, 71000 Sarajevo; tel. and
fax (33) 206-492; fax (33) 206-492; e-mail
info@arhivbih.gov.ba; internet www.arhivbih
.gov.ba; f. 1947, present name 1965; national
archive; 11,000 m of documents from the
14th century to the present; 20,000 vols; Dir
Prof. MATKO KOVAČEVIĆ; publ. *Glasnik.*

Arhiv Federacije Bosne i Hercegovine
(Archive of the Federation of Bosnia and
Herzegovina): Reisa Čauševića 6, 71000
Sarajevo; tel. (33) 214-481; fax (33) 556-905;
e-mail info@arhivfbih.gov.ba; internet www
.arhivfbih.gov.ba; f. 1994; entity archive;
activities incl. archival processing and preservation, devt of archival service; Dir ADA-
MIRA JERKOVIĆA.

Biblioteka Grada Sarajeva (Sarajevo City
Library): Mis Irbina 4, 71000 Sarajevo; tel.
(33) 444-580; fax (33) 265-030; e-mail info@
bgs.ba; internet www.bgs.ba; f. 1948; colln,
restoration, preservation and processing of
professional library materials, old and rare
books; promotion of information systems;
300,000 vols; Pres. RAMO KOLAR; Dir MESUD
SMAJIĆ.

Gazi Husrevbegova biblioteka (Gazi Hus-
rav-Bey Library): Hamdije Kreševljakovića
58, 71000 Sarajevo; tel. (33) 658-143; fax (33)
205-525; e-mail ghbibl@bih.net.ba; internet
www.ghbibl.com.ba; f. 1537; Oriental library;
80,000 vols, incl. 11,000 Islamic MSS; Pres.
AHMET ALIBAŠIĆ; Dir Dr MUSTAFA JAHIĆ; Sec.
HAMIDA KARČIĆ; publs *Anali Gazi Husrevbe-
gove biblioteke, Katalog arapskih, turskih i
perzijskih rukopisa.*

Historijski Arhiv Sarajevo (Sarajevo Historical Archives): Alipašina 19, 71000 Sarajevo; tel. (33) 223-281; fax (33) 209-737;
e-mail has@arhivsa.ba; internet www
.arhivsa.ba; f. 1948; archive of the canton and
city of Sarajevo; 3,000 m of documents; spec.
colln of Ottoman MSS; 20,000 vols; Dir Prof.
TONČI GRBELJA; publ. *Glas Arhiva Grada
Sarajeva.*

Nacionalna i univerzitetska biblioteka
Bosne i Hercegovine (National and University Library of Bosnia and Herzegovina):
Zmaja od Bosne 8B, 71000 Sarajevo; tel. (33)
275-301; fax (33) 218-431; e-mail nubbih@
nub.ba; internet www.nub.ba; f. 1945, destroyed 1992, reconstructed 1995; nat. deposit

library; nat. agency for ISSN and ISMN; nat.
bibliography centre; centre for permanent
education of librarians; nat. centre for
cooperative online bibliographic and information system and service; supports univ.
research, educational and scientific work;
500,000 vols; Dir Dr ISMET OVČINA.

Zemaljski Muzej Bosne i Hercegovine,
Biblioteka (National Museum of Bosnia and
Herzegovina, Library): Zmaja od Bosne 3,
71000 Sarajevo; tel. (33) 586-321; fax (33)
262-710; e-mail z.muzej@zemaljskimuzej.ba;
internet www.zemaljskimuzej.ba; f. 1888,
present bldg 1913; archaeology, ethnology
and natural sciences; 250,000 vols; Chief
Librarian OLGA LALEVIĆ; publ. *Glasnik
Zemaljskog muzeja BiH* (scientific reports of
the museum of Bosnia and Herzegovina; 3
series: Archaeology, Ethnology, Natural History, in Bosnian and English).

Travnik

Kantonalni-Županijski Arhiv Travnik
(Cantonal and County Archive, Travnik): ul.
Školska bb., 72000 Travnik; tel. (30) 511-580;
fax (30) 518-979; f. 1954; 8,900 m of documents; Dir Prof. JASMINA HOPIĆ.

Tuzla

Arhiv Tuzlanskog kantona (Archives of
Tuzla Canton): ul. Franje Ledera 1, 75000
Tuzla; tel. (35) 252-620; fax (35) 252-620;
e-mail arhiv.tk@bih.net.ba; internet www
.arhivtk.com.ba; f. 1954 as Archive of Tuzla,
present name 1966; 1,380 m of documents
from all periods; 20,000 vols; Dir Dr IZET
ŠABOTIĆ; publ. *Archival Practice.*

Narodna i Univerzitetska Biblioteka
'Derviš Sušić' Tuzla (Public and University
Library Derviš Sušić, Tuzla): Mihajla i Živka
Crnogorčevića 7, 75000 Tuzla; tel. (35) 272-
626; fax (35) 266-343; e-mail nubtz@nubtz
.ba; internet www.nubtz.ba; f. 1946, present
status 1986; gen. reference colln; works in
science and arts, literature, history and
philosophy, domestic and foreign rarities,
doctoral and masters papers, serial publs;
200,000 vols, 10,000 periodicals; Dir ENISA
ŽUNIĆ.

Zenica

Opća Biblioteka Zenica (Zenica Public
Library): Skolska ul. 6, 72000 Zenica; tel.
(32) 407-600; fax (32) 407-664; e-mail
biblioze@biblioze.ba; internet www.biblioze
.ba; f. 1954; 78,000 vols; Dir MIDHAT KASAP;
Sec. RASMA SEHIC.

Museums and Art Galleries

Banja Luka

Muzej savremene umjetnosti Republike
Srpske (Museum of Contemporary Art of
Republika Srpska): Trg Srpskih Junaka 2,
78000 Banja Luka; tel. (51) 215-364; fax (51)
215-366; e-mail galrs@inecco.net; internet
www.msurs.org; f. 1971; history, archae-
ology, ethnography, history of art, contem-
porary art, natural history of Republika
Srpska; library of 5,500 vols, 500 journals;
Dir LJILJANA LABOVIC-MARINKOVIC; Man.
MILICA RADOJIČIĆ; Curators BRANKA ŠESTIĆ,
DANKA DAMJANOVIC, NIKOLA GALIC, LANA
PAVLOVIC, LJILJANA P. MISIRLIC, SARITA VUJ-
KOVIĆ; publ. *Zbornik* (irregular).

Bihać

Muzej Unsko-sanskog Kantona (Una-
Sana Canton Museum): ul. 5 Korpusa 2,
77000 Bihać; tel. (37) 229-743; f. 1953;
archaeology, history, natural history, ethnography; attached museums: Kapetanova

kula (The Captain's Tower), Museum of the
first Session of AVNOJ; Dir Dr DŽAFER MAHMU-
TOVIĆ.

Bijeljina

Muzej Semberija (Semberija Museum):
Karadjordjeva 1, 76300 Bijeljina; tel. (65)
401-293; fax (65) 471-625; e-mail mbabic@
rstel.net; f. 1970; archaeology, history, ethnography; 5,000 artefacts, 2,000 photographs; Resić collns of ceramics, tapestries
by Milica Zorić-Colaković; library of 5,000
vols; Dir MIRKO BABIĆ.

Doboj

Regionalni Muzej Doboj (Doboj Regional
Museum): ul. Vidovdanska br. 4, Doboj; tel.
(32) 231-220; f. 1956; 16,000 items; archaeology, history, ethnography, photography;
Dir DOBRILA BIJELIĆ.

Fojnica

Franjevački Samostan Fojnica (Franciscan Monastery Fojnica): 4 Angels Fra Zviz-
dovića pp. 45, 71270 Fojnica; tel. (30) 832-
081; fax (30) 832-082; e-mail info@samostan
.ba; internet www.samostan.ba; spec. colln of
church clothes embroidered with gold,
bishops' clothing and footwear, Roman and
Greek coins; documents relating to the
Franciscan order, Fojnica monastery and
Fojnica incl. inventories and parish registers,
Ottoman land-related documents, 156 documents in Bosnian Cyrillic and 3,000 Turkish
documents; Bosnian ecclesiastical and secular history, education, diaries and autograph
letters; library of 12,500 vols, incl. 13
incunabula, Fojnica Arms book, 19th century
periodicals; Guardian Fra JANKO LJUBOS.

Krešovo

Franjevački Samostan Krešovo (Franciscan Monastery, Krešovo): 71260 Krešovo; tel.
(87) 806-075; f. 1767; library of 17,000 vols,
92 periodicals; Guardian Fra MATO CVIJET-
KOVIĆ.

Mostar

Muzej Hercegovine (Museum of Herzegovina): Bajatova br. 4, 88000 Mostar; tel. (61)
707-307; fax (36) 551-602; e-mail muzej
.herc@bih.net.ba; internet www
.muzejhercegovine.com; f. 1950; archaeology,
history, ethnography, art, numismatics; Dir
ZDRAVKO ZVONIĆ; publ. *Kingdom Magazine.*

Prijedor

Muzej Kozara (Kozara Museum): Nikole
Pašića, 79101 Prijedor; tel. (62) 221-334; f.
1953; regional museum; archaeology, history,
ethnography, art; collns incl. 400 paintings of
the Prijedor school, 900 archeological
exhibits, 5th century Celtic-Illyrian helmets,
400 artefacts from the Kozara region, 2,000
documents relating to the Second World War;
Dir MILENKO RADIVOJEC.

Sarajevo

Ars Aevi—Museum of Contemporary Art
Sarajevo: Centar Skenderija, Dom mladih,
Terezija bb., 71000 Sarajevo; tel. (33) 216-
919; fax (33) 216-927; e-mail arsaevi@arsaevi
.ba; internet www.arsaevi.ba; f. 1992; contributed works of approx. 120 int. artists
form the Ars Aevi Colln; Gen. Dir ENVER
HADŽIOMERSPAHIĆ; Exec. Dir AMILA ROMOVIĆ.

Historijski Muzej Bosne i Hercegovine
(Historical Museum of Bosnia and Herzegovina): Zmaja od Bosne 5, 71000 Sarajevo; tel.
and fax (33) 656-629; fax (33) 656-629; e-mail
histmu@bih.net.ba; internet www.muzej.ba;
f. 1945, present name 1993, present bldg
1963; history since medieval times; archive
material, objects, academic library, documentation centre (300,000 vols); colln of 2,600

BOTSWAN/

The Higher Education System

Tertiary education is provided by the University of Botswana (which was attended by 15,725 students in 2005) and the Francistown College of Technical and Vocational Education. There are also technical and vocational training centres, including the Botswana College of Agriculture, the Botswana Institute of Administration and Commerce, the Botswana Polytechnic and the Institute of Development Management. The University of Botswana was founded in 1963 as the University of Basutoland (now Lesotho), Bechuanaland (now Botswana) and Swaziland at Roma, in Lesotho. It became the University of Botswana, Lesotho and Swaziland (UBLS) following the independence of Botswana and Lesotho in 1966, and has been known under its current name since 1982. The University of Botswana is funded mainly by the Government and receives some income from students' fees. The Tertiary Education Council is the principal body regulating higher

education in
programmes
private instit
Admission
Botswana G
local variant
either first
language. Th
which compr
degree is the
sity technical
provided by
wana, with
Certificates.
In 2008 ten
to set up the
Technology, c

Regulatory Bodies

GOVERNMENT

Ministry of Education: PMB 005, Gaborone; tel. 3655400; fax 3655458; e-mail moe.webmaster@gov.bw; internet www.moe.gov.bw/moe/index.html; Min. JACOB NKATE.

Ministry of Youth, Sports and Culture: Gaborone; Min. Maj.-Gen. MOENG PHETO.

Learned Societies

GENERAL

Botswana Society: POB 71, Gaborone; tel. 3919745; e-mail botsoc@info.bw; internet www.botsoc.org.bw; f. 1968, in association with the National Museum and Art Gallery, to encourage knowledge and research on Botswana in all fields; 100 mems; Chair. Dr JOSEPH TSONOPE; Exec. Sec. RAPELANG TSEBE; Vice-Chair. Prof. FRED MORTON; publ. *Botswana Notes and Records* (1 a year).

BIBLIOGRAPHY, LIBRARY SCIENCE AND MUSEOLOGY

Botswana Library Association: POB 1310, Gaborone; tel. 3552295; fax 3957291; f. 1978; 60 mems; Chair. F. M. LAMUSSE; Sec. A. M. MBANGIWA; publs *Botswana Journal of Library and Information Science* (2 a year), *Journal*.

LANGUAGE AND LITERATURE

Alliance Française: POB 1817, Gaborone; tel. 3951650; fax 3584433; e-mail af.gaborone@info.bw; internet www.ibis.bw/~all.francaise/; offers courses and exams in French language and culture and promotes cultural exchange with France.

British Council: British High Commission Bldg, Queen's Rd, The Mall, POB 439, Gaborone; tel. 3953602; fax 3956643; e-mail general.enquiries@britishcouncil.org.bw; internet www.britishcouncil.org/botswana; offers courses and exams in English language and British culture and promotes cultural exchange with the UK; Dir DAVID KNOX.

Research Institute

NATURAL SCIENCES

Physical Sciences

Geological Survey of Botswana: P
Bag 14, Lobatse; tel. 5330327; fax 53
internet www.gov.bw/government/g
.htm; f. 1948; library of 2,000 vols
periodicals; Dir TIYAPO NGWISANYI;
Bibliography of the Geology of Bot
(every 5 years), *Bulletin*, *District Mem*

Libraries and Archive

Gaborone

**Botswana National Archives
Records Services:** Khama Crescent,
ernment Enclave, POB 239, Gaboron
3911820; fax 3908545; e-mail kramo
gov.bw; f. 1967; central govt, district,
business and private archives since c.
audiovisual and machine-readable ar
records management for central gov
tricts and parastatal orgs; oral tra
programmes; educational programme
exhibitions; 14,000 vols; Dir KAGO RAM
Sr Archivist C. T. NENGOMASHA; Librar
R. ADEKANMBI; publ. *Archives Library*
sions List.

Botswana National Library Servic
vate Bag 0036, Gaborone; tel. 395228
3901149; f. 1968; nationwide public l
service; also acts as a nat. library
deposit); 282,383 vols; 23 br. librar
mobile libraries; 286 book box service
64 village reading rooms; Dir CONSTA
MODISE; publs *National Bibliograp*
Botswana (3 a year), *Quarterly Acce*
List, Statistical Bulletin.

Museums and Art Galleries

Gaborone

**National Museum, Monuments an
Gallery:** Independence Ave, Private
00114, Gaborone; tel. 3974616; fax 39

69011-970 Manaus, AM; tel. (92) 621-0300; fax (92) 621-0322; internet www.cpaa.embrapa.br; f. 1975; rubber and oil palm research.

Centro de Pesquisa Agroflorestal da Amazônia Oriental: Travessa Dr Enéas Pinheiro s/n, Bairro do Marco, 66095-100 Belém, PA; tel. (91) 276-6333; fax (91) 276-0323; internet www.cpatu.embrapa.br; f. 1975.

Centro de Pesquisa Agroflorestal de Rondônia: Rodovia BR 364, km 5.5, 78970-900 Porto Velho, RO; tel. (69) 216-6500; fax (69) 216-6543; f. 1975.

Centro de Pesquisa Agroflorestal de Roraima: BR 174, km 08, Distrito Industrial, 69301-970 Boa Vista, RR; tel. (95) 626-7125; fax (95) 626-7104; internet www.cpafrr.embrapa.br; f. 1981.

Centro de Pesquisa Agroflorestal do Acre: Rodovia BR 364, km 14, 69908-970 Rio Branco, AC; tel. (68) 212-3200; fax (68) 212-3284; internet www.cpafac.embrapa.br; f. 1976.

Centro de Pesquisa Agroflorestal do Amapá: Rodovia Juscelino Kubitschek, km 05, (Macapá/Fazendinha), 68903-000 Macapá, AP; tel. (96) 241-1551; fax (96) 241-1480; internet www.cpafap.embrapa.br.

Centro de Pesquisa Agropecuária de Clima Temperado: Rodovia BR 392 km 78, 9° Distrito de Pelotas, 96001-970 Pelotas, RS; tel. (532) 275-8100; fax (532) 275-8221; internet www.cpact.embrapa.br; f. 1975; research on temperate fruit and vegetable crops and food technology.

Centro de Pesquisa Agropecuária do Meio Norte: Av. Duque de Caxias 5.650, Bairro Buenos Aires, 64006-220 Teresina, PI; tel. (86) 225-1141; fax (86) 225-1142; internet www.cnpmn.embrapa.br.

Centro de Pesquisa Agropecuária do Oeste: Rodovia BR 163, km 253.6, 79804-970 Dourados, MS; tel. (67) 425-5122; fax (67) 425-0811; internet www.cpao.embrapa.br; f. 1976.

Centro de Pesquisa Agropecuária do Pantanal: Rua 21 de Setembro 1880, 79320-900 Corumbá, MS; tel. (67) 233-2430; fax (67) 233-1011; internet www.cpap.embrapa.br; research on beef cattle and pasture land.

Centro de Pesquisa Agropecuária dos Cerrados: BR 020 km 18, Rodovia Brasília/Fortaleza, 73301-970 Planaltina, DF; tel. (61) 388-9898; fax (61) 389-9879; internet www.cpac.embrapa.br; f. 1975.

Centro de Pesquisa Agropecuária dos Tabuleiros Costeiros: Av. Beira Mar 3250, 49025-040 Aracaju, SE; tel. (79) 226-1300; fax (79) 226-6145; internet www.cpatc.embrapa.br; f. 1974.

Centro de Pesquisa Agropecuária do Trópico Semi-Árido: Rodovia BR 428 km 152, Zona Rural, 56300-000 Petrolina, PE; tel. (87) 3862-1711; fax (87) 3862-1744; internet www.cpatsa.embrapa.br; f. 1975.

Centro de Pesquisa de Pecuária dos Campos sul Brasileiros: Rodovia 153, km 595, Vila Industrial, Zona Rural, 96400-970 Bagé, RS; tel. (32) 42-8499; fax (32) 42-4395; internet www.cppsul.embrapa.br; f. 1975.

Centro de Pesquisa de Pecuária do Sudeste: Rodovia Washington Luiz km 234, 13560-970 São Carlos, SP; tel. (16) 261-5611; fax (16) 261-5754; internet www.cppse.embrapa.br; f. 1975.

Centro Nacional de Pesquisa de Agrobiologia: Rodovia Rio/São Paulo km 47, BR 465, 23851-970 Seropédica, RJ; tel. (21) 2682-1500; fax (21) 2682-1230; internet www.cnpala.embrapa.br.

Centro Nacional de Pesquisa de Agroindústria Tropical (CNPAT): Rua Dra Sara Mesquita 2270, Bairro Pici, 60511-110 Fortaleza, CE; tel. (85) 299-1800; fax (85) 299-1803; internet www.cnpat.embrapa.br.

Centro Nacional de Pesquisa de Algodão: Rua Osvaldo Cruz 1143, Bairro Centenário, 58107-720 Campina Grande, PB; tel. (83) 341-3608; fax (83) 322-7751; internet www.cnpa.embrapa.br; f. 1975; research on cotton.

Centro Nacional de Pesquisa de Arroz e Feijão: Rodovia Goiânia a Nova Veneza km 12, 75375-000, Santo Antônio de Góias, GO; tel. (62) 533-2110; fax (62) 533-2100; internet www.cnpaf.embrapa.br; f. 1975; research on beans, cowpeas and rice.

Centro Nacional de Pesquisa de Caprinos: Fazenda Três Lagoas/Estrada Sobral/Groaíras km 4, 62010-970 Sobral, CE; tel. (88) 3112-7400; fax (88) 3112-7455; e-mail adriana@cnpc.embrapa.br; internet www.cnpc.embrapa.br; f. 1975; research on goats; Gen. Dir Dr EVANDRO VASCONCELOS HOLANDA Jr; Deputy Gen. Dir Dr MARCO AURELIO DELMONDES BOMFIM.

Centro Nacional de Pesquisa de Embrapa Solos: Rua Jardim Botânico 1024, 22460-000 Rio de Janeiro, RJ; tel. (21) 2179-4500; fax (21) 2274-5291; internet www.cnps.embrapa.br; f. 1974; soil survey and conservation.

Centro Nacional de Pesquisa de Florestas: Estrada da Ribeira km 111, CP 319, 83411-000 Colombo, PR; tel. (41) 666-1313; fax (41) 666-1276; internet www.cnpf.embrapa.br; f. 1978; forest research.

Centro Nacional de Pesquisa de Gado de Corte: Rodovia BR 262 km 04, CP 154, 79002-970 Campo Grande, MS; tel. (67) 3368-2000; fax (67) 3368-2150; internet www.cnpgc.embrapa.br; f. 1976; research on beef cattle.

Centro Nacional de Pesquisa de Gado de Leite: Rua Eugênio do Nascimento 610, Bairro Dom Bosco, 36038-330 Juiz de Fora, MG; tel. (32) 3249-4700; fax (32) 3249-4701; internet www.cnpgl.embrapa.br; f. 1976; dairy research.

Centro Nacional de Pesquisa de Hortaliças: Rodovia BR 060 Brasília-Anápolis km 09, Fazendo Tamandué, 70359-970 Brasília; tel. (61) 385-9000; fax (61) 556-5744; internet www.cnph.embrapa.br; f. 1975; vegetable research.

Centro Nacional de Pesquisa de Mandioca e Fruticultura Tropical (National Research Center for Cassava and Tropical Fruits): Rua EMBRAPA s/n, 44380-000 Cruz das Almas, Bahia; tel. (75) 3312-8007; fax (75) 3312-8097; e-mail chgeral@cnpmf.embrapa.br; internet www.cnpmf.embrapa.br; f. 1975; research on cassava and tropical fruits, with emphasis on banana, pineapple, citrus, papaya, passion fruit, barbados cherry, mango and some regional native fruits; Head Dr DOMINGO HAROLDO REINHARDT.

Centro Nacional de Pesquisa de Milho e Sorgo: Rodovia MG 424, km 65, 35701-970, Sete Lagoas, MG; tel. (31) 3779-1000; fax (31) 3779-1088; internet www.cnpms.embrapa.br; f. 1975; research on maize and sorghum; library of 5,500 vols, 65 periodicals; Head Dr ANTÔNIO FERNANDINO C. BAHIA F.

Centro Nacional de Pesquisa de Monitoramento e Avaliaçao de Impacto Ambiéntal – CNPMA: Rodovia SP 340, km 127.5, Bairro Tanquinho Velho, 13820-000 Jaguariúna, SP; tel. (19) 3867-8700; fax (19) 3867-8740; internet www.cnpma.embrapa.br.

Centro Nacional de Pesquisa de Soja: Rodovia Carlos João Strass (Londrina/Warta), Acesso Orlando Amaral, Distrito de Warta, 86001-970 Londrina, PR; tel. (43) 3371-6000; fax (43) 3371-6100; internet www.cnpso.embrapa.br; f. 1975; research on soya beans and sunflowers.

Centro Nacional de Pesquisa de Suínos e Aves: Rodovia BR 153, km 110, Vila Tamanduá, 89700-000 Concórdia, SC; tel. (49) 442-8555; fax (49) 442-8559; internet www.cnpsa.embrapa.br; f. 1975; research on pigs and poultry; library of 4,000 vols, 800 periodicals.

Centro Nacional de Pesquisa de Tecnologia Agroindustrial de Alimentos: Av. das Americas 29501-B, Guaratiba, 23020-470 Rio de Janeiro, RJ; tel. (21) 2410-9500; fax (21) 2410-1090; internet www.ctaa.embrapa.br; f. 1971; food science and technology centre.

Centro Nacional de Pesquisa de Trigo: Rodovia BR 285 km 174, 99001-970 Passo Fundo, RS; tel. (54) 311-3444; fax (54) 311-3617; internet www.cnpt.embrapa.br; f. 1974; wheat research centre.

Centro Nacional de Pesquisa e Desenvolvimento de Instrumentação Agropecuária: Rua XV de Novembro 1452, Centro, 13561-160 São Carlos, SP; tel. (16) 274-2477; fax (16) 272-5958; internet www.cnpdia.embrapa.br.

Centro Nacional de Pesquisa Tecnológica em Informática para a Agricultura: Cidade Universitária Zeferino Vaz, Campus da Universidade Estadual de Campinas—UNICAMP, Bairro de Barão Geraldo, 13083-970 Campinas, SP; tel. (19) 3789-5700; fax (19) 3789-5711; internet www.cnptia.embrapa.br.

Centro Nacional de Recursos Genéticos e Biotecnologia: Parque Estacão Biológico s/n, Plano Piloto (final W-3 Norte), 70770-900 Brasília, DF; tel. (61) 448-4700; fax (61) 448-3624; internet www.cenargem.embrapa.br; f. 1976.

Embrapa Uva e Vinho: Rua Livramento 515, 95700-000 Bento Gonçalves, RS; tel. (54) 3455-8000; fax (54) 3451-2792; e-mail sac@cnpuv.embrapa.br; internet www.cnpuv.embrapa.br; f. 1975; research and devt in viticulture, temperate fruit and the wine industry; 165 mems; library of 10,000 vols, 531 journal titles; Gen. Dir Dr LUCAS DA RESSURREICAO GARRIDO.

Núcleo de Monitoramento Ambiental de Recursos Naturais por Satélite: Av. Dr Júlio Soares de Arruda 803, Parque São Quirino, 13088-300 Campinas, SP; tel. (19) 3256-6030; fax (19) 3254-1100; internet www.cnpm.embrapa.br.

Instituto Agronômico (Institute of Agronomy): Av. Barão de Itapura 1481, CP 28, 13012-970 Campinas, SP; tel. (19) 3231-5422; fax (19) 3231-4943; e-mail iacdir@iac.sp.gov.br; internet www.iac.sp.gov.br; f. 1887; basic and applied research on plants, soils, environment, farming methods and agricultural machinery; Divs: agricultural engineering, biology, experimental stations, food plants, industrial plants, soil; Technical Scientific Information Service; library of 200,000 vols; 20 experimental stations in the State of São Paulo; Gen. Dir Dr MARCO ANTÔNIO TEIXEIRA ZULLO; publs *Bragantia* (2 a year), *O Agronômico* (irregular).

Instituto Brasileiro do Meio Ambiente e dos Recursos Naturais Renováveis (IBAMA) (Brazilian Institute for the Environment and Renewable Natural Resources): SCEN trecho 2, Edifício Sede Ibama, 70818-900 Brasília, DF; tel. (61) 316-1205; fax (61) 226-5094; internet www.ibama.gov.br; f. 1989; library of 65,000 vols; Pres. Dr MARCUS LUIZ BARROSO BARROS.

Instituto de Economia Agrícola (Agricultural Economics Institute): Av. Miguel Stefano 3900, Água Funda, CP 68029, 04301-903 São Paulo, SP; tel. (11) 5067-0526; fax (11) 5073-4062; e-mail iea@iea.sp.gov.br; internet www.iea.sp.gov.br; f. 1942; affiliated to São Paulo Secretariat of Agriculture and Provision; provides information for state and federal govts and other interested bodies; library of 70,000 vols, 2,700 periodicals; Dir Dr VALQUÍRIA DA SILVA; publs *Agricultura em São Paulo* (irregular), *Informações Econômicas* (12 a year), *Informações Estatística da Agricultura* (1 a year).

Instituto de Zootecnia (Institute of Animal Science and Pastures): Rua Heitor Penteado 56, CP 60, 13460-000 Nova Odessa, SP; tel. (19) 3466-9400; fax (19) 3466-6415; e-mail diretoria@iz.sp.gov.br; internet www.iz.sp .gov.br; f. 1905; 92 researchers; beef cattle, dairy cattle, goats, information science, pastures, pigs, reproduction and genetics, sheep, water buffaloes; library of 10,710 vols, 1,610 periodicals; Dir-Gen. ANTONIO ALVARO DUARTE DE OLIVEIRA; publs *Boletim de Indústria Animal* (2 a year), *Boletim Tecnicos*.

Instituto Florestal (Estado de São Paulo) (São Paulo State Forestry Institute): Rua do Horto 931, CP 1322, 02377-000 São Paulo, SP; tel. (11) 6231-8555 ext. 2100; fax (11) 6132-5767; e-mail nuinfo@iflorest.sp.gov .br; internet www.iflorestsp.br; f. 1896; 1,107 staff; library of 7,500 vols, 2,000 periodicals; Dir MARIA CECÍLIA WEY DE BRITO; publs *Revista do Instituto Florestal* (2 a year), *Revista IF-Serie Registros* (irregular).

Organização Nacional de Proteção Fitossanitária (ONPF) (National Plant Protection Organization): Departamento de Sanidade Vegetal, Ministério da Agricultura, Pecuária e Abastecimento, Esplanada dos Ministérios, Bloco D, Anexo B, Sala 303-B, Brasília, DF; tel. (61) 3218-2675; fax (61) 3224-3874; e-mail dsv@agricultura.gov.br; internet www.agricultura.gov.br; f. 2005; Dir JOSÉ GERALDO BALDINI RIBEIRO.

ECONOMICS, LAW AND POLITICS

Centro de Estatística e Informações (Statistics and Information Centre): Centro Administrativo da Bahia, Av. 435 4A, 41750-300 Salvador, BA; tel. (71) 371-9665; fax (71) 371-9664; f. 1983; statistics, natural resources, economic indicators; library of 15,448 vols; Dir RENATA PROSERPIO; publ. *Bahia Análise e Dados* (every 4 months).

EDUCATION

Instituto Nacional de Estudos e Pesquisas Educacionais (National Institute for Educational Studies and Research): INEP/MEC, Esp. dos Ministérios, Bloco L, Anexos I e II (4° andar), 70047-900 Brasília, DF; internet www.inep.gov.br; f. 1938; 130 mems; library of 50,000 vols, 985 periodicals; Pres. Dr MARIA HELENA GUIMARÃES DE CASTRO; publs *Bibliografia Brasileira de Educação*, *Em Aberto*, *Revista Brasileira de Estudos Pedagógicos*.

HISTORY, GEOGRAPHY AND ARCHAEOLOGY

Fundação Instituto Brasileiro de Geografia e Estatística (Brazilian Institute of Geography and Statistics): Av. Franklin Roosevelt 166, 20021-120 Rio de Janeiro, RJ; internet www.ibge.gov.br; f. 1936; produces and analyzes statistical, geographical, cartographic, geodetic, demographic, socio-economic, natural resources and environmental information; Pres. EDUARDO PEREIRA NUNES; publs *Anuário Estatístico do Brasil*, *Revista Brasileira de Estatística*, *Revista Brasileira de Geografia*.

MEDICINE

Fundacão 'Oswaldo Cruz' (Oswaldo Cruz Foundation): Av. Brasil 4365, Manguinhos, CP 926, 21045-900 Rio de Janeiro, RJ; tel. (21) 2598-4242; fax (21) 2270-7444; e-mail ferreirj@fiocruz.br; internet www.fiocruz.br; f. 1900; infectious and parasitic diseases, entomology, epidemiology, history of science, immunology, public health; tropical medicine, virology; library of 800,000 vols, 2,000 current periodicals; Pres. Dr PAULO MARCHIORI BUSS; publs *Cadernos de Saúde Pública* (4 a year), *História, Ciências, Saúde—Manguinhos* (3 a year), *Memórias* (6 a year).

Instituto 'Adolfo Lutz': Av. Dr Arnaldo 355, Pacaembú, 01246-902 São Paulo, SP; fax (11) 3085-3505; f. 1892; Central Laboratory of Public Health for the State of São Paulo; library of 50,000 vols, incl. periodicals; Dir.-Gen. CRISTIANO CORRÊA DE AZEVEDO MARQUES; publ. *Revista*.

Instituto 'Benjamin Constant': Av. Pasteur 350/368, Urca, 22290-240 Rio de Janeiro, RJ; tel. (21) 3478-4442; fax (21) 3478-4442; e-mail dirgeral@ibc.gov.br; internet www.ibc.gov.br; f. 1854; educational institute for the blind; library: braille and general library of 15,000 vols; Dir ÉRICA DESLANDES MAGNO OLIVEIRA; publs *Pontinhos* (4 a year), *Revista Benjamin Constant*, *Revista Brasileira para Cegos* (4 a year).

Instituto Brasileiro de Estudos e Pesquisas de Gastroenterologia (IBE-PEGE): Rua Dr Seng 320, Bairro da Bela Vista, 01331-020 São Paulo; tel. (11) 3288-2119; fax (11) 3289-2768; f. 1963; study and research in gastroenterology, nutrition and psychosomatic medicine; postgraduate courses; library of 10,000 vols; Pres. Prof. JOSÉ FERNANDES PONTES; Vice-Pres. Dr JOSÉ VICENTE MARTINS CAMPOS; publ. *Arquivos de Gastroenterologia* (4 a year).

Instituto Butantan (Butantan Institute): Av. Vital Brasil 1500, CP 65, 05503-900 São Paulo, SP; tel. (11) 3726-7222; fax (11) 3726-1505; e-mail instituto@butantan.gov.br; internet www.butantan.gov.br; f. 1901; library of 96,000 vols on ophiology and biomedical sciences; famous snake farm; Public Health Institute for research and the production of vaccines, sera, etc.; also research in genetics, virology, pathology, etc.; Hospital Vital Brasil (snake, spider and scorpion accidents); Dir OTÁVIO AZEVEDO MERCADANTE.

Instituto de Saúde (Institute of Health): Rua Santo Antonio 590, Bela Vista, 01314-000 São Paulo, SP; tel. (11) 3293-2244; internet www.isaude.sp.gov.br; f. 1969; degenerative diseases, dermatology, hansenology, nutrition, ophthalmology, organization and supervision of study, phthisiology, research and activities in the fields of mother and child care; library: see Libraries; Dir-Gen. Dr EDMUR F. PASTORELO; publ. *Boletim* (3 a year).

Instituto Evandro Chagas (MS-Fundação Nacional de Saúde): Rodovia BR-316 km 7 s/n, Levilândia, 67030-000 Ananindeua, PA; tel. (91) 3214-2213; fax (91) 3214-2214; e-mail contato@iec.pa.gov.br; internet www .iec.pa.gov.br; f. 1936; research in bacteriology, parasitology, pathology, virology, mycology, medical entomology, human ecology and environment; library of 50,000 vols, 134 current periodicals, 4,000 reprints; Dir ELISABETH CONCEIÇÃO DE OLIVEIRA SANTOS; publ. *Revista Pan-Amazônica de Saúde*.

Instituto Nacional de Cancer, Coordenação de Pesquisa: Rua André Cavalcanti 37/2 andar-Centro, 20231-050 Rio de Janeiro, RJ; tel. (21) 3233-1414; fax (21) 3233-1355; internet www.inca.org.br; f. 1958; cell biology, experimental oncology, genetics, molecular biology, pharmacology; Head of Research Dra MARISA BREITENBACH.

Instituto Oscar Freire (Oscar Freire Institute): Rua Teodoro Sampaio 115, 05405-000 São Paulo, SP; tel. (11) 3085-9677; fax (11) 3085-9677; f. 1918; for instruction and research in forensic medicine; assoc. with Univ. of São Paulo; library of 4,200 vols; Chair. Prof. Dr CLÁUDIO COHEN.

Instituto Pasteur: Av. Paulista 393, 01311-000 São Paulo, SP; tel. (11) 3288-00-88; fax (11) 3289-08-31; e-mail pasteur@pasteur .saude.sp.gov.br; internet www.pasteur .saude.sp.gov.br; f. 1903; practical measures and theoretical studies aimed at preventing rabies in humans; 28 staff; library of 5,000 vols and 1,083 periodicals; Technical Dir NEIDE TAKAOKA.

Instituto 'Penido Burnier': Rua Dr Mascarenhas 249, POB 284, 13020-050 Campinas, SP; tel. (19) 3232-5866; fax (19) 3233-4492; e-mail penido@penidoburnier.com.br; f. 1920; anaesthesiology, ophthalmology, otolaryngology; library of 11,585 vols; Chief Librarians Dr HILTON DE MELLO E OLIVEIRA, VANDA REGINA SILVA JUCÁ; publ. *Arquivos IPB* (2 a year).

NATURAL SCIENCES

General

Centro de Ciências, Letras e Artes (Science, Letters and Arts Centre): Rua Bernardino de Campos 989, 13010-151, Campinas, SP; tel. (19) 3231-2567; e-mail ccla@ccla.org .br; internet www.ccla.org.br; f. 1901; library of 120,000 vols; museum and art gallery attached; Pres. Eng. MARINO ZIGGIATTI; Gen. Sec. Dr EDUARDO DA ROCHA E SILVA; Librarian Prof. DUILIO BATTISTONI FILHO; publ. *Revista*.

Conselho Nacional de Desenvolvimento Científico e Tecnológico (CNPq) (National Council of Scientific and Technological Development): SEPN 507, Bloco B, Ed. Sede CNPq, 70740-901 Brasília, DF; tel. (61) 2108-9000; fax (61) 2108-9394; internet www.cnpq.br; f. 1951; an agency of the Ministério da Ciência e Tecnologia; Pres. MARCO ANTONIO ZAGO.

Institut de Recherche pour le Développement (IRD): CP 7091, Lago Sul, 71619-970 Brasília, DF; SHIS, QL 16, Conj. 4, Casa 8, Lago Sul, 71640-245 Brasília, DF; tel. (61) 3248-5323; fax (61) 3248-5378; e-mail bresil@ ird.fr; internet www.brasil.ird.fr; f. 1979; headquarters of the Brazilian delegation to Latin America; missions at various univs and research institutes; See main entry under France; Delegate to Brazil JEAN-LOUP GUYOT.

Instituto Nacional de Pesquisas da Amazônia (National Research Institute for Amazonia): Av. André Araújo 2936, Aleixo, 69060-001 Manaus, AM; tel. (92) 3643-3377; fax (92) 3643-3095; internet www.inpa.gov.br; f. 1954; agronomics, biology, ecology, forestry, medicine, technology, and special projects; 1,003 staff; library of 48,000 items; herbarium; wood collection; Dir ADALBERTO LUIS VAL; publ. *Acta Amazônica* (4 a year).

Biological Sciences

Campo de Santana: Praça da República s/n, Centro, 20211-360 Rio de Janeiro, RJ; tel. (21) 2323-3500; internet www.rio.rj.gov.br/fpj/cposantana.htm; laid out 1870 by Auguste F. M. Glaziou, who collected 23,000 plants,

9052; fax (61) 223-5137; e-mail cibec@inep
.gov.br; internet www.inep.gov.br/cibec; f.
1981; 21,000 vols, 844 periodicals; specialized
library on education; Dir ÉRICA MÁSSIMO
MACHADO.

**Instituto Brasileiro de Informação em
Ciência e Tecnologia (IBICT):** SAS
Quadra 05, Lote 06, Bloco H, 5° andar,
70070-912 Brasília, DF; tel. (61) 3217-6360;
fax (61) 3217-6490; internet www.ibict.br; f.
1954 as IBBD, renamed 1976; coordinates
scientific and technical information services
throughout the country; provides technical
assistance, and training; maintains the following databases available for public access,
through the Nat. Telecommunications Network: *ACERVO*(library and information science, holds records from 1982 to present,
updated daily), *BASES*(directory of Brazilian
databases from 1989), *BEN*(directory of
Brazilian instns in science and technology,
updated daily), *BPS*(union catalogue of serials publications, updated daily), *CIENTE*(s-
cientific and technological policy, updated
daily), *EMPRESAS*(directory of software
instns), *EVENTOS*(current meetings,
updated daily), *FILMES*(Films and videos
in science and technology from 1988 to
present), *TESES*(theses and dissertations
from 1984 to present, updated daily); runs a
postgraduate course in information science
and a spec. course on scientific documentation; 205,000 vols; Dir (vacant); publ. *Ciência
da Informação* (3 a year).

Curitiba

**Biblioteca Central da Universidade Fed-
eral do Paraná** (University of Paraná
Library): CP 19051, Rua General Carneiro
370/380, Centro, 81351-990 Curitiba, PR; tel.
(41) 3360-5000; fax (41) 3360-5400; e-mail
bc@ufpr.br; internet www.ufpr.br; f. 1956;
350,000 vols; 13 specialized libraries; Dir
LIGIA ELIANA SETENARESKI.

Biblioteca Pública do Paraná (Paraná
Public Library): Rua Cândido Lopes 133,
80020-901 Curitiba, PR; tel. (41) 3221-4900;
fax (41) 225-6883; e-mail bppgeral@pr.gov.br;
internet www.bpp.pr.gov.br; f. 1954; 480,000
vols, 6,000 periodicals; Dir MARILENE ZICAR-
ELLI MILARCH.

Florianópolis

**Biblioteca Pública do Estado de Santa
Catarina** (Santa Catarina State Public
Library): Rua Tenete Silveira 343, Centro,
88010-301 Florianópolis, SC; tel. (48) 3028-
8063; fax (48) 3028-8061; e-mail biblio@fcc.sc
.gov.br; f. 1854; 110,000 vols; collections of
rare books, Braille and talking books; Dir
ISABELA SALUM FETT.

Fortaleza

**Biblioteca Pública Governador Menezes
Pimentel** (Ceará Public Library): Av. Presidente Castelo Branco 255, Centro, CEP
60010-000, Fortaleza, CE; tel. (85) 3101-
2546; fax (85) 3101-2544; e-mail bpublica@
secult.ce.gov.br; internet www.secult.ce.gov/
br; f. 1867 as a provincial library; 100,000
vols, incl. books, periodicals, rare books,
video cassettes, spoken books, Braille books
and CD-ROMs; Man. MARIA HELENA LYRA.

**Biblioteca Universitária da Universi-
dade Federal do Ceará:** Campus do Pici
s/n, CP 6025, 60451-970 Fortaleza, CE; tel.
(85) 3366-9506; fax (85) 3366-9513; internet
www.biblioteca.ufc.br; f. 1958, renamed
1982; 164,429 vols; Dir FRANCISCO JONATAN
SOARES.

João Pessoa

Biblioteca Pública do Estado da Paraíba
(Paraíba Public Library): Rua General Osório
253, Centro, 58000-000 João Pessoa, PB; tel.

(83) 3218-4194; f. 1859; 10,000 vols; Dir
MARIA RODRIGUES DA SILVA.

Manaus

Biblioteca Pública do Estado (Amazonas
Public Library): Rua Barroso 57, Centro,
69010-050 Manaus, AM; tel. (92) 3637-6660;
e-mail bpublica@culturamazonas.am.gov.br;
internet www.culturamazonas.am.gov.br;
100,000 vols; Dir SHARLES SILVA DA COSTA.

Niterói

**Biblioteca Pública do Estado do Rio de
Janeiro** (Public Library of the State of Rio):
Av. Presidente Vargas 1261, Centro, 20071-
004 Rio de Janeiro, RJ; tel. (21) 2224-6184;
fax (21) 2252-6810; e-mail bibliotecapublica@
bperj.rj.gov.br; internet www.bperj.rj.gov.br;
f. 1873; attached to the State Office of
Culture; possesses rare early works, newspapers and valuable first editions; 80,000
vols, notably dictionaries, encyclopedias, reference books; Gen. Dir ANA LIGIA MEDEIROS.

Ouro Preto

Biblioteca Dr Amaro Lanari Júnior
(Library of the Ouro Preto School of Mines):
Campus Universitário, Morro do Cruzeiro,
35400-000 Ouro Preto, MG; tel. (31) 559-
1508; e-mail bibem@sisbin.ufop.br; internet
www.em.ufop.br/bibliotecas.php; f. 1876;
50,000 vols, 1,900 periodicals; Librarian
JORDANA RABELLO SOARES; publ. *Revista*.

Pelotas

Biblioteca Pública Pelotense (Public
Library): Praça Coronel Pedro Osório 103,
96015-010 Pelotas, RS; tel. (53) 3222-3856;
fax (53) 3222-3856; f. 1875; 150,000 vols;
museum, cultural exhibition; Pres. JOAQUIM
SALVADOR COELHO PINHO.

Petrópolis

**Biblioteca Central Municipal Gabriela
Mistral** (Municipal Library): Praça Visconde
de Mauá 305, Centro, 25685-380 Petrópolis,
RJ; tel. (24) 2247-3745; fax (24) 2247-3727;
e-mail biblioteca@petropolis.rj.gov.br;
internet www.petropolis.rj.gov.br; f. 1871;
140,000 vols; incorporates archive of
300,000 documents concerning admin. history of Petrópolis; Librarian MARIA HELENA
DE AVELLAR PALMA.

Porto Alegre

**Biblioteca Central da Universidade Fed-
eral do Rio Grande do Sul:** Av. Paulo
Gama 110, Térreo da Reitoria, 90046-900
Porto Alegre, RS; tel. (51) 3316-3065; fax (51)
3316-3984; e-mail bcentral@bc.ufrgs.br;
internet www.biblioteca.ufrgs.br; f. 1971; 32
br. libraries; 1,044,830 vols; Dir VIVIANE
CARRION CASTANHO.

**Biblioteca Pública do Estado do Rio
Grande do Sul** (Rio Grande do Sul State
Public Library): Rua dos Andradas, 736,
Centro, Porto Alegre, RS; tel. (51) 3224-
5045; fax (51) 3225-9411; e-mail bpe@via-rs
.net; internet www.bibliotecapublica.rs.gov
.br; f. 1871; 775,863 vols; Dir MORGANA
MARCON.

Recife

**Biblioteca Central da Universidade Fed-
eral de Pernambuco:** Av. Prof. Moraes
Rego 1235, Cidade Universitária, 50670-901
Recife, PE; tel. (81) 2126-8094; fax (81) 2126-
8090; e-mail bcufpe@ufpe.br; internet www
.ufpe.br; f. 1968; 405,291 vols (incl. all
departmental libraries), 8,603 periodicals; a
regional centre for the nat. bibliographic
network organized by the Instituto Brasileiro
de Informação em Ciência e Tecnologia (*q.v.*);
Dir ADELAIDE LIMA; publs *BC-informa* (12 a
year), *Sumários de Periódicos* (12 a year).

**Biblioteca Pública do Estado de Per-
nambuco** (Pernambuco State Public
Library): Rua João Lira s/n, Santo Amaro
50050-550 Recife, PE; tel. (81) 3423-8446;
e-mail arles@educacao.pe.gov.br; internet
www.biblioteca.pe.gov.br; f. 1852; 250,000
vols, 350,000 periodicals; Dir CLEA DUBEUX
PINTO PIMENTEL.

Rio de Janeiro

Arquivo Nacional (National Archives): Rua
Azeredo Coutinho 77, 20230-170 Rio de
Janeiro, RJ; tel. (21) 2252-2617; fax (21)
2232-8430; e-mail diretorgeral@
arquivonacional.gov.br; internet www
.arquivonacional.gov.br; f. 1838; specializes
in history of Brazil, technique of archives and
legislation; 28,000 vols; 45 shelf-km of documents; Dir-Gen. JAIME ANTUNES DA SILVA;
publs *BIBA*, *Revista Acervo*.

**Biblioteca Bastos Tigre da Associação
Brasileira de Imprensa** (Library of Brazilian Press Association): Rua Araújo Porto
Alegre 71, 12° andar, 20030-010 Rio de
Janeiro, RJ; tel. 2262-9822; fax 2262-3893;
e-mail abi@abi.org.br; f. 1908; 40,473 vols,
6,788 periodical titles; Dir MAURÍCIO AZÊDO.

**Biblioteca da Sociedade Brasileira de
Cultura Inglesa:** Rua São Clemente 258 –
3°, 4° e 5° andares, Botafogo, 22260-000 Rio
de Janeiro, RJ; tel. (21) 2528-8700; fax (21)
2535-4141; internet www.culturainglesa.net;
f. 1934; 3 brs; 34,000 vols; Head Librarian
MARIA DE FÁTIMA BORGES GONÇALVES; publ.
Library News.

**Biblioteca do Centro Cultural Banco do
Brasil** (Library of the Banco do Brasil Cultural Centre): Rua Primeiro de Março 66, 5°
andar, Centro, 20010-000 Rio de Janeiro, RJ;
tel. (21) 3808-2030; fax (21) 3808-0216; f.
1931; social sciences, literature and arts;
100,000 vols; special collections: rare books,
Brazilian music and folklore; Dir KLEUBER DE
PAIVA PEREIRA.

Biblioteca do Exército (Army Library):
Palácio Duque de Caxias, Ala Marcílio Dias
(3° andar), Centro, 20221-260 Rio de Janeiro;
tel. (21) 2519-5726; fax (21) 2519-5569;
e-mail bibliex@bibliex.com.br; internet www
.bibliex.com.br; f. 1881; 60,000 vols; general
collections to supply cultural needs of the
army; Dir Cel LUIZ EUGÊNIO DUARTE PEIXOTO;
publs *Revista A Defesa Nacional* (3 a year),
Revista do Exército Brasileiro (3 a year),
Revista Militar de Ciência e Tecnologia (3 a
year).

**Biblioteca do Instituto dos Advogados
Brasileiros** (Library of Lawyers' Institute):
Av. Marechal Câmara 210, 5° andar, Centro,
20020-080 Rio de Janeiro, RJ; tel. (21) 2240-
3921; fax (21) 2240-3173; internet www
.iabnacional.org.br; f. 1897; 32,000 vols; Dir
ROBERTO DE BASTOS LELIS.

**Biblioteca do Ministério da Fazenda no
Estado do Rio de Janeiro** (Library of the
Ministry of Finance of the Rio de Janeiro State):
Av. Presidente Antônio Carlos 372, 12°
andar, sala 1238, Centro, 20020-010 Rio de
Janeiro, RJ; tel. (21) 3805-4285; e-mail
biblioteca.rj.gra@fazenda.gov.br; f. 1943 by
incorporation of various departmental librar-
ies; 145,000 vols, 100 current periodicals;
Librarian KATIA APARECIDA TEIXEIRA DE OLI-
VEIRA; publs *A Legislação Tributária no
Brasil*, *Informe*.

**Biblioteca do Ministério das Relações
Exteriores no Rio de Janeiro** (Library of
the Ministry of Foreign Affairs in Rio de
Janeiro): Palácio Itamaraty, Av. Marechal
Floriano 196, Centro, 20080-002 Rio de
Janeiro, RJ; tel. (21) 2253-5730; f. 1906;
history; 270,000 vols including periodicals;
rare books; Dir SONIA DOYLE; (See also under
Brasília.).

Biblioteca do Mosteiro de S. Bento (Library of the St Benedict Monastery): Caixa Postal 2666, 20001-970 Rio de Janeiro, RJ; tel. (21) 2206-8100; fax (21) 2263-5679; e-mail msbrj@osb.org.br; f. 1600; 125,000 vols; Librarian D. MIGUEL VEESER; also in the towns of São Paulo, Salvador (Bahia) and Olinda; publs *Pergunte e Responderemos*, *Liturgia e Vida*.

Biblioteca Nacional (National Library): Av. Rio Branco 219-39, 20040-008 Rio de Janeiro, RJ; tel. (21) 262-8255; fax (21) 220-4173; e-mail infobn@bn.br; internet www.bn.br; f. 1810 with 60,000 vols from the Real Biblioteca brought to Brazil by the Royal Family of Portugal in 1808; 9m. documents; spec. cllns: Col. De Angelis (Brazilian and Paraguayan History), Col. Tereza Cristina Maria (donated by Emperor D. Pedro II, 1891), Col. Alexandre Rodrigues Ferreira (description with illustrations of travels in Amazônia by A. R. Ferreira, 1783–1792); Pres. PEDRO CORREA DO LAGO; publ. *Anais da Biblioteca Nacional*.

Biblioteca Popular do Leblon-Vinicius de Moraes: Av. Bartolomeu Mitre 1297, Gávea, 22431-000, Rio de Janeiro, RJ; tel. (21) 2294-1598; f. 1954; 8,000 vols; Dir MARIA LEONICE DE ALMEIDA.

Biblioteca Pública de Copacabana: Av. N.S. de Copacabana 817, Copacabana, 22050-002 Rio de Janeiro, RJ; tel. (21) 2255-0081; e-mail biblicopa@pcrj.rj.gov.br; f. 1954; 29,706 vols; Dir ANA MARIA COSTA DESLANDES.

Fundação Casa de Rui Barbosa (Rui Barbosa Foundation): Rua S. Clemente 134, 22260-000 Rio de Janeiro, RJ; tel. (21) 2537-0036; fax (21) 2537-1114; e-mail mario@rb.gov.br; internet www.casaruibarbosa.gov.br; f. 1930, became Foundation 1966; includes a centre for research in law, philology and history, a centre of Brazilian literature (over 50,000 documents), a documentation centre, with a library, Rui Barbosa archive, a microfilm laboratory and a paper restoration laboratory; museum and auditorium; 100,000 vols; Pres. MARIO BROCKMANN MACHADO; Exec. Dir LUIZ EDUARDO CONDE.

Fundação Instituto Brasileiro de Geografia e Estatística – Centro de Documentação e Disseminação de Informações, Divisão de Biblioteca e Acervos Especiais: Rua General Canabarro 706, Térreo Maracanà, 20271-201 Rio de Janeiro, RJ; fax (21) 2142-4933; e-mail ibge@ibge.gov.br; internet www.ibge.gov.br; f. 1977; documentation and dissemination of research and studies in geoscience, environment, demography, social and economic indicators, national accounts, statistics; 48,000 vols, 2,105 periodicals, 20,000 maps, 115,000 photographs; Dir MARIA TERESA PASSOS BASTOS.

Serviço de Documentação da Marinha (Documentation Service of the Navy): Praça Barão de Ladário (Ilha das Cobras), Centro, 20091-000 Rio de Janeiro, RJ; tel. (21) 3870-6721; fax (21) 3870-6716; e-mail admin@sdm.mar.mil.br; internet www.sdm.mar.mil.br; f. 1943; maritime history of Brazil; includes a naval museum and archives; naval library of 110,000 vols; Dir CMG LUIS HENRIQUE DE AZEVEDO BRAGA; publ. *Revista Marítima Brasileira* (3 a year).

Sistema de Bibliotecas e Informação da Universidade Federal do Rio de Janeiro (Library and Information System of the Federal University of Rio de Janeiro): Av. Pasteur 250, Urca, Rm 106, 22295-900 Rio de Janeiro, RJ; tel. (21) 2295-1595 ext. 219; fax (21) 2295-1397; e-mail paulamello@sibi.ufrj.br; internet www.sibi.ufrj.br; f. 1989; coordinates 43 brs; maintains mem. of the

Nat. Catalogue of Periodicals Online; 1,567,330 vols, 3,237,673 periodicals; Dir PAULA MARIA ABRANTES COTTA DE MELLO.

Rio Grande

Biblioteca Rio-Grandense (Rio Grande Library): Rua General Osório 454, Bairro Centro, 96200-400 Rio Grande, RS; tel. (53) 231-2842; e-mail contato@bibliotecariograndense.com.br; internet bibliotecariograndense.com.br; f. 1846; 400,000 vols, 7,600 maps; Pres. Dr JOÃO MARINONIO CARNEIRO LAGES; Dir Dr GILBERTO M. CENTENO CARDOSO.

Rio Negro

Biblioteca Pública Municipal Prof. Wenceslau Muniz (Municipal Library): Rua Getúlio Vargas 680, Centro, 83880-000 Rio Negro, PR; tel. (47) 645-1311; fax (47) 645-1311; e-mail sec.cultura@rno.matrix.com.br.

Salvador

Biblioteca do Gabinete Português de Leitura (Portuguese Reading Room and Library): Praça da Piedade s/n, Centro, 40060-300, Salvador, BA; tel. (71) 3329-3060; fax (71) 3329-1299; f. 1863; 15,000 vols; Librarian AGNÚBIA OLIVEIRA.

Biblioteca Pública do Estado da Bahia (Bahia State Central Library): Rua Gen. Labatut 27, Barris, 40010-100 Salvador, BA; tel. (71) 3328-4555; fax (71) 3328-4555; f. 1811, name changed 1984; 114,698 vols; Dir LÍDIA MARIA BASTISTA BRANDÃO.

São José dos Campos

Biblioteca Pública 'Cassiano Ricardo' ('Cassiano Ricardo' Public Library): Rua XV de Novembro 99, Centro, 12210-070 São José dos Campos, SP; tel. (12) 3921-6330; f. 1968; 70,000 vols and 8,500 periodicals; Dir ANA ELISABETE MARTINELLI GODINHO.

São Luís

Biblioteca Pública Benedito Leite (Benedito Leite Public Library): Praça do Panteon s/n, Centro, 65020-430 São Luís, MA; tel. (98) 3232-9730; fax (98) 3232-9688; e-mail sebpbpbl@cultura.ma.gov.br; f. 1829; 38 mems; 45,000 vols; collns of more than 15,000 engravings, and newspapers since 1821; Dir JOSEANE MARIA DE SOUZA; Librarian ROBERTO TAMARA.

São Paulo

Arquivo do Estado de São Paulo (São Paulo State Archives): Rua Voluntários da Pátria 596, Santana, 02010-000 São Paulo, SP; tel. (11) 6221-2850; fax (11) 6221-4785; e-mail supervisao@arquivoestado.sp.gov.br; internet www.arquivoestado.sp.gov.br; f. 1721; 45,000 vols; 10,000 files of loose documents; 1m. images (negatives, photographs, postcards, caricatures and illustrations); State records, collections of rare books, MSS, periodicals, maps and plans; Dir Dr FAUSTO COUTO SOBRINHO; publ. *Revista Histórica* (print and online, 12 a year).

Biblioteca do Conservatório Dramático e Musical de São Paulo (Library of Academy of Music and Drama): Av. Conselheiro Crispiniano 378, 01037-000 São Paulo, SP; tel. (11) 3337-2111; fax (11) 223-9231; e-mail cdmsp@cdmsp.edu.br; f. 1906; 30,000 vols; Dir Dr LUÍS CORRÊA FRAGOSO; Sec. JOSÉ RAYMUNDO LOBO.

Biblioteca do Instituto de Saúde (Health Institute Library): Rua Santo Antônio 590, Bela Vista, 01314-000 São Paulo, SP; tel. (11) 3293-2244; internet www.isaude.sp.gov.br; f. 1969; 41,000 vols, valuable collection of works, reviews, maps on dermatology and Hansen's disease, and rare works since 1600; Librarian ASTRID B. WIESEL.

Biblioteca 'George Alexander' (George Alexander Library): Rua da Consolação 896, Prédio 02, Higienópolis, 01302-907 São Paulo, SP; tel. (11) 3236-8302; fax (11) 3236-8302; e-mail biblio.per@mackenzie.com.br; internet www.mackenzie.com.br; f. 1870 as Mackenzie Library, present name 1926; 246,342 vols; Dir KAO SHIN.

Biblioteca Municipal Mário de Andrade (Municipal Library): Rua da Consolação 94, 01302-000 São Paulo, SP; tel. (11) 3241-5630; fax (11) 3259-5728; f. 1925; municipal library; 344,000 vols and 11,000 journal titles; incorporates former Biblioteca Pública do Estado de São Paulo; specialized collections of 40,000 rare editions and MSS, 25,000 drawings and art books, 5,500 maps; microfilms, legislation and multimedia sections; Dir of Municipal Library LUÍS FRANCISCO CARVALHO FILHO; publ. *Revista da Biblioteca Mário de Andrade*.

BIREME—Centro Latino-Americano e do Caribe de Informação em Ciências da Saúde (Latin American and Caribbean Centre on Health Sciences Information): Rua Botucatu 862 São Paulo, SP; tel. (11) 5576-9801; fax (11) 5575-8868; e-mail bireme@bireme.org; internet www.bireme.org; f. 1967 under the auspices of the Pan American Health Organization to promote a regional network of health libraries and information centres; aims to index all health literature produced in the region; provides bibliographic searches, document delivery, training, etc.; coordinates and promotes the Virtual Health Library (VHL); coordinates the Latin American and Caribbean Network of Libraries on Health Sciences; 400,000 issues of scientific journals, 3,500 current periodicals, 3,000 discontinued periodicals; Dir ABEL LAERTE PACKER; publ. *LILACS / CD-ROM* (3 a year).

British Council Library and Information Centre: Rua Ferreira Araújo, 741 terreo Pinheiros, 05428-000 São Paolo SP; tel. (11) 2126-7560; fax (11) 2126-7564; e-mail centro.info@britishcouncil.org.br; 7,000 vols; Library and Customer Services Officer ANA LUIZA MATTOS.

Discoteca Oneyda Alvarenga: Centro Cultural São Paulo, Rua Vergueiro 1000, Paraíso, 01504-000 São Paulo, SP; tel. (11) 3397-4071; internet www.centrocultural.sp.gov.br/discoteca.asp; f. 1935; study and diffusion of Brazilian and int. classical, folk and popular music; colln of 75,000 records, 2,500 CDs, 400 periodical titles; museum of folklore; 62,000 music scores and 11,000 books; Dir JÉSSICA A. M. BARRETO.

Sistema Integrado de Bibliotecas da Universidade de São Paulo (São Paulo University Integrated Library System): Av. Prof. Luciano Gualberto, Trav. J, 374-1 andar, 05508-010 São Paulo, SP; tel. (11) 3091-1573; fax (11) 3091-1567; e-mail dtsibi@usp.br; internet www.usp.br/sibi; f. 1981; 43 libraries, with 7,762,103 vols; Technical Dir ELIANA AZEVEDO MARQUES.

Vitória

Arquivo Público Estadual do Espírito Santo: Rua Pedro Palácios 76, Cidade Alta, 29015-160 Vitória, ES; tel. (27) 3223-7524; fax (27) 3223-2952; e-mail ape@coplag.es.gov.br; f. 1855.

Biblioteca Municipal Adelpho Poli Monjardim: Escola de Teatro e Dança, Av. Jerônimo Monteiro, Centro, Vitória, ES; tel. (27) 3381-6925; f. 1941; 14,800 vols.

Rector: ARISTIDES CIMADON
Library of 180,099 vols, 21,633 periodicals
Number of teachers: 766
Number of students: 13,645

UNIVERSIDADE DO SUL DE SANTA CATARINA

Av. José Acácio Moreira 787, Bairro Dehon, 88704-900 Tubarão, SC
Telephone: (48) 621-3000
Fax: (48) 621-3036
E-mail: unisul@unisul.br
Internet: www.unisul.br
Founded 1967
Municipal control
Academic year: March to November
Rector: GERSON LUIZ JONER DA SILVA
Vice-Rector: SEBASTIÃO SALÉSIO HERDT
Library of 161,346 vols
Number of teachers: 1,641
Number of students: 23,113
Publication: *Jornal* (10 a year).

UNIVERSIDADE SANTA CECÍLIA

Rua Oswaldo Cruz 277, Boqueirão, 11045-907 Santos, SP
Telephone: (13) 3202-7100
Fax: (13) 3234-5297
Internet: www.unisanta.br
Founded 1961
Private control
Academic year: February to December
Chancellor: Dr MILTON TEIXEIRA
Pres.: Dra LÚCIA M. TEIXEIRA FURLANI
Vice-Pres.: Profa MARIA CECÍLIA P. TEIXEIRA
Rector: Dra SÍLVIA ÂNGELA TEIXEIRA PEN-TEADO
Academic Pro-Rector: Profa ZULEIKA DE A. SENGER GONÇALVES
Admin. Pro-Rector: Dr MARCELO PIRILO TEIX-EIRA
Community Pro-Rector: Prof. AQUELINO J. VASQUES
Pro-Rector for Univ. Devt: Profa EMÍLIA MARIA PIRILO
Gen. Sec.: WALDIR GRAÇA
Chief Librarian: ANA MARIA RACCIOPI SIL-VEIRA
Library of 84,000 vols
Number of teachers: 640
Number of students: 13,000
Publications: *Ceciliana*, *Revista de Estudo*

COORDINATORS

Bandeirante I Campus: Profa ROSINHA GAR-CIA DE SIQUEIRA VIEGAS
Bandeirante II Campus: Profa CARMEN LÚCIA TABOADA DE CARVALHO
Santa Cecília Campus: Profa LÚCIA MARIA TEIXEIRA FURLANI, Dr MARCELO TEIXEIRA, Profa MARIA CECÍLIA TEIXEIRA

DEANS

Faculty of Arts and Communication: Prof. A. J. VASQUES
Faculty of Civil Engineering: Eng. A. DE SALLES PENTEADO
Faculty of Chemical Engineering: Eng. A. DE SALLES PENTEADO
Faculty of Commercial and Administrative Sciences: Prof. A. PORTO PIRES
Faculty of Dance: Prof. L. RACCINI
Faculty of Dentistry: Dr R. G. DE SIQUEIRA VIEGAS
Faculty of Education and Human Sciences: Prof. C. M. BAFFA
Faculty of Industrial Engineering: Eng. A. E. P. FIGUEIREDO
Faculty of Law: Dr R. MEHANNA KHAMIS
Faculty of Physical Education: Prof. V. A. TABOADA DE CARVALHO RAPHAELLI

Faculty of Sciences and Technology: Prof. R. PATELLA

UNIVERSIDADE DE SANTA CRUZ DO SUL

Av. Independência 2293, Bairro Universi-tário, 96815-900 Santa Cruz do Sul, RS
Telephone: (51) 3717-7300
Fax: (51) 3717-1855
E-mail: info@unisc.br
Internet: www.unisc.br
Founded 1964
Rector: VILMAR THOMÉ
Vice-Rector: JOSÉ ANTÔNIO PASTORIZA FON-TOURA
Pro-Rector for Admin.: Prof. JAIME LAUFER
Pro-Rector for Extension and Community Relations: Profa ANA LUISA TEIXEIRA DE MENEZES
Pro-Rector for Planning and Institutional Devt: Prof. JOÃO PEDRO SCHMIDT
Pro-Rector for Research and Graduate Courses: Prof. LIANE MÄHLMANN KIPPER
Pro-Rector for Undergraduate Courses: Profa CARMEN LÚCIA DE LIMA HELFER
Library of 26,000
Number of teachers: 548
Number of students: 10,668

UNIVERSIDADE FEDERAL DE SANTA MARIA

Campus Universitário–Camobi, 97105-900 Santa Maria, RS
Telephone: (55) 220-8000
Fax: (55) 220-8001
E-mail: sai@adm.ufsm.br
Internet: www.ufsm.br
Founded 1960
Federal control
Academic year: March to December (2 semes-ters)
Dean: Prof. FELIPE MARTINS MÜLLER
Vice-Dean: Prof. DALVAN JOSÉ REINERT
Pro-Rector for Admin.: ANDRÉ LUIS KIELING RIES
Pro-Rector for Extension: Prof. JOÃO RODOL-PHO FLÔRES
Pro-Rector for Planning: CHARLES JACQUES PRADE
Pro-Rector for Postgraduates and Research: Prof. HELIO LEÃES HEY
Pro-Rector for Student Affairs: Prof. JOSÉ FRANCISCO SILVA DIAS
Pro-Rector for Undergraduates: Prof. ORLANDO FONSECA
Librarian: MARIA INEZ FIGUEIREDO FIGAS
Library of 177,490 vols
Number of teachers: 1,444
Number of students: 18,490 (13,322 under-graduate, 2,262 postgraduate, 2,906 at Technical High School)
Publications: *Animus Revista Interameri-cana de Comunicação Mediática*, *Ciência e Ambiente*, *Ciência e Natura*, *Ciência Rural*, *Extensão Rural*, *Revista Brasilerira de Agroameteorologia*

DIRECTORS OF CENTRES

Arts and Letters: Prof. EDEMUR CASANOVA
Education: Profa HELENISE SANGOI ANTUNES
Health Sciences: Prof. PAULO AFONSO BUR-MANN
Natural and Exact Sciences: Profa MARTHA BOHRER ADAIME
Rural Science: Prof. THOMÉ LOVATO
Social and Human Sciences: Prof. ROGÉRIO FERRER KOFF
Sports Research Centre: Prof. CARLOS BOLLI MOTA
Technology: Prof. EDUARDO RIZZATTI

ATTACHED INSTITUTES

Faculty of Nursing: Av. Presidente Vargas 2777, 97100 Santa Maria, RS; Dir Ir NOEMI LUNARDI.
Faculty of Philosophy, Sciences and Letters: Rua Andradas 1614, 97100 Santa Maria, RS; Dir Profa MARIA A. MARQUES.

UNIVERSIDADE SANTA ÚRSULA

Rua Fernando Ferrari 75, Botafago, 22231-040 Rio de Janeiro, RJ
Telephone: (21) 2554-2500
E-mail: reitoria@usu.br
Internet: www.usu.br
Founded 1938
Rector: MARIA DO CARMO BITTENCOURT
Library of 123,000 vols, 2,128 periodicals
Number of teachers: 425
Number of students: 7,639

UNIVERSIDADE DE SANTO AMARO

Rua Prof. Enéas de Siqueira Neto 340, Jardim das Imbuias, 04829-300 São Paulo, SP
Telephone: (11) 2141-8619
Internet: www.unisa.br
Founded 1968 as Instituição de Ensino Superior; current name 1994
Private control
Rector: DARCI GOMES DO NASCIMENTO
Vice-Rector: JOSÉ DOUGLAS DALLORA
Library of 57,000 vols, 700 periodicals
Number of teachers: 505
Number of students: 7,789

UNIVERSIDADE CATÓLICA DE SANTOS

Rua Euclides da Cunha 241, Pompéia, 11065-902 Santos, SP
Telephone: (13) 3205-5555
E-mail: secgeral@unisantos.com.br
Internet: www.unisantos.com.br
Founded 1986
Rector: Profa MARIA HELENA DE ALMEIDA LAMBERT
Library of 58,000 vols, 945 periodicals
Number of teachers: 537
Number of students: 7,015

UNIVERSIDADE METROPOLITANA DE SANTOS

Rua da Constituição 374, Vila Mathias, 11015-470 Santos, SP
Telephone: (13) 3226-3400
E-mail: infounimes@unimes.com.br
Internet: www.unimes.com.br
Founded 1968 as Centro de Estudos Uni-ficados Bandeirante; current name 1985
Private control
Rector: Profa RENATA GARCIA DE SIQUEIRA VIEGAS
Pro-Rector for Academic Affairs: Profa VERA APARECIDA TABOADA DE CARVALHO RAPHAELLI
Library of 59,000 vols, 233 periodicals
Number of teachers: 405
Number of students: 5,034

UNIVERSIDADE FEDERAL DE SÃO CARLOS

Rodovia Washington Luiz, km 235, Monjo-linho, CP 676, 13565-905 São Carlos, SP
Telephone: (16) 260-8111
Fax: (16) 261-4846
E-mail: reitoria@ufscar.br
Internet: www.ufscar.br

Founded 1970
Federal control
Language of instruction: Portuguese
Academic year: March to December
Campuses in São Carlos, Sorocaba and Araras
Chancellor: PAULO RENATO DE SOUZA
Rector: Prof. Dr TARGINO DE ARAÚJO FILHO
Vice-Rector: Prof. Dr PEDRO MANOEL GALETTI, Jr
Chief Admin. Officer: Profa Dra NANCY V. F. DE ALMEIDA
Librarian: LIGIA MARIA SILVA D SOUZA
Number of teachers: 874
Number of students: 11,372
Publications: *Cadernos de Terapia ocupacional*, *Revista Brasileira de Fisioterapia*, *Revista Gestão e Produção*, *Revista Olhar*, *Revista Universitária do Audiovisual*

DIRECTORS

Araras Campus:

Institute of Agricultural Sciences: Prof. Dr NORBERTO ANTONIO LAVORENTTI

São Carlos Campus:

Institute of Biological and Health Sciences: Prof. Dr JOSÉ EDUARDO DOS SANTOS
Institute of Education and Human Sciences: Profa Dra WANDA AP. M. HOFFMANN
Institute of Sciences and Technology: Prof. Dr ERNESTO ANTONIO URQUIETA GONZALEZ

UNIVERSIDADE DE SÃO FRANCISCO

Av. São Francisco de Assis 218, Jd. São José, 12916-900 Bragança Paulista, SP
Telephone: (11) 4034-8170
Internet: www.usf.com.br
Founded 1976, university status 1985
Private control
Language of instruction: Portuguese
Academic year: February to December
Rector: Fr GILBERTO
Vice-Rector: Fr JOSÉ ANTÔNIO CRUZ DUARTE
Pro-Rector for Academic Affairs and Institutional Devt: LEILA PAGNOZZI
Pro-Rector for Admin. Affairs: PAULO CUNHA
Pro-Rector for Community Affairs: EVANDRO RIBEIRO
Gen. Sec.: PAULO POZEBON
Librarian: IVANI BENASSI
Library of 132,000 vols, 1,200 periodicals
Number of teachers: 821
Number of students: 17,561
Publications: *Anais do Encontro de Iniciação Científica e Pesquisadores* (1 a year), *Cadernos do IFAN* (4 a year), *InformIP-PEX* (12 a year), *Informativo USF* (12 a year), *Semeando* (12 a year)

DIRECTORS

Câmpus de Bragança Paulista (Av. São Francisco de Assis 218, CP 163, 12900-000 Bragança Paulista, SP):

Faculty of Dentistry: Prof. ROSSINE AMORIM MACIEL
Faculty of Economics and Administration: Profa HILDA MARIA C. BARROSO BRAGA
Faculty of Law: Prof. JOSÉ NICOLA JANNUZZI
Faculty of Medicine: Prof. SÉRGIO LUIZ MARTIN NARDY
Faculty of Pharmacy: Prof. EDSON RODRIGUES
Faculty of Philosophy, Sciences and Literature: Prof. MIGUEL HENRIQUE RUSSO

Câmpus de Itatiba (Rua Alexandre Rodrigues Barbosa 45, 13251-900 Itatiba, SP):

Faculty of Administrative and Exact Sciences: Prof. FÁBIO ALEXANDRE GAION CASOTTI
Faculty of Engineering: Prof. WERNER MERTZIG
Faculty of Human Sciences: Profa CARMEM BEATRIZ RODRIGUES FABRIANI

Câmpus de São Paulo (Rua Hannemann 352, Pari, 03031-040 São Paulo, SP):

Faculty of Business and Administration: Prof. LUIZ MAURÍCIO DE ANDRADE DA SILVA
Faculty of Education and Social Sciences: Prof. MARINO ANTONIO SEHNEN
Faculty of Law: Prof. MARLON WANDER MACHADO

ATTACHED INSTITUTES

Franciscan Institute of Anthropology: Dir Fr ORLANDO BERNARDI.

Institute for Graduate Research and Extension: Dir Profa JOSIANE MARIA DE FREITAS TONELOTTO.

UNIVERSIDADE SÃO JUDAS TADEU

Rua Taquari 546, Mooca, 03166-000 São Paulo, SP
Telephone: (11) 2799-1677
E-mail: webmaster@saojudas.br
Internet: www.usjt.br
Founded 1985
Private control
Rector: Prof. JOSÉ CHRISTIANO A. SILVA MESQUITA
Library of 70,000 vols, 2,066 periodicals
Number of teachers: 733
Number of students: 18,410

UNIVERSIDADE SÃO MARCOS

Rua Clóvis Bueno de Azevedo 176, Ipiranga, 04266-040 São Paulo, SP
Telephone: (11) 3491-0500
Fax: (11) 6163-0978
E-mail: info@smarcos.br
Internet: www.smarcos.br
Founded 1970
Private control
Rector: ERNANI BICUDO DE PAULA
Library of 73,000 vols, 347 periodicals
Number of teachers: 309
Number of students: 8,164

UNIVERSIDADE DE SÃO PAULO

Cidade Universitária, Rua da Reitoria 109, 05508-900 São Paulo, SP
Telephone: (11) 3091-1000
Fax: (11) 3815-5665
E-mail: gr@usp.br
Internet: www.usp.br
Founded 1934
State control
Academic year: March to November
Rector: Prof. Dra SUELY VILELA
Vice-Rector: Prof. Dr FRANCO MARIA LAJOLO
Pro-Rector for Culture and Univ. Extension: Prof. Dr RUY ALBERTO CORREA ALTAFINE
Pro-Rector for Postgraduate Studies: Prof. Dr ARMANDO CORBANI FERRAZ
Pro-Rector for Research: Prof. Dra MAYANA ZATZ
Pro-Rector for Undergraduate Studies: Profa Dra SELMA GARRIDO PIMENTA
Sec.-Gen.: Profa Dra MARIA FIDELA DE LIMA NAVARRO
Library: see Libraries and Archives
Number of teachers: 5,434
Number of students: 81,179

Publications: *Boletim de Botânica* (1 a year), *Boletim IG/USP—Série Científica* (1 a year), *Brazilian Journal of Veterinary Research and Animal Science* (6 a year), *Educação e Pesquisa—FE* (2 a year), *Estilos da Clínica* (2 a year), *Pesquisa Odontológica Brasileira* (4 a year), *Revista Brasileira de Ciências Farmacêuticas—IQ/FCF* (3 a year), *Revista Brasileira de Oceanografia* (2 a year), *Revista da Escola de Enfermagem* (4 a year), *Revista da Faculdade de Direito* (1 a year), *Revista de Administração* (4 a year), *Revista de Fisioterapia* (2 a year), *Revista de Psicologia USP* (2 a year), *Revista de Saúde Pública* (6 a year), *Revista de Terapia Ocupacional* (4 a year), *Revista do Instituto de Medicina Tropical de SP* (6 a year), *Revista do Museu de Arqueologia e Etnologia* (1 a year), *Revista Paulista de Educação Física* (2 a year), *Revista USP* (4 a year), *Scientia Agrícola—ESALQ* (4 a year), *Sinopses—FAU* (irregular)

DEANS

Faculty of Animal Husbandry and Food Engineering (Pirassununga): Prof. Dr HOLMER SAVASTANO Jr
Faculty of Architecture and Town Planning: Prof. Dr SYLVIO BARROS SAWAYA
Faculty of Dentistry: Prof. Dr CARLOS DE PAULA EDUARDO
Faculty of Dentistry (Bauru): Prof. Dr LUIZ FERNANDO PEGORARO
Faculty of Dentistry (Ribeirão Preto): Prof. Dr OSWALDO LUIZ BEZZON
Faculty of Economics, Administration and Accounting: Prof. Dr CARLOS ROBERTO AZZONI
Faculty of Economics, Administration and Accounting (Ribeirão Preto): Prof. Dr RUDINEI TONETO J\Jr
Faculty of Education: Profa Dra SONIA TERESINHA DE SOUSA PENIN
Faculty of Law: Prof. Dr JOÃO GRANDINO RODAS
Faculty of Law (Ribeirão Preto): Prof. Dr IGNÁCIO MARIA POVEDA VELASCO
Faculty of Medicine: Prof. Dr MARCOS BOULOS
Faculty of Medicine (Ribeirão Preto): Prof. Dr BENEDITO CARLOS MACIEL
Faculty of Pharmaceutical Sciences: Prof. Dr JORGE MANCINI FILHO
Faculty of Pharmaceutical Sciences (Ribeirão Preto): Prof. Dr AUGUSTO CÉSAR CROPANESE SPADARO
Faculty of Philosophy, Literature and Human Sciences: Profa Dra SANDRA MARGARIDA NITRINI
Faculty of Philosophy, Sciences and Literature (Ribeirão Preto): Prof. Dr SEBASTIÃO DE SOUSA ALMEIDA
Faculty of Public Health: Prof. Dr CHESTER LUIZ GALVÃO CÉSAR
Faculty of Veterinary Medicine and Zootechnics: Prof. Dr JOSÉ ANTONIO VISINTIN
Institute of Biomedical Sciences: Prof. Dr LUIZ ROBERTO GIORGETTI DE BRITTO
Institute of Biosciences: Profa Dra WELLINGTON BRAZ CARVALHO DELITTI
Institute of Chemistry: Prof. Dr HANS VIERTLER
Institute of Chemistry (São Carlos): Prof. Dr EDSON ANTONIO TICIANELLI
Institute of Geophysics, Astronomy and Atmospheric Sciences: Profa Dra MÁRCIA ERNESTO
Institute of Geosciences: Prof. Dr COLOMBO CELSO GAETA TASSINARI
Institute of Mathematical Sciences and Computing Systems (São Carlos): Prof. Dr JOSÉ ALBERTO CUMINATO
Institute of Mathematics and Statistics: Prof. Dr PAULO DOMINGOS CORDARO
Institute of Oceanography: Prof. Dr ANA MARIA S. PIRES VANIN

Pro-Rector for Research and Postgraduate: Prof. Og Francisco Fonseca de Souza
Pro-Rector for Undergraduate: Prof. José Benício Paes Chaves
Chief Admin. Officer: Prof. Vicente de Paula Lelis
Dir of Library: Doris Magna de Avelar Oliveira
Number of teachers: 786
Number of students: 9,584 (incl. 815 at high school level)
Publications: *Boletim Técnico de Extensão, Economia Rural* (6 a year), *Jornal da UFV* (12 a year), *Revista Brasileira de Armazenamento, Revista Brasileira de Zootecnia* (6 a year), *Revista Ceres* (6 a year), *Revista de Ciências Humanas* (2 a year), *Revista de Educação Física* (2 a year), *Revista de Engenharia na Agricultura* (12 a year), *Revista Gláuks* (2 a year), *Revista Oikos* (2 a year)

DIRECTORS
Agricultural Sciences Centre: Prof. Maurinho Luiz dos Santos
Biological and Health Sciences Centre: Prof. Ricardo Junqueira del Carlo
Engineering and Technological Sciences Centre: Prof. Luiz Aurelio Raggi
Human Sciences and Liberal Arts Centre: Prof. Adriel Rodrigues de Oliveira

Colleges
GENERAL

Centro de Ensino Unificado de Brasília: SEPN 707/907, Campus do UniCEUB, Brasília, DF; tel. 340-1878; fax 340-1578; e-mail biblioteca@uniceub.br; internet www.uniceub.br; f. 1968; controls Ciências e Letras do Distrito Federal, Contábeis e Administrativas do Distrito Federal, Faculdade de Ciências da Educacão, Faculdade de Ciências da Saudé, Faculdade de Direito do Distrito Federal, Faculdade de Ciências Econômicas,Faculdade de Ciências Exatas e Tecnologia, Faculdade de Ciências Sociais e Aplicadas, Faculdade de Filosofia; library: 22,000 vols; 710 teachers; 14,000 students; Rector Dr João Herculino de Souza Lopes; publs *Universitas—Biociencias* (2 a year), *Universitas—Jus* (2 a year), *Universitas—Psicologia* (2 a year).

Centro Universitário do Distrito Federal (UDF): SEP/SUL, Eq. 704/904, Conjunto A, 70390-045 Brasília, DF; tel. (61) 3704-8888; e-mail udf@udf.edu.br; internet www.unidf.edu.br; f. 1967; graduate courses in accountancy, administration, advertising, economics, education, information systems, international relations, journalism, law, politics; library: 42,000 vols; 950 teachers; 33,000 students; Pres. Rezende Ribeiro de Rezende.

Centro Universitário Moura Lacerda: Rua Padre Euclides 995, Campos Elíseos, 14085-420 Ribeirão Preto, SP; tel. (16) 2101-1010; fax (16) 2101-1024; internet www.mouralacerda.edu.br; f. 1923; graduate courses in computing and mathematics, accountancy, administration, architecture and town planning, agronomy, civil, economics, education, fashion, electronic and production engineering, international relations, languages and literature, law, philosophy, physical education, social communication, and veterinary medicine; postgraduate courses incl. MBA; campuses in Ribeirão Preto, Jaboticabal and Sertãozinho; library: 50,000 vols; Rector Prof. Dr Glauco Eduardo Pereira Cortez.

Centro Universitário Salesiano de São Paulo—Unidade de Ensino de Lorena: Rua Dom Bosco 284, Centro, 12600-000 Lorena, SP; tel. (12) 3153 2033; fax (12) 3152 1299; internet www.unisal-lorena.br; f. 1985; courses in administration, computer science, education, geography, history, Internet systems technology, law, mathematics, philosophy, psychology, tourism, technology in hotel management; library: 60,000 vols; Dir Dilson Passos Junior; Sec. Getulino do Espírito Santo Maciel; publs *Revista Ciência e Tecnologia, Revista de Ciências da Educação, Revista Jurídica Direito e Paz.*

Faculdades ASMEC: Av. Dr Professor Antônio Eufrâsio de Tôledo 100, Jardim dos Ypês, 37570-000 Ouro Fino, MG; tel. (35) 3441-1616; e-mail asmec@asmec.br; internet www.asmec.br; f. 1972; run by Associação Sul Mineira de Educação e Cultura; courses in administration, agricultural environmental management, biology, chemistry, education, geography, hotel management, languages and literature, mathematics, nursing, nutrition, physical education, systems analysis and development, tourism; 23 teachers; 1,437 students; library: 8,306 vols, 3,522 periodicals; Gen. Coordinator Bel. Guilherme Bernardes Filho; publ. *Signum.*

Faculdades Integradas Hebraico Brasileira Renascença: Rua Prates 790, Bom Retiro, 01121-000 São Paulo; tel. (11) 3311-0778; fax (11) 3311-0778; e-mail faculdade.br@renascenca.br; internet www.renascenca.br/faculdade; f. 1975; attached to the Sociedade Hebraico Brasileira Renascença; languages of instruction: Portuguese, English, Spanish, Hebrew; academic year January to December 2 terms); library: 41,157 vols, 868 periodicals, 164 video cassettes, 839 theses; 72 teachers; 1,107 students; Dir-Gen. Prof. Bernardo Zweiman Abrão.

Faculdades Oswaldo Cruz: Rua Brigadeiro Galvão 540, Barra Funda, São Paulo, SP; tel. 3825-4266; fax 3825-4266 ext. 236; e-mail faculdades@oswaldocruz.br; internet www.oswaldocruz.br; f. 1966; library: 36,565 vols; 328 teachers; 4,895 students; Dir Carlos Eduardo Quirino Simões de Amorim; Librarian Valdenise Machado Ribeiro Fidelis.

Constituent Institutions:

Escola Superior de Química: Rua Brigadeiro Galvão 540, Prédio I 7° andar, Barra Funda, São Paulo, SP; tel. 3825-4266 ext. 258; fax 3825-4266 ext. 236; e-mail esq@oswaldocruz.br; internet www.oswaldocruz.br; f. 1966; 76 teachers; 1,313 students; courses in engineering, industrial chemistry; Dir Prof. Victor Abou Nehmi.

Faculdade de Ciências Administrativas, Econômicas e Contábeis: Rua Brigadeiro Galvão 540, Prédio I 7° andar, Barra Funda, São Paulo, SP; tel. 3825-4266 ext. 245; fax 3825-4266 ext. 236; e-mail ocfaec@oswaldocruz.br; internet www.oswaldocruz.br; f. 1974; 98 teachers; 2,257 students; courses in accountancy, economics, and management; Dir Prof. Dr Oduvaldo Cardoso.

Faculdade de Ciências Farmacêuticas e Bioquímicas: Rua Brigadeiro Galvão 540, Prédio I 7° andar, Barra Funda, São Paulo, SP; tel. 3825-4266 ext. 259; fax 3825-4266 ext. 236; e-mail farmacia@oswaldocruz.br; internet www.oswaldocruz.br; f. 1981; courses in biochemistry and pharmacy; 70 teachers; 504 students; Dir Prof. Paulo Roberto Miele.

Faculdade de Filosofia, Ciências e Letras: Rua Brigadeiro Galvão 540, Prédio I 7° andar, Barra Funda, São Paulo, SP;

tel. 3825-4266 ext. 243; fax 3825-4266 ext. 236; e-mail ffcl@oswaldocruz.br; internet www.oswaldocruz.br; f. 1969; 84 teachers; 821 students; courses in chemistry, mathematics, pedagogy, physics, Portuguese; Dir Prof. Victor Abou Nehmi.

ECONOMICS, POLITICAL SCIENCE, SOCIOLOGY

Centro Universitário Fundação Santo André: Av. Príncipe de Gales 821, 09060-650 Santo André, SP; tel. (11) 4979-3300; fax (11) 440-2048; internet www.fsa.br; f. 1954; supported by the Fundação Santo André; faculties of economics and administration; engineering; languages and literature, philosophy, sciences; graduate courses in education and MBA; library: 19,340 vols; Rector Prof. Dr Oduvaldo Cacalano.

Escola de Administração de Emprêsas de São Paulo da Fundação Getúlio Vargas: Av. 9 de Julho 2029, Bela Vista, 01313-902 São Paulo, SP; tel. (11) 3281-7777; e-mail mtereza.fleury@fgv.br; internet www.eaesp.fgvsp.br; f. 1954; library: 70,000 books, 1,200 periodicals; business and public administration; 250 teachers; 4,616 students; Dir Maria Tereza Leme Fleury; publs *Relatórios de Pesquisa, Revista de Administração de Emprêsas.*

Faculdade de Ciências Sociais Aplicadas do Sul de Minas Gerais: Av. Presidente Tancredo de Almeida Neves 45, Itajubá, MG; tel. (35) 3629-5700; fax (35) 3629-5705; internet www.facesm.br; f. 1965; courses in accountancy, administration and economics; Dir Prof. Guilherme Garnett.

Faculdade de Ciências Políticas e Econômicas de Cruz Alta: Rua Andrade Neves 308, Cruz Alta, RS; f. 1955; independent; library: 4,605 vols; Dir Dario Silveira Netto.

Faculdade Estadual de Ciências Econômicas de Apucarana: Av. Minas Gerais 5021, 86800-970 Apucarana, PR; tel. (43) 3423-7277; fax (43) 3423-7277; internet www.fecea.br; f. 1959; state school; accounting, administration, economics, human sciences, quantitative methods; Dir Prof. Vanderley Ceranto.

Instituto Rio Branco: Ministério das Relações Exteriores, Setor de Administração Federal Sul, Quadra 5–Lotes 2/3, 70170-900 Brasília, DF; tel. (61) 3411-9804; fax (61) 3411-9828; e-mail irbr@mre.gov.br; internet www.irbr.mre.gov.br; f. 1945; official Brazilian Diplomatic Academy; 2-year graduate courses; also courses for foreign students; Dir Min. Andre Mattoso Maia Amado.

Instituto Universitário de Pesquisas do Rio de Janeiro: Rua da Matriz 82, Botafogo, 22260-100, Rio de Janeiro, RJ; tel. (21) 2266-8300; fax (21) 2286-7146; e-mail webmaster@iuperj.br; internet www.iuperj.br; f. 1969; research and graduate training in political science and sociology; 18 teachers; library: 20,000 vols; Exec. Dir José Maurício Domingues; publs *Cadernos de Sociologia e Política* (every 2 years), *Contributions to the History of Concepts* (2 a year), *Dados* (4 a year).

LAW

Faculdade de Direito Cândido Mendes: Rua da Assembléia, 10, sala 416, Centro, Rio de Janeiro, RJ; tel. (21) 2531-2000 ext. 217; e-mail fdcm@candidomendes.edu.br; f. 1953; course in law; library: 10,000 vols; Dir Prof. José Baptista de Oliveira Junior; publ. *Dados.*

Faculdade de Direito de São Bernardo do Campo: Rua Java 425, Jardim do Mar,

CP 180, 09750-650 São Bernardo do Campo, SP; tel. and fax 4123-0222; e-mail diretoria@ direitosbc.br; internet www.direitosbc.br; f. 1964; library: 27,000 vols; 57 teachers; 2,486 students; Dir LUIZ ANTONIO MATTOS PIMENTA ARAÚJO.

Faculdade de Direito de Sorocaba: Rua Dra Ursulina Lopes Torres 123, Vergueiro, 18100 Sorocaba, SP; tel. (15) 2105-1234; fax (15) 2105-1234; internet www.fadi.br; f. 1957; library: 10,000 vols; Dir Dr HELIO ROSA BALDY; publ. *Revista*.

MEDICINE

Escola de Farmácia e Odontologia de Alfenas: Rua Gabriel Monteiro da Silva 714, 37130-000 Alfenas, MG; tel. (35) 3299-1062; fax (35) 3299-1063; e-mail grad@efoa.int.br; f. 1914; graduate courses in biochemical and applied pharmacy, biological sciences and nutrition, dentistry, general nursing and obstetrics; 127 teachers; library: 16,059 vols; Dean Prof. MACIRO MANOEL PEREIRA; publ. *Revista*.

Faculdade de Medicina do Triângulo Mineiro: Rua Frei Paulino 30, 38025-180 Uberaba, MG; tel. (34) 3318-5004; fax (34) 3312-1487; e-mail diretoria@diretoria.fmtm .br; internet www.fmtm.br; f. 1953; 185 teachers; 1,383 students; Dir Prof. EDSON LUIZ FERNANDES.

TECHNICAL

Centro Universitário de Lins: Av. Nicolau Zarvos 1925, Jardim Aeroporto, 16401-371 Lins, SP; tel. (14) 3533-3200; fax (14) 3533-3248; internet www.unilins.edu.br; f. 1961; courses in administration, business automation engineering, engineering (civil, computer, electromechanical, electronic, environmental, information), executive secretaryship, information systems, marketing, mechatronics, nursing, social services, technology (in industrial chemistry, in Internet systems, in management processes, in systems analysis); 50 teachers; 650 students; Rector MILTON LÉO; Vice-Rector EDGAR PAULO PASTORELLO.

Centro Universitário do Instituto Mauá de Tecnologia: Praça Mauá, CEP 09580-900, São Caetano do Sul, SP; tel. (11) 4239-3000; fax (11) 4239-3041; e-mail ceum@maua .br; internet www.maua.br; f. 1961; civil, chemical, electrical, environmental and food engineering, mechanical, industrial, mechatronics and packaging technology; library: 60,000 vols; 250 teachers; 4,000 students; Dir OTAVIO DE MATTOS SILVARES.

Escola Superior de Desenho Industrial: Rua Evaristo da Veiga 95, Rio de Janeiro 20031-040; tel. (21) 2240-1790; fax (21) 2240-1890; e-mail diretoria@esdi.uerj.br; internet www.esdi.uerj.br; f. 1962; state school, affiliated to Univ. do Estado do Rio de Janeiro; courses in product and graphic design; 34 teachers; 160 students; Dean GABRIEL PATROCÍNIO.

Faculdade de Ciências de Barretos: Av. Prof. Roberto Frademonte 389, Aeroporto, 14783-226 Barretos, SP; tel. (17) 322-6411; fax (17) 322-6205; e-mail faciba@seb.br; f. 1969; chemistry, food engineering and processing, mathematics, physics; library: 13,300 vols; Prin. LUIZA MARIA PIERINI MACHADO.

Faculdade de Engenharia de Barretos: c/o Fundacão Educacional de Barretos, Av. Prof. Roberto Frade Monte 389, CP 16, 14783-226 Barretos, SP; tel. (17) 3322-6411;

fax (17) 3322-6205; e-mail dirgeral@feb.br; internet www.feb.br; f. 1965; part of the Fundação Educacional de Barretos; civil, food and electrical engineering; library: 14,000 vols; 202 teachers; 2,000 students; Academic Dir PATRICIA HELENA RODRIGUES DE SOUZA; Vice-Dir Dr OLIVIO CARLOS NASCIMENTO SOUTO.

Instituto Militar de Engenharia: Praça General Tibúrcio 80, Praia Vermelha, 22290-270 Rio de Janeiro, RJ; tel. (21) 2546-7080; internet www.ime.eb.br; f. 1792, present name 1959; undergraduate, Masters and doctoral courses in sciences and engineering; 200 teachers; 500 students; library: 20,000 vols; Dir-Gen. EMILIO CARLOS ACOCELLA.

Instituto Nacional de Telecomunicações (INATEL): Av. João de Camargo 510, 37540-000 Santa Rita do Sapucaí, MG; tel. (35) 3471-9200; fax (35) 3471-9314; e-mail inatel@ inatel.br; internet telecom.inatel.br; f. 1965; electrical engineering (electronics and telecommunications); library: 13,000 vols; Dir Prof. PEDRO SERGIO MONTI.

Instituto Tecnológico de Aeronáutica: Praça Mal. do Ar Eduardo Gomes 50, Vila das Acácias, 12228-900 São José dos Campos, SP; tel. (12) 3947-5731; fax (12) 3941-3500; e-mail reitor@ita.br; internet www.ita.br; f. 1950; divs of aeronautical engineering, civil and basic engineering, computer engineering, electronic engineering, echanical engineering,; 130 teachers; 800 students; library: 98,841 vols and reports, 135,000 microforms, 2,182 periodicals, 5,000 electronic publs; Rector Prof. MICHAL GARTENKRAUT; Dean Prof. FERNANDO TOSHINORI SAKANE; Admin. Officer Cel. DINO ISHIKURA; publ. *Produção Técnico Científica*.

Instituto Tecnológico e Científico 'Roberto Rios' (INTEC): Av. Prof. Roberto Frade Monte 389, Bairro Aeroporto, 14783-226 Barretos, SP; tel. (17) 3321-6411; fax (17) 3322-6205; e-mail intec@feb.br; internet www.feb.br/intec; f. 1981; courses in administration and business, chemistry, civil engineering, dentistry, electricity and electrical engineering, English, environment, foreign trade, gastronomy, graphic design, health sciences, hotel management, industrial automation, informatics and computer engineering, logistics, networks and infrastructure, safety at work, Web design, welding; Dir Dr GERALDO NUNES CORRÊA.

Universidade Federal Rural da Amazônia: CP 917, 66077-530 Belém, PA; tel. (91) 274-4518; fax (91) 274-4518; e-mail biblioteca@ufra.edu.br; internet www.ufra .edu.br; f. 1951; agronomy, fisheries engineering, forestry and veterinary studies, zootechnics; library: 18,000 vols, 1,343 periodicals; 118 teachers; 1,900 students; Dir Dr MANOEL MALHEIROS TOURINHO; publs *Cartilhas Didáticas* (irregular), *Informe Didático* (irregular), *Informe Técnico* (irregular), *Livros Técnicos* (irregular), *O Trimestre*, *Revista de Ciências Agrárias* (2 a year).

Schools of Art and Music

Centro de Letras e Artes da UNIRIO: Av. Pasteur 436, Urca, 22290-240 Rio de Janeiro, RJ; tel. (21) 2295-2548; fax (21) 2295-1043; internet www.unirio.br/cla; f. 1969; 4-year course in theatre and music, Masters course in theatre and Brazilian music; 96 teachers; 850 students; library: 25,000 vols, 7,000 scores, 3,000 records; Dean EDIR EVANGELISTA GANDRA; Dirs AUSONIA BERNARDES MON-

TEIRO, NEREIDA DE ASSIS NOGUEIA DE MOURA RANGEL.

Conservatório Brasileiro de Música: Av. Graça Aranha 57, 12° andar, Castelo, 20030-002 Rio de Janeiro; tel. (21) 3478-7600; fax (21) 240-6131; e-mail cbm@cbm-musica.org .br; internet www.cbm-musica.org.br; f. 1936; undergraduate and postgraduate courses; library: 6,000 vols; Gen. Dir CECILIA CONDE; publ. *Revista Pesquisa e Música*.

Conservatório Dramático e Musical de São Paulo: Av. Conselheiro Crispiniano 378, 01037-000 São Paulo; tel. (11) 3337-2111; fax (11) 223-9231; e-mail cdmsp@cdmsp.edu.br; f. 1906; library: 30,000 vols; Dir JÚLIO DA CRUZ NAVEGA NETO (acting).

Escola de Artes Visuais (School of Visual Arts): Rua Jardim Botânico 414, Parque Lage, 22461-000 Rio de Janeiro, RJ; tel. (21) 2538-1879; fax (21) 2538-1879; e-mail eav@ eavparquelage.org.br; internet www .eavparquelage.org.br; f. 1975; linked administratively to the State Dept of Culture; courses in art theory and history, computer art, drawing, painting, photography, sculpture, video cassettes; library: 5,500 vols; 40 teachers; 1,200 students; Dir REYNALDO ROELS, Jr.

Escola de Música da Universidade Federal do Rio de Janeiro: Rua do Passeio 98, Lapa, 20021-290 Rio de Janeiro, RJ; tel. (21) 240-1391; fax (21) 240-1591; f. 1848; 77 teachers; 478 students; library: 100,000 vols of music; museum of 90 antique instruments; Dir Prof. JOSÉ ALVES; Librarian DOLORES BRANDÃO DE OLIVEIRA; publ. *Revista Brasileira de Música* (irregular).

Attached to the School:

Centro de Pesquisas Folclóricas: Rio de Janeiro; f. 1943; collns of traditional music on records; Dir Prof. SAMUEL MELLO ARAÚJO, Jr.

Escola de Música e Belas Artes do Paraná: Rua Emiliano Perneta 179, 80010-050 Curitiba, PR; tel. (41) 3026-0029; fax (41) 3017-2070; e-mail secretaria@embap.pr.gov .br; internet www.embap.pr.gov.br; f. 1948; library: 2,350 vols, also tapes, records; musical instruments, plastic arts, singing; Dir ANNA MARIA LACOMBE FEIJÓ.

Faculdade de Belas Artes de São Paulo: Rua Edmundo Juventino Fuentes 160 (apt 12), Edif. Torino, 03280-000 São Paulo, SP; tel. (11) 6946-1255; fax (11) 6946-1255; f. 1925; architecture, town planning, industrial arts and design, painting, sculpture, etc.; 130 teachers; library: 10,000 vols; Dir PAULO ANTONIO GOMES CARDIM.

Faculdade Santa Marcelina—(FASM): Rua Dr Emílio Ribas 89, Perdizes, 05006-020 São Paulo, SP; tel. (11) 3824-5800; fax (11) 3824-5818; e-mail fasm@fasm.edu.br; internet www.fasm.edu.br; f. 1929; art education, composition, electric-acoustic music, fashion design, international relations, marketing administration, music, musical instruments, nursing, singing, visual arts,; 169 teachers; 1,700 students; library: 50,000 vols; Pres. FILOMENA MARIA PEDONE; Dir ÂNGELA RIVERO.

Fundação Armando Alvares Penteado: Rua Alagoas 903, Higienópolis, 01242-902 São Paulo; tel. (11) 3662-7000; internet www .faap.br; f. 1947; undergraduate, graduate and extension courses; 1,120 teachers; 12,000 students; Pres. CELITA PROCOPIO DE CARVALHO; Exec. Dir Dr ANTONIO BIAS BUENO GUILLON.

BRUNEI

The Higher Education System

The Universiti Brunei Darussalam (founded in 1985) is the principal institution of higher education. A second university, the Universiti Islam Sultan Sharif Ali, was founded in 2007 to offer Islamic education. In the same year the status of the Seri Begawan Training College for Teachers of Islamic Religion was upgraded when it became the Seri Begawan University College for Teachers of Islamic Religion. Malay is the official language of instruction, but courses are also taught in English and Arabic (especially Islamic education). The Ministry of Education is responsible for higher education.

Students with adequate 'A' Level passes are eligible for entry to the Universiti Brunei Darussalam or other tertiary institutions or to be awarded scholarships to study abroad. The Institut Teknologi Brunei provides courses leading to a Higher National certificate (part-time) or a National Diploma (full-time). Bachelors degrees at the Universiti Brunei Darussalam last for four to six years and programmes operate on a US-style 'credit' system, with a minimum number required for graduation. In 2005 there were 4,242 students enrolled in higher education institutions.

Regulatory and Representative Bodies

GOVERNMENT

Ministry of Culture, Youth and Sports: Simpang 336-17, Jalan Kebangsaan, Bandar Seri Begawan BA 1210; tel. 2380667; fax 2380235; e-mail info@kkbs.gov.bn; internet www.kkbs.gov.bn; Min. Pehin Dato' Haji MOHAMMAD BIN DAUD.

Ministry of Education: Old Airport Rd, Jalan Berakas, Bandar Seri Begawan BB 3510; tel. 2382233; fax 2380050; e-mail feedback@moe.edu.bn; internet www.moe .gov.bn; Min. Pehin Dato' Haji ABDUL RAHMAN TAIB.

ACCREDITATION

National Accreditation Council: 2nd Floor, Block B, Ministry of Education, Old Airport Rd , Berakas BB 3510; tel. (2) 381133 ext 2209; fax (2) 381238; e-mail mkpk@moe .edu.bn; internet www.moe.gov.bn/ departments/accreditation; f. 1990; ensures and maintains the quality and standard of educational credentials; considers and evaluates the status and quality of qualifications awarded by local and overseas instns; Sec. OTHMAN BIN HAJI SIMBRAN.

Learned Societies

LANGUAGE AND LITERATURE

Alliance Française: No 29, Simpang 130-15, Jalan Telanai, Bandar Seri Begawan BA2312; tel. (2) 654245; fax (2) 652214; e-mail alliancefr@brunet.bn; internet www .afbrunei.com; offers courses and exams in French language and culture and promotes cultural exchange with France.

British Council: 2nd Fl., Block D, Yayasan Complex, Sultan Haji Hassanal Bolkiah Jalan Pretty, Bandar Seri Begawan BS 8711; tel. (2) 237742; fax (2) 237392; e-mail all.enquiries@bn.britishcouncil.org; internet www.britishcouncil.org/brunei; offers courses and exams in English language and British culture and promotes cultural exchange with the UK; Dir AMANDA GRIFFITHS.

Research Institutes

AGRICULTURE, FISHERIES AND VETERINARY SCIENCE

Brunei Agricultural Research Centre, Department of Agriculture: Dept of Agriculture, Ministry of Industry and Primary Resources, Jalan Tutong, Kilanas BF 2520; tel. (2) 661894; fax (2) 661354; e-mail barc001@brunet.bn; internet www.brunet .bn/gov/doa/barc.htm; f. 1984, present name since 1995; 100 mems; Head of Div. Pengiran Hajah ROSIDAH BINTI PENGIRAN HAJI METUSSIN.

HISTORY, GEOGRAPHY AND ARCHAEOLOGY

Brunei History Centre: Ministry of Culture, Youth and Sports, BS 8610 Bandar Seri Begawan; tel. (2) 240166; fax (2) 241958; e-mail sejarah@brunet.bn; internet www .history-centre.gov.bn; f. 1982; govt dept under the Ministry of Culture, Youth and Sports; research on Brunei's history and genealogies, and history of Brunei's Sultan, royal families, and state dignitaries; Dir Haji MOHAMED JAMIL AL-SUFRI; publs Pusaka (Heritage, 2 a year), Darussalam (The Abode of the Peace, 1 a year).

Library

Bandar Seri Begawan

Language and Literature Bureau Library: Jalan Elizabeth II, Bandar Seri Begawan; tel. (2) 235501; f. 1961; reference and lending facilities open to the public; 300,000 vols in Malay and English; one central and 4 full-time brs; 5 mobile units; Chief Librarian Haji ABU BAKAR BIN HAJI ZAINAL; publs Accessions List, indexes.

Museums and Art Galleries

Bandar Seri Begawan

Brunei Museum: Jalan Kota Batu, Bandar Seri Begawan BD 1510; tel. (2) 244545; fax (2) 242727; e-mail bmdir@brunet.bn; internet www.museums.gov.bn; f. 1965; ethnographical, historical, archaeological displays; natural history, oriental arts and cultural heritage collns; library of 77,813 vols, Borneo colln of 2,492 vols, 63,927 local publs; legal depository for Brunei; Dir Haji MATASSIM BIN HAJI JIBAH; publs Berita Muzium (4 a year), Brunei Darussalam National Bibliography (1 a year), Brunei Museum Journal (1 a year).

Constitutional History Gallery: Jalan Sultan, Bandar Seri Begawan BD 1510; tel. (2) 238360; fax (2) 242727; f. 1984; Dir Pengiran Haji HASHIM BIN PENGIRAN HAJI MOHAMED JADID.

Malay Technology Museum:; tel. (2) 242861; fax (2) 242727; e-mail bmethno@ brunet.bn; internet www.museums.gov.bn; f. 1988; exhibitions of traditional industries and handicrafts, Malay traditional technologies, research on Brunei indigenous ethnic groups; Curator of Ethnography PUDARNO BIN BINCHIN; Musuem Officer JAHRANI BTE HAJI ABAS; Musuem Officer SHARIANA BTE HAJI NAIM; publ. The Brunei Museum Journal.

Royal Regalia Building: Jalan Sultan, Bandar Seri Begawan BS 8610; tel. (2) 238360; fax (2) 242727; internet www .museums.gov.bn/bangunan2.htm; f. 1992; Dir Haji MATASSIM BIN HAJI JIBAH.

Universities

UNIVERSITI BRUNEI DARUSSALAM

Jalan Tungku Link, Gadong BE 1410

Telephone: (2) 463001

Fax: (2) 463015

Internet: www.ubd.edu.bn

Founded 1985, the Sultan Hassanal Bolkiah Teachers' College was integrated into the Univ. in 1988; the Institute of Islamic Studies was integrated into the Univ. in 1999, the School of Nursing was integrated into the Univ. in 2008

State control

Languages of instruction: Malay, English

Academic year: August to December, January to May (2 semesters)

Chancellor: HM Sultan Haji HASSANAL BOLKIAH MU'IZZADDIN WADDAULAH

Pro-Chancellor: HRH Crown Prince Pengiran MUDA HAJI AL-MUHTADEE BILLAH

Vice-Chancellor: Dr Haji ZULKARNAIN HANAFI

Registrar and Sec.: Dr Haji SITI ZULIANA ABD SAMAD

Chief Librarian: HAJI AWG SUHAIMI BIN HAJI ABDUL KARIM

Library of 341,533 vols

Number of teachers: 619

Number of students: 3,649

Publications: *Jare* (1 a year), *Tinjauan* (1 a year), *Ungkayah* (4 a year)

DEANS

Faculty of Arts and Social Science: Dr MOHD GARY JONES
Faculty of Business, Economics and Policy Studies: Dr ROGER LAWREY
Faculty of Science: Dr JIMMY LIM CHEE MING
Academy of Brunei Studies: Dr SITI NOR-KHALBI
Communication and Technology Centre: Dr YONG CHEE TUAN
Educational Technology Centre: Dr HANAPI BIN MOHAMAD
Institute of Medicine: Dr ANITA BINURUL ZAHRINA AZIZ
Language Centre: Dr YABIT ALAS
Postgraduate Studies and Research: Assoc. Prof. Dr TAN KHA SHENG
Sultan Hassanal Bolkiah Institute of Education: Dr HAJAH ROMAIZAH
Sultan Haji Omar Ali Saifuddien Institute of Islamic Studies: Dr NUROL HUDA

UNIVERSITI ISLAM SULTAN SHARIF ALI (UNISAA)

Jalan Tungku, Gadong BE 1410
Telephone: (2) 463001 ext 1435
Fax: (2) 463065
Internet: www.unissa.edu.bn

Founded 2007
State control

Rector: Pengiran Dato' Seri Setia Dr Haji MOHAMMAD BIN PENGIRAN HAJI ABD RAHMAN
Permanent Academic Advisor: Prof. Dato' Dr MUNIR YAACOB
Registrar: Haji TARIP BIN HAJI MAT YASSIN
Bursar: Haji SULAIMAN BIN LATIP
Dean of Student Affairs: Pengiran Haji SAIFUL BAHRIN BIN PENGIRAN HAJI KULA

DEANS

Faculty of Arabic Language and Islamic Civilization: Prof. Madya Dr ARIF KARKHI ABUKHUDAIRI
Faculty of Business and Management Science: (vacant)
Faculty of Shariah and Law: Dr AYMAN ABDEL RAOUF SALEH
Faculty of Usuluddin: Dr SABER AHMAD TAHA

Colleges

There are Adult Education Centres attached to colleges and schools.

Institut Teknologi Brunei: Tungku Link, Gadong, Bandar Seri Begawan 1410; tel. (2) 461020; fax (2) 461035; internet www.itb.edu.bn; f. 1986; B/TEC HND and BEng courses; library: 35,000 vols; 83 teachers; 483 students; Dir Haji MOHAMED YUSRA BIN HAJI ABDUL HALIM; Registrar Haji MOHAMMAD BIN HAJI HIDUP; Librarian Hajah PUSPARAINI BINTI HAJI THANI.

Jefri Bolkiah College of Engineering: POB 63, Kuala Belait 6000; internet www.brunet.bn/php/chongrms/jbcehome.htm; f. 1970; craft, technical, mathematics and English courses; 78 teachers; 350 students; Principal MICHAEL LIM (acting).

Seri Begawan Religious Teachers' College: Bandar Seri Begawan.

Sultan Saiful Rijal Technical College: POB 914, Simpang 125, Jalan Muara; tel. (2) 331077; fax (2) 343207; e-mail mtssr@brunet.bn; internet www.mtssr.edu.bn; f. 1985; eng. and business courses; 195 teachers; 1,000 students; Dir Pengiran SUHAIMI BIN PENGIRAN HAJI BAKAR (acting).

BULGARIA

The Higher Education System

Higher education is supported by the State through the aegis of the Ministry of Education, Youth and Science. During the mid-1990s the higher education system was extensively reorganized, with a degree system introduced and many foundations renamed. Higher education is governed by the Higher Education Act (amended 1999, 2001 and 2004) and the Academic Degrees and Titles Act (amended 1999). In 2007/08 there were 26,169 students enrolled in colleges and in 2009 there were 246,523 enrolled in 43 universities and equivalent institutions. In mid-1999 tuition fees for university students were introduced.

Admission to higher education is on the basis of the Diploma of Completed Secondary Education and successful entrance examinations. Institutions are allowed to set their own criteria for admission. Under the 2001 and 2004 amendments to the Higher Education Act, Bulgaria has implemented the Bologna Process. The principal undergraduate degree is the Bachelors, which requires four years of study culminating in defence of a thesis. There is also a range of Diploma and Diploma Specialist programmes. The Masters degree requires five years of study (or one more year after the Bachelors) ending with either state examinations or defence of a thesis. Finally, there are three types of Doctorate, each requiring at least three years of study following the Masters: Doctors, Doctor of Sciences, and Doctor Honoris Causa.

Vocational and technical training is mostly implemented at the secondary-school level. The National Evaluation and Accreditation Agency is responsible for evaluating and accrediting institutions of higher education.

Regulatory and Representative Bodies

GOVERNMENT

Ministry of Culture: 'Al. Stamboliiski' Blvd 17, 1040 Sofia; tel. (2) 94-00-900; fax (2) 981-81-45; e-mail press@mc.government.bg; internet www.mc.government.bg; Min. VEZHDI LETIF RASHIDOV.

Ministry of Education, Youth and Science: St Prince Dondukov 2A, 1000 Sofia; tel. (2) 921-77-44; fax (2) 988-26-93; e-mail press_mon@minedu.government.bg; internet www.minedu.government.bg; Min. SERGEY IGNATOV.

ACCREDITATION

ENIC/NARIC Bulgaria: National Centre for Information and Documentation (NACID), 52 A G. M. Dimitrov Blvd, 1125 Sofia; tel. (2) 817-38-55; fax (2) 971-31-20; e-mail naric@nacid.bg; internet www.enic-naric.net/index.aspx?c=bulgaria; Exec. Dir Dr VANYA GRASHKINA.

National Evaluation and Accreditation Agency: 125 Tsarigradsko shose Blvd, Bldg 5, 4th Fl., N Wing, 1113 Sofia; tel. (2) 807-78-11; fax (2) 971-20-68; e-mail info@neaa.government.bg; internet www.neaa.government.bg; statutory body for evaluation, accreditation and monitoring of quality in higher education instns and scientific orgs; 11 mems: 1 chair., 6 reps from higher education instns, 1 from the Bulgarian Acad. of Sciences, 1 from the Nat. Centre of Agricultural Science, 2 reps from the Min. of Education, Youth and Science; Chair. Prof. Dr IVAN PANAYOTOV; Deputy Chair. Prof. DANAIL LAZAROV DANAILOV; Chief Exec. Assoc. Prof. PATRICIA GEORGIEVA.

NATIONAL BODY

Bulgarian Rectors' Conference: Agricultural Univ., 12 Mendeleev Blvd, 4000 Plovdiv; tel. (32) 65-42-00; fax (32) 63-31-57; e-mail rector@au-plovdiv.bg; internet www.au-plovdiv.bg; Rector Prof. Dr DIMITAR GREKOV; Pres. Prof. Dr YORDANKA KUZMANOVA.

Learned Societies

GENERAL

Bulgarian Academy of Sciences: 1040 Sofia; tel. (2) 979-53-33; fax (2) 981-72-62; e-mail presidentbas@cu.bas.bg; internet www.bas.bg; f. 1869 as Bulgarian Learned Society, present name 1911; attached research institutes: see Research Institutes; 224 mems (62 academicians, 89 corresp., 73 foreign); library of 1,956,465 vols; see Libraries and Archives; Pres. STEFAN VODENICHAROV; Vice-Pres. Acad. ANGEL GALABOV; Vice-Pres. Sr Dr NIKOLAI MILOSHEV; Sec. Assoc. Dr RAYA KUNCHEVA; Gen. Scientific Sec. Prof. STEFAN HADJITODOROV; publs *Balgaristika/Bulgarica* (2 a year), *Comptes rendus de l'Académie Bulgare des Sciences* (12 a year), *Spisanie na Balgarskata Akademija na Naukite* (Journal of the Bulgarian Academy of Sciences), various spec. publs on science and the arts.

Bulgarian Comparative Education Society: Faculty of Primary and Preschool Education, Blvd Shipchenski prohod 69A, 1574 Sofia; tel. (2) 97-06-240; fax (2) 872-23-21; e-mail npopov@fnpp.uni-sofia.bg; internet bces.home.tripod.com; f. 1991; promotes historical, methodological and practical aspects of comparative education; organizes and supports research; cooperates with scholars, research orgs, instns, societies in Bulgaria and abroad; Pres. Dr Hab. NIKOLAY POPOV.

National Centre of Health Informatics: Acad. Iv. Geshov Blvd 15, 1431 Sofia; tel. (2) 951-53-02; fax (2) 951-52-38; e-mail office@nchi.government.bg; internet www.nchi.government.bg; specialized authority of the Min. of Healthcare; provides necessary information on healthcare; Dir Assoc. Prof. Dr CHRISTIAN GRIVA; Deputy Dir Eng. PETER AMUDJEV; Deputy Dir KRASSIMIRA DIKOVA; publs *Zdraveopazvane*, *Public Health Statistics* (1 a year).

Union of Publishers in Bulgaria: Alabin St 58, 1000 Sofia; tel. (2) 921-42-04; fax (2) 921-42-31; e-mail office@sib.bg; internet www.sib.bg; f. 2000; non-governmental assn that defends the freedom of the press, the independence of journalists and encourages their work so that society is objectively informed; 22 mems; Chair. TOSHO TOSHEV; Exec. Dir DESSISLAVA BINEVA.

Union of Scientists in Bulgaria: 39 Madrid Blvd., 2nd Fl., 1505 Sofia; tel. (2) 944-11-57; fax (2) 944-15-90; e-mail science@usb-bg.org; internet www.usb-bg.org; f. 1944; works in the area of science and research, education, innovations, environment, health care, information, informatics and information technologies, int. cooperation, social assistance, tourism and recreation; 4,000 mems; Pres. Prof. DAMYAN DAMYANOV; Vice-Pres. Prof. ANGEL POPOV; publs *Nauka* (6 a year), *Science* (6 a year).

AGRICULTURE, FISHERIES AND VETERINARY SCIENCE

Scientific and Technical Union of Specialists in Agriculture: G. Rakovski 108, 1000 Sofia; tel. (2) 987-65-13; fax (2) 987-93-60; f. 1965; Pres. Prof. V. VALOV; Sec. DIMITAR RADULOV; publ. *Buletin Vnedreni Novosti*.

Soil Resources Agency: Shose Bankia 7, 1331 Sofia; tel. (2) 824-87-98; fax (2) 824-02-39; e-mail soilsurv@mail.netplus.bg; internet www.soils-bg.org; f. 1959; analytical research of soil; verifies the quality of agricultural land, and applies finding in legal cases; assesses deterioration risks posed by erosion, contamination, salinity, acidity/alkalinity and bogginess; cartographic information and reports; creation and maintenance of the State Digital Map of Soil and Agricultural Land Grades and Soil Resource Geographical Information System, both overseen by the Min. of Agriculture and Forestry; Exec. Dir DAMIAN MIHALEV; Gen. - Sec. TSENKA CHERNOGOROVA.

ARCHITECTURE AND TOWN PLANNING

Union of Architects in Bulgaria: Krakra St 11, 1504 Sofia; tel. (2) 943-83-21; fax (2) 943-83-49; e-mail sab@bularch.org; internet www.bularch.org; f. 1965; non-profit assocn; protects professional interests of its mems; develops and extends its professional cooperation with the Chamber of the Architects in Bulgaria and other related Bulgarian, foreign and int. orgs in the area of architecture; creates, distributes and protects cultural values; organizes cultural and educational activities; synchronizes architectural activities with int. professional practice; public discussions, qualification and re-qualification of the mems in area of architecture; devt of architectural education; documentation and protection of monuments; library of 6,000 vols; 2,200 mems; Pres. Arch. GEORGI BAKALOV; Vice-Pres. Arch. ILKO NIKOLOV; Chair. SPIRIDON GANEV; publs *Architecture* (6 a year), *Bulgarian Architect* (information bulletin, 26 a year).

ECONOMICS, LAW AND POLITICS

Bulgarian Association of Criminology: Vitosha 2, 1000 Sofia; tel. (2) 987-47-51; fax (2) 986-22-70; f. 1986; Pres. Assoc. Prof. Y. BOYADZHIEVA.

Bulgarian Association of International Law: H. C. Belite Brezi, Bldg 6, ap. 31, 1680 Sofia; tel. (2) 859-68-26; fax (2) 869-19-79; e-mail m.ganev@mail.bg; f. 1962; 60 mems; Pres. Prof. ALEXANDER YANKOV; Vice-Pres. Prof. EMIL KONSTANTINOV; Sec.-Gen. Prof. MARGARIT GANEV; publ. *Trudove po Mezhdunarodno Pravo* (every 3 years).

Union of Economists: G. Rakovski 108, 1000 Sofia; tel. (2) 987-18-47; fax (2) 984-43-215; f. 1968; Pres. Assoc. Prof. S. ALEXANDROV; Sec. I. POPOV; publ. *Bjuletin*.

FINE AND PERFORMING ARTS

Union of Bulgarian Actors: 12 Narodno Sabranie Sq., 1000 Sofia; tel. (2) 987-07-25; fax (2) 988-11-78; e-mail office@uba.bg; internet www.uba.bg; f. 1921 as Union of Bulgarian Artists; artistic trade union org. that represents the interests of its members in front of their employers and state authorities; library of 6,000 vols; 600 mems; Chair. HRISTO MUTAFCHIEV; Assist Sec. VELISLAVA SMILIANOVA; publ. *Teatar*.

Union of Bulgarian Artists: Shipka St 6, 1504 Sofia; tel. (2) 944-37-11; fax (2) 946-02-12; e-mail info@sbhart.com; internet www .sbhart.com; f. 1893 as Society for Supporting the Arts in Bulgaria, present name 1953; protects the interests of its members and promotes Bulgarian visual culture nationally and internationally; 2,700 mems; library of 9,000 vols; Chair. Prof. IVAYLO MIRCHEV; Vice-Chair. BOYKO MITKOV; publs *Dekorativno Izkustvo*, *Promishlena Estetika* (Information Bulletin, in Bulgarian only).

Union of Bulgarian Composers: ul. Ivan Vazov, 1000 Sofia; tel. (2) 988-15-60; fax (2) 987-43-78; e-mail mail@ubc-bg.com; internet www.ubc-bg.com; f. 1933 as Contemporary Music Society, present name 1954; encourages composers to use traditional music and recreate it in artistic forms; promotes closer relationships among composers; creates better work conditions for composers; assists financially challenged composers; preserves the memory of composers of merit; 230 mems; library of 25,280 books, scores and recordings; Pres. VELISLAV ZAIMOV; Vice-Pres. STEFAN ILIEV.

Union of Bulgarian Film Makers: Dondukov Blvd 67, 1504 Sofia; tel. and fax (2) 946-10-69; e-mail sbfd@sbfd-bg.com; internet www.filmmakersbg.org; f. 1934; creative professional org; promotes devt of film and audio-visual arts in Bulgaria; 907 mems; Pres. IVAN PAVLOV; Admin. Sec. RENI ZLATANOVA; publ. *KINO* (6 a year).

HISTORY, GEOGRAPHY AND ARCHAEOLOGY

Bulgarian Geographical Society: Tsar Osvoboditel 15, 1000 Sofia; tel. (2) 985-82-61; fax (2) 944-64-87; f. 1918; Pres. Prof. P. V. PETROV; Sec. L. TSANKOVA; publs *Geoecologija, Geografija, Geografijata Dnes*.

Union of Numismatic Societies: Veliko Tarnovo; tel. (62) 2-37-72; f. 1964; 9,000 mems; Pres. G. HARALAMPIEV; Sec. H. HARITONOV; publ. *Revue Numismatica* (4 a year).

LANGUAGE AND LITERATURE

Alliance Française: Dragan Tsankov St 34A, BP 1015, 4000 Plovdiv; tel. (3) 263-13-42; fax (3) 263-48-07; e-mail afbg@afbg.org; internet www.afbg.org; f. 1904; offers courses and exams in French language and culture and promotes cultural exchange with France; attached offices in Blagoevgrad, Burgas, Kazanlak, Pleven, Stara Zagora, Varna and Veliko Tarnovo; library of 17,000 vols, 40 periodicals, 950 videocassettes, 600 audios, 350 CDs, 105 CD-ROMs; Dir TÉOPHANA BRADINSKA-ANGELOVA; publ. *Alliances* (2 a year).

Balkanmedia Association: Luibotran 96, 1407 Sofia,; tel. (2) 980-70-85; fax (2) 87-16-98; e-mail balkanmedia@internet-bg.net; f. 1990; ind. non-profit org. for mass media and communication culture in the Balkan countries; 36 assoc. mems (from all Balkan countries); Pres. ROSEN MILEV; publ. *Balkanmedia*.

British Council: Krakra St 7, 1504 Sofia; tel. (2) 942-43-44; fax (2) 942-42-22; e-mail bc .sofia@britishcouncil.bg; internet www .britishcouncil.org/bulgaria; f. 1991; offers courses and exams in English language and British culture; promotes cultural exchange with the UK; teaching centre; library of 20,000 vols, 80 periodicals; Dir IAN STEWART.

Bulgarian Philologists' Society: Moskovska 13, 1000 Sofia; tel. (2) 986-25-61; e-mail vessie@biscom.net; f. 1977; Pres. Prof. S. HADZHIKOSEV; Editor-in-Chief Prof. Dr BOIAN VALTCHEV; publ. *Ezik i literatura* (4 a year).

Goethe-Institut: Budapesta St 1, POB 1384, 1000 Sofia; tel. (92) 939-01-00; fax (92) 939-01-99; e-mail info@sofia.goethe.org; internet www.goethe.de/sofia; f. 1989; offers courses and exams in German language and culture; promotes cultural exchange with Germany; library of 10,000 vols; Dir Dr RUDOLF BARTSCH; Sec. OLYA MATEEVA.

Society of Aesthetes and Art and Literary Critics: Krakra 21, 1000 Sofia; f. 1970; Pres. (vacant); Sec. (vacant).

Union of Bulgarian Journalists: ul. Graf Ignatiev 4, 1000 Sofia; tel. (2) 987-28-08; fax (2) 988-30-47; f. 1944; 5,500 mems; Pres. MILEN VALKOV.

Union of Bulgarian Writers: Pl. Slavejkova 2A, 1000 Sofia; tel. (2) 88-00-31; fax (2) 88-06-85; f. 1913; 495 mems; Pres. N. HAITOV; publs *Bulgarian Writer, Plamak, Slavejche*.

Union of Translators in Bulgaria: Slavic 29, 5th Fl., 1000 Sofia; tel. (2) 986-45-00; fax (2) 981-09-60; e-mail office@bgtranslators .org; internet www.bgtranslators.org; f. 1974; non-profit org.; represents and defends the professional and creative rights of its mems; raises the quality of translation; Bureau translation translates about 46 languages; Chair. MARIA PETKOVA; Sec. IVO PANOV; publ. *Panorama*.

MEDICINE

Bulgarian Society of Neurosciences: Zdrave 2, 1431 Sofia; tel. (2) 51-86-23; fax (2) 51-87-83; f. 1987; Pres. Prof. V. OVCHAROV.

Bulgarian Society for Parasitology: Tzar Osvoboditel Blvd 1, 1000 Sofia; tel. (2) 979-23-13; fax (2) 71-01-07; e-mail ieppcom@bas .bg; internet bsparasitology.org; f. 1965 as Soc. of Parasitologists in Bulgaria, present name 1999; conducts research on parasitological aspects of biology, human and veterinary medicine, agriculture and forestry; organizes annual meetings, lectures; Pres. OLGA POLYAKOVA-KRUSTEVA; Sec. IVAN TODEV; Treas. Dr ISKRA RAYNOVA.

Bulgarian Society of Sports Medicine and Kinesitherapy: Dept of Sports Medicine, National Sports Academy, Studentski grad, 1700 Sofia; tel. (2) 962-04-58; e-mail bsssmk@abv.bg; f. 1953; 200 mems; Pres. Assoc. Prof. IVAN MAZNEV; Vice-Pres. Dr VALENTIN MATEV; Sec. Dr MARIELA SIRAKOVA; publ. *Sport i Nauka* (12 a year).

Union of the Bulgarian Medical Societies: Nat. Centre of Public Health Protection, 12th Fl., room 19, 15, Akad. Ivan Geshov Blvd, 1431 Sofia; tel. (2) 954-11-56; fax (2) 80-56-410; e-mail snmd@rtb-mu.com; internet www.medunion-bg.org; f. 1968; promotes research and contributes to maintaining high professional qualities among medical professionals by developing a modern system for continuous medical training; 12,000 mems, 64 mem. socs; Pres. Assoc. Prof TODOR POPOV; Vice-Pres. Prof. RADKA ARGIROVA; Sec-Gen. Prof. SEVDALIN NACHEV; Sec. Prof. RADOSLAV GYRCHEV; publ. *Modern Medicine* (4 a year).

NATURAL SCIENCES

Biological Sciences

Bulgarian Botanical Society: c/o Institute of Botany, Acad. G. Bonchev St., Blvd 23, 1113 Sofia; tel. (2) 871-82-59; fax (2) 71-90-32; e-mail botinst@bio.bas.bg; internet www .bio.bas.bg; f. 1923; Pres. (vacant); Sec. M. ANCHEV.

Bulgarian Society of Natural History: D. Zankov 8, 1164 Sofia; tel. (2) 66-65-94; f. 1896; 1,000 mems; Pres. Prof. D. VODENICHAROV; Sec. S. DIMITROVA; publ. *Priroda i Znanie* (10 a year).

Mathematical Sciences

Union of Bulgarian Mathematicians: Acad. G. Bonchev Blvd 8, 1113 Sofia; tel. (2) 873-80-76; fax (2) 872-11-89; e-mail smb .sofia@gmail.com; internet www.math.bas .bg/smb; f. 1898; 2,000 mems; Pres. Prof. Dr ST. DODUNEKOV; Sec. Dr S. GROZDEV; publ. *Mathematics and Education in Mathematics* (1 a year).

Physical Sciences

Bulgarian Geological Society: Akad. G. Bonchev Str., Bldg 24, 1113 Sofia; tel. (2) 97-93-472; fax 87-246-38; e-mail radnac@ geology.bas.bg; internet www.bgd.bg; f. 1925; contributes to the geological studies and protection of the geological heritage of Bulgaria; promotes the activities of its mems and of nat. geology; cooperates with similar nat. and foreign orgs; enhances geological education and professional growth of geologists; protects the professional interests of geoscientists of different generations; supports and helps the competent govt institutions on problems related to the progress of Bulgarian geology; serves as a social corrective of state policy in the field of geology; organizes seminars, confs and geological field trips; 320 mems; library: more than 21,000 books and journals; Pres. Dr RADOSLAV NAKOV; Vice-Pres. Assoc. Prof. Dr EUGENIA TARASOVA; Sec. Assoc. Prof. Dr DARIA IVANOVA; Treas. Dr MOMCHIL DYULGEROV; publ. *Review of the Bulgarian Geological Society* (3 a year).

Union of Physicists in Bulgaria: 5 James Bourchier Blvd, 1164 Sofia; tel. (2) 62-76-60; fax (2) 962-52-76; e-mail upb@phys.uni-sofia .bg; internet www.phys.uni-sofia.bg/~upb/ main.html; f. 1971 as Bulgarian Physical Society, present name and status 1989; Pres. Prof. Dr MATEY DRAGOMIROV MATEEV; Exec. Sec. PENKA GANCHEVA LAZAROVA; publ. *Bulgarian Journal of Physics*.

PHILOSOPHY AND PSYCHOLOGY

Bulgarian Pedagogical Society: Shipchenski prohod 69A, 1547 Sofia,; tel. (2) 72-08-93; f. 1975; Pres. Prof. G. BIZHKOV.

Bulgarian Philosophical Association: Tzar Osvoboditel Blvd 15, Sofia Univ., 1504 Sofia; tel. and fax (88) 838-30-73; e-mail ivan_kaltchev@yahoo.com; f. 1968; 320 mems; Pres. Prof. IVAN KALCHEV; Sec. R. KRIKORIAN; publs *Filosofia* (Philosophy, 12 a year), *Filosofski Alternativi* (Philosophical Alternatives, 12 a year), *Filosofski Forum* (Philosophical Forum, 4 a year), *Filosofski Vestnik* (Philosophical News, 4 a year).

Society of Bulgarian Psychologists: Liulin Planina 14, POB 1333, 1606 Sofia; tel. (2) 54-12-95; f. 1969; provides consultation and assistance to its members, institutions and citizens of the country on the ethical issues of the activities of the psychologists; develops and applies corrective and disciplinary procedures for investigating and reaching decisions in cases of complaints against its members; Pres. Prof. D. GRADEV; Sec. ZH. BALEV; publ. *Balgarsko Spisanie po Psikhologija.*

RELIGION, SOCIOLOGY AND ANTHROPOLOGY

Bulgarian Sociological Association: Institute of Sociology, Bulgarian Acad. of Sciences, 13A Moskovska St., 1000 Sofia; tel. (2) 980-98-92; fax (2) 52-24-07; e-mail bsa@sociology.bas.bg; internet www.bsa-bg.org; f. 1959 as Sociological Assn, present name 1969; professional non-profit org.; carries out theoretical and empirical research, teaching and publishing activities in the field of sociology in Bulgaria; conducts congresses, confs. and seminars; Pres. PEPKA BOYADZHIEVA; Sec. DIANA NENKOVA; publ. *Sociological Problems* (4 a year).

TECHNOLOGY

Bulgarian Astronautical Society: Moskovska St 6, POB 799, 1000 Sofia; tel. (2) 979-33-50; e-mail bas@space.bas.bg; f. 1957; astronautics and aeronautics; 300 mems; library of 3,000 vols; Pres. Prof. P. GETSOV; Scientific Sec. Prof. E. ALEXANDROVA.

Federation of the Scientific-Technical Unions in Bulgaria: 108 G. S. Rakovsky St, POB 431, 1000 Sofia; tel. (2) 987-72-30; fax (2) 987-93-60; e-mail info@fnts-bg.org; internet www.fnts-bg.org; f. 1893 as Bulgarian Engineering-Architectural Asscn, present name 1992; non-profit asscn; organizes congresses, confs, symposia, seminars and workshops; participates in the drafting of laws and other normative documents related to science and technology; carries out qualification activity through its Centre for Professional Education and Qualification; 10,000 mems; Pres. Acad. V. SGUREV; publ. *Nauka i Obshestvo* (Scientific newspaper); publ. *Technosphera* (Scientific journal).

Scientific and Technical Union of Civil Engineering: G. Rakovski 108, 1000 Sofia; tel. (2) 988-53-03; fax (2) 987-93-60; f. 1965; Pres. Dr E. MILCHEV; Sec. M. RUSEVA; publs *Stroitel 2000, Stroitelstvo.*

Scientific and Technical Union of Forestry: G. Rakovski 108, 1000 Sofia; tel. (2) 88-36-83; fax (2) 987-93-60; e-mail ntsl@mail.bg; f. 1965; Pres. V. BREZIN; Sec. S. SAVOV; publs *Celuloza i Hartija, Darvoobrabotvashta i mebelna Promislenost.*

Scientific and Technical Union of Mining, Geology and Metallurgy: G. Rakovski 108, 1000 Sofia; tel. (2) 87-57-27; fax (2) 986-13-79; e-mail nts-mdgm@speedbg.net; f. 1965; Pres. Prof. V. STOYANOV; Sec. V. GENEVSKI; publs *Metalurgija, Rudodobiv.*

Scientific and Technical Union of Power Engineers: G. Rakovski 108, 5th Fl., Office 505, 1000 Sofia; tel. (2) 88-41-58; fax (2) 87-93-60; e-mail energy@fnts-bg.org; internet www.ntse-bg.org; f. 1965; carries out vocational training activities and supports the devt of creative ideas and initiatives of its members; participates in the devt and discussion of laws, regulations, rules, instructions and other regulations on energy, environment, protecting people from harmful effects and the protection of tangible property against damage and destruction resulting from the use of energy; conducts scientific and technical events; Pres. Prof. S. BATOV; Sec. Eng. D. TOMOV; publ. *Energetika.*

Scientific and Technical Union of Textiles, Clothing and Leather: G. Rakovski 108, 1000 Sofia; tel. (2) 88-16-41; fax (2) 987-93-60; f. 1965; Pres. Prof. E. KANTCHEV; Sec. I. MECHEV; publs *Kozhi i Obuvki, Tektil i obleklo.*

Scientific and Technical Union of the Food Industry: G. Rakovski 108, 1000 Sofia; tel. (2) 87-47-44; fax (2) 987-93-60; e-mail hvp_magazine@go.com; f. 1965; Pres. A. PETROV; Sec. TODOROV; publ. *Hranitelna promishlenost.*

Scientific and Technical Union of Transport: G. Rakovski 108, 1000 Sofia,; tel. (2) 958-10-36; fax (2) 87-93-60; f. 1965; participates in policy making in the field of transport research and technological devt; Pres. K. ERMENKOV; Sec. ST. GAIDAROV; publs *Patishta, Zelezopaten Transport.*

Scientific and Technical Union of Water Affairs in Bulgaria: G. Rakovski 108, 1000 Sofia; tel. (2) 988-53-03; fax (2) 987-93-60; f. 1965; Pres. Prof. A. MALINOV; Sec. MARGARITA SJAROVA; publ. *Vodno delo.*

Scientific-Technical Union of Mechanical Engineering: 108 Rakovsky, 1000 Sofia; tel. (2) 987-72-90; fax (2) 986-22-40; e-mail nts-bg@mech-ing.com; internet www.mech-ing.com; f. 1965; supports the industrial devt of Bulgaria; protects and represents the professional, intellectual and social interests of its members; 900 mems; Pres. Prof. GEORGI POPOV; Gen. Sec. DAMIAN DAMIANOV; publ. *International Virtual Journal—Machinery, Technology, Materials* (12 a year).

Union of Chemists in Bulgaria: G. Rakovski 108, 1000 Sofia; tel. and fax (2) 987-58-12; e-mail chem@fnts-bg.org; internet www.unionchem.org; f. 1901; non-profit org.; scientific and technical work; nat. and int. scientific confs. and symposia; Pres. Prof. VENKO NIKOLAEV BESHKOV; Sec. Eng. NAYDEN HRISTOV NAYDENOV; publ. *Bulgarian Chemistry and Industry* (4 a year).

Union of Electronics, Electrical Engineering and Telecommunications: G. Rakovski 108, 1000 Sofia; tel. (2) 987-97-67; fax (2) 987-93-60; e-mail ceec@mail.bg; internet ceec.fnts-bg.org; f. 1965; non-profit org.; scientific and technical events; confs, symposia, seminars, roundtables, discussions; devt of draft laws, regulations, programmes; training activities; int. cooperation; 1,300 mems; Chair. Prof. Dr IVAN STOYANOV YATCHEV; Deputy-Pres. Assoc. Prof. TODOROV SEFERIN MIRCHEV; Exec. Dir Prof. Dr IVAN VASILEV NIKOLOV; publ. *Elektrotechnica i Elektronica* (12 a year).

Union of Surveyors and Land Managers: G. 108 Rakovski, POB 431, 1000 Sofia; tel. (2) 987-58-52; fax (2) 987-93-60; e-mail geodesy_union@fnts-bg.org; internet geodesy.fnts-bg.org; f. 1922; protects interests of the surveying profession; organises int. and nat. symposia, confs, seminars, nat. and regional meetings and publishes proceedings and materials of such events; 200 mems; Pres.

Prof. Dr Ing. G. MILEV; Sec. ST. BOGDANOV; publ. *Geodesija, Kartografija, Zemeustrojstvo* (6 a year).

Research Institutes
AGRICULTURE, FISHERIES AND VETERINARY SCIENCE

Agricultural Institute: Blvd Simeon Veliki 3, 9700 Shumen; tel. (54) 83-04-48; fax (54) 83-04-55; e-mail agr_inst@abv.bg; internet www.zemedelskiinstitut-shumen.com; f. 2000, merger of Institute of Buffalo, Institute of Pig Breeding and the Institute of Sugar Beet; research activity in stockbreeding; library of 10,900 vols; Dir TSONKA PEEVA; publs *Bulgarian Journal of Agricultural Science, Genetica i selectija* (4 a year), *Zhivotnovadni Nauki* (8 a year).

Barley Research Institute: 8400 Karnobat; tel. 27-31; fax (559) 58-47; f. 1925; library of 17,000 vols; Dir Assoc. Prof. I. MIHOV.

Canning Research Institute: V. Aprilov 154, 4000 Plovdiv; tel. (32) 95-13-52; fax (32) 95-22-86; e-mail office@canri.org; internet www.canri.org; f. 1962, present status 1974; develops and transfers new technologies and products in canning industry; library of 19,000 vols; Assoc. Dr Dr PAVLINA GEORGIEVA PARASKOVA; Vice-Assoc. Dir Dr GEORGE LEONIDOV BEKYAROV.

Central Medical Veterinary Research Institute: P. Slaveykov 15, 1606 Sofia; tel. (2) 952-12-77; fax (2) 952-53-06; e-mail director@iterra.net; f. 1901; Dir Prof. Dr S. P. MARTINOV.

Cotton and Durum Wheat Research Institute: 55 G. Dimitrov St, 6200 Chirpan; tel. and fax (416) 31-33; e-mail iptp@abv.bg; internet www.iptp-chirpan.org; f. 1925, now part of the Nat. Centre of Agricultural Sciences at the Min. of Agriculture and Food Supply; breeding of high yielding and high-quality cotton and durum wheat cultivars; devt of cotton and durum wheat cultivation technologies and elements of technologies for main field crops cultivation under irrigation and in dry conditions; laboratory and field experiments with various crops, machinery, fertilizers, pesticides, growth regulators and defoliants; study of technological parameters of cotton fibre and durum wheat grain; information provision; laboratory analysis of soil and plant samples; seed-production of cotton and durum wheat; 124 mems; library of 16,000 vols; Dir Assoc. Dr NELI VALKOVA; Scientific Sec. Assoc. Dr GALIA DIMITROVA PANAYOTOVA.

Dairy Research Institute: 3700 Vidin; tel. 2-32-04; fax 3-46-32; f. 1959; library of 8,000 vols; Dir A. KOZHEV; publs *Advanced Experience* (2 a year), *Dairy Abstracts Bulletin* (12 a year).

Fisheries Industry Institute: Industrialna 3, 8000 Burgas; tel. (56) 84-05-22; fax (56) 4-03-31; f. 1965; Dir Dr ZH. NECHEV.

Forest Research Institute: 132, St. Kliment Ohridski Blvd, 1756 Sofia; tel. (2) 962-04-42; fax (2) 962-04-47; e-mail forestin@bas.bg; internet www.fribas.org; f. 1928; attached to Bulgarian Acad. of Sciences; library of 39,000 vols; Dir Prof. ALEXANDER HARALANOV ALEXANDROV; Deputy-Dir Prof. HRISTO IVANOV TSAKOV; Scientific Sec. Prof. BOYAN NIKOLOV ROSSNEV; publs *Nauka za gorata* (Forest Science, 4 a year), *Silva Balcanica* (2 a year).

Freshwater Fisheries Research Institute: V. Levski 248, 4003 Plovdiv; tel. (32) 55-60-33; fax (32) 55-39-24; f. 1978; Dir G. GROZEV.

Fruit-Growing Research Institute: 12 Ostromila, 4004 Plovdiv; tel. (32) 69-23-49; fax (32) 67-08-08; e-mail instov@infotel.bg; internet fruitgrowinginstitute.com; f. 1950, present name 1952; attached to Agricultural Acad. at the Min. of Agriculture and Food Supply; research, incl. breeding, genetic resources and biotechnology, fruit growing technologies; extension activities; service in the field of fruit growing; Dir Prof. ARGIR ZHIVONDOV; Deputy - Dir ZARYA RANKOVA; Scientific Sec. PETYA GERCHEVA.

Institute for Plant Genetic Resources 'K.Malkov': 4122 Sadovo (Plovdiv District); tel. and fax (32) 62-90-26; f. 1902 as an agricultural experimental station; attached to Nat. Centre for Agrarian Research at Min. of Agriculture and Food Supply; plant genetic resources programme; offers free germplasm exchange, registration and free storage of plant accessions; library of 30,000 vols; Dir Prof. LILIA KRASTEVA.

Institute for the Control of Foot and Mouth Disease and Dangerous Infections: Trakia 75, 8800 Sliven; tel. (44) 2-20-39; fax (44) 2-26-42; f. 1974; Dir R. KASABOV.

Institute of Agricultural Economics: Tsarigradsko Shosse 125, Unit 1, 1113 Sofia; tel. (2) 971-00-14; fax (2) 971-00-13; e-mail office@iae-bg.com; internet www.iae-bg.com; f. 1935; research and devt in economics, org., sociology, ecology and management of agriculture and food–beverage industry; library of 10,850 vols, 5,560 periodicals; Dir RUMEN GROZDANOV POPOV; Deputy Dir QNKA PETRAKIEVA DIMITROVA-SLAVOVA.

Institute of Agriculture: Sofjisko shose St, 2500 Kyustendil; tel. (78) 52-26-12; fax (78) 52-40-36; e-mail iz_kn@av.bg; internet iz-kyustendil.org; f. 1929; attached to Agricultural Acad. of Min. of Agriculture and Food Supply; research instn for investigation of theoretical and practical problems in agriculture; introduction of Bulgarian and foreign achievements in the area; assistance to the growers; library of 9,000 vols; Dir Prof. Dr DIMITAR DOMOZETOV; Deputy Dir Assoc. Dr ILIYANA RADOMIRSKA; Scientific Sec. Assoc. Prof. Dr VENERA TASEVA.

Institute of Animal Science: 2232 Kostinbrod; tel. and fax (721) 68943; e-mail inst_anim_sci@abv.bg; internet www.iasbg .hit.bg; f. 1950 as part of Bulgarian Agricultural Acad.; attached to Nat. Centre of Agricultural Sciences (Min. of Agriculture and Food Supply); basic and applied research in genetics, animal and bee breeding and selection, reproduction, nutritive physiology and biochemistry, feeding technology of farm animals, ecology and quality of animal production; library of 25,200 vols; Dir Assoc. Prof. Dr LAZAR KOZELOV; Deputy-Dir of science and Scientific Sec. Assoc. Prof. Dr MAIA IGNATOVA.

Institute of Cattle and Sheep Breeding: 6000 Stara Zagora; tel. (42) 4-10-76; fax (42) 4-71-48; f. 1942; Dir Prof. GEKO GEKOV.

Institute of Fisheries and Aquaculture: Primorski 4, Blvd 4, POB 72 9000 Varna; tel. (52) 23-18-52; fax (52) 25-78-76; f. 1932; attached to Nat. Center of Agricultural Sciences (Min. for Agriculture and Food Supply); library of 24,000 vols; Dir Dr P. KOLAROV; publ. Proceedings (1 a year).

Institute of Forage Crops-Pleven: Gen.-Vladimir Vazov 89 St, 5800 Pleven; tel. (64) 80-58-82; fax (64) 80-58-81; e-mail ifc@elsoft .com; internet www.ifc-pleven.org; f. 1954; attached to Agricultural Acad.; nat. centre for complex scientific and applied researches and devt activities, advises and trains in the field of breeding of forage production, crop technology and animal nutrition; Dir Assoc.

Prof. Dr TODOR SIMEONOV KERTIKOV; Scientific Sec. Dr ANELIYA ILIEVA KATOVA.

Institute of Grains and Feed Industry: Kostinbrod 2, 2232 Sofia 2; tel. (721) 20-84; fax (721) 20-84; f. 1965; library of 9,050 vols, 16 periodicals; Dir M. MACHEV.

Institute of Soil Science 'Nikola Poushkarov': Shousse Bankya 7, 1080 Sofia; tel. (2) 824-61-41; fax (2) 824-89-37; e-mail soil@mail.bg; internet www.iss-poushkarov.org; f. 1947; attached to Agricultural Acad.; research, conservation and restoration of soil resources; management of agriculture and ecosystems; Dir Prof. Dr METODI TEOHAROV; Deputy Dir for Scientific Activities Assoc. Prof. BOZIDAR GEORGIEV; Deputy Dir for Consultancy, Contract and Innovation Activities Assoc. Prof. Dr VICTOR KRUMOV; Scientific Sec. Prof. Dr DIMITRANKA STOICHEVA; publs Journal of Balkan Ecology (in English, 4 a year), Soil Science, Agrochemistry and Ecology (in Bulgarian with English abstract, 6 a year).

Institute of Soya Bean Growing: POB 8, 5200 Pavlikeni; tel. (610) 22-75; fax (610) 25-41; f. 1925; Dir Dr G. GEORGIEV.

Institute of Viticulture and Oenology: Kala tepe 1, 5800 Pleven; tel. (64) 2-21-61; fax (64) 2-64-70; f. 1902 as State Control Station in Viticulture and Oenology, present name 1944; Dir Prof. P. ABRASHEVA.

Institute of Water Problems: Acad. G. Bonchev St, Bl.1 1113 Sofia; tel. (2) 72-25-72; fax (2) 72-25-77; e-mail santur@iwp.bas.bg; internet www.iwp.bas.bg; f. 1963; attached to Bulgarian Acad. of Sciences; carries out theoretical and applied investigations and develops methods, models, software, technologies and installations concerning water resource use and protection; 73 mems; Dir Prof. Eng. OHANES SANTOURDJIAN; Scientific Sec. Assoc. Prof. Dr. Eng. IGOR NIAGOLOV; publ. Vodni Problemi (Water Problems, 1 a year).

Institute of Wheat and Sunflower 'Dobroudja': General Toshevo, 9520 Dobrich Dist.; tel. (58) 2-74-54; fax (58) 2-63-64; f. 1940; library of 32,000 vols; Dir Prof. Dr PETER IVANOV.

Maize Research Institute: 3230 Knezha; tel. (9132) 22-11; fax (9132) 27-11; f. 1924; Dir Assoc. Prof. K. ANGELOV.

Maritsa Vegetable Crops Research Institute: Brezovsko shose St 32, 4000 Plovdiv; tel. (32) 95-12-27; fax (32) 96-01-77; e-mail balkanvegetables@gmail.com; f. 1930; attached to Bulgarian Agricultural Acad.; library of 20,500 vols; research emphasizes-vegetable quality by improving biological value and sensory characteristics, pest and disease resistance, high temperature and drought tolerance; Dir Assoc. Prof. Dr MASHEVA STOYKA PETKOVA.

National Wine and Spirituous Beverages Research Institute: Tsar Boris 3rd 134, 1618 Sofia,; tel. (2) 818-49-50; fax (2) 855-40-09; e-mail office@wineinbg.org; internet www.wineinbg.org; f. 1952; research incl. chemistry and microbiology of wine and spirituous beverages production; Exec. Dir CHRISTO BOEVSKY.

'Obraztsov Chiflik' Institute of Agriculture and Seed Science: 7007 Ruse; tel. (82) 22-57-34; fax (82) 22-58-98; e-mail izsruse@elits.rousse.bg; f. 1905; Dir Dr. GENKA PATENOVA.

Plant Protection Institute: 35 Panayot Volov St, 2230 Kostinbrod, POB 238; tel. (721) 660-61; fax (721) 660-62; e-mail protection@infotel.bg; internet www.ppi-bg .org; f. 1936, present location 1961; depts of biological and integrated pest control, entomology and radiobiology, prognosis, toxicol-

ogy, phytopatology and plant immunity, herbology; library of 15,343 vols (incl. 6,744 books, 2,573 periodicals, 6,026 magazines); Dir Assoc. Prof. Dr OLIA EVTIMOVA KARADJOVA; Deputy Dir Assoc. Prof. Dr GANKA STANCHEVA BAEVA; Scientific Sec. Assoc. Prof. Dr HRISTINA TODOROVA KRUSTEVA.

Regional Veterinary Institute: Nezavisimost III, 4000 Plovdiv; tel. (32) 26-08-68; fax (32) 22-33-67; f. 1936; library of 10,000 vols; Dir D. ARNAUDOV.

Regional Veterinary Institute: Slavjanska 5, 5000 Veliko Tarnovo,; tel. 2-16-69; fax 2-16-69; f. 1932; library of 11,840 vols; Dir Assoc. Prof. V. RADOSLAVOV.

Regional Veterinary Research Institute and Centre: Slavyanska 58, 6000 Stara Zagora; tel. (42) 2-67-32; fax (42) 2-31-15; f. 1931; Dir Assoc. Prof. N. NIKOLOV.

Research Institute for Irrigation, Drainage and Hydraulic Engineering: Tsar Boris III 136, 1618 Sofia; tel. (2) 56-30-01; fax (2) 55-41-58; e-mail riidhe@bgcict.acad .bg; f. 1953; library of 18,000 vols; Dir Asst Prof. Dr PLAMEN PETKOV; publ. Proceedings (every 3 years).

Research Institute for Land Reclamation and Agricultural Mechanization: St Bansko shosse 3, IMM, 1331 Sofia; tel. (2) 825-71-70; fax (2) 824-78-42; e-mail imm_2001@mail.bg; internet www .e-imm2001-ncan-bg.com; f. 1949; nat. centre for strategic and applied research, extension and training in the fields of irrigated agriculture and mechanization of crop husbandry and animal breeding.; 135 mems; library of 22,000 vols; Dir Assoc. Prof. Dr NIKOLAY MINKOV MARKOV; Deputy Dir Assoc. Prof. Dr NELI ILIEVA GADJALSKA; Scientific Sec. Assoc. Prof. Dr GEORGI DIMITROV KOSTADINOV; publ. Agricultural Engineering (scientific journal, 6 a year).

Research Institute for Roses, Aromatic and Medicinal Plants: Blvd Osvobojdenie 49, 6100 Kazanlak; tel. (431) 2-20-39; fax (431) 4-10-83; f. 1907; library of 3,600 vols; Dir Dr GEORGE CHAUSHEV.

Research Institute of Mountain Stockbreeding and Agriculture: V. Levski 281, 5600 Trojan; tel. (670) 6-28-02; fax (670) 5-30-32; e-mail rimsa@mail.bg; internet www .rimsa.eu; f. 1978; Dir Prof. Dr MARIN METODIEV TODOROV.

Scientific and Production Enterprise with Sugar Beet Research Institute 'Prof. Ivan Ivanov': Carev Brod, 9747 Shumen Dist.; tel. (54) 5-51-02; fax (54) 5-69-06; f. 1926; Dir Assoc. Prof. S. KRASTEV.

Scientific and Production Institute for Veterinary Preparations 'Vetbiopharm': 3000 Vraca; tel. 4-94-81; fax 4-75-30; f. 1942; library of 5,000 vols; Dir Dr T. NIKOLOV.

Tobacco and Tobacco Products Institute: 4108 Plovdiv; tel. (32) 67-23-64; fax 77-51-56; f. 1944; library of 40,000 vols; Dir Dr ELENA APOSTOLOVA; publ. Bulgarian Tobacco (6 a year).

Veterinary Institute of Immunology Ltd: Bakareno shose 1, 1360 Sofia; tel. (2) 26-31-70; fax (2) 26-24-85; f. 1942; Pres. Prof. Dr STEFANOV.

ARCHITECTURE AND TOWN PLANNING

Centre for Architectural Studies: 1, Akad. G. Bonchev St, 1113 Sofia; tel. and fax (2) 72-46-20; e-mail danizen@iwt.bas.bg; internet www.bas.bg/arch; f. 1949 as Institute for Urbanism and Architecture, present name 1995; attached to Bulgarian Acad. of Sciences; history of architecture and urban planning from ancient period to modern times, architectural stylistic influences, and comparative studies in the larger context of Balkan and European architecture, continuity in architectural traditions through the ages; new ideas in Europe and their impact on world architecture; preservation of architectural heritage and devt of cultural tourism; Dir Prof. Dr KONSTANTIN BOJADJIEV; Research Sec. Dr ANTON GOUGOV.

National Centre for Regional Development and Housing Policy: Alabin 14–16, 1000 Sofia; tel. (2) 980-03-08; fax (2) 980-03-12; f. 1960; library of 9,000 vols; Dir-Gen. Dr V. GARNIZOV; publ. *Series for the Municipalities* (6 a year).

ECONOMICS, LAW AND POLITICS

Institute for Legal Studies: St Serdika 4 1000 Sofia; tel. (2) 987-49-02; fax (2) 989-25-97; e-mail ipn_ban@bas.bg; internet www.ipn-bg.org; f. 1947; attached to Bulgarian Acad. of Sciences; research, activities and training in the field of law; library of 34,187 titles, 20,586 books and 13,601 periodicals; Dir Dr VESSELIN TZANKOV; Deputy Dir Dr VELINA TODOROVA; Scientific Sec. GERGANA MARINOVA (acting); publ. *Pravna Misal* (4 a year).

Institute of Economics: Aksakov St 3, 1040 Sofia; tel. (2) 810-40-10; fax (2) 988-21-08; e-mail ineco@iki.bas.bg; internet www.iki.bas.bg; f. 1949; attached to Bulgarian Acad. of Sciences; nat. research centre for theoretical and scientific-applied studies and training of scientific experts in economy; library of 40,000 vols; Dir Dr MITKO ATANASOV DIMITROV; Scientific Sec. ISKRA BOGDANOVA CHRISTOVA; publs *Ikonomicheska Misal* (6 a year), *Ikonomicheski Izsledvania* (4 a year), *Economic Thought* (1 a year), *Economic Studies* (4 a year).

Research Institute of Forensic Sciences and Criminology: POB 934, 1000 Sofia; tel. (2) 987-82-10; fax (2) 987-82-10; e-mail int.27@mvr.bg; f. 1968; forensic science and criminology studies; Dir Prof. K. BOBEV; publs *News Bulletin* (3 a year), *Scientific Proceedings* (1 a year).

EDUCATION

National Institute for Education – Centre For Higher Education Research: 125 Tsarigradsko shose, Blvd 5, 1113 Sofia; tel. 71-72-24; fax 70-20-62; f. 1996; non-profit org.; supports educational policy, strategy and priorities for change and enhancement of Bulgarian education in the perspective of the wider European integration; library of 100,000 vols; Head Dr. ROSITZA PENKOVA; publ. *Strategies for Policy in Science and Education*.

FINE AND PERFORMING ARTS

Institute of Art Studies: Krakra 21, 1000 Sofia; tel. (2) 944-24-14; fax (2) 943-30-92; e-mail office@artstudies.bg; internet musicart.imbm.bas.bg; f. 1947; attached to Bulgarian Acad. of Sciences; carries out studies on ancient, medieval and contemporary art and culture; focuses on collecting and preserving art documentation as well as the analysis of art phenomena, both professional and vernacular, associated with the Bulgarian legacy and its role in the construction of European culture; library of 45,000 vols; Dir Assoc. Prof. Dr ALEXANDER YANAKIEV; publs *Art Studies Quarterly* (4 a year), *Bulgarian Musicology* (4 a year).

HISTORY, GEOGRAPHY AND ARCHAEOLOGY

Archaeological Institute: Saborna 2, 1000 Sofia; tel. (2) 988-44-06; fax (2) 988-24-05; e-mail naim@naim.bg; internet www.naim.bg; f. 1921; research into prehistory, classical antiquity and the middle ages; attached to Bulgarian Acad. of Sciences; Dir Prof. VASIL NIKOLOV; publs *Archaeology* (4 a year), *Reports* (irregular).

Centre for Population Studies: Acad. G. Bonchev St, Bldg 6, 6th Fl., 1113 Sofia; tel. (2) 979-30-30; fax (2) 870-53-03; e-mail cps@cc.bas.bg; internet cps.bas.bg; f. 2002 fmrly Institute of Demography; attached to Bulgarian Acad. of Sciences; nat. unit for theoretical and applied demographic studies; research on is the population of Bulgaria; aim of identifying the laws and determinants of its evolution as well as population strategy and policy concerns within the context of European integration and the global devt trend; Dir Assoc. Prof. Dr GENOVEVA MIHOVA (acting); Scientific Sec. Dr KREMENA BORISSOVA-MARINOVA; publ. *Naselenie*.

Institute of Balkan Studies: 45 Moskovska St, 1000 Sofia; tel. and fax (2) 980-62-97; e-mail balkani@cl.bas.bg; internet www.cl.bas.bg/balkan-studies; f. 1964; attached to Bulgarian Acad. of Sciences; researches on the historical past and contemporary devt of the Balkan states, as well as on issues in the cultural, demographic and linguistic heritage of the Balkan nations; library of 27,000 vols; Dir Prof. Dr AGOP GARABED GARABEDYAN; Deputy Dir Prof. Dr LILIANA VIDENOVA SIMEONOVA; Scientific Sec. Prof. Dr ROUMIANA LACHEZAROVA STANTCHEVA; publ. *Études Balkaniques* (4 a year).

Institute of Geography: Acad. G. Bonchev St, Blvd 3, 1113 Sofia; tel. and fax (2) 870-02-04; e-mail geograph@bas.bg; f. 1950; attached to Bulgarian Acad. of Sciences; provides scientific services to the nat., regional, and municipal govts of Bulgaria in the fields of sustainable regional devt, nature protection, and raising the quality of geographic education; library of 17,000 vols; 43 mems, 30 scientists; Dir Dr MARIYANA NIKOLOVA; Deputy Dir Prof. Dr CHAVDAR MLADENOV; Sec. Assoc. Prof. ZOYA MATEEVA; publ. *Problems of Geography* (4 a year).

Institute of History: Shipchenski prokhod 52 Blvd, Block 17, 1113 Sofia; tel. (2) 870-85-13; fax (2) 870-21-91; e-mail ihistory@ihist.bas.bg; internet www.ihist.bas.bg; f. 1947; attached to Bulgarian Acad. of Sciences; works in the field of theoretical and specialized problems of Bulgarian nat., political, social, religious and cultural history from the establishment of the Bulgarian state to the present day, as well as on problems of world history and int. relations; 104 mems; library of 50,000 vols; Dir Acad. Prof. Dr GEORGI MARKOV; Deputy Dir Prof. Dr VALERY STOYANOW; Scientific Sec. Assoc. Prof. Dr IVAN TANCHEV; publs *Bulgarian Historical Review* (2 a year), *Istoritcheski Pregled* (3 a year).

Prof. Alexander Fol Centre of Thracian Studies: 13 Moskovska St, 1000 Sofia; tel. and fax (2) 988-15-59; e-mail thracologia@abv.bg; internet www.thracologia.org; f. 1972 as Institute of Thracology; attached to Bulgarian Acad. of Sciences; Thracian history, culture and language; library of 6,000 vols; Dir Prof. KIRIL YORDANOV; Scientific Sec. Prof. Dr IRINA SHOPOVA; publ. *Orpheus* (Journal of Indo-European and Thracian studies, 1 a year).

LANGUAGE AND LITERATURE

Cyrillo-Methodian Research Centre: POB 432, Moskovska St 13, 1000 Sofia; tel. (2) 987-02-61; fax (2) 986-69-62; e-mail kmnc@bas.bg; internet www.kmnc.bg; f. 1914 as Clement Commission, present name 1980; attached to Bulgarian Acad. of Sciences; comprehensive study and publishing of the translated and original works of Cyril and Methodius, the Slavonic, Greek and Latin sources on the Cyrillo-Methodian activities; Dir Assoc. Prof. Dr SVETLINA NIKOLOVA; Deputy Dir Assoc. Prof. Dr SLAVIA BARLIEVA; Scientific Sec. Assoc. Prof. Dr TATYANA MOSTROVA; publs *Kirilo-Metodievski studii* (Cyrillo-Methodian Studies, 1 a year), *Palaeobulgarica/Starobalgaristica* (4 a year).

Institute for Literature: 52, Blvd Shipchenski prohod, Bldg 17, 7th and 8th Fls, 1113 Sofia; tel. and fax (2) 971-70-56; e-mail director@ilit.bas.bg; internet www.ilit.bas.bg; f. 1948; attached to Bulgarian Acad. of Sciences; researches on Bulgarian literature from the Middle Ages to the present day, in its theoretical, historical, cultural and comparative aspects; library of 114,795 vols; Dir Assoc. Prof. Dr RAYA KUNTCHEVA; Deputy Dir Assoc. Prof. Dr VIHREN CHERNOKOZHEV; Scientific Sec. Assoc. Prof. Dr ELKA TRAYKOVA; publs *Literaturna misal* (literary thought, print and online, 2 a year), *Scripta & e-Scripta* (journal of interdisciplinary medieval studies, 1 a year), *Starobulgarska literatura* (old bulgarian literature).

Institute for the Bulgarian Language: 52 Shipchenski prohod, Blvd Block 17, 1113 Sofia; tel. and fax (2) 72-23-02; e-mail ibe@ibl.bas.bg; internet www.ibl.bas.bg; f. 1942, present name 2004; fundamental and applied research on diverse aspects of Bulgarian language; attached to Bulgarian Acad. of Sciences; Dir Dr VASSIL RAINOV; Deputy Dir Dr ELKA MIRCHEVA; Deputy Dir Dr SVETLA KOEV; Scientific Sec. Dr PETYA KOSTADINOVA; publs *Bulgarian Language*, *Linguistique Balkanique*.

MEDICINE

Centre of Physiotherapy and Rehabilitation: Ovcha Kupel 2B, 1618 Sofia; tel. 56-28-24; fax 55-30-23; f. 1949; Dir Assoc. Prof. P. NIKOLOVA; publ. *Journal*.

Institute of Obstetrics and Gynaecology: Zdrave 2, 1431 Sofia; tel. (2) 51-72-200; fax (2) 51-70-92; f. 1976; library of 2,000 vols; 110 mems; Exec. Dir Assoc. Prof. V. ZLATKOV; publs *Akusherstvo i Ginekologia* (Obstetrics and Gynaecology, 12 a year), *Problems of Obstetrics and Gynaecology* (1 a year).

MHATEM 'N.I. Pirogov': 21 Totleben Blvd, 1606 Sofia; tel. (2) 52-10-77; fax (2) 951-62-68; f. 1951 fmrly Institute 'N.I. Pirogov'; Chair. MATEY MATEEV; Dir DIMITAR RADENKOVSKI; Deputy Finance Dir ANGELO DRENOV; Deputy Admin. Dir LUDMIL DJUNKOV; Deputy - Medical Dir PLAMEN STEFANOV; publ. *Emergency Medicine* (magazine).

National Center of Infectious and Parasitic Diseases: 26 Yanko Sakazov Blvd, 1504 Sofia; tel. (2) 944-69-99; fax (2) 943-30-75; e-mail ncipd@ncipd.org; internet www.ncipd.org; f. 1972; courses in epidemiology, microbiology, virology, parasitology and immunology and allergology; training; Dir Prof. HRISTO TASKOV; Vice-Dir Prof. Dr MIRA KOJOUHAROVA; publs *Infektologiya*, *Problems of Infectious and Parasitic Diseases*.

National Centre of Haematology and Transfusiology: Darvenica, Plovdivsko Pole 6, 1756 Sofia; tel. and fax (2) 9701-235; e-mail tlissitchkov@yahoo.com; f. 1948; Dir Prof. Dr T. LISICHKOV; publ. *Clinical and Transfusional Haematology*.

National Centre of Public Health Protection: Akad. Ivan Ev. Geshov Blvd 15, 1431 Sofia; tel. (2) 805-62-61; fax (2) 954-11-14; e-mail ncphp@ncphp.government.bg; internet www.ncphp.government.bg; f. 2005 by merger of Nat. Centre of Hygiene, Medical Ecology and Nutrition and Nat. Centre of Public Health; 244 mems; research and devt, expert consultancy, methodological and training activities in the field of public health protection; assessment of health risks from occupational and environmental factors, personal behaviour and lifestyle, health promotion and integral diseases prevention, analytical and control services; base org. and coordinator for nat. and int. programmes and projects on public health protection; base for postgraduate and continuation training; library of 32,000 vols; Dir Assoc. Prof. STEFKA PETROVA; publ. *Bulgarian Journal of Public Health* (4 a year).

National Centre of Radiobiology and Radiation Protection: Sv. G. Sofijski, Blvd 3, House 7, 1606 Sofia; tel. (2) 862-60-36; fax (2) 862-10-59; e-mail ncrrp@ncrrp.org; internet www.ncrrp.org; f. 1963; research, education and training, monitoring and control on occupationally exposed persons and radiological equipment, methodology, diagnostics and prophylaxis of radiation injury, emergency at nuclear accident sites; Dir Prof. Dr RADOSTINA GEORGIEVA (acting).

National Drug Institute: Blvd Yanko Sakazov 26, 1504 Sofia; tel. (2) 943-40-46; fax (2) 943-44-87; e-mail ndi@bg400.bg; f. 1949; registration, analysis and control of drugs; Dir Dr BORISLAV BORISOV.

National Heart Hospital: Konoviza Str. 65, 1309 Sofia; tel. (2) 822-33-49; fax (2) 921-15-61; e-mail cardiosurgery@abv.bg; f. 1972; Dir Dr L. BOYADZHIEV.

National Oncological Centre: Plovdivsko Pole 6, 1756 Sofia; tel. (2) 72-06-54; fax (2) 72-06-51; f. 1952; library of 22,000 vols; Dir Prof. I. CHERNOZEMSKI; publ. *Oncology* (4 a year).

State Institute of Endocrinology and Gerontology: Dame Gruev 6, 1303 Sofia; tel. (2) 987-72-01; fax (2) 87-41-45; f. 1972; Dir Prof. B. LOZANOV.

University Clinical Centre of Gastroenterology – Sofia: UMBAL 'Tsaritsa Giovanna— ISUL', 8 St Bialo more, 1527 Sofia; tel. (2) 943-22-77; fax (2) 43-26-64; e-mail hirurgi@isul.eu; internet www.kcg.medfac-sofia.eu; f. 1959; Dir Prof. Dr DAMIAN DAMIANOV.

University Clinical Dialysis Centre—Sofia: 1st 'St Georgi Sofiiski' Blvd, 1431 Sofia; tel. (2) 923-04-63; fax (2) 923-06-91; e-mail firstkhd_org@yahoo.com; internet www.kcd.medfac-sofia.eu; f. 1967; attached to Clinic of Urology at the Chair of Surgery in the Medical Univ.—Sofia; researches on haemodialysis, peritoneal dialysis and related complications; Head Assoc. Prof. Dr DIANA HRISTOVA YONOVA-IVANCHEVA.

NATURAL SCIENCES

Biological Sciences

Acad. M. Popov Institute of Plant Physiology: Acad. G. Bonchev St, Bldg 21, 1113 Sofia; tel. (2) 979-26-06; fax (2) 873-99-52; e-mail karanov@obzor.bio21.bas.bg; internet www.bio21.bas.bg/ipp; f. 1948 as Institute of Biology, present name 1964; attached to Bulgarian Acad. of Sciences; depts of experimental algology, mineral nutrition and water relations, photosynthesis, plant stress molecular biology, regulation of plant growth and devt; Dir Prof. Dr LOZANKA POPOVA-STAEVSKA; Vice-Dir Prof. Dr KLIMENTINA DEMIREVSKA; Vice-Dir Assoc. Prof. Dr SNEZHANA DONCHEVA; Scientific Sec. Assoc. Prof. Dr LILIANA MASLENKOVA; publ. *General and Applied Plant Physiology*.

Central Laboratory of General Ecology: 2 Yurii Gagarin St, 1113 Sofia; tel. (2) 873-61-37; fax (2) 870-54-98; e-mail ecolab@ecolab.bas.bg; internet www.ecolab.bas.bg; f. 1996, fmrly Institute of Ecology; attached to Bulgarian Acad. of Sciences; conducts basic

research for a better understanding of biodiversity and ecosystem functioning and applied research for understanding the mechanisms and drivers of change in biodiversity, assessing and minimising the negative impacts of human activities on ecosystems, and ensuring integrated environmental management in relation to the conservation of natural resources; library of 8,500 vols; Dir Assoc. Prof. Dr VALKO BISSERKOV; Scientific Sec. Dr GERGANA VASILEVA.

Centre for Biomedical Engineering: Bldg 105 Acad G. Bonchev St, 1113 Sofia; tel. (2) 870-03-26; fax (2) 872-37-87; e-mail clbme@clbme.bas.bg; internet www.clbme.bas.bg; f. 1994; attached to Bulgarian Acad. of Sciences; depts of analysis and processing of biomedical signals and data, analysis and modelling the excitability of biological structures, biomedical informatics, modelling and optimization of bioprocess systems, QSAR and molecular modelling; Dir Prof. Dr MIKHAIL MATVEEV; Deputy Dir Prof. Dr IVAYLO CHRISTOV; Scientific Sec. Assoc. Prof. Dr TANIA PENCHEVA; publ. *Bioautomation* (print and online).

Institute of Biophysics: Acad. G. Bonchev St, Bldg 21, 1113 Sofia; tel. (2) 971-22-64; fax (2) 971-24-93; e-mail biophys@obzor.bio21.bas.bg; internet www.bio21.bas.bg/ibf; f. 1967, present name and status 1994; attached to Bulgarian Acad. of Sciences; research in biophysics, biochemistry, cellular biology, motor control and muscle electrophysiology; Dir Prof. ANDON KOSSEV; Deputy Dir Prof. ALBENA MOMCHILOVA-PANKOVA; Deputy Dir Prof. IANA TSONEVA; Scientific Sec. Assoc. Prof. MAYA VELITCHKOVA; publ. *Journal of Geometry and Symmetry in Physics* (4 a year).

Institute of Botany: Acad. Georgi Bonchev St, Bldg 23, 1113 Sofia; tel. (2) 871-82-59; fax (2) 871-90-32; e-mail botinst@bio.bas.bg; internet www.bio.bas.bg/botany; f. 1947; attached to Bulgarian Acad. of Sciences; research in floristic, taxonomic and chemotaxonomic, phytocoenological and ecological, phytogeographical and resource-oriented, historical, anatomical and embryological, biotechnological fields; library of 24,974 vols, 1,5611 periodicals, 9363 books; 98 mems; Dir Prof. Dr DIMITAR PEEV; Deputy Dir Assoc. Prof. Dr DIMITAR IVANOV; Scientific Sec. Assoc. Prof. Dr ANNA GANEVA; publ. *Phytologia Balcanica* (3 a year).

Institute of Experimental Morphology and Anthropology with Museum: Acad. G. Bonchev bl. 25, 1113 Sofia; tel. (2) 979-23-40; fax (2) 871-90-07; e-mail iemabas@bas.bg; internet www.iema.bas.bg; f. 1953 as Institute of Morphology, present name 1995; attached to Bulgarian Acad. of Sciences; investigation of contemporary problems in the field of experimental morphology, cell biology and anthropology; 84 mems; Dir Prof. Dr YORDAN YORDANOV; Deputy Dir Prof. Dr NINA ATANASSOVA; Scientific Sec. Assoc. Prof. DIMITAR KADIYSKY; publs *Acta Morphologica et Anthropologica* (1 a year), *Journal of Anthropology* (1 a year).

Institute of Experimental Pathology and Parasitology: 25 Acad. G. Bonchev St, 1113 Sofia; tel. (2) 872-24-26; fax (2) 871-01-07; e-mail ieppcom@bas.bg; internet www.iepp.bas.bg; f. 1995 by merger of Institute of Gen. and Comparative Pathology (f. 1948) and Institute of Parasitology (f. 1954); attached to Bulgarian Acad. of Sciences; fundamental and applied research in the fields of pathology and parasitology important to human and veterinary medicine; Dir Prof. Dr ILIA BANKOV; Deputy - Dir Assoc. Prof. Dr YANA MIZINSKA-BOEVSKA; Scientific Sec. Assoc. Prof. Dr EVELINA SHIKOVA-

LEKOVA; publ. *Experimental Pathology and Parasitology* (4 a year).

Institute of Genetics 'Acad. Doncho Kostoff': Tsarigradsko Shose, 13 Km, 1113 Sofia; tel. (2) 974-62-28; fax (2) 978-55-16; e-mail genetika@bas.bg; internet ig.bas.bg; f. 1910 present name 1987; attached to Bulgarian Acad. of Sciences; promotes genetic science and devt; library of 27,069 vols; Dir Prof. Dr KOSTADIN GECHEFF; Deputy Dir Assoc. Prof. Dr LUBOMIR MANOLOV; Deputy Dir Assoc. Prof. Dr ZHIVKO DANAILOV; Scientific Sec. Assoc. Prof. Dr GANKA GANEVA; publ. *Genetics and Breeding* (2 a year).

Institute of Molecular Biology 'Roumen Tsanev': Acad. G. Bonchev St, Bldg 21, 1113 Sofia; tel. and fax (2) 872-80-50; internet www.bio21.bas.bg/imb; f. 1947 as a laboratory of cytology and cytochemistry at the Institute of Applied and Developmental Biology, present status 1960, present name 1979; attached to Bulgarian Acad. of Sciences; research and training in the field of molecular biology and biochemistry; 97 mems; library of 5,000 vols; Dir Prof. ILYA GEORGIEV PASHEV (acting); Deputy Dir Assoc. Prof. G. NACHEVA (acting); Scientific Sec. Assoc. Prof. K. GRANCHAROV (acting).

Institute of Physiology: Acad. G. Bonchev Bldg 23, 1113 Sofia,; tel. (2) 71-91-08; fax (2) 71-91-09; f. 1947; attached to Bulgarian Acad. of Sciences; Dir Prof. R. RADOMIROV.

Institute of the Biology and Immunology of the Reproduction – Acad. 'K. Bratanov': 73 Tsarigradsko Shose Blvd, 1113 Sofia; tel. (2) 971-13-95; fax (2) 872-00-22; e-mail ibir@abv.bg; internet ibir.bas.bg; f. 1938 as Institute for Artificial Insemination and Breeding Diseases, present name 1994; attached to Bulgarian Acad. of Sciences; fundamental and applied research in the field of animal and human reproductive biology and immunology; Dir Assoc. Prof. MARGARITA MOLLOVA; Deputy Dir Assoc. Prof. DIMITRINKA KACHEVA; Scientific Sec. Assoc. Prof. MARIA STAMENOVA.

Institute of Zoology: 1 Tsar Osvoboditel Blvd, 1000 Sofia; tel. (2) 988-51-15; fax (2) 988-28-97; e-mail zoology@zoology.bas.bg; internet www.zoology.bas.bg; f. 1947, by merger of Zoology and Entomology depts of fmr Royal Institutes of Natural Sciences; attached to Bulgarian Acad. of Sciences; depts of biology and ecology of terrestrial animals, experimental zoology, faunology and zoogeography, hydrobiology, protozoology, taxonomy; library of 15,000 vols, 27,000 periodicals and journals; Dir Prof. Dr PARASKEVA MICHAILOVA; Deputy Dir Assoc. Prof. Dr NASKO ATANASSOV; Scientific Sec. Assoc. Prof. Dr SNEJANA GROZEVA; publs *Acta Zoologica Bulgarica* (3 a year), *Catalogus Faunae Bulgaricae* (1 a year), *Fauna bulgarica* (1 a year).

Stephan Angeloff Institute of Microbiology: Acad. G. Bonchev St 26, 1113 Sofia; tel. 979-31-57; fax 870-01-09; e-mail micb@microbio.bas.bg; internet www.microbio.bas.bg; f. 1947 as Institute of Microbiology; attached to Bulgarian Acad. of Sciences; depts of extremophilic bacteria, immunology, microbial biochemistry, microbial genetics, microbial biosynthesis and biotechnology, microbial ecology, morphology of microorganisms and electron microscopy, mycology, pathogenic bacteria, virology; 121 mems; Dir Prof. Dr ANGEL S. GALABOV; Deputy Dir Assoc. Prof. Dr HRISTO NAJDENSKI; Deputy Dir Assoc. Prof. Dr LUBKA DOUMANOVA; Scientific Sec. Prof. Dr MARIA B. ANGELOVA.

Mathematical Sciences

Institute of Mathematics and Informatics: Acad. Georgi Bonchev St, Block 8, 1113

Sofia; tel. (2) 979-38-28; fax (2) 971-36-49; e-mail office@math.bas.bg; internet www .math.bas.bg; f. 1947; attached to Bulgarian Acad. of Sciences; researches and trainsspecialists and exercises long-range, consistent policy related to the fundamental trends in the devt of mathematics, computer science and information technologies; Dir Prof. STEFAN DODUNEKOV; Deputy Dir Assoc. Prof. RADOSLAV PAVLOV; Deputy Dir Prof. OLEG MUSKAROV; Scientific Sec. Assoc. Prof. ANDREY ANDREEV; publs Serdica Journal of Computing, Fractional Calculus and Applied Analysis, Mathematica Balkanica, Mathematica Plus, Physico-Mathematical Journal, Pliska, Serdica Mathematical Journal (4 a year).

Physical Sciences

Central Laboratory of Geodesy: Acad. G. Bonchev Bldg 1, 1113 Sofia; tel. and fax (2) 872-08-41; e-mail clgdimi@argo.bas.bg; internet clg.cc.bas.bg; f. 1948; attached to Bulgarian Acad. of Sciences; research in estimation theory and statistics, geodetic astronomy, global, regional and local geodynamics, space geodesy, physical and mathematical geodesy,; library of 10,000 vols; Dir Assoc. Prof. Dr DIMITAR DIMITROV; Deputy Dir and Scientific Sec. Assoc. Prof. Dr IVAN GEORGIEV; publ. Geodesy (2 a year).

Central Laboratory of Optical Storage and the Processing of Information: 101, Acad. G. Bonchev St, POB 95, 1113 Sofia; tel. (2) 871-00-18; fax (2) 871-91-65; e-mail clospi@optics.bas.bg; internet www.optics .bas.bg; f. 1975; attached to Bulgarian Acad. of Sciences; media and methods for optical and digital holographic recording, optical and digital processing of information clusters and images as well as devt of sensors and measurement equipment for optical metrology; Dir Prof. Dr VENTSESLAV SAINOV; Deputy Dir Assoc. GEORGI MINTCHEV; Deputy Dir KALOYAN ZDRAVKOV; Scientific Sec. Assoc. Prof. Dr ELENA STOYKOVA.

Central Laboratory of Photoprocesses 'Acad. Jordan Malinowski': Acad. G. Bonchev St, Bldg 109, 1113 Sofia; tel. and fax (2) 872-00-73; e-mail clf@clf.bas.bg; internet www.clf.bas.bg; f. 1967; attached to Bulgarian Acad. of Sciences; research the interaction of condensed matter with light and other irradiations, its application for the devt of new media for information recording, nanotechnologies, optoelectronics, infrared and integral optics, sensor technique; Dir Assoc. Prof. Dr NIKOLAY SPIRIDONONOV STARBOV; Deputy Dir for Research and Devt Assoc. Prof. BORISLAV MEDNIKAROV; Scientific Sec. Assoc. Prof. Dr VESSELINA NIKOLOVA PLATIKANOVA.

Central Laboratory of Solar Energy & New Energy Sources: 72 Tarigradsko Shose Blvd, 1784 Sofia; tel. (2) 877-84-48; fax (2) 875-40-16; e-mail solar@phys.bas.bg; internet www.senes.bas.bg; f. 1977; attached to Bulgarian Acad. of Sciences; specializes in the field of photovoltaics research; 44 mems; Dir Assoc. Prof. Dr PETKO VITANOV; Scientific Sec. Assoc. Prof. Dr MARUSHKA SENDOVA-VASSILEVA.

Geological Institute 'Strashimir Dimitrov': Acad. G. Bonchev St Bldg 24, 1113 Sofia; tel. (2) 872-35-63; fax (2) 872-46-38; e-mail geolinst@geology.bas.bg; internet www.geology.bas.bg; f. 1947; attached to Bulgarian Acad. of Sciences; basic and applied research studies of the geoenvironment of the Bulgarian territory aiming to support the sustainable devt of contemporary society and harmonic safe control of the issues associated with geohazards; library of 73,000 vols; Dir Assoc. Prof. Dr DONCHO KARASTANEV; Deputy Dir for Int. and Information Activities Assoc. Prof. Dr RADOSLAV NAKOV; Admin. Dir ROSIZA DIMITROVA; Scientific Sec. Prof. Dr KRISTALINA STOYKOVA; publs Geologica Balcanica (4 a year), Geochemistry, Mineralogy and Petrology (1 a year), Review of the Bulgarian Geological Society (3 a year).

Georgi Nadjakov Institute of Solid State Physics: 72, Tsarigradsko Shose Blvd, 1784 Sofia; tel. (2) 875-80-61; fax (2) 975-36-32; e-mail director@issp.bas.bg; internet www .issp.bas.bg; f. 1972, present name 1982; attached to Bulgarian Acad. of Sciences; fundamental and applied research in fields of laser physics, condensed matter physics, microelectronics, spectroscopy and optics; Dir Acad. Prof. Dr ALEXANDER G. PETROV; Deputy Dir Assoc. Prof. Dr STEFAN ANDREEV; Deputy Dir Assoc. Prof. Dr VASSIL ; Scientific Sec. Assoc. Prof. Dr MARINA PRIMATAROWA.

Institute of Catalysis: Acad. G. Bonchev St, Bldg 11, 1113 Sofia; tel. (2) 979-35-63; fax (2) 71-29-67; e-mail icatalys@ic.bas.bg; internet www.ic.bas.bg; f. 1983; attached to Bulgarian Acad. of Sciences; theory and practice of catalysis; elaboration of new catalysts; devt of new catalytic processes; investigation of the kinetics and mechanism of catalytic processes; creation of models of catalytic processes and elementary acts; research and devt of technologies for catalyst manufactures; coordination of the research activities in the field of catalysis in Bulgaria; 78 mems; Dir Prof. Dr SLAVCHO RAKOVSKY; Deputy Dir Prof. Dr SONIA DAMYANOVA; Scientific Sec. Assoc. Prof. Dr ALEXANDER ELIYAS; Deputy Scientific Sec. Assoc. Prof. Dr ELINA MANOVA; publs Proceedings of the International Symposium on Electron Paramagnetic Resonance, Proceedings of the International Symposium on Heterogeneous Catalysis.

Institute of Electrochemistry and Energy Systems: Acad. G. Bonchev St, Bldg 10, 1113 Sofia; tel. (2) 872-25-45; fax (2) 872-25-44; e-mail stoynov@bas.bg; internet www.bas.bg/cleps; f. 1967 as Central Laboratory of Electrochemical Power Sources; attached to Bulgarian Acad. of Sciences; depts of electrocatalysis and electrocrystallization, electrochemistry of biocatalytic and metal-air systems, electrochemistry of lead-acid batteries, electrochemical methods, electrochemical scientific instrumentation, lithium systems electrochemistry, nanoscaled materials, solid state electrolytes; Dir Prof. ZDRAVKO STOYNOV; Vice-Dir Dr ALEXANDER POPOV; Vice-Dir Assoc. Prof. Dr PROKOPI ANDREEV; Scientific Sec. Assoc. Prof. Dr ANASTASIA KAISHEVA; publs Bulgarian Chemical Communications, ICIS (online).

Institute of General and Inorganic Chemistry: Acad. Georgi Bonchev St, Bldg 11, 1113 Sofia; tel. (2) 872-48-01; fax (2) 870-50-24; e-mail info@svr.igic.bas.bg; internet www.bas.bg; f. 1960; attached to Bulgarian Acad. of Sciences; Dir Prof. KONSTANTIN HADJIIVANOV; Vice-Dir Prof. ELISAVETA IVANOVA; Vice-Dir Assoc. Prof. PLAMEN STEFANOV; Scientific Sec. Assoc. Prof. EKATERINA ZHECHEVA.

Institute of Geophysics 'Acad. L. Krastanov': Acad G. Bonchev St, Block 3, 1113 Sofia; tel. (2) 971-26-77; fax (2) 971-30-05; e-mail office@geophys.bas.bg; internet www .geophys.bas.bg; f. 1960; attached to Bulgarian Acad. of Sciences; researches physics of the solid Earth and the Earth's environment; activities incl. protection of the population and risk mitigation of unfavourable natural phenomena and disasters; facilitates sustainable devt and use of the natural and raw-material resourcesof Bulgaria; provides nat. authorities with expert geophysical information; 133 mems; Dir Dr NIKOLAY MILOSHEV; Deputy Dir Dr SV. NIKOLOVA; Deputy Dir Dr D. SOLAKOV; Scientific Sec. Dr DORA PANCHEVA; publ. Bulgarian Geophysical Journal (4 a year).

Institute of Mechanics: Acad. G. Bonchev St, Bldg 4, 1113 Sofia; tel. (2) 979-64-20; fax (2) 870-74-98; e-mail office@imbm.bas.bg; internet www.imbm.bas.bg; f. 1977, present name 1993; attached to Bulgarian Acad. of Sciences; theoretical and experimental research, consultation and experts' reports, metrology measurements, construction of scientific devices and education of highly qualified specialists in theoretical and applied mechanics, biomechanics and mechatronics; main fields of research incl. mechanics of multibody systems, solid mechanics, fluid mechanics and biomechanics; 135 mems, 100 scientists; library of 7,000 vols; Dir Dr EMIL SAMUIL MANOACH; Vice-Dir Dr NINA CHRISTOVA PESHEVA; Scientific Sec. SLAVTCHO GUERGUIEV SLAVTCHEV; publs Journal of Theoretical and Applied Mechanics (online), Series of Biomechanics.

Institute of Nuclear Research and Nuclear Energy: Tsarigradsko Shose Blvd 72, 1784 Sofia; tel. (2) 974-37-61; fax (2) 975-36-19; e-mail inrne@inrne.bas.bg; internet www.inrne.bas.bg; f. 1972; attached to Bulgarian Acad. of Sciences; scientific research and applications of nuclear science and technologies and studies of their interactions with the environment; Dir Prof. Dr JORDAN STAMENOV; Deputy Dir Assoc. Prof. Dr MITKO GAIDAROV; Deputy Dir Assoc. Prof. Dr PAVLIN PETKOV GRUDEV; Scientific Sec. Assoc. Prof. Dr ANNA ANDREEVA DAMIANOVA; publ. Proceedings of the International School on Nuclear Physics.

Institute of Oceanology 'Fridtjof Nansen': POB 152, 9000 Varna; located at: First May Street 40, 9000 Varna; tel. (52) 37-04-86; fax (52) 37-04-83; e-mail office@io-bas.bg; internet www.io-bas.bg; f. 1973 as Institute for Marine Research and Oceanology; attached to Bulgarian Acad. of Sciences; research in the field of biology, chemistry, coastal dynamics and underwater investigations, geology, ecology marine physics; consulting and expert services; training; library of 10,000 vols; 104 mems; Dir Dr ATANAS PALAZOV; Deputy Dir Dr VESELIN PEICHEV; Dr SNEZHANA MONCHEVA; Deputy Dir for Admin. CVETAN SIRAKOV; Scientific Sec. Dr GALINA SHTEREVA; publ. Proceedings (irregular).

Institute of Organic Chemistry with Centre of Phytochemistry: Acad. G. Bonchev St, Bldg 9, 1113 Sofia; tel. (2) 960-61-12; fax (2) 870-02-25; e-mail iochem@ orgchm.bas.bg; internet www.orgchm.bas.bg; f. 1960; attached to Bulgarian Acad. of Sciences; focuses on clarifying the relationship between synthesis, structure and reactivity of organic compounds; isolation, determination of structure and practical application of natural compounds; determination of structure and the function of proteins, enzymes and peptides; study of the thermal and catalytic transformations of hydrocarbons; Dir Prof. BOJIDAR TCHORBANOV; Deputy Dir Assoc. Prof. JORDAN TSENOV; Deputy Dir Assoc. Prof. Dr BORYANA DAMYANOVA; Scientific Sec. Assoc. Prof. Dr ILIJANA TIMTCHEVA.

Institute of Polymers: Acad. G. Bonchev St, Block 103-A, 1113 Sofia; tel. and fax (2) 870-03-09; e-mail instpoly@polymer.bas.bg; internet www.polymer.bas.bg; f. 1960; attached to Bulgarian Acad. of Sciences; research and education in macromolecular sciences relevant to devt and application of polymers and polymeric materials; Dir Prof.

Dr KOLIO TROEV; Deputy Dir Assoc. Prof. Dr DARINKA CHRISTOVA; Scientific Sec. Assoc. Prof. Dr NELI KOSEVA.

National Institute of Meteorology and Hydrology: Blvd Tsarigradsko chaussee 66, 1784 Sofia; tel. (2) 975-39-96; fax (2) 988-44-94; e-mail office@meteo.bg; internet www.bas .bg; f. 1954; attached to Bulgarian Acad. of Sciences; Dir-Gen. Assoc. Prof. GEORGI KORTCHEV; Deputy Dir-Gen. Assoc. Prof. Dr VALERY SPIRIDONOV; Deputy Dir-Gen. Assoc. Prof. Dr PETIO SIMEONOV; Scientific Sec. Assoc. Prof. Dr STAYTCHO KOLEV; publ. *Bulgarian Journal of Meteorology and Hydrology.*

Rostislaw Kaischew Institute of Physical Chemistry: Acad. G. Bonchev St, Bldg 11, 1113 Sofia; tel. (2) 872-75-50; fax (2) 971-26-88; e-mail physchem@ipc.bas.bg; internet www.ipc.bas.bg; f. 1958; attached to Bulgarian Acad. of Sciences; interface colloid science phase formation, crystal growth, electrochemical deposition and metal dissolution; electrochemically obtained materials and corrosion processes; amorphous materials; 102 mems; Dir Prof. Dr IVAN KRASTEV; Deputy Dir Prof. ELENA MILEVA; Scientific Sec. Assoc. Prof. MARIA PETROVA.

Rozhen National Astronomical Observatory: POB 136, 4700 Smoljan; tel. and fax (301) 985-356; internet www.nao-rozhen.org; f. 1981; attached to Institute of Astronomy, Bulgarian Acad. of Sciences; fundamental studies in the field of astronomy and astrophysics; library of 5,000 vols; Deputy Dir Dr ANASTAS STINKOV.

Space Research Institute: Moskovska 6, POB 799, 1000 Sofia; tel. (2) 988-35-03; fax (2) 981-33-47; e-mail office@space.bas.bg; internet www.space.bas.bg; f. 1975; attached to Bulgarian Acad. of Sciences; fundamental and applied investigations in space physics, astrophysics, image processing, remote sensing, life sciences, scientific equipment; preparation and realisation of experiments in the region of space investigation and usage from the board of automatic and navigated spacecrafts; investigation on control systems, air- and spacecrafts and equipment for them; activity for creation of cosmic materials and technologies and their transfer in the nat. economy; Dir Prof. Dr PETER STEFANOV GETZOV; Scientific Sec. Prof. GARO MARDIROSSIAN; publ. *Aerospace Research in Bulgaria* (1 a year).

Solar-Terrestrial Influences Laboratory: Block 3 Acad. Georgi Bonchev St, 1113 Sofia; tel. (2) 870-02-29; fax (2) 870-01-78; internet www.stil.bas.bg; f. 1990; attached to Bulgarian Acad. of Sciences; fundamental space research and its application in solar-terrestrial physics; in situ and remote investigation of the geospace, planets and interplanetary space; study of global change and ecosystems and heliobiology and telemedicine and eHealth; Dir Prof. TSVETAN PANTALEEV DACHEV; Deputy Dir Dr DOYNO IVANOV PETKOV; Chair., Scientific Council PETER VELINOV; Scientific Sec. IRINA MITKOVA STOILOVA; publs *Advances in Space Research, Comptes Rendus de l'Académie Bulgare des Sciences, Journal of Atmospheric and Solar-Terrestrial Physics.*

PHILOSOPHY AND PSYCHOLOGY

Institute for Philosophical Research: 6 Patriarh Evtimij Blvd, 1000 Sofia; tel. and fax (2) 981-07-91; e-mail office@ philosophybulgaria.org; internet www .philosophybulgaria.org; f. 1945, as Institute of Philosophy and Education; Institute of Philosophy 1952–88; Institute of Philosophical Sciences 1988–95; present name 1995; attached to Bulgarian Acad. of Sciences;

depts of aesthetics and cultural studies, anthropology and religious studies, ethics and bioethics, history of philosophy, logic, ontology and epistemology, philosophy of science, social philosophy; library of 32,952 vols, incl. 24,929 books and 8,023 periodicals; 65 mems; Dir Prof. Dr VASSIL PRODANOV; Scientific Sec. Assoc. Prof. Dr VESSELIN PETROV; publs *Balkan Journal of Philosophy* (2 a year), *Philosophical Alternatives* (6 a year).

Institute of Psychology: Acad. G. Bonchev St, Bldg 6, Fl. 5, 1113 Sofia; tel. and fax (2) 870-32-17; e-mail bozhi@ipsyh.bas.bg; internet www.ipsyh.bas.bg; f. 1973 as Laboratory of Psychology, present name 1990; attached to Bulgarian Acad. of Sciences; studies the theoretical and practical problems of contemporary psychology; Dir Prof. Dr BOZHIDAR DIMITROV; Deputy Dir Assoc. Prof. DIMITER SHTETINSKY; Scientific Sec. Assoc. Prof. Dr ELIANA PENCHEVA; publ. *Psychological Research.*

RELIGION, SOCIOLOGY AND ANTHROPOLOGY

Ethnographic Institute and Museum: Moskovska 6A, 1000 Sofia; tel. (2) 987-41-91; fax (2) 980-11-62; internet hs41.iccs.bas .bg; f. 1947, present name 1949; attached to Bulgarian Acad. of Sciences; explores different aspects of Bulgarian traditional culture; works on the ethnological problems connected with the role and the specific features of the Bulgarian traditional and modern culturefrom Slavonic and Balkan perspectives; some aspects of the ethnic devt and ethnic relations between Bulgarians, Christians and Moslems; Dir Assoc. Prof. R. POPOV; publs *Bulgarska Etnologia* (Bulgarian Ethnology), *Ethnologia Balkanica* (1 a year).

Institute of Folklore: Acad. G. Bonchev St., Bldg 6, 1113 Sofia; tel. (2) 71-36-43; fax (2) 870-42-09; e-mail folklor@bas.bg; internet www.folklor.bas.bg; f. 1973; attached to Bulgarian Acad. of Sciences; interdisciplinary research; documents Bulgarian nominations for the UNESCO Representative List of Elements of Intangible Cultural Heritage; library of 4,200 vols, 73 periodicals; Dir Prof. Dr MILA SANTOVA; Scientific Sec. Assoc. Prof. Dr VALENTINA GANEVA-RAJCHEVA; publ. *Bulgarian Folklore* (4 a year).

Institute of Sociology: 13A Moskovska St, 1000 Sofia; tel. (2) 980-90-86; fax (2) 980-58-95; e-mail info@sociology-bg.org; internet sociology-bg.org; f. 1968; attached to Bulgarian Acad. of Sciences; conducts theoretical and applied research in the fields of social communities, social stratification and social mobility, social pathology, sociology of labour, orgs. and politics, sociology of education, science and technologies, ethno-sociology, sociology of religions and everyday life, regional and global devt; Dir Prof. Dr DIMITAR VELKOV DIMITROV; Deputy Dir Prof. Dr VALENTINA ILIEVA ZLATANOVA; Scientific Sec. Assoc. Prof. Dr ANNA IVANOVA MANTAROVA; publ. *Sociological Problems* (4 a year).

TECHNOLOGY

'Acad. Emil Djakov' Institute of Electronics: 72, Tsarigradsko Shose Blvd, 1784 Sofia; tel. (2) 875-00-77; fax (2) 975-32-01; e-mail die@ie.bas.bg; internet www.ie-bas.dir .bg; f. 1963; attached to Bulgarian Acad. of Sciences; applied physics and eng. such as high-tech material fabrication, treatment and analysis, nanoscience and nanotechnologies, nanoelectronics, photonics, optoelectronics, quantum optics, environmental monitoring, biomedical photonics; Dir Assoc. Prof. Dr RADOMIR ENIKOV; Deputy Dir Assoc.

Prof. Dr SANKA GATEVA; Deputy Dir Assoc. Prof. Dr NIKOLAY NEDIALKOV; Scientific Sec. Assoc. Prof. Dr KATIA VUTOVA.

Central Laboratory of Applied Physics: 59 St Petersburg Blvd, 4000 Plovdiv; tel. (32) 63-50-19; fax (32) 63-28-10; e-mail ipfban@ mbox.digsys.bg; internet www.bas.bg/ plovdiv; f. 1979 as Laboratory of Applied Physics, present status and name 1995; attached to Bulgarian Acad. of Sciences; scientific investigation, research and devt work and production in the field of electronics, micro- and optoelectronics, semiconductor sensors and sensor devices and production technologies; Dir Assoc. Prof. Dr ROUMEN KAKANAKOV; Deputy Dir Assoc. Prof. Dr MINKO NESHEV; Scientific Sec. Assoc. Prof. LYDIA BEDIKIAN.

Central Laboratory of Mechatronics and Instrumentation: Acad G. Bonchev, Bldg 1, 1113 Sofia; tel. and fax (2) 872-35-71; internet www.clmi.bas.bg; f. 1994; attached to Bulgarian Acad. of Sciences; research on design, analysis, devt of mechatronic and control systems, robots, specialized and unique devices; Dir Assoc. Prof. TANIO TANEV; Vice-Dir Assoc. Prof. GENCHO STAJNOV; Acdemic Sec. Assoc Prof. VASSIL TRENEV.

Central Laboratory of Mineralogy and Crystallography 'Acad. Ivan Kostov': Acad. Georgi Bonchev St, Bldg 107, 1113 Sofia; tel. (2) 979-70-55; fax (2) 979-70-56; e-mail mincryst@interbgc.com; internet www .clmc.bas.bg; f. 1995; attached to Bulgarian Acad. of Sciences; basic studies and applied research; consulting; expertise service and analytic activities; practical applications of scientific results and training of highly qualified specialists in the field of mineralogy and crystallography; investigation and modelling of natural and technogenic mineral systems; Dir Dr ZHELYAZKO DAMYANOV; Deputy Dir Dr LUDMIL KONSTANTINOV; Scientific Sec. Dr MIHAIL TARASSOV.

Central Laboratory of Physico-Chemical Mechanics: Georgi Bonchev St, Bldg 1, 1113 Sofia; tel. (2) 871-81-82; fax (2) 870-34-33; e-mail clphchm@clphchm.bas.bg; internet www.clphchm.bas.bg; f. 1972; attached to Bulgarian Acad. of Sciences; nat. coordinator of research in the field of mechanics and technology of non-metallic composite materials for constructions; Dir Assoc. Prof. Dr NIKOLAY BAROVSKY; Asst Dir Eng. ILIYA KRASTEV; Scientific Sec. Prof. Dr RUMIANA KOTSILKOVA; publs *Physico-Chemical Mechanics* (2 a year), *Non-Metallic Composite Materials* (2 a year).

Central Laboratory of Seismic Mechanics and Earthquake Engineering: Acad. G. Bonchev St, Bldg 3, 1113 Sofia; tel. and fax (2) 971-24-07; e-mail clsmseeof@geophys.bas .bg; internet www.clsmee.geophys.bas.bg; f. 1982; attached to Bulgarian Acad. of Sciences; seismic risk assessment of urban areas, buildings and structures; monitors strong ground motion; reduces the effects of earthquakes; elaborates standard documents for design and construction in seismic regions; trains scientific and engineering specialists and improves public earthquake knowledge; Dir Assoc. Prof. Eng. SVETOSLAV SIMEONOV; Vice-Dir Assoc. Prof. Dr Eng. DIMITAR STEFANOV; Scientific Sec. Assoc. Prof. Dr Eng. KIRIL HDJIYSKI.

Institute of Chemical Engineering: Acad. G. Bonchev St, Bldg 103, 1113 Sofia; tel. (2) 870-20-88; fax (2) 870-75-23; e-mail ichemeng@bas.bg; internet www.bas.bg/ iceng; f. 1973, present name 1986; attached to Bulgarian Acad. of Sciences; nat. research centre for chemical engineering and bioengineering science; Dir Prof. Dr VENKO BESCH-

KOV; Scientific Sec. Assoc. Prof. Dr TSVETAN SAPUNDZHIEV.

Institute of Computer and Communication Systems: Acad. G. Bonchev St, Bldg 2, 1113 Sofia; tel. (2) 871-90-97; fax (2) 872-39-05; e-mail diana@iccs.bas.bg; internet iccsweb.isdip.bas.bg; f. 1964 as Institute of Engineering Cybernetics; attached to Bulgarian Acad. of Sciences; comprises 7 depts: architecture of computer and communication systems, dependable computer and communication systems, hierarchical systems, integrated systems for digital processing of information, intelligent computer technologies, real-time control systems, software engineering; Dir Assoc. Prof. Dr ZLATOLILIA ILCHEVA (acting); Scientific Sec. Assoc. Prof. Dr DIMITER LAKOV; publ. *Proceedings of ICCS-BAS.*

Institute of Control and Systems Research 'Saint Apostle and Gospeller Matthew': Acad. G. Bonchev St, Bldg 2, POB 79, 1113 Sofia; tel. (2) 873-26-14; fax (2) 870-33-61; internet www.icsr.bas.bg; f. 1994; attached to Bulgarian Acad. of Sciences; depts of multisensors and robotic systems, knowledge-based control systems, adaptive and robust control hybrid systems and management, modelling and control of ecological systems, and scientific research, applications and training; Dir Prof. Dr CHAVDAR ROUMENIN; Deputy Dir Assoc. Prof. Dr DIMITAR NEDIALKOV; Deputy Dir Assoc. Prof. Dr HRISTO VARBANOV; Scientific Sec. Assoc. Prof. Dr MAYA IGNATOVA.

Institute of Information Technologies: Acad. G. Bonchev St., Block 2, 1113 Sofia; tel. and fax (2) 872-04-97; e-mail office@iit.bas.bg; internet www.iit.bas.bg; f. 1994; attached to Bulgarian Acad. of Sciences; investigates and develops approaches, methods and tools in the modern information technology areas with applications for real problem solving; Dir Assoc. Prof. Dr GEORGI GLUHCHEV (acting); Deputy Dir Assoc. Prof. Dr BOYAN METEV; Deputy Dir Assoc. Prof. Dr IVAN MUSTAKEROV; Scientific Sec. Assoc. Prof. Dr DANAIL DOCHEV; publs *Cybernetics and Information Technologies, IIT Working Papers, Problems of Engineering Cybernetics and Robotics.*

Institute of Laser Technology: Galichitsa 33A, 1326 Sofia; tel. 68-89-13; fax 68-89-13; f. 1980; Dir Assoc. Prof. I. KHRISTOV.

Institute of Metal Science 'Acad. A. Balevski': Shipchenski prohod 67, 1574 Sofia; tel. (2) 462-62-00; fax (2) 462-63-00; e-mail imst@bgcict.acad.bg; internet www.ims.bas.bg; f. 1967; attached to Bulgarian Acad. of Sciences; fundamental and applied research in the field of metal science and heat treatment, casting, crystallization, structure and properties of metals, alloys and composites on metal base, plasticity and fracture of materials, interaction of gases and metal and non-metal materials, production of high nitrogen steels under high pressures, physics and mechanics of welding processes, ceramics and composites, thermal electric and magnetohydraulic processes in molten metals, ecologically appropriate processes and machines for the production of novel materials and products; Dir Prof. STEFAN VODENICHAROV; Vice-Dir Prof NIKOLAY POPOV; Assoc. Prof TODOR STOYCHEV; Scientific Sec. Prof IVAN PARSHOROV; publ. *Journal of Materials Science and Technology* (4 a year).

ISOMATIC Labs Ltd: 4, Andrey Lyapchev Blvd, 1797 Sofia; tel. (2) 877-45-96; fax (2) 975-30-32; e-mail isomatic@isomatic.com; internet www.isomatic.com; f. 1992; robotics, electronics; Dir Assoc. Prof. G. NACHEV.

Technological Institute of Agricultural Engineering: Blvd Lipnitsa 106, 7005 Ruse; tel. (82) 44-19-21; fax (82) 45-93-82; f. 1962; Dir T. KAYRIAKOV.

Libraries and Archives

Burgas

Library PK Yavorov: Blvd A. Bogoridi 21, 8000 Burgas; tel. and fax (56) 84-27-53; e-mail rl_bourgas@burglib.org; internet www.burglib.org; f. 1888; 560,000 vols; Dir NATALIA KOTSEVA.

Plovdiv

Ivan Vazov National Library: Avksentii Veleshki 17, 4000 Plovdiv; tel. (32) 65-49-01; fax (32) 65-49-02; e-mail nbiv@libplovdiv.com; internet www.libplovdiv.com; f. 1879; 1,313,000 vols, 1,100 periodical titles, 336 MSS, 4,134 incunabula; Dir RADKA KOLEVA; Vice-Dir DIMITAR MINEV; publ. *Plovdivski Kraj* (1 a year).

Ruse

'Lyuben Karavelov' Regional Library: D. Korsakov 1, 7000 Ruse; tel. (82) 82-01-26; fax (82) 82-01-34; e-mail libruse@libruse.bg; internet www.libruse.bg; f. 1888; 700,000 vols; Dir RUMIAN GANCHEV.

Shumen

Public Library 'Stilian Chilingirov': Slavianski Blvd 19, 9700 Shumen; tel. 87-73-32; e-mail libshumen@abv.bg; internet www.libshumen.org; f. 1922; 720,000 vols; Dir Z. KUKUSHKOVA.

Sofia

Archives State Agency: Moskovska 5, 1000 Sofia; tel. (2) 940-01-01; fax (2) 980-14-43; e-mail daa@archives.government.bg; internet www.archives.government.bg; f. 1951; administers 2 central and 6 regional archives; 34,800 vols, 140 periodicals; Chair. Prof. Dr GEORGI BAKALOV; Vice-Chair. PLAMEN GEORGIEV; Vice-Chair. DANIEL HADJIEV; publs *Archival Guides, The records speak* (bilingual, French and Bulgarian), *Arhiven pregled* (4 a year), *Izvestiya na daržavnite arhivi* (2 a year).

British Council Library and Information Centre: Krakra St 7, Sofia; tel. (2) 942-43-44; fax (2) 942-42-22; e-mail bc.sofia@britishcouncil.bg; internet www.britishcouncil.bg; promotes the teaching of English language, organizes exams and training courses; 7,000 vols; Dir (vacant).

Central Agricultural Library: Tsarigradsko shose Blvd 125, Block 1, 1113 Sofia; tel. (2) 870-41-61; fax (2) 870-80-78; e-mail csb@abv.bg; internet cnti.hit.bg/cal.htm; f. 1952, present status 1962; attached to Institute of Agricultural Information; documentation centre of nat. and int. literature of the agriculture and forestry industry; 449,483 vols; Dir Assoc. Prof. Dr SIMONA RALCHEVA; Head of library MARGARITA STAMATOVA; publs *Agricultural Economics and Management, Agricultural Engineering, Agricultural Science, Animal Science, Bulgarian Journal Of Agricultural Science, Plant Science, Soil Science Agrochemistry and Ecology.*

Central Library of the Bulgarian Academy of Sciences: 1, 15 Noemvri St, 1040 Sofia; tel. (2) 987-89-66; fax (2) 986-25-00; e-mail library@cl.bas.bg; internet www.cl.bas.bg; f. 1869; 1,905,253 vols; maintains the book stock of the Central Library and of the 49 special libraries of the acad.; provides information services for the scientific potential of BAS and the country; Dir Assoc. Dr DINCHO KRASTEV; Deputy Dir SABINA ANEVA;

publs *Bulgaristika / Bulgarica, Informatsionen biuletin, Problemi na spetsialnite biblioteki–tematichen sbornik.*

Central Medical Library: St Sofia D. 1, 1431 Sofia; tel. (2) 952-31-71; fax (2) 851-82-65; e-mail mlib@medun.acad.bg; internet www.medun.acad.bg; f. 1918; 25 affiliated libraries; medicine, dental medicine, pharmacy and health-care; scientific research and education; exchange of information resources with local and int. scientific instns and orgs; interlibrary loans; publishing and editorial activities; 524,777 vols; Dir Dr LYDIA TACHEVA; publs *Abstracts of Bulgarian Scientific Medical Literature, Acupuncture, Acta medica Bulgaria* (in English, 2 a year), *Alergology, Clinical Immunology & Clinical Laboratory* (in Bulgarian), *Bulgarian medical journal* (in Bulgarian, 4 a year), *Cardiovascular Diseases* (in Bulgarian), *General Medicine* (in English and Bulgarian, 4 a year), *Medical review* (4 a year), *Nursing* (in Bulgarian), *Pediatrics & Infectious diseases* (in Bulgarian), *Obstetrics and Gynecology, Scripta periodica* (in English, 4 a year), *Surgery* (in Bulgarian).

Central Scientific Technical Library at the National Centre for Information and Documentation: NACID, Blvd MD. GM Dimitrov 50, 1125 Sofia; tel. (2) 817-38-41; e-mail ctb@nacid-bg.net; internet www.nacid.bg; f. 1962; collects, stores and makes available various types of Bulgarian and foreign publs incl. monographs, reference books, encyclopaedias, dictionaries, magazines and periodicals, bibliographic and referral issues, reports from scientific confs held nationally and internationally, and dissertations; 119,000 vols, 13,000 titles of journals and periodicals, bibliographic publs, 75,000 reports of scientific confs, 18,000 UN reports, 10,000 dissertations, 103,000 co literatures, 600 CD-ROMs, DVDs, scientific and technical translations; Dir VALENTINA SLAVCHEVA; publ. *Advances in Bulgarian Science.*

Central State Archives: Moskovska 5, 1000 Sofia; tel. (2) 940-01-04; fax (2) 980-14-43; e-mail cda@archives.government.bg; internet www.archives.government.bg; f. 1952; 110,000 files, documenting the activities of state instns, political parties, state and private cos and enterprises, from the mid-19th century to recent times; personal papers of eminent Bulgarians; Dir GEORGI CHERNEV.

Centre for European Studies: G. M. Dimitrov 52A, 1125 Sofia; tel. and fax (2) 971-24-11; e-mail ces@mail.cesbg.org; f. 1990; European Documentation Centre receiving all official publs of EC; Dir I. SHIKOVA; publ. *Europa* (12 a year).

Institute of Agricultural Information (with Central Agricultural Library): Tsarigradsko shose 125, Bldg 1, 1113 Sofia; tel. (2) 870-55-58; fax (2) 870-80-78; e-mail agrolib@abv.bg; f. 1961; library and information services in agriculture; Dir Assoc. Prof. SIMONA RALCHEVA; publ. *Bulgarian Journal of Agricultural Science.*

Library of the UBA: 6 Slavyanska St, Sofia; tel. (2) 987-38-72; e-mail library@uba.bg; internet www.uba.bg; plays and drama materials from the end of the 19th and beginning of the 20th centuries; open to mems; 6,000 vols; Librarians IVANKA SHINDAROVA; Librarian VESELA PAVLOVA; publs *Homo Ludens, Theatre magazine.*

National Centre for Information and Documentation (at the Ministry of Industry): G. M. Dimitrov Blvd 52A, 1125 Sofia; tel. (2) 817-38-24; fax (2) 971-31-20; e-mail secretary@nacid.bg; internet www.nacid.bg; f. 1993; attached to Min. of Education, Youth and Science; management models, structure, control and resources ensuring of popular education, higher education, youth and science systems; information products and services in the field of education and science; 4,650,000 vols; Gen. Dir J. KHLEBAROV; CEO VANIA GRASHKINA; publs *Advances in Bulgarian Science* (in English, 1 a year), *Infoswjat* (in Bulgarian, 4 a year), *Scientific and Technical Publications in Bulgaria* (in English, 4 a year).

Scientific Archives of the Bulgarian Academy of Sciences: 15 Noemvri 1, 1040 Sofia; tel. (2) 988-40-46; fax (2) 981-66-29; e-mail archiv1@cl.bas.bg; internet archiv.cl .bas.bg; f. 1947; MSS and 110,000 scientific dossiers; historical archives containing valuable documents on the history of the Bulgarian state; Head Assoc. Prof. S. PINTEV.

Sofia City Library: 4 Slaveikov Sq., 1000 Sofia; tel. (2)986-21-69; fax (2) 988-22-36; e-mail libsofdir@libsofia.bg; internet www .libsofia.bg; f. 1898, present status 2000; personal library of Dr Constantin Stoilov and Sofia local history colln; 932,428 vols (incl. 866,867 books, 31,304 periodicals, 8,182 black and white drawings, 1,954 maps, 9,075 scores, 13,579 sound records, 269 official editions, 1,833 slides and films and 260 pictures); 9,121 mems; Dir MIHAIL BELCHEV.

St. St. Cyril and Methodius National Library: Blvd Vasil Levski 88, 1037 Sofia; tel. (2) 988-28-11; fax (2) 843-54-95; e-mail nl@nationallibrary.bg; internet www .nationallibrary.bg; f. 1878, present bldg 1953; holds Slavonic and foreign language MSS, incunabula, rare and valuable edns, Bulgarian historical archives, maps and graphics, official publs, music publs and recordings, foreign books and periodicals, reference books, specialized collns, dept of Oriental collns; 255 staff; 2,863,754 vols and periodicals, 5,536 MSS, 34,187 old and rare publs, 290,093 maps, prints and portraits, 85,418 scores and gramophone records, 292,437 patents and standards, 3,114,876 archival documents; archive of Bulgarian printed material; nat. ISBN and ISSN agency; spec. archive of documents from the period of Ottoman rule, feudalism and the Bulgarian nat. revival; research institute in library science; Dir Prof. Dr BORYANA HRISTOVA; Deputy Dir for Admin. Business SPAS DAMYANOV; Deputy Dir for Library ANETA DONCHEVA; Sec. VIOLETA BOZHKOVA; publs *Biblioteca Journal* (6 a year), *Proceedings* (1 a year).

University Library: 1 Hristo Smirnenski Blvd, 1046 Sofia; tel. (2) 866-52-74; fax (2) 865-68-63; e-mail lib@uacg.bg; internet www .uacg.bg; f. 1942; holds MSS, theses, gray literature, microfilms, spec. colln of art and graphics albums, reference books and encyclopaedias in Bulgarian, English, French, German, Italian, Polish, Russian, Spanish and other Slavonic languages covering areas of architecture, art, agricultural sciences, economics, environmental sciences, geodesy, mathematics, physics, philosophy, political and social sciences, technics; 450,000 vols; Dir PERSIDA TOMOVA RAFAILOVA.

University Library 'St Kliment Ohridski': Tsar Osvoboditel Blvd 15, 1504 Sofia; tel. (2) 846-75-84; fax (2) 846-71-70; e-mail lsu@libsu.uni-sofia.bg; internet www .libsu.uni-sofia.bg; f. 1888; print and electronic library and information services, database access, interlibrary and international interlibrary loans; copying and microfiche services and electronic document delivery services; 2,001,000 vols; Dir Dr ANNA ANGELOVA; Deputy Dir BILIANA YAVRUKOVA; Sec. BISTRA DRAGOLOVA.

Stara Zagora

Regional Library: Tsar Kalojan 50, 6000 Stara Zagora; tel. (42) 64-81-31; e-mail lib-sz@prolink.bg; f. 1954; 419,000 vols; Dir SNEZANA MARINOVA.

Rodina Library: Ruski Blvd 17, 6000 Stara Zagora; tel. (42) 63-01-13; fax (42) 60-39-50; e-mail lib@rodina-bg.org; internet www .rodina-bg.org; f. 1860; 300,000 vols.

Varna

'Pencho Slaveykov' Public Library—Varna: Slivnitsa Blvd 34, 9000 Varna; tel. (52) 65-91-36; e-mail office@libvar.bg; internet www.libvar.bg; f. 1883; depository of Bulgarian nat. literature since 1945; 773,000 vols; Man. Dir EMILIYA STANEVA-MILKOVA.

Veliko Tărnovo

P. R. Slaveykov Regional Public Library: 2 Ivanka Boteva St, 5000 Veliko Tărnovo; tel. and fax (62) 62-02-08; e-mail prs@libraryvt.com; internet www.libraryvt .com; f. 1889; third nat. depository library; 586,873 vols; Dir IVAN ALEXANDROV; Deputy Dir KALINA IVANOVA.

Vidin

Regional library 'Mihalacky Gergiev': Bdintzi pl. 1, Vidin; tel. and fax (94) 60-17-04; e-mail libvidin@vidin.net; internet www .libvidin.net; f. 1863; 282,624 vols of books, periodicals, musical and graphic publs, audiovideo cassettes, CDs, maps.

Museums and Art Galleries

Blagoevgrad

Blagoevgrad Regional History Museum: kvartal Varosha, ul. Rila 1, 2700 Blagoevgrad; tel. (73) 88-53-70; fax (73) 88-53-73; e-mail im_bld@yahoo.com; f. 1951; archaeology, ethnography, fine arts, history, natural history; library of 16,500 vols; Dir K. GRANCHAROVA.

Burgas

Regional Historical Museum, Burgas: Slavianska St 69, 8000 Burgas; tel. (56) 82-03-44; fax (56) 84-25-88; e-mail main@ burgasmuseums.bg; internet www .burgasmuseums.bg; f. 1912, present status 2000; organizes research and study of cultural heritage; Dir TSONYA DRAZHEVA; publs *Bulletin* (1 a year), *Bulletin of Museums of Southeast Bulgaria* (1 a year).

Dobrich

Regional Museum of History: 18 Konstantin Stoilov St, p. k. 131, 9300 Dobrich; tel. and fax (58) 60-32-56; e-mail rim_dobrich@abv.bg; internet museum-dobrich.net; f. 1953; holds 150,000 items; depts of archaeology; ethnography; literature and art; modern history, nat. revival period, nature; library of 20,000 vols; Dir DIANA BORISOVA; publ. *Dobrudja* (1 a year).

Haskovo

Regional Museum of History: Pl. Svoboda, 6300 Haskovo; tel. 62-42-37; fax 62-42-37; internet haskovomuseum.com; f. 1952; Dir G. GRAMATIKOV.

Kalofer

Hristo Botev National Museum: Khr. Botev 5, 4370 Kalofer; tel. and fax (3133) 22-71; e-mail musei_botev@abv.bg; f. 1944; birthplace of Hristo Botev, poet, revolutionary and rebel against Ottoman rule; objects and clothes showing Bulgarian life in the past; exhibit of rose oil and lace production; Dir A. NIKOLOVA.

Karlovo

'Vasil Levski' Museum – Karlovo: Gen. Kartsov St 57, 4300 Karlovo; tel. and fax (335) 934-89; e-mail v_levski_museum@mail .orbitel.bg; internet www.vlevskimuseum-bg .org; f. 1937; named after Vasil Levski (1837–73), founder of the Revolutionary Cttee of, which liberated Bulgaria from Ottoman rule; consists of Levski's birth house, an exhibition hall with personal items, photographs, documents and works of art; and a memorial chapel in which the hair of Vasil Levski is preserved; Dir DORA CHAUSHEVA.

Kazanlak

Shipka-Buzludza National Park Museum: P. R. Slavejkov 8, 6100 Kazanlak; tel. (431) 6-29-18; fax (431) 6-24-95; e-mail shipkamuseum@mail.bg; internet www .shipkamuseum.org; f. 1956; monuments connected with the liberation of Bulgaria from Ottoman rule; Dir D. DANCHO.

Lovech

Regional Museum of History: Todor Kirkov St 1, 5500 Lovech; tel. (68) 60-13-82; e-mail imlovech@yahoo.com; internet www .lovechmuseum.hit.bg; f. 1895; holds 70,000 exhibits; restoration and conservation activities; photography services; exhibition area for temporary exhibits; Dir IVAN LALEV.

Montana

Regional Museum of History: Tsar Boris III 2, 3400 Montana,; tel. 2-84-81; fax 2-25-36; f. 1953; Dir U. DERAKCHIISKA.

Pazardzhik

Regional Museum of History: Pl. K. Velichkov 15, 4400 Pazardzhik; tel. (34) 44-31-13; fax (34) 44-31-44; e-mail museumpz@ yahoo.com; internet www.rimpazar.hit.bg; f. 1911; House Museum of Constantine Velichkov; also incl. historical and ethnographic collns; library of 11,000 vols; Dir BORIS EMILOV HADJIYSKI; publ. *Homeland* (every 2 years).

Stanislav Dospevsky Art Gallery: Pl. K. Velichkov 15, 4400 Pazardzhik; tel. 44-41-52; f. 1963; Dir DOYCHEV.

Pernik

Regional Museum of History: Fizkulturna 2, 2300 Pernik; tel. (76)60-31-18; e-mail muzeum@rotop.com; f. 1954; sections of archaeology, ethnography, labour movement, socialistic devt, mine and coal devt; Dir O. ASPROV.

Pleven

Regional Historical Museum: Stoyan Zaimov 3, 5800 Pleven; tel. and fax (64) 82-26-23; e-mail plevenmuseum@dir.bg; internet www.plevenmuseum.dir.bg; f. 1903 as Archaeological Society, present location 1984, present name and status 2000; gen. history with a natural science section; units: archeology, history of Bulgaria from 15th to 19th century, modern history, ethnography, nature, stocks and scientific records, public relations, studio for restoration and conservation, photo-laboratory, library; basic museum colln over 180, 000 items; library of 14,122 vols; Dir PETER BANOV; publ. *Museum Studies in North-Western Bulgaria* (1 a year).

Plovdiv

Archaeological Museum: Saedinenie Sq. 1, 4000 Plovdiv; tel. and fax (32) 63-31-06;

e-mail ram.plovdiv@gmail.com; internet www.archaeologicalmuseumplovdiv.org; f. 1882, present status 1920; colln of 100,000m. artefacts related to the history of Plovdiv, prehistoric, Thracian, ancient Greek, Roman medieval, Bulgarian revival art; numismatic colln; library of 13,000 vols; Dir A. PEYKOV; publs *Pulpudeva, Year book of the Archaeological Museum.*

City Gallery of Fine Arts: 'Saborna' St 14A, 4000 Plovdiv; tel. (32) 63-53-22; e-mail ghgpl@abv.bg; f. 1952; collects, treasures, and popularizes some of the best works of the Bulgarian fine arts (painting, graphic art, sculpture, applied arts, photography, icon collection, and Mexican art); holds a colln of 6,900 items; Dir KRASIMIR LINKOV.

Ethnographic Museum: Dr Chomakov 2, 4000 Plovdiv; tel. (32) 62-52-57; fax (32) 62-71-32; f. 1917; exhibits traditional material and spiritual culture of the population of Plovdiv and Rodopi; Dir Dr A. YANKOV.

Historical Museum – Plovdiv: Pl. Šaedinenie 1, 4000 Plovdiv; tel. (32) 26-99-55; e-mail ssh@historymuseumplovdiv.com; internet www.historymuseumplovdiv.com; f. 1951; collects, preserves and popularizes historical evidences from the past of Plovdiv and Plovdiv region from 15th to 20th century; Dir SHIVACHEV STEFAN.

Natural Science Museum: Chr. G. Danov 34, 4000 Plovdiv; tel. (32) 63-30-96; f. 1955; collns in palaeontology, mineralogy, botany; freshwater aquarium with decorative fishes and a few amphibians; colln of Rhodope minerals; library of 7,820 vols; Dir I. BASAMAKOV.

Rila

Rila Monastery National Museum: Rilski Monastir, 2643 Rila (Sofia District); tel. (70) 54-22-08; fax (70) 54-33-83; e-mail rila_monastery@abv.bg; internet www .rilamonastery.pmg-blg.com; f. 1961; Bulgarian art and architecture during the Ottoman period, Bulgarian history and history of the monastery; Dir P. MITEV.

Ruse

Regional Museum of History: Sq Al. Batenberg 3, POB 60, 7000 Ruse; tel. (82) 82-50-02; fax (82) 82-50-06; e-mail pr@ museumruse.com; internet www .museumruse.com; f. 1904; archaeology, ethnography, history of Bulgaria, modern and contemporary history, nature; colln of 130,000 items; library of 15,340 vols; Dir Dr NIKOLAY NENOV; publ. *Izvestija.*

Shumen

Regional Museum of History – Shumen: 17 Slavianski Blvd, 9700 Shumen; tel. and fax (54) 5-74-10; e-mail museum_shumen@ abv.bg; internet www.museum-shumen .psit35.net; f. 1904; incl. 6 archaeological reserves and preserved sites; maintains main exhibition in Shumen city museum and 7 smaller museums, specialising in history and/or archaeology of the region; 20 Soc. of the Museum Friends; library of 25,000 vols; Dir GEORGI MAYSTORSKI; publs *Proceedings of the Museum of History, Shumen* (Vols 1–12, 1960–2006), *Yearbook of the museums of N Bulgaria* (Vols 1–20, 1975–95).

Sofia

Boyana Church National Museum: 1–3 Boyansko Ezero St, 1616 Sofia; tel. and fax (2) 959-29-66; e-mail nmbc@mail.orbitel.bg; internet www.boyanachurch.org; f. 1947; medieval orthodox painting; Dir MARIANA HRISTOVA-TRIFONOVA.

Dimitr Blagoev Museum: L. Koshut 34, 1606 Sofia; tel. (2) 52-31-45; f. 1948; house of the founder of the Bulgarian Social-Democratic Party, containing documents and personal effects; Dir R. RUSSEV.

Georgi Dimitrov National Museum: Opalchenska 66, 1303 Sofia; tel. (2) 32-01-49; f. 1951; Dir VERA DICHEVA.

Ivan Vazov Memorial House: I. Vazov 10, 1000 Sofia; tel. (2) 88-12-70; f. 1926; house in which the Bulgarian poet lived; colln of personal belongings such as clothes, books, presents and awards; his workroom is preserved in its original state; Curator I. BACHEVA.

National Ethnographical Museum: Moskovska 6A, 1000 Sofia; tel. (2) 988-41-91; fax (2) 980-11-62; e-mail eim_bas@mail.bg; internet ethnography.cc.bas.bg; f. 1978; contains elements of Renaissance, Baroque Vienna, reminiscent of French palaces of the 18th century; library of 22,221 vols; Dir Prof. Dr RACHKO POPOV; Deputy Dir Dr HOPE TENEVA; Sec. Prof. Dr ELYA TSANEVA; publs *Bulgarian Ethnology, Ethnologia Balcanica* (1 a year).

National Gallery of Decorative Arts: Blvd Cerni vrah 2, 1421 Sofia; tel. (2) 963-07-58; fax (2) 963-07-48; f. 1976; works from the 1950s to the present; library of 2,000 vols; Dir ZDRAVKO MAVRODIEV.

National Institute of Archaeology and Museum: Saborna St 2, 1000 Sofia; tel. (2) 988-24-06; fax (2) 988-24-05; e-mail naim@ naim.bg; internet www.naim.bg; f. 1892; attached to Bulgarian Acad. of Sciences; permanent exhibitions on prehistory, classical antiquity and the middle ages; temporary exhibitions; Dir Dr MARGARITA VAKLINOVA; Deputy Dir Dr LYUDMIL VAGALINSKI; Deputy Dir Dr BISTRA BOZHKOVA; Sec. Dr DIANA GERGOVA; publs *Annual, Archaeology* (4 a year).

National Museum of Bulgarian Literature: ul. Rakovski 138, 1000 Sofia; tel. (2) 988-24-93; f. 1976; Dir DZH. KAMENOV.

National Museum of Ecclesiastical History and Archaeology: Pl. Sv. Nedelya 19, 1000 Sofia; tel. (2) 89-01-15; Dir N. KHADZHIEV.

National Museum of History: 16 Vitoshko lale St, 1000 Sofia; tel. (2) 955-42-80; fax (2) 955-76-02; e-mail nim1973@abv.bg; internet www.historymuseum.org; f. 1973, present location 2000; more than 650,000 exhibits, incl. colln from Paleolithic, Neolithic, Chalcolithic, Bronze , Iron, Roman, Middle–Late Middle ages; numismatics, adornments, jewellery, embroideries, weapons, uniforms and civil clothes and accessories, traditional clothes, applied and fine arts, documents from the nat. revival, modern history of Bulgaria, also maps, printed materials, manufacture samples; 1 br.; Dir Assoc. Prof. Dr BOZHIDA DIMITROV; Deputy Dir Dr IVAN HRISTOV.

National Museum of Military History: Cherkovna St 92, 1505 Sofia; tel. (2) 946-18-05; fax (2) 946-18-06; e-mail m.museum@bol .bg; internet www.militarymuseum.bg; f. 1916; attached to Min. of Defence; more than 1,000,000 artefacts; collects and registers Bulgarian and European military artefacts (arms, uniforms, flags, photographs, etc.); maintains two military mausolea in Sofia; 2 brs in Varna and 1 br. in Krumovo; library of 15,000 vols; Dir Dr PETKO YOTOV; Deputy Dir Dr SONIA PENKOVA; publ. *Bulletin* (1 a year).

National Natural History Museum: Tsar Osvoboditel Blvd 1, 1000 Sofia; tel. (2) 987-41-95; fax (2) 988-28-94; internet www .nmnhs.com; f. 1889 as Royal Prince's Natural History Museum; attached to Bulgarian Acad. of Sciences; 1m. specimens and samples incl. 460 mammal species, 1,990 bird species, reptile and amphibian colln, 480,000 specimens of insects and over 300,000 specimens of other invertebrates; colln also incls mineral species from around the world and more than 30,000 samples of fossil invertebrates; br. at Asenovgrad; library of 7,887 vols of periodicals, 2,427 books; Dir Assoc. Prof. Dr ALEXI POPOV; Scientific Sec. Assoc. Prof. Dr PAVEL STOEV; publ. *Historia naturalis bulgarica* (1 a year).

National Polytechnical Museum: Opulchenska 66, 1303 Sofia; tel. (2) 931-80-18; fax (2) 931-40-46; e-mail polytechnic@abv.bg; internet www.polytechnicmuseum.org; f. 1968; science and technology; library of 10,000 vols; Dir Dr EKATERINA TSEKOVA; publs *Annual of the National Polytechnical Museum, Technitartché.*

Sofia Art Gallery: 1 Gen. Gurko St, 1000 Sofia; tel. (2) 987-21-81; fax (2) 980-00-71; e-mail adelinafileva@sghg.bg; internet www .sghg.bg; f. 1928, present name and status 1952, present location 1973; conserves, maintains and studies art heritage; modern Bulgarian art; Dir Dr ADELINA FILEVA; Chief Curator Dr MARIA VASSILEVA.

Sofia Museum of History: Exarh Yossif 27, 1000 Sofia; tel. (2) 983-37-55; fax (2) 983-53-51; e-mail p_mitanov@yahoo.com; f. 1952; library of 16,000 vols.

Sopot

Ivan Vazov Museum – Sopot: Vasil Levski 1, 4330 Sopot; tel. (3134) 86-50; fax (3134) 76-60; e-mail vazov-muzeum@ sopot-municipality.com; internet www .vazovmuseum.com; f. 1935; birthplace of the writer (1850–1921); Dir C. NEDELCHEVA.

Stara Zagora

Regional Museum of History: 42 Ruski Blvd, 6000 Stara Zagora; tel. (42)91-92-06; fax (42) 91-94-27; e-mail rim@museum .starazagora.net; internet museum .starazagora.net; f. 1907, present name and status 1953; sections of archeology, Bulgarian history, folklore, numismatics; library of 7,600 books and periodicals; Dir Assoc. Prof. Dr EUGENIA IVANOVA.

Trjavna

Museum of Wood Carving and Icon Painting: Captain Dyado Nikola Sq. 7, 5350 Tryavna; tel. (677) 22-78; e-mail tryavna_museum@mail.bg; internet www .tryavna-museum.com; f. 1963; library of 4,535 vols; Dir JULIA NINOVA (acting).

Trojan

Museum of Folk Craft and Applied Arts: Pl. Vazrashdane, P.B. 46, 5600 Trojan; tel. 2-20-62; f. 1962; library of 2,700 vols; Dir T. TOTEVSKI; publ. *Cultural and Historical Inheritance of Trojan Region* (1 a year).

Varna

Regional Museum of History: Blvd Maria Luisa 41, 9000 Varna; tel. (52) 68-10-12; fax (52) 68-10-25; internet www.varna-bg.com; f. 1906; br. open-air museums: Roman Baths, Aladzha Monastery, 'Stone Forest' Nat. Park; library of 25,000 vols; Dir Dr VALENTIN PLETNYOV; publ. *Izvestija na narodniya muzei Varna* (1 a year).

Veliko Tărnovo

National Museum of Architecture: Ivan Vazov 35, POB 281, 5000 Veliko Tarnovo; tel. (62) 63-05-87; f. 1979; library of 4,600 vols; Man. Dir T. TEOPHILOV.

Regional Museum of History – Veliko Tărnovo: Nikola Pikolo St 6, 5000 Veliko Tărnovo; tel. and fax (62) 63-69-54; e-mail rimvt@abv.bg; internet www.museumvt.com;

f. 1871; comprises Archaeological Museum, Museum of the Bulgarian Revival and Constituent Assembly, Museum of Contemporary History, Museum of Prison, Sarafkina's House, Slaveikov House, Architectural reserve 'Arbanasi', Konstantsalieva's House, Museum of History in the town of Kilifarev, Philip Totyo House, Archaeological reserve 'Nicopolis ad Istrum', Ethnographic complex 'Osenarska reka'; library of 12,000 vols; Dir IVAN TZAROV; publ. *Bulletin* (1 a year).

Vidin

Historical Museum: Tsar Simeon Veliki St 13, 3700 Vidin; tel. (94) 60-17-10; e-mail museumvd@mail.bg; internet museum-vidin .domino.bg; f. 1910; units of archaeology, numismatics, ethnography, modern history, recent history, Bulgarian history (15th to 19th century); library of 4,600 vols; Dir A. BANOVA.

Vratsa

Regional Museum of History: Pl. Hr. Boteva 2, 3000 Vratsa; tel. (92) 2-03-73; f. 1952; Dir I. RAJKINSKY.

Universities

AGRAREN UNIVERSITET PLOVDIV
(Agricultural University Plovdiv)

12 Mendeleev Blvd, 4000 Plovdiv

Telephone: (32) 65-42-00
Fax: (32) 63-31-57
E-mail: inter@au-plovdiv.bg
Internet: www.au-plovdiv.bg

Founded 1945, present status and name 2001
State control
Academic year: October to June

Rector: Assoc. Prof. Dr DIMITAR GREKOV
Pro-Rectors: Prof. IVANKA LECHEVA, Assoc. Prof. CHRISTINA YANCHEVA, Assoc. Prof. VASKO KOPRIVLENSKI
Chief Admin. Officer: VELICHKO RODOPSKI
Chief Librarian: E. ANASTASOVA

Number of teachers: 212
Number of students: 2,950

Publications: *Agricultural Sciences* (2 a year), *Scientific Works of the Agricultural University Plovdiv* (4 a year)

DEANS

Faculty of Agronomy: Assoc. Prof. Dr BOZHIN BOZHINOV
Faculty of Economics: Assoc. Prof. Dr GEORGI DZHELEPOV
Faculty of Plant Protection and Agroecology: Assoc. Prof. Dr YANKO DIMITROV
Faculty of Viticulture and Horticulture: Assoc. Prof. Dr ANGEL IVANOV

PROFESSORS

ALADJADJIYAN, ANNA, Physics
CHOLAKOV, DIMITAR, Horticulture
IVANOV, KRASIMIR, Chemistry
KAMBUROVA, MERI, Chemistry
KOUZMANOVA, IORDANKA, Microbiology
LECHEVA, IVANKA, Entomology
MANDRADZHIEV, SAVA, Agricultural Machanization
PANDELIEV, SLAVCHO, Viticulture
SPASOV, VELICHKO, Crop Farming
STOYKOV, ALEKSI, Animal Sciences
SVETLEVA, DIANA, Plant Genetics

AMERIKANSKI UNIVERSITET V BULGARIA
(American University in Bulgaria)

1 Georgi Izmirliev Sq., 2700 Blagoevgrad
Telephone: (73) 88-83-06
Fax: (73) 88-83-99

Internet: www.aubg.bg
Founded 1991
Private control
Language of instruction: English
Academic year: August to May

Pres.: DAVID HUWILER
Chair.: GERARD D. VAN DER SLUYS
Chief Admin. Officer: DAVID DURST
Dean of Students: LYDIA KRISE
Assoc. Dean for Academic Affairs: STEVEN SULLIVAN
Assoc. Dean for College of Business: DUDLEY BLOSSOM
Registrar: EVELINA TERZIEVA

Number of teachers: 70
Number of students: 827

Publication: *AUBG Today* (newsletter, 3 a year)

Academic depts: arts, languages and literature; business management; computer science; economics; European studies, history, and political science/int. relations; journalism/mass communication; mathematics and science

PROFESSORS

BRADY, D.
CHRISTOZOV, D.
DURST, D.
FEDHILA, H.
FOULDS, L.
GALLETLY, J.
GREGORY, A.
MATEEV, M.
MIREE, L.
MUTAFCHIEV, L.
NAQVI, N.
POPOV, A.
STEFANOVICH, M.
STOYTCHEV, O.
TOPYAN, K.

BURGAS PROF. ASSEN ZLATAROV UNIVERSITY
(Burgas 'Prof. Assen Zlatarov' University)

Blvd Prof. Yakimov 1, 8010 Burgas

Telephone: (56) 86-00-41
Fax: (56) 88-02-49
E-mail: office@btu.bg
Internet: www.btu.bg

Founded 1963 as Higher Institute of Chemical Technology, present name 1995
State control
Language of instruction: English
Academic year: September to July

Rector: Prof. PETKO PETKO
Assoc. Vice Rector: PIPEVA PETRANKA
Vice-Rector for Education): Prof. NIKOLAY RALEV
Vice-Rector for Quality Control: Prof. YONKA BALTADJIEVA
Vice-Rector for Scientific Research and Business: Prof. BOGDAN BOGDANOV
Rector for Int. Cooperation and SDK: Prof. MAGDALENA MAGDALENA
Registrar: IVAN MARKOV
Librarian: IRENA MARKOVSKA

Library of 160,000 vols
Number of teachers: 206
Number of students: 3,918

Publication: *Godishnik*

DEANS

Faculty of Science: Dr RADOSTIN KUTSAROV
Faculty of Social Sciences: Dr IVAN DIMITROV
Faculty of Technical Sciences: Prof. ENCHO BALBOLOV

BURGASKI SVOBODEN UNIVERSITET
(Burgas Free University)

San Stefano St 62, 8000 Burgas

Telephone: (56) 900-400
Fax: (56) 813-912
E-mail: maria@bfu.bg
Internet: www.bfu.bg

Founded 1991
Private control

Pres.: Prof. Dr PETKO CHOBANOV
Rector: Prof. Dr VASIL YANKOV
Vice-Rector for Academic Affairs: Assoc. Prof. Dr MILEN BALTOV
Vice-Rector for Research and Int. Cooperation: Prof. Dr GALYA HRISTOZOVA
Registrar: DARINA DIMITROVA
Librarian: DIANA ADAMOVA

Library of 62,000 vols
Number of teachers: 615
Number of students: 7,000

Publications: *Business Directions, Juridical Collection* (2 a year), *University Annual*

DEANS

Faculty for Business Studies: Prof Dr PETKO CHOBANOV
Faculty for Computer Science, Engineering and Natural Studies: Prof. DIMITAR YUDOV
Faculty for Humanities: Assoc. Prof. Dr EVELINA DINEVA
Faculty for Legal Studies: Assoc. Prof. Dr MOMYANA GUNEVA

PROFESSORS

(some professors teach in more than one faculty)

Faculty for Business Studies:
GROZDANOV, B. K.
STANKOV, P. C.
YANKOV, V. N.

Faculty for Computer Science, Engineering and Natural Sciences:
JUDAH, D. D.
LAZAROV, A. D.
STAMOVA, I. M.

Faculty for Humanities:
HRISTOZOV, G. M.
LUKOVA, K. G.

Faculty for Legal Studies:
DRAGIEV, A. D.
ENCHEV, T. T.
IVANOV, I. V.
KYNDEVA-SPIRIDO, E. V.
ZLATAREV, E. N.

HIMIKO TEHNOLOGIČEN I METALURGIČEN UNIVERSITET
(University of Chemical Technology and Metallurgy)

St Kliment Ohridski Blvd 8, 1756 Sofia

Telephone: (2) 81-63-120
Fax: (2) 868-54-88
E-mail: rectorat@uctm.edu
Internet: www.uctm.edu

Founded 1945 as Dept of the State Polytechnic, present name 1995, present status 1998
State control
Language of instruction: Bulgarian, some subjects in English, French, German
Academic year: September to July

Rector: Prof. Dr BORIS STEFANOV
Sec.: Dr LUDMIL FACHIKOV
Vice-Rector for Education: Prof. Dr KALINA MUTAFCHIEVA
Vice-Rector for Research and Int. Cooperation: Prof. Dr BORIS STEFANOV
Chief Admin. Officer: Prof. Dr ASSEN PETKOV
Librarian: MAIA PENCHEVA

Library of 66,000 vols

Number of teachers: 371
Number of students: 3,667
Publication: *Godishnik, now Journal of the University of Chemical Technology and Metallurgy* (4 a year, in English)

DEANS

Faculty of Chemical and Systems Engineering: Prof. PAWN KUMANOVA DJAMBOVA
Faculty of Chemical Technology: Prof. Eng. VLADIMIR BOJINOV
Faculty of Metallurgy and Materials: Prof. Dr IVAN GRUEV AHMAKOV
Department of Chemical Sciences: Dr MARIA MACHKOVA
Department of Humanities: Prof. VENTSISLAV GAVRILOV
Department of Physico-Mathematical and Engineering Sciences: Assoc. Prof. ALEXANDER ALEXANDROV
College of Technology: Dr SENYA TERZIEVA

PROFESSORS

Department of Chemical Sciences:
  DUKOV, I., Inorganic Chemistry
  GIRGINOV, A., Physical Chemistry
  VELEVA, S., Physical Chemistry
Department of Humanities (tel. (2) 816-34-90; e-mail marianao@uctm.edu):
  ILIEVA, M., Education Quality
Department of Physico-Mathematical and Technical Sciences:
  HADJOV, K., Applied Mechanics
  PANEV, S., Applied Mechanics
  SHOILEV, N., Electrotechnology and Electronics
Faculty of Chemical and Systems Engineering:
  VELEV, K., Automation of Industry
  VUCHKOV, I., Automation of Industry
  YONCHEV, H., Automation of Industry
Faculty of Chemical Technology:
  DISHOVSKI, N., Polymer engineering
  DOMBALOV, I., Technology of Inorganic Compounds
  GRANCHAROV, I., Technology of Inorganic Compounds
  RAICHEV, R., Electrochemistry and Corrosion
  SIMEONOV, N., Textile Chemistry
  VLADKOVA, T., Polymer Engineering
Faculty of Metallurgy and Materials Science:
  ANGELOVA, D., Plastic Deformation and Heat Treatment of Metals
  KOJUHAROV, V., Silicate Technology

LESOTEHNIČESKI UNIVERSITY
(University of Forestry)

Kl. Ohridski 10, 1756 Sofia
Telephone: (2) 862-16-82
Fax: (2) 862-28-30
Internet: www.ltu.bg
Founded as an ind. institute 1953
State control
Academic year: September to June (2 terms)
Rector: Prof. NINO PETKOV NINOV
Vice-Rectors: Prof. VESELIN STAMENOV BREZINA, Dr RUMEN IGNATOV TOMOV, Dr PETER ZHELEV STOYANOV
Registrar: (vacant)
Librarian: JULIANA JOSIFOVA
Number of teachers: 350
Number of students: 3,500
Publications: *Forest Ideas, Management and Sustainable Development, Propagation of Ornamental Plants, Woodworking and Furniture Production*

DEANS

Faculty of Business Administration: Prof. IVAN PETROV PALIGOROV
Faculty of Forestry: Dr CHRISTOPHER MILKO MILEV,
Faculty of Forestry Industry: Prof. NENO IVANOV TRICHKOV
Faculty of Veterinary Medicine: Prof. DOROTHEA HRISANOVA
Postgraduate Centre: Prof. EK. PAVLOVA

PROFESSORS

ASPARUCHOV, K., Harvesting Machinery and Technology
DIMITROV, E., Basis of Forestry
DINKOV, B., Wood Technology
GENCHEVA, S., Ecology and Conservation, Soil Science
GERASIMOV, Sv., Zoology
GRIGOROV, P., Sawing of Timber
KAVALOV, A., Furniture Technology
KOLAROV, D., Plant Physiology
KOVACHEV, G., Veterinary Medicine
KULELIEV, J., Planting Trees and Flowers
KYUCHUKOV, G., Furniture Construction
MICHOV, I., Forest Mensuration
PAVLOV, D., Phytocenology
PAVLOVA, Ek., Ecology
PUCHALEV, G., Organization and Planting in Landscape Architecture
RAICHEV, A., Thermodynamics, Heat and Mass Transfer
SHECHTOV, Ch., Automation of Technological Processes
SHKTILYANOVA, El., Floriculture
TASEV, G., Machinery and Technology in Agronomy
VAKAZELOV, I., Dendrology
VIDELOV, H., Hydrothermal Treatment of Wood
YOROVA, K., Soil Science
YOSIFOV, N., Particle-Board Technology

MEDICINSKI UNIVERSITET PLEVEN
(Medical University Pleven)

Kliment Ohridski St 1, 5800 Pleven
Telephone: (64) 88-41-00
Fax: (64) 80-16-03
E-mail: rector@mu-pleven.bg
Internet: www.mu-pleven.bg
Founded 1974
State control
Academic year: September to June
Rector: Prof. Dr GRIGOR GORTCHEV
Vice-Rector for Education: Assoc. Prof. Dr PETYO BOCHEV
Vice-Rector for European Integration and International Cooperation: Assoc. Prof. Dr ANGELIKA VELKOVA
Vice-Rector for Quality of Education and Accreditation: Assoc. Prof. Dr VENETA LYUBENOVA SHOPOVA
Vice-Rector for Science and Research: Assoc. Prof. Dr MARIA SREDKOVA
Vice-Chancellor for Student Affairs: Prof. PETYO BOCHEV
Vice-Rector for Therapeutic Activities: Assoc. Prof. Dr IVAN LALEV
Chief Librarian: VALENTINA ICHEVA
Library of 82,287 vols, 90 periodicals
Number of teachers: 307
Number of students: 1,555
Publication: *Journal of Biomedical and Clinical Research*

DEANS

College of Medical Science: Assoc. Prof. Dr PAVLINA YORDANOVA (Dir)
Department of Language and Specialized Training: Assoc. Prof. MARIA ALEXANDROVA (Dir)
Faculty of Health Care: Assoc. Prof. Dr DIMITAR STOYKOV

Faculty of Medicine: Assoc. Prof. Dr DIMITAR GOSPODINOV
Faculty of Public Health: Assoc. Prof. Dr GENA GRANCHAROVA

MEDICINSKI UNIVERSITET PLOVDIV
(Medical University of Plovdiv)

15-A Vassil Aprilov Blvd, 4002 Plovdiv
Telephone: (32) 60-22-07
Fax: (32) 60-25-34
E-mail: rector@meduniversity-plovdiv.bg
Internet: www.meduniversity-plovdiv.bg
Founded 1945 as VMI
Academic year: September to May (2 terms)
Rector: Assoc. Prof. Dr GEORGI PASCALEV
Vice-Rector for Admin. and Economic Affairs: Dipl. Eng. RADKO STEFANOV
Vice-Rector for Research and Devt: TONKA VASSILEVA
Library of 170,000 vols
Number of teachers: 636
Number of students: 3,800
Publication: *Folia Medica* (4 a year)

DEANS

Dept for Specialized Medical Education: Dir: Assoc. Prof. D. MILIEVA
Faculty of Dental Medicine: Assoc.Prof. St. VLADIMIROV
Faculty of Medicine: Prof. ILIA YOVCHEV
Faculty of Pharmacy: Assoc. Prof. LUDMIL LUKANOV
Faculty of Public Health: Prof. Dr ZHELYAZKO HRISTOV
Medical College: Dir: Assoc. Prof. N. KRASTEVA

MEDICAL UNIVERSITY 'PROF. DR. PARASKEV STOYANOV'

'Marin Drinov' St 55, 9002 Varna
Telephone and fax (52) 67-70-20
E-mail: uni@asclep.muvar.acad.bg
Internet: www.mu-varna.bg
Founded 1961
Academic year: September to June
Rector: Prof. Dr ANELIA KLISSAROVA
Vice-Rector for Science and Research: Assoc. Prof. ROSEN MADJOV
Vice-Rector for Student Affairs: Assoc. Prof. NEGRIN NEGREV
Vice-Rector for Univ. Hospital Coordination and Postgraduate Education: Assoc. Prof. JANETA GEORGIEVA
Chief Librarian: P. A. MILEVA
Library of 200,000 vols
Number of teachers: 382 (172 full profs and assoc. profs, 210 asst profs and lecturers)
Number of students: 2,360
Publications: *Biomedical Reviews* (1 a year), *Bulgarska koloproktologia* (2 a year), *Scripta Scientifica Medica* (1 a year), *Syrtse i Byal Drob* (Heart and Lung, in Bulgarian and English, 4 a year)

DEANS

Faculty of Dental Medicine: Assoc. Prof. Dr VASIL GOSPODINOV SVISTAROV
Faculty of Medicine: Assoc. Prof. Dr MARINKA TASHKOVA PENEVA
Faculty of Pharmacy: Assoc. Prof. Dr DIMITAR DIMITROV ATANASOV
Faculty of Public Health: Assoc. Prof. Dr STOYANKA CVETKOVA POPOVA
Medical College of Dobrich: Assoc. Prof. Dr N. SPASOVA (Head)
Medical College of Shumen: Assoc. Prof. Dr N. STOYNOV (Head)
Medical College of Varna: Assoc. Prof. Dr HRISTO GANCHEV (Dir)

MEDICINSKI UNIVERSITET SOFIA
(Medical University Sofia)

D. Nestorov 15, 1431 Sofia
Telephone: (2) 952-37-91
Fax: (2) 953-28-16
E-mail: glavsec@mu-sofia.bg
Internet: mu-sofia.bg

Founded 1972 as the Acad. of Medicine, by merger of fmr Higher Medical Institute and the medical research institutes; present name and status 1995
State control
Academic year: September to June

Rector: Prof. VANYO MITEV
Pro-Rector for International Integration: Prof. ANDON FILCHEV
Pro-Rector for Scientific Affairs: Prof. GUENKA PETROVA
Pro-Rector for Students Education: Prof. SASHKA POPOVA
Pro-Rector for Post-graduate Education: Assoc. Prof. VASSIL DIMITROV
Sec.: Prof. Dr ELI GEORGIEVA NIKOLOVA
Gen.-Sec.: Assoc. Prof, ALEKSEI ALEKSEEV
Chief Admin. Officer: KHRISTO ANACHKOV
Librarian: Dr DABCHEV
Library of 50,000
Number of teachers: 1,408
Number of students: 5,308
Publication: *Acta Medica Bulgarica* (2 a year)

DEANS

Faculty of Dental Health: Prof. Dr DOAN ZIA
Faculty of Medicine: Prof. MARIN MARINOV
Faculty of Nursing: Assoc. Prof. K. YURUKOVA
Faculty of Pharmacy: Assoc. Prof. NIKOLAY LAMBOV
Faculty of Public Health: Prof. Dr RUMENOV SASHKA POPOVA
Faculty of Stomatology: Prof. B. INDZHOV
Free Faculty: Assoc. Prof. N. VRABCHEV

MINNO-GEOLOŽKI UNIVERSITET 'SV. IVAN RILSKI'
(University of Mining and Geology 'St Ivan Rilski')

Studentski grad Hristo Botev St, Sofia
Telephone: (2) 806-03-00
Fax: (2) 962-49-40
E-mail: maillist-mgu@mgu.bg
Internet: www.mgu.bg
Founded 1953
Academic year: October to June (2 terms)
Rector: Prof. Dr IVAN VLADOV MILEV
Vice-Rector for Academic Performance and Quality of Training: NIKOLAI IVANOV DZHERAHOV
Vice-Rector for Research and Int. activities: VENTSISLAV IVANOV SIMEONOV
Registrar: S. IVANOV
Librarian: K. DRAGANOVA
Library of 90,000 vols, 61,000 books, 29,000 periodicals
Number of teachers: 230
Number of students: 2,500
Publication: *Godishnik* (1 a year)

DEANS

Faculty of Geological Prospecting: Dr RADI GEORGIEV RADICHEV
Faculty of Mining Electromechanics: Dr KANCHO IVANOV YORDANOV
Faculty of Mining Technology: Prof. LUBEN IVANOV TOTEV

DIRECTORS

Department of Humanities: MONIKA STOYANOVA HRISTOVA

PROFESSORS

Faculty of Geological Prospecting (tel. (2) 962-72-70 ext. 207; e-mail radirad@mgu.bg):
  GROUDEV, S., Environmental Science
  STAVREV, P., Applied Geophysics
Faculty of Mining Electromechanics (tel. 262-72-28):
  DONCHEV, S., Theory of Mechanics
  FETVADJIEV, G., Mechanization of Mines
Faculty of Mining Technology (tel. (2) 962-72-20 ext. 206; e-mail ltotev@abv.bg):
  KOLEV, K., Rock Mechanics
  KUZEV, L., Mineral Processing
  METODIEV, M., Mineral Processing
  MICHAYLOV, M., Mine Ventilation
  VISOKOV, G., Chemistry
Department of Humanities (tel. (2) 962-72-20 ext. 324):
  STAMATOV, A., Philosophy

NATIONAL MILITARY UNIVERSITY 'VASIL LEVSKI'

Blvd 76, 5006 Veliko Tărnovo
Telephone: (62) 61-88-22
Fax: (62) 61-88-99
E-mail: nvu@nvu.bg
Internet: www.nvu.bg
Founded 1878, present name and status 2002
Library of 149,111 vols.

NOV BULGARKI UNIVERSITET
(New Bulgarian University)

Ovcha Kupel 21, Montevideo St, 1618 Sofia
Telephone and fax (2)8110247
Fax: (2) 8110260
E-mail: info@nbu.bg
Internet: www.nbu.bg
Founded 1990
Private control
Languages of instruction: Bulgarian, French, English
Rector: Assoc. Prof. Dr LJUDMIL GEORGIEV
Vice-Rector for Educational Activities and Accreditation: Assoc. Prof. PLAMEN BOCHKOV
Vice-Rector for Research Activities: Assoc. Prof. Dr LJUDMIL GEORGIEV
Vice-Rector for Int. Affairs and Public Relations: Prof. TOLYA STOITSOVA
Vice-Rector for Quality, Assessment and Attestation: Assoc. Prof. MORIS GRINBERG
Library of 162,300 vols, 1,800 reference works, 480 periodicals
Number of teachers: 500
Number of students: 12,000
Publications: *Kant, Praven Pregled, Sledva*

DEANS

Graduate School: Prof. Dr MARIN MARINOV
School of Basic Education: Assoc. Prof. NIKOLAY ARABADZIYSKI
Undergraduate School: Prof. ATANAS BLIZNAKOV

PLOVDIVSKI UNIVERSITET 'PAISII HILENDARSKI'
(Plovdiv University 'Paisii Hilendarski')

24 Tsar Asen St, 4000 Plovdiv
Telephone: (32) 26-13-63
Fax: (32) 63-50-49
E-mail: ir@uni-plovdiv.bg
Internet: www.uni-plovdiv.bg
Founded 1961, fmrly 'Paisii Hilendarski' Higher Pedagogical Institute, Plovdiv; present status and name 1972
Academic year: October to June
Rector: Prof. IVAN KUTSAROV

Vice-Rector for Univ. Management: MARIYANA MIHAYLOVA
Registrar: D. BOIKOV
Dir of Library: MILKA YANKOVA
Library of 280,000 vols
Number of teachers: 561 (34 full profs, 167 assoc. profs and 360 asst profs
Number of students: 12,500 (7,500 full-time and 5,000 part-time students)
Publications: *Journal Plovdiv University, Nauchni Trudove*

DEANS

Faculty of Biology: Prof. AT. DONEV
Faculty of Chemistry: Prof. AT. VENKOV
Faculty of Economics: Assoc. Prof. M. MIHAILOVA
Faculty of Law: Prof. G. PETROVA
Faculty of Mathematics and Computer Science: Prof. D. MEKEROV
Faculty of Pedagogics: Assoc. Prof. P. RADEV
Faculty of Philology: Prof. IV. KUTSAROV
Faculty of Physics: Prof. G. MEKISHEV

PROFESSORS

ALEKSANDROV, A.
ANDREEV, G.
ANGELOV, A.
ANGELOV, P., Zoology
ATANASOV, A., Theoretical Physics
BACHVAROV, G.
BALABANOV, N., Nuclear Physics
DIMITROV, R., Technology of Inorganic Chemistry
DRUMEVA, E.
FUTEKOV, L., Analytical Chemistry
GOLEMINOV, C.
GOLEVA, P.
GRUEV, B.
IVANOV, A., Microbiology
IVANOV, S., Technology of Organic Chemistry
JENKINS, D.
KARTALOV, A.
KATSARKOVA, V.
KIRYAKOV, I.
KOLAROV, N.
KUTSAROV, I., Morphology of Modern Bulgarian Language
KUZMANOVA, A.
LAZAROV, K.
MIHAYLOVA, M.
MIHOVSKI, S.
MINKOV, I., Plant Physiology
MITEV, D., Zoology
MOLLOV, T., Algebra
MRACHKOV, V.
NIKOLOVA, M.
PAPANOV, G.
PETROV, P.
POPCHEV, I.
POPOV, P.
SAPAREV, O.
SAPKOVA, I.
SAVOV, E.
TSEKOV, G.
VELCHEV, N., Physics of Dielectrics
VENKOV, A.
YORDANOV, Y

RUSENSKI UNIVERSITET 'ANGEL KANCHEV'
('Angel Kanchev' University of Ruse)

Studentska St 8, 7017 Ruse
Telephone: (82) 88-84-65
Fax: (82) 84-57-08
E-mail: secretary@uni-ruse.bg
Internet: www.ru.acad.bg
Founded 1954 as Institute of Mechanization and Electrification of Agriculture; became Angel Kanchev Higher Technical School 1982 and Angel Kanchev Technical Univ. of Ruse 1990; present name 1995
State control
Academic year: September to July

311

Rector: Assoc. Prof. Dr HRISTO BELOEV
Vice-Rector for Admission and Degree Programmes: Assoc. Prof. Dr BORISLAV ANGELOV
Vice-Pres. for European Integration and Int. Relations: Assoc. Prof. Dr NIKOLAY MIHAYLOV
Vice-Rector for Scientific and Staff Devt: Assoc. Prof. Dr ANGEL SMRIKAROV
Sec.-Gen.: Assoc. Prof. Dr IORDAN NIKOLOV
Dir of the Int. Relations Dept: Assoc. Prof. Dr KIRIL BARZEV
Dir of Library: Mag. Prof. EMILIA KIRILOVA LEHOVA

Library of 395,000 vols, incl. 323,000 books, 41,000 periodicals
Number of teachers: 600
Number of students: 7,700

Publication: *Nauchni Trudove*

DEANS

Faculty of Agricultural Mechanisation: Assoc. Prof. PLAMEN KANGALOV
Faculty of Automative and Transport Engineering: Assoc. Prof. ROSSEN PETROV IVANOV
Faculty of Business and Management: Prof. EMIL GEORGIEV TRIFONOV
Faculty of Electrical Engineering, Electronics and Automation: Assoc. Prof. MIHAIL PETKOV ILIEV
Faculty of Law: Assoc. Prof. Dr EMIL MINGOV
Faculty of Mechanical and Manufacturing Engineering: Assoc. Prof. VALENTIN GAGOV
Faculty of Pedagogy: Prof. MARGARITA STEFANOVA TEODOSEVA
Faculty of Pedagogy (Silistra): Assoc. Prof. Dr ILIANA GORANOVA
Faculty of Postgraduate Studies and Further Education: Assoc. Prof. Dr IULIAN MLADENOV

DIRECTORS

Branch of the Univ. (Razgrad): Assoc. Prof. MILUVKA STANCHEVA
Branch of the Univ. (Silistra): Assoc. Prof. DIMO DIMOV

PROFESSORS

Faculty of Agricultural Mechanization:
ENCHEV, K.
GUZHGULOV, G.
MITKOV, A.
ORLOEV, N.
PARASHKEVOV, I.

Faculty of Automotive and Transport Engineering:
ANDREEV, D.
ILIEV, L.
LIUBENOV, SL.
NENOV, P.
SIMEONOV, D.

Faculty of Business and Management:
PAPAZOV, KR.

Faculty of Electrical Engineering, Electronics and Automatics:
ANDONOV, K.

Faculty of Law:
MICHEV, N.

Faculty of Mechanical and Manufacturing Engineering:
IVANOV, V.
KANEV, M.
POPOV, G.
TOMOV, B.
VELCHEV, S.
VITLIEMOV, VL.

Faculty of Pedagogy:
KOZHUKHAROV, K.

Faculty of Pedagogy (Silistra) (Albena 1, POB 103, 7500 Silistra):
NEDEV, L.

SHUMENSKI UNIVERSITET 'EPISKOP KONSTANTIN PRESLAVSKI' (Bishop Konstantin Preslavski University of Shumen)

Universitetska St 115, 9712 Shumen
Telephone: (54) 83-04-95
Fax: (54) 83-03-71
E-mail: rector@shu-bg.net
Internet: www.shu-bg.net
Founded 1971
Academic year: September to June

Chair.: Dr KINA VACHKOVA
Deputy Chair.: Dr SONIA BABEV
Rector: Prof. Dr Hab. MARGARITA GEORGIEVA
Vice-Rector of Academic Affairs: Assoc. Prof. DIMCHO STANKOV
Vice-Rector of Accreditation: Assoc. Prof. BOGDANA GEORGIEVA
Vice-Rector of Int. Relations: Assoc. Prof. RUMYANA TODOROVA
Vice Rector of Research and Projects: Assoc. Prof. DRAGOMIR MARCHEV
Library Dir: MARIANA PETEVA

Library of 362,568 vols
Number of teachers: 448
Number of students: 7,389

Publication: *Godishnik* (1 a year)

DEANS

Faculty of Education: Prof. Dr Hab. GEORGI KOLEV
Faculty of Humanities: Prof. Dr Hab. IVELINA SAVOVA
Faculty of Mathematics and Computer Science: Assoc. Prof. RUSANKA D. PETROVA
Faculty of Natural Sciences: Assoc. Prof. DOBROMIR ENCHEV
Faculty of Technical Sciences: Assoc. Prof. IVAN CONEV

SOFIISKI UNIVERSITET 'SVETI KLIMENT OHRIDSKY' (Sofia University 'St Kliment Ohridsky')

Tsar Osvoboditel Blvd 15, 1504 Sofia
Telephone: (2) 930-82-00
Fax: (2) 946-02-55
Internet: www.uni-sofia.bg
Founded 1888 as High School, granted charter 1909
State control
Academic year: September to June (2 terms)

Rector: Prof. IVAN ILCHEV
Asst Rector: KALIN STANUKOV
Vice-Rector for Economic and Investment Affairs: Prof. IVAN KOLEV PETKOV
Vice-Rector for Information Affairs and Admin.: Assoc. Prof. ZHELYU DECHEV VLADIMIROV
Vice-Rector for Scientific and Int. Projects: Prof. NEDYU IVANOV POPIVANOV
Vice-Rector for Student Affairs: Assoc. Prof. MARIYA DELOVA SHISHINYOVA
Vice-Rector for Student Affairs: NEDYALKA IGNATOVA VIDEVA
Dir for Int. Relations: R. GRIGOROV
Sec.: R. STANIMIROVA
Dir of Library: Prof. ZH. STOYANOV

Library: see under Libraries
Number of teachers: 1,608
Number of students: 25,454

Publication: *Godishnik*

DEANS

Faculty of Biology: Dr BOZHIDAR GALUTSOV
Faculty of Chemical Engineering: Prof. TONY GEORGIEV SPASOV
Faculty of Classical and Modern Philology: Prof. PETYA YANEVA
Faculty of Economics: Prof. GEORGI CHOBANOV

Faculty of Education: Prof. IVAYLO TEPAVICHAROV
Faculty of Geology and Geography: Assoc. Prof. PETAR SLAVEIKOV
Faculty of History: Prof. PLAMEN DIMITROV MITEV
Faculty of Journalism: Dr TOTKA MONOVA
Faculty of Law: Dr TENCHO KOLEV DUNDOV
Faculty of Mathematics and Information Science: Prof. IVAN SOSKOV
Faculty of Primary and Pre-School Education: Prof. BOZHIDAR ANGELOV
Faculty of Philosophy: Prof. ALEXANDER DIMCHEV
Faculty of Physics: Prof. DIMITAR MARVAKOV
Faculty of Slavonic Philology: Prof. PANAYOT KARAGYOZOVA
Faculty of Theology: Dr EMIL TRAICHEV
Medical Faculty: Dr LYUBOMIR SPASSOV

PROFESSORS

Faculty of Biology:
BOZHILOVA, E., Botany
IVANOVA, I., Plant Physiology
KIMENOV, G., Plant Physiology
KOLEV, D., Biochemistry
MARGARITOV, N., Hydrobiology and Ichthyology
MINKOV, I., Human and Animal Physiology
TEMNISKOVA, D., Botany
VLAHOV, S., General and Industrial Microbiology

Faculty of Chemistry:
ALEKSANDROV, S., Analytical Chemistry
BONCHEV, P., Analytical Chemistry
DOBREV, A., Organic Chemical Technology
FAKIROV, S., Organic Chemical Technology
GALABOV, B., Organic Chemical Technology
IVANOV, I., Physical Chemistry
KALCHEVA, B., Organic Chemical Technology
KOSTADINOV, K., Inorganic Chemical Technology
LAZAROV, D., Inorganic Chemical Technology
MARKOV, P., Organic Chemistry
PANAYOTOV, I., Physical Chemistry
PETROV, B., Organic Chemical Technology
PETSEV, N., Organic Chemistry
PLATIKANOV, D., Physical Chemistry
RADOEV, B., Physical Chemistry
TOSHEV, B., Physical Chemistry

Faculty of Classical and Modern Philology:
ALEKSIEVA, B., English Philology
BOEV, E., Eastern Languages
BOGDANOV, B., Classical Philology
BOYADZHIEV, D., Classical Philology
DAKOVA, N., German Philology
DELIIVANOVA, B., German Philology
GALABOV, P., Romance Philology
KANCHEV, I., Ibero-Romance Philology
PARASHKEVOV, B., German Philology
PETKOV, P., German Philology
SHURBANOV, A., English Philology

Faculty of Economics:
BEHAR, H., History of Economics
SERGIENKO, R., General Economic Theory

Faculty of Geology and Geography:
BACHVAROV, M., Geography of Tourism
ESKENAZI, G., Mineralogy, Petrology and Economic Geology
KANCHEV, D., Economic Geography
MANDOV, G., Geology and Palaeontology
PETROV, P., Geography

Faculty of History:
BAKALOV, G., Byzantine History
DIMITROV, I., Bulgarian History
DRAGANOV, D., Modern History
GEORGIEV, V., Bulgarian History
GEORGIEVA, I., Ethnography
GETOV, L., Archaeology
GYUZELEV, V., Bulgarian History
ILIEV, I., Modern History

LALKOV, M., Modern History
NAUMOV, G., Bulgarian History
NIKOLOV, J., Medieval History
OGNYANOV, L., Bulgarian History
PANTEV, A., Modern History
POPOV, D., Ancient History and Thracian Studies
SEMKOV, M., Modern History
TACHEVA, M., Ancient History and Thracian Studies
TRIFONOV, S., Modern History

Faculty of Journalism:
DIMITROV, V., Radio Journalism
KARAIVANOVA, P., Journalism
PANAYOTOV, F., History of Journalism
SEMOV, M., Theory of Journalism

Faculty of Law:
BOYCHEV, G., Theory of State Law
GERDZHIKOV, O., Civil Law
MIHAYLOV, D., Criminal Law
PAVLOVA, M., Civil Law
PETKANOV, G., Finance Law
POPOV, P., Civil Law
SREDKOVA, K., Civil Law
STOYCHEV, S., Constitutional and Administrative Law
TSANKOVA, TS., Civil Law
ZAHAROV, V., Theory of State Law
ZIDAROVA, I., International Law

Faculty of Mathematics and Information Science:
BOYANOV, B., Numerical Analysis and Algorithms
DENCHEV, R., Complex Analysis and Topology
GENCHEV, T., Differential Equations
HADZHIIVANOV, N., Education in Mathematics and Computer Sciences
HOROSOV, E., Differential Equations
HRISTOV, E., Complex Analysis and Topology
LILOV, L., Analytical Mechanics
MARKOV, K., Continuous Media Mechanics
POPIVANOV, N., Differential Equations
SKORDEV, D., Mathematical Logic and Applications
STANILOV, G., Education in Mathematics and Computer Sciences
TROYANSKI, S., Mathematical Analysis
ZAPRYANOV, Z., Continuous Media Mechanics

Faculty of Pedagogy:
ANDREEV, M., Didactics
BOYCHEVA, V., History of Pedagogy
DIMITROV, L., Theory of Education
PAVLOV, D., Didactics
STOYANOV, P., History of Pedagogy
VASILEV, D., Didactics

Faculty of Philosophy:
ALEKSANDROV, P., History of Psychology
ANDONOV, A., Philosophy
BOYADZHIEV, T., History of Philosophy
DESEV, L., Social Psychology
DINEV, V., Philosophical Anthropology
FOL, A., History of Culture
GENCHEV, N., History of Culture
GERGOVA, A., Book Science
GINEV, V., Theory of Culture
GRADEV, D., Social Psychology
KARASIMEONOV, G., Political Science
KRUMOV, K., Social Psychology
MIHAILOVSKA, E., Sociology
MITEV, P. E., Political Science
NESHEV, K., Ethics
PETKOV, K., Sociology
RADEV, R., History of Philosophy
SIVILOV, L., Epistemology
STEFANOV, I. I., Sociology
VASILEV, N., Philosophy
VENEDIKOV, Y., Sociology
ZNEPOLOSKY, I., Theory of Culture

Faculty of Physics:
APOSTOLOV, A., Solid State Physics

DENCHOV, G., Geophysics
DINEV, S., Quantum Electronics
GEORGIEV, G., Quantum Electronics
ILIEV, M., Condensed Matter Physics
IVANOV, G., Astronomy
KAMENOV, P., Nuclear Physics and Energetics
KUTSAROV, S., Electronics
LALOV, I., Condensed Matter Physics
LUKYANOV, A., Nuclear Physics and Energetics
MARTINOV, N., Condensed Matter Physics
MATEEV, M., Theoretical Physics
NIKOLOV, N., Plasma Physics
PANCHEV, S., Meteorology and Geophysics
POPOV, A., Semiconductor Physics
SALTIEV, S., Quantum Electronics
SLAVOV, B., Quantum and Nuclear Physics
ZAHARIEV, Z., Theoretical Physics
ZHELYASKOV, I., Plasma Physics

Faculty of Primary and Pre-School Education:
BALTADZHIEVA, A., Special Education
BIZHKOV, G., Primary Education
DOBREV, Z., Special Education
KOLEV, J., Primary Education
PETROV, P., Primary Education
RADEVA, B., Anatomy
TSVETKOV, D., Primary Education
ZDRAVKOVA, S., Primary Education

Faculty of Slavonic Philology:
BIOLCHEV, B., Slavonic Literature
BOEVA, L., Russian Literature
BOYADZHIEV, T., Bulgarian Language
BOYADZHIEV, Z., Linguistics
BRESINSKI, S., Bulgarian Language
BUNDZHALOVA, B., Russian Language
BUYUKLIEV, I., Slavonic Linguistics
CHERVENKOVA, I., Russian Language
CHOLAKOV, Z., Bulgarian Literature
DIMCHEV, K., Teaching Methods of Bulgarian Language and Literature
DOBREV, I., Studies on Cyril and Methodius
GEORGIEV, N., Theory of Literature
HADZHIKOSEV, S., Theory of Literature
MINCHEVA, A., Studies on Cyril and Methodius
NITSOLOVA, R., Bulgarian Language
PASHOV, P., Bulgarian Language
PAVLOV, I., Slavonic Literature
PAVLOVA, R., Russian Language
POPIVANOV, L., Theory of Literature
POPOVA, V., Bulgarian Language
RADEVA, V., Bulgarian Language
TROEV, P., Russian Literature
VASILEV, M., Bulgarian Literature
VIDENOV, M., Bulgarian Language
YANEV, S., Bulgarian Literature
YOTOV, T., Russian Language

Faculty of Theology:
DENEV, I., Practical Theology
HUBANCHEV, A., Christian Philosophy
KIROV, T., Moral Theology
KOEV, T., Dogmatics
MADZHUROV, N., Christian Philosophy
POPTODOROV, R., Canon Law
SHIVAROV, N., Old Testament Studies
SLAVOV, S., Old Testament Studies
STOYANOV, H., Church History

TEHNIČESKI UNIVERSITET GABROVO
(Technical University of Gabrovo)

4 Hadzhi Dimităr, 5300 Gabrovo
Telephone: (66) 82-77-77
Fax: (66) 80-11-55
E-mail: info@tugab.bg
Internet: www.tugab.bg
Founded 1964 as Higher Mechanical and Electrical Engineering Institute of Gabrovo; present name 1990
Academic year: September to June

Rector: Assoc. Prof. DESHKA MARKOVA
Vice-Rector for Research: Assoc. Prof. RAYCHO ILARIONOV
Vice-Rector for Staff Qualification and Int. Cooperation: Assoc. Prof. LYUBOMIR LAZOV
Vice-Rector for Studies: Assoc. Prof. HRISTO HRISTOV
Registrar: NIKOLAY MIRAZCHIEV
Number of teachers: 240
Number of students: 7,219
Publication: *Journal* (2 a year)

DEANS

Faculty of Economics: Assoc. Prof. Dr ANYUTA GEORGIEVA NIKOLOVA
Faculty of Electrical Engineering and Electronics: Assoc. Prof. Dr ANATOLIY TRIFONOV ALEXANDROV
Faculty of Mechanical and Precision Engineering: Assoc. Prof. Dr GEORGI EVSTATIEV RASHEV

TEHNIČESKI UNIVERSITET SOFIA
(Technical University of Sofia)

Blvd Kliment Ohridski 8, 1000 Sofia
Telephone: (2) 965-21-11
Fax: (2) 868-32-15
E-mail: office_tu@tu-sofia.bg
Internet: www.tu-sofia.bg
Founded 1945, present name 1995
Academic year: September to June

Rector: Prof. Prof. KAMEN VESELINOV
Vice-Rector for Academic Affairs: Prof. GEORGI MIHOV SLAVCHEV
Vice-Rector for Academic Staff and Coordination: Dr LYUBOMIR IVANOV MECHKAROV
Vice-Rector for Scientific and Applied activities: Prof. NIKOLA GEORGIEV KALOYANOV
Chief-Sec.: VALENTIN DIMITROV IVANOV
Librarian: A. DIMITROVA
Library of 153,517 vols
Number of teachers: 1,309
Number of students: 14,190
Publication: *Nov Tehničeski Avangard* (12 a year)

DEANS

Department of Applied Physics: Prof. UZUNOV IVAN MITEV
Department of Physical Education and Sports: Assoc. Prof. IVAN YORDANOV BOZOV
Department of Telecommunications: Assoc. Prof. VLADIMIR KOSTADINOV PULKOVO
Department of Transportation: Assoc. Prof. TEODOSI PETROV EVTIMOV
DCHEOPL: ANTONIA SLAVEYKOV VELKOVA
Faculty of Applied Mathematics and Information Science: Prof. Eng. KETI GEORGIEVA PEEVA
Faculty of Automation: Assoc. Prof. DIMITAR PETKOV DIMITROV
Faculty of Computer Systems and Control: Assoc. Prof. OGNYAN NAKOV NAKOV
Faculty of Electrical Engineering: Assoc. Prof. VASIL SPASOV GOSPODINOV
Faculty of Electronics and Electronic Technologies: Prof. Dr Eng. MARIN HRISTOV HRISTOV
Faculty of German Engineering Education and Industrial Management: Prof. STEFANOV STEFAN ANGELOV
Faculty of Machine Technology: Assoc. Prof. LUBOMIR DIMITROV VANKOV
Faculty of Management: Prof. G. TSVETKOV
Faculty of Mechanical Engineering Technology: Assoc. Prof. Dr YORDAN GENOV GENOV
Faculty of Power Engineering and Power Machines: Assoc. Prof. YORDANOV VASIL YANEV
English - Language Faculty of Engineering: Assoc. Prof. T. TASHEV

French - Language Faculty of Electrical Engineering: Assoc. Prof. IVAN MOMCHILOV MOMCHEV

TEHNIČESKI UNIVERSITET VARNA
(Technical University of Varna)

Studenska 1, POB 10, 9010 Varna

Telephone: (52) 30-24-44

Fax: (52) 30-27-71

E-mail: rectorat@ms3.tu-varna.acad.bg

Internet: www.tu-varna.bg

Founded 1962 as Institute of Mechanics and Electrics, present name in 1990

Academic year: September to July

Rector: Assoc. Prof. OBED AZARIAH

Vice-Rector for Academic Affairs: Assoc. Prof. STOYANOV DISHKO

Vice-Rector for Accreditation and Devt: Prof. Prof. DIMITAR SVETLOZAROV

Vice-Rector for Int. Cooperation and Integration: Assoc Prof. SAVA VASILEV

Vice-Rector for Science and Applied Scientific Research: Dr IVAN VASILEV

Registrar: DIMITAR DIMITRAKIEV

Librarian: D. DIMITROVA

Library of 231,800 vols

Number of teachers: 450

Number of students: 6,500

Publications: *Acta Universitatis Pontica Euxinus* (2 a year), *Annual Proceedings*

DEANS

Department of Foreign Languages: Assoc. Prof. Dr MILENA ALEKSANDROVA PALIY

Faculty of Computing and Automation: Assoc. Prof. Dr PETER IANTONOV

Faculty of Electrical Engineering: Assoc. Prof. Dr MARIA IVANOVA MARINOVA

Faculty of Electronics: Assoc. Prof. Dr JORDAN KOLEV

Faculty of Mechanical Engineering and Technology: Assoc. Prof. Dr ANGEL DIMITROV

Faculty of Marine Sciences and Ecology: Assoc. Prof. Dr ATANAS STEFANOV KRUSHEV

Faculty of Shipbuilding: Assoc. Prof. Dr NIKOLA IVANOV PETROV

PROFESSORS

ALEXANDROV, Z., Theory of Machinery
DIMITROV, D., Electrical Apparatus
GEORGIEV, V., Theoretical Electrical Engineering
GRADINAROV, P., Theoretical Mechanics
IVANOV, I., Law
JOSIFOV, R., Marine Engineering
KANDEVA, E., Law
KOLEV, P., Shipbuilding
KOTSEVA, E., Law
MILANOV, ZH., Law
MILKOV, V., Engineering Mechanics
MINCHEV, N., Engineering Mechanics
MUTAFCHIEV, S., Government
NEDEV, A., Heat Technology
PILEV, D., Transport Machinery and Technology
RUSEV, I., Biology
RUSEV, R, Materials Science
SERAFIMOV, M., Internal Combustion Engine
SHISHKOV, A., Law
SOTIROV, L., Computer Engineering
STAVREV, D., Physical Metallurgy and Metals Engineering
STOYANOV, V., Internal Combustion Engines
VLADIMIROV, R., Law
ZAHAROV, V., Law

TRAKIJSKI UNIVERSITET
(Trakia University)

Student's campus, 6000 Stara Zagora

Telephone: (42) 67-02-04

Fax: (42) 67-20-09

E-mail: rector@uni-sz.bg

Internet: www.uni-sz.bg

Founded 1995, following merger of Higher Institute of Animal Sciences and Veterinary Medicine and Higher Institute of Medicine

State control

Languages of instruction: Bulgarian, English

Academic year: September to July

Rector: Prof. Dr IVAN STANKOV

Asst Rector: Assoc. Prof. Dr DOBRI YARKOV

Vice-Rector for Admin., Economical and Information Activities: Assoc. Prof. Dr IVAN VASHIN

Vice-Rector for Scientific Research and Int. Activities: Prof. Dr VESELINA GADJEVA

Vice-Rector for Student Affairs: Assoc. Prof. Dr KINA SIVKOVA

Chief-Sec.: Assoc. Prof. Dr TSONKA KASNAKOVA

Librarian: J. DAKOVSKA

Library of 360,000 vols, monographs, reference books, books and scientific periodicals

Number of teachers: 646

Number of students: 4,000

Publications: *Bulgarian Journal of Veterinary Medicine* (4 a year), *Pro Otology* (4 a year), *Trakia Journal of Sciences* (biomedical sciences and social sciences series, 4 a year)

DEANS

Bulgarian-German Farmers' College: Assoc. Prof. Dr A. ANTONOV (Dir)

Department of Information and In-service Teacher Training: Assoc. Prof. Dr GALYA KOZHUHAORVA

Faculty of Agriculture: Prof. RADOSLAV SLAVOV

Faculty of Medicine: Prof. Dr MAYA VLADOVA GULUBOVA

Faculty of Veterinary Medicine: Prof. Dr DINKO DINEV

Medical College, Haskovo: Dr D. KOSTOV (Dir)

Medical College, Sliven: K. HALACHEVA (Dir)

Medical College, Stara Zagora: Dr K. KOSTOV (Dir)

Technical College, Yambol: Assoc. Prof. KR. GEORGIEVA (Dir)

UNIVERSITET PO ARHITEKTURA, STROITELSTVO I GEODEZIA
(University of Architecture, Civil Engineering and Geodesy)

H. Smirnenski 1, 1046 Sofia

Telephone: (2) 963-52-45

Fax: (2) 865-68-63

E-mail: aceint@uacg.bg

Internet: www.uacg.bg

Founded 1942 as Higher Institute of Architecture and Civil Engineering, present name 1990

State control

Academic year: September to June

Rector: Assoc. Prof. Dr DOBRIN DENEV DENEV

Vice-Rector for Academic Affairs: Assoc. Prof. Dr KRASIMIR VELKOV PETROV

Vice-Rector for Int. Relations and Postgraduate Qualification: Assoc. Prof. Dr BOYAN MILCHEV GEORGIEV (acting)

Vice-Rector for Management and Devt of Material and Technical Equipment: Assoc. Prof. Dr M. RILSKI

Vice-Rector for Research and Design Affairs: Assoc. Prof. Dr BOGOMIL VESELINOV PETROV

Vice-Rector for Social and Living Affairs: Assoc. Prof. Dr PETAR TODOROV PENEV

Asst Rector: Eng. DIMITAR NIKOLAEV VITANOV

Registrar: S. VASILEVA

Librarian: P. RAFAILOVA

Library of 450,000 vols

Number of teachers: 531 (372 full-time, 159 part-time)

Number of students: 3,300

Publication: *Annals* (1 a year)

DEANS

Department of Applied Linguistics and Physical Culture: BORISLAV NIKOLOV KOLEV

Faculty of Architecture: Assoc. Prof. Dr NEDYALKO IVANOV BONCHEV

Faculty of Geodesy: Assoc. Prof. Dr SLAVEIKO GOSPODINOV

Faculty of Hydrotechnology: Assoc. Prof. Dr STEFAN PARVANOV MODEV

Faculty of Structural Engineering: Prof. TZVETI DAKOV DAKOVSKI

Faculty of Transportation Engineering: Assoc. Prof. Dr STOYO PETKOV TODOROV

PROFESSORS

Faculty of Architecture (tel. (2) 865-31-48; fax (2) 865-68-63; e-mail far@uacg.bg):

DIMITROV, S., Urban Planning
HARALAMPIEV, H., Drawing and Modelling
KRASTEV, T., History of Architecture
TROEVA, D., Urban Planning

Faculty of Geodesy (tel. (2) 866-22-01; fax (2) 866-22-01; e-mail fgs@uacg.bg):

VALEV, G., Geodesy

Faculty of Hydrotechnology (tel. (2) 865-66-48; fax (2) 865-68-63; e-mail fhe@uacg.bg):

ARSOV, R., Water Supply and Sewerage
DIMITROV, G., Water Supply and Sewerage
KALINKOV, P., Water Supply and Sewerage
MARADJIEVA, M., Hydraulics and Hydrology
MLADENOV, K., Theoretical Mechanics

Faculty of Structural Engineering (tel. (2) 865-66-74; fax (2) 865-66-74; e-mail dean_fce@uacg.bg):

BARAKOV, T., Reinforced Concrete Structures
BAYCHEV, I., Building Mechanics
DAKOV, D., Steel, Timber and Plastic Structures
DRAGANOV, N., Steel, Timber and Plastic Structures
GOSPODINOV, G., Building Mechanics
JANCHULEV, A., Organization and Economics of Construction
KIROV, N., Building Technology and Mechanization
NAZARSKI, D., Building Materials and Insulation
STAJKOV, P., Steel, Timber and Plastic Structures

Faculty of Transportation Engineering (tel. (2) 865-50-79; fax (2) 865-68-63; e-mail fte@uacg.bg):

DOULEVSKI, E., Bridges, Tunnels, Harbours
GICHEV, T., Mathematics
KONSTANTINOV, M., Mathematics
TRIFONOV, I., Road Engineering

UNIVERSITET PO HRANITELNI TECHNOLOGII
(University of Food Technology)

Maritsa Blvd 26, 4000 Plovdiv

Telephone: (32) 64-30-05

Fax: (32) 64-41-02

E-mail: uft@uft-plovdiv.bg

Internet: www.uft-plovdiv.bg

Founded 1953 as Higher Institute of Food and Flavour Industries, present name 2003

State control

Academic year: September to July

Rector: Prof. Dr Eng. GEORGE IVANOV VALTCHEV

Vice-Chancellor for Student Affairs and Quality of Training: Prof. Dr GEORGE TODOROV SOMOV

Deputy-Rector for Science Activity and Staff Potential: Prof. Prof. KOSTADIN VASILEV VASILEV

Deputy-Rector for Int. Cooperation and Public Relations: Prof. Prof. ZHELYAZKO ILIEV SIMOV

Registrar: VOLODYA KAMENOV

Head of Accounts: PENKA PETROVA

Librarian: IVANKA KUNEVA

Library of 150,000 vols

Number of teachers: 222

Number of students: 2,546

Publications: *Scientific Journals in Food Technology* (irregular), *Scientific Works of UFT* (1 a year)

DEANS

Economic Faculty: Assoc. Prof. Dr JORDANKA ALEXIEVA

Technical Faculty: Prof. Dr Eng. MILCHO ANGELOV

Technological Faculty: Prof. Dr Eng. ALBENA STOYANOVA

PROFESSORS

Economic Faculty:

KONAREV, A., Organization and Management

STAMOV, S., Catering and Tourism

ZLATEV, T., Ecology and Environmental Safety

Technical Faculty:

DICHEV, S., Refrigeration

GEORGIEV, A., Automatics, Information and Control Equipment

LAMBREV, A., Technical Equipment in the Food Industry

Technological Faculty:

KABSEV, J., Technology of Fish and Fish Products

MARINOV, M., Beverage Technology

MURGOV, I., Microbiology

OBRETENOV, T., Organic Chemistry

VASILEV, K., Technology of Meat and Fish

UNIVERSITET ZA NACIONALNO I SVETOVNO STOPANSTVO
(University of National and World Economics)

Studentski grad 'Hristo Botev', 1700 Sofia

Telephone: (2) 819-52-11

Fax: (2) 962-39-03

E-mail: secretary@unwe.acad.bg

Internet: www.unwe.acad.bg

Founded 1920

Academic year: October to July

Rector: Prof. Dr. BORISLAV BORISOV

Vice-Rector: Assoc. Prof. Dr VALENTIN KISIMOV

Vice Rector for Continuing Education and Training: Assoc. Prof. Dr MARCHO MARKOV

Vice-Rector for Education in Masters Degree Programmes and Distant Learning: Assoc. Prof. Dr VESELKA PAVLOVA

Vice-Rector for Scientific Research and Int. Projects: Prof. Dr PLAMEN MISHEV

Librarian: DESISLAVA STEFANOVA STEFANOVA

Library of 465,443 vols

Number of teachers: 531

Number of students: 19,556

Publications: *Alternativi* (12 a year), *Trudove* (2 a year)

DEANS

Business Faculty: Assoc. Prof. Dr YORDANKA YOVKOVA

Economics College: Prof. H. KARAKASHEV (Dir)

Faculty of Applied Informatics and Statistics: Assoc. Prof. Dr VALENTIN GOEV

Faculty of Economic Industries: Asst Prof. V. ZLATEV

Faculty of Economics and Infrastructure: Prof. Dr HRISTO PURVANOV

Faculty of Finance and Accounting: Assoc. Prof. Dr OGNYAN SIMEONOV

Faculty of General Economics: Assoc. Prof. Dr ATANAS KAZAKOV

Faculty of International Economics and Politics: Dr GEORGI GENOV

Faculty of Law: Prof. Dr HRISTINA BALABANOVA

Faculty of Management and Administration: Assoc. Prof. Dr VELINA BALEVA

Institute for Postgraduate Studies: Assoc. Prof. B. NEDELCHEVA (Dir)

PROFESSORS

Faculty of Economic Industries:

GEORGIEV, I., Industrial Business

ILIEV, I., Industrial Business

KANCHEV, I., Agrarian Business

TODOROV, K., Industrial Business

Faculty of Economics:

BORISOV, B., Economics of Intellectual Property

KOLEV, B., Sociology

MIRKOVICH, K., Economics

NIKOV, A., Economic Psychology and Economic Pedagogy

YANKOV, G., Politology

Faculty of Economics and Infrastructure:

IVANOV, T., Economics of National Defence and Security

KARAKASHEV, H., Public Administration

LULANSKY, P., Economics of the Social and Cultural Sphere

VASILEV, E., Economics of Transport

Faculty of Finance and Accounting:

MLADENOV, M., Finance

STEFANOVA, P., Finance

Faculty of International Economics and Politics:

BOEVA, B., International Economics

MARINOV, V., International Economics

MIHOV, N., French Language

Faculty of Law:

BALABANOVA, H., Law

BOIANOV, G., Law

KARANIKOLOV, L., Law

KORENZOV, L., Law

SUKAREVA, Z., Law

VASILEV, A., Law

Faculty of Management and Informatics:

BOGINOV, N., Mathematics

GEROV, A., Forecasting and Planning

MANOV, V., Forecasting and Planning

VLADIMIROVA, K., Marketing

UNIVERSITY OF TRANSPORT 'TODOR KABLESHKOV'

Geo Milev St 158, 1574 Sofia

Telephone: (2) 970-92-40

Fax: (2) 970-92-42

E-mail: office@vtu.bg

Internet: www.vtu.bg

Founded 1922 as State Railway School, present name and status 2000

State control

Rector: Prof. Dr PETAR KOLEV KOLEV

Vice-Rector for Educational Activities: Assoc. Prof. Dr RUMEN KOSTADINOV ULUTCHEV

Vice-Rector for Research and Business Activities: Prof. Dr NENCHO GEORGIEV NENOV

Library of 50,000 vols

DEANS

Faculty of Machinery and Construction Technologies in Transport: Assoc. Prof. Dr VALENTIN ALEKSANDROV NIKOLOV

Faculty of Telecommunications and Electrical Equipment in Transport: Assoc. Prof. Dr IVAN KOSTADINOV MILENOV

Faculty of Transport Management: Assoc. Prof. Dr TOSHO TRIFONOV KACHAUNOV

VARNENSKI SVOBODEN UNIVERSITET
(University of Economics—Varna)

77 Kniaz Boris I Blvd, 9002 Varna

Telephone: (52) 66-02-12

Fax: (52) 23-56-80

E-mail: u_otdel@ue-varna.bg

Internet: www.ue-varna.bg

Founded 1920 as Higher School of Commerce

State control

Academic year: September to June

Rector: Prof. Dr KALYU IVANOV DONEV

Vice Rector for Academic Affairs: Assoc. Prof. Dr PLAMEN BLAGOV ILIEV

Vice Rector for IC and Public Relations: Assoc. Prof. Dr BLAGO ANGELOV BLAGOEV

Vice Rector for PSC and Finance: Assoc. Prof. Dr NIKOLA MILEV BAKALOV

Vice Rector for Research: Assoc. Prof. Dr ZOJA KOSTOVA MLADENOVA

Registrar: Dr S. IVANOV

Librarian: Mag. T. TSANEVA

Library of 270,000 vols

Number of teachers: 262

Number of students: 8,202

Publications: *Economic Research* (3 a year), *Godishnik, Izvestya*

DEANS

Faculty of Computer Science: Prof. MARIA ZAPRIANOVA KASHEVA

Faculty of Economics: Assoc. Prof. Dr STOYAN ANDREEV STOYANOV

Faculty of Finance and Accounting: Assoc. Prof. NADIA KOSTOVA ENCHEVA

Faculty of Management: Prof. APOSTLE ATANASOV APOSTOLOV

PROFESSORS

ATANASOV, B., Econometrics

DIMITROV, G., Economics of Building

DOCHEV, D., Mathematics

DONEV, K., Auditing

GENOV, G., Accountancy

ILIEV, P., Computer Sciences

KARAMFILOV, Z., Informatics

KOTSEV, T., Finance and Credit

KOVACHEV, Z., Economics

MIKHAILOV, P., Economics

MINCHEV, S., Organic Chemistry

SALOVA, N., Economics and Organization of Trade

VELIKO TĂRNOVSKI UNIVERSITET 'SV. KIRIL I METODII'
(St Cyril and St Methodius University of Veliko Tărnovo)

Teodosii Tarnovo St 2, 5003 Veliko Tărnovo

Telephone: (62) 61-83-77

Fax: (62) 62-80-23

E-mail: mbox@uni-vt.bg

Internet: www.uni-vt.bg

Founded 1963, fmrly 'Kiril i Metodii' Higher Pedagogical Institute, Univ. Status 1971

Academic year: October to June

Rector: Prof. Dr Hab. PLAMEN ANATOLIEV LEGKOSTUP

Vice-Rector: Assoc. Prof. Dr MARIYA MINKOVA PAVLOVA

Vice-Rector: Assoc. Prof. Dr BAGRELIA SABCHEVA BORISOVA

Vice-Rector for Education: Assoc. Prof. Dr PETKO STEFANOV PETKOV
Sec.-Gen.: OLEG YANKOV BOZHANOV
Admin. Officer: OLEG BOZHANOV
Dir of Library: Assoc. Prof. Dr SAVA YORDANOV VASILEV
Library of 380,000 vols, 42,000 periodicals, rare and valuable books, electronic and other materials
Number of teachers: 853
Number of students: 12,000
Publications: *Archives of Historical and Geographical Research* (4 a year), *Epochi* (4 a year), *Pir* (1 a year), *Proglas* (4 a year), *Works of the University* (1 a year)

DEANS

Faculty of Arts: Prof. Dr ANTOANETA ANGELOVA ANCHEVA
Faculty of Economics: Prof. Dr Hab. GEORGI STEFANOV IVANOV
Faculty of Education: Assoc. Prof. Dr ZHIVKO TRIFONOV KARAPENCHEV
Faculty of History: Assoc. Prof. Dr ANDREY ANDREEV
Faculty of Law: Assoc. Prof. Dr TSVETAN GEORGIEV SIVKOV
Faculty of Modern Languages: Assoc. Prof. Dr BAGRELIA SABCHEVA BORISSOVA BORISOVA
Faculty of Orthodox Theology: Assoc. Prof. Dr DIMITAR MARINOV KIROV
Faculty of Philosophy: Assoc. Prof. Dr VIHREN YANAKIEV BUZOV

VISSHE UCHILISHTE PO ZASTRAKHOVANE I FINANSI (VUZF University)

zh.k. Ovcha Kupel, ul. Gusla No.1, 1618 Sofia
Telephone: (2) 401-58-12
Fax: (2) 401-58-21
E-mail: office@vuzf.bg
Internet: www.vuzf.bg
Founded 2002
Private control
Pres.: Dr GRIGORII VAZOV
Vice-Pres.: CLOVER SMILKOVA
Exec. Dir: RADOSTIN VAZOV
Deputy Rector for Educational Activities and Quality Management: Prof. YORDAN HRISTOSKOV
Deputy Rector for Research and Devt and Institutional Relations: Prof. KOSTADIN KOSTADINOV

Courses in finance; insurance and social insurance; management and marketing.

YUGOZAPADEN UNIVERSITET 'NEOFIT RILSKI' (Southwest University 'Neofit Rilski')

Ivan Michailov St 66, 2700 Blagoevgrad
Telephone: (73) 88-55-05
Fax: (73) 88-55-16
E-mail: info @swu. bg
Internet: www.swu.bg
Founded 1976
State control
Academic year: September to July
Chair.: Prof. Dr ILIA GYUDZHENOV
Rector: Prof. Dr IVAN MIRCHEV
Vice-Rector for Credential Activity, Publs and Information Infrastructure: Prof. Dr IVAN MIRCHEV
Vice-Rector for Int. Relations: Asst Prof. Dr DOBRINKA GEORGIEVA
Vice-Rector for Research and Devt, Practical Training and Professional Qualifications: Assoc. Prof. Dr DIMITAR DIMITROV
Vice-Rector for Teaching: Assoc. Prof. Dr ZDRAVKO GARGAROV
Library of 155,000 vols

Number of teachers: 1,000
Number of students: 10,000

DEANS

Faculty of Arts: Prof. Dr RUMEN POTEROV
Faculty of Economics: Assoc. Prof. Dr CHAVDAR NIKOLOV
Faculty of Law and History: Prof. Dr SOFKA MATEEVA
Faculty of Mathematics and Natural Sciences: Assoc. Prof. Dr BORISLAV YURUKOV
Faculty of Pedagogy: Assoc. Prof. Dr RUSSI RUSSEV
Faculty of Philology: Dr ANTHONY STOILOV
Faculty of Philosophy: Assoc. Prof. GEORGI APOSTOLOV
Faculty of Public Health and Sports: Assoc. Prof. STOIAN IVANOV
Technical College: Assoc. Prof. IVANKA GEORGIEVA (Dir)

Academies and Institutes

Akademija za Muzikalno i Tanzovo Izkustvo (Academy of Music and Dance): T. Samodumov 2, 4025 Plovdiv; tel. (32) 22-83-11; fax (32) 63-16-68; f. 1972; academic year September to July; 105 teachers; 972 students; Rector Assoc. Prof. VASILKA YONCHEVA; Pro-Rector Assoc. Prof. LYUBEN DOSEV; Pro-Rector Prof. SNEJANA SIMEONOVA; Pro-Rector Prof. MILCHO VASILEV; Sec.-Gen. (Man.) K. MECHEV; Librarian V. PAVLOVA; publ. *Collection of Articles* (1 a year).

Bulgaria–Romania Interuniversity Europe Centre: 55 Alexandrovska St, 7000 Ruse; tel. (82) 82-56-67; fax (82) 82-56-62; e-mail brie-bg@ru.acad.bg; internet www.brie.ru.acad.bg; f. 2001 operates through collaboration between the Rusenski Universitet 'Angel Kanchev' and the Academia de Studii Economice (see Romania chapter); attached to Rusenski Universitet 'Angel Kanchev'; offers postgraduate degrees in European studies.

College of Economics and Administration: Blvd Kuklensko Rd 13, Plovdiv; tel. (32) 26-69-35; e-mail ceabul@yahoo.co.uk; internet www.ceabul.net; f. 2003; Chair. Prof. DIMITAR KOSTOV; Rector GEORGI MANOLOV.

College of Tourism: Park Ezero, 8000 Burgas; tel. (56) 85-81-84; fax (56) 81-37-61; e-mail cot@cot.bse.bg; internet www.btu.bg; f. 1967 as Institute of Int. Tourism, present name 1997; attached to Burgas Prof. Assen Zlatarov Univ.; Dir Prof. A. KOKINOV.

European College of Economics and Management: 18 Zadruga St, 4004 Plovdiv; tel. and fax (32) 67-23-62; e-mail office@ecem.org; internet www.ecem.org; f. 2001; offers courses in accountancy and control, business administration, corporate economics, tourist hospitality management; 2,000 students; Pres. Prof. Dr MARIANA MIHAILOVA; Rector Assoc. Prof. Dr TSVETAN KOLEV; Vice-Rector Prof. Dr MARIA KAPITANOVA; Chief Sec. Dr TSVETAN KOTSEV.

G. S. Rakovski National Defence Academy: Evlogi and Hristo Georgiev No. 82, 1504 Sofia; tel. (2) 922-65-10; fax (2) 944-16-57; e-mail rectorrdsc@md.government.bg; internet rdsc.md.government.bg; f. 1912; higher education and scientific research on issues of nat. security and defence; library: 420,000 vols in Academic Library and 250,000 books in Military History Library; 1,000 students; Commandant Major Gen. GEORGI TANEV GEORGIEV; publ. *Military Journal* (10 a year).

Higher School 'Agricultural College ' Plovdiv: Dunav Blvd 78, 4003 Plovdiv; tel.

(32) 96-03-60; fax (32) 96-04-06; e-mail agri_college@mail.bg; internet www.agricollege.com; f. 1992, present name 1997, present status 2003; agrotechnologies; technologies in horticulture and wine-production; economics of tourism; alternative tourism; agrarian economics; business administration; Rector Assoc. Prof. Dr Eng. DIMITAR DIMITROV; Vice-Rector Assoc. Prof. Dr DIMITAR IV. DIMITROV; Vice-Rector Assoc. Prof. Dr PETAR PETROV; Vice-Rector Assoc. Prof. Dr MARIANA IVANOVA.

Higher School – College Telematics: St Parchevich 26, 6000 Stara Zagora; tel. and fax (42) 63-02-06; e-mail coppk@abv.bg; internet www.telematika-college.com; f. 1989; offers professional courses and specialized language courses, incl. English, French, German, Spanish, Italian, Russian; 470 mems; Rector Prof. Dr CHRISTO SANTULOV.

Higher State School 'College of Telecommunications and Post': Studentski grad 1 Academic Stefan Mladenov St, 1700 Sofia; tel. (2) 862-28-93; fax (2) 806-22-27; e-mail rector@hctp.acad.bg; internet www.hctp.acad.bg; f. 1922; Rector Assoc. Prof. Dr IVAN KURTEV; Deputy Rector for Educational Process Assoc. Prof. TATYANA DAMGOVA; Deputy Rector of PGS and SR Assoc. Prof. Dr STEFAN POPOV.

International University College: Bulgaria St 3, 9300 Dobrich; tel. (58) 65-56-20; fax (58) 60-57-60; e-mail dobrich@vumk.eu; internet www.vumk.eu; f. 1992; library: 12,500 vols; 1,400 students; Rector Prof. TODOR RADEV; Vice-Rector KLARA DIMITROVA; Academic Dir STANISLAV IVANOV; publ. *The European Journal of Tourism Research*.

Medical College: 69 Stefan Stambolov Blvd, 8000 Burgas; tel. (56) 85-81-50; fax (56) 81-32-95; e-mail medcollege@bginfo.net; internet www.btu.bg; f. 1950 as Medical School, present name 1997; attached to Burgas Prof. Assen Zlatarov Univ.; specializes in health care and pharmacy; Dir Asst Prof. M. STOICHEVA.

Ministry of the Interior Academy: c/o Ministry of Interior, 29 Shesti Septemvri St, 1000; tel. (2) 982-50-00; internet www.mvr.bg; f. 2002; attached to Min. of Interior; training state officials, incl. faculties of security, police, fire and emergency safety; organizes nat. and int. confs, seminars and research.

N. Y. Vaptsarov Naval Academy: 73 V. Drumev St, 9026 Varna; tel. (52) 552-228; fax (52) 303-163; e-mail public-rel@naval.acad.bg; internet www.naval-acad.bg; f. 1881 as Machine School for the Navy, present name 1949; trains specialists for the Navy and for the merchant marine in all areas of maritime life; research and devt; Commandant Captain DIMITAR ANGELOV.

National Music Academy 'Prof.Pancho Vladigerov': e-mail sagitta@dma.acad.bg E. Georgiev 94, 1505 Sofia; tel. (2) 943-34-00; fax (2) 944-14-54; internet www.nma.bg; f. 1921, fmrly State Academy of Music, present name 2006; academic year September to June; Faculties of instrumentation, musical theory, composition and conducting, and vocal studies; 220 teachers; 995 students; Rector Prof. Dr DIMITAR MOMCHILOV MOMCHILOV; Vice-Rector for Training's Methodical and Scientific Research Activity Prof. Dr PRAVDA ATANASOVA GORANOV; Vice-Rector for Art Activities and Academic Orchestra Work Prof ANATOLY DOBREV KRASTEV; Vice-Rector for Academic Opera Theatre and Art Activities of the Vocal Faculty Prof. ILKA BORISOVA POPOVA; Dir of Library Dr ELIZABETH PETKOVA; publ. *Godishnik*.

National Sports Academy 'Vassil Levski': Studentski grad, 1700; tel. (2) 962-

04-58; fax (2) 62-90-07; internet www.nsa.bg; f. 1942 as Higher School for Physical Education, present name 1999; faculties of physiotherapy, physical education, teachers and coaches training; Rector Prof. Dr LACHEZAR DIMITROV; Vice-Rector for Education Assoc. Prof. Dr PENCHO GESHEV; Vice-Rector for Int. Relations and European Integration Prof. Dr DANIELA DASHEVA; Vice-Rector for Accreditation and Quality of Education Assoc. Prof. Dr DIMITAR MIHAILOV; Vice-Rector for Science Prof. Dr PETAR BONOV; Vice-Rector for Social and Economic Affairs Prof. Dr KIRIL ANDONOV.

Nacionalna Akademija za Teatralno i Filmovo Izkustvo (National Academy of Theatre and Film Arts): G. S. Rakovski St 108A, 1000 Sofia; tel. (2) 923-12-25; fax (2) 989-73-89; e-mail natfiz@bitex.com; internet natfiz.bg; f. 1948; academic year October to July; offers drama theatre acting, puppet theatre acting, physical theatre, drama theatre directing, puppet theatre directing, stage and screen design; screen arts and stage arts management; incl. faculties of screen arts and stage arts; library: 60,000 vols; 87 teachers; 560 students; Rector Prof. Dr STANISLAV SEMERDJIEV; Registrar STOYAN EVTIMOV; Sec. ILIANA DIMITROVA; Librarian EMILIA BALDZHIYSKA; publ. *108A Magazine.*

Nacionalna Hudojestvena Akademija (National Academy of Art): 1 Shipka St, 1000 Sofia; tel. (2) 988-17-01; fax (2) 987-33-28; e-mail art_academy@yahoo.com; internet www.nha-bg.org; f. 1896, reorganized as an acad. 1995; academic year October to May; offers courses in fine and applied arts, design, conservation and restoration and history and theory of art; 131 teachers; 800 students; Rector Prof. SVETOSLAV KOKALOV; Vice-Rector for Education and Scientific Activities Prof. SVILEN STEFANOV; Vice-Rector for Exhibition and Artistic Activities Prof. ANNA BOYADJIEVA; Vice-Rector for Int. Relations Prof. MITKO DINEV; Librarian DARINKA DIUKMEDJIEVA; publ. *The Art of Drawing* (1 a year).

Pedagogical College in Pleven: c/o Veliko Tărnovski Universitet 'Sv. Kiril i Metodii', T. Tarnovo 2, 5003 Veliko Tărnovo; tel. (62) 61-83-33; fax (62) 62-80-23; internet www.uni-vt.bg; attached to St Cyril and St Methodius Univ. of Veliko Tarnovo; Dir Assoc. Prof. YORDAN MITEV.

Stopanska Akademija 'D. A. Tsenov' ('D. A. Tsenov' Academy of Economics): St Em. Chakarov 2, 5250 Svishtov; tel. (631) 6-62-46; fax (631) 6-09-78; e-mail rectorat@uni-svishtov.bg; internet www.uni-svishtov.bg; f. 1936 as D. A. Tsenov Higher School of Commerce, present name 1995; State control; academic year September to July; offers courses in economic accounting, finance, management and marketing, production and commercial business; library: 192,748 vols of periodicals, 200,000 vols of books, 15 int. databases; 274 teachers; 12,300 students; Rector Assoc. Prof. Dr VELICHKA ADAMOV IONOV; Vice-Rector for BA Training and Financial Policy Dr GEORGI MARINOV GERGANOVA; Vice-Rector for Social, and Student Information Policy Dr LYUBEN MARINOV KRAEV; Vice-Rector for Research and Int. Cooperation SARKIS AGOP SARKISYAN; Admin. Sec. CNEZHANA DIMITROVA GENKOV; Chief Admin. Officer V. TANEV; Dir of Library ANKA PETKOVA TANEVA; publs *Biznes—Upravlenie* (4 a year), *Dialogue* (online, 4 a year), *Economic World Library* (6 a year), *Narodnostopanski Arhiv* (4 a year).

Technical College: Prof. Yakimov Blvd 1, 8010 Burgas; tel. and fax (56) 88-12-31; e-mail barzov@btu.bg; internet www.btu.bg; f. 1986 as Institute of Mechanical and Electrical Engineering, present name 1997; attached to Burgas Prof. Assen Zlatarov Univ.; machinery and equipment construction, transport equipment and technologies, electrotechnics, electronics, computer systems and technologies, marketing; Dir Prof. P. BARZOV.

Technical College of Lovech: Gr. Lovech, POB 5500, St C Saev 31, Lovech; tel. (68) 60-39-29; fax (68) 60-39-25; e-mail tklovech@mail.bg; internet www.tklovech.org; f. 1990; attached to Tehničeski Universitet Gabrovo; Dir Assoc. Prof. Dr VASIL KOCHEVSKI.

Theatre College 'Luben Groys': Sq. 'Bulgaria' 1, NDK, Admin. Bldg, 12th Fl., Suite 7A, 1000 Sofia; tel. (2) 986-20-25; fax (2) 916-61-65; e-mail lgroys_college@yahoo.com; internet www.lgrois.50megs.com; f. 1991.

Vratsa College of Education: c/o Veliko Tărnovski Universitet 'Sv. Kiril i Metodii, T. Tarnovo No. 2, 5003 Veliko Tărnovo; tel. (62) 61-83-33; fax (62) 62-80-23; e-mail ; internet www.uni-vt.bg; attached to St Cyril and St Methodius Univ. of Veliko Tarnovo; Dir Assoc. Prof. YORDAN YOTOV.

BURKINA FASO

The Higher Education System

Higher education in Burkina Faso dates from the establishment of a teacher-training institute in 1965 which, after several name changes, became known as the Université de Ouagadougou (UO) in 1972. In addition to the UO there is a polytechnic university at Bobo-Dioulasso and an institute of teacher training at Koudougou; there are also 11 private institutions. The number of students enrolled at tertiary-level institutions in 2006/07 was 33,500. The two state-run universities are government-funded, with additional financial resources provided by bilateral or multilateral agreements and the universities' own revenue streams. Higher education is the responsibility of the Ministry of Secondary and Higher Education and Scientific Research.

The UO and Université Polytechnique de Bobo-Dioulasso have similar, five-tier administrative structures consisting of a Board of Directors, a University Assembly, a University Council, institutions and departments. The Board of Directors consists of representatives from the government ministries, the institution's administrative staff, trade unions' representatives, academic staff and students. The University Assembly decides university policy and is summoned by the Rector at least twice a year. Its members are drawn from the Directors, teaching, administrative and technical staff, students and representatives from government ministries. The Rector (or Chancellor) runs the university with the aid of the Vice-Chancellors and a Secretary-General. Finally, institutions are administered by Directors, who report directly to the Rector.

Admission to higher education is based on the award of the Baccalauréat or Bachelier du second degré. Higher education awards are arranged in three cycles. The first cycle lasts two years and leads to award of the Diplôme d'Études Universitaires Générales (DEUG), Premier Cycle d'Études Médicales (PCEM), Diplôme Universitaire d'Études Littéraires (DUEL), Diplôme Universitaire d'Études Scientifiques (DUES) or Diplôme Universitaire de Technologie. The second cycle lasts one year after the first cycle for the Licence degree, two years for the Maîtrise or three years for Diplôme d'Ingénieur. Finally, the third cycle comprises doctoral-level studies. The Diplôme d'Études Supérieures Spécialisées (DESS) or the Diplôme d'Études Approfondies (DEA) are awarded after one-year courses in subjects such as mathematics, biology, chemistry, law, economics and linguistics, and the Doctorat de Troisième Cycle or Doctorat de Spécialité are awarded following two further years of study after the DEA. In addition to higher education awards, the main vocational award is the Diplôme, which requires two years of study.

Regulatory Bodies

GOVERNMENT

Ministry of Culture, Tourism and Communication: 03 BP 7007, Ouagadougou 03; tel. 50-33-09-63; fax 50-33-09-64; e-mail mcat@cenatrin.bf; internet www.culture.gov .bf; Min. PHILIPPE SAWADOGO.

Ministry of Secondary and Higher Education and Scientific Research: 03 BP 7047, Ouagadougou 03; tel. 50-32-45-67; fax 50-32-61-16; e-mail laya.saw@messrs.gov.bf; internet www.messrs.gov.bf; Min. Prof. JOSEPH PARÉ.

Research Institutes

GENERAL

Centre National de la Recherche Scientifique et Technologique: BP 7047, Ouagadougou 03; tel. 50-32-46-48; fax 50-31-50-03; internet www.cnrst.bf; f. 1950, 1968 incorporated into Ministère de l'Education Nationale, 1978 into Ministère de l'Enseignement Supérieur et de la Recherche Scientifique; basic and applied research in humanities, social sciences, natural sciences, agriculture, energy, medicine; library of 20,000 vols; 102 researchers; Dir-Gen. BASILE L. GUISSOU; publs *Sciences et Technique* (2 a year), *CNRST-Information* (6 a year), *Eurêka* (4 a year).

Institut de Recherche pour le Développement (IRD): BP 182, Ouagadougou 01; tel. 50-30-67-37; fax 50-31-03-85; internet www.ird.bf; f. 1968; hydrology, geography, agronomy, botany, medical entomology, economics, demography, anthropology, pedology, ethnology, geology, sociology; Dir JEAN-PIERRE GUENGANT; (see main entry under France).

AGRICULTURE, FISHERIES AND VETERINARY SCIENCE

Centre de Coopération Internationale en Recherche Agronomique pour le Développement (CIRAD): Ave du Président Kennedy, BP 596, Ouagadougou 01; tel. 50-30-70-70; fax 50-30-76-17; e-mail jacques.pages@cirad.fr; f. 1963; natural resource management and environmental protection; improved crop and livestock production; agroeconomics; remote sensing and geographical information systems; agrifoods; 15 research staff; Regional Dir for continental West Africa JACQUES PAGÈS; publ. *Rapport scientifique* (1 a year).

Institut de l'Environnement et de Recherches Agricoles: BP 8645, Ouagadougou 04; tel. 50-34-71-12; fax 50-34-02-71; e-mail inera.direction@fasonet.bf; f. 1978; research in arable and livestock farming, forestry, agricultural machinery, natural resources, management and farming systems; library of 2,500 vols, 2,500 documents; Dir Prof. HAMIDOU BOLY; publ. *Science et Technique* (2 a year).

EDUCATION

Institut Pédagogique du Burkina: BP 7043, Ouagadougou; tel. 50-33-63-63; f. 1976 by the Min. of Nat. Education, for the devt of methods and courses in primary education; library of 16,000 vols (Min. of Education Library); 150 staff; Dir Gen. JUSTINE TAPSOBA; publ. *Action, Réflexion et Culture* (8 a year).

TECHNOLOGY

Bureau de Recherches Géologiques et Minières (BRGM): BP 86, Ouagadougou; tel. 50-33-50-42; (see main entry under France).

Libraries and Archives

Ouagadougou

Bibliothèque Nationale du Burkina: 03 LP 7007, Ouagadougou 03; tel. 50-32-63-63; internet www.culture.gov.bf/site_ministere/ m.c.a.t/ministere/ministere_sr_bn.htm; f. 1988; under Min. of Culture, Arts and Tourism; Dir-Gen. ABEL NADIE.

Centre National des Archives: Présidence du Faso, BP 7030, Ouagadougou; tel. 50-33-61-96; fax 50-31-49-26; f. 1970; Dir DIDIER E. OUEDRAOGO.

Museum

Ouagadougou

Musée National: 08 BP 11186, Ouagadougou; located at: Ave Oubritenga, Ouagadougou; tel. 50-30-73-89; fax 50-31-25-09; internet www.culture.gov.bf/site_ministere/ textes/etablissements/etablissements_mu-seenational.htm; f. 2003; 4,000 artefacts; Dir Prof. ALIMATA SAWADOGO.

Universities

UNIVERSITÉ POLYTECHNIQUE DE BOBO-DIOULASSO

01 BP 1091, Bobo-Dioulasso 01

Telephone: 20-98-06-35

Fax: 20-98-25-77

E-mail: hamidou.boly@yahoo.fr

Internet: www.univ-bobo.bf

Founded 1997

State control

Academic year: October to July

Pres.: Prof. HAMIDOU BOLY

Vice-Pres. for Teaching and Pedagogic Innovation: Prof. MARIE YVES THÉODORE TAPSOBA

Vice-Pres. for Research, Prospective and Int. Cooperation: Prof. ANTOINE N. SOME
Dir for Int. Cooperation: Dr IRÉNÉE SOMDA
Number of teachers: 101
Number of students: 2,048

DIRECTORS

Ecole Supérieure d'Informatique: Prof. M'BI KABORE
Institut du Développement Rural: Dr HASSAN BISMARCK NACRO
Institut des Sciences Exactes et Appliquées: Dr SADO TRAORE
Institut des Sciences de la Nature et de la Vie: Prof. JULIETTE DIALLO-TRANCHOT
Institut des Sciences de la Santé: Prof. ROBERT T. GUIGUEMDE
Institut Universitaire de Technologie: Dr BETABOALÉ NAHON

UNIVERSITÉ DE OUAGADOUGOU

03 BP 7021, Ouagadougou 03
Telephone: 50-30-70-64
Fax: 50-30-72-42
E-mail: info@univ-ouaga.bf
Internet: www.univ-ouaga.bf
Founded 1969, univ. status 1974

Academic year: October to June
State control
Language of instruction: French
Pres.: JOSEPH PARÉ
Vice-Press: JEAN COULIDIATY, GUSTAVE KABRÉ, FRANÇOIS RENÉ TALL
Sec.-Gen.: MAMIDOU KONE
Librarian: MAÏMOUNA SANOKO
Library of 70,000 vols
Number of teachers: 395
Number of students: 21,309

Publications: *Annales* (2 a year), *Cahiers du Centre d'Etudes, de Documentation et de Recherches Economiques et Sociales* (4 a year), *Revue burkinabé de Droit* (2 a year)

DEANS

Faculty of Economics and Management Sciences: DEMBO GADIAGA
Faculty of Health Sciences: MAMADOU SAWADOGO
Faculty of Law and Politics: G. AUGUSTIN LOADA
Faculty of Letters, Arts, Humanities and Social Sciences: ROSAIRE BAMA, JUSTIN KOUTABA

Faculty of Science and Technology: MARTIN LOMPO

Colleges

Centre d'Etudes Economiques et Sociales d'Afrique Occidentale (CESAO): BP 305, Bobo-Dioulasso; tel. 20-97-10-17; fax 20-97-08-02; e-mail cesao.bobo@fasonet.bf; f. 1960; areas of study incl. the enhancement of rural orgs on an institutional level, the promotion of women, faith and humanity, community health, admin. of the devt of rural communities, environment and land admin., savings and investments in rural areas, devt projects; 16 staff; library: 14,000 vols and 77 periodicals; Dir ROSALIE OUOBA; publ. *Construire Ensemble* (6 a year).

Ecole Inter-Etats d'Ingénieurs de l'Equipement Rural (EIER): BP 7023, Ouagadougou 03; tel. 50-30-20-53; fax 50-31-27-24; f. 1968 by governments of 14 francophone African states; 3-year postgraduate diploma course; hydraulics, civil engineering, refrigeration technology, sanitary engineering; Dir MICHEL GUINAUDEAU.

BURUNDI

The Higher Education System

The main institution of higher education is the Université du Burundi, founded in 1973 following a merger of several institutions, including the Université Officielle de Bujumbura. In 2004/05 17,061 students were enrolled in higher education. The main language of instruction is French. The Minister of Higher Education and Scientific Research is responsible for higher education, although the Université du Burundi enjoys a relative degree of autonomy. There is also a growing private higher education sector.

The Diplôme des Humanités Complètes is the standard secondary education qualification required for admission to higher education. Undergraduate education consists of three stages: the Candidature is a programme of general studies lasting two years; the Diplôme de Licence requires a further two years of study; and in medicine the professional title Docteur en Médecin is awarded after four years of study following the Candidature. The main postgraduate qualification is the Diplôme d'Études Approfondies.

Several institutes of the Université du Burundi also offer higher vocational education, usually courses of three to four years leading to the award of the Diplôme d'Ingénieur Technicien.

Regulatory Bodies

GOVERNMENT

Ministry of Higher Education and Scientific Research: Bujumbura; Min. Dr SAÏDI KIBEYA.

Ministry of Youth, Sports and Culture: Bujumbura; tel. 22226822; Min. JEAN-JACQUES NYENIMIGABO.

Research Institutes

AGRICULTURE, FISHERIES AND VETERINARY SCIENCE

Institut des Sciences Agronomiques du Burundi: BP 795, Bujumbura; tel. 22223390; fax 22225798; e-mail isabu@usan-bu.net; internet www.asareca.org/naris/isabu; f. 1962; agronomical research and farm management; library of 11,500 vols, 120 periodicals; Dir-Gen. Dr JEAN NDIKURANA.

MEDICINE

Laboratoire Médical: Bujumbura; devoted to clinical analyses, physio-pathological research and nutritional studies.

NATURAL SCIENCES

Physical Sciences

Centre National d'Hydrométéorologie: Bujumbura; Dir E. KAYENGAYENGE.

TECHNOLOGY

Direction Générale de la Géologie et des Mines: Ministère de l'Energie et des Mines, BP 745, Bujumbura; tel. 22222278; fax 22223538; Dir-Gen. Dr AUDACE NTUNGICIMPAYE.

Libraries and Archives

Bujumbura

Archives nationales du Burundi: Ministère de la Jeunesse, de la Culture et des Sports, BP 1095 Rohero II, Bujumbura; located at: ave Kunkiko, Bujumbura; tel. 22225051; fax 22226231; 26,000 vols; Dir NICODÈME NYANDWI.

Bibliothèque de l'Université: BP 1320, Bujumbura; tel. 22222857; f. 1961; 192,000 vols, 554 periodicals; Chief Librarian THARLISSE NSABIMANA.

Museums and Art Galleries

Bujumbura

Musée Vivant de Bujumbura: Ministère de la Jeunesse, de la Culture et des Sports, BP 1095 Rohero II, Bujumbura; located at: ave Kunkiko, Bujumbura; tel. 22226852; f. 1977; part of Centre de Civilisation Burundaise attached to Ministry of Youth, Culture and Sport; reflects the life of the Burundi people in all its aspects; incl. a reptile house, aquarium, aviary, traditional Rugo dwelling, open-air theatre, fishing museum, botanical garden, herpetology centre, musical pavilion, and crafts village; Dir EMMANUEL NIRAGIRA.

Gitega

Musée National de Gitega: 223 Magarama (Pl. de la Révolution), BP 110, Gitega; tel. 22402359; fax 22219295; e-mail jmapfarakora@yahoo.fr; f. 1955; history, archaeology, ethnography, arts, folk traditions, arms; library: in process of formation (200 vols); Curator JACQUES MAPFARAKORA.

University

UNIVERSITÉ DU BURUNDI

BP 1550, Bujumbura
Telephone: 2242353
Fax: 2223288
E-mail: rectorat@ub.edu.bi
Internet: www.ub.edu.bi
Founded 1973, present name 1980
Academic year: October to September
Pres. of Admin. Ccl: MARC RWABAHUNGU
Rector: Prof. ALEXANDRE HATUNGIMANA
Vice-Rector: Prof. JACQUES BUKURU
Academic Dir: Prof. SYLVIE HATUNGIMANA
Admin. and Finance Dir: VÉNÉRAND NIZIGIYIMANA
Research Dir: Prof. VESTINE NTAKARUTIMANA
Librarian: VENANT BUSHUBIJE
Number of teachers: 239
Number of students: 8,545
Publications: *Actes de la Conférence des Universités des Etats Membres de la CEPGL* (1 a year), *Actes de la Semaine de l'Université* (1 a year), *Le Flambeau* (1 a year), *Le Héraut* (6 a year), *Revue de l'Université* (4 a year)

DEANS

Faculty of Agriculture: BONAVENTURE NIYOYANKANA
Faculty of Applied Sciences: JOSEPH NZEYIMANA
Faculty of Economic and Administrative Sciences: PASCAL RUTAKE
Faculty of Law: STANISLAS MAKOROKA
Faculty of Letters and Humanities: MELCHIOR NTAHONKIRKIYE
Faculty of Medicine: FRANÇOIS XAVIER BUYOYA
Faculty of Psychology and Education: PAUL NKUNZIMANA
Faculty of Sciences: DÉO DOUGLAS NIYONZIMA

DIRECTORS

Higher Technical Institute: THÉOPHILE NDIKUMANA
Institute of Education: DOMITIEN NIZIGIYIMANA
Institute of Physical Education and Sports: THARCISSE NIYONZIMA

Colleges

Centre Social et Éducatif: Bujumbura; f. 1957; courses in crafts, photography, mechanics; 75 students.

École Supérieure de Commerce du Burundi: BP 1440, Bujumbura; tel. 22224520; f. 1982; 304 students; library: 1,200 vols; Dir PIERRE NZEYIMANA.

Institut Supérieur d'Agriculture: BP 35, Gitega; tel. 22242335; f. 1983; under Min. of Nat. Education; courses in tropical agriculture, stockbreeding, agricultural engineering, food technology; 213 students; Dir (vacant); publ. *Revue des Techniques Agricoles Tropicales* (2 a year).

Institut Supérieur de Techniciens de l'Aménagement et de l'Urbanisme: BP 2720, Bujumbura; tel. 22223694; f. 1983; under the Min. of Public Works and Urban Development; 103 students; library: 863 vols; Dir SALVATOR NAHIMANA.

Lycée Technique: Bujumbura; f. 1949; training apprentices, craftsmen and professional workers; 4 workshops: mechanics, masonry, carpentry, electrical assembling; 450 students.

CAMBODIA

The Higher Education System

The oldest institution of higher education is the Royal University of Phnom-Penh, founded in 1960. The higher education system was greatly affected by the coup of 1975 and the Khmer Rouge regime (1975–79), but has enjoyed a renaissance in recent years with the restoration of pre-Khmer Rouge institutions and foundation of private establishments. Other public institutions of higher education now include universities of agriculture, fine arts and health sciences.

To gain admission to higher education students must possess the Diploma of Upper Secondary Education and pass the competitive national entrance examination. Higher education lasts for up to eight years, including undergraduate and postgraduate study. Until 1993 the most common undergradu-ate qualification was the Diploma of Higher Education, but since then several other equivalent degree titles have emerged. In 2009 there were 76 higher education institutions; 33 of them were public and 43 were private. There were 168,003 students studying in graduate and postgraduate programmes, and there were 11,694 state public students. The Ministry of Education, Youth and Sport (MoEYS) sent 415 students to study overseas and 51 graduates were from overseas. MoEYS admitted 56 foreign students to study in the local universities.

Technical and vocational educational and training courses are one to three years in length, and the Department of Technical Vocational Education and Training (DTVET) has established criteria for certificate- and Diploma-level studies.

Regulatory and Representative Bodies

GOVERNMENT

Ministry of Culture and Fine Arts: 227 blvd Norodom, Phnom-Penh; tel. (23) 217645; fax (23) 725749; e-mail mcfa@cambodia.gov.kh; internet www.mcfa.gov.kh; Minister Prince SISOVAT PANARA SIRIVUDH.

Ministry of Education, Youth and Sport: 80 blvd Norodom, Phnom-Penh; tel. (23) 217253; fax (23) 212512; e-mail moeys@everyday.com.kh; internet www.moeys.gov.kh; Minister KOL PHENG.

ACCREDITATION

Accreditation Committee of Cambodia: 3/F, Bldg No. 134, cnr of Monivong and Kampuchea Krom Blvd, Phnom-Penh; tel. (23) 224620; fax (23) 725743; internet www.acc.gov.kh; f. 2003; assures and works to improve the quality of higher education instns in Cambodia; meets int. standards through accreditation; Chair. SOK AN.

Learned Societies

GENERAL

UNESCO Office Phnom-Penh: POB 29, Phnom-Penh; located at: House 38, Samdech Sothearos Blvd, Phnom-Penh; tel. (23) 426726; fax (23) 426163; e-mail phnompenh@unesco.org; internet www.un.org.kh/unesco; Dir ETIENNE CLEMENT.

AGRICULTURE, FISHERIES AND VETERINARY SCIENCE

Cambodian Society of Agriculture: c/o CIAP, POB 01, Phnom-Penh; located at: CIAP, 29 Km Highway 3, Phnom-Penh; internet www.bigpond.com.kh/users/ciap/csa.htm; f. 1998; attached to Cambodia-IRRI-Australia Project; 144 mems; Pres. MAK SOLIENG; Sec. TOUCH SAVY; publs *Bulletin* (3 a year), *Cambodian Journal of Agriculture* (irregular).

HISTORY, GEOGRAPHY AND ARCHAEOLOGY

Authority for the Protection and Management of Angkor and the Region of Siem Reap (APSARA): 187 Pasteur St, Chaktomuk, Daun Penh, Phnom-Penh; tel. (23) 720315; fax (23) 990185 Angkor Preservation Compound, Siem Reap; tel. (63) 760080; fax (63) 760080; e-mail apsara-admin@camnet.com.kh; internet www.autoriteapsara.org; f. 1995; depts of administration, monuments and archaeology 1, monuments and archaeology 2, urbanism and urban planning, Angkor tourist devt, water and forest, demography, public order and cooperation; publs *Journal* (12 a year), *Udaya—Journal of Khmer Studies* (irregular).

Royal Angkor Foundation: POB 255, 1241 Budapest, Hungary; tel. (1) 3224270; fax (1) 3224270; e-mail angkor@hu.inter.net; internet www.angkor.iif.hu; f. 1992; safeguards the monuments and relics of the ancient Khmer civilization, establishing projects and gathering data; Hon. Co-Pres. HM NORODOM SIHANOUK (King of Cambodia), ÁRPÁD GÖNCZ (former Pres. of Hungary); Chair. of Supervisory Board GÁBOR BARTA.

NATURAL SCIENCES

Biological Sciences

Parks Society of Cambodia: POB 2680, Phnom-Penh; located at: 280B, Street 146, Group 32, Sangkat Toek Laaok II, Khan Toul Kork, Phnom-Penh; tel. (16) 813700; e-mail vibolparkssociety@hotmail.com; internet parkssociety-cambodia.netfirms.com; NGO responsible for community development, environmental education and the preservation of 10 wildlife reserves, 7 national parks, 3 protected landscapes and 3 multiple-use areas.

RELIGION, SOCIOLOGY AND ANTHROPOLOGY

Buddhist Association: c/o Buddhist Institute Library, POB 1047, Phnom-Penh.

Research Institutes

ECONOMICS, LAW AND POLITICS

Cambodia Development Resource Institute: POB 622, Phnom-Penh; 56 St 315, Tuol Kork, Phnom-Penh; tel. (23) 881701; fax (23) 880734; internet www.cdri.org.kh; f. 1990; centre for Peace and Devt programme; research in macroeconomic policy, rural livelihoods, governance and decentralization, natural resources and the environment, poverty analysis and monitoring; library of 15,250 vols, 100 periodicals; Dir LARRY STRANGE; Coordinator of the Centre for Peace and Devt ROMDUOL HUY; publs *Annual Development Review* (1 a year), *Cambodia Development Review* (4 a year), *Flash Report on the Cambodian Economy* (12 a year).

Cambodian Institute for Cooperation and Peace: POB 1007, Phnom-Penh; Phum Paung Peay, Sangkat Phnom-Penh Thmey, Khan Sen Sok, Phnom-Penh; tel. (12) 819953; fax (16) 982559; e-mail cicp@everyday.com.kh; internet www.cicp.org.kh; f. 1994; affiliated with ASEAN Institutes of Strategic and International Studies; library of 4,000 vols in Khmer, English and French; Admin. SOTHEARA CHHORN.

Cambodian Institute of Human Rights: POB 550, 30, St 57, Sangk at Boeung Keng Kong 1, Khan Chamcar Morn, Phnom-Penh; tel. (23) 210596; fax (23) 362739; e-mail chir@camnet.com.kh; f. 1993 by UN Transitional Authority in Cambodia; Dir KASSIE NEOU.

Centre for Social Development: POB 1346, Phnom-Penh; House 19, St 57, Sangkat Boeung Trabek, Keng Kang I Khan Chamkar Mon, Phnom-Penh; tel. and fax (23) 364735; internet www.bigpond.com.kh/users/csd; f. 1995; aims to promote democratic values through research, training, advocacy and debate; Pres. CHEA VANNATH; publ. *Bulletin* (12 a year).

MEDICINE

National Institute of Public Health: POB 1300, Phnom-Penh; tel. (23) 880345; fax (23) 880346; e-mail nphri@camnet.com.kh; internet www.camnet.com.kh/nphri; attached to Min. of Health; advises on govt policy and trains senior staff.

RELIGION, SOCIOLOGY AND ANTHROPOLOGY

World Buddhism Association for Development, Cambodia Regional Center: 11c, Rd 1986, Sangkat Phnom-Penh, Termei, Khan Kussey Keo, Phnom-Penh; tel. (23) 368506.

Libraries and Archives
Phnom-Penh

Documentation Centre of Cambodia: POB 110, Phnom-Penh; 70E, King Norodom Sihanouk Blvd, Phnom-Penh; tel. (23) 211875; fax (23) 210358; e-mail dccam@online.com.kh; internet www.dccam.org; f. 1995, as field office of the Cambodian Genocide Program at Yale University, USA; became fully autonomous instn in 1997; information resource centre on the Khmer Rouge regime; Dir YOUK CHHANG.

National Archives of Cambodia: POB 1109, Phnom-Penh; tel. (23) 430582; e-mail archives.cambodia@camnet.com.kh; internet www.camnet.com.kh/archives.cambodia; records of Résidence Supérieure du Cambodge (French colonial administration), 1863–1954; post-colonial govt collns; records of Khmer Rouge regime and 1979 genocide tribunal; periodicals and newspapers in French, Khmer, Vietnamese and Chinese.

National Library of Cambodia: Street 92, Daun Penh District, Phnom-Penh; tel. and fax (23) 430609; f. 1924; 103,635 vols; special collection of original palm-leaf manuscripts, 700 manuscript titles on microfilm; French Indo-China collection; Dir KHLOT VIBOLLA; publ. *Books-in-Print Cambodia*.

Museums and Art Galleries
Phnom-Penh

Museum of Genocide: Tuol Svay Prey Gymnasium, 103rd St, Phnom-Penh; f. 1979; fmr school converted into prison in 1975 after capture of Phnom-Penh by Khmer Rouge, and used as interrogation, torture and execution facility; following fall of the Khmer Rouge in 1979, converted into a museum depicting crimes of the regime.

National Museum of Arts: POB 2341, Phnom-Penh; located at: 13 Street, Phnom-Penh; tel. (23) 24369; f. 1920; main galleries dedicated to bronzes, sculpture, ethnography and ceramics; Dir KHUN SAMEN.

Universities

ROYAL ACADEMY OF CAMBODIA

Campus 2, Federation of Russia Boulevard, Sangkat Tuk Laak 1, Khan Tuol Kok, Phnom-Penh 12156
POB 2070, Phnom-Penh
Telephone: (23) 890180
Fax: (23) 221408
E-mail: hacademy@camnet.com.kh
Internet: www.rac.edu.kh
Founded 1965; disbanded 1975 due to civil war; re-established 1997
Languages of instruction: Khmer, English

State control; attached to Office of the Council of Ministers
Academic year: October to June
Library of 10,000 vols
Pres.: LOK CHUUTEAR KLOT THIDA
Under-General Secretary (Administration and Finance): CHHUN SUM BUN
Under-General Secretary (Training and Research): CHEA NENG

Offers a range of masters and doctoral programmes; promotes research in all major academic areas and organises scientific forums.

SUB-INSTITUTES

Institute of Biology, Medicine and Agriculture: tel. (12) 835306; Dir Dr SAM SOPHEAN.

Institute of Culture and Fine Arts: tel. (12) 733336; Dir Dr CHHAY YIHEANG.

Institute of Humanities and Social Sciences: tel. (11) 919044; Dir Dr ROS CHANTRABOT.

Institute of National Language: tel. (12) 836040; Dir (vacant).

Institute of Science and Technology: tel. (11) 951849; Dir Dr CHAN PORN.

ROYAL UNIVERSITY OF AGRICULTURE

POB 2696, Chamkar Daung, Phnom-Penh
Telephone: (23) 219829
Fax: (23) 219690
E-mail: rua@forum.org.kh
Founded 1964, university status since 1999
Number of teachers: 217
Number of students: 1,097
Rector: NARETH CHAN
Vice-Rector: MUNY PHAT

DEANS

Agricultural Economics and Rural Development: BORA KATHY
Agricultural Technology and Management: BUNTHAN NGO
Agro-Industry: SOK KUNTHY
Agronomy: SOPHAL CHOUNG
Animal Science and Production: PITH LOAN CHUM
Fisheries: CHHOUK BORIN
Forestry: MONIN VON
Information Technology and Telecommunications: MAO NARA
Land Management and Administration: MAK VISAL

ROYAL UNIVERSITY OF FINE ARTS

Street No. 70, Phnom-Penh
Telephone: (23) 910703
Founded 1965, closed 1975, re-opened as School of Fine Arts 1980, original name and status restored 1993
Rector: KEOUN TUK
Vice-Rector and Dean of Choreographic Arts: CHHIENG PROEUNG

Faculties: archaeology, architecture and urban studies, choreographic arts, music, plastic arts.

ROYAL UNIVERSITY OF LAW AND ECONOMICS

Preah Monivong, Phnom-Penh 12305
Telephone: (23) 211565
Fax: (23) 214953
E-mail: fle@khmerson.com
Founded 1948 as National Institute of Law, Politics and Economics; incorporated into the University of Phnom-Penh as Faculty of Law and Economics 1957; independent university status 2003
Language of instruction: Khmer
State control
Academic year: October to July
Number of teachers: 266 (84 full-time, 112 visiting Cambodian lecturers and 70 foreign visiting lecturers)
Number of students: 4,802
Rector: YUOK NGOY (acting)
Faculties of economics and management; law; public administration; Graduate Schools of law and economics and management.

ROYAL UNIVERSITY OF PHNOM-PENH

Confederation of Russia Blvd, Khan Tuol Kork, Phnom-Penh
Telephone: (12) 812017
Fax: (23) 880116
E-mail: pitch@camnet.com.kh
Internet: www.rupp.edu.kh
Founded 1960 as Khmer Royal University, re-named Phnom-Penh University 1970, closed 1975–1979, re-opened 1980, current name 1996
State control
Languages of instruction: Khmer, English, French
Academic year: September to June
Rector: Prof. PIT CHAMNAM
Vice-Rector: LAV CHHIV EAV
Vice-Rector: Dr NETH BAROM
Librarian: SEN SENG
Library of 39,000 vols
Number of teachers: 225
Number of students: 6,500

DEANS

Faculty of Science: HANG CHANTHON
Faculty of Social Science and Humanities: MONH SARY
Institute of Foreign Languages: Dr MAO SOKAN

UNIVERSITY OF HEALTH SCIENCES

Monivong Blvd, Phnom-Penh
Telephone: (23) 430732
Fax: (23) 430129
Rector: KIM PO VOU.

CAMEROON

The Higher Education System

As a result of Cameroon's mixed colonial heritage, there are separate education systems in the former British and French-administered regions. East Cameroon was a French colony from 1916 to 1960, when it became independent and was known as Republic of Cameroon. A merger with the smaller, British-run provinces of Southern Cameroon in the same year led to the creation of United Republic of Cameroon. The official name of the country, Republic of Cameroon, was adopted in 1984. British and French-inspired educational systems now operate in the respective former provinces, and English and French are now the respective official languages of instruction. The Université de Yaoundé I (formerly Federal University of Cameroon) was established in 1962 and operates on a decentralized principle, with five regional campuses, each devoted to a different field of study. Five new state universities were created by Presidential decree in 1993: Buea, Douala, Dschang, Ngaoundéré and Yaoundé II. The Ministry of Education is responsible for maintaining standards in both the public and private higher education sectors. In 2003 seven private institutions signed 'creation agreements' with the Ministry of Education, which initiate the process by which universities seek authorization for establishment.

Chancellors are government appointees and are the executive heads of universities. The Chancellor oversees the appointments of Deans of faculty, Heads of department and Directors of professional schools in consultation with the Vice-Chancellor. The Governing Council is presided over by the Vice-Chancellor, and includes the Deans, Directors, members of the academic staff and representatives from government and labour organizations.

Admission to university requires the Baccalauréat or two GCE Advanced level examinations and four GCE Ordinary level examinations. University education is broken up into three cycles, the first two at undergraduate level and the third at postgraduate level. The first cycle comprises two- or three-year diploma programmes (Diplômes), notably the Diplôme d'Etudes Universitaires Générales (DEUG, two years) and Diplôme d'Etudes Professionnelles Approfondies (three years). The second cycle programmes last for a further one or two years. Awards at this level include the Licence, Bachelors, Maîtrise and Diplôme. The Licence usually requires one year of study after the first cycle, and the Maîtrise two years. The third cycle consists of doctoral studies: two to four years of study after the Maîtrise for the Doctorat du Troisième Cycle; and five years for the award of Doctorat d'Etat.

There are seven universities, six of which are state-owned. There were 120,300 students enrolled at the state-owned universities in 2005/06. Specialist institutions also offer vocational education and technical training in several fields; the most common awards are diplomas.

In 2010 the Ministry of Higher Education announced that from 2011 Cameroon students will be offered scholarships for study at Masters level by Australia and at postgraduate level by New Zealand.

Regulatory Bodies

GOVERNMENT

Ministry of Culture: Quartier Hippodrome, Yaoundé; tel. 2222-6579; fax 2223-6579; Minister AMA TUTU MUNA.

Ministry of Higher Education: Blvd du 20 Mai, BP 1739, Yaoundé; tel. 2222-1907; fax 2222-9724; e-mail elmfouou@yahoo.com; internet www.minesup.gov.cm; Minister Prof. JACQUES FAME NDONGO; Minister Prof. DOMINIQUE MVOGO; publ. *SupInfos* (Note de Conjoncture; Annuaire Statistique).

Ministry of Scientific Research and Innovation: Yaoundé; tel. 2222-1334; fax 2222-1336; e-mail info@minresi.net; internet www.minresi.net; f. 2004; Minister Dr MADELEINE TCHUINTÉ.

Learned Societies

GENERAL

UNESCO Office Yaoundé: POB 12909, Yaoundé; Immeuble Stamatiades, 2e étage, Yaoundé; tel. 2222-5763; fax 2222-6389; e-mail yaounde@unesco.org; internet www.unesco.org/fr/yaounde; f. 1991; designated Cluster Office for Cameroon, Chad and Central African Republic; 19 mems; Dir BERNARD HADJADJ.

LANGUAGE AND LITERATURE

Alliance Française: BP 441, Ngaoundéré; tel. and fax 2225-1826; e-mail alliance.ngaoundere@free.fr; internet alliance.ngaoundere.free.fr; offers courses and exams in French language and culture and pro-motes cultural exchange with France; attached teaching offices in Bamenda, Buea, Dschang, Garoua and L'Adamaoua; Dir JACQUES LE JOLLEC.

British Council: Immeuble Christo, Ave Charles de Gaulle, BP 818 Yaoundé; tel. 2221-1696; fax 2221-5691; e-mail bc-yaounde@britishcouncil.cm; internet www.britishcouncil.org/cameroon; teaching centre; offers courses and exams in English language and British culture and promotes cultural exchange with the UK; attached teaching centre in Douala; Dir JENNY SCOTT; Teaching Centre Man. TOM HINTON.

Goethe-Institut: Quartier Bastos, BP 1067, Yaoundé; tel. 2221-4409; fax 2221-4419; e-mail goethe.il@camnet.cm; internet www.goethe.de/af/yao/deindex.htm; offers courses and exams in German language and culture and promotes cultural exchange with Germany; library of 6,000 vols; Dir ANDREA JACOB.

Research Institutes

GENERAL

Instituts du Ministère de l'Enseignement Supérieur: BP 1457, Yaoundé; tel. 2227-2983; 5 univ. institutes and 5 research institutes; archaeology, botany and vegetal biology, demography, economics, geography, hydrology, nutrition, medical entomology, psycho-sociology, soil science; Sec.-Gen. PIERRE OWONO ATEBA; publs *Annales* (4 a year, in 4 series: languages and literature, human sciences, law, economics), *Revue Science et Technique* (4 a year, in 3 series: agriculture, health sciences, human sciences).

Institut de Recherche pour le Développement (IRD): Représentation ORSTOM, BP 1857, Yaoundé; tel. 2220-1508; fax 2220-1854; e-mail orstyde@ird.uninet.cm; internet www.ird.fr; f. 1944; anthropology, cell biology, demography, geography, hydrology, ecology, linguistics, medical entomology, ornithology, pedology, sedimentology, ornithology, sociology; see main entry under France; Representative FRANÇOIS RIVIÈRE.

Institut des Sciences Humaines: Yaoundé; f. 1979; part of Min. of Higher Education; Dir W. NDONGKO.

AGRICULTURE, FISHERIES AND VETERINARY SCIENCE

Humid Forest Ecoregional Center: BP 2008, Nkolbisson, Yaoundé; tel. 2223-2644; f. 1980; forestry research; 170 staff (14 researchers); Dir A. M. MAINO.

Institut de la Recherche Agronomique: BP 2123, Yaoundé; tel. 2223-2644; f. 1979; part of Min. of Higher Education; agriculture, agronomy, botany, entomology, phytopathology, pedology; 6 research centres, 16 stations; 314 staff; library of 2,600 vols, 2,500 brochures, 450 periodicals; Dir Dr J.-A. AYUK-TAKEM; publs *Mémoires et Travaux de l'IRA*, *Science et Technique (Series Sciences agronomiques et zootechniques* (4 a year).

Institut de Recherches pour les Huiles et Oléagineux (IRHO): BP 243, Douala; f. 1949; See main entry under France; Dir J. N. REGAUD.

Institut des Recherches Zootechniques et Vétérinaires (IRZV): BP 1457, Yaoundé; tel. and fax 2223-2486; f. 1974; part of Min. of

Higher Education; research on livestock, fisheries and wildlife, and environment; library of 1,800 vols, 358 periodicals; Dir Dr JOHN TANLAKA BANSER; publ. *Science and Technology Review*.

ECONOMICS, LAW AND POLITICS

Institut de Formation et de Recherche Démographiques: BP 1556, Yaoundé; tel. 2222-2471; fax 2222-6793; f. 1972 with the cooperation of the UN; ECA Executing Agency; training and research on demographic phenomena and their links with economic and social factors; library of 17,000 vols; Dir AKOTO ELIWO; publ. *Annales* (3 a year).

Institut des Relations Internationales du Cameroun (IRIC): BP 1637, Yaoundé; tel. and fax 2231-0305; e-mail iric@uycdc.uninet.cm; f. 1971 by the Federal Government, the Carnegie Endowment for International Peace, the Swiss Division for Technical Cooperation and others; a bilingual, postgraduate institute for education, training and research in diplomacy and int. studies, attached to the Univ. of Yaoundé II; library of 65,000 vols; Dir Dr JEAN-EMMANUEL PONDI; Sec.-Gen. SAMUEL ENOH BESONG; publ. *Cameroon Review of International Studies* (1 a year).

EDUCATION

Centre National d'Education: Yaoundé; f. 1979; part of Min. of Higher Education; Dir E. BEBEY.

HISTORY, GEOGRAPHY AND ARCHAEOLOGY

Institut National de Cartographie: BP 157, Ave Mgr.-Vogt, Yaoundé; tel. 2222-2921; fax 2223-3954; e-mail inc@incsdncmr.undp .org; f. 1945; cartography, geography, GIS and remote sensing; Dirs PAUL MOBY ETIA, MICHEL SIMEU KAMDEM.

LANGUAGE AND LITERATURE

Centre Régional de Recherche et de Documentation sur les Traditions Orales et pour le Développement des Langues Africaines (CERDOTOLA): BP 479, Yaoundé; tel. 2230-3144; fax 2230-3189; e-mail cerdotola@yahoo.com; f. 1978; research on African languages, oral literature, traditional music, traditional medicine, traditional arts, African history, African anthropology; 20 mem. countries; library in process of formation; Exec. Sec. Prof. CHARLES BINAM BIKOI.

MEDICINE

Institut de Recherches Médicales et d'Etudes des Plantes Médicinales: Yaoundé; tel. 2223-1361; f. 1979; 250 staff; library of 1,000 vols, 50 periodicals; Dir A. ABONDO; publs *Cahiers, Science et Technique* (series *Sciences Médicales*).

NATURAL SCIENCES

Physical Sciences

Direction de la Météorologie Nationale: 33 rue Ivy, BP 186, Douala; tel. and fax 3342-1635; f. 1934; Dir EMMANUEL EKOKO ETOU-MANN; publs *Annales climatologiques* (irregular), *Bulletin agrométéorologique décadaire*, *RCM: Résumé climatologique mensuel* (12 a year), *Résumé mensuel du Temps* (12 a year).

TECHNOLOGY

Compagnie Française pour le Développement des Fibres Textiles (CFDT): BP 1699, Douala; brs at Garoua, Maroua, Mora, Touboro and Kaele; textile research.

Institut de Recherches Géologiques et Minières: POB 4110, Yaoundé; tel. and fax 2221-0316; f. 1979; Dir GEORGES E. EKODECK.

Libraries and Archives

Bamenda

British Council Learning and Information Centre: Bamenda Urban Council Library, Commercial Ave, POB 622,; tel. 3336-2011; fax 3336-2022; e-mail anyeoscar@yahoo.co.uk; f. 1995; jtly run with Bamenda Urban Ccl; library; learning and information centre; conducts exams; 15,000 vols; Information Officer EMMANUEL NGANG.

Yaoundé

Archives Nationales: BP 1053, Yaoundé; tel. 2223-0078; fax 2223-2010; f. 1952; conserves and classifies all documents relating to the Republic; 15,000 vols; Dir AMADOU POKEKO.

Bibliothèque Nationale du Cameroun: Ministère de la Culture, Yaoundé; tel. and fax 2223-7002; 64,000 vols; Dir NGOTOBO NGOTOBO.

Museums and Art Galleries

Bamenda

International Museum and Library— Akum: POB 389, Bamenda, Northwest Province; f. 1948; local and foreign artefacts of interest to researchers and students of sociology, anthropology and archaeology; brasswork, paintings, beaded work, clay figures, animal skins, masks, postage stamps, iron work, sculpture, stools, traditional costumes, films and books; Curator PETER S. ATANGA.

Kumbo-Nso

Musa Heritage Gallery (Mus'Art): POB 21, Kumbo, Northwest Prov.; Bamfem Quarter, street above STS, Kumbo, Northwest Prov.; tel. 7707-7651; e-mail musartgallery@ yahoo.com; internet www.musartgallery.info .ms; f. 1996; named after Cameroonian artists Daniel and John Musa; arts and crafts of the Western Grassfields region of Cameroon; 400 artefacts; Dir MANGONG PETER MUSA.

Universities

UNIVERSITÉ DE BUÉA

POB 63, Buea
Telephone: 3332-2134
Fax: 3343-2508
Internet: www.cm.refer.org/edu/ram3/ univers/ubuea/ubuea.htm
Founded 1977 (opened 1986) as Buea University Centre; present name and status 1992
State control
Languages of instruction: English, French, Spanish
Academic year: September to June
Chancellor: Dr PETER AGBOR TABI
Pro-Chancellor: Prof. VICTOR ANOMAH NGU
Vice-Chancellor: Dr DOROTHY L. NJEUMA
Deputy Vice-Chancellor for Control: Prof. SAMMY BEBAN CHUMBOW
Deputy Vice-Chancellor for Research and Cooperation: Prof. SAMSON ABANGMA
Deputy Vice-Chancellor for Teaching: Prof. VINCENT P. K. TITANJI
Registrar: Dr HERBERT NGANJO ENDELEY

Librarian: ROSEMARY SHAFACK
Library of 35,000 vols
Number of teachers: 93 full-time
Number of teachers: 115 part-time
Number of students: 3,300
Publication: *Epasa Moto* (1 a year)

DEANS

Faculty of Arts: Prof. EMMANUEL GWAN ACHU
Faculty of Education: Dr GRACE EWENE
Faculty of Health Sciences: Dr THEODOSA McMOLI
Faculty of Science: Dr NZUMBE MESAPE NTOKO
Faculty of Social and Management Sciences: Prof. CORNELIUS LAMBI

CONSTITUENT INSTITUTE

Advanced School of Translators and Interpreters (ASTI): Dir Dr ETIENNE ZÉ AMVELA.

UNIVERSITÉ CATHOLIQUE DE L'AFRIQUE CENTRALE

BP 11628, Yaoundé
Telephone: 2223-7400
Fax: 2223-7402
E-mail: ucac.icy-nk@camnet.cm
Internet: www.cm.refer.org/edu/ram3/ univers/ucac/ucac.htm
Founded 1989
Private Control (Catholic Church)
Languages of instruction: English, French
Academic year: October to July
Rector: Abbé OSCAR EONE EONE
Vice-Rector: Abbé OLIVIER MASSAMBA LOU-BELO
Sec.-Gen.: JOSEPH KONO OWONA
Dir of Devt and Cooperation: GILLES NOUD-JAG
Head Librarian: Dr PATRICK ADESO (acting)
Library of 39,341 vols
Number of teachers: 90 and 240 assoc. lecturers
Number of students: 1,692
Publication: *Cahiers de l'U.C.A.C.* (1 a year)

DEANS

Faculty of Social Sciences and Management: Prof. Dr JACQUES FDRY
Faculty of Theology: Père Dr ANTOINE BABÉ
School of Nursing: Soeur RENÉE GEOFFRAY

DIRECTORS

Dept of Canon Law: Fr ALFRED NOTHUM
Dept of Philosophy: Fr CLAUDE PAIRAULT

UNIVERSITÉ DE DOUALA

BP 2701, Douala
Telephone: 3340-6415
Fax: 3340-1134
E-mail: ud@camnet.com
Internet: www.cm.refer.org/edu/ram3/ univers/udla/udla.htm
Founded 1977
State control
Languages of instruction: English, French
Academic year: October to July
Rector: Prof. MAURICE TCHUENTE
Deputy Rector: Prof. ROGER GABRIEL NLEP
Sec.-Gen.: THÉRÈSE WANGUE
Librarian: JEREMIE NSANGOU
Number of teachers: 140
Number of students: 6,500
Publications: *Arts Review* (1 a year), *Revue de Sciences Economiques et de Management* (4 a year), *Technologie et Développement* (every 2 years).

CONSTITUENT INSTITUTES

Ecole Normale Supérieure de l'Enseignement Technique: BP 1872, Douala; Dir Dr NDEH NTOMAMBANG NINGO.

Ecole Supérieure des Sciences Economiques et Commerciales: BP 1931, Douala; Dir Dr ROBERT BILONGO.

Faculté des Lettres et des Sciences Humaines: BP 3132, Douala; Dean Prof. SYLVESTRE BOUELET IVAHA.

Faculté des Sciences: BP 24157, Douala; Dean Prof. THÉOPHILE NGANDO MPONDO.

Faculté des Sciences Economiques et de Gestion Appliquée: BP 4032, Douala; Dean Prof. BLAISE MUKOKO.

Faculté des Sciences Juridiques et Politiques: BP 4982, Douala; Dean Dr LEKENE DONFACK.

Institut Universitaire de Technologie: BP 8698, Douala; Dir Dr AWONO ONANA.

UNIVERSITÉ DE DSCHANG

POB 96, Dschang
Telephone: 3345-1092
Fax: 3240-1134
Founded 1993
State control
Languages of instruction: English, French
Academic year: October to July
Rector: Prof. ANACLET FOMETHE
Vice-Rector for Inspection: Prof. LAURE PAULINE FOTSO
Vice-Rector for Research and Cooperation: Prof. JOHN MUCHO NGUNDAM
Vice-Rector for Teaching: Prof. ONGLA JEAN
Sec.-Gen.: Prof. MARTHE ISABELLE ATANGANA ABOLO
Librarian: DJIDERE VALÈRE
Number of teachers: 330
Number of students: 14,000
Publications: *Les Echos* (law and politics, 4 a year), *NKA* (arts and humanities, 2 a year), *Sciences et Développement* (agriculture, 2 a year)

DEANS

Faculty of Agronomy and Agricultural Sciences: Dr MANGELI YACOUBA
Faculty of Economics and Management Sciences: Prof. TAFAH EDOKAT OKI EDWARD
Faculty of Law and Political Science: Prof. FRANÇOIS ANOUKAHA
Faculty of Letters and Social Sciences: Prof. CHARLES ROBERT DIMI
Faculty of Sciences: Prof. PIERRE TANE
Fotso Victor Institute of Technology: MÉDARD FOGUE

UNIVERSITÉ DE NGAOUNDÉRÉ

BP 454, Ngaoundéré
Telephone: 2222-5741
Fax: 3333-0643
E-mail: rectorat_ngaoundere@yahoo.fr
Founded 1977, opened 1982; present name since 1993
State control
Accredited by Ministry of Higher Education
Languages of instruction: English, French
Academic year: October to July
Rector: Prof. PAUL-HENRI AVZAM ZOLLO
Vice-Rector for Control and Internal Evaluation: Prof. DAVID BEKOLLE
Vice-Rector for Research and Cooperation and Relations with the Business World: Prof. JOSEPH G. KAYEM
Vice-Rector for Teaching, Professionalisation and Devt of Information Technology: Prof. BOUBA OUMAROU
Sec.-Gen.: Prof. ANDRÉ TIENTCHEU NJIAKO
Library of 60,000 vols

Number of teachers: 300
Number of students: 14,000
Publications: *Annales de la Faculté des Arts, Lettres et Sciences Humaines* (1 a year), *Ngaounderé-Apropos* (social science review, 1 a year)

DEANS

Faculty of Arts and Humanities: Dr IYA MOUSSA
Faculty of Economics and Management Science: Prof. VICTOR TSAPI
Faculty of Law and Political Science: Prof. ANDRÉ AKAM AKAM
Faculty of Science: Prof. ISMAIL NGOUNOUNO
Institute of Technology: Dr ALI AHMED
School of Agro-Industrial Sciences: Prof. CARL M. F. MBOFUNG (Dir)
School of Veterinary Medicine and Animal Science: Prof. ANDRÉ ZOLLY PAGNA

PROFESSORS

Faculty of Economics and Management Science:
    FEUDJO, J. R.
    TSAPI, V.
Faculty of Law and Political Science:
    AKAM AKAM, A.
    TIENTCHEU NJIAKO, A.
Faculty of Science:
    AMVAM ZOLLO, P.-H.
    BEKOLLÉ, D.
    LOURA BENGUELLA, B.
    MAPONGMETSEM, P. M.
    NGO BUM, E.
    NGOUNOUNO, I.
    OUMAROU, B.
    TCHUENGUEM FOHOUO, F. N.
School of Agro-Industrial Sciences:
    DZUDIE, T.
    KAMGA, R.
    KAPSEU, C.
    KAYEM, J.
    MBOFUNG, C. M. F.
    NGASSOUM, M. B.
    TCHIEGANG, C.

UNIVERSITÉ DE YAOUNDÉ I

BP 337, Centre Province, Yaoundé
Telephone: 2222-0744
Fax: 2223-5388
E-mail: cdc@uycdc.uninet.cm
Founded 1962
State control
Languages of instruction: English, French
Academic year: October to July
Rector: JEAN TABI-MANGA
Vice-Rector for Inspection: MAURICE AURÉLIEN SOSSO
Vice-Rector for Research and Cooperation: (vacant)
Vice-Rector for Teaching: MAURICE AURÉLIEN SOSSO
Sec.-Gen.: ELIE-CLAUDE NDJITOYAP NDAM
Librarian: ALEXIS EYANGO MOUEN
Library of 90,000 vols
Number of teachers: 929
Number of students: 20,343
Publications: *Annales de la Faculté des Lettres*, *Annales de la Faculté des Sciences*, *Sosongo* (Cameroon review of the arts, annual), *Syllabus* (review of the Ecole Normale Supérieure)

DEANS

Faculty of Arts: Prof. EMMANUEL GWAN ACHU
Faculty of Medicine and Biomedical Science: Prof. AMOUGOU AKOA
Faculty of Sciences: Prof. MAURICE A. SOSSO

DIRECTORS

Ecole Normale Supérieure: MATHIEU FRANÇOIS MINYONO NKODO
Ecole Nationale Supérieure Polytechnique: AYINA OHANDJA

FACULTIES AND DEPARTMENTS

Faculty of Arts: POB 755, Yaoundé; depts of African Languages and Linguistics, art and archaeology, English, foreign language-sliterature and civilization, French, geography, German, history, Negro-African literature, philosophy, psychology, sociology, Spanish.

Faculty of Medicine and Biomedical Science: POB 8290, Yaoundé; tel. 2223-1226; fax 2223-1841; depts of anatomy and pathology, biomedical sciences, clinical sciences, gynaecology and obstetrics, internal medicine, medical imagery and radiotherapy, ophthalmology, paediatrics, public health, physiology, stomatology, surgery.

Faculty of Science: POB 812, Yaoundé; tel. 2223-5660; depts of animal biology and physiology, biochemistry, computer science, earth sciences, inorganic chemistry, mathematics, organic chemistry, physics, plant biology and physiology.

Ecole Normale Supérieure: POB 47, Yaoundé; tel. 2222-4934; fax 2222-0913; depts of biology, chemistry, education, English, French, history and geography, languages, mathematics, philosophy, physics).

Ecole Nationale Supérieure Polytechnique: POB 8290, Yaoundé; tel. 2223-1226; fax 2223-1841; depts of civil engineering and town planning, computer engineering, electrical engineering, mathematics, physics and chemistry.

UNIVERSITÉ DE YAOUNDÉ II

POB 18, Soa
Telephone: 7220-1154
Fax: 7799-1423
E-mail: info@univ-yde2.org
Internet: www.univ-yde2.org
Founded 1993
State Control
Academic year: October to July
Rector: Prof. JEAN TABI MANGA
Vice-Rector for Academic Affairs: Prof. PAUL GÉRARD POUGOUÉ
Vice-Rector for Inspection: Prof. PIERRE OWONA ATEBA
Vice-Rector for Research and Cooperation: Prof. ADOLPHE MINKOA SHE
Sec.-Gen.: Dr LISETTE ELOMO NTONGA (acting)
Number of teachers: 271
Number of students: 13,768
Publications: *African Review of Political Strategy* (1 a year), *Cameroon Review of International Relations* (2 a year), *Fréquence Sud* (2 a year), *Les Cahiers de l'IFORD* (52 a year), *Revue Africaine des Sciences Economiques et de Gestion* (2 a year), *Revue Africaine des Sciences Juridiques* (2 a year)

DEANS

Faculty of Economics and Management: Prof. GEORGES KOBOU
Faculty of Law and Political Science: Prof. VICTOR-EMMANUEL BOKALLI

DIRECTORS

Advanced School of Mass Communication: Prof. LAURENT-CHARLES BOYOMO ASSALA
Institute for Demographic Training and Research: ÉLIE JUSTIN OUÉDRAOGO
International Relations Institute of Cameroon: Prof. NARCISSE MOUELLE KOMBI

PROFESSORS

Faculty of Economics and Management:
BEKOLO, E. B.
GANKOU, J. M.
NDJIEUNDE, G.
TOUNA, M.

Faculty of Law and Political Science:
ALETUM, M. T.
ANOUKAHA, F.
KONTCHOU, K. A.
MINKOA, S. A.
NGWAFOR, É. N.
NTAMARK, P. Y.
OWONA, J.
POUGOUE, P. G.

Advanced School of Mass Communication:
BOYOMO, A. L. C.
CHINJI, K. F.
FAME, N.

International Relations Institute of Cameroon:
OYONO, D.

ATTACHED INSTITUTES

Centre for Study and Research in Economics and Management: tel. 2223-7389; fax 2223-7912; Coordinator Assoc. Prof. SÉRAPHIN FOUDA.

Centre for Study and Research in International Community Law: tel. 2221-4234; fax 2231-3509; Coordinator Assoc. Prof. MAURICE KAMTO.

Colleges

Ecole Nationale d'Administration et de Magistrature: BP 7171, Yaoundé; tel. 2223-1308; f. 1959; training for public admin.; library: 11,000 vols; 85 teachers (10 full-time, 75 part-time); 1,063 students; Dir. V. MOUTTAPA.

Institut d'Administration des Entreprises: BP 337, Yaoundé; 150 students; Dir G. NDJIEUNDE.

CANADA

The Higher Education System

Under legislation passed in 1982, the 10 provinces and three territories enjoy autonomy over higher education; however, the Council of Ministers of Education Canada was created by the provincial and territorial ministers of education to take collective decisions in the national interest. The Association of Universities and Colleges of Canada (AUCC) is the national organization of university executive heads. There are over 200 public and private institutes authorised to offer degrees. Most are conferred by universities and their affiliated and federated institutions, as well as colleges of applied science and technology. Conservatories and some community colleges are also authorised to offer degrees. There are 113 university-level institutions in the 10 Canadian provinces, 90 of which are public universities and 23 are university colleges federated or affiliated with another university. There are no universities in Canada's three territories. In 2006/07 an estimated 1,059,912 students were enrolled in post-secondary education (not including the Northwest Territories, Nunavut Territory and Yukon Territory). The official languages of Canada are French and English, but English is the language of instruction in most universities except in the province of Québec, where French is used.

The standard administrative structure for a university consists of two governing bodies, a Board of Governors or Regents and a Senate or Academic Council. In addition, a Vice-Chancellor, President, Principal or Rector is responsible for administrative and academic management. Higher education funding varies according to the province or territory in question. The only consistent admissions criteria for university include possession of the secondary school equivalent or, in Québec, the Collège d'enseignement général et professionnel (CEGEP); otherwise, universities are free to set their own criteria.

Though there may be provincial or territorial peculiarities, the university degree system conforms to the Bachelors/Masters/Doctorate schema. The Bachelors (Baccalaureat in Québecois) is a three- to four-year programme the format of which varies from institution to institution, with some following the US-style credits system. Some Bachelors programmes include an element of research and are known as Honours. Following Bachelors are Masters (Maîtrise) programmes of two years, which fall into two classifications: Taught and Research. Finally, the qualification Doctor of Philosophy (PhD, or Philosophiae Doctor) requires three- to five-years' study following the Masters.

Post-secondary technical and vocational education is provided by community and professional colleges; the most common qualifications are the Certificate and Diploma, the latter requiring two- to three-years' study.

There is no central system of accreditation for post-secondary institutions in Canada, only for certain programmes within these institutions. However, procedures and regulations are in place in each province and territory that provide ongoing assessment of the overall quality equivalent to 'accreditation' as it is commonly understood. The Canadian Education and Training Accreditation Commission (CETAC) provides a voluntary system of non-governmental self-regulation of Canada's private post-secondary institutions. There is also the Association of Accrediting Agencies of Canada which provides a national network of professional education accrediting bodies.

Regulatory and Representative Bodies

GOVERNMENT

Council of Ministers of Education, Canada/Conseil des Ministres de l'Éducation (Canada) (CMEC): Suite 1106, 95 St Clair Ave W, Toronto, ON M4V 1N6; tel. (416) 962-8100; fax (416) 962-2800; e-mail info@cmec.ca; internet www.cmec.ca; f. 1967; intergovernmental body of which all 13 provinces and territories are mems; forum to discuss policy issues; mechanism through which to undertake activities, projects and initiatives in areas of mutual interest; means by which to consult and cooperate with nat. education orgs and the federal govt; instrument to represent the education interests of the provinces and territories internationally; provides leadership in education at the pan-Canadian and int. levels and contributes to the fulfilment of the constitutional responsibility for education conferred on provinces and territories; governed by an Agreed Memorandum approved by all mems; current funding C\$7.5m. per year, of which provinces and territories provide C\$5.7m. through base amount, calculated according to the population of each province and territory, and additional amounts for specific projects and initiatives; Chair. KELLY LAMROCK.

National Research Council Canada: Bldg M58, 1200 Montréal Rd, Ottawa, ON K1A 0R6; tel. (613) 993-9101; fax (613) 952-9907; e-mail info@nrc-cnrc.gc.ca; internet www.nrc.ca; f. 1916; carries out research and devt in engineering, information technology, life sciences, physical sciences, technology and industry support; Pres. Dr PIERRE COLOUMBE; Sec.-Gen. MARIELLE PICHÉ.

ACCREDITATION

Association of Accrediting Agencies of Canada/Association des Agences d'Agrément du Canada: POB 370, 1-247 Barr St, Renfrew, ON K7V 1J6; tel. (613) 432-9491; fax (613) 432-6840; e-mail info@aaac.ca; internet www.aaac.ca; f. 1994; pursues excellence in standards and processes of accreditation to foster the highest quality of professional education; 35 mems; Chair. MARLENE WYATT.

Canadian Education and Training Accreditation Commission (CETAC): Suite 101, 267 Adelaide St W, Toronto, ON M5H 1Y3; tel. (416) 875-8629; fax (416) 977-5612; e-mail info@accreditations.ca; internet www.accreditations.ca; f. 1984; responsible for institutional accreditation of private post-secondary institutions in Canada; provides nat. accrediting service with established nat. standards; Nat. Commissioner BILL RICHES; Nat. Commissioner CAROL LOWTHERS; Nat. Commissioner CHRISTOPHER HOPE; Nat. Commissioner FRANK T. MIOSI; Nat. Commissioner F. RICK KLEIMAN; Nat. Commissioner MICHAEL BARRETT; Nat. Commissioner MONIKA OEPKES; Nat. Commissioner NELLIE BURKE; Nat. Commissioner ROSEMARY BOYD.

Canadian Information Centre for International Credentials (CICIC): Canadian ENIC, 95 St Clair Ave W, Suite 1106, Toronto ON M4V 1N6; tel. (416) 962-9725; fax (416) 962-2800; e-mail info@cicic.ca; internet www.cicic.ca; f. 1990; unit of the Ccl of Mins. of Education, Canada (CMEC); collects, organizes, and distributes information; acts as a nat. clearing house and referral service to support the recognition of Canadian and international educational and occupational qualifications; promotes int. mobility by advocating wider recognition of higher education and professional qualifications; Nat. Coordinator YVES BEAUDIN; Admin. Officer NOELLINE IP YAM; Project Man. ERIC SCHVARTZ.

NATIONAL BODIES

Association of Atlantic Universities/Association des Universités de l'Atlantique: Suite 403, 5657 Spring Garden Rd, Halifax, NS B3J 3R4; tel. (902) 425-4230; fax (902) 425-4233; e-mail info@atlanticuniversities.ca; internet www.atlanticuniversities.ca; f. 1964; mems: 17 univs in the Atlantic region of Canada and in the W Indies, which offer programmes leading to a degree or have degree-granting status; Exec. Dir PETER HALPIN; Dir of Operations CORINA KENT.

Association of Canadian Community Colleges/Association des Collèges Communautaires du Canada (ACCC): Suite 200, 1223 Michael St N, Ottawa, ON K1J 7T2; tel. (613) 746-2222; fax (613) 746-6721; e-mail info@accc.ca; internet www.accc.ca; f. 1972; nat. voluntary membership org. to represent colleges and institutes to govt, business and industry, both in Canada and worldwide; interacts with fed. depts and agencies on the mems' behalf; links college capabilities to nat. industries; organizes conferences and workshops for college staff, students and board mems to facilitate networking and participation in nat. and int. activities such as sector studies, awards programmes and linkages; Pres. and CEO JAMES KNIGHT.

Association of Registrars of the Universities and Colleges of Canada (ARUCC)/ Association des Registraires des Universités et Collèges du Canada: c/o France Myette, Sec. Treas., ARUCC, Univ. de Sherbrooke, 2500 Blvd de l'Université, Sherbrooke QC J1K 2R1; tel. (819) 821-7685; fax (819) 821-7966; e-mail france.myette@ usherbrooke.ca; internet www.arucc.unb.ca; f. 1964; approx. 182 mem. instns; mems incl. registrars, admission dirs, student records managers, student services managers and other personnel in the areas of student advice and counselling, student financial aid and student placement; Pres. DAVID HINTON.

Association of Universities and Colleges of Canada (AUCC): 350 Albert St (Suite 600), Ottawa, ON K1R 1B1; tel. (613) 563-1236; fax (613) 563-9745; e-mail info@aucc .ca; internet www.aucc.ca; f. 1911; represents Canadian public and private, not-for-profit univs and univ.-degree level colleges; 95 univ. mems; Pres. and CEO PAUL DAVIDSON; Chair. J.-L. MICHEL BELLEY.

Canadian Bureau for International Education/Bureau Canadien de l'Education Internationale: 220 Laurier Ave W, Suite 1550, Ottawa, ON K1P 5Z9; tel. (613) 237-4820; fax (613) 237-1073; e-mail info@ cbie.ca; internet www.cbie.ca; f. 1966 to promote int. devt and inter-cultural understanding through a broad range of educational activities in Canada and abroad; 3 divs: research, devt and membership, scholarships and awards, centre for central and Eastern Europe; library of 300 vols and journals; 120 institutional mems; Chair. Dr ROBERT MCCULLOCH; publ. *E-Internationalist* (irregular).

Canadian Network for Innovation in Education (CNIE)/Réseau Canadien pour l'Innovation en Éducation (RCIE): Suite 204, 260 Dalhousie St, Ottawa, ON K1N 7E4; tel. (613) 241-0018; fax (613) 241-0019; e-mail cnie-rcie@cnie-rcie.ca; internet www.cnie-rcie.ca; f. 2007; nat. org. of professionals committed to excellence in the provision of innovation in education in Canada; holds annual conference; 600 mems; Pres. RAYMOND WHITLEY; Dir of Admin. TIM HOWARD; publs *Journal of Distance Education* (3 a year), *Canadian Journal of Learning and Technology* (3 a year).

Learned Societies

GENERAL

Académie des Lettres du Québec: CP 8888, Succursale Centre-ville, Montréal, QC H3C 3P8; tel. (514) 987-3000; fax (514) 987-8484; e-mail secretariat@ academiedeslettresduquebec.ca; internet academiedeslettresduquebec.ca; f. 1944 (fmrly Académie canadienne-française) for the promotion of the French language and culture in Canada; 42 chairs; 38 mems; Pres. JACQUES ALLARD; publ. *Les Ecrits* (3 a year).

Canadian Council for International Co-operation/Conseil Canadien pour la Coopération Internationale: 1 Nicholas St, Suite 300, Ottawa, ON K1N 7B7; tel. (613) 247-7007; fax (613) 241-5302; internet

www.ccic.ca; f. 1968 (fmrly Overseas Institute of Canada, f. 1961); coordination centre for voluntary agencies working in int. devt; 115 mems; Chair. JEAN-PIERRE MASSÉ; publs *Directory of Canadian NGOs, Newsletter* (6 a year).

Royal Canadian Academy of Arts: 401 Richmond St West (Suite 375), Toronto, ON M5V 3A8; tel. (416) 408-2718; fax (416) 408-2286; e-mail rcaarts@interlog.com; internet www.rca-arc.ca; f. 1880; visual arts; Pres. ALISON HYMAS.

Royal Canadian Institute: 700 University Ave, H7-D, Toronto, ON M5G 1X6; tel. (416) 977-2983; fax (416) 962-7314; internet www .royalcanadianinstitute.org; f. 1849; aims to increase public understanding of science; 800 mems; Pres. M. JANE PHILLIPS; Sec. PIPPA WYSONG; Treasurer HAROLD H. HARVEY.

Royal Society of Canada: 170 Waller St, Ottawa, ON K1N 9B9; tel. (613) 991-6990; fax (613) 991-6996; e-mail info@rsc.ca; internet www.rsc.ca; f. 1882; 1,800 Fellows; academies of Arts (I), Humanities (II) and Science (III); Pres. YVAN GUINDON; Hon. Sec. ROBERT MAJOR; publs *RSC News* (3 a year), *Présentations* (1 a year), *Proceedings* (1 a year).

AGRICULTURE, FISHERIES AND VETERINARY SCIENCE

Agricultural Institute of Canada: Suite 900, 280 Albert St, Ottawa, ON K1P 5G8; tel. (613) 232-9459; fax (613) 594-5190; internet www.aic.ca; f. 1920 to organize and unite all workers in scientific and technical agriculture and to serve as a medium where progressive ideas for improvements in agricultural education, investigation, publicity and extension work can be discussed and recommended for adoption; represents 6,500 scientists and agrologists; publs *Canadian Journal of Animal Science* (4 a year), *Canadian Journal of Plant Science* (4 a year), *Canadian Journal of Soil Science* (4 a year).

Canadian Forestry Association: 185 Somerset St West, Suite 203, Ottawa, ON K2P 0J2; tel. (613) 232-1815; fax (613) 232-4210; e-mail cfa@canadianforestry.com; internet www.canadianforestry.com; f. 1900; conservation org. providing educational materials and programmes to raise awareness of the wise use of forest, wildlife and water resources; 354 mems; Pres. BARRY WAITO; General Manager DAVE LEMKAY.

Canadian Society of Animal Science: Suite 900, 280 Albert St, Ottawa, ON K1P 5G8; tel. (613) 232-9459; fax (613) 594-5190; internet www.csas.net; part of the Agricultural Institute of Canada (*q.v.*); f. 1925 to provide opportunities for discussion of problems, improvement and coordination of research, extension and teaching and to encourage publication of scientific and educational material relating to animal and poultry industries; holds annual meetings, produces occasional papers and presents awards to members; 550 mems; Pres. DUANE MCCARTNEY; Sec.-Treas. CHRISTIANE GIRARD; publs *Canadian Journal of Animal Science* (4 a year), *CSAS Newsletter* (4 a year, mems only).

Canadian Veterinary Medical Association/Association Canadienne des Médecins Vétérinaires: 339 Booth St, Ottawa, ON K1R 7K1; tel. (613) 236-1162; fax (613) 236-9681; e-mail kallen@ cvma-acmv.org; internet www.cvma-acmv .org; f. 1948; 4,000 mems; publs *Canadian Journal of Veterinary Research* (4 a year), *Canadian Veterinary Journal* (12 a year).

ARCHITECTURE AND TOWN PLANNING

Canadian Society of Landscape Architects/Association des Architectes Paysagistes du Canada: POB 13594, Ottawa, ON K2K 1X6; tel. (613) 622-5520; fax (613) 622-5870; e-mail info@csla.ca; internet www.csla .ca; f. 1934; 1,100 mems, a federation of seven component asscns; Exec. Dir FRAN PAUZÉ; publs *Bulletin* (6 a year), *Landscapes/Paysages* (4 a year).

Royal Architectural Institute of Canada: 55 Murray St, Suite 330, Ottawa, ON K1N 5M3; tel. (613) 241-3600; fax (613) 241-5750; e-mail info@raic.org; internet www .raic.org; f. 1908; 3,500 mems; Pres. CHRIS FILLINGHAM; Exec. Dir JON F. HOBBS; publs *Bulletin* (online, 12 a year), *Update/En Bref* (4 a year).

BIBLIOGRAPHY, LIBRARY SCIENCE AND MUSEOLOGY

ASTED (Association pour l'Avancement des Sciences et des Techniques de la Documentation) Inc. (Association for the advancement of documentation sciences and techniques): 2065 rue Parthenais, Bureau 387, Montréal, QC H2X 3T1; tel. (514) 281-5012; fax (514) 281-8219; e-mail info@asted .org; internet www.asted.org; f. 1973; a professional organization of libraries, librarians and library technicians; 500 mems; Pres. SYLVIE THIBAULT (acting); Exec. Dir FRANCIS FARLEY-CHEVRIER (acting); publs *Documentation et bibliothèques* (4 a year), *Nouvelles de l'ASTED* (online only).

Bibliographical Society of Canada: POB 575, Postal Station P, Toronto, ON M5S 2T1; e-mail gretagolick@rogers.com; internet www.library.utoronto.ca/bsc; f. 1946; 300 mems; Pres. ANNE DONDERTMAN; Sec. GRETA GOLICK; publs *Bulletin* (2 a year), *Papers/Cahiers* (2 a year).

Canadian Association of Law Libraries: POB 1570, Kingston, ON K7L 5C8; tel. (613) 531-9338; fax (613) 531-0626; e-mail office@ callacbd.ca; internet www.callacbd.ca; f. 1961 to promote law librarianship, to develop and increase the usefulness of Canadian law libraries, and to foster a spirit of cooperation among them, to provide a forum for meetings and to cooperate with other similar orgs; 500 mems; Pres. JANINE MILLER; Administrative Officer ELIZABETH HOOPER; publs *CALL Newsletter* (5 a year), *Canadian Law Library* (5 a year).

Canadian Library Association: 328 Frank St, Ottawa, ON K2P 0X8; tel. (613) 232-9625; fax (613) 563-9895; e-mail info@cla .ca; internet www.cla.ca; f. 1946; 3,000 mems; Pres. STEPHEN ABRAM; Exec. Dir DON BUTCHER.

Canadian Museums Association/Association des Musées Canadiens: 280 Metcalfe, Suite 400, Ottawa, ON K2P 1R7; tel. (613) 567-0099; fax (613) 233-5438; e-mail info@museums.ca; internet www.museums .ca; f. 1947; advancement of public museums and art galleries services in Canada; 2,000 mems; Exec. Dir JOHN G. MCAVITY; publ. *Muse* (6 a year).

ECONOMICS, LAW AND POLITICS

Canadian Bar Association: 500–865 Carling Ave, Ottawa, ON K1S 5S8; tel. (613) 237-1988; fax (613) 237-0185; e-mail info@cba .org; internet www.cba.org; f. 1914 to promote the administration of justice and uniformity of legislation throughout Canada, and to promote a high standard of legal education, training and ethics; 38,000 mems; Pres. D. KEVIN CARROL; Exec. Dir. JOHN HOYLES; Treasurer WAYNE ONCHULENKO;

publs *The Canadian Bar Review, The National*.

Canadian Economics Association: c/o Frances Woolley, Dept of Economics, Carleton Univ., 1125 Colonel By Dr., Ottawa, ON K1S 5B6; e-mail frances_woolley@carleton.ca; internet www.economics.ca; f. 1967; non-partisan asscn promoting the advancement of economic knowledge through the encouragement of study and research, the issuing of publs and the furtherance of free and informed discussion of economic questions; 1,400 mems; Pres. GERARD GAUDET; Sec.-Treas. FRANCES WOOLLEY; publs *Canadian Journal of Economics/Revue Canadienne d'Economique, Canadian Public Policy/ Analyse de Politique.*

Canadian Institute of Chartered Accountants: 277 Wellington St W, Toronto, ON M5V 3H2; tel. (416) 977-3222; fax (416) 977-8585; internet www.cica.ca; f. 1902; professional and examining body; 70,000 mems; Chair. ALAIN BENEDETT; Pres. and CEO KEVIN J. DANCEY; publ. *CA Magazine* (12 a year).

Canadian Institute of International Affairs: Suite 302, 205 Richmond St W, Toronto, ON M5V 1V3; tel. (416) 977-9000; fax (416) 977-7521; e-mail mailbox@ciia.org; internet www.ciia.org; f. 1928; 1,400 mems in 15 brs; library of 8,000 vols; Chair. The Hon. ROY MACLAREN; Pres. and CEO DOUGLAS GOOLD; publs *Behind the Headlines, International Journal* (4 a year), *Canadian Foreign Relations Index* (CD-ROM, 1 a year; online, 12 a year).

Canadian Political Science Association/ Association Canadienne de Science Politique: 260 Dalhousie St, Suite 204, Ottawa, ON K1N 7E4; tel. (613) 562-1202; fax (613) 241-0019; e-mail cpsa-acsp@ cpsa-acsp.ca; internet www.cpsa-acsp.ca; f. 1913; organizes annual conference; awards prizes; runs the Parliamentary Internship Programme and Ontario Legislative Internship Programme; 1,500 mems; Administrator MICHELLE HOPKINS; publ. *Canadian Journal of Political Science/Revue canadienne de science politique* (4 a year).

EDUCATION

Canadian Education Association/Association Canadienne d'Education: 317 Adelaide St W, Suite 300, Toronto, ON M5V 1P9; tel. (416) 591-6300; fax (416) 591-5345; e-mail info@cea-ace.ca; internet www.cea-ace.ca; f. 1891; 300 mems; Chair. CAROLE OLSEN; Vice Chair. LYNNE ZUCKER; CEO PENNY MILTON; publs *Bulletin* (12 a year), *CEA Handbook/Ki-es-Ki* (1 a year), *Education Canada* (4 a year).

Canadian Society for the Study of Education: Suite 204, 260 Dalhousie St, Ottawa, ON K1N 7E4; tel. (613) 241-0018; fax (613) 241-0019; e-mail csse-scee@csse.ca; internet www.csse.ca; f. 1972 to enhance educational research in Canada; holds annual conference; 1,000 mems; Dir of Admin. TIM G. HOWARD; publ. *Canadian Journal of Education* (4 a year).

FINE AND PERFORMING ARTS

Canada Council for the Arts/Conseil des Arts du Canada: POB 1047, 350 Albert St, Ottawa, ON K1P 5V8; tel. (613) 566-4365; fax (613) 566-4390; internet www.canadacouncil.ca; f. 1957; the Council provides grants and services to professional Canadian artists and arts organizations; maintains secretariat for Canadian Commission for UNESCO; administers Public Lending Right Comm. and Canada Council Art Bank; administers Killam Program of prizes and fellowships to Canadian research scholars, and recognizes

achievement through a number of prizes, including Governor General's Literary Awards, Molson Prizes and Glenn Gould Prize; 90% state-funded; 11 mems; Chair. JOSEPH L. ROTMAN; Vice-Chair. SIMON BRAULT; Dir ROBERT SIRMAN.

Canadian Film Institute: 2 Daly Ave, Suite 120, Ottawa, ON K1N 6E2; tel. (613) 232-6727; fax (613) 232-6315; f. 1935 to encourage and promote the study, appreciation and use of motion pictures and television in Canada; division of Cinémathèque Canada; operates CFI Film Library, renting 6,500 educational films and videocassettes; cinema; Canadian Centre for Films on Art; hosts Ottawa International Animation Festival; Dir TOM McSORLEY.

Canadian Music Centre (Centre de Musique Canadienne): 20 St Joseph St, Toronto, ON M4Y 1J9; tel. (416) 961-6601; fax (416) 961-7198; e-mail info@musiccentre.ca; internet www.musiccentre.ca; f. 1959; 700 mems; library of 20,000 vols, 15,000 scores; for the collection and promotion, in Canada and abroad, of music by contemporary Canadian composers; produces Canadian concert recordings (Centrediscs); Exec. Dir ELISABETH BIHL.

Sculptors' Society of Canada: c/o Studio 204, 60 Atlantic Ave, Toronto, ON M6K 1X9; 500 Church St, Toronto, ON M4Y 2C8; tel. (647) 435-5858; e-mail gallery@cansculpt .org; internet www.sculptorssocietyofcanada .org; f. 1928; Pres. JUDI MICHELLE YOUNG; Vice-Pres. RICHARD MCNEILL; Treasurer D. PAOLINI.

Society of Composers, Authors and Music Publishers of Canada (SOCAN): 41 Valleybrook Drive, Toronto, ON M3B 2S6; tel. (416) 445-8700; fax (416) 445-7108; e-mail socan@socan.ca; internet www.socan .ca; f. 1990; copyright collective for the communication and performance of musical works; licenses music in Canada; distributes royalties to its members for the use of their music overseas; offices in Dartmouth, Edmonton, Toronto, Montréal, Vancouver, Toronto; 80,000 mems; Pres. PIERRE-DANIEL RHEAULT; publs *Music Means Business/Le Rhytme de vos Affaires* (2 a year), *Words & Music/Paroles & Musique* (4 a year).

Visual Arts Ontario: 1153A Queen St West, Toronto, ON M6J 1J4; tel. (416) 591-8883; fax (416) 591-2432; e-mail info@vao.org; internet www.vao.org; f. 1973; federation of professional artists; 3,600 mems; Exec. Dir HENNIE L. WOLFF; publs *Agenda* (4 a year), *Hidden Agenda* (8 a year).

HISTORY, GEOGRAPHY AND ARCHAEOLOGY

Canadian Association of Geographers: Dept of Geography, McGill Univ., 425-805 Sherbrooke St W, Montréal, QC H3A 2K6; tel. (514) 398-4946; fax (514) 398-7437; e-mail cag@geog.mcgill.ca; internet www .cag-acg.ca; f. 1951; 800 mems; Pres. CHRIS SHARPE; Sec.-Treas. ALAN NASH; publs *The CAG Newsletter* (6 a year), *The Canadian Geographer* (4 a year), *The Directory* (1 a year).

Canadian Historical Association/Société Historique du Canada: 501-130 Albert St, Ottawa, ON K1P 5G4; tel. (613) 233-7885; fax (613) 567-3110; e-mail cha-shc@cha-shc .ca; internet www.cha-shc.ca; f. 1922, to encourage historical research and public interest in history; 1,200 mems; Annual Meeting Awards; Prizes Affiliated Committees Advocacy; Exec. Coordinator Dr MICHEL DUQUET (acting); publs *Bulletin* (3 a year), *Canada's Ethnic Groups* (2 a year), *Historical Booklets* (2 a year), *Journal of the CHA/*

Revue de la SHC (1 a year), *Register of Dissertations/Répertoire des thèses* (online).

Château Ramezay Museum/Musée du Château Ramezay: 280 Notre Dame E, Old Montréal, QC H2Y 1C5; tel. (514) 861-3708; fax (514) 861-8317; e-mail info@ chateauramezay.qc.ca; internet www .chateauramezay.qc.ca; f. 1895; 250 mems; library of 8,000 books; Dir ANDRÉ J. DELISLE; Sec. SUZANNE LALUMIÈRE; publ. *La Lettre de Ramezay* (Ramezay Letter, 3 a year).

Genealogical Association of Nova Scotia: 3045 Robie St, Suite 222, Halifax, NS B3K 4P6; tel. (902) 454-0322; e-mail gans@ chebucto.ns.ca; internet www.chebucto.ns .ca/recreation/gans; f. 1982; 1,000 mems; Pres. JANICE FRALIC-BROWN; publ. *The Nova Scotia Genealogist* (3 a year).

Genealogical Institute of the Maritimes (Institut Généalogique des Provinces Maritimes): POB 36022, Canada Post Postal Office, 5675 Spring Garden Rd, Halifax, NS B3J 1G0; internet nsgna.ednet.ns.ca/gim; f. 1983; education and research in genealogy; offers certification and registration of individuals undertaking genealogical research for the public; 44 mems.

Institut d'Histoire de l'Amérique Française: 261 Bloomfield Ave, Montréal, QC H2V 3R6; tel. (514) 278-2232; fax (514) 271-6369; e-mail ihaf@ihaf.qc.ca; internet www .ihaf.qc.ca; f. 1946; 1,000 mems; Pres. Prof. ALAIN BEAULIEU; Sec. Prof. BRIGITTE CAULIER; publ. *Revue d'histoire de l'Amérique française* (4 a year).

Ontario Historical Society: 34 Parkview Ave, Willowdale, ON M2N 3Y2; tel. (416) 226-9011; fax (416) 226-2740; e-mail ohs@ ontariohistoricalsociety.ca; internet www .ontariohistoricalsociety.ca; f. 1888; 300 affiliated societies; 3,000 mems; Exec. Dir PATRICIA K. NEAL; publs *OHS Bulletin* (5 a year), *Ontario History* (2 a year).

Royal Canadian Geographical Society: 1155 Lola St, Suite 200, Ottawa ON K1K 4C1; tel. (613) 745-4629; fax (613) 744-0947; e-mail rcgs@rcgs.org; internet www.rcgs.org; f. 1929; 204,000 mems; Pres. GISELE JACOB; publ. *Canadian Geographic* (10 a year).

Royal Nova Scotia Historical Society: POB 2622, Halifax, NS B3J 3P7; internet nsgna.ednet.ns.ca/rnshs/; f. 1878; history, biography, social studies of provincial past; 350 mems; Pres. JUDITH FINGARD; Sec. R. BARBOUR; publs *Collections* (irregular), *Journal* (1 a year).

Société Généalogique Canadienne Française: 3440 rue Davidson, Montréal, QC H1W 2Z5; tel. (514) 527-1010; fax (514) 527-0265; e-mail info@sgcf.com; internet www .sgcf.com; f. 1943; studies and publications on the origins and history of French Canadian families since 1615; 3,400 mems; library of 21,300 books, 3,000,000 cards on marriages, 4,500 microfilms; Pres. GISÈLE MONARQUE; Dir-Gen. MICHELINE PERREAULT; publ. *Mémoires* (4 a year).

Waterloo Historical Society: c/o Kitchener Public Library, 85 Queen St N, Kitchener, ON N2H 2H1; tel. (519) 743-0271 ext. 252; fax (519) 743-1261; e-mail whs@whs.ca; internet www.whs.ca; f. 1912; 275 mems; local history; colln at Kitchener Public Library, ON; Sec. AMANDA BONNEY.

LANGUAGE AND LITERATURE

Alliance Française: 352 MacLaren St, Ottawa, ON K2P 0M6; tel. (613) 234-9470; fax (613) 233-1559; internet www.af.ca; offers courses and examinations in French language and culture and promotes cultural exchange with France; attached offices in Calgary, Edmonton, Halifax, Mississauga,

Moncton, North York, Regina, Saskatoon, Toronto, Vancouver, Victoria and Winnipeg; Dir ALAIN LANDRY.

British Council: British High Commission, 80 Elgin St, Ottawa, ON K1P 5K7; tel. (514) 886-5863; e-mail education.enquiries@ca .britishcouncil.org; internet www .britishcouncil.org/canada; promotes education in and cultural exchange with the UK; attached office in Montréal; Dir MARTIN ROSE.

Canadian Authors Association: Box 419, Campbellford, ON K0L 1L0; tel. (705) 653-0323; fax (705) 653-0593; e-mail admin@ canauthors.org; internet www.canauthors .org; f. 1921; 600 mems; administers awards; annual conference; workshops and seminars; Pres. JOAN EYOLFSON CADHAM; publ. *The Canadian Writer's Guide* (irregular).

Canadian Linguistic Association/Association Canadienne de Linguistique: Département d'Études Françaises, University of Toronto, Toronto, ON M5S 1J4; fax (416) 926-1300; internet www.chass.utoronto .ca/~cla-acl; f. 1954 to advance the study of linguistics and languages in Canada; 220 mems; Pres. JOHN ARCHIBALD; Sec. MARTHA McGINNIS; Treas. MARGUERITE MACKENZIE; publ. *The Canadian Journal of Linguistics/ La Revue Canadienne de Linguistique* (4 a year).

Goethe-Institut: 418 Sherbrooke Est, Montréal, QC H2L 1J6; tel. (514) 499-0159; fax (514) 499-0905; e-mail info@montreal.goethe .org; internet www.goethe.de/montreal; f. 1962; offers courses and examinations in German language and culture and promotes cultural exchange with Germany; attached centres in Ottawa and Toronto; library of 7,000 vols, 20 periodicals, incl. German newspapers, magazines, CDs and DVDs; Dir MECHTILD MANUS.

PEN Canada: 24 Ryerson Ave, Suite 301, Toronto, ON M5T 2P3; tel. (416) 703-8448; fax (416) 703-3870; e-mail pen@pencanada .ca; f. 1982; international literary association; 125 mems; Pres. ELLEN SELIGMAN; Vice-Pres. CHARLES FORAN.

MEDICINE

Academy of Medicine: c/o Library and Information Services, Univ. Health Network, Toronto General Hospital, 200 Elizabeth St, EN1-418, Toronto, ON M5G 2C4; tel. (416) 340-3259; fax (416) 340-4384; f. 1907; history of medicine; Librarian MARGARET ALIHARAN.

Canadian Association for Anatomy, Neurobiology and Cell Biology/Association Canadienne d'Anatomie, de Neurobiologie et de Biologie Cellulaire: c/o Dr MICHAEL KAWAJA, Dept of Anatomy and Cell Biology, Queen's University, Kingston, ON K7L 3N6; tel. (613) 533-2864; fax (613) 533-2566; e-mail kawajam@post.queensu.ca; f. 1956; 147 mems; Pres. Dr RIC DEVON; Sec. Dr MICHAEL KAWAJA; publ. *The Bulletin* (1 a year).

Canadian Association of Optometrists: 234 Argyle Ave, Ottawa, ON K2P 1B9; tel. (613) 235-7924; fax (613) 235-2025; e-mail info@opto.ca; internet www.opto.ca; f. 1948; Pres. Dr KIRSTEN NORTH; Dir-Gen. GLENN CAMPBELL; Sec.-Treasurer Dr PAUL GENEAU; publ. *The Canadian Journal of Optometry/ La Revue Canadienne d'Optométrie* (4 a year).

Canadian Dental Association: 1815 Alta Vista Drive, Ottawa, ON K1G 3Y6; tel. (613) 523-1770; fax (613) 523-7736; e-mail reception@cda-adc.ca; internet www.cda-adc .ca; f. 1902; Pres. Dr LOUIS DUBÉ; publs *Communiqué* (6 a year), *Journal* (11 a year).

Canadian Lung Association: 3 Raymond St, Suite 300, Ottawa, ON K1R 1A3; tel. (613) 569-6411; fax (613) 569-8860; e-mail info@lung.ca; internet www.lung.ca; f. 1900; 10 provincial member associations (Alberta, British Columbia, Québec, Nova Scotia, Saskatchewan, Manitoba, New Brunswick, Newfoundland and Labrador, Ontario, Prince Edward Island), 1 territorial association (North West Territories); associated professional societies: Canadian Thoracic Society, Canadian Physiotherapy Cardio-Respiratory Society, Canadian Nurses' Respiratory Society, Respiratory Therapy Society; publ. *Canadian Respiratory Journal* (8 a year).

Canadian Medical Association: 1867 Alta Vista Drive, Ottawa, ON K1G 3Y6; fax (613) 236-8864; e-mail pubs@cma.ca; internet www .cma.ca; f. 1867; 60,000 mems; Pres. Dr COLIN MACMILLAN; Sec.-Gen. WILLIAM THOLL; Hon. Treas. Dr JOHN RAPIN; publs *Canadian Association of Radiologists Journal* (6 a year), *Canadian Journal of Emergency Medicine* (4 a year), *Canadian Journal of Rural Medicine* (4 a year), *Canadian Journal of Surgery* (6 a year), *Canadian Medical Association Bulletin* (26 a year), *Canadian Medical Association Journal—CMAJ* (25 a year), *Health Care News* (12 a year), *Journal of Psychiatry and Neuroscience* (5 a year), *Strategy Magazine*.

Canadian Paediatric Society (Société Canadienne de Pédiatrie): 100–2204 Walkley Rd, Ottawa, ON K1G 4G8; tel. (613) 526-9397; fax (613) 526-3332; e-mail info@cps.ca; internet ww.cps.ca; f. 1923; 2,000 mems; Pres. C. ROBIN WALKER; publ. *Paediatrics and Child Health* (6 a year).

Canadian Pharmacists Association: 1785 Alta Vista Drive, Ottawa, ON K1G 3Y6; tel. (613) 523-7877; fax (613) 523-0445; e-mail cpha@pharmacists.ca; internet www .pharmacists.ca; f. 1907; 9,000 mems; Pres. GARTH McCUTCHEON; publs *Compendium of Non Prescription Products* (English only), *Compendium of Pharmaceuticals and Specialties* (English and French edns, 1 a year), *Patient Self-Care* (English only), *Therapeutic Choices* (English only).

Canadian Physiological Society: c/o Canadian Federation of Biological Societies, 305-1750 Courtwood Crescent, Ottawa, ON K2C 2B5; tel. (613) 225-8889; fax (613) 225-9621; internet www.cps.cfbs.org; f. 1936; 300 mems; Pres. Dr CHRIS CHEESEMAN; Sec. Dr C. ELAINE CHAPMAN; Treas. Dr DOUG JONES; publ. *The Canadian Journal of Physiology and Pharmacology* (12 a year).

Canadian Psychiatric Association/Association des Psychiatres du Canada: 141 Laurien Ave West, Suite 701, Ottawa, ON K1P 5J3; tel. (613) 234-2815; fax (613) 234-9857; e-mail cpa@cpa-apc.org; internet www .cpa-apc.org; f. 1951 to promote research into psychiatric disorders and foster high standards of professional practice in clinical care, education and research; 2,950 mems; Chair. Dr BLAKE WOODSIDE; Chief Exec. Officer ALEX SAUNDERS; publ. *The Canadian Journal of Psychiatry* (12 a year).

Canadian Public Health Association: 400-1565 Carling Ave, Ottawa, ON K1Z 8R1; tel. (613) 725-3769; fax (613) 725-9826; e-mail info@cpha.ca; internet www.cpha.ca; f. 1910; represents public health in Canada with links to int. public health community; 1,150 mems; Chair. Dr CORY NEUDORF; CEO DEBRA LYNKOWSKI; publ. *Canadian Journal of Public Health* (6 a year, and online at cjph.cpha.ca).

Canadian Society for Nutritional Sciences: c/o Dr SUSAN WHITING, Div. Nutrition & Dietetics, College of Pharmacy & Nutri-

tion, 110 Science Place, Univ. of Saskatchewan, Saskatoon, SK S7N 5C9; internet www .nutritionalsciences.ca; f. 1957 to extend knowledge of nutrition by research, discussion of research reports, and exchange of information; 340 mems; Pres. SUSAN WHITING; Sec. GUYLAINE FERLAND; publ. *Nutrition/ Forum de Nutrition* (2 a year).

Pharmacological Society of Canada: c/o Dept of Physiology and Pharmacology, M216 Medical Sciences Bldg, Univ. of Western Ontario, London, ON N6A 5C1; e-mail robert.mcneill@usask.ca; internet www .physpharm.med.uwo.ca; f. 1956; 320 mems; Pres. Dr J. ROBERT McNEILL; Sec. Dr FIONA PARKINSON; publ. *Canadian Journal of Physiology and Pharmacology*.

Royal College of Physicians and Surgeons of Canada: 774 Echo Dr., Ottawa, ON K1S 5N8; tel. (613) 730-8177; fax (613) 730-8830; e-mail info@rcpsc.edu; internet rcpsc.medical.org; f. 1929; sets standards for postgraduate medical education of specialists in Canada; accredits postgraduate specialist education programmes; acts as nat. examining body to certify medical, surgical and laboratory specialists; offers a professional devt programme; 39,270 mems; CEO Dr ANDREW PADMOS; publ. *Royal College Outlook* (4 a year).

NATURAL SCIENCES
General

Association Francophone pour le Savoir (Acfas): 425 rue de la Gauchetière Est, Montréal, QC H2L 2M7; tel. (514) 849-0045; fax (514) 849-5558; e-mail acfas@acfas.ca; internet www.acfas.ca; f. 1923; aims to popularize science by means of lectures, meetings, awards, publications; 6,000 mems; Pres. CLAIRE V. DE LA DURANTAYE; publs *Découvrir* (6 a year), *Les Cahiers de l'Acfas* (2–3 a year).

Nova Scotian Institute of Science: Ocean Nutrition Canada, 1721 Lower Water St, Halifax, NS B3J 1S5; internet www.chebucto .ns.ca; f. 1862; monthly lecture series; 300 mems; Pres. Dr ARCHIE McCULLOCH; Vice-Pres. CAROLYN BIRD; Sec. TRUMAN LAYTON; publ. *Proceedings* (irregular).

Biological Sciences

Canadian Phytopathological Society: c/o Joanne McWilliams, KW Neatby Bldg, Agriculture & Agri-Food Canada, 960 Carling Ave, Ottawa, ON K1A 0C6; internet www .cps-scp.ca; f. 1929; 500 mems; Pres. RICHARD MARTIN; Sec. DEENA ERRAMPALLI; publs *Canadian Journal of Plant Pathology* (4 a year), *News* (4 a year).

Canadian Society for Cellular and Molecular Biology: Centre de recherche, Hôtel-Dieu de Québec, 11 Côte du Palais, Quebec, QC G1R 2J6; internet www.csbmcb .ca; f. 1966; 400 mems; Pres. Dr DAVID ANDREWS; Sec. C. CASS; publ. *Bulletin* (3 a year).

Canadian Society for Immunology: c/o Immunology Research Group, University of Calgary, 2500 University Drive NW, Calgary, AB T2N 1N4; tel. (403) 492-0712; fax (403) 439-3439; f. 1966; 400 mems; Pres. Dr JOHN SCHRADER; Sec. and Treas. Dr DONNA CHOW; publ. *Bulletin* (irregular).

Canadian Society of Microbiologists/ Société Canadienne des Microbiologistes: c/o Canadian Federation of Biological Societies, 305-1750 Courtwood Crescent, Ottawa, ON K2C 2B5; tel. (613) 225-8889; fax (613) 225-9621; e-mail info@csm-scm.org; internet www.csm-scm.org; f. 1951; 500 mems; Man. WAFAA ANTONIOUS; publs *CSM*

Newsletter (3 a year), *Programme and Abstracts* (1 a year).

Cercles des Jeunes Naturalistes: 4101 Sherbrooke est, Suite 262, Montréal, QC H1X 2B2; tel. (514) 252-3023; fax (514) 254-8744; e-mail cjn@cam.org; internet www.cjn .cam.org; f. 1931; 1,500 mems; Pres.-Gen. YVES BREAULT; Dir LAURE BOUCHARD; publs *Les Naturalistes* (4 a year), *Nouvelles CJN* (12 a year).

Entomological Society of Canada: 393 Winston Ave, Ottawa, ON K2A 1Y8; tel. (613) 725-2619; fax (613) 725-9349; e-mail entsoc .can@bellnet.ca; internet esc-sec.org; f. 1863; 500 mems, 7 affiliated regional socs; Pres. Dr MAYA EVENDEN; Sec. Dr ANNABELLE FIRLEJ; publ. *The Canadian Entomologist* (6 a year).

Genetics Society of Canada/Société de Génétique du Canada: c/o E. K. Consulting, 53 Slalom Gate Rd, Collingwood, ON L9Y 5B1; tel. (613) 232-9459; fax (613) 594-5190; internet www.life.biology.mcmaster.ca/ gsc; f. 1956; 425 mems; Pres. VIRGINIA WALKER; Treasurer JOHN BELL; Sec. CAROLYN J. BROWN; publs *Bulletin* (4 a year), *Genome* (6 a year).

Manitoba Naturalists Society: 401–63 Albert St, Winnipeg, MB R3B 1G4; tel. (204) 943-9029; fax (204) 943-9029; e-mail mns@escape.ca; internet www .manitobanature.ca; f. 1920; 1,500 mems; Pres. LARRY DE MARCH; Exec. Dir GORDON FARDOE; publ. *Bulletin* (10 a year).

Société de Protection des Plantes du Québec: c/o Secretary, 1643 Chemin des Lacs, Vincent Phillion, Station de recherches agricoles, CP 480, Saint-Faustin-Lac carré, QC J0T 1J2; e-mail ltartier@sympatico.ca; internet www.sppq.qc.ca; f. 1908; 225 mems; Pres. DANNY RIOUX; Sec. LÉON TARTIER; Treas. GAÉTAN BOURGEOIS; publs *Echos phytosanitaires* (4 a year), *Phytoprotection* (3 a year).

Société Linnéenne du Québec: 1040 Belvédère, Sillery, QC G1S 3G3; tel. (418) 683-2432; fax (418) 683-2893; internet ecoroute .uqcn.qc.ca/group/slq; f. 1929; 800 mems; natural history; Pres. JEAN-PAUL L'ALLIER; Dir AGATHE SAVARD; publ. *Le Linnéen* (4 a year).

Vancouver Natural History Society: POB 3021, Vancouver, BC V6B 3X5; tel. (604) 737-3074; fax (604) 876-3313; e-mail mgrcoope@interchange.ubc.ca; internet www .naturalhistory.bc.ca/vhns; f. 1918; aims to promote interest in nature, conserve natural resources, protect endangered species and ecosystems; 900 mems; Pres. CYNTHIA CRAMPTON; publ. *Discovery* (2 a year).

Mathematical Sciences

Canadian Mathematical Society/Société Mathématique du Canada: 105-1785 Alta Vista Dr., Ottawa, ON K1G 3Y6; tel. (613) 733-2662; fax (613) 733-8994; e-mail office@ cms.math.ca; internet www.cms.math.ca; f. 1945, inc. 1979; promotes the discovery, learning and application of mathematics; 960 mems; Pres. ANTHONY LAU; Exec. Dir and Sec. Dr JOHAN RUDNICK; Treas. DAVID RODGERS; publs *Canadian Journal of Mathematics* (6 a year), *Canadian Mathematical Bulletin* (4 a year), *CMS Notes* (6 a year), *CRUX with Mayhem* (8 a year).

Physical Sciences

Canadian Association of Physicists/ Association Canadienne des Physiciens et Physiciennes: MacDonald Bldg (Suite 112), 150 Louis Pasteur, Ottawa, ON K1N 6N5; tel. (613) 562-5614; fax (613) 562-5615; e-mail cap@physics.uottawa.ca; internet www.cap.ca; f. 1945; 2,000 mems; Pres. Dr MICHAEL R. MORROW; Exec. Dir. FRANCINE M.

FORD; Sec. and Treasurer Dr RICHARD HODGSON; publ. *Physics in Canada* (6 a year).

Canadian Meteorological and Oceanographic Society/Société Canadienne de Météorologie et d'Océanographie: Station 'D', POB 3211, Ottawa, ON K1P 6H7; tel. (613) 990-0300; fax (613) 990-1617; e-mail execdir@cmos.ca; internet www.cmos .ca; f. 1977; 800 mems; Pres. Dr BILL CRAWFORD; Exec. Dir Dr IAN D. RUTHERFORD; publs *Atmosphere-Ocean* (4 a year), *CMOS Bulletin SCMO* (6 a year), *Congress Program and Abstracts* (1 a year).

Canadian Society of Biochemistry, Molecular and Cellular Biology/Société Canadienne de Biochimie et de Biologie Moléculaire et Cellulaire: c/o Dr E. R. Tustanoff, Dept of Biochemistry, University of Western Ontario, London, ON N6A 5C1; tel. (519) 471-1961; fax (519) 661-3175; e-mail etustan@uwo.ca; f. 1958; 1,000 mems; Pres. Dr J. ORLOWSKI; Sec. Dr E. R. TUSTANOFF; publ. *Bulletin* (1 a year).

Canadian Society of Petroleum Geologists: 540 Fifth Ave SW (Suite 160), Calgary, AB T2P 0M2; tel. (403) 264-5610; fax (403) 264-5898; e-mail cspg@cspg.org; internet www.cspg.org; f. 1927; 3,400 mems; Pres. CRAIG LAMB; Business Man. TIM HOWARD; publs *Bulletin of Canadian Petroleum Geology* (4 a year), *Reservoir* (11 a year).

Chemical Institute of Canada: 130 Slater St, Suite 550, Ottawa, ON K1P 6E2; tel. (613) 232-6252; fax (613) 232-5862; e-mail info@ cheminst.ca; internet www.cheminst.ca; f. 1945; 27 local sections, 16 subject divisions, 116 student chapters and 3 constituent societies—Canadian Society for Chemical Engineering, the Canadian Society for Chemical Technology and the Canadian Society for Chemistry; Exec. Dir ROLAND ANDERSSON; publs *Canadian Chemical News* (10 a year), *Canadian Journal of Chemical Engineering* (6 a year).

Geological Association of Canada: c/o Dept of Earth Sciences, Rm ER4063, Memorial University of Newfoundland, St John's, NL A1B 3X5; tel. (709) 737-7660; fax (709) 737-2532; e-mail gac@mun.ca; internet www .gac.ca; f. 1947 to advance the science of geology and related fields of study and to promote a better understanding thereof throughout Canada; 2,500 mems; Pres. Dr STEPHEN JOHNSTON; Sec.-Treas. Dr TOBY RIVERS; publs *Geolog* (4 a year), *Geoscience Canada* (4 a year).

Society of Chemical Industry (Canadian Section): 247 Ridgewood Rd, Toronto, ON M1C 2XC; tel. (416) 708-8924; fax (416) 281-8691; internet www.soci.org; f. 1902; fosters contact between chemical industry, universities and govt; rewards achievement in industry and universities; promotes international contact; 150 mems; Administrator BETH GALLOWAY.

Spectroscopy Society of Canada/Société de Spectroscopie du Canada: POB 332, Stn A, Ottawa, ON K1N 8V3; internet www .globalserve.net/~ssccan; f. 1957; 350 mems; provides the annual Herzberg Award, the Barringer Research Award and an award to the Youth Science Foundation; Pres. DIANE BEAUCHEMIN; Sec. TERESA SWITZER; publ. *Canadian Journal of Analytical Sciences and Spectroscopy.*

The Royal Astronomical Society of Canada: 203-4920 Dundas St W, Toronto, ON M9A 1B7; tel. (416) 924-7973; fax (416) 924-2911; e-mail nationaloffice@rasc.ca; internet www.rasc.ca; f. 1890; 29 centres; 4,400 mems; Exec. Sec. JO TAYLOR; publs *Journal* (6 a year), *Observers' Handbook* (1 a year).

PHILOSOPHY AND PSYCHOLOGY

Canadian Philosophical Association/ Association Canadienne de Philosophie: Saint Paul Univ., 223 Main St, Ottawa, ON K1S IC4; tel. (613) 236-1393; fax (613) 782-3005; e-mail acpa@ustpaul.ca; internet www .acpcpa.ca; f. 1958 to promote philosophical scholarship in Canada and to represent Canadian philosophers; 800 mems; Exec. Dir LOUISE MOREL; publ. *Dialogue: Canadian Philosophical Review / Revue canadienne de philosophie* (French and English, 4 a year).

Canadian Psychological Association/ Société Canadienne de Psychologie: 151 Slater St, Suite 205, Ottawa, ON K1P 5H3; tel. (613) 237-2144; fax (613) 237-1674; e-mail cpa@cpa.ca; internet www.cpa.ca; f. 1939; 4,500 mems; Exec. Dir Dr JOHN C. SERVICE; publs *Canadian Journal of Behavioural Science* (4 a year), *Canadian Journal of Experimental Psychology* (4 a year), *Canadian Psychology* (4 a year), *Psynopsis* (4 a year).

RELIGION, SOCIOLOGY AND ANTHROPOLOGY

Association for the Advancement of Scandinavian Studies in Canada (AASSC): 643 University College, Winnipeg, MB R3T 2M8; tel. (204) 474-6628; fax (204) 261-5764; f. 1982; 120 mems; Pres. JOHN TUCKER; Sec. KATHY HANSON; publs *Newsbulletin* (2 a year), *Scandinavian-Canadian Studies* (1 a year).

Canadian Association of African Studies/Association Canadienne des Etudes Africaines: CAAS/ACÉA Administrator, 4-17E Old Arts Bldg University of Alberta, Edmonton, AB T6G 2E6; fax (780) 492-9125; e-mail caas@ualberta.ca; internet www.arts .ualberta.ca/~caas; f. 1970; 310 mems; promotion of the study of Africa in Canada; aims to improve the Canadian public's knowledge and awareness of Africa; provides a link between Canadian and African scholarly and scientific communities; Admin. LOUISE ROLINGHER; publ. *Canadian Journal of African Studies / Revue Canadienne des Etudes Africaines* (3 a year).

Canadian Association for Latin American and Caribbean Studies/Association Canadienne des Etudes Latino-Américaines et des Caraïbes: CALACS c/o Dept of History, Univ. of Windsor, Windsor ON N9B 3P4; tel. (514) 253-3000; fax (514) 971-3610; e-mail calacs@uwindsor.ca; internet www.can-latam.org; f. 1969; 300 mems; Pres. JUANITA DE BARROS; Treas. STEVEN PALMER; publ. *Canadian Journal of Latin American and Caribbean Studies* (2 a year).

Canadian Society of Biblical Studies: c/o Michele Murray, Dept of Religion, Bishop's University, Lennoxville, QC J1M 1Z7; tel. (819) 822-9600; e-mail mmurray@ubishops .ca; internet www.ccsr.ca/csbs; f. 1933; the promotion of scholarship in Biblical studies; 287 mems; Pres. DAVID HAWKIN; Exec. Sec. M. MURRAY; publ. *Bulletin* (1 a year).

TECHNOLOGY

Canadian Academy of Engineering/Académie Canadienne du Génie: 180 Elgin St, Suite 1100, Ottawa, ON K2P 2K3; tel. (613) 235-9056; fax (613) 235-6861; e-mail acadeng@ccpe.ca; internet www .acad-eng-gen.ca; f. 1987; assesses the changing needs of Canada and the technical resources that can be applied to them; sponsors programmes to meet these needs; provides independent and expert advice on matters of national importance concerning engineering; highlights exceptional engineering achievements; works by cooperation with national and international academies; 260 mems; Pres. RON NOLAN; Sec. and Treas. Dr JOHN McLAUGHLIN; Exec. Dir PHILIP COCK-SHUTT; publ. *Newsletter* (4 a year).

Canadian Aeronautics and Space Institute: 1685 Russell Rd, Unit 1R, Ottawa, ON K1G 0N1; tel. (613) 234-0191; fax (613) 234-9039; e-mail casi@casi.ca; internet www.casi .ca; f. 1954; 2,000 mems; Pres. P. WHYTE; Exec. Dir I. ROSS; publ *Canadian Aeronautics and Space Journal* (4 a year), *Canadian Journal of Remote Sensing* (4 a year).

Canadian Council of Professional Engineers: 180 Elgin St (Suite 1100), Ottawa, ON K2P 2K3; tel. (613) 232-2474; fax (613) 230-5759; e-mail info@ccpe.ca; internet www.ccpe.ca; f. 1936; coordinating body for 12 Provincial and Territorial Licensing Bodies; total membership of constituent associations 152,000; CEO MARIE LEMAY.

Canadian Electricity Association: 1155 rue Metcalfe, bureau 1120, Montréal, QC H3B 2V6; tel. (514) 866-6121; fax (514) 866-1880; e-mail info@canelect.ca; internet www .canelect.ca; f. 1891; represents Canada's electric utility industry; 35 corporate utilities, 38 corporate manufacturers, 109 assoc. cos, 2,500 individual mems; Pres. H. R. KONOW; publs *Connections* (10 a year), *Electricity* (1 a year), *Reports* (various).

Canadian Institute of Mining, Metallurgy and Petroleum: Xerox Tower, Suite 1210, 3400 de Maisonneuve Blvd West, Montréal, QC H3Z 3B8; tel. (514) 939-2710; fax (514) 939-2714; e-mail cim@cim.org; internet www.cim.org; f. 1898; 10,500 mems; Pres. WARREN HOLMES; Exec. Dir JEAN VAVREK; publs *CIM Bulletin* (10 a year), *CIM Directory* (1 a year), *CIM Reporter* (2 a year), *Journal of Canadian Petroleum Technology* (10 a year).

Engineering Institute of Canada: 1295 Hwy 2E, Kingston, ON K7L 4V1; tel. (613) 547-5989; fax (613) 547-0195; e-mail info@ eic-ici.ca; internet www.eic-ici.ca; f. 1887; 16,000 mems and 13 mem. socs; Pres. Prof. Dr KERRY ROWE; Exec. Dir B. JOHN PLANT.

Research Institutes

GENERAL

Alberta Innovates—Technology Futures: 250 Karl Clark Rd, Edmonton, AB T6N 1E4; tel. (780) 450-5111; fax (780) 450-5333; internet www.arc.ab.ca; f. 1921; develops and commercializes technologies to give clients a competitive advantage; provides solutions globally to the agriculture, life sciences, energy, environment, forestry and manufacturing sectors; library of 40,000 vols, 3,500 reports, 450 current periodicals; CEO GARY ABACH; publ. *R & D Newsletter* (3 a year).

InNOVAcorp: 101 Research Drive, Woodside Industrial Park, Dartmouth, NS B2Y 4T6; tel. (902) 424-8670; fax (902) 424-4679; e-mail corpcomm@innovacorp.ns.ca; f. 1995; library of 20,000 vols; assists firms based in Nova Scotia to develop and market products, particularly in the fields of advanced engineering, information technology and oceans technology; CEO Dr ROSS McCURDY; publ. *Progress Report* (4 a year).

National Research Council of Canada/ Conseil National de Recherches Canada: 1200 Montréal Rd, Bldg M-58, Ottawa, ON K1A 0R6; tel. (613) 993-9101; fax (613) 952-9907; e-mail info@nrc-cnrc.gc .ca; internet www.nrc-cnrc.gc.ca; f. 1916; integrated science and technology agency of the federal govt; provides scientific and technological information through Canada

Institute for Scientific and Technical Information and industrial support through Industrial Research Assistance Programme; research carried out by 16 research institutes linked to 3 technology groups: biotechnology, information and telecommunications technologies, and manufacturing technologies; Pres. MICHAEL RAYMONT (acting); Sec.-Gen. PAT MORTIMER; publs *Biochemistry and Cell Biology* (6 a year), *Environmental Reviews* (4 a year), *Genome* (6 a year), *Canadian Geotechnical Journal* (6 a year), *Canadian Journal of Botany* (12 a year), *Canadian Journal of Chemistry* (12 a year), *Canadian Journal of Civil Engineering* (6 a year), *Canadian Journal of Earth Sciences* (12 a year), *Canadian Journal of Fisheries and Aquatic Sciences* (12 a year), *Canadian Journal of Forest Research* (12 a year), *Canadian Journal of Microbiology* (12 a year), *Canadian Journal of Physics* (12 a year), *Canadian Journal of Physiology and Pharmacology* (12 a year), *Canadian Journal of Zoology* (12 a year).

North-South Institute: 55 Murray St, Suite 200, Ottawa, ON K1N 5M3; tel. (613) 241-3535; fax (613) 241-7435; e-mail nsi@ nsi-ins.ca; internet www.nsi-ins.ca; f. 1976; policy-relevant research on issues of relations between industrialized and developing countries; library of 10,000 vols, 300 periodicals; Pres. Dr ROY CULPEPER; publs *Canadian Development Report* (1 a year), *Review* (newsletter, 2 a year).

Nunavut Research Institute: POB 1720, Iqaluit, NU X0A 0H0; tel. (867) 979-7279; fax (867) 979-7109; e-mail slcnri@nunanet.com; internet pooka.nunanet.com/~research; f. 1978; present name 1995; br. in Igloolik; publ. *Research Compendium* (1 a year).

Process Research ORTECH Corporation: 2350 Sheridan Park Dr., Mississauga, ON L5K 2T4; tel. (905) 822-4941; fax (905) 822-9537; e-mail info@processortech.com; internet www.processortech.com; f. 1928 as Ontario Research Foundation, privatized 1999; contract research in areas of mining, metallurgical, recycling and chemical industries; library of 10,000 vols; Pres. Dr R. SRIDHAR.

RPC (Research and Productivity Council): 921 College Hill Rd, Fredericton, NB E3B 6Z9; tel. (506) 452-1212; fax (506) 452-1395; e-mail info@rpc.ca; internet www.rpc .ca; f. 1962; professional and technical services to help industry develop new products and innovative solutions to operating problems; depts incl. chemical and biotechnical services, engineering materials and diagnostics, food, fisheries and aquaculture, inorganic analytical services, product innovation, and process and environmental technology; library: information centre with 21,000 vols, 250 periodicals, inter-library loan services, access to on-line databases; Exec. Dir Dr P. LEWELL.

Saskatchewan Research Council: 125-15 Innovation Blvd, Saskatoon, SK S7N 2X8; tel. (306) 933-5400; fax (306) 933-7446; e-mail info@src.sk.ca; internet www.src.sk .ca; f. 1947; assists the population of Saskatchewan in strengthening the economy and securing the environment by means of research, development and the transfer of innovative scientific and technological solutions, applications and services; library: library (Information Services) of 25,000 vols, 5,500 in-house publs and 300 periodicals; Pres. and CEO LAURIER SCHRAMM.

Vizon SciTech Inc.: BC Research Complex, 3650 Wesbrook Mall, Vancouver, BC V6S 2L2; tel. (604) 224-4331; fax (604) 224-0540; internet www.vizonscitech.com; f. 1944 as British Columbia Research Inc. (BCRI), pre-

sent name 2004; conducts technological research in fields of applied biology, applied chemistry, engineering-physics.

AGRICULTURE, FISHERIES AND VETERINARY SCIENCE

Canadian Forest Service: Ottawa, ON K1A 0E4; f. 1899; forest production, tree improvement, forest statistics and the environmental aspects of forestry, pests, fire, carbon monitoring, industrial competitiveness; supports FPInnovations (see Research Institutes, Technology) and research at Canadian forestry schools; Asst Deputy Minister JIM FARRELL; publs *Annual State of Canada's Forests*, *CFS Research Notes*, *Forestry Technical Reports*, *Information Reports Digest*.

Research Establishments:

Great Lakes Forestry Centre: Box 490, 1219 Queen St East, Sault Ste Marie, ON P6A 5M7; Dir-Gen. E. KONDO.

Laurentian Forestry Centre: 1055 rue du P.E.P.S., BP 10380, Ste-Foy, QC G1V 4C7; tel. (418) 648-5847; fax (418) 648-7317; Dir-Gen. N. LAFRENIÈRE.

Maritimes Forestry Service: Box 4000, Fredericton, NB E3B 5P7; Dir-Gen. H. OLDHAM.

Northern Forestry Centre: 5320 122nd St, Edmonton, AB T6H 3S5; Dir-Gen. G. MILLER.

Pacific Forestry Centre: 506 West Burnside Rd, Victoria, BC V8Z 1M5; Dir-Gen. C. WINGET.

Dominion Arboretum: Bldg 72, Central Experimental Farm, Ottawa, ON K1A 0C6; tel. (613) 995-3700; fax (613) 992-7909; f. 1886; part of Agriculture Canada; evaluation of woody plants for cold hardiness and adaptability; display area of 35 ha; special living collections; Dir Dr H. DAVIDSON.

MEDICINE

Canadian Institutes of Health Research: Room 97, 160 Elgin St, Ottawa, ON K1A 0W9; tel. (613) 941-2672; fax (613) 954-1800; e-mail info@cihr.ca; internet www.cihr.ca; f. 2000; aims to make Canadian health services and products more effective and to strengthen the health care system; Pres. Dr ALAN BERNSTEIN; publs *Communiqué* (in English and French, 4 a year), *Report of the President* (1 a year).

Cancer Care Ontario: 620 University Ave, Suite 1500, Toronto, ON M5G 2L7; tel. (416) 971-9800; fax (416) 971-6888; e-mail publicaffairs@cancercare.on.ca; internet www.cancercare.on.ca; f. 1943; prevention, diagnosis, treatment, supportive care, education and research in cancer; Pres. and CEO Dr TERRENCE SULLIVAN; publ. *Cancer Care*.

Dentistry Canada Fund: 427 Gilmour Street, Ottawa, ON K2P 0R5; tel. (613) 236-4763; fax (613) 236-3935; e-mail information@dcf-fdc.ca; internet www.dcf-fdc .ca; f. 1902; charity promoting oral health; Pres. and Chair. Dr BERNARD DOLANSKY; Exec. Dir RICHARD MUNRO.

Canadian Cancer Society Research Institute: Suite 200, 10 Alcorn Ave, Toronto, ON M4V 3B1; tel. (416) 961-7223; fax (416) 961-4189; e-mail ccsri@cancer.ca; internet www.cancer.ca/research; f. 1947; research grant-awarding agency; Pres. and CEO Dr PETER GOODHAND; publs *Annual Scientific Report*, *NCIC CBCRI Breast Cancer Bulletin*, *NCIC Update*.

NATURAL SCIENCES

General

Arctic Institute of North America: Univ. of Calgary, 2500 University Dr., NW, Calgary, AB T2N 1N4; tel. (403) 220-7515; fax (403) 282-4609; e-mail arctic@ucalgary.ca; internet www.arctic.ucalgary.ca; f. 1945, became inst. of Univ. of Calgary 1979; multidisciplinary research on physical, biological and social sciences; library of 40,000 vols; Exec. Dir BENOIT BEAUCHAMP; publ. *Arctic* (4 a year).

International Development Research Centre: POB 8500, 150 Kent St, Ottawa, ON K1G 3H9; tel. (613) 236-6163; fax (613) 238-7230; e-mail info@idrc.ca; internet www.idrc.ca; f. 1970 by Act of the Canadian Parliament; to support research in the developing regions of the world in the fields of environment and natural resources; information sciences and systems; health science; social science; training and research utilization; library of 60,000 vols, 5,000 serials, 1,000 pamphlets and annual reports; Pres. Dr DAVID M. MALONE; publ. *IDRC Bulletin* (12 a year).

Natural Sciences and Engineering Research Council of Canada (NSERC): 350 Albert St, Ottawa, ON K1A 1H5; tel. (613) 995-5992; fax (613) 992-5337; e-mail comm@nserc.ca; internet www.nserc.ca; f. 1978; a Crown corporation of the federal Government reporting to Parliament through the Minister of Industry; supports both basic university research through research grants and project research through partnerships of universities with industry, as well as the advanced training of highly qualified people in both areas; Pres. TOM BRZUSTOWSKI; publ. *NSERC Contact* (newsletter).

Biological Sciences

Huntsman Marine Science Centre: 1 Lower Campus Rd, St Andrews, NB E5B 2L7; tel. (506) 529-1200; fax (506) 529-1212; e-mail huntsman@huntsmanmarine.ca; internet www.huntsmanmarine.ca; f. 1969 with the cooperation of universities and the federal Government; mems incl. several Canadian univs, Fisheries and Oceans Canada, National Research Council of Canada, New Brunswick Depts of Education and of Fisheries and Aquaculture, corporations, organizations and individuals; research and teaching in marine sciences and coastal biology; marine education courses for elementary, high school and univ. groups; centre includes public aquarium with local flora and fauna and Atlantic Reference Centre, which houses a zoological and botanical museum reference colln; Dir W. D. ROBERTSON; publ. *Newsletter (In Depth)* (4 a year).

Jardin botanique de Montréal: 4101 Sherbrooke St East, Montréal, QC H1X 2B2; tel. (514) 872-1400; fax (514) 872-3765; e-mail jardin_botanique@ville.montreal.qc.ca; internet www.ville.montreal.qc.ca/jardin; f. 1931; 22,000 plant species and cultivars, 30 thematic gardens; educational, conservation and research activities; affiliated botanical and horticultural socs; library of 27,000 vols on botany, horticulture, landscaping and natural sciences and 60,000 vols of periodicals (500 titles); Botanist-Librarian CELINE ARSENEAULT; publs *Index Seminum* (every 2 years), *Quatre-temps* (Amis du Jardin botanique, 4 a year).

Physical Sciences

Algonquin Radio Observatory: c/o Natural Resources Canada, Geodetic Survey Div., 615 Booth St, Room 440, Ottawa, ON K1A 0E9; tel. (613) 996-4410; fax (613) 995-3215; f. 1959; operated by the National Research Council; includes 150 ft-diameter radiotelescope completed in 1966.

David Dunlap Observatory of the University of Toronto: POB 360, Station A, Richmond Hill, ON L4C 4Y6; tel. (905) 884-2112; fax (905) 884-2672; f. 1935; 50 mems; library of 30,000 vols; Assoc. Dir SLAVEK RUCINSKI.

Dominion Astrophysical Observatory: 5071 West Saanich Rd, Victoria, BC V9E 2E7; tel. (250) 363-0001; fax (250) 363-0045; f. 1918; part of Nat. Research Ccl Herzberg Inst. of Astrophysics; 70 mems; library of 20,000 vols; Dir Dr JAMES E. HESSER.

Geological Survey of Canada: 601 Booth St, Ottawa, ON K1A 0E8; tel. (613) 996-3919; fax (613) 943-8742; e-mail ess-esic@nrcan-rncan.gc.ca; internet gsc.nrcan.gc.ca; f. 1842; part of Natural Resources Canada; regional centres in Dartmouth, NS, Ste-Foy, QC, Calgary, AB, Vancouver and Sidney, BC, and associated with Iqaluit, NU, Nunavut Geoscience Centre, NU; nat. geoscience agency providing geological information on Canada's landmass and near-offshore regions to support the sustainable devt of the nation's natural resources, to help mitigate against loss from natural disasters and to inform about environmental stewardship and health issues; carries out studies and provides information relating to bedrock geology at the surface or at depth, and the derived surficial deposits that characterize the geological regions of Canada; carries out research assisted by airborne and ground-based mapping of physical properties of these geological materials; has information on mineral deposits of Canada, including exploration guidelines and techniques, and on mineral potential for land-use planning and policy formulation; provides information and advice on natural hazards and terrain stability influenced by permafrost, glaciation and geomorphology, with spec. emphasis on public safety and the environment; has information on coastal and offshore marine geoscience, hazards and environmental quality of these extensive regions; has geological, geochemical and geophysical information on the coastal zone, seabed, onshore and offshore sedimentary basins and crustal processes; has information on Canada's marine continental margins for UN Convention on Law of the Sea; has geoscience knowledge about oil, gas, coal, coalbed methane and gas hydrate resources throughout Canada, both onshore and offshore; has information on climate change evidence, glaciers, ice caps, glacial history, glacial deposits and drift prospecting; has information on groundwater resources and the sustainability of aquifers for potable water; library services; major cartographic service; has extensive publishing programme for geological, geophysical and geochemical maps and reports; Asst Deputy Min. MARK COREY; publ. *GSC Information Circular*.

Toronto Biomedical NMR Centre: Dept of Medical Genetics and Microbiology, University of Toronto Medical Sciences Building, Rm 1233, Toronto, ON M5S 1A8; fax (416) 978-6885; f. 1970; a national centre for high field NMR spectroscopy servicing industry, universities and the Government; Dir Dr A. A. GREY.

RELIGION, SOCIOLOGY AND ANTHROPOLOGY

Canadian Federation for the Humanities and Social Sciences: Suite 415, 151 Slater St, Ottawa, ON K1P 5H3; tel. (613) 238-6112; fax (613) 238-6114; e-mail fedcan@fedcan.ca; internet www.fedcan.ca; f. 1941; Exec. Dir PAUL LEDWELL.

International Center for Research on Language Planning/Centre International de Recherche en Aménagement Linguistique: Pavillon De Koninck, Cité Universitaire, Sainte-Foy, QC G1K 7P4; tel. (418) 656-3232; f. 1967; basic research on language planning, description of oral and written Québec French, new information technologies, learning of a second language; 19 researchers, 80 graduate students, 4 staff; library of 6,000 vols, 50 periodicals; Exec. Dir D. DESHAIES.

Social Sciences and Humanities Research Council of Canada/Conseil de Recherches en Sciences Humaines du Canada: 350 Albert St, POB 1610, Ottawa, ON K1P 6G4; tel. (613) 992-0691; fax (613) 992-1787; e-mail info@sshrc-crsh.gc.ca; internet www.sshrc-crsh.gc.ca; f. 1977 to promote research and advanced training in the social sciences and humanities; offers grants for basic and applied research; doctoral and postdoctoral fellowships; scholarly publishing journals and conferences; Pres. Dr CHAD GAFFIELD.

TECHNOLOGY

Atomic Energy of Canada, Ltd (AECL): 2251 Speakman Drive, Mississauga, ON L5K 1B2; tel. (905) 823-9040; fax (905) 823-6120; internet www.aecl.ca; f. 1952; development of economic nuclear power, scientific research and development in the nuclear energy field, and marketing of nuclear reactors; Chair. J. RAYMOND FRENETTE; Pres. and CEO ROBERT VAN ADEL.

Attached Laboratories:

AECL Research, Chalk River Laboratories: Chalk River, ON K0J 1J0; f. 1944; nuclear reactors (NRU, NRX, Pool Test Reactor and ZED-2), Tandem Accelerating Super Conducting Cyclotron, equipment for nuclear research and engineering development.

AECL Research, Whiteshell Laboratories: Pinawa, MB R0E 1L0; f. 1960; I-10/1 Accelerator, Underground Research Laboratory, equipment for nuclear research and engineering development.

BC Advanced Systems Institute: 1048, 4720 Kingsway, Burnaby, BC V5H 4N2; tel. (604) 438-2752; fax (604) 438-6564; e-mail asi@asi.bc.ca; internet www.asi.bc.ca; f. 1986; promotes research and development in high technology areas such as microelectronics and artificial intelligence; Pres. and CEO VICTOR JONES.

Canada Centre for Inland Waters/Centre Canadien des Eaux Intérieures: 867 Lakeshore Rd, POB 5050, Burlington, ON L7R 4A6; tel. (905) 336-4981; fax (905) 336-6444; f. 1967; jt freshwater research complex of the Depts of Environment and Fisheries and Oceans; freshwater environmental and fisheries research and monitoring; 600 mems; cooperative management by cttee of institutional dirs.

Attached Research Institutes:

Bayfield Institute: 867 Lakeshore Rd, POB 5050, Burlington, ON L7R 4A6; under Dept of Fisheries and Oceans; comprises: Great Lakes Laboratory for Fisheries and Aquatic Sciences; Fisheries and Habitat Management; Canadian Hydrographic Service; Small Craft Harbours br.; and support for shipping. Together with the Freshwater Research Institute in Winnipeg, it provides the federal Fisheries and Oceans programme for the Central and Arctic Region.

National Water Research Institute: 867 Lakeshore Rd, POB 5050, Burlington, ON L7P 3M1; tel. (905) 336-4675; fax (905) 336-6444; e-mail nwriscience.liaison@ec.gc.ca; internet www.nwri.ca; component of Environment Canada's Science and Technology br.; Canada's largest freshwater research facility; staff incl. aquatic ecologists, environmental chemists, hydrologists, modellers, limnologists, physical geographers, research technicians, toxicologists, and experts in linking water science to environmental policy; operates 2 main centres: the larger at the Canada Centre for Inland Waters on the shores of the Great Lakes in Burlington, ON; the other at the National Hydrology Research Centre, in the heart of the Canadian Prairies in Saskatoon, SK; also has staff located in Gatineau, QC; Fredericton, NB; and Victoria, BC; works with other govt depts, univs and research orgs to address a variety of water-related issues; conducts a comprehensive programme of ecosystem-based research and devt in the aquatic sciences, generating and disseminating scientific knowledge needed to resolve environmental issues of regional, nat. or int. significance to Canada; brs focus on aquatic ecosystem impacts, protection and management research, science liaison, monitoring and research support; also comprises the Nat. Laboratory for Environmental Testing (NLET) and (since 1974) the program office for the UN's Global Environment Monitoring System (GEMS/Water); 300 mems; library of 58,000 vols, 105 print journals, 105 online journals; Dir-Gen. Dr JOHN H. CAREY; publ. *NWRI Contributions*.

FPInnovations—Forintek Division: Head Office and Western Laboratory, 2665 East Mall, Vancouver, BC V6T 1W5; tel. (604) 224-3221; fax (604) 222-5690; Eastern Laboratory, 319 rue Franquet, Sainte-Foy, QC G1P 4R4; f. 1979 (fmrly Forintek Canada Corp.); solid wood products research; Pres. PIERRE LAPOINTE; Corp. Sec. NORINE YOUNG.

Institute for Aerospace Studies: 4925 Dufferin St, Toronto, ON M3H 5T6; tel. (416) 667-7700; fax (416) 667-7799; e-mail info@utias.utoronto.ca; internet www.utias.utoronto.ca; f. 1949; attached to Univ. of Toronto; undergraduate and graduate studies; research in aerospace science and engineering, and associated fields; serves industrial research and development needs in government and industry; facilities for experimental and computational research; library of 80,000 vols; Dir Prof. D. W. ZINGG; publ. *Progress Report* (1 a year).

Pulp and Paper Research Institute of Canada (Paprican): 570 Blvd St-Jean, Pointe-Claire, QC H9R 3J9; tel. (514) 630-4100; fax (514) 630-4134; e-mail info@paprican.ca; internet www.paprican.ca; f. 1925; pulp and paper research, contract research and technical services; postgraduate training programme in cooperation with McGill University and University of British Columbia; library of 20,000 vols; Pres. and CEO J. D. WRIGHT; Sec. and Treasurer LUCIE LAPOINTE.

Libraries and Archives

Alberta

Calgary Public Library: 616 Macleod Trail SE, Calgary, AB T2G 2M2; tel. (403) 260-2600; fax (403) 237-5393; e-mail dearlibrary@calgarypubliclibrary.com; internet www.calgarypubliclibrary.com; f. 1912; 2.4 million

items; 16 brs; special sections on petroleum; Dir GERRY MEEK.

City of Edmonton Archives: 10440 108th Ave, Edmonton, AB T5H 3Z9; tel. (780) 496-8711; fax (780) 496-8732; internet www.edmonton.ca/archives; f. 1971; reference library of 10,000 vols, also MSS, newspapers, slides, city records, photographs and maps of the city; Man. (vacant).

Edmonton Public Library: 7 Sir Winston Churchill Square, Edmonton, AB T5J 2V4; tel. (780) 496-7000; fax (780) 496-7097; internet www.epl.ca; f. 1913; 16 brs; 1,766,809 print items, 242,934 audiovisual items; Dir of Libraries LINDA C. COOK.

Glenbow Library and Archives: 130—9 Ave SE, Calgary, AB T2G 0P3; tel. (403) 268-4204; fax (403) 232-6569; e-mail library@glenbow.org; internet www.glenbow.org; f. 1955; 80,000 vols, 700,000 photographs and a large collection of manuscript materials, chiefly on western and northern Canada.

Legislature Library: 216 Legislature Bldg, 10800 97th Ave, Edmonton, AB T5K 2B6; tel. (780) 427-2473; fax (780) 427-6016; e-mail library@assembly.ab.ca; internet www.assembly.ab.ca/lao/library; f. 1906; 425,000 vols; parliamentary library; extensive colln of most Alberta weekly newspapers; Legislature Librarian SANDRA E. PERRY; publs *New Books in the Library* (10 a year), *Selected Periodical Articles List* (10 a year).

Parkland Regional Library: 5404 56 Ave, Lacombe, AB T4L 1G1; tel. (403) 782-3850; fax (403) 782-4650; e-mail rsheppard@prl.ab.ca; internet www.prl.ab.ca; f. 1959; network of 50 public libraries and 48 school libraries in central Alberta; Dir RONALD SHEPPARD.

Provincial Archives of Alberta: 8555 Roper Rd, Edmonton, AB T6E 5W1; tel. (780) 427-1750; fax (780) 427-4646; e-mail paa@gov.ab.ca; internet culture.alberta.ca/archives/default.aspx; f. 1963; holdings incl. non-current Alberta govt records, private papers, church records, municipal records, photographs, taped oral history interviews, films, video cassettes and maps pertaining to the history of Alberta; regular exhibitions; reference library colln with focus on W Canadiana, local/community histories and archival literature (12,000 vols); Exec. Dir and Provincial Archivist LESLIE LATTA-GUTHRIE.

University of Alberta Library: 5-07 Cameron Library, Edmonton, AB T6G 2J8; tel. (403) 492-3790; fax (403) 492-8302; f. 1909; 4,809,303 vols, 3,690,989 microforms; Chief Librarian ERNIE INGLES; Dir KAREN ADAMS; publ. *Library Editions* (2 a year).

University of Calgary Library: 2500 University Drive NW, Calgary, AB T2N 1N4; tel. (403) 220-5953; fax (403) 282-1218; e-mail libinfo@ucalgary.ca; internet library.ucalgary.ca; f. 1966; 7,678,394 items (2,540,294 print items, 3,528,108 microforms, 1,430,467 maps and aerial photographs, 179,525 audiovisual items), 2,917 m of archives; University Librarian H. THOMAS HICKERSON.

British Columbia

British Columbia Archives: 655 Belleville St, Victoria, BC V8W 9W2; tel. (250) 387-1952; fax (250) 387-2072; e-mail access@bcarchives.gov.bc.ca; internet www.bcarchives.gov.bc.ca; f. 1893; 71,000 items of printed material, 7,000 linear metres of MSS and government records, 5,000,000 photographs, 9,000 paintings, 35,000 maps, charts and architectural plans, 25,000 hours of sound recordings, 4,000 cans of moving images; Provincial Archivist GARY A. MITCHELL.

Fraser Valley Regional Library: Admin. Centre, 34589 Delair Rd, Abbotsford, BC V2S 5Y1; tel. (604) 859-7141; fax (604) 852-5701; internet www.fvrl.ca; f. 1930; 24 brs, Outreach Services; 900,000 vols, 10,000 talking books, also incl. electronic resources DVDs, CDs, e-books; CEO ROB O'BRENNAN.

Greater Victoria Public Library: 735 Broughton St, Victoria, BC V8W 3H2; tel. (250) 382-7241; fax (250) 382-7125; internet www.gvpl.ca; f. 1864; 940,749 vols; CEO SANDRA ANDERSON.

Legislative Library: Parliament Bldgs, Victoria, BC V8V 1X4; tel. (250) 387-6510; fax (250) 356-1373; e-mail llbc.ref@leg.bc.ca; internet www.llbc.leg.bc.ca; f. 1863; 200,000 vols; Dir PETER GOURLAY.

Public Library InterLINK: 7252 Kingsway, Lower level, Burnaby, BC V5E 1G3; tel. (604) 517-8441; fax (604) 517-8410; e-mail info@interlinklibraries.ca; internet www.interlinklibraries.ca; f. 1994; a federation of 18 autonomous public libraries sharing resources and services and providing open access to all mem. libraries; spec. services: audiobooks for the visually impaired (46,056 vols), multilingual books, staff training video cassettes, children's educational video cassettes; Man. of Operations RITA AVIGDOR; Exec. Dir MICHAEL BURRIS.

Simon Fraser University, W. A. C. Bennett Library: 8888 University Blvd, Burnaby, BC V5A 1S6; tel. (604) 291-3265; fax (604) 291-3023; e-mail libhelp@sfu.ca; internet www.lib.sfu.ca; f. 1965; 1,214,111 vols, 937,181 microforms; University Librarian LYNN COPELAND.

University of British Columbia Library: 1961 East Mall, Vancouver, BC V6T 1Z1; tel. (604) 822-6375; fax (604) 822-3893; internet www.library.ubc.ca; f. 1915; 14 brs; 5,500,000 vols, 65,000 print and electronic serial subscriptions, 261,000 e-books, 5,200,000 microforms; Univ. Librarian Dr W. PETER WARD.

Vancouver Island Regional Library: 6250 Hammond Bay Rd, Box 3333, Nanaimo, BC V9R 5N3; tel. (250) 758-4697; fax (250) 758-2482; internet virl.bc.ca; f. 1936; 37 brs; 1,172,571 vols; Exec. Dir PENNY GRANT.

Vancouver Public Library: 350 West Georgia St, Vancouver, BC V6B 6B1; tel. (604) 331-3603; fax (604) 331-4080; e-mail info@vpl.ca; internet www.vpl.ca; f. 1887; 2,641,444 vols; 22 brs; City Librarian PAUL WHITNEY.

Vancouver School of Theology Library: 6050 Chancellor Blvd, Vancouver, BC V6T 1X3; tel. (604) 822-9430; fax (604) 822-9372; e-mail gmcleod@vst.edu; internet www.vst.edu; f. 1971; 85,000 vols; Library Dir GILLIAN MCLEOD.

Manitoba

Archives of Manitoba: 200 Vaughan St, Winnipeg, MB R3C 1T5; tel. (204) 945-3971; fax (204) 948-2008; e-mail archives@gov.mb.ca; internet www.gov.mb.ca/archives/index.html; f. 1884; 5,500 linear ft private MSS, 65,000 linear ft Manitoba government and court records, 8,000 linear ft Hudson's Bay Co Archives records, 130,000 architectural drawings, 1,200,000 photographs, 32,000 maps, 300 paintings, 5,500 prints and drawings, 7,000 sound records; special collections: Red River Settlement and Red River Disturbance, Lt-Governors' papers, Winnipeg General Strike, Canadian Airways Ltd, archives of the Ecclesiastical Province of Rupert's Land, records of local govts and school divisions, Archives of Manitoba legal and judicial history; Archivist of Manitoba GORDON DODDS.

Legislative Library of Manitoba: Rm 100, 200 Vaughan St, Winnipeg, MB R3C 1T5; tel. (204) 945-4330; fax (204) 948-1312; e-mail legislative_library@gov.mb.ca; internet www .manitoba.ca/leglib; f. 1870; 1.4m. items; special collns: Canadian, Western Canadian and Manitoba history, economics, political and social sciences, urban, rural and ethnic language newspapers of Manitoba, govt publs; Legislative Librarian SUSAN BISHOP; publs *Monthly Checklist of Manitoba Government Publications* (online), *Selected New Titles* (10 a year, online).

Manitoba Culture, Heritage and Tourism—Public Library Services Branch: 300-1011 Rosser Ave, Brandon, MB R7A 0L5; tel. (204) 726-6590; fax (204) 726-6868; e-mail pls@gov.mb.ca; f. 1972; 50,000 vols, 10,000 e-books; Dir (vacant); publ. *Manitoba Public Library Statistics* (1 a year).

Manitoba Law Library Inc., Great Library: 331–408 York Ave, Winnipeg, MB R3C 0P9; tel. (204) 945-1958; fax (204) 948-2138; internet www.cbsc.org; f. 1877; attached to Law Society of Manitoba; 50,000 vols; Librarian R. GARTH NIVEN.

University of Manitoba Libraries: Winnipeg, MB R3T 2N2; tel. (204) 474-9881; fax (204) 474-7583; e-mail marina_webster@ umanitoba.ca; internet www.umanitoba.ca/ libraries; f. 1877; collections supporting 18 faculties and 4 schools; special collections: Slavic, Icelandic; 2,000,000 vols, 520,000 government publications, 157,500 other print items (maps, performance music, textbook collection, etc.), 2,700,000 microforms, 31,000 audiovisual items, 9,000 serial titles; Dir CAROLYNNE PRESSER.

New Brunswick

Mount Allison University Libraries and Archives: Mount Allison Univ., 49 York St, Sackville, NB E4L 1C6; tel. (506) 364-2562; fax (506) 364-2617; e-mail bgnassi@mta.ca; internet www.mta.ca/library; f. 1840; 454,000 vols, 515,000 microforms, 282,000 documents; Univ. Librarian BRUNO GNASSI.

Bibliothèque Champlain (Université de Moncton): 12 Ave de l'Université, Moncton, NB E1A 3E9; tel. (506) 858-4012; fax (506) 858-4086; internet www.umoncton.ca/ umcm-bibliotheque-champlain; f. 1965; gen. academic collns; 618,077 vols, 1,336 current periodicals; Head Librarian ALAIN ROBERGE.

Harriet Irving Library: Univ. of New Brunswick, POB 7500, Fredericton, NB E3B 5H5; tel. (506) 453-4740; fax (506) 453-4595; e-mail library@unb.ca; internet www.lib.unb .ca; f. 1790; 1,141,807 vols and 3,103,813 (equivalent vols) microforms; Dir of Libraries JOHN D. TESKEY.

Legislative Library: Box 6000, Fredericton, NB E3B 5H1; tel. (506) 453-2338; fax (506) 444-5889; e-mail library.biblio-info@ gnb.ca; f. 1841; 35,000 vols; Librarian MARGARET PACEY.

Provincial Archives of New Brunswick: POB 6000, Fredericton, NB E3B 5H1; tel. (506) 453-2122; fax (506) 453-3288; e-mail provincial.archives@gnb.ca; internet archives.gnb.ca; f. 1968; 25,000 ft of govt and private textual documents, 250,000 photographs, 300,000 cartographic and architectural documents, 4,600 hours audio recordings, 1,800 video cassettes and films, 60,000 microfiches, 14,000 reels microfilm; 19,425 m, 339,355 photos, 374,908 maps, plans, and drawings, 25,000 microfilm, 551 items documentary art; Provincial Archivist MARION BEYEA.

Newfoundland and Labrador

Newfoundland and Labrador Public Libraries: 48 St George's Ave, Stephenville, NL A2N 1K9; tel. (709) 643-0900; fax (709) 643-0925; internet www.nlpl.ca; f. 1934; 1,300,000 vols at 96 libraries; provides public library services incl. books, magazines, newspapers, large-print and spoken-word books, DVDs computers with free internet access, digital cameras; Exec. Dir SHAWN TETFORD.

The Rooms Corporation of Newfoundland and Labrador—The Rooms Provincial Archives Division: POB 1800, St John's, NL A1C 5P9; 9 Bonaventure Ave, St John's, NL A1C 5P9; tel. (709) 757-8030; fax (709) 757-8031; e-mail archives@therooms .ca; internet www.therooms.ca; f. 1960, refounded 2005; provincial govt archives, genealogical colln, cartographic and architectural archives, sports archives, film and still images; Provincial Archivist, Newfoundland and Labrador and Dir, The Rooms Provincial Archives Division GREG WALSH.

Provincial Resource Library: Arts and Culture Centre, St John's, NL A1B 3A3; tel. (709) 737-3946; fax (709) 737-2660; f. 1934; Newfoundland Collection open to the public; backup resource library for the provincial system; 181,604 vols (incl. Newfoundland Collection); Man. MICHELLE WALTERS.

Queen Elizabeth II Library: Memorial University of Newfoundland, St John's, NL A1B 3Y1; tel. (709) 737-7428; fax (709) 737-2153; e-mail rhellis@mun.ca; internet www .library.mun.ca; f. 1925; 1,724,807 vols, 1,977,982 microform units; Librarian RICHARD H. ELLIS.

Nova Scotia

Angus L. Macdonald Library: St Francis Xavier Univ., POB 5000, Antigonish, NS B2G 2W5; tel. (902) 867-2267; fax (902) 867-5153; internet library.stfx.ca; f. 1853; 762,000 vols; special collection: Celtic history, literature and language; Librarian LYNNE MURPHY; publ. *The Antigonish Review* (4 a year).

Dalhousie University Libraries: Halifax, NS B3H 4H8; tel. (902) 494-3601; internet www.library.dal.ca; f. 1844,000 vols; University Librarian WILLIAM R. MAES.

Halifax Regional Library: 60 Alderney Dr., Dartmouth, NS B2Y 4P8; tel. (902) 490-5744; fax (902) 490-5762; internet www .halifaxpubliclibraries.ca; f. 1996; 898,532 books (fiction, non-fiction, reference, rapid read, multilingual), 51,202 periodicals, 41,099 CDs, 55,471 DVDs, 30,816 video cassettes, 8,440 cassettes, 5,613 talking books; CEO JUDITH HARE.

Nova Scotia Archives and Records Management: 6016 University Ave, Halifax, NS B3H 1W4; tel. (902) 424-6060; fax (902) 424-0628; e-mail nsarm@gov.ns.ca; internet www .gov.ns.ca/nsarm; f. 1929; provincial govt records; family, political, personal and business papers; maps, plans, charts; photographs, paintings; microfilmed files of leading newspapers; film, television and sound archives; research library of 50,000 titles; Dir of Public Services LOIS YORKE; Provincial Archivist (vacant).

Nova Scotia Legislative Library: Province House, 1726 Hollis St, Halifax, NS B3J 2P8; tel. (902) 424-5932; fax (902) 424-0220; e-mail murphymf@gov.ns.ca; internet www .gov.ns.ca/legislature/library; f. 1862; Nova Scotiana Collection; 170,000 vols; Librarian MARGARET MURPHY; publ. *Publications of the Province of Nova Scotia* (12 a year and 1 a year).

Vaughan Memorial Library, Acadia University: POB 4, 50 Acadia St, Wolfville, NS B4P 2P6; tel. (902) 585-1249; fax (902) 585-1748; internet library.acadiau.ca; f. 1843; 800,000 vols and govt documents; Univ. Librarian SARA LOCHHEAD.

Nunavut Territory

Nunavut Public Library Services: POB 189A, Iqaluit, NU X0A 0H0; tel. (867) 979-5400; fax (867) 979-1373; e-mail nuic@gov.nu .ca; br. libraries in Arctic Bay, Arviat, Baker Lake, Cambridge Bay, Clyde River, Igloolik, Kugluktuk, Pangnirtung, Pond Inlet and Rankin Inlet.

Branch Library:

Iqaluit Centennial Library: POB 189A, Iqaluit, NU X0A 0H0; tel. (867) 979-5400; fax (867) 979-1373; e-mail gov@gov.nu.ca; T. H. Manning archival collection of polar materials; Librarian TORI-LYNNE EVANS.

Ontario

Canada Institute for Scientific and Technical Information: 1200 Montréal Rd, M-55, Ottawa, ON K1A 0R6; tel. (613) 998-8544; fax (613) 993-7619; e-mail info .cisti@nrc-cnrc.gc.ca; internet cisti-icist .nrc-cnrc.gc.ca; operated by National Research Council Canada; f. 1974, fmrly National Science Library; focal point of a national scientific and technical information network; resources of over 50,000 serial titles are made available through loan, copies and consultation; information services include operation of a national computerized current awareness service and an online table of contents service (CISTI SOURCE), Customized Literature Search Service providing custom bibliographies on requested topics, MEDLARS coordinator for Canada; Dir Gen. BERNARD DUMOUCHEL.

Canadian Agriculture Library: Sir John Carling Bldg, Agriculture and Agri-Food Canada, Ottawa, ON K1A 0C5; tel. (613) 759-7068; fax (613) 759-6643; internet www .agr.gc.ca/cal; f. 1910; 1,000,000 vols, 22,200 serials; specializes in agriculture, biology, biochemistry, economics, entomology, food sciences, plant science, veterinary medicine; serves 24 field libraries; Dir DANIELLE JACQUES.

Carleton University Library: 1125 Colonel By Drive, Ottawa, ON K1S 5B6; tel. (613) 520-2735; fax (613) 520-2750; e-mail university.librarian@carleton.ca; internet www.library.carleton.ca; f. 1942; 1,782,483 vols, 10,486 serial subscriptions, 1,513,714 items (microforms, maps, audiovisual items), 12,025 electronic journals; Librarian MARTIN FOSS.

Departmental Library, Indian and Northern Affairs Canada: Ottawa, ON K1A 0H4; tel. (819) 997-0811; fax (819) 953-5491; e-mail reference@ainc-inac.gc.ca; internet www.ainc-inac.gc.ca; f. 1966; 100,600 vols, 20,000 bound periodicals, 2,000 rare books, 3,500 government documents, 3,000 microfilm reels, incl. records relating to Indian Affairs; service to Native people, researchers, libraries; br. in Gatineau, Québec; Chief Librarian JULIA FINN.

Earth Sciences Information Centre: 601 Booth St, Ottawa, ON K1A 0E8; tel. (613) 996-3919; fax (613) 943-8742; e-mail esic@ nrcan.ac.ca; internet www.nrcan.gc.ca/ess/ esic; f. 1842; component of Natural Resources Canada; interlibrary loans, online retrospective searching; 400,000 vols, 260,000 geological maps; Head of ESIC Services PAULINE MCDONALD (acting).

Hamilton Public Library: 55 York Blvd, POB 2700, Station A, Hamilton, ON L8N 4E4; tel. (905) 546-3200; fax (905) 546-3202; e-mail kroberts@hpl.ca; internet www.hpl .hamilton.on.ca; f. 1889; special collections of local history, Canadiana to 1950, govt documents; 1,492,467 vols and 1,876 periodicals; 24 br. libraries; 2 bookmobiles; Chief Librarian KEN ROBERTS.

John W. Graham Library, University of Trinity College: 6 Hoskin Ave, Toronto, ON M5S 1H8; tel. (416) 978-2653; fax (416) 978-2797; internet www.trinity.utoronto.ca; f. 1851; 200,000 vols; spec. collns: Anglican Church of Canada Colln, Churchill Colln, G8 Colln, SPCK Colln, Strachan Colln, W. Speed Hill Colln (works of Richard Hooker), Upjohn-Waldie Colln (works of Eric Gill and other fine printing); Nicholls Librarian and Dir of Graham Library LINDA WILSON CORMAN.

Library and Archives Canada: 395 Wellington St, Ottawa, ON K1A 0N4; tel. (613) 996-5115; fax (613) 995-6274; e-mail reference@lac-bac.gc.ca; internet www .collectionscanada.gc.ca; f. 2004, following merger of National Library of Canada (f. 1953) and National Archives of Canada (f. 1872); incl. Canadian Postal Archives; depository of all Canadian publs, public records and historical material; 71,000 films and documentaries, 2.5m. architectural drawings, plans and maps, 21.3m. photographic images, 270,000 hours of audio and visual recordings, 343,000 works of art, Canadian sheet music and 200,000 recordings related to music in Canada, Canadian postal archive, medals, seals, posters and coats of arms, nat., provincial and territorial newspapers, periodicals, MSS, microforms and theses, more than 1m. portraits of Canadians; Librarian and Archivist Dr DANIEL CARON; publ. *Annual Review*.

Library of Parliament: Ottawa, ON K1A 0A9; tel. (613) 995-1166; fax (613) 992-1269; e-mail info@parl.gc.ca; internet www.parl.gc .ca; f. 1867; 407,500 vols in integrated systems, 510,000 microforms; Parliamentary Librarian WILLIAM YOUNG; publs *Quorum* (1 a day, during session), *Radar* (1 a day, during session), *Current Issue Reviews* (12 a year), *Research Publications* (12 a year).

Library of the Pontifical Institute of Mediaeval Studies: 4th Floor, 113 St Joseph St, Toronto, ON M5S 1J4; tel. (416) 926-7146; e-mail pims.library@utoronto.ca; internet www.pims.ca; f. 1929; principal research resource for the Institute's Mellon Fellows, postdoctoral candidates for the Licence in Medieval Studies, and for the faculty and doctoral students of the Univ. of Toronto's Centre for Medieval Studies; 120,000 vols, 210 periodicals, 15 MSS codices, 300 MSS charters, 10,000 folios of MSS on photostats, 250,000 folios of MSS on microfilm; Pres. RICHARD. ALWAY; Dir JONATHAN. BENGTSON.

London Public Library: 251 Dundas St, London, ON N6A 6H9; tel. (519) 661-4600; fax (519) 663-5396; internet www.lpl.london .on.ca; f. 1894; 982,581 vols, 110,813 non-book materials; CEO SUSANNA HUBBARD KRIMMER.

McMaster University Libraries: 1280 Main St West, Hamilton, ON L8S 4L6; tel. (905) 525-9140; fax (905) 546-0625; e-mail libinfo@mcmaster.ca; internet www .mcmaster.ca/library; f. 1887; 1,717,799 vols, 1,488,305 microform items, 175,000 non-print items, 10,976 linear metres archival material, 6,292 serial subscriptions; contains among others Vera Brittain archives, Bertrand Russell archives and 18th-century colln; Librarian GRAHAM R. HILL.

National Defence Headquarters Library: 101 Colonel By Drive, Ottawa, ON K1A 0K2; tel. (613) 995-2213; fax (613) 995-8176; internet www.collectionscanada .ca; f. 1903; library services, inter-library loans, information retrieval; 30,000 vols incl. military Canadiana; Librarian J. BRIAN GRIER.

Natural Resources Canada, Headquarters Library: 580 Booth St, Ottawa, ON K1A 0E4; tel. (613) 996-8282; fax (613) 992-7211; internet www.nrcan-rncan.gc.ca; f. 1958; 65,000 vols and bound periodicals, 3,000 reports; mineral and energy economics, policy, taxation, legislation and statistics, energy conservation; Dir S. E. HENRY.

Ontario Legislative Library: Legislative Bldg, Queen's Park, Toronto, ON M7A 1A9; tel. (416) 325-3900; fax (416) 325-3925; f. 1867; 58,440 monograph titles; Exec. Dir (vacant).

Ottawa City Archives: 1st Floor, Bytown Pavilion, 111 Sussex Drive, Ottawa, ON K1N 1J1; tel. (613) 580-2424; e-mail archives@ ottawa.ca; f. 1976; repository of public records of civic administration and other historical material; special collections: genealogy, heraldry, local railroad history; City Archivist DAVE BULLOCK.

Ottawa Public Library/Bibliothèque Publique d'Ottawa: 120 Metcalfe St, Ottawa, ON; tel. (613) 580-2940; fax (613) 567-4013; e-mail feedback@ biblioottawalibrary.ca; internet www .biblioottawalibrary.ca; f. 1906; 2,500,000 vols; City Librarian BARBARA CLUBB.

Philatelic Collections, Library and Archives Canada: 550 Blvd de la Cité, Gatineau, QC K1A 0N4; tel. (613) 996-5115; fax (613) 995-6274; internet www .collectionscanada.gc.ca/philately-postal; f. 1988 fmrly Canadian Postal Archives; acquisition, preservation, description of philatelic records and related material; Manager PASCAL LEBLOND.

Queen's University Library: Miller Hall, 36 Union St, Kingston, ON K7L 5C4; tel. (613) 533-2519; fax (613) 533-6362; internet library.queensu.ca; f. 1842; 2,380,675 vols, 3,792,624 other items; Univ. Librarian PAUL WIENS; Curator MARK BADHAM.

Supreme Court of Canada Library: 301 Wellington St, Ottawa, ON K1A 0J1; tel. (613) 996-8120; fax (613) 952-2832; e-mail library@scc-csc.gc.ca; internet www.scc-csc .gc.ca; 200,000 vols; Dir ROSALIE FOX.

Toronto Public Library: 789 Yonge St, Toronto, ON M4W 2G8; tel. (416) 393-7131; internet www.tpl.toronto.ca; 99 brs; 1,200,000 vols; City Librarian JOSEPHINE BRYANT; publ. *What's On* (4 a year).

University of Ottawa Library Network: 65 University Private, Ottawa, ON K1N 6N5; tel. (613) 562-5883; fax (613) 562-5195; internet www.biblio.uottawa.ca; f. 1848; library contains more than 4.5m. items incl. more than 1,250,000 monographs, 19,000 current periodicals, 1,900,000 microforms; tens of thousands of music scores, sound recordings and audiovisual items; hundreds of thousands of slides, aerial photographs, maps and govt publications; electronic resources; University Chief Librarian LESLIE WEIR.

University of Toronto Libraries: Toronto, ON M5S 1A5; tel. (416) 978-8580; fax (416) 978-7653; e-mail utweb@library.utoronto.ca; internet www.library.utoronto.ca; f. 1891; 10,342,574 vols, 32,485 serials, 5,372,000 microforms, 1,695,060 other non-book items (maps, sound recordings, audiovisual, manuscript titles, aerial photographs, etc.), 32,912 online journals; Chief Librarian CAROLE MOORE.

University of Waterloo Library: 200 University Ave, Waterloo, ON N2L 3G1; tel. (519) 888-4567; fax (519) 888-4320; f. 1957; 2,006,887 vols, 1,707,697 microfiches, 7,017 periodicals, 13,011 online periodicals; University Librarian K. MARK HASLETT; publ. *Bibliography* (irregular).

University of Western Ontario Libraries: London, ON N6A 3K7; tel. (519) 661-2111; internet www.lib.uwo.ca; f. 1878; 3,546,496 vols, 9,756 print serials subscriptions; 480,985 ebooks, 54,790 electronic journals; 4,062,350 microforms; 1,823,011 audio, video graphic and other spec. materials; Univ. Librarian JOYCE C. GARNETT.

Victoria University Library (E. J. Pratt Library): 71 Queen's Park Crescent East, Toronto, ON M5S 1K7; tel. (416) 585-4471; fax (416) 585-4591; e-mail victoria.library@ utoronto.ca; internet library.vicu.utoronto .ca; f. 1836; 275,000 vols; spec. collns: humanities (gen.), religions and theology; Northrop Frye, S. T. Coleridge, William Blake and his contemporaries, Hogarth Press, Tennyson, V. Woolf, Bloomsbury Group, Wesleyana, Norman Jewison Archive, E. J. Pratt; George Baxter (books and prints); 19th-century Canadian Poetry, French and French-Canadian Literature (Rièse colln); folklore; Senator Keith Davey; posters (Paris riots of 1968); contemporary poets; University archives; Chief Librarian Dr ROBERT C. BRANDEIS.

Prince Edward Island

Confederation Centre Public Library: Box 7000, Charlottetown, PE C1A 8G8; tel. (902) 368-4642; fax (902) 368-4652; e-mail ccpl@gov.pe.ca; internet www.library.pe.ca; f. 1773; 72,000 vols; Chief Librarian TRINA O'BRIEN LEGGOTT.

Prince Edward Island Public Library Service: POB 7500, 89 Red Head Rd, Morell, PE C0A 1S0; tel. (902) 961-7320; fax (902) 961-7322; e-mail plshq@gov.pe.ca; internet www.library.pe.ca; f. 1933; 371,000 vols in regional system of 26 public libraries; Provincial Librarian KATHLEEN EATON.

Public Archives and Records Office of Prince Edward Island: POB 1000, Charlottetown, PE C1A 7M4; tel. (902) 368-4290; fax (902) 368-6327; e-mail archives@gov.pe .ca; internet www.gov.pe.ca/cca; f. 1964; Provincial Archivist JILL MacMICKEN-WILSON.

Québec

Bibliothèque de l'Assemblée Nationale du Québec: Edifice Pamphile-Lemay, Québec, QC G1A 1A3; tel. (418) 643-4408; fax (418) 646-3207; e-mail bibliotheque@assnat .qc.ca; internet www.assnat.qc.ca; f. 1802; law and legislation, political science, parliamentary procedure, history, official publications of Québec, newspapers; 955,000 vols; Chief Librarian PHILIPPE SAUVAGEAU; publs *Bulletin* (4 a year), *Débats de l'Assemblée législative 1867–1962* (irregular), *Journal des débats: index* (irregular).

Bibliothèque de la Compagnie de Jésus: Collège Jean-de-Brébeuf, L. B4–25, 3200 Chemin Côte-Ste-Catherine, Montréal, QC H3T 1C1; tel. (514) 342-9342; f. 1882; books from the 16th to the 18th centuries, Canadiana; philosophy, scripture, theology; 195,000 vols; Dir C.-R. NADEAU.

Bibliothèque de l'Université Laval: Cité Universitaire, Québec, QC G1K 7P4; tel. (418) 656-5344; fax (418) 656-7897; internet www.bibl.ulaval.ca; f. 1852; 5,000,000 vols, 24,422 periodicals, 19,500 films, 140,000 maps; Dir Dr SYLVIE DELORME; publ. *Répertoire des vedettes-matière* (CD-ROM, 2 a year).

Bibliothèques de l'Université de Montréal: CP 6128, Succursale Centre-ville, Montréal, QC H3C 3J7; tel. (514) 343-6905; fax (514) 343-6457; e-mail biblios@bib .umontreal.ca; internet www.bib.umontreal .ca; f. 1928; 3,106,971 vols, 21,087 current periodicals, 1,650,557 microforms, 189,164 audiovisual documents; Dir of Libraries JEAN-PIERRE CÔTÉ.

Bibliothèque de Montréal: 1210 Sherbrooke Est, Montréal, QC H2L 1L9; tel. (514) 872-5171; fax (514) 872-1626; internet www2.ville.montreal.qc.ca/biblio; f. 1902; 2,102,600 vols, of which 51,700 books, 20,757 pamphlets, 43,900 pictures and photographs, 1,547 maps, 3,035 slides and 99,200 microforms related to Canada and its history; 23 brs, 1 sound-recording library and 1 bookmobile; Dir JACQUES PANNETON.

Bibliothèque et Archives Nationales du Québec: 2275 rue Holt, Montréal, QC H2G 3H1; tel. (514) 873-1100; fax (514) 873-9312; e-mail info@banq.qc.ca; internet www.banq .qc.ca; f. 1967; merged with Archives Nationales du Québec (f. 1920) 2006; 4m. vols; Conservation Centre and Grande Bibliothèque in Montréal; 9 archive centres (Chicoutimi, Gatineau, Montréal, Québec, Rimouski, Rouyn-Noranda, Sept-Iles, Sherbrooke,Trois-Rivières); Chair and CEO LISE BISSONNETTE; publ. *A rayons ouverts* (4 a year).

CAIJ—Montréal: Palais de Justice, 17e étage, 1 rue Notre-Dame est, local 17.50, Montréal, QC H2Y 1B6; tel. (514) 866-2057; fax (514) 879-8592; e-mail mlaforce@caij.qc .ca; f. 1828; 100,000 vols; Librarian MIREILLE LAFORCE.

Concordia University Libraries: 1455 de Maisonneuve Blvd West, Montréal, QC H3G 1M8; tel. (514) 848-2424; fax (514) 848-2882; e-mail judya@alcor.concordia.ca; internet library.concordia.ca; f. 1974; 2,730,000 vols; Univ. Librarian GERALD BEASLEY.

Fraser-Hickson Institute Library: c/o 25 Wolseley Ave S, Montréal, QC H4X 1V3; tel. (514) 489-5301; e-mail frances@fraserhickson .qc.ca; internet www.fraserhickson.qc.ca; f. 1870; 150,000 vols; colln of archives of the Mercantile Library Asscn (Montréal); library currently closed and in storage, pending move to a new site; Chief Librarian FRANCES W. ACKERMAN; Reader Services Man. ISABEL RANDALL.

McGill University Libraries: 3459 McTavish St, Montréal, QC H3A 1Y1; tel. (514) 398-4734; fax (514) 398-7356; e-mail doadmin .library@mcgill.ca; internet www.mcgill.ca/ library; f. 1855; 13 libraries, 3.6m. vols, 49,897 current periodicals, 1,782,148 microtexts, 676,373 govt documents; Dir JANINE SCHMIDT; Assoc. Dir, Planning and Resources DIANE KOEN.

Osler Library: McGill Univ., McIntyre Medical Sciences Bldg, 3655 Promenade Sir William Osler, 3rd Fl., Montréal, QC H3G 1Y6; tel. (514) 398-4475; fax (514) 398-5747; e-mail osler.library@mcgill.ca; internet www .mcgill.ca/osler-library; f. 1929; history of medicine and allied sciences; 97,219 vols; History of Medicine Librarian PAMELA MILLER.

Saskatchewan

Regina Public Library: 2311 12th Ave, Regina, SK S4P 3Z5; tel. (306) 777-6000; fax (306) 949-7260; internet www.reginalibrary .ca; f. 1908; 9 brs; 665,928 items; Library Dir JEFF BARBER; publs @ *the Library* (6 a year), *Community Information Catalogue*, *Regina Public Library Film Catalogue*, *RPL Theatre Calendar* (6 a year).

Saskatchewan Legislative Library: 234-2405 Legislative Dr., Regina, SK S4S 0B3; tel. (306) 787-2276; fax (306) 787-1772; e-mail reference@legassembly.sk.ca; internet www.legassembly.sk.ca/leglibrary; f. 1878, present name 1905; 152,500 vols, approx. 522,000 sheets of microfiche; 6,300 reels of microfilm; 3,200 CD-ROMs; 760 audio, video and film recordings; social sciences, law and history; noted for its colln of govt documents and W Canadiana; Legislative Librarian MELISSA BENNETT; publ.

Checklist of Saskatchewan Government Publications (12 a year).

Saskatchewan Provincial Library: 1945 Hamilton St, Regina, SK S4P 2C8; tel. (306) 787-2972; fax (306) 787-2029; internet www .learning.gov.sk.ca/provinciallibrary; f. 1953; coordinates library services in the province; 97,000 vols, specializing in library science, multilingual books and last copy fiction; Provincial Librarian JOYLENE CAMPBELL.

Saskatoon Public Library System: 311 23rd St East, Saskatoon, SK S7K 0J6; tel. (306) 975-7558; fax (306) 975-7542; internet www.saskatoonlibrary.ca; f. 1913; 7 brs; 828,641 vols, 12,790 audio cassettes, 22,456 video cassettes, 68,189 CDs, 36,171 DVDs, 3,362 talking books; local history room; Dir of Libraries ZENON ZUZAK.

University of Saskatchewan Libraries: 3 Campus Dr., Saskatoon, SK S7N 5A4; tel. (306) 966-5927; fax (306) 966-5932; internet www.library.usask.ca; f. 1909; main library and 6 brs with 1,871,000 vols, 15,423 current journals, 3,054,000 items on microform, 427,902 govt documents and pamphlets, Adam Shortt colln of Canadiana, Conrad Aiken colln of Published works; Russell Green music MSS; Dir of Libraries F. WINTER.

Wapiti Regional Library: 145 12th St East, Prince Albert, SK S6V 1B7; tel. (306) 764-0712; fax (306) 922-1516; e-mail wapiti@ panet.pa.sk.ca; f. 1950; 55 brs; 508,000 vols; Regional Dir JOHN MURRAY (acting).

Museums and Art Galleries

Alberta

Art Gallery of Alberta: 2 Sir Winston Churchill Sq., Edmonton, AB T5J 2C1; tel. (780) 422-6223; fax (780) 426-3105; e-mail info@youraga.ca; internet www.youraga.ca; f. 1924; Canadian and int. drawing, painting, printmaking, sculpture and photography; devt and presentation of original exhibitions of contemporary and historical art from Alberta, Canada and around the world; art education and public programmes; colln of more than 6,000 objects; exhibits, preservation of art and visual culture; Exec. Dir TONY LUPPINO; Deputy Dir CATHERINE CROWSTON.

Banff Park Museum: Box 900, Banff, AB T1L 1K2; tel. (403) 762-1558; fax (403) 762-1565; e-mail banff.vrc@pc.gc.ca; internet www.parkscanada.gc.ca/lnh-nhs/ab/banff/ index-e.asp; f. 1895; natural and human history of the park; Historic Sites Supervisor STEVE MALINS.

Buffalo Nations Museum: 1 Birch Ave (Box 850), Banff, AB T1L 1A8; tel. (403) 762-2388; fax (403) 760-2803; e-mail buffalonations@telus.net; f. 1951 as Luxton Museum; promotes education and awareness of the Northern Plains and Canadian Rockies Indians; natural history exhibits; Pres. HAROLD HEALY.

Department of Earth and Atmospheric Sciences Museum, University of Alberta: Edmonton, AB T6G 2E3; tel. (780) 492-2518; fax (780) 492-2030; internet easweb.eas .ualberta.ca; f. 1912; geology, meteorites, mineralogy, invertebrate and vertebrate palaeontology, stratigraphy; Collections and Museums Administrator A. J. LOCOCK.

Glenbow Museum: 130—9 Ave SE, Calgary, AB T2G 0P3; tel. (403) 268-4100; fax (403) 265-9769; e-mail glenbow@glenbow.org; internet www.glenbow.org; f. 1966; western Canadian and foreign cultural history, ethnology, military history, mineralogy and art;

library of 100,000 vols, archives of 1,250,000 photos and negatives; Pres. Dr ROBERT R. JANES; Chair., Board of Governors ROBERT G. PETERS; publ. *Experience* (3 a year).

Medicine Hat Museum and Art Gallery: 1302 Bomford Crescent, Medicine Hat, AB T1A 5E6; tel. (403) 502-8580; fax (403) 502-8589; e-mail mhmag@medicinehat.ca; internet www.city.medicine-hat.ab.ca/ cityservices/museum; f. 1967; cultural and natural history, palaeontology, and primitive peoples representative of south-east Alberta; art gallery; monthly exhibits by Canadian and international artists.

Royal Alberta Museum: 12845 102nd Ave, Edmonton, AB T5N 0M6; tel. (780) 453-9100; fax (780) 454-6629; internet www .royalalbertamuseum.ca; f. 1967; Alberta history, geology, natural history; Exec. Dir CHRIS ROBINSON (acting).

Royal Tyrrell Museum of Palaeontology: POB 7500, Highway 838 Midland Provincial Park, Drumheller, AB T0J 0Y0; tel. (403) 823-7707; fax (403) 823-7131; e-mail tyrrell .info@gov.ab.ca; internet www .tyrrellmuseum.com; f. 1985; colln, research, display and interpretation of fossils as evidence for history of life, with emphasis on famous dinosaur fauna of Alberta; resource management, vertebrate and invertebrate palaeontology, palynology, sedimentology, stratigraphy, taphonomy, preparation, illustration, administration; library of 50,000 vols, special biographical collection on Joseph Burr Tyrrell; 110,000 catalogued fossil specimens; field station in Dinosaur Provincial Park; UNESCO World Heritage Site; Dir BRUCE G. NAYLOR.

British Columbia

H. R. MacMillan Space Centre: 1100 Chestnut St, Vancouver, BC V6J 3J9; tel. (604) 738-7827; fax (604) 736-5665; e-mail tcromwell@spacecentre.ca; internet www .spacecentre.ca; f. 1988; administers the H. R. MacMillan Space Centre, H. R. MacMillan Planetarium and Gordon Southam Observatory; multimedia astronomy shows, laser shows, exhibitions, Observatory activities, lectures; 1,000 mems; Exec. Dir ROB APPLETON; publ. *Starry Messenger* (4 a year).

Helmcken House Museum: c/o Royal BC Museum, 675 Belleville St, Victoria, BC V8W 9W2; tel. (250) 356-7226; fax (250) 356-8197; internet www.royalbcmuseum.bc.ca; house built in 1852 for the surgeon Dr J. S. Helmcken (1824–1920); historic medical colln; Curator of Human History, Royal BC Museum LORNE HAMMOND.

Museum of Northern British Columbia: 100 First Ave W, Prince Rupert, BC V8J 1A8; tel. (250) 624-3207; fax (250) 627-8009; e-mail mnbc@citytel.net; internet www .museumofnorthernbc.com; f. 1924; exhibits cover 10,000 years of human habitation, incl. First Nations culture, local pioneer history and natural history; art gallery; library of 800 vols (50 rare); Dir ROBIN WEBER; Curator SUSAN MARSDEN.

Royal British Columbia Museum: 675 Belleville St, Victoria, BC V8W 9W2; tel. (250) 356-7226; fax (250) 356-8197; e-mail reception@royalbcmuseum.bc.ca; internet www.royalbcmuseum.bc.ca; f. 1886; contains reference collections and exhibits pertaining to natural history and human history of BC; CEO PAULINE RAFFERTY; publ. *Discovery* (newsletter, 3 a year).

Vancouver Art Gallery: 750 Hornby St, Vancouver, BC V6Z 2H7; tel. (604) 662-4700; fax (604) 682-1086; e-mail info@ vanartgallery.bc.ca; internet www .vanartgallery.bc.ca; f. 1931; Canadian and foreign art by contemporary artists and major historical figures; library of 25,000 vols; Dir KATHLEEN BARTELS; publ. *Members' Newsletter* (3 a year).

Vancouver Maritime Museum: 1905 Ogden Ave, Vancouver, BC V6J 1A3; tel. (604) 257-8300; fax (604) 737-2621; internet www.vmm.bc.ca; f. 1958; maritime history, local and international heritage vessels, RCMP *St Roch* Arctic patrol vessel, school programmes, lectures and summer festivals; library of 10,000 vols; Exec. Dir JAMES P. DELGADO; publ. *Signals* (4 a year).

Manitoba

Manitoba Museum of Man and Nature: 190 Rupert Ave, Winnipeg, MB R3B 0N2; tel. (204) 956-2830; fax (204) 942-3679; e-mail info@manitobamuseum.ca; f. 1965; human and natural history of Manitoba; planetarium; 'Touch the Universe' interactive science centre; library of 26,000 vols; Exec. Dir CLAUDETTE LECLERC; publ. *Happenings* (6 a year).

Winnipeg Art Gallery: 300 Memorial Blvd, Winnipeg, MB R3C 1V1; tel. (204) 786-6641; fax (204) 788-4998; e-mail inquiries@wag.mb .ca; internet www.wag.mb.ca; f. 1912; exhibitions, lectures, films, performing arts, education programmes; library of 24,000 vols; Dir (vacant).

New Brunswick

Beaverbrook Art Gallery: POB 605, Fredericton, NB E3B 5A6; tel. (506) 458-8545; fax (506) 459-7450; e-mail emailbag@ beaverbrookartgallery.org; internet www .beaverbrookartgallery.org; f. 1959; paintings; 18th-, 19th- and 20th-century English and continental paintings; 19th- and 20th-century Canadian paintings; 18th- and 19th-century English porcelain; English sculptures; medieval and Renaissance furniture, tapestries; Man., Outreach and Communications LAURIE GLENN NORRIS; publ. *Tableau* (3 a year).

Fort Beauséjour (Fort Cumberland National Historic Site of Canada): 111 Fort Beauséjour Rd, Aulac, NB E4L 2W5; tel. (506) 364-5080; fax (506) 536-4399; e-mail fort.beausejour@pc.gc.ca; internet www.pc.gc .ca/lhn-nhs/nb/beausejour/default.asp; f. 1926; semi-restored ruins of star-shaped fort overlooking the Bay of Fundy, built by the French in 1751 to defend their interests in the Isthmus of Chignecto, Acadia; renamed Fort Cumberland by the British; reinforced for the War of 1812, abandoned in 1835 and declared a nat. historic site in 1926; barracks, underground casemates and stone foundations overlooking the Bay of Fundy, the Tantramar marshes and extensive dykes; attached museum and visitor centre; Supervisor, Heritage Presentation JULIETTE MCLEOD.

Miramichi Natural History Museum: 149 Wellington St, Chatham NB E1N 1L7; fax (506) 773-6509; f. 1880; Curator KEN WEATHERBY.

New Brunswick Museum: 277 Douglas Ave, Saint John, NB E2K 1E5; tel. (506) 643-2300; fax (506) 643-2360; e-mail nbmuseum@nbm-mnb.ca; internet www .nbm-mnb.ca; f. 1842; archives, library, fine art, decorative art, natural science and history; Dir JANE FULLERTON.

York-Sunbury Historical Society Museum: POB 1312, Fredericton, NB E3B 5C8; tel. (506) 455-6041; fax (506) 458-8741; e-mail yorksun@nbnet.nb.ca; f. 1932; domestic and military exhibits of Fredericton and area; housed in British Officers' Quarters of 1840; Exec. Dir KATE MOSSMAN.

Newfoundland and Labrador

The Rooms Corporation of Newfoundland and Labrador—Provincial Museum Division and Art Gallery Division: POB 1800, St John's, NL A1C 5P9; 9 Bonaventure Ave, St John's, NL A1C 5P9; tel. (709) 757-8020 (museum); tel. (709) 757-8040 (art gallery); fax (709) 757-8021 (museum); fax (709) 757-8041 (art gallery); e-mail information@therooms.ca; internet www .therooms.ca; f. 2005; colln of over 8,000 works from historical, contemporary, international, crafts and folk art; Canadian works, including a Jean-Paul Riopelle; more than 1m. archeological items and natural history specimens; native artifacts; the world's largest Beothuk colln; Dir of Provincial Museum ANNE CHAFE; Dir of Provincial Art Gallery SHIELA PERRY.

Subsidiary Museums:

Mary March Regional Museum and Loggers' Exhibit: Grand Falls–Windsor, NL; tel. (709) 292-4522; fax (709) 292-4526; e-mail pwells@nf.aibn.com; internet www .nfmuseum.com; Curator PENNY WELLS.

Southern Newfoundland Seamen's Museum: Grand Bank, NL; tel. (709) 832-1484; fax (709) 832-2053; e-mail gwcrews@nf.aibn.com; internet www .nfmuseum.com; Curator GERALD CREWS.

Nova Scotia

Art Gallery of Nova Scotia: 1723 Hollis St, POB 2262, Halifax, NS B3J 3C8; tel. (902) 424-7542; fax (902) 424-7359; internet www .agns.gov.ns.ca; f. 1975; paintings, drawings, sculpture, prints, collection of Nova Scotia folk art; Dir and Chief Curator JEFFREY SPALDING.

Fort Anne National Historic Site and Museum: POB 9, Annapolis Royal, NS B0S 1A0; tel. (902) 532-2321; fax (902) 532-2232; e-mail information@pc.gc.ca; internet www .pc.gc.ca; f. 1917; Superintendent Operations THERESA BUNBURY.

Fortress of Louisbourg National Historic Site: 259 Park Service Rd, Louisbourg, NS B1C 2L2; tel. (902) 733-2280; fax (902) 733-2362; e-mail louisbourg.info@pc.gc.ca; internet fortress.uccb.ns.ca; f. 1963; reconstruction and restoration project, including 18th-century period rooms and museum complex; archives and library collections of 18th-century French and North American colonial material; District Dir CAROL WHITFIELD.

Maritime Museum of the Atlantic: 1675 Lower Water St, Halifax, NS B3J 1S3; tel. (902) 424-7890; fax (902) 424-0612; e-mail mmalibry@gov.ns.ca; internet museum.gov .ns.ca/mma/; f. 1982; naval and merchant shipping history; *Titanic* and Halifax explosion exhibitions; small boat collection; collection of 20,000 photographs and 5,000 books; Dir MICHAEL MURRAY.

Nova Scotia Museum of Natural History: 1747 Summer St, Halifax, NS B3H 3A6; tel. (902) 424-7370; fax (902) 424-0560; internet nature.museum.gov.ns.ca; f. 1868; collections, research and exhibits relating to natural history of Nova Scotia; Dir D. L. BURLESON.

Ontario

Art Gallery of Hamilton: 123 King St West, Hamilton, ON L8P 4S8; tel. (905) 527-6610; fax (905) 577-6940; e-mail info@ artgalleryofhamilton.com; internet www .artgalleryofhamilton.com; f. 1914; 9,000 works, mainly Canadian paintings, sculpture and graphics; also art from the USA, UK and other European countries; library of 2,000 vols; Pres. and CEO LOUISE DOMPIERRE; publ. *Insights* (members' magazine, 3 a year).

Art Gallery of Ontario: 317 Dundas St W, Toronto, ON M5T 1G4; tel. (416) 979-6648; internet www.ago.net; f. 1900; European and N American art since 15th century; Inuit art in all forms; Henry Moore; research; library of 250,000 vols; Dir and CEO MATTHEW TEITELBAUM; Dir, Collns and Research DENNIS REID; publ. *Art Matters Magazine* (4 a year).

Canada Science and Technology Museum Corporation: POB 9724, Station T, Ottawa, ON K1G 5A3; tel. (613) 991-6090; fax (613) 990-3636; e-mail info@technomuses .ca; internet technomuses.ca; f. 1967; shows Canada's role in science and technology through displays such as: steam locomotives, vintage cars, cycles, carriages, household appliances, computers, communications and space technology, model ships, and through experiments, demonstrations, special exhibitions and educational programmes and an evening astronomy programme; the Corporation also includes the Canada Aviation Museum and the Canada Agriculture Museum; Pres. and CEO DENISE AMYOT; publs *Collection Profile* (also in electronic edn, 11 a year), *Curator's Choice* (also in electronic edn, irregular), *Material History Review* (2 a year).

Canadian Museum of Nature: POB 3443 Station D, Ottawa, ON K1P 6P4; tel. (613) 566-4700; fax (613) 364-4763; e-mail questions@mus-nature.ca; internet www .nature.ca; f. 1912; research and collns in the areas of botany, evolution, mineralogy, palaeobiology and zoology; houses the Centre for Traditional Knowledge, National Herbarium, the Biological Survey of Canada and the Canadian Centre for Biodiversity; library of 36,000 vols, 2,000 periodical titles (200 active subscriptions); Pres. and CEO JOANNE DICOSIMO.

Collingwood Museum: POB 556, 45 St Paul St, Collingwood, ON L9Y 4B2; tel. (705) 445-4811; fax (705) 445-9004; e-mail museum@collingwood.ca; internet www .collingwood.ca/museum; f. 1904; exhibits, children's programming, adult lectures, display, programming, research, special events; Supervisor SUSAN WARNER.

Dundurn Castle: 610 York Blvd, Hamilton, ON L8R 3H1; tel. (905) 546-2872; fax (905) 546-2875; former home of Sir Allan MacNab, Prime Minister of United Province of Canada 1854–56, built 1834, restored 1967; guided tours, special exhibits, period demonstrations; Curator WILLIAM NESBITT.

Jordan Historical Museum of the Twenty: 3802 Main St, Jordan, ON L0R 1S0; tel. (905) 562-5242; fax (905) 562-7786; f. 1953; a collection illustrating life in the Twenty Mile Creek area since 1776; Curator HELEN BOOTH.

Marine Museum of Upper Canada: Exhibition Place, Toronto, ON M5T 1R5; tel. (416) 392-1765; fax (416) 392-1767; e-mail can-thb@immedia.ca; f. 1959; operated by the Toronto Historical Board; preserves and interprets the marine history of Toronto, Toronto Harbour and Lake Ontario; collections include 1932 steam tug *Ned Hanlan* in dry dock; Curator JOHN SUMMERS.

Museum London: 421 Ridout St N, London, ON N6H 5H4; tel. (519) 661-0333; fax (519) 661-2559; e-mail ramurray@museumlondon .ca; internet www.museumlondon.ca; f. 1940; 25,000 historical artefacts, incl. paintings, prints, drawings and sculptures; undertakes collection and conservation of fine art and artefacts; exhibitions, lectures, films, workshops, tours and live performances; 900 mems; Exec. Dir BRIAN MEEHAN; publ. *At the Museum* (4 a year).

National Arts Centre: 53 Elgin St, Box 1534, Station B, Ottawa, ON K1P 5W1; tel. (613) 947-7000; fax (613) 996-9578; e-mail info@nac-cna.ca; internet www.nac-cna.ca; f. 1969; consists of Southam Hall (2,300 seats), theatre (950 seats), studio (300 seats), 4th stage (140 seats); resident 60-mem. NAC orchestra, English and French theatre, dance, opera, workshops, artist devt; 700 performances a year; Chair. JULIA FOSTER; Pres. and CEO PETER HERRNDORF.

National Gallery of Canada: 380 Sussex Drive, POB 427 Station A, Ottawa, ON K1N 9N4; tel. (613) 990-1985; fax (613) 993-4385; e-mail info@gallery.ca; internet national .gallery.ca; f. 1880; largest collection of Canadian art in the world; collns incl. large and important prints and drawings colln; historical and contemporary Canadian and international photography colln; Canadian art colln; Inuit colln; European colln; large contemporary colln; site incl. Canadian Museum of Contemporary Photography; operates largest travelling exhibition program in North America; library of 275,000 vols; Dir PIERRE THÉBERGE; publs *National Gallery of Canada Review* (1 a year), *Vernissage* (4 a year).

Ontario Science Centre: 770 Don Mills Rd, Toronto, ON M3C 1T3; tel. (416) 696-1000; fax (416) 696-3124; e-mail webmaster@osc.on .ca; internet www.ontariosciencecentre.ca; f. 1969; more than 600 exhibits in all fields of science and technology; library of 11,000 vols; CEO LESLEY LEWIS; Dir, Visitor Experience RICHARD VIEIRA.

Queen's University Museums: Miller Hall, Union St, Kingston, ON K7L 3N6; geology dept, tel. (613) 533-6767, f. 1901, Curator M. H. BADHAM; biology dept, tel. (613) 533-6160, f. 1880, Curator A. A. CROWDER; anatomy dept, tel. (613) 533-2600, f. 1854, Curator Dr M. G. JONEJA.

Royal Ontario Museum: 100 Queen's Park, Toronto, ON M5S 2C6; tel. (416) 586-8000; fax (416) 586-5863; e-mail info@rom.on.ca; internet www.rom.on.ca; f. 1912 opened in March 1914; affiliated to the Univ. of Toronto; decorative arts, natural history, anthropology and archaeology, and Canadian historical art; library of 175,000 vols; spec. collns 5,000 vols; Dir WILLIAM THORSELL; publ. *ROM: The Magazine of the Royal Ontario Museum* (3 a year).

Attached Institution:

George R. Gardiner Museum of Ceramic Art: 111 Queen's Park, Toronto, ON M5S 2C7; tel. (416) 586-8080; fax (416) 586-8085; e-mail mail@gardinermuseum .com; internet gardinermuseum.com; f. 1984.

Stephen Leacock Museum: Old Brewery Bay, 50 Museum Rd, Orillia, ON; tel. (705) 329-1908; fax (705) 326-5578; e-mail leacock@mail.transdata.ca; internet www .transdata.ca/~leacock; f. 1957; summer home, correspondence, manuscripts, personal effects of Stephen Butler Leacock 1869–1944; Curator DAPHNE MAINPRIZE.

Tom Thomson Memorial Art Gallery: 840 1st Ave West, Owen Sound, ON N4K 4K4; tel. (519) 376-1932; fax (519) 376-3037; e-mail sreid@e-owensound.com; internet www.tomthomson.org; f. 1967; Tom Thomson paintings, memorabilia; changing exhibitions of historic and contemporary art; Dir and Curator STUART REID; publ. *Newsletter* (4 a year).

Upper Canada Village: R. R. 1, Morrisburg, ON K0C 1X0; tel. (613) 543-3704; fax (613) 543-2847; internet www .uppercanadavillage.com; f. 1961; living historical site; 45 restored buildings portraying a rural community c. 1866; library of 5,000 vols; special collection of 19th-century archival materials including family and business records, photographs and social history documents from the region of eastern Ontario; Man. DAVE DOBBIE (acting).

Prince Edward Island

Confederation Centre Art Gallery and Museum: 145 Richmond St, Charlottetown, PE C1A 1J1; tel. (902) 628-6111; fax (902) 566-4648; e-mail artgallery@ confederationcentre.com; internet www .confederationcentre.com; f. 1964; nat. colln of 15,000 works of Canadian art since 19th century: paintings, drawings, prints, sculpture and photography; Harris Colln (paintings, drawings, MSS and records of Robert Harris, 1849–1919); temporary exhibitions on historical research and the contemporary artist; Dir JON TUPPER; Registrar and Curatorial Man. KEVIN RICE.

Québec

Canadian Museum of Civilization: 100 Laurier St, POB 3100, Station B, Gatineau, QC K1A 0M8; tel. (819) 776-7173; fax (819) 776-7152; e-mail library@civilization.ca; internet www.civilization.ca; f. 1856; archaeology, ethnology, folk culture studies, history of Canada, linguistics, physical anthropology,; study collns open to qualified researchers and gen. public; incl. Archaeological Survey of Canada, Canadian Children's Museum, Canadian Centre for Folk Culture Studies, Canadian Ethnology Service, Canadian Postal Museum, Canadian War Museum and other elements; library of 200,000 vols, of which 70,000 accessible to public; Pres. and CEO Dr VICTOR RABINOVITCH.

Centre Canadien d'Architecture/Canadian Centre for Architecture: 1920 rue Baile, Montréal, QC H3H 2S6; tel. (514) 939-7000; fax (514) 939-7020; e-mail ref@cca.qc .ca; internet www.cca.qc.ca; f. 1979 as a non-profit org., recognized as a museum in 1989; research centre and museum; aims to advance knowledge and promote public understanding of architecture, its history, theory, practice, and role in soc., through study programmes, exhibitions, publications, seminars, lectures and internships; library of 215,000 printed monographs (incl. rare books); 5,000 runs of periodicals, a number of spec. collns; architecture-related artefacts (such as toys and souvenir models); ephemera; Founding Dir and Pres. of the Board PHYLLIS LAMBERT.

Insectarium de Montréal: 4581 rue Sherbrooke Est, Montréal, QC H1X 2B2; tel. (514) 872-1400; fax (514) 872-0662; e-mail insectarium@ville.montreal.qc.ca; internet www.ville.montreal.qc.ca/insectarium; f. 1990; colln of 160,000 insects; Dir ANNE CHARPENTIER.

McCord Museum of Canadian History: 690 Sherbrooke St West, Montréal, QC H3A 1E9; tel. (514) 398-7100; fax (514) 398-5045; e-mail info@mccord.mcgill.ca; internet www .musee-mccord.qc.ca; f. 1921; museum of Canadian social history with collns of Canadian ethnology, costumes, decorative arts, drawings, documents, paintings, prints, toys; Notman Photographic Archives containing 800,000 glass plates and prints; Exec. Dir Dr VICTORIA DICKENSON.

Montréal Biodôme: 4777 ave Pierre-de-Coubertin, Montréal, QC H1V 1B3; tel. (514) 868-3000; fax (514) 868-3065; e-mail biodome@ville.montreal.qc.ca; internet www .biodome.qc.ca; f. 1992; museum of the environment; live collns, containing more than 4,800 animals of 230 species, and 750 plants species in four recreated ecosystems found in the Americas; housed in the velodrome used for the 1976 Olympic Games; Dir RACHEL LÉGER.

Montréal Museum of Fine Arts: 1379 and 1380 Sherbrooke St West, Montréal, QC H3G 2T9; tel. (514) 285-1600; fax (514) 844-6042; e-mail webmaster@mbamtl.org; internet www.mmfa.qc.ca; f. 1860; permanent collection of paintings (European and Canadian), sculptures, decorative arts and drawings; art from Asia, Africa and Oceania; library: over 90,000 vols and slide library; Pres. BRIAN M. LEVITT; Dir NATHALIE BONDIL; publ. *M* (3 a year).

Musée d'Art Contemporain de Montréal: 185 St Catherine St W, Montréal, QC H2X 3X5; tel. (514) 847-6226; fax (514) 847-6291; e-mail info@macm.org; internet www.macm .org; f. 1964; exhibits contemporary Québecois, Canadian and international art; organizes multimedia events, art videos, art workshops, lectures; library of 38,000 vols and exhibition catalogues, 713 periodicals, 8,000 visual archives, 1,000 video cassettes and audio items, 12,000 artists' files and bibliographic database; Dir MONIQUE GAUTHIER; Chief Curator PAULETTE GAGNON; publ. *Le Magazine*.

Musée de l'Amérique Française (Museum of French North America): 9 rue de la Vieille-Université, CP 460, succ., Haute-Ville, QC G1R 4R7; tel. (418) 528-0157; fax (418) 692-5206; e-mail archives@mcq.org; internet www.mcq.org; f. 1806, as Musée du Séminaire de Québec, present name 1983; attached to Musée de la Civilisation complex; art and history of French North America; library of 180,000 vols; Museum Dir DANIELLE POIRÉ; Archives Dir PIERRE BAIL.

Musée du Québec/Musée National des Beaux-Arts du Québec: Parc des Champs de Bataille, Québec, QC G1R 5H3; tel. (418) 643-2150; fax (418) 646-3330; e-mail info@ mnba.qc.ca; internet www.mnba.qc.ca; f. 1933; paintings, sculptures, drawings, prints, photographs, decorative art objects, interior design pieces; colln of 24,000 items relating to Québecois art and artists; Exec. Dir Dr JOHN R. PORTER.

Planétarium de Montréal: 1000 rue Saint-Jacques Ouest, Montréal, QC H3C 1G7; tel. (514) 872-4530; fax (514) 872-8102; e-mail info@planetarium.montreal.qc.ca; internet www.planetarium.montreal.qc.ca; f. 1966; astronomy, meteorite colln, museum; Dir PIERRE LACOMBE.

Redpath Museum: 859 Sherbrooke St West, Montréal, QC H3A 2K6; tel. (514) 398-4086; fax (514) 398-3185; e-mail marie .laricca@mcgill.ca; internet www.mcgill.ca/ redpath; f. 1882; natural history, geology, mineralogy, palaeontology, anthropology, herpetology, vertebrate and invertebrate zoology; Dir DAVID GREEN.

Saskatchewan

MacKenzie Art Gallery: 3475 Albert St, Regina, SK S4S 6X6; tel. (306) 522-4250; fax (306) 569-8191; e-mail mackenzie@uregina .ca; internet www.mackenzieartgallery.ca; f. 1954; permanent colln of Canadian historical and contemporary art, int. art since the 19th century, permanent colln displays and travelling exhibitions; public programmes; library: Resource Centre of 3,500 vols; Exec. Dir STUART REID; Curator TIMOTHY LONG; publs *At the MacKenzie* (3 a year), *@ the MacKenzie* (online, 12 a year).

Mendel Art Gallery and Civic Conservatory (Saskatoon Gallery and Conservatory Corporation): 950 Spadina Crescent East, POB 569, Saskatoon, SK S7K 3L6; tel. (306) 975-7610; fax (306) 975-7670; e-mail mendel@mendel.ca; internet www.mendel

.ca; f. 1964; Canadian and int. art, exhibitions, permanent colln; library of 10,000 vols; Exec. Dir and CEO RICHARD MOLDENHAUER (acting); publ. *Folio* (4 a year).

Musée Ukraina Museum: POB 26072, Saskatoon, SK S7K 8C1; tel. (306) 244-4212; fax (306) 384-6310; e-mail ukrainamuseum@sasktel.net; internet www .mumsaskatoon.com; f. 1953; ethnographic collns representing the spiritual, material and folkloric culture of Ukraine; Pres. PATRICIA MIALKOWSKY.

Prince Albert Historical Museum: 10 River St East, Prince Albert, SK S6V 8A9; tel. (306) 764-2992; e-mail historypa@citypa .com; internet www.historypa.com; f. c. 1887 as Saskatchewan Institute, disbanded 1891 when records and artefacts destroyed by fire, re-formed 1923 as Prince Albert Historical Soc.; run by Prince Albert Historical Soc. (also operates the Diefenbaker House Museum, the Evolution of Education Museum and the Rotary Museum of Police and Corrections); local historical exhibits, early settlement, pioneers, Indian life, education, law enforcement; colln of memorabalia relating to Canadian Prime Minister John Diefenbaker; maintains Bill Smiley Archives (12,000 documents, 20,000 photographs and negatives, relating to Prince Albert and area; available for research); Pres. H. S. MAY; Man. JAMES BENSON.

Royal Saskatchewan Museum: College Ave and Albert St, Regina, SK S4P 3V7; tel. (306) 787-2815; fax (306) 787-2820; internet www.gov.sk.ca/rsm; f. 1906; Earth Sciences Gallery depicts 2.5 billion years of Saskatchewan's geological history; First Nations Gallery traces 12,000 years of aboriginal history and culture; Paleo Pit interactive gallery; Megamunch, a roaring robotic Tyrannosaurus rex; Life Sciences Gallery features the flora, fauna and landscapes of Saskatchewan's diverse ecoregions; Dir DAVID BARON.

Saskatchewan Western Development Museum: 2935 Melville St, Saskatoon, SK S7J 5A6; tel. (306) 934-1400; fax (306) 934-4467; e-mail info@wdm.ca; internet www .wdm.ca; f. 1949; exhibit brs at N Battleford, Moose Jaw, Saskatoon, and Yorkton; colln associated with the settlement of the Canadian W; agricultural machinery, early transport and household items; annual summer shows; library: George Shepherd Library of 15,000 historical vols; Exec. Dir DAVID KLATT; publ. *Sparks off the Anvil* (6 a year).

Universities and Colleges

ACADIA UNIVERSITY

15 University Ave, Wolfville, NS B4P 2R6
Telephone: (902) 542-2201
Fax: (902) 585-1072
E-mail: ask.acadia@acadiau.ca
Internet: www.acadiau.ca
Founded 1838
Provincial control
Language of instruction: English
Academic year: September to April
Chancellor: ARTHUR IRVING
Pres.and Vice-Chancellor: Dr RAY IVANY
Academic Vice-Pres.: Dr CYRUS MACLATCHY (acting)
Vice-Pres. for Finance and Transport: GARY DRAPER
Vice-Pres. for Growth and Operations: DOV BERCOVICI
Sr Dir of Communications and Public Affairs: SCOTT ROBERTS
Registrar: ROSEMARY JOTCHAM (acting)
Librarian: SARAH LOCHHEAD

Library: see Libraries and Archives
Number of teachers: 211 full-time, 37 part-time
Number of students: 3,100 full-time, 380 part-time

DEANS

Faculty of Arts: Dr BRUCE MATTHEWS
Faculty of Professional Studies: Dr GARY NESS (acting)
Faculty of Pure and Applied Sciences: Dr PAUL CABILIO (acting)
Faculty of Theology: Dr HARRY GARDNER
Research and Graduate Studies: Dr TOM ELLIS

PROFESSORS

ARCHIBALD, T., Mathematics
ASH, S., Business Administration
ASHLEY, T. R.
BAILET, D., French
BALDWIN, D., History
BARR, S. M., Geology
BAWTREE, M., English
BEDINGFIELD, E. W., Recreation and Kinesiology
BEST, J., French
BISSIX, G., Recreation and Kinesiology
BOOTH, P., Classics
BOWEN, K., Sociology
CABILIO, P., Mathematics
CAMERON, B. W., Geology
CONRAD, M. R., History
DABORN, G. R., Biology
DADSWELL, M., Biology
DAVIES, J. E., Economics
DAVIES, R. A., English
FISHER, S. F., Music
GRIFFITH, B., Education
HERMAN, T. B., Biology
HOBSON, P., Economics
HORVATH, P., Psychology
JOHNSTON, E. M., Nutrition
LATTA, B., Physics
LEITER, M. P., Psychology
LOOKER, E. D., Sociology
MACLATCHY, C. S., Physics
MCLEOD, W., Kinesiology
MATTHEWS, B., History
MOODY, B. M., History
MOUSSA, H., Economics
MULDNER, T., Computer Science
NESS, G., Recreation and Kinesiology
OGILVIE, K. K., Chemistry
OLIVER, L., Computer Science
O'NEILL, P. T. H., Psychology
PARATTE, H. D., French
PIPER, D., Education
PYRCZ, G. E., Political Science
RAESIDE, R. P., Geology
RIDDLE, P. H., Music
ROSCOE, J. M., Chemistry
ROSCOE, S., Chemistry
SACOUMAN, R. J., Sociology
SPARKMAN, R., Business
STEWART, I., Political Science
STEWART, R., English
STILES, D. A., Chemistry
SUMARAH, J., Education
SYMON, S., Psychology
TOEWS, D. P., Biology
TOMEK, I., Computer Science
TOWNLEY, P., Economics
TRITES, A. A., Theology
TRUDEL, A., Computer Science
TUGWELL, M., Economics
VAN WAGONER, N. A., Geology
VERSTRAETE, B. C., Classics
WILSON, R. S., Theology

AFFILIATED COLLEGE

Acadia Divinity College: Wolfville; f. 1968; on campus; under direction of Atlantic United Baptist Convention; degrees granted by the University; Principal L. MCDONALD.

UNIVERSITY OF ALBERTA

Edmonton, AB T6G 2M7
Telephone: (780) 492-3113
Fax: (780) 492-7172
E-mail: info@ualberta.ca
Internet: www.ualberta.ca
Founded 1908
Provincial control
Language of instruction: English (Faculté Saint-Jean: French)
Academic year: September to August
Chancellor: JOHN FERGUSON
Pres. and Vice-Chancellor: Dr R. D. FRASER
Vice-Pres. for Academic Affairs and Provost: Dr CARL G. AMRHEIN
Vice-Pres. for External Affairs: SUSAN L. GREEN
Vice-Pres. for Facilities and Operations: DON HICKEY
Vice-Pres. for Finance and Administration: PHYLLIS CLARK
Vice-Pres. for Research: Dr R. GARY
Associate Vice-Pres. for Learning Support Systems and Dir of Libraries: E. INGLES
Associate Vice-Pres. and Registrar: C. BYRNE (acting)
Library: see Libraries
Number of teachers: 1,500
Number of students: 37,000
Publications: *Calendar* (1 a year), *Folio* (26 a year), *Report of the Board of Governors of the University of Alberta* (1 a year), *The New Trail* (4 a year)

DEANS AND DIRECTORS

Faculty of Agriculture, Forestry and Home Economics: IAN N. MORRISON
Faculty of Arts: DANIEL WOOLF
Faculty of Business: M. PERCY
Faculty of Education: Dr FERN SNART (acting)
Faculty of Engineering: DAVID T. LYNCH
Faculty of Extension: Dr CHERYL MCWATTERS
Faculty of Graduate Studies and Research: MARK R. T. DALE
Faculty of Law: DAVID PERCY
Faculty of Medicine and Dentistry: D. L. J. TYRELL
Faculty of Nursing: Prof. GENEVIEVE I. GRAY
Faculty of Pharmacy and Pharmaceutical Sciences: FRANCO M. PASUTTO
Faculty of Physical Education and Recreation: Dr MICHAEL MAHON
Faculty of Rehabilitation Medicine: ALBERT M. COOK
Faculty of Science: GREGORY J. TAYLOR
Augustana Faculty: ROGER I. EPP
Faculté St-Jean: M. ARNAL
School of Library and Information Studies: A. ALTMAN
School of Native Studies: Dr ELLEN BIELAWSKI

AFFILIATED COLLEGES

North American Baptist College: 11525-23 Ave, Edmonton, AB T6J 4T3; affiliated since 1988; offers first-year courses in liberal arts; Pres. Dr M. DEWEY.

St Joseph's College: Edmonton, AB T6G 2J5; affiliated 1926; Roman Catholic; courses in philosophy and Christian theology; Pres. T. SCOTT.

St Stephen's College: Edmonton, AB T6G 2J6; affiliated 1909; theological school of United Church of Canada; offers its own courses to degree level and certain courses open to students of the University; Principal G. ROGER.

ATHABASCA UNIVERSITY

1 Univ. Dr., Athabasca, AB T9S 3A3
Telephone: (780) 675-6100
Fax: (780) 675-6145

Internet: www.athabascau.ca

Founded 1970

Provincial control

Open univ. providing undergraduate and Masters-level courses for adult, non-residential students, with emphasis on distance and online education

Language of instruction: English

Chair., Governing Ccl: JOY ROMERO

Pres.: Dr FRITS PANNEKOEK (acting)

Vice-Pres. for Academic Affairs: Dr MARGARET HAUGHE

Vice-Pres. for Advancement: Dr LORI VAN ROOIZEN

Registrar: JIM DARCY

Librarian: S. SCHAFER

Library of 143,261

Number of teachers: 258

Number of students: 31,250

Publications: *Aurora* (interviews with leading thinkers and writers), *Electronic Journal of Sociology, Globalization, IRRODDL* (research for Open and Distance Learning), *Radical Pedagogy, Sport and the Human Animal, Theory and Science, Trumpeter*

DIRECTORS

Centre for Computing and Information Systems: KINSHUK

Centre for Distance Education: Dr MOHAMED ALLY

Centre for Global and Social Analysis: DAVID GREGORY

Centre for Graduate Education in Applied Psychology: Dr SANDRA COLLINS

Centre for Innovative Management: ALEX KONDRA

Centre for Language and Literature: VERONICA THOMPSON

Centre for Learning Accreditation: DIANNE CONRAD (acting)

Centre for Nursing and Health Studies: Dr DONNA ROMYN

Centre for Psychology: TREVOR GILBERT

Centre for Science: NORMAN TEMPLE

Centre for State and Legal Studies: JAY SMITH

Centre for Work and Community Studies: LYNDA ROSS

Centre for World and Indigenous Knowledge and Research: PRISCILLA CAMPEAU

School of Business: DAVID ANNAND

BISHOP'S UNIVERSITY

Sherbrooke, QC J1M 1Z7

Telephone: (819) 822-9600

Fax: (819) 822-9661

E-mail: recruitment@ubishops.ca

Internet: www.ubishops.ca

Founded 1843, constituted a univ. by Royal Charter 1853

Academic year: September to May

Language of instruction: English

Chancellor: SCOTT GRIFFIN

Prin.: MICHAEL GOLDBLOOM

Vice-Prin.: Dr MICHAEL CHILDS

Vice-Prin. for Admin. and Finance: HELENE ST AMAND

Registrar and Sec.-Gen.: RUTH SHEERAN

Librarian: WENDY DURRANT

Dean of Student Affairs: BRUCE STEVENSON

Number of teachers: 109 full-time

Number of students: 2,850

Publication: *Journal of Eastern Township Studies* (2 a year)

DEANS

School of Arts and Sciences: Dr JAMIE CROOKS

School of Education: Dr CATHERINE BEAUCHAMP

Williams School of Business: Dr STEVE HARVEY

BRANDON UNIVERSITY

270 18th St, Brandon, MB R7A 6A9

Telephone: (204) 727-9762

Fax: (204) 728-7340

E-mail: president@brandonu.ca

Internet: www.brandonu.ca

Founded 1899; gained full autonomy July 1967

Public control

Language of instruction: English

Academic year: September to April

Chancellor: H. CHAMP

Pres.: Dr DEBORAH POFF

Vice-Pres. for Academic and Research: Dr SCOTT GRILLS

Vice-Pres. for Admin. and Finance: SCOTT J. B. LAMONT

Registrar: Dr LAWRENCE VAN BEEK

Librarian: L. BURRIDGE

Number of teachers: 170

Number of students: 3,200 (full- and part-time)

Publications: *Abstracts of Native Studies, Canadian Journal of Native Studies, Cross Cultural Psychology Bulletin, Ecclectica, Journal of Rural and Community Development*

DEANS AND DIRECTORS

Faculty of Arts: Dr G. BRUCE STRANG

Faculty of Education: JERRY STORIE

Faculty of Science: JANET S. WRIGHT

School of Health Studies: Dr DEAN CARE

School of Music: Dr MICHAEL KIM

Department of Rural Development: Dr ROBERT ANNIS (acting)

First Nations and Aboriginal Counselling Programme: ANDREA HINCH-BOURNS

UNIVERSITY OF BRITISH COLUMBIA

Vancouver, BC V6T 1Z1

Telephone: (604) 822-2211

Fax: (604) 822-5785

E-mail: presubc@interchange.ubc.ca

Internet: www.ubc.ca

Founded 1908

Academic year: September to August

Chancellor: ALLAN MCEACHERN

Pres. and Vice-Chancellor: MARTHA C. PIPER

Vice-Pres. for Academics and Provost: LORNE A. WHITEHEAD

Vice-Pres. for Administration and Finance: T. SUMNER

Vice-Pres. for External and Legal Affairs: DENNIS PAVLICH

Vice-Pres. for Research: (VACANT)

Vice-Pres. for Students: BRIAN SULLIVAN

Registrar: R. A. SPENCER

Librarian: CATHERINE QUINLAN

Number of teachers: 1,870

Number of students: 31,331

Publications: *BC Asian Review* (1 a year), *BC Studies* (4 a year), *BC Studies: The British Columbian Quarterly* (4 a year), *Canadian Journal of Botany* (4 a year), *Canadian Journal of Civil Engineering* (6 a year), *Canadian Journal of Women and the Law* (1 a year), *Canadian Literature* (4 a year), *PRISM International* (4 a year), *University Calendar* (winter and summer), *Yearbook of International Law*

DEANS

Faculty of Agricultural Sciences: M. QUAYLE

Faculty of Applied Science: M. ISAACSON

Faculty of Arts: NANCY GALLINI

Faculty of Commerce and Business Administration: DANIEL F. MUZYKA

Faculty of Dentistry: E. H. K. YEN

Faculty of Education: ROB TIERNEY

Faculty of Forestry: JOHN N. SADDLER

Faculty of Graduate Studies: FRIEDA GRANOT

College of Health Disciplines: JOHN H. V. GILBERT (Principal)

Faculty of Law: MARY ANNE BOBINSKI

Faculty of Medicine: GAVIN STUART

Faculty of Pharmaceutical Sciences: ROBERT D. SINDELAR

Faculty of Science: JOHN W. HEPBURN

DIRECTORS OF SCHOOLS

School of Architecture: C. MACDONALD

School of Audiology and Speech Science: Prof. JUDITH R. JOHNSTON

School of Community and Regional Planning: Prof. W. E. REES

School of Family and Nutritional Sciences: Prof. A. MARTIN-MATTHEWS

School of Human Kinetics: PETER CROCKER (acting)

School of Journalism: DONNA LOGAN

School of Library, Archival and Information Studies: Prof. EDIE RASMUSSEN

School of Music: JESSE READ

School of Nursing: SALLY THORNE

School of Rehabilitation Sciences: LESLEY BAINBRIDGE

School of Social Work and Family Studies: GRAHAM RICHES

PROFESSORS

Faculty of Agricultural Sciences

Department of Agroecology:

BLACK, A.
CHANWAY, C.
CHENG, K.
CHIENG, S.-T.
COPEMAN, R.
CRONK, Q.
ELLIS, B.
ISMAN, M.
JOLLIFFE, P.
LAVKULICH, L.
MCKINLEY, S.
MYERS, J.
RAJAMAHENDRAN, R.
SCHREIER, H.
SHACKLETON, D.
TAYLOR, I.
UPADHYAYA, M.
WEARY, O.

Department of Community and the Environment:

CONDON, P.
PATERSON, D.
QUAYLE, M.

Department of Food, Nutrition and Health:

BARR, S.
CHENG, K.
DURANCE, T.
KITTS, D.
LI-CHAN, E.
THOMPSON, J.
VAN VUUREN, H.
VERCAMMEN, J.

Faculty of Applied Science

Department of Chemical and Biological Engineering:

BERT, J.
BOWEN, B.
CHIENG, S.
DUFF, S.
ENGLEZOS, P.
GRACE, J.
HATZIKIRIAKOS, S.
JIM JIM, C.
KEREKES, R.
LO, K.
OLOMAN, C.
PIRET, J.
SMITH, K.

WATKINSON, P.

Department of Civil Engineering:

ADEBAR, P.
BANTHIA, N.
FANNIN, R.
FOSCHI, R.
HALL, E.
HALL, K. J.
ISSACSON, M.
LAWRENCE, G.
MAVINIC, D.
MINDESS, S.
NAVIN, F.
RUSSELL, A.
SEXSMITH, R.
STEIMER, S.

Department of Electrical and Computer Engineering:

DAVIES, M.
DUMONT, G.
IVANOV, A.
JAEGER, N.
KRISHNAMURTHY, V.
LAWRENCE, P.
LEUNG, C.
LEUNG, V.
PULFREY, D.
SALEH, R.
WARD, R.

Department of Mechanical Engineering:

ALTINTAS, Y.
CALISAL, S.
CHERCHAS, D.
DE SILVA, C.
EVANS, R.
GADALA, M.
GREEN, S.
HILL, P.
HODGSON, M.
HUTTON, S.
RAJAPAKSE, N.
SALCUDEAN, M.
SASSANI, F.
SCHAJER, G.
YELLOWLEY, I.

Department of Metals and Materials Engineering:

DREISINGER, D.
POURSARTIP, A.
REED, R.
TROCZYNSKI, T.
TROMANS, D.

Department of Mining Engineering:

MEECH, J.
SCOBLE, M.
WILSON, W.

Faculty of Arts

Department of Anthropology:

MATSON, R.
MILLER, B.

Department of Art History, Visual Art and Theory:

COHODAS, M.
EDER, R.
GUILBAUT, S.
LUM, K.
O'BRIAN, J.
WATSON, S.
WINDSOR-LISCOMBE, R.

Department of Asian Studies:

DUKE, M.
NOSCO, P.
OBEROI, H.
SCHMIDT, J.
TAKASHIMA, K.-I.

Department of Classical, Near Eastern and Religious Studies:

BARRETT, A. A.
HARDING, P.
SULLIVAN, S.
TODD, R.

WILLIAMS, E.

Department of Economics:

COPELAND, B.
DIEWERT, E.
ESWARAN, M.
EVANS, R.
GREEN, D.
KOTWAL, A.
LEMIEUX, T.
PATERSON, D.
REDISH, A.
RIDDELL, C.

Department of French, Hispanic and Italian Studies:

BOCCASSINI, D.
HODGSON, R.
MCEACHERN, J.
RAOUL, V.
SARKONAK, R.
TESTA, C.
URRELLO, A.

Department of Geography:

BARNES, T.
CHURCH, M.
GREGORY, D.
HIEBERT, D.
LEY, D.
MCCLUNG, D.
MCKENDRY, I.
OKE, T.
PRATT, G.
ROBINSON, J.
SLAYMAKER, O.
STEYN, D.
STULL, R.
WYNN, G.

Department of Germanic Studies:

MORNIN, E.
PETERSEN, K.
PETRO, P.
STENBERG, P.

Department of History:

FRIEDRICHS, C.
KRAUSE, P.
LARY, D.
NEWELL, D.
RAY, A.
UNGER, R.
WARD, P.

Department of Linguistics:

PULLEYBLANK, D.
STEMBERGER, J.
VATIKIOTIS-BATESON, E.

School of Music:

BENJAMIN, W.
BERINAUM, M.
BUTLER, G.
CHATMAN, S.
COOP, J.
DAWES, A.
HAMEL, K.
READ, J.
SHARON, R.
TENZER, M.

Department of Philosophy:

BEATTY, J.
IRVINE, A.
RUSSELL, P.
SAVITT, S.
SCHABAS, M.
WILSON, C.

Department of Political Science:

JOB, B.
JOHNSTON, R.
LASELVA, S.
MARANTZ, P.
MAUZY, D.
RESNICK, P.
TENNANT, P.
TUPPER, A.
WALLACE, M.

Department of Psychology:

ALDEN, L.
CHANDLER, M.
COREN, S.
DUTTON, D.
ENNS, J.
GORZALKA, B.
GRAF, P.
HAKSTIAN, R.
LEHMAN, D.
LINDEN, W.
PINEL, J.
TEES, R.
WALKER, L.
WARD, L.
WERKER, J.

Department of Sociology:

CREESE, G.
CURRIE, D.
ELLIOTT, B.
ERICSON, R.
GUPPY, N.
JOHNSON, G.
JOPPKE, C.
MATTHEWS, D.

Department of Theatre, Film and Creative Writing:

ALDERSON, S.
DURBACH, E.
GARDINER, R.
MCWHIRTER, G.
MAILLARD, K.
WASSERMAN, J.

Faculty of Dentistry

Department of Oral Biological and Medical Sciences:

BRUNETTE, D.
CLARK, C.
DIEWERT, V.
DONALDSON, D.
HANNAM, A.
LARJAVA, H.
LOWE, A.
OVERALL, C.
UITTO, V.-J.
YEN, E.

Department of Oral Health Sciences:

CLARK, C.
DIEWERT, V.
HANNAM, A.
LOWE, A.
MCENTEE, M.

Faculty of Education

Faculty of Curriculum Studies:

CHALMERS, F. G.
ERICKSON, G.
GASKELL, P.
IRWIN, R.
KINDLER, A.
PETERAT, L.
PIRIE, S.

Department of Educational and Counselling Psychology, and Special Education:

AMUNDSON, N.
ARLIN, M.
BORGEN, W.
BUTLER, D.
DANILUK, J.
KAHN, S.
LONG, B.
PORATH, M.
SIEGEL, L.
WESTWOOD, M.
YOUNG, R.
ZUMBO, B.

Department of Educational Studies:

ADAM-MOODLEY, K.
BARMAN, J.
BOSHIER, R.
BROWN, D.
FISHER, D.

KELLY, D.
PRATT, D. D.
ROMAN, L.
RUBENSON, K.
SCHUETZE, H.
SHIELDS, C.
SORK, T.
STRONG-BOAG, V.
UNGERLEIDER, C. S.

Faculty of Forestry:

AVRAMIDIS, S.
BARKER, J.
BARRETT, D.
BUNNELL, F.
CHAFWAY, C.
EL-KASSABY, Y.
EVANS, P.
FANNIN, J.
GUY, R.
HALEY, D.
HOBERG, G.
INNES, J.
KIMMINS, J.
KLINKA, K.
MCLEAN, J.
MARTIN, K.
MURTHA, P.
RITLAND, K.
RUDDICK, J.
VAN DER KAMP, B.

Faculty of Law:

BAKAN, J.
BLACK, W.
BLOM, J.
BOYD, S.
BOYLE, C.
BURNS, P.
ELLIOT, R.
FARQUHAR, K.
GRANT, I.
JACKSON, M.
LEBARON, L. M.
MCDOUGALL, B.
PATERSON, R.
PAVLICH, D.
PUE, W.
SHEPPARD, A.
WEILER, J.
YOUNG, C.

Faculty of Medicine

Department of Anatomy:

BRESSLER, B.
CHURCH, J.
CRAWFORD, B.
EMERMAN, J.
NAUS, C.
OVALLE, W.
SLONECKER, C.
VOGL, A.
WEINBERG, J.

School of Audiology and Speech Sciences:

JOHNSTON, J.
STAPELLS, D.

Department of Biochemistry and Molecular Biology:

BRAYER, G.
BROWNSEY, R.
CULLIS, P.
DEDHAR, S.
FINLAY, B.
MACGILLIVRAY, R.
MCINTOSH, L.
MACKIE, G.
MAUK, A.
MOLDAY, R.
ROBERGE, M.
SADOWSKI, I.

Department of Family Practice:

BASSETT, K.
BATES, J.
CALAM, B.
DONNELLY, M.

GRAMS, G.
GRZYBOWSKI, S.
KHAN, K.
KLEIN, M.
KUHL, D.
LIVINGSTONE, V.
MCKENZIE, D.
SCOTT, I.
TAUNTON, J.
WHITESIDE, C.
WIEBE, C.
WOOLLARD, R.

Department of Healthcare and Epidemiology:

BARER, M.
BLACK, C.
HERTZMAN, C.
KAZANJIAN, A.
KENNEDY, S.
MATHIAS, R.
SCHECHTER, M.
SHEPS, S.
SINGER, J.
TESCHKE, K.

Faculty of Medical Genetics:

BURGESS, M.
EAVES, C.
FIELD, L.
FRIEDMAN, J.
HALL, J.
HIETER, P.
JEFFERIES, W.
JURILOFF, D.
KAY, R.
MCGILLIVRAY, B.
MCMASTER, W.
MAGER, D.
ROSE, A.
SADOVNICK, A.

Department of Medicine:

ABBOUD, R.
BAI, T.
BEATTIE, B.
BIRMINGHAM, C.
BOWIE, W.
BRUNHAM, R.
CAIRNS, J.
CALNE, D.
CHOW, A.
EAVES, A.
EISEN, A.
ESDAILE, J.
FLEETHAM, J.
FREEMAN, H.
HO, V.
HUMPHRIES, R.
KEOWN, P.
KERR, C.
LAM, S.
LUI, H.
MCLEAN, D.
MANCINI, G.
MONTANER, J.
OGER, J.
OSTROW, D.
PAGE, G.
PARÉ, P.
PATY, D.
PELECH, S.
PRIOR, J.
QUAMME, G.
RABKIN, S.
REINER, N.
RIVERS, J.
ROAD, J.
RUSSELL, J.
SCHELLENBERG, R.
SCHRADER, J.
SCHULZER, M.
STEIN, H.
STEINBRECHER, U.
STIVER, H.
STOESSL, J.
SUTTON, R.

TSUI, J.
WALLEY, K.
WANG, Y.
WONG, N.
WRIGHT, J.
YEUNG, M.

Department of Physiology:

BAIMBRIDGE, K.
BUCHAN, A.
FEDIDA, D.
MCINTOSH, C.
NAUS, C. C.
PEARSON, J

Department of Radiology:

COOPERBERG, P.
CULHAM, G.
LI, D.
LYSTER, D.
MACKAY, A.
MÜLLER, N.
MUNK, P.

Department of Surgery:

WARNOCK, G.

Faculty of Science

Department of Botany:

DEWREEDE, R.
DOUGLAS, C.
GANDERS, F.
GLASS, A.
GREEN, B.
GRIFFITHS, A.
MADDISON, W.
TAYLOR, F.
TAYLOR, I.
TOWERS, G.
TURKINGTON, R.

Department of Chemistry:

ANDERSEN, R.
BLADES, M.
BROOKS, D.
BURNELL, E.
COMISAROW, M.
DOLPHIN, D.
DOUGLAS, D.
FLEMING, D.
FRYZUK, M.
FYFE, C.
GERRY, M.
HEPBURN, J.
HERRING, G.
LEGZDINS, P.
MCINTOSH, L.
MITCHELL, K.
ORVIG, C.
PATEY, G.
PIERS, E.
SAWATZKY, G.
SCHEFFER, J.
SHAPIRO, M.
SHERMAN, J.
SHIZGAL, B.
STORR, A.
TANNER, M.
WITHERS, S.

Department of Computer Science:

ASCHER, U.
BOOTH, K.
CONDON, A.
FRIEDMAN, J.
KICZALES, G.
KIRKPATRICK, D.
KLAWE, M.
LAKSHMANAN, L.
LITTLE, J.
LOWE, D.
MACKWORTH, A.
NG, R.
PAI, D.
PIPPENGER, N.
POOLE, D.
ROSENBERG, R.
WOODHAM, R.

Department of Earth and Ocean Sciences:
ANDERSEN, R.
BOSTOCK, M.
BUSTIN, M.
CLARKE, G.
CLOWES, R.
FLETCHER, K.
GROAT, L.
HARRISON, P.
HEALEY, M.
HSIEH, W.
HUNGR, O.
INGRAM, G.
OLDENBURG, D.
RUSSELL, K.
SMITH, L.
SMITH, P.
STEYN, D.
STULL, R.
TAYLOR, M.
ULRYCH, T.
WEIS, D.

Department of Mathematics:
ANSTEE, R.
BLUMAN, G.
BOYD, D.
CARRELL, J.
FOURNIER, J.
GHOUSSOUB, N.
LAM, K.
LOEWEN, P.
MACDONALD, J.
MARCUS, B.
PEIRCE, A.
PERKINS, E.
SEYMOUR, B.
SJERVE, D.
SLADE, G.
WARD, M.

Department of Microbiology and Immunology:
HANCOCK, R. E. W.
JEFFERIES, W. A.
KRONSTAD, J. W.
SMIT, J.
SPIEGELMAN, G.
TEH, H.-S.
WEEKS, G.

Department of Statistics:
HARRY, J.
HECKMAN, N.
PETKAU, J.
VAN EEDEN, C.
ZAMAR, R.
ZIDEK, J.

Department of Zoology:
ADAMSON, M.
BERGER, J.
BLAKE, R.
BROCK, H.
GASS, C.
GOSLINE, J.
GRIGLIATTI, T.
JONES, D.
MILSOM, W.
MOERMAN, D.
MYERS, J.
PAULY, D.
PITCHER, T.
RANDALL, D.
SCHLUTER, D.
SINCLAIR, T.
SMITH, J.
SNUTCH, T.
STEEVES, J.
TETZLAFF, W.
WALTERS, C.

Sauder School of Business
Division of Accounting:
FELTHAM, G.
SIMUNIC, D.

Division of Finance:
GIAMMARINO, R.
HAMILTON, S.
HEINKEL, R.
KRAUS, A.
LEVI, M.

Division of Law:
WAND, Y.

Division of Marketing:
GRIFFIN, D.
WEINBERG, C.

Division of Operations and Logistics:
ATKINS, D.
GRANOT, D.
GRANOT, F.
McCORMICK, T.
OUM, T.
PUTERMAN, M.
QUEYRANNE, M.
ZHANG, A.
ZIEMBA, W.

Division of Strategy and Business Economics:
ANTWEILER, W.
BOARDMAN, A.
BRANDER, J.
FRANK, M.
HELSLEY, R.
NAKAMURA, M.
NEMETZ, P.
ROSS, T.
SPENCER, B.
VERTINSKY, I.
WINTER, R.

School of Architecture:
BROCK, L.
COLE, R.
CONDON, P.
MACDONALD, C.
PATKAU, P.
WAGNER, G.
WALKEY, R.
WOJTOWICZ, J.

School of Human Kinetics:
CROCKER, P.
FRANKS, I.
McKENZIE, D.
RHODES, E.
TAUNTON, J.

School of Journalism:
LOGAN, D.

School of Library, Archival and Information Studies:
DURANTI, L.
HAYCOCK, K.
RASMUSSEN, E.

School of Nursing:
ACORN, S.
ANDERSON, J.
BOTTORFF, D.
CARTY, E.
HILTON, A.
JOHNSON, J.
PATERSON, B.
THORNE, S.

School of Social Work and Family Studies:
CHRISTENSEN, C.
MARTIN-MATHEWS, A.
PERLMAN, D.
RUSSELL, M.
WHITE, J.

THEOLOGICAL COLLEGES
Carey Hall and Carey Theological College: 5920 Iona Drive, Vancouver, BC V6T 1J6; tel. 224-4308; internet www .careytheologicalcollege.ca; Baptist; Principal Dr B. F. STELCK.
Regent College: 5800 University Boulevard, Vancouver, BC V6T 2E4; tel. 224-

3245; internet www.regent-college.edu; trans-denominational; Pres. ROD WILSON.
St Andrew's Hall: 6040 Iona Drive, Vancouver, BC V6T 2E8; tel. (604) 822-9720; Presbyterian; Dean Rev. B. J. FRASER.
St Mark's College: 5935 Iona Drive, Vancouver, BC V6T 1J7; tel. 224-3311; internet www.stmarkscollege.ca; Roman Catholic; Principal Dr JOHN D. DENNISON.
Vancouver School of Theology: 6000 Iona Drive, Vancouver, BC V6T 1L4; tel. (604) 228-9031; fax (604) 228-0189; internet www .vst.edu; an ecumenical school of theology, incorporated 1971; continues work of the Anglican Theological College of BC and Union College of BC; provides theological education for laymen, for future clergy and for graduates in theology; Principal Dr KENNETH MACQUEEN.

BROCK UNIVERSITY
500 Glenridge Ave, St Catharines, ON L2S 3A1

Telephone: (905) 688-5550
Fax: (905) 688-2789
E-mail: regist@brocku.ca
Internet: www.brocku.ca

Founded 1964
Provincial control
Academic year: September to April
Language of instruction: English

Chancellor: NED GOODMAN
Pres. and Vice-Chancellor: JACK LIGHTSTONE
Provost and Vice-Pres. for Academics: R. T. BOAK
Vice-Pres. for Admin.: STEVEN PILLAR
Registrar: BARB DAVIS
Librarian: M. GROVE

Library: Library of 1,559,824 items
Number of teachers: 592
Number of students: 17,453

Publications: *Calendar* (1 a year), *Surgite* (4 a year)

Depts of applied language studies, biochemistry, biological sciences, biophysics, biotechnology, business—accounting, business—finance, operations and information systems, business—marketing, international business and strategy, business—organizational behaviour, human resource management, entrepreneurship and ethics, business economics, Canadian studies, chemistry, child and youth studies, classics, communications, popular culture and film, community health sciences, computer science, computing and business, dramatic arts, earth sciences, economics, education—adult education, education—centre for continuing teacher education, education—graduate and undergraduate studies, education—pre-service education, English language and literature, geography, great books/liberal studies, history, interactive arts and sciences, intercultural studies, international political economy, mathematics, medieval and renaissance studies, modern languages, literatures and cultures, music, neuroscience, nursing, oenology and viticulture, philosophy, physical education and kinesiology, physics, political science, psychology, recreation and leisure studies, sociology, sport management, studies in art and culture, tourism and environment, visual arts, women's studies

DEANS
Faculty of Business: MARTIN KUSY
Faculty of Education: JAMES HEAP
Faculty of Humanities: ROSEMARY HALE
Faculty of Physical Education and Recreation: JOHN CORLETT
Faculty of Science and Mathematics: IAN BRINDLE

Faculty of Social Sciences: DAVID SIEGEL
Faculty of Graduate Studies: MARILYN ROSE

UNIVERSITY OF CALGARY

2500 University Drive NW, Calgary, AB T2N 1N4

Telephone: (403) 220-5110
Fax: (403) 282-7298
E-mail: reginfo@ucalgary.ca
Internet: www.ucalgary.ca

Founded 1945 as a br. of the University of Alberta; gained full autonomy 1966
Language of instruction: English
Academic year: July to June

Chancellor: W. J. WARREN
Pres. and Vice-Chancellor: HARVEY WEINGARTEN
Provost and Vice-Pres. for Academic Affairs: R. B. BOND
Vice-Pres. for External Relations: R. COONEY
Vice-Pres. for Finance and Services: M. W. MCADAM
Vice-Pres. for Research and International Affairs: D. R. SALAHUB
Registrar: D. B. JOHNSTON
Director, Information Resources: A. DAVIS (acting)
Chief Information Officer for Information Technologies: H. A. ESCHE
Chief Development Officer: G. D. DURBENIUK
Number of teachers: 2,410 (1,569 full-time, 841 part-time)
Number of students: 27,928 (23,414 full-time, 4,514 part-time)
Publications: *Abstracts of English Studies, Arctic Journal* (Arctic Institute of North America), *Ariel: Review of International English Literature, Calgary Alumni, Canadian Energy Research Institute publs* (irregular), *Canadian Ethnic Studies, Canadian and International Education* (2 a year), *Canadian Journal of Law and Society* (1 a year), *Canadian Journal of Philosophy* (4 a year), *Classical Views—Echos du monde classique, International Journal of Man-Machine Studies* (12 a year), *Journal of Child and Youth Care, Journal of Comparative Family Studies, Journal of Educational Thought* (3 a year), *University Gazette* (26 a year)

DEANS

Faculty of Communication and Culture: K. SCHERF
Faculty of Education: A. V. LaGRANGE
Faculty of Engineering: S. C. WIRASINGHE
Faculty of Environmental Design: B. R. SINCLAIR
Faculty of Fine Arts: A. CALVERT
Faculty of Graduate Studies: W. L. VEALE
Faculty of Humanities: R. J. SMITH
Faculty of Kinesiology: R. F. ZERNICKE
Faculty of Law: P. A. HUGHES
Faculty of Medicine: D. G. GALL
Faculty of Nursing: M. E. CLINTON
Faculty of Science: P. M. BOORMAN
Faculty of Social Sciences: S. J. RANDALL
Faculty of Social Work: G. ROGERS
Haskayne School of Business: M. A. GRANDIN
Continuing Education: J. W. HUMPHREY (Dir)

PROFESSORS

ADDICOTT, J. F., Biological Sciences
ADDINGTON, D. E. N., Psychiatry
AGOPIAN, E. E., Music
ANDREWS, J. W., Division of Applied Psychology
ARCHER, C. I., History
ARCHER, D. P., Anaesthesia and Clinical Neurosciences
ARCHER, K. A., Political Science
ARCHIBALD, J. A., Linguistics

ARMSTRONG, G. D., Microbiology and Infectious Diseases
ARTHUR, N. M., Division of Applied Psychology
ASTLE, W. F., Surgery
ATKINSON, M. H., Medicine
AUER, R. N., Clinical Neurosciences and Pathology and Laboratory Medicine
AUSTIN, C. D., Social Work
BACK, T. G., Chemistry
BANKES, N. D., Law
BARCLAY, R. M. R., Biological Sciences
BARKER, K. E., Computer Science
BARRY, D., Political Science
BAUWENS, L., Mechanical Engineering
BECH-HANSEN, N. T., Medical Genetics and Surgery
BECKER, W. J., Clinical Neurosciences and Medicine
BEHIE, L. A., Chemical and Petroleum Engineering
BELENKIE, I., Medicine
BELL, A. G., Music
BELL, D. M., Music
BELYEA, B., English
BENEDIKTSON, H., Pathology and Laboratory Medicine
BENNETT, S., English
BENTLEY, L. R., Geology and Geophysics
BERCUSON, D. J., History
BERSHAD, D. L., Art
BEZDEK, K., Mathematics and Statistics
BIDDLE, F. G., Paediatrics and Biochemistry and Molecular Biology and Medical Genetics
BINDING, P. A., Mathematics and Statistics
BIRSS, V. I., Chemistry
BISZTRICZKY, T., Mathematics and Statistics
BLAND, B. H., Psychology
BOND, R. B., English
BOS, L. P., Mathematics and Statistics
BOSETTI, B. L., Education
BOWAL, P. C., Haskayne School of Business
BOYCE, J. R., Economics
BRADLEY, J., Computer Science
BRANNIGAN, A., Sociology
BRANT, R. F., Community Health Sciences
BRAY, R. C., Surgery
BRENKEN, B. A., Mathematics and Statistics
BRENT, D. A., Communication and Culture
BROWDER, L. W., Biochemistry and Molecular Biology and Oncology
BROWN, C. A., Law
BROWN, C. B., Medicine, Oncology, Biochemistry and Molecular Biology
BROWN, J. L. S., Environmental Design
BROWN, J. S., Music
BROWN, K., French, Italian and Spanish
BROWN, R. J., Geology and Geophysics
BROWN, T. G., Civil Engineering
BROWNELL, A. K. W., Clinical Neurosciences and Medicine
BRUCE, C. J., Economics
BRUEN, A. A., Mathematics and Statistics
BRUTON, L. T., Electrical and Computer Engineering
BULLOCH, A. G. M., Physiology and Biophysics
BURET, A. G., Biological Sciences
BURGESS, E. D., Medicine
BURKE, M. D., Mathematics and Statistics
BUTZNER, J. D., Paediatrics
CAIRNCROSS, J. G., Clinical Neurosciences
CAIRNS, K. V., Division of Applied Psychology
CAMERON, E., Art
CAMPBELL, G. W., French, Italian and Spanish
CAMPBELL, N. R. C., Medicine
CANNON, M. E., Geomatics Engineering
CARTER, S. A., History
CAVEY, M. J., Biological Sciences
CERI, H., Biological Sciences
CHACONAS, G., Biochemistry, Molecular Biology, Microbiology and Infectious Diseases
CHADEE, K., Microbiology and Infectious Diseases

CHANG, K.-W., Mathematics and Statistics
CHEN, S. R. W., Physiology, Biophysics, Biochemistry and Molecular Biology
CHINNAPPA, C. C., Biological Sciences
CHIVERS, T., Chemistry
CHUA, J. H., Haskayne School of Business
CHURCH, D. L., Pathology and Laboratory Medicine and Medicine
CHURCH, J. R., Economics
CLARK, A. W., Pathology and Laboratory Medicine and Clinical Neurosciences
CLARK, P. D., Chemistry
CLARKE, M. E., Paediatrics and Psychiatry
CLEVE, R. E., Computer Science
COCKETT, J. R. B., Computer Science
COELHO, V. A., Music
COLE, W. C., Pharmacology and Therapeutics
COLEMAN, H. D. J., Social Work
COLIJN, A. W., Computer Science
COLLINS, D. G., Social Work
COLLINS, J. R., Mathematics and Statistics
CONLY, J. M., Pathology and Laboratory Medicine
COOK, F. A., Geology and Geophysics
COOPER, F. B., Political Science
COPPES, M. J., Oncology and Paediatrics
CORENBLUM, B., Medicine
COUCH, W. E., Mathematics and Statistics
COWIE, R. L., Medicine and Community Health Sciences
CROSS, J. C., Biochemistry, Molecular Biology, Obstetrics and Gynaecology
CURRY, B., Pathology and Laboratory Medicine and Clinical Neurosciences
DAIS, E. E., Law
DANSEREAU, E. D. M., French, Italian and Spanish
DAVIES, J. M., Anaesthesia
DAVIES, W. K. D., Geography
DAVIS, R. C., English
DAVISON, J. S., Physiology and Biophysics
DAY, R. L., Civil Engineering
DEACON, P. G., Art
DELONG, K. G., Music
DEWEY, D. M., Paediatrics
DICKIN, J. P., Faculty of Communication and Culture
DICKINSON, J. A., Family Medicine and Community Health Sciences
DOBSON, K. S., Psychology
DORT, J. C., Surgery
DOWTY, A., Political Science
DRAPER, D. L., Geography
DUCKWORTH, K., Geology and Geophysics
DUGAN, J. S., Drama
DUGGAN, M. A., Pathology, Laboratory Medicine, Obstetrics and Gynaecology
DUNN, J. F., Radiology, Physiology and Biophysics
DUNSCOMBE, P. B., Oncology
DYCK, R. H., Psychology
EAGLE, C. J., Anaesthesia
EATON, B. C., Economics
EBERLY, W. M., Computer Science
EDWARDS, M. V., Music
EGGERMONT, J. J., Physiology and Biophysics and Psychology
EINSIEDEL, E. F., Communications and Culture
EL-BADRY, M. M., Civil Engineering
EL-GUEBALY, M. A., Psychiatry
EL-SHEIMY, N. M., Geomatics Engineering
ELHAJJ, R. S., Computer Science
ELLIOTT, R. J., Haskayne School of Business
ELOFSON, W. M., History
EMES, C. G., Kinesiology
ENGLE, J. M., Music
ENNS, R. E. G., Mathematics and Statistics
EPSTEIN, M., Mechanical and Manufacturing Engineering
ERESHEFSKY, M. F., Philosophy
ESLINGER, L. M., Religious Studies
FACCHINI, P. J., Biological Sciences
FARFAN, P. C. M., Drama and English
FATTOUCHE, M. T., Electrical and Computer Engineering

FAUVEL, O. R., Mechanical and Manufacturing Engineering
FEDIGAN, L. M., Anthropology
FERRIS, J. R., History
FEWELL, J. E., Obstetrics and Gynaecology, Paediatrics and Physiology and Biophysics
FICK, G. H., Community Health Sciences
FLANAGAN, T. E., Political Science
FLETCHER, W. A., Clinical Neurosciences and Surgery
FONG, T. C., Radiology
FORD, G. T., Medicine
FOREMAN, C. L., Music
FOREMAN, K. J., Drama
FOUTS, G. T., Psychology
FRANCIS, R. D., History
FRANK, A. W., Sociology
FRANK, C. B., Surgery
FRENCH, R. J., Physiology and Biophysics
FRIDERES, J. S., Sociology
FRIESEN, J. W., Faculty of Education
FRITZLER, M. J., Medicine, Biochemistry and Molecular Biology
FUJITA, D. J., Biochemistry and Molecular Biology
GABOR, P. A., Social Work
GAISFORD, J. D., Economics
GEDAMU, L., Biological Sciences
GETZ, D. P., Haskayne School of Business
GHALI, W. A., Medicine and Community Health Sciences
GHANNOUCHI, F., Electrical and Computer Engineering
GHENT, E. D., Geology and Geophysics
GILES, W. R., Physiology and Biophysics and Medicine
GILL, B., French, Italian and Spanish
GILL, M. J., Medicine
GILLIS, A. M., Medicine
GORDON, D. V., Economics
GORDON, T. M., Geology and Geophysics
GOREN, H. J., Biochemistry and Molecular Biology
GORESKY, G. V., Anaesthesia and Paediatrics
GRAHAM, J. R., Social Work
GRAVEL, R. A., Cell Biology and Anatomy
GREEN, F. H. Y., Pathology and Laboratory Medicine
GREENBERG, S., Computer Science
GU, P., Mechanical and Manufacturing Engineering
GUPTA, A., Management
HABIBI, H. R., Biological Science
HAGEN, N. A., Oncology and Medicine
HAJI, I. H., Philosophy
HALL, B. L., Social Work
HANLEY, D. A., Medicine
HANLEY, P. J., Medicine
HARASYM, P. H., Office of Medical Education and Community Health Sciences
HARDER, L. D., Biological Sciences
HARDING, T. G., Chemical and Petroleum Engineering
HARPER, T. L., Environmental Design
HART, D. A., Microbiology and Infectious Diseases, Medicine
HARTMAN, F. T., Civil Engineering
HASLETT, J. W., Electrical and Computer Engineering
HAWE, H. P., Community Health Sciences
HAWKES, R. B., Cell Biology and Anatomy
HAWKINS, R. W., Communication and Culture
HEBERT, Y. M., Faculty of Education
HECKEL, W., Greek and Roman Studies
HELMER, J. W., Archaeology
HENDERSON, C. M., Geology and Geophysics
HERMAN, R. J., Medicine
HERWIG, H. H., History
HERZOG, W., Kinesiology
HETTIARATCHI, J. P. A., Civil Engineering
HEXHAM, I. R., Religious Studies
HEYMAN, R. D., Faculty of Education
HIEBERT, B. A., Division of Applied Psychology
HILLER, H. H., Sociology

HO, M., Microbiology, Infectious Diseases and Medicine
HODGINS, D. C., Psychology
HOGAN, D. B., Medicine and Clinical Neurosciences and Community Health Sciences
HOLLENBERG, M. D., Pharmacology and Therapeutics
HU, B., Clinical Neurosciences, Cell Biology and Anatomy
HUBER, R. E., Biological Sciences
HUGHES, M. E., Law
HULL, R. D., Medicine
HULLIGER, M., Clinical Neurosciences and Physiology and Biophysics
HUNT, J. D., Civil Engineering
HUSHLAK, G. M., Art
HYNES, M. F., Biological Sciences
IRVINE-HALLIDAY, D., Electrical and Computer Engineering
ISMAEL, J. S., Social Work
ISMAEL, T. Y., Political Science
JACOB, J. C., Faculty of Education
JADAVJI, T., Microbiology and Infectious Diseases and Paediatrics
JAMESON, E., History
JARDINE, D. W., Faculty of Education
JARRELL, J. F., Obstetrics and Gynaecology
JEJE, A. A., Chemical and Petroleum Engineering
JENNETT, P. A., Office of Medical Education and Community Health Sciences
JIRIK, F. R., Biochemistry and Molecular Biology
JOHNSON, E. A., Biological Sciences
JOHNSON, J. M., Obstetrics and Gynaecology
JOHNSTON, R. H., Electrical and Computer Engineering
JOHNSTON, R. N., Biochemistry and Molecular Biology
JOLDERSMA, H., Germanic, Slavic and East Asian Studies
JONES, A. R., Medicine and Oncology
JONES, D. C., Faculty of Education
JONES, V. J., Haskayne School of Business
JORDAN, W. S., Music
JOY, M. M., Religious Studies
JULLIEN, G. A., Electrical and Computer Engineering
KALBACH, M. H., Sociology
KALER, K. V. I., Electrical and Computer Engineering
KANTZAS, A., Chemical and Petroleum Engineering
KAPLAN, B. J., Paediatrics
KARGACIN, G. J., Physiology and Biophysics
KARIM, G. A., Mechanical and Manufacturing Engineering
KATZENBERG, M. A., Archaeology
KAUFFMAN, S. A., Biological Sciences, Physics and Astronomy
KAWAMURA, L. S., Religious Studies
KEAY, B. A., Chemistry
KEENAN, T. P., Environmental Design
KEITH, D. W., Chemical and Petroleum Engineering and Economics
KEITH, R. C., Political Science
KELLNER, J. D., Paediatrics, Microbiology and Infectious Diseases
KEREN, M., Communication and Culture and Political Science
KERTZER, A. E., English
KERTZER, J. M., English
KLASSEN, J., Pathology and Laboratory Medicine and Medicine
KLINE, D. W., Psychology
KLINE, T. J., Psychology
KNEEBONE, R. D., Economics
KNOLL, R. J., Law
KNOPFF, R., Political Science
KNUDTSON, M. L., Cardiac Sciences and Medicine
KOOPMANS, H. S., Physiology and Biophysics and Psychology
KOOYMAN, B. P., Archaeology
KOSTYNIUK, R. P., Art
KRAUSE, F. F., Geology and Geophysics

KREBES, E. S., Geology and Geophysics
KUBES, P., Physiology and Biophysics and Medicine
KURTZ, S. M., Education
LACHAPELLE, G. J., Geomatics Engineering
LAFLAMME, C., Mathematics and Statistics
LAFRENIÈRE, R., Surgery
LAI, D. W. L., Social Work
LAING, W. J. H., Art
LAMOUREUX, M. P., Mathematics and Statistics
LANGE, I. R., Obstetrics and Gynaecology
LARTER, S. R., Geology and Geophysics
LAU, D. C. W., Medicine
LAWTON, D. C., Geology and Geophysics
LEAHY, D. A., Physics and Astronomy
LEE, S. S., Medicine
LEE, T. G., Environmental Design
LEES-MILLER, S. P., Biochemistry and Molecular Biology
LEON, L. J., Electrical and Computer Engineering
LEUNG, H. K. Y., Electrical and Computer Engineering
LEVIN, G. J., Music
LEVY, J. C., Law
LEVY, R. M., Environmental Design
LEWKONIA, R. M., Medicine and Paediatrics and Medical Genetics
LINES, L. R., Geology and Geophysics
LOUIE, T. J., Medicine, Microbiology and Infectious Diseases
LOUTZENHISER, R. D., Pharmacology and Therapeutics
LOVE, J. A., Environmental Design
LUCAS, A. R., Law
LUKASIEWICZ, S. A., Mechanical and Manufacturing Engineering
LUKOWIAK, K., Physiology and Biophysics
LYTTON, J., Biochemistry, Molecular Biology, Physiology and Biophysics
MCCALLUM, P. M., English
MCCAULEY, F. E. R., Biological Sciences
MCCLELLAND, R. W., Social Work
MCCONNELL, C. S., Art
MCCREADY, W. O., Religious Studies
MCCULLOUGH, D. T., Drama
MACDONALD, D. L., English
MCGHEE, J. D., Biochemistry and Molecular Biology
MCGILLIS, R. F., English
MCGILLIVRAY, M. D., English
MACINTOSH, B. R., Kinesiology
MACINTOSH, J. J., Philosophy
MCKENZIE, K. J., Economics
MCKEOUGH, A. M., Division of Applied Psychology
MCKINNON, J. G., Surgery and Oncology
MCMORDIE, M. J., Environmental Design, Communication and Culture
MCMULLAN, W. E., Haskayne School of Business
MACNAUGHTON, W. K., Physiology and Biophysics
MCRAE, R. N., Economics
MCWHIR, A. R., English
MAES, M. A., Civil Engineering
MAHER, P. M., Haskayne School of Business
MAHONEY, K. E., Law
MAINI, B. B., Chemical and Petroleum Engineering
MAINS, P. E., Biochemistry and Molecular Biology
MANDIN, H., Medicine
MARTIN, R. H., Paediatrics and Medical Genetics
MARTIN, S. L., Law
MARTINUZZI, R., Mechanical and Manufacturing Engineering
MASH, E. J., Psychology
MATO, D., Art
MAURER, F. O., Computer Science
MEDDINGS, J. B., Medicine
MEEUWISSE, W. H., Kinesiology
MEHROTRA, A. K., Chemical and Petroleum Engineering

MEHTA, S. A., Chemical and Petroleum Engineering
MIDHA, R., Clinical Neurosciences
MILONE, E. F., Physics and Astronomy
MINTCHEV, M. P., Electrical and Computer Engineering
MITCHELL, D. B., Communication and Culture
MITCHELL, I., Paediatrics
MITCHELL, L. B., Cardiac Science and Medicine
MITCHELL, S. H., Education
MOAZZEN-AHMADI, N., Physics and Astronomy
MOCQUAIS, P. Y. A., French, Italian and Spanish
MODY, C. H., Medicine, Microbiology and Infectious Diseases
MOHAMAD, A. A., Mechanical and Maufacturing Engineering
MOLLIN, R. A., Mathematics and Statistics
MOORE, R. G., Chemical and Petroleum Engineering
MORCK, D. W., Biological Sciences
MORTON, F. L., Political Science
MUELLER, J. H., Division of Applied Psychology
MUNRO, M. C., Haskayne School of Business
MURPHREE, J. S., Physics and Astronomy
MURRAY, R. W., Linguistics
MURRAY, S. C., Kinesiology
MUZIK, I., Civil Engineering
MYLES, S. T., Surgery and Clinical Neurosciences
NATION, J. G., Obstetrics and Gynaecology and Oncology
NAULT, B. R., Haskayne School of Business
NEU, D. E., Haskayne School of Business
NEUFELDT, A. H., Faculty of Education
NEUFELDT, R. W., Religious Studies
NICHOLSON, W. K., Mathematics and Statistics
NIELSON, N., Haskayne School of Business
NIGG, B. M., Kinesiology
NKEMDIRIM, L. C., Geography
NORTON, P. G., Family Medicine
NOSAL, M., Mathematics and Statistics
NOSEWORTHY, T. W., Community Health Sciences
OETELAAR, G. A., Archaeology
OKONIEWSKI, M., Electrical and Computer Engineering
OSBORN, G. D., Geology and Geophysics
OSLER, M. J., History
PARKER, J. R., Computer Science
PATTISON, D. R. M., Geology and Geophysics
PAUL, R., Chemistry
PEREIRA ALMAO, P. R., Chemical and Petroleum Engineering
PERL, A. D., Political Science
PERREAULT, J. M., English
PIERS, W. E., Chemistry
PINEO, G. F., Medicine and Oncology
PITTMAN, Q. J., Physiology and Biophysics
POLLAK, P. T., Medicine, Cardiac Sciences, Pharmacology and Therapeutics
PONAK, A. M., Haskayne School of Business
PONTING, J. R., Sociology
POON, M.-C., Medicine and Paediatrics
POST, J. R., Biological Sciences
POWELL, D. G., Family Medicine
PRICE, G. D., Music
PROUD, D., Physiology and Biophysics
PRUSINKIEWICZ, P., Computer Science
PYRCH, T., Social Work
RABIN, H. R., Microbiology, Infectious Diseases and Medicine
RADTKE, H. L., Psychology
RAFFERTY, N. S., Law
RAMRAJ, V. J., English
RANGACHARI, P. K., Pharmacology and Therapeutics
RANGAYYAN, R. M., Electrical and Computer Engineering
RASPORICH, B. J., Communication and Culture

RATTNER, J. B., Cell Biology and Anatomy and Biochemistry and Molecular Biology and Oncology
RAY, D. I., Political Science
RAYMOND, S., Archaeology
REID, D. M., Biological Sciences
REMMERS, J. E., Medicine, Physiology and Biophysics
REVEL, R. D., Environmental Design
REYNOLDS, J. D., Physiology, Biophysics and Medicine
RIABOWOL, K. T., Biochemistry and Molecular Biology
RIEDIGER, C. L., Geology and Geophysics
RITCHIE, J. R. B., Haskayne School of Business
ROBERTSON, S. E., Division of Applied Psychology
ROHLEDER, T. R., Haskayne School of Business
ROKNE, J. G., Computer Science
RONSKY, J. L., Mechanical and Manufacturing Engineering
RORSTAD, O. P., Medicine
ROSS, W. A., Environmental Design
ROTH, S. H., Pharmacology and Therapeutics, and Anaesthesia
ROTHERY, M. A., Social Work
ROUNTHWAITE, H. I., Law
ROWNEY, J. I. A., Haskayne School of Business
ROWSE, J. G., Economics
RUDY, S. A., English
RUHE, G., Computer Science and Electrical and Computer Engineering
RUSSELL, A. P., Biological Sciences
SAINSBURY, R. S., Psychology
SAMUELS, M. T., Division of Applied Psychology
SANDERS, B. C., Physics and Astronomy
SANDS, G. W., Mathematics and Statistics
SANTAMARIA, P., Microbiology and Infectious Diseases
SARNAT, H. B., Paediatrics, Clinical Neurosciences Pathology and Laboratory Medicine
SAUER, N. W., Mathematics and Statistics
SAUNDERS, I. B., Law
SAUVE, R. S., Paediatrics and Community Health Sciences
SCHACHAR, N. S., Surgery
SCHNETKAMP, P. P. M., Biochemistry and Molecular Biology, and Physiology and Biophysics
SCHRYVERS, A. B., Microbiology and Infectious Diseases
SCHULZ, R. A., Haskayne School of Business
SCHWARZ, K.-P., Geomatics Engineering
SCIALFA, C. T., Psychology
SCOLLNIK, D. P. M., Mathematics and Statistics
SCOTT, R. B., Paediatrics
SEGAL, E. L., Religious Studies
SENSEN, C. W., Biochemistry and Molecular Biology
SERLETIS, A., Economics
SESAY, A. B., Electrical and Computer Engineering
SETTARI, A., Chemical and Petroleum Engineering
SEVERSON, D. L., Pharmacology and Therapeutics
SHAFFER, E. A., Medicine
SHANTZ, D. H., Religious Studies
SHAPIRO, B. L., Education
SHARKEY, K. A., Physiology and Biophysics
SHAW, W. J. D., Mechanical and Manufacturing Engineering
SHELDON, R. S., Medicine
SHIELL, A. M., Community Health Sciences
SHRIVE, N. G., Civil Engineering
SICK, G. A., Haskayne School of Business
SIDERIS, M. G., Geomatics Engineering
SIMMINS, G., Art
SINGHAL, N., Paediatrics
SMART, A., Anthropology

SMART, P. J., Anthropology
SMITH, D. D. B., History
SMITH, D. G., Geography
SMITH, D. J., Kinesiology
SMITH, F. R., Physiology and Biophysics
SMITH, G. B., Drama
SMITH, M. R., Electrical and Computer Engineering
SNIATYCKI, J. Z., Mathematics and Statistics
SNYDER, F. F., Paediatrics, Medical Biochemistry and Medical Biology
SOKOL, P. A., Microbiology and Infectious Diseases
SPENCER, R. J., Geology and Geophysics
SPRATT, D. A., Geology and Geophysics
STALKER, M. A., Law
STAM, H. J., Psychology
STAMP, R. M., Education
STAUM, M. S., History
STELL, W. K., Cell Biology and Anatomy and Surgery
STEWART, R. R., Geology and Geophysics
STOCKING, J. R., Art
STOREY, D. G., Biological Sciences
STOUGHTON, N. M., Haskayne School of Business
SUCHOWERSKY, O., Clinical Neurosciences
SUTHERLAND, C. T., Communication and Culture
SUTHERLAND, F. R., Surgery and Oncology
SUTHERLAND, G. R., Clinical Neurosciences
SUTHERLAND, L. R., Medicine and Community Health Sciences
SVRCEK, W. Y., Chemical and Petroleum Engineering
SWAIN, M. G., Medicine
SYED, N. I. S., Cell Biology, Anatomy, Physiology and Biophysics
TARAS, D., Communication and Culture
TARAS, D. G., Haskayne School of Business
TAY, R. S. T., Civil Engineering
TAYLOR, A. R., Physics and Astronomy
TAYLOR, M. S., Economics
TEMPLE, W. J., Surgery and Oncology
TER KEURS, H. E. D., Cardiac Sciences, Medicine, Physiology and Biophysics
TESKEY, G. C., Psychology
TESKEY, W. F., Geomatics Engineering
THOMAS, R. E., Family Medicine
THOMPSON, D. A. R., Environmental Design
THURSTON, W. E., Community Health Sciences
TIELEMAN, D. P., Biological Sciences
TOEWS, J. A., Psychiatry
TOMM, K. M., Psychiatry
TOOHEY, P. G., Greek and Roman Studies
TREBBLE, M. A., Chemical and Petroleum Engineering
TRIGGLE, C. R., Pharmacology and Therapeutics
TRUTE, B., Social Work and Nursing
TSENKOVA, S., Environmental Design
TURNER, L. E., Electrical and Computer Engineering
TURNER, R. W., Cell Biology, Anatomy, Physiology and Biophysics
TUTTY, L. M., Social Work
TYBERG, J. V., Cardiac Sciences, Medicine, Physiology and Biophysics
UNGER, B. W., Computer Science
URBANSKI, S. J., Pathology and Laboratory Medicine
VANBALKOM, W. D., Education
VAN DER HOORN, F. A., Biochemistry and Molecular Biology
VANDERSPOEL, J., Greek and Roman Studies
VAN DE SANDE, J. H., Biochemistry and Molecular Biology
VAN HERK, A., English
VAN ROSENDAAL, G. M. A., Medicine
VEALE, W. L., Physiology and Biophysics
VERBEKE, A. C. M., Haskayne School of Business
VERHOEF, M. J., Community Health Sciences and Medicine
VICKERS, J. N., Kinesiology

VINOGRADOV, O., Mechanical and Manufacturing Engineering
VIOLATO, C., Community Health Sciences
VIZE, P. D., Biological Sciences
VOGEL, H. J., Biological Sciences
VOORDOUW, G., Biological Sciences
VREDENBURG, H., Haskayne School of Business
WAISMAN, D. M., Biochemistry and Molecular Biology
WALKER, D. C., French, Italian and Spanish
WALKER, S., Environmental Design
WALL, A. J., French, Latin and Spanish
WALLACE, J. L., Physiology and Biophysics, and Pharmacology and Therapeutics and Medicine
WALLS, W. D., Economics
WALSH, M. P., Biochemistry and Molecular Biology
WAN, R. G., Civil Engineering
WANG, Y., Electrical and Computer Engineering
WANNER, R. A., Sociology
WARNICA, J. W., Cardiac Sciences and Medicine
WATERS, N. M., Geography
WEBBER, C. F., Education
WEISS, S., Cell Biology and Anatomy and Pharmacology and Therapeutics
WESTRA, H. J., Greek and Roman Studies
WHITE, T. H., Haskayne School of Business
WHITELAW, W. A., Medicine
WIEBE, S., Clinical Neurosciences, Paediatrics and Community Health Sciences
WIERZBA, I., Mechanical and Manufacturing Engineering
WILLIAMS, H. C., Mathematics and Statistics
WILLIAMSON, C. L., Computer Science
WILMAN, E. A., Economics
WILSON, M. G., Social Work
WINCHESTER, W. I. S., Education
WONG, N. C. W., Medicine
WONG, R. C. K., Civil Engineering
WONG, S. L., Biological Sciences
WOODROW, P., Art
WOODROW, R. E., Mathematics and Statistics
WOODS, D. E., Microbiology and Infectious Diseases
WRIGHT, L. M., Nursing
WU, P. P. C., Geology and Geophysics
WYVILL, B. L. M., Computer Science
YACOWAR, M., Art
YANG, X. J., Germanic, Slavic and East Asian Studies
YAU, A. W., Physics and Astronomy
YEUNG, E. C. J., Biological Sciences
YONG, V. W., Oncology and Clinical Neurosciences
YOON, J. W., Microbiology and Infectious Diseases and Paediatrics
YOUNG, D. B., Biochemistry, Molecular Biology and Oncology
ZAMPONI, G. W., Physiology, Biophysics, Pharmacology and Therapeutics
ZANZOTTO, L., Civil Engineering
ZAPF, M. K., Social Work
ZEKULIN, N. G. A., Germanic, Slavic and East Asian Studies
ZIEGLER, T., Chemistry
ZOCHODNE, D. W., Clinical Neurosciences
ZVENGROWSKI, P. D., Mathematics and Statistics

CAPE BRETON UNIVERSITY

POB 5300, 1250 Grand Lake Rd, Sydney, NS
B1P 6L2

Telephone: (902) 563-1330
Fax: (902) 563-1371
E-mail: registrar@capebretonu.ca
Internet: www.capebretonu.ca

Founded 1974
State control
Language of instruction: English
Academic year: September to April

Chancellor: ANNETTE VERSCHUREN
Pres. and Vice-Chancellor: JOHN HARKER
Vice-Pres. for Academic and Research: Dr ANTHONY SECCO
Vice-Pres. for Devt: Dr KEITH BROWN
Vice-Pres. for Finance and Operations: GORDON MACINNIS
Vice-Pres. Student Services and Registrar: ALEXIS MANLEY
Dean of Research: Dr HARVEY JOHNSTONE
Library of 532,290 vols, 800 periodicals
Number of teachers: 153
Number of students: 3,600

Depts of education, mathematics, physics and geology, nutrition, nursing, psychology, public health

DEANS

School of Arts and Community Studies: Dr J. ARTHUR TUCKER
School of Business Studies: JOHN MACKINNON
School of Education, Health, and Wellness: Dr JANE LEWIS
School of Science and Technology: Dr ALLEN BRITTEN

ATTACHED RESEARCH INSTITUTES

The mailing address is that of the University

Beaton Institute: repository of Cape Breton social, economic, political and cultural history; Dir WENDY ROBICHEAU.

Children's Rights Centre: f. 1996; conducts research and provides public education on children's rights; monitors implementation of UN Children's Rights Convention in Nova Scotia and Canada; Co-Dir Prof. KATHERINE COVELL; Co-Dir Prof. BRIAN HOWE.

Community Economic Development Institute: f. 1996 to provide support, training, policy advice and research in community economic development; Dir Dr GERTRUDE MACINTYRE.

CARLETON UNIVERSITY

1125 Colonel By Drive, Ottawa, ON K1S 5B6
Telephone: (613) 520-2600
Fax: (613) 520-3847
E-mail: infocarleton@carleton.ca
Internet: www.carleton.ca

Founded 1942
Provincial control
Language of instruction: English
Academic year: September to May

Chancellor: MARC GARNEAU
Pres. and Vice-Chancellor: Dr RICHARD VAN LOON
Vice-Pres. for Academic Affairs and Provost: ALAN HARRISON
Vice-Pres. for Advancement: LUCINDA BOUCHER
Vice-Pres. for Finance and Administration: DUNCAN WATT
Vice-Pres. for Research: FERIDUN HAMDULLAHPUR
Asst Vice-Pres. for Development and Alumni: SERGE ARPIN
Asst Vice-Pres. for Enrolment Management: SUSAN GOTTHEIL
Librarian: MARTIN FOSS
Library: see Libraries and Archives
Number of teachers: 786
Number of students: 22,535
Publications: *Research and Works* (4 a year), *The President's Report* (1 a year)

DEANS

Faculty of Arts and Social Science: MICHAEL SMITH
Faculty of Engineering: SAMI MAHMOUD
Faculty of Public Affairs and Management: KATHERINE GRAHAM
Faculty of Science: JEAN-GUY GODIN

Faculty of Graduate Studies and Research: ROGER BLOCKLEY

CHAIRS AND DIRECTORS

Faculty of Arts and Social Science (330 Paterson Hall, 1125 Colonel By Drive, Ottawa, ON K1S 5B6; tel. (613) 520-2355; fax (613) 520-4481; internet www.carleton .ca/fass):

  Canadian Studies: F. ROCHER
  English Language and Literature: R. HOLTON
  Environmental Studies: N. DOUBLEDAY
  French: C. DOUTRELEPONT
  Geography: S. DALBY
  History: E. P. FITZGERALD
  Humanities: S. WILSON
  Interdisciplinary Studies: K. ARNUP
  Philosophy: J. DRYDYK
  Psychology: J. LOGAN (acting)
  Sociology and Anthropology: C. GORDON
  Studies in Art and Culture: B. GILLIINGHAM (acting)
  Women's Studies: P. RANKIN
  Centre for Applied Language Studies: I. PRINGLE

Faculty of Engineering (3010 Minto Centre, 1125 Colonel By Drive, Ottawa, ON K1S 5B6; tel. (613) 520-5790; fax (613) 520-7481; internet www.carleton.ca/ engineeringdesign):

  Architecture: G. HAIDER
  Civil and Environmental Engineering: G. HARTLEY (acting)
  Electronics: L. ROY
  Industrial Design: L. FRANKEL
  Mechanical and Aerospace Engineering: R. BELL
  Systems and Computer Engineering: R. GOUBRAN

Faculty of Public Affairs and Management (D391 Loeb Building, 1125 Colonel By Drive, Ottawa, ON K1S 5B6; tel. (613) 520-3741; fax (613) 520-3742; e-mail melanie_thompson@ carleton.ca; internet www.carleton.ca/pam):

  Business: V. KUMAR
  Criminology and Criminal Justice: B. WRIGHT
  Economics: A. RITTER
  European and Russian Studies: P. DUTKIEWICZ
  International Affairs: F. HAMPSON
  Journalism and Communication: C. DORNAN
  Law: C. SWAN
  Political Economy: R. MAHON
  Political Science: C. BROWN
  Public Administration: L. PAL
  Social Work: C. LUNDY

Faculty of Science (3239 Herzberg Laboratories, 1125 Colonel By Drive, Ottawa, ON K1S 5B6; tel. (613) 520-4388; fax (613) 520-4389; e-mail odscience@ccs.carleton.ca; internet www.carleton.ca/science):

  Biochemistry: M. SMITH
  Biology: J. CHEETHAM
  Chemistry: G. BUCHANAN
  Computational Sciences: L. COPLEY
  Computer Science: D. HOWE
  Earth Sciences: C. SCHROEDER-ADAMS
  Environmental Science: D. WIGFIELD
  Geography: S. DALBY
  Integrated Science Studies: I. MUNRO
  Mathematics and Statistics: C. GARNER
  Physics: P. KALYNDAK
  Psychology: J. LOGAN

CONCORDIA UNIVERSITY

Sir George Williams Campus, 1455 de Maisonneuve Blvd West, Montréal, QC H3G 1M8

Loyola Campus, 7141 Sherbrooke St West, Montréal, QC H4B 1R6

Telephone: (514) 848-2424
Fax: (514) 848-3494
Internet: www.concordia.ca

Founded 1974 by merger of Sir George Williams University (established 1948) and Loyola College (incorporated 1899)
Provincial control
Language of instruction: English
Academic year: May to April

Chancellor and University Secretariat: ERIC MOLSON
Pres. and Vice-Chancellor: Prof. FREDERICK H. LOWY
Provost: DAVID GRAHAM
Vice Provost for Academic Affairs: ROBERT M. ROY
Vice Provost for Academic Relations: RAMA BHAT
Vice-Provost for Teaching and Learning: OLLIVIER DYENS
Exec. Dir for Office of the Pres.: GARY MILTON
Registrar: LINDA HEALEY
Director of Libraries: GERALD BEASLEY

Library: see Libraries and Archives
Number of teachers: 1,837 (884 full-time, 953 part-time)
Number of students: 31,175
Publications: *Canadian Jewish Studies* (1 a year), *Canadian Journal of Irish Studies* (2 a year), *Canadian Journal of Research in Early Childhood Education* (2 a year), *Journal of Canadian Art History/Annales d'Histoire de L'art Canadien* (2 a year), *Journal of Religion and Culture* (1 a year), *Revue de l'Institut Simone de Beauvoir Institute Review* (1 a year)

DEANS

Faculty of Arts and Science: BRIAN LEWIS
Faculty of Engineering and Computer Science: ROBIN DREW
Faculty of Fine Arts: CATHERINE WILD
John Molson School of Business: SANJAY SHARMA
School of Graduate Studies and Research: BINA FREIWALD (Dir)

DIRECTORS

Applied Psychology Centre: M. DUGAS
Centre for the Arts in Human Development: P. ABRAMI
Centre for Building Studies: R. ZMEUREANU
Centre for Canadian-Irish Studies: M. KENNEALLY
Centre for Community and Ethnic Studies: D. SALEE
Centre for Continuing Education: M. SANG
Centre for Digital Arts: J. CEZAR
Centre for Human Relations and Community Studies: S. DINAN
Centre for Industrial Control: (vacant)
Centre for International Academic Cooperation: B. SAHNI
Centre for Mature Students: R. OPPENHEIMER
Centre for Native Education: M. TREMBLAY
Centre for Research in Human Development: L. SERBIN
Centre for Signal Processing and Communications: M. N. S. SWAMY
Centre for Structural and Functional Genomics: M. GUEST
Centre for Studies in Behavioural Neurobiology: B. WOODSIDE
Centre for the Study of Learning and Performance: (vacant)
Centre for Teaching and Learning Services: O. ROVINESCU

Concordia Centre for Broadcasting Studies: G. NIELSEN
Concordia Centre for Composites: S. V. HOA
Concordia Centre for Pattern Recognition and Machine Intelligence: C. Y. SUEN
Concordia Centre for Small Business and Entrepreneurial Studies: A. IBRAHIM
Concordia Computer-Aided Vehicle Engineering: I. STIHARU
Concordia Institute for Aerospace Design and Innovation: H. MOUSTAPHA
Concordia Institute for Information Systems Engineering: R. DSSOULI
Interuniversity Centre for Algebraic Computation: H. KISILEVSKY
Montrèal Institute for Genocide and Human Rights Studies: F. CHALK, K. JONASSOHN

DALHOUSIE UNIVERSITY

Halifax, NS B3H 4H6

Telephone: (902) 494-2450
Fax: (902) 494-1630
E-mail: registrar@dal.ca
Internet: www.dal.ca

Founded 1818; merged with Technical Univ. of Nova Scotia 1997
Private control
Language of instruction: English
Academic year: September to August

Chancellor: Dr FRED FOUNTAIN
Pres. and Vice-Chancellor: THOMAS D. TRAVES
Vice-Pres. for Academic and Provost: A.SHAVER
Vice-Pres. for External: F. DYKEMAN
Vice-Pres. for Finance and Admin: K. BURT
Vice-Pres. for Research: M. CRAGO
Vice-Pres. for Student Services: BONNIE NEUMAN
Registrar: ASA KACHAN
Librarian: W. MAES

Library: see Libraries
Number of teachers: 1,860 (full- and part-time)
Number of students: 11,600 full-time, 3,700 part-time, 1,180 international

DEANS

Faculty of Architecture: C. MACY
Faculty of Arts and Social Sciences: M. E. BINKLEY
Faculty of Computer Science: M. SHEPHERD
Faculty of Dentistry: T. BORAN
Faculty of Engineering: J. LEON
Faculty of Graduate Studies: C. WATTERS
Faculty of Health Professions: WILLIAM WEBSTER
Faculty of Law: PHILLIP SAUNDERS
Faculty of Management: D. WHEELER (acting)
Faculty of Medicine: H. COOK (acting)
Faculty of Science: M. LEONARD

PROFESSORS

Faculty of Architecture (tel. (902) 494-3971; fax (902) 423-6672; e-mail arch.office@dal.ca; internet archplan.dal.ca):

CAVANAGH, E., Architecture
GRANT, J., Planning
KROEKER, R., Architecture
MacKAY-LYONS, B., Architecture
MACY, C., Architecture
PALERMO, F., Planning
POULTON, M., Planning
PROCOS, D., Architecture
WANZEL, J., Architecture

Faculty of Arts and Social Sciences (tel. (902) 494-1440; fax (902) 494-1957; e-mail fass@dal.ca):

APOSTLE, R., Sociology and Social Anthropology
AUCOIN, P. C., Political Science
BAKVIS, H., Political Science
BARKER, W., English

BARKOW, J. H., Sociology and Social Anthropology
BAXTER, J., English
BAYLIS, F., Philosophy
BEDNARSKI, H. E., French
BINKLEY, M. E., Sociology and Social Anthropology
BOARDMAN, R., Political Science
BURNS, S., Philosophy
CAMPBELL, R. M., Philosophy
CROWLEY, J. E., History
CURRAN, J. V., German (Chair.)
DAVIS, J., Political Science
DE MEO, P., French
DIEPEVEEN, L. P., English
FURROW, M. M., English
HANKEY, W., Classics (King's)
HANLON, G., History
HARVEY, F., Political Science
HUEBERT, R., English
KIRK, J. M., Spanish
LI, T. J., Sociology and Social Anthropology
LUCKYJ, C., English
MARTIN, R., Philosophy
MIDDLEMISS, D., Political Science
NEVILLE, C., History (Chair.)
OORE, I., French
OVERTON, D. R., Theatre
PARPART, J., International Development Studies
PEREIRA, N. G. O., History and Russian
PERINA, P., Theatre
RUNTE, H. R., French
SHAW, T. W., Political Science
SCHOTCH, P., Philosophy
SCHROEDER, D., Music
SCHWARZ, H. G., German
SCULLY, S., Classics
SERVANT, G. W., Music
SHERWIN, S., Philosophy
SMITH, J., Political Science (Chair.)
STARNES, C. J., Classics (King's)
STONE, M. I., English
TETREAULT, R., English
THIESSEN, V., Sociology and Social Anthropology
TRAVES, T., History
VINCI, T., Philosophy
WAINWRIGHT, J. A., English and Canadian Studies
WATERSON, K., French

Faculty of Computer Science (tel. (902) 494-2093; fax (902) 492-1517):

BODORIK, P.
BORWEIN, J.
BROWN, J. I.
COX, P.
FARRAG, A.
GENTLEMAN, M.
GRUNDKE, E.
HITCHCOCK, P.
JOST, A.
KEAST, P.
MacDONALD, N.
MILOS, E.
RAU-CHAPLIN, A.
RIORDAN, D.
SAMPALLI, S.
SCRIMGER, J. N.
SHEPHERD, M.
SLONIM, J.
WACH, G.
WATTERS, C. R.

Faculty of Dentistry (tel. (902) 494-2824; fax (902) 494-2527):

LEE, J. M., Applied Oral Sciences
LONEY, R., Dental Clinical Sciences
PRECIOUS, D. S., Oral and Maxillofacial Science
PRICE, R. B. T., Dental Clinical Science
RYDING, H. A., Applied Oral Sciences (Acting Chair.)
SUTOW, E. J., Applied Oral Sciences

Faculty of Engineering (tel. (902) 494-3267; fax (902) 429-3011; e-mail dean .engineering@dal.ca):

ALI, N. A., Civil Engineering
ALLEN, P., Mechanical Engineering
AL-TAWEEL, A., Chemical Engineering
AMYOTTE, P., Chemical Engineering
BASU, P., Mechanical Engineering
BEN-ABDALLAH, N., Biological Engineering (Head)
CADA, M., Electrical and Computer Engineering
CALEY, W. F., Mining and Metallurgical Engineering
CHEN, Z., Electrical and Computer Engineering
CHUANG, J. M., Mechanical Engineering
EL-HAWARY, M., Electrical and Computer Engineering
EL-MASRY, E., Electrical and Computer Engineering (Head)
FELS, M., Chemical Engineering
FENTON, G., Engineering Mathematics
GHALY, A., Biological Engineering
GILL, T., Food Science and Technology
GREGSON, P., Electrical and Computer Engineering
GUNN, E., Industrial Engineering
GUPTA, Y., Chemical Engineering (Head)
HUGHES, F. L., Electrical and Computer Engineering
ISLAM, M., Civil Engineering
KALAMKAROV, A., Mechanical Engineering
KEMBER, G., Engineering Mathematics
KIPOUROS, G., Mining and Metallurgical Engineering
KUJATH, M., Mechanical Engineering
MILITZER, J., Mechanical Engineering
PAULSON, A. T., Food Science and Technology
PEGG, M., Chemical Engineering
PHILLIPS, W., Engineering Mathematics (Head)
RAHMAN, M., Engineering Mathematics
ROBERTSON, W., Engineering Mathematics
ROCKWELL, M., Mining and Metallurgical Engineering
SANDBLOM, C., Industrial Engineering
SATISH, M., Civil Engineering
SPEERS, R. A., Food Science and Technology (Head)
TROTTIER, J.-F., Civil Engineering
UGURSAL, M., Mechanical Engineering
WATTS, K., Biological and Mechanical Engineering
YEMENIDJIAN, N., Mining and Metallurgical Engineering (Head)
ZOU, D. H., Mining and Metallurgical Engineering

Faculty of Health Professions (tel. (902) 494-3327; fax (902) 494-1966; internet healthprofessions.dal.ca):

School of Health and Human Performance:
HOLT, L. E.
LYONS, R. F.
MALONEY, T.
SINGLETON, J.
UNRUH, A.

School of Health Services Administration:
MCINTYRE, L.
NESTMAN, L.
RATHWELL, T. (Dir)

School of Nursing:
BUTLER, L. (Dir)
DOWNE-WAMBOLDT, B. (Dir)
KEDDY, B. A.

School of Occupational Therapy:
TOWNSEND, E. (Dir)

College of Pharmacy:
SKETRIS, I.
YEUNG, P. K. F.

School of Physiotherapy:
KOZEY, C. L.
MAKRIDES, L. (Dir)
TURNBULL, G. I.

Maritime School of Social Work:
DIVINE, D.
WIEN, F. C.

Faculty of Law (tel. (902) 494-3495; fax (902) 494-1316; e-mail lawinfo@dal.ca):

ARCHIBALD, B.
BLACK, V.
DEVLIN, R.
KAISER, H. A.
KINDRED, H. M.
MCCONNELL, M. L.
MACKAY, A. W.
POTHIER, D. L.
THOMAS, P.
THOMPSON, D. A. R.
THORNHILL, E. M. A.
VANDERZWAGG, D.
WOODMAN, F. L.
YOGIS, J. A.

Faculty of Management (tel. (902) 494-2582; fax (902) 494-1195; internet www .management.dal.ca):

School of Business Administration:
BROOKS, M. R.
CONRAD, J.
DUFFY, J.
FOOLADI, I.
MACLEAN, L. C.
MCNIVEN, J. D.
MEALIEA, L. W.
OPPONG, A.
ROSSON, P.
SANKAR, Y.
SCHELLINCK, D. A.

School of Public Administration:
AUCOIN, P. C.
BAKVIS, H.
BROWN, M. P.
MCNIVEN, J. D.
SIDDIQ, F.
SULLIVAN, K.
TRAVES, T.

School of Resource and Environmental Studies:
COHEN, F. G.
CÔTÉ, R.
DUINKER, P. (Dir)
WILLISON, J. H.

Faculty of Medicine (tel. (902) 494-6592; fax (902) 494-7119; e-mail dean.medicine@dal .ca; internet www.medicine.dal.ca):

ALDA, H., Psychiatry
ALEXANDER, D., Surgery
ALLEN, A. C., Paediatrics, Obstetrics and Gynaecology
ANDERSON, D. R., Medicine, Community Health and Epidemiology
ANDERSON, P. A., Urology
ANDERSON, R., Microbiology and Immunology
ARMSON, A., Obstetrics and Gynaecology
ATTIA, E., Surgery
BARNES, S., Physiology and Biophysics, Ophthalmology
BASKETT, T., Obstetrics and Gynaecology
BAYLIS, F., Bioethics
BENSTED, T., Medicine
BITTER-SUERMANN, H., Surgery
BLAY, J., Pharmacology
BONJER, H. J., Surgery
BORTOLUSSI, R., Paediatrics
BRECKENRIDGE, W. C., Biochemistry
BROWN, M. G., Community Health and Epidemiology
BRYSON, S., Paediatrics
BYERS, D., Paediatrics
CAMERON, I., Family Medicine
CAMFIELD, C., Paediatrics

CAMFIELD, P. R., Paediatrics
CASSON, A., Surgery and Pathology
CHAUHAN, B., Ophthalmology, Physiology and Biophysics
CLEMENTS, J. C., Biomedical Engineering
COHEN, M. M., Paediatrics
CONNOLLY, J., Medicine
COOK, H. W., Paediatrics
COONAN, T., Anaesthesia (Head)
COWDEN, E., Medicine (Head)
COX, J., Medicine
CROCKER, J. F. S., Paediatrics
CROLL, R. P., Physiology and Biophysics
CRUESS, A. F., Ophthalmology (Chair.)
CURRIE, R. W., Anatomy and Neurobiology
DANIELS, C., Diagnostic Radiology
DEVITT, H., Anaesthesia
DOANE, B. K., Psychiatry
DOOLEY, J., Paediatrics
DOOLITTLE, W. F., Biochemistry
DOWNIE, J. W., Pharmacology
DUCHARME, J., Emergency Medicine
DUNCAN, R., Microbiology and Immunology
DUNPHY, B., Obstetrics and Gynaecology
FARRELL, S., Obstetrics and Gynaecology
FERNANDEZ, L. A. V., Medicine
FERRIER, G. R., Pharmacology
FINE, A., Physiology and Biophysics
FINLEY, G. A., Anaesthesia
FINLEY, J. P., Paediatrics
FORWARD, K., Pathology, Medicine, Microbiology and Immunology
FOX, R. A., Medicine
FRANK, B. W., Division of Medical Education
FRENCH, A., Biomedical Engineering, Physiology and Biophysics
GARDNER, M. J., Medicine
GAJEWSKI, J., Urology
GASS, D. A., Family Medicine
GOLDBLOOM, R., Paediatrics
GRAVES, G., Obstetrics and Gynaecology (Head)
GRAY, M. W., Biochemistry (Head)
GREER, W., Pathology
GREGSON, P., Biomedical Engineering
GROSS, M., Surgery
GRUNFIELD, E., Medicine, Community Health and Epidemiology
GUERNSEY, D. L., Pathology, Physiology, Biophysics and Ophthalmology
HAASE, D. A., Medicine
HALL, R., Anaesthesia and Pharmacology
HALPERIN, S., Paediatrics
HANDA, S. P., Medicine
HANLY, J. G., Medicine
HAYES, V., Family Medicine
HEATHCOTE, J. G., Ophthalmology and Pathology (Head)
HIRSCH, D., Medicine and Psychiatry
HOLNESS, R. O., Surgery
HOPKINS, D. A., Anatomy and Neurobiology
HORACEK, B. M., Physiology, Biophysics and Biomedical Engineering
HORACKOVA, M., Physiology and Biophysics
HOSKIN, D. W., Microbiology, Immunology, and Pathology
HOWLETT, S., Pharmacology
HUGENHOLZ, H., Surgery
HUNG, O. R., Anaesthesia and Pharmacology
HYNDMAN, J. C., Surgery
IMRIE, D., Anaesthesia
ISA, N. N., Obstetrics and Gynaecology
ISSEKUTZ, A., Paediatrics and Pathology
ISSEKUTZ, T. B., Paediatrics, Microbiology, Immunology and Pathology
JAMIESON, C. G., Surgery
JOHNSTON, B. L., Medicine, Community Health and Epidemiology
JOHNSTON, G. C., Microbiology and Immunology (Head)
JOHNSTONE, D. E., Medicine
KAZIMIRSKI, J., Division of Medical Education
KELLS, C., Medicine

KELLY, M., Pharmacology
KELLY, M. E., Ophthalmology
KENNY, N. P., Paediatrics and Bioethics and Division of Medical Education
KHANNA, V. N., Medicine
KIBERD, B. A., Medicine
KIRBY, R. L., Medicine and Biomedical Engineering
KISELY, S. R., Community Health and Epidemiology, Psychiatry
KRONICK, J., Paediatrics (Head)
KUTCHER, S., Psychiatry
LAIDLAW, T., Division of Medical Education
LANGILLE, D. B., Community Health and Epidemiology
LANGLEY, G. R., Medicine
LAROCHE, G. R., Ophthalmology
LAWEN, J. G., Urology
LAZIER, C. B., Biochemistry
LEBLANC, R. P., Ophthalmology
LEBRON, G., Diagnostic Radiology
LEE, M., Applied Oral Sciences and Biomedical Engineering
LEE, P. W. K., Microbiology, Immunology and Pathology
LEE, T., Microbiology, Immunology and Pathology
LEIGHTON, A. H., Psychiatry
LESLIE, R. A., Anatomy, Neurobiology and Psychiatry (Head)
LO, C. D., Diagnostic Radiology
LUDMAN, H., Paediatrics
MACAULAY, R., Pathology
MACDONALD, A. S., Surgery
MACDONALD, N., Paediatrics
MCDONALD, T. F., Physiology and Biophysics
MCGRATH, P. J., Paediatrics, Psychiatry and Psychology
MACLACHLAN, R., Family Medicine (Head)
MACLEAN, L. D., Community Health and Epidemiology
MCMILLAN, D., Paediatrics
MAHONY, D. E., Microbiology and Immunology
MALATJALIAN, D. A., Pathology and Medicine
MANN, K. V., Division of Medical Education
MANN, O. E., Medicine
MARSHALL, J., Pathology, Microbiology and Immunology
MASSOUD, E., Surgery
MAXNER, C. E., Medicine and Opthalmology
MEINERTZHAGEN, I., Psychology, Physiology and Biophysics
MENDEZ, I., Surgery
MILLER, R. A., Medicine
MILLER, R. M., Diagnostic Radiology
MORRIS, I. R., Anaesthesia
MORRIS, S. F., Surgery
MOSHER, D., Medicine
MOSS, M. A., Pathology (Head)
MURPHY, P., Physiology and Biophysics (Head)
MURRAY, T. J., Medicine
NACHTIGAL, M., Pharmacology
NASHON, B. J., Surgery and Urology
NASSAR, B. A., Pathology, Medicine and Urology
NEUMANN, P. E., Anatomy and Neurobiology
NORMAN, R., Urology (Head)
O'NEILL, B., Medicine, Community Health and Epidemiology
PADMOS, M., Medicine
PALMER, F. B. ST. C., Biochemistry (Head)
PARKHILL, W. S., Surgery
PELZER, D., Physiology and Biophysics and Division of Medical Education
PETERSON, T., Medicine and Pharmacology
PHILLIPS, S., Medicine
POLLAK, T., Medicine
POULIN, C., Community Health and Epidemiology
POWELL, C., Medicine

PURDY, R. A., Medicine
RAMSEY, M., Ophthalmology
RASMUSSON, D., Physiology and Biophysics
RENTON, K. W., Pharmacology
RO, H., Biochemistry
ROBERTSON, G. S., Pharmacology and Psychiatry
ROBERTSON, H. A., Pharmacology and Medicine (Head)
ROBINSON, K. S., Medicine
ROCKER, G., Medicine
ROCKWOOD, K., Medicine
ROWDEN, G., Pathology and Medicine
ROWE, R. C., Medicine
RUSAK, B., Psychiatry, Psychology and Pharmacology
RUTHERFORD, J., Anatomy and Neurobiology
SADLER, R. M., Medicine
SAWYNOK, J., Pharmacology
SCHLECH, W., Medicine
SEMBA, K., Anatomy and Neurobiology
SHUKLA, R. C., Anaesthesia
SIMPSON, D., Medicine
SINCLAIR, D., Emergency Medicine
SINGER, R. A., Biochemistry
STANISH, W. D., Surgery
STEWART, R. D., Anaesthesia, Emergency Medicine and Division of Medical Education
STEWART, S., Psychology
STOKES, A., Psychiatry (Acting Head)
STOLTZ, D. B., Microbiology and Immunology
STONE, R. M., Surgery (Head)
STROINK, G., Biomedical Engineering
STUTTARD, C., Microbiology and Immunology
SULLIVAN, J., Surgery
TURNBULL, G. K., Medicine
VAN DEN HOF, M., Obstetrics and Gynaecology
VANZANTEN, S., Medicine, Community Health and Epidemiology
VAUGHN, P., Division of Medical Education
WALLACE, C. J. A., Biochemistry
WALSH, N., Pathology
WARD, T., Paediatrics
WASSERSUG, R. J., Anatomy and Neurobiology
WEAVER, D., Medicine and Biomedical Engineering
WEST, M. L., Medicine
WILKINSON, M., Physiology, Biophysics, Obstetrics and Gynaecology
WOLF, H. K., Physiology and Biophysics
WRIGHT, J. R., Pathology, Surgery and Biomedical Engineering
YABSLEY, R. H., Surgery

Faculty of Science (tel. (902) 494-2373; fax (902) 494-1123; e-mail science@dal.ca; internet www.science.dal.ca):

BARRESI, J., Psychology
BEAUMONT, C., Oceanography
BENTZEN, P., Biology and Oceanography
BOUDREAU, B. P., Oceanography (Chair.)
BOWEN, A. J., Oceanography
BOYD, R. J., Chemistry (Chair.)
BRADFIELD, F. M., Economics
BROWN, J., Mathematics and Statistics
BROWN, R. E., Psychology
BRYSON, S. E., Psychology
BURFORD, N., Chemistry
BURNELL, D. J., Chemistry
BURTON, P., Economics
CAMERON, T. S., Chemistry
CAMFIELD, C., Psychology
CHATT, A., Chemistry
CLARKE, D. B., Earth Sciences
CLEMENTS, J., Mathematics and Statistics
COLEY, A., Mathematics and Statistics, Physics
CONNOLLY, J. F., Psychology
COXON, J. A., Chemistry
CROLL, R. P., Biology

CULLEN, J., Oceanography
DAHN, J. R., Chemistry and Physics
DARVESH, S., Chemistry
DASGUPTA, S., Economics
DILCHER, K., Mathematics and Statistics
DUNHAM, P. J., Psychology
DUNLAP, R., Physics
FENTRESS, J. C., Biology
FIELD, C. A., Mathematics and Statistics
FINLEY, G. A., Psychology
FOURNIER, R. O., Oceanography
FREEDMAN, W., Biology (Chair.)
GABOR, G., Mathematics and Statistics
GELDART, D. J., Physics
GIBLING, M. R., Earth Sciences (Chair.)
GRANT, J., Oceanography
GREATBATCH, R., Oceanography and Physics
GRINDLEY, B., Chemistry
GUPTA, R. P., Mathematics and Statistics
HALL, B. K., Biology
HAMILTON, D. C., Mathematics and Statistics
HAY, A., Oceanography
HILL, P. S., Oceanography
HILLS, E. L., Biology
HUTCHINGS, J. A., Biology
ISCAN, T., Economics
IVERSON, S. J., Biology
JAMIESON, R. A., Earth Sciences
JERICHO, M. H., Physics
JOHNSTON, M. O., Biology
KAY-RAINING BIRD, E., Psychology
KEAST, P., Mathematics and Statistics (Chair.)
KLEIN, R. M., Psychology
KREUZER, H. J., Physics
KUSALIK, P. G., Chemistry
KWAK, J. C., Chemistry
LANE, P. A., Biology
LEE, R., Biology
LEONARD, M. L., Biology
LESSER, B., Economics (Chair.)
LEWIS, M., Oceanography
LOLORDO, V. M., Psychology
LOUDEN, K. E., Oceanography
LYONS, R., Psychology
MCGRATH, P. J., Psychology
MCMULLEN, P., Psychology
MACRAE, T., Biology
MEINERTZHAGEN, I. A., Psychology
MITCHELL, D. E., Psychology
MOORE, C. L., Psychology
MOORE, R. M., Oceanography
MORIARTY, K., Mathematics and Statistics, and Physics
MYERS, R. A., Biology
NOWAKOWSKI, R., Mathematics and Statistics
O'DOR, R. K., Biology
OSBERG, L. S., Economics
PACEY, P. D., Chemistry
PARÉ, R., Mathematics and Statistics
PATON, B. E., Physics
PATRIQUIN, D. G., Biology
PHILLIPS, D., Psychology
PHIPPS, S. A., Economics
PINCOCK, J. A., Chemistry
POHAJDAK, B., Biology
RAJORA, O. P., Biology
REYNOLDS, P. H., Earth Sciences and Physics
ROBERTSON, H., Psychology
RUDDICK, B., Oceanography
RUSAK, B., Psychology and Psychiatry
SCHEIBLING, R., Biology
SCOTT, D., Earth Sciences
SEMBA, K., Psychology
SHAW, S., Psychology
STEWART, S., Psychology
STROINK, G., Physics (Chair.)
SUTHERLAND, W. R., Mathematics and Statistics
TAN, K. K., Mathematics and Statistics
TAYLOR, K., Mathematics and Statistics

THOMPSON, K., Mathematics and Statistics, and Oceanography
WACH, G. D., Earth Sciences
WALDE, S., Biology
WEAVER, D. F., Chemistry and Division of Neurology
WENTZELL, P. D., Chemistry
WHITE, M. A., Chemistry and Physics
WHITEHEAD, H., Biology
WILLISON, J. H. M., Biology and Resource, Environmental Studies
WOOD, R. J., Mathematics and Statistics
WRIGHT, J. M., Biology
XU, K., Economics
ZWANZIGER, J. W., Chemistry and Physics

Henson College of Continuing Education (tel. (902) 494-2526; fax (902) 494-6875; e-mail henson-info@dal.ca):

BENOIT, J.
FRASER, L.
NOVACK, J.

COLLÈGE DOMINICAIN DE PHILOSOPHIE ET DE THÉOLOGIE

96 Empress Ave, Ottawa, ON K1R 7G3
Telephone: (613) 233-5696
Fax: (613) 233-6064
Internet: www.collegedominicain.com
Founded 1909 as 'Studium Generale' of Order of Friars Preachers in Canada; present name 1967
Private control
Languages of instruction: French, English
Academic year: September to April

Chancellor: YVON POMERLEAU
President and Regent of Studies: GABOR CSEPREGI
Vice-Presidents: MAXIME ALLARD MICHEL GOURGES
Registrar: HERVÉ TREMBLAY
Librarian: MARTIN LAVOIE

Library of 120,000 vols, 500 periodicals
Number of teachers: 25
Number of students: 635 (127 full-time, 508 part-time)

DEANS

Faculty of Theology: MARIE-THÉRÈSE NADEAU
Faculty of Philosophy: EDUARDO ANDUJAR
Institute of Pastoral Theology: DENIS GAGNON (Chair.)

UNIVERSITY OF GUELPH

Guelph, ON N1G 2W1
Telephone: (519) 824-4120
Fax: (519) 766-9481 (for undergraduate studies); (519) 766-0843 (for graduate studies)
Internet: www.uoguelph.ca
Founded 1964 from Ontario Agricultural College, Ontario Veterinary College and Macdonald Institute, formerly affiliated to the University of Toronto
Private/Provincial control
Language of instruction: English
Three semester system

Chancellor: L. M. ALEXANDER
Pres. and Vice-Chancellor: ALASTAIR SUMMERLEE
Provost and Vice-Pres. for Academic Affairs: MAUREEN MANCUSO (acting)
Vice-Pres. for Alumni Affairs and Development: PAMELLA HEALEY (acting)
Vice-Pres. for Finance and Administration: NANCY SULLIVAN
Vice-Pres. for Research: ALAN WILDEMAN
Vice-Provost and Chief Academic Officer: MICHAEL NIGHTINGALE
Librarian: M. RIDLEY

Library: Library of over 2.5m. vols
Number of teachers: 750
Number of students: 14,000

Publications: *Graduate Calendar, President's Report, Undergraduate Calendar*

DEANS

College of Arts: JACQUELINE MURRAY
College of Biological Science: MICHAEL EMES
College of Physical and Engineering Science: PETER TREMAINE
College of Social and Applied Human Sciences: ALUN JOSEPH
Ontario Agricultural College: CRAIG PEARSON
Ontario Veterinary College: A. H. MEEK
Faculty of Environmental Sciences: M. R. MOSS
Faculty of Graduate Studies: ISOBEL HEATHCOTE

UNIVERSITY OF KING'S COLLEGE

Halifax, NS B3H 2A1
Telephone: (902) 422-1271
Fax: (902) 423-3357
E-mail: admissions@ukings.ns.ca
Internet: www.ukings.ca
Founded 1789 by United Empire Loyalists; granted Royal Charter 1802; entered into asscn with Dalhousie University 1923
Language of instruction: English
Academic year: September to May

Chancellor: MICHAEL MEIGHEN
Pres. and Vice-Chancellor: WILLIAM BARKER
Vice-Pres.: CHRISTOPHER ELSON
Registrar: E. YEO
Bursar: G. G. SMITH
Librarian: H. DRAKE PETERSEN

Number of teachers: 51
Number of students: 1,137
Publication: *The Hinge* (1 a year)

PROFESSORS

BARKER, W., English
BISHOP, M., French
BURNS, S. A. M., Philosophy
CROWLEY, J., History
HANKEY, W. J., Classics
HUEBERT, R., English
KIMBER, S., Journalism
STARNES, C. J., Classics
VINCI, T., Philosophy

LAKEHEAD UNIVERSITY

Oliver Rd, Thunder Bay, ON P7B 5E1
Telephone: (807) 343-8110
Fax: (807) 343-8023
E-mail: commun@lakeheadu.ca
Internet: www.lakeheadu.ca
Founded 1965; previously est. as Lakehead College of Arts, Science and Technology, 1956, and Lakehead Technical Institute, 1946
Academic year: September to April

Chancellor: LORNE G. EVERETT
Pres.: FREDERICK F. GILBERT
Provost and Vice-Pres. for Academic Affairs: Dr LAURIE HAYES
Vice-Pres. for Admin. and Finance: MICHAEL PAWLOWSKI
Vice-Pres. for Advancement: JOHN SINGER
Vice-Pres. for Research: Dr RUI WANG
Registrar: (vacant)
Librarian: ANNE DEIGHTON

Number of teachers: 240
Number of students: 7,900

DEANS

Faculty of Business Administration: Dr BAHRAM DADGOSTAR
Faculty of Education: Dr JOHN O'MEARA
Faculty of Engineering: Dr HENRI T. SALIBA
Faculty of Forestry and Forest Environment: REINO PULKKI
Faculty of Graduate Studies: JANE CROSSMAN (acting)

Faculty of Health and Behavioural Sciences: Dr DAVID TRANTER
Faculty of Medicine: Dr ROGER STRASSER
Faculty of Science and Environmental Studies: Dr ANDREW DEAN
Faculty of Social Sciences and Humanities: Dr GILLIAN SIDDALL

LAURENTIAN UNIVERSITY OF SUDBURY

935 Ramsey Lake Rd, Sudbury, ON P3E 2C6
Telephone: (705) 675-1151
Fax: (705) 675-4891
E-mail: admission@laurentian.ca
Internet: www.laurentian.ca
Founded 1960
Provincially assisted, non-denominational
Languages of instruction: French, English(certain depts offer parallel courses in both languages)
Academic year: September to April

Pres.: JUDITH WOODSWORTH
Vice-Pres. for Admin.: ROBERT F. BOURGEOIS
Academic Vice-Pres. for Anglophone Affairs: SUSAN SILVERTON
Academic Vice-Pres. for Francophone Affairs: HARLEY D'ENTREMONT
Registrar: RON SMITH
Dir of Library: LIONEL BONIN
Dir for Centre for Continuing Education: DENIS MAYER
Dirfor Div. of Physical Education: ROGER COUTURE
Dir for Graduate Studies and Research: PAUL COLILLI

Number of teachers: 377 (full-time)
Number of students: 9,100

Depts of anthropology, behavioural neuroscience, biology, classical studies, commerce and administration, earth science, education (English), education (French), English, environmental earth science, ethics studies, film studies, folklore, geography, history, liberal science, mathematics and computer science, midwifery, modern languages and literatures, music, native human services, native studies, nursing, philosophy, physics and astronomy, political science, psychology, radiation therapy, religious studies, social work, sociology, sport psychology, sports administration

DEANS

Humanities and Social Sciences: JOHN ISBISTER
Management: HUGUETTE BLANCO
Professional Schools: ANNE-MARIE MAWHINEY
Sciences and Engineering: PATRICE SAWYER

CONSTITUENT INSTITUTIONS

Algoma University College: 1520 Queen St E, Sault Ste Marie, ON P6A 2G4; internet www.algomau.ca; Pres. C. ROSS; Registrar D. MARASCO.

Collège Universitaire de Hearst: Hearst, ON P0L 1N0; internet www.univhearst.edu; f. 1952; Rector R. TREMBLAY; Registrar J. DOUCET.

FEDERATED UNIVERSITIES

Huntington University: Ramsey Lake Rd, Sudbury, ON P3E 2C6; f. 1960; related to United Church of Canada; Pres.-Principal KEVIN MCCORMICK; Registrar A. HOOD.

Thorneloe University: Ramsey Lake Rd, Sudbury, ON P3E 2C6; Provost S. ANDREWS; Registrar I. MACLENNAN.

University of Sudbury: Ramsey Lake Rd, Sudbury, ON P3E 2C6; f. 1957; conducted by the Jesuit Fathers; Pres. ANDRII KRAWCHUK; Registrar L. BEAUPRÉ.

UNIVERSITÉ LAVAL

Québec, QC G1V 0A6
Telephone: (418) 656-2131
Fax: (418) 656-5920
E-mail: accueil@sg.ulaval.ca
Internet: www.ulaval.ca

Founded 1852; Royal Charter signed December 1852, Pontifical Charter 1876, Provincial Charter 1970
Language of instruction: French
Academic year: September to August

Rector: DENIS BRIÈRE
Vice-Rector for Academic Int. Activities: BERNARD GARNIER
Vice-Rector for Admin. and Finances: JOSÉE GERMAIN
Vice-Rector for Human Resources: MICHEL BEAUCHAMP
Deputy Vice-Rector for Research and Creation: CHRISTIANE PICHÉ
Vice-Rector for Research and Creation: EDWIN BOURGET
Dean of Graduate Studies: MARIE AUDETTE
Dir of Undergraduate Studies: SERGE TALBOT
Dir of Continuing Education: PIERRE DIONNE
Sec.-Gen.: MONIQUE RICHER
Registrar: DANIELLE FLEURY
Librarian: SILVIE DELORME

Library: see Libraries and Archives
Number of teachers: 1,587
Number of students: 37,295 (24,415 full-time, 12,880 part-time)

Publications: *Didaskalia* (2 a year, education), *Cahiers de Droit* (law), *Cahiers de Géographie du Québec* (geography), *Cahiers de Recherche* (1 a year, economics), *CRIRES* (education), *Communication* (mass communication), *Anthropologie et Sociétés* (anthropology), *Ecoscience* (biology), *Ethnologies* (1 a yearjournal of Canadian folklore studies), *Études Littéraires* (3 a year, literature), *Études Internationales* (4 a year, international studies), *Études Inuits* (2 a year, Inuit studies), *Recherches Féministes* (feminism), *Relations Industrielles* (industrial relations), *Revue Scientifique* (education), *Langues et Linguistique* (linguistics), *L'Année Francophone Internationale (L'AFI)* (literary), *Laval Théologique et Philosophique* (theology and philosophy), *Les Cahiers du Journalisme* (journalism), *Service Social* (online, social work), *Recherches Sociographiques* (1 a year, Quebec studies), *Rédiger* (1 a year, technical writing), *Revue d'Histoire Intellectuelle de l'Amérique Française* (12 a year), *Visio* (history)

DEANS AND DIRECTORS

Faculty of Administrative Sciences: ROBERT W. MANTHA
Faculty of Agriculture and Food Sciences: JEAN-PAUL LAFOREST
Faculty of Dentistry: ANDRÉ FOURNIER
Faculty of Education: MARCEL MONETTE
Faculty of Forestry and Geomatics: ROBERT BEAUREGARD
Faculty of Law: PIERRE LEMIEUX
Faculty of Letters: THIERRY BELLEGUIC
Faculty of Medicine: PIERRE JACOB DURAND
Faculty of Music: PAUL CADRIN
Faculty of Nursing Sciences: DIANE MORIN
Faculty of Pharmacy: JEAN-PIERRE GRÉGOIRE
Faculty of Philosophy: LUC LANGLOIS
Faculty of Sciences and Engineering: GUY GENDRON
Faculty of Social Sciences: FRANÇOIS BLAIS
Faculty of Theology and Religious Sciences: MARC PELCHAT
Faculty of Urban Planning, Architecture and Visual Arts: RICHARD PLEAU
Québec Institute of Higher International Studies: PAUL GAUTHIER

PROFESSORS

Faculty of Administrative Sciences (Pavillon Palasis-Prince, Bureau 1322, Québec, QC G1K 7P4; tel. (418) 656-2180; fax (418) 656-2624; e-mail fsa@fsa.ulaval.ca; internet www.fsa.ulaval.ca):

AUDET, M., Management
BANVILLE, C., Management Information Systems
BEAULIEU, M.-C., Finance and Insurance
BÉDARD, J., Accounting (Sciences)
BÉLIVEAU, D., Marketing
BELLEMARE, G., Finance and Insurance
BERGERON, F., Management Information Systems
BERNIER, G., Finance and Insurance
BHERER, H., Management
BLAIS, R., Management
BOCTOR, F. F., Operations and Decision Systems
BOIRAL, O., Management
BOULAIRE, C., Marketing
BOURDEAU, L., Management
BRUN, J.-P., Management
CARPENTIER, C., Accounting (School)
CAYER, M., Management
CORMIER, E., Accounting (School)
COULOMBE, D., Accounting (Sciences)
D'AVIGNON, G. R., Operations and Decision Systems
DES ROSIERS, F., Management
DIONNE, P., Management
FISCHER, P. K., Finance and Insurance
GARAND, D. J., Management
GARNIER, B., Management
GASCON, A., Operations and Decision Systems
GASSE, Y., Management
GAUTHIER, A., Operations and Decision Systems
GAUVIN, S., Marketing
GENDRON, M., Finance and Insurance
GOSSELIN, M., Accounting (School)
GRISÉ, J., Management
HASKELL, N., Marketing
KETTANI, O., Operations and Decision Systems
KISS, L. N., Operations and Decision Systems
LACASSE, N., Management
LAI, V. S., Finance and Insurance
LAMOND, B., Operations and Decision Systems
LANDRY, R., Management
LANG, P., Operations and Decision Systems
LEE-GOSSELIN, H., Management
LESCEUX, D., Marketing
LETARTE, P.-A., Management
MANTHA, R. W., Management Information Systems
MARTEL, A., Operations and Decision Systems
MOFFET, D., Finance and Insurance
MONTREUIL, B., Operations and Decision Systems
NADEAU, L., Accounting (School)
NADEAU, R., Operations and Decision Systems
PAQUETTE, S., Accounting (Sciences)
PARÉ, P.-V., Accounting (School)
PASCOT, D., Management Information Systems
POULIN, D., Management
PRÉMONT, P. E., Management Information Systems
RENAUD, J., Operations and Decision Systems
RIDJANOVIC, D., Management Information Systems
RIGAUX-BRICMONT, B., Marketing
ROY, M.-C., Management Information Systems
ROY, M.-J., Management
SAINT PIERRE, J., Finance and Insurance
SEROR, ANN C., Management
SU, Z., Management
SURET, J.-M., Accounting (School)
VERNA, G., Management
VÉZINA, R., Marketing
ZINS, M., Marketing

Faculty of Agriculture and Food Sciences (Pavillon Paul-Comtois, Bureau 1122, Québec, QC G1K 7P4; tel. (418) 656-3145; fax (418) 656-7806; e-mail fsaa@fsaa.ulaval.ca; internet www.fsaa.ulaval.ca):

ALLARD, G., Plant Science
AMIOT, J., Food Science and Nutrition
ANGERS, P., Food Science and Nutrition
ANTOUN, H., Soils and Agricultural Engineering
ARUL, J., Food Science and Nutrition
ASSELIN, A., Plant Science
BAILEY, J. L., Animal Sciences
BEAUCHAMP, C. J., Plant Science
BEAUDOIN, P., Agricultural Economics and Consumer Sciences
BEAUDRY, M., Food Science and Nutrition
BÉLANGER, R., Plant Science
BELZILE, F., Plant Science
BENHAMOU, N., Plant Science
BERGERON, R., Animal Sciences
BERNIER, J.-F., Animal Sciences
BLACKBURN, M., Soils and Agricultural Engineering
BRODEUR, J., Plant Science
CAILLIER, M., Soils and Agricultural Engineering
CALKINS, P., Agricultural Economics and Consumer Sciences
CAREL, M., Agricultural Economics and Consumer Sciences
CARON, J., Soils and Agricultural Engineering
CASTAIGNE, F., Food Science and Nutrition
CESCAS, M. P., Soils and Agricultural Engineering
CHALIFOUR, F. P., Plant Science
CHAREST, P.-M., Plant Science
CHOUINARD, Y., Animal Sciences
COLLIN, J., Plant Science
DANSEREAU, B., Plant Science
DEBAILLEUL, G., Agricultural Economics and Consumer Sciences
DESJARDINS, Y., Plant Science
DESPRES, J.-P., Food Science and Nutrition
DESROSIERS, T., Food Science and Nutrition
DION, P., Plant Science
DOSTALER, D., Plant Science
DOYEN, M., Agricultural Economics and Consumer Sciences
DUFOUR, J. C., Agricultural Economics and Consumer Sciences
EMOND, J.-P., Soils and Agricultural Engineering
FLISS, I., Food Science and Nutrition
FORTIN, J., Soils and Agricultural Engineering
GALIBOIS, I., Food Science and Nutrition
GALLICHAND, J., Soils and Agricultural Engineering
GAUTHIER, S., Food Science and Nutrition
GERVAIS, J.-P., Agricultural Economics and Consumer Services
GOSSELIN, A., Plant Science
GOUIN, D., Agricultural Economics and Consumer Sciences
GOULET, J., Food Science and Nutrition
JACQUES, H., Food Science and Nutrition
KARAM, A., Soils and Agricultural Engineering
LACHANCE, M. J., Agricultural Economics and Consumer Sciences
LAFOREST, J.-P., Animal Sciences
LAGACÉ, R., Soils and Agricultural Engineering
LAMARCHE, B., Food Science and Nutrition
LAMBERT, R., Agricultural Economics and Consumer Sciences
LAPOINTE, G., Food Science and Nutrition

LARUE, B., Agricultural Economics and Consumer Sciences
LAVERDIÈRE, M.-R., Soils and Agricultural Engineering
LEFRANÇOIS, M., Animal Sciences
LEMIEUX, S., Food Science and Nutrition
LEROUX, G., Plant Science
LEVALLOIS, R., Agricultural Economics and Consumer Sciences
LOCONG, A., Food Science and Nutrition
MAKHLOUF, J., Food Science and Nutrition
MARQUIS, A., Soils and Agricultural Engineering
MARTEL, R., Food Science and Nutrition
MARTIN, F., Agricultural Economics and Consumer Sciences
MICHAUD, D., Plant Science
MORISSET, M., Agricultural Economics and Consumer Sciences
OLIVIER, A., Plant Science
OUELLET, D., Food Science and Nutrition
PAQUIN, P., Food Science and Nutrition
PARENT, D., Animal Science
PARENT, L. E., Soils and Agricultural Engineering
PELLERIN, D., Animal Sciences
PERRIER, J.-P., Agricultural Economics and Consumer Sciences
PICARD, G., Food Science and Nutrition
POTHIER, F., Animal Science
POULIOT, Y., Food Science and Nutrition
RATTI, C., Soils and Agricultural Engineering
RIOUX, J.-A., Plant Science
ROBITAILLE, J., Agricultural Economics and Consumer Sciences
ROCHEFORT, L., Plant Science
ROMAIN, R., Agricultural Economics and Consumer Sciences
ROY, D., Food Science and Nutrition
ST-LOUIS, R., Agricultural Economics and Consumer Sciences
SIRARD, M.-A., Animal Science
SUBIRADE, M., Food Science and Nutrition
THÉRIAULT, R., Soils and Agricultural Engineering
TURGEON, S., Food Science and Nutrition
TURGEON-O'BRIEN, H., Food Science and Nutrition
VOHL, J.-C., Food Science and Nutrition
VUILLEMARD, J.-C., Food Science and Nutrition
WEST, E. G., Agricultural Economics and Consumer Sciences
ZEE, J., Food Science and Nutrition

Faculty of Architecture, Planning and Visual Arts (Édifice du Vieux-Séminaire de Québec, 1 Côte de la Fabrique, Bureau 2230, Québec, QC G1R 3V6; tel. (418) 656-2546; fax (418) 656-3325; e-mail faaav@faaav.ulaval.ca; internet www.faaav.ulaval.ca):

BLAIS, M., Architecture
CARRIER, M., Planning
CASAULT, A., Architecture
CHAINE, F., Visual Arts
CLOUTIER, L., Visual Arts
COSSETTE, M. A., Visual Arts
CÔTÉ, P., Architecture
DEMERS, C., Architecture
DESPRÉS, C., Architecture
DUBÉ, C., Planning
GIRARD, G., Visual Arts
JEAN, M., Visual Arts
LAVOIE, C., Planning
LEE-GOSSELIN, M., Planning
LEMIEUX, R., Visual Arts
MALENFANT, N., Visual Arts
MILL, R., Visual Arts
NAYLOR, D., Visual Arts
PICHÉ, D., Architecture
PLEAU, R., Architecture
POTVIN, A., Architecture
POULIOT, S., Visual Arts
ROCHON, A., Visual Arts
RODRIGUEZ-PINZON, M., Planning

TEYSSOT, G., Architecture
THÉRIAULT, M., Planning
TREMBLAY, G.-H., Architecture
VACHON, E., Architecture
VACHON, G., Architecture
VILLENEUVE, P., Planning
ZWIEJSKI, J., Architecture

Faculty of Dentistry (Pavillon de Médecine Dentaire, Bureau 1615, Québec, QC G1K 7P4; tel. (418) 656-2247; fax (418) 656-2720; e-mail fmd@fmd.ulaval.ca; internet www.ulaval.ca/fmd):

BASTIEN, R.
BERNARD, C.
CARON, C.
CHMIELEWSKI, W.
FOURNIER, A.
GAGNON, G.
GAGNON, P.
GAUCHEN, H.
GIASSON, L.
GOULET, J.-P.
GRENIER, D.
LACHAPELLE, D.
MORAND, M.-A.
MORIN, S.
NICHOLSON, L.
PAYANT, L.
PERUSSE, R.
PROULX, M.
ROBERT, D.
ROUABHIA, M.
ROY, S.
VALOIS, M.

Faculty of Education (Pavillon des Sciences de l'Éducation, Québec, QC G1K 7P4; tel. (418) 656-3062; fax (418) 656-7347; e-mail fse@fse.ulaval.ca; internet www.fse.ulaval.ca):

ARRIOLA-SOCOL, M., Foundations and Interventions in Education
BÉLANGER, J.-D., Teaching and Learning Studies
BOISCLAIR, A., Teaching and Learning Studies
BOIVIN, M.-D., Foundations and Interventions in Education
BOUCHARD, P., Foundations and Interventions in Education
BOURASSA, B., Foundations and Interventions in Education
CARDIN, J.-F., Teaching and Learning Studies
CARDU, H., Foundations and Interventions in Education
CLOUTIER, R., Foundations and Interventions in Education
DEBLOIS, L., Teaching and Learning Studies
DENIGER, M.-A., Foundations and Interventions in Education
DÉSAUTELS, J., Teaching and Learning Studies
DESGAGNÉ, S., Teaching and Learning Studies
DIAMBOMBA, M., Foundations and Interventions in Education
DIONNE, J., Teaching and Learning Studies
DRAPEAU, S., Foundations and Interventions in Education
DROLET, J.-L., Foundations and Interventions in Education
FOUNTAIN, R. M. B., Teaching and Learning Studies
FOURNIER, G., Foundations and Interventions in Education
FOURNIER, J.-P., Teaching and Learning Studies
GAGNON, J., Physical Education
GAGNON, R., Teaching and Learning Studies
GAULIN, C., Teaching and Learning Studies
GAUTHIER, C., Teaching and Learning Studies

GERVAIS, F., Teaching and Learning Studies
GIASSON, J., Teaching and Learning Studies
GUAY, F., Foundations and Interventions in Education
GUERETTE, C., Teaching and Learning Studies
GUILBERT, L., Teaching and Learning Studies
HAMEL, T., Foundations and Interventions in Education
JACQUES, M., Teaching and Learning Studies
JEANRIE, C., Foundations and Interventions in Educations
JEFFREY, D., Teaching and Learning Studies
KASZAP, M., Teaching and Learning Studies
LACHANCE, L., Foundations and Interventions in Education
LAFERRIÈRE, T., Teaching and Learning Studies
LANDRY, C., Foundations and Interventions in Education
LAPOINTE, C., Foundations and Interventions in Education
LAROCHELLE, M., Teaching and Learning Studies
LAROSE, S., Teaching and Learning Studies
LE BOSSE, Y., Foundations and Interventions in Education
LECLERC, C., Foundations and Interventions in Education
LEGAULT, M., Teaching and Learning Studies
MARANDA, M.-F., Foundations and Interventions in Education
MARCOUX, Y., Foundations and Interventions in Education
MARTEL, D., Physical Education
MASSOT, A., Foundations and Interventions in Education
MOISSET, J.-J., Foundations and Interventions in Education
MONETTE, M., Foundations and Interventions in Education
MURA, R., Teaching and Learning Studies
NADEAU, G.-A., Physical Education
PAGÉ, P., Teaching and Learning Skills
PELLETIER, P., Teaching and Learning Skills
PLANTE, J., Foundations and Interventions in Education
RATTE, J., Foundations and Interventions in Education
ROY-BUREAU, L., Teaching and Learning Skills
ROYER, E., Teaching and Learning Studies
ST-LAURENT, L., Teaching and Learning Studies
SAMSON, J., Physical Education
SAVARD, C., Physical Education
SIMARD, C., Teaching and Learning Studies
SIMARD, D., Teaching and Learning Skills
SPAIN, A., Foundations and Interventions in Education
TALBOT, S., Physical Education
THERIAULT, G., Physical Education
TROTTIER, C., Foundations and Interventions in Education
VALOIS, P., Foundations and Interventions in Education
VINCENT, S., Teaching and Learning Skills
ZIARKO, H., Teaching and Learning Skills

Faculty of Forestry and Geomatics (Pavillon Abitibi-Price, Bureau 1151, Québec, QC G1K 7P4; tel. (418) 656-3880; fax (418) 656-3177; e-mail ffg@ffg.ulaval.ca; internet www.ffg.ulaval.ca):

ALLARD, M., Geography
BAUCE, E., Wood and Forest Sciences
BEAUDOIN, M., Wood and Forest Sciences
BEAULIEU, B., Geomatics

BEAUREGARD, R., Wood and Forest Sciences
BÉDARD, Y., Geomatics
BÉGIN, J., Wood and Forest Sciences
BÉGIN, Y., Geography
BÉLANGER, L., Wood and Forest Sciences
BELLEFLEUR, P., Wood and Forest Sciences
BERNIER, L., Wood and Forest Sciences
BHIRY, N., Geography
BOULIANNE, M., Geomatics
BOUSQUET, J., Wood and Forest Sciences
BOUTHILLER, L., Wood and Forest Sciences
BRIÈRE, D., Wood and Forest Sciences
CAMIRÉ, C., Wood and Forest Sciences
CHEVALLIER, J.-J., Geomatics
CLOUTIER, A., Wood and Forest Sciences
CONDAL, A., Geomatics
DESROCHERS, A., Wood and Forest Sciences
DESSUREAULT, M., Wood and Forest Sciences
EDWARDS, G., Geomatics
FILION, L., Geography
FORTIN, Y., Wood and Forest Sciences
GODBOUT, C., Wood and Forest Sciences
HERNANDEZ PENA, R., Wood and Forest Sciences
LALONDE, M., Wood and Forest Sciences
LEBEL, L., Wood and Forest Sciences
LOWELL, K., Wood and Forest Sciences
MARGOLLIS, H., Wood and Forest Sciences
MERCIER, G., Geography
MUNSON, A., Wood and Forest Sciences
PICHÉ, Y., Wood and Forest Sciences
PIENITZ, R., Geography
PLAMONDON, A. P., Wood and Forest Sciences
PLANTE, F., Geomatics
POTHIER, D., Wood and Forest Sciences
RIEDL, B., Wood and Forest Sciences
RUEL, J.-C., Wood and Forest Sciences
ST-HILAIRE, M., Geography
SANTERRE, R., Geomatics
STEVANOVIC, J. T., Wood and Forest Sciences
THIBEAULT, J.-R., Wood and Forest Sciences
TREMBLAY, F., Wood and Forest Sciences
VIAU, A., Geomatics

Faculty of Law (Pavillon Charles-DeKoninck, Bureau 2407, Québec, QC G1K 7P4; tel. (418) 656-2131 ext. 6134; fax (418) 656-7230; e-mail fd@fd.ulaval.ca; internet www.ulaval.ca/fd):

ARBOUR, M.
BELLEAU, M.-C.
BOUCHARD, C.
BRETON, R.
BROCHU, F.
COTE-HARPER, G.
CRÊTE, R.
DELEURY, E.
DESLAURIERS, J.
DUPLE, N.
FERLAND, D.
GARDNER, D.
GIROUX, L.
GOUBAU, D.
HALLEY, P.
ISSALYS, P.
LANGEVIN, L.
LAQUERRE, P.
LAREAU, A.
LAUZIÈRE, L.
LEMIEUX, D.
LEMIEUX, P.
MANGANAS, A.
MELKEVILL, B.
NORMAND, S.
OTIS, G.
PRUJINER, A.
RAINVILLE, P.
ROUSSEAU, G.
TREMBLAY, G.
TURGEON, J.

Faculty of Letters (Pavillon Charles-De Koninck, Bureau 3254, Québec, QC G1K 7P4; tel. (418) 656-3460; fax (418) 656-2019; e-mail fl@fl.ulaval.ca; internet www.fl.ulaval.ca):

AUGER, P., Languages and Linguistics
AUGER, R., History
BACZ, B., Languages and Linguistics
BAKER, P., History
BAUDOU, A., Literature
BEAUCHAMP, M., Information and Communication
BEAUDET, M.-A., Literature
BEAUSOLEIL, P., Information and Communication
BELANGER, R., History
BELLEGUIC, T., Literature
BERNIER, J., History
BISAILLON, J., Languages and Linguistics
BOISVERT, L., Languages and Linguistics
BOIVIN, A., Literature
BORGONOVO, C., Languages and Linguistics
BOULANGER, J.-C., Languages and Linguistics
CARANI, M., History
CARDIN, M., History
CAULIER, B., History
CHARRON, J., Information and Communication
CLERC, I., Information and Communication
COSSETTE, J. C., Information and Communication
CUMMINS, S., Languages and Linguistics
DAGENAIS, B., Information and Communication
DAIGLE, J., History
DAVIAULT, A., Literature
DE BONVILLE, J., Information and Communication
DE KONINCK, Z., Languages and Linguistics
DE LA GARDE, R., Information and Communication
DEMERS, F., Information and Communication
DEMERS, G., Languages and Linguistics
DESDOUITS, A.-M., History
DESHAIES, D., Languages and Linguistics
DOLAN, C., History
DUBÉ, P., History
DUFFLEY, P., Languages and Linguistics
DUMONT, F., Literature
ESPANOL, E. M., Languages and Linguistics
FAITELSON-WEISER, S., Languages and Linguistics
FINETTE, L., Literature
FORTIER, A.-M., Literature
FORTIN, M., History
FYSON, D., History
GAGNÉ, M., Literature
GARON, L., Information and Communication
GAUTHIER, G., Information and Communication
GRENIER, D., History
GRIGNON, M., History
GUEVEL, Z., Languages and Linguistics
GUILBERT, L., History
HÉBERT, C., Literature
HERMON, E., History
HUMMEL, K., Languages and Linguistics
HUOT, D., Languages and Linguistics
HUOT-LEMONNIER, F., Languages and Linguistics
JOLICOEUR, L., Languages and Linguistics
JUNEAU, M., Languages and Linguistics
KAREL, D., History
KEGLE, C., Literature
KOSS, B. J., History
KUGLER, M., Information and Communication
LABERGE, A., History
LACHARITÉ, D. P., Languages and Linguistics
LADOUCEUR, J., Languages and Linguistics
LAPOINTE, M., History

LAVIGNE, A., Information and Communication
LEBEL, E., Information and Communication
LEMELIN, B., History
LEMIEUX, J., Information and Communication
LÉTOURNEAU, J., History
LOWE, R., Languages and Linguistics
LUKIC, R., History
MANNING, A., Languages and Linguistics
MARCHAND, J., Information and Communication
MARTIN, P., Languages and Linguistics
MATHIEU, J., History
MERCIER, A., Literature
MOORE, E., History
MOSER VERREY, M., Literature
MOUSSETTE, M., History
NAKOS, D., Languages and Linguistics
NGUYEN-DUY, V., Information and Communication
NIQUETTE, M., Information and Communication
OUELLET, J., Languages and Linguistics
PAQUETTE, G., Information and Communication
PAQUOT, A., Languages and Linguistics
PARADIS, C., Languages and Linguistics
PARKS, S. E., Languages and Linguistics
PELLETIER, E., Literature
PERELLI-CONTOS, I., Literature
PERESTRELO, F., Languages and Linguistics
PICARD, J.-C., Information and Communication
PIETTE, C., History
POIRIER, C., Languages and Linguistics
PONTBRIAND, J.-N., Literature
PRÉVOST, P., Languages and Linguistics
RIVET, J., Information and Communication
ROY, L., Literature
SADETSKY, A., Languages and Linguistics
ST-GELAIS, R., Literature
SAINT JACQUES, D., Literature
SAUVAGEAU, F., Information and Communication
THENON, L., Literature
THÉRY, C., Literature
THOMAS, N. H., Literature
TREMBLAY, G., Geography
TURGEON, L., History
VALLIÈRES, M., History
VAN DER SCHWEREN, E., Literature
VERREAULT, C., Languages and Linguistics
VINCENT, D., Languages and Linguistics
WATINE, T., Information and Communication

Faculty of Medicine (Pavillon Ferdinand-Vandry, Bureau 1214, Québec, QC G1K 7P4; tel. (418) 656-5245; fax (418) 656-2501; e-mail fmed@fmed.ulaval.ca; internet www.fmed.ulaval.ca):

ABDOUS, B., Social and Preventive Medicine
AKOUM, A., Obstetrics and Gynaecology
ALARY, M., Social and Preventive Medicine
ALLEN, T., Family Medicine
AMZICA, F., Anatomy and Physiology
AUBIN, M., Family Medicine
AUDETTE, M., Medical Biology
AUGER, F., Surgery
AYOTTE, P., Social and Preventive Medicine
BACHELARD, H., Medicine
BACHVAROV, D., Medicine
BAIRAM, A., Paediatrics
BAIRATI, I., Surgery
BARDEN, N., Anatomy and Physiology
BASTIDE, A., Obstetrics and Gynaecology
BEAUCHAMP, D., Medical Biology
BEAUCHEMIN, J.-P., Family Medicine
BEAULIEU, A., Medicine
BEDARD, P., Medicine
BÉLANGER, A., Anatomy and Physiology
BÉLANGER, A. Y., Rehabilitation
BÉLANGER, L., Medical Biology

BERGERON, J., Obstetrics and Gynaecology
BERGERON, M. G., Medical Biology
BERGERON, R., Family Medicine
BERNARD, P.-M., Social and Preventive Medicine
BERNATCHEZ, J.-P., Psychiatry
BERNIER, V., Medical Biology
BILODEAU, A., Family Medicine
BISSONNETTE, E., Medicine
BLANCHET, J., Obstetrics and Gynaecology
BLONDEAU, F., Family Medicine
BLONDEAU, L., Medicine
BOGATY, P., Medicine
BOIVIN, G., Medical Biology
BORGEAT, P., Anatomy and Physiology
BOUCHARD, J.-P., Medicine
BOUCHER, F., Paediatrics
BOULAY, M. R., Social and Preventive Medicine
BOULET, L.-P., Medicine
BOURBONNAIS, R., Rehabilitation
BOURGOIN, S.-G., Anatomy and Physiology
BRAILOVSKY, C. A., Family Medicine
BRASSARD, N., Obstetrics and Gynaecology
BRISSON, C., Social and Preventive Medicine
BRISSON, J., Social and Preventive Medicine
CABANAC, M., Anatomy and Physiology
CANDAS, B., Anatomy and Physiology
CAPADAY, C., Anatomy and Physiology
CARRIÈRE, M., Rehabilitation
CARUSO, M., Medical Biology
CHAHINE, M., Medicine
CHAKIR, J., Medicine
CHARRON, J., Medical Biology
CLOUTIER, A., Paediatrics
CORBEIL, J., Anatomy and Physiology
CORMIER, Y., Medicine
CÔTÉ, C., Rehabilitation
CÔTÉ, J., Anaesthesiology
CÔTÉ, L., Medicine
COUET, J., Medicine
CUSAN, L., Anatomy and Physiology
DE KONINCK, M., Social and Preventive Medicine
DE KONINCK, Y., Psychiatry
DE SERRES, G., Medical Biology
DE WALS, P., Social and Preventive Medicine
DELAGE, R., Medicine
DERY, P., Paediatrics
DESCHÊNES, M., Anatomy and Physiology
DESHAIES, Y., Anatomy and Physiology
DESLAURIERS, J., Surgery
DESMEULES, M., Medicine
DEWAILLY, F., Social and Preventive Medicine
DIONNE, C., Rehabilitation
DIONNE, F. T., Social and Preventive Medicine
DODIN, S. D., Obstetrics and Gynaecology
DOILLON, C., Surgery
DORÉ, F. M., Medicine
DORVAL, J., Paediatrics
DOUVILLE, Y., Surgery
DROLET, G., Medicine
DUMESNIL, J.-G., Medicine
DURAND, P.-J., Social and Preventive Medicine
FAURE, R., Paediatrics
FLAMAND, L., Anatomy and Physiology
FOREST, J.-C., Medical Biology
FORTIER, M.-A., Obstetrics and Gynaecology
FORTIN, J.-P., Social and Preventive Medicine
FRADET, Y., Surgery
FRÉMONT, P., Rehabilitation
FRENETTE, J., Family Medicine and Rehabilitation
GAGNON, F., Psychiatry
GAILIS, L., Medicine
GERMAIN, L., Surgery
GERVAIS, M., Rehabilitation

GIRARD, J. E., Social and Preventive Medicine
GLENN, J., Medical Biology
GOSSELIN, J., Anatomy and Physiology
GOVINDAN, M. J., Anatomy and Physiology
GRAVEL, C., Psychiatry
GUAY, G., Medicine
GUÉRIN, S., Anatomy and Physiology
GUIDOIN, R., Surgery
HANCOCK, R., Medical Biology
HUDON, C., Paediatrics
HUOT, J., Medicine
JEANNOTTE, L., Medical Biology
JOBIN, J., Medicine
JULIEN, J.-P., Anatomy and Physiology
JULIEN, P., Medicine
KHANDJIAN, E. W., Medical Biology
KINKEAD, R., Paediatrics
KINGMA, J. G., Medicine
L'ARRIÈRE, M., Rehabilitation
LABBÉ, J., Paediatrics
LABBÉ, R., Medical Biology
LABELLE, Y., Medical Biology
LABERGE, C., Medicine
LABRECQUE, M., Family Medicine
LABRIE, C., Anatomy and Physiology
LABRIE, F., Anatomy and Physiology
LACASSE, Y., Medicine
LAFRAMBOISE, R., Paediatrics
LAGACÉ, R., Medical Biology
LAGASSE, P.-P., Social and Preventive Medicine
LAJOIE, P., Social and Preventive Medicine
LALANNE, M., Medical Biology
LAMBERT, R. D., Obstetrics and Gynaecology
LAMONTAGNE, R., Family Medicine
LANDRY, J., Medicine
LANGELIER, M., Medicine
LANGLOIS, S., Medicine
LANIVIÈLE, R., Medicine
LAROCHELLE, L., Anatomy and Physiology
LATULIPPE, L., Medicine
LAVIOLETTE, M., Medicine
LAVOIE, J., Medical Biology
LEBEL, M., Medicine
LEBLANC, R., Social and Preventive Medicine
LEBLOND, P., Medicine
LECLERC, P., Medical Biology
LEDUC, Y., Family Medicine
LELIÈVRE, M., Paediatrics
LEMAY, A., Obstetrics and Gynaecology
LETARTE, R., Medical Biology
LEVALLOIS, P., Social and Preventive Medicine
LEVESQUE, D., Medicine
LÉVESQUE, R., Medical Biology
LIN, S.-X., Anatomy and Physiology
LUU, T. V., Anatomy and Physiology
McFADYEN, B. J., Rehabilitation
MAHEUX, R., Obstetrics and Gynaecology
MALOUIN, F., Rehabilitation
MALTAIS, F., Medicine
MARCEAU, F., Medicine
MARCEAU, N., Medicine
MARCHAND, R., Anatomy and Physiology
MARCOUX, H., Family Medicine
MARCOUX, S., Social and Preventive Medicine
MARETTE, A., Anatomy and Physiology
MARTINEAU, R., Medical Biology
MAUNSELL, E., Social and Preventive Medicine
MAURIEGE, P., Social and Preventive Medicine
MAZIADE, M., Psychiatry
MERETTE, C., Psychiatry
MEYER, F., Social and Preventive Medicine
MIRAULT, M.-E., Medicine
MOFFET, H., Rehabilitation
MONTGRAIN, N., Psychiatry
MORISSETTE, J., Anatomy and Physiology
MOSS, T., Medical Biology
MOURAD, M. W., Medicine
MURTHY, M.-R.-V., Medical Biology

NACCACHE, P.-H., Medicine
NADEAU, A., Medicine
NADEAU, L., Medical Biology
NOREAU, L., Rehabilitation
OUELLETTE, M., Medical Biology
PAINCHAUD, G., Psychiatry
PAPADOPOULO, B., Medical Biology
PARENT, A., Anatomy and Physiology
PELLETIER, G.-H., Anatomy and Physiology
PERUSSE, L., Social and Preventive Medicine
PHILIPPE, E., Anatomy and Physiology
PIBAROT, P., Medicine
PIEDBOEUF, B., Paediatrics
POIRIER, D., Anatomy and Physiology
POIRIER, G., Medical Biology
POMERLEAU, G., Psychiatry
POUBELLE, P., Medicine
POULIN, R., Anatomy and Physiology
PUYMIRAT, J., Medicine
RATTÉ, C., Psychiatry
RAYMOND, V., Anatomy and Physiology
RICHARD, D., Anatomy and Physiology
RICHARDS, C. L., Rehabilitation
RIOUX, F., Medicine
RIVEST, S., Anatomy and Physiology
ROBERGE, C., Medical Biology
ROBICHAUD, L., Rehabilitation
ROUILLARD, C., Medicine
ROULEAU, J., Medicine
ROUSSEAU, F., Medical Biology
ROY, M., Obstetrics and Gynaecology
SALESSE, C., Otorhinolaryngology and Ophthalmology
SATO, M., Anatomy and Physiology
SATO, S., Medical Biology
SAUCIER, D., Family Medicine
SAVARD, P., Medicine
SEGUIN, C., Anatomy and Physiology
SERIES, F., Medicine
SHAH, G., Medical Biology
SIMARD, J., Anatomy and Physiology
STERIADE, M., Anatomy and Physiology
SULLIVAN, R., Obstetrics and Gynaecology
TALBOT, J., Medical Biology
TANGUAY, R., Medicine
TEASDALE, N., Social and Preventive Medicine
TESSIER, P., Medical Biology
TETREAULT, S., Rehabilitation
TETU, B., Medical Biology
THIVIERGE, J., Psychiatry
TREMBLAY, A., Social and Preventive Medicine
TREMBLAY, J.-P., Anatomy and Physiology
TREMBLAY, M. J., Medical Biology
TREMBLAY, Y., Obstetrics and Gynaecology
TRUDEL, L., Rehabilitation
VENRREAULT, R., Social and Preventive Medicine
VERRET, S., Paediatrics
VEZINA, M., Social and Preventive Medicine
VILLENEUVE, E., Psychiatry
VINCENT, C., Rehabilitation
VINCENT, M., Medicine

Faculty of Music (Pavillon Louis-Jacques-Casault, Bureau 3312, Québec, QC G1K 7P4; tel. (418) 656-7061; fax (418) 656-7365; e-mail mus@mus.ulaval.ca; internet www.ulaval.ca/mus):

BOULET, M.-M.
CADRIN, P.
DUCHARME, M.
LAFLAMME, S.
MASSON-BOURQUE, C.
MATHIEU, L.
PAPILLON, A.
PARENT, N.
PINSON, J.-P.
RINGUETTE, R.
ROBERGE, M.-A.
STUBER, U.
TEREBESI, G.

Faculty of Nursing Sciences (Pavillon Paul-Comtois, Bureau 4106, Québec, QC G1K 7P4; tel. (418) 656-3356; fax (418) 656-7747; e-mail fsi@fsi.ulaval.ca; internet www.ulaval.ca/fsi):

BLONDEAU, D.
CÔTÉ, E.
DALLAIRE, C.
EBACHER, M.-F.
FILLION, L.
GODIN, G.
HAGAN, L.
LEPAGE, L.
MORIN, D.
O'NEILL, M.
PATENAUDE, L.
PELLETIER, L.
PROVENCHER, H.
VIENS, C.

Faculty of Pharmacy (Pavillon Ferdinand-Vandry, Bureau 2241, Québec, QC G1K 7P4; tel. (418) 656-3211; fax (418) 656-2305; e-mail pha@pha.ulaval.ca; internet www.pha.ulaval.ca):

BEAULAC-BAILLARGEON, L.
BELANGER, P. M.
CASTONGUAY, A.
DALEAU, P.
DESGAGNÉ, M.
DI PAOLO-CHENEVERT, T.
DIONNE, A.
DORVAL, M.
GRÉGOIRE, J.-P.
GUILLEMETTE, C.
JUHASZ, J.
MOISAN, J.
RICHER, M.
TREMBLAY, M.
VÉZINA, C.

Faculty of Philosophy (Pavillon Félix-Antoine-Savard, Bureau 644, Québec, QC G1K 7P4; tel. (418) 656-2244; fax (418) 656-7267; e-mail fp@fp.ulaval.ca; internet www.fp.ulaval.ca):

BÉGIN, L.
BILODEAU, R.
BOSS, G.
CUNNINGHAM, H.-P.
DE KONINCK, T.
KNEE, P.
LAFLEUR, C.
LANGLOIS, L.
NARBONNE, J.-M.
PARIZEAU, M.-H.
PELLETIER, Y.
RICARD, M.-A.
SASSEVILLE, M.
THIBAUDEAU, V.
TOURNIER, F.

Faculty of Sciences and Engineering (Pavillon Alexandre-Vachon, Bureau 1033, Québec, QC G1K 7P4; tel. (418) 656-2163; fax (418) 656-5902; e-mail fsg@fsg.ulaval.ca; internet www.fsg.ulaval.ca):

ADAM, L., Actuarial Science
AIT-KADI, D., Mechanical Engineering
AMIOT, P. L., Physical Engineering and Optics
ANCTIL, F., Civil Engineering
ANDERSON, A., Biology
AUGER, M., Chemistry
BARBEAU, C., Chemistry
BARIBEAU, L., Mathematics and Statistics
BARRETTE, C., Biology
BASTIEN, J., Civil Engineering
BAZIN, C., Mining, Metallurgical and Materials Engineering
BEAUDOIN, G., Geology and Geological Engineering
BEAULIEU, D., Civil Engineering
BEAULIEU, J.-M., Computer Science
BEAUPRÉ, D., Civil Engineering
BÉDARD, D., Actuarial Science

BÉDARD, G., Physical Engineering and Optics
BELISLE, C., Mathematics and Statistics
BELKHITER, N., Computer Science
BERGEVIN, R., Electrical and Computer Engineering
BERNATCHEZ, L., Biology
BORRA, E. F., Physical Engineering and Optics
BOUCHARD, C., Civil Engineering
BOUDREAU, D., Chemistry
BOUKOUVALAS, J., Chemistry
BOURBONNAIS, Y., Biochemistry and Microbiology
BOUSMINA, M. M., Chemical Engineering
BRISSON, J., Chemistry
BUI, M. D., Computer Science
CARDOU, A., Mechanical Engineering
CARMICHAEL, J.-P., Mathematics and Statistics
CASSIDY, C., Mathematics and Statistics
CASSIDY, D. P., Geology and Geological Engineering
CHAIB-DRAA, B., Computer Science
CHARLET, G., Chemistry
CHÊNEVERT, R., Chemistry
CHIN, S. L., Physical Engineering and Optics
CHOUINARD, J.-Y., Electrical and Computer Engineering
CLOUTIER, C., Biology
COSSETTE, H., Actuarial Science
CROS, J., Electrical and Computer Engineering
CURODEAU, A., Mechanical Engineering
D'AMOURS, S., Mechanical Engineering
DARVEAU, A., Biochemistry and Microbiology
DE CHAMPLAIN, A., Mechanical Engineering
DE KONINCK, J.-M., Mathematics and Statistics
DEL VILLAR, R., Mining, Metallurgical and Materials Engineering
DESBIENS, A., Electrical and Computer Engineering
DESCHÊNES, C., Mechanical Engineering
DESHARNAIS, J., Computer Science
DESLAURIERS, N., Biochemistry and Microbiology
DODSON, J., Biology
DORÉ, G., Civil Engineering
DUBE, L. J., Physical Engineering and Optics
DUBÉ, D., Mining, Metallurgical and Materials Engineering
DUCHESNE, J., Geology and Geological Engineering
DUGUAY, M.-A., Electrical and Computer Engineering
DUMAS, G., Mechanical Engineering
DUPUIS, C., Computer Science
DUSSAULT, P., Biochemistry and Microbiology
FAFARD, M., Civil Engineering
FORIERO, A., Civil Engineering
FORTIER, L., Biology
FORTIER, P., Electrical and Computer Engineering
FORTIER, R., Geology and Geological Engineering
FORTIN, A., Mathematics and Statistics
FRENETTE, M., Biochemistry and Microbiology
FYTAS, K., Mining, Metallurgical and Materials Engineering
GAKWAYA, A., Mechanical Engineering
GALSTIAN, T., Physics, Physical Engineering and Optics
GALVEZ-CLOUTIER, R., Civil Engineering
GANGULY, U. S., Electrical and Computer Engineering
GARNIER, A., Chemical Engineering
GAUTHIER, G., Biology
GELINAS, P. J., Geology and Geological Engineering

GENDRON, G., Mechanical Engineering
GENEST, C., Mathematics and Statistics
GERVAIS, J.-J., Mathematics and Statistics
GHALI, E., Mining, Metallurgical and Materials Engineering
GHAZZALI, N., Mathematics and Statistics
GIGUÈRE, M., Actuarial Science
GLOVER, P., Geology and Geological Engineering
GOSSELIN, C., Mechanical Engineering
GOUDREAU, S., Mechanical Engineering
GOULET, V., Actuarial Science
GOURDEAU, F., Mathematics and Statistics
GRANDJEAN, B., Chemical Engineering
GRENIER, D., Electrical and Computer Engineering
GUDERLEY, H., Biology
GUENETTE, R., Mathematics and Statistics
GUERTIN, M., Biochemistry and Microbiology
GUILLOT, M., Mechanical Engineering
HADJIGEORGIOU, J., Mining, Metallurgical and Materials Engineering
HEBERT, R., Geology and Geological Engineering
HIMMELMAN, J., Biology
HODGSON, B. R., Mathematics and Statistics
HODOUIN, D., Mining, Metallurgical and Materials Engineering
HOULE, G., Biology
HUOT, J., Biology
JACQUES, M., Actuarial Science
JOHNSON, L. E., Biology
JONCAS, G., Physics, Physical Engineering and Optics
KALIAGUINE, S., Chemical Engineering
KIRKWOOD, D., Geology and Geological Engineering
KNYSTAUTAS, E., Physics, Physical Engineering and Optics
KONRAD, J.-M., Civil Engineering
KRETSCHMER, D., Mechanical Engineering
KROEGER, H., Physics, Physical Engineering and Optics
LACROIX, R., Chemical Engineering
LAPOINTE, L., Biology
LARACHI, F., Chemical Engineering
LAROCHE, G., Mining, Metallurgical and Materials Engineering
LAROCHELLE, J., Biology
LAROCHELLE, S., Electrical and Computer Engineering
LAURENDEAU, D., Electrical and Computer Engineering
LAVOIE, M. C., Biochemistry and Microbiology
LEBOEUF, D., Civil Engineering
LECLERC, M., Chemistry
LEDUY, A., Chemical Engineering
LE HUY, H., Electrical and Computer Engineering
LEMAY, J., Mechanical Engineering
LEMIEUX, C., Biochemistry and Microbiology
LEMIEUX, G., Biochemistry and Microbiology
LEROUEIL, S., Civil Engineering
LESSARD, P., Civil Engineering
LESSARD, R. A., Physics, Physical Engineering and Optics
LEVASSEUR, M., Biology
LÉVEILLÉ, G., Actuarial Science
LÉVESQUE, B., Mechanical Engineering
LÉVESQUE, C., Mathematics and Statistics
LOCAT, J., Geology and Geological Engineering
LUONG, A., Actuarial Science
MCBREEN, P. H., Chemistry
MCCARTHY, N., Physics, Physical Engineering and Optics
MACIEL, Y., Mechanical Engineering
MALDAGUE, X., Electrical and Computer Engineering
MANOUZI, H., Mathematics and Statistics
MARCEAU, E., Actuarial Science

MARCHAND, J., Civil Engineering
MARCHAND, M., Computer Science
MARCHAND, P., Computer Science
MARLEAU, L., Physics, Physical Engineering and Optics
MARTEL, H., Physics, Physical Engineering and Optics
MASSE, J.-C., Mathematics and Statistics
MATHIEU, P., Physics, Physical Engineering and Optics
MINEAU, G., Computer Science
MOINEAU, S., Biochemistry and Microbiology
MORSE, B., Civil Engineering
MOULIN, B., Computer Sciences
NGUYEN-DANG, T.-T., Chemistry
PALLOTTA, D., Biology
PAQUETTE, N., Biology
PARASZCZAK, J., Mining, Metallurgical and Materials Engineering
PARIZEAU, M., Electrical and Computer Engineering
PAYETTE, S., Biology
PEZOLET, M., Chemistry
PHILIPPIN, G., Mathematics and Statistics
PICARD, A., Civil Engineering
PICHÉ, M., Physics, Physical Engineering and Optics
PIERRE, R., Mathematics and Statistics
PIGEON, M., Civil Engineering
PINEAULT, S., Physics, Physical Engineering and Optics
PLANETA, S., Mining, Metallurgical and Materials Engineering
POMERLEAU, A., Electrical and Computer Engineering
POULIN, R., Mining, Metallurgical and Materials Engineering
RANCOURT, D., Mechanical Engineering
RANSFORD, T.-J., Mathematics and Statistics
RICHARD, M. J., Mechanical Engineering
RITCEY, A.-M., Chemistry
RIVEST, L.-P., Mathematics and Statistics
ROBERT, C., Physics, Physical Engineering and Optics
ROBERT, J.-L., Civil Engineering
ROCHELEAU, M., Geology and Geological Engineering
RODRIGUE, D., Chemical Engineering
ROY, C., Chemical Engineering
ROY, D., Physics, Physical Engineering and Optics
ROY, P.-H., Biochemistry and Microbiology
ROY, R., Physics, Physical Engineering and Optics
RUSCH, L. A., Electrical and Computer Engineering
SEGUIN, M. K., Geology and Geological Engineering
SERODES, J.-B., Civil Engineering
SHENG, Y., Physics, Physical Engineering and Optics
TARASIEWICZ, R., Mechanical Engineering
TAWBI, N., Computer Science
TÊTU, M., Electrical and Computer Engineering
THERRIEN, R., Geology and Geological Engineering
TOURIGNY, N., Computer Science
TREMBLAY, P., Electrical and Computer Engineering
TREMBLAY, R., Physics, Physical Engineering and Optics
TURCOTTE, J., Chemistry
TURMEL, M., Biochemistry and Microbiology
VADEBONCOEUR, C., Biochemistry and Microbiology
VALLÉE, R., Physics, Physical Engineering and Optics
VIAROUGE, P., Electrical and Computer Engineering
VINCENT, W. F., Biology
VO VAN, T., Mining, Metallurgical and Materials Engineering

VOYER, N., Chemistry
WITZEL, B., Physics, Physical Engineering and Optics
ZACCARIN, A., Electrical and Computer Engineering

Faculty of Social Sciences (Pavillon Charles-DeKoninck, Bureau 3456, Québec, QC G1K 7P4; tel. (418) 656-2615; fax (418) 656-2114; e-mail fss@fss.ulaval.ca; internet www.fss.ulaval.ca):

ARCAND, B., Anthropology
AUDET, M., Industrial Relations
BACCIGALUPO, A., Political Science
BAKARY, T., Political Science
BARIBEAU, J., Psychology
BARITEAU, C., Anthropology
BARLA, P., Economics
BARRE, A., Industrial Relations
BEAUCHAMP, C., Sociology
BEAUDREAU, B. C., Economics
BEAUDRY, M., Social Work
BÉLANGER, G., Economics
BÉLANGER, J., Industrial Relations
BÉLANGER, L., Political Science
BERNARD, J.-T., Economics
BERNIER, C., Industrial Relations
BERNIER, J., Industrial Relations
BLAIS, F., Political Science
BLOUIN, R., Industrial Relations
BOISVERT, J.-M., Psychology
BOIVIN, J., Industrial Relations
BOIVIN, M., Psychology
BOLDUC, D., Economics
BOUCHER, N., Social Work
BOUSQUET, N., Sociology
BRETON, G., Political Science
CARMICHAEL, B., Economics
CHALIFOUX, J.-J., Anthropology
CLAIN, O., Sociology
CLOUTIER, R., Psychology
COMEAU, Y., Social Work
CONSTANTANOS, C., Economics
CÔTÉ, P., Political Science
COUILLARD, M.-A., Anthropology
CRÊTE, J., Political Science
DAGENAIS, H., Anthropology
DAMANT, D., Social Work
DARVEAU-FOURNIER, L., Social Work
DECALUWE, B., Economics
DELAGE, D., Sociology
DEOM, E., Industrial Relations
DERRIENNIC, J.-P., Political Science
DESÈVE, M., Sociology
DESROCHERS, S., Psychology
DESSY, S. E., Economics
DIGUER, L., Psychology
DOMPIERRE, J., Industrial Relations
DORAIS, L.-J., Anthropology
DORAIS, M., Social Work
DORÉ, F.-Y., Psychology
DRAINVILLE, A., Political Science
DUCLOS, J.-Y., Economics
DUFORT, F., Psychology
DUHAIME, G., Sociology
DUMAIS, A., Sociology
DUMONT, S., Social Work
ELBAZ, M., Anthropology
EVERETT, J., Psychology
FOREST, P. G., Political Science
FORTIN, A., Sociology
FORTIN, B., Economics
FORTIN, C., Psychology
FORTIN, D., Social Work
GAGNÉ, O., Sociology
GAUTHIER, J., Psychology
GENEST, S., Anthropology
GILES, A. J., Industrial Relations
GINGRAS, A.-M., Political Science
GISLAIN, J.-J., Industrial Relations
GONZALEZ, P., Economics
GORDON, S. F., Economics
GOSSELIN, G., Political Science
GOULET, S., Psychology
GRONDIN, S., Psychology
GUAY, L., Sociology

HERVOUET, G., Political Science
HUDON, R., Political Science
HUNG, N. M., Economics
HURTUBISE, Y., Social Work
IMBEAU, L., Political Science
KHALAF, L. A., Economics
KIROUAC, G., Psychology
LABRECQUE, M.-F., Anthropology
LACOMBE, S., Sociology
LACOUTURE, Y., Psychology
LACROIX, G., Economics
LADOUCEUR, R., Psychology
LAFLAMME, G., Industrial Relations
LAFLAMME, R., Industrial Relations
LAFLEUR, G.-A., Political Science
LAFOREST, G., Political Science
LAMONDE, F., Industrial Relations
LAMOUREUX, D., Political Science
LANDREVILLE, P., Psychology
LANGLOIS, L., Industrial Relations
LANGLOIS, S., Sociology
LAPOINTE, P.-A., Industrial Relations
LAUGRAND, F. B., Anthropology
LAVALLÉE, M., Psychology
LAVOIE, F., Psychology
LEBLANC, G., Economics
LINDSAY, J., Social Work
LORANGER, M., Psychology
MACE, G., Political Science
MARCOUX, R., Sociology
MASSÉ, R., Anthropology
MERCIER, J., Industrial Relations
MERCIER, J., Political Science
MERCURE, D., Sociology
MONTREUIL, S., Industrial Relations
MOREL, S., Industrial Relations
MORIN, C.-M., Psychology
NORMANDIN, L., Psychology
PAQUIN, L., Economics
PELLETIER, R., Political Science
PEPIN, M., Psychology
PETRY, F., Political Science
PICHÉ, C., Psychology
POCREAU, J.-B., Psychology
POIRIER, S., Anthropology
ROLAND, M., Economics
SABOURIN, S., Psychology
SAILLANT, F., Anthropology
SAINT-ARNAUD, P., Sociology
SAINT-YVES, A., Psychology
SAMSON, L., Economics
SAVARD, J., Psychology
SENECAL, C., Psychology
SEXTON, J., Industrial Relations
SHEARER, B., Economics
SIMARD, J.-J., Sociology
SIMARD, M., Social Work
TESSIER, L., Social Work
TESSIER, R., Psychology
THWAITES, J., Industrial Relations
TRUCHON, M., Economics
TRUDEL, F., Anthropology
TURCOTTE, D., Social Work
TURMEL, A., Sociology
VAN AUDENRODE, M., Economics
VEILLETTE, D., Sociology
VEZINA, A., Social Work
VÉZINA, J., Psychology
VINET, A., Industrial Relations
ZYLBERBERG, J., Political Science

Faculty of Theology and Religious Studies (Pavillon Félix-Antoine-Savard, Bureau 832, Québec, QC G1K 7P4; tel. (418) 656-3576; fax (418) 656-3273; e-mail ftsr@ftsr.ulaval.ca; internet www.ftsr.ulaval.ca):

AUBERT, M.
BRODEUR, R.
CÔTÉ, L.
CÔTÉ, P.-R.
COUTURE, A.
FARRELL, S. E.
FAUCHER, A.
FORTIN, A.
HURLEY, R.
KEATING, B.

LEMIEUX, R.
MAGER, R.
PAINCHAUD, L.
PASQUIER, A.
PELCHAT, M.
POIRIER, P.-H.
RACINE, J.
ROBERGE, R. M.
ROUTHIER, G.
VIAU, M.

UNIVERSITY OF LETHBRIDGE

4401 University Dr., Lethbridge, AB T1K 3M4

Telephone: (403) 320-5700
Fax: (403) 329-5159
E-mail: inquiries@uleth.ca
Internet: www.uleth.ca
Founded 1967
Provincial control
Language of instruction: English
Academic year: September to April (2 semesters), also summer sessions
Chancellor: ROBERT HIRONAKA
Pres. and Vice-Chancellor: WILLIAM HENRY CADE
Provost and Vice-Pres. for Academic Affairs: SEAMUS O'SHEA
Vice-Pres. for Finance and Admin.: NANCY WALKER
Registrar: LESLIE LAVERS
Chief Librarian: JUDY HEAD
Number of teachers: 248 full-time
Number of students: 8,230
Library of 498,000 vols
Publication: *Annual Calendar*

DEANS

Faculty of Arts and Science: CHRISTOPHER NICOL
Faculty of Education: Dr JANE O'DEA
Faculty of Management: Dr JOHN USHER
School of Fine Arts: C. SKINNER
School of Health Sciences: LYNN BASFORD
School of Graduate Studies: ALAM SHAMSUL

McGILL UNIVERSITY

845 Sherbrooke St West, Montréal, QC H3A 2T5

Telephone: (514) 398-4455
Fax: (514) 398-3594
Internet: www.mcgill.ca
Founded 1821 by legacy of Hon. James McGill
Provincial control
Language of instruction: English
Academic year: September to May (2 terms)
Chancellor: H. ARNOLD STEINBERG
Prin. and Vice-Chancellor: HEATHER MUNROE-BLUM
Provost and Vice-Prin. for Academic: LUC VINET
Deputy Provost and Chief Information Officer: ANTHONY C. MASI
Vice-Prin. for Admin. and Finance: Prof. MORTY YALOVSKY
Vice-Prin. for Devt and Alumni Relations: NANCY WELLS
Vice-Prin. for Research: Dr LOUISE PROULX
Sec.-Gen.: ROBIN GELLER
Registrar and Exec. Dir of Admissions, Recruitment and Registrar's Office: S. FRANKE
Dir of Libraries: FRANCES GROEN
Library: see Libraries
Number of teachers: 5,428 (full-time and part-time)
Number of students: 30,580 (full-time and part-time)
Publications: *McGill Journal of Education* (3 a year), *McGill Journal of Medicine* (2 a year), *McGill Journal of Middle East Studies* (1 a year), *McGill Reporter* (6 a year), *McGill University Health Centre. Annual Report, The McGill Journal of Political Economy* (1 a year), *The McGill Journal of Political Studies* (1 a year), *The McGill Law Journal* (4 a year), *MUHC Ensemble*

DEANS

Faculty of Agricultural and Environmental Sciences: Dr DEBORAH BUSZARD
Faculty of Arts: Prof. JOHN HALL
Faculty of Dentistry: Dr JAMES LUND
Faculty of Education: ROGER SLEE
Faculty of Engineering: JOHN E. GRUZLESKI
Faculty of Law: NICHOLAS KASIRER
Faculty of Management: GERALD H. B. ROSS
Faculty of Medicine: Dr ABRAHAM FUKS
Faculty of Music: DON MCLEAN
Faculty of Religious Studies: BARRY B. LEVY
Faculty of Science: ALAN SHAVER
Graduate and Postdoctoral Studies: MARTHA CRAGO
Centre for Continuing Education: ROBIN ELEY
Dean of Students: Dr BRUCE SHORE

DIRECTORS OF SCHOOLS

Architecture: D. COVO
Communication Sciences and Disorders: S. R. BAUM
Computer Science: D. THÉRIEN
Dietetics and Human Nutrition: K. GRAY-DONALD
Environment: N. ROULET
Graduate School of Library and Information Studies: J. BEHESHTI
Nursing: S. E. FRENCH
Physical and Occupational Therapy: R. DYKES
Social Work: WENDY THOMSON
Urban Planning: D. BROWN

CHAIRS OF DEPARTMENTS

Faculty of Agricultural and Environmental Sciences (including School of Dietetics and Human Nutrition) (21111 Lakeshore Rd, Ste Anne de Bellevue, QC H9X 3V9; tel. (514) 398-7928; fax (514) 398-7968; e-mail studentinfo@macdonald.mcgill.ca; internet www.mcgill.ca/macdonald):

Agricultural Economics: J. C. HENNING
Agricultural and Biosystems Engineering: G. S. V. RAGHAVAN
Animal Science: X. ZHAO
Biosource Engineering: R. KOK
Food Science and Agricultural Chemistry: W. D. MARSHALL
Natural Resource Sciences: B. CÔTÉ
Plant Science: M. FORTIN

Faculty of Arts (Dawson Hall, 853 Sherbrooke St W, Montréal, QC H3A 2T6; tel. (514) 398-4210; fax (514) 398-8102; e-mail adviser.artsci@mcgill.ca; internet www.mcgill.ca/arts):

Anthropology: M. BISSON
Art History and Communication Studies: W. STRAW
East Asian Studies: G. FONG
Economics: C. GREEN
English: M. KILGOUR
French Language and Literature: F. RICARD
German Studies: K. BAUER
Hispanic Studies: J. PÉREZ-MAGALLÓN
History: B. LEWIS
Italian: L. KROHA
Jewish Studies: E. ORENSTEIN
Linguistics: L. WHITE
Philosophy: R. P. BUCKLEY
Political Science: C. MANFREDI
Russian and Slavic Studies: P. M. AUSTIN
Sociology: S. STRAGGENBORG

Faculty of Education (3700 McTavish St, Montréal, QC H3A 1Y2; tel. (514) 398-7042; fax (514) 398-4679; e-mail sao.education@mcgill.ca; internet www.education.mcgill.ca):

Educational and Counselling Psychology: S. P. LAJOIE (acting)
Integrated Studies: A. W. PARÉ
Kinesiology and Physical Education: H. PERRAULT

Faculty of Engineering (Macdonald Engineering Bldg, 3rd Floor, 817 Sherbrooke St, Montréal, QC H3A 2K6; tel. (514) 398-7257; fax (514) 398-7379; e-mail information@engineering.mcgill.ca; internet www.mcgill.ca/engineering):

Chemical Engineering: R. J. MUNZ
Civil Engineering and Applied Mechanics: D. MITCHELL
Electrical and Computer Engineering: D. LOWTHER
Mechanical Engineering: A. K. MISRA
Mining Metals and Materials Engineering: R. A. L. DREW

Faculty of Medicine (6th Floor, McIntyre Medical Bldg, Promenade Sir William Osler, Montréal, QC H3G 1Y6; tel. (514) 398-3515; fax (514) 398-3595; e-mail recep.med@mcgill.ca; internet www.medicine.mcgill.ca):

Anaesthesia: F. CARLI
Anatomy and Cell Biology: J. J. M. BERGERON
Biochemistry: D. Y. THOMAS
Biomedical Engineering: R. E. KEARNEY
Epidemiology and Biostatistics: R. FUHRER
Family Medicine: M. DAWES
Human Genetics: D. S. ROSENBLATT
Medicine: D. GOLTZMAN
Microbiology and Immunology: G. J. MATLASHEWSKI
Neurology and Neurosurgery: R. J. RIOPELLE
Obstetrics and Gynaecology: S. L. TAN
Oncology: G. BATIST
Ophthalmology: M. N. BURNIER, JR
Otolaryngology: M. D. SCHLOSS
Paediatrics: H. J. GUYDA
Pathology: C. COMPTON
Pharmacology and Therapeutics: H. ZINGG
Physiology: A. SHRIER
Psychiatry: J. PARIS
Radiation Oncology: C. R. FREEMAN
Surgery: J. L. MEAKINS

Faculty of Music (Strathcona Music Bldg, Room E203, 555 Sherbrooke St W, Montréal, QC H3A 1E3; tel. (514) 398-4535; fax (514) 398-8061; e-mail undergradadmissions.music@mcgill.ca; internet www.mcgill.ca/music):

Performance: G. FOOTE
Theory: W. WOSZCZYK

Faculty of Science (Dawson Hall, 853 Sherbrooke St W, Montréal, QC H3A 2T6; tel. (514) 398-4210; fax (514) 398-8102; e-mail adviser.artsci@mcgill.ca; internet www.mcgill.ca/science):

Anatomy and Cell Biology: J. J. M. BERGERON
Atmospheric and Oceanic Sciences: J. R. GYAKUM
Biochemistry: D. Y. THOMAS
Biology: P. F. LASKO
Chemistry: R. B. LENNOX
Earth and Planetary Sciences: A. MUCCI
Geography: G. O. EWING
Mathematics and Statistics: K. GOWRISANKAREN
Microbiology and Immunology: G. J. MATLASHEWSKI
Pharmacology and Therapeutics: H. ZINGG
Physics: M. GRANT
Physiology: A. SHRIER
Psychology: K. B. J. FRANKLIN

Centre for Continuing Education (688 Sherbrooke St W, 11th Floor, Montréal, QC H3A 3R1; tel. (514) 398-6200; fax (514) 398-4448; e-mail info@conted.mcgill.ca; internet www .mcgill.ca/conted):

Career and Management Studies: P. MARTUCCI

Education: B. WALKER

General Studies: P. MARTUCCI (acting) (Dir)

Translation Studies: J. ARCHIBALD

INCORPORATED COLLEGES AND CAMPUSES

Macdonald Campus: 21111 Lakeshore Rd, Ste Anne de Bellevue, QC H9X 3V9; site of the Faculty of Agricultural and Environmental Sciences, the School of Dietetics and Human Nutrition and the School of Environment.

Royal Victoria College: Montréal; nonteaching; provides residential accommodation for women students; Warden F. TRACY.

AFFILIATED BODIES

Montreal Diocesan Theological College: 3473 University St, Montréal, QC H3A 2A8; Prin. J. M. SIMONS.

Presbyterian College: 3495 University St, Montréal, QC H3A 2A8; Prin. J. VISSERS.

United Theological College: 3521 University St, Montréal, QC H3A 2A9; Prin. P. JOUDREY.

McMASTER UNIVERSITY

Hamilton, ON L8S 4L8

Telephone: (905) 525-9140

Fax: (905) 527-0100

Internet: www.mcmaster.ca

Founded 1887 in Toronto; moved to Hamilton 1930

Private control

Language of instruction: English

Academic year: September to April

Chancellor: M. M. HAWKRIGG

Pres. and Vice-Chancellor: Prof. PETER J. GEORGE

Provost and Vice-Pres. for Academic Affairs: K. NORRIE

Vice-Pres. for Admin.: K. BELAIRE

Vice-Pres. for Health Sciences: J. KELTON

Vice-Pres. for Research: M. SHOUKRI

Registrar: L. ARIANO

Librarian: G. R. HILL

Library: see Libraries

Number of teachers: 1,025 full-time

Number of students: 17,775 full- and part-time

Publications: *Journal of the Bertrand Russell Archives* (4 a year), *McMaster University Library Research News, The Research Bulletin* (12 a year)

DEANS

Faculty of Engineering: M. ELBESTAWI

Faculty of Health Sciences: J. KELTON

Faculty of Humanities: N. RAHIMIEH

Faculty of Science: P. SUTHERLAND

Faculty of Social Sciences: S. J. ELLIOTT

School of Business: P. BATES

Graduate Studies: L. FINSTEN (acting)

Principal of the Divinity College: S. PORTER

PROFESSORS

Faculty of Engineering:

BAETZ, B. W., Civil Engineering

BEREZIN, A. A., Engineering Physics

CAPSON, D. W., Electrical and Computer Engineering

CASSIDY, D. T., Engineering Physics

CHANG, J. S., Engineering Physics

DEEN, M. J., Electrical and Computer Engineering

DICKSON, J. M., Chemical Engineering

DRYSDALE, R. G., Civil Engineering

ELBESTAWI, M. A., Mechanical Engineering

FRANEK, F., Computing and Software

GARLAND, W. J., Engineering Physics

GERSHMAN, A. B., Electrical and Computer Engineering

GHOBARAH, A., Civil Engineering

HAUGEN, H., Engineering Physics

HRYMAK, A. N., Chemical Engineering

IRONS, G. A., Materials Science and Engineering

JANICKI, R., Computing and Software

JESSOP, P. E., Engineering Physics

JOHARI, G. P., Materials Science and Engineering

KITAI, A. H., Engineering Physics

KLEIMAN, R. N., Engineering Physics

KREYMAN, K., Computing and Software

LOUTFY, R., Chemical Engineering

LUO, Z.-Q., Electrical and Computing Engineering

LUXAT, J. C., Engineering Physics

MACGREGOR, J. F., Chemical Engineering

MAIBAUM, T., Computing and Software

MARLIN, T. E., Chemical Engineering

MASCHER, P., Engineering Physics

PARNAS, D. L., Computing and Software

PELTON, R. H., Chemical Engineering

PETRIC, A., Materials Science and Engineering

PIETRUSZCZAK, S., Civil Engineering

PRESTON, J. S., Engineering Physics

QIAO, S., Computing and Software

REILLY, J. P., Electrical and Computer Engineering

SIVAKUMARAN, K. S., Civil Engineering

SMITH, P. M., Electrical and Computer Engineering

STOLLE, D. F. E., Civil Engineering

SZABADOS, B., Electrical and Computer Engineering

SZYMANSKI, T. H., Electrical and Computer Engineering

TAYLOR, P. A., Computing and Software

TERLAKY, T., Computing and Software

THOMPSON, D. A., Engineering Physics

TODD, T. D., Electrical and Computer Engineering

TSANIS, I. K., Civil Engineering

VLACHOPOULOS, J. A., Chemical Engineering

WEAVER, D. S., Mechanical Engineering

WILKINSON, D. S., Materials Science and Engineering

WONG, K. M., Electrical and Computer Engineering

WOOD, P. E., Chemical Engineering

WU, X., Electrical and Computer Engineering

XU, G., Materials Science and Engineering

ZHU, S., Chemical Engineering

ZIADA, S., Mechanical Engineering

ZUCKER, J. I., Computing and Software

Faculty of Health Sciences:

ADACHI, R., Medicine

ANDREWS, D. W., Biochemistry

ANTONY, M., Psychiatry

ANVARI, M., Surgery

ARNOLD, A., Medicine

ARSENAULT, L., Pathology

ARTHUR, H. M., School of Nursing

ATKINSON, S. A., Paediatrics

BALL, A. K., Pathology

BARR, R. D., Paediatrics

BAUMANN, M. A., School of Nursing

BELBECK, L. W., Pathology

BIRCH, S., Clinical Epidemiology and Biostatistics

BLAJCHMAN, M, Pathology

BOYLE, M. H., Psychiatry

BROWNE, R. M., School of Nursing

BUCHANAN, M. R., Pathology

BUTLER, R. G., Pathology

CAPONE, J. P., Biochemistry

CHAMBERS, L. W., Clinical Epidemiology and Biostatistics

CHEN, V., Pathology

CHERNESKY, M., Paediatrics

CHIRAKAL, R., Radiology

CHURCHILL, D. N., Medicine

CILISKA, D. K., School of Nursing

COATES, G., Radiology

COBLENTZ, C., Radiology

COLLINS, S. M., Medicine

CONNOLLY, S. J., Medicine

COOK, D. J., Medicine

CRANKSHAW, D. J., Obstetrics and Gynaecology

CROITORU, K., Medicine

CUNNINGHAM, C., Psychiatry

DAYA, S., Obstetrics and Gynaecology

DENBURG, J. A., Medicine

DENBURG, S. D., Psychiatry

DICENSO, A., School of Nursing

FAHNESTOCK, M., Psychiatry

FARGAS-BABJAK, A., Anaesthesia

FERNANDES, C., Medicine

FIRNAU, G., Radiology

GAFNI, A. J., Clinical Epidemiology and Biostatistics

GAULDIE, J., Pathology

GERBER, G. E., Biochemistry

GERSTEIN, H. C., Medicine

GINSBERG, J. S., Medicine

GOLDSMITH, C. H., Clinical Epidemiology and Biostatistics

GROVER, A. K., Medicine

GROVES, D., Pathology

GUPTA, R. S., Biochemistry

GUYATT, G. H., Clinical Epidemiology and Biostatistics

HARNISH, D. G., Pathology

HARVEY, J. T., Surgery

HASSELL, J. A., Biochemistry

HATTON, M. W. C., Pathology

HAYNES, R. B., Clinical Epidemiology and Biostatistics

HEIGENHAUSER, G. J. F., Medicine

HENRY, J., Psychiatry

HOLDER, D. A., Medicine

HOLLAND, F. J., Paediatrics

HUCKER, S. J., Psychiatry

HUGHES, D., Obstetrics

HUIZINGA, J. D., Medicine

HUNT, R. H., Medicine

HUTCHISON, B. G., Family Medicine

ISSENMAN, R. M., Paediatrics

JORDANA, M., Pathology

KARMALI, M. A., Pathology

KATES, N., Psychiatry

KAUFMAN, K. J., Family Medicine

KEARON, C., Medicine

KELTON, J. G., Pathology

KILLIAN, K. J., Medicine

KIRBY, J., Medicine

KIRPALANI, H., Paediatrics

KWAN, C. Y., Medicine

LATIMER, E. J., Family Medicine

LAW, M. C., Rehabilitation Science

LEE, R. M. K. W., Anaesthesia

LEVINE, M., Clinical Epidemiology and Biostatistics

LEVITT, C. A., Family Medicine

LONN, E., Medicine

LUDWIN, D., Medicine

LUKKA, H., Medicine

McDERMOTT, M. R., Pathology

MACMILLAN, H., Psychiatry

MACPHERSON, A., Medicine

MAHONY, J., Pathology

MAJUMDAR, B., School of Nursing

McKELVIE, R., Medicine

MANDELL, L., Medicine

MAZUREK, M., Medicine

McQUEEN, M., Pathology

MEYER, R., Medicine

MISHRA, R. K., Psychiatry

MOAYYEDI, P., Medicine

MOHIDE, P. T., Obstetrics and Gynaecology

MOLLOY, D. W., Medicine

MORILLO, C., Medicine
MUGGAH, H. F., Obstetrics and Gynaecology
NAHMIUS, C., Radiology
NEAME, P., Pathology
NEVILLE, A., Medicine
NIEBOER, E., Biochemistry
NILES, L. P., Psychiatry
NORMAN, G. R., Clinical Epidemiology and Biostatistics
O'BYRNE, P., Medicine
OFOSU, F., Pathology
OROVAN, W. L., Surgery
PAES, B. A., Paediatrics
PANJU, A., Medicine
PATTERSON, C. J. S., Medicine
PATTERSON, M., Radiology
PERDUE, M. H., Pathology
PINELLI, J. M., School of Nursing
RADHI, J., Pathology
RATHBONE, M. P., Medicine
RICHARDS, C. D., Pathology
RIDDELL, R., Radiology
RONEN, G. M., Paediatrics
ROSENBAUM, P. L., Paediatrics
ROSENFELD, J. M., Pathology
ROSENTHAL, K. L., Pathology
ROTSTEIN, C. M. F., Medicine
RUSTHOVEN, J., Medicine
RYAN, E., Psychiatry
SALAMAS, S., Pathology
SCHMIDT, B. K., Paediatrics
SCHULMAN, S., Medicine
SEARS, M. R., Medicine
SEGGIE, J., Psychiatry
SHANNON, H. S., Clinical Epidemiology and Biostatistics
SHARMA, A., Medicine
SMAILL, F., Pathology
SNIDER, D., Pathology
SOLOMON, P., School of Rehabilitation Science
SOMERS, S., Radiology
STEER, P., Paediatrics
STEINER, M., Psychiatry
STODDART, G. L., Clinical Epidemiology and Biostatistics
STRATFORD, P., School of Rehabilitation Science
SUR, R., Medicine
SWINSON, R. P., Psychiatry
SZATMARI, P., Psychiatry
SZECHTMAN, H., Psychiatry
TEO, K., Medicine
TOUGAS, G., Medicine
TURNBULL, J. D., Medicine
TURPIE, I. D., Medicine
UPTON, A. R. M., Medicine
VAN DER SPUY, R., Medicine
VERMA, D. K., Family Medicine
VICKERS, J. D., School of Nursing
WALKER, I. R., Medicine
WALTER, S. D., Clinical Epidemiology and Biostatistics
WARKENTIN, T., Pathology
WATTS, J. L., Paediatrics
WAYE, J., Pathology
WEBBER, C., Radiology
WEITZ, J., Medicine
WESSEL, J., Rehabilitation Science
WHELAN, D., Paediatrics
WHITTON, A., Medicine
WITELSON, S. F., Psychiatry
WRIGHT, G. D., Biochemistry
YANG, D. S. C., Biochemistry
YOUNG, E., Pathology
YOUNGLAI, E. V., Obstetrics and Gynaecology
YUSUF, S., Medicine
ZHOROV, B., Biochemistry

Faculty of Humanities:
ADAMSON, J., English
AHMED, A., French
ALLEN, B. G., Philosophy
ALSOP, J. D., History

ARTHUR, R. T. W., Philosophy
BAYARD, C. A., French
BOWERBANK, S., English
CLARK, D. L., English
CROSTA, S., French
DUNBABIN, K. M. D., Classics
FERNS, H. J., English
GAUVREAU, J. M., History
GIROUX, H., English and Communications Studies
GOELLNICHT, D. C., English
GRIFFIN, N. J., Philosophy
HITCHCOCK, D. L., Philosophy
JEAY, M. M., French
JONES, H., Classics
KACZYNSKI, B. M., History
KING, J., English
KOLESNIKOFF, N., Modern Languages and Linguistics
MAGINNIS, H. B. J., School of the Arts
MURGATROYD, P., Classics
NELLES, H. V., History
O'CONNOR, M. E., English
OSTOVICH, H. M., English
RAHIMIEH, N., English and Comparative Literature
RAPOPORT, P., School of the Arts
RENWICK, W., School of the Arts
SILCOX, M., English
STROINSKA, M., Modern Languages and Linguistics
WALMSLEY, P., English
WALUCHOW, W. J., Philosophy
WEAVER, J. C., History
YORK, L. M., English

Faculty of Science:
ALAMA, S., Mathematics and Statistics
ALLAN, L. G., Psychology
BAIN, A. D., Chemistry
BALAKRISHNAN, N., Mathematics and Statistics
BARBIER, J. R. H., Chemistry
BECKER, S., Psychology
BENNETT, P., Psychology
BERLINSKY, A. J., Physics and Astronomy
BRONSARD, L., Mathematics and Statistics
BROOK, M. A., Chemistry
CHETTLE, D. R., Physics and Astronomy
CHOUINARD, V. A., School of Geography and Geology
COUCHMAN, H. M., Physics and Astronomy
CRAIG, W., Mathematics and Statistics
DALY, M., Psychology
DE CATANZARO, D. A., Psychology
DICKIN, A. P., School of Geography and Geology
DRAKE, J. J., School of Geography and Geology
ELLIOTT, S. J., School of Geography and Geology
EYLES, C. H., School of Geography and Geology
EYLES, J. D., School of Geography and Geology
FENG, S., Mathematics
FINAN, T. M., Biology
GAULIN, B. D., Physics and Astronomy
GOLDING, B., Biology
GREEDAN, J. E., Chemistry
GUAN, P., Mathematics and Statistics
HALL, F. L., School of Geography and Geology
HAMBLETON, I., Mathematics and Statistics
HARRIS, R. S., School of Geography and Geology
HARRIS, W. E., Physics and Astronomy
HART, B. T., Mathematics and Statistics
HIGGS, P. G., Physics and Astronomy
HITCHCOCK, A. P., Chemistry
HOPPE, F. M., Mathematics and Statistics
HURD, T. R., Mathematics and Statistics
JACOBS, J. R., Biology
KALLIN, C., Physics and Astronomy
KANAROGLOU, P. S., School of Geography and Geology

KOLASA, J., Biology
KOLSTER, M., Mathematics and Statistics
LEIGH, W. J., Chemistry
LEVY, B. A., Psychology
LEWIS, T. L., Psychology
LIAW, K. L., School of Geography and Geology
LUKE, G. M., Physics and Astronomy
MCCARRY, B. E., Chemistry
MACDONALD, P. D. M., Mathematics and Statistics
MAURER, D. M., Psychology
MIN-OO, M., Mathematics and Statistics
MOORE, G. H., Mathematics and Statistics
MORRIS, W. A., School of Geography and Geology
MOTHERSILL, C. E., Medical Physics and Applied Radiological Science
MURPHY, K. M., Psychology
NICAS, A. J., Mathematics and Statistics
NURSE, C. A., Biology
O'DONNELL, M. J., Biology
PUDRITZ, R. E., Physics and Astronomy
RACINE, R. J., Psychology
RAINBOW, A. J., Biology
ROLLO, C. D., Biology
SAWYER, E. T., Mathematics and Statistics
SCHELLHORN, H., Biology
SCHROBILGEN, G. J., Chemistry
SEKULER, A., Psychology
SHI, A., Physics and Astronomy
SIEGEL, S., Psychology
SINGH, R. S., Biology
STOVER, H., Chemistry
SUTHERLAND, P., Physics and Astronomy
TERLOUW, J. K., Chemistry
TRAINOR, L. J., Psychology
VALERIOTE, M. A., Mathematics and Statistics
VENUS, D., Physics and Astronomy
VIVEROS-AGUILER, R., Mathematics and Statistics
WANG, M. Y. K., Mathematics and Statistics
WELCH, D. L., Physics and Astronomy
WERETILNYK, E. A., Biology
WERSTIUK, N. H., Chemistry
WILSON, C. D., Physics and Astronomy
WILSON, M. I., Psychology
WOLKOWICZ, G. S. K., Mathematics and Statistics
WOO, M. K., School of Geography and Geology
WOOD, C. M., Biology
YIP, P. C. Y., Mathematics and Statistics

Faculty of Social Sciences:
ARCHIBALD, W. P., Sociology
ARONSON, J. H., School of Social Work
BLIMKIE, C. J. R., Kinesiology
BROWN, R. A., Social Work
CAIN, R., Social Work
CANNON, A., Anthropology
CARROLL, B. A., Political Science
CHAN, K. S. Y., Economics
COLARUSSO, J. J., Anthropology
COLEMAN, W. D., Political Science
COOPER, M. O., Anthropology
CUNEO, C. J., Sociology
DENTON, M. A., Gerontology
DOOLEY, M. D., Economics
ELLIOTT, D., Kinesiology
FEIT, H. A., Anthropology
FINSTEN, L., Anthropology
FOX, J. D., Sociology
HERRING, D. A., Anthropology
HICKS, A. L., Kinesiology
HURLEY, J. E., Economics
JACEK, H. J., Political Science
JONES, S. R. G., Economics
KROEKER, P. T., Religious Studies
KUBURSI, A. A., Economics
LEACH, J. E., Economics
LEE, T. D., Kinesiology
LEVITT, C. H., Sociology
LEWCHUK, W., Economics

LEWIS, T. J., Political Science
McCARTNEY, N., Kinesiology
MAGEE, L. J., Economics
MENDELSON, A., Religious Studies
MESTELMAN, S., Economics
MIALL, C., Sociology
MULLER, R. A., Economics
PORTER, T., Political Science
RACINE, J., Economics
RICE, J. J., School of Social Work
RODMAN, W. L., Anthropology
SALE, D. G., Kinesiology
SATZEWICH, V., Sociology
SAUNDERS, S. R., Anthropology
SCARTH, W. M., Economics
SCHULLER, E. M., Religious Studies
SHAFFIR, W. B., Sociology
SPENCER, B. G., Economics
SPROULE-JONES, M. H., Political Science
STARKES, J., Kinesiology
STEIN, M. B., Political Science
STUBBS, R. W., Political Science
VEALL, M. R., Economics
WATT, M. S., School of Social Work
WHITE, P. G., Kinesiology
YATES, C. A. B., Political Science

School of Business:

ABAD, P. L., Management Science and Information Systems
AGARWAL, N. C., Human Resources and Management
BABA, V., Business
BART, C. K., Marketing
CHAMBERLAIN, T. W., Finance and Business Economics
CHEUNG, C. S., Finance and Business Economics
COOPER, R. G., Marketing
DEAVES, R., Finance and Business Economics
HACKETT, R. D., Human Resources and Management
KLEINSCHMIDT, E. J., Marketing
KWAN, C. C. Y., Finance and Business Economics
MEDCOF, J. W., Human Resources and Management
MILTENBURG, J. G., Management Science and Information Systems
MOUNTAIN, D. C., Finance and Business Economics
PARLAR, M., Management Science and Information Systems
ROSE, J. B., Human Resources and Management
SHEHATA, M. M., Accounting
STEINER, G., Management Science and Information Systems
WESOLOWSKY, G. O., Management Science and Information Systems
YUAN, Y., Management Science and Information Systems
ZEYTINOGLU, F. I., Human Resources and Management

Divinity College (1280 Main St, W, Hamilton, ON L8S 4R1; tel. (905) 525-9140 ext. 24401; fax (905) 577-4782; internet www.macdiv.ca):

HORNSELL, M. J. A., Old Testament and Hebrew
LONGENECKER, R. N., New Testament
PORTER, S. E., New Testament

ATTACHED RESEARCH INSTITUTES

Centre for Electrophotonic Materials and Devices: Hamilton; research and development; Dir Dr D. A. THOMPSON.

R. Samuel McLaughlin Centre for Gerontological Health Research: Hamilton; research, training and promotion of health and preventive care for the elderly; organizes conferences; publishes reports; Dir Dr L. W. CHAMBERS.

Centre for Health Economics and Policy Analysis: Hamilton; research, consultation, education, liaison; organizes conferences, etc.; publishes health policy commentaries and research reports; Coordinator Dr J. HURLEY.

Centre for Peace Studies: Hamilton; research, graduate and undergraduate courses, seminars, lectures, conferences and other projects in the area of international peace; Dir Dr G. PURDY.

Gerontology Programme: Hamilton; f. 1979; a multidisciplinary unit to promote and develop research and educational programmes on aging; Dir Dr M. DENTON.

McMaster Institute for Energy Studies: Hamilton; f. 1980 to encourage communication between researchers in different fields of energy study; Dir Dr DEAN MOUNTAIN; publ. *Newsletter* (3 a year).

Institute of Environment and Health: Hamilton; research, health surveys and health assessments, identification and evaluation of hazards, development of preventive policies and strategies and of educational programmes; participation in community-based environment and health initiatives; conducts workshops and seminars; Dir Dr B. NEWBOLD (acting).

Brockhouse Institute for Materials Research: Hamilton; research in the chemistry, engineering, metallurgy and physics of solid materials is supplemented through this multidisciplinary unit; principal areas: lattice dynamics, kinetics and diffusion, mechanical properties, microelectric and electro-optic devices, optical materials, phase transformations, thermodynamics, radiation damage, structure determination, surfaces and catalysis; Dir Dr J. S. PRESTON.

Institute of Polymer Production Technology: Hamilton; provides a facility and environment in which University staff and technical personnel from industry can do research and development on process technology for polymer production; Dir (vacant).

Office of International Affairs: Hamilton; coordinates institutional international activities; provides leadership in international education and research, and in the provision of professional services by McMaster personnel to the global community; includes Centre for International Health; Dir Dr M. W. L. CHAN.

UNIVERSITY OF MANITOBA

Winnipeg, MB R3T 2N2
Telephone: (204) 474-8880
Fax: (204) 474-7536
E-mail: registrar@umanitoba.ca
Internet: www.umanitoba.ca

Founded 1877
Language of instruction: English
Academic year: September to April (2 terms)
Chancellor: Dr WILLIAM NORRIE
President and Vice-Chancellor: Dr DAVID T. BARNARD
Vice-Pres. for Academic and Provost: JOANNE C. KESELMAN
Vice-Pres. for Admin.: DEBORAH McCALLUM
Vice-Pres. for External: ELAINE GOLDIE
Vice-Pres. for Research: DIGVIR JAYAS (acting)
Dir of Libraries: C. PRESSER

Library of 2,000,000 vols
Number of teachers: 1,142
Number of students: 26,800

DEANS

Faculty of Agricultural and Food Sciences: Dr MICHAEL TREVAN
Faculty of Architecture: Dr DAVID R. WITTY
Faculty of Arts: RICHARD SIGURDSON
Faculty of Dentistry: ANTHONY IACOPINO

Faculty of Education: JOHN WIENS
Faculty of Engineering: DOUGLAS RUTH
Faculty of Graduate Studies: Dr TONY SECCO
Faculty of Environment: LESLIE KING
Faculty of Human Ecology: R. BIRD
Faculty of Law: HARVEY SECTER
Faculty of Management: J. L. GRAY
Faculty of Medicine: B. K. E. HENNEN
Faculty of Nursing: D. M. GREGORY
Faculty of Pharmacy: D. COLLINS
Faculty of Physical Education and Recreation Studies: D. W. HRYCAIKO
Faculty of Science: Dr MARK WHITMORE
Faculty of Social Work: BOB MULLALY

DIRECTORS

School of Agriculture: D. FLATEN
School of Art: D. AMUNDSON
School of Dental Hygiene: S. LAVIGNE
School of Medical Rehabilitation: J. COOPER (Overall Dir: E. ETCHEVERRY (Occupational Therapy: GISELE PEREIRA (Physical Therapy, acting)
School of Music: DALE LONIS
Continuing Education Division: A. PERCIVAL

PROFESSORS

Faculty of Agricultural and Food Sciences:
BALLANCE, G. M., Plant Science
BJARNASON, H., Agribusiness and Agricultural Economics
BLANK, G., Food Science
BOYD, M. S., Agribusiness and Agricultural Economics
BRITTON, M. G., Biosystems Engineering
BRÛLÉ-BABEL, A. L., Plant Science
CAMPBELL, L. D., Animal Science
CENKOWSKI, S., Biosystems Engineering
CONNOR, M. L., Animal Science
DRONZEK, B. L., Plant Science
ENTZ, M., Plant Science
GALLOWAY, T. D., Entomology
GOH, T. B., Soil Science
GUENTER, W., Animal Science
HILL, R. D., Plant Science
HOLLEY, R. A., Food Science
HOLLIDAY, N. J., Entomology
JAYAS, D. S., Biosystems Engineering
KRAFT, D. F., Agribusiness and Agricultural Economics
MACKAY, P. A., Entomology
MACMILLAN, J. A., Agribusiness and Agricultural Economics
McVETTY, P. B. E., Plant Science
MUIR, W. E., Biosystems Engineering
PRITCHARD, M. K., Plant Science
RACZ, G. J., Soil Science
REMPHREY, W. R., Plant Science
ROUGHLEY, R. E., Entomology
SCANLON, M. G., Food Science
SCARTH, R., Plant Science
VESSEY, J. K., Plant Science
WITTENBERG, K. M., Animal Science
ZHANG, Q., Biosystems Engineering

Faculty of Architecture:
COX, M. G., Interior Design
MACDONALD, R. I., Environmental Design
NELSON, C., Landscape Architecture
RATTRAY, A. E., Landscape Architecture
THOMSEN, C. H., Landscape Architecture

Faculty of Arts:
ALBAS, D. C., Sociology
ANNA, T. E., History
ARNASON, D. E., English
BAILEY, P. C., History
BARBER, D. G., Geograpy
BRIERLEY, J. S., Geography
BUMSTED, J. M., History
BUTEUX, P. E., Political Studies
CAMERON, N. E., Economics
CHERNOMAS, R., Economics
COMACK, A. E., Sociology
COOLEY, D. O., English
COSMOPOULOS, M. B., Classics

DEAN, J. M., Economics
DEBICKI, M., Political Studies
DeLUCA, R., Psychology
EATON, W. O., Psychology
FERGUSON, B. G., History
FINLAY, J. L., History
FINNEGAN, R. E., English
FORTIER, P., French, Spanish and Italian
FRIESEN, G. A., History
GERUS, O. W., History
GONICK, C. W., Economics
GORDON, D. K., French, Spanish and Italian
GREENFIELD, H. J., Anthropology
GRISLIS, E., Religion
HALLI, S. S., Sociology
HELLER, H., History
HINZ, E. J., English
HUM, D., Economics
JOHNSON, C. G., English
JUDD, E. R., Anthropology
KENDLE, J. E., History
KESELMAN, H. J., Psychology
KESELMAN, J. C., Psychology
KINNEAR, E. M., History
KINNEAR, M. S. R., History
KULCHYSKI, P., Native Studies
KWONG, J., Sociology
LeBow, M. D., Psychology
LEVENTHAL, L. Y., Psychology
LINDEN, E. W., Sociology
LOBDELL, R. A., Economics
LOXLEY, J., Economics
McCANCE, D., Religion
McCARTHY, D. J., Philosophy
MARTIN, D. G., Psychology
MARTIN, G. L., Psychology
MATHESON, C., Philosophy
NAHIR, M., Linguistics
NICHOLS, J. D., Linguistics
NICKELS, J. B., Psychology
NORTON, W., Geography
OAKES, J. E., Native Studies
O'KELL, R. P., English
PEAR, J. J., Psychology
PERRY, R. P., Psychology
PHILLIPS, P. A., Economics
RAMU, G. N., Sociology
REA, J. E., History
REMPEL, H., Economics
ROBERTS, L., Sociology
RUBENSTEIN, H., Anthropology
SCHAFER, A. M., Philosophy
SCHLUDERMANN, E. H., Psychology
SCHLUDERMANN, S., Psychology
SEGALL, A., Sociology
SHAVER, R. W., Philosophy
SHKANDRIJ, M., German and Slavic Studies
SIMPSON, W., Economics
SINGER, M., Psychology
SMIL, V., Geography
SMITH, G. C., Geography
SPRAGUE, D. N., History
STAMBROOK, F. G., History
STEIMAN, L. B., History
SZATHMÁRY, J. E., Anthropology
TAIT, R. W., Psychology
THOMAS, P. G., Political Studies
TODD, D., Geography
TOLES, G. E., English
WALZ, E. P., English
WATERMAN, A. M. C., Economics
WEIL, H. S., English
WIEST, R. E., Anthropology
WILLIAMS, D. L., English
WILSON, L. M., Psychology
WOLF, K., Icelandic
WOLFART, H. C., Linguistics
WORTLEY, J. T., History

Faculty of Dentistry:

BHULLAR, R. P.
BOWDEN, G. H. W.
DAWES, C.
DE VRIES, J.
FLEMING, N.

HAMILTON, I. R.
KARIM, A. C.
LAVELLE, C. L. B.
LOVE, W. B.
SCOTT, J. E.
SINGER, D. L.
SUZUKI, M.
WILTSHIRE, W.

Faculty of Education:

BARTELL, R., Educational Administration, Foundations and Psychology
CAP, O., Curriculum, Teaching and Learning
CHINIEN, C., Curriculum, Teaching and Learning
CLIFTON, R. A., Postsecondary Studies, Educational Administration, Foundations and Psychology
FREEZE, D. R., Educational Administration, Foundations and Psychology
GREGOR, A. D., Postsecondary Studies, Educational Administration, Foundations and Psychology
HARVEY, D. A., Curriculum, Teaching and Learning
HLYNKA, L. D., Curriculum, Teaching and Learning
JENKINSON, D. H., Curriculum, Teaching and Learning
KESELMAN, J. C., Educational Administration, Foundations and Psychology
KIRBY, D. M., Postsecondary Studies
LEVIN, B., Educational Administration, Foundations and Psychology
LONG, J. C., Educational Administration, Foundations and Psychology
MAGSINO, R., Educational Administration, Foundations and Psychology
MORPHY, D. R., Postsecondary Studies
PERRY, R. P., Postsecondary Studies
POROZNY, G. H. J., Curriculum, Teaching and Learning
ROBERTS, L. W., Postsecondary Studies
SCHULZ, W. E., Educational Administration, Foundations and Psychology
SEIFERT, K. L., Educational Administration, Foundations and Psychology
STAPLETON, J. J., Educational Administration, Foundations and Psychology
STINNER, A. O., Curriculum, Teaching and Learning
STRAW, S. B., Curriculum, Teaching and Learning
YOUNG, J. C., Educational Administration, Foundations and Psychology
ZAKALUK, B. L., Curriculum, Teaching and Learning

Faculty of Engineering:

BALAKRISHNAN, S., Mechanical and Industrial
BASSIM, M. N., Mechanical and Industrial
BRIDGES, G. E. J., Electrical and Computer
BURN, D. H., Civil and Geological
CAHOON, J. R., Mechanical and Industrial
CARD, H. C., Electrical and Computer
CHATURVEDI, M. C., Mechanical and Industrial
CIRIC, I. M. R., Electrical and Computer
CLAYTON, A., Civil and Geological
GOLE, A. M., Electrical and Computer
GRAHAM, J., Civil and Geological
KINSNER, W., Electrical and Computer
LAJTAI, E. Z., Civil and Geological
LEHN, W., Electrical and Computer
McLAREN, P. G., Electrical and Computer
McLEOD, R. D., Electrical and Computer
MARTENS, G. O., Electrical and Computer
MENZIES, R. W., Electrical and Computer
MUFTI, A. A., Civil and Geological
OLESZKIEWICZ, J. A., Civil and Geological
ONYSHKO, S., Electrical and Computer
PAWLAK, M., Electrical and Computer
POLYZOIS, D., Civil and Geological
POPPLEWELL, N., Mechanical and Industrial

RAGHUVEER, M. R., Electrical and Computer
RUTH, D. W., Mechanical and Industrial
SEBAK, A., Electrical and Computer
SEPEHRI, N., Mechanical and Industrial
SHAFAI, L., Electrical and Computer
SHAH, A. H., Civil and Geological
SHWEDYK, E., Electrical and Computer
SOLIMAN, H. M., Mechanical and Industrial
STIMPSON, B., Civil and Geological
STRONG, D., Mechanical and Industrial
THOMSON, D. J., Electrical and Computer
THORNTON-TRUMP, A. B., Mechanical and Industrial
WOODBURY, A. D., Civil

Faculty of Human Ecology:

BERRY, R. E., Family Studies
BIRD, R. P., Foods and Nutrition
BOND, J. B., Family Studies
ESKIN, N. A. M., Foods and Nutrition
HARVEY, C. D. H., Family Studies

Faculty of Law:

ANDERSON, D. T.
BUSBY, K.
DEUTSCHER, D.
ESAU, A.
GUTH, D. J.
HARVEY, D. A. C.
IRVINE, J. C.
McGILLIVRAY, A.
NEMIROFF, G.
OSBORNE, P. H.
PENNER, R.
SECTER, H. L.
SNEIDERMAN, B.
STUESSER, L.
VINCENT, L.

Faculty of Management:

BARTELL, M., Business Administration
BECTOR, C. R., Business Administration
BHATT, S. K., Business Administration
BRUNING, E. R., Marketing
BRUNING, N. S., Business Administration
ELIAS, N. S., Accounting and Finance
FROHLICH, N., Business Administration
GODARD, J. H., Business Administration
GOOD, W. S., Marketing
GOULD, L. I., Accounting and Finance
GRAY, J. L., Business Administration
HILTON, M. W., Accounting and Finance
HOGAN, T. P., Business Administration
McCALLUM, J. S., Accounting and Finance
NOTZ, W. W., Business Administration
OWEN, B. E., Business Administration
ROSENBLOOM, E. S.
STARKE, F. A., Business Administration

Faculty of Medicine:

ADAMSON, I. Y. R., Pathology
ANDERSON, J., Human Anatomy and Cell Science
ANGEL, A., Medicine and Physiology
AOKI, F. Y., Continuing Medical Education, Medical Microbiology, Medicine, Pharmacology and Therapeutics
ARNETT, J. L., Clinical Health Psychology and Continuing Medical Education
ARTHUR, G., Biochemistry and Medical Genetics
BAKER, S., Medicine
BARAGAR, F., Medicine
BARAKAT, S., Psychiatry
BARAL, E., Medicine, Radiology
BARWINSKY, J., Cardiothoracic Surgery
BEBCHUK, W., Psychiatry
BECKER, A., Paediatrics and Child Health
BEGLEITER, A., Medicine, Pharmacology and Therapeutics
BERCZI, I., Immunology
BLACK, G., Surgery
BLAKLEY, B., Otolaryngology
BOOTH, F., Paediatrics and Child Health
BORODITSY, R., Obstetrics, Gynaecology and Reproductive Sciences

BOSE, D., Anaesthesia, Medicine, Pharmacology and Therapeutics
BOSE, R., Pharmacology and Therapeutics
BOW, E., Medical Microbiology
BOWDEN, G. H., Medical Microbiology
BOWMAN, D. M., Medicine
BOWMAN, W. D., Paediatrics and Child Health
BRANDES, L. J., Medicine, Pharmacology and Therapeutics
BRISTOW, G. K., Anaesthesia
BRUNHAM, R. C., Medical Microbiology, Medicine, Obstetrics, Gynaecology and Reproductive Sciences
BRUNI, J. E., Human Anatomy and Cell Science
CARR, I., Pathology
CARTER, S. A., Medicine and Physiology
CASIRO, O., Paediatrics and Child Health
CATTINI, P., Physiology, Pharmacology and Therapeutics
CHERNICK, V., Paediatrics and Child Health
CHOY, P. C., Biochemistry and Molecular Biology
CHUDLEY, A. E., Continuing Medical Education, Human Genetics, Paediatrics and Child Health
COOMBS, C., Medical Microbiology
COOPER, J., Community Health Sciences
CRAIG, D. B., Anaesthesia
CRISTANTE, L., Surgery
CUMMING, G. R., Paediatrics and Child Health
DANZINGER, R. G., General Surgery
DAVIE, J. R., Biochemistry and Molecular Biology
DEAN, H., Paediatrics and Child Health
DUBO, H. I. C., Medicine
DUKE, P. C., Anaesthesia
EL-GABALAWY, H., Medicine
EVANS, J. A., Community Health Sciences, Human Genetics, Paediatrics and Child Health
FERGUSON, C. A., Paediatrics and Child Health
FINE, A., Medicine
FORESTER, J., Medicine
FORGET, E., Community Health Sciences
GARTNER, J., Immunology, Pathology
GEIGER, J., Pharmacology and Therapeutics
GERRARD, J. M., Paediatrics and Child Health
GLAVIN, G., Pharmacology and Therapeutics
GORDON, R., Radiology
GREENBERG, C. R., Human Genetics, Paediatrics and Child Health
GREWAR, D. A. I., Family Medicine, Paediatrics and Child Health
GUIJON, F., Obstetrics, Gynaecology and Reproductive Sciences
HALL, P. F., Obstetrics, Gynaecology and Reproductive Sciences
HAMERTON, J. L., Paediatrics and Child Health
HAMMOND, G. W., Medical Microbiology, Medicine
HARDING, G. M., Medical Microbiology, Medicine
HARVEY, D. A., Community Health Sciences
HASSARD, T. H., Community Health Sciences
HAVENS, B., Community Health Sciences
HAYGLASS, K. T., Immunology
HELEWA, M., Obstetrics, Gynaecology and Reproductive Sciences
HERSHFIELD, E. A., Community Health Sciences
HERSHFIELD, E. S., Medicine
HOESCHEN, R., Medicine
HOGAN, T. P., Community Health Sciences
HORNE, J. M., Community Health Sciences
HOSKING, D., Surgery

HUDSON, R., Anaesthesia
HUGHES, K. R., Physiology
IRELAND, D. J., Otolaryngology
JAY, F. T., Medical Microbiology
JEFFERY, J., Medicine
JOHNSTON, J. B., Medicine
JORDAN, L. M., Physiology
KARDAMI, E., Human Anatomy and Cell Science
KATZ, P., Psychiatry
KAUFERT, J. M., Community Health Sciences
KAUFERT, P. A., Community Health Services
KAUFMAN, B. J., Medicine
KEPRON, M. W., Medicine
KIRK, P. J., Family Medicine
KIRKPATRICK, J. R., Continuing Medical Education, General Surgery
KREPART, G. V., Obstetrics, Gynaecology and Reproductive Sciences
KROEGER, E. A., Physiology
KRYGER, M., Medicine
LaBELLA, F. S., Pharmacology and Therapeutics
LATTER, J., Medicine
LAUTT, W. W., Pharmacology and Therapeutics
LeJOHN, H. B., Human Genetics
LERTZMAN, M., Continuing Medical Education, Medicine
LEVI, C. S., Radiology
LEVITT, M., Medicine
LIGHT, B., Medicine
LIGHT, R. B., Medical Microbiology
LONGSTAFFE, S., Paediatrics and Child Health
LYONS, E. A., Radiology, Obstetrics, Gynaecology and Reproductive Sciences
McCARTHY, D. S., Medicine
McCLARTY, B., Radiology
McCLARTY, G. A., Medical Microbiology
McCOSHEN, J. A., Obstetrics, Gynaecology and Reproductive Sciences
McCREA, D. A., Physiology
McCULLOUGH, D. W., Continuing Medical Education, Otolaryngology
MacDOUGALL, B., Medicine
McILWRAITH, R., Clinical Health Psychology
McKENZIE, J. K., Community Health Sciences
MAKSYMIUK, A., Medicine
MINK, G., Medicine
MINUK, G. Y., Medicine, Pharmacology and Therapeutics
MOFFATT, M. E., Community Health Services, Paediatrics and Child Health
MOWAT, M., Biochemistry and Medical Genetics
MURPHY, L. C., Biochemistry and Molecular Biology, Medicine
MURPHY, L. J., Medicine and Physiology
MURRAY, R., Community Health Sciences
MUTCH, A., Anaesthesia
NAGY, J. I., Physiology
NAIMARK, A., Physiology
NANCE, D. M., Pathology
NICOLLE, L., Medicine, Medical Microbiology
OEN, K., Paediatrics and Child Health
OLWENY, C., Medicine
O'NEIL, J. D., Community Health Sciences
ONG, B. Y., Anaesthesia
OPPENHEIMER, L., General Surgery
ORR, F. W., Pathology
PANAGIA, V., Human Anatomy and Cell Science, Physiology
PARKINSON, D., Neurosurgery
PASTERKAMP, H., Paediatrics and Child Health
PATERSON, J. A., Human Anatomy and Cell Science
PEELING, J., Pharmacology and Therapeutics
PEELING, W. J., Radiology

PENNER, B., Medicine
PENNER, S. B., Pharmacology and Therapeutics
PETTIGREW, N., Pathology
PIERCE, G. N., Physiology
PLUMMER, F. A., Medical Microbiology, Medicine
POSTL, B., Community Health Sciences, Paediatrics and Child Health
POSTUMA, R., General Surgery
RAMSEY, E., Surgery
REED, M. H., Continuing Medical Education, Paediatrics and Child Health, Radiology
RENNIE, W., Orthopaedic Surgery
RHODES, R., Pathology
RIESE, K. T., General Surgery and Otolaryngology
RIGATTO, H., Paediatrics and Child Health, Obstetrics, Gynaecology and Reproductive Sciences
ROBERTS, D., Medicine
RONALD, A. R., Community Health Sciences, Medical Microbiology, Medicine
ROOS, L. L., Community Health Sciences
ROOS, N. P., Community Health Sciences
ROY, R., Clinical Health Psychology
RUSH, D., Medicine
SCHACTER, B., Medicine
SCHROEDER, M., Paediatrics and Child Health
SESHIA, M. M. K., Obstetrics, Gynaecology and Reproductive Sciences, Paediatrics and Child Health
SHEFCHY, S., Physiology
SHIU, R. P. C., Physiology
SHOJANIA, A. M., Medicine, Paediatrics and Child Health, Pathology
SIMONS, F. E. R., Immunology, Paediatrics and Child Health
SIMONS, K., Paediatrics and Child Health
SINGAL, P. K., Physiology
SITAR, D., Medicine, Pharmacology and Therapeutics
SMYTH, D. D., Continuing Medical Education, Pharmacology and Therapeutics
SMYTHE, D., Medicine
SNEIDERMAN, B. M., Community Health Sciences
STANWICK, R. S., Community Health Sciences
STEPHENS, N. L., Physiology
STRANC, M. F., Plastic Surgery
SZATHMÁRY, E. J. E., Human Genetics
TENENBEIN, M., Community Health Sciences, Medicine, Pharmacology and Therapeutics, Paediatrics and Child Health
THLIVERIS, J. A., Human Anatomy and Cell Science
THOMSON, I., Anaesthesia
UNRUH, H. W., Surgery
VRIEND, J., Human Anatomy and Cell Science
WALKER, J., Clinical Health Psychology
WARREN, C. P. W., Continuing Medical Education, Medicine
WARRINGTON, R. J., Immunology and Medicine
WEST, M., Surgery
WILKINS, J. A., Immunology, Medicine, Medical Microbiology
WILLIAMS, T., Medical Microbiology, Paediatrics and Child Health
WOODS, R. A., Human Genetics
WRIGHT, J. A., Biochemistry and Molecular Biology
WROGEMANN, K., Biochemistry and Molecular Biology, Human Genetics
YASSI, A., Community Health Sciences
YOUNES, M., Medicine
YOUNG, T. K., Community Health Sciences
ZELINSKI, T., Biochemistry and Medical Genetics

Faculty of Nursing:

BEATON, J. I.
DEGNER, L. F.
GREGORY, D. M.

Faculty of Pharmacy:

BRIGGS, C. J.
COLLINS, D.
GRYMONPRE, R.
HASINOFF, B.
SIMONS, K. J.
TEMPLETON, J. F.
ZHANEL, G.

Faculty of Physical Education and Recreation Studies:

ALEXANDER, M. J. L.
DAHLGREN, W. J.
GIESBRECHT, G.
HARPER, J.
HRYCAIKO, D. W.
JANZEN, H. F.
READY, A. E.

Faculty of Science:

ABRAHAMS, M., Zoology
AITCHISON, P. W., Mathematics
ARNASON, A. N., Computer Science
AYRES, L. D., Geological Sciences
BALDWIN, W. G., Chemistry
BARBER, R. C., Physics and Astronomy
BELL, M. G., Mathematics
BERRY, T. G., Mathematics
BIRCHALL, J., Physics and Astronomy
BLUNDEN, P., Physics and Astronomy
BOOTH, J. T., Botany
BREWSTER, J. F., Statistics
BUTLER, M., Microbiology
CHARLTON, J. L., Chemistry
CHENG, S. W., Statistics
CHOW, A., Chemistry
CLARK, G. S., Geological Sciences
COLLENS, R. J., Computer Science
DAVISON, N. E., Physics and Astronomy
DICK, T. A., Zoology
DOOB, M., Mathematics
DUCKWORTH, H. W., Chemistry
EALES, J. G., Zoology
ELIAS, R. J., Geological Sciences
ENS, W., Physics and Astronomy
FALK, W., Physics and Astronomy
FU, J. C., Statistics
GERHARD, J. A., Mathematics
GHAHRAMANI, F., Mathematics
GRATZER, G., Mathematics
GUO, B., Mathematics
GUPTA, C. K., Mathematics
GUPTA, N. D., Mathematics
HALDEN, N. M., Geological Sciences
HAWTHORNE, F. C., Geological Sciences
HOSKINS, J. A., Computer Science
HOSKINS, W. D., Mathematics
HRUSKA, F. E., Chemistry
HUEBNER, E., Zoology
HUNTER, N. R., Chemistry
JAMIESON, J. C., Chemistry
JANZEN, A. F., Chemistry
KELLY, D., Mathematics
KENKEL, N. C., Botany
KING, P. R., Computer Science
KLASSEN, G. R., Microbiology
KOCAY, W. L., Computer Science
KRAUSE, G., Mathematics
LAKSER, H., Mathematics
LAST, W. M., Geological Sciences
LOEWEN, P. C., Microbiology
LOLY, P. D., Physics and Astronomy
MACARTHUR, R. A., Zoology
McKINNON, D. M., Chemistry
MACPHERSON, B. D., Statistics
MAEBA, P. Y., Microbiology
MEEK, D. S., Computer Science
MENDELSOHN, N. S., Mathematics
MOON, W., Geological Sciences
MORRISH, A. H., Physics and Astronomy
O'NEIL, J. D. J., Chemistry
OSBORN, T. A., Physics and Astronomy

PADMANABHAN, R., Mathematics
PAGE, J. H., Physics and Astronomy
PAGE, S. A., Physics and Astronomy
PARAMESWARAN, M. R., Mathematics
PLATT, C., Mathematics
PUNTER, D., Botany
RIEWE, R. R., Zoology
ROBINSON, G. G. C., Botany, Environmental Science Program
ROSHKO, R. M., Physics and Astronomy
SAMANTA, M., Statistics
SCHAEFER, T., Chemistry
SCUSE, D. H., Computer Science
SEALY, S. G., Zoology
SECCO, A. S., Chemistry
SHARMA, K. S., Physics and Astronomy
SHERRIFF, B. L., Geological Sciences
SHIVAKUMAR, P. N., Mathematics
SICHLER, J., Mathematics
SOUTHERN, B. W., Physics and Astronomy
STANTON, R. G., Computer Science
STEWART, J. M., Botany
SUZUKI, I., Microbiology
SVENNE, J. P., Physics and Astronomy
TABISZ, G. C., Physics and Astronomy
TELLER, J. C., Geological Sciences
THOMAS, R. S. D., Mathematics
TRIM, D. W., Mathematics
VAN OERS, W. T. H., Physics and Astronomy
VAN REES, G. H. J., Computer Science
WALLACE, R., Chemistry
WALTON, D. J., Computer Science
WESTMORE, J. B., Chemistry
WIENS, T. J., Zoology
WILLIAMS, G., Physics and Astronomy
WILLIAMS, H. C., Computer Science
WILLIAMS, J. J., Mathematics
WOODS, R. G., Mathematics
WRIGHT, J. A., Microbiology
ZETNER, P. W., Physics and Astronomy

Faculty of Social Work:

FUCHS, D. M.
ROY, R.
TRUTE, B.

School of Art:

AMUNDSON, D. O.
BAKER, M. C.
FLYNN, R. K.
HIGGINS, S. B.
McMILLAN, D. S.
PURA, W. P.
SAKOWSKI, R. C.
SCOTT, C. W.

School of Dental Hygiene:

BOWDEN, G. H. W.
DAWES, C.
FLEMING, N.
HAMILTON, I. R.
JAY, F.
KARIM, A. C.
LAVELLE, C. L. B.
SCOTT, J. E.
SINGER, D. L.

School of Medical Rehabilitation:

ANDERSON, J., Occupational Therapy
COOPER, J. E., Occupational Therapy
LOVERIDGE, B., Physical Therapy

School of Music:

ENGBRECHT, H.
JENSEN, K.
LONIS, D.
WEDGEWOOD, R.

Continuing Education Division:

PERCIVAL, A.

ATTACHED INSTITUTE

Natural Resources Institute: Dir Dr C. EMDAD HAQUE.

AFFILIATED COLLEGES

St Andrew's College: 29 Dysart Rd, Winnipeg, MB R3T 2M7; tel. (204) 474-8995; fax (204) 474-7624; f. 1964 (Ukrainian Orthodox Church); Principal V. OLENDER.

St Boniface College: 200 Cathedral Ave, St Boniface, MB R2H 0H7; tel. (204) 233-0210; fax (204) 237-3240; f. 1818 (Roman Catholic); Rector P. RUEST.

St John's College: 400 Dysart Rd, Winnipeg, MB R3T 2M5; tel. (204) 474-8531; fax (204) 474-7610; f. 1849 (Anglican); Warden and Vice-Chancellor Dr J. HOSKINS.

St Paul's College: 430 Dysart Rd, Winnipeg, MB R3T 2M6; tel. (204) 474-8575; fax (204) 474-7620; f. 1926 (Roman Catholic); Rector J. J. STAPLETON.

University College: 500 Dysart Rd, Winnipeg, MB R3T 2M8; tel. (204) 474-9522; fax (204) 474-7589; Provost G. WALZ.

MEMORIAL UNIVERSITY OF NEWFOUNDLAND

POB 4200, Elizabeth Ave, St John's, NL A1C 5S7

Telephone: (709) 737-8000
Fax: (709) 737-4569
Internet: www.mun.ca

Founded 1925 by Provincial Government as Memorial University College, university status 1949
Academic year: September to August (3 terms)
Language of instruction: English
Chancellor: J. CROSBIE
Pres. and Vice-Chancellor: A. MEISON
Vice-Pres. for Academic and Pro Vice-Chancellor: E. SIMPSON
Vice-Pres. for Admin.: W. W. THISTLE
Vice-Pres. for Research: K. KEOUGH
Prin., Sir Wilfred Grenfell College: A. FOWLER
Registrar: G. W. COLLINS
Librarian: R. ELLIS
Number of teachers: 1,367
Number of students: 16,000
Publications: *Canadian Folklore Canadien* (2 a year), *Communicator* (4 a year), *Culture and Tradition* (1 a yea), *Echos du Monde Classique/Classical Views* (3 a year), *Gazette* (26 a year), *Labour/Le Travail* (2 a year), *Luminus* (3 a year), *Newfoundland Quarterly* (4 a year), *Regional Language Studies* (1 a year), *Research Matters* (3 a year), *The Muse* (52 a year)

DEANS AND DIRECTORS

Faculty of Arts: T. MURPHY
Faculty of Business Administration: GARY GORMAN
Faculty of Education: ALICE COLLINS
Faculty of Engineering and Applied Science: Dr M. R. HADDARA
Faculty of Human Kinetics: Dr COLIN HIGGS
Faculty of Medicine: (vacant)
Faculty of Science: W. DAVIDSON
School of Continuing Education: H. WEIR
School of Graduate Studies: G. KEALEY
School of Music: TOM GORDON
School of Nursing: M. BEATON
School of Pharmacy: C. LOOMIS (acting)
School of Social Work: E. DOW

PROFESSORS

Faculty of Arts:

ALLEN, T. J.
BATH, A. J., Geography
BELL, D. N., Religious Studies
BELL, T. J., Physical Geography
BISHOP, N. B., French and Spanish
BORNSTEIN, C., Philosophy
BRADLEY, J., Linguistics
BRANIGAN, P., Linguistics
BROWN, S. C., Anthropology
BUBENIK, V., Linguistics

BUTLER, K., Physical Geography
BUTRICA, J., Classics
BYRNE, P., English
CATTO, N. R., Physical Geography
CHADWICK, A., French and Spanish
CHERWINSKI, W. J., History
CLARKE, S., Linguistics
CLOSE, D., Philosophy
CROCKER, S., Religious Studies
CULLUM, L., Religious Studies
DEAL, M., Anthropology
DEN OTTER, A. A., History
DEROCHE, M., Religious Studies
DYCK, C., Linguistics
EDINGER, E., Physical Geography
FEEHAN, J. P., Economics
FELT, L. F., Sociology
FISCHER, L., History
GRAHAM, D. E., French and Spanish
HARGER-GRINLING, V. A., French and Spanish
HARRIS, P. F., Linguistics
HART, P., History
HAWKIN, D. J., Religious Studies
HILL, R., Sociology
HILLER, J. K., History
HOUSE, J. D., Sociology
JACOBS, J. D., Geography
JOHNSTONE, F., Sociology
JONES, G. P., English
KENNEDY, J. C., Anthropology
LAI, T. T. L., Philosophy
LATUS, A., Philosophy
LEYTON, E. H., Anthropology
LYNDE, D., English
MCKENZIE, M., Linguistics
MANNION, J. J., Geography
MAXWELL, D. V., Philosophy
MAY, J. D., Economics
NARVAÉZ, P., Folklore
NICHOL, D. W., English
NICHOL, K., Geography
NURSE, D., Linguistics
O'DEA, S., English
O'DWYER, B., English
PANJABI, R. K., History
PARKER, K. I., Religious Studies
PARKER, M., Classics
PETERS, H., English
POCIUS, G., Folklore
PORTER, J., Religious Studies
RAINEY, L., Religious Studies
RENOUF, P., Anthropology
ROLLMAN, H., Religious Studies
ROSENBERG, N., Folklore
ROY, N., Economics
RYAN, S., History
SCHRANK, B., English
SCHRANK, W. E., Economics
SHARPE, C., Geography
SHAWYER, A. J., Geography
SHORROKS, G., English Language and Literature
SHUTE, M., Religious Studies
SIMMS, A., Geography
SIMMS, E., Geography
SIMPSON, E., Philosophy
SMITH, P., Folklore
STAFFORD, A., Philosophy
STAVELEY, M., Geography
STOREY, C., Economic Geography
TANNER, A., Anthropology
THOMSPON, D., Philosophy
TSOA, E., Economics
TUCK, J. A., Anthropology
WHITE, R. W., Geography
WOOD, C., Geography

Faculty of Business Administration:
BARNES, J. G., Marketing
FASERUK, A. J., Business Administration
KUBIAK, W., Quantitative Methods
PARSONS, J., Information Systems
SAHA, S., Organizational Behaviour
SEXTY, R. W., Management and Policy
SKIPTON, M. D., Management and Policy

SOOKLAL, L. R., Human Resource Management and Organizational Theory
STEWART, D. B., Business Administration
WITHEY, M. J., Organizational Behaviour

Faculty of Education:
BARRELL, B., Education
BROWN, J., Education
BURNABY, B. J., Education
CAHILL, M., Education
CANNING, P., Education
CROCKER, R. K., Education
DOYLE, C. P., Education
GARLIE, N. W., Education
GLASSMAN, M. S., Education
HADLEY, N. H., Education
JEFFREY, G. H., Education
KELLEHER, R. R., Education
KELLY, U., Education
KENNEDY, W., Education
KIM, K. S., Education
MANN, B. L., Education
NESBIT, W. C., Education
OLDFORD-MATCHIM, J., Education
ROBERTS, B. A., Education
SHARPE, D. B., Education
SINGH, A., Education
STEVENS, K., Education
TRESLAN, D., Education

Faculty of Engineering and Applied Sciences:
ABDI, M., Mechanical Engineering
ADLURI, S., Civil Engineering
AHMED, M. H., Electrical and Computer Engineering
BASS, D. W., Mathematics and Statistics and Engineering
BOOTON, M., Mechanical Engineering
BOSE, N., Engineering
BRUCE-LOCKHART, M., Engineering
CLAUDE, D., Engineering
COLES, C., Civil Engineering
GEORGE, G., Electrical and Computer Engineering
GILL, E., Electrical and Computer Engineering
GOSINE, R., Electrical and Computer Engineering
HADDARA, M. M. R., Engineering
HAWBOLDT, K., Civil Engineering
HEYS, H., Electrical and Computer Engineering
HINCHEY, M., Mechanical Engineering
HUSAIN, T., Engineering
IQBAL, T., Electrical and Computer Engineering
JEYASURYA, B., Electrical and Computer Engineering
JORDAAN, I. J., Ocean Engineering
KHAN, F., Mechanical Engineering
KREIN, L., Mechanical Engineering
LI, C., Electrical and Computer Engineering
LYE, L., Engineering
MALONEY, C., Electrical and Computer Engineering
MASEK, V., Electrical and Computer Engineering
NIEFER, R., Engineering
NORVELL, T., Electrical and Computer Engineering
O'YOUNG, S., Electrical and Computer Engineering
PETERS, D., Electrical and Computer Engineering
POPESCU, R., Engineering
QUAICOE, J., Electrical and Computer Engineering
RAHMAN, M., Electrical and Computer Engineering
SABIN, G., Mechanical Engineering
SESHADRI, R., Mechanical Engineering
SHARAN, A., Mechanical Engineering
SHARP, J. J., Engineering
SHIROKOFF, J., Mechanical Engineering
SWAMIDAS, A. S. J., Engineering
VEITCH, B., Engineering

WILLIAMS, F., Engineering
Faculty of Medicine:
BEAR, J. C., Medicine (Genetics)
BROSNAN, J. T., Biochemistry and Medicine
BROSNAN, M. E., Biochemistry and Medicine
CARAYANNIOTIS, G., Medicine and Endocrinology
CORBETT, D. R., Medicine
GADAG, V., Biostatistics
GILLESPIE, L. L., Oncology
HANSEN, P. A., Medicine
HERZBERG, G. R., Biochemistry and Medicine
HOEKMAN, T., Biophysics
HOOVER, R., Biochemistry
HULAN, H., Biochemistry
KEOUGH, K., Biochemistry
LIEPINS, A., Medicine (Cell Sciences)
MARTIN, A. M., Biochemistry
MICHALAK, T. I., Medicine
MICHALSKI, C. J., Medicine (Molecular Biology)
MOODY-CORBETT, F., Physiology
NEUMAN, R. S., Medicine (Pharmacology)
PATER, A., Medicine (Molecular Biology)
PATERNO, G., Medicine (Oncology)
RAHIMTULA, A. D., Biochemistry and Medicine
SCOTT, T. M., Medicine (Anatomy)
VASDEV, S. C., Medicine (Biochemistry)
WEST, R., Pharmacy and Medicine

Faculty of Science:
ADAMEC, R. E., Psychology
ADAMS, R. J., Psychology
AFANASSIEV, I., Physics
AKSU, A. E., Earth Sciences
ANDERSON, R., Psychology
ANDREWS, E., Psychology
ANDREWS, T., Physics
ARLETT, C., Psychology
BARTHA, M., Computer Science
BARTLETT, R., Statistics
BODWELL, G. J., Chemistry
BOURGAULT, D., Physics
BRIDSON, J., Chemistry
BROWN, J. A., Psychology
BRUNNER, H., Mathematics and Statistics
BURDEN, E., Earth Sciences
BURRY, J. H., Mathematics
BURTON, D., Biology
BURTON, M., Biology
BUTTON, C., Psychology
CALON, T. J., Earth Sciences
CARR, S. M., Biology
CHO, C. W., Physics
CLOUTER, M. J., Physics
COLBO, M. H., Biology
COLLINS, M., Biology
COURAGE, M., Psychology
CURNOE, S., Physics
DABINETT, P., Biology
DAVIDSON, W. S., Biochemistry, Molecular Biology
DEBRUYN, J. R., Physics
DEYOUNG, B., Physics
DRIEDZIC, W., Biochemistry, Molecular Biology
DUNBRACK, R. L., Biochemistry, Molecular Biology
DUNNING, G., Earth Sciences
EDDY, R. H., Mathematics and Statistics
EDINGER, E., Biology
EVANS, J., Psychology
FAHRAEUS-VAN RAE, G., Biology
FINNEY-CRAWLEY, J., Biology
FLETCHER, G. L., Ocean Sciences Centre (Biology)
GALE, J. E., Earth Sciences
GAMPERL, K., Biology
GARDNER, G., Biology
GASKILL, H. S., Mathematics
GEORGHIOU, P., Chemistry
GIEN, T. T., Physics
GILLARD, P., Computer Science

GOODAIRE, E. G., Mathematics and Statistics
GOSSE, V., Psychology
GOW, J., Biology
GRANT, M. J., Psychology
GREEN, J. M., Biology
GREEN, J. M., Psychology
HADDEN, K., Psychology
HAEDRICH, R. L., Ocean Sciences Centre (Biology)
HALL, J., Earth Sciences
HANNAH, E., Psychology
HANNAH, T. E., Psychology
HARLEY, C. A., Psychology
HEATH, P. R., Mathematics and Statistics
HERMANUTZ, L., Biology
HISCOTT, R. N., Earth Sciences
HODYCH, J. P., Earth Sciences
HOOPER, R., Biology
HURICH, C. A., Earth Sciences
INDARES, A.-D., Earth Sciences
INNES, D., Biology
JABLONSKI, C. R., Chemistry
JENNER, G., Earth Sciences
JONES, I., Biology
JONES, I., Psychology
KNOECHEL, R., Biology
LAGOWSKI, J., Physics
LARSON, D. J., Biology
LEE, D., Biology
LEITCH, A. M., Earth Sciences
LEWIS, J. C., Physics
LIEN, J., Psychology
LOADER, C. E., Chemistry
LUCAS, C. R., Chemistry
McKIM, W., Psychology
MADDIGAN, R., Psychology
MALSBURY, C., Psychology
MARTIN, G., Psychology
MASON, R. A., Earth Sciences
MEYER, R., Earth Sciences
MILLER, E., Psychology
MILLER, H. G., Earth Sciences
MILLER, T., Biology
MINIMIS, G., Computer Science
MOESER, S., Psychology
MONTEVECCHI, W. A., Psychology
MORROW, M. R., Physics
MURRIN, F., Biology
MYERS, J. S., Earth Sciences
NARAYANASWAMI, P. P., Mathematics and Statistics
PARMENTER, M. M., Mathematics and Statistics
PARSONS, J., Biology
PARSONS, J., Computer Science
PATEL, T. R., Biochemistry and Biology
PENNEY, C. G., Psychology
PETERSEN, C., Psychology
PICKUP, P. G., Chemistry
PODUSKA, K., Physics
POIRIER, R., Chemistry
QUINLAN, G. M., Earth Sciences
QUIRION, G., Physics
RABINOWITZ, F. M., Psychology
REVUSKY, B., Psychology
RICH, N. H., Physics
RIVERS, C. J. S., Earth Sciences
ROSE, B., Psychology
ROSE, G., Marine Institute
SCHNEIDER, D. C., Ocean Sciences Centre
SCOTT, P., Biology
SHAWYER, B. L. R., Mathematics and Statistics
SHERRICK, M., Psychology
SIWEI, L., Computer Science
SKINNER, D., Psychology
SLAWINSKI, M., Earth Sciences
SMITH, F., Physics
SNELGROVE, P., Biology
STAVELY, B. E., Biology
STEIN, A. R., Chemistry
STENSON, G. B., Psychology
STOREY, A. E., Psychology
SUMMERS, D., Mathematics and Statistics

SUTRADHAR, B. C., Mathematics and Statistics
SYLVESTER, P. J., Earth Sciences
TANG, J., Computer Science
THOMPSON, R. J., Ocean Sciences Centre
VOLKOFF, H., Biology
VIDYASANKAR, K., Computer Science
WADLEIGH, M., Earth Sciences
WALSH, D., Physics
WANG, C. A., Computer Science
WARKENTIN, I., Psychology
WHITEHEAD, J. P., Physics
WHITMORE, M. D., Physics
WHITTICK, A., Biology
WILSON, M., Earth Sciences
WILTON, D. H. C., Earth Sciences
WRIGHT, J. A., Earth Sciences
WROBLEWSKI, J. S., Ocean Sciences Centre (Physics)
ZEDEL, L., Physics
ZUBEREK, W. M., Computer Science

School of Nursing:
LARYEA, M., Nursing

School of Pharmacy:
WEST, R., Pharmacy

UNIVERSITÉ DE MONCTON

Moncton, NB E1A 3E9
Telephone: (506) 858-4000
Fax: (506) 858-4585
E-mail: info@umoncton.ca
Internet: www.umoncton.ca
Founded 1864 as St Joseph's Univ., name changed 1963
Language of instruction: French
Public control
Academic year: September to April
Campuses also in Edmundston and Shippagan
Chancellor: LOUIS R. COMEAU
Rector: YVON FONTAINE
Vice-Rector for Academic Research: NEIL BOUCHER
Vice-Rector for Edmundston Campus: PAUL ALBERT
Vice-Rector for Human Resources and Admin.: NASSIR EL-JABI
Vice-Rector for Shippagan Campus: JOCELYNE ROY VIENNEAU
Sec.-Gen.: LYNNE CASTONGUAY (acting)
Librarian: ALAIN ROBERGE
Number of teachers: 390 full-time
Number of students: 6,219 (5,029 full-time, 1,190 part-time)
Publication: La Revue

DEANS
Moncton Campus:
Faculty of Administration: GASTON LeBLANC
Faculty of Arts and Social Sciences: ISABELLE McKEE-ALLAIN
Faculty of Education: JEAN-FRANÇOIS RICHARD
Faculty of Engineering: PAUL A. CHIASSON
Faculty of Higher Studies and Research: SOUAD H'MIDA
Faculty of Sciences: CHARLES BOURQUE
Faculty of Forestry: JEAN-MARIE BINOT
Faculty of Law: SERGE ROUSSELLE
Faculty of Health Sciences and Community Services: PAUL-EMILE BOURQUE

DIRECTORS
Edmundston Campus:
Academic Services: JACQUES PAUL COUTURIER
Arts and Letters: BLANCA NAVARRO-PARDIÑAS
Business Administration: FRANCOIS BOUDREAU
Education: PIERRETTE FORTIN
Human Sciences: LUC VIGNEAULT
Sciences: LUC FRENETTE
School of Nursing: FRANCE L. MARQUIS

Moncton Campus:
School of Kinesiology and Recreology: HUBERT ROUSSEL
School of Nursing: SYLVIE ROUBICHAUD-EKSTRAND
School of Nutrition and Home Economics: SLIMANE BELBRAOUET
School of Psychology: DOUGLAS FRENCH
School of Social Work: JEAN-MARC BÉLANGER
Shippagan Campus:
Arts and Human Sciences: BENOIT FERRON
Management: ZINE KHELIL
Nursing: SUZANNE OUELLET
Sciences: ELISE MAYRAND

UNIVERSITÉ DE MONTRÉAL

CP 6128, Succursale Centre-ville, Montréal, QC H3C 3J7
Telephone: (514) 343-6111
Fax: (514) 343-5976
E-mail: international@umontreal.ca
Internet: www.umontreal.ca
Founded 1878
Public control
Language of instruction: French
Academic year: September to August
Chancellor: ANDRÉ BISSON
Rector: LUC VINET
Executive Vice-Rector: MICHEL TRAHAN
Vice-Rector for Human Resources: GISÉLE PAINCHAUD
Vice-Rector for Planning: FRANÇOIS DUCHESNEAU
Vice-Rector for Research: ALAIN CAILLÉ
Vice-Rector for Undergraduate Education and Continuing Education: MARYSE RINFRET-RAYNOR
Gen. - Sec.: MICHEL LESPÉRANCE
Registrar: FERNAND BOUCHER
Dir of Finances: ANDRÉ RACETTE
Librarian: JEAN-PIERRE CÔTÉ
Library: see Libraries and Archives
Number of teachers: 6,150
Number of students: 54,465
Publications: L'Actualité Economique, Criminologie, Cahiers du Centre d'études de l'Asie de l'Est, Cahiers d'Histoire, Cinémas, CIRCUIT (North American modern music), Collection Tiré à part (School of Industrial Relations), Études françaises, La Gazette des Sciences mathématiques du Québec, Géographie physique et Quaternaire, Gestion, Le Médecin vétérinaire du Québec, META, Journal des traducteurs, Paragraphes, Revue Juridique Thémis, Revue des Sciences de l'Education, Sociologie et sociétés, Surfaces, Théologiques

DEANS
Faculty of Arts and Sciences: J. HUBERT
Faculty of Continuing Education: J.-M. BOUDRIAS (Administrator)
Faculty of Dental Medicine: CLAUDE LAMARCHE
Faculty of Education Sciences: M. CRESPO (acting)
Faculty of Environment Design: IRÉNE CINQ-MARS
Faculty of Graduate Studies: LOUIS MAHEU
Faculty of Law: J. FRÉMONT
Faculty of Medicine: P. VINAY
Faculty of Music: RÉJEAN POIRIER
Faculty of Nursing: CÉLINE GOULET
Faculty of Pharmacy: JACQUES TURGEON
Faculty of Theology: JEAN-MARC CHARRON
Faculty of Veterinary Medicine: RAYMOND S. ROY

PROFESSORS

Faculty of Arts and Sciences

Department of Anthropology:
BEAUCAGE, P.
BERNIER, B.
BIBEAU, G.
CHAPAIS, B.
CHAPDELAINE, C.
CLERMONT, N.
LEAVITT, J.
MEINTEL, D.
MULLER, J.-C.
PANDOLFI, M.
PARADIS, L. I.
SMITH, P.
THIBAULT, P.
TOLSTOY, P.
VERDON, M.

Department of Biology:
ANCTIL, M.
BOISCLAIR, D.
BOUCHARD, A.
BROUILLET, L.
CABANA, T.
CAPPADOCIA, M.
CARIGNAN, R.
HARPER, P.-P.
LEGENDRE, P.
MOLOTCHNIKOFF, S.
MORSE, D.
PINEL-ALLOUL, B.
SAINI, H. S.
SIMON, J.-P.

Department of Chemistry:
BEAUCHAMP, A. L.
BERTRAND, M.
BRISSE, F.
CARRINGTON, T.
CHARETTE, A.
D'AMBOISE, M.
DUGAS, H.
DUROCHER, G.
ELLIS, T. H.
HANESSIAN, S.
HUBERT, J.
LAFLEUR, M.
REBER, C.
ST-JACQUES, M.
WINNIK, F. M.
WUEST, J. D.
ZHU, J.

Department of Classical and Medieval Studies:
FASCIANO, D.

Department of Communication:
CARON, A. H.
GIROUX, L.
LAFRANCE, A. A.
RABOY, M.

Department of Comparative Literature:
CHANADY, A.
GUÉDON, J.-C.
KRYSINSKI, W.
MOSER, W.

Department of Computing Sciences and Operational Research:
ABOULHAMID, E. M.
BRASSARD, G.
CERNY, E.
DSSOULI, R.
FERLAND, J. A.
FLORIAN, M.
FRASSON, C.
GENDREAU, M.
JAUMARD, B.
LAPALME, G.
L'ÉCUYER, P.
MCKENZIE, P.
MARCOTTE, P.
MEUNIER, J.
NGUYEN, S.
POTVIN, J.-Y.

STEWART, N.
VAUCHER, J.

School of Criminology:
BROCHU, S.
BRODEUR, J.-P.
CUSSON, M.
LANDREVILLE, P.
OUIMET, M.
TREMBLAY, P.
TRÉPANIER, J.

Department of Demography:
LAPIERRE-ADAMCYK, E.
PICHÉ, V.

Department of Economics:
BOSSERT, W.
BOYER, M.
BRONSARD, C.
DUDLEY, L.
DUFOUR, J.-M.
GAUDET, G.
GAUDRY, M. J. I.
HOLLANDER, A.
LACROIX, R.
MARTENS, A.
MARTIN, F.
MONTMARQUETTE, C.
POITEVIN, M.
RENAULT, É.
VAILLANCOURT, F.

School of Educational Psychology:
CHARLEBOIS, P.
GAGNON, C.
LARIVÉE, S.
LEBLANC, M.
NORMANDEAU, S.
VAN GIJSEGHEM, H.
VITARO, F.

Department of English Studies:
MARTIN, R. K.

Department of French Studies:
BEAULIEU, J.-P.
CAMBRON, M.
GAUVIN, L.
HÉBERT, F.
LAFLÈCHE, G.
LAROSE, J.
MELANÇON, R.
MICHAUD, G.
NEPVEU, P.
PIERSSENS, M.
SOARE, A.
VACHON, S.

Department of Geography:
BRYANT, C. R.
CAVAYAS, F.
COFFEY, W.
COMTOIS, C.
COMTOIS, P.
COURCHESNE, F.
DE KONINCK, R.
FOGGIN, P. M.
GANGLOFF, P.
GRAY, J. T.
MANZAGOL, C.
MAROIS, C.
RICHARD, P. J. H.
ROY, A. G.
SINGH, B.
THOUEZ, J.-P.

Department of Geology:
BOUCHARD, M. A.
MARTIGNOLE, J.
TRZCIENSKI, W. E.

Department of History:
ANGERS, D.
BOGLIONI, P.
DICKINSON, J. A.
HUBERMAN, M.
KEEL, O.
LÉTOURNEAU, P.
LUSIGNAN, S.

MORIN, C.
PERREAULT, J. Y.
RABKIN, Y.
RAMIREZ, B.
ROUILLARD, J.
SUTTO, C.

Department of History of Art:
DE MOURA SOBRAL, L.
DUBREUIL, N.
GAUDREAULT, A.
KRAUSZ, P.
LAFRAMBOISE, A.
LAMOUREUX, J.
LAROUCHE, M.
LHOTE, J.-F.
MARSOLAIS, G.
NAUBERT-RISER, C.
TOUSIGNANT, S.
TRUDEL, J.

School of Industrial Relations:
BOURQUE, R.
BROSSARD, M.
CHICHA, M.-T.
COUSINEAU, J.-M.
DOLAN, S.
DURAND, P.
GUÉRIN, G.
MURRAY, G.
SIMARD, M.
TRUDEAU, G.

School of Library and Information Sciences:
BERTRAND-GASTALDY, S.
COUTURE, C.
DESCHATELETS, G.
LAJEUNESSE, M.
SAVARD, R.

Department of Linguistics and Translation:
CONNORS, K.
CORMIER, M. C.
FORD, A.
HOSINGTON, B.
JAREMA-ARVANITAKIS, G.
KITTREDGE, R.
MEL'ČUK, I. A.
MÉNARD, N.
MORIN, J.-Y.
MORIN, Y.-C.
NUSELOVICI NOUSS, A.
PATRY, R.
ST-PIERRE, P.
SCHULZE-BUSACKER, E.
SINGH, R.

Department of Literature and Modern Languages:
BOUCHARD, J.
PECK, J.
RÄKEL, H.-H.

Department of Mathematics and Statistics:
ARMINJON, P.
BÉLAIR, J.
BENABDALLAH, K.
BILODEAU, M.
BRUNET, R.
CLÉROUX, R.
DELFOUR, M.
DUFRESNE, D.
FRIGON, M.
GAUTHIER, P.
GIRI, N. C.
GIROUX, A.
HUSSIN, V.
JOFFE, A.
LALONDE, F.
LÉGER, C.
LEPAGE, Y.
LESSARD, S.
PATERA, J.
PERRON, F.
RAHMAN, Q. I.
REYES, G.
ROSENBERG, I.
ROUSSEAU, C.
ROY, R.

SABIDUSSI, G.
SAINT-AUBIN, Y.
SANKOFF, D.
SCHLOMIUK, D.
TURGEON, J.
WINTERNITZ, P.
ZAIDMAN, S.

Department of Philosophy:

BAKKER, E. J.
BODEÜS, R.
DUCHESNEAU, F.
GAUTHIER, Y.
GRONDIN, J.
LAGUEUX, M.
LAURIER, D.
LEPAGE, F.
LÉVESQUE, C.
PICHÉ, C.
ROY, J.
SEYMOUR, M.

Department of Physics:

BASTIEN, P.
CAILLÉ, A.
CARIGNAN, C.
COCHRANE, R. W.
DEMERS, S.
FONTAINE, G.
GOULARD, B.
LAPOINTE, J.-Y.
LAPRADE, R.
LEONELLI, R.
LÉPINE, Y.
LEROY, C.
LESSARD, L.
LEWIS, L. J.
LONDON, D.
MICHAUD, G.
MOFFAT, A.
MOISAN, M.
ROORDA, S.
TARAS, P.
TEICHMANN, J.
VINCENT, A.
WESEMAEL, F.
ZACEK, V.

Department of Politics:

BÉLANGER, A.-J.
BERNIER, G.
BLAIS, A.
BOISMENU, G.
CLOUTIER, É.
DION, S.
DUQUETTE, M.
ÉTHIER, D.
FAUCHER, P.
FORTMANN, M.
JENSON, J.
MONIÈRE, D.
NADEAU, R.
NOËL, A.
SOLDATOS, P.
THÉRIEN, J.-P.

Department of Psychology:

BERGERON, J.
BOUCHARD, M.-A.
BRUNET, L.
CLAES, M.
COMEAU, J.
COSSETTE-RICARD, M.
CYR, M.
DAVID, H.
DOYON, J.
DUBÉ, L.
FAVREAU, O.
FORTIN, A.
GRANGER, L.
HACCOUN, R.
HODGINS, S.
LASRY, J.-C.
LASSONDE, M.
LECOMTE, C.
LEPORE, F.
MATHIEU, M.
NADEAU, L.

PAGÉ, M.
PERETZ, I.
PERRON, J.
ROBERT, M.
SABOURIN, M.
SAVOIE, A.
STRAVYNSKI, A.
TREMBLAY, R. E.
WRIGHT, J.
ZAVALLONI, M.

School of Social Work:

BERNIER, D.
CHAMBERLAND, C.
GROULX, L. H.
LEGAULT, G.
MAYER, R.
PANET-RAYMOND, J.
RINFRET-RAYNOR, M.
RONDEAU, G.

Department of Sociology:

BERNARD, P.
FOURNIER, M.
HAMEL, J.
HAMEL, P.
HOULE, G.
JUTEAU, D.
LAURIN, N.
McALL, C.
MAHEU, L.
RACINE, L.
RENAUD, J.
RENAUD, M.
ROCHER, G.
SALES, A.
VAILLANCOURT, J.-G.

Faculty of Dental Medicine

Department of Dental Prosthesis:

BALTAJIAN, H.
BOUDRIAS, P.
LAMARCHE, C.
PRÉVOST, A.
TACHÉ, R.

Department of Oral Health:

CHARLAND, R.
JULIEN, M.
KANDELMAN, D.
LAVIGNE, G.
MASSEREDJIAN, V.
REMISE, C.
TURGEON, J.
WECHSLER, M.

Department of Stomatology:

DONOHUE, W. B.
DUNCAN, G.
DUPUIS, R.
DUQUETTE, P.
FOREST, D.
LEMAY, H.
MICHAUD, M.
NANCI, A.

Faculty of Education Sciences

Department of Curriculum and Instruction:

BEER-TOKER, M.
CHARLAND, J.-P.
GAGNÉ, G.
LEMOYNE, G.
PAINCHAUD, G.
PARET, M.-C.
PIERRE, R.
RETALLACK-LAMBERT, N.
SAINT-JACQUES, D.
THÉRIEN, M.
VAN GRUNDERBEECK, N.

Department of Education and Educational
Administration Studies:

AJAR, D.
BOURGEAULT, G.
BRASSARD, A.
CHENÉ, A.
CRESPO, M.
DUPUIS, P.
JOFFE-NICODÈME, A.

LESSARD, C.
PELLETIER, G.
PROULX, J.-P.
TARDIF, M.
TRAHAN, M.
VAN DER MAREN, J.-M.

Department of Psychopedagogy and
Andragogy:

COMEAU, M.
DUFRESNE-TASSÉ, C.
GAUDREAU, J.
LANGEVIN, J.
LÉVESQUE, M.
MARCHAND, L.
TREMBLAY, N.

Faculty of Environmental Design

School of Architecture:

ADAMCZYK, G.
DALIBARD, J.
DAVIDSON, C. H.
MARSAN, J.-C.

School of Industrial Design:

CAMOUS, R. F.
FINDELI, A.
LECLERC, A.

Department of Kinesiology:

ALAIN, C.
ALLARD, P.
GAGNON, M.
GARDINER, P. F.
LABERGE, S.
LAVOIE, J.-M.
LÉGER, L.
PÉRONNET, F.
PROTEAU, L.

School of Landscape Architecture:

CINQ-MARS, I.
JACOBS, P.
LAFARGUE, B.
POULLAOUEC-GONIDEC, P.

Institute of Urbanism:

BARCELO, A.-M.
BLANC, B.
BOISVERT, M. A.
CARDINAL, A.
GARIÉPY, M.
LESSARD, M.
McNEIL, J.
PARENTEAU, R.
SOKOLOFF, B.
TRÉPANIER, M.-O.

Faculty of Law:

BENYEKHLEF, K.
BICH, M.-F.
BOISVERT, A.-M.
BRISSON, J.-M.
CHEVRETTE, F.
CIOTOLA, P.
CÔTÉ, P.-A.
CÔTÉ, P. P.
CRÉPEAU, F.
DESLAURIERS, P.
DUMONT, H.
FABIEN, C.
FRÉMONT, J.
GAGNON, J. D.
GOLDSTEIN, G.
GRUNING, D.
HÉTU, J.
KNOPPERS, B. M.
LABRÈCHE, D.
LAJOIE, A.
LAMONTAGNE, D.-C.
LEFEBVRE, G.
LEROUX, T.
LLUELLES, D.
MACKAAY, E.
MOLINARI, P.
NEUWAHI, N.
PINARD, D.
POPOVICI, A.
ROCHER, G.

TALPIS, J.
TREMBLAY, A.
TREMBLAY, L.
TRUDEL, P.
TURP, D.
VIAU, L.
WOEHRLING, J.

Faculty of Medicine
Department of Anaesthesiology:
BLAISE, G.
DONATI, F.
HARDY, J.-F.

Department of Biochemistry:
BOILEAU, G.
BOUVIER, M.
BRAKIER-GINGRAS, L.
BRISSON, N.
CRINE, P.
DAIGNEAULT, R.
DESGROSEILLERS, L.
LANG, F. B.
ROKEACH, L. A.
SKUP, D.
SYGUSCH, J.

Department of Family Medicine:
BEAULIEU, M.-D.
MILLETTE, B.

Department of Health Administration:
BÉLAND, F.
BLAIS, R.
CHAMPAGNE, F.
CONTANDRIOPOULOS, A.-P.
DENIS, J.-L.
DUSSAULT, G.
LAMARCHE, P.
SICOTTE, C.
TILQUIN, C.

Department of Medicine:
AYOUB, J.
BICHET, D.
BRADLEY, E.
BRAZEAU, P.
BUTTERWORTH, R. F.
CARDINAL, J.
CHIASSON, J.-L.
D'AMOUR, P.
DELESPESSE, G. J. T.
DUQUETTE, P.
GOUGOUX, A.
GRASSINO, A.
HALLÉ, J.-P.
HAMET, P.
HUET, M.
LACROIX, A.
LAPLANTE, L.
LECOURS, A. R.
LE LORIER, J.
MALO, J.-L.
MARLEAU, D.
MARTEL-PELLETIER, J.
MATTE, R.
MES-MASSON, A.-M.
NADEAU, R.
NATTEL, S.
PELLETIER, J.-P.
PERREAULT, C.
POITRAS, P.
POMIER-LAYRARGUES, G.
RASIO, E.
SARFATI, M.
SÉNÉCAL, J.-L.
TREMBLAY, J.
VINAY, P.

Department of Microbiology and Immunology:
AUGER, P.
COHEN, É.
DE REPENTIGNY, L.
HALLENBECK, P.
LEMAY, G.
MENEZES, J. P. C. A.
MONTPLAISIR, S.

MORISSET, R.
SEKALY, R.-P.

Department of Nutrition:
DELISLE, H.
DES ROSIERS, C.
GARREL, D.
GAVINO, V.
HOUDE-NADEAU, M.
LÉVY, E.
POEHLMAN, É.
PRENTKI, M.
SERRI, O.
SIMARD-MAVRIKAKIS, S.
VAN DE WERVE, G.

Department of Obstetrics and Gynaecology:
BÉLISLE, S.
DROUIN, P.

Department of Occupational and Environmental Health:
CARRIER, G.
CHAKRABARTI, S. K.
GÉRIN, M.
KRISHNAN, K.
VIAU, C.
ZAYED, J.

Department of Ophthalmology:
BOISJOLY, H.
LABELLE, P.

Department of Paediatrics:
ALVAREZ, F.
BARD, H.
CHEMTOB, S.
FOURON, J.-C.
FRAPPIER, J.-Y.
GAGNAN-BRUNETTE, M.
GAUTHIER-CHOUINARD, M.
LABUDA, D.
LACROIX, J.
LAMBERT, M.
LAPOINTE, N.
RASQUIN-WEBER, A.-M.
ROBITAILLE, P.
ROUSSEAU, É.
SEIDMAN, E.
TEASDALE, F.
VANASSE, M.
VAN VLIET, G.
WEBER, M.
WILKINS, J.

Department of Pathology and Cellular Biology:
BENDAYAN, M.
CHARTRAND, P.
DESCARRIES, L.
GIROUX, L.
KESSOUS, A.
LATOUR, J.-G.
SCHÜRCH, W.

Department of Pharmacology:
CARDINAL, R.
DE LÉAN, A.
DUMONT, L.
DU SOUICH, P.
ÉLIE, R.
GASCON-BARRÉ, M.
LAMBERT, C.
LAROCHELLE, P.
LAVOIE, P.-A.
MOMPARLER, R.
YOUSEF, I.

Department of Physiology:
ANAND-SRIVASTAVA, M.
BERGERON, M.
BERTELOOT, A.
BILLETTE, J.
CASTELLUCCI, V.
COUTURE, R.
DE CHAMPLAIN, J.
DREW, T. B.
FELDMAN, A. G.
GULRAJANI, R.
KALASKA, J. F.

LACAILLE, J.-C.
LAMARRE, Y.
LAVALLÉE, M.
LEBLANC, A.-R.
MAESTRACCI, D.
MALO, C.
READER, T. A.
ROBERGE, F.
ROSSIGNOL, S.
SAUVÉ, R.
SMITH, A.

Department of Preventive and Social Medicine:
BRODEUR, J.-M.
DASSA, C.
FOURNIER, P.
LABERGE-NADEAU, C.
LAMBERT, J.
MAHEUX, B.
PHILIPPE, P.
PINEAULT, R.
POTVIN, L.
SÉGUIN, L.
SIEMIATYCKI, J.

Department of Psychiatry:
AMYOT, A.
CHOUINARD, G.
LALONDE, P.
LEMAY, M.-L.
MONDAY, J.
MONTPLAISIR, J. Y.
SAUCIER, J.-F.
WEISSTUB, D. N.

Department of Radiology, Radio-Oncology and Nuclear Medicine:
BRETON, G.
LAFORTUNE, M.
SAMSON, L.

School of Rehabilitation:
ARSENAULT, B.
BOURBONNAIS, D.
CHAPMAN, C. E.
DUTIL, É.
FERLAND, F.
FORGET, R.
GAUTHIER-GAGNON, C.
GRAVEL, D.
WEISS-LAMBROU, R.

School of Speech Pathology and Audiology:
GAGNÉ, J.-P.
GETTY, L.
JOANETTE, Y.
LE DORZE, G.
SKA, B.

Department of Surgery:
BEAUCHAMP, G.
BERNARD, D.
CAOUETTE-LABERGE, L.
CARRIER, M.
CHARLIN, B.
DALOZE, P.
DUBÉ, S.
DURANCEAU, A.
LABELLE, H.
PAGÉ, P.
PAQUIN, J.-M.
RIVARD, C.-H.
ROBIDOUX, A.
SMEESTERS, C.
VALIQUETTE, L.
WASSEF, R.

Faculty of Music:
BELKIN, A.
DESROCHES, M.
DURAND, M.
EVANGELISTA, J.
GUERTIN, M.
LEFEBVRE, M.-T.
LEROUX, R.
LONGTIN, M.
NATTIEZ, J.-J.
PANNETON, I.

PICHÉ, J.
POIRIER, R.
RIVEST, J.-F.
SMOJE, D.
VAILLANCOURT, L.

Faculty of Nursing:
DUCHARME, F.
DUQUETTE, A.
GAGNON, L.
GOULET, C.
GRENIER, R.
KÉROUAC, S.
REIDY, M.
RICARD, N.

School of Optometry:
BEAULNE, C.
CASANOVA, C.
FAUBERT, J.
KERGOAT, H.
LOVASIK, J. V.
PTITO, M.
SIMONET, P.

Faculty of Pharmacy:
ADAM, A.
BESNER, J.-G.
BISAILLON, S.
BRAZIER, J.-L.
CARTILIER, L.
GAGNÉ, J.
LAURIER, C.
MCMULLEN, J.-N.
MAILHOT, C.
ONG, H.
TURGEON, J.
VARIN, F.
WINNIK, F.
YAMAGUCHI, N.

Faculty of Theology:
DUHAIME, J.
NADEAU, J.-G.
PETIT, J.-C.

Faculty of Veterinary Medicine
Department of Clinical Sciences:
BLAIS, D.
BONNEAU, N. H.
BOUCHARD, É.
BRETON, L.
CARRIER, M.
CÉCYRE, A. J.
CHALIFOUX, A.
COUTURE, Y.
CUVELLIEZ, S.
D'ALLAIRE, S.
DI FRUSCIA, R.
DUBREUIL, P.
LAMOTHE, P. J.
LAROUCHE, Y.
LAVERTY, S.
LAVOIE, J.-P.
MARCOUX, M.
PARADIS, M.
VAILLANCOURT, D.
VRINS, A.

Department of Pathology and Microbiology:
BIGRAS-POULIN, M.
DROLET, R.
DUBREUIL, D.
EL AZHARY, Y.
FAIRBROTHER, J. M.
FONTAINE, M.
GIRARD, C.
GOTTSCHALK, M.
HAREL, J.
HIGGINS, R.
JACQUES, M.
LALLIER, R.
LARIVIÈRE, S.
MITTAL, K. R.
MORIN, M.
ROY, R. S.
SCHOLL, D. T.
SILIM, A. N.

Department of Veterinary Biomedicine:
BARRETTE, D.
BISAILLON, A.
DALLAIRE, A.
DEROTH, L.
GOFF, A. K.
LARIVIÈRE, N.
LUSSIER, J. G.
MURPHY, B. D.
SILVERSIDES, D. W.
SIROIS, J.
SMITH, L. C.
TREMBLAY, A. V.

AFFILIATED INSTITUTIONS

Ecole des Hautes Etudes Commerciales: 3000, chemin de la Côte-Sainte-Catherine, Montréal, QC H3T 2A7; tel. (514) 340-6000; f. 1907; Dir JEAN-MARIE TOULOUSE.

Ecole Polytechnique: 2500 ch. de Polytechnique, Montréal, QC H3T 1J4; tel. (514) 340-4711; f. 1873; Dir RÉJEAN PLAMONDON.

MOUNT ALLISON UNIVERSITY

Sackville, NB E4L 1E4

Telephone: (506) 364-2600
Fax: (506) 364-2262
E-mail: ldillman@mta.ca
Internet: www.mta.ca

Founded 1839
Private control
Language of instruction: English
Academic year: September to May

Chancellor: JOHN BRAGG
Pres. and Vice-Chancellor: Dr ROBERT CAMPBELL
Provost and Vice-Pres. for Academics and Research: Dr STEPHEN MCCLATCHIE
Vice-Pres. for Admin. and Finance: D. J. STEWART
Registrar: CHRIS PARKER
Librarian: BRUNO GNASSI

Library of 1,200,000 vols
Number of teachers: 130
Number of students: 2,250

DEANS

Faculty of Arts: Dr HANS VANDERLEEST
Faculty of Science: Dr JEFF OLLERHEAD
Faculty of Social Sciences: Dr ROB SUMMERBY-MURRAY

PROFESSORS

AIKEN, R., Biology
BAERLOCHER, F. J., Biology
BAKER, C., Mathematics and Computer Science
BEATTIE, M., Mathematics and Computer Science
BEATTIE, R., Mathematics and Computer Science
BELKE, T., Psychology
BLAGRAVE, M., English
BOGAARD, P., Philosophy
BURKE, R., Fine Arts
COHEN, I., Classics
CRAIG, T., English
FLEMING, B., Sociology
FOX, M., Geography and Environment
HAWKES, B., Physics
HOLOWNIA, T., Fine Arts
HUDSON, R., Commerce
HUNT, W., Political Science
IRELAND, R., Biology
KACZMARSKA, I., Biology
MACMILLAN, C., English
POLEGATO, R., Commerce
ROSEBRUGH, B., Mathematics and Computer Science
STEWART, J. M., Biochemistry
STRAIN, F., Economics
TUCKER, M., Political Science
VARMA, P., Physics

VERDUYN, C., English
VOGAN, N., Music
WESTCOTT, S., Chemistry

MOUNT SAINT VINCENT UNIVERSITY

Halifax, NS B3M 2J6

Telephone: (902) 457-6117
Fax: (902) 457-6498
E-mail: admissions@msvu.ca
Internet: www.msvu.ca

Founded 1925
Language of instruction: English
Academic year: September to April, 2 summer sessions

Chancellor: MARY LOUISE BRINK
Pres. and Vice-Chancellor: Dr SHEILA A. BROWN
Vice-Pres. for Academics: Dr DONNA WOOLCOTT
Vice-Pres. for Admin.: AMANDA WHITEWOOD
Registrar: J. LYNNE THERIAULT
Univ. Librarian: LILLIAN BELTAOS

Number of teachers: 232 (151 full-time, 81 part-time)
Number of students: 4,500

Publications: *Atlantis* (4 a year), *Folia Montana*, *The Connection* (12 a year)

DEANS

Arts and Sciences: Dr SHEVA MEDJUCK
Professional Studies: Dr MARY LYON
Student Affairs: Dr CAROL HILL

UNIVERSITY OF NEW BRUNSWICK

UNB Fredericton POB 4400, Fredericton, NB E3B 5A3

Telephone: (506) 453-4666
Fax: (506) 453-4599

UNB Saint John 100 Tucker Park Rd, POB 5050 Saint John NB E2L 4L5

Telephone: (506) 648-5500
Fax: (506) 648-5691
E-mail: qc2@unb.ca
Internet: www.unb.ca

Established 1785
Provincial control
Language of instruction: English
Academic year: September to May

Chancellor: RICHARD CURRIE
Pres.: JOHN MCLAUGHLIN
Vice-Pres. for Academic Affairs and Fredericton Campus: Dr ANTHONY SECCO (acting)
Vice-Pres. for Finance and Corporate Services: DANIEL V. MURRAY
Vice-Pres. for Research: Dr GREGORY S. KEALEY
Vice-Pres. (Saint John Campus): Dr ROBERT MACKINNON
Comptroller: LARRY GUITARD
Secretary: STEPHEN STROPLE
Registrar: TOM BUCKLEY
Director (Development and Donor Relations): SUSAN MONTAGUE
Librarian: JOHN TESKEY

Number of teachers: 679
Number of students: 10,880 (9,430 full-time, 1,450 part-time)

Publications: *Acadiensis*, a historical journal of the Atlantic provinces (2 a year), *Experience UNB* (1 a year), *Fiddlehead* (short stories and poetry, quarterly), *Graduate Studies Calendar*, *International Fiction Review*, *Research Inventory* (1 a year), *Studies in Canadian Literature* (3 a year), *Summer School Calendar*, *Undergraduate Calendar*

DEANS

Fredericton Campus:
Faculty of Administration: DANIEL COLEMAN
Faculty of Arts: Dr JAMES S. MURRAY (acting)

Faculty of Computer Science: ALI GHORBANI
Faculty of Education: SHARON RICH (acting)
Faculty of Engineering: DAVID COLEMAN
Faculty of Forestry and Environmental Management: IAN METHVEN (acting)
Faculty of Kinesiology: TERRY R. HAGGERTY
Faculty of Law: PHILIP BRYDEN
Faculty of Nursing: CHERYL GIBSON
Faculty of Science: ALLAN SHARP
School of Graduate Studies: GWEN DAVIES (acting)

Saint John Campus:

Faculty of Arts: Dr JOANNA EVERITT
Faculty of Business: REGENA FARNSWORTH (acting)
Faculty of Science, Applied Science and Engineering: Dr RUTH SHAW

PROFESSORS

Fredericton Campus:

Faculty of Administration:

ABEKAH, J.
ANGELES, R.
ARCELUS, F. J.
ASKANAS, W.
BETTS, N.
BOOTHMAN, B.
COLEMAN, D.
DU, D.
DUNNETT, J.
DUPLESSIS, D.
EISELT, H. A.
FLINT, D.
GAUDES, A.
GRANT, S.
HINTON, J.
KABADI, S.
LAUGHLAND, A. R.
LIM, W.
MAHER, E.
MAHER, R.
MITRA, D.
NAIR, K. P. K.
NASIEROWSKI, W.
NEVERS, R.
OTCHERE, I.
OTUTEYE, E.
OUYANG, M.
POST, P.
RAHIM, M. A.
RASHID, M.
RITCHIE, P.
ROY, J. A.
SHARMA, B.
SHEPPARD, R. G.
SIMYAR, F.
SRINIVASAN, G.
THOMAS, M. E.
TOLLIVER, J.
TRENHOLM, B.
WHALEN, H.
WIELMAKER, M.
ZULUAGA, L.

Faculty of Arts:

AHERN, D., Philosophy
ALLEN, J. G., Political Science
ALMEH, R., Sociology
ANDREWS, J., English
AUSTIN, D., English
BALL, J., International Development Studies
BALL, J. C., English
BEDFORD, A., International Development Studies
BEDFORD, D., Law and Society
BEDFORD, D., Women's Studies
BEDFORD, D. W., Political Science
BLACK, D., Anthropology
BONNETT, J., History
BOWDEN, G., Sociology
BRANDER, J. R. G., Economics
BROWN, A., French
BROWN, A., Women's Studies
BROWN, J. S., History

BYERS, E. S., Psychology
CAMPBELL, G., History
CANITZ, A. E., English
CARRIERE, M., French
CHARRON, D., French
CHARTERS, D., History
CICHOCKI, W., French
CLARK, D. A., Psychology
CONRAD, M., History
COOK, B. A., Economics
CULVER, K., Law in Society
CULVER, K., Philosophy
CUPPLES, B. W., Philosophy
DAVIES, G., English
D'ENTREMONT, B., Psychology
DICKSON, V., Economics
DOERKSEN, D., English
DONALDSON, A. W., Psychology
DUECK, C., Culture and Language Studies
DUPLESSIS, D., Law in Society
FALKENSTEIN, L., English
FARNWORTH, M., Economics
FERGUSON, B., Economics
FIELDS, D. L., Psychology
FRANK, D., History
GANTS, D. L., English
GEYSSEN, J. W., Classics and Ancient History
HAMLING, A., Women's Studies
HARRISON, D., Sociology
HIEW, C. C., Psychology
HORNE, C., Linguistics
HORNOSTY, J., Women's Studies
HORNOSTY, J. M., Sociology
HOWE, J. M., Sociology
JARMAN, M., English
KEALEY, G. S., History
KEALEY, L., History
KENNEDY, S., History
KERR, W., Classics and Ancient History
KERR, W., Law in Society
KLINCK, A., English
KUFELDT, K., Sociology
LACHAPELLE, D., Psychology
LANTZ, V., Economics
LARMER, R., Philosophy
LAUTARD, E. H., Sociology
LAW, S., Economics
LEBLANC, D., French
LECKIE, R., English
LEMIRE, B., History
LEMIRE, B. J., History
LEVINE, L., Economics
LINTON, M., Culture and Language Studies
LOREY, C., Culture and Language Studies
LOVELL, P. R., Anthropology
LOW, J., Sociology
McDONALD, T., Economics
McFARLAND, J., International Development Studies
McGAW, R. L., Economics
McTAVISH, L., Women's Studies
MARTIN, R., English
MIEDEMA, B., Sociology
MILLS, M. J., Classics and Ancient History
MILNER, M., History
MITRA, K., International Development Studies
MULLALY, E. J., English
MURRAY, J., Classics and Ancient History
MURRAY, J. S., Classics and Ancient History
MURRAY, K., Political Science
MURRELL, D., Economics
MYATT, A. E., Economics
NASON-CLARK, N., Sociology and Women's Studies
NEILL, W., Philosophy
NEILSON, L., Law in Society
PAPPONET-CANTAT, C., Anthropology and International Development Studies
PARENTEAU, W. M., History
PASSARIS, C. E., Economics
PIERCEY, D., Psychology
PLAICE, E., Anthropology
PLOUDE, R. J., English

POOL, G., International Development Studies
POOL, G. R., Anthropology
POULIN, C., Law in Society
POULIN, C., Psychology
POULIN, C., Women's Studies
RAHMANIAN, A., Philosophy
REHORICK, D. A., Sociology
REID, A., Culture and Language Studies
REZUN, M., Economics, International Development Studies and Political Science
RIDEOUT, V., Sociology
RIMMER, M. P., English
ROBBINS, W., Women's Studies
ROBBINS, W. J., English
ROBINSON, G. B., Psychology
ROWCROFT, J. E., Economics
SCHERF, K., English
SHANNON, C., Women's Studies
SIGURDSON, R., Political Science
SPINNER, B., Psychology
STOPPARD, J. M., Psychology
TASIC, V., Linguistics
THOMPSON, D. G., History
TRYPHONOPOULOS, D., English
TURNER, R. S., History
VAN DEN HOONAARD, W. C., Sociology
VIAU, R., French
VILLIARD, P., Linguistics
WAITE, G. K., History
WHITEFORD, G., International Development Studies
WIBER, M., Anthropology
WISNIEWSKI, L. J., Sociology
WORKMAN, T., Anthropology

Faculty of Computer Science:

BHAVSAR, V. C.
COOPER, R. H.
DEDOUREK, J. M.
DESLONGCHAMPS, G.
DU, W.
EVANS, P.
FRITZ, J.
GHORBANI, A. A.
HORTON, J. D.
KENT, K.
KURZ, B. J.
MACNEIL, D. G.
NICKERSON, B. G.
WASSON, W. D.
ZHANG, H.

Faculty of Education:

ALLEN, P., Adult and Vocational Education
BERRY, K., Educational Foundations
BEZEAU, L., Educational Foundations
BURGE, E., Adult and Vocational Education
CASHION, M., Educational Foundations
CLARKE, G. M., Curriculum and Instruction
COOPER, T. G., Curriculum and Instruction
EYRE, L., Health Education
GILL, B., Educational Administration
HUGHES, A. S., Curriculum and Instruction
LEAVITT, R., Curriculum and Instruction
MYERS, S., Health Education
NASON, P. N., Curriculum and Instruction
OTT, H. W., Educational Foundations
PAUL, L., Curriculum and Instruction
PAZIENZA, J., Curriculum and Instruction
RADFORD, K., Curriculum and Instruction
REHORICK, S., Curriculum and Instruction
SEARS, A., Curriculum and Instruction
SMALL, M. S., Curriculum and Instruction
SOUCY, D. A., Curriculum and Instruction
STEVENSON, M., Electrical and Computer Engineering
STEWART, J. (acting), Educational Foundations
SULLENGER, K., Science Education
WHITEFORD, G., Curriculum and Instruction
WILLMS, J. D., Educational Foundations

Faculty of Engineering:

BENDRICH, G., Chemical Engineering

BIDEN, E., Mechanical Engineering
BISCHOFF, P. H., Civil Engineering
BONHAM, D. J. (acting), Mechanical Engineering
CHANG, L., Electrical and Computer Engineering
CHAPLIN, R. (acting), Chemical Engineering
CHAPLIN, R. A. (acting), Chemical Engineering
COLEMAN, D. J., Geodesy and Geomatics
COLPITTS, B. (acting), Electrical and Computer Engineering
COUTURIER, M. (acting), Chemical Engineering
DARE, P., Geodesy and Geomatics (Chair)
DAWE, J. L. (acting), Civil Engineering
DIDUCH, C. (acting), Electrical Engineering
DORAISWAMI, R., Electrical Engineering
EIC, M., Chemical Engineering
HILL, E. F. (acting), Electrical Engineering
HUDGINS, B., Electrical and Computer Engineering
HUSSEIN, E. (acting), Mechanical Engineering
INNES, J. D., Civil Engineering
IRCHA, M. C., Civil Engineering
LANGLEY, R. B. (acting), Geodesy and Geomatics Engineering
LEE, Y. C., Geodesy and Geomatics
LEWIS, J. E., Electrical Engineering
LISTER, D., Chemical Engineering
LOVELY, D., Electrical and Computer Engineering
LOWRY, B. (acting), Chemical Engineering
LUKE, D. M. (acting), Electrical Engineering
LYON, D., Mechanical Engineering
MCLAUGHLIN, J. D. (acting), Geodesy and Geomatics Engineering
MAYER, L., Geodesy and Geomatics Engineering
NI, Y., Chemical Engineering
NICHOLS, S. E. (acting), Geodesy and Geomatics
PARKER, P. A. (acting), Electrical Engineering
ROGERS, R. J., Mechanical Engineering
SHARAF, A. M. M., Electrical Engineering
SOUSA, A. C. M., Mechanical Engineering
SULLIVAN, P., Mechanical Engineering
TAYLOR, J. H. (acting), Electrical Engineering
TERVO, R., Electrical and Computer Engineering
THOMAS, M. D. A. (acting), Civil Engineering
VALSANGKAR, A. J. (acting), Civil Engineering
VANICEK, P., Geodesy and Geomatics Engineering
WAUGH, L. M., Civil Engineering

Faculty of Forestry and Environmental Management:

AFZAL, M. (acting)
ARP, P. A.
BECKLEY, T.
BOURQUE, C.
CHUI, Y.
CUNJAK, R.
CURRY, A.
DAUGHERTY, D.
DIAMOND, T.
ERDLE, T.
FORBES, G.
JAEGER, D.
JORDAN, G.
KEPPIE, D. M.
KERSHAW, J.
KRASOWSKI, M.
LANTZ, V.
LEBLON, B.
MACLEAN, D.
MENG, C.-H.
QUIRING, D. T. W.

ROBAK, E. W.
ROBERTS, M. R.
SAVIDGE, R.
SCHNEIDER, M. H.
SERGEANT, B.
SMITH, I.
ZUNDEL, P.

Faculty of Kinesiology:

BURKARD, J.
HAGGERTY, T. R.
PATON, G. A.
SEXSMITH, J.
STEVENSON, C. L.
WRIGHT, P. H.

Faculty of Law:

BELL, D. G.
BIRD, R. W.
BLADON, G. L.
CHATERJEE, A.
DORE, K. J.
FLEMING, D. J.
GOCHNAUER, M. L.
KUTTNER, T. S.
LAFOREST, A.
MCCALLUM, M. E.
MCEVOY, J. P.
MATHEN, C.
PEARLSTON, K.
PENNEY, S.
SIEBRASSE, N.
TOWNSEND, D.
VEITCH, E.
WILLIAMSON, J. R.

Faculty of Nursing:

ERICSON, P.
GETTY, G.
GIBSON, C.
GILBEY, V. J. U.
LEWIS, K.
OUELLET, L.
RUSH, K. L.
STORR, G.
WIGGINS, N.
WUEST, J.

Faculty of Science:

ADAM, A. G., Chemistry
BALCOLM, B., Chemistry
BANERJEE, P. K., Mathematics and Statistics
BARCLAY, D. W., Mathematics and Statistics
BROSTER, B., Geology
CASHION, P. J., Biology
CHERNOFF, W. W., Mathematics and Statistics
COOMBS, D. H., Biology
COOPER, R., Chemistry
CWYNAR, L., Biology
CULP, J., Biology
CUNJAK, R., Biology
DESLONGCHAMPS, G., Chemistry
DIAMOND, A., Biology
DILWORTH, T. G., Biology
FORBES, G., Biology
GEGENBERG, J., Mathematics and Statistics
HAMZA, A., Mathematics and Statistics
HUSAIN, V., Mathematics and Statistics
INGALLS, C., Mathematics and Statistics
JONES, C., Mathematics and Statistics
KEPPIE, D. M., Biology (also under Faculty of Forestry and Environmental Management)
LENTZ, D., Geology
LINTON, C., Physics
LYNCH, W. H., Biology
MCKELLAR, R., Mathematics and Statistics
MAGEE, D., Chemistry
MARCHAND, E., Mathematics and Statistics
MASON, G. R., Mathematics and Statistics
MATTAR, S., Chemistry
MONSON, B. R., Mathematics and Statistics
MUREIKA, R. A., Mathematics and Statistics
NEVILLE, J., Chemistry

NI, Y., Chemistry
PASSMORE, J., Chemistry
PICKERILL, R. K., Geology
RIDING, R. T., Biology
ROSS, W. R., Physics
SAUNDERS, G., Biology
SEABROOK, W. D., Biology
SHARP, A. R., Physics
SIVASUBRAMANIAN, P., Biology
SPRAY, J., Geology
THAKKAR, A., Chemistry
TIMOTHY, J. G., Physics
TINGLEY, D., Mathematics and Statistics
TUPPER, B. O. J., Mathematics and Statistics
TURNER, T. R., Mathematics and Statistics
VILLEMURE, G., Chemistry
WHITE, J. C., Geology
WHITTAKER, J. R., Biology
WILLIAMS, P. F., Geology
YOO, B. Y., Biology

Saint John Campus:

Faculty of Arts:

BELANGER, L., French
BEST, L., Psychology
BOTH, L., Psychology
BRADLEY, M. T., Psychology
CAMPBELL, M. A., Psychology
CAVALIERE, P. A., History
CHILDS, J., Economics
DARTNELL, M., Political Science
DESSERUD, D., Political Science
DI TOMMASO, E., Psychology
DONNELLY, F., History and Politics
EVERITT, J., Political Science
GENDREAU, P., Psychology
GODDARD, M. J., Psychology
HILL, R., Economics
HILL, V., French
HYSON, S., Political Sciences
JEFFREY, L., Political Sciences
KABIR, M., Social Science
LINDSAY, D., History
MARQUIS, G., History
MOIR, R., Economics
MOSHIRI, S., Economics
NKUNZIMANA, O., French
PONS-RIDLER, S., Humanities and Languages
RIDLER, N. B., Social Science
SELIM, M., Economics
SNOOK, B., Psychology
TAUKULIS, H., Psychology
TONER, P., History and Politics
WHITNEY, R., History
WILSON, A., Psychology

Faculty of Business:

CHALYKOFF, J.
DAVIS, C. H.
DAVIS, G.
GILBERT, E.
MINER, F. C.
PIKE, E.
ROUMI, E.
STERNICZUK, H.
WANG, S.
WONG, J.

Faculty of Science, Applied Science and Engineering:

ALDERSON, H., Mathematical Sciences
ALDERSON, T., Mathematical Sciences
BECKETT, B. A., Physical Sciences
BOONE, C., Engineering
BUCHANAN, J., Nursing (non-professorial Head, acting)
CHOPIN, T., Biology
CHRISTIE, J., Engineering
COTTER, G. T., Engineering (Head)
DE'BELL, K., Mathematical Sciences
FEICHT, A., Chemistry (Chair.)
GAREY, L. E., Mathematics, Statistics and Computer Science
GUPTA, R. D., Mathematics, Statistics and Computer Science

HALCROW, K., Biology
HAMDAN, M., Mathematics, Statistics and Computer Science
HUMPHRIES, R., Physical Sciences
KAMEL, M. T., Mathematics, Statistics and Computer Science
KAYSER, M., Physical Sciences
LEUNG, C.-H., Physical Sciences
LITVAK, M. K., Biology
LOGAN, A., Physical Sciences
McCULLUM, D., Engineering
MACDONALD, B., Biology
MacLATCHY, D., Biology
MAHANTI, P., Computer Science and Applied Statistics
NUGENT, L., Nursing
PRASAD, R. C., Engineering
PUNNEN, A., Mathematical Sciences
RILEY, E., Engineering
ROCHETTE, R., Biology
SHAW, R., Computer Science and Applied Statistics
SOLLOWS, K., Engineering
STOICA, G., Mathematical Sciences
TERHUNE, J. M., Biology
THOMPSON, C., Computer Science and Applied Statistics (Chair.)
WAGSTAFF, J., Physical Sciences
WALTON, B., Engineering
WILSON, L., Physical Sciences
XU, L.-H., Physical Sciences

ATTACHED COLLEGES

Renaissance College: Dean Dr PIERRE ZUNDEL.

Saint John College: e-mail sjcol@unbsj.ca.

FEDERATED UNIVERSITY

St Thomas University: Fredericton, NB; f. 1910; Pres. DANIEL O'BRIEN.

NIPISSING UNIVERSITY

100 College Drive, Box 5002, North Bay, ON P1B 8L7

Telephone: (705) 474-3450
Fax: (705) 495-1772
E-mail: liaison@nipissingu.ca
Internet: www.nipissingu.ca

Founded 1967 as Nipissing College, affiliated to Laurentian University of Sudbury; merged with North Bay Teachers' College 1973; became independent, under current name, 1992

Academic year: September to August

Chancellor: DAVID B. LIDDLE
Pres.: Dr DENNIS R. MOCK
Vice-Pres. of Admin. and Finance: VICKY PAINE-MANTHA
Vice-Pres. of Academic Affairs and Research: Dr. PETER RICKETTS
Dean of Arts and Science: Dr CRAIG COOPER
Dean of Applied and Professional Studies: Dr. RICK VANDERLEE
Dean of Education: Dr RON WIDERMAN
Registrar: ANDREA ROBINSON
Executive Director of Library Services: BRIAN NETTLEFOLD

Number of teachers: 170
Number of students: 7,170

UNIVERSITY OF NORTHERN BRITISH COLUMBIA

3333 University Way, Prince George, BC V2N 4Z9

Telephone: (250) 960-5555
Fax: (250) 960-5543
E-mail: registrar-info@unbc.ca
Internet: www.unbc.ca

Founded 1990; full opening 1994
Language of instruction: English
Academic year: September to May (2 semesters)

Chancellor: Dr ALEX MICHALOS
Pres.: Dr GEORGE IWAMA
Provost: Dr MARK DALE
Vice-Pres. for Admin. and Finance: EILEEN BRAY
Vice-Pres. for Research: Dr GAIL FONDAHL
Registrar: JOHN DeGRACE
Univ. Librarian: NANCY BLACK (acting)
Number of teachers: 178 (full-time); 204 (part-time)
Number of students: 4,177

DEANS

College of Arts, Social and Health Sciences: Dr JOHN YOUNG
College of Science and Management: Dr WILLIAM McGILL
Graduate Programs: Dr IAN HARTLEY
Student Success and Enrolment Management: Dr PAUL MADAK

NOVA SCOTIA AGRICULTURAL COLLEGE

Truro, NS B2N 5E3

Telephone: (902) 893-6722
Fax: (902) 895-5529
E-mail: reg@nsac.ns.ca
Internet: www.nsac.ns.ca

Founded 1905

Under the direction of the Nova Scotia Department of Agriculture and Marketing

President: Dr PHILIP HICKS
Vice-Pres. for Academics: Dr BRUCE GRAY
Vice-President for Admin.: Dr BERNIE MAC-DONALD
Registrar: T. DOLHANTY
Librarian: B. R. WADDELL
Library of 19,000 vols
Number of teachers: 69
Number of students: 900

Publication: *NSAC College Calendar*.

NSCAD UNIVERSITY

5163 Duke St, Halifax, NS B3J 3J6

Telephone: (902) 422-7381
Fax: (902) 425-2420
E-mail: admissions@nscad.ca
Internet: www.nscad.ca

Founded 1887
Academic year: September to April
Pres.: DAVID B. SMITH
Snr Vice-Pres. for Academic Affairs and Research: KENN HONEYCHURCH
Vice-Pres. for Finance and Administration: PETER FLEMMING
Registrar: LAURELLE LeVERT
Library Dir: ILGA LEJA
Library of 50,000 vols, 220 art periodicals, 140,000 colour slides, large holding of films and video cassettes (incl. Canada Council Art Bank colln)
Number of teachers: 53
Number of students: 1,100 (800 full-time, 300 part-time)

Depts of craft, design, fine art, foundation, graduate studies, historical and critical studies, media art

Fine art studios in painting, sculpture, printmaking, ceramics, weaving, video, film, woodworking and metalworking, textiles, fashion, jewellery, photography, digital media; undergraduate programmes include: Bachelor of Arts with major in art history; Bachelor of Design with majors in interdisciplinary design or international major in graphic design, and Bachelor of Fine Arts with majors in interdisciplinary pre-teacher education, ceramics, film, fine art, intermedia, jewellery design and metalwork, photography and textiles; current graduate-level programmes: Master of Design, Master of

Design International and Master of Fine Arts.

UNIVERSITY OF OTTAWA

550 Cumberland St, Ottawa, ON K1N 6N5

Telephone: (613) 562-5700
Fax: (613) 562-5103
Internet: www.uottawa.ca

Founded 1848
Independent, Provincially assisted
Languages of instruction: French, English
Academic year: September to August (undergraduate 2 semesters, graduate 3 terms)

Chancellor: HUGUETTE LABELLE
Pres. and Vice-Chancellor: ALLAN ROCK (acting)
Vice-Pres. for Academic Affairs: ROBERT MAJOR
Vice-Pres. for Research: MONA NEMER
Vice-Pres. for Resources: VICTOR SIMON
Vice-Pres. for Univ. Relations: (vacant)
Asst Vice-Pres. for Strategic Enrolment Management and Registrar: FRANÇOIS CHAPLEAU
Sec.-Gen.: PIERRE-YVES BOUCHER
Librarian: LESLIE WEIR

Library: see under Libraries and Archives
Number of teachers: 1,737 (936 full-time, 801 part-time)
Number of students: 36,460 (29,800 full-time, 6,660 part-time)

DEANS

Faculty of Arts: GEORGE LANG
Faculty of Education: MARIE JOSÉE BERGER
Faculty of Engineering: CLAUDE LAGUE
Faculty of Health Sciences: DENIS PRUD'-HOMME
Faculty of Law: SEBASTIAN GRAMMOND (Acting Dean, Civil Law: BRUCE FELDTHUSEN (Common Law)
Faculty of Medicine: JACQUES E. BRADWEJN
Faculty of Science: ANDRÉ DABROWSKI
Faculty of Social Sciences: FRANCOIS HOULE
Faculty of Graduate and Post-doctoral Studies: GARY SLATER
Telfer School of Management: MICHEÁL J. KELLY

PROFESSORS

Faculty of Arts (internet www.uottawa.ca/academic/arts):

BARBIER, J. A., History
BEHIELS, M. D., History
BERTHIAUME, P., French Literature
BRISSET, A., Translation and Interpretation
BURGESS, R., Classics
CARLSON, D., English
CASTILLO DURANTE, D., French Literature
CHILDS, D., English Literature
CHOQUETTE, R., Religious Studies
CLAYTON, J. D., Russian
CRAM, R., Music
DAIGLE, J.-G., History
DAVIS, D. F., History
DE BRUYN, F., English
DELISLE, J., Translation and Interpretation
DONSKOV, A., Russian
EGERVARI, T., Visual Arts
FERGUSON, S., Communication
FERRIS, I., English
FLOYD, C., Music
FORGET, D., French Literature
FRENCH, H. M., Geography
FROEHLICH, A. J. P., Theatre
GAFFIELD, C. M., History
GAJEWSKI, K., Geography
GELLMAN, S., Music
GEURTS, M.-A., Geography
GILBERT, A., Geography
GIROU-SWIDERSKI, M., French Literature
GOLDENBERG, N., Religious Studies

GOODLUCK, H., Linguistics
GRISE, Y., French Literature
HIRSCHBUHLER, P., Linguistics
HUNTER, D. G., Philosophy
IMBERT, P. L., French Literature
JARRAWAY, D., English Literature
JOHNSON, P. G., Geography
KILMER, M. F., Classics and Religious Studies
KUNSTMANN, P. M. F., French Literature
LABELLE, N., Music
LA BOSSIÈRE, C. R., English Literature
LACHANCE, P. F., History
LAFON, D., French Literature
LANGLOIS, A., Geography
LAPIERRE, A., Linguistics
LAURIOL, B., Geography
LEMELIN, S., Music
LEPAGE, Y. G., French Literature
LEVY, P., Communication
LEWKOWICZ, A. G., Geography
LONDON, A., English Literature
LUGG, A. M., Philosophy
LYNCH, G., English
MAKARYK, I. R., English
MANGANIELLO, D., English
MAYNE, S., English
MERKLEY, P., Music
MOSER, W., Modern Languages and Literature
MOSS, J., English
MUNOZ-LICERAS, J., Modern Languages and Literature
PIVA, M., History
POPLACK, S., Linguistics
PUMMER, R. E., Religious Studies
RADLOFF, B., English
RAMPTON, D. P., English
REID, L., Visual Arts
RIVERO, M. L., Linguistics
ROBERTS, R. P., Translation and Interpretation
RUANO DE LA HAZA, J., Modern Languages and Literature
STROCCHI, L. G., Modern Languages and Literature
SEGUIN, H., Second Language Institute
STAINES, D., Arts
STICH, K. P., English
STOLARIK, M. M., History
VAILLANCOURT, P.-L., French Literature
VANDENDORPE, C., French Literature
VILLA, B. L., History
VON MALTZAHN, N., English
WELLAR, B. S., Geography
WESCHE, M. B., Centre for Second Language Learning
WILSON, K. G., English
YARDLEY, J. C., Classics

Faculty of Education (internet www.uottawa .ca/academic/education):

BÉLAIR, L.
BERGER, M.-J.
BOURDAGES, J. J.
COOK, S.
COUSINS, B.
FORGETTE-GIROUX, R.
FORTIN, J.-C.
GAGNE, E.
GIROUX, A.
HERRY, Y.
JEFFERSON, A. L.
LAVEAULT, D.
LEBLANC, R. N.
MACDONALD, C.
MASNY, D.
MICHAUD, J. P.
ST-GERMAIN, M.
TAYLOR, M.

Faculty of Engineering (internet www.eng .uottawa.ca):

ABOULNASR, T. T., Engineering
ADAMOWSKI, K., Civil Engineering
CHENG, S.-C., Mechanical Engineering
DHILLON, B. S., Engineering Management

DROSTE, R. L., Civil Engineering
EVGIN, E., Civil Engineering
FAHIM, A. E., Mechanical Engineering
GARDNER, N. J., Civil Engineering
GARGA, V. K., Civil Engineering
HADDAD, Y. M., Mechanical Engineering
HALLETT, W. L. H., Mechanical Engineering
KENNEDY, K. J., Civil Engineering
LIANG, M., Mechanical Engineering
MCLEAN, D. D., Chemical Engineering
MUNRO, M. B., Mechanical Engineering
NARBAITZ, R. M., Civil Engineering
NEALE, G. H., Chemical Engineering
NECSULESCU, D.-S., Engineering Management
REDEKOP, D., Mechanical Engineering
SAATCIOGLU, M., Civil Engineering
TANAKA, H., Engineering
TAVOULARIS, S., Mechanical Engineering
THIBAULT, J., Chemical Engineering
TOWNSEND, D. R., Civil Engineering

School of Information Technology and Engineering:

BOCHMANN, G. V.
CADA, M.
CHOUINARD, J.-Y.
DELISLE, G. Y.
DUBOIS, E.
GEORGANAS, N. D.
GIBBONS, D.-T.
HALL, T.
IONESCU, D.
KARMOUCH, A.
MCNAMARA, D. A.
MATWIN, S. J.
MOUFTAH, H. T.
OROZCO, B.-L.
PETRIU, E.
PROBERT, R. L.
RAYMOND, J.
SKUCE, D. R.
STOJMENOVIC, I.
SZPAKOWICZ, S.
URAL, H.
YANG, O. W.
YONGACOGLU, A. M.

Faculty of Health Sciences
School of Human Kinetics:

HARVEY, J.
LAMONTAGNE, M.
ORLICK, T. D.
RAIL, G.
ROBERTSON, G. E.
TRUDEL, P.

School of Nursing:

CRAGG, E. C.
EDWARDS, N.
FOTHERGILL-BOURBONNAIS, F.
O'CONNOR, A.

School of Rehabilitation Sciences:

DURIEUX-SMITH, A., Audiology and Speech-language Pathology

Faculty of Law (internet www.uottawa.ca/ academic/droit-law):

Civil Law Section:

ARCHAMBAULT, J.-D.
BEAULNE, J.
BELLEAU, C.
BISSON, A.-F.
BOIVIN, M.
BOUDREAULT, M.
BRAEN, A.
DUPLESSIS, Y.
EMANUELLI, C.
GRONDIN, R.
JODOUIN, A.
LACASSE, J.-P.
MORIN, M.
PELLETIER, B.
PROULX, D.
VINCELETTE, D.

Common Law Section:

DES ROSIERS, N.
JACKMAN, M.
KRISHNA, V.
MCRAE, D. M.
MAGNET, J. E.
MANWARING, J. A.
MENDES, E. P.
MORSE, B. W.
PACIOCCO, D. M.
PERRET, L.
RATUSHNY, E. J.
RODGERS, S.
SHEEHY, E.
SULLIVAN, R.
ZWEIBEL, E.

Faculty of Management:

ADJAOUD, F.
CALVET, A. L.
CARO, D. H. J.
DE LA MOTHE, J.
DOUTRIAUX, J.
GANDHI, D. K.
GOH, S.
HENAULT, G. M.
HENIN, C. G.
JABES, J.
KELLY, M. J.
KERSTEN, G.
KINDRA, G. S.
LANE, D.
MANGA, P.
MICHALOWSKI, W.
NASH, J. C.
SIDNEY, J. B.
WRIGHT, D. J.
ZEGHAL, D.
ZUSSMAN, D.

Faculty of Medicine (internet www.uottawa .ca/academic/med):

ALTOSAAR, I., Biochemistry, Microbiology and Immunology
ANDERSON, P. J., Biochemistry, Microbiology and Immunology
BAENZIGER, J., Biochemistry, Microbiology and Immunology
BERNATCHEZ-LEMAIRE, I., Cellular and Molecular Medicine (Pharmacology)
BROWN, E., Biochemistry, Microbiology and Immunology
CHAN, A. C., Biochemistry, Microbiology and Immunology
CHEN, Y., Epidemiology and Community Medicine
CHEUNG, D. W., Cellular and Molecular Medicine (Pharmacology)
DE BOLD, A. J., Pathology and Laboratory Medicine
DILLON, J. R., Biochemistry, Microbiology and Immunology
DIMOCK, K. D., Biochemistry, Microbiology and Immunology
FRANKS, D., Pathology and Laboratory Medicine
FRYER, J. N., Cellular and Molecular Medicine (Anatomy)
GELFAND, T., History of Medicine
GIBB, W., Obstetrics and Gynaecology
HACHE, R. J. G., Medicine
HAKIM, A. M., Medicine
HÉBERT, R., Medicine
HINCKE, M., Cellular and Molecular Medicine (Anatomy)
JASMIN, B. J., Cellular and Molecular Medicine (Physiology)
KACEW, S., Cellular and Molecular Medicine (Pharmacology)
KRANTIS, A., Cellular and Molecular Medicine (Physiology)
KREWSKI, D., Medicine
LABOW, R., Surgery
LEMAIRE, S., Cellular and Molecular Medicine (Pharmacology)
MCBURNEY, M. W., Medicine

McDowell, I. W., Epidemiology and Community Medicine

Maler, Leonard, Cellular and Molecular Medicine (Anatomy)

Marcel, Y. L., Pathology and Laboratory Medicine

Marshall, K. C., Cellular and Molecular Medicine (Physiology)

Milne, R. W., Pathology and Laboratory Medicine

Mussivand, T. F., Surgery

Nair, R. C., Epidemiology and Community Medicine

Parry, D. J., Cellular and Molecular Medicine (Physiology)

Peterson, L. M., Cellular and Molecular Medicine (Physiology)

Rousseaux, Colin, Cellular and Molecular Medicine

St John, R. K., Medicine

Sattar, S. A., Biochemistry, Microbiology and Immunology

Spasoff, R. A., Epidemiology and Community Medicine

Staines, W., Cellular and Molecular Medicine (Anatomy)

Tanphaichitr, N., Obstetrics and Gynaecology

Tsang, B. K., Obstetrics and Gynaecology

Tuana, B. S., Cellular and Molecular Medicine (Pharmacology)

Walker, P., Medicine

Wells, G., Medicine

Yao, Z., Biochemistry, Microbiology and Immunology

Faculty of Science (internet www.science.uottawa.ca):

Alvo, M., Mathematics and Statistics

Arnason, J. T., Biology

Bao, X., Physics

Brabec, T., Physics

Bonen, L., Biology

Burgess, W. D., Mathematics and Statistics

Castonguay, C., Mathematics and Statistics

Chapleau, F., Biology

Clark, I. B., Earth Sciences

Currie, D. J., Biology

Dabrowski, A. R., Mathematics and Statistics

Detellier, C. G., Chemistry

Durst, T., Chemistry

Fallis, A. G., Chemistry

Fenwick, J. C., Biology

Fowler, A., Earth Sciences

Gambarotta, S., Chemistry

Giordano, T., Mathematics and Statistics

Handelman, D. E., Mathematics and Statistics

Hattori, K., Earth Sciences

Hickey, D. A., Biology

Hodgson, R. J. W., Physics

Ivanoff, G. B., Mathematics and Statistics

Joos, B., Physics

Kaplan, H., Chemistry

LaLonde, A. E., Earth Sciences

Lean, D. R., Biology

Longtin, A., Physics

McDonald, D. R., Mathematics and Statistics

Moon, T. W., Biology

Morin, A., Biology

Neher, E., Mathematics and Statistics

Perry, S. F., Biology

Pestov, V., Mathematics and Statistics

Philogène, B. J. R., Biology

Racine, M. L., Mathematics and Statistics

Rancourt, D., Physics

Richeson, D., Chemistry

Rossman, W., Mathematics and Statistics

Roy, D., Mathematics and Statistics

Sankoff, D., Mathematics and Statistics

Sayari, A. H., Chemistry

Scaiano, J. C., Chemistry

Scott, P. J., Mathematics and Statistics

Stadnik, Z., Physics

Teitelbaum, H., Chemistry

Veizer, J., Earth Sciences

Faculty of Social Sciences (internet www.uottawa.ca/academic/socsci):

Andrew, C. P., Political Science

Beauchesne, L., Criminology

Cardinal, L., Political Science

Cellard, A., Criminology

Chossudovsky, M., Economics

Coulombe, S., Economics

Crelinsten, R., Criminology

da Rosa, V. M. P., Sociology

Denis, A. B., Sociology

Denis, S., Political Science

Gabor, T., Criminology

Grenier, G., Economics

Hastings, J. R., Criminology

Havet, J. L., Sociology

Laczko, L., Sociology

Laux, J. K., Political Science

Lavoie, M., Economics

Los, M. J., Criminology

Mellos, K., Political Science

Moggach, D., Political Science

Murphy, R. J., Sociology

Pires, A., Criminology

Poulin, R., Sociology

Roberts, J., Criminology

Seccareccia, M., Economics

Tahon, M.-B., Sociology

Thériault, J. Y., Sociology

Tremblay, M., Political Science

Waller, I., Criminology

School of Psychology:

Bielajew, C.

Campbell, K. B.

Cappeliez, P.

Clement, R.

Firestone, P.

Flynn, R.

Fouriezos, G.

Girodo, M.

Hunsley, J.

Johnson, S.

Ledingham, J.

Lee, C.

LeMyre, L.

Merali, Z.

Messier, C.

Mook, B.

Pelletier, L.

Ritchie, P.

Sarrazin, G.

Schneider, B.

Tougas, F.

Whiffen, V.

Younger, A.

School of Social Work:

Coderre, C.

Home, A. M.

St-Amand, N.

Tougas, F.

FEDERATED UNIVERSITY

Saint Paul University: 223 Main St, Ottawa, ON K1S 1C4; internet www.ustpaul.ca; Rector Rev. Prof. Dale Schlitt

DEANS

Faculty of Canon Law: Rev. Roch Pagé

Faculty of Human Sciences: Jean-Guy Goulet

Faculty of Theology: Rev. David Perrin

PROFESSORS

Faculty of Canon Law:

Huels, J.

Mendonça, Rev. A.

Morrisey, Rev. F. G.

Page, R.

Faculty of Human Sciences:

Bégin, B.

Daviau, P.

Goulet, J.-G.

Meier, A.

Mooren, T.

Rigby, P.

Faculty of Theology:

Coyle, J. K.

Dumais, Rev. M.

Martínez de Pisón, R.

Melchin, K.

Pambrun, J.

Peelman, Rev. A.

Provencher, Rev. M. N.

Schlitt, Rev. D. M.

Van den Hengel, Rev. J.

Walters, G.

UNIVERSITY OF PRINCE EDWARD ISLAND

550 University Ave, Charlottetown, PE C1A 4P3

Telephone: (902) 566-0439

Fax: (902) 566-0795

E-mail: registrar@upei.ca

Internet: www.upei.ca

Founded 1969 by merger of St Dunstan's University (f. 1855) and Prince of Wales College (f. 1834)

Academic year: September to May

Chancellor: Norman Webster

Pres. and Vice-Chancellor: H. Wade MacLauchlan

Vice-Pres. for Academic Devt: Vianne Timmons

Vice-Pres. for Finance and Facilities: Garry G. Bradshaw

Registrar: Karen Smythe

Univ. Librarian: Lynn Murphy

Library: see Libraries

Number of teachers: 192 full-time

Number of students: 3,410 full-time

DEANS

Faculty of Arts: Richard Kurial

Faculty of Business Administration: Dr Roberta MacDonald

Faculty of Education: Dr Graham Pike

Faculty of Nursing: Dr Irene Coulson

Faculty of Science: Dr Roger Gordon

Faculty of Veterinary Medicine: Dr Timothy Ogilvie

UNIVERSITÉ DU QUÉBEC

475 rue de l'Eglise, Québec, QC G1K 9H7

Telephone: (418) 657-3551

Fax: (418) 657-2132

E-mail: info-uq@uqss.uquebec.ca

Internet: www.uquebec.ca

Founded 1968

Language of instruction: French

Pres.: Pierre Moreau

Vice-Pres. for Admin. and Finance: Louis Gendreau

Vice-Pres. for Teaching and Research: Daniel Coderre

Sec.-Gen.: Michel Quimper

Dir of Public Relations: (vacant)

Librarian: (vacant)

Library: Library (network) of 2,340,000 vols

Number of teachers: 2,200

Number of students: 84,700

Publications: *Inventaire de la Recherche Subventionnée et Commanditée* (1 a year), *Réseau* (4 a year).

CONSTITUENT INSTITUTIONS

Université du Québec en Abitibi-Témiscamingue

445 blvd de l'Université, Rouyn-Noranda, QC J9X 5E4

Telephone: (819) 762-2922
Fax: (819) 797-4727
E-mail: registraire@uqat.ca
Internet: www.uqat.uquebec.ca

Founded 1981 as Centre d'etudes universitaires, name changed 1984

Rector: JULES ARSENAULT
Vice-Rector for Resources: L. BERGERON
Vice-Rector for Teaching and Research: ROGER CLAUX
Registrar: N. MURPHY
Dir of Services: N. MURPHY
Sec.-Gen.: J. TURGEON
Librarian: A. BÉLAND

Library of 201,000 vols
Number of teachers: 75
Number of students: 911 full-time
Number of students: 1,932 part-time

Université du Québec à Chicoutimi

555 blvd de l'Université, Chicoutimi, QC G7H 2B1

Telephone: (418) 545-5011
Fax: (418) 545-5049
E-mail: regist@uqac.ca
Internet: www.uqac.ca

Founded 1969
State control
Language of instruction: French
Academic year: September to April

Rector: MICHEL BELLEY
Sec.-Gen.: MARTIN CÔTÉ
Registrar: CLAUDIO ZOCCASTELLO
Librarian: GILLES CARON

Library of 250,000 vols
Number of teachers: 225
Number of students: 6,500 (3,200 full-time, 3,300 part-time)

Publication: *UQACtualité* (4 a year).

Université du Québec en Outaouais

CP 1250, Succursale Hull, Gatineau, QC J8X 3X7

Telephone: (819) 595-3900
Fax: (819) 595-1835
E-mail: registraire@uqo.ca
Internet: www.uqo.ca

Founded 1970
Language of instruction: French
Academic year: September to June

Rector: JEAN VAILLANCOURT
Sec.-Gen.: LUC MAURICE
Registrar: ROBERT BONDAZ
Librarian: HÉLÈNE LAROUCHE

Library of 210,000 vols
Number of teachers: 184
Number of students: 5,492 (2,884 full-time, 2,608 part-time)

Publication: *Savoir Outaouais* (3 a year).

Université du Québec à Montréal

CP 8888, Succ. Centre-ville, Montréal, QC H3C 3P8

Telephone: (514) 987-3000
Fax: (514) 987-3009
E-mail: registrariat@uqam.ca
Internet: www.regis.uqam.ca

Founded 1969

Rector (vacant)
Vice-Rector for Academics and Research: LYNN DRAPEAU
Vice-Rector for Academic Services and Technological Devt: MICHEL ROBILLARD

Vice-Rector for Human Resources and Admin. Affairs: ALAIN DUFOUR
Vice-Rector for Partnership and External Affairs: PAULE LEDUC (acting)
Vice-Rector for Strategic and Financial Planning and Gen. Sec.: LOUISE DANDURAND
Registrar: CLAUDETTE JODOIN
Librarian: JEAN-PIERRE CÔTÉ

Library of 2,388,000 vols
Number of teachers: 903
Number of students: 37,395 (18,406 full-time, 18,989 part-time)

Université du Québec à Rimouski

300 Allée des Ursulines, Rimouski, QC G5L 3A1

Telephone: (418) 723-1986
Fax: (418) 724-1525
E-mail: uqar@uqar.uquebec.ca
Internet: wer.uqar.qc.ca

Founded 1969
State control
Academic year: September to April (2 semesters)

Rector: PIERRE COUTURE
Vice-Rector for Admin. and Human Resources: J.-N. THÉRIAULT
Vice-Rector for Teaching and Research: MICHEL RINGUET
Sec.-Gen.: M. BOURASSA
Librarian: GASTON DUMONT

Library of 334,600 vols
Number of teachers: 172
Number of students: 2,100 full-time, 2,300 part-time

Publication: *UQAR-Info* (6 a year).

ATTACHED CENTRE

Oceanography Centre: Dir V. KOUTI-TONSKY.

Université du Québec à Trois-Rivières

3351 blvd des Forges, CP 500, Trois-Rivières, QC G9A 5H7

Telephone: (819) 376-5045
Fax: (819) 376-5012
E-mail: crmultiservice@uqtr.ca
Internet: www.uqtr.ca

Founded 1969
Provincial control
Academic year: September to April

Rector: GHISLAIN BOURQUE
Vice-Rector for Admin. and Finance: RENÉ GARNEAU
Sec.-Gen.: ANDRÉ GABIAS
Registrar: NORMAND SHAFFER

Library of 500,000 vols
Number of teachers: 352
Number of students: 11,427 (6,650 full-time, 4,777 part-time)

Publication: *En Tête*.

Ecole Nationale d'Administration Publique

555 blvd Charest Est, Québec, QC G1K 9E5

Telephone: (418) 641-3000
Fax: (418) 641-3060

Founded 1969

Dir-Gen.: PIERRE DE CELLES

Library of 90,000 vols
Number of teachers: 59
Number of students: 1,143

Ecole de Technologie Supérieure

1100 rue Notre-Dame Ouest, Montréal, QC H3C 1K3

Telephone: (514) 396-8800
Fax: (514) 396-8950
Internet: www.etsmtl.ca

Founded 1974

Dir-Gen.: YVES BEAUCHAMP

Library of 65,000 vols
Number of teachers: 126

INRS-Institut Armand-Frappier

531 blvd des Prairies, Laval, QC H7V 1B7

Telephone: (450) 687-5010

Founded 1938

Dir-Gen.: ALAIN FOURMIER

Library of 10,000 vols
Number of teachers: 45
Number of students: 170

Human, animal, environmental health (immunity, infectious diseases, cancer, epidemiology, biotechnologies, toxicology, pharmacodiomistry sciences.

Institut National de la Recherche Scientifique

490 de la Couronne, Québec, QC G1K 9A9

Telephone: (418) 654-2500
Fax: (418) 654-2525
Internet: www.inrs.ca

Founded 1969

Dir-Gen.: DANIEL CODERRE

Library of 58,000 vols
Number of teachers: 154
Number of students: 619 (558 full-time, 61 part-time)

Télé-université

Tour de la Cité, 2600 blvd Laurier, 7e étage, Québec, QC G1V 4V9

Telephone: (418) 657-2262

Founded 1972

Dir-Gen.: A. MARREC

Library of 12,000 vols
Number of teachers: 35
Number of students: 5,716 (258 full-time, 5,458 part-time)

Distance-learning programmes.

QUEEN'S UNIVERSITY AT KINGSTON

Kingston, ON K7L 3N6

Telephone: (613) 545-2000
Fax: (613) 545-6300
E-mail: liaison@post.queensu.ca
Internet: www.queensu.ca

Founded 1841
Language of instruction: English
Academic year: September to May (2 terms)

Chancellor: PETER LOUGHEED
Rector: MICHAEL KEALY
Vice-Chancellor and Prin.: Dr W. C. LEGGETT
Vice-Prin. for Academics: Dr S. FORTIER
Vice-Prin. for Advancement: Dr G. N. HOOD
Vice-Prin. for Health Sciences: Dr M. C. WALKER
Vice-Prin. for Operations and Finance: Dr D. L. ANDERSON
Vice-Prin. for Research: Dr B. J. HUTCHINSON
Registrar: JO-ANNE BECHTHOLD
Chief Librarian: PAUL WIENS

Number of teachers: 1,158
Number of students: 17,510

Publication: *Queen's Quarterly* (4 a year)

DEANS

Faculty of Applied Science: T. J. HARRIS
Faculty of Arts and Sciences: R. A. SILVERMAN
Faculty of Education: R. BRUNO-JOFRÉ
Faculty of Health Sciences: M. C. WALKER
Faculty of Law: A. HARVISON YOUNG
School of Business: DAVID SAUNDERS
School of Graduate Studies and Research: R. J. ANDERSON

PROFESSORS

Some staff teach in more than one faculty

Faculty of Applied Science (Ellis Hall, Kingston, ON K7L 3N6; tel. (613) 533-2055; fax (613) 533-6500; e-mail appsci@post.queensu.ca; internet appsci.queensu.ca):

AITKEN, G. J. M., Electrical and Computer Engineering
ANDERSON, R. J., Mechanical Engineering
ARCHIBALD, J. F., Mining Engineering
BEAULIEU, N. C., Electrical and Computer Engineering
BIRK, A. M., Mechanical Engineering
BOYD, J. D., Materials and Metallurgical Engineering
BRYANT, J. T., Mechanical Engineering
CAMERON, J., Materials and Metallurgical Engineering
CAMPBELL, T. I., Civil Engineering
CARTLEDGE, J. C., Electrical and Computer Engineering
DANESHMEND, L. K., Mining Engineering
DAUGULIS, A. J., Chemical Engineering
GRANDMAISON, E. W., Chemical Engineering
HALL, K., Civil Engineering
HAMACHER, V. C., Electrical and Computer Engineering
HARRIS, T. J., Chemical Engineering
JESWIET, J., Mechanical Engineering
JORDAN, M. P., Mechanical Engineering
KAMPHUIS, J. W., Civil Engineering
KORENBERG, M., Electrical and Computer Engineering
KRSTIC, V. D., Materials and Metallurgical Engineering
KUEPER, B., Civil Engineering
MCKINNON, S. D., Mining Engineering
MCLANE, P. J., Electrical and Computer Engineering
MITCHELL, R. J., Civil Engineering
MOUFTAH, H. T., Electrical and Computer Engineering
MULVENNA, C. A., Mechanical Engineering
NEUFELD, R. J., Chemical Engineering
OOSTHUIZEN, P. H., Mechanical Engineering
PICKLES, C. A., Materials and Metallurgical Engineering
POLLARD, A., Mechanical Engineering
ROSE, K., Civil Engineering
SAIMOTO, S., Materials and Metallurgical Engineering
SEN, P. C., Electrical and Computer Engineering
SMALL, C. F., Mechanical Engineering
SURGENOR, B. W., Mechanical Engineering
TAVARES, S. E., Electrical and Computer Engineering
TURCKE, D. J., Civil Engineering
VAN DALEN, K., Civil Engineering
WATT, W. E., Civil Engineering
WYSS, U. P., Mechanical Engineering
YEN, W.-T., Mining Engineering

Faculty of Arts and Science (Mackintosh-Corry Hall, Room F300, Kingston, ON K7L 3N6; tel. (613) 533-2470; fax (613) 533-2067; internet www.queensu.ca/artsci):

AARSSEN, L. W., Biology
AKENSON, D. H., History
AKL, S. G., Computing and Information Science
ATHERTON, D. L., Physics
BAIRD, M. C., Chemistry
BAKAN, A. B., Political Studies
BAKHURST, D., Philosophy
BANTING, K. G., Politics
BEACH, C. M., Economics
BECKE, A. D., Chemistry
BENINGER, R. J., Psychology
BERG, M., English
BERGIN, J., Economics
BERMAN, B. J., Politics
BERNHARDT, D., Economics

BICKENBACH, J. E., Philosophy
BLY, P. A., Spanish and Italian
BOADWAY, R. W., Economics
BOAG, P. T., Biology
BOGOYAVLENSKIJ, O. I., Mathematics and Statistics
BROWN, R. S., Chemistry
BURKE, F., Film
CALLE-GRUBER, M., French
CAMPBELL, H. E. A., Mathematics and Statistics
CARMICHAEL, D. M., Geological Sciences
CARMICHAEL, H. L., Economics
CASTEL, B., Physics
CHRISTIANSON, P., History
CLARK, A. H., Geology
CONAGHAN, C. M., Politics
CORDY, J. R., Computing and Information Science
CRAWFORD, R. G., Computing and Information Science
CRUSH, J., Geography
CUDDY, L. L., Psychology
DALRYMPLE, R. W., Geology
DAVIDSON, R., Economics
DE CAEN, D. J. P., Mathematics and Statistics
DIXON, J. M., Geology
DONALD, M. W., Psychology
DUNCAN, M. J., Physics
DU PREY, P. D., Art
ELTIS, D., History
ERDAHL, R. M., Mathematics and Statistics
ERRINGTON, E. J., History
FINLAYSON, J., English
FISHER, A., Music
FLATTERS, F. R., Economics
FLETCHER, R., Physics
FORTIER, S., Chemistry
FOX, M. A., Philosophy
FROST, B. J., Psychology
GEKOSKI, W. L., Psychology
GERAMITA, A. V., Mathematics and Statistics
GILBERT, R. E., Geography
GLASGOW, J., Computing and Information Science
GOHEEN, P. G., Geography
GREGORY, A. W., Economics
GREGORY, D. A., Mathematics and Statistics
GUNN, J. A. W., Politics
HAGEL, D. K., Classics
HAGLUND, D. G., Politics
HAMILTON, R., Sociology
HAMM, J.-J. N., French
HANES, D. A., Physics
HARRISON, J. P., Physics
HARTWICK, J. M., Economics
HELLAND, J., Art
HELMSTAEDT, H., Geology
HENRIKSEN, R. N., Physics
HERZBERG, A. M., Mathematics and Statistics
HEYWOOD, J. C., Art
HIRSCHORN, R. M., Mathematics and Statistics
HODSON, P. V., Biology
HOLDEN, R. R., Psychology
HOLMES, J., Geography
HUGHES, I., Mathematics and Statistics
HUNTER, B. K., Chemistry
JAMES, N. P., Geology
JEEVES, A. H., History
JIRAT-WASIVTYNSKI, V., Art
JOHNSTONE, I. P., Physics
JONKER, L. B., Mathematics and Statistics
KALIN, R., Psychology
KANI, E., Mathematics and Statistics
KILPATRICK, R. S., Classics
KNAPPER, C., Psychology
KNOX, V. J., Psychology
KOBAYASHI, A., Women's Studies
KYMLICKA, W., Philosophy
KYSTER, T. K., Geology
LAKE, K. W., Physics

LAYZELL, D. B., Biology
LEDERMAN, S., Psychology
LEGGETT, W. C., Biology
LEIGHTON, S. R., Philosophy
LELE, J. K., Politics
LESLIE, J. R., Physics
LESLIE, P. M., Politics
LEVISON, M., Computing and Information Science
LEWIS, F. D., Economics
LINDSAY, R. C. L., Psychology
LOBB, R. E., English
LOCK, F. P., English
LOGAN, G. M., English
LOVELL, W. G., Geography
LYON, D., Sociology
MACARTNEY, D. H., Chemistry
MCCAUGHEY, J. H., Geography
MCCOWAN, J. D., Chemistry
MCCREADY, W. D., History
MCDONALD, A. B., Physics
MCINNIS, R. M., Economics
MCKAY, I. G., History
MACKINNON, J. G., Economics
MCLATCHIE, W., Physics
MACLEAN, A. W., Psychology
MACLEOD, A. M., Philosophy
MCTAVISH, J. D., Art
MALCOLMSON, R. W., History
MANUTH, V., Art
MARSHALL, W. L., Psychology
MEWHORT, D., Psychology
MILNE, F., Economics
MINGO, J. A., Mathematics and Statistics
MONKMAN, L. G., English
MONTGOMERIE, R. D., Biology
MOORE, E. G., Geography
MORRIS, G. P., Biology
MUIR, D. W., Psychology
MURTY, M. R. P., Mathematics and Statistics
NARBONNE, G. M., Geology
NATANSOHN, A. L., Chemistry
O'NEILL, P. J., German
ORZECH, M., Mathematics and Statistics
OSBORNE, B. S., Geography
OVERALL, C. D., Philosophy
PAGE, S. C., Politics
PALMER, B. D., History
PEARCE, G. R. F., Sociology
PEARCE, T. H., Geology
PENTLAND, C. C., Politics
PERLIN, G. C., Politics
PETERS, R. D., Psychology
PIKE, R. M., Sociology
PLANT, R. L., Drama
PLAXTON, W. C., Biology
PRACHOWNY, M. F. J., Economics
PRADO, C. G., Philosophy
PRITCHARD, J., History
QUINSEY, V. L., Psychology
RASULA, J., English
RAY, A., Economics
REEVE, W. C., German
RIDDELL, J. B., Geography
ROBERTS, L. G., Mathematics and Statistics
ROBERTSON, B. C., Physics
ROBERTSON, R. J., Biology
ROBERTSON, R. M., Biology
ROSENBERG, M. W., Geography
SACCO, V. F., Sociology
SAYER, M., Physics
SCHROEDER, F. M., Classics
SHENTON, R. W., History
SILVERMAN, R. A., Sociology
SKILLICORN, D. B., Computing and Information Science
SMITH, G. S., History
SMITH, G. W., Economics
SMOL, J., Biology
SNIDER, D. L., Sociology
SNIECKUS, U. A., Chemistry
SPARKS, G. R., Economics
STAYER, J. M., History
STEVENSON, J. M., Physical and Health Education

STONE, J. A., Chemistry
STOTT, M. J., Physics
SYPNOWICH, C., Philosophy
SZAREK, W. A., Chemistry
TAYLOR, D. R., Physics
TAYLOR, P. D., Mathematics and Statistics
TENNENT, R. D., Computing and Information Science
THOMSON, C. J., Geology
TINLINE, R. R., Geography
VANLOON, G. W., Chemistry
VERNER, J. H., Mathematics and Statistics
WALKER, V. K., Biology
WANG, S., Chemistry
WARDLAW, D. M., Chemistry
WARE, R., Economics
WEISMAN, R. G., Psychology
WIEBE, M. G., English
WOLFE, L. A., Physical and Health Education
YOUNG, P. G., Biology
YUI, N., Mathematics and Statistics
ZAMBLE, E., Psychology
ZAREMBA, E., Physics
ZUK, I. B., Education
ZUREIK, E. T., Sociology

Faculty of Education (tel. (613) 533-6205; fax (613) 533-6203; e-mail regoff@educ.queensu.ca; internet educ.queensu.ca):

HUTCHINSON, N. L.
KIRBY, J. R.
MUNBY, A. H.
O'FARRELL, L.
RUSSELL, T.
UPITIS, R. B.
WILSON, R. J.

Faculty of Health Sciences (tel. (613) 533-2544; fax (613) 533-6884; e-mail jeb8@post.queensu.ca; internet meds.queensu.ca):

ADAMS, M. A., Pharmacology and Toxicology
ANASTASSIADES, T. P., Medicine
ANDREW, R. D., Anatomy and Cell Biology
ARBOLEDA-FLOREZ, J. E., Psychiatry
ASTON, W. P., Microbiology and Immunology
BENNETT, B. M., Pharmacology and Toxicology
BIRTWHISTLE, R. V., Family Medicine
BOEGMAN, R. J., Pharmacology and Toxicology
BRIEN, J. F., Pharmacology and Toxicology
BRUNET, D. G., Medicine
BURGGRAF, G. W., Medicine
BURKE, S. O., School of Nursing
CARSTENS, E. B., Microbiology and Immunology
CHAPLER, C. K., Physiology
CLARK, A. F., Biochemistry
COLE, S. P. C., Pathology
COTE, G. P., Biochemistry
CRUESS, A. F., Ophthalmology
DA COSTA, L. R., Medicine
DAGNONE, L. E., Emergency Medicine
DAVIES, P. L., Biochemistry
DEELEY, R. G., Pathology
DELISLE, G. J., Microbiology and Immunology
DEPEW, W. T., Medicine
DOW, K. E., Paediatrics
DUFFIN, J. M., Health Sciences
DWOSH, I. L., Medicine
EISENHAUER, E. A., Radoncology
ELCE, J. S., Biochemistry
ELLIOTT, B. E., Pathology
FERGUSON, A. V., Physiology
FISHER, J. T., Physiology
FLYNN, T. G., Biochemistry
FORD, P. M., Medicine
FORKERT, P. G., Anatomy and Cell Biology
FROESE, A. B., Anaesthesia
GORWILL, R. H., Obstetrics and Gynaecology
HALL, S. F., Otolaryngology
HEATON, J. P. W., Urology

HOLDEN, J. J. A., Psychiatry
HUDSON, R. W., Medicine
JACKSON, A. C., Medicine
JARRELL, K. F. J., Microbiology and Immunology
JHAMANDAS, K., Pharmacology and Toxicology
JONEJA, M. G., Anatomy and Cell Biology
JONES, G., Biochemistry
KAN, F. W. K., Anatomy and Cell Biology
KISILEVSKY, R., Pathology
KROPINSKI, A. M., Microbiology and Immunology
LAMB, M. W., School of Nursing
LAWSON, J. S., Psychiatry
LILLICRAP, D. P., Pathology
LUDWIN, S. K., Pathology
MCCREARY, B., Psychiatry
MAK, A. S., Biochemistry
MANLEY, P. N., Pathology
MASSEY, T. E., Pharmacology and Toxicology
MERCER, C. D., Surgery
MILNE, B., Anaesthesia
MORALES, A., Urology
MUNT, P. W., Medicine
NAKATSU, K., Pharmacology and Toxicology
NESHEIM, M. E., Biochemistry
NICKEL, J. C., Urology
NOLAN, R. L., Diagnostic Radiology
O'CONNOR, H. M., Emergency Medicine
O'DONNELL, D. E., Medicine
OLNEY, S. J., Rehabilitation Therapy
PANG, S. C., Anatomy and Cell Biology
PATER, J. L., Community Health and Epidemiology
PATERSON, W. G., Medicine
PICHORA, D. R., Surgery
POOLE, R. K., Microbiology and Immunology
PROSS, H. F., Microbiology and Immunology
RACZ, W. J., Pharmacology and Toxicology
RAPTIS, L. H., Microbiology and Immunology
REID, R. L., Obstetrics and Gynaecology
REIFEL, C., Anatomy and Cell Biology
RICHMOND, F. J., Physiology
RIOPELLE, R. J., Medicine
ROSE, P. K., Physiology
SHANKS, G. L., Rehabilitation Medicine
SHIN, S. H., Physiology
SHORTT, S. E. D., Community Health and Epidemiology
SIMON, J. B., Medicine
SINGER, M. A., Medicine
SMITH, B. T., Paediatrics
SZEWCZUK, M. R., Microbiology and Immunology
WALKER, D. M. C., Emergency Medicine
WEAVER, D. F., Medicine
WHERRETT, B. A., Paediatrics
WIGLE, R. D., Medicine
WILSON, C. R., Family Medicine

Faculty of Law (Macdonald Hall, Kingston, ON K7L 3N6; tel. (613) 533-2220; fax (613) 533-6611; e-mail llb@gsilver.queensu.ca; internet gsilver.queensu.ca/law):

ADELL, B. L.
ALEXANDROWICZ, G. W.
BAER, M. G.
BALA, N. C.
CARTER, D. D.
DELISLE, R. J.
EASSON, A. J.
HARVISON YOUNG, A.
LAHEY, K. A.
MAGNUSSON, D. N.
MANSON, A. S.
MULLAN, D. J.
SADINSKY, S.
STUART, D. R.
WEISBERG, M. A.

School of Business (Dunning Hall, Kingston, ON K7L 3N6; tel. (613) 533-2330; fax (613)

533-2013; e-mail info@business.queensu.ca; internet business.queensu.ca):

ANDERSON, D. L.
ARNOLD, S. J.
BARLING, J. I.
COOPER, W. H.
DAUB, M. A. C.
GALLUPE, R. B.
GORDON, J. R. M.
JOHNSON, L. D.
MCKEEN, J. D.
MORGAN, I. G.
NEAVE, E. H.
NIGHTINGALE, D. V.
NORTHEY, M. E.
PETERSEN, E. R.
RICHARDSON, A. J.
RICHARDSON, P. R.
RUTENBERG, D. P.
TAYLOR, A. J.
THORNTON, D. B.

School of Policy Studies (tel. (613) 533-6555; fax (613) 533-6606; e-mail policy@policy.queensu.ca; internet gsilver.queensu.ca/sps):

LEISS, W.
WILLIAMS, T. R.

School of Urban and Regional Planning (tel. (613) 533-2188; fax (613) 533-6905; e-mail williamj@post.queensu.ca; internet info.queensu.ca/surp):

LEUNG, H. L.
QADEER, M. A.
SKABURSKIS, A.

AFFILIATED COLLEGE

Queen's Theological College: Kingston, ON K7L 3N6; f. 1841; Prin. Rev. H. E. LLEWELLYN.

REDEEMER UNIVERSITY COLLEGE

777 Garner Rd East, Ancaster, ON L9K 1J4

Telephone: (905) 648-2131
Fax: (905) 648-2134
E-mail: adm@redeemer.on.ca
Internet: www.redeemer.on.ca

Founded 1976; became Redeemer College 1980; university status 1982; present name 2000

Committed to the advancement of Reformed Christian education in all academic disciplines
Language of instruction: English
Private control
Academic year: September to May
Pres.: Dr JUSTIN COOPER
Vice-Pres. for Academics: Dr JACOB ELLENS
Vice-Pres. for Administration and Finance: BILL VAN STAALDUINEN
Registrar: RICHARD WIKKERINK
Librarian: JANNY EIKELBOOM

Library: Library of 100,000 items
Number of teachers: 40
Number of students: 800

FACULTY DIVISION HEADS

Faculty of Arts and Foundations: Dr DOUGLAS LONEY
Faculty of Sciences and Social Sciences: Dr DOUGLAS NEEDHAM

UNIVERSITY OF REGINA

3737 Wascana Pkwy, Regina, SK S4S 0A2

Telephone: (306) 585-4111
Fax: (306) 337-2525
E-mail: admissions.office@leroy.cc.uregina.ca
Internet: www.uregina.ca

Founded 1974 (previously Regina Campus, Univ. of Saskatchewan)
Provincial control
Language of instruction: English

Academic year: September to April (2 terms)

Chancellor: Dr WILLIAM F. READY

Vice-Chancellor and Pres.: Dr VIANNE TIM-
MONS

Vice-Pres. for Academic Affairs: Dr GARY
BOIRE

Vice-Pres. for Admin.: DAVID BUTTON

Vice-Pres. for External Relations: BARBARA
POLLOCK

Vice-Pres. for Research and Int. Affairs: Dr
DAVID GAUTHIER

Univ. Sec.: ANNETTE REVET

Registrar: JUDY CHAPMAN

Librarian: CAROL HIXSON

Library: 2.4m. items incl. 655,000 print and
electronic vols and periodicals, 626,110
govt publs (incl. 296,000 in microform),
918,000 other items in microform; colln of
recordings and materials in other media

Number of teachers: 468

Number of students: 12,170 (9,210 full-time;
2,969 part-time)

Publications: *Carillon* (12 a year), *Degrees* (2
a year), *Wascana Review* (2 a year)

DEANS

Faculty of Arts: Dr THOMAS CHASE

Faculty of Business Admin.: ANNE LAVAK

Faculty of Education: Dr JAMES MCNINCH

Faculty of Engineering: Dr PAITOON TONTI-
WACHWUTHIKUL

Faculty of Fine Arts: Dr SHEILA PETTY

Faculty of Kinesiology and Health Studies:
Dr CRAIG CHAMBERLIN

Faculty of Science: Dr KATHERINE BERGMAN

Faculty of Social Work: Dr DAVID SCHANTZ

Faculty of Graduate Studies and Research:
Dr ROD KELLN

Centre for Continuing Education: Dr HARVEY
KING (Dir)

PROFESSORS

ALFANO, DENNIS P., Psychology
ANDERSON, LEONA, Religious Studies
ANDERSON, ROBERT, Business Admin.
ASHTON, NEIL W., Biology
ASMUNDSON, GORDON, Kinesiology and
Health Studies
AUSTIN, BRYAN J., Business Admin.
BERGMAN, KATHERINE, Geology
BLACKSTONE, MARY, Theatre
BLAKE, RAYMOND, History
BRENNAN, WILLIAM, History
BRIGHAM, R. MARK, Biology
BROAD, DAVID, Social Work
CHAN, CHRISTINE, Engineering
CHANNING, LYNN, Music
CHAPCO, WILLIAM, Biology
CHERLAND, MEREDITH, Education
CHOW, SUI, Psychology
CONWAY, JOHN, Sociology and Social Studies
CRUIKSHANK, JANE, Social Work
DAI, LIMING, Engineering
DIAZ, HARRY, Sociology and Social Studies
DOLMAGE, ROD, Education
DONG, MINGZHE, Engineering
DRURY, SHADIA, Philosophy, Political Science
DURST, DOUG, Social Work
EVANS, DENNIS, Visual Arts
FARENICK, DOUGLAS, Mathematics and Stat-
istics
FISHER, J. C., Mathematics
GAUTHIER, DAVID, Geography
GILLIGAN, BRUCE, Mathematics
GINGRICH, PAUL, Sociology and Social Studies
GRIFFITHS, JOHN, Music
GU, YONGAN, Engineering
HADJISTAVROPOULOS, HEATHER, Psychology
HADJISTAVROPOULOS, THOMAS, Psychology
HAMILTON, HOWARD, Computer Science
HANDEREK, KELLY, Theatre
HANSEN, PHILLIP, Philosophy
HART, PAUL, Education
HAYFORD, ALISON, Sociology

HEINRICH, KATHERINE, Mathematics and
Statistics
HOWARD, WILLIAM, English
HUANG, GUO, Engineering
HUBER, GARTH, Physics
IDEM, RAPHAEL, Engineering
ITO, JACK, Business Admin.
JEFFREY, BONNIE, Social Work
JIN, YEE-CHUNG, Engineering
JOHNSON, SHANTHI, English
KELLN, RODNEY, Chemistry and Biochemistry
KESTEN, CYRIL, Education
KIPLING BROWN, ANN, Education
KIRKLAND, STEPHEN, Mathematics and Stat-
istics
KNUTTILA, K. MURRAY, Sociology and Social
Studies
KORTÉ, HERBERT, Philosophy
LAVACK, ANNE, Business Admin.
LEAVITT, PETER, Biology
LEDREW, JUNE, Kinesiology and Health Stud-
ies
LEESON, HOWARD, Political Science
LENTON-YOUNG, GERALD, Theatre
LOLOS, GEORGE, Physics
LOUIS, CAMERON, English
MCINTOSH, RICHARD, Mathematics and Stat-
istics
MACLENNAN, RICHARD, Justice Studies
MAEERS, MHAIRI (VI), Education
MAGUIRE, BRIEN, Computer Science
MALLOY, DAVID, Kinesiology and Health
Studies
MARCHILDON, GREGORY, Johnson-Shoyama
Graduate School of Public Policy
MASLANY, GEORGE, Social Work
MATHIE, EDWARD, Physics
MISSKEY, WILLIAM, Systems Engineering
PALMER, RONALD, Electronic Systems Engin-
eering
PAPANDREOU, ZISIS, Physics
PARANJAPE, RAMAN, Electronic Systems
Engineering
PAUL, ALEXANDER, Geography
PETTY, SHEILA, Media Studies
PFEIFER, JEFFREY, Justice, Psychology
PICKARD, GARTH, Education
PITSULA, JAMES, History
QING, HAIRUO, Geology
RAUM, J. RICHARD, Music
RENNIE, MORINA, Business Admin.
ROBINSON, ANNABEL, Classics
RUDDICK, NICHOLAS, English
SAUCHYN, DAVID, Geography
SAXTON, LAWRENCE, Computer Science
SHAMI, JEANNE, English
SHARMA, SATISH, Systems Engineering
SMYTHE, WILLIAM, Psychology
SOIFER, ELDON, Philosophy
STARK, CANNIE, Psychology
STREIFLER, LEESA, Visual Arts
SZABADOS, BELA, Philosophy
TOMKINS, JAMES, Mathematics
TONTIWACHWUTHIKUL, PAITOON, Engineering
TYMCHAK, MICHAEL, Education
WALL, KATHLEEN, English
WATKINSON, AILSA, Social Work
WEE, ANDREW, Chemistry and Biochemistry
WIDDIS, RANDY, Geography
YAKEL, NORM, Education
YANG, XUE-DONG, Computer Science
YAO, YIYU, Computer Science
ZHANG, CHANG, Computer Science
ZIARKO, WOJCIECH, Computer Science

FEDERATED COLLEGES

Campion College: 3737 Wascana Parkway,
Regina, SK S4S 0A2; tel. (306) 586-4242; fax
(306) 359-1200; e-mail campion.college@
uregina.ca; internet www.campioncollege.sk
.ca; f. 1917; library of 50,000 vols; Pres. B.
FIORE; Academic Dean Dr SAMIRA MCCARTHY.

First Nations University of Canada: 1
First Nations Way, Regina, SK S4S 7K2; tel.
(306) 790-5950; fax (306) 790-5994; e-mail

info@firstnationsuniversity.ca; internet www
.firstnationsuniversity.ca; f. 1975; library of
55,200 vols, incl. the Eeniwuk Colln of 5,000
titles, supporting research in native studies;
Pres. CHARLES PRATT (acting); Vice-Pres. for
Academic Affairs Dr BERNIE SELINGER.

Luther College: Regina, SK S4S 0A2; tel.
(306) 585-5444; fax (306) 585-5267; e-mail
lutherreg@uregina.ca; internet www
.luthercollege.edu; f. 1913; Pres. Dr BRUCE
PERLSON; Academic Dean Dr MARY VETTER.

ATTACHED INSTITUTES

**Canadian Institute for Peace, Justice
and Security:** tel. (306) 585-4779; fax (306)
585-4815; internet www.uregina.ca/arts/
cipjs; Dir Dr JEFFREY PFEIFER.

Canadian Plains Research Center: tel.
(306) 585-4758; fax (306) 585-4699; e-mail
canadian.plains@uregina.ca; internet www
.cprc.caRegina; Exec. Dir Dr DAVID GAU-
THIER.

Centre for Academic Technologies: tel.
(306) 337-2400; fax (306) 337-2401; e-mail
cat@uregina.ca; internet www.uregina.ca/
cat/home.html; Dir Dr VI MAEERS.

Institut Français: Regina; tel. (306) 585-
4828; fax (306) 585-5183; e-mail institut@
uregina.ca; internet institutfrancais.uregina
.ca/home.htm; Dir DOMINIQUE SARNY.

**Organizational and Social Psychology
Research Unit:** tel. (306) 585-5268; fax
(306) 585-4827; e-mail cannie.stark@uregina
.ca; internet uregina.ca/~starkc; Dir CANNIE
STARK.

**Saskatchewan Institute of Public Pol-
icy:** Univ. of Regina, College Avenue Campus, Regina, SK S4S 0A2; tel. (306) 585-5777;
fax (306) 585-5780; e-mail sipp@uregina.ca;
internet www.uregina.ca/sipp; Dir IAN
PEACH.

**Saskatchewan Instructional Develop-
ment and Research Unit of the Faculty
of Education:** tel. (306) 585-4537; e-mail
contactus@education.uregina.ca; internet
education.uregina.ca/index.php?id=38; f.
1985; Dir Dr MICHAEL TYMCHAK.

**Saskatchewan Population Health and
Evaluation Research Unit (SPHERU):**
tel. (306) 585-5674; fax (306) 585-5694;
e-mail spheru@uregina.ca; internet www
.spheru.ca; Dir Dr GEORGE MASLANY (acting).

Social Policy Research Unit: Faculty of
Social Work, Univ. of Regina, Regina, SK
S4S 0A2; tel. (306) 585-5643; fax (306) 585-
5408; e-mail social.policy@uregina.ca; Dir Dr
GARSON HUNTER.

Teaching Development Centre: Dir J.
MCNINCH.

ROYAL MILITARY COLLEGE OF
CANADA

POB 17000 Stn Forces, Kingston, ON K7K
7B4

Telephone: (613) 541-6000
Fax: (613) 542-3565
E-mail: liaison@rmc.ca
Internet: www.rmc.ca

Founded 1876

Languages of instruction: English, French
Academic year: September to May

Chancellor and Pres.: The Minister of
National Defence
Commandant: Brig. Gen. J. M. J. LECLERC
Prin. and Director of Studies: Dr J. S. COWAN
Registrar: Cdr DEBORAH A. WILSON
Director of Cadets: Col W. N. PETERS
Chief Librarian: B. CAMERON

Library of 380,000 vols
Number of teachers: 174

Number of students: 865 (760 undergraduate, 105 graduate)

DEANS AND CHAIRMEN OF DIVISIONS

Arts: Dr J. J. SOKOLSKY
Engineering: Dr J. A. STEWART
Science: Dr R. F. MARSDEN
Continuing Studies: Dr M. F. BARDON
Graduate Studies and Research: Dr B. J. FUGERE

PROFESSORS

AKHRAS, G., Civil Engineering
AL-KHALILI, D., Electrical Engineering
ALLARD, P. E., Electrical Engineering
AMAMI, M., Business Administration
AMPHLETT, J. C., Chemistry
ANTAR, Y., Electrical Engineering
BARDON, M. F., Mechanical Engineering
BARRETT, A. J., Mathematics
BATALLA, E., Physics
BATHURST, R. J., Civil Engineering
BEATY, A., Civil Engineering
BENABDALLAH, H., Mechanical Engineering
BENESCH, R., Mathematics
BENNETT, L., Chemistry and Chemical Engineering
BENSON, M., French Studies
BONESS, R. J., Mechanical Engineering
BONIN, H. W., Chemical Engineering
BONNYCASTLE, S., English
BRADLEY, P., Military Psychology and Leadership
BUCKLEY, J., Physics
BUI, T., Chemistry and Chemical Engineering
BUSSIERES, P., Mechanical Engineering
CHAUDHRY, M. L., Mathematics
CHIKHANI, A. Y., Electrical Engineering
CONSTANTINEAU, P., Politics and Economics
CREBER, K., Chemistry and Chemical Engineering
DAVIES BOUCHARD, S., Continuing Studies
DEPLANCHE, D., Electrical and Computer Engineering
DREIZIGER, N. A. F., History
DUNNETT, P., Political and Economic Science
DuQUESNAY, D., Mechanical Engineering
EDER, W. E., Mechanical Engineering
ERKI, M., Civil Engineering
ERRINGTON, J., History
FAROOQ, M., Electrical Engineering
FINAN, J., Politics and Economics
FJARLIE, E. J., Mechanical Engineering
FUGERE, J., Mathematics and Computer Science
GAGNON, Y., Politics and Economics
GAUTHIER, N., Physics
GERVAIS, R., Mathematics
GODARD, R., Mathematics and Computer Science
GRAVEL, P., Mathematics and Computer Science
HADDAD, L., Mathematics and Computer Science
HASSAN-YARI, H., Politics and Economics
HAYCOCK, R. G., History
HEFNAWI, M., Electrical and Computer Engineering
HURLEY, W., Business Administration
ION, A., History
ISAC, G., Mathematics and Computer Science
JENKINS, A. L., Engineering Management
KLEPAK, H., History
LABBE, M., Mathematics and Computer Science
LABONTE, G., Mathematics
LACHAINE, A. R., Physics
LAGUEUX, P.-A., French Studies
LAPLANTE, J. P., Chemistry
LEWIS, B., Chemistry and Chemical Engineering
LUCIUK, L., Politics and Economics
McDONOUGH, L., Politics and Economics
MCKERCHER, B., History
MALONEY, S., War Studies

MANN, R. F., Chemical Engineering
MOFFATT, W. C., Mechanical Engineering
MONGEAU, B., Electrical Engineering
MUKHERJEE, B. K., Physics
NEILSON, K. E., History
NOEL, J.-M., Physics
POTTIER, R. H., Chemistry
QUILLARD, G., French Studies
RACEY, T. J., Physics
RANGANATHAN, S., Mathematics
REIMER, K., Chemistry and Chemical Engineering
ROBERGE, P. R., Chemistry
ROCHON, P., Physics
ST PIERRE, A., Business Administration
SCHURER, C., Physics
SEGUIN, G., Electrical Engineering
SHEPARD, T., Electrical Engineering
SHOUCRI, R. M., Mathematics
SIMMS, B. W., Engineering Management
SOKOLSKY, J. J., Political Science
SRI, P. S., English
STACEY, M., Physics
STEWART, A., Civil Engineering
TARBOUCHI, M., Electrical and Computer Engineering
THOMPSON, W. T., Chemical Engineering
TORRIE, G. M., Mathematics
TREDDENICK, J. M., Economics
VINCENT, T. B., English
WEIR, R. D., Chemical Engineering
WHELAU, D., Mathematics and Computer Science
WHITEHORN, A. J., Political Science
WILSON, J. D., Electrical Engineering

ROYAL ROADS UNIVERSITY

2005 Sooke Rd, Victoria, BC V9B 5Y2
Telephone: (250) 391-2511
Fax: (250) 391-2500
E-mail: learn.more@royalroads.ca
Internet: www.royalroads.ca

Founded 1995

Pres. and Vice-Chancellor: Dr ALLAN CAHOON
Vice-Pres. for Academic Affairs and Provost: Dr PETER MEEKISON (acting)
Vice-Pres. and Chief Information Officer: DAN TULIP
Vice-Pres. for University Relations: ROBERTA MASON (acting)
Vice-Pres. for RRU Foundation and Chief Devt Officer: DAN SPINNER
Univ. Librarian: (vacant)
Number of students: 3,000

DEANS

Faculty of Management: Dr PEDRO MARQUEZ
Faculty of Social and Applied Science: Dr JIM BAYER
Faculty of Tourism and Hotel Management: Dr NANCY ARSENAULT

RYERSON UNIVERSITY

350 Victoria St, Toronto, ON M5B 2K3
Telephone: (416) 979-5000
Fax: (416) 979-5221
E-mail: international@ryerson.ca
Internet: www.ryerson.ca

Founded 1948 as Ryerson Institute of Technology; became Ryerson Polytechnical Institute 1964 and Ryerson Polytechnic University 1993; present name 2001
Provincial control
Language of instruction: English
Academic year: September to April

Chancellor: G. RAYMOND CHANG
Pres. and Vice-Chancellor: SHELDON LEVY
Provost and Vice-Pres. for Academics Affairs: Dr ALAN SHEPARD
Vice-Provost for Academics: Dr MEHMET ZEYTINOGLU (acting)

Vice-Pres. for Admin. and Finance: LINDA GRAYSON
Vice Pres. for Research and Innovation: Dr TAS VENETSANOPOULOS
Vice-Provost for Faculty Affairs: Dr MICHAEL DEWSON
Vice Provost for Students: Dr HEATHER LANE VETERE
Vice-Pres. for Univ. Advancement: ADAM KAHAN
Vice Provost for Univ. Planning Office: Dr PAUL STENTON
Registrar: KEITH ALNWICK
Chief Librarian: MADELEINE LEFEBVRE

Number of teachers: 771
Number of students: 24,475 (full-time)

DEANS

Faculty of Arts: Dr CARLA CASSIDY
Faculty of Business: TOM KNOWLTON
Faculty of Communication and Design: Dr DANIEL DOZ (acting)
Faculty of Community Services: Dr USHA GEORGE
Faculty of Engineering, Architecture and Science: Dr MOHAMED LACHEMI
School of Graduate Studies: Dr MAURICE YEATES
Ted Rogers School of Management: Dr KEN JONES
The G. Raymond Chang School of Continuing Education: Dr GERVAN FEARON

UNIVERSITÉ SAINTE-ANNE

Church Point, NS B0W 1M0
Telephone: (902) 769-2114
Fax: (902) 769-2930
E-mail: admission@ustanne.ednet.ns.ca
Internet: www.usainteanne.ca

Founded 1890
Language of instruction: French
Academic year: September to April

Chancellor: JEAN-LOUIS ROY
President: Dr ANDRÉ ROBERGE
Vice-Pres. for Academics: Dr NEIL BOUCHER
Registrar: MURIELLE COMEAU
Librarian: CÉCILE POTHIER-COMEAU

Library of 84,000 vols
Number of teachers: 37
Number of students: 400

Publication: *Port Acadie* (1 a year).

ST FRANCIS XAVIER UNIVERSITY

POB 5000, Antigonish, NS B2G 2W5
Telephone: (902) 867-3931
Fax: (902) 867-5153
E-mail: pr@stfx.ca
Internet: www.stfx.ca

Founded 1853
Language of instruction: English
Academic year: September to May

Chancellor: Most Rev. RAYMOND LAHEY
President: Dr SEAN E. RILEY
Vice-Pres. for Academic Affairs: Dr RON JOHNSON
Vice-Pres. for Administration: RAMSAY DUFF
Vice-Pres. for Student Services: JANA LUKER
Vice-Pres. for University Advancement: PETER FARDY
Vice-Pres. and Director of Coady International Institute: M. COYLE
Director of University Extension: R. WEHRELL
Registrar: J. STARK
Librarian: LYNNE MURPHY

Library: see Libraries and Archives
Number of teachers: 200
Number of students: 5,200 (4,200 full-time, 1,000 part-time)

Publications: *Antigonish Review* (literary), *Xavieran Annual*, *Xavieran Weekly*

DEANS

Faculty of Arts: M. McGillivray
Faculty of Science: E. McAlduff

PROFESSORS

ANDERSON, A., Earth Sciences
AQUINO, M., Chemistry
ASPIN, M., Modern Languages
BALDNER, S., Philosophy
BECK, J., Chemistry
BELTRAMI, H., Earth Sciences
BERNARD, I., Education
BICKERTON, J., Political Science
BIGELOW, A., Psychology
BILEK, L., Human Kinetics
BROOKS, G. P., Psychology
BUCKLAND-NICKS, J., Biology
CALLAGHAN, T., Psychology
CLANCY, P., Political Science
DeMONT, E., Biology
DEN HEYER, K., Psychology
DOSSA, S. A., Political Science
DUNCAN, C. M., Business Administration
EDWARDS, J., Psychology
EL-SHEIKH, S., Economics
GALLANT, C. D., Mathematics, Statistics and
   Computer Science
GALLANT, L., Business Administration
GALLANT, M., Human Kinetics
GARBARY, D., Biology
GERGE, A., Music
GERRIETS, M., Economics
GILLIS, A., Nursing
GRANT, J., Education
GRENIER, Y., Political Science
HARRISON, J. F., Political Science
HENKE, P., Psychology
HOGAN, M. P., History
HOLLOWAY, S., Political Science
HUNTER, D., Physics
JACKSON, W., Sociology and Anthropology
JACONO, J., Nursing
JAN, N., Physics
JOHNSON, R. W., Psychology
KLAPSTEIN, D., Chemistry
KOCAY, V., Modern Languages
LANGILLE, E., Modern Languages
LIENGME, B., Chemistry
McALDUFF, E., Chemistry
MacCAULL, W., Mathematics, Statistics and
   Computer Science
MacDONALD, B., Religious Studies
MacDONALD, M. Y., Religious Studies
MacEACHERN, A., Mathematics, Statistics
   and Computer Science
MacFARLANE, E., Nursing
McGILLIVRAY, M., English
MacINNES, D., Sociology and Anthropology
MADDEN, R. F., Business Administration
MARAGONI, G., Chemistry
MARQUIS, P., English
MARSHALL, W. S., Biology
MELCHIN, M., Earth Sciences
MENSCH, J., Philosophy
MILNER, P., English
MURPHY, J. B., Earth Sciences
NACZK, M., Human Nutrition
NASH, R., Sociology and Anthropology
NEWSOME, G. E., Biology
NILSEN, K., Celtic Studies
NORRIS, J., Education
ORR, J., Education
PALEPU, R., Chemistry
PHILLIPS, P., History
PHYNE, J., Anthropology and Sociology
QUIGLEY, A., Adult Education
QUINN, J., Mathematics, Statistics and Com-
   puter Science
QUINN, W. R., Engineering
RASMUSSEN, R., Human Kinetics
SCHUEGRAF, E. J., Mathematics, Statistics
   and Computer Science
SEYMOUR, N., Biology
SMITH, D., English
SMITH, G., Music

SMITH-PALMER, T., Chemistry
STANLEY-BLACKWELL, L., History
STEINITZ, M. O., Physics
SWEET, W., Philosophy
TAYLOR, J., English
TRITES, G., Information Systems
WALLBANK, B., Physics
WANG, P., Mathematics, Statistics and Com-
   puter Science
WEHRELL, R., Extension
WILPUTTE, E., English
WOOD, D., English
WRIGHT, E., Psychology

ATTACHED INSTITUTE

Coady International Institute: POB 5000,
Antigonish, NS B2G 2W5; tel. (902) 867-
3960; f. 1959; runs leadership and organization development programmes with peoples
of Third World countries; diploma and certificate courses in Canada, also training
courses and projects overseas; library of
7,000 vols, 90 periodicals; Dir M. COYLE;
publ. *Newsletter* (2 a year).

SAINT MARY'S UNIVERSITY

923 Robie St, Halifax, NS B3H 3C3

Telephone: (902) 420-5400
E-mail: public.affairs@smu.ca
Internet: www.smu.ca

Founded 1802
Academic year: September to May

Chancellor: Archbishop TERRENCE PRENDER-
   GAST
Vice-Chancellor: Rev. CLAUDE CHAMPAGNE
Pres.: J. COLIN DODDS
Vice-Pres. for Academics and Research: Dr
   TERRY MURPHY
Vice-Pres. for Administration: GABRIELLE
   MORRISON
Vice Pres. for Finance: LARRY CORRIGAN
Registrar: Dr ELIZABETH A. CHARD
Librarian: MADELEINE LEFEBVRE

Number of teachers: 525
Number of students: 8,535 (6,309 full-time,
   2,230 part-time)

DEANS

Faculty of Arts: Dr ESTHER E. ENNS
Faculty of Graduate Studies and Research:
   Dr KEVIN VESSEY (acting)
Faculty of Science: Dr DAVID RICHARDSON
Sobey School of Business: Dr AL MICIAK

PROFESSORS

AMIRKHALKHAI, S., Economics
ARYA, P. L., Economics
BARRETT, G., Sociology
BOWLBY, P., Religious Studies
BOYLE, W. P., Engineering
CATANO, V. M., Psychology
CHAMARD, J. C., Management
CHARLES, A., Finance and Management Sci-
   ence
CHENG, T., Accounting
CHESLEY, G. R., Accounting
CHRISTIANSEN-RUFFMAN, L., Sociology and
   Women's Studies
CLARKE, D., Astronomy and Physics
CONE, D., Biology
DAR, A., Economics
DARLEY, J., Psychology
DAS, H., Management
DAVIS, S., Anthropology
DEUPREE, R., Astronomy and Physics
DIXON, P., Finance and Management Science
DOAK, E. J., Economics
DODDS, J. C., Finance and Management
   Science
DOSTAL, J., Geology
ELSON, C., Chemistry
EMMS, R., Modern Languages and Classics
ERICKSON, P. A., Anthropology
FARRELL, A., Modern Languages and Classics

FITZGERALD, P., Management
GORMAN, B., Accounting
GUENTHER, D., Astronomy and Physics
HAIGH, E., History
HARTNELL, B., Mathematics and Computing
   Science
HARVEY, A., Economics
HILL, K., Psychology
HOWELL, C. D., History and Atlantic Canada
   Studies
KATZ, W., English
KELLOWAY, K., Management and Psychology
KIANG, M.-J., Mathematics and Computing
   Science
KIM, C., Marketing
KONAPASKY, R., Psychology
LANDES, R., Political Science
LARSEN, M. J., English
LEE, E., Finance and Management Science
LINGRAR, P., Mathematics and Computing
   Science
McCALLA, R., Geography
MacDONALD, M., Economics and Women's
   Studies
MacDONALD, R. A., English
McGEE, H., Anthropology
McMULLEN, J., Sociology
MICIAK, A., Marketing
MILLAR, H., Finance and Management Sci-
   ence
MILLS, A., Management
MILLWARD, H., Geography
MITCHELL, G., Astronomy and Physics
MORRISON, J. H., History and Asian Studies
MUIR, P., Mathematics
MUKHOPADHYAY, A. K., Economics
MURPHY, J., Religious Studies
OWEN, V., Geology
PARKER, R., English
PENDSE, S., Management
PE-PIPER, G., Geology
RAND, J., Biology
REID, J. G., History, Atlantic Canada Studies
RICHARDSON, D. H. S., Biology
SASTRY, V., Engineering
SEAMEN, A., English
SIDDIQUI, Q., Geology
STRONGMAN, D., Biology and Forensic Science
SWINGLER, D., Engineering
TARNAWSKI, V., Engineering
THOMAS, G., English
TURNER, D. G., Astronomy and Physics
TWOMEY, R. J., History
VAUGHAN, K., Chemistry
VELTMEYER, H., Sociology, International
   Development Studies
VESSEY, K., Biology
WAGAR, T., Management
WEIN, S., Philosophy
YOUNG, N., Accounting

UNIVERSITY OF SASKATCHEWAN

105 Administration Pl., Saskatoon, SK S7N
5A2

Telephone: (306) 966-1212
Fax: (306) 966-6730
E-mail: askus@usask.ca
Internet: www.usask.ca

Founded 1907; 2-campus institution 1967
   (Saskatoon and Regina); legislation was
   passed in 1974 creating 2 separate univs
State control
Language of instruction: English
Academic year: September to August

Pres. and Chancellor: R. P. MACKINNON
Provost and Vice-Pres. for Academic Affairs:
   BRETT FAIRBAIRN
Vice-Pres. for Finance and Resources:
   RICHARD FLORIZONE
Vice-Pres. for Research: KAREN CHAD
Univ. Sec.: LEA PENNOCK
Registrar: K. McINNES
Librarian: F. WINTER
Number of teachers: 1,091

Number of students: 20,113

DEANS

College of Agriculture and Bioresources: G. J. SCOLES (acting)
College of Arts and Science: J. R. DILLON
College of Commerce: G. E ISAAC
College of Dentistry: G. S. USWAK (acting)
College of Education: C. REYNOLDS
College of Engineering: J. A. KOZINSKI
College of Graduate Studies and Research: T. B. WISHART
College of Kinesiology: C. D. RODGERS
College of Law: W. B. COTTER
College of Medicine: W. ALBRITTON
College of Nursing: J. SAWATZKY (acting)
College of Pharmacy and Nutrition: D. K. GORECKI
College of Veterinary Medicine: C. S. RHODES

DIRECTOR

School of Physical Therapy: E. L. HARRISON

PROFESSORS

ADAMS, G. P., Veterinary Biomedical Sciences
AKKERMAN, A., Geography
ALBRITTON, W. L., Paediatrics
ALLEN, A. L., Veterinary Pathology
ALTMAN, M., Economics
ANDERSON, D. W., Soil Science
ANGEL, J. F., Biochemistry
ANSDELL, K. M., Geological Sciences
ARCHIBOLD, O. W., Geography
ATKINSON, M., Political Studies
AXWORTHY, C. S., Law
BAILEY, J. V., Large Animal Clinical Sciences
BAKER, C. G., Dentistry
BARANSKI, A. S., Chemistry
BARBER, E. M., Agricultural and Bioresource Engineering
BARBER, S. M., Large Animal Clinical Sciences
BARBOUR, S. L., Civil Engineering
BARTH, A. D., Large Animal and Clinical Sciences
BASINGER, J. F., Geological Sciences
BATTISTE, M., Educational Foundations
BAXTER-JONES, A. D. G., Kinesiology
BELL, K. T. M., Art and Art History
BELL, L. S., Art and Art History
BERENBAUM, S. L., Nutrition and Dietetics
BERGSTROM, D. J., Mechanical Engineering
BETTANY, J. R., Soil Science
BIDWELL, P. M., Languages and Linguistics
BILSON, R. E., Law
BINGHAM, W., Paediatrics
BLACKSHAW, S. L., Psychiatry
BLAKLEY, B. R., Veterinary Biomedical Sciences
BOLTON, R. J., Electrical and Computer Engineering
BONHAM-SMITH, P. C., Biology
BORSA, J., Women's and Gender Studies
BORTOLOTTI, G. R., Biology
BOWDEN, M. A., Law
BOWEN, R. C., Psychiatry
BOYD, C. W., Management and Marketing
BRAWLEY, L., Kinesiology
BREMNER, M., Mathematics and Statistics
BRENNA, D. S., Drama
BRETSCHER, P. A., Microbiology and Immunology
BROOKE, J. A., Mathematics and Statistics
BROWN, W. J., Agricultural Economics
BROWN, Y. M. R., Nursing
BUCHANAN, F. C., Animal and Poultry Science
BUGG, J. D., Mechanical Engineering
BUNT, R. B., Computer Science
BURBRIDGE, B., Medical Imaging
BURNELL, D., History
BURTON, R. T., Mechanical Engineering
BUTLER, L., Nursing
CALDER, R. L., English
CAMPBELL, D. C., Anaesthesia
CAMPBELL, J., Psychology

CAMPBELL, J. R., Veterinary Large Animal Science
CARD, C. E., Veterinary Large Animal Science
CARD, R. T., Medicine
CARR-STEWART, S., Educational Admin.
CARTER, JR, J. A., Computer Science
CASSON, A., Psychiatry
CHAD, K., Kinesiology
CHAPMAN, D., Anatomy and Cell Biology
CHARTRAND, P., Law
CHEDRESE, P. J., Obstetrics, Gynaecology and Reproductive Sciences
CHIBBAR, R. N., Plant Sciences
CHILIBECK, P., Kinesiology
CHILTON, N., Biology
CHIRINO-TREJO, J. M., Veterinary Microbiology
CHIVERS, D. P., Biology
CLARKE, P. L., Industrial Relations and Organizational Behaviour
CLASSEN, H. L., Animal and Poultry Science
COCKCROFT, D. W., Medicine
COOLEY, R. W., English
COOPER-STEPHENSON, K. D., Law
CORCORAN, M., Anatomy and Cell Biology
COTTER, W. B., Law
COTTON, D. J., Medicine
COULMAN, B. E., Plant Science
CROSSLEY, D. J., Philosophy
CROWE, T. G., Agricultural and Bioresource Engineering
CSAPO, G., Music
CUMING, R. C. C., Law
CUSHMAN, D. O., Economics
DABNI, C. B., Management and Marketing
DAKU, B. L. F., Electrical and Computer Engineering
DALAI, A. K., Chemical Engineering
D'ARCY, C., Psychiatry
DAVIS, A. R., Biology
DAVIS, G. R., Physics and Engineering Physics
DAYTON, E. B., Philosophy
DE BOER, D. H., Geography
DELBAERE, L. T. J., Biochemistry
DENHAM, W. P., English
DENIS, W. B., Sociology
DESAUTELS, M., Physiology
DEUTSCHER, T. B., History
DEVON, R. M., Anatomy and Cell Biology
DICK, R., Physics and Engineering Physics
DICKINSON, H. D., Sociology
DICKSON, G., Nursing
DILLON, J. R., Biology
DODDS, D. E., Electrical and Computer Engineering
DOUCETTE, J. R., Anatomy and Cell Biology
DOWLING, P. M., Veterinary Biomedical Sciences
DUGGLEBY, W. D., Nursing
DUKE, T., Small Animal Clinical Sciences
DUST, W., Surgery
DYCK, L. E., Psychiatry
DYCK, R. F., Medicine
EAGER, D. L., Computer Science
ECHEVARRIA, E. C., Economics
ELLIS, J. A., Veterinary Microbiology
ENGLAND, G. J., Industrial Relations and Organization Behaviour
ENTWISTLE, G., Accounting
ERVIN, A. M., Religious Studies and Anthropology
FAIRBAIRN, B. T., History
FARIED, S. O., Electrical and Computer Engineering
FAULKNER, R. A., Kinesiology
FERGUSON, L. M., Nursing
FINDLAY, L. M., English
FLANNIGAN, R. D., Law
FLYNN, M., Educational Psychology and Special Education
FORSYTH, G. W., Veterinary Biomedical Sciences
FOWLER, D. B., Plant Sciences
FOWLER-KERRY, S. E., Nursing

FRANKLIN, S., Geography
FULTON, M. E., Agricultural Economics
FURTAN, W. H., Agricultural Economics
GANDER, R. E., Electrical and Computer Engineering
GEORGE, G. N., Geological Sciences
GERMIDA, J. J., Soil Science
GIESY, J. P., Veterinary Biomedical Sciences
GINGELL, S. A., English
GOLDIE, H. A., Microbiology and Immunology
GOPALAKRISHNAN, V., Pharmacology
GORDON, J. R., Veterinary Microbiology
GORECKI, D. K. J., Pharmacy
GRAHAM, B. L., Medicine
GRAHN, B. H., Small Animal Clinical Sciences
GRANT, P. R., Psychology
GRAY, R. S., Agricultural Economics
GREER, J. E., Computer Science
GRIEBEL, R. W., Surgery
GUSTA, L. V., Plant Sciences
GUSTHART, J. L., Kinesiology
GUTWIN, C., Computer Science
HAIGH, J. C., Veterinary Large Animal Sciences
HAINES, D. M., Veterinary Microbiology
HAINES, L. P., Educational Psychology and Special Education
HAMILTON, D. L., Veterinary Biomedical Sciences
HANDY, J. R., History
HARDING, A. J., English
HARRIS, D. I., Music
HARRIS, R. L., English
HARRISON, E. L., Physical Therapy
HARVEY, B. L., Plant Sciences
HAUG, M. D., Civil and Geological Engineering
HAYES, S. J., Microbiology and Immunology
HEMMINGS, S. J., Medicine
HENDERSON, J. R., English
HENDRY, M. J., Geological Sciences
HERTZ, P. B., Mechanical Engineering
HIEBERT, L. M., Veterinary Biomedical Sciences
HILL, G. A., Chemical Engineering
HIROSE, A., Physics and Engineering Physics
HOBBS, J. E., Agricultural Economics
HOEPPNER, V. H., Medicine
HOLM, F. A., Plant Sciences
HOOVER, J. N., Dentistry
HOWARD, S. P., Microbiology and Immunology
HOWE, E. C., Economics
HUBBARD, J. W., Pharmacy
HUCL, P. J., Plant Sciences
HULL, P. R., Medicine
HURST, T. S., Medicine
IRVINE, D., Family Medicine
ISAAC, G., Management and Marketing
ISH, D., Law
JACKSON, M. L., Veterinary Pathology
JELINSKI, M. D., Large Animal Clinical Sciences
JOHNSTON, G. H. F., Surgery
JUURLINK, B. H. J., Anatomy and Cell Biology
KALRA, J., Pathology
KASAP, S. O., Electrical and Computer Engineering
KASIAN, G. F., Paediatrics
KEIL, J. M., Computer Science
KEITH, R. G., Surgery
KELLY, I. W., Educational Psychology and Special Education
KENT, C. A., History (Acting Head)
KERR, W. A., Agricultural Economics
KERRICH, R. W., Geological Sciences
KHACHATOURIANS, G. G., Applied Microbiology and Food Science
KHANDELWAL, R. L., Medical Biochemistry
KIRK, A., Medicine
KOLB, N. R., Physics and Engineering Physics
KOLBINSON, D. A., Diagnostic and Surgical Sciences
KONCHAK, P. A., Dentistry
KORDAN, B., Political Studies

KORINEK, V. J., History
KOUSTOV, A. V., Physics and Engineering Physics
KOZINSKI, J. A., Chemical Engineering
KRAHN, J., Pathology
KREYSZIG, W. K., Music
KRONE, P. H., Anatomy and Cell Biology
KUHLMANN, F.-V., Mathematics and Statistics
KUHLMANN, S., Mathematics and Statistics
KULSHRESHTHA, S. N., Agricultural Economics
KULYK, W. M., Anatomy and Cell Biology
KUSALIK, A. J., Computer Science
LAARVELD, B., Animal and Poultry Science
LAFERTÉ, S., Biochemistry
LEE, J. S., Biochemistry
LEHMKUHL, D. M., Biology
LEIGHTON, F. A., Veterinary Pathology
LEPNURM, R., Management and Marketing
LI, P. S., Sociology
LI, X. M., Psychiatry
LLEWELLYN, E. J., Physics and Engineering Physics
LOH, L. C., Medical Biochemistry
LONG, R. J., Industrial Relations and Organization Behaviour
LOW, N. H., Applied Microbiology and Food Science
LOWRY, N., Paediatrics
LUCAS, R. F., Economics
MAAKA, R., Native Studies
McCALLA, G. I., Computer Science
McCROSKY, C., Electrical and Computer Engineering
MacDONALD, M. B., Nursing
MacDOUGALL, B., Native Studies
McKAY, G., Pharmacy
MACKINNON, J. C., History
McKINNON, J. J., Animal and Poultry Science
MacKINNON, R. P., Law
McLENNAN, B. D., Biochemistry
MacLENNAN, J., Professional Communication in Engineering
McMULLEN, L. M., Psychology
McNEILL, D., Music
MAJEWSKI, M., Chemistry
MANSON, A. H., Physics and Engineering Physics
MAPLETOFT, R. J., Large Animal and Clinical Sciences
MARCINIUK, D. D., Medicine
MARTIN, J. R., Mathematics and Statistics
MARTZ, L. W., Geography
MATHESON, T. J., English
MAULÉ, C. P., Agricultural and Bioresource Engineering
MEHTA, M. D., Sociology
MERRIAM, J. B., Geological Sciences
MESSIER, F., Biology
MEYER, D. A., Archaeology
MICHELMANN, H. J., Political Studies
MIDDLETON, D., Veterinary Pathology
MIKET, M. J., Mathematics and Statistics
MILLER, J. R., History
MISRA, V., Veterinary Microbiology
MOEWES, A., Physics and Engineering Physics
MONTURE, P. A., Sociology
MOULDING, M. B., Restorative and Prosthetic Dentistry
MUHAJARINE, N., Community Health and Epidemiology
MUIR, G. D., Veterinary Biomedical Sciences
NAZARALI, A. J., Pharmacy
NEUFELD, E. M., Computer Science
NORMAN, K. E., Law
OGLE, K. D., Family Medicine
OLATUNBOSUN, O. A., Obstetrics, Gynaecology and Reproductive Sciences
OLFERT, M. R., Agricultural Economics
OVSENEK, N. C., Anatomy and Cell Biology
PACKOTA, G. V., Dentistry
PAINTER, M., Management and Marketing
PAN, Y., Geological Sciences
PARKINSON, D. J., English

PATERSON, P. G., Nutrition and Dietetics
PATTERSON, W., Geology
PATO, M. D., Medical Biochemistry
PATRICK, G. W., Mathematics and Statistics
PEDRAS, M. S. C., Chemistry
PENG, D.-Y., Chemical Engineering
PENNOCK, D. J., Soil Science
PETERNELJ-TAYLOR, C. A., Nursing
PETRIE, L., Veterinary Large Animal Sciences
PFEIFER, K., Philosophy
PHARR, J. W., Veterinary Anaesthesiology, Small Animal Clinical Sciences
PHILLIPS, B., Management and Marketing
PHILLIPS, F., Accounting
PHILLIPS, P. W. B., Political Studies
PIERSON, R. A., Obstetrics, Gynaecology and Reproductive Sciences
POLLEY, L. R., Veterinary Microbiology
POMEROY, J., Geography
POOLER, J. A., Geography
POPKIN, D. R., Obstetrics, Gynaecology and Reproductive Sciences
POST, K., Small Animal Clinical Sciences
PRATT, B. R., Geological Sciences
PROCTOR, L. F., Curriculum Studies
PUGSLEY, T. S., Chemical Engineering
PYWELL, R. E., Physics and Engineering Physics
QUALTIERE, L. F., Pathology
QUIGLEY, T. L., Law
RALPH, E. G., Curriculum Studies
RANGACHARYULU, C., Physics and Engineering Physics
RANK, G. H., Biology
RAWLINGS, N. C., Veterinary Biomedical Sciences
REED, M. G., Geography
REEDER, B. A., Community Health and Epidemiology
REEVES, M. J., Civil and Geological Engineering
REGNIER, R. H., Educational Foundations
RELKE, D., Women's and Gender Studies
REMILLARD, A. J., Pharmacy
RENAUT, R. W., Geological Sciences
RENIHAN, P. J., Educational Administration
REYNOLDS, C., Educational Administration
RHODES, C. S., Large Animal Clinical Sciences
RICHARDSON, J. S., Pharmacology
ROESLER, W. J., Biochemistry
ROMO, J. T., Plant Sciences
ROSAASEN, K. A., Agricultural Economics
ROSENBERG, A. M., Paediatrics
ROSSER, B. W. C., Anatomy and Cell Biology
ROSSNAGEL, B. G., Crop Development Centre
ROWLAND, G. G., Plant Sciences
RUDACHYK, L., Physical Medicine and Rehabilitation (Acting Head)
RUTLEDGE HARDING, S., Pathology
ST LOUIS, L. V., Economics
SALT, J. E., Electrical and Computer Engineering
SANKARAN, K., Paediatrics
SAWATZKY, J. E., Nursing
SAWHNEY, V. K., Biology
SAXENA, A., Pathology
SCHISSEL, B., Sociology
SCHMUTZ, S. M., Animal and Poultry Science
SCHOENAU, G. J., Mechanical Engineering
SCHONEY, R. A., Agricultural Economics
SCHREYER, D., Anatomy and Cell Biology
SCHWIER, R. A., Curriculum Studies
SCOLES, G. J., Plant Sciences
SEMCHUK, K. M., Nursing
SHAND, P. J., Applied Microbiology and Food Science
SHANTZ, S., Art and Art History
SHARMA, R. K., Pathology
SHERIDAN, D. P., Medicine
SHEVCHUK, Y. M., Pharmacy
SHMON, C. L., Small Animal Clinical Sciences
SHOKER, A., Medicine
SIMKO, E., Veterinary Pathology
SINGH, B., Veterinary Biomedical Sciences
SINGH, J., Veterinary Biomedical Sciences

SINHA, B. M., Religious Studies
SMART, M. E., Small Animal Clinical Sciences
SMITH, B. L., Nursing
SMOLYAKOV, A., Physics and Engineering Physics
SOFKO, G. J., Physics and Engineering Physics
SOTEROS, C. E., Mathematics and Statistics
SPARKS, G. A., Civil and Geological Engineering
SPINK, K. S., Kinesiology
SRINIVASON, R., Mathematics and Statistics
STAMLER, L. R. L., Nursing
STEELE, T. G., Physics and Engineering Physics
STEER, R. P., Chemistry
STEEVES, J. S., Political Studies
STEPHANSON, R. A., English
STEWART, L., History
STEWART, N. J., Nursing
STOICHEFF, R. P., English
STOOKEY, J. M., Veterinary Large Animal Sciences
STORY, D. C., Political Studies
SULAKHE, P. V., Physiology
SUTHERLAND, J. K., Restorative and Prosthetic Dentistry
SUVEGES, L. G., Pharmacy
SZMIGIELSKI, J., Mathematics and Statistics
SZYSZKOWSKI, W., Mechanical Engineering
TAKAYA, K., Electrical and Computer Engineering
TANNOUS, G. F., Finance and Management Science
TAYLOR, S. M., Small Animal Clinical Sciences
TEMPIER, R., Psychiatry
TEPLITSKY, P. E., Restorative and Prosthetic Dentistry
THACKER, P. A., Animal and Poultry Science
THOMLINSON, W., Physics and Engineering Physics
THOMPSON, V. A., Psychology
THORNHILL, J. A., Physiology
THORPE, D. J., English
TOWNSEND, H. G. G., Veterinary Internal Medicine
TREMBLAY, M., Kinesiology
TYLER, R. T., Applied Microbiology and Food Science
TYMCHATYN, E. D., Mathematics and Statistics
VAIDYANATHAN, G., Accounting
VAN REES, K. C. J., Soil Science
VANDENBERG, A., Plant Sciences
VANDERVORT, L. A., Law
VERGE, V. M. K., Anatomy and Cell Biology
VON BAEYER, C. L., Psychology
WAISER, W. A., History
WALDNER, C. L., Large Animal Clinical Sciences
WALDRAM, J. B., Psychology
WALKER, E. G., Anthropology and Archaeology
WALKER, K. D., Educational Administration
WALLEY, F. L., Soil Science
WALTZ, W. L., Chemistry
WARD, A., Curriculum Studies
WARD, D. E., Chemistry
WARRINGTON, R. C., Biochemistry
WASON-ELLAM, L., Curriculum Studies
WATSON, L. G., Mechanical Engineering
WAYGOOD, E. B., Biochemistry
WEST, N. H., Physiology
WETZEL, K. W., Industrial Relations and Organizational Behaviour
WHITE, G. N., Family Medicine
WHITING, S. J., Nutrition and Dietetics
WICKETT, R. E. Y., Educational Foundations
WILSON, D. G., Veterinary Large Animal Sciences
WILSON, T. W., Medicine
WISHART, T. B., Psychology
WOBESER, G. A., Veterinary Pathology
WOODHOUSE, H., Educational Foundations
WORMITH, J. S., Psychology

WOROBETZ, L. J., Medicine
WOTHERSPOON, T. L., Sociology
XIAO, C., Physics and Engineering Physics
XIAO, W., Microbiology and Immunology
YONG-HING, K., Surgery
YU, P. H., Psychiatry
ZELLO, G. A., Nutrition and Dietetics
ZHANG, C., Mechanical Engineering
ZICHY, F. A., English
ZIOLA, B., Pathology

FEDERATED COLLEGE
St Thomas More College: 1437 College Dr., Saskatoon, SK. S7N 0W6; Pres. Rev. G. SMITH.

AFFILIATED COLLEGES
Briercrest College: 510 College Dr., Caronport, SK S0H 0S0; Pres. Rev. D. UGLEM.

Central Pentecostal College: 1303 Jackson Ave, Saskatoon, SK S7H 2M9; Pres. Rev. D. STILLER.

College of Emmanuel and St Chad: 1337 College Dr., Saskatoon, SK S7N 0W6; Principal Rev. W. D. DELLER.

Gabriel Dumont College: Exec. Dir C. RACETTE.

Lutheran Theological Seminary: 114 Seminary Crescent, Saskatoon, SK S7N 0X3; Pres. D. E. BUCK.

St Andrew's College: 1121 College Dr., Saskatoon, SK S7N 0W3; Pres. T. FAULKER.

St Peter's College: POB 10, Muenster, SK S0K 2Y0; Pres. G. KOBUSSEN.

UNIVERSITÉ DE SHERBROOKE

2500 Blvd de l'Université, Sherbrooke, QC J1K 2R1

Telephone: (819) 821-7000
Fax: (819) 821-7966
E-mail: information@courrier.usherb.ca
Internet: www.usherbrooke.ca

Founded 1954
Private control
Language of instruction: French
Academic year: September to May

Chancellor: H. E. Mgr JEAN-MARIE FORTIER (Catholic Archbishop of Sherbrooke)
Rector: BRUNO-MARIE BÉCHARD
Vice-Rector for Admin.: LUCE SAMOISETTE
Vice-Rector for Personnel and Students: JEAN DESCLOS
Vice-Rector for Research: EDWIN BOURGET
Vice-Rector for Studies: DENIS MARCEAU
Sec.-Gen.: MARTIN BUTEAU
Registrar: FRANCE MYETTE
Librarian: SYLVIE BELZILE

Library of 1,676,000 vols
Number of teachers: 1,750 (650 full-time, 1,100 part-time)
Number of students: 22,272 (11,259 full-time, 11,013 part-time)

DEANS
Faculty of Administration: ROGER NOËL
Faculty of Applied Sciences: RICHARD J MARCEAU
Faculty of Education: CÉLINE GARANT
Faculty of Law: LOUIS MARQUIS
Faculty of Letters and Human Sciences: BERNARD CHAPUT
Faculty of Medicine: RÉJEAN HÉBERT
Faculty of Physical Education and Sport: PAUL DESHAIES
Faculty of Sciences: JEAN GOULET
Faculty of Theology, Ethics and Philosophy: MICHEL DION

PROFESSORS
Faculty of Administration
Accountancy:
BEAUCHESNE, A.

COMTOIS, J.
GODBOUT, R.
JOLIN, M.
LEMIEUX, P.
MENARD, P.
MORIN, R.
MORIN, R. J.
NOËL, R.

Finance:
BEN-AMOR, A.
GARANT, J.-P.
GARNIER, G.
GUÉRIN, F.
PAGE, J.
PRÉFONTAINE, J.
PREZEAU, C.

Management:
BERGERON, J.-L.
COUPAL, M.
LAFLAMME, M.
LEONARD, H.
PETIT, A.
PRÉVOST, P.
ROBIDOUX, J.
ROY, A. F.
TURCOTTE, P.

Marketing:
BOIVIN, Y.
D'ASTOUS, A.
VALENCE, G.

Quantitative Methods:
BASTIN, E.
BEAUDOIN, P.-H.
INGHAM, J.
MALTAIS, G.
THEORET, A.

Faculty of Applied Sciences
Chemical Engineering:
BOULOS, M.
BROADBENT, A. D.
CHORNET, E.
DEKEE, D.
GRAVELLE, D.
JONES, P.
THÉRIEN, N.

Civil Engineering:
AITCIN, P.-C.
BALLIVY, G.
BRUNELLE, P.-E.
GALLEZ, B.
JOHNS, K. C.
LAHOUD, A.
LEFEBVRE, D.
LEFEBVRE, G. A.
LEMIEUX, P.
LUPIEN, C.
MORIN, J.-P.
NARASIAH, S. K.
NEALE, K. W.
ROHAN, K.

Electrical Engineering and Computer Engineering:
ADOUL, J.-P.
AUBÉ, G.
BÉLAND, B.
BOUTIN, N.
DALLE, D.
DELISLE, J.
DENIS, G.
DUVAL, F.
GOULET, R.
LEROUX, A.
MORISSETTE, S.
RICHARD, S.
THIBAULT, R.

Mechanical Engineering:
BOURASSA, P.-A.
GALANIS, N.
LANEVILLE, A.
MASSOUD, M.
MERCADIER, Y.

NICOLAS, J.
PROULX, D.
ROY, C.
VAN HOENACKER, Y.

Faculty of Education
Counselling and School Administration:
DUPONT, P.
LAFLAMME, CL.
LIMOGES, J.
MARCEAU, D.
MASSE, D.
REID, A.

Pedagogy:
CORMIER, R. A.
HARVEY, V.
HIVON, R.
ROBIDAS, G.
SCHOLER, M.
SERRE, F.
STRINGER, G.

Pre-School and Primary Education:
LAFONTAINE, L.
MARTEL, G.
ROY, G.-R.
THÉRIEN, L.

Special Education:
HADE, D.
LEFEBVRE, R.
OTIS, R.
POULIN, G.
RHEAULT, M.
TARDIF, J.

Faculty of Law:
ANCTIL, J.
BERGERON, J.-G.
BLACHE, P.
BOISCLAIR, C L.
CHARRON, C.
CODÈRE, D.
DUBÉ, J.-L.
DUBÉ, M.
GAGNON, J.
KOURI, R.-P.
LAVOIE, J.-M.
MELANSON, J.
PATENAUDE, P.
PEPIN, R.
PHILIPS-NOOTENS, S.
POIRIER, M. Z.
RATTI, N.
TÉTRAULT, R.

Faculty of Letters and Human Sciences
Economics:
ASCAH, L.-G.
BASTIEN, R.
DAUPHIN, R.
HANEL, P.
LARIN, G.-N.
PELLETIER, G.-R.
ROY, G.
WENER, N.

Geography and Remote Sensing:
BONN, F.
CHOQUETTE, R.
DUBOIS, J.-M.
GAGNON, R.
GWYN, H.
MORIN, D.
NADEAU, R.
PAQUETTE, R.
POULIN, A.
POULIOT, M.

Human Sciences:
BLAIS, M.
CHAPUT, B.
CHOTARD, J.-R.
DE BUJANDA, J.-M.
DUMONT, M.
GAGNON, M.
GIROUX, L.
LACHANCE, A.-L.

LAPERRIÈRE, G.
LEGAULT, G.
LUC, L.
VALCKE, L.
VANDAL, G.

Letters and Communications:

BEAUCHEMIN, N.
BONENFANT, J.
DUPUIS, H.
FOREST, J.
GIGUÈRE, R.
GIROUX, R.
HÉBERT, P.
JONES, D.-G.
LÉARD, J.-M.
MALUS, A.
MARTEL, P.
MICHON, J.
PAINCHAUD, L.
SIROIS, A.
SUTHERLAND, R.
THEORET, M.
TREMBLAY, R.
VINET, M. T.

Psychology:

CHARBONNEAU, C.
LECLERC, G.
L'ECUYER, R.
NORMANDEAU, A.
PAYETTE, M.
ST-ARNAUD, Y.

Social Service:

ALARY, J.
LEFRANÇOIS, R.
MALAVOY, M.

Faculty of Medicine

Anaesthesia:

LAMARCHE, Y.
TÉTREAULT, J. P.

Anatomy and Cellular Biology:

BRIÈRE, N.
CALVERT, R.
MENARD, D.
NEMIROVSKY, M.-S.
NIGAM, V.-N.

Biochemistry:

BASTIN, M.
DE MÉDICIS, M.-E.
DUPUIS, G.
GIBSON, D.
GRANT, A.
LEHOUX, J.-G.
TAN, L.

Biophysics and Physiology:

PAYET, M. D.
RUIZ-PETRICH, E.
SCHANNE, O.
SEUFERT, W. D.

Cardiovascular and Thoracic Surgery:

TEIJEIRA, F. J.

Community Health:

BÉLAND, R.
IGLESIAS, R.
VOBECKY, J.
VOBECKY, J. S.

Diagnostic Radiology:

BRAZEAU-LAMONTAGNE, L.
SCHMUTZ, G.

Family Medicine:

BERNIER, R.
CAUX, R.
GRAND'MAISON, P.

General Surgery:

DEVROEDE, G.
RIOUX, A.

Medicine:

BARON, M., Internal Medicine
BEAUDRY, R., Gastroenterology
BEGIN, R., Pneumology

BELLABARBA, D., Endocrinology
BÉNARD, B., Endocrinology
CÔTÉ, M., Cardiology
DUMAIS, B., Cardiology
HADDAD, H., Gastroenterology
LONGPRÉ, B., Haematology
LUSSIER, A., Rheumatology
MARCOUX, J.-A., Infectious Diseases
MÉNARD, D. B., Gastroenterology
MÉNARD, H., Rheumatology
MONTAMBAULT, P., Nephrology
NAWAR, T., Nephrology
PÉPIN, J.-M., Internal Medicine
PIGEON, G., Nephrology
PLANTE, A., Internal Medicine
PLANTE, G.-E., Nephrology
REIHER, J., Neurology
ROCHON, M., Haematology
ROULEAU, J. L., Cardiology
TÉTREAULT, L., Internal Medicine

Microbiology:

BOURGAUX, D.
BOURGAUX, P.
THIRION, J.-P.
WEBER, J.

Nuclear Medicine and Radiobiology:

JAY-GERIN, J.-P.
SANCHE, L.
VAN LIER, J.

Nursing Sciences:

CHARTIER, L.
LALANCETTE, D.

Obstetrics and Gynaecology:

AINMELK, Y.
BLOUIN, D.
GAGNER, R.

Ophthalmology:

BRUNETTE, J.-R.

Orthopaedic Surgery:

DES MARCHAIS, J. E.

Otorhinolaryngology:

CHARLIN, B.

Paediatrics:

BUREAU, M. A.
LANGLOIS, L.
LEMIEUX, B.
PARÉ, C.
ROLA-PLESZCZYNSKI, M.

Pathology:

COTÉ, R. A.
LAMARCHE, J.
MADARNAS, P.
MASSÉ, S.

Pharmacology:

ESCHER, E.
REGOLI, G.
SIROIS, P.

Faculty of Physical Education and Sport:

BISSONNETTE, R.
CUERRIER, J.-P.
DEMERS, P. J.
DESHAIES, P.
GAUTHIER, P.
LEMIEUX, G.-B.
NADEAU, M.
NADON, R.
OUELLET, J.-G.
QUENNEVILLE, G.
ROY, R.
ROYER, D.
THERRIEN, R.
VANDEN-ABEELE, J.

Faculty of Sciences

Biology:

BEAUDOIN, A.
BEAUMONT, G.
BÉCHARD, P.
BERGERON, J.-M.
CYR, A.

LEBEL, D.
MATTON, P.
MORISSET, J.-A.
O'NEIL, L.-C.
ROBIN, J.

Chemistry:

BANDRAUK, A. D.
BROWN, G. M.
CABANA, A.
DESLONGCHAMPS, P.
GIGUÈRE, J.
JERUMANIS, S.
JOLICOEUR, C.
LESSARD, J.
MÉNARD, H.
MICHEL, A.
PELLETIER, G.-E.
RUEST, L.

Mathematics and Computer Science:

ALLARD, J.
BAZINET, J.
BELLEY, J.-M.
BOUCHER, C.
BRISEBOIS, M.
COLIN, B.
CONSTANTIN, J.
COURTEAU, B.
CUSTEAU, G.
DUBEAU, F.
DUBOIS, J.
FOURNIER, G.
GIROUX, G.
HAGUEL, J.
KRELL, M.
LEDUC, P.-Y.
MORALES, P.
SAINT-DENIS, R.
SAMSON, J.-P.

Physics:

AUBIN, M.
BANVILLE, M.
CAILLÉ, A.
CARLONE, C.
CARON, L. G.
JANDL, S.
LEMIEUX, A.
SIMARD, P.-A.
TREMBLAY, A. M.

Faculty of Theology, Ethics and Philosophy:

BÉDARD, A.
BOISVERT, L.
MELANÇON, L.
OUELLET, F.
RACINE, L.
VACHON, L.
VAILLANCOURT, R.

SIMON FRASER UNIVERSITY

8888 University Dr., Burnaby, BC V5A 1S6
Telephone: (604) 291-3111
E-mail: sfumpr@sfu.ca
Internet: www.sfu.ca
SFU Vancouver: 515 West Hastings St, Vancouver, BC V6B 5K3
Telephone: (604) 291-5000
Fax: (604) 291-5060
Internet: www.sfu.ca
SFU, Surrey: 250, 13450 102 Ave, Surrey, BC V3T 2W1
Telephone: (778) 782-7500
Fax: (778) 782-7488
Internet: www.sfu.ca
Founded 1963
Provincial control
Language of instruction: English
Academic year: September to August (3 terms of 4 months each)

Chancellor: Dr BRANDT C. LOUIE
Pres. and Vice-Chancellor: Dr MICHAEL STEVENSON

Academic Vice-Pres. and Provost: Dr J. H. WATERHOUSE
Vice-Pres. for Finance and Admin.: P. HIBBITTS
Vice-Pres. for Research: Dr B. M. PINTO
Vice-Pres. for Univ. Relations: Dr W. GILL
Registrar and Sr Dir, Enrolment Services: K. ROSS
Dean of Library Services: L. COPELAND
Library of 1,000,000 vols
Number of teachers: 730 (faculty status)
Number of students: 25,000
Publications: *Canadian Journal of Communication* (4 a year), *International History Review* (4 a year), *West Coast Line* (3 a year)

DEANS

Faculty of Applied Sciences: Dr B. S. LEWIS
Faculty of Arts: Dr J. T. PIERCE
Faculty of Business Administration: Dr C. E. LOVE
Faculty of Education: KRIS MAGNUSSON
Faculty of Science: Dr M. PLISCHKE (acting)
Continuing Studies: Dr J. C. YERBURY
Graduate Studies: Dr J. C. DRIVER

PROFESSORS

Faculty of Applied Sciences (9861 Applied Sciences Building, Burnaby; tel. (604) 291-4724; fax (604) 291-5802; internet fas.sfu.ca):

School of Communication:

ANDERSON, R. S.
GRUNEAU, R.
HACKETT, R. A.
HARASIM, L. M.
KLINE, S.
LABA, M.
LEWIS, B. S.
LORIMER, R. M.
RICHARDS, W. D.
TRUAX, B. D.

School of Computing Science:

ATKINS, M. S.
BHATTACHARYA, B. K.
BURTON, F. W.
CAMERON, R. D.
DAHL, V.
DELGRANDE, J. P.
FUNT, B. V.
HADLEY, R. F.
HAN, J. W.
HELL, P.
HOBSON, R. F.
KAMEDA, T.
LI, Z. N.
LIESTMAN, A. L.
LUK, W. S.
PETERS, J. G.
POPOWICH, F.
SHERMER, T. C.
YANG, Q.

School of Engineering Science:

BIRD, J. S.
BOLOGNESI, C. R.
CAVERS, J. K.
CHAPMAN, G. H.
DILL, J. C.
GRUVER, W. A.
GUPTA, K. K.
HARDY, R. H. S.
HO, P. K. M.
HOBSON, R. F.
JONES, J. D.
LEUNG, A. M.
PARAMESWARAN, M.
PAYANDEH, S.
RAWICZ, A. H.
SAIF, M.
STAPLETON, S. P.
SYRZYCKI, M.

School of Kinesiology:

BAWA, P. N. S.

DICKINSON, J.
FINEGOOD, D. T.
GOODMAN, D.
HOFFER, J. A.
MACKENZIE, C. L.
MACLEAN, D. R.
MARTENIUK, R. G.
MORRISON, J. B.
PARKHOUSE, W. S.
ROSIN, M.
TIBBITS, G.

School of Resource and Environmental Management Programme:

DE LA MERE, W. K.
GILL, A. M.
GOBAS, F.
PETERMAN, R. M.
WILLIAMS, P. W.

Faculty of Arts (6168 Academic Quadrangle, Burnaby; tel. (604) 291-4414; fax (604) 291-3033; internet www.sfu.ca/arts):

Archaeology:

BURLEY, D. V.
DRIVER, J. C.
FLADMARK, K. R.
GALDIKAS, B. M. F.
HAYDEN, B. D.
NANCE, J. D.
NELSON, D. E.
SKINNER, M. F.

School for the Contemporary Arts:

ALOI, S. A.
DIAMOND, M.
GOTFRIT, M. S.
MACINTYRE, D. K.
SNIDER, G.
TRUAX, B. D.
UNDERHILL, O.

School of Criminology:

BOYD, N. T.
BRANTINGHAM, P. J.
BRANTINGHAM, P. L.
BROCKMAN, J.
BURTCH, B.
CHUNN, D. E.
CORRADO, R. R.
FAITH, K.
GORDON, R. M.
GRIFFITHS, C. T.
JACKSON, M. A.
LOWMAN, J.
MENZIES, R. J.
VERDUN-JONES, S. N.

Economics:

ALLEN, D. W.
BOLAND, L. A.
CHANT, J. F.
DEVORETZ, D. J.
DEAN, J. W.
DOW, G.
EASTON, S. T.
HARRIS, R. G.
JONES, R. A.
KENNEDY, P. E.
MAKI, D. R.
MUNRO, J. M.
OLEWILER, N. D.
SCHMITT, N.
SPINDLER, Z. A.

English:

COE, R. M.
DELANY, P.
DELANY, S.
DJWA, S.
GERSON, C.
MEZEI, K.
MIKI, R. A.
STOUCK, D.
STURROCK, J.

French:

DAVISON, R.
FAUQUENOY, M. C.

VISWANATHAN, J.

Geography:

BAILEY, W. G.
GILL, A. M.
HAYTER, R.
HICKIN, E. J.
PIERCE, J. T.
ROBERTS, A. C. B.
ROBERTS, M. C.

Gerontology Program:

GUTMAN, G.
WISTER, A. V.

History:

BOYER, R. E.
CLEVELAND, W. L.
DEBO, R. K.
DUTTON, P. E.
FELLMAN, M. D.
GAGAN, D. P.
HUTCHINSON, J. F.
JOHNSTON, H. J. M.
LITTLE, J. I.
PARR, J.
STEWART, M. L.
STUBBS, J. O.

Humanities:

ANGUS, I.
DUGUID, S.
DUTTON, P. E.
MEZEI, K.
WALLS, J. W.

Latin American Studies:

BROHMAN, J. A C.

Linguistics:

GERDTS, D. B.
MCFETRIDGE, P.
ROBERTS, E. W.
SAUNDERS, R.

Philosophy:

HANSON, P. P.
JENNINGS, R. E.
ZIMMERMAN, D.

Political Science:

COHEN, L. J.
COHN, T. H.
COVELL, M. A.
ERICKSON, L. J.
GRIFFIN COHEN, M. G.
HOWLETT, M.
MCBRIDE, S.
MEYER, P.
ROSS, D. A.
SMITH, P. J.
STEVENSON, H. M.
WARWICK, P. V.

Psychology:

ALEXANDER, B. K.
BOWMAN, M. L.
HART, S. D.
KIMBALL, M.
KREBS, D. L.
MCFARLAND, C. G.
MISTLBERGER, R.
MORETTI, M. M.
ROESCH, R. M.
WHITTLESEA, B. W. A.

Sociology and Anthropology:

DYCK, N.
GEE, E.
HOWARD, M.
KENNY, M.
MACLEAN, D. R.

Women's Studies:

GRIFFIN COHEN, M. G.
KIMBALL, M. M.
STEWART, M. L.
WENDELL, S.

Faculty of Business Administration (3302 Lohn Building, Burnaby; tel. (604) 291-

3708; fax (604) 291-4920; internet www.bus
.sfu.ca):

CHOO, E. U.
CLARKSON, P. M.
FINLEY, D. R.
GRAUER, R. R.
LOVE, C. E.
MAUSER, G. A.
MEREDITH, L. N.
PINFIELD, L. T.
POITRAS, G.
RICHARDS, J. G.
SHAPIRO, D. M.
TUNG, R. L.
VINING, A. R.
WATERHOUSE, J. H.
WEDLEY, W. C.
WEXLER, M. N.
WYCKHAM, R. G.
ZAICHKOWSKY, J. L.

Faculty of Education (8622 Education Building, Burnaby; tel. (604) 291-3395; fax (604)
291-3203; internet www.educ.sfu.ca):

BAILIN, S.
BARROW, R.
CASE, R.
DE CASTELL, S. C.
EGAN, K.
GEVA-MAY, I.
GRIMMETT, P. P.
MAMCHUR, C. M.
MARTIN, J.
OBADIA, A. A.
RICHMOND, S.
TOOHEY, K
WINNE, P. H.
WONG, B. Y. L.
ZAZKIS, R.

Faculty of Science (P9451 Shrum Science
Centre, Burnaby; tel. (604) 291-4590; fax
(604) 291-3424; internet www.sfu.ca/
~science):

Biological Sciences:
ALBRIGHT, L. J.
BECKENBACH, A. T.
BORDEN, J. H.
BRANDHORST, B. P.
CRESPI, B. J.
DILL, L. M.
FARRELL, A. P.
GRIES, G. J.
HAUNERLAND, N. H.
LAW, F. C. P.
MATHEWES, R. W.
PUNJA, Z. K.
RAHE, J. E.
ROITBERG, B. D.
WINSTON, M. L.
YDENBERG, R. C.

Chemistry:
BENNET, A. J.
CORNELL, R. B.
D'AURIA, J. D.
GAY, I. D.
HILL, R. H.
HOLDCROFT, S.
JONES, C. H. W.
MALLI, G. L.
PERCIVAL, P. W.
PINTO, B. M.
POMEROY, R. K.
RICHARDS, W. R.
SEN, D.
SLESSOR, K. N.

Earth Sciences:
HICKIN, E. J.
ROBERTS, M. C.

Mathematics:
BERGGREN, J. L.
BORWEIN, J. M.
BORWEIN, P. B.
BROWN, T. C.
GRAHAM, G. A. C.

HELL, P.
LACHLAN, A. H.
LEWIS, A. S.
REILLY, N. R.
RUSSELL, R. D.
SHEN, C. Y.

Molecular Biology and Biochemistry:
BAILLIE, D. L.
BRANDHORST, B. P.
CORNELL, R. B.
DAVIDSON, W. S.
HONDA, B. M.
RICHARDS, W. R.
SEN, D.
SMITH, M. J.

Physics:
BALLENTINE, L. E.
BECHHOEFER, J. L.
BOAL, D. H.
BOLOGNESI, C. R.
CLAYMAN, B. P.
CROZIER, E. D.
ENNS, R. H.
FRINDT, R. F.
HEINRICH, B.
KAVANAGH, K. L.
KIRCZENOW, G.
PLISCHKE, M.
SCHEINFEIN, M. R.
THEWALT, M. L. W.
TROTTIER, H. D.
VETTERLI, M.
WATKINS, S.

Statistics and Actuarial Science:
LOCKHART, R. A.
MacLEAN, D. R.
ROUTLEDGE, R. D.
SCHWARZ, C. J.
SITTER, R. R.
SWARTZ, T. B.

ATTACHED INSTITUTES

Behavioural Ecology Research Group:
tel. (604) 291-3664; f. 1989; Dir Dr L. M. DILL.

**Canadian Centre for Studies in Publish-
ing:** tel. (604) 291-5240; fax (604) 291-5239; f.
1987; Dir Dr R. M. LORIMER.

Centre for Coastal Studies: tel. (604) 291-
4653; fax (604) 291-3851; Dir Dr P. GALLA-
GHER.

Centre for Education, Law and Society:
tel. (604) 291-4484; fax (604) 291-3203; f.
1984; Dir Dr W. CASSIDY.

**Centre d'Études Francophones Québec-
Pacifique:** tel. (604) 291-3544; fax (604) 291-
5932; Dir Dr G. POIRIER.

**Centre for Experimental and Construct-
ive Mathematics:** tel. (604) 291-5617; fax
(604) 291-4947; f. 1993; Dir Dr J. BORWEIN.

Centre for Innovation in Management:
tel. (604) 291-4183; fax (604) 291-5833; Dir
Dr E. LOVE.

Centre for Labour Studies: tel. (604) 291-
5827; fax (604) 291-3851; Dir Dr M. LEIER.

**Centre for Policy Research on Science
and Technology:** tel. (604) 291-5116; fax
(604) 291-5165; f. 1996; Dir R. SMITH.

Centre for Restorative Justice: fax (604)
291-4140; f. 2001; Dirs Dr R. M. GORDON, Dr
E. ELLIOTT.

Centre for Scientific Computing: tel.
(604) 291-4819; fax (604) 291-4947; Dir Dr
R. RUSSELL.

Centre for Scottish Studies: tel. (604) 291-
5515; fax (604) 291-4504; Dir Dr S. DUGUID.

**Centre for the Study of Government and
Business:** fax (604) 291-5122; e-mail csgb@
csgb.ubc.ca; internet www.csgb.ubc.ca; Co-
Dirs Dr T. ROSS, Dr A. R. VINING.

Centre for Systems Science: tel. (604) 291-
4588; fax (604) 291-4424; Dir Dr S. ATKINS.

**Centre for Tourism Policy and
Research:** tel. (604) 291-3103; fax (604)
291-4968; f. 1989; Dir Dr P. W. WILLIAMS.

Chemical Ecology Research Group: tel.
(604) 291-3646; fax (604) 291-3496; f. 1981;
Dir Dr J. H. BORDEN.

**Community Economic Development
Centre:** tel. (604) 291-5849; fax (604) 291-
5473; e-mail cedc@sfu.ca; internet www.sfu
.ca/cedc; f. 1989; Dir Dr M. ROSELAND.

**Cooperative Resource Management
Institute:** tel. (604) 291-4683; fax (604)
291-4986; f. 1998; Dir R. PETERMAN.

Criminology Research Centre: tel. (604)
291-4040; fax (604) 291-4140; f. 1978; Dir Dr
W. GLACKMAN.

**David Lam Centre for International
Communication:** tel. (604) 291-5021; fax
(604) 291-5112; f. 1989; Dir Dr J. W. WALLS.

The Dialogue Institute.

**Feminist Institute for Studies on Law
and Society:** f. 1990; Co-Dirs Dr D. CHUNN,
Dr W. CHAN.

Gerontology Research Centre: tel. (604)
291-5062; fax (604) 291-5066; f. 1982; Dir Dr
G. GUTMAN.

**Institute for Canadian Urban Research
Studies:** tel. (604) 291-3515; fax (604) 291-
4140; Dir Dr P. L. BRANTINGHAM.

Institute of Governance Studies: tel.
(604) 291-4994; fax (604) 291-4786; Dir P. J.
SMITH.

Institute for the Humanities: tel. (604)
291-5516; fax (604) 291-5788; Dir Dr D.
GRAYSTON.

**Institute of Micromachine and Micro-
fabrication Research:** tel. (604) 291-4971;
fax (604) 291-4951; Dir Dr A. M. PARAMES-
WARAN.

**Institute for Studies in Criminal Justice
Policy:** tel. (604) 291-4040; fax (604) 291-
4140; f. 1980; Dir Dr M. A. JACKSON.

**Institute for Studies in Teacher Educa-
tion:** tel. (604) 291-4937; fax (604) 291-3203;
Co-Dirs P. GRIMMETT, Dr M. F. WIDEEN.

**International Centre for Criminal Law
Reform and Criminal Justice Policy:** tel.
(604) 822-9875; fax (604) 822-9317; f. 1991;
Exec. Dir F. M. GORDON.

**Logic and Functional Programming
Group:** tel. (604) 291-3426; fax (604) 291-
3045; f. 1990; Dir Dr V. DAHL.

**Mental Health, Law and Policy Insti-
tute:** tel. (604) 291-3370; fax (604) 291-3427;
f. 1991; Dir Dr R. ROESCH.

**Pacific Institute for the Mathematical
Sciences:** tel. (604) 291-4376; fax (604) 268-
6657; f. 1996; Dir Dr P. BORWEIN.

**Research Institute on South-Eastern
Europe:** tel. (604) 291-5597; fax (604) 291-
5837; Dir Dr A. GEROLYMATOS.

**Tri-University Meson Facility (TRI-
UMF):** tel. (604) 222-1047 ext. 6258; Dir Dr
A. SHOTTER.

**Western Canadian Universities Marine
Biological Station (Bamfield):** tel. (250)
728-3301; fax (250) 728-3452; f. 1969; Dir Dr
A. N. SPENCER.

**W. J. VanDusen BC Business Studies
Institute:** tel. (604) 291-4183; fax (604) 291-
5833; f. 1982; Dir Dr E. LOVE.

UNIVERSITY OF TORONTO

215 Huron St, Toronto, ON M5S 1A1
Telephone: (416) 978-2011
Fax: (416) 978-5572
Internet: www.utoronto.ca
Founded 1827
Language of instruction: English

Provincially supported, assisted by private funds

Academic year: September to May (May to August, summer session)

Chancellor: The Hon. DAVID R. PETERSON

Pres.: DAVID NAYLOR

Vice-Pres. and Chief Advancement Officer: DAVID PALMER

Vice-Pres. and Provost: CHERYL MISAK

Vice-Pres. for Business Affairs: CATHERINE RIGGALL

Vice-Pres. for Human Resources and Equity: ANGELA HILDYARD

Vice-Pres. for Research: PAUL YOUNG

Vice-Pres. for University Relations: JUDITH WOLFSON

Vice-Pres. and Prin., University of Toronto at Mississauga: IAN ORCHARD

Vice-Pres. and Prin., University of Toronto at Scarborough: FRANCO VACCARINO

Chief Librarian: CAROLE MOORE

Library: see Libraries and Archives

Number of teachers: 3,362

Number of students: 75,760 full-time

Publications: *Bulletin, Calendars, The Graduate, President's Report, Undergraduate Admission Handbook*

DEANS AND DIRECTORS

Faculty of Applied Science and Engineering: CRISTINA AMON

Faculty of Architecture, Landscape and Design: GEORGE BAIRD

Faculty of Arts and Science: MERIC GERTLER (acting)

Faculty of Dentistry: DAVID MOCK

Faculty of Forestry: C. T. SMITH

Faculty of Information: SEAMUS ROSS

Faculty of Law: MAYO MORAN

Faculty of Medicine: CATHERINE WHITESIDE

Faculty of Music: RUSSELL HARTEN BERGER

Faculty of Nursing: SIOBAN NELSON

Faculty of Pharmacy: K. WAYNE HINDEMARSH

Faculty of Social Work: CHERYL REGEHR

Institute of Studies in Education: JANE GASKELL

School of Continuing Studies: MARILYNN BOOTH

School of Graduate Studies: SUSAN PFEIFFER

School of Physical Education and Health: B. KIDD

Joseph L. Rothman School of Management: ROGER MARTIN

PROFESSORS

N.B.—In the following list staff members of colleges are indicated thus: Erindale Coll. (E), New Coll. (N), St Michael's Coll. (M), Scarborough Coll. (S), Trinity Coll. (T), University Coll. (C), Victoria Univ. (V)

Faculty of Applied Science and Engineering:

AARABI, P., Electrical and Computer Engineering

ABDELRAHMAN, T., Electrical and Computer Engineering

ADAMS, B. J., Civil Engineering

AITCHISON, J., Electrical and Computer Engineering

ALLEN, D., Chemical Engineering

BALKE, S. T., Chemical Engineering

BAWDEN, W., Civil Engineering

BIDLEMAN, T., Chemical Engineering

BIRKEMOE, P. C., Civil Engineering

BONERT, R., Electrical and Computer Engineering

BOOCOCK, D. G. B., Chemical Engineering

BOULTON, P. I. P., Electrical Engineering

BYER, P. H., Civil Engineering

CHAFFEY, C. E., Chemical Engineering

CHARLES, M. E., Chemical Engineering

CHENG, Y., Chemical Engineering

CHOW, P., Electrical and Computer Engineering

CLUETT, W., Chemical Engineering

COBBOLD, R. S. C., Institute of Biomedical Engineering

COLLINS, M. P., Civil Engineering

CORMACK, D. E., Chemical Engineering

COYLE, T., Chemical Engineering

CURRAN, J. H., Civil Engineering

DAVIES, S., Electrical and Computer Engineering

DAVISON, E. J. A., Electrical Engineering

DAWSON, F., Electrical and Computer Engineering

DEWAN, S. B., Electrical Engineering

DIAMOND, M., Chemical Engineering

DIOSADY, L. L., Chemical Engineering

EDWARDS, E., Chemical Engineering

EIZENMAN, M., Electrical and Computer Engineering

ERB, U., Materials Science

EVANS, G., Chemical Engineering

FARNOOD, R., Chemical Engineering

FOULKES, F. R., Chemical Engineering

FOX, M. S., Industrial Engineering

FRANCIS, B. A., Electrical Engineering

FRECKER, R., Electrical and Computer Engineering

FULTHORPE, R., Chemical Engineering

GOLDENBERG, A. A., Mechanical Engineering

GULACK, P., Electrical and Computer Engineering

HATZINAKOS, D., Electrical and Computer Engineering

HERMAN, P., Electrical and Computer Engineering

HOOTON, R., Civil Engineering

IRAVANI, M. R., Electrical and Computer Engineering

JACOBSEN, H.-A., Electrical and Computer Engineering

JAMES, D. F., Mechanical Engineering

JARDINE, A. K. S., Industrial Engineering

JIA, C., Chemical Engineering

JOY, M., Electrical and Computer Engineering

KARNEY, B., Civil Engineering

KAWAJI, M., Chemical Engineering

KIRK, D. W., Chemical Engineering

KONRAD, A., Electrical and Computer Engineering

KORTSCHOT, M., Chemical Engineering

KSCHISCHANG, F., Electrical and Computer Engineering

KUHN, D., Chemical Engineering

KUNOV, H., Biomedical Engineering

KWONG, R. H., Electrical Engineering

LAVERS, J. D., Electrical Engineering

LEE, E. S., Electrical Engineering

LEHN, P., Electrical and Computer Engineering

LEON-GARCIA, A., Electrical Engineering

LI, D., Mechanical Engineering

LO, H.-K., Electrical and Computer Engineering

LUUS, R., Chemical Engineering

McKAGUE, A., Chemical Engineering

MANDELIS, A., Mechanical Engineering

MANN, S., Electrical and Computer Engineering

MARTIN, K., Electrical Engineering

MEASURES, R. M., Aerospace Studies

MEGUID, S. A., Mechanical Engineering

MILLER, E. J., Civil Engineering

MIMS, C. A., Chemical Engineering

MOHANTY, B., Civil Engineering

OJHA, M., Chemical Engineering

PACKER, J. A., Civil Engineering

PARADI, J., Chemical Engineering

PARK, C., Mechanical Engineering

PASUPATHY, S. P., Electrical Engineering

PEROVIC, D., Materials Science

REEVE, D. W., Chemical Engineering

ROSE, J., Electrical and Computer Engineering

SAIN, M., Chemical Engineering

SALAMA, C. A. T., Electrical Engineering

SANTERRE, J., Chemical Engineering

SARGENT, E., Electrical and Computer Engineering

SAVILLE, B., Chemical Engineering

SEFTON, M. V., Chemical Engineering

SEMLYEN, A., Electrical and Computer Engineering

SEVCIK, K., Electrical and Computer Engineering

SHEIKH, S. A., Civil Engineering

SHOICHET, M., Chemical Engineering

SLEEP, B., Civil Engineering

SMITH, K. C., Electrical Engineering

SMITH, P. W., Electrical Engineering

SODHI, R., Engineering

SOUSA, E., Electrical and Computer Engineering

TERZOPOULOS, D., Electrical and Computer Engineering

TRAN, H. N., Chemical Engineering

TRASS, O., Chemical Engineering

TURKSEN, I. B., Industrial Engineering

VECCHIO, F. J., Civil Engineering

VENETSANOPOULOS, A. N., Electrical Engineering

VENTER, R. D., Mechanical Engineering

VRANESIC, Z. G., Electrical Engineering

WALLACE, J. S., Mechanical Engineering

WANG, Z., Materials Science

WANIA, F., Chemical Engineering

WARD, C. A., Mechanical Engineering

WONHAM, W. M., Electrical Engineering

WOODHOUSE, K., Chemical Engineering

WRIGHT, P. M., Civil Engineering

YAN, N., Chemical Engineering

YIP, C., Chemical Engineering

YOUNG, R., Civil Engineering

ZAKY, S. G., Electrical Engineering

ZANDSTRA, P., Chemical Engineering

ZUKOTYNSKI, S., Electrical Engineering

Faculty of Architecture, Landscape and Design:

CORNEIL, C. S.

EARDLEY, A.

Faculty of Arts and Science:

ABBATT, J., Chemistry

ABOUHAIDAR, M. G., Botany

ABRAHAM, R. G., Astronomy and Astrophysics

ACCINELLI, R. D., History

ADLER, E., Political Science

AIVAZIAN, V. A., Economics

ALLOWAY, T. M., Psychology

ANDERSON, G. M., Geology

ANDERSON, J. B., Botany

ARNHEIM, C., Geography

ARTHUR, J. G., Mathematics

ASTER, S., History

ASTINGTON, J., English

BACCHUS, F., Computer Science

BAILEY, D. C., Physics

BAILEY, R. C., Physics

BAIRD, J., English

BAKER, M., Economics

BAKICH, O., Slavic Languages and Literature

BALDUS, B., Sociology

BARNES, C. J., Slavic Languages and Literature

BARRETT, F. M., Zoology

BARRETT, S. C. H., Botany

BARZDA, V., Physics

BASHKEVIN, S., Political Science

BEINER, R. S., Political Science

BENJAMIN, D., Economics

BERGER, C. C., History

BERKOWITZ, M. K., Economics

BEWELL, A., English

BIERSTONE, E., Mathematics

BINNICK, R. I., Linguistics

BIRGENEAU, R. J., Physics

BISZTRAY, G., Slavic Languages and Literature

BLAKE, T., Botany

BLANCHARD, P. H., History

BLAND, J. S., Mathematics

BLISS, J. M., History
BLOOM, T., Mathematics
BODDY, J., Anthropology
BODEMANN, M., Sociology
BOLTON, C. T., Astronomy
BOND, J., Astronomy and Astrophysics
BOONSTRA, R., Life Sciences
BORODIN, A. B., Computer Science
BOTHWELL, R., History
BOURNE, L. S., Geography
BOYD, M., Sociology
BRAUN, A., Political Science
BRITTON, J., Geography
BROOK, T. J., History, East Asian Studies
BROOKS, D. R., Zoology
BROWN, I. R., Zoology
BROWN, J. R., Philosophy
BROWN, R. M., Humanities
BROWNLEE, J. S., East Asian Studies
BRUDNER, A., Political Science
BRUMER, P. W., Chemistry
BRYAN, R. B., Geography
BRYANT, J., Sociology
BRYM, R. J., Sociology
BUCHWEITZ, R., Mathematics
BUNCE, M., Geography
BURKE, J. F., Spanish and Portuguese
BURTON, F. D., Anthropology
CAMERON, D. R., Political Science
CANFIELD, J. V., Philosophy
CAPOZZI, R., Italian Studies
CARLBERG, R. G., Physical Sciences
CARR, J. L., Economics
CASAS, F. R., Economics
CHAMBERLIN, J. E., English
CHEETHAM, M., Fine Art
CHEN, J., Geography
CHIN, J., Chemistry
CHING, J. C., Religious Studies
CLARKE, W. H., Astronomy
CLIVIO, G. P., Italian Studies
CODE, R. F., Physics
COOK, S. A., Computer Science
CORMAN, B., English Literature
CORNEIL, D. G., Mathematics, Computer Science
CRAWFORD, G., Anthropology
CRUDEN, S., Geology
CUMMINS, W. R., Botany
CUNNINGHAM, F. A., Philosophy, Political Science
DANESI, M., Italian Studies
DAY, R. B., Political Economy
DE KERCKHOVE, D., French
DE QUEHEN, A. H., English
DE SOUSA, R., Philosophy
DEL JUNCO, A., Mathematics
DENGLER, N. G., Botany
DENNY, M. G. S., Economics
DENT, J., History
DESAI, R. C., Physics
DEWAR, M., Classics
DEWEES, D. N., Political Economy
DIAMOND, M., Geography
DION, P.-E., Near Eastern Studies
DONALDSON, D., Chemistry
DONNELLY, M. W., Political Science, East Asian Studies
DRUMMOND, J. R., Physics
DUNLOP, D. J., Physics
EDWARDS, E., Botany
EDWARDS, R. N., Physics
EISENBICHLER, K., Italian
ELLIOTT, G. A., Mathematics
ENRIGHT, W. H., Mathematics, Computer Science
ERICKSON, B. H., Sociology
ESPIE, G., Botany
EVANS, M. J., Statistics
EYLES, N., Physical Sciences
FAIG, M., Economics
FALKENHEIM, V. C., Political Science, East Asian Studies
FARRAR, D., Chemistry
FENNER, A., German
FIUME, E., Computer Science

FOOT, D. K., Economics
FORBES, H. D., Political Science
FORGUSON, L. W.
FRANCESCHETTI, A., Italian Studies
FRIEDLANDER, J. B., Mathematics
FRIEDMANN, H. B., Sociology
FUSS, M. A., Economics
GAD, G. H. K., Geography
GALLOWAY, J. H., Geography
GARTNER, R. I., Sociology
GEORGES, M., Chemistry
GERTLER, M. S., Geography
GERVERS, M., History
GILLIS, A. R., Sociology
GITTINS, J., Geology
GOERING, J., History
GOLDSTEIN, M., Mathematics
GOLDSTICK, D., Philosophy
GOTLIEB, C., Computer Science
GOURIEROUX, C., Economics
GRAHAM, I. R., Mathematics
GREENWOOD, B., Geography
GREENWOOD, B., Geology
GREER, A. R., History
GREINER, P. C., Mathematics
GRIFFEN, P. A., Physics
GROSS, M. R., Zoology
GUNDERSON, M. K., Economics
GWYNNE, D. T., Biology
HAGAN, J. L., Sociology
HALLS, H. C., Geological Sciences
HANNIGAN, J., Sociology
HANSELL, R. I. C., Zoology
HARVEY, D., Geography
HARVEY, E., Sociology
HARVEY, E. R., English
HAYHOE, R., East Asian Studies
HEALEY, A., English
HEATH, M. C., Botany
HEHNER, E. C. R., Computer Science
HELMSTADTER, R. J., History
HIGGINS, V. J., Botany
HIGGS, D. C., History
HINTON, G. E., Computer Science
HIRST, G., Computer Science
HOLDOM, B., Physics
HORGEN, P. A., Botany
HORI, K., Physics
HORTON, S., Economics
HOWARD, K., Geology
HOWARD, P. J., English
HOWELL, N., Sociology
HOWSON, S. K., Social Sciences
HUTCHEON, L. A., English
INGHAM, J. N., History
INWOOD, B. C., Classics, Philosophy
ISRAEL, M., History
IVRII, V., Mathematics
JAAKSON, R., Geography
JACKSON, H., English
JACKSON, K. R., Computer Science
JACOBS, A. E., Physics
JEFFREY, L., Mathematics
JELLINEK, M., Physics
JEPSON, A. D., Computer Science
JOHN, S., Physics
JOHNSON, W. M. L. A., Fine Art
JOHNSTON, A., English
JONES, A., Classics
JONES, C. L., Sociology
JUMP, G. V., Economics
JURDJEVIC, V., Mathematics
KAPRAL, R. E., Chemistry
KAPRANOV, M., Mathematics
KAY, L., Chemistry
KEE, H.-K., Physics
KEITH, W. J., English
KERVIN, J. B., Sociology
KEY, A. W., Physics
KHESIN, B., Mathematics
KHOVANSKII, A., Mathematics
KIM, H., Mathematics
KIM, Y.-B., Physics
KLAUSNER, D. N., English
KLEIN, M. A., History
KLUGER, R. H., Chemistry

KOFMAN, L., Astronomy
KRAMER, C. E., Slavic Languages and Literature
KRIEGER, P., Physics
KRULL, U., Chemistry
KUKLA, A., Psychology, Philosophy
LAMBEK, M. J., Anthropology
LANCASHIRE, A. C., English
LANCASHIRE, D. I., English
LANTZ, K. A., Slavic Languages and Literature
LAUTENS, M., Chemistry
LEDUC, L., Political Science
LEE, M. J., Physics
LEE, R. B., Anthropology
LEGGATT, A. M., English
LEHMAN, A. B., Computer Science
LEVESQUE, H. J., Computer Science
LO, H.-K., Physics
LOGAN, R., Physics
LORIMER, J. W., Mathematics
LUKE, M., Physics
LUONG, H. V., Anthropology, East Asian Studies
LUSTE, G. J., Physics
LYNN, R., East Asian Studies
LYUBICH, M., Mathematics
MCCLELLAND, R. A., Chemistry
MCDONALD, P., Chemistry
MCILWRAITH, T., Geography
MAGEE, J., Classics
MAGILL, D. W., Sociology
MAGNUSSON, L., English
MAGOCSI, P. R., Political Science
MALLOCH, D. W., Botany
MANNERS, I., Chemistry
MARGORIBANKS, R., Physics
MARTIN, J. F., Physics
MARTIN, P. G., Astronomy
MATHEWSON, G. F., Political Economy
MATHON, R. A., Mathematics, Computer Science
MATUS, J., English
MELINO, A., Economics
MENDELSOHN, E., Mathematics, Computer Science
MENDELZON, A. O., Computer Science
MENZINGER, M., Chemistry
MERRILEES, B., French
MIALL, A. D., Geology
MICHELSON, W., Sociology
MIKHALKIN, G., Mathematics
MILKEREIT, B., Physics
MILLER, R., Chemistry
MILLER, R., Physics
MILMAN, P., Mathematics
MIMS, C., Chemistry
MINTZ, J., Economics
MIRON, J. R., Geography
MITROVICHA, J. X., Physics
MOCHNACKI, S., Astronomy
MOGGRIDGE, D. E., Economics
MOORE, G., Physics
MORGAN, K. P., Philosophy
MORRIS, G. K., Zoology
MORRIS, R., Chemistry
MORRIS, S. W., Physics
MORRISON, J. C., Philosophy
MUNK, L., English
MUNRO, D. S., Geography
MURNAGHAN, F., Mathematics
MURRAY, H., English
MURRAY, N., Astronomy
MURTY, V., Mathematics
MYLES, J., Sociology
MYLOPOULOS, J., Computer Science
NACHMAN, A., Mathematics
NEDELSKI, J., Political Science
NETTERFIELD, B., Physics
NEUMAN, S., English
NOYES, J. K., German
O'DAY, D., Zoology
O'DONNELL, P. J., Physics
OLIVER, W. A., French
ORCHARD, A., English
ORCHARD, I., Zoology

ORR, R. S., Physics
ORWIN, C. L., Political Science
OSBORNE, M., Economics
O'TOOLE, R., Sociology
OZIN, G. A., Chemistry
PANGLE, T. L., Political Science
PATERSON, J. M., French
PAULY, P., Political Science, Economics
PEET, A., Physics
PELTIER, W. R., Physics
PERCY, J. R., Astronomy
PERRON, P., French
PIETROPAOLO, D., Italian
PITASSI, T., Computer Science
POLANYI, J. C., Chemistry
POPPITZ, E., Physics
POWELL, J., Chemistry
PRIESTLEY, L. C., East Asian Studies
PRUESSEN, R. W., History
PUGLIESE, G., Italian
RACKOFF, C. W., Computer Science
RAYSIDE, D. M., Political Science
REDEKOP, M., English
REIBETANZ, J. H., English
REID, D., Fine Art
REID, F. J., Economics
REISZ, R. R., Zoology
REITZ, J. G., Sociology
RELPH, T., Geography
REPKA, J. S., Mathematics
RICE, K. D., Linguistics
RICHARDSON, D. S., Fine Art
RISING, J. D., Zoology
ROBIN, P. Y., Geological Science
ROSENTHAL, J., Mathematics
ROSENTHAL, P., Mathematics
ROSSOS, A., History
RUBINOFF, A., Political Science
RUTHERFORD, P., History
SALAFF, J. W., Sociology
SANDBROOK, K. R. J., Political Science
SANDERS, G., East Asian Studies
SAVARD, P., Physics
SCHWARTZ, D. V., Political Science
SCOTT, S. D., Geology
SEAGER, W. E., Philosophy
SEAQUIST, E. R., Astronomy
SEARY, P. D., English
SECO, L., Mathematics
SELICK, P., Mathematics
SELIGER, F., German
SEVCIK, K. C., Computer Science
SHAW, W. D., English
SHEN, V., East Asian Studies
SHEPHERD, T., Physics
SHERK, A., Mathematics
SHERWOOD LOLLAR, B., Geology
SHI, S., Economics
SHUB, M., Mathematics
SIGMON, B. A., Anthropology
SILCOX, P., Political Science
SIMEON, R., Political Science, Law
SIOW, A., Economics
SIPE, J. E., Physics
SKOGSTAD, G. D., Political Science
SMITH, J. J. B., Zoology
SMYTH, D., History
SOECKI, S., English
SOHM, P. L., Fine Art
SOLOMON, P. H., Political Science
SOLOMON, S., Political Science
SPOONER, E. T., Geology
SPRULES, W. G., Zoology
STATT, B., Physics
STEIN, J., Political Science
STEINBERG, A., Physics
STERNBERG, R., Spanish and Portuguese
STEVENS, P., English
STREN, R. E., Political Science
STRONG, K., Physics
SULEM, C., Mathematics
SULLIVAN, R., English
SUMNER, L. W., Philosophy
TAILLEFER, L., Physics
TALL, F. D., Mathematics
TANNER, J., Sociology

TANNY, S., Mathematics
TEICHMAN, J., Political Science
TEPPERMAN, L. J., Sociology
TERZOPOLOUS, D., Computer Science
THOMPSON, J. C., Chemistry
THOMPSON, M., Chemistry
THOMPSON, R. P., Philosophy
THOMSON, L., English
THYWISSEN, J., Physics
TOBE, S. S., Zoology
TOWNSEND, D., English
TREBILOCK, M., Economics
TREFLER, D., Economics
TRISCHUK, W., Physics
TROTT, D., French
TUOHY, C., Political Science
TURNER, D. H., Anthropology
URQUHART, A. I. F., Philosophy
VAN DRIEL, H. M., Physics
VIPOND, R., Political Science
VIRAG, B., Mathematics
WAGLE, N. K., History
WALKER, M. B., Physics
WATERHOUSE, D. B., East Asian Studies
WEI, J., Physics
WEINRIB, L., Political Science
WEISS, W. A., Mathematics
WELLMAN, B. S., Sociology
WESTGATE, J. A., Geology
WHEATON, B., Sociology
WHITE, G., Political Science
WHITE, R. R., Geography
WHITTINGTON, S. G., Chemistry
WILLIAMS, D. D., Life Sciences
WILSON, F. F., Philosophy
WOLFE, D., Political Science
WOOLDRIDGE, T. R., French
WORTMAN, D. B., Computer Science
YOUNG, R. P., Geology
YOUSON, J. H., Zoology
YU, E., Computer Science
ZIMMERMAN, A. M., Zoology

Faculty of Dentistry:

BENNICK, A.
DAVIES, J.
DEPORTER, D. A.
ELLEN, R. P.
FERRIER, J. M.
FREEMAN, E.
HEERSCHE, J. N. M.
LEAKE, J. L.
LEVINE, N.
LEWIS, D. W., Community Dentistry
LOCKER, D.
McCOMB, D.
McCULLOCH, C. A.
MAIN, J. H. P., Oral Pathology
MAYHALL, J. T.
MELCHER, A. H.
MOCK, D.
PILLIAR, R. M.
SANDHAM, H. J.
SESSLE, B. J.
SODEK, J.
SYMINGTON, J. M.
TEN CATE, A. R.
TENENBAUM, H. C.
WATSON, P. A.
ZARB, G. A., Prosthodontics

Faculty of Law:

BEATTY, D. M.
BENSON, P.
BRUDNER, A.
BRUNÉE, J.
CHAPMAN, B.
COOK, R.
COSSMAN, B.
DANIELS, R.
DEWEES, D.
DICKENS, B.
DYZENHAUS, D.
FLOOD, C.
FRIEDLAND, M.
GREEN, A.
HAGAN, J.

JANISCH, H.
LANGILLE, B.
LEE, I.
MACKLEM, P.
NEDELSKY, J.
PHILLIPS, J.
RÉAUME, D.
RIPSTEIN, A.
ROACH, K.
ROGERSON, C.
SIMEON, R.
SOSSIN, R.
TREBILOCK, M.
WADDAMS, S.
WEINRIB, E.
WEINRIB, L.

Faculty of Medicine:

ABEL, S., Otolaryngology
ACKERMANN, U., Physiology
ADAMSON, S., Obstetrics and Gynaecology, Paediatrics
ADELI, K., Pathobiology
ANDERSON, G. H., Nutrition and Food Sciences
ANDREWS, B. J., Medical Genetics and Microbiology
ANDRULIS, I., Pathobiology, Microbiology
ARCHER, M. C., Nutritional Studies
ARROWSMITH, C., Immunology
ASA, S., Pathobiology
ATWOOD, H. L., Physiology
AUBIN, J., Medical Biophysics
AXELRAD, A. A., Medical Biophysics
BAINES, A. D., Clinical Biochemistry
BAKER, R. R., Medicine
BARKER, G., Anaesthesia
BAUMAL, R., Pathology
BAZETT-JONES, D., Biochemistry
BELIK, J., Paediatrics
BENCHIMOL, S., Medical Biophysics
BENSON, L., Paediatrics
BERGERON, C., Pathobiology
BEVAN, D., Anaesthesia
BHAVNANI, B., Obstetrics and Gynaecology
BIGGAR, W. D., Paediatrics
BISSONETEE, B., Anaesthesia
BLAKE, J., Obstetrics and Gynaecology
BLANCHETTE, V., Paediatrics
BLENCOWE, B., Medical Research, Microbiology
BLUMENTHAL, A., Pathobiology
BOCKING, A., Obstetrics and Gynaecology, Physiology
BOGGS, J., Pathobiology
BOGNAR, A., Microbiology
BOHN, D., Anaesthesia
BOONE, C., Medical Research
BOONSTRA, R., Zoology, Physiology
BOUFFET, E., Paediatrics
BOYD, N., Medical Biophysics
BRESLIN, C., Ophthalmology
BRET, P.
BRONSKILL, M., Immunology
BROWN, D., Otolaryngology
BRUBAKER, P., Physiology
BRUNTON, J., Pathobiology
BUNCIC, R., Ophthalmology
BURNHAM, W. M., Pharmacology
BURNS, P., Medical Biophysics
BUSTO, U., Pharmacology
BUTANY, J., Pathobiology
BUTLER, D., Physiology
BYRICK, R., Anaesthesia
CAMERMAN, N., Biochemistry
CAMPBELL, J. B., Microbiology
CARLEN, P. L., Medicine
CASPER, R. F., Obstetrics and Gynaecology
CHALLIS, J., Physiology and Obstetrics
CHAMBERLAIN, D., Pathobiology
CHAN, H. S., Biochemistry
CHAN, S. L., Paediatrics
CHAN, V. L., Microbiology
CHARLTON, M. P., Physiology
CHETTY, R., Pathobiology
CHIANG, L., Pathobiology

CHITAYAT, D., Paediatrics
CHUNG, F. F., Anaesthesia
CLARKE, D., Biochemistry
CLARKE, J. T. R., Paediatrics
COATES, A., Paediatrics, Physiology
COLE, D., Pathobiology
COLE, P., Otolaryngology
COLGAN, T., Pathobiology
COVENS, A., Obstetrics and Gynaecology
CRUZ, T., Pathobiology
CRYSDALE, W. S., Otolaryngology
CUNNANE, S., Nutritional Sciences
CUNNINGHAM, A., Medical Biophysics
DANEMAN, A., Medical Imaging
DANEMAN, D., Paediatrics
DANSKA, J., Medical Biophysics
DEBER, C. M., Medical Biophysics
DEBONI, U., Physiology
DENNIS, J., Pathobiology
DE PETRILLO, A. D., Obstetrics and Gynaecology
DIAMANDIS, E., Pathobiology
DIAMANT, N. E., Physiology
DICK, J. E., Microbiology
DIRKS, F., Medicine
DIRKS, P., Medicine
DIXON, W., Ophthalmology
DORIAN, P., Pharmacology
DOSCH, H., Paediatrics
DOSTROVSKY, J. O., Physiology
DRUCKER, D. J., Pathobiology
DRUTZ, H., Obstetrics and Gynaecology
DUBE, I., Pathobiology
DUFFIN, J., Anaesthesia
DULLIN, J., Medical Biophysics
DURIE, P., Paediatrics
EASTERBROOK, M., Ophthalmology
EDWARDS, A., Medical Research, Microbiology
ELLEN, R., Pathobiology
ELLIS, D., Otolaryngology
EMILI, A., Medical Research, Microbiology
FARINE, D., Obstetrics and Gynaecology
FELDMAN, B. M., Paediatrics
FELDMAN, F., Ophthalmology
FERNIE, G. R., Surgery
FIEDBERG, J., Otolaryngology
FISH, E., Medical Biophysics
FISHER, R. H. G., Family and Community Medicine
FONG, I., Pathobiology
FORNASIER, V., Pathobiology
FORSTNER, G. G., Paediatrics
FORSTNER, J., Biochemistry
FOSTER, F. S., Medical Biophysics
FOX, A., Medical Imaging
FOX, G., Anaesthesia
FRECKER, R., Biomedical Engineering
FREEDMAN, J., Pathobiology
FREEDMAN, M., Paediatrics
FREEDOM, R., Paediatrics
FREEDOM, R., Pathobiology
FREEMAN, J., Otolaryngology
FRIESEN, J., Medical Research
FROM, L., Medicine
GALLIE, B., Ophthalmology
GALLINGER, S., Pathobiology
GANOZA, M. C., Medical Research
GARE, D., Obstetrics and Gynaecology
GARIÉPY, J., Medical Biophysics
GARVEY, M. B., Medicine
GEARY, D., Paediatrics
GEORGE, S., Pharmacology
GILDAY, D., Medical Imaging
GOLDMAN, B. S., Surgery
GOLDSTEIN, M. B., Medicine
GOTLIEB, A. I., Pathology
GRANT, D., Pharmacology
GREENBERG, G. R., Medicine
GREENBERG, M. L., Paediatrics
GREENBLATT, J. F., Medical Research
GREENWALD, M., Paediatrics
GREENWOOD, C., Nutritional Sciences
GRINSTEIN, S., Biochemistry
GRYNPAS, M., Pathobiology
GUHA, A., Medical Biochemistry

GULLANE, P. J., Otolaryngology
GURD, J., Biochemistry
HALLIDAY, W., Pathobiology
HAMPSON, D., Pharmacology
HANLEY, W., Paediatrics
HANNA, M., Pathobiology
HANNAH, M., Obstetrics and Gynaecology
HARRISON, R., Otolaryngology
HASLAM, R., Paediatrics
HAWKE, M., Pathobiology, Otolaryngology
HAY, J. B., Immunology
HEDLEY, D., Medical Biophysics
HEERSCH, J., Pharmacology
HELM, T., Paediatrics
HENKELMAN, R. M., Medical Biophysics
HERSCHORN, S., Urology
HILL, R., Medical Biophysics
HILLIARD, R., Paediatrics
HINEK, A., Pathobiology
HO PING KONG, Medicine
HOWELL, P., Biochemistry
HUGHES, T., Medical Research
HUNT, J. W., Medical Biophysics
HYDE, M., Otolaryngology
IKURA, M., Medical Biophysics
INABA, T., Pharmacology
INGLES, C. J., Medical Research
ISCOVE, N., Medical Biochemistry
ISENMAN, D. E., Biochemistry
JEEJEEBHOY, K. N., Medicine
JOHNSSTON, K. W., Vascular Surgery
JOHNSTON, M., Pathobiology
JORGENSEN, A. O., Anatomy and Cell Biology
JOTHY, S., Pathobiology
JULIUS, M., Medical Biophysics
KAHN, H. (acting), Pathobiology
KAIN, K., Pathobiology
KALNINS, V. I., Histology
KANDEL, R., Pathobiology
KAPLAN, D., Medical Genetics
KARMALI, M., Pathobiology
KAY, L., Biochemistry
KEELEY, F., Biochemistry, Pathobiology
KERBEL, R., Medical Biophysics, Pathobiology
KHANNA, J. M., Pharmacology
KHOKHA, R., Medical Biophysics, Pathobiology
KISH, S., Pharmacology
KLIP, A., Biochemistry, Paediatrics
KOREN, G., Paediatrics, Pharmacology
KOVACS, K., Pathobiology
KRAFT, S., Ophthalmology
KRAFTCHIK, B., Paediatrics
KRAICER, J., Physiology
KRAUSE, H., Medical Research
KUCHARCZYK, W., Radiology
KUKSIS, A., Medical Research
KUNOV, H., Otolaryngology
LANGER, B., Surgery
LANGILLE, B. L., Pathology
LAWEE, D. H., Family and Community Medicine
LEPOCK, J., Medical Biophysics
LETARTE, M., Medical Biophysics
LEVY, G. A., Medicine
LEWIS, P. N., Biochemistry
LI, R.-K., Pathobiology
LICKLEY, L., Physiology
LICKRISH, G., Obstetrics and Gynaecology
LIEBGOTT, B., Anatomy
LIEW, C. C., Clinical Biochemistry
LINGWOOD, C., Biochemistry
LIU, F.-F., Medical Biophysics, Physiology
LIVINGSTONE, R. A., Obstetrics and Gynaecology
LOGAN, W. J., Paediatrics
LOW, D., Pathobiology
LYE, S., Obstetrics and Gynaecology
MACDONALD, J. F., Physiology
MCGEER, A., Pathobiology
MCGRAIL, S., Otolaryngology
MCINNES, R. R., Paediatrics
MACKAY, M., Biomedical Communications
MCKEE, N., Plastic Surgery

MACLENNAN, D. H., Medical Research
MAHURAN, D., Pathobiology
MAK, T.-W., Medical Biophysics
MARKS, A., Neurobiology
MARSDEN, P., Medical Biophysics, Pathobiology
MARSHALL, V. W., Behavioural Science
MAZER, C. D., Anaesthesia
MESSNER, H., Medical Biophysics
MICKLE, D., Pathobiology
MICKLEBOROUGH, L., Cardiac Surgery
MILGRAM, N., Pharmacology
MILLER, F., Physiology
MINDEN, M., Medical Biophysics
MOCK, D., Pathobiology
MOSCARELLO, M., Pathobiology
MORAN, L., Biochemistry
MORAN, M. F., Medical Research
MORGAN, J. E., Obstetrics and Gynaecology
MORTIMER, C. B., Ophthalmology
MROSOVSKY, N., Physiology
NAG, S., Pathobiology
NAGY, A., Medical Genetics
NARANJO, C. A., Pharmacology
NEDZELSKI, J. M., Otolaryngology
NOBLE, W. H., Anaesthesia
NOYEK, A. M., Otolaryngology
O'BRIEN, P., Pharmacology
O'BRODOVICH, H., Paediatrics, Physiology
O'DOWD, B., Pharmacology
OHASHI, P., Medical Biophysics
OHLSSON, A., Paediatrics
OKEY, A. B., Pharmacology
OLIVIERI, N., Paediatrics
OPAS, M., Pathobiology
ORSER, B., Anaesthesia, Physiology
OSMOND, D. H., Physiology
OTTENSMEYER, F. P., Medical Biophysics
PACE-ASCIAK, C., Pharmacology
PAI, E., Biochemistry
PAIGE, C., Medical Biophysics
PANG, C., Physiology
PANG, K., Pharmacology
PANTALONY, D., Pathobiology
PAPPO, A., Paediatrics
PAPSIN, F. R., Obstetrics and Gynaecology
PARKER, J., Ophthalmology
PARKER, J. D., Pharmacology
PAVLIN, C., Ophthalmology
PENCHARZ, P., Paediatrics
PENN, L., Medical Biophysics
PENNINGER, J., Medical Biophysics
PERLMAN, M., Paediatrics
PETERS, W. J., Plastic Surgery
PINKERTON, P. H., Pathology
PLEWES, D., Medical Biophysics
POST, M., Pathobiology, Physiology
PRITZKER, K., Pathobiology
PRUD'HOMME, G., Pathobiology
PULLEYBLANK, D. E., Biochemistry
RABINOVITCH, M., Paediatrics
RACHLIS, A., Pathobiology
RAJALAKSHMI, S., Pathobiology
RAUTH, A., Medical Biophysics
READ, S. E., Paediatrics, Pathobiology
REGAN, M., Ophthalmology
REITHMEIER, R., Biochemistry
RENLUND, R., Physiology
REZNICK, R., General Surgery
RICHARDSON, C., Medical Biophysics
RIDDELL, R., Pathobiology
RITCHIE, J. W. K., Obstetrics and Gynaecology
ROBERTS, E., Paediatrics
ROBINSON, G., Psychiatry
ROIFMAN, C., Paediatrics
ROSE, D., Medical Biophysics
ROTSTEIN, O. D., Surgery
ROWLANDS, J. A., Medical Biophysics
RUTKA, J., Pathobiology
SADOWSKI, P. D., Medical Genetics, Pathobiology
SARMA, D., Pathobiology
SAUDER, D. N., Medicine
SCHATZKER, J., Surgery
SCHIMMER, B. P., Medical Research

SCHLICHTER, L., Physiology
SCHMITT-ULMS, G., Pathobiology
SCULLY, H., Cardiac Surgery
SEGALL, J., Biochemistry, Medical Genetics
SEIDELMAN, W. E., Family and Community Medicine
SELLERS, E. M., Pharmacology
SERMER, M., Obstetrics and Gynaecology
SESSLE, B., Dentistry
SETH, A., Pathobiology
SHAH, C. P., Preventive Medicine and Biostatistics
SHARPE, J. A., Otolaryngology
SHEAR, N., Pharmcology
SHEK, P., Pathobiology
SHERMAN, P., Paediatrics, Pathobiology
SHIER, R. M., Obstetrics and Gynaecology
SHIME, J., Obstetrics and Gynaecology
SHULMAN, H. S., Radiology
SHULMAN, M. J., Immunology, Medical Genetics
SILVERMAN, M., Medicine
SIMOR, A., Pathobiology
SIU, C. H., Medical Research
SLINGER, P., Anaesthesia
SNEAD, III, O. C., Paediatrics
SODEK, J., Biochemistry
SOLE, M. J., Medicine
SONNENBERG, H., Physiology
SPEAKMAN, J., Ophthalmology
SQUARE, P., Speech-Language Pathology
SQUIRE, J., Pathobiology
STEIN, H., Ophthalmology
STEINER, G., Medicine
STEWART, D. J., Pathobiology
STEWART, P. A., Anatomy and Cell Biology
SUN, A., Physiology
TALLETT, S., Paediatrics
TANNOCK, I., Medical Biophysics
TANSWELL, A., Paediatrics
TATOR, C. H., Surgery
TAYLOR, G., Pathobiology
TAYLOR, I. M., Anatomy
TEMPLETON, D. M., Pathobiology
TENENBAUM, H., Pathobiology
TerBRUGGE, K., Medical Imaging
THOMPSON, L., Nutrition
THORNER, P., Pathobiology
TIMMER, V., Botany
TOMLINSON, D., Otolaryngology
TRIMBLE, W. S., Biochemistry
TRITCHLER, D., Medical Biophysics
TROPE, G., Ophthalmology
TSAO, M., Medical Biophysics, Pathobiology
TWEED, D., Physiology
UETECHT, J., Pharmacology
VAN DER KOOY, D. J., Anatomy and Cell Biology
VAN NOSTRAND, P., Otolaryngology
VAN TOL, H., Pharmacology
VAS, S., Pathobiology
VELLEND, H., Medicine
VRANIC, M., Physiology
WADDELL, J. P., Surgery
WALFISH, P. G., Otolaryngology
WANG, Y.-T., Pathobiology
WANLESS, I., Pathobiology
WARSH, J., Pharmacology
WEISBROD, G., Medical Imaging
WEISER, W., Medical Imaging
WEITZMAN, S., Paediatrics
WEKSBERG, R., Paediatrics
WELLS, J., Pharmacology
WELLS, P., Pharmacology
WILLIAMS, D., Biochemistry
WILLINSKY, R., Medical Imaging
WILSON, B., Medical Biophysics
WILSON, G., Pathobiology
WILSON, S., Medical Imaging
WILSON-PAUWELS, L., Biomedical Communications
WITTNICH, C., Cardiac Surgery
WOJTOWICZ, J., Physiology
WOLEVER, T., Nutritional Sciences
WONG, J. T. F., Biochemistry

WONG, P.-Y., Pathobiology
WONG, S., Medical Biophysics
WOOD, L., Medical Biophysics
WOOD, M., Medical Imaging
WOODGETT, J., Medical Biophysics
WOOLRIDGE, N., Biomedical Communications
WU, T. W., Clinical Biochemistry
YAFFE, M., Medical Biophysics
YIP, C. C., Medical Research
YOO, S.-J., Medical Imaging
ZAMEL, N., Otolaryngology
ZHOU, M., Physiology

Faculty of Music:

ARMENIAN, R., Director of Orchestral Activities
HARTENBERGER, R., Percussion, Graduate Coordinator
HATZIS, C., Composition
HAWKINS, J., Theory and Composition
LAUFER, E. C., Music Theory
MacDONALD, L., Voice Studies
SHAND, P. M., Music Education

Faculty of Nursing:

GALLOP, R.
HILLAN, E.
HODNETT, E.
McKEEVER, P.
O'BRIEN-PALLAS, L.
PRINGLE, D.
STEVENS, B.

Faculty of Pharmacy:

O'BRIEN, P. J.
PANG, K. S.
PERRIER, D. G.
ROBINSON, J. B.
SEGAL, H.
STIEB, E. W., History of Pharmacy
THIESSEN, J. J.
UETRECHT, J. P.

Faculty of Social Work:

BARBER, J.
BOGO, M.
HULCHANSKI, D.
LIGHTMAN, E.
McDONALD, L.
NEYSMITH, S.
SHERA, W.

Joseph L. Rothman School of Management:

AIVAZIAN, V., Finance
AMBURGEY, T. (acting), Strategic Management
AMERNIC, J. (acting), Accounting
BAUM, J. (acting), Strategic Management
BEATTY, D. (acting), Strategic Management
BERKOWITZ, M. (acting), Finance
BERMAN, O. (acting), Operations Management
BIRD, R. (acting), Economics
BOOTH, L. (acting), Finance
BORINS, S. (acting), Public Management
BREAN, D. (acting), Business Economics
BROOKS, L. (acting), Business Ethics and Accounting
CALLEN, J. (acting), Accounting
D'CRUZ, J. (acting), Strategic Management
DOBSON, W. (acting), International Business
DUAN, J.-C. (acting), Finance
EVANS, M. (acting), Organizational Behaviour
FELDMAN, M. (acting), Business Economics
FLECK, J. (acting), Business Government Relations
GOLDEN, B. (acting), Strategic Management
GUNZ, H. (acting), Organizational Behaviour
HALPERN, P. (acting), Finance
HORSTMANN, I. (acting), Business Economics
HUGHES, P. (acting), Strategic Management, Space Systems

HULL, J. (acting), Finance
HYATT, D. (acting), Business Economics
KIRZNER, E. (acting), Finance
KOLODNY, H. (acting), Organizational Behaviour
LATHAM, G. (acting), Organizational Effectiveness
McCURDY, T. (acting), Finance
MARTIN, R. (acting), Strategic Management
MENZEFRICKE, U. (acting), Operations Management
MINTZ, J. (acting), Taxation
MITCHELL, A. (acting), Marketing
MOORTHY, S. (acting), Marketing
ONDRACK, D. (acting), Organizational Behaviour
PAULY, P. (acting), Economics
SMIELIAUSKAS, W. (acting), Accounting
SOMAN, D. (acting), Marketing
STARK, A. (acting), Strategic Management
STRANGE, W. (acting), Urban Economics
TOMBAK, M. (acting), Technology Management
TREFLER, D. (acting), Business Economics
WHITE, A. (acting), Finance
WHYTE, G. (acting), Organizational Behaviour
WILSON, T. (acting), Economics

Ontario Institute for Studies in Education:

ACKER, S. (acting), Sociology and Equity Studies in Education, Theory and Policy Studies in Education
ASTINGTON, J., Human Development
BECK, C., Curriculum, Teaching and Learning
BIEMILLER, A. J.
BOGDAN, D., Theory and Policy and Studies in Education
BOYD, D., Theory and Policy Studies in Education
COLE, A., Adult Education
CONNELLY, M., Curriculum, Teaching and Learning
CORTER, C. M.
CUMMING, A., Curriculum, Teaching and Learning
CUMMINS, J., Curriculum, Teaching and Learning
DARROCH-LOZOWSKI, V., Curriculum, Teaching and Learning
DAVIE, L., Curriculum, Teaching and Learning
DEI, G., Sociology and Equity Studies in Education
DIAMOND, P.
EICHLER, M., Sociology and Equity Studies in Education
FARRELL, J., Curriculum, Teaching and Learning, Theory and Policy Studies in Education
GASKELL, J., Sociology and Equity Studies in Education
GEVA, E., Curriculum, Teaching and Learning
GUTTMAN, M. A., Counselling Psychology
HANNAY, L., Curriculum, Teaching and Learning
HARVEY, E., Sociology and Equity Studies in Education
HAYHOE, R., Theory and Policy Studies in Education
HELLER, M., Sociology and Equity Studies in Education
HODSON, D., Curriculum, Teaching and Learning
JENKINS, J., Human Development
JORDAN, A., Curriculum, Teaching and Learning
KEATING, D., Human Development
KNOWLES, J. G., Adult Education
LABRIE, N., Curriculum, Teaching and Learning
LANG, D., Theory and Policy Studies in Education

LAPKIN, S., Curriculum, Teaching and Learning
LEITHWOOD, K., Theory and Policy Studies in Education
LENSKYJ, H., Sociology and Equity Studies in Education
LEVINE, D., Theory and Policy Studies in Education
LEWIS, M., Human Development
LIVINGSTONE, D., Sociology and Equity Studies in Education
MCLEAN, R., Curriculum, Teaching and Learning
MIEZITIS, S., Teacher Education
MILLER, J., Curriculum, Teaching and Learning
MISGELD, D., Theory and Policy Studies in Education
MOORE, C., Human Development
NG, R., Adult Education, Sociology and Equity Studies in Education
O'SULLIVAN, E., Adult Education
OATLEY, K., Human Development
OLSON, D., Human Development
PASCAL, C., Theory and Policy Studies in Education
PIERSON, R. R., Sociology and Equity Studies in Education
PIRAN, N., Counselling Psychology
PORTELLI, J., Theory and Policy Studies in Education
QUARTER, J., Adult Education
ROSS, J., Curriculum, Teaching and Learning
RYAN, J., Theory and Policy Studies in Education
SCARDAMALIA, J., Curriculum, Teaching and Learning
SIMON, R., Curriculum, Teaching and Learning
SKOLNIK, M., Theory and Policy Studies in Education
SPADA, N., Curriculum, Teaching and Learning
STANOVICH, K., Curriculum, Teaching and Learning
STERMAC, L., Counselling Psychology
SWAIN, M., Curriculum, Teaching and Learning
THIESSEN, D., Curriculum, Teaching and Learning
TROPER, H., Theory and Policy Studies in Education
VOLPE, R., Human Development
WIENER, J., Human Development
WILLOWS, D., Curriculum, Teaching and Learning
WILSON, D., Curriculum, Teaching and Learning, Theory and Policy Studies in Education

School of Graduate Studies:
ANGENOT, M., Comparative Literature
BEATTIE, J. M., Criminology
BOND, R. J., Theoretical Astronomy
BRYDEN, R., Drama
COHEN, J. S., Graduate Studies
DOOB, A. N., Criminology
HACKING, I. M., History and Philosophy of Science and Technology
HARIANTO, F., International Studies
HEALEY, A. D., Medieval Studies
HERNANDEZ, C., International Studies
KAISER, N., Theoretical Astronomy
LEVERE, T. H., History and Philosophy of Science and Technology
MARKER, L. L., Drama
MARTIN, P. G., Theoretical Astronomy
NESSELROTH, P. W., Comparative Literature
PESANDO, J. E., Policy Analysis
RIGG, A. G., Medieval Studies
SHEARING, C. D., Criminology
STENNING, P. C., Criminology
STOCK, B. C., Comparative Literature
TREMAINE, S. D., Theoretical Astronomy

VALVERDE, M. V., Criminology
WINSOR, M. P., History and Philosophy of Science and Technology

School of Physical Education and Health:
COREY, P.
DONNELLY, P.
FERNIE, G.
GOODE, R.
JACOBS, I.
LEITH, L.
LENSKYJ, H.
MCCLELLAND, J.
MCKEE, N.
PLYLEY, M.
VOLPE, R.

UNIVERSITY COLLEGES

Erindale College/University of Toronto at Mississauga: 3359 Mississauga Rd North, Mississauga, ON L5L 1C6; tel. 828-5211; f. 1964; Prin. IAN ORCHARD.

Innis College: 2 Sussex Ave, Toronto, ON M5S 1J5; tel. 978-7023; fax 978-5503; internet www.utoronto.ca/innis; f. 1964; Prin. F. CUNNINGHAM.

New College: 300 Huron St, Toronto, ON M5S 3JO; tel. 978-2461; fax 978-0554; internet utt2.library.utoronto.ca/www/new_college/index.htm; f. 1962; Pres. DAVID KLANDFIELD.

Scarborough College: 1265 Military Trail, Scarborough, ON M1C 1A4; tel. 287-8872; f. 1964; Prin. R. P. THOMPSON.

University College: 15 King's College Circle, Toronto, ON M5S 3H7; tel. 978-3170; f. 1853; Prin. PAUL J. PERRON.

Woodsworth College: 117–119 St George St, Toronto, ON M5S 1A9; tel. 978-2411; fax 978-6111; e-mail info@wdw.utoronto.ca; f. 1974; Prin. N. M. MELTZ.

FEDERATED UNIVERSITIES

University of St Michael's College: 81 St Mary St, Toronto, ON M5S 1J4; tel. (416) 926-1300; f. 1958; conducted by the Basilian Fathers; Pres. Dr ANNE ANDERSON.

University of Trinity College: 6 Hoskin Ave, Toronto, ON M5S 1H8; tel. (416) 978-2522; f. 1851; Vice-Chancellor and Provost R. PAINTER.

Victoria University, Toronto: 73 Queen's Park Cres., Toronto, ON M5S 1K7; tel. (416) 585-4524; f. 1836; Pres. E. KUSHNER.

FEDERATED COLLEGES

Emmanuel College: 75 Queen's Park Cres., Toronto, ON M5S 1K7; tel. (416) 585-4540; f. 1928; United Church of Canada theological college; Prin. JOHN HOFFMAN.

Knox College: 59 St George St, Toronto, ON M5S 2E5; tel. (416) 978-4500; Presbyterian theological college; Prin. Rev. Dr RAYMOND HUMPHRYES (acting).

Regis College: 15 St Mary St, Toronto, ON M4Y 2R5; tel. (416) 922-5474; f. 1930; Roman Catholic theological college (Society of Jesus); Pres. Rev. JOHN E. COSTELLO.

Wycliffe College: 5 Hoskin Ave, Toronto, ON M5S 1H7; tel. (416) 979-2870; Anglican theological college; Prin. Rev. H. S. HILCHEY (acting).

AFFILIATED INSTITUTES

Massey College: University of Toronto, Toronto, ON M5S 2E1; tel. (416) 978-2895; f. 1963; residential college for graduates and senior scholars engaged in research; Master J. S. DUPRE.

Pontifical Institute of Medieval Studies: 59 Queen's Park Cres. East, Toronto, ON M5S 2C4; affiliated to Univ. of St Michael's College; grants degrees in its own right,

offering pontifical Licentiate in Medieval Studies (MSL) and Doctorate in Medieval Studies (MSD); Pres. Prof. M. DIMNIK.

TRENT UNIVERSITY

1600 West Bank Drive, Peterborough, ON K9J 7B8

Telephone: (705) 748-1332
Fax: (705) 748-1629
E-mail: liaison@trentu.ca
Internet: www.trentu.ca

Founded 1963
Language of instruction: English
Academic year: September to April (2 semesters with reading periods intervening; summer sessions also available)

Chancellor: Dr ROBERTA BONDAR
Pres. and Vice-Chancellor: BONNIE M. PATTERSON
Vice-Pres. for Academic Affairs and Provost: SUSAN APOSTLE-CLARK
Vice-Pres. for Administration: DON O'LEARY
Vice-Pres. for External Relations and Advancement: DIANNE LISTER
Registrar: SUSAN SALUSBURY
Senior Director of Public Affairs: DON CUMMING
University Librarian: ROBERT F. CLARKE
Number of teachers: 467 (325 full-time, 142 part-time)
Number of students: 8,050 undergraduates (6,688 full-time, 1,362 part-time), 277 postgraduates

DEANS

Faculty of Arts and Science: CHRISTINE MCKINNON
Faculty of Graduate Studies: DOUGLAS EVANS

PROFESSORS

ARVIN, M. C., Economics
BANDYOPADHYAY, P., Comparative Development Studies
BERRILL, D., School of Education
BERRILL, M., Biology
BISHOP, J., Business Administration
BRUNGER, A. G., Geography
BUTTLE, J., Geography
CHOUDRY, S., Economics
COGLEY, J. G., Geography
CONOLLY, L. W., English Literature
CURTIS, D. C. A., Economics
DAWSON, P. C., Physics
DELLAMORA, R. J., English Literature and Cultural Studies
DILLON, P., Environmental Studies, Chemistry
EVANS, D., Environmental Studies
EVANS, W., Environmental Studies, Physics
FEKETE, J. A., English Literature, Cultural Studies
FOX, M., Environmental Studies, Biology
HAGMAN, R. S., Anthropology
HEALY, P. F., Anthropology
HEITLINGER, A., Sociology
HURLEY, R., Computer Studies, Science
HUXLEY, C. V., Sociology and Comparative Development Studies
JAMIESON, S., Anthropology
JOHNSTON, G. A., English Literature
JONES, E. H., History
JURY, J. W., Physics and Computer Studies
KANE, S., English Literature, Cultural Studies
KATZ, S., Sociology
KEEFER, S., English Literature
KENNETT, D. J., Psychology
KINZL, K. H., Ancient History and Classics
KITCHEN, H. M., Economics
LAFLEUR, P., Geography
LASENBY, D. C., Biology
LEM, W., International Development Studies and Women's Studies
LEWARS, E. G., Chemistry

MCCASKILL, D. N., Native Studies
MCKENNA-NEWMAN, C., Geography
MCKINNON, C., Philosophy
MAXWELL, E. A., Mathematics
METCALFE, C., Environmental Studies
MILLOY, J., Native Studies and History
MITCHELL, O. S., English Literature
MORRISON, D. R., International Development Studies
NADER, G. A., Geography
NEUFELD, J. E., English Literature
NEUMANN, M., Philosophy
NOL, E., Biology
NORIEGA, T. A., Hispanic Studies
PAEHLKE, R. C., Political Studies, Environmental Studies
PALMER, B., Canadian Studies
PARNIS, M., Chemistry
PATTERSON, B., Business Administration
PETERMAN, M., English Literature
PICKEL, A., Political Studies
POLLOCK, Z., English Literature
POOLE, D. G., Mathematics
REKER, G. T., Psychology
SANGSTER, J., History and Women's Studies
SHEININ, D., History
SLAVIN, A. J., Physics
SMITH, C. T., Psychology
SO, J. K.-F., Anthropology
STANDEN, S. D., History
STOREY, I. C., Ancient History and Classics
STRUTHERS, J. E., Canadian Studies, History
SUTCLIFFE, J., Biology
SVISHCHEV, I., Chemistry
TAMPLIN, M., Anthropology
TAYLOR, C., Geography
TAYLOR, G., History
TINDALE, C., Philosophy
TOPIC, J. R., Anthropology
TORGERSON, D., Environmental and Resource Studies
TROMLY, F. B., English Literature
WADLAND, J. H., Canadian Studies
WALDEN, K., History
WERNICK, A. L., Cultural Studies
WHITE, B., Biology
WINOCUR, G., Psychology
ZHOU, B., Mathematics

TRINITY WESTERN UNIVERSITY

7600 Glover Rd, Langley, BC V2Y 1Y1
Telephone: (604) 888-7511
Fax: (604) 513-2061
E-mail: suderman@twu.ca
Internet: www.twu.ca
Founded 1962, university status 1985
Private control
Language of instruction: English
Academic year: September to April

Pres.: Dr JONATHAN RAYMOND
Provost: Dr DENNIS JAMESON
Vice-Pres. for Academic Affairs: Dr DENNIS JAMESON
Vice-Pres. for Advancement: DAVID COONS
Vice-Pres. for Finance: DALE CLARK
Assoc. Provost for Student Life: SHELDON LOEPPKY
Registrar: GRANT MCMILLAN
Librarian: TED GOSHULAK

Library of 430,000 items
Number of teachers: 305 (165 full-time, 140 part-time)
Number of students: 3,500

DEANS

Faculty of Humanities and Social Sciences: Dr ROBERT BURKINSHAW
Faculty of Natural and Applied Sciences-Graduate School of Theological Studies: Dr KEN RADANT, Dr KA YIN LEUNG
School of Arts, Media and Culture: Dr DAVID SQUIRES
School of Business and Economics: ANDREA SOBERG

School of Graduate Studies: Dr WILLIAM ACTON
School of Human Kinetics: Dr BLAIR WHITMARSH

UNIVERSITY OF VICTORIA

POB 1700, Victoria, BC V8W 2Y2
Telephone: (250) 721-7211
Fax: (250) 721-7212
E-mail: ucom@uvic.ca
Internet: www.uvic.ca
Founded 1963
Language of instruction: English
Provincial control
Academic year: September to April

Chancellor: MURRAY FARMER
Pres. and Vice-Chancellor: Dr DAVID H. TURPIN
Vice-Pres. for Academic Affairs and Provost: Prof. JAMIE CASSELS
Vice-Pres. for External Relations: Dr VALERIE KUEHNE
Vice-Pres. for Finance and Operations: GAYLE GORRILL
Vice-Pres. for Research: Dr HOWARD BRUNT
University Sec.: Dr JULIA EASTMAN
Admin. Registrar: LYNDA WALLACE-HULECKI
University Librarian: MARNIE SWANSON

Number of teachers: 790
Number of students: 19,646

Publications: *Calendar* (1 a year), *Malahat Review*

DEANS

Faculty of Business: Dr ALI DASTMALCHIAN
Faculty of Education: Dr TED RIECKEN
Faculty of Engineering: Dr THOMAS TIEDJE
Faculty of Fine Arts: Dr SARAH BLACKSTONE
Faculty of Graduate Studies: Dr AARON DEVOR
Faculty of Human and Social Development: Dr MARY ELLEN PURKIS (acting)
Faculty of Humanities: Dr ANDREW RIPPIN
Faculty of Law: Prof. DONNA GRESCHNER (acting)
Faculty of Science: Dr THOMAS PEDERSON
Faculty of Social Sciences: Dr PETER KELLER

PROFESSORS

AGATHOKLIS, P., Electrical and Computer Engineering
ANDERSON, J., Educational Psychology and Leadership Studies
ANDRACHUK, G. P., Hispanic and Italian Studies
ANTONIOU, A., Electrical and Computer Engineering
ARMITAGE, A., Social Work
AUSIO, J., Biochemistry and Microbiology
AVIO, K. L., Economics
BACHOR, D. G., Psychological Foundations
BALFOUR, W. J., Chemistry
BARCLAY, J. A., Mechanical Engineering
BARNES, C., Earth and Ocean Sciences
BARNES, G. E., Child and Youth Care
BASKERVILLE, P. A., History
BAVELAS, J. B., Psychology
BEDESKI, R. E., Political Science
BENNETT, C., Political Science
BENOIT, C., Sociology
BERRY, E. I., English
BEST, M. R., English
BHARGAVA, V. K., Electrical and Computer Engineering
BHAT, A. K. S., Electrical and Computer Engineering
BLANK, K., English
BOAG, D. A., Faculty of Business
BOHNE, C., Chemistry
BORNEMANN, J., Electrical and Computer Engineering
BORROWS, J., Law
BRADLEY, K. R., Classics

BRENER, R., Visual Arts
BROWNING-MOORE, A., Music
BRUNT, H., Nursing
BRYANT, D., Pacific and Asian Studies
BUB, D., Psychology
BUCKLEY, J. T., Biochemistry and Microbiology
BURKE, R. D., Biology
CAMPBELL, M., Human and Social Development
CARROLL, W. K., Sociology
CASSELS, J. L., Law
CASSWELL, D. G., Law
CELONA, J., Music
CHAPMAN, R., Earth and Ocean Sciences
CHAPPELL, N. L., Sociology
COBLEY, E., English
COCKAYNE, E. J., Mathematics and Statistics
COOPERSTOCK, F. I., Physics and Astronomy
COWARD, H. G., History
CROIZIER, L., Writing
CROIZIER, R. C., History
CUNNINGHAM, J. B., Public Administration
CUTT, J., Public Administration
DEARDEN, P., Geography
DEVOR, H., Sociology
DIACU, F., Mathematics and Statistics
DIMOPOULOS, N., Electrical and Computer Engineering
DIPPIE, B. W., History
DIXON, R. A., Psychology
DJILALI, N., Mechanical Engineering
DOBELL, A. R., Public Administration
DOCHERTY, D., Physical Education
DONALD, L. H., Anthropology
DONG, Z., Mechanical Engineering
DOST, S., Mechanical Engineering
DYSON, L., Psychological Foundations
EDWARDS, A. S., English
EL GUIBALY, F. H., Electrical and Computer Engineering
ENGINEER, M., Economics
ESLING, J., Linguistics
FELLOWS, M., Computer Science
FERGUSON, G. A., Law
FLEMING, T., Education
FOSS, J., Philosophy
FOSTER, H., Law
FOSTER, H. D., Geography
FOWLER, R., Social and Natural Sciences
FRANCE, H., Psychological Foundations
FYLES, T. M., Chemistry
GALAMBOS, N., Psychology
GALLAGHER, Nursing
GALLOWAY, J., Law
GARRETT, C., Physics, Earth and Ocean Sciences
GARTRELL, D., Sociology
GIBSON-WOOD, C., History in Art
GIFFORD, R. D., Psychology
GILES, D. E., Economics
GILLIN, M., Law
GLICKMAN, B., Biology
GOOCH, B. N. S., English
GOUGH, T. E., Chemistry
GRANT, P. J., English
GREGORY, P. T., Biology
GULLIVER, A., Electrical and Computer Engineering
HALL, B., Curriculum and Instruction
HANLEY, B., Curriculum and Instruction
HARKER, W. J., Education
HARRINGTON, D., Chemistry
HARRIS, C., Communication and Social Foundations
HARTWICK, F. D. A., Physics and Astronomy
HARVEY, A., Psychological Foundations
HAWRYSHYN, C., Biology
HEDLEY, R. A., Sociology
HILLS, M., Nursing
HOCKING, M., Chemistry
HODGINS, J., Creative Writing
HOEFER, W. J. R., Electrical and Computer Engineering
HOGYA, G., Theatre
HORITA, R. E., Physics and Astronomy

HORSPOOL, R. N., Computer Science
HOWE, B. L., Physical Education
HOWELL, R. G., Law
HUENEMANN, R. W., Faculty of Business
HULTSCH, D. F., Psychology
ILLNER, R., Mathematics and Statistics
ISHIGURO, E. E., Biochemistry and Microbiology
JOHNSON, T. D., Education
JONES, J. C. H., Economics
KAMBOURELI, S., English
KAY, W. W., Biochemistry and Microbiology
KEELER, R., Physics and Astronomy
KELLER, A., English
KELLER, P., Geography
KERBY-FULTON, K., English
KESS, J. F., Linguistics
KINDERMAN, W., Music
KIRLIN, R. L., Electrical and Computer Engineering
KLUGE, E.-H., Philosophy
KOENIG, D., Sociology
KOOP, B., Biology
KREBS, H., Music
KUEHNE, V., Child and Youth Care
KWOK, H. H. L., Electrical and Computer Engineering
LAI, D. C.-Y., Geography
LANGFORD, J. W., Public Administration
LAPPRAND, M., French Language and Literature
LAZAREVICH, G., Music
LEADBEATER, B., Psychology
LEEMING, D. J., Mathematics and Statistics
LIDDELL, P., Germanic Studies
LIEDTKE, W. W., Education
LINDSAY, D., Psychology
LISCOMB, K., History in Art
LIVINGSTON, N., Biology
LONERGAN, S. C., Geography
LU, W.-S., Electrical and Computer Engineering
MCCANN, L., Geography
MCDAVID, J. C., Public Administration
MCDORMAN, T., Law
MCDOUGALL, I., Music
MCLAREN, A. G., History
MCLAREN, J. P. S., Law
MACGREGOR, J. N., Public Administration
MACPHERSON, G. R. I., History
MAGNUSSON, W., Political Science
MALONEY, M. A., Law
MANNING, E. G., Computer Science, Electrical and Computer Engineering
MARTIN-NEWCOMBE, Y., Communication and Social Foundations
MASSON, M. E. J., Psychology
MATEER, C., Psychology
MAYFIELD, M., Education
MAZUMDER, A., Biology
M'GONIGLE, R., Environmental Studies
MIERS, C. R., Mathematics and Statistics
MILLER, D., Computer Science
MISRA, S., Biochemistry and Microbiology
MITCHELL, D. H., Anthropology
MITCHELL, R. H., Chemistry
MOEHR, J. R., Health Information Service
MOLZAHN, A., Nursing
MORE, B. E., Music
MORGAN, C. G., Philosophy
MOSK, C. A., Economic Relations with Japan
MULLER, H., Computer Science
MURPHY, P., Communication and Social Foundations
MUZIO, J. C., Computer Science
MYRVOLD, W., Computer Science
NANO, F., Biochemistry and Microbiology
NEILSON, W. A. W., Law
NG, I., Business
NICHOLS, D., Physical Education
NIEMANN, O., Geography
OGMUNDSON, R., Sociology
OLAFSON, R. W., Biochemistry and Microbiology
OLESKY, D., Computer Science
OLESON, J. P., Classics

OSBORNE, J., History in Art
PAETKAU, V., Biochemistry
PEARSON, T. W., Biochemistry and Microbiology
PENCE, A. R., Child and Youth Care
PFAFFENBERGER, W. E., Mathematics and Statistics
PHILLIPS, J., Mathematics and Statistics
PICCIOTTO, C. E., Physics and Astronomy
PINDER, W. C., Business
PORTEOUS, J. D., Geography
PRINCE, M. J., Social Policy
PRITCHET, C. J., Physics
PROTTI, D. J., Health Information Science
PROVAN, J. W., Mechanical Engineering
PUTNAM, I., Mathematics and Statistics
RANGER, L., Music
REED, W. J., Mathematics and Statistics
REID, R. G. B., Biology
REITSMA-STREET, M., Child and Youth Care
RICKS, F. A. S., Child and Youth Care
RIEDEL, W. E., Germanic Studies
RING, R. A., Biology
ROMANIUK, P., Biochemistry and Microbiology
ROTH, E., Anthropology
ROTH, W.-M., Social and Natural Sciences
ROY, P., History
RUSKEY, F., Computer Science
RUTHERFORD, M., Economics
SAGER, E. W., History
ST PETER, C., Women's Studies
SCARFE, C. D., Physics and Astronomy
SCHAAFSMA, J., Economics
SCHAARSCHMIDT, G. H., Slavonic Studies
SCHOFIELD, J. A., Economics
SCHULER, R., English
SCHWANDT, E., Music
SCOBIE, S. A. C., English
SERRA, M., Computer Science
SHERWOOD, N., Biology
SHRIMPTON, G., Greek and Roman Studies
SMITH, D., Geography
SOUROUR, A. R., Mathematics and Statistics
SRIVASTAVA, H. M., Mathematics and Statistics
STEPANENKO, Y., Mechanical Engineering
STEPHENSON, P. H., Anthropology
STOBART, S. R., Chemistry
STORCH, J., Nursing
STOREY, V., Communication and Social Foundations
STRAUSS, E., Psychology
STRONG, D. F., Earth and Ocean Sciences
STUCHLY, M., Electrical and Computer Engineering
SYMINGTON, R. T. K., Germanic Studies
THALER, D., French Language and Literature
THATCHER, D. S., English
TUCKER, J., English
TULLER, S., Geography
TULLY, J., Political Science
TUNNICLIFFE, V. J., Earth and Ocean Sciences
TURNER, N., Environmental Studies
UHLEMANN, M. R., Education
VALGARDSON, W. D., Creative Writing
VAN DEN DRIESSCHE, R., Biology
VAN EMDEN, M., Computer Science
VAN GYN, G., Physical Education
VANCE, J. H., Education
VANDENBERG, D. A., Physics
VICKERS, G. W., Mechanical Engineering
VOGT, B., Music
VON ADERKAS, P., Biology
WADGE, W. W., Computer Science
WALDRON, M. A., Law
WALKER, R. B. J., Political Science
WALTER, G. R., Economics
WAN, P. C., Chemistry
WARBURTON, R., Sociology
WATTON, A., Physics and Astronomy
WEAVER, A., Earth and Ocean Sciences
WELCH, S. A., History in Art
WENGER, H. A., Physical Education
WHITICAR, M., Earth and Ocean Sciences

WILL, H. J., Public Administration
WILLIAMS, T., English
WILSON, J., Political Science
WOLFF, R., Business
WOON, YUEN-FONG, Pacific Asian Studies
WU, Z., Sociology
WYNAND, D., Creative Writing
YORE, L. D., Education
YOUDS, R., Visual Arts
YOUNG, J., Philosophy
ZIELINSKI, A., Electrical and Computer Engineering
ZIMMERMAN, D., History
ZUK, W., Arts in Education

UNIVERSITY OF WATERLOO

Waterloo, ON N2L 3G1

Telephone: (519) 888-4567 ext. 33614
Fax: (519) 746-8088
E-mail: registrar@uwaterloo.ca
Internet: www.uwaterloo.ca

Founded 1957
Provincially supported
Language of instruction: English
Academic year: September to April (Cooperative programmes September to August, Summer Session July to August)

Chancellor: PREM WATSA
Pres. and Vice-Chancellor: DAVID L. JOHNSTON
Vice-Pres. for Academic Affairs and Provost: FERIDUN HAMDULLAHPUR
Vice-Pres. for Admin. and Finance: DENNIS E. HUBER
Vice-Pres. for Univ. Relations: MEG BECKEL
Vice-Pres. for Univ. Research: GEORGE DIXON
Assoc. Provost for Academic and Student Affairs: BRUCE MITCHELL
Assoc. Provost for Graduate Studies: SUE HORTON
Assoc. Provost for Human Resources and Student Services: JANET PASSMORE
Assoc. Provost for Information Systems and Technology: ALAN GEORGE
Registrar: KEN A. LAVIGNE
Univ. Librarian: MARK HASLETT
Library: 2m. vols
Number of teachers: 1,062 (full-time and part-time)
Number of students: 30,861 (full-time and part-time)
Publications: *Alternatives* (6 a year), *Environments Journal* (3 a year), *New Quarterly*

DEANS

Faculty of Applied Health Sciences: ROGER MANNELL
Faculty of Arts: KEN COATES
Faculty of Engineering: Prof. ADEL SEDRA
Faculty of Environmental Studies: Dr H. S. (DEEP) SAINI
Faculty of Mathematics: THOMAS COLEMAN
Faculty of Science: TERRY MCMOHAN

FEDERATED UNIVERSITY

St Jerome's University: Waterloo, ON N2L 3G3; f. 1864; federated 1960; Roman Catholic, conducted by the Congregation of the Resurrection; Pres. D. PERRIN.

AFFILIATED COLLEGES

Conrad Grebel University College: Waterloo, ON N2L 3G6; f. 1961; Mennonite; Pres. H. PAETKAU.

Renison University College: Waterloo, ON N2L 3G4; f. 1959, affiliated 1960; Anglican; Prin. G. CARTWRIGHT.

St Paul's University College: Waterloo, ON N2L 3G5; f. 1962; United Church of Canada; Prin. G. BROWN.

UNIVERSITY OF WESTERN ONTARIO

1151 Richmond St, Suite 2, London, ON N6A 5B8

Telephone: (519) 661-2111
Fax: (519) 661-3710
E-mail: reg-admissions@uwo.ca
Internet: www.uwo.ca

Founded 1878
Academic year: September to April

Chancellor: JOHN THOMPSON
Pres. and Vice-Chancellor: Dr PAUL DAVEN-PORT
Vice-Pres. for Academic Affairs and Provost: Dr FRED LONGSTAFFE
Vice-Pres. for Admin.: GITTA KULCZYCKI
Vice-Pres. for External Relations: Dr TED GARRARD
Vice-Pres. for Research: Dr TED HEWITT
Vice-Provost for Academic Programmes and Students and Registrar: Dr JOHN DOERKSEN
Vice-Provost for Policy, Academic Planning and Faculty: Dr ALAN WEEDON
University Librarian: JOYCE GARNETT

Library of 3,546,496 vols
Number of teachers: 1,357 full-time
Number of students: 37,335 (33,503 full-time, 3,832 part-time)

Publications: *Alumni Gazette* (magazine, 3 a year), *Dental Journal*, *Gazette* (student daily bulletin), *Mediations*, *Medical Journal*, *Reflections*, *The Business Quarterly*, *The President's Report*, *The Science Terrapin*, *Western News* (52 a year, newspaper)

DEANS

Faculty of Arts and Humanities: Dr D. PENNEE
Faculty of Education: Dr JULIA O' SULLIVAN
Faculty of Engineering: Dr G. K. KNOPF
Faculty of Health Sciences: Dr J. WEESE
Faculty of Information and Media Studies: Dr T. CARMICHAEL
Faculty of Law: Prof. I. HOLLOWAY
Don Wright Faculty of Music: Dr ROBERT WOOD
Faculty of Science: Dr D. WARDLAW (acting)
Faculty of Social Science: Dr B. TIMNEY
Richard Ivey School of Business: C. STEPHENSON
School of Graduate and Postdoctoral Studies: Dr L. MILLER
Schulich School of Medicine and Dentistry: Dr C. P. HERBERT

PROFESSORS

Faculty of Arts and Humanities (tel. (519) 661-3043; fax (519) 661-3640; internet www.uwo.ca/arts):

ADAMS, S. J., English
BELL, J. L., Philosophy
BENTLEY, D. M. R., English
BRENNAN, S., Philosophy (Head)
BROWN, C. G., Classical Studies (Head)
BROWN, H., Philosophy
BRUSH, K., Visual Arts
CROWTHER, N. B., Classical Studies
DAVEY, F. W., English
DEMOPOULOS, W. G., Philosophy
ELLIOTT, B., Visual Arts
ESTERHAMMER, A., English, Modern Languages and Literatures
FALKENSTEIN, L., Philosophy
GEDALOF, A., Film Studies
GITTINGS, C., Film Studies (Head)
GOLDSCHLAGER, A. J., French
GRODEN, M. L., English
HARPER, W. L., Philosophy
HOFFMASTER, C. B., Philosophy
KNEALE, J. D., English (Head)
KREISWIRTH, M., English
LEE, A. M., Women's Studies (Head)
LENNON, T. M., Philosophy
LEONARD, J., English

LITTLEWOOD, A. R., Classical Studies
MAHON, P., Visual Arts (Head)
MARRAS, A., Philosophy
MAYNARD, P. L., Philosophy, Visual Arts
MURISON, L., Classical Studies
POOLE, R., English
PURDY, A., French
RAJAN, T., English
RANDALL, M., French
SOMERSET, J. A. B., English
TENNANT, J., French (Head)
THOMSON, C., French

Faculty of Education (tel. (519) 661-3182; internet www.uwo.ca/edu):

CUMMINGS, A.
DICKINSON, G. M.
LESCHIED, A.
MAJHANOVICH, S. E. W.
PEARSON, A. T.

Faculty of Engineering (tel. (519) 661-2128; internet www.eng.uwo.ca):

ADAMIAK, K., Electrical and Computer
BADDOUR, R. E., Civil and Environmental
BARTLETT, F. M. P., Civil and Environmental
BASSI, A., Chemical and Biochemical
BERRUTI, F., Dean's Office, Chemical and Biochemical
BRIENS, C. L., Chemical and Biochemical
DE LASA, H., Chemical and Biochemical
EL NAGGAR, H., Civil and Environmental
FLORYAN, J. M., Mechanical and Materials
GREASON, W. D., Electrical and Computer
HONG, H. P., Civil and Environmental
JIANG, J., Electrical and Computer
JOHNSON, J. A., Mechanical and Materials
JUTAN, A., Chemical and Biochemical
KARAMANEV, D., Chemical and Biochemical
KHAYAT, R. E., Mechanical and Materials
KNOPF, G. K., Mechanical and Materials
PATEL, R. V., Electrical and Computer
ROHANI, S., Chemical and Biochemical
SHANG, J. Q., Civil and Environmental
SHINOZAKI, D. M., Mechanical and Materials
SIDHU, T. S., Electrical and Computer
SIMONOVIC, S., Civil and Environmental
SINGH, A. V., Mechanical and Materials
VANFUL, E., Civil and Environmental
ZHU, J., Chemical and Biochemical

Faculty of Health Sciences (tel. (519) 661-4249; internet www.uwo.ca/fhs):

BAKA, R., Kinesiology
BELCASTRO, A. N., Kinesiology
BUCKOLZ, E., Kinesiology
CARRON, A. V., Kinesiology
DOYLE, P., Communication Sciences and Disorders
FORCHUK, C., Nursing
GARLAND, J., Physical Therapy
GOLDENBERG, D., Nursing
HALL, C. R., Kinesiology
IWASIW, C., Nursing
JAMIESON, D., Communication Sciences and Disorders
JOHNSON, C. S., Kinesiology
LASCHINGER, H., Nursing
LEMON, P., Kinesiology
McWILLIAM, C., Nursing
MEIER, K. V., Kinesiology
MORROW, L. D., Kinesiology
MYERS, A. M., Kinesiology
NOBLE, E., Kinesiology
ORCHARD, C., Nursing (Head)
OVEREND, T., Physical Therapy (Head)
PATERSON, D. H., Kinesiology
PICHÉ, L. A., Kinesiology
SALMONI, A., Kinesiology (Head)
SEEWALD, R. C., Communication Sciences and Disorders
SEMOTIUK, D., Kinesiology
SUMSION, T., Occupational Therapy (Head)
TREVITHICK, J. R., Kinesiology
TRUJILLO, S., Health Sciences (Head)

VANDERVOORT, A. A., Physical Therapy
WATSON, R., Communication Sciences and Disorders (Head)
WEESE, W. J., Kinesiology

Faculty of Information and Media Studies (tel. (519) 661-3542; fax (519) 661-3506; internet www.fims.uwo.ca):

BABE, R. E.
CRAVEN, T. C.
HARRIS, R. M.
PARR, J.
ROSS, C. L.
SPENCER, D.
VAUGHAN, L. Q.
WILKINSON, M. A.

Faculty of Law (tel. (519) 661-3346; fax (519) 850-2412; internet www.law.uwo.ca):

BARTON, P. G.
BROWN, C.
EDGAR, T.
HOLLAND, W. H.
HOLLOWAY, I.
HOVIUS, B.
McLAREN, R. H.
MERCER, P.
SOLOMON, R.
USPRICH, S. J.
WELLING, B.

Don Wright Faculty of Music (tel. (519) 661-2043; fax (519) 661-3531; e-mail music@uwo.ca; internet www.music.uwo.ca):

BRACEY, J. P., Music Performance Studies
FISKE, H., Music Education
GRIER, J., Music History
HEARD, A., Theory and Composition
KOPROWSKI, P. P., Theory and Composition
McKAY, J., Music Performance Studies (Head)
NOLAN, C., Theory and Composition (Head)
PARKS, R. S., Theory and Composition
TOFT, R. E., Music History (Head)
WOODFORD, P., Music Education (Head)

Faculty of Science (tel. (519) 661-3040; e-mail science@uwo.ca; internet www.uwo.ca/sci):

BAILEY, R., Biology
BAINES, K. M., Chemistry (Head)
BAIRD, N. C., Chemistry
BARRON, J. L., Computer Science
BATTISTA, J., Medical Biophysics (Head)
BAUER, M. A., Computer Science (Head)
BELLHOUSE, D. R., Statistical and Actuarial Sciences
BOIVIN, A., Mathematics
BRANDL, C., Biochemistry (Head)
CAMPBELL, K., Epidemiology and Biostatistics (Head)
CASS, F. P. A., Mathematics
CAVENEY, S., Biology
CORLESS, R. M., Applied Mathematics; Computer Science; Philosophy (Head, Applied Mathematics)
COTTAM, M. G., Physics and Astronomy
DAY, A. W., Biology
DEAN, P. A. W., Chemistry
DEBRUYN, J. R., Physics and Astronomy (Joint Head)
EATON, D. W. S., Earth Sciences
ELIAS, V. W., Applied Mathematics
ESSEX, G. C., Applied Mathematics
FENTON, M. B., Biology (Head)
FLORYAN, J. M., Applied Mathematics
GUTHRIE, J. P., Chemistry and Biochemistry
HEINICKE, A. G., Mathematics
HICOCK, S. R., Earth Sciences
HOCKING, W. K., Physics and Astronomy
HOLT, R. A., Physics and Astronomy
HUANG, Y., Chemistry
HUNER, J. A., Biology
JARDINE, J. F., Mathematics
JEFFREY, D. J., Applied Mathematics
JIN, J., Earth Sciences
JONES, B. L., Physics and Astronomy (Joint Head)

JÜRGENSEN, H., Computer Science
JUTAN, A., Applied Mathematics
KANE, R. M., Mathematics (Head)
KANG, C. Y., Biology
KERR, M. A., Chemistry
KHALKHALI, M., Mathematics
KOVAL, S. F., Earth Sciences, Microbiology and Immunology
KRISHNA, P., Biology
KULPERGER, R. J., Statistical and Actuarial Sciences
LACHANCE, M. A., Biology, Microbiology and Immunology
LAU, L. W. M., Physics and Astronomy
LEAIST, D. G., Chemistry
LEHMAN, M., Anatomy and Cell Biology (Head)
LENNARD, W. N., Physics and Astronomy
LIPSON, R. H., Chemistry
LONGSTAFFE, F. J., Earth Sciences
LUTFIYYA, H., Earth Sciences
McKEON, D. G. C., Applied Mathematics
McLEOD, A. I., Statistical and Actuarial Sciences
McNEIL, J. N., Biology
MADHAVJI, J. W., Computer Science
MARTIN, R. R., Chemistry
MERCER, R. E., Computer Science
MILLAR, J. S., Biology
MILNES, P., Mathematics
MINÀC, J., Mathematics
MIRANSKY, V. A., Applied Mathematics
MITTLER, S., Physics and Astronomy
NESBITT, H. W., Earth Sciences (Head)
NORTON, P. R., Chemistry
PAYNE, N. C., Chemistry
PLINT, A. G., Earth Sciences
PODESTA, R. B., Biology
POTTER, P., History of Medicine (Head)
PROVOST, S., Statistical and Actuarial Sciences
PUDDEPHATT, R. J., Chemistry
RAY, A. K., Applied Mathematics
RENNER, L. E., Mathematics
RILEY, D. M., Mathematics
ROHANI, S., Applied Mathematics
ROSNER, S. D., Physics and Astronomy
RYLETT, R. J., Physiology and Pharmacology (Head)
SECCO, R. A., Earth Sciences
SHAM, T. K., Chemistry
SHAW, G. S., Biochemistry and Chemistry
SHOESMITH, D. W., Chemistry
SICA, R. J., Physics and Astronomy
SINGH, M. R., Physics and Astronomy
SINGH, S. M., Biology
STANFORD, D. A., Statistical and Actuarial Sciences
STILLMAN, M. J., Chemistry
TRICK, C. G., Biology
USSELMAN, M. C., Chemistry
VALVANO, M., Microbiology and Immunology (Head)
WATT, S., Computer Science
WEEDON, A. C., Chemistry
WORKENTIN, M. S., Chemistry
WREN, J. C., Chemistry
YU, P., Applied Mathematics
YU, S., Computer Science
ZHANG, K., Computer Science
ZINKE-ALLMANG, M., Physics and Astronomy

Faculty of Social Science (tel. (519) 661-2053; fax (519) 661-3868; internet www.ssc.uwo .ca):

ABELSON, D., American Studies (Joint Head)
ABELSON, D., Political Science (Head)
ALLAHAR, A., Sociology
ALLEN, N., Psychology
ASHMORE, P. E., Geography
AVERY, D. H., History
AVISON, W. R., Sociology
BEAUJOT, R. P., Sociology
BHATIA, K. B., Economics

BOYER, R. S., Economics
BURGESS, D. F., Economics
CAIN, D. P., Psychology
CARROLL, M., Sociology
CHEN, X., Psychology
CHHEM, R. K., Anthropology
CLARK, S., Sociology
CODE, W. R., Geography
CONNIDIS, I. A., Sociology
CÔTE, J. E., Sociology
CREIDER, C., Linguistics (Joint Head)
CREIDER, C. A., Anthropology (Head)
CYBULSKI, J. S., Anthropology
DARNELL, R., First Nations Studies (Joint Head)
DAVENPORT, P., Economics
DAVIES, J. B., Economics
ELLIS, C., Anthropology
EMERY, G., History
ESSAS, V., Psychology
FISHER, W. A., Psychology
FLEMING, K., Management and Organizational Studies (Head)
FLEMING, M., Political Science
FORSTER, B., History (Head)
GARDINER, M., Sociology
GOODALE, M., Psychology
GRABB, E. G., Sociology
GREEN, M. B., Geography
HAMPSON, E., Psychology
HARSHMAN, R., Psychology
HEAP, D., Linguistics (Joint Head)
HELE, K., First Nations Studies (Joint Head)
HERNANDEZ-SAENZ, L. M., Latin American Studies (Head)
HEWITT, W. E., Sociology
JOHNSTON, A., American Studies (Joint Head)
KATZ, A. N., Psychology
KAVALIERS, M., Psychology
KELLOW, M., International Relations (Head)
KING, R. H., Geography
KNIGHT, J., Economics
KUIPER, N. A., Psychology
LUCKMAN, B. H., Geography
LUPKER, S. J., Psychology
McBEAN, G., Geography, Political Science
McDOUGALL, J. N., Political Science
McQUILLAN, K., Sociology
McRAE, K., Psychology
MARTIN, R. A., Psychology
MAXIM, P. S., Sociology
MEYER, J. P., Psychology
MOLTO, J. E., Anthropology
MORAN, G., Psychology
NEUFELD, R. W. J., Psychology
OLSON, J. M., Psychology
OSSENKOPP, K.-P., Psychology (Head)
PAUNONEN, S. V., Psychology
PEREZ, A., Political Science
RIDDELL-DIXON, E., Political Science
ROBINSON, C. M. G. F., Economics
ROLLMAN, G. B., Psychology
RUSHTON, J. P., Psychology
SANCTON, A. B., Political Science
SELIGMAN, C., Psychology
SHATZMILLER, M., History
SHERRY, D., Psychology
SHRUBSOLE, D., Geography (Head)
SLIVINSKI, A., Economics (Head)
SMART, C. C., Geography
SORRENTINO, R. M., Psychology
SPENCE, M. W., Anthropology
TIMNEY, B. N., Psychology
VERNON, P. A., Psychology
VERNON, R. A., Political Science
WANG, J., Geography
WHALLEY, J., Economics
WHITE, C., Anthropology
WHITE, J., Sociology (Head)
WHITEHEAD, P. C., Sociology
WINTROBE, R. S., Economics
YOUNG, R. A., Political Science

Richard Ivey School of Business (tel. (519) 661-3485; e-mail info@ivey.uwo.ca; internet www.ivey.uwo.ca):

ATHANASSAKOS, G.
BEAMISH, P. W.
BELL, P. C.
CONKLIN, D. W.
DAWAR, N.
DEUTSCHER, T. H.
FISHER, R. J.
FOERSTER, S. R.
GANDZ, J.
HARDY, K. G.
HATCH, J. E.
HENDRICKS, K. B.
HIGGINS, C. A.
HOWELL, J. M.
KALYMON, B.
KONRAD, A. M.
ROTHSTEIN, M. G.
SCHAAN, J. L.
SHACKEL, D. S. J.
VAN DEN BOSCH, M. B.
WHITE, R. W.
WILSON, J. G.
WYNANT, L.

Schulich School of Medicine and Dentistry (tel. (519) 661-3459; internet www.med.uwo .ca):

ADAMS, P. C., Medicine
ALBORES, A., Physiology and Pharmacology
ANG, L. C., Pathology
ARNOLD, J. M. O., Medicine
AVISON, W. R., Paediatrics; Epidemiology and Biostatistics
BAILEY, S. I., Surgery
BALL, E. H., Biochemistry
BANTING, D. W., Dentistry
BARR, R. M., Medicine
BATTISTA, J. J., Oncology
BAUMAN, G., Oncology (Head)
BELL, D. A., Medicine
BEND, J. R., Pathology
BERTRAND, M. A., Obstetrics and Gynaecology
BLAKE, P. G., Medicine
BOLLI, P., Medicine
BORRIE, M. J., Medicine
BOUGHNER, D. R., Medicine
BOURNE, R. B., Surgery
BRANDL, C. J., Biochemistry
BRIDGER, W. A., Biochemistry
BROWN, J. B., Family Medicine
BROWN, J. D., Clinical Neurological Sciences
BROWN, J. E., Medicine
CANHAM, P. B., Medical Biophysics
CECHETTO, D. F., Anatomy and Cell Biology
CERNOVSKY, Z. Z., Psychiatry
CHACONAS, G., Biochemistry
CHAMBERS, A. F., Oncology
CHAN, F. P., Anatomy and Cell Biology
CHANG, D. C. H., Anaesthesia and Perioperative Medicine (Head)
CHERIAN, G. M., Pathology
CHHEM, R. K., Diagnostic Radiology and Nuclear Medicine
CIRIELLO, J., Physiology and Pharmacology
CLARK, W. F., Medicine
COLCLEUGH, R. G., Surgery
COOK, M. A., Physiology and Pharmacology
COOK, R. A., Biochemistry
COOKE, J. D., Physiology and Pharmacology
CORDY, P. E., Medicine
CUNNINGHAM, I. A., Diagnostic Radiology and Nuclear Medicine
DALEY, T. D., Pathology
DEKABAN, G. A., Microbiology and Immunology
DELOVITCH, T. L., Microbiology and Immunology
DENSTEDT, J. D., Surgery (Head)
DIXON, S. J., Physiology and Pharmacology

DONNER, A. P., Epidemiology and Biostatics
DREYER, J. F., Medicine
DRIEDGER, A. A., Medicine
DROST, D. J., Diagnostic Radiology and Nuclear Medicine
DUNN, S. D., Biochemistry
EDMONDS, M. W., Medicine
ELLIS, C. G., Medical Biophysics
FEIGHTNER, J. W., Family Medicine
FELDMAN, R. D., Medicine
FENSTER, A., Diagnostic Radiology and Nuclear Medicine
FERGUSON, G. G., Clinical Neurological Sciences
FINNIE, K. J. C., Medicine
FISHER, W. A., Medicine
FISMAN, S. N., Psychiatry (Head)
FLINTOFF, W., Microbiology and Immunology
FLUMERFELT, B. A., Anatomy and Cell Biology
FOWLER, P. J., Surgery
FRAHER, L. J., Medicine
FREEMAN, T., Family Medicine (Head)
FREWEN, T. C., Paediatrics (Head)
GAGNON, R., Obstetrics and Gynaecology
GARCIA, B. M., Pathology (Head)
GEORGE, C. F. P., Medicine
GERACE, R. V., Medicine
GILBERT, J. J., Pathology
GIROTTI, M. J., Surgery
GIRVAN, D. P., Surgery
GLOOR, G. B., Biochemistry
GOODALE, M. A., Physiology and Pharmacology
GRANT, C. W., Biochemistry
GUENTHER, L. C., Medicine
GUPTA, M. A., Psychiatry
HAASE, P., Anatomy and Cell Biology
HACHINSKI, V., Clinical Neurological Sciences
HAHN, A. F. G., Clinical Neurological Sciences
HAMMOND, J. R., Physiology and Pharmacology
HAMPSON, E., Psychiatry
HAN, V. K. M., Paediatrics
HANIFORD, D. B., Biochemistry
HARRIS, K. A., Surgery
HAYES, K. C., Physical Medicine and Rehabilitation
HEGELE, R. A., Medicine
HENNING, J. L., Physiology and Pharmacology
HERBERT, C. P., Family Medicine
HILL, D. J., Medicine
HOBBS, B. B., Diagnostic Radiology and Nuclear Medicine
HODSMAN, A. B., Medicine
HOFFMASTER, C. B., Family Medicine
HOLLIDAY, R. L., Surgery
HOLLOMBY, D. J., Medicine (Head)
HOOPER, P., Ophthalmology (Head)
HORE, J., Physiology and Pharmacology
HOWARD, J. M., Paediatrics
HRAMIAK, I. M., Medicine
HRYCYSHYN, A. W., Anatomy and Cell Biology
HUANG, G., Physiology and Pharmacology
HUFF, M. W., Medicine
HUMEN, D. P., Medicine
HUNTER, G. K., Dentistry
HURST, L. N., Surgery
JAFFE, P. G., Psychiatry
JAIN, S. C., Psychiatry
JAMIESON, D. G., Medicine
JEVNIKAR, A. M., Medicine
JOHNSON, C., Medicine
JOHNSON, K. C., Epidemiology and Biostatics
JONES, D. L., Physiology and Pharmacology
JUNG, J. H., Paediatrics
KANG, C. Y., Microbiology and Immunology
KARLIK, S. J., Diagnostic Radiology and Nuclear Medicine

KARMAZYN, M., Physiology and Pharmacology
KENNEDY, T. G., Physiology and Pharmacology
KIDDER, G. M., Physiology and Pharmacology
KIERNAN, J. A., Anatomy and Cell Biology
KING, G. J., Surgery
KIRK, M. E., Pathology
KLEIN, G. J., Medicine
KOGON, S. L., Dentistry
KOREN, G., Paediatrics; Medicine
KOROPATNICK, D. J., Oncology
KOSTUK, W. J., Medicine
KRONICK, J. B., Medicine
KVIETYS, P. R., Physiology
LAIRD, D. W., Anatomy and Cell Biology
LAJOIE, G., Biochemistry
LAMPE, H. B., Otolaryngology
LANNIGAN, R., Microbiology and Immunology
LEASA, D. J., Medicine
LEE, D. H., Diagnostic Radiology and Nuclear Medicine
LEE, T. Y., Diagnostic Radiology and Nuclear Medicine
LEFCOE, M. S., Diagnostic Radiology and Nuclear Medicine
LELLA, J. W., History of Medicine
LEUNG, L. W. S., Clinical Neurological Sciences
LEWIS, J. F., Medicine
LINDSAY, R. M., Medicine
LO, T. C., Biochemistry
LOWNIE, S., Clinical Neurological Sciences (Joint Head)
MCCARTHY, G. M., Dentistry
MCCORMACK, D. G., Medicine
MCDONALD, J. W., Medicine
MCFADDEN, D. G., Microbiology and Immunology
MCFADDEN, R. G., Medicine
MCGRATH, P. A., Paediatrics
MCKENZIE, F. N., Surgery
MCLACHLAN, R. S., Clinical Neurological Sciences
MACRAE, D. L., Otolaryngology (Joint Head)
MAO, Y., Epidemiology and Biostatics
MAROTTA, J. T., Clinical Neurological Sciences
MENDONCA, J., Psychiatry
MENKIS, A. H., Surgery
MILLWARD, S. F., Diagnostic Radiology and Nuclear Medicine
MORRIS, V. L., Microbiology
MUIRHEAD, J. M., Medicine
MURKIN, J. M., Anaesthesia and Perioperative Medicine
NARAYANAN, N., Physiology and Pharmacology
NATALE, R., Obstetrics and Gynaecology
NEUFELD, R. W. J., Psychiatry
NICHOLSON, R. L., Diagnostic Radiology and Nuclear Medicine
NICOLLE, D. A., Opthalmology
NISKER, J. A., Obstetrics and Gynaecology
NORMAN, R. M. G., Psychiatry
NORRIS, J. W., Clinical Neurological Sciences
NOVICK, R. J., Surgery
PARNES, L. S., Otolaryngology
PATERSON, N. A. M., Medicine
PAYTON, K. B., Medicine
PERSAD, E., Psychiatry
PETERS, T. M., Diagnostic Radiology and Nuclear Medicine
PETERSEN, N. O., Biochemistry
POTTER, P. M. J., History of Medicine and Science
POZNANSKY, M. J., Biochemistry
PRABHAKARAN, V. M., Biochemistry
PRATO, F. S., Diagnostic Radiology and Nuclear Medicine
RALLEY, F. E., Anaesthesia and Perioperative Medicine

RALPH, E. D., Medicine
RANKIN, R. N., Diagnostic Radiology and Nuclear Medicine (Head)
REID, G., Microbiology and Immunology
REYNOLDS, R. P., Medicine
RICE, G. P. A., Clinical Neurological Sciences
RICHARDSON, B. S., Obstetrics and Gynaecology (Head)
RIEDER, M J., Paediatrics
RODGER, N. W., Medicine
RORABECK, C. H., Surgery
ROTH, J. H., Surgery
RUTLEDGE, F. S., Medicine
RUTT, B. K., Diagnostic Radiology and Nuclear Medicine
RYLETT, R. J., Physiology and Pharmacology
SANDHU, H. S., Dentistry (Head)
SANGSTER, J. F., Family Medicine
SHAW, G. S., Biochemistry
SHERAR, M. D., Oncology
SHKRUM, M. J., Pathology
SHOUKRI, M. M., Epidemiology and Biostatics
SHUM, D. T. W., Pathology
SILCOX, J. A., Obstetrics and Gynaecology
SIMS, S. M., Physiology and Pharmacology
SINGH, B., Microbiology and Immunology
SINGHAL, S. K., Microbiology and Immunology
SOLIMAN, G. L., Medicine
SPENCE, J. D., Clinical Neurological Sciences
STEWART, M. A., Family Medicine
STILLER, C. R., Medicine
STRONG, M. J., Clinical Neurological Sciences (Joint Head)
TAVES, D. H., Diagnostic Radiology and Nuclear Medicine
TEASELL, R. W., Physical Medicine and Rehabilitation (Head)
TEPPERMAN, B. L., Physiology and Pharmacology
THOMPSON, R. T., Diagnostic Radiology and Nuclear Medicine
TRICK, C. G., Microbiology and Immunology
TYML, K., Medical Biophysics
URBAIN, J. L. C. P., Diagnostic Radiology and Nuclear Medicine
VALVANO, M. A., Microbiology and Immunology
VAN DYK, J., Oncology
VILIS, T., Physiology and Pharmacology
VILOS, G., Obstetrics and Gynaecology
VINGILIS, E. R., Family Medicine
WALL, W. J., Surgery
WEAVER, L. C., Physiology and Pharmacology
WESTON, W., Family Medicine
WEXLER, D., Medicine
WHITE, D. J., Surgery
WILLIAMSON, P. C., Psychiatry
WILLIS, N. R., Ophthalmology
WILSON, J. X., Physiology and Pharmacology
WISENBERG, G., Medicine
WRIGHT, E., Otolaryngology (Joint Head)
WRIGHT, J. G., Epidemiology and Biostatistics
WYSOCKI, G. P., Pathology
YANG, K., Obstetrics and Gynaecology
YEE, R., Medicine
YOUNG, G. B., Clinical Neurological Sciences
ZAMIR, M., Medical Biophysics
ZHONG, Z., Surgery

AFFILIATED INSTITUTIONS

Brescia University College: 1285 Western Rd, London, ON N6G 1H2; internet www.uwo.ca/brescia; f. 1919; arts subjects; Principal T. TOPIC

PROFESSORS

SNYDER, J., Philosophy
TOPIC, T., Anthropology

Huron University College: 1349 Western Rd, London, ON N6G 1H3; internet www .huronuc.on.ca; f. 1863; arts and theological college; Principal Dr R. LUMPKIN

PROFESSORS

BLOCKER, J. S., History
CRIMMINS, J. E., Political Science
HAMILTON, G., Theology
HYLAND, P., English
MCCARTHY, D. R., English
READ, C., History
SCHACHTER, J. P., Philosophy
XU, D., Economics

King University College: 266 Epworth Ave, London, ON N6A 2M3; e-mail kings@ uwo.ca; internet www.uwo.ca/kings; f. 1912 (Seminary), 1955 (College); seminary and college of arts; Principal Dr GERALD KILLAN

PROFESSORS

BAHCHELI, T., Political Science
BARUSS, I., Psychology
BROWN, H., Philosophy and Religious Studies
BROWN, J., Social Work
COMPTON-BROUWER, R., History
GORASSINI, D. R., Psychology
HARMAN, L., Sociology
IRVING, A., Social Work
KILLAN, G., History
KOPINAK, K., Sociology
LELLA, J. W., Sociology
MACGREGOR, D., Sociology
O'CONNOR, T., Religious Studies
PATERSON, G. H., English
PRIEUR, M. R., Religious Studies
SKINNER, N. F., Psychology
WERSTINE, P., English

WILFRID LAURIER UNIVERSITY

75 University Ave, Waterloo, ON N2L 3C5
Telephone: (519) 884-1970
Fax: (519) 886-9351
Internet: www.wlu.ca

Founded 1911; formerly Waterloo Lutheran University; name changed 1973
Language of instruction: English
State control
Academic year: September to April (2 terms)

Chancellor: BOB RAE
Pres. and Vice-Chancellor: Dr MAX BLOUW
Vice-Pres. for Academic Affairs: Dr DEBORAH MACLATCHY
Vice-Pres. for Finance and Admin.: JIM BUTLER
Registrar: Dr JOHN METCALFE
Librarian and Archivist: SHARON BROWN

Number of teachers: 838 (410 full-time, 428 part-time)
Number of students: 14,750 (12,700 full-time, 2,050 part-time)
Publications: *Anthropologica* (2 a year), *Canadian Bulletin of Medical History/ Bulletin Canadien D'histoire de la Médecine* (2 a year), *Canadian Social Work Review/Revue Canadienne de Service Social* (2 a Year), *Dialogue: Canadian Philosophical Review/Revue Canadienne de Philosophie* (4 a year), *Leisure/Loisive* (4 a year), *Studies in Religion/Sciences Religieuses* (4 a year), *Toronto Journal of Theology* (4 a year), *Topia: A Canadian Journal of Cultural Studies* (2 a year)

DEANS

Faculty of Arts and Science: Dr ROBERT CAMPBELL
Faculty of Graduate Studies: Dr ADELE REINHARTZ

Faculty of Music: Dr CHARLES MORRISON
Faculty of Science: Dr ARTHUR SZABO
Faculty of Social Work: Prof. LUKE FUSCO
School of Business and Economics: Dr SCOTT CARSON
Waterloo Lutheran Seminary: Dr RICHARD CROSSMAN

UNIVERSITY OF WINDSOR

Windsor, ON N9B 3P4
Telephone: (519) 253-3000
Fax: (519) 973-7050
E-mail: registr@uwindsor.ca
Internet: www.uwindsor.ca

Founded 1857
Provincially assisted
Language of instruction: English
Academic year: September to May (2 semesters)

Chancellor: Dr EDWARD LUMLEY
Vice-Chancellor and Pres.: Dr ALAN WILDEMAN
Vice-Pres. for Admin. and Finance: STEPHEN WILLETTS
Vice-Pres. for University Advancement: MICHAEL SALTER (acting)
Provost and Vice-Pres. for Academics: Prof. NEIL GOLD
Vice-Provost for Students and Registrar: Prof. BRIAN MAZER (acting)
Librarian: GWENDOLYN EBBETT

Number of teachers: 428 (full-time)
Number of students: 16,180 (full-time and part-time)
Publications: *Review*, *The Lance* (52 a year), *Windsor University Magazine* (4 a year)

DEANS

Faculty of Arts and Social Science: Dr CECIL HOUSTON
Faculty of Education: Dr PAT ROGERS
Faculty of Engineering: Dr GRAHAM T. READER
Faculty of Human Kinetics: Dr ROBERT BOUCHER
Faculty of Law: Prof. BRUCE ELMAN
Faculty of Nursing: Dr ELAINE DUFFY
Faculty of Science: Dr MARLYS KOSCHINSKY
Faculty of Graduate Studies and Research: Dr JIM FRANK
Odette School of Business: Dr ALLAN CONWAY

PROFESSORS

Faculty of Arts:

AMORE, R. C., Political Sciences
ATKINSON, C. B., English
BABE, R. E., Communication Studies
BALANCE, W. D., Psychology
BAXTER, I., Visual Arts
BÉLANGER, S., Visual Arts
BERTMAN, S., Classical Studies
BIRD, H. W., Classical Studies
BLAIR, J. A., Philosophy
BROOKS, S., Political Science
BROWN-JOHN, C. L., Political Science
BUTLER, E. G., Music
CASSANO, P., French
COHEN, J. S., Psychology
DEANGELIS, J. R., Visual Arts
DEVILLERS, J. P., French
DILWORTH, T. R., English
DITSKY, J. M., English
GOLD SMITH, S. B., Visual Arts
HANSON, J., Music
HAWKINS, F. R., Social Work
HOLOSKO, M. J., Social Work
HOUSEHOLDER, R., Music
KING, J. N., Religious Studies
KINGSTONE, B. D., French
KLINCK, D. M., History
LAKHAN, V. C., Geography
LINTON, J. M., Communication Studies
MCCRONE, K. E., History

MACKENDRICK, L. K., English
MADY KELLY, D., Dramatic Art
MURRAY, J., History
PAGE, J. S., Psychology
PALMER, D., Music
PHIPPS, A. G., Geography
PINNELL, W. H., Dramatic Art
REYNOLDS, D. V., Psychology
ROMSA, G. H., Geography
ROURKE, B. P., Psychology
SCHNEIDER, F. W., Psychology
SODERLUND, W. C., Political Science
STARETS, M., French
STEBELSKY, I., Geography
TRENHAILE, A. S., Geography
VAN DEN HOVEN, A., French
WARREN, B., Dramatic Art
WHITNEY, B., Religious Studies
WINTER, J. P., Communication Studies

Faculty of Education:

CRAWFORD, W. J. I.
KUENDIGER, E.
LAING, D. A.
MORTON, L.
WILLIAMS, N. H.

Faculty of Engineering:

AHMADI, M., Electrical Engineering
ALFA, A. S., Industrial Engineering and Manufacturing Systems Engineering
ALPAS, A. T., Mechanical, Automotive and Materials Engineering
ASFOUR, A. A., Civil and Environmental Engineering
BEWTRA, J. K., Civil and Environmental Engineering
BISWAS, N., Civil and Environmental Engineering
BUDKOWSKA, B. B., Cultural and Environmental Engineering
DUTTA, S. P., Industrial Engineering and Manufacturing Systems Engineering
EL MARAGHY, H., Industrial Engineering and Manufacturing Systems Engineering
EL MARAGHY, W., Industrial Engineering and Manufacturing Systems Engineering
FRISE, P. R., Mechanical, Automotive and Materials Engineering
HEARN, N., Civil and Environmental Engineering
KWAN, H. K., Electrical Engineering
LASHKARI, R. S., Industrial Engineering and Manufacturing Systems Engineering
MADUGULA, M. K. S., Civil and Environmental Engineering
MILLER, W. C., Electrical Engineering
NORTH, W., Mechanical, Automotive and Materials Engineering
RAJU, G. R. G., Electrical Engineering
RANKIN, G. W., Mechanical, Automotive and Materials Engineering
READER, G. T., Mechanical, Automotive and Materials Engineering
SID-AHMED, M., Electrical Engineering
SOLTIS, J., Electrical Engineering
TABOUN, S., Industrial Engineering and Manufacturing Systems Engineering
WANG, H., Industrial Engineering and Manufacturing Systems Engineering
WATT, D. F., Mechanical, Automotive and Materials Engineering
WILSON, N. W., Mechanical, Automotive and Materials Engineering

Faculty of Human Kinetics:

BOUCHER, R. L., Athletics and Recreational Studies
MARINO, W., Kinesiology
OLAFSON, G. A., Kinesiology
SALTER, M. A., Kinesiology
WEESE, W. J., Kinesiology

Faculty of Law:

BERRYMAN, J.

BOGART, W. A.
BUSHNELL, I. S.
CARASCO, E. F.
CONKLIN, W.
ELMAN, B.
GOLD, N.
IRISH, M.
MAZER, B. M.
MENEZES, J. R.
MOON, R. J.
MURPHY, P. T.
STEWART, G. R.
WEST, J. L.
WILSON, L. C.
WYDRZYNSKI, C. J.

Faculty of Science
(Some professors are also attached to the Faculty of Engineering)

AL-AASM, I. S., Earth Sciences
ANGLIN, P., Economics
AROCA, R., Chemistry and Biochemistry
ATKINSON, J. B., Physics
BANDYOPADHYAY, S., Computer Science
BARRON, R. M., Mathematics and Statistics
BAYLIS, W. E., Physics
BRITTEN, D. J., Mathematics and Statistics
CAMERON, W. S., Nursing
CARON, R. J., Mathematics and Statistics
CARTY, L., Nursing
CHANDNA, O. P., Mathematics and Statistics
CIBOROWSKI, J. J. H., Biological Sciences
COTTER, D. A., Biological Sciences
DRAKE, G. W., Physics
DRAKE, J. E., Chemistry and Biochemistry
FACKRELL, H. B., Biological Sciences
FAN, Y., Economics
FORTUNE, J. N., Economics
FROST, R. A., Computer Science
FUNG, K. Y., Mathematics and Statistics
GENCAY, R., Economics
GILLEN, W. J., Economics
GLASS, E. N., Physics
HAFFNER, G. D., Biological Sciences
HUDEC, P. P., Earth Sciences
KALONI, P. N., Mathematics and Statistics
KENT, R. D., Computer Science
LEMIRE, F. W., Mathematics and Statistics
LOEB, S. J., Chemistry and Biochemistry
LOVETT DOUST, J. N., Biological Sciences
LOVETT DOUST, L., Biological Sciences
McCONKEY, J. W., Physics
McDONALD, J. F., Mathematics and Statistics
McINTOSH, J. M., Chemistry and Biochemistry
MacISAAC, H. J., Biological Sciences
MAEV, R. G., Physics
MUTUS, B., Chemistry and Biochemistry
PAUL, S. R., Mathematics and Statistics
SALE, P. F., Biological Sciences
SIMPSON, F., Earth Sciences
SMITH, T. E., Earth Sciences
STEPHAN, D. W., Chemistry and Biochemistry
STRICK, J. C., Economics
SUH, S. C., Economics
TAYLOR, N. F., Chemistry and Biochemistry
THOMAS, B. C., Nursing
THOMAS, D., Biological Sciences
TRACY, D. S., Mathematics and Statistics
TUREK, A., Earth Sciences
WARNER, A., Biological Sciences
WONG, C. S., Mathematics and Statistics
ZAMANI, N. G., Mathematics and Statistics

Odette School of Business Administration:
ANDIAPPAN, P.
ANEJA, Y. P.
ARMSTRONG-STASSEN, M.
BRILL, P. H.
CHANDRA, R.
DICKINSON, J. R.

FARIA, A. J.
FIELDS, M.
HUSSEY, R.
KANTOR, J.
LAM, W. P.
MORGAN, A.
OKECHUKU, C.
PUNNETT, B. J.
SINGH, J.
TEMPLER, A.
THACKER, J. W.
WITHANE, S.

FEDERATED UNIVERSITY
Assumption University: 400 Huron Church Rd, Windsor, ON; Pres. Rev. U. E. PARÉ.

AFFILIATED COLLEGES
Canterbury College: 172 Patricia Rd, Windsor, ON; Principal D. T. A. SYMONS.
Holy Redeemer College: Cousineau Rd, Windsor, ON; Principal Rev. R. CORRIVEAU.
Iona College: Sunset Ave, Windsor, ON; Principal Rev. D. G. GALSTON.

UNIVERSITY OF WINNIPEG

515 Portage Ave, Winnipeg, MB R3B 2E9
Telephone: (204) 786-7811
Fax: (204) 786-8656
Internet: www.uwinnipeg.ca
Founded 1871; University status 1967
Controlled jointly by the Government of Manitoba and the United Church of Canada
Language of instruction: English
Academic year: September to April
Chancellor: H. SANDFORD RILEY
Vice-Chancellor and Pres.: LLOYD AXWORTHY
Vice-Pres. for Academic Affairs: BRIAN STEVENSON (acting)
Vice-Pres. for Finance and Admin.: BILL BALAN
University Sec.: R. A. KINGSLEY
Dir of Registrarial Services: N. LATOCKI
Librarian: W. R. CONVERSE
Number of teachers: 232
Number of students: 9,010 (6,230 full-time; 2,780 part-time)

DEANS
Faculty of Arts: DAVID FITZPATRICK
Faculty of Business and Economics: MICHAEL BENARROCH
Faculty of Continuing Education: ERIN STEWART
Faculty of Education: KEN McCLUSKEY
Faculty of Science: RODNEY HANLEY
Faculty of Theology: JAMES CHRISTIE
The Collegiate: ROBERT BEND

PROFESSORS
ABD-EL-AZIZ, Chemistry
ABIZADEH, S., Economics
BAILEY, D. A., History
BASILEVSKY, A., Statistics
BECKER, G., Psychology
BOTTERILL, C., Sport Psychology
BRADBURY, H., Psychology
BROWN, J., History
BROWN, W., Economics
BURLEY, D., History
CARLYLE, W. J., Geography
CARTER, T., Geography
CHAN, F. Y., Business Computing
CHEAL, D. J., Sociology
CLARK, J., Psychology
CLOUTIS, E., Geography
DANNEFAER, S., Physics
DAY, P., Religious Studies
DONG, X.-Y., Economics
EVANS, M., English
FEHR, B., Psychology

FORBES, S., Biology
FRIESEN, K., Chemistry
GINSBERG, J., Mathematics
GOLDEN, M., Classics
GRANT, H., Economics
GRANZBERG, G., Anthropology
GREENHILL, P., Women's Studies
HARVEY, C. J., French Studies
HATHOUT, S., Geography
HOWLADER, H., Statistics
HUEBNER, J., Biology
IZYDORCZYK, Z., English
KERR, D. P., Physics
KHAN, R. A., Political Science
KOBES, R., Physics
KUNSTATTER, G., Physics
KYDON, D. W., Physics
LEHR, J., Geography
LEO, C., Political Science
McCORMACK, A. R., History
McCORMACK, R., History
McDOUGALL, I., Classics
McINTYRE, M., Psychology
MAYS, A., Education
MEADWELL, K., French Studies
MEIKLEJOHN, C., Anthropology
MILLS, A., Political Science, Anthropology
MOODIE, G. E. E., Biology
NNADI, J., French Studies
NODELMAN, P. M., English
NORTON, R., Psychology
NOVEK, J., Sociology
PARAMESWARAN, U., English
PEELING, J., Chemistry
PIP, E., Biology
POLYZOI, E., Education
RANNIE, W., Geography
ROCKMAN, G., Psychology
RODRIGUEZ, L., French
SCHAEFER, E., Psychology
SCOTT, G., Geography
SELWOOD, J., Geography
SPIGELMAN, M., Psychology
STANIFORTH, R., Biology
STONE, D. Z., History
STRUB, H., Psychology
TOMCHUK, E., Physics
TOMLINSON, G., Chemistry
VISELLI, S., French Studies
WIEGAND, M., Biology
WRIGHT, C., Political Science
YOUNG, R. J., History

ATTACHED INSTITUTES
Institute of Urban Studies: 515 Portage Ave, Winnipeg; Dir JINO DISTASIO.
Menno Simons College: 515 Portage Ave, Winnipeg; Pres. EARL DAVEY.

YORK UNIVERSITY

4700 Keele St, Toronto, ON M3J 1P3
Telephone: (416) 736-2100
Fax: (416) 736-5700
Internet: www.yorku.ca
Founded 1959, independent 1965
Public control
Language of instruction: English (Glendon College: English and French)
Academic year: September to April
Chancellor: ROY McMURTRY
President and Vice-Chancellor: MAMDOUH SHOUKRI
President and CEO York University Foundation and Vice-President (Development): PAUL MARCUS
Vice-President for Academics: SHEILA EMBLETON
Vice-President for Finance and Administration: GARY BREWER
Vice-President for Research and Innovation: STAN SHAPSON
Vice-President for Students and Alumni: ROBERT J. TIFFIN
Univ. Sec. and Gen. Counsel: HARRIET LEWIS

Number of teachers: 1,415 (full-time)
Number of students: 52,290
Publications: *Profiles* (4 a year), *York Gazette* (37 a year)

DEANS

Faculty of Education: ALICE PITT
Faculty of Environmental Studies: BARBARA RAHDER (acting)
Faculty of Fine Arts: BARBRA SELLERS-YOUNG
Faculty of Liberal Arts and Professional Studies: MARTIN SINGER
Faculty of Pure and Applied Science: GILLIAN E. WU
Faculty of Graduate Studies: DOUGLAS PEERS
Osgoode Hall Law School: PATRICK J. MONAHAN
Schulich School of Business: DEZSO HORVATH
Glendon College: KENNETH MCROBERTS (Principal)

PROFESSORS

Faculty of Education:

BRITZMAN, D. P.
BUNCH, G.
EWOLDT, C.
HESHUSIUS, L.
PIPER, T. C.
ROGERS, P. K.
SHAPSON, S.

Faculty of Environmental Studies:

BELL, D. V. J.
DALY, G. P.
FOUND, W. C.
GREER-WOOTTEN, B.
HOMENUCK, H. P. M.
SPENCE, E. S.
VICTOR, P. A.
WEKERLE, G. R.
WILKINSON, P. F.

Faculty of Fine Arts:

BIELER, T., Visual Arts
MÉTRAUX, G. P. R., Visual Arts
MORRIS, P., Film and Video
RUBIN, D., Theatre
SANKARAN, T., Music
TENNEY, J., Music
THURLBY, M., Visual Arts
TOMCIK, A., Visual Arts
WHITEN, T., Visual Arts

Faculty of Liberal Arts and Professional Studies:

ABRAMSON, M., Mathematics and Statistics
ADELMAN, H., Philosophy
ANISEF, P., Sociology
APPELBAUM, E., Economics
ARMSTRONG, C., History
ARMSTRONG, P., Sociology
ARTHUR, R. G., Humanities
AXELROD, P., Social Science
BARTEL, H., Administrative Studies
BAYEFSKY, A. F., Political Science
BEER, F. F., English
BIALYSTOK, E., Psychology
BIRBALSINGH, F. M., English
BLUM, A. F., Sociology
BORDESSA, R., Geography
BROWN, M. G., Humanities
BURNS, R. G., Mathematics and Statistics
BUTLER, G. R., Humanities
CALLAGHAN, B., English
CARLEY, J., English
CHAMBERS, D., Physical Education
CODE, L. B., Philosophy
COHEN, D., English
COTNAM, J., French Studies
COWLES, M. P., Psychology
CUFF, R. D., History
CUMMINGS, M. J., English
DANZIGER, L., Economics
DARROCH, A. G. L., Sociology
DAVIES, D. I., Social Science and Sociology
DAVIS, C. A., Physical Education
DEWITT, D. B., Political Science

DONNENFELD, S., Economics
DOSMAN, E. J., Political Science
DOW, A. S., Mathematics and Statistics
DRACHE, D., Political Science
DROST, H., Economics
EGNAL, M. M., History
EHRLICH, S. L., Languages, Literatures and Linguistics
ELLENWOOD, W. R., English
EMBLETON, S. M., Languages, Literatures and Linguistics
ENDLER, N. S., Psychology
FAAS, E., Humanities
FANCHER, R. E., Psychology
FICHMAN, M., Humanities
FLEMING, S. J., Psychology
FLETCHER, F. J., Political Science
FLETT, G. L., Psychology
FOWLER, B. H., Physical Education
FREEMAN, D. B., Geography
FROLIC, M. B., Political Science
GILL, S., Political Science
GLEDHILL, N., Physical Education
GRAY, P. T., Humanities
GRAYSON, J. P., Sociology
GREEN, B. S., Sociology
GREEN, L. J. M., Philosophy
GREENBERG, L., Psychology
GREENGLASS, E. R., Psychology
GREER-WOOTTEN, B., Geography
GUIASU, S., Mathematics and Statistics
GUY, G. R., Languages, Literatures and Linguistics
HABERMAN, A., Humanities
HARRIES-JONES, P., Anthropology
HARRIS, L. R., Psychology
HATTIANGADI, J. N., Philosophy
HEIDENREICH, C., Geography
HELLMAN, J., Political Science and Social Science
HELLMAN, S., Political Science
HERREN, M., Classics and Humanities
HILL, A. R., Geography
HOBSON, D. B., Humanities
HOFFMAN, R. C., History
HRUSKA, K. C., Mathematics and Statistics
INNES, C., English
IRVINE, W. D., History
JARVIE, I. C., Philosophy
KANYA-FORSTNER, A. S., History
KAPLAN, H., Political Science and Social Science
KATER, M. H., History
KATZ, E., Economics
KING, R. E., Languages, Literatures and Linguistics
KLEINER, I., Mathematics and Statistics
KOCHMAN, S. O., Mathematics and Statistics
KOHN, P. M., Psychology
LANDA, J. T., Economics
LANPHIER, C. M., Sociology
LENNOX, J. W., English
LEVY, J., Nursing
LEYTON-BROWN, D., Political Science
LIGHTMAN, B. V., Humanities
LIPSIG-MUMMÉ, C., Social Science
LOVEJOY, P. E., History
LUXTON, M., Social Science
MCROBERTS, K. H., Political Science
MADRAS, N. N., Mathematics and Statistics
MAHANEY, W. C., Geography
MAIDMAN, M. P., History
MALLIN, S. B., Philosophy
MANN, S. N., History
MASON, S. N., Humanities
MASSAM, B. H., Geography
MASSAM, H., Mathematics and Statistics
MENDELSOHN, D. J., Languages, Literatures and Linguistics
MOUGEON, R., French Studies
MULDOON, M. E., Mathematics and Statistics
MURDIE, R. A., Geography

NAGATA, J., Anthropology
NELLES, H. V., History
NOBLE, D., Social Science
NORCLIFFE, G. B., Geography
NORTH, L., Political Science
O'BRIEN, G. L., Mathematics and Statistics
OKADA, R., Psychology
OLIN, P., Mathematics and Statistics
OLIVER, P. N., History
ONO, H., Psychology
PANITCH, L., Political Science
PELLETIER, J. M., Mathematics and Statistics
PEPLER, D. J., Psychology
PLOURDE, C., Economics
POLKA, B., Humanities
POPE, R. W. F., Languages, Literatures and Linguistics
PROMISLOW, S. D., Mathematics and Statistics
PYKE, S., Psychology
RADFORD, J. P., Geography
REGAN, D. M., Psychology
RENNIE, D. L., Psychology
ROBBINS, S. G., Physical Education
RODMAN, M. C., Anthropology
ROGERS, N. C. T., History
SALISBURY, T., Mathematics and Statistics
SAUL, J. S., Social Science
SHANKER, S. G., Philosophy
SHTEIR, A. B., Humanities
SHUBERT, A., History
SILVERMAN, M., Anthropology
SIMMONS, H., Political Science
SIMPSON-HOUSLEY, P., Geography
SMITHIN, J. N., Economics
SOLITAR, D., Mathematics and Statistics
STAGER, P., Psychology
STEINBACH, M. J., Psychology
STEPRANS, J., Mathematics and Statistics
SUBTELNY, O., History and Political Science
THOLEN, W., Mathematics and Statistics
UNRAU, J. P., English
VAN ESTERIK, P., Anthropology
WAKABAYASHI, B. T., History
WATSON, W. S., Mathematics and Statistics
WEISS, A. I., Computer Science and Mathematics
WHITAKER, R., Political Science
WHITELEY, W. J., Mathematics and Statistics
WILSON, B. A., Humanities
WONG, M., Mathematics and Statistics
WOOD, J. D., Geography
WU, J., Mathematics and Statistics

Faculty of Pure and Applied Science:

ALDRIDGE, K. D., Earth and Atmospheric Science
ARJOMANDI, E., Computer Science
BARTEL, N. H., Physics and Astronomy
BOHME, D. K., Chemistry
CAFARELLI, E. D., Physical Education
CALDWELL, J. J., Natural Science, Physics and Astronomy
CANNON, W. H., Physics and Astronomy
COLMAN, B., Biology
COUKELL, M. B., Biology
DAREWYCH, J. W., Physics and Astronomy
DAVEY, K. G., Biology
DE ROBERTIS, M. M., Physics and Astronomy
DYMOND, P. W., Computer Science
FENTON, M. B., Biology and Environmental Science
FILSETH, S. V., Chemistry
FORER, A., Biology
FREEDHOFF, H. S., Physics and Astronomy
GLEDHILL, N., Physical Education
GOODINGS, J. M., Chemistry
HARRIS, G. W., Chemistry
HASTIE, D. R., Chemistry
HEATH, I. B., Biology
HEDDLE, J. A. M., Biology

HILLIKER, A. J., Biology
HOLLOWAY, C. E., Chemistry
HOOD, D. A., Physical Education
HOPKINSON, A. C., Chemistry
HORBATSCH, M., Physics and Astronomy
INNANEN, K. A., Physics and Astronomy
JARRELL, R. A., Natural Science
JARVIS, G. T., Earth and Atmospheric Science
KONIUK, R., Physics and Astronomy
LAFRAMBOISE, J. G., Physics and Astronomy
LEE-RUFF, E., Chemistry
LEVER, A. B. P., Chemistry
LEZNOFF, C. C., Chemistry
LICHT, L. E., Biology and Environmental Science
LIU, J. W. H., Computer Science
LOGAN, D. M., Biology and Natural Science
LOUGHTON, B. G., Biology
McCALL, M., Physics and Astronomy
McCONNELL, J. C., Earth and Atmospheric Science
McQUEEN, D. J., Biology and Environmental Science
MALTMAN, K. R., Mathematics and Statistics
MILLER, J. R., Physics and Astronomy
PACKER, L. D. M., Biology
PEARLMAN, R. E., Biology
PRINCE, R. H., Physics and Astronomy
RUDOLPH, J., Chemistry
SALEUDDIN, A. S. M., Biology
SAPP, J. A., Biology
SHEPHERD, G. G., Earth and Atmospheric Science
SIU, K. W. M., Chemistry
SMYLIE, D. E., Earth and Atmospheric Science
STAUFFER, A. D., Mathematics and Statistics, Physics and Astronomy
STEEL, C. G., Biology
TAYLOR, P. A., Earth and Atmospheric Science
TOURLAKIS, G., Computer Science
TSOTSOS, J. K., Computer Science
WEBB, R. A., Biology

Osgoode Hall Law School:
ARTHURS, H. W.
BROOKS, W. N.
GEVA, B.
GRAY, R. J. S.
HASSON, R. A.
HATHAWAY, J. C.
HOGG, P. W.
HUTCHINSON, A. C.
McCAMUS, J. D.
MANDEL, M. G.
MONAHAN, P. J.
MOSSMAN, M. J.
RAMSAY, I. D.
SALTER, R. L.
SLATTERY, B.
VAVER, D.
WATSON, G. D.
WILLIAMS, S. A.
ZEMANS, F. H.

Schulich School of Business:
BURKE, R. J., Organizational Behaviour, Industrial Relations
BUZACOTT, J., Management Science
COOK, W. D., Management Science
CRAGG, A. W., Business Ethics
DERMER, J. D., Policy
FENWICK, I. D., Marketing
HEELER, R. M., Marketing
HORVATH, D., Policy
LITVAK, I. A., Policy
McKELLAR, J., Real Property Development
McMILLAN, C. J., Policy
MORGAN, G. H., Organizational Behaviour, Industrial Relations
OLIVER, C. E., Organizational Behaviour, Industrial Relations
PAN, Y., International Business

PETERSON, R., Policy
PRISMAN, E., Finance
ROBERTS, G. S., Finance
ROSEN, L. S., Accounting
THOMPSON, D. N., Marketing
TRYFOS, P., Management Science
WHEELER, D. C., Business and Sustainability
WILSON, H. T., Policy
WOLF, B. M., Economics

Glendon College:
ABELLA, I. M., History
ALCOCK, J., Psychology
BAUDOT, A., French Studies
DOOB, P. B., English
GENTLES, I. J., History
HORN, M. S. D., History
KIRSCHBAUM, S. J., Political Science
KLEIN-LATAUD, C., Translation
MAHANT, E., Political Science
MORRIS, R. N., Sociology
MOYAL, G. J. D., Philosophy
OLSHEN, B. N., English and Multidisciplinary Studies
ONDAATJE, P. M., English
SHAND, G. B., English
TATILON, C., French Studies
TWEYMAN, S., Philosophy
WALLACE, R. S., English
WHITFIELD, A., Translation

ATTACHED INSTITUTES

Canadian Centre for German and European Studies: 230 York Lanes, York University, 4700 Keele St, Toronto, ON M3J 1P3; Dir J. PECK.

Centre for Atmospheric Chemistry: 006 Steacie Science, York University, 4700 Keele St, Toronto, ON M3J 1P3; Dir G. W. HARRIS.

Centre for Feminist Research: 228 York Lanes, York University, 4700 Keele St, Toronto, ON M3J 1P3; Dir D. KHAYATT.

Centre for Health Studies: 214 York Lanes, York University, Toronto, ON M3J 1P3; Dir G. D. FELDBERG.

Centre for International and Security Studies: 375 York Lanes, York University, 4700 Keele St, Toronto, ON M3J 1P3; Dir D. B. DEWITT.

Centre for Jewish Studies: 260 Vanier College, York University, 4700 Keele St, Toronto, ON M3J 1P3; Dir M. G. BROWN.

Centre for Practical Ethics: 102 McLaughlin, York University, 4700 Keele St, Toronto, ON M3J 1P3; Dir D. SHUGARMAN.

Centre for Public Law and Public Policy: 435 Osgoode, York University, 4700 Keele St, Toronto, ON M3J 1P3; Dir P. J. MONAHAN.

Centre for Refugee Studies: 322 York Lanes, York University, 4700 Keele St, Toronto, ON M3J 1P3; Dir P. PENZ.

Centre for Research in Earth and Space Science: 249 Petrie Science Building, York University, 4700 Keele St, Toronto, ON M3J 1P3; Dir G. SHEPHERD.

Centre for Research on Latin America and the Caribbean: 240 York Lanes, York University, Toronto, ON M3J 1P3; Dir V. PATRONI.

Centre for Research on Work and Society: 276 York Lanes, York University, Toronto, ON M3J 1P3; Dir C. LIPSIG-MUMMÉ.

Centre for the Study of Computers in Education: S869 Ross, York University, 4700 Keele St, Toronto, ON M3J 1P3; Dir R. D. OWSTON.

Centre for Vision Research: 103 Farquharson, York University, 4700 Keele St, Toronto, ON M3J 1P3; Dir J. TSOTSOS.

Joint Centre for Asia Pacific Studies: 270 York Lanes, York University, 4700 Keele St, Toronto, ON M3J 1P3; Dir B. FROLIC.

LaMarsh Centre for Research on Violence and Conflict Resolution: 217 York Lanes, York University, 4700 Keele St, Toronto, ON M3J 1P3; Dir D. J. PEPLER.

Nathanson Centre for the Study of Organized Crime and Corruption: 321A Osgoode, York University, 4700 Keele St, Toronto, ON M3J 1P3; Dir M. BEARE.

Robarts Centre for Canadian Studies: 227 York Lanes, York University, 4700 Keele St, Toronto, ON M3J 1P3; Dir D. DRACHE.

York Centre for Applied Sustainability: 355 Lumbers, York University, 4700 Keele St, Toronto, ON M3J 1P3; Dir D. BELL.

York Institute for Social Research: 242A Schulich School of Business, York University, 4700 Keele St, Toronto, ON M3J 1P3; Dir M. ORNSTEIN.

Schools of Art and Music

Alberta College of Art and Design: 1407 14th Ave NW, Calgary, AB T2N 4R3; tel. (403) 284-7600; fax (403) 289-6682; e-mail admissions@acad.ca; internet www.acad.ab .ca; f. 1926; 100 teachers; 1,000 students; library: 28,578 vols and collection of 124,845 slides, 75 periodical titles; 4-year Degree and Diploma programmes in Visual Arts and Design; Pres. LANCE CARLSON.

Banff Centre: POB 1020, Banff, AB T1L 1H5; tel. (403) 762-6100; fax (403) 762-6444; internet www.banffcentre.ca; f. 1933; offers programmes in arts (aboriginal arts, audio, press, new media, creative electronic environment, dance, media and visual arts, music, opera, theatre, writing, curatorial practice), leadership development, aboriginal leadership and management, mountain culture, environmental issues; Pres. and CEO MARY E. HOFSTETTER; Senior Vice-President, Programming JOANNE MORROW; Vice-President and CFO J. A NUTT.

Conservatoire de Musique de Montréal: 4750 ave Henri-Julien, Montréal, QC H2T 2C8; tel. (514) 873-4031; fax (514) 873-4601; e-mail cmm@mcc.gouv.qc.ca; internet www .mcc.gouv.ca/conservatoire/montreal.htm; f. 1942; a government-controlled institution, largest of a network of 7 in Québec Province; 76 teachers; 340 students; library: 58,000 books and scores, 125 rare books, 20 MSS, 10,000 recordings and 80 periodicals; Dir ISOLDE LAGACÉ.

Conservatoire de Musique de Québec: 270 rue St-Amable, Québec, QC G1R 5G1; tel. (418) 643-2190; fax (418) 644-9658; e-mail cmq@mcc.gouv.qc.ca; internet www .mcc.gouv.gc.ca/conservatoire/quebec.htm; f. 1944; 50 teachers; 250 students; library: 68,000 vols, recordings, scores and periodicals; Dir GUY CARMICHAEL.

Maritime Conservatory of Performing Arts: 6199 Chebucto Rd, Halifax, NS B3L 1K7; tel. (902) 423-6995; fax (902) 423-6029; e-mail mconservatory@ns.sympatico.ca; f. 1887; 80 teachers; 1,200 students; Dir Dr IFAN WILLIAMS.

Ontario College of Art and Design: 100 McCaul St, Toronto, ON M5T 1W1; tel. (416) 977-6000; fax (416) 977-6006; internet www .ocad.on.ca; f. 1876; library: 24,000 vols, 225 periodical subscriptions, 44,000 pictures, 70,000 slides, etc.; post-secondary education in fine art and design; 200 teachers; 2,329 students; Pres. RON SHUEBROOK; Exec. Vice-Pres. PETER CALDWELL; Financial Aids and Awards Officer KELLY DICKINSON; Dir of Library JILL PATRICK.

Royal Canadian College of Organists: 204 St George St, Suite 204, Toronto, ON M5R 2N5; tel. (416) 929-6400; fax (416) 929-

2265; e-mail rcco@the-wire.com; internet www.rcco.ca; f. 1909; Pres. F. ALAN REESOR; Vice-Pres. PATRICIA WRIGHT; Treas. DON TIMMINS; publs *Organ Canada* (4 a year), *The American Organist* (12 a year, in asscn with American Guild of Organists).

Royal Conservatory of Music: 273 Bloor St West, Toronto ON M5S 1W2; tel. (416) 408-2824; fax (416) 408-3096; e-mail communityschool@rcmusic.ca; internet www .rcmusic.ca; f. 1886; 350 teachers; 10,000 students; Pres. PETER C. SIMON; Deans JEFF MELANSON, RENNIE REGEHR.

CAPE VERDE

The Higher Education System

Cape Verde has little history of higher education. During five centuries of colonial rule in the archipelago Portugal did not draft any known plans for the establishment of a university for Cape Verde. After independence the number of students enrolled in secondary education increased markedly, and the demand for higher education began to be addressed with the creation of several institutes of higher studies to train teachers and health workers. Most Cape Verdeans studied abroad; in 2002/03 there were 1,743 Cape Verdean students studying at overseas universities. However, the cost of foreign study was high. Thus, as domestic demand increased throughout the 1990s, more concrete plans were made for establishing a university. The Universidade Jean Piaget de Cabo Verde was founded in 2002; in 2005/06 there were 4,567 students in higher education. There is also a higher institute of engineering and marine science, and in 2007 the first professional training centre for mechanics, metalworkers, plumbers, and electricians was opened.

Regulatory Bodies

GOVERNMENT

Ministry of Culture: Praia, Santiago; tel. 261-05-67; Minister MANUEL MONTEIRO DA VEIGA.

Ministry of Education and Higher Education: Palácio do Governo, Várzea, CP 111, Praia, Santiago; tel. 261-05-09; fax 261-27-64; internet www.minedu.cv; Minister FILOMENA DE FÁTIMA RIBEIRO VIEIRA MARTINS.

Learned Society

LANGUAGE AND LITERATURE

Alliance Française: Rua de Santo Antonio, CP 37, Mindelo; tel. 232-11-49; fax 232-11-48; e-mail afmsvcapvert@cvtelecom.cv; internet www.afmindelo.n3.net; offers courses and exams in French language and culture and promotes cultural exchange with France.

Research Institute

ECONOMICS, LAW AND POLITICS

Instituto Nacional de Estatistica de Cabo Verde (Cape Verde National Statistical Institute): CP 116, Praia, Santiago; tel. 261-38-27; e-mail inecv@mail.telecom.cv;

internet www.ine.cv; Pres. FRANCISCO FERNANDES TORRES.

Library

Praia

Biblioteca de Assembleia Nacional (National Assembly Library): Achada de Santo António, CP 20-A, Praia, Santiago; tel. 262-32-90; fax 262-26-60; internet www.parlamento.cv/biblioteca; f. 1985; 5,000 vols, 100 periodicals; Dir ALBERTINA GRAÇA.

University

UNIVERSIDADE JEAN PIAGET DE CABO VERDE

Campus Universitário da Cidade da Praia, CP 775, Cidade de Praia, Santiago

Telephone: 262-90-85
Fax: 262-90-89
E-mail: info@caboverde.ipiaget.cv
Internet: www.unipiaget.cv

Founded 2001; attached to Instituto Piaget, Portugal
Academic year: October to July

Rector: Prof. Dr ESTELA PINTO RIBEIRA LAMAS
Vice-Rector: Prof. Dr JORGE SOUSA BRITO

Gen. Administrator: Prof. Dr DAVID RIBEIRO LAMAS

Number of teachers: 50
Number of students: 650

Courses in architecture, business information, chemistry and physics teaching, civil construction engineering, communications science, hotel and tourism management, education science, economics and management, English language and literature teaching, information systems and engineering, mathematics teaching, nursing, pharmaceutical sciences, physiotherapy, professional education, Portuguese language and literature teaching psychology, sociology.

College

Instituto Superior de Engenharia e Ciências do Mar (ISECMAR) (Higher Institute of Engineering and Marine Science): CP 163, Ribeira de Julião, São Vicente; tel. 232-65-61; fax 232-65-63; e-mail info@isecmar.cv; internet www.isecmar.cv; f. 1984; depts of electrical and mechanical engineering, electronic and computer engineering, marine biology and aquatic research, natural and human sciences, nautical sciences; Pres. ELISA FERREIRA SILVA.

CENTRAL AFRICAN REPUBLIC

The Higher Education System

Until the late 1960s higher education was closely linked to the former colonial power, France, from which the Central African Republic (CAR) had gained its independence in 1960. Students either travelled to France to study or attended the Foundation for Higher Education in Central Africa, established by the French to serve the CAR, Gabon, Chad and the Republic of Congo. The state-run Université de Bangui was founded in 1969 and remains the CAR's only university. The provision of state-funded higher education was severely disrupted during the 1990s and early 2000s, owing to the inadequacy of financial resources. The Ministry of Education oversees higher education. In 2006/07 there were 4,462 students in further and higher education.

The University Council is the administrative and executive body of the Université de Bangui, and the Rector is the institutional head. All appointments and promotions are based on recommendations made to the Minister of Education by the University Council.

The secondary school Baccalauréat or Diplôme de Bachelier de l'Enseignement du Second Degré are the main criteria for admission to university. Higher education awards are divided into two cycles. The first cycle results in the award of a Diplôme for which two years of study in an area of specialization (general studies, literature, science, economics, law) are required. The second cycle lasts for a year following this and leads to the award of the Licence degree, after which an additional year of study results in award of a Maîtrise degree. The only doctoral qualification awarded by Université de Bangui is the Doctorat en Médecine, which requires six years of study. The Université de Bangui also offers vocational education.

The higher education system in the CAR is beset by numerous and complex challenges. For decades, various governments have failed to provide adequate funding for the education system or regular and decent pay for its workers. Strikes by students and professors have led to the shortening of academic years. The system suffers severe deficiencies in quality and does not satisfy real labour-market demand. It remains to be seen whether the National Plan for the Development of Education, to be implemented during 2000–10, will be adequately funded.

Regulatory Body

GOVERNMENT

Ministry of National Education: BP 791, Bangui; tel. 61-08-38; Minister CHARLES-ARMEL DOUBANE.

Learned Society

LANGUAGE AND LITERATURE

Alliance Française: cnr Rue de L'Industrie/Rue Du Poitou, BP 971, Bangui; tel. 61-49-41; fax 61-90-72; e-mail afbangui@yahoo.fr; offers courses and exams in French language and culture and promotes cultural exchange with France.

Research Institutes

AGRICULTURE, FISHERIES AND VETERINARY SCIENCE

Centre d'Études sur la Trypanosomiase Animale: BP 39, Bouar; stations at Bewiti, Sarki; annexe at Bambari.

Institut de Recherches Agronomiques de Boukoko (Agricultural Research Institute): BP 44, M'Baiki, Boukoko; f. 1948; research into tropical agriculture and plant diseases, fertilization and entomology; library of 2,740 vols; Dir M. GONDJIA.

Institut d'Études Agronomiques d'Afrique Centrale: École Nationale des Adjoints Techniques d'Agriculture de Wakombo, BP 78, M'Baiki; affiliated to Université de Bangui; Dir R. ELIARD.

ECONOMICS, LAW AND POLITICS

Département des études de population à l'Union Douanière et Économique de l'Afrique Centrale: BP 1418, Bangui; tel. 61-45-77; f. 1964; Dir JEAN NKOUNKOU.

MEDICINE

Institut Pasteur: BP 983, Bangui; tel. 61-45-76; fax 61-08-66; e-mail ipb@pasteur.cf; f. 1961; research on viral haemorrhagic fevers, polio virus, tuberculosis, HIV/AIDS and simian retroviruses; WHO Regional Centre for poliomyelitis in Africa; 110 researchers; Dir Dr ALAIN LE FAOU.

NATURAL SCIENCES

Station Expérimentale de la Maboké: par M'Baiki; f. 1963 under the direction of the Muséum National d'Histoire Naturelle, Paris; studies in the protection of materials in tropical regions, anthropology, botany, entomology, mycology, parasitology, protection of natural resources, virology, zoology; Dir (vacant).

RELIGION, SOCIOLOGY AND ANTHROPOLOGY

Mission sociologique du Haut-Oubangui: BP 68, Bangassou; f. 1954; sociological and archaeological study of societies and cultures from the CAR, especially from the Gbaya, Nzakara and Zandé countries; historical maps and sociological documents; Head Prof. E. DE DAMPIERRE; publ. *Recherches oubanguiennes*.

TECHNOLOGY

Institut National de Recherches Textiles et Cultures Vivrières: BP 17, Bambari; Dir GABRIEL RAMADHANE-SAÏD.

Library

Bangui

Bibliothèque Universitaire de Bangui: BP 1450, Bangui; tel. 61-20-00; f. 1980; 26,000 vols, 600 periodicals (Central Library); 9,144 vols (École Normale Supérieure); 5,240 vols, 168 periodicals (Faculty of Health Sciences); Dir JOSEPH GOMA-BOUANGA.

University

UNIVERSITÉ DE BANGUI

Ave des Martyrs, BP 1450, Bangui
Telephone: 61-20-00
Fax: 61-78-90
Internet: ww.univ-bangui.info
Founded 1969
Language of instruction: French
Academic year: October to June

Rector: FAUSTIN TOUADÉRA
Vice-Rector: JOSEPH MABINGUI
Sec.-Gen.: GABRIEL NGOUANDJITANGA
Librarian: JOSEPH NGOMA-BOUANGA
Library: See Libraries and Archives
Number of teachers: 243
Number of students: 6,474

Publications: *Annales de l'Université de Bangui Wambesso, Espace francophone, Revue d'Histoire et d'Archéologie Centrafricaine*

DEANS

Faculty of Health Science: Prof. MAMADOU NESTOR NALI
Faculty of Law and Economics: DAMIENNE NANARE
Faculty of Letters and Humanities: GABRIEL NGOUANDJI-TANGA
Faculty of Science and Technology: Lic. MABOUA BARA

Colleges

École Centrale d'Agriculture: Boukoko.

École Nationale d'Administration et de la Magistrature (ENAM) (National School of Administration and Judiciary): BP 1450, Bangui; tel. 61-04-88; state control under Sec.-Gen. of Govt; f. as school for future civil students and magistrates; curriculum now oriented to workshops for benefit of public-sector workers; Dir-Gen. ISAAC EDGAR BENAM.

École Nationale des Arts: BP 349, Bangui; f. 1966; dance, dramatic art, music and plastic arts.

École Territoriale d'Agriculture: Grimari.

CHAD

The Higher Education System

The main institution of higher education is the Université de N'Djamena, which was founded as the Université de Tchad in 1971 and adopted its current name in 1994. In addition, there are several technical colleges. Some 10,468 students were enrolled at further and higher education institutions in 2004/05.

Higher education in Chad is influenced by the French model, in which universities are under direct government supervision. The Ministry of Higher Education, Scientific Research and Professional Training oversees research activities through the National Committee of Scientific and Technical Research. The ministry has power over most education institutions in which teaching and research activities are performed. Some specialized institutions are supervised by other ministries. In 1990 the Government adopted a development strategy entitled Education-Formation-Emploi (EFE—Education-Training-Employment). The strategy, made up of five programmes corresponding to five sectors of the education system, sought to improve the education system's efficiency and increase access to education. It focused on teacher training, curriculum design and the rationalization of management. The Government was committed to improving the management of public resources in an attempt to meet structural adjustment programmes, and directed its attention to investment and basic education. As a result, inadequate resources were allocated to higher education. EFE strategists decided to increase student enrolment, particularly to scientific and technological disciplines. The resulting growth served only to exacerbate existing imbalances. The implementation of EFE strategy has since stalled owing to a lack of resources, and the reforms have yet to yield satisfactory results.

The Baccalauréat is required for admission to university. University-level education consists of two cycles. The first cycle involves two years of study and leads to one of three diplomas, depending on the student's area of specialization: Diplôme Universitaire de Lettres Modernes (humanities), Diplôme Universitaire de Sciences (sciences) and Diplôme Universitaire de Sciences Juridiques, Economiques et de Gestion (social sciences). The second cycle leads to the award of the Licence after one year of study following the award of the Diplôme, and the Maîtrise after a further one or two years of study. The Baccalauréat is also required for admission to non-university higher education and professional training courses.

Regulatory Bodies

GOVERNMENT

Ministry of Culture and the Arts: BP 892, N'Djamena; tel. 52-40-97; fax 52-65-60; Minister DILLAH LUCIENNE.

Ministry of Higher Education, Scientific Research and Professional Training: BP 743, N'Djamena; tel. 51-61-58; fax 51-92-31; Minister Dr OUMAR IDRISS AL-FAROUK.

Research Institutes

AGRICULTURE, FISHERIES AND VETERINARY SCIENCE

Institut de Recherches du Coton et des Textiles Exotiques (IRCT): BP 764, N'Djamena; f. 1939; cotton research (agronomy, entomology and genetics); Head of station at Bebedja M. RENOU; Regional Dir M. YEHOUESSI.

Laboratoire de Recherches Vétérinaires et Zootechniques de Farcha: BP 433, N'Djamena; tel. 52-74-75; fax 52-83-02; f. 1952; veterinary and stock-breeding research and production of vaccines; training; library of 3,500 vols; Dir Dr HASSANE MAHAMAT HASSANE.

EDUCATION

Centre de Recherche, des Archives et de Documentation, Commission nationale pour l'UNESCO: BP 731, N'Djamena; Sec.-Gen. Dr KHALIL ALIO; publ. COMNAT: Bulletin d' Information.

RELIGION, SOCIOLOGY AND ANTHROPOLOGY

Institut National des Sciences Humaines: BP 1117, N'Djamena; tel. 51-62-68; f. 1961; anthropology, ethno-sociology, geography, history, linguistics, oral traditions, palaeontology, prehistory, proto-history, social sciences, sociolinguistics, sociology social sciences; 6 researchers; library of 1,000 vols and 400 archive documents; Dir MOUKTHAR DJIBRINE MAHAMAT; Gen. Sec. DJONG-YANG OÜANLARBO; publ. Revue de Tchad.

Museum

N'Djamena

Musée National: BP 638, N'Djamena; tel. 51-33-75; fax 51-60-94; f. 1963; attached to Institut National des Sciences Humaines (see above); 100 collections; in process of reformation; depts of ethnography, palaeontology, prehistory and archaeology, scientific archives; Dir DJAMIL MOUSSA NENE.

University

UNIVERSITÉ DE N'DJAMENA (UNDJ)

BP 1117, Ave Mobutu, N'Djamena
Telephone: 51-44-44
Fax: 51-45-81
E-mail: rectorat@intnet.td
Internet: www.undt.info
Founded 1971 as Université de Tchad; present title 1994
State control

Languages of instruction: French, Arabic
Academic year: October to June
Rector: Prof. RODOUMTA KOINA
Vice-Rector: ZAKARIA KHIDIR FADOUL
Sec.-Gen.: MAHAMAT ADOUM DOUTOUM
International Relations Officer: GILBERT LAWANE
Librarian: MAHAMAT SALEH
Library of 30,000 vols
Number of teachers: 203
Number of students: 5,183
Publication: Annuaire

DEANS

Faculty of Arts and Human Sciences: AHMED N'GARE
Faculty of Exact and Applied Sciences: AHMAT CHARFADINE
Faculty of Health Sciences: DJADA DJIBRINE ATIM
Faculty of Law and Economics: BENJAMEN DJIKOLOUM BENAN (acting)

Colleges

Ecole Nationale d'Administration: BP 768, N'Djamena; f. 1963; set up by the Government and controlled by an Administrative Council to train students as public servants; Dir N. GUELINA.

Institut Supérieur des Sciences de l'Education: BP 473 N'Djamena; tel. 51-44-87; fax 51-45-50; f. 1992; depts of teacher training for primary education, teacher training for secondary education and teacher training for technical and professional education; Dir MAYORE KARYO.

CHILE

The Higher Education System

There are three types of higher education institution in Chile: public and private universities (universidad publica and universidad privada), professional institutes (instituto profesional) and centres of technical training. In 2007 there were 753,398 students in tertiary education.

Students require the Licencia de Educación Media to be admitted to university, and state-funded universities must hold an entrance examination (Prueba de Aptitud Academica). There are three levels of university qualifications in Chile, one undergraduate and two postgraduate. Undergraduates study for three to five years for the Bachiller (Bachelors), Licenciado or a professional degree. Postgraduates study for two years following the Licenciado to receive the Magister, and then for a further three years for the Doctorado.

Technical and vocational training is coordinated by Instituto Nacional de Capitación Profesional, which administers and accredits qualifications and institutions. Entrance requirements are the same as those for university-level education. Centres of technical training award the title of Técnico Superior in fields of professional education; professional institutes offer training programmes of four to five years, leading to award of a professional title; and universities award the title of Ingeniero de Ejecucion after four years of full-time study in different fields. Two universities, Universidad de Santiago de Chile and Universidad Técnica 'Federico Santa Maria', offer courses requiring three years of full-time study and leading to the title of Técnico Universitario.

As a MERCOSUR member state Chile is a participant of El Mecanismo Experimental de Acreditación de Carreras del MERCOSUR which has so far accredited Chilean degrees in agronomy, medicine and engineering. At the national level the Comisión Nacional de Acreditación de Pregrado was established in 1999 to ensure national standards are met at undergraduate level. The accreditation process consists of both the accreditation of degrees as well as institutions and is voluntary. Technical committees of university academics assess the standard of degrees. The Comisión Nacional de Acreditación de Posgrado was established in 1999 to monitor standards of postgraduate degrees.

Since 2008 Chile has earned a vast revenue from its copper mines. From this it has paid for many Chileans to earn graduate degrees abroad. It has also spent millions of dollars on improving its state universities and developing programmes in the humanities, arts, and social sciences—partly in a bid to attract foreign students and professors.

Regulatory and Representative Bodies

GOVERNMENT

Ministry of Education: Alameda 1371, 7°, Santiago; tel. (2) 3904000; fax (2) 3800317; internet www.mineduc.cl; Minister MÓNICA JIMÉNEZ.

National Commission for Culture and the Arts: San Camilo 262, Santiago; tel. (2) 5897824; internet www.consejodelacultura.cl; Minister PAULINA URRUTIA FERNÁNDEZ.

ACCREDITATION

Comisión Nacional de Acreditación (National Accreditation Commission): Avda Ricardo Lyon 1532, Providencia, Santiago; tel. (2) 6201100; fax (2) 6201120; e-mail contacto@cnachile.cl; internet www.cnachile.cl; f. 2006; ind. body set up to verify and promote the quality of univs, professional institutes and self-governing technical training centres, and of the courses and programmes they offer; 13 mems; Pres. EMILIO RODRÍGUEZ PONCE; Exec. Sec. Dr GONZALO ZAPATA LARRAÍN.

Consejo Nacional de Educación (National Council of Education): Marchant Pereira 844, Providencia, Santiago; tel. (2) 3413412; fax (2) 2254616; e-mail consulta@consejo.cl; internet www.consejo.cl; f. 1990, fmrly known as Consejo Superior de Educación, reorganised and present name 2009; accredits new univs, professional institutes and technical training centres; promotes devt of research on higher education; Head of Research and Public Information RODRIGO DIAZ; Exec. Sec. DANIELA TORRE GRIGGS; publs *Revista Calidad en la Educación* (2 a year), *Serie Seminarios Internacionales* (1 a year).

NATIONAL BODY

Consejo de Rectores de las Universidades Chilenas (Council of Rectors of Chilean Universities): Alameda 1371, 4° piso, Casilla 14798, Santiago; tel. (2) 6964286; fax (2) 6988436; e-mail cruch@cruch.cl; internet www.cruch.cl; f. 1954; coordinates the academic activities of its mem. instns, develops policies aimed at enhancing higher-education activities, promotes changes in laws regulating univ. studies and student financial aid; 25 mem. univs; Pres. YASNA PROVOSTE CAMPILLAY; Gen. Sec. CARLOS LORCA AUGER; publ. *Anuario Estadístico* (Statistical Yearbook, 1 a year).

Learned Societies

GENERAL

Instituto de Chile: Almirante Montt 453, 6500445 Santiago; tel. (2) 6854400; internet www.institutodechile.cl; f. 1964; promotes cultural, humanistic and scientific studies; Pres. SERVET MARTÍNEZ AGUILERA; Gen. Sec. MARINO PIZARRO PIZARRO; publ. *Anales*.

Constituent Academies:

Academia Chilena de Bellas Artes (Chilean Academy of Fine Arts): Almirante Montt 453, 6500445 Santiago; tel. (2) 6854418; fax (2) 6337460; e-mail acchbear@ctcinternet.cl; internet www.institutodechile.cl/bellasartes; f. 1964; 40 mems (28 academicians, 11 corresp., 1 hon.); Pres. SANTIAGO VERA RIVERA; Sec. RAMÓN NÚÑEZ VILLARROEL; publ. *Boletín*.

Academia Chilena de Ciencias (Chilean Academy of Sciences): Almirante Montt 454, Santiago; tel. (2) 4812841; fax (2) 4812843; internet www.academia-ciencias.cl; f. 1964; 36 Academicians; 21 corresp.; 5 hon. Academicians; promotes research in pure and applied sciences; Pres. SERVET MARTÍNEZ AGUILERA; Sec. FRANCISCO HERVE ALLAMAND; publs *Boletín* (irregular), *Figuras señeras de la Ciencia en Chile* (irregular).

Academia Chilena de Ciencias Sociales, Políticas y Morales (Chilean Academy of Social, Political and Moral Sciences): Almirante Montt 454, 6500445 Santiago; tel. (2) 6854416; fax (2) 6385802; e-mail acchcsso@ctcinternet.cl; internet www.institutodechile.cl/cienciassociales; f. 1964; 36 mems; library of 7,000 vols; Pres. JOSÉ LUIS CEA EGAÑA; Sec. JAIME ANTÚNEZ ALDUNATE; publs *Boletín* (3 a year), *Anales* (1 a year), *Folletos*.

Academia Chilena de la Historia (Chilean Academy of History): Almirante Montt 454, 6500445 Santiago; tel. (2) 6854414; fax (2) 6399323; e-mail acchhist@tie.cl; internet www.institutodechile.cl/historia; f. 1933; 36 mems; library of 2,500 vols; Pres. JOSÉ MIGUEL BANOS FRANCO; Sec. RICARDO COUYOUMDJIAN BERGAMALI; publs *Boletín de la Academia* (1 a year), *Archivo de D. Bernardo O'Higgins* (irregular).

Academia Chilena de la Lengua (Chilean Academy of Language): Almirante Montt 453, 6500445 Santiago; tel. (2) 6854413; fax (2) 6640776; e-mail acadchileng@terra.cl; internet www.institutodechile.cl/lengua; f. 1885; fmrly Academia Chilena; corresp. mem. of the Real Academia Española, Madrid; 36 mems; Dir ALFREDO MATUS OLIVIER; Sec. JOSÉ LUIS SAMANIEGO ALDAZÁBAL; publ. *Boletín de la Academia Chilena*.

Academia Chilena de Medicina (Chilean Academy of Medicine): Almirante Montt 453, 6500445 Santiago; tel. (2) 6854417; fax (2) 6388205; e-mail acchmed@tie.cl; internet www.institutodechile.cl/medicina; f. 1964; 75 Academicians; 45 hon. foreign mems; library of 900 vols; Pres. ALEJANDRO GOIC

GOIC; Sec. RODOLFO ARMAS MERINO; publs *Boletín, Proceedings on the Chilean History of Medicine.*

UNESCO Office Santiago and Regional Bureau for Education in Latin America and the Caribbean/Oficina Regional de Educación de la UNESCO para América Latina y el Caribe: Casilla 127, Correo 29, Santiago; Calle Enrique Delpiano 2058, Providencia, Santiago; tel. (2) 4724600; fax (2) 6551046; e-mail santiago@unesco.org; internet www.unesco.org/santiago; f. 1963; dissemination of knowledge, formulation of public policy guidelines, provision of advisory services and technical support to countries of the region, promotion of dialogue, exchange and cooperation; Dir JORGE SEQUEIRA.

AGRICULTURE, FISHERIES AND VETERINARY SCIENCE

Colegio de Ingenieros Forestales de Chile A.G.: San Isidro 22, Of. 503, Santiago Centro; tel. (2) 6393289; fax (2) 6395280; e-mail jsalas@surnet.cl; internet www.cifag .cl; f. 1982; 350 mems; Pres. JAIME SALAS ARANCIBIA; publs *Actas de las Jornadas Forestales* (2 a year), *Renarres* (6 a year).

Sociedad Agronómica de Chile (Agronomical Society of Chile): Calle MacIver 120, Of. 36, Casilla 4109, Santiago; tel. (2) 6384881; fax (2) 6384881; e-mail sociedad .agronomica.chile@gmail.com; internet www .sach.cl; f. 1910; 1,900 mems; library of 1,600 vols; Pres. HORST BERGER; Sec. CHRISTEL OBERPAUR; publ. *Simiente* (3 a year).

Sociedad Chilena de Producción Animal A.G.: c/o Sra Carmen Gallo S., Facultad de Ciencias Veterinarias, Universidad Austral de Chile, Casilla 567, Valdivia; tel. (45) 215706, ext. 299; e-mail mdiaz@inia.cl; internet www.sochipa.cl; f. 1979; 115 mems; Pres. CARMEN GALLO S.; Sec./Treas. DANTE PINOCHET T.

Sociedad Nacional de Agricultura (National Society of Agriculture): Tenderini 187, 8320232 Santiago; tel. (2) 5853300; fax (2) 5853370; e-mail comunicaciones@sna.cl; internet www.sna.cl; f. 1838; library of 3,500 vols; research in agricultural, social and economic problems; controls a plant genetics experimental station and a broadcasting chain with stations in several cities; register of pedigree cattle kept; technical assistance to farmers; annual international and agricultural show since 1869, and home show since 1980; Pres. LUIS SCHMIDT MONTES; Gen. Sec. JUAN PABLO MATTE F.; publs *Revista El Campesino, El Vocero, Informe Semanal.*

ARCHITECTURE AND TOWN PLANNING

Colegio de Arquitectos de Chile (Chilean College of Architects): Av. Libertador B. O'Higgins 115, Santiago; tel. (2) 6398744; fax (2) 6398769; e-mail central@coarq.com; internet www.arqchile.cl; f. 1942 for all Chilean and foreign architects working in Chile; 5,500 mems; library of 2,000 vols, 2,500 journals; Pres. JOSÉ RAMÓN UGARTE; Gen. Man. ERICO LUEBERT CID; publs *Revista CA* (4 a year), *Boletín* (12 a year), *Bienal de Arquitectura* (every 2 years), *Congreso Nacional de Arquitectos* (every 2 years).

BIBLIOGRAPHY, LIBRARY SCIENCE AND MUSEOLOGY

Colegio de Bibliotecarios de Chile, AG: Diagonal Paraguay 383, Depto 122, Torre 11, Santiago; tel. (2) 2225652; fax (2) 6355023; e-mail cbc@uplink.cl; internet www .bibliotecarios.cl; f. 1969; 1,891 mems; Pres. MARCIA MARINOVIC SIMUNOVIC; Sec. ANA MARÍA PINO YÁÑEZ; publs *Eidisis* (4 a year), *Documento de Trabajo* (irregular).

ECONOMICS, LAW AND POLITICS

Servicio Médico Legal (Forensic Medicine Service): Avda La Paz 1012, Independencia, Santiago; tel. (2) 7823500; internet www.sml .cl; f. 1915; attached to Min. of Justice; advises tribunals on forensic medicine; 305 mems; library of 800 vols; Dir Dr PATRICIO BUSTOS; publs *Monografías Servicio Médico Legal* (3 a year), *Revista de Medicina Legal* (3 a year).

FINE AND PERFORMING ARTS

Asociación Plástica Latina Internacional de Chile (APLICH) (Chilean International Plastic Arts Association): Avda P. de Valdivia 1781, Casilla 177, Correo 29, Santiago; tel. (2) 2233444; fax (2) 2233444; internet www.mnba.cl; f. 1990; Pres. ALICIA ARGANDOÑA R.; Sec.-Gen. SERGIO JUZAM NUMAN; publ. *APLICH al Día.*

HISTORY, GEOGRAPHY AND ARCHAEOLOGY

Instituto Geográfico Militar (Military Geographical Institute): Nueva Santa Isabel 1640, Santiago; tel. (2) 4606800; fax (2) 4606918; e-mail igm@igm.cl; f. 1922; 400 mems; library of 4,000 vols, 25,000 maps; Dir GDB PABLO GRAN LÓPEZ; publ. *Revista Terra Australis* (1 a year).

Sociedad Chilena de Historia y Geografía (Chilean Society of History and Geography): Casilla 1386, Santiago; Calle Londres 65, Santiago; tel. (2) 6382489; f. 1911; 304 mems; 13 hon.; 70 corresp.; library of 12,600 vols; Pres. SERGIO MARTÍNEZ BOEZA; Vice-Pres. ISIDOROVOZQUEZ DE ACUÑA; Sec.-Gen. ROBERTO COBO DE LA MOZA; publs *Revista Chilena de Historia y Geografía,* related works.

LANGUAGE AND LITERATURE

Alliance Française: Casilla 94, Las Condes, Santiago; Lycée Antoine de Saint-Exupéry, Av. Luis Pasteur 5418, Vitacura, Santiago 10; tel. (2) 8278200; fax (2) 2183287; e-mail serge.buenaventes@lafase.cl; internet www .lafase.cl; offers courses and exams in French language and culture and promotes cultural exchange with France; attached teaching offices in Concepción, Curico, Osorno, Renaca, Santiago, Valparaíso; Head SERGE BUENAVENTES.

British Council: Eliodoro Yáñez 832, Providencia, Santiago; tel. (2) 4106900; fax (2) 4106929; e-mail info@britishcouncil.cl; internet www.britishcouncil.cl; offers courses and exams in English language and British culture and promotes cultural exchange with the UK; Dir SARAH BARTON.

Goethe-Institut: Esmeralda 650, Santiago; tel. (2) 5711950; fax (2) 5711999; e-mail info@ santiago.goethe.org; internet www.goethe .de/ins/cl/sao/esindex.htm; f. 1961; offers courses and exams in German language and culture and promotes cultural exchange with Germany; library of 8,500 vols; Dir JUDITH MAIWORM; Dir REINHARD MAIWORM.

Sociedad Chilena de Lingüística (Chilean Linguistics Society): Casilla 394, Santiago 11; tel. (41) 2203001; internet www .sochil.cl; f. 1971; over 100 mems; Pres. Dr BERNARDO RIFFO; Dir Dr PILAR ALVAREZ-SANTULLANO; publ. *Actas.*

MEDICINE

Colegio de Químico-Farmacéuticos y Bioquímicos de Chile (College of Pharmacists and Biochemists): Casilla 1136, Santiago; Merced 50, Santiago; tel. (2) 6392505; fax (2) 6399780; internet www .colegiofarmaceutico.cl; f. 1942; 2,500 regional councils in 13 main towns; Pres.

Dr ELMER TORRES CORTÉS; Sec. Dra MARÍA ANGÉLICA SÁNCHEZ VOGEL; publ. *Revista.*

Sociedad Chilena de Cancerología y Hematología: Calle Pérez Valenzuela 1520, Of. 502, Providencia, Santiago; tel. (2) 2358357; fax (2) 2051914; internet www .cancersoc.cl; f. 1954; 142 mems; Pres. Dr RAMÓN BAEZA B.; Gen. Sec. Dr MAURICIO CAMUS A.; publ. *Revista Chilena de Cancerología* (4 a year).

Sociedad Chilena de Cardiología y Cirugía Cardiovascular: Alfredo Barros Errázuriz 1954, Oficinas 1601, Providencia, Santiago; tel. (2) 2690076; fax (2) 2690207; e-mail sochicar@entelchile.net; internet www .sochicar.cl; f. 1949; Pres. Dr FERNANDO LANAS ZANETTI; publ. *Revista.*

Sociedad Chilena de Dermatología y Venereología: Vitacura 5250, Oficina 202, Vitacura, Santiago; tel. (2) 3781301; fax (2) 3781302; internet www.sochiderm.cl; f. 1938; Pres. Dr ENRIQUE MULLINS; Gen. Sec. Dra IRENA ARAYA.

Sociedad Chilena de Endocrinología y Metabolismo: Bernarda Morín 488, 2° piso, Providencia, Santiago; tel. (2) 2230386; fax (2) 7535556; e-mail sochem@sochem.cl; internet www.sochem.cl; f. 1961; Pres. Dr GILBERTO PÉREZ PACHECO; Sec.-Gen. Dra VERÓNICA ARAYA QUINTANILLA.

Sociedad Chilena de Enfermedades Respiratorias: Santa Magdalena 75, Oficina 701, Providencia, Santiago; tel. (2) 2316292; fax (2) 2443811; e-mail ser@ serchile.cl; internet www.serchile.cl; f. 1930; 410 mems; Pres. Dr MANUEL BARROS; Sec. Dra VIVIANA LEZANA; publs *Boletín Informativo* (12 a year), *Revista Chilena de Enfermedades Respiratorias* (4 a year).

Sociedad Chilena de Gastroenterología: El Trovador 4280, Of. 909, Las Condes, Santiago; tel. (2) 3425004; fax (2) 3425005; e-mail schgastr@tie.cl; internet www .socgastro.cl; f. 1938; Pres. Dr FERNANDO FLUXÁ GARCÍA; Exec. Secs Dr FRANCISCO LÓPEZ KOSTNER, Dra PAULA VIAL CERDA; publs *Gastroenterologia Latinoamericana, Normas de Diagnóstico en Enfermedades Digestivas.*

Sociedad Chilena de Inmunología: Av. Independencia 1027, Santiago 7; tel. (2) 9786347; fax (2) 9786979; e-mail info@ sochin.cl; internet www.sochin.cl; f. 1972; 55 active mems; Pres. Dr ÁNGEL OÑATE CONTRERAS; Sec. Biol. DARWIN SÁEZ POBLETE.

Sociedad Chilena de Obstetricia y Ginecología: Román Díaz 205, Oficina 205, Providencia, Santiago; tel. (2) 2350133; fax (2) 2351294; e-mail sochog@entelchile.net; internet www.sochog.cl; f. 1935; 350 mems; Pres. Dr LUIS MARTINEZ; Sec. Dr MAURICIO CUELLO; publ. *Revista Chilena de Obstetricia y Ginecología* (online, 6 a year).

Sociedad Chilena de Oftalmología: Casilla 16197, Correo 9, Providencia, Santiago; tel. (2) 2185950; fax (2) 2185950; e-mail sochioft@tie.cl; internet www.sochiof.cl; f. 1931; 600 mems; library of 625 vols; spec. colln of video cassettes; Pres. Dr ALEJANDRO SIEBERT E.; Sec. Dr JAVIER CORVALÁN R.; publs *Archivos Chilenos de Oftalmología* (2 a year), *Boletín Informativo* (12 a year).

Sociedad Chilena de Ortopedia y Traumatología: Evaristo Lillo 78, Of. 81, Las Condes, Santiago; tel. (2) 2072151; fax (2) 2069820; e-mail schot@schot.cl; internet www.schot.cl; f. 1949; 508 mems; library of 500 vols; Pres. Dr IGNACIO DOCKENDORFF B.; Sec.-Gen. Dr JORGE VERGARA L.; publ. *Revista Chilena de Ortopedia y Traumatología* (4 a year).

Sociedad Chilena de Pediatría: CP 6841638, Casilla 593, Correo 11, Santiago;

Alcade Eduardo Castillo Velasco 1838, Ñuñoa, Santiago; tel. (2) 2371598; fax (2) 2380046; e-mail contacto@sochipe.cl; internet www.sochipe.cl; f. 1922; 1,230 mems; Pres. Dr OSCAR HERRERA GONZÁLEZ; Sec. Dr CARLOS SAIEH ANDONIE.

Sociedad Chilena de Reumatología: Bernarda Morin 488, Providencia, Santiago; tel. (2) 7535545; fax (2) 2693394; e-mail info@ sochire.cl; internet www.sochire.cl; f. 1950; Pres. Dr GONZALO ASTORGA P.; Sec. Dr ALBERTO VALDÉS S.; publ. *Boletín* (4 a year).

Sociedad de Farmacología de Chile: Casilla 70.000, Santiago 7; Av. Independencia 1027, Santiago 7; tel. (2) 6786050; fax (2) 7774216; internet www.sofarchi.cl; f. 1979; 88 mems; Pres. Dra GABRIELA DÍAZ-VÉLIZ.

Sociedad de Neurocirugía de Chile: Esmeralda 678 (2° piso interior), Santiago; tel. (2) 6334149; fax (2) 6391085; e-mail neurocirugia@tie.cl; internet www .neurocirugia.cl; f. 1957; 100 mems; Sec. Dr JEANNETTE VAN SCHUERBECK P.; publ. *Revista Chilena de Neurocirugía* (2 a year).

Sociedad de Neurología, Psiquiatría y Neurocirugía de Chile: Calle Carlos Silva V 1292, Plaza Las Lilas, Providencia, Casilla 251, Correo 35, Santiago; tel. (2) 2329347; fax (2) 2319287; e-mail secretariagral@123.cl; internet www.sonepsyn.cl; f. 1932; Pres. Dr ENRIQUE JADRESIC; publ. *Revista Chilena de Neuro-Psiquiatría* (4 a year).

Sociedad Médica de Concepción (Concepción Medical Society): Casilla 60-C, Concepción; f. 1886; Pres. Dr ENRIQUE BELLOLIOZ; publ. *Anales Médicos de Concepción*.

Sociedad Médica de Santiago (Santiago Medical Society): Casilla 168, Correo Tajamar, Santiago; tel. (2) 7535500; fax (2) 7535599; e-mail smschile@smschile.cl; internet www.smschile.cl; f. 1869; 1,600 mems; library: 50 periodical titles; Pres. Dr HECTOR UGALDE PRIETO; Sec. Dr SYLVIA ECHÁVARRI; publ. *Revista Médica de Chile* (12 a year).

Sociedad Odontológica de Concepción: Casilla 2107, Concepción; f. 1924; 300 mems; Pres. Dr EDUARDO NAVARETE; Sec. Dr SERGIO ESQUERRÉ S.; publ. *Anuario*.

NATURAL SCIENCES

General

Academia Chilena de Ciencias Naturales (Chilean Academy of Natural Sciences): Almirante Montt 454, Santiago; tel. (2) 6441030; fax (2) 6332129; f. 1926; Pres. Dr HUGO GUNCKEL L.; Sec. HANS NIEMEYER F.; publ. *Anales*.

Asociación Científica y Técnica de Chile (Scientific and Technical Association of Chile): Carlos Antúnez 1885, Dpto 205, Santiago; tel. (2) 2354137; f. 1965; 22 mems; Pres. HÉCTOR CATHALIFAUD ARGANDOÑA; Sec.-Gen. ELENA TORRES SEGUEL.

Corporación para el Desarrollo de la Ciencia: Marcoleta 250, Casilla 10332, Santiago; f. 1978; Pres. FERNANDO DÍAZ A.; Sec.-Gen. HÉCTOR CATHALIFAUD A.; publ. *Revista CODECI*.

Sociedad Científica Chilena 'Claudio Gay' (Chilean Scientific Society): Casilla 2974, Santiago; tel. (2) 7455066; fax (2) 7455176; e-mail ugartepena@itn.cl; f. 1955; 45 mems; library of 5,000 vols; Dir ALFREDO UGARTE-PEÑA.

Biological Sciences

Sociedad de Microbiología de Chile: Canadá 253, piso 3 Of. F, Santiago; tel. (2) 2093503; fax (2) 2258427; e-mail socbiol@ manquehue.net; internet somich .biologiachile.cl; f. 1964; 194 mems; Pres.

MICHAEL SEEGER PFEIFFER; Sec. GINO CORSINI ACUÑA; publ. *Acta Microbiológica* (2 a year).

Sociedad Chilena de Entomología (Entomological Society): POB 21132, Santiago 21; tel. (2) 6804635; fax (2) 6804602; internet www.insectachile.cl; f. 1922; 170 mems; library of 4,000 periodicals; Pres. Dra FRESIA ESTER ROSAS A.; Sec. Ing. Agr. JOSÉ MONDACA E.; publ. *Revista Chilena de Entomología* (1 a year).

Sociedad de Biología de Chile: Canadá 253 depto F, Santiago; tel. (2) 2093503; fax (2) 2258427; e-mail socbiol@biologiachile.cl; internet www.biologiachile.cl; f. 1928; 565 mems; Pres. Dr MARCO TULIO NÚÑEZ; Sec. Dr CHRISTIAN GONZÁLEZ; publs *Biological Research* (2 a year), *Revista Chilena de Historia Natural* (4 a year), *Noticiario* (12 a year).

Sociedad de Genética de Chile: Almirante Montt 454, Santiago; tel. and fax (2) 6387046; e-mail sochigen@adsl.tie.cl; internet www .sochigen.cl; f. 1964; 100 mems; Pres. Dra LUCÍA CIFUENTES OVALLE; Sec.-Gen. Prof. PATRICIA PEREZ-ALZOLA; publs *Biological Research*, *Revista Chilena de Historia Natural*.

Sociedad de Vida Silvestre de Chile (Chilean Wildlife Society): c/o Claudia Gil, Casilla 18, Valdivia; tel. (63) 215846; e-mail svsch@surnet.cl; internet svsch.ceachile.cl; f. 1975; 300 mems; Pres. CLAUDIA GIL; Exec. Sec. ROCIO SANHUEZA; publs *Gestión Ambiental* (1 a year), *Enlace* (1 a year).

Mathematical Sciences

Sociedad de Matemática de Chile: Canadá 253, departamento F, Providencia, Santiago; tel. (2) 2489260; fax (2) 2489260; internet www.somachi.cl; f. 1976; 250 mems; Pres. RUBÍ RODRÍGUEZ MORENO; Sec. MANUEL ELGUETA DEDES; publ. *Boletín* (irregular).

Physical Sciences

Asociación Chilena de Astronomía y Astronáutica: Casilla 3904, Santiago 1; tel. (2) 6327556; f. 1957; union of amateur astronomers; arranges courses and lectures; astronomy, astrophotography, radioastronomy, telescope-making; owns the observatory of Mt Pochoco, near Santiago; 350 mems; library of 1,000 vols; Pres. JODY TAPIA NUÑEZ; Sec. BIANCA DINAMARCA FIERRO; publ. *Boletín ACHAYA* (12 a year).

Asociación Chilena de Sismología e Ingeniería Antisísmica (Chilean Association of Seismology and Earthquake Engineering): Blanco Encalada 2002, piso 4, Santiago; tel. (2) 978-4372; fax (2) 689-2833; e-mail mmualin@ing.uchile.cl; internet www .achisina.cl; f. 1963; Pres. Dr PATRICIO RUIZ.

Comisión Chilena de Energía Nuclear: Amunátegui 95, Casilla 188-D, Santiago; tel. (2) 4702500; fax (2) 4702570; e-mail oirs@ cchen.cl; internet www.cchen.gov.cl; f. 1964; library of 9,000 vols; research, devt and applications of the pacific uses of nuclear energy; Pres. ROBERTO HOJMAN-GUIÑERMAN; Exec. Dir Ing. FERNANDO LOPEZ-LIZANA; publ. *Nucleotécnica* (1 a year).

Comité Oceanográfico Nacional (CONA): Casilla 324, Valparaíso; tel. (32) 2266520; fax (32) 2266522; e-mail cona@shoa .cl; internet www.cona.cl; f. 1971; 29 mem. instns; coordinates oceanographic activities in the country; Pres. Capt. FERNANDO MINGRAM; Exec. Sec. ALEJANDRO CABEZAS; publ. *Ciencia y Tecnología del Mar* (1 a year).

Liga Marítima de Chile (Chilean Maritime League): Casilla 1345, Valparaíso; Avda Errázuriz 471, 2° piso, Valparaíso; tel. (32) 2235280; fax (32) 2255179; e-mail ligamar@ terra.cl; internet www.ligamar.cl; f. 1914; runs course in nautical education; Pres.

Rear Admiral ERI SOLIS OYARZÚN; Exec. Dir Captain ENRIQUE TRUCCO DELÉPINE; 1,350 mems; brs in Iquique, Tocopilla, Santiago, Concepción, Tomé, Valdivia, Puerto Montt and Punta Arenas; publ. *Mar* (1 a year).

Sociedad Chilena de Física: c/o Dr Juan Carlos Retamal, Casilla 307, Correo 2, Santiago; c/o Dr Juan Carlos Retamal, Depto de Física, Universidad de Santiago de Chile, Av. Ecuador 3493 Estación Central, Santiago; tel. (2) 7191200; fax (2) 7769596; e-mail jretamal@lauca.usach.cl; internet fisica .usach.cl; f. 1965; 250 mems; Pres. Dr JUAN CARLOS RETAMAL; Sec. Dr LUIS ROA; publ. *Boletín* (12 a year).

Sociedad Chilena de Fotogrametría y Percepción Remota: Instituto Geográfico Militar, Nueva Santa Isabel 1640, Santiago; tel. (2) 6968221; fax (2) 6988278; e-mail igm@ igm.cl; library of 4,000 vols, 25,000 maps; Pres. JUAN VIDAL GARCÍA-HUIDOBRO; Sec. Tcl. JUAN GUTIÉRREZ PALACIOS.

Sociedad Chilena de Química: Casilla de Correo 2613, Concepción; tel. (41) 227815; fax (41) 235819; e-mail schq@surnet.cl; internet www.schq.cl; f. 1945; 1,000 mems; library of 1,500 vols and 400 periodicals; Pres. Dr GALO CÁRDENAS; Sec. Dr JUAN GODOY; publ. *Boletin* (4 a year).

Sociedad de Bioquímica de Concepción: Casilla 237, Escuela de Química y Farmacia y Bioquímica, Concepción; f. 1957; Pres. MARIO POZO LÓPEZ; Sec. FROILÁN HERNÁNDEZ CARTES.

Sociedad de Bioquímica y Biología Molecular de Chile: c/o Dr Marcelo López Lastra, Laboratorio de Virología Molecular, Facultad de Medicina, Pontificia Universidad Católica, Marcoleta 391, Santiago; tel. (2) 3548182; fax (2) 6387457; e-mail malopez@ med.puc.cl; internet www.sbbmch.cl; f. 1974; 130 mems; Pres. Dr XAVIER JORDANA DE BUEN; Sec. Dr MARCELO LÓPEZ LASTRA.

Sociedad Geológica de Chile: Valentin Letelier 20, Oficina 401, Santiago; tel. (2) 6712415; fax (2) 6980481; e-mail info@ sociedadgeologica.cl; internet www .sociedadgeologica.cl; f. 1962; 434 mems; Pres. FRANCISCO HERVÉ; Sec. CÉSAR ARRIAGADA; publs *Comunicaciones* (1 a year), *Revista Geológica de Chile* (2 a year).

TECHNOLOGY

Asociación Interamericana de Ingeniería Sanitaria y Ambiental: Barros Errázuriz 1954, Piso 10, Of. 1007, Providencia, Santiago; tel. (2) 2690085; fax 02) 2690087; e-mail aidischi@aidis.cl; f. 1979; Pres. Ing. ALEX CHECHILNITZKY Z.; Sec. JULIO HEVIA MEDEL; publ. *Revista* (4 a year).

Colegio de Ingenieros de Chile, AG: Avda Santa María 0508, Casilla 13745, Santiago; tel. (2) 4221140; fax (2) 4221012; e-mail colegio@ingenieros.cl; internet www .ingenieros.cl; f. 1958; professional engineering asscn; 23,000 mems; Pres. Eng. FERNANDO GARCÍA CASTRO; Gen. Man. Eng. PEDRO TORRES OJEDA; publs *C.I. Informa* (12 a year), *Ingenieros* (4 a year).

Instituto de Ingenieros de Chile (Institute of Chilean Engineers): Casilla 487, Santiago; San Martín 352, Santiago; tel. (2) 6984028; fax (2) 6971136; e-mail iing@iing.cl; internet www.iing.cl; f. 1888; 800 mems; library of 2,100 vols; Pres. MATEO BUDINICH DIEZ; Sec. CARLOS TAPIA ILLANES; publs *Revista Chilena de Ingeniería, Anales*.

Instituto de Ingenieros de Minas de Chile: Encomenderos 260 Of. 31, Casilla 14668, Correo 21, Santiago; tel. (2) 2461615; fax (2) 2466387; e-mail iimch@entelchile.net; f. 1930; 1,200 mems; Pres. MARCO ANTONIO

ALFARO; Sec. MANUEL VIERA; publ. *Minerales* (6 a year).

Sociedad Chilena de Tecnología en Alimentos (Chilean Society of Food Technology): Echaurren 149, Santiago; tel. (2) 6966236; fax (2) 6974780; e-mail sochital@lauca.usch.cl; internet www.geocities.com/sochital; f. 1963; publ. *Alimentos* (4 a year).

Sociedad Nacional de Minería (National Society of Mining): Ave Apoquindo 3000 (5° piso), Las Condes, Santiago; tel. (2) 8207000; fax (2) 8207053; e-mail sonami@sonami.cl; internet www.sonami.cl; f. 1883; library of 20,000 digital reports, 20,000 plans, 5,000 spec. documents; Pres. ALBERTO SALAS MUÑOZ; Vice-Pres. RAMÓN JARA A; Vice-Pres. PATRICIO CÉSPEDES GUZMÁN; Gen. Sec. HÉCTOR PÁEZ BARAZA; publ. *Boletín Minero*.

Research Institutes

AGRICULTURE, FISHERIES AND VETERINARY SCIENCE

Estación Experimental 'Las Vegas' de la Sociedad Nacional de Agricultura (National Agricultural Society Experimental Station): c/o Sociedad Nacional de Agricultura, Casilla 40-D, Tenderini 187, Santiago; f. 1924; library of 1,000 vols; Dir RAÚL MATTE VIAL; publ. *El Campesino* (12 a year).

Instituto de Fomento Pesquero (Fishery Research Institute): Blanco 839, Valparaíso; tel. (32) 322000; fax (32) 322345; e-mail direccion@ifop.cl; internet www.ifop.cl; f. 1964 for research into fisheries and aquaculture, and to support the regulation of a sustainable marine environment; 400 mems; library of 9,000 vols; Dir GUILLERMO MORENO PAREDES; publ. *Boletín Bibliográfico* (12 a year).

Instituto de Investigaciones Agropecuarias: Casilla 439, Correo 3, Santiago; tel. (2) 5417223; fax (2) 5417667; f. 1964; conducts research on plant and livestock production, horticulture, viticulture, oenology, field crops; 170 research workers; library: see Libraries; Pres. FERNANDO MUJICA CASTILLO; National Dir FRANCISCO GONZÁLEZ DEL RÍO; Dir of Carillanca Agricultural Experiment Station ADRIÁN CATRILEO S.; Dir of Intihuasi Agricultural Experiment Station ALFONSO OSORIO U.; Dir of La Platina Agricultural Experiment Station JORGE VALENZUELA BARNECH; Dir of Kampenaike Agricultural Experiment Station RAÚL LIRA F.; Dir of Quilamapu Agricultural Experiment Station HERNÁN ACUÑA P.; Dir of Remehue Agricultural Experiment Station FRANCISCO LANUZA A.; Dir of Tamel-aike Agricultural Experiment Station HERNÁN FELIPE ELIZALDE; publs *Agricultura Técnica* (4 a year), *Bibliografía Agrícola Chilena* (1 a year), *Boletín Técnico* (irregular), *Memoria Anual*, *Tierra Adentro* (6 a year).

Instituto Forestal (Forestry Institute): Casilla 109 c, Concepción; Camino a Coronel Km 7.5, Concepción; tel. (41) 2853260; fax (41) 2853260; e-mail info@infor.cl; internet www.infor.cl; f. 1961; research and advice in all aspects of forestry; library of 8,000 vols; Exec. Dir MARTA ABALOS ROMERO; publs *Boletín Estadístico, Ciencia e Investigación Forestal, Documento de Divulgación, Informe Técnico*.

ECONOMICS, LAW AND POLITICS

Instituto Latinoamericano y del Caribe de Planificación Económica y Social (ILPES) (Latin American and Caribbean Institute for Economic and Social Planning): Edif. Naciones Unidas, Avda Dag Hammarskjöld s/n, Vitacura, Casilla 1567, San-

tiago; tel. (2) 2102507; fax (2) 2066104; e-mail anaser@eclac.cl; internet www.ilpes.cl; f. 1962; permanent body within the Economic Comm. for Latin America and the Caribbean (ECLAC), which in turn forms part of the UN; supports mem. countries in their strategic planning and management of public affairs, by providing training, advisory and research services; library of 60,000 vols, documents and periodicals; Dir JUAN CARLOS RAMIREZ; publs *Cuadernos del ILPES, ILPES Bulletin*.

Instituto Nacional de Estadísticas (National Statistical Institute): Casilla 498, Correo 3, Santiago; Avda Pdte. Bulnes 418, Santiago; tel. (2) 3667766; fax (2) 6712169; e-mail ine@ine.cl; internet www.ine.cl; f. 1843; library of 16,104 vols; Dir MARIANA SCHKOLNIK CHAMUDES; publs *Compendio Estadístico* (1 a year), *Indicadores Mensuales* (12 a year), *Metodologías*, *Revista Estadística y Economía* (2 a year).

EDUCATION

Centro de Investigación y Desarrollo de la Educación (CIDE): Erasmo Escala 1825, Santiago; tel. (2) 8897100; fax (2) 6718051; e-mail cide@reuna.cl; internet www.cide.cl; f. 1965; attached to the Universidad Alberto Hurtado; aims to provide education relevant to the basic needs of the people; research into education and the family, education and work, education and social values; library of 50,000 vols, 7,000 documents; Pres. FERNANDO MONTES MATTE; Dir JUAN EDUARDO GARCÍA-HUIDOBRO.

Latin American Information and Documentation Network for Education (REDUC): Casilla 13608, Santiago; tel. (2) 6987153; fax (2) 6718051; e-mail reduc@cide.cl; internet www.reduc.cl; f. 1977; network of different educational research institutions; aims to disseminate information on education for research and policy making; 27 mem. instns; documentation centre of 20,000 research summaries; Dir GONZALO GUTIÉRREZ; publ. *Databases* (online).

HISTORY, GEOGRAPHY AND ARCHAEOLOGY

Instituto de Investigaciones Arqueológicas y Museo 'R.P. Gustavo Le Paige, S.J.': San Pedro de Atacama; tel. (55) 851002; fax (55) 851066; e-mail museospa@ucn.cl; f. 1985; affiliated to the Universidad Católica del Norte, Antofagasta; research in archaeology and anthropology; postgraduate courses (MA and PhD); library of books, 5,000 periodicals; Dir Dr AGUSTÍN LLAGOSTERA M.; publ. *Estudios Atacameños* (irregular).

MEDICINE

Instituto de Medicina Experimental del Servicio Nacional de Salud (Institute of Experimental Medicine of the National Health Service): Avda Irarrázaval 849, Casilla 3401, Santiago; tel. (2) 2497930; f. 1937; affiliated to WHO; physiology, neuroendocrinology and cancer research; maintains tumour bank, available for use by other research centres; 15 mems; library of 6,800 vols; Dir Dr SERGIO YRARRÁZAVAL; Chief Sec. Mrs BERTA IRIBARRA.

Instituto de Salud Pública de Chile (Chilean Public Health Institute): Av. Marathon 1000, Ñuñoa, Santiago; tel. (2) 3507321; fax (2) 3507578; internet www.ispch.cl; f. 1980; centre for vaccine production, national control of pharmaceutical, food and cosmetic products, and for coordination of national network of health laboratories; 600 mems; library of 9,142 vols (Central Scientific Library 3,600 vols; Centre of Occupational

Health and Air Pollution Library 5,542 vols); Dir JORGE SÁNCHEZ VEGA; publs *Boletín informativo de medicamentos, Manual de Bioseguridad, Manuales de Procedimiento de Laboratorio Clínico, Laboratorio al día*.

NATURAL SCIENCES

General

Centro de Información de Recursos Naturales (CIREN) (Centre for Information on Natural Resources): Av. Manuel Montt 1164, Providencia, 7501556 Santiago; tel. (2) 2008900; fax (2) 2008914; e-mail ciren@reuna.cl; internet www.ciren.cl; f. 1964; a privately run corporation; gathers data and provides a central information service in the areas of climate, soil, water, fruit production, afforestation, mining, agricultural resources; holds a land-owners register; library of 11,000 vols, 150 journals; Exec. Dir RODRIGO FRANCISCO ALVAREZ SEGUEL.

Physical Sciences

Comité Nacional de Geografía, Geodesía y Geofísica (National Geographical, Geodetic and Geophysical Committee): Nueva Santa Isabel 1640, Santiago; tel. (2) 4606800; fax (2) 4606978; e-mail igm@igm.cl; f. 1935 to encourage and coordinate research in the fields mentioned; 119 mems; Dirs PABLO GRAN LÓPEZ, LUIS ALEGRÍA MATTA, JUAN GUTTIÉREZ PALACIOS.

Dirección Meteorológica de Chile (Meteorological Bureau): Casilla 140, Sucursal Matucana, Estación Central, Santiago; Av. Portales 3450, Estación Central, Santiago; tel. (2) 4364538; fax (2) 4378212; e-mail dimetche@meteochile.cl; internet www.meteochile.cl; f. 1884; library of 3,000 vols; Dir Col NATHAN MAKUC; publs *Anuario Agrometeorológico, Anuario Meteorológico, Boletín Agrometeorológico* (12 a year), *Boletín de Radiación Ultravioleta, Boletín Climatologico* (12 a year), *Informe Solarimetrico Semestral de Radiación e Insolación*.

European Southern Observatory (ESO): Casilla 19001, Correo 19, Avda Alonso de Córdova 3107, Vitacura, Santiago; tel. (2) 4633000; fax (2) 4633101; internet www.sc.eso.org/santiago/science; f. 1962; ESO is the European organization for astronomical research in the southern hemisphere; ESO operates 3 observational sites in the Chilean Atacama Desert: the Very Large Telescope (VLT), is located on Paranal, a 2600-m high mountain south of Antofagasta; several medium-sized optical telescopes are operated at La Silla, 600 km north of Santiago, at 2400-m altitude; a new submillimetre telescope (APEX) is in operation at the 5000-m high Llano de Chajnantor, near San Pedro de Atacama; a large number of 12-m submillimetre antennas (ALMA) are currently under development; ESO Representative and Head of Science Office in Chile FELIX MIRABEL.

Instituto Antártico Chileno: Luis Thayer Ojeda 814, Casilla 16521, Correo 9, Santiago; tel. (2) 2310105; fax (2) 2320440; e-mail inach@inach.cl; internet www.inach.cl; f. 1963; a centre for technological and scientific development on matters relating to the Antarctic and adjacent ecosystems; 43 mems; library of 4,100 vols, 400 periodicals; Dir OSCAR PINOCHET DE LA BARRA; publs *Boletín Antártico Chileno* (2 a year), *Serie Científica* (1 a year).

Instituto Isaac Newton (Isaac Newton Institute): Casilla 8–9, Correo 9, Santiago; tel. (2) 2172013; fax (2) 2172352; e-mail inewton@terra.cl; internet www.ini.cl; f. 1978; promotes astronomy in 9 Eastern European and Eurasian countries; Dir GONZALO ALCAINO; publs *Astronomical Journal*

(10 a year), *Astronomy and Astrophysics* (70 a year), *Astrophysical Journal* (10 a year).

Observatorio Astronómico Nacional (National Astronomical Observatory): Universidad de Chile, Departamento de Astronomía, Biblioteca, Casilla 36-D, Santiago 1; tel. (2) 2294002; fax (2) 2294101; e-mail biblio@das.uchile.cl; internet www.das.uchile.cl; f. 1852; attached to the Universidad de Chile; Repsold Meridian circle, Transit instrument, Gauthier refractor astrograph, Heyde visual refractor, Danjon astrolabe and Zeiss transit instruments; astronomical station at Cerro El Roble; library of 7,247 vols; Dir MARÍA TERESA RUIZ.

Observatorio Interamericano de Cerro Tololo (Cerro Tololo Inter-American Observatory): Casilla 603, La Serena; tel. (51) 205200; fax (51) 205212; internet www.ctio.noao.edu; f. 1963; astronomical observation of stars only observable in the southern hemisphere; library of 21,405 vols; Dir Dr ALISTAIR R. WALKER.

Servicio Hidrográfico y Oceanográfico de la Armada de Chile (Hydrographic and Oceanographic Service of the Chilean Navy): Errazuriz 254, Playa Ancha, Valparaíso; tel. (32) 266666; fax (32) 266542; e-mail shoa@shoa.cl; internet www.shoa.cl; f. 1874; hydrographic surveys, nautical charts and publications, oceanography, maritime safety, national oceanographic data centre; library of 12,000 vols; Dir Capt. ROBERTO GARNHAM P.; publs *Anuario Hidrográfico* (1 a year), *Derroteros de la Costa de Chile*, *Noticias a los Navegantes* (12 a year), *Tablas de Marea de la Costa de Chile* (1 a year).

Servicio Nacional de Geología y Minería: Casilla 10465, Santiago; tel. (2) 7375050; fax (2) 7372026; e-mail msuarez@sernageomin.cl; internet www.sernageomin.cl; f. 1981; geoscience and mining; library of 30,000 vols, 15,000 aerial photographs, 200 satellite photographs, 600 periodical titles, 6,000 maps; Nat. Dir PATRICIO CARTAGENA; publ. *Revista Geológica de Chile* (2 a year).

RELIGION, SOCIOLOGY AND ANTHROPOLOGY

Instituto Latinoamericano de Doctrina y Estudios Sociales: Almirante Barroso 6, Casilla 14446, Correo 21, Santiago; tel. (2) 6714072; fax (2) 6986873; f. 1965 for the study, dissemination and renewal of social thought within the Church; teaching and research in economics and social sciences; in-service courses for teachers and professionals; 54 mems; Exec. Vice-Dir R. P. GONZALO ARROYO; publs *DOCLA*, *Revista de Análisis Económico*, *Persona y Sociedad*.

TECHNOLOGY

Comisión Nacional de Investigación Científica y Tecnológica (CONICYT) (National Commission for Scientific and Technological Research): Canadá 308, Providencia, Santiago; tel. (2) 3654400; fax (2) 6551396; internet www.conicyt.cl; f. 1969; government agency in charge of studying, planning and proposing national scientific and technological policy to the govt and developing, promoting and improving science and technology; mem. of ICSU; mem. of FID; library of 4,500 vols; Pres. VIVIAN HEYL CHIAPPINI; Dir of Scientific Information PATRICIA E. MUÑOZ PALMA; publs *C & T* (electronic edition only, 12 a year), *Series Bibliografías*, *Series Directorios*, irregular study reports, documentation reports, *Series Información y Documentación*, *Panorama Científico* (12 a year).

Instituto de Investigaciones y Ensayes de Materiales (IDIEM), Universidad de Chile (Institute for Materials Research and Testing): Plaza Ercilla 883, Santiago; tel. (20 9784151; fax (2) 6983166; e-mail idiem@idiem.uchile.cl; f. 1898; library of 8,000 vols; Dir FERNANDO YAÑEZ URIBE.

Instituto Nacional de Normalización (National Institute of Standardization): Matías Cousiño 64 piso 6, Santiago; tel. (2) 4458800; e-mail info@inn.cl; internet www3.inn.cl; f. 1944; library: 160,000 technical standards; Exec. Dir SERGIO TORO GALLEGUILLOS.

Libraries and Archives

Concepción

Universidad de Concepción, Dirección de Bibliotecas: Barrio Universitario, Casilla 1807, 160-C, Correo 3, Concepción; tel. (41) 234985; fax (41) 244796; f. 1919; 425,250 vols, 6,315 periodicals; Dir DIETER OELKER LINK.

Santiago

Archivo Nacional (National Archive): Miraflores 50, Santiago; tel. (2) 3605213; fax (2) 6325735; e-mail archivo.nacional@dibam.cl; internet www.dibam.cl/archivo_nacional; f. 1927; incl. historic and public administration collns; Dir MARÍA EUGENIA BARRIENTOS.

Biblioteca Central, Instituto de Investigaciones Agropecuarias: Casilla 439 Correo 3, CP 7083150, Santiago; tel. (2) 7575223; fax (2) 5464668; internet alerce.inia.cl; f. 1947; 18,000 vols, 31,800 documents and papers incl. Chilean colln, 675 current periodicals, 9,764 Chilean univ. theses; Head Librarian SONIA ELSO; publs *Agricultura Técnica* (4 a year, online), *Bibliografía Agrícola Chilena* (online only), *Boletín INIA* (irregular), *Collection Libros INIA* (irregular), *Serie Actas* (irregular), *Tierra Adentro* (6 a year).

Biblioteca del Congreso Nacional (Congress Library): Huérfanos 1117, 2° piso, Clasificador Postal 1199, Santiago; tel. (2) 2701700; fax (2) 2701766; internet www.congreso.cl/biblioteca; f. 1883; 1,000,000 vols and 5,600 periodicals on law, social sciences, politics and economics, human sciences and literature; 13,500 leaflets, 12,000 rare books, 1,353 maps and topographical charts, 4,000,000 Chilean press cuttings; official depository for international organizations, legal depository for national publs; open to the public; Dir XIMENA FELIÚ SILVA; Asst Dir ALICIA ROJAS ESTIBIL; publs *Serie Estudios*, *Alerta Informativa*, *Temas de Actualidad*, *Visión Semanal*.

Biblioteca Nacional de Chile (National Library): Av. Libertador Bernardo O'Higgins 651, Santiago; tel. (2) 3605200; fax (2) 6380461; e-mail biblioteca.nacional@bndechile.cl; internet www.dibam.cl/biblioteca_nacional; f. 1813; 3,500,000 vols, 75,000 MSS, 83 incunabula; Dir MARTA CRUZ-COKE M.; publs *Bibliografía Chilena* (1 a year), *Mapocho* (2 a year), *Referencias Críticas sobre autores Chilenos*, bibliographies, catalogues.

Dirección del Sistema de Bibliotecas de la Universidad de Santiago de Chile: Schatchtebeck 4, Ex-Avenida Oriente, Estación Central, Santiago; tel. (2) 7182603; fax (2) 7763516; e-mail ximena.sobarzo@usach.cl; internet www.biblioteca.usach.cl; f. 1979; 292,175 vols; Dir XIMENA SOBARZO SÁNCHEZ.

Pontificia Universidad Católica de Chile, Sistema de Bibliotecas: Campus San Joaquín, Vicuña Mackenna 4860, Casilla 306, Correo 22, Santiago; tel. (2) 6864615; fax (2) 6865852; f. 1901; 10 university libraries; 1,587,518 vols; Dir MARÍA LUISA ARENAS FRANCO.

Sistema de Servicios de Información y Bibliotecas de la Universidad de Chile (SISIB): Av. Diagonal Paraguay 265, Oficina 703, Santiago; tel. (2) 9782583; fax (2) 9782574; e-mail sisib@uchile.cl; internet www.uchile.cl; f. 1843, reorganized 1936; contains more than 3m. vols, comprising donations from Canada, the UK, the USA and Spain, and from private collections, including those of Pedro Montt and Pablo Neruda; collection of periodicals comprising 14,500 titles, with over 500,000 issues; there are 49 libraries in the University; Dir GABRIELA ORTÚZAR FONTT.

Valdivia

Sistema de Bibliotecas, Universidad Austral de Chile: Correo 2, Valdivia; tel. (63) 221290; fax (63) 221360; e-mail biblio@uach.cl; internet www.biblioteca.uach.cl; f. 1962; 147,000 vols, 1,600 periodicals; specializes in science; Dir LUIS VERA CARTES.

Valparaíso

Biblioteca Central de la Universidad Técnica 'Federico Santa María': Avda España 1680, Edificio U, Valparaíso; tel. (32) 2654147; e-mail casa.central@bib.utfsm.cl; internet www.bib.utfsm.cl; f. 1926; 110,000 vols, 2,400 periodicals; audiovisual material: cassettes, video cassettes, maps, microfilms, slides; specializes in science and technology; Dir ALEX ARELLANO CALZADILLA; publs *Gestión tecnológica* (4 a year), *Scientia: Serie A Mathematical Sciences*, *USM Noticias* (12 a year).

Biblioteca de la Pontificia Universidad Católica de Valparaíso: Avda Brasil 2950, Casilla 4059, Valparaíso; tel. (32) 2273261; fax (32) 2273183; e-mail abustos@ucv.cl; internet biblioteca.ucv.cl; f. 1928; 248,000 vols; Dir ATILIO BUSTOS; publs *Biblioteca Agora*, *Electronic Journal of Biotechnology*, *Fondo de Etnomusicologia Margot Loyola Palacios*.

Biblioteca Publica No. 1 'Santiago Severin' de Valparaíso: Plaza Simón Bolívar, Valparaíso; tel. (32) 213375; fax (32) 213375; f. 1873; incl. a colln of historical books on Chile and America and a colln of 17th- to 19th-century books; 94,149 vols, 166,814 periodicals; Dir YOLANDA SOTO VERGARA.

Museums and Art Galleries

Angol

Museo Dillman S. Bullock: Casilla 8-D, Angol; Km 5 Camino Angol–Collipulli, Angol; tel. (45) 712395; fax (45) 719303; e-mail museodbullock@yahoo.es; f. 1946; general local flora and fauna; extensive local archaeological colln; library of 5,000 vols; undertakes research, scientific expeditions; Dir ALBERTO E. MONTERO.

Antofagasta

Museo Regional de Antofagasta: Bolívar No 188, Casilla 746, Antofagasta; tel. (55) 227016; fax (55) 221109; e-mail museoantof@terra.cl; f. 1984; archaeology, history, ethnography, geology; small library; Curator IVO KUZMANIĆ PIEROTIĆ.

Arica

Museo Arqueológico San Miguel de Azapa: Facultad de Ciencias Sociales Administrativas y Económicas, Depto de Arqueología y Museología, Casilla 6-D, Arica;

tel. (58) 205555; fax (58) 205552; e-mail masma@uta.cl; internet www.uta.cl/masma; f. 1967; Univ. museum, belonging to the dept of anthropology; exhibits communicate univ. research on pre-Columbian, colonial and modern native people; library of 8,000 vols; Dir Dr MARIETTA ORTEGA PERRIER (acting); publs *Chungara* (Chilean anthropology, 2 a year), *Cuadernos de Trabajo* (irregular).

Cañete

Museo Folklórico Araucano de Cañete 'Juan A. Ríos M.': Casilla 28, Cañete; f. 1968; to conserve, exhibit and research the Mapuche culture from its origins to contact with Spanish culture; to recreate the environment which Valdivia saw in 1552 when he built the Tucapel Fort (near the museum); anthropological research of the native Mapuche settlements which still exist; archaeological excavations in the surrounding area; library of 2,000 vols; Curator GLORIA CÁRDENAS TRONCOSO.

Concepción

Museo de Historia Natural de Concepción (Concepción Natural History Museum): Maipú 2359, Plaza Acevedo, Concepción; tel. (41) 2310932; fax (41) 2310932; e-mail musconce@surnet.cl; internet www.dibam.cl/sdm_mr_concepcion; f. 1902; library of 6,732 vols; Dir MARCO SÁNCHEZ AGUILERA; publ. *Comunicaciones del Museo de Concepción.*

Museo de Hualpén (Hualpén Museum): Camino Desembocadura s/n, Hualpén; tel. (41) 2426399; f. 1882; collns of Greek, Roman and Egyptian archaeology; Chilean arms and numismatic collns; Oriental art; Chilean and American folk arts; Chilean archaeology; 18th- and 19th-century furniture; Dir MARTÍN DOMÍNGUEZ.

Copiapó

Museo Regional de Atacama: Casilla 134, Copiapó; Atacama 98, Copiapó; tel. (52) 212313; fax (52) 212313; e-mail museo.atacama@dibam.cl; internet www.dibam.cl/sdm_mr_atacama; f. 1973; archaeology, mineralogy, ecology and history; library of 15,000 vols; Dir MIGUEL CERVELLINO.

Iquique

Museo Antropológico de Iquique: c/o Universidad Arturo Prat de Iquique, Calle Grumete Volado 127, Iquique; f. 1987; attached to the Centro de Estudios del Desierto of the University; permanent exhibition showing the cultural devt of the people of the region from 10,000 BC to AD 1900; research in archaeology, rural devt of farming communities, history and ethnography; specialized library; Dir Arq. ÁLVARO CAREVIC RIVERA; publ. research findings.

Museo Regional de Iquique: Calle Baquedano 951, Iquique; tel. (57) 411214; fax (57) 413278; e-mail ftellezc@gmail.com; attached to the Dept of Social Development of the Municipality of Iquique; f. 1960; permanent exhibition of regional archaeology, ethnography and history; Dir FRANCISCO TÉLLEZ CANCINO.

La Serena

Museo Arqueológico de La Serena (La Serena Archaeological Museum): Calle Cordovez esq. Cienfuegos s/n, La Serena; tel. (51) 224492; fax (51) 550423; e-mail muarse@entelchile.net; internet www.dibam.cl/sdm_m_laserena; f. 1943; sections on archaeology, prehistory, physical anthropology, colonial history, ethnology and palaeontology; library of 23,000 vols, 18,043 slides, 28,150 photographs; Dir GONZALO AMPUERO B.

Linares

Museo de Arte y Artesanía de Linares: Casilla Postal 280, Linares; Avda Valentín Letelier 572, Linares; tel. (73) 210662; fax (73) 210662; e-mail mulin@ctcinternet.cl; internet www.dibam.cl/sdm_maya_linares; f. 1966; arts and crafts from the Inca period to the present; valuable collections including unique clay miniatures; collection of Huaso implements; ceramics; exhibition of history and people of Linares; conferences, lectures, films; Dir PATRICIO ACEVEDO LAGOS.

Ovalle

Museo del Limari: Covarrubias esq. Antofagasta, Casilla 59, Ovalle; tel. (53) 620029; fax (53) 620029; e-mail mdlim@ctcinternet.net.cl; internet www.mdlim.cl; f. 1963; archaeology (esp. local); Curator DANIELA SERANI ELLIOTT.

Puerto Williams

Museo 'Martín Gusinde': Aragay 1, Puerto Williams, Isla Navarino, XII Región de Magallanes, Antártica Chilena; tel. and fax (61) 621043; e-mail pgrendi@yahoo.com; internet www.dibam.cl; f. 1975; situated on Navarino Island; history and geography of the southernmost archipelagos of the Americas; aboriginal culture, flora, fauna and minerals of the area; library of 500 vols; Curator PAOLA GRENDI ILHARREBORDE.

Punta Arenas

Museo Regional de Magallanes: Centro Cultural Braun-Menéndez, Hernando de Magallanes 949, Punta Arenas; tel. (61) 244216; fax (61) 221387; f. 1983, fmrly Museo de la Patagonia, f. 1967; Patagonian history; library: specialized 3,500 vols; Dir MAURICIO QUERCIA.

Museo Salesiano 'Maggiorino Borgatello' (Salesian Museum 'Maggiorino Borgatello'): Av. Bulnes 336, Casilla 347, Punta Arenas; tel. (61) 221001; e-mail musborga@tnet.cl; internet www.museomaggiorinoborgatello.cl; f. 1893; scientific and ethnographical (notable relics of extreme South American and Tierra del Fuegan tribes), patagonic history, antarctic continent vision, petroleum industry; library of 2,000 vols; Scientific Dir Prof. SALVATORE CIRILLO DAMA.

Santiago

Museo Chileno de Arte Precolombino: Casilla 3687, Bandera 361, Santiago; tel. (2) 6887348; fax (2) 6972779; f. 1981 by the council of Santiago City and the Fundación Familia Larraín Echenique; 2,000 items of pre-Columbian art and 1,000 items in ethnographic collns from Mapuche and Aymara cultures; textiles, ceramics, metal work, stone sculptures; large colln of photographs, slides, video and audio cassettes; laboratory for textile and pottery conservation; laboratory for archaeological research; research on pre-Columbian music, rock art, Tiahuanaco, Aymara, Atacama and Araucanian cultures, prehistoric architecture, Andean textiles and symbolism; educational programmes; music archive; library of 6,000 vols, 500 periodicals, spec. colln of pre-Columbian art, conservation and archaeology; Dir CARLOS ALDUNATE DEL SOLAR; publs *Boletín* (1 a year), catalogue of exhibitions (irregular).

Museo de Arte Colonial de San Francisco: Alameda Bernardo O'Higgins 834, Santiago; tel. (2) 6398737; fax (2) 6398737; e-mail museosanfrancisco@museosanfrancisco.tie.cl; internet www.museosanfrancisco.cl; f. 1968 by the Franciscan Order; 16th–19th century art (esp. 17th-century paintings); the life of St Francis depicted in 22 pictures; the life of San Diego de Alcalá depicted in 35 pictures; also other religious works of art, furniture, icons, embroidery, sculpture, carving, woodwork and metalwork; Dir ROSA PUGA D.

Museo de Arte Contemporáneo (Contemporary Art Museum): Parque Forestal frente a Calle Mosqueto, Santiago; tel. (2) 6395486; fax (2) 6394945; internet www.uchile.cl/mac; f. 1947; contemporary and fine arts; Dir FRANCISCO BRUGNOLI BAILONI.

Museo de Arte Popular Americano (Museum of American Folk Art): Compañía 2691, Casilla 2100, Universidad de Chile, Santiago; tel. (2) 6821481; fax (2) 6821481; e-mail mapa@uchile.cl; internet www.mapa.uchile.cl; f. 1943; objects of American folk art in pottery, basketware, wood and metal, Araucanian silverware; Dir NURY GONZALEZ.

Museo de Historia Natural de San Pedro Nolasco (Natural History Museum): MacIver 341, Santiago; f. 1922; library of 58,000 vols; spec. collns: Claudio Gay, G. Cuvier, A. E. Brehrm, Ch. Darwin.

Museo de la Educación Gabriela Mistral: Chacabuco 365, Santiago Centro; tel. (2) 6818169; e-mail museodelaeducacion@gmail.com; internet www.museodelaeducacion.cl; f. 1941, was closed to the public between 1981 and 2006; permanent exhibition on Chilean educational history; central themes of heritage and memory; interactive space for recreational learning; organizes seminars, workshops and training in subjects such as education, culture and soc.; library of 1,600 vols, photographic archive of 6,000 images; Dir Dr MARÍA ISABEL ORELLANA RIVERA.

Museo Histórico Nacional (National Historical Museum): Palacio de la Real Audiencia, Plaza de Armas, Casilla 9764, Santiago; tel. (2) 6381411; fax (2) 6331815; e-mail bdevose@oris.renib.cl; internet www.museohistoriconacional.cl; f. 1911; pre-Hispanic period to the present; costume, iconographic, arms, arts and crafts, and numismatic collections; dept of education; research in textile, paper and photographic restoration; library of 12,000 vols; Dir BARBARA DE VOS EYZAGUIRRE.

Museo Nacional de Bellas Artes (National Museum of Fine Arts): Parque Forestal s/n, Casilla 3209, Correo Central, Santiago; tel. (2) 6391946; fax (2) 6393297; e-mail milan.ivelic@mnba.cl; internet www.dibam.cl; f. 1880; paintings, engravings, etchings and sculpture, Chilean and European paintings; library of 15,000 vols; Dir MILAN IVELIC.

Museo Nacional de Historia Natural (National Museum of Natural History): Casilla 787, Santiago; tel. (2) 6804603; fax (2) 6804602; e-mail webmaster@mnhn.cl; internet www.mnhn.cl; f. 1830; depts of zoology, entomology, hydrobiology, botany, mineralogy, palaeontology, anthropology, museology, education; Curator MARÍA ELIANA RAMÍREZ CASALI; publs *Boletín*, *Noticiario mensual.*

Talca

Museo O'Higginiano y de Bellas Artes de Talca: 1 Norte No. 875, Talca; tel. (71) 210428; fax (71) 227330; e-mail museodetalca@gmail.com; internet www.dibam.cl/sdm_moba_talca; f. 1964; paintings, sculpture, Chilean history, archaeology, religious artefacts, antique furniture, arms; library of 430 vols; video cassettes; Dir ALEJANDRO MORALES YAMAL; publ. *La Casona durante la Colonia.*

Temuco

Museo Regional de la Araucania (Araucania Museum): Avda Alemania 084, Casilla 481, Temuco; tel. (45) 730062; fax (45) 730064; f. 1940; opened to the public 1943;

archaeological, artistic and ethnographic exhibits of the Araucanian, or Mapuche, Indians of South Chile, and others relating to the conquest, pacification and colonization of Araucania, as well as the history of Temuco city itself; maintains research section; library: specialized library of 886 vols about Mapuche culture and regional history; 1,400 reprints and maps of Mapuche reservations and foreign colonization; Dir HÉCTOR ZUMAETA ZÚÑIGA; publ. *Bulletin*.

Valdivia

Museo Histórico y Antropológico 'Mauricio Van de Maele': Los Laureles s/n, Isla Teja, Valdivia; tel. (63) 212872; fax (63) 212872; e-mail secmuseologica@uach.cl; internet www.uach.cl/direccion/museologica; f. 1967; attached to Universidad Austral de Chile; centre for Conservation of historical monuments, archaeology, museums and historical archives; undertakes teaching, research, training of museum staff, conservation, museology; library of 3,000 vols, 4,000 photographs; Dir LEONOR ADÁN A.

Valparaíso

Museo de Historia Natural de Valparaíso (Natural History Museum): Calle Condell 1546, Valparaíso; tel. (32) 2544840; fax (32) 2544843; e-mail contacto@mhnv.cl; internet www.dibam.cl/sdm_mhn_valpo; f. 1876; natural sciences and anthropology; library of 3,000 vols; Dir CRISTIAN BECKER ALVAREZ; publ. *Anales*.

Vicuña

Museo Gabriela Mistral de Vicuña: Calle Gabriela Mistral 759, Casilla 50, Vicuña; tel. (51) 411223; fax (51) 412524; e-mail mgmistral@entelchile.net; f. 1971 to preserve the cultural legacy of the poet Gabriela Mistral (Nobel prize for Literature 1945); documents, photographs and personal effects; replica of birthplace of poet, talks, films, music; library of 6,000 vols; Dir RODRIGO IRIBARREN AVILÉS; publ. *Boletín*.

Viña del Mar

Museo Comparativo de Biología Marina: Facultad de Ciencias del Mar y Recursos Naturales, Universidad de Valparaíso, Casilla 5080 Reñaca; tel. (32) 507820; fax (32) 507859; e-mail ricardo.bravo@uv.cl; f. 1955; echinoderms, molluscs and other invertebrates; algae and marine lichens from the coastal regions of the SE Pacific; library for the students of marine biology and oceanic engineering; Curator Dr RICARDO BRAVO; publ. *Revista de Biología Marina y Oceanografía*.

Universities and Technical Universities

UNIVERSIDAD DE ANTOFAGASTA

Avda Angamos 601, Antofagasta
Telephone: (55) 637325
Fax: (55) 637102
E-mail: rectoria@uantof.cl
Internet: www.uantof.cl
Founded 1981
State control
Language of instruction: Spanish
Academic year: March to January
Rector: LUIS ALBERTO LOYOLA MORALES
Vice-Rector for Academic Affairs: HERNÁN BAEZA KUROKI
Vice-Rector for Finance: CARLOS RIVERA DANTAGNAN
Gen. Sec.: MACARENA SILVA BOGGIANO

Dir of Teaching: NELSON HERRERA AVILA
Gen. Dir of Student Affairs: DOMINGO GÓMEZ PARRA
Dir of Admin. and Financial Affairs: OSCAR MORALES CASTILLO
Dir of Computing: RICHARDS ROJAS ARQUERO
Dir of Extension and Communications: CÉSAR TRABUCCO SWANECK
Dir of Graduate Affairs: MARÍA ELISA TABOADA MENESES
Dir of Legal Affairs: FERNANDO FERNÁNDEZ DE LA CERDA
Dir of Studies and Development: INGRID JAMETT ARANDA
Dir of Research: CARLOS RIQUELME SALAMANCA
Librarian: NORMA MONTERREY
Number of teachers: 320
Number of students: 6,067
Publications: *Estudios Oceanológicos, Hombre y Desierto, Innovación*

DEANS

Faculty of Basic Sciences: GUILLERMO MONDACA
Faculty of Education and Human Sciences: JUAN PANADES VARGAS
Faculty of Engineering: PEDRO CÓRDOVA
Faculty of Health Sciences: MARCOS CIKUTOVIC
Faculty of Law: DOMINGO CLAPS
Faculty of Marine Resources: HERNAN BAEZA

ATTACHED INSTITUTES

Instituto del Desierto: research in energy and water resources of Atacama desert; agriculture and solar energy in the desert; Dir RENÉ CONTRERAS.

Instituto de Investigaciones Antropológicas: research in archaeology, anthropology, linguistics and literature of North Chile; Dir PATRICIO NÚÑEZ.

Instituto de Investigaciones Oceanológicas: research in marine life of northern coast of Chile; Dir LUIS RODRIGUEZ.

UNIVERSIDAD ARTURO PRAT

Avda Arturo Prat 2120, Iquique
Telephone: (57) 441208
Fax: (57) 394393
E-mail: j.torres@cec.unap.cl
Internet: www.unap.cl
Founded 1984
State control
Language of instruction: Spanish
Academic year: March to December
Rector: CARLOS MERINO PINOCHET
Vice-Rector for Academic Affairs: CÉSAR ARANCIBIA CÓRDOVA
Admin. Dir: CARLOS LADRIX OSÉS
Librarian: ROBERTO JIMÉNEZ RAMÍREZ
Number of teachers: 500
Number of students: 5,300

UNIVERSIDAD DE ATACAMA

Copayapu 485, Copiapó
Telephone: (52) 206500
Fax: (52) 212662
Internet: www.uda.cl
Founded 1981
State control
Language of instruction: Spanish
Academic year: March to December
Rector: JUAN IGLESIAS DÍAZ
Vice-Rector: GABRIELA PRADO PRADO
Gen. Sec.: TERESA REYES ASPILLAGA
Librarian: MARIANELA VIVANCO CORTÉS
Number of teachers: 95
Number of students: 2,950

Publications: *Revista de Derecho de Aguas* (1 a year), *Revista de Derecho de Minas* (1 a year), *Revista de Ingeniería* (1 a year)

DEANS

Faculty of Engineering: CELSO ARIAS M.
Faculty of Humanities and Education: OSCAR PAINÉAN BUSTAMANTE
Faculty of Law: RODRIGO PÉREZ LISICIC
Faculty of Natural Sciences: RENÉ MAURELIA GÓMEZ

ATTACHED INSTITUTES

Instituto Asistencia a la Minería: Casilla 240, Copiapó; tel. (52) 212006; fax (52) 212662; Dir JUAN NAVEA DANTAGNAN.

Instituto de Investigaciones Científicas y Tecnológicas: Casilla 240, Copiapó; tel. (52) 218770; fax (52) 218770; Dir GERMÁN CÁCERES ARENAS.

Instituto Derecho de Minas y Aguas: Moneda 673, 8° piso, Santiago; tel. (2) 6328290; fax (2) 6383452; Dir ALEJANDRO VERGARA BLANCO.

Instituto Tecnológico: Casilla 240, Copiapó; tel. (52) 206755; fax (52) 206756; e-mail timur.padilla@uda.cl; internet www.tecnologico.uda.cl; Dir TIMUR PADILLA BOCIC.

UNIVERSIDAD DEL BÍOBÍO

Avda Collao 1202, Casilla 5-C, Concepción
Telephone: (41) 261200
Fax: (41) 313897
E-mail: rector@ubiobio.cl
Internet: www.ubiobio.cl
Founded 1988
State control
Language of instruction: Spanish
Academic year: March to December
Campus also at Avda Andrés Bello s/n, Chillán
Rector: HILARIO HERNÁNDEZ GURRUCHAGA
Pro-Rector for Chillán Campus: FELIX MARTÍNEZ RODRÍGUEZ
Vice-Rector for Academic Affairs: HÉCTOR GAETE FERES
Vice-Rector for Financial Affairs: CLAUDIO ROJAS MIÑO
Sec.-Gen.: RICARDO PONCE SOTO
Dir for Int. Liaison: ALDO A. BALLERINI
Number of teachers: 603
Number of students: 8,986
Publications: *Arquitecturas del Sur* (3 a year), *Cuadernos de Edificación en Madera* (3 a year), *Maderas: Ciencia y Tecnología* (2 a year), *Memoria Anual Institucional* (1 a year), *Mercado de suelo de Concepción* (3 a year), *Proyección UBB*, *Theoria* (1 a year), *Tiempo y Espacio* (1 a year)

DEANS

Faculty of Architecture, Construction and Design: RICARDO HEMPEL HOLZAPFEL
Faculty of Business Management: LUIS CONTRERAS VILLAR
Faculty of Education and Humanities (Chillán): MARCO AURELIO REYES COCA
Faculty of Engineering: PETER BACKHOUSE ERAZO
Faculty of Health and Food Sciences: NORA PLAZA CEBALLOS
Faculty of Sciences: JORGE PLAZA DE LOS REYES ZAPATA

UNIVERSIDAD DE CHILE

Avda Bernardo O'Higgins 1058, Casilla 10-D, Santiago
Telephone: (2) 6781003
Fax: (2) 6781012
Internet: www.uchile.cl

Founded 1738 as Universidad Real de San Felipe; inaugurated 1843 as Universidad de Chile
State control
Academic year: March to December
Rector: LUIS A. RIVEROS C.
Pro-Rector: LUIS BAHAMONDE BRAVO
Academic Vice-Rector: MARIO SAPAG-HAGAR

Library: see Libraries and Archives
Number of teachers: 2,775 (including all branch institutions)
Number of students: 24,822

Publications: *Actualidad Universitaria* (12 a year), *Anales de la Universidad de Chile* (1 a year), *Anuario Astronómico* (1 a year), *Bizantion Nea Hellas*, *Boletín Chileno de Parasitología* (4 a year), *Boletín de Filología* (2 a year), *Boletín Interamericano de Educación Musical* (1 a year), *Comentarios sobre la Situación Económica*, *Cuadernos de Ciencia Política* (4 a year), *Cuadernos de Historia* (1 a year), *Desarrollo Rural* (2 a year), *Estudios Internacionales* (4 a year), *Ocupación y Desocupación Encuesta Nacional* (2 a year), *Política* (2 a year), *Revista Chilena de Antropología* (1 a year), *Revista Chilena de Historia del Derecho*, *Revista Chilena de Humanidades* (1 a year), *Revista Comunicaciones en Geología* (1 a year), *Revista de Derecho Económico*, *Revista de Derecho Público*, *Revista Económica y Administración* (4 a year), *Revista de Filosofía* (1 a year), *Revista Musical Chilena* (2 a year), *Revista Psiquiátrica Clínica* (1 a year), *Terra Aridae* (2 a year), *U Noticias* (12 a year)

DEANS
Faculty of Agriculture: MARIO SILVA G.
Faculty of Architecture and Town Planning: MANUEL FERNÁNDEZ HECHENLEITNER
Faculty of Chemical and Pharmaceutical Sciences: LUIS NÚÑEZ
Faculty of Dentistry: JOSÉ MATAS COLOM
Faculty of Economic and Administrative Sciences: NASSIR SAPAG
Faculty of Fine Arts: LUIS MERINO MONTERO
Faculty of Forestry: GUILLERMO JULIO A.
Faculty of Law: ANTONIO BASCUÑAN V.
Faculty of Medicine: Dr JORGE LAS HERAS
Faculty of Philosophy and Humanities: MARÍA ISABEL FLISHFISCH
Faculty of Physical and Mathematical Sciences: VÍCTOR PÉREZ VERA
Faculty of Sciences: CAMILO QUEZADA BOUEY
Faculty of Social Sciences: FERNANDO DURÁN
Faculty of Veterinary Sciences and Cattle Breeding: SANTIAGO URCELAY

ATTACHED INSTITUTES
Clinical Hospital of the University of Chile: Avda Santos Dumont 999, Santiago; Dir Dr ITALO BRAGHETTO.

Institute of International Studies: Condell 249, Santiago; Dir JEANETTE IRIGOIN.

Institute of Nutrition and Food Technology: Avda José Pedro Alessandri 5540, Santiago; Dir FERNANDO VIO.

Institute of Public Affairs: María Guerrero 940, Santiago; Dir OSVALDO SUNKEL.

UNIVERSIDAD DE LA FRONTERA

Avda Francisco Salazar 01145, Casilla 54-D, Temuco
Telephone: (45) 325000
Fax: (45) 325950
E-mail: ufro-tco@ufro.cl
Internet: www.ufro.cl
Founded 1981
State control
Academic year: March to December (2 semesters)

Rector: SERGIO BRAVO ESCOBAR
Vice-Rector for Academic Affairs: JUAN MANUEL FIERRO BUSTOS
Vice-Rector for Admin. and Finance: SERGIO CARTER FUENTEALBA
Sec.-Gen.: RICARDO HERRERA LARA
Library Dir: ROBERTO ARAYA NAVARRO

Number of teachers: 645
Number of students: 8,735

Publications: *Cubo* (1 a year), *Chilean Review of Biological Medical Sciences* (2 a year), *International Journal of Morphology* (4 a year), *Vertientes UFRO* (4 a year), *Revista Educación y Humanidades* (education and humanities, 1 a year), *Revista Investigaciones en Educación* (educational research, 1 a year), *Memoria Institucional* (1 a year), *Lengua y Literatura Mapuche* (2 a year), *Revista Médica del Sur* (medicine, 2 a year), *Revista Nuestra Muestra* (2 a year)

DEANS
Faculty of Agricultural and Forestry Sciences: ALIRO CONTRERAS NOVOA
Faculty of Education and Humanities: CARLOS DEL VALLE ROJAS
Faculty of Engineering and Administration: PLINIO DURÁN GARCIÁ
Faculty of Medicine: EDUARDO HEBEL WEISS

PROFESSORS
Faculty of Agricultural and Forestry Sciences (Francisco Salazar 01145; tel. (45) 325630; fax (45) 325634; e-mail aliroc@ufro.cl; internet www.agrofor.ufro.cl):
MARÍN, P., Forestry Sciences
SORIANO, R., Agricultural Production
VENEGAS, J., Agricultural Sciences and Natural Resources

Faculty of Education and Humanities (Francisco Salazar 01145; tel. (45) 325370; fax (45) 325379; e-mail hcarrasc@ufro.cl; internet educacionyhumanidades.ufro.cl):
CHÁVEZ, J., Social Sciences
FELMER, L., Psychology
MÉNDEZ, I., Education
RIBERA, E., Language, Literature and Communication
SALAZAR, C., Physical Education, Sports and Recreation
TRABOL, H., Social Work

Faculty of Engineering and Administration (Arturo Prat 321; tel. (45) 325800; fax (45) 325810; e-mail decing@ufro.cl; internet fica.ufro.cl/web):
BARRA, M., Chemical Sciences
BARRERA, A., Mathematics Engineering
BRACHMANN, C., Chemical Engineering
BRICEÑO, I., Electrical Engineering
JARA, F., Administration and Economy
SALAZAR, G., Systems Engineering
SANHUEZA, M., Physical Sciences
VEGA, H., Mathematics and Statistics
VILLASEÑOR, M., Mechanical Engineering
VON-BISCHOFFSHAUSEN, G., Civil Engineering

Faculty of Medicine (Manuel Montt 112; tel. (45) 325700; fax (45) 325710; e-mail decanmed@ufro.cl; internet www.med.ufro.cl):
ARAYA ORÓSTICA, J., Pathology
CONCHA, S., Medicine (specialized)
CORTES, H., Public Health
ESPINOZA, B., Basic Sciences
FERNÁNDEZ, L., Paediatrics and Infant Surgery
FERNÁNDEZ, R., Integral Odontology
FREDES, E., Surgery and Traumatology
FRENE, E., Internal Medicine
FUENTES, L., Mental Health and Psychiatry
GONZÁLEZ, M., Pre-clinical Sciences
VALLEJOS, C., Obstetrics and Gynaecology

UNIVERSIDAD DE LA SERENA

Avda Raúl Bitrán Nachary s/n, La Serena
Telephone: (51) 204000
Fax: (51) 204310
E-mail: uls@userena.cl
Internet: www.userena.cl
Founded 1981
State control
Academic year: March to December
Rector: Dr NIBALDO AVILÉS PIZARRO
Vice-Rector for Academic Affairs: Dr JORGE CATALÁN AHUMADAS
Vice-Rector for Admin.: Dra MARÍA MARCELA AGUIRRE SALGADO
Gen. Dir of Student Affairs: HERNÁN CORTÉS OLIVARES
Sec.-Gen.: Prof. CALIXTO VEAS GAZ
Int. Liaison Officer: Dr RICARDO CASTILLO BOZO
Librarian: Lic. MARÍA A. CALABACERO JIMÉNEZ

Number of teachers: 554
Number of students: 7,694

Publications: *Revista Actas de Logos* (1 a year), *Revista Crisalida* (1 a year), *Revista Humus* (1 a year), *Revista de Investigación y Desarrollo* (1 a year), *Revista Logos* (1 a year), *Revista Omnibus* (1 a year), *Revista Temas de Educación* (1 a year)

DEANS
Faculty of Economics and Business: Dra LUPERFINA ROJAS ESCOBAR
Faculty of Engineering: Dr Ing. ALBERTO CORTÉS ÁLVAREZ
Faculty of Humanities: Dra MARÍA ZÚNIGA CARRASCO
Faculty of Sciences: Dr GUSTAVO LABBÉ MORALES

UNIVERSIDAD DE LOS LAGOS

Casilla 933, Osorno
Avda Alcalde Fuchslocher 1305, Osorno
Telephone: (64) 333000
Fax: (64) 333374
E-mail: rectoria@ulagos.cl
Internet: www.ulagos.cl
Founded 1993; fmrly Instituto Profesional de Osorno
State control
Academic year: March to December
Rector: RAÚL AGUILAR GATICA
Vice-Rector for Academic Affairs: IVÁN NAVARRO
Vice-Rector for Admin. and Finance: JUAN ABELLO ROMERO
Vice-Rector for Corporate Management: ALEJANDRO SANTIBÁÑEZ HANDSCHUH
Vice-Rector for Planning and Devt: DANIEL LÓPEZ STEFONI
Gen. Sec.: BRUNO CÁRDENAS
Librarian: EDUARDO BARROS BARROS

Number of teachers: 261 (143 full-time, 118 part-time)
Number of students: 3,635

Publications: *Alpha* (humanities), *Biota* (aquatic sciences), *Leader* (social sciences).

UNIVERSIDAD DE MAGALLANES

Casilla 113-D, Punta Arenas
Telephone: (61) 212945
Fax: (61) 219276
Internet: www.umag.cl
Founded 1964 (previously branch of Universidad Técnica del Estado)
State control
Language of instruction: Spanish
Academic year: begins in March
Rector: Dr VÍCTOR FAJARDO MORALES
Vice-Rector for Academic Affairs: LUIS OVAL GONZÁLEZ

Sec.-Gen.: Francisco Soto Piffault
Librarian: Iluminanda Rojas Palacios
Number of teachers: 168
Number of students: 3,200
Publications: *Anales del Instituto de la Patagonia, Austrouniversitaria*

DEANS

Faculty of Economics and Law: Luis Poblete Davanzo
Faculty of Engineering: Juan Oyarzo Pérez
Faculty of Humanities, Social Sciences and Health Sciences: Juan Yudikis Preller
Faculty of Sciences: Octavio Lecaros Palma

ATTACHED INSTITUTE

Instituto de la Patagonia: Avda Bulnes 01890, Casilla 113-D, Punta Arenas; tel. 217173; fax 212973; f. 1969; scientific, cultural and social development of the South American region; Dir Claudio Venegas Canelo.

UNIVERSIDAD DE PLAYA ANCHA

Edificio Puntángeles, piso 6, Av. Playa Ancha 850, Playa Ancha, Valparaíso
Telephone: (32) 2500100
E-mail: mbaxman@upla.cl
Internet: www.upla.cl
Founded 1948
Languages of instruction: Spanish, English, French, German
State control
Academic year: March to December
Rector: Patricio Sanhueza Vivanco
Pro-Rector: Carmen Ibañez Castillo
Vice-Rector for Academic Affairs: Rolando Tiemann
Vice-Rector for Admin. and Financial Affairs: Eduardo Faivovich
Vice-Rector for Development: Luis Bork
Gen. Sec.: Ginette Bobillier
Librarian: Maria Eugenia Olguin Steenbecker
Number of teachers: 328
Number of students: 3,700
Publications: *Diálogos Educacionales, Diccionario Ejemplificado de Chilenismos, Nueva Revista del Pacífico, Notas Históricas y Geográficas, Proyección Universitaria, Revista de Orientación, Visiones Científicas*

DEANS

Faculty of Art: Alberto Teichelmann Shuttleton
Faculty of Education: René Flores Castillo
Faculty of Humanities: Juan Saavedra A.
Faculty of Natural and Exact Sciences: Juan Camus
Faculty of Physical Education: Elías Marín Valenzuela

UNIVERSIDAD DE SANTIAGO DE CHILE

Avda. Libertador Bernardo O'Higgins 3363, Santiago
Telephone: (2) 7180000
Internet: www.usach.cl
Founded 1849 as Escuela de Artes y Oficios; renamed as Universidad Técnica del Estado 1947; present name 1981
State control
Language of instruction: Spanish
Academic year: March to December
Rector: Dr Juan Manuel Zolezzi Cid
Vice-Rector for Academic Affairs: Rodrigo Vidal
Vice-Rector for Finances and Management: Juan Pablo Aguirre

Vice-Rector for Research and Devt: Dr Mauricio Escudey
Sec.-Gen.: Gustavo Robles
Gen. Dir for Communications: Margarita Pastene
Dir of Int. Relations: Maria Fernanda Contreras
Academic Registrar: Enrique San Juan
Librarian: María Isabel Parra
Library of 241,478
Number of teachers: 1,145
Number of students: 20,344
Publications: *Avances en Investigación y Desarrollo, Educación en Ingeniería, Mantención e Industria* (4 a year), *Boletín APYME* (6 a year), *Comunicación Universitaria, Contribuciones Científicas y Tecnológicas, Cuadernos de Humanidades*

DEANS

Faculty of Administration and Economics: Silvia Ferrada
Faculty of Chemistry and Biology: Juan Luis Gautier
Faculty of Engineering: Ramón Blasco
Faculty of Humanities: Carmen Norambuena
Faculty of Medicine: José Luis Cárdenas
Faculty of Sciences: Samuel Navarro
Faculty of Technology: Laura Almendares
School of Architecture: Carlos Richards
School of Journalism: Margarita Pastene Valladares
School of Psychology: Emilio Moyano Díaz
Undergraduate Programme: Leopoldo Sáez Godoy

ATTACHED RESEARCH INSTITUTES

Centre for Innovation and Technology transfer: e-mail mariateresa.santander@usach.cl; Dir Maria Teresa Santander.

Centre for Innovation developments in Education: e-mail fidel.oteiza@usach.cl; Dir Fidel Oteiza.

Centre for Research in Creativity and Higher Education: e-mail mario.letelier@usach.cl; Dir Mario Letelier.

Centre for Studies in Science and Food Technology: e-mail claudio.martinez@usach.cl; Dir Claudio Martínez.

Institute for Advanced Studies: e-mail cristian.parker@usach.cl; Dir Cristian Parker.

UNIVERSIDAD DE TALCA

2 Norte 685, Talca
Telephone: (71) 200101
Fax: (71) 228054
Internet: www.utalca.cl
Founded 1981
State control
Language of instruction: Spanish
Academic year: March to December
Rector: Dr Juan Antonio Rock Tarud
Vice-Rector for Academic Affairs: Luis Huerta
Vice-Rector for Cultural Affairs: Pedro Zamorano Pérez
Vice-Rector for Devt: Juan Pablo Prieto Cox
Vice-Rector for Finance and Admin.: Patricio Ortúzar Ruiz
Vice-Rector for Student Affairs: Paulina Arroyo Urrizola
Sec.-Gen.: Ricardo Sánchez Venegas
Librarian: Raúl Ravanal
Number of teachers: 522 (248 full-time, 274 part-time)
Number of students: 7,989
Publications: *Acontecer* (12 a year), *Ius et Praxis* (2 a year), *Panorama Socio Económico* (1 a year), *Revista de Estudios Constitucionales, Revista de Estudios Seriados en Gestión de Salud, Revista Neuma,*

Revista Interamericana de Ambiente y Turismo (Riat), Universum (1 a year)

DEANS

Faculty of Agronomy: Hernán Paillán
Faculty of Business Administration: Claudio Rojas Miño
Faculty of Engineering: Claudio Tenreiro Leiva
Faculty of Forestry Sciences: Juan Franco de la Jara
Faculty of Health Sciences: Carlos Gigoux Castellón
Faculty of Juridical and Social Sciences: Jorge del Picó Rubio
Faculty of Psychology: Emilio Moyano Díaz

DIRECTORS

Faculty of Agronomy (Avda Lircay s/n, Casilla 721, Talca; tel. (71) 200210; fax (71) 200362):
  School of Agronomy: Paula Manríquez Novoa

Faculty of Business Administration (Avda Lircay s/n, Casilla 727, Talca; tel. (71) 200310; fax (71) 200358):
  Graduate School: Patricio Sánchez Campos
  School of Business Data Processing: Andrés Ruiz-Tagle Avendaño
  School of Commercial Engineering: Tamara Tigero Richards
  School of Public Bookkeeping and Auditing: José Salas Ávila

Faculty of Engineering (Camino Los Niches s/n Km 1, , Curico; tel. (75) 201700; fax (75) 325958):
  School of Bioinformatics: José Antonio Reyes Suárez
  School of Civil and Industrial Engineering: Carlos Toledo
  School of Civil Engineering in Computation: Federico Meza
  School of Construction: Leonardo Rischmoller Delgado
  School of Mechanical Engineering: Oscar Fuentes Márquez
  School of Mechatronics Engineering: Mario Fernández Fernández

Faculty of Forestry Sciences (Avda Lircay s/n, Casilla 727, Talca; tel. (71) 200442; fax (71) 200440):
  School of Forestry Engineering: Marcia Vásquez Sandoval

Faculty of Health Sciences (Avda Lircay s/n, Casilla 727, Talca; tel. (71) 201667; fax (71) 201668):
  School of Dentistry: Ivonne Bustos
  School of Medical Technology: Silvia Vidal Flores
  School of Medicine: Verónica Mujica
  School of Physiotherapy: Ramón Valdés Moya
  School of Speech: Exequiel Plaza T.

Faculty of Juridical and Social Sciences (Avda Lircay s/n, Casilla 727, Talca; tel. (71) 200299; fax (71) 200410):
  School of Law: Iván Obando Camino

Faculty of Psychology (Avda Lircay s/n, Casilla 727 Talca; tel. (71) 200299; fax (71) 200410):
  School of Psychology: Nadia Ramos

Faculty of Architecture (Avda Lircay s/n, Casilla 727 Talca; tel. (71) 201539; fax (71) 201539):
  School of Architecture: Germán Valenzuela B.

Faculty of Design (Avda Lircay s/n, Casilla 727, Talca; tel. (71) 200200; fax (71)200225):
  School of Design: Jaime Parra Marchant

School of Music (Avda Lircay s/n, casilla 727, Talca; tel. (71) 201539; fax (71) 201766):

School of Music: MIRTA BUSTAMANTE MÁRQUEZ

UNIVERSIDAD DE TARAPACÁ

Gral Velásquez 1775, Casilla 7-D, Arica
Telephone: (58) 205100
Fax: (58) 232135
E-mail: rec@uta.cl
Internet: www.uta.cl
Founded 1981
State control
Language of instruction: Spanish
Academic year: March to December
Library of 80,242 vols, 499 periodicals
Rector: EMILIO RODRIGUEZ PONCE
Vice-Rector for Academic Affairs: ARTURO FLORES FRANULIC
Vice-Rector for Finance and Admin.: MANUEL DOSONO MUÑOZ
Librarian: INÉS RODRÍGUEZ RIQUELME
Library of 73,300 vols, 622 periodicals
Number of teachers: 237
Number of students: 7,474
Publications: *Chungará* (2 a year), *Diálogo Andino* (2 a year), *Idesia* (2 a year), *Limite* (1 a year), *Revista Facultad de Ingeniería* (1 a year), *Revista de Fisica* (1 a year)

DEANS

Faculty of Agronomy: EUGENIO DOUSSOULIN ESCOBAR
Faculty of Education and Humanities: CARLOS HERRERA SAAVEDRA
Faculty of Engineering: JORGE BENAVIDES SILVA
Faculty of Sciences: HUGO BRAVO AZLAN
Faculty of Social Sciences, Business Administration and Economics: SERGIO PULIDO ROCCATAGLIATA

PROFESSORS

Faculty of Engineering:

ARACENA PIZARRO, D.
BARRAZA SOTOMAYOR, B.
BECK FERNÁNDEZ, H.
BENAVIDES SILVA, J.
BORJAS MONTERO, R.
BUSTOS ANDREU, H.
CAMPOS TRONCOSO, J.
COHEN HORNICKEL, W.
CORREA ARANEDA, E.
DÍAZ ROJAS, H.
DURÁN ARRIAGADA, R.
ESPINOZA VALLEDOR, J.
ESTUPIÑAN PULIDO, E.
FERNÁNDEZ MAGGI, M.
FIGUEROA PÉREZ, H.
FLORES CONDORI, C.
FUENTES HEINRICH, E.
FUENTES ROMERO, R.
GALLEGOS ARAYA, A.
GÁLVEZ SOTO, E.
GODOY RAMSAY, J.
GONZÁLEZ ARAYA, A.
GUÍRRIMAN CARRASCO, R.
HARNISCH VELOSO, I.
JERALDO CASTRO, A.
MARCHIONI CHOQUE, I.
MENDIZABAL JIMÉNEZ, H.
MUÑOZ ESPINOSA, J.
OSSANDON DÍAZ, H.
OSSANDON NUÑEZ, Y.
OVALLE CUBILLOS, R.
PAZ SEGURA, G.
PEDRAJA REJAS, L.
PONCE LÓPEZ, E.
RAMÍREZ VARAS, I.
RODRÍGUEZ ESTAY, A.
SANHUEZA HORMAZABAL, R.
SANZ CANTILLANA, T.
SAPIAÍN ARAYA, R.

TARQUE COSSIO, S.
TORRES ORTÍZ, E.
TORRES SILVA, H.
VALDÉS GONZÁLEZ, H.
VALDIVIA PINTO, R.
VERGARA DÍAZ, J.
VILLALOBOS ABARCA, J.
VILLANUEVA AGUILA, J.
VILLARROEL GONZÁLEZ, C.
ZAMORANO LUCERO, M.

Faculty of Sciences:

ALVAREZ INOSTROZA, L.
BARRIENTOS NUÑOZ, V.
BELTRAN BARRIOS, R.
BOGGIONI CASANOVA, S.
BÓRGUEZ BENITT, CELIA
BRAVO AZLÁN, H.
CABALLERO PETTERSEN, H.
CABELLO FERNÁNDEZ, G.
CALISTO PÉREZ, H.
CAMPOS ORTEGA, H.
CANDIA ANDRADE, M.
CARO ARAYA, M.
CASTRO SANTANDER, F.
CISTERNAS RIVEROS, M.
CORNEJO PONCE, L.
CORRALES MUÑOZ, J.
CORTÉS GAJARDO, W.
CRUZ MARINO, A.
ESPINOZA NAVARRO, O.
FERNÁNDEZ CARVAJAL, I.
FLORES ARAYA, J.
FLORES FRANCULIC, A.
GALAZ LEIVA, S.
GLASS SADIA, B.
GONZÁLEZ FLORES, M.
HERNÁNDEZ VILLASECA, L.
LAIME CONDORI, D.
LAVÍN BECERRA, L.
LAZO NÚÑEZ, E.
LEA RODRÍGUEZ, L.
LEIVA SAJURIA, C.
LOBATO ACOSTA, I.
LÓPEZ PERIC, H.
LORCA PIZARRO, S.
MARTÍN GARCÍA, E.
MEDINA DÍAZ, M.
MENESES VERA, C.
MONTALVO VILLALBA, M.
MOSCOSO ZÁRATE, D.
NARANJO GÁRATE, A. M.
OLIVARES TOLEDO, V.
O'NELL SEQUEIRA, M.
ORTEGA ARAYA, A.
ORTEGA ROJAS, A.
PACHÁ BUSTAMENTE, A.
PALLEROS SANTOS, M.
PEDREROS AVENDAÑO, M.
PÉREZ MORETTI, N.
QUELOPANA DEL VALLE, A.
QUIOZA PALOMINOS, S.
REYES RUBILAR, T.
REY MAS, V.
RIVAS AVILA, M.
ROJAS ESPINOZA, E.
ROJAS TRONCOSO, M.
ROMÁN FLORES, H.
SANHUEZA COLLINAO, M.
UBEDA DE LA CERDA, C.
VALENZUELA ESTRADA, M.
VASQUEZ ROJAS, M. I.
VILAXA OLCAY, A.
VILLANUEVA DÍAZ, H.
VILLEGAS BRAVO, J.
ZÚÑIGA AGUIRRE, J.
ZÚÑIGA SALAS, P.

Faculty of Social Sciences, Business Studies and Administration:

ALBURQUENQUE ELIASH, M.
ALFONSO VARGAS, J.
ALFRED ALFARO, F.
ALVAREZ ROSALES, N.
BARRIENTOS BORDOLI, I.
BELMONTE SCHWARZBAUM, E.
BERNAL PERALTA, J.

BRIONES MORALES, L.
BUSSENIUS RISCO, J. C.
CABRALES GÓMEZ, F.
CAYO RIOS, G.
CHACAMA RODRÍGUEZ, J.
CHAIGNEAU ORFANOZ, S.
CISTERNAS ARAPIO, B.
CONTRERAS CORDANO, M.
CÓRDOVA GONZÁLEZ, J.
CUADRA PERALTA, A.
DONOSO MUÑOZ, M.
ESPINOZA VERDEJO, A.
FERREIRA REYES, R.
FIGUEROA GUACHALLA, M.
FLORES TAPIA, E.
GONZÁLEZ CORTÉS, H.
GUTIÉRREZ SAMOHOD, A.
HENRIQUEZ AGUILERA, A.
JIMÉNEZ QUÑONES, P.
KARMELIC PAVLOV, V.
LEAL SOTO, F.
LeBLANC VALENZUELA, L.
MUÑIZ OVALLE, I.
MUÑOZ ABELLA, G.
NAVARRETE ALVAREZ, M.
OCHOA DE LA MAZA, O.
PALMA QUIROZ, A.
PARRA SUAZO, O.
PERALTA MONTECINOS, J.
PULIDO ROCCATAGLIATA, S.
RAMÍREZ HUANCA, D.
RODRÍGUEZ PONCE, E.
ROMERO ROMERO, J.
RUÍZ LARRAL, C.
SALAS PALACIOS, R.
SANTORO VARGAS, C.
STANDEN RAMÍREZ, V.
STOREY MEZA, R.
ULLOA TORRES, H.
VIERA CASTILLO, D.

UNIVERSIDAD DE VALPARAÍSO

Casilla 123-V, Valparaíso
Telephone: (32) 2507000
Fax: (32) 2507143
Internet: www.uv.cl
Founded 1981; previously br. of Univ. of Chile
State control
Academic year: 2 terms, beginning March and August
Rector: ALDO SALVADOR VALLE ACEVEDO
Pro-Rector: OSVALDO CORRALES
Academic Dir-Gen.: OSVALDO BADENIER BUSTAMENTE
Sec.-Gen.: OSVALDO ENRIQUE CORRALES JORQUERA
Number of teachers: 1,189 (322 full-time, 867 part-time)
Number of students: 17,951
Publications: *Boletín Micológico*, *Revista de Biología Marina*, *Revista de Ciencias Sociales*

DEANS

Faculty of Architecture: JUAN LUIS MORAGA LACOST
Faculty of Dentistry: Dr OSVALDO BADENIER BUSTAMANTE
Faculty of Economics and Administration: RICARDO BARRIL VILLALOBOS
Faculty of Humanities: CARLOS MARTEL LLANO
Faculty of Law and Social Sciences: ALBERTO BALBONTÍN RETAMALES
Faculty of Marine Sciences and Natural Resources: GERARDO LEIGHTON SOTOMAYOR
Faculty of Medicine: Dr DAVID SABAH JAIME,
Faculty of Pharmacy: MARÍA SOLEDAD LOBOS SALVO
Faculty of Sciences: LUÍS MALDONADO CORTÉS

UNIVERSIDAD METROPOLITANA DE CIENCIAS DE LA EDUCACIÓN

Av, Jose Pedro Alessandri 774, Nunoa, Santiago
Telephone: (2) 2412400
Fax: (2) 2412723
E-mail: prensa@umce.cl
Internet: www.umce.cl
Founded 1889

Rector: JESÚS GONZÁLEZ
Vice-Rector: MAXIMINO FERNANDEZ FRAILE
Dir of Admin.: ROSANA SPROVERA MANRIQUEZ
Librarian: MARÍA ISABEL BRUCE

Number of teachers: 440
Number of students: 4,800
Publications: *Academia, Acta Entomológica chilena, Dimensión histórica de Chile, Educación Física*

DEANS

Faculty of Arts and Physical Education: MILTON COFRE ILUFFI
Faculty of Basic Sciences: MAFALDA SCHIAP-PACASSE COSTA
Faculty of History, Geography and Literature: SILVIA VYHMEISTER TZSCHABRAN
Faculty of Philosophy and Education: JAIME ARAOS SAN MARTIN

UNIVERSIDAD TECNOLÓGICA METROPOLITANA

Calle Dieciocho 161, Casilla 9845, Santiago
Telephone: (2) 7877500
Internet: www.utem.cl
Founded 1981 as Instituto Profesional de Santiago; present name 1993

Rector: HAYDÉE GUTIÉRREZ VILCHES
Vice-Rector for Academic Affairs: JUAN JOSÉ NEGRONI VERA
Vice-Rector for Admin. and Financial Affairs: GERMÁN MOLINA CHÁVEZ
Vice-Rector for Technology Transfer and Extension: MARIO TORRES ALCAYAGA
Gen. Sec.: PATRICIO BASTÍAS ROMÁN
Librarian: XIMENA SÁNCHEZ STAFORELLI

Number of teachers: 458
Number of students: 5,600
Publications: *Anuario Investigación del Departamento de Humanidades, Boletín Investigación del Departamento de Humanidades* (4 a year), *Trilogía*

DEANS

Faculty of Administration and Economics: ENRIQUE MATURANA LIZARDI
Faculty of Building and Town and Country Planning: ÁLVARO TORREALBA LÓPEZ
Faculty of Engineering: ARTURO OTT VILLA
Faculty of Humanities and Social Communication Technology: EDUARDO CAMPOS KAHLER
Faculty of Natural Sciences, Mathematics and the Environment: BEATRIZ GÓMEZ HERNÁNDEZ

Private Universities with Public Funding

PONTIFICIA UNIVERSIDAD CATÓLICA DE CHILE
(Catholic University of Chile)

Casilla 114-D, Alameda 340, Santiago
Telephone: (2) 6862415
Fax: (2) 2223116
E-mail: soporte@puc.cl
Internet: www.puc.cl
Founded 1888
Private control

Academic year: March to December

Grand Chancellor: Exmo Rmo Mons. FRANCISCO JAVIER ERRÁZURIZ OSSA
Vice-Grand Chancellor: Pbro ANDRÉS ARTEAGA
Rector: PEDRO PABLO ROSSO
Pro-Rector: JUAN IGNACIO VARAS
Vice-Rector: NICOLÁS VELASCO
Gen. Sec.: RAÚL MADRID
Dir of Distance Education: RICHARD WARNER
Librarian: MARÍA LUISA ARENAS
Library: see Libraries and Archives
Number of teachers: 2,100 (1,300 full-time, 800 part-time)
Number of students: 18,000
Publications: *Revista Humanitas* (every 2 years), *Revista Universitaria* (4 a year)

DEANS

Faculty of Agronomy: GUILLERMO DONOSO HARRIS
Faculty of Architecture and Fine Arts: JUAN JOSÉ UGARTE
Faculty of Biological Sciences: RENATO ALBERTINI BARTOLAMEOLLI
Faculty of Chemistry: LUIS HERNÁN TAGLE DOMÍNGUEZ
Faculty of Communication: FRANCISCA ALESSANDRI
Faculty of Economics and Management Sciences: FRANCISCO ROSENDE RAMÍREZ
Faculty of Education: GONZALO UNDURRAGA
Faculty of Engineering: HERNÁN DE SOLMINIHAC
Faculty of History, Geography and Political Sciences: RENÉ MILLAR
Faculty of Law: ARTURO YIRRAZAVAL
Faculty of Mathematics: GUILLERMO MARSHALL
Faculty of Medicine: GONZALO GREBE
Faculty of Philosophy: LUIS FLORES
Faculty of Physics: RICARDO RAMÍREZ LEIVA
Faculty of Social Sciences: PEDRO MORANDÉ COURT
Faculty of Theology: R.-P. SAMUEL FERNÁNDEZ

BRANCH CAMPUS

Sede Regional de Villarrica: Casilla 111; Dir Mons. PAUL WEVERING WEIDEMANN.

PONTIFICIA UNIVERSIDAD CATÓLICA DE VALPARAÍSO

Avda Brasil 2950, Casilla 4059, Valparaíso
Telephone: (32) 2273000
Fax: (32) 2212746
E-mail: rector@ucv.cl
Internet: www.ucv.cl
Founded 1928
Private control
Languages of instruction: Spanish, English
Academic year: March to December

Chancellor: Mgr GONZALO DUARTE GARCÍA DE CORTÁZAR
Rector: Prof. ALFONSO MUGA NAREDO
Vice-Rector for Academic and Student Affairs: EDUARDO ARAYA LEUPÍN
Vice-Rector for Admin. and Financial Affairs: CLAUDIO ELÓRTEGUI RAFFO
Vice-Rector for Devt Affairs: SALVADOR ZAHR MALUK
Vice-Rector for Research and Advanced Studies: SERGIO MARSHALL GONZÁLEZ
Sec.-Gen.: ALAN BRONFMAN VARGAS
Registrar: PAULA DROGUETT MEGE
Librarian: ATILIO BUSTOS GONZÁLEZ
Library: see Libraries and Archives
Number of teachers: 490
Number of students: 12,676
Publications: *Electronic Journal of Biotechnology* (online), *Revista de Derecho* (online), *Revista de Estudios Histórico-Jurídicos* (online), *Revista Geográfica de Valparaíso* (online), *Revista Investigaciones Marinas* (online), *Revista Perspectiva Educacional, Revista Philosophica, Revista Signos* (online)

DEANS

Faculty of Agronomy: PEDRO UNDURRAGA MARTÍNEZ
Faculty of Architecture: SALVADOR ZAHR MALUK
Faculty of Basic Sciences and Mathematics: ARTURO MENA LORCA
Faculty of Economics and Admin.: RODRIGO NAVIA CARVALLO
Faculty of Engineering: PAULINO ALONSO RIVAS
Faculty of Law and Social Sciences: ALEJANDRO GUZMÁN BRITO
Faculty of Natural Resources: ELEUTERIO YAÑEZ RODRÍGUEZ
Faculty of Philosophy and Education: BALDOMERO ESTRADA TURRA
Institute of Religious Studies: MARÍA INÉS CONCHA

UNIVERSIDAD AUSTRAL DE CHILE
(Southern University of Chile)

Independencia 641, Valdivia
Telephone: (63) 221277
Fax: (63) 293045
Internet: www.uach.cl
Founded 1954
Private control
Language of instruction: Spanish
Academic year: March to December

Rector: Dr VÍCTOR CUBILLOS GODOY
Vice-Rector for Academic Affairs: Dr OSCAR GALINDO
Vice-Rector for Economic and Admin. Affairs: AGUSTÍN QUEVEDO GODOY
Sec.-Gen.: CARLOS CARNEVALI DICKINSON
Dir of Extension: Prof. ARTURO ESCOBAR VALLEDOR
Dir of Postgraduate Studies: Dr FERNANDO MEDEL SALAMANCA
Dir of Public Relations: VIELLA SHIPLEY
Dir of Research and Development: Dr ERNESTO ZUMELZU DELGADO
Dir of Student Affairs: Prof. ANGÉLICA AGUILAR VIVAR
Dir of Undergraduate Studies: Prof. PATRICIO ALTAMIRANO VALENCIA
Registrar: MARIA C. BARRIGA RAMÍREZ

Library: see Libraries and Archives
Number of teachers: 832
Number of students: 8,785
Publications: *Agro Sur, Archivos de Medicina Veterinaria, Bosque, English Notes, Estudios Filológicos, Estudios Pedagógicos* (1 a year), *Medio Ambiente*

DEANS

Faculty of Agriculture: RENÉ ANRIQUE G.
Faculty of Economic and Administrative Sciences: EDMUNDO BOREL CH.
Faculty of Engineering Sciences: FREDY RÍOS MARTÍNEZ
Faculty of Fishery and Oceanography: RENATO WESTERMEIER H.
Faculty of Forestry Sciences: ANDRES IROUMÉ A.
Faculty of Juridical and Social Sciences: JUAN CARLOS FERRADA
Faculty of Medicine: CLAUS GROB B.
Faculty of Philosophy and Humanities: CARLOS AMTMANN M.
Faculty of Sciences: EDUARDO QUIROZ REYES
Faculty of Veterinary Science: FERNANDO WITTWER M.

UNIVERSIDAD CATÓLICA DE LA SANTÍSIMA CONCEPCIÓN

Caupolicán 491, Concepción
Telephone: (41) 246175
Fax: (41) 212318
E-mail: ucsc@ucsc.cl
Internet: www.ucsc.cl
Founded 1991
Private control; financially supported by the State

Rector: FERNANDO JIMÉNEZ LARRAÍN
Sec.-Gen.: ROLANDO GUTIÉRREZ GONZÁLEZ
Vice-Rector for Academic Affairs: EDUARDO SOUPER ESPINOSA
Vice-Rector for Financial and Admin. Affairs: GABRIEL HIDALGO AEDO

Library of 73,000 vols, 2,311 periodicals
Number of teachers: 263
Number of students: 5,979

DEANS

Faculty of Economics and Administration: JORGE ALAN CLEVELAND
Faculty of Education: FERNANDO SOTO SOTO
Faculty of Engineering: HUBERT MENNICKENT MENA
Faculty of Law: FERNANDO SAENGER GIANONI
Faculty of Medicine: Dr ALVARO LLANCAQUEO VALERI
Faculty of Science: Dr RAMÓN AHUMADA B.

DIRECTORS

School of Journalism: MARIO URZÚA ARACENA
Theological Centre: Dr JUAN CARLOS INOSTROZA LANAS

ATTACHED INSTITUTE

Instituto Tecnológico: Colón 2766, Talcahuano; tel. (41) 735070; fax (41) 735078; internet it.ucsc.cl; Rector FERNANDO JIMÉNEZ LARRAIN.

UNIVERSIDAD CATÓLICA DEL MAULE

Avda San Miguel 3605, CP 617 Talca
Telephone: (71) 203300
Fax: (71) 241767
E-mail: webmaster@hualo.ucm.cl
Internet: www.ucm.cl
Founded 1991
Private control; financially supported by the State

Rector: Dr CLAUDIO ROJAS MIÑO
Vice-Rector for Academic Affairs: HERNÁN MAUREIRA PAREJA
Vice-Rector for Finance and Admin.: MARIANO VARAS HERNÁNDEZ
Sec.-Gen.: ORLANDO ARAVENA AGUILERA

Library of 46,700 vols, 227 periodicals
Number of teachers: 183
Number of students: 5,628

DEANS

Faculty of Agrarian and Forestry Sciences: CLAUDIO RODRÍGUEZ FIGUEROA
Faculty of Education: MARCELO ROMERO MÉNDEZ
Faculty of Engineering: GUSTAVO LEDEZMA MATURANA
Faculty of Health Sciences: HÉCTOR FIGUEROA MARÍN
Faculty of Religion and Philosophy: JAMES MORIN ST ONGE

UNIVERSIDAD CATÓLICA DEL NORTE

Avda Angamos 0610, Casilla 1280, Antofagasta
Telephone: (55) 355002
Fax: (55) 355093
E-mail: mcamus@ucn.cl

Internet: www.ucn.cl
Founded 1956
Language of instruction: Spanish
Private control
Academic year: March to December
Chancellor: Most Rev. PABLO LIZAMA RIQUELME
Rector: MISAEL CAMUS IBACACHE
Vice-Rector for Academic Affairs: JOSE FERNANDO VIAL VALDES
Vice-Rector for Coquimbo Campus: LUÍS MONCAYO MARTÍNEZ
Vice-Rector for Economic Affairs: JORGE ALBERTO TABILO ALVAREZ
Gen. Sec.: VICTORIA GONZÁLEZ STUARDO
Head of Admissions Office: OLGA MARIA VALDES DE LA TORRE
Librarian: SERGIO ARCE MOLINA

Library of 113,222 vols
Number of teachers: 372
Number of students: 10,324

Publications: *Boletín de Educación, Cuadernos de Arquitectura, Estudios Atacameños, Norte: Revista divulgacíon de ciencias, tecnologia y cultura* (science, technology and culture), *Revista de Derecho, Revista Proyecciones, Revista Reflejos, Revista Vertiente, Tercer Milenio*

DEANS

Antofagasta Campus (tel. (55) 355000; fax (55) 355093):

   Faculty of Architecture, Civil Engineering and Construction: PABLO REYES FRANZANI
   Faculty of Economics: ANGEL GOMEZ MORALES
   Faculty of Engineering and Sciences: PABLOS REYES FRANZANI
   Faculty of Humanities: JAIME BARRIENTOS DELGADO
   Faculty of Sciences: JULIO VASQUEZ CASTRO

Coquimbo Campus (Larrondo 1281, Coquimbo; tel. (51) 209701; fax (51) 209707):

   Faculty of Marine Sciences: EXEQUIEL GONZÁLEZ BALBONTÍN

UNIVERSIDAD CATÓLICA DE TEMUCO

Manuel Montt 56, 15-D Temuco
Telephone: (45) 205205
Fax: (45) 234126
E-mail: dara@uct.cl
Internet: www.uct.cl
Founded 1991
Private control; financially supported by the State
Academic year: March to November

Rector: MÓNICA JIMÉNEZ DE LA JARA
Vice-Rector for Academic Affairs: ALIRO BÓRQUEZ RAMÍREZ
Vice-Rector for Finance and Admin.: PEDRO BAKOVIC VIÑALS

Library of 43,560 vols, 4,100 periodicals
Number of teachers: 213
Number of students: 4,854

DEANS

Faculty of Agricultural and Forestry Sciences: MARCO ANTONIO FERNÁNDEZ NAVARRETE
Faculty of Agriculture and Veterinary Sciences: ROLANDO VEGA AGUAYO
Faculty of Arts, Humanities and Social Sciences: MARIO SAMANIEGO SASTRE
Faculty of Education: RENÉ MORGAN MELGOSA
Faculty of Science: OSVALDO RUBILAR ALARCÓN
Institute of Theological Studies: JUAN LEONELLI LEONELLI (Dir)
School of Law: RODRIGO COLOMA CORREA (Dir)

ATTACHED RESEARCH INSTITUTES

Centre of Sociocultural Studies: tel. (45) 205626; fax (45) 205626; e-mail tduran@uct.cl; Dir Dra TERESA DURÁN PÉREZ.
Centre of Sustainable Development: tel. (45) 205629; fax (45) 205626; e-mail cds@uct.cl; Dir Dr ANDRÉS YURJEVIC MARSCHAL.
Institute of Regional Studies: tel. (45) 205685; fax (45) 205626; e-mail artufilu@uct.cl; Dir ARTURO HERNANDEZ SALLÁS.

UNIVERSIDAD DE CONCEPCIÓN

Casilla 160-C, Correo 3, Concepción
Telephone: (41) 204000
Fax: (41) 227455
E-mail: foro@udec.cl
Internet: www.udec.cl
Founded 1919
Private control
Language of instruction: Spanish
Academic year: March to January

Rector: SERGIO LAVANCHY MERINO
Vice-Rector for Academic Affairs: ERNESTO FIGUEROA HUIDOBRO
Vice-Rector for Financial Affairs and Personnel: ALBERTO LARRAÍN PRAT
Gen. Sec.: RODOLFO WALTER DÍAZ
Library Dir: OLGA MORA MARDONES

Number of teachers: 1,410
Number of students: 16,800

Publications: *Acta Literaria, Agro-Ciencia* (2 a year), *Atenea* (science, art and literature, 12 a year), *Gayana, Informativo de Rectoría—PANORAMA* (public relations), *Revista de Derecho* (4 a year), *RLA—Revista de Lingüística Aplicada*

DEANS

Faculty of Agricultural Engineering: JOSÉ REYES AROCA
Faculty of Agriculture: ALFREDO VERA M.
Faculty of Architecture: RICARDO UTZ BARRIGA
Faculty of Biological Sciences: CARLOS GONZÁLEZ CORREA
Faculty of Chemical Sciences: BERNABÉ RIVAS QUIRÓZ
Faculty of Dentistry: FERNANDO ESCOBAR MUÑOZ
Faculty of Economic and Administrative Sciences: JUAN SAAVEDRA GONZÁLEZ
Faculty of Education: ABELARDO CASTRO HIDALGO
Faculty of Engineering: JOEL ZAMBRANO VALENCIA
Faculty of Forestry Sciences: FERNANDO DRAKE ARANDA
Faculty of Humanities and Art: EDUARDO NÚÑEZ CRISOSTO
Faculty of Law and Social Sciences: SERGIO CARRASCO DELGADO
Faculty of Medicine: OCTAVIO ENRÍQUEZ LORCA
Faculty of Natural Sciences and Oceanography: FRANKLIN CARRASCO VASQUEZ
Faculty of Pharmacy: CARLOS CALVO MONFIL
Faculty of Physical Sciences and Mathematics: JOSÉ SÁNCHEZ HENRÍQUEZ
Faculty of Social Sciences: EDUARDO AQUEVEDO SOTO
Faculty of Veterinary Medicine: RUBÉN PÉREZ FERNÁNDEZ

UNIVERSIDAD TÉCNICA 'FEDERICO SANTA MARÍA'

Avda España 1680, Casilla 110V, Valparaíso
Telephone: (32) 654246
Fax: (32) 654443
E-mail: consultas@utfsm.cl
Internet: www.utfsm.cl
Founded 1926

Private control
Language of instruction: Spanish
Academic year: March to January

Rector: ADOLFO ARATA ANDREANI
Vice-Rector for Academic Affairs: DANIEL ALKALAY LOWITT
Vice-Rector for Economic and Admin. Affairs: GIOVANNI PESCE SANTANA
Sec.-Gen.: FRANCISCO GHISOLFO ARAYA
Library Dir: MARÍA EUGENIA LAULIÉ
Library: see Libraries and Archives
Number of teachers: 456 (237 full-time, 219 part-time)
Number of students: 9,311
Publications: *Gestión Tecnológica* (2 a year), *Revista Industrias* (4 a year), *Scientia* (1 a year).

BRANCH CAMPUSES

Campus Rancagua: Gamero 212, Rancagua; Dir SERGIO ESTAY VILLALÓN.

Campus Santiago: Avda Santa María 6400, Vitacura, Santiago; Dir SERGIO OLAVARRÍA SIMONSEN.

Sede José Miguel Carrera: Avda Federico Santa María 6090, Viña del Mar; Dir ROSENDO ESTAY MARTÍNEZ.

Sede Rey Balduino de Bélgica: Avda Alemparte 943, Talcahuano; Dir ALEX ERIZ SOTO.

Private Universities

UNIVERSIDAD ADOLFO IBÁÑEZ

Balmaceda 1625, Recreo, Viña del Mar
Telephone: (32) 2503500
E-mail: paula.fernandez@uai.cl
Internet: www.uai.cl
Founded 1953
Private control
Language of instruction: Spanish
Academic year: March to December
Rector: ANDRÉS BENÍTEZ
Vice-Rector for Academic Affairs: RAFAEL MACHERONE
Vice-Rector for Economic and Admin. Affairs: CATALINA BOBENRIETH
Gen. Sec.: AGUSTÍN ANTOLA
Dean of Undergraduates: COLIN ROGERS
Librarian: MARÍA ZINA JIMÉNEZ
Number of teachers: 46 full-time
Number of students: 1,444
Publications: *Cuadernos Jurídicos* (3 a year), *Informe Económico* (4 a year), *INTUS LEGERE: Anuario de Filosofía, Historia y Letras* (1 a year)

DEANS

Faculty of Engineering and Science: ALEJANDRO JADRESIC
Faculty of Law: RODRIGO CORREA
Faculty of Liberal Arts: LUCÍA SANTA CRUZ
School of Government: LEONIDAS MONTES
School of Journalism: ASCANIO CAVALLO
School of Management: ALFONSO GÓMEZ
School of Psychology: JORGE SANHUEZA

UNIVERSIDAD CENTRAL

Toesca 1783, Santiago
Telephone: (2) 5826000
E-mail: guia@ucentral.cl
Internet: www.ucentral.cl
Founded 1982
Private control
Language of instruction: Spanish
Academic year: March to January
Rector: LUIS LUCERO ALDAY
Vice-Rector for Academic Affairs: LUIS MERINO MONTERO

Vice-Rector for Admin.: JUAN IGNACIO CARVALLO MARÍN
Vice-Rector for Communication: RAFAEL GARAY PITA
Vice-Rector for Finance: SERGIO ÁLVAREZ MONTOYA
Vice-Rector for Institutional Devt: SILVANA COMINETTI COTTI-COMETTI
Gen. Sec.: OMAR AHUMADA MORA
Librarian: NELLY CORNEJO MENESES
Number of teachers: 662
Number of students: 6,177
Publications: *Boletín Informativo, Parthenon* (2 a year), *Perspectiva, Revista de Arquitectura, Revista de Derecho, Revista de Psicología, Universidad y Sociedad*

DEANS

Faculty of Architecture and Town and Country Planning: ELIANA ISRAEL JACARD
Faculty of Communications: BERNARDO DE LA MAZA BAÑADOS
Faculty of Economics and Administration: HUMBERTO VEGA FERNÁNDEZ
Faculty of Education: SELMA SIMONSTEIN FUENTES
Faculty of Law and Social Sciences: ÁNGELA CATTAN ATALA
Faculty of Physical Sciences and Mathematics: SERGIO QUEZADA GONZÁLEZ
Faculty of Politics and Public Administration: ALDO CASSINELLI CAPURRO
Faculty of Social Sciences: LUIS GAJARDO IBÁÑEZ

ATTACHED RESEARCH CENTRES

Centre of Economic and Administrative Research: San Ignacio 414, Santiago; tel. (2) 6954010; fax (2) 6727377; Dir CARLOS RETAMAL UMPIERREZ.

Centre of Housing Research: José Joaquin Prieto 10001, Casilla 6D, San Bernardo; tel. (2) 5585311; fax (2) 5270323; Dir ALFONSO RAPOSO MOYANO.

Centre of Juridical Research: Lord Cochrane 417, Santiago; tel. (2) 6957533; fax (2) 6727377; Dir RUBEN CELIS RODRIGUEZ.

UNIVERSIDAD DIEGO PORTALES

Avda Manuel Rodríguez Sur 415, Santiago 8370179
Telephone: (2) 6762000
Fax: (2) 6762112
E-mail: admsion@udp.cl
Internet: www.udp.cl
Founded 1982
Rector: MANUEL MONTT
Provost: FRANCISCO JAVIER CUADRA
Vice-Rector for Academic Affairs and Research: CARLOS PEÑA
Vice-Rector for Admin., Finance and Devt: HORACIO RÍOS
Dir of Communications and Admission: BÁRBARA FASANI
Librarian: PAULINA GODOY
Number of teachers: 1,208
Number of students: 10,930
Publications: *El Portaliano, Noticias Académicas*

DEANS

Faculty of Architecture, Design and Art: MATHÍAS KLOTZ
Faculty of Business: MIGUEL LÉON
Faculty of Communication: ANDRÉS VELASCO
Faculty of Engineering: MIGUEL LÉON
Faculty of Health Sciences: FERNANDO MÖNCKEBERG
Faculty of Humanities: CARMEN FARIÑA
Faculty of Human Sciences and Education: JUAN PABLO TORO

Faculty of Industrial Engineering and Data Processing: LUIS COURT
Faculty of Law: ANDRÉS CUNEO

UNIVERSIDAD GABRIELA MISTRAL

Avda Ricardo Lyon 1177, Providencia, Santiago
Telephone: (2) 4144545
Internet: www.ugm.cl
Founded 1981
Academic year: March to January
Rector: ALICIA ROMO ROMÁN
Vice-Rector for Academic Affairs: RICARDO RIESCO JARAMILLO
Vice-Rector for Admin. and Finance: ESTANISLAO GALOFRÉ TERRASA
Librarian: CARMEN BUSQUETS
Number of teachers: 450
Number of students: 3,500

UNIVERSIDAD PEREZ ROSALES

Brown Norte 290, Ñuñoa, Santiago Metropolitana
Telephone: (2) 7571300
Fax: (2) 2238825
E-mail: unitec@uvipro.cl
Internet: www.upper.cl
Founded 1992
Private control
Rector: KARIN RIEDEMANN H.
Sec.-Gen.: ELISA CASTRO P.
Vice-Rector for Academic Affairs: CECILIA IBARRA M.
Vice-Rector for Teaching and Research: MÓNICA HERRERA P.
Dir of Extension Studies and Humanities: PÍA MONTALVA D.
Head Librarian: CLAUDIA GILARDONI.

UNIVERSIDAD SAN SEBASTIÁN

Campus Las Tres Pascualas, General Cruz 1577, Concepción
Telephone: (41) 2400000
E-mail: concepcion@uss.cl
Internet: www.uss.cl
Founded 1989
Private control
Academic year: March to December
Rector: GUIDO ALFREDO MELLER MAYR
Vice-Rector for Academic Affairs: JAIME TORREALBA CUBILLOS
Vice-Rector for Communications: ADOLFO UGARTE ALONSO
Vice-Rector for Devt: LUIS CORDERO BARRERA
Vice-Rector for Economic and Admin. Affairs: LUIS ERNESTO VIDELA BERGUECIO
Vice-Rector for Quality Assurance: KIYOSHI FUKUSHI MANDIOLA
Gen. Sec.: SANDRA GUZMÁN MARTÍNEZ
Librarian: MARGARITA VALDERRAMA CÁCERES
Library of 6,000 vols
Number of teachers: 174
Number of students: 1,714

DEANS

Faculty of Architecture, Art and Design: CRISTIÁN BOZA DÍAZ
Faculty of Dentistry: SERGIO CASTRO ALFARO
Faculty of Economics and Business: ERIK HAINDL
Faculty of Education: JORGE JIMÉNEZ ESPINOZA
Faculty of Engineering and Technology: JUAN BENNETT URRUTIA
Faculty of Health: FERNANDO QUIROGA DUBORNAIS
Faculty of Law: ARMANDO CARTES MONTORY
Faculty of Medicine and Nursing: Dr JAIME SEPÚLVEDA C.

Faculty of Social Services: CARMEN BONNEFOY DIBARRART

Faculty of Veterinary Medicine: NORBERTO BUTENDIECK BURATTINI

Colleges

Escuela Militar del Libertador Bernardo O'Higgins: Los Militares 4500, Las Condes, Santiago; tel. (2) 6615012; fax (2) 6615397; internet www.escuelamilitar.cl; f. 1817 (by General O'Higgins); 90 military instructors and officials, 80 civilian instructors; 700 students; library: 25,000 vols; Dir Col HUMBERTO OVIEDO ARRIAGADA; Librarians OSCAR CORNEJO C., JUAN CARLOS MEDINA V.; publs *Armas y Servicio, Memorial del Ejército, Revista 'Cien Aguilas'* (1 a year).

Facultad Latinoamericana de Ciencias Sociales (FLACSO): Avda Dag Hammarskjold 3269, Vitacura, Santiago; tel. (2) 2900200; fax (2) 2900263; e-mail flacso@flacso.cl; internet www.flacso.cl; f. 1957; postgraduate training and research centre for Latin America; library: 30,000 vols, 710 periodicals; 16 teachers; 60 students; Dir CLAUDIO FUENTES SAAVEDRA; Librarian MARÍA INÉS BRAVO; publ. *Fuerzas Armadas y Sociedad* (3 a year).

Instituto Agrícola Metodista 'El Vergel' (Methodist Agricultural Institute): Casilla 2-D, Angol; tel. (45) 712103; fax (45) 711202; f. 1919; ornamental plant nursery, fruit nursery, fruit garden, dairy, cattle ranch, apiculture, tourism, workshops, packing; museum; Administrator Rev. MARIO MAYER.

PEOPLE'S REPUBLIC OF CHINA

The Higher Education System

Some of the oldest institutions of higher education in the world are to be found in the People's Republic of China (for example, Hunan University dates back to the establishment of Yuelu Academy in 976). Higher education is dominated by state institutions, although some private universities have been established in recent years, and administration reflects the centralized nature of the State. During the 1950s a number of higher education establishments were designated 'key' institutions and received better staff, facilities and funding. The term 'key institution' is now officially defunct but is still used to denote the highest-rated institutions. The Cultural Revolution (1966–76) led to radical changes in the higher education system, as entrance examinations and continuous assessment were abolished; however, many of the changes were later reversed (the National University Entrance Examination was re-introduced in 1977). Following university unrest in 1989, including the Tianenman Square protests in Beijing, students were required to undergo a year of political 'training' prior to university. Further reforms were launched in 1992, under which institutions were given greater autonomy in decision-making. There was also a trend towards mergers that led to a decrease in the number of higher education institutions, from 1,984 in 1998 to 1,731 in 2004, but this had increased to 1,908 in 2007. In 2008 a total of 20.2m. students were enrolled in higher education. A new higher education reform programme was launched in early 2000, with the aim of modernizing courses and teaching materials and improving pedagogy.

Performance in the National University Entrance Examination, which was re-instated in 1977 following the Cultural Revolution, represents the main criteria for admission to higher education. Additionally, students may be required to undergo political education and perform some form of industrial or agricultural labour. The examination is conducted on a national basis and students are examined in five core subjects. A score in the range of 550–600 will gain admission to university. The university degree system consists of Xueshi (Bachelors), Shoshi (Masters) and Boshi (Doctorate). Bachelors degree courses last four years and conform to one of the 249 programmes defined by the Ministry of Education. In 1989 it was announced that selection of postgraduate students would also be on the basis of 'moral' and physical fitness. A Masters degree requires two to three years of further study after the Bachelors, including research and submission of a thesis. The Doctorate is awarded after three years of study following the Masters and concludes with submission and defence of a thesis.

Diplomas from technical and vocational education at tertiary level are available from a number of different types of institution, and usually require two to three years of study. Institutions offering technical and vocational education include vocational technology colleges, vocational universities, radio and television universities (Dianda) and spare-time universities (Yeda). Vocational education is supervised by the Department of Education and Labour.

Regulatory and Representative Bodies

GOVERNMENT

Ministry of Culture: 10 Chaoyangmen Bei Jie, Dongcheng Qu, Beijing 100020; tel. (10) 65551432; fax (10) 65551433; e-mail webmaster@whb1.ccnt.com.cn; internet www .ccnt.com.cn; Minister SUN JIAZHENG.

Ministry of Education: 37 Damucang Hutong, Xidan, Beijing 100816; tel. (10) 66096114; fax (10) 66011049; e-mail webmaster@moe.edu.cn; internet www.moe .edu.cn; Minister ZHOU JI.

FUNDING

China Scholarship Council: Level 13, Building A3 No. 9, Chegongzhuang Ave, Beijing 100044; tel. (10) 66093900; fax (10) 88393620; e-mail webmaster@csc.edu.cn; internet www.csc.edu.cn; f. 1994; attached to Ministry of Education; provides financial assistance to Chinese citizens wishing to study abroad and to foreign citizens wishing to study in China; Chair. ZHANG XINSHENG; Sec.-Gen. ZHANG XIUQIN.

NATIONAL BODY

China Education Association for International Exchange: 37 Damucang Hutong, Xicheng Dist., Beijing 100816; 160 Fuxingmen Nei Dajie, Beijing 100031; tel. (10) 66416080; fax (10) 66411885; e-mail info@ ceaie.edu.cn; internet chn.ceaie.edu.cn; f. 1981; 145 mem. instns; not-for-profit org. conducting int. educational exchanges; Pres. Prof. LIU BIN; Sec.-Gen. JIANG BO.

Learned Societies

GENERAL

Chinese Academy of Sciences: 52 San Li He Rd, Beijing 100864; tel. (10) 68597289; fax (10) 68512458; internet www.cas.ac.cn; f. 1949; academic divs of chemistry, earth sciences, information technical sciences, life sciences and medicine, mathematics and physics, technological sciences; 633 mems; 13 foreign mems; attached research institutes: see Research Institutes; library: libraries: see Libraries and Archives; Pres. Prof. Dr-Ing. LU YONGXIANG; Vice-Pres ZHAN WENLONG, DING ZHONGLI, YIN HEJUN; Sec.-Gen. Prof. ZHU XUAN.

Chinese Academy of Social Sciences: 5 Jianguomen Nei Da Jie, Beijing 100732; tel. (10) 65137744; fax (10) 65138154; internet www.cass.net.cn; f. 1977; attached research institutes: see Research Institutes; Pres. WANG WEIGUANG; Sec.-Gen. ZHU JINCHANG.

UNESCO Office Beijing: Waijiaogongyu 5-13-3, Jianguomenwai Compound, Beijing 100600; tel. (10) 65322828; fax (10) 65324854; e-mail beijing@unesco.org; internet www.unescobeijing.org; designated Cluster Office for People's Republic of China, Democratic People's Republic of Korea, Japan, Mongolia and Republic of Korea; Dir YASUYUKI AOSHIMA.

AGRICULTURE, FISHERIES AND VETERINARY SCIENCE

China Society of Fisheries: 31 Minfeng Lane, Beijing 100032; tel. (10) 66020794; fax (10) 66062346; 15,000 mems; library of 12,000 vols; Pres. ZHANG YANXI; publs *Journal of Fisheries of China, Marine Fisheries,* *Freshwater Fisheries, Deep-sea Fisheries, Scientific Fish Farming.*

Chinese Academy of Agricultural Sciences: 30 Bai Shi Qiao Rd, Beijing 100081; tel. (10) 62174433; fax (10) 62174142; f. 1957; 40 attached research institutes; library of 650,000 vols, 7,000 periodicals; Pres. LU FEIJIE; publs *Acta Agronomica Sinica, Acta Horticulturae Sinica, Acta Phyliphulacica Sinica.*

Chinese Academy of Forestry: Wan Shou Shan, 100091 Beijing; tel. (10) 62582211; fax (10) 62584229; f. 1958; 4,700 mems; attached research institutes: see Research Institutes; library of 400,000 vols; Pres. JIANG ZEHUI; publs *Chemistry and Industry of Forest Products, China Forestry Abstracts, Foreign Forest Product Industry Abstracts, Foreign Forestry Abstracts, Forestry Research, Forestry Science and Technology, Scientia Silvae Sinicae, Wood Industry, World Forestry Research.*

Chinese Agricultural Economics Society: Agro-Exhibition, Beijing; Pres. CAI ZIWEI.

Chinese Association of Agricultural Science Societies: Ministry of Agriculture and Fisheries, 11 Nongzhanguan Nanli, Beijing 100026; f. 1917; Pres. HONG FUZENG; Sec.-Gen. LI HUAIZHI.

Chinese Sericulture Society: Sibaidu, Zhenjiang, Jiangsu 212018; tel. (511) 5616661; fax (511) 5622507; f. 1963; 10,000 mems; library of 50,000 vols; Pres. XIANG ZHONGHUAI; Sec.-Gen. ZHUANG DAHUAN; publ. *Sericultural Science* (4 a year).

Chinese Society for Horticultural Science: 12 Zhongguancun Nandajie, Beijing 100081; tel. (10) 68919528; fax (10) 62174123; e-mail ivfcaas@public3.bta.net.cn;

f. 1930; 3,000 mems; Pres. ZHU DEWEI; publ. *Acta Horticulturae Sinica* (6 a year).

Chinese Society of Agricultural Machinery: 1 Beishatan, Deshengmen Wai, Beijing 100083; tel. (10) 64882231; fax (10) 64883508; e-mail bhmetecj@public3.bta.net .cn; f. 1963; 26,245 mems; library of 1,500,000 vols; Pres. LI SHOUREN; Sec.-Gen. GAO YUANEN; publs *China Agricultural Mechanization* (6 a year), *Farm Machinery* (12 a year), *Rural Mechanization* (6 a year), *Tractor and Automobile Drivers* (6 a year), *Transactions of the Chinese Society of Agricultural Machinery* (4 a year).

Chinese Society of Forestry: Wanshoushan, Beijing 100091; tel. (10) 62889817; fax (10) 62888312; f. 1917; 75,000 mems; Pres. LIU YUHE; publ. *Scientia Silvae Sinicae* (6 a year).

Chinese Society of Tropical Crops: Baodao Xincun, Danzhou, Hainan; tel. (898) 23300157; fax (898) 23300157; e-mail scutafao@yahoo.com; f. 1978; 4,474 mems; library of 250,000 vols; Jt Chairs ZENG YUZHUANG, YU RANGSHUI; Sec.-Gen. ZHENG WENRONG; publ. *Chinese Journal of Tropical Crops* (4 a year).

Crop Science Society of China: Institute of Crop Breeding and Cultivation, 30 Bai Shi Qiao Rd, Beijing 100081; tel. (10) 68918616; fax (10) 68975212; f. 1961; 22,000 mems; Pres. WANG LIANZHENG; Sec.-Gen. CHEN XIN-HUA; publs *Acta Agronomica Sinica* (6 a year), *Crops* (6 a year).

Soil Science Society of China: POB 821, Nanjing 210008; tel. (25) 86881532; fax (25) 86881538; e-mail sssc@issas.ac.cn; f. 1945; academic exchange; publication; scientific popularization; education and training; consultation for decision-making; technical service; int. cooperation; talents recommendation, reward and recognition; 17,600 mems; Pres. Prof. ZHOU JIANMIN; Vice Sec.-Gen. WEIDONG YAN; Prof. XIN JIANG; publs *Acta Pedologica Sinica* (6 a year), *Journal of Soil and Water Conservation*, *Journal of Soil Science* (6 a year), *Pedosphere* (6 a year).

ARCHITECTURE AND TOWN PLANNING

Architectural Society of China: 9 Sanlihe Rd, Beijing 100835; tel. (10) 88082238; fax (10) 88082222; e-mail asc@mail.cin.gov.cn; f. 1953; 30,000 mems; library of 25,000 vols; Pres. SONG CHUNHUA; publs *Architectural Journal* (12 a year), *Architectural Knowledge* (12 a year), *Journal of Building Structure* (6 a year).

Chinese Society for Urban Studies: Bai Wanzhuang, Beijing 100835; tel. (10) 68393424; fax (10) 68313149; e-mail zhaibh@mail.cin.gov.cn; internet www .urbanstudies.org.cn; f. 1984; part of Min. of Construction; 30,000 mems; Pres. ZHOU GANSHI; Sec.-Gen. GU WENXUAN; publ. *Urban Studies* (6 a year).

BIBLIOGRAPHY, LIBRARY SCIENCE AND MUSEOLOGY

Chinese Archives Society: 21 Fengshen Hutong, Beijing; tel. (10) 66175130; fax (10) 66183636; f. 1981; 74 institutional mems, 7,252 individual mems; Chair. SHEN ZHEN-GLE; publ. *Archive Science Study* (4 a year).

Chinese Association of Natural Science Museums: 126 Tian Qiao South St, Beijing 100050; tel. (10) 67024431; fax (10) 67021254; f. 1979; 1,200 individual mems; 320 group mems; Sec.-Gen. XIE YENGHUAN; publ. *China Nature* (6 a year, jtly with Beijing Natural History Museum and China Wildlife Conservation Association).

Chinese Society of Library Science: 39 Bai Shi Qiao Rd, Beijing 100081; tel. (10) 68415566 ext. 5563; fax (10) 68419271; f. 1979; 10,150 mems; Pres. LIU DEYOU; publ. *Journal of Library Science in China* (in Chinese, every 2 months).

ECONOMICS, LAW AND POLITICS

China Law Society: 6 Xizhi Men Nan Da Jie, Beijing 100035; tel. (10) 66150114; fax (10) 66182128; f. 1982; ind. academic instn for study of the Chinese socialist legal system; 523 corporate mems; 100,000 individual mems; library of 40,000 vols, incl. China Catalogue of Law Books; Pres. REN JIANXIN; Sec.-Gen. SONG SHUTAO; publs *China Law Yearbook*, *Democracy and Law Journal*, *Law of China*.

Chinese Association for European Studies: 5 Jiannei, Beijing 100732; tel. (10) 65138428; f. 1981; 1,000 mems; Chair. Prof. QIU YUANLUN; publ. *European Studies* (every 2 months, co-edited with Inst. of West European Studies).

Chinese Association of Political Science: c/o Chinese Academy of Social Sciences, 5 Jianguomennei Ave, Beijing; tel. (10) 65125048; f. 1980; asscn of workers in the field of political science; 1,025 mems; Pres. JIANG LIU; Sec.-Gen. ZHANG ZHIRONG; publs *Political Science Abroad* (6 a year), *Studies in Political Science* (6 a year).

Chinese Legal History Society: Law Dept, Beijing University, Haidian District, Beijing 100871; tel. (10) 62561166; f. 1979; studies history of Chinese and foreign legal systems; 300 mems; Pres. Prof. ZHANG GUOHUA; Chief Sec. RAO XINXIAN; publs *Communications of Legal History*, *Review of Legal History*.

Chinese Research Society for the Modernization of Management: c/o China Association for Science and Technology, Sanlihe, Xijiao, Beijing; tel. (10) 68318877 ext. 524; f. 1978; Pres. XIE SHAOMING; publ. *Modernization of Management*.

Chinese Society of the History of International Relations: 12 Poshangcun, Haidian District, Beijing; Pres. WANG SHENGZU.

EDUCATION

Chinese Education Society: 35 Damucang Lane, Beijing 100816; Pres. ZHANG CHENG-XIAN.

HISTORY, GEOGRAPHY AND ARCHAEOLOGY

Chinese Historical Society: 5 Jianguomennei St, Beijing 100732.

Chinese Society for Future Studies: 32 Baishiqiao Rd, Haidian District, Beijing 100081; f. 1979; 1,000 mems; CEO DU DAGONG; publ. *Future and Development* (4 a year).

Chinese Society of Geodesy, Photogrammetry and Cartography: Baiwanzhuang, Beijing; tel. (10) 68992229; f. 1959; 3,000 mems; Pres. Prof. WANG ZHIZHUO; Sec.-Gen. Prof. YANG KAI; publ. *Acta Geodetica et Cartographica Sinica*.

Chinese Society of Oceanography: 10 Fuxingmenwai, Beijing; Pres. PENG DEQING.

Geographical Society of China: No. A11, Datun Rd, Beijing 100101; tel. (10) 64870663; fax (10) 64889598; e-mail gsc@igsnrr.ac.cn; internet www.gsc.org.cn; f. 1909; 31 provincial divs; special comms: cartography, climatology, economic geog., environmental geog. and chemical geog., geographical information systems, geomorphology and quaternary studies, historical geog., human geog., hydrography, marine geog., medical geog., physical geog., quantative geog., sustained agricul-

ture and rural development, tourist geog., urban geog., world geog.; working comms: academic affairs, edition and publication, geographical education, international scientific and technical cooperation (China National Committee for International Geographical Union—IGU), popularization of geographical knowledge, young geographers; br. socs: coastal open region, Changjang river research, desert research, environmental remote sensing, glaciology and geocryology, mountain research; geographical construction in the arid and semi-arid region; 18,900 mems; Pres. LU DADAO; Sec.-Gen. ZHANG GUOYOU; publs *Acta Geographica Sinica* (6 a year), *China National Geography* (12 a year), *Economic Geography* (6 a year), *Historical Geography* (4 a year), *Human Geography* (6 a year), *Journal of Geographical Sciences* (English edition, 4 a year), *Journal of Glaciology and Geocryology* (6 a year), *Journal of Mountain Science* (6 a year), *Journal of Remote Sensing* (6 a year), *World Regional Studies* (4 a year).

LANGUAGE AND LITERATURE

Alliance Française: 18 Gongtixilu, Guangcai Guojigongyu, Chaoyang District, Beijing 100020; tel. (10) 65532678; fax (10) 65532718; e-mail info.beijing@afchine.org; internet www.alliancefrancaise.org.cn; offers courses and exams in French language and culture and promotes cultural exchange with France; attached teaching centres in Chengdu, Guangzhou, Nanjing, Shanghai and Wuhan.

British Council: Cultural and Education Section, British Embassy, 4th Fl., Landmark Bldg Tower 1, 8 North Dongsanhuan Rd, Chaoyang District, 100004 Beijing; tel. (10) 6590-6903; fax (10) 6590-0977; e-mail enquiry@britishcouncil.org.cn; internet www .britishcouncil.org/china; offers courses and exams in English language and British culture and promotes cultural exchange with the UK; attached offices in Shanghai, Guangzou and Chongqing; Dir and Cultural Counsellor MICHAEL O'SULLIVAN.

Chinese Writers' Association: 2 Shatanbeijie, Beijing 100720; 20,000 mems; Chair. BA JIN; publs include *People's Literature* (12 a year), *Chinese Writers* (6 a year), *Literature and Arts* (52 a year, newspaper), *Minority Literature* (12 a year), *Poetry* (12 a year).

Goethe-Institut: Cyber Tower, Bldg B, 17th Fl., No. 2, Zhong Guan Cun South Ave, Haidian District, Beijing 100086; tel. (10) 82512909; fax (10) 82512903; e-mail info@ peking.goethe.org; internet www.goethe.de/ os/pek/deindex.htm; offers courses and exams in German language and culture and promotes cultural exchange with Germany; attached centres in Shanghai; library of 10,000 vols; Dir DR ULRICH NOWAK.

MEDICINE

China Academy of Traditional Chinese Medicine: 18 Beixincang, Dongzhimennei, Beijing 100700; tel. (10) 64014411 ext. 2435; fax (10) 64016387; f. 1955; 12 attached research institutes; library of 300,000 vols; Pres. FU SHIYUAN; publs *Chinese Acupuncture and Moxibustion*, *Chinese Journal of Integrated Traditional and Western Medicine*, *Journal of Traditional Chinese Medicine*.

China Association of Traditional Chinese Medicine: A4 Yinghualu, Hepingli Dongjie, Beijing 100029; tel. (10) 64212828; fax (10) 64220867; f. 1979; 80,000 mems; Chair. CUI YULI; Gen. Sec. (vacant); publ. *China Journal of Traditional Chinese Medicine* (6 a year).

China Association of Zhenjiu (Acupuncture and Moxibustion): 18 Beixincang Dongcheng Qu, Beijing 100700; tel. (10) 64030611; f. 1979; 13,000 mems; Pres. HU XIMING; Sec.-Gen. LI WEIHENG; publ. *Chinese Acupuncture and Moxibustion*.

Chinese Academy of Medical Sciences and Peking Union Medical College: 9 Dongdan Santiao, Beijing 100730; tel. 553447; fax 5124876; f. 1917 (College), 1956 (Academy); the two instns have a single governing body; attached research institutes: see Research Institutes; Pres. Dr BA DENIAN; publ. *Chinese Medical Sciences Journal*.

Chinese Anti-Cancer Association: 52 Fucheng, Haidian District, Beijing 100036; tel. (10) 88148749; fax (10) 88148749; e-mail yuhui@caca.org.cn; internet www.caca.org.cn; f. 1985; 40,000 mems; Pres. Dr XU GUANGWEI; publs *Cancer Rehabilitation* (6 a year), *Chinese Journal of Cancer Biotherapy* (4 a year), *Chinese Journal of Cancer Research* (4 a year), *Chinese Journal of Clinical Oncology* (12 a year), *Journal of Practical Oncology* (6 a year), *Research on Prevention and Treatment of Cancer* (6 a year).

Chinese Anti-Tuberculosis Society: 42 Dung-si-xi-da St, Beijing; tel. 553685; Pres. HUANG DINGCHEN; publ. *Bulletin* (4 a year).

Chinese Association for Mental Health: 5 An Kang Hutong, De Wai, Beijing 100088; tel. (10) 82085385; fax (10) 62359838; e-mail camh@camh.org.cn; internet www.camh.org.cn; f. 1985; 30,000 mems; Pres. CAI ZHUOJI; Sec.-Gen. LI ZHANJIANG; publs *Chinese Journal of Clinical Psychology* (4 a year), *Chinese Journal of Health Psychology* (6 a year), *Chinese Mental Health Journal* (12 a year).

Chinese Association of Integrated Traditional and Western Medicine: 18 Beixincang, Dongzhimennei, Beijing; tel. (10) 64010688; fax (10) 64010688; f. 1981; 20,000 mems; Pres. CHEN KEJI; Sec.-Gen. CHEN SHIGUI; publ. *Chinese Journal of Integrated Traditional and Western Medicine* (12 a year in Chinese, 4 a year in English).

Chinese Medical Association: 42 Dongsi Xidajie, Beijing; tel. 551943; tel. (10) 65265331; fax (10) 65265331; f. 1915; library of 80,000 vols; Pres. BAI XIQING; publs *Chinese Journal of Internal Medicine* (12 a year), *Chinese Journal of Surgery* (12 a year), *Chinese Medical Journal* (English edition, 12 a year), *National Medical Journal of China* (12 a year).

Chinese Nursing Association: 42 Dongsi Xidajie, Beijing 100710; tel. (10) 65265331; fax (10) 65265331; f. 1909; Pres. ZENG XIYUAN; publ. *Chinese Journal of Nursing* (12 a year).

Chinese Nutrition Society: Guang'an Men, Xuanwu District, Beijing 100053; tel. (10) 83554781; fax (10) 83554780; e-mail mm@cnsoc.org; internet www.cnsoc.org; f. 1981; 7,026 mems; Pres. GE KEYOU; publ. *Acta Nutrimenta* (Chinese and English, 4 a year).

Chinese Pharmaceutical Association: A38 Lishi Rd N., Beijing 100810; tel. (10) 68316576; f. 1907; Pres. QI MAIJIA.

Chinese Pharmacological Society: 1 Xian Nong Tan St, Beijing 100050; tel. (10) 63013366 ext. 404; fax (10) 63017757; f. 1979; Pres. ZHANG JUNTIAN; Sec.-Gen. Prof. LIN ZHIBIN; publs *Acta Pharmacologica Sinica*, *Chinese Journal of Pharmacology and Toxicology*, *Chinese Pharmacological Bulletin*, *Pharmacology and Clinics of Chinese Materia Medica*.

NATURAL SCIENCES
General

China Association for Science and Technology (CAST): 3 Fuxing, Beijing 100863; tel. (10) 68571898; fax (10) 68571897; internet www.cast.org.cn; f. 1958; almost all societies in China are affiliated members; organizes academic exchanges, int. conferences and in-service training for scientists, engineers and technicians; library of 50,000 vols; Pres. ZHOU GUANGZHAO.

Chinese Society for Oceanology and Limnology: 7 Nanhai Rd, Qingdao 266071; tel. (532) 2879062 ext. 3402; fax (532) 2870882; f. 1950; 7,000 mems; Pres. QIN YUNSHAN; Sec.-Gen. ZHOU MINGJIANG; publs *Chinese Journal of Oceanology and Limnology* (4 a year, in English), *Oceanologia et Limnologia Sinica* (6 a year, in Chinese).

Chinese Society of the History of Science and Technology: 137 Chao Nei St, Beijing 100010; tel. (10) 64043989; fax (10) 64017637; f. 1980; 1,500 mems; Pres X. ZEZONG, LU YONGXIANG; publs *China Historical Materials of Science and Technology* (4 a year), *Studies in the History of Natural Sciences* (4 a year).

National Natural Science Foundation of China (NSFC): Beijing; tel. (10) 62327001; e-mail bic@nsfc.gov.cn; internet www.nsfc.gov.cn; depts of chemical sciences, earth sciences, eng. and materials science, information sciences, life sciences, management sciences, mathematical and physical sciences; does not have any research entities; directs, coordinates and financially supports basic research and applied basic research, identifies and fosters scientific talents, promotes science and technology; receives research proposals from univs and other institutions, prepares peer reviews and sessions of evaluation panels; provides advisory services on major issues related to the nat. strategic devt of basic and applied basic research in China; supports activities of nat. professional science foundations; develops cooperative relations with scientific orgs in other countries; Pres. CHEN YIYU; Vice-Pres WANG JIE, SHEN WENQING, SUN JIAGUANG, SHEN YAN, YAO JIANNIAN; publ. *Guide to Programs* (1 a year).

Biological Sciences

Biophysical Society of China: 15 Datun Rd, Chaoyang District, 100101 Beijing; tel. (10) 64889869; fax (10) 64871293; e-mail bscott@sun5.ibp.ac.cn; internet bsc.org.cn; f. 1980; 2,300 mems; Pres. Prof. ZHAO NANMING; Sec.-Gen. Prof. SHEN XUN; publs *Acta Biophysica Sinica* (4 a year), *Progress in Biochemistry and Biophysics* (6 a year).

Botanical Society of China: 20 Naxincun, Xiangshan, Beijing 100093; tel. (10) 62591431; fax (10) 62591431; e-mail bsco@public.bta.net.cn; 15,000 mems; Pres. KUANG TINGYUN; publs *Acta Botanica Sinica* (12 a year), *Acta Phytoecologica et Geobotanica Sinica* (4 a year), *Acta Phytotaxonomica* (6 a year), *Bulletin of Biology* (12 a year), *Chinese Bulletin of Botany* (4 a year), *Plants* (6 a year).

China Zoological Society: 19 Zhong Guan Cun Lu, Beijing; tel. (10) 62552368; fax (10) 62552368; e-mail czs@panda.ioz.ac.cn; f. 1934; 11,600 mems; Pres. CHEN DAYUAN; publs *Acta Arachnologica Sinica* (2 a year), *Acta Parasitologica et Medica Entomologica Sinica* (4 a year), *Acta Theriologica Sinica* (4 a year), *Acta Zoologica Sinica* (6 a year), *Acta Zootaxonomica Sinica* (4 a year), *Chinese Journal of Zoology* (6 a year).

Chinese Association for Physiological Sciences: 42 Dongsixidajie, Beijing 100710; Pres. CHEN MENGQIN.

Chinese Association of Animal Science and Veterinary Medicine: 33 Nongfengli, Dongdaqiao, Chao Yang District, Beijing 100020; tel. (10) 65005934; fax (10) 65005670; e-mail caavxshb@public.bta.net.cn; f. 1936; 50,000 mems; Pres. WU CHANGXIN; Sec.-Gen. YAN HANPING; publs *Chinese Journal of Animal and Veterinary Sciences*, *Chinese Journal of Animal Science*, *Chinese Journal of Veterinary Medicine*.

Chinese Society for Anatomical Sciences: 42 Dongsi Xidajie, Beijing 100710; tel. (10) 65133311 ext. 247; fax (10) 65123754; f. 1920; 3,000 mems; Pres. XU QUNYUAN; Sec.-Gen. LIU BIN; publs *Acta Anatomica Sinica* (4 a year), *Chinese Journal of Anatomy* (4 a year), *Chinese Journal of Clinical Anatomy* (4 a year), *Chinese Journal of Histochemistry and Cytochemistry* (4 a year), *Journal of Neuroanatomy* (4 a year), *Progress of Anatomical Sciences* (4 a year).

Chinese Society for Microbiology: Zhongguancun, Beijing 100080; tel. (10) 62554677; fax (10) 62554677; e-mail chenggs@sun.im.ac.cn; f. 1952; Pres. WEN YUNMEI; publs *Acta Microbiologica Sinica*, *Acta Mycologica Sinica*, *Chinese Journal of Biotechnology*, *Chinese Journal of Virology*, *Chinese Journal of Zoonoses*, *Microbiology*.

Chinese Society of Biochemistry and Molecular Biology: 15 Datun Rd, Chao Yang District, Beijing 100101; tel. (10) 64889859; fax (10) 64872026; internet csbmb.ibp.ac.cn; f. 1979; 1,000 mems; Pres. C. L. TSOU; Sec.-Gen. J. M. ZHOU; publs *Chemistry of Life* (6 a year), *Chinese Journal of Biochemistry and Molecular Biology* (6 a year).

Chinese Society of Environmental Sciences: 115 Xizhimennei Nanxiaojie, Beijing; tel. (10) 661006; f. 1979; 20 industrial/corporate mems; 22,000 individual mems; Pres. LI JINGZHAO; Sec.-Gen. QU GEPING; publs *China Environmental Management*, *China Environmental Science*, *Environmental Chemistry*, *Environmental Engineering*.

Chinese Society of Plant Physiology: 300 Fongling Rd, Shanghai; tel. (21) 64042090; fax 64042385; f. 1963; 4,000 mems; Chair. Prof. TANG ZHANGCHENG; publs *Acta Phytophysiologica Sinica* (4 a year), *Plant Physiology Communications* (6 a year).

Ecological Society of China: 19 Zhongguancun Lu, Beijing 100080; tel. (10) 62565694; fax (10) 62562775; f. 1979; 5,500 mems; Pres. Prof. WANG ZUWANG; Sec.-Gen. Prof. WANG RUSONG; publs *Acta Ecologica Sinica* (6 a year), *Journal of Applied Ecology* (4 a year), *Journal of Ecology* (6 a year).

Entomological Society of China: 19 Zhongguancun Lu, Haidian, Beijing 100080; tel. (10) 62565687; fax (10) 62630062; e-mail wangmm@panda.ioz.ac.cn; f. 1944; 11,000 mems; Pres. ZHANG GUANGXUE; Gen. Sec. LI DIANMO; publs *Acta Entomologica Sinica* (in Chinese), *Acta Parasitologica et Medica* (in Chinese), *Acta Zootaxonomia Sinica* (in Chinese), *Entomological Knowledge* (in Chinese), *Entomologia Sinica* (in Chinese).

Genetics Society of China: Bldg 917, Datun Rd, Andingmenwai, Beijing 100101; tel. (10) 64919944; fax (10) 64914896; f. 1978; 400 nat. mems, 6,600 mems of local socs; Pres. LI ZHENSHENG; Sec.-Gen. CHEN SHOUYI; publs *Acta Genetica Sinica*, *Hereditas* (6 a year).

Palaeontological Society of China: 39 E. Beijing Rd, Nanjing 210008; tel. (25) 3612664; fax (25) 3357026; f. 1929; 1,230 mems; Pres. MU XINAN; Sec.-Gen. SUN GE; publ. *Acta Palaeontologica Sinica* (4 a year).

Mathematical Sciences

Chinese Mathematical Society: c/o Institute of Mathematics, Chinese Academy of Sciences, Beijing 100080; tel. (10) 62551022; fax (10) 62568356; e-mail cms@math08.math.ac.cn; f. 1935; Pres. K. C. CHANG; Sec.-Gen. LI WENLIN.

Physical Sciences

Acoustical Society of China: 17 Zhongguancun St, Beijing 100080; tel. (10) 62553765; fax (10) 62553898; f. 1985; 3,030 mems; Pres. CHEN TONG; Sec.-Gen. HOU CHADHUAN; publs *Acta Acustica* (6 a year), *Applied Acoustics* (4 a year), *Chinese Journal of Acoustics* (4 a year, English version of *Acta Acustica*).

Chinese Academy of Meteorological Sciences: 7 Block 11, Hepingli, Beijing; tel. (10) 64211631; fax (10) 64218703; attached research institutes: see Research Institutes.

Chinese Aerodynamics Research Society: POB 2425, Beijing; Pres. ZHUANG GENGGAN.

Chinese Astronomical Society: Purple Mountain Observatory, Nanjing, Jiangsu 210008; tel. (25) 3302147; fax (25) 3301459; f. 1922; 1,611 mems; Pres. FANG CHENG; publs *Acta Astronomica Sinica* (4 a year), *Acta Astrophysica Sinica* (4 a year).

Chinese Chemical Society: POB 2709, Beijing 100080; tel. (10) 62564020; fax (10) 62568157; f. 1932; Pres. XI FU; publs *Acta Chimica Sinica* (12 a year), *Chinese Journal of Chemistry* (6 a year).

Chinese Geological Society: 26 Baiwanzhuang, Beijing 100037; fax 68310894; f. 1922; 71,000 mems; Pres. ZHANG HONGREN; Sec.-Gen. ZHAO XUN; publs *Acta Geologica Sinica*, *Geological Review*.

Chinese Geological Survey: 45 Fu Wai St, Beijing 100037; tel. (10) 58584680; fax (10) 58584681; e-mail netcenter@mail.cgs.gov.cn; internet www.cgs.gov.cn; f. 1959; attached to Ministry of Land and Resources; responsible for the centralized deployment and implementation of China's basic, public and strategic geological investigation and mineral exploration; provides basic geological information and data for the national economy; attached institutes: see Research Institutes; Dir-Gen. MENG XIANLAI; publs *Acta Geologica Sinica*, *Bulletin*, *Geological Review*.

Chinese Geophysical Society: Institute of Geophysics, POB 9701, Beijing 100101; tel. (10) 64889027; fax (10) 64871995; f. 1948; 4,000 mems; Pres. LIU GUANGDING; Sec.-Gen. ZHU RIXIANG; publ. *Acta Geophisica Sinica* (6 a year).

Chinese High-Energy Physics Society: POB 918, Beijing 100039; tel. 68235910; fax 68213374; e-mail zhouxb@alpha02.ihep.ac.cn; internet www.ihep.ac.cn; f. 1981; 962 mems; Chair. DAI YUANBEN; Sec.-Gen. HUANG TAO; publs *High Energy Physics and Nuclear Physics* (12 a year), *Modern Physics* (6 a year).

Chinese Meteorological Society: 46 Zhongguancun South Ave, Beijing 100081; tel. 68407634; fax 6840682; e-mail cmsams@cms1924.org; internet www.cms1924.org; f. 1924; 21,000 mems; Pres. Prof. Dr QIN DAHE (acting); Sec.-Gen. WANG CHUNYI; publs *Acta Meteorologica Sinica* (24 a year, in English), *Meteorological Knowledge* (12 a year, in Chinese).

Chinese Nuclear Physics Society: POB 275-50, Beijing 102413; tel. (10) 69358003; fax (10) 69357787; e-mail zhusy@ciae.ac.cn; internet www.cnps.ac.cn; f. 1979; 600 mems;

Pres. Prof. HUANQIAO ZHANG; Sec.-Gen. Prof. SHENGYUN ZHU; publ. *Nuclear Physics Review* (4 a year).

Chinese Nuclear Society: POB 2125, Beijing 100822; tel. (10) 68531473; fax (10) 68527188; internet www.ns.org.cn; f. 1980; 8,894 mems; Pres. WANG NAIYAN; publ. *Chinese Journal of Nuclear Science and Technology*.

Chinese Physical Society: POB 603, Beijing 100080; tel. (10) 82649019; fax (10) 82649019; e-mail cps@aphy.iphy.ac.cn; internet www.cps-net.org; f. 1932; attached to Chinese Association for Science and Technology; 42,000 mems; Pres. YANG GUO-ZHEN; Sec.-Gen. WANG EN-GE; publs *Acta Physica Sinica* (12 a year, in Chinese), *Chinese Journal of Chemical Physics* (6 a year, in Chinese), *Chinese Physics* (12 a year, in English), *Chinese Physics Letters* (12 a year, in English), *College Physics* (12 a year, in Chinese), *Communications in Theoretical Physics* (12 a year, in English), *Physics Teaching* (12 a year, in Chinese), *Progress in Physics* (4 a year, in Chinese), *Wuli* (Physics, 12 a year, in Chinese).

Chinese Society for Mineralogy, Petrology and Geochemistry: 46 Guanshui Rd, Guiyang 550002, Guizhou Province; tel. and fax (851) 5895823; e-mail csmpg@vip.skleg.cn; internet www.gyig.ac.cn/society; f. 1978; 6,500 mems; library of 10,000 vols and periodicals; Pres. OUYANG ZIYUAN; publs *Acta Mineralogica Sinica* (4 a year), *Acta Petrologica Sinica* (4 a year), *Bulletin of Mineralogy, Petrology and Geochemistry* (4 a year), *Chinese Journal of Geochemistry* (4 a year, in English), *Geochemica* (6 a year), *Journal of Paleography* (4 a year).

Chinese Society for Rock Mechanics and Engineering: POB 9825, Beijing, 100029; tel. and fax (10) 82998163; e-mail csrme@163.com; internet www.csrme.com; f. 1985; 14 Corporate mems; 554 individual mems; Pres. Prof. QIAN QIHU (acting); Sec.-Gen. Prof. WU FAQUAN; publs *Chinese Journal of Rock Mechanics and Engineering* (in Chinese), *Chinese Journal of Underground Space and Engineering* (in Chinese), *Journal of Rock Mechanics and Geotechnical Engineering* (in English), *News of Rock Mechanics and Engineering* (4 a year, in Chinese).

Chinese Society of Space Research: 1 Second Southern Ave, Zhongguancun, Beijing 100080; tel. (10) 62559882; f. 1980; Pres. Prof. WANG XIJI; publ. *Chinese Journal of Space Science* (4 a year).

Seismological Society of China: 5 Minzu Daxue Nanlu, Beijing 100081; tel. (10) 68417858; f. 1979; 1,250 mems; Pres. Prof. ZHANG GUOMIN; publ. *Acta Seismologica Sinica* (4 a year, in Chinese and English edns).

PHILOSOPHY AND PSYCHOLOGY

Chinese Psychological Society: Institute of Psychology, Chinese Academy of Sciences, Datun Rd, Jia 10 Hao, Chaoyang District, Beijing 100101; tel. and fax (10) 64855830; e-mail xuehui@psych.ac.cn; internet www.cpsbeijing.org; f. 1921; organizes annual conference on various topics by branch committees; National Congress of Psychology every two years; open lectures to public; promotion of psychological science through the internet; seminars organized for professionals in other fields; 2,000 mems; Pres. Prof. KAN ZHANG; Sec.-Gen. Prof. YUFANG YANG; publs *Acta Psychologica Sinica* (6 a year), *Psychological Science* (6 a year).

RELIGION, SOCIOLOGY AND ANTHROPOLOGY

Chinese Sociological Research Society: c/o Chinese Academy of Social Sciences, 5 Jianguomennei Da Jie, Beijing; f. 1979; Pres. FEI XIAOTONG; Exec. Sec. WANG KANG.

Chinese Study of Religion Society: Xi'anmen Ave, Beijing; Pres. REN JIYU.

TECHNOLOGY

Chemical Industry and Engineering Society of China: POB 911, Beijing; tel. 466025; f. 1922; 40,000 mems; Pres. YANG GUANGQI; Sec.-Gen. YIN DELIN; publs *Huagong Jinzhan* (Chemical Engineering Progress, 6 a year), *Huagong Xuebao* (Journal of Chemical Engineering, 4 a year).

China Coal Society: Hepingli, Beijing 100013; tel. (10) 84262776; fax (10) 84261671; f. 1962; 53,000 mems; Pres. FAN WEITANG; Sec.-Gen. PAN HUIZHENG; publs *Journal* (irregular), *Modern Miners* (12 a year).

China Computer Federation: POB 2704, Beijing 100080; tel. (10) 62562503; fax (10) 62567485; e-mail ccf@ns.ict.ac.cn; internet www.ccf.org.cn; f. 1962; fmrly Chinese Information Processing Soc.; 40,000 individual mems; Chair. ZHANG XIAOXIANG; Sec.-Gen. CHEN SHUKAI; publs *Chinese Journal of Advanced Software Research*, *Chinese Journal of Computers*, *Journal of Computer Science and Technology* (in English), *Journal of Computer-aided Design and Computer Graphics*, *Journal of Software*.

China Electrotechnical Society: 46 Sanlihe Rd, POB 2133, Beijing 100823; tel. (10) 68595358; fax (10) 68511242; e-mail cesintl@public.bta.net.cn; internet www.ces.org.cn; f. 1981; 50,000 mems; Pres. WU XIAOHUA; Sec.-Gen. DUAN RUICHUN; publs *Electrical Engineering* (12 a year), *Transactions of China Electrotechnical Society* (12 a year).

China Energy Research Society: 54 San Li He Rd, Beijing 100863; tel. (10) 68511816; fax (10) 68511816; f. 1981; 18,000 mems; Pres. HUANG YICHENG; Sec.-Gen. BAO YUNQIAO; publ. *Guide to World Energy* (52 a year).

China Engineering Graphics Society: POB 85, Beijing 100083; tel. (10) 82317091; fax (10) 82326420; Pres. TANG RONGXI; publ. *Computer Aided Drafting, Design and Manufacturing* (4 a year).

China Fire Protection Association: 5th Floor, Fire Station, 19A Huawei XiLi, Chaoyang District, Beijing 100021; China Fire, 48, Banbuqiao Road, Xuanwu Beijing 100054; tel. (10) 51232677; fax (10) 51232676; e-mail english@china-fire.org; internet www.china-fire.com; f. 1984; 30,000 mems; Pres. SUN LUN; publs *Fire Protection in China*, *Fire Science and Technology*, *Fire Technique and Products Information*.

China Society for Scientific and Technical Information: 15 Fuxinglu, Beijing; tel. (10) 68014024; fax (10) 68014025; internet www.cssti.org.cn; f. 1964; organizes academic activities about information science and technology; 13,000 mems; Pres. WU HENG; publ. *Journal of the China Society for Scientific and Technical Information* (6 a year).

Chinese Abacus Association: Sidaokou, Xizhimenwai, Shidaokou, Beijing; tel. 896275; f. 1979; 500,000 mems; Pres. ZHU XI-AN; Sec.-Gen. HU JING; publs *Chinese Abacus* (12 a year), *Chinese Abacus News* (12 a year).

Chinese Academy of Engineering (CAE): POB 3847, Beijing 100038; 3 Fuxing Rd, Beijing; tel. (10) 68530187; fax (10)

68519694; internet www.cae.ac.cn; f. 1994; 616 Academicians; Pres. XU KUANGDI; Sec. HE ZHONGWEI.

Chinese Academy of Space Technology: 31 Baishiqiao, POB 2417, Beijing 100081; tel. (10) 68379439; fax (10) 68378237; 4 mems; attached research institutes: see Research Institutes; Pres. QI FAREN.

Chinese Association of Automation: POB 2728, 100080 Beijing; tel. (10) 62544415; fax (10) 62620908; e-mail wangh@iamail.ia.ac .cn; internet www.gongkong.com; f. 1961; 40,000 mems; Pres Prof. CHEN HANFU, Prof. YANG JIACHI, Prof. DAI RUWAI; publs *Acta Automatica Sinica* (6 a year), *Automation Panorama* (6 a year), *Pattern Recognition and Artificial Intelligence* (4 a year), *Information and Control* (6 a year), *Robot* (6 a year).

Chinese Ceramic Society: Bai Wan Zhuang, Beijing 100831; tel. (10) 68313364; fax (10) 68313364; f. 1945; 30,000 mems; Pres. WANG YANMOU; Sec.-Gen. JIANG DONGHUA; publs *Bulletin of the Chinese Ceramic Society* (6 a year), *Journal of the Chinese Ceramic Society* (6 a year).

Chinese Civil Engineering Society: Bai Wan Zhuang, POB 2500, 100835 Beijing; tel. (10) 68311313; fax (10) 68313669; f. 1953; Pres. MAO YISHENG; Sec.-Gen. ZHAO XICHUN; publ. *Civil Engineering Journal.*

Chinese Hydraulic Engineering Society: 2-2 Baiguang Rd, Beijing 100053; tel. (10) 63202171; fax (10) 63202154; e-mail ches@ mwr.gov.cn; internet www.hwcc.gov.cn; f. 1931; 93,309 mems; Pres. ZHU ERMING; Sec.- Gen. FENG GUANGZHI; publ *China Rural Water and Hydropower* (12 a year), *Journal of Hydraulic Engineering* (12 a year), *Journal of Sediment Research* (12 a year).

Chinese Light Industry Society: B22 Fuchengmenwai Ave, Beijing 100037; tel. 894147; f. 1979; Pres. JI LONG.

Chinese Mechanical Engineering Society: 11th Fl., Bldg 4, Zhuyu Int., 9 Shouti S Rd, Haidian Dist., Beijing 100048; tel. (10) 68799038; fax (10) 68799050; e-mail headquarters@cmes.org; internet www.cmes .org; f. 1936; 180,000 mems; Pres. Dr LU RONGXIANG; Gen. Sec. ZHANG YAN-MIN; publs *Chinese Journal of Mechanical Engineering* (6 a year, 4 a year, in English), *China Mechanical Engineering* (52 a year, in Chinese), *Journal of Mechanical Engineering* (12 a year, in Chinese).

Chinese Petroleum Society: POB 766, Liu Pu Kang, Beijing 100724; tel. (10) 62095615; fax (10) 62014787; f. 1979; academic asscn of petroleum engineers; 60,000 mems; library: 20,000 books, 560 periodicals; Pres. JIN ZHONGCHAO; Sec.-Gen. LU JIMENG; publ. *Acta Petrolei Sinica* (Exploration and Development, and Refining and the Petrochemical Industry, each edition 4 a year).

China Railway Society: 10 Fuxing Rd, POB 2499, Beijing; e-mail yangzm25@yahoo .com.cn; internet www.crs.org.cn; f. 1978; railway transport, construction and rolling stock manufacture; academic exchanges, technological consultation, technical research and devt; 78,000 mems; Chair. SUN YONGFU; Sec.-Gen. LU CHANGQING; publs *Railway Journal, Railway Knowledge.*

Chinese Society for Metals: 46 Dongsi Xidajie, Beijing 100711; tel. (10) 65133322; fax (10) 65124122; e-mail csmoffice@csm.org .cn; internet www.csm.org.cn; f. 1956; 100,000 mems; library of 50,000 vols, 20,000 serials, 1,270 periodicals; Pres. WENG YUQ- ING; Sec.-Gen. LI WENXIU; publs *Acta Metallurgica Sinica* (i12 a year, n Chinese; 6 a year, in English), *China Metallurgy* (6 a

year), *Iron and Steel* (12 a year), *Journal of Materials Science and Technology* (6 a year).

Chinese Society of Aeronautics and Astronautics: 5 Liangguochang Rd, Dong-cheng District, Beijing 100010; tel. (10) 84923943; fax (10) 84923942; internet www .csaa.org.cn; f. 1964; 21,800 mems; Pres. LIU GAOZHUO; Sec.-Gen. ZHANG JUEN; publs *Acta Aeronautica et Astronautica Sinica* (6 a year), *Aerospace Knowledge* (12 a year), *Chinese Journal of Aeronautics* (4 a year), *Journal of Aeronautical Materials* (6 a year), *Journal of Aerospace Power* (6 a year), *Model Airplane* (6 a year).

Chinese Society of Astronautics (CSA): POB 838, Beijing 100830; 2 Yue Tan Beixiao Tie, Beijing; tel. (10) 68768622; fax (10) 68768624; e-mail csa_heinlein@yahoo.com .cn; internet www.csaspace.org.cn/heinlein/ hlindex-en.htm; f. 1979; 10,000 mems; Pres. LIU JIYUAN; Sec.-Gen. Prof. YANG, JUNHUA; publs *Space Exploration, Journal.*

Chinese Society of Electrical Engineering: 1 Lane 2, Baiguang Rd, Beijing 10076; Pres. ZHANG FENGXIANG.

Chinese Society of Engineering Thermophysics: POB 2706, Zhong Guan Cun, Beijing; f. 1978; 5,000 mems; Sec.-Gen. Prof. XU JIANZHONG; publ. *Journal of Engineering Thermophysics* (4 a year).

Chinese Society of Naval Architects and Marine Engineers: POB 817, Beijing; tel. (10) 68340527; fax (10) 68313380; f. 1943; Pres. WANG RONGSHENG; Sec.-Gen. WANG SHOUDAO; publs *Naval and Merchant Ships* (12 a year), *Shipbuilding of China* (4 a year, contents and abstracts), *Ship Engineering* (6 a year).

Chinese Society of Theoretical and Applied Mechanics (CSTAM): 15 Zhong-Guan-Cun, Beijing 100080; tel. (10) 62559588; fax (10) 62561284; e-mail cstam@ sun.ihep.ac.cn; internet www.cstam.org.cn; f. 1957; 21,000 mems; Dir Prof. BAI YILONG; publs *Acta Mechanica Sinica* (6 a year, in English 4 a year), *Acta Mechanica Solida Sinica* (6 a year, in English 4 a year), *Engineering Mechanics* (4 a year), *Explosion and Shock Waves* (4 a year), *Journal of Computational Mechanics* (4 a year), *Journal of Experimental Mechanics* (4 a year), *Mechanics and Practice* (6 a year).

Chinese Textile Engineering Society: 3 Middle St, Yanjing Li, East Suburb, Beijing 100025; tel. (10) 65016537; fax (10) 65016538; f. 1930; 60,000 mems; Pres. JI GUOBIAO.

Nonferrous Metals Society of China: B12, Fuxing Rd, Beijing 100814; tel. (10) 63971451; fax (10) 63965399; e-mail nfsoc@ public.bta.net.cn; internet www.nfsoc.org.cn; f. 1984; 39,000 mems; Pres. KANG YI; Sec.-Gen. NIU YINJIAN; publs *Journal of Nonferrous Metals* (4 a year, with English Abstracts), *Journal of Rare Metals* (4 a year, with English version), *Transactions of Nonferrous Metals Society of China* (4 a year, with English version).

Society of Automotive Engineers of China: 46 Fucheng Rd, Beijing 100036; tel. (10) 68121894; fax (10) 68125556; f. 1963; 1,520 mems; Pres. ZHANG XINGYE; publs *Auto Fan* (12 a year), *Automotive Engineering* (6 a year).

Systems Engineering Society of China: Institute of Systems Science, Zhongyguancun, Beijing 100080; tel. 62541827; fax 62568364; internet www.amss.iss.ac.cn.sesc; f. 1980; 3,000 individual mems; 150 collective mems; Pres. CHEN, GUANGYA; Sec.-Gen. WANG, SHOUYANG; publs *Journal of Systems Science and Systems Engineering* (4 a year, in English), *Journal of Transportations Sys-*

tems Engineering and Information Technology (4 a year, in English), *Systems Engineering* (4 a year), *Systems Engineering—Theory and Practice* (12 a year).

Research Institutes
AGRICULTURE, FISHERIES AND VETERINARY SCIENCE

Chinese Research Institute of the Wood Industry: Wan Shou Shan, Beijing 100091; attached to Chinese Acad. of Forestry.

Forest Economics Research Institute: He Ping Li, Beijing; tel. 64210476; attached to Chinese Acad. of Forestry.

Forest Resource and Insect Research Institute: Kunming, Yunnan Province; attached to Chinese Acad. of Forestry.

Forestry Research Institute: Wan Shou Shan, Beijing 100091; tel. (10) 62888862; fax (10) 62872015; e-mail lumz@www.caf.ac.cn; internet nic6.forestry.ac.cn; f. 1953; attached to Chinese Acad. of Forestry; research into silviculture, tree cultivation, soil science, agroforestry, prevention of desertification, ornamental plants, biotechnology; 148 mems; Dir Prof. Dr LU MENG ZHU; publ. *Forest Research* (6 a year).

Institute of Agricultural Meteorology: 7 Block 11, Hepingli, Beijing; attached to Chinese Acad. of Meteorological Sciences.

Institute of Soil Science: POB 821, Nanjing 210008; tel. 7712572; fax 3353590; f. 1953; attached to Chinese Acad. of Sciences; library of 110,000 vols; Dir Prof. ZHAO QIGUO; publs *Acta Pedologica Sinica, Advance of Soil Science, Pedosphere, Soils, Soil Science Research Report.*

Sub-Tropical Forestry Research Institute: Fuyang, Zhejiang Province 311400; attached to Chinese Acad. of Forestry; Dir YANG PEISHOU.

Tropical Forestry Research Institute: Longdong, Guangzhou, Guandong Province 510520; attached to Chinese Acad. of Forestry.

BIBLIOGRAPHY, LIBRARY SCIENCE AND MUSEOLOGY

State Archives Bureau of China: 21 Feng Sheng Hutong, Beijing; tel. 665797; Dir FENG ZIZHI; publ. *Archival Work* (12 a year).

ECONOMICS, LAW AND POLITICS

Academy of Marxism of the Chinese Academy of Social Sciences: Rd Jianguo-mennei Da jie, No. 5, Beijing; e-mail wangzb@cass.org.cn; internet myy.cass.cn; f. 1980; attached to Chinese Acad. of Social Sciences; Dir SU SHAOZHI; publs *International Thought Review* (in English), *Marxism Digest* (in Chinese), *Study of Marxism* (in Chinese).

Economics Institute: 2 Yuetanxiaojie N., Fuchengmenurai, Beijing 100836; tel. (10) 895323; attached to Chinese Acad. of Social Sciences; Dir ZHAO RENWEI.

Industrial Economics Institute: 2 Yue-tanbeixiao Street, Fuchengmenwai, Beijing 100836; f. 1978; attached to Chinese Acad. of Social Sciences; Dir ZHOU SHULIAN.

Institute of American Studies: 3 Zhang-zizhong Rd, Beijing 100007; tel. (10) 64039046; fax (10) 64000021; internet ias .cass.cn; f. 1981; attached to Chinese Acad. of Social Sciences; Dir HUANG PING; publ. *American Studies Quarterly.*

Institute of East European, Russian and Central Asian Studies: 3 Zhangzhizhong Rd, Beijing 100007; tel. 64014020; f. 1976;

attached to Chinese Acad. of Social Sciences; library of 60,000 vols, 280 periodicals; Dir Li JINGJIE.

Institute of European Studies: 5 Jianguomennei Ave, Beijing 100732; tel. (10) 65138428; fax (10) 65125818; e-mail ies@cass.net.cn; internet europeanstudies.org; f. 1980; attached to Chinese Acad. of Social Sciences; Dir Prof. ZHOU HONG; publ. *Chinese Journal for European Studies* (6 a year).

Institute of Latin American Studies: POB 1113, Beijing; tel. (10) 64014009; fax (10) 64014011; f. 1961; attached to Chinese Acad. of Social Sciences; Dir Li MINGDE.

Institute of West Asian and African Studies: 3 Zhangzhizhong Rd, Beijing 100007; f. 1961; attached to Chinese Acad. of Social Sciences; Dir-Gen Prof. YANG GUANG; publ. *West Asia and Africa* (6 a year).

Japanese Studies Institute: Dong Yuan, 3 Zhangzhizhong Rd, Beijing 100007; f. 1980; attached to Chinese Acad. of Social Sciences; Dir HE FANG.

Law Institute: 15 Shatan St N., Beijing 100720; tel. 64014045; f. 1958; attached to Chinese Acad. of Social Sciences; Dir WANG JIAFU.

Political Science Institute: Shatan Bei Jie, Beijing 100720; f. 1981; attached to Chinese Acad. of Social Sciences; Dir YAN JIAQI.

Quantitative and Technical Economics Institute: 5 Jianguomennei Ave, Beijing 100732; tel. (10) 65137561; fax (10) 65125895; e-mail tswang@mx.cei.gov.cn; internet www.iqte-cass.org; f. 1982; attached to Chinese Acad. of Social Sciences; Dir WANG TONGSAN; publ. *Quantitative and Technical Economics* (12 a year).

Rural Development Institute: Ritan Rd, Beijing; tel. (10) 65275067; fax (10) 65137559; internet www.cass.net.en/chinese/s04-nfs/s04-nfs.htm; f. 1978; attached to Chinese Acad. of Social Sciences; Dir Prof. ZHANG XIAOSHAN; publs *Chinese Rural Economy* (12 a year), *Chinese Rural Survey* (6 a year).

Taiwan Studies Institute: 15 Poshangcun, Haidian District, Beijing 100091; tel. (10) 62883311; fax (10) 62880285; f. 1984; attached to Chinese Acad. of Social Sciences; Dir XU SHIQUAN; publ. *Taiwan Studies* (4 a year).

Trade, Finance and Material Supply Institute: 2 Yuetanbeixiao St, Beijing 100836; attached to Chinese Acad. of Social Sciences; Dir ZHANG ZHUOYUAN.

World Economy and Politics Institute: 5 Jianguomennei Ave, Beijing 100732; attached to Chinese Acad. of Social Sciences; Dir PU SHAN.

HISTORY, GEOGRAPHY AND ARCHAEOLOGY

Archaeology Institute: 27 Wangfujing Ave, Beijing 100710; f. 1950; attached to Chinese Acad. of Social Sciences; Dir WANG ZHONGSHU.

Changchun Institute of Geography: 16 Gongnong Rd, Changchun 130021, Jilin Province; tel. (431) 5652931; fax (431) 5652931; f. 1958; attached to Chinese Acad. of Sciences; Dir Prof. HE YAN.

Chinese Academy of Surveying and Mapping, National Bureau of Surveying and Mapping: 16 Bei Tai Ping Lu, Beijing 100039; tel. (10) 68212277; fax (10) 68218654; f. 1959; library of 50,000 vols; Dir LIU XIANLIN; publs *Remote Sensing Information, Trends in Science and Technology of Surveying and Mapping*.

History (Chinese) Institute: 5 Jianguomennei Ave, Beijing 100732; attached to Chinese Acad. of Social Sciences; Dir LI XUEQIN.

History (Modern Chinese) Institute: 1 Dongcheng Lane, Wangfu Ave, Beijing 100006; tel. (10) 555400; attached to Chinese Acad. of Social Sciences; Dir WANG QINGCHENG.

History (World) Institute: 1 Dongcheng Lane, Wangfu Ave, Beijing 100006; f. 1964; attached to Chinese Acad. of Social Sciences; Dir ZHANG CHUNNIAN.

Institute of Geography: Bldg 917, Datun Rd, Anwai, Beijing 100101; tel. (10) 64914841; fax (10) 64911844; f. 1940; attached to Chinese Acad. of Sciences; library of 90,000 vols; Dir Prof. ZHENG DU; publ. *Geographical Research* (4 a year).

LANGUAGE AND LITERATURE

Applied Linguistics Institute: 51 Nanxiao Street, Chaoyangmennei, Beijing 100010; tel. (10) 557146; f. 1984; attached to Chinese Acad. of Social Sciences; Dir CHEN YUAN.

Chinese Literature Institute: 5 Jianguomennei Ave, Beijing 100732; attached to Chinese Acad. of Social Sciences; Dir LIU ZAIFU.

Foreign Literature Institute: 5 Jianguomennei Ave, Beijing 100732; attached to Chinese Acad. of Social Sciences; Dir ZHANG YU.

Institute of Ethnic Literature: 5 Jianguomennei Ave, Beijing 100732; tel. (10) 65138025; fax (10) 65134585; e-mail iel-scholarship@cass.org.cn; internet www.ilnm.cass.net.cn; f. 1981; attached to Chinese Acad. of Social Sciences; Dirs TANG XIAOGING, CHAO GEJIN; publ. *Studies of Ethnic Literature* (4 a year).

Institute of Linguistics: 5 Jianguomenei Dajie, Beijing 100732; tel. (10) 65737403; fax (10) 65737403; f. 1950; attached to Chinese Acad. of Social Sciences; Dir SHEN JIAXUAN; publs *Contemporary Linguistics, Dialects, The Chinese Language and Writing*.

Journalism Institute: 2 Jintai Rd W., Chaoyang District, Beijing 100026; attached to Chinese Acad. of Social Sciences; Dir SUN XUPEI.

MEDICINE

Biomedical Engineering Institute: POB (25) 204, Tianjing 300192; fax (22) 361095; attached to Chinese Acad. of Medical Sciences; Deputy Dir WANG PENGYAN.

Blood Transfusion Institute: Renmin Rd N., Chengdu, Sichuan 61008; tel. (28) 332125; fax (28) 332125; attached to Chinese Acad. of Medical Sciences; Dir YANG CHENGMIN.

Cancer Institute and Hospital: Faculty of Oncology, Peking Union Medical College, Panjiayuan, Chaoyang District, Beijing 100021; tel. (10) 67781331; fax (10) 67713359; attached to Chinese Acad. of Medical Sciences; Dir DONG ZHIWEI.

Cardiovascular Diseases Institute: A167 Beilishi Rd, Beijing 100037; tel. (10) 68314466; fax (10) 68313012; e-mail fuwaih@public.bta.net.cn; attached to Chinese Acad. of Medical Sciences; Dir GAO RUNLIN.

Clinical Medicine Institute: 1 Shuaifuyuan Lane, Beijing 100730; tel. (10) 65127733; fax (10) 65124875; attached to Chinese Acad. of Medical Sciences; Dir LU ZHADLIN.

Dermatology Institute: 12 Jiangwangmiao St, Nanjing, Jiangsu 210042; tel. (25) 5411040; fax (25) 5414477; attached to

Chinese Acad. of Medical Sciences; Dir YE SHUNZHANG.

Haematology Institute: 228 Nanjing Rd, Tianjing 300020; tel. (22) 707939; fax (22) 706542; attached to Chinese Acad. of Medical Sciences; Dir HAO YUSHU.

Health School: Badachu, Xishan, Beijing 100041; tel. 68862233; fax 68864137; attached to Chinese Acad. of Medical Sciences; Dir CHI XINGQIU.

Institute of Basic Medical Sciences: 5 Dongdan Santiao, Beijing 100005; tel. (10) 65134466; fax (10) 65124876; e-mail zheng@public3.bta.net.cn; attached to Chinese Acad. of Medical Sciences; Dir ZHENG DEXIAN.

Institute of Laboratory Animal Science: 5 Pan Jia Yuan Nan Li, Chao Yang District, Beijing 100021; fax (10) 67780683; attached to Chinese Acad. of Medical Sciences; Dir LIU YINONG.

Institute of Microcirculation: 5 Dongdan Santiao, Beijing 100005; tel. (10) 65126407; fax (10) 62015012; f. 1984; attached to Chinese Acad. of Medical Sciences; Dir Prof. XIU RUIJUAN.

Institute of Plastic Surgery: Badachu, Beijing 100041; tel. (10) 68874826; fax (10) 68864137; f. 1957; attached to Chinese Acad. of Medical Sciences; library of 20,000 vols; Dir Prof. SONG YEGUANG; publ. *Chinese Journal of Plastic Surgery and Burns*.

Materia Medica Institute: 1 Xiannongtan St, Beijing 100050; tel. (10) 63013366; fax (10) 63017757; attached to Chinese Acad. of Medical Sciences; Dir ZHANG JUNTIAN.

Medical Biology Institute: Huahongdong, Kunming, Yunnan 650160; f. 1959; attached to Chinese Acad. of Medical Sciences.

Medical Biotechnology Institute: 1 Tiantanxili, Beijing 100050; tel. (10) 757315; fax (10) 63017302; attached to Chinese Acad. of Medical Sciences; Dir ZHANG ZHIPING.

Medicinal Plant Development Institute: 151 Ma Lian Wa North Rd, Haidian District, Beijing 100094; tel. (10) 62896288; fax (10) 62899715; e-mail implad@implad.ac.cn; internet www.implad.ac.cn; f. 1983; attached to Chinese Acad. of Medical Sciences; library of 30,000 vols; Dir Prof. CHEN SHILIN.

Radiation Medicine Institute: POB 71, Tianjin 300192; attached to Chinese Acad. of Medical Sciences.

Shanghai Institute of Materia Medica: 294 Tai-Yuan Rd, Shanghai 200031; tel. (21) 64311833; fax (21) 64370269; f. 1932; attached to Chinese Acad. of Sciences; development of new drugs; library of 80,000 vols, 600 current periodicals; Dir CHEN KAIXIAN; publ. *Acta Pharmocologica Sinica*.

NATURAL SCIENCES
General

Fujian Institute of Research on the Structure of Matter: Xihe, Fuzhou, Fujian 350002; tel. (591) 3714517; fax (591) 3714946; f. 1960; attached to Chinese Acad. of Sciences; library of 75,000 vols; Dir Prof. HUANG JINSHUN; publ. *Journal on Structural Chemistry* (6 a year).

Institute of Oceanology: 7 Nanhai Rd, Qingdao 266071; tel. (532) 2879062; fax (532) 2870882; e-mail iocas@ms.qdio.ac.cn; f. 1950; attached to Chinese Acad. of Sciences; library of 180,000 vols; Dir XIANG JIANHAI; publs *Chinese Journal of Oceanology and Limnology* (4 a year, in English), *Marine Sciences* (6 a year, in Chinese), *Oceanologia et Limnologia Sinica* (6 a year, Chinese), *Studia Marina Sinica* (Chinese with English abstracts, 1 a year).

Institute of the History of Natural Sciences: 137 Chao Nei St, Beijing 100010; tel. (10) 64043989; fax (10) 64017637; e-mail ihns_2008_@ihns.ac.cn; internet www.ihns.ac.cn; f. 1957; attached to Chinese Acad. of Sciences; library of 150,000 vols; Dir Prof. DUN LIU; publs *China Historical Materials of Science and Technology* (4 a year), *Studies in the History of Natural Sciences* (4 a year).

Qinghai Institute of Salt Lakes: 7 Xinning Rd, Xinning, Qinghai Province 810008; tel. 44306; fax 46002; f. 1965; attached to Chinese Acad. of Sciences; library of 85,000 vols; Dir LIU DEJIANG; publ. *Journal of Salt Lake Science*.

South China Sea Institute of Oceanology: 164 West Xingang Rd, Guangzhou 510301; tel. (20) 84452227; fax (20) 84451672; internet www.scsio.ac.an; f. 1959; attached to Chinese Acad. of Sciences; library of 95,546 vols; Dir Dr SHI PING; publs *Journal of Tropical Oceanology* (6 a year), *Nanhai Studia Marina Sinica* (irregular, Chinese with English abstracts).

Biological Sciences

Institute of Applied Ecology: POB 417, Shenyang 110015; tel. (24) 3902096; fax (24) 3843313; f. 1954; attached to Chinese Acad. of Sciences; library of 95,000 vols; Dir SUN TIEHANG; publs *Chinese Journal of Applied Ecology*, *Chinese Journal of Ecology*.

Institute of Biophysics: 15 Datun Rd, Chaoyang District, Beijing 100101; tel. (10) 62022029; fax (10) 62027837; attached to Chinese Acad. of Sciences; Dir WANG SHURONG.

Institute of Botany: 141 Xizhimen Wai St, Beijing 100044; attached to Chinese Acad. of Sciences; Dir ZHANG XINSHI.

Institute of Developmental Biology: POB 2707, Beijing; fax 62561269; f. 1980; attached to Chinese Acad. of Sciences; specializes in biotechnology of fish and mammals; Dir YAN SHAOYI.

Institute of Genetics and Developmental Biology: Datun Rd, Andingmenwai, Beijing 100101; tel. (10) 64889331; fax (10) 64856610; e-mail genetics@genetics.ac.cn; internet www.genetics.ac.cn; attached to Chinese Acad. of Sciences; Dir Prof. JIAYANG LI.

Institute of Hydrobiology: Luojiashan, Wuhan 430072, Hubei Province; tel. (27) 68780789; fax (27) 68780123; e-mail zhh@ihb.ac.cn; internet www.ihb.ac.cn; f. 1930; attached to Chinese Acad. of Sciences; freshwater ecology, fisheries, biotechnology and molecular biology, aquatic environment protection; library of 70,000 vols; fish museum; Dir Dr. GUI JIANFANG; publ. *Acta Hydrobiologica Sinica* (6 a year).

Institute of Microbiology: 13 Beiyitiao, Zhongguancun, Haidian District, Beijing 100080; tel. (10) 62552178; fax (10) 62560912; e-mail gaof@im.ac.cn; internet www.im.ac.cn; f. 1958; attached to Chinese Acad. of Sciences; 380 mems; Dir Prof. GEORGE F. GAO; publs *Acta Microbiologica Sinica* (6 a year), *Chinese Journal of Biotechnology* (6 a year), *Microbiology* (6 a year), *Mycosystema* (4 a year).

Institute of Vertebrate Palaeontology and Palaeo-Anthropology: Academia Sinica, Beijing; f. 1929; attached to Chinese Acad. of Sciences; Dir QIU ZHANXIANG.

Institute of Zoology: Chinese Academy of Sciences, 19 Zhongguancun Rd, Haidian, Beijing 100080; tel. (10) 62552219; fax (10) 62565689; e-mail ioz@panda.ioz.ac.cn; internet panda.ioz.ac.cn; attached to Chinese Acad. of Sciences; Dir Prof. HUANG DAWEI; publs *Acta Entomologica Sinica* (4 a year),

Acta Zoologica Sinica (6 a year), *Acta Zootaxonomica Sinica* (4 a year), *Chinese Journal of Entomology* (6 a year), *Chinese Journal of Zoology* (6 a year), *Entomologica Sinica* (4 a year, in English).

Kunming Institute of Zoology: Kunming 650223, Yunnan Province; tel. (871) 5140390; fax (871) 5151823; f. 1959; attached to Chinese Acad. of Sciences; library of 180,000 vols; Dir SHI LIMING; publ. *Zoological Research* (4 a year).

Nanjing Institute of Geology and Palaeontology: 39 East Beijing Rd, Chi-Ming-Ssu, Nanjing 210008, Jiangsu Province; tel. (25) 7714437; fax (25) 3357026; f. 1951; attached to Chinese Acad. of Sciences; library of 26,000 vols; Dir MU XINAN; publs *Acta Micropalaeontologica Sinica* (4 a year), *Acta Palaeobotanica et Palynologica Sinica* (irregular), *Acta Palaeontologica Sinica* (4 a year), *Bulletin* (irregular), *Journal of Stratigraphy* (4 a year), *Memoirs* (irregular), *Palaeontologia Cathayana*, *Palaeontologia Sinica* (irregular), *Palaeontological Abstracts* (4 a year), *Palaeoworld* (irregular).

Research Centre for Environmental Sciences: POB 2871, 18 Shuangqing Rd, Haidian, Beijing 100085; tel. and fax (10) 62923549; e-mail zhb@rcees.ac.cn; internet www.rcees.cas.cn; f. 1975; attached to Chinese Acad. of Sciences; 392 ; library of 20,000 vols; Dir Dr QU JIUHUI; publs *Acta Ecologica Sinica* (12 a year), *Acta Scientiae Circumstantiae* (12 a year, with English abstracts), *Asian Journal of Ecotoxicology* (6 a year), *Chinese Journal of Environmental Engineering* (12 a year), *Huanjing Huaxue* (Environmental Chemistry, 6 a year), *Huanjing Kexue* (Environmental Sciences, 12 a year), *Journal of Environmental Sciences* (12 a year).

Shanghai Institute of Biochemistry: Chinese Academy of Sciences, 320 Yue-Yang Rd, Shanghai 200031; tel. (21) 64374430; fax (21) 64338357; attached to Chinese Acad. of Sciences; Dir Prof. LI BOLIANG.

Shanghai Institute of Cell Biology: 320 Yue-Yang Rd, Shanghai; tel. (21) 64315030; fax (21) 64331090; e-mail jhc@sunm.shcnc.ac.cn; f. 1950; attached to Chinese Acad. of Sciences; Dir Dr GUO LI-HE; publs *Acta Biologiae Experimentalis Sinica*, *Cell Research*, *Chinese Journal of Cell Biology*.

Shanghai Institute of Entomology: 225 Chongqing S. Rd, Shanghai 200025; tel. (21) 3282039; f. 1959; attached to Chinese Acad. of Sciences; Dir CHEN YUANGUANG.

Shanghai Institute of Physiology: 320 Yue-Yang Rd, Shanghai; tel. (21) 64370080; fax (21) 64332445; f. 1944; attached to Chinese Acad. of Sciences; library of 150,000 vols; Dir XIONG-LI YANG; publ. *Acta Physiologica Sinica* (in Chinese with English abstract, every 2 months).

Shanghai Institute of Plant Physiology: 300 Fongling Rd, Shanghai 200032; tel. (21) 64042090; fax (21) 64042385; f. 1944; attached to Chinese Acad. of Sciences; library of 150,000 vols; Dir Prof. Z. C. TANG.

South China Institute of Botany: Wushan, Guangzhou, 510650 Guangdong Province; tel. 87705626; f. 1929; attached to Chinese Acad. of Sciences; library of 59,000 vols; botanic garden, herbarium and arboretum; Dir LIANG CHENGYE; publs *Acta Botanica Austro Sinica*, *Journal of Tropical and Sub-tropical Botany* (4 a year).

Xishuangbanna Tropical Botanical Garden: Menglun, Mengla County, Yunnan 666303; tel. (Jinghong) 905; f. 1959; attached to Chinese Acad. of Sciences; library of 50,000 vols; Dir Prof. XU ZAIFU; publs *Collected Research Papers on Tropical Botany* (1 a year), *Tropical Plants Research* (4 a year).

Mathematical Sciences

Institute of Applied Mathematics: Academia Sinica, Box 2734, Beijing 100080; tel. (10) 62562939; fax (10) 62541689; f. 1979; attached to Chinese Acad. of Sciences; Dir ZHANG XIANGSUN.

Institute of Mathematics: Zhongguancun, Beijing 100080; attached to Chinese Acad. of Sciences; Dir YANG LE.

Physical Sciences

562 Comprehensive Geological Brigade: Yanqiaozhen 101601, Sanhe County, Hebei; attached to Chinese Acad. of Geological Sciences.

Beijing Observatory: Zhongguancun, Beijing 100080; attached to Chinese Acad. of Sciences; Dir WANG SHOUGUAN.

Changchun Institute of Applied Chemistry: 109 Stalin St, Changchun, Jilin Province; tel. (431) 5682801; fax (431) 5685653; f. 1948; attached to Chinese Acad. of Sciences; library of 120,000 vols; Dir Prof. WANG ERKANG; publs *Analysis Chemistry* (12 a year), *Applied Chemistry* (6 a year).

Changchun Institute of Physics: 1 Yan An Rd, Changchun 130021, Jilin Province; tel. (431) 5952215; fax (431) 5955378; f. 1958; attached to Chinese Acad. of Sciences; luminescence and its application, integrated optics; library of 69,800 vols; Dir JIN YIXIN; publs *Chinese Journal of Liquid Crystal and Displays* (4 a year), *Chinese Journal of Luminescence* (4 a year).

Chengdu Institute of Geology and Mineral Resources: 101 Renmin N. Rd, Chengdu 610082, Sichuan; attached to Chinese Acad. of Geological Sciences.

Chinese Institute of Atomic Energy: POB 275, Beijing; tel. 69357487; fax 69357008; f. 1958; attached to Chinese Acad. of Sciences; Dir Prof. SUN ZUXUN; publs *Atomic Energy Science and Technology* (6 a year), *Chinese Journal of Nuclear Physics* (4 a year), *Isotopes* (4 a year), *Journal of Nuclear and Radiochemistry* (4 a year).

Cold and Arid Regions Environmental and Engineering Research Institute: 260 Donggang Rd W., Lanzhou 730000, Gansu Province; tel. (931) 8818203; fax (931) 8885241; f. 1965; attached to Chinese Acad. of Sciences; library of 546,246 vols, 23,968 periodicals; Dir Prof. CHENG GUODONG; publs *Journal of Glaciology and Geocryology* (in Chinese, 4 a year), *Plateau Meteorology* (in Chinese, 4 a year), *Journal of Desert Research* (in Chinese, 4 a year).

Commission for the Integrated Survey of Natural Resources: POB 9717, Beijing 100101; tel. (10) 64889797; fax (10) 64914230; f. 1956; attached to Chinese Acad. of Sciences; co-ordinates the integrated survey teams for the exploitation, utilization, conservation and evaluation of natural resources; multi-disciplinary research; library of 40,096 vols; Dir Prof. CHENG SHENGKUI; publs *Journal of Natural Resources* (with English abstracts, 4 a year), *Resources Science* (6 a year).

Dalian Institute of Chemical Physics: 161 Zhongshan Rd, Dalian; tel. 3631841; fax 363426; f. 1949; attached to Chinese Acad. of Sciences; library of 70,000 vols; Dir YUAN QUAN; publs *Chinese Journal of Chromatography* (6 a year), *Journal of Catalysis* (4 a year).

Guangzhou Institute of Chemistry: Academia Sinica, Guangzhou 510650; tel. (20) 85231815; fax (20) 85231119; e-mail cyha@gic.ac.cn; internet www.gic.ac.cn; f. 1958; attached to Chinese Acad. of Sciences; 270 mems; library of 80,000 vols; Dir CHENGYONG HA; publs *Guangzhou Chemistry* (4 a year),

Journal of Cellulose Science and Technology (4 a year).

Institute for the Application of Remote Sensing Information: Changsha 410114, Hunan; attached to Chinese Acad. of Geological Sciences.

Institute of Acoustics: 17 Zhongguancun St, Beijing 100080; tel. (10) 62553765; fax (10) 62553898; e-mail lig@mail.ioa.ac.cn; internet www.ioa.ac.cn; f. 1964; attached to Chinese Acad. of Sciences; Dir LI QIHU.

Institute of Atmospheric Physics: Qijiahezi, Beijing 100029; tel. (10) 64919693; fax (10) 62028604; f. 1928; attached to Chinese Acad. of Sciences; library of 55,000 vols and periodicals; Dir Prof. ZENG QINGCUN; publs *Advances in Atmospheric Sciences* (4 a year), *Chinese Journal of Atmospheric Sciences* (4 a year), *Collected Papers of the Institute of Atmospheric Physics* (in Chinese), *Scientia Atmospherica Sinica* (in Chinese).

Institute of Atmospheric Sounding: 7 Block 11, Hepingli, Beijing; attached to Chinese Acad. of Meteorological Sciences.

Institute of Chemistry: Zhongguancun, Haidian District, Beijing; tel. (10) 282281; fax (10) 62569564; f. 1956; attached to Chinese Acad. of Sciences; library of 100,000 vols; Dir Prof. HU YADONG.

Institute of Climatology: 7 Block 11, Hepingli, Beijing; attached to Chinese Acad. of Meteorological Sciences.

Institute of Geochemistry: Chinese Academy of Sciences, 73 Guanshui Rd, Guiyang, Guizhou 550002; tel. (851) 5895095; fax (851) 5895574; f. 1966; attached to Chinese Acad. of Sciences; library of 150,000 vols; Dir LIU CONGQIANG; publs *Acta Mineralogica Sinica* (4 a year), *Bulletin of Mineralogy, Petrology and Geochemistry* (4 a year), *Chinese Journal of Geochemistry* (4 a year, in English), *Geology-Geochemistry* (4 a year).

Institute of Geology: 26 Baiwanzhuang Rd, Beijing 100037; attached to Chinese Acad. of Geological Sciences.

Institute of Geomechanics: Fahuasi, Beijing 100081; tel. (10) 68412303; fax (10) 68422326; f. 1956; attached to Chinese Acad. of Geological Sciences; Pres. Prof. WU GANGUO; publ. *Journal of Geomechanics* (4 a year).

Institute of Geophysics: A-11 Datun Rd, Chao Yang District, Beijing 100101; tel. (10) 64871497; attached to Chinese Acad. of Sciences; Dir ZHENG TIANYU.

Institute of Geotectonics: Academia Sinica, Changsha, Hunan Province 410013; tel. (731) 8859150; fax (731) 8859137; internet www.csig.ac.cn; f. 1961; attached to Chinese Acad. of Sciences; library of 36,000 vols; Dir CHEN GUODA; publ. *Geotectonica et Metallogenia* (4 a year).

Institute of High Energy Physics: POB 918, Beijing 100039; tel. (10) 68219643; fax (10) 68213374; e-mail mail@ihep.ac.cn; internet www.ihep.ac.cn; f. 1973; attached to Chinese Acad. of Sciences; Dir Prof. CHEN HESHENG; publs *High Energy Physics and Nuclear Physics* (12 a year), *Modern Physics* (6 a year).

Institute of Karst Geology: 40 Seven Stars Rd, Guilin 541104, Guangxi; attached to Chinese Acad. of Geological Sciences.

Institute of Mesoscale Meteorology: 7 Block 11, Hepingli, Beijing; attached to Chinese Acad. of Meteorological Sciences.

Institute of Metal Research: Academia Sinica, 72 Wenhua Rd, Shenyang 110015; tel. (24) 3843531; fax (24) 3891320; f. 1953; attached to Chinese Acad. of Sciences; library of 85,000 vols, 2,300 periodicals; publs *Acta Metallurgica Sinica* (12 a year), *Journal of*

Materials Science and Technology (6 a year), *Materials Science Progress* (6 a year).

Institute of Mineral Deposits: 26 Baiwanzhuang Rd, Beijing 100037; attached to Chinese Acad. of Geological Sciences.

Institute of Photographic Chemistry: Academia Sinica, Bei Sha Tan, Beijing 100101; tel. (10) 62017061; fax (10) 62029375; f. 1975; attached to Chinese Acad. of Sciences; library of 32,000 vols; Dir CHEN-HO TUNG; publ. *Photographic Science and Photochemistry*.

Institute of Physics: Zhongguancun, Haidian District, Beijing 100080; fax 282271; attached to Chinese Acad. of Sciences; Dir YANG GUOZHEN.

Institute of Process Engineering: 1 Beiertiao, Zhongguancun, Beijing; fax (10) 62561822; internet www.ipe.ac.cn; f. 1958; attached to Chinese Acad. of Sciences; library of 171,500 vols; Dir Prof. JINGHAI LI; publs *Chinese Journal of Process Engineering* (6 a year), *Chinese Journal of Spectroscopy Laboratory* (6 a year), *Computer and Applied Chemistry* (6 a year).

Institute of Rock and Mineral Analysis: 26 Baiwanzhuang Rd, Beijing 100037; tel. (10) 68311550; fax (10) 68320365; f. 1978; attached to Chinese Acad. of Geological Sciences.

Institute of Space Physics: Zhongguancun, Beijing 100080; tel. (10) 288052; attached to Chinese Acad. of Sciences.

Institute of Synoptic and Dynamic Meteorology: 7 Block 11, Hepingli, Beijing; attached to Chinese Acad. of Meteorological Sciences.

Institute of the Corrosion and Protection of Metals: Academia Sinica, 62 Wencui Rd, Shenyang 110015; tel. 3894313; fax 3894149; f. 1982; attached to Chinese Acad. of Sciences; library of 7,000 vols, 500 journals; Dir Prof. WU WEITAO; publ. *Corrosion Science and Protection Technology* (4 a year).

Institute of Theoretical Physics: Academia Sinica, POB 2735, Beijing 100080; tel. (10) 62555058; fax (10) 62562587; f. 1978; attached to Chinese Acad. of Sciences; library of 10,000 vols; Dir OU-YANG ZHONG CAN; publ. *Communications in Theoretical Physics* (12 a year, in English).

Institute of Weather Modification: 7 Block 11, Hepingli, Beijing; attached to Chinese Acad. of Meteorological Sciences.

Lanzhou Institute of Physics: POB Lanzhou 94; attached to Chinese Acad. of Space Technology.

Nanjing Institute of Geology and Mineral Resources: 534 Zhongshan E. Rd, Nanjing 210016, Jiangsu; tel. (25) 84600446; e-mail njcgs@cgs.gov.cn; internet www.nanjing.cgs.gov.cn; f. 1962; 320 mems; attached to Chinese Geological Survey; publ. *Resources Survey and Environment*.

Purple Mountain Observatory: 2 West Beijing Rd, Nanjing 210008, Jiangsu; tel. (25) 3300818; fax (25) 3300818; f. 1934; attached to Chinese Acad. of Sciences; library of 36,000 vols; Dir LIU BENQUI; publs *Acta Astronomica Sinica* (4 a year), *Publications of Purple Mountain Observatory*.

Shaanxi Astronomical Observatory: POB 18, Lintong, Xian; tel. (29) 3890326; fax (29) 3890196; f. 1966; attached to Chinese Acad. of Sciences; library of 3,500 vols; Dir Prof. LI ZHIGANG; publ. *Time and Frequency* (12 a year).

Shanghai Astronomical Observatory: 80 Nandan Rd, Shanghai 200030; tel. (21) 64384522; fax (21) 64384618; internet www .center.shao.ac.cn; f. 1872; attached to Chinese Acad. of Sciences; library of 80,000 vols;

Dir Prof. ZHAO JUNLIANG; publs *Annals of Shanghai Observatory*, *Progress in Astronomy* (4 a year).

Shanghai Institute of Metallurgy: Chinese Academy of Sciences, 865 Changning Rd, Shanghai 200050; tel. (21) 2511070; fax (21) 2513510; f. 1928; attached to Chinese Acad. of Sciences; Dir ZOU SHICHANG.

Shanghai Institute of Nuclear Research: POB 800-204, Shanghai 201800; tel. (21) 59553998; fax (21) 59553021; f. 1959; attached to Chinese Acad. of Sciences; Dir Prof. YANG FUJIA; publs *Journal of Radiation Research and Radiation Processing* (4 a year), *Nuclear Science and Techniques* (4 a year), *Nuclear Technology* (12 a year, in Chinese).

Shanghai Institute of Organic Chemistry: 345 Fenglin Lu, Shanghai 200032; tel. (21) 64163300; fax (21) 64166128; internet www.sioc.ac.cn; f. 1950; attached to Chinese Acad. of Sciences; library of 300,000 vols; Dir Prof. JIANG BIAO; publs *Acta Chimica Sinica* (12 a year, in Chinese), *Chinese Journal of Chemistry* (12 a year, in English), *Organic Chemistry* (12 a year, in Chinese).

Shenyang Institute of Geology and Mineral Resources: Beiling Ave, Shenyang 110032, Liaoning; attached to Chinese Acad. of Geological Sciences.

Southwestern Institute of Physics: POB 15, Leshan, 614007 Sichuan; POB 432, Chengdu 610041, Sichuan; tel. (28) 2932304 (Chengdu); fax (28) 2932202 (Chengdu); e-mail wb@swip.ac.cn; f. 1965; attached to China National Nuclear Corporation; controlled nuclear fusion and application of intermediate technology; library of 150,000 vols, 630 periodicals; Dir Prof. PAN CHUANHONG; publ. *Nuclear Fusion and Plasma Physics* (4 a year).

Tianjin Institute of Geology and Mineral Resources: 4 8th Rd, Dazhigu, Tianjin, 300170; tel. (22) 24314386; fax (22) 24314292; f. 1962; attached to Chinese Acad. of Geological Sciences; Dir LU SONGNIAN; publ. *Progress in Precambrian Research* (4 a year).

Xi'an Institute of Geology and Mineral Resources: 160 Eastern to Youyi Rd, Xian 710054, Shaanxi; attached to Chinese Acad. of Geological Sciences.

Yichang Institute of Geology and Mineral Resources: POB 502, Yichang 443003, Hubei; attached to Chinese Acad. of Geological Sciences.

Yunnan Observatory: POB 110, Kunming 650011; fax (871) 3911845; e-mail ynao@ public.km.yn.cn; f. 1972; attached to Chinese Acad. of Sciences; library of 35,000 vols; Dir Prof. TAN HUISONG; publ. *Publications of Yunnan Observatory* (4 a year).

PHILOSOPHY AND PSYCHOLOGY

Institute of Psychology: POB 1603, Beijing 100101; tel. (10) 64919520; fax (10) 64872070; e-mail yangyf@psych.ac.cn; f. 1951; attached to Chinese Acad. of Sciences; library of 145,000 vols, 1,500 periodicals; Dir Dr YANG YUFANG; publs *Acta Psychologica Sinica* (4 a year), *Journal of Developments in Psychology* (4 a year).

Philosophy Institute: 5 Jianguomennei Ave, Beijing 100732; f. 1977; attached to Chinese Acad. of Social Sciences; Dir XING FONSI.

RELIGION, SOCIOLOGY AND ANTHROPOLOGY

Institute of Population and Labour Economics: 5 Jianguo Mennei Ave, Beijing 100732; tel. (10) 85195417; fax (10)

85195427; e-mail iple@cass.org.cn; internet iple.cass.cn; f. 1980; attached to Chinese Acad. of Social Sciences; 48 mems; library of 10,000 vols; Dir Prof. FANG CAI; publs *China Labour Economics* (4 a year), *Population Science of China* (6 a year).

Institute of World Religions: 5 Jianguo Mennei St, Beijing 100732; tel. (10) 65138523; f. 1964; attached to Chinese Acad. of Social Sciences; Dir Prof. WU YUNGUI; publs *Studies on World Religions* (4 a year), *World Religious Culture* (4 a year).

Nationalities Studies Institute: Baishiqiao, Beijing; attached to Chinese Acad. of Social Sciences; Dir ZHAONA SITU.

Sociology Institute: 5 Jianguomennei Ave, Beijing 100732; f. 1979; attached to Chinese Acad. of Social Sciences; Dir HE JIANZHANG.

TECHNOLOGY

Beijing Institute of Control Engineering: POB 729, Beijing 100080; attached to Chinese Acad. of Space Technology.

Beijing Institute of Spacecraft Systems Engineering: POB 9628, Beijing 100086; attached to Chinese Acad. of Space Technology.

Changchun Institute of Optics and Fine Mechanics: 112 Stalin St, Changchun, Jilin Province; tel. 684692; fax 682346; f. 1950; attached to Chinese Acad. of Sciences; Dir WANG JIAQI; publ. *Optics and Precision Engineering* (6 a year).

Chemical Processing and Forest Products Utilization Research Institute: Longpan Rd, Nanjing, Jiangsu Province; attached to Chinese Acad. of Forestry.

China Coal Research Institute: 5 Qingniangou Rd, Hepingli, Beijing 100013; tel. (10) 84262809; fax (10) 84261671; internet www.ccri.ac.cn; f. 1957; Dir Prof. Dr ZHANG YUZHUO; publs *Coal Science and Technology* (12 a year, in Chinese), *Journal of China Coal Society* (12 a year, in Chinese; 2 a year, in English).

China National Space Administration: POB 2940, Beijing; 8 Fucheng Rd, Haidian District, Beijing 100037; tel. (10) 68516733; fax (10) 68516732; internet www.cnsa.gov.cn; coordinates and implements national space policy and development of space science, technology and industry, and arranges bilateral technical and scientific programmes, incl. launch of space probes; Administrator LUAN ENJIE.

China State Bureau of Technical Supervision (CSBTS): POB 8010, Beijing; tel. 62025835; fax 62031010; f. 1988; research and development for national standards and quality control; colln of nat. standards from 56 countries; Dir-Gen. ZHU YULI; publs *Standards Journal*, *Technical Supervision Journal*.

Institute of Automation: Zhong Guan Cun, Haidian District, Beijing; tel. (10) 62551397; fax (10) 62545229; f. 1956; attached to Chinese Acad. of Sciences; Dir HU FENGFENG; publs *Acta Automatica Sinica* (6 a year, in Chinese), *Chinese Journal of Automation* (4 a year, in English).

Institute of Coal Chemistry: POB 165, Taiyuan 030001, Shaanxi Province; tel. (351) 4041267; fax (351) 4041153; f. 1954; attached to Chinese Acad. of Sciences; Dir Prof. ZHONG BING; publ. *Journal of Fuel Chemistry and Technology* (4 a year).

Institute of Computer Technology: 6 Kexueyuan Nan Lu, Haidian District, Beijing 100080; tel. (10) 62565533; fax (10) 62567724; e-mail wgao@ict.ac.cn; internet www.ict.ac.cn; f. 1956; attached to Chinese Acad. of Sciences; Dir GAO WEN; publs *Computer Research and Development, Journal of Computer-aided Design and Graphics, Journal of Computer Science and Technology*.

Institute of Computer Technology: 24 Section 2, Sanhao St, Shenyang 110001, Liaoning; tel. 7705360; fax 7705319; attached to Chinese Acad. of Sciences; Dir CONG GUANGMIN.

Institute of Electronics: 17 Zhong Guan Cun Rd, POB 2702, Beijing 100080; tel. 62554424; fax 62567363; internet www.ie.ac.cn; f. 1956; attached to Chinese Acad. of Sciences; library of 35,000 vols; Dir Prof. YIN HEJUN; publs *Journal of Electronics and Information Technology* (12 a year, in Chinese), *Journal of Electronics (China)* (6 a year, in English).

Institute of Engineering Mechanics: 9 Xuefu Rd, Harbin 150080; tel. 6662901; fax 6664755; e-mail iem@public.hr.hl.cn; f. 1954; attached to China Seismological Bureau; earthquake and safety engineering; library of 110,000 vols; Dir QUIMIN FENG; publs *Earthquake Engineering and Engineering Vibration* (4 a year), *Journal of Natural Disasters* (4 a year), *World Information on Earthquake Engineering* (4 a year).

Institute of Engineering Thermophysics: 12B Zhongguancun Rd, Beijing; tel. 62554126; f. 1980; attached to Chinese Acad. of Sciences; Dir CAI RUIXIAN; publ. *Journal of Engineering Thermodynamics* (4 a year).

Institute of Hydrogeology and Engineering Geology: Zhengding County 050303, Hebei; attached to Chinese Acad. of Geological Sciences.

Institute of Mechanics: 15 Zhongguancun Rd, Beijing 100080; attached to Chinese Acad. of Sciences; Dir ZHENG ZHEMIN.

Institute of Meteorological Instrument Calibration: 7 Block 11, Hepingli, Beijing; attached to Chinese Acad. of Meteorological Sciences.

Institute of Optics and Electronics: POB 350, Shuangliu, Chengdu, Sichuan Province; tel. and fax (28) 85100341; e-mail dangban@ioe.ac.cn; internet www.ioe.cas.cn; f. 1970; attached to Chinese Acad. of Sciences; library of 90,000 vols; Dir Prof. ZHANG YUDONG; publ. *Opto-Electronics Engineering* (12 a year).

Institute of Semiconductors: POB 912, Beijing 100083; tel. (10) 288131; fax (10) 62562389; f. 1960; attached to Chinese Acad. of Sciences; Dir WANG QIMING.

Institute of Systems Science: 1A Nansi St, Zhongguancun, Beijing 100080; tel. (10) 62541830; fax (10) 62568364; internet www.iss.ac.cn; f. 1979; attached to Chinese Acad. of Sciences; Dir Prof. XIAO-SHAN GAO; publs *Journal of Systems Science and Complexity, Journal of Systems Science and Mathematics* (4 a year), *Journal of Systems Science and Systems Engineering* (6 a year).

Science and Technology Development Corporation: 26 Baiwanghuang Rd, Beijing 100037; attached to Chinese Acad. of Geological Sciences.

Shanghai Institute of Ceramics: 1295 Ding Xi Rd, Shanghai 200050; tel. (21) 62512990; fax (21) 62513903; internet www.sic.ac.cn; f. 1959; attached to Chinese Acad. of Sciences; library of 80,000 vols; Dir SHI ERWEI; publ. *Journal of Inorganic Materials* (6 a year).

Shanghai Institute of Optics and Fine Mechanics: POB 800-211, Shanghai, 201800; tel. (21) 69918000; fax (21) 69918800; internet www.siom.ac.cn; attached to Chinese Acad. of Sciences; laser science and technology; Dir Prof. ZHU JIANQING; publs *Acta Optica Sinica* (12 a year, in Chinese), *Chinese Journal of Lasers* (12 a year, in Chinese), *Chinese Optics Letters* (12 a year, in English).

Shanghai Institute of Technical Physics: 500 Yutian Rd, Shanghai 200083; tel. (21) 65420850; fax (21) 63248028; e-mail sitp@mail.sitp.ac.cn; internet www.sitp.ac.cn; f. 1958; attached to Chinese Acad. of Sciences; infrared technology and physics, optoelectronics and remote sensing; library of 40,000 vols; Dir WANG JIANYU; publ. *Chinese Journal of Infrared and Millimetre Waves* (6 a year).

Xian Institute of Optics and Precision Mechanics: Xian, Shaanxi; tel. (29) 5261376; fax (29) 5261473; f. 1962; attached to Chinese Acad. of Sciences; library of 120,000 vols; Dir Prof. ZHAO BAOCHANG; publ. *Acta Photinica Sinica* (6 a year).

Xian Institute of Space Radio Technology: POB 165, Xian 710000; tel. (29) 5290500; fax (29) 5290588; f. 1965; attached to Chinese Acad. of Space Technology.

Zhengzhou Institute of the Multi-Purpose Utilization of Mineral Resources: 26 Funu Rd, Zhengzhou 450006, Henan Province; tel. (371) 8984974; fax (371) 8984942; f. 1956; attached to Chinese Acad. of Geological Sciences; library of 200,000 vols; Dir Prof. Dr ZHANG KEREN; publ. *Conservation and Utilization of Mineral Resources* (6 a year).

Libraries and Archives

Baoding

Hebei University Library: 2 Hezuo Rd, Baoding, Hebei Province; tel. (312) 5022922 ext. 417; fax (312) 5022648; f. 1921; 1,960,000 vols, 3,923 current periodicals; 3,000 back copies; special collection: 4,397 vols of Chinese ancient books, incl. local chronicles and family trees; Dir LOU CHENGZHAO; publ. *Journal of Hebei University*.

Beijing

Beijing Normal University Library: Xinjiekouwai Dajie, Beijing 100875; tel. (10) 62208163; fax (10) 62200567; f. 1902; 2,700,000 vols, 14,436 periodicals; rich collection of thread-bound Chinese ancient books, incl. 1,500 titles of remarkable editions, 2,800 titles of local chronicles, 1,300 series; Dir YIU TIANCHI.

Capital Library: 15 Guozijian St, Dongcheng District, Beijing; tel. (10) 64040905; fax (10) 64040905; f. 1913; municipal library; 2,574,000 vols, 142,000 current periodicals; spec. collns incl. traditional opera, folk customs; Dir JIN PEILIN.

Central Archives of China: Wenquan, Haidian District, Beijing; tel. (10) 62556611; f. 1959; revolutionary historical archives from the May 4th Movement of 1919 to the founding of the People's Republic in 1949, and archives of CPC and central government offices; 8,000,000 files; Curator WANG GANG; publs *CPC Documents, Central Archives of China Series, Collection of PCC Documents*, etc.

Centre for Documentation and Information, Chinese Academy of Social Sciences: 5 Jianguomennei Ave, Beijing 100732; tel. and fax (10) 65126393; e-mail kyc-tsg@cass.org.cn; internet www.lib.cass.org.cn; f. 1985; attached to Chinese Acad. of Social Sciences; administrates Chinese Society of Social Sciences Information; 2,400,000 vols; Dir YANG PEICHAO; publs *Social Sciences Abroad* (6 a year), *Diogenes* (in Chinese, 2 a year).

First Historical Archives of China: Palace Museum inside Xihuamen, Beijing 100031; tel. (10) 63096487; fax (10) 63096489; f. 1925; 10,000,000 files; historical archives of Ming and Qing Dynasties; Curator XING YONGFU; publ. *Historical Archives* (4 a year).

Institute of Medical Information: 3 Yabaolu, Chaoyang District, Beijing 100020; tel. (10) 65122340; fax (10) 85626057; e-mail qianq@imicams.ac.cn; internet www.library .imicams.ac.cn; f. 1958; attached to Chinese Acad. of Medical Sciences and Peking Union Medical Coll.; Dir Prof. DAI TAO.

Institute of Meteorological, Scientific and Technical Information: 7 Block 11, Hepingli, Beijing; attached to Chinese Acad. of Meteorological Sciences.

Institute of Scientific and Technical Information of China (ISTIC): 15 Fu Xing Lu, POB 3827, Beijing 100038; tel. (10) 68514020; fax (10) 68514025; f. 1956; 18,000,000 items from China and abroad, incl. research reports, conference proceedings, periodicals, patents, standards, catalogues and samples and audiovisual material; Dir-Gen. ZHU WEI; publs *Journal of Scientific and Technical Information*, *Review of World Inventions*, *Scientific and Technical Trends Abroad*.

Institute of Scientific and Technological Information on Forestry: Wan Shou Shan, Beijing 100091; tel. (10) 62889713; fax (10) 62882317; internet www.lknet.forestry.ac.cn; f. 1964; attached to Chinese Acad. of Forestry; Deputy Director LI WEIDONG.

Library of the Chinese Academy of Sciences: 33 Beisihuanxilu, Zhongguancun, Beijing 100080; tel. (10) 82626684; fax (10) 82626600; e-mail office@mail.las.ac.cn; internet www.las.ac.cn; f. 1950; 5,200,000 vols, 8,636 current periodicals, 51,000 reports of conference proceedings; spec. collns incl. local chronicles, collected works of the Ming and Qing Dynasties, 40,000 rubbings from stone tablets, 600,000 rare books, 28 web-based databases, 38 CD-rom databases; Chief Deputy Dir ZHANG XIAOLIN; publs *Chinese Biotechnology* (12 a year), *Chinese Mathematical Abstracts* (6 a year), *Chinese Physical Abstracts* (6 a year), *High Technology and Industrialization* (12 a year), *Library and Information Service* (12 a year), *New Technology of Library and Information Service* (12 a year), *Progress in Chemistry* (6 a year), *R&D Information* (12 a year), *Science and Technology International* (12 a year).

Medical Library: 9 Dongdan Santiao, Beijing 100730; tel. 65127733; attached to Chinese Acad. of Medical Sciences; Dir LU RUSHAN.

National Library of China: 33 Zhongguancun Nandajie, Haidian District, Beijing 100081; tel. (10) 88545023; fax (10) 68419271; e-mail interco@publicf.nlc.gov.cn; internet www.nlc.gov.cn; f. 1909; 22,000,000 vols, 21,000 current periodicals, 1,100,000 microforms and audiovisual items; spec. collns incl. 291,696 vols of rare books of imperial libraries in the Southern Song, Ming and Qing dynasties; all kinds of Chinese publs incl. those in minority languages; foreign books, periodicals and newspapers, UN publs and govt publs of certain countries; blockprinted editions, books of rubbings, and other antique items; Dir Prof. REN JIYU; publs *Documents* (4 a year), *Journal of the National Library of China* (4 a year), *National Bibliography*.

Peking University Library: Haidian District, Beijing 100871; tel. (10) 62751051; fax (10) 62761008; e-mail office@lib.pku.edu.cn; internet www.lib.pku.edu.cn; f. 1902; 5,736,401 books, 708,424 vols of bound periodicals, spec. colln: 1,600,000 vols of threadbound Chinese ancient books, incl. 200,000 vols of rare books, 70,000 rubbings, copy of *Complete Works of Shakespeare* (publ. 1623), Dante's *Divine Comedy* (publ. 1896), and plays by Schiller, 529,446 vols of eBooks, 47,010 electronic journal titles, 466 databases.; Dir Prof. QIANG ZHU; publ. *Journal of Academic Libraries* (6 a year).

Renmin University of China Library: 175 Haidian Rd, Beijing; tel. 62511371; fax 62566374; f. 1937; 2,500,000 vols, 2,400 current periodical titles, 400,000 back copies; publs on philosophy, politics, law, economics, etc.; rich collection of philosophy of Marxism, law, economics, modern and contemporary history of China; special collection: Chinese revolutionary documents in liberated and base areas, ancient rare books of Song, Yuan, Ming and Qing Dynasties (2,400 titles); 154 staff; Dir Prof. YANG DONGLIANG; publs *Index to the Complete Works of Marx and Engels, Classification of the Renmin University of China Library, Index to the ancient rare books of RUC Library*.

Tsinghua University Library: Qinghuayuan, West Suburb, Beijing 100084; tel. (10) 62782137; fax (10) 62781758; e-mail tsg@mail.lib.tsinghua.edu.cn; internet www .lib.tsinghua.edu.cn; f. 1911; 2,500,000 vols, 15,495 periodicals (foreign 5,902); spec. collns: Chinese ancient books 30,000 titles (300,000 vols), including rare editions, only existing copies and handcopies, 3,000 titles (30,000 vols); collns of acad. books and periodicals, conference literature, engineering historical data, local chronicles, collected papers on spec. subjects, major abstract journals, complete set of nearly 200 foreign periodicals; Dir XUE FANGYU; publs *Science Report, Tsinghua Journal* (Natural Sciences and Social Sciences edns), *Tsinghua University Selections of Scientific Theses*.

Changchun

Jilin Provincial Library: 10 Xinmin Ave, Changchun, Jilin Province; tel. 5643796; f. 1958; 2,700,000 vols; Dir JIN ENHUI; publ. *Research in Library Science* (6 a year).

Jilin University Library: 117 Jiefang Rd, Changchun 130023, Jilin Province; tel. 8923189; f. 1946; 2,154,000 vols, 3,078 current periodicals, 299,808 back copies; special collection: local chronicles, clan trees, Asian Series, documents of Manchurian railways; Dir Prof. WANG TONGCHE.

Northeast Normal University Library: 138 Renmin St, Changchun, Jilin Province; tel. 5684174; f. 1946; 2,300,000 vols, 4,000 current periodicals, 11,600 back copies; publs from time of the War of Resistance Against Japan, rare Chinese ancient books; Dir SUN ZHONGTIAN; publ. *Jilin Libraries of Colleges and Universities* (4 a year).

Changsha

Hunan Provincial Library: 38 Shaoshan Rd, Changsha, Hunan Province; tel. 25653; f. 1904; 3,090,000 vols, 130,000 bound vols of periodicals, 900,000 ancient books.

Chengdu

Sichuan Provincial Library: 6 Lu Zongfu, Chengdu 610016, Sichuan Province; tel. (28) 6659219; f. 1940; 3,760,000 vols, 13,485 periodicals, historical material; Dir WANG ENLAI (acting); publ. *Librarian* (6 a year).

Chongqing

Chongqing Library: 1 Changjiang Rd A, Chongqing, Sichuan Province; tel. 54832; f. 1947; 3,137,198 vols, 690,183 bound periodicals, 65,514 technical reports, 35,000 antique books, historical documents, UN publs; Dir LI PUJIE.

Dalian

Dalian City Library: 7 Changbai, Xigang District, Dalian, Liaoning Province; tel. (411) 3630033; fax (411) 3623796; f. 1907; 2,000,000 vols, 5,502 periodicals; 700 ancient books; Dir LIU ZHENWEI.

Fuzhou

Fujian Provincial Library: 37 Dongfanghong Dajie St, Fuzhou, Fujian Province; tel. 31604; f. 1913; 2,200,000 vols, 4,350 current periodicals, historical material; spec. collns incl. data on Taiwan and Southeast Asia.

Guangzhou

South China Teachers' University Library: Shipai, Tianhe District, Guangzhou, Guangdong Province; tel. 774911; 1,600,000 vols, over 3,000 current periodicals, 7,145 back copies; special collection: 180,000 vols of Chinese ancient books, incl. 1,025 titles of local chronicles; 106 staff; Deputy Dir YANG WEIPING.

Zhongshan Library of Guangdong Province: 211 Wenming Rd, Guangzhou, Guangdong Province; tel. 330676; f. 1912; 3,300,000 vols, 6,000 current periodicals, historical documents; spec. collns incl. research materials on Dr Sun Yat-sen; Dir HUANG JUNGUI; publs *Journal of Guangdong Libraries* (4 a year), *Library Tribune* (4 a year).

Guilin

Guilin Library of Guangxi Zhuang Autonomous Region: 15 North Ronghu Rd, Guilin, Guangxi Zhuang Autonomous Region; tel. 223494; f. 1909; 1,380,000 vols, 15,275 current periodicals, historical material; Deputy Dir YANG JIANHONG; publs *Catalogue of Guangxi Local Documents, Catalogue of Materials on Guangxi Minority Study* (vols 1–2).

Guiyang

Guizhou Provincial Library: 31 Beijing Rd, Guiyang, Guizhou Province; tel. 25562; f. 1937; 1,270,000 vols, 5,000 periodicals, historical material; publs *Chronological Table of the Historical Calamities of Guizhou Province, Collected Papers on the Mineral Products of Guizhou Province, Journal* (4 a year).

Hangzhou

Zhejiang Provincial Library: 38 Shuguang Rd, Hangzhou 310007, Zhejiang Province; tel. (571) 87999812; fax (571) 87995860; e-mail bgs@zjlib.net.cn; internet www.zjlib .net.cn; f. 1900; 4,210,000 vols, 7,526 current periodicals; Chief Officer CHENG XIAOLIAN; publ. *Library Science Research and Work* (4 a year).

Hankou

Wuhan Library: 86 Nanjing Rd, Hankou, Hubei Province; tel. 24334; f. 1953; 1,400,000 vols, 2,018 periodicals, 200,000 ancient books, historial material.

Harbin

Heilongjiang Provincial Library: No 218 Changjiang Rd, Nangang Dist., Harbin 150090, Heilongjiang Province; tel. (451) 85990586; fax (451)-85990587; e-mail hljstsg@sina.com; f. 1958; 2,928,193 vols, 2,371,484 books; 133,693 ancient books; 6,602 rare books; 438,675 newspapers and periodicals; 35,866 audiovisual documents and microcopies; 82,168 other documents; spec. collns incl. Russian publs, 1920s–1940s Japanese publs; Dir GAO WENHUA; publ. *Library Development* (12 a year).

Hefei

Anhui Provincial Library: 38 Wuhu Rd, Hefei, Anhui Province; tel. 257602; f. 1913; 2,108,608 vols, 5,400 current periodicals, 30,000 antique books, historical documents; Dir WANG BAO SHENG; publs *Bulletin of Anhui Libraries* (4 a year), *Library Work* (4 a year).

Huhhot

Nei Monggol Autonomous Region Library (Inner Mongolia Autonomous Region Library): People's Park, Huhhot 010020, Nei Monggol Autonomous Region; tel. 27948; f. 1950; 1,260,000 vols, 2,131 current periodicals; spec. collns incl. Mongolia; Dir ZHANG XIANGTANG; publ. *Nei Monggol Library Work* (4 a year, in Mongolian and Chinese).

Jinan

Shandong Provincial Library: 275 Daminhu Rd, Jinan, Shandong Province; tel. 612338; f. 1908; 3,500,000 vols, 3,500 periodicals, ancient books, historical documents.

Shandong University Library: Jinan, Shandong Province; tel. 803861; f. 1901; 2,000,000 vols, 3,000 current periodicals, 260,000 back copies; 77% of holdings are on liberal arts; special collection: rare books, rubbings from stone inscriptions, calligraphy and paintings, revolutionary documents; 118 staff; Dir Prof. XU WEN-TIAN.

Kunming

Yunnan Provincial Library: 2 South Cuihu Rd, Kunming, Yunnan Province; tel. 5298; f. 1950; 2,150,000 vols, 7,172 periodicals, historical material.

Lanzhou

Gansu Provincial Library: 250 Binghedong Rd, Lanzhou, Gansu Province; tel. 28982; f. 1916; 2,400,000 vols, historical material; spec. collns incl. Imperial Library of Qianlong; Dir PAN YINSHENG; publ. *Library and Information* (4 a year).

Nanchang

Jiangxi Provincial Library: 160 North Hongdu Rd, Nanchang, Jiangxi Province; tel. (791) 8517065; f. 1920; 2,200,000 vols, 6,600 periodicals, historical material; publ. *Journal of the Jiangxi Society of Library Science* (4 a year).

Nanjing

Nanjing Library: 66 Chengxian St, Nanjing, Jiangsu Province; tel. (25) 57717619; fax (25) 83372163; e-mail ntbgs@sina.com; internet www.jslib.com.cn; f. 1907; 7,790,000 vols, 8,000 current periodicals, 1,700,000 ancient books; Exec. Dir MA NING; publ. *New Century Library* (6 a year).

Nanjing University Library: 22 Hankou Rd, Nanjing 210093, Jiangsu Province; tel. (25) 3592943; fax (25) 3592943; internet lib .nju.edu.cn; f. 1902; 3,560,000 vols, 5,000 current periodicals, 566,400 bound vols of periodicals; systematic colln of literature, history, philosophy, economics, law, mathematics, physics, chemistry, astronomy, geology, geography, meteorology, environmental science, computer science, biology and medicine, in Chinese and foreign languages; fairly complete colln of reference books from most countries, colln of major retrieval serials; spec. colln: 1,452 titles of rare books (Song, Yuan, Ming and Qing Dynasties), 10,000 sheets of rubbings from stone inscriptions, many paintings, MSS and handcopies, 4,600 titles (40,000 vols) of local chronicles, mainly of Jiangsu and Sichuan Provinces, also books on orientalism, bibliography and archae-

ology; Dir Prof. ZHANG YIBING; publ. *Journal of Serials Management and Research* (2 a year).

Second Historical Archives of China: 309 East Zhongshan Rd, Nanjing, Jiangsu Province; tel. 4409996; f. 1951; archive material of the Republic of China (1912–49); 1,740,000 files, 246,000 periodicals; Curator XU HAO; publs *Collected Archives Series of the History of the Republic of China*, *Republican Archives* (4 a year).

Nanning

Guangxi Zhuang Autonomous Region Library: 61 Minzu Dadao, Nanning, Guangxi Zhuang Autonomous Region; tel. 5860297; fax 5860297; e-mail gxlib@mail.nn .gx.cn; internet www.gxlib.org.cn; f. 1931; 2,050,000 vols, 4,575 current periodicals; Dir WANG XUEGUANG; publ. *Library World* (4 a year).

Shanghai

East China Normal University Library: 3663 North Zhongshan Rd, Shanghai; tel. (21) 62579196; f. 1951; 2,640,000 vols, 5,187 current periodicals, 237,000 back copies; notable collns on pedagogy, psychology, geography, classical philosophy, local histories and bibliography; the earliest edns of thread-bound Chinese ancient books are those of the Song Dynasty and of foreign books (publ. 1630); rubbings from stone inscriptions; Dir WANG XIJING; publ. *Library Information* (12 a year).

Fudan University Library: 220 Handan Rd, Shanghai 200433; tel. (21) 65643162; fax (21) 65649814; f. 1918; 3,500,000 vols, incl. remarkable editions of Chinese ancient books; special collections: 709 different editions of *The Books of Songs* and 3,000 titles of collected works of famous writers of Qing Dynasty; Dir Prof. QIN ZENG-FU.

Shanghai Library: Huaihai Rd, Shanghai; tel. (21) 3273176; fax (21) 3278493; f. 1952; 8,200,000 vols, 14,449 periodicals, 152,270 technical reports, early MSS, historical material, microforms, audio-visual material; Dir ZHU QING ZHO; publs *Catalog of Chinese Series* (1959), *Contents of Modern Chinese Journals*, *Catalog of Shanghai Library Collections of Local Histories*, *Catalog of Works and Translations by Guo Moruo*, *National Index of Newspapers and Periodicals*.

Shenyang

Liaoning Provincial Library: Shenyang, Liaoning Province; f. 1948; 1,923,366 vols, 13,307 periodicals.

Taiyuan

Shanxi Provincial Library: 1 Wenguan Lane, South Jiefang Rd, Taiyuan, Shanxi Province; f. 1918; 1,700,000 vols, 9,900 periodicals.

Tianjin

Nankai University Library: 94 Weijin Rd, Tianjin 300071; tel. (22) 23502410; fax (22) 23505633; e-mail tsg@nankai.edu.cn; internet www.lib.nankai.edu.cn; f. 1919; 3,145,805 vols, 3,349 current periodicals, 511,159 bound copies of periodicals; spec. colln: 2,000 titles of rare books, 4,000 titles of local chronicles, 10,000 reference books, complete set of 100 periodicals with back issues of more than 50 years, 5,946 audiovisual items, 1,689 multimedia CD-ROMs, 51 databases; Dir Prof. YAN SHIPING; publs *Catalog of Rare Books Held by Nankai University Library*, *Catalog of Thread-Bound Ancient Books Held by Nankai University Library*.

Tianjin Library: 12 Chengdedao Rd, Heping District, Tianjin; tel. (22) 315171; f. 1907; 2,800,000 vols, 3,900 current periodicals,

500,000 ancient books; Dir DONG CHANGXU; publ. *Library Work and Research* (4 a year).

Urumqi

Xinjiang Library: 11 South Xinhua Rd, Urumqi, Xinjiang Uygur Autonomous Region; f. 1946; 546,800 vols, 3,723 periodicals, historical documents; spec. collns incl. books in Xinjiang nationality languages.

Wuhan

Central China Teachers' University Library: Mt Guizishan, Wuhan, Hubei Province; tel. 72631; f. 1951; 1,255,000 vols, 6,486 periodicals.

Hubei Provincial Library: 45 Wuluo Rd, Wuchang District, Wuhan 430060, Hubei Province; tel. 871284; f. 1904; 2,605,000 vols, 930,000 vols of periodicals, 50,000 antique books; Dir XIONG JINSHAN; publ. *Library & Information Science Tribune* (4 a year).

Wuhan University Library: Mt Luojiashan, Wuhan, Hubei Province; tel. 7872290; fax 7872290; f. 1913; 2,900,000 vols, 6,000 current periodicals, 300,000 back copies; rich collection of works on basic theories, and newspapers and periodicals published before 1949; special collection: 180,000 vols of thread-bound local chronicles, over 500 titles of rare books of Yuan, Ming and Qing Dynasties; 141 staff; Dir SHEN JIWU.

Xiamen

Xiamen University Library: 422 Siming Nan Rd, Xiamen, Fujian Province; tel. (592) 2186127; fax (592) 2182360; e-mail xiaodh@ xmu.edu.cn; internet library.xmu.edu.cn; f. 1921; 2,400,000 vols, 6,000 current periodicals, 90,000 back copies; publs on natural and social sciences, especially economics, biology, chemistry, and data on Southeast Asia and Taiwan; Dir CHEN MINGGUANG.

Xian

Shaanxi Provincial Library: 146 Xi Ave, Xian, Shaanxi Province; f. 1909; 2,300,000 vols.

Shaanxi Teachers' University Library: Wujiafen, South Suburb, Xian 710062, Shaanxi Province; tel. 711946, ext. 248; f. 1953; 1,884,487 vols, 2,628 current periodicals, 6,116 back copies; as one of the largest university libraries of Northwest China, it has a fairly rich colln of publs on philosophy, social sciences, literature, linguistics and philology, natural sciences, and thread-bound remarkable editions of Chinese ancient books, local chronicles, 7,000 sheets of rubbings from bronze and stone tablets of the Zhou, Qing, Han and Tang Dynasties, el-hi textbooks and materials on pedagogy; 119 staff; Exec. Dir WANG KEJUN.

Xian Jiaotong University Library: Xianning Rd, Xian, Shaanxi Province 710049; tel. (29) 3268102; fax (29) 3237910; f. 1896; 1,840,000 vols, 4,373 current periodicals, 9,000 back copies; systematic collection of scientific and technical publs, complete sets of 15 world-famous sci-tech periodicals having a history of over 100 years; 143 staff; Dir Prof. LI RENHOU.

Xining

Qinghai Provincial Library: 44 Jiefang Rd, Xining, Qinghai Province; f. 1935; 1,354,000 vols, 2,819 periodicals; publ. *Libraries in Qinghai* (4 a year).

Yinchuan

Ningxia Library: Tongxin Rd N, Yinchuan, Ningxia Hui Autonomous Region; f. 1958; 1,300,000 vols.

Zhengzhou

Henan Provincial Library: 150 Song Shan Nan Rd, Zhengzhou, Henan Province; tel. (371) 7972396; f. 1909; 2,360,000 vols, 4,419 current periodicals, 700,000 antique books, historical material; Dir TONG JIYONG; publ. *Journal of Henan Libraries* (4 a year).

Museums and Art Galleries

Beijing

Arthur M. Sackler Museum of Art and Archaeology: Peking University, School of Archaeology and Museology, Beijing 100871; tel. (10) 62751667; fax (10) 62751667; f. 1993; attached to Peking Univ.; Dir Prof. ZHAO HUI.

Beijing Lu Xun Museum: Ritiao, Gongmenkou, Beijing; Curator LI HELIN.

Beijing Natural History Museum: 126 Tianqiao South St, Beijing; tel. (10) 67024431; fax (10) 67021254; e-mail bnhm@public3.bta.net.cn; internet www.bnhm.org.cn; f. 1951; library of 50,000 vols; Dir AI CHUNCHU; publs *China Nature* (with English contents, jtly with the China Wildlife Conservation Asscn, the Chinese Asscn of Natural Science Museums and Beijing Natural History Museum), *Memoirs* (with English abstract).

China Art Gallery: 1 Wu Si St, East City District, Beijing; tel. (10) 64016234; f. 1958; traditional Chinese painting and sculpture; library of 13,700 vols; Dir LIU KAIQU.

Geological Museum of China: 15 Yangrouhutong, Xisi, Beijing 100034; tel. (10) 66557402; fax (10) 66557477; e-mail ngmc@public2.bta.net.cn; f. 1916; Dir CHENG LIWEI.

Military Museum of the Chinese People's Revolution: 9 Fuxing Rd, Beijing 100038; tel. (10) 68014441; f. 1958; Curator QIN XINGHAN; publ. *Military History* (6 a year).

National Museum of China: 16 East Chang'an Ave, Beijing 100006; tel. (10) 65118983; fax (10) 65118923; e-mail webmaster@chnmuseum.cn; internet www.chnmuseum.cn; f. 2003 by merger of National Museum of Chinese History (f. 1912) and National Museum of the Chinese Revolution (f. 1950); ancient Chinese historical artefacts and documents since prehistoric times; modern Chinese art and history since 1840; archaeology, history and art; Dir LU ZHANGSHEN; publs *Journal of National Museum of China, Modern China and Cultural Relics*.

Palace Museum: 4 Jingshan Qian Jie, Beijing 100009; tel. (10) 65132255; fax (10) 65123119; internet www.dpm.org.cn; f. 1925; paintings, ceramics, bronzes, jades, applied arts, calligraphy, carvings, coins, furniture, arms, decorative arts, musical instruments, clocks, seals, toys; library of 700,000 vols; Dir ZHENG XINMIAO; publs *Forbidden City* (6 a year), *Palace Museum Journal* (6 a year).

Quanzhou

Quanzhou Museum for Overseas Communications History: Quanzhou City, Fujian Province; tel. (595) 226655; f. 1959; Chinese foreign trade and China's int. relations in the fields of culture, science and religion; Curator WANG LIANMAO; publ. *Research into Overseas Communications History* (published jointly with the China Society of Research on Overseas Communications History, 2 a year).

Shanghai

Shanghai Museum: 201 Ren Min Da Dao, Shanghai 200003; tel. (21) 63723500; fax (21) 63728522; e-mail webmaster@shanghaimuseum.net; internet www.shanghaimuseum.net; f. 1952; library of 200,000 vols; Dir CHEN XIEJUN.

Universities and Colleges

ANHUI UNIVERSITY

3 Feixi Rd, Hefei 230039, Anhui

Telephone: (551) 5106114

Fax: (551) 5107999

Internet: www.ahu.edu.cn

Founded 1928

Academic year: September to July

President: HUAN DEKUAN

Vice-Presidents: WEI SUI, YI YOU MIN, LAN XI JIE, WU LIANG

Heads of Graduate Dept: ZHU SHI QUN, WANG XING HAI

Librarian: XU JUN DA

Number of teachers: 1,100

Number of students: 26,787

Publications: *Anhui University Law Review* (2 a year), *Hui Study* (1 a year), *Journal of Anhui University* (natural sciences, 6 a year), *Journal of Anhui University* (philosophy and social science, 6 a year)

DEANS

Business Administration: ZHOU YA NA
Chinese: TAO XIN MIN
Economics: RONG ZHAO ZI
Electrical Science and Technology: CHEN JUN NING
Foreign Studies: HUANG QING LONG
History: WU CHUN MEI
Law: LI MING FA
Life Science: LI JIN HUA
Management: XIE YANG QUN
Mathematics and Computing Science: JIANG WEI
Philosophy: LI XIA
Physics and Material Science: SHI SHOU HUA

PROFESSORS

BA, ZHAO LIN, Chinese
CAO, ZHUO LIANG, Physics and Material Science
CHEN, DAO GUI, Chinese
CHEN, GUI JING, Mathematics and Computing Science
CHEN, HUA YOU, Mathematics and Computing Science
CHEN, JUN NING, Electrical Science and Technology
CHEN, QIN, Life Science
CHEN, SHENG QING, Law
CHEN, ZHANG JIN, Physics and Material Science
CHENG, JING RONG, Physics and Material Science
DOU, REN SHENG, Physics and Material Science
DU, XIAN NENG, Mathematics and Computing Science
DU, PENG CHENG, Business Administration
FAN, YI ZHENG, Mathematics and Computing Science
FANG, BIN, Electrical Science and Technology
FANG, QING QING, Physics and Material Science
FANG, XIANG ZHENG, Physics and Material Science
FENG, YI MING, Economics
GAO, QING WEI, Electrical Science and Technology
GE, CHUANG LI, Electrical Science and Technology

GE, LI FENG, Electrical Science and Technology
GU, RONG BAO, Mathematics and Computing Science
GU, ZU DAO, Chinese
GUAN, XIN LIN, Business Administration
GUO, JIAN YOU, Physics and Material Science
HAN, JIA HUA, Physics and Material Science
HE, JIA QING, Life Science
HU, GUO GUANG, Physics and Material Science
HU, MAO LIN, Mathematics and Computing Science
HU, SHU HE, Mathematics and Computing Science
HU, YAN JUN, Electrical Science and Technology
HUANG, PEI, Life Science
JIA, HAI JI, Economics
JIANG, WEI, Mathematics and Computing Science
KE, DAO MING, Electrical Science and Technology
KONG, FAN CHAO, Mathematics and Computing Science
LI, CAI FU, Management
LI, JIN HUA, Life Science
LI, MING FA, Law
LI, SHOU SHEN, Economics
LI, XIA, Philosophy
LI, XIAO HUI, Electrical Science and Technology
LI, XIU SONG, History
LI, YU CHENG, Life Science
LIU, XIN FANG, History
LOU, PING, Physics and Material Science
LU, QIN YI, History
LU, RONG SHAN, Economics
LU, YING BIN, Economics
MA, REN JIE, Management
MA, XIU SHUI, Electrical Science and Technology
MING, JUN, Electrical Science and Technology
REN, KAI, Philosophy
RONG, ZHAO ZI, Economics
SHENG, YE SHOU, Life Science
SHENG, ZHAO XUAN, Mathematics and Computing Science
SHI, FU YUAN, Electrical Science and Technology
SHI, SHOU HUA, Physics and Material Science
SHI, XIANG QIAN, Philosophy
SUN, YI KAI, Philosophy
SUN, YU FA, Electrical Science and Technology
SUN, ZHAO QI, Physics and Material Science
TANG, HUA QUAN, Chinese
TANG, QI XUE, History
TAO, XIN MIN, Chinese
WANG, DA MING, Chinese
WANG, DAO MING, Economics
WANG, DAO QING, Chinese
WANG, HUI, Management
WANG, LIANG LONG, Mathematics and Computing Science
WANG, RONG, Law
WANG, XIN YI, History
WANG, YI PING, Life Science
WANG, YIN HAI, Physics and Material Science
WANG, YONG DE, Chinese
WANG, YU, Life Science
WEI, WEI, Economics
WEN, CHUN RU, Philosophy
WU, CHUN MEI, History
WU, JIA RONG, Chinese
XIAO, JIAN, Mathematics and Computing Science
XIAO, YA ZHONG, Life Science
XIE, YANG QUN, Management
XIONG, XIAO QI, Economics
XU, CHANG QING, Mathematics and Computing Science
XU, CHENG ZHI, Chinese
XU, JIAN HUA, Mathematics and Computing Science

Xu, Jun Da, Philosophy
Xu, Zai Guo, Chinese
Xu, Zhang Cheng, Physics and Material Science
Yan, Peng Fei, Mathematics and Computing Science
Yang, Fang Zhi, Economics
Yang, Shang Jun, Mathematics and Computing Science
Yang, Xiao Li, Chinese
Yao, Xue Biao, Physics and Material Science
Ye, Liu, Physics and Material Science
Yi, You Min, Physics and Material Science
Yong, Xi Qi, Mathematics and Computing Science
Yu, Ben Li, Physics and Material Science
Yue, Fang Sui, Chinese
Yue, Jie Xian, Philosophy
Zeng, Fan Yin, Economics
Zha, Xiang Dong, Life Science
Zhang, Bu Chang, Life Science
Zhang, Jian Feng, Economics
Zhang, Jin Xi, History
Zhang, Lu Gao, Chinese
Zhang, Neng Wei, Philosophy
Zhang, Qi You, Chinese
Zhang, Zi Xia, History
Zheng, Ming Zhen, Philosophy
Zhou, Huai Yu, History
Zhou, Li Zhi, Life Science
Zhou, Nan, Law
Zhou, Sheng Ming, Physics and Material Science
Zhou, Ya Na, Business Administration
Zhou, Zhi Yuan, History
Zhou, Zhong Ze, Life Science
Zhu, Shi Qun, Philosophy
Zhu, Xue Shan, Law
Zhu, Zong Yan, Economics

BEIJING BROADCASTING UNIVERSITY

Ding Fu Zhuang St, Chao Yang District, Beijing 10024
Telephone: (10) 65779319
Fax: (10) 65779134
Internet: www.cuc.edu.cn
Founded 1954
Min. of Education control
Academic year: August to July
Pres.: Liu Ji Nan
Number of teachers: 772
Number of students: 28,000
Publications: *Asia Media and Communication Studies* (1 a year), *Journal of Beijing Broadcasting University* (modern communication, 4 a year), *Journal of Beijing Broadcasting University* (natural science, 4 a year), *Media Studies* (irregular)

DEANS
Advertising Studies: Huang Sheng Min
Animation: Lu Sheng Zhan
Film and Television Arts: Li Xing Guo
Information Engineering and Science: Li Jian Zeng
International Communication: Xu Qin Yuan
Journalism and Communication: Ding Jun Jie
Literature: Miao Di
Media Management: Zan Yan Quan
Presentation Art: Li Xiao Hua
Social Sciences: Gao Hui Ran
Television: Gao Xiao Hong

PROFESSORS
Bi, Gen Hui, Film and Television Arts
Cai, Chao Shi, Information Engineering
Cai, Guo Fen, International Communication
Cai, Wen Mei, Journalism and Communication
Cao, Lu, Journalism and Communication
Cao, Qing Rui, Film and Television Arts

Chen, Bian Zhi, International Communication
Chen, Jing Sheng, Broadcasting
Chen, Wei Xing, International Communication
Chen, Yuan Meng, International Communication
Ding, Jun Jie, Journalism and Communication
Dong, Hua Miao, Film and Television Arts
Du, Han Feng, Literature
Feng, Song Che, Social Sciences
Fu, Jun Qing, Journalism and Communication
Gao, Fu An, Film and Television Arts
Gao, Fu An, Media Management
Gao, Xiao Hong, Television
Guan, Ling, Film and Television Arts
Guo, Zhen Zhi, Television
Ha, Yan Qiu, Journalism and Communication
He, Lan, International Communication
He, Su Liu, Television
He, Xiao Bing, Film and Television Arts
Hou, Min, Broadcasting
Huang, Jing Hua, Advertising Studies
Huang, Zhi Xun, Information Engineering
Huo, Wen Li, Television
Jia, Fou, Animation
Jiang, Xiu Hua, Information Engineering
Jin, Gui Rong, Film and Television Arts
Ke, Hui Xin, Journalism and Communication
Lei, Yue Jie, Journalism and Communication
Li, Dong, Information Engineering
Li, Jian Zeng, Information Engineering
Li, Jian Zeng, Science
Li, Sheng Li, Film and Television Arts
Li, Xing Guo, Film and Television Arts
Li, Zeng Rui, Information Engineering
Li, Zeng Rui, Science
Li, Zuo Feng, Literature
Liang, Ming, Film and Television Arts
Liang, Yi Gao, Journalism and Communication
Liang, Zheng Li, Media Management
Lin, Zheng Bao, Information Engineering
Liu, Jian Bo, Information Engineering
Liu, Jing Lin, Journalism and Communication
Liu, Li Wen, Literature
Liu, Li Wen, Film and Television Arts
Liu, Shu Liang, Film and Television Arts
Liu, Ting, Film and Television Arts
Liu, Ye Yuan, Film and Television Arts
Lu, Gui Zhen, Information Engineering
Lu, Jian, Film and Television Arts
Lu, Sheng Zhan, Animation
Lu, Ying Kun, Film and Television Arts
Luo, Li, Broadcasting
Mao, Zhi Ji, Information Engineering
Miao, Di, Literature
Ni, Xue Li, Film and Television Arts
Pan, Ye, Film and Television Arts
Peng, Hui Guo, Animation
Pu, Zhen Yuan, Literature
Qin, Yu Ming, Television
Ren, Su Qin, Social Sciences
Ren, Yuan, Television
Sheng, Qin, Information Engineering
Shi, Min Yong, Animation
Shi, Xu Sheng, Film and Television Arts
Song, Pei Yi, Film and Television Arts
Song, Pei Yi, Media Management
Wang, Chun Zhi, Information Engineering
Wang, Hong, Television
Wang, Ming Ya, Film and Television Arts
Wang, Wei, International Communication
Wang, Wu Lu, Journalism and Communication
Wang, Xiao Hong, Television
Wang, Ya Ping, Animation
Wei, Yong Zheng, Social Sciences
Wu, Yin, Television
Wu, Yu, Broadcasting
Xing, Xin, Broadcasting

Yang, Feng Jiao, Television
Yang, Lei, Information Engineering
Yang, Lu Ping, Television
Yang, Xiao Lu, Film and Television Arts
Yao, Xiao Ou, Literature
Ye, Feng Ying, Television
You, Fei, Film and Television Arts
Yuan, Qing Feng, Film and Television Arts
Zan, Yan Quan, Media Management
Zeng, Xiang Min, Television
Zeng, Zhi Hua, Broadcasting
Zhang, Fen Zhu, Film and Television Arts
Zhang, Ge Dong, Film and Television Arts
Zhang, Gui Zhen, International Communication
Zhang, Jing, Literature
Zhang, Jun, Animation
Zhang, Qi, Information Engineering
Zhang, Shu, Journalism and Communication
Zhang, Xiao Feng, Social Sciences
Zhang, Yan, Film and Television Arts
Zhang, Yan, Journalism and Communication
Zhang, Yong Hui, Information Engineering
Zhang, Yu Hua, Film and Television Arts
Zhao, Shu Ping, Television
Zhao, Xiao Guang, Literature
Zhao, Yu Ming, Journalism and Communication
Zhong, Tao, Literature
Zhong, Yi Qian, Advertising Studies
Zhou, Hong Guo, Media Management
Zhou, Hua Bin, Film and Television Arts
Zhou, Jing Bo, Film and Television Arts
Zhou, Yong, Film and Television Arts
Zhou, Yue Liang, Film and Television Arts

BEIJING UNIVERSITY OF AERONAUTICS AND ASTRONAUTICS

37 Xueyuan Rd, Beijing 100083
Telephone: (10) 62017251
Fax: (10) 62028356
Internet: www.buaa.edu.cn
Founded 1952
Controlled by the aviation industries of China
Languages of instruction: Chinese, English
Academic year: September to August
Number of teaching and research staff: 2,300
Pres.: Prof. Shen Shituan
Vice-Pres: Prof. Deng Xueying, Xu Congwei, Fei Binjun, Wu Zhe
Dir, Int. Academic Exchange: Cui Deyu
Librarian: Prof. Jin Maozhong
Library of 1,100,000 vols, 98,000 periodicals
Number of students: 12,600 (2,000 postgraduate)
Publications: *Acta Aeronautica et Astronautica Sinica* (12 a year), *Acta Materiae Compositae Sinica* (4 a year), *Aerospace Knowledge* (12 a year), *China Aeronautical Education* (4 a year), *College English* (6 a year), *DADDM* (2 a year), *Journal* (4 a year), *Journal of Aerospace Power* (4 a year), *Journal of Engineering Graphics* (2 a year), *Model World* (4 a year)

DEPARTMENTAL DEANS
Automatic Control: Prof. Li Xingshan
Computer Sciences and Engineering: Prof. Jin Maozhong
Electronic Engineering: Prof. Zhang Xiaolin
Flying Vehicle Design and Applied Mechanics: Prof. Wang Jinjun
Foreign Languages: Prof. Li Baokun
Manufacturing Engineering: Prof. Tang Xiaoqing
Materials Science and Engineering: Prof. Xu Huibin
Mechanical and Electrical Engineering: Prof. Yang Zongxu
Propulsion: Prof. Li Qihan
Systems Engineering: Prof. Yang Weimin

PRINCIPALS

Flying College: Prof. WANG XIAOWAN (Exec. Dir)
Graduate School: Prof. DENG XUEYING
School of Astronautics: Prof. ZHANG ZHEN-PENG
School of Continuing Education: Prof. WANG BAORAI
School of Haidian Applied Technology: Prof. LIU TIANSHEN
School of Humanities and Social Sciences: Prof. SHENG SHUREN (Dean)
School of Management: Prof. JIANG XIESHENG
School of Science: Prof. GUAN KEYING (Dean)

BEIJING UNIVERSITY OF BUSINESS AND TECHNOLOGY

33 Fu-cheng Rd, Beijing 100037
Telephone: (10) 68904774
Fax: (10) 68417834
Founded 1950
Academic year: September to July
Pres.: Prof. SU ZHIPING
Vice-Pres: LI ZHONG, LIU XIUSHENG, LI DIA-NFU, WANG ZHONGDE, PAN BANGJIN, NI ZHIHENG
Librarian: GAO YUNZHI
Number of teachers: 700
Number of students: 14,000 (400 graduate)
Publications: *Commercial Economy Research* (12 a year), *Correspondence Department Report* (4 a year), *Journal* (6 a year).

BEIJING UNIVERSITY OF CHEMICAL TECHNOLOGY

15 Bei San Huan East Rd, Chao Yang District, Beijing 100029
Telephone: (10) 64434820
Fax: (10) 64423089
E-mail: office@buct.edu.cn
Internet: www.buct.edu.cn
Founded 1958
Academic year: September to July
Pres.: WANG ZI GAO
Vice-Pres: DING JU YUAN, WANG GUI, ZHAO SU ZHEN, ZUO YU
Head of Graduate Dept: FU ZHI FENG CO
Librarian: ZHANG YU CHUAN
Number of teachers: 1,800
Number of students: 16,900
Publications: *Journal of Beijing University of Chemical Technology* (natural sciences, 6 a year), *Journal of Beijing University of Chemical Technology* (social science, 4 a year)

DEANS

College of Chemical Engineering: ZHANG ZE YAN
College of Economics and Management: YAO FEI
College of Information Science and Technology: ZHAO HENG YONG
College of Life Sciences and Technology: TAN TIAN WEI
College of Literature and Law: FU YU LONG
College of Machine Electricity Engineering: WANG KUI SHENG
College of Materials Science and Engineering: YU DING SHENG
College of Science: JIANG GUANG FENG
Professional Technology Institute: XU XI TANG

PROFESSORS

CAO, LIU LIN, Information Science and Technology
CAO, ZHI QING, Machine Electricity Engineering
CHEN, BIAO HUA, Chemical Conligeers
CHEN, CHANG SHU, Literature and Law
CHEN, JIAN FENG, Chemical Engineering
CHEN, XIAO CHUN, Chemical Engineering
CHEN, YAO QI, Literature and Law
CHEN, ZHONG LI, Literature and Law
CUI, WEI QI, Literature and Law
DANG, ZHI MIN, Materials Science and Engineering
DUAN, XUE, Science
FENG, LIAN XUN, Machine Electricity Engineering
GAO, ZHENG MING, Chemical Engineering
GENG, XIAO ZHEN, Machine Electricity Engineering
GUO, FEN, Chemical Engineering
GUO, KAI, Chemical Engineering
HAI, RE TI, Chemical Engineering
HE, JING, Science
HUA, YOU QING, Materials Science and Engineering
HUANG, LI, Materials Science and Engineering
HUANG, MIN LI, Materials Science and Engineering
HUANG, MING ZHI, Materials Science and Engineering
HUANG, XIONG BIN, Chemical Engineering
JI, SHENG FU, Chemical Engineering
JIANG, BO, Machine Electricity Engineering
JIN, RI GUANG, Materials Science and Engineering
LI, CHANG JIANG, Science
LI, CHUN XI, Chemical Engineering
LI, DIAN QING, Science
LI, HANG QUAN, Materials Science and Engineering
LI, HONG GUANG, Information Science and Technology
LI, QI FANG, Materials Science and Engineering
LI, QUN SHENG, Chemical Engineering
LI, WU SI, Economics and Management
LI, XIAO YU, Materials Science and Engineering
LI, XIU JIN, Chemical Engineering
LI, YUE CHENG, Chemical Engineering
LI, ZHI LIN, Materials Science and Engineering
LIU, FENG XIN, Information Science and Technology
LIU, HUI, Chemical Engineering
LIU, JIE, Materials Science and Engineering
LIU, KUN YUAN, Chemical Engineering
LIU, WEI, Chemical Engineering
MA, YUN YU, Life Sciences and Technology
MAO, BING QUAN, Science
MO, DE JU, Information Science and Technology
PAN, LI DENG, Information Science and Technology
PANG, YAN BIN, Information Science and Technology
QIAN, CAI FU, Machine Electricity Engineering
QIAO, JIN LIANG, Materials Science and Engineering
QU, YI XIN, Chemical Engineering
SHENG, WEI YONG, Literature and Law
SONG, HUAI HE, Materials Science and Engineering
SU, HAI JIA, Life Sciences and Technology
SUN, JUN, Economics and Management
TAN, TIAN WEI, Life Sciences and Technology
WANG, FANG, Life Sciences and Technology
WANG, JIAN HONG, Chemical Engineering
WANG, JIAN LIN, Information Science and Technology
WANG, KUI SHENG, Machine Electricity Engineering
WANG, MING MING, Economics and Management
WANG, WEN CHUAN, Chemical Engineering
WANG, XUE WEI, Information Science and Technology
WANG, ZI GAO, Chemical Engineering
WEI, GANG, Materials Science and Engineering
WEI, JIE, Materials Science and Engineering
WU, CHONG GUANG, Information Science and Technology
WU, DE ZHEN, Materials Science and Engineering
WU, GANG, Materials Science and Engineering
WU, XIANG ZHI, Chemical Engineering
WU, YI XIAN, Materials Science and Engineering
XIONG, RONG CHUN, Materials Science and Engineering
XU, CHUN CHUN, Materials Science and Engineering
XU, GUANG JUN, Economics and Management
XU, HONG, Machine Electricity Engineering
XU, PENG HUA, Machine Electricity Engineering
YANG, QI, Science
YANG, RU, Materials Science and Engineering
YANG, WANG TAI, Materials Science and Engineering
YANG, WEN SHENG, Science
YANG, YUAN YI, Science
YANG, ZU RONG, Chemical Engineering
YAO, FEI, Economics and Management
YIN, DENG XIANG, Literature and Law
YU, DING SHENG, Materials Science and Engineering
YUAN, DE YU, Literature and Law
YUAN, QI PENG, Life Sciences and Technology
ZHANG, JING CHANG, Science
ZHANG, LI QUN, Materials Science and Engineering
ZHANG, MEI LING, Machine Electricity Engineering
ZHANG, MING GUO, Literature and Law
ZHANG, PENG, Life Sciences and Technology
ZHANG, WEI DONG, Chemical Engineering
ZHANG, XING YING, Materials Science and Engineering
ZHANG, YING KUI, Economics and Management
ZHANG, YU CHUAN, Materials Science and Engineering
ZHANG, ZE YAN, Chemical Engineering
ZHAO, BAO YUAN, Economics and Management
ZHAO, HENG YONG, Information Science and Technology
ZHAO, SHU QING, Information Science and Technology
ZHAO, SU HE, Materials Science and Engineering
ZHEN, DAN XING, Chemical Engineering
ZHONG, CHONG LI, Chemical Engineering
ZHOU, HENG JIN, Materials Science and Engineering
ZHU, QUN XIONG, Information Science and Technology

BEIJING UNIVERSITY OF CHINESE MEDICINE

11 East Rd, Bei San Huan, Chao Yang District, Beijing 100029
Telephone: (10) 64213841
Fax: (10) 64213817
Internet: www.bjucmp.edu.cn
Founded 1956
Min. of Education control
Academic year: September to July
Pres.: ZHENG SHOU ZE
Vice-Pres: QIAO WANG ZHONG, WANG QING GUO, WEI TIAO MAO, XU XIAO
Heads of Graduate Dept: TU YA, WANG WEI
Librarian: ZHANG QI CHENG
Number of teachers: 2,705
Number of students: 9,925
Publications: *Chinese Medicine Education* (6 a year), *Journal of Beijing University of Chinese Medicine* (6 a year), *Journal of*

Beijing University of Chinese Medicine
(clinical studies, 4 a year)

DEANS

College of Acupuncture: GU SHI ZE
College of Basic Medicine: GUO XIA ZHEN
College of Chinese Traditional Medicine: LI
JIA SHI
College of Nursing: ZHANG MEI
Network Education College: YU YONG JIE

PROFESSORS

BAI, LING MIN, Chinese and Western Medicine
CHEN, JIA XU, Chinese Medicine (Diagnostics)
CHEN, LI XIN, Chinese and Western Medicine
CHEN, MING, Basic Medicine
CHEN, SHU CHANG, Chinese Medicine (Surgery)
CHEN, XIN YI, Chinese and Western Medicine
FENG, QIAN JIN, Chinese and Western Medicine
FU, YAN LING, Basic Medicine
GAO, XUE MIN, Chinese Medicine (Clinical)
GAO, YAN BING, Chinese Medicine
GAO, YING, Chinese Medicine
GU, LI GANG, Chinese and Western Medicine
GU, SHI ZE, Acupuncture
GUO, WEI QIN, Chinese Medicine
GUO, XIA ZHEN, Basic Medicine
GUO, YA JIAN, Chinese Medicine (Traditional)
HAO, RUI FU, Chinese Medicine
HAO, WANG SHAN, Basic Medicine
HOU, JIA YU, Chinese Medicine (Traditional)
HU, LI SHENG, Chinese and Western Medicine
HUANG, QI FU, Chinese and Western Medicine
JI, SHAO LIANG, Chinese Medicine (Diagnostics)
JIANG, LI SHENG, Basic Medicine
JIANG, LIANG GUO, Chinese Medicine
JIN, GUANG LIANG, Basic Medicine
JIN, ZHE, Chinese and Western Medicine
LI, FENG, Chinese Medicine (Diagnostics)
LI, GUO ZHANG, Chinese and Western Medicine
LI, JIA SHI, Chinese Medicine (Traditional)
LI, JIN XIANG, Chinese Medicine
LI, NAI QING, Chinese and Western Medicine
LI, PENG TAO, Chinese and Western Medicine
LI, RI QING, Chinese Medicine (Surgery)
LI, SHI FAN, Basic Medicine
LI, XUE WU, Acupuncture
LI, YU HANG, Basic Medicine
LI, YUN GU, Chinese Medicine (Traditional)
LIANG, RONG, Chinese Medicine (Diagnostics)
LIN, QIAN, Chinese and Western Medicine
LIU, JIN MING, Chinese Medicine
LIU, TIAN JUN, Acupuncture
LIU, TONG HUA, Chinese Medicine
LIU, YAN CHI, Basic Medicine
LU, WEI XING, Chinese and Western Medicine
LU, YUN RU, Chinese Medicine (Traditional)
LU, ZHAO LIN, Basic Medicine
LV, REN HE, Chinese Medicine
MENG, QING GANG, Basic Medicine
NIU, JIAN ZHAO, Chinese and Western Medicine
NIU, XIN, Chinese and Western Medicine
QIAO, YAN JIANG, Chinese Medicine (Traditional)
QIU, QUAN YING, Chinese and Western Medicine
QU, SHUANG QING, Basic Medicine
REN, TIAN CHI, Chinese Medicine (Traditional)
SHI, REN BIN, Chinese Medicine (Traditional)
SONG, NAI GUANG, Basic Medicine
SU, JING, Basic Medicine
SUN, JIAN NING, Chinese Medicine (Traditional)
SUN, YING LI, Chinese and Western Medicine
TANG, QI SHENG, Chinese Medicine

TANG, YI PENG, Chinese and Western Medicine
TIAN, DE LU, Chinese Medicine
TIAN, JING ZHOU, Chinese Medicine
TU, YA, Acupuncture
WANG, HONG TU, Basic Medicine
WANG, JI FENG, Chinese and Western Medicine
WANG, QI, Basic Medicine
WANG, QING GUO, Basic Medicine
WANG, SHUO REN, Chinese and Western Medicine
WANG, TIAN FANG, Chinese Medicine (Diagnostics)
WANG, WEI, Chinese and Western Medicine
WANG, WEN QUAN, Chinese Medicine (Traditional)
WANG, XIN YUE, Chinese Medicine
WANG, YU LAI, Chinese Medicine
WEI, LU XUE, Chinese Medicine (Traditional)
WU, WEI PING, Chinese Medicine
XIAO, PEI GEN, Chinese Medicine (Traditional)
XU, LIN, Chinese and Western Medicine
XU, QIU PING, Chinese Medicine (Traditional)
YAN, JI LAN, Basic Medicine
YAN, JIAN HUA, Basic Medicine
YAN, YU NING, Chinese Medicine (Traditional)
YAN, ZHENG HUA, Chinese Medicine (Clinical)
YANG, JING XIANG, Chinese Medicine
YANG, SHU PENG, Chinese Medicine (Traditional)
YE, YONG AN, Chinese Medicine
ZHANG, BING, Chinese Medicine (Clinical)
ZHANG, QI CHENG, Basic Medicine
ZHANG, YAN SHENG, Chinese Medicine (Surgery)
ZHANG, YUN LING, Chinese Medicine
ZHAO, JI PING, Acupuncture
ZHAO, JIN XIN, Chinese Medicine
ZHOU, PING AN, Chinese Medicine
ZHOU, YI HUAI, Chinese Medicine

BEIJING FILM ACADEMY

Xi Tu Cheng Lu 4, Haidian District, Beijing 100088

Telephone: 62012132
Internet: www.bfa.edu.cn

Founded 1950

Pres.: SHEN SONGSHENG
Vice-Pres: XIE FEI, MENG HAIFENG
Deputy Librarians: CHEN WENJING, LU SHIPING

Library of 150,000 vols
Number of teachers: 273
Number of students: 286 (29 postgraduate)
Publication: *Journal*.

BEIJING FOREIGN STUDIES UNIVERSITY

2 North Xisanhuan Ave, Haidian District, Beijing 100089

Telephone: (10) 68916215
Fax: (10) 68423144
E-mail: bwxzb@bfsu.edu.cn
Internet: bfsu.edu.cn

Founded 1941
Academic year: September to July

Chancellor: Prof. CHEN NAIFANG
Vice-Chancellors: Prof. YANG XUEYI, Prof. Dr HE QIXIN, Prof. ZHONG MEISUN, Prof. ZHOU LIE

Library of 600,000 vols
Number of teachers: 700
Number of students: 10,000

Publications: *Foreign Language Teaching and Research, Foreign Literatures, International Forum, Soviet Art and Literature.*

BEIJING FORESTRY UNIVERSITY

Xiaozhuang, Haidian District, Beijing 100083

Telephone: 62338279
Fax: 62325071
Internet: www.bjfu.edu.cn

Founded 1952

Rector: Prof. HE QINGTANG
Registrar: Prof. ZHOU XINCHEN
Librarian: Prof. GAO RONGFU

Library of 560,000 vols
Number of teachers: 700
Number of students: 3,500

BEIJING JIAOTONG UNIVERSITY

Shang Yuan Cun, Xi Zhi Men Wai, Hai Ding District, Beijing 100044

Telephone: (10) 51688421
Fax: (10) 62245827
Internet: www.njtu.edu.cn

Founded 1921
Academic year: September to July

Pres.: TAN ZHEN HUI
Vice-Pres: CHEN FENG, LI XUE WEI, NING BIN, WANG JIA QIONG
Head of Graduate Department: WANG YONG SHENG
Librarian: SHA SHU LI

Number of teachers: 2,500
Number of students: 15,000

Publication: *Journal* (6 a year)

DEANS

School of Civil Engineering and Architecture: XU ZHAO YI
School of Computer and Information Technology: RUAN QIU QI
School of Economy and Management: WANG JIA QIONG
School of Electrical Engineering: ZHENG QIONG LIN
School of Electronics and Information Engineering: ZHANG SI DONG
School of Humanities and Social Science: GUO HAI YUN
School of Mechanical, Electronic and Control Engineering: SUN SHOU GUANG
School of Science: ZHANG PING ZHI
School of Traffic and Transportation: SUN QUAN XIN

PROFESSORS

BI, YING, Humanities and Social Science
CHANG, YAN XUN, Science
CHEN, CHANG JIA, Electronics and Information Engineering
CHEN, HOU JIN, Electronics and Information Engineering
CHEN, JING YAN, Economy and Management
CHEN, SHI RONG, Humanities and Social Science
CHEN, SHU MIN, Humanities and Social Science
CHEN, XI SHENG, Economy and Management
CHEN, YIN HANG, Electronics and Information Engineering
CHENG, ZHEN WEI, Science
DENG, ZHEN BO, Science
DING, HUI PING, Economy and Management
DONG, BAO TIAN, Traffic and Transportation
DU, YAN LIANG, Mechanical Engineering
FAN, YU, Electrical Engineering
FANG, YUE FA, Mechanical Engineering
FENG, QI BO, Science
FENG, YAN QUAN, Science
FENG, YU MIN, Electronics and Information Engineering
GAO, WEN, Humanities and Social Science
GAO, YU CHEN, Civil Engineering and Architecture
GAO, ZI YOU, Traffic and Transportation
GUAN, KE YING, Science

GUAN, ZHONG LIANG, Economy and Management
HAN, BAO MING, Traffic and Transportation
HAO, RONG TAI, Electrical Engineering
HE, QING FU, Mechanical Engineering
HE, SHI WEI, Traffic and Transportation
HOU, YAN BIN, Science
HOU, ZHONG SHENG, Electronics and Information Engineering
HU, SI JI, Traffic and Transportation
HUANG, LEI, Economy and Management
HUANG, MEI, Electrical Engineering
HUANG, SHI HUA, Science
JI, JIA LUN, Traffic and Transportation
JIA, LI, Mechanical Engineering
JIA, LI MIN, Traffic and Transportation
JIA, YUAN HUA, Traffic and Transportation
JIANG, JIU CHUN, Electrical Engineering
JIANG, ZHONG HAO, Science
JIN, XIN MIN, Electrical Engineering
JIN, ZONG ZE, Mechanical Engineering
JU, SONG DONG, Economy and Management
LI, CHENG SHU, Electronics and Information Engineering
LI, DE CAI, Mechanical Engineering
LI, PEI XUAN, Economy and Management
LI, QIANG, Mechanical Engineering
LI, SI ZE, Science
LI, WEN XING, Economy and Management
LI, XUE WEI, Economy and Management
LIN, BO LIANG, Traffic and Transportation
LIN, DAI DAI, Economy and Management
LIU, CHANG BIN, Economy and Management
LIU, JIAN KUN, Civil Engineering and Architecture
LIU, JUN, Traffic and Transportation
LIU, KAI, Traffic and Transportation
LIU, KUN HUI, Science
LIU, MING GUANG, Electrical Engineering
LIU, WEI NING, Civil Engineering and Architecture
LIU, YAN PEI, Science
LIU, YAN PING, Economy and Management
LIU, YI SHENG, Economy and Management
LIU, ZUO YI, Traffic and Transportation
LV, YONG BO, Traffic and Transportation
MA, JIAN JUN, Traffic and Transportation
MAO, BAO HUA, Traffic and Transportation
NIE, YU XIN, Science
NING, TI GANG, Electronics and Information Engineering
NU, YI HONG, Economy and Management
OU, GUO LI, Economy and Management
QIAO, CHUN SHENG, Civil Engineering and Architecture
QU, HONG XIANG, Mechanical
RONG, CHAO HE, Economy and Management
SHA, FEI, Electronics and Information Engineering
SHANG, PENG JIAN, Science
SHAO, CHUN FU, Traffic and Transportation
SHEN, JIN SHENG, Traffic and Transportation
SHENG, XIN ZHI, Science
SHI, DING HUAN, Traffic and Transportation
SHI, MEI XIA, Economy and Management
SHI, ZHI FEI, Civil Engineering and Architecture
SHI, ZHONG HENG, Civil Engineering and Architecture
SONG, SHOU XIN, Economy and Management
SUN, QUAN XIN, Traffic and Transportation
SUN, SHOU GUANG, Mechanical Engineering
TAN, ZHEN HUI, Electronics and Information Engineering
TANG, TAO, Electronics and Information Engineering
TANG, TAO, Electronics and Information Engineering
TANG, ZHEN MIN, Electronics and Information Engineering
WANG, JIA QIONG, Economy and Management
WANG, JUN HONG, Electronics and Information Engineering
WANG, LI DE, Electrical Engineering
WANG, LIAN JUN, Civil Engineering and Architecture

WANG, MENG SHU, Civil Engineering and Architecture
WANG, WEI, Electrical Engineering
WANG, XI SHI, Electronics and Information Engineering
WANG, YAN YONG, Traffic and Transportation
WANG, YAO QIU, Economy and Management
WANG, YI, Electrical Engineering
WANG, YONG SHENG, Science
WANG, YUAN FENG, Civil Engineering and Architecture
WANG, YUE SHENG, Civil Engineering and Architecture
WEI, QING CHAO, Civil Engineering and Architecture
WEI, XUE YE, Electronics and Information Engineering
WU, CHONG QING, Science
WU, LIU, Science
XIA, HE, Civil Engineering and Architecture
XIAO, GUI PING, Traffic and Transportation
XIE, JI LONG, Mechanical Engineering
XIN, SHU MING, Mechanical Engineering
XIU, NAI HUA, Science
XU, TAO BO, Economy and Management
XU, YU GONG, Mechanical Engineering
XU, ZHAO YI, Civil Engineering and Architecture
YAN, FENG PING, Electronics and Information Engineering
YAN, GUI PING, Civil Engineering and Architecture
YAN, HONG SEN, Mechanical Engineering
YANG, HAO, Traffic and Transportation
YANG, QIN SHAN, Civil Engineering and Architecture
YANG, QING XIN, Mechanical Engineering
YANG, SHAO PU, Mechanical Engineering
YANG, ZHAO XIA, Traffic and Transportation
YAO, BIN, Economy and Management
YAO, PEI JI, Economy and Management
YAO, QIAN FENG, Civil Engineering and Architecture
YE, SHU JUN, Economy and Management
YI, XIANG YONG, Traffic and Transportation
YU, LEI, Traffic and Transportation
YU, QING, Traffic and Transportation
YUAN, LU QU, Economy and Management
YUAN, ZHEN ZHOU, Traffic and Transportation
ZHA, JIAN ZHONG, Mechanical, Electronic and Control Engineering
ZHAN, HE SHENG, Economy and Management
ZHANG, CHAO, Traffic and Transportation
ZHANG, GUO WU, Traffic and Transportation
ZHANG, HONG KE, Electronics and Information Engineering
ZHANG, HONG RU, Civil Engineering and Architecture
ZHANG, LEI, Economy and Management
ZHANG, LI, Electrical Engineering
ZHANG, LIN CHANG, Electronics and Information Engineering
ZHANG, LU XIN, Civil Engineering and Architecture
ZHANG, MING YU, Economy and Management
ZHANG, QIU SHENG, Economy and Management
ZHANG, SI DONG, Electronics and Information Engineering
ZHANG, WEN JIE, Economy and Management
ZHANG, XI, Traffic and Transportation
ZHANG, XI QING, Science
ZHANG, XIAO DONG, Electrical Engineering
ZHANG, XIAO QING, Electrical Engineering
ZHANG, XING CHEN, Traffic and Transportation
ZHANG, YI HUANG, Electrical Engineering
ZHANG, YU XIN, Traffic and Transportation
ZHANG, YUN TONG, Economy and Management
ZHANG, ZHI WEN, Traffic and Transportation
ZHANG, ZHONG YI, Traffic and Transportation
ZHANG, ZI MAO, Civil Engineering and Architecture

ZHAO, CHENG GAN, Civil Engineering and Architecture
ZHAO, JIAN, Economy and Management
ZHENG, QIONG LIN, Electrical Engineering
ZHONG, YAN, Traffic and Transportation
ZHOU, LEI SHAN, Traffic and Transportation
ZHOU, XI DE, Electrical Engineering
ZHOU, YU HUI, Electrical Engineering
ZHU, HENG JUN, Mechanical Engineering
ZHU, HONG, Science
ZHU, JIA SHAN, Traffic and Transportation
ZHU, XI, Civil Engineering and Architecture
ZHU, XIAO NING, Traffic and Transportation

BEIJING LANGUAGE AND CULTURE UNIVERSITY

15 Xue Yuan Rd, Hai Ding District, Beijing 100083

Telephone: (10) 82303035
Fax: (10) 82303903
Internet: www.blcu.edu.cn

Founded 1962
State control
Academic year: September to July

Pres: QU DELIN
Vice-Pres: HUO MINGJIE, LIN GUOLI
Head of Graduate Dept: QU DE NING
Librarian: ZHANG YAN FENG

Number of teachers: 700
Number of students: 8,000

Publications: *Chinese Culture Research* (4 a year), *Learning Chinese* (12 a year), *World Chinese Teaching* (4 a year)

DEANS

College of Chinese Language: LI LI CHENG
College of Foreign Languages: ZHU WEN JUN
College of Humanities and Social Sciences: CHEN JUAN
College of Information Sciences: SONG ROU
Financial Department: LIU KE

PROFESSORS

CHEN, JUAN, Humanities and Social Sciences
CUI, XI LIANG, Humanities and Social Sciences
DU, DAO MING, Humanities and Social Sciences
FAN, LI, Foreign Languages
FANG, MING, Humanities and Social Sciences
HAN, DE MIN, Humanities and Social Sciences
HAN, JING TAI, Humanities and Social Sciences
HU, YU LONG, Foreign Languages
HUANG, ZHUO YUE, Humanities and Social Sciences
JIAO, FENG, Information Sciences
LI, LI CHENG, Chinese Language
LI, YANG, Chinese Language
LI, YAN SHU, Foreign Languages
LI, TIE CHENG, Humanities and Social Sciences
LI, WEI, Finance
LIANG, XIAO SHENG, Humanities and Social Sciences
LIU, XUN, Humanities and Social Sciences
LIU, GUI LONG, Information Sciences
LIU, KE, Finance
LV, WEN HUA, Humanities and Social Sciences
MA, SHU DE, Chinese Language
MA, ZHEN SHENG, Humanities and Social Sciences
NING, YI ZHONG, Foreign Languages
QIU, MING, Foreign Languages
SHEN, ZHI JUN, Chinese Language
SHI, DING GUO, Humanities and Social Sciences
SONG, ROU, Information Sciences
WANG, YE XIN, Chinese Language
WANG, ZHEN YA, Foreign Languages
XU, SHU AN, Humanities and Social Sciences

YAN, CHUN DE, Humanities and Social Sciences
ZHENG, GUI YOU, Humanities and Social Sciences
ZHENG, WANG PENG, Humanities and Social Sciences
ZHU, WEN JUN, Foreign Languages

BEIJING MEDICAL UNIVERSITY

38 Xue Yuan Lu, Northern Suburb, Beijing 100083
Telephone: (10) 62091334
Fax: (10) 62015681
E-mail: dxb@mail.bjmu.edu.cn
Internet: www.bjmu.edu.cn
Founded 1912
Languages of instruction: Chinese, English
Academic year: August to July (2 terms)
19 Research institutes, 11 research centres and 6 affiliated hospitals
Pres.: WANG DEBING
Vice-Pres: CHENG BOJI, HAN QIDE, LIN JIUX-IANG, LU ZHAOFENG, WEI LIHUI, WANG YU
Dean for Education: (vacant)
Director of Libraries: LIAN ZHIJIAN
Library of 730,000 vols, 66,500 periodicals
Number of teachers: 3,721
Number of students: 6,274
Publication: *Journal* (6 a year)

DEANS

First School of Medicine: Prof. ZHANG YOU-KANG
School of Basic Medicine: Prof. JIA HONGTI
School of Mental Health: Prof. CUI YUHUA
School of Nursing: Prof. ZHENG XIUXIA
School of Oral Medicine: Prof. YU GUANGYAN
School of Pharmacy: Prof. ZHANG LIHE
School of Public Health: Prof. LI LIMING
Second School of Medicine: Prof. LU HOUSHAN
Third School of Medicine: HOU KUANYONG

BEIJING METALLURGICAL MANAGEMENT INSTITUTE

Guan Zhuang Chao Yang District, Beijing
Telephone: (10) 65762934
Fax: (10) 65762807
Founded 1984
Pres.: MA DEQING
Vice-Pres: HUANG ZHENGYU, LI YAN
Librarian: ZHAO ZONGDE
Library of 70,000 vols
Number of teachers: 126
Number of students: 1,700

BEIJING NORMAL UNIVERSITY

Xinjiekouwai St 19, Beijing 100875
Telephone: (10) 62207960
Fax: (10) 62200074
E-mail: ipo@bnu.edu.cn
Internet: www.bnu.edu.cn
Founded 1902
State control
Academic year: September to July
12 Colleges
Pres.: YUAN GUIREN
Vice-Pres: SHI PEIJUN, DONG QI, ZHENG JUNLI, XIE WEIHE, DAI JIAGANG, ZHENG SHIQU
Librarian: Prof. JIANG LU
Library: see Libraries
Number of teachers: 1,900
Number of students: 16,400 (8,400 full-time, 8,000 part-time)
Publications: *Comparative Education Review* (12 a year), *Foreign Language Teaching in Schools* (12 a year), *Journal* (Natural Science edn, 4 a year; Social Science edition, 6 a year), *Journal of Historiography* (12 a year).

BEIJING UNIVERSITY OF POSTS AND TELECOMMUNICATIONS

10 Xi Tu Cheng Rd, Haidian District, Beijing 100088
Telephone: (10) 62282628
Fax: (10) 62281774
E-mail: faoffice@bupt.edu.cn
Internet: www.bupt.edu.cn
Founded 1954
Under control of Min. of Posts and Telecommunications
Academic year: September to July
Pres.: ZHU XIANGHUA
Vice-Pres: LIN JINTONG, ZHONG YIXIN, ANG XIUFEN, ZHANG YINGHAI, RENG XIAOMIN, MI JIANHU
Chief Administrative Officer: WANG CHENG-CHU
Librarian: MA ZIWEI
Library of 700,000 vols
Number of teachers: 800
Number of students: 8,000
Publications: *Academic Journal of BUPT* (4 a year), *Journal of China University of Posts and Telecommunications*

DEANS

Correspondence College: ANG XIUFEN
Fuzhou Extension: ANG XIUFEN
Graduate School: SONG JUNDE
Management Humanities College: TANG SHOULIAN
Telecommunications College: LIN JINTONG

ATTACHED RESEARCH INSTITUTES

BUPT-BNR (Nortel China) Advanced Telecommunications R&D Centre: 10 Xi Tu Cheng Rd, Beijing 100088; Dir (China) ZHU QILIANG.
Institute of Communications and Optoelectronic Information Processing: 10 Xi Tu Cheng Rd, Beijing 100088; optical fibres, optical wave guides, holography and optical information processing; Dir XU DAXIONG.
Research Institute: 10 Xi Tu Cheng Rd, Beijing 100088; communications systems and networks, information theory and processing, signal processing, artificial intelligence, neural networks and applications; Dir WU WEILING.

BEIJING SPORT UNIVERSITY

Zhong Guan Cun, Hai Ding District, Beijing 100084
Telephone: (10) 62989047
Fax: (10) 62989289
Internet: www.bupe.edu.cn
Founded 1953
State control
Academic year: September to July
Pres.: YANG HUA
Vice-Pres: ZHONG BIN SHU, HE ZHEN WEN, CHI JIAN
Head of Graduate Depnt: CHI JIAN
Librarian: LIU CAI XIA
Number of teachers: 5,000
Number of students: 540
Publications: *China Method of Body Mechanics* (2 a year), *China School Sport* (6 a year), *Journal* (4 a year)

DEANS

School of Gym Education: ZHOU DIAN MIN
School of Gym Management: QIN CHUN LIN
School of Human Sport: XIE MIN HAO
School of Sports Coaching: YUAN ZUO SHENG
School of Wu Shu: LIU BAO CAI

PROFESSORS

GUI, XIANG, Wu Shu
JIN, JI CHUN, Human Sport Science

JIN, YING HUA, Gym Management
LIU, DA QING, Sports Coaching
MEN, HUI FENG, Wu Shu
MENG, WEN DI, Gym Management
QI, GUO YING, Gym Education
QIN, CHUN LIN, Gym Management
SU, PI REN, Gym Education
SUN, BAO LI, Gym Management
WANG, MIN XIANG, Gym Education
WANG, QIAN, Gym Education
WANG, RUI YUAN, Human Sport Science
WANG, WEI, Sports Coaching
XIA, HUAN ZHEN, Gym Education
XIE, MIN HAO, Human Sport Science
XIONG, XIAO ZHENG, Gym Management
XU, SHENG HONG, Sports Coaching
YAO, XIA WEN, Gym Education
YUAN, DAN, Gym Management
YUAN, ZUO SHENG, Sports Coaching
ZHANG, GUANG DE, Wu Shu
ZHAO, LIAN JIA, Gym Education
ZHOU, DENG SONG, Gym Education
ZHU, RUI QI, Wu Shu

BEIJING INSTITUTE OF TECHNOLOGY

7 Bai Shi Giao, Hai Ding District, Beijing 100081
Telephone: (10) 68914246
Fax: (10) 68468035
Internet: www.bit.edu.cn
Founded 1940
State control
Academic year: September to July
Pres: KUANG JINGMING
Vice-Pres: HOU GUANGMING, LI ZHIXIANG, YANG BIN, ZHAO CHANGLU
Head of Graduate Dept: KUANG JINGMING
Librarian: CAO SHU REN
Number of teachers: 3,000
Number of students: 31,000
Publications: *Journal of Beijing Institute of Technology* (natural sciences, 6 a year), *Journal of Beijing Institute of Technology* (social sciences, 6 a year)

DEANS

School of Chemical Engineering and Materials: ZHOU, TONG LAI
School of Computers and Control: HOU, CHAO ZHEN
School of Design Art: ZHANG, NAI REN
School of Humanities and Social Sciences: XI, QIAO JUAN
School of Information Engineering: WANG, YUE
School of Management and Economics: WANG, XIU CUN
School of Mechatronic Engineering: LIU, LI
School of Science and Technology: XU, WEN GUO
School of Software: WANG, SHU WU
School of Vehicle and Transport Engineering: XU, CHUN GUANG

PROFESSORS

AN, JIAN PING, Information and Communication Engineering
BA, YAN ZHU, Optics Engineering
BAI, CHUN HUA, Mechatronic Engineering
BI, SHI HUA, Mechatronic Engineering
CAI, HONG YAN, Material Science and Engineering
CAO, GEN RUI, Apparatus Science and Technology
CAO, YUAN DA, Computer Science and Technology
CHAI, RUI JIAO, Mechatronic Engineering
CHEN, DONG SHENG, Vehicle and Transport Engineering
CHEN, HUI YAN, Vehicle and Transport Engineering

CHEN, JIA BIN, Control Science and Engineering
CHEN, JIE, Control Science and Engineering
CHEN, SHU FENG, Electronic Science and Technology
CHEN, SI ZHONG, Vehicle and Transport Engineering
CHEN, XIANG GUANG, Control Science and Engineering
CUI, ZHAN ZHONG, Mechatronic Engineering
DA, YA PING, Control Science and Engineering
DING, HONG SHENG, Vehicle and Transport Engineering
DONG, YU PING, Material Science and Engineering
DOU, LI HUA, Control Science and Engineering
DU, ZHI MING, Mechatronic Engineering
FAN, NING JUN, Mechatronic Engineering
FAN, TIAN YOU, Applied Mathematics
FAN, XIAO ZHONG, Computer Science and Technology
FEI, YUAN CHUN, Electronic Science and Technology
FENG, CHANG GEN, Mechatronic Engineering
FENG, SHUN SHAN, Mechatronic Engineering
FU, MENG YING, Control Science and Engineering
GAN, REN CHU, Management Science and Engineering
GAO, BEN QING, Electronic Science and Technology
GAO, CHUN QING, Electronic Science and Technology
GAO, MEI GUO, Information and Communication Engineering
GAO, SHI QIAO, Engineering Mechanics
GAO, ZHI YUN, Optics Engineering
GE, WEI GAO, Applied Mathematics
GE, YUN SHAN, Vehicle and Transport Engineering
GOU, BING CONG, Electronic Science and Technology
GU, LIANG, Vehicle and Transport Engineering
GU, ZHI MIN, Computer Science and Technology
GUO, QIAO, Control Science and Engineering
HAN, BAO LING, Vehicle and Transport Engineering
HAN, BO TANG, Management Science and Engineering
HAN, FENG, Mechatronic Engineering
HAN, YUE QIU, Information and Communication Engineering
HE, PEI KUN, Information and Communication Engineering
HOU, CHAO ZHEN, Control Science and Engineering
HOU, GUANG MING, Management Science and Engineering
HU, CHANG WEN, Chemistry
HU, GENG KAI, Solid Mechanics
HUANG, FENG LEI, Mechatronic Engineering
HUANG, RUO, Vehicle and Transport Engineering
JIA, YUN DE, Computer Science and Technology
JIAO, QING JIE, Mechatronic Engineering
JIAO, YONG HE, Vehicle and Transport Engineering
KANG, JING LI, Mechatronic Engineering
KONG, LING JIA, Vehicle and Transport Engineering
KONG, ZHAO JUN, Management Science and Engineering
KUANG, JING MING, Information and Communication Engineering
LI, JIA ZE, Electronic Science and Technology
LI, JIAN, Management Science and Engineering
LI, JIN LIN, Management Science and Engineering
LI, KE JIE, Mechatronic Engineering
LI, LIN, Apparatus Science and Technology

LI, PING, Mechatronic Engineering
LI, SHI YI, Apparatus Science and Technology
LI, SHI YI, Mechatronic Engineering
LI, XIAO LEI, Vehicle and Transport Engineering
LI, ZHI XIANG, Management Science and Engineering
LIAO, NING FANG, Optics Engineering
LIN, YI, Vehicle and Transport Engineering
LIU, LI, Mechatronic Engineering
LIU, YU SHU, Computer Science and Technology
LIU, ZAO ZHEN, Control Science and Engineering
LIU, ZAO ZHEN, Mechatronic Engineering
LIU, ZHAO DU, Vehicle and Transport Engineering
LIU, ZHI WEN, Information and Communication Engineering
LONG, TENG, Information and Communication Engineering
LONG, XIN PING, Mechatronic Engineering
LU, GUANG SHU, Material Science and Engineering
LU, XIN, Electronic Science and Technology
LUO, WEI XIONG, Information and Communication Engineering
LUO, YUN JUN, Material Science and Engineering
MA, BAO HUA, Mechatronic Engineering
MA, BIAO, Vehicle and Transport Engineering
MA, CHAO CHEN, Vehicle and Transport Engineering
MA, SHU YUAN, Apparatus Science and Technology
MAI, XIAO QING, Mechatronic Engineering
MAO, ER KE, Information and Communication Engineering
MEI, FENG XIANG, Applied Mathematics
NING, GUO QIANG, Optics Engineering
NING, JIAN GUO, Mechatronic Engineering
NING, JIAN GUO, Solid Mechanics
OU, YU XIANG, Material Science and Engineering
PENG, ZHENG GUANG, Control Science and Engineering
QI, ZAI KANG, Mechatronic Engineering
QUAN, WEI QI, Optics Engineering
REN, XUE MEI, Control Science and Engineering
SHA, DING GUO, Apparatus Science and Technology
SHAO, BIN, Chemistry
SHENG, TING ZHI, Information and Communication Engineering
SHI, FENG, Computer Science and Technology
SHI, FU GUI, Applied Mathematics
SONG, HAN TAO, Computer Science and Technology
SONG, ZHEN GUO, Mechatronic Engineering
SUI, SHU YUAN, Mechatronic Engineering
SUN, FENG CHUN, Vehicle and Transport Engineering
SUN, GUANG CHUAN, Information and Communication Engineering
SUN, LIANG, Applied Mathematics
SUN, YE BAO, Vehicle and Transport Engineering
SUN, YU NAN, Electronic Science and Technology
TAN, HUI MIN, Mechatronic Engineering
TAN, HUI MIN, Material Science and Engineering
TAO, RAN, Information and Communication Engineering
WANG, BO, Control Science and Engineering
WANG, FU CHI, Material Science and Engineering
WANG, GUO YU, Vehicle and Transport Engineering
WANG, JIAN ZHONG, Mechatronic Engineering
WANG, PEI LAN, Mechatronic Engineering
WANG, QING LIN, Control Science and Engineering

WANG, SHUN TING, Control Science and Engineering
WANG, XIAO LI, Vehicle and Transport Engineering
WANG, XIAO MO, Information and Communication Engineering
WANG, XING WEN, Mechatronic Engineering
WANG, YONG TIAN, Optics Engineering
WANG, YU, Control Science and Engineering
WANG, YUE, Information and Communication Engineering
WU, QI ZONG, Management Science and Engineering
WU, QING HE, Control Science and Engineering
WU, SI LIANG, Information and Communication Engineering
WU, WEN HUI, Material Science and Engineering
XIA, EN JUN, Management Science and Engineering
XIANG, CHANG LE, Vehicle and Transport Engineering
XIE, JING HUI, Optics Engineering
XING, JIAN GUO, Electronic Science and Technology
XU, GENG GUANG, Mechatronic Engineering
XU, XIAO WEN, Electronic Science and Technology
XU, XING ZHONG, Applied Mathematics
XUE, WEI, Optics Engineering
YAN, JI XIANG, Electronic Science and Technology
YANG, JUN, Engineering Mechanics
YANG, RONG JIE, Material Science and Engineering
YANG, SHU YIN, Mechatronic Engineering
YAO, XIAO XIAN, Mechatronic Engineering
YI, JIANG, Mechatronic Engineering
YU, XIN, Electronic Science and Technology
YUAN, SHI HUA, Vehicle and Transport Engineering
ZENG, FENG ZHANG, Management Science and Engineering
ZENG, QING XUAN, Mechatronic Engineering
ZHAN, SHOU YI, Computer Science and Technology
ZHANG, CHENG NING, Vehicle and Transport Engineering
ZHANG, CHUN LIN, Vehicle and Transport Engineering
ZHANG, FU JUN, Vehicle and Transport Engineering
ZHANG, JING LIN, Mechatronic Engineering
ZHANG, PING, Mechatronic Engineering
ZHANG, QI, Mechatronic Engineering
ZHANG, QIANG, Management Science and Engineering
ZHANG, QING MING, Engineering Mechanics
ZHANG, TONG ZHUANG, Vehicle and Transport Engineering
ZHANG, WEI ZHENG, Vehicle and Transport Engineering
ZHANG, YONG FA, Solid Mechanics
ZHANG, YOU TONG, Vehicle and Transport Engineering
ZHANG, YU HE, Control Science and Engineering
ZHANG, YUN HONG, Chemistry
ZHAO, CHANG LU, Vehicle and Transport Engineering
ZHAO, CHANG MING, Electronic Science and Technology
ZHAO, DA ZUN, Optics Engineering
ZHAO, HONG KANG, Electronic Science and Technology
ZHAO, XING QI, Material Science and Engineering
ZHAO, YUE JIN, Apparatus Science and Technology
ZHEN, LIAN, Mechatronic Engineering
ZHENG, HONG FEI, Vehicle and Transport Engineering
ZHENG, LIAN, Control Science and Engineering

ZHONG, QIU HAI, Control Science and Engineering
ZHOU, JIAN, Applied Mathematics
ZHOU, LI WEI, Optics Engineering
ZHOU, TONG LAI, Chemistry
ZHU, DONG HUA, Management Science and Engineering
ZUO, ZHEN XING, Vehicle and Transport Engineering

BEIJING UNIVERSITY OF TECHNOLOGY

100 Ping Le Yuan, Chao Yang District, Beijing 100226
Telephone: (10) 67392239
Fax: (10) 67392675
Internet: www.bjpu.edu.cn
Founded 1960
Academic year: September to July
Pres: FAN, BO YUAN
Vice-Pres: HOU, YI BIN
Head of Graduate Dept: JIANG, YI JIAN
Librarian: FEI, REN YUAN
Number of teachers: 1,100
Number of students: 26,000
Publication: *Journal* (4 a year)

DEANS

College of Applied Science: ZHANG, ZHONG ZHAN
College of Architecture Engineering: HUO, DA
College of Computer Science: ZHANG, SHU JIE
College of Economics and Management: LI, JING WEN
College of Electronic Information and Control Engineering: WANG, PU
College of Energy and Environmental Engineering: MA, CHONG FANG
College of Foreign Languages: WANG, FU XIANG
College of Humanities and Social Sciences: LU, XUE YI
College of Life Science and Bio-Engineering: ZENG, YI
College of Material Science and Engineering: NIE, ZHA REN
College of Mechanical Engineering and Applied Electronics Technology: YANG, JIAN WU
College of Software Engineering: HOU, YI BIN

PROFESSORS

BAO, CHANG CHUN, Electronic Information and Control Engineering
CAO, WANG LIN, Architecture Engineering
CHEN, GUANG HUA, Material Science and Engineering
CHEN, JIAN XIN, Electronic Information and Control Engineering
CHEN, YANG ZHOU, Electronic Information and Control Engineering
CHENG, CAO ZONG, Applied Science and Physics
CHENG, SHUI YUAN, Energy and Environmental Engineering
CUI, PING YUAN, Electronic Information and Control Engineering
DAI, HONG XING, Energy and Environmental Engineering
DI, RUI HUA, Computer Science
DU, XIU LI, Architecture Engineering
DUAN, JIAN MIN, Electronic Information and Control Engineering
FEI, REN YUAN, Mechanical Engineering and Applied Electronics Technology
GUO, BAI NING, Computer Science
HAN, FU RONG, Economics and Management
HE, CUN FU, Mechanical Engineering and Applied Electronics Technology
HE, HONG, Energy and Environmental Engineering
HE, RUO QUAN, Architecture Engineering

HE, ZI NIAN, Energy and Environmental Engineering
HOU, BI HUI, Applied Science and Physics
HOU, YI BIN, Computer Science
HUANG, LU CHENG, Economics and Management
HUANG, TI YUN, Economics and Management
HUO, DA, Architecture Engineering
JIANG, YI JIE, Applied Science and Physics
KANG, BAO WEI, Electronic Information and Control Engineering
KANG, TIAN FANG, Energy and Environmental Engineering
LEI, YONG PING, Material Science and Engineering
LI, DE SHENG, Mechanical Engineering and Applied Electronics Technology
LI, GANG, Laser Engineering
LI, HUI MING, Economics and Management
LI, JING WEN, Economics and Management
LI, SHOU MEI, Applied Science and Physics
LI, XIAO YAN, Material Science and Engineering
LI, ZHEN BAO, Architecture Engineering
LI, ZHI GUO, Electronic Information and Control Engineering
LIAO, HU SHENG, Computer Science
LIU, CHUN NIAN, Computer Science
LIU, XIAO MING, Architecture Engineering
LIU, YOU MING, Applied Science and Physics
LIU, ZHONG LIANG, Energy and Environmental Engineering
LU, XUE YI, Economics and Management
MA, CHONG FANG, Energy and Environmental Engineering
MA, GUO YUAN, Energy and Environmental Engineering
NIE, ZHA REN, Material Science and Engineering
PENG, YONG ZHEN, Energy and Environmental Engineering
REN, FU TIAN, Architecture Engineering
REN, ZHEN HAI, Energy and Environmental Engineering
RUAN, XIAO GANG, Electronic Information and Control Engineering
SHANG, DE GUANG, Mechanical Engineering and Applied Electronics Technology
SHE, YUAN BIN, Energy and Environmental Engineering
SHENG, GUANG DI, Electronic Information and Control Engineering
SHENG, LAN SUN, Electronic Information and Control Engineering
SHI, YAO WU, Material Science and Engineering
SONG, ROU, Computer Science
SUI, YUN KANG, Mechanical Engineering and Applied Electronics Technology
TAO, LIAN JIN, Architecture Engineering
TAO, SHI QUAN, Applied Science and Physics
WAN, SU CHUN, Architecture Engineering
WANG, DA YONG, Applied Science and Physics
WANG, DAO, Energy and Environmental Engineering
WANG, GUANG TAO, Architecture Engineering
WANG, LI, Applied Science and Physics
WANG, PU, Electronic Information and Control Engineering
WANG, SONG GUI, Applied Science and Physics
WU, BIN, Mechanical Engineering and Applied Electronics Technology
WU, GUO WEI, Economics and Management
WU, WU CHEN, Electronic Information and Control Engineering
WU, YONG LUN, Mechanical Engineering and Applied Electronics Technology
XIA, DING GUO, Energy and Environmental Engineering
XUE, LIU GEN, Applied Science and Physics
XUE, SU GUO, Architecture Engineering
YAN, HUI, Material Science and Engineering
YAN, WEI MING, Architecture Engineering
YANG, HONG RU, Applied Science and Physics
YAO, HAI LOU, Applied Science and Physics

YI, BAO CAI, Computer Science
YIN, SHU YAN, Mechanical Engineering and Applied Electronics Technology
YIN, SHU YAN, Material Science and Engineering
YU, JIAN, Energy and Environmental Engineering
YU, KUAN XIN, Applied Science and Physics
YU, YUE QING, Mechanical Engineering and Applied Electronics Technology
ZENG, YI, Energy and Environmental Engineering
ZHANG, AI LIN, Architecture Engineering
ZHANG, HONG BIN, Computer Science
ZHANG, HONG BIN, Electronic Information and Control Engineering
ZHANG, HUI HUI, Mechanical Engineering and Applied Electronics Technology
ZHANG, JIE, Energy and Environmental Engineering
ZHANG, JIU JIE, Material Science and Engineering
ZHANG, WANG RONG, Electronic Information and Control Engineering
ZHANG, WEI, Mechanical Engineering and Applied Electronics Technology
ZHANG, WEN XIONG, Material Science and Engineering
ZHANG, YI GANG, Architecture Engineering
ZHANG, ZE, Applied Science and Physics
ZHANG, ZHEN HAI, Applied Science and Physics
ZHANG, ZHI GANG, Applied Science and Physics
ZHANG, ZHONG ZHAN, Applied Science and Physics
ZHONG, NING, Computer Science
ZHONG, RU GANG, Energy and Environmental Engineering
ZHOU, DA SEN, Energy and Environmental Engineering
ZHOU, MEI LING, Material Science and Engineering
ZHOU, WEI, Architecture Engineering
ZHOU, XI YUAN, Architecture Engineering
ZHOU, YU WEN, Energy and Environmental Engineering
ZONG, GANG, Economics and Management
ZUO, TIE XUN, Applied Science and Physics
ZUO, TIE YONG, Material Science and Engineering

CAPITAL NORMAL UNIVERSITY

105 Xi San Huan, Beijing 100037
Telephone: (10) 68900974
Fax: (10) 68902539
Internet: www.cnu.edu.cn
Founded 1954
Bureau of Education of Beijing
Academic year: September to July
Pres.: XIANG YUAN XU
Vice-Pres: HUI LI GONG, JIAN CHENG LIU, JIAN SHE ZHOU, WAN LIANG WANG
Head of Graduate Dept: JING HE LIANG
Librarian: YUE HU
Number of teachers: 1,147
Number of students: 24,905 (12,786 full-time, 12,119 part-time)
Publications: *Education Art* (12 a year), *Journal of Capital Normal University (Natural Sciences Edition)* (4 a year), *Journal of Capital Normal University (Social Sciences Edition)* (6 a year), *Language Teaching in Middle School* (12 a year), *Middle School Math* (12 a year)

DEANS

College of Biology: HE YIKUN
College of Education: MEN FANHUA
College of Environmental Resources and Tourism: GONG HUILI
College of Fine Arts: SUN ZHIJUN
College of Foreign Languages: YANG YANG

College of Information Technology: WANG WANSEN
College of International Culture: LIU XIAO-TIAN
College of Music: YANG QING
College of Political Sciences and Law: WANG SHUMENG
Department of Chemistry: ZHANG ZHUOYONG
Department of Educational Technology: AI LUN
Department of History: SONG JIE
Department of Mathematics: ZHENG CHONGYOU
Department of Physics: ZHANG CUNLIN
Elementary Education College: WANG ZHIQIU
Physical Teaching and Research Section: SUN JIANHUI
School of Literature: WU SHIJING
Teaching and Research Division of Marxism: LI SONGLIN
University English Teaching and Research Division: XIE FUZHI

PROFESSORS

AN, YUFENG, Political Sciences and Law
BI, LUO, Environmental Resources and Tourism
CAI, TUANYAO, Biology
CHANG, RUILUN, Fine Arts
CHEN, XINXIA, Political Sciences and Law
CHI, YUNFEI, History
DAI, LIN, Fine Arts
DIAO, YONGZHA, Marxism
DONG, ZHONGXUN, Fine Arts
DU, XIAOSHI, Music
DU, XIXIAN, Fine Arts
FAN, YANNING, Political Sciences and Law
FANG, PING, Education
FANG, YAN, Physics
FU, HUA, Environmental Resources and Tourism
GONG, HUILI, Environmental Resources and Tourism
GU, XUEXIN, Chemistry
HAO, CHUNWEN, History
HE, YIKUN, Biology
HUANG, MEIYING, Music
HUO, LONGGUANG, Mathematics
JIN, QIONGHUA, Chemistry
LAN, WEI, Political Sciences and Law
LEI, DA, Music
LI, AIGUO, Fine Arts
LI, FULI, Physics
LI, JIAYANG, Biology
LI, SHUPEI, Mathematics
LI, SONGLIN, Marxism
LI, XIA, Chemistry
LI, YARU, Marxism
LIAN, SHAOMING, History
LIANG, JINGHE, History
LIN, LI, Foreign Languages
LIU, DACHUN, Mathematics
LIU, LIMIN, Foreign Languages
LU, XIAOMING, Chemistry
MENG, FANHUA, Education
NIE, YUEYAN, Political Sciences and Law
NING, HONG, Education
NING, KE, History
QI, SHIRONG, History
QIU, YUNHUA, Literature
REN, DONG, Biology
SHAO, HUIBO, Chemistry
SHEN, JINGLING, Physics
SHI, SHENGMING, Mathematics
SHUI, SHUFENG, Political Sciences and Law
SONG, JIE, History
SUN, ZHIJUN, Fine Arts
TAN, FENGTAI, Education
TANG, CHONGQIN, Music
TAO, DONGFENG, Literature
TIAN, BAO, Education
WANG, ANGUO, Music
WANG, CHANGCHUN, Education
WANG, DESHENG, Literature
WANG, GUANGMING, Literature
WANG, JIANPING, Education

WANG, LU, Educational Technology
WANG, SHIPING, Physics
WANG, SHUMENG, Political Sciences and Law
WANG, SHUQIN, Political Sciences and Law
WANG, ZHIQIU, Elementary Education
WEI, GUANGQI, History
WEN, LISHU, Political Sciences and Law
WU, JIANGPING, Mathematics
WU, SHIJING, Literature
XIA, JIGUO, History
XIA, LIMIN, Political Sciences and Law
XIE, CHENGREN, History
XING, HONGJUN, Physics
XING, YONGFU, Education
XU, PEIJUN, Physics
XU, YUZHEN, Education
YANG, QING, Music
YANG, SHENGPING, Political Sciences and Law
YANG, YANG, Foreign Languages
YANG, YUE, Biology
YE, XIAOBING, History
YIN, LIPING, Biology
YIN, TIELIANG, Music
YIN, WEIPING, Mathematics
ZHAN, LIJUAN, Music
ZHANG, CUNLIN, Physics
ZHANG, GUOLI, Music
ZHANG, JUNDA, Education
ZHANG, YONGHUA, Chemistry
ZHANG, ZHUOYONG, Chemistry
ZHAO, XUEZHI, Mathematics

CAPITAL MEDICAL UNIVERSITY

10 Xitoutiao, You Anmen, Fengtai Dist., Beijing 100069

Telephone: (10) 83911199
Fax: (10) 83911194
E-mail: guohechu@ccmu.edu.cn
Internet: www.ccmu.edu.cn

Founded 1960
Academic year: September to July

Pres.: LU ZHAOFENG
Vice-Pres.: FAN QI
Vice-Pres.: WANG XIAOMIN
Vice-Pres.: WANG YUHUI
Vice-Pres.: WANG SONGLING
Vice-Pres.: XIAN FUHUA
Head of Graduate Dept: LU ZHAOFENG
Librarian: WANG JIEZHEN

Number of teachers: 2,500

Publications: *Journal* (4 a year), *School of Public Health* (4 a year)

DEANS

Biomedical Engineering Institute: LIU ZHICHENG
Eighth Faculty of Clinical Medicine: XI XIUMING
Faculty of Mental Health: CAI ZHUOJI
Faculty of Nursing: LI SHUJIA
Faculty of Obstetrics and Gynaecology: CHEN BAOYING
Faculty of Paediatrics: LI ZHONGZHI
Faculty of Rehabilitation: YOU HONG
Faculty of Stomatology: ZHENG SUN
Fifth Faculty of Clinical Medicine: DAI JIANPING
First Faculty of Clinical Medicine: ZHANG JIAN
Fourth Faculty of Clinical Medicine: LIU HONGBO
Ninth Faculty of Clinical Medicine: ZHAO CHUNHUI
School of Basic Medical Sciences: CHEN TIEJUN
School of Chemical Biology and Pharmaceutical Sciences: PENG SHIQI
School of Chinese Traditional Medicine: QI FANG
School of Health Administration and Education: LIANG WANNIAN
School of Public Health and Family Medical Science: WANG WEI

Second Faculty of Clinical Medicine: GAO DONGCHEN
Sixth Faculty of Clinical Medicine: ZHANG GUANGZHAO
Third Faculty of Clinical Medicine: GAO JUZHONG

PROFESSORS

AN, WEI, School of Basic Medical Sciences
AN, YUNQING, School of Basic Medical Sciences
BAI, YUXING, Faculty of Stomatology
CAI, ZHUOJI, Faculty of Mental Health
CHANG, XHIWEN, Fourth Faculty of Clinical Medicine
CHE, NIANCONG, School of Chinese Traditional Medicine
CHEN, BAOTIAN, Sixth Faculty of Clinical Medicine
CHEN, BAOYING, Faculty of Obstetrics and Gynaecology
CHEN, BIAO, First Faculty of Clinical Medicine
CHEN, HAIYING, School of Chinese Traditional Medicine
CHEN, HUIDE, Third Faculty of Clinical Medicine
CHEN, HUIRU, Fourth Faculty of Clinical Medicine
CHEN, JUN, School of Basic Medical Sciences
CHEN, SHAN, Fourth Faculty of Clinical Medicine
CHEN, TIEJUN, School of Basic Medical Sciences
CHEN, XUESHI, Faculty of Mental Health
CHEN, YILIN, First Faculty of Clinical Medicine
CHEN, YINGCHUN, Sixth Faculty of Clinical Medicine
CHEN, YUPING, Sixth Faculty of Clinical Medicine
CHEN, ZHAN, Sixth Faculty of Clinical Medicine
CUI, GUOHUI, School of Chemical Biology and Pharmaceutical Sciences
CUI, SHUQI, School of Public Health and Family Medical Science
DAI, JIANPING, Fifth Faculty of Clinical Medicine
DAI, XINGHUA, Faculty of Obstetrics and Gynaecology
DAO, HONG, School of Public Health and Family Medical Science
DING, BOTAN, Faculty of Rehabilitation
DING, ZONGYI, Faculty of Paediatrics
DONG, PEIQING, Sixth Faculty of Clinical Medicine
DONG, ZONGJUN, First Faculty of Clinical Medicine
DU, FENGHE, Fifth Faculty of Clinical Medicine
DU, LINDONG, Second Faculty of Clinical Medicine
DUAN, YANPING, School of Chinese Traditional Medicine
DUAN, ZHONGPING, Ninth Faculty of Clinical Medicine
FAN, DONGPO, Fifth Faculty of Clinical Medicine
FAN, MING, School of Basic Medical Sciences
FAN, XUNMEI, Faculty of Paediatrics
FANG, DEYUN, First Faculty of Clinical Medicine
GAO, BAOQIN, Fifth Faculty of Clinical Medicine
GAO, CHUNJIN, Third Faculty of Clinical Medicine
GAO, DONGCHEN, Second Faculty of Clinical Medicine
GAO, FENG, Faculty of Obstetrics and Gynaecology
GAO, JUZHONG, Third Faculty of Clinical Medicine
GAO, MINGZHE, Sixth Faculty of Clinical Medicine
GAO, PEIYI, Fifth Faculty of Clinical Medicine

GAO, WENZHU, Faculty of Rehabilitation
GAO, XIULAI, School of Basic Medical Sciences
GAO, YIMIN, School of Chinese Traditional Medicine
GUAN, DELIN, Third Faculty of Clinical Medicine
GUO, AIMIN, School of Public Health and Family Medical Science
GUO, SONG, Faculty of Mental Health
GUO, XIUHUA, School of Public Health and Family Medical Science
HAN, DEMIN, Fourth Faculty of Clinical Medicine
HAN, LING, Sixth Faculty of Clinical Medicine
HE, YAN, Fifth Faculty of Clinical Medicine
HU, DAYI, Third Faculty of Clinical Medicine
HU, YAMEI, Faculty of Paediatrics
HU, YINYUAN, Faculty of Rehabilitation
HUA, QI, First Faculty of Clinical Medicine
HUANG, JIEYING, Second Faculty of Clinical Medicine
HUANG, SHUZHEN, Faculty of Mental Health
JI, SHURONG, Faculty of Rehabilitation
JIA, HONGTI, School of Basic Medical Sciences
JIA, JIANPING, First Faculty of Clinical Medicine
JIA, JIDONG, Second Faculty of Clinical Medicine
JIANG, BING, School of Health Administration and Education
JIANG, TAO, Fifth Faculty of Clinical Medicine
JIANG, WENHUA, First Faculty of Clinical Medicine
JIANG, ZAIFANG, Faculty of Paediatrics
JIANG, ZUONING, Faculty of Mental Health
JIN, RUI, Ninth Faculty of Clinical Medicine
JU, LIRONG, School of Public Health and Family Medical Science
LI, BIN, Fourth Faculty of Clinical Medicine
LI, CUIYING, Faculty of Stomatology
LI, FEI, First Faculty of Clinical Medicine
LI, HONGPEI, Fifth Faculty of Clinical Medicine
LI, JIANPING, School of Health Administration and Education
LI, KUNCHENG, First Faculty of Clinical Medicine
LI, LIN, First Faculty of Clinical Medicine
LI, LIN, School of Health Administration and Education
LI, PING, Sixth Faculty of Clinical Medicine
LI, REN, Third Faculty of Clinical Medicine
LI, SHUJIA, Faculty of Nursing
LI, SHUREN, Second Faculty of Clinical Medicine
LI, XIA, Biomedical Engineering Institute
LI, YONGJIE, First Faculty of Clinical Medicine
LI, YUJING, Faculty of Stomatology
LI, ZHI'AN, Sixth Faculty of Clinical Medicine
LI, ZHIZIA, Fourth Faculty of Clinical Medicine
LI, ZHONGZHI, Faculty of Paediatrics
LIAN, SHI, First Faculty of Clinical Medicine
LIANG, WANNIAN, School of Health Administration and Education
LING, FENG, First Faculty of Clinical Medicine
LIU, BIN, Fourth Faculty of Clinical Medicine
LIU, CHANGGUI, Second Faculty of Clinical Medicine
LIU, HONGBO, Fourth Faculty of Clinical Medicine
LIU, HONGGANG, Fourth Faculty of Clinical Medicine
LIU, JINGZHONG, Third Faculty of Clinical Medicine
LIU, LEI, Fourth Faculty of Clinical Medicine
LIU, NONG, School of Basic Medical Sciences
LIU, WEIZHEN, School of Basic Medical Sciences
LIU, XICHENG, Faculty of Paediatrics
LIU, YONGBIN, Faculty of Rehabilitation
LIU, ZHICHENG, Biomedical Engineering Institute
LONG, JIE, Fifth Faculty of Clinical Medicine

LU, HUIZHANG, First Faculty of Clinical Medicine
LU, SHIQI, School of Basic Medical Sciences
LUAN, GUOMING, Fifth Faculty of Clinical Medicine
LUO, SHIQI, Fifth Faculty of Clinical Medicine
LUO, SHUQIAN, Biomedical Engineering Institute
MA, BINRONG, Biomedical Engineering Institute
MA, CHANGSHENG, Sixth Faculty of Clinical Medicine
MA, DAQING, Second Faculty of Clinical Medicine
MA, DONGLI, Fourth Faculty of Clinical Medicine
MENG, XU, Sixth Faculty of Clinical Medicine
NI, JIAYI, First Faculty of Clinical Medicine
PAN, JULI, Faculty of Stomatology
PENG, SHIQI, School of Chemical Biology and Pharmaceutical Sciences
QI, FANG, School of Chinese Traditional Medicine
QI, YING, Fourth Faculty of Clinical Medicine
QIAN, YING, School of Chinese Traditional Medicine
QIAO, ZHIHENG, Faculty of Rehabilitation
QU, RENYOU, Third Faculty of Clinical Medicine
SHE, KUNLING, Faculty of Paediatrics
SHEN, LUHUA, Second Faculty of Clinical Medicine
SHEN, YIN, Faculty of Paediatrics
SHI, SHENGGEN, Faculty of Stomatology
SHI, XIAOLIN, School of Basic Medical Sciences
SHI, XIANG'EN, Fifth Faculty of Clinical Medicine
SHI, YUYING, Fourth Faculty of Clinical Medicine
SONG, MAOMIN, Fifth Faculty of Clinical Medicine
SONG, WEIXIAN, Fourth Faculty of Clinical Medicine
SUN, BAOZHEN, Fourth Faculty of Clinical Medicine
SUN, BO, Fifth Faculty of Clinical Medicine
SUN, JIANBANG, First Faculty of Clinical Medicine
SUN, YANQING, Sixth Faculty of Clinical Medicine
SUN, ZHENG, Faculty of Stomatology
TANG, XHAOQU, School of Basic Medical Sciences
TIAN, XHU'EN, Faculty of Mental Health
WANG, BANGKANG, Faculty of Stomatology
WANG, BAOGUO, Fifth Faculty of Clinical Medicine
WANG, CHEN, Third Faculty of Clinical Medicine
WANG, DEXIN, Second Faculty of Clinical Medicine
WANG, ENXHEN, Fifth Faculty of Clinical Medicine
WANG, HUILING, Sixth Faculty of Clinical Medicine
WANG, JIE, Fifth Faculty of Clinical Medicine
WANG, PEIYAN, Third Faculty of Clinical Medicine
WANG, SONGLING, Faculty of Stomatology
WANG, SUQIU, Fifth Faculty of Clinical Medicine
WANG, TIANYOU, Second Faculty of Clinical Medicine
WANG, XHONGCHENG, Fifth Faculty of Clinical Medicine
WANG, WEI, School of Public Health and Family Medical Science
WANG, WENWEI, Fourth Faculty of Clinical Medicine
WANG, XHENFU, Fourth Faculty of Clinical Medicine
WANG, XHIGANG, Second Faculty of Clinical Medicine
WANG, XIAOLIANG, School of Chemical Biology and Pharmaceutical Sciences

WANG, XIAOMIN, School of Basic Medical Sciences
WANG, XIAOYAN, School of Health Administration and Education
WANG, YADONG, School of Health Administration and Education
WANG, YIZHEN, Fifth Faculty of Clinical Medicine
WANG, YONGJUN, Fifth Faculty of Clinical Medicine
WANG, YU, Second Faculty of Clinical Medicine
WANG, ZHONGGAO, First Faculty of Clinical Medicine
WENG, XINAHI, Third Faculty of Clinical Medicine
WENG, YONGZHEN, Faculty of Mental Health
WU, AINGHUA, Sixth Faculty of Clinical Medicine
WU, FENGYI, Third Faculty of Clinical Medicine
WU, HAO, Ninth Faculty of Clinical Medicine
WU, MINYUAN, Faculty of Paediatrics
WU, SHUZENG, Sixth Faculty of Clinical Medicine
WU, XUESHI, Sixth Faculty of Clinical Medicine
WU, ZHAOSU, Sixth Faculty of Clinical Medicine
XI, XIUMING, Eighth Faculty of Clinical Medicine
XIANG, XIUKUN, Fourth Faculty of Clinical Medicine
XIAO, RONG, School of Public Health and Family Medical Science
XU, QUNYAN, School of Basic Medical Sciences
XUE, MING, School of Health Administration and Education
YANG, BAOQIN, School of Chinese Traditional Medicine
YANG, HUI, School of Basic Medical Sciences
YANG, JINKUI, Fourth Faculty of Clinical Medicine
YANG, SHAOXU, Fifth Faculty of Clinical Medicine
YANG, SHENGHUI, Faculty of Stomatology
YANG, YUNPING, Faculty of Mental Health
YAO, CHONGHUA, Sixth Faculty of Clinical Medicine
YAO, TIANQIAO, Sixth Faculty of Clinical Medicine
YOU, HONG, Faculty of Rehabilitation
YOU, KAITAO, Third Faculty of Clinical Medicine
YU, CHUNJIANG, First Faculty of Clinical Medicine
YU, ZELI, Fourth Faculty of Clinical Medicine
YUAN, ZHENGGUO, School of Chinese Traditional Medicine
YUE, YUN, Third Faculty of Clinical Medicine
ZHAN, ZHENTING, Faculty of Stomatology
ZHANG, BINXI, Fourth Faculty of Clinical Medicine
ZHANG, CHANGHUAI, Second Faculty of Clinical Medicine
ZHANG, FENGXIAN, Third Faculty of Clinical Medicine
ZHANG, GUANGZHAO, Sixth Faculty of Clinical Medicine
ZHANG, HONGYU, Third Faculty of Clinical Medicine
ZHANG, JIAN, First Faculty of Clinical Medicine
ZHANG, JIGU, Faculty of Mental Health
ZHANG, JINCAI, Faculty of Stomatology
ZHANG, JINRONG, Sixth Faculty of Clinical Medicine
ZHANG, JINZHE, Faculty of Paediatrics
ZHANG, JIZHI, Faculty of Mental Health
ZHANG, PENGTIAN, Second Faculty of Clinical Medicine
ZHANG, QIUHAN, First Faculty of Clinical Medicine
ZHANG, SHIJI, Faculty of Mental Health

ZHANG, SHUMIN, School of Chinese Traditional Medicine
ZHANG, SHUWEN, Second Faculty of Clinical Medicine
ZHANG, YU, First Faculty of Clinical Medicine
ZHANG, YUHAI, Second Faculty of Clinical Medicine
ZHANG, ZHAOGUANG, Sixth Faculty of Clinical Medicine
ZHANG, ZHAOQI, Sixth Faculty of Clinical Medicine
ZHANG, ZHITAI, Sixth Faculty of Clinical Medicine
ZHAO, CHUNHUI, Ninth Faculty of Clinical Medicine
ZHAO, DONG, Sixth Faculty of Clinical Medicine
ZHAO, JIZONG, Fifth Faculty of Clinical Medicine
ZHAO, MING, School of Chemical Biology and Pharmaceutical Sciences
ZHAO, YADU, Fifth Faculty of Clinical Medicine
ZHAO, YI, Second Faculty of Clinical Medicine
ZHAO, YUANLI, Fifth Faculty of Clinical Medicine
ZHENG, BANGHE, Fourth Faculty of Clinical Medicine
ZHENG, JIE, School of Basic Medical Sciences
ZHENG, YI, Faculty of Mental Health
ZHOU, BING, Fourth Faculty of Clinical Medicine
ZHOU, QIWEN, Sixth Faculty of Clinical Medicine
ZHOU, YAOTING, School of Chinese Traditional Medicine
ZHOU, YUJIE, Sixth Faculty of Clinical Medicine
ZHU, XINPING, School of Basic Medical Sciences

CENTRAL ACADEMY OF ARTS AND DESIGN

34 North Dong Huan Rd, Beijing 100020
Telephone: (10) 65026391
Founded 1956
Pres.: CHANG SHANA
Vice-Pres: WANG MING ZHI, YANG YONG SHAN, WANG ZHONG XIN
Library Dir: QIU CHENGDE
Library of 170,000 vols
Number of teachers: 240
Number of students: 900 (36 postgraduates)
Publications: *College Journal* (12 a year), *Decoration* (4 a year), *Reference on Arts and Crafts* (12 a year).

CENTRAL UNIVERSITY OF FINANCE AND ECONOMICS

39 Xue Yuan Nan Rd, Beijing 100081
Telephone: (10) 62289132
Fax: (10) 62289132
E-mail: wlb@cufe.edu.cn
Internet: www.cufe.edu.cn
Founded 1949
Min. of Education control
Academic year: September to July
Pres.: WANG GUANGQIAN
Vice-Pres: CHEN MING, LI JUNSHENG, WANG GUOHUA, YUAN DONG
Head of Graduate Dept: QI LAN
Librarian: HAN ZHIPING
Number of teachers: 500
Number of students: 14,000 (6,800 full-time, 7,200 part-time)
Publication: *Journal of the Central University of Finance and Economics* (12 a year)

DEANS
Business School: SUN GUOHUI

College of Culture and Communication: WANG QIANG
Department of Athletics Economy and Management: GAO HAN
Department of Economic Mathematics: CHEN WENDENG
Department of Foreign Languages: WANG XIAOHONG
Department of Insurance: HAO YANSU
Department of Investment Economics: WANG YAOQI
Department of Sociology: LI ZHIJUN
School of Accountancy: MENG YAN
School of Economics: JIN ZHESONG
School of Finance: SHI JIANPING
School of Information: WANG LUBIN
School of Law: GAN GONGEN
School of Public Finance and Administration: MA HAITAO

PROFESSORS
BAO, XIAOGUANG, Culture and Communication
CHEN, WENDENG, Economic Mathematics
CUI, XINJIAN, Business
DONG, CHENGZHANG, Information
GAN, GONGEN, Law
HAN, FULING, Finance
HAO, YANSU, Insurance
HOU, RONGHUA, Economics
HUO, PEI, Finance
HUO, QIANG, Finance
JIANG, WEIZHUANG, Public Finance and Administration
JIANG, XIAN, Economics
JIN, ZHESONG, Economics
LAN, CUIPAI, Law
LI, BAOREN, Public Finance and Administration
LI, JIAN, Finance
LI, JIXIONG, Insurance
LI, JUNSHENG, Public Finance and Administration
LI, SHUANG, Accountancy
LI, XIAOLIN, Insurance
LI, YAN, Public Finance and Administration
LI, ZHIJUN, Sociology
LIAO, SIPING, Culture and Communication
LIU, HENG, Public Finance and Administration
LIU, HONGXIA, Accountancy
LIU, YANG, Economics
MA, HAITAO, Public Finance and Administration
MENG, YAN, Accountancy
MIAO, RUNSHENG, Accountancy
PAN, JINSHENG, Finance
PAN, SHENGCHU, Information
QI, HUAIJIN, Accountancy
QI, LAN, Economics
SHI, JIANPING, Finance
SHI, SHULIN, Law
SUN, BAOWEN, Information
SUN, GUOHUI, Business
WANG, GUOHUA, Public Finance and Administration
WANG, JINYING, Business
WANG, JUNCAI, Accountancy
WANG, KEJING, Economics
WANG, LUBIN, Information
WANG, PEIZHEN, Finance
WANG, QIANG, Culture and Communication
WANG, RUIHUA, Accountancy
WANG, YONGJUN, Public Finance and Administration
WANG, YONGPING, Accountancy
WEI, ZHENXIONG, Accountancy
WEN, QIAN, Economics
WU, ZHENZHI, Finance
XI, SHUQIN, Accountancy
XU, SHANHUI, Finance
XU, XIANGYU, Investment Economics
YANG, JINGUANG, Accountancy
YANG, ZHIQING, Public Finance and Administration
YAO, SUI, Finance

ZHANG, BIQIONG, Finance
ZHANG, LIQIN, Finance
ZHANG, SHUJUN, Business
ZHANG, TIEGANG, Economics
ZHAO, LIFENG, Economics
ZHAO, XUEHENG, Public Finance and Administration

CENTRAL ACADEMY OF FINE ARTS

8 Hua Jia Di Nan Jie, Chaoyang District, Beijing 100102
Telephone: (10) 64771018
Fax: (10) 64771136
Internet: www.cafa.com.cn
Founded 1950
Min. of Education control
Academic year: September to July
Pres.: PAN GONGKAI
Vice-Pres.: FAN DIAN
Head of Graduate Department: CHU DI
Librarian: SHEN JIANDONG
Number of teachers: 141
Number of students: 1,000
Publications: *Art Research* (4 a year), *World Art* (4 a year)

DEANS
Art History Department: YIN JINAN
Art Education Department: JIN JIAZHEN
Chinese Painting Department: TIAN LIMING
First-year Foundation Programme: WEN GUOZHANG
Mural Painting Department: SUN JINGBO
Oil Painting Department: DAI SHIHE
Printmaking Department: SU XINPING
School of Architecture: LU PINJING
School of Design: WANG MIN
School of Humanities: YIN JINAN
Sculpture Department: SUI JIANGUO

PROFESSORS
CAO, LI, Mural Painting
CHAO, GE, Oil Painting
CHEN, WENYI, Mural Painting
DAI, SHIHE, Oil Painting
DING, YILIN, Oil Painting
FAN, DI'AN, Humanities
GAO, RONGSHENG, Printmaking
HONG, PENGSHENG, Humanities
HU, JIANCHENG, Oil Painting
HU, WEI, Chinese Painting
HU, YUE, Architecture
HUANG, WEI, Architecture
LI, LINZUO, Mural Painting
LU, SHENGZHONG, Oil Painting
LU, PINJING, Architecture
LUO, SHIPING, Humanities
MA, LU, Oil Painting
QIU, ZHENZHONG, Chinese Painting
SU, XINPING, Printmaking
SUI, JIANGUO, Sculpture
SUN, JIABO, Sculpture
SUN, JINGBO, Mural Painting
TAN, PING, Design
TANG, YONGLI, Chinese Painting
TIAN, LIMING, Chinese Painting
WANG, MIN, Design
WANG, YONG, Chinese Painting
WEN, GUOZHANG, First-year Foundation Program
WU, CHANGJIANG, Printmaking
YIN, JINAN, Art History
ZHOU, ZHIYU, Design

CENTRAL CHINA NORMAL UNIVERSITY (HUAZHONG NORMAL UNIVERSITY)

152 Luoyu Rd, Wuhan 430079, Hubei
Telephone: (27) 67868133
E-mail: wwww@ccnu.edu.cn
Internet: www.ccnu.edu.cn
Founded 1903

Min. of Education control
Academic year: September to July
Pres.: MA MING
Vice-Pres: HUANG YONGLING, LE GUANGZHOU, LI ZONGKAI, PANG XIANGNONG, YANG ZHENGNONG
Librarian: ZUO BIN
Number of teachers: 1,200
Number of students: 20,000
Publications: *Foreign Literature Studies* (6 a year), *Journal of Central China Normal University* (humanities and social science, 6 a year), *Journal of Central China Normal University* (natural sciences, 6 a year)

DEANS

College of Networking Academy: ZHANG YOULIANG
Department of Computer Science: TAN LIANSHENG
Department of Information Management: WANG XUEDONG
Department of Information Technology: ZHANG GUOPING
Department of Sociology: JIANG LIHUA
School of Chemistry: YANG GUANGFU
School of City and Environmental Science: ZENG JUXIN
School of Economics: CAO YANG
School of Foreign Language and Literature: ZHANG WEIYOU
School of History and Culture: WANG YUDE
School of Life Science: CHEN QICAI
School of Literature: LI XIANGNONG
School of Management: WU JINSHENG
School of Mathematics and Statistics: DENG YINBIN
School of Music: TIAN XIAOBAO
School of Physics and Technology: WANG ENKE
School of Political Science and Law: LIN JIAN

PROFESSORS

BAI, GUOZHONG, Information Management
CAI, JINQUAN, History and Culture
CAI, XU, Physics and Technology
CAO, YANG, Economics
CHEN, CHUANLI, Mathematics and Statistics
CHEN, GUOSHENG, Life Science
CHEN, HONGWEI, Foreign Language and Literature
CHEN, JIANXIAN, Literature
CHEN, JISHENG, Physics and Technology
CHEN, QICAI, Life Science
CHEN, QUN, Mathematics and Statistics
CHEN, YIN'E, Sociology
CHEN, YOULIN, Foreign Language and Literature
CHU, ZEXIANG, Literature
DAI, JIANYE, Literature
DENG, HONGGUANG, History and Culture
DENG, XIANRUI, City and Environmental Science
DENG, YINBIN, Mathematics and Statistics
DING, MINGWU, Chemistry
DING, YIHUA, History and Culture
FENG, GANG, Computer Science
FU, HUIHUA, Life Science
GAO, HUAPING, Literature
GONG, SHENGSHENG, City and Environmental Science
GU, YONGXING, History and Culture
GU, ZHIHUA, History and Culture
GUO, JUN, Foreign Language and Literature
GUO, TUOYING, Mathematics and Statistics
HAN, KEFANG, Physics and Technology
HAN, XUNGUO, Music
HE, BAIGEN, City and Environmental Science
HE, HONGWU, Chemistry
HE, JIANMING, History and Culture
HE, SUI, Mathematics and Statistics
HE, TINGTING, Computer Science
HE, XUEFENG, Sociology
HONG, HUAZHU, Life Science
HOU, FUDE, Physics and Technology

HU, JINZHU, Computer Science
HU, XIANGMING, Physics and Technology
HU, YAMIN, Literature
HU, ZONGQIU, Chemistry
HUA, XIANFA, Foreign Language and Literature
HUANG, HUAWEN, History and Culture
HUANG, QINGYANG, Life Science
HUANG, WANHUI, Computer Science
HUANG, XIAOQUN, Foreign Language and Literature
HUANG, XINTANG, Physics and Technology
HUANG, YONGLIN, Literature
HUANG, ZHENGBO, History and Culture
HUANG, ZHONGLIAN, Foreign Language and Literature
JIA, YA, Physics and Technology
JIA, ZHIJIE, Physics and Technology
JIN, BOXIN, City and Environmental Science
JIN, CONG, Computer Science
JING, CAIRUI, City and Environmental Science
LI, BANGJI, Computer Science
LI, GAOXIANG, Physics and Technology
LI, JIALIN, Physics and Technology
LI, JIAQING, City and Environmental Science
LI, JIARONG, Physics and Technology
LI, QIRONG, History and Culture
LI, TAOSHENG, Mathematics and Statistics
LI, WENXIN, Life Science
LI, XIANGNONG, Literature
LI, XIAOYAN, Computer Science
LI, XINGRUN, Life Science
LI, XUEBAO, Life Science
LI, YADAN, Foreign Language and Literature
LI, ZHIYANG, Physics and Technology
LI, ZHONGHUA, Chemistry
LIANG, MIAOYUAN, Computer Science
LIAO, MEIZHEN, Foreign Language and Literature
LIAO, ZHANRU, Chemistry
LIN, DELI, Life Science
LIU, ANHAI, Literature
LIU, FENG, Physics and Technology
LIU, GUSHENG, History and Culture
LIU, LIANSHOU, Physics and Technology
LIU, SHAOJUN, History and Culture
LIU, SHENGHUA, Chemistry
LIU, SHENGJIA, City and Environmental Science
LIU, SHENGXIANG, Life Science
LIU, SHOUHUA, Literature
LIU, WEI, History and Culture
LIU, WU, Physics and Technology
LIU, XIANLONG, Mathematics and Statistics
LIU, YONGHONG, Foreign Language and Literature
LIU, ZHAOJIE, Chemistry
LOU, CEQUN, Information Management
LU, GUANGHAN, Chemistry
LU, WUQIANG, City and Environmental Science
LUO, BANGCHENG, Mathematics and Statistics
LUO, DEHUI, History and Culture
MA, CHENGWU, Literature
MA, MIN, History and Culture
MENG, DAZHONG, Physics and Technology
MOU, JIMEI, Physics and Technology
NIE, ZHENDAO, Foreign Language and Literature
PENG, CHANGZHENG, History and Culture
PENG, JIANXIN, Life Science
PENG, NANSHENG, History and Culture
QIU, BAOSHENG, Life Science
QIU, ZIHUA, Literature
SHAO, QINGYU, City and Environmental Science
SHEN, JIE, Sociology
SHEN, ZHENGYU, Literature
SU, BAIMEI, Foreign Language and Literature
SUN, WENXIAN, Literature
TAN, BANGHE, Literature
TAN, CHUANFENG, City and Environmental Science
TAN, HONG, Mathematics and Statistics
TAN, LIANSHENG, Computer Science

TANG, CHENGCHUN, Physics and Technology
TAO, JIAYUAN, City and Environmental Science
TIAN, SONGQING, City and Environmental Science
WAN, JIAN, Chemistry
WANG, ENKE, Physics and Technology
WANG, GUOSHENG, Literature
WANG, GUOXIU, Life Science
WANG, LIHUA, Sociology
WANG, MANJUN, Literature
WANG, QINGSHENG, Literature
WANG, QIZHOU, Literature
WANG, WEIJUN, Information Management
WANG, XIANPEI, Literature
WANG, XUEDONG, Information Management
WANG, YANGANG, Chemistry
WANG, YOUNIAN, Literature
WANG, YUDE, History and Culture
WANG, YUFENG, Life Science
WANG, ZELONG, Literature
WEI, CHANGHUA, Computer Science
WU, GANG, Life Science
WU, QI, History and Culture
WU, YI, Sociology
WU, YUANFANG, Physics and Technology
XIA, MINGYUAN, Mathematics and Statistics
XIA, XIAOBIN, Life Science
XIANG, JIQUAN, Sociology
XIAO, DEBAO, Computer Science
XIE, MINYU, Mathematics and Statistics
XIN, FUYI, Literature
XIN, LAISHUN, History and Culture
XIONG, TIEJI, History and Culture
XIU, DIAO, Literature
XU, QIAOLI, City and Environmental Science
XU, SENLIN, Mathematics and Statistics
XU, ZUHUA, Literature
YAN, CHANGHONG, History and Culture
YAN, GUOZHENG, Mathematics and Statistics
YAN, SHAOXIANG, History and Culture
YANG, BAOLIANG, City and Environmental Science
YANG, CHANG, History and Culture
YANG, CHUNBIN, Physics and Technology
YANG, GUANGFU, Chemistry
YANG, SHAO, Life Science
YANG, SHUANGHUA, Computer Science
YANG, XU, Life Science
YAO, WEIJUN, History and Culture
YI, HONGGEN, Foreign Language and Literature
YOU, LIRONG, Sociology
YU, GUANGMING, City and Environmental Science
YU, ZEHUA, Life Science
ZENG, JUXIN, City and Environmental Science
ZENG, LIANMAO, City and Environmental Science
ZENG, QINGQIANG, Foreign Language and Literature
ZHAN, CHANGGUO, Chemistry
ZHAN, ZHENGKUN, Chemistry
ZHANG, AIDONG, Chemistry
ZHANG, CHANGNIAN, Music
ZHANG, FAN, Information Management
ZHANG, GUOPING, Physics and Technology
ZHANG, KAIQUAN, History and Culture
ZHANG, LIDE, Physics and Technology
ZHANG, LONGSHENG, Foreign Language and Literature
ZHANG, QUANMING, History and Culture
ZHANG, SANXI, Literature
ZHANG, SHAOYAN, Economics
ZHANG, WEIYOU, Foreign Language and Literature
ZHANG, YINGLIN, Foreign Language and Literature
ZHANG, YONGJIAN, Literature
ZHANG, YUNENG, Literature
ZHANG, ZHENGMING, History and Culture
ZHAO, YIJUN, Life Science
ZHENG, QUAN, Mathematics and Statistics
ZHENG, XIAOPING, Physics and Technology
ZHOU, DAICUI, Physics and Technology

ZHOU, GUOLIN, History and Culture
ZHOU, JIYUAN, Life Science
ZHOU, XIAOMING, Literature
ZHOU, ZHENGRONG, Mathematics and Statistics
ZHOU, ZONGKUI, Sociology
ZHU, CHANGJIANG, Mathematics and Statistics
ZHU, CHUANFANG, Chemistry
ZHU, XINDE, Chemistry
ZHU, YING, History and Culture
ZOU, SHANGHUI, City and Environmental Science
ZUO, BIN, Sociology

CENTRAL CONSERVATORY OF MUSIC

43 Bao Jia St, Beijing 100031
Telephone: (10) 66425598
Fax: (10) 66413138
E-mail: ccom@ccom.edu.cn
Internet: www.ccom.edu.cn

Founded 1950
Min.of Culture control
Academic year: September to July
Pres.: WANG CIZHAO
Vice-Pres: LI XU, LIU KANGHUA, XU CHANG-JUN, ZHOU HAIHONG
Head of Graduate Dept: WANG CIZHAO
Librarian: ZHOU HAIHONG

Number of teachers: 278
Number of students: 1,665

Publication: *Haihong Journal of the Central Conservatory of Music* (4 a year)

DEANS

Composition Department: TANG JIANPING
Conducting Department: YU FENG
General Education Department: LIANG JING
Music Education Department: GAO JIANJIN
Musicology Department: ZHANG BOYU
Orchestral Instruments Department: LIU PEIYAN
Piano Department: YANG MING
Traditional Instruments Department: ZHAO HANYANG
Voice and Opera Department: LIU DONG

PROFESSORS

BIAN, MENG, Piano
CAI, ZHOANGDE, Musicology
CHEN, BIGANG, Piano
CHEN, DANBU, Composition
CHEN, ZIMIN, Musicology
CHENG, DA, Voice and Opera
DU, MINGXIN, Composition
DU, TAIHANG, Piano
DUAN, PINGTAI, Composition
GAO, JIANJIN, Music Education
GUI, XILI, Traditional Instruments
GUO, SHUZHEN, Voice and Opera
GUO, WENJING, Composition
HAN, XIAOMING, Orchestral Instruments
HAN, ZHIHONG, Piano
HAN, ZHONGJIE, Conducting
HE, RONG, Orchestral Instruments
HEI, HAITAO, Voice and Opera
HU, SHIXI, Voice and Opera
HU, ZHIHOU, Traditional Instruments
HUANG, HE, Traditional Instruments
HUANG, PEIYING, Piano
HUANG, XIAOHE, Musicology
LI, GUANGHUA, Traditional Instruments
LI, HENG, Traditional Instruments
LI, JITI, Composition
LI, MENG, Traditional Instruments
LI, QIFENG, Piano
LI, XIANGTING, Traditional Instruments
LI, XINCHANG, Voice and Opera
LI, YINGHUA, Musicology
LI, ZHENGUI, Traditional Instruments
LIANG, DANA, Orchestral Instruments
LIANG, NING, Voice and Opera

LIN, SHICHENG, Traditional Instruments
LIN, YAXIONG, Musicology
LIU, CHANGFU, Traditional Instruments
LIU, DONG, Voice and Opera
LIU, LIN, Composition
LIU, PEIYAN, Orchestral Instruments
LIU, YUAN, Composition
LUO, ZHONGRONG, Composition
MA, HONGHAI, Voice and Opera
PAN, BIXIN, Musicology
PAN, CHUN, Piano
PENG, KANGLIANG, Voice and Opera
PINI, YAXUO, Voice and Opera
SHENG, LIHONG, Composition
SONG, JIN, Musicology
TAI, ER, Piano
TANG, JIANPING, Composition
TIAN, LIANTAO, Musicology
WANG, CIZHAO, Musicology
WANG, SHUHE, Musicology
WANG, XIANLIN, Voice and Opera
WANG, XIUFENG, Voice and Opera
WANG, YAOLING, Orchestral Instruments
WU, SHIKAI, Composition
WU, ZHUQIANG, Composition
XIE, HUAZHEN, Piano
XU, CHANGJUN, Composition
XU, XIN, Conducting
YANG, HONGNIAN, Conducting
YANG, JUN, Piano
YANG, MING, Piano
YAO, HENGLU, Composition
YE, XIAOGANG, Composition
YU, FENG, Conducting
YU, RUNYANG, Musicology
YU, SUXIAN, Composition
YU, ZHIGANG, Musicology
YUAN, JINGFANG, Musicology
ZHANG, BOYU, Musicology
ZHANG, JIANYI, Voice and Opera
ZHANG, LIPING, Voice and Opera
ZHANG, QIAN, Musicology
ZHANG, SHAO, Traditional Instruments
ZHAO, BIXUAN, Voice and Opera
ZHAO, DENGYING, Voice and Opera
ZHAO, HANYANG, Traditional Instruments
ZHAO, RUILIN, Orchestral Instruments
ZHENG, XIAOYING, Conducting
ZHENG, ZHUXIANG, Musicology
ZHONG, ZILIN, Musicology
ZHOU, GUANGREN, Piano
ZHOU, HAIHONG, Musicology
ZHOU, QINGQING, Musicology
ZHU, DUN, Orchestral Instruments
ZHU, YIBING, Orchestral Instruments

CENTRAL UNIVERSITY FOR NATIONALITIES

27 Nan Da Rd, Zhong Guan Village, Haidian District, Beijing 100081
Telephone: (10) 68932544
Fax: (10) 68932544
E-mail: cunofficexz@sina.com
Internet: www.cun.edu.cn

Founded 1951
State Ethnic Affairs Commission control
Academic year: September to July
Pres.: RONG SHIXIANG
Vice-Pres: AI'BI BULA, CHEN LI, GUO WEIPING, HUANG FENGXIAN, JIN YASHENG, REN ZHONGXIA, YAN YUMING
Head of Graduate Dept: CHEN LI
Librarian: LI DELONG

Number of teachers: 700
Number of students: 13,000

Publications: *Journal of The Central University for Nationalities* (natural sciences, 4 a year), *Journal of The Central University for Nationalities* (philosophy and social sciences, 6 a year)

DEANS

School of Arts: YIN HUILI

School of Education: WANG JUN
School of Ethnology and Sociology: YANG SHENGMIN
School of Foreign Language: HE KEYONG
School of Law: ZHU JING'AN
School of Literature, Journalism and Communication: BAI WEI
School of Management: LI JUNQING
School of Music: MENG XINYANG
College of Dance: SU ZIHONG
College of Economics: LIU YONGJI
College of Life and Environment Science: FENG JINZHAO
College of National Minorities: LI JINFANG
College of Science and Engineering: FENG JINZHAO
Department of History: LI HONGBIN
Department of Philosophy and Religion: GONG YUKUAN
Department of Physics: WEI XIAOKANG
Preparatory Department: SONG TAICHENG
Research Institute of Tibet: BANBAN DUOJIE

PROFESSORS

BAI, RUNSHENG, Literature, Journalism and Communication
BAI, WEI, Literature, Journalism and Communication
BAI, YINTAI, National Minority Study
BANBAN, DUOJIE, Tibetan Studies
BI, MUXUN, Literature, Journalism and Communication
BU, ZHONGJIAN, Philosophy and Religion
CHEN, CHANGPING, Ethnology and Sociology
CHEN, FANGYING, Science and Engineering
CHEN, JIANJIAN, Tibetan Studies
CHEN, NAN, History
CUI, GUANZHI, Science and Engineering
DALI, ZHABU, History
DING, HONG, Ethnology and Sociology
DING, SHIQING, National Minority Study
FENG, JINZHAO, Life and Environment Science
FENG, JINZHAO, Science and Engineering
FU, CHENGZHOU, Literature, Journalism and Communication
FU, YIXIN, Education
GEN, SHIMIN, National Minority Study
GENG, YUFANG, Tibetan Studies
GESANG, DUNZHU, Tibetan Studies
GESANG, JUMIAN, Tibetan Studies
GONG, YUKUAN, Philosophy and Religion
HA, JINGXIONG, Education
HAMITI, TIEMUER, National Minority Study
HASHI, E'ERDUN, National Minority Study
HE, JINRUI, Philosophy and Religion
HE, KEYONG, Foreign Languages
HE, QIMIN, Philosophy and Religion
HE, WEI, Science and Engineering
HU, SHAOHUA, History
HU, ZHENHUA, National Minority Study
HUANG, KAI, Science and Engineering
HUOXIGE, TAOKETAO, National Minority Study
JI, YONGHAI, National Minority Study
JIAO, YUGUO, Life and Environment Science
JIN, RIGUANG, Music
LI, BINQUAN, Tibetan Studies
LI, GUIZHI, History
LI, HONGBIN, History
LI, JINFANG, National Minority Study
LI, JUNQING, Management
LI, KUI, Arts
LI, XINCHANG, Music
LI, YAN, National Minority Study
LI, YAN, Law
LIN, JING, Music
LIU, BINGJIANG, Arts
LIU, JIANMING, Literature, Journalism and Communication
LIU, JINZHEN, Science and Engineering
LIU, YONGJI, Economics
LIU, YONGZHOU, Literature, Journalism and Communication
LU, SHAO'EN, Music
MEN, DUHU, National Minority Study

MENG, XINYANG, Music
PIAO, CHANGTIAN, Music
SHANG, YANBIN, History
SHAO, XIANSHU, Ethnology and Sociology
SHEN, JIA, Music
SONG, RUBU, National Minority Study
SU, ZIHONG, Dance
TAO, LIPAN, Literature, Journalism and Communication
TENG, XING, Education
WANG, JUN, Education
WANG, RAO, Tibetan Studies
WANG, TIANJIN, Economics
WANG, YUANXIN, National Minority Study
WANG, ZHONGHAN, History
WANGMEN, TIEGA, National Minority Study
WEI, FENGRONG, Science and Engineering
WU, LIJI, National Minority Study
XIAO, XIURONG, Management
XING, FUCHON, Science and Engineering
XING, LI, Literature, Journalism and Communication
XU, LUYA, Foreign Languages
XU, SHOUCHUN, Science and Engineering
XU, WANBANG, Ethnology and Sociology
XU, YONGZHI, History
XU, YONGZHI, Management
YANG, CONG, Economics
YANG, ROOMING, Life and Environment Science
YANG, SHENGMIN, Ethnology and Sociology
YAO, NIANCI, History
YIN, HUILI, Arts
YU, KESEN, Literature, Journalism and Communication
YU, QIMING, Philosophy and Religion
ZENG, SHIQI, National Minority Study
ZHANG, GONGJIN, National Minority Study
ZHANG, GUANGHUA, Science and Engineering
ZHAO, KANG, Tibetan Studies
ZHAO, SHILIN, Philosophy and Religion
ZHOU, LI, Management
ZHOU, RUNNIAN, Tibetan Studies
ZHU, JING'AN, Law
ZHU, ZHENGYUAN, Science and Engineering

CENTRAL SOUTH UNIVERSITY

Chang Sha 410083, Hunan
Telephone: (731) 8879225
Fax: (731) 8830308
E-mail: csuweb@mail.csu.edu.cn
Internet: www.csu.edu.cn

Founded 1952
Academic year: September to July

Pres.: HUANG BOYUN
Vice-Pres: CHEN QIYUAN, CHEN ZHIYA, HU TIEHUI, LI GUIYUAN, QIU GUANZHOU
Head of Graduate Dept: LIU YILUN
Librarian: FANG ZHENG

Publications: *International Chinese Nursing Journal* (4 a year), *Journal of Central South University* (6 a year), *Journal of Central South University* (medical sciences, 6 a year), *Journal of Central South University* (social sciences, 6 a year), *Transactions of Nonferrous Metals Society of China* (6 a year)

DEANS

School of Basic Medical Sciences: WEN JIFANG
School of Business: CHEN XIAOHONG
School of Chemistry and Chemical Engineering: HUANG KELONG
School of Civil Engineering and Architecture: YU ZHIWU
School of Energy and Power Engineering: ZHOU DIAOMIN
School of Fine Arts: DAI DUAN
School of Foreign Languages: TU GUOYUAN
School of Geoscience and Environmental Engineering: DAI TAGEN
School of Info-Physics and Geomatics Engineering: TANG JINGTIAN

School of Information Science and Engineering: GUI WEIHUA
School of Law: QI DUOJUN
School of Literature: OU YANG YOUQUAN
School of Materials Science and Engineering: YI DANQING
School of Mathematical Sciences and Computing Technology: ZOU JIEZHONG
School of Mechanical and Electrical Engineering: WU YUNXIN
School of Medical Technology and Information: GUO QULIAN
School of Metallurgic Science and Engineering: LI JIE
School of Nursing: HE GUOPING
School of Pharmaceutical Sciences: LI YUANJIAN
School of Physics, Sciences and Technology: YANG BINGCHU
School of Politics and Public Administration: LI JIANHUA
School of Public Health: XIAO SHUIYUAN
School of Resources Processing and Bioengineering: HU YUEHUA
School of Resources and Safety Engineering: LI XIBING
School of Stomatology: JIAN XINCHUN
School of Traffic and Transportation Engineering: SHI FENG

PROFESSORS

CAI, HONGWEI, Medical Technology and Information
CAI, ZIXING, Information Science and Engineering
CAO, JIAN, Physics, Sciences and Technology
CAO, XING, Business
CHANG, YETIAN, Medical Technology and Information
CHEN, FANGPING, Medical Technology and Information
CHEN, FENG, Materials Science and Engineering
CHEN, HAIBO, Mathematical Sciences and Computing Technology
CHEN, HUANXIN, Civil Engineering and Architecture
CHEN, HUANXIN, Energy and Power Engineering
CHEN, JIAN'ER, Information Science and Engineering
CHEN, KANGHUA, Powder Metallurgy
CHEN, LIQUAN, Chemistry and Chemical Engineering
CHEN, QIYUAN, Chemistry and Chemical Engineering
CHEN, SHIZHU, Materials Science and Engineering
CHEN, SONGQIAO, Information Science and Engineering
CHEN, XIAOHONG, Business
CHEN, XIAOQING, Chemistry and Chemical Engineering
CHEN, XIAOSONG, Mathematical Sciences and Computing Technology
CHEN, XIUFANG, Civil Engineering and Architecture
CHEN, YIZHUANG, Politics and Public Administration
CHEN, YUEWU, Foreign Languages
CHEN, YUXIANG, Bioscience and Technology
CHEN, ZHENXING, Chemistry and Chemical Engineering
CHEN, ZHIGANG, Information Science and Engineering
CHEN, ZHONGWEN, Foreign Languages
DAI, BINXIANG, Mathematical Sciences and Computing Technology
DAI, DUAN, Fine Arts
DAI, GONGLIAN, Civil Engineering and Architecture
DENG, CHAO, Business
DENG, DEHUA, Civil Engineering and Architecture
DENG, FEIYAOI, Chemistry and Chemical Engineering

DENG, HANWU, Pharmaceutical Sciences
DENG, RUIJIAO, Nursing
DENG, TIANSHENG, Business
DU, YONG, Powder Metallurgy
FAN, XIANGRU, Business
FAN, XIANLONG, Foreign Languages
FAN, XIAOHUI, Resources Processing and Bioengineering
FAN, XIAOPING, Information Science and Engineering
FANG, LIGANG, Civil Engineering and Architecture
FANG, PING, Medical Technology and Information
FANG, YUNXIANG, Pharmaceutical Sciences
FANG, ZHENG, Chemistry and Chemical Engineering
FENG, QIMING, Resources Processing and Bioengineering
FU, HELIN, Civil Engineering and Architecture
GAN, SIQING, Mathematical Sciences and Computing Technology
GAN, WEIPING, Materials Science and Engineering
GAO, YANG, Business
GONG, FAN, Chemistry and Chemical Engineering
GONG, YANPING, Business
GU, JINGHUA, Resources Processing and Bioengineering
GU, YINGYING, Chemistry and Chemical Engineering
GUAN, LUXIONG, Chemistry and Chemical Engineering
GUI, WEIHUA, Information Science and Engineering
GUO, GUANGHUA, Physics, Sciences and Technology
GUO, QULIAN, Medical Technology and Information
GUO, SHAOHUA, Civil Engineering and Architecture
GUO, XIANGRONG, Civil Engineering and Architecture
HAN, JINGQUAN, Foreign Languages
HAN, QINGLAN, Business
HAN, XULI, Information Science and Engineering
HAN, XULI, Mathematical Sciences and Computing Technology
HE, BOQUAN, Resources Processing and Bioengineering
HE, GUOPING, Nursing
HE, HONGBO, Physics, Sciences and Technology
HE, HONGQU, Business
HE, JISHAN, Business
HE, XUEWEI, Literature
HE, YUNBO, Foreign Languages
HOU, MANLING, Chemistry and Chemical Engineering
HOU, ZHENTING, Mathematical Sciences and Computing Technology
HU, HUIPING, Chemistry and Chemical Engineering
HU, HUOSHENG, Information Science and Engineering
HU, KAI, Politics and Public Administration
HU, WEIXIN, Bioscience and Technology
HU, YUEHUA, Resources Processing and Bioengineering
HU, ZHENHUA, Business
HUANG, BOYUN, Materials Science and Engineering
HUANG, FANGLIN, Civil Engineering and Architecture
HUANG, JIAN, Chemistry and Chemical Engineering
HUANG, JIANBO, Business
HUANG, JIANREN, Foreign Languages
HUANG, KELONG, Chemistry and Chemical Engineering
HUANG, LANFANG, Chemistry and Chemical Engineering

HUANG, PEIYUN, Materials Science and Engineering
HUANG, PEIYUN, Powder Metallurgy
HUANG, QIZHONG, Powder Metallurgy
HUANG, SHENGSHENG, Resources Processing and Bioengineering
HUANG, YANPING, Politics and Public Administration
HUANG, YONG'AN, Foreign Languages
HUANG, ZHUCHENG, Resources Processing and Bioengineering
HUO, GUOJING, Civil Engineering and Architecture
HUO, YAOHUI, Powder Metallurgy
JIA, WEIJIA, Information Science and Engineering
JIAN, XINCHUN, Stomatology
JIANG, DONGJIU, Nursing
JIANG, DONGMEI, Nursing
JIANG, JINZHI, Chemistry and Chemical Engineering
JIANG, SHAOJIAN, Energy and Power Engineering
JIANG, TAO, Resources Processing and Bioengineering
JIANG, XINHUA, Information Science and Engineering
JIANG, YIMIN, Physics, Sciences and Technology
JIANG, YUREN, Chemistry and Chemical Engineering
JIN, ZHANPENG, Materials Science and Engineering
LAN, XIAOJUN, Medical Technology and Information
LENG, WUMING, Civil Engineering and Architecture
LI, BAIQING, Foreign Languages
LI, DENGQING, Medical Technology and Information
LI, HE, Energy and Power Engineering
LI, HONGJIAN, Physics, Sciences and Technology
LI, HUANDE, Pharmaceutical Sciences
LI, JIANHUA, Politics and Public Administration
LI, JIE, Chemistry and Chemical Engineering
LI, JUNPING, Mathematical Sciences and Computing Technology
LI, LIANG, Civil Engineering and Architecture
LI, LIPING, Business
LI, MINGSHENG, Business
LI, SONGREN, Resources Processing and Bioengineering
LI, XIAOBIN, Energy and Power Engineering
LI, XIAORU, Chemistry and Chemical Engineering
LI, XIBIN, Powder Metallurgy
LI, XUE, Mathematical Sciences and Computing Technology
LI, YANGCHENG, Mathematical Sciences and Computing Technology
LI, YANGSHENG, Fine Arts
LI, YANLIN, Foreign Languages
LI, YIBING, Information Science and Engineering
LI, YIBING, Physics, Sciences and Technology
LI, YIMIN, Powder Metallurgy
LI, YIZHI, Business
LI, YUANGAO, Chemistry and Chemical Engineering
LI, YUANJIAN, Pharmaceutical Sciences
LI, ZIRU, Business
LIANG, HONG, Chemistry and Chemical Engineering
LIANG, LAIYIN, Business
LIANG, XIMING, Information Science and Engineering
LIANG, YIZENG, Chemistry and Chemical Engineering
LIAO, SHENGMING, Civil Engineering and Architecture
LIAO, SHENGMING, Energy and Power Engineering
LIU, AIDONG, Business

LIU, BAOCHEN, Civil Engineering and Architecture
LIU, CHANGQING, Chemistry and Chemical Engineering
LIU, DONGRONG, Business
LIU, GUOPING, Information Science and Engineering
LIU, JIAJIA, Chemistry and Chemical Engineering
LIU, JIANSHE, Resources Processing and Bioengineering
LIU, KAIYU, Chemistry and Chemical Engineering
LIU, LIHANG, Politics and Public Administration
LIU, LIYING, Pharmaceutical Sciences
LIU, MINGJING, Foreign Languages
LIU, QINGTAN, Civil Engineering and Architecture
LIU, SHIJUN, Chemistry and Chemical Engineering
LIU, SUQIN, Chemistry and Chemical Engineering
LIU, WEIJUN, Mathematical Sciences and Computing Technology
LIU, XIAOCHUN, Medical Technology and Information
LIU, XINXING, Resources Processing and Bioengineering
LIU, XIONGFEI, Physics, Sciences and Technology
LIU, YANPING, Bioscience and Technology
LIU, YAZHENG, Business
LIU, YEXIANG, Energy and Power Engineering
LIU, YIRONG, Mathematical Sciences and Computing Technology
LIU, YONGHE, Medical Technology and Information
LIU, YONGMEI, Business
LIU, YOUNIAN, Chemistry and Chemical Engineering
LIU, ZAIMING, Mathematical Sciences and Computing Technology
LIU, ZEMIN, Literature
LIU, ZHIYI, Materials Science and Engineering
LIU, ZHUMING, Materials Science and Engineering
LUO, AIJING, Medical Technology and Information
LUO, AN, Information Science and Engineering
LUO, DAYONG, Information Science and Engineering
LUO, JIAOWAN, Mathematical Sciences and Computing Technology
LUO, WENDONG, Physics, Sciences and Technology
LUO, XIAOLING, Business
LUO, XINXING, Business
LUO, XUEGANG, Basic Medical Sciences
LUO, YIMING, Chemistry and Chemical Engineering
LUO, ZIQIANG, Basic Medical Sciences
LU, HAIBO, Powder Metallurgy
LU, XICHEN, Politics and Public Administration
LU, YAOHUAI, Politics and Public Administration
MA, CHENGYIN, Chemistry and Chemical Engineering
MAN, RUILIN, Chemistry and Chemical Engineering
MAO, XUANGUO, Literature
MEI, MEIZHI, Energy and Power Engineering
MENG, ZE, Foreign Languages
NIU, YINJIAN, Resources Processing and Bioengineering
OU YANG, YOUQUAN, Literature
PAN, QINGLIN, Materials Science and Engineering
PANG, CHUNYAO, Chemistry and Chemical Engineering
PEN, JINDING, Foreign Languages
PENG, JIEYING, Stomatology

PENG, LIMIN, Civil Engineering and Architecture
PENG, PINGYI, Politics and Public Administration
PENG, XIAOQI, Energy and Power Engineering
PENG, XIAOQI, Physics, Sciences and Technology
PENG, YUELIN, Mathematical Sciences and Computing Technology
QIAN, DONG, Chemistry and Chemical Engineering
QIN, XIAOQUN, Basic Medical Sciences
QIU, KEQIANG, Chemistry and Chemical Engineering
QIU, YUNREN, Chemistry and Chemical Engineering
QU, LONG, Chemistry and Chemical Engineering
QU, XUANHUI, Powder Metallurgy
RAO, QIUHUA, Civil Engineering and Architecture
RAO, YUELEI, Business
REN, FENGLIAN, Chemistry and Chemical Engineering
REN, JIFAN, Literature
RUAN, JIANMING, Powder Metallurgy
SHE, XIEBIN, Foreign Languages
SHEN, CHAOHONG, Business
SHEN, MEILAN, Mathematical Sciences and Computing Technology
SHEN, QUNTAI, Information Science and Engineering
SHI, RONGHUA, Information Science and Engineering
SHI, ZHANGMING, Energy and Power Engineering
SHU, WANGEN, Chemistry and Chemical Engineering
SI, SHIHUI, Chemistry and Chemical Engineering
SONG, HUIPING, Bioscience and Technology
SU, YUCHANG, Materials Science and Engineering
SUN, XIANGMING, Fine Arts
SUN, ZHENQIU, Mathematical Sciences and Computing Technology
TAN, DAREN, Medical Technology and Information
TAN, GUANXZHENG, Information Science and Engineering
TAN, MENGQUN, Basic Medical Sciences
TAN, XIPEI, Politics and Public Administration
TAN, YUNJIE, Foreign Languages
TANG, HONG'E, Civil Engineering and Architecture
TANG, RUIREN, Chemistry and Chemical Engineering
TANG, XIANHUA, Mathematical Sciences and Computing Technology
TANG, YOUGEN, Chemistry and Chemical Engineering
TANG, ZHANGUI, Stomatology
TAO, XINLU, Nursing
TU, GUOYUAN, Foreign Languages
TU, LING, Stomatology
WAN, ZHONG, Mathematical Sciences and Computing Technology
WANG, DIANZUO, Resources Processing and Bioengineering
WANG, GUOSHUN, Business
WANG, HANQING, Energy and Power Engineering
WANG, HUI, Chemistry and Chemical Engineering
WANG, JIABAO, Mathematical Sciences and Computing Technology
WANG, JIANQIANG, Business
WANG, JIANXIU, Chemistry and Chemical Engineering
WANG, JIGUI, Medical Technology and Information
WANG, LINGSEN, Powder Metallurgy
WANG, MENGJUN, Civil Engineering and Architecture

WANG, MING'AN, Medical Technology and Information

WANG, MINGMING, Nursing

WANG, MINGPU, Materials Science and Engineering

WANG, SHIPING, Basic Medical Sciences

WANG, SHUHUA, Resources Processing and Bioengineering

WANG, XIAOCHUN, Medical Technology and Information

WANG, XINGHUA, Civil Engineering and Architecture

WANG, YAN, Chemistry and Chemical Engineering

WANG, YIJUN, Information Science and Engineering

WANG, YONGHE, Civil Engineering and Architecture

WANG, YUECHUAN, Literature

WANG, ZHANGHUA, Literature

WANG, ZHIFA, Materials Science and Engineering

WANG, ZHIZHONG, Mathematical Sciences and Computing Technology

WEI, RENYONG, Information Science and Engineering

WEN, JIFANG, Basic Medical Sciences

WEN, YUSONG, Civil Engineering and Architecture

WU, JINMING, Business

WU, KUN, Mathematical Sciences and Computing Technology

WU, LIANGGANG, Business

WU, LIXIANG, Basic Medical Sciences

WU, XIANCHENG, Politics and Public Administration

XIA, CHANGQING, Materials Science and Engineering

XIA, JIAHUI, Bioscience and Technology

XIA, JINLAN, Resources Processing and Bioengineering

XIANG, SHU, Mathematical Sciences and Computing Technology

XIAO, LIMING, Foreign Languages

XIAO, TIEJIAN, Politics and Public Administration

XIAO, XIANZHONG, Basic Medical Sciences

XIAO, XIAODAN, Medical Technology and Information

XIAO, XU, Business

XIAO, ZEQIANG, Energy and Power Engineering

XIE, RUHE, Energy and Power Engineering

XIE, XIAOLI, Stomatology

XIE, YOUJUN, Civil Engineering and Architecture

XIONG, LUMAO, Politics and Public Administration

XIONG, XIANG, Powder Metallurgy

XIONG, YAN, Pharmaceutical Sciences

XU, HUI, Physics, Sciences and Technology

XU, JICHENG, Materials Science and Engineering

XU, QINGSONG, Mathematical Sciences and Computing Technology

XU, ZHISHENG, Civil Engineering and Architecture

YAN, AIMIN, Business

YAN, ZHEN, Literature

YANG, BINGCHU, Physics, Sciences and Technology

YANG, CHANGXIN, Information Science and Engineering

YANG, CHANGYING, Foreign Languages

YANG, DONGLIANG, Chemistry and Chemical Engineering

YANG, GUOLIN, Civil Engineering and Architecture

YANG, HUAMING, Resources Processing and Bioengineering

YANG, JUNSHENG, Civil Engineering and Architecture

YANG, SHOUKANG, Foreign Languages

YANG, WEIWEN, Business

YANG, XINRONG, Information Science and Engineering

YANG, ZHANHONG, Chemistry and Chemical Engineering

YE, BOLONG, Civil Engineering and Architecture

YE, HONGQI, Chemistry and Chemical Engineering

YE, MEIXIN, Civil Engineering and Architecture

YI, DANQING, Energy and Power Engineering

YI, JIANHONG, Powder Metallurgy

YI, MAOZHONG, Powder Metallurgy

YIN, ZHIMIN, Materials Science and Engineering

YIN, ZHOULAN, Chemistry and Chemical Engineering

YU, DEQUAN, Literature

YU, PING, Basic Medical Sciences

YU, SHENGHUA, Mathematical Sciences and Computing Technology

YU, SHOUYI, Information Science and Engineering

YU, ZHIWU, Civil Engineering and Architecture

YUAN, DONGYUAN, Physics, Sciences and Technology

YUAN, JINGEN, Civil Engineering and Architecture

YUAN, LEPING, Business

YUAN, MINGLIANG, Resources Processing and Bioengineering

YUAN, XIUGUI, Mathematical Sciences and Computing Technology

YUE, YIDING, Business

ZENG, CHANGQIU, Politics and Public Administration

ZENG, DONGMING, Chemistry and Chemical Engineering

ZENG, QINGFU, Basic Medical Sciences

ZENG, QINGREN, Basic Medical Sciences

ZENG, QINGYUAN, Civil Engineering and Architecture

ZENG, SUMIN, Materials Science and Engineering

ZENG, YUHUA, Nursing

ZENG, ZHICHENG, Basic Medical Sciences

ZHANG, CHENGPING, Foreign Languages

ZHANG, CONGYI, Foreign Languages

ZHANG, HANJUN, Mathematical Sciences and Computing Technology

ZHANG, HONGYAN, Mathematical Sciences and Computing Technology

ZHANG, HUAILIANG, Fine Arts

ZHANG, JIANXIANG, Basic Medical Sciences

ZHANG, JIASHENG, Civil Engineering and Architecture

ZHANG, JINGSHENG, Resources Processing and Bioengineering

ZHANG, JINRU, Chemistry and Chemical Engineering

ZHANG, LONGKUAN, Foreign Languages

ZHANG, NAN, Civil Engineering and Architecture

ZHANG, PINGMIN, Chemistry and Chemical Engineering

ZHANG, QINGJIN, Resources Processing and Bioengineering

ZHANG, QISEN, Civil Engineering and Architecture

ZHANG, QUAN, Energy and Power Engineering

ZHANG, SENKUAN, Foreign Languages

ZHANG, SHIMIN, Chemistry and Chemical Engineering

ZHANG, SIQI, Materials Science and Engineering

ZHANG, TAIMING, Chemistry and Chemical Engineering

ZHANG, TAISHAN, Information Science and Engineering

ZHANG, XINGXIAN, Foreign Languages

ZHANG, XINMIN, Materials Science and Engineering

ZHANG, XU, Foreign Languages

ZHANG, YAOJUN, Foreign Languages

ZHAO, WANGDA, Civil Engineering and Architecture

ZHAO, YAOLONG, Information Science and Engineering

ZHENG, ZHIQIAO, Materials Science and Engineering

ZHENG, ZHOUSHUN, Mathematical Sciences and Computing Technology

ZHON, HONG, Chemistry and Chemical Engineering

ZHONG, MEIZUO, Medical Technology and Information

ZHONG, SHI'AN, Chemistry and Chemical Engineering

ZHONG, YOUXUN, Literature

ZHOU, CHAOYANG, Civil Engineering and Architecture

ZHOU, CHUNSHAN, Chemistry and Chemical Engineering

ZHOU, DEBI, Chemistry and Chemical Engineering

ZHOU, DIAOMIN, Energy and Power Engineering

ZHOU, FEIMENG, Chemistry and Chemical Engineering

ZHOU, JICHENG, Physics, Sciences and Technology

ZHOU, KECHAO, Powder Metallurgy

ZHOU, KESHENG, Physics, Sciences and Technology

ZHOU, LIUXI, Foreign Languages

ZHOU, MINGDA, Chemistry and Chemical Engineering

ZHOU, NAIJUN, Energy and Power Engineering

ZHOU, PIN, Energy and Power Engineering

ZHOU, QIAN, Energy and Power Engineering

ZHOU, SHIQIONG, Civil Engineering and Architecture

ZHOU, TAO, Chemistry and Chemical Engineering

ZHU, DEQING, Resources Processing and Bioengineering

ZHU, KAICHENG, Physics, Sciences and Technology

ZHU, NIANQIONG, Nursing

ZHUANG, JIANMING, Resources Processing and Bioengineering

ZOU, BEIJI, Information Science and Engineering

ZOU, JIEZHONG, Mathematical Sciences and Computing Technology

ZUO, TIEYONG, Materials Science and Engineering

CHANG'AN UNIVERSITY

Nan Er Huan Rd, Xian 710064, Shaanxi

Telephone: (29) 82334104

Fax: (29) 85261532

Internet: www.xahu.edu.cn

Founded 2000

Min. of Education control

Academic year: September to July

Pres.: ZHOU XU HONG

Vice-Pres: LI YUN JI, LIU BO QUAN, LIU JIAN CHAO, MA JIAN

Head of Graduate Dept: LU PENG MIN

Librarian: SHA AI MIN

Number of teachers: 3,438

Number of students: 36,383

Publications: *Automobile Racing Driver* (12 a year), *China Journal of Highway and Transport* (4 a year), *Journal of Chang'an University* (architecture and environmental sciences, 6 a year), *Journal of Chang'an University* (natural sciences, 6 a year), *Journal of Chang'an University* (philosophy and social sciences, 6 a year), *Journal of Earth Sciences and Environment* (4 a year), *Journal of Traffic and Transportation Engineering* (4 a year), *Road Machinery and Construction Mechanization* (12 a year)

DEANS

School of Construction Machinery: FENG ZHONG XU
School of Economics and Management: ZHOU GUO GUANG
School of Humanities and Social Science: LIU JI FA
School of Science: FENG JIAN HU
College of Applied Technology: HU XUE MEI
College of Construction Engineering: WANG YI HONG
College of Earth Science and Land Resources Management: LI YONG
College of Environmental Science and Engineering: WANG WEN KE
College of Foreign Languages: LI MIN QUAN
College of Geology Engineering and Geomatics: PENG JIAN MIN
College of Highway Engineering: XU YUE
College of Information Engineering: HE YI QU

PROFESSORS

CHEN, DE CHUAN, Highway Management
CHEN, HONG, Traffic Engineering
CHEN, KUAN MIN, Traffic Engineering
CHEN, ZHI XIN, Geology Engineering and Geomatics
CHEN, ZHONG DA, Highways
DAI, JING LIANG, Highways
DONG, QIAN LI, Economics and Management
DOU, MING JIAN, Highway Disaster Prevention and Cure
DU, DONG JU, Geology Engineering and Geomatics
FAN, WEN, Geology Engineering and Geomatics
FENG, JIAN HU, Science
FENG, ZHEN YU, Science
FENG, ZHONG XU, Construction Machinery
GUAN, WEI XING, Environmental Science and Engineering
GUO, YUAN SHU, Information Engineering
HAN, SEN, Highways
HAO, PEI WEN, Highways
HAO, XIAN WU, Bridges
HE, AN MING, Science
HE, SHUANG HAI, Bridges
HE, YI QU, Information Engineering
HU, DA LIN, Bridges
HU, YONG BIAO, Construction Machinery
HU, YUE, Bridges
HU, ZHAO TONG, Bridges
HUANG, PING MIN, Bridges
JIANG, CHANG YI, Earth Science and Land Resources Management
JIAO, SHENG JIE, Construction Machinery
JU, YONG FENG, Information Engineering
LEI, SHENG YOU, Geognosy and Tube Engineering
LI, PEI CHENG, Environmental Science and Engineering
LI, QING CHUN, Geology Engineering and Geomatics
LI, XIU, Geology Engineering and Geomatics
LI, YONG, Earth Science and Land Resources Management
LI, YUN FENG, Environmental Science and Engineering
LI, ZI QING, Bridges
LIU, BAO JIAN, Geognosy and Tube Engineering
LIU, JI FA, Humanities and Social Science
LIU, JIAN XIN, Bridges
LIU, LAI JUN, Bridges
LIU, YONG JIAN, Bridges
LONG, SHUI GEN, Construction Machinery
LU, KANG CHENG, Geognosy and Tube Engineering
LU, PENG MIN, Construction Machinery
MA, JIANG MING, Science
MA, RONG GUO, Traffic Engineering
MA, TIAN SHAN, Economics and Management
MAO, YAN LONG, Geology Engineering and Geomatics

MEN, YU MING, Geology Engineering and Geomatics
NI, WANG KUI, Geology Engineering and Geomatics
PEI, XIAN ZHI, Earth Science and Land Resources Management
PENG, JIAN MIN, Geology Engineering and Geomatics
QIAN, ZHUANG ZHI, Earth Science and Land Resources Management
SHA, AI MIN, Highways
SHEN, AI QIN, Highways
SHI, YONG MIN, Highway Management
SONG, YI FAN, Bridges
SU, SHENG RUI, Geology Engineering and Geomatics
TAN, CHENG QIAN, Geology Engineering and Geomatics
TIAN, WEI PING, Highway Disaster Prevention and Cure
WANG, BIN GANG, Highways
WANG, HU, Science
WANG, WEN KE, Environmental Science and Engineering
WANG, XIAO MOU, Geognosy and Tube Engineering
WANG, XUAN CANG, Highway Management
WEI, GUANG SHENG, Science
WU, XIAO GUANG, Highway Management
XIA, YONG XU, Geognosy and Tube Engineering
XIE, YONG LI, Geognosy and Tube Engineering
XU, HAI CHENG, Economics and Management
XU, JING LIANG, Road Reconnaissance
XUE, CHUN JI, Earth Science and Land Resources Management
YAN, BAO JIE, Traffic Engineering
YANG, BIN CHENG, Bridges
YANG, SHAO WEI, Road Reconnaissance
YANG, XIAO HUA, Geognosy and Tube Engineering
YANG, XING KE, Earth Science and Land Resources Management
YI, GUAN SHENG, Science
ZHANG, CHAO, Highways
ZHANG, DENG LIANG, Highways
ZHANG, JUN, Geology Engineering and Geomatics
ZHANG, QIN, Geology Engineering and Geomatics
ZHANG, ZHI QIANG, Geology Engineering and Geomatics
ZHAO, FA SHUO, Geology Engineering and Geomatics
ZHE, XUE SEN, Geognosy and Tube Engineering
ZHENG, CHUAN CHAO, Highways
ZHENG, NAN XIANG, Highways
ZHOU, GUO GUANG, Economics and Management
ZHOU, WEI, Traffic Engineering
ZHOU, XU HONG, Bridges
ZHU, GUANG MING, Geology Engineering and Geomatics

CHANGCHUN UNIVERSITY OF EARTH SCIENCES

6 Ximinzhu St, Changchun, 130026 Jilin

Telephone: (431) 822391

Founded 1952

Languages of instruction: Chinese, English, Russian, Japanese

Academic year: September to January, March to July

Chancellor: Prof. ZHANG YIXIA
Vice-Chancellors: LIU BAOREN, MA ZHIHONG, Prof. SHUN YUNSHENG
Librarian: XIANG TIANYUAN

Library of 800,000 vols
Number of teachers: 830
Number of students: 3,890

Publications: Geology of the World, Journal.

CHANGCHUN INSTITUTE OF POSTS AND TELECOMMUNICATIONS

20 Nanhu St, Changchun, Jilin Province 130012

Telephone: 5171220

Fax: 5176342

Founded 1947

Controlled by the Ministry of the Information Industry
Language of instruction: Chinese
Academic year: September to July

Pres.: SUN MUQIAN
Registrar: LIU YAN
Librarian: YU JIE

Library of 380,000 vols
Number of teachers: 407
Number of students: 2,125 (and 2,005 corresponding students)

Publication: Journal of Changchun Institute of Posts and Telecommunications.

CHENGDU UNIVERSITY OF TECHNOLOGY

1st East Third Rd, Chenghua, Erxianqiao, Chengdu 610059, Sichuan

Telephone: (28) 84078898

Internet: www.cdut.edu.cn

Founded 1956

Provincial control

Academic year: September to July

Pres.: LIU JIADUO
Vice-Pres: HUANG RUNQIU, NI SHIJUN, TAN SHUMIN, WANG YINGCHUAN
Librarian: LI YONG

Library of 1,170,000 vols
Number of teachers: 2,021
Number of students: 25,000

Publications: Computing Techniques for Geophysical Exploration (4 a year), Journal (6 a year), Journal of Geological Hazards and Environment Preservation (4 a year), Journal of Mineralogy and Petrology (4 a year), Scientific and Technological Management of Land and Resources (6 a year)

DEANS

College of Applied Techniques and Automation Engineering: GE LIANGQUAN
Commercial College: LI YUSHENG
College of Energy Resources: ZHANG SHAONAN
College of Environment and Civil Engineering: XU QIANG
College of Foreign Languages and Cultures: LUO YIJUN
College of Geosciences: SUN CHUANMIN
College of Humanities and Law: LI QUANHUI
College of Information Engineering: WANG XUBEN
College of Information Management: GUO KE
College of Materials and Bioengineering: WANG LING
Australian Institute of Tourism and Hospitality: LI YUSHENG

PROFESSORS

CAO, JINWEN, College of Information Management
CAO, JUNXING, College of Information Engineering
CHEN, BUKE, College of Energy Resources
CHEN, CHANGQUAN, College of Information Management
CHEN, HONGDE, Geosciences College
CHEN, JUNMING, Australian Institute of Tourism and Hospitality
CHEN, WANJIANG, Commercial College
CHENG, XIA, Commercial College
DENG, LIN, College of Information Engineering
DENG, TIANLONG, College of Materials and Bioengineering
DING, ZHAOYU, Network Education College

FAN, BIWEI, College of Materials and Bioengineering
FANG, FANG, College of Applied Techniques and Automation Engineering:
FENG, WENGUANG, College of Energy Resources
FU, GUANGHAI, Commercial College
FU, RONGHUA, College of Environment and Civil Engineering
FU, RULIN, College of Information Engineering
GE, LIANGQUAN, College of Applied Techniques and Automation Engineering:
GU, XUEXIANG, Geosciences College
GUO, JIANG, College of Information Engineering
GUO, KE, College of Information Management
HE, MINGSHENG, College of Applied Techniques and Automation Engineering:
HE, ZHENGWEI, Geosciences College
HE, ZHENHUA, College of Information Engineering
HONG, ZHIQUAN, College of Information Engineering
HU, GUANGMANG, College of Information Engineering
HU, YUANLAI, College of Information Management
HUANG, DILONG, College of Information Engineering
HUANG, JIJUN, Geosciences College
HUANG, RUNQIU, College of Environment and Civil Engineering
HUANG, SIJING, Geosciences College
JIA, SUYUAN, College of Environment and Civil Engineering
KONG, FANJING, College of Foreign Languages and Cultures
KUANG, JIANCHAO, College of Information Management
LI, HONGMU, College of Applied Techniques and Automation Engineering:
LI, JUCHU, College of Applied Techniques and Automation Engineering:
LI, LIANGMING, Commercial College
LI, LUMING, College of Information Engineering
LI, QUANHUI, College of Humanities and Law
LI, RUI, College of Information Engineering
LI, SHUSHENG, College of Environment and Civil Engineering
LI, TIANBIN, College of Environment and Civil Engineering
LI, WUQUAN, College of Foreign Languages and Cultures
LI, YUSHENG, Commercial College
LI, ZHENGWEN, College of Information Engineering
LI, ZHEQIN, College of Environment and Civil Engineering
LI, ZHIQUAN, College of Information Engineering
LIE, DEXIN, College of Environment and Civil Engineering
LIN, LI, Geosciences College
LIU, DENGZHONG, Geosciences College
LIU, HANCHAO, College of Environment and Civil Engineering
LIU, HONGJUN, College of Information Management
LIU, JIADUO, Geosciences College
LIU, MAOCAI, College of Information Management
LIU, SHUGEN, College of Energy Resources
LIU, XIANFAN, Geosciences College
LU, KUN, College of Applied Techniques and Automation Engineering:
LU, ZHENGYUAN, College of Energy Resources
LUO, MEI, College of Applied Techniques and Automation Engineering:
LUO, RUNTIAN, College of Foreign Languages and Cultures
LUO, SHENGXIAN, College of Information Engineering

LUO, YIJUN, College of Foreign Languages and Cultures
MA, RUNZE, Geosciences College
MA, YUXIAO, College of Applied Techniques and Automation Engineering:
MIAO, FANG, College of Information Engineering
NI, SHIJUN, College of Applied Techniques and Automation Engineering:
PENG, DAJUN, College of Energy Resources
QIE, JINLING, College of Information Engineering
QIU, KEHUI, College of Materials and Bioengineering
REN, GUANGMING, College of Environment and Civil Engineering
SHA, JICHANG, College of Information Management
SHENG, ZHONGMING, College of Energy Resources
SHI, HE, Geosciences College
SHI, ZHEJIN, College of Energy Resources
SUN, CHUANMIN, Geosciences College
SUN, SHUXIA, Network Education College
TAN, JIANXIONG, Geosciences College
TANG, JUXING, Geosciences College
TIAN, JINGCHUN, Geosciences College
TONG, CHUNHAN, College of Applied Techniques and Automation Engineering:
TUO, XIANGUO, College of Information Engineering
WAN, XINNAN, College of Environment and Civil Engineering
WANG, CHENGSHAN, Geosciences College
WANG, HONGFENG, Geosciences College
WANG, HONGHUI, College of Energy Resources
WANG, HUIZHOU, College of Foreign Languages and Cultures
WANG, LANSHENG, College of Environment and Civil Engineering
WANG, LING, College of Materials and Bioengineering
WANG, MOHUI, College of Materials and Bioengineering
WANG, SHITIAN, College of Environment and Civil Engineering
WANG, XIAOCHUN, College of Environment and Civil Engineering
WANG, XINZHUANG, College of Information Management
WANG, XUBEN, College of Information Engineering
WANG, YUNCHENG, College of Energy Resources
WANG, YUNSHENG, College of Environment and Civil Engineering
WANG, ZAIQI, College of Foreign Languages and Cultures
WEI, GUIMING, College of Information Management
WEN, CHUNQI, Geosciences College
WU, SHAN, Geosciences College
XI, DASHUN, College of Information Engineering
XIAN, YUANFU, Geosciences College
XIANG, YANG, College of Energy Resources
XIAO, CIXUN, College of Information Engineering
XING, WENXIANG, College of Information Management
XU, GUOSHENG, College of Energy Resources
XU, MO, College of Environment and Civil Engineering
XU, QIANG, College of Environment and Civil Engineering
YAN, HELIN, Geosciences College
YANG, SHAOGUO, College of Information Engineering
YANG, WUNIAN, Geosciences College
YANG, ZHENGXI, Geosciences College
YI, GUAN, College of Applied Techniques and Automation Engineering:
YI, HAISHENG, Geosciences College
YIN, HUIAN, College of Materials and Bioengineering

ZHANG, CHENGJIANG, College of Applied Techniques and Automation Engineering:
ZHANG, QICHUN, College of Materials and Bioengineering
ZHANG, SHAONAN, College of Energy Resources
ZHANG, ZUOYUAN, College of Environment and Civil Engineering
ZHAO, BING, Geosciences College
ZHAO, QIHUA, College of Environment and Civil Engineering
ZHAO, XIAFEI, College of Energy Resources
ZHAO, XIGUI, College of Energy Resources
ZHAO, ZESONG, Commercial College
ZHEN, HUAN, College of Foreign Languages and Cultures
ZHEN, MINGHUA, Geosciences College
ZHEN, RONGCAI, Geosciences College
ZHONG, BENSHAN, College of Information Engineering
ZHONG, YONGJIAN, Commercial College
ZHOU, JIAJI, College of Information Engineering
ZHOU, RONGSHENG, College of Applied Techniques and Automation Engineering:
ZHOU, SICHUN, College of Applied Techniques and Automation Engineering:
ZHOU, XIXIANG, College of Information Engineering
ZHU, CHUANGYE, Geosciences College
ZHU, JIESHOU, College of Information Engineering

CHENGDU UNIVERSITY OF TRADITIONAL CHINESE MEDICINE

37 Shierqiao Rd, Chengdu 610075
Telephone: (28) 87784542
Fax: (28) 87784606
E-mail: wsc@cdutcm.edu.cn
Internet: www.cdutcm.edu.cn
Founded 1956
State control
Languages of instruction: Chinese, English
Academic year: September to August
Pres.: Prof. ZHU BIDE
Vice-Pres: FU CHUNHUA LIANG FANRONG LUO CAIGUI, XIE KEQING
Chief Administrative Officer: XU, LIAN
Librarian: JIANG YONGGUANG

Library of 602,000 vols
Number of teachers: 1,678
Number of students: 10,095

Publications: *Academic Journal* (4 a year), *Higher Education Research into Traditional Chinese Medicine* (4 a year).

CHINA AGRICULTURAL UNIVERSITY

2 West of Yuanmingyuan Rd, Haidian District, Beijing 100094
Telephone: (10) 62732394
Fax: (10) 62732872
Internet: www.cau.edu.cn
Founded 1905
Academic year: September to July
Pres.: CHEN ZHANGLIANG
Vice-Pres: FU ZETIAN, JIANG SHUREN, MA JIANSHENG, SUN QIXIN, TAN XIANGYONG, ZHANG DONGJUN
Head of Graduate Department: CHEN ZHANGLIANG
Librarian: ZHANG QUAN

Number of teachers: 1,170
Number of students: 18,425

Publications: *Chinese Journal of Veterinary Medicine*, *Journal* (natural sciences, 6 a year)

DEANS

College of Agronomy and Biotechnology: DAI JINGRUI

College of Animal Science and Technology: LI DEFA

College of Biology Science: WU WEIHUA

College of Economic Management: WANG XIUQING

College of Food Science and Nutritional Engineering: LUO YUNBO

College of Humanities and Development: LI XIAOYUN

College of Information and Electrical Engineering: YANG RENGANG

College of Resource and Environment: ZHANG FUSUO

College of Science: JIAO QUNYING

College of Veterinary Medicine: WANG MING

College of Water Conservation and Civil Engineering: WANG FUJUN

College of International Studies: MENG FANXI

PROFESSORS

AO, GUANGMING, Biological Sciences

CAI, WANZHI, Agronomy and Biotechnology

CAO, YIPING, Resources and the Environment

CAO, ZHIPING, Resources and the Environment

CHANG, JINSHI, Water Conservation and Civil Engineering

CHEN, BAOFENG, Economic Management

CHEN, BU, Agronomy and Biotechnology

CHEN, HUANWEI, Resources and the Environment

CHEN, JIA, Biological Sciences

CHEN, JIANPING, Resources and the Environment

CHEN, MIN, Food Science and Nutritional Engineering

CHEN, QINGYUN, Agronomy and Biotechnology

CHEN, SANFENG, Biological Sciences

CHEN, SHAOJIANG, Agronomy and Biotechnology

CHEN, WENXIN, Biological Sciences

CHEN, YONGFU, Biological Sciences

CHEN, ZHANGLIANG, Agronomy and Biotechnology

CHENG, XU, Agronomy and Biotechnology

CUI, JIANYUN, Food Science and Nutritional Engineering

CUI, SHENG, Biological Sciences

CUI, ZONGJUN, Agronomy and Biotechnology

DAI, JINGRUI, Agronomy and Biotechnology

DENG, NAIYANG, Science

DENG, XIMIN, Agronomy and Biotechnology

DUAN, CHANGQING, Food Science and Nutritional Engineering

FENG, GONG, Humanities and Development

FENG, GU, Resources and the Environment

FENG, KAIWEN, Economic Management

FENG, SHAOYUAN, Water Conservation and Civil Engineering

FU, ZHIYI, Science

GAO, JUNPING, Agronomy and Biotechnology

GAO, QIJIE, Humanities and Development

GAO, WANGSHENG, Agronomy and Biotechnology

GAO, XIWU, Agronomy and Biotechnology

GAO, YANXIANG, Food Science and Nutritional Engineering

GONG, LIMIN, Animal Science and Technology

GONG, YUANSHI, Resources and the Environment

GONG, ZHIZHONG, Biological Sciences

GUO, SHUNTANG, Food Science and Nutritional Engineering

GUO, XIQING, Information and Electrical Engineering

GUO, YANGDONG, Agronomy and Biotechnology

GUO, YUHAI, Agronomy and Biotechnology

GUO, YUYUAN, Agronomy and Biotechnology

GUO, ZEJIAN, Agronomy and Biotechnology

HAN, BEIZHONG, Food Science and Nutritional Engineering

HAN, CHENGGUI, Agronomy and Biotechnology

HAN, JIANGUO, Animal Science and Technology

HAN, YUZHEN, Biological Sciences

HAN, ZHENHAI, Agronomy and Biotechnology

HAO, JINMIN, Resources and the Environment

HE, GUANGWEN, Economic Management

HE, XIURONG, Economic Management

HOU, CAIYUN, Food Science and Nutritional Engineering

HU, XIAOSONG, Food Science and Nutritional Engineering

HU, YUEGAO, Agronomy and Biotechnology

HUANG, GUANHUA, Water Conservation and Civil Engineering

HUANG, WEIDONG, Food Science and Nutritional Engineering

HUANG, WENBIN, Science

HUANG, YUANFANG, Resources and the Environment

HUANG, ZHIYONG, Agronomy and Biotechnology

JI, BAOPING, Food Science and Nutritional Engineering

JI, CHENG, Animal Science and Technology

JI, HAIYAN, Information and Electrical Engineering

JIA, WENSUO, Agronomy and Biotechnology

JIA, ZHIHAI, Animal Science and Technology

JIAN, HENG, Agronomy and Biotechnology

JIANG, RONGFENG, Resources and the Environment

JIANG, SHUREN, Science

JIANG, WEIBO, Food Science and Nutritional Engineering

JIAO, QUNYING, Science

JIAO, SHIYAN, Animal Science and Technology

KANG, DINGMING, Agronomy and Biotechnology

KANG, SHAOZHONG, Water Conservation and Civil Engineering

KE, BINGSHENG, Economic Management

LEI, TINGWU, Water Conservation and Civil Engineering

LENG, PING, Agronomy and Biotechnology

LI, BAOGUO, Resources and the Environment

LI, BAOMING, Water Conservation and Civil Engineering

LI, CHONGJIU, Science

LI, CHUNJIAN, Resources and the Environment

LI, DAWEI, Biological Sciences

LI, DEFA, Animal Science and Technology

LI, GENGLONG, Economic Management

LI, GUANGYONG, Water Conservation and Civil Engineering

LI, GUOHUI, Science

LI, GUOXUE, Resources and the Environment

LI, HUAIFANG, Agronomy and Biotechnology

LI, JI, Resources and the Environment

LI, JIANMIN, Agronomy and Biotechnology

LI, JIANQIANG, Agronomy and Biotechnology

LI, JIANSHENG, Agronomy and Biotechnology

LI, JILUN, Biological Sciences

LI, LITE, Food Science and Nutritional Engineering

LI, LONG, Resources and the Environment

LI, MINZAN, Information and Electrical Engineering

LI, NAN, Science

LI, NING, Biological Sciences

LI, OU, Humanities and Development

LI, PING, Economic Management

LI, SHAOKUN, Agronomy and Biotechnology

LI, SHENGLI, Animal Science and Technology

LI, SHUHUA, Agronomy and Biotechnology

LI, WEIJIONG, Resources and the Environment

LI, XIAOLIN, Resources and the Environment

LI, XIAOYUN, Humanities and Development

LI, XUEFENG, Science

LI, YAN, Biological Sciences

LI, YING, Biological Sciences

LI, ZANDONG, Biological Sciences

LI, ZHAOHU, Agronomy and Biotechnology

LI, ZICHAO, Agronomy and Biotechnology

LIAN, LINSHENG, Animal Science and Technology

LIAN, ZHENGXING, Animal Science and Technology

LIN, CONG, Water Conservation and Civil Engineering

LIN, DEGUI, Veterinary Medicine

LIN, QIMEI, Resources and the Environment

LIN, SHAN, Resources and the Environment

LIU, GUOJIE, Agronomy and Biotechnology

LIU, GUOQIN, Biological Sciences

LIU, LIMING, Resources and the Environment

LIU, QINGCHANG, Agronomy and Biotechnology

LIU, YONGGONG, Humanities and Development

LIU, ZHIYONG, Agronomy and Biotechnology

LOU, CHENGHOU, Biological Sciences

LU, FENGJU, Economic Management

LU, JUAN, Economic Management

LU, YAHAI, Resources and the Environment

LU, ZHIGUANG, Resources and the Environment

LUO, YUNBO, Food Science and Nutritional Engineering

MA, CHANGWEI, Food Science and Nutritional Engineering

MA, CHENGWEI, Water Conservation and Civil Engineering

MAO, DARU, Resources and the Environment

MENG, FANXI, International College

MENG, QINGXIANG, Animal Science and Technology

MI, GUOHUA, Resources and the Environment

MIN, SHUNGENG, Science

NIU, TIANGUI, Food Science and Nutritional Engineering

PAN, SHENQUAN, Agronomy and Biotechnology

PAN, XUEBIAO, Resources and the Environment

PENG, YOULIANG, Agronomy and Biotechnology

QIAO, JUAN, Economic Management

QIAO, ZHONG, Economic Management

QIN, FU, Economic Management

QIN, YAODONG, Resources and the Environment

REN, DONGTAO, Biological Sciences

REN, FAZHENG, Food Science and Nutritional Engineering

REN, LI, Resources and the Environment

REN, SHUMEI, Water Conservation and Civil Engineering

SHEN, DEZHONG, Resources and the Environment

SHEN, JIANZHONG, Veterinary Medicine

SHEN, ZUORUI, Agronomy and Biotechnology

SHI, DAZHAO, Agronomy and Biotechnology

SHI, JIEPING, Food Science and Nutritional Engineering

SHI, YUANCHUN, Resources and the Environment

SONG, YUAN, Biological Sciences

SU, DECHUN, Resources and the Environment

SU, ZHEN, Biological Sciences

SUN, BAOQI, Agronomy and Biotechnology

SUN, CHUANQING, Agronomy and Biotechnology

SUN, JUNSHE, Food Science and Nutritional Engineering

SUN, QIXIN, Agronomy and Biotechnology

SUN, YURUI, Information and Electrical Engineering

SUN, ZHEN, Resources and the Environment

TAN, XIANGYONG, Economic Management

TENG, GUANGHUI, Water Conservation and Civil Engineering

TIAN, WEIMING, Economic Management

WANG, AIGUO, Animal Science and Technology

WANG, BIN, Biological Sciences

WANG, CHUDUAN, Animal Science and Technology

WANG, DEHAI, Humanities and Development

WANG, FANG, Animal Science and Technology

WANG, FUJUN, Water Conservation and Civil Engineering
WANG, GUOYING, Biological Sciences
WANG, HEXIANG, Biological Sciences
WANG, HONGGUANG, Agronomy and Biotechnology
WANG, HUANHUA, Information and Electrical Engineering
WANG, HUAQI, Agronomy and Biotechnology
WANG, HUIMIN, Agronomy and Biotechnology
WANG, JIANHUA, Agronomy and Biotechnology
WANG, JINGGUO, Resources and the Environment
WANG, KU, Information and Electrical Engineering
WANG, MAO, Biological Sciences
WANG, MING, Veterinary Medicine
WANG, PU, Agronomy and Biotechnology
WANG, SHIPING, Food Science and Nutritional Engineering
WANG, SHOUCAI, Agronomy and Biotechnology
WANG, TAO, Biological Sciences
WANG, XIUQING, Economic Management
WANG, XUECHEN, Biological Sciences
WANG, YIMING, Information and Electrical Engineering
WEN, BOYING, Information and Electrical Engineering
WO, YUMING, Animal Science and Technology
WU, PING, Information and Electrical Engineering
WU, WEIHUA, Biological Sciences
WU, WENLIANG, Resources and the Environment
XIA, GUOLIANG, Biological Sciences
XIAO, HAIFENG, Economic Management
XIAO, XINGGUO, Biological Sciences
XIE, GUANGHUI, Agronomy and Biotechnology
XIN, XIAN, Economic Management
XU, HUIYUAN, Economic Management
XU, MINGLIANG, Agronomy and Biotechnology
XU, XUEFENG, Agronomy and Biotechnology
XUE, WENTONG, Food Science and Nutritional Engineering
YAN, TAILAI, Information and Electrical Engineering
YANG, DING, Agronomy and Biotechnology
YANG, HANCHUN, Veterinary Medicine
YANG, JIANCHANG, Agronomy and Biotechnology
YANG, MINGHAO, Information and Electrical Engineering
YANG, NING, Animal Science and Technology
YANG, PEILING, Water Conservation and Civil Engineering
YANG, QIULIN, Economic Management
YANG, RENGANG, Information and Electrical Engineering
YANG, XIAOBING, Agronomy and Biotechnology
YANG, ZHIFU, Resources and the Environment
YE, JINGZHONG, Humanities and Development
YE, ZHIHUA, Agronomy and Biotechnology
YI, MINGFANG, Agronomy and Biotechnology
YU, HUAIJIANG, Humanities and Development
YU, JIALIN, Biological Sciences
YU, RUIPING, Veterinary Medicine
YU, ZHENRONG, Resources and the Environment
YUAN, MING, Biological Sciences
ZANG, RIHONG, Economic Management
ZENG, SHENMING, Animal Science and Technology
ZENG, SHIMAI, Agronomy and Biotechnology
ZHAI, ZHIXI, Agronomy and Biotechnology
ZHANG, BAOGUI, Resources and the Environment
ZHANG, CONG, Resources and the Environment
ZHANG, DAPENG, Biological Sciences

ZHANG, FENGRONG, Resources and the Environment
ZHANG, FUSUO, Resources and the Environment
ZHANG, KEJIA, Veterinary Medicine
ZHANG, LONG, Agronomy and Biotechnology
ZHANG, QIN, Animal Science and Technology
ZHANG, QINGWEN, Agronomy and Biotechnology
ZHANG, RUAN, Animal Science and Technology
ZHANG, SHAOYING, Food Science and Nutritional Engineering
ZHANG, SHUQIU, Biological Sciences
ZHANG, WEI, Information and Electrical Engineering
ZHANG, XIAOMING, Animal Science and Technology
ZHANG, ZHENGHE, Economic Management
ZHANG, ZHENXIAN, Agronomy and Biotechnology
ZHANG, ZHONGJUN, Agronomy and Biotechnology
ZHANG, ZHONGZHI, Veterinary Medicine
ZHAO, DEMING, Veterinary Medicine
ZHAO, GUANGYONG, Animal Science and Technology
ZHAO, LIANGJUN, Agronomy and Biotechnology
ZHAO, MING, Agronomy and Biotechnology
ZHENG, DAWEI, Resources and the Environment
ZHENG, HANG, Biological Sciences
ZHOU, HE, Animal Science and Technology
ZHU, DAOLIN, Resources and the Environment
ZHU, DEHAI, Information and Electrical Engineering
ZHU, DEJU, Resources and the Environment
ZHU, QIZHEN, Humanities and Development
ZHU, SHIEN, Animal Science and Technology
ZUO, QIANG, Resources and the Environment
ZUO, TING, Humanities and Development

CHINA CENTRAL INSTITUTE OF FINE ARTS

5 Xiaowei hutong, East District, Beijing 100730
Telephone: (10) 65254731
Founded 1950 by merger of National Beijing College of Art and Fine Arts Department of North China United University

Pres.: JIN SHANGYI
Deputy Pres: DU JIAN, YE YUZHONG
Librarian: TANG CHI

Library: over 170,000 vols (25,000 in foreign languages), 8,500 vols periodicals
Number of teachers: 164
Number of students: 519 (incl. 28 postgraduates)

CHINA FOREIGN AFFAIRS UNIVERSITY

24 Zhanlan Rd, Xicheng, Beijing 100037
Internet: www.cfau.edu.cn
Founded 1955
Academic year: September to July

President: WU JIANMING
Vice-Presidents: QIN YAQING, QU XING
Head of Graduate Department: ZHENG QIRONG
Vice-Librarian: JIAN LEYI

Library of 23,500
Number of teachers: 170
Number of students: 1,600

Publication: *Journal* (4 a year)

DEANS

English: FAN SHOUYI
Foreign Affairs: ZHANG LILI
International Economics: JIANG RUIPING
International Law: JIN KESHENG

PROFESSORS

CHU, GUANGYOU, English
FAN, SHOUYI, English
HUANG, JINQI, English
JIANG, RUIPING, International Economics
QIN, YAQING, English
QU, XING, Foreign Affairs
REN, XIAOPING, English
SU, HAO, Foreign Affairs
WANG, SHAOREN, English
XIONG, ZHIYONG, Foreign Affairs
YANG, XUEYAN, English
YUAN, SHIBING, English
ZHANG, LILI, Foreign Affairs
ZHANG, YITING, English
ZHENG, QIRONG, Foreign Affairs

CHINA UNIVERSITY OF GEOSCIENCES (WUHAN)

Yujiashan, 388 Lumo Rd, Wuhan 430074 Hubei
Telephone: (27) 87481030
Fax: (27) 87481030
E-mail: xb@dns.cug.edu.cn
Internet: www.cug.edu.cn
Founded 1952
Academic year: September to July

Pres.: ZHANG, JINGAO
Vice-Pres: OUYANG JIANPING, WANG YANXIN, XING XIANGQIN, YAO SHUZHEN

Library of 1,167,000 vols, 3,852 periodicals
Number of teachers: 2,800
Number of students: 23,600

Publications: *Chinese Journal of Engineering Geophysics, Earth Science, Geological Science and Technology Information, Journal of China University of Geosciences* (in English and Chinese), *Journal of Geoscience Translations*

21 Colleges which offer 49 Bachelors degree courses, 65 Masters degree courses and 30 doctoral courses.

CHINA MEDICAL UNIVERSITY

Bei Er Rd, He Ping District, Shenyang 110001, Liaoning
Telephone: (24) 23265491
Fax: (24) 23261169
Internet: www.cmu.edu.cn
Founded 1931
Provincial Dept of Education control
Academic year: September to July

Pres.: ZHAO QUN
Vice-Pres: HAN MINTAN, HE QINCHENG, SUN BAOZHI, ZHAO LIKUI
Head of Graduate Dept: ZHAO QUN
Librarian: NENG DIZHI

Number of teachers: 6,126
Number of students: 19,602 (11,094 full-time, 8,508 part-time)

Publications: *Chinese Journal of Health Statistics* (6 a year), *Chinese Journal of Practical Ophthalmology* (12 a year), *Journal* (6 a year), *Journal of China Clinical Medical Imaging* (4 a year), *Liaoning Journal of Pharmacy and Clinical Remedies* (4 a year), *Liaoning Journal of Practical Diabetology* (4 a year), *Paediatric Emergency Medicine* (4 a year), *Practical Journal for Rural Doctors* (6 a year), *Progress of Anatomical Sciences* (4 a year), *Progress in Japanese Medicine* (12 a year)

DEANS

Faculty of Forensic Medicine: WANG BAOJIE
First Clinical College and First Affiliated Hospital: LI JIGUANG
College of Basic Medical Sciences: BAI SHULING
College of Nursing: LI XIAOHAN

College of Public Health: SUN GUIFAN
Department of Information Management and Information Systems: ZHAO YUHONG
Department of Social Science: GUO SHUYING
School of Pharmacy: JIN XIN
School of Stomatology and Affiliated Stomatological Hospital: AI HONGJUN
Second Clinical College and Second Affiliated Hospital: GUO QIYONG
Third Clinical College and Third Affiliated Hospital: XU JIANJUN
Fourth Clinical College and Fourth Affiliated Hospital: HAN JIANPING

PROFESSORS

AI, HONGJUN, Stomatology
AN, XHUNLI, Basic Medical Sciences
BAI, SHULING, Basic Medical Sciences
BAO, ZHONGXIAO, Basic Medical Sciences
CAI, JINGYUAN, First Clinical College
CAI, JIQUN, Basic Medical Sciences
CAI, YUAN, Public Health
CAI, ZHIDAO, First Clinical College
CAO, YAMING, Basic Medical Sciences
CHANG, TIANHUI, Basic Medical Sciences
CHEN, HONGDUO, First Clinical College
CHEN, JUNQING, First Clinical College
CHEN, LIANG, First Clinical College
CHEN, SHUZHENG, Second Clinical College
CHEN, YUHUA, Basic Medical Sciences
CHU, HANG, First Clinical College
CUI, JIANJUN, Second Clinical College
CUI, LEI, Information Management and Information Systems
DAI, XIANWEI, Second Clinical College
DENG, XIANGDONG, First Clinical College
DENG, YAN, Stomatology
DING, LUOLAN, First Clinical College
DING, MEI, Forensic Medicine
DONG, XIAOJIE, Basic Medical Sciences
DONG, YULAN, Basic Medical Sciences
DU, XUEBIN, Social Science
DUAN, ZHIQUAN, First Clinical College
FAN, GUANGYU, First Clinical College
FAN, SHUDUO, Basic Medical Sciences
FANG, JINWU, First Clinical College
FANG, XIUBIN, Basic Medical Sciences
FU, BAOYU, First Clinical College
GAO, DIANWEN, Second Clinical College
GU, CHUNJIU, First Clinical College
GUAN, DAWEI, Forensic Medicine
GUO, DUISHAN, Second Clinical College
GUO, SHUYING, Social Science
HAN, JIANPING, Fourth Clinical College
HAN, YUKUN, Second Clinical College
HE, AN'GUANG, First Clinical College
HE, QINCHENG, Information Management and Information Systems
HE, SANGUANG, First Clinical College
HE, XIUQIN, First Clinical College
HONG, JIAKANG, Basic Medical Sciences
HONG, YANG, Basic Medical Sciences
HOU, XIANGMING, First Clinical College
HUANG, JIANQUN, First Clinical College
JI, SHIJUN, Second Clinical College
JIA, XINSHAN, Basic Medical Sciences
JIANG, RUOLAN, First Clinical College
JIN, CHUNLIAN, Basic Medical Sciences
JIN, WANBAO, Basic Medical Sciences
JIN, XIN, Pharmacy
LI, FUCAO, Basic Medical Sciences
LI, HOUWEN, First Clinical College
LI, JIGUANG, First Clinical College
LI, JINMING, Basic Medical Sciences
LI, LIYUN, First Clinical College
LI, SHAOYING, First Clinical College
LI, SHUQIN, Second Clinical College
LI, XIAOHAN, Nursing
LI, XINGYUAN, Second Clinical College
LI, XIULLING, First Clinical College
LI, YAN, Second Clinical College
LI, YUQUAN, Second Clinical College
LI, ZHENCHUN, Stomatology
LI, ZHENG, Second Clinical College
LI, ZHI, Basic Medical Sciences
LI, ZHUQIN, First Clinical College

LIU, CHUNRONG, First Clinical College
LIU, ENJIE, Basic Medical Sciences
LIU, ENQING, Second Clinical College
LIU, GUOLIANG, First Clinical College
LIU, HONGQIN, Second Clinical College
LIU, JUHUI, Forensic Medicine
LIU, JUNTING, Forensic Medicine
LIU, JUNTING, Pharmacy
LIU, LANQING, Second Clinical College
LIU, LIMIN, Forensic Medicine
LIU, SHUJIE, Stomatology
LIU, XIUMEI, First Clinical College
LIU, YANG, Public Health
LIU, YINGMIN, Second Clinical College
LIU, ZHENLIN, Public Health
LU, CHANGLONG, Basic Medical Sciences
LU, JINGMING, Second Clinical College
LU, SHENGMIN, Second Clinical College
MENG, FANHAO, Pharmacy
MU, HUACHUN, Basic Medical Sciences
PAN, YAPING, Stomatology
PAN, ZHIMIN, First Clinical College
PANG, XINING, Basic Medical Sciences
PEI, ZHUGUO, Second Clinical College
PIAO, AIYING, Second Clinical College
QIU, XUESHAN, Basic Medical Sciences
QU, MIN, First Clinical College
REN, CHONG, First Clinical College
SHEN, KUI, First Clinical College
SHI, LIDE, Basic Medical Sciences
SHI, YUXIU, Basic Medical Sciences
SONG, FANGJI, First Clinical College
SONG, JIJIE, Basic Medical Sciences
SONG, JINDAN, Basic Medical Sciences
SONG, MIN, Basic Medical Sciences
SUN, GUIFAN, Public Health
SUN, GUIYUAN, Basic Medical Sciences
SUN, JIANCHUN, Second Clinical College
SUN, KAILAI, Basic Medical Sciences
SUN, LIGUANG, Basic Medical Sciences
TANG, HAO, Basic Medical Sciences
TIAN, XUSHENG, Basic Medical Sciences
WANG, BAOJIE, Forensic Medicine
WANG, CHUN, Fourth Clinical College
WANG, DEWEN, Forensic Medicine
WANG, DEZHI, Second Clinical College
WANG, ENHUA, Basic Medical Sciences
WANG, GUIZHEN, Basic Medical Sciences
WANG, HAIPENG, Basic Medical Sciences
WANG, HAIYI, Second Clinical College
WANG, HE, Basic Medical Sciences
WANG, HONGDA, First Clinical College
WANG, HUAILIANG, Basic Medical Sciences
WANG, HUIZHEN, Second Clinical College
WANG, LIANYING, Second Clinical College
WANG, LIJUN, Second Clinical College
WANG, LIYU, Social Science
WANG, MINGQIAN, Second Clinical College
WANG, SHUBAO, First Clinical College
WANG, SHULAN, First Clinical College
WANG, TIE, Second Clinical College
WANG, WEILIN, Second Clinical College
WANG, XINGDUO, First Clinical College
WANG, XUEYING, Second Clinical College
WANG, YANFENG, Second Clinical College
WANG, YUXIN, Stomatology
WANG, ZHAOGUAN, Second Clinical College
WANG, ZHAOYUAN, Stomatology
WEI, KELUN, Second Clinical College
WU, BAOMIN, Second Clinical College
WU, HUAZHANG, Social Science
WU, JINGTIAN, First Clinical College
WU, KEGUANG, Second Clinical College
WU, YIJIANG, Fourth Clinical College
WU, YINGYU, Second Clinical College
WU, ZHENHUA, Second Clinical College
XIE, HUIFANG, Second Clinical College
XU, ZHAOFA, Public Health
XU, ZHENXING, First Clinical College
XUE, XINDONG, Second Clinical College
XUE, YIXUE, Basic Medical Sciences
YANG, GUORUI, First Clinical College
YANG, JUN, Public Health
YANG, SHILIN, Second Clinical College
YANG, XIANGHONG, Basic Medical Sciences
YANG, XIAODONG, Stomatology

YANG, YUXIU, First Clinical College
YAO, XINGJIA, Public Health
YIN, HONGNIAN, First Clinical College
YIN, SHUGUO, Second Clinical College
YU, BINGXHI, Basic Medical Sciences
YU, RUNJIANG, First Clinical College
YUAN, ZHUANG, Second Clinical College
ZENG, DINGYIN, First Clinical College
ZHA, HONGYAN, Basic Medical Sciences
ZHANG, DAORONG, Basic Medical Sciences
ZHANG, GANZHONG, First Clinical College
ZHANG, HAIPENG, Basic Medical Sciences
ZHANG, HONG, Basic Medical Sciences
ZHANG, JIAXING, Second Clinical College
ZHANG, JINGRONG, First Clinical College
ZHANG, LIFENG, Basic Medical Sciences
ZHANG, SHULAN, Second Clinical College
ZHANG, XUE, Basic Medical Sciences
ZHAO, CHONGZHI, Second Clinical College
ZHAO, GUIZHEN, Second Clinical College
ZHAO, GUOGUI, Second Clinical College
ZHAO, LIJUAN, First Clinical College
ZHAO, SHUFENG, Basic Medical Sciences
ZHAO, SHUXIA, Second Clinical College
ZHAO, YKUN, Basic Medical Sciences
ZHAO, YUHONG, Information Management and Information Systems
ZHONG, MING, Stomatology
ZHOU, BAOSEN, Public Health
ZHOU, WEI, Social Science
ZHOU, XIJING, First Clinical College
ZHOU, YONGDE, Second Clinical College
ZHU, LIPING, Basic Medical Sciences

CHINA UNIVERSITY OF MINING AND TECHNOLOGY

Xuzhou, 221008 Jiangsu
Telephone: (516) 3885745
Fax: (516) 3888682
Internet: www.cumt.edu.cn

Founded 1909
State control
Academic year: September to July

Pres.: Prof. XIE HEPING
Vice-Pres: Prof. GE SHIRONG, Prof. KE WENJIN, Prof. LUO CHENG XUAN, Prof. SUNG XUEFENG, Prof. WANG JIANPING, Prof. WANG YUEHAN
Registrar: Prof. XING YONGCHANG
Dir of Int. Div.: ZHENG ZHENKANG
Librarian: Prof. TANG YI

Library of 330,000 vols
Number of teachers: 3,817
Number of students: 30,942

Publication: *Journal* (4 a year in Chinese, 2 a year in English)

HEADS OF ACADEMIC DIVISIONS

College of Adult Education: ZHANG FUSHENG
College of Applied Science and Technology: FAN ZHONGQI
Department of Physical Education: CHI ZHONGJUN
School of Architecture and Civil Engineering: ZHOU GUOQING
School of Chemical Engineering: LIU JIONGTIAN
School of Computer Science and Technology: XIA SHIXIONG
School of Environment and Spatial Informatics: HAN BAOPING
School of Foreign Studies: YANG SHU
School of Information and Electrical Engineering: JIANG JIANGUO
School of Mechatronic and Materials Engineering: DUAN XIONG
School of Mineral and Energy Resources Engineering: CAI QINGXIANG
School of Resources and Geoscience: LIN JIAN
School of Management: NIE RUI
School of Politics, Literature and Law: WANG YAN
School of Science: MIAO XIEXIN

CHINA UNIVERSITY OF PETROLEUM

2 North Rd, Dongying 257061, Shandong
Telephone: (546) 8392241
Fax: (546) 7366374
Internet: www.hdpu.edu.cn
Founded 1953
State control
Academic year: September to July
President: TONG ZHAOQI
Vice-Presidents: SHAN HONGHONG, SUN HAI-FENG, TONG XINHUA, WANG RUIHE, ZHA MING
Head of Graduate Department: WANG RUIHE
Librarian: ZHANG ZHONGXUE

Number of teachers: 1,000
Number of students: 23,500

Publication: *Journal of China University of Petroleum* (6 a year)

DEANS

College of Architecture, Transport and Storage Engineering: ZHANG GUOZHONG
College of Chemistry and Chemical Engineering: JIN YOUHAI
College of Computer and Communication Engineering: DUAN YOUXIANG
College of Economic Administration: ZHANG ZAIXU
College of Foreign Languages: LUAN SHUWEN
College of Geo-Resources and Information: YIN XINGYAO
College of Humanities and Social Science: XIA CHONGYA
College of Information and Control Engineering: TIAN XUEMING
College of Mathematics and Computer Science: LI WEIGUO
College of Mechanical and Electronic Engineering: QI MINGXIA
College of Petroleum Engineering: YAO JUN
College of Physical Education: WEI RULI
College of Physics, Science and Technology: GUAN JITENG

PROFESSORS

BAI, LIANPING, Information and Control Engineering
CHAO, KE, Humanities and Social Science
CHEN, GANGHUA, Geo-Resources and Information
CHEN, JIANMIN, Petroleum Engineering
CHEN, SHIYUE, Geo-Resources and Information
CHEN, YUEMING, Petroleum Engineering
CHENG, YUANFANG, Petroleum Engineering
DAI, JUNSHENG, Geo-Resources and Information
DU, JINLIANG, Humanities and Social Science
FAN, YIREN, Geo-Resources and Information
FANG, JIANHUI, Physics, Science and Technology
GAO, YIFA, Petroleum Engineering
GUAN, ZHICHUAN, Petroleum Engineering
GUANG, JITENG, Physics, Science and Technology
HAN, ZHIYONG, Petroleum Engineering
HE, LIMIN, Architecture, Transport and Storage Engineering
JIA, RUIGAO, Physics, Science and Technology
JIANG, HUA, Humanities and Social Science
JIANG, YOULU, Geo-Resources and Information
JIANG, ZAIXING, Geo-Resources and Information
JIN, QIANG, Geo-Resources and Information
LI, GUOHUA, Physical Education
LI, HANLIN, Geo-Resources and Information
LI, MINGZHONG, Petroleum Engineering
LI, SHURONG, Information and Control Engineering
LI, WEIGUO, Mathematics and Computational Science
LI, YUANCHENG, Physics, Science and Technology

LI, YUXING, Architecture, Transport and Storage Engineering
LI, ZHAOMIN, Petroleum Engineering
LI, ZILI, Architecture, Transport and Storage Engineering
LIANG, JINGUO, Architecture, Transport and Storage Engineering
LIN, CHENGYAN, Geo-Resources and Information
LIU, HUIQING, Petroleum Engineering
LIU, RUNHUA, Information and Control Engineering
LIU, ZHAN, Geo-Resources and Information
LUAN, SHUWEN, Foreign Languages
MA, XIGENG, Information and Control Engineering
MEN, FUDIAN, Physics, Science and Technology
QIU, SHIWEI, Architecture, Transport and Storage Engineering
QIU, ZHENGSONG, Petroleum Engineering
SHAN, YIXIAN, Information and Control Engineering
SHEN, ZHONGHOU, Petroleum Engineering
SHU, HENGMU, Architecture, Transport and Storage Engineering
SONG, DESHENG, Foreign Languages
SUN, BAOJIANG, Petroleum Engineering
SUN, JIANMENG, Geo-Resources and Information
SUN, XIULI, Foreign Languages
TIAN, XUEMIN, Information and Control Engineering
WAN, JIANHUA, Geo-Resources and Information
WANG, HUAQIN, Foreign Languages
WANG, JIANJUN, Humanities and Social Science
WANG, QINGTING, Foreign Languages
WANG, RUIHE, Petroleum Engineering
WANG, SHUTING, Foreign Languages
WANG, WEIFENG, Geo-Resources and Information
WANG, YANJIANG, Information and Control Engineering
WANG, YONGGANG, Geo-Resources and Information
XIA, CHONGYA, Humanities and Social Science
XING, LIANJUN, Physical Education
XU, MINGHAI, Architecture, Transport and Storage Engineering
XU, YIJI, Petroleum Engineering
XUE, SHIFENG, Architecture, Transport and Storage Engineering
YAN, XIANGZHEN, Architecture, Transport and Storage Engineering
YANG, DEWEI, Architecture, Transport and Storage Engineering
YANG, SHAOCHUN, Geo-Resources and Information
YANG, WEI, Physics, Science and Technology
YAO, JUN, Petroleum Engineering
YIN, XINGYAO, Geo-Resources and Information
YU, RANGANG, Architecture, Transport and Storage Engineering
YU, ZHAOXIAN, Physics, Science and Technology
YUAN, HONGCHAN, Foreign Languages
ZHAN, YONGLIANG, Architecture, Transport and Storage Engineering
ZHANG, GUOZHONG, Architecture, Transport and Storage Engineering
ZHANG, JIASHENG, Information and Control Engineering
ZHANG, QI, Petroleum Engineering
ZHANG, RONGHUA, Humanities and Social Science
ZHANG, ZHAOHUI, Information and Control Engineering
ZHAO, FULIN, Petroleum Engineering
ZHAO, XIUTAI, Petroleum Engineering
ZHAO, XIYU, Humanities and Social Science
ZHAO, YONGJUN, Geo-Resources and Information

ZHENG, JINWU, Information and Control Engineering
ZHONG, JIANHUA, Geo-Resources and Information
ZHOU, DETIAN, Humanities and Social Science
ZHOU, XIAOJUN, Petroleum Engineering
ZHOU, YAOQI, Geo-Resources and Information

CHINA PHARMACEUTICAL UNIVERSITY

Xuan Wu Men, Yan Zi Ji, Nanjing 210009, Jiangsu
Telephone: (25) 3271319
Fax: (25) 3271101
Internet: www.cpu.edu.cn
Founded 1936
Min. of Education Control
Academic year: September to July
Pres.: WU XIAOMING
Vice-Pres: LI FENGWEN, PAN YUJIAN, WANG GUANGJI, ZHANG XIAOLIAN
Head of Graduate Dept: CHU MINZUO
Librarian: MA SHIPING

Library of 700,000 vols
Number of teachers: 610
Number of students: 8,880

Publications: *Journal of China Pharmaceutical University* (6 a year), *Medical Evolution* (6 a year), *Medicine Annual of China*, *Medicine Education* (4 a year)

DEANS

Basic Institute: TAO LU
Department of Foreign Languages: DU HUI
Institute of Physical Education: WANG YONGTAO
School of Biological Pharmacy: WANG WEN
School of Economics and Economic School of International Medicine: GU HAI
Schools of Medicine and Chinese Traditional Medicine: KONG LINGYI

PROFESSORS

DAI, DEZAI, Medicine
GAO, SHANLIN, Chinese Traditional Medicine
GAO, XIANGDONG, Biological Pharmacy
GU, HAI, Economic School of International Medicine
HU, YUZHU
HUA, WEIYI, Medicine
HUANG, WENLONG, Medicine
JI, HUI, Medicine
JI, MIN, Medicine
KONG, LINGYI, Chinese Traditional Medicine
LIANG, JINGYU, Chinese Traditional Medicine
LIU, JINGJING, Biological Pharmacy
LIU, WENYING, Medicine
LIU, XIAODONG, Chinese Traditional Medicine
LIU, XIAODONG, Medicine
MA, SHIPING, Chinese Traditional Medicine
NI, KUNYI
PENG, SIXUN, Medicine
PING, QINENG, Medicine
QIAN, ZHIYU, Medicine
SHAO, RONG, Economic School of International Medicine
SHEN, ZILONG, Biological Pharmacy
TU, SHUCI, Medicine
WANG, GUANGJI, Medicine
WANG, QIUJUAN, Medicine
WANG, WEN, Biological Pharmacy
WU, WUTONG, Biological Pharmacy
WU, XIAOMING, Medicine
XI, TAO, Biological Pharmacy
XIANG, BINGREN
YANG, ZHONGLIN, Chinese Traditional Medicine
YE, WENCAI, Chinese Traditional Medicine
YOU, QIDONG, Medicine
YU, BOYANG, Chinese Traditional Medicine
ZHANG, LUYONG, Medicine
ZHANG, YIHUA, Medicine

ZHANG, ZHENGHANG, Medicine
ZHOU, JIANPING, Medicine
ZHU, DANNI, Chinese Traditional Medicine
ZHU, JIABI, Medicine

CHINA UNIVERSITY OF POLITICAL SCIENCE AND LAW

Yuanyuan Rd, Chang Ping, Beijing 102249
Telephone: (10) 69745577
Fax: (10) 82228531
Internet: www.cupl.edu.cn
Founded 1952
State control
Academic year: September to July
President: XU XIANMING
Vice-Presidents: JIE ZHANYUAN, MA KANGMEI, ZHANG BAOSHENG, ZHANG GUILIN, ZHANG LIUHUA
Head of Graduate Department: ZHU YONG
Librarian: ZENG ERSHU
Number of teachers: 1,400
Number of students: 21,325
Publications: *Journal of China University of Political Science and Law (Tribune of Political Science and Law)* (6 a year), *Journal of Comparative Law* (6 a year)

DEANS

School of American and Comparative Law: XU CHUANXI
Business School: SUN XUANZHONG
Criminal and Judicial School: WANG MU
School of Foreign Languages: LI LI
School of German and Comparative Law: MI JIAN
International Law School: WANG CHUANLI
Law School: MA HUAIDE
School of Political and Public Management: ZHU WEIJIU

PROFESSORS

CAI, DINGJIAN, Law
CAI, TUO, Political and Public Management
CHE, HU, American and Comparative Law
CHEN, GUANGZHONG, Procedural Law
CHEN, HONGTAI, Political and Public Management
CHEN, LIJUN, Law
CHENG, XIAOXIANG, International Law
CONG, RIYUN, Political and Public Management
CUI, YONGDONG, Law
DING, MEI, German and Comparative Law
DONG, SHUJUN, Criminal and Judicial Law
DU, XINLI, International Law
DUAN, DONGHUI, International Law
FAN, CHONGYI, Procedural Law
FENG, XIA, International Law
GAO, JIAWEI, German and Comparative Law
GU, YONGZHONG, Procedural Law
HAO, WEIHUA, American and Comparative Law
HE, JIAHONG, Procedural Law
HONG, DAODE, Criminal and Judicial Law
HOU, TINGZHI, Business School
HU, WENZHENG, Business School
HUANG, DAOXIU, Foreign Languages
HUANG, YISI, Foreign Languages
JIANG, RUJIAO, International Law
JIAO, HONGCHANG, Law
JIAO, MEIZHEN, Foreign Languages
LANG, PEIJUAN, Law
LE, GUOAN, Criminal and Judicial Law
LI, JUQIAN, International Law
LI, LI, Foreign Languages
LI, MING, Research of Legal Historiography
LI, WEI, International Law
LI, XIAO, Business School
LIN, QIAN, Research of Legal Historiography
LIU, BANGHUI, Criminal and Judicial Law
LIU, CHANGMIN, Political and Public Management
LIU, GENJU, Criminal and Judicial Law

LIU, GUANGAN, Research of Legal Historiography
LIU, HONGYING, Law
LIU, JINGUO, Law
LIU, JUNSHENG, Political and Public Management
LIU, LI, International Law
LIU, MU, Criminal and Judicial Law
LIU, SHANCHUN, Law
LIU, SHEN, Law
LONG, MENGHUI, Foreign Languages
MA, CHENGYUAN, International Law
MA, HUAIDE, Law
MA, ZHIBING, Research of Legal Historiography
MI, JIAN, German and Comparative Law
MO, SHIJIAN, International Law
PAN, QIN, Criminal and Judicial Law
PENG, YANAN, American and Comparative Law
QI, DONGXIANG, American and Comparative Law
QI, XIANGQUAN, International Law
QU, CHAOLI, Political and Public Management
QU, XINJIU, Criminal and Judicial Law
RUAN, QILIN, Criminal and Judicial Law
SHI, XIAOLI, International Law
SHI, YAJUN, Political and Public Management
SHU, GUOYING, German and Comparative Law
SONG, YINGHUI, Procedural Law
SUN, XUANZHONG, Business School
WANG, CHUANLI, International Law
WANG, JIANCHENG, Procedural Law
WANG, JIANXIN, Political and Public Management
WANG, JIE, Law
WANG, MU, Criminal and Judicial Law
WANG, RENBO, Law
WANG, SHUNAN, Criminal and Judicial Law
WU, MINGYANG, Business School
XIAO, JIANHUA, Procedural Law
XIN, CHONGYANG, International Law
XU, CHUANXI, American and Comparative Law
XU, HAIMING, International Law
XU, HAOMING, German and Comparative Law
XU, SHIHONG, Institute of Legal Ancient Books Arrangement
XUAN, ZENGYI, International Law
XUE, GANGLING, Law
YANG, FAN, Business School
YANG, FAN, International Law
YANG, RONGXIN, Procedural Law
YANG, YANG, Political and Public Management
YANG, YUGUAN, Procedural Law, German and Comparative Law
YUE, LILING, German and Comparative Law
ZHANG, GUILIN, Political and Public Management
ZHANG, GUOJUN, Business School
ZHANG, JINFAN, Research of Legal Historiography
ZHANG, LI, International Law
ZHANG, LIYING, International Law
ZHANG, SHENG, Law
ZHANG, SHUYI, Law
ZHANG, XIAOMU, International Law
ZHANG, ZHONGQIU, Research of Legal Historiography
ZHAO, BAOCHENG, Criminal and Judicial Law
ZHAO, WEI, International Law
ZHAO, XIANGLIN, International Law
ZHAO, YIMIN, International Law
ZHENG, XIANWEN, Institute of Legal Ancient Books Arrangement
ZHENG, YONGLIU, German and Comparative Law
ZHOU, JIANHAI, International Law
ZHOU, ZHONGHAI, International Law
ZHU, JIANGENG, International Law
ZHU, WEIJIU, Political and Public Management
ZHU, YONG, Research of Legal Historiography

ZHU, ZIQIN, International Law

CHINA CENTRAL RADIO AND TELEVISION UNIVERSITY

160 Fuxing Men Nei St, Beijing 100031
Telephone: (10) 66412407
Fax: (10) 66419025
E-mail: fao@crtvu.edu.cn
Internet: www.crtvu.edu.cn
Founded 1979 on the 'open university' principle
State control
Academic year: September to July
44 Provincial campuses, 961 br. schools
Pres.: ZHANG YAOXUE
Vice-Pres: RUAN ZHIYONG, SUN LUYI, YAN BING, YU YUNXIU
Library Dir: SUN LUYI
Library of 100,000 vols (CRTVU), 32,869,000 vols (provinces)
Number of teachers: 188 full-time, 565 part-time (CRTVU)
Number of teachers: 42,500 full-time, 31,500 part-time (provinces)
Number of students: 2,300,000
Publication: *Distance Education in China* (6 a year).

CHINESE TRADITIONAL OPERA COLLEGE

3 Li Ren St, Xuan Wu District, Beijing 100054
Telephone: 33-5156
Founded 1978
Pres.: YU LIN
Vice-Pres: GE SHILIANG, ZHU WENXIANG
Librarian: LIU SHIYUAN
Library of 150,000 vols
Number of teachers: 246
Number of students: 329
Publication: *Traditional Opera Art* (4 a year).

CHONGQING UNIVERSITY

Chongqing, Sichuan Province 630044
Telephone: (23) 65102449
Fax: (23) 65316656
E-mail: fao@cqu.edu.cn
Internet: www.cqu.edu.cn
Founded 1929
State control
Languages of instruction: Chinese, English
Academic year: February to January
Pres.: LIN FEI
Vice-Pres.: WU ZHONGFU
Chief Admin. Officer: CHEN DEWEN
Librarian: TANG YIKE
Number of teachers: 2,000
Number of students: 14,000
Publication: *Journal* (6 a year)

DEANS

College of Business Administration: YANG XIUTAI
College of Chemical Engineering: GAN GUNANGZHONG
College of Electronic Information Engineering: CAO ZEHAN
College of Foreign Languages: JIANG ZHIWEN
College of Resources and Environmental Engineering: LI XIAOHONG
College of Trade and Law: HE RONGWEI

CHONGQING UNIVERSITY OF MEDICAL SCIENCES

1 Medicine Rd, Yu Zhong, Chongqing 400046
Telephone: (23) 68804034
Internet: www.cqums.edu.cn

Founded 1956
Academic year: September to July
Pres.: LEI HAN
Vice-Pres: DENG SHIXIONG, DONG ZHI, HUANG AILONG, WANG LIHUA, XIE PENG
Librarian: LU CHANGHONG
Library of 570,000 vols
Number of teachers: 4,374
Number of students: 8,923

Publications: *Chinese Journal of Hepatology* (6 a year), *Journal of Chongqing Medical University* (6 a year), *Journal of Paediatric Pharmacy* (6 a year), *Journal of Ultrasound in Clinical Medicine* (6 a year), *Research in Medical Education* (6 a year)

DEANS

College of Basic Medicine: WANG YAPING
Department of Biomedical Engineering: WANG ZHIBIAO
Department of Medical Examining: TU ZHIGUANG
Department of Medical Imaging: REN HONG
Department of Reproductive Medical Science: WANG YINGXIONG
Institute of Humanity and Social Science: FENG ZHEYONG

PROFESSORS

CHEN, SHOUTIAN, Medical Imaging
CONG, YULONG, Medical Examining
DAI, YONG, Medical Examining
DONG, ZHI, Pharmacy
FENG, ZHEYONG, Humanities and Social Science
HU, GUOHU, Basic Medicine
JIANG, JIKAI, Medical Examining
KANG, GEFEI, Medical Examining
LEI, PEIYING, Medical Imaging
LEI, XIAOKUN, Humanities and Social Science
LI, HUIZHI, Pharmacy
LI, QINGEN, Pharmacy
LI, SHAOLIN, Basic Medicine
LIU, DAWEI, Preventive Medicine
LUO, JIA, Medical Imaging
LUO, YUNPENG, Basic Medicine
LU, CHANGHONG, Basic Medicine
MI, CAN, Basic Medicine
NING, BAODONG, Basic Medicine
PENG, HUIMING, Basic Medicine
QIU, ZONGYING, Pharmacy
QUAN, XUEMO, Medical Imaging
REN, HONG, Medical Imaging
SONG, FANGZHOU, Basic Medicine
SUN, SHANQUAN, Basic Medicine
TANG, SIJIE, Basic Medicine
TANG, WEIXUE, Basic Medicine
TU, ZHIGUANG, Medical Examining
WANG, RUIHUA, Preventive Medicine
WANG, WEIWEI, Basic Medicine
WANG, YANG, Preventive Medicine
WANG, YAPING, Basic Medicine
WANG, YINGXIONG, Reproductive Medical Science
WANG, ZHIBIAO, Biomedical Engineering
WANG, ZHIGANG, Medical Imaging
WU, FENG, Biomedical Engineering
XIANG, LIKE, Basic Medicine
XIE, ZHENGXIANG, Basic Medicine
YANG, ZHENGWEI, Basic Medicine
YANG, ZHIBANG, Basic Medicine
YI, YONGFENG, Basic Medicine
YU, YU, Basic Medicine
ZHANG, NENG, Basic Medicine
ZHAO, JIANNONG, Medical Imaging
ZHENG, ZHAOCHUN, Basic Medicine
ZHOU, CHENGHE, Pharmacy
ZHOU, JIANZHONG, Medical Imaging
ZHOU, QIXIN, Basic Medicine
ZHU, DAOYIN, Basic Medicine

DALIAN MARITIME UNIVERSITY

1 Linghai Rd, Dalian 116026, Liaoning Province
Telephone: (411) 84727149
Fax: (411) 84727874
E-mail: iceodmu@gmail.com
Internet: www.dlmu.edu.cn
Founded 1909
State control
Academic year: September to July
Pres.: Prof. WU ZHAOLIN
Vice-Pres: Dr SUN LICHENG, Dr SUN PEITING, WEN XIAOQIN
Registrar: WANG YUEHUI
Librarian: PANG FUWEN
Number of teachers: 728
Number of students: 12,722

Publications: *Higher Education Research in Areas of Communications* (2 a year), *Journal* (6 a year), *Liaoning Navigation* (4 a year), *World Shipping* (6 a year)

DEANS

Adult Education College: DING YONG
Automation and Electrical Engineering College: WANG XINGCHEN
Business College: FAN HOUMING
Computer Science and Technology College: ZHANG WEISHI
Electronic Information College: ZHANG SHUFANG
Environmental Science and Engineering College: DING YONGSHENG
Humanities and Social Sciences College: FENG WENHUA
International Cooperation College: ZHANG SHIPPING
Law College: QU GUANGQING
Marine Engineering College: REN GUANG
Navigation College: DONG FANG
Shipping Management College: YANG ZHAN

DALIAN UNIVERSITY OF TECHNOLOGY (DUT)

2 Linggong Rd, Ganjingzi District, Dalian 116023, Liaoning
Telephone: (411) 4678300
Fax: (411) 4708116
E-mail: dut@dlut.edu.cn
Internet: www.dlut.edu.cn
Founded 1949 as Dalian Institute of Technology
State control
Academic year: September to July
Units incl. 14 schools, 50 research institutes and 4 Nat. Key Laboratories
Pres.: Prof. CHENG GENGDONG
Vice-Pres: Prof. JIANG DEXUE, Prof. KONG XIANJING, Prof. SHEN HONGSHU, Prof. WANG LIANSHENG, Prof. XUE GUANG
Librarian: XIE MAOZHAO
Library of 1,840,000 vols, 8,000 periodicals
Number of teachers: 1,297
Number of students: 22,344 (incl. 5,883 postgraduate)

Publications: *Journal* (6 a year), *Journal of Computational Mechanics* (4 a year), *Journal of Mathematical Research and Exposition* (4 a year), *Journal of Social Sciences* (4 a year).

DAQING PETROLEUM INSTITUTE

Daqing 151400, Heilongjiang
Telephone: (459) 4653232
Fax: (459) 7332415
Internet: www.dqpi.net
Founded 1960
State control
Academic year: September to July
Pres.: LIU YANG

Vice-Pres: LIU YONG JIAN, LU YAN FANG, SONG ZHI CHEN, YANG XIAO LONG
Number of teachers: 1,762
Number of students: 10,000

Publications: *Journal* (4 a year), *Petroleum Industry Technology* (4 a year)

DEANS

College of Building Construction Engineering: SUN JIAN GANG
College of Computing and Information Technology: MA RUI MIN
College of Continuing Education: ZHAO JIN LIN
College of Earth Sciences: SHI SHANG MING
College of Economics and Management: SHAO QIANG
College of Electricity and Information Engineering: DUAN YU BO
College of Electronic Engineering: WANG MING JI
College of Foreign Languages: QIU XUE HE
College of Humanities: KUAN JIN LIN
College of Mathematics: WANG SHOU TIAN
College of Mechanical Science and Engineering: WANG ZUN CE
College of Oil Engineering Institute: CUI HAI QING

PROFESSORS

AI, CHI, Oil Engineering
BAI, XING HUA, Earth Sciences
CAO, YU QUAN, Electricity and Information Engineering
CHANG, YU LIAN, Mechanical Science and Engineering
CHEN, TAO PING, Oil Engineering
CHEN, XUE MEI, Mechanical Science and Engineering
CUI, HAI QING, Oil Engineering
CUI, ZHEN HUA, Mechanical Science and Engineering
DAI, GUANG, Mechanical Science and Engineering
DU, HONG LIE, Earth Sciences
DUAN, YU BO, Electricity and Information Engineering
FAN, HONG FU, Oil Engineering
FU, GUANG, Earth Sciences
FU, GUANG JIE, Electricity and Information Engineering
GAO, BING KUN, Electricity and Information Engineering
GUO, YU FENG, Electronic Engineering
HAN, GUO YOU, Mechanical Science and Engineering
HAN, HONG SHENG, Oil Engineering
HAO, WEN SEN, Mechanical Science and Engineering
JIA, WEN JU, Computing and Information Technology
JIA, ZHEN QI, Oil Engineering
JIANG, MING HU, Mechanical Science and Engineering
JIN, SHAO XIAN, Electronic Engineering
KANG, WANG LI, Oil Engineering
KONG, LING BIN, Mathematics
LI, BAO YAN, Mechanical Science and Engineering
LI, CHUN SHENG, Computing and Information Technology
LI, CONG XIN, Computing and Information Technology
LI, JIE, Earth Sciences
LI, XIAO PING, Mathematics
LI, YAN JIE, Mathematics
LING, JING LONG, Earth Sciences
LIU, JU BAO, Mechanical Science and Engineering
LIU, SU LIN, Mechanical Science and Engineering
LIU, TIE NAN, Electricity and Information Engineering
LIU, XIAO YAN, Earth Sciences
LIU, YANG, Oil Engineering

LIU, YI KUN, Oil Engineering
LIU, YONG JIAN, Oil Engineering
LU, LING JIE, Computing and Information Technology
LU, SHUANG FANG, Earth Sciences
LU, YAN FANG, Earth Sciences
MA, RUI MIN, Computing and Information Technology
MA, SHI ZHONG, Earth Sciences
NUAN, QING DE, Mechanical Science and Engineering
REN, FU SHAN, Mechanical Science and Engineering
REN, WEI JIAN, Electricity and Information Engineering
SHAO, QIANG, Economics and Management
SHI, SHANG MING, Earth Sciences
SONG, KAO PING, Oil Engineering
SONG, YU LING, Humanities
SUN, BO TAO, Foreign Languages
SUN, JIAN GANG, Building Construction Engineering
SUN, YAN BIN, Economics and Management
SUN, YU XUE, Oil Engineering
TANG, GUO WEI, Computing and Information Technology
WANG, DE MING, Oil Engineering
WANG, HENG JIU, Economics and Management
WANG, JING QI, Earth Sciences
WANG, MING JI, Electronic Engineering
WANG, SHOU TIAN, Mathematics
WANG, WEN GUANG, Earth Sciences
WANG, XIU MING, Earth Sciences
WANG, ZUN CE, Mechanical Science and Engineering
WU, WEN XIANG, Oil Engineering
XIA, HUI FENG, Oil Engineering
XU, BU YUN, Mechanical Science and Engineering
XU, SHAO HUA, Computing and Information Technology
YAN, TIE, Oil Engineering
YI, ZHI AN, Computing and Information Technology
ZENG, ZHAO YING, Mathematics
ZHANG, CHANG HAI, Mathematics
ZHANG, DA WEI, Oil Engineering
ZHANG, JI HUA, Foreign Languages
ZHANG, JING, Earth Sciences
ZHANG, YONG HONG, Mechanical Science and Engineering
ZHANG, YU BIN, Mechanical Science and Engineering
ZHAO, WEI MIN, Mechanical Science and Engineering
ZHAO, ZI GANG, Oil Engineering
ZHOU, QING LONG, Mechanical Science and Engineering
ZHU, JUN, Mechanical Science and Engineering

DONGBEI UNIVERSITY OF FINANCE AND ECONOMICS

217 Jianshan St, Shahekou District, Dalian 116025
Telephone: (411) 4691503
Fax: (411) 4691862
E-mail: dufe1952@pub.dl.inpta.net.cn
Internet: www.dufe.edu.cn

Founded 1952
State control
Languages of instruction: Chinese, English
Academic year: September to July
President: Prof. YU YANG
Vice-Presidents: Prof. GUO CHANGLU, Assoc. Prof. LIU JIANMIN, Prof. QIU DONG
President's Assistant: Assoc. Prof. ZHOU LIANSHENG
Librarian: ZHANG LI

Library of 900,000 vols
Number of teachers: 561
Number of students: 11,815 (incl. 5,678 correspondence)

Publication: *Research on Finance and Economics Issues*

HEADS OF SCHOOLS
School of Accountancy: Prof. LIU YONGZE
School of Adult Education: Prof. CONG JIZENG
School of Business Management: Prof. LIU QINGYUAN
School of Finance and Taxation: Prof. MA GOUQIANG
School of Hotel Management: Assoc. Prof. LI LI
School of International Chinese: Assoc. Prof. ZHANG WENFENG

DONGHUA UNIVERSITY

1882 West Yan-An Rd, Shanghai 200051
Telephone: 62197533
Fax: 62194722
Internet: www.dhu.edu.cn

Founded 1951 as East China Textile Institute of Science and Technology, re-named China Textile University 1985, current name 1999
Academic year: September to July
Pres.: Prof. SHAO SHIHUANG
Vice-Pres: Prof. JIN JIAYOU, Prof. HU XUE-CHAO, Prof. TAN DEZHONG, Prof. XUE YOUYI, Prof. ZHU SHIGEN
Registrar: Prof. ZHANG JIAYU
Librarian: Prof. YU MING

Library of 810,000 vols and periodicals
Number of teachers: 903
Number of students: 12,081

Publications: *Journal* (6 a year, English edn 2 a year), *Textile Technology Overseas* (6 a year)

HEADS OF COLLEGES
Art and Design Institute: Prof. HUANG YUANQING
College of Textile Science and Technology: Prof. ZHU SUKANG
College of Chemistry and Chemicals: Prof. DAI JINJIN
College of Mechanical Engineering: Prof. WANG SHENZE
College of Information Science and Technology: Prof. SONG LIQUN
College of Science: Prof. XIE HANKUN
College of Humanities: ZHANG YI
College of Environmental Science and Engineering: Prof. XI DANLI
College of Materials Science and Engineering: Prof. CHEN YANMO
College of Foreign Languages: Prof. SHEN BAIYAO
Fashion Institute: Prof. ZHANG WEIYUAN
Glorious Sun School of Business Management: Prof. SUN JUNKANG

EAST CHINA NORMAL UNIVERSITY

3663 Zhongshan Rd North, Shanghai 200062
Telephone: (21) 62233333
Fax: (21) 62576217
E-mail: webmaster@ecnu.edu.cn
Internet: www.ecnu.edu.cn

Founded 1951
Controlled by the Min. of Education
Academic year: September to July (two semesters)
Pres.: WANG JIANPAN
Vice-Pres: DU GONGZHUO, MA QINRONG, TANG MINGJIAN, WANG TIEXIAN, YE JIANNONG, YU LIZHONG
Librarian: HUANG XIUWEN

Library of 3,535,000 vols
Number of teachers: 1,647
Number of students: 19,108

Publications: *Applied Probability and Statistics* (4 a year), *East Europe and Central Asia Today* (6 a year), *Journal of Educational Science* (4 a year), *Journal of Natural Sciences* (4 a year), *Journal of Philosophy and Social Sciences* (6 a year), *Psychological Science* (6 a year), *Research into the Theory of Ancient Literature* (irregular), *Theoretical Studies in Literature and Art* (6 a year), *World Geography Research* (2 a year)

DEANS
College of Continuing Education: SUN JIANMING
College of Educational Administration: MA QINRONG
Graduate School: YU LIZHONG
International College of Chinese Culture: WANG TIEXIAN
School of Business: JIN RUNGUI
School of Chemistry and Life Science: XU HONGFA
School of Educational Science and Technology: DING GANG
School of Foreign Languages: ZHANG CHUNBO
School of Humanities: FENG SHAOLEI
School of Literature and Art: HONG BENJIAN
School of Pre-School and Special Education: NIE YOULI
School of Resources and Environmental Science: CHEN ZHONGYUAN
School of Science and Engineering: WANG ZUGENG

EAST CHINA UNIVERSITY OF SCIENCE AND TECHNOLOGY

130 Meilong Rd, Shanghai 200237
Telephone: 4775678
Fax: 4777138
Internet: www.ecust.edu.cn

Founded 1952 (until 1993, East China University of Chemical Technology)

Depts of applied mathematics, applied physics, automatic control and electronic engineering, biochemical engineering, business management, chemical engineering, chemistry, computer science, environmental engineering, English for business, fine chemicals technology, foreign languages, industrial design, inorganic materials, management engineering, mechanical engineering, petroleum processing, polymer materials, social science; research Institutes of agrochemical bioregulators, applied chemistry, applied mathematics, biomedical engineering, bioreactors (national laboratory) chemical engineering, chemical environmental engineering, chemical physics, chemical reaction engineering (joint laboratory), culture, economic development, fine chemicals technology, heterogeneous reaction engineering (national laboratory), higher education, industrial automation, industrial design, inorganic chemical technology, inorganic materials, Marxism and ideological education, materials science, petroleum processing, process equipment and pressure vessels, speciality chemicals, technical chemical physics

Pres.: Prof. WANG XINGYU
Vice-Pres: Prof. DAI GANCE, LIN ZHUYUAN, Prof. ZHANG DONGSHAN, Prof. ZHU ZIBIN

Library of 1,240,000 vols, 4,500 periodicals in 11 languages
Number of teachers: 1,841
Number of students: 8,322

Publication: *Journal* (6 a year).

FUDAN UNIVERSITY

220 Handan Rd, Shanghai 200433
Telephone: (21) 65642222
Internet: www.fudan.edu.cn

Founded 1905, present status 2000, following merger with Shanghai Medical Univ.

State control
Languages of instruction: Chinese, English
Academic year: September to July (2 semesters)
Pres.: Prof. WANG, SHENGHONG
Vice-Pres: CAI, DAFENG WANG, WEIPING XUE, MINGYANG XU MINZHI XU, ZHONG YANG, YULIANG ZHANG, YIHUA ZHENG, ZUKANG ZHOU, LUWEI
Librarian: Prof. QIN ZENGFU
Library of 4,330,000 vols
Number of teachers: 2,400
Number of students: 28,800 undergraduates and 1,620 postgraduates
Publications: *Fudan Natural Sciences Journal*, *Fudan Social Sciences Journal*, *Mathematics Annals Acta* (6 a year)

DEANS

School of Cultural Relics and Museum Science: Prof. ZHUANG XICHANG
School of Economics: Prof. HONG YUANPENG
School of Journalism: Prof. DING GANLIN
School of Life Science: Prof. LI YUYANG
School of Management: Prof. ZHENG SHAOLIAN
School of Technological Science: Prof. YUAN QU

FUJIAN AGRICULTURAL AND FORESTRY UNIVERSITY

Jinshan, Fujian Province, 350002
Telephone: (591) 3741721
Fax: (591) 3741251
Internet: www.fjau.edu.cn
Founded 1936
State control
Language of instruction: Chinese
Pres.: Prof. LU LIUXIN
Vice-Pres: PAN TINGGUO, Prof. YE SHANGQING, YOU MINSHENG
Librarian: HU FANPING
Library of 560,000 vols
Number of teachers: 843
Number of students: 3,880
Publications: *Current Communications on Overseas Agricultural Science and Technology*, *Journal of Entomology in Eastern China*, *Journal of Fujian Agricultural University*, *Overseas Agricultural Science: Sugarcane*, *Wuyi Science*

HEADS OF COLLEGES

College of Adult Education: YE YICHUN
College of Animal Science: HUANG YIFAN
College of Crop Science: LIN YANQUAN
College of Economics and Trade: HUANG JIANCHENG

FUJIAN MEDICAL UNIVERSITY

88 Jiaotong Rd, Fuzhou, Fujian 350004
Telephone: (591) 3568821
Internet: www.fjmu.edu.cn
Founded 1937
Pres.: Prof. WU ZHONGFU
Vice-Pres: LIN KEHUA, LUO GUEILIN
Head of Postgraduate Dept: KANG YUANYUAN
Librarian: HUANG HUISHANG
Library of 258,448 vols
Number of teachers: 398
Number of students: 2,306
Publications: *Journal*, *Medical Education Study*.

FUJIAN NORMAL UNIVERSITY

8 Shang San Rd, Cang Shan Section, Fuzhou 350007, Fujian
Telephone: (591) 83456156
Fax: (591) 83425154

Internet: www.fjtu.edu.cn
Founded 1907
Dept of Education of Fujian control
Academic year: September to July
Pres.: LI JIANPING
Vice-Pres: HUANG HANSHENG, LI MIN, WANG ZHENGLU, WANG WENDING, ZHENG YISHU
Head of Graduate Department: LI JIANPING
Librarian: WAN BAOCHUAN
Number of teachers: 2,500
Number of students: 30,000
Publications: *Journal* (natural sciences, 6 a year), *Journal* (philosophy and social sciences, 6 a year), *Mathematics of Fujian Middle School* (6 a year)

DEANS

College of Physical Education and Sports Science: MEI XUEXIONG
School of Bioengineering: LI MIN
School of Chemistry and Material Science: HU BINGHUAN
School of Economy: LI JIANJIAN
School of Educational Sciences and Technology: YU WENSEN
School of Foreign Languages: LIN DAJIN
School of Geographical Sciences: YANG YUSHENG
School of Humanities: CHEN QINGYUAN
School of Law: GUO TIEMIN
School of Mathematics and Computer Science: LI YONGQING
School of Media: YAN CHUNJUN
School of Music: ZHENG JINYANG
School of Physics and Optoelectronic Technology: XIE SHUSEN
School of Public Administration: HE YILUN
School of Society and History: LIN JINSHUI
School of Software: WENG ZUMAO
School of Tourism: ZHENG YAOXIN

PROFESSORS

CAI, XIULING, Economics
CHAI, YUPING, Public Administration
CHEN, GUIRONG, Public Administration
CHEN, GUORUI, Physical Education and Sports Science
CHEN, HUOPING, Educational Sciences and Technology
CHEN, JUNQIN, Physical Education and Sports Science
CHEN, KAI, Foreign Languages
CHEN, LIANGYUAN, Humanities
CHEN, QINGYUAN, Humanities
CHEN, RONG, Physical Education and Sports Science
CHEN, SHAOHUI, Economics
CHEN, SHAOPING, Chemistry and Material Science
CHEN, TIECHENG, Physical Education and Sports Science
CHEN, WEIZHEN, Foreign Languages
CHEN, YIPING, Bioengineering
CHEN, YONGCHUN, Public Administration
CHEN, YOUQIANG, Bioengineering
CHEN, ZEPING, Humanities
CHEN, ZHENG, Economics
CHENG, LIGUO, Educational Sciences and Technology
DAI, CONGTENG, Foreign Languages
DAI, XIANQUN, Society and History
DU, CHANGZHONG, Foreign Languages
GANG, SONG, Bioengineering
GAO, JIANMIN, Bioengineering
GU, YEPING, Humanities
GUO, TIEMIN, Economics
HE, YILUN, Public Administration
HONG, MING, Educational Sciences and Technology
HONG, YANGUO, Bioengineering
HU, BINGHUAN, Chemistry and Material Science
HU, CANGZE, Society and History
HU, ZHIGANG, Chemistry and Material Science

HUANG, AILING, Educational Sciences and Technology
HUANG, GUANGYANG, Educational Sciences and Technology
HUANG, GUOSHENG, Society and History
HUANG, GUOXIONG, Public Administration
HUANG, HANSHENG, Physical Education and Sports Science
HUANG, JIANZHONG, Bioengineering
HUANG, JIAYE, Economics
HUANG, RENXIAN, Educational Sciences and Technology
HUANG, ZHIGAO, Physics and Optoelectronic Technology
LAN, XUEFEI, Music
LI, HONGCAI, Physics and Optoelectronic Technology
LI, JIANJIAN, Economics
LI, JIANPING, Economics
LI, MIN, Bioengineering
LI, RONGBAO, Foreign Languages
LI, SHUZHEN, Public Administration
LI, XIANGMIN, Public Administration
LIAN, CHENGYE, Society and History
LIAN, RONG, Educational Sciences and Technology
LIN, BENCHUN, Foreign Languages
LIN, DAJIN, Foreign Languages
LIN, GUOPING, Society and History
LIN, JING, Educational Sciences and Technology
LIN, JINHUO, Chemistry and Material Science
LIN, JINSHUI, Society and History
LIN, LIN, Bioengineering
LIN, QING, Economics
LIN, SHANLANG, Economics
LIN, XIUGUO, Public Administration
LIN, ZHANG, Foreign Languages
LIN, ZIHUA, Economics
LIU, HUIYU, Society and History
LIU, JIANQIU, Bioengineering
LIU, RONGFANG, Chemistry and Material Science
LIU, YAMENG, Foreign Languages
LIU, YONGGENG, Humanities
MAO, NING, Bioengineering
MEI, XUEXIONG, Physical Education and Sports Science
PAN, XINHE, Humanities
PAN, YUTENG, Public Administration
QIAO, JIANZHONG, Music
QIU, LING, Foreign Languages
QIU, YISHEN, Physics and Optoelectronic Technology
QIU, YONGQU, Educational Sciences and Technology
SHI, QIAOQIN, Bioengineering
SU, XIAOQING, Physical Education and Sports Science
SU, ZHENFANG, Public Administration
SUN, SHAOZHEN, Humanities
TAN, XUEXHUN, Humanities
TANG, WENJI, Society and History
WANG, GUOHONG, Bioengineering
WANG, HANMIN, Humanities
WANG, JIANDE, Society and History
WANG, KE, Humanities
WANG, YAOHUA, Music
WANG, ZHENGLU, Society and History
WANG, ZHIBO, Public Administration
WEN, RI, Society and History
WENG, JIABAO, Chemistry and Material Science
WENG, YINTAO, Humanities
WENG, ZUMAO, Computer Software
WU, YOUGEN, Economics
WU, ZONGHUA, Chemistry and Material Science
XI, YANG, Humanities
XIAO, HUASHAN, Bioengineering
XIE, BIZHEN, Society and History
XIE, SHUSEN, Physics and Optoelectronic Technology
XU, HONGFENG, Physical Education and Sports Science

XU, MING, Educational Sciences and Technology

XU, YONG, Physics and Optoelectronic Technology

YAN, CHUNJUN, Humanities

YAN, YOUWEI, Educational Sciences and Technology

YANG, KONGCHI, Educational Sciences and Technology

YANG, MINGRU, Bioengineering

YANG, XINHUA, Public Administration

YANG, YUSHENG, Geographical Sciences

YANG, ZHAOFENG, Bioengineering

YE, YIDUO, Educational Sciences and Technology

YOU, YONGLONG, Bioengineering

YU, GECHUN, Public Administration

YU, WENSEN, Educational Sciences and Technology

YUAN, SHUQI, Geographical Sciences

ZENG, CONGSHENG, Geographical Sciences

ZHAN, GUANQUN, Society and History

ZHANG, DINGHUA, Bioengineering

ZHANG, HANJIN, Physical Education and Sports Science

ZHANG, HUARONG, Economics

ZHANG, WENGONG, Chemistry and Material Science

ZHANG, YANDING, Bioengineering

ZHEN, XIAOHUA, Society and History

ZHENG, DAXIAN, Geographical Sciences

ZHENG, JINYANG, Music

ZHENG, YI, Bioengineering

ZHENG, YOUXIAN, Public Administration

ZHU, HEJIAN, Geographical Sciences

ZHU, JIAN, Economics

ZHU, JINZI, Bioengineering

ZHU, LING, Humanities

ZHUANG, HUIRU, Bioengineering

ZHUANG, TAO, Foreign Languages

ZUAN, ZHENGFANG, Public Administration

FUZHOU UNIVERSITY

523 Industry Rd, Fuzhou 350002, Fujian

Telephone: (591) 3739513

Fax: (591) 3713866

Internet: www.fzu.edu.cn

Founded 1958

Academic year: September to July

President: WU MIN SHENG

Vice-Presidents: CHEN GUO NAN, FAN GENG HUA, FANG ZHEN ZHENG, FU XIAN ZHI

Heads of Graduate Department: LIN SHU WEN, LIU SONG QING

Librarian: ZHANG WEN DE

Number of teachers: 1,200

Number of students: 20,000

Publications: *Journal* (natural sciences, 6 a year), *Journal* (philosophy, 4 a year)

DEANS

Napier College: XIE LIU HUI

School of Biological Science and Technology: RAO PING FAN

School of Civil Engineering and Architecture: CHEN BAO CHUN

School of Electric Engineering and Automation: CHEN BAO CHUN

School of Environment and Resources: XU HAN QIU

School of Foreign Languages: WU SONG JIANG

School of Humanities and Social Sciences: LIN YI

School of Law: CHEN QUAN SHENG

School of Management: CHEN GUO HONG

School of Materials Sciences and Engineering: CHEN XIAN SHENG

School of Mathematics and Computer Science: WANG XIAO DONG

School of Mechanical Engineering: GAO CHENG HUI

School of Physics and Information Engineering: YU LUN

School of Public Management: WANG JIAN

School of Software: FAN GENG HUA

School of Zhi Cheng: TANG YI ZHU

Sunshine College: CHEN GONG LIN

PROFESSORS

CAI, JIN DING, Electrical Engineering and Automation

CHEN, BAO CHUN, Civil Engineering and Architecture

CHEN, CHONG, Electrical Engineering and Automation

CHEN, FU JI, Public Management

CHEN, GUO HONG, Management

CHEN, LE SHAN, Mechanical Engineering

CHEN, LI, Mechanical Engineering

CHEN, RONG SI, Management

CHEN, SEN, Civil Engineering and Architecture

CHEN, SHU MEI, Mechanical Engineering

CHEN, XIAN SHENG, Materials Science and Engineering

CHEN, XIAO WEI, Foreign Languages

CHEN, XIN, Physics and Information Engineering

CHEN, XIN SHU, Civil Engineering and Architecture

DU, MING, Electrical Engineering and Automation

FANG, ZHEN ZHENG, Civil Engineering and Architecture

GAO, CHENG HUI, Mechanical Engineering

GUO, ZONG REN, Electrical Engineering and Automation

HU, JI RONG, Management

HU, XIAO RONG, Civil Engineering and Architecture

HUANG, KE AN, Management

HUANG, SHU ZHANG, Management

HUANG, WEN XIN, Management

HUANG, YAO ZHI, Mechanical Engineering

HUANG, ZHI GANG, Management

JIAN, WEN BIN, Environment and Resources

LAN, ZHAO HUI, Mechanical Engineering

LEI, DE SEN, Public Management

LIN, GUO RONG, Mechanical Engineering

LIN, QIANG, Physics and Information Engineering

LIN, SHU WEN, Mechanical Engineering

LIN, TONG, Mechanical Engineering

LIN, YI, Humanities and Social Sciences

LIN, YING XING, Management

LIN, YOU WEN, Management

LIN, YUAN QING, Management

LIU, MING HUA, Environment and Resources

LIU, YAN BIN, Mechanical Engineering

PAN, YAN, Management

PENG, DA WEN, Civil Engineering and Architecture

QI, KAI, Civil Engineering and Architecture

QIAN, KUANG WU, Materials Science and Engineering

QIU, GONG WEI, Electrical Engineering and Automation

RAO, PING FAN, Biological Science and Technology

RUAN, YU ZHONG, Materials Science and Engineering

SHENG, FEI MIN, Environment and Resources

SU, KAI XIONG, Physics and Information Engineering

SUN, QIU BI, Management

TANG, DE PING, Materials Science and Engineering

TANG, DIAN, Materials Science and Engineering

TANG, LI HONG, Public Management

TANG, NING PING, Electrical Engineering and Automation

WANG, JIAN, Public Management

WANG, QIN MIN, Physics and Information Engineering

WANG, WEI YI, Management

WANG, YING MING, Public Management

WANG, ZHONG LAI, Biological Science and Technology

WU, HAN GUANG, Electrical Engineering and Automation

WU, SONG JIANG, Foreign Languages

WU, XING NAN, Humanities and Social Sciences

XI, YONG QIN, Public Management

XIE, ZHI XIN, Civil Engineering and Architecture

XU, DOU DOU, Humanities and Social Sciences

XU, HAN QIU, Environment and Resources

YANG, FU WEN, Electrical Engineering and Automation

YANG, XIAO XIANG, Mechanical Engineering

YE, ZHONG HE, Mechanical Engineering

YEA, ZHONG, Management

YU, LUN, Physics and Information Engineering

YUAN, BING LING, Humanities and Social Sciences

ZHANG, BAI, Management

ZHANG, BEI MIN, Electrical Engineering and Automation

ZHANG, QI SHAN, Management

ZHANG, MAO XUN, Mechanical Engineering

ZHANG, QI SHAN, Mechanical Engineering

ZHANG, QIONG, Materials Science and Engineering

ZHANG, YE, Management

ZHENG, JIAN LAN, Civil Engineering and Architecture

ZHENG, SHI BIAO, Physics and Information Engineering

ZHENG, ZHEN, Civil Engineering and Architecture

ZHENG, ZHEN FEI, Civil Engineering and Architecture

ZHOU, RUI ZHONG, Civil Engineering and Architecture

ZHOU, XIAO LIANG, Management

ZHU, YONG CHUN, Civil Engineering and Architecture

ZHU, ZU PING, Mechanical Engineering

GANSU AGRICULTURAL UNIVERSITY

1 Yingmencun, Nanning District, Lanzhou 730070, Gansu Province

Telephone: (931) 7631125

Fax: (931) 7631125

E-mail: wujp@public.lz.gs.cn

Internet: www.gsau.edu.cn

Founded 1958

Academic year: September to July

President: Prof. WANG DI

Vice-Presidents: LAN YUZHEN, Prof. LI ZHENXIAO, LU JIANHUA

Director of Foreign Affairs: Prof. WU JIANPING

Librarian: LIU XI

Library of 500,000 vols

Number of teachers: 600

Number of students: 5,000 (125 postgraduates)

Publications: *Journal of Grassland and Turf* (4 a year), *University Journal* (12 a year)

DEANS

Agricultural Business and Trade: WANG CENGLIN

Agricultural Machinery and Engineering: WU JIANMING

Agronomy: LI WEI

Animal Science: CUI XIAN

Basic Courses: YUAN TONGSHENG

Food Science: YU QUNLI

Forest Science: JIANG ZHIRONG

Grassland Science: CAO ZHIZHONG

Horticulture: YU JIHUA

Plant Protection: ZHANG XINGHU

Social Science: SHANG ZHENHAI

Soil Chemistry: SHI YINGFU

Veterinary Science: LIU YING

Water Conservation: CHENG ZIYONG

GUANGDONG COLLEGE OF MEDICINE AND PHARMACY

40 Guang Han Zhi, Haizhu District, Guangzhou, Guangdong Province 510224

Telephone: 4429040

Founded 1978

President: Prof. Du Qi Zhang (acting)

Vice-Presidents: Cheng Shenghao, Li Ting-jie

Librarian: Liao Ming Qing

Library of 160,000 vols

Number of teachers: 300

Number of students: 1,800

Publication: *Journal*

PROFESSORS

Fenghe, H., Pharmacology
Fengming, Z., Epidemiology
Jincheng, H., Pharmaceutical Chemistry
Jingxian, J., Internal Medicine
Jingzhi, H., Human Parasitology
Jipeng, L., Pharmacognosy
Muxian, L., Biochemistry
Pusheng, W., Traditional Chinese Medicine
Qihua, W., Human Anatomy
Qiyun, Y., Phytochemistry
Qizhang, D., Pharmacology
Shide, S., Statistics
Yiyuan, Z., Dermatology
Zhicheng, C., Hygiene
Zhuhua, L., Microbiology

GUANGXI NORMAL UNIVERSITY

Yan Shan, Gui Lin 541004, Guangxi

Telephone: (773) 5812081

Fax: (773) 5812383

Internet: www.gxnu.edu.cn

Founded 1932

Min. of Education control

Academic year: September to July

President: Liang Hong

Vice-Presidents: Lan Changzhou, Liu Jianbing, Liu Muren, Wang Jie, Yi Zhong, Zhong Ruitian

Librarian: Yao Qian

Library of 2,060,000 vols

Number of teachers: 1,043

Number of students: 40,000

Publication: *Journal of Guangxi Normal University* (4 a year)

DEANS

College of Foreign Studies: Liu Zhaozhong
College of Life Science: Qin Xinming
College of Politics and Public Management: Tan Peiwen
College of Physics and Information Technology: Wang Qiang
Department of Resources and Environmental Science: He Xingcun
Educational Science College: Gao Jinling
School of Chemistry and Chemical Engineering: Liang Fupei
School of Culture and Tourism: Zhou Zuoming
School of Law and Business: Luo Zhisong
School of Sports: Liang Zhuping

PROFESSORS

Cai, Changzhuo, International Culture and Education
Chen, Hongjiang, Politics and Public Management
Chen, Jitang, Foreign Studies
Chen, Qin, Politics and Public Management
Chen, Xiongzhuan, Culture and Tourism
Chen, Zhaobin, Physical Education
Chen, Zhenfeng, Chemistry and Chemical Engineering
Cui, Tianshun, Resources and Environmental Science

Cui, Yaodong, Mathematics and Computer Science
Deng, Biyang, Chemistry and Chemical Engineering
Deng, Peiming, Mathematics and Computer Science
Ding, Changming, Mathematics and Computer Science
Feng, Cunhua, Mathematics and Computer Science
Guo, Liliang, Physical Education
He, Linxia, Culture and Tourism
He, Xianglin, Foreign Studies
He, Xingcun, Resources and Environmental Science
Hu, Dalei, Chinese Studies
Huang, Binlian, Physics and Information Technology
Huang, Chengming, Life Science
Huang, Jieshan, Social Sciences
Huang, Ruixiong, Social Sciences
Huang, Shen, Physical Education
Huang, Weilin, Chinese Studies
Huang, Zhusheng, Law and Business
Jiang, Guocheng, Life Science
Jiang, Shihui, Educational Science
Jiang, Yiming, Chemistry and Chemical Engineering
Lei, Rei, Chinese Studies
Li, Dunxiang, Law and Business
Li, Fubo, Chinese Studies
Li, Honghan, Educational Science
Li, Jiang, Chinese Studies
Li, Lailong, Chinese Studies
Li, Lu, Educational Science
Li, Xiao, Foreign Studies
Li, Yi, Resources and Environmental Science
Li, Zhiqing, Physical Education
Liang, Fupei, Chemistry and Chemical Engineering
Liang, Hong, Chemistry and Chemical Engineering
Liang, Zhuping, Physical Education
Liao, Guowei, Chinese Studies
Lin, Fengmin, Social Sciences
Lin, Shimin, Mathematics and Computer Science
Liu, Muren, Physics and Information Technology
Liu, Xiaolin, Culture and Tourism
Liu, Xingjun, Chinese Studies
Liu, Ying, International Culture and Education
Liu, Zhaozhong, Foreign Studies
Lu, Xiao, Physics and Information Technology
Lu, Yutai, Foreign Studies
Luo, Guilie, Mathematics and Computer Science
Luo, Xiaoshu, Physics and Information Technology
Luo, Xingkai, Physics and Information Technology
Luo, Zhisong, Law and Business
Mai, Yongxiong, Chinese Studies
Mo, Daocai, Chinese Studies
Mo, Qixun, Chinese Studies
Po, Jinze, Foreign Studies
Qi, Peifang, Politics and Public Management
Qin, Yongsong, Mathematics and Computer Science
Qin, Zixiong, Physics and Information Technology
Que, Zhen, Chinese Studies
Ren, Guanwen, Culture and Tourism
Shen, Jiazhuang, Chinese Studies
Shi, Guiyu, Life Science
Su, Guifa, Chemistry and Chemical Engineering
Sun, Jianyuan, Chinese Studies
Tan, Deqing, Chinese Studies
Tan, Peiwen, Politics and Public Management
Tan, Zhaoyi, Culture and Tourism
Tang, Dehai, Educational Science

Tang, Fucheng, Mathematics and Computer Science
Tang, Gaoyuan, Foreign Studies
Tang, Ling, Culture and Tourism
Tang, Zhaoqing, Life Science
Teng, Dingming, Chinese Studies
Tong, Guangzheng, Law and Business
Wang, Chaoyuan, Chinese Studies
Wang, Chengming, Mathematics and Computer Science
Wang, Defu, Social Sciences
Wang, Deming, Chinese Studies
Wang, Jie, Chinese Studies
Wang, Qiang, Physics and Information Technology
Wang, Xiangjun, Politics and Public Management
Wang, Zhiying, Chinese Studies
Wei, Han, Foreign Studies
Weng, Jiaqiang, Physics and Information Technology
Wu, Dianhua, Mathematics and Computer Science
Xie, Xiang, Physical Education
Xu, Jiwang, Foreign Studies
Xu, Xuefu, Educational Science
Xu, Xueying, Educational Science
Xue, Yuegui, Life Science
Yan, Xiaowei, Mathematics and Computer Science
Yang, Liyan, Law and Business
Yang, Qigui, Mathematics and Computer Science
Yang, Shanchao, Mathematics and Computer Science
Yang, Shujie, Chinese Studies
Yang, Yongbing, Physics and Information Technology
Yang, Yongliang, Physical Education
Yao, Dailiang, Chinese Studies
Ye, Yongji, Arts Department
Yi, Xing, Politics and Public Management
Yi, Zhong, Mathematics and Computer Science
Yin, Lingling, Physical Education
Yu, Ping, Mathematics and Computer Science
Yuan, Binye, Foreign Studies
Zhang, Liqun, Chinese Studies
Zhang, Mingfei, Chinese Studies
Zhang, Shichao, Mathematics and Computer Science
Zhao, Shulin, Chemistry and Chemical Engineering
Zhong, Ruitian, Politics and Public Management
Zhou, Liangren, Foreign Studies
Zhou, Quanlin, Foreign Studies
Zhou, Shanyi, Life Science
Zhou, Shizhong, Law and Business
Zhu, Congbin, Culture and Tourism
Zhu, Junqiang, Law and Business
Zhu, Shouxing, Chinese Studies

GUANGXI TRADITIONAL CHINESE MEDICAL UNIVERSITY

179 Mingxiudong Rd, Nanning, Guangxi

Telephone: (771) 3137577

Fax: (771) 317517

Internet: www.gxtcmu.edu.cn

Founded 1956

President: Prof. Wei Guikang

Vice-Presidents: Prof. Li Weitai, Assoc. Prof. Zhu Hua, Assoc. Prof. Den Jiagang

Librarian: Li Jianguang

Library of 300,000 vols

Number of teachers: 296

Number of students: 1,849

Publications: *Guangxi Journal of Traditional Chinese Medicine, Study in Higher Education of Traditional Chinese Medicine.*

GUANGXI UNIVERSITY

10 Xixiangtang Rd, Nanning, Guangxi Zhuang Autonomous Region 530004
Telephone: (771) 3832391
Fax: (771) 3823743
E-mail: gxugjc@public.nn.gx.cn
Internet: www.gxu.edu.cn
Founded 1928
State control
Academic year: September to June
Pres.: Prof. TANG JILIANG
Registrar: Prof. FU ZHENFANG
Librarian: Prof. CHEN DAGUANG
Library of 2,020,000 vols
Number of teachers: 1,735
Number of students: 17,290
Publication: *Guangxi University Journal*

DEANS

College of Adult Education: Prof. HE BAO-CHONG
College of Agronomy: Prof. MO TIANYAN
College of Animal Science and Technology: Prof. YANG NIANSHENG
College of Biological Technology and Sugar Industrial Engineering: Prof. LU JIAJIONG
College of Business: Prof. LIU CHAOMING
College of Culture and Mass Communication: Prof. LIANG YANG
College of Chemistry and Chemical Engineering: Prof. TONG ZHANGFA
College of Civil Engineering: Prof. YAN LIUBIN
College of Computer Science and Information Technology: Prof. LI TAOSHEN
College of Electrical Engineering: Prof. LU ZUPEI
College of Forestry: Prof. JIN DAGANG (Exec. Vice-Dean)
College of Foreign Languages: Prof. ZHOU YI
College of Law: Prof. MENG QINGUO
College of Mechanical Engineering: Prof. LI SHANGPING
College of Natural Resources and the Environment: Prof. MA SHAOJIAN
College of Sciences: Prof. XI HONGJIAN
College of Social Sciences and Management: Prof. XIE SHUN
Department of Physical Education: Prof. XU MINGRONG
Department of Teacher Training: Prof. WANG HAIYIN (Vice-Dean)

GUANGZHOU UNIVERSITY

248 Guang Yuan Zhong Rd, Guangzhou 510405
Telephone: (20) 86394493
Fax: (20) 86370350
E-mail: faogzu@21cn.com
Internet: www.gzhu.edu.cn
Founded 1983, merged with 8 other institutions of higher education 2000
Academic year: September to July
President: Prof. LIN WEIMING
Vice-Presidents: Prof. CHEN WANPENG, Prof. LI XUNGUI, Prof. LONG SHAOFENG, Prof. SHU YANG, Prof. XU CIRONG, Prof. YU GUOYANG
Director of Academic Affairs: Prof. YU QICAI
Director of Academic Research: Prof. XIAN QIAOLING
Director of the Institute for Higher Education Research: Prof. HUANG JIAQUAN
Director of the International Office: Prof. LI YI
Director of Postgraduate Affairs: Prof. YAO PO
Library Director: Prof. ZHANG BAIYING
Library of 182,000 vols
Number of teachers: 2,372
Number of students: 31,333
Publication: *Journal* (12 a year).

GUANGZHOU UNIVERSITY OF TRADITIONAL CHINESE MEDICINE

12 Airport Rd, Guangzhou 510405, Guangdong
Telephone: (20) 36588233
Fax: (20) 36585258
Internet: www.gzhtcm.edu.cn
Founded 1956
Department of Education of Guangdong control
Academic year: September to July
President: FENG XINSONG
Vice-Presidents: CHEN YINGHUA, LI JIANJUN, LIN PEICHENG, WANG NINGSHENG, XU ZHIWEI
Head of Graduate Department: QIU SHIJUN
Librarian: LI JIAN
Number of teachers: 1,025
Number of students: 3,000

Publications: *Journal* (6 a year), *New Journal of Traditional Chinese Medicine* (12 a year), *Traditional Chinese Drug Research and Clinical Pharmacology* (6 a year)

DEANS

First School of Medicine: DENG TIETAO
School of Acupuncture and Massage: CAI TIEQU
School of Basic Medical Sciences: CHEN QUN
School of Chinese Traditional Medicine: CHEN WEIWEN
School of Economy and Administration: QIU HONGZHONG
School of Information Technology: CHEN SU
School of Nursing: HE YANPING
Second School of Medicine: LU YUBO
Third School of Medicine: ZHUANG HONG

PROFESSORS

CAI, TIEQU, Acupuncture and Massage
CHEN, DACAN, Medicine
CHEN, JINGHE, Medicine
CHEN, JIPAN, Medicine
CHEN, QUN, Basic Medical Sciences
CHEN, SU, Information Technology
CHEN, WEIWEN, Chinese Traditional Medicine
CHEN, XHAOFENG, Basic Medical Sciences
CHEN, ZHIQIANG, Medicine
CHENG, YI, Chinese Traditional Medicine
DENG, TIETAO, Medicine
GAO, YOUHENG, Chinese Traditional Medicine
HUANG, SHAOYING, Medicine
I, JIEFEN, Basic Medical Sciences
JIN, RUI, Medicine
LAI, WEN, Basic Medical Sciences
LAI, XINSHENG, Acupuncture and Massage
LI, HANJIN, Basic Medical Sciences
LI, JINGBO, Basic Medical Sciences
LI, RENXIAN, Medicine
LI, RI, Chinese Traditional Medicine
LI, WANYAO, Acupuncture and Massage
LI, WEI, Chinese Traditional Medicine
LI, WEIMIN, Chinese Traditional Medicine
LI, YIWEI, Nursing
LIANG, SONGMIN, Chinese Traditional Medicine
LIN, LI, Chinese Traditional Medicine
LIU, HUANLAN, Basic Medical Sciences
LIU, JUN, Medicine
LIU, SHICHANG, Medicine
LIU, XIAOBIN, Basic Medical Sciences
LUO, RONGJING, Basic Medical Sciences
LUO, YUNJIAN, Medicine
LU, YUBO, Medicine
OU, YONGXIN, Basic Medical Sciences
OUYANG, HUIQING, Medicine
PAN, YI, Basic Medical Sciences
PENG, SHENGQUAN, Medicine
QIU, HEMING, Medicine
QIU, HONGZHONG, Economy and Administration
WANG, HONGQI, Basic Medical Sciences

WU, MIMAN, Basic Medical Sciences
WU, QINGHE, Chinese Traditional Medicine
XIONG, MANQI, Medicine
XU, HONGHUA, Chinese Traditional Medicine
XU, NENGGUI, Acupuncture and Massage
XU, ZHIWEI, Basic Medical Sciences
YANG, SHUNYI, Acupuncture and Massage
YANG, ZHIMIN, Medicine
YUAN, HAO, Medicine
ZHANG, HONG, Acupuncture and Massage
ZHANG, JIAWEI, Acupuncture and Massage
ZHOU, DAIHAN, Medicine
ZHOU, LILING, Chinese Traditional Medicine
ZHUANG, LIXING, Acupuncture and Massage

GUIZHOU UNIVERSITY

Guiyang, Guizhou
Telephone: (851) 3851187
Fax: (851) 3851381
Founded 1958 as Guizhou University as successor to institution that had been disbanded in 1953; merged with Guizhou Renmin University (Guizhou People's University) 1993
Colleges: agriculture, arts, biotechnology, humanities, science and engineering, vocational training
Chancellor: XU CAODONG
Vice-Chancellor: LIU CHAOZHENG
Number of teachers: 2,800
Number of students: 10,000

GUIZHOU UNIVERSITY OF TECHNOLOGY

Caijiaguan, Guiyang 550003, Guizhou Province
Telephone: (851) 4731641
Fax: (851) 4731649
E-mail: fao@gut.gy.gz.cn
Founded 1958
Academic year: September to July
President: HU GUOGEN
Registrar: WANG YI
Secretary-General: YUAN HUAJUN
Librarian: HE LIQUAN
Library of 520,000 vols, 1,500 periodicals
Number of teachers: 780
Number of students: 8,000
Publication: *Journal* (6 a year).

HANGZHOU UNIVERSITY OF COMMERCE

29 Jiao Gong Rd, Hangzhou, Zhejiang 310035
Telephone: (571) 8071024
Fax: (571) 8053079
E-mail: huc1@zjpta.net.cn
Internet: www.hzic.edu.cn
Founded 1911
Under control of Min. of Internal Trade
Academic year: February to July, September to January
President: Prof. HU ZUGUANG
Vice-Presidents: DING ZHENGZHONG, HU WEIMIN, Prof. WANG GUANGMING, ZHANG JIANPING, ZHOU DAJUN
Chief Administrative Officer: KE LI
Librarian: ZHU SHANGWU
Library of 620,000 vols
Number of teachers: 326
Number of students: 5,100 full-time, 3,600 part-time
Publications: *Academic Periodical, Economics and Business Administration*.

HARBIN INSTITUTE OF ELECTRICAL TECHNOLOGY

53 Daqing Rd, Harbin, Heilongjiang 150040

Telephone: (451) 6221000

Fax: (451) 51623

Founded 1950

Academic year: September to July

Pres.: HE LIAN

Vice-Pres: BAO SHAOXUAN, LIANG YUANHUA, ZHOU SHICHANG

Registrar: LU MINGJUAN

Librarian: BAO SHAOXUAN

Library of 270,000 vols

Number of teachers: 537

Number of students: 2,015 (incl. 95 post-graduates)

Publication: *Journal* (4 a year).

HARBIN ENGINEERING UNIVERSITY

145 Nantong Street, Harbin, Heilongjiang 150001

Telephone: (451) 2519212

Fax: (451) 2533090

E-mail: heu@public.hr.hl.cn

Internet: www.hrbeu.edu.cn

Founded 1953

Academic year: September to July

President: Prof. QIU CHANGHUA

Secretary of the University Party Committee: LIU ZHIGANG

Library of 900,000 vols

Number of teachers: 2,200

Number of students: 23,000

Publications: *Applied Science and Technology*, *Journal of HEU*, *Overseas Science and Technology*.

HARBIN MEDICAL UNIVERSITY

194 Nan Gang Section, Xue Fu Rd, Harbin 150086, Heilongjiang

Telephone: (451) 86671349

Fax: (451) 86671349

Internet: www.hrbmu.edu.cn

Founded 1926

Department of Education of Heilongjiang Province control

Academic year: September to July

President: YANG BAOFENG

Vice-Presidents: CAO DEPIN, LI YUKUI, LIU WENCHUAN, WO ZHENZHONG

Head of Graduate Department: ZHANG BAOX-ING

Librarian: YUE WEIPING

Number of teachers: 1,151

Number of students: 9,228 (6,414 full-time, 2,814 part-time)

Publications: *Chinese Journal of Endemiology* (6 a year), *Journal* (6 a year)

DEANS

Branch of Harbin Medical University: ZHANG SHIXUE

Department of Bioinformatics: LI XIA

First School of Medicine: ZHOU JIN

School of Basic Medical Sciences: FU SONGBIN

School of Mouth Cavity Medical Science: ZHANG BIN

School of Nursing: LI JIANFENG

School of Pharmacy: ZHU DALING

School of Public Health: SUN CHANGHAO

Second School of Medicine: ZHANG QIFAN

PROFESSORS

AI, MINGLI, Medicine

BAI, XINZHI, Medicine

BAO, XIUZENG, Pharmacy

BAO, YONGPING, Public Health

BI, WENSHU, Medicine

BI, ZHENGGANG, Medicine

CHEN, BINGQING, Public Health

CHEN, GENGXIN, Medicine

CHEN, LI, Public Health

CHEN, SHUXIANG, Medicine

CHEN, XIUJIE, Pharmacy

CHENG, DEQING, University Branch

CHENG, LIHA, Medicine

CHENG, ZHI, Basic Medical Sciences

CHI, ZIANG, Medicine

CUI, HAO, Medicine

CUI, HONGBIN, Public Health

CUI, LIANBIN, Medicine

CUI, SHI, Medicine

CUI, YUNPU, Medicine

DAI, HAIBIN, Medicine

DAI, QINSHUN, Medicine

DAI, ZE, University Branch

DU, XIUXHEN, Medicine

DU, ZHIMIN, Pharmacy

FAN, LIHUA, Public Health

FU, LU, Medicine

FU, SHIYING, Medicine

FU, SONGBIN, Basic Medical Sciences

GAO, GUANGMING, Dentistry

GAO, GUANGXIN, University Branch

GAO, RUIJU, Medicine

GAO, SHANLING, Medicine

GONG, LINGTAO, University Branch

GU, SUYI, Medicine

GUAN, JINGMING, Medicine

GUAN, YONGMEI, Medicine

GUAN, ZHENZHONG, Medicine

GUO, LUNSHU, University Branch

GUO, ZHENG, Bioinformatics

HAN, DE'EN, Medicine

HAN, DEWEN, University Branch

HAN, FENGPING, Medicine

HAN, MINGZI, Medicine

HAN, XIANGYANG, Medicine

HAO, LI, University Branch

HONG, FENGYANG, Medicine

HONG, WANQING, Medicine

HU, SHUANGJIU, Medicine

HU, XIAOCHEN, Medicine

HUANG, YONGLIN, Medicine

HUANG, ZHENGSONG, Medicine

JI, YUBIN, Pharmacy

JI, ZHUANZHEN, University Branch

JIA, GUODONG, Medicine

JIANG, GUIQIN, Medicine

JIANG, HONGCHI, Medicine

JIANG, LIJING, Medicine

JIANG, XUEHAI, Medicine

LI, BAIXIANG, Public Health

LI, BANQUAN, Medicine

LI, BAOJIE, Medicine

LI, BAOXIN, Pharmacy

LI, BIN, Medicine

LI, BO, Basic Medical Sciences

LI, CHANGXHUN, Medicine

LI, CHUNMING, Medicine

LI, HEYU, Medicine

LI, JIANFENG, Nursing

LI, JIXUE, Medicine

LI, KANG, Public Health

LI, PEILING, Medicine

LI, QIUJIE, Nursing

LI, SHULIN, Medicine

LI, WEIMIN, Medicine

LI, XIA, Bioinformatics

LI, XIA, Pharmacy

LI, XIAOYUN, Medicine

LI, XIULAN, Medicine

LI, YURONG, Basic Medical Sciences

LI, ZHIXU, Medicine

LI, ZUNYI, Medicine

LIN, XUESONG, University Branch

LIN, YIJIA, Medicine

LIU, BAOLIN, Public Health

LIU, BOSONG, Medicine

LIU, DEXIANG, University Branch

LIU, ENZHONG, Medicine

LIU, FENGJI, Medicine

LIU, FENGZHI, Pharmacy

LIU, HAITANG, Medicine

LIU, HONG, Dentistry

LIU, HONGYUAN, Public Health

LIU, JINJIE, University Branch

LIU, RUIHAI, Public Health

LIU, SHUDE, Medicine

LIU, TIEFU, Medicine

LIU, WENZHU, Medicine

LIU, XIANJUN, Medicine

LIU, YUFENG, Medicine

LIU, ZHICHENG, Public Health

LOU, GUIRONG, Medicine

LU, DAGUANG, Medicine

LU, LEI, Medicine

LU, MINGJUN, Public Health

MA, YINGJI, Medicine

MENG, FANCHAO, Medicine

MENG, HUANBIN, Medicine

QI, YOUCHENG, Medicine

QIAO, GUOFENG, Pharmacy

QIN, HUADONG, Medicine

QIU, FENGQIN, Medicine

QIU, ZHONGYI, Medicine

QU, RENHAI, Medicine

QU, XIUFEN, Medicine

QUAN, HUDE, Public Health

SANG, YIMIN, Medicine

SHENG, YUCHEN, Medicine

SHI, YUZHI, Medicine

SI, ZHUANG, Medicine

SONG, CHUNFANG, Medicine

SONG, CUIPING, Medicine

SONG, ZHIMIN, University Branch

SUN, AHIBO, Medicine

SUN, CHANGHAO, Public Health

SUN, GANG, University Branch

SUN, JIANPING, Pharmacy

SUN, KAOXIANG, Pharmacy

SUN, KEMIN, Medicine

SUN, XIANCHAO, Medicine

SUN, YUNQIAO, Medicine

TAN, TIEZHENG, Medicine

TAN, WENHUA, Medicine

TIAN, SULI, Medicine

WANG, BINYOU, Public Health

WANG, BOWEN, Medicine

WANG, CAIXIA, University Branch

WANG, CHUNXIANG, Medicine

WANG, FUJING, Medicine

WANG, GUIZHAO, Medicine

WANG, GUOQING, Medicine

WANG, HUIMIN, Medicine

WANG, JINGHUA, Medicine

WANG, JINGHUA, University Branch

WANG, JUNCHENG, Medicine

WANG, LI, University Branch

WANG, LING, Pharmacy

WANG, LINGSHAN, Medicine

WANG, MENGXUE, Medicine

WANG, MINGJUN, Medicine

WANG, NAIQIAN, Medicine

WANG, SHENGFA, Medicine

WANG, SHOUREN, Medicine

WANG, TAIHE, Medicine

WANG, XIAOFENG, Medicine

WANG, XIUFAN, Medicine

WANG, ZHIBANG, Medicine

WANG, ZHIGUO, Pharmacy

WEI, LINYU, Medicine

WU, DEQUAN, Medicine

WU, KUN, Public Health

WU, LIJIE, Public Health

WU, LINHUA, Pharmacy

WU, QUNHONG, Public Health

WU, YONGWEN, Medicine

XI, ZHENSHAN, Medicine

XING, JIE, University Branch

XU, JUNRU, Medicine

XU, LINSHENG, Medicine

XU, XUGUANG, Medicine

YANG, BAOFENG, Pharmacy

YANG, FUMING, Medicine

YANG, SHIXHUN, Medicine

YANG, WEILIANG, Medicine

YANG, XUEWEI, Medicine

YAO, LI, Medicine

YE, YUANZHU, Medicine

YIN, HUIQING, Medicine

YIN, KESEN, University Branch

YIN, XIAOQIAN, Medicine
YU, BO, Medicine
YU, DANPING, Medicine
YU, JINGHAI, Pharmacy
YU, JINGYUAN, Medicine
YU, WEIGANG, Medicine
YU, WEIPING, Public Health
YU, XIUXIAN, University Branch
YU, ZHONGSHU, Medicine
YUAN, XIZHEN, University Branch
YUAN, FENG, Medicine
YUE, WU, Medicine
ZHANG, BAOKU, Medicine
ZHANG, BIN, Dentistry
ZHANG, FENGMING, Basic Medical Sciences
ZHANG, JUN, University Branch
ZHANG, MINGWEN, Medicine
ZHANG, PENG, Medicine
ZHANG, QIFAN, Medicine
ZHANG, SHUQI, Basic Medical Sciences
ZHANG, SHUTAO, Medicine
ZHANG, TINGDONG, Medicine
ZHANG, XIANGLI, University Branch
ZHANG, XIAOXIAN, Medicine
ZHANG, XICHEN, University Branch
ZHANG, XINYING, Medicine
ZHANG, XIUQI, Medicine
ZHANG, XIYU, Medicine
ZHANG, YAN, Medicine
ZHANG, YINA, Medicine
ZHANG, YUCHENG, Medicine
ZHANG, YUCHUN, Medicine
ZHANG, ZHONGYI, Public Health
ZHAO, CHANGJI, Medicine
ZHAO, SHUZHEN, Medicine
ZHAO, YASHUANG, Public Health
ZHAO, ZHIHAI, Medicine
ZHONG, ZHENYU, Medicine
ZHOU, JIN, Medicine
ZHOU, WENXUE, Medicine
ZHOU, XIAOMING, Medicine
ZHOU, YUQOI, University Branch
ZHOU, ZHONGFANG, Medicine
ZHU, DALING, Pharmacy
ZHU, GUICHUN, Medicine
ZHU, QUAN, Medicine
ZHU, SHUYING, Medicine
ZHU, SIHE, Medicine
ZHU, XIUYING, Medicine
ZHU, YAN, Medicine

HARBIN NORMAL UNIVERSITY

1 Danan Rd, Liming District, Harbin 150080, Heilongjiang
Telephone: (451) 86376222
Internet: www.hrbnu.edu.cn
Founded 1951
Academic year: September to July
President: CHEN SHUMING
Vice-Presidents: FU DAOBIN, FU JUNLONG, LU YUSUN, SUN FUGUANG, WANG XUANZHANG, WANG ZHONGQIAO
Librarian: GUO SHIMING
Library of 3,340,000 vols
Number of teachers: 3,695
Number of students: 31,835
Publications: *Continuing Education Research* (6 a year), *Heilongjiang Researches on Higher Education* (6 a year), *Natural Science Journal of Harbin Normal University* (6 a year), *Northern Forum* (6 a year)

DEANS

College of Arts: LU XUSUN
College of Computer Science and Mathematics: WANG YUWEN
College of Education Science and Technology: ZHAO HENIN
College of Life and Environment: ZHAO WENGE
College of Literature: GUO CONGLIN

College of Physics and Chemistry: LU SHUCHENG
College of Politics, Law and Economics Management: XU XIAOFENG
College of Sports Sciences: LIU ZHONGWU
Foreign Language Institute: JIANG TAO

PROFESSORS

CHEN, SHUTAO, Computer Science and Mathematics
DAI, BOQING, Physics and Chemistry
FENG, SUYUN, Literature
FU, DAOBIN, Literature
GAO, HUIMING, Arts
GE, YUNCHENG, Physics and Chemistry
GE, ZHIYI, Literature
GUO, CONGLIN, Literature
HUA, DEZUN, Life and Environment
LI, CHANGYU, Literature
LI, JILIN, Life and Environment
LU, SHUCHENG, Physics and Chemistry
LU, YUSUN, Arts
LUO, ZHENYA, Literature
SONG, WEN, Computer Science and Mathematics
SUN, MUTIAN, Literature
TAO, YABIN, Arts
TIAN, GUOWEI, Life and Environment
WANG, LISAN, Arts
WANG, TONGCHANG, Education Science and Technology
WANG, XUANZHANG, Physics and Chemistry
WANG, YUWEN, Computer Science and Mathematics
WANG, ZHONGQIAO, Literature
XU, GUOLIN, Physics and Chemistry
XU, HENGYONG, Physics and Chemistry
XU, XIANGLING, Life and Environment
XU, XIAOFENG, Literature
YU, LIJIE, Life and Environment
ZHANG, JINGCHI, Literature
ZHANG, JUNMING, Politics, Law and Economics Management
ZHANG, YONGZHENG, Computer Science and Mathematics
ZHAO, HENIN, Education Science and Technology
ZHAO, YUNLONG, Arts
ZHOU, JINXIAN, Literature

HARBIN UNIVERSITY OF SCIENCE AND TECHNOLOGY

57 Xuefu Rd, Nan Gang, Harbin 150080, Heilongjiang
Telephone: (451) 86390114
Internet: www.hrbust.edu.cn
Founded 1953
Academic year: September to July
President: ZHAO QI
Vice-Presidents: DU GUANGCUN, LI DAYONG, TENG CUNXIAN, WU JUNFENG, ZHAO HONG
Head of Graduate Department: ZHEN MINLI
Librarian: CHEN JIE
Library of 173,800 vols
Number of teachers: 2,379
Number of students: 19,907
Publications: *Electric Machines and Control* (4 a year), *Journal* (6 a year), *Science, Technology and Management* (6 a year)

DEANS

College of Applied Science: CUI YUNAN
College of Chemistry and Environmental Engineering: LIU BO
College of Computer and Control Science: QIAO PEILI
College of Electrical and Electronic Engineering: WEI XINLAO
College of International Culture Education: ZHAO DAWEI
College of Material Science and Engineering: GUO ERJUN

College of Observation Technology and Communications Engineering: YU XIAOYANG
Foreign Language Institute: LUI LIQUN
School of Economics and Management: XIU GUOYI
School of Law: ZHANG YING
School of Mechanical Engineering: SHAO JUNPENG
Software College: LIU SHENGHUI

PROFESSORS

CHEN, DEYUN, Computer and Control Science
CHEN, DONGYAN, Applied Science
CHEN, GUANGHAI, Applied Science
CHEN, RONGDUO, Economics and Management
CHEN, YUQUAN, Mechanical Engineering
CUI, YUNAN, Applied Science
DENG, CAIXIA, Applied Science
DU, DESHENG, Computer and Control Science
DU, KUNMEI, Electrical and Electronic Engineering
DUAN, TIEQUN, Mechanical Engineering
FAN, JINGYUN, Material Science and Engineering
FAN, YONG, Material Science and Engineering
GAO, ANBANG, Mechanical Engineering
GAO, CHANGYUAN, Economics and Management
GAO, ZHONGWEN, Computer and Control Science
GE, BAOJUN, Electrical and Electronic Engineering
GE, JIANGHUA, Mechanical Engineering
GUO, ERJUN, Material Science and Engineering
GUO, JIANYING, Observation Technology and Communications Engineering
HE, ZHONGXIAO, Computer and Control Science
HU, BAOXIA, Computer and Control Science
JI, DONGHAI, Applied Science
JI, ZHESHENG, Material Science and Engineering
JING, XU, Computer and Control Science
KONG, FANLIANG, Applied Science
LEI, QINGQUAN, Electrical and Electronic Engineering
LI, DAYONG, Material Science and Engineering
LI, DONGMEI, Applied Science
LI, FENGZHEN, Material Science and Engineering
LI, GECHENG, Computer and Control Science
LI, HONGXIA, Economics and Management
LI, LEI, Economics and Management
LI, QUANLI, Computer and Control Science
LI, WEILI, Electrical and Electronic Engineering
LI, YUMING, Chemistry and Environmental Engineering
LI, ZHENJIA, Mechanical Engineering
LI, ZHONGHUA, Electrical and Electronic Engineering
LIANG, JINGXI, Economics and Management
LIANG, YANPING, Electrical and Electronic Engineering
LIN, JIAQI, Applied Science
LIU, BO, Chemistry and Environmental Engineering
LIU, RUNTAO, Applied Science
LIU, SHENGHUI, Computer and Control Science
LIU, WEIJUN, Mechanical Engineering
LIU, WENLI, Electrical and Electronic Engineering
LIU, XIANLI, Mechanical Engineering
LIU, XINGJIA, Mechanical Engineering
LUO, XIAOGUANG, Economics and Management
MA, HONGFEI, Economics and Management
MA, HUAIJIAN, Observation Technology and Communications Engineering
MENG, DAWEI, Electrical and Electronic Engineering

PAN, ZHUANGYUAN, Applied Science
QI, LIANGQUN, Economics and Management
QIAO, PEILI, Computer and Control Science
REN, FUJUN, Mechanical Engineering
SHAO, JUNPENG, Mechanical Engineering
SHAO, TIEZHU, Economics and Management
SHI, LIANSHENG, Material Science and Engineering
SONG, JIASHENG, Economics and Management
SONG, RUNBIN, Material Science and Engineering
SUI, XIULING, Mechanical Engineering
SUN, FENGLIAN, Material Science and Engineering
SUN, LIJIONG, Computer and Control Science
SUN, MINGSONG, Computer and Control Science
SUN, QUANYING, Mechanical Engineering
SUN, XIAOJUN, Chemistry and Envirnomental Engineering
TAN, GUANGYU, Mechanical Engineering
TENG, CUNXIAN, Economics and Management
WAN, GUOQIN, Material Science and Engineering
WANG, HONGQI, Economics and Management
WANG, LIPING, Material Science and Engineering
WANG, MUKUN, Observation Technology and Communications Engineering
WANG, PEIDONG, Computer and Control Science
WANG, TONG, Mechanical Engineering
WANG, XUAN, Applied Science
WANG, XUDONG, Electrical and Electronic Engineering
WANG, YIJIE, Applied Science
WANG, YUDONG, Economics and Management
WEI, XINLAO, Electrical and Electronic Engineering
WEN, JIABIN, Electrical and Electronic Engineering
WU, HONGBO, Economics and Management
WU, JUNFENG, Computer and Control Science
WU, YUBIN, Material Science and Engineering
WU, ZHONGYANG, Computer and Control Science
XIAOXU, Material Science and Engineering
XIU, GUOYI, Economics and Management
XU, LI, Mechanical Engineering
XU, XIAOCUN, Mechanical Engineering
YANG, JIAXIANG, Electrical and Electronic Engineering
YANG, MINGGUI, Mechanical Engineering
YIN, JINGHUA, Applied Science
YOU, BO, Mechanical Engineering
YU, HUILI, Mechanical Engineering
YU, LI, Economics and Management
YU, XIAOYANG, Observation Technology and Communications Engineering
YU, YANDONG, Material Science and Engineering
YUAN, JIANXIONG, Mechanical Engineering
ZHAI, LILI, Economics and Management
ZHANG, CUNXI, Electrical and Electronic Engineering
ZHANG, CUNYI, Mechanical Engineering
ZHANG, DECHENG, Economics and Management
ZHANG, GUOJIE, Economics and Management
ZHANG, JIAZHEN, Mechanical Engineering
ZHANG, LIYONG, Observation Technology and Communications Engineering
ZHANG, XIANYOU, Material Science and Engineering
ZHANG, XIAOHONG, Electrical and Electronic Engineering
ZHANG, YONGDE, Mechanical Engineering
ZHANG, YONGJUN, Mechanical Engineering
ZHANG, ZHONGMING, Mechanical Engineering
ZHAO, DAWEI, Economics and Management
ZHAO, HONG, Electrical and Electronic Engineering
ZHAO, XINLUO, Economics and Management

ZHEN, DIANCUN, Electrical and Electronic Engineering
ZHEN, MINLI, Mechanical Engineering

HARBIN INSTITUTE OF TECHNOLOGY

92 West Dazhi St, Harbin 150001, Heilongjiang

Telephone: (451) 6412114
Fax: (451) 6221048
Internet: www.hit.edu.cn

Founded 1920
Pres.: Prof. YANG SHIQIN
Vice-Pres: LIU JIAQU, SHI GUANGJI, WANG SHUGUO, WANG ZUWEN, ZHANG DACHENG
Librarian: SHI HUILAI

Library of 1,000,000 vols
Number of teachers: 2,300
Number of students: 14,843 (incl. 2,652 postgraduates)

Publications: *Higher Engineering Education*, *Journal*, *Metal Science and Technology*, *Studying Computers*, *Technology of Energy Conservation*

DEANS

School of Astronautics: Prof. JIA SHILOU
School of Computer and Electrical Engineering: Prof. HONG WENXUE
School of Electric Mechanical Engineering: Prof. WANG SHUGUO
School of Energy Science and Engineering: Prof. WANG ZUWEN
School of Humanities and Social Sciences: Prof. JIANG ZHENHUA
School of Management: LI YIJUN
School of Materials Science and Engineering: Prof. ZHAO LIANCHENG
School of Science: Prof. GENG WANZHEN

HEBEI MEDICAL UNIVERSITY

361 Zhongshan East Rd, Shijiazhuang City, Hebei Province 050017

Telephone: (311) 6048177
Fax: (311) 6048177
E-mail: fad@hebmu.edu.cn
Internet: www.hebmu.edu.cn

Founded 1915
Academic year: September to July

President: WEN JINKUN
Vice-Presidents: DUAN HUIJUN, JI HAIJIN, WANG RUNTIAN, WANG GENGXIN, WANG YANTIAN, ZHANG ZHANKUI
Head of Graduate School: CONG BIN
Librarian: MO ZHENYUN

Library of 541,000 vols
Number of teachers: 887
Number of students: 12,753

Publications: *Chinese Journal of Ultrasonography* (12 a year), *Clinical Focus* (6 a year), *Journal* (6 a year).

HEBEI UNIVERSITY

1 Hezuo Rd, Baoding 071002, Heibei

Telephone: (312) 5079709
E-mail: hbu@mail.hbu.edu.cn
Internet: www.hbu.edu.cn

Founded 1921
Hebei Province control
Academic year: September to July

President: WANG HONGRUI
Vice-Presidents: HA MINGHU, LI SHUANGYIN, SUN HANWEN, SUN JINGYUAN, WEI SUI
Head of Graduate College: HA MINGHU
Librarian: LI ZHENGANG

Library of 3,170,000 vols
Number of teachers: 2,500
Number of students: 47,500

Publications: *Journal* (natural sciences, 6 a year), *Journal* (philosophy and social sciences, 6 a year)

DEANS

College of Arts: YANG WENHUI
College of Chemistry and Environment Science: MA FENGRU
College of Economics: GU LIUBAO
College of Education: HE GUOQIN
College of Electronic and Information Engineering: WANG PEIGUANG
College of Foreign Languages: LI ZUOWEN
College of Industry and Commerce: WANG HONGRUI
Faculty of Journalism and Communication: BAI GUI
College of Life Science: REN GUODONG
College of Literature: LI JINSHAN
College of Machinery and Civil Engineering: ZHANG JIANHUI
College of Management: SUN JIANFU
College of Mathematics and Computer Studies: WANG XIZHAO
College of Medicine: YANG GENGLIANG
College of Physics and Technology: HAN LI
College of Political Science and Law: LIU ZHIGANG
College of Quality and Technical Supervision: LI XIAOTING

PROFESSORS

BA, XINWU, Chemistry and Environment Science
BAI, GUI, Journalism and Communication
BAI, SHUQIN, Political Science and Law
BI, WUQIN, Political Science and Law
BIAN, ZHAOLING, Management
CAI, HAIBO, Arts
CAO, MINGLUN, Foreign Languages
CAO, RU, Journalism and Communication
CAO, YUPING, Life Science
CHEN, JUNYING, Education
CHEN, SHUANGXIN, Arts
CHEN, ZHIGUO, Economics
CHENG, CHANGYU, Economics
CHENG, XINXUAN, Management
DING, JIHUI, Machinery and Civil Engineering
DING, XIAOZHENG, Journalism and Communication
DONG, LIFANG, Physics and Technology
DONG, ZHENGXIN, Economics
DU, HAO, Journalism and Communication
DU, YOUJUN, Journalism and Communication
FANG, BAOAN, Management
FANG, YOULIANG, Machinery and Civil Engineering
FENG, XIUQI, Education
FENG, YULONG, Life Science
FU, SONGTAO, Education
GAO, JUNGANG, Chemistry and Environment Science
GAO, SHUJUN, Management
GU, LIUBAO, Economics
GU, XIAOHUA, Management
GU, ZHONGLIANG, Arts
GUO, BAOZENG, Electronic and Information Engineering
GUO, FULIANG, Literature
GUO, JIAN, Arts
GUO, JIAN, Industry and Commerce
GUO, SHIXIN, Economics
GUO, XUYUAN, Literature
HAN, CHENGWU, Literature
HAN, LI, Physics and Technology
HAN, PANGSHAN, Arts
HAN, PANSHAN, Literature
HAN, XIUJING, Economics
HE, GUOQIN, Education
HE, XUELI, Life Science
HE, ZHIPU, Arts
HOU, GUANYING, Journalism and Communication
HOU, YUHUA, Management
HU, NING, Arts

HU, YAN, Management
HUA, ZHUXIN, Industry and Commerce
HUANG, GENGZHUO, Arts
HUANG, PENGZHANG, Management
JIAN, MIN, Arts
JIANG, JIANYUN, Literature
JIANG, JIZHI, Life Science
JIANG, LIHUA, Economics
JIAO, GUOZHANG, Journalism and Communication
JIAO, MAOLIN, Literature
JIE, YONGJUN, Arts
KAN, ZHENRONG, Life Science
KANG, SHUSHENG, Economics
KANG, XIANJIANG, Life Science
KONG, LINGHONG, Political Science and Law
LI, FANGHUA, Electronic and Information Engineering
LI, GANSHUN, Economics
LI, GUOHUA, Literature
LI, HEPING, Political Science and Law
LI, HUARUI, Literature
LI, JINSHAN, Literature
LI, JINZHENG, Literature
LI, JITAI, Chemistry and Environment Science
LI, LINJIE, Economics
LI, RENKAI, Literature
LI, SHU, Economics
LI, SHUANGJIE, Economics
LI, SHUQI, Machinery and Civil Engineering
LI, SUMIN, Education
LI, TONGSHUANG, Chemistry and Environment Science
LI, WENCAI, Literature
LI, WENXIU, Machinery and Civil Engineering
LI, XIAOTING, Quality and Technical Supervision
LI, XIAOWEI, Physics and Technology
LI, YAHONG, Journalism and Communication
LI, YANAN, Journalism and Communication
LI, YANBIN, Arts
LI, ZUOWEN, Foreign Languages
LIANG, SUZHEN, Political Science and Law
LIAO, XIANGRU, Life Science
LIU, CUIYING, Management
LIU, HUIWEN, Journalism and Communication
LIU, JINZHONG, Literature
LIU, JINZHU, Arts
LIU, SIJIN, Literature
LIU, YONGRUI, Education
LIU, YUKAI, Literature
LIU, ZHIGANG, Political Science and Law
LIU, ZHIQIANG, Physics and Technology
LIU, ZHIQIANG, Electronic and Information Engineering
LU, HONGPING, Economics
LU, MINGFANG, Physics and Technology
LU, ZIZHENG, Journalism and Communication
MA, CHENGLIAN, Journalism and Communication
MA, YANLING, Management
MAO, ZHUOLIANG, Foreign Languages
MEI, BAOSHU, Arts
MENG, SHIEN, Management
PEI, GUIFEN, Economics
PENG, YINGCAI, Physics and Technology
PENG, YINGCAI, Electronic and Information Engineering
QI, YI, Arts
QIAO, YUNXIA, Journalism and Communication
REN, GUODONG, Life Science
RONG, XINFANG, Foreign Languages
SONG, DENGYUAN, Electronic and Information Engineering
SONG, RUITIAN, Physics and Technology
SONG, YAOWU, Education
SUN, HANWEN, Chemistry and Environmental Science
SUN, SHENGCUN, Journalism and Communication
SUN, ZHIZHONG, Economics

TAO, DAN, Journalism and Communication
TIAN, JIANMING, Literature
TIAN, JUNFENG, Mathematics and Computer Science
WANG, BAOXING, Education
WANG, HONGRUI, Electronic and Information Engineering
WANG, HONGRUI, Industry and Commerce
WANG, JINYING, Economics
WANG, JUNJIE, Journalism and Communication
WANG, JUNLI, Life Science
WANG, PEIGUANG, Electronic and Information Engineering
WANG, QIN, Economics
WANG, SHUHUI, Management
WANG, WENLI, Electronic and Information Engineering
WANG, XIZHAO, Mathematics and Computer Science
WANG, YANLING, Journalism and Communication
WANG, YINSHUN, Physics and Technology
WANG, ZHENCHAO, Electronic and Information Engineering
WU, GENGZHEN, Journalism and Communication
WU, HONGCHENG, Education
WU, YAQING, Economics
WU, YONGZHEN, Management
XIE, CHANGFA, Education
XIONG, RENWANG, Arts
XU, JINGZHI, Physics and Technology
XU, MING, Journalism and Communication
XUE, KEMIU, Literature
YANG, BAOZHONG, Literature
YANG, GENGLIANG, Chemistry and Envirnoment Science
YANG, GENGLIANG, Medicine
YANG, WENHUI, Arts
YANG, XIUGUO, Journalism and Communication
YANG, XUEXIN, Industry and Commerce
YAO, ZIHUA, Chemistry and Environment Science
ZHANG, DAOCHUAN, Life Science
ZHANG, DEQIANG, Chemistry and Environment Science
ZHANG, JIANHUI, Machinery and Civil Engineering
ZHANG, LIPING, Life Science
ZHANG, LIXIN, Education
ZHANG, RISHENG, Education
ZHANG, SHUANGCAI, Management
ZHANG, WEI, Journalism and Communication
ZHANG, WENCHUAN, Arts
ZHANG, YANJING, Political Science and Law
ZHANG, YUKE, Economics
ZHAO, YANYAN, Medicine
ZHEN, SHUQING, Political Science and Law
ZHENG, YUNLONG, Physics and Technology
ZHENG, ZHITING, Literature
ZHU, BAOCHENG, Life Science
ZHU, MINGSHENG, Life Science

HEBEI UNIVERSITY OF ECONOMICS AND TRADE

Wu Qi Rd, Shijiazhuang, Hebei Province 050061

Telephone: (311) 6039189
Fax: (311) 6039123
Internet: www.heuet.edu.cn

Founded 1982

President: YU RENGANG
Vice-Presidents: CUI YUANMIN, HU BAOZHONG, HU DONGYANG, MAZHI ZHONG, WU SHENGCHEN, YAO JINGGUAN
Librarian: MA KE

Library of 250,000 vols
Number of teachers: 900
Number of students: 10,000

Publication: *Economics and Management.*

HEBEI NORMAL UNIVERSITY

265 Huadong Rd, Shijiazhuang 030002, Hebei
Internet: www.hebtu.edu.cn

Founded 1902
Academic year: September to July

President: SU BAORONG
Vice-Presidents: JIANG CHUNLAN, LI YOUCHENG, LU JUNHENG, WANG CHANGHUA, ZHEN SHIJUN
Librarian: JIAO ZHILAN

Number of teachers: 3,438
Number of students: 36,185

Publication: *Journal* (4 a year)

DEANS

College of Education Science: LU ZHONGYI
College of Foreign Languages: PAN BINXIN
College of Law and Political Science: ZHANG JILIANG
College of Life Science: DUANG XIANGLIN
College of Literature: XING JILIANG
College of Mathematics and Information: DENG MINGLI
College of Physics: LIU JIANJUN
College of Resources and the Environment: WANG WEI

PROFESSORS

BAI, ZIMING, Foreign Languages
CHANG, CONGQIAN, Foreign Languages
CHEN, CHAO, Literature
CHEN, HUI, Literature
CHENG, RUZHEN, Mathematics and Information
CUI, JIYIN, Literature
CUI, ZHIYUAN, Literature
DENG, MINGLI, Mathematics and Information
DI, ZHAOYING, Mathematics and Information
DING, REN, Mathematics and Information
DONG, JUNMIN, Foreign Languages
DU, JIANZHENG, Education Science
DUAN, XIAOYING, Foreign Languages
DUAN, ZHEREN, Foreign Languages
FAN, SHUCHENG, Law and Political Science
GAO, SHUNSHENG, Mathematics and Information
GAO, SUOGANG, Mathematics and Information
GAO, TING, Mathematics and Information
GAO, XINFA, Resources and Environment Science
GAO, YUANXIANG, Resources and Environment Science
GAO, ZHIHUAI, Foreign Languages
GE, JINGFENG, Resources and Environment Science
GU, ZHONGQUAN, Foreign Languages
GUI, DINGKANG, Foreign Languages
GUO, BAOLIANG, Literature
GUO, QUNYING, Foreign Languages
HE, ANBAO, Foreign Languages
HE, LIANFA, Mathematics and Information
HU, WENLIANG, Resources and Environment Science
HU, YINGTONG, Foreign Languages
HUANG, HONGQUAN, Foreign Languages
HUANG, HONGXU, Foreign Languages
HUANG, HUAFANG, Resources and Environment Science
JIANG, CHUNLAN, Mathematics and Information
KANG, QINDE, Mathematics and Information
LEI, JIANGUO, Mathematics and Information
LI, SHIJU, Law and Political Science
LI, SUO, Literature
LI, TIANGUI, Law and Political Science
LI, XILONG, Literature
LI, YANNIAN, Literature
LI, ZHENGSHUAN, Foreign Languages
LIANG, YI, Foreign Languages
LIANG, ZHIHE, Mathematics and Information
LIE, WUJUN, Mathematics and Information
LIU, HONG, Education Science

LIU, HUANQUN, Foreign Languages
LIU, MING, Education Science
LIU, SHITIAN, Law and Political Science
LIU, YAN, Resources and Environment Science
LIU, ZHONGMING, Law and Political Science
LU, ZHONGYI, Education Science
LU, ZI, Resources and Environment Science
MA, HENGJUN, Literature
MA, RENHUI, Resources and Environment Science
MA, YUN, Literature
MENG, GUOHUA, Foreign Languages
MI, JUSHENG, Mathematics and Information
NAN, YUESHENG, Resources and Environment Science
PAN, BINXIN, Foreign Languages
QIAN, JINPING, Resources and Environment Science
QIAO, YUYING, Mathematics and Information
SHI, GUOXING, Education Science
SHI, JINGXIU, Literature
SU, BAORONG, Literature
TANG, GUOZENG, Law and Political Science
TIAN, XIUYUN, Law and Political Science
WANG, CHANGHUA, Literature
WANG, DELIN, Education Science
WANG, FENGMIN, Law and Political Science
WANG, FUISHENG, Foreign Languages
WANG, JIANXUN, Foreign Languages
WANG, WEI, Resources and Environment Science
WANG, XIN, Education Science
WANG, YANYING, Mathematics and Information
WANG, ZHENCHANG, Foreign Languages
WU, WEIREN, Foreign Languages
WU, XIUHUA, Literature
WU, ZHENGDE, Mathematics and Information
XIAO, GUIQING, Law and Political Science
XING, JIANCHANG, Literature
XU, JIANPING, Literature
XU, QINGHAI, Resources and Environment Science
YAN, KELE, Education Science
YANG, CHUNHONG, Mathematics and Information
YANG, DONG, Literature
YANG, TONGYONG, Literature
YI, SHENGLEI, Foreign Languages
YI, WEI, Foreign Languages
ZHAI, HONGCHANG, Education Science
ZHAN, YUANJIE, Resources and Environment Science
ZHANG, CHENGZONG, Resources and Environment Science
ZHANG, GUOYING, Foreign Languages
ZHANG, JI, Law and Political Science
ZHANG, JILIANG, Law and Political Science
ZHANG, JUNCAI, Literature
ZHANG, JUNHAI, Resources and Environment Science
ZHANG, WENXIANG, Law and Political Science
ZHANG, YIWEN, Resources and Environment Science
ZHANG, YOUHUI, Mathematics and Information
ZHANG, ZHENGGUO, Mathematics and Information
ZHANG, ZILONG, Mathematics and Information
ZHENG, ZHENFENG, Literature
ZHUANG, BIAO, Literature

HEFEI UNIVERSITY OF TECHNOLOGY

59 Tunxi Rd, Hefei, Anhui Province 230009

Telephone: (551) 4655210
Fax: (551) 4651517
Internet: www.hfut.edu.cn

Founded 1945
15 Depts
President: CHEN XINZHAO

Vice-Presidents: LIU GUANGFU, TANG JIAN, WANG DEZE, XU HUIPENG, ZHENG ZHIXIANG
Registrar: ZHOU XU
Librarian: SUN XUANYIN

Number of teachers: 4,513
Number of students: 18,216

Publications: *Engineering Mathematics, Forecasting, Journal, Teaching and Study of Industrial Automation, Techniques Abroad, Tribology Abroad.*

HEILONGJIANG UNIVERSITY OF CHINESE MEDICINE

24 Dongli Section He Ping Rd, Harbin 150040, Heilongjiang

Telephone: (451) 82118254
Fax: (451) 82193031
Internet: www.hljucm.net

Founded 1959
Academic year: September to July

President: KUANG HAIXUE
Vice-Presidents: CHENG WEI, LI BINGZHI, LI JINGXIAO, WANG XIJUN
Head of Graduate Department: NING XIE
Librarian: YOU YANJUN

Number of teachers: 370
Number of students: 5,002 (4,817 full-time, 185 part-time)

Publications: *Acts of Chinese Medicine and Pharmacology* (6 a year), *Information on Traditional Chinese Medicine* (6 a year), *Journal of Clinical Acupuncture and Moxibustion* (12 a year)

DEANS

First School of Medicine: TIAN ZHENKUN
School of Basic Medical Sciences: LI YI
School of Human Sciences: TONG ZILIN
School of Pharmacy: LI YONGJI
Second School of Medicine: SUN ZHONGREN

PROFESSORS

AN, LIWEN, Medicine
CHEN, HONGBIN, Basic Medical Sciences
CHENG, WEIPING, Medicine
DAI, TIECHENG, Medicine
DONG, QINGPING, Medicine
DU, XIAOWEI, Pharmacy
DUAN, FUJIN, Basic Medical Sciences
GAO, QUANGUO, Basic Medical Sciences
GONG, ZHANYUE, Medicine
GU, JIALE, Medicine
HAN, BO, Medicine
HOU, LIHUI, Medicine
HUI, XIULI, Medicine
JIA, GUIZHI, Pharmacy
JIANG, DEYOU, Basic Medical Sciences
JIN, SHUYING, Basic Medical Sciences
KANG, GUANGSHENG, Basic Medical Sciences
KUANG, HAIXUE, Pharmacy
LI, JINGXIA, Medicine
LI, LINGGEN, Medicine
LI, QIUHONG, Pharmacy
LI, TINGLI, Pharmacy
LI, YADONG, Basic Medical Sciences
LI, YAN, Medicine
LI, YANBING, Pharmacy
LI, YI, Basic Medical Sciences
LI, YONGJI, Pharmacy
LIU, HANDE, Human Sciences
LIU, HUASHENG, Basic Medical Sciences
LIU, JIANQIU, Medicine
LIU, JILI, Human Sciences
LIU, YUANZHANG, Medicine
LU, BINGWEN, Basic Medical Sciences
LUO, HONGSHI, Medicine
MA, YINGLI, Pharmacy
MENG, RI, Pharmacy
NIE, YUNAHENG, Medicine
QU, JIE, Human Sciences
QUAN, HONG, Pharmacy
SONG, LIQUN, Medicine
SU, LIANJIE, Pharmacy

SU, YUNMING, Basic Medical Sciences
SUN, HUI, Pharmacy
SUN, WEIZHENG, Medicine
SUN, ZHONGREN, Medicine
TIAN, ZHENKUN, Medicine
TIAN, ZHENKUN, Pharmacy
TONG, ZILIN, Human Sciences
WANG, DEMIN, Medicine
WANG, DONG, Pharmacy
WANG, FEI, Basic Medical Sciences
WANG, GANG, Medicine
WANG, HEPING, Pharmacy
WANG, JIANMING, Pharmacy
WANG, LI, Basic Medical Sciences
WANG, TIECE, Basic Medical Sciences
WANG, XIAXIAN, Basic Medical Sciences
WANG, XIJUN, Pharmacy
WANG, XING, Medicine
WANG, XUEHUA, Basic Medical Sciences
WANG, YUMEI, Medicine
WANG, YUXI, Medicine
WU, BOYAN, Basic Medical Sciences
XIE, JINGRI, Medicine
YAN, JING, Pharmacy
YU, JIABIN, Pharmacy
YU, XIAOHONG, Basic Medical Sciences
ZHANG, FULI, Basic Medical Sciences
ZHANG, YOUTANG, Basic Medical Sciences
ZHANG, ZHIMIN, Basic Medical Sciences
ZHAO, WENJING, Basic Medical Sciences
ZHOU, DECHEN, Basic Medical Sciences
ZHOU, LING, Medicine
ZHOU, MIN, Basic Medical Sciences
ZHOU, WI, Medicine
ZHOU, YABIN, Medicine
ZHU, YONGZHI, Medicine
ZHU, ZHIZHEN, Basic Medical Sciences

HENAN COLLEGE OF TRADITIONAL CHINESE MEDICINE

1 Jinshui Rd, Zhengzhou 450008, Henan

Telephone: (371) 65962930
Fax: (371) 65962930
E-mail: haiwai@hactcm.edu.cn
Internet: www.henantcm.net

Founded 1958
State control
Language of instruction: Chinese, English
Academic year: September to July

Pres.: Prof. PENG BO
Vice-Pres.: Prof. LI JIANSHENG
Librarian: LAI QIANKAI

Library of 800,000 vols
Number of teachers: 2,421
Number of students: 10,000

Publications: *Henan Traditional Chinese Medicine* (12 a year), *Journal* (6 a year)

PROFESSORS

CHEN, R. F., Internal Medicine
DING, Y., Paediatrics
FENG, M. Q., Traditional Chinese Medicine
GAO, T. S., Traditional Chinese Medicine
HOU, S. L., Traditional Materia Medica
JI, C. R., Traditional Materia Medica
LI, X. W., Traditional Chinese Medicine
LI, Z. H., Traditional Chinese Medicine
LI, Z. S., Internal Medicine
LOU, D. F., Traditional Chinese Medicine for Traumatology
LU, S. C., Qigong
MA, Z. H., Traditional Chinese Medicine
SHANG, C. C., Traditional Chinese Medicine
SHAO, J. M., Acupuncture
SHI, G. Q., Traditional Chinese Medicine
SHUN, L. H., Acupuncture
SUN, C. Q., Physiology
SUN, H. B., Parasitology
SUN, J. Z., Internal Medicine
TANG, S., Traditional Chinese Medicine
WANG, A. B., History of Traditional Chinese Medicine
WANG, R. K., Diagnostics

WANG, Y. M., Pharmaco-Chemistry
YANG, L. Y., Anatomy
YANG, Y. S., Traditional Materia Medica
ZHANG, G. Q., Traditional Materia Medica
ZHENG, J. M., Traditional Chinese Medicine
for Paediatrics

HENAN UNIVERSITY

Ming Lun Rd, Kaifeng 475001, Henan
Internet: www.henu.edu.cn

Founded 1912

Academic year: September to July

President: GUAN AIHE
Vice-Presidents: GUO TIANBANG, HUANG YABIN, LU KEPING, SHI QUANSHENG, WANG FAZENG, ZHAO GUOXIANG
Librarian: LI JINGWEN

Number of teachers: 3,600
Number of students: 240,000

Publications: *Chinese Quarterly Journal of Mathematics, Journal* (6 a year), *Journal of Henan University Chemical Research* (4 a year), *Quarterly Journal of Pure and Applied Mathematics*

DEANS

Faculty of History and Culture: ZHANG QIANHONG
College of Arts: ZHAO WEIMING
College of Civil Engineering: BAO PENG
College of Communication and Journalism: LI JIANWEI
College of Economics: DI MINGZAI
College of Environmental Planning: QIN YAOCHEN
College of Foreign Languages: ZHANG KEDING
College of Life Science: SONG CHUNPENG
College of Medicine: MA YUANFANG
School of Business Administration: WEI CHENGLONG
School of Chemistry Engineering: CUI YUAN-CHENG
School of Computer and Information Engineering: LIU XIANSHENG
School of Mathematics and Information Science: LI QISHENG
School of Physics and Information Optoelectronics: ZHANG WEIFENG

PROFESSORS

CHEN, CHANGYUAN, History and Culture
CHEN, JIAHAI, Arts
CHEN, SHOUXIN, Mathematics and Information Science
CHENG, MINGSHENG, History and Culture
DI, MINGZHAI, Economics
DING, SHENGYAN, Environmental Planning
DING, SHENGYAN, Life Science
DONG, FACAI, Life Science
GAO, HAILIN, History and Culture
GAO, JIANGUO, Economics
GAO, JIANHUA, Environmental Planning
GONG, LIUZHU, History and Culture
GU, YUZONG, Physics and Information Optoelectronics
HOU, XUN, Physics and Information Optoelectronics
HU, CHANGLIU, Mathematics and Information Science
HU, CONGE, Mathematics and Information Science
HU, YUXIN, Life Science
HUANG, YABIN, Physics and Information Optoelectronics
JIA, XINGQIN, Mathematics and Information Science
JIA, YUYING, History and Culture
JU, QINGLIN, Arts
LI, CHENGDE, History and Culture
LI, GUANGYI, History and Culture
LI, GUOQIANG, Mathematics and Information Science
LI, JIANWEI, Communication and Journalism
LI, JIE, Business Administration

LI, MING, History and Culture
LI, QISHENG, Mathematics and Information Science
LI, RUI, Mathematics and Information Science
LI, SUOPING, Life Science
LI, YONGWEN, Environmental Planning
LI, YUJIE, History and Culture
LI, ZHENHONG, History and Culture
LIN, JIAKUN, History and Culture
LIU, BINSHAN, Foreign Languages
LIU, HONG, Arts
LIU, JIANZHONG, Business Administration
LIU, KUNTAI, History and Culture
LU, ZHENGUANG, Communication and Journalism
MA, JIANHUA, Environmental Planning
MA, LING, Arts
MA, XIAOQUAN, History and Culture
MAO, HAITAO, Physics and Information Optoelectronics
MIAO, CHANGHONG, Environmental Planning
MIAO, CHENG, Life Science
MIAO, SHUMEI, History and Culture
MO, YUJUN, Physics and Information Optoelectronics
NIU, JIANQIANG, History and Culture
OU, ZHENGWEN, History and Culture
QI, LING, Economics
QIAN, HUAISUI, Environmental Planning
QIN, MINGZHOU, Environmental Planning
QIN, YAOZHEN, Environmental Planning
SANG, FUDE, Life Science
SHAN, LUN, Life Science
SONG, CHUNPENG, Life Science
SONG, YINGLI, Communication and Journalism
SU, KEWU, Economics
SUN, QIULIN, Environmental Planning
TAN, CHENGLIN, Environmental Planning
TANG, GUIQIN, Arts
WAN, SONGYU, History and Culture
WANG, CHANGSHUN, Physics and Information Optoelectronics
WANG, CHUMING, Economics
WANG, FAZHENG, Environmental Planning
WANG, JILIN, History and Culture
WANG, JINGYE, Communication and Journalism
WANG, JINXIAN, Business Administration
WANG, XINGYU, Business Administration
WANG, YANFA, Arts
WANG, ZHANGUO, Physics and Information Optoelectronics
WANG, ZHENDUO, Communication and Journalism
WEI, CHENGLONG, Economics
WEI, QIANZHI, History and Culture
WENG, YOUWEI, History and Culture
WU, TAO, History and Culture
WU, XUELI, Foreign Languages
XU, XINGYA, Economics
YAN, ZHAOXIANG, History and Culture
YANG, HAIJUN, Communication and Journalism
YANG, XUEZHI, Mathematics and Information Science
YAO, BOHUA, Mathematics and Information Science
YAO, YINGTING, History and Culture
YI, GUOSHENG, Physics and Information Optoelectronics
YI, QIXIANG, History and Culture
YU, BAOLONG, Physics and Information Optoelectronics
YU, JINFU, Economics
ZHANG, DEZONG, History and Culture
ZHANG, JIATAI, History and Culture
ZHANG, JIN, Foreign Languages
ZHANG, KUN, Economics
ZHANG, MINGLIANG, Mathematics and Information Science
ZHANG, QIANHONG, History and Culture
ZHANG, QIUZHOU, History and Culture
ZHANG, RUFA, Communication and Journalism

ZHANG, TAIHAI, Business Administration
ZHANG, TIANDING, Communication and Journalism
ZHANG, WEIFENG, Physics and Information Optoelectronics
ZHANG, XINGMAO, Economics
ZHANG, XIUYING, Business Administration
ZHANG, ZHONGLIANG, Communication and Journalism
ZHANG, ZHONGSUO, Physics and Information Optoelectronics
ZHAO, BINDONG, Environmental Planning
ZHAO, BUYUN, History and Culture
ZHAO, JIANGUO, Communication and Journalism
ZHAO, WEIMING, Arts
ZHAO, ZHENQIAN, Arts
ZHAO, ZHIFA, Economics
ZHENG, HUISHENG, History and Culture
ZHOU, BAOZHU, History and Culture
ZHU, SHAOHOU, History and Culture

HOHAI UNIVERSITY

1 Xikang Rd, Nanjing 210098
Telephone: (25) 3323777
Fax: (25) 3315375
Internet: www.hhu.edu.cn

Founded 1915 (fmrly East China Technical Univ. of Water Resources), name changed 1985

State control

Languages of instruction: Chinese, English

Academic year: September to July

President: Prof. JIANG HONGDAO
Vice-Presidents: Prof. LIU XINREN, Prof. JIN ZHONGQING, Prof. ZHANG CHANG
Librarian: DONG TINGSONG

Number of teachers: 1,343
Number of students: 8,000

Publications: *Advances in the Science and Technology of Water Resources, Economics of Water Resources, Journal, Journal of Higher Education, Water Resources Protection*

DEANS

College of Civil Engineering: Prof. ZHUO JIASHOU
College of Computer and Information Engineering: Assoc. Prof. ZHU YAOLONG
College of Electrical Engineering: Prof. YANG JINTANG
College of Harbour, Waterway and Coastal Engineering: Prof. ZHANG CHANGKUAN
College of Mechanical and Electrical Engineering: Prof. JIN YAHE
College of International Industry and Commerce: Assoc. Prof. ZHANG YANG
College of Technical Economics: Prof. ZHENG CHUIYONG
College of Water Conservancy and Hydro-power Engineering: Prof. SUO LISHENG
College of Water Resources and Environment: Prof. WANG HUIMIN

HUAQIAO UNIVERSITY

Quanzhou 362011, Fujian
Telephone: (595) 2693630
Fax: (595) 2681940
E-mail: wsc@hqu.edu.cn
Internet: www.hqu.edu.cn

Founded 1960

State control

Academic year: starts September

Pres.: Prof. WU CHENGYE
Vice-Pres: Assoc. Prof. GUAN YIFAN, Prof. GUO HENGQUN, Assoc. Prof. LI JIMIN
Registrar: Prof. HONG SHANGREN
Librarian: Prof. ZHANG WEIBIN

Library of 775,449 vols, 16,235 periodicals
Number of teachers: 542 (full-time)
Number of students: 12,000

Publications: *Journal of Huaqiao University* (Natural science and social science editions, 4 a year, in Chinese), *Research in Higher Education by Overseas Chinese* (in Chinese, 2 a year)

DEANS

College of Economic Management: Prof. YE MINGQIANG
College of Electromechanical Engineering and Automation: Prof. XU XIPENG
College of Foreign Languages: Assoc. Prof. WANG HUAIHUI
College of Information Science and Engineering: Prof. GUO HENGQUN
College of Materials Science and Engineering: Prof. WU JIHUAI
College of Teaching Chinese as a Foreign Language: Assoc. Prof. LI HONG
Fujian Conservatory of Music: Prof. CAI JIKUN

HUAZHONG AGRICULTURAL UNIVERSITY

Shizhishan, Wuhan 430070, Hubei
Telephone: (27) 87282026
Fax: (27) 87396057
E-mail: fao@mail.hzau.edu.cn/en.htm
Internet: www.hzau.edu.cn
Founded 1898, present name 1985
State control
Languages of instruction: Chinese, English
Academic year: September to July
Pres.: ZHANG DUANPIN
Vice-Pres: CHEN HUANCHUN, GAO CHI, LI GUIFANG, LI MINGJIA, LIU GUIYOU, WANG CHUANXIN, XIE CONGHUA
Librarian: WAN JIQIN
Library of 620,000 vols
Number of teachers: 2,215
Number of students: 15,000

Publication: *Journal* (4 a year)

DEANS

College of Adult Education: ZHANG DUANPIN
College of Animal Husbandry and Veterinary Science: BI DINGREN
College of Arts and Humanities and Social Science: LI CHONGGUANG
College of Basic Sciences: CHEN CHANGSHUI
College of Economics and Trade: WANG YAPENG
College of Engineering and Technology: ZHANG YANLIN
College of the Fishing Industry: XIE CONGXIN
College of Food Science and Technology: PAN SIYI
College of Horticulture and Forestry Science: BAO MANZHU
College of Land Management: WANG YAPENG
College of Life Sciences and Technology: ZHANG QIFA
College of Plant Science and Technology: ZHANG XIANLONG
College of Resources and Environment: CAI CHONGFA

HUAZHONG UNIVERSITY OF SCIENCE AND TECHNOLOGY

1037 Luoyu Rd, Wuhan 430074, Hubei
Telephone: (27) 87542157
Fax: (27) 87547063
E-mail: chengrw@126.com
Internet: www.hust.edu.cn
Founded 1953
Academic year: September to July
President: Prof. FAN MINGWU
Vice-Presidents: Prof. CAO SHUQIN, Prof. DING HANCHU, Prof. DING LIEYUN, Prof. FENG XIANGDONG, Prof. FENG YOUMEI, Prof. HUANG GUANGYING, Prof. LI PEIGEN, Prof.

LIU XIANJUN, Prof. WANG CHENG, Prof. XIANG JIZHOU
Librarian: Assoc. Prof. WU JINWEI
Library of 2,070,000 vols, 550,000 vols of periodicals in Chinese and foreign languages
Number of teachers: 4,000
Number of students: 50,000

Publications: *Applied Mathematics, China's Organic Chemistry and Cellular Chemistry, Chinese Medicine Digest* (detection and clinical), *Clinical Cardiology, Clinical Gastroenterology, Clinical Haematology, Clinical Otolaryngology, Clinical Urology, Clinic Emergency, Foreign Medicine and Molecular Biology, Foreign Medicine* (social medicine), *Gastroenterology in Combined Traditional Chinese Medicine and Western Medicine, HUST Journal* (in separate natural sciences, social sciences and medical sciences editions), *Hydroelectric Energy, Internal Emergency, Journal of Higher Education, Journal of Solid State Mechanics, Linguistics Study, Medicine and Society, New Architecture, Nursing, Practice of Radiology, Radiant Diagnosis* (Chinese medical digest), *Research in Higher Education of Engineering, Sino–German Tumour Clinic*

DEANS

School of Architecture and Urban Planning: Prof. YUAN PEIHUANG
School of Civil Engineering and Mechanics: Prof. CHEN CHUANYAO
School of Computer Science and Technology: Prof. LU ZHENGDIAN
School of Economics: Prof. XU CHANGSHENG
School of Education: Prof. ZHANG YINGQIANG
School of Electrical and Electronics Engineering: Prof. GU CHENGLIN
School of Energy and Power Engineering: Prof. LIU WEI
School of Environmental Science and Engineering: Prof. SHEN YUNFENG
School of Humanities: Prof. ZHANG SHUGUANG
School of Hydropower and Information Engineering: Prof. WU ZHONGRU
School of Information Technology and Engineering: Prof. HUANG DEXIU
School of Journalism and Information Communication: Prof. WU TINGJUN
School of Law: Prof. LUO YUZHONG
School of Life Science and Technology: Prof. LUO QINGMING
School of Management: Prof. ZHANG JINLONG
School of Materials Science and Engineering: Prof. LI DEQUN
School of Mechanical Science and Engineering: Prof. SHAO XINYU
School of Public Administration: Prof. XIA SHUZHANG
School of Science: Prof. YE ZHAOHUI
School of Software Engineering: Prof. CHEN CHUANBO
School of Traffic Science and Engineering: Prof. ZHAO YAO
Tongji Medical School: Prof. XIANG JIZHOU

HUBEI UNIVERSITY

11 Xueyuan Rd, Wuchang, Wuhan 430062, Hubei
Telephone: (27) 88663896
E-mail: xiaoban@hubu.edu.cn
Internet: www.hubu.edu.cn
Founded 1931
Hubei Province control
Academic year: September to July
President: WU CHUANXI
Vice-Presidents: GU HAOSHUANG, LI JINHE, YAN MINGMING, ZHOU JIMING
Librarian: ZHANG WEIHUA
Library of 1,520,000 vols

Number of teachers: 1,000
Number of students: 12,700
Publications: *Acta Arachnologica Sinica* (2 a year), *Chinese Journal of Colloids and Polymers* (4 a year), *Journal* (4 a year), *Journal of the Adult Education College of Hubei University* (6 a year)

DEANS

Faculty of Arts: LUN ZUNMING
Faculty of Chemistry and Materials Science: WANG SHIMIN
Faculty of Education: JIN GUOPING
Faculty of Foreign Studies: XU QIUMEI
Faculty of History and Culture: GUO YING
Faculty of Philosophy: DAI MAOTANG
Institute of Physics and Electronic Technology: WANG HAO
School of Business: LIU JIANPING
School of Life Science: CHEN JIAN
School of Resources and the Environment: LI ZHAOHUA

PROFESSORS

BIAN, XIANGYI, Arts
CAO, WANQIANG, Physics and Electronic Technology
CHAN, SHAOHUA, Physics and Electronic Technology
CHANG, SHIYUAN, Chemistry and Materials Science
CHEN, PEIZHI, Chemistry and Materials Science
CHEN, QIUHUI, Mathematics and Computer Science
CHEN, TIANYOU, Business
CHEN, YIHAN, Physics and Electronic Technology
CHEN, YOUQING, Education
CHEN, ZHIHUI, Physics and Electronic Technology
CHEN, ZHUXING, Chemistry and Materials Science
CHENG, CHONGZHEN, Business
CHENG, SIHUI, Education
CHENG, YUANFA, Physics and Electronic Technology
DAI, MAOTANG, Philosophy
FENG, CHUANQI, Chemistry and Materials Science
FENG, HAO, Business
GAO, LU, History and Culture
GONG, GUIFANG, Foreign Studies
GONG, QUN, Philosophy
GU, HAOSHUANG, Physics and Electronic Technology
GU, PEI, History and Culture
GUAN, RONG, Chemistry and Materials Science
GUO, KANGSONG, Arts
GUO, YING, History and Culture
HAN, HUA, Education
HE, PEIXIN, Chemistry and Materials Science
HU, SHUGUANG, Chemistry and Materials Science
HUANG, SHIQIANG, Chemistry and Materials Science
HUANG, YUEHUI, Arts
JIANG, CHANG, Philosophy
JIANG, TAO, Chemistry and Materials Science
JIN, CONG, Mathematics and Computer Science
JIN, KEZHONG, Arts
LEI, TINAN, Education
LI, JUANWEN, Business
LI, JUANWEN, Resources and the Environment
LI, LUOQING, Mathematics and Computer Science
LI, YAN, Chemistry and Materials Science
LI, ZHAOHUA, Resources and the Environment
LI, ZONGRONG, Mathematics and Computer Science
LIU, CHUANE, Arts

LIU, HEGUO, Mathematics and Computer Science
LIU, JIANPING, Business
LIU, SHENGWU, Arts
LIU, ZHUNMING, Arts
LOU, ZHAOWEN, Chemistry and Materials Science
LU, DEPING, Chemistry and Materials Science
LU, ZHILU, Foreign Studies
QIN, ZHAOGUI, History and Culture
SHAO, CHANGGUI, Physics and Electronic Technology
SHI, JINPING, Business
SHU, HUAI, Arts
SONG, KEFU, Arts
TAN, SHUKUI, Business
TIAN, FANJI, Mathematics and Computer Science
TU, HUAIZHANG, Arts
WAN, CHANGGAO, Mathematics and Computer Science
WANG, HAO, Physics and Electronic Technology
WANG, HONGLING, Business
WANG, JIAZHI, Foreign Studies
WANG, SHENGFU, Chemistry and Materials Science
WANG, SHIMIN, Chemistry and Materials Science
WANG, YANG, History and Culture
WANG, ZHENGXIANG, Resources and the Environment
WU, CHUANXI, Mathematics and Computer Science
WU, MIN, Mathematics and Computer Science
XIA, QINGHUA, Chemistry and Materials Science
XIAN, KEN, Mathematics and Computer Science
XIANG, SONG, Foreign Studies
XIAO, DE, Business
XIAO, WEIDONG, Chemistry and Materials Science
XIE, FEIHOU, Education
XIE, JUFANG, Physics and Electronic Technology
XU, QIUMEI, Foreign Studies
XU, XUEJUN, Education
XU, ZHUSHUN, Chemistry and Materials Science
YAN, CUIE, Chemistry and Materials Science
YAN, MEIFU, Education
YAN, MINGMING, Education
YAN, XUEJUN, Business
YANG, JIANBO, Arts
YANG, YAOKUN, Philosophy
YE, YONG, Chemistry and Materials Science
YI, HONGCHUAN, Arts
YOU, WULI, Foreign Studies
ZHANG, BICHENG, Chemistry and Materials Science
ZHANG, HESHENG, Chemistry and Materials Science
ZHANG, JIANMING, Business
ZHANG, QINGZONG, Foreign Studies
ZHANG, TIANJIN, Physics and Electronic Technology
ZHAO, SHAOYI, Mathematics and Computer Science
ZHENG, YUMEI, Mathematics and Computer Science
ZHOU, DEJUN, History and Culture
ZHOU, HAO, Foreign Studies
ZHOU, TAOSHENG, Physics and Electronic Technology
ZHU, JIANZHEN, History and Culture
ZHU, WEIMING, Arts

HUNAN AGRICULTURAL UNIVERSITY

Fu Rong District, Chang Sha 410128, Hunan
Telephone: (731) 4618001

Fax: (731) 4611473
Internet: www.hunau.net
Founded 1951
Academic year: September to July
President: ZHOU QINGMING
Vice-Presidents: BO LIANYANG, FU SHAOHUI, LU XIANGYANG, PENG KEQIN, ZHU YINGSHENG
Librarian: XIAO QIMING
Library of 909,600 vols
Number of teachers: 978
Number of students: 34,259
Publications: *Crop Research* (4 a year), *Journal* (4 a year)

DEANS

College of Bio-Safety Science and Technology: GAO BIDA
College of Economics Management: ZENG WEI
College of Engineering Technology: SUN SONGLIN
College of Resources and the Environment: DUAN JIANNAN
College of Science: RAO LIQUN
Faculty of Food Science and Technology: XIA YANBIN
School of Agriculture: WANG GUOHUAI
School of Literature: QU LINYAN
Institute of Computing and Information Engineering: SHEN YUE

PROFESSORS

BO, LIANYANG, Bio-Safety Science and Technology
CHEN, JINXIANG, Agriculture
CUI, GUOXIAN, Agriculture
DAI, LIANGYING, Bio-Safety Science and Technology
DENG, FANGMING, Food Science and Technology
DUAN, JIANNAN, Resources and the Environment
FANG, ZHI, Resources and the Environment
GAO, BIDA, Bio-Safety Science and Technology
GAO, YINGWU, Engineering Technology
GUAN, CHUNYUN, Agriculture
GUO, QINGQUAN, Agriculture
HUANG, HUANG, Agriculture
HUANG, YIHUAN, Food Science and Technology
HUANG, ZHENGQUAN, Literature
LAO, LIQUN, Science College
LI, FINGJUN, Bio-Safety Science and Technology
LI, XINGHUI, Food Science and Technology
LI, XUN, Agriculture
LIAO, BOHAN, Resources and the Environment
LIAO, XIAOLAN, Bio-Safety Science and Technology
LIU, DEHUA, Food Science and Technology
LIU, GUOHUA, Agriculture
LIU, QIANG, Resources and the Environment
LIU, ZHONGHUA, Food Science and Technology
LIU, ZHONGSONG, Agriculture
LUO, JUNWU, Food Science and Technology
LUO, KUAN, Bio-Safety Science and Technology
MA, MEIHU, Food Science and Technology
OU YANG, XIRONG, Agriculture
PENG, XILIN, Literature
QU, LINYAN, Literature
RONG, XIANGMING, Resources and the Environment
SHENG, XIAOBANG, Agriculture
SHI, ZHAOPENG, Food Science and Technology
SHUN, HUANLIANG, Agriculture
TAN, JICAI, Food Science and Technology
TAN, JICAI, Bio-Safety Science and Technology
TAN, XINGHE, Food Science and Technology
TANG, CHUYU, Engineering Technology
TANG, QIYUAN, Agriculture

TU, LIAOMEI, Agriculture
WANG, GUOHUAI, Agriculture
WANG, GUOLIANG, Agriculture
WANG, GUOPING, Bio-Safety Science and Technology
WEN, LIZHANG, Bio-Safety Science and Technology
WU, LIYOU, Bio-Safety Science and Technology
XI, YANBIN, Food Science and Technology
XIA, YANBIN, Food Science and Technology
XIAO, QIMING, Bio-Safety Science and Technology
XIAO, TIEGUANG, Bio-Safety Science and Technology
YAN, HEHONG, Agriculture
YANG, RENBIN, Resources and the Environment
YANG, WEILI, Food Science and Technology
YANG, ZHIJIAN, Agriculture
ZENG, FUSHENG, Economics Management
ZENG, QINGRU, Resources and the Environment
ZHANG, FUQUAN, Agriculture
ZHANG, XIWEI, Economics Management
ZHANG, YANGZHU, Resources and the Environment
ZHOU, DONGSHENG, Agriculture
ZHOU, JIHENG, Agriculture
ZHOU, MEILAN, Agriculture
ZHOU, QINGMING, Agriculture
ZHU, QI, Food Science and Technology

HUNAN UNIVERSITY

Yule, Changsha 410082
Telephone: (731) 8822745
Fax: (731) 8824525
Internet: www.hunu.edu.cn
Founded 976 as Yuelu Academy; became Hunan Institute of Higher Education 1903, Hunan University 1926, Hunan National University 1937, South-Central Institute of Civil Engineering 1953, Hunan Institute of Technology between 1953 and 1959, and Hunan University 1959; merged with Hunan College of Finance and Economics 2000
State control
President: WANG KEMING
Library of 2,380,000 vols
Number of teachers: 1,563
Number of students: 34,000

HUNAN MEDICAL UNIVERSITY

88 Xiang Ya Rd, Changsha, 410078 Hunan
Telephone: (731) 4471347
Fax: (731) 4471339
Internet: hmu.hypermart.net
Founded 1914
Academic year: September to July
President: Prof. HU DONGXU
Vice-Presidents: Prof. CHEN ZHUCHU, Prof. HU TIEHUI, Prof. SUN ZHENGQIU, Prof. TIAN YONGQUAN, Prof. WU ZHONGQI, Prof. ZHOU HONGHAO
Librarian: Assoc. Prof. LIU XIACHUN
Library of 560,000 vols
Number of teachers: 652 (full-time)
Number of students: 3,846 (incl. 585 postgraduates)
Publications: *Bulletin* (6 a year), *Chinese Journal of Endoscopy* (4 a year), *Chinese Journal of General Surgery* (6 a year), *Chinese Journal of Otolaryngological and Craniosacral Surgery, Chinese Journal of Psychology* (4 a year), *Higher Medical Education Management* (4 a year), *Journal of Applied Uro-Surgery* (4 a year), *Journal of Foreign Medicine* (sections on Psychiatry, Neurology and Neurosurgery, and Physiology and Pathology), *Journal of Medical Degree and Postgraduate Educa-*

tion (4 a year), *Journal of Modern Medicine* (12 a year)

DIRECTORS

1st Affiliated Hospital (Clinical Medicine): TIAN YONGQUAN
2nd Affiliated Hospital (Clinical Medicine): LIAO ERYUAN
3rd Affiliated Hospital (Clinical Medicine): LIU XUNYANG
Faculty of Basic Medical Sciences: WEN JIFANG
Faculty of Laboratroy Research: CHEN ZHENGYAN
Faculty of Library and Information Sciences: LIU XIAOCHUN
Faculty of Mental Health: CHEN YUANGUANG
Faculty of Nursing: ZHOU CHANGJU
Faculty of Pharmacology: TANG GUISHAN (Deputy Dir)
Faculty of Preventive Medicine: TANG HONGZHUAN (Deputy Dir)
Faculty of Stomatology: JIAN XINCHUN

PROFESSORS

BAI XIANXIN, Radiology
CAO PING, Internal Medicine (Haematology)
CAO YA, Tumour Molecular Biology
CAO ZHIHAN, Internal Medicine (Kidney Diseases)
CHA GUOZHANG, Clinical Microbiology and Immunology
CHEN DAOJING, General Surgery
CHEN FANGPING, Internal Medicine (Haematology)
CHEN FUWEN, Dermatology
CHEN GANREN, Internal Medicine (Cardiology)
CHEN QIZHI, Anaesthesiology
CHEN SHENGXI, Cardiac Surgery
CHEN SHUZHEN, Microbiology
CHEN YUANGUANG, Psychiatry
CHEN ZHENGYAN, Clinical Biochemistry
CHEN ZHUCHU, Tumour Cellular Biology
CHENG RUIXUE, Pathology
DENG HANWU, Pharmacology
DENG HANXIANG, Biology and Medical Genetics
FAN JUNYUAN, Organic Chemistry
FANG PING, Library and Information Sciences
FU YINYU, Orthopaedic Surgery
GAO JIESHENG, Internal Medicine (Rheumatology)
GONG GUANGFU, Cardiac Surgery
GUO SHISHI, Immunology
GUO ZHAOGUI, Clinical Pharmacology
HAN FENGXIA, Biology
HAN XIUYUN, Internal Medicine (Endocrinology)
HU DONGXU, Cardiac Surgery
HU FUZEN, General Surgery
HU GUOLING, Infectious Diseases
HU JIANGUO, Cardiac Surgery
HU MANLING, Health Chemistry
HU TIEHUI, Cardiac Surgery
HU WEIXIN, Tumour Molecular Biology
HUANG GANCHU, Physics and Chemistry
HUANG XUN, Uro-Surgery
HUANG YIMING, Nutritious Food and Health
HUANG ZHAOMIN, Rebabilitation
HUANG ZHENNAN, Health Statistics
JI LONGZHEN, Internal Medicine (Kidney Diseases)
JIAN XINCHUN, Stomatology
JIANG DEZHAO, Haemophysiology
JIANG XIANZHEN, Uro-Surgery
JIANG YOUQIN, Ophthalmology
JIN YIQIANG, Chinese Traditional Medicine
LI DETAI, Radiology
LI GUIYUAN, Molecular Biology
LI HEJUN, Orthopaedic Surgery
LI JIABANG, Chinese Traditional Medicine
LI JUNCHENG, Physiology
LI LUYUN, Medical Genetics
LI RUIZHEN, Ultrasound Diagnosis
LI XINGQUN, Chinese Traditional Medicine

LI XUERONG, Medical Psychology
LI YUANJIAN, Pharmacology
LIAO ERYUAN, Internal Medicine (Endocrinology)
LIN QIUHUA, Gynaecology and Obstetrics
LIU LIHOU, Anatomy
LIU REN, Uro-Surgery
LIU XIAOCHUN, Library and Information Sciences
LIU XUNYANG, General Surgery
LIU YUNSHENG, Neurosurgery
LIU ZHIRAN, Dermatology
LU BINGQING, Neurology
LU GUANGXIU, Biology and Genetics
LU HANBO, Internal Medicine (Haematology)
LU WENNENG, General Surgery
LU XINSHENG, General Surgery
LU YONGDE, Otorhinolaryngology
LU YINZHU, Internal Medicine (Cardiovascular Diseases)
LUO JIAN, Internal Medicine (Kidney Diseases)
LUO XUEGANG, Anatomy
LUO XUEHONG, Emergency Medicine
MA CHUANTAO, Cardiovascular Physiology
MA ENQING, Burns Medicine
OU YANG KE, Infectious Diseases
OU YANG ZHITING, General Surgery
PAN AIYIN, Isotopes in Medicine
QI FAN, Uro-Surgery
QI SHUSHAN, Internal Medicine (Cardiology)
QI ZHENHUA, Internal Medicine (Haematology)
SHEN PENGFEI, Uro-Surgery
SHEN ZIHUA, Stomatology
SONG HUIPING, Biochemistry
SU JIANZHI, Isotopes in Medicine
SU XIANSHI, Infectious Diseases
SUN MING, Internal Medicine (Cardiovascular Diseases)
SUN XIUHONG, Physiology
SUN ZHENGQIU, Health Statistics
TANG DEMING, Infectious Diseases
TANG MINGDE, Environmental Health
TAO ZHENGDE, Otorhinolaryngology
TIAN YONGQUAN, Otorhinolaryngology
WANG LIZHUANG, Emergency Medicine
WANG QIRU, Haemophysiology
WANG ZHONGLIN, Internal Medicine (Cardiology)
WEN JIFANG, Pathology
WU ESHENG, Internal Medicine (Respiratory Diseases)
WU ZHONGQI, Medical Hyperbaric Oxygen
XIE DINGHUA, Otorhinolaryngology
XIA JIAHUI, Biology and Medical Genetics
XIAO JIANYUN, Otorhinolaryngology
XIE ZHAOXIA, Internal Medicine (Haematology)
XU LILI, Gynaecology and Obstetrics
XU XIUHUA, Infection
XU YOUHENG, Haemophysiology
YANG DESEN, Psychiatry
YANG QIDONG, Neurology
YANG YUJIA, Paediatrics
YAO KAITAI, Experimental Oncology
YE YIYAN, Paediatrics
YI XINYUAN, Parasitology
YI ZHUWEN, Paediatrics
YIN BANGLIAN, Cardiac Surgery
YIN BENYI, Internal Medicine (Cardiology)
YOU JIALU, Pathophysiology
YU XIAOLIANG, Paediatrics
YUAN XIANRUI, Neurosurgery
ZENG XIANFANG, Parasitology
ZHANG GUANGSEN, Internal Medicine (Haematology)
ZHANG XICHUN, Internal Medicine (Digestive Diseases)
ZHANG YANGDE, General Surgery
ZHANG YANXIAN, Pathology
ZHOU CHANGJU, Gynaecology and Obstetrics
ZHAO SHUIPING, Internal Medicine (Cardiology)
ZHAO SHUYING, Children's Health
ZHOU HONGHAO, Pharmacology

ZHOU JIANGNAN, Orthopaedic Surgery
ZHU JIMING, Histology and Embryology
ZHU WEIGUANG, Chinese Traditional Medicine

HUNAN NORMAL UNIVERSITY

36 Lu Shan Rd, He Xi, Changsha 410081, Hunan

Telephone: (731) 8883131
Fax: (731) 8851226
E-mail: study@hunnu.edu.cn
Internet: www.hunnu.edu.cn

Founded 1938
Min. of Education control
Academic year: September to July

President: LIU XIANG RONG
Vice-Presidents: GONG WEI ZHONG, JIANG JI CHENG, LIANG SONG PING, ZHOU JING MING
Heads of Graduate Department: CHEN JIAN CHU, SHI OU
Librarian: YAN ZHAO HUI
Number of teachers: 1,000
Number of students: 22,000

Publications: *Ancient Chinese Research* (4 a year), *Chinese Literature Research* (4 a year), *Consumer Economy* (4 a year), *Journal* (education science, 6 a year), *Journal* (medicine, irregular), *Journal* (social science, 6 a year), *Life Science Research* (4 a year), *Modern Law* (4 a year)

DEANS

School of Chemistry and Chemical Engineering: XIE QING JI
School of Education Science: ZHANG CHUAN SUI
School of Foreign Languages: HUANG ZHEN DING
School of International Chinese Culture: JI XUE FENG
School of Law: JIANG XIN MIAO
School of Life Science: WU XIU SHAN
School of Literature: TAN GUI LIN
School of Mathematics and Computer Science: DONG XIN HAN
School of Medicine: FU XIAO HUA
School of Physical Education: LI YAN LING
School of Tourism: XIE JUN GUI
College of Commerce: LIU MAO SONG
Department of Computer Education: WANG LU YA

PROFESSORS

CAI, XUE BING, Law
CHEN, BO, Chemistry and Chemical Engineering
CHEN, CHUAN MIAO, Mathematics and Computer Science
CHEN, HUAN GEN, Mathematics and Computer Science
CHEN, JIA QIN, Life Science
CHEN, LIANG BI, Life Science
CHEN, YUN LIANG, Law
CHEN, ZE, Life Science
CHEN, ZUO HONG, Life Science
CUI, ZHEN HUA, International Chinese Culture
DENG, HONG WEN, Life Science
DENG, LE, Life Science
DENG, LE, Chemistry and Chemical Engineering
DENG, XUE JIAN, Life Science
DONG, XIN HAN, Mathematics and Computer Science
DU, XUE TANG, Mathematics and Computer Science
FANG, KUI, Mathematics and Computer Science
FU, PENG, Life Science
FU, ZAI HUI, Chemistry and Chemical Engineering
GU, YONG GENG, Mathematics and Computer Science

GUO, JING YUN, Mathematics and Computer Science
HAO, SAN RU, Computer Education
HE, DING SHENG, Chemistry and Chemical Engineering
HOU, YAO PING, Mathematics and Computer Science
HUANG, JIAN PING, Computer Education
HUANG, YI NONG, Tourism
HUANG, YUAN QIU, Mathematics and Computer Science
JI, XUE FENG, International Chinese Culture
JIANG, XIAN FU, Law
JIANG, XIAO CHENG, Life Science
JIANG, XIN MIAO, Law
JIN, GUANG HUI, Physical Education
JIN, ZU JUN, Mathematics and Computer Science
LENG, GANG SONG, Mathematics and Computer Science
LI, AI NIAN, Law
LI, FANG CHENG, Life Science
LI, HAI TAO, Chemistry and Chemical Engineering
LI, JIAN ZONG, Life Science
LI, SHUANG YUAN, Law
LI, XIAN BO, Law
LI, YAN LING, Physical Education
LI, ZE LIN, Chemistry and Chemical Engineering
LIANG, SONG PING, Life Science
LIU, HONG, Mathematics and Computer Science
LIU, KE MING, Life Science
LIU, MING YAO, Life Science
LIU, SHAO JUN, Life Science
LIU, YING DI, Life Science
LIU, YUN, Life Science
LIU, ZHEN XIU, Mathematics and Computer Science
LUO, CHEN, Life Science
MA, MING, Chemistry and Chemical Engineering
MA, WEI PING, Physical Education
NUAN, SHENG, Life Science
PENG, XIAN JING, Life Science
QIAN, GUANG MING, Mathematics and Computer Science
QIN, ZHENG DI, Computer Education
QIU, MENG SHENG, Life Science
QIU, XI MIN, Chemistry and Chemical Engineering
QU, FU DONG, Tourism
QUAN, HUI YUN, Mathematics and Computer Science
REN, JI CUN, Chemistry and Chemical Engineering
SHEN, JIAN HUA, Mathematics and Computer Science
SHEN, WEN XUAN, Mathematics and Computer Science
SHI, SHAO RONG, Physical Education
SHI, XIAN LIANG, Mathematics and Computer Science
SHI, YING GUANG, Mathematics and Computer Science
SUN, HONG TAO, Physical Education
TAN, PING PING, Physical Education
WANG, BAO HE, Life Science
WANG, GUI GUO, Law
WANG, GUO QIU, Mathematics and Computer Science
WANG, HONG QUAN, Life Science
WANG, LU YA, Computer Education
WANG, XIAN CHUN, Life Science
WANG, XIAN TAO, Mathematics and Computer Science
WU, XIU SHAN, Life Science
XIA, LI QIU, Life Science
XIANG, KAI NAN, Mathematics and Computer Science
XIAO, BEI GENG, Law
XIAO, XIAO MING, Chemistry and Chemical Engineering
XIE, JING YUN, Life Science
XIE, JUN GUI, Tourism

XIE, QING JI, Chemistry and Chemical Engineering
XU, CHUN XIAO, Tourism
XU, DA, Mathematics and Computer Science
XU, FEI XIONG, Tourism
XU, MAN CAI, Chemistry and Chemical Engineering
XU, MENG LIANG, Life Science
YAN, HENG MEI, Life Science
YANG, XIANG QUN, Mathematics and Computer Science
YANG, XIN JIAN, Mathematics and Computer Science
YAO, SHOU ZHUO, Chemistry and Chemical Engineering
YI, CHANG MIN, Life Science
YIN, DA ZHONG, Life Science
YIN, DONG HONG, Chemistry and Chemical Engineering
YUAN, WU ZHOU, Life Science
ZENG, YUE, Chemistry and Chemical Engineering
ZHANG, BAI ZHEN, Physical Education
ZHANG, JIAN, Life Science
ZHANG, TIAN XIAO, Life Science
ZHANG, XUAN JIE, Life Science
ZHANG, YAO, Mathematics and Computer Science
ZHANG, ZHI GUANG, Life Science
ZHENG, YAN, Tourism
ZHENG, YUAN MIN, Law
ZHOU, GONG JIAN, Life Science
ZHOU, JIAN SHE, Physical Education
ZHOU, TIE JUN, Physical Education
ZHOU, XIN YI, Computer Education
ZHU, QI DING, Mathematics and Computer Science

INNER MONGOLIA UNIVERSITY

235 Daxue West Rd, Huhehaote 010021, Inner Mongolia
Telephone: (471) 4992241
Fax: (471) 4951761
Internet: www.imu.edu.cn
Founded 1957
Academic year: September to July
President: XU RIGAN
Vice-Presidents: CHEN GUOQING, HU GEJILETU, LI YANJUN, LIANG XIXIA, TONG GUOQING
Head of Graduate Department: LIANG XIXIA
Librarian: A LATANCANG

Number of teachers: 1,447
Number of students: 20,000

Publications: *Journal* (humanities and social sciences, 6 a year), *Journal* (natural sciences, 6 a year), *Journal* (philosophy and social sciences, 6 a year)

DEANS

Academy of Mongolian Studies: BAI YINMENDE
College of Art: LI YULIN
College of Chemistry and Chemical Engineering: SU HAIQUAN
College of Computer Science: GAO GUANGLAI
College of Continuing Education: FU WENJUN
College of Economics and Management: GUO XIAOCHUAN
College of Foreign Languages: LI KANING
College of Humanities: QIAN JIANMEI
College of Life Science: YANG JIE
College of Physical Education: YU ZHIHAI
College of Public Administration: JIN HAIHE
College of Science and Technology: BAN SHILIANG
College of Vocational Technology: CHAI JINYI
School of Law: DING WENYING

PROFESSORS

A, LATANCANG, Science and Technology
BAI, XUELIANG, Life Science
BAN, SHILIANG, Science and Technology

BAO, QINGDE, Humanities
BAO, WENHAN, Humanities
BO, YINHUI, Humanities
BU, LINBEILE, Mongolian Studies
BU, RENBATU, Mongolian Studies
CHEN, GUOQING, Science and Technology
CHEN, YOUZUN, Law
CONG, ZHIJIE, Public Administration
DU, LIKE, Humanities
EN, HE, Mongolian Studies
GE, RILETU, Mongolian Studies
GUO, XIAOCHUAN, Economics and Management
HAO, WEIMIN, Mongolian Studies
HE, JIANG, Life Science
HU, TINGMAO, Life Science
JIA, GUISHENG, Public Administration
JIN, HAIHE, Public Administration
LANG, BAORU, Humanities
LI, HONG, Science and Technology
LI, QIANZHONG, Science and Technology
LI, SHUXIN, Humanities
LI, XIAOCHUN, Humanities
LIAN, ZIXIN, Public Administration
LIANG, XIXIA, Science and Technology
LIU, AIHUA, Public Administration
LIU, CHENG, Mongolian Studies
LIU, LIHUA, Public Administration
LIU, XIN, Public Administration
LUO, LIAOFU, Science and Technology
MA, JI, Humanities
MA, ZHANXIN, Economics and Management
MENG, BIN, Economics and Management
MENG, HUIJUN, Economics and Management
MING, YUE, Public Administration
NIU, JIANMING, Life Science
NIU, JINGZHONG, Humanities
QING, GEERTAI, Mongolian Studies
QUAN, FU, Mongolian Studies
REN, WEIDE, Public Administration
REN, YUFENG, Humanities
SHI, ZHENGJI, Humanities
SUN, JIONG, Science and Technology
SUN, KAIMIN, Public Administration
TONG, CHUAN, Life Science
WANG, HONGYAN, Law
WANG, MEICUI, Economics and Management
WANG, YAN, Economics and Management
WANG, YINGCHUN, Life Science
WU, QILATU, Mongolian Studies
WU, YINGJI, Life Science
WU, YUNNA, Public Administration
XU, RIGAN, Life Science
YANG, CHI, Life Science
YANG, JIE, Life Science
YANG, XINMIN, Science and Technology
YU, ZHIHAI, Public Administration
YUN, GUOHONG, Science and Technology
ZHANG, CUIZHEN, Public Administration
ZHANG, FENGMING, Law
ZHANG, ZHIZHONG, Public Administration
ZHAO, MIN, Public Administration
ZHEN, XIUYU, Humanities
ZHOU, QINGSHU, Mongolian Studies

INNER MONGOLIA AGRICULTURAL UNIVERSITY

Xinjian East Rd, Beyong Nanmen, Huhehaote 010018, Inner Mongolia
Telephone: (471) 4301576
Fax: (471) 4301530
Internet: www.imau.edu.cn
Founded 1952
Provincial control
Academic year: September to July
President: LI CHANGYOU
Vice-Presidents: HOU XIANZHI, LI JINQUAN, REN QIANG, WANG LINHE, ZHENG JUNBAO
Library of 750,000 vols
Number of teachers: 1,010
Number of students: 18,800

Publication: *Journal* (4 a year)

DEANS

College of Agriculture: YU ZHUO
College of Animal Science and Animal Medicine: LI JINQUAN
College of Biology Engineering: ZHOU HUANMIN
College of Computing and Information Engineering: PEI XICHUN
College of Ecology and the Environment: WANG MINQIU
College of Economics Management: XIU CHANGBO
College of Forestry: ZHANG QIULIANG
College of Forestry Engineering: WANG XIAOLIANG
College of Humanities and Social Sciences: GAO CHAO
College of Mechanical and Electrical Engineering: WANG CHUNGUANG
College of Water Conservancy and Civil Engineering: JI BAOLIN

PROFESSORS

AN, SHOUQIN, Forestry
AO, CHANGJIN, Animal Science and Medicine
AO, RIGELE, Animal Science and Medicine
BAI, SHULAN, Forestry
CAO, GUIFANG, Animal Science and Medicine
CHANG, JINBAO, Forestry
CHAO, LUNBAGEN, Water Conservancy and Civil Engineering
CHEN, YAXIN, Water Conservancy and Civil Engineering
CUI, ZHIGUO, Animal Science and Medicine
DAO, ERJI, Animal Science and Medicine
DE, LIGEERSANG, Food Science and Engineering
DOU, WEIGUO, Mechanical and Electrical Engineering
DU, WENLIANG, Mechanical and Electrical Engineering
FAN, MINGSHOU, Agriculture
FENG, LIN, Forestry
GA, ERDI, Animal Science and Medicine
GAO, CHAO, Humanities and Social Sciences
GE, RILE, Forestry
GUANG, PINGYUAN, Animal Science and Medicine
GUO, LIANSHENG, Ecology and the Environment
GUO, LIANSHENG, Forestry
HE, YINFENG, Food Science and Engineering
HOU, XIANZHI, Animal Science and Medicine
HU, HEBATEER, Animal Science and Medicine
JIN, SHUGUANG, Animal Science and Medicine
LI, CHANGYOU, Water Conservancy and Civil Engineering
LI, JINQUAN, Animal Science and Medicine
LI, LIANGUO, Agriculture
LI, PEIFENG, Animal Science and Medicine
LI, QINGFENG, Ecology and the Environment
LI, YUNZHANG, Animal Science and Medicine
LIU, DEFU, Ecology and the Environment
LIU, KELI, Agriculture
LIU, YONG, Economics Management
LIU, ZHENGYI, Animal Science and Medicine
MA, SHUOSHI, Mechanical and Electrical Engineering
MA, XUEEN, Animal Science and Medicine
MANG, LAI, Animal Science and Medicine
MO, LIGEN, Biology Engineering
PANG, BAOPING, Agriculture
PEI, XICHUN, Computer and Information Engineering
QI, TONGCHUN, Mechanical and Electrical Engineering
QIAO, CHEN, Agriculture
QIAO, GUANGHUA, Economics Management
QIAO, LING, Animal Science and Medicine
QIN, HUA, Food Science and Engineering
SAI, YINCHAOKETU, Biology Engineering
SHANG, SHIYOU, Mechanical and Electrical Engineering
SHENG, XIANGDONG, Water Conservancy and Civil Engineering

SHENG, ZHIYI, Animal Science and Medicine
SHI, HAIBIN, Water Conservancy and Civil Engineering
SI, YA, Humanities and Social Sciences
TAN, PENZHEN, Humanities and Social Sciences
TIAN, DE, Mechanical and Electrical Engineering
TIAN, ZIHUA, Agriculture
TONG, SHUMIN, Mechanical and Electrical Engineering
WAN, TAO, Biology Engineering
WANG, BINXIU, Economics Management
WANG, CHUNGUANG, Mechanical and Electrical Engineering
WANG, CHUNJIE, Animal Science and Medicine
WANG, HAOFU, Humanities and Social Sciences
WANG, LAI, Biology Engineering
WANG, LIMING, Forestry
WANG, LINHE, Ecology and the Environment
WEN, HENG, Water Conservancy and Civil Engineering
WU, NI, Animal Science and Medicine
WU, SHUQING, Animal Science and Medicine
XIU, CHANGBO, Economics Management
XU, ZHIXIN, Ecology and the Environment
XUE, HERU, Computer and Information Engineering
YAN, SUMEI, Animal Science and Medicine
YAN, WEI, Ecology and the Environment
YAN, WEI, Forestry
YANG, BAOSHOU, Animal Science and Medicine
YANG, MINGSHAO, Mechanical and Electrical Engineering
YANG, XIAOYE, Animal Science and Medicine
YAO, FENGTONG, Economics Management
YAO, YUNFENG, Ecology and the Environment
YU, ZHUO, Agriculture
YUAN, XIUYING, Forestry
YUN, JINGFENG, Ecology and the Environment
YUN, XINGFU, Agriculture
YUN, YUEHUA, Humanities and Social Sciences
ZHANG, DEMIAN, Mechanical and Electrical Engineering
ZHANG, HEPING, Food Science and Engineering
ZHANG, LILING, Animal Science and Medicine
ZHANG, QIULIANG, Forestry
ZHANG, SHAOYING, Agriculture
ZHANG, XINLING, Economics Management
ZHANG, ZHIYI, Mechanical and Electrical Engineering
ZHAO, GENBAO, Computingr and Information Engineering
ZHAO, SHIJIE, Mechanical and Electrical Engineering
ZHAO, YUANFENG, Economics Management
ZHAO, ZHENHUA, Animal Science and Medicine
ZHAO, ZHIGONG, Animal Science and Medicine
ZHOU, HUANMIN, Animal Science and Medicine
ZHOU, HUANMIN, Biology Engineering

INNER MONGOLIA UNIVERSITY FOR NATIONALITIES

22 Huolinhe Rd, Tongliao 028043, Inner Mongolia
Telephone: (475) 8313292
Fax: (475) 8218937
Internet: www.imun.edu.cn
Founded 1960
Academic year: September to July
Pres.: WANG DINGZHU
Vice-Pres.: LIU ZONGRUI, MA GUOWEN, PAN XIANG, XIAO JIANPING
Head of Graduate Department: XING PENGNIN
Librarian: DONG SHALI

Library of 700,000 vols
Number of teachers: 2,262
Number of students: 31,271
Publications: *Journal* (natural sciences; 6 a year in Chinese, 2 a year in Mongolian), *Journal* (social sciences, 6 a year)

DEANS

College of Arts: (vacant)
College of Education Science: (vacant)
College of Law and History: PU FANDA
College of Literature: XU WENHAI
College of Mathematics and Computer Science: (vacant)
College of Mongolian Medicine: BA GENNA
College of Mongolian Studies: (vacant)
College of Sports: (vacant)

PROFESSORS

A, GULA, Mongolian Medicine
AN, GUANBU, Mongolian Medicine
BA, GENNA, Mongolian Medicine
BA, RIGEQI, Mongolian Medicine
BAI, YANMANDULA, Mongolian Medicine
PU, FANDA, Law and History
XUN, WENHAI, Literature
YANG, AMING, Mongolian Medicine

JIANGNAN UNIVERSITY

1800 Lihu Rd, Wuxi 214122, Jiangsu
Telephone: (510) 85913623
Fax: (510) 85913622
Internet: www.jiangnan.edu.cn
Founded 1902
State control
Academic year: September to July
Pres.: CHEN JIAN
Vice-Presidents: FENG BIAO, JIANG ZHONGPING, LOU GUODONG, WANG WU, ZHU TUO
Head of Graduate Department: ZHANG HAO
Librarian: ZHANG YIXIN
Number of teachers: 1,504
Number of students: 19,600
Publication: *Journal of Southern Yangtze University* (editions: food and biotechnology, natural sciences, humanities and social science, 6 a year; beverage and frozen food industry, 4 a year)

DEANS

Department of Art: WANG JIANYAN
Department of Civil Engineering: HUA YUAN
Department of International Studies: GUO XIHUA
Department of Physical Education: YANG RONGLIN
School of Biotechnology: XU YAN
School of Business: FU XIANZHI
School of Chemical and Materials Engineering: FANG YUN
School of Communication and Control Engineering: JI ZHICHENG
School of Continuing Education: HUANG ZHENGMING
School of Design: GUO WEIMIN
School of Education: CHEN MINGXUAN
School of Food Science and Technology: ZHANG HAO
School of Foreign Studies: DONG JIANQIAO
School of Information Technology: WANG SHITONG
School of Law and Politics: ZHU TONGDAN
School of Literature: XU XINGHAI
School of Mechanical Engineering: ZHANG QIUJU
School of Medicine: LI HUAZHONG
School of Science: (vacant)
School of Textiles and Clothing: FANG KUANJUN

PROFESSORS

CAO, GUANGQUN, Chemical and Materials Engineering

CHEN, ANJUN, Mechanical Engineering
CHEN, JIAN, Biotechnology
CHEN, JIONG, Literature
CHEN, ZHENGXING, Food Science and Technology
DENG, ZIMEI, Law and Politics
DING, WEIGUO, Commerce
DING, XIAOLIN, Food Science and Technology
DONG, YUZI, Information Technology
DU, GUOCHENG, Biotechnology
FANG, HANWEN, Literature
FANG, KUANJUN, Textiles
FENG, BIAO, Food Science and Technology
GAO, WEIDONG, Textiles
GE, MINGQIAO, Textiles
GU, GUOXIAN, Biotechnology
GU, WENYING, Food Science and Technology
GU, YAOLIN, Information Technology
GU, YIFAN, Literature
GUO, SHIDONG, Food Science and Technology
HUANG, HUANCHU, Law and Politics
HUANG, WEINING, Food Science and Technology
HUANG, ZHIHAO, Literature
HUANG, ZHONGJING, Law and Politics
JIANG, BO, Food Science and Technology
JIANG, CHENGYONG, Literature
JIN, JIAN, Biotechnology
JIN, QIRONG, Biotechnology
JIN, ZHENGYU, Food Science and Technology
LE, GUOWEI, Food Science and Technology
LI, HUAZHONG, Biotechnology
LI, SHIGUO, Mechanical Engineering
LI, WEIJIANG, Biotechnology
LIU, HUANMING, Law and Politics
LUN, SHIYI, Biotechnology
MA, JIANGUO, Food Science and Technology
MA, QIFAN, Commerce
MAO, ZHONGGUI, Biotechnology
MENG, QING-EN, Law and Politics
PAN, BEILEI, Food Science and Technology
QIU, AIYONG, Food Science and Technology
QUAN, WENHAI, Biotechnology
SHAO, JIYONG, Commerce
SHI, YONGHUI, Food Science and Technology
SIMA, NAN, Literature
SUN, HONG, Literature
SUN, YANTANG, Information Technology
SUN, ZHIHAO, Biotechnology
SUN, ZHOUNIAN, Literature
TANG, JIAN, Food Science and Technology
TAO, BOHUA, Literature
TAO, WENYI, Biotechnology
WANG, SHITONG, Information Technology
WANG, WU, Biotechnology
WANG, YONGFENG, Literature
WANG, ZHANG, Food Science and Technology
WANG, ZHENGXIANG, Biotechnology
WANG, ZHIWEI, Mechanical Engineering
WU, GE, Commerce
WU, GEMING, Literature
WU, PEIZONG, Biotechnology
WU, XIANZHANG, Biotechnology
XIA, WENSHUI, Food Science and Technology
XIE, ZHENRONG, Law and Politics
XU, WENBO, Information Technology
XU, XINGHAI, Literature
XU, YAN, Biotechnology
XU, ZHENGYUAN, Information Technology
YAO, HUIYUAN, Food Science and Technology
YAO, JINMING, Literature
YU, SHIYING, Food Science and Technology
YUAN, HUIXIN, Mechanical Engineering
YUAN, ZHENHUI, Law and Politics
ZENG, YOUXIN, Commerce
ZHANG, GENYI, Food Science and Technology
ZHANG, HEGUAN, Commerce
ZHANG, JIWEN, Information Technology
ZHANG, KECHANG, Biotechnology
ZHANG, MIN, Food Science and Technology
ZHANG, QIUJU, Mechanical Engineering
ZHANG, XINCHANG, Mechanical Engineering
ZHANG, XINGYUAN, Biotechnology
ZHANG, XIQING, Mechanical Engineering
ZHANG, YIXIN, Information Technology
ZHANG, YONGXIN, Literature

ZHANG, YUZHONG, Mechanical Engineering
ZHAO, GUANGAO, Biotechnology
ZHAO, JIANGUO, Biotechnology
ZHAO, YONGWU, Mechanical Engineering
ZHOU, HUIMING, Food Science and Technology
ZHOU, QING, Biotechnology
ZHOU, WUCHUN, Literature
ZHU, TONGDAN, Law and Politics
ZHU, ZHIFENG, Textiles
ZHUGE, HONGYUN, Literature
ZHUGE, JIAN, Biotechnology

JIANGSU UNIVERSITY

301 Xuefu Rd, Zhenjiang 212013, Jiangsu
Telephone: (511) 8780048
Fax: (511) 8791785
Internet: www.ujs.edu.cn

Founded 2001
Academic year: September to July
President: YANG JICHANG
Vice-Presidents: CAO YOUQING, SONG JINGZHANG, SONG YUQING, SUN YUKUN, XU HUAXI, YUAN SHOUQI, YUAN YINNAN, ZHAO JIEWEN
Head of Graduate Department: MAO HANPING
Librarian: SONG SHUNLIN

Number of teachers: 900
Number of students: 26,320

Publication: *Journal* (6 a year, editions: higher education, medicine, natural sciences, social sciences)

DEANS

College of Adult Education: XIN JUNKANG
Faculty of Science: TIAN LIXIN
School of Art Education: ZHU ZHENGLUN
School of Automotive and Traffic Engineering: CAI YIXI
School of Biological and Environmental Engineering: WU CHUNDU
School of Chemistry and Chemical Engineering: XIE JIMIN
School of Computer Science and Telecommunications: JU SHIGUANG
School of Electrical and Information Engineering: LIU GUOHAI
School of Energy Resources and Power Engineering: YANG MINGUAN
School of Foreign Languages: LUO XINMIN
School of Humanities and Social Sciences: DA YUANYI
School of Industrial and Business Administration: MEI QIANG
School of Materials Engineering: (vacant)
School of Mechanical Engineering: LI PINGPING
School of Medical Technology: XU WENRONG
School of Medicine: XU HUAXI
School of Normal Education: CHEN LIN
School of Pharmacy: XU XIMING

PROFESSORS

BAO, BINGHAO, Mechanical Engineering
CAI, LAN, Mechanical Engineering
CHEN, CUIYING, Mechanical Engineering
CHEN, GUOXIANG, Humanities and Social Sciences
CHEN, JIN, Mechanical Engineering
CHEN, LIZHEN, Business Administration
CHEN, ZHAOZHANG, Electrical and Information Engineering
CHEN, ZHIGANG, Materials Engineering
CHENG, LI, Electrical and Information Engineering
CHENG, XIANYI, Computer Science and Telecommunications
CHENG, XIAONONG, Materials Engineering
CHONG, KAI, Materials Engineering
DAI, QIXUN, Materials Engineering
DING, GUILIN, Mechanical Engineering
DING, JIANNING, Mechanical Engineering
DONG, DEFU, Humanities and Social Sciences
FAN, MING, Business Administration

GE, XIAOLAN, Mechanical Engineering
GU, JINAN, Mechanical Engineering
HE, YOUSHI, Business Administration
HE, ZHIGUO, Art
HUANG, GENLIANG, Materials Engineering
HUANG, XIQUAN, Medical Technology
JIN, LIFU, Humanities and Social Sciences
JU, SHIGUANG, Computer Science and Telecommunications
KONG, YUSHENG, Business Administration
LEI, YUCHENG, Materials Engineering
LI, BOQUAN, Mechanical Engineering
LI, CHANGSHENG, Mechanical Engineering
LI, DETAO, Energy Resources and Power Engineering
LI, PINGPING, Mechanical Engineering
LI, XINCHENG, Mechanical Engineering
LI, YAOMING, Mechanical Engineering
LI, ZHENGMING, Electrical and Information Engineering
LIN, HONGYI, Energy Resources and Power Engineering
LIU, AIZHEN, Foreign Languages
LIU, FENGYING, Computer Science and Telecommunications
LIU, GUOHAI, Electrical and Information Engineering
LIU, JIANYI, Business Administration
LIU, QIUSHENG, Business Administration
LU, ZHANGPING, Mechanical Engineering
LU, ZHENGNAN, Business Administration
LUO, DEFU, Materials Science and Engineering
LUO, TIGAN, Energy Resources and Power Engineering
LUO, XINMIN, Materials Engineering
LUO, ZHIGAO, Mechanical Engineering
MA, LVZHONG, Mechanical Engineering
MAO, HANPING, Mechanical Engineering
MEI, QIANG, Business Administration
QI, HONG, Energy Resources and Power Engineering
QIAO, ZHAOHUA, Humanities and Social Science
QIU, BAIJING, Mechanical Engineering
REN, NAIFEI, Mechanical Engineering
SHAO, HONGHONG, Materials Engineering
SHAO, SHIHE, Medical Technology
SHEN, XIANGQIAN, Materials Engineering
SHI, GUOHONG, Business Administration
SI, NAICHAO, Materials Engineering
SONG, SHUNLIN, Computer Science and Telecommunications
SONG, XINNAN, Energy Resources and Power Engineering
SONG, YUQING, Computer Science and Telecommunications
SUN, JIAGUANG, Computer Science and Telecommunications
SUN, YUKUN, Electrical and Information Engineering
WANG, CUNTANG, Mechanical Engineering
WANG, GANG, Computer Science and Telecommunications
WANG, GUICHENG, Mechanical Engineering
WANG, QIAN, Energy Resources and Power Engineering
WANG, SHULIN, Mechanical Engineering
WANG, SHUQI, Materials Engineering
WANG, ZE, Energy Resources and Power Engineering
WEI, QI, Energy Resources and Power Engineering
WEN, JIANLONG, Energy Resources and Power Engineering
WU, YANYOU, Mechanical Engineering
XIAO, TIEJUN, Computer Science and Telecommunications
XIE, GANG, Humanities and Social Sciences
XU, HUAXI, Medical Technology
XU, WENRONG, Medical Technology
XU, XIMING, Pharmacy
YANG, JICHANG, Mechanical Engineering
YANG, MINGUAN, Energy Resources and Power Engineering
YANG, PING, Mechanical Engineering

YAO, GUANXIN, Business Administration
ZHAN, YONGZHAO, Computer Science and Telecommunications
ZHANG, BINGSHENG, Humanities and Social Sciences
ZHANG, JIAN, Business Administration
ZHANG, RONGBIAO, Electrical and Information Engineering
ZHANG, YONGKANG, Mechanical Engineering
ZHANG, ZHUMEI, Humanities and Social Sciences
ZHAO, BUHUI, Electrical and Information Engineering
ZHAO, DEAN, Electrical and Information Engineering
ZHAO, JIN, Business Administration
ZHAO, XICANG, Business Administration
ZHAO, YANPING, Business Administration
ZHAO, YUTAO, Materials Engineering
ZHOU, HONG, Medical Technology
ZHOU, JIANZHONG, Mechanical Engineering
ZHOU, JUN, Mechanical Engineering
ZHOU, TIANJIAN, Medical Technology
ZHOU, ZHICHU, Humanities and Social Sciences
ZHU, HUANGQIU, Electrical and Information Engineering
ZHU, WEIXING, Electrical and Information Engineering
ZUO, RAN, Energy Resources and Power Engineering

JIANGXI AGRICULTURAL UNIVERSITY

Meiling, Nanchang, Jianxi Province 330045
Internet: www.jxau.edu.cn

Founded 1980

President: Prof. LUO MING

Library: over 400,000 vols
Number of teachers: 530
Number of students: 2,900

Publication: *Journal*

Departments of agricultural economics, agronomy, animal husbandry and veterinary science, farm engineering, forestry, horticulture, plant protection.

JILIN UNIVERSITY

10 Qianwei Rd, Changchun 130012

Telephone: (431) 5166885
Fax: (431) 5166570
E-mail: fsc@jlu.edu.cn
Internet: www.jlu.edu.cn

Founded 1946, merged in 2001 with Jilin University of Technology (f. 1955), Norman Bethune University of Medical Sciences (f. 1939), Changchun University of Science and Technology (f. 1951) and Changchun Institute of Posts and Telecommunications (f. 1947), to form new Jilin University

Academic year: September to July (2 semesters).

Colleges: philosophy and sociology; literature and arts; foreign languages; art; physical education; economics; law; administration studies; management studies; economics and information; mathematics; physics; chemistry; life sciences; machinery and engineering; motor car engineering; materials science and engineering; transport; biology and agricultural engineering; electronics and engineering; communications engineering; computer science and technology; geological sciences; geological exploration and information technology; construction engineering; environment and resources; public health sciences; clinical medicine; stomatology; pharmacy; nursing

Pres.: LIU ZHONGSHU
Head of Graduate School: QIU SHILUN
Librarian: BAO CHENGGUAN

Library of 2,510,000 vols
Publications: *Chemical Research in Chinese Universities* (Chinese and English edns), *Higher Education Research and Practice*, *Journal of Demography*, *Journal of Historical Studies*, *Journal of Natural Science*, *Legal Systems and Social Development*, *Mathematics of Northeastern China*, *Modern Japanese Economy*, *Northeast Asian Forum*.

JINAN UNIVERSITY

601 Huangpu West Rd, Guangzhou 510632, Guangdong

Telephone: (20) 85220010
E-mail: officex@jnu.edu.cn
Internet: www.jnu.edu.cn

Founded 1906
Academic year: September to July

President: LIU RENHUAI
Vice-Presidents: HU JUN, JI ZONGAN, JIA YIMIN, JIANG SHUZHUO, LU DAXIANG, WANG HUA, YE QIN
Head of Graduate Department: GU WEIFANG
Librarian: ZHU LINA

Number of teachers: 1,477
Number of students: 22,000

Publications: *Chinese Journal of Pathophysiology* (6 a year), *Ecological Science* (4 a year), *Economic Front* (12 a year), *Jinan Higher Education Research* (6 a year), *Journal* (6 a year), *Journal of the College of Chinese Language and Culture of Jinan University* (4 a year), *South-east Asian Studies* (6 a year)

DEANS

College of Chinese Language and Culture: BAO CHAO
College of Continuing Education: HAO ZHAOZHOU
College of Economics: LIU SHAOBO
College of Foreign Studies: LIANG DONGHUA
College of Information Science and Technology: BO YUANHUAI
College of Journalism and Communication: CAI MINGZE
College of Liberal Arts: SUN WEIMING
College of Life Science and Technology: ZHOU TIANHONG
College of Pharmacy: ZHANG RONGHUA
College of Science and Engineering: ZHANG YONGLIN
International School: SUN BOHUA
Management School: SUI GUANGJUN
Medical School: SU BAOGUI
School of Law: ZHOU XIANZHI
Shenzhen College of Tourism: LIU ZEPENG
Zhuhai Special Economic Zone College: HU JUN

PROFESSORS

AO, NINGJIAN, Life Science and Technology
CAI, JIYE, Life Science and Technology
CAI, MINGZE, Journalism and Communication
CAO, BAOLIN, Liberal Arts
CAO, YUNHUA, Law
CHEN, CHUSHENG, Liberal Arts
CHEN, EN, Economics
CHEN, QIAOZHI, Law
CHEN, WEIMING, Liberal Arts
CHEN, XIAOJIN, Liberal Arts
CHEN, XINGDAN, Science and Engineering
CHEN, XUEMEI, Economics
CHEN, YINYUAN, Life Science and Technology
CHEN, YONGLIANG, Economics
CHENG, GUOBIN, Liberal Arts
DENG, QIAOBIN, Chinese
DONG, JIANXIN, Management
DONG, TIANCE, Journalism and Communication
DU, JINMIN, Finance

DUAN, SHUNSHAN, Life Science and Technology
FEI, YONG, Liberal Arts
FENG, BANGYAN, Economics
FENG, XIAOYUN, Economics
GAO, WEINONG, Liberal Arts
GAO, YINGJUN, Science and Engineering
GONG, WEIPING, Economics
GU, GUOYAO, Finance
GUO, SHUHAO, Life Science and Technology
HAN, BOPING, Life Science and Technology
HAN, ZHAOZHOU, Statistics
HE, WENTAO, Finance
HONG, AN, Life Science and Technology
HU, JUN, Management
HU, JUN, Zhuhai SEZ College
HU, SHIZHEN, Economics
HUANG, DEHONG, Management
HUANG, YAOXIONG, Life Science and Technology
JI, MANHONG, Liberal Arts
JI, ZONG-AN, Liberal Arts
JIA, YIMIN, Liberal Arts
JIANG, DUXIAO, Life Science and Technology
JIANG, SHUZHUO, Chinese
JIN, LAHUA, Science and Engineering
LI, BOQIAO, Law
LI, GUISHENG, Life Science and Technology
LI, WEI, Life Science and Technology
LI, YIJUN, Life Science and Technology
LI, YUFANG, Economics
LIN, FUYONG, Zhuhai SEZ College
LIN, LIQIONG, Economics
LIN, RUPENG, Journalism and Communication
LING, WENQUAN, Management
LIU, DEXUE, International Economics and Trade
LIU, JIALIN, Journalism and Communication
LIU, JIANPING, Statistics
LIU, JIESHENG, Life Science and Technology
LIU, RENHUAI, Science and Engineering
LIU, SHAOBO, Finance
LIU, SHAOJIN, Chinese
LIU, YIN, Law
LIU, YINGLIANG, Life Science and Technology
LIU, ZHENGGANG, Liberal Arts
LIU, ZHENGWEN, Life Science and Technology
LU, JUNHUA, Pharmacy
MA, MINGDA, Liberal Arts
MA, QIUFENG, Journalism and Communication
MA, ZHIRONG, Zhuhai SEZ College
MEI, LINHAI, Economics
NIU, DESHENG, Economics
OUYANG, JIANMING, Life Science and Technology
PAN, SHANPEI, Life Science and Technology
PANG, QICHANG, Science and Engineering
QIU, SHUSEN, Liberal Arts
RAO, PENGZI, Chinese
SHAO, JINGMIN, Chinese
SU, BAOHE, Zhuhai SEZ College
SU, DONGWEI, Finance
SUI, GUANGJUN, Management
SUN, BOHUA, International School
SUN, DONGCHUAN, Zhuhai SEZ College
SUN, HANXIAO, Pharmacy
TAN, TIAN, Journalism and Communication
TAN, YUE, Finance
TANG, KAIJIAN, Liberal Arts
TANG, SHUNQING, Life Science and Technology
TANG, SHUZE, Science and Engineering
WANG, CONG, Finance
WANG, FUCHU, Economics
WANG, HUA, Management
WANG, LIEYAO, Liberal Arts
WANG, XIANGPING, Zhuhai SEZ College
WANG, XINMIN, Liberal Arts
WANG, YANKUN, Chinese
WANG, YIFEI, Pharmacy
WANG, YING, Life Science and Technology
WEI, ZHONGLIN, Liberal Arts
WEN, BEIYAN, Law
WU, CHAOBIAO, Statistics

WU, JIANG, Economics
WU, LIGUANG, International Economics and Trade
WU, XIANZHONG, Management
XIA, HONGSHENG, Management
XIANG, JUNJIAN, Life Science and Technology
XIE, QINAN, Statistics
XU, SHIHAI, Life Science and Technology
YANG, QIGUANG, Liberal Arts
YANG, XING, Finance
YANG, YING, Economics
YANG, YUFENG, Life Science and Technology
YAO, XINSHENG, Pharmacy
YE, CHUNLING, Pharmacy
YE, WENCAI, Pharmacy
YIN, HUA, Science and Engineering
YIN, PINGHE, Life Science and Technology
YU, DINGCHENG, Economics
YU, RONGMIN, Pharmacy
YU, YOULONG, Science and Engineering
ZENG, JIANXIONG, Journalism and Communication
ZENG, YAOYING, Life Science and Technology
ZHAN, BOHUI, Chinese
ZHANG, JIE, International Economics and Trade
ZHANG, QIFAN, Liberal Arts
ZHANG, QIZHONG, Life Science and Technology
ZHANG, RONGHUA, Pharmacy
ZHANG, SENWEN, Science and Engineering
ZHANG, SHIJUN, Liberal Arts
ZHANG, XIAOHUI, Liberal Arts
ZHANG, YAOHUI, Zhuhai SEZ College
ZHANG, YONGLIN, Science and Engineering
ZHANG, YUANMING, Life Science and Technology
ZHANG, YUCHUN, Liberal Arts
ZHANG, ZIYONG, Life Science and Technology
ZHAO, JIAMIN, Finance
ZHENG, WENJIE, Life Science and Technology
ZHONG, JINGANG, Science and Engineering
ZHOU, CHANGREN, Life Science and Technology
ZHOU, LIXIN, Life Science and Technology
ZHOU, TIANHONG, Life Science and Technology
ZHOU, XIANZH, Law
ZHU, CHENGPING, Liberal Arts
ZHU, WEIJIE, Life Science and Technology

KUNMING MEDICAL COLLEGE

84 Renmin Xilu, Kunming 650031, Yunnan
Telephone: (871) 5339224
Fax: (871) 5311542
Internet: www.kmmc.edu.cn
Founded 1956
Academic year: September to January, March to August
Pres.: Prof. LIANG LIQUAN
Vice-Pres: Prof. CHEN DECHANG, Prof. WANG ZICANG, ZHANG CHAO
Chief Administrative Officer: JIANG RUNSHENG
Library of 170,000 vols, 1,659 periodicals
Number of teachers: 1,200
Number of students: 2,789 (including 118 postgraduates)

KUNMING UNIVERSITY OF SCIENCE AND TECHNOLOGY

1 Wenchangxiang, Kunming 650093, Yunnan
Telephone: (871) 5144212
Fax: (871) 5158622
Internet: www.kmust.edu.cn
Founded 1954
Academic year: September to July
Pres.: Prof. ZHANG WENBIN
Vice-Pres: Prof. HE TIANCHUN, Prof. TAO HENGCHANG, Prof. XIANG NAIMING
Asst Pres.: Prof. SUN JIALIN

Registrar: Prof. ZHOU RONG
Librarian: Prof. LIU ZHONGHUA
Library of 1,100,000 vols
Number of teachers: 800
Number of students: 8,000
Publications: *Journal, Research in Higher Education in KUST, Science and Technology in KUST*

HEADS OF COLLEGES

College of Adult Education: Prof. XU BAOZHONG
College of Management and Economy: Prof. YANG BAOJIAN
College of Social Science and Art: LI XUEYOU

LANZHOU UNIVERSITY

222 Tianshui Nanlu, 730000 Lanzhou, Gansu Province
Telephone: 8912126
Fax: 8625576
Internet: www.lzu.edu.cn
Founded 1909
Academic year: September to July (2 semesters)
Pres.: ZHOU XUHONG
Vice-Pres.: AN LIZHE
Vice-Pres.: CHEN FAHU
Vice-Pres.: GAN HUI
Vice-Pres.: JING TAO
Vice-Pres.: XU SHENGCHENG
Dir for Pres. Office: ZHANG ZHENGGUO
Librarian: SHA YONGZHONG
Number of teachers: 1,779
Number of students: 28,358
Publications: *Collections of Articles on Dunhuang Studies, Historical and Geographical Review of Northwest China.*

LIAONING UNIVERSITY

66 Chongshan Middle Rd, Shenyang 110036, Liaoning
Telephone: (24) 86842756
Fax: (24) 62202013
E-mail: office@lnu.edu.cn
Internet: www.lnu.edu.cn
Founded 1948
Ministry of Education control
Academic year: September to July
President: CHENG WEI
Vice-Presidents: LIU ZHICHAO, MU HUAIZHONG, ZANG SHULIANG, ZHANG WEI
Head of Graduate Department: XU PING
Librarian: YANG XIAOJUN
Number of teachers: 1,200
Number of students: 23,000
Publications: *Journal* (natural sciences, 4 a year), *Journal* (philosophy and social sciences, 6 a year), *Research of Japan* (4 a year)

DEANS

Asia-Australia College of Business: ZHOU JIE
College of Adult Education: MA YONGJUN
College of Business Management: GAO CHUANG
College of Chemistry and Engineering: SONG XIMING
College of Cultural Communication: GAO KAIZHENG
College of Economics: LIN MUXI
College of Foreign Languages: CHEN FENG
College of Higher Professional Techniques: YU ZHONGCHENG
College of Information Science and Technology: SHI XIANGBIN
College of Law: YANG SONG
College of Philosophy and Public Administration: SHAO XIAOGUANG
College of Radio, Film and Television: HU GUANGHUI

Faculty of Environmental Science: LI FAYUN
Faculty of History: DING HAIBIN
Faculty of Life Sciences: ZHOU RENQING
Faculty of Mathematics: DAI TIANMIN
Faculty of Physics: GUO YONGXIN
Sun Wah International Business School: CHENG WEI

PROFESSORS

BI, XIAOHUI, Philosophy and Public Administration
CHE, WEIYI, Mathematics
CHEN, CHUNGUANG, Information Science and Technology
CHEN, FENG, Foreign Languages
CHEN, XIN, Chemistry and Engineering
DAI, BOXUN, Business Management
DAI, TIANMIN, Mathematics
DING, HAIBIN, History
DING, NING, Information Science and Technology
DONG, SHOUYI, History
DONG, WENCHENG, Cultural Communication
FANG, BAOLIN, Business Management
GAO, CHUANG, Business Management
GAO, KAIZHENG, Cultural Communication
GAO, YANGKUI, Foreign Languages
GU, KUIXIANG, History
GUO, HUOXUN, Philosophy and Public Administration
GUO, JIE, Law
GUO, WENSHENG, Chemistry and Engineering
GUO, YONGXIN, Physics
HAO, JIANSHE, Law
HU, YUHAI, History
JIA, SHUFENG, Foreign Languages
JIAO, RUNMING, History
JIN, LISHUN, Business Management
LI, CHUNGUANG, History
LI, JUEXIAN, Mathematics
LI, LIPING, Information Science and Technology
LI, TIEMIN, Life Sciences
LI, YONGCHANG, History
LIN, MUXI, Economics
LIU, DUCAI, Law
LIU, FULIN, Mathematics
LIU, LIGANG, Business Management
LIU, WEIZHI, Cultural Communication
LIU, XINGZHI, Chemistry and Engineering
LU, JIERONG, Philosophy and Public Administration
LU, DIANZHEN, Chemistry and Engineering
LU, FANG, Mathematics
LU, GUOCHEN, Philosophy and Public Administration
LUO, JUNBO, Mathematics
MA, LIJUAN, Foreign Languages
NIU, BIN, Information Science and Technology
PENG, HAORONG, Business Management
QI, LIQUAN, Chemistry and Engineering
QI, ZHENGHUI, History
QIN, YONGLU, Information Science and Technology
QU, DELAI, Cultural Communication
REN, JI, Law
SHAO, XIAOGUANG, Philosophy and Public Administration
SHEN, GUIFENG, Physics
SHEN, HONGDA, Business Management
SHI, XIANGBIN, Information Science and Technology
SHI, YING, Law
SONG, XIMING, Chemistry and Engineering
SUN, HONGLIE, Mathematics
SUN, LI, Law
TANG, XIAOHUA, Business Management
TIAN, YUFENG, Information Science and Technology
TU, GUANGSHE, Cultural Communication
WANG, CHUNFEI, Cultural Communication
WANG, CHUNRONG, Cultural Communication
WANG, JUN, Chemistry and Engineering
WANG, QIUYU, Life Sciences
WANG, WEI, Cultural Communication

WANG, WEIFAN, Mathematics
WANG, WENCI, Foreign Languages
WANG, XIANGFENG, Cultural Communication
WU, CHUNYU, Physics
WU, WENZHONG, Foreign Languages
WU, XINJIE, Physics
XIAO, SHENG, Business Management
XING, ZHIREN, Law
XU, HAOGUANG, Cultural Communication
XU, ZHIGANG, Cultural Communication
XUE, JIANSHENG, Information Science and Technology
YANG, JIAZHEN, Chemistry and Engineering
YANG, LINRUI, Law
YANG, MING, Law
YANG, SONG, Law
YU, ZHONGZHUO, Business Management
ZANG, SHULIANG, Chemistry and Engineering
ZENG, XIAOFEI, Life Sciences
ZHANG, CHENGHUA, Physics
ZHANG, FENG, Chemistry and Engineering
ZHANG, JIE, History
ZHANG, LIZHEN, History
ZHANG, XIANGDONG, Chemistry and Engineering
ZHANG, YOUHUI, Information Science and Technology
ZHAO, BINGGUI, Law
ZHAO, DEZHI, Philosophy and Public Administration
ZHAO, GUOXING, Information Science and Technology
ZHAO, LINGHE, Cultural Communication
ZHENG, YONGFAN, Mathematics
ZHOU, FEI, Philosophy and Public Administration
ZHOU, RENQING, Life Sciences
ZHU, MINGLUN, Cultural Communication
ZUO, ZHICHENG, Foreign Languages

LIAONING NORMAL UNIVERSITY

Da Lian 116029, Liaoning
Telephone: (411) 2158235
Internet: www.lnnu.edu.cn
Founded 1951
Provincial control
Academic year: September to July

President: QU QINGBIAO
Vice-Presidents: HAN ZHENGLIN, QU WEI
Librarian: ZHAO YUNSHENG
Library of 1,330,000 vols
Number of teachers: 1,897
Number of students: 25,200
Publication: *Journal* (6 a year)

DEANS

College of the City and Environment: LIN XIANSENG
College of Education: FU WEILI
College of Film and Television Art: GAO GUANGFU
College of Foreign Languages: MA YANGGANG
College of History and Tourism: XIE JINGFANG
College of Law: YU PEILIN
College of Life Science: HOU HESHENG
College of Literature: WANG WEIPING
College of Management: ZHAO ZHONGWEN
College of Physics and Electronic Technology: PAN FENG
College of Politics: SHI YIJUN
College of Sports: HE MINXUE
Faculty of Chemistry and Chemical Engineering: JIAO QIANGZHU
School of Mathematics: HAN YOUFA

PROFESSORS

BI, ZHIGUO, Politics
CAI, MIN, Education
CHANG, JINCHANG, History and Tourism
CHANG, RUOSONG, Education
CHEN, DACHAO, Education
CHEN, LIU, Literature

CHEN, TUYUN, Mathematics
CHENG, XIAOGUANG, Foreign Languages
DIAO, YANBIN, Literature
DONG, GUANGCAI, Foreign Languages
DONG, XUEDONG, Mathematics
DU, LIN, Literature
DU, RUIZHI, Mathematics
DU, XINGZHI, History and Tourism
FAN, YINGHENG, Chemistry and Chemical Engineering
FANG, HONGXIAO, Life Science
FENG, CHUNLIANG, Chemistry and Chemical Engineering
FU, WEILI, Education
GAO, BO, Management
HAN, YOUFA, Mathematics
HAN, YUCHANG, Education
HE, MINXUE, Sports
HOU, HESHENG, Life Science
HOU, LIN, Life Science
HU, ZHENKAI, Education
HUANG, BIN, Sports
JIANG, HUA, Life Science
JIN, CHENGJI, Sports
JIN, HONGYUAN, Education
JIN, RENSHU, Management
LI, CHUNLIN, Literature
LI, JINXIANG, Chemistry and Chemical Engineering
LI, LAIZHI, Management
LI, RENXI, Life Science
LI, TIANJIAN, Mathematics
LI, XUGUANG, Foreign Languages
LI, YAOZHENG, City and Environment Studies
LI, YINGJUN, Chemistry and Chemical Engineering
LIANG, GUIZHI, Literature
LIANG, SHUSHENG, Physics and Electronic Technology
LIN, HUA, Sports
LIN, XIANSHENG, City and Environment Studies
LIU, FANFU, Foreign Languages
LIU, FUGENG, Foreign Languages
LIU, PEIHAN, Politics
LIU, WANQI, Law
LIU, WEN, Education
LIU, XIUCHUN, Politics
LIU, ZHEQING, Mathematics
LUAN, WEIXIN, City and Environment Studies
LU, FENGYING, Law
LU, GUOFENG, Sports
MA, DONGYU, History and Tourism
MA, JIANSHENG, Education
MA, JUNSHAN, Literature
MA, YOUHUI, Life Science
MENG, DEXIU, Foreign Languages
MENG, ZHAOYUAN, Politics
NIU, SHUYUN, Chemistry and Chemical Engineering
PAN, FENG, Physics and Electronic Technology
QI, GUOYING, Physics and Electronic Technology
QU, GUANG, Literature
QU, JIANWU, Politics
QU, QINGBIAO, Politics
QU, WEI, Foreign Languages
SANG, DEJING, Life Science
SHI, LEI, Chemistry and Chemical Engineering
SHI, YIJUN, Politics
SHUN, RENAN, Chemistry and Chemical Engineering
SHUN, YUANGANG, Education
SONG, HUA, History and Tourism
TAO, YANG, Foreign Languages
TIAN, GUANGLIN, History and Tourism
WANG, BING, Foreign Languages
WANG, CHANGSHENG, Chemistry and Chemical Engineering
WANG, GUANLIN, Life Science
WANG, HONG, Sports
WANG, JIPENG, Literature
WANG, LI, Literature
WANG, QIHUA, Life Science

WANG, QINGJIAN, Mathematics
WANG, WEIPING, Literature
WANG, XIUWU, Life Science
WANG, XIUXIANG, Sports
WANG, YAOGUANG, Sports
WANG, YI, Literature
WANG, ZHIWEN, Physics and Electronic Technology
WEI, HUAZHONG, Education
WU, DESHENG, Literature
WU, ZHIHUA, Life Science
XIE, JINGFANG, History and Tourism
XIE, LIN, Mathematics
XIE, MINGJIE, Life Science
XU, YINGJUN, Foreign Languages
YAN, BANGYI, Literature
YAN, ZHILI, Sports
YANG, HONG, Life Science
YANG, LIZHU, Education
YANG, MING, Education
YANG, XIAO, Education
YANG, XIUXIANG, Politics
YANG, YINGJIE, History and Tourism
YANG, ZHONGZHI, Chemistry and Chemical Engineering
YI, HUAINING, City and Environment Studies
YOU, WANSHENG, Chemistry and Chemical Engineering
YU, BING, Literature
YU, DAHUA, History and Tourism
YU, PEILING, Law
YU, WENQIAN, Sports
YUAN, XUEHAI, Mathematics
YUE, ZHONGXING, Physics and Electronic Technology
ZHANG, AIJUN, Politics
ZHANG, GUICHUN, Education
ZHANG, GUIREN, Politics
ZHANG, LIHUA, Education
ZHANG, NINGSHENG, Education
ZHANG, QI, Education
ZHANG, SHUMIN, Chemistry and Chemical Engineering
ZHANG, WEIDONG, Life Science
ZHANG, XIAONING, Foreign Languages
ZHANG, YAOGUANG, City and Environment Studies
ZHAO, YI, History and Tourism
ZHAO, YUBAO, History and Tourism
ZHAO, ZHENYING, History and Tourism
ZHAO, ZHONGWEN, Management
ZHONG, GUIQING, City and Environment Studies
ZHOU, DANHONG, Chemistry and Chemical Engineering
ZHOU, WEI, Life Science
ZHOU, XIAOYAN, Education
ZHOU, ZHIQIANG, Politics
ZHU, NINGBO, Education
ZHU, ZHIJUN, Politics

LIAONING TECHNICAL UNIVERSITY

Fu Xin 3350461, Liaoning
Internet: www.lntu.edu.cn
Founded 1958
State control
Academic year: September to July

Constituent colleges and departments in the following areas: resources and environmental engineering; business management; mechanical engineering; architecture and civil engineering; software; technology and economics; geomatics engineering; mechanics and engineering sciences; electrical engineering; electrical and information engineering; materials science and engineering; foreign languages; journalism and communication; politics and law

President: SHI JINFENG
Vice-Presidents: MA ZHUANG, PAN YISHAN, SHAO LIANGBIN, WANG JIREN, ZHANG SHUSEN, ZHANG ZUOGANG
Head of Graduate Department: LIANG BING
Librarian: LIE JIE

Number of teachers: 1,349
Number of students: 25,000

Publications: *Journal* (natural sciences, 6 a year), *Journal* (social sciences, 4 a year)

PROFESSORS

FU, XINGWU, Electrical Engineering
GUO, FENGYI, Electrical Engineering
HUI, XIAOWEI, Electrical and Information Engineering
LI, WEIDONG, Electrical Engineering
LI, XIAOZHU, Electrical Engineering
LI, YIJIE, Electrical and Information Engineering
LI, ZHENGZHONG, Geomatics Engineering
LIU, JIANHUI, Electrical and Information Engineering
LU, SHIKUI, Electrical Engineering
MENG, QINGCHUN, Electrical Engineering
QIAO, YANGWEN, Geomatics Engineering
SONG, WEIDONG, Geomatics Engineering
SUN, JINGUANG, Electrical and Information Engineering
SUN, PENGYONG, Electrical and Information Engineering
WANG, JIAGUI, Geomatics Engineering
WANG, YUFENG, Electrical Engineering
XING, BAOJUN, Electrical Engineering
YE, JINGLOU, Electrical and Information Engineering
YE, JINGLOU, Electrical Engineering
ZHAO, GUOCAI, Electrical Engineering
ZHAO, GUOQIANG, Electrical Engineering
ZHU, HUA, Electrical Engineering

NANCHANG UNIVERSITY

235 Nanjing East Rd, Nanchang 330047, Jiangxi
Telephone: (791) 8305499
Fax: (791) 8305835
Internet: www.ncu.edu.cn

Founded 1940
State control
Academic year: September to July

President: ZHOU WENBIN
Vice-Presidents: CHENG YANGGUO, FU MINGFU, GAN XIAOQING, LI JIANMIN, LIU SANQIU, SHAO HONG, XIE MINGYONG
Head of Graduate Department: LI MING
Librarian: HE XIAOPING

Number of teachers: 1,253
Number of students: 45,000

Publications: *Journal* (engineering and technology, 4 a year), *Journal* (humanities and social sciences, 6 a year), *Journal* (natural sciences, 4 a year)

DEANS

Centre for Public Administration Programmes: TAO XUERONG
College of Architectural Engineering: GUI GUOQING
College of Art and Design: XIONG MANLING
College of Information Engineering: CHEN KEN
College of Life Sciences: ZHU YOULIN
College of Mechanics and Engineering: LIU HESHENG
College of Natural Science: LIU NIANHUA
College of Science and Technology: HE JIESHAN
College of Software: LU XIAOYONG
School of Chemistry and Materials Science: ZHOU LANG
School of Economics and Management: YIN JIDONG
School of Environmental Science and Engineering: HU ZHAOJI
School of Foreign Languages: FANG KEPING
School of Humanities and Social Sciences: LI DONGNI

PROFESSORS

BAO, ZHONGXU, Mechanics and Engineering
CAO, DEHE, Humanities and Social Sciences
CAO, YUSHENG, Life Sciences
CHEN, DONGYOU, Humanities and Social Sciences
CHEN, XINLING, Humanities and Social Sciences
DENG, SHUILAN, Economics and Management
DENG, ZEYUAN, Life Sciences
FU, XIAOLONG, Art and Design
GAO, GUOZHEN, Mechanics and Engineering
GAO, YINYU, Life Sciences
GONG, LIANSHOU, Humanities and Social Sciences
GU, XINGBIN, Humanities and Social Sciences
GU, ZHENGSHI, Mechanics and Engineering
HE, CHENGHONG, Mechanics and Engineering
HE, YUN, Economics and Management
HU, PING, Humanities and Social Sciences
HU, QING, Humanities and Social Sciences
HU, ZHAOJI, Environmental Science and Engineering
HUANG, JIHUA, Mechanics and Engineering
HUANG, XIJIA, Economics and Management
HUANG, XINJIAN, Economics and Management
JIANG, BOQUAN, Environmental Science and Engineering
JIANG, SHUISHENG, Mechanics and Engineering
JIN, LAHUA, Environmental Science and Engineering
LI, CHENGGUI, Humanities and Social Sciences
LI, DONGNI, Humanities and Social Sciences
LI, SHENGMEI, Humanities and Social Sciences
LI, XIANTAN, Economics and Management
LIN, BO, Environmental Science and Engineering
LIU, HESHENG, Mechanics and Engineering
LIU, LUNXIN, Humanities and Social Sciences
LIU, NIANHUA, Natural Science
LIU, QIJING, Environmental Science and Engineering
LIU, RENSHENG, Humanities and Social Sciences
LIU, WEIDONG, Mechanics and Engineering
LIU, XIAOHONG, Environmental Science and Engineering
LIU, XIAOQIN, Art and Design
LIU, YING, Mechanics and Engineering
LU, BINGFU, Humanities and Social Sciences
LU, SHENGPING, Art and Design
LU, XIANFENG, Mechanics and Engineering
LU, XIAOYONG, Economics and Management
LU, XIXING, Humanities and Social Sciences
MA, WEI, Economics and Management
NI, YONGNIAN, Life Sciences
PENG, DIYUN, Economics and Management
QIU, ZUMIN, Environmental Science and Engineering
RUAN, RONGSHENG, Life Sciences
SUN, RISHENG, Environmental Science and Engineering
SUN, YONG, Art and Design
WAN, FANGZHEN, Humanities and Social Sciences
WAN, JINBAO, Environmental Science and Engineering
WANG, DEBAO, Humanities and Social Sciences
WANG, LIANGSHENG, Art and Design
WANG, XIANGYANG, Art and Design
WANG, ZHEPING, Humanities and Social Sciences
WEI, LI, Economics and Management
WEN, SHIHUA, Humanities and Social Sciences
WU, LUSHEN, Mechanics and Engineering
WU, XIAOWEI, Humanities and Social Sciences
XIAO, ANKUN, Mechanics and Engineering
XIE, MINGYONG, Life Sciences

XIE, YONG, Economics and Management
XIN, YONG, Mechanics and Engineering
XIONG, JIANXIN, Art and Design
XIONG, MANLING, Art and Design
XIONG, RUIWEN, Mechanics and Engineering
XIONG, XIANGHUI, Mechanics and Engineering
XU, YANG, Life Sciences
YANG, GUOTAI, Mechanics and Engineering
YANG, MINGLANG, Art and Design
YANG, XUECHUN, Mechanics and Engineering
YANG, XUEPIN, Humanities and Social Sciences
YAO, YAPING, Humanities and Social Sciences
YI, PING, Humanities and Social Sciences
YIN, JIDONG, Economics and Management
YIN, XINGFAN, Humanities and Social Sciences
YING, YULONG, Life Sciences
YU, RANGYAO, Humanities and Social Sciences
YUAN, LIHUA, Humanities and Social Sciences
ZHAN, ZHIYOU, Humanities and Social Sciences
ZHANG, HUA, Mechanics and Engineering
ZHANG, NING, Natural Science
ZHANG, RENMU, Humanities and Social Sciences
ZHANG, SHENGYANG, Humanities and Social Sciences
ZHANG, YUMING, Economics and Management
ZHANG, YUSHENG, Humanities and Social Sciences
ZHANG, ZHIYONG, Humanities and Social Sciences
ZHAO, LIQIU, Economics and Management
ZHENG, DIANMO, Environmental Science and Engineering
ZHENG, WEIXIAN, Life Sciences
ZHENG, XIANGQING, Economics and Management
ZHENG, XIAOJIANG, Humanities and Social Sciences
ZHOU, GUOFA, Environmental Science and Engineering
ZHOU, PINGYUAN, Humanities and Social Sciences
ZHOU, SHU, Art and Design
ZHOU, TIANRUI, Mechanics and Engineering
ZHOU, WENBIN, Environmental Science and Engineering
ZHOU, YAOWANG, Humanities and Social Sciences
ZHU, CHUANXI, Natural Science

NANJING UNIVERSITY

22 Hankou Rd, Nanjing 210093, Jiangsu
Telephone: (25) 3593186
Fax: (25) 3302728
Internet: www.nju.edu.cn

Founded 1902
State control
Language of instruction: Chinese
Academic year: September to June

President: JIANG SHUSHENG
Vice-Presidents: CHEN JUN, HON YINXING, MIN TIEJUN, SHIN JIANJUN, ZHANG DALIANG, ZHANG YIBIN
Librarian: QIAN CHENGDAN

Number of teachers: 2,400
Number of students: 27,000

Publications: *Approximation Theory and its Application, Contemporary Foreign Literature, Geology in Higher Education, Journal* (humanities and social sciences), *Journal* (natural sciences), *Journal of Computer Science, Journal of Inorganic Chemistry, Mathematics in Higher Education, Mathematics Review* (2 a year), *Progress in Physics, Research in Higher Education*

DEANS

Adult Education School: WANG JIANQIANG
Graduate School: CHEN CHONGQING
International Business School: ZHAO SHUMING
Medical School: HAN XIAODONG
School of Chemistry and Chemical Engineering: PAM YI
School of Foreign Studies: WANG SHOUREN
School of Geoscience: WANG YING
School of Humanities: DONG JIAN
School of Intensive Instruction in Sciences and Liberal Arts: LU DEXIN
School of Law: SHAO JIANDONG (acting)
School of Life Science: ZHANG HONGZU
School of Natural Sciences: GONG CHANGDE
School of Technology: SUN ZHONGXIU

NANJING UNIVERSITY OF AERONAUTICS AND ASTRONAUTICS

29 Yudao Rd, Nanjing 210016, Jiangsu
Telephone: (25) 4892424
Fax: (25) 4891512
E-mail: office@nuaa.edu.cn
Internet: www.njmu.edu.cn

Founded 1952
Academic year: September to July

President: HU HAIYAN
Vice-Presidents: CHEN XIACHU, LIANG DEWANG, NIE HONG, WANG GUINONG, WANG YONGLIANG, WU QINGXIAN, WU YIZHAO
Head of Graduate Department: HU HAIYAN
Librarian: HUANG YINHUI
Number of teachers: 1,300
Number of students: 22,725

Publication: *Journal* (6 a year)

DEANS

College of Advanced Vocational Education: JIANG WEI
College of Aerospace Engineering: XU XIWU
College of Art: LIU CANMING
College of Automation Engineering: LIU JIANYE
College of Civil Aviation: SHEN YUANKANG
College of Economics and Management: LIU SIFENG
College of Energy and Power Engineering: ZHANG JINGZHOU
College of Humanities and Social Sciences: WANG YAN
College of Information Science and Technology: BEN DE
College of Material Science and Engineering: TAO JIE
College of Mechanical Engineering: ZHU DI
College of Natural Sciences: YAN XIAOHONG

PROFESSORS

AI, JUN, Aerospace Engineering
AN, YUKUN, Natural Sciences
ANG, HAISONG, Aerospace Engineering
BAO, MING, Aerospace Engineering
BAO, MINGBAO, Humanities and Social Sciences
CAI, QIMING, Economics and Management
CAO, YUNFENG, Automation Engineering
CHANG, HAIPING, Energy and Power Engineering
CHE, GUANGJI, Art
CHEN, DA, Material Science and Engineering
CHEN, DAOLIAN, Automation Engineering
CHEN, GUOPING, Aerospace Engineering
CHEN, HONGQUAN, Aerospace Engineering
CHEN, HUAIHAI, Aerospace Engineering
CHEN, QI, Economics and Management
CHEN, QIAN, Aerospace Engineering
CHEN, RENLIANG, Aerospace Engineering
CHEN, SONGCAN, Information Science and Technology
CHEN, WEI, Energy and Power Engineering
CHEN, XIN, Automation Engineering

CHEN, ZHILIANG, Aerospace Engineering
DANG, YAOGUO, Economics and Management
DENG, ZHIQUAN, Automation Engineering
DING, QIULIN, Information Science and Technology
DING, YUNLIANG, Aerospace Engineering
DU, JIDA, Aerospace Engineering
FAN, YINHE, Energy and Power Engineering
FANG, XIANDE, Aerospace Engineering
GAN, MINLIANG, Civil Aviation
GAO, DEPING, Energy and Power Engineering
GAO, DEPING, Civil Aviation
GAO, ZHENG, Aerospace Engineering
GE, NING, Energy and Power Engineering
GONG, CHUNYING, Automation Engineering
GU, HONGBIN, Civil Aviation
GU, ZHIMING, Natural Sciences
GU, ZHONGQUAN, Aerospace Engineering
GUAN, DE, Aerospace Engineering
GUO, RONGWEI, Energy and Power Engineering
GUO, WANLIN, Aerospace Engineering
HAN, JINGLONG, Aerospace Engineering
HE, JIANGSHENG, Humanities and Social Sciences
HE, JIANPING, Material Science and Engineering
HU, HAIYAN, Aerospace Engineering
HU, JUN, Energy and Power Engineering
HU, MINGHUA, Civil Aviation
HU, MINGMIN, Aerospace Engineering
HUANG, HULIN, Energy and Power Engineering
HUANG, JINQUAN, Energy and Power Engineering
HUANG, MINGGE, Aerospace Engineering
HUANG, SHENGGUO, Civil Aviation
HUANG, SHULA, Art
HUANG, ZAIXING, Aerospace Engineering
HUANG, ZHENGXIN, Humanities and Social Sciences
JI, HONGHU, Energy and Power Engineering
JIANG, BIN, Automation Engineering
JIANG, KESHEN, Economics and Management
LI, BANGYI, Economics and Management
LI, DONG, Humanities and Social Sciences
LI, NAN, Economics and Management
LI, PENGTONG, Natural Sciences
LI, SHUNMING, Energy and Power Engineering
LI, ZIQUAN, Material Science and Engineering
LI, ZONGZHI, Humanities and Social Sciences
LIAN, QIANGUI, Humanities and Social Sciences
LIANG, DAKAI, Aerospace Engineering
LIANG, DEWANG, Energy and Power Engineering
LIU, CANMING, Art
LIU, RENPEI, Material Science and Engineering
LIU, SIFENG, Economics and Management
LIU, WEIHUA, Aerospace Engineering
LIU, XIANBIN, Aerospace Engineering
LIU, YIPING, Economics and Management
LIU, YU, Information Science and Technology
LU, LIZHI, Humanities and Social Sciences
MA, JIE, Humanities and Social Sciences
MENG, FANCHAO, Humanities and Social Sciences
MIAO, JIANJUN, Humanities and Social Sciences
MING, XIAO, Aerospace Engineering
NIE, HONG, Aerospace Engineering
NING, XUANXI, Economics and Management
PENG, CAN, Economics and Management
QIAN, XIAOLIN, Information Science and Technology
RUAN, XINBO, Automation Engineering
SHENG, SONGBO, Natural Sciences
SHI, YUNLONG, Humanities and Social Sciences
SONG, BAOYIN, Aerospace Engineering
SONG, YINGDONG, Energy and Power Engineering

SUN, JIANGUO, Energy and Power Engineering
SUN, JIUHOU, Aerospace Engineering
SUN, LIANGXIN, Aerospace Engineering
TAN, QINGMEI, Humanities and Social Sciences
TANG, DENGBIN, Aerospace Engineering
TAO, JIE, Material Science and Engineering
TONG, MINGBO, Aerospace Engineering
WANG, CAIYONG, Art
WANG, HUAMING, Aerospace Engineering
WANG, JIANDONG, Information Science and Technology
WANG, KAIFU, Aerospace Engineering
WANG, LUJIE, Humanities and Social Sciences
WANG, XINWEI, Aerospace Engineering
WANG, YAN, Humanities and Social Sciences
WANG, YONGLIANG, Aerospace Engineering
WEI, MINXIANG, Energy and Power Engineering
WEN, WEIDONG, Energy and Power Engineering
WU, DAIZHAO, Aerospace Engineering
WU, DINGMIN, Humanities and Social Sciences
WU, WENLONG, Aerospace Engineering
XIA, HONGSHAN, Civil Aviation
XIA, PINQI, Aerospace Engineering
XIAO, JUN, Material Science and Engineering
XIAO, PING, Humanities and Social Sciences
XIE, SHAOJUN, Automation Engineering
XING, YAN, Automation Engineering
XIONG, KE, Aerospace Engineering
XU, DAZHUAN, Information Science and Technology
XU, GUOHUA, Aerospace Engineering
XU, JINFA, Aerospace Engineering
XU, QIANG, Humanities and Social Sciences
XU, ZONGZE, Information Science and Technology
YANG, LILI, Art
YAO, WEIXING, Aerospace Engineering
YE, ZHIFENG, Energy and Power Engineering
YIN, HONGYOU, Natural Sciences
YU, XIONGQING, Aerospace Engineering
YU, XIWU, Aerospace Engineering
YUAN, SHENFANG, Aerospace Engineering
YUE, QIN, Natural Sciences
ZHANG, BUREN, Humanities and Social Sciences
ZHANG, CHENGLIN, Aerospace Engineering
ZHANG, GUODAI, Natural Sciences
ZHANG, JINGZHOU, Energy and Power Engineering
ZHANG, KUNYUAN, Energy and Power Engineering
ZHANG, LINGMI, Aerospace Engineering
ZHANG, LUMING, Natural Sciences
ZHANG, ZENGCHANG, Aerospace Engineering
ZHAO, CHUNSHENG, Aerospace Engineering
ZHAO, JIANXING, Energy and Power Engineering
ZHAO, MIN, Automation Engineering
ZHAO, NING, Aerospace Engineering
ZHAO, YOUQUN, Energy and Power Engineering
ZHENG, QI, Art
ZHENG, SHIJIE, Aerospace Engineering
ZHOU, CHUANRONG, Aerospace Engineering
ZHOU, DEQUN, Economics and Management
ZHOU, JIANJIANG, Information Science and Technology
ZHOU, LI, Aerospace Engineering
ZHU, JIANYING, Civil Aviation
ZHU, JINDONG, Humanities and Social Sciences
ZHU, JINFU, Civil Aviation
ZHU, WUJIA, Information Science and Technology
ZHU, ZHAODA, Information Science and Technology
ZUO, HONGFU, Civil Aviation

NANJING AGRICULTURAL UNIVERSITY

1 Weigang Rd, Nanjing 210095, Jiangsu
Telephone: (8625) 84395366
Internet: www.njau.edu.cn
Founded 1952
Ministry of Education control
Academic year: September to July
President: ZHENG XIAOBO
Vice-Presidents: CAO WEIXING, QU FUTIAN, SUN JIAN, WANG YAONAN, XU XIANG, ZHOU GUANGHONG
Librarian: GAO RONGHUA
Number of teachers: 2,400
Number of students: 24,000
Publications: *Agricultural Education of China* (6 a year), *Agricultural History of China* (4 a year), *Animal Husbandry and Veterinary Science* (6 a year), *Chinese Animal Products and Food* (6 a year), *Journal* (natural sciences, 4 a year), *Journal* (social sciences, 4 a year)

DEANS

College of Adult Education: XU XIANG
College of Agronomy: WAN JIANMIN
College of Animal Science and Technology: WANG TIAN
College of Economics and Management: ZHONG FUNING
College of Engineering: DING WEIMIN
College of Food Science and Technology: LU ZHAOXIN
College of Foreign Studies: XU XIANG
College of Horticulture: XILIN HOU
College of Humanities and Social Sciences: WANG SIMING
College of Information Science and Technology: GAO RONGHUA
College of International Education: YAN ZHIMING
College of Life Sciences: XU LANGLAI
College of Plant Protection: HAN ZHAOJUN
College of Public Management (incorporating College of Land Management): (vacant)
College of Resources and Environmental Sciences: SHEN QIRONG
College of Science: YANG CHUNLONG
College of Veterinary Medicine: ZOU SIXIANG
Graduate School: ZHENG XIAOBO

PROFESSORS

BAO, ENDONG, Veterinary Medicine
BIAN, XINMIN, Agronomy
CAI, QINGSHENG, Agronomy
CAI, QINGSHENG, Life Sciences
CAO, WEIXING, Agronomy
CHEN, FUYAN, Veterinary Medicine
CHEN, JIE, Veterinary Medicine
CHEN, JINFENG, Horticulture
CHEN, MAO, Humanities and Social Sciences
CHEN, QIUSHENG, Veterinary Medicine
CHEN, WANMING, Economics and Management
CHEN, WEIHUA, Veterinary Medicine
CHEN, WENLIN, Humanities and Social Sciences
CHEN, XIAOMIN, Resources and Environmental Sciences
CHENG, CHUNYOU, Foreign Languages
CHU, BAOJIN, Economics and Management
DAI, HAOGUO, Plant Protection
DENG, ZHAOCHUN, Foreign Languages
DING, WEIMIN, Engineering
DONG, MINGSHENG, Food Science and Technology
DONG, SHUANGLIN, Plant Protection
GAI, JUNYI, Agronomy
GAO, GUANG, Land Science
GE, JIQI, Land Management
GONG, YIQIN, Horticulture
GU, HUANZHANG, Economics and Management
GU, ZHENXIN, Food Science and Technology

GUAN, HENGLU, Humanities and Social Sciences
GUO, JIANHUA, Plant Protection
GUO, QIAOSHENG, Horticulture
GUO, SHIRONG, Horticulture
GUO, WEIMING, Horticulture
HAN, ZHAOJUN, Plant Protection
HONG, XIAOYUE, Plant Protection
HOU, GUANGXU, Foreign Languages
HOU, HANQING, Information Science and Technology
HOU, JIAFA, Veterinary Medicine
HOU, XILIN, Horticulture
HU, FENG, Resources and Environmental Sciences
HU, JINBO, Humanities and Social Sciences
HU, QIUHUI, Food Science and Technology
HU, YUANLIANG, Veterinary Medicine
HUANG, KEHE, Veterinary Medicine
HUANG, SHUIQING, Information Science and Technology
HUANG, WEIYI, Resources and Environmental Sciences
HUANG, YAO, Resources and Environmental Sciences
HUI, FUPING, Humanities and Social Sciences
JI, CHANGYING, Engineering
JIANG, HANHU, Food Science and Technology
JIANG, MINGYI, Life Sciences
JIANG, PING, Veterinary Medicine
LAN, YEQING, Land Science
LEI, ZHIHAI, Veterinary Medicine
LI, BAOPING, Plant Protection
LI, SHUNPENG, Resources and Environmental Sciences
LI, XIANGRUI, Veterinary Medicine
LI, YANGHAN, Agronomy
LI, YUEYUN, Economics and Management
LIANG, YONGCHAO, Resources and Environmental Sciences
LIN, MAOSONG, Plant Protection
LIU, BAOJIN, Economics and Management
LIU, DAJUN, Agronomy
LIU, DEHUI, Resources and Environmental Sciences
LIU, HONGLIN, Animal Science and Technology
LIU, LEI, Information Science and Technology
LIU, YOULIANG, Agronomy
LIU, YOUZHAO, Land Management
LIU, ZHAOPU, Resources and Environmental Sciences
LU, CHENGPING, Veterinary Medicine
LU, DAXIN, Engineering
LU, ZHAOXIN, Food Science and Technology
LU, ZUOMEI, Agronomy
LUO, WEIHONG, Agronomy
MA, KAI, Horticulture
MENG, LING, Plant Protection
MENG, LINGJIE, Economics and Management
NIU, YOUQI, Information Science and Technology
OU, MINGHAO, Land Management
PAN, GENXIN, Resources and Environmental Sciences
PAN, JIANJUN, Resources and Environmental Sciences
PENG, JISHENG, Humanities and Social Sciences
PENG, ZENGQI, Food Science and Technology
QIANG, SHENG, Agronomy
QIANG, SHENG, Life Sciences
QIN, LIJUN, Foreign Languages
QU, FUTIAN, Land Management
SHEN, JINLIANG, Plant Protection
SHEN, QIRONG, Resources and Environmental Sciences
SHEN, YIXIN, Animal Science and Technology
SHEN, YONGLIN, Veterinary Medicine
SHEN, ZHENGUO, Agronomy
SHEN, ZHENGUO, Life Sciences
SHENG, BANGYUE, Humanities and Social Sciences
SUN, HANGSHENG, Economics and Management

SUN, JIN, Resources and Environmental Sciences
TANG, YIZU, Agronomy
TU, KANG, Food Science and Technology
WANG, GENLIN, Animal Science and Technology
WANG, GUOJIE, Veterinary Medicine
WANG, HUAIMING, Economics and Management
WANG, JIANMIN, Agronomy
WANG, JINSHENG, Plant Protection
WANG, KAI, Economics and Management
WANG, KERONG, Plant Protection
WANG, LINYUN, Animal Science and Technology
WANG, RONG, Economics and Management
WANG, SIMING, Humanities and Social Sciences
WANG, TIAN, Animal Science and Technology
WANG, WANMAO, Land Management
WANG, XIAOHUA, Engineering
WANG, XIAOLONG, Veterinary Medicine
WANG, YINQUAN, Foreign Languages
WANG, YUQUAN, Land Science
WHONG, ZHIWEI, Resources and Environmental Sciences
WU, QINSHENG, Horticulture
WU, YIDONG, Plant Protection
WU, YULIN, Economics and Management
XIE, ZHUANG, Animal Science and Technology
XU, JIANHUA, Plant Protection
XU, LIANGLAI, Life Sciences
XU, LIREN, Veterinary Medicine
XU, XIANG, Economics and Management
XU, YIWEN, Humanities and Social Sciences
YAN, HUOQI, Humanities and Social Sciences
YAN, PEISHI, Animal Science and Technology
YANG, HONG, Land Science
YANG, LIANFANG, Plant Protection
YANG, LIGUO, Animal Science and Technology
YANG, MINGMIN, Land Science
YANG, QIANG, Veterinary Medicine
YANG, QING, Life Sciences
YANG, SHIHU, Agronomy
YANG, ZHIMIN, Life Sciences
YE, YIGUANG, Economics and Management
YIN, WENQING, Engineering
YING, RUIYAO, Economics and Management
YU, DEYUE, Agronomy
ZHAI, BAOPING, Plant Protection
ZHANG, BING, Economics and Management
ZHANG, CHUNLAN, Resources and Environmental Sciences
ZHANG, FANG, Humanities and Social Sciences
ZHANG, GUOTAI, Agronomy
ZHANG, HAIBIN, Veterinary Medicine
ZHANG, HONGSHENG, Agronomy
ZHANG, JINGSHUN, Economics and Management
ZHANG, RONGXIAN, Agronomy
ZHANG, SHAOLING, Horticulture
ZHANG, SHUXIA, Veterinary Medicine
ZHANG, TIANZHEN, Agronomy
ZHANG, WEIQIANG, Engineering
ZHANG, ZHEN, Horticulture
ZHAO, RUQIAN, Veterinary Medicine
ZHENG, XIAOBO, Plant Protection
ZHENG, YONGHUA, Food Science and Technology
ZHONG, FUNING, Economics and Management
ZHOU, GUANGHONG, Food Science and Technology
ZHOU, LIXIANG, Resources and Environmental Sciences
ZHOU, MINGGUO, Plant Protection
ZHOU, SHUDONG, Economics and Management
ZHOU, YINGHENG, Economics and Management
ZHU, JUN, Life Sciences
ZHU, SIHONG, Engineering
ZHU, WEIYUN, Animal Science and Technology
ZHU, YUELIN, Horticulture

ZONG, LIANGGANG, Resources and Environmental Sciences
ZOU, SIXIANG, Veterinary Medicine

NANJING UNIVERSITY OF ECONOMICS

128 Tielubeijie, Nanjing 210003
Telephone: (25) 3418207
Fax: (25) 3418207
Internet: www.njue.edu.cn
Founded 1956, present status 1981
State control
Academic year: September to July
President: Dr XU CONGCAI
Vice-Presidents: GAO YADONG, LI SHIHUA, WANG JIAXIN, WANG SUITING, ZHANG ZHENGGANG
Librarian: DING DAKE
Library: over 500,000 vols
Number of teachers: 565
Number of students: 5,600 (incl. correspondence courses 3,000)
Publication: *Journal of Nanjing University of Economics.*

NANJING FORESTRY UNIVERSITY

9 Xinzhuang, Longpan Rd, Nanjing 210037, Jiangsu
Telephone: (25) 85427131
Fax: (25) 85412389
E-mail: interpro@njfu.edu.cn
Internet: www.njfu.edu.cn
Founded 1952
President: Prof. YU SHIYUAN
Vice-Presidents: Prof. CAI FULIANG, Prof. ZHANG SHUQAN, Prof. SHI JISEN
Librarian: LIU XIUHUA
Library of 600,000 vols
Number of teachers: 731
Number of students: 4,000 (incl. 274 postgraduates)
Publications: *Bamboo Research, China Forestry Science and Technology, Forestry Energy Conservation, Interior Design and Construction, Journal of Nanjing Forestry University*

HEADS OF COLLEGES AND DEPARTMENTS
Adult Education: Prof. GUAN SUQI
Basic Courses Division: Assoc. Prof. WEI SHUGUANG
Chemical Engineering: Prof. AN XINNAN
Civil Engineering: Prof. ZHAO CHEN
Forest Economics and Management: Prof. CHEN GUOLIANG
Forest Resources and Environment: Prof. CAO FULIANG
Graduate Studies: Prof. YE JIANREN
Mechanical and Electronic Engineering: Prof. ZHOU YONGZHAO
Social Sciences Division: Assoc. Prof. WANG GUOPIN
Wood Science and Technology: Prof. TAN SHOUXIA

PROFESSORS
CHEN GUOLIANG, Forest Economics
CHEN ZHI, Chemical Processing of Forest Products
HUA YUKUN, Wood Processing
LI ZHONGZHENG, Chemical Processing of Forest Products
SHEN GUANFU, Forest Mechanics
SU JINYUN, Forest Engineering
XIONG WENYUE, Forest Ecology
ZHU ZHENGDE, Forest Botany

NANJING MEDICAL UNIVERSITY

140 Hanzhong Rd, Nanjing 210029, Jiangsu
Telephone: (25) 6649141
Fax: (25) 6612696
E-mail: xiaoban@njmu.edu.cn
Internet: www.njmu.edu.cn
Founded 1934
Academic year: September to July
President: CHEN QI
Vice-Presidents: HU GANG, HUANG JUN, QU ZHAOMIN, XU YAOCHU, WANG XINRU
Librarian: ZHANG ZHENGHUI
Library of 1,040,330 vols
Number of teachers: 1,148
Number of students: 7,283
Publications: *Jiangsu Medical Journal* (12 a year), *Journal* (6 a year), *Journal of Clinical Neurology* (6 a year)

DEANS
First Clinical Medical College: HUANG JUN
Second Clinical Medical College: LIU HUI
Third Clinical Medical College: (vacant)
School of Basic Medical Science: ZHU CHANGLIANG
School of Health Policy and Management: MENG GUOXIANG
School of Medicine: ZHU DONGYA
School of Nursing: CUI YAN
School of Public Health: ZHOU JIANWEI

PROFESSORS
BI, ZHIGANG, Clinical Medicine I
BIAN, JIAYI, Medicine
CAI, YI, Clinical Medicine II
CAO, KEJIANG, Clinical Medicine I
CHANG, YI, Clinical Medicine II
CHEN, GUANGMING, Clinical Medicine I
CHEN, GUOYU, Clinical Medicine I
CHEN, RONGHUA, Clinical Medicine II
CHEN, XIWEI, Basic Medical Science
CHEN, YIJIANG, Clinical Medicine I
CHEN, YULIAN, Public Health
CHENG, YUNLIN, Clinical Medicine I
DE, WEI, Basic Medical Science
DING, JIONG, Basic Medical Science
DING, XINSHENG, Clinical Medicine I
FAN, QINHE, Clinical Medicine I
FAN, WEIMING, Clinical Medicine I
FU, CHENGZHANG, Clinical Medicine I
FU, ZHENG, Clinical Medicine I
HU, GUANG, Basic Medical Science
HU, QIN, Medicine
HU, WEIXING, Clinical Medicine I
HUANG, JUN, Clinical Medicine I
HUANG, ZHUHU, Clinical Medicine I
LI, GUOPING, Clinical Medicine I
LI, JIANAN, Clinical Medicine I
LI, JUN, Clinical Medicine II
LI, SHENGNAN, Basic Medical Science
LI, YUEHUA, Basic Medical Science
LI, ZUOHAN, Clinical Medicine II
LIU, CHAO, Clinical Medicine I
LIU, JIAYIN, Clinical Medicine I
LIU, QIZHAN, Public Health
LIU, XUNLIANG, Clinical Medicine I
LU, FENGXIANG, Clinical Medicine I
LUO, DAN, Clinical Medicine I
MA, WENZHU, Clinical Medicine I
MENG, GUOXIANG, Health Policy and Management
MIAO, YI, Clinical Medicine I
NI, CHUNHUI, Public Health
QI, XIAOHONG, Basic Medical Science
SHUN, NANXIONG, Clinical Medicine I
SHUN, YUJIE, Basic Medical Science
TANG, LINGFANG, Public Health
WANG, DEFANG, Clinical Medicine I
WANG, HEMIN, Basic Medical Science
WANG, HONG, Clinical Medicine I
WANG, SHOULIN, Public Health
WANG, XIAOYUN, Clinical Medicine I
WANG, XINRU, Public Health
WANG, XUEHAO, Clinical Medicine I
WANG, YINGWEI, Basic Medical Science
WANG, YONG, Basic Medical Science
WANG, YUBIN, Clinical Medicine I
WEI, BAIQI, Medicine
WU, HAIWEI, Basic Medical Science
WU, HONGFEI, Clinical Medicine I
WU, JINCHANG, Clinical Medicine I
WU, WENXI, Clinical Medicine I
WU, ZHENGYAN, Clinical Medicine I
XIAO, HANG, Public Health
XU, QUNWEI, Medicine
XU, XINRONG, Clinical Medicine I
YIN, KAISHENG, Clinical Medicine I
ZHANG, FUMIN, Clinical Medicine I
ZHANG, HAIDI, Clinical Medicine I
ZHANG, JINAN, Clinical Medicine I
ZHANG, QI, Public Health
ZHANG, YIDONG, Clinical Medicine II
ZHANG, ZHENGDONG, Public Health
ZHANG, ZHONGNAN, Clinical Medicine I
ZHAO, ZHIQUAN, Clinical Medicine I
ZHOU, JIANWEI, Public Health
ZHOU, XUEMIN, Medicine
ZHOU, ZUOMING, Basic Medical Science
ZHU, CHANGLIANG, Basic Medical Science
ZHU, DONGYA, Medicine
ZHU, GUOQING, Basic Medical Science
ZHU, WENYUAN, Clinical Medicine I

NANJING INSTITUTE OF METEOROLOGY

114 Pancheng New Street, Nanjing 210044, Jiangsu
Telephone: 8731102
Fax: 7792648
E-mail: nimemail@nim02.njim.edu.cn
Internet: www.njim.edu.cn
Founded 1960
State control
Languages of instruction: Chinese, English
Academic year: September to July
President: SUN ZHAOBO
Vice-President: LU WEISONG
Dean: ZHAO XUEYU
Chief Administrative Officer: XU KAI
Librarian: PANG XINGUO
Library of 500,000 vols
Number of teachers: 450
Number of students: 8,000
Publications: *Journal* (4 a year), *Meteorological Education and Science and Technology* (4 a year).

NANJING NORMAL UNIVERSITY

122 Ninghai Rd, Nanjing 210097, Jiangsu
Telephone: (25) 3720999
Fax: (25) 3706565
Internet: www.njnu.edu.cn
Founded 1902
Provincial govt control
Academic year: September to August
President: Prof. GONG PIXIANG
Vice-Presidents: Prof. CHEN GUOJUN, Prof. CHEN LINGFU, Prof. HUANG TAO, Prof. LU BINGSHOU, Prof. TU GUOHUA, Prof. WANG XIAOPENG, Prof. ZHU XIAOMAN
Dean of Postgraduate Studies: PAN BAIQI
Librarian: WU JIN
Library of 1,650,000 vols
Number of teachers: 1,100
Number of students: 7,000 (incl. 430 postgraduates)
Publications: *Fine Arts Education in China, Periodicals of Nanjing Normal University* (social sciences, natural sciences), *References for Educational Research*, text books.

NANJING UNIVERSITY OF POSTS AND TELECOMMUNICATIONS

66 Xin Mofan Ma Lu, Nanjing 210003, Jiangsu
Telephone: (25) 3492038
Fax: (25) 3492349
E-mail: nupt@njupt.edu.cn

Internet: www.njupt.edu.cn
Founded 1942
Academic year: September to July
President: XIE LING
Vice-Presidents: TANG JINTU, YIE ZHANGZHAO, ZHANG SHUNYI, ZHANG XIAOQIANG
Librarian: YANG ZHUYING
Library: over 600,000 vols
Number of teachers: 768
Number of students: 7,970 (4,300 undergraduates, 270 postgraduates, 3,400 correspondence)
Publications: *Journal of Social Science, NUPT Periodical*

PROFESSORS

BI HOUJIE, Image Communications
CAO WEI, Microwave Communications
CHEN TINGBIAO, Information Engineering
CHEN XI SHENG, Telecommunications Engineering
FENG GUANGZENG, Satellite Communications
HU JIANZHANG, Information Engineering
JU TI, Computer Engineering Science
KAN JIAHAI, Mathematics
LI BIAOQING, Telecommunications Engineering
LUO CHANGLONG, Computer Science
MEI ZHUOCHUN, Communication and Electronic Systems
MI ZHENGKUN, Communications Engineering
QI YUSHENG, Mobile Communication
QIN TINGKAI, Electrical Engineering
SHEN JINLONG, Computer Communication
SHEN YUANLONG, Electrical Engineering
SUN JINLUN, Communications Engineering
TANG JIAYI, Computer Science
WANG SHAOLI, Computer Communication
WANG SHUOPING, Electrical Engineering
WU XINYU, Electrical Engineering
WU ZHIZHONG, Electrical Engineering
XU CHENGQI, Telecommunications Engineering
YANG ZHUYING, Electrical Engineering
YIE ZHANGZHAO, Mathematics
YU ZHAOMIN, Information Engineering
ZHANG LIJUN, Telecommunications Engineering
ZHANG SHUNYI, Computer Communications
ZHANG XIAOQIANG, Communication Systems
ZHANG ZHIYONG, Electrical Engineering
ZHANG ZONGCHENG, Information Engineering
ZHENG BAOYU, Telecommunications Engineering
ZHU XIUCHANG, Information Engineering

NANJING UNIVERSITY OF SCIENCE AND TECHNOLOGY

200 Xiao Lingwei, Nanjing, 210094 Jiangsu
Telephone: (25) 84315567
Internet: www.njust.edu.cn
Founded 1953
Min. of Industry and Information Technology
Academic year: September to July
Chair., Univ. Council: GENFU CHEN
President: XIAOFENG WANG
Vice-Presidents: DAQING MA, GANG LIU, SHANZHI YANG, WENYU SONG, XIN WANG, YIMIN XUAN, YINKANG XIANG
Head of Graduate Department: XIN WANG
Librarian: MIN ZHAO
Number of teachers: 1,466
Number of students: 20,283
Publications: *Higher Education Digest* (12 a year), *Journal* (natural sciences, 6 a year), *Journal* (social sciences, 6 a year), *Journal of Ballistics* (4 a year), *Journal of Explosive Materials* (6 a year), *Journal of Optoelectronic Information* (6 a year)

DEANS

Department of Foreign Languages: QUAN ZHANG
Department of Materials Science and Engineering: JINCHUN MEI
School of Adult Education: YUNLEI ZHANG
School of Automation: YUMING BO
School of Chemical Engineering: LIANJUN WANG
School of Computer Science: ZHENMIN TANG
School of Economics and Management: GUANGPING HUI
School of Electronic Engineering and Optoelectronic Technology: QIAN CHEN
School of Humanities and Social Sciences: JIANPING QIAN
School of International Education: WANG QINYOU
School of Joint Education: YUZHEN KE
School of Mechanical Engineering: YONG HE
School of Natural Science: XIAOPING YANG
School of Power Engineering: HAO WANG
Vocational and Technical College: ZHANG YUEXIN

PROFESSORS

AN, LICHAO, Chemical Engineering
BO, LIANFA, Electronic Engineering and Optoelectronic Technology
BO, YUMING, Automation Engineering
CAI, CHUN, Chemical Engineering
CAO, CONGYONG, Mechanical Engineering
CHANG, BENKANG, Electronic Engineering and Optoelectronic Technology
CHEN, GUANG, Materials Science and Engineering
CHEN, GUOLIANG, Materials Science and Engineering
CHEN, HEJUAN, Mechanical Engineering
CHEN, LEI, Electronic Engineering and Optoelectronic Technology
CHEN, QIAN, Electronic Engineering and Optoelectronic Technology
CHEN, QINGWEI, Automation Engineering
CHEN, RUSHAN, Electronic Engineering and Optoelectronic Technology
CHEN, YANRU, Electronic Engineering and Optoelectronic Technology
CHENG, YI, Chemical Engineering
CUI, CHONG, Materials Science and Engineering
DAI, YUEWEI, Automation Engineering
DENG, KAIMING, Natural Science
DU, YULAN, Economics and Management
DUAN, QIJUN, Mechanical Engineering
FAN, BAOCHUN, Power Engineering
FAN, XINMIN, Materials Science and Engineering
FANG, DAGANG, Electronic Engineering and Optoelectronic Technology
FANG, ZHIJIE, Chemical Engineering
FANG, ZILIANG, Mechanical Engineering
FENG, JUNWEN, Economics and Management
GAN, LIREN, Economics and Management
GEN, JIHUI, Power Engineering
GONG, GUANGRONG, Mechanical Engineering
GU, KEQIU, Mechanical Engineering
GU, XIAOHUI, Mechanical Engineering
GUO, ZHI, Automation Engineering
HAN, YUQI, Economics and Management
HAN, ZHIJUN, Economics and Management
HAN, ZIPENG, Power Engineering
HAO, JIANCHU, Chemical Engineering
HE, ANZHI, Natural Science
HE, QIHUAN, Chemical Engineering
HE, YONG, Mechanical Engineering
HE, ZHAOJI, Humanities and Social Sciences
HOU, XIAOXIA, Automation Engineering
HOU, YUANLONG, Mechanical Engineering
HU, KAIJIE, Humanities and Social Sciences
HU, WEILI, Automation Engineering
HUANG, JIN-AN, Automation Engineering
HUANG, YINSHENG, Chemical Engineering
HUANG, ZHENGYA, Chemical Engineering
HUI, JUNMING, Chemical Engineering

HUI, XIAOHUA, Electronic Engineering and Optoelectronic Technology
JIANG, JIANFANG, Automation Engineering
JIANG, LIPING, Electronic Engineering and Optoelectronic Technology
JIANG, RENYUAN, Mechanical Engineering
JIN, ZHONG, Computer Science
KANG, XIAODONG, Economics and Management
LAN, SHAOHUA, Computer Science
LI, BAOMING, Power Engineering
LI, CHENGJUN, Chemical Engineering
LI, DONGBO, Mechanical Engineering
LI, FENGSHENG, Chemical Engineering
LI, HONGCHANG, Chemical Engineering
LI, HUIZHONG, Materials Science and Engineering
LI, XIANGYIN, Natural Science
LI, XIAONING, Mechanical Engineering
LI, XINGGUO, Electronic Engineering and Optoelectronic Technology
LI, YAJUN, Mechanical Engineering
LI, YING, Mechanical Engineering
LI, ZHENHUA, Natural Science
LIANG, RENJIE, Mechanical Engineering
LIU, DABIN, Chemical Engineering
LIU, FENGYU, Computer Science
LIU, HONGYING, Chemical Engineering
LIU, JIACONG, Chemical Engineering
LIU, KUI, Humanities and Social Sciences
LIU, ZHONG, Electronic Engineering and Optoelectronic Technology
LIU, ZULIANG, Chemical Engineering
LOU, LANGHONG, Materials Science and Engineering
LU, CHUNXU, Chemical Engineering
LU, JIAN, Natural Science
LU, JINHUI, Electronic Engineering and Optoelectronic Technology
LU, LUDE, Chemical Engineering
LU, MING, Chemical Engineering
LUO, GUOWEI, Electronic Engineering and Optoelectronic Technology
MA, DAWEI, Mechanical Engineering
MA, YIZHONG, Economics and Management
MENG, YINGJUN, Electronic Engineering and Optoelectronic Technology
MOU, SHANXIANG, Electronic Engineering and Optoelectronic Technology
NI, OUQI, Chemical Engineering
NI, XIAOWU, Natural Science
PAN, GONGPEI, Chemical Engineering
PAN, RENMING, Chemical Engineering
PAN, ZHENGWEI, Mechanical Engineering
PENG, JINHUA, Chemical Engineering
PENG, XINHUA, Chemical Engineering
PU, XIONGZHU, Mechanical Engineering
QIAN, JIANPING, Automation Engineering
QIAN, LINFANG, Mechanical Engineering
SHEN, PEIHUI, Mechanical Engineering
SHEN, RUIQI, Chemical Engineering
SHENG, ANDONG, Automation Engineering
SHI, LIANJIE, Materials Science and Engineering
SHI, TIANHUA, Economics and Management
SHI, XIANGQUAN, Electronic Engineering and Optoelectronic Technology
SONG, YAOLIANG, Electronic Engineering and Optoelectronic Technology
SUN, GUIXIANG, Humanities and Social Sciences
SUN, HUAIJIANG, Computer Science
SUN, JIANPING, Economics and Management
SUN, JINSHENG, Automation Engineering
SUN, JINTAO, Electronic Engineering and Optoelectronic Technology
SUN, YAMIN, Computer Science
SUN, YU, Mechanical Engineering
TAN, LEBIN, Mechanical Engineering
TANG, ZHENMIN, Computer Science
TAO, CHUNKAN, Electronic Engineering and Optoelectronic Technology
WANG, DAYONG, Humanities and Social Sciences
WANG, FENGYUN, Chemical Engineering
WANG, HUAKUN, Mechanical Engineering

WANG, JIANXIN, Electronic Engineering and Optoelectronic Technology
WANG, JIANYU, Automation Engineering
WANG, JINGTAO, Materials Science and Engineering
WANG, JUNDE, Chemical Engineering
WANG, KEHONG, Materials Science and Engineering
WANG, LIANGGUO, Natural Science
WANG, LIANGMING, Power Engineering
WANG, LIANGMO, Mechanical Engineering
WANG, LIANJUN, Chemical Engineering
WANG, NAIYAN, Chemical Engineering
WANG, SHUMEI, Computer Science
WANG, XIAOMING, Mechanical Engineering
WANG, XIN, Chemical Engineering
WANG, YUSHI, Mechanical Engineering
WANG, ZESHAN, Chemical Engineering
WANG, ZHIQUAN, Automation Engineering
WEI, YUNYANG, Chemical Engineering
WEI, ZHIHUI, Natural Science
WEN, CHUNSHENG, Power Engineering
WU, HUIZHONG, Computer Science
WU, JIANG, Materials Science and Engineering
WU, JUNJI, Power Engineering
WU, XIAOBEI, Automation Engineering
XIA, DESHEN, Computer Science
XIAO, HEMING, Chemical Engineering
XIONG, DANGSHENG, Materials Science and Engineering
XU, FUMING, Chemical Engineering
XU, HOUQIAN, Power Engineering
XU, JIANCHENG, Mechanical Engineering
XU, JIANZHONG, Electronic Engineering and Optoelectronic Technology
XU, MING, Chemical Engineering
XU, MINGYOU, Power Engineering
XU, SHENGYUAN, Automation Engineering
XU, WANHE, Mechanical Engineering
XU, ZHENXIANG, Chemical Engineering
XU, ZHILIANG, Automation Engineering
XUAN, YIMIN, Power Engineering
XUE, HENGXIN, Economics and Management
XUE, XIAOZHONG, Power Engineering
YAN, LIANHE, Chemical Engineering
YANG, CHENGWU, Power Engineering
YANG, DETONG, Materials Science and Engineering
YANG, SHUIYANG, Humanities and Social Sciences
YANG, SHULIN, Chemical Engineering
YANG, XIAOPING, Natural Science
YANG, XUJIE, Chemical Engineering
YANG, ZHENYU, Computer Science
YAO, JUN, Humanities and Social Sciences
YE, YOUPEI, Computer Science
YIN, XIAOCHUN, Natural Science
YIN, ZHENGZHOU, Mechanical Engineering
YU, ANPING, Economics and Management
YU, YONGGANG, Power Engineering
YUAN, JUNTANG, Mechanical Engineering
YUAN, YAXIONG, Power Engineering
ZHANG, BAOMIN, Electronic Engineering and Optoelectronic Technology
ZHANG, CHI, Chemical Engineering
ZHANG, FENG, Power Engineering
ZHANG, FUXIANG, Mechanical Engineering
ZHANG, GONGXUAN, Computer Science
ZHANG, HONG, Computer Science
ZHANG, MINGYAN, Economics and Management
ZHANG, SHAOFAN, Power Engineering
ZHANG, TIE, Mechanical Engineering
ZHANG, XI, Mechanical Engineering
ZHANG, XIAOBING, Power Engineering
ZHANG, YOULIANG, Mechanical Engineering
ZHANG, YUE, Mechanical Engineering
ZHANG, YUEJUN, Chemical Engineering
ZHANG, ZHONGLIN, Economics and Management
ZHANG, ZHONGXIONG, Electronic Engineering and Optoelectronic Technology
ZHAO, BAOCHANG, Chemical Engineering
ZHAO, CHUNXIA, Computer Science

ZHAO, HUICHANG, Electronic Engineering and Optoelectronic Technology
ZHENG, JIANGUO, Mechanical Engineering
ZHONG, QIN, Chemical Engineering
ZHOU, BOSEN, Materials Science and Engineering
ZHOU, KEDONG, Mechanical Engineering
ZHOU, SHUGE, Electronic Engineering and Optoelectronic Technology
ZHOU, WEILIANG, Chemical Engineering
ZHOU, XIANZHONG, Automation Engineering
ZHU, JINAN, Mechanical Engineering
ZHU, RIHONG, Electronic Engineering and Optoelectronic Technology
ZHU, XIANCHEN, Economics and Management
ZHU, XIAOHUA, Electronic Engineering and Optoelectronic Technology
ZOU, YUN, Automation Engineering

NANJING UNIVERSITY OF TECHNOLOGY

Gu Lou Section, 5 New Model Rd, Nanjing 210009, Jiangsu
Telephone: (25) 83587018
Fax: (25) 83587636
E-mail: xiaoban@njut.edu.cn
Internet: www.njuct.edu.cn
Founded 1902
Department of Education of Jiangsu Province control
Academic year: September to July
President: OU YANG PINGKAI
Vice-Presidents: SHU FANG, SUN CHUANSONG, SUN WEIMIN SUN, WANG JINMING, XU NANPING, ZAI JINMIN, ZHU YAO
Head of Graduate Department: HAN PINGFANG
Librarian: ZHANG ZHENGHUI
Number of teachers: 1,000
Number of students: 23,000
Publications: *Journal* (natural sciences, 6 a year), *Journal* (social sciences, 4 a year)

DEANS

College of Architecture and Urban Planning: WU JILIANG
College of Artistic Design: LIU WEIQING
College of Automation: LIN JINGUO
College of Chemistry and Chemical Engineering: XU NANPING
College of Civil Engineering: CHEN GUOXING
College of Economics and Management: HE HONGJIN
College of Foreign Languages and International Exchange: YIN FULIN
College of Information Science and Engineering: YANG XIAOJIAN
College of Law and Politics: LI BIN
College of Life Sciences and Pharmaceutical Engineering: ZHOU HUA
College of Management Science and Engineering: NIE QIBO
College of Materials Science and Engineering: XU ZHONGZI
College of Mechanical and Power Engineering: TU SHANDONG
College of Sciences: YU BIN
College of Urban Construction, Safety and Environmental Engineering: JIANG JUNCHENG

PROFESSORS

CAI, RUIYING, Information Science and Engineering
CAI, ZHIFU, Mechanical and Power Engineering
CEI, CHENGJIAN, Information Science and Engineering
CHEN, BIAO, Mechanical and Power Engineering
CHEN, CHANGLIN, Chemistry and Chemical Engineering
CHEN, GUOXING, Civil Engineering

CHEN, HONGLING, Chemistry and Chemical Engineering
CHEN, SU, Chemistry and Chemical Engineering
CHEN, XIANYI, Materials Science and Engineering
CUI, KEQING, Mechanical and Power Engineering
CUI, QUN, Chemistry and Chemical Engineering
DAI, SHUHE, Mechanical and Power Engineering
DENG, MIN, Materials Science and Engineering
FAN, YIQUAN, Chemistry and Chemical Engineering
GONG, JIANMING, Mechanical and Power Engineering
GONG, YANFENG, Urban Construction, Safety and Environmental Engineering
GU, BOQIN, Mechanical and Power Engineering
GU, HEPING, Chemistry and Chemical Engineering
GUAN, GUOFENG, Chemistry and Chemical Engineering
GUO, LUCUN, Materials Science and Engineering
HE, HONGJIN, Economics and Management
HE, JIAPENG, Urban Construction, Safety and Environmental Engineering
HUANG, PEI, Chemistry and Chemical Engineering
HUANG, YOUDIAO, Mechanical and Power Engineering
HUANG, ZHENREN, Mechanical and Power Engineering
JIAN, MIAOFU, Materials Science and Engineering
JIANG, JUNCHENG, Urban Construction, Safety and Environmental Engineering
JIANG, JUNCHENG, Mechanical and Power Engineering
JIN, SUMIN, Mechanical and Power Engineering
JIN, WANQIN, Chemistry and Chemical Engineering
LI, BIN, Law and Politics
LI, DONGXU, Materials Science and Engineering
LI, LIQUAN, Materials Science and Engineering
LI, XIANGYING, Foreign Languages and International Exchange
LI, YONGSHENG, Mechanical and Power Engineering
LIN, JINGUO, Automation
LIN, XIAO, Chemistry and Chemical Engineering
LING, XIANG, Mechanical and Power Engineering
LIU, WEIQING, Artistic Design
LIU, XIAOQIN, Chemistry and Chemical Engineering
LIU, ZHONGWEN, Chemistry and Chemical Engineering
LU, JINGUI, Information Science and Engineering
LU, LEI, Materials Science and Engineering
LU, WEILIAN, Automation
LU, XIAOHUA, Chemistry and Chemical Engineering
LU, XIAOPING, Chemistry and Chemical Engineering
LU, YINONG, Materials Science and Engineering
MA, GONGXUN, Mechanical and Power Engineering
MA, ZHENGFEI, Chemistry and Chemical Engineering
PAN, YU, Management Science and Engineering
PAN, ZHIHUA, Materials Science and Engineering
QIAO, XU, Chemistry and Chemical Engineering

QIU, TAI, Materials Science and Engineering
SHEN, LINJIANG, Sciences
SHEN, SHIMING, Mechanical and Power Engineering
SHEN, XIAODONG, Materials Science and Engineering
SHI, JUN, Chemistry and Chemical Engineering
SHI, MEIREN, Chemistry and Chemical Engineering
SUN, WEIMIN, Civil Engineering
TANG, MINGSHU, Materials Science and Engineering
TU, SHANDONG, Mechanical and Power Engineering
WANG, HUI, Information Science and Engineering
WANG, JUN, Chemistry and Chemical Engineering
WANG, TINGWEI, Materials Science and Engineering
WANG, YANRU, Chemistry and Chemical Engineering
WANG, YONGPING, Architecture and Urban Planning
WANG, ZHUOJUN, Law and Politics
WEI, PING, Life Sciences and Pharmaceutical Engineering
WEI, WUJI, Materials Science and Engineering
WU, CHENGZHEN, Materials Science and Engineering
WU, JILIANG, Architecture and Urban Planning
XIAO, WANRU, Sciences
XU, NANPING, Chemistry and Chemical Engineering
XU, YANHUA, Urban Construction, Safety and Environmental Engineering
XU, ZHONGZI, Materials Science and Engineering
YAN, SHENG, Materials Science and Engineering
YANG, XIANNING, Chemistry and Chemical Engineering
YANG, XIAOJIAN, Information Science and Engineering
YAO, CHENG, Sciences
YAO, HUQING, Chemistry and Chemical Engineering
YAO, XIAO, Materials Science and Engineering
YEI, XUCHU, Materials Science and Engineering
YIN, CHENBO, Mechanical and Power Engineering
YIN, FULIN, Foreign Languages and International Exchange
YIN, XIA, Mechanical and Power Engineering
YU, BIN, Sciences
YUN, ZHI, Chemistry and Chemical Engineering
ZENG, CHONGYU, Chemistry and Chemical Engineering
ZENG, YANWEI, Materials Science and Engineering
ZHANG, GANDAO, Life Sciences and Pharmaceutical Engineering
ZHANG, HONG, Mechanical and Power Engineering
ZHANG, JUN, Materials Science and Engineering
ZHANG, LIJING, Urban Construction, Safety and Environmental Engineering
ZHANG, LIXIONG, Chemistry and Chemical Engineering
ZHANG, QITU, Materials Science and Engineering
ZHANG, SHAOMING, Materials Science and Engineering
ZHANG, WEI, Materials Science and Engineering
ZHANG, YAMING, Chemistry and Chemical Engineering
ZHAO, HESHENG, Architecture and Urban Planning

ZHAO, SHILIN, Materials Science and Engineering
ZHAO, YINGKAN, Automation
ZHENG, FENGQIN, Mechanical and Power Engineering
ZHOU, CHANGYU, Mechanical and Power Engineering
ZHOU, HUA, Life Sciences and Pharmaceutical Engineering
ZHU, DUNRU, Chemistry and Chemical Engineering
ZHU, HONG, Materials Science and Engineering
ZHU, XURONG, Chemistry and Chemical Engineering
ZHUANG, JUN, Mechanical and Power Engineering

NANJING UNIVERSITY OF TRADITIONAL CHINESE MEDICINE

282 Hanzhong Rd, Nanjing 210029, Jiangsu
Telephone: (25) 86798005
Fax: (25) 86798009
Internet: www.njutcm.edu.cn
Founded 1954
Academic year: September to July
President: XIANG PING
Vice-Presidents: CHEN DIPING, LIU SHENLIN, WU MIANHUA
Librarian: JI WENHUI
Library of 4,320,000 vols
Number of teachers: 1,308
Number of students: 6,000
Publication: *Journal* (6 a year)

DEANS

College of Basic Medicine: ZHANG MINGQIN
College of Pharmacy: DING ANWEI
First Clinical Medical College: (vacant)
Second Clinical Medical College: LI ZHONGREN
School of Commercial Management and Trade: (vacant)
School of Foreign Languages: (vacant)

PROFESSORS

BIAN, HUIMIN, Pharmacy
CAI, BAOCHANG, Pharmacy
CHEN, JIANWEI, Pharmacy
DING, ANWEI, Pharmacy
DING, SHUHUA, Clinical Medicine
FANG, TAIHUI, Pharmacy
GUO, LIWEI, Pharmacy
HUANG, YAOZHOU, Pharmacy
LI, XIANG, Pharmacy
LIU, HANQING, Pharmacy
PENG, GUOPING, Pharmacy
QIN, MINGZHU, Pharmacy
WANG, SHOUCHUAN, Clinical Medicine
WU, DEKANG, Pharmacy
WU, HAO, Pharmacy
YAN, DAONAN, Clinical Medicine
YU, XIAOWEI, Clinical Medicine
ZHOU, FUYI, Clinical Medicine
ZHU, QUAN, Pharmacy

ATTACHED RESEARCH INSTITUTES

Adult Education College.
Botanical Refinement Engineering Research Centre: Dir GUO LIWEI.
College of International Education.
Jiangsu Province Research and Development Centre for Marine Pharmaceuticals: Dir WU HAO.

NANKAI UNIVERSITY

94 Weijin Rd, Tianjin 300071
Telephone: (22) 23508208
Fax: (22) 23502208
E-mail: xb@office.nankai.edu.cn
Internet: www.nankai.edu.cn

Founded 1919
Academic year: September to July
President: Prof. HOU ZIXIN
Vice-Presidents: CHEN HONG, CHEN XUEQI, CHEN YONGCHUAN, GENG YUNQI, PANG JINJU, ZHANG JING
Librarian: Prof. YAN SHIPING
Library of 2,900,000 vols
Number of teachers: 1,465
Number of students: 23,000

Publications: *Journal* (4 a year), *Nankai Economics Studies* (6 a year), *Nankai Journal* (6 a year), *Nankai Management Review* (6 a year)

DEANS

College of Adult Education: Prof. JING HONGGANG
College of Chemistry: Prof. GUAN NAIJIA
College of Chinese Language and Culture: Prof. SHI FENG
College of Economics: Prof. ZHOU LIQUN
College of Economics and Societal Development: Prof. HOU ZIXIN
College Environmental Science and Engineering: Prof. ZHU TAN
College of Foreign Languages and Literature: Prof. WANG JIANYI
College of History: Prof. LI ZHIAN
College of Ideological and Cultural Education: Prof. LI YI
College of Information Science and Technology: Prof. WU GONGYI
College of International Business: Prof. LI WEIAN
College of Law and Political Science: Prof. ZHU GUANGLEI
College of Life Sciences: Prof. GENG YUNQI
College of Literature: Prof. CHEN HONG
College of Mathematics: Prof. LONG YIMING
College of Medicine: Prof. ZHU TIANHUI
College of Modern Distance Education: Prof. LEI ZONGBAO
College of Occupational Technology: Prof. SU LICHUN
College of Physics: Prof. XU JINGJUN
Software College: Prof. HUANG YALOU
Teda College: Prof. XIAN GUOMING

PROFESSORS

College of Chemistry (tel. (22) 23508470; fax (22) 23502458; e-mail hxx@office.nankai.edu.cn):

Department of Chemistry:

BU XIANHE, Inorganic Chemistry
CAI ZUNSHENG, Physical Chemistry
CAO YURONG, Organic Chemistry
CHENG JINPEI, Inorganic Chemistry
CHENG PENG, Inorganic Chemistry
DENG GUOCAI, Inorganic Chemistry
GUAN NAIJIA, Physical Chemistry
HE JIAQI, Inorganic Chemistry
HE XIWEN, Analytical Chemistry
HU QINGMEI, Organic Chemistry
HUANG JIAXIAN, Polymer Chemistry
HUANG WEIPING, Inorganic Chemistry
HUANG ZHIRONG, Analytical Chemistry
JIANG ZONGHUI, Inorganic Chemistry
LI FANGXING, Polymer Chemistry
LIAO DAIZHENG, Inorganic Chemistry
LIN HUAKUAN, Physical Chemistry
LIU YU, Physical Chemistry
MENG JIBEN, Organic Chemistry
SHEN HANXI, Inorganic Chemistry
SHEN PANWEN, Analytical Chemistry
SONG LICHENG, Organic Chemistry
WANG BAIQUAN, Organic Chemistry
WANG XINSHENG, Organic Chemistry
WANG YONGMEI, Organic Chemistry
WU SHIHUA, Inorganic Chemistry
XU SHANSHENG, Organic Chemistry
YAN SHIPING, Inorganic Chemistry
YAN XIUPING, Analytical Chemistry
YANG GUANGMING, Inorganic Chemistry

YANG XIULIN, Physical Chemistry
YIN LIHUA, Inorganic Chemistry
YOU YINGCAI, Polymer Chemistry
YUAN MANXUE, Physical Chemistry
ZHANG BAOLONG, Organic Chemistry
ZHANG BAOSHEN, Polymer Chemistry
ZHANG GUIZHU, Analytical Chemistry
ZHANG ZHIHUI, Physical Chemistry
ZHAO HONGXI, Physical Chemistry
ZHAO ZUEZHANG, Physical Chemistry
ZHU CHANGYING, Polymer Chemistry
ZHU SHOURONG, Physical Chemistry
ZHU XIAOQING, Organic Chemistry
ZHU ZHIANG, Physical Chemistry
ZUO JU, Polymer Chemistry
ZUO YUMIN, Organic Chemistry

Department of Materials Chemistry:

CHE YUNXIA, Inorganic Chemistry
CHEN JUN, Materials Chemistry
CHEN TIEHONG, Physical Chemistry
GAO XUEPING, Materials Chemistry
LIU SHUANGXI, Physical Chemistry
SONG DEYING, Materials Chemistry
SUN BO, Inorganic Chemistry
TAO KEYI, Physical Chemistry
XIANG SHOUHE, Physical Chemistry
YAN JIE, Materials Chemistry
YUAN HUATUNG, Materials Chemistry
ZHENG WENJUN, Physical Chemistry

College of Chinese Language and Culture
(tel. (22) 23501687; fax (22) 23501687; e-mail
hy@office.nankai.edu.cn):

CUI JIANXIN, Modern Chinese
GUO JIMAO, Modern Chinese
SHI FENG, Chinese Linguistics
SHI XIANGDONG, Ancient Chinese

College of Economics (tel. (22) 23508981; fax
(22) 23500261; e-mail jjxy@office.nankai.edu
.cn):

Department of Economics:

HE ZILI, Comparative Economics
JIA GENLIANG, Development Economics
JING WEIMIN, Transitional Economics
LIU CHUNBIN, Agro-economics
LIU JUNMIN, Macroeconomics and Virtual
Economics
WANG SHUYING, Industrial Economics
WEN HAICHI, Labour Economics
ZHANG RENDE, Comparative Economics
ZHANG SHIQING, Macroeconomics and
Microeconomics
ZHANG TONGYU (acting), Political Economy
ZHAO JIN, History of Economics
ZHU GUANGHUA, Political Economy

Department of Finance:

LI ZHIHUI, International Finance
LIU YUCAO, International Finance
MA JUNLU, International Finance

Department of International Economics and
Trade:

GAO LEYONG, International Economic The-
ories, International Investment
LI KUNWANG, Theory and Policy of Inter-
national Trade
LIU ZHONGLI, International Trade Manage-
ment
TONG JIADONG, International Trade, Eco-
nomics of International Integration
XUE JINGXIAO, International Economics,
Japanese Economy
YANG CANYING, Open Economy
ZHANG ZHICHAO, Public Finance, Economics
of Development

Department of Risk Management and
Insurance:

JIANG SHENGZHONG, Research, Insurance
Management
LIU MAOSHAN, Research, Insurance Eco-
nomics
XIAO YUNRU, Research, Actuarial Math-
ematics

College of Environmental Science and Engineering (tel. (22) 23508807; fax (22) 23508936;
e-mail hjxy@office.nankai.edu.cn):

Department of Environmental Engineering
and Management:

BAI ZHIPENG, Air Pollution Chemistry,
Environmental Risk Assessment
LIU MAO, Environmental Safety Assess-
ment
WAN QISHAN, Water Pollution Control
ZHU TAN, Environmental Planning and
Management
ZHUANG YUANYI, Environmental Engineer-
ing

Department of Environmental Science:

CHEN FUHUA, Environmental Chemistry
DAI SHUGUI, Environmental Chemistry
FU XUEQI, Environmental Chemistry
HU GUOCHEN, Environmental Biology
HUANG GUOLAN, Environmental Chemistry
JIN ZHAOHUI, Environmental Chemistry
SUN HONGWEN, Environmental Chemistry,
Environmental Pollution Control
ZHANG BAOGUI, Environmental Chemistry,
Analytic Chemistry
ZHU LIN, Environmental Biology

College of Foreign Languages and Literature
(tel. (22) 23509292; fax (22) 23500497; e-mail
wyxy@office.nankai.edu.cn):

Department of English Language and
Literature:

CHANG YAOXIN, English Literature
CUI YONGLU, English Translation
GU QI'NAN, English Literature
JIANG HUASHANG, English Literature
LIU SHICONG, English Translation
SU LICHANG, English Linguistics
MA QIUWU, English Linguistics
WANG HONGYIN, English Translation
WANG WENHAN, English Literature
WEI RONGCHENG, English Literature
YAN QIGANG, English Literature
ZHANG MAIZENG, English Linguistics

Department of General Literature:

LI JINGYU, English Language
SUO JUNMEI, English Language
WANG SHIBIN, English Language
XUE CHEN, English Language
ZHANG JUNZHI, English Language
ZHANG WENQI, English Language
ZHOU SHUJIE, English Language

Department of Japanese Language and
Literature:

LIU GUIMIN, Japanese Literature and Lin-
guistics
WANG JIANYI, Japanese Literature and
Linguistics

Department of Western Languages and
Literature:

CHEN XI, Comparative Linguistics
YAN GUODONG, Sino-Russian Cultural
Relations, Comparative Culture
ZHANG ZHITING, French Literature

College of History (tel. (22) 23508422; fax
(22) 23501637; e-mail lizhian@nankai.edu
.cn):

Department of History:

CHANG JIANHUA, Ancient Chinese History
CHEN ZHENJIANG, Modern and Contempor-
ary Chinese History
CHEN ZHIQIANG, Ancient and Medieval
World History
FENG ERKANG, Ancient Chinese History
HA QUAN'AN, Ancient and Medieval World
History
HOU JIE, Modern and Contemporary Chi-
nese History
JIANG PEI, Modern and Contemporary
Chinese History
JIANG SHENGLI, Historiography
LI ZHI'AN, Ancient Chinese History

LI XISUO, Modern and Contemporary Chi-
nese History
LIN HEKUN, Modern and Contemporary
World History
LIU MIN, Ancient Chinese History
LIU ZEHUA, Ancient Chinese History
MA SHILI, Modern and Contemporary
World History
SUN LIQUN, Ancient Chinese History
WANG DUNSHU, Ancient and Medieval
World History
WANG XIANMING, Modern and Contempor-
ary Chinese History
XU TAN, Ancient Chinese History
ZHANG FENTIAN, Ancient Chinese History
ZHANG GUOGANG, Ancient Chinese History

Department of Philosophy:

CHANG JIAN, Western Philosophy
CHEN YANQING, Marxist Philosophy
CUI QINGTIAN, Logical Philosophy
HAN QIANG, Chinese Philosophy
LI NA, Logical Philosophy
LI JIANSHANG, Scientific and Technological
Philosophy
LI XIANGHAI, Chinese Philosophy
LIU WENYING, Chinese Philosophy
LU YANG, Aesthetics
REN XIAOMING, Logical Philosophy
WANG NANSHI, Marxist Philosophy
XUE FUXING, Aesthetics
YAN MENGWEI, Marxist Philosophy

Department of Relics and Museum Studies:

LIU YI, Museology
ZHU FENGHAN, Ancient Chinese History

College of Ideological and Cultural Education
(tel. (22) 23507985; fax (22) 23507985; e-mail
jyxy@office.nankai.edu):

CAO JIE, Marxist Theories and Ideological
and Political Education
DING JUN, Political Economics
DOU AIZHI, History of the Chinese Com-
munist Party
LI JIANSONG, Political Economics
LI YI, Marxist Philosophy
LIU JINGQUAN, History of the Chinese
Communist Party
SHAO YUNRUI, History of the Chinese Com-
munist Party
WANG YUANMING, Marxist Philosophy
WU DONGSHENG, Marxist Theories and
Ideological and Political Education
YANG YONGZHI, Theoretical Thoughts of
Deng Xiaopin
ZHANG HONGGUANG, Scientific and Techno-
logical Philosophy
ZHAO TIESUO, History of the Chinese Com-
munist Party

College of Information Science and Technology (tel. (22) 23505705; fax (22) 23509054;
e-mail xxxy@office.nankai.edu.cn):

CHANG SHENGJIANG, Optical Information
Processing
CHEN WENJU, Nonlinear Optical Physics
and Materials Optoelectronics for
Optical Information
DONG YUANYI, Photonics Technology and
Modern Optical Communication
FANG ZHILIANG, Optical Information Pro-
cessing
FU RULIAN, Laser and Biomedical Optics
GENG XINHUA, Photo-electronic Technology
and Applications
HAN WEIHENG, Computer Software
LIN MEIRONG, Nonlinear Optical Physics
and Materials, Optoelectronics for
Optical Information
LIU FULAI, Optical Information Processing
MU GUOGUANG, Optical Information Pro-
cessing
SHEN JINYUAN, Optical Information Pro-
cessing
SUN YUN, Photo-electronic Materials and
Technology

SUN ZHONGLI, Photo-electronic Technology, Semiconductor Materials and Devices

TANG GUOQING, Molecular Electronic Spectroscopy and Biomedical Photomaps

WANG QINGREN, Pattern Recognition and Intelligent Systems

WANG ZHAOQI, Optical Information Processing

WANG ZONGPAN, Photo-electronic Technology and Applications

XIONG SHAOZHEN, Optoelectronic Devices and Technology, Display Electronics

YUAN SHUZHONG, Fibre Communication and Fibre Sensors

ZHAI HONGCHEN, Institute of Modern Optics

ZHANG GUILAN, Nonlinear Optical Physics and Materials

ZHANG YANXIN, Optical Information Processing, Neural Networks and Pattern Recognition

ZHAO QIDA, Fibre Communication and Fibre Sensors

ZHU XIAONONG, Applications of Femtosecond Laser Science and Technology

Department of Automation:

CHEN QIUSHUANG, Job Shop Schedule Systems, DEDS System

CHEN ZENGQIANG, Adaptive, Predictive and Intelligent Control

SUN YONGHUA, Adaptive Control Systems

TU FENGSHENG, Integrated Computer Manufacturing Systems

WANG XIUFENG, Modelling and Identification, Financial Decision Support Systems

WANG ZHIBAO, Financial Decision Support Systems

YUAN ZHUZHI, Adaptive and Predictive Control, Intelligent Communication

Department of Communications Engineering:

LI WENCHEN, Radio Communications

WU YUE, Radio Communications

Department of Computer Science and Technology:

BAI GANG, Pattern Recognition

LI QINGCHENG, Embedded Operating Systems

LIU JING, Computer Architecture

LU ZHICAI, Intelligent Control and Communication Networks

SUN GUIRU, Software Engineering

WU GONGYI, Computer Networks

YANG YULU, Computer Architecture

YUAN XIAOJIE, Database Technology, Data Warehousing, Data Mining

ZHU YAOTING, Multimedia Technology and Network Teaching

Department of Electronic Information Science and Technology:

LI WEIXIANG, Systems and System Design

YAN SHAOLIN, Superconductor Electronics, Communications Science and Technology

YANG WENXIA, Net Communication

Department of Electronic Science and Technology:

FANG LAN, Superconductivity, Electronics

SHAO SHUMIN, Vacuum Science and Technology, Functional Materials and Devices

Department of Microelectronics:

JIA XIANGLUAN, VLSI and System Design

NIU WENCHENG, Transducer Technology and Systems

NIU XIUQING, VLSI and System Design

QIN SHICAI, VLSI and System Design

College of International Business (tel. (22) 23500603; fax (22) 23501039; e-mail alison41@eyou.com):

Department of Accounting:

FENG YANQI, International Accounting

LIU ZHIYUAN, Managerial Accounting

ZHOU XIAOSU, Financial Accounting

Department of Financial Management:

QI YINFENG, Corporate Finance

WANG QUANXI, Corporate Finance

Department of Human Resource Management:

LI WINJIAN, Human Resource Management

WU GUOCUN, Human Resource Management, Human Resource Development

XIE JINYU, Human Resource Management, Strategic Human Resource Management

Department of Information Systems and Management:

YAN JIANYUAN, Management Information Systems, Logistics Management

Department of International Business:

HAN JINGLUN, Management

JIA LANXIANG, Management

LI FEI, Management

LI GUOJING, Management

QI ANBANG, Management

WANG YINGJUN, Management

ZHANG YULI, Management

Department of Library Science:

LIU YUZHAO, Library Management

WANG ZHIJIN, Library Management

Department of Marketing:

FAN XIUCHENG, Service Marketing Management

HAN DECHANG, Marketing

WU XIAOYUN, Global Marketing Management

Department of Tourism Management:

LI TIANYUAN, Tourism Marketing

QI SHANHONG, Tourism Business Management

WANG JIAN, Tourism Development

College of Law and Political Science (tel. (22) 23501400; fax (22) 23500327; e-mail fzxy@nankai.edu.cn; internet nkfzxy.my163.com):

Department of Law:

BAI HUA, Theory of Law

FU SCHICHENG, Administrative Law

HOU XINYI, Theory of Law

HU SHIKAI, Theory of Law

LI YUNWU, Forensic Medicine

QI DAOMENG, Environmental Law

ZHAO ZHENGQUN, Administrative Law

ZHU JINGAN, International Private Law

Department of Political Science:

CAI TUO, International Relations

GE QUAN, Political Science

SHEN YAPING, Public Administration

WANG ZHENGYI, International Relations

YANG LONG, Political Science

YIN YANJUN, International Relations

ZHANG RUIZHUANG, International Relations

ZHU GUANGLEI, Political Science

Department of Sociology:

GUAN XINPING, Social Policy

HOU JUNSHENG, Applied Sociology

LIU JUNJUN, Applied Sociology

PENG HUAMIN, Social Work

WANG CHUHUI, Applied Sociology

WANG XINJIAN, Social Psychology

YUE GUOAN, Social Psychology

College of Life Sciences (tel. (22) 23501846; fax (22) 23508800; e-mail sky@office.nankai.edu.cn):

Department of Biochemistry:

CAO YOUJIA, Biochemistry and Molecular Biology, Signals Transduction and Apoptosis

CHEN QIMIN, Microbiology and Molecular Genetics, Molecular Virology

DU RONGQIAN, Molecular Biology

GENG YUNQI, Molecular Virology

HUANG XITAI, Biochemistry and Molecular Biology, Structure of Nucleic Acids and Gene Chips

WANG NINGNING, Plant Molecular Biology

WANG SHUFANG, Plant Physiology

WANG YONG, Plant Molecular Biology

YE LIHONG, Protein Biochemistry

YU ZIRAN, Purification and Characterization of Human Growth Hormones Expressed in Insect Cells

YU XINDA, Gene Engineering in Eukaryotic Cells

Department of Biology:

BU WENJUN, Zoological Systematics

CHEN QIANG, Biosensors, Biophysical Chemistry

CHEN RUIYANG, Cytogenetics

GAO YUBAO, Botany and Plant Ecology

LI HOUHUN, Insect Taxonomy, Zoogeography

LIU ANXI, Animal Physiology and Biochemistry

QIU ZHAOZHI, Zootaxy and Parasitology

SONG WENQIN, Molecular Cytogenetics

WANG XINHUA, Systematic Zoology

ZHENG LEYI, Zoological Systematics

Department of Microbiology:

BAI GANG, Molecular Immunology

DIAO HUXIN, Study of Petroleum Microorganisms

LIU FANG, Microbiological Sources and Molecular Biology

LIU RULIN, Microbiology

REN GAIXIN, Insect Microbiology

WANG LEI, Bacterial Genetics and Evolution

XING LAIJUN, Modern Mycology

YANG WENBO, Resource Bacteriology and Engineering

College of Literature (tel. (22) 23508247; fax (22) 23508247; e-mail chinese@wxy.nankai.edu.cn; internet www.nankai.chinese.edu.cn):

Department of Art Design:

XUE YI, Art Design

Department of Basic Cultural Education:

NING JIAYU, Ancient Chinese Literature

Department of Chinese Language and Literature:

CHEN HONG, Ancient Chinese Literature

HONG BO, Ancient Chinese

LI JIANGUO, Ancient Chinese Literature

LIU LILI, Literature and Art Science

LU SHENGJIANG, Ancient Chinese Literature

LUO ZONGQIANG, Ancient Chinese Literature

MA QINGZHU, Modern Chinese

MENG ZHAOLIAN, Ancient Chinese Literature

NING JIAYU, Ancient Chinese Literature

PENG XIUYIN, Literature and Art Science

QIAO YIGANG, Modern and Contemporary Chinese Literature

SHI FENG, Experimental Phonetics

SUN CHANGWU, Ancient Chinese Literature

TAO MUNING, Ancient Chinese Literature

WANG LIXIN, Comparative and World Literature

WANG ZHIGENG, Comparative and World Literature

XING KAI, Languages and Literature of Ethnic Minorities in China

XU XIANGLIN, Ancient Chinese Literature

ZENG XIAOYU, Languages and Literature of Ethnic Minorities in China

ZHANG YI, Ancient Chinese Literature

ZHOU JIAN, Modern Chinese

Department of Eastern Art:

CHEN YUPU, Chinese Painting
FAN ZENG, Chinese Painting
HAN CHANGLI, Chinese Painting
SHEN QUAN, Chinese Painting

Department of Mass Communication:

LUO DERONG, Editorial and Publishing Science
ZHAO HANG, Editorial and Publishing Science

College of Mathematics (tel. (22) 23501233; fax (22) 23506423; e-mail longym@nankai.edu.cn; internet www.math.nankai.edu.cn):

Department of Financial Information and Technology:

CHEN WANYI, Control Theory, Financial Mathematics
WANG GONGSHU, Applied Statistics
WANG HONG, Control Theory

Department of Information and Probability:

FU FANGWEI, Coding Theory, Bioinformation
GUO JUNYI, Stochastic Process, Risk Theory
LIANG PU, Coding Theory, Bioinformation
SHEN SHIYI, Coding Theory, Bioinformation
WANG YONGJIN, Probability, Stochastic Process
WU RONG, Probability, Stochastic Process
ZHOU XINGWEI, Harmonic Analysis, Wavelet Analysis

Department of Mathematics:

DENG SHAOQIANG, Lie Groups and Lie Algebras
DING GUANGGUI, Functional Analysis
GU PEI, Algebra, Group Metahomomorphisms
GUO JINGMEI, Differential Topology
HOU ZIXIN, Lie Groups and Lie Algebras
HUANG YUMIN, Partial Differential Equations
LIANG KE, Lie Groups and Lie Algebras
LIN JINKUN, Algebraic Topology
LIU CHUNGEN, Nonlinear Analysis
MENG DAOJI, Basic Mathematics, Algebra, Lie Therapy

Department of Scientific Computing and Applied Software:

HU JIANGWEI, Numerical Mathematics
TIAN CHUNSONG, Numerical Mathematics

Department of Statistics:

WANG ZHAOJUN, Experimental Design, Statistical Process Control
ZHANG RUNCHU, Experimental Design, Multivariate Analysis, Applied Statistics

College of Medicine (tel. (22) 23509842; fax (22) 23509842; e-mail zhuth@nankai.edu.cn):

LIU WEN, Anatomy
ZHU TIANHUI, Medical Genetics

College of Physics (tel. (22) 23501490; fax (22) 23501490; e-mail physics@nankai.edu.cn; internet www.physics.nankai.edu.cn):

Department of Physics:

CAI CHONGHAI, Evaluation of Nuclear Data
CHEN TIANLUN, Nonlinear Dynamics, Partial Physics Theory
DING DATONG, Nuclear Magnetic Resonance, Computational Materials, Mesoscopic Physics
GAO CHENGQUN, Nuclear Physics
HU BEILAI, Statistical Physics, Plasma Physics
HUANG WUQUN, Nonlinear Dynamics
LI BAOHUI, Nuclear Magnetic Resonance, Computational Physics
LI XUEQIAN, Phenomenology of High Energy Physics
LU ZHENQIU, Inverse Scattering Physics and Imaging Techniques
LUO MA, Perturbative Chromodynamic Power Electronics

MENG XINHE, Particle Physics and the Universe, Mesoscopic Physics
NING PINGZHI, Nuclear Physics
SHEN HONG, Nuclear Physics
WEN JINGSONG, Micro-atmospheric Science Suspension Mechanics
ZHOU WENZHUANG, Crystallology
ZHU YAPING, X-Ray Crystallology

Department of Optical and Electrical Science:

LÜ FUYUN, Photoelectron Laser and Modern Optical Communication
LÜ KECHENG, Photoelectron Laser and Modern Optical Communication
SHENG QIUQIN, Opto-electronics and Optical Fibre Communication, Optical Sensors

Department of Biophysical Science:

YANG WENXIU, Cellular and Molecular Informatics, Cellular and Membrane Biophysics

Software College (tel. (22) 23500526; fax (22) 23500526; e-mail cs@nankai.edu.cn; internet www.cs.nankai.edu.cn):

HUANG YALOU, Intelligent Robot Systems, Intelligent Information Processes

Department of Physical Education (tel. (22) 23502801; e-mail tyb@office.nankai.edu.cn):

WANG YUZHU, Track and Field
XING CHUNGUI, Volleyball
YANG XIANGDONG, Basketball (Dir)
ZHAO SHIJIE, Track and Field

Institute of Ancient Chinese Culture Studies (tel. (22) 23509662; fax (22) 23508247; e-mail chinese@wxy.nankai.edu.cn; internet www.nankai.chinese.edu.cn):

YE JIAYING, Ancient Chinese Literature and Culture

Institute of Economics (tel. (22) 23503997; fax (22) 23501254; e-mail zhoulq@public.tpt.tj.cn):

CAO ZHENLIANG, Regional Economic Theory
CHEN ZHONGSHENG, Socialist Economic Theory
LIU XIN, Capitalist Economic Theory
PANG JINJU, Socialist Economic Theory
WANG YURU, History of Modern Economic Development
ZHOU BING, Socialist Economic Theory
ZHOU LIQUN, Socialist Economic Theory

Institute of Elemento-Organic Chemistry (tel. (22) 23508629; fax (22) 23503438; e-mail yss@office.nankai.edu.cn):

CHEN RUYU, Organic Chemistry
CHENG JUNRAN, Organic Chemistry
FANG JIANXIN, Organic Chemistry
GAO RUYU, Organic Chemistry
HAN JIAXIANG, Organic Chemistry
HUANG RUNQIU, Organic Chemistry
LI JING, Organic Chemistry
LI JINSHAN, Organic Chemistry
LI SHUZHENG, Organic Chemistry
LI ZHENGMING, Organic Chemistry
LIAO RENAN, Organic Chemistry
LIU HUAYIN, Organic Chemistry
LIU LUNZU, Organic Chemistry
TANG CHUCHI, Organic Chemistry
WANG GUANGYUAN, Organic Chemistry
XIE QINGLAN, Organic Chemistry
YANG HUAZENG, Organic Chemistry
ZHANG ZHENGZHI, Organic Chemistry
ZHANG ZUXIN, Organic Chemistry
ZHENG JIANU, Organic Chemistry
ZHOU QILIN, Organic Chemistry

Institute of History (tel. (22) 23508903; fax (22) 23508903; e-mail lg433@eyou.com):

BAI XINLIANG, Ancient Chinese History
DU JIAJI, Ancient Chinese History
LIN YANQING, Ancient Chinese History
NAN BINGWEN, Ancient Chinese History
WANG MAOHE, Ancient Chinese History

Institute of International Economic Law (tel. (22) 23500694; fax (22) 23500327; e-mail shixuey@fm365.com; internet www.nkfzxy.my163.com):

CHENG BAOKU, International Economic Law
SHI XUEYING, International Economic Law

Institute of International Economics (tel. (22) 23508291; fax (22) 23502437; e-mail iitnk@office.nankai.edu.cn):

CHEN LIGAO, Open Economy
DAI JINPING, International Finance
LI RONGLIN, International Trade
QIU LICHENG, International Investment and Business
TENG WEIZAO, International Investment and Business
XIANG GUOMING, International Investment and Business
ZHANG CHENG, International Investment and Business
ZHANG XIAOTONG, Econometrics
ZHANG YANGUI, International Investment and Business

Institute of Modern Research Management (tel. (22) 23508439; fax (22) 23503690; e-mail nkimm@public.tpt.tj.cn):

LE WEIAN, Corporate Governance
ZHANG JINCHENG, Service Management and Strategic Management

Institute of Mathematics (tel. (22) 23501029; fax (22) 23501532; e-mail nim@nankai.edu.cn):

CHEN YONGCHUAN, Combinatorics
FANG FUQUAN, Geometric Topology
FU LEI, Algebraic Geometry
GE MOLIN, Theoretical Physics
LI XUELIANG, Theory of Graphs and Combinatorial Optimizations
LONG YIMING, Nonlinear Analysis
ZHANG WEIPING, Differential Geometry
ZHOU XINGWEI, Harmonic Analysis, Wavelet Analysis

Institute of Molecular Biology (tel. (22) 23501846; fax (22) 23508800; e-mail sky@office.nankai.edu.cn):

CAI BAOLI, Biodegradation and Biotechnology
GAO CAICHANG, Biochemistry and Molecular Biology
LI MINGGANG, Plant Molecular Biology
QIAO MINGQIANG, Molecular Microbiology and Microbial Technology
YU YAOTING, Biomaterials and Enzyme Engineering
ZHANG JINHONG, Enzyme Engineering and Biomedical Materials
ZHANG JU, Medical Genetics
ZHENG JIANYU, Molecular Biology
ZHANG XIAODONG, Tumour Molecular Biology

Institute of Modern Optics (tel. (22) 23502275; fax (22) 23503690; e-mail xxxy@office.nankai.edu.cn):

CHANG SHENGJIANG, Optical Information Processing
CHEN WENJU, Nonlinear Optical Physics and Materials
DONG XIAOYI, Photonics Technology and Modern Optical Communication
FANG ZHILIANG, Optical Engineering
FU RULIAN, Laser and Biomedical Optics
KAI GUIYUN, Fibre Communications and Fibre Sensors
LIN MEIRONG, Nonlinear Optical Physics and Materials
LIU FULAI, Optical Engineering
MU GUOGUANG, Optical Information Processing
SHEN JINYUAN, Optical Information Processing
TANG GUOQING, Molecular Electronic Spectroscopy and Biomedicine Photomaps

WANG ZHAOQI, Optical Information Processing

YUAN ZHUZHONG, Fibre Communications and Fibre Sensors

ZHAI HONGCHEN, Optical Information Processing, Optics Engineering

ZHANG GUILAN, Nonlinear Optical Physics and Materials

ZHANG YANXIN, Optical Information Processing Neural Networks and Pattern Recognition

ZHAO QIDA, Fibre Communications and Fibre Sensors

ZHU XIAONONG, Applications of Femtosecond Laser Science and Technology

Institute of Photoelectronics (tel. (22) 23502778; fax (22) 23502778; e-mail xxxy@office.nankai.edu.cn):

GENG XINHUA, Photoelectronic Technology and Applications

SUN YAN, Photoelectronic Materials and Technology

SUN ZHONGLIN, Photoelectronic Technology, Semiconductor Materials and Devices

WANG ZONGPAN, Photoelectronic Technology and Applications

XIONG SHAOZHEN, Optoelectronic Devices and Technology, Display Electronics

Institute of Polymer Chemistry (tel. (22) 23501386; fax (22) 23503510; e-mail gfzs@office.nankai.edu.cn):

HE BINGLIN, Polymer Chemistry

HUANG WENQIANG, Polymer Chemistry

LI CHAOXING, Polymer Chemistry

LI CHENXI, Polymer Chemistry

LI HONG, Polymer Chemistry

MA JIANBIAO, Polymer Chemistry

MI HUAIFENG, Biochemistry

SHI LINQI, Polymer Chemistry

SHI ZUOQING, Polymer Chemistry

WANG GUOCHANG, Polymer Chemistry

WU QIANG, Polymer Chemistry

YAN HUSHENG, Polymer Chemistry

YUAN ZHI, Polymer Chemistry

ZHANG BANGHUA, Polymer Chemistry

ZHANG ZHENGPU, Polymer Chemistry

Institute of Population and Development (tel. (22) 23508012; fax (22) 23501773; e-mail rks@office.nankai.edu.cn):

LI JIANMIN, Economics of Population and Labour

TAN LIN, Economics of Population and Labour

YUAN XIN, Economics of Population and Labour

APEC Study Centre (tel. (22) 23501573; fax (22) 23500035; e-mail apecnk@office.nankai.edu.cn):

GONG ZHANKUI, Regional Economic Cooperation, International Trade and Investment

Chinese Philology Research Centre (tel. (22) 23507855; fax (22) 23508247; e-mail chinese@wxy.nankai.edu.cn; internet www.nankai.chinese.edu.cn):

HE LEYUE, Chinese Philology

XIANG GUANGZHONG, Chinese Philology

ZHAO XIANCUO, Chinese Philology

Photonics Research Centre (tel. (22) 23503697; fax (22) 23501490; e-mail zhangcp@nankai.edu.cn; internet www.physics.nankai.edu.cn):

LIU SIMIN, Nonlinear Optics, Solid Spectrum

TIAN JIANGUO, Photonics

XU JINGJUN, Condensed Matter Physics and Photonic Devices

ZHANG CHUNPING, Photonics and Biomedical Photonics

ZHANG GUANGYIN, Solid Spectrum, Photonics and Laser Physics

Transnational Studies Centre (tel. (22) 23505235; fax (22) 23502437; e-mail ctsnk@office.nankai.edu.cn):

CHEN LIGAO, Open Economy

DAI JINPING, International Finance

QIU LICHENG, International Investment and Business

XIAN GUOMING, International Investment and Business

ZHANG CHENG, International Investment and Business

ZHANG XIAOTONG, Econometrics

ZHANG YANGUI, International Investment and Business

NINGXIA MEDICAL COLLEGE

Sheng Li South Rd, Yinchuan 750004, Ningxia

Telephone: (951) 4095934

Internet: www.nxmc.edu.cn

Founded 1958

Academic year: September to July

President: SHUN TAO

Vice-Presidents: CHEN SHENGCHUN, DAI XIUYING, LI ZHENGZHI, SHI WEIZHONG, ZHANG JIANZHONG

Head of Graduate Department: LI ZHENGZHI

Librarian: WANG HUIFANG

Library of 200,000 vols

Number of teachers: 811

Number of students: 7,500

Publication: *Journal* (6 a year)

DEANS

School of Nursing: ZHANG LIN

School of Pharmacy: ZHANG DONGNIN

Department of Basic Medicine: WANG YANRONG

Department of Chinese Medicine: NIU YANG

Department of Clinical Medicine: WANG HUIXING

Department of Dentistry: MA MING

Department of Public Health: SONG QIRU

PROFESSORS

GAO, WENHUA, Public Health

HOU, LINGLING, Chinese Medicine

HU, SANGPING, Basic Medicine

JIANG, HOUWEN, Chinese Medicine

JIN, ZHIJUN, Public Health

LI, YUCHUN, Chinese Medicine

LI, ZHENGZHI, Public Health

LIU, XIUFANG, Public Health

QIAN, LIQUN, Public Health

SONG, QIRU, Public Health

WANG, YANRONG, Basic Medicine

WANG, ZHONGJIU, Chinese Medicine

WEN, RUNLING, Public Health

ZHANG, YUJIE, Chinese Medicine

ZHANG, ZHENXIANG, Public Health

ZHU, YUDONG, Chinese Medicine

NORTH CHINA ELECTRIC POWER UNIVERSITY

204 Qingnian Rd, Baoding 071003, Hebei

Telephone: (312) 5024952

Fax: (312) 5028483

Internet: www.ncepu.edu.cn

Founded 1958

State control

President: LIU JI ZHEN

Vice-Presidents: AN LIAN SUO, LEI YING QI, LI HE MING, PENG ZHEN ZHONG

Heads of Graduate Department: AN LIAN SUO, DING CHANG FU

Librarian: KONG ZHENGHUI

Number of teachers: 2,348

Number of students: 20,000

Publications: *Electric Power Higher Education* (4 a year), *Electric Power Information* (4 a year), *Electric Power Record* (4 a year), *Journal* (4 a year), *Modern Electric Power* (6 a year)

DEANS

Department of English: DAI ZHONG XIN

School of Adult Education: AN LIAN SUO

School of Applied Mathematics: LU ZHAN HUI

School of Applied Physics: ZHANG XIAO HONG

School of Automation: (vacant)

School of Computer Science and Technology: ZHU YONG LI

School of Dynamical Engineering: YANG YONG PING

School of Economic Management: QI JIAN XUN

School of Electrical and Communications Engineering: (vacant)

School of Electrical Engineering: CUI XIANG

School of Environmental Engineering: ZHAO YI

School of Humanity and Social Sciences: LI JU YING

School of Mechanical Engineering: (vacant)

School of Physical Education: YAN GUO QIANG

PROFESSORS

AI, XIN, Electrical Engineering

BAO, HAI, Electrical Engineering

CAO, CHUN MEI, Applied Physics

CHEN, SHENG JIAN, Computer Science and Technology

CHEN, WU, Computer Science and Technology

CHEN, YING MIN, Environmental Engineering

CUI, XIANG, Electrical Engineering

DAI, ZHONG XIN, English Department

DONG, XING HUI, Computer Science and Technology

DU, JIAN GUO, Computer Science and Technology

FANG, LU GUANG, Physical Education

FENG, HUI, Environmental Engineering

GUAN, RONG HUA, Applied Physics

GUO, LEI, English Department

HE, YONG GUI, Economics and Management

HU, MAN YIN, Environmental Engineering

HU, ZHI GUANG, Environmental Engineering

HUANG, YUAN SHENG, Economics and Management

JIA, ZHENG YUAN, Economics and Management

JIANG, GEN SHAN, Applied Physics

LI, JU YING, Humanities and Social Sciences

LI, QI, Applied Physics

LI, QUAN HUA, Physical Education

LI, SHOU XIN, Environmental Engineering

LIN, BI YING, Computer Science and Technology

LIU, ZHI YUAN, Humanities and Social Sciences

LU, FANG CHENG, Electrical Engineering

LU, ZHAN HUI, Applied Mathematics

MA, XIN SHUN, Applied Mathematics

NIU, DONG XIAO, Economics and Management

QI, JIAN XUN, Economics and Management

SUN, JIAN GUO, Computer Science and Technology

SUN, WEI, Economics and Management

WAN, SHI WEI, Applied Physics

WANG, BAO YI, Computer Science and Technology

WANG, CUI RU, Computer Science and Technology

WANG, JING MIN, Economics and Management

WANG, MIN, Humanities and Social Sciences

WU, KE HE, Computer Science and Technology

XIAO, XIANG NING, Electrical Engineering

XING, MIAN, Applied Mathematics

YAN, GUO QIANG, Physical Education

YANG, QI XUN, Electrical Engineering

YI, LIAN QING, Environmental Engineering

YI, ZENG QIAN, Applied Physics

YUAN, YONG TAO, Environmental Engineering

ZHANG, SHENG HAN, Environmental Engineering

ZHANG, TIAN XIN, Humanities and Social Sciences

ZHANG, XIAO HONG, Applied Physics

ZHANG, XU ZHEN, Humanities and Social Sciences

ZHANG, ZHEN SHENG, Environmental Engineering

ZHAO, WEN XIA, Applied Mathematics

ZHAO, YI, Environmental Engineering

ZHENG, GU PING, Computer Science and Technology

ZHU, LING, Electrical Engineering

ZHU, YONG LI, Computer Science and Technology

NORTHEAST FORESTRY UNIVERSITY

26 Hexing Rd, Harbin 150040, Heilongjiang
Telephone: (451) 2190015
Fax: (451) 2110146
E-mail: faob@public.hr.hl.cn
Internet: www.nefu.edu.cn
Founded 1952
Academic year: September to July
President: Prof. LI JIAN
Vice-Presidents: Prof. CHAO JUN, Assoc. Prof. CHEN WENBIN, Assoc. Prof. HU WANYI, Prof. HUO JIANYU, Prof. YANG CHUANPING
Dean of Graduate School: FAN DELIN
Librarian: LIN XISHENG
Library of 570,000 vols
Number of teachers: 846
Number of students: 5,482 (incl. 307 postgraduates)
Publications: *Bulletin of Botany Research* (4 a year), *Chinese Wildlife* (4 a year), *Forest Fire Protection* (4 a year), *Forestry Finance and Accounting* (12 a year), *Forestry Research in Northern China* (4 a year, in English), *Journal of Northeast Forestry University* (4 a year, in English), *Science of Logging Engineering* (6 a year)

HEADS OF COLLEGES AND DEPARTMENTS

College of Civil Engineering: Prof. ZHANG YINGE
College of Electromechanical Engineering: Prof. LI DONGSHENG
College of Foreign Languages: Prof. LIU MENLAN
College of Forest Products: Prof. WANG FENGHU
College of Forest Resources and Environment: Prof. WANG FENGYOU
College of Humanities: Prof. WANG YAOXIAN
College of Information and Computer Engineering: WANG NIHONG
College of Landscape Architecture: Prof. ZHUO LIHUAN
College of Transportation: Prof. WANG LIHAI
College of Wildlife Resources: Prof. JIA JINGBO
Correspondence College: CAO XIAOGUANG
Department of Physical Education: Prof. MO SHONGSHAN
Normal College: Prof. SONG YE

PROFESSORS

DING, B., Silviculture
GE, M., Wood Science, Wood Chemistry
HU, Y., Forest Entomology
HUANG, Q., Plan Statistics
JIANG, M., Forestry Economics
LI, G., Forest Resources
LI JIAN, Wood Science and Technology, Wood Surface Chemistry
LI JINGWEN, Ecosystems, Community Ecology
LIU, G., Financial Accounting
LU, R., Wood and Composites Technology and Manufacturing

MA, J., Wildlife Management, Natural Reserves
MA, L., Forest Machinery
NIE, S., Phytocommunity Ecology, Phytotaxonomy
SHAO, L., Forest Disease Epidemiology, Taxonomy of Pathogenic Fungi
SHI, J., Forest Engineering
WANG, F., Ecosystems, Community Ecology
WANG, Y., Ecosystems, Physical and Chemical Ecology
WANG, Z., High Yield Forests
XIAN, K., Forest Protection, Water and Soil Conservation
XIANG, C., Taxonomy of Pathogenic Fungi, Management of Forest Diseases
YUE, S., Pest Control
ZHOU, X., Ecosystems, Economic Ecology
ZHOU, Y., Phytocommunity Ecology, Phytotaxonomy
ZHU, G., Forestry Vehicles, Sawing Equipment
ZU, Y., Unlinear Phytoecology

NORTHEASTERN UNIVERSITY

No. 11, Lane 3, Wenhua Lu, Heping District, Shenyang, 110006 Liaoning
Telephone: (24) 3893000
Fax: (24) 3892454
E-mail: neu@ramm.neu.edu.cn
Internet: www.neu.edu.cn
Founded 1923 as Northeastern University; became Northeast University of Technology in 1950; reverted to former name in 1993
Controlled by Ministry of Metallurgical Industry
Academic year: September to July (2 semesters)
President: HE JICHENG
Vice-Presidents: LIU JIREN, WANG ZHI, YANG PEIZHEN, WANG QIYI, WANG WANSHAN, ZHOU GUANGYOU
Provost: Prof. DUAN YUEHU
Dean of General Affairs: Assoc. Prof. MENG QINGXIAN
Librarian: Prof. YANG HUAI
Library of 1,650,000 vols
Number of teachers: 1,950
Number of students: 18,814 undergraduates, 1,807 postgraduates
Publications: *Basic Automation, China Engineer, Control and Decision, Economics and Management of Metallurgical Enterprise, Journal*

DEANS

Adult Education School: Prof. ZHAO LIANGZHEN
College of Business Administration: Prof. BI MENGLIN
College of Gold Metallurgy: Prof. YANG LI
College of Humanities and Law: Prof. PENG DINGAN
College of Information Science and Engineering: Prof. GU SHUSHENG
College of Materials and Metallurgical Engineering: Prof. HAO SHIMING
College of Mechanical Engineering: Prof. WANG DEJUN
College of Resources and Civil Engineering: Prof. CHEN BAOZHI
Graduate School: Prof. HE JICHENG
Liaoning Branch: Prof. MAO TIANYU
Qinhuangdao Branch: Prof. WANG ZHENFAN

NORTHWEST UNIVERSITY

Tai Bai Bei Lu, Xian 710069, Shaanxi
Telephone: (29) 8302344
Fax: (29) 7232733
Internet: www.nwu.edu.cn
Founded 1912

Academic year: September to August.
President: Prof. HAO KEGANG
Vice-Presidents: CHEN ZONGXING, LIU SHUNKANG, WANG JIAN, WANG SHUANCAI
Librarian: Prof. ZHOU TIANYOU
Library: Library of 1.6 million vols
Number of teachers: 1,135
Number of students: 10,466 (incl. 571 postgraduates)
Publications: *Journal* (arts and social science, natural sciences, 4 a year), *Literature of the Tang Dynasty, Middle East, Studies in Higher Education, Studies in the History of North Western China*.

NORTHWESTERN POLYTECHNICAL UNIVERSITY

Xian 710072, Shaanxi
Telephone: (29) 8493119
Fax: (29) 8491000
E-mail: office@nwpu.edu.cn
Internet: www.nwpu.edu.cn
Founded 1938
State control
Languages of instruction: Chinese, English
Academic year: September to July (2 semesters).
Honorary President: Prof. JI WENMEI
President: Prof. JIANG CHENGYU
Vice-Presidents: Prof. GAO DEYUAN, Prof. WANG RUNXIAN, Prof. WANG WEI, Prof. YUAN JIANPING
Dean of Studies: Prof. WAN XIANPENG
Director of Foreign Affairs: Prof. TANG HONG
Librarian: Prof. GOU WENXUAN
Number of teachers: 1,400

Number of students: 28,000, incl. 5,160 postgraduates
Publications: *Journal of Theoretical and Applied Mechanics* (4 a year), *Mechanical Science and Engineering* (4 a year), *University Journal* (4 a year)

DEANS

College of Continuing Education: Prof. WEI SHENGMIN
College of Marine Engineering: SONG BAOWEI
College of Astronautics: Prof. ZHOU JUN
College of Civil Aviation Engineering: Prof. SUN QIN
College of Materials Science: Prof. LI HEJUN
College of Management: Prof. YE ZHENGYIN
Graduate School: Prof. JIANG CHENGYU
School of Mechatronic Engineering: Prof. ZHANG DINGHUA

PROFESSORS

AI, J. L., Aircraft Design
AN, J. W., Aircraft Automatic Control
BAI, C. R., Aerodynamics
CAI, W. D., Computer Application
CAI, Y. H., Aero-engines
CAO, C. N., Physics
CHEN, C. L., Physics
CHEN, G. D., Mechanics
CHEN, K. A., Noise Control
CHEN, M., Gyroscope and Inertial Navigation
CHEN, S. L., Flight Mechanics
CHEN, Z., Metallic Materials and Heat Treatment
CHENG, G., Signal Measuring and Instruments
CHENG, L. F., Physical Metallurgy
CHU, W. L., Aero-engines
CUI, Y. Z., China Revolutionary History
DAI, G. Z., Theory and Application of Automatic Control
DANG, J. B., Solid Mechanics
DENG, Z. C., Mechanics
DING, X. Q., Applied Mathematics

DUAN, Z. M., Signal Circuit and Systems Engineering
FAN, D., Aero-engines
FAN, M. F., China Revolutionary History
FAN, X. D., High Polymer Material
FAN, X. Y., Computer Application
FANG, Q., Flight Mechanics
FANG, Z. D., Mechanical Engineering
FENG, D., Traditional Chinese Painting
FENG, J. L., Linguistics (Japanese)
FU, H. Z., Physical Metallurgy
FU, L. Z., Mathematics
GAN, X. Y., Linguistics (English)
GAO, D. Y., Computer Science and Engineering
GAO, M. T., Drafting
GAO, X. G., Command Systems Engineering
GAO, Z. H., Aerodynamics
GE, W. J., Machinery Design and Manufacturing
GOU, D. B., Track and Field Sports
GOU, W. X., Solid Mechanics
GU, L. X., Guided Missile Design
GUO, H. Z., Metal Forming
GUO, L., Intelligent Signal Processing
GUO, X. P., Physical Metallurgy
HAO, C. Y., Space Vehicle Design
HE, C. A., Theory and Application of Automatic Control
HE, E. M., Aircraft Control
HE, G. Q., Rocket Engine
HE, H. C., Computer and Artificial Intelligence
HE, M. Y., Signal Circuit and Systems Engineering
HE, W. P., Space Flight Manufacturing Engineering
HE, X. S., General Mechanics
HE, Y. Y., Automatic Control
HU, X. L., Physical Chemistry
HU, Z. G., Computer Software
HUANG, J. G., Applied Electronic Technology
HUANG, Q. Q., Structure Intensity
HUANG, W. D., Physical Metallurgy
JIANG, C. Y., Space Flight Manufacturing Engineering
JIANG, D. W., Applied Mathematics
JIANG, J. S., Structural Mechanics
JIANG, Z. J., Computer Software
JIAO, G. Q., Solid Mechanics
JIE, W. Q., Physical Metallurgy
JIN, B. S., Mechanics of Materials
JING, Z. R., Electronic Engineering
KANG, F. J., Automatic Control
KANG, R. K., Machinery Manufacturing
LAI, X. X., Dialectics of Nature
LEI, Y., Signal Processing
LI, B. X., Rocket Engines
LI, E. P., Physics
LI, F. G., Metal Plasticity Processing
LI, F. W., Aerodynamics
LI, H. J., Metallic Materials and Heat Treatment
LI, H. L., Physical Metallurgy
LI, H. X., Aerodynamics
LI, J. L., Mathematics
LI, J. Z., Political Economy
LI, K. Z., Metallic Materials and Heat Treatment
LI, M. Q., Metal Forming
LI, S. J., Magnetos
LI, S. P., Plasticity Processing
LI, T. H., Materials Processing
LI, W. H., Computer Applications
LI, W. J., Aircraft Design
LI, X. Q., Drafting
LI, Y., Space Flight Manufacturing Engineering
LI, Y. J., Guided Missile Automatic Control
LI, Y. L., Fracture Mechanics
LI, Y. Z., Applied Polymer Science
LI, Z. H., Computer Software
LI, Z. S., Underwater Technology
LIAN, B. W., Radio Communication
LIAN, X. C., Aero-engines

LIANG, G. Q., Space Flight Manufacturing Engineering
LIANG, G. Z., Physical and Chemistry Experiment
LIANG, S. X., Equipment Management
LIAO, M. F., Aero-engines Intensity
LIN, H., Electric Technology
LIU, B., Aero-engines
LIU, B. M., Metal Plasticity Processing
LIU, D., Solid Mechanics
LIU, G., Mechanical Design
LIU, J. H., Welding
LIU, L., Physical Metallurgy
LIU, W. G., Electrical Machinery and Control
LIU, X. L., Aircraft Automatic Control
LIU, Z. T., Metallic Materials and Heat Treatment
LU, B. T., Metallic Materials and Heat Treatment
LU, C. D., Machinery Manufacturing
LU, G. Z., Aircraft Structure Intensity
LU, J. C., Automatic Control
LU, S., Engine Structure Intensity
LU, Z. Z., Solid Mechanics
LUO, C. R., Physics
LUO, X. B., Mathematics
MA, R. Q., Electric Engineering
MA, X. Q., Space Flight Manufacturing Engineering
MA, Y. L, Underwater Acoustics Engineering
MAO, G. W., Rocket Engines
MENG, B. A., Track and Field Sports
MENG, J. M., Linguistics (English)
MO, R., Computer Design
MU, D. J., Theory and Application of Automatic Control
NING, R. C., High Polymer Material
NIU, P. C., Mathematics
OU, Y. J., Applied Mathematics
PAN, J. Y., Management Engineering
PAN, Q., Automatic Control
PEI, C. M., Signal Processing
QI, L. H., Metal Art
QI, S. H., High Polymer Material
QIAN, Z. B., Hot Motive Equipment of the Torpedo
QIAO, S. R., Metallic Materials and Heat Treatment
QIAO, Z. D., Computational Aerodynamics
QIN, X. S., Machinery Manufacturing
QIN, Y. Y., Gyroscope and Inertial Navigation
QING, H. Y., Chemistry
QU, S. R., Drafting
REN, X. M., Aero-engines
SHEN, J., Physical Metallurgy
SHI, H. S., Radio Communication
SHI, K. M., Linguistics (German)
SHI, X. F., Administration
SHI, X. H., Mechanical Engineering
SHI, X. Q., Linguistics (French)
SHI, Y. K., Electrical Equipment
SHI, Y. M., Applied Mathematics
SHI, Y. Y., Ergonomics
SHI, Z. K., Theory and Application of Automatic Control
SONG, B. F., Aircraft Design
SONG, B. W., Machinery Manufacturing
SONG, Z. M., Applied Physics
SU, C. W., Applied Mathematics
SU, K. H., Chemistry
SUN, C., Signal Processing
SUN, G. Z., Drafting
SUN, J. C., Applied Acoustics and Noise Control Engineering
SUN, Q., Aircraft Design
SUN, S. D., Machinery Manufacturing
TANG, G. P., Mathematics
TANG, H., Personnel Management
TANG, S., Flight Mechanics
TANG, Y. Z., Aircraft Automatic Control
TAO, H., Space Flight Manufacturing Engineering
TIAN, C. S., Metallic Materials and Heat Treatment
TIAN, Z., Mathematics
TONG, S. R., Equipment Management

TONG, X. Y., Aircraft Design
TU, Q. P., Signal Processing
WAN, X. P., Aircraft Design
WANG, B., Physics
WANG, J., Linguistics (English)
WANG, J. B., Aircraft Manufacture Engineering
WANG, J. F., Financial Accounting
WANG, L., Rocket Engines
WANG, L. D., Physics
WANG, R. M., Compound Materials
WANG, R. X., Numerically Controlled Machine Tools
WANG, S. M., Basic Electrical Training
WANG, S. M., Mechanics
WANG, W., Aircraft Automatic Control
WANG, X. M., Automatic Control and Computer Application
WANG, Y. C., Hot Motive Equipment of the Torpedo
WANG, Y. M., Underwater Acoustics Engineering
WANG, Y. S., Radio Technology
WANG, Z. S., Motive Equipment Control Engineering
WEI, B. B., Physical Metallurgy
WEI, F., Mechanics of Materials
WEI, S. M., Ergonomics
WENG, Z. Q., Navigation Systems
WU, D. Y., Heat Energy Engineering
WU, H., Aero-engines
WU, J., Computer Software
WU, J. J., Space Flight Manufacturing Engineering
WU, X. G., Torpedo Control
WU, Z. Y., Armoured Concrete Systems
XI, D. K., Aerodynamics
XI, S. M., Metallic Materials and Heat Transfer
XIAO, Y. L., Mathematics
XIE, F. Q., Metal Surface Corrosion
XIN, K., Linguistics (English)
XU, D. M., Torpedo Automatic Control
XU, J. D., Microwave and Antenna Technology
XU, M., Aerodynamics
XU, W., Applied Mathematics
XU, Y. D., Physical Metallurgy
XU, Z., Applied Mathematics
YAN, J., Aircraft Navigation Control
YAN, J. G., Automatic Control
YANG, G. C., Physical Metallurgy
YANG, H., Space Flight Technology
YANG, H. C., Computer Design
YANG, J., Aircraft Automatic Control
YANG, N. D., Systems Engineering
YANG, S. Q., Welding
YANG, Y. F., Linguistics (English)
YANG, Y. N., Aerodynamics
YANG, Y. Q., Metallic Materials and Heat Transfer
YANG, Y. S., Electrical Technology
YANG, Z. C., Solid Mechanics
YANG, Z. Y., Computer Applications
YAO, Z. K., Metal Forming
YE, Z. L., Applied Mathematics
YE, Z. Y., Aerodynamics
YU, H. X., Radio Communication
YUAN, J. P., Flight Mechanics
YUAN, W. Z., Machinery Manufacturing
YUAN, Z. K., Dialectics of Nature
YUE, Z. F., Aircraft Design
ZHANG, A., Command Systems Engineering
ZHANG, B. Q., Aerodynamics
ZHANG, D., Guided Missile Design
ZHANG, D. H., Ergonomics
ZHANG, D. S., Structural Mechanics
ZHANG, H. C., Theory and Application of Automatic Control
ZHANG, H. F., Thermal and Solar Energy Engineering
ZHANG, H. G., Linguistics (German)
ZHANG, H. S., Signal Circuit and Systems Engineering
ZHANG, K. S., Solid Mechanics
ZHANG, K. Y., Applied Mathematics

ZHANG, L. T., Physical Metallurgy
ZHANG, Q. X., Physical Metallurgy
ZHANG, Q. Y., High Polymer Material
ZHANG, S. S., Equipment Engineering
ZHANG, W. G., Aircraft Navigation Control
ZHANG, W. H., Space Flight Manufacturing Engineering
ZHANG, X. A., Building Structure
ZHANG, X. K., Space Flight Manufacturing Engineering
ZHANG, X. M., Detonator Technology
ZHANG, Y. M., Torpedo Design
ZHANG, Y. Y., Computer Software
ZHANG, Y. Z., Automatic Control
ZHAO, J. L., Modern Optics Application
ZHAO, J. W., Sound Electronic Engineering of Water
ZHAO, R. C., Signal and Graph Processing
ZHAO, S. Z., Machinery Manufacturing
ZHAO, X. A., Linguistics (English)
ZHAO, X. M., Mathematics
ZHAO, X. P., Solid Mechanics
ZHAO, Y. S., General Mechanics
ZHAO, Z. W., Computer Software
ZHI, B. S., Automatic Control
ZHI, X. Z., General Mechanics
ZHOU, D. Y., Command Systems Engineering
ZHOU, J., Aircraft Navigation Control
ZHOU, J. H., Analysis and Design of Control Systems
ZHOU, Q., Automatic Control
ZHOU, W. C., Physical Metallurgy
ZHOU, X. S., Computer Applications
ZHOU, Y. H., Physical Metallurgy
ZHOU, Z., Flight Mechanics
ZHU, H. R., Heat Energy Engineering
ZHU, J. Q., Aero-engines
ZHU, M. Q., Measurement Control in Mechanical Engineering
ZHU, X. P., Automatic Control
ZHU, Y. A., Computer Applications
ZOU, G. R., Materials Processing Engineering

PEKING UNIVERSITY

5 Yiheyuan Rd, Haidian, Beijing 100871
Telephone: (10) 62752114
Fax: (10) 62751207
Internet: www.pku.edu.cn
Founded 1898
Languages of instruction: Chinese, English
Academic year: September to June

President: XU ZHIHONG
Vice-Presidents: CHEN ZHANGLIANG, CHI HUISHENG, HAN QIDE, HAO PING, HE FANGCHUAN, LII ZHAOFENG, LIN JIUXIANG, LIN JUNJING, MIN WEIFANG
Registrar: LI KE'AN
Librarian: DAI LONGJI

Library of 4,610,000 vols
Number of teachers: 4,537
Number of students: 55,000

Publication: *Peking University Academic Journal.*

PEKING UNION MEDICAL COLLEGE

9 Dong Dan San Tiao, Dongcheng District, Beijing 100730
Telephone: (10) 65295912
Fax: (10) 65133086
E-mail: liudp@pumc.edu.cn
Internet: www.pumc.edu.cn
Founded 1917
Academic year: September to July

President: LIU DEPEI
Vice-Presidents: HE WEI, LIU QIAN, LU CHONGMEI, QI KEMING, SONG XUEMIN
Head of Graduate Department: LIU DEPEI
Librarian: WANG ZHAOLING

Number of teachers: 3,328

Publications: *Acta Academiae Medicinae Sinicae* (6 a year), *Bilingual Journal of Medicine International* (6 a year), *Chinese Chemical Letters* (12 a year), *Journal of Asian Natural Products Research* (4 a year)

DEANS

Cancer Hospital: ZHAO PING
Fu Wai Hospital: HU SHENGSHOU
Institute of Materia Medica: WANG XIAOLIANG
Institute of Medical Biology Technology: JIANG JIANDONG
Orthopaedic Surgery Hospital: QI KEMING
Peking Union Medical College Hospital: LIU QIAN
School of Basic Medical Sciences: ZHENG DEXIAN
School of Nursing: SHEN NING

PROFESSORS

BAO, XIULAN, Peking Union Medical College Hospital
CAI, BOQIANG, Peking Union Medical College Hospital
CAI, LIXING, Peking Union Medical College Hospital
CAI, WEIMING, Cancer Hospital
CAO, JIMIN, School of Basic Medical Sciences
CHEN, CUANXIA, Peking Union Medical College Hospital
CHEN, DECHANG, Peking Union Medical College Hospital
CHEN, GUOZHANG, Orthopaedic Surgery Hospital
CHEN, HONGSHAN, Institute of Medical Biology Technology
CHEN, JIE, Peking Union Medical College Hospital
CHEN, TINGYUAN, Peking Union Medical College Hospital
CHEN, XI, Fu Wai Hospital
CHU, DATONG, Cancer Hospital
DAI, JINGLEI, Cancer Hospital
DAI, YUHUA, Peking Union Medical College Hospital
DONG, JINGWU, Peking Union Medical College Hospital
DONG, YI, Peking Union Medical College Hospital
FAN, JINCAI, Orthopaedic Surgery Hospital
FANG, DEFU, School of Basic Medical Sciences
FANG, QI, Peking Union Medical College Hospital
GAO, JUZHEN, Cancer Hospital
GAO, RUNLIN, Fu Wai Hospital
GU, DAZHONG, Cancer Hospital
GU, DONGFENG, Fu Wai Hospital
GUAN, YAN, Peking Union Medical College Hospital
GUANG, YAO, Peking Union Medical College Hospital
GUI, LAI, Orthopaedic Surgery Hospital
GUO, HUIYUAN, Institute of Medical Biology Technology
GUO, YUZHEN, Peking Union Medical College Hospital
HA, XIANGWEN, Cancer Hospital
HAO, YUZHI, Cancer Hospital
HE, ZHAMA, Fu Wai Hospital
HE, ZHUGEN, Cancer Hospital
HONG, FENGYI, Cancer Hospital
HONG, WANJUN, Cancer Hospital
HU, JINGQUN, Cancer Hospital
HU, SHENGSHOU, Fu Wai Hospital
HUANG, GUOJUN, Cancer Hospital
HUANG, HANYUAN, Peking Union Medical College Hospital
HUANG, LIANG, Institute of Materia Medica
HUANG, XIZHEN, Peking Union Medical College Hospital
HUANG, YIRONG, Cancer Hospital
HUI, RUTAI, Fu Wai Hospital
JI, BAOHUA, Peking Union Medical College Hospital
JI, XIAOCHENG, Peking Union Medical College Hospital

JIANG, JIANDONG, Institute of Medical Biology Technology
JIANG, MING, Peking Union Medical College Hospital
JIANG, XIUFANG, Peking Union Medical College Hospital
JIANG, ZHUMING, Peking Union Medical College Hospital
JIAO, HAIYAN, Peking Union Medical College Hospital
JIN, LAN, Peking Union Medical College Hospital
LI, CHANGLING, Cancer Hospital
LI, DIANDONG, Institute of Medical Biology Technology
LI, HANHONG, Peking Union Medical College Hospital
LI, JIAXIU, Cancer Hospital
LI, KUI, Cancer Hospital
LI, LIHUAN, Fu Wai Hospital
LI, LING, Cancer Hospital
LI, LONGYU, Peking Union Medical College Hospital
LI, QINGHONG, Cancer Hospital
LI, SENKAI, Orthopaedic Surgery Hospital
LI, TAISHENG, Cancer Hospital
LI, ZEJIAN, Peking Union Medical College Hospital
LIANG, XIAOTIAN, Institute of Materia Medica
LIANG, ZHIQUAN, School of Basic Medical Sciences
LIU, DAWEI, Peking Union Medical College Hospital
LIU, DEPEI, School of Basic Medical Sciences
LIU, FUSHENG, Cancer Hospital
LIU, GENTAO, Institute of Materia Medica
LIU, JINGSHENG, School of Basic Medical Sciences
LIU, LIYING, Cancer Hospital
LIU, QIAN, Peking Union Medical College Hospital
LIU, RUIXUE, Peking Union Medical College Hospital
LIU, SHUFAN, Cancer Hospital
LIU, TONGHUA, Peking Union Medical College Hospital
LIU, XINFAN, Cancer Hospital
LIU, YULING, Institute of Materia Medica
LIU, YUQING, Fu Wai Hospital
LIU, ZHONGXUN, Institute of Medical Biology Technology
LOU, ZHIXIAN, Institute of Medical Biology Technology
LU, CHONGMEI, School of Nursing
LU, NING, Cancer Hospital
LU, WEIXUAN, Peking Union Medical College Hospital
LUO, HUIYUAN, Peking Union Medical College Hospital
LUO, WEICI, Peking Union Medical College Hospital
MIAO, YANJUN, Cancer Hospital
OU YANG, HAN, Cancer Hospital
PAN, QINJING, Cancer Hospital
PAN, YANRUO, Peking Union Medical College Hospital
PU, JIELIN, Fu Wai Hospital
QI, KEMING, Orthopaedic Surgery Hospital
QI, MEIFU, Peking Union Medical College Hospital
QI, YONGFA, Cancer Hospital
QIANG, TUNAN, Cancer Hospital
QIAO, SHUBIN, Fu Wai Hospital
QIN, DEXING, Cancer Hospital
QIU, GUIXING, Peking Union Medical College Hospital
QIU, HUIZHONG, Peking Union Medical College Hospital
REN, YUZHU, Peking Union Medical College Hospital
SHAO, YONGFU, Cancer Hospital
SHEN, NING, School of Nursing
SHI, MULAN, Cancer Hospital
SHI, YUANKAI, Cancer Hospital
SONG, ZONGLU, Peking Union Medical College Hospital

SU, XUEZENG, Cancer Hospital
SUN, GENGTIAN, Cancer Hospital
SUN, JIANHENG, Cancer Hospital
SUN, LI, Cancer Hospital
SUN, LIXHONG, Fu Wai Hospital
SUN, NIANGU, Peking Union Medical College Hospital
SUN, YAN, Cancer Hospital
SUN, YINGLONG, Fu Wai Hospital
TANG, BANGCI, Peking Union Medical College Hospital
TANG, PINGZHANG, Cancer Hospital
TANG, WEISONG, Peking Union Medical College Hospital
TU, GIYI, Cancer Hospital
WANG, DANHUA, Peking Union Medical College Hospital
WANG, JIAQI, Orthopaedic Surgery Hospital
WANG, JINWAN, Cancer Hospital
WANG, LIANGJUN, Cancer Hospital
WANG, LUHUA, Cancer Hospital
WANG, MEI, Cancer Hospital
WANG, QILU, Cancer Hospital
WANG, SHIZHEN, Peking Union Medical College Hospital
WANG, XHISHI, Peking Union Medical College Hospital
WANG, XIAOMING, School of Basic Medical Sciences
WANG, YIPENG, Peking Union Medical College Hospital
WEI, MIN, Peking Union Medical College Hospital
WU, AIRU, Cancer Hospital
WU, NING, Cancer Hospital
WU, NING, Peking Union Medical College Hospital
WU, YANGFENG, Fu Wai Hospital
XI, ZHI, Cancer Hospital
XU, BINGHE, Cancer Hospital
XU, BINGZE, Cancer Hospital
XU, CHENGSU, School of Basic Medical Sciences
XU, GUOZHEN, Cancer Hospital
XU, JINGQIN, Peking Union Medical College Hospital
XU, LETIAN, Peking Union Medical College Hospital
XU, ZHENGANG, Cancer Hospital
YANG, GONGHUAN, School of Basic Medical Sciences
YANG, LIN, Cancer Hospital
YANG, YAOJIN, Fu Wai Hospital
YANG, ZIBIN, School of Basic Medical Sciences
YE, QIBIN, Peking Union Medical College Hospital
YIN, WEIBO, Cancer Hospital
YOU, KAI, Peking Union Medical College Hospital
YU, DEQUAN, Institute of Materia Medica
YU, GAOZHI, Cancer Hospital
YU, GUORUI, Cancer Hospital
YU, HONGZHAO, Cancer Hospital
YU, MENGXUE, Peking Union Medical College Hospital
YU, XHIHAO, Cancer Hospital
YUE, JILIANG, Orthopaedic Surgery Hospital
ZENG, XIAOFENG, Peking Union Medical College Hospital
ZENG, XUAN, School of Basic Medical Sciences
ZHAN, RUGANG, Cancer Hospital
ZHANG, BAONING, Cancer Hospital
ZHANG, DAWEI, Cancer Hospital
ZHANG, DECHANG, School of Basic Medical Sciences
ZHANG, DECHAO, Cancer Hospital
ZHANG, DELI, Peking Union Medical College Hospital
ZHANG, FENCHUN, Peking Union Medical College Hospital
ZHANG, HONGXING, Cancer Hospital
ZHANG, HUILAN, Fu Wai Hospital
ZHANG, JIANXI, Peking Union Medical College Hospital
ZHANG, SHIYUAN, Peking Union Medical College Hospital

ZHANG, WENHUA, Cancer Hospital
ZHANG, XHIXIAN, Cancer Hospital
ZHANG, XIANGRU, Cancer Hospital
ZHANG, XUE, School of Basic Medical Sciences
ZHANG, YOUJU, Peking Union Medical College Hospital
ZHANG, ZHENHAN, Peking Union Medical College Hospital
ZHANG, ZHIPING, Institute of Medical Biology Technology
ZHAO, MIN, Orthopaedic Surgery Hospital
ZHAO, PING, Cancer Hospital
ZHAO, SHIHUA, Fu Wai Hospital
ZHAO, SHIMIN, Peking Union Medical College Hospital
ZHAO, YAN, Peking Union Medical College Hospital
ZHAO, YUPEI, Peking Union Medical College Hospital
ZHEN, YONGSU, Institute of Medical Biology Technology
ZHENG, DEXIAN, School of Basic Medical Sciences
ZHONG, SHOUGUANG, Peking Union Medical College Hospital
ZHOU, JICHANG, Cancer Hospital
ZHOU, QIAN, Peking Union Medical College Hospital
ZHOU, XHUNWU, Cancer Hospital
ZHOU, YANMIN, Peking Union Medical College Hospital
ZHU, CHUANQIU, Peking Union Medical College Hospital
ZHU, DAHIA, School of Basic Medical Sciences
ZHU, GUANGJI, School of Basic Medical Sciences
ZHU, JUN, Fu Wai Hospital
ZHU, LI, Peking Union Medical College Hospital
ZHU, WENLING, Peking Union Medical College Hospital
ZHU, XIAODONG, Fu Wai Hospital
ZHUANG, HONGXING, Orthopaedic Surgery Hospital
ZHUI, YUANYU, Peking Union Medical College Hospital

QINGHAI NATIONALITIES COLLEGE

25 Ba Yi Rd, Xining 810007, Qinghai
Telephone: 76803
Founded 1949
Pres: DUO JIE JIAN ZAN
Vice-Pres: SHAO DESHAN, Assoc. Prof. YU DEYUAN, ZHUO MA CAI DAN
Librarian: YAO KERANG
Library of 550,000 vols
Number of teachers: 330
Number of students: 1,572
Publications: *Journal of Qinghai Nationalities Institute*, *Qinghai Nationalities Research*

PROFESSORS

FENG, Y., Theory of Arts
HU, A., Ancient Chinese
MI, Y., History of Chinese
ZHU, K., Modern Literature

QUFU NORMAL UNIVERSITY

57 Jingxuanxi Rd, Qufu 273165, Shandong
Telephone: (537) 4458831
Fax: (537) 4455669
Internet: www.qfnu.edu.cn
Founded 1955
Academic year: September to July
President: TIAN DEQUAN
Librarian: DU YU
Library of 1,880,000 vols
Number of teachers: 2,200
Number of students: 42,000

Publications: *Journal* (4 a year), *Qilu Journal* (6 a year)

DEANS

College of Literature: XUE YONGWU
College of Mathematics Science: (vacant)

PROFESSORS

CHEN, KESHOU, Literature
CHEN, QINGPING, Literature
DAN, CHENGBIN, Literature
GAO, SHANGQU, Literature
LIU, FENGGUANG, Literature
LIU, XINSHENG, Literature
LIU, YAOJIN, Literature
PU, ZHAOLIN, Literature
QIAN, JIAQING, Literature
TANG, XUENING, Literature
XU, ZHENGUI, Literature
XUE, YONGWU, Literature
ZHANG, LIANRANG, Literature
ZHANG, QUANZHI, Literature
ZHAO, DONGSHUAN, Literature
ZHAO, LIMING, Literature
ZHENG, JIEWEN, Literature

ATTACHED RESEARCH INSTITUTE
Adult Education College: Dir DU YIDE.

RENMIN UNIVERSITY OF CHINA

39 Haidian Rd, Haidian District, Beijing 100872
Telephone: (10) 62563399
Fax: (10) 62566374
Internet: www.ruc.edu.cn
Founded 1937
State control
Academic year: starts September
President: LI WENHAI
Vice-Presidents: DU HOUWEN, LI KANGTAI, LI SHAOGONG, LUO GUOJIE, MA SHAOMENG, YANG DEFU, ZHENG HANGSHENG
Librarian: DAI YI
Number of teachers: 1,595
Number of students: 14,289 (incl. 1,284 postgraduates)
Publications: *Archival News* (6 a year), *Economic Theory and Business Management*, *Information Service News*, *International Journalism World* (4 a year), *Learned Journal of the People's University of China* (6 a year), *Population Research, Teaching and Research*, *The History of Qing Dynasty Research Newsletter*.

SHAANXI NORMAL UNIVERSITY

199 Chang'an South Rd, Xian 710062, Shaanxi
Telephone: (29) 85308992
Fax: (29) 85307025
Internet: www.snnu.edu.cn
Founded 1944
Ministry of Education control
Academic year: September to July
President: FANG YU
Vice-Presidents: XIAO ZHENGHONG, ZHANG JIANXIANG, ZHAO BIN, ZHOU DEMING
Head of Graduate Department: LI JIKAI
Librarian: YANG ENCHENG
Number of teachers: 2,600
Number of students: 40,000
Publications: *Journal* (natural sciences, quarterly), *Journal* (philosophy and social sciences, 6 a year)

DEANS

College of Arts: HU YUKANG
College of Chemistry and Materials Science: ZHANG CHENGXIAO
College of Chinese Language and Literature: LI XIJIAN

College of Computer Science: FENG DEMIN
College of Educational Science: YOU XUJUN
College of Food Engineering: CHEN JINPING
College of Foreign Languages: MA ZHENYI
College of Further Education: JIA WENXING
College of History and Civilization: JIA ERQIANG
College of International Business: LI ZHONGMIN
College of Life Sciences: WANG ZHEZHI
College of Mathematics and Information Science: WU JIANHUA
College of News and Media: LIU LU
College of Physical Education: LI ZHENBIN
College of Physics and Information Technology: ZHAO WEI
College of Political Economy: WANG ZHENYA
College of Teachers and Administrators: GONG JIANGUO
College of Tourism and the Environment: HUANG CHUNCHANG
e-College: LU JIURU

PROFESSORS

CAO, HAN, Computer Science
CAO, HUAIXIN, Mathematics and Information Science
CAO, WEIAN, History and Civilization
CHANG, JINCANG, History and Civilization
CHEN, FENG, History and Civilization
CHEN, JINPING, Life Science
CHEN, JINPING, Food Engineering
CHEN, XIAORUI, Educational Science
CHEN, YASHAO, Chemistry and Materials Science
DANG, HUAIXING, Chinese Language and Literature
DU, HONGKE, Mathematics and Information Science
DU, JIULIN, Physics and Information Technology
DU, WENYU, History and Civilization
DUAN, YUFENG, Food Engineering
FANG, YU, Chemistry and Materials Science
FENG, DEMING, Computer Science
FENG, WENLOU, Chinese Language and Literature
FU, SHAOLIANG, Chinese Language and Literature
GUO, MIN, Computer Science
GUO, QINNA, Chinese Language and Literature
HAO, WENWU, Educational Science
HE, JUHOU, Computer Science
HU, ANSHUN, Chinese Language and Literature
HU, DAODAO, Chemistry and Materials Science
HU, JI, History and Civilization
HU, MANCHENG, Chemistry and Materials Science
HUANG, QIN-AN, Mathematics and Information Science
HUANG, YUAN, Life Science
HUO, SONGLIN, Chinese Language and Literature
HUO, YOUMING, Chinese Language and Literature
JI, GUOXING, Mathematics and Information Science
JIA, ERQIANG, History and Civilization
LI, BAOLIN, Chemistry and Materials Science
LI, BAOXIN, Chemistry and Materials Science
LI, GUOQING, Educational Science
LI, HONGWU, Educational Science
LI, HUISHI, Mathematics and Information Science
LI, JIANFENG, Food Engineering
LI, JIKAI, Chinese Language and Literature
LI, QUANLU, Physics and Information Technology
LI, SHENGGANG, Mathematics and Information Science
LI, WANSHE, Mathematics and Information Science
LI, XIJIAN, Chinese Language and Literature

LI, YONGFANG, Physics and Information Technology
LI, YONGMING, Mathematics and Information Science
LI, YUMIN, History and Civilization
LI, ZHEN, Chinese Language and Literature
LIAN, ZHENMIN, Life Science
LIANG, DAOLI, Chinese Language and Literature
LIN, SHUYU, Physics and Information Technology
LIU, FENGDAO, Chinese Language and Literature
LIU, JING, Chinese Language and Literature
LIU, LU, News and Media
LIU, PENG, Physics and Information Technology
LIU, XINKE, Educational Science
LIU, XINPING, Mathematics and Information Science
LIU, ZHAOTIE, Chemistry and Materials Science
LIU, ZONGHUAI, Chemistry and Materials Science
LU, JIURU, Chemistry and Materials Science
LUO, ZENGRU, Mathematics and Information Science
MA, GEDONG, Chinese Language and Literature
MA, ZHENDUO, Foreign Languages
MIAO, RUNCAI, Physics and Information Technology
NIU, YONG, Physics and Information Technology
QIU, GUOYONG, Computer Science
QIU, NONGXUE, Food Engineering
QIU, XUENONG, Life Science
QU, YAJUN, Chinese Language and Literature
REN, YI, Life Science
RUN, QINGSHENG, Chinese Language and Literature
SHANG, ZHIYUAN, Physics and Information Technology
SHE, XIAOPING, Life Science
SUN, RUNGUANG, Physics and Information Technology
TANG, YIGONG, History and Civilization
TIAN, CHENRUI, Life Science
TIAN, JIANRONG, Educational Science
WANG, BO, Chemistry and Materials Science
WANG, CHENRUI, Food Engineering
WANG, GUOJUN, Mathematics and Information Science
WANG, HUI, History and Civilization
WANG, SHUANGHUAI, History and Civilization
WANG, WENLIANG, Chemistry and Materials Science
WANG, XIAOAN, Life Science
WANG, XIAOMING, Computer Science
WANG, XILI, Computer Science
WANG, XIN, Physics and Information Technology
WANG, YINGZONG, Physics and Information Technology
WANG, YINHUI, Computer Science
WANG, ZHEZHI, Life Science
WANG, ZHIWU, Chinese Language and Literature
WEI, GENGYUAN, Chinese Language and Literature
WEI, JIANGUO, Chinese Language and Literature
WEI, JUNFA, Chemistry and Materials Science
WU, BAOWEI, Mathematics and Information Science
WU, HONGBO, Mathematics and Information Science
WU, JIANHUA, Mathematics and Information Science
WU, YANSHENG, Chinese Language and Literature
WU, ZHENQIANG, Computer Science
XI, GENGSI, Life Science
XIAO, ZHENGHONG, History and Civilization

XING, XIANGDONG, Chinese Language and Literature
XUE, PINGSHUAN, History and Civilization
YANG, CUNTANG, History and Civilization
YANG, ENCHENG, Chinese Language and Literature
YANG, HEQING, Chemistry and Materials Science
YANG, HONGKE, Chinese Language and Literature
YANG, WANMIN, Physics and Information Technology
YANG, ZUPEI, Chemistry and Materials Science
YIN, SHENGPING, History and Civilization
YOU, XILIN, Chinese Language and Literature
YOU, XUQUN, Educational Science
YUAN, LIN, History and Civilization
ZANG, ZHEN, History and Civilization
ZHANG, CHENGXIAO, Chemistry and Materials Science
ZHANG, GUOJUN, Chinese Language and Literature
ZHANG, JIANHUA, Mathematics and Information Science
ZHANG, JIANMIN, Physics and Information Technology
ZHANG, JIANZHONG, Mathematics and Information Science
ZHANG, MAORONG, History and Civilization
ZHANG, XIAOLING, Chemistry and Materials Science
ZHANG, XINKE, Chinese Language and Literature
ZHANG, XUEZHONG, Chinese Language and Literature
ZHANG, YUHU, Chemistry and Materials Science
ZHANG, ZHIQI, Chemistry and Materials Science
ZHANG, ZHUJUN, Chemistry and Materials Science
ZHAO, BIN, Mathematics and Information Science
ZHAO, SHICHAO, History and Civilization
ZHAO, WANGQIN, Chinese Language and Literature
ZHENG, XINGWANG, Chemistry and Materials Science
ZHENG, ZHEMIN, Life Science
ZHOU, TIANYOU, History and Civilization

SHAANXI UNIVERSITY OF SCIENCE AND TECHNOLOGY

49 Renmin West Rd, Xianyang 712081, Shaanxi

Telephone: (910) 3579500
Fax: (910) 3579700
Internet: www.sust.edu.cn

Founded 1958
Academic year: September to July

President: LUO HONGJIE
Vice-Presidents: CAO JUJIANG, CUI JIHUA, SHEN YIDING, ZHANG MEIYUN
Head of Graduate Department: ZHANG XIAOLEI
Librarian: GAO DONGQIANG

Number of teachers: 900
Number of students: 18,000

Publications: *The Future* (6 a year), *Journal* (6 a year)

DEANS

College of Chemistry and Chemical Engineering: ZHANG GUANGHUA
College of Computer and Information Engineering: CHEN HUA
College of Design: YANG JUNSHUN
College of Electrical and Electronic Engineering: MENG YANJING
College of Electromechanical Engineering: DANG XINAN

College of Life Sciences and Engineering: CHEN HE
College of Management: YAN YUJIE
College of Materials Science and Engineering: WANG XIUFENG
College of Paper Manufacture Engineering: ZHANG MEIYUN
College of Resources and the Environment: MA JIANZHONG
College of Science: LIN XIAOLIN
College of Vocational Technology (Xian): LI WENHAN
College of Vocational Technology (Xianyan): ZHANG WEIPING
Department of Foreign Languages: LI XIAO-HONG

PROFESSORS

CHEN, HE, Life Sciences and Engineering
CHEN, HUA, Computer and Information Engineering
CHEN, JUNZHI, Chemistry and Chemical Engineering
CHEN, MANRU, Design
CHEN, TAILUN, Science
CHENG, FENGXIA, Resources and the Environment
DANG, HONGSHE, Electrical and Electronic Engineering
DANG, SISHAN, Science
DANG, XIN-AN, Electromechanical Engineering
DONG, WENBIN, Life Sciences and Engineering
DU, RUIQING, Foreign Languages
GAN, JIANZHI, Design
GONG, TAISHENG, Resources and the Environment
HOU, ZAIEN, Science
LI, GUOXING, Science
LI, LINSHENG, Chemistry and Chemical Engineering
LI, XI, Electrical and Electronic Engineering
LI, XIAORUI, Chemistry and Chemical Engineering
LI, ZHONGJIN, Chemistry and Chemical Engineering
LIN, XIAOLIN, Computer and Information Engineering
LIU, SHUXING, Life Sciences and Engineering
LU, JIALI, Life Sciences and Engineering
LU, XINGFANG, Resources and the Environment
LUO, CANGXUE, Life Sciences and Engineering
LUO, HONGJIE, Materials Science and Engineering
MA, JIANZHONG, Resources and the Environment
MENG, YANJING, Electrical and Electronic Engineering
MIAO, HONGYAN, Materials Science and Engineering
NING, DUO, Electrical and Electronic Engineering
QI, XIANGJUN, Life Sciences and Engineering
QIANG, XIHUAI, Resources and the Environment
SHAN, JINGMIN, Design
SHEN, YIDING, Chemistry and Chemical Engineering
SONG, HONGXIN, Life Sciences and Engineering
SUN, YU, Electrical and Electronic Engineering
TIAN, SANDE, Life Sciences and Engineering
WANG, DEZHONG, Design
WANG, FENG, Materials Science and Engineering
WANG, HONGRU, Resources and the Environment
WANG, JIANGEN, Resources and the Environment
WANG, LIANJIE, Life Sciences and Engineering

WANG, MENGXIAO, Electrical and Electronic Engineering
WANG, QUANJIE, Resources and the Environment
WANG, XIUFENG, Materials Science and Engineering
WANG, XUECHUAN, Resources and the Environment
XU, JIANZHONG, Foreign Languages
XU, MUDAN, Life Sciences and Engineering
YANG, JIANZHOU, Chemistry and Chemical Engineering
YANG, JUNSHUN, Design
YU, CONGZHEN, Resources and the Environment
YU, DAYUAN, Electrical and Electronic Engineering
ZHANG, CHUANBO, Resources and the Environment
ZHANG, GUANGHUA, Chemistry and Chemical Engineering
ZHANG, XIAOLEI, Resources and the Environment
ZHANG, ZHENGXI, Computer and Information Engineering
ZHENG, ENRANG, Electrical and Electronic Engineering
ZHOU, LIAN, Materials Science and Engineering
ZHU, ZHENFENG, Materials Science and Engineering

SHANDONG UNIVERSITY

Shanda Nanlu, Shandong 250100, Jinan
Telephone: (531) 8364701
Fax: (531) 8565657
Internet: www.sdu.edu.cn

Founded 1901
Ministry of Education control
Academic year: September to July

President: ZHAN TAO
Vice-Presidents: FAN HONGJIAN, FANG HONGJIAN, HU JIACHEN, LI CHENGJUN, WANG QILONG, YU XIUPING, ZHANG YONGBING
Head of Graduate Department: WANG QILONG
Librarian: SU WEIZHI

Number of teachers: 3,154
Number of students: 50,000

Publications: *Folk Custom Research* (4 a year), *Journal of Literature, History and Philosophy* (6 a year), *Journal of Shandong University* (editions: philosophy and social sciences; natural sciences; health science; engineering science, 6 a year), *Studies of Zhouyi* (6 a year), *Young Thinker* (6 a year)

DEANS

School of Business Administration: XU XIANGYI
School of Chemistry and Chemical Engineering: JIANG JIANZHUANG
School of Civil Engineering: CAO SHENGLE
School of Computer Science and Technology: MENG XIANGXU
School of Continuing Education: ZHUANG PING
School of Control Science and Engineering: JIA LEI
School of Dentistry: YANG PISHAN
School of Economics: ZANG XUHENG
School of Electrical Engineering: ZHAO JIANGUO
School of Energy and Power Engineering: PAN JIHONG
School of Environmental Science and Engineering: GAO BAOYU
School of Fine Arts: LI XIAOFENG
School of Foreign Languages and Literature: WANG SHOUYUAN
School of History and Culture: WANG YUJI

School of Information Science and Engineering: YUAN DONGFENG
School of Law: CHEN JINZHAO
School of Life Sciences: QU YINBO
School of Literature and Journalism: CHEN YAN
School of Marxist Theory of Education: ZHOU XIANGJUN
School of Materials Science and Engineering: JIANG MINHUA
School of Mathematics: LIU JIANYA
School of Mechanical Engineering: LI JIANFENG
School of Medicine: ZHANG YUN
School of Nursing: LOU FENGLAN
School of Pharmacy: LOU HONGXIANG
School of Philosophy and Social Development: FU YOUDE
School of Physics and Microelectronics: XIE SHIJIE
School of Political Science and Public Administration: LIU YUAN
School of Public Health: ZHAOS ZHONGTANG

PROFESSORS

BAI, ZENGLIANG, Life Sciences
BAO, SITAO, Literature and Journalism
BAO, XIAOMING, Life Sciences
BAO, YIFEI, Civil Engineering
BIAN, XIUFANG, Materials Science and Engineering
BU, YUXIANG, Chemistry and Chemical Engineering
CAI, LUZHONG, Information Science and Engineering
CAI, ZHENGTING, Chemistry and Chemical Engineering
CAO, CHENGBO, Chemistry and Chemical Engineering
CAO, QINGJIE, Mathematics
CAO, SHENGLE, Civil Engineering
CHAO, ZHONGCHEN, History and Culture
CHEN, CHUANZHONG, Materials Science and Engineering
CHEN, DAIRONG, Chemistry and Chemical Engineering
CHEN, GUANJUN, Life Sciences
CHEN, HONG, Foreign Languages and Literature
CHEN, JIGUANG, Civil Engineering
CHEN, KAOSHAN, Life Sciences
CHEN, LIANBI, Medicine
CHEN, QINGLAI, Civil Engineering
CHEN, SHANGSHENG, History and Culture
CHEN, SHAOZHU, Mathematics
CHEN, SHENHAO, Chemistry and Chemical Engineering
CHEN, XIAO, Chemistry and Chemical Engineering
CHEN, XISHEN, Materials Science and Engineering
CHEN, YAN, Literature and Journalism
CHEN, ZENGJING, Mathematics
CHEN, ZHIJUN, Business Administration
CHEN, ZIAN, History and Culture
CHENG, XINGKUI, Physics and Microelectronics
CHENG, ZHAOLIN, Mathematics
CHI, ZHENMING, Life Sciences
CONG, YAPING, Foreign Languages and Literature
CUI, DAYONG, History and Culture
CUI, XI, Public Health
CUI, XING, Medicine
CUI, ZHAOJIE, Environmental Science and Engineering
DING, RONGGUI, Business Administration
DING, SHILIANG, Physics and Microelectronics
DING, SHILIANG, Chemistry and Chemical Engineering
DING, YUANMING, Philosophy and Social Development
DUAN, QI, Mathematics
EHRLICH, M. A., Philosophy and Social Development
FAN, JINXUE, Law

FAN, XIULING, Business Administration
FANG, HUI, History and Culture
FANG, LEI, Political Science and Public Administration
FENG, DACHENG, Chemistry and Chemical Engineering
FENG, DIANMEI, Law
FENG, MEILI, Nursing
FENG, SHENGYU, Chemistry and Chemical Engineering
FU, YONGJUN, Philosophy and Social Development
FU, YOUDE, Philosophy and Social Development
GAN, YING, Business Administration
GAO, BAOYU, Chemistry and Chemical Engineering
GAO, BAOYU, Environmental Science and Engineering
GAO, JIANGUO, Philosophy and Social Development
GAO, PEIJI, Life Sciences
GAO, RUWEI, Physics and Microelectronics
GAO, YINGMAO, Medicine
GAO, ZHENMING, Information Science and Engineering
GE, BENYI, Literature and Journalism
GENG, HAORAN, Materials Science and Engineering
GENG, JIANHUA, Literature and Journalism
GENG, ZUNJING, Civil Engineering
GONG, YAOQIN, Medicine
GU, LUANZHAI, History and Culture
GU, QINGMIN, Medicine
GU, YUEZHU, Chemistry and Chemical Engineering
GUAN, SHAOJI, History and Culture
GUAN, XIAOJUN, Materials Science and Engineering
GUO, DAJUN, Mathematics
GUO, JIDE, Foreign Languages and Literature
GUO, YANLI, Literature and Journalism
HAN, SHENGHAO, Physics and Microelectronics
HAO, AIYOU, Chemistry and Chemical Engineering
HAO, JINGCHENG, Chemistry and Chemical Engineering
HE, MAO, Physics and Microelectronics
HE, ZHONGHUA, Philosophy and Social Development
HONG, XIAOGUANG, Computer Science and Technology
HOU, WANGUO, Chemistry and Chemical Engineering
HOU, XUEYUAN, Information Science and Engineering
HU, JIFAN, Physics and Microelectronics
HU, PEICHU, Mathematics
HU, WEICHENG, Medicine
HU, WEIQING, History and Culture
HU, WENRONG, Environmental Science and Engineering
HU, XINSHENG, History and Culture
HU, ZHENGMING, Business Administration
HUANG, FAYOU, Literature and Journalism
HUANG, FENG, Life Sciences
HUANG, QINGZHI, Political Science and Public Administration
HUANG, SHENG, Civil Engineering
HUANG, WANHUA, Literature and Journalism
HUANG, XIRONG, Chemistry and Chemical Engineering
JI, AIGUO, Pharmacy
JI, FAHAN, Literature and Journalism
JI, PEIRONG, Political Science and Public Administration
JI, YUNXIA, Foreign Languages and Literature
JIA, LEI, Control Science and Engineering
JIA, ZHIPING, Computer Science and Technology
JIANG, BAOFA, Public Health
JIANG, JIANZHUANG, Chemistry and Chemical Engineering

JIANG, MINHUA, Materials Science and Engineering
JIANG, QINGLI, Environmental Science and Engineering
JIANG, SHENG, History and Culture
JIANG, SHOULI, Mathematics
JIANG, YONG, Philosophy and Social Development
JIN, WENRUI, Chemistry and Chemical Engineering
KONG, FANJIN, Literature and Journalism
KONG, JIAN, Life Sciences
KONG, LINGREN, History and Culture
LI, CHUANLIN, Computer Science and Technology
LI, DAIBIN, Control Science and Engineering
LI, DAXING, Mathematics
LI, FENGXIAN, Environmental Science and Engineering
LI, GANZUO, Chemistry and Chemical Engineering
LI, GUOJUN, Mathematics
LI, HONGWEI, Life Sciences
LI, HUA, Physics and Microelectronics
LI, JIANFENG, Literature and Journalism
LI, JIE, Public Health
LI, JINGZHOU, Computer Science and Technology
LI, JINYU, Physics and Microelectronics
LI, JUN, Business Administration
LI, MUSEN, Materials Science and Engineering
LI, QIN, Philosophy and Social Development
LI, QINGZHONG, Computer Science and Technology
LI, QIQIANG, Control Science and Engineering
LI, SHAOMING, Foreign Languages and Literature
LI, SHUCAI, Civil Engineering
LI, WEI, History and Culture
LI, XIAO, History and Culture
LI, XIAOYAN, Chemistry and Chemical Engineering
LI, XUEQING, Computer Science and Technology
LI, XUEZHEN, Foreign Languages and Literature
LI, YAJIANG, Materials Science and Engineering
LI, YUCHEN, Computer Science and Technology
LI, YUEZHONG, Life Sciences
LI, ZHENZHONG, Medicine
LI, ZHONGYOU, Materials Science and Engineering
LIANG, HUIXING, Law
LIANG, ZUOTANG, Physics and Microelectronics
LIAO, QUN, Literature and Journalism
LIE, JIE, Philosophy and Social Development
LIE, JIE, Computer Science and Technology
LIN, JIANQIANG, Life Sciences
LIN, JUREN, Philosophy and Social Development
LIN, LU, Mathematics
LIN, MING, Law
LIN, XINYING, Public Health
LIU, BAOYU, Law
LIU, CHENGBO, Chemistry and Chemical Engineering
LIU, FENGJUN, History and Culture
LIU, GANG, Business Administration
LIU, GUIZHEN, Mathematics
LIU, HONGWEI, Business Administration
LIU, JIANYA, Mathematics
LIU, JIAZHUANG, Mathematics
LIU, JU, Information Science and Engineering
LIU, KAI, Medicine
LIU, LUPENG, Philosophy and Social Development
LIU, PING, History and Culture
LIU, RONGXING, Computer Science and Technology
LIU, SHIGUO, Law

LIU, SHUMEI, Foreign Languages and Literature
LIU, SHUTANG, Control Science and Engineering
LIU, SHUWEI, Medicine
LIU, TIANLU, History and Culture
LIU, XIANXI, Medicine
LIU, XINLI, Philosophy and Social Development
LIU, YIHUA, Physics and Microelectronics
LIU, YU-AN, Political Science and Public Administration
LIU, YUFENG, History and Culture
LIU, YUNGANG, Control Science and Engineering
LIU, YUTIAN, Electrical Engineering
LIU, ZHAOLI, Mathematics
LIU, ZHAOXU, Nursing
LIU, ZHENQIAN, Foreign Languages and Literature
LIU, ZHIYU, Medicine
LIU, ZONGLIN, Chemistry and Chemical Engineering
LOU, FENGLAN, Nursing
LOU, HONGXIANG, Pharmacy
LU, JUNWEI, History and Culture
LU, WEIZHONG, Foreign Languages and Literature
LU, YAO, History and Culture
LUAN, FENGSHI, History and Culture
LUO, FUTENG, Literature and Journalism
MA, FENGSHU, Political Science and Public Administration
MA, GUANGHAI, Philosophy and Social Development
MA, HONGLEI, Physics and Microelectronics
MA, JUN, Computer Science and Technology
MA, LIXIAN, Medicine
MA, LONGQIAN, Literature and Journalism
MA, RUIFANG, Literature and Journalism
MA, SHAOHAN, Mathematics
MEI, LIANGMO, Physics and Microelectronics
MENG, LIRONG, Computer Science and Technology
MENG, XIANGCAI, History and Culture
MENG, XIANGXU, Computer Science and Technology
MIAO, JUNYING, Life Sciences
MIAO, QINGHAI, Physics and Microelectronics
MIAO, RUNTIAN, Philosophy and Social Development
MIAO, XINGWEI, Foreign Languages and Literature
MIN, GUANGHUI, Materials Science and Engineering
MO, WENCHUAN, Business Administration
NING, FEI, Computer Science and Technology
NIU, YUNQING, Literature and Journalism
PAN, AILING, Business Administration
PANG, SHOUYING, Literature and Journalism
PENG, SHIGE, Mathematics
PENG, YUHUA, Information Science and Engineering
PENG, ZHIZHONG, Business Administration
QI, GUIJIE, Business Administration
QI, YANPING, Law
QIAN, ZENGYI, Literature and Journalism
QIAO, YIZHENG, Control Science and Engineering
QIAO, YOUMEI, History and Culture
QU, YINBO, Life Sciences
REN, DENGYI, Materials Science and Engineering
REN, QUAN, Information Science and Engineering
REN, XIANGHONG, History and Culture
RUI, HONGXING, Mathematics
SHANG, QINGSEN, Civil Engineering
SHANG, YU, Philosophy and Social Development
SHAO, LIHUA, Public Health
SHENG, YUQI, Literature and Journalism
SHI, BING, Computer Science and Technology
SHI, KAIQUAN, Mathematics
SHI, LIANYUN, Business Administration
SHI, YUMING, Mathematics

SONG, GANG, Medicine
SUI, QINGMEI, Control Science and Engineering
SUN, DEJUN, Chemistry and Chemical Engineering
SUN, HONGJIAN, Chemistry and Chemical Engineering
SUN, JILIN, Literature and Journalism
SUN, KANGNING, Materials Science and Engineering
SUN, NAZHENG, Mathematics
SUN, SIXIU, Chemistry and Chemical Engineering
SUN, TONGJING, Control Science and Engineering
SUN, WENSHENG, Medicine
SUN, XINQIANG, Law
SUN, YINGCHUN, Foreign Languages and Literature
SUN, ZIMEI, Literature and Journalism
TAN, HAOZHE, Literature and Journalism
TAN, SHIBAO, History and Culture
TAN, YEBANG, Chemistry and Chemical Engineering
TANG, ZIHENG, Literature and Journalism
TIAN, GUOHUI, Control Science and Engineering
TIAN, XUELEI, Materials Science and Engineering
WAN, JIANCHENG, Computer Science and Technology
WANG, CHENGRUI, Physics and Microelectronics
WANG, CHUNLEI, Physics and Microelectronics
WANG, DEGANG, Business Administration
WANG, FENGSHAN, Pharmacy
WANG, FUTAI, Business Administration
WANG, HAIYANG, Computer Science and Technology
WANG, HUAIJING, Medicine
WANG, JIANMIN, Political Science and Public Administration
WANG, JIANWU, Chemistry and Chemical Engineering
WANG, JIAYE, Mathematics
WANG, JIEZHEN, Public Health
WANG, JINFENG, Physics and Microelectronics
WANG, JINXING, Life Sciences
WANG, JIYANG, Materials Science and Engineering
WANG, JUNJU, Foreign Languages and Literature
WANG, KEMING, Physics and Microelectronics
WANG, KEMING, Materials Science and Engineering
WANG, LILI, Foreign Languages and Literature
WANG, LIPING, Law
WANG, PEIYUAN, Literature and Journalism
WANG, PENG, Life Sciences
WANG, PING, Literature and Journalism
WANG, QILONG, Chemistry and Chemical Engineering
WANG, QING, Civil Engineering
WANG, QINGYOU, Information Science and Engineering
WANG, QUANJUAN, Civil Engineering
WANG, RENQING, Life Sciences
WANG, RUBIN, Pharmacy
WANG, SHANBO, Philosophy and Social Development
WANG, SHAOXING, Political Science and Public Administration
WANG, SUMEI, Public Health
WANG, TIANHONG, Life Sciences
WANG, WEI, Mathematics
WANG, WENCHENG, Literature and Journalism
WANG, WENQIAO, Mathematics
WANG, XIAOSHU, Literature and Journalism
WANG, XIAOYI, History and Culture
WANG, XIAOYUN, Mathematics
WANG, XINCHUN, Philosophy and Social Development
WANG, XINGYUAN, Business Administration

WANG, XINNIAN, Physics and Microelectronics
WANG, XUEDIAN, History and Culture
WANG, YIMING, Business Administration
WANG, YOUZHI, Civil Engineering
WANG, YUJI, History and Culture
WANG, YUZHEN, Control Science and Engineering
WANG, ZHIFU, Materials Science and Engineering
WANG, ZHIYU, Public Health
WANG, ZHOUMING, Literature and Journalism
WANG, ZUNONG, Life Sciences
WANG, ZUOCHENG, Materials Science and Engineering
WEI, ZHONGLI, Mathematics
WEN, SHULIN, Materials Science and Engineering
WU, AIHUA, Business Administration
WU, JIAN, Chemistry and Chemical Engineering
WU, RUNTING, Literature and Journalism
WU, XIAOJUAN, Information Science and Engineering
WU, YAOHUA, Control Science and Engineering
WU, YOUSHI, Materials Science and Engineering
WU, ZHEN, Mathematics
XIA, GUANGMIN, Life Sciences
XIA, HAIRUI, Physics and Microelectronics
XIA, YUEYUAN, Physics and Microelectronics
XIANG, FENGNING, Life Sciences
XIAO, JINMING, Law
XIAO, MIN, Life Sciences
XIAO, XIA, Foreign Languages and Literature
XIE, HONGXIANG, Literature and Journalism
XIE, HUI, Law
XIE, KEQIN, Public Health
XIE, QUBING, Physics and Microelectronics
XIE, SHIJIE, Physics and Microelectronics
XIONG, ZHIPING, Civil Engineering
XU, BIN, Materials Science and Engineering
XU, CHAO, Literature and Journalism
XU, DONG, Materials Science and Engineering
XU, GUIFA, Public Health
XU, GUIYING, Chemistry and Chemical Engineering
XU, MINGYU, Mathematics
XU, PING, Life Sciences
XU, QIULIANG, Computer Science and Technology
XU, WENFANG, Pharmacy
XU, XIANGYI, Business Administration
XU, YANSHENG, Civil Engineering
YAN, BINGGANG, Philosophy and Social Development
YANG, DANPING, Mathematics
YANG, HUIXIN, Business Administration
YANG, JINGHE, Chemistry and Chemical Engineering
YANG, LIANZHONG, Mathematics
YANG, LUHUI, Political Science and Public Administration
YANG, RUIZHI, Literature and Journalism
YANG, XUEJIN, Business Administration
YANG, YANZHAO, Chemistry and Chemical Engineering
YI, HONGXUN, Mathematics
YIN, YANSHENG, Materials Science and Engineering
YU, GUANG, Business Administration
YU, GUANGHAI, History and Culture
YU, HONGXIA, Public Health
YU, XIUPING, Medicine
YUAN, DONGFENG, Information Science and Engineering
YUAN, SHISHUO, Literature and Journalism
YUAN, YIRANG, Mathematics
YUE, QINGYAN, Environmental Science and Engineering
ZENG, GUANGZHOU, Computer Science and Technology
ZENG, ZHENYU, History and Culture
ZHAN, TAO, Mathematics

ZHANG, CAIMING, Computer Science and Technology
ZHANG, CHANGKAI, Life Sciences
ZHANG, CHENGHUI, Control Science and Engineering
ZHANG, CHUNGUANG, Chemistry and Chemical Engineering
ZHANG, CHUNLING, Public Health
ZHANG, HENG, Medicine
ZHANG, HUAZHONG, Computer Science and Technology
ZHANG, JIANYE, Medicine
ZHANG, JINLONG, History and Culture
ZHANG, JUREN, Life Sciences
ZHANG, KELI, Literature and Journalism
ZHANG, LIHENG, History and Culture
ZHANG, LINING, Medicine
ZHANG, NAIJIAN, Physics and Microelectronics
ZHANG, PEILIN, Physics and Microelectronics
ZHANG, PEIZHONG, Civil Engineering
ZHANG, QINGFAN, Control Science and Engineering
ZHANG, QINGZHU, Pharmacy
ZHANG, RUILIN, Physical Education
ZHANG, SHUNHUA, Mathematics
ZHANG, SHUXUE, History and Culture
ZHANG, SHUZHENG, Literature and Journalism
ZHANG, TAO, History and Culture
ZHANG, TIQIN, Business Administration
ZHANG, XIEN, Political Science and Public Administration
ZHANG, XINGYU, Information Science and Engineering
ZHANG, XIUMEI, Medicine
ZHANG, XIWEI, History and Culture
ZHANG, XUEJUN, Literature and Journalism
ZHANG, XUEYAO, Physics and Microelectronics
ZHANG, YULIN, Control Science and Engineering
ZHANG, YUZHEN, Life Sciences
ZHANG, YUZHONG, Life Sciences
ZHAO, AIGUO, History and Culture
ZHAO, BINGXIN, Business Administration
ZHAO, GUOQUN, Materials Science and Engineering
ZHAO, JIANGUO, Electrical Engineering
ZHAO, JINGHUA, Business Administration
ZHAO, SHENGZI, Information Science and Engineering
ZHAO, WEIMIN, Medicine
ZHAO, XIAOFAN, Life Sciences
ZHAO, ZHONGTANG, Public Health
ZHENG, CHUN, Literature and Journalism
ZHENG, FENGLAN, Literature and Journalism
ZHENG, LIQIANG, Chemistry and Chemical Engineering
ZHENG, PEIXIN, History and Culture
ZHENG, XUNZUO, Literature and Journalism
ZHONG, MAIYING, Control Science and Engineering
ZHONG, WEILIE, Physics and Microelectronics
ZHOU, GENYAN, Medicine
ZHOU, GUANGYUAN, History and Culture
ZHOU, HONGXING, Mathematics
ZHOU, LAIXIANG, Literature and Journalism
ZHOU, XIAOYU, History and Culture
ZHU, DAMING, Computer Science and Technology
ZHU, RUIFU, Materials Science and Engineering
ZHU, WEISHEN, Civil Engineering

SHANDONG AGRICULTURAL UNIVERSITY

61 Dai Zong St, Taian 271018, Shandong
Telephone: (538) 8242291
Fax: (538) 8226399
E-mail: xb@sdau.cdu.cn
Internet: www.sdau.edu.cn

Founded 1906
Department of Education of Shandong control
Academic year: September to July

President: WEN FUJIANG
Vice-Presidents: DONG SHUTING, YAO LAI-
CHANG, ZHANG JINGHE, ZHANG XIANSHENG
Head of Graduate Department: WANG ZHEN-
LIN
Librarian: ZHANG XIANQI
Number of teachers: 1,151
Number of students: 20,000
Publications: *Journal* (natural sciences, 4 a
year), *Journal* (social sciences, 4 a year),
*Shandong Journal of Animal Husbandry
and Veterinary Science* (6 a year)

DEANS

College of Agricultural Resources and Envir-
onment: SHI YANXI
College of Agronomy: WANG HONGGANG
College of Animal Technology: TAN JINGHE
College of Chemistry and Materials Science:
ZHOU JIE
College of Economy and Management: HU
JILIAN
College of Food Science and Engineering:
DONG HAIZHOU
College of Foreign Languages: LI ZHILING
College of Forestry: MU ZHIMEI
College of Horticulture: WANG XIUFENG
College of Humanities and Law: SUN YAN-
QUAN
College of Hydrology and Civil Engineering:
LIU FUSHENG
College of Information Science and Technol-
ogy: WANG YUNCHENG
College of Life Sciences: ZHENG CHENGCHAO
College of Mechanical and Electronic Engin-
eering: ZHENG WEI
College of Plant Protection: LI DUOCHUAN
College of Science: ZHOU JIE

PROFESSORS

AI, SHIYUN, Chemistry and Materials Science
CAI, TONGJIE, Animal Technology
CHANG, WEISHAN, Animal Technology
CHEN, XUESEN, Horticulture
CHENG, SHUHAN, Information Science and
Technology
CUI, DECAI, Life Sciences
CUI, WEI, Humanities and Law
CUI, WEIZHENG, Forestry
CUI, YANSHUN, Animal Technology
CUI, ZHIZHONG, Animal Technology
DIAO, YOUXIANG, Animal Technology
DING, AIYUN, Plant Protection
DING, SHIFEI, Information Science and Tech-
nology
DONG, HAIZHOU, Food Science and Engineer-
ing
DONG, JINLING, Economy and Management
DONG, SHUTING, Agronomy
DU, SHOUJUN, Humanities and Law
FAN, WEIXING, Animal Technology
FAN, ZHICHENG, Horticulture
FENG, CHENGMING, Electromechanical Engin-
eering
FENG, YONGJUN, Agricultural Resources and
Environment
GAO, HUA, Information Science and Technol-
ogy
GAO, HUA, Science
GAO, HUIYUAN, Life Sciences
GAO, QINGRONG, Agronomy
GAO, RONGQI, Agronomy
GUANGLIANG, DONGYE, Agricultural
Resources and Environment
GUO, HUABEI, Information Science and Tech-
nology
GUO, HUABEI, Science
GUO, XINMIN, Electromechanical Engineering
HA, YIMING, Science
HE, MINGRONG, Agronomy
HU, CHANGHAO, Agronomy
HU, JILIAN, Economy and Management
HU, YANJI, Agronomy
JIANG, LIN, Chemistry and Materials Science
JIANG, YONGBIN, Economy and Management

JIN, XIANG, Chemistry and Materials Science
KANG, JINGFENG, Electromechanical Engin-
eering
KONG, LINGRANG, Agronomy
LI, ANFEI, Agronomy
LI, DEQUAN, Life Sciences
LI, DUOCHUAN, Plant Protection
LI, FUCHANG, Animal Technology
LI, JIRONG, Horticulture
LI, JIYE, Hydrology and Civil Engineering
LI, QIANG, Plant Protection
LI, QINGQI, Agronomy
LI, RUXIN, Electromechanical Engineering
LI, TONGSHU, Animal Technology
LI, XIANGDONG, Agronomy
LI, XIANGDONG, Plant Protection
LI, XIANLI, Horticulture
LI, ZENGJIA, Agronomy
LI, ZHAOHUI, Plant Protection
LI, ZHENSHENG, Plant Protection
LIANG, XUETIAN, Hydrology and Civil Engin-
eering
LIN, HAI, Animal Technology
LIN, HONGXIAO, Hydrology and Civil Engin-
eering
LIN, QUANYE, Forestry
LING, CHENGHOU, Electromechanical Engin-
eering
LIU, CHUANBAO, Hydrology and Civil Engin-
eering
LIU, CHUNSHENG, Agricultural Resources and
Environment
LIU, FUSHENG, Hydrology and Civil Engin-
eering
LIU, KAIQI, Plant Protection
LIU, LIANWE, Science
LIU, LIANWEI, Chemistry and Materials Sci-
ence
LIU, SHIDANG, Animal Technology
LIU, XIAOGUANG, Plant Protection
LIU, YAN, Foreign Languages
LIU, ZHONGXIANG, Animal Technology
LU, FUSUI, Chemistry and Materials Science
LU, FUSUI, Science
LUO, WANCHUN, Plant Protection
MA, SHUSHENG, Hydrology and Civil Engin-
eering
MENG, QINGWEI, Life Sciences
MENG, XIANGDONG, Horticulture
MIAO, LIANG, Information Science and Tech-
nology
MU, LIYI, Plant Protection
MU, ZHIMEI, Forestry
NIE, JUNHUA, Agricultural Resources and
Environment
PANG, QINGJIANG, Hydrology and Civil Engin-
eering
PEIZHENG, ZHANG, Food Science and Engin-
eering
QI, SHUJUN, Foreign Languages
QU, XIANGJIN, Science
SHAN, LUN, Agronomy
SHEN, XIANG, Horticulture
SHI, JIANMIN, Economy and Management
SHI, PEI, Agronomy
SHI, YANXI, Agricultural Resources and
Environment
SHU, HUAIRUI, Horticulture
SHUHAN, CHENG, Science
SONG, JIANCHENG, Agronomy
SU, LANZHEN, Agronomy
SUN, MINGGAO, Forestry
SUN, XUGEN, Forestry
SUN, YANQUAN, Humanities and Law
SUN, ZHONGXU, Horticulture
TAN, JINGHE, Animal Technology
TIAN, BO, Plant Protection
TIAN, JICHUN, Agronomy
TIAN, QIZHUO, Agronomy
WAN, JIACHUAN, Economy and Management
WAN, YONGSHAN, Agronomy
WANG, DECHUN, Economy and Management
WANG, HANZHONG, Life Sciences
WANG, HONGGANG, Agronomy
WANG, HONGMO, Economy and Management

WANG, HUIMING, Electromechanical Engin-
eering
WANG, KAIYUN, Plant Protection
WANG, LIQIN, Horticulture
WANG, SHUYING, Animal Technology
WANG, XIANZE, Life Sciences
WANG, XIUFENG, Horticulture
WANG, YUNCHENG, Information Science and
Technology
WANG, YUNCHENG, Science
WANG, ZELI, Life Sciences
WANG, ZHENLIN, Agronomy
WANG, ZHONGHUA, Animal Technology
WEI, JIANGCHUN, Plant Protection
WEN, FUJIANG, Life Sciences
XING, SHIYAN, Forestry
XU, HONGFU, Plant Protection
XU, KUN, Horticulture
XU, WEIAN, Plant Protection
XUE, XINGLI, Economy and Management
XUESONG, HUANG, Food Science and Engin-
eering
YAN, YANCHUN, Life Sciences
YAN, ZHENYUAN, Hydrology and Civil Engin-
eering
YANG, DI, Humanities and Law
YANG, HONGQIANG, Horticulture
YANG, JIHUA, Forestry
YANG, QUANMING, Animal Technology
YANG, XUECHENG, Economy and Management
YANG, ZAIBIN, Animal Technology
YIN, XIANGCHU, Plant Protection
YIN, XUNHE, Animal Technology
YIN, YANPING, Agronomy
YU, SONGLIE, Agronomy
YU, XIANCHANG, Horticulture
YU, YIMIN, Hydrology and Civil Engineering
YU, YUANJIE, Agronomy
YU, ZHENWEN, Agronomy
YUE, YONGSHENG, Animal Technology
ZENG, YONGQING, Animal Technology
ZHAI, HENG, Horticulture
ZHANG, CHUNQING, Agronomy
ZHANG, GUANGMIN, Plant Protection
ZHANG, LIANGCHENG, Hydrology and Civil
Engineering
ZHANG, MIN, Agricultural Resources and
Environment
ZHANG, TIANYU, Plant Protection
ZHANG, XIANSHENG, Life Sciences
ZHANG, XIAOHUI, Electromechanical Engin-
eering
ZHANG, ZHIGUO, Agricultural Resources and
Environment
ZHAO, GENGXING, Agricultural Resources and
Environment
ZHAO, HONGKUN, Animal Technology
ZHAO, LANYONG, Forestry
ZHAO, TANFANG, Agronomy
ZHENG, CHENGCHAO, Life Sciences
ZHENG, GUOSHENG, Life Sciences
ZHOU, JIE, Chemistry and Materials Science
ZHOU, JIE, Science
ZHOU, YANPING, Economy and Management
ZHU, FENGGANG, Chemistry and Materials
Science
ZHU, FENGGANG, Science
ZHU, LUSHENG, Agricultural Resources and
Environment
ZHU, RUILIANG, Animal Technology
ZOU, QI, Life Sciences

SHANDONG INSTITUTE OF ECONOMICS

4 East Yanzishan Rd, Jinan 250014, Shandong

Telephone: (531) 8934161
Internet: www.china-sd.com/business/sdjjxy/
home2e.htm
Founded 1958

President: Prof. HU JIJIAN
Vice-Presidents: LI RENQUAN, Prof. LIU SHI-
FAN, Prof. REN HUI
Librarian: LI ZIRUI

Number of teachers: 322
Number of students: 2,118
Publications: *Accountant, Shandong Economy, Statistics and Management.*

SHANDONG NORMAL UNIVERSITY

88 Wen Hua East Rd, Jinan 250014, Shangdong
Telephone: (531) 6180018
Fax: (531) 6180017
E-mail: xiaoban@sdnu.edu.cn
Internet: www.sdnu.edu.cn
Founded 1950
Provincial control
Academic year: September to July
President: ZHAO YANXIU
Vice-Presidents: QI WANXUE, TANG BO, WANG ZHAOLIANG, WANG ZHIMIN, ZHANG QINGGANG
Head of Graduate Department: ZHANG WEIJUN
Librarian: SHEN DAGUANG
Number of teachers: 1,150
Number of students: 37,300 (24,300 fulltime, 13,000 part-time)
Publications: *China Population, Resources and Environment* (6 a year), *Journal* (humanities and social sciences, 6 a year), *Journal* (natural sciences, 4 a year), *Journal of the School of Foreign Languages of Shandong Teachers' University* (4 a year), *Shandong Foreign Languages Journal* (6 a year)

DEANS

College of Broadcasting: MENG XIANGZENG
College of Chemistry, Chemical Engineering and Materials Science: DONG YUBIN
College of Chinese Language and Literature: ZHOU JUNPING
College of Educational Science: ZHANG WENXIN
College of Fine Arts: KONG XINMIAO
College of Foreign Languages: YANG MIN
College of History, Culture and Social Development: WANG WEI
College of Information and Management: LIU XIYU
College of Legal Science: HAN YUGUI
College of Life Sciences: AN LIGUO
College of Mathematical Science: FU XILIN
College of Music: ZHANG ZHUN
College of Physical Education: YU TAO
College of Physics and Electronics: WANG CHUANKUI
College of Population, Resources and the Environment: REN JIANLAN

PROFESSORS

AN, LIGUO, Life Sciences
BI, HUALIN, Chemistry, Chemical Engineering and Materials Science
CAI, JINLING, Chemistry, Chemical Engineering and Materials Science
CAO, CHUNCHUN, Foreign Languages
CAO, DAOPING, Life Sciences
CAO, MINGHAI, Chinese Language and Literature
CHEN, DEZHAN, Chemistry, Chemical Engineering and Materials Science
CHEN, HAIHONG, History, Culture and Social Development
CHEN, HUANZHEN, Mathematical Science
CHEN, QING, Broadcasting
CHEN, XIULAN, Physics and Electronics
CHEN, YIMING, Music
CHENG, DAOPING, Population, Resources and the Environment
CHENG, JIEMIN, Population, Resources and the Environment
CHENG, XHUANFU, Physics and Electronics
DAI, SHIJUN, Chinese Language and Literature

DENG, HONGMEI, Chinese Language and Literature
DIAO, PEIJUN, Legal Science
DONG, SHAOKE, Chinese Language and Literature
DONG, YUBIN, Chemistry, Chemical Engineering and Materials Science
DU, GUICHEN, Chinese Language and Literature
FAN, XIJUN, Physics and Electronics
FU, HAILUN, Mathematical Science
FU, RONGRU, Life Sciences
FU, XILIN, Mathematical Science
GAO, FENGQIANG, Educational Science
GAO, HUA, Foreign Languages
GAO, JINGZHEN, Mathematical Science
GAO, TIEJUN, Physics and Electronics
GAO, YIQING, Fine Arts
GUO, CHENGSHAN, Physics and Electronics
GUO, GENSHENG, Broadcasting
HAN, HONGFEI, Physical Education
HAN, MEI, Population, Resources and the Environment
HAN, YUGUI, Legal Science
HE, JIAMEI, Population, Resources and the Environment
HE, JINGLIANG, Physics and Electronics
HONG, XUEBIN, Broadcasting
HOU, FULIN, Life Sciences
HOU, KANGWEI, Music
HUANG, MINGSHUI, Music
JI, GUANGMAO, Chinese Language and Literature
JIANG, CHONGQIU, Chemistry, Chemical Engineering and Materials Science
JIANG, ZHENCHANG, Chinese Language and Literature
JIANG, ZHONGYING, Broadcasting
JIANG, ZIWEN, Mathematical Science
KONG, XINMIAO, Fine Arts
LI, AIHUA, Legal Science
LI, HONGRUI, Chemistry, Chemical Engineering and Materials Science
LI, HUAIXIANG, Chemistry, Chemical Engineering and Materials Science
LI, JIAN, Physics and Electronics
LI, LAIZHONG, Chemistry, Chemical Engineering and Materials Science
LI, PING, Population, Resources and the Environment
LI, QIAN, Mathematical Science
LI, SHIZHENG, Mathematical Science
LI, TAOXIN, Educational Science
LI, XIAOLIN, Chemistry, Chemical Engineering and Materials Science
LI, XUEMIN, Mathematical Science
LI, YANXHU, Chinese Language and Literature
LI, YUJIANG, Population, Resources and the Environment
LI, YUNLONG, Life Sciences
LI, ZHIHUA, Chemistry, Chemical Engineering and Materials Science
LIANG, FANZHEN, Chemistry, Chemical Engineering and Materials Science
LIN, SHENGLU, Physics and Electronics
LIU, CHUNYING, Foreign Languages
LIU, FANG'AI, Information and Management
LIU, FENGLING, Chemistry, Chemical Engineering and Materials Science
LIU, HAIYAN, Educational Science
LIU, HONG, Information and Management
LIU, PEIYU, Information and Management
LIU, TAO, Physical Education
LIU, WENXIAN, Physics and Electronics
LIU, XIAOLIAN, Physical Education
LIU, XIYU, Information and Management
LIU, YANSHENG, Mathematical Science
LIU, ZAISHENG, Music
LU, HONG, Broadcasting
MA, SHUNYE, Mathematical Science
MA, YONGQING, Legal Science
MAN, BAOYUAN, Physics and Electronics
MENG, XIANGZENG, Broadcasting
NIE, QINGXIANG, Physics and Electronics
QI, WANXUE, Educational Science

QU, MINGWEN, Foreign Languages
QU, WENGUANG, Mathematical Science
QUAN, CHAOLU, Educational Science
REN, JIANLAN, Population, Resources and the Environment
SHENG, DAZHONG, Chemistry, Chemical Engineering and Materials Science
SHI, JINGMIN, Chemistry, Chemical Engineering and Materials Science
SHI, ZHIQIANG, Chemistry, Chemical Engineering and Materials Science
SONG, FENGGUANG, Fine Arts
SONG, JIGUO, Fine Arts
SONG, LILI, Music
SUN, LEI, Mathematical Science
SUN, XIHUA, Population, Resources and the Environment
TANG, BO, Chemistry, Chemical Engineering and Materials Science
TANG, BO, Life Sciences
TANG, NING, Music
TIAN, JIANGUO, Mathematical Science
TIAN, SHUFENG, Broadcasting
TONG, DIANMIN, Physics and Electronics
WAN, GUANGXIA, Legal Science
WANG, BAOSHAN, Life Sciences
WANG, BING, Educational Science
WANG, CHUANKUI, Physics and Electronics
WANG, HONGJIAN, Chemistry, Chemical Engineering and Materials Science
WANG, HONGQI, Chinese Language and Literature
WANG, HUAIYOU, Chemistry, Chemical Engineering and Materials Science
WANG, HUAXUE, Chinese Language and Literature
WANG, KUIYONG, Information and Management
WANG, QINGXIN, Foreign Languages
WANG, SHENGHAI, Physical Education
WANG, WANSEN, Chinese Language and Literature
WANG, WEI, History, Culture and Social Development
WANG, YOUBANG, Population, Resources and the Environment
WANG, ZEXIN, Chemistry, Chemical Engineering and Materials Science
WANG, ZHIMING, Chinese Language and Literature
WEI, JIAN, Chinese Language and Literature
WEI, WEI, Educational Science
WU, QINGFENG, Chinese Language and Literature
WU, QUANYUAN, Population, Resources and the Environment
WU, YIQIN, Chinese Language and Literature
XIA, ZHIFANG, Chinese Language and Literature
XIANG, YANG, Music
XIAO, LONGFU, Foreign Languages
XU, CHANGJUN, Music
XU, QINGPU, Legal Science
XU, QINGRU, Music
XU, XINZHAI, Mathematical Science
XU, YAOTONG, Population, Resources and the Environment
YAN, BAOQIANG, Mathematical Science
YANG, GUOLIANG, Physical Education
YANG, MIN, Foreign Languages
YANG, SHOUSEN, Chinese Language and Literature
YU, JINJIANG, Foreign Languages
YU, QUANXUN, Physics and Electronics
YU, TAO, Physical Education
ZHANG, CONGSHAN, Broadcasting
ZHANG, ENYI, Broadcasting
ZHANG, FUJI, Legal Science
ZHANG, GUORONG, Chemistry, Chemical Engineering and Materials Science
ZHANG, HUI, Life Sciences
ZHANG, JINGHUAN, Educational Science
ZHANG, JINPING, Broadcasting
ZHANG, QINGGANG, Physics and Electronics
ZHANG, QINGHUA, Chinese Language and Literature

ZHANG, SHUFENG, Educational Science
ZHANG, SHUQIN, Foreign Languages
ZHANG, WENXIN, Educational Science
ZHANG, XIJIE, Fine Arts
ZHANG, YUFEN, Mathematical Science
ZHANG, YUHONG, Life Sciences
ZHANG, ZHIDE, Chemistry, Chemical Engineering and Materials Science
ZHANG, ZHULU, Population, Resources and the Environment
ZHANG, ZHUN, Music
ZHAO, CHENGFU, Educational Science
ZHAO, JIAN, Population, Resources and the Environment
ZHAO, JIE, Physics and Electronics
ZHAO, QINGUO, Fine Arts
ZHAO, QINGZHEN, Information and Management
ZHAO, YANXIU, Life Sciences
ZHENG, MINGCHUN, Information and Management
ZHENG, XINQI, Population, Resources and the Environment
ZHOU, BO, Chinese Language and Literature
ZHOU, JUNPING, Chinese Language and Literature
ZHOU, ZHICHEN, Chemistry, Chemical Engineering and Materials Science
ZHU, DEFA, Chinese Language and Literature
ZHU, JUNKONG, Physics and Electronics
ZHUANG, WAN, Mathematical Science
ZHUANG, WENZHONG, Life Sciences
ZHUO, ZHUANG, Physics and Electronics

SHANGHAI INTERNATIONAL STUDIES UNIVERSITY

550 Dalian Rd West, Shanghai 200083
Telephone: (21) 65360599
Fax: (21) 65313756
E-mail: oisasisu@mail.online.sh.cn
Internet: www.shisu.edu.cn
Founded 1949
Academic year: September to July
President: DAI WEIDONG
Vice-Presidents: SHENG YULIANG, TAN JINGHUA, WU YOUFU, ZHU JIANGUO
Head of Graduate Department: FENG QINGHUA
Librarian: ZHU LEI
Number of teachers: 300
Number of students: 8,300
Publications: *Educational Technology for Foreign Language Teaching* (6 a year), *Journal* (6 a year), *The Arab World* (6 a year)

DEANS

College of Eastern Languages: LU PEIYONG
College of International Business Administration: LIN XUNZI
College of International Cultural Exchange: XU BAOMEI
College of International Education: SHI HUILI
College of Japanese Culture and Economy: PI XIGENG
College of Journalism and Communication: HU SHUZHONG
College of the English Language: SHI ZHIKANG
College of the Russian Language: ZHENG TIWU
College of Western Language and Literature: WEI MAOPING
Graduate Institute of Interpretation and Translation: CHAI MINGJIONG
School of Law: YU JIANHUA

PROFESSORS

CAI, YOUSHENG, Western Language and Literature
CAO, DEMING, Western Language and Literature

CHAI, MINGJIONG, Graduate Institute of Interpretation and Translation
CHEN, HUIZHONG, International Cultural Exchange
CHEN, XIAOCHUN, Western Language and Literature
DAI, HUIPING, Graduate Institute of Interpretation and Translation
DAI, WEIDONG, English
DOU, HUI, Law
DU, YUNDE, Graduate Institute of Interpretation and Translation
FENG, QINGHUA, English
HE, ZHAOXIONG, English
HU, LONG, Journalism and Communication
HU, SHUZHONG, Journalism and Communication
LI, WEIPING, English
LU, JINGSHENG, Western Language and Literature
LU, LOUFA, Graduate Institute of Interpretation and Translation
LU, PEIYONG, Eastern Languages
LU, YONGCHANG, Russian
LU, GUANGDAN, English
MEI, DEMING, English
PI, XIGENG, Japanese Culture and Economy
QIAN, PEIXIN, Western Language and Literature
QIU, MAORU, English
SHEN, YUCHENG, Japanese Culture and Economy
SHI, HUILI, International Education
SHI, ZHIKANG, English
SHI, ZHIKANG, Graduate Institute of Interpretation and Translation
SHU, SHENGPENG, Western Language and Literature
TAN, JINGHUA, Japanese Culture and Economy
WEI, MAOPING, Western Language and Literature
WU, DAGANG, Japanese Culture and Economy
WU, DINGBO, English
XIE, TIANZHEN, Graduate Institute of Interpretation and Translation
XU, YULONG, English
YANG, JINHUA, International Cultural Exchange
YU, JIANHUA, Law
ZHANG, SHIHUA, Western Language and Literature
ZHANG, WEILIANG, English
ZHANG, YONGHUA, Journalism and Communication
ZHANG, ZHUXIN, Journalism and Communication
ZHENG, TIWU, Russian
ZHOU, PING, Japanese Culture and Economy
ZHOU, SHEN, English
ZHOU, WENJU, Eastern Languages

SHANGHAI JIAOTONG UNIVERSITY

1954 Hua Shan Rd, Shanghai 200030
Telephone: (21) 62812444
Fax: (21) 62821369
Internet: www.sajtu.edu.cn
Founded 1896
Academic year: September to July
President: XIE SHENGWU
Vice-Presidents: BAI TONGSHUO, SHENG HUANYE, SHEN WEIPING, XU XIAOMING, YE QUYUAN, ZHANG SHENGKUN
Director of President's Office: ZHANG WEI
Librarian: CHEN ZHAONEN
Library of 1,826,000 vols
Number of teachers: 2,889
Number of students: 13,882 (incl. 2,831 postgraduates)
Publication: *Journal* (6 a year, also in English)

HEADS OF SCHOOLS

Department of Physical Education: SUN QILING
Department of Plasticity Technology: RUAN XUEYU
School of Chemistry and Chemical Engineering: TANG XIAOZHENG
School of Civil Engineering and Mechanics: LIU ZHENGXING
School of Electric Power Engineering: HOU ZHIJIAN
School of Electronics and Information Technology: XI YUGENG
School of Foreign Languages: ZHENG SHUTANG
School of Humanities and Social Sciences: YE DUNPING
School of Life Sciences and Technology: TANG ZHANGCHENG
School of Machinery Engineering: YAN JUNQI
School of Management: ZHANG XIANG
School of Materials Science and Engineering: WU JIANSHENG
School of Naval Architecture and Ocean Engineering: LI RUNPEI
School of Power and Energy Resources Engineering: XU JIJUN
School of Science: SHI ZHONGCI

SHANGHAI NORMAL UNIVERSITY

100 Guilin Rd, Nanjing 200234, Jiangsu
Telephone: (21) 64322881
Fax: (21) 64360512
Internet: www.shtu.edu.cn
Founded 1954
Academic year: September to July
President: YU LIZHONG
Vice-Presidents: JIANG WEIYI, LIU ZHIGANG, LU JIANPING, XIANG JIAXIANG
Librarian: CAO XU
Library of 2,600,000 vols
Number of teachers: 1,181
Number of students: 40,000
Publications: *Chinese University Academic Abstracts* (6 a year), *Journal* (6 a year)

DEANS

Architecture Engineering College: LIU JIANXIN
Engineering College of Machinery and Electronics Information: LIN XIAOYUN
Fine Arts College: XU WANGYAO
Life and Environmental Sciences College: LI HEXING
Mathematics and Science College: ZHANG JIZHOU
School of Arts: XIE JING
School of Commerce: FU HONGCHUN
School of Education: LU JIAMEI
School of European Culture and Trade: MAO XUNCHENG
School of Foreign Languages: GU DAXIN
School of Law and Politics: SHANG HONGRI
School of Literature: SUN XUN
School of Music: DAI DINGCHENG
Sports College: LU CHANGYA

PROFESSORS

CAI, LONGQUAN, Foreign Languages
CAO, TONG, Life and Environmental Sciences
CAO, XU, Literature
CEN, GUOZHEN, Education
CHEN, KEJIAN, Law and Politics
CHEN, MINGZHENG, Arts
CHEN, WEI, Literature
CHEN, WEIPING, Law and Politics
CHENG, XINGHUA, Foreign Languages
CHENG, ZHEHUAN, Law and Politics
DAI, DINGCHENG, Music
DENG, MINGDE, Foreign Languages
FAN, KAITAI, Literature
FAN, WUYUN, Literature
FANG, GUANGCHANG, Law and Politics

FEI, HELIANG, Mathematics and Science
FU, HONGCHUN, Commerce
GAN, FENG, Law and Politics
GAO, HUIZHU, Law and Politics
GAO, JIANHUA, Mathematics and Science
GU, DAXI, Foreign Languages
GU, HAIGEN, Education
HE, YUNFENG, Law and Politics
HONG, XIAOXIA, Law and Politics
HUANG, BAOHUA, Literature
JIA, HUANZHEN, Arts
JIANG, CHUANGUANG, Law and Politics
KANG, AISHI, Arts
LI, HEXING, Life and Environmental Sciences
LI, JIAHOU, Arts
LI, SHENG, Law and Politics
LI, SHI, Literature
LI, WEIHUI, Commerce
LI, WEIMING, Sports
LI, XIAOYUN, Machinery and Electronics Information Engineering
LI, YIZHEN, Life and Environmental Sciences
LI, ZHIGUO, Commerce
LIU, DANQING, Literature
LIU, JIANXIN, Architecture
LIU, YANYAN, Law and Politics
LU, CHANGYA, Sports
LU, JIAMEI, Education
LU, RUOPING, Arts
LU, RUZHAN, Literature
MA, DELING, Law and Politics
MEI, ZIHAN, Literature
MI, ZHENG, Arts
QI, LUYANG, Literature
REN, ZHONGLUN, Literature
SHANG, HONGRI, Law and Politics
SHAO, YONG, Literature
SHEN, HEBO, Life and Environmental Sciences
SHI, YONGBING, Mathematics and Science
SHUN, XUN, Literature
SUN, JINGRAO, Literature
SUN, XUSHENG, Sports
SUN, YUWEI, Law and Politics
TAN, WEIGUO, Foreign Languages
TANG, LIXING, Literature
TAO, BENYI, Literature
WANG, CUIYING, Sports
WANG, GUORONG, Mathematics and Science
WANG, JIREN, Literature
WANG, TIANQU, Literature
WANG, XIAODUN, Literature
WANG, XINQIU, Foreign Languages
WANG, YANMING, Mathematics and Science
WEI, SHIXIAN, Arts
WENG, MINHUA, Literature
WU, HONGLIN, Arts
WU, JINGDONG, Law and Politics
WU, JUNMING, Life and Environmental Sciences
WU, QUANXI, Life and Environmental Sciences
WU, XIAQIN, Life and Environmental Sciences
XIA, HUIXIAN, Education
XIE, LIMIN, Education
XU, SHIYI, Literature
XU, WEIHONG, Arts
XUE, HESHENG, Commerce
XUE, SIJIA, Life and Environmental Sciences
YAN, GWENHU, Literature
YANG, DONG, Sports
YANG, JIANLONG, Literature
YANG, ZHONGHUA, Mathematics and Science
YANG, ZHONGNAN, Life and Environmental Sciences
YE, HUANIAN, Foreign Languages
YE, HUANIAN, Literature
YU, XIBING, Life and Environmental Sciences
YUAN, BING, Literature
YUAN, FENG, Law and Politics
YUE, RONGXIAN, Mathematics and Science
ZHANG, JIZHOU, Mathematics and Science
ZHANG, ZIQIANG, Machinery and Electronics Information Engineering
ZHAO, XIAONAN, Arts

ZHENG, KELU, Literature
ZHOU, GENYU, Life and Environmental Sciences
ZHOU, ZHONGZHI, Law and Politics
ZHU, SHUNQUAN, Mathematics and Science
ZHU, XIANSHENG, Literature

SHANGHAI SECOND MEDICAL UNIVERSITY

280 South Chongqing Rd, Shanghai 200025
Telephone: (21) 63846590
Fax: (21) 63842916
Internet: www.shsmu.edu.cn
Founded 1952
Languages of instruction: Chinese, English, French
Academic year: September to July
Chancellor: FAN GUANRONG
Vice-Chancellors: Prof. CHEN ZHIXING, Prof. QIAN GUANXIANG, Prof. ZHUANG MENGHU, Assoc. Prof. ZHU ZHENGGANG
Registrar: Prof. CAI WEI
Librarian: Assoc. Prof. ZHANG WENHAO
Library of 420,000 vols
Number of teachers: 3,379
Number of students: 5,000
Publications: *Chinese Journal of Endocrinology and Metabolism* (in Chinese), *Journal of Clinical Paediatrics* (in Chinese), *Journal of Shanghai Second Medical University* (in Chinese and English), *Shanghai Journal of Immunology* (in Chinese)

DEANS

College of Basic Medical Sciences: Prof. LU YANG
Department of Social Sciences: XIANG YANG
Faculty of Clinical Medicine in Ren Ji Hospital: Prof FAN GUANRONG
Faculty of Clinical Medicine in Rui Jin Hospital: Prof. LI HONGWEI
Faculty of Clinical Medicine in No. 6 People's Hospital: Prof. LIN FAXIONG
Faculty of Paediatrics and Clinical Medicine in Xin Hua Hospital: Prof. SHEN XIAOMIN
Junior Medical College in Bao Gang Hospital: JUN SHENGJI
Health School: Assoc. Prof. WU XIANGQIAN
School of Stomatology: Prof. ZHANG ZHIYUAN

SHANGHAI TIEDAO UNIVERSITY

450 Zhennan Lu, Shanghai 200333
Telephone: (21) 2506812
Fax: (21) 2506812
Internet: www.shtdu.edu.cn
Founded 1995 by merger of Shanghai Institute of Railway Technology and Shanghai Railway Medical College
State control
Academic year: September to July (2 terms)
Pres.: Prof. CHEN GUANMAO
Vice-Pres: Prof. LI MENG, Prof. MA WENZENG, Prof. MAO YONGJIANG, Assoc. Prof. SUN ZHANG, Prof. XU LONG, Prof. ZHU GUANGJIE
Registrar: Prof. MIAO RUNSHEN
Librarian: Prof. WU WENQI
Library of 850,000 vols, 2,900 periodicals
Number of teachers: 1,164
Number of students: 6,354
Publication: *Journal*

PROFESSORS

AI, Y., Hygienics
CAI, N., Physiology
CAI, T., Surgery
CHAO, X., Bridge, Tunnel and Structural Engineering
CHEN, D. L., Dermatology
CHEN, D. Y., Fluid Drive
CHEN, H., Mechanical Engineering

CHEN, J., Railway Locomotives and Rolling Stock
CHEN, S., Railway Locomotives and Rolling Stock
CHENG, S., Pathology
DENG, N., Internal Medicine
DU, Q., Electrification and Automation
FAN, P., Mechanical Engineering
FENG, Z. Q., Histology and Embryology
FENG, Z. Z., Railway Vehicles
GONG, J., Railway Locomotives and Rolling Stock
GUO, D. F., Railway Location and Construction
GUO, D. P., Orthopaedics
HOU, H., Neuropathology
HU, B., Anatomy
HU, K., Bridge, Tunnel and Structural Engineering
HU, M., Computer Communication
HUA, W., English
HUANG, S., Transport Management
JI, L., Transport Management
JIANG, E., Internal Combustion Engines
LE, S., Stomatology
LI, D., Surgery
LI, H., Mathematics
LI, J., Ophthalmology
LI, M., Applied Computer Technology
LI, S., Internal Medicine
LI, Y., Mechanics
LIN, Z., Ultrasonic Diagnosis
LIU, C., Internal Medicine
LIU, Q., Hydraulic Pressure Technology
LIU, X., Railway Automation
LIU, Y., Electrical Appliances
LIU, Z., Paediatrics
LU, G., Civil Engineering
LU, Y., Civil Engineering
NIE, C., Fluid Drive and Control
PAN, K., Stomatological Surgery
PENG, Y. O., Economics
QI, W., Internal Combustion Engines
QIU, W., Medical Genetics
REN, J., Transport Management
RUAN, Y., Computer Engineering
SHAO, B., Power Electronics Technology
SHEN, P., Railway Locomotives and Rolling Stock
SHEN, Z., Infectious Diseases
SHI, S., Stomatology
SONG, J., Anaesthesia
SUN, P., Surgery
SUN, Q., Railway Location and Construction
SUN, S., Parasitology
SUN, Y., Laboratory Testing
TAN, B., Mechanical Engineering
TAO, S., Computer Engineering
TAO, Z., Fluid Drive
TONG, D., Wheel-rail System
WANG, B., Applied Computer Technology
WANG, B., Surgery
WANG, D., Telecommunications
WANG, F., Railway Vehicles
WANG, Q., Railway Electrification and Automation
WANG, R., Mathematics
WANG, W., Railway Engineering
WANG, Y., Biochemistry
WU, F., Telecommunications
WU, J., Railway Location and Construction
WU, W. Q., Transport Signals and Control
WU, W. Y., Psychiatry
WU, X., Railway Location and Construction
WU, Z. K., Electrical Appliances
WU, Z. R., Civil Engineering
XIA, Y., Mechanics
XIONG, W., Mechanics
XU, T., Mechanics
YANG, G., Mechanics
YANG, H. C., Histology and Embryology
YANG, H. Y., Transport Management
YANG, X., Civil Engineering
YE, E., Hygienics
YIN, L., Mechanics
YU, W., Pharmacology

YUAN, S., Stomatology
ZHANG, D. X., Railway Locomotives and Rolling Stock
ZHANG, D. Z., Railway Locomotives and Rolling Stock
ZHANG, J., Gynaecology and Obstetrics
ZHANG, S. C., Stomatology
ZHANG, S. J., Telecommunications and Information Processing
ZHANG, W. C., Civil Engineering
ZHANG, X., Mechanics
ZHANG, Y. J., Electrical Technology
ZHANG, Y. Z., Internal Medicine
ZHANG, Z., Railway Locomotives and Rolling Stock
ZHAO, S., Politics
ZHENG, G., Stomatology
ZHENG, T., Power Electronics Technology
ZHOU, Z., Stomatological Surgery
ZHU, J., Railway Location and Construction
ZHU, M., Mechanics
ZHU, P., Theoretical Physics
ZHU, X., Mathematics
ZONG, G., Structural Engineering

SHANGHAI UNIVERSITY OF FINANCE AND ECONOMICS

777 Guoding Rd, Shanghai 200433
Telephone: (21) 65903505
Fax: (21) 65100561
Internet: www.shufe.edu.cn

Founded 1917
Ministry of Education control
Academic year: September to July

President: TAN MIN
Vice-Presidents: CONG SHUHAI, HUANG LINFANG, SUN ZHENG, WANG HONGWEI, ZHOU ZHONGFEI
Head of Graduate Department: FENG ZHENGQUAN
Librarian: LI XIAOYE
Number of students: 20,000

Publications: *Economics and Management of Foreign Countries* (12 a year), *Higher Education of Finance and Economics* (4 a year), *Journal* (6 a year), *Journal of Finance and Economics* (12 a year)

DEANS

Department of Foreign Languages: WANG XIAOQUN
Department of Information Management: LIU LANJUAN
Department of Physical Education: CHEN XIAO
Department of Statistics: HAN XIAOLIANG
School of Accountancy: CHEN XINYUAN
School of Applied Mathematics: CHEN QIHONG
School of Economics: TIAN GUOQIANG
School of Finance: DAI GUOQIANG
School of Humanities: ZHANG XIONG
School of International Business Management: SUN HAIMING
School of Law: ZHOU ZHONGFEI
School of MBA Programmes: LUO ZUWANG
School of Public Economy Administration: JIANG HONG

PROFESSORS

BIAN, ZUWU, Statistics
CHANG, NING, Statistics
CHAO, GANGLING, Marketing
CHE, WEIHAN, International Economics
CHEN, HUIQIN, Statistics
CHEN, QIHONG, Applied Mathematics
CHEN, QIJIE, Marketing
CHEN, WENHAO, Accountancy
CHEN, XIAO, Physical Education
CHEN, XINKANG, Marketing
CHEN, XINYUAN, Accountancy
CHEN, YUN, Public Economy Administration
CHENG, ENFU, Economics

CHU, MINWEI, Public Economy Administration
CHU, YIYUN, Accountancy
CONG, SHUHAI, Public Economy Administration
DAI, GUOQIANG, Banking
DING, BANGKAI, Law
DONG, FENGGU, Statistics
DOU, JIANMING, Statistics
DU, XUNCHENG, Economics
FEI, FANGYU, International Finance
GAN, CHUNHUI, Industry Economics
GU, GUIDING, Applied Mathematics
GU, GUOZHU, Humanities
GUO, SHIZHENG, Public Economy Administration
GUO, YUDAN, International Trade
HAN, QING, Economics
HAN, XIAOLIANG, Statistics
HE, JIANMIN, Tourism Management
HE, YUCHANG, Economics
HU, JINGBEI, Economics
HU, YIJIAN, Public Economy Administration
HU, YIMING, Accountancy
HU, YONGGANG, Economics
HUO, WENWEN, Finance
JIANG, HONG, Public Economy Administration
JIANG, YIHONG, Accountancy
JIN, DEHUAN, Finance
LAN, YISHENG, International Trade
LI, XIAOYE, Humanities
LI, XIAOYU, Statistics
LI, XIN, Economics
LIANG, ZHIAN, Applied Mathematics
LIAO, YINLIN, Statistics
LIN, JUE, International Economics
LIU, HANLIANG, Statistics
LIU, LIJUAN, Resource Management
LIU, YONGMING, Banking
LU, PINYUE, Humanities
LU, SHIMIN, Banking
LU, WANZHONG, Statistics
LUO, ZUWANG, Humanities
MA, GUOXIAN, Public Economy Administration
MI, WENZHAN, Humanities
PAN, FEI, Accountancy
PEI, YIRAN, Humanities
PENG, JIAQIANG, Humanities
QI, ZHIXIANG, Humanities
QU, WEIDONG, International Finance
SHAO, JIANLI, Statistics
SHENG, BANGHE, Humanities
SHI, BINGCHAO, Banking
SHI, XIQUAN, International Finance
SU, JUNHE, Statistics
SUN, HAIMING, Industry Economics
SUN, YUNWU, Statistics
SUN, ZHENG, Accountancy
TAN, MIN, Economics
TAN, ZHENG, Information Management
TAO, TINGFANG, Tourism Management
WANG, DEFA, Statistics
WANG, HONGWEI, Public Economy Administration
WANG, HUILING, Statistics
WANG, LIMING, Statistics
WANG, LIYA, Foreign Languages
WANG, SONGNIAN, Accountancy
WANG, XIAOMING, Statistics
WANG, XIAOQUN, Foreign Languages
WANG, XINXIN, Marketing
WANG, XUEMIN, Statistics
WANG, YU, Business Management
WU, LONGSHENG, Resource Management
XI, JUNYANG, International Finance
XIA, JIANMING, Business Management
XIE, ZHIGANG, Finance
XU, DAJIAN, Humanities
XU, GUOXIANG, Statistics
XU, JIANPING, Humanities
XU, JINLIANG, Finance
XU, ZHENDAN, Accountancy
XUE, HUACHENG, Information Management
YAN, GUANGHUA, Business Management

YANG, DAKAI, Public Economy Administration
YANG, GONGPU, Industry Economics
YANG, JUNCHANG, Public Economy Administration
YANG, NAN, Statistics
YIN, CHENGYUAN, Applied Mathematics
YING, SHICHANG, Finance
YOU, JIARONG, Accountancy
YU, DINGWEI, Statistics
YU, ZHIYOU, Finance
YUAN, HONGQI, Accountancy
YUE, YAOXING, International Trade
ZAN, TINGQUAN, Information Management
ZHANG, CHUN, Accountancy
ZHANG, JUE, Humanities
ZHANG, MIAO, Statistics
ZHANG, MING, Accountancy
ZHANG, MINGFANG, Statistics
ZHANG, XIONG, Humanities
ZHANG, YAN, Humanities
ZHANG, YAOTING, Economics
ZHANG, YINJIE, Economics
ZHAO, JIANYONG, Accountancy
ZHAO, XIAOJU, Banking
ZHAO, XIAOLEI, Economics
ZHAO, XIAOSHENG, Foreign Languages
ZHOU, ZHONGFEI, Law
ZHU, BAOHUA, Economics
ZHU, GUOHUA, Industry Economics
ZHU, JIANZHONG, Statistics
ZHU, MINGXIONG, Statistics
ZHU, PINGFANG, Economics
ZHU, RONGEN, Accountancy
ZHU, YINGPING, Humanities
ZHU, ZHONGDI, International Economics

SHANGHAI UNIVERSITY

1220 Xin Zha Rd, Shanghai 200041
Telephone: (21) 2553062
Fax: (21) 2154780
Internet: www.shu.edu.cn

Founded 1983

Chancellor: Prof. WANG SHENGHONG
Deputy Chancellor: Prof. LIN JIONGRU
Vice-Chancellors: Prof. CAO ZHONGXIAN, Prof. LI MINGZHONG
University Dean: Prof. WENG SHIRONG
University Coordinator for Foreign Affairs and International Programmes: ZHONG GUOXIANG

Number of teachers: 1,200, incl. 296 profs
Number of students: 7,500

Publications: *Journal, Secretariat, Sociology*

PRESIDENTS

College of Business: Prof. JIANG JIAJUN
College of Engineering: Prof. MA GUOLIN
College of Fine Arts: Prof. LI TIANXIANG
College of International Business: Prof. LU GUANQUAN
College of Liberal Arts: Prof. WANG XIMEI
College of Political Science: Prof. WANG XIMEI

SHANTOU UNIVERSITY

243 University Rd, Shantou 515063, Guangdong

Telephone: (754) 2902350
Fax: (754) 2510509
Internet: www.stu.edu.cn

Founded 1981
Provincial control
Academic year: September to July

President: XU XIAOHU
Vice-Presidents: LI YUGUANG, WU GUANGGUO, XIANG BING, XIAO ZELI, ZHENG YI
Head of Graduate Department: WANG ZHAN
Librarian: HUANG TING

Number of teachers: 630
Number of students: 12,868 (8,254 full-time, 4,614 part-time)

Publications: *Chinese Literature* (6 a year), *Journal* (4 a year), *Journal* (humanities and social sciences edition, 6 a year), *Journal* (natural science edition, 4 a year)

DEANS

College of Business: XUE YUNKUI
College of Engineering: GONG LEIGUANG
College of Law: ZHOU WEI
College of Literature: FENG SHANG
College of Medicine: LI YUGUANG
College of Science: LI DAN
Department of Physical Education: XU BIN
Department of Social Science: CHENG JIAMING
School of Art and Design: JIN DAIQIANG
School of Journalism and Communication: CHEN WANYING

PROFESSORS

CAO, BINGYUAN, Science
CHEN, FANGJING, Literature
CHEN, GUOQIANG, Science
CHEN, HANWEN, Business
CHEN, HONGLIN, Science
CHEN, MAOHUAI, Medicine
CHEN, WANYING, Journalism and Communication
CHEN, YAN, Art and Design
CHENG, JIAMING, Social Science
DING, XIAOJUN, Medicine
DING, ZHAOKUN, Science
DU, DANMING, Business
DU, GANGJIAN, Law
DU, LUNLUN, Literature
DUAN, MINGKE, Medicine
FANG, JIE, Science
GAO, KUNSHAN, Science
GONG, LEIGUANG, Engineering
GUO, XIANGUO, Medicine
GUO, XISHEN, Science
HAN, YALI, Science
HANG, JIAN, Art and Design
HE, SHAOHENG, Medicine
HERFORD, P. M., Journalism and Communication
HU, XINGRONG, Journalism and Communication
HUANG, CHANGJIANG, Science
HUANG, DONGYANG, Medicine
HUANG, XUELAN, Law
HUANG, YAN, Business
HUANG, YUANMING, Science
HUO, XIA, Medicine
JIANG, XUEWU, Medicine
JIN, DAIQIANG, Art and Design
KONG, KANGMEI, Medicine
LAN, SHENG, Science
LI, DAN, Science
LI, ENMIN, Medicine
LI, GUICANG, Literature
LI, KANGSHENG, Medicine
LI, PING, Law
LI, QING, Art and Design
LI, SHENGPING, Engineering
LI, YUGUANG, Medicine
LIN, FURONG, Science
LIN, SHUNCHAO, Medicine
LIU, JIANBIN, Engineering
LIU, XIAOHUA, Science
LOU, ZENGJIAN, Science
LUO, WENHONG, Medicine
MA, WENHUI, Science
MAI, JIEHUA, Science
MO, YAN, Literature
NI, ZHENHUA, Engineering
QI, DAQING, Business
QI, WEILI, Medicine
QIAN, SHUANRU, Medicine
QIAN, ZHIQIANG, Art and Design
QIN, DANIAN, Medicine
QIU, HANYING, Medicine
QIU, QINGCHUN, Science
SHEN, MINFEN, Engineering
SHI, GANGGANG, Medicine
SU, MIN, Medicine
TIAN, DONGPING, Medicine

WANG, CHEN, Medicine
WANG, FUREN, Literature
WANG, HUIGE, Medicine
WANG, JUNMING, Science
WANG, SHOUZHI, Art and Design
WANG, YINHE, Science
WANG, ZIYUAN, Science
WU, GUANGFUO, Science
WU, JIANXHONG, Medicine
WU, RENHUA, Medicine
WULAN, HASHI, Science
XIANG, BING, Business
XIAO, TAN, Science
XIE, HUICAI, Engineering
XIE, ZHUANGNING, Engineering
XU, JIANHENG, Medicine
XU, LUHANG, Law
XU, XIAOHU, Medicine
XU, ZONGLING, Business
XUE, YUNKUI, Business
YANG, SHOUZHI, Science
YANG, ZHONGQIANG, Science
YE, RUISONG, Science
YIN, YEGAO, Science
YUAN, ZHOU, Journalism and Communication
ZHAO, XIAOHUA, Engineering
ZHENG, XHIPEI, Medicine
ZHENG, YI, Engineering
ZHOU, WEI, Law

SHANXI AGRICULTURAL UNIVERSITY

Taigu 030801, Shaanxi
Telephone: (354) 6288211
Fax: (354) 6222942
E-mail: sxauxb@sxau.edu.cn
Internet: www.sxau.edu.cn
Founded 1950
Provincial control
Academic year: September to July
President: DONG CHANGSHENG
Vice-Presidents: CUI KEYONG, WANG JUNDONG, YUE WENBIN
Librarian: KANG CHENGYE

Number of teachers: 602
Number of students: 7,300

Publications: *Journal* (natural sciences, 4 a year), *Journal* (social sciences, 4 a year), *Study of Agriculture in Higher Education* (6 a year)

DEANS

College of Adult Education: REN JIAYAN
College of Agriculture: LI SHENGCAI
College of Animal Technology: LI HONGQUAN
College of Economics and Trade: (vacant)
College of Engineering Technology: (vacant)
College of Food Science and Engineering: HAO LIPING
College of Forestry: (vacant)
College of Horticulture: REN JIAYAN
College of Life Sciences: (vacant)
College of Resources and Environmental Science: SUN TAISEN
College of Social Science: (vacant)
Department of Modern Education and Technology: (vacant)

PROFESSORS

BAI, ZHONGKE, Resources and Environmental Science
CHANG, MINGCHANG, Food Science and Engineering
DONG, CHANGSHENG, Animal Technology
FAN, WENHUA, Resources and Environmental Science
HAN, JUCAI, Agriculture
HAO, JIANPING, Agriculture
HAO, LIN, Food Science and Engineering
HAO, LIPING, Food Science and Engineering
HE, YUNCHUN, Agriculture
HONG, JIANPING, Resources and Environmental Science

LI, BINGLIN, Agriculture
LI, HONGQUAN, Animal Technology
LI, SHENGCAI, Agriculture
LIN, DAYI, Resources and Environmental Science
LIU, HUIPING, Agriculture
LU, XIN, Resources and Environmental Science
MA, LIZHEN, Food Science and Engineering
PANG, QUANHAI, Animal Technology
SUN, TAISEN, Resources and Environmental Science
TANG, CHAOZHONG, Animal Technology
WANG, HONGFU, Agriculture
WANG, JUNDONG, Animal Technology
WANG, RUFU, Food Science and Engineering
WANG, SHENGUI, Resources and Environmental Science
WANG, YUGUO, Agriculture
WANG, ZHIRUI, Animal Technology
WANG, ZHIYA, Resources and Environmental Science
WEN, WEIYE, Animal Technology
WU, CAI-E, Food Science and Engineering
XIE, YINGHE, Resources and Environmental Science
YANG, JINZHONG, Agriculture
YANG, WUDE, Agriculture
ZHANG, HENG, Resources and Environmental Science
ZHAO, LIZHI, Agriculture

SHANXI UNIVERSITY

36 Wu Cheng Rd, Taiyuan 030006, Shaanxi
Telephone: (351) 7010944
Fax: (351) 7011981
E-mail: xiaoban@sxu.edu.cn
Internet: www.sxu.edu.cn
Founded 1902
Provincial control
Academic year: September to July
President: GUICHUN GUI
Vice-Presidents: JIA SUOTANG, LIU WEIQI, LIU ZHENSHENG, QI FENG, XING LONG
Head of Graduate Department: GAO CE
Librarian: LI JIALIN

Number of teachers: 1,105
Number of students: 18,817 (11,905 full-time, 6,912 part-time)

Publications: *Acta Sinica Quantum Optica* (philosophy and social sciences, 4 a year), *Journal* (natural sciences, 4 a year), *Journal* (philosophy and social sciences, 4 a year), *Journal of Teachers' College of Shanxi University* (4 a year), *Shanxi Library Journal* (6 a year)

DEANS

College of Fine Arts: WANG ERXI
College of Music: WANG LIANG
College of Physical Education: WANG LIANG
College of Physics and Electronics Engineering: LIANG JIUQING
Department of History: LI SHUJI
Department of Mathematics: LI SHENGJIA
School of Chemistry and Engineering: ZHAO YONGXIANG
School of Chinese Language and Literature: QIAO QUANSHENG
School of Computer Science and Information Technology: LIANG JIYE
School of Economics: LIU JIANSHENG
School of Education Science: HOU HUAIYIN
School of Environmental Science and Resources: GUO DONGSHENG
School of Foreign Languages: NIE JIANZHONG
School of Law: WANG JIJUN
School of Life Science and Technology: MA ENBO
School of Management: CAO LIJUN
School of Philosophy and Sociology: QIAO RUIJIN

School of Political Science and Public Administration: LI LUQU

PROFESSORS

AN, XIMENG, Philosophy and Sociology
BI, FUSHENG, Philosophy and Sociology
CAO, LIJUN, Management
CHEN, JINSHENG, Law
CHEN, SHIBIN, Music
CHEN, ZHAOBIN, Chemistry and Engineering
CHENG, RENGAN, History
DENG, BING, Chemistry and Engineering
DONG, CHUAN, Chemistry and Engineering
DONG, YUMING, Law
FAN, WENBIAO, Environmental Science and Resources
FAN, YINGFANG, Chemistry and Engineering
GAO, XING, Music
GONG, RONGDE, Fine Arts
GUO, DONGSHENG, Environmental Science and Resources
GUO, GUICHUN, Philosophy and Sociology
GUO, YUXIANG, Fine Arts
HAN, JIANRONG, Life Science and Technology
HAN, XIANGMING, Education Science
HAN, ZHIMO, Fine Arts
HAO, JIANGRUI, Physics and Electronics Engineering
HONG, LIANGZHEN, Chinese Language and Literature
HOU, HUAIYIN, Education Science
HU, JIANHUA, Physical Education
HU, MINGLIANG, Foreign Languages
HUANG, FENGCHUN, Chemistry and Engineering
HUANG, SHUPING, Chemistry and Engineering
JIA, LIANFENG, Physics and Electronics Engineering
JIA, SHUOTANG, Physics and Electronics Engineering
JIA, XINCHUN, Mathematics
JIA, XIUYING, Foreign Languages
JIN, WEIJUN, Chemistry and Engineering
KANG, JINSHENG, Chinese Language and Literature
LAI, YUNZHONG, Physics and Electronics Engineering
LAN, HUANG, Chinese Language and Literature
LI, DEREN, Fine Arts
LI, FUYI, Mathematics
LI, JIANYING, Physical Education
LI, JINLONG, Physical Education
LI, LUQU, Political Science and Public Administration
LI, RUINING, Physics and Electronics Engineering
LI, SHENGJIA, Mathematics
LI, SHUJI, History
LI, WENDE, Chemistry and Engineering
LI, YUE'E, Foreign Languages
LI, ZHENGMIN, Chinese Language and Literature
LI, ZHIQIANG, Economics
LI, ZHONGHAO, Physics and Electronics Engineering
LIANG, JIAHUA, Management
LIANG, JIUQING, Physics and Electronics Engineering
LIANG, JIYE, Computer Science and Information Technology
LIANG, LIPING, Political Science and Public Administration
LIANG, ZHANDONG, Mathematics
LIU, BO, Chemistry and Engineering
LIU, CHAO, Music
LIU, GUIHU, Chinese Language and Literature
LIU, HAILIANG, Foreign Languages
LIU, HONGBING, Music
LIU, JIANSHENG, Economics
LIU, SHUQING, Chinese Language and Literature
LIU, WENSEN, Physics and Electronics Engineering

LIU, XHENSHENG, Chemistry and Engineering
LIU, XIAOHUI, Life Science and Technology
LIU, XIAOLI, Physical Education
LIU, YEPING, Fine Arts
LIU, ZHENSHENG, Chemistry and Engineering
MA, AIPING, Law
MA, ENBO, Life Science and Technology
MA, GUIBIN, Chemistry and Engineering
MA, HAILIANG, Foreign Languages
MA, WEIHUA, Law
MA, YONGMING, Chemistry and Engineering
MA, YUSHAN, History
MENG, ZIQIANG, Life Science and Technology
MIAO, DUOQIAN, Mathematics
NIE, HONGYIN, Chinese Language and Literature
NIE, YIXIN, Physics and Electronics Engineering
PAN, JINGHAO, Chemistry and Engineering
PAN, QING, Physics and Electronics Engineering
PANG, RENJI, Foreign Languages
PEI, CHENGFA, Economics
PEI, CHENGFA, Management
PENG, KUIXI, Physics and Electronics Engineering
PENG, YUNYE, Law
QIAO, DECAI, Physical Education
QIAO, QUANSHENG, Chinese Language and Literature
QIAO, RUIJIN, Philosophy and Sociology
QIN, XUEMEI, Chemistry and Engineering
REN, JIANGUO, Chemistry and Engineering
SHI, YAN, Physical Education
SHUANG, SHAOMIN, Chemistry and Engineering
SONG, BINGYAN, Philosophy and Sociology
SU, CHUNSHENG, Chinese Language and Literature
TIAN, YANNI, Chemistry and Engineering
WANG, HAI, Physics and Electronics Engineering
WANG, JIJUN, Law
WANG, JUNMIN, Physics and Electronics Engineering
WANG, LAN, Life Science and Technology
WANG, LIANG, Music
WANG, RONGSHENG, History
WANG, SHIYING, Mathematics
WANG, XIANMING, History
WANG, YI, Law
WANG, YINTIAN, History
WANG, YUANZHI, Law
WANG, ZHENGREN, Foreign Languages
WEI, GUANHLAI, History
WU, GAOSHOU, Philosophy and Sociology
WU, MIN, Political Science and Public Administration
WU, MINZHONG, Political Science and Public Administration
XIA, XHIXHONG, Chemistry and Engineering
XIANG, LILING, Management
XIE, CHANGDE, Physics and Electronics Engineering
XIE, JIAOLIANG, Life Science and Technology
XIE, SHULIAN, Life Science and Technology
XIE, YINGPING, Life Science and Technology
XING, LONG, History
XU, BINGSHENG, Chinese Language and Literature
XU, GENQI, Mathematics
XU, YONGMIN, Philosophy and Sociology
YAN, FENGWU, Chinese Language and Literature
YAN, JURANG, Mathematics
YANG, BINSHENG, Chemistry and Engineering
YANG, JUPING, History
YANG, LIAN, Chinese Language and Literature
YANG, PIN, Chemistry and Engineering
YANG, SUPING, Life Science and Technology
YI, HUILAN, Life Science and Technology
YU, GUODONG, Foreign Languages
YUE, QIANHOU, History
ZHANG, CUIYING, Management
ZHANG, FENG, Life Science and Technology

ZHANG, HENG, Chinese Language and Literature
ZHANG, JINGSHI, Education Science
ZHANG, JINTUN, Environmental Science and Resources
ZHANG, KUANSHOU, Physics and Electronics Engineering
ZHANG, MIN, Chinese Language and Literature
ZHANG, MINGYUAN, Fine Arts
ZHANG, RU, Chinese Language and Literature
ZHANG, RUIRONG, Music
ZHANG, SHENGWAN, Chemistry and Engineering
ZHANG, TIANCAI, Physics and Electronics Engineering
ZHANG, XIAOGE, Music
ZHANG, XINWEI, Management
ZHANG, YIXIAN, Life Science and Technology
ZHANG, ZHAO, Chemistry and Engineering
ZHANG, ZHUANGHUA, Life Science and Technology
ZHAO, AIMIN, Mathematics
ZHAO, JIANGUO, Chinese Language and Literature
ZHAO, RUIMIN, History
ZHAO, XIAOJUN, Law
ZHAO, YONGXIANG, Chemistry and Engineering
ZHAO, YUXIA, Philosophy and Sociology
ZHAO, ZHAOMING, Life Science and Technology
ZHOU, GUOSHENG, Physics and Electronics Engineering

SHENYANG AGRICULTURAL UNIVERSITY

120 Dongling Rd, Shenyang 110161, Liaoning

Telephone: (24) 88421121
Fax: (24) 88417415
Internet: www.syau.edu.cn

Founded 1952
Academic year: September to July

Pres.: ZHANG YULONG
Vice-Pres.: LI TIANLAI
Vice-Pres.: LIU GUANGLIN
Vice-Pres.: MENG QINGCHENG
Head of Graduate Dept: JIN BAOLIAN
Librarian: DUAN YUXI

Number of teachers: 859
Number of students: 20,105

Publications: *Chinese Journal of Soil Science* (6 a year), *Higher Agricultural Education* (12 a year), *Journal* (natural sciences, 6 a year), *Journal* (social sciences, 4 a year), *Journal of Pig Rearing* (6 a year), *New Agriculture* (12 a year)

DEANS

College of Agronomy: CAO MINJIAN
College of Biological Science and Technology: ZHANG LIJUN
College of Economics and Trade: FANG TIANKUN
College of Engineering: LI CHENGHUA
College of Food Science: LIU CHANGJIAN
College of Forestry: LIU MINGGUO
College of Horticulture: LI ZUOXUAN
College of Information and Electrical Engineering: PU ZAILIN
College of Land and the Environment: WANG QIUBING
College of Plant Protection: FU JUNFAN
College of Practical Technology: YANG YINSHAN
College of Science and Technology: (vacant)
College of Veterinary Science: HU JIANMING
College of Water Resources: WANG TIELIANG

PROFESSORS

BEI, NAXIN, Plant Protection

BIAN, QUANLIAN, Veterinary Science
CAO, MINJIAN, Agronomy
CAO, YUANYIN, Plant Protection
CAO, ZHIQIANG, Agronomy
CHEN, ENFENG, Land and the Environment
CHEN, JIE, Plant Protection
CHEN, WENFU, Agronomy
CHEN, XIAOFEI, Water Resources
CHEN, XISHI, Land and the Environment
CHEN, ZHENWU, Agronomy
CHENG, GUOHUA, Biological Science and Technology
CHENG, YULAI, Food Science
CHI, DAOCAI, Water Resources
CONG, BIN, Plant Protection
DAI, PENGJUN, Economics and Trade
DONG, WENXUAN, Horticulture
DU, GUANGMING, Horticulture
DU, SHAOFAN, Veterinary Science
DUAN, YUXI, Plant Protection
FANG, TIANKUN, Economics and Trade
FENG, HUI, Horticulture
FU, JUNFAN, Plant Protection
GAO, DESAN, Biological Science and Technology
GAO, GUOPING, Forestry
GAO, XINGLIAN, Engineering
GUAN, LIANZHU, Land and the Environment
GUO, XIUWU, Horticulture
GUO, YUHUA, Agronomy
HAN, XIAORI, Land and the Environment
HE, JUNSHI, Water Resources
HE, LILI, Horticulture
HOU, LIBAI, Agronomy
HU, JIANMIN, Veterinary Science
HUANG, RUIDONG, Agronomy
HUI, SHURONG, Basic Education
JI, JIANWEI, Information and Electrical Engineering
JI, MINGSHAN, Plant Protection
JI, MINGXI, Water Resources
JI, SHUJUAN, Food Science
JIANG, QILIANG, Plant Protection
LAN, QINGGAO, Economics and Trade
LI, BAOFA, Engineering
LI, BAOHUA, Basic Education
LI, BAOJIANG, Horticulture
LI, BINGCHAO, Basic Education
LI, CHENGHUA, Engineering
LI, GUOJIE, Insititue of Higher Education
LI, JIANNAN, Biological Science and Technology
LI, TIANLAI, Horticulture
LI, XINHUA, Food Science
LI, YONGKUI, Engineering
LI, YUXIA, Basic Education
LI, ZUOXUAN, Horticulture
LIANG, CHENGHUA, Land and the Environment
LIANG, JINGYI, Plant Protection
LIN, GUOLIN, Land and the Environment
LIU, CHANGJIANG, Food Science
LIU, MINGGUO, Forestry
LIU, RONGHOU, Engineering
LIU, ZHIHENG, Plant Protection
LIU, ZHONGQIN, Economics and Trade
LU, GUOZHONG, Plant Protection
LU, JIE, Economics and Trade
LU, SHUXIA, Biological Science and Technology
LUO, GUANGBIN, Veterinary Science
MAO, TAO, Food Science
MENG, XIANJUN, Food Science
MI, YONGNING, Water Resources
NIU, SHEN, Centre for Analysis and Testing
PU, ZAILIN, Information and Electrical Engineering
QIN, LI, Biological Science and Technology
QIU, LICHUN, Engineering
REN, WENTAO, Engineering
SHEN, XIANGQUN, Horticulture
SHI, ZHENSHENG, Agronomy
SI, LONGTING, Horticulture
SUN, JUNDE, Land and the Environment
TANG, YONG, Biological Science and Technology

WANG, BOLUN, Agronomy
WANG, CHUNPING, Economics and Trade
WANG, HONGPING, Plant Protection
WANG, HUICHENG, Engineering
WANG, JINGKUAN, Land and the Environment
WANG, JINMIN, Agronomy
WANG, LIXUE, Water Resources
WANG, QINGXIANG, Agronomy
WANG, QIUBING, Land and the Environment
WANG, SHAOBIN, Agronomy
WANG, XIAOQI, Plant Protection
WANG, XUEYING, Biological Science and Technology
WEI, YUTANG, Horticulture
WU, LUPING, Horticulture
WU, YUANHUA, Plant Protection
XIAO, SHENGAN, Social Science
XIE, FUTI, Agronomy
XU, XIAOMING, Physical Education
XU, ZHENGJIN, Agronomy
YAN, HONGWEI, Forestry
YANG, GUIQIN, Veterinary Science
YANG, SHOUREN, Agronomy
YANG, YONG, Information and Electrical Engineering
YI, YANLI, Land and the Environment
YIN, MINGFANG, Forestry
YU, ZHONGTAO, Social Science
ZHAI, YINLI, Economics and Trade
ZHANG, BAOSHI, Agronomy
ZHANG, KAIBIN, Horticulture
ZHANG, LIJUN, Biological Science and Technology
ZHANG, LONGBU, Agronomy
ZHANG, SHUSHEN, Plant Protection
ZHANG, XIURAN, Information and Electrical Engineering
ZHANG, YONGMING, Social Science
ZHANG, YULIN, Social Science
ZHANG, YULONG, Land and the Environment
ZHANG, ZHIHONG, Horticulture
ZHANG, ZULI, Engineering
ZHAO, YUJUN, Veterinary Science
ZHOU, BAOLI, Horticulture
ZHOU, HONGFEI, Agronomy
ZHOU, QILONG, Information and Electrical Engineering
ZHOU, YANMING, Centre for Analysis and Testing

SHENZHEN UNIVERSITY

Nanhai Rd 3688, 518060 Shenzhen Guangdong
Telephone and fax (755) 26534940
E-mail: szufao@szu.edu.cn
Internet: www.szu.edu.cn
Founded 1983
State control
Academic year: September to July
Pres.: ZHANG BIGONG
Vice-Pres.: DU HONGBIAO
Vice-Pres.: LI FENGLIANG
Vice-Pres.: Prof. LI YONGHUA
Vice-Pres.: Prof. RUAN SHUANGCHEN
Vice-Pres.: Prof. XING FENG
Vice-Pres.: Prof. XING MIAO
Registrar: XU CHEN
Librarian: HUANG WEIPING
Library: 3.8m. vols, incl. 2.69m. journals and books, 1.26m. e-books
Number of teachers: 1,221
Number of students: 28,000
Publications: *Shenzhen University Journal* (social sciences and humanities), *Shenzhen University Journal* (natural sciences), *World Architecture Review*

DEANS

Department of English: Prof. CAO YIAJUN
Faculty of Adult Education: Prof. YANG ZHONGXIN
Faculty of Architecture and Civil Engineering: Prof. XU ANZHI

Faculty of Art: Prof. LIAO XINGQIAO
Faculty of Arts: Prof. YU LONGYU
Faculty of Economics: Prof. CAO LONGQI
Faculty of Engineering Technology: Prof. ZHU QIN
Faculty of Golf Sport and Management: Prof. LIN ZUJI
Faculty of Information Engineering: Prof. YONG ZHENGZHENG
Faculty of Science: Prof. SHU QIQING
Sports Department: Prof. CHEN XIAORONG
Teachers' College: Prof. ZHANG BIGONG

SICHUAN AGRICULTURAL UNIVERSITY

12 Xinkang Rd, Yaan 625014, Sichuan
Telephone: (835) 2882233
Fax: (835) 2883166
Internet: www.sicau.edu.cn
Founded 1906 as Sichuan Tong Sheng Agricultural School, subordinated to Nat. Sichuan Univ. in 1935, present name 1985
Academic year: September to July
Pres.: WEN XINTIAN
Vice-Pres: REN ZHENGLONG, YANG WENYU, ZHANG QIANG, ZHENG YOULIANG, ZHU QING
Librarian: XIA JIMING
Library of 2,000,000 vols
Number of teachers: 1,500
Number of students: 28,000
Publication: *Journal* (4 a year)
Schools and Faculties: agronomy, animal science, economical management in agriculture and forestry, environmental engineering, forestry and grass science, humanities and social sciences, information and engineering technology, land resource management, life science, plant protection, veterinary science, vocational technology; Further Education College.

SICHUAN UNION UNIVERSITY

Jiuyanqiao, Chengdu 610064, Sichuan
Telephone: (28) 5412233
Fax: (28) 5410187
E-mail: scuu@sun.scuu.cdnet.edu.cn
Founded 1994 by merger of Sichuan University and Chengdu University of Science and Technology
State control
Language of instruction: Chinese
Academic year: September to July
Pres.: LU TIECHENG
Vice-Pres.: CHEN JUNKAI
Vice-Pres.: LIU YINGMING
Vice-Pres.: LI ZHIQIANG
Vice-Pres.: LONG WEI
Vice-Pres.: YANG JIRUI
Vice-Pres.: ZHANG YIZHENG
Registrar: XIAO DINGQUAN
Librarians: CAI SHUXIAN, FENG ZESI, LIU YINGMING
Library of 3,650,000 vols
Number of teachers: 3,660
Number of students: 19,150
Publications: *Journal of Atomic and Molecular Physics, Oil-field Chemistry, Polymeric Material Science and Technology, Religion Studies, Sichuan Union University Journal of Natural Science, Sichuan Union University Journal of Social Science, Sichuan Union University Journal of Engineering Science, South Asian Studies Quarterly*

DEANS

College of Chemical Science and Engineering: ZHU JIAHUA
College of Economics and Management: CHEN GAOLIN

College of Energy Resources Science and Engineering: (vacant)
College of Fine Art: DENG SHENGQING
College of Foreign Languages: (vacant)
College of Humanities: CAO SHUNQING
College of Information Science and Engineering: TAO FUZHOU
College of Journalism: QIU PEIHUANG
College of Law: TANG LEI
College of Life Sciences and Engineering: CHEN FANG
College of Light Science and Engineering: WU DACHENG
College of Manufacturing Science and Engineering: (vacant)
College of Materials Science and Engineering: GU YI
College of Sciences: (vacant)
College of Urban and Rural Construction and Environmental Protection: LUO TEJUN
School of Adult Education and Vocational Education: WANG ZHONGMING

SICHUAN UNIVERSITY

24 South Section 1, Yihuan Rd, Chengdu 610065, Sichuan
Telephone: (28) 85402443
Fax: (28) 85403260
Internet: www.scu.edu.cn
Founded 1896
State control
Academic year: September to July
Pres.: ZHAO YANXIU
Vice-Presidents: LI ZHIQIANG, LIU YINGMING, TANG DENGXUE, XIE HEPING, YANG JIRUI, ZHANG WEIGUO, ZHAO ZHAODA
Head of Graduate Department: LIU YINGMING
Librarian: LI BINGYAN
Library of 4,847,300 vols
Number of teachers: 1,035
Number of students: 44,003
Publication: *Journal* (edns: natural sciences, 6 a year; engineering, 12 a year; medicine, 4 a year; philosophy and social sciences, 4 a year)

DEANS

College of Art: (vacant)
College of Chemistry: HU CHANG WEI
College of Economics and Management: ZHOU GUANG YAN
College of Foreign Languages and Cultures: SHI JIAN
College of Literature and Journalism: CAO SHUNQING
College of Mathematics: LI AN MIN
College of Physical Science and Technology: GONG MIN
College of Politics: WANG GUO MIN
College of Polymer Science and Engineering: YANG MING BO
College of Software Engineering: ZHOU JI LIU
College of Water Resources and Hydropower: LIANG CHUAN
School of Architecture and the Environment: FAN YU BO
School of Chemistry and Engineering: ZHU JIA HUA
School of Community and Sanitation: MA XIAO
School of Computer Science and Engineering: (vacant)
School of Electricity and Electronic Information: ZHAO ZHUO YAO
School of History and Culture: WANG TING ZHI
School of Law: (vacant)
School of Life Sciences: CHEN FANG
School of Manufacturing Science and Engineering: YIN GUO FU
School of Materials Science and Engineering: (vacant)
School of Physical Education: TANG CHENG

School of Pre-Clinical and Forensic Medicine: HOU YI PING
School of Tourism: (vacant)
West China College of Stomatology: ZHOU XUE DONG
West China School of Pharmacy: ZHANG ZHI RONG

PROFESSORS

AI, NAN SHAN, Architecture and the Environment
AO, FAN, Foreign Languages and Cultures
CAO, GUANG FU, Mathematics
CAO, YI PING, Electronics and Information Engineering
CAO, YI, Life Sciences
CAO, YU RONG, Politics
CENG, ZONG YONG, Life Sciences
CHEN, DAO BANG, Pre-Clinical and Forensic Medicine
CHEN, DE BEN, Chemistry
CHEN, GAO LIN, Economics and Management
CHEN, GUO DI, Pre-Clinical and Forensic Medicine
CHEN, HONG CHAO, Chemistry
CHEN, JIAN KANG, Water Resources and Hydropower
CHEN, JUN KAI, Architecture and the Environment
CHEN, KANG YANG, Law
CHEN, QIAN DE, Architecture and the Environment
CHEN, QIAO, Pre-Clinical and Forensic Medicine
CHEN, TIAN LANG, Chemistry
CHEN, WEN JUN, Chemistry
CHEN, YONG GE, Law
CHEN, ZE FANG, Chemistry
CHEN, ZHONG RONG, Foreign Languages and Cultures
CHENG, LI, Tourism
CHENG, XI LIN, Foreign Languages and Cultures
DAI, ZONG KUN, Electronics and Information Engineering
DAN, DE ZHONG, Architecture and the Environment
DENG, XIAO KANG, Pre-Clinical and Forensic Medicine
DENG, ZHEN HUA, Pre-Clinical and Forensic Medicine
DOU, HOU SONG, Chemistry
FAN, HONG, Architecture and the Environment
FAN, YU BO, Architecture and the Environment
FANG, GUO ZHEN, Chemistry
FANG, SHU XIN, History and Culture
FENG, YI JUN, Chemistry
FENG, ZE HUI, Foreign Languages and Cultures
FU, HE JIAN, Chemistry
FU, HUA LONG, Life Sciences
GAO, CHUN HUA, Manufacturing Science and Engineering
GAO, RONG, Life Sciences
GU, BIN, Life Sciences
GU, ZHONG BI, Electronics and Information Engineering
GUAN, PENG, Pre-Clinical and Forensic Medicine
HE, CHANG RONG, Water Resources and Hydropower
HE, JIANG DA, Water Resources and Hydropower
HE, JING XU, Law
HE, PEI YU, Electronics and Information Engineering
HE, PING, Foreign Languages and Cultures
HE, QING, History and Culture
HE, XING JIN, Life Sciences
HE, YA PING, Pre-Clinical and Forensic Medicine
HE, YU EN, Chemistry
HOU, XIAN DENG, Chemistry
HU, HUO ZHEN, Life Sciences

HU, JIA YUAN, Chemistry
HU, JUN MEI, Pre-Clinical and Forensic Medicine
HUANG, DE CHANG, Economics and Management
HUANG, FA LUN, Mathematics
HUANG, GUANG LIN, Chemistry
HUANG, NAN JING, Mathematics
HUANG, NIAN CI, Electricity and Electronic Information
HUANG, NING, Pre-Clinical and Forensic Medicine
HUANG, SHAN, Electricity and Electronic Information
HUANG, YING, Pre-Clinical and Forensic Medicine
JIANG, BO, Chemistry
JIANG, CHENG FA, Chemistry and Engineering
JIANG, WEN JU, Architecture and the Environment
JIN, MING, Law
JING, DONG, Electricity and Electronic Information
JU, XIAO MING, Water Resources and Hydropower
KANG, ZHEN HUANG, Architecture and the Environment
KE, JI GUI, Foreign Languages and Cultures
LEI, YONG XUE, Politics
LI, AN MIN, Mathematics
LI, BO HUAI, Tourism
LI, DE YU, Architecture and the Environment
LI, FANG, Chemistry
LI, FU HAI, Economics and Management
LI, GUO CHENG, Electricity and Electronic Information
LI, HONG, Pre-Clinical and Forensic Medicine
LI, HUI, Chemistry and Engineering
LI, JIAN MING, Chemistry and Engineering
LI, JIAO, Foreign Languages and Cultures
LI, JIE, Politics
LI, JU CAI, Chemistry
LI, KE FENG, Water Resources and Hydropower
LI, LIANG, Pre-Clinical and Forensic Medicine
LI, MENG LONG, Chemistry
LI, PING, Law
LI, RUI XIANG, Chemistry
LI, SHI YAN, Economics and Management
LI, TAO, History and Culture
LI, XIAO SONG, Infrastructure and Sanitation
LI, YAO ZHONG, Chemistry
LI, YING BI, Pre-Clinical and Forensic Medicine
LI, YING, Chemistry
LI, ZAN, Law
LI, ZHANG ZHENG, Architecture and the Environment
LI, ZHI SHU, Computer Science and Engineering
LI, ZHONG FU, Mathematics
LI, ZHONG MING, Polymer Science and Engineering
LIANG, BING, Chemistry and Engineering
LIANG, JI HUA, Mathematics
LIANG, YUAN DI, Economics and Management
LIAO, LIN CHUAN, Pre-Clinical and Forensic Medicine
LIN, BI GUO, Foreign Languages and Cultures
LIN, DA QUAN, Manufacturing Science and Engineering
LIU, CHANG JUN, Electronics and Information Engineering
LIU, DONG QUAN, Software Engineering
LIU, FEI PENG, Electricity and Electronic Information
LIU, GUANG ZHONG, Economics and Management
LIU, JIA YONG, Electronics and Information Engineering
LIU, LI MIN, Foreign Languages and Cultures
LIU, MIN, Pre-Clinical and Forensic Medicine

LIU, NIAN, Electricity and Electronic Information
LIU, QI CHAO, Software Engineering
LIU, RONG ZHONG, Manufacturing Science and Engineering
LIU, SHAN JUN, Water Resources and Hydropower
LIU, SHENG QING, Manufacturing Science and Engineering
LIU, TIAN QI, Electricity and Electronic Information
LIU, TING HUA, Polymer Science and Engineering
LIU, YI FEI, History and Culture
LIU, YU SHENG, Electricity and Electronic Information
LONG, JIAN ZHONG, Electronics and Information Engineering
LONG, KUI, Foreign Languages and Cultures
LONG, WEI, Manufacturing Science and Engineering
LONG, YUN FANG, Infrastructure and Sanitation
LONG, ZONG ZHI, Law
LUO, DI LUN, Foreign Languages and Cultures
LUO, LIN, Water Resources and Hydropower
LUO, LIN, Architecture and the Environment
LUO, MAO KANG, Mathematics
LUO, MEI MING, Chemistry
LUO, SU QIONG, Infrastructure and Sanitation
LUO, TE JUN, Architecture and the Environment
LUO, WAN BO, Computer Science and Engineering
LUO, XIANG LIN, Polymer Science and Engineering
LV, GUANG HONG, Computer Science and Engineering
LV, TAO, Mathematics
MA, HONG, Mathematics
MA, LI TAI, Foreign Languages and Cultures
MENG, YAN FA, Life Sciences
MU, CHUN LAI, Mathematics
NIE, GANG, Politics
NING, YUAN ZHONG, Electricity and Electronic Information
PEI, JUE MIN, Architecture and the Environment
PENG, BANG BEN, History and Culture
PENG, LIAN GANG, Mathematics
QI, JIAN GUO, Pre-Clinical and Forensic Medicine
QIN, SHI LUN, Architecture and the Environment
QIU, WANG SHENG, Foreign Languages and Cultures
QU, ZHAO YANG, Pre-Clinical and Forensic Medicine
SHI, JIAN, Foreign Languages and Cultures
SHI, YING PING, Tourism
SHU, QIN, Electricity and Electronic Information
SONG, HANG, Chemistry and Engineering
SONG, WEI, Economics and Management
SUN, CHENG JUN, Infrastructure and Sanitation
SUN, JIN QUAN, History and Culture
SUN, QI, Mathematics
TAN, DA LU, Architecture and the Environment
TAN, XIAO PING, Architecture and the Environment
TAN, YANG, Pre-Clinical and Forensic Medicine
TANG, JIA LING, Polymer Science and Engineering
TANG, LEI, Law
TANG, NING JIU, Computer Science and Engineering
TANG, YA, Architecture and the Environment
TAO, LI, Economics and Management
TU, SHANG YIN, Foreign Languages and Cultures

TU, YUAN ZHAO, Electricity and Electronic Information
WAN, JIA YI, Chemistry
WANG, DAO HUI, Electricity and Electronic Information
WANG, FAN, Pre-Clinical and Forensic Medicine
WANG, GUO MIN, Politics
WANG, JIAN PING, Law
WANG, LEI, Pre-Clinical and Forensic Medicine
WANG, LI, Water Resources and Hydropower
WANG, LI, Life Sciences
WANG, QI ZHI, Architecture and the Environment
WANG, QING YUAN, Architecture and the Environment
WANG, SHU YU, Foreign Languages and Cultures
WANG, XIAO LU, Foreign Languages and Cultures
WANG, YA JING, Pre-Clinical and Forensic Medicine
WANG, YING HAN, Polymer Science and Engineering
WANG, ZHEN XUE, Electronics and Information Engineering
WEI, XIN PING, Water Resources and Hydropower
WEI, ZHONG HAI, Politics
WEN, CHU AN, Foreign Languages and Cultures
WU, JIANG, Chemistry
WU, JIN, Pre-Clinical and Forensic Medicine
WU, QING, Pre-Clinical and Forensic Medicine
WU, XIAN HONG, Foreign Languages and Cultures
WU, ZHI HUA, Polymer Science and Engineering
XIA, SU LAN, Chemistry and Engineering
XIANG, TAO, Pre-Clinical and Forensic Medicine
XIANG, ZHAO YANG, Law
XIAO, AN FU, Foreign Languages and Cultures
XIAO, SHEN XIU, Chemistry
XIAO, XU, Politics
XIE, BANG HU, Polymer Science and Engineering
XIONG, FENG, Architecture and the Environment
XU, DAO YI, Mathematics
XU, HENG, Life Sciences
XU, LAN, Electronics and Information Engineering
XUE, YING, Chemistry
YANG, FANG JU, Pre-Clinical and Forensic Medicine
YANG, GANG, Polymer Science and Engineering
YANG, HONG GENG, Electricity and Electronic Information
YANG, HONG YU, Computer Science and Engineering
YANG, JIANG, Economics and Management
YANG, JIE, Chemistry
YANG, JUN LIU, Architecture and the Environment
YANG, SHI WEN, History and Culture
YANG, SUI QUAN, Law
YANG, WAN QUAN, Electronics and Information Engineering
YANG, WU NENG, Foreign Languages and Cultures
YANG, YI, Manufacturing Science and Engineering
YANG, YI, Life Sciences
YANG, ZHEN ZHI, Tourism
YANG, ZHENG GUANG, Politics
YE, GUANG DOU, Polymer Science and Engineering
YI, DAN, Foreign Languages and Cultures
YI, XU FU, Pre-Clinical and Forensic Medicine

YIN, HUA QIANG, Architecture and the Environment
YIN, YONG XIANG, Chemistry and Engineering
YOU, XIAN GUI, Chemistry and Engineering
YU, JIAN HUA, Architecture and the Environment
YU, ZHONG DE, Software Engineering
YUAN, DAO HUA, Computer Science and Engineering
YUAN, DE CHENG, Foreign Languages and Cultures
YUAN, DE QI, Chemistry
YUAN, LI HUA, Chemistry
YUAN, PENG, Water Resources and Hydropower
YUAN, YONG MING, Chemistry
YUAN, ZHI RUN, Architecture and the Environment
YUE, LI MIN, Pre-Clinical and Forensic Medicine
ZENG, CHENG MING, Life Sciences
ZENG, LING FU, Infrastructure and Sanitation
ZHANG, CHAO, Electricity and Electronic Information
ZHANG, DAI RUN, Electricity and Electronic Information
ZHANG, DE XUE, Mathematics
ZHANG, GUANG KE, Water Resources and Hydropower
ZHANG, HONG WEI, Computer Science and Engineering
ZHANG, HUA, Electricity and Electronic Information
ZHANG, JIAN ZHOU, Computer Science and Engineering
ZHANG, KE RONG, Infrastructure and Sanitation
ZHANG, LIN, Water Resources and Hydropower
ZHANG, PIN, Pre-Clinical and Forensic Medicine
ZHANG, WEI NIAN, Mathematics
ZHANG, WEI, Pre-Clinical and Forensic Medicine
ZHANG, XIN PEI, Architecture and the Environment
ZHANG, XU, Mathematics
ZHANG, YI ZHONG, Electricity and Electronic Information
ZHANG, YONG KUI, Chemistry and Engineering
ZHAO, CHANG SHEN, Polymer Science and Engineering
ZHAO, CHENG YU, Life Sciences
ZHAO, SHI PING, Manufacturing Science and Engineering
ZHAO, YUN, Life Sciences
ZHENG, CHANG YI, Chemistry
ZHENG, HUA, Politics
ZHONG, SHU LIN, Chemistry
ZHONG, YIN PING, Polymer Science and Engineering
ZHOU, AN MIN, Electronics and Information Engineering
ZHOU, BO, Architecture and the Environment
ZHOU, BU XIANG, Electricity and Electronic Information
ZHOU, GUANG YA, Foreign Languages and Cultures
ZHOU, JI LIU, Software Engineering
ZHOU, JIAN LUE, Chemistry
ZHOU, LI MING, Pre-Clinical and Forensic Medicine
ZHOU, WEI, Law
ZHOU, XUE, Pre-Clinical and Forensic Medicine
ZHOU, YI, Tourism
ZHU, HUI, Foreign Languages and Cultures
ZHU, XIN MIN, Economics and Management
ZHU, YUN MIN, Mathematics
ZHUANG, CHENG SAN, Computer Science and Engineering
ZUO, WEI MIN, Law

SOOCHOW UNIVERSITY

1 Shi Xin St, Suzhou 215006, Jiangsu
Internet: www.suda.edu.cn

Founded 1900
Academic year: September to July

Pres.: QIAN PEIDE
Vice-Presidents: BAI LUN, GE JIANYI, ZHANG XUEGUANG, ZHU XIULIN
Head of Graduate Department: ZHU SHIQUN
Librarian: WANG GUOPING

Library of 3,320,000 vols
Number of teachers: 1,200
Number of students: 32,300

Publication: *Journal of Suzhou University* (editions: engineering sciences, medical science, 6 a year; natural sciences, philosophy and social science, 4 a year)

DEANS

College of Politics and Public Management: ZHOU KEZHEN
Institute of Pollution and Public Health: TONG JIAN
Material Engineering Institute: CHEN GUOQIANG
School of Agricultural Science and Technology: SHEN WEIDE
School of Chemistry and Chemical Engineering: JI SHUNJUN
School of Computer Science and Technology: ZHU QIAOMING
School of Electronic Information: ZHAO HEMING
School of Foreign Languages: WANG LABAO
School of Life Sciences: ZHANG XUEGUANG
School of Literature Department: LUO SHIJIN
School of Mathematical Sciences: WANG LABAO
School of Mechanical and electronic Engineering: RUI YANNIAN
School of Medicine: WU AIQIN
School of Physical Education and Sports: WANG JIAHONG
School of Social Science: WANG LABAO

PROFESSORS

BAO, SHIQIAO, Medicine
CAO, YONGLUO, Mathematical Sciences
CAO, YONGLUO, Mechanical and Electronic Engineering
CHEN, LINSEN, Computer Science and Technology
CHEN, QINGGUAN, Mechanical and Electronic Engineering
CHEN, ZIXING, Medicine
CUI, ZHIMING, Mechanical and Electronic Engineering
FENG, ZHIHUA, Mechanical and Electronic Engineering
FU, GEYAN, Mechanical and Electronic Engineering
GAO, FANGYING, Social Science
GAO, QI, Medicine
GU, ZHENLUN, Medicine
GU, ZONGJIANG, Medicine
GUI, SHIHE, Mechanical and Electronic Engineering
HONG, FASHUI, Life Sciences
HU, HUACHENG, Medicine
HUA, RENDE, Art
HUANG, QIANG, Medicine
JIANG, WENKAI, Physical Education and Sports
JIANG, XINGHONG, Medicine
JIN, WEIXING, Social Science
LAN, QING, Medicine
LI, DECHUN, Medicine
LIANG, JUN, Art
LIAO, LIANGYUN, Art
LIU, CHUNFENG, Medicine
LIU, ZHIHUA, Medicine
LU, HUIMIN, Medicine
LU, JIAN, Social Science
MA, WEIZHONG, Literature

QIAN, HAIXIN, Medicine
QIN, ZHENGHONG, Medicine
RUI, YANNIAN, Mechanical and Electronic Engineering
SHEN, YULIANG, Mathematical Sciences
SHEN, ZHENYA, Medicine
SHI, GUANGYU, Mechanical and Electronic Engineering
SHI, SHIHONG, Mechanical and Electronic Engineering
SONG, HUICHUN, Life Sciences
SUN, JUNYING, Medicine
SUN, MINZHI, Physical Education and Sports
TANG, TIANSI, Medicine
TANG, ZHENGPEI, Social Science
TANG, ZHINGMING, Mathematical Sciences
TIAN, JIUMAI, Physical Education and Sports
TU, YIFENG, Chemistry and Chemical Engineering
WAN, JIEQIU, Commerce
WANG, GUANGWEI, Commerce
WANG, GUOPING, Social Science
WANG, JIAHONG, Physical Education and Sports
WANG, ZHAOYUE, Medicine
WEI, XIANGDONG, Social Science
WEN, DUANGAI, Medicine
WU, DEPEI, Medicine
WU, HAORONG, Medicine
WU, JINCHANG, Medicine
XIA, CHAOMING, Medicine
XIA, CHUNLIN, Medicine
XU, HAOWEN, Physical Education and Sports
XUE, YONGQUAN, Medicine
YAN, CHUNYIN, Medicine
YANG, JICHENG, Medicine
YANG, XIANGJUN, Medicine
YIN, YUNXING, Mechanical and Electronic Engineering
YU, HONGBING, Mathematical Sciences
YU, TONGYUAN, Social Science
YU, ZHENG, Social Science
ZANG, ZHIFEI, Social Science
ZHANG, LIN, Physical Education and Sports
ZHANG, MING, Social Science
ZHANG, PENGCHUAN, Art
ZHANG, RI, Medicine
ZHANG, SHIMING, Medicine
ZHANG, XIQING, Medicine
ZHANG, XUEGANG, Life Sciences
ZHANG, XUEGUANG, Life Sciences
ZHANG, ZHAOYU, Social Science
ZHAO, ZENGYAO, Commerce
ZHONG, KANGMIN, Mechanical and Electronic Engineering
ZHOU, DAI, Medicine
ZHOU, JIANPENG, Chemistry and Chemical Engineering
ZHU, CONGBING, Social Science
ZHU, JIANG, Life Sciences
ZHUGE, HONGXIANG, Medicine
ZHUGE, KAI, Art

SOUTH CHINA AGRICULTURAL UNIVERSITY

Wushan, Guangzhou 510642, Guangdong
Telephone: (20) 85280007
Fax: (20) 85282693
E-mail: office@scau.edu.cn
Internet: www.scau.edu.cn

Founded 1909
State (provincial) control
Academic year: September to July

Pres.: Prof. LUO SHIMING
Vice-Pres.: Prof. CHEN BEIGUANG
Vice-Pres.: Assoc. Prof. CHEN CHANGSHENG
Vice-Pres.: Prof. LUO XIWEN
Librarian: YE JINGHUA

Library of 700,000 vols
Number of teachers: 753
Number of students: 12,501

Publications: *Journal* (4 a year), *Poultry Husbandry and Disease Control* (12 a year), *Guangdong Agricultural Sciences* (jtly published with Guangdong Acad. of Agricultural Science, 12 a year)

DEANS

College of Adult Education: Prof. NIU BAOJUN
College of Biotechnology: Prof. PENG XINXIANG
College of Economics and Trade: Prof. LI DASHENG
College of Forestry: Prof. CHEN XIMU
College of Liberal Arts: Prof. ZHANG WENFANG
College of Resources and Environment: Prof. LI HUAXING
College of Science: Prof. ZHANG GUOQUAN
Department of Agronomy: Prof. ZHANG GUIQUAN
Department of Animal Medicine: Prof. ZENG ZHENLING
Department of Animal Science: Prof. FENG DINGYUAN
Department of Food Science: Assoc. Prof. LI BIN
Department of Horticulture: Assoc. Prof. CHEN RIYUAN
Department of Physical Education: Assoc. Prof. WANG CHANGQING
Department of Sericulture: Assoc. Prof. XU XINGYAO
Polytechnic College: Prof. OU YINGGANG

PROFESSORS

BI, Y. Z., Animal Nutrition and Immunology
CAO, Y., Silkworm Biotechnology
CHEN, B.G., Forest Ecology
CHEN, D. C., Pomology
CHEN, W. K., Insect Toxicology
CHEN, W. X., Post-harvest Physiology of Fruit and Vegetables
CHEN, X. M., Plant Systematics and Evolution
CHEN, Y. S., Animal Genetics and Breeding
CHEN, Y. Q., Food Biochemistry
CHEN, Z. L., Veterinary Medicine
CHEN, Z. Q., Crop Genetics and Breeding
FAN, H. Z., Plant Pathology
FAN, X. L., Soil Chemistry
FENG, D. Y., Animal Nutrition and Feed Science
FENG, Q. H., Veterinary Medicine
FU, C., Economic Policy and Development
FU, W. L., Animal Physiology
GAO, X. B., Plant Pathology
GU, D. J., Insect Ecology
GUO, Z. F., Plant Physiology and Molecular Biology
HONG, T. S., Agricultural Mechanization
HUANG, B. Q., Insecticide
HUANG, H. B., Fruit Tree Physiology
HUANG, Q. Y., Veterinary Microbiology
HUANG, X. Y., Food Nutrition
HUANG, Z. L., Biochemistry
JI, Z. L., Agricultural Product Storage and Processing
JIAN, Y. Y., Plant Biotechnology
JIANG, H., Agricultural Economics and Management
JIANG, Z. D., Plant Pathology
KONG, X. M., Veterinary Pathology
LAN, S. F., Ecological Energy and Value of Energy
LI, B. T., Plant Taxonomy
LI, D. S., Economics of Agricultural Engineering
LI, G. Q., Veterinary Parasitology
LI, H. X., Soil Science
LI, J. P., Soil Chemistry
LI, K. F., Wood Science
LI, M. Q., Plant Physiology
LI, Z. L., Crop Cultivation
LIANG, G. W., Insect Ecology
LIANG, J. N., Crop Cultivation
LIAO, Z. W., Soil Science and the Environment
LIN, J. R., Silkworm Genetics and Breeding
LIN, S. Q., Pomology

LIN, Y. G., Genetic Engineering
LU, Y. G., Plant Genetics
LUO, B. L., Agricultural Economics and Management
LUO, F. H., Forest Management
LUO, S. M., Agroecology
LUO, X. W., Agricultural Mechanization
MEI, M. T., Plant Biotechnology
OU, Y. G., Agricultural Engineering
PAN, Q. H., Plant Pathology
PANG, X. F., Insect Ecology and Taxonomy
PENG, X. X., Plant Physiology and Molecular Biology
REN, S. X., Insect Ecology
SUN, Y. M., Food Chemistry
TAN, Z. W., Plant Genetics and Breeding
TIE, L. Y., Fashion Design
WAN, B. H., Plant Genetics and Breeding
WANG, D. L., Tea Science
WANG, J., Forest Pathology
WANG, S. Z., Landscape Gardening
WANG, Z. S., Animal Ecology
WANG, Z. Z., Plant Pathology
WEN, S. M., Agricultural Economics and Management
WU, H., Botany
WU, Q. T., Agricultural Environment Protection
XIAO, H. G., Plant Pathology
XIN, C. A., Poultry Disease
XU, F. C., Plant Physiology
XU, H. H., Insect Toxicology
XU, X. Y., Silkworm Pathology
YAN, X. L., Plant Nutrition
YANG, G. F., Animal Genetics and Breeding
YANG, Y. S., Genetic Engineering
ZENG, L., Insect Ecology
ZENG, Z. L., Veterinary Pharmacology
ZHANG, G. Q., Crop Genetics and Breeding
ZHANG, T. L., Agricultural Mechanization
ZHANG, W. F., Agricultural Economics and Management
ZHANG, X. Q., Animal Genetics and Breeding
ZHANG, Y. H., Agricultural Economics and Management

SOUTH CHINA NORMAL UNIVERSITY

Shipai, Guangzhou 510631, Guangdong
Telephone: (20) 85210169
Fax: (20) 85210991
Internet: www.scnu.edu.cn
Founded 1933
Academic year: September to July
Pres.: WANG GUOJIAN
Vice-Presidents: HU SHEJUN, HUANG LIYA, LI YONGJIE, LIU MING, MO LEI, QIAN XIANBIN, WU YINGMIN
Head of Graduate Department: XIAO HUA
Librarian: ZHU JIANLIANG
Number of teachers: 2,400
Number of students: 60,600
Publications: *High School Physics Education* (12 a year), *Journal* (6 a year), *Journal of Physical Education* (6 a year), *Oriental Culture* (6 a year)

DEANS

College of Economics and Management: LI YONGJIE
College of Educational Information Technology: XU FUYING
College of Foreign Languages: (vacant)
College of Humanities: KE HANLING
College of International Culture: LI SHENGBING
College of Life Sciences: MA GUANGZHI
College of Optoelectronics Technology: LIU SONGHAO
College of Physics and Telecommunications Engineering: LIU QIONGFA
College of Politics and Law: HU ZEHONG
College of Sports Science: ZHOU AIGUANG
Department of Art: HUANG LIYA

Department of Chemistry: ZENG HEPING
Department of Computer Science: BAO SUSU
Department of Geography: XU XIANGJUN
Department of Mathematics: HUANG ZHIDA
Department of Music: CHENG JIANPING
Department of Tourism Management: GAN QIAOLIN
School of Continuing Education: HUANG ZHIYING
School of Education Science: MO LEI

PROFESSORS

BAO, ZONGTI, Physics and Telecommunications Engineering
BIN, JINHUA, Life Sciences
CHANG, HONGSEN, Physics and Telecommunications Engineering
CHEN, HAO, Physics and Telecommunications Engineering
CHEN, HUOWANG, Computer Science
CHEN, JUNFANG, Physics and Telecommunications Engineering
CHEN, QI, Sports Science
CHEN, XIANGLIN, Life Sciences
CHEN, XINMIN, Economics and Management
CHEN, YAOSHENG, Economics and Management
CHEN, YONGSHAO, Mathematics
CHEN, YUQUN, Mathematics
CHEN, ZHANGHE, Life Sciences
DENG, SHUXUN, Sports Science
DING, SHIJIN, Mathematics
DING, XIN, Educational Information Technology
DONG, WULUN, Economics and Management
FANG, XINGQI, Economics and Management
FENG, YOUHE, Mathematics
GAN, QIAOLIN, Tourism Management
GAO, SHIAN, Mathematics
HAO, XUANMING, Sports Science
HE, ZHENGJIANG, Physics and Telecommunications Engineering
HU, LIAN, Physics and Telecommunications Engineering
HU, XIAOMING, Sports Science
HUANG, KUANROU, Sports Science
HUANG, LIREN, Mathematics
HUANG, WENFANG, Life Sciences
HUANG, YUSHAN, Sports Science
LI, DONGFENG, Life Sciences
LI, HONGQING, Life Sciences
LI, JIANYING, Economics and Management
LI, JIDONG, Economics and Management
LI, KEDONG, Educational Information Technology
LI, LING, Life Sciences
LI, SHAOSHAN, Life Sciences
LI, SHIJIE, Mathematics
LI, WEISHAN, Chemistry
LI, WEN, Mathematics
LI, YIJUN, Sports Science
LI, YONGJIE, Economics and Management
LI, YUNLIN, Educational Information Technology
LIN, CHANGHAO, Mathematics
LIN, YONG, Economics and Management
LING, JIANGHUAI, Economics and Management
LIU, BOLIAN, Mathematics
LIU, CHENGYI, Sports Science
LIU, QIONGFA, Physics and Telecommunications Engineering
LIU, SONGHAO, Optoelectronics
LIU, YUQIANG, Mathematics
LU, YUANZHEN, Sports Science
MO, LEI, Education Science
PAN, RUICHI, Life Sciences
PENG, BIYU, Economics and Management
SANG, XINMIN, Educational Information Technology
SHEN, WENHUAI, Mathematics
SUN, DAOCHUN, Mathematics
SUN, RUYONG, Life Sciences
TAN, HUA, Sports Science
TANG, SHANGYONG, Mathematics
TANG, ZAIXIN, Economics and Management

TANG, ZHILIE, Physics and Telecommunications Engineering
TONG, QINGXI, Geography
WANG, ANLI, Life Sciences
WANG, LINQUAN, Mathematics
WANG, QIAN, Sports Science
WANG, WEINA, Life Sciences
WANG, XIAOJING, Life Sciences
WENG, PEIXUAN, Mathematics
WU, CHAOLIN, Economics and Management
XIA, HUA, Physics and Telecommunications Engineering
XIAO, GUOQIANG, Sports Science
XIAO, PENG, Life Sciences
XIONG, JIANWEN, Physics and Telecommunications Engineering
XIONG, JINCHENG, Mathematics
XU, FUYING, Educational Information Technology
XU, JIE, Life Sciences
XU, XIAOYANG, Sports Science
XU, XUAN, Chemistry
YANG, WENXUAN, Sports Science
YANG, YONGHUA, Economics and Management
YE, QINGSHENG, Life Sciences
YI, FAHUAI, Mathematics
YU, YING, Chemistry
YUANG, GUANLING, Physics and Telecommunications Engineering
ZENG, HEPING, Chemistry
ZHENG, ZHI, Chemistry
ZHANG, JIANWU, Economics and Management
ZHANG, JUNPENG, Physics and Telecommunications Engineering
ZHANG, MOUCHENG, Mathematics
ZHANG, ZHIYONG, Sports Science
ZHAO, XUEZENG, Economics and Management
ZHOU, AIGUANG, Sports Science
ZHU, JIANJUN, Life Sciences
ZUO, ZAISHI, Mathematics

SOUTH CHINA UNIVERSITY OF TECHNOLOGY

Wushan, Guangzhou 510641, Guangdong
Telephone: (20) 87110000
Fax: (20) 85516386
Internet: www.scut.edu.cn
Founded 1952
State control
Academic year: September to July
Pres.: LIU HUANBIN
Vice-Pres: HAN DAJIAN, HUANG SHISHENG, JIA XINZHEN, LIU SHUDAO, CHEN NIANQIANG
Registrar: LIN YANGSU
Librarian: LI JIANBIN
Library of 1,350,000 vols
Number of teachers: 2,200
Number of students: 14,000
Publications: *Control Theory and Applications*, *Journal*

DEANS

School of Adult Education: WU MAN
School of Business Administration: SUN DONGCHUAN
School of Chemical Engineering: CHEN HUANQIN
School of Electrical Communication: ZHU XUEFENG
School of Electric Power: WU JIE
School of Light Chemical Engineering and Food Engineering: GAO DAWEI
School of Materials Science and Engineering: JIA DEMIN

SOUTHEAST UNIVERSITY

Si Pai Lou 2, Nanjing 210096
Telephone: (25) 83792412
Fax: (25) 83615736
E-mail: oic@seu.edu.cn
Internet: www.seu.edu.cn

Founded 1902
State control
Pres.: Prof. YI HONG
Vice-Pres.: Prof. LIU BO
Vice-Pres.: Prof. PU YUEPU
Vice-Pres.: Prof. ZHAO QIMAN
Vice-Pres.: Prof. HU MINQIANG
Vice-Pres.: Prof. ZHENG JIAMAO
Vice-Pres.: Prof. SHEN JIONG
Vice-Pres.: Prof. WANG BAOPING
Library: c. 3.3m. vols
Number of teachers: 2,269
Number of students: 41,090
Publication: *Journal*

DIRECTORS

Chien-shiung Wu College: Prof. LI AIQUN
College of Continuing Education: ZHUANG BAOJIE
College of Integrated Circuits: Prof. SHI LONGXING
College of International Students: Prof. HUANG KAI
Department of Mathematics: Prof. LIU JIJUN
Department of Physics: Prof. YANG YONGHONG
Department of Physical Education: Prof. CAI XIAOBO
Research Institute of SEU in Changzhou: Prof. LIU JINGNAN
Research Institute of SEU in Suzhou: HU MINQIANG
School of Architecture: Prof. WANG JIANGUO
School of Arts: Prof. WANG TINGXIN
School of Automation: Prof. FEI SHUMIN
School of Biological Science and Medical Engineering: Prof. GU NING
School of Computer Science and Engineering: Prof. LUO JUNZHOU
School of Chemistry and Chemical Engineering: Prof. LIN BAOPING
School of Civil Engineering: Prof. WU GANG
School of Economics and Management: Prof. XU KANGNING
School of Electrical Engineering: Prof. HUANG XUELIANG
School of Electronic Science and Engineering: Prof. SHI LONGXING
School of Energy and Environment: Prof. JIN BAOSHENG
School of Foreign Languages: Prof. LI XIAOXIANG
School of Humanities: Prof. FAN HEPING
School of Information Science and Engineering: Prof. YOU XIAOHU
School of Instrument Science and Engineering: Prof. SONG AIGUO
School of Material Science and Engineering: Prof. PAN YE
School of Mechanical Engineering: Prof. TANG WENCHENG
School of Medicine: Prof. TENG GAOJUN
School of Public Health: Prof. LIU PEI
School of Transportation: Prof. WANG WEI

SOUTH WESTERN UNIVERSITY OF FINANCE AND ECONOMICS

55 Guanghua St, Chengdu 610074, Sichuan
Telephone: (28) 7352937
Fax: (28) 7352355
Internet: www.swufe.edu.cn
Founded 1950
State control
Academic year: September to July
Pres.: WANG YUGUO
Vice-Presidents: FENG XIDE, LIU CAN, ZHAO DEWU
Head of Graduate Department: ZHAO ZHENXIAN
Librarian: LIU FANGJIAN
Library of 1,000,000 vols
Number of teachers: 1,300
Number of students: 14,000

Publications: *Finance and Economics* (6 a year), *The Economist*

DEANS

Department of Economical Mathematics: XIANG KAILI
School of Accounting: PENG SHAOBING
School of e-Commerce: PU GUOQUAN
School of Economics: LI PING
School of Economic Information Engineering: SHAOBING SONG
School of Finance: YIN MENGBO
School of Insurance: AI SUNLIN
School of International Business: CHENG MINXUAN
School of Law: GAO JINKANG
School of Public Administration: YIN QINGSHUANG
School of Public Finance and Taxation: WANG GUOQING
School of Statistics: SHI DAIMIN

PROFESSORS

AI, SUNLIN, Insurance
CAI, CHUN, Accounting
CAO, TINGGUI, Finance
CHEN, MINGLI, Law
CHEN, SUYU, Law
CHEN, YONGSHENG, Finance
CHEN, YUANHONG, Accounting
CHENG, MINXUAN, International Business
CHENG, QIAN, Public Finance and Taxation
DENG, GUANJUN, e-Commerce
DING, RENZHONG, Economics
DU, ZHIHAN, Economic Mathematics
FAN, XINGJIAN, Accounting
FENG, JIAN, Accounting
FENG, XIDE, Economics
FENG, YADONG, Law
FU, DAIGUO, Accounting
FU, HONGCHUN, Economics
GAO, JINKANG, Law
GUO, FUCHU, Accounting
HE, ZERONG, Finance
JIANG, LING, Economics
JIANG, YUMEI, Law
KUANG, SONG, Economic Information Engineering
LI, NANCHENG, Statistics
LI, PING, Economics
LI, SHI, Statistics
LIN, WANXIANG, Accounting
LIN, YI, Insurance
LIU, CAN, Economics
LIU, RONG, Public Finance and Taxation
LIU, SHIBAI, Economics
MA, XIAO, Public Finance and Taxation
MU, LIANGPING, Economics
NI, KEQIN, Finance
PAN, XUEMO, Accounting
PANG, HAO, Statistics
PENG, SHAOBING, Accounting
REN, ZHIJUN, Economics
SHEN, XIAOMEI, Public Administration
SHI, DAIMIN, Statistics
SUN, RONG, Insurance
TU, KAIYI, International Business
WANG, GUOQING, Public Finance and Taxation
WANG, XIANGXI, e-Commerce
WANG, YONGXI, Economics
WANG, YUGUO, Economics
WANG, ZHIAN, Accounting
XIANG, KAILI, Economic Mathematics
XIANG, RONGMEI, Statistics
XIE, JIANMIN, e-Commerce
XIE, SHENGZHI, Economic Information Engineering
XIE, ZHILONG, e-Commerce
XING, QIANGGUO, Public Administration
XU, LANG, Statistics
YIN, MENGBO, Finance
YIN, QINGSHUANG, Public Administration
YIN, YINPIN, Public Finance and Taxation
YIN, ZHONGMING, International Business
YUAN, WENPING, Economics

YUE, CAISHEN, Law
ZENG, KANGLIN, Finance
ZENG, XIAOLING, Accounting
ZHANG, HEJIN, Finance
ZHANG, KUANHAI, Economic Information Engineering
ZHANG, QIAOYUN, Finance
ZHANG, WEI, Economics
ZHANG, XINCAI, e-Commerce
ZHAO, DEWU, Accounting
ZHENG, JINGJI, Economics
ZHONG, CHENG, e-Commerce
ZHOU, GUANGDA, Statistics
ZHOU, HONGYUAN, Finance
ZHOU, QIHAI, Economic Information Engineering
ZHOU, XIAOLIN, Public Finance and Taxation
ZHU, MINGXI, Public Finance and Taxation
ZHUO, ZHI, Insurance

SOUTHWEST JIAOTONG UNIVERSITY

111 North 1, Er Huan Rd, Chengdu 610031, Sichuan
Telephone: (28) 87600114
Fax: (28) 87600502
Internet: www.swjtu.edu.cn
Founded 1896
State control
Academic year: September to July
Pres.: ZHOU BENKUAN
Vice-Presidents: CHEN ZHIJIAN, HUANG QING, JIANG GEFU, LIN ANLIN, PU DEZHANG, YANG LIZHONG
Head of Graduate Department: HUANG QING
Librarian: DONG DEZHEN
Number of teachers: 1,961
Number of students: 20,000
Publication: *Journal* (natural sciences, in Chinese and English, 6 a year)

DEANS

College of Foreign Languages: XIA WEIRONG
College of Traffic and Transportation: ZHANG DIANYE
Faculty of Software: WU GUANG
School of Art and Communication: WANG SHUNHONG
School of Architecture: QIU JIAN
School of Civil Engineering: LI QIAO
School of Computer Science and Communications Engineering: FAN PINGZHI
School of Economics and Management: JIA JIANMIN
School of Electrical Engineering: LI QUNZHEN
School of Environmental Science and Engineering: LIU BAOJUN
School of Material Science and Engineering: HUANG NAN
School of Mechanical Engineering: XU MINGHENG

PROFESSORS

CAI, HUAI, Computer Science and Communications Engineering
CAI, YING, Civil Engineering
CEN, MINYI, Civil Engineering
CHE, HUIMIN, Civil Engineering
CHEN, JUNYING, Material Science and Engineering
CHEN, XIANGDONG, Computer Science and Communications Engineering
CHEN, XIAOCHUAN, Electrical Engineering
CHENG, QIANGONG, Civil Engineering
DAI, GUANGZE, Material Science and Engineering
DENG, RONGGUI, Civil Engineering
DENG, YOUQIANG, Economics and Management
DENG, YUCAI, Civil Engineering
DIAO, MINGBI, Economics and Management
FAN, HONG, Computer Software
FAN, LILI, Economics and Management

FAN, PINGZHI, Computer Science and Communications Engineering
FANG, XUMING, Computer Science and Communications Engineering
FENG, BO, Material Science and Engineering
FENG, QUANYUAN, Computer Science and Communications Engineering
FENG, XIAOYUN, Electrical Engineering
FU, YONGSHENG, Environmental Science and Engineering
GAO, BO, Civil Engineering
GAO, LONGCHANG, Economics and Management
GAO, SHIBIN, Electrical Engineering
GUAN, BAOSHU, Civil Engineering
GUO, JIN, Computer Science and Communications Engineering
GUO, YAOHUANG, Economics and Management
HE, CHUAN, Civil Engineering
HE, DAKE, Computer Science and Communications Engineering
HE, GUANGHAN, Civil Engineering
HU, HOUTIAN, Civil Engineering
HU, PEI, Economics and Management
HU, XIEWEN, Civil Engineering
HUANG, DENGSHI, Economics and Management
HUANG, DINGFU, Civil Engineering
HUANG, NAN, Material Science and Engineering
HUANG, ZEWEN, Material Science and Engineering
JIA, JIANMIN, Economics and Management
JIA, ZHIYONG, Economics and Management
JIANG, GUANLU, Civil Engineering
JIANG, QI, Material Science and Engineering
JIANG, SHIZHONG, Civil Engineering
JIN, WEIDONG, Electrical Engineering
LAO, YUANCHANG, Civil Engineering
LENG, YONGXIANG, Material Science and Engineering
LI, CHENGHUI, Civil Engineering
LI, CHENGZHONG, Computer Science and Communications Engineering
LI, JUN, Economics and Management
LI, QIAO, Civil Engineering
LI, QUNZHEN, Electrical Engineering
LI, XIAOHONG, Material Science and Engineering
LI, YADONG, Civil Engineering
LI, YONGSHU, Civil Engineering
LI, YUANFU, Civil Engineering
LI, ZHI, Electrical Engineering
LIAO, HAILI, Civil Engineering
LIU, DAN, Environmental Science and Engineering
LIU, HANWEI, Material Science and Engineering
LIU, XUEYI, Civil Engineering
LIU, ZHENGPING, Civil Engineering
LU, CHANGJIANG
LU, HELIN, Civil Engineering
LU, YANG, Civil Engineering
LU, ZHENQIN, Civil Engineering
LUO, BIN, Computer Science and Communications Engineering
LUO, YUANLIANG, Economics and Management
MA, YONGQIANG, Computer Science and Communications Engineering
MOU, RUIFANG, Environmental Science and Engineering
PAN, WEI, Computer Science and Communications Engineering
PENG, DAIYUAN, Computer Science and Communications Engineering
PENG, QIYUAN, Traffic and Transportation
PU, JINHUI, Civil Engineering
QI, TAIYUE, Civil Engineering
QIAN, DONGSHENG, Civil Engineering
QIANG, YONGJIU, Civil Engineering
QIU, WENGE, Civil Engineering
QUE, YANJUN, Civil Engineering
SHI, BENSHAN, Economics and Management
SU, BIN, Computer Software

SUN, LINFU, Civil Engineering
TANG, XIAOHU, Computer Science and Communications Engineering
WAN, FUGUANG, Civil Engineering
WANG, BEN, Electrical Engineering
WANG, CHENGZHANG, Economics and Management
WANG, JIN, Material Science and Engineering
WANG, JUNSHI, Material Science and Engineering
WANG, MINGNIAN, Civil Engineering
WANG, PING, Civil Engineering
WANG, QIAN, Economics and Management
WANG, YONG, Material Science and Engineering
WONG, JIE, Material Science and Engineering
WU, GUANG, Civil Engineering
WU, GUANG, Environmental Science and Engineering
WU, GUANG, Computer Software
WU, GUANGNING, Electrical Engineering
WU, ZHENYE, Economics and Management
XIA, WEIRONG, Foreign Languages
XIAO, JIAN, Electrical Engineering
XIE, QIANG, Civil Engineering
XU, JIANPING, Electrical Engineering
YAN, CHUANPENG, Material Science and Engineering
YANG, BANGCHENG, Material Science and Engineering
YANG, CHUAN, Material Science and Engineering
YANG, JIMEI, Economics and Management
YANG, LIZHONG, Civil Engineering
YANG, LIZHONG, Environmental Science and Engineering
YANG, PING, Material Science and Engineering
YANG, SHUNSHENG, Environmental Science and Engineering
YANG, YONGGAO, Computer Software
YAO, LINGKAN, Civil Engineering
YE, ZIRONG, Economics and Management
YI, SIRONG, Civil Engineering
YIN, ZHIBEN, Computer Science and Communications Engineering
YIN, ZHIBEN, Computer Software
ZENG, HUASANG, Computer Science and Communications Engineering
ZHANG, CUIFANG, Computer Science and Communications Engineering
ZHANG, DIANYE, Traffic and Transportation
ZHANG, JIANQIANG, Environmental Science and Engineering
ZHANG, JIASHU, Computer Science and Communications Engineering
ZHANG, JICHUN, Civil Engineering
ZHANG, KUNLUN, Electrical Engineering
ZHANG, WEI, Economics and Management
ZHANG, XIYAN, Material Science and Engineering
ZHAO, LEI, Civil Engineering
ZHAO, RENDA, Civil Engineering
ZHAO, SHANRUI, Civil Engineering
ZHAO, YUGUANG, Civil Engineering
ZHENG, KAIFENG, Civil Engineering
ZHOU, DEPEI, Civil Engineering
ZHOU, GUOHUA, Economics and Management
ZHOU, RONGHUI, Computer Science and Communications Engineering
ZHOU, SHAOBING, Material Science and Engineering
ZHOU, ZHONGRONG, Material Science and Engineering
ZHOU, ZUOWAN, Material Science and Engineering
ZHU, BING, Civil Engineering
ZHU, CHANGJIN, Computer Science and Communications Engineering
ZHU, DEGUI, Material Science and Engineering
ZHU, FENG, Electrical Engineering
ZHU, WENHAO, Material Science and Engineering
ZHUANG, SHENGXIAN, Electrical Engineering

SOUTHWEST PETROLEUM UNIVERSITY

Chengdu, Nanchong 637001, Sichuan
Telephone: (817) 2642301
Internet: aa.swpu.edu.cn/en

Founded 1958
Provincial control
Academic year: September to July
President: DU ZHIMIN
Vice-Presidents: CHEN CICHANG, SUN YIPING, ZHAO JINZHOU, ZHOU MAO
Librarian: REN HAO
Library of 1,473,000 vols
Number of teachers: 888
Number of students: 15,951

Publications: *Higher Petroleum Education* (4 a year), *Journal* (4 a year)

DIRECTORS

College of Computer Science: CHEN WENBIN (DEPUTY DIR)
College of Electronics and Information Engineering: DU JIAN
Department of Basic Experimental Education: LAI TIANHUA
Department of Foreign Languages: LONG SHIWEN
Department of Physical Education: YANG XUEMING
School of Civil Engineering and Architecture: YAO ANLING
School of Chemistry and Chemical Engineering: HUANG ZHIYU
School of Continuing Education: DENG YU
School of Economics and Management: LIU XIANTAO
School of Humanities and Social Sciences: YANG BOWEN
School of Law: SUN PING
School of Materials Science and Engineering: ZENG MINGYOU
School of Mechanical Engineering: LIANG ZHENG
School of Petroleum Engineering: ZHANG LIEHUI
College of Resources and Environment Engineering: ZHAN FAN
School of Sciences: XIE XIANGJUN
School of Vocational and Technical Education: DENG HONGBO

PROFESSORS

BENG, JUN, Resources and the Environment
CHEN, JINGSHAN, Petroleum Exploration
CHEN, PING, Petroleum Engineering
CHENG, SHIQI, Resources and the Environment
DENG, JIANMING, Petroleum Engineering
DU, ZHIMIN, Petroleum Engineering
DUAN, DARONG, Electronic Information
GUO, XIAOYANG, Petroleum Engineering
HONG, QINYU, Deposition
HU, XINGQI, Electronic Information
HUANG, BINGGUANG, Petroleum Engineering
HUANG, LINJI, Petroleum Engineering
HUANG, ZHIYU, Electronic Information
JIANG, PING, Resource Science and Engineering
KANG, YILI, Petroleum Engineering
LI, BINGYUAN, Petroleum Engineering
LI, CHANGJUN, Petroleum Engineering
LI, CHUANLIANG, Petroleum Engineering
LI, CHUNFU, Resource Science and Engineering
LI, QIAN, Petroleum Engineering
LI, SHILUN, Petroleum Engineering
LI, YINGCHUAN, Petroleum Engineering
LI, YUN, Petroleum Engineering
LI, ZHIPING, Petroleum Engineering
LIAN, ZHANGHUA, Petroleum Engineering
LIANG, ZHENG, Resource Science and Engineering
LIAO, XIMING, Resources and the Environment

LIEHUI, Petroleum Engineering
LIU, CHONGJIAN, Petroleum Engineering
LUO, MINGGAO, Resources and the Environment
LUO, PINGYA, Petroleum Engineering
MA, DEKUN, Resource Science and Engineering
PU, XIAOLIN, Petroleum Engineering
QIN, QIRONG, Resources and the Environment
SHEN, ZHAOGUO, Survey and Exploration of Mineral Products
SHI, TAIHE, Petroleum Engineering
SUN, LIANGTIAN, Petroleum Engineering
WANG, TINDONG, Resources and the Environment
WANG, XINZHI, Resources and the Environment
WANG, YUAN, Petroleum Engineering
YAN, QIBIN, Survey and Exploration of Mineral Products
YANG, SHIGUANG, Electronic Information
YAO, ANLIN, Building Engineering
YUAN, ZONGMING, Petroleum Engineering
ZHANG, BAILIN, Resources and the Environment
ZHANG, FAN, Resources and the Environment
ZHANG, MINGHONG, Resource Science and Engineering
ZHANG, PENG, Resource Science and Engineering
ZHANG, TINSHAN, Resources and the Environment
ZHAO, JINZHOU, Petroleum Engineering
ZHAO, LIQIANG, Petroleum Engineering
ZHAO, LIZHI, Electronic Information
ZHOU, KAIJI, Petroleum Engineering

SOUTHWEST UNIVERSITY OF POLITICAL SCIENCE AND LAW

2 Zhuangzhi Rd, Shapingba, Chongqing 400031

Telephone: (23) 65382114
Fax: (23) 65383284
Internet: www.swupl.edu.cn
Founded 1953
Academic year: September to July
President: LONG ZONGZHI
Vice-Presidents: FU ZITANG, LI CHUNRU, LIU JUN, WANG JIANHUA
Head of Graduate Department: YANG SHUMING
Librarian: ZOU YULI

Library of 800,000 vols
Number of teachers: 1,000
Number of students: 20,000

Publications: *Contemporaneity Law School* (6 a year), *Journal* (6 a year)

DEANS

School of Administration: CAO DAYOU
School of Administrative Law: (vacant)
School of Applied Law: LI WEI
School of Civil and Business Law: ZHAO WANYI
School of Criminology: GUAN GUANGCHENG
School of Economic and Trade Law: TANG QINGYANG
School of Economics: LIU LUJI
School of Foreign Languages: SONG LEI
School of Law: CHEN ZHONGLIN
School of Media: ZHAO ZHONGJI
School of Politics and Public Affairs: RAN ZHI

PROFESSORS

BAI, SHENG, Administration
CAO, DAYOU, Administration
CHANG, YI, Law
CHEN, JINQUAN, Administrative Law
CHEN, WEI, Civil and Business Law
CHEN, ZHONGLIN, Law
DENG, RUIPING, Economic and Trade Law
FU, ZITANG, Economic and Trade Law

FU, ZITANG, Law
GAO, SHAOXIAN, Law
GUAN, GUANGCHENG, Criminology
HAN, TIANSEN, Economic and Trade Law
HU, GUANGZHI, Economic and Trade Law
HU, RUKUI, Politics and Public Affairs
HU, SHICHENG, Criminology
HUI, YIN, Environment and International Law
LAI, DAQING, Economic and Trade Law
LI, CHANGQI, Economic and Trade Law
LI, JINRONG, Economic and Trade Law
LI, KAIGUO, Civil and Business Law
LI, PEIZE, Law
LI, SHENGYU, Administrative Law
LI, WEI, Law Application
LI, YONGSHENG, Law
LI, ZUJUN, Law
LIAO, ZHONGHONG, Law
LIN, RUIYING, Politics and Public Affairs
LIU, LUJI, Economics
LIU, XIANGSHU, Economic and Trade Law
LONG, ZONGZHI, Law
LU, DAIFU, Economic and Trade Law
RAN, ZHI, Politics and Public Affairs
REN, ZUYAO, Economics
SHI, HUIRONG, Civil and Business Law
SONG, LEI, Foreign Languages
SONG, YUBO, Administration
SUN, CHANGYONG, Law
TIAN, PINGAN, Law
WAN, YINGZHONG, Economics
WANG, LIRONG, Law
WANG, SHIHU, Civil and Business Law
WANG, XUEHUI, Administrative Law
WEN, ZHENGBANG, Administrative Law
WU, YUE, Economic and Trade Law
XIAO, YUNSHU, Foreign Languages
XU, JINGCUN, Law
XU, MINGYUE, Economic and Trade Law
YANG, SHUMING, Economic and Trade Law
YU, RONGGEN, Law
ZENG, DAIWEI, Administrative Law
ZENG, FANYUE, Politics and Public Affairs
ZHANG, GENG, Civil and Business Law
ZHANG, QIAN, Administrative Law
ZHANG, SHIDI, Media
ZHANG, YUMIN, Civil and Business Law
ZHAO, MING, Administrative Law
ZHAO, WANYI, Civil and Business Law
ZHAO, XUEQING, Economic and Trade Law
ZHAO, ZHONGJI, Media
ZHENG, CHUANKUN, Administrative Law
ZHONG, MINGZHAO, Economic and Trade Law
ZHU, JIANHUA, Law
ZUO, KAIDA, Politics and Public Affairs

SUN YAT-SEN UNIVERSITY

135 Xingang Rd, Guangzhou 510275, Guangdong

Telephone: (20) 84111583
Fax: (20) 84039173
E-mail: adpo@sysu.edu.cn
Internet: www.sysu.edu.cn
Founded 1924
State control
Academic year: September to July
President: HUANG DAREN
Vice-Pres.: CHEN RUZHU
Vice-Pres.: CHEN WEILING
Vice-Pres.: CHEN YUCHUAN
Vice-Pres.: LIANG QINGYIN
Vice-Pres.: LI PING
Vice-Pres.: WANG JIANPING
Vice-Pres.: XU JIARUI
Vice-Pres.: XU NINGSHENG
Vice-Pres.: XU YUANTONG
Vice-Pres.: YAN GUANGMEI
Vice-Pres.: YU SHIYOU
Librarian: CHENG HUANWEN

Library of 4,170,000 vols
Number of teachers: 7,700
Number of students: 41,000

Publications: *Journal* (natural sciences and social sciences edns, each 4 a year), *Journal of the Graduates*, *Pearl River Delta Economy*, *South China Population*

HEADS OF SCHOOLS

College of Continuing Education: Prof. ZHAO GUODU
Graduate School: Prof. HUANG DAREN
Guang Hua School of Stomatology: Prof. LING JUNQI
Lingnan (University) College: Prof. SHU YUAN
School of Business: Prof. WEI MINGHAI
School of Chemistry and Chemical Engineering: Prof. CHEN XIAOMING
School of Environmental Science and Engineering: Prof. SUN XIAOMING
School of Foreign Languages: Prof. HUANG GUOWEN
School of Geographical Science and Planning: Prof. BAO JIGANG
School of Humanities: Prof. CHEN CHUNSHENG
School of Information Science and Technology: Prof. HUANG JIWU
School of Law and Political Science: Prof. REN JIANTAO
School of Life Sciences: Prof. XU ANLONG
School of Mathematics and Computational Science: Prof. ZHU XIPING
School of Physics and Engineering: Prof. XU NINGSHENG
School of Nursing: Prof. YOU LIMING
School of Overseas Educational Exchange: Prof. XU NINGSHENG
School of Pre-Clinical Medicine: Prof. XIE FUKANG
School of Public Health: LING WENHUA

SUN YAT-SEN UNIVERSITY OF MEDICAL SCIENCES

74 Zhongshan Rd II, Guangzhou 510089, Guangdong

Telephone: 778223
Fax: (20) 765679
Internet: www.gzsums.edu.cn
Founded 1866
State control
Languages of instruction: Chinese, English
Pres.: LU GUANGQI
Vice-Pres.: GU JIANHUI
Vice-Pres.: TAN XUCHANG
Vice-Pres.: ZHU JIAKAI
Vice-Pres.: ZHUO DAHONG
Librarian: HUANG RUXUEN

Library of 545,900 vols
Number of teachers: 1,101
Number of students: 3,825 (incl. 489 postgraduates)

Publications: *Academic Journal, Cancer, Chinese Journal of Microsurgery, Chinese Journal of Nephrology, Chinese Journal of Neurology and Psychiatry, Family Doctor, New Chinese Medicine, Ophthalmic Science*

DEANS

Faculty of Stomatology: REN CAI-NIAN
First School of Clinical Medicine: XIAO GUANHUI
School of Basic Sciences: LI GUIYUN
School of Public Health: CHENG CHENZHANG
Second School of Clinical Medicine: ZHANG XUMING
Third School of Clinical Medicine: GU CAIRAN

There are 8 research institutes, 30 research laboratories, an attached ophthalmic centre, 4 hospitals, and an affiliated school of nursing

TAIYUAN UNIVERSITY OF TECHNOLOGY

West Fen River Park, Taiyuan, Shanxi
Telephone: (351) 6010140
Fax: (351) 6041236
Internet: www.tyut.edu.cn
E-mail: xiaoban@tyut.edu.cn
Founded 1902
Academic year: September to July
President: XIE KECHANG
Vice-Presidents: GUO MINTAI, HAO JIANG-
GONG, HU BOYAN, LU MING, LU ZHENGUANG,
MA FUCHANG, XU BINGSHE
Head of Graduate Department: LING KAI-
CHENG
Librarian: WANG SHENGKUN
Library of 1,830,000 vols
Number of teachers: 1,506
Number of students: 15,659
Publications: *Coal Transformation* (4 a year),
Journal (natural sciences, 6 a year; social
sciences, 4 a year), *Journal of Social
Science of Shanxi High Schools* (12 a
year), *Journal of Systemic Dialectics* (4 a
year)

DEANS

College of Architecture and Environmental
Engineering: (vacant)
College of Chemical Engineering and Tech-
nology: (vacant)
College of Economics Management: NIU
CHONGHUAI
College of Electrical and Power Engineering:
BU QINGHUA
College of Humanities: (vacant)
College of Information Engineering: XIE
KEMING
College of Materials Science and Engineer-
ing: XU BINGSHE
College of Mechanical Engineering: (vacant)
College of Mining Engineering: KANG LIXUN
College of Science: (vacant)
College of Textile Engineering and Arts:
(vacant)

PROFESSORS

BU, QINGHUA, Electrical and Power Engin-
eering
CHEN, JUNJIE, Information Engineering
DUAN, FU, Information Engineering
DUAN, KANGLIAN, Mining Engineering
FANG, JINGHUA, Electrical and Power Engin-
eering
GUO, YONGYI, Mining Engineering
HAN, FUCHUN, Electrical and Power Engin-
eering
JIA, XIAOCHUAN, Electrical and Power Engin-
eering
KANG, LIXUN, Mining Engineering
LI, XUEZHONG, Mining Engineering
NIU, CHONGHUAI, Economics Management
REN, PINGZHAO, Electrical and Power Engin-
eering
SONG, JIANCHENG, Electrical and Power
Engineering
TIAN, QUZHEN, Mining Engineering
WANG, HANBIN, Economics Management
ZHANG, JIANPING, Economics Management
ZHAO, YIFANG, Mining Engineering
ZHAO, YUHUAI, Electrical and Power Engin-
eering

TIANJIN CONSERVATORY OF MUSIC

57 11th Meridian Rd, Hedong District,
Tianjin 300171
Telephone: (22) 412882
Internet: www.tjcm.edu.cn
Founded 1958
Pres.: Prof. YANG JINHAO (acting)
Vice-Pres: Prof. CHEN JIXU
Vice-Pres: Assoc. Prof. SHI WEIZHENG

Vice-Pres: Assoc. Prof. XU YONGKUN
Librarian: Assoc. Prof. WANG ZHIJIAN
Library of 99,106 vols, 20,000 records
Number of teachers: 178
Number of students: 344 (incl. 9 postgradu-
ates)
Publication: *Music Study and Research* (4 a
year)

DEANS

Chinese Traditional Music: Assoc. Prof. SONG
GUOSHENG
Composition: Prof. CHEN ENGUANG
Education: Assoc. Prof. YANG LIZHONG
Orchestra: Prof. YAN ZHENGPING
Vocal: Assoc. Prof. XIA ZHONGHENG

TIANJIN MEDICAL UNIVERSITY

22 Qi Xiang Tai Rd, Heping District, Tianjin
300070
Telephone: (22) 341234
Fax: (22) 319429
Internet: www.tijmu.edu.cn
Founded 1951
Pres.: WU XIANZHONG
Vice-Pres.: CUI YITAI
Vice-Pres.: FANG PEIHUA
Vice-Pres.: LI JINGFU
Vice-Pres.: XING KEHAO
Chief Librarian: BAI JINGWEN
Library of 284,000 vols
Number of teachers: 761
Number of students: 1,883
Publications: *Foreign Medicine* (4 a year),
Journal of Tianjin Medical College (4 a
year), *Medical Education Research* (2 a
year), *Medical Inquiry* (6 a year), *Medical
Translation* (4 a year)

CHAIRMEN

Biomedical Engineering: LI YUANMING
Medicine: ZHANG NAIXIN
Nursing: ZOU DAOHUI
Public Health: LAI ZEMIN
Stomatology: SHI SHUJUN

PROFESSORS

Dermatology:
FU ZHIYI
SHEN JIANMING
Endocrinology:
LI LIANGE
MA LIYUN
PANG ZHILING
Internal Medicine:
CHENG YUQIAN
DU WENBIN
HUANG NAIXIA
HUANG TIGANG
HUANG XIANGQIAN
SHI YUSHU
WANG PEIXIAN
YIN WEI
ZHOU JINTAI
Isotope:
FANG PEIHUA
LU TIZHANG
ZHENG MIAORONG
Neurology:
CHEN SHIJUN
PU PEIYU
JIANG DEHUA
XUE QINGCHENG
YANG LUCHUN
Obstetrics and Gynaecology:
JIAO SHUZHU
ZHAI ZHANCAN
Ophthalmology:
SONG GUOXIANG
WANG YANHUA

YING SHIHAO
YUAN JIAQING
ZHANG LIANJING
Otorhinolaryngology:
GUO QIXIN
WANG YANYOU
YAN CHENGXIAN
Paediatrics:
HUANG HONGHAI
LIU YUJI
Radiology:
HE NENGSHU
LIAN ZHONGCHENG
LI JINGXUE
WU ENHUI
YANG TIANEN
ZHAO CHANGJIANG
Stomatology:
HOU ZHIYAN
SUN XUEMIN
Surgery:
DAI ZHIHUA
DONG KEQUAN
GUO SHIFU
LI QINGRUI
LIU ZIKUAN
SHENG XIKUN
WANG PENGZHI
WU XIANZHONG
YU SONGTING

TIANJIN NORMAL UNIVERSITY

241 Weijing Rd, Tianjin 300074
Telephone: (22) 23540025
Fax: (22) 23541665
E-mail: msk@mail.tjnu.edu.cn
Internet: www.tjnu.edu.cn
Founded 1958
Academic year: September to July
Pres.: GAO YUBAO
Vice-Presidents: WANG GUILIN, WANG YAOJIN,
XU JIANDONG
Library of 2,140,000 vols
Number of teachers: 2,113
Number of students: 30,000
Publication: *Journal* (4 a year)

DEANS

College of Basic Education: WANG GONGLIANG
College of Biology and Chemistry: GU BIN-
HONG
College of Chemistry and Environment Sci-
ence: (vacant)
College of Computer and Information Engin-
eering: (vacant)
College of Economics: (vacant)
College of Education Science: GAO HENGLI
College of Foreign Languages: GU GANG
College of History and Culture: HOU JIANXIN
College of Literature: MENG ZHAOYI
College of Management: (vacant)
College of Mathematics: (vacant)
College of News and Communication: LIU
WEIDONG
College of Physical Culture and Science:
ZHANG JINNIAN
College of Physics and Electronic Informa-
tion: CHANG XIANGRONG
College of Politics and Public Administration:
GAO JIAN
Institute of Arts: SHUN GUANGJUN

PROFESSORS

BA, XINSHENG, History and Culture
BAO, YUANKAI, Arts
BI, GUANGJI, Physics and Electronic Informa-
tion
CHANG, SHIYAN, Politics and Public Adminis-
tration
CHEN, SHANGWEI, Politics and Public Admin-
istration

CHEN, XU, Biology and Chemistry
CHEN, YAN, Literature
CHEN, YUANLONG, Arts
CUI, FENGFU, Mathematics
DING, WEIMING, Economics
DONG, SIDAI, Politics and Public Administration
DUO, LIAN, Biology and Chemistry
FENG, JINCHENG, Biology and Chemistry
GAO, HENGWEN, Literature
GAO, JIAN, Politics and Public Administration
GAO, JIE, Management
GE, LUNHONG, Foreign Languages
GONG, ZUOMING, Chemistry and Environment Science
GU, BINHONG, Biology and Chemistry
GU, GANG, Foreign Languages
GU, WEIQING, Management
GUO, JIAN, Mathematics
GUO, QINGZHU, Foreign Languages
HAO, GUISHENG, Politics and Public Administration
HAO, JINKU, Biology and Chemistry
HE, CHENGQUAN, Chemistry and Environment Science
HONG, SONGLING, Economics
HOU, JIANXIN, History and Culture
HOU, RUNSHENG, Physical Culture and Science
LI, BAOYI, Mathematics
LI, DAPENG, Literature
LI, HUA, Literature
LI, JIECHUAN, History and Culture
LI, LONGZHU, Management
LI, PEIWU, Chemistry and Environment Science
LI, XUEZHI, History and Culture
LI, YI, Physics and Electronic Information
LI, YIJIN, Literature
LI, YUNXING, Foreign Languages
LI, ZHENGANG, Physics and Electronic Information
LIAO, QIBING, Physical Culture and Science
LIU, CHUNMAO, Management
LIU, DONGHUA, Biology and Chemistry
LIU, HONG, Economics
LIU, LILI, Biology and Chemistry
LIU, QIANG, Biology and Chemistry
LIU, SHIMING, Politics and Public Administration
LIU, WEIDONG, News and Communication
LIU, XIANGJUN, Biology and Chemistry
LIU, XIAOLAN, Biology and Chemistry
LIU, YUZHEN, Foreign Languages
LONG, XIUQING, History and Culture
LU, GUANGYUAN, Physics and Electronic Information
MA, DEPU, Politics and Public Administration
MA, JUNMING, History and Culture
MA, RUIJIANG, History and Culture
MA, YI, News and Communication
MAO, JIANYAO, Mathematics
MENG, ZHAOYI, Literature
MIU, FANGMING, Biology and Chemistry
PAN, RONG, History and Culture
PANG, ZHUOHENG, History and Culture
PENG, JINRONG, Economics
PENG, YONGKANG, Biology and Chemistry
PING, HUIYUAN, Literature
RONG, CHANGHAI, Politics and Public Administration
SHEN, LAIFAN, Arts
SHUN, HUIMIN, Economics
SHUN, QIFENG, Arts
SONG, CHANGLI, Literature
SONG, YI, Arts
TIAN, QINGJUN, Physics and Electronic Information
WAN, QUAN, Economics
WAN, TANGMING, Literature
WANG, FU, Arts
WANG, GUANGMING, Mathematics
WANG, GUOSHOU, Literature
WANG, JIANING, Foreign Languages
WANG, JINGAN, Biology and Chemistry
WANG, JINLING, Biology and Chemistry

WANG, TONGQI, Politics and Public Administration
WANG, XINHUA, Economics
WANG, XIUGE, Politics and Public Administration
WANG, YAN, Basic Education College
WANG, YAPING, History and Culture
WANG, YONGCHENG, Physics and Electronic Information
WANG, YUBEN, Mathematics
WANG, ZHENYING, Biology and Chemistry
WEI, WENYUAN, Mathematics
WEI, ZIGUANG, Biology and Chemistry
WU, CHUNHUA, Politics and Public Administration
XIA, XIAOYANG, Physics and Electronic Information
XIAO, LIJUN, History and Culture
XU, DATONG, Politics and Public Administration
XU, DELING, Economics
XU, LIMIAO, Chemistry and Environment Science
XU, RONGKUN, Arts
XU, YONGLONG, Management
XU, ZHELIN, Mathematics
YAN, YONGXIN, Management
YANG, JIALING, Biology and Chemistry
YANG, XIYUN, History and Culture
YOU, ZHEQING, Physics and Electronic Information
YU, JINCHENG, Politics and Public Administration
ZENG, YUEXIN, Physics and Electronic Information
ZHAI, CHANGMING, Politics and Public Administration
ZHANG, FUYE, Arts
ZHANG, JIER, Mathematics
ZHANG, JINGNIAN, Physical Culture and Science
ZHANG, LINJIE, Literature
ZHANG, QIYING, Economics
ZHANG, WENHUI, Biology and Chemistry
ZHANG, XIN, Biology and Chemistry
ZHANG, ZHIYONG, Physics and Electronic Information
ZHAO, DENGYING, Arts
ZHAO, JIE, Physics and Electronic Information
ZHAO, LIMING, Literature
ZHAO, LIZHU, Foreign Languages
ZHENG, LIANBING, Biology and Chemistry
ZHONG, YUXIU, Foreign Languages
ZHU, SHAOHONG, Mathematics

TIANJIN POLYTECHNIC UNIVERSITY

63 Chenglinzhuang Rd, Hedong District, Tianjin 300160
Telephone: (22) 24528000
Fax: (22) 24528001
E-mail: zxb@tjpu.edu.cn
Internet: www.tjpu.edu.cn
Founded 1958
Academic year: September to July
Pres.: Prof. ZHANG, HONGWEI
Vice-Pres.: Prof. JIANG XIUMING
Vice-Pres.: Prof. XIAO CHANGFA
Vice-Pres.: Assoc. Prof. YANG HONG
Vice-Pres.: YANG JIDI
Dirs of Int. Office: Prof. CHENG BOWEN, Prof. LI YUXIANG
Librarian: HANG GUANGFENG
Library of 700,000 vols, 2,100 periodicals
Number of teachers: 1,086
Number of students: 23,600
Publication: *Journal* (6 a year)

HEADS OF SCHOOLS AND COLLEGES

College of Adult Education: Prof. YANG XIULAN
College of Vocational Technology: Prof. YANG, XIULAN

School of Accounting: Prof. WEI, YAPING
School of Art Design: Prof. XU, DONG
School of Computer Technology and Automation: Prof. HANG, QUIRI
School of Economics: Prof. ZHAO, HONG
School of Foreign Languages: Assoc. Prof. YU, XIAODAN
School of Humanities and Law: Prof. ZHANG, CHUNHONG
School of Information and Communications Engineering: Prof. MIAO, CHANYUN
School of International Culture: Prof. LI YUXIANG
School of Management: Assoc. Prof. WU, ZHONGYUAN
School of Material Science and Chemical Engineering: Prof. CHENG, LI
School of Mechanical and Electronic Engineering: Prof. WU BAOLIN
School of Science: Prof. SUN MINGZHU
School of Textiles and Clothing: Prof. WANG, RUI
Institute of Function Fibre: Prof. MA, YAJING
Institute of Laser Processing: Prof. YANG, XICHEN
Institute of Membrane Technology: Prof. LI, XINMIN
Institute of Textile Composite Material: Prof. LI, JIALU
There are 38 research institutes and laboratories

TIANJIN UNIVERSITY

92 Weijin Rd, Tianjin 300072
Telephone: (22) 27406148
Fax: (22) 23358706
Internet: www.tju.edu.cn
Founded 1895
State control
Academic year: August/September to July (2 semesters)
Pres.: Prof. SHAN PING
Vice-Pres.: Prof. GAO WENXIN
Vice-Pres.: Prof. HU XIAOTANG
Vice-Pres.: Prof. KOU JISONG
Vice-Pres.: Prof. WANG YULIN
Vice-Pres.: Prof. YU DAOYIN
Sec.-Gen.: Prof. SU QUANZHONG (Deputy)
Dean of Studies: Prof. CHEN RONGJIN
Chief for Gen. Affairs: Prof. LI JINPU
Librarian: Prof. YANG JIACHENG
Library of 1,740,000 vols, 148,854 periodicals
Number of teachers: 2,438
Number of students: 18,000
Publications: *Collection of Research Achievements, Journal* (4 a year), various departmental publs

DEANS

Graduate School: Prof. YU DAOYIN
School of Adult Education: Prof. CHEN RONGJIN
School of Architecture: Prof. ZHANG QI
School of Chemical Engineering: Prof. ZHAO XUEMING
School of Constructional Engineering: Prof. GU XIAOLU
School of Electrical Automation and Energy Resources Engineering: Prof. SUNG YUGENG
School of Electronic Information Engineering: RING RUNTAO
School of Letters: Assoc. Prof. LIU YUSHAN
School of Management: Prof. ZHANG SHIYING
School of Materials Science and Engineering: Prof. LI JIAJUN
School of Mechanical Engineering: Prof. ZHANG CE
School of Petrochemical Engineering: Prof. CHEN HONGFANG (Dir)
School of Precision Instruments and Opto-Electronics Engineering: Prof. JIN SHIJIU
School of Sciences: JIANG ENYONG

TIANJIN UNIVERSITY OF COMMERCE

East Entrance of Jinba Road, Beichen District, Tianjin 300134
Telephone: (22) 26667666
Fax: (22) 26675789
Internet: www.tjuc.edu
Founded 1980
President: Prof. LIU SHUHAN

Library of 400,000 vols, 1,817 periodicals
Number of teachers: 839
Number of students: 15,000

Publication: *University Journal*

DEANS

College of Administration: ZHANG GUOWANG
College of Biological Technology and Food Science: PANG GUANGCHANG
College of Economy and Trade: BAI LING
College of Information Engineering: LIU DUO
College of International Exchange: KOU XIAOXUAN
College of Law and Politics: SHI RUIJIE
College of Mechanical Engineering: (vacant)
College of Science: YU YILIANG
College of Tourism Administration: WANG WENJUN
School of Foreign Languages: PAUL CHILTON

TIANJIN UNIVERSITY OF LIGHT INDUSTRY

1038 Dagu Nanlu, Tianjin 300222
Telephone: (22) 8340538
Fax: (22) 8341536
E-mail: tjili@tju.edu.cn
Founded 1958
State control
Languages of instruction: Chinese, English
Pres.: TAN GUOMIN
Vice-Pres: CHANG RUXIANG
Vice-Pres: LI JUN
Vice-Pres: XU MINLIANG
Vice-Pres: YANG SHUHUI
Chief Admin. Officer: LI ZHENG

Library of 450,000 vols
Number of teachers: 552
Number of students: 5,109

Publication: *Journal*

Divs of applied liberal arts and sciences, biotechnology and food technology, chemistry and chemical engineering, industrial art engineering, management and systems engineering, mechanical and electrical engineering.

TIBET UNIVERSITY

Lhasa, Tibet Autonomous Region
Telephone: (891) 6324482
E-mail: master@utibet.edu.cn
Internet: www.utibet.edu.cn
Founded 1951, as Tibet Cadres School, current name and status 1985, based on Tibet Teachers' College
State control
Library of 22,000 vols
Number of teachers: 320
Number of students: 1,400

Main degree areas: Tibetan language, Chinese and English, politics and history, mathematics and physics, chemistry, biology and geography, Tibetan art and music, economics and management.

TONGJI MEDICAL UNIVERSITY

13 Hang Kong Lu, Wuhan, Hubei 430030
Telephone: (27) 83692777
Fax: (27) 3643050
Internet: www.tjmu.edu.cn

Founded 1907
State control
Languages of instruction: Chinese, English, German
Academic year: September to July
Chancellor: Prof. LIU SHUMAO
Pres.: Prof. XUE DELIN
Vice-Pres.: Prof. LI GUOCHENG
Vice-Pres.: Prof. LIU SHENGYUAN
Vice-Pres.: Prof. WANG CAIYUAN
Vice-Pres.: Prof. WANG XIMING
Vice-Pres.: Prof. WANG ZUQIN
Vice-Pres.: Prof. WEN LIYANG
Registrar: Prof. LUO WUJIN
Librarian: Prof. XU FENGYING (Deputy Librarian)

Library of 400,000 vols
Number of teachers: 2,692
Number of students: 7,962

Publications: *Acta Universitatis Medicinae Tongji* (Chinese and English, 6 a year), *China Higher Medical Education* (Chinese, 6 a year), *Journal* (Chinese, 4 a year), various departmental publs

DIRECTORS

College of Basic Medicine: Prof. SHI YOU'EN
College for Continuing Medical Education: Prof. XIANG CHUNTING
College of Pharmacy: Prof. TIAN SHIXIONG
College of Public Health: Prof. CHEN XUEMIN
Faculty of Foreign Languages: Prof. ZHANG HONGQING
Faculty of Forensic Medicine: Prof. QIN QISHENG
Faculty of Maternal and Child Health: Prof. LIU XIAOXIAN
Faculty of Medical Library and Information Sciences: Prof. LI DAOPING (Deputy Dir)
Faculty of Paediatrics: Prof. HONG GUANGXIANG
Faculty of Social Sciences: Prof. HU JICHUN
First College of Clinical Medicine: (vacant)
Second College of Clinical Medicine: Prof. HONG GUANG XIANG

TONGJI UNIVERSITY

1239 Siping Rd, Shanghai 200092
Telephone: (21) 65982200
Fax: (21) 65983803
Internet: www.tongji.edu.cn
Founded 1907
Pres.: PEI GANG
Vice-Pres.: CHEN YIYI
Vice-Pres.: CHEN XIAOLONG
Vice-Pres.: DONG QI
Vice-Pres.: JIANG CHANGJUN
Vice-Pres.: LI YONGSHENG
Vice-Pres.: WU JIANG
Vice-Pres.: ZHENG HUIQIANG
Librarian: SHEN JINHUA

Number of teachers: 6,350 6350 (incl. 645 profs)
Number of students: 77,516 (incl. 14,312 postgraduates)

Publications: *Tongji Journal*, several technical publications

DEANS

College of Architecture and Urban Planning: CHEN BINZHAO
College of Computer Science: XUAN GUORONG
College of Economics and Management: HUANG YUXIANG
College of Environmental Engineering: LIU SUIQING
College of Humanities and Law: DENG WEIZHI
College of Mechanical Engineering: MAO QINGXI
College of Structural Engineering: FAN LICHU
Graduate School: WU QIDI

Professional Education and Correspondence School: WU QIDI
Sino-German School: WU QIDI

TSINGHUA UNIVERSITY

1 Qinghuayuan, Beijing 100084
Telephone: (10) 62782015
Fax: (10) 62770349
E-mail: lbzhz@mail.tsinghua.edu.cn
Internet: www.tsinghua.edu.cn
Founded 1911 as Tsinghua Xuetang; renamed Tsinghua School 1912; university section added 1925; became National Tsinghua University 1928; re-structured 1952
Academic year: September to July
Pres.: Prof. GU BINGLIN
Vice-Pres: Prof. CEN ZHANGZHI
Vice-Pres: Prof. GONG KE
Vice-Pres: Prof. KANG KEJUN
Vice-Pres: Prof. WANG JINSONG
Vice-Pres: Prof. ZHANG FENGCHANG
Provost: Prof. WANG JINSONG
Librarian: XUE FANGYU

Number of teachers: 2,877
Number of students: 26,312 (incl. 12,135 graduate)

Publication: *Tsinghua Science and Technology* (6 a year)

DEANS

Academy of Art and Design: Prof. WANG MINGZHI
Graduate School: Prof. GU BINGLIN
Institute of Nuclear and New Energy Technology: Prof. ZHANG ZUOYIN
School of Aerospace: WANG YONGZHI
School of Architecture: Prof. QIN YOUGUO
School of Civil Engineering: Prof. YUAN SI
School of Economics and Management: Prof. ZHAO CHUNJUN
School of Humanities and Social Sciences: Prof. LI QIANG
School of Information Science and Technology: Prof. GONG KE
School of Journalism and Communication: Prof. FAN JINGYI
School of Law: Prof. WANG CHENGUANG
School of Mechanical Engineering: Prof. GUO ZENGYUAN
School of Medicine: Prof. WU JIEPING
School of Public Policy and Management: Prof. CHEN QINGTAI
School of Sciences: Prof. ZHOU GUANGZHAO
Teaching and Research Division of Physical Education: Prof. CHEN WEIQIANG

UNIVERSITY OF ELECTRONIC SCIENCE AND TECHNOLOGY OF CHINA

4 North Jian She Rd, Chengdu 610054, Sichuan
Telephone: (28) 3202353
Fax: (28) 3202365
E-mail: whfu@uestc.edu.cn
Internet: www.uestc.edu.cn
Founded 1956
Academic year: September to July
Pres.: Prof. LIU SHENGGANG
Dir of the International Office: Prof. FU WENHAO
Librarian: Prof. WU WEIGONG

Library of 1,000,000 vols
Number of teachers: 1,380
Number of students: 20,000 (2,000 postgraduate)

Publication: *University Journal* (6 a year)

Eight colleges, 16 departments, 10 research institutes, and 6 centres.

UNIVERSITY OF INTERNATIONAL BUSINESS AND ECONOMICS

10 Hui Xin East St, Chao Yang District, Beijing, 100029

Telephone: (10) 64492001
E-mail: zhaoban@uibe.edu.cn
Internet: www.uibe.edu.cn

Founded 1951
State control
Academic year: September to July

President: CHEN ZHUN MIN
Vice-Presidents: HU FU YIN, LIU YA, WANG ZHENG FU, XU ZI JIAN
Heads of Graduate Department: YANG CHANG CHUN, YANG FENG HUA
Librarian: QIU XIAO HONG

Number of teachers: 1,600
Number of students: 20,000

Publications: *International Trade Problem Research* (4 a year), *Japanese Study and Research* (4 a year), *Journal* (6 a year), *Logistics World* (4 a year)

DEANS

Institute of Executive Development: XU ZI JIAN
International College of Excellence: CEHN SU DONG
Haier Business School: ZHANG XIN MIN
School of Continuing Education: XIE YI BIN
School of Finance: WU JUN
School of Foreign Studies: YANG YAN HONG
School of Higher Vocational Education: XIE WEI FANG
School of Humanities and Politic Administration: ZHENG JUN TIAN
School of Information Technology and Management Engineering: CHEN JIN
School of Insurance: CHEN XIN
School of International Business and Economics: ZHANG XIN MIN
School of International Education: (vacant)
School of International Studies: LI PING
School of International Trade and Economics: LIN GUI JUN
School of Law: SHENG SI BAO
School of Long-Distance Education: XIE YI BIN
School of Physical Education: LI FENG QIAO
Sino-American School of International Management: LIU BAO CHENG
Sino-French School of International Management: LIU BAO CHENG
Sino-German Institute: CHEN JIAN PING

PROFESSORS

BAI, SHU QIANG, International Trade and Economics
CHANG, LI, International Studies
CHANG, YU TIAN, International Studies
CHE, HONG BO, Humanities and Political Administration
CHEN, GONG HE, Information Technology and Management Engineering
CHEN, JIAN PING, Chinesisch-Deutsches Institut
CHEN, JIN, Information Technology and Management Engineering
CHEN, XIN, Insurance
DU, QI HUA, International Trade and Economics
FAN, LI BO, International Business and Economics
FENG, LI CHENG, International Trade and Economics
FU, HUI FEN, International Business and Economics
GE, TIE YING, Foreign Studies
GUO, FEI, International Trade and Economics
GUO, MING HUA, Chinesisch-Deutsches Institut
HAN, QI, International Trade and Economics
HUANG, JING YANG, Insurance

JIA, HUAI QIN, International Business and Economics
JIA, WEN HAO, International Studies
JIANG, PING, International Business and Economics
JIANG, XIAN JING, International Studies
JIN, BING YUN, Foreign Studies
KONG, SHU HONG, International Trade and Economics
LI, AI WEN, Foreign Studies
LI, BO JIE, Chinesisch-Deutsches Institut
LI, DA FENG, Information Technology and Management Engineering
LI, PING, International Studies
LI, QING, International Trade and Economics
LI, SHI, International Trade and Economics
LI, XIAO, Information Technology and Management Engineering
LIANG, PEI, International Trade and Economics
LIN, GUI JUN, International Trade and Economics
LIN, HAN QUAN, International Business and Economics
LIU, SHU LIN, International Trade and Economics
LIU, YUAN, International Trade and Economics
LIU, ZI AN, International Business and Economics
LU, JIN YONG, International Trade and Economics
LU, YONG, Foreign Studies
MA, CHUN GUANG, International Business and Economics
MEN, MING, International Trade and Economics
RONG, ZHEN, Humanities and Political Administration
SANG, BAI CHUAN, International Trade and Economics
SHENG, SI BAO, Law
SHENG, SU PING, International Studies
SHI, YAN PING, International Trade and Economics
TANG, YI HONG, International Trade and Economics
WANG, EN MIAN, International Studies
WANG, GUAN FU, International Studies
WANG, JIAN, International Trade and Economics
WANG, LIN SHENG, International Trade and Economics
WANG, SHAO XI, International Trade and Economics
WANG, TIAN QING, Foreign Studies
WANG, XIAO LIN, International Trade and Economics
WANG, XIU LI, International Business and Economics
WANG, ZHENG FU, Chinesisch-Deutsches Institut
WU, FEN, International Studies
WU, GE, International Business and Economics
WU, JUN, Finance
XI, NING HUA, Information Technology and Management Engineering
XU, YONG BIN, Foreign Studies
XU, ZI JIAN, International Business and Economics
XUE, RONG JIU, International Trade and Economics
YANG, CHANG CHUN, International Trade and Economics
YANG, YAN HONG, Foreign Studies
YAO, LI PING, Foreign Studies
YE, DONG YA, International Trade and Economics
YU, LI JUN, International Studies
YU, XU LIAN, International Business and Economics
ZHANG, JIAN PING, International Business and Economics
ZHANG, JIE, International Business and Economics

ZHANG, JING, Foreign Studies
ZHANG, MI, Foreign Studies
ZHANG, WEI, International Trade and Economics
ZHANG, XIN MIN, International Business and Economics
ZHANG, ZUO QI, Information Technology and Management Engineering
ZHAO, JUN, International Business and Economics
ZHAO, ZHONG XIU, International Trade and Economics
ZHENG, JUN TIAN, Humanities and Political Administration
ZHU, KAI, Foreign Studies
ZHU, MING XIA, International Trade and Economics

UNIVERSITY OF INTERNATIONAL RELATIONS

12 Po Shang Cun, Hai Ding District, Beijing 250014

Telephone: (10) 62861310
Fax: (10) 62861660
Internet: www.uir.edu.cn

Founded 1949
Academic year: September to July
Number of teachers: 1,000

Schools: culture and communication, English language, Japanese and French language, law, Marxism and Leninism, national economy, national politics, science and technology information, continuing education.

UNIVERSITY OF SCIENCE AND TECHNOLOGY BEIJING

30 Xueyuan Lu, Beijing 100083

Telephone: (10) 62332312
Fax: (10) 62327283
Internet: www.ustb.edu.cn

Founded 1952, present name 1988

Pres.: Prof. YANG TIANJUN
Vice-Pres.: Prof. XU JINWU
Head of Foreign Relations: LIU YONGCAI

Library of 837,000 vols
Number of teachers: 2,849
Number of students: 5,122 undergraduates, 1,424 graduates

Publications: *Higher Education Research, Journal of UST Beijing.*

UNIVERSITY OF SCIENCE AND TECHNOLOGY OF CHINA

96 Jinzhai Rd, Hefei 230026

Telephone: (551) 3601000
Fax: (551) 3631760
E-mail: iao@ustc.ac.cn
Internet: www.ustc.edu.cn

Founded 1958 by Chinese Academy of Sciences
Academic year: September to January, March to July

President: ZHU QINGSHI
Vice-Presidents: CHENG YI, HOU JIANGUO, LI DING, LI GUODONG, XU WU
Secretary-General: WANG KEQIANG
Director of Foreign Affairs: ZHANG MENGPING

Library of 1,620,000 vols, 230,000 periodicals
Number of teachers: 3,500
Number of students: 13,186

Publications: *Chinese Journal of Low Temperature Physics, Education and Modernization, Experimental Mechanics, Journal, Journal of Chemical Physics.*

WEST CHINA CENTRE OF MEDICAL SCIENCES

17 Renminnanlu 3 Duan, Chengdu, Sichuan 610044
Telephone: (28) 85501047
Fax: (28) 85502321
E-mail: dff@wcums.ecu.cn
Internet: www.wcums.edu.cn
Founded 1910
State control; attached to Sichuan Union University
Languages of instruction: Chinese, English
Academic year: September to January, February to July
Pres.: XIE HEPING
Vice-Pres.: BAO LANG
Vice-Pres.: LI HONG
Vice-Pres.: ZHANG ZHAODA
Chief Admin. Officer: BU HONG
Librarian: LI BINYAN

Library of 650,000 vols
Number of teachers: 1,057
Number of students: 4,998

Publications: *Chinese Journal of Medical Genetics, Chinese Journal of Ocular Fundus Diseases, Chinese Journal of Reparative and Reconstructive Surgery, Journal of West China University of Medical Sciences, Modern Preventive Medicine, West China Journal of Pharmaceutical Sciences, West China Journal of Stomatology, West China Medical Journal*

DEANS

School of Basic Medical Sciences: Dr HOU YIPING
School of Continued Education: Dr HUO TINGFU
School of Medicine: Dr SHI YINGKANG
School of Pharmacy: WANG FENGPENG
School of Public Health: Dr MA XIAO
School of Stomatology: Dr ZHOU XUEDONG

DISTINGUISHED PROFESSORS

Faculty of Forensic Medicine:

WU MEIYUN, Forensic Medicine

School of Basic Medical Sciences:

BAO LANG, Pathophysiology
CAI MEIYING, Immunology
CHEN HUAIQING, Biomedical Engineering
CHEN JUNJIE, Biochemistry
CHEN MANLING, Biochemistry
DAI BAOMIN, Pathophysiology
FU MINGDE, Biochemistry
HU XIAOSHU, Parasitology
LI RUIXIANG, Anatomy
LIU BINGWEN, Biochemistry
LU ZHENSHAN, Histology and Embryology
OU KEQUN, Histology and Embryology
WANG BOYAO, Pathophysiology
WU LIANGFANG, Histology and Embryology
ZHU BIDE, Histology and Embryology

School of Pharmacy:

LI TUN, Pharmaceutics
LIAO GONGTIE, Pharmaceutics
LU BIN, Pharmaceutics
WANG FENGPENG, Chemistry of Natural Medicinal Products
WANG XIANKAI, Pharmaceutical Chemistry
WENG LINGLING, Pharmaceutical Chemistry
XU MINGXIA, Pharmaceutical Chemistry
ZHENG HU, Pharmaceutical Chemistry
ZHONG YUGONG, Pharmaceutical Chemistry

School of Public Health:

LI CHANGJI
LI XIAOSONG, Health Statistics
NI ZONGZAN
PENG SHUSHENG, Nutrition and Food Hygiene
SUN MIANLING, Environmental Health

WANG RUISHU, Nutrition and Hygiene
WANG ZHIMING, Occupational Health and Occupational Diseases
WU DESHENG, Environmental Health
YANG SHUQIN, Health Statistics
ZHANG CHAOWU
ZHANG CHENLIE, Occupational Health and Occupational Diseases

School of Stomatology:

CAO YONGLIE, Orthodontics
DU CHUANSHI, Prosthodontics
LI BINGQU, Oral Medicine
LI SHENWEI, Maxillofacial Surgery
LIU TIANJIA, Oral Medicine
LUO SONGJIAO, Orthodontics
MAO ZHUYI, Maxillofacial Surgery
WANG DAZHANG, Maxillofacial Surgery
WANG HANZHANG, Maxillofacial Surgery
WEI ZHITONG, Orthodontics
WEN YUMING, Maxillofacial Surgery
YUE SONGLING, Oral Medicine
ZHANG YUNHUI, Oral Medicine
ZHAO YUNFENG, Orthodontics
ZHOU XIUKUN, Orthodontics

West China School of Medicine:

CAO ZEYI, Obstetrics and Gynaecology
CAO ZHONGLIANG, Infectious Diseases
CHEN WENBIN, Internal Medicine
DENG XIANZHAO, Genito-Urinary Surgery
FANG QIANXUN, Ophthalmology
GAO LIDA, Neural Surgery
HU TINGZE, Paediatric Surgery
HUANG DEJIA, Diagnostic Imaging
HUANG MINGSHENG, Psychiatry and Mental Health
LEI BINGJUN, Infectious Diseases
LI GANDI, Pathology
LI XIUJUN, Internal Medicine
LIAO QINGKUI, Paediatrics
LIN DAICHENG, Otolaryngology
LIU XIEHE, Psychiatry and Mental Health
LUO CHENGREN, Ophthalmology
LUO CHUNHUA, Paediatrics
MIN PENGQIU, Diagnostic Imaging
OUYANG QIN, Gastroenterology
PENG ZHILAN, Obstetrics and Gynaecology
SHEN WENLU, General Surgery
SHI YINGKANG, Cardiological Surgery
TANG TIANZHI, Nuclear Medicine
TANG ZEYUAN, Paediatrics
WANG SHILANG, Obstetrics and Gynaecology
WANG ZENGLI, Internal Medicine
WEI FUKANG, Paediatric Surgery
XIAO LUJIA, General Surgery
YAN LUNAN, General Surgery
YAN MI, Ophthalmology
YANG GUANGHUA, Pathology
YANG YURU, Genito-Urinary Surgery
YANG ZHIMING, Orthopaedics
ZHANG ZIZHONG, Medical Genetics
ZHANG ZHAODA, General Surgery
ZHAO LIANSAN, Infectious Diseases

WUHAN UNIVERSITY

Wuhan 430072, Hubei
Telephone: (27) 87882547
Fax: (27) 87882661
E-mail: wupo@whu.edu.cn
Internet: www.whu.edu.cn
Founded 1893
Academic year: September to July
Pres.: Prof. LIU JINGNAN
Vice-Pres.: Prof. CHEN ZHAOFANG
Vice-Pres.: Prof. HUANG CONGXIN
Vice-Pres.: Prof. HU DEKUN
Vice-Pres.: Prof. LI QINGQUAN
Vice-Pres.: Prof. LIU JINGNAN
Vice-Pres.: Prof. LI WENXIN
Vice-Pres.: Prof. LONG XIAOLE
Vice-Pres.: Prof. WU JUNPEI
Secretary-General: Prof. REN XINNIAN

Director of Foreign Affairs Office: Assoc. Prof. PENG YUANJIE
Librarian: Prof. YAN JINWEI
Number of teachers: 5,000
Number of students: 40,000

Publications: *Economic Review* (6 a year), *French Studies* (every 2 years), *Journal* (humanities edn, in Chinese; social sciences edn, in Chinese; natural sciences edn, in English; engineering edn, in Chinese; information sciences edn, in English and Chinese; medical science edn, in Chinese), *Journal of Analytical Science* (6 a year), *Journal of Audiology and Speech Pathology* (4 a year), *Journal of Mathematical Medicine* (6 a year), *Journal of Mathematics* (4 a year), *Knowledge of Library Information* (4 a year), *Law Review* (6 a year), *Stroke and Nervous Diseases* (4 a year), *Writing* (12 a year)

DEANS

Business: Prof. ZHOU MAORONG
Chemistry and Molecular Science: Prof. PANG DAIWEN
Civil Engineering: Prof. ZHU YIWEN
Computer Science: Prof. HE YANXIANG
Dynamics and Mechanics: Prof. WU QINGMING
Electrical Engineering: Prof. CHEN YUNPING
Foreign Languages: Prof. WANG XIUZHEN
Geomatics: Prof. LI JIANCHENG
Humanities: Prof. GUO QIYONG
Information Management (Library and Information Science): Prof. MA FEICHENG
International Relations: (vacant)
Journalism and Communications: Prof. LUO YICHENG
Law: Prof. ZENG LINGLIANG
Life Science: Prof. HE GUANGCUN
Materials Science and Engineering: (vacant)
Mathematics and Probability: Prof. CHEN HUA
Medicine: Prof. FAN MINGWEN
Pharmacy: (vacant)
Photoelectronics and Information Service: Prof. KE HENGYU
Physics: Prof. SHI JING
Political Science and Management: Prof. TAN JUNJIU
Public Health: (vacant)
Public Management: Prof. DENG DASONG
Remote Sensing and Information Engineering: Prof. WANG YOUCHUAN
Resources and Environmental Science: Prof. LIU YAOLIN
Stomatology: Prof. FAN MINGWEN
Urban Studies: Prof. ZHAO BING
Water Resources and Hydropower Engineering: Prof. TAN GUANGMING

WUHAN UNIVERSITY OF TECHNOLOGY

122 Luoshi Rd, Wuhan 430070, Hubei
Telephone: (27) 87658253
Internet: www.whut.edu.cn
Founded 1945
State control
Academic year: September to July
Pres.: ZHOU ZUDE
Vice-Presidents: CHEN DONGSHENG, LI HAIYING, TAO DEXIN, YAN XINGPING, ZHANG LIANMENG, ZHANG QINGJIE
Librarian: XIAO JINSHENG

Library of 2,720,000 vols
Number of teachers: 2,400
Number of students: 37,000

Publication: *Journal* (editions: management and information engineering; material sciences (in English); social sciences; transportation science and engineering)

Schools: economics, material science and engineering, literature and law, international studies, arts and design, natural sciences, resources and environmental engineering, mechatronic engineering, automotive engineering, automation, computer science and technology, information engineering, civil engineering and architecture, transportation, navigation, energy and power engineering, management sciences; Deps: logistics engineering, humanities, chemical engineering, physical education, Institutes: continuing education, network education

PROFESSORS

CAI, CHANGXIU, Mechanical Design and Theory
CHANG, ZHIHUA, Automotive Engineering
CHEN, BINKANG, Ship-Building and Marine Structure Design
CHEN, DINGFANG, Manufacturing Engineering and Automation
CHEN, GONGYU, Management Science and Engineering
CHEN, GUOHONG, Management Science and Engineering
CHEN, MINGZHAO, Marine Engineering
CHEN, TIEQUN, Automotive Engineering
CHEN, WEN, Material Physics and Chemistry
CUI, KERUN, Marine Engineering
DENG, CHUNAN, Automotive Engineering
DENG, MINGRAN, Management Science and Engineering
FENG, ENDE, Ship-Building and Marine Structure Design
FU, ZHENGYI, Material Processing Engineering
GAO, XIAOHONG, Marine Engineering
GONG, WENQI, Mineralogy
GU, BICHONG, Mechanical Design and Theory
HU, RONGQIANG, Mechanical Design and Theory
HU, SHUGUANG, Material Science and Engineering
HU, SHUHUA, Management Science and Engineering
JIANG, CANGRU, Structural Engineering
JIANG, DESHENG, Material Science and Engineering
JIANG, ZHENGFENG, Mechanical Design and Theory
LI, BIQING, Management Science and Engineering
LI, GANGYAN, Mechanical Design and Theory
LI, HAIYING, Management Science and Engineering
LI, LAYUAN, Transportation Information Engineering and Control
LI, QIANG, Material Physics and Chemistry
LI, SHIPU, Material Science and Engineering
LI, ZHIMING, Mechanical Design and Theory
LI, ZHUOQIU, Structural Engineering
LIN, QITAI, Mineralogy
LIN, ZONGSHOU, Material Science and Engineering
LIU, GUOXIN, Management Science and Engineering
LIU, HANXING, Material Physics and Chemistry
LIU, ZUOMING, Mechanical Design and Theory
LIU, ZUYUAN, Fluid Mechanics
LU, KAISHENG, Marine Engineering
LU, LING, Transportation Information Engineering and Control
MEI, BINGCHU, Material Processing Engineering
MO, YIMIN, Mechanical Design and Theory
NAN, CEWEN, Material Physics and Chemistry
OU YANG, SHIXI, Material Science and Engineering
PAN, CHUNXU, Material Processing Engineering
PENG, SHAOMIN, Structural Engineering
QU, WEILIAN, Structural Engineering
SHEN, CHENWU, Ship-Building and Marine Structure Design

SUN, GUOZHENG, Mechanical Design and Theory
TAO, DEXIN, Manufacturing Engineering and Automation
WAN, JUNKANG, Management Science and Engineering
WANG, CENGFANG, Ship-Building and Marine Structure Design
WANG, DEXUN, Fluid Mechanics
WANG, JIEDE, Ship-Building and Marine Structure Design
WANG, LUNKANG, Fluid Mechanics
WANG, SHAOMEI, Mechanical Design and Theory
WANG, ZHONGFAN, Automotive Engineering
WU, BOLIN, Material Physics and Chemistry
WU, DAIHUA, Structural Engineering
XIA, YUANYOU, Structural Engineering
XIAO, HANLIANG, Application Engineering for Load-Carrying Equipment
XIAO, JINSHENG, Marine Engineering
XIE, KEFAN, Management Science and Engineering
XIONG, QIANXING, Transportation Information Engineering and Control
XUE, YIYU, Automotive Engineering
YAN, SHILIN, Structural Engineering
YAN, XINGPING, Application Engineering for Load-Carrying Equipment
YAN, YUHUA, Material Physics and Chemistry
YANG, MINGZHONG, Mechanical Design and Theory
YUAN, CHUXIONG, Mineralogy
YUAN, RUNZHANG, Material Science and Engineering
ZHANG, LEWEN, Fluid Mechanics
ZHANG, LIANMENG, Material Processing Engineering
ZHANG, QINGJIE, Material Science and Engineering
ZHANG, SHIXIONG, Mineralogy
ZHANG, YOULING, Automotive Engineering
ZHANG, ZHONGPU, Mechanical Design and Theory
ZHAO, XIUJIAN, Material Physics and Chemistry
ZHONG, LUO, Structural Engineering
ZHOU, YICHEN, Marine Engineering
ZHOU, ZAOJIAN, Ship-Building and Marine Structure Design
ZHOU, ZUDE, Manufacturing Engineering and Automation
ZHU, MEIQI, Ship-Building and Marine Structure Design
ZHU, RUIGENG, Mineralogy
ZHU, XICHAN, Automotive Engineering

XIAMEN UNIVERSITY

422 Siming Rd S, Xiamen 361005, Fujian
Telephone: (592) 2182229
Fax: (592) 2086526
E-mail: xmupo@xmu.edu.cn
Internet: www.xmu.edu.cn
Founded 1921
Academic year: September to July
Pres.: CHEN CHUANHONG
Vice-Pres.: PAN SHIMO
Vice-Pres.: SUN SHIGANG
Vice-Pres.: WU SHUIPENG
Vice-Pres.: ZHU CONGSHI
Foreign Affairs Office: SU ZIXING
Registrar: YANG BING
Librarian: CHEN MINGGUANG
Library of 2,180,000 vols
Number of teachers: 2,589
Number of students: 12,125
Publications: *China's Social Economics* (4 a year), *Xiamen University Journal* (philosophy and social sciences edn and natural sciences edn, both 4 a year)

DEANS
Adult Education College: YANG YOUTING

College of Art Education: WU PEIWEN
College of Economics: QIU HUABING
College of Foreign Languages and Cultures: LIAN SHUNENG
College of Humanities: CHEN ZHIPING
College of Life Science: PEN XUANXIAN
Medical College: LIN YANLIN
Overseas Education College: ZHAN XINLI
School of Chemistry and Chemical Engineering: WAN HUILIN
School of Computer and Information Engineering: CHEN HUIHUANG
School of Law: LIAO YIXIN
School of Management: WU SHILONG
School of Oceanography and Environment: YAN DONGXING
School of Physics and Machinery Electronic Engineering: CHEN JINCAN
Vocational Technical College: YANG SHENYUN

HEADS OF DEPARTMENTS AND INSTITUTES

College of Art Education (tel. (592) 2182404; fax (592) 2181499):
Fine Arts: HE SHIYANG
Music: YANG ZHEN

College of Economics (tel. (592) 2181387):
Economics: CHEN YONGZHI
Finance and Banking: LEI GENGQIANG
International Trade: ZHANG DINGZHONG
Planning and Statistics: DAI YIYI

College of Foreign Languages and Cultures (tel. (592) 2186380; fax (592) 2182476):
Asian and European Language and Literature: FENG SHOULONG
Foreign Languages: ZHANG LILONG
Foreign Language Teaching: GUO YONGHUI

College of Humanities (tel. (592) 2181932):
Chinese: ZHU SHUIYONG
History: DAI YIFENG
Journalism and Communication: ZHU JIANQIANG
Philosophy: CHEN XICHENG
Sociology: ZHANG YOUQIN

College of Life Science (tel. (592) 2185360; fax (592) 2186392):
Biology: HUANG HEQING

School of Chemistry and Chemical Engineering (tel. (592) 2182430):
Chemical Engineering: LI QINGBIAO
Chemistry: ZHU YAXIAN
Materials: FENG ZUDE

School of Computer and Information Engineering (tel. (592) 2183127):
Architecture: LING SHIDE
Automation: CAI JIANLI
Computing: LU WEI
Electronic Engineering: XIE TINGGUI

School of Law (tel. (592) 2186653):
Law: XU CONGLI
Politics: ZHU RENXIAN

School of Management (tel. (592) 2182873):
Accounting: CHEN HANWEN
Business Administration: SHEN WEITAO

School of Oceanography and Environment (tel. (592) 2183064):
Oceanography: PAN WEIRAN

School of Physics and Machinery Electronic Engineering (tel. (592) 2182454; fax (592) 2189426):
Electronic Engineering for Machinery: ZHU LIMIAO
Physics: LIN GUOXING

XIAN INTERNATIONAL STUDIES UNIVERSITY

437 South Changan Rd, Xian 710061, Shaanxi
Telephone: (29) 85309274
Fax: (29) 85261350

Internet: www.xisu.edu.cn
Founded 1952
Provincial control
Academic year: September to July
President: Du Ruiqing
Vice-Presidents: Chu Chu, Hu Xishe, Liu Yuelian
Head of Graduate Department: Yang Xiwen
Librarian: Yang Yongcai
Library of 901,000 vols
Publications: *Foreign Language Education* (6 a year), *Human Geography* (6 a year), *Journal of Xian Foreign Languages Institute* (4 a year)

DEANS

Department of French: Zhang Ping
Department of German: Wen Renbai
School of Audiovisual Communication: Qin Yaming
School of Culture and Communication: Hu Ruihua
School of Eastern Languages and Culture: Zhang Sehngyu
School of Economics: Pan Huixia
School of Tourism: Dang Jinxue

PROFESSORS

Dang, Jinxue, Tourism
Feng, Guang, Audiovisual Communication
Gao, Yaoting, German Studies
Hu, Ruihua, Culture and Communication
Li, Qiuquan, Tourism
Lin, Kai, Audiovisual Communication
Liu, Jianqiang, Eastern Languages and Culture
Ma, Yongping, Eastern Languages and Culture
Wang, Xingzhong, Tourism
Wang, Xinrong, Eastern Languages and Culture
Wei, Genyuan, Audiovisual Communication
Wen, Renbai, German Studies
Yao, Baorong, Tourism
Yuan, Jianping, Russian Studies
Zhang, Baoning, Culture and Communication
Zhang, Cong, Culture and Communication
Zhang, Shengyu, Eastern Languages and Culture
Zheng, Mingjiang, Culture and Communication

XIAN JIAOTONG UNIVERSITY

28 West Xianning Rd, Xian 710049
Telephone: (29) 2668234
Fax: (29) 3234781
E-mail: mailxjtu@xjtu.edu.cn
Internet: www.xjtu.edu.cn
Founded 1896
State control
Academic year: September to July (two semesters)
Pres.: Zheng Nanning
Registrar: Li Nenggui
Admin. Officer: Liu Bin
Librarian: Zhou Jingen
Number of teachers: 3,241
Number of students: 26,410 (incl. 5,504 postgraduate)
Publications: *Applied Mechanics* (4 a year), *Engineering Mathematics* (4 a year), *Journal* (4 a year), *Journal of Economic Sciences* (4 a year), *Journal of Medical Sciences* (4 a year), *Journal of Social Sciences* (4 a year)

DEANS

Graduate School: Xu Tongmo
School of Accountancy: Xhang Tianxi
School of Architectural Engineering and Mechanics: Chen Yiheng
School of Continuing Education: Sun Bi

School of Economics and Finance: Xue Mouhong
School of Electrical and Communications Engineering: Zhu Shihua
School of Electrical Engineering: Wang Zhaoan
School of Energy and Power Engineering: Hui Shen
School of Environmental and Chemical Engineering: Cheng Guangxu
School of Foreign Languages: Bai Yongquan
School of Humanities and Social Science: Liu Yongfu
School of Life Sciences and Technology: Wan Mingxi
School of Management: Xi Youmin
School of Materials Science and Engineering: Xu Kewei
School of Mechanical Engineering: Xing Jiandong
School of Medical Science: Yan Jianqun
School of Network Education: Yu Dehong
School of Science: Xu Zongben
School of Stomatology: (vacant)
There are 64 research institutes and 126 research laboratories

XIAN MEDICAL UNIVERSITY

205 Zhuquedajie, Nanjiao, Xian 710061, Shaanxi
Telephone: (29) 5261609
Fax: (29) 5267364
E-mail: mail1@irix.xamu.edu.cn
Founded 1937
Controlled by Ministry of Health
Language of instruction: Chinese
Academic year: September to January, March to July (3-year, 4-year, 5-year and 7-year courses)
Pres.: Prof. Ren Huimin
Vice-Pres.: Prof. Chen Hengyuan
Vice-Pres.: Prof. Fan Xiaoli
Library Dir: Ma Xingfu
Number of teachers: 4,972
Number of students: 4,000
Publications: *Abstracts of Medicine, Academic Journal of Xian Medical University* (Chinese and English editions), *Journal, Journal of Audio-Visual Medical Education, Journal of Children's Health, Journal of Chinese Medical Ethics, Journal of Maternity and Child Health Overseas, Journal of Medical Education in Northwest China, Journal of Medical Geography Overseas, Journal of Modern TCM* (Traditional Chinese Medicine), *Journal of Pharmacy in Northwest China, P.R. China* (dermatology)

DEANS

First Clinical Medical School: Pan Chengen
Second Clinical Medical School: Chen Junchang
Pre-clinical Medical School: Gao Hongde
Secondary Health School: Ni Kai
School of Stomatology: Hu Yongsheng
School of Pharmacy: Yang Shimi
School of Forensic Medicine: Li Shengbin
School of Public Health: Yan Hong
School of Social Medicine: Li Jinsuo
School of Adult Training: Feng Xinzhou
Faculty of Biomedical Engineering: Jin Jie
Faculty of Health Administration: Gao Jianmin
Faculty of Foreign Languages: Bai Yongquan
Faculty of Maternal and Child Care: Zhang Minghui
Faculty of Nursing: Shao Weiwei

PROFESSORS

Bai Yongquan, English
Chen Junchang, Surgery

Cui Changzong, Internal Medicine
Deng Yunshan, Dermatology
Diao Guixiang, Pathology
Ding Dongning, Chemistry
Ding Huiwen, Cardiology
Dong Lei, Digestive Medicine
Fang Xiaoli, Physiology
Feng Xueliang, Internal Medicine
Feng Yinqun, Orthopaedics
Gu Jianzhang, Paediatrics
Guo Yingchun, Cardiology
He Langchong, Pharmaceutical Analysis
Hu Guoying, Isotopes
Hu Haobo, Health Administration
Hu Yongsheng, Stomatology
Ji Zongzheng, Surgery
Jin Jie, Physics
Kong Xiangzhen, Pathophysiology
Lei Liquan, Pathophysiology
Lei Xiaoying, Ultrasonic
Li Guowei, Surgery
Li Rong, Oncology
Li Shuxi, Digestive Medicine
Li Yiming, Surgery
Li Yingli, Pharmacognosy
Li Zhe, Parasitology
Li Zhongmin, Internal Medicine
Liu Hongtao, English
Liu Huixi, Gynaecology and Obstetrics
Liu Jinyan, Internal Medicine
Liu Shanxi, Internal Medicine
Liu Xiaogong, Surgery
Liu Zhiquan, Internal Medicine
Lu Guilin, Gynaecology and Obstetrics
Lu Zhuoren, Cardiology
Ma Aiqun, Internal Medicine
Ma Xiuping, Endocrine Medicine
Mei Jun, Physiology
Men Boyuan, Epidemics
Nan Xunyi, Urology
Pan Chengen, Surgery
Pang Zhigong, Analytical Chemistry
Pian Janping, Health Care of Children
Qin Zhaoyin, Surgery
Qiu Shudong, Histology and Embryology
Qu Xinzhong, Gynaecology and Obstetrics
Ren Huimin, Anatomy
Ruan Meisheng, Stomatology
Shi Jingsen, Surgery
Shi Wei, Neurology
Song Tianbao, Histology and Embryology
Su Min, Pathological Anatomy
Sun Naixue, Ophthalmology
Tan Shengshun, Dermatology
Tan Tinghua, Physical Chemistry
Wang Baoqi, Inorganic Chemistry
Wang Bingwen, Pharmacology
Wang Hui, History of the Communist Party
Wang Jingui, Physical Education
Wang Kunzheng, Orthopaedics
Wang Qiang, Stomatology
Wang Shichen, Internal Medicine
Wang Shiying, Stomatology
Wang Xueliang, Epidemics
Wang Zezhong, Radiology
Wang Ziming, Urology
Wu Yingyun, Respiratory Medicine
Xu Wenyou, Pharmacology
Yang Dingyi, Internal Medicine
Yang Guangfu, Radiological Diagnosis
Ye Pingan, Anaesthesiology
Yu Bolang, Medical Image Diagnosis
Yuan Bingxiang, Pharmacology
Yue Jinsheng, Infectious Diseases
Zhang Ahui, Chemistry
Zhang Huaan, Pharmacology
Zhang Minghui, Gynaecology and Obstetrics
Zhang Quanfa, Cardiology
Zhang Shulin, Infectious Diseases
Zhang Yonghao, Parasitology
Zhang Zhefang, Radiology
Zhao Genran, Anatomy
Zhao Junyong, Biochemistry
Zhao Zhongrong, Radiology
Zhu Hongliang, Otorhinolaryngology
Zhu Jiaqing, Cardiology

XIAN PETROLEUM INSTITUTE

18 Dian Zi Er Lu, Xian 710061, Shaanxi
Telephone: (29) 5253253
Fax: (29) 5263449

Founded 1958

Controlled by National Petroleum Corporation

Language of instruction: English

President: LIN RENZI
Vice-Presidents: XIN XIXIAN, XUE ZHONGTIAN, YANG ZHENGYI
Registrar: WANG XIAOQUAN
Librarian: XIE KUN

Library of 280,000 vols, 2,000 periodicals
Number of teachers: 558
Number of students: 4,000

Publications: *Journal* (natural science and social science editions), *Petroleum Library and Information*, *Supervision of Petroleum Industry Technology*

PROFESSORS

CHEN XIAOZHENG, Petroleum Economics
FU XINGSHENG, Earth Strata Slope Angles, Well-Logging Methods and Instruments
GAO CHENGTAI, Well-testing
GAO JINIAN, Applied Electric-Hydraulic Control Technology
HU QI, Petroleum Instruments
LI DANG, Mechanism of High-Energy Gas Fracturing
LU JIAO, Petroleum Instruments
PANG JUFENG, Physics and Nuclear Well Logging
SHENG DICHENG, Walking Beam Pumping Units
WANG JIAHUA, Computers
WANG SHIQING, Mechanical Engineering
WANG YIGONG, Management Systems of Petroleum Machinery
WU KUN
WU YIJIONG, Pumping Wells
ZHANG SHAOHUAI, Drilling
ZHANG ZONGMING, Petroleum Tectonics of China
ZHAO GUANGCHANG, Economics and Management

XIAN UNIVERSITY OF ARCHITECTURE AND TECHNOLOGY

13 Yanta Rd, Xian 710055, Shaanxi
Telephone: (29) 2202121
Fax: (29) 5522471
E-mail: jianda@webmail.xauat.edu.cn
Internet: www.xauat.edu.cn

Founded 1956

Academic year: September to July

Pres.: Prof. XU DELONG
Vice-Pres: Prof. DUAN ZHISHAN, Prof. GAN ANSHENG, Prof. WANG XIAOCHANG, Assoc. Prof. MA JIANHUA
Head of the Graduate School: Assoc. Prof. YUAN SHOUQIAN
Librarian: Prof. LIU JIAPING

Library of 1,000,800 vols
Number of teachers: 2,100
Number of students: 22,518

Publications: *Journal* (4 a year), *Science and Technology of Xian University of Architecture and Technology* (4 a year), *Study of Higher Education*

HEADS OF COLLEGES AND DEPARTMENTS

College of Architecture: Prof. LIU KECHENG
College of Civil Engineering: Prof. BAO GUOLIANG
College of Environmental and Municipal Engineering: Prof. WANG XIAOCHANG
College of Management: Prof. LUO FUZHOU
College of Metallurgy Engineering: Prof. LAN XINZHE

College of Information and Auto-control Engineering: Prof. ZHAO WENJING
College of Mechanical and Electrical Engineering: Prof. ZHANG XIAOLONG
College of Materials Science and Engineering: Prof. XU QIMING
College of Humanities and Chinese Literature: Prof. ZHANG TONGLE
College of Science: Prof. LI DONGLIANG
College of Environmental Arts: Prof. YANG HAOZHONG
College of Vocational Technology: Prof. LI HUIMIN
Department of Foreign Studies: Assoc. Prof. TANG YIFAN

XIAN UNIVERSITY OF SCIENCE AND TECHNOLOGY

58 Yanta Rd, Mid Sector, Xian 710054, Shaanxi
Telephone: (29) 5583033
Fax: (29) 5583719
E-mail: iecc@xust.sn.cn
Internet: www.xust.sn.cn

Founded 1958

Academic year: September to July

President: Prof. CHANG XINTAN
Vice-President: Prof. HAN JIANGSHUI
Vice-President: Prof. LU JIANJUN
Vice-President: Prof. MA HONGWEI
Vice-President: Prof. YANG GENGSHE
Librarian: Prof. WANG TINGMAN

Library of 580,000 vols
Number of teachers: 750
Number of students: 14,200

Publications: *Higher Education Research* (6 a year), *Journal* (12 a year), *Scientech Talent Market* (6 a year).

XIAN UNIVERSITY OF TECHNOLOGY

5 Jinhua Rd (South), Xian 710048, Shaanxi
Telephone: (29) 82312541
Fax: (29) 83230026
E-mail: xzb@mail.xaut.edu.cn
Internet: www.xaut.edu.cn

Founded 1949; until 1993, Shaanxi Institute of Mechanical Engineering

Joint Ministry of Education and Provincial control

Academic year: September to July

President: Prof. CHEN ZHIMING
Vice-President: Prof. CUI DUWU
Vice-President: Prof. FU YOUMING
Vice-President: Prof. LIU DING
Vice-President: Prof. ZHANG MIAOFENG
Librarian: Prof. SHI JUNPING

Library of 800,000 vols
Number of teachers: 1,050
Number of students: 26,200

Publications: *Foundry Technology* (6 a year), *Journal of Shaanxi Water Power* (4 a year), *Journal of Xian University of Technology* (4 a year)

DEANS

Faculty of Automation Engineering and Information Science: Prof. GAO YONG
Faculty of Computer Science and Engineering: Prof. ZHANG YIKUN
Faculty of Humanities and Social Sciences: Prof. LI QINGMING
Faculty of Management: Prof. DANG XINHUA
Faculty of Materials Science and Engineering: Prof. FAN ZHIKANG
Faculty of Mechanical Engineering: Prof. LI YAN
Faculty of Printing and Packaging Engineering: Prof. WANG JIAMIN
Faculty of Science: Prof. HE QINXIANG
Faculty of Water Conservancy and Hydroelectric Power: Prof. LUO XINGQI

Polytechnic College: Prof. WANG HUI

XIANGTAN UNIVERSITY

Yanggutang, Xiangtan 411105, Hunan
Telephone: (732) 8292130
Fax: (732) 8292282
E-mail: ecc@xtu.edu.cn
Internet: www.xtu.edu.cn

Founded 1975

State control

Language of instruction: Chinese

Pres.: Prof. LUO HE'AN

Number of teachers: 1,309
Number of students: 31,600

Publications: *Journal* (social science and natural science editions), *Journal* (philosophy and social sciences series, 6 a year), *Journal* (natural science series, 4 a year), *Transaction of Chinese Verse* (4 a year).

XIDIAN UNIVERSITY

2 South Tai Bai Rd, Xian 710071, Shaanxi
Telephone: (29) 8202221
Fax: (29) 8201620
E-mail: master@xidian.edu.cn
Internet: www.xidian.edu.cn

Founded 1937

State control

Academic year: September to July

President: DUAN BAOYAN
Vice-Presidents: CAO TIANSHUN, CHEN YONG, HAO YUE, LI RUFENG, YU NANNAN
Librarian: FAN LAIYAO

Library of 860,000 vols
Number of teachers: 1,900
Number of students: 15,000

Publication: *Journal* (editions: physical and social sciences)

DEANS

School of Computer Science and Engineering: WU BO
School of Economics and Management: ZHAO PENGWEI
School of Electronic Engineering: JIAO LICHENG
School of Humanities: ZHAO BOFEI
School of Mechatronics: JIA JIANYUAN
School of Science: WU ZHENSEN
School of Technical Physics: AN YUYING
School of Telecommunications Engineering: LI JIANDONG

PROFESSORS

BAI, BAOMING, Telecommunications Engineering
CAI, XIQIAO, Software Engineering
CHEN, BOXIAO, Electronic Engineering
CHEN, JIANJUN, Mechatronic Engineering
CHEN, PING, Computer Science and Engineering
DUAN, ZHENHUA, Computer Science and Engineering
FENG, DAZHENG, Electronic Engineering
FU, FENGLIN, Telecommunications Engineering
GAO, XINBO, Electronic Engineering
GAO, YOUXING, Computer Science and Engineering
GONG, JIEMIN, Software Engineering
GONG, SHUXI, Electronic Engineering
GUO, BAOLONG, Mechatronic Engineering
HU, QIYING, Economics and Management
HUANG, LIYU, Electronic Engineering
JI, HONGBING, Electronic Engineering
JIA, JIANYUAN, Mechatronic Engineering
JIANG, ZHEXIN, Economics and Management
JIAO, LICHENG, Electronic Engineering
JIAO, YONGCHANG, Electronic Engineering
LI, BINGBING, Telecommunications Engineering

LI, HUA, Economics and Management
LI, WEIYING, Telecommunications Engineering
LI, YUSHAN, Electronic Engineering
LI, ZHIWU, Mechatronic Engineering
LIANG, CHANGHONG, Electronic Engineering
LIU, FANG, Computer Science and Engineering
LIU, HONGWEI, Electronic Engineering
LIU, HONGWEI, Science
LIU, JIAN, Software Engineering
LIU, MING, Mechatronic Engineering
LIU, QIZHONG, Electronic Engineering
LIU, ZHIJING, Computer Science and Engineering
MA, JIANFENG, Computer Science and Engineering
MA, JINPING, Electronic Engineering
NIU, ZHONGQI, Electronic Engineering
QIU, YANG, Mechatronic Engineering
QIU, YUANYING, Mechatronic Engineering
REN, ZHICHUN, Economics and Management
SHI, GUANGMING, Electronic Engineering
SUN, XIAOZI, Electronic Engineering
WANG, ANMIN, Economics and Management
WANG, BAOSHU, Computer Science and Engineering
WANG, JIALI, Mechatronic Engineering
WANG, LI, Software Engineering
WEN, XIAONI, Economics and Management
WEN, YOUKUI, Economics and Management
WEN, ZHENGZHONG, Mechatronic Engineering
WU, SHUNJUN, Electronic Engineering
XIE, YONGJUN, Electronic Engineering
XING, MENGDAO, Electronic Engineering
XU, CHUNXIANG, Economics and Management
XU, GUOHUA, Economics and Management
XU, LUPING, Electronic Engineering
YANG, WANHAI, Electronic Engineering
ZENG, PING, Computer Science and Engineering
ZENG, XINGWEN, Telecommunications Engineering
ZHANG, FUSHUN, Electronic Engineering
ZHANG, HUI, Telecommunications Engineering
ZHANG, JUNYING, Computer Science and Engineering
ZHANG, PING, Mechatronic Engineering
ZHANG, SHIXUAN, Electronic Engineering
ZHANG, SHOUHONG, Electronic Engineering
ZHANG, YONGRUI, Mechatronic Engineering
ZHAO, GUOQING, Electronic Engineering
ZHAO, KE, Mechatronic Engineering
ZHAO, PENGWEI, Economics and Management
ZHAO, WEI, Economics and Management
ZHAO, WENPING, Economics and Management
ZHAO, YIGONG, Electronic Engineering
ZHI, BOQING, Mechatronic Engineering
ZHOU, WEI, Mechatronic Engineering

XINJIANG UNIVERSITY

14 Sheng Li Rd, Urumqi 830046, Xinjiang Uygur Autonomous Region
Telephone: (991) 8582221
Fax: (991) 8581249
E-mail: wsc@xju.edu.cn
Founded 1924; merged with Xinjiang Engineering Institute 2000
Academic year: September to July
Rector: ANIWER AMUT
Vice-Rector: AZHAT SULITAN
Vice-Rector: TASHPLAT TYIP
Vice-Rector: ZHANG XIAOFAN
Librarian: WANG KAIYUAN
Library of 1,330,000 vols
Number of teachers: 1,830
Number of students: 39,000 (incl. 784 postgraduate)
Publication: *Xinjiang University Journal* (natural sciences and social sciences versions)

Teaching units: College of Adult Education; College of Chemistry and Chemical Engineering; College of Construction Engineering; College of Electrical Engineering; College of Foreign Languages; College of Information Science and Engineering; College of Liberal Arts; College of Mechanical Engineering; College of Science and Technology; Department of Physics; Department of Textile Engineering; Institute of Life Sciences and Technology; Institute of Mathematics and Systematic Science; Institute of Resources and Environmental Science; Higher Vocational and Technical College; School of Economics and Management; School of Law

Research Institutes: Institute of Altaic Study; Institute of Applied Chemistry; Institute of Architectural Design; Institute of Arid Ecology; Institute of Central Asian Culture; Institute of Demography; Institute of Economics; Institute of Mathematical Theory.

YANBIAN UNIVERSITY

88 977 Gongyuan Rd, Yanji 133002, Jilin
Telephone: (433) 2713167
Fax: (433) 2719618
Internet: www.ybu.edu.cn
Founded 1949
Provincial control
Academic year: September to July
President: JIN BINMIN
Vice-Presidents: GAI TONGXIANG, LI SHUIJIN, PIAO YONGHAO, YU YONGHE
Head of Graduate Department: CUI XIONGHAN
Librarian: HAN ZHE
Library of 1,400,000 vols
Number of teachers: 1,345
Number of students: 16,447
Publications: *Chinese Studies*, *Collection of Papers on Korean Issues*, *Collection of Papers on Korean Nationality*, *Collection of Papers on North and South Korean Studies*, *Dongjiang* ('Eastern Border'), *Journal* (editions: agricultural, medical, sciences and engineering and social science), *Oriental Philosophy Research*

DEANS

College of Agriculture: ZHANG SHOUFA
College of Art: JIANG GUANGXUN
College of Chinese Language and Culture: (vacant)
College of Economics and Management: XUAN DONGRI
College of Foreign Languages: (vacant)
College of Medicine: CUI JIONGMO
College of Nursing: JIN DONGXU
College of Pharmacy: CUI JIONGMO
College of Physical Education: LIU QIXIAO
College of Science and Engineering: WU XUE
College of Science and Technology: WU XUE
Normal College: CUI CHENGRI
School of Law: CHEN ZHENMING

PROFESSORS

AN, GUOFENG, Chinese Language and Culture
BAI, HONGAI, Foreign Languages
CAI, MEIHUA, Normal College
CAO, XIULING, Chinese Language and Culture
CHEN, YANQIU, Agriculture
CUI, CHENGXUE, Normal College
CUI, RONGYI, Science and Technology
CUI, SHENGYUN, Science and Technology
CUI, TAIJI, Chinese Language and Culture
CUI, YONGCHUN, Art
FANG, HAOFAN, Normal College
FANG, MEISHAN, Art
FANG, NANZHU, Agriculture
FEI, HONGGEN, Normal College
FU, WEIJIE, Agriculture

GU, GUANGRUI, Science and Technology
GUO, ZHENPING, Science and Technology
HE, YUNPENG, Law
HUANG, ZHENJI, Chinese Language and Culture
JIANG, HAISHUN, Law
JIANG, JIJIAN, Agriculture
JIANG, LONGFAN, Normal College
JIANG, RISHAN, Science, Technology and Engineering
JIANG, YONGZHE, Physical Education
JIANG, YUN, Normal College
JIN, BINGHUO, Normal College
JIN, BINGMIN, Normal College
JIN, CHENGGAO, Normal College
JIN, CHUNZHI, Physical Education
JIN, DONGRI, Science and Technology
JIN, HAIGUO, Agriculture
JIN, HELU, Law
JIN, HEWAN, Pharmacy and Nursing
JIN, HEYAN, Normal College
JIN, HUALIN, Economics and Management
JIN, HUXIONG, Normal College
JIN, JIANGLONG, Agriculture
JIN, JISHI, Normal College
JIN, JUNCHENG, Art
JIN, KUANXIONG, Normal College
JIN, LONGZHE, Physical Education
JIN, QIANGYI, Normal College
JIN, XIANGHUA, Chinese Language and Culture
JIN, XINGGUANG, Agriculture
JIN, XINGSAN, Art
JIN, XUECHUN, Law
JIN, YINGXIONG, Physical Education
JIN, YONGCHUN, Law
JIN, YONGHAO, Science and Technology
JIN, YONGSHOU, Foreign Languages
JIN, YUANZHE, Medicine
JIN, ZHEHUA, Normal College
JIN, ZHEHUI, Foreign Languages
JIN, ZHENGYI, Normal College
JIN, ZHEZHU, Normal College
LI, AISHUN, Art
LI, BAOQI, Law
LI, CHUNYU, Pharmacy and Nursing
LI, GUANFU, Normal College
LI, MINDE, Foreign Languages
LI, MINZI, Art
LI, SHANJI, Science and Technology
LI, SHENGLONG, Art
LI, WUJI, Foreign Languages
LI, YUNJUN, Science and Technology
LI, ZONGXUN, Normal College
LIAN, ZHEMAN, Science and Technology
LIN, CHENGHU, Foreign Languages
LIN, JINSHU, Economics and Management
LIU, XIANHU, Agriculture
LU, CHENG, Agriculture
LU, LONGSHI, Agriculture
MA, JINKE, Normal College
MENG, FANPING, Medicine
NAN, CHENGYU, Foreign Languages
PAN, CHANGHE, Normal College
PIAO, CHENGXIAN, Economics and Management
PIAO, XIUHAO, Economics and Management
PU, SHIZHEN, Law
PU, TAIZHU, Normal College
PU, XIANGFAN, Science and Technology
PU, YUMING, Normal College
PU, ZHE, Medicine
PU, ZHENGYANG, Normal College
QU, BOHONG, Agriculture
QUAN, LONGHUA, Foreign Languages
QUAN, XUEXI, Normal College
QUAN, YU, Foreign Languages
QUAN, ZONGXUE, Science and Technology
SHAO, JINGBO, Science and Technology
SUN, DEBIAO, Normal College
SUN, DONGZHI, Medicine
SUN, SHU, Medicine
TIAN, GUANRONG, Science, Technology and Engineering
WANG, GUIFEN, Science and Technology

Wang, Keping, Chinese Language and Culture
Wang, Xiaobo, Normal College
Wei, Zhifang, Normal College
Wen, Zhaohai, Normal College
Wu, Minggen, Agriculture
Wu, Xue, Science, Technology and Engineering
Xiang, Kiaming, Art
Xu, Ji, Normal College
Xu, Mingzhe, Normal College
Xu, Wenyi, Medicine
Xu, Yuanxian, Law
Xuan, Dongri, Economics and Management
Yan, Changguo, Agriculture
Yin, Bingzhu, Science, Technology and Engineering
Yin, Taishun, Law
Yu, Chunhai, Normal College
Yu, Chunxi, Foreign Languages
Yu, Yancun, Normal College
Zhang, Jingzhong, Normal College
Zhang, Min, Agriculture
Zhang, Shou, Science and Technology
Zhang, Shoufa, Agriculture
Zhang, Zhenai, Foreign Languages
Zhao, Enhua, Physical Education
Zhao, Jingchun, Foreign Languages
Zhao, Lianhua, Science and Technology
Zheng, Dahao, Agriculture
Zheng, Rinan, Normal College
Zheng, Xianri, Foreign Languages
Zheng, Yongzhen, Normal College
Zhou, Zhiyuan, Normal College

YANGZHOU UNIVERSITY

88 Daxue Rd South, Yangzhou 225009, Jiangsu
Telephone: (514) 7971850
Fax: (514) 7352262
Internet: www.yzu.edu.cn
Founded 1902
Provincial control
Academic year: September to July
President: Guo Rong
Vice-Presidents: Fang Hongjin, Feng Chaonian, Hu Jiaxing, Liu Chao, Yang Jiadong, Zhou Xinguo
Head of Graduate Department: Yuan Jianli
Librarian: Zhang Zhenghui
Number of teachers: 2,000
Number of students: 46,000 (30,000 full-time, 16,000 part-time)
Publications: *Journal* (editions: higher education study, humanities and social sciences, 6 a year; agricultural and life sciences, natural sciences, 4 a year), *Journal of Taxation College of Yangzhou University* (4 a year)

DEANS
Guangling College: Liu Yanqing
School of Agriculture: Wang Yulong
School of Animal Science and Technology: Chen Guohong
School of Architectural Science and Engineering: Liu Ping
School of Arts: Zhang Meilin
School of Biological Sciences and Biotechnology: Jiao Xin'an
School of Chemistry and Chemical Engineering: Hu Xiaoya
School of Chinese Language and Literature: Yao Wenfang
School of Economics: Jiang Naihua
School of Educational Science and Technology: Chen Jialiln
School of Environmental Science and Engineering: Feng Ke
School of Foreign Languages: Yu Hongliang
School of Information Engineering: Chen Ling
School of Law: Jiao Fumin

School of Management: Chen Yao
School of Mathematical Sciences: Wang Hongyu
School of Mechanical Engineering: Zhou Yiping
School of Medicine: Tang Yao
School of Physical Education: Tong Zhaogang
School of Physical Science and Technology: Chen Xiaobing
School of Social Development: Zhou Jianchao
School of Tourism and Food Science: Lu Xinguo
School of Veterinary Science: Qin Aijian
School of Water Conservation and Hydraulic Engineering: Chen Jiankang

PROFESSORS
Ban, Jiqing, Chinese Language and Literature
Bao, Zhenqiang, Information Engineering
Bi, Qiao, Physical Science and Technology
Cai, Chuanren, Mathematical Science
Cao, Jinhua, Social Development
Chang, Hong, Animal Science and Technology
Chen, Guohong, Animal Science and Technology
Chen, Jialiln, Educational Science and Technology
Chen, Jiankang, Water Conservancy and Hydraulic Engineering
Chen, Jianmin, Biological Sciences and Biotechnology
Chen, Ling, Information Engineering
Chen, Rongfa, Mechanical Engineering
Chen, Xiaobing, Physical Science and Technology
Chen, Xiaoming, Management
Chen, Yao, Management
Cheng, Jilin, Water Conservancy and Hydraulic Engineering
Cheng, Yong, Veterinary Science
Chou, Baoyun, Water Conservancy and Hydraulic Engineering
Chou, Zhigang, Physical Education
Chu, Xun, Water Conservancy and Hydraulic Engineering
Dai, Xhiyi, Agriculture
Diao, Shuren, Social Development
Ding, Jiatong, Animal Science and Technology
Ding, Li, Medicine
Dong, Guoyan, Chinese Language and Literature
Er, Rongben, Chinese Language and Literature
Fan, Ming, Management
Fang, Hongyuan, Water Conservancy and Hydraulic Engineering
Fang, Wenli, Foreign Languages
Fei, Xun, Social Development
Feng, Ke, Environmental Science and Engineering
Feng, Yongshan, Medicine
Gao, Huiming, Medicine
Gao, Song, Veterinary Science
Ge, Xiaoqun, Medicine
Gu, Feng, Chinese Language and Literature
Gu, Nong, Chinese Language and Literature
Gu, Ruixia, Tourism and Food Science
Gu, Shiliang, Agriculture
Guo, Xia, Chemistry and Chemical Engineering
He, Daren, Physical Science and Technology
Hu, Jingguo, Physical Science and Technology
Hu, Rong, Medicine
Hu, Xiaoya, Chemistry and Chemical Engineering
Hu, Xuenong, Information Engineering
Hu, Xueqin, Economics
Hua, Changyou, Social Development
Huang, Cheng, Economics
Huang, Qian, Medicine

Huang, Qiang, Chinese Language and Literature
Huang, Shucheng, Economics
Huang, Shucheng, Tourism and Food Science
Huo, Wanli, Arts
Ji, Mingchun, Medicine
Ji, Suyue, Mathematical Science
Jiang, Naihua, Economics
Jiao, Fumin, Law
Jiao, Wenfeng, Social Development
Jiao, Xin'an, Biological Sciences and Biotechnology
Jin, Yingen, Biological Sciences and Biotechnology
Jin, Yu, Physical Education
Li, Bichun, Animal Science and Technology
Li, Changji, Chinese Language and Literature
Li, Cunhua, Information Engineering
Li, Guoli, Medicine
Li, Houda, Veterinary Science
Li, Jianji, Veterinary Science
Li, Jinyu, Animal Science and Technology
Li, Shihao, Agriculture
Liang, Jiansheng, Biological Sciences and Biotechnology
Lin, Zhigui, Mathematical Science
Liu, Chao, Water Conservancy and Hydraulic Engineering
Liu, Cheng, Social Development
Liu, Gang, Management
Liu, Hong, Chinese Language and Literature
Liu, Moxiang, Medicine
Liu, Ping, Architectural Science and Engineering
Liu, Xiufan, Veterinary Science
Liu, Yan, Architectural Science and Engineering
Liu, Yanqing, Medicine
Liu, Yongjun, Physical Science and Technology
Liu, Zhuhan, Mathematical Science
Liu, Zongping, Veterinary Science
Lu, Jianfei, Agriculture
Lu, Linguang, Water Conservancy and Hydraulic Engineering
Lu, Xinguo, Tourism and Food Science
Mao, Yuyang, Tourism and Food Science
Mo, Yueping, Information Engineering
Pan, Xhaowei, Physical Education
Piao, Ping, Medicine
Qiang, Jianya, Tourism and Food Science
Qiang, Jing, Medicine
Qiang, Zhonghao, Economics
Qin, Aijian, Veterinary Science
Qin, Xingfang, Economics
Shao, Yaochun, Physical Science and Technology
Shen, Jie, Information Engineering
Shi, Mingyi, Medicine
Shi, Yongfan, Physical Education
Su, Peiqing, Medicine
Sun, Guorong, Biological Sciences and Biotechnology
Sun, Huaichang, Veterinary Science
Tian, Hanyun, Chinese Language and Literature
Tong, Zhaogang, Physical Education
Wang, Bao'an, Veterinary Science
Wang, Handong, Veterinary Science
Wang, Hongrong, Animal Science and Technology
Wang, Hongyu, Mathematical Science
Wang, Jianjun, Medicine
Wang, Jun, Chinese Language and Literature
Wang, Linsuo, Water Conservancy and Hydraulic Engineering
Wang, Longtai, Mechanical Engineering
Wang, Qingren, Social Development
Wang, Xingchi, Management
Wang, Xinglong, Animal Science and Technology
Wang, Yeming, Architectural Science and Engineering

WANG, YONGPING, Chinese Language and Literature
WANG, YONGPING, Social Development
WANG, YOUPING, Biological Sciences and Biotechnology
WANG, YULONG, Agriculture
WANG, ZHAOLONG, Biological Sciences and Biotechnology
WANG, ZONGYUAN, Veterinary Science
WEI, JUN, Physical Education
WEI, SHANHAO, Chinese Language and Literature
WEI, WANHONG, Biological Sciences and Biotechnology
WU, JIAN, Management
WU, SHANZHONG, Social Development
WU, YANTAO, Veterinary Science
WU, ZHOUWEN, Chinese Language and Literature
XIAO, SHUFENG, Chinese Language and Literature
XIONG, DEPING, Economics
XU, DEMING, Chinese Language and Literature
XU, JIANZHONG, Chinese Language and Literature
XU, LICHUN, Medicine
XU, MINGLIANG, Biological Sciences and Biotechnology
XU, WEIPING, Social Development
XU, YIMIN, Veterinary Science
YAN, JUN, Physical Education
YANG, BENHONG, Social Development
YANG, JIADONG, Economics
YANG, QIANPU, Social Development
YANG, SHUHE, Mechanical Engineering
YAO, WENFANG, Chinese Language and Literature
YIN, SHIXUE, Environmental Science and Engineering
YIN, XINCHUN, Information Engineering
YU, HAIPENG, Economics
YUAN, JIANLI, Architectural Science and Engineering
YUAN, XINMING, Water Conservancy and Hydraulic Engineering
ZENG, LI, Mechanical Engineering
ZHANG, HONGCHENG, Agriculture
ZHANG, HONGLIANG, Chinese Language and Literature
ZHANG, HONGQUAN, Medicine
ZHANG, JUN, Physical Education
ZHANG, MIANG, Chemistry and Chemical Engineering
ZHANG, MINLI, Architectural Science and Engineering
ZHANG, PEIJIAN, Medicine
ZHANG, QIJUN, Chinese Language and Literature
ZHANG, QING, Law
ZHANG, RUIHONG, Mechanical Engineering
ZHANG, TIANPING, Information Engineering
ZHANG, ZHENGANG, Medicine
ZHAO, GUOQI, Animal Science and Technology
ZHAO, ZONGFANG, Agriculture
ZHOU, JIANCHAO, Social Development
ZHOU, MINGYAO, Water Conservancy and Hydraulic Engineering
ZHOU, XIAOXIA, Medicine
ZHOU, XINTIAN, Social Development
ZHOU, YIPING, Mechanical Engineering
ZHOU, YIPING, Social Development
ZHU, XIASHI, Chemistry and Chemical Engineering
ZHU, YONGZE, Medicine
ZHUANG, LIN, Social Development

YANSHAN UNIVERSITY

438 Hebei Ave, Qinhuangdao 066004, Hebei
Telephone: (335) 8057100
Fax: (335) 8051148
E-mail: headmaster@ysu.edu.cn
Internet: www.ysu.edu.cn
Founded 1960

Provincial control
Academic year: September to July
President: LIU HONGMIN
Vice-Presidents: KONG XIANGDONG, LI QIANG, LIU BIN, WANG YONGCHANG, XING GUANGZHONG, YANG YULIN
Head of Graduate Department: ZHAO YONGSHENG
Librarian: ZHANG FUCHENG
Library of 600,000 vols
Number of teachers: 1,321
Number of students: 28,000
Publication: *Journal* (editions: natural science, philosophy and social sciences, 4 a year)

DEANS
College of Civil Engineering and Mechanics: (vacant)
College of Economic Administration: YUAN YE
College of Electrical Engineering: GUAN XINPING
College of Environmental and Chemical Engineering: BAI MINGHUA
College of Fine Art: ZHANG JIAXIN
College of Foreign Languages: (vacant)
College of Humanities and Law: WU YONG
College of Information Science and Engineering: KONG LINGFU
College of Material Science and Engineering: TIAN YONGJUN
College of Mechanical Engineering: ZHANG QING
College of Science: JIN XILI

PROFESSORS
AN, ZIJUN, Mechanical Engineering
BAI, MINGHUA, Environmental and Chemical Engineering
BI, WEIHONG, Information Science and Engineering
CHANG, DANHUA, Information Science and Engineering
CUI, YUNQI, Mechanical Engineering
DONG, HONGXUE, Foreign Languages
DONG, SHIMIN, Mechanical Engineering
DU, FENGSHAN, Mechanical Engineering
FANG, BAOGUO, Humanities and Law
GAO, DIANKUI, Mechanical Engineering
GAO, DIANRONG, Mechanical Engineering
GAO, FENG, Mechanical Engineering
GAO, SHIYOU, Mechanical Engineering
GAO, YINGJIE, Mechanical Engineering
GONG, JING'AN, Mechanical Engineering
GUO, BAOFENG, Mechanical Engineering
GUO, JINGFENG, Information Science and Engineering
GUO, XIJUAN, Information Science and Engineering
HAN, DECAI, Mechanical Engineering
HAN, PEIFU, Information Science and Engineering
HAN, XIAOJUAN, Mechanical Engineering
HOU, LANTIAN, Information Science and Engineering
HU, GUODONG, Mechanical Engineering
HU, ZHANQI, Mechanical Engineering
HUANG, ZHEN, Mechanical Engineering
HUI, JIXING, Humanities and Law
JIANG, SHIPING, Mechanical Engineering
JIANG, WANLU, Mechanical Engineering
JIN, ZHENLIN, Mechanical Engineering
JING, TIANFU, Material Science and Engineering
KONG, LINGFU, Information Science and Engineering
KONG, XIANGDONG, Mechanical Engineering
LI, BAODONG, Humanities and Law
LI, FULIANG, Humanities and Law
LI, JINLIANG, Mechanical Engineering
LI, JIUTONG, Mechanical Engineering
LI, KUIYING, Material Science and Engineering
LI, QIANG, Mechanical Engineering

LI, WEIMIN, Mechanical Engineering
LI, XIANKUI, Mechanical Engineering
LI, YUPENG, Mechanical Engineering
LIAN, JIACHUANG, Mechanical Engineering
LIU, GUOHUA, Information Science and Engineering
LIU, HONGMIN, Mechanical Engineering
LIU, RIPING, Material Science and Engineering
LIU, XIPING, Mechanical Engineering
LIU, YONGSHAN, Information Science and Engineering
LIU, ZEQUAN, Foreign Languages
LIU, ZHUBO, Mechanical Engineering
LU, XIUCHUN, Mechanical Engineering
LU, YI, Mechanical Engineering
NIE, SHAOMIN, Mechanical Engineering
PAN, MINGHAN, Information Science and Engineering
PENG, YAN, Mechanical Engineering
QIAO, CHANGSUO, Mechanical Engineering
QIN, SIJI, Mechanical Engineering
REN, YUNLAI, Mechanical Engineering
SHEN, GUANGXIAN, Mechanical Engineering
SHEN, LIMIN, Information Science and Engineering
SHEN, XIAOMEI, Humanities and Law
SHENG, YIPING, Environmental and Chemical Engineering
SHI, RONG, Mechanical Engineering
SONG, GUOSEN, Information Science and Engineering
SUN, HUIXUE, Mechanical Engineering
SUN, XUGUANG, Mechanical Engineering
TANG, JINGLIN, Mechanical Engineering
WANG, CHENGRU, Information Science and Engineering
WANG, FUSHENG, Foreign Languages
WANG, HAIRU, Mechanical Engineering
WANG, JUN, Mechanical Engineering
WANG, QINGXUE, Humanities and Law
WANG, XINSHENG, Information Science and Engineering
WANG, YIQUN, Mechanical Engineering
WANG, YONGCHANG, Mechanical Engineering
WEI, LIBO, Humanities and Law
WEN, DESHENG, Mechanical Engineering
WU, XIAOMING, Mechanical Engineering
WU, YONG, Humanities and Law
WU, YUEMING, Mechanical Engineering
XIAO, HONG, Mechanical Engineering
XU, CHENGQIAN, Information Science and Engineering
XU, HONGXIANG, Mechanical Engineering
XU, LIZHONG, Mechanical Engineering
XU, RUI, Material Science and Engineering
YANG, YULIN, Mechanical Engineering
YE, DEQIAN, Information Science and Engineering
YU, DESHENG, Information Science and Engineering
YU, DONGLI, Material Science and Engineering
YU, ENLIN, Mechanical Engineering
YU, JIANPING, Foreign Languages
YU, RONGJIN, Information Science and Engineering
YU, YUFENG, Information Science and Engineering
ZHANG, HAI, Mechanical Engineering
ZHANG, LIYING, Mechanical Engineering
ZHANG, QING, Mechanical Engineering
ZHANG, QISHENG, Mechanical Engineering
ZHANG, TAO, Mechanical Engineering
ZHANG, TONGYI, Mechanical Engineering
ZHANG, WEIDONG, Foreign Languages
ZHANG, WENZHI, Mechanical Engineering
ZHANG, ZHONGYI, Humanities and Law
ZHAO, JINGYI, Mechanical Engineering
ZHAO, JUN, Mechanical Engineering
ZHAO, TIESHI, Mechanical Engineering
ZHAO, YONGHE, Mechanical Engineering
ZHAO, YONGSHENG, Mechanical Engineering
ZHENG, SHENGXUAN, Information Science and Engineering
ZHOU, CHAO, Mechanical Engineering

ZHOU, QINGTIAN, Mechanical Engineering
ZHU, GUANGRONG, Humanities and Law
ZOU, MUCHANG, Information Science and
Engineering

YANTAI UNIVERSITY

Yantai 264005, Shandong
Telephone: (535) 6888995
Fax: (535) 6888801
Internet: www.ytu.edu.cn
Founded 1984
State control
Languages of instruction: Chinese, English
Pres.: ZHANG JIANYI
Registrar: LU XUEMING
Librarian: SUN JILIANG
Library of 40,000 vols
Number of teachers: 450
Number of students: 3,839

Publication: *Journal*

Degree programmes in applied mathematics,
applied physics, architecture, biochemical
engineering, chemical engineering, Chinese
language and literature, electronics and
computing, finance and economics and management, fisheries industry, foreign languages and literature, industrial and civil
engineering, international business, law,
machine design and manufacture, physical
education.

YUNNAN FINANCE AND TRADE INSTITUTE

Shangmacun, North Suburb, Kunming
650221, Yunnan
Telephone: (871) 5122394
Fax: (871) 5163384
Founded 1981
President: Prof. WU JIANAN
Presidents: Assoc. Prof. MA GUANGBI, WU
TANXUE, YANG LIZHI
Registrar: ZHOU ANFAN
Librarian: LIU SHUNDE
Library of 280,000 vols
Number of teachers: 289
Number of students: 2,620

Publications: *Foreign Economic Theory and
Administration, Journal.*

YUNNAN INSTITUTE FOR THE NATIONALITIES

420 Huanchengbei Rd, Kunming 650031,
Yunnan
Telephone: (871) 5154308
Fax: (871) 5154304
Internet: www.ynni.edu.cn
Founded 1951
State control

Languages of instruction: Chinese, English,
Thai, Burmese and some minority languages
Academic year: September to July
Pres.: ZHAO JIAWEN
Vice-Presidents: HUANG HUIKUN, PU TONGJIN,
ZHAO JUNSHAN
Chief Admin. Officer: DI HUAYI
Librarian: DUAN SHENG'OU
Library of 430,000 vols, 28 special collns
Number of teachers: 385
Number of students: 4,969

Publication: *Journal* (social sciences edn and
science edn, 4 a year).

YUNNAN UNIVERSITY

2 North Cuihu Rd, Kunming 650091, Yun-
nan
Telephone: (871) 5148533
Fax: (871) 5153832
Internet: www.ynu.edu.cn

Founded 1923
State control
Academic year: September to July
President: Prof. WU SONG
Vice-Presidents: Prof. WANG RONG, Prof.
HONG PINJIE, Prof. LIN CHAOMIN, Prof. NI
HUIFANG, Prof. ZHANG KEQIN, Prof. CHEN
SHIBO
Registrar: Prof. YANG JIAHE
Librarian: Prof. WANG WENGGUAN
Library of 1,170,000 vols
Number of teachers: 888
Number of students: 7,160

Publication: *The Ideological Front* (6 a year)

PROFESSORS

Dianchi School (tel. (871) 5172513):
    WU JIANGUO, Chemistry

School of Adult Education (tel. (871)
5147702):
    DU CHAO, Analytical Chemistry
    SHI PENGFEI, Ancient Chinese Literature
    WANG JIALIN, Analytical Chemistry
    WANG SHIDONG, Fluxional Dynamic Sys-
    tems

School of Computer Science (tel. (871)
5031597):
    LI TAILING, Electronic Circuits and Com-
    munication
    LI TIANMU, Electronics and Information
    Systems
    LIU WEIYI, Fuzzy Database Theory
    TIAN ZHILIANG, Management Operating
    Systems
    ZHENG WENXING, Correspondence

School of Development Research (tel. (871)
5031453):
    CHEN LIN, Systems Engineering
    LIAO HONGZHI, Systems Engineering
    MAO YUGONG, Management Science
    XIAO XIAN, History of International Rela-
    tions
    YANG MANSU, History of International
    Relations
    YANG SHOUCHUANG, Ethnic History

School of Economics (tel. (871) 5033613):
    CHEN JIANBO, Economic Statistics
    GUO SHUHUA, Finance
    HONG HUAXI, Economics
    HU QIHUI, Economics
    JIN RONG, Economics
    LI DEPU, Economics
    LU ZHAOHE, Demology
    MA JUN, Accountancy
    PAN JIANXING, Mathematical Statistics
    SHI BENZHI, Investment
    SHI LEI, Economic Statistics
    SUN WENSHUANG, Mathematical Statistics
    WANG XUEREN, Economics
    XU GUANGYUAN, Economics
    YENG XIANMING, Finance
    ZHANG JIANHUA, Foreign Trade
    ZHANG JIN, Economic Statistics
    ZHU YINGGENG, Ideological History of West-
    ern Economics

School of Foreign Languages (tel. (871)
5033629):
    GONG NINGZHU, Lao, Vietnamese
    LI JIGANG, English
    XU FENG
    ZHANG XINHE, English

School of Humanities (tel. (871) 5033607):
    JIN DANYUAN, Aesthetics
    LI CONGZONG, Modern Literature
    LI JIABIN, Ancient World History
    LI YAN, History of the Chinese Feudal
    Economy
    LIN CHAOMIN, Ethnic History
    QIAO CHUANZAO, Writing
    SUN QINHUA, Literary Language
    TANG MIN, Modern World History

WANG KAILIAN, Classical Chinese Lan-
    guage
    XU KANGMING, Modern World History
    YANG ZHENKUN, Modern Literature
    YOU ZHONG, History of Chinese Minorities
    ZHANG FUSAN, Ethnic and Folk Literature
    ZHANG GUOQING, Classical Chinese Writ-
    ings
    ZHANG XINCHANG, History and Archives of
    Chinese Minorities
    ZHU HUIRONG, Historical Geography

School of Law (tel. (871) 5184816):
    CHEN ZIGUO, Civil Law
    XU ZHISHAN, Constitution

School of Life Sciences and Chemistry (tel.
(871) 5031412):
    DAI SHUSHAN, Physics and Chemistry
    HE SENQUAN, Organic Chemistry
    HONG PINJIE, Microwave Plasma
    HU ZHIHAO, Botany
    HUANG SUHUA, Botany
    LI LIANG, Organic Chemistry
    LI QIREN, Plant Cell Engineering
    LIU FUCHU, Organic Chemistry
    LIU SONGYU, Analytical Chemistry
    LIU XINHUA, Soil Ecology
    TAO YUANQI, Quantum Organic Chemistry
    WANG CHANGYI, Organic Chemistry
    XU QIHENG, Analytical Chemistry
    YANG CHUNJIN, Inorganic Chemistry
    YANG PIPENG, Organic Chemistry
    YIN JIANGUO, Inorganic Chemistry
    ZAN RUIGUANG, Cell Biology
    ZHENG ZHUO, Microbiology
    ZUO YANGXIAN, Invertebrates

School of Public Administration (tel. (871)
5033609):
    CHEN GUOXING, Socialism
    CUI YUNWU, Public Administration
    GAO LI, Ethics
    HOU YIHONG, Management Psychology
    JIANG ZIHUA, Politics
    JIN ZIQIANG, Current Chinese Politics
    KUANG ZHIMING, Politics
    LI BIN, Philosophy
    LIU JIAZHI, Philosophy
    LIU YUNHANG, Aesthetics
    WANG YANBING, Sociology
    XIONG SIYUAN, Economics
    YANG JIQIONG, Current Chinese Politics
    ZENG JIAN, Dialectics
    ZHOU PING, Politics

School of Tourism and Business Administration (tel. (871) 5034561):
    GUANG NINGSHEN, Tourism Administration
    LI HAO, Tourism Administration
    LIU XUEYU, Business Management
    TIAN WEIMING, Tourism Administration
    WANG JIANPIN, Econometrics
    XUE QUNHUI, Tourism Administration
    YANG GUIHUA, Tourism Administration
    ZHANG MINGAN, Business Management
    ZHANG XIAOPIN, English

School of Sciences (tel. (871) 5032012):
    CAO KEFEI, Physics
    CHEN ZHONGZHANG, Physics
    CONG LIANLI, Earth Sciences
    GUO SHICANG, Earth Sciences
    GUO XIAOJIANG, Mathematics
    GUO YUQI, Mathematics
    HE DAMING, Earth Sciences
    HE XIANGPANG, Mathematics
    HU JIAFU, Earth Sciences
    HU WENGUO, Physics
    JU JIANHUA, Earth Sciences
    LI JIANPIN, Mathematics
    LI YAOTANG, Mathematics
    LI YONGKUN, Mathematics
    LIN LIZHONG, Physics
    LIU ZHENGRONG, Mathematics
    LUO YAOHUANG, Physics
    MEI DONGCHENG, Physics
    PENG KUANGDING, Physics

PENG SHOULI, Physics
TANG XINGHUA, Mathematics
TIEN XINSHI, Physics
WANG WEIGUO, Earth Sciences
WEN XIAOMIN, Physics
WU XINGHUI, Material Sciences
XIE YINGQI, Atmospheric Science, Mathematics
YAN GUANGXIONG, Mathematics
YAN HUASHENG, Earth Sciences
YANG DEQING, Physics
YANG HUAKANG, Mathematics
YANG XUESHENG, Earth Sciences
YANG YU, Material Sciences
ZHANG LI, Physics
ZHANG ZHONGMIN, Physics
ZHAO XIAOHUA, Mathematics
ZHENG BAOZHONG, Material Sciences
ZHENG XIYIN, Mathematics
ZHOU QING, Physics

ZHEJIANG UNIVERSITY

38 Zheda Rd, Hangzhou 310027, Zhejiang

Telephone: (571) 87951846
Fax: (571) 87951358
E-mail: zupo@zju.edu.cn
Internet: www.zju.edu.cn

Founded 1897; merged with Hangzhou University, Zhejiang Agricultural University and Zhejiang Medical University 1998
State control
Languages of instruction: Chinese, English(-for foreign students)
Academic year: September to June

Pres.: Prof. PAN YUNHE
Exec. Vice-Pres.: Prof. NI MINGJIANG
Vice-Pres.: Prof. BU FANXIAO
Vice-Pres.: Prof. CHU, JIAN
Vice-Pres.: Prof. HU JIANMIAO
Vice-Pres.: Prof. LAI MAODE
Vice-Pres.: Prof. SI, JIANMIN
Vice-Pres.: Prof. ZHU, JUN
Dir of Int. Programmes Office: Prof. QIU JIZHEN
Librarian: ZHU HAIKANG

Number of teachers: 3,285
Number of students: 90,475 (43,222 full-time, 30,571 part-time, 16,682 distance learning)

Publications: *Applied Mathematics of Chinese Universities* (in Chinese and English), *Applied Psychology* (in Chinese), *China Higher Medical Education* (in Chinese), *Engineering Design* (in Chinese), *Journal of Zhejiang University (Agricultural and Life Sciences)* (in Chinese), *Journal of Zhejiang University (Humanities and Social Science)* (in Chinese), *Journal of Zhejiang University (Medicine)* (in Chinese), *Journal of Zhejiang University (Natural Science)* (in Chinese), *Journal of Zhejiang University (Sciences)* (in Chinese and English), *Materials Science and Engineering* (in Chinese), *Management Engineering* (in Chinese), *Population and Eugenics* (in Chinese), *Practical Oncology* (in Chinese), *Spatial Structures* (in Chinese)

Chu Kechen College, Distance Learning School, Graduate School, School of Adult Education, International College, School of Advanced Studies, School of Agriculture and Biotechnology (depts of agronomy, applied biosciences, horticulture, plant protection, tea science), School of Animal Sciences (depts of Animal science, special animal science, veterinary medicine), School of Biomedical Engineering and Instrument Science (depts of biomedical engineering, instrumentation science and engineering), School of Biosystems Engineering and Food Science (depts of biosystems engineering, food and nutrition science), School of Civil Engineering and Architecture (depts of architecture, civil engineering, regional and urban planning, water conservation and ocean engineering), School of Computer Science (also known as School of Software technology—depts of computer science and engineering, digital media and network technology, industrial design), School of Economics (depts of economics, finance and banking, international economics and trade, public administration and public finance), School of Education (depts of education, physical education), School of Electrical Engineering (applied electronics, electrical engineering, systems science and engineering), School of Environmental and Resource Sciences (depts of environmental science, environmental engineering, land management, natural resource science), School of Humanities (depts of arts, philosophy, Chinese language and literature, information resources and management, journalism and communication studies, international cultural studies, history, sociology), School of Information Science and Engineering (depts of control science and engineering, optical engineering, information and electronic engineering), School of International Studies (depts of english language and literature, eastern and western languages and literatures, linguistics), School of Law (depts of law, political science and public administration, ideological and political education), School of Life Sciences (depts of biological sciences, biotechnology), School of Management (depts of management science and engineering, business administration, tourism, administration, agricultural economics and management), School of Materials Science and Chemical Engineering (depts of chemical and biochemical engineering, materials science and engineering, polymer science and engineering), School of Mechanical and Energy engineering (depts of mechanical engineering, energy engineering, mechanics), School of Medicine (depts of stomatology, basic medical sciences, public health and preventive medicine, nursing and 1st, 2nd and 3rd depts of clinical medicine), School of Medicine (depts of basic medical sciences, 1st, 2nd and 3rd depts of clinical medicine, nursing, public health and preventive medicine, stomatology), School of Pharmaceutical Sciences (dept of chinese traditional pharmacy, pharmacy), School of Sciences (depts of mathematics, physics, chemistry, earth sciences, psychology and behavioural sciences), School of Vocational Technical Education.

ZHEJIANG UNIVERSITY OF TECHNOLOGY

District 6, Zhaohui Xincun, Hangzhou 310032, Zhejiang

Telephone: (571) 88320114
Fax: (571) 88320272
E-mail: webmaster@zjut.edu.cn
Internet: www.zjut.edu.cn

Founded 1953
Academic year: September to July

Pres.: Prof. SHEN YINCHU
Vice-Pres: Prof. MA CHUN'AN
Vice-Pres: Prof. XIAO RUIFENG
Vice-Pres: Prof. XUAN YONG
Vice-Pres: Prof. ZHANG LIBIN
Librarian: Prof. HE LIMIN

Library of 1,002,000 vols
Number of teachers: 2,600
Number of students: 18,000

Publication: *Journal* (separate editions for natural sciences and social sciences, each 6 a year)

DEANS

College of Architecture and Civil Engineering: Prof. ZHENG JIANJUN
College of Arts and Humanities: Prof. SUN LIPING
College of Biological and Environmental Engineering: Prof. CHEN JIANMENG
College of Business Administration: Prof. CHENG HUIFANG
College of Chemical Engineering: Prof. JI JIANBING
College of Electrical and Mechanical Engineering: Prof. CHAI GUOZHONG
College of Foreign Languages: Prof. LIAO FEI
College of Information Engineering: Prof. CAI JIAMEI
College of Law: Prof. ZHANG XU
College of Pharmaceutical Sciences: Prof. QIAN JUNQING
College of Sciences: Prof. CHENG CHENG
College of Vocational and Technical Education: Prof. DU SHIGUI

ZHENGZHOU UNIVERSITY

100 Kexue St, Zhengzhou 450001, Henan

Telephone: (371) 7763036
Fax: (371) 7763036
E-mail: headmaster@zzu.edu.cn
Internet: www.zzu.edu.cn

Founded 1956
Provincial control
Academic year: September to July

President: SHEN CHANGYU
Vice-Presidents: GAO DANYING, JIAO LIUCHENG, SONG MAOPING, XU ZHENLU, ZHENG YULING
Head of Graduate Department: ZHU CHENGSHEN
Librarian: ZHANG LEISHUN

Library of 3,900,000 vols
Number of teachers: 2,200
Number of students: 44,000

Publication: *Journal* (editions: science, natural sciences, 4 a year; philosophy and social science, medical science, 6 a year)

DEANS

College of Nursing: (vacant)
College of Public Health: HU DONGSHENG
College of Chemical Engineering: WEI XINLI
Department of Bioengineering: KANG QIAOZHEN
Department of Chemistry: LIU HONGMIN
Department of History and Archaeology: JIANG JIANSHE
Department of Management Engineering: (vacant)
Department of Mathematics: CHEN SHAOCHUN
Department of Music: GONG WEI
School of Applied Technology: LI SHUXIN
School of Basic Medical Science: DONG ZIMING
School of Civil Engineering: LIU LIXIN
School of Economics: DU SHUYUN
School of Education: WANG ZONGMIN
School of Electrical Engineering: CHEN TIEJUN
School of Environment and Water Conservancy: WANG FUMING
School of Foreign Languages: SHEN NANA
School of Information Management: KE PING
School of Journalism and Communication: DONG GUANGAN
School of Law: TIAN TUCHENG
School of Liberal Arts: ZHANG HONGSHENG
School of Materials Science and Engineering: GUAN SHAOKANG
School of Mechanical Engineering: ZHANG LUOMING
School of Physical Education: WU LANYING
School of Pharmacy: RAO YAOGANG
School of Physical Science and Technology: LI YUXIAO

School of Public Administration: (vacant)
School of Tourism Management: MAO ANFU
Institute of Physical Science and Technology: WANG ZHONGYONG

PROFESSORS

AN, GUOLOU, History and Archaeology
AN, YUHUI, Basic Medical Science
CAO, SHAOKUI, Materials Science and Engineering
CEN, SHAOCHENG, Mechanical Engineering
CHAN, JIE, Basic Medical Science
CHEN, HUAI, Civil Engineering
CHEN, JINGBO, Materials Science and Engineering
CHEN, JINZHOU, Materials Science and Engineering
CHEN, TAN, Public Health
CHEN, TIEJUN, Electrical Engineering
CHEN, YILANG, Chemical Engineering
CHENG, BAOSHAN, Law
CUI, JING, Basic Medical Science
CUI, JINGBIN, Basic Medical Science
CUI, LIUXIN, Public Health
CUI, XIULING, Chemistry
DONG, GUANGAN, Journalism and Culture
DONG, MINGMIN, Bioengineering
DONG, QIWU, Chemical Engineering
DONG, ZIMING, Basic Medical Science
DU, CHENXIA, Chemistry
DU, SHUYUN, Economic School
DU, XIANTANG, Bioengineering
DUAN, GUANGCAI, Public Health
FAN, MING, Information Engineering
FAN, XIQING, Physical Science and Technology
FAN, YAOTING, Chemistry
FANG, WENJI, Chemical Engineering
FENG, DONGQING, Electrical Engineering
FENG, LIYUN, Public Health
FU, CHUNJING, Basic Medical Science
FU, RUNFANG, Basic Medical Science
GAO, JIANHUA, Chemistry
GAO, JINFENG, Electrical Engineering
GAO, XIAOQUN, Basic Medical Science
GAO, ZHENGYAO, Physical Science and Technology
GONG, JUNFANG, Chemistry
GUAN, HUILING, Mechanical Engineering
GUAN, SHAOKANG, Materials Science and Engineering
GUAN, XINXIN, Chemistry
GUO, SHILING, Chemical Engineering
GUO, XIANJI, Chemistry
GUO, YANCHUN, Chemistry
GUO, YINGJIAN, Foreign Languages
GUO, YIQUN, Chemistry
GUO, YUANCHENG, Civil Engineering
HAN, GUOHE, History and Archaeology
HAN, JIE, Mechanical Engineering
HAN, QIAO, Chemistry
HAN, WEICHENG, Chemistry
HE, ZHANHANG, Chemistry
HOU, HONGWEI, Chemistry
HOU, ZONGYUAN, Law
HU, DONGSHENG, Public Health
HU, JIANLI, Chemistry
HUA, SHAOJIE, Mechanical Engineering
HUO, YUPING, Physical Science and Technology
JIA, HANDONG, Chemistry
JIA, XIAOLIN, Materials Science and Engineering
JIANG, DENGGAO, Chemical Engineering
JIANG, JIANCHU, Law
JIANG, JIANSHE, History and Archaeology
JIANG, MAYUN, Education
JIANG, YUANLI, Chemical Engineering
KE, PING, Information Management
LI, DAWANG, Civil Engineering
LI, GANG, Chemistry
LI, HAIMEI, Materials Science and Engineering
LI, JIANJUN, Chemistry
LI, JIANKE, Bioengineering
LI, LIMIN, Chemistry

LI, TIAN, Civil Engineering
LI, WENJIE, Public Health
LI, XIAOWEN, Basic Medical Science
LI, XINFA, Materials Science and Engineering
LI, YINGDAN, Public Health
LI, YUEBAI, Basic Medical Science
LI, YUXIAO, Physical Science and Technology
LI, ZHIMIN, Public Health
LI, ZHONGJUN, Chemistry
LIANG, ERJUN, Physical Science and Technology
LIANG, FENGRONG, Law
LIAO, XINCHENG, Chemistry
LIN, LIN, Chemistry
LIU, DAZHUANG, Chemical Engineering
LIU, DEFA, Law
LIU, GUOJI, Chemical Engineering
LIU, HONGMIN, Chemistry
LIU, HONGXIA, Chemistry
LIU, HUALIAN, Public Health
LIU, JINDUN, Chemical Engineering
LIU, JINXIA, Chemistry
LIU, LIXIN, Civil Engineering
LIU, MINYING, Materials Science and Engineering
LIU, PU, Chemistry
LIU, SHOUCHANG, Chemistry
LIU, XIANGWEN, Law
LIU, XIANLIN, Electrical Engineering
LIU, XINTIAN, Materials Science and Engineering
LIU, YUNBO, Foreign Languages
LU, MEIYI, History and Archaeology
LU, SONGYUE, Law
LU, TAIFENG, Law
LU, WENGE, Public Health
LU, XINGUANG, Materials Science and Engineering
LU, ZUHUI, Physical Science and Technology
LUO, DAPENG, Public Health
MA, SHENGGANG, Mechanical Engineering
MA, XIAOJIAN, Chemical Engineering
MAO, LUYUAN, Materials Science and Engineering
MIAO, HUIQING, Economic School
MIAO, LIANYING, Law
NING, JINCHENG, Law
NING, ZHENHUAN, Physical Science and Technology
NIU, YUNYIN, Chemistry
PEI, BINGNAN, Information Engineering
PEI, YINGXIN, Public Health
QI, YUANMING, Bioengineering
QIAO, HAILING, Basic Medical Science
QIN, GUANGYONG, Physical Science and Technology
QU, CHUANZHI, Basic Medical Science
QU, LINGBO, Chemistry
RAO, YAOGANG, Pharmacy
REN, BAOZENG, Chemical Engineering
REN, CUIPING, Chemistry
SHEN, GUIMING, Law
SHEN, KAIJU, Law
SHEN, NANA, Foreign Languages
SHEN, NINGFU, Materials Science and Engineering
SHEN, XIANZHANG, Electrical Engineering
SHEN, XIAOCHENG, Bioengineering
SHI, JIE, Chemistry
SHI, MAOSHENG, Law
SHI, QIUZHI, Chemistry
SHI, XUEZHONG, Public Health
SHUI, TINGLIANG, Chemical Engineering
SONG, MAOPING, Chemistry
SU, JINGXIANG, Information Engineering
SU, YUNLAI, Chemistry
SUN, PEIQIN, Chemical Engineering
SUN, YUFU, Materials Science and Engineering
TAN, XINMIN, Education
TANG, KEYONG, Materials Science and Engineering
TANG, MINGSHENG, Chemistry
TAO, JINGCHAO, Chemistry
TIAN, TUCHENG, Law
TONG, LIPING, Civil Engineering

WANG, DONGWEI, Civil Engineering
WANG, FENG, Law
WANG, FUAN, Chemical Engineering
WANG, GUANGLONG, Chemical Engineering
WANG, GUOLING, Education
WANG, HONGXING, Chemistry
WANG, HONGYING, Materials Science and Engineering
WANG, JIE, Electrical Engineering
WANG, JINGWU, Materials Science and Engineering
WANG, LIANFENG, Law
WANG, LIDONG, Bioengineering
WANG, MINCAN, Chemistry
WANG, MINGCHEN, Basic Medical Science
WANG, XIANGYU, Chemistry
WANG, XIKE, Materials Science and Engineering
WANG, XINGGUANG, History and Archaeology
WANG, XINLING, Civil Engineering
WANG, YAN, Chemical Engineering
WANG, YUDONG, Materials Science and Engineering
WANG, YUNZHI, History and Archaeology
WANG, ZHONGQUAN, Basic Medical Science
WANG, ZHONGYONG, Information Engineering
WEI, XINLI, Chemical Engineering
WU, FENG, Basic Medical Science
WU, MIN, Public Health
WU, MINGJIAN, Chemical Engineering
WU, XIAOLING, Mechanical Engineering
WU, YANGJIE, Chemistry
WU, YIMING, Public Health
WU, YOULIN, Physical Science and Technology
XIAO, GUOXING, Law
XIAO, QIANGANG, Law
XU, HAISHENG, Chemical Engineering
XU, QILOU, Civil Engineering
XU, QUN, Materials Science and Engineering
XU, SHUN, Chemistry
XU, XIUCHENG, Chemical Engineering
XU, YAN, Chemistry
XU, YOULI, History and Archaeology
XUE, CHANGGUI, Basic Medical Science
XUE, LEXUN, Bioengineering
YAN, SUQING, Public Health
YANG, CHANGCHUN, Chemistry
YANG, GUANYU, Chemistry
YANG, JIUJUN, Materials Science and Engineering
YANG, SHENGLI, Basic Medical Science
YANG, TIANYU, History and Archaeology
YANG, YUANHUI, Electrical Engineering
YE, BAOXIAN, Chemistry
YE, YANGDONG, Information Engineering
YU, XIANGDONG, History and Archaeology
YU, YANGUANG, Information Engineering
YUAN, SIGUO, Chemical Engineering
YUAN, ZULIANG, History and Archaeology
ZENG, ZHIPING, Chemical Engineering
ZHANG, AFANG, Materials Science and Engineering
ZHANG, BAOLIN, Chemical Engineering
ZHANG, BINGLIN, Physical Science and Technology
ZHANG, GUOSHUO, History and Archaeology
ZHANG, HAOQIN, Chemical Engineering
ZHANG, HENG, Mechanical Engineering
ZHANG, HONGQUAN, Public Health
ZHANG, HONGYUN, Chemistry
ZHANG, JIANMIN, Chemistry
ZHANG, LINNA, Mechanical Engineering
ZHANG, MINFU, History and Archaeology
ZHANG, PING, Basic Medical Science
ZHANG, QIAN, Basic Medical Science
ZHANG, QINXIAN, Basic Medical Science
ZHANG, RUI, Materials Science and Engineering
ZHANG, RUIQIN, Chemistry
ZHANG, SHUSHENG, Chemistry
ZHANG, SHUYUAN, Chemistry
ZHANG, XIUQUAN, Law
ZHANG, XUHUA, History and Archaeology
ZHANG, YADONG, Chemical Engineering
ZHANG, ZHAO, Basic Medical Science

ZHANG, ZHIHONG, Information Engineering
ZHAO, JIANWEN, Law
ZHAO, QINGXIANG, Materials Science and Engineering
ZHAO, WENEN, Chemical Engineering
ZHAO, XINGTAI, Education
ZHAO, YUFEN, Chemistry
ZHENG, YONGFU, History and Archaeology
ZHOU, CAIRONG, Chemical Engineering
ZHOU, CHUXIAN, Chemistry
ZHOU, DAPENG, Chemistry
ZHOU, PENG, Information Engineering
ZHOU, QINGLEI, Information Engineering
ZHOU, YUANFANG, Public Health
ZHU, CHENGSHEN, Materials Science and Engineering
ZHUANG, LEI, Information Engineering
ZHUANG, YINFENG, Materials Science and Engineering

ZHONGNAN UNIVERSITY OF ECONOMICS AND LAW

114 Wu Luo Rd, Wuhan 430064, Hubei
Telephone: (27) 88044332
Fax: (27) 88044339
E-mail: xz@znufe.edu.cn
Internet: www.znufe.edu.cn

Founded 1948
Academic year: September to July
President: WU HANDONG
Vice-Presidents: LI HANCHANG, TAN YOUTU, ZHANG ZHONGHUA, ZHAO LINGYUN
Head of Graduate Department: ZHU YANFU
Librarian: HU YUANMIN

Number of teachers: 1,173
Number of students: 35,200

Publications: *Journal* (6 a year), *Studies in Law and Business* (6 a year)

DEANS

School of Accounting: LUO FEI
School of Banking and Insurance: ZU XINGRONG
School of Business Administration: ZHANG XINGUO
School of Economics: LU XIANXIANG
School of Finance and Public Administration: YANG CANMING
School of Foreign Languages: XIE QUN
School of Humanities: WANG YUCHEN
School of Information Science: YANG YUNYAN
School of Journalism and Mass Media: YIN XIULIN
School of Law: QI WENYUAN
School of Public Administration: ZHAO MAN
School of Public Security: YANG ZONGHUI

PROFESSORS

CAI, HONG, Law
CAI, LING, Economics
CAO, SHIQUAN, Law
CHAO, LONGQI, Banking and Insurance
CHEN, CHIBO, Business Administration
CHEN, DAJIE, Finance and Public Administration

CHEN, GUANGYAN, Finance and Public Administration
CHEN, JINLIANG, Law
CHEN, XIAOJUN, Law
CHENG, LIHUA, Humanities
CHENG, QIZHI, Economics
CHENG, QUANMING, Finance and Public Administration
CUI, MINGXIA, Law
DAI, WUTANG, Economics
DU, XINGCHAI, Economics
DUAN, NINGHUA, Information Science
FAN, ZHONGXI, Law
FANG, SHIRONG, Law
GU, YUANQING, Economics
GUO, DAOYANG, Accounting
HU, XIANSHUN, Information Science
HUANG, SHIPING, Humanities
JIA, QIYU, Information Science
JIANG, HAISU, Business Administration
KU, KEJIAN, Business Administration
LEI, XINGHU, Law
LI, CHANGQING, Banking and Insurance
LI, DAMING, Finance and Public Administration
LI, DAORONG, Humanities
LI, GEFEI, Banking and Insurance
LI, GUANGZHONG, Accounting
LI, JIANXUN, Public Security
LI, MAONIAN, Information Science
LI, NAINZHAO, Banking and Insurance
LI, QINGZHI, Public Security
LI, WEINING, Economics
LI, XIANPEI, Business Administration
LI, XUANJU, Information Science
LIANG, YUXIA, Law
LIN, HANCHUAN, Economics
LIU, DAHONG, Law
LIU, KEFENG, Humanities
LIU, LIELONG, Economics
LIU, LUANSHENG, Humanities
LIU, MAOLIN, Law
LIU, SIHUA, Economics
LIU, TENGHONG, Information Science
LIU, XIANFAN, Humanities
LU, XIANXIANG, Economics
LU, ZHONGMEI, Law
LUO, FEI, Accounting
LUO, SHENGBAO, Business Administration
MEI, ZIHUI, Banking and Insurance
MOU, BINGHUA, Information Science
NI, PINGSONG, Finance and Public Administration
NIE, HUAMING, Banking and Insurance
OUYANG, XUCHU, Business Administration
PANG, FENGXI, Finance and Public Administration
PENG, XINGLV, Business Administration
PENG, YONGXING, Information Science
PENG, ZHENGHUI, Law
QI, WENYUAN, Law
QIN, YOUTU, Law
QIU, JIAWU, Information Science
QU, GUANGQIN, Law
SHEN, BENZHU, Law
SHONG, QINGHUA, Banking and Insurance
SU, SHAOZHI, Economics

SUN, XIAOFU, Law
SUN, XIAOMEI, Humanities
TANG, GUOPING, Accounting
TANG, WEIBEN, Economics
TANG, WUYUN, Economics
TONG, ZHIWEI, Law
WAN, HOUFEN, Business Administration
WANG, FULIN, Humanities
WANG, JUNPING, Public Security
WANG, QUANXIN, Law
WANG, SHOU'AN, Information Science
WANG, XINGYUAN, Information Science
WU, GUANGBING, Economics
WU, HANGDONG, Law
WU, JUNPEI, Finance and Public Administration
WU, LIANLIAN, Humanities
WU, YIJUN, Business Administration
WU, ZHIZHONG, Law
XIA, CHENGCAI, Accounting
XIA, XINYUAN, Economics
XIA, YONG, Law
XIONG, SHENGXU, Business Administration
XU, DUNKAI, Economics
XU, GUOXIN, Economics
XU, JIANGUO, Finance and Public Administration
XU, RENZHANG, Finance and Public Administration
YAN, DEYU, Accounting
YAN, LIDONG, Business Administration
YAN, QIZHONG, Business Administration
YAN, RICHU, Information Science
YANG, CANMING, Finance and Public Administration
YANG, JIAZHI, Economics
YANG, KAIHAN, Information Science
YANG, YUNYAN, Humanities
YANG, ZONGHUI, Public Security
YAO, HUIYUAN, Economics
YAO, LI, Law
YE, QING, Finance and Public Administration
YU, XIYAN, Business Administration
YU, ZONGQI, Humanities
YUAN, JICHENG, Humanities
ZENG, QINGWEI, Information Science
ZHAN, CAILI, Accounting
ZHANG, CHAOQUN, Finance and Public Administration
ZHANG, FULIN, Humanities
ZHANG, HUAIFU, Finance and Public Administration
ZHANG, LONGPING, Accounting
ZHANG, SHIJING, Humanities
ZHANG, SHUZHEN, Law
ZHANG, YU, Public Security
ZHANG, YUANHUANG, Public Security
ZHANG, ZHENGLING, Humanities
ZHAO, LINGYU, Economics
ZHAO, MAN, Finance and Public Administration
ZHENG, ZHUJUN, Law
ZHOU, JUN, Banking and Insurance
ZHU, HAIFANG, Accounting
ZHU, YANFU, Economics
ZOU, LIGANG, Law
ZU, XINGRONG, Banking and Insurance

HONG KONG

Regulatory and Representative Bodies

GOVERNMENT

Education Bureau: 15th Fl., Wu Chung House, 213 Queen's Rd E, Wan Chai; tel. (852) 28910088; fax (852) 28930858; e-mail edbinfo@edb.gov.hk; internet www.edb.gov .hk; Sec. for Education MICHAEL M. Y. SUEN; Permanent Sec. for Education RAYMOND H. C. WONG.

Leisure and Cultural Services Department: Leisure and Cultural Services HQ, 1–3 Pai Tau St, Sha Tin; tel. (852) 24145555; fax (852) 26030642; e-mail enquiries@lcsd .gov.hk; internet www.lcsd.gov.hk; attached to Home Affairs Bureau; Dir BETTY FUNG CHING SUK-YEE; Deputy Dir for Cultural Services CHUNG LING-HOI; Deputy Dir for Leisure Services BOBBY CHENG KAM-WING.

ACCREDITATION

Hong Kong Council for Accreditation of Academic & Vocational Qualifications: 10th Fl., Cambridge House, Taikoo Pl., 979 King's Rd, Quarry Bay; tel. (852) 36580000; fax (852) 28459910; e-mail info@hkcaavq.edu .hk; internet www.hkcaavq.edu.hk; f. 1990; Chair. Dr YORK LIAO; Exec. Dir Prof. YIU-KWAN FAN.

NATIONAL BODIES

Heads of Universities Committee: The Hong Kong Polytechnic Univ., Hung Hom, Kowloon; tel. (852) 27665168; fax (852) 23631349; e-mail pphucom@polyu.edu.hk; internet www.polyu.edu.hk; Convenor Prof. WAY KUO.

Hong Kong Examinations and Assessment Authority: Southorn Centre, 12th–14th Fl., 130 Hennessy Rd, Wan Chai; tel. (852) 36288833; fax (852) 36288088; e-mail tsa1@hkeaa.edu.hk; internet www.hkeaa .edu.hk; 17 mems; Chair. EDDIE NG HAK-KIM; Deputy Chair. HUI CHIN-YIM; Sec.-Gen. Dr FRANCIS CHEUNG.

University Grants Committee: 7th Fl., Shui On Centre, 6–8 Harbour Rd, Wan Chai; tel. (852) 25243987; fax (852) 28451596; e-mail ugc@ugc.edu.hk; internet www.ugc .edu.hk; f. 1965; 30 mems; Chair. Hon. LAURA M. CHA; Sec.-Gen. MICHAEL V. STONE.

Vocational Training Council: VTC Tower, 27 Wood Rd, Wan Chai; tel. (852) 28361000; fax (852) 28380667; e-mail vtcmailbox@vtc .edu.hk; internet www.vtc.edu.hk; f. 1982; 13 mem. instns; Chair. Hon. ANDREW LEUNG KWAN-YUEN; Exec. Dir Dr CARRIE WILLIS.

Learned Societies

GENERAL

Royal Asiatic Society Hong Kong Branch: PO Box 3864, Central; tel. and fax (852) 28137500; e-mail info@ royalasiaticsociety.org.hk; internet www .royalasiaticsociety.org.hk; f. 1847, re-established 1959; encourages history, arts, science and literature in relation to Asia, particularly Hong Kong and China and their cultures; lectures and social activities; 720 mems (incl. 150 overseas mems); library of 5,500 books, 140,000 index cards; Pres. ROBERT NIELD; Vice-Pres. Dr ELIZABETH SINN; Vice-Pres. PETER STUCKEY; Hon. Sec. DAVID McKELLAR; Hon. Treas. Dr PETER HALLIDAY; Hon. Librarian JULIA CHAN; publ. *Journal of the Hong Kong Branch of the Royal Asiatic Society* (1 a year).

BIBLIOGRAPHY, LIBRARY SCIENCE AND MUSEOLOGY

Hong Kong Library Association: POB 10095, Gen. Post Office; e-mail hkla@hkla .org; internet www.hkla.org; f. 1958; promotes librarianship; offers professional growth, networking and community service; develops policies promoting provision of information and library services in Hong Kong; 694 mems; Pres. JIM CHANG; Vice-Pres. SIDNEY CHENG; Hon. Sec IRIS YUEN; Hon. Treas. PATTI CHEUNG; publs *Journal* (irregular), *Newsletter* (3 a year).

University of Hong Kong Museum Society: Univ. Museum and Art Gallery, Univ. of Hong Kong, 94 Bonham Rd, Pokfulam; tel. (852) 22415500; fax (852) 25469659; e-mail info@hkums.com; internet www.hkums.com; f. 1988; attached to Univ. of Hong Kong; supports the Univ. of Hong Kong Museum and Art Gallery; promotes Chinese arts and antiquities; sponsors art and educational programmes in the community; 500 mems; Chair. BONNIE KWAN HUO; Vice-Chair. YVONNE CHOI; Sec. WINNIE TONG; Treas. AUDY MAK; publ. *MVSE News* (5 a year).

ECONOMICS, LAW AND POLITICS

Hong Kong Institute of Certified Public Accountants: 37th Fl., Wu Chung House, 213 Queen's Rd E, Wan Chai; tel. (852) 22877228; fax (852) 28656603; e-mail hkicpa@hkicpa.org.hk; internet www.hkicpa .org.hk; f. 1973, fmrly Hong Kong Society of Accountants; registers and grants practising certificates to Certified Public Accountants in Hong Kong; mems earn description Certified Public Accountant and designatory letters CPA; assures the quality of entry into the profession through its postgraduate CPA Qualification Programme; promulgates financial reporting, auditing and ethical standards in Hong Kong; 28,000 mems; 13,000 students; Pres. WILSON FUNG; Vice-Pres. FOOK AUN CHEW; Vice-Pres. PHILIP TSAI WING CHUNG; Chief Exec. and Registrar WINNIE C. W. CHEUNG; publs *APlus* (12 a year), Technical bulletin, guides and other publs online.

Hong Kong Management Association: 14th Fl., Fairmont House, 8 Cotton Tree Dr., Central; tel. (852) 25266516; fax (852) 28684387; e-mail hkma@hkma.org.hk; internet www.hkma.org.hk; f. 1960; non-profit org.; offers management training courses, management consultancy services, library information, seminars, forums, awards and competitions; 12,000 mems; Chair. Hon. DAVID K. P. LI; Deputy Chair. Dr DENNIS SUN; Deputy Chair. HENRY H. L. FAN; Deputy Chair. Dr IAN FOK; Dir-Gen. Dr ELIZABETH S. C. SHING; publ. *The Hong Kong Manager* (4 a year).

The Law Society of Hong Kong: 3rd Fl., Wing On House, 71 Des Voeux Rd, Central; tel. (852) 28460500; fax (852) 28450387; e-mail sg@hklawsoc.org.hk; internet www .hklawsoc.org.hk; f. 1907; professional assn for solicitors in Hong Kong; ensures compliance by solicitors with relevant laws, codes, regulations and practice directions; supports and protects the character, status and interests of solicitors; 6,122 mems; Pres. HUEN WONG; Vice-Pres. JUNIUS K. Y. HO; Vice-Pres. DIETER YIH; Sec.-Gen. RAYMOND C. K. HO; Deputy Sec.-Gen. HEIDI K.P. CHU; publ. *Hong Kong Lawyer*.

LANGUAGE AND LITERATURE

Alliance Française: 1st and 2nd Fl., 123 Hennessy Rd, Wan Chai; tel. (852) 25277825; fax (852) 28653478; e-mail afinfo@ alliancefrancaise.com.hk; internet www .alliancefrancaise.com.hk; f. 1953; offers courses and examinations in French language and culture and promotes cultural exchange with France; Pres. R. A. V. RIBERO; Dir-Gen. JEAN-PIERRE DUMONT; Treas. THIERRY MÉQUILLET; publ. *Paroles*.

British Council: 3 Supreme Court Rd, Admiralty; tel. (852) 29135100; fax (852) 29135102; e-mail enquiries@britishcouncil .org.hk; internet www.britishcouncil.org.hk/ index.asp; f. 1948; teaching centre; offers courses and examinations in English language and British culture and promotes cultural exchange with the UK; Dir RUTH GEE; Deputy Dir, Teaching Centre GEORGINA PEARCE.

Goethe-Institut: 14th Fl., Hong Kong Arts Centre, 2 Harbour Rd, Wan Chai; tel. (852) 28020088; fax (852) 28024363; e-mail info@ hongkong.goethe.org; internet www.goethe .de/hongkong; f. 1963; offers courses and examinations in German language and culture and promotes cultural exchange with Germany; library of 7,400 vols, incl. audio-visual materials; Dir MICHAEL MÜLLER-VERWEYEN; Deputy Dir and Head of Language Courses MARTIN BODE; Head of Library and Information Service GABRIELE SANDER.

Hong Kong Chinese Speaking PEN Centre: Flat F, 4th Fl., Tower 6, Jubilant Pl. 99, Paucheung St, Kowloon; f. 1955; 92 mems; library of 1,600 vols; Pres. YU HOI FU; Sec. S. B. TENG; publ. *PEN News* (52 a year, in Chinese).

MEDICINE

Hong Kong Medical Association: Duke of Windsor Social Service Bldg, 5th Fl., 15 Hennessy Rd; tel. (852) 25278285; fax (852) 28650943; e-mail hkma@hkma.org; internet www.hkma.org; f. 1920, fmrly Hong Kong Chinese Medical Assn; promotes welfare and protects the lawful interests of the medical profession; promotes cooperation with nat. and int. medical socs; works for the advancement of medical science; 8,400 mems; Pres. Dr TSE HUNG HING; Vice-Pres. Dr ALVIN CHAN YEE SHING; Vice-Pres. Dr CHIN CHOW PAK; Hon. Sec. Dr ERNIE LO CHI FUNG; Hon. Treas. Dr CHI CHU LEUNG; Chief Exec. YVONNE LEUNG; publs *HKMA News* (12 a year), *Hong Kong Medical Journal* (6 a year), *HKMA CME Bulletin* (12 a year).

Research Institute

MEDICINE

Institute of Chinese Medicine: 2nd and 3rd Fl., Science Centre E Block, Chinese Univ. of Hong Kong, Sha Tin, New Territories; tel. (852) 31634370; fax (852) 26035248; e-mail icm@cuhk.edu.hk; internet www.icm .cuhk.edu.hk/icm/en; f. 2000, fmrly Chinese Medicinal Material Research Centre; attached to Chinese Univ. of Hong Kong; conducts scientific research to modernize, commercialize and promote Chinese medicine; sections in clinical trials, drug devt, standardization and safety of Chinese medicine, natural products; Chair. Prof. JACK CHENG; Dir Prof. P. C. LEUNG; Dir Prof. K. P. FUNG.

NATURAL SCIENCES

Physical Sciences

Hong Kong Observatory: 134A Nathan Rd, Kowloon; tel. (852) 29268200; fax (852) 23119448; e-mail mailbox@hko.gov.hk; internet www.hko.gov.hk; f. 1883, renamed Royal Observatory, Hong Kong 1912, original name restored 1997; attached to the Govt of the Hong Kong Special Administrative Region; govt dept that operates weather forecasting, cyclone warning and other meteorological and geophysical services; library of 40,000 vols; Dir Dr BOO-YING LEE; publs *Daily Weather Chart, Hong Kong Observatory Almanac* (1 a year), *Hong Kong Observatory Calendar, Hong Kong Tide Tables* (1 a year), *Monthly Weather Summary, Occasional papers* (irregular), *Summary of Meteorological Observations in Hong Kong* (1 a year), *Tropical Cyclones* (1 a year), *Technical Notes* (irregular), *Technical Notes (local)* (irregular).

Libraries and Archives

Hong Kong

University Library System: Tin Ka Ping Bldg 2 Fl., Sha Tin, New Territories; tel. (852) 26097305; fax (852) 26036952; e-mail library@cuhk.edu.hk; internet www.lib.cuhk .edu.hk; f. 1963; attached to Chinese Univ. of Hong Kong; coordinates the collns and services of the Univ. Library (f. 1965) and the 7 br. libraries; spec. collns: Careers colln; CUHK theses submitted since 1967; Chinese Overseas colln; History of Medicine of Hong Kong, China and the Asia-Pacific region; Hong Kong Govt documents; Hong Kong Studies; Instructional Materials colln; Modern Chinese Drama colln; rare Chinese books from the Yuan to the Qing dynasties; 2,194,000 vols incl. 986,479 vols of books and bound journals in East Asian languages, 1,307,891 vols of books and bound journals in Western languages, more than 13,000 active print serials, 100,000 e-journals, 1.2m. e-books, 580 e-databases; Univ. Librarian Dr COLIN STOREY; Deputy Librarian RITA WONG; publ. *Annotated Bibliography of Rare Books in the CUHK Libraries.*

Hong Kong Central Library: 66 Causeway Rd, Causeway Bay; tel. (852) 31501234; fax (852) 28815500; e-mail hkcl_ref@lcsd.gov.hk; internet www.hkpl.gov.hk/english/aboutus/ aboutus_hkcl/aboutus_hkcl_intro/aboutus_ hkcl_intro.html; f. 2001; attached to Hong Kong Public Libraries, Leisure and Cultural Services Dept; 2.3m. vols; largest library facility in the Hong Kong Public Libraries system; depository library for publs of Asian Devt Bank, European Union, ILO, Int. Maritime Org., UN, UNESCO, World Bank, World Trade Org. and World Food Programme.

Pao Yue-kong Library–Hong Kong Polytechnic University: Hung Hom, Kowloon; tel. (852) 27666863; fax (852) 27658274; e-mail lbinf@polyu.edu.hk; internet www.lib .polyu.edu.hk; f. 1972 as The University Library, present name 1995; inter-library loan and document delivery services; reference and personal information consultancy services, information skills workshops, online information literacy programmes; 1,270,911 monographs, 247,328 series bound vols, 646 electronic databases, 32,603 full-text e-journal titles, 225,033 e-books and 249 electronic learning programmes; spec. collns: Industrial Standards (online, 55,967 vols); Slide Colln (260,398 items); local TV programmes (24,913); digital images (online, 47,211); audio-visual material (63,960 items); 387,643 microfiches; 2,394 reels of microfilm; PolyU examination paper database, PolyU course scheme database, PolyU electronic theses, Hongkongiana online, video-on-demand, online audio libraries, newspaper clippings image database; Univ Librarian STEVE O'CONNOR; publ. *Directory of Professional Associations and Learned Societies in Hong Kong.*

Hong Kong Public Libraries: c/o Hong Kong Central Library, Moreton Terrace, Causeway Bay; tel. (852) 29210208; e-mail enquiries@lcsd.gov.hk; internet www.hkpl .gov.hk; f. 1962; attached to Leisure and Cultural Services Dept; promotes literary arts and literary research in Hong Kong; cultivates public interest in creative writing and literary research; encourages literary writing and cultural exchange; central reference library of 6 subject depts; toy library; a young adult library; exhibition gallery and lecture theatre; provides a network of 66 br. libraries and 10 mobile libraries; 12.47m. items, incl. books, audiovisual materials, newspapers, periodicals, CD-ROM databases, microforms and maps.

Public Records Office: 3rd Fl., Hong Kong Public Records Bldg, 13 Tsui Ping Rd, Kwun Tong, Kowloon; tel. (852) 21957700; fax (852) 28046413; e-mail proinfo@grs.gov.hk; internet www.info.gov.hk/pro; f. 1972; attached to Govt Records Service (f. 1997); 22,000 Hong Kong Govt publs; newspapers colln, photographs colln, map colln; 800,000 archival records and library items.

University of Hong Kong Libraries: 4th Fl. Main Library, Univ. of Hong Kong Pokfulam; tel. (852) 28592203; fax (852) 28589420; e-mail hkulref@hkucc.hku.hk; internet www.lib.hku.hk; f. 1912; main library and 6 brs; spec. collns incl. Hong Kong Colln, Morrison Colln, Hong Kong Tourist Asscn Colln, Republic of China Govt Publs, Taiwan Studies Univ. of Hong Kong Theses; 2,730,000 print vols in East Asian and Western languages, 9,760 current print journals, 57,860 e-journals on subscription, 1,900,000 e-books and substantial holdings of audiovisual items and materials in microform; Librarian Dr ANTHONY W. FERGUSON; Deputy Librarian PETER SIDORKO.

Museums and Art Galleries

Hong Kong

Art Museum: Institute of Chinese Studies, Chinese Univ. of Hong Kong, Sha Tin, New Territories; tel. (852) 26097416; fax (852) 26035366; e-mail artmuseum@cuhk.edu.hk; internet www.cuhk.edu.hk/ics/amm; f. 1971; attached to Institute of Chinese Studies, Chinese Univ. of Hong Kong; collects, preserves, researches and exhibits artefacts representing the rich art and cultural heritage of ancient and pre-modern China; promotes Chinese culture and heritage; facilitates academic exchange between China and the West; collaborates with univ. dept of Fine Arts for practice in museology and teaching in art history.

Hong Kong Film Archive: 50 Lei King Rd, Sai Wan Ho; tel. (852) 27392100; fax (852) 23115229; e-mail hkfa@lcsd.gov.hk; internet www.filmarchive.gov.hk; f. 1993; attached to Leisure and Cultural Services Dept; acquires and conserves films made in Hong Kong; catalogues and maintains archival colln; provides information related to cinema and the Hong Kong film industry; organizes thematic retrospectives, exhibitions, symposia and seminars on cinema; publ. *Oral History Series.*

Hong Kong Heritage Museum: 1 Man Lam Rd, Sha Tin; tel. (852) 21808188; fax (852) 21808111; e-mail hkhm@lcsd.gov.hk; internet www.heritagemuseum.gov.hk; attached to Leisure and Cultural Services Dept; colln of local history relics, natural history relics, performing art relics, folk art and popular culture artefacts (toys and comics); art colln: contemporary art, design and Chinese fine art (Chinese paintings, calligraphy and Chinese antiquities); houses 6 permanent galleries: Orientation Theatre, New Territories Heritage Hall, Cantonese Opera Heritage Hall, T. T. Tsui Gallery of Chinese Art, Chao Shao-an Gallery, Children's Discovery Gallery and 6 thematic galleries; 3 br. museums: Hong Kong Railway Museum (Tai Po), Sam Tung Uk Museum (Tsuen Wan), Sheung Yiu Folk Museum (Sai Kung); publ. *Hong Kong Heritage Museum Newsletter* (4 a year).

Hong Kong Maritime Museum: Ground Fl., Murray House, Stanley Plaza, Stanley; tel. (852) 28132322; fax (852) 28138033; e-mail info@hkmaritimemuseum.org; internet www.hkmaritimemuseum.org; non-profit org.; stimulates public interest in ships and the sea particularly the South China coast and adjacent seas; promotes the growth of Hong Kong as a major port and int. maritime centre; 2 galleries: ancient and modern displaying c. 500 exhibits incl. ceramics, ships models, paintings, trade goods and ships manifests; Chair. ANTHONY J. HARDY; Dir Dr STEPHEN DAVIES; Exec. Man. and Curator CATALINA CHOR.

Hong Kong Museum of Art: 10 Salisbury Rd, Tsim Sha Tsui, Kowloon; tel. (852) 27210116; fax (852) 27237666; e-mail enquiries@lcsd.gov.hk; internet www.lcsd .gov.hk/hkma; f. 1962, present bldg 1991; attached to Leisure and Cultural Services Dept; 15,000 art objects; Chinese antiquities, incl. the Henry Yeung colln; historical paintings, prints and drawings of Hong Kong, Macao and China, incl. Chater, Sayer, Law and Ho Tung colls; contemporary works by local artists; Chinese paintings and calligraphy, incl. the Xubaizhai Colln; 1 br. museum: Museum of Tea Ware; Chief Curator CHRISTINA CHU.

Branch Museum:

> **Museum of Tea Ware:** 10 Cotton Tree Dr., Central; tel. (852) 28690690; fax (852) 28100021; f. 1984; displays famous Yixing teapots; conducts tea gatherings and lecture programmes to promote ceramic art and Chinese tea drinking culture.

Hong Kong Museum of History: 100 Chatham Rd South, Tsimshatsui, Kowloon; tel. (852) 27249042; fax (852) 27249090; e-mail hkmh@lcsd.gov.hk; internet hk .history.museum; f. 1962 as City Museum and Art Gallery, present status and name 1975, present location 1998; attached to Leisure and Cultural Services Dept; archaeology, ethnography, natural history and history of Hong Kong; historical photographs and documents; postal history and numismatics colln; brs at Lei Cheng Uk Han Tomb Museum, Law Uk Folk Museum, Hong Kong Museum of Coastal Defence, Dr. Sun Yat-sen Museum and Fireboat Alexander Grantham Exhibition Gallery; permanent exhibition: 'The Hong Kong Story'; Chief Curator ESA LEUNG KIT-LING; publ. *Newsletter* (4 a year).

Branch Museums:

Dr Sun Yat-sen Museum: 7 Castle Rd, Central; tel. (852) 23676373; fax (852) 35800498; e-mail sysm@lcsd.gov.hk; internet hk.drsunyatsen.museum; f. 2006; life and career of Dr Sun Yat-sen; Hong Kong's role in reform movements and revolutionary activities in the 19th–20th centuries; 2 permanent exhibitions display historical artefacts.

Fireboat Alexander Grantham Exhibition Gallery: Quarry Bay Park; tel. (852) 23677821; fax (852) 35800498; displays unique fire fighting artefacts; documents marine rescue work in Hong Kong.

Hong Kong Museum of Coastal Defence: 175 Tung Hei Rd, Shau Kei Wan; tel. (852) 25691500; fax (852) 25691637; e-mail hkmcd@lcsd.gov.hk; internet hk.coastaldefence.museum; f. 2000, fmrly the Lei Yue Mun Fort; preserves and presents 600 year history of coastal defence in Hong Kong.

Law Uk Folk Museum: 14 Kut Shing St, Chai Wan; tel. (852) 28967006; fax (852) 27249090; 18th-century Hakka village house.

Lei Cheng Uk Han Tomb Museum: 41 Tonkin St, Sham Shui Po, Kowloon; tel. (852) 23862863; fax (852) 23612105; f. 1988 declared as gazetted monument, tomb discovered 1955; tomb closed to public; displays pottery and bronze wares excavated from the tomb, texts, graphics, photos, maps, videos models of the tomb; 2 exhibitions 'Lei Cheng Uk Han Tomb' and 'Han Culture in South China'.

Hong Kong Science Museum: 2 Science Museum Rd, Tsim Shat Tsui E, Kowloon; tel. (852) 27323232; fax (852) 23112248; e-mail enquiries@hk.science.museum; internet hk .science.museum; f. 1991; attached to Leisure and Cultural Services Dept; 500 exhibits on permanent display, temporary thematic exhibitions; 16 galleries; education and extension activities; lecture hall and spec. rental exhibition hall; Chief Curator MICHAEL WONG HING-IAN; Sr Man. KATHLEEN MA KA-LIN; publ. *Newsletter* (4 a year).

Hong Kong Space Museum: 10 Salisbury Rd, Tsim Sha Tsui, Kowloon; tel. (852) 27210226; fax (852) 23115804; e-mail spacem@space.lcsd.gov.hk; internet hk.space .museum; f. 1980; attached to Leisure and Cultural Services Dept; promotes interest in astronomy and related sciences by exhibitions, lectures, films, Omnimax and sky shows; 100 staff; library of 1,700 vols, also films and videos; Curator CHAN KI HUNG; publs *Astrocalendar* (1 a year), *Newsletter* (4 a year).

Hong Kong Visual Arts Centre: 7A Kennedy Rd, Central; tel. (852) 25213008; fax (852) 25014703; internet www.lcsd.gov.hk/ce/ museum/apo/en/vac.html; f. 1992; attached to Art Promotion Office, Leisure and Cultural Services Dept; provides studios for trained artists practising in the fields of sculpture, printmaking and ceramics; organizes art activities incl. workshops, exhibitions,

demonstrations, lectures and artist-in-residence programmes.

Ping Shan Tang Clan Gallery and Heritage Trail Visitors Centre: Hang Tau Tsuen, Ping Shan, Yuen Long, New Territories; tel. (852) 26171959; fax (852) 26170925; internet www.lcsd.gov.hk/ce/ museum/monument/en/ping_shan.php; f. 1993 as Ping Shan Heritage Trail, present name and staus 2007, converted from the Old Ping Shan Police Station built in 1899; attached to Antiquities and Monuments Office, Leisure and Cultural Services Dept; displays various relics belonging to members of the Tang Clan who personally relate their history, customs and cultural life; introduces monuments and bldgs along the Ping Shan Heritage Trail; spec. thematic exhibitions on history and culture of the New Territories.

University Museum and Art Gallery: Univ. of Hong Kong, 94 Bonham Rd, Pokfulam; tel. (852) 22415500; fax (852) 25469659; e-mail museum@hkusua.hku.hk; internet www.hku.hk/hkumag/main.html; f. 1953 as Fung Ping Shan Museum of Chinese Art and Archaeology, present name and bldg 1996; attached to Univ. of Hong Kong; 1,000 items of Chinese antiquities, ceramics, bronzes and paintings; colln incl. items dating from the Neolithic period to the Qing dynasty; bronze colln incl. works from the Shang to the Tang dynasties; largest colln of Yuan dynasty Nestorian crosses in the world; carvings in jade, wood and stone; colln of Chinese oil paintings; attached tea gallery promotes Chinese tea culture; Dir YEUNG CHUN-TONG; Curator for Art TINA YEE-WAN PANG; Curator for History ANITA YIN-FONG WONG.

Universities

CHINESE UNIVERSITY OF HONG KONG

Sha Tin, New Territories
Telephone: (852) 26097000
Fax: (852) 26035544
E-mail: cpr@cuhk.edu.hk
Internet: www.cuhk.edu.hk

Founded 1963
Public control
Languages of instruction: Chinese, English
Academic year: August to July
Chancellor: CHIEF EXEC. OF THE HONG KONG SPEC. ADMIN. REGION
Chair. of Council: EDGAR W. K. CHENG
Vice-Chancellor and Pres.: LAWRENCE J. LAU
Provost: Prof. BENJAMIN WAH
Pro-Vice-Chancellor: Prof. HENRY N. C. WONG
Pro-Vice-Chancellor: Prof. CHING PAK-CHUNG
Pro-Vice-Chancellor: Prof. JACK C. Y. CHENG
Pro-Vice-Chancellor: Prof. KENNETH YOUNG
Pro-Vice-Chancellor: Prof. MICHAEL K. M. HUI
Univ. Dean of Students: Prof. DENNIS NG
Registrar: ERIC S. P. NG
Sec.: JACOB S. K. LEUNG
Treas.: ROGER K. H. LUK
Librarian: COLIN STOREY

Library: see Libraries and Archives
Number of teachers: 1,283
Number of students: 13,513

Publications: *Annals of Contemporary Diagnostic Pathology* (1 a year), *Asian Anthropology* (1 a year), *Asian Economic Journal* (1 a year), *Asian Journal of Counselling* (2 a year), *Asian Journal of English Language Teaching* (1 a year), *Asian Journal of Mathematics* (4 a year), *The China Review* (2 a year), *Chinese Academic Jour-*

nal (every 2 years), *Chinese Language Newsletter* (4 a year), *Comparative Literature and Culture* (1 a year), *Communications in Information and Systems* (4 a year), *Crosslinks in English Language Teaching* (every 2 years), *Education Journal* (2 a year), *Educational Research Journal* (2 a year), *Geographic Information Sciences* (2 a year), *Global Chinese Journal on Computers in Education* (2 a year), *Journal of Basic Education* (2 a year), *Journal of Chinese Philosophy and Culture* (2 a year), *Journal of Chinese Studies* (1 a year), *Journal of Contemporary Chinese Education* (2 a year), *Journal of Translation Studies* (2 a year), *Methods and Application of Analysis* (4 a year), *Phenomenology and the Human Sciences* (1 a year), *Renditions* (2 a year), *Southeast Asia Bulletin of Mathematics* (6 a year), *Twenty-first Century* (6 a year)

DEANS

Faculty of Arts: Prof. HSIUNG PING-CHEN
Faculty of Business Administration: Prof. WONG TAK-JUN
Faculty of Education: Prof. JOHN C. K. LEE
Faculty of Engineering: Prof. C. P. WONG
Faculty of Medicine: Prof. TAI-FAI FOK
Faculty of Science: Prof. NG CHEUK-YIU
Faculty of Social Science: Prof. PAUL S. N. LEE
Graduate School: Prof. WONG WING-SHING

PROFESSORS

BAKER, H. D. R., Humanities
BANIASSAD, E., Architecture
BOND, M. H., Psychology
CHAN, A. T. C., Clinical Ontology
CHAN, H. C., Physiology
CHAN, J. C. N., Medicine and Therapeutics
CHAN, K. L., Medicine and Therapeutics
CHAN, K. M., Orthopaedics and Traumatology
CHAN, N. H., Statistics
CHAN, R. H. F., Mathematics
CHEN, H. C., Psychology
CHENG, J. C. Y., Orthopaedics and Traumatology
CHEUNG, F. M. C., Psychology
CHEUNG, S. H. N., Chinese Language and Literature
CHING, P. C., Electronic Engineering
CHIU, H. F. K., Psychiatry
CHO, C. H., Pharmacology
CHOW, M. S. S., Pharmacy
CHUNG, T. K. H., Obstetrics and Gynaecology
COCKRAM, C. S., Medicine and Therapeutics (Medicine)
FAURE, D., History
FOK, T. F., Paediatrics
FUNG, K. P., Biochemistry
GIN, T., Anaesthesia and Intensive Care
GRIFFITHS, S., Public Health
HAZLETT, C. B., Medical Education
HO, S. S., Community and Family Medicine
HUI, M. K. M., Marketing
KEMBER, D. R., Learning Enhancement
KUNG, H. F., Virology
LAM, D. S. C., Ophthalmology and Visual Sciences
LANG, L. H. P., Finance
LAU, J. W. Y., Surgery
LAU, K. S., Mathematics
LAU, L. J., Economics
LAU, L. W. M., Physics (Materials Science)
LAU, S. K., Sociology
LAW, S. K., Management
LEE, K. H., Marketing
LEE, L. O. F., Humanities
LEE, R. P. L., Sociology
LEE, S. S., Infectious Diseases
LEE, S. Y., Statistics
LEE, T. T., Information Engineering
LEE, V. H. L., Pharmacy

LEUNG, Y., Geography and Resource Management (Geography)
LEUNG, Y. S., History
LI, R. S. Y., Information Engineering
LIN, C., Information Engineering, Electronic Engineering (Photonics)
LIU, P. W., Economics
LO, D. Y. M., Chemical Pathology
LO, L. N. K., Educational Admin. and Policy
McCONVILLE, M., Law
McNAUGHT, C. M., Learning Enhancement
MIRRLEES, J. A., Distinguished Professor-at-Large
NG, H. K., Anatomical and Cellular Pathology
NG, P. C., Paediatrics
NGAN, K. N., Electronic Engineering
PARKER, D. H., English
POON, W. S., Surgery
SHUN, K. L., Philosophy
SO, B. K. L., History
SO, J. F. S., Fine Arts
SUN, S. S. M., Biology
SUNG, J. J. Y., Medicine and Therapeutics
TANG, K. L., Social Work
VAN HASSELT, C. A., Surgery (Otorhinolaryngology)
WONG, H. N. C., Chemistry
WONG, K. S., Medicine and Therapeutics
WONG, L. K. P., Translation
WONG, T. J., Accountancy
WONG, W. S., Information Engineering
WOO, J., Medicine and Therapeutics (Medicine)
WU, C., Chemistry
XIE, Z., Chemistry
XIN, Z. P., Mathematics
XU, L., Computer Science and Engineering
XU, Y., Automation and Computer-Aided Engineering
YANG, C. N., Distinguished Professor-at-Large
YAO, A. C. C., Distinguished Professor-at-Large
YAO, D. D. W., Systems Engineering and Engineering Management
YAU, S. T., Distinguished Professor-at-Large
YEUNG, C. K., Surgery
YEUNG, W. H., Information Engineering
YEW, D. T. W., Anatomy
YIM, A. P. C., Surgery
YOUNG, K., Physics
YOUNG, L., Finance
YUM, P. T. S., Information Engineering
ZHANG, J., Economics
ZHOU, X., Systems Engineering and Engineering Management

CITY UNIVERSITY OF HONG KONG

83 Tat Chee Ave, Kowloon
Telephone: (852) 34427654
Fax: (852) 27881167
E-mail: webmaster@cityu.edu.hk
Internet: www.cityu.edu.hk
Founded 1984 as City Polytechnic of Hong Kong; present name and status 1994
Autonomous control, financed by the Univ. Grants Committee
Language of instruction: English
Academic year: September to August
Pres.: Prof. WAY KUO
Provost: CHI-HOU CHAN (acting)
Vice-Pres. for Devt and External Relations: RODERICK S. C. WONG
Vice-Pres. for Research and Technology: Prof. HORACE H. S. IP (acting)
Vice-Pres. for Student Affairs: Prof. PAUL KWAN-SING LAM (acting)
Librarian: Prof. C. C. CHENG (acting)
Library of 908,500 vols of books, 195,000 vols of bound periodicals, 3,000 print serials
Number of teachers: 1,138 (923 full-time, 215 part-time)

Number of students: 18,558 (11,651 full-time, 6,907 part-time)
Publications: Bulletin (3 a year), CityU Today (12 a year), Linkage (12 a year), Research Report (1 a year)

DEANS

Chow Yei Ching School of Graduate Studies: Prof. HORACE H. S. IP (acting)
College of Business: Prof. KWOK-KEE WEI
College of Humanities and Social Sciences: Prof. MARTIN PAINTER (acting)
College of Science and Engineering: Prof. EDWIN Y. B. PUN (acting)
School of Creative Media: Prof. JEFFERY SHAW
School of Energy and Environment: Prof. JOHNNY C. L. CHAN
School of Law: Prof. GUI GUO WANG

HONG KONG BAPTIST UNIVERSITY

Kowloon Tong, Kowloon
Telephone: (852) 34117400
Fax: (852) 23387644
E-mail: aaco@hkbu.edu.hk
Internet: www.hkbu.edu.hk
Founded 1956
State control
Languages of instruction: English, Chinese
Academic year: September to June
Pres. and Vice-Chancellor: Prof. ALBERT CHAN
Vice-Pres. for Academic Affairs: Prof. FRANKLIN LUK
Vice-Pres. for Admin. and Sec.: ANDY LEE SHIU CHUEN
Vice-Pres. for Research and Institutional Advancement: Prof. TSOI AH-CHUNG
Academic Registrar: Dr TONG CHONG-SZE
Librarian: Dr TERRY WEBB
Library of 1,045,530 vols, 132,586 audio-visual materials and microforms, 221,990 e-books, 34,644 e-journals, 3,901 serials, 210 e-databases
Number of teachers: 561 (full-time)
Number of students: 8,720
Publications: Contemporary Historical Review (4 a year), Journal of the History of Christianity in Modern China (1 a year), Journal of Physical Education and Recreation (2 a year), Sino Humanitas (2 a year)

DEANS

Academy of Visual Arts: Prof. WAN QINGLI
Faculty of Arts: Prof. CHUNG LING
Faculty of Science: Prof. RICK WONG
Faculty of Social Sciences: Prof. ARIAN BAILEY
School of Business: Prof. STEPHEN Y. L. CHEUNG
School of Communication: Prof. XINSHU ZHAO (acting)
School of Continuing Education: Dr SIMON WONG
School of Chinese Medicine: Prof. LIU LIANG
Graduate School: Prof. TANG TAO (Dir)

HONG KONG POLYTECHNIC UNIVERSITY

Yuk Choi Rd, Hung Hom, Kowloon
Telephone: (852) 27665333
Fax: (852) 27643374
E-mail: paadmin@inet.polyu.edu.hk
Internet: www.polyu.edu.hk
Founded 1937 as Govt Trade School, became Hong Kong Technical College 1947 and Hong Kong Polytechnic 1972, present name and status 1994
Autonomous control, financed by the Univ. Grants Cttee
Language of instruction: English
Academic year: September to August
Chancellor: CHIEF EXEC. OF THE HONG KONG SPEC. ADMIN. REGION

Pres.: Prof. TIMOTHY W. TONG
Deputy Pres. and Provost: PHILIP C. H. CHAN
Vice-Pres. for Academic Devt: Prof. WALTER W. YEUN
Vice Pres. for Institutional Advancement and Partnership: Prof. ANGELINA YUEN
Vice Pres. for Int. and Exec. Education: Prof. JUDY TSUI
Vice-Pres. for Management: Prof. THOMAS K. S. WONG
Vice-Pres. for Research Devt: Prof. ALBERT S.C. CHAN
Univ. Librarian: BARRY BURTON
Library: see Libraries and Archives
Number of teachers: 3,089 full-time
Number of students: 28,702
Publication: University Calendar (1 a year)

DEANS

College of Professional and Continuing Education: Prof. PETER P. YUEN
Faculty of Applied Science and Textiles: Prof. K. Y. WONG
Faculty of Business: Prof. HOWARD DAVIES (acting)
Faculty of Communication: Prof. T. P. LEUNG
Faculty of Construction and Land Use: Prof. JIN-GUANG TENG
Faculty of Engineering: Prof. ALEX WAI
Faculty of Health and Social Sciences: Prof. GEORGE WOO
Faculty of Humanities: Prof. HUANG CHU-REN

HONG KONG UNIVERSITY OF SCIENCE AND TECHNOLOGY

Clear Water Bay, Kowloon
Telephone: (852) 23586000
Fax: (852) 23580537
E-mail: ophkust@ust.hk
Internet: www.ust.hk
Founded 1988, first student intake 1991
State control
Language of instruction: English
Academic year: September to July
Chancellor: CHIEF EXEC. OF THE HONG KONG SPEC. ADMIN. REGION
Pres.: Prof. Dr TONY F. CHAN
Vice-Pres. for Academic Affairs: Prof. Dr SHIU YUEN CHENG (acting)
Vice-Pres. for Admin. and Business: Prof. Dr YUK-SHAN WONG
Vice-Pres. for Research and Devt: Prof. Dr MATTHEW YUEN (acting)
Dir. for Language Centre: Dr GREGORY C. A. JAMES
Dir. for Research Centre: Prof. ROLAND T. CHIN
Dir. for Library: Dr SASMSON SOONG
Library of 660,000 print vols, colln of media resources, 26,000 electronic and print journals, e-books, databases and digital resources
Number of teachers: 489
Number of students: 9,515
Publications: Academic Calendar, HKUST Newsletter

DEANS

Business and Management: Prof. LEONARD K. CHENG
Engineering: Prof. KHALED BEN LETAIEF
Humanities and Social Science: Prof. JAMES Z. LEE (acting)
Science: Prof. MICHAEL M. T. LOY (acting)
Undergraduate Education: KAR YAN TAM

PROFESSORS

ADAVAL, R., Marketing
ALTMAN, M., Physics
ARYA, S., Computer Science and Engineering
AU, O., Electronic and Computer Engineering
BAARK, E., Environment

BAARK, E., Social Science
BANFIELD, D., Biology
BARFORD, J., Chemical and Biomolecular Engineering
BEN LETAIEF, K., Electronic and Computer Engineering
BENSAOU, B., Computer Science and Engineering
BERMAK, A., Electronic and Computer Engineering
CAI, L., Mechanical Engineering
CAI, N., Industrial Engineering and Logistics Management
CAI, Y., Social Science
CAO, X., Electronic and Computer Engineering
CHAN, A., Biochemistry
CHAN, C., Chemical and Biomolecular Engineering
CHAN, C., Civil and Environmental Engineering
CHAN, C., Environment
CHAN, C., Humanities
CHAN, C., Physics
CHAN, K., Finance
CHAN, K., Humanities
CHAN, G., Computer Science and Engineering
CHAN, H., Physics
CHAN, K., Mathematics
CHAN, M., Electronic and Computer Engineering
CHAN, T., Computer Science and Engineering
CHAN, T., Mathematics
CHANG, C., Civil and Environmental Engineering
CHANG, H., Mathematics
CHAO, C., Mechanical Engineering
CHAO, M., Management
CHASNOV, J., Mathematics
CHATTOPADHYAY, P., Management
CHAU, Y., Chemical and Biomolecular Engineering
CHEN, B., Mathematics
CHEN, G., Chemical and Biomolecular Engineering
CHEN, G., Civil and Environmental Engineering
CHEN, J., Humanities
CHEN, K., Accounting
CHEN, K., Electronic and Computer Engineering
CHEN, K., Mathematics
CHEN, L., Humanities
CHEN, L., Computer Science and Engineering
CHEN, P., Accounting
CHEN, P., Electronic and Computer Engineering
CHEN, S., Economics
CHEN, T., Accounting
CHEN, Y., Social Science
CHENG, J., Civil and Environmental Engineering
CHENG, L., Economics
CHENG, R., Electronic and Computer Engineering
CHENG, S., Computer Science and Engineering
CHENG, S., Mathematics
CHEUNG, K., Information Systems, Business Statistics and Operations Management
CHEUNG, M., Civil and Environmental Engineering
CHEUNG, S., Computer Science and Engineering
CHEUNG, S., Humanities
CHEUNG, Z., Biochemistry
CHEW, S., Economics
CHIANG, Y., Mathematics
CHIGRINOV, V., Electronic and Computer Engineering
CHIN, R., Computer Science and Engineering
CHO, H., Social Science
CHOI, C., Biology
CHOI, D., Finance
CHONG, J., Social Science

CHONG, K., Humanities
CHOW, K., Biology
CHUNG, A., Computer Science and Engineering
CHUNG, K., Biochemistry
CLARK, T., Information Systems, Business Statistics and Operations Management
COOK, D., Economics
DAI, W., Chemistry
DALTON, A., Marketing
DASGUPTA, S., Finance
DING, C., Computer Science and Engineering
DING, F., Finance
DING, X., Social Science
DU, D., Finance
DU, S., Physics
DUCLOS, R., Marketing
FARH, L., Management
FENG, W., Biochemistry
FOREMAN, B., Physics
FU, F., Humanities
FUNG, J., Environment
FUNG, J., Mathematics
FUNG, P., Electronic and Computer Engineering
FUNG, Y., Humanities
GALLI, M., Marketing
GAN, J., Environment
GAN, J., Finance
GAN, J., Mathematics
GAO, F., Chemical and Biomolecular Engineering
GAO, Y., Mechanical Engineering
GEORGE, E., Management
GHIDAOUI, M., Civil and Environmental Engineering
GOLIN, M., Computer Science and Engineering
GONG, Y., Management
GOONETILLEKE, R., Industrial Engineering and Logistics Management
GOYAL, V., Finance
GU, L., Computer Science and Engineering
GUO, L., Marketing
GUO, Z., Chemistry
HA, A., Information Systems, Business Statistics and Operations Management
HAMDI, M., Computer Science and Engineering
HAN, L., Social Science
HAN, Y., Physics
HARRISON, P., Environment
HAYNES, R., Chemistry
HE, J., Management
HE, W., Social Science
HE, X., Mathematics
HELSEN, K., Marketing
HILARY, G., Accounting
HO, S., Biology
HO, V., Humanities
HOLZ, C., Social Science
HONG, J., Industrial Engineering and Logistics Management
HONG, J., Marketing
HORNER, A., Computer Science and Engineering
HOSSAIN, T., Economics
HSIEH, C., Accounting
HSING, I., Chemical and Biomolecular Engineering
HSU, C., Accounting
HSU, C., Mechanical Engineering
HU, I., Information Systems, Business Statistics and Operations Management
HU, J., Mathematics
HUA, X., Economics
HUANG, A., Accounting
HUANG, H., Electronic and Computer Engineering
HUANG, J., Mathematics
HUANG, P., Biology
HUANG, X., Chemistry
HUANG, Z., Management
HUI, D., Chemical and Biomolecular Engineering
HUI, K., Accounting

HUI, K., Information Systems, Business Statistics and Operations Management
HUNG, C., Humanities
IP, N., Biochemistry
JAISINGH, J., Information Systems, Business Statistics and Operations Management
JAMES, L., Information Systems, Business Statistics and Operations Management
JIA, G., Chemistry
JIANG, W., Industrial Engineering and Logistics Management
JING, B., Mathematics
JONEJA, A., Industrial Engineering and Logistics Management
JU, N., Finance
KARHADE, P., Information Systems, Business Statistics and Operations Management
KATAFYGIOTIS, L., Civil and Environmental Engineering
KI, W., Electronic and Computer Engineering
KIKKERT, G., Civil and Environmental Engineering
KIM, J., Mechanical Engineering
KIM, K., Economics
KIM, S., Computer Science and Engineering
KO, R., Biochemistry
KU, A., Social Science
KUANG, J., Civil and Environmental Engineering
KUNG, J., Social Science
KURSUN, V., Electronic and Computer Engineering
KWOK, H., Electronic and Computer Engineering
KWOK, J., Computer Science and Engineering
KWOK, Y., Mathematics
LAI, E., Economics
LAI, K., Biochemistry
LAM, D., Mechanical Engineering
LAM, H., Chemical and Biomolecular Engineering
LAM, J., Chemistry
LAU, A., Civil and Environmental Engineering
LAU, A., Environment
LAU, A., Mathematics
LAU, D., Biology
LAU, K., Electronic and Computer Engineering
LAU, S., Biology
LAU, V., Electronic and Computer Engineering
LEA, C., Electronic and Computer Engineering
LEE, C., Industrial Engineering and Logistics Management
LEE, D., Computer Science and Engineering
LEE, J., Social Science
LEE, K., Biology
LEE, N., Industrial Engineering and Logistics Management
LEE, O., Biology
LEE, R., Mechanical Engineering
LEE, Y., Mechanical Engineering
LENG, Y., Mechanical Engineering
LENNOX, C., Accounting
LEUNG, C., Civil and Environmental Engineering
LEUNG, S., Economics
LEUNG, S., Mathematics
LEUNG, P., Physics
LEUNG, W., Chemistry
LI, B., Computer Science and Engineering
LI, J., Management
LI, J., Mathematics
LI, K., Mathematics
LI, N., Biology
LI, Q., Information Systems, Business Statistics and Operations Management
LI, W., Mathematics
LI, X., Chemistry
LI, Y., Information Systems, Business Statistics and Operations Management
LI, Z., Civil and Environmental Engineering
LI, Z., Electronic and Computer Engineering

LI, Z., Mechanical Engineering
LIANG, C., Biochemistry
LIN, F., Computer Science and Engineering
LIN, N., Physics
LIN, Y., Social Science
LIN, Z., Chemistry
LING, S., Mathematics
LIU, H., Biology
LIU, H., Environment
LIU, G., Humanities
LIU, L., Finance
LIU, Q., Industrial Engineering and Logistics Management
LIU, T., Humanities
LIU, Y., Computer Science and Engineering
LO, A., Information Systems, Business Statistics and Operations Management
LO, H., Civil and Environmental Engineering
LO, I., Civil and Environmental Engineering
LOCHOVSKY, F., Computer Science and Engineering
LORTZ, R., Physics
LOY, M., Physics
LU, Z., Humanities
LUI, F., Economics
LUO, Q., Computer Science and Engineering
LUONG, H., Electronic and Computer Engineering
MA, J., Humanities
MA, J., Social Science
MACKAY, P., Finance
MAK, B., Computer Science and Engineering
MAK, H., Industrial Engineering and Logistics Management
MARKLE, A., Management
MCKAY, M., Electronic and Computer Engineering
MCKAY, G., Chemical and Biomolecular Engineering
MENG, G., Mathematics
MI, Y., Chemical and Biomolecular Engineering
MILLER, A., Biology
MOK, P., Electronic and Computer Engineering
MOW, W., Electronic and Computer Engineering
MOY, A., Mathematics
MU, M., Mathematics
MUKHOPADHYAY, A., Marketing
MUPPALA, K., Computer Science and Engineering
MURCH, R., Electronic and Computer Engineering
MUTHUKRISHNAN, A., Marketing
NASON, E., Management
NG, C., Civil and Environmental Engineering
NG, K., Humanities
NG, K., Chemical and Biomolecular Engineering
NG, S., Information Systems, Business Statistics and Operations Management
NG, T., Physics
NG, W., Computer Science and Engineering
NI, L., Computer Science and Engineering
NI, S., Finance
NOVOSELOV, K., Accounting
PALOMAR, D., Electronic and Computer Engineering
PAPADIAS, D., Computer Science and Engineering
PATCHELL, G., Environment
PATCHELL, G., Social Science
PENG, H., Biology
PING GAO, P., Chemical and Biomolecular Engineering
PONG, T., Computer Science and Engineering
POON, A., Electronic and Computer Engineering
POON, R., Biochemistry
QI, R., Biochemistry
QI, X., Industrial Engineering and Logistics Management
QIAN, P., Biology
QIAN, T., Mathematics
QIU, H., Mechanical Engineering

QIU, L., Electronic and Computer Engineering
QU, H., Computer Science and Engineering
QU, J., Electronic and Computer Engineering
QUAN, L., Computer Science and Engineering
RENNEBERG, R., Chemistry
SANDER, P., Computer Science and Engineering
SAUTMAN, B., Social Science
SEASHOLES, M., Finance
SEN, R., Finance
SENGUPTA, J., Marketing
SHANG, C., Civil and Environmental Engineering
SHAO, Q., Mathematics
SHARIF, N., Social Science
SHEN, H., Computer Science and Engineering
SHEN, V., Computer Science and Engineering
SHENG, P., Physics
SHI, B., Electronic and Computer Engineering
SHI, L., Electronic and Computer Engineering
SHIMOKAWA, S., Social Science
SHUM, S., Information Systems, Business Statistics and Operations Management
SIN, J., Electronic and Computer Engineering
SIN, R., Information Systems, Business Statistics and Operations Management
SING, M., Social Science
SO, A., Social Science
SO, M., Information Systems, Business Statistics and Operations Management
SO, R., Industrial Engineering and Logistics Management
SOU, I., Physics
STAM, W., Management
SULLIVAN, B., Management
SUN, J., Humanities
SUN, Q., Mechanical Engineering
SZETO, K., Physics
TAI, C., Computer Science and Engineering
TAKEUCHI, R., Management
TAM, K., Information Systems, Business Statistics and Operations Management
TAM, K., Social Science
TAM, W., Physics
TANAKA, M., Economics
TANG, B., Chemistry
TANG, C., Computer Science and Engineering
TANG, K., Mechanical Engineering
TANG, Z., Physics
THONG, J., Information Systems, Business Statistics and Operations Management
TONG, P., Physics
TSANG, S., Biochemistry
TSANG, D., Electronic and Computer Engineering
TSENG, M., Industrial Engineering and Logistics Management
TSIM, K., Biology
TSUI, C., Electronic and Computer Engineering
TSUNG, F., Industrial Engineering and Logistics Management
TU, J., Social Science
TUNG, Y., Civil and Environmental Engineering
VISARIA, S., Economics
WAN, J., Biochemistry
WAN, X., Information Systems, Business Statistics and Operations Management
WANG, G., Civil and Environmental Engineering
WANG, H., Management
WANG, J., Civil and Environmental Engineering
WANG, J., Physics
WANG, N., Physics
WANG, P., Economics
WANG, S., Accounting
WANG, S., Economics
WANG, W., Biology
WANG, X., Humanities
WANG, X., Mathematics

WANG, X., Physics
WANG, Y., Civil and Environmental Engineering
WANG, Y., Economics
WEI, K., Finance
WEI, Z., Biochemistry
WEN, W., Physics
WEN, Z., Biochemistry
WILLIAMS, I., Chemistry
WONG, A., Electronic and Computer Engineering
WONG, E., Management
WONG, G., Physics
WONG, J., Biology
WONG, K., Physics
WONG, L., Humanities
WONG, M., Electronic and Computer Engineering
WONG, M., Mathematics
WONG, M., Physics
WONG, R., Computer Science and Engineering
WONG, R., Social Science
WONG, S., Humanities
WONG, W., Biochemistry
WONG, Y., Biology
WONG, Y., Biochemistry
WU, D., Computer Science and Engineering
WU, H., Chemistry
WU, J., Mechanical EngineeringWU, L., Mathematics
WU, X., Social Science
WU, Y., Chemistry
WU, Z., Biochemistry
XIA, J., Biochemistry
XIANG, Y., Marketing
XIANG, Y., Mathematics
XIE, D., Economics
XIE, Y., Biology
XIJUN HU, X., Chemical and Biomolecular Engineering
XU, B., Chemistry
XU, C., Computer Science and Engineering
XU, J., Economics
XU, J., Electronic and Computer Engineering
XU, K., Mathematics
XU, S., Information Systems, Business Statistics and Operations Management
XU, Y., Information Systems, Business Statistics and Operations Management
XUE, H., Biochemistry
YAN, M., Mathematics
YAN, Y., Chemistry
YANG, H., Civil and Environmental Engineering
YANG, Q., Computer Science and Engineering
YANG, S., Chemistry
YANG, Z., Physics
YAO, S., Mechanical Engineering
YE, W., Mechanical Engineering
YEE, A., Humanities
YEUNG, K., Chemical and Biomolecular Engineering
YEUNG, D., Computer Science and Engineering
YI, K., Computer Science and Engineering
YIK, M., Social Science
YIP, K., Humanities
YIU, C., Humanities
YOU, H., Accounting
YU, J., Chemistry
YU, J., Environment
YU, M., Information Systems, Business Statistics and Operations Management
YU, S., Information Systems, Business Statistics and Operations Management
YU, T., Mechanical Engineering
YU, W., Electronic and Computer Engineering
YUAN, G., Electronic and Computer Engineering
ZHANG, M., Humanities
YUEN, M., Mechanical Engineering
ZANG, A., Accounting
ZENG, B., Electronic and Computer Engineering

ZHANG, C., Computer Science and Engineering
ZHANG, C., Finance
ZHANG, G., Accounting
ZHANG, H., Information Systems, Business Statistics and Operations Management
ZHANG, J., Industrial Engineering and Logistics Management
ZHANG, L., Civil and Environmental Engineering
ZHANG, M., Accounting
ZHANG, M., Biochemistry
ZHANG, M., Information Systems, Business Statistics and Operations Management
ZHANG, N., Computer Science and Engineering
ZHANG, Q., Computer Science and Engineering
ZHANG, R., Industrial Engineering and Logistics Management
ZHANG, T., Mechanical Engineering
ZHANG, X., Civil and Environmental Engineering
ZHANG, Y., Accounting
ZHANG, Z., Physics
ZHAO, J., Civil and Environmental Engineering
ZHAO, T., Mechanical Engineering
ZHAO, Y., Marketing
ZHENG, S., Information Systems, Business Statistics and Operations Management
ZHENG, R., Information Systems, Business Statistics and Operations Management
ZHOU, R., Marketing
ZHU, G., Biochemistry
ZHU, J., Management
ZHU, K., Industrial Engineering and Logistics Management
ZHU, Y., Mathematics
ZHU, Y., Social Science
ZHU, X., Humanities
ZHU, T., Economics
ZWEIG, D., Social Science

LINGNAN UNIVERSITY

8 Castle Peak Rd, Tuen Mun, New Territories
Telephone: (852) 26168888
Fax: (852) 24638363
E-mail: prinfo@ln.edu.hk
Internet: www.ln.edu.hk
Founded 1888 as Christian College in China, as Lingan College Co Ltd 1967, self-accrediting status 1998, present name 1999
Academic year: September to August
Chancellor: Hon DONALD YAM-KUEN TSANG
Pres.: Prof. CHAN YUK-SHEE
Vice-Pres.: Prof. SEADE JESÚS
Comptroller: HERDIP SINGH
Dean of Students: Prof. LEE HUNG-KAI
Registrar: LOK-WOOD MUI
Univ. Librarian: FREDERICK NESTA
Library of 300,000 vols
Number of teachers: 226
Number of students: 4,879

DEANS

Faculty of Arts: NATHAN PAISLEY LIVINGSTON
Faculty of Business: Prof. KOON-HUNG CHAN
Faculty of Social Sciences: Prof. DAVID ROSSER PHILLIPS

OPEN UNIVERSITY OF HONG KONG

30 Good Shepherd St, Homantin, Kowloon
Telephone: (852) 27112100
Fax: (852) 27150760
E-mail: infoctr@ic.ouhk.edu.hk
Internet: www.ouhk.edu.hk
Founded 1989 as Open Learning Institute of Hong Kong, present location 1996, present name and status 1997

Public control
Chancellor: Hon. CHIEF EXEC. OF THE HONG KONG SPEC. ADMIN. REGION
Pres.: Prof. JOHN LEONG CHI-YAN
Vice-Pres. for Academic Affairs: Prof. DANNY WONG
Vice-Pres. for Technology and Devt: Prof. LEUNG CHUN-MING
Registrar: LEE SHU WING
Librarian: MOK WONG WAI-MAN

Library of 500,000 vols, 133,000 printed and multimedia items, 20,200 e-books, 980 printed serials, 18,200 electronic serials
Number of teachers: 590 full-time, 1,060 part-time
Number of students: 17,000 (full-time and distance learning)

DEANS

School of Arts and Social Sciences: Prof. TAM KWOK-KAN
School of Business and Administration: Prof. IP YIU-KEUNG
School of Education and Languages: YVONNE FUNG SHI YUK-HANG
School of Science and Technology: Prof. HO KIN CHUNG

UNIVERSITY OF HONG KONG

Pokfulam Rd, Pokfulam
Telephone: (852) 28592111
Fax: (852) 28582549
E-mail: cpao@hku.hk
Internet: www.hku.hk
Founded 1912
Academic year: September to June
Chancellor: CHIEF EXEC. OF THE HONG KONG SPEC. ADMIN. REGION
Pro-Chancellor: Dr The Hon. DAVID LI KWOK PO
Vice-Chancellor and Pres.: Prof. LAP-CHEE TSUI
Provost: Prof. RICHARD WONG YUE CHIM
Pro-Vice-Chancellor and Vice-Pres. for Infrastructure: Prof. JOHN GRAHAM MALPAS
Pro-Vice-Chancellor and Vice-Pres. for Research: Prof. PAUL TAM KWONG HANG
Pro-Vice-Chancellor and Vice-Pres. for Staffing: Prof. JOSEPH LEE HUN WEI
Pro-Vice-Chancellor and Vice-Pres. for Teaching and Learning: Prof. AMY TSUI BIK MAY
Pro-Vice-Chancellor and Vice-Pres. for Univ. Relations: Prof. SHEW-PING CHOW
Treas.: PAUL CHOW MAN YIU (acting)
Registrar: HENRY WAI WING KUN
Librarian: Dr A. W. FERGUSON

Number of teachers: 860 full-time
Number of students: 23,400

Publications: *Bulletin* (3–4 a year), *Centennial Campus Newsletter* (4 a year), *Convocation Newsletter* (4 a year), *Journal of Oriental Studies* (2 a year)

DEANS

Faculty of Architecture: Prof. RALPH LERNER
Faculty of Arts: Prof. LOUIE KAM HUNG (acting)
Faculty of Business and Economics: Prof. ERIC C. CHANG (acting)
Faculty of Dentistry: Prof. L. P. SAMARANAYAKE
Faculty of Education: Prof. SHIRLEY GRUNDY
Faculty of Engineering: Prof. CHEW WENG CHO
Faculty of Law: Prof. JOHANNES CHAN MAN MUN
Faculty of Medicine: Prof. LEE SUM-PING
Faculty of Science: Dr KWOK SUN
Faculty of Social Sciences: Dr IAN HOLLIDAY

PROFESSORS

ABERNETHY, A. B., Human Performance

AU, T. K. F., Psychology
BRAY, T. M., Education
BURNS, J. P., Politics and Public Administration
CHAN, D. K. O., Zoology
CHAN, M. M. W., Medicine
CHAN, V. N. Y., Medicine
CHANG, E. C., Business
CHAU, K. W., Real Estate and Construction
CHE, C. M., Chemistry
CHEAH, K. S. E., Biochemistry
CHENG, K. M., Education
CHENG, K. S., Physics
CHIN, F. Y. L., Computer Science and Information Systems
CHO, C. H., Pharmacology
CHOW, N. W. S., Social Work and Social Administration
CHOW, S. P., Orthopaedic Surgery
CHWANG, A. T. Y., Mechanical Engineering
DUGGAN, B. J., Mechanical Engineering
FAN, S. T., Surgery
FANG, H. H. P., Civil Engineering
FREWER, R. J. B., Architecture
FUNG, P. C. W., Medicine
GHAI, Y. P., Law
GOLDSTEIN, L., Philosophy
HAGG, E. U. O., Dentistry
HANSEN, C., Philosophy
HEDLEY, A. J., Community Medicine
HO, P. C., Obstetrics and Gynaecology
IP, M. S. M., Medicine
JIM, C. Y., Geography
KO, R. C. C., Zoology
KUMANA, C. R., Medicine
KUNG, H., Molecular Biology
LAI, C. L., Medicine
LAI, K. N., Medicine
LAM, E., Botany
LAM, K. S. L., Medicine
LAM, S. K., Medicine
LAM, T. H., Community Medicine
LAM, W. K., Medicine
LAU, A. H. L., Business
LAU, C. P., Medicine
LAU, Y. L., Paediatrics and Adolescent Medicine
LEE, C. F., Civil Engineering
LEE, J. H. W., Civil Engineering
LI, V. O. K., Electrical and Electronic Engineering
LI, W. K., Statistics and Actuarial Science
LIANG, R. H. S., Medicine
LIE KEN JIE, M. S. F., Chemistry
LO, C. M., Surgery
LUK, K. D. K., Orthopaedic Surgery
MALPAS, J. G., Earth Sciences
MAN, R. Y. K., Mathematics
MOK, N., Mathematics
NG, T. S., Electrical and Electronic Engineering
NUNAN, D. C., English Centre
SAMARANAYAKE, L. P., Dentistry
SHERRIN, C. H., Professional Legal Education
TAM, P. K. H., Surgery
TAMBLING, J. C. R., Comparative Literature
TANG, S. W., Psychiatry
TIDEMAN, H., Dentistry
TONG, H., Statistics
TSE, D. K. C., Business
TSUI, A. B. M., Education
WEI, W. I., Surgery
WONG, J., Surgery
WONG, R. Y. C., Economics and Finance
WONG, S. L., Sociology
WU, F. F., Electrical and Electronic Engineering
YAM, V. W. W., Chemistry
YANG, E. S., Electrical and Electronic Engineering
YEH, A. G. O., Urban Planning and Environmental Management
YUEN, K. Y., Microbiology
ZHANG, F., Physics

Colleges

Chung Chi College: Taipo Rd, New Territories; tel. (852) 26098009; e-mail ccc@cuhk .edu.hk; internet www.cuhk.edu.hk/ccc; f. 1951, present location 1956, present status 1963; attached to Chinese Univ. of Hong Kong; depts of arts, business administration, education, engineering, law, medicine, science and social science; 2,807 students; Head Prof. YUEN-SANG LEUNG; Dean of Gen. Education Prof. KWOK-NAM LEUNG; Dean of Students Prof. WING-PING FONG; Librarian KEVIN LEUNG; publs *Chung Chi Alumni* (4 a year, electronic), *Chung Chi Campus Newsletter*.

New Asia College: Sha Tin, New Territories; tel. (852) 26097609; fax (852) 26035418; e-mail nac@cuhk.edu.hk; internet www3 .cuhk.edu.hk/na; f. 1949 as Asia Evening College of Arts and Commerce, present name 1950, present status and location 1973; attached to Chinese Univ. of Hong Kong; 2,800 students; Head Prof. HENRY WONG; Dean of Gen. Education Prof. S. O. CHAN; Dean of Students Prof. MARIA S. M. TAM; publs *Ch'ien Mu Lectures in History and Culture* (monograph series), *New Asia College Academic Bulletin, New Asia Life Monthly*.

United College: 2nd Fl., Tsang Shiu Tim Bldg, Chinese Univ. of Hong Kong, Sha Tin, New Territories; tel. (852) 26097575; fax (852) 26035412; e-mail unitedcollege@cuhk .edu.hk; internet www2.cuhk.edu.hk/uc; f. 1956 by merger of five colleges: Canton Overseas, Kwang Hsia, Wah Kiu, Wen Hua and Ping Jing College of Accountancy, present status 1959, present location 1971; attached to Chinese Univ. of Hong Kong; faculties of arts, business administration, education, engineering, law, medicine, science and social science; 2,931 students; Head Prof. FUNG KWOK-PUI; Dean of Gen. Education Prof. JIMMY C. M. YU; Dean of Students

Prof. STEPHEN H. S. WONG; Librarian YIFENG WU; publs *United College Alumni Newsletter* (4 a year), *United Bulletin, United We Advance*.

Shaw College: LG1, Wen Lan Tang; tel. (852) 26097363; fax (852) 26035427; e-mail shaw-college@cuhk.edu.hk; internet www5 .cuhk.edu.hk/shaw; f. 1990; attached to Chinese Univ. of Hong Kong; Head Prof. JOSEPH J. Y. SUNG; Dean of Gen. Education Prof. HO PUI-YIN; Dean of Students Prof. FREEDOM Y. K. LEUNG; publs *Shaw Link, Shaw Net*.

Maritime Services Training Institute: 23 Castle Peak Rd, Tai Lam Chung, Tuen Mun, New Territories; tel. (852) 24583833; fax (852) 24400308; e-mail msti@vtc.edu.hk; internet www.vtc.edu.hk/vtc/web/template/ about_the_centr.jsp?fldr_id=498; f. 1988; attached to Vocational Training Ccl; programmes for new entrants and professionals in marine-related and shore-based industry.

Hong Kong Design Institute: Planning Team Office, Room 735, VTC Tower, 27 Wood Rd, Wan Chai; tel. (852) 28361912; fax (852) 35204185; e-mail hkdi@vtc.edu.hk; internet www.hkdi.edu.hk; f. 2007; attached to Vocational Training Ccl; depts of designs, engineering, fashion and textiles, printing and digital media, toy design and multimedia exhibition design; at present all programmes are delivered at IVE campuses; new HKDI campus at Tiu Keng Leng opens in 2010–11; Exec. Dir Dr CARRIE WILLIS; publ. *D. I Winners*.

Hong Kong Academy for Performing Arts: 1 Gloucester Rd, Wan Chai; tel. (852) 25848500; fax (852) 28024372; e-mail aso@ hkapa.edu; internet www.hkapa.edu; f. 1984, present status 1992; schools of dance, drama, film and television, music, theatre and entertainment arts and Chinese traditional theatre; library: 18,000 vols of Chinese books, 48,000 vols of English books, 1,900

books in other languages, 25,000 music scores, 36,000 audiovisual items, 329 printed journals, 2,100 titles in archives, 600 slide sets and kits, 7,400 electronic plays, 5,200 e-books, 1,300 electronic journal titles, 40 reference and aggregator databases; 453 teachers (79 full-time, 374 part-time); 749 students; Pres. CHIEF EXEC. OF THE HONG KONG SPEC. ADMIN. REGION; Dir Prof. KEVIN THOMPSON; Assoc. Dir for Admin. and Registrar Dr HERBERT HUEY; Assoc. Dir for Operations PHILIP SODEN; Librarian LING WAI-KING; publ. *Dramatic Arts* (1 a year).

Hong Kong Institute of Education: 10 Lo Ping Rd, Tai Po, New Territories; tel. (852) 29488888; fax (852) 29486000; e-mail info@ ied.edu.hk; internet www.ied.edu.hk; f. 1994 by merger of four colleges of education and the Institute of Language in Education, present location 1997, self-accrediting status 2004; faculties of arts and sciences, education studies, languages; library: 605,914 vols; 412 teachers; 7,153 students; Pres. Prof. ANTHONY B. L. CHEUNG; Vice-Pres. for Academic Affairs Prof. LEE WING ON; Vice-Pres. for Admin. Prof. CHRIS MONG CHAN; Vice-Pres. for Research and Devt Prof. CHENG YIN CHEONG; publs *Education Focus, Education Matters, Joy of Learning* (bilingual magazine).

IVE Morrison Hill: 6 Oi Kwan Rd, Wan Chai; tel. (852) 25745321; fax (852) 25729847; e-mail csivemh@vtc.edu.hk; internet www.vtc.edu.hk/ti/mhti/homepage/ english; f. 1969, fmrly Morrison Hill Technical Institute; attached to Vocational Training Ccl; depts of business administration, construction, information and communications technology, real estate and facilities management; library: 50,000 books, 200 periodicals; 300 full-time teachers; 6,260 students; Prin. DANIEL KWOH KAI HING.

MACAO

Regulatory Body

NATIONAL BODY

Gabinete de Apoio ao Ensino Superior (Tertiary Education Services Office): Calçada de St Agostinho 19, Edif. Nam Yue, 13° a 15° Andares; tel. (853) 28345403; fax (853) 28318401; e-mail info@gaes.gov.mo; internet www.gaes.gov.mo; f. 1992; govt dept in charge of higher education affairs under the leadership of the Sec. for Social Affairs and Culture; formulates policies for the devt of higher education; helps in the evaluation of higher education instns; Dir Prof. CHAN PAK-FAI; publs *Data of Higher Education in Macao (Numbers of Staff and Students)* (1 a year, in Chinese, online version in English), *Higher Education Bursaries* (1 a year, in Chinese), *Guidebook for Higher Education in Macao* (1 a year, in Chinese), *Q&A: Studying in a Higher Education Institution of Macao* (1 a year, simplified Chinese).

Learned Societies

GENERAL

Fundação Macau (Macao Foundation): Ave da República 6; tel. (853) 28966777; fax (853) 28968658; e-mail info@fm.org.mo; internet www.fmac.org.mo; conducts research on cultural, social, economic, educational, scientific, academic, philanthropic activities for the promotion of Macao; Pres. CHUI SAI ON; Pres. for Admin. VITOR NG.

ARCHITECTURE AND TOWN PLANNING

Architects Association of Macau:tel. (853) 28703458; fax (853) 28704089; e-mail info@macaoarchitects.com; internet www .macaoarchitects.com; f. 1980 as Macau Association of Architects in Private Practice, present name 1988; Dir EDDIE Y. K. WONG; Gen-Sec. JOY TIN TIN CHOI.

ECONOMICS, LAW AND POLITICS

Associação de Ciências Sociais de Macau (Macao Society of Social Sciences): Estrada Adolfo Loureiro 3A, Edif. Tak On, 3rd Floor A, POB 957; tel. (853) 28319880; fax (853) 28319880; f. 1985; studies and serves the society of Macao; 40 mems; Pres. HUANG WEI-WEN; Sec. CHEONG CHOK FU; publ. *Huo Keng* (Mirror of Macao, 2 a year).

FINE AND PERFORMING ARTS

Instituto Cultural do Governo da R. A. E. de Macau (Cultural Affairs Bureau): Praça do Tap Seac, Edif. do Instituto Cultural; tel. (853) 83996699; fax (853) 28366899; e-mail postoffice@icm.gov.mo; internet www.icm.gov.mo; f. 1982, fmrly Cultural Institute of Macao, reorganized to present status 1994; cultural studies; classes for music, drama and ballet; promotion of cultural events; also oversees the Macao

Historical Archives, the Macao Central Library and the Macao Museum; Pres. Dra HEIDI HO; publ. *Revista de Cultura* (in English, Chinese and Portuguese, 4 a year).

LANGUAGE AND LITERATURE

Alliance Française: 4/F Travessa do Bom Jesus R/C; tel. (853) 28965342; fax (853) 28962697; e-mail info.macao@afchine.org; internet www.alliancefrancaise.org.mo; f. 1987; offers courses and examinations in French language and culture and promotes cultural exchange with France; 11 mems; Pres. JOAQUIM JORGE PERESTRELO NETO VALENTE; Dir (vacant); Head of Studies PATRICIA BERTONECHE.

MEDICINE

Nurses Association of Macao: Ave Macao 1-1B, E Sunrise House 2-D Block; tel. (853) 28525614; fax (853) 28581787; e-mail naom@macau.ctm.net; internet www.naom.org.mo; f. 1986; improves professional standards of care and promotes basic rights of nurses; 650 mems; Pres. LI XUE-PING; Vice-Pres. SHU-CHEN HUANG; Chair. TIAN JIE BING; Sec.-Gen. MAO XIAONI.

Research Institutes

GENERAL

Instituto Ricci de Macau (Macau Ricci Institute): Ave Cons. Ferreira de Almeida 95-E; tel. (853) 28532536; fax (853) 28568274; e-mail info@riccimac.org; internet www.riccimac.org; f. 1999, present status 1999; non-profit org.; studies and research dedicated to fostering mutual understanding between China and the world community; library of 10,198 Chinese books, 7,782 Western books, 343 periodicals; Dir ARTUR WARDEGA; Vice-Dir LUÍS SEQUEIRA; Gen.-Sec. JERÓNIMO HUNG; Sec. SANDY LEI HAO WENG; publs *Chinese Cross Currents* (in Chinese and English, 4 a year), *Macau Ricci Institute Studies*.

ECONOMICS, LAW AND POLITICS

Social, Economic and Public Policy Research Centre: Rua de Luís Gonzaga Gomes; tel. (853) 85996267; fax (853) 28704200; e-mail cepes@ipm.edu.mo; internet www.ipm.edu.mo/cepes; f. 2007; attached to Macao Polytechnic Institute; research areas incl. gambling industry of Macao, devt of economy, society, govt and public policy in Macao; provides consultancy services to Macao Spec. Admin. Region Govt; Exec. Deputy Dir Prof. CHEN QINGYUN.

MEDICINE

Institute of Chinese Medical Sciences: c/o Univ. of Macao, Ave Padre Tomás Pereira SJ, Taipa; tel. (853) 83974698; fax (853) 28841358; e-mail icms.enquiry@umac.mo; internet www.umac.mo/icms; f. 2002; attached to Univ. of Macao; develops postgraduate education; trains management and scientific research professionals in medical science; researches in medicine and pharmacology; networks with int. instns and orgs; promotes traditional Chinese medicine; Dir YITAO WANG.

Macau Institute for Applied Research in Medicine and Health: Macau Univ. of Science and Technology, Ave Wai Long, Taipa; tel. (853) 88972633; fax (853) 28822799; e-mail miar@must.edu.mo; internet www.mustf-miar.org.mo; attached to Macau Univ. of Science and Technology; provides educational service, clinical practice and various biological research and devt for the Faculty of Chinese Medicine (Macau

Univ. of Science and Technology); also provides a platform in Macao for biotechnology industrialization, modernization and internationalization of Chinese medicine; Dir Dr TIMOTHY MING WAI CHAN; Deputy Dir Dr BRAD W. C. LAU.

Libraries and Archives

Macao

Arquivo Histórico de Macau (Macao Historical Archives): Praca do Tap Seac, Edif. do Instituto Cultural; tel. (853) 28592919; fax (853) 28561495; e-mail info.ah@icm.gov.mo; internet www.archives.gov.mo; f. 1952 as Macao Gen. Archives, renamed and restructured 1979; attached to Instituto Cultural do Governo da R.A.E. de Macau (Cultural Affairs Bureau); promotes research; holds govt gazettes, original records, microfilms of rare works on Macao's history and Portugal's relations with the Far East; 7,000 vols; Dir MARIE IMELDA MACLEOD; publ. *Boletim do Arquivo Histórico de Macau*.

Biblioteca Central de Macau (Macao Central Library): Ave Conselheiro Ferreira de Almeida 89A-B; tel. (853) 28567576; fax (853) 28318756; e-mail info.bc@icm.gov.mo; internet www.library.gov.mo; f. 1895; attached to Instituto Cultural do Governo da R.A.E. de Macau (Cultural Affairs Bureau); public network of main library and 6 brs; gen. colln; Chinese Books (Sir Robert Ho Tung); highlights traditional culture and encourages leisure reading through reading activities, exhibitions and lectures; participates in Library Week; 550,000 vols; Dir TANG, MEI LIN; publs *Boletim Bibliográfico de Macau, Boletim de Literatura Infantil, Boletim Bibliográfico de Literatura Portuguesa*.

Biblioteca da Ilha Verde (Ilha Verde Library): Ave de Concórdia 281, 4th Floor Edif. 'May Fair Garden' II Fase; tel. (853) 28225783; fax (853) 28225474; internet www.library.gov.mo/pt/general/library_3.aspx; f. 1995; attached to Macao Central Library; cultural and educational centre for dissemination of entertainment and information; 34,000 vols of monographs, 2,400 multimedia material, 72 newspaper titles and 435 journals.

Biblioteca de Coloane (Library of Coloane): Rua de 5 de Outubro, Coloane; tel. and fax (853) 28882254; internet www.library.gov.mo/pt/general/library_5.aspx; f. 1983; attached to Macao Central Library; 8,700 vols of monographs, 16 newspaper titles and 59 magazine titles.

Biblioteca de Mong Há (Mong Ha Library): Bairro de Mong Há, near the Pavilion de Mong Ha; tel. (853) 28317288; fax (853) 28481963; internet www.library.gov.mo/pt/general/library_4.aspx; f. 1988; attached to Macao Central Library; 21,000 vols incl. monographs, 51 journal titles and 229 magazines.

Biblioteca do Edifício do IACM (IACM Building Library): Ave de Almeida Ribeiro 163, Edif. do IACM; tel. (853) 28572233; fax (853) 28312772; internet www.library.gov.mo/pt/general/library_6.aspx; f. 1929 fmrly Biblioteca do Leal Senado; attached to Macao Central Library; spec. collns incl. historical and scholarly works on China and Portuguese rule in the Far East and Africa; 30,000 vols, 19,000 monographs, 22 journals, 99 newspapers.

Biblioteca Sir Robert Ho Tung (Sir Robert Ho Tung Library): Largo do Sto. Agostinho 3; tel. (853) 28377117; fax (853) 28314456; internet www.library.gov.mo/pt/general/library_2.aspx; f. 1958; attached to Macao Central Library; largest public library

in Macao; 100,000 vols, incl. 5,000 ancient Chinese books, 79,924 other books, 4,925 multimedia materials, 74 journals, 732 magazines, 23 newspaper titles; Librarian SAM CHAN FAI; publ. *Boletim Bibliográfico de Macau*.

Museums and Art Galleries

Macao

Macao Tea Culture House: Lou Lim Ieoc Garden, Ave do Conselheiro Ferreira de Almeida; tel. (853) 28827103; fax (853) 28827102; e-mail dic@iacm.gov.mo; internet www.iacm.gov.mo/museum; f. 2005; attached to Civic and Municipal Affairs Bureau; represents China's tea culture; Macao's role in the history of Chinese tea propagation and trade.

Macau Maritime Museum: 1 Largo do Pagode da Barra; tel. (853) 28595481; fax (853) 28512160; e-mail museumaritimo@marine.gov.mo; internet www.museumaritimo.gov.mo; f. 1987, present bldg 1990; plans and drawings of old Portuguese vessels such as ships of war, merchant ships and fishing vessels; photographs dating from 1920; library of 2,500 vols.

Museu das Comunicações (Communications Museum): Estrada D. Maria II 7; tel. (853) 28718570; fax (853) 28718018; e-mail info@macao.communications.museum; internet macao.communications.museum; f. 2006; stimulates interest in philatelic colln, stamp colln; promotes Macao philately and scientific and technical knowledge of telecommunications.

Museu de Arte de Macau (Macao Museum of Art): Centro Cultural de Macau, Ave Xian Xing Hai s/n Nape; tel. (853) 287919814; fax (853) 28751317; e-mail artmuseum@iacm.gov.mo; internet www.artmuseum.gov.mo; f. 1999; attached to Civil and Municipal Affairs Bureau; collns incl. Shi Wan ceramics, Chinese painting and calligraphy, historical pictures, Macao contemporary art, ceramics and stoneware excavated from Heisha in Macao, seal cutting from Guangdong, Western historical paintings, poster design, photographic works; attached auditorium and library; Dir CHAN HOU SENG.

Museu de Macau (Museum of Macao): Praceta do Museu de Macau 112; tel. (853) 28357911; fax (853) 28358503; e-mail info.mm@icm.gov.mo; internet www.macaumuseum.gov.mo; f. 1998; attached to Instituto Cultural do Governo da R.A.E. de Macau; promotes understanding and interest in Macao's history and cultural heritage; creates and develops collns related to archaeology, history, natural history, ethnography and ethnology; serves as a centre for learning through research and study; preserves and records materials of historical and cultural significance; library of 3,000 vols; Dir CHAN IENG HIN; publ. *Museum of Macao* (magazine).

Nature and Agriculture Museum: Seac Pai Van Park, Coloane Island; tel. (853) 28870277; fax (853) 28870271; e-mail decn@iacm.gov.mo; internet nature.iacm.gov.mo.

Temporary Exhibition Gallery of the Civic and Municipal Affairs Bureau (IACM): Ave Almeida Ribeiro 163, 'Leal Senado' Bldg; tel. (853) 89884100; internet www.iacm.gov.mo/museum; f. 1985; attached to Civic and Municipal Affairs Bureau; housed in historically significant 'Leal Senado' bldg; exhibits works of local and Chinese artists.

Universities

UNIVERSIDADE DE CIÊNCIA E TECNOLOGIA DE MACAU
(Macau University of Science and Technology)

Avenida Wai Long, Taipa
Telephone: (853) 28881122
Fax: (853) 28880022
E-mail: enquiry@must.edu.mo
Internet: www.must.edu.mo
Founded 2000
Private control
Chancellor: Dr LIU CHAK WAN
Rector: Prof. XU AO AO
Vice Rector: Acad. LIU REN HUAI
Vice Rector: Prof. CHAN LAI KOW
Registrar: Prof. KEITH ROBERT BARCLAY MORRISON
Univ. Librarian: Prof. DAI LONG JI
Library of 100,000 vols, 15,000 periodicals, electronic database

DEANS

Faculty of Arts and Humanities: Dr CHEN NAI CHI
Faculty of Chinese Medicine: Prof. XIANG PING
Faculty of Health Sciences: Prof. LAM WAI KEI
Faculty of Information Technology: Prof. DING LI YA
Faculty of International Tourism: Prof. ALIANA LEONG MAN WAI
Faculty of Law: Prof. MI JIAN
Faculty of Management and Administration: Prof. CHAN LAI KOW
School of Graduate Studies: Prof. TANG HUNG LIAN

UNIVERSIDADE DE MACAU
(University of Macao)

Ave Padre Tomás Pereira, Taipa
Telephone: (853) 28831622
Fax: (853) 28831694
E-mail: info@umac.mo
Internet: www.umac.mo
Founded 1981 as Univ. of East Asia, present name 1991
State control
Languages of instruction: Chinese, Portuguese, English
Academic year: September to June
Chancellor: CHIEF EXEC. OF MACAO SPEC. ADMIN. REGION
Rector: Prof. WEI ZHAO
Vice-Rector for Academic Affairs: Prof. SIMON SHUN MAN HO
Vice-Rector for Admin.: Dr ALEX LAI IAT LONG
Vice-Rector for Research: Prof. RUI PAULO DA SILVA MARTINS
Librarian: Dr PAUL POON WAH TUNG
Library: 3m. vols, 300,000 periodicals, 13,000 vols old Chinese edns, 1m. ebooks, 35,000 online journals
Number of teachers: 407
Number of students: 6,791
Publications: *Boletim da Faculdade de Direito* (in Chinese and Portuguese, 2 a year), *Journal of Macau Studies* (6 a year)

DEANS

Faculty of Business Administration: Prof. JACKY YUK CHOW SO
Faculty of Education: Prof. GEORGE CHENG CHUN WAI
Faculty of Law: Prof. ZENG LINGLIANG
Faculty of Science and Technology: Prof. PHILIP CHEN CHUN LUNG

Faculty of Social Sciences and Humanities: Prof. HAO YUFAN
Honours College: Prof. MOK KAI MENG
Institute of Chinese Medical Sciences: Prof. WANG YI TAO

Colleges

Instituto de Formação Turística (Institute for Tourism Studies): Colina de Mong-Há; tel. (853) 28561252; fax (853) 28519058; e-mail iftpr@ift.edu.mo; internet www.ift.edu .mo; f. 1995, governed by Sec. for Social Affairs and Culture of the Macao Spec. Admin. Region Govt; offers degree programmes in heritage, hospitality, tourism, tourism event and tourism retail, marketing management; Pres. Prof. FANNY VONG.

Instituto Polytécnico de Macau (Macao Polytechnic Institute): Rua Luis Gonzaga Gomes; tel. (853) 28578722; fax (853) 28308801; e-mail webadmin@ipm.edu.mo; internet www.ipm.edu.mo; f. 1991; programmes in Chinese–English translation and interpretation, Chinese–Portuguese translation and interpretation, accounting and finance, computer studies, design, e-commerce, management, music, nursing and biomedical science, public administration, physical education and sports, social work, visual arts; 500 teachers; 2,800 students; Pres. Prof. LEI HEONG IOK; Vice-Pres. Prof. YIN LEI; Sec.-Gen. RAYMOND CHAN; publs *Journal of MPI* (in Chinese and English, 4 a year), *Journal of Sino-Western Cultural Studies* (2 a year).

CHINA (TAIWAN)

The Higher Education System

Until 1947 Taiwan was governed from the mainland China; however, in 1947 the Chinese communists came to power in Beijing, and the National Government was forced to remove itself to Taipei, the capital of Taiwan, where it established the 'Republic of China'. The population is mainly Chinese in origin, and the official language is Mandarin (Guoyu); Taiwanese, Hakka and English are also spoken. Most universities have been founded since the establishment of the Republic of China, but some were formerly mainland institutions that either relocated during the Communist takeover or were refounded; these include Fu-Jen Catholic University (founded in 1925 in Beijing), National Central University (originally based in Nanking), National Chiao Tung University (founded in 1896 in Shanghai), National Tsing Hua University (founded in 1911 in Beijing), and Soochow University (founded in 1900 in the mainland province of Jiangsu). In 2008/09 there were 162 universities, junior colleges and independent colleges, most of which offer postgraduate facilities; total enrolment in higher education in that year was 1,337,455 students. In 1987 the nine teachers' junior colleges were upgraded to teachers' colleges. These admit senior secondary graduates for a four-year course. High-school teachers are trained at normal universities. Higher education is highly centralized and the Constitution places great emphasis on the importance of education. The higher education system is based on the US model.

The Ministry of Education supervises the Universities and Colleges Joint Entrance Examination, which is required for admission to higher education. Students, however, may also gain admission through two other methods, either by applying directly to the institution in question and meeting that institution's entry requirements, or through recommendation on grounds of academic excellence.

Junior colleges, which provide two- or five-year Junior College Diploma programmes, are the first level of higher education. Two-year junior colleges admit graduates from Senior and Senior Vocational High Schools, while five-year junior colleges accept students from Junior High Schools. The majority of junior colleges are privately-run. Institutes of technology operate on a similar basis: two-year institutes admit junior college graduates and four-year institutes admit senior vocational school graduates. There are also 'Open' universities which specialize in adult education.

The Bachelors degree is the main university undergraduate qualification, and usually lasts four years, although specialist programmes such as dentistry and medicine may take six or seven years. At postgraduate level, the Masters degree requires one to four years' study, while the final qualification, the Doctorate, requires two to seven years' study following the Masters. Technical and vocational education and training is provided by senior vocational schools and junior colleges. Periods of study vary between two to five years.

Regulatory Bodies

GOVERNMENT

Bureau of International Cultural and Educational Relations: Ministry of Education, 13F, 5 Syujhou Rd, Jhongjheng District, Taipei 100; tel. (2) 23565608; fax (2) 23976978; e-mail cschang@mail.moe.gov.tw; internet english.moe.gov.tw; f. 1947; assists colleges and univs to enter into academic co-operation with foreign instns of higher learning; sponsors int. scholar exchange programs; organizes bilateral conferences on higher education; encourages Taiwan specialists, academics and doctoral students to participate in int. academic conferences abroad; provides Taiwan Scholarships to encourage exceptional foreign students to pursue degrees in Taiwan; works with govts, cultural and educational instns and commercial enterprises to obtain scholarships for Taiwan students; Dir-Gen. Dr CHIN-SHENG CHANG.

Ministry of Education: 5 Chung Shan South Rd, Taipei 10051; tel. (2) 23566051; fax (2) 23976978; internet www.moe.gov.tw; Minister TU CHENG-SHENG.

Research, Development and Evaluation Commission: 6/F, 2-2 Chi Nan Rd, Sec. 1, Taipei 10051; tel. (2) 23419066; fax (2) 23969990; e-mail service@rdec.gov.tw; internet rdec.gov.tw; Minister SHIH NING-JYE.

Learned Societies

GENERAL

Academia Sinica: 128 Academia Rd, Section 2, Nankang, Taipei 11529; tel. (2) 27822120; fax (2) 27853847; internet www .sinica.edu.tw; f. 1928; 220 mems; attached research institutes: see Research Institutes; library of 2,236,000 vols; Pres. Dr YUAN-TSEH LEE; Dir-Gen. Dr YIH-HSIUNG YEH; Chief of Secretariat Dr CHI-CHIUNG LO; publs *Bulletin of the Institute of Mathematics*, *Botanical Bulletin* (4 a year), *Zoological Studies* (4 a year), *Academia Economic* (papers), *Academia Sinica* (2 a year), *Asia-Major* (2 a year), *Asia-Pacific Forum* (4 a year), *Bulletin of the Institute of Ethnology*, *Bulletin of the Institute of History and Philosophy*, *Bulletin of the Institute of Modern History* (4 a year), *Disquisitions of the Past and Present* (2 a year), *EurAmerica Quarterly*, *Journal of Social Sciences and Philosophy*, *Language and Linguistics* (4 a year), *Mathmedia* (4 a year), *Newsletter for Modern Chinese History* (2 a year), *Research on Women in Chinese History* (1 a year), *Statistica Sinica* (4 a year), *Taiwan Economic Forecasts and Plicies Academia Economic Papers*, *Taiwan Historical Research* (2 a year), *Taiwan Journal of Anthropology* (2 a year), *Taiwanese Sociological Review* (2 a year).

China Academy: Hwa Kang, Yang Ming Shan; f. 1966; private instn for sinological studies, consisting of 20 academic asscns and research institutions and Chinese and foreign mems; 591 acads, 312 hon. acads, 1,815 fellows; library of 450,000 vols; Pres. CHANG CHI-YUN; Sec.-Gen. PAN WEI-HO; publs *Sino-American Relations* (in English, 4 a year), *Beautiful China Pictorial Monthly* (bilingual Chinese and English), *Sinological Monthly* (Chinese), *Sinological Quarterly* (Chinese), *Renaissance Monthly* (Chinese), *Chinese Culture* (in English, 4 a year).

China National Association of Literature and the Arts: 4 Lane 22, Nuigpo St W, Taipei.

China Society: 7 Lane 52, Wenchow St, Taipei; f. 1960; centre for Chinese studies; 100 mems; Pres. Dr CHEN CHI-LU; publ. *Journal* (1 a year).

AGRICULTURE, FISHERIES AND VETERINARY SCIENCE

Agricultural Association of China: 14 Wenchow St, Taipei; tel. (2) 23636681; f. 1917; mems: 159 instns, 2,554 individuals; Pres. TSONG-SHIEN WU; publ. *Journal* (4 a year).

Chinese Forestry Association: 2 Sec. 1, Hang-chow South Rd, Taipei 100; tel. (2) 33221299; fax (2) 33221099; e-mail cfa@forest .gov.tw; internet www.forestry.org.tw; f. 1967; 1,219 mems; Chair. JEN-TEH YEN; publ. *Quarterly Journal of Chinese Forestry*.

BIBLIOGRAPHY, LIBRARY SCIENCE AND MUSEOLOGY

Library Association of China: c/o National Central Library, 20 Chungshan S. Rd, Taipei 10001; tel. (2) 23312475; fax (2) 23700899; e-mail lac@ncl.edu.tw; internet www.lac.org.tw; f. 1953; 2,037 mems; Pres. CHAO-CHEN CHEN; Sec.-Gen. WEI PENG; publs *Journal of Library and Information Science Research* (2 a year), *Library Association of the Republic of China (Taiwan) e-NEWs* (12 a year), *Newsletter* (2 a year).

ECONOMICS, LAW AND POLITICS

Chinese National Foreign Relations Association: 3rd Floor, 94 Nanchang St, Sec. 1, Taipei; Pres. HUANG KUO-SHU.

National Bar Association: 124 Chungking South Rd, Sec. 1, Taipei.

HISTORY, GEOGRAPHY AND ARCHAEOLOGY

Academia Historica (Academy of History): 406 Sec. 2, Pei Yi Rd, Hsintien, Taipei; tel. (2)

22175500; fax (2) 22170317; internet www
.drnh.gov.tw; f. 1947; responsible for
researching and compiling material on Taiwanese national history; 175 mems; library
of 10,000,000 items (nat. archives, books,
documents); Pres. CHANG YEN HSIEN; Sec.-
Gen. Prof. LI CHUNG KUANG; publs *Bulletin* (2
a year), *Journal* (2 a year).

LANGUAGE AND LITERATURE

British Council: 2F-1, 106 XinYi Rd, Sec. 5,
Taipei 110; tel. (2) 87221000; fax (2)
87860985; e-mail enquiries@britishcouncil
.org.tw; internet www.britishcouncil.org/
taiwan; teaching centre; offers courses and
exams in English language and British culture and promotes cultural exchange with
the UK; attached office in Kaohsiung; Dir
GORDON SLAVEN.

Chinese Language Society: c/o Taiwan
Normal University, Hoping East Rd, Taipei;
f. 1953; Dir MAO TZU-SHUI; publ. *Chinese
Language Monthly*.

MEDICINE

Chinese Medical Association: 201 Shih-
Pai Rd, Sec. II, Taipei; f. 1915; 1,672 mems;
Pres. Dr KWANG-JUEI LO; Sec.-Gen. Dr YANG-
TE TSAI; publ. *Chinese Medical Journal* (12 a
year).

NATURAL SCIENCES

Mathematical Sciences

Chinese Statistical Association: 1 Nan
Chung Rd, Sec. 1, Taipei; f. 1941; 1,082
mems; Pres. C. C. LEE; publ. *Chinese Statistical Journal*.

**Mathematical Society of the Republic of
China:** Dept of Mathematics, National
Cheng Kung University, Tainan 70101; fax
(6) 2743191; Pres. LEE YUH-JIA; Sec. HUANG
YOUNG-YE.

Physical Sciences

Chemical Society: POB 1-18, Nankang,
Taipei 115; tel. (2) 27898574; fax (2)
26530440; e-mail ccswww@gate.sinica.edu
.tw; internet www.ccs.sinica.edu.tw; f. 1932;
3,000 mems; Sec.-Gen. LING-KANG LIU; publs
Hua Hsueh (in Chinese, 4 a year), *Journal*
(in English, 6 a year).

**Committee on the Promotion of the
Peaceful Uses of Atomic Energy:** 110
Yenping South Rd, Taipei; Pres. MILTON J.
T. SHIEH.

Physical Society of China: POB 23-30,
Taipei.

PHILOSOPHY AND PSYCHOLOGY

**Confucius-Mencius Society of the
Republic of China:** 45 Nanhai Rd, Taipei;
f. 1960; spreads knowledge about Confucius
and Mencius, seeks the improvement of
public morals and the creation of a better
society; 3,900 mems; Chair. Dr CHEN LI-FU;
Sec. HUA CHUNG-LIN; publ. *Confucius-Mencius Monthly*, *Journal of Confucius-Mencius
Society*.

RELIGION, SOCIOLOGY AND ANTHROPOLOGY

Chinese Association for Folklore: 422
Fulin Rd, POB 68-1292, Shihlin, Taipei; f.
1932; Chinese and Asian folklore; 47 mems;
library of 1,000 vols and MSS; Chair. Prof.
LOU TSU-KUANG; Sec. AMY LOU.

TECHNOLOGY

**Chinese Institute of Civil and Hydraulic
Engineering:** 4th Fl., 1 Jen Ai Rd, 2 Taipei;
tel. (2) 23926325; fax (2) 23964260; e-mail
ciche@ciche.org.tw; internet www.ciche.org

.tw; f. 1973; 7,500 mems; Pres. YU CHENG;
publs *Journal of Civil and Hydraulic Engineering* (4 a year), *Journal of the Chinese
Institute of Civil and Hydraulic Engineering*
(4 a year).

Chinese Institute of Engineers: Fl. 3, No.
1 Ren-ai Rd, Sec. 2, Taipei 100; tel. (2)
23925128; fax (2) 23973003; e-mail
secretariat@cie.org.tw; internet www.cie.org
.tw; f. 1912; 11,501 mems; library of 7,334
vols, 60 periodicals; Sec. FENZA CHIANG; publs
Journal of the Chinese Institute of Engineers
(7 a year), *Newsletter* (4 a year), *Transactions*
(6 a year).

Research Institutes

GENERAL

**National Institute for Compilation and
Translation:** 179 Heping E Rd, Sector 1, Da-
An District, Taipei City 10644; tel. (2)
33225558; fax (2) 33225559; e-mail
trcnews@mail.nict.gov.tw; internet www.nict
.gov.tw; f. 1932; translates foreign books,
examines and approves textbooks, standardizes scientific and technical terms; 75
mems; library of 100,000 vols; Dir-Gen; PAN
WEN-CHUNG; publs *Compilation and Translation Review* (print and online), *Journal of
Textbook Research* (print and online).

AGRICULTURE, FISHERIES AND VETERINARY SCIENCE

Council of Agriculture: 37 Nanhai Rd,
Taipei; tel. (2) 23812991; fax (2) 23310341;
e-mail coa@mail.coa.gov.tw; internet www
.coa.gov.tw; f. 1984; govt agency under the
Exec. Yuan, with ministerial status; administers nat. agriculture, forestry, fisheries,
livestock farming and food; 300 mems;
library of 18,000 vols; Minister Dr WU-
HSIUNG CHEN.

Taiwan Agricultural Research Institute:
189 Chung-Cheng Rd, Wan-Feng, Wu-Feng,
Taichung; tel. (4) 3302301; fax (4) 3338162;
e-mail mwf-doc@wufeng.tari.gov.tw; internet
www.tari.gov.tw; f. 1895; insect colln; Dir LIN
CHIEN-YIH; publ. *Journal of Agricultural
Research of China* (4 a year).

Taiwan Fisheries Research Institute:
199 Hou-Ih Rd, Keelung 220; tel. (2)
24622101; fax (2) 24629388; f. 1933; library
of 16,000 vols; Dir-Gen. I-CHIU LIAO; publs
Journal, research reports.

Taiwan Forestry Research Institute: 53
Nan-Hai Rd, Taipei, 10066; tel. (2) 23039978;
fax (2) 23142234; e-mail service@serv.tfri.gov
.tw; internet www.tfri.gov.tw; f. 1985; 376
mems; library of 33,000 vols; Dir HEN-BIAU
KING; Sec.-Gen. KUO-CHUAN LIN; publ. *Journal of Forest Science* (4 a year).

Taiwan Sugar Research Institute: 54
Sheng Chan Rd, Tainan; tel. (6) 2671911;
fax (6) 2685425; e-mail tsc02@taisugar.com
.tw; f. 1902; supported by Taiwan Sugar
Corpn; library of 46,800 vols; Dir LONG-HUEI
WANG; publs *Extension Bulletin*, *Report* (in
Chinese, 4 a year, English summary), *Tech-
nical Bulletin*.

ECONOMICS, LAW AND POLITICS

**Co-operative League of the Republic of
China:** 11-2 Fu Chow St, Taipei; tel. (2)
23219343; fax (2) 23517918; f. 1940; cooperative business research and education;
Chair. YANG CHIA-LIN; Exec. Dir/Sec.-Gen.
HSU WEN-FU; publs *CLC Co-operative News*
(1 a year), *Co-operative Economics* (4 a year).

Institute of Economics: c/o Academia
Sinica, Nankang, Taipei 11529; tel. (2)
27822791; fax (2) 27853946; internet www

.sinica.edu.tw/~econ; attached to Academia
Sinica; Dir Dr CHUNG-MING KUAN; f. 1962;
publs *Academia Economic Papers* (4 a year),
Taiwan Economic Forecast and Policy (2 a
year).

FINE AND PERFORMING ARTS

National Taiwan Arts Education Center:
47 Nan Hai Rd, Taipei; tel. (2) 23110574; fax
(2) 23122555; internet www.arte.gov.tw; f.
1957; in charge of the research, extension
and guidance of art education in Taiwan; Dir
JOSEPH TSU-SHENG WU; publs *Journal of
Aesthetic Education* (6 a year), *Newsletter of
Arts Education* (12 a year), *The International
Journal of Arts Education* (2 a year).

HISTORY, GEOGRAPHY AND ARCHAEOLOGY

Institute of History and Philology: c/o
Academia Sinica, Nankang, Taipei 11529;
tel. (2) 27829555; fax (2) 27868834; internet
www.ihp.sinica.edu.tw/english; attached to
Academia Sinica; Dir Prof. TUNG-KUEI KUAN.

Institute of Modern History: c/o Academia
Sinica, Nankang, Taipei 11529; tel. (2)
27824166; attached to Academia Sinica; Dir
Prof. KO-WU HUANG; Sec. SHU-LING CHIANG.

MEDICINE

**Institute of Biomedical Sciences, Pre-
paratory Office:** c/o Academia Sinica, Nankang, Taipei 11529; attached to Academia
Sinica; Dir Dr CHENG-WEN WU.

NATURAL SCIENCES

General

National Science Council: 106 Ho-ping E
Rd, Section 2, Taipei 106; tel. (2) 27377981;
fax (2) 27377672; e-mail klchou@nsc.gov.tw;
internet www.nsc.gov.tw; f. 1959; br. of central govt; promotes nat. science and technology devt, supports academic research and
establishes industrial parks; Sr Systems
Coordinator K.L. CHOU; publs *East Asian
Science, Technology and Society* (in English,
4 a year), *Indicators of Science and Technology* (in Chinese and English, 1 a year),
*International Journal of Science and Math-
ematics Education* (in English, 4 a year),
Journal of Biomedical Science (in English, 6
a year , open access journal since January
2009), *National Science Council Review* (in
English and Chinese, 1 a year), *Science
Development* (in Chinese, 12 a year).

Biological Sciences

**Central Laboratory of Molecular Biol-
ogy, Preparatory Office:** c/o Academia
Sinica, Nankang, Taipei 11529; attached to
Academia Sinica; Dir Dr CHIEN HO.

Institute of Biological Chemistry: c/o
Academia Sinica, Nankang, Taipei 11529;
attached to Academia Sinica; Dir Dr WEN-
CHANG CHANG (acting).

Institute of Botany: c/o Academia Sinica,
Nankang, Taipei 11529; tel. (2) 27899590; fax
(2) 27827954; e-mail boplshaw@ccvax.sinica
.edu.tw; internet www.botany.sinica.edu.tw;
f. 1929; attached to Academia Sinica; Dir Dr
JEI-FU SHAW; publ. *Botanical Bulletin of
Academia Sinica* (4 a year).

Institute of Zoology: c/o Academia Sinica,
Nankang, Taipei 11529; attached to Academia Sinica; Dir Dr JEN-LEIH WU.

Mathematical Sciences

Institute of Mathematics: c/o Academia
Sinica, Nankang, Taipei 11529; attached to
Academia Sinica; Dir Dr KO-WEI LIH.

Institute of Statistical Science: c/o Academia Sinica, 128 Academia Rd Sec. 2, Taipei

115 29; tel. (2) 27835611; fax (2) 27831523; internet www.stat.sinica.edu.tw; f. 1982; attached to Academia Sinica; 40 mems; Dir Dr KER-CHAU LI; publ. *Statistica Sinica* (4 a year).

Physical Sciences

Atomic Energy Council: 67 Lane 144, Keelung Rd, Sec. 4, Taipei 106; tel. (2) 23634180; fax (2) 23635377; f. 1955; govt agency for the peaceful application of atomic energy; library of 11,000 vols, deposit library at the National Tsing Hua Univ. of 36,000 vols and 424,000 microcards; Chair. Dr YIH-YUN HSU; Sec.-Gen. KUANG-CHI LIU; publs *Nuclear Climate* (12 a year), *Nuclear Science Journal* (6 a year).

Central Geological Survey: POB 968, Taipei 100; tel. (2) 29462793; fax (2) 29429291; e-mail cgs@linx.moeacgs.gov.tw; internet www.moeacgs.gov.tw; f. 1946; library of 50,000 vols and periodicals; Dir CHAO-CHUNG LIN; publs *Bulletin*, *Ti-Chih* (geology, 2 a year); maps.

Institute of Atomic and Molecular Sciences, Preparatory Office: c/o Academia Sinica, Nankang, Taipei 11529; attached to Academia Sinica; Dir Dr CHAO-TIN CHANG.

Institute of Chemistry: c/o Academia Sinica, Nankang, Taipei 11529; attached to Academia Sinica; Dir Dr SUNNEY I. CHAN.

Institute of Earth Sciences; e-mail april@ earth.sinica.edu.tw Academia Sinica, Nankang, Taipei 11529; tel. (2) 27839910; fax (2) 27839871; attached to Academia Sinica; Dir Dr BOR-MING JAHN.

Institute of Information Science: c/o Academia Sinica, Nankang, Taipei 11529; attached to Academia Sinica; Dir Dr YUE-SUN KUO (acting).

Institute of Nuclear Energy Research: POB 3, Lung-Tan 32500; tel. (2) 3651717; fax (3) 4711064; f. 1968; research in peaceful uses of atomic energy; Dir Dr HSIA DER-YU (acting); publ. *INER report series*.

Institute of Physics: c/o Academia Sinica, Nankang, Taipei 11529; attached to Academia Sinica; Dir Dr TUNG-MIN HO (acting).

PHILOSOPHY AND PSYCHOLOGY

Sun Yat-sen Institute for Social Sciences and Philosophy: c/o Academia Sinica, Nankang, Taipei 11529; tel. (2) 27821693; fax (2) 27854160; e-mail issp@www.issp.sinica.edu .tw; internet www.issp.sinica.edu.tw; f. 1981; attached to Academia Sinica; Dir Dr ANGELA KI CHE LEUNG; publ. *Journal of Social Sciences and Philosophy* (4 a year).

RELIGION, SOCIOLOGY AND ANTHROPOLOGY

Institute of Ethnology: c/o Academia Sinica, Nankang, Taipei 11529; tel. (2) 26523300; fax (2) 26523436; e-mail tja@gate .sinica.edu.tw; internet www.sinica.edu.tw/ ioe; f. 1955; attached to Academia Sinica; main field of research: social and cultural anthropology; Dir Prof. HUANG SHU-MIN; publs *Field Materials*, *Taiwan Journal of Anthropology* (2 a year).

Institute of European and American Studies: Academia Sinica, Nankang, Taipei 11529; attached to Academia Sinica; Dir Dr WEN-CHING HO; publ. *EurAmerica* (4 a year).

TECHNOLOGY

Industrial Technology Research Institute: 195 Chung Hsing Rd, Sec. 4, Chu-Tung, Hsinchu; tel. (35) 820100; fax (35) 820045; f. 1973; library of 130,000 vols; Pres. Dr OTTO C. C. LIN; publs *CFC Newsletter*, *Chemical Industry Notes*, *Electro-optics*

Development Journal, *Energy-Resources and Environment* (in Chinese, 4 a year), *Materials and Society*, *Mechatronics Journal*, *Metrology Information* (in Chinese, 6 a year), *Mining Technology*, *MRL Bulletin of Research and Development* (in English, 2 a year), *Opto-Electronics and Systems*, *Reports of Center for Measurement Standards* (in Chinese, 12 a year), *Superconductor Applications News*, *UCL Chemical Information Digest*.

Research Laboratories:

Centre for Aviation and Aerospace: Hsinchu; Dir Dr RICHARD Y. H. LIN.

Centre for Industrial Safety and Health Technology: Hsinchu; Dir Dr ADA W. S. MA.

Centre for Measurement Standards: Hsinchu; Dir Dr CHANG HSU.

Centre for Pollution Control Technology: Hsinchu; Dir Dr LING-YUAN CHEN.

Computer and Communication Research Laboratories: Hsinchu; Dir Dr STEVEN CHENG.

Electronics Research and Service Organization: Hsinchu; Dir Dr DAVID C. T. HSING.

Energy and Resources Laboratories: Hsinchu; Dir Dr ROBERT J. YANG.

Materials Research Laboratories: Hsinchu and Kaohsiung; Dir Dr LI-CHUNG LEE.

Mechanical Industry Research Laboratories: Hsinchu; Dir Dr C. RICHARD LIU.

Opto-Electronics and Systems Laboratories: Hsinchu; Dir Dr MIN-SHYONG LIN.

Union Chemical Laboratories: Hsinchu; Dir Dr JOHN-SEE LEE.

National Bureau of Standards: Ministry of Economic Affairs, 3rd Floor, 185 Hsinhai Rd, Sec. 2, Taipei 106; tel. (2) 27380007; fax (2) 27352656; f. 1947; nat. standards, weights and measures, patents, trademarks; library of 20,000 vols, 500 periodicals; Dir-Gen. MING-BANG CHEN; publs *Catalogue of Chinese National Standards* (1 a year), *Chinese National Standards* (irregular), *Official Gazette for Patents* (36 a year), *Official Gazette for Standards* (12 a year), *Official Gazette for Trademarks* (24 a year).

Libraries and Archives

Tainan

National Cheng Kung University Library: 1 Ta Hsueh Rd, Tainan 70101; tel. (6) 2757575 ext. 65701; fax (6) 2378232; internet www.lib.ncku.edu.tw; f. 1927; 1,685,049 vols, 12,676 periodicals; Dir MING-TZONG YANG; publs *Bulletin* (4 a year), *Newsletter* (12 a year).

Taipei

Agricultural Science Information Center: POB 7-636, Taipei 106; tel. (2) 23626222; internet www.asic.org.tw; f. 1977; 11,000 vols, 638 periodicals, databases; Dir WAN-JIUN WU.

Dr Sun Yat-sen Library: 2F, 505 Jen Ai Rd, Sec. 4, Taipei; tel. (2) 27297030; fax (2) 27582460; f. 1929; 299,345 vols on Dr Sun Yat-sen's writings and studies on San Min Chu Yih and modern Chinese history; Curator SHAW MING-HUANG; publ. *Modern China* (6 a year).

Fu Ssu-nien Library, Institute of History and Philology: 130 Yen Chiu Yuan Rd, Sec. 2, Nankang, Taipei 11521; tel. (2) 27829555 ext. 136; fax (2) 27868834; f. 1928;

420,000 vols, 3,000 periodicals; spec. collns incl. 33,889 stone and bronze rubbings, 13,100 folk plays, 310,000 cabinet records of Ming and Ch'ing dynasties; Dir JUEI-HSIU WU.

National Central Library: 20 Chung Shan South Rd, Taipei 100; tel. (2) 23619132; fax (2) 23110155; internet www.ncl.edu.tw; f. 1933; 2,555,069 items incl. 190,000 rare books, stone rubbings; historical material; maintains centre for Chinese studies; Dir Dr CHUANG FANG-JUNG; publs *Chinese National Bibliography* (12 a year), *Index to Chinese Periodicals* (4 a year), *NCL Bulletin* (2 a year), *NCL Newsletter* (in English, 2 a year), *NCL News Bulletin* (4 a year).

Branch Library:

Taiwan Branch Library, National Central Library: 1 Hsinshen South Rd, Sec. 1, Taipei; tel. (2) 27724724; internet www.ncltb.edu.tw; f. 1915; 592,023 vols; spec. collns incl. Taiwan and Southern Asia; Dir LIN WEI-JEI; publs *Catalogue of Materials for the Blind, Catalogue of NCL Taiwan Branch Collection on Southeast Asia, Catalogue on China in Japanese Languages, Catalogue on China in Western Languages, Index to Taiwan-Related Periodical Literature collected in NCL Taiwan Branch, List of Non-Chinese Serials in NCL Taiwan Branch, The Annotative Catalogue of Taiwan Documents, Union Catalogue of Taiwan-Related Bibliographies*.

National War College Library: Yangmingshan, Taipei; 156,639 vols on political subjects; Librarian LO MOU-PIN.

Parliamentary Library, Legislative Yuan: 1 Chung Shan S Rd, Taipei 10051; tel. (2) 23585278; fax (2) 23585290; internet npl.ly.gov.tw; f. 1947; gen. reference, govt publs, legal documents; 231,060 vols; Dir Dr SHOW-RONG WANG; publs *Chinese legislative news review index* (12 a year), *Chinese legislative news reviews series* (irregular), *Code Amendment Cyclopedia* (irregular), *Code and reference book catalogue* (irregular), *Code resource pathfinder* (6 a year), *Collection of Interpellation Records* (irregular), *Gazette, Index to Chinese Legislative Literature* (6 a year), *Index to Legal Periodicals* (irregular), *Index of Legislative Records* (every 3 years), *LEGISIS thesaurus* (irregular), *Legislative Decision Support Service* (12 a year), *Legislative Microform Catalog* (irregular), *Library Communications Quarterly*, *Newsletter of books and documentation* (4 a year), *Proceedings and Serials catalogue* (irregular), *Selective abstracts of US Congressional Records* (irregular), *Selected Dissemination of Information Series* (6 a year), *Subject Guide to Chinese Code* (irregular), *The Legislative Yuan Library Catalogue* (irregular).

Taipei City Library: 46 Chinan Rd, Sec. 2, Taipei; f. 1952; 125,000 vols; 4 brs; Dir CHIH-SHIH YANG; publ. *Taipei Municipal Library Annals*.

Museums and Art Galleries

Kaohsiung

Kaohsiung Museum of Fine Arts: 80 Meishukuan Rd, Kaohsiung; tel. (7) 5550331; fax (7) 5550307; e-mail service@ kmfa.gov.tw; internet www.kmfa.gov.tw; f. 1994; Dir PEI-NI BEATRICE HSIEH.

Taichung

National Taiwan Museum of Fine Arts: 2, Sec. 1, Wu Chuan West Rd, Taichung 403;

tel. (4) 23723552; fax (4) 23721195; e-mail artnet@art.ntmofa.gov.tw; internet www .ntmofa.gov.tw; f. 1986; mostly works of Taiwan artists; library of 70,000 vols; Dir TSAI-LANG HUANG; publs *Journal of National Taiwan Museum of Fine Arts* (4 a year), *Newsletter* (6 a year).

Taipei

Chinese Postal Museum: 45 Chungking South Rd, Sec. 2, Taipei 100; tel. (2) 23945185; fax (2) 23518773; e-mail musol@ mail.post.gov.tw; internet www.post.gov.tw/ museum.htm; f. 1966; library of 27,000 vols; Dir SUSAN TENG-KUEI YU.

Hwa Kang Museum: 55 Hwa Kang Rd, Chinese Culture Univ., Yang Ming Shan, Taipei 111; tel. (2) 28610511 ext 17601; fax (2) 28621918; e-mail cuch@staff.pccu.edu.tw; internet www2.pccu.edu.tw/cuch; f. 1971; Chinese folk arts, pottery, porcelain, calligraphy and paintings; Dir MARGARET CHEN LEE.

National Museum of History: 49 Nan Hai Rd, Taipei 10066; tel. (2) 23610270; fax (2) 23610171; internet www.nmh.gov.tw; f. 1955; Chinese and Taiwanese historical and archaeological artefacts; library of 30,000 vols; Dir YUNG-CHUAN HUANG; publs *Bulletin of the National Museum of History* (in Chinese, 12 a year), *Journal of the National Museum of History* (in Chinese, 2 a year).

National Palace Museum: Wai-shuanghsi, Shih-lin, Taipei; tel. (2) 28812021; fax (2) 28821440; internet www.npm.gov.tw; f. 1925; colln consists chiefly of historic and archaeological treasures brought from mainland China; library of 155,136 vols, 624 periodical titles, 200,907 rare books, 395,335 Ch'ing documents; Dir SHIH SHOU-CHIEN; publs *National Palace Museum Monthly of Chinese Art* (12 a year), *Research Quarterly* (4 a year).

National Taiwan Museum: 2 Siang-yang Rd, Taipei 100; tel. (2) 23822699; fax (2) 23822684; e-mail ntmmail@ntm.gov.uk; internet www.ntm.gov.uk; f. 1908; anthropology, earth sciences, zoology and botany; Dir HSIAO TSUNG-HUANG; publs *Journal of Taiwan Museum* (in English), *Taiwan Natural Science*.

National Taiwan Science Education Center: 41 Nan Hai Rd, Taipei; tel. (2) 23116734; f. 1958; planetarium, science exhibitions, lectures and films; Dir SHIH-BEY CHEN; publ. *Science Study Monthly*.

Shung Ye Museum of Formosan Aborigines: 282 Chishan Rd Section 2, Shi-Lin Dist, Taipei 11143; tel. (2) 28412611; fax (2) 28412615; e-mail shungye@gate.sinica.edu .tw; internet www.museum.org.tw; f. 1994; holds a collection of artefacts of Taiwan's indigenous peoples; promotes understanding between ethnic groups and undertakes research and preservation of Aboriginal cultural works; Museum Curator and Dir ERIC H. Y. YU.

Taipei Astronomical Museum: 363 Kee-Ho Rd, Taipei 111; tel. (2) 28314551; fax (2) 28314405; e-mail tam001@tam.gov.tw; internet www.tam.gov.tw; f. 1996; Pres. GUO-GUANG CIOU; Gen. Sec. CHING-HSIUNG WANG; publs *Astronomical Almanac* (1 a year), *Report on Sunspot Observations* (1 a year), *Taipei Skylight* (4 a year).

Taipei Fine Arts Museum: 181, Sec. 3, Zhong Shan N. Rd, Taipei 10461; tel. (2) 25957656; fax (2) 25944104; e-mail info@tfam .gov.tw; internet www.tfam.gov.tw; f. 1983; modern art; Dir TSAI-LANG HSIAO (acting); publs *Journal* (2 a year), *Modern Art* (6 a year).

Universities

CHINESE CULTURE UNIVERSITY

55 Hwa Kang Rd, Yang Ming Shan, Taipei
Telephone: (2) 28610511
Fax: (2) 28615031
Internet: www.pccu.edu.tw

Founded 1962
Private control
Pres.: LIN TSAI-MEI

Library of 630,000 vols, 3,500 periodicals
Number of teachers: 531
Number of students: 20,013

Colleges of agriculture, arts, business, engineering, foreign languages and literature, journalism and mass communication, law, liberal arts, science; graduate and evening schools.

CHUNG YUAN CHRISTIAN UNIVERSITY

Chung Li
Telephone: (3) 4563171
Fax: (3) 4563160
Internet: www.cycu.edu.tw

Founded 1955
Private control
Academic year: August to July
Pres.: Dr SAMUEL K. C. CHANG

Library of 250,000 vols
Number of teachers: 12,491
Number of students: 11,798

Publications: *Chung Yuan Journal, CYCU News*

Colleges of business, design, engineering, science; evening dept.

FENG CHIA UNIVERSITY

100 Wenhwa Rd, Seatwen, Taichung 40724
Telephone: (4) 24517250
Fax: (4) 24514907
E-mail: linkages@fcu.edu.tw
Internet: www.fcu.edu.tw

Founded 1961
Private control
Languages of instruction: Chinese, English
Academic year: September to June
Pres.: AN-CHI LIU
Vice-Pres.: YUAN-TONG LEE
Sec.-Gen.: HAI-PING HSIEH
Chief Librarian: HSIANG-HOO CHING

Library of 590,000 vols
Number of teachers: 1,107
Number of students: 19,124 (17,517 undergraduate, 1,607 postgraduate)

Publications: *Accounting Journal, Architecture Quarterly, Banking and Insurance, Civil Engineering Journal, Computer Science, Co-operative Research, FCU Weekly, Finance Research, Industrial Engineering, International Trade, Mechanical Engineering, Statistics Journal, Textile Science*

DEANS

College of Business: PAO-LONG CHANG
College of Construction and Devt: BING-JEAN LEE
College of Continuing Education: YOU-REN SHIAU
College of Engineering: TONG-MIIN LIOU
College of Humanities and Social Studies: YEN CHU
College of Information and Electrical Engineering: CHUANG-CHIEN CHIU
College of Sciences: TAI-LEE HU

DIRECTORS OF GRADUATE INSTITUTES

Accounting and Taxation: YU-CHI LIN
Aeronautical Engineering: WEN-SHYONG KOU

Applied Mathematics: JIANN-CHERNG YANG
Architecture and Urban Planning: MEI-JUNG LAI
Automatic Control Engineering: CHERN-SHENG LIN
Business Administration: MEI-YANE CHUNG
Chemical Engineering: CHYI-TSONG CHEN
Chinese Literature: JIANN-HWA SONG
Civil and Hydraulic Engineering: YU-MIN KANG
Communications Engineering: CHENG-HO HSIN
Economics: CHI-CHU CHOU
Electrical and Communications Engineering: CHUANG-CHIEN CHIU
Electrical Engineering: CHANG-CHOU HWANG
Electronic Engineering: WEN-LUH YANG
Environmental Science and Engineering: JYA-JYUN YU
Finance: CHE-PENG LIN
History and Cultural Heritage Management: CHIH-CHIA HU
Industrial Engineering: ANGUS JEANG
Information Engineering: DON-LIN YANG
Insurance: GOW-NING YUAN
International Trade: TING-JI LIN
Land Management: JING-CHZI HSIEH
Materials Science: HSIN-CHIH LIN
Mechanical Engineering: JIN-HUANG HUANG
Optical Physics: YING-TE LEE
Statistics and Actuarial Science: WOAN-SHU CHEN
Textiles Engineering: TIEN-WEI SHYR
Traffic and Transportation Engineering and Management: TA-YIN HU

FU-JEN CATHOLIC UNIVERSITY

510 Chungcheng Rd, Hsin-Chuang, Taipei
Telephone: (2) 29031111 ext. 3016
Fax: (2) 29017391
E-mail: fjuweb@mails.fju.edu.tw
Internet: www.fju.edu.tw

Founded 1925 in Beijing; re-opened in Taiwan 1961
Academic year: August to July
Pres.: Dr JOHN NING-YUEAN LEE
Vice-Pres: Dr PERRY C. CHIU, Dr PETER SHANG-SHING CHOU, Rev. LOUIS GENDRON
Sec.-Gen.: JOHN SHIANG-YANG HWANG
Dean of Academic Affairs: Dr YIU-LUNG CHEN
Dean of General Affairs: Prof. ZERMAN HU
Dean of Research and Devt: Dr SHIH-MING KO
Dean of Student Affairs: Dr HUNG YAN CHEN
Registrar: TZU-CHI LI
Librarian: Dr H. H. CHENG

Library of 828,000 vols
Number of teachers: 1,591
Number of students: 23,658

Publications: *Catholic Observer, Fu Jen Philosophical Studies, Fu Jen Studies* (4 a year)

DEANS

College of Fine Arts: Dr MING-JIAN FANG
College of Foreign Languages: Dr NICHOLAS KOSS
College of Human Ecology: Dr SHAU-YEN HUANG
College of Law: Dr AH-YEE LEE
College of Liberal Arts: Dr THOMAS FU-BEING CHEN
College of Management: Dr DENG-YUAN HUANG
College of Medicine: Dr VINCENT HAN-SUN CHIANG
College of Science and Engineering: Dr JOSEPH L. G. HWA
Holistic Education Center: Dr DAMIANUS JEN-LUNGKAO
School of Continuing Education: Dr CAJUS CHI-CHI LIN

NATIONAL CENTRAL UNIVERSITY

Chung-Li 320
Telephone: (3) 4227151
Fax: (3) 4226062
Internet: www.ncu.edu.tw

Founded 1968 as re-establishment of National Central University (Nanking)
Academic year: February to January

Pres.: Prof. CHAO-HAN LIU
Vice-Pres.: KUANG-FU CHENG
Dean of Academic Affairs: KUAN-CHING LEE
Dean of General Affairs: EDMOND LIU-WU HOURNG
Dean of Research and Devt: WEI-LING CHIANG
Dean of Student Affairs: DYI-HWA TSENG
Dir of Secretariat: JIEN-MING JUE
Librarian: CHIEU-YIUG WANG
Number of teachers: 450
Number of students: 7,813
Publications: *Bulletin of Geophysics* (2 a year), *Journal of Humanities East/West* (2 a year)

DEANS

College of Earth Sciences: YI-BEN TSAI
College of Engineering: KUO-SHONG WANG
College of Information Technology and Electrical Engineering: SHING-TSAAN HUANG
College of Liberal Arts: JEH-HANG LAI
College of Management: JING-TWEN CHEN
College of Science: WING-HUEN IP

NATIONAL CHENGCHI UNIVERSITY

64 Zhinan Rd Sec. 2, Wenshan 116, Taipei
Telephone: (2) 29379611
E-mail: www@nccu.edu.tw
Internet: www.nccu.edu.tw

Founded 1927, univ. status 1946; state-funded
Language of instruction: Chinese
Academic year: September to July (2 semesters)

Pres.: JEI-CHENG CHENG
Dean of Academic Affairs: CHIN-YUE TUNG
Dean of General Affairs: MICHAEL KWAN
Dean of Student Affairs: LING-TAI CHOU
Librarian: OU-LAN HU
Library of 2,289,000 vols
Number of teachers: 948 (full- and part-time)
Number of students: 11,554

DEANS

College of Commerce: SE-HWA WU
College of Communication: VEN-HWEI LO
College of Foreign Languages: CHAO-MING CHEN
College of International Affairs: DENG-KER LEE
College of Law: HSIU-HSIUNG LIN
College of Liberal Arts: HSIN-CHUAN HO
College of Science: LONG-YI TSAI
College of Social Sciences: AN-PANG KAO

NATIONAL CHENG KUNG UNIVERSITY

1 Ta-Hsueh Rd, Tainan 70101
Telephone: (6) 2757575
Fax: (6) 2368660
E-mail: em50000@mail.ncku.edu.tw
Internet: www.ncku.edu.tw

Founded 1931 as Tainan Technical College, renamed Taiwan Provincial College of Engineering 1946, present name 1971
State control
Language of instruction: Chinese, some English
Academic year: September to June

Pres.: Dr CHIANG KAO
Dean of Academic Affairs: Dr YAN-KUIN SU

Registrar: SHIN-FU HUANG
Librarian: Dr JEN-FA MIN

Number of teachers: 1,200
Number of students: 19,000

Publications: *Bulletin of National Cheng Kung University* (1 a year), *Journal of National Cheng Kung University* (1 a year)

DEANS

College of Design: Dr MING-FU HSU
College of Electrical Engineering and Computer Science: Dr CHING-TING LI
College of Engineering: Dr WEN-TENG WU
College of Liberal Arts: Dr KAO-PING CHANG
College of Management Science: Dr WANN-YIH WU
College of Medicine: Dr RUEY-JEN SUNG
College of Sciences: Dr SHU-CHENG YU
College of Social Sciences: Dr JENN-YEU CHEN

Graduate institutes are attached to the College of Engineering, the College of Liberal Arts, the College of Management Science, the College of Medicine, the College of Sciences and the College of Social Sciences

NATIONAL CHIAO TUNG UNIVERSITY

1001 Ta Hsueh Rd, Hsinchu
Telephone: (35) 712121
Fax: (35) 721500
Internet: www.nctu.edu.tw

Founded 1896, re-established in Hsinchu 1958
Languages of instruction: Chinese, English
Academic year: August to July (2 semesters)

President: Dr CHI-FU DEN
Dean of Academic Affairs: Dr LONG-ING CHEN
Dean of General Affairs: Dr CHUNG-BIAU TSAY
Dean of the Research and Development Council: Dr CHUNG-YU WU
Dean of Student Affairs: Dr FU-WHA HAN
Chief Secretary: Prof. HSIN-SEN CHU
Registrar: Assoc. Prof. CHIN-SHYONG CHEN
Chief Librarian: Dr RUEI-CHUAN CHANG
Library of 170,329 vols, 2,373 periodicals
Number of teachers: 415 (full-time)
Number of students: 4,896

Publications: *Chiao Ta Management Review*, *List of Publications of Faculty Members*, abstracts of papers and research reports

DEANS

College of Electrical Engineering and Computer Science: Dr CHE-HO WEI
College of Engineering: Dr TAI-YAN KAM
College of Management: Dr PAO-LONG CHANG
College of Science: Dr DER-SAN CHUU

DIRECTORS OF GRADUATE INSTITUTES

Applied Arts (Design and Music): Dr MING-CHUEN CHUANG
Applied Chemistry: Dr CHAIN-SHU HSU
Applied Mathematics: Dr GERARD J. CHANG
Biological Science and Technology: Dr CHENG ALLEN CHANG
Civil Engineering: Dr YUNG-SHOW FANG
Communication Engineering: Dr CHUNG-JU CHANG
Communication Studies: Dr SHIN-MIN CHEN
Computer and Information Science: Dr RONG-HONG JAN
Computer Science and Information Engineering: Dr SHU-YUEN HWANG
Control Engineering: Dr DER-CHERNG LIAW
Electronics: Dr TAN-FU LEI
Electro-Optical Engineering: Dr CI-LING PAN
Electrophysics: Dr MING-CHIH LEE
Environmental Engineering: Dr JEHNG-JUNG KAO
Industrial Engineering: Dr CHAO-TON SU
Information Management: Dr CHI-CHUN LO
Management Science: Dr SOUSHAN WU
Management Technology: Dr SHANG-JYH LIU

Materials Science and Engineering: Dr TZENG-FENG LIU
Mechanical Engineering: Dr HSIN-SEN CHU
Physics: Dr JSIN-FU JIANG
Statistics: Dr CHAO-SHENG LEE
Traffic and Transportation: Dr YUAN-CHING HSU

DIRECTORS OF RESEARCH CENTRES

Center for Telecommunications Research: Dr SIN-HORNG CHEN
Computer Center: Dr RUEI-CHUAN CHANG
Microelectronics and Information Science and Technology Research Center: Dr MING SZE
National Nano Device Center: Dr CHUN-YEN CHANG
Semiconductor Research Center: (vacant)

NATIONAL CHUNG HSING UNIVERSITY

250 Kuokuang Rd, Taichung
Telephone: (4) 2872991
Fax: (4) 2853813
Internet: www.nchu.edu.tw

Founded 1961

Pres.: Dr CHENG-CHANG LI
Sec.-Gen.: MU-CHIOU HUANG
Librarian: WOEI LIN

Number of teachers: 980
Number of students: 17,625

DEANS

College of Agriculture: MING-TSAO CHEN
College of Engineering: SHIH-SHYN WU
College of Law and Commerce: SEN-TIAN WU
College of Liberal Arts: CHUNG-HSUAN TUNG
College of Life Science: SCHENG-MING TSCHEN
College of Science: TENG-KUEI YANG

HEADS OF INSTITUTES

Institute of Agricultural Biotechnology: FENG-NAN HOU
Institute of Agricultural Extension and Education: CHING-YING HUANG
Institute of Biochemistry: JUNGYIE KAO
Institute of Computer Science: SYING-JYAN WANG
Institute of Library and Information Science: WOEI LIN
Institute of Materials Engineering: FUN-SHENG SHEIU
Institute of Molecular Biology: LIANG-JWU CHEN
Institute of Natural Resource Management: DAIGEE SHAW
Institute of Urban Planning: HSUEH-TAO CHIEN
Institute of Veterinary Microbiology: LONG-HUW LEE
Institute of Veterinary Pathology: CHENG-I LIU

NATIONAL OPEN UNIVERSITY

172 Chung Cheng Rd, Lu Chow, Taipei 24702
Telephone: (2) 22829355
Fax: (2) 22831721
E-mail: elec007@mail.nou.edu.tw
Internet: www.nou.edu.tw

Founded 1986
Language of instruction: Chinese
Academic year: September to June

Pres.: Dr SHENG-SHIUNG HUANG
Registrar: LI-CHI HSIEH
Dean of Academic Affairs: Dr CHIA-SHING YANG

Number of teachers: 2,037 (88 full-time, 1,949 part-time)
Number of students: 40,000

Publication: *National Open University Learning Journal* (every 2 weeks)

CHAIRMEN OF DEPARTMENTS
Arts in Commerce: JIN-HO YUAN
General Affairs: TSAI HSIANG-HUEI
General Studies: SZE-LU NA
Instructional Media: DWO-YAN CHANG
Liberal Arts: YUAN-JEN FANG
Living Sciences: WEN-CHIN CHOU
Management and Information: SUNG-BO CHEN
Public Administration: SHIH-PEI LAI
Research and Development: JUDY HUANG
Social Sciences: JEHNG OUYANG
Student Affairs: JESSE C. CHOU

NATIONAL PINGTUNG UNIVERSITY OF SCIENCE AND TECHNOLOGY

1 Hseuh-Fu Rd, Nei Pu Hsiang, Pingtung Hsien 912

Telephone: (8) 7703660
Fax: (8) 7702226
E-mail: choumasa@mail.npust.edu.tw
Internet: www.npust.edu.tw

Founded 1954 as Taiwan Provincial Institute of Agriculture; became National Pingtung Institute of Agriculture 1981 and National Pingtung Polytechnic Institute 1991; present name and status 1997

Pres.: CHANG-HUNG CHOU

Library of 227,198 vols
Number of teachers: 324
Number of students: 9,000

Publication: *Bulletin* (1 a year)

Colleges of agriculture, engineering, management and humanities, social sciences.

NATIONAL TAIWAN NORMAL UNIVERSITY

162 East Ho Ping Rd, Sec. 1, Taipei 10610
Telephone: (2) 23625101
Fax: (2) 23922673
Internet: www.ntnu.edu.tw

Founded 1946
Language of instruction: Chinese
State control
Academic year: August to July (2 semesters)

Pres.: MAW-FA CHIEN
Vice-Pres.: CHUNG-YANG TSAI
Sec.-Gen.: HSI-PING WANG
Dean of General Affairs: DAR-CHIN RAU
Dean of Internship Supervision and Placement
Dean of Research and Devt: LILLIAN MEEI-JIN HUANG
Dean of Students: HU-HSIUNG LI
Dean of Studies: C. H. GEORGE KAO
Registrar: AN-PAN LIN
Library Dir: HARRY LIANG

Number of teachers: 1,131
Number of students: 9,716

Publications: *A-V Education* (6 a year), *Bulletin*, *NTNU Alumni* (12 a year), *Secondary Education* (6 a year), graduate institutional and departmental journals

DEANS
College of Education: WU-TIEN WU
College of Fine and Applied Arts: CHING-LANG CHANG
College of Liberal Arts: WEN-HSING WU
College of Sciences: CHU-NAN CHANG
College of Sports and Recreation: YAO-HUI CHIEN
College of Technology: LUNG-SHERN LEE
Extension Division: SUZ-WEI YANG

NATIONAL TAIWAN OCEAN UNIVERSITY

2 Pei-Ning Rd, Keelung
Telephone: (2) 24622192
Fax: (2) 24623563

Internet: www.ntou.edu.tw

Founded 1953 (formerly National Taiwan College of Marine Science and Technology)
Academic year: August to July

Pres.: ROBERT R. HWANG
Vice-Pres.: KUO-TIEN LEE
Dean of Academic Affairs: CHING-FONG CHANG
Dean of General Affairs: YU-HSING CHAO
Dean of Research and Devt: DENG-FWU HWANG
Dean of Student Affairs: JEUN-LEN WU
Librarian: CHIN-HWA HU

Library of 200,000 vols, 2,000 periodicals
Number of teachers: 325
Number of students: 7,731

Publication: *Journal of Marine Science and Technology* (4 a year)

DEANS OF COLLEGES
Engineering: YOUNG-ZEHR KEHR
Life and Resource Science: SHANN-TZONG JIANG
Maritime Science: YEN-HORNG TSUEI
Science: CHAO-SHING LEE
Technology Science: RONG-HUA YEH

NATIONAL TAIWAN UNIVERSITY

1 Roosevelt Rd, Section 4, Taipei 10617
Telephone: (2) 3366-3366
Fax: (2) 2362-7651
E-mail: secretor@ntu.edu.tw
Internet: www.ntu.edu.tw

Founded 1928 during the Japanese occupation as the Taihoku Imperial Univ.; taken over and renamed by Chinese Govt in 1945
Language of instruction: Chinese
Academic year: August to July (2 semesters)

Pres.: SI-CHEN LEE
Vice-Pres. for Academic Affairs: TAI-JEN GEORGE CHEN
Vice-Pres. for Admin. Affairs: TZONG-HO BAU
Vice-Pres. for Financial Affairs: MING-JE TANG
Dean of Academic Affairs: BEEN-HUANG CHIANG
Dean of International Affairs: TUNG SHEN
Dean of Research and Devt: JI-WANG CHERN
Dean of Student Affairs: JOYCE YEN FENG
Library Dir: SHIUE-HUA CHEN

Library of 3,000,000 vols
Number of teachers: 3,509
Number of students: 33,416

Publications: *Acta Botanica Taiwania, Acta Geologica Taiwanica, Acta Oceanographica Taiwanica*

DEANS
College of Bio-Resources and Agriculture: BAO-JI CHEN
College of Electrical Engineering: SOO-CHANG PEI
College of Engineering: HUAN-JANG KEH
College of Law: MING-CHENG TSAI
College of Liberal Arts: MING-CHENG TSAI
College of Life Science: JU-FANG LUO
College of Management: MAO-WEI HUNG
College of Medicine: PAN-CHYR YANG
College of Public Health: DUNG-LIANG JIANG
College of Science: CHING-HUA LO
College of Social Sciences: YUNG-MAU CHAO
School of Dentistry: CHUN-PIN LIN
School of Professional and Continuing Studies: RUEI-SHIANG GUO
School of Veterinary Medicine: JEN-SHIUAN LIOU

DIRECTORS OF GRADUATE INSTITUTES
Accounting: SHU-HSING LI
Agricultural Chemistry: DAR-YUAN LEE
Agricultural Economics: SHIH-HSUN HSU
Agronomy: YUN-MING PONG
Anatomy and Cell Biology: KUO-SHYAN LU

Animal Science and Technology: LEANG-SHIN WU
Anthropology: YUAN-CHAO TUNG
Applied Mechanics: MAO-KUEN KUO
Applied Physics: YEE-BOB HSIUNG
Art History: MING-LIANG HSIEH
Astrophysics: YEE-BOB HSIUNG
Atmospheric Sciences: CHUN-CHIEH WU
Biochemical Sciences: GEEN-DONG CHANG
Biochemistry and Molecular Biology: LU-PING CHOW
Bioenvironmental Systems Engineering: HUNG-PIN HUANG
Bio-Industrial Mechatronics Engineering: TA-TE LIN
Bio-Industry Communication and Development: ER-ROU LAI
Biomedical Electronics and Bioinformatics: PAI-CHI LI
Biomedical Engineering: TAI-HORNG YOUNG
Biotechnology: HUU-SHENG LUR
Building and Planning: CHU-JOE HSIA
Business Administration: SHU-CHENG STEVE CHI
Chemical Engineering: LI-JEN CHEN
Chemistry: PI-TAI CHOU
Chinese Literature: YU-YU JENG
Civil Engineering: KUO-CHUN CHANG
Clinical Dentistry: CHUN-PIN LIN
Clinical Laboratory Sciences and Medical Biotechnology: CHUN-NAN LEE
Clinical Medicine: PEI-JER CHEN
Clinical Pharmacy: FE-LIN LIN
Communications Engineering: HUEI WANG
Computer Science and Information Engineering: YUH-DAUH LYUU
Drama and Theatre: WEI-JAN CHI
Economics: CHIEN-FU CHOU
Electrical Engineering: JENN-GWO HWU
Electronics Engineering: SHEY-SHI LU
Engineering Science and Ocean Engineering: JING-FA TSAI
Entomology: CHENG-JEN SHIH
Environmental Engineering: SHIAN-CHEE WU
Environmental Health: GEN-SHUH WANG
Epidemiology: WEN-CHUNG LEE
Finance: MING-SHEN TANG
Fisheries Science: WANN-NIAN TZENG
Food Science and Technology: AN-I YEH
Foreign Languages and Literature: YAN-WING LEUNG
Forensic Medicine: YAO-CHANG CHEN
Forestry and Resource Conservation: HANN-CHUNG LO
Geography: SUE-CHING JOU
Geosciences: HONGEY CHEN
Health Care Organization Administration: MING-CHIN YANG
Health Policy and Management: LAN LEE
History: HUAI-CHEN KAN
Horticulture: YANN-JOU LIN
Immunology: PING-NING HSU
Industrial Engineering: ARGON CHEN
Information Management: CHING-CHIN CHERN
Interdisciplinary Legal Studies: TAY-SHENG WANG
International Business: HSIOU-WEI LIN
Japanese Language and Literature: SHING-CHING SHYU
Journalism: DENNIS WENG-JENG PENG
Law: MING-CHENG TSAI
Library and Information Science: CLARENCE TSA-KANG CHU
Linguistics: HINTAT CHEUNG
Materials Science and Engineering: JER-REN YANG
Mathematics: GERARD-JENNHWA CHANG
Mechanical Engineering: SHUO-HUNG CHANG
Microbiology: SHOW-LIN CHEN
Microbiology and Biochemistry: TZU-MING PAN
Molecular and Cellular Biology: HUAI-JEN TSAI
Molecular Medicine: FANG-JEN LEE
Musicology: YING-FEN WANG

National Development: RONG-JEO CHIU
Networking and Multimedia: YI-PING HUNG
Nursing: LIAN-HUA HUANG
Occupational Medicine and Industrial Hygiene: TSUN-JEN CHENG
Occupational Therapy: KEH-CHUNG LIN
Oceanography: LING-YUN CHIAO
Oral Biology: YEN-PING KUO
Pathology: CHUNG-WU LIN
Pharmacology: CHING-CHOW CHEN
Pharmacy: SHOEI-SHENG LEE
Philosophy: HSIAO-CHIH SUN
Photonics and Optoelectronics: SHENG-LUNG HUANG
Physical Therapy: SUH-FANG JENG
Physics: YEE-BOB HSIUNG
Plant Biology: KAI-WUN YEH
Plant Pathology and Microbiology: CHAO-YING CHEN
Political Science: TSAI-TSU SU
Political Science and Engineering: WEN-CHANG CHEN
Preventive Medicine: WEI-CHU CHIE
Psychology: LI-JEN WENG
Physiology: KUO-CHU CHANG
Public Health: WEI-JIAN CHEN
Social Work: YEUN-WEN KU
Sociology: HOLIN LIN
Taiwan Literature: CHIA-LING MEI
Toxicology: SHING-HWA LIU
Veterinary Clinical Science: LI-SEN YEH
Veterinary Medicine: ZHEN-XUAN LIU
Zoology: JIUN-HONG CHEN

NATIONAL TAIWAN UNIVERSITY OF SCIENCE AND TECHNOLOGY

43 Keelung Rd, Sec. 4, Taipei
Telephone: (2) 27376101
Fax: (2) 27376107
E-mail: president@mail.ntust.edu.tw
Internet: www.ntust.edu.tw
Founded 1974
Academic year: August to July (2 semesters)
Pres.: SHUN-TYAN CHEN
Dean of Studies: CHENG-SEEN HO

Library of 279,326 vols
Number of teachers: 315
Number of students: 8,106

NATIONAL TSING HUA UNIVERSITY

101, Sec. 2, Kuang Fu Rd, Hsinchu 30013
Telephone: (3) 5715131
Fax: (3) 5710582
E-mail: presid@my.nthu.edu.tw
Internet: www.nthu.edu.tw
Founded 1911, re-founded 1956
Language of instruction: Chinese
Academic year: August to July
Pres.: WEN-TSUEN CHEN
Librarian: HSIAO-CHIN HSIEH

Number of teachers: 604
Number of students: 11,381

Publication: *Tsing Hua Journal of Chinese Studies* (Chinese literature and community science, 4 a year)

DEANS

College of Electrical Engineering and Computer Science: JYUO-MIN SHYU
College of Engineering: HONG HOCHENG
College of Humanities and Social Sciences: WEI-AN CHANG
College of Life Science: RONG-LONG PAN
College of Nuclear Science: CHIN PAN
College of Science: HUAN-CHIU KU
College of Technology Management: CHIN-TAY SHIH
Commission of General Education: HWAI-PWU CHOU

SOOCHOW UNIVERSITY

70 Linhsi Rd, Shihlin, Taipei 111
Telephone: (2) 28819471
Fax: (2) 28829310
E-mail: secretary@scu.edu.tw
Internet: www.scu.edu.tw
Founded 1900
Private control
Languages of instruction: Chinese, English
Academic year: September to June (2 semesters)
Pres.: CHAO-SHUIAN LIU
Vice-Pres.: CHUN-MEI MA
Vice-Pres. for Academic Affairs: MAO-TING CHIEN
Registrar: CHENG-TSUN LIN
Librarian: YUAN-JEE DING
Library of 692,767 vols
Number of teachers: 1,149 (including part-time teachers)
Number of students: 15,085

Publications: *Journal of Chinese Studies* (1 a year), *Journal of Economics and Business* (4 a year), *Journal of Foreign Languages and Cultures* (1 a year), *Journal of History* (1 a year), *Journal of Japanese Language Teaching* (1 a year), *Journal of Mathematics* (1 a year), *Journal of Philosophical Studies* (2 a year), *Journal of Political Science* (2 a year), *Journal of Sociology* (2 a year), *Law Review* (2 a year)

DIRECTORS

School of Arts and Social Sciences: SIU-KEUNG WONG
School of Business: YUNG-HO CHIU
School of Foreign Languages and Cultures: TSONG-MINN LIN
School of Law: WEI-DA PAN
School of Science: HIN-CHUNG WONG
Extension School: PING-WEN LIN

TAIPEI NATIONAL UNIVERSITY OF THE ARTS

1 Hsueh Yuan Rd, Kuan-Tu, Taipei 112
Telephone: (2) 28961000
Fax: (2) 28945124
E-mail: www@www.tnua.edu.tw
Internet: www.tnua.edu.tw
Founded 1982 as National Institute of the Arts; university status 2004
Library of 300,000 vols
Number of teachers: 127
Number of students: 1,726
Pres.: Dr KUN-LIANG CHIU

Publications: *Arts Review* (1 a year), *Guandu Music Journal* (2 a year), *Journal of Cultural Resources* (1 a year), *Taipei Theatre Journal* (2 a year)

DEANS

Faculty of Culture Resources: HUI-CHENG LIN
Faculty of Dance: CHUNG-SHIUAN CHANG
Faculty of Fine Art: CHANG-HU LIN
Faculty of Music: HWANG-LONG PAN
Faculty of Theatre: MING-TE CHUNG

TAMKANG UNIVERSITY

151 Ying-Chuan Rd, Tamsui, Taipei 25137
Telephone: (2) 26215656
Fax: (2) 26237384
Internet: www.tku.edu.tw
Founded 1950 (formerly Tamkang College of Arts and Sciences)
Private control
Languages of instruction: Chinese, English
Academic year: August to July
Pres.: Dr HORNG-JINH CHANG
Vice-Pres. for Academic Affairs: Dr CHAO-KANG FENG

Vice-Pres. for Admin.: Dr FLORA CHIA-I CHANG
Sec.-Gen.: Dr TUN-LI CHEN
Dean of Academic Affairs: Dr HIS-JEN FU
Dean of General Affairs: Prof. CHING-JEN HUNG
Dean of Student Affairs: Dr HUAN-CHAO KEH
Librarian: Prof. HONG-CHU HUANG

Library of 753,911 vols, 6,901 periodicals
Number of teachers: 2,033
Number of students: 26,600

Publications: *Educational Media and Library Science, International Journal of Information and Management Science, Journal of Future Studies, Tamkang Journal, Tamkang Journal of International Affairs, Tamkang Mathematics, Tamkang Review*

DEANS OF COLLEGES

Business: Dr JONG-RONG CHIOU
Engineering: Dr SHI-CHIH CHU
Foreign Languages and Literature: Dr YAOFU LIN
International Studies: Dr WOU WEI
Liberal Arts: Dr SHIH-HSION HUANG
Management: Dr LIANG-YU OUYANG
Science: Dr KAN-NAN CHEN
Technocracy: Prof. HSIN-FU TSAI
Extension Education Centre: Prof. YAO-LUNG HAN

DIRECTORS OF GRADUATE INSTITUTES

Accounting: Dr CHEN-LI HUANG
Aerospace Engineering: Dr TZENG-YUAN CHEN
American Studies: Dr I-HSIN CHEN
Applied Statistics: Dr JONG-WUU WU
Architecture: Prof. HOANG-ELL JENG
Chemical Engineering: Dr KUO-JEN HWANG
Chemistry: Dr HUEY-CHUEN KAO
Chinese Literature: Dr PO-YUAN KAO
China Studies: Dr ANDY W. Y. CHANG
Civil Engineering: Dr CHO-SEN WO
Educational Media Library Science: Dr JEONG-YEOU CHIU
Educational Technology: Dr CHIEN-HUA WANG
Electrical Engineering: Dr JEN-CHIUN CHIANG
European Studies: Dr TZUNG-JEN TSAI
History: Dr TZENG-CHYUAN LIOU
Industrial Economics: Dr JIUNN-RONG CHIOU
Information Engineering: Dr KUO-CHEN SHIH
Information Management: Dr CHEN-CHUNG HUANG
International Affairs and Strategic Studies: Dr MING-HSIEN WONG
International Business: Dr JYH-HORNG LIN
Japanese Studies: Dr CHANG-HUEI LIU
Latin-American Studies: Dr KWO-WEI KUNG
Management Science: Dr PEI-CHI LEE
Mass Communication: Dr SHU-HUA CHANG
Mathematics: Dr CHIN-MEI KAU
Mechanical Engineering: Dr FENG-HUI YEH
Money, Banking and Finance: Dr GIN-CHUNG LIN
Physics: Dr WAY-FAUNG PONG
Public Administration: Dr MING-SIANG CHEN
Slavic Studies: Dr ALEXANDER PISAREV
South-east Asian Studies: Dr JUO-YU LIN
Transportation Management: Dr HSIAO-HSIEN LUO
Water Resources and Environmental Engineering: Dr PO-CHIEN LU
Western Languages and Literature: Dr CHUN-CHUNG LIN

TUNGHAI UNIVERSITY

181 Taichung Harbour Rd, Sec. 3, Taichung 40704
Telephone: (4) 23590200
Fax: (4) 23590361
E-mail: kpwang@mail.thu.edu.tw
Internet: www.thu.edu.tw

Founded 1955 under the auspices of the United Board for Christian Higher Education in Asia

Languages of instruction: Chinese, English

Academic year: September to July (2 semesters)

President: KANG-PEI WANG

Dean of Academic Affairs: CHENG-TUNG LIN

Dean of General Affairs: I-CHAO HSIAO

Dean of Student Affairs: HUNG-DER FU

Librarian: CHUNG-LIN LU

Number of teachers: 826

Number of students: 14,500

Publications: *The Vineyard, Tunghai Bulletin, Tunghai Journal, Tunghai News*

DEANS

College of Agriculture: TSUN-CHUNG TSAI

College of Arts: HAI-YUN HUANG

College of Engineering: JEN-TENG TSAI

College of Management: TSAI-DING LIN

College of Science: CHING-SHENG CHEN

College of Social Sciences: JENN-HWAN WANG

Colleges and Institutes

China Medical College: 91 Hseuh Shih Rd, Taichung 404; tel. (4) 2057153; f. 1958; private control; two campuses (in Taichung and Peikang), six graduate institutes, 12 undergraduate schools, Chiang Kai-shek Medical Center, two teaching hospitals; 625 staff; 4,666 students; Pres. MASON CHEN.

Kaohsiung Medical University: 100 Shih Chuan 1st Rd, Kaohsiung 807; tel. (7) 3117820; fax (7) 3212062; internet www .kmu.edu.tw; f. 1954; private control; colleges of medicine, dental medicine, pharmacy, nursing, health sciences, life sciences; undergraduate division of 19 schools; 12 postgraduate institutes; 7 research centres: health and social services, industrial hygiene, gender studies, tropical medicine, orthopaedics, genomics, proteomics; 428 teachers; 6,106 students; library: 175,802 vols, 2,970 periodicals; Pres. Dr GWO-JAW WANG; publ. *Kaohsiung Journal of Medical Sciences* (12 a year).

National Kaohsiung University of Applied Sciences: 415 Chien-Kung Rd, Kaohsiung 807; tel. (7) 3814526; fax (7) 3838435; f. 1963; depts of accounting, applied foreign languages, business administration, chemical, civil, cultural industries development, electrical, electronic, finance, human resource development, industrial management, information management, international trade, mechanical, mould- and die-making engineering, taxation and finance, tourism; graduate institutes of civil engineering and disaster prevention, commerce, electrical energy and control, electronic and information engineering, finance and information, mechanical and precision engineering, tourism management; library: 171,674 vols; 415 teachers; 10,727 students; Pres. Dr REN-YIH LIN; publ. *Journal* (1 a year).

Taipei Institute of Technology: 3, Sec. 1, Shin-sheng South Rd, Taipei; f. 1912; 8,973 students; library: 112,000 vols; Pres. Dr CHIH TANG.

Taipei Medical College: 250 Wu Hsing St, Taipei; tel. (2) 27361661; fax (2) 27362824; f. 1960; private control; undergraduate and graduate programmes; 568 teachers; 4,208 students; library: 83,000 vols; Pres. CHUNG-HONG HU; Vice-Pres. MEEI-SHIOW LU; Dean of Studies KUANG-YANG HSU; publ. *Journal* (2 a year).

Tatung University: 40 Chungshan N Rd, Sec. 3, Taipei; tel. (2) 25925252; fax (2) 25941371; e-mail registrar@ttu.edu.tw; internet www.ttu.edu.tw; f. 1956; private control; depts of applied mathematics, bioengineering, business management, chemical engineering, computer science and engineering, electrical engineering, industrial design, information management, materials engineering, mechanical engineering; graduate institutes in electro-optical engineering and communications engineering; 200 teachers; 2,500 students; library: 159,683 vols; Pres. T. S. LIN; Dean of Studies JAN-CHEN HONG.

School of Art and Music

National Taiwan College of Arts: Panchiao, Taipei; tel. (2) 22722181; fax (2) 29687563; internet www.ntca.edu.tw; f. 1955; Chinese music, cinema, dance, drama, fine arts, graphic arts, industrial arts, music, painting, radio and television, sculpture; 364 teachers; 2,300 students; library: 104,000 vols; Pres. MING-SHEAN WANG.

COLOMBIA

The Higher Education System

The Roman Catholic Church pioneered higher education in Colombia, with the establishment of the Pontificia Universidad Javeriana in 1622, and remained the driving force behind universities until the 1930s. In 1994 the Educational Law (No. 115) put the Ministry of National Education in charge of public and private education. In 2002 there were an estimated 321 higher education institutes (including universities) in Colombia. In 2006/07 some 1,372,700 students were enrolled in higher education. Other university-level institutions include centros, corporaciones, escuelas, fundaciones, institutos and colegios.

Admission to higher education is on the basis of the secondary school certificate (Bachillerato) and, from March 2000, a new version of the State Higher Education Entrance Examination. The basic university degree structure consists of Licenciado (equivalent to Bachelors), Magister (Masters) and Doctorado (Doctorate) degrees. Undergraduates study for four to five years for the Licenciado or professional title. At postgraduate level the Diploma de Especialización (Diploma of Specialization) requires one to four years of study, usually in a professional or applied discipline. The Magister is awarded after two years of study following Licenciado, while a Doctorado requires two to three years of study in an area of specialization.

Public and private institutos tecnológicas (technical institutes) offer post-secondary technical and vocational education. The title Técnico Profesional Intermedio is awarded after two years of study following the Bachillerato, and a Título de Tecnólogo or a Técnico de Alto Nivel is awarded by technical institutes and some universities after three years of study. Another qualification is the Tecnólogo Especializado, which requires two years of study.

Regulatory and Representative Bodies

GOVERNMENT

Ministry of Culture: Calle 8, No 6-97, Bogotá, DC; tel. (1) 3424100; fax (1) 3421721; e-mail servicioalcliente@mincultura.gov.co; internet www.mincultura.gov.co; Minister PAULA MARCELA MORENO ZAPATA.

Ministry of National Education: Centro Administrativo Nacional (CAN), Of. 501, Calle 45, Avda El Dorado, Bogotá, DC; tel. (1) 2222800; fax (1) 2224578; e-mail dci@mineducacion.gov.co; internet www.mineducacion.gov.co; Minister CECILIA MARÍA VÉLEZ WHITE.

ACCREDITATION

Consejo Nacional de Acreditación (National Accreditation Council): Calle 19 No. 6-68 Piso 17, Bogotá; tel. (1) 3411050; fax (1) 2863416; e-mail cna@cna.gov.co; internet www.cna.gov.co; f. 1992; 7 academic mems; directs and organizes the accreditation of programmes and instns; Coordinator HAROLD JOSÉ RIZO OTERO.

FUNDING

Instituto Colombiano de Crédito Educativo y Estudios Técnicos en el Exterior (ICETEX) (Colombian Institute for Educational Loans and Advanced Studies Abroad): Carrera 3a, No. 18–24, Apdo Aéreo 5735, Bogotá; tel. (1) 2867780; fax (1) 2843510; f. 1950; provides undergraduate and postgraduate grants; selects Colombian students for foreign scholarships, and finances foreign postgraduate students in Colombia; information and documentation centres; library of 15,000 vols; Dir Dr CARLOS A. BURITICÁ GIRALDO.

NATIONAL BODIES

Asociación Colombiana de Universidades (Colombian Universities Association): Calle 93 No. 16–43, Bogotá; tel. (1) 6231580; fax (1) 2185098; e-mail ascun@ascun.org.co; internet www.ascun.org.co; f. 1957; 70 mem univs; Pres. Monseñor LUIS FERNANDO RODRÍGUEZ VELÁSQUEZ; Sec.-Gen. Dr CARLOS HERNANDO FORERO ROBAYO.

Instituto Colombiano para el Fomento de la Educación Superior (ICFES) (Colombian Institute for the Promotion of Higher Education): Calle 17 No. 3-40, Bogotá; tel. (1) 3387338; e-mail direcciondelicfes@icfes.gov.co; internet www.icfes.gov.co; attached to Min. of Nat. Education; assesses the Colombian educational system at all levels; implements policies to promote higher education and assessment; promotes the devt of research in higher education instns; Dir MARGARITA PEÑA BORRERO; Gen. Sec. GENISBERTO LÓPEZ CONDE.

Learned Societies

GENERAL

Academia Colombiana de la Lengua (Colombian Academy): Apdo Aereo 13922, Bogotá; f. 1871; corresp. of the Real Academia Española (Madrid); 29 mems; 50 corresp. and hon. mems; library of 40,000 vols; Dir JAIME POSADA DÍAZ; Exec. Sec. JAIME BERNAL LEONGÓMEZ; publ. Boletín.

Casa de la Cultura de la Costa (House of Caribbean Coast Culture): Carrera 3, No. 19–60, Of. 401, Bogotá; tel. (1) 2433898; f. 1981; study centre for development of the Colombian coastal regions and int. Caribbean studies; mems: 36 companies and individuals, 86 congressmen from the coast; library of 2,000 vols; Pres. MARCO ANTONIO CONTRERAS; Sec. GERARDO MORA MEDINA; publ. Revista Caribe Internacional (12 a year).

AGRICULTURE, FISHERIES AND VETERINARY SCIENCE

Sociedad de Agricultores de Colombia (Colombian Farmers' Society): Carrera 7 No. 24–89, 44° piso, Apdo Aéreo 3638, Bogotá; tel. (1) 2821989; fax (1) 2844572; internet www.sac.org.co; f. 1871; consultative body for the Government; 400 mems; library of 5,500 vols, 435 periodical titles; Pres. RAFAEL MEJIA LÓPEZ; Sec. RICARDO SÁNCHEZ LÓPEZ; publs Documentos Independientes, El Editorial Agrario (irregular), Revista Nacional de Agricultura (4 a year).

BIBLIOGRAPHY, LIBRARY SCIENCE AND MUSEOLOGY

Asociación Colombiana de Bibliotecarios (ASCOLBI) (Colombian Association of Librarians): Calle 10, No. 3–16, Apdo Aéreo 30883, Bogotá; tel. (1) 2694219; f. 1942; 1,200 mems; Pres. SAUL SANCHEZ TORO; Gen. Sec. B. N. CARDONA DE GIL; publ. Boletín (4 a year).

Centro Regional para el Fomento del Libro en América Latina y el Caribe (CERLALC) (Regional Centre for the Promotion of Books in Latin America and the Caribbean): Calle 70 No. 9–52, Apdo Aéreo 57348, Bogotá; tel. (1) 3217501; fax (1) 3217503; internet www.cerlalc.com; f. 1972 by UNESCO and Colombian govt, later joined by most states in the area; promotes production and circulation of books, and development of libraries; provides training; promotes protection of copyright; 21 mem. countries; library of 5,600 documents, 100 periodicals; Dir ALMA BYINGTON DE ARBOLEDA; publs Boletín Informativo CERLALC (4 a year), El Libro en América Latina y el Caribe (4 a year).

Fundación para el Fomento de la Lectura—(FUNDALECTURA): Dg 40A bis No. 16–46, Apdo 48902, Bogotá; tel. (1) 3201511; fax (1) 2877071; e-mail contactenos@fundalectura.org.co; internet www.fundalectura.org; f. 1984; promotion of reading, and children's and juvenile literature; library of 40,200 vols; Dir CARMEN BARVO; publs Nuevas Hojas de Lectura (3 a year), Revista Latinoamericana de Literatura Infantil y Juvenil (online at www.relalij.com, 2 a year).

ECONOMICS, LAW AND POLITICS

Academia Colombiana de Jurisprudencia (Colombian Academy of Jurisprudence): Carrera 9 No. 74–08, Oficina 203, Bogotá; tel. (1) 2124315; f. 1894; 50 mems; Pres. HERNANDO MORALES M.; publs Anuario, Revista (2 a year).

Sociedad Colombiana de Economistas: Carrera 20 No. 36–41, Apdo Aéreo 8429, Bogotá; tel. (1) 2459637; f. 1957 to promote the improvement of the teaching of economic sciences and economics as a profession, for the economic and social development of the country; 5,500 mems; library of 25,000 vols; Pres. Dr SERGIO ENTRENA LÓPEZ; publ. *Revista* (6 a year).

HISTORY, GEOGRAPHY AND ARCHAEOLOGY

Academia Antioqueña de Historia (Antioquia Academy of History): Carrera 43, Nos 53–37, Apdo Aéreo 7175, Medellín; tel. (942) 395576; f. 1903; 60 mems; Pres. JAIME SIERRA GARCÍA; Sec. ALICIA GIRALDO GÓMEZ; publs *Bolsilibros, Repertorio Histórico* (3 a year).

Academia Boyacense de Historia (Boyaca Academy of History): Casa del Fundador, Tunja; tel. (9792) 3441; f. 1905; publication and encouragement of historical, literary and anthropological studies in Boyaca; 30 mems; library of 1,000 vols, 600 MSS from the period 1539–1860; Pres. JAVIER OCAMPO LÓPEZ; Sec. RAMÓN CORREA; publ. *Repertorio Boyacense* (2 a year).

Academia Colombiana de Historia (Colombian Academy of History): Calle 10 No. 8–95, Apdo Aéreo 14428, Bogotá; f. 1902; 40 mems excluding Colombian and foreign corresp. mems; library of 45,000 vols; Pres. Dr GERMÁN ARCINIEGAS; Sec. ROBERTO VELANDIA; Library Dir Dr RAFAEL SERRANO CAMARGO; publ. *Boletín de Historia y Antigüedades*.

Academia de la Historia de Cartagena de Indias (Cartagena Academy of History): Casa de la Inquisición, Plaza Bolívar, Cartagena; tel. (59) 645432; f. 1918; 24 mems, and 48 Colombian, and 48 foreign corresponding mems; library of 10,000 vols; special collections on the history of Cartagena and Colombia; Pres. DONALDO BOSSA HERAZO; Sec.-Gen. CELEDONIO PIÑERES DE LA ESPRIELLA; publ. *Boletín Historial* (4 a year).

Sociedad Bolivariana de Colombia: Calle 19A No 4–40E, Apdo 11812, Bogotá; tel. (1) 2431166; f. 1924; 20 hon. mems; library of 1,000 vols, specialized bibliography on Simón Bolívar; Pres. Col ALBERTO LOZANO; publ. *Revista Bolivariana* (3 a year).

Sociedad Geográfica de Colombia (Colombian Geographical Society): Observatorio Astronómico Nacional, Apdo 2584, Bogotá; tel. (1) 2348893; f. 1903; 40 mems; Pres. CLEMENTE GARAVITO; Sec. RAFAEL CONVERS PINZON; publs *Boletín* (3 a year), *Cuadernos de Geografía Colombiana*; branch socs in Barranquilla, Medellín, Pasto, Sibundoy, Tunja.

LANGUAGE AND LITERATURE

Alliance Française: Carrera 7a 84–72, Bogotá; tel. (1) 2563197; fax (1) 6556045; e-mail alfradir@neutel.com.co; internet www.alianzafrancesa.org.co; offers courses and examinations in French language and culture and promotes cultural exchange with France; attached teaching offices in Armenia, Barranquilla, Bogatá-Centro, Bucuramanga, Cali, Cartagena, Manizales, Medellín, Pereira, Popayán and Santa Marta.

British Council: Carrera 9 No. 76–49, piso 5, Bogotá DC; tel. (1) 3259090; fax (1) 3259091; e-mail customer.services@britishcouncil.org.co; internet www.britishcouncil.org/colombia; offers courses and examinations in English language and British culture and promotes cultural exchange with the UK; separate teaching centre in Bogotá; library of 7,500 vols, 60 periodicals; Dir ROBERT NESS.

Goethe-Institut: Carrera 7, No. 81–57, Bogotá; tel. (1) 2547600; fax (1) 2127167; e-mail vl@bogota.goethe.org; internet www.goethe.de/hn/bog/deindex.htm; offers courses and examinations in German language and culture and promotes cultural exchange with Germany; Dir FOLCO NÄTHER.

Instituto Caro y Cuervo: Carrera 10 No. 4–69, Apdo Aéreo 51502, Bogotá; tel. (1) 3422121; fax (1) 2170243; e-mail contactenos@caroycuervo.gov.co; internet www.caroycuervo.gov.co; f. 1942; attached to Min. of Culture; Hispanic philology and literature; library of 102,491 vols, 102,000 vols of periodicals; Dir HERNANDO CABARCAS ANTEQUERA; Sec.-Gen. LILIANA RIVERA ORJUELA; publs *Aguas Vivas, Anuario Bibliográfico Colombiano, Archivo Epistolar Colombiano, Atlas Linguístico-Etnográfico de Colombia, Biblioteca de Publicaciones del Instituto, Biblioteca Colombiana, Biblioteca 'Ezequiel Uricoechea', Clásicos Colombianos, Cuadernos del Seminario Andrés Bello, Diccionario de Construcción y Régimen de la Lengua Castellana, Filólogos Colombianos, La Granada Entreabierta, Litterae, Noticias Culturales* (6 a year), *Poesia Rescatada, Thesaurus* (3 a year).

PEN Internacional, Colombia: Calle 88, 11A-20, Apdo 302, Bogotá; tel. (1) 6919627; e-mail pencolombia@cable.net.co; f. 1936; 50 mems; library of 1,000 vols; Pres. Emeritus Dr CECILIA BALCÁZAR; Pres. ENRIQUE SANTOS-MOLANO; Sec.-Gen. Prof. RUBÉN DARÍO FLÓREZ.

MEDICINE

Academia Nacional de Medicina de Colombia (Colombian National Academy of Medicine): Carrera 7 No. 69–05, Bogotá; tel. (1) 3458890; fax (1) 2128670; e-mail acadmed@cable.net.co; internet www.fepafem.org/anm; f. 1873; 557 mems; library of 10,000 vols; Pres. Dr JUAN MENDOZA-VEGA; Perm. Sec. Dr HERNANDO GROOT; publs *Medicina* (4 a year), *Temas Médicos* (1 a year).

Asociación Colombiana de Facultades de Medicina (Colombian Association of Medical Faculties): Apdo 53751, Calle 39a 28–63, Bogotá; tel. (1) 3686711; f. 1959 to further higher education and research in medicine; divisions of Education, Evaluation, Health and Social Security, Information; membership: 24 medical faculties (institutional mems), 4,500 individuals, 7 affiliated mems; library of 3,500 vols, 100 periodicals and audiovisual materials; Pres. JOSE MARIA MAYA; Exec. Dir. JULIO ENRIQUE OSPINA; publs *Boletín del Centro de Etica Médica y Bioética, Boletín de Medicamentos y Terapéutica* (4 a year), *Cuadernos de Actualización Médica Permanente, Gaceta Médica, Revista de ASCOFAME*.

Asociación Colombiana de Fisioterapía: Carrera 23 No. 47–51, Of. 3N-06-D, Bogotá; tel. (1) 2876106; f. 1953; 950 mems; library of 300 vols; Pres. ELISA JARAMILLO DE LOPEZ; Exec. Sec. CLARA INES DE AMAYA; publ. *Revista* (1 a year).

Asociación Colombiana de Psiquiatría: Carrera 18 No. 84–87, Oficina 403, Bogotá; tel. (1) 2561148; fax (1) 2563549; e-mail acp@psiquiatria.org.co; internet www.psiquiatria.org.co; f. 1961; 854 mems; Pres. Dr CARLOS ALBERTO MIRANDA BASTIDAS; Sec. Dr RAMÓN EDUARDO LOPERA LOPEA; publs *Cuadernos de Psiquiatría Enlace* (4 a year), *Revista Colombiana de Psiquiatría* (4 a year).

Asociación Colombiana de Sociedades Científicas: Cra. 16a 77-11, Oficina 404, Santafé de Bogotá; tel. (1) 5311226; fax (1) 2367483; e-mail sociedadsc@col.net.co; internet www.sociedadescientificas.com; f. 1957, present name 1970; health sciences; 3,692 mems; Exec. Dir Dr FABIO LOAIZA D.; publ. *Boletín* (4 a year).

Capitolo Colombiano de las Federaciones Latinoamericanas de Asociaciones de Cancer (Colombian Chapter of Latin American Cancer Asscns): Clínica del Country, Carrera 15 No. 84–13, Bogotá; tel. (1) 2361168; f. 1983; Pres. CALIXTO NOGUERA.

Federación Médica Colombiana: Carrera 7 No. 82–66, Oficinas 218/219, Bogotá; fax (1) 8050073; e-mail federacionmedica colombiana@encolombia.com; internet www.encolombia.com/federamedicolom.htm; f. 1935; Pres. Dr SERGIO ISAZA VILLA; Sec. SERGIO ROBLEDA RIAGA; publ. *Directorio Médico Asistencial* (1 a year).

Instituto Nacional de Medicina Legal y Ciencias Forenses (National Institute of Legal Medicine and Forensic Sciences): Calle 7a, A 12–61, Santafé de Bogotá; tel. (1) 233854; f. 1914; staff of 800; library of 30,000 vols; Dir RICARDO MORA IZQUIERDO; publ. *Revista*.

Sociedad Colombiana de Cardiología (Colombian Cardiological Society): Avda 19 No. 97-31 Of. 401, Apdo Aéreo 1875, Bogotá; tel. (1) 6234603; fax (1) 6234603; f. 1950; 245 mems; Pres. Dr RICARDO ROZO URIBE; Sec. Dra MARGARITA BLANCO DE ESCOBAR; publ. *Revista SCC* (4 a year).

Sociedad Colombiana de Cirugía Ortopédica y Traumatología: Calle 134 No. 7B-83, Oficina 201, Bogotá; tel. (1) 6257445; fax (1) 6257417; e-mail secretaria@sccot.org.co; internet www.sccot.org.co; f. 1946; 961 mems; Pres. Dr NICOLÁS RESTREPO; Gen. Sec. Dr FERNANDO HELO; publ. *Carta de Ortopédica* (12 a year).

Sociedad Colombiana de Obstetricia y Ginecología: Carrera 23, No. 39–82, Apdo Aéreo 34188, Bogotá; tel. (1) 2681485; f. 1943; 300 mems; library of 1,000 vols; Pres. Dr JAIME FERRO CAMARGO; Vice-Pres. Dra MARIA TERESA PERALTA ABELLO; Sec.-Gen. Dr PIO IVÁN GÓMEZ SÁNCHEZ; publ. *Revista Colombiana de Obstetricia y Ginecología* (4 a year).

Sociedad Colombiana de Patología: Dpto de Patología, Universidad del Valle, Cali; f. 1955; to improve all aspects of pathology studies; 155 mems; Pres. Dr EDGAR DUQUE; Sec. and Treas. Dr JOSÉ A. DORADO.

Sociedad Colombiana de Pediatría (Colombian Paediatrics Society): Avdo 4 Norte, No. 16–23, Apdo 3124, Cali; tel. (2) 611407; fax (2) 673614; f. 1917; 150 mems; library of 2,300 vols; Pres. CESAR A. VILLAMIZAR LUNA; Sec. ALBERTO LEVY F.; publs *Acta Pedriatrica Colombiana, Pediatría* (4 a year).

Sociedad Colombiana de Radiología (Radiological Society): Carrera 13a No. 90–18, Of. 208, Bogotá; tel. (1) 6183895; fax (1) 6183775; f. 1945; 400 mems; library of 3,000 vols, collections of journals; Pres. CAYO DUARTE; Sec. PATRICIA CASTRO S.

NATURAL SCIENCES

General

Academia Colombiana de Ciencias Exactas, Físicas y Naturales (Colombian Academy of Exact, Physical and Natural Sciences): Carrera 28a, No. 39A–63, Apdo Aéreo 44763, Bogotá DC; tel. (1) 2683290; fax (1) 2443486; internet www.accefyn.org.co; f. 1933; 40 active mems (98 corresp., 6 hon.); Pres. JAIME RODRIGUEZ LARA; Sec. JOSÉ A. LOZANO; publ. *Revista* (4 a year).

Biological Sciences

Sociedad Colombiana de Biología: Calle 73 No. 10–10, Apartamento 301, Bogotá; Pres Dr GONZALO MONTES; Sec. MARGARET ORDÓÑEZ SMITH.

Mathematical Sciences

Sociedad Colombiana de Matemáticas: Apdo Aéreo 2521, Bogotá 1; tel. (1) 3165000 ext.13232; f. 1955; 800 mems; library of 7,000 vols; Pres LEONARDO RENDÓN ARBELÁEZ; publs *Lecturas Matemáticas, Revista Colombiana de Matemáticas.*

Physical Sciences

Sociedad Colombiana de Ciencias Químicas: Univ. Nacional de Colombia, sede, Unidad Camilo Torres, Bloque C Modulo 7, Oficina 202, Bogotá; tel. (1) 2216920; fax (1) 3150751; e-mail info@socolquim.com; internet www.socolquim.com; f. 1941 to promote chemical research in Colombia, to uphold professional ethical standards, to serve as an advisory body for public and private orgs, to maintain relations with similar instns at home and abroad; 350 mems; Pres. FABIAN PARADA ALFONSO; Vice-Pres. BARBARA MORENO MURILLO; Sec. MYRIAM MUNOZ; Treas. CESAR SIERRA AVILA; publ. *Química e Industria* (2 a year).

TECHNOLOGY

Asociación Colombiana de Industrias Gráficas—ANDIGRAF (Graphic Industry National Association): Carrera 4a No. 25B–46, Apdo Aéreo 45243, Bogotá; tel. (1) 2819611; f. 1975; 200 company mems; Pres. JOSE GRANADA RODRIGUEZ; publs *Boletín Informativo* (12 a year), *Colombia Gráfica* (1 a year).

Asociación Colombiana de Informática y Comunicaciones (Colombian Association of Information Technology and Communication): Avda Estación 5B Norte, 73 Oficina 205, Santiago de Cali; tel. (2) 6675595; e-mail acvcsurocci@telesat.com.co; internet www.acvc.org.co; f. 1970; 400 company mems; library of 1,500 documents; Pres. JOSE GUILLERMO JARAMILLO G.; Exec. Dir CESAR AUGUSTO SALAZAR U.; publs *ACUC Noticias* (6 a year), *Boletín El Usuario* (52 a year), *Catálogo Nacional de Software—Guía de Servicios Informáticos* (1 a year).

Sociedad Colombiana de Ingenieros (Colombian Society of Engineers): Carrera 4, No. 10–41, Apdo 340, Bogotá; tel. (1) 2862200; fax (1) 2816229; f. 1887; 2,000 mems; library of 5,000 vols; Pres. HERNANDO MONROY VALENCIA; Exec. Dir SANTIAGO HENAO PÉREZ; publ. *Anales de Ingeniería* (4 a year).

Research Institutes

GENERAL

Instituto Colombiano para el Desarrollo de la Ciencia y la Tecnología 'Francisco José de Caldas' (Colciencias): Transversal 9a No. 133–28, Apdo Aéreo 051580, Santafé de Bogotá; tel. (1) 2169800; fax (1) 6251788; f. 1968 to promote scientific and technical development; coordinates and finances projects; library of 15,000 vols, 225 periodicals, 10,000 databases; Dir LUIS FERNANDO CHAPARRO OSORIO; Sec.-Gen. JUAN RICARDO MORALES ESPINEL; publs serials: *Carta de Colciencias* (12 a year), *Colombia Ciencia y Tecnología* (4 a year).

AGRICULTURE, FISHERIES AND VETERINARY SCIENCE

Instituto Colombiano Agropecuario (Colombian Agricultural and Livestock Institute): Apdo Aéreo 7984, Calle 37 No. 8–43 (4° y 5° pisos), Bogotá; tel. (1) 2855520; fax (1) 2884169; internet www.iica-saninet/ica/ica.htm; f. 1962 to promote, coordinate and carry out research, teaching and develop-

ment in agriculture and animal husbandry; library: see Libraries and Archives; Dir-Gen. ALVARO JOSÉ ABISAMBRA ABISAMBRA; publ. *Informe Anual.*

ECONOMICS, LAW AND POLITICS

Centro de Estudios sobre Desarrollo Económico (Centre for Economic Development Studies): Universidad de los Andes, Carrera 1E No. 18A–10, Apdo Aéreo 4976, Bogotá; tel. (1) 3324495; fax (1) 3324492; e-mail infocede@uniandes.edu.co; internet economia.uniandes.edu.co; f. 1958; library of 35,000 vols; Dir ROBERTO STEINER; publ. *Desarrollo y Sociedad* (2 a year).

Departamento Administrativo Nacional de Estadística (National Statistics Department): Transversal 45 No. 26–70 Interior 1 CAN, Apdo Aéreo 80043, Bogotá; tel. (1) 5978300; fax (1) 5978384; e-mail dane@dane.gov.co; internet www.dane.gov.co; f. 1953; library of 12,000 vols, 850 periodicals received; Dir CÉSAR AUGUSTO CABALLERO REINOSO; publs *Anuario de Comercio Exterior* (1 a year), *Anuario de Industria Manufacturera* (1 a year), *Atlas Sociodemigráfico de Colombia, Bases de Contabilidad, Boletín Mensual de Estadística* (12 a year), *Colombia Estadística, Cuentas Nacionales de Colombia, DIVIPOLA, Estudios Censales, Indicadores de Coyuntura, Metodología Cuentas Departamentales, Mujeres con Hijos Habitantes de la Calle, Plan Estadístico de Cundinamarca.*

EDUCATION

Centro de Investigación y Educación Popular: Carrera 5 No 33A–08, Apdo 25916, Bogotá; tel. (1) 2858977; fax (1) 2879089; f. 1962; private, non-profit org. specializing in social sciences education, and analysis of the Colombian system; library of 25,000 vols; Dir Dr MAURICIO GARCIA-DURAN; publs *Cien Días* (4 a year), *Controversia* (2 a year).

Instituto Colombiano para el Fomento de la Educación Superior: Calle 17 No. 3–40, Apdo Aéreo 6319, Bogotá; tel. (1) 2819311; fax (1) 2868045; e-mail snies@icfes.gov.co; f. 1968; branch of the Min. of National Education; govt body supervising the running of higher education; coordinates the country's distance education system; library: documentation centre specializing in higher, distance and 'open' education, and nat. film colln: 9,200 vols, 2,500 documents, 2,527 periodicals, 1,015 films, audiovisual items and video cassettes; Dir LUIS CARLOS MUÑOZ URIBE; publs *Estadísticas de la Educación Superior, Memorias de Eventos Científicos, Revista ICFES* (irregular).

HISTORY, GEOGRAPHY AND ARCHAEOLOGY

Instituto Colombiano de Antropología e Historia (Colombian Institute of Anthropology and History): Calle 12 No. 2–41, Apdo Aéreo 407, Bogotá; tel. (1) 3418849; fax (1) 2811051; f. 1941; research in fields of history, archaeology and anthropology; oversees cultural, archaeological and anthropological patrimony of Colombia, and administers national archaeological parks; publishes editions of 'Flora of the Botanic Expedition' of the New Kingdom of Granada; library of 30,000 vols (open to public); Dir MARÍA VICTORIA URIBE-ALARCÓN; publs *Fronteras de la Historia* (1 a year), *Revista Colombiana de Antropología* (1 a year).

Instituto Geográfico 'Agustín Codazzi': Apdo 6721, Carrera 30 No. 48–51, Santafé de Bogotá; tel. (1) 3694053; fax (1) 3694099; e-mail webpage@igac.gov.co; internet www.igac.gov.co; f. 1935; prepares topographical,

cadastral, sectional, national, and agricultural maps of the country, and geophysical, cadastral and geodetic surveys; prepares geographical studies of Colombia; library of 10,000 vols; Dir IVAN DARIO GOMEZ GUZMÁN.

MEDICINE

Instituto Nacional de Cancerología: Calle 1, No. 9–85, Bogotá 1; tel. (1) 3342474; fax (1) 3341844; e-mail biblioteca@incancerologia.gov.co; internet www.incancerologia.gov.co; f. 1934; diagnosis, therapy, control, teaching and research in cancer; adviser instn to Min. of Health, designs and implements national policies and programmes to control the spread of cancer; library of 26,000 vols; Dir-Gen. CARLOS VICENTE RADA ESCOBAR; publ. *Revista Colombiana de Cancerología.*

Instituto Nacional de Salud (National Institute of Health): Avda el Dorado Carrera 50, Apdo Aéreo 80334, Bogotá; tel. (1) 2221059; fax (1) 2220194; f. 1968; library of 10,000 vols, 500 periodicals; Dir Dr MOISES WASSERMAN; publs *Biomédica, Boletín Epidemiológico, Informe Quincenal de Casos y Brotes de Enfermedades* (26 a year).

NATURAL SCIENCES

Biological Sciences

Instituto de Ciencias Naturales (Institute of Natural Sciences): Universidad Nacional de Colombia, Apdo 7495, Bogotá; tel. (1) 3165305; fax (1) 3165365; e-mail inscien_bog@unal.edu.co; internet www.icn.unal.edu.co; f. 1936 to conduct scientific research; 3 main sections: botany, zoology and archaeology; library of 8,000 vols; Dir GLORIA GALEANO; publs *Biblioteca José Jerónimo Triana, Caldasia, Fauna de Colombia, Flora de Colombia.*

Instituto de Investigaciones Marinas de Punta de Betín 'José Benito Vives de Andreis' (INVEMAR): Apdo Aéreo 1016, Santa Marta; tel. (327) 211380; fax (327) 211377; f. 1963; institute of Colciencias (*q.v.*); aims to study and preserve the marine wildlife of the Colombian Caribbean; library of 10,000 vols; Dir Dra LEONOR BOTERO; publ. *Anales.*

Physical Sciences

Observatorio Astronómico Nacional (National Astronomical Observatory): Carrera 8, Calle 8, Apdo Aéreo 2584, Bogotá; tel. (1) 2423786; f. 1803; library of 3,000 vols; Dir JORGE ARRAS DE GREIFF; publs *Anuario del Observatorio*, occasional publications.

TECHNOLOGY

Instituto Colombiano de Geologia y Mineria (INGEOMINAS) (Institute for Research and Information in the Geosciences, Mining, the Environment and Nuclear Physics): Diagonal 53, No. 34–53, Apdo Aéreo 4865, Bogotá; tel. (1) 2221811; fax (1) 2220797; internet www.ingeominas.gov.co; f. 1940 as National Geological Survey, name changed 1969; library of 6,000 books, 104 current periodicals, 2,400 technical reports; Dir Dr JULIAN VILLARRUEL TORO; publs *Boletín de Actividad Sismica, Boletín Geológico* (3 vols, 1 a year), *Boletin de Vocanes Colombianos, Informe de Actividades Anuales, Revista Ingeominas.*

Instituto Colombiano de Normas Técnicas y Certificación (ICONTEC): Carrera 37, No. 52–95, Bogotá; tel. (1) 6078888; fax (1) 2221435; e-mail cliente@icontec.org.co; internet www.icontec.org.co; f. 1963; 1,200 mems; library of 800,000 vols; Exec. Dir Ing. FABIO TOBÓN; Admin. Dir RICARDO TOBO; publ. *Normas y Calidad* (4 a year).

Instituto Colombiano del Petróleo (Colombian Petroleum Institute): Autopista Piedecuesta Km 7, Apdo Aereo 4185, Bucaramanga; tel. (57) 76445420; fax (57) 76445444; internet www.icp.ecopetrol.com .co; exploration and development of oil reserves; library of 19,000 vols, 500 periodicals and newspapers, 1,000 audiovisual items, 8,000 documents; Dir JAIME CADAVID CALVO; publ. *GT & F Magazine*.

Instituto de Ciencias Nucleares y Energías Alternativas (Institute for Nuclear Sciences and Alternative Energy): Avda Eldorado, Carrera 50, Apdo Aéreo 8595, Santafé de Bogotá, DC; tel. (1) 2220071; fax (1) 2220173; f. 1959 to study the application of atomic and nuclear energy for peaceful uses, the development of alternative energy sources and the efficient use of energy; library of 18,000 vols, 60 periodicals, 70,000 reprints, 120,000 microforms; Dir Dr CESAR HUMBERTO ARIAS PABON.

Libraries and Archives

Barranquilla

Biblioteca Pública Departamental Meira Delmar: Calla 38, No. 38B–21, Barranquilla; tel. (95) 3307020; e-mail baguilar@ atlantico.gov.co; internet www.cultura .atlantico.gov.co/biblioteca.asp; f. 1923; 40,000 vols; Dir BEATRIZ EUGENIA AGUILAR CADAVID.

Bello

Biblioteca del Marco Fidel Suárez: Avda Suárez, Bello, Antioquia; tel. (942) 750774; f. 1957; public library and regional centre; 2,615 vols; Dir WALTER GIL.

Bogotá

Archivo Nacional de Colombia: Archivo General de la Nación, Calle 24 No. 5–60, 4° piso, Bogotá; tel. (1) 416015; f. 1868; 40,600 vols and 3,135 metres of documents; Dir JORGE PALACIOS PRECIADO; publs *Catálogos*, *Revista*.

Biblioteca Agropecuaria de Colombia: Inst. Colombiano Agropecuario, Apdo Aéreo 240142, Santafé de Bogotá; tel. (1) 3443000 ext. 1253; fax (1) 3443000 ext. 1248; e-mail fsalazar@corpoica.org.co; internet www .corpoica.org.co; f. 1954; 46,000 vols devoted to agriculture and livestock, 46,300 pamphlets, 1,900 journals, 29,560 documents, 170 maps, 150 audiovisual titles, 497 tapes; Dir FRANCISCO SALAZAR ALONSO.

Biblioteca Central de la Pontificia Universidad Javeriana: Carrera 7a, No. 41-00, Bogotá; tel. (1) 3208320 ext. 2132; fax (1) 2850973; f. 1931; 287,000 vols; Dir LUZ MARIA CABARCAS SANTOYA.

Biblioteca 'Luis-Angel Arango' del Banco de la República (Bank of the Republic Library): Carrera 5 No. 11–68, Apdo Aéreo 3531, Bogotá; tel. (1) 3431202; fax (1) 2863551; e-mail wbiblio@banrep.gov .co; internet www.lablaa.org; f. 1932; includes Museo Botero and Museo de Artes del Banco de la Republica; 1,050,000 vols, 23,000 periodicals, 14,000 maps, 102,000 slides, 4,000 original works of art, 25,000 sound recordings, 9,000 video recordings; Dir JORGE ORLANDO MELO; publ. *Boletín Cultural y Bibliográfico* (3 a year).

Biblioteca Nacional de Colombia (National Library): Calle 24, No. 5–60, Apdo 27600, Bogotá; tel. (1) 3414029; fax (1) 3414030; f. 1777; 800,000 vols, 22,000 periodicals; rare book section (28,000 vols); Dir CARLOS JOSÉ REYES POSADA; publ. *Revista Senderos*.

Biblioteca Seminario Conciliar de San José (Library of the San José Seminary): Carrera 7 No. 94–80, Bogotá 8; tel. (1) 6440405; fax (1) 2181096; e-mail semmayorbogota@hotmail.com; internet www.seminariobogota.org; f. 1581; 40,000 vols specializing in philosophy and theology; Dir Rev. CESAR BARACALDO VEGA.

Dirección de Bibliotecas—Sede Bogotá, Universidad Nacional de Colombia: Ciudad Universitaria, Apdo Aéreo 14490, Santafé de Bogotá; tel. and fax (1) 3165000; e-mail jensanchezsal@unal.edu.co; internet www.sinab.unal.edu.co/bog; f. 1867; 900,000 vols; Dir JENNIFER SÁNCHEZ SALAZAR.

División de Documentación e Información Educativa, Ministerio de Educación Nacional (Educational Documentation and Information Division, Ministry of National Education): Avda El Dorado, CAN, Bogotá; tel. (1) 222800; coordinates the Educational Documentation and Information Sub-system, the School Libraries National Programme and runs the National Educational Documentation Centre; 10,000 vols, 300 pamphlets, 6,000 documents, 300 periodicals; Dir MARY LUZ ISAZA; publs *Correo Educativo, Memorias del Ministro de Educación al Congreso Nacional* (1 a year).

Calí

Biblioteca Centenario: Avda Colombia Cl. 4 Oeste, Calí; tel. (2) 8932908; f. 1910; 22,000 vols; Dir ORIETTA LOZANO.

Biblioteca Departamental de Calí: Calle 14 Norte No 9–45, Calí; tel. (2) 6613018; fax (2) 6618214; 54,000 vols; Dir ELISA INÉS ARBOLEDA MAYORK.

Cartagena

Centro de Información y Documentación Biblioteca Fernández de Madrid, Universidad de Cartagena: Centro Cra. 6 No.36–100, Cartagena; tel. (95) 6646182; fax (95) 6697778; f. 1827; 50,000 vols; Librarian LUIS EDUARDO ESPINAL A.

Manizales

Biblioteca Central, Universidad de Caldas: Apdo Aéreo 275, Calle 65 No. 26-10, Manizales, Caldas; tel. (968) 861250 ext. 115; fax (968) 862520; internet biblio.ucaldas.edu .co; f. 1958; 53,000 vols, 5,500 documents, 1,300 periodicals; Librarian SAUL SANCHEZ TORO; publs *HIPSIPILA – Revista Cultural de la Universidad* (2 a year), *Revista de Agronomía* (4 a year), *Revista de Educación Física y Recreación* (2 a year), *Revista de Medicina Veterinaria y Zootecnia* (2 a year), *Revista de la Universidad de Caldas* (2 a year).

Biblioteca Pública Municipal: Calle 23 No. 20–30, Manizales; tel. (968) 831697; f. 1931; 8,100 vols; Librarian NELLY AGUIRRE DE FIGUEROA.

Medellín

Biblioteca de la Universidad Pontificia Bolivariana: Apdo Aéreo 56006, Medellín; tel. (4) 4159075; fax (4) 4118513; internet biblio.upb.edu.co; f. 1936; 139,000 vols, 3,000 periodicals, 12,779 pamphlets, 150,000 audiovisual records; Librarian Lic. OLGA BEATRIZ BERNAL LONDOÑO; publs *Comunicación UPB, Cuestiones Teológicas, Revista de la Facultad de Derecho y Ciencias Políticas, Revista de la Facultad de Filosofía, Revista de la Facultad de Medicina, Revista de la Facultad de Trabajo Social, Revista Universidad Pontificia Bolivariana*.

Biblioteca Pública Piloto de Medellín (Pilot Public Library of Medellín): Carrera 64 con Calle 50 No. 50–32, Apdo Aéreo 1797, Medellín; tel. (4) 2302422; fax (4) 2305389; f. 1954 under the auspices of UNESCO; 85,000 vols; spec. collns: Antioquia and Antioquian authors, UNESCO depository; Dir GLORIA INES PALOMINO L.

Departamento de Bibliotecas, Universidad de Antioquia: Apdo Aéreo 1226, Medellín; tel. (4) 2105140; fax (4) 2116939; internet biblioteca.udea.edu.co; f. 1935; 13 br. libraries; 662,000 vols, 7,000 periodicals; Dir NORA HELENA LÓPEZ CALLE; publs *Ex-Libris* (4 a year), *Leer y Releer* (4 a year).

Popayán

Departamento de Bibliotecas, Universidad del Cauca: Apdo Nacional 113, Calle 5 No 4–70, Popayán; tel. (2) 8209800; internet biblio.unicauca.edu.co; f. 1827; 70,000 vols; Dir JOSÉ MARÍA SERRANO PRADA; publs *Catálogo del Archivo Central del Cauca, Boletín Bibliográfico, Boletín Informativo, Cuadernos de Medicina, Boletín del Comité de Investigaciones Científicas, Revista Cátedra*.

Tunja

Universidad Pedagógica y Tecnológica de Colombia, Biblioteca Central, Tunja: Apdo Aéreo 1234, Tunja; tel. (98) 400668; f. 1932; 68,000 vols; 1,800 periodical titles; spec. collns: theses, Fondo E. Posada, rare books, learned works; Dir BARBARA MARTIN MARTIN; publs *Lista de Canje, Apuntes del CENES, Educación y Ciencia, Cuadernos de Linguística hispánica-UPTC, Agricultura y Ciencia, Perspectiva Proceso Salud-Enfermedad, Inquietud Empresarial, Revista Facultad de Ingeniería, Revista de Ciencias Sociales*.

Museums and Art Galleries

Bogotá

Casa Museo 'Jorge Eliécer Gaitán': Calle 42, No. 15–23, Bogotá; tel. (1) 2450368; fax (1) 2879093; f. 1948; collection relating to the history of Bogotá; run by the Centro Jorge Eliécer Gaitán; Dir GLORIA GAITÁN.

Casa Museo Quinta de Bolívar (Bolívar Museum): Calle 20, No. 2–91 Este, Bogotá; tel. (1) 3366419; fax (1) 3366410; e-mail quintadebolivar@excite.com; f. 1919 in the country house occupied by Simón Bolívar from 1820 to 1830, where relics of the Liberator and his epoch are exhibited; is administered by the Ministry of Culture and the Sociedad de Mejoras y Ornato de Bogotá; Dir DANIEL CASTRO BENÍTEZ.

Jardín Botánico de Bogotá 'José Celestino Mutis': Calle 63 No. 68–95, Bogotá; tel. (1) 4377060; fax (1) 6305075; e-mail bogotanico@jbb.gov.co; internet www.jbb.gov .co; f. 1955; research and conservation of biodiversity in the Andean ecosystem; library of 6,000 vols; Dir HERMAN MARTÍNEZ GÓMEZ; Gen. Sec EDNA PATRICIA RANGEL BARRAGÁN; publ. *Pérez-Arbelaezia* (2 a year).

Museo Colonial (Museum of the Colonial Period): Carrera 6, No. 9–77, Bogotá; tel. (1) 3416017; fax (1) 2866768; e-mail colonial@ mincultura.gov.co; f. 1942; paintings, sculpture, furniture, gold and silver work, drawings, etc., of the Spanish colonial period (16th, 17th and 18th centuries); library of 1,000 vols in education dept; installed in a building erected by the Jesuits in 1604 to house the first Javeriana University; Dir CONSTANZA TOQUICA CLAVIJO; publ. *Cuadernos de Estudio* (1 a year).

Museo del Oro (Gold Museum): Calle 16 No. 5–41, Parque de Santander, Bogotá; tel. (1)

3431414; fax (1) 2847450; e-mail wmuseo@
banrep.gov.co; internet www.banrep.gov.co/
museo/home.htm; f. 1939; 36,000 pre-Columbian gold objects representing the gods,
myths, and customs of the Quimbaya,
Muisca, Tairona and other native Indian
cultures; Dir CLARA ISABEL BOTERO CUERVO.

Museo Nacional (National Museum): Carrera 7, No. 28–66, Bogotá; tel. (1) 3342129;
fax (1) 3347447; e-mail info@museonacional
.gov.co; internet www.museonacional.gov.co;
f. 1823; archaeology, ethnology, history since
Spanish conquest; collections of portraits,
arms, banners, medals, coins, ceramics, fine
arts; theatre; exhibition gallery; Dir ELVIRA
CUERVO DE JARAMILLO.

Museo Nacional de Antropología
(National Museum of Anthropology): Calle
8, No. 8-87, Bogotá; tel. (1) 2462481; fax (1)
2330960; f. 1941; ceramics, stone carvings,
gold objects, textiles, etc., from all districts of
Colombia; is a department of the Instituto
Colombiano de Antropología; Dir MYRIAM
JIMENO SANTOYO; publs *Informes Antropológicos*, *Revista Colombiana de Antropología*.

Medellín

**Museo de Ciencias Naturales del Cole-
gio de San José** (Natural Science Museum):
Apdo Aéreo 1180, Medellín; f. 1913; natural
history in general, zoology, botany, mineralogy, anthropology; library of 500 vols and
1,000 magazines; Dir H. MARCO A. SERNA D.;
publs *Avancemos* (12 a year), *Boletín Cultural* (4 a year), *El Colombiano* (1 a day),
catalogues.

**Museo Filatélico del Banco de la Repúb-
lica:** Edif. Banco de la República, Parque de
Berrió, Medellín; tel. (4) 5767400; fax (4)
2515488; e-mail grincogo@banrep.gov.co; f.
1977; collns of Colombian postage stamps,
and stamps from other countries; Dir GON-
ZALO RINCÓN GÓMEZ; publ. *Revista*.

Museo Universitario: Universidad de Antioquia, Apdo Aéreo 1226, Medellín; tel. (4)
2105180; fax (4) 2638282; internet quimbaya
.udea.edu.co/~museo; f. 1942; sections:
anthropology, university history, natural sciences, visual arts, the human being, interactive exhibition; Dir ROBERTO L. OJALVO
PRIETO; publ. *Códice* (scientific and cultural
journal).

Roldanillo

Museo Omar Rayo: Calle 8a, 8–53, Rolda-
nillo, Valle del Cauca; tel. (92) 2298623; fax
(92) 2297290; e-mail museorayo@hotmail
.com; internet www.museorayo.net; f. 1976,
opened 1981; run by Fundación Museo Rayo;
specializes in modern works on or with
paper, fundamentally graphic art and design,
by Latin American artists or those working
in Latin America; a large collection has been
donated by the artist Omar Rayo; library of
2,003 vols; Pres. of Foundation and Dir-Gen.
OMAR RAYO REYES; publ. *Ediciones Embalaje*.

National Universities

ESCUELA SUPERIOR DE ADMINISTRACIÓN PÚBLICA

Apdo Aéreo 29745, Diagonal 40 No. 46A–37,
Santafé de Bogotá
Telephone: (1) 2224700
Fax: (1) 2224356
Internet: www.esap.edu.co
Founded 1958
State control
Academic year: February to November
Dir-Gen.: SAMUEL OSPINA MARÍN

Academic Deputy Dir: TITO ANTONIO HUERTAS
PORRAS
Admin. Deputy Dir: GUILLERMO LEÓN REY
Sec.-Gen.: GERMÁN PUENTES GONZÁLEZ
Librarian: MARÍA CRISTINA ESCOBAR DE ARA-
NGO
Library of 27,000 vols
Number of teachers: 91
Number of students: 905
Publications: *Administración y Desarrollo* (2
a year), *Documentos ESAP*

DEANS

Faculty of Advanced Studies: OCTAVIO BAR-
BOSA CARDONA
Faculty of Political and Administrative Sci-
ences: TITO ANTONIO HUERTAS PORRAS

POLITÉCNICO COLOMBIANO JAIME ISAZA CADAVID

Carrera 48 No. 7–151, Avenida Las Vegas
Medellín- Colombia-Suramé
Telephone: (574) 3197900
Fax: (574) 2680067
E-mail: rectoria@elpoli.edu.co
Internet: www.politecnicojic.edu.co
Founded 1964
State control
Rector: Dr JUAN CAMILO RUIZ PÉREZ
Sec.-Gen.: IVÁN ECHEVERRI VALENCIA
Vice-Rector for Admin.: JUAN GUILLERMO
VILLADA ARANGO
Vice-Rector for Extension: GILBERTO GIRALDO
BUITRAGO
Vice-Rector for Teaching and Research: GIO-
VANI OROZCO ARBELÁEZ
Number of teachers: 880
Number of students: 13,500
Regional campus in Rionegro

DEANS

Faculty of Administration: FABIO TORRES
LOZANO
Faculty of Basic, Social and Human Sciences:
ELMER JOSÉ RAMÍREZ MACHADO
Faculty of Engineering: JAIRO MIGUEL VER-
GARA ÁVILA

DIRECTORS

School of Agriculture: JAIME LEÓN BOTERO
AGUDELO
School of Audiovisual Communication: JOSÉ
SAMUEL ARANGO MARTÍNEZ
School of Physical Education, Recreation and
Sport: GONZALO JARAMILLO HERNÁNDEZ

UNIVERSIDAD DE ANTIOQUIA

Apdo Aéreo 1226, Ciudad Universitaria,
Medellín, Antioquia
Telephone: (4) 2105020
Fax: (4) 2638282
E-mail: wwwmgr@www.udea.edu.co
Internet: www.udea.edu.co
Founded 1822
State control
Academic year: January to November
Rector: ALBERTO URIBE CORREA
Vice-Rector for Academic Affairs: GUILLERMO
LONDOÑO RESTREPO
Vice-Rector for Admin.: ALVARO PÉREZ ROL-
DÁN
Vice-Rector for Extension: MARGARITA BERRÍO
DE RAMOS
Vice-Rector for Gen. Affairs: MARTINIANO
JAIME CONTRERAS
Vice-Rector for Research: Dr GUSTAVO VALEN-
CIA RESTREPO
Sec.-Gen.: ANA LUCÍA HERRERA GÓMEZ
Librarian: NORA ELENA LÓPEZ
Library: see Libraries and Archives
Number of teachers: 1,043

Number of students: 21,337
Publications: *Revista Estudios de Derecho* (2
a year), *Revista Iatreia* (4 a year), *Revista
Lecturas de Economia* (2 a year), *Revista
Universidad de Antioquia* (4 a year)

DEANS AND DIRECTORS

Faculty of Arts: CLARA MÓNICA ZAPATA JAR-
AMILLO
Faculty of Communications: EDISON DARÍO
NEIRA PALACIO
Faculty of Dentistry: CARLOS MARIO URIBE
SOTO
Faculty of Economics: MAURICIO ALVIAR
RAMÍREZ
Faculty of Education: CARLOS ARTURO SOTO
LOMBANA
Faculty of Engineering: CARLOS ARROYAVE
POSADA
Faculty of Exact and Natural Sciences:
NÉSTOR LÓPEZ ARISTIZÁBAL
Faculty of Law and Political Science: MARTA
NUBIA VELÁSQUEZ RICO
Faculty of Medicine: LUIS JAVIER CASTRO
NARANJO
Faculty of Nursing: ASTRID ELENA VALLEJO
RICO
Faculty of Pharmaceutical Chemistry:
AMANDA INÉS MEJÍA GALLÓN
Faculty of Social and Human Sciences: LUZ
STELLA CORREO BOTERO
Faculty of Veterinary Medicine and Animal
Husbandry: LUIS JAVIER ARROYAVE MOR-
ALES
Institute of Philosophy: ALFONSO MONSALVE
SOLÓRZANO
Institute of Physical Education and Sports:
ALAIN PEDRO BUSTAMANTE SIMÓN
Institute of Political Sciences: MANUEL
ALBERTO ALONSO ESPINAL
Institute of Regional Studies: DIEGO HERRERA
GÓMEZ
National Faculty of Public Health: OSCAR
SIERRA RODRÍGUEZ
School of Bacteriology and Clinical Labora-
tory: ANGELA MARÍA ARANGO RAVE
School of Languages: ADRIANA GONZÁLEZ
MONCADA
School of Nutrition and Dietetics: DORA
NICOLASA GÓMEZ CIFUENTES

ATTACHED INSTITUTE

**Escuela Interamericana de Biblioteco-
logía** (Interamerican School of Librarianship): Apdo Aéreo 1307, Medellín; f. 1956;
training in librarianship to postgraduate
level; technical assistance on administration
and organization of information centres and
libraries; 15 staff (10 full-time; 5 part-time);
292 students; library of 16,000 vols; Dir
MARÍA TERESA MÚNERA TÓRRES; publ. *Revista
Interamericana de Bibliotecología*.

UNIVERSIDAD DE CALDAS

Apdo Aéreo 275, Calle 65 No. 26-10, Mani-
zales, Caldas
Telephone: (68) 861250 ext. 114
Fax: (68) 8862732
E-mail: biblio@ucaldas.edu.co
Internet: www.ucaldas.edu.co
Founded 1943
State control
Academic year: February to December (2
semesters)
Rector: CARLOS-ENRIQUE RUIZ RESTREPO
Vice-Rector for Academic Affairs: PEDRO NEL
GARCÍA QUICENO
Registrar: CARLOS ALBERTO RUIZ VILLA
Librarian: SAUL SÁNCHEZ TORO
Library: see Libraries and Archives
Number of teachers: 488
Number of students: 3,620

Publications: *Altamira* (fine arts, 1 a year), *Boletín Científico Museo de Historia* (1 a year), *Cuadernos Filósofos Literarios* (1 a year), *IDEE Revista* (education, 2 a year), *Revista Luna Azul* (ecology, 2 a year)

DEANS

Faculty of Agriculture: Dr GERMÁN GÓMEZ LONDOÑO
Faculty of Arts and Humanities: Dr JUAN CARLOS YEPES OCAMPO
Faculty of Engineering: Dra ADELA MARÍA CEBALLOS PEÑALOZA
Faculty of Exact and Natural Sciences: Dr MARCO TULIO JARAMILLO S.
Faculty of Health Sciences: Dr LUIS FERNANDO URIBE VARGAS
Faculty of Juridical and Social Sciences: Dra MARÍA ROCÍO CIFUENTES PATIÑO

UNIVERSIDAD DE CARTAGENA

Apdo Aéreo 1382, Cartagena, Bolívar
Telephone: (59) 654480
Fax: (59) 650426
Internet: www.unicartagena.edu.co
Founded 1827
State control
Academic year: February to December
Pres. of the Council: Dr GUILLERMO PANIZA RICARDO
Rector: Dra BEATRIZ BECHARA DE BORGE
Academic Vice-Rector: Dr JAIME BARRIOS AMAYA
Admin. Dir: Dr CLARET BERMUDEZ CORONEL
Chief Admin. Officer: Dr EDGAR REY SINNING
Librarian: PERLA ECHEVERRI LEMA
Library: see Libraries and Archives
Number of teachers: 560
Number of students: 4,310
Publications: *Boletín Informativo, Revista Ciencia, Revista Facultad de Medicina, Revista Facultad de Economía, Prospecto Universidad, Tecnología y Educación*

DEANS

Faculty of Dentistry: Dr LUIS ALVAREZ GARCIA
Faculty of Economics: Dr GUILLERMO QUINTANA SOSSA
Faculty of Engineering: Dr ALVARO CUBAS MONTES
Faculty of Law: Dr ALCIDES ANGULO PASSOS
Faculty of Medicine: Dr ROBERTO GUERRERO FIGUEROA
Faculty of Nursing: Lic. YADIRA FERREIRA DE SIERRA
Faculty of Pharmaceutical Chemistry: Dra THELMA DEL CASTILLO DE SALAZAR
Faculty of Social Work: Lic. NATACHA MORILLO DE RODRIGUEZ

UNIVERSIDAD DE CÓRDOBA

Apdo Aéreo 354, Carretera a Cereté, Km 5, Montería, Córdoba
Telephone: (4) 7904050
Internet: www.unicordoba.edu.co
Founded 1964
Academic year: April to March
Rector: Dr CLAUDIO SÁNCHEZ PARRA
Academic Vice-Rector: Dr EFRAIN PASTOR NIEVES
Admin. Dir: Dr ALVARO VIDAL OROZCO
Library Dir: CARLOS HENAO TORO
Number of teachers: 270
Number of students: 2,493
Publications: *Revista, Trabajos de Grado presentados en la Universidad*

DEANS

Faculty of Agricultural Engineering: Dr MAXIMILIANO ESPINOSA PERALTA

Faculty of Education: Dr JOSÉ MORALES MANCHEGO
Faculty of Nursing: Dra GISELLE FERRER FERRER
Faculty of Science: Dr AQUILES GONZÁLEZ SALAZAR
Faculty of Veterinary Medicine and Animal Husbandry: Dr FRANCISCO AGUILAR MADERA

UNIVERSIDAD DE CUNDINAMARCA

Diagonal 18 No. 20–29, Fusagasugá, Cundinamarca
Telephone: (91) 8672144
Fax: (91) 8677898
E-mail: rectoria@udecund.edu.co
Internet: www.udecund.edu.co
Founded 1969
State control
Rector: Dr ALFONSO SANTOS MONTERO.

UNIVERSIDAD DE LA AMAZONIA

Avda Circunvalación Barrio El Porvenir, Florencia, Caquetá
Telephone: (98) 4340851
Fax: (98) 4358231
E-mail: rectoria@uniamazonia.edu.co
Internet: www.uniamazonia.edu.co
Founded 1971 as Instituto Tecnológico Universidad Surcolombiana; present name and status 1982
State control
Rector: Dr OSCAR VILLANUEVA ROJAS
Sec.-Gen.: MEYER HURTADO PARRA
Number of students: 4,000

DEANS

Faculty of Accountancy: (vacant)
Faculty of Agricultural Sciences: Mgr OSCAR ALFREDO MORELES GAMBOA
Faculty of Basic Sciences: JOSE ANTONIO MARÍN PEÑA
Faculty of Education: (vacant)
Faculty of Engineering: Ing. JULIO CESAR LUNA
Faculty of Law: LUIS FERNANDO URREGO CARVAJAL

UNIVERSIDAD DE LA GUAJIRA

Apdo Aéreo 172, Riohacha
Internet: www.uniguajira.edu.co
Founded 1976
State control
Academic year: February to July, August to November
Rector: FRANCISCO JUSTO PÉREZ VAN-LEENDEN
Vice-Rector: ROSALBA CUESTA LÓPEZ
Chief Admin. Officer: CRISTÓBAL VEGA GUTIÉRREZ
Librarian: MARINELA MENGUAL MEZA
Number of teachers: 107
Number of students: 1,258
Publications: *Anuario Estadístico, Revista Universidad de La Guajira, WOUMMAINPA*

DEANS

Faculty of Business Administration: ISIDORO OSPINO MERIÑO
Faculty of Education: JOSÉ CLEMENTE MARTÍNEZ
Faculty of Industrial Engineering: JAIRO SALCEDO DAVILA

UNIVERSIDAD DE LOS LLANOS

Km 11 Vía Puerto López, Villavicencio, Meta
Telephone: (98) 6698000
Fax: (98) 6698602
E-mail: rectoria@unillanos.edu.co

Internet: www.unillanos.edu.co
Founded 1974 as Universidad Tecnológica de Los Llanos Orientales; present name and status 1992
State control
Academic year: February to December
Rector: CARLOS ENRIQUE GARZÓN GONZÁLEZ
Sec.-Gen.: RUTH CHAVEZ A.
Library of 10,000 vols
Number of teachers: 120
Number of students: 1,345
Publications: *Boletín, Boletín Estadístico, Catálogo*
Faculties of animal husbandry and natural resources, basic sciences, health sciences, humanities.

UNIVERSIDAD DE NARIÑO

Ciudad Universitaria Torobajo, Pasto, Nariño
Telephone: (27) 7313605
Fax: (27) 7313605
Internet: www.udenar.edu.co
Founded 1827 as Colegio Provincial by General Francisco de Paula Santander; later named Colegio Académico; university status 1964
First degree courses
Rector: JAIRO MUÑOZ HOYOS
Vice-Rector: JAMIE HERNAN CABRERA
Vice-Rector for Admin.: VICENTE PARRA
Vice-Rector for Research, Postgraduates and Int. Relations: CARLOS CORDOBA
Dir of Planning: ARMANDO MUÑOZ
Gen. Sec.: JUAN ANDRES VILLOTA RAMOS
Librarian: SEGUNDO BURBANO L.
Library: central library of 10,000 vols; agronomy library of 15,000 vols
Number of teachers: 700
Number of students: 8,000
Publications: *Awarca, Foro Universitario, Revista de Ciencias Agrícolas Meridiano, Revista de Investigaciones, Revista de Zootecnia*

DEANS

Faculty of Agroindustrial Engineering: NELSON ARTURO
Faculty of Agronomy: GERMÁN ARTEAGA MENESES
Faculty of Arts: ALVARO ZAMBRANO
Faculty of Economics and Administration: LUIS ALBERTO ARCOS
Faculty of Education: ALVARO TORRES
Faculty of Engineering: JAIRO GUERRERO GARCÍA
Faculty of Human Sciences: CARLOS SANTAMARIA
Faculty of Law: MANUEL CORAL PABON
Faculty of Natural Sciences and Mathematics: ARSENI HIDALGO TROYA
Faculty of Stockbreeding: HECTOR FABIO VALENCIA

UNIVERSIDAD DE PAMPLONA

Ciudad Universitaria 'El Buque', Pamplona, Santander del Norte
Telephone: (7) 5685303
Fax: (7) 5682750
E-mail: rectoria@unipamplona.edu.co
Internet: www.unipamplona.edu.co
Founded 1960, univ. status 1970
State control
Academic year: February to December
Rector: ÁLVARO GONZÁLEZ JOVES
Vice-Rector for Academic Affairs: LUIS ALBERTO GUALDRÓN SÁNCHEZ
Vice-Rector for Research: YOLANDA ALBARRACÍN CONTRERAS

Vice-Rector for Social Devt: LUIS GUSTAVO ARAQUE
Admin. Dir: JAIRO AGUSTÍN ACEVEDO BAUTISTA
Sec.-Gen.: ROSALBA OMAÑA BONILLA
Number of teachers: 215 (145 full-time, 70 part-time)
Number of students: 4,560
Publications: *Bistua* (natural and technological sciences, 2 a year), *Faria* (arts and humanities, 2 a year), *Zulima* (business and economics, 2 a year)

DEANS

Arts and Humanities: FLOR DELIA PÚLIDO C.
Business and Economics: JAIRO DEL CARMEN OLMOS S.
Education: INÉS ROMERO MARTÍNEZ
Health: PEDRO LEON PEÑARANDA L.
Natural and Technological Sciences: JAIRO ALONSO MENDOZA SUÁREZ

UNIVERSIDAD DE SUCRE

Apdo Aéreo 406, Cra. 28 No. 5-267, Sincelejo, Sucre
Telephone: (52) 821240
Fax: (52) 821240
Internet: www.unisucre.edu.co
Founded 1977
State control
Academic year: February to December
Rector: GUSTAVO VERGARA ARRÁZOLA
Chief Admin. Officer: VICTOR RAÚL CASTILLO JIMÉNEZ
Sec.-Gen.: AMIRA VALDÉS ALTAMAR
Librarian: IRMA OCHOA DE FONSECA
Library of 12,000 vols
Number of teachers: 65
Number of students: 910

DEANS

Faculty of Engineering: PABLO ALFONSO CARO RETTIZ
Faculty of Health Sciences: CARMEN CECILIA ALVIS DE PUENTES
Faculty of Sciences and Humanities: CARMEN PAYARES PAYARES
Faculty of Stockbreeding: JULIO ALEJANDRO HERNÁNDEZ

UNIVERSIDAD DEL ATLÁNTICO

Km 7 Vía Puerto Colombia, Apdo Aéreo 1890, Barranquilla, Atlántico
Telephone: (5) 3599458
Internet: www.uniatlantico.edu.co
Founded 1941
Undergraduate courses
Rector: ANA SOFÍA MESA DE CUERVO
Sec.-Gen.: ROBERTO NORIEGA
Librarian: EDUARDO PINZON
Number of teachers: 845
Number of students: 17,910
Publications: *Cuadernos de literatura del Caribe e Hispanoamérica Nº 4*, *Economía*, *Historia Caribe Vol. iv Nº 12*

DEANS

Faculty of Architecture: WILSON ANNICHIARICCO
Faculty of Economics: FERNANDO CABARCAS CHARRIS
Faculty of Education: JANETH TOVAR GUERRA
Faculty of Fine Arts: GUILLERMO CARBO RONDEROS
Faculty of Law and Political Science: GUILLERMO CARBO RONDEROS
Faculty of Nutrition and Dietetics: SONIA SAAVEDRA ARENAS
Faculty of Pharmacy and Chemistry: CLARA FAY VARGAS LASCARRO

UNIVERSIDAD DEL CAUCA

Apdo Nacional 113, Calle 5 No. 4–70, Popayán, Cauca
Telephone: (2) 8209900
E-mail: rectoria@ucauca.edu.co
Internet: www.unicauca.edu.co
Founded 1827
State control
Academic year: January to December
Rector: RAFAEL EDUARDO VIVAS LINDO
Vice-Rector for Academic Affairs: KONNY ELIZABETH CAMPO SARZOSA
Vice-Rector for Culture and Welfare: EVIALRA CASTRILLÓN
Vice-Rector for Research: JUAN MARTÍN VELASCO M.
Pres. of Supreme Council: TEMISTOCLES ORTEGA
Gen. Sec.: GUILLERMO MUÑOZ VELÁSQUEZ
Admin. Dir: JOSÉ MARÍA ARBOLEDA CASTRILLÓN
Planning Head: CÉSAR OSORIO VERA
Library Dir: AMPARO PRADO
Library: see Libraries and Archives
Number of teachers: 600
Number of students: 7,000

DEANS

Faculty of Accountancy, Administration and Economics: Dr ENRIQUE PEÑA FORERO
Faculty of Arts: Lic. MATILDE CHÁVEZ DE TOBA
Faculty of Civil Engineering: Ing. MARGARITA POLANCO
Faculty of Education Sciences: Dr GERARDO NAUNDORF SAEZ
Faculty of Electronic Engineering: Ing. FRANCISCO J. TERÁN CUARAN
Faculty of Health Sciences: JAIME A. NATES BURBANO
Faculty of Humanities: Dr HÉCTOR ORTEGA BURBANO
Faculty of Law, Political and Social Sciences: Dr ALVARO HURTADO TEJADA

DIRECTORS OF POSTGRADUATE INSTITUTES

Accounting: LUIS A. COLVO
Civil Engineering: Ing. FERNANDO HURTADO
Electronics and Telecommunications: Ing. PEDRO VERA VERA
Health Sciences: ALONSO RUIZ PEREA
Human Sciences: LUCIANO RIVERA
Law: CARLOS IGNACIO MOSQUERA U.

UNIVERSIDAD DEL MAGDALENA

Carrera 32 No. 22-08, Santa Marta, Magdalena
Telephone: (57) 4301692
Fax: (57) 4303621
E-mail: vicedocencia@unimagdalena.edu.co
Internet: www.unimag.edu.co
Founded 1958
State control
Academic year: February to December (2 semesters)
Rector: Dr RUTHBER ESCORCIA CABALLERO
Librarian: MILVIDA SUÁREZ
Library of 67,506 vols
Number of teachers: 772
Number of students: 9,163
Publications: *Revista Agronómica*, *Revista Económica*, *Revista Facultad Ingeniería Pesquera*

DEANS

Basic Sciences: MIGUEL CANTILLO
Economic and Managerial Sciences: JAIME MORÓN
Education: ERICK HERNÁNDEZ
Engineering: GERARDO ANGULO
Health Sciences: GUILLERMO TROUT

UNIVERSIDAD DEL PACÍFICO

Avda Simón Bolívar 54 A-10, Buenaventura
E-mail: info@unipacifico.edu.co
Telephone: (92) 2439789
Fax: (92) 2431461
Internet: www.unipacifico.edu.co
Founded 1988
State control
Rector: Dr OMAR BARONA MURILLO
Sec.-Gen.: Dra MARIA CARMELA QUIÑONEZ.

UNIVERSIDAD DEL QUINDÍO

Cra. 15, Cl. 12N, Avda Bolívar, Apdo Aéreo 460, Armenia, Quindío
Telephone: (7) 460112
Fax: (7) 460222
Internet: www.uniquindio.edu.co
Founded 1960
State control
Academic year: February to June, August to November
Rector: ALFONSO LONDOÑO OROZCO
Vice-Rector for Academic Affairs: ORLANDO SALAZAR SALAZAR
Vice-Rector for Admin.: CLARA INES ARISTIZABAL ROA
Sec.-Gen.: FRANCELINE BARRERO
Dean of Research Committee: PATRICIA LANDAZURY
Registrar: NELLY RESTREPO SÁNCHEZ
Librarian: Lic. MIRYAM GARCIA
Library of 26,250 vols
Number of teachers: 844
Number of students: 12,320
Publications: *Revista Facultad de Formación Avanzada e Investigaciones*, *Revista de la Universidad del Quindío*

DEANS

Faculty of Agro-cultural Industry Sciences: JAIME BOTERO
Faculty of Basic and Technological Sciences: EDUARDO ARANGO
Faculty of Civil Engineering: JOSE FENANDO ECHEVERRY
Faculty of Education and Pedagogy: DARIO ALVAREZ
Faculty of Health Sciences: ROBERTO STEFAN
Faculty of Human Sciences: WILLIAM GARCIA
Faculty of Management and Economics Sciences: FABIOLA RESTREPO

UNIVERSIDAD DEL TOLIMA

Apdo Aéreo No. 546, Santa Elena, Ibagué, Tolima
Telephone: (98) 2649219
Fax: (98) 2644869
E-mail: ut@ut.edu.co
Internet: www.ut.edu.co
Founded 1945
State control
Academic year: January to December
Rector: JESÚS RAMÓN RIVERA BULLA
Vice-Rector for Academic Affairs: JOSÉ HERMAN MUÑOZ ÑUNGO
Vice-Rector for Admin.: LUIS EVELIO GUZMÁN DIAZ
Vice-Rector for Devt and Educational Resources: FABIO ALFONSO SANDOVAL PATARROYO
Registrar: LUZ ANGELA CALLE BARRERO
Librarian: CIELO URUEÑA LOZANO
Number of teachers: 201
Number of students: 10,130
Publication: *Revista Panorama Universitario*

DEANS

Faculty of Agricultural Engineering: CARLOS ANTONIO RIVERA BARRERO

Faculty of Business Administration: GERMÁN
RUBIO GUERRERO
Faculty of Educational Science: LUIS ALBERTO
MALAGÓN PLATA
Faculty of Forestry Engineering: RAFAEL
VARGAS RÍOS
Faculty of Health Sciences: FRANCIA HELENA
DE BETANCOURTH
Faculty of Science: RAMIRO URIBE KAFFURE
Faculty of Technology: ALBERTO MEJÍA
RENGIFO
Faculty of Veterinary Medicine and Zootech-
nics: FRANCISCO SEGURA CANIZALES
Institute of Distance Education: LUCÍA
DURÁN PINILLA

UNIVERSIDAD DEL VALLE

Ciudad Universitaria, Meléndez, Apdo Aéreo
25360, Apdo Nacional 439, Calí, Valle del
Cauca
Telephone: (2) 392310
Fax: (2) 398484
Internet: www.univalle.edu.co
Founded 1945
State control
Academic year: January to June, August to
December
Rector: JAIME E. GALARZA SANCLEMENTE
Vice-Rector for Academic Affairs: CARLOS E.
DULCEY BONILLA
Vice-Rector for Admin.: Dr ALBERTO LOPEZ
SANCHEZ
Vice-Rector for Research: Dr HUMBERTO REY
VARGAS
Vice-Rector for Univ. Welfare: Dra CECILIA
MADRIÑAN POLO
Library Dir: Lic. ISABEL ROMERO DE DULCEY
Library of 267,656 vols
Number of teachers: 962
Number of students: 14,640 (9,640 full-time;
5,000 part-time)
Publications: *Boletín Socioeconómico, Colom-
bia Médica, Cuadernos de Administración,
Historia y Espacio, Heurística, Humboltia,
Fin de Siglo, La Palabra, Lenguaje, Praxis
Filosófica, Planta Libre, Pliegos Adminis-
trativos, Poligramas, Revista de Ciencias,
Revista Estomatología, Revista Universi-
dad del Valle*

DEANS

Faculty of Administrative Science: Dr BER-
NARDO BARONA
Faculty of Architecture: Dr CARLOS ENRIQUE
DULCEY BONILLA E.
Faculty of Economics and Social Sciences: Dr
LUGARDO ALVAREZ AGUDELO
Faculty of Education: Dr MARIO DIAZ
Faculty of Engineering: Dr SILVIO DELVASTO
Faculty of Health: Dr HECTOR RAUL ECHA-
VARRIA ABAD
Faculty of Humanities: Dr HUMBERTO VÉLEZ
RAMÍREZ
Faculty of Science: Dr LUIS FERNANDO CASTRO

UNIVERSIDAD DISTRITAL 'FRANCISCO JOSÉ DE CALDAS'

Carrera 7, No. 40–53, Bogotá
Telephone: (1) 3239300
Fax: (1) 3239300 ext. 2002
E-mail: spral@udistrital.edu.co
Internet: www.udistrital.edu.co
Founded 1950
Number of teachers: 600
Number of students: 7,200
Rector: LUIS CARLOS MOLINA MARIÑO
Faculties of education and science; engineer-
ing; environment and natural resources;
technology.

UNIVERSIDAD FRANCISCO DE PAULA SANTANDER

Avda Gran Colombia 12E–96, Barrio Colsag,
Apdo Aéreo 1055, Cúcuta, Norte de San-
tander
Telephone: (75) 753172
Internet: www.ufps.edu.co
Founded 1962
State control
Affiliated to the Universidad Nacional
Undergraduate courses
Chancellor: PATROCINIO ARARAT DÍAZ
Sec.-Gen.: ALVARO ORLANDO PEDROZA ROAJS
Admin. Dir: HÉCTOR MIGUEL PARRA LÓPEZ
Academic Vice-Chancellor: JOSÉ LUIS TOLOSA
CHACÓN
Librarian: GLORIA MATILDE MELO SALCEDO
Library of 5,000 vols
Number of teachers: 350
Number of students: 6,500

DEANS

Faculty of Basic Sciences: JOSÉ LUIS MAL-
DONADO
Faculty of Business Studies: JOSÉ RAMÓN
VARGAS TOLOSA
Faculty of Education, Arts, Humanities and
Sciences: RICARDO GARCIA
Faculty of Engineering: HUGO ALBERTO POR-
TILLA DUARTE
Faculty of Environmental Sciences: CIRO
ESPINOSA
Faculty of Health Sciences: FANNY MARTINEZ

UNIVERSIDAD INDUSTRIAL DE SANTANDER

Apdo Aéreo 678, Bucaramanga, Santander
Telephone: (7) 6344000
Internet: www.uis.edu.co
Founded 1947
Academic year: February to June, August to
December
Rector: JORGE GÓMEZ DUARTE
Vice-Rector for Academic Affairs: GERMÁN
OLIVEROS VILLAMIZAR
Vice-Rector for Admin.: HUMBERTO PRADILLA
ARDILA
Sec.-Gen.: Dra LILIA AMANDA PATIÑO DE CRUZ
Research Dir: LUIS ALFONSO MALDONADO
CERÓN
Librarian: ESPERANZA MÉNDEZ BRAVO
Number of teachers: 455
Number of students: 9,684

DEANS

Faculty of Distance Education: GLORIA INÉS
MARÍN MUÑOZ
Faculty of Health: GERMAN GAMARRA HER-
NÁNDEZ
Faculty of Human Sciences: EMILIA ACEVEDO
DE ROMERO
Faculty of Physical/Chemical Sciences: CAR-
LOS JULIO MONSALVE MORENO
Faculty of Physical/Mechanical Sciences:
ROBERTO MARTÍNEZ ANGEL
Faculty of Sciences: AUGUSTO LÓPEZ ZAGARRA

UNIVERSIDAD MILITAR NUEVA GRANADA

Carrera 11 No. 101-80, Bogotá
Telephone: (1) 2757300
Fax: (1) 2159689
E-mail: rectoria@santander.umng.edu.co
Internet: www.umng.edu.co
Founded 1982
State control
Rector: Brig. Gen. ADOLFO CLAVIJO ARDILA
Vice-Rector for Academic Affairs: Dra
BLANCA PATRICIA BARRERO DE RIVERA

Vice-Rector for Admin.: Col WLADISLAO REIN-
OSO MARIN
Vice-Rector for General Affairs: Maj. Gen.
JAIME HUMBERTO CORTES P.
Vice-Rector for Research: Dr GUILLERMO
MONSALVO.

UNIVERSIDAD NACIONAL ABIERTA Y A DISTANCIA

Calle 14 sur No. 14–23, Bogotá
Telephone: (1) 3443700
Fax: (1) 3444120
E-mail: sgeneral@unad.edu.co
Internet: www.unad.edu.co
Founded 1981 as Unidad Universitaria del
Sur de Bogotá; current name and status
1997
State control
Academic year: February to December
Rector: Dra JAIME LEAL AFANADOR
Vice-Rector for Academic Affairs: LETICIA
ESCOBAR CEDANO
Vice-Rector for Finance and Admin.: SEHIFAR
BALLESTEROS MORENO
Sec.-Gen.: ROBERTO SALAZAR RAMOS

DEANS

Faculty of Administrative Sciences: ROQUE
JULIO RODRIGUEZ PARRA
Faculty of Agricultural Sciences: DOMINGO
ALIRIO MONTAÑO ARIAS
Faculty of Basic Sciences and Engineering:
JOSE HUMBERTO GUERRERO RODRIGUEZ
Faculty of Social, Human and Educational
Sciences: CARLOS BERNAL GRANADOS

UNIVERSIDAD NACIONAL DE COLOMBIA

Ciudad Universitaria, Apdo Aéreo 14490,
Bogotá
Telephone: (1) 3165000
Fax: (1) 2219891
E-mail: secgener@unal.edu.co
Internet: www.unal.edu.co
Founded 1867
Academic year: February to December
Campuses in Manizales, Medellín, Palmira,
Arauca, San Andrés and Leticia
Rector: MARCO PALACIOS
Vice-Rector for Arauca Campus: MARÍA SARA
MEJÍA DE TAFUR
Vice-Rector for Manizales Campus: GERMAN
PALACIO CASTAÑEDA
Vice-Rector for Medellín Campus: JORGE
EDUARDO HURTADO GÓMEZ
Vice-Rector for Leticia Campus: ADRIANA
SANTOS MARTÍNEZ
Vice-Rector for Palmira Campus: ARGEMIRO
ECHEVERRY CANO
Vice-Rector for San Andrés Campus: ALEXIS
DE GREIFF
Library: see Libraries and Archives
Number of teachers: 3,055
Number of students: 43,159
Publications: *Acta Bibliográfica, Agronomía
Colombiana, Alimentos, Anuario Colom-
biano de Historia, Anuario del Observa-
torio Astronómico Nacional, Boletín de
Matemáticas, Caldasia* (natural science),
Cuadernos de Economía, Forma y Función
(philology and languages), *Geografía Geo-
logía Colombiana, Ideas y Valores, Inge-
niería e Investigación, Lozania* (natural
science), *Maguaré* (anthropology), *Mutisia*
(natural science), *Revistas* (Faculty publications)

DEANS

Faculty of Agronomy: FABIO LEYVA BARÓN
Faculty of Arts: FERNANDO MONTENEGRO
LIZARRALDE
Faculty of Dentistry: GLADYS NÚÑEZ BARRERA

Faculty of Economics: LUIS IGNACIO AGUILAR
Faculty of Engineering: JULIO COMENARES MONTAÑEZ
Faculty of Humanities: GERMAN MELENDEZ ACUÑA
Faculty of Law and Political and Social Sciences: ADOLFO SALAMANCA CORREA
Faculty of Medicine: JAIME GALLEGO ARBELÁEZ
Faculty of Nursing: CLARA BEATRIZ SÁNCHEZ HERRERA
Faculty of Science: MOISES WASSERMAN LERNER
Faculty of Veterinary Science and Animal Husbandry: RAMÓN FAYAD NAFAH

OTHER CAMPUSES

Medellín Campus: Apdo Aéreo 568, Medellín

DEANS

Faculty of Architecture: OCTAVIO URIBE TORO
Faculty of Humanities: CATALINA REYES CÁRDENAS
Faculty of Mining: GONZALO JIMÉNEZ CALAD
Faculty of Sciences: MARIO ARIAS ZABALA
Faculty of Stockbreeding: DIEGO HOYOS DUQUE

Manizales Campus: Carrera 27 No. 64-60, Manizales

DEANS

Faculty of Architecture and Engineering: JOSÉ JAIRO BOTERO ANGEL
Faculty of Science and Administration: GONZALO DE JESÚS SÁNCHEZ

Palmira Campus: Apdo Aéreo 237, Palmira

DEANS

Faculty of Stockbreeding: EUGENIO ESCOBAR HANRIQUE

UNIVERSIDAD PEDAGÓGICA NACIONAL

Apdo Aéreo 75144, Calle 73, No. 11–73, Santafé de Bogotá
Telephone: (1) 3473562
Fax: (1) 3473535
Internet: www.pedagogica.edu.co
Founded 1955
State control
Languages of instruction: Spanish, English
Academic year: January to December (2 semesters)
Rector: Dr ADOLFO RODRÍGUEZ BERNAL
Vice-Rector for Academic Affairs: Dr MANUEL ERAZO PARGA
Vice-Rector for Admin.: Dr HERNÁN VÁSQUEZ ROCHA
Librarian: Dr CAMILO ROJAS LEÓN
Number of teachers: 660
Number of students: 4,190
Publications: *Pedagogica y Saberes, Revista Colombiana de Educación*

DEANS

Faculty of Education: Dra MYRIAM PARDO TORRES
Faculty of Humanities: Dra GLORIA RINCÓN CUBIDES
Faculty of Science and Technology: Dr RAFAEL HUMBERTO RAMÍREZ GIL

ATTACHED INSTITUTE

Instituto Pedagógico Nacional: Calle 127 No. 12A-20, Santafé de Bogotá; 2,178 students; Dir LUIS ERNESTO OJEDA SUÁREZ.

UNIVERSIDAD PEDAGÓGICA Y TECNOLÓGICA DE COLOMBIA

Apdo Aéreo 1094 y 1234, Carretera Central del Norte, Tunja, Boyacá
Telephone: (8) 7422175
Fax: (8) 7424311
Internet: www.uptc.edu.co
Founded 1953
State control
Academic year: February to December
Rector: OLMEDA VARGAS HERNÁNDEZ
Vice-Rector for Academic Affairs: MANUEL FRANCISCO CAICEDO RUIZ
Vice-Rector for Admin.: FRANCISCO MANOSALVA CERON
Sec.-Gen.: NUBIA ELENA PEDRAZA VARGAS
Librarian: BARBARÁ MARTÍN MARTÍN
Number of teachers: 520
Number of students: 15,850

Publications: *Acción Pedagógica* (education, 2 a year), *Agenda P & G* (planning and management, 2 a year), *Agrodesarrollo* (agriculture, 2 a year), *Anuario de Investigaciones* (research, 1 a year), *Apuntes del Cenes* (economics and business administration, 2 a year), *Boletín de Acuerdos* (2 a year), *Boletín UPTC en Cifras* (university statistics, annual), *Ciencia en Desarrollo* (science, 2 a year), *Ciencia y Agricultura* (2 a year), *Cuadernos de Lingüística* (Hispanic linguistics, 1 a year), *EPG Geografía* (2 a year), *Matemáticas y Educación* (2 a year), *Observatorio Urbano* (project management, 3 a year), *Pensamiento y Acción* (2 a year), *Perspectiva Geográfica* (2 a year), *Perspectiva Salud y Enfermedad* (health sciences, 2 a year), *Revista Metalurgia y Ciencia de Materiales* (2 a year), *Terra Nostra* (project management, 4 a year)

DEANS AND DIRECTORS

Faculty of Agricultural Sciences: MAGNOLIA DEL PILAR CANO ORTIZ
Faculty of Economics and Business Administration: VÍCTOR HERMES BARRERA GODOY
Faculty of Education: ANA MARGARITA SANTAFÉ CALDERÓN
Faculty of Engineering: LUIS EDUARDO VARGAS CARMONA
Faculty of Health Sciences: CARLOS ALBERTO JIMÉNEZ ESPINEL
Faculty of Law and Social Sciences: GERMÁN BERNAL CAMACHO
Faculty of Sciences: CARLOS NORBERTO GÓMEZ GÓMEZ
Sectional Faculty, Chiquinquirá: MANUEL HUMBERTO RESTREPO DOMÍNGUEZ
Sectional Faculty, Duitama: ALVARO CALVACHE ARCHILA
Sectional Faculty, Sogamoso: RAFAEL BALCAZAR COLLO
Institute of Open Learning and Correspondence Courses: FAUSTO RENAN MASTRODOMENICO CORREDOR
Centre of Educational Research: MARÍA NUBIA ROMERO BALLEN

UNIVERSIDAD POPULAR DEL CÉSAR

Apdo Aéreo 590, Sede Balneario Hurtado, Valledupar, César
Telephone: (95) 5736203
Fax: (95) 5735877
E-mail: univer@teleupar.net.co
Internet: www.unicesar.edu.co
Founded 1973 as Instituto Tecnológico del César; present name and status 1976
State control
Academic year: February to December (2 semesters)
Rector: Dr OSCAR PACHECO HERNANDEZ
Library of 17,000 vols

Faculties of Business Administration, Economics and Accountancy, Education, Engineering and Technology, Health Sciences, and Law, Politics and Social Sciences.

UNIVERSIDAD SURCOLOMBIANA

Avda Pastrana Borrero con Carrera 1A, Neiva, Huila
Telephone: (88) 745444
Internet: www.usurcolombia.com
Founded 1970
State control
Academic year: February to December
Rector: ALVARO LOZANO OSORIO
Vice-Rector for Academic Affairs: CARLOS BOLIVAR BONILLA
Vice-Rector for Admin.: MARIA BEATRIZ PAVA MARÍN
Chief Admin. Officer: EFRAÍN POLANÍA VIVAS
Sec.: JOSÉ PIAR IRIARTE VELILLA
Librarian: LUIS ALFREDO PINTO
Number of teachers: 450
Number of students: 4,500

DEANS

Faculty of Accountancy and Administration: ALFONSO MANRIQUE MEDINA
Faculty of Educational Science: FABIO LOSADA PÉREZ
Faculty of Engineering: ALFONSO ORTÍZ
Faculty of Medicine and Health: ANTONIO ACEVEDO A.

UNIVERSIDAD TECNOLÓGICA DE PEREIRA

Apdo Aéreo 97, Pereira, Risaralda
Telephone: (6) 63213292
Fax: (6) 63215839
E-mail: relint@utp.edu.co
Internet: www.utp.edu.co
Founded 1958
State control
Academic year: February to December
Rector: LUIS ENRIQUE ARANGO JIMÉNEZ
Vice-Rector for Academic Affairs: GERMÁN LÓPEZ QUINTERO
Vice-Rector for Admin.: FERNANDO NOREÑA JARAMILLO
Registrar: DIEGO OSORIO
Gen. Sec.: CARLOS ALFONSO ZULUAGA ARANGO
Librarian: MARGARITA FAJARDO
Library of 30,000 vols, 1,400 periodicals
Number of teachers: 700
Publications: *Revista de Ciencias Humanas* (3 a year), *Revista Médica de Risaralda*, *Scientia et Technica* (2 a year)

DEANS

Faculty of Basic Sciences: JOSÉ GÓMEZ ESPÍNDOLA
Faculty of Education: Licda MARÍA TERESA ZAPATA SALDARRIAGA
Faculty of Electrical Engineering and Computer Science: Ing. OMAR IVÁN TREJOS BURITICÁ
Faculty of Environmental Sciences: Dr SAMUEL DARIO GUZMÁN LÓPEZ
Faculty of Fine Arts and Humanities: JUAN HUMBERTO GALLEGO RAMÍREZ
Faculty of Industrial Engineering: Ing. WILSON ARENAS VALENCIA
Faculty of Mechanical Engineering: Ing. WALDO LIZCANO ARIAS
Faculty of Medicine: Dr SAMUEL EDUARDO TRUJILLO HENAO
Faculty of Technology: Ing. JOSÉ REINALDO MARÍN BETANCOURTH

UNIVERSIDAD TECNOLÓGICA DEL CHOCÓ 'DIEGO LUIS CÓRDOBA'

Carrera 2a, No. 25–22, Quibdó, Chocó
Telephone: (57) 711589
Internet: www.utch.edu.co

Founded 1972
State control
Academic year: February to June

Rector: HECTOR D. MOSQUERA BENITEZ
Vice-Rector for Academic Affairs: ALVARO GIRALDO GOMEZ
Vice-Rector for Admin.: VICTOR RAUL MOSQUERA BENITEZ
Registrar: LEONILA BLANDÓN ASPRILLA
Librarian: ZAHILY SARRAZOLA MARTINEZ

Number of teachers: 125
Number of students: 1,500

Publications: Libros Tecnicos en diferentes areas del Conocimieto, Obras Literarias

DEANS

Faculty of Education: EFRAIN MORENO RODRI-GUEZ
Faculty of Health and Social Security: MELIDA MORENO MURILLO
Faculty of Technology: LORENZO PORTOCAR-RERO SIERRA

Private Universities

FUNDACIÓN UNIVERSIDAD CENTRAL

Carrera 5a No. 21–38, Bogotá
North Bogotá branch: Calle 75 No. 15–91, Bogotá
Telephone: (1) 3134537
Fax: (1) 3134720
E-mail: webpage@ucentral.edu.co
Internet: www.ucentral.edu.co

Founded 1966
Academic year: January to December

Rector: Dr RUBÉN AMAYA REYES
Vice Rector for Academic Affairs: Dra GLORIA RINCÓN CUBIDES
Vice Rector for Admin. and Finance: Dr FERNANDO ALVAREZ MORALES
Sec.-Gen.: Dr BILLY ESCOBAR PÉREZ

Number of teachers: 700
Number of students: 12,000

Publications: Cuadernos del Cine Club (2 a year), Hojas Universitarias (2 a year), Magazin Mercadológico (2 a year), Nómadas (2 a year), NotiCentral (4 a year)

Faculties of accounting, business administration, economics, electronic engineering, industrial engineering, marketing and advertising, mechanical engineering, musical studies, social communication and journalism, systems engineering, water resources and environmental engineering; postgraduate programmes.

FUNDACIÓN UNIVERSIDAD DE BOGOTÁ 'JORGE TADEO LOZANO'

Apdo Aéreo 34185, Carrera 4, No. 22–61, Bogotá
Telephone: (1) 3341777
Fax: (1) 2826197
E-mail: btadeo12@andinet.lat.net
Internet: www.utadeo.edu.co

Founded 1954
Private control
Academic year: February to December (2 semesters)

Pres.: GUILLERMO RUEDA MONTAÑA
Rector: EVARISTO OBREGON GARCES
Vice-Rector for Academic Affairs: JUAN MANUEL CABALLERO PRIETO

Vice-Rector for Admin.: FANNY MESTRE DE GUTIERREZ
Vice-Rector for Postgraduate Studies: MIGUEL BERMUDEZ PORTOCARRERO
Sec.-Gen.: OSCAR AZUERO RUIZ
Librarian: MARIA CONSUELO MONCADA CAMACHO

Number of teachers: 1,020
Number of students: 11,500

Publications: Agenda cultural, Ecotropica, La Tadeo, Tadeísta

DEANS

Faculty of Agriculture and Stockbreeding Administration: INES ELVIRA TAMARA
Faculty of Agrology: Dr TOMAS LEON SICARD
Faculty of Business Administration: Dra CONSUELO VIDAL DE BRUGGEMAN
Faculty of Computer Science: JUAN ORLANDO LIZCANO
Faculty of Economic Sciences: JOAQUIN FLOREZ TRUJILLO
Faculty of Fine Arts: NATALIA GUTIERREZ E.
Faculty of Food Technology: JANETH LUNA
Faculty of Geographic Engineering: Dr JAIME VILLAREAL MORALES
Faculty of Graphic Design: Dra PASTORA CORREA DE AMAYA
Faculty of Industrial Design: Dr FERNANDO CORREA MUÑOZ
Faculty of Interior Design: Dr DICKEN CASTRO DUQUE
Faculty of International Commerce: HUGO VILLAMIL P.
Faculty of International Relations: ESTHER LOZANO DE REY
Faculty of Law: CAMILO NOGUERA
Faculty of Marine Biology: IVAN REY CARRASCO
Faculty of Marketing: JESUS ANTONIO POVEDA
Faculty of Public Accountancy: Dra GENOVEVA CAMACHO DE CONSTAIN
Faculty of Publicity: Dr CHRISTIAN SCHRADER
Faculty of Social Communication: Dr MARGOTH RICCI DE GOSSAIN
Food Business Management: PEDRO LUIS JIMENEZ
Health Services Management: ALFONSO LEON CANCINO
International Business Management: CIRO AREVALO Y.
Workers' Health: LEONARDO CAÑON ORTEGON

DIRECTORS

Agro-industrial Marketing: ISMAEL PEÑA DIAZ
Commercial Logistics: JORGE URIBE ROLDAN
History and Fine-Art Criticism: FRANCISCO GIL TOVAR
International Relations: DIEGO URIBE VARGAS
Marketing Management: ALEJANDRO SCHNARCH KIRBERG
Regional Development Planning: CARLOS A. GONZALEZ PARRA

PONTIFICIA UNIVERSIDAD JAVERIANA

Carrera 7 No. 40–76, Apdo Aéreo 56710, Bogotá
Telephone: (1) 3208320
Fax: (1) 2853348
E-mail: puj@javeriana.edu.co
Internet: www.javeriana.edu.co

Founded 1622 by the Jesuit Fathers; re-established 1931, present status 1937
Academic year: January to November (2 semesters)

Grand Chancellor: Fr P.-H. KOLVENBACH
Vice-Grand Chancellor: Fr GABRIEL IGNACIO RODRÍGUEZ
Rector: Fr GERARDO REMOLINA
Vice-Rector for Academic Affairs: Dr JAIRO H. CIFUENTES

Vice-Rector for Admin.: Ing. ROBERTO ENRIQUE MONTOYA
Vice-Rector for Univ. Affairs: Fr MIGUEL ROZO
Rector for Calí Section: Fr JOAQUÍN SÁNCHEZ
Sec.-Gen.: Fr JAIME BERNAL
Library: see Libraries and Archives
Number of teachers: 3,958
Number of students: 28,611

Publications: Cuadernos de Agroindustria y Economía Rural, Cuadernos de Administración, Ingeniería y Universidad, Memoria y Sociedad, Papel Político, Revista Ibero-Latinoamericana de Seguros, Signo y Pensamiento (2 a year), Theologica Xaveriana, Universitas Canonica, Universitas Economica, Universitas Humanistica, Universitas Jurídica, Universitas Médica (4 per year), Universitas Odontologica, Universitas Philosophica, Universitas Psychologica (2 a year), Universitas Scientiarum

DEANS

Faculty of Architecture: Arq. ALVARO BOTERO
Faculty of Arts: M. JUAN ANTONIO CUÉLLAR
Faculty of Canon Law: Dr RAFAEL GÓMEZ
Faculty of Communication and Language: Dr JÜRGEN HORLBECK
Faculty of Dentistry: Dr ALEJANDRO ZAPATA
Faculty of Economic and Administrative Sciences: Dr GUILLERMO GALÁN
Faculty of Economic and Administrative Sciences (in Calí): Dr BERNARDO BARONA
Faculty of Education: Dr JOSÉ BERNARDO TORO
Faculty of Engineering: Ing. FRANCISCO JAVIER REBOLLEDO
Faculty of Engineering (in Calí): Dr JORGE FRANCISCO ESTELA
Faculty of Environmental and Rural Studies: Dr LUIS MIGUEL RENJIFO
Faculty of Humanities and Social Sciences (in Calí): Dr ESTEBAN OCAMPO
Faculty of Law: Fr LUIS FERNANDO ALVAREZ
Faculty of Medicine: Dr IVAN SOLARTE
Faculty of Nursing: Dra ROSAURA CORTÉS DE TÉLLEZ
Faculty of Philosophy: Dr ALFONSO FLÓREZ
Faculty of Psychology: Dra ANGELA MARÍA ROBLEDO
Faculty of Political Sciences and International Relations: Dra CLAUDIA DANGOND
Faculty of Sciences: Dra ANGELA UMAÑA
Faculty of Social Sciences: Dra CONSUELO URIBE
Faculty of Theology: Fr VÍCTOR MARTÍNEZ
Department of Languages: Dra NELLY ESPERANZA TORRES

UNIVERSIDAD AUTÓNOMA DE BUCARAMANGA

Calle 48, 39-234, Apdo Aéreo 1642, Bucaramanga
Telephone: (97) 6436161
Fax: (97) 6474488
E-mail: mcamargoa@unab.edu.co
Internet: www.unab.edu.co

Founded 1952
Private control
Academic year: January to November

Pres.: Dr ALBERTO MONTOYA PUYANA
Vice-Pres. for Academic Affairs: Dra EULALIA GARCIA
Vice-Pres. for Admin.: Dr GILBERTO RAMIREZ
Dir of Int. Relations: MARIA T. CAMARGO
Librarian: ELENA UVAROVA

Library of 65,664 vols, 3,099 journals
Number of teachers: 454
Number of students: 7,362

Publications: Periódico 15, Revista Cuestiones, Revista Facultad de Contaduría, Revista Medunab, Revista Prospectiva,

Revista Reflexiones, Revista Temas Socio-Jurídicos

DEANS

Faculty of Accountancy: FERNANDO CHAPARRO
Faculty of Business Administration: JUAN CARLOS HEDERICH MARTÍNEZ
Faculty of Business Psychology: LILIANA STELLA QUIÑONEZ TORRES
Faculty of Communication: IVAN DARIO MONTOYA
Faculty of Economics: CATHERINNE GIOHANNA MÉDINA ARÉVALO
Faculty of Education: AMPARO GALVIS DE ORDUZ
Faculty of Energy Engineering: GERMAN OLIVEROS
Faculty of Finance Engineering: MARTHA INES BLANCO
Faculty of Hospitality and Tourism Administration: ALVARO MORALES
Faculty of Law: JORGE CASTILLO RUGELES
Faculty of Marketing Engineering: LUIS ALFREDO ROJAS
Faculty of Mechanical and Electronic Engineering: GERMAN OLIVEROS
Faculty of Medicine: LUZ MARINA CORSO
Faculty of Music: JESÚS ALBERTO REY MARIÑO
Faculty of Nursing: OLGA GOMEZ
Faculty of Systems Engineering: WILSON BRICEÑO PINEDA
Faculty of Visual Arts Production: CARLOS ACOSTA

UNIVERSIDAD AUTÓNOMA LATINOAMERICANA

Carrera 55 (Tenerife) No. 49–51, Apdo 3455, Medellín
Telephone: (4) 5112199
Fax: (4) 5123418
E-mail: info@unaula.edu.co
Internet: www.unaula.edu.co
Founded 1966
Private control with state supervision
Academic year: February to November
President: Dr LUCIANO SANÍN ARROYAVE
Rector: Dr JAIRO URIBE ARANGO
Vice-Rector for Academic Affairs: Dr ANÍBAL VÉLEZ MUÑOZ
Vice-Rector for Admin.: Dr JOSÉ RAÚL JARAMILLO RESTREPO
Sec.-Gen.: Dr ÁLVARO OCHOA MORALES
Registrar: Dr VICENTE IGLESIAS ESCORCE
Librarian: Dr ALONSO GUILLERMO MERINO G.
Number of teachers: 250
Number of students: 2,000
Publications: *Actividad Contable* (1 a year), *Apuntes de Economía* (1 a year), *Boletín Informativo* (12 a year), *Círculo de Humanidades* (4 a year), *Ratio Juris* (2 a year), *Revista Unaula* (1 a year), *Sociología* (1 a year), *Visión Autónoma* (2 a year)

DEANS

Faculty of Accountancy: Dr JORGE ALBERTO SÁNCHEZ GIRALDO
Faculty of Economics: Dr ÁLVARO JAVIER CORREA VÉLEZ
Faculty of Education and Social Sciences: Dr FERNANDO CORTÉS GUTIÉRREZ
Faculty of Industrial Engineering: Dr ANÍBAL VÉLEZ MUÑOZ
Faculty of Law: Dr FERNANDO SALAZAR MEJÍA
Faculty of Sociology: Dr FRANCISCO MÚNERA DUQUE
Faculty of Postgraduate Studies: Dr HÉCTOR ORTIZ CAÑAS

UNIVERSIDAD CATÓLICA DE MANIZALES

Apdo 357, Carrera 23 No. 60–63, Manizales
Telephone: (68) 860019

Fax: (68) 860575
E-mail: sucatomz@col2.telecom.co
Internet: www.ucatolicamz.edu.co
Founded 1954
Private control
Academic year: February to June, July to November
Rector: JUDITH LEON GUEVARA
Vice-Rector for Admin.: Sis. CECILIA GOMEZ JARAMILLO
Vice-Rector for Higher Teaching: SILVIO CARDONA GONZALEZ
Vice-Rector for Planning and Devt: JORGE OSWALDO SANCHEZ BUITRAGO
Vice-Rector for Professional Teaching: GLORIA ARRIETA DE PLATA
Vice-Rector for Research: MARCO FIDEL CHICA LASSO
Vice-Rector for Univ. Environment: Sis. BEATRIZ PATINO GARCIA
Registrar: FANNY CASTELLANOS TORO
Librarian: GABRIEL DEL ROSARIO
Number of teachers: 248
Number of students: 2,567
Publications: *Boletín Informativo*, *Protocolo*, *Revista de Investigaciones*.

UNIVERSIDAD CATÓLICA POPULAR DEL RISARALDA

Avda de las Américas, Frente al Parque Metropolitano del Café, Apdo Aéreo 2435, Pereira
Telephone: (96) 3127722
Fax: (96) 3127613
E-mail: ucpr@ucpr.edu.co
Internet: www.ucpr.edu.co
Founded 1975
Private control
Academic year: January to November
Grand Chancellor: Mgr FABIO SUESCÚN MUTIS
Rector: Fr ALVARO EDUARDO BETANCUR JIMÉNEZ
Vice-Rector: Dr JAIME MONTOYA FERRER
Admin. Dir: Dr HÉCTOR FABIO LONDOÑO PARRA
Librarian: Dra JUDITH GÓMEZ GÓMEZ
Number of teachers: 250
Number of students: 1,850
Publication: *Páginas de la UCPR* (5 a year)

DEANS

Faculty of Architecture: Dr EDGAR SALOMÓN CRUZ MORENO
Faculty of Business Administration: Dr ARIEL GALVIS GONZÁLEZ
Faculty of Industrial Design: Dra CARMEN ADRIANA PÉREZ CARDONA
Faculty of Industrial Economics: Dr HEDMAN ALBERTO SIERRA SIERRA
Faculty of Psychology: Dra BEATRIZ MARÍN LONDOÑO
Faculty of Religious Studies: Dr HÉCTOR CÓRDOBA VARGAS
Faculty of Social Communication and Journalism: Dra CRISTINA BOTERO SALAZAR

UNIVERSIDAD DE LA SABANA

Km 21, Autopista Norte de Bogotá D.C., Apdo Aéreo 140013, Bogotá
Telephone: (1) 8615555
Fax: (1) 8614220
E-mail: universidad.de.la.sabana@unisabana.edu.co
Internet: www.unisabana.edu.co
Founded 1979
Private control
Languages of instruction: Spanish, English
Academic year: February to November
Chancellor: JAVIER ECHEVARRÍA RODRÍGUEZ
Rector: Dr ALVARO MENDOZA RAMIREZ

Vice-Rector for Academic Affairs: Dra LILIANA OSPINA DE GUERRERO
Vice-Rector for Institutional Devt: Dra LAURA ELVIRA POSADA NÚÑEZ
Vice-Rector for Univ. Welfare: Dra MERCEDES SINISTERRA POMBO
Registrar: LUZ ANGELA VANEGAS
Sec.-Gen.: Dr JAVIER MOJICA SÁNCHEZ
Head of Admin.: Dr MAURICIO ROJAS PÉREZ
Academic Sec.: Dra LUZ ANGELA VANEGAS DE SÁNCHEZ
Librarian: Dra NELLY VÉLEZ SIERRA
Number of teachers: 491
Number of students: 8,872
Publications: *Pensamiento y Cultura* (1 a year), *Persona y Bioética* (1 a year)

DEANS

Faculty of Economic and Business Sciences: Dr HERNÁN DARÍO SIERRA ARANGO
Faculty of Education: Dra JULIA GALOFRE CANO
Faculty of Engineering: Dra GLORIA GONZÁLEZ MARIÑO
Faculty of Law: Dr OBDULIO VELÁSQUEZ OSADA
Faculty of Medicine: Dr EDUARDO BORDA CAMACHO
Faculty of Nursing: Dra LEONOR PARDO NOVOA
Faculty of Psychology: Dra MARÍA EUGENIA DE BERMÚDEZ
Faculty of Social Communication and Journalism: Dr CESAR MAURICIO VELÁSQUEZ OSSA

UNIVERSIDAD DE LA SALLE

Apdo Aéreo 28638, Bogotá
Telephone: (1) 2842606
Fax: (1) 2815064
Internet: www.lasalle.edu.co
Founded 1964
Academic year: February to May
Rector: Bro. JOSE VICENTE HENRY VALBUENA
Vice-Rector for Academic Affairs: Bro. LUIS HUMBERTO BOLÍVAR RODRÍGUEZ
Vice-Rector for Admin.: Dr ORLANDO ORTIZ PEÑA
Vice-Rector for Promotion and Human Devt: Bro. JOSE ANTONIO RODRÍGUEZ OTERO
Sec.-Gen.: Dr JUAN GUILLERMO DURÁN MANTILLA
Librarian: Dr NAPOLEÓN MUÑOZ NEDA
Number of teachers: 1,000
Number of students: 11,300
Publications: *Ciencia Animal*, *Ensayo en Administración*, *Reflejos*

DEANS

Faculty of Accountancy: Dr JESÚS MARÍA PEÑA BERMÚDEZ
Faculty of Agricultural Administration: Dr CARLOS ARTURO GONZÁLEZ
Faculty of Architecture: Dr TOMÁS FERNANDO URIBE
Faculty of Business Administration: Dr JESÚS SANTOS AMAYA
Faculty of Civil Engineering: Dr MIGUEL ORTEGA RESTREPO
Faculty of Economics: Dr SEBASTIÁN ARANGO FONNEGRA
Faculty of Education: Dra LUZ AMPARO MARTÍNEZ R.
Faculty of Food Engineering: LUIS FELIPE MAZUERA
Faculty of Library Science and Archives: Dr HUGO NOEL PARRA FLÓREZ
Faculty of Optometry: Dr CARLOS HERNANDO MENDOZA
Faculty of Philosophy and Letters: Dr LUIS ENRIQUE RUÍZ LÓPEZ
Faculty of Sanitary Engineering: Dr CAMILO H. GUÁQUETA R.

Faculty of Social Work: Dra ROSA MARGARITA VARGAS
Faculty of Stockbreeding: Dr GERMÁN SERRANO QUINTERO
Faculty of Veterinary Medicine: Dr GONZALO LUQUE FORERO
Division of Advanced Training: Dr FELIPE REYES DE LA VEGA

UNIVERSIDAD DE LOS ANDES

Carrera 1, No. 18A-70, Bogotá
Telephone: (1) 3394949
Fax: (1) 3324448
E-mail: uniandes@uniandes.edu.co
Internet: www.uniandes.edu.co
Founded 1948
Private control
Accredited by Consejo Nacional de Acreditación (CNA)
Languages of instruction: Spanish, English
Academic year: January to December
Pres.: ALBERTO GUTIÉRREZ
Rector: CARLOS ANGULO
Vice-Rector for Academic Affairs: JOSÉ RAFAEL TORO
Vice-Rector for Admin.: CONSUELO CARRILLO
Vice-Rector for Research: JOSÉ LUIS VILLAVECES
Sec.-Gen.: MARÍA TERESA TOBÓN
Registrar: ALEJANDRO RICO RESTREPO
Librarian: ANGELA MARÍA MEJÍA DE RESTREPO
Library of 409,700 vols
Number of teachers: 1,147 (full- and part-time)
Number of students: 14,200

Publications: *Colombia Internacional* (4 a year), *Hipótesis* (2 a year), *Historia Crítica* (2 a year), *Nota Uniandina* (2 a year), *Revista de Estudios Sociales* (2 a year), *Revista de Ingeniería* (2 a year)

DEANS

Faculty of Admin.: MARÍA LORENA GUTIÉRREZ
Faculty of Architecture and Design: WILLIE DREWS
Faculty of Arts and Humanities: CLAUDIA MONTILLA
Faculty of Economics: ALEJANDRO GAVIRIA
Faculty of Engineering: ALAIN GAUTHIER
Faculty of Law: EDUARDO CIFUENTES
Faculty of Medicine: MARIO BERNAL
Faculty of Sciences: JOSÉ ROLANDO ROLDÁN
Faculty of Social Sciences: CARL LANGEBAEK

UNIVERSIDAD DE MEDELLÍN

Apdo Aéreo 1983, Carrera 87 No. 30–65, Belén Los Alpes, Medellín, Antioquia
Telephone: (4) 3405555
Fax: (4) 3414913
Telephone: udem@guayacan.udem.edu.co
Internet: www.udem.edu.co
Founded 1950
Academic year: February to December
Rector: NÉSTOR HINCAPIÉ VARGAS
Sec.-Gen.: RAFAEL SOSA
Admin. Dir: MARIA TRINIDAD PINEDA CUERVO
Academic Dir: VICENTE ALBÉNIZ LACLAUSTRA
Dir of Postgraduate Studies: CARLOS TULIO MONTOYA HERRERA
Librarian: MARTA LUZ TAMAYO PALACIO
Number of teachers: 623
Number of students: 8,801

Publications: *Revista Con-Textos* (2 a year), *Revista Universidad de Medellín* (2 a year)

DEANS

Faculty of Administrative Sciences: JORGE LEÓN JARAMILLO MOLINA
Faculty of Civil Engineering: ARTURO ALBERTO ARISMENDY JARAMILLO

Faculty of Communication and Corporate Relations: LUIS MARIANO GONZALEZ AGUDELO
Faculty of Educational Sciences: JAIRO PÉREZ ARROYAVE
Faculty of Environmental Engineering: JUAN CARLOS BUITRAGO BOTERO
Faculty of Industrial Economy: JAIRO PÉREZ ARROYAVE
Faculty of Law: JUAN CARLOS VASQUEZ RIVERA
Faculty of Public Accountancy: ESTELLA SABA LOPEZ
Faculty of Statistics and Informatics: MARTA CECILIA MEZA PELÁEZ
Faculty of Systems Engineering: MARTA CECILIA MESA

UNIVERSIDAD DE SAN BUENAVENTURA

Trans. 26, No. 172-08, Apdo Aéreo 50679, Bogotá, D.C.
Telephone: (1) 6671090
Fax: (1) 6773003
Internet: www.usbbog.edu.co
Founded 1708, University status 1961
Private control
Academic year: February to November
Rector Gen.: Fr LUIS JAVIER URIBE MUÑOZ
Sec.-Gen.: Fr LUIS ARMANDO ROMERO GAONA.

CAMPUSES

Bogotá, D.C. Campus

Transversal 26, No. 172–08, Apdo Aéreo 75010, Bogotá
Telephone: (1) 6671090
Fax: (1) 6773003
Internet: www.usbbog.edu.co
Rector: Fr PABLO CASTILLO NOVA
Academic Dir: Dr BLANCA DE PINILLA
Admin. Dir: Dr RENÁN RODRIGUEZ CÁRDENAS
Librarian: Lic. JOSÉ BUELVAS
Number of teachers: 400
Number of students: 4,000

Publications: *Franciscanum* (3 a year), *Ingenium* (2 a year), *Itinerario Educativo* (3 a year), *Management* (2 a year)

DEANS

Faculty of Business Sciences: Dr JORGE GALEANO
Faculty of Education: Dr LUIS JAVIER CLARO
Faculty of Engineering: Ing. JAIME LEAL
Faculty of Gerontology: Dr OMAR PEÑA
Faculty of Philosophy: Fr MIGUEL ANGEL BUILES
Faculty of Psychology: Dr CLEMENCIA RAMÍREZ
Faculty of Theology: Fr FERNANDO GARZÓN

Calí Campus

La Umbría, Carretera a Pance, Apdo Aérero 25162, Calí
Telephone: (23) 552007
Fax: (23) 552006
Internet: www.usb.edu.co
Rector: Fr LUIS JAVIER URIBE MUÑOZ
Academic Dir: Dr DELIO MERINO ESCOBAR
Admin. Dir: Dr FRANCISCO VELASCO VELEZ
Librarian: CICILIA LIBREROS
Number of teachers: 360
Number of students: 5,041

Publications: *Architectura*, *Boletín Institucional* (26 a year), *Derecho* (2 a year), *Economía* (2 a year), *Educación* (2 a year), *Contaduria* (2 a year), *Ingeniería de Sistemas* (2 a year)

DEANS

Faculty of Accountancy: Dr JUAN GUILLERMO OCAMPO

Faculty of Agroindustrial Engineering: Dr RAÚL SALAZAR
Faculty of Architecture: Dr JUAN MARCO ANGEL
Faculty of Business Administration: Dr DIDIER NAVARRO
Faculty of Economics: Dr FRANCISCO JOSÉ RIZO
Faculty of Education: Dr OCTAVIO CALVACHES
Faculty of Electronic Engineering: Dr HAROLD PEDROZA
Faculty of Industrial Engineering: Dr ARTURO HERNÁNDEZ
Faculty of Law: Dr JORGE LUIS ROMERO
Faculty of Psychology: Dr JOEL OTERO
Faculty of Systems Engineering: Dr RICARDO LLANO

Cartagena Campus

Calle Real de Ternera, Apdo Aéreo 7833, Cartagena
Telephone: (53) 610465
Fax: (53) 630943
Internet: www.usbctg.edu.co
Rector: Fr ALBERTO MONTEALEGRE GONZÁLEZ
Academic Dir: Dr NICANOR ESPINOSA
Admin. Dir: Dr SILVIO MONTIEL
Sec.-Gen.: Fr MARIO RAMOS
Number of teachers: 68
Number of students: 961

DEANS

Faculty of Accountancy: Dr DEMÓSTENES BARRIOS
Faculty of Architecture: Dr GUSTAVO LEMAITRE
Faculty of Bacteriology: Dr LOURDES BENITEZ
Faculty of Business Administration: Dr LUIS MOSQUERA
Faculty of Chemical Engineering: Dr IGNACIO BURGOS
Faculty of Food Engineering: Dr MAYRA AYUZ
Faculty of Law: Dr HERNANDO URIBE
Faculty of Physical Therapy: Dra SANDRA DÍAZ
Faculty of Psychology: Dr BERTHA NUÑEZ
Faculty of Systems Engineering: Dr JORGE BUSTOS

Medellín Campus

Carrera 56c No. 51–90, Apdo Aéreo 5222-7370, Medellín
Telephone: (4) 5113600
Fax: (4) 2316191
Internet: www.usb-med.edu.co
Rector: Fr HERNANDO ARIAS RODRÍGUEZ
Admin. Dir: Dr EDGAR HINCAPIÉ
Sec.-Gen.: Fr ANDRÉS BOTERO
Number of teachers: 249
Number of students: 2,640

DEANS

Faculty of Architecture: Dr MARCO BAQUERO
Faculty of Business Science: Dr HERNÁN ARIAS
Faculty of Education: Dr LUIS ALBERTO RADA
Faculty of Engineering: Dr JESÚS LONDOÑO
Faculty of Law: Dr JUAN SÁNCHEZ
Faculty of Psychology: Dr ENRIQUE ARBELÁEZ
Faculty of Sociology: Dr GUILLERMO RIVERA

UNIVERSIDAD DEL NORTE

Km 5 Via Puerto Colombia, Barranquilla, Atlántico, Apdo Aéreo 1569-51820
Telephone: (5) 3509509
Fax: (5) 3598852
E-mail: webmaster@uninorte.edu.co
Internet: www.uninorte.edu.co
Founded 1966
Languages of instruction: Spanish, English
Academic year: January to December
Rector: JESÚS FERRO BAYONA

Vice-Rector for Academic Affairs: ALBERTO ROA VARELO
Vice-Rector for Admin.: ALMA LUCÍA DIAZ GRANADOS
Dean of Students: GINA PEZZANO
Dir, International Cooperation and Devt: CARMEN H. JIMENEZ DE PEÑA
Librarian: LUIS TARAZONA
Library of 89,238 vols, 1232 periodicals
Number of teachers: 855
Number of students: 10,721

Publications: *Derecho* (2 a year), *Eidos* (2 a year), *Ingenieria y Desarollo* (2 a year), *Investigacion y Desarrollo* (4 a year), *Pensamiento y Gestion* (2 a year), *Psicología desde el Caribe* (2 a year), *Revista Salud Uninorte* (2 a year)

DEANS

Division of Administrative Sciences: DIEGO CARADONA MADARIAGA
Division of Basic Sciences: JOACHIM HAHN
Division of Engineering: JAVIER PAEZ SAAVEDRA
Division of Health Sciences: HERNANDO BAQUERO LATOME
Division of Humanities and Social Sciences: JOSE AMAR AMAR
Division of Law: SILVIA GLORIA DE VIVO
Institute of Studies in Economics: LEONOR JARAMILLO DE CERTAIN

UNIVERSIDAD DEL ROSARIO – COLEGIO MAYOR DE NUESTRA SEÑORA DEL ROSARIO

Calle 14, No. 6-25, Bogotá
Telephone: (1) 2970200
Fax: (1) 2818583
E-mail: orelaint@urosario.edu.co
Internet: www.urosario.edu.co
Founded 1653
Private control
Languages of instruction: Spanish, English
Academic year: February to November
Rector: Dr HANS-PETER KNUDSEN QUEVEDO
Vice-Rector: Dr JOSÉ MANUEL RESTREPO ABONDANO
Sec.-Gen.: Dr LUIS ENRIQUE NIETO A.
Librarian: Dra MARGARITA LISOWSKA
Library of 62,735 vols, 2,143 periodicals, 16,267 e-books, 99 databases
Number of teachers: 1,044 (251 full-time, 134 half-time, 659 part-time)
Number of students: 13,382 (7,423 undergraduates, 5,959 graduates)
Publications: *Revista Desafíos, Revista de Economía del Rosario, Revista Estudios Sociojurídicos, Revista Universidad—Empresa* (2 a year)

DEANS

Faculty of Business: LUIS FERNANDO RESTREPO PUERTA
Faculty of Economics: HERNÁN JARAMILLO SALAZAR
Faculty of Human Development: LEONARDO PALACIOS SÁNCHEZ
Faculty of Human Sciences: FRANCISCO RODRIGUEZ LATORRE
Faculty of International Relations: EDUARDO BARAJAS SANDOVAL
Faculty of Law: ALEJANDRO VENEGAS FRANCO
Faculty of Medicine: LEONARDO PALACIOS SÁNCHEZ
Faculty of Political Science: EDUARDO BARAJAS SANDOVAL
Faculty of Science and Mathematics: LEONARDO PALACIOS SÁNCHEZ

UNIVERSIDAD EAFIT

Avda Las Vegas, Carrera 49 No. 7 Sur-50, Medellín
Telephone: (4) 2619600
Fax: (4) 2664284
Internet: www.eafit.edu.co
Founded 1960
Private control
Academic year: January to December
Rector: JUAN LUIS MEJÍA ARANGO
Registrar: MARÍA EUGENIA HOYOS
Academic Provost: MAURICIO VÉLEZ U.
Librarian: MARÍA CRISTINA RESTREPO LÓPEZ
Library of 40,000 vols
Number of teachers: 759
Number of students: 8,000

Publications: *AD Minister* (2 a year), *Cuadernos de Investigación, Eafitense* (12 a year), *Ecos de Economía* (2 a year), *Lúdica* (social communication), *Nuevo Foro Penal* (3 a year), *Revista Universidad Eafit* (4 a year), *Ruido Blanco* (2 a year), *Yesca y Pedernal* (4 a year)

DEANS

School of Administration and Accountancy: FRANCISCO LÓPEZ G.
School of Engineering: ALBERTO RODRÍGUEZ G.
School of Law: HUGO ALBERTO CASTAÑO Z.
School of Sciences and Humanities: LUCIANO ANGEL T.

UNIVERSIDAD EXTERNADO DE COLOMBIA

Calle 12, No. 1–17 Este, Bogotá
Telephone: (1) 3420288
Fax: (1) 2843769
E-mail: uextpub3@impsat.net.co
Internet: www.uexternado.edu.co
Founded 1886
Private control
Academic year: February to December
Rector: Dr FERNANDO HINESTROSA
Sec.-Gen.: Dr HERNANDO PARRA NIETO
Librarian: Dra LINA ESPITALETA DE VILLEGAS
Number of teachers: 639
Number of students: 7,000

Publications: *Boletín Tiempo y Turismo, Contexto* (4 a year), *Colección de Estudios en Derecho Penal—Cuadernos de Conferencias y Artículos* (3 a year), *Derecho del Estado* (2 a year), *Derecho Económico, Derecho Penal y Criminología* (3 a year), *Derecho y Vida, Documentos para la Historia del Constitucionalismo Colombiano* (2 a year), *Filosofía del Derecho* (4 a year), *Lúdica* (social communication), *Revista de Derecho Privado* (2 a year), *Revista de Economía Institucional, Notas de Coyuntura Económica, Oasis—Observatorio de Análisis de los Sistemas Internacionales, Revista Zero, Temas de Derecho Público* (4 a year)

DEANS

Faculty of Business Administration: Dra DIANA CABRERA
Faculty of Economics: Dr MAURICIO PÉREZ
Faculty of Education: Dra MIRYAM OCHOA PIEDRAHITA
Faculty of Finance, Government and International Relations: Dr ROBERTO HINESTROSA
Faculty of Furniture Restoration: Dra HELENA WIESNER
Faculty of Hotel Management and Tourism: Dr LUIS CARLOS CRUZ CORTÉS
Faculty of Law: Dr FERNANDO HINESTROSA
Faculty of Public Finance: Dr HERNANDO PÉREZ DURÁN

Faculty of Social Communication and Journalism: Dr MIGUEL MÉNDEZ CAMACHO
Faculty of Social Sciences and Humanities: Dra LUCERO ZAMUDIO

UNIVERSIDAD ICESI

Calle 18 122–135, Calí, Valle del Cauca
Telephone: (2) 5552334
Fax: (2) 5552345
E-mail: wwwmgr@icesi.edu.co
Internet: www.icesi.edu.co
Founded 1979
Private control
Language of instruction: Spanish
Pres.: FRANCISCO PIEDRAHITA
Sec.-Gen.: MARÍA CRISTINA NAVIA K.
Librarian: MARTA CECILIA LORA
Number of teachers: 260
Number of students: 2,580 (2,124 undergraduates, 456 graduates)
Publications: *Estudios Gerenciales* (3 a year), *Innovando* (52 a year), *Precedente* (3 a year), *Revista Interacción* (3 a year), *Sistemas y Telemática* (52 a year)

DEANS

Faculty of Economics and Administration: Dr HÉCTOR OCHOA DÍAZ
Faculty of Engineering: Dr HENRY ARANGO
Faculty of Law and Social Sciences: Dr LELIO FERNANDEZ

UNIVERSIDAD INCCA DE COLOMBIA

Apdo Aéreo 14817, Bogotá
Telephone: (2) 865200
Fax: (2) 824932
Internet: www.unincca.edu.co
Founded 1955
Private control
Academic year: January to December
Rector: Dra LEONOR GARCIA DE ANDRADE
Vice-Rector: Dra MARUJA GARCIA DE CORDOBA
Vice-Rector for Admin.: Dr JORGE ROJAS ALARCON
Academic Registrar: Dr MOISES NAJAR SANABRIA
Gen. Sec.: Dr JOSE LUIS ROBAYO LEON
Librarian: MARTHA ISABEL ANGEL GIRALDO
Number of teachers: 520
Number of students: 6,700

DEANS

Faculty of Basic and Natural Sciences: Mgr OVER QUINTERO CASTILLO
Faculty of Economic and Management Sciences: JULIO SILVA COLMENARES
Faculty of Human and Social Sciences: Mgr MESTOR BRAVO SALINAS
Faculty of Judicial and State Sciences: Dr OSCAR DUEÑAS RUIZ
Faculty of Postgraduate Studies: Mgr GERMAN PACHON OVALLE
Faculty of Technical and Engineering Sciences: Ing. Sis. MARIO MARTINEZ ROJAS

UNIVERSIDAD LA GRAN COLOMBIA

Carrera 6a, No. 13–40, Apdo Aéreo 7909, Bogotá
Telephone: (1) 2868200
Fax: (1) 2828386
E-mail: rectorjg@colomsat.net.co
Internet: www.ugrancolombia.edu.co
Founded 1953
Private control
Academic year: January to November (2 semesters)
Rector: JOSÉ GALAT NOUMER
Vice-Rector: RAFAEL BELTRAN BAJARANO
Gen. Sec.: RAÚL PACHECO BLANCO
Librarian: CONSTANZA GOMEZ DE NOVOA

Number of teachers: 661
Number of students: 9,650

DEANS

Faculty of Accountancy: JOSE DONADO UCROS
Faculty of Architecture: LUIS ALFREDO QUIÑONES SARMIENTO
Faculty of Civil Engineering: MANUEL RICARDO RUIZ ROMERO
Faculty of Economics: VICTOR MANUEL PEREZ ARGUELLEZ
Faculty of Law: CARLOS FREDY NAVIA PALACIOS
Faculty of Postgraduate Courses and Continuing Education: SERAFIN CRISANTO PEÑA MURCIA
Faculty of Sciences: AURA FELISA PEÑA

UNIVERSIDAD LIBRE DE COLOMBIA
(Colombia Free University)

Calle 8 No. 5–80, Bogotá
Telephone: (1) 2820389
Fax: (1) 2823580
Internet: www.unilibre.edu.co
Founded 1923
Rector: FERNANDO DJANON RODRIGUEZ
Number of teachers: 2,500
Number of students: 32,000
Faculties of accountancy, business administration, economics, education, engineering, law, medicine; campuses in Barranquilla, Calí, Cartagena, Cúcuta, Pereira, Socorro.

UNIVERSIDAD LIBRE, SECCIONAL DE PEREIRA

Apdo Aéreo 1330, Calle 40 No. 7–30, Pereira
Telephone: (63) 366025
Internet: www.ulibrepei.edu.co
Founded 1971
Academic year: February to December
Rector: JAIME ARIAS LOPEZ
Librarian: LUZ MARIA HINCAPIE
Number of teachers: 121
Number of students: 1,311
Publication: Boletín del Centro de Investigaciones (4 a year)

DEANS

Faculty of Economics: BERNARDO VÁSQUEZ CORREA
Faculty of Law: RODRIGO RIVERA CORREA

UNIVERSIDAD PONTIFICIA BOLIVARIANA

Apdo Aéreo 56006, Circular 1a No. 70–01, Medellín, Antioquia
Telephone: (4) 4159015
Fax: (4) 2502080
E-mail: secretaria@logos.upb.edu.co
Internet: www.upb.edu.co
Founded 1936
Private control
Academic year: January to December
Chancellor: Mgr ALBERTO GIRALDO JARAMILLO
Rector: Mgr GONZALO RESTREPO RESTREPO
Vice-Rector for Academic Affairs: JORGE IVÁN RAMÍREZ AGUIRRE
Vice-Rector for Admin. and Finance: Econ. OSCAR VELÁSQUEZ URIBE
Vice-Rector for Pastoral Affairs: Mgr CARLOS LUQUE AGUILERA
Sec.-Gen.: Abog. CARMEN HELENA CASTAÑO CARDONA
Library Dir: OLGA BEATRIZ BERNAL LONDOÑO
Library: see Libraries and Archives
Number of teachers: 1,746
Number of students: 7,462
Publications: Administración UPB (1 a year), Boletín de Programación de Radio Boli-

variana (6 a year), Comunicación Social UPB (1 a year), Escritos (philosophy, irregular), Cuestiones Teológicas y Filosóficas (2 a year), Pensamiento Humanista (1 a year), Revista Contaminación Ambiental (2 a year), Revista de la Facultad de Derecho y Ciencias (1 a year), Revista de la Facultad de Trabajo Social UPB (1 a year), Revista de Medicina UPB (2 a year), Revista Universidad Pontificia Bolivariana (2 a year)

DEANS

School of Advertising: MARÍA PATRICIA VÉLEZ BERNAL
School of Architecture: Arq. CARLOS MARIO RODRÍGUEZ
School of Basic Science: Ing. BERNARDO LOPERA VILLA
School of Business Administration: Admor. ÁLVARO GÓMEZ FERNÁNDEZ
School of Chemical Engineering: Ing. MARÍA ELENA SIERRA VÉLEZ
School of Communications: JORGE ALBERTO VELÁSQUEZ BETANCUR
School of Design, Philosophy and Humanities: RESTREPO POSADA CLEMENCIA
School of Divinity: GUILLERMO LEÓN ZULETA SALAS
School of Economics: Econ. ROBERTO ZAPATA VILLEGAS
School of Education: Mgr OLGA OSORIO RAMÍREZ
School of Electrical Engineering: Ing. MARISOL OSORIO CÁRDENAS
School of Electronic Engineering: Ing. MARISOL OSORIO CÁRDENAS
School of Humanities: Mgr. CARLOS LUQUE AGUILERA
School of Law: Abog. JOSÉ ALFREDO TAMAYO JARAMILLO
School of Mechanical Engineering: Ing. JORGE MANRIQUE HENAO
School of Medicine: MARTA BETANCUR GÓMEZ
School of Nursing: GLORIA ANGEL JIMÉNEZ
School of Philosophy: ALVARO MURILLO CASTAÑO
School of Psychology: JAIRO RESTREPO RINCÓN
School of Social Work: OLGA CECILIA OSPINA DE GIRALDO
School of Textile Engineering: Ing. JORGE MANIQUE HENAO
Graduate School: Ing. AUGUSTO URIBE MONTOYA

UNIVERSIDAD SANTIAGO DE CALÍ

Apdo Aéreo 4102, Calle 5 No. 62-00 (Pampalinda), Calí, Valle del Cauca
Telephone: (2) 5183000
Fax: (2) 5516567
E-mail: secgener@usaca.edu.co
Internet: www.usc.edu.co
Founded 1958
Private control
Languages of instruction: Spanish, English
Academic year: January to December
Rector: HEBERT CELÍN NAVAS
Vice-Rector: JOSÉ IGNACIO ZAMUDIO FRANCO
Admin. Dir: CARLOS JULIO BARRERO SANMIGUEL
Dir for Univ. Welfare: WILSON LÓPEZ ARAGÓN
Gen. Sec.: JORGE ELIÉCER TAMAYO MARULANDA
Academic Registrar: LUZ MARIA CANO ARIAS
Library Dir: JAVIER SALDARRIAGA ARANGO
Number of teachers: 1,368
Number of students: 13,469

UNIVERSIDAD SANTO TOMÁS

Carrera 9, No. 51–11, Bogotá
Telephone: (1) 3484141
Fax: (1) 5740383
E-mail: admisiones@correo.usta.edu.co

Internet: www.usta.edu.co
Founded 1580; restored 1965
Academic year: February to December
Rector: Fr EDUARDO GONZÁLEZ GIL
Vice-Rector for Academic Affairs: Fr FAUSTINO CORCHUELO ALFARO
Vice-Rector for Admin.: Fr VICENTE BECERRA REYES
Sec.-Gen.: HÉCTOR FABIO JARAMILLO SANTAMARIA
Librarian: Fr ADALBERTO CARDONA GÓMEZ
Library of 69,800 vols
Number of teachers: 660
Number of students: 12,961
Publications: Análisis, Cuadernos de Filosofía Latinoamericana, Revista Activos, Revista de Psicología, Revista Ciencia, Tecnología y Ambiente (science, technology and the environment, 2 a year), Revista CIFE, Revista Interamericana de Investigación, Educación y Pedagogía (research and education, 2 a year)

DEANS

Faculty of Civil Engineering: Ing. CARLOS ALBA MENDOZA
Faculty of Economics: Dr GILBERTO ENRIQUE HERAZO CUETO
Faculty of Electronic Engineering: Ing. CLAUDIA PATRICIA PÉREZ ROMERO
Faculty of Law: Dra LUZ AMPARO SERRANO QUINTERO
Faculty of Mechanical Engineering: JORGE ENRIQUE HERRERA FLAUTERO
Faculty of Philosophy: ALBERTO CÁRDENAS PATIÑO
Faculty of Physical Culture, Entertainment and Sports: PATRICIA CASALLAS REYES
Faculty of Psychology: EMILIO ESPEJO MOLANO
Faculty of Public Accounting: FERNANDO ARTURO RODRÍGUEZ MARTÍNEZ
Faculty of Social Communication: P. ADALMIRO ARIAS AGUDELO
Faculty of Sociology: RICARDO ARTURO ARIZA LÓPEZ
Faculty of Telecommunications Engineering: MAURICIO SAMUDIO LIZCANO

POSTGRADUATE INSTITUTES

Administration: Dir HERNÁN BOJACÁ MARTÍN.
Administration and Management of Quality Systems: Dir GERMÁN DARÍO MARÍN SEGURA.
Administrative Law: Dir MARIA EUGENIA SAMPER.
Business and Commercial Law: Dir HERNANDO ACOSTA RODRÍGUEZ.
Clinical and Family Psychology: Dir JAIRO ESTUPIÑAN MOJICA.
Economics: Dir DANILO TORRES REINA.
Electronic Instrumentation: Dir LUIS ALFONSO INFANTE.
Family Law: Dir LUZ AMPARO SERRANO QUINTERO.
Finance: Dir HERNÁN BOJACÁ MARTÍN.
Health Auditing: Dir Dr CARLOS IVÁN RODRÍGUEZ MELO.
International Business Management: Dir Dr JAVIER OSWALDO GUECHA MARIÑO.
Juridical Psychology: Dir FERNANDO DÍAZ COLORADO.
Latin-American Philosophy: Dir CARMENZA NEIRA.
Management of Health and Social Security Institutions: Dir Dr CARLOS IVÁN RODRÍGUEZ MELO.
Penal Law: Dir YESID REYES ALVARADO.

Political Sociology and Governmental Administration: Dir Dra ANA MEDINA DE RUÍZ.

Public Accounting: Dir TAYRON ROA VARGAS.

Socioeconomic Planning: Dir Dr DIEGO GIRALDO SAMPER.

Strategic Management of Financial Institutions: Dir DANILO TORRES REINA.

Systematic Family Supervision: Dir JAIRO ESTUPIÑAN MOJICA.

Systems Auditing: Dir Dr JAVIER OSWALDO GUECHA MARIÑO.

Tax Auditing: Dir TAYRON ROA VARGAS.

Technical Management of Electronic Engineering Projects: Dir LUIS ALFONSO INFANTE.

OTHER CAMPUSES

Bucaramanga Campus

Carrera 18, No. 9–27, Apdo Aéreo 75010, Bucaramanga

Telephone: (976) 712970
Fax: (976) 717067
E-mail: ustabuca@coll.telecom.com.co
Internet: www.usta.edu.co
Academic year: February to December

Sectional Rector: Fr CARLOS ARTURO DÍAZ RODRÍGUEZ

Vice-Rector for Academic Affairs: Fr PEDRO JOSÉ DÍAZ CAMACHO

Vice-Rector for Admin.: Fr JESÚS ANTONIO CEBALLOS GIRALDO

Gen. Sec.: Dr JOSÉ PABLO SANTAMARÍA
Library of 46,887 vols
Number of teachers: 423
Number of students: 4,500

Publications: *Iusticia* (law, 2 a year), *Temas* (humanities, 2 a year)

Tunja Campus

Calle 1, No. 11–64, Apdo Aéreo, Tunja
Telephone: (8) 7445847
Fax: (8) 7445851
E-mail: rectoria@ustatunja.edu.co
Internet: www.usta.edu.co
Academic year: January to December

Sectional Rector: Fr JOSÉ ANTONIO BALAGUERA CEPEDA

Vice-Rector for Academic Affairs: Fr SAMUEL ELIAS FORERO BUITRAGO

Vice-Rector for Admin.: Fr CARLOS ARIEL BETANCOURT OSPINA

Gen. Sec. (vacant)
Library of 6,800 vols
Number of teachers: 114
Number of students: 1,500

Publications: *Colecciones Investigando* (1 a year), *Iter Veritatis* (2 a year), *Principia Iuris* (2 a year).

Schools of Art and Music

Conservatorio de Música de la Universidad del Atlántico: Calle 68, No. 53–45, Apdo Aéreo 1890, Barranquilla; f. 1939; 21 teachers; 400 students; Dir Prof. GUNTER RENZ.

Conservatorio Nacional de Música (National Conservatory of Music): Dpto de Música, Facultad de Artes, Universidad Nacional, Bogotá; fax (1) 3681551; f. 1882 as Academia Nacional de Música, present name 1910; basic and university-level courses; 60 teachers; 900 students; library: 11,000 vols, scores and records; Dir LUIS E. AGUDELO.

Conservatorio del Tolima: Calle 9, No. 1–18, Apdo Aéreo 615, Ibagué; tel. (82) 639139; fax (82) 615378; internet www.bundenet.com/umusical; f. 1906; 121 teachers; 1,295 students; library: 3,216 vols; Rector IVETTE JOSEFINA GARDEAZABAL MICOLTA.

Escuela de Música: Universidad de Nariño, Calle 21 No. 23-90, Pasto, Nariño; Dir FAUSTO MARTINEZ.

Escuela de Pintura y Artes Plásticas: Universidad del Atlántico, Calle 68, No. 53–54, Barranquilla; f. 1961; teaching of plastic arts; staff of 11; library: 1,900 vols; Dir Dr EDUARDO VIDES CELIS.

Instituto Musical de Cartagena: Apdo Aéreo No. 17–67, Cartagena, Bolívar; f. 1890; 12 teachers; 340 students; library: 1,500 vols; Dir Prof. JIRI PITRO M.

COMOROS

The Higher Education System

The Comoros declared their independence from France in 1975. French is one of the official languages, along with Comorian and Arabic. For many years higher education in the Comoros was limited to a number of programmes in teacher training, agriculture and health sciences at colleges and schools. Many students left the Comoros to study abroad; the World Bank estimated that 1,000 students did so in 1995. The Government provided scholarships for these students, but relied on funds from international donors to do so. The islands' first university, the Université des Comores, opened in December 2003 and 2,600 students were enrolled there in 2005/06.

Illiteracy, especially among females, poses serious difficulties for the Comoros (as in many African countries). The development of higher education is hampered by the absence of a viable primary and secondary education system. In the Comoros more than one-third of school-age children have no access to six-year formal education; of those who do have access only one-tenth continue to lower-secondary education. Enrolment levels at primary, secondary and post-secondary education are estimated at 64%, 11% and just 2%, respectively.

Regulatory Body

GOVERNMENT

Ministry of National Education, Higher Education and Research: Moroni; Minister ABDOURAHIM SAÏD BACAR.

Research Institute

AGRICULTURE, FISHERIES AND VETERINARY SCIENCE

Institut National de la Recherche pour L'Agriculture, La Pêche et l'Environ-ment (INRAPE): Moroni; tel. 736688; fax 736357; agricultural and environmental research; Dir-Gen. ABOUBACAR ALLAOUI.

Library

Moroni

Centre National de Documentation et de Recherche Scientifique (CNDRS): BP 169, Moroni; tel. 744187; fax 744189; f. 1979; incorporates the national library and archives, national museum and research centre (human and natural sciences); Dir Dr DJAFFAR MMADI.

University

UNIVERSITÉ DES COMORES

Route de la corniche BP 2585, Moroni
Telephone: 734227
E-mail: univ_com@snpt.km
Internet: www.univ-comores.com
Founded 2003
State control
Pres.: MOHAMED RACHADI.

DEMOCRATIC REPUBLIC OF THE CONGO

The Higher Education System

Prior to independence from Belgium in 1960, the country was known as Belgian Congo. Following independence it became the Democratic Republic of the Congo, and then Zaire in 1971; in 1997 the name reverted to Democratic Republic of the Congo. The oldest university is the Université de Kinshasa (formerly Université Lovanium), which was founded in 1954 by the Université Catholique de Louvain (Belgium). Between 1971 and 1981 the Université de Kinshasa was merged with the Université de Kisangani (formerly the Protestant-run Université Libre du Congo, founded 1963) and the Université de Lubumbashi (founded 1955) to form the National University of Zaire (UNAZA). Since 1981 these three state-run universities have reverted to autonomous institutions. There are also private universities at Kinshasa, Bas-Congo, Bakavu, Butembo and Goma. Other institutions of higher education include technical institutes and teaching institutes. In 2002/03 there were an estimated 60,341 students in tertiary education.

In 1997 the former ministries of primary, secondary, technical and higher education were merged into a supra-Ministry of National Education. As a result of the prolonged civil conflict, government funding for education was effectively suspended, contributing to a decline in enrolment. In 2002 an emergency programme for education, with an estimated cost of US $101m., was introduced to restore access to basic education. Administration of higher education is split between government ministries: the Ministry of Finance controls budget allocation; the Ministry of the Civil Service controls personnel; and the Ministry of Planning oversees the use of human resources. Senior administrative and academic figures, such as the Rector and heads of department, are appointed by the President and/or the Minister of National Education.

The Diplôme d'Etat d'Etudes Secondaires du Cycle Long is required for admission to university education. University degree programmes are divided into three cycles. The first cycle lasts three years and leads to the award of Graduat; the second cycle lasts two to three years and results in the award of the Licence, though some programmes, such as medicine and veterinary medicine, may require longer; and the third cycle is a two- to four-year programme of postgraduate study resulting in either Diplôme d'Études Spéciales (DES) or Diplôme de Spécialiste. Doctorates in agriculture are also available.

Technological and teaching-training institutes attached to universities provide three-year courses of higher vocational education, leading to the award of the Gradué.

Regulatory Bodies

GOVERNMENT

Ministry of Culture and the Arts: BP 8541, Kinshasa 1; tel. (12) 31005; Minister ESDRAS KAMBALE.

Ministry of Higher and University Education and Scientific Research: Kinshasa; Minister LÉONARD MASUGA RUGAMIRA.

Learned Societies

GENERAL

UNESCO Office Kinshasa: Immeuble Losonia, Blvd du 30 juin, POB 7248, Kinshasa; tel. 8848253; fax 8848252; e-mail kinshasa@unesco.org; Head of Office CATHERINE OKAI.

BIBLIOGRAPHY, LIBRARY SCIENCE AND MUSEOLOGY

Association des Archivistes, Bibliothécaires et Documentalistes: BP 805, Kinshasa 11; f. 1973, to assist the Government in the planning and organization of archives, libraries and documentation centres; professional training and seminars.

HISTORY, GEOGRAPHY AND ARCHAEOLOGY

Société des Historiens: BP 7246, Lubumbashi; f. 1974; attached to Min. of Higher Education and Scientific Research; aims to bring about a better understanding of the nation's past; to organize meetings, etc. for historians; to preserve the national archives, works of art, and archaeological remains; Pres. Prof. NDAYWEL È NZIEM; Sec.-Gen. Prof. Dr TSHIBANGU MUSAS KABET; publs *Etudes d'Histoire Africaine* (1 a year), *Likundoli* (2 a year).

LANGUAGE AND LITERATURE

Alliance Française: 11, Ave Lubefu, Commune de la Gombe, BP 5404, Kinshasa 10; tel. 8803221; fax 8804707; offers courses and exams in French language and culture and promotes cultural exchange with France; attached teaching centres in Boma, Bukavu, Kananga, Kikwit, Kisangani, Lubumbashi and Matadi.

Research Institutes

GENERAL

Centre de Recherche en Sciences Humaines (CRSH): BP 3474, Kinshasa/Gombe; f. 1985 by fusion of IRS and ONRD; administration, economics, education, history, law, linguistics, literature, philosophy, psychology, social sciences, sociology; 94 research mems; library of 4,000 vols and 12,000 periodicals; Dir-Gen. MAKWALA MA MAVAMBU YE BEDA; publs *Cahier Zaïrois de Recherche en Sciences Humaines* (4 a year), *IRS—Information*.

AGRICULTURE, FISHERIES AND VETERINARY SCIENCE

Institut National pour l'Etude et la Recherche Agronomique (INERA): BP 2037, Kinshasa 1; tel. 32332; f. 1933; agronomical study and research; 2,250 staff; library of 38,428 vols; Pres. Dr Ir. MASIMANGO NDYANABO; publs *Bulletin Agricole du Zaïre* (2 a year), *Bulletin Agroclimatologique* (1 a year), *Info-INERA* (12 a year), *Programme d'Activités* (1 a year).

HISTORY, GEOGRAPHY AND ARCHAEOLOGY

Institut Géographique: 106 Blvd du 30 Juin, BP 3086, Kinshasa-Gombe; f. 1949; geodetic, topographical, photogrammetric and cartographic studies; small library; Dir-Gen. Major LUBIKU LUSIENSE BELANI.

MEDICINE

Institut de Médecine Tropicale: BP 1697, Kinshasa; f. 1899; clinical laboratory serving Hôpital Mama Yemo with reference laboratory functions for other medical services in Kinshasa; Dir Dr DARLY JEANTY.

NATURAL SCIENCES

Biological Sciences

Institut Congolais pour la Conservation de la Nature: BP 868, Kinshasa 1; tel. 31401; f. 1925; 2,295 staff; library of 2,500 vols; Man. Dir EULALIE BASHIGE; publ. *Revue Leopard*.

TECHNOLOGY

Bureau de Recherches Géologiques et Minières (BRGM): BP 1974, Kinshasa 1; copper mining; see main entry under France; Dir G. VINCENT.

Centre de Recherches Géologiques et Minières: 44 Ave des Huileries, BP 898, Kinshasa 1; tel. 99-28-982; e-mail crgm@cedesurk.refer.org; f. 1939; staff of 120 undertake mineral exploration and geological mapping; library of 7,305 vols; Dir-Gen. Prof. NTOMBI MUEN KABEYA; publ. *Revue* (52 a year).

Commissariat Général à l'Energie Atomique: BP 868-184, Kinshasa XI; f. 1959; scientific research in peaceful applications of atomic energy; 140 staff; library of 3,000 vols; Commissary Gen. Prof. MALU WA KALENGA; publs *Bulletin d'Information Scientifique et Technique* (4 a year), *Rapport de Recherche* (1 a year).

Libraries and Archives

Kinshasa

Archives Nationales: BP 3428, 42A Ave de la Justice, Kinshasa-Gombe; tel. 31083; f. 1947; 3,000 vols; Curator KIOBE LUMENGA-NESO.

Bibliothèque Centrale de l'Université de Kinshasa: BP 125, Kinshasa 11; f. 1954; 300,000 vols; Chief Librarian (vacant); publs *Liste des Acquisitions*, *Nouvelles du Mont Amba* (52 a year).

Bibliothèque Publique: BP 410, Kinshasa; f. 1932; 24,000 vols; Librarian B. MONGU.

Kisangani

Bibliothèque Centrale de l'Université de Kisangani: BP 2012, Kisangani; tel. 2948; f. 1963; 90,000 vols; Chief Librarian MUZILA LABEL KAKES.

Lubumbashi

Bibliothèque Centrale de l'Université de Lubumbashi: POB 2896, Lubumbashi; f. 1955; 300,000 vols, 1,000 periodicals, 500,000 microfiches and microfilms; Librarian MUBADI SULE MWANANSUKA; publs *Cahiers Philosophiques Africains* (6 a year), *Lettres*, *Likundoli* (irregular), *Séries A*.

Museums and Art Galleries

Kananga

Musée National de Kananga: 160 Ave Kinkole, BP 612, Kananga.

Kinshasa

Musée National de Kinshasa: BP 4249, Kinshasa.

Lubumbashi

Musée National de Lubumbashi: BP 2375, Lubumbashi.

Universities

UNIVERSITÉ DE KINSHASA

BP 127, Kinshasa 11

Telephone: 30123

Internet: www.unikin.cd

Founded 1954 as the Université Lovanium by the Université Catholique de Louvain in collaboration with the Government; reorganized 1971 and 1981

Language of instruction: French

Academic year: October to July

Rector: BOGUO MAKELI

Sec.-Gen.: KAPETA NZOVU

Library: see Libraries and Archives

Number of teachers: 536

Number of students: 5,800

Publications: *Annales* (faculty publs, 2 a year), *Cahiers Economiques et Sociaux* (4 a year)

DEANS

Faculty of Economics: KINTAMBO MAFUKU
Faculty of Law: KISAKA KIA KOY
Faculty of Medicine: Dr NGALA KENDA
Faculty of Pharmacy: MULUMBA BIPI
Faculty of Sciences: MUKANA WA MURANA
Polytechnic Faculty: ANDRE DE BOECK

ATTACHED RESEARCH INSTITUTES

Centre de Cardiologie.

Centre de Recherches pour le Développement.

Centre de Recherche pour l'Exploitation de l'Energie Renouvelable (CREER).

Centre de Recherche Interdisciplinaire pour le Droit de l'Homme.

Centre Interdisciplinaire d'Etudes et de Documentation Politiques (CIE-DOP).

Centre Interdisciplinaire pour le Développement et l'Education Permanente (CIDEP): BP 2307, Kinshasa 1; training courses in management; branches at Kisangani, Lubumbashi and Karanga; politics and administration, commerce, social sciences, applied education, applied technology; 1,785 students; Sec.-Gen. MBULAMOKO ZENGE MOVOAMBE.

Institut d'Etudes et de Recherche Historique du Temps Présent.

Institut de Recherches Economiques et Sociales (IRES): BP 257, Kinshasa 11; Dir ILUNGA ILUKAMBA.

Institut des Sciences et Techniques de l'Information (ISTI): BP 14.998, Kinshasa 1; first degrees and doctorates; 15 staff; 103 students; Dir-Gen. MALEMBE TAMANDIAK.

Institut Supérieur d'Arts et Métiers (ISAM): BP 15.198, Kinshasa 1; f. 1968; management training for the clothing industry; 18 staff, 101 students; Dir OMONGA OKAKO DENEWADE.

Institut Supérieur de Commerce, Kinshasa: BP 16.596, Kinshasa 1; 37 staff; 600 students; Dir-Gen. PANUKA D'ZENTEMA.

Institut Supérieur des Bâtiments et Travaux Publics (IBTP): BP 4.731, Kinshasa 2; 83 staff; 916 students; Dir-Gen. BUTASNA BU NIANGA.

Institut Supérieur de Techniques Appliquées (ISTA): BP 6593, Kinshasa 31; tel. 20727; f. 1971; technical training; 513 staff; 5,814 students; library of 3,443 vols, 2,486 periodicals, 2,789 dissertations; Dir-Gen. Prof. MUKANA WA MUANDA.

Institut Supérieur des Techniques Médicales (ISTM): BP 774, Kinshasa 11; tel. 22113; f. 1981; 80 staff, 1,005 students; Dir-Gen. Dr PHAKA MBUMBA.

Laboratoire d'Analyses des Médicaments et des Aliments.

UNIVERSITÉ DE KISANGANI

BP 2012, Kisangani

Telephone: 2152

Founded 1963; present name 1981

State control

Language of instruction: French

Academic year: October to July (three terms)

Rector: MWABILA MADELA

Admin. Sec.: GUDIJIGA A. GIKAPA

Academic Sec.: BOKULA MOISO

Budget Administrator: LINDONGA TEMELE-ZEMAKA

Library: see Libraries and Archives

Number of teachers: 216

Number of students: 2,439

Publication: *Le Cahier du CRIDE*

Faculties of administration, medicine, political science, science, social sciences.

ATTACHED RESEARCH INSTITUTES

Bureau Africain des Sciences de l'Education (BASE): BP 14, Kisangani; Dir A. S. MUNGALA.

Centre de Recherche Interdisciplinaire pour le Développement de l'Education (CRIDE): BP 1386, Kisangani; Dir KALALA NKUDI.**

Institut Facultaire des Sciences Agronomiques (IFA): BP 1232, Kisangani; f. 1973; first degrees and doctorates in agriculture; 38 teachers; 683 students; library of 7,141 vols, 14,574 periodicals; Rector Dr Ir Prof. MAMBANI BANDA; publ. *Annales*.

Institut Supérieur de Commerce, Kisangani: BP 2.012, Kisangani; Dir KABAMBI MULAMBA.

Institut Supérieur d'Etudes Agronomiques de Bengamisa: BP 202, Kisangani; 31 staff; 328 students; Dir-Gen. LUMPUNGU KABAMBA.

UNIVERSITÉ DE LUBUMBASHI

BP 1825, Lubumbashi

Telephone: 225285

E-mail: unilu@unilu.net

Internet: www.unilu.ac.cd

Founded 1955; reorganized 1971 and 1981

Language of instruction: French

State control

Academic year: October to July (October–February, March–July)

Rector: Prof. KAUMBA LUFUNDA

Sec.-Gen. for Academic Affairs: Prof. HUIT MULONGO

Sec.-Gen. for Admin.: CHABU MUMBA

Chief Librarian: SUKA MUBADI

Number of teachers: 442

Number of students: 13,158

Publications: *Cahiers Philosophiques Africains*, *Cahiers d'Études Politiques et Sociales* (2 a year), *Études d'Histoire Africaine* (2 a year), *Likundoli* (2 a year), *Mitunda* (African cultures, 2 a year), *Prospective et Perspective* (2 a year), *Recherches Linguistiques et Littéraires* (2 a year), various faculty publs

DEANS

Faculty of Agricultural Science: Prof. MICHEL NGONGO LUHEMBWE
Faculty of Economics: Prof. KASANGANA MWALABA
Faculty of Law: Prof. MALEMBA M. N'SAKILA
Faculty of Letters: Prof. KASHALA KAPALOWA
Faculty of Medicine: Prof. MUTETA WA PA MANDA
Faculty of Psychology and Pedagogy: (vacant)
Faculty of Sciences: Prof. BYAMUNGU BIN RUSANGIZA
Faculty of Social, Administrative and Political Sciences: Prof. ELENGESA NDUNGUNA
Faculty of Veterinary Medicine: Prof. KASHALA KAPAWOLA
Polytechnic Faculty: Prof. KALENGA NGOY

AFFILIATED RESEARCH INSTITUTES

École Supérieur de Commerce (ESC): Dir Prof. KIZOBO O'OBWENG O.

École Supérieure d'Ingénieur (ESI): Dir Prof. NGOIE NSENGA.

Institut Supérieur d'etudes Sociales de Lubumbashi: BP 825, Lubumbashi 1; tel. 4315; f. 1956; 18 full-time staff, 785 students; Dir KITENGE YA.

Institut Supérieur de Statistique (ISS): BP 2471, Lubumbashi (Shaba); tel. 3905; f. 1967; 72 staff, 700 students; library of 3,000 vols, 10 periodicals; Dir-Gen. Prof. Dr MBAYA KAZADI; Sec.-Gen. for Academic Affairs Prof. Dr ANYENYOLA WELO; Sec.-Gen. for Admin. Lic. BIHINI YANKA; publ. *Annales*.

Institut Supérieur des Techniques Médicales: Dir Prof. MALONGA KAJ.

UNIVERSITÉ DE MBUJI-MAYI
(University of Mbuji-Mayi)

BP 225 Ave de l'Université, Campus de Tshikama, Dibindi, Mbuji-Mayi, Kasaï Oriental

Telephone: 8854890

Fax: 8854111

E-mail: univmayi@yahoo.fr

Internet: www.fundp.ac.be/~itshiman/um/html

Founded 1990

Private Control (Catholic Church)

Language of instruction: French

Academic year: November to July

Rector: RAPHAËL MBOWA KALENGAYI

Library of 14,000 vols, 75 periodicals

Number of teachers: 134

Number of students: 904

Faculties of applied science, economics, human medicine and law.

UNIVERSITÉ KONGO

BP 202, Mbanza-Ngungu, Bas-Congo

Telephone: 232132

Founded 1990 as University de Bas-Zaïre

Private Control

Language of instruction: French

Rector: Prof. B. LUTULALA MUMPHASI

Sec.-Gen.for Academic Affairs: Prof. PHUKU PHUATI

Sec.-Gen. for Admin.: F. KITUBA MAKUNSA

Number of teachers: 154

Number of students: 816

DEANS

Faculty of Agronomy: Prof. K. MAFWILA

Faculty of Economics and Management: Prof. KAMIANTAKO MIYAMWENI

Faculty of Law: Prof. K. BUKA

Faculty of Literature and Social Communication: (vacant)

Faculty of Medicine: Prof. Dr MBANZULU PITA

Polytechnic Faculty: Prof. PHUKU PHUATI

Colleges

Académie des Beaux-Arts (ABA): BP 8.349, Kinshasa 1; 44 staff; 248 students; Dir BEMBIKA NKUNKU.

Institut National des Arts (INA): BP 8332, 1 Ave du Commerce, Zone en Gombé, Kinshasa 1; 72 staff; 147 students; Dir Prof. BAKOMBA KATIK DIONG.

REPUBLIC OF CONGO

The Higher Education System

Higher education was established while the Republic of Congo was under French administration (it was then part of French Equatorial Africa), through the foundation of an Institute for Advanced Studies and a Centre for Advanced Administrative and Technical Studies. Following independence in 1960 the Fondation de l'Enseignement Supérieur en Afrique Centrale was created, which comprised several centres and schools. It was dissolved in 1971 and in the same year the Université de Brazzaville was inaugurated; in 1977 it adopted its current name, Université Marien-Ngouabi. In 2000 there were some 20,000 students enrolled at the Université Marien-Ngouabi, which is the only state university. In 2002/03 the total number of students in further and higher education was estimated at 12,456. Public education exists at two levels: university and non-university. Private initiatives are also increasingly moving into the higher education system, providing mainly technical and professional training in subjects such as business management. Some Congolese students also attend further education establishments abroad. In September 2004 the World Bank approved a grant of US $20m. to assist with the reconstruction of the country's educational sector, which had been severely damaged by years of civil conflict.

The four types of higher educational establishment—public and private universities, training schools and institutions of continuing education—are stipulated in the 1990 law related to education, which was modified by the November 1995 law (008/90) defining the organizational structures of the Congolese educational system. This law also stipulates a number of depositions, among them equality in access, free public education, the Government's responsibility for the organization of education and the recognition of the private sector.

Admissions to the Université Marien-Ngouabi are determined by ministerial decree. Generally, the university accepts candidates of Congolese nationality and foreigners holding a high school degree (baccalauréat) or its equivalent in return for an application fee. University-level qualifications are divided into two cycles: first, either the Diplôme Universitaire d'Etudes Littéraires (DUEL) in arts and humanities or the Diplôme Universitaire d'Etudes Scientifiques (DUES) in the sciences is awarded after two years of study; second, the Licence is awarded after an additional two years of study after DUEL/DUES, with an option of studying a further two years for the Diplôme des Etudes Supérieures (DES). There are no Masters or doctoral programmes. There are also professional institutes and schools which award the DES, usually after two-year courses of study.

Regulatory Bodies

GOVERNMENT

Ministry of Culture and the Arts: BP 20480, Brazzaville; tel. 81-02-35; fax 81-40-25; Minister JEAN-CLAUDE GAKOSSO.

Ministry of Higher Education: Ancien Immeuble de la Radio, BP 169, Brazzaville; tel. 81-08-15; fax 81-52-65; Minister HENRI OSSEBI.

Ministry of Scientific Research and Technical Innovation: Ancien Immeuble de la Radio, Brazzaville; tel. 81-03-59; Minister PIERRE ERNEST ABANDZOUNOU.

Ministry of Technical Education and Vocational Training: BP 2076, Brazzaville; tel. 81-17-27; fax 81-56-82; e-mail metp_cab@yahoo.fr; Minister PIERRE MICHEL NGUIMBI.

Learned Societies

GENERAL

Union Panafricaine de la Science et de la Technologie (UPST): Ave E. P. Lumumba, BP 2339, Brazzaville; tel. 83-65-35; fax 83-21-85; f. 1987; coordinates research into scientific and technological devt; 409 mem. instns (asscns, academies, socs and research institutes); Pres. Prof. EDWARD S. AYENSU; publ. *Nouvelles de l'UPST* (4 a year).

LANGUAGE AND LITERATURE

PEN Centre of Congo: BP 2181, Brazzaville; tel. 81-36-01; fax 81-36-01; Pres. E. B. DONGALA.

Research Institutes

GENERAL

Direction Générale de la Recherche Scientifique et Technique: BP 2499, Brazzaville; tel. 81-06-07; f. 1966; spec. commissions for industrial and technological sciences, medical science, natural sciences, social sciences and agricultural sciences; library of 4,500 vols; Dir-Gen. Prof. MAURICE ONANGA; publ. *Sciences et Technologies*.

Institut de Recherche pour le Développement (IRD): BP 1286, Zone Industrielle, Pointe-Noire; tel. 94-02-38; fax 94-39-81; f. 1950; biological and physical oceanography, botany, nematology, pedology, plant ecology, plant physiology; library; see main entry under France; Dir LAURENT VEYSSEYRE.

Institut de Recherche pour le Développement (IRD–DGRST): BP 181, Brazzaville; tel. 83-26-80; fax 83-29-77; f. 1947; bioclimatology, botany, demography and sociology, entomology, hydrology, medical epidemiology, microbiology, nutrition, phytopathology, soil science; library of 16,000 vols; see main entry under France; Dir C. REICHENFELD.

AGRICULTURE, FISHERIES AND VETERINARY SCIENCE

Centre de Recherche Forestière du Littoral: BP 764, Pointe-Noire; tel. and fax 94-39-12; f. 1992; forestry research; Dir Dr MAURICE DIABANGOUAYA.

Centre d'Etudes sur les Resources Végétales (CERVE): BP 1249, Brazzaville; tel. 81-21-83; f. 1985; attached to Min. of Scientific Research; catalogues plant species of the Congo; promotes traditional phytotherapy; develops indigenous and exotic fodder plants; library of 100 vols; Dir Prof. LAURENT TCHISSAMBOU.

Station Fruitière du Congo: BP 27, Loudima; f. 1963; Dir C. MAKAY.

HISTORY, GEOGRAPHY AND ARCHAEOLOGY

Centre de Recherche Géographique et de Production Cartographique: Ave de l'OUA, BP 125, Brazzaville; tel. 81-07-80; f. 1945; attached to Min. of Scientific Research and Technical Innovation; library of 2,786 vols; Dir F. ELONGO.

MEDICINE

Direction de la Médecine Préventive: BP 236, Brazzaville; tel. 81-43-51; f. 1978; attached to Ministry of Health and Social Affairs; responsible for carrying out policy on endemo-epidemic illnesses; 98 staff; Dir Dr RÉNÉ CODDY-ZITSAMELE; publ. various reports and research papers.

TECHNOLOGY

Centre de Recherche et d'Initiation des Projets de Technologie (CRIPT): BP 97, Brazzaville; tel. 51-44-95; fax 81-03-30; f. 1986; under the Min. of Scientific Research and Technical Innovation; aims to develop farming and forestry, to promote the creation of industry, to set up projects concerned with industrial science and technology, and to adapt imported technology for local requirements; Dir Dr GASTON GABRIEL ELLALY.

Libraries and Archives

Brazzaville

Bibliothèque Nationale Populaire: BP 1489, Brazzaville; tel. 83-34-85; f. 1971; 15,000 vols (7,000 in brs); Dir PIERRE MAYOLA.

Bibliothèque des Sciences de la Santé et Centre de Documentation/AFRO Health Sciences Library and Documentation Centre: BP 6, Brazzaville; tel. 241-39425; fax 241-39673; f. 1952; 7,000 vols; Librarian MARIE-PAULE KABORE.

Bibliothèque Universitaire, Université Marien-Ngouabi: BP 2025, Brazzaville; tel. 83-14-30; f. 1992; 78,000 vols; Chief Librarian INNOCENT MABIALA; publs *Cahiers congolais d'anthropologie et d'histoire, Cahiers de la Jurisprudence, Congolaise de Droit, Revue.*

Centre d'Information des Nations Unies: BP 1018, Ave Foch, Brazzaville; tel. 83-50-90; fax 83-61-40; f. 1983; affiliated to UN Dept of Information in New York; 4,378 vols (mostly NGO publs); Dir ISMAEL A. DIALLO; publs *Notes d'Information,* monthly list of acquisitions.

Museums and Art Galleries

Brazzaville

Musée National: BP 994, Brazzaville; tel. 81-03-30; f. 1965; ethnographic colln and nat. history; library of 285 vols; Dir JEAN GILBERT JULES KOULOUFOUA.

Kinkala

Musée Régional André Grenard Matsoua: BP 85, Kinkala; tel. 85-20-14; f. 1978; under the Min. of Culture and the Arts; ethnography; 5 staff; library; Curator BIVINGOU-NZEINGUI.

Pointe Noire

Musée Régional Ma-Loango Diosso: BP 1225, Pointe-Noire; tel. 94-15-79; f. 1982;

attached to Min. of Culture and the Arts; collects historical, ethnographical, scientific, artistic materials as a source of information on Congolese culture; Curator JOSEPH KIMFOKO-MADOUNGOU.

University

UNIVERSITÉ MARIEN-NGOUABI

BP 69, Brazzaville
Telephone: 81-01-41
Fax: 81-01-41
Founded 1961 as Centre d'Etudes Administratives et Techniques Supérieur; became Université de Brazzaville 1971; present name 1977
State control
Language of instruction: French
Rector: CHARLES MBALAWA GOMBE
Library: see Libraries and Archives
Number of teachers: 550
Number of students: 15,844
Publications: *Annales, DIMI, Mélanges, Revue médicale du Congo, Sango* (6 a year)

DEANS

Faculty of Arts and Humanities: PAUL NZETE
Faculty of Economics: HERVÉ DIATA
Faculty of Health Sciences: GEORGES MOYEN
Faculty of Law: BERNARD TCHICAYA
Faculty of Science: JEAN MOALI

DIRECTORS OF SCHOOLS

Ecole Normale d'Administration et de Magistrature (ENAM): CYRIAQUE AYON-BOUE
Ecole Normale Supérieur (ENS): ROSALIE KAMA NIAMAYOUA
Ecole Normale Supérieure de l'Enseignement Technique (ENSET): BERNARD MABIALA

ATTACHED INSTITUTES

Institut de Développement Rural (IDR): BP 69, Brazzaville; f. 1976; Dir PAUL YOKA.

Institut Supérieur d'Education Physique et Sportive (ISEPS): BP 1100, Brazzaville; f. 1976; Dir BERNARD PACKA TCHISSAMBOU.

Institut Supérieur de Gestion: BP 2469, Brazzaville; f. 1976; Dir FRANÇOIS SITA.

Colleges

Collège d'Enseignement Technique Agricole: BP 30, Sibiti; f. 1943; Dir JEAN BOUNGOU.

Collège Technique, Commercial et Industriel de Brazzaville (et Centre d'Apprentissage): Brazzaville; f. 1959; Dir HUBERT CUOPPEY.

Ecole Supérieure Africaine des Cadres des Chemins de Fer (Higher School for Railway Engineers): Brazzaville; f. 1977; management and technical courses.

COSTA RICA

The Higher Education System

The Universidad de Costa Rica is the oldest institution of higher education in Costa Rica. It was founded in 1843 by the Roman Catholic Church as Universidad de Santo Tomás, closed in the 1880s and refounded under its current name in 1940. The Ministry of Education controls the formal education system through the aegis of the Consejo Superior de Educación (Higher Council of Education). The supervisory body of public universities is the Consejo Nacional de Rectores (National Council of Rectors). Private universities are under the control of the Consejo Nacional de Educación Superior de Universidades Privadas (National Council of Higher Education for Private Universities).

The administrative structure of a university consists of an Asamblea General (legislative body), Concejo Universitario (board of directors), Rectoría (president) and Vicerrectorías (vice-presidents). Faculties are the top academic divisions, and are subdivided into departments. There are also attached research centres and institutes.

The Bachiller or Bachillerato is the main undergraduate qualification, for which a student is required to accrue 120–144 credits over four to five years; an additional 30–36 credits lead to the award of the Licenciado. At postgraduate level, following Bachiller or Bachillerato, a Maestría is awarded after two years of study or 60–72 credits. Finally, the Doctorado requires three-and-a-half years of study or 100–120 credits (including those accrued for the Maestría). In 2004/05 there were 110,717 students enrolled in higher education.

Technical and vocational education is offered by public and private 'para-universities'. Courses last for two to three years and lead to the award of the Diplomado or Técnico Superior.

Regulatory and Representative Bodies

GOVERNMENT

Ministry of Culture, Youth and Sport: Avdas 3 y 7, Calles 11 y 15, frente al parque España, San José; tel. 2221-3806; fax 2221-1759; e-mail mcarballo@mcj.go.cr; internet www.mcjdcr.go.cr; Minister MARÍA ELENA CARBALLO.

Ministry of Public Education: Edif. Antigua Embajada, Apdo 10087, 1000 San José; tel. 2258-3745; fax 2258-3745; e-mail contraloriaservicios@mep.go.cr; internet www.mep.go.cr; Minister LEONARDO GARNIER.

ACCREDITATION

Sistema Nacional de Acreditación de la Educación Superior (SINAES) (National System of Accreditation in Higher Education): Apdo 1174-1200 Pavas, San José; tel. 2290-3325, ext. 3317; fax 2290-8653; e-mail sinaes@sinaes.ac.cr; internet www.sinaes.ac.cr; f. 1999; Pres. GUILLERMO VARGAS SALAZAR; Vice-Pres. Dra SONIA MARTA MORA ESCALANTE.

NATIONAL BODY

Consejo Nacional de Rectores (CONARE) (National Council of Rectors): Apdo 1174-1200, San José; tel. 2290-3325; fax 2296-5626; e-mail conare@conare.ac.cr; internet www.conare.ac.cr; f. 1974; responsible for co-ordinating decision-making regarding the state university education system; composed of the rectors of the Universidad de Costa Rica, Instituto Tecnológico de Costa Rica, Universidad Nacional and Universidad Estatal a Distancia; Pres. OLMAN SEGURA BONILLA.

Learned Societies

GENERAL

UNESCO Office San José: Apdo 220-2120, San Francisco de Guadalupe, San José; Paseo Colon, Avda 1 bis, Calle 28, Casa Esquinera 2810, San José; tel. 2258-7625; fax 2258-7458; e-mail san-jose@unesco.org; designated Cluster Office for Costa Rica, El Salvador, Guatemala, Honduras, Mexico, Nicaragua and Panama; Dir ALEJANDRO ALFONZO.

HISTORY, GEOGRAPHY AND ARCHAEOLOGY

Academia de Geografía e Historia de Costa Rica (Costa Rican Academy of Geography and History): Apdo 4499, 1000 San José; tel. 2234-7629; fax 2234-7629; f. 1940; 32 mems; Pres. Dra MARÍA EUGENIA BOZZOLI; Sec. EUGENIA IBARRA; publ. *Anales*.

LANGUAGE AND LITERATURE

Academia Costarricense de la Lengua (Costa Rican Academy of Language): Apdo 157, 1002 Paseo de los Estudiantes, San José; internet www.acl.ac.cr; f. 1923; corresp. of the Real Academia Española (Madrid); 18 mems; Dir ALBERTO F. CAÑAS ESCALANTE; Sec. FERNANDO DURÁN AYANEGUI; publ. *Boletín*.

Alliance Française: Avda 7, Calle 5, Apdo 10195, 1000 San José; tel. 2222-2283; fax 2233-5819; e-mail alcultfr@racsa.co.cr; internet www.alianzafr.ac.cr; offers courses and exams in French language and culture and promotes cultural exchange with France; Dir PATRICK LACOMBE.

MEDICINE

Colegio de Médicos y Cirujanos de Costa Rica: Sabana Sur, San José; tel. 2232-3433; fax 2232-2406; e-mail info@medicos.sa.cr; internet www.medicos.sa.cr; f. 1857 to promote the devt of the medical profession through medical research, interchange between mem. asscns and cooperation with nat. and int medical authorities; 45 mem. asscns; Pres. Dr ARTURO ROBLES ARIAS; Sec. Dr ABDÓN CASTRO BERMÚDEZ; publs *Acta Médica Costarricense* (4 a year), *Medicine, Vida y Salud*.

Member Associations:

Asociación Costarricense de Cardiología (Costa Rican Cardiology Association): Apdo 527, Pavas, San José; tel. 2253-8868; fax 2272-4214; f. 1978; 36 mems; library of 50 vols; Pres. Dr ANDRES BENAVIDES SANTOS.

Asociación Costarricense de Cirugía (Costa Rican Surgery Association): POB 548, 1000 San José; tel. 2231-0301; fax 2233-4165; f. 1954; 150 mems; Pres. Dr EDUARDO FLORES MONTERO; Sec. Dr LUIS MORALES ALFARO.

Asociación Costarricense de Medicina Interna (Association of Internal Medicine): Hospital San Juan de Díos, San José; tel. 2257-5252; fax 2235-1308; Pres. Dr RODOLFO LEAL VEGA.

Asociación Costarricense de Pediatría (Costa Rican Paediatrics Association): Apdo 1654, 1000 San José; tel. 2221-6821; fax 2221-6821; e-mail acope@hnn.sa.cr; f. 1951; organizes nat. conference annually in October; 370 mems; Pres. Dr EFRAÍN ARTAVIA LORÍA; Sec. Dra JULIA FERNÁNDEZ MONGE; publ. *Acta Pediátrica Costarricense*.

Asociación de Obstetricia y Ginecología de Costa Rica (Obstetrics and Gynaecology Association): Apdo 1011–1116, La Y Griega, San José; tel. 8911-4555; fax 2227-3300; e-mail rmontielarios@gmail.com; internet www.aogcr.com; f. 1956; 220 mems; Pres. Dr CAM LIM BADILLA.

Research Institutes

GENERAL

Consejo Nacional para Investigaciones Científicas y Tecnológicas (CONICIT): Apdo 10318, 1000 San José; tel. 2224-4172; fax 2225-2673; e-mail conicit@conicit.go.cr; internet www.conicit.go.cr; f. 1973; promotes devt of science and technology; makes available funds for research; works in cooperation with the Min. of Nat. Planning and Min. of Science and Technology; library of 3,500 vols; spec. colln: UNISIST program; Pres. Dr RONALD MELÉNDEZ; Exec. Sec. Lic. ALVARO BORBÓN; publ. *Memoria Anual CONICIT*.

AGRICULTURE, FISHERIES AND VETERINARY SCIENCE

Centro Agronómico Tropical de Investigación y Enseñanza (CATIE): 7170 Turrialba; tel. 2558-2000; fax 2558-2060; e-mail comunicacion@catie.ac.cr; internet www.catie.ac.cr; f. 1973 by the IICA and the Costa Rican Govt as a non-profit-making scientific and educational asscn for research and graduate education in devt, conservation and the sustainable use of natural resources in Belize, Colombia, Costa Rica, Dominican

Republic, El Salvador, Guatemala, Honduras, Mexico, Nicaragua, Panama and Venezuela; library of 92,000 vols, 5,000 current periodicals; Dir Dr PEDRO FERREIRA ROSSI; publs *Informe Anual*, *Revista Manejo Integrado de Plagas* (plant protection and public health, 4 a year), *Revista Agroforestería en las Américas*, *Revista Forestal Centroamericana*.

ECONOMICS, LAW AND POLITICS

Instituto Latinoamericano de las Naciones Unidas para la Prevención del Delito y Tratamiento del Delincuente (ILANUD) (UN Latin American Institute for Crime Prevention and Treatment of Offenders): Apdo 10071, 1000 San José; tel. 2257-5826; fax 2233-7175; e-mail ilanud@ilanud.or.cr; internet www.ilanud.or.cr; f. 1975 as a UN regional agency; training, advice and research in the fields of law and criminology, crime prevention and treatment of offenders; specialized library and data bank for int. use; arranges symposia, ministerial meetings; projects include standardization of criminal statistics, human rights in the admin. of justice, female and juvenile crime, 'white-collar' crime; Dir Dr ELÍAS CARRANZA; publ. *ILANUD* (2 a year).

Instituto Nacional de Estadística y Censos: Apdo 10163, 1000 San José; de la Rotonda de La Bandera, 450 metros oeste, Calle Los Negritos, Edificio Ana Lorena, Mercedes de Montes de Oca, San José; tel. 2280-9280; fax 2224-2221; e-mail informacion@inec.go.cr; internet www.inec.go.cr; f. 1883; 250 mems; library of 8,500 items; Dir Licda MARÍA ELENA GONZÁLEZ QUESADA; publs *Anuario Estadístico de Costa Rica* (1 a year), *Cifras Básicas sobre Fuerza de Trabajo* (1 a year), *Cifras Básicas sobre Pobreza e Ingresos* (1 a year), *Costa Rica: Cálculo de Población por Provincia, Cantón y Distrito* (2 a year), *Costo de la Canasta Básica de Alimentos* (12 a year), *Encuesta de Hogares de Propósitos Múltiples, Módulo de Empleo* (1 a year), *Estadísticas de Comercio Exterior* (2 a year), *Estadísticas de la Construcción* (2 a year), *Estadísticas Vitales: Población, Nacimientos, Defunciones, Matrimonios* (1 a year), *Indicadores Demográficos* (1 a year), *Índice de Precios al Consumidor* (12 a year), *Índices de Precios de los Insumos Básicos de la Industria de la Construcción* (12 a year), *Mortalidad Infantil y Evolución Reciente* (2 a year).

EDUCATION

Fundación Omar Dengo: Apdo 1032-2050, 1000 San José; tel. 2527-6000; fax 2527-6010; e-mail info@fod.ac.cr; internet www.fod.ac.cr; f. 1987 to promote the economic, social and human development of Costa Rica, implementing innovative programs to improve the quality of education; Pres. ALFONSO GUTIÉRREZ; publ. *Estado de la Nación* (irregular).

HISTORY, GEOGRAPHY AND ARCHAEOLOGY

Instituto Geográfico Nacional: Apdo 2272, 1000 San José; Avda 20, Calle 5/7, San José; tel. 2523-2630; fax 2221-0087; e-mail lbenavides@mopt.go.cr; internet www.mopt.go.cr/ign; f. 1944; library of 3,000 vols; Dir MAX LOBO HERNÁNDEZ.

MEDICINE

Centro Internacional de Investigación y Adiestramiento Médico de la Universidad del Estado de Louisiana (Louisiana State University International Centre for Medical Research and Training): Apdo 10155, 1000 San José; tel. 2280-5149; fax 2224-7236; e-mail icmrtlsu@sol.racsa.co.cr; f.

1962; research on viral diseases; library of 4,000 vols; Dir Dr RONALD B. LUFTIG.

Instituto Costarricense de Investigación y Enseñanza en Nutrición y Salud (Institute of Research and Teaching in Nutrition and Health): Apdo 4, Tres Ríos, Cartago; La Unión, Cartago; tel. 2279-9911; fax 2279-5546; e-mail msolis@inciensa.sa.cr; internet www.inciensa.sa.cr; f. 1977; attached to Min. of Health and affiliated to the University of Costa Rica; library of 4,500 vols; Dir LISSETTE NAVAS ALVARADO; publ. *Boletín INCIENSA* (3 a year).

NATURAL SCIENCES

Biological Sciences

Organization for Tropical Studies: Apdo 676, 2050 San Pedro; tel. 2524-0607; fax 2524-0608; e-mail cro@ots.ac.cr; internet www.ots.ac.cr; f. 1963; promotes education, research and the responsible use of natural resources in the tropics; operates 3 biological stations: Las Cruces, incorporating Wilson Botanical Garden (premontane forest), Palo Verde (dry forest) and La Selva (tropical wet forest); consortium of 58 univs and research instns in the USA, Latin America and Australia; library of 10,000 vols, 50 current periodicals; Dir Dr JORGE JIMÉNEZ; publ. *Liana* (in Spanish and English edns, each 2 a year).

Tropical Science Centre: Apdo 83870, 1000 San José; tel. 2253-3267; fax 2253-4963; e-mail cct@cct.or.cr; internet www.cct.or.cr; f. 1962; private non-profit asscn; research and training in tropical science; consultation on tropical ecology, land use capability and planning, environmental assessments; biological reserve and field station at Monteverde Cloud Forest; library of 7,000 vols; Exec. Dir JULIO CALVO ALVARADO; publ. *Occasional Paper Series* (irregular).

Physical Sciences

Instituto Meteorológico Nacional: Apdo 5583, 1000 San José; Frente a Antiguo Emergencias del Hospital Calderón Guardia, Barrio Aranjuez, San José; tel. 2222-5616; fax 2223-1837; e-mail imn@imn.ac.cr; internet www.imn.ac.cr; f. 1888; climatology, hydrometeorology, agrometeorology, synoptic and aeronautical meteorology; Dir PAULO MANSO SAYAO; publ. *Boletín Meteorológico* (12 a year).

TECHNOLOGY

Comisión de Energía Atómica de Costa Rica (National Atomic Energy Commission): Edif. Galerías del Este, 3°, Apdo 6681, 1000 San José; tel. 2224-1591; fax 2224-1293; e-mail coatom@racsa.co.cr; internet sibdi.bldt.ucr.ac.cr/cea; f. 1969; Pres. PATRICIA MORA RODRÍGUEZ; Dir LILLIANA SOLÍS DÍAZ.

Libraries and Archives

San José

Archivo Nacional de Costa Rica: Apdo 41-2020, Zapote, San José; 900 metros sur y 150 oeste de Plaza del Sol Curridabat, San José; tel. 2283-1400; fax 2234-7312; e-mail ancost@ice.co.cr; internet www.archivonacional.go.cr; f. 1881; 5,000 vols, 8.5 shelf-km of documents; Dir-Gen. Lic. VIRGINIA CHACÓN ARIAS; publs *Archívese* (bulletin, 4 a year), *Cuadernillos del Archivo Nacional* (irregular), *Revista del Archivo Nacional* (1 a year).

Biblioteca Instituto Diplomático: Apdo 10027, 1000 San José; tel. 2223-7555; fax 2257-8401; e-mail biblioteca@rree.go.cr; internet www.rree.go.cr; f. 1991; attached to Min. of Foreign Affairs; int. affairs, diplo-

macy, foreign policy, law; 20,000 vols historical memories, official diary, texts; Librarian LUIS GONZÁLEZ CALVO; publ. *Revista Costarricense de Política Exterior*.

Biblioteca 'Mark Twain'–Centro Cultural Costarricense-Norteamericano: Apdo 1489, 1000 San José; tel. 2207-7574; fax 2224-1480; e-mail bibmarktwain@cccncr.com; internet www.cccncr.com; f. 1945; 18,000 vols and documents; Librarian ANDREA SOLIS; publ. *CCCNoticias* (6 a year).

Biblioteca Nacional Miguel Obregón Lizano: Apdo 10008, 1000 San José; Calles 15 y 17, Av. 3 y 3B, San José; tel. 2221-2436; fax 2223-5510; e-mail dibinacr@racsa.co.cr; internet www.mcjdcr.go.cr/sistema_bibliotecas/biblioteca_nac.html; f. 1888; 270,000 vols; Dir GUADALUPE RODRIGUEZ MÉNDEN; publ. *Bibliografía Nacional*.

Centro de Información 'Alvaro Castro Jenkins': Avda Central y Primera, Calles 2 y 4, San José; tel. 2243-4460; fax 2243-4583; e-mail centroinf@bccr.fi.cr; internet www.bccr.fi.cr/ci; f. 1950; attached to the Central Bank; specializes in economics; 43,028 vols; Librarian DEYANIRA VARGAS DE BONILLA.

Departamento de Servicios Bibliotecarios, Documentación e Información de la Asamblea Legislativa: Apdo 75-1013, San José; tel. 2243-2394; fax 2243-2400; e-mail jvolio@congreso.aleg.go.cr; internet www.asamblea.go.cr/biblio; f. 1953; social sciences; 40,000 vols, 800 periodicals; Dir Lic. JULIETA VOLIO GUEVARA; publs *C. R. Leyes, decretos* (index of Costa Rican legislation, 12 a year), *Revista Parlamentaria* (4 a year).

Sistema de Bibliotecas, Documentación e Información: Ciudad Universitaria Rodrigo Facio, 2060 San Pedro de Montes de Oca, San José; tel. 2253-6152; fax 2234-2809; e-mail mbriceno@sibdi.ucr.ac.cr; internet sibdi.bldt.ucr.ac.cr; f. 1946; attached to Univ. de Costa Rica; 443,853 vols, 13,425 periodicals, 48,059 theses, 23,212 audiovisual items, 5,615 maps and atlases; Dir Licda MA. EUGENIA BRICEÑO MEZA.

Museums and Art Galleries

Alajuela

Museo Histórico Cultural Juan Santamaría: Apdo 785, 4050 Alajuela; tel. 2441-4775; fax 2441-6926; e-mail mhcjscr@ice.co.cr; internet www.museojuansantamaria.go.cr; f. 1974; attached to Min. of Culture, Youth and Sport; 19th-century colln; library of 2,000 vols; Dir Prof. RAÚL AGUILAR PIEDRA; publ. *11 de Abril: Cuadernos de Cultura*.

San José

Museo de Arte Costarricense: Apdo 378, Fecosa 1009, San José; Parque Metropolitano de La Sabana, San José; tel. 2222-7155; fax 2222-7247; e-mail info@musarco.go.cr; internet www.musarco.go.cr; attached to Ministry of Culture, Youth and Sport; f. 1977; collects and exhibits representative works of Costa Rican art; promotes artistic work through workshops and grants; supervision and preservation of state art collections; library of 5,000 vols; Dir ELIZABETH BARQUERO.

Museo Indígeno (Native Museum): Seminario Central, San José; f. 1890; library of 40,000 vols; Dir Rev. WALTER E. JOVEL CASTRO.

Museo Nacional de Costa Rica: Apdo 749, 1000 San José; Calle 17, Avda Central y 2, San José; tel. 2257-1433; fax 2233-7427; e-mail informacion@museocostarica.go.cr;

internet www.museocostarica.go.cr; f. 1887; gen. museum: pre-Columbian art, colonial and republican history, nat. herbarium, natural history, culture; library of 70,000 vols; Dir MELANIA ORTIZ VOLIO; publs *Brenesia* (natural sciences), *Trees and Seeds from the Neotropics*, *Vínculos* (anthropology, 2 a year).

Affiliated Museums:

Museo de Insectos: Faculty of Agricultural Sciences, Univ. de Costa Rica, San Pedro, San José; internet www.miucr.ucr.ac.cr; f. 1962; 1m. specimens of butterflies and other insects.

Museo de Zoología: Dpto de Biología, Univ. de Costa Rica, San José; mammals, herpetology, fish; small library.

Universities

ESCUELA DE AGRICULTURA DE LA REGION TROPICAL HÚMEDA (UNIVERSIDAD EARTH)

Apdo Postal 4442 SJ, San José

Telephone: 2713-0000
Fax: 2713-0001
E-mail: admision@earth.ac.cr
Internet: www.earth.ac.cr

Founded 1986
Private control
Academic year: January to December
Pres. and Rector: Dr JOSÉ A. ZAGLUL SLON
Provost: Dr JAMES B. FRENCH
Rector: Dr JOSÉ A. ZAGLUL SLON
Vice-Pres. for Admin. and Finance: Ing. ALEX MATA
Librarian: JOSÉ RUPERTO ARCE

Library of 35,000 vols
Number of teachers: 40
Number of students: 400

Courses in agricultural engineering.

UNIVERSIDAD AUTÓNOMA DE CENTRO AMERICA

Apdo 7637-1000, San José
Campus Los Cipreses, 1 km al Norte del Servicentro La Galera, Curridabat, San José

Telephone: 2272-9100
Fax: 2271-2046
E-mail: info@uaca.ac.cr
Internet: www.uaca.ac.cr

Founded 1976
Private control
Language of instruction: Spanish
Academic year: January to December (3 terms)

Rector: Lic. GUILLERMO MALAVASSI VARGAS
Chancellor: GONZALO GALLEGOS J.
Vice-Chancellor: LISETTE MARTÍNEZ L.
Registrar: PABLO ARCE
Librarian: JULISSA MÉNDEZ M.

Number of teachers: 250
Number of students: 5,000

Publications: *Acta Académica* (2 a year), *Ordenanzas y Anuario Universitario.*

CONSTITUENT COLLEGES

Colegio Andrés Bello: Apdo 2393-2050, San Pedro, San José; tel. 2272-9102; fax 2271-3839; e-mail abello@uaca.ac.cr; Dean Lic. HERBERTH SASSO.

Colegio de Ciencias Clorito Picado: 2393-2050, San Pedro, San José; tel. 2272-9100; fax 2271-3839; e-mail ccp@uaca.ac.cr.

Colegio Iñigo de Loyola: Apdo 12345-1000, San José; tel. 2225-5413; fax 2225-5413; Dean ELIO BURGOS.

Colegio Leonardo da Vinci: Apdo 44-1009, San José; tel. 2290-2552; fax 2290-2728;

e-mail davinci@racsa.co.cr; Dean TERESITA BONILLA.

Collegium Academicum: Apdo 2393-2050, San Pedro, San José; tel. 2272-9102; fax 2271-3839; e-mail academicum@uaca.ac.cr; Dean GASTÓN CERTAD.

Stvdivm Generale Costarricense: Apdo 7651-1000, San José; tel. 2271-2100; fax 2271-2015; e-mail stvdivm@uaca.ac.cr; Dean Lic. MARIO GRANADOS.

UNIVERSIDAD DE COSTA RICA

Ciudad Universitaria 'Rodrigo Facio', San Pedro de Montes de Oca, San José

Telephone: 2207-4000
Fax: 2224-8214
E-mail: consultas.odi@ucr.ac.cr
Internet: www.ucr.ac.cr

Founded 1843, refounded 1940
Autonomous control
Language of instruction: Spanish
Academic year: March to November

Rector: Dra YAMILETH GONZÁLEZ GARCÍA
Vice-Rector for Admin.: Dr HERMANN HESS
Vice-Rector for Research: Dr HENNING JENSEN PENNINGTON
Vice-Rector for Student Life: MSc ALEJANDRINA MATA
Vice-Rector for Teaching: Dra LIBIA HERRERO URIBE
Registrar: Sr JORGE RECOBA VARGAS (acting)
Librarian: Lic. AURORA ZAMORA GONZÁLEZ (acting)

Library: see Libraries and Archives
Number of teachers: 3,800
Number of students: 28,986

DEANS

Faculty of Agronomy: Dr MANUEL ZELEDÓN
Faculty of Dentistry: Dr FERNANDO SAÉNZ FORERO
Faculty of Economics: Dr JUSTO AGUILAR FONG
Faculty of Education: ALEJANDRINA MATA SEGREDA
Faculty of Engineering: Ing. FERNANDO SILESKY GUEVARA
Faculty of Fine Arts: Dr LUIS DIEGO HERRA RODRÍGUEZ
Faculty of Law: Dr RAFAEL GONZÁLEZ BALLAR
Faculty of Letters: M. L. ENRIQUE MARGERY PEÑA
Faculty of Medicine: Dr GUIDO ULATE
Faculty of Microbiology: Dr MARIO CHAVES VILLALOBOS
Faculty of Pharmacy: Dra LIDIETTE FONSECA GONZÁLEZ
Faculty of Science: Dr OLDEMAR RODRÍGUEZ ROJAS
Faculty of Social Sciences: Dr ROBERTO SALOM ECHEVERRIA (acting)
Graduate Studies: Dra MAIA PÉREZ YGLESIAS

There are 21 research institutes attached to the various faculties.

REGIONAL CENTRES

Centro Regional del Atlántico: internet www.sa.ucr.ac.cr; Dir Ing. CARLOS CALVO PINEDA.

Centro Regional de Guanacaste: Dir Ing. RAFAEL MONTERO ROJAS.

Centro Regional de Limón: Dir Dr ENRIQUE ZAPATA DUARTE.

Centro Regional del Occidente: internet www.so.ucr.ac.cr; Dir Dr ELIAM CAMPOS BARRANTES.

Centro Regional del Pacífico: internet www.srp.ucr.ac.cr; Dir SUSAN CHEN MOK.

UNIVERSIDAD EMPRESARIAL DE COSTA RICA

Apdo 12640-1000, San José

Telephone: 2253-5952
Fax: 2225-5141
E-mail: info@unem.edu
Internet: www.unem.edu

Founded 1992 as International Postgraduate School affiliated with Universidad de San Jose; became independent and adopted present name 1997
Private control
Languages of instruction: Spanish, English
Academic year: January to December

Rector: Dr RAFAEL ANGEL PÉREZ CORDOVA
Registrar: ELAINE PÉREZ
Librarian: RODOLFO MARTÍNEZ

Number of teachers: 62
Number of students: 895

Publication: *Gazetta Empresarial*

Faculties of administrative sciences, biological sciences, education and humanities, psychology and behavioural sciences, social sciences, postgraduate studies; school of languages.

UNIVERSIDAD ESTATAL A DISTANCIA (Open University)

Apdo 474, 2050 San Pedro de Montes de Oca, San José

Telephone: 2527-2000
Fax: 2253-4990
Internet: www.uned.ac.cr

Founded 1977
State control
Language of instruction: Spanish
Academic year: March to November

Rector: RODRIGO ARIAS CAMACHO
Academic Vice-Rector: JOSÉ LUIS TORRES
Exec. Vice-Rector: LUIS GUILLERMO CARPIO MALAVASSI
Vice-Rector for Planning: SILVIA ABDELNOUR ESQUIVEL
Dir of Information Technology, and Communications: MSc VIGNY ALVARADO CASTILLO
Librarian: RITA LEDEZMA

Number of teachers: 235
Number of students: 12,000

DIRECTORS

School of Business Administration: RODOLFO TACSAN CHEN
School of Education: (vacant)
School of Exact and Natural Sciences: Ing. OLMAN DÍAZ SÁNCHEZ
School of Social Sciences and Humanities: GERARDO ESQUIVEL MONGE

There are 28 regional centres where students can register, receive instruction, sit examinations and use library facilities

UNIVERSIDAD FIDELITAS

Apdo 8063-1000, San José

Telephone: 2253-0262
Fax: 2253-2186
E-mail: informacion@ufidelitas.ac.cr
Internet: www.ufidelitas.ac.cr

Founded 1980 as Collegium Fidélitas; present name 1994
Private control

Rector: JESÚS MERINO SERNA
Gen. Man.: MIGUEL MARÍN VALENCIANO

Courses in advertising design, business administration, civil engineering, computer systems engineering, electrical engineering, electromechanical engineering, industrial engineering, law, pre-school education, psychology, public finance, teaching of English.

UNIVERSIDAD INTERNACIONAL DE LAS AMERICAS

Apdo 1447–1002, San José

Barrio Aranjuez, Calle 23 (Avenidas 7 y 7bis), El Carmen, San José

Telephone: 2258-0220

Fax: 2222-3216

E-mail: correo@uia.ac.cr

Internet: www.uia.ac.cr

Founded 1986

Private control

Library of 25,000 vols

Schools of administration, advertising, computer engineering, dentistry, education, electromechanical engineering, industrial engineering, international business, international relations, journalism, languages, law, medicine, pharmacy, public finance, tourism.

UNIVERSIDAD LATINA DE COSTA RICA

Apdo 1561-2050, San Pedro, San José

Telephone: 2283-2611

Fax: 2225-2801

Internet: www.ulatina.ac.cr

Founded 1981

Private control

Rector: ARTURO JOFRÉ VARTANIÁN

Vice-Rector for Academic Affairs: LUIS ALBERTO CHAVES MONGE

Campuses in Cañas, Grecia, Guápiles, Limón, Palmares, Paso Canoas, Puntarenas, San Isidro del General, Santa Cruz and Turrialba

Courses in economics and business administration, education, tourism and environmental science, engineering and architecture, health sciences, social sciences.

UNIVERSIDAD LATINOAMERICANA DE CIENCIA Y TECNOLOGIA (ULACIT)

Apdo 10235, 1000 San José

Telephone: 2523-4000

Fax: 2523-4028

E-mail: info@ulacit.ac.cr

Internet: www.ulacit.ac.cr

Founded 1987

Private control

Academic year: January to December

Campuses in San José and in Panama City (Panama)

Pres.: SYLVIA CASTRO

Vice-Pres. for Academic Affairs: JOHN BROWN

Vice-Pres. for Admin.: JUSTO PARDO

Vice-Pres. for Student Affairs: ALEJANDRA QUIRÓS

Registrar: FLORY SOLANO

Librarian: LIGIA GONZALEZ

Library of 25,000 vols

Number of teachers: 275

Number of students: 4,500

DEANS

School of Business Administration: JUAN RICARDO WONG

School of Computer Sciences: WILBERTH MOLINA

School of Dentistry: Dr RAFAEL PORRAS

School of Education: Lic. NIDIA GUTIÉRREZ

School of Industrial Engineering: ORLANDO TORRES

School of Law: Lic. MARIANELA NÚÑEZ PIEDRA

School of Psychology: Lic. MARJORIE BARQUERO

Graduate School: ROSMERY HERNÁNDEZ

UNIVERSIDAD NACIONAL

Apdo 86-3000, Heredia

Telephone: 2261-0101

Fax: 2237-7593

E-mail: jmora@una.ac.cr

Internet: www.una.ac.cr

Founded 1973

State control

Language of instruction: Spanish

Academic year: February to November

Rector: Dra SONIA MARTA MORA ESCALANTE

Vice-Rector for Academic Affairs: Dr CARLOS LÉPIZ JIMÉNEZ

Vice-Rector for Devt: MARCO TULIO FALLAS DÍAZ

Vice-Rector for Student Affairs: HERIBERTO VALVERDE CASTRO

Library Dir: Lic. MARGARITA GARCÍA

Number of teachers: 1,200

Number of students: 12,000

Publications: *ABRA* (2 a year), *Relaciones Internacionales* (4 a year), *Repertorio Americano* (2 a year), *Revista Ciencias Ambientales*, *Revista de Historia* (2 a year), *Uniciencia* (2 a year), *Vida Silvestre Neotropical* (2 a year)

DEANS

Faculty of Earth and Sea Sciences: Dr MARÍA DE LOS ANGELES ALVAREZ FERNÁNDEZ

Faculty of Exact and Natural Sciences: Dr LUIS MANUEL SIERRA SIERRA

Faculty of Health Sciences: Dr PEDRO UREÑA BONILLA

Faculty of Philosophy and Letters: JORGE ALFARO PERÉZ

Faculty of Social Sciences: JOSÉ CARLOS CHINCHILLA COTO

Centre of General Studies: Dr CARLOS ARAYA GUILLÉN

Centre for Research and Teaching in Education: IRMA ZÚÑIGA LEÓN

Centre for Research, Teaching and Extension in Fine Arts: ELSA FLORES MONTERO

Brunca Regional Centre: Lic. JUAN RAFAEL MORA CAMACHO

UNIVERSIDAD DE SAN JOSE

Apdo 7446, 1000 San José

Telephone: 2218-0747

E-mail: info@usanjose.ac.cr

Internet: www.usanjose.ac.cr

Founded 1976 as Colegio Académicum; present name and status 1992

Private control

Language of instruction: Spanish

Academic year: January to December (3 terms)

Rector: MANUEL SANDI MURILLO

Registrar: Lic. RÓGER SEGNINI ESQUIVEL

Librarian: JOSÉ SEGNINI

Number of teachers: 175

Number of students: 1,800

Publication: *Revista Universitaria*

Schools of business administration, computer science, education and psychology, humanities, international trade, law, social science; international postgraduate school.

UNIVERSIDAD VERITAS

Apdo 1380–1000, San José

Telephone: 2283-4747

Fax: 2225-2907

E-mail: info@uveritas.ac.cr

Internet: www.uveritas.ac.cr

Private control

Academic year: January to December (3 semesters)

Rector: Ing. JOSÉ JOAQUIN SECO

Number of teachers: 95

Number of students: 1,100

Faculties of art, architecture and design.

Colleges

INCAE Business School: Apdo 960, 4050 Alajuela; tel. 2437-2200; fax 2433-9101; e-mail library@incae. edu; internet www .incae.edu/es/biblioteca/sistema-bibliotecas/ costa-rica/crbiblio.php; f. 1964 in Nicaragua with technical assistance from Harvard Univ.; Costa Rica campus opened 1983; (See also under Nicaragua); 2-year MBA programmes in English and Spanish; exec. education programmes; management research and consulting; library: 32,600 vols in fields of business admin., economic devt, natural resources, tourism and Latin American economic and social conditions; Rector Dr ARTURO CONDO; Librarian Lic. THOMAS BLOCH.

Instituto Centroamericano de Administración Pública (ICAP): Apdo 10025-1000, 100 sur, 75 oste de la Heldería Pop's, Curridabat, San José; tel. 2234-1011; fax 2225-2049; e-mail info@icap.ac.cr; internet www.icap.ac.cr; f. 1954 as Escuela Superior de Administración Pública (ESAPAC) by a jt project of the govts of Costa Rica, El Salvador, Guatemala, Honduras and Nicaragua (Panama incorporated 1961); Masters degree programmes in public management; training courses for managers and technical personnel; advisory services; Centre for Information Technology; Dir Dr HUGO ZELAYA CÁLIX; publ. *Revista Centroamerica de Administración Pública* (2 a year).

Instituto Tecnológico de Costa Rica: Apdo 159-7050 Cartago; tel. 2552-5333; fax 2551-5348; e-mail archivo@itcr.ac.cr; internet www.itcr.ac.cr; f. 1971; State control; language of instruction: Spanish; academic year February to December; Rector EUGENIO TREJOS; Vice-Rector for Academic Affairs Dr LUIS GERARDO MEZA CASCANTE; Vice-Rector for Academic Services and Students JEANNETTE BARRANTES M.; Vice-Rector for Admin. JOSÉ RAFAEL HIDALGO; Vice-Rector for Research and Extension Dr JUAN FERNANDO ALVAREZ CASTRO; Registrar WILLIAM VIVES BRENES; Librarian CRISTINA GÓMEZ MOLINA; depts of agricultural engineering, agricultural management engineering, agronomy, architecture and town planning, biology, business administration, chemistry, computer science, communication, construction engineering, culture and sport, electromechanical engineering, electronic engineering, forestry engineering, industrial design, industrial production engineering, materials science and engineering, mathematics, physics; safety and hygiene at work, social sciences; library: 54,000 vols; 455 teachers; 6,000 students; publs *Comunicación* (2 a year), *Espacio Virtual de la Física*, *Kurú: Revista Forestal*, *Revista Virtual Matemática Educación e Internet*, *Tecnología en Marcha* (3 a year).

CÔTE D'IVOIRE

The Higher Education System

Côte d'Ivoire was a province in French West Africa before gaining its independence in 1960. The Université de Cocody in Abidjan is the oldest university, founded in 1958 as Centre d'Enseignement Supérieur d'Abidjan; in 1964 it became the Université Nationale de Côte d'Ivoire, and it acquired its current name in 1995. There are also two other universities, at Abodo-Adjamé (also in Abidjan) and at Bouaké. Some 96,681 students were enrolled in tertiary education in 1998/99. Education in the north of the country was badly disrupted following the failed coup in 2002. The Ministry of Higher Education and Scientific Research oversees the universities. There are also two administrative bodies, the Council of Higher Education Teaching and the Standing Board of Higher Education Teaching. The universities are run by Councils.

The Baccalauréat is the secondary school qualification required for admission to university. After the first two years of undergraduate studies, a diploma is awarded based on the academic path being followed: arts and humanities (Diplôme Universitaire d'études Littéraires—DUEL), sciences (Diplôme Universitaire d'études Scientifiques—DUES), law (Diplôme Universitaire d'études Juridiques—DUEJ), economics (Diplôme Universitaire d'études Economiques Générales—DUEEG) or general studies (Diplôme d'études Universitaires Générales—DEUG). After the Diplôme, a further year of study leads to the Licence. However, five years of study are required for the Diplôme d'Ingénieur. At postgraduate level, the Maîtrise is awarded following one year of study after the Licence. A further year of study leads to the Diplôme d'études Approfondies (DEA). A final year of postgraduate study results in the award of either the Diplôme d'études Supérieures or the Doctorat de Spécialité de Troisième Cycle. Vocational and technical education is provided by several schools and institutes.

Regulatory Bodies

GOVERNMENT

Ministry of Culture and Francophone Affairs: 22e étage, Tour E, Tours Administratives, BP V39, Abidjan; tel. 20-21-40-34; fax 20-21-33-59; e-mail culture.ci@ci.refer.org; Minister KOMOÉ AUGUSTIN KOUADIO.

Ministry of Higher Education and Scientific Research: 20e étage, Tour C, Tours Administratives, BP V151, Abidjan; tel. 20-21-57-73; fax 20-21-22-25; Minister IBRAHIMA CISSÉ.

Learned Societies

LANGUAGE AND LITERATURE

Alliance Française: AFI N'Gokro, BP 1899, Yamoussoukro; tel. and fax 30-64-25-30; e-mail afi_yakro@yahoo.fr; offers courses and exams in French language and culture and promotes cultural exchange with France; attached teaching offices in Abengourou, Korhogo and San Pedro.

Goethe-Institut: Cocody, Rue C27, par Ave C16 Jean Mermoz prolongée, BP 982, Abidjan; tel. 22-44-14-22; fax 22-44-96-89; e-mail verw@abidjan.goethe.org; internet www.goethe.de/af/abi/deindex.htm; offers courses and exams in German language and culture and promotes cultural exchange with Germany; library of 7,750 vols; Dir FRIEDRICH ENGELHARDT.

Research Institutes

GENERAL

Institut de Recherche pour le Développement (IRD): Rue du Chevalier de Clieu, Zone 4, 15 BP 917, Abidjan 15; tel. 21-24-37-79; fax 21-24-65-04; e-mail rep@ird.ci; internet www.ird.ci; f. 1946; health education, economic development, environmental management; (see main entry under France); Rep. ALAIN MORLIÈRE.

AGRICULTURE, FISHERIES AND VETERINARY SCIENCE

Centre de Co-opération Internationale en Recherche Agronomique pour le Développement (CIRAD): see entry in Burkina Faso:

Centre National de Recherche Agronomique (CNRA) (National Centre for Agricultural Research): Adiopodoumé, KM17 Route de Dabou, 01 POB 1740, Abidjan 01; tel. 23-47-24-24; fax 23-47-24-11; e-mail info@cnra.ci; internet www.cnra.ci; f. 1998; 140 mems; Dir-Gen. Dr KOFFI SIE; publ. *CNRA-Info* (4 a year).

ECONOMICS, LAW AND POLITICS

Centre Ivoirien de Recherches et d'Etudes Juridiques: Blvd Latrille, opp. Eglise St Jean, Cocody 01, BP 3811, Abidjan; tel. 22-44-60-54; f. 1973; strategic research into problems affecting the judiciary in Côte d'Ivoire; Dir KOMENAN ZAPKA.

Centre de Recherche et d'Action pour la Paix (CERAP): 08 BP 2088, Abidjan 08; tel. 22-40-47-20; fax 22-44-84-38; e-mail iddh@cerap-inades.org; internet www.cerap-inades.org; f. 1962 by the Soc. of Jesus to promote the devt of newly ind. countries; research and training in human rights, peace, politics, economics; 60 mems; library of 50,000 vols, 230 periodicals; Gen. Dir DENIS MAUGENEST; publs *Débats: Courrier d'Afrique de l'Ouest* (12 a year), *La Lettre de l'IDDH, Bulletin sur les Droits de l'homme en Afrique de l'Ouest* (4 a year).

MEDICINE

Institut Pasteur de Côte d'Ivoire: 01 BP 490, Abidjan 01; tel. 23-45-33-92; fax 23-45-76-23; f. 1972; research laboratories for the study of viral diseases, including yellow fever, poliomyelitis, rabies, influenza, hepatitis, HIV/AIDS; clinical analysis laboratories used by the Centre Hospitalier Universitaire, Cocody; small library in process of formation; Dir MIREILLE DOSSO.

Institut Pierre Richet: BP1500, Bouaké; tel. 30-63-37-46; fax 30-63-27-38; e-mail ipr@ird.ci; f. 1973; research into tropical endemic diseases, incl. malaria, sleeping sickness, dengue fever and yellow fever; part of l'Organisation de Co-opération et de Co-ordination de la Lutte contre les Grandes Endémies en Afrique de l'Ouest (OCCGE); training on 2 levels: technician in medical entomology, and medical entomologist; missions and field studies carried out as required by member countries of OCCGE; library containing spec. colln and field data; Dir P. CARNEVALE.

NATURAL SCIENCES

General

Centre de Recherches Océanographiques: 29 rue des Pêcheurs, BP V18, Abidjan; tel. 21-35-50-14; fax 21-35-11-55; e-mail abe@cro.ird.ci; internet www.refer.ci/ivoir_ct/rec/cdr/cro/accueil.htm; f. 1958; biological oceanography, hydrobiology, physics and chemistry; 40 staff; library of 30,000 vols; Dir Dr JACQUES ABE; publs *Archives Scientifiques, Journal Ivoirien d'Océanologie et de Limnologie.*

Physical Sciences

Station Géophysique de Lamto: BP 31, N'Douci; tel. 31-62-90-95; fax 31-62-92-20; e-mail lamtogeo@aviso.ci; f. 1962; atmospherical and climatological, seismological, infrared studies; Dir Prof. MAMADOU FOFANA; publ. *Bulletin of Teleseisms* (52 a year).

RELIGION, SOCIOLOGY AND ANTHROPOLOGY

Centre des Sciences Humaines: BP 1600, Abidjan; f. 1960; ethnological and sociological research, especially in the cultural and religious field; museology, conservation, exhibitions; Dir Dr B. HOLAS; see also Musée des Civilisations.

TECHNOLOGY

Bureau de Recherches Géologiques et Minières (BRGM): 01 BP 1335, Abidjan 01; gold-mining stations at Ity, Bondoukou, Fetekio, Yaouré, Toulepleu.

Société pour le Développement Minier de la Côte d'Ivoire (SODEMI): 01 BP 2816, 31 blvd Latrille Abidjan 01; tel. 22-44-29-95; fax 22-44-08-21; e-mail sodemi@aviso.ci; f. 1962; carries out a programme of geological and geophysical minerals prospecting; mineral mining; library of 5,435 vols, 28 current periodicals, 2,556 geological or prospecting reports, 3,500 topographic and geological maps; Dir-Gen. J. N'ZI.

Libraries and Archives

Abidjan

Archives de Côte d'Ivoire: BP V126, Abidjan; tel. 20-32-41-58; f. 1913; Dir (vacant).

Bibliothèque Centrale de la Côte d'Ivoire: BP 6243, Abidjan-Treichville; f. 1963; a service of the Ministry of National Education; public lecture service; 14,000 vols; founded with help of UNESCO; Librarian P. ZELLI ANY-GRAH.

Bibliothèque Centrale de l'Université de Cocody: BP V34, Abidjan 01; tel. 22-44-08-47; f. 1963; 95,000 vols, 1,650 periodicals; Librarian FRANÇOISE N'GORAN.

Bibliothèque du Centre Culturel Français: 01 BP 3995, 01 Abidjan; tel. 20-22-56-28; fax 20-22-71-32; 32,014 vols (adult library), 6,352 vols (children's library), and 5,000 vols in African Documentation section; 197 periodicals and reviews; Dir MICHEL JANNIN; Librarian GÉRARD AUDOUIN.

Bibliothèque Nationale: BP V180, Abidjan; tel. 20-21-38-72; f. 1968; scientific library of 75,000 vols and 135 current periodicals; part of the former centre of the Institut Français d'Afrique Noire; Dir COFFIE TIBURCE; publ. *Bibliographie de la Côte d'Ivoire* (1 a year).

Museum

Abidjan

Musée des Civilisations: BP 1600, Abidjan 01; fmrly Musée de la Côte d'Ivoire; exhibits of ethnographical, sociological, artistic and scientific nature; attached to the Centre des Sciences Humaines; Dir MEMEL SILVIE KASSI.

Universities

UNIVERSITÉ D'ABOBO-ADJAMÉ

BP 801, Abidjan 02
Telephone: 22-37-81-22
Fax: 22-37-81-18
E-mail: abobo-adj@abobo.edu.ci
Internet: www.abobo.edu.ci

Founded 1957 as Centre d'Enseignement Supérieur; became part of Université Nationale de Côte-d'Ivoire 1964; independent status and present name 1992
State control

Pres.: ETIENNE EHOUAN EHILÉ
Library of 14,000
Number of teachers: 50
Number of students: 5,000

Units of bsic sciences, food technology and higher education; school of health sciences; centres for advanced training and ecology.

UNIVERSITÉ DE BOUAKÉ

BP V 18, Bouaké 01
Telephone: 30-63-48-57
Fax: 30-63-59-84
Internet: www.refer.ci/ivoir_ct/edu/sup/uni/bke/accueil.htm

Founded 1960; became part of Université Nationale de Côte-d'Ivoire 1964; independent status 1994
State control

Pres.: FRANÇOIS KOUAKOU N'GUESSAN
Sec.-Gen.: GERMAIN ADJA-DIBY

Units of communication, environment and society, economics and development, higher education, law, administration and development and medical sciences; centres for development research and lifelong education.

UNIVERSITÉ DE COCODY

BP V34, Abidjan 01
Telephone: 22-44-90-00
Fax: 22-44-14-07
E-mail: acceuil@ucocody.ci
Internet: www.ucocody.ci

Founded 1958 as the Centre d'Enseignement Supérieur d'Abidjan; became part of Université Nationale de Côte d'Ivoire 1964; present name 1995
State control
Language of instruction: French
Academic year: September to July

Pres.: CÉLESTIN TÉA GOKOU
Gen. Sec.: JÉRÔME TOTO BALOUBI
Librarian: FRANÇOISE N'GORAN
Number of teachers: 1,081
Number of students: 37,500
Publications: *En-Quête* (Humanities), *Repères* (Humanities), *Revues Médicales* (4 a year), *Revues Sociales* (2 a year)

DEANS

Faculty of Biosciences: VALENTIN N'DOUBA
Faculty of Construction Engineering and Technology: MARIE-CHANTAL KOUASSI-GOFFRI
Faculty of Criminology: ZÉPHIRIN BOLIGA
Faculty of Earth Sciences and Mining Resources: JEAN BIENI
Faculty of Economics Sciences: GILBERT-MARIE AKE NGBO
Faculty of Human and Social Sciences: IGNACE ZASSELI BIAKA
Faculty of Information, Art and Communication: AUGUSTE AGHI BAHI
Faculty of Language, Literature and Civilization: FRANÇOIS ASSI ADOPO
Faculty of Law: DJEDRO MELEDJE
Faculty of Mathematics and Computer Science: KONIN KOUA
Faculty of Medicine: ISIDORE MOHÉNOU DIOMANDE
Faculty of Odontostomatology: SIAKA TOURÉ
Faculty of Pharma: ANGLADE KLA MALAN

PROFESSORS

Faculty of Biosciences:

ACHY SEKA, A., Atmospheric Physics
AIDARA, D.
ASSA, A.
BOKRA, Y.
DEGNY, E.
DJAKOURE, A. L.
EBBY, N.
EHILE, E. E.
HONENOU, P.
KAMENAN, A.
KOPOH, K.
KOUAKOU, G.
KOUASSI, N., Zoology
KRA, G.
LOROUGNON, G.
N'DIAYE, A. S., Cell Biology
NEZIT, P., Mathematics
N'GUESSAN, Y. T., Organic Chemistry
OFFOUMOU, A. M.
SERI, B.
TOURE, S., Mathematics
TOURE, V., Organic Chemistry

Faculty of Economic Sciences:

ATSAIN, A.
ALLECHI, M.
KOULIBALY, M.

Faculty of Language, Literature and Civilization:

ANO, N., Oral Literature
BOKA, M., The African Novel in French
DIBI, K., Metaphysical Philosophy
HAUHOUOT, A., Geography
KODJO, N., History
KOMENAN, A. L., Philosophy
KONATE, Y., Philosophy
KONE BONI, T., Philosophy
LEZOU, D. G., The Francophone African Novel South of the Sahara, Semiotics
M'BRA, E., History
N'DA, P., The Francophone Novel
NIAMKET, K., Philosophy
NIANGORAN, B., Ethnology
SEMI-BI, Z., History
TANO, J., Differential Psychology

Faculty of Law:

BLEOU, D. M., Public Law
DEGNI-SEGUI, R., Public Law
ISSA, S., Private Law
SARASSORO, H., Private Law
WODIE, V. F., Public Law
YAO-N'DRE, P., Public Law

Faculty of Medicine:

ANDOH, J.
ATTIA, Y. R.
BAMBA, M.
BEDA, Y. B.
BOUHOUSSOU, K. M.
COULIBALY, O. A.
DAGO, A. B. A.
DJEDJE, M.
DOSSO, B. M.
EHOUMAN, A.
GADEGBEKU, A. S.
KADIO, A.
KANGA, J. M.
KANGA, M.
KEITA, A. K.
KONE, N.
KOUAKOU, N. M.
KOUAME, K. J.
LAMBIN, Y.
MOBIOT, M. L.
N'DORI, R.
N'DRI, K. D.
N'GUESSAN, K. G.
NIAMKET, E. K.
ODEHOURI, K. P.
ODI, A. M.
ROUX, C.
SANGARE, A.
SANGARE, I. S.
SOMBO, M. F.
TIMITE ADJOUA, M.
WAOTA, C.
WELFFENS-EKRA, C.

Faculty of Odontostomatology:

ANGOA, Y.
BAKAYOKO, L. R.
BROU, K. E.
EGNANKOU, K.
ROUX, H.
TOURE, S.

Faculty of Pharmacy:

BAMBA, M.
KONE, M.
MARCY, R.
OUATTARA, L.
YAPO, A. E.

DIRECTORS

Institute of African History of Art and Archaeology: ZAN SEMI-BI
Institute of African Literature and Aesthetics: (vacant)
Institute of Applied Linguistics: ASSY ADOPO
Institute of Ethnosociology: (vacant)
Institute of Teacher-Training and Teaching Research: ADOU AKA

Centre for Architectural and Urban Research: (vacant)

Centre for Communication Teaching and Research: REGINA SERIE TRAORE

University Centre for French Studies: N'GUESSAN KOUASSI

Colleges

Académie Régionale des Sciences et Techniques de la Mer: BP V158, Abidjan; tel. 20-37-18-23; f. 1975 by 17 African countries; merchant shipping, training for radio officers, marine management; library; Dir-Gen. AKA ADOU.

Ecole Nationale d'Administration: BP V 20, Abidjan; tel. 22-41-52-25; fax 22-41-49-63; e-mail ena@globe.access.net; f. 1960; 954 students; library: 11,676 vols, 15 periodicals; Dir GUILLAUME KOUACOU DJAH.

Ecole Nationale des Postes et Télécommunications: BP 1501, Abidjan; tel. 21-25-54-94; fax 21-25-99-05.

Ecole Nationale Supérieure de Statistique et d'Economie Appliquée: Cnr Blvd François Mitterand and Blvd des Grandes Ecoles, Campus Universitaire de Cocody, 08 BP3, Abidjan 08; tel. 22-44-08-40; fax 22-44-39-88; e-mail ensea@ensea.ed.ci; internet www.ensea.refer.ci; f. 1961; 20 teachers; 120 students; library: 13,268 vols; Dir KOFFI N'GUESSAN.

Ecole Nationale Supérieure des Travaux Publics: BP 1083, Yamoussoukro; tel. 30-64-01-00; fax 30-64-03-06; f. 1963; comprises l'Ecole Préparatoire, l'Ecole Nationale Supérieure des Ingénieurs, le Centre de Formation Continue, Ecole Nationale des Techniciens Supérieurs; library: 60,000 vols; 97 teachers; 567 students; Dir SYLVAIN KACOU.

Ecole Supérieure d'Agronomie: BP 1313, Yamoussoukro; tel. 30-64-07-70; fax 30-64-17-49; e-mail esayakro@africaonline.ci; f. 1965; training of agricultural managers; research into agricultural production; 75 teachers; 600 students; library: 6,000 vols; Dir Dr KAMA BERTÉ.

Ecole Supérieure Interafricaine de l'Electricité/Interafrican Electrical Engineering College: BP 311, Bingerville; tel. 22-40-33-12; fax 22-40-35-07; f. 1979; bilingual (English and French) training to graduate level in electrical engineering for students sponsored by power-supply authorities or private companies from all over Africa; Dir-Gen. ABDOU KARIM DIAGNE.

Institut National Polytechnique Félix Houphouët-Boigny: BP 1093, Yamoussoukro; tel. 30-64-05-41; fax 30-64-04-06; f. 1975; technical and vocational training; comprises Ecole de Formation Continue et de Perfectionnement des Cadres, Ecole Supérieure d'Agronomie, Ecole Supérieure de Commerce et d'Administration d'Entreprises, Ecole Supérieure d'Industrie, Ecole Supérieure des Travaux Publics; library: 20,000 vols; 350 teachers; 3,500 students; Dir-Gen. ADO GOSSAN; publs *Akounda* (1 a year), *Leader* (4 a year).

CROATIA

The Higher Education System

Before gaining independence in 1991 Croatia was a federal republic of the former Yugoslavia. The oldest university is Sveučilište u Zagreb (University of Zagreb), which was founded in 1669. Higher education is administered according to the Higher Education Law of 1996, and is the responsibility of the Ministry of Science, Education and Sports. In 2007/08 a total of 143,410 students were enrolled at 115 institutions of higher education in Croatia, including seven universities (in Zagreb, Rijeka, Osijek, Zadar, Pula, Dubrovnik and Split). In 2008 the Dubrovnik International University was founded.

Higher education institutions set their own admissions requirements, with the approval of the Ministry of Science, Education and Sports. Students are usually required to possess the requisite secondary school qualifications and sit an entrance exam. In 2001 Croatia signed up to the Bologna agreement and will have implemented most prescribed changes by 2010; the traditional undergraduate degrees, the Vise Obrazovanje (two to three years' study) and Visoko Obrazovanja (four to six years' study), have been phased out in favour of the Bachelors (four years). Study for a Magistar (Masters degree) in either arts or science subjects includes a magistarski rad (Masters thesis). The Doctorate is the highest postgraduate qualification, study for which includes the research and defence of a doktorski rad (doctoral thesis).

Tertiary-level technical and vocational education consists of one- to four-year programmes in industrial, trade, and craft occupations. Students who complete a postgraduate course in art at a polytechnic may attain the professional title of Master of Arts in accordance with a separate law.

Both higher education institutions and study programmes must undergo an evaluation process in order to be accredited for operation in Croatia. The request for accreditation is submitted to the Ministry in charge of Higher Education, which requests a recommendation from the National Council for Higher Education.

Regulatory and Representative Bodies

GOVERNMENT

Ministry of Culture: Runjaninova 2, HR-10000 Zagreb; tel. (1) 4866-666; fax (1) 4866-280; e-mail kabinet@min-kulture.hr; internet www.min-kulture.hr; Min. BOŽO BIŠKUPIĆ.

Ministry of Science, Education and Sports: Donje Svetice 38, HR-10000 Zagreb; tel. (1) 4569-000; fax (1) 4594-301; e-mail office@mzos.hr; internet www.mzos.hr; Min, RADOVAN FUCHS.

ACCREDITATION

ENIC/NARIC Croatia: Croatian ENIC/NARIC Office, Donje Svetice 38/5, HR-10000 Zagreb; tel. (1) 6274-888; fax (1) 6274-889; e-mail enic@azvo.hr; internet www.azvo.hr/default.aspx?sec=110; f. 2004; information centre for academic mobility and recognition of foreign higher education qualifications; part of European Network of nat. information centres on recognition and mobility; Head of Office MARINA CVITANUSIC.

NATIONAL BODIES

Agencija za znanost i visoko obrazovanje (Agency for Science and Higher Education): Donje Svetice 38/5, HR-10000 Zagreb; tel. (1) 6274-800; fax (1) 6274-801; e-mail ured@azvo.hr; internet www.azvo.hr; f. 2004; legal entity which autonomously and independently performs activities within the scope and authorities determined under the Scientific Activity and Higher Education Act, the Act on Quality Assurance in Higher Education and Science and the Act on Recognition of Foreign Educational Qualifications; activities incl. quality assurance and improvement in higher education and science; full mem of Int. Network for Quality Assurance Agencies in Higher Education since 2006; Pres Prof. MILE DŽELALIJA; Dir Prof. JASMINA HAVRANEK (acting).

Hrvatska akademska i istraživačka mreža (CARNet) (Croatian Academic and Research Network): Josipa Marohnića 5, HR-10000 Zagreb; tel. (1) 6661-616; fax (1) 6661-615; e-mail ured@carnet.hr; internet www.carnet.hr; f. 1991; attached to Min. of Science, Education and Sports; develops advanced information technology and infrastructure for the academic and research community to improve higher education and to promote the design, introduction and implementation of new technologies in Croatia; 250 mem. instns in 382 locations; Chair. of the Board Prof. Dr MARIO KOVAČ; CEO ZVONIMIR STANIĆ.

Rektorski zbor (Rectors' Conference): Trg maršala Tita 14, HR-10000 Zagreb; tel. (1) 4564-012; fax (1) 4830-602; e-mail rc@unizg.hr; internet www.unizg.hr/rz; promotes implementation of the Bologna Declaration; Pres. Prof. Dr GORDANA KRALIK; Sec.-Gen. Prof. Dr BRANKO JEREN.

Vijeće Veleučilišta i Visokih škola Hrvatske (Croatian Council of Institutions of Higher Professional Education): Martićeva 13, HR-10000 Zagreb; tel. (1) 5495-762; fax (1) 5495-769; e-mail vijece@zvu.hr; f. 2002; Pres. Prof. Dr MARKO JELIĆ.

Learned Societies

GENERAL

Društvo za Proučavanje i Unapredenje Pomorstva (Society for Research and Promotion of Maritime Sciences): Riva 16/V, POB 301, HR-51000 Rijeka; tel. (51) 334-210; fax (51) 334-210; e-mail dpuprh@inet.hr; f. 1962; research divided in 9 sections: economics, ethnology, history, law, literature, medicine, natural sciences, nautical sciences, technology; 323 elected mems; Pres. Prof. Dr BLANKA KESIĆ; Sec Dr DUŠAN VRUS; publ. Pomorski Zbornik (Maritime Annals, 1 a year).

Hrvatska Akademija Znanosti i Umjetnosti (Croatian Academy of Sciences and Arts): Zrinski trg 11, HR-10000 Zagreb; tel. (1) 4895-111; fax (1) 4819-979; e-mail kabpred@hazu.hr; internet www.hazu.hr; f. 1861; depts of fine arts, literature, mathematical, medical sciences, music, natural sciences, philology, physical and chemical sciences, social sciences, technical sciences; 146 mems; 14 scientific councils and 6 committees; 160 full, 100 assoc. and 160 corresp. mems; library: see Libraries and Archives; Pres. MILAN MOGUŠ; Vice-Pres. PAVLE DEŠPALJ; Vice-Pres. ALICA WERTHEIMER-BALETIĆ; Gen. Sec. SLAVKO CVETNIĆ; publs Ljetopis, Rad (Memoirs).

BIBLIOGRAPHY, LIBRARY SCIENCE AND MUSEOLOGY

Hrvatsko Knjižničarsko Društvo (Croatian Library Association): c/o National and University Library, Hrvatske bratske zajednice 4, HR-10000 Zagreb; tel. and fax (1) 6159-320; fax (1) 6159-320; e-mail hkd@nsk.hr; internet www.hkdrustvo.hr; f. 1940; promotes library services and the profession of librarianship; publishes journals and other literature; organizes professional meetings; creates library legislation; promotes devt of libraries and general literacy; raises public awareness of the need to preserve and protect cultural heritage; 1,200 mems; Pres. ZDENKA SVIBEN; Vice-Pres. ANICA SABARIĆ; Vice-Pres. BRUNO DOBRIĆ; Sec. SANJA ŽUNIĆ; Treas. VESNA GOLUBOVIĆ; publs HKD Novosti (4 a year, online), Vjesnik bibliotekara Hrvatske (4 a year).

Hrvatsko Muzejsko Društvo (Croatian Museum Association): c/o Muzej za umjetnost i obrt, Trg Maršala Tita 10, HR-10000 Zagreb; tel. (1) 4851-808; fax (1) 4851-977; e-mail hmd@hrmud.hr; internet www.hrmud.hr; f. 1946 as Association of the Employees and Associates of Museums, Galleries and Conservation Institutes in People's Republic of Croatia, present name 1998; non-profit org.; promotes growth and advancement of museum profession and protects the common interests of museum workers; 500 mems; Pres. DUBRAVKA OSREČKI JAKELIĆ; Sec. DORA BOŠKOVIĆ; publ. News of Museum Custodians and Conservators of Croatia (4 a year).

EDUCATION

Hrvatski pedagoško-književni zbor (Croatian Pedagogic—Literary Association): trg Maršala Tita 4, HR-10000 Zagreb; tel. (1) 4855-713; fax (1) 4810-396; e-mail hpkz@zg.t-com.hr; internet www.hpkz-napredak.hr; f. 1871; brs in Slavonski Brod, Križevci, Vukovar, Dubrovnik, Split, Petrinja, Sibenik and Zagreb; 2,000 mems; Pres. VESNA BUDINŞKI; Vice-Pres. NEVIO ŠETLÆ; Sec. KRISTINA ŠNI-DARŠIĆ-VLAŠIĆ; publ. *Napredak* (4 a year).

HISTORY, GEOGRAPHY AND ARCHAEOLOGY

Geografija (Croatian Geographic Society): Marulićev trg 19, POB 595 HR-10000 Zagreb; tel. (1) 4895-402; fax (1) 4895-451; e-mail geografija.hr@gmail.com; internet www .geografija.hr; f. 1897; 600 mems; library of 6,550 vols, 9,570 in spec. collns; Pres. ALEKSANDAR LUKIĆ; publs *Geografski glasnik* (1 a year), *Geografski horizont* (4 a year).

Hrvatsko numizmatičko društvo (Croatian Numismatic Society): Habdelićeva 2, POB 181, HR-10000 Zagreb; tel. (1) 431-426; internet www .hrvatskonumizmatickodrustvo.hr; f. 1928; 500 mems; library of 1,600 vols; Pres. DAMIR KOVAČ; Sec. Prof. BORIS PRISTER; Sec. BER-ISLAV KOPAC; publs *Numizmatičke vijesti* (1 a year), *Numizmatika, Obol* (1 a year).

LANGUAGE AND LITERATURE

Alliance Française: Ante Kovačića 4, HR-10000 Zagreb; tel. and fax (1) 4818-292; e-mail alliance-francaise@zg.htnet.hr; internet www.alliance-francaise.hr; offers courses and examinations in French language and culture and promotes cultural exchange with France; attached offices in Dubrovnik and Split.

British Council: Illica 12, PP55, HR-10001 Zagreb; tel. (1) 4899-500; fax (1) 4833-955; e-mail zagreb.info@britishcouncil.hr; internet www.britishcouncil.hr; offers courses and examinations in English language and British culture and promotes cultural exchange with the UK; library of 7,500 vols, 60 periodicals, 2,500 DVDs; Dir ROY CROSS.

Goethe-Institut: ul. Grada Vukovara 64, HR-10000 Zagreb; tel. (1) 6195-000; fax (1) 6274-355; e-mail info@zagreb.goethe.org; internet www.goethe.de/ms/zag/deindex .htm; offers courses and examinations in German language and culture and promotes cultural exchange with Germany; library of 10,000 vols, 20 periodicals; Dir JULIANE STEGNER; Head Librarian MAJA ANTUNOVIĆ.

MEDICINE

Hrvatskog Liječničkog Zbora (Croatian Medical Association): Šubićeva ul. 9, HR-10000 Zagreb; tel. (1) 4693-300; fax (1) 4655-066; e-mail tajnistvo@hlz.hr; internet www .hlz.hr; f. 1874; 26 regional brs, 121 mem. şocs, 10,400 individual mems; Pres. Prof. Dr ŽELJKO METELKO; Vice-Pres. Prof. Dr ZELJKO KRZNARIĆ, HRVOJE PEZO; Gen. Sec. Prof. Dr TOMISLAV BOŽEK; publs *Acta Stomatologica Croatica*, *Liječničke Novine* (Medical News), *Liječnički Vjesnik* (Medical Journal).

Hrvatsko Farmaceutsko Društvo (Croatian Pharmaceutical Society): Masarykova 2, HR-10000 Zagreb; tel. (1) 4872-849; fax (1) 4872-853; e-mail hfd-fg-ap@zg.t-com.hr; internet www.hfd-fg.hr; f. 1858, present name 1946; asscn of pharmacists to improve professional and scientific work in the field of pharmacy in Croatia; 1,040 mems; library of 2,000 vols; Chair. KREŠIMIR RUKAVINA; publs *Acta Pharmaceutica* (4 a year), *Farmaceutski glasnik* (12 a year).

NATURAL SCIENCES

General

Hrvatsko Prirodoslovno Društvo (Croatian Society of Natural Sciences): Frankopanska 1/I, POB 258, HR-10001 Zagreb; tel. (1) 4831-224; fax (1) 4831-223; e-mail hpd@

hpd.hr; internet www.hpd.hr; f. 1885; organizes meetings and scientific platforms for the promotion of natural sciences; Pres. Prof. Dr NIKOLA LJUBEŠIĆ; Vice-Pres. MLADEN JURAČIĆ; Sec. Dr LIDIJA SUMAN; publs *Periodicum Biologorum* (scientific journal with papers on biomedicine and biochemistry, 6 a year), *Priroda* (Nature, 12 a year).

TECHNOLOGY

Hrvatski Savez Građevinskih Inženjera (Croatian Association of Civil Engineers): Berislavićeva 6, HR-10000 Zagreb; tel. (1) 4872-498; fax (1) 4828-053; e-mail dgiz@zg .t-com.hr; internet www.hsgi.org; f. 1970; promotes scientific research work in the field of architecture; organizes lectures, conferences and symposia; 3,017 mems; library of 5,000 vols; Chief Officer Prof. Dr Ing. ERVIN NONVEILLER; publ. *Gradevinar* (online at www.casopis-gradjevinar.hr).

Research Institutes

GENERAL

Zavod za povijest i filozofiju znanosti u Zagrebu (Institute for the History and Philosophy of Science in Zagreb): Ante Kovačića 5, HR-10000 Zagreb; tel. (1) 4698-231; internet info.hazu.hr/zavod_za_povijest_i_filozofiju_znanosti; f. 1992 by merger of The Institute for Te History of Natural, Mathematical and Medical Sciences (f. 1960) and the Institute for the Philosophy of Science and Peace; attached to Hrvatske Akademije Znanosti i Umjetnosti (Croatian Academy of Sciences and Arts); comprises divs for the history of natural and mathematical sciences, philosophy of science and history of medical sciences; incorporates Institute of the History of Pharmacy of the Croatian Pharmaceutical Society, Institute for the History of Medicine, Medical Faculty, University of Zagreb, Cabinet for the History of Veterinary Medicine, Museum of the Society of Physicians of Croatia and Institute for the Philosophy of Sciences; scientific institution to foster research into the history of science, especially that of the Croats; plans to study problems of methodology, to organize at Zagreb higher education the study of the history of science, to collaborate with analogous institutes at home and abroad; library of 8,000 vols; Dir Prof. Dr ŽARKO DADIĆ; publ. *Rasprave i Gradja za Povijest Nauka* (1 a year).

Zavod za Znanstveni i Umjetnički u Splitu (Institute for Scientific and Artistic Work in Split): Trg Braće Radića 7, POB 100, HR-42000 Split; tel. (21) 348-599; fax (21) 348-599; e-mail hazu.zavod.split@st.t-com .hr; internet info.hazu.hr/zavod_za_znanstveni_i_umjetnicki_rad_u_s-plitu; f. 1925 as Institute of Maritime and Social Sciences, reconstituted to present status 1981; attached to Hrvatske Akademije Znanosti i Umjetnosti (Croatian Academy of Sciences and Arts); performs scientific and other expert research in the areas of the humanities, social and bio-technical sciences (history, archaeology, viticulture, wine production, ecological food production and tourism); initiates and organises scientific meetings, symposia, exhibitions; publishes the results of scientific work and research; library of 6,000 vols; Hon. Dir Prof. Dr DAVORIN RUDOLF; publ. *Adrias*.

AGRICULTURE, FISHERIES AND VETERINARY SCIENCE

Institut za oceanografiju i ribarstvo (Institute of Oceanography and Fisheries):

Šetalište Ivana Meštrovića 63, HR-21000 Split; tel. (21) 408-000; fax (21) 358-650; e-mail office@izor.hr; internet www.izor.hr; f. 1930; conducts research in hydrography, geology, marine biology, mariculture and fishery technology, marine fisheries, ichthyology, mariculture and fishery technology, oceanography; postgraduate study in fisheries; has a hatchery and a research vessel; library of 15,000 vols; Dir Dr IVONA MARASOVIĆ; Pres. of Scientific Council Dr IVICA VILIBIĆ; publs *Acta Adriatica, Notes*.

Poljoprivredni Institut Osijek (Osijek Agricultural Institute): Južno Predgrade 17, POB 334, HR-31001 Osijek; tel. (31) 515-501; fax (31) 515-509; e-mail institut@poljinos.hr; internet www.poljinos.hr; f. 1916; agricultural and scientific research into breeding of wheat, barley, corn, soybeans, sunflowers and alfalfa; 160 mems; library of 5,380 vols; Dir Dr ZVONIMIR ZDUNIĆ; publ. *Poljoprivreda* (Agriculture, 2 a year).

ARCHITECTURE AND TOWN PLANNING

Kabinet za Arhitekturu i Urbanizam (Cabinet for Architecture and Urban Planning): Hebrangova 1, HR-10000 Zagreb; tel. (1) 4825-406; e-mail arlikum@hazu.hr; internet info.hazu.hr/kabinet_za_arhitekturu_i_urbanizam; f. 1952; attached to Arhiv za lLikovne Umjetnosti Hrvatska Akademija Znanosti i Umjetnosti (Fine Art Archives of the Croatian Academy of Sciences and Arts); scientific study of the history of architecture and town planning and methods of protection, conservation and presentation of monuments; holds seven collns: catalogue colln, author files, exhibition files, periodicals colln, artist's correspondence, personal archives, archives of art societies and photograph colln; 5 mems; library of 2,000 vols, 30 periodicals; Hon. Dir VELIMIR NEIDHARDT; publs *Bulletin Razreda za likovne umjetnosti* (2 a year), *Monographs* (irregular), *Rad JAZU* (irregular).

BIBLIOGRAPHY, LIBRARY SCIENCE AND MUSEOLOGY

City Institute for Protection of Cultural and Natural Monuments: Kuševićeva 3, HR-10000 Zagreb; tel. (1) 6101-970; fax (1) 6101-896; e-mail zastita.spomenika@zagreb .hr; f. 1910; attached to Min. of Culture; library of 12,050 vols, photo colln of 54,000 negatives, 10,000 charts; Head DORIS KAŽ-MIR; publ. *Godišnjak zaštite spomenika kulture Hrvatske* (Yearbook of Protection of Croatian Cultural Monuments).

Hrvatski restauratorski zavod (Croatian Conservation Institute): Nike Grskovica 23, HR-10000 Zagreb; tel. (1) 4684-599; fax (1) 4683-289; e-mail uprava@h-r-z.hr; internet www.h-r-z.hr; f. 1997 by merger of Institute for the Conservation of Objects of Art (f. 1948) and the Conservation Institute of Croatia (f. 1966); restoration of and research into the conservation of paintings, historic architecture, wooden sculpture, furniture, stucco, stone, mosaics, wall paintings, architectural monuments, paper and leather, textiles, metal and other archaeological finds; underwater archaeological research; 360 mems; Dir Prof. FERDINAND MEDER.

Regionalni zavod za zaštitu spomenika kulture (Regional Institute for the Protection of Historic Monuments): Poljudsko šetalište 15, POB 191, HR-21000 Split; tel. (21) 342-327; f. 1854; library of 12,000 vols and periodicals, 130,000 photographs and negatives; Dir Dr JOŠKO BELAMARIĆ; Sec. NEIRA STOJANAC; publ. *Prilozi povijesti umjetnosti u Dalmaciji*.

ECONOMICS, LAW AND POLITICS

Institute for International Relations: POB 303, ul. Lj. Farkaša Vukotinovića 2/II, HR-10000 Zagreb; tel. (1) 4877-460; fax (1) 4828-361; e-mail ured@irmo.hr; internet www.imo.hr; f. 1963 as Africa Research Institute, name changed to Institute for Developing Countries 1971, present name and status 1996; attached to Min. of Science, Education and Sports; interdisciplinary study of devt processes and economic and int. relations, and cooperation in the field of economics, culture, science, environmental protection and politics; organizes seminars, int. conferences and specialist training programmes; library of 9,000 vols, 400 periodicals; Chair. MLADEN ANDRLIĆ; Dir Dr SANJA TIŠMA; publs *Croatian International Relations Review* (4 a year, in English), *Culturelink* (3 a year and special issue in English), *Euroscope* (6 a year, in Croatian).

Jadranski zavod (Adriatic Institute): Frane Petrića 4/1, HR-10000 Zagreb; tel. (1) 481-20733; fax (1) 481-2703; e-mail jz@hazu.hr; internet www.hazu.hr/jzavod; f. 1945, inc. as research institute of Yugoslav Academy of Sciences and Arts (now Croatian Academy of Sciences and Arts) 1948, renamed Institute of Maritime Law, History and Economics 1974, present bldg 1992, present name 1994; attached to Hrvatske Akademije Znanosti i Umjetnosti (Croatian Academy of Sciences and Arts); maritime law and the law of the sea, with particular emphasis on the carriage of goods by sea, maritime safety, insurance, protection of the marine environment and maritime delimitations; library of 10,000 book titles, 117 periodicals, 2,500 documents; 7 mems; Dir Prof. Emeritus VLADIMIR-DJURO DEGAN; Sec. VLATKA ŽIVOJNOVIĆ; publ. *Poredbeno pomorsko pravo* (Comparative Maritime Law, in English and Croatian, 1 a year).

LANGUAGE AND LITERATURE

Leksikografski Zavod 'Miroslav Krleža' ('Miroslav Krleža' Lexicographic Institute): Frankopanska 26, HR-10000 Zagreb; tel. (1) 4800-398; fax (1) 4800-399; e-mail lzmk@lzmk.hr; internet www.lzmk.hr; f. 1951; collects and processes MSS for encyclopaedic, lexicographic, bibliographic, monographic and other scientific edns; publishes results of research and cooperates with similar institutions abroad; 10,000 contributors, specialists in all fields; library: specialized library of 35,000 vols; Dir-Gen. Prof. BOGIŠIĆ BLAISE; Dir BRUNO KRAGIĆ.

Staroslavenski institut (Old Church Slavonic Institute): Demetrova 11, HR-10000 Zagreb; tel. (1) 4851-380; fax (1) 4851-377; e-mail info@stin.hr; internet www.stin.hr; f. 1902 as Old Church Slavonic Academy, present name 1952; research of the Croatian Glagolitic heritage: language, literature and palaeography; library of 20,000 vols, 11,820 book titles, 482 periodicals; Dir. Dr MARICA ČUNČIĆ; Sec. MARINA ŠANTIĆ; publ. *Slovo* (1 a year).

MEDICINE

Institut za medicinska istraživanja i medicinu rada (Institute for Medical Research and Occupational Health): Ksaverska cesta 2, POB 291, HR-10001 Zagreb; tel. (1) 4673-188; fax (1) 4673-303; e-mail uprava@imi.hr; internet mimi.imi.hr; f. 1947 as Institute of Occupational Hygiene; ind. status 1958, present name 1959; attached to Min. of Science, Education and Sports; conducts research on working and living environment, hygiene, health and dissemination of knowledge on industrial hygiene, environmental pollution and radiation; seeks to implement research results in industry and runs a number of projects of national interest; scientists of the institute teach in postgraduate and undergraduate programmes, primarily at the University of Zagreb; 149 mems; library of 8,000 books, 75 journals; Dir Dr ANA LUCIĆ VRDOLJAK; Chair. VLASTA DREVENKAR; publ. *Arhiv za higijenu rada i toksilologiju* (Archives of Industrial Hygiene and Toxicology, in English and Croatian, 4 a year).

NATURAL SCIENCES

General

Institut 'Rudjer Bošković' (Rudjer Bošković Institute): Bijenička cesta 54, POB 1016, HR-10000 Zagreb; tel. (1) 4561-111; fax (1) 4680-084; e-mail info@irb.hr; internet www.irb.hr; f. 1950; attached to Univ. of Osijek, Univ. of Rijeka and Univ. of Zagreb; research in physics (biophysics, medical, nuclear and atomic, theoretical), chemistry (biochemistry, organic and physical), biology (biomedicine, molecular biology), electronics; marine research centres in Rovinj and Zagreb; 82 laboratories; library of 37,000 vols, 760 print journals and access to 16000 electronic journals; Dir-Gen. Dr DANICA RAMLJAK; Sec. JADRANKA KUČAN; Head of Library BOJAN MACAN.

Biological Sciences

Bureau for Nature Conservation: Ilica 44/II, HR-10000 Zagreb; tel. (1) 432-022; fax (1) 431-515; f. 1961; photographic colln of 12,200 negatives, 12,000 photographs and 1,240 colour slides; 16 mems; library of 5,400 vols; Dir Prof. Dr MIHO MILJANIĆ.

Physical Sciences

Državni hidrometeorološki zavod (Meteorological and Hydrological Service): Grič 3, HR-10000 Zagreb; tel. (1) 4565-666; fax (1) 4851-901; e-mail dhmz@cirus.dhz.hr; internet meteo.hr; f. 1947; meteorology, climatology, ecological studies, hydrology; maintains Marine Meteorological Centre in Split; library of 7,000 vols, 45 periodicals; Dir IVAN CACIĆ; publs *Bilten* (meteorological and hydrological bulletin, 12 a year), *Croatian Meteorological Journal* (1 a year).

RELIGION, SOCIOLOGY AND ANTHROPOLOGY

Institut za Društvena Istraživanja Zagreb (Institute for Social Research Zagreb): Amruševa 11/II, HR-10000 Zagreb; tel. (1) 4810-264; fax (1) 4810-263; e-mail idiz@idi.hr; internet www.idi.hr; f. 1964; attached to Univ. of Zagreb; research in all fields of sociology, social anthropology, psychology; library of 16,400 vols and periodicals; Dir. RUŽA FIRST-DILIĆ; publs *Revija za Sociologiju* (Sociology Review), *Sociologija Sela* (Rural Sociology, 4 a year).

Institut za etnologiju i folkloristiku (Institute of Ethnology and Folklore Research): Šubićeva 42, HR-10000 Zagreb; tel. (1) 4596-700; fax (1) 4596-709; e-mail institut@ief.hr; internet maief.ief.hr; f. 1948 as Institute of Folk Art; 185,000 items of archives and documentation; spec. colln of ethnographic materials: 1,800 text collns and music annotations, 19 dance collns, 374 kinetograms, 57 drawing collns with 2,000 panels, 3,300 tape recordings (music recordings and narratives); record library (770 sound recordings); photo and slide library (4,700 items); 970 video cassettes and 51 films; library of 28,100 vols, 19,000 books and offprints, 9,100 bound periodicals; Dir IVAN LOZICA; Sec. SANJA LESIĆ; Librarian ANAMARIJA STARCEVIC-STAMBUK; publs *Narodna Umjetnost* (2 a year), *Nova etnografija* (Series).

TECHNOLOGY

Končar–Institut za elektrotehniku d.d. (Končar–Electrical Engineering Institute): Fallerovo šetalište 22, HR-10002 Zagreb; tel. (1) 3667-315; fax (1) 3667-317; e-mail info@koncar-institut.hr; internet www.koncar-institut.hr; f. 1991; research and devt division within Končar Group of companies; research and devt in all fields of electrical engineering; library of 30,000 vols, 350 periodicals; Chair. Dr STJEPAN CAR.

Libraries and Archives

Dubrovnik

Znanstvena knjižnica Dubrovnik (Scientific Library of Dubrovnik): Cvijete Zuzorić 4, HR-20000 Dubrovnik; tel. (20) 323-911; fax (20) 323-767; e-mail znanstvena@dkd.hr; internet www.dkd.hr; f. 1936; 267,000 vols, 7,000 vols of periodicals, 77 incunabula, 928 MSS, 10,490 books belonging to the Republic of Dubrovnik up to 1808 (Old Ragusina), collection of 14,000 vols (New Ragusina); Chief Officer MIRJANA URBAN.

Pula

Sveučilišna knjižnica u Puli (University Library of Pula): Herkulov prolaz 1, HR-52100 Pula; tel. (52) 213-888; fax (52) 214-603; e-mail skpu@unipu.hr; internet www.unipu.hr; f. 1861; 2,730 mems; publicly accessible central library for the Juraj Dobrila Univ. of Pula; Antonio Smareglia memory room; 200,000 vols, 120,000 periodicals; spec. collns: the Istrian area, Austro-Hungarian Naval Library (20,000 vols); Marine Library: 20,731 vols (131,716 monographs, 6,655 journals, annals and newspapers); 100 vols of incunabula and books from the 16th and 17th centuries; 2,400 audio recordings, 541 maps, postcards and plaques; Dir TIJANA BARBIĆ DOMAZET; publ. *Nova Istra* (literary review, 4 a year).

Rijeka

Sveučilišna knjižnica Rijeka (University Library Rijeka): Dolac 1, POB 132, HR-51000 Rijeka; tel. (51) 336-911; fax (51) 332-006; e-mail ravnatelj@svkri.hr; internet www.svkri.hr; f. 1949 as Scientific Library of Rijeka, present name and status 1979; legal deposit library; spec. collns of material on the Primorsko-Goranska region and on the Glagolitic script; repository of Univ. of Rijeka publs and dissertations; 300,000 vols, 16,000 online magazines, heritage colln: 100,000 vols; Dir SENKA TOMLJANOVIĆ.

Split

Sveučilišna knjižnica u Splitu (Split University Library): Ruđera Boškovića 31, HR-21000 Split; tel. (21) 434-800; fax (21) 434-801; e-mail svkst@svkst.hr; internet www.svkst.hr; f. 1903; 3,000 mems; material on Split and the surrounding area; 400,000 vols, 12,000 periodicals, 700 MSS, 5,000 rare books, maps and atlases, sheet music, sound recordings and graphic material; Dir Prof. PETAR KROLO; Head Librarian SANJA BRBORA.

Varaždin

Gradska knjižnica i čitaonica 'Metel Ožegović' (City Library 'Metel Ožegović'): Trg Slobode 8A, HR-42000 Varaždin; tel. and fax (42) 212-767; e-mail gknjizmo@vz.htnet.hr; internet library.foi.hr/metel; f. 1838; 190,000 vols; Dir MARIO ŠOŠTARIĆ; Deputy Dir JASMINKA ŠTIMAC.

Zadar

Znanstvena Knjižnica Zadar (Research Library of Zadar): Ante Kuzmanića bb, HR-23000 Zadar; tel. (23) 211-365; fax (23) 312-129; e-mail zkzd@zkzd.hr; internet www .zkzd.hr; f. 1855 as Biblioteca Comunale Paravia; deposit library; spec. colln: Dalmatica (20,000 vols); 815,000 vols, collns incl. 372 parchments, 34 incunabula, 1,140 MSS, 1,460 rare books, 236 Masters and Doctoral theses, colln of 2,398 photographs and 300 negatives on glass plates, 2,250 maps and atlases, 2,250 music scores; Dir MIRO GRUBIĆ; Sr Librarian MILENKA BUKVIĆ; publ. *Knjižno blago Naučne biblioteke u Zadru continued as Knjižno blago Znanstvene knjižnice Zadar.*

Zagreb

Hrvatski državni arhiv (Croatian State Archives): Marulićev trg 21, HR-10000 Zagreb; tel. (1) 4801-999; fax (1) 4829-000; e-mail hda@arhiv.hr; internet www.arhiv.hr; f. 1643; records of central govt archives, other public instns and nat. cinematographic production; incl. 24,000 linear m of records since 10th century, concerning the history of Croatia; 20,000 km of film; 160,000 vols, 90,000 books, 70,000 magazines and newspapers, 600,000 photographs; Dir Dr STJEPAN ĆOSIĆ; publs *Arhivski vjesnik* (Archives Bulletin), *Fontes. Izvori za hrvatsku povijest* (Fontes. Sources for Croatian history).

Knjižnica Hrvatske akademije znanosti i umjetnosti (Library of the Croatian Academy of Sciences and Arts): Strossmayerov trg 14, HR-10000 Zagreb; tel. (1) 4895-113; fax (1) 4895-134; e-mail library@hazu.hr; internet knjiznica.hazu.hr; f. 1867; 400,000 vols, 1,000 current periodicals; Dir VEDRANA JURIĆIĆ.

Knjižnice Grada Zagreba (Zagreb City Libraries): Starčevićev trg 6, HR-10000 Zagreb; tel. (1) 4572-344; fax (1) 4572-089; e-mail kgz@kgz.hr; internet www.kgz.hr; f. 1967 beginning of library network with merger of City Library of Zagreb and Silvije Strahimir Kranjčević Library; network of public libraries; comprises the City Library of Zagreb (f. 1907) and the Božidar Adžija Library (f. 1927) both holding the largest collns, the County Research and Development Department, 12 br. libraries with a network of 31 attached brs in 45 locations; bookmobile service; Dir DAVORKA BASTIĆ; publ. *Književni petak* (Literary Friday, f. 1955).

Nacionalna i sveučilišna knjižnica u Zagrebu (National and University Library in Zagreb): Ul. Hrvatske bratske zajednice 4, POB 550, HR-10000 Zagreb; tel. (1) 6164-111; fax (1) 6164-186; e-mail nsk@nsk.hr; internet www.nsk.hr; f. 1611, present name 1874, present bldg 1995; generates and organizes Croatian nat. colln of library holdings and supervises acquisition of publs on the nat. level, and on behalf of the Univ. of Zagreb; acts as the nat. bibliographic office; keeps and renews/updates the library's holdings in accordance with int. programme; promotes Croatian books and other publs; performs bibliographic and information activities, incl. inter-library lending; performs scientific research in the area of librarianship and information science; is also involved in publishing, exhibition and promotional activities; 2.5m. vols; average annual acquisition: 12,000 books, 4,800 magazines and newspapers, 8,800 gen. items and 1,000 pieces of electronic material; spec. collns: MSS and old books, print colln, music and map collns; Chair. MILIVOJ ZENIĆ; Dir-Gen. Prof. TIHOMIL MAŠTROVIĆ; Sr Librarian Dr SLAVKO HARNI; publ. *Hrvatska bibliografija* (Croatian Bibliography, 12 a year).

Museums and Art Galleries

Dubrovnik

Dubrovacki muzeji (Dubrovnik Museums): Pred dvorom 3, HR-20000 Dubrovnik; tel. (20) 321-422; fax (20) 322-096; internet www .mdc.hr/dubrovnik; f. 1872 as the Dubrovnik Regional Museum; comprised of 6 museums; Head Dir PAVICA VILAC.

Attached Museums:

Archaeological Museum: Brace Andrijica 7, Dubrovnik; tel. (20) 324-041; e-mail dubrovacki.muzeji1@du.t-com.hr; internet www.mdc.hr/dubrovnik/nj/arheoloski; f. 1991; reference library; museums holdings divided into the prehistoric, antique, early medieval collns, colln from 13th century to the 1667 earthquake, Egyptian, vase and coin collns; Dir ROMANA MENALO.

Cultural Historical Museum: Kneževdvor 1, Dubrovnik; tel. (20) 321-422; fax (20) 322-096; internet www.mdc.hr/dubrovnik/nj/kulturnopovijesni; Rector's palace: seat of govt and residence of the Prince (Rector) of the Dubrovnik Republic; colln of paintings, ceramics, icons, metalwork, textiles, furniture, glassware, photography and photographic material; Sr Curator LJILJANA IVUSIC; Sr Curator RENATA ANDJUS.

Ethnographic Museum—The 'Rupe' Museum: Od Rupa 3, Dubrovnik; tel. (20) 412-545; internet www.mdc.hr/dubrovnik/nj/etnografski; f. 1991; 5,000 exhibits on permanent display; collns incl. traditional folk costumes, folklore, textiles, lace; Dir MIRJANA ZEC.

Marin Drzic House: Siroka ul. 7, Dubrovnik; tel. (20) 420-490; internet www.mdc .hr/dubrovnik/nj/marindrzic; f. 1989; theatrical museum, scientific-documentary institute and exhibition space; collns of posters, programmes and photographs of Marin Drzic's plays in Croatia and abroad; display of post-modern installations reconstructing the Renaissance period during which Drzic lived; puppets, posters and stage props; audio guides with excerpts from Drzic texts; Dir IVANA JASIC.

Maritime Museum: St John's Fortress, HR-20000 Dubrovnik; tel. (20) 323-904; fax (20) 322-096; internet www.mdc.hr/dubrovnik/nj/pomorski; f. 1941, admin by Yugoslav Acad. of Arts and Sciences 1949, present status 1987; Dubrovnik's maritime past; ship models from the 17th, 18th and 19th centuries; flags, cannons and other weapons, figureheads, nautical instruments and log books; library of rare books and archival materials; library of 10,027 vols; Dir Prof. ĐIVO BAŠIĆ; Curator Prof. LJERKA DUNATOV; Curator Prof. ANA KAZNACIC.

Modern History Museum: ul. Brace Andrijica 7, Dubrovnik; tel. (20) 429-461; internet www.mdc.hr/dubrovnik/nj/suvremenapovijest; f. 1956; colln of documents from the Second World War, memoirist writings on the Croatian Homeland War; Dir Prof. VARINA JURICA TURK.

Dubrovnik Umjetnička Galerija (Museum of Modern Art Dubrovnik): Frana Supila 23, HR-20000 Dubrovnik; tel. (20) 426-590; fax (20) 432-114; e-mail info@ugdubrovnik.hr; internet www.ugdubrovnik .hr; f. built between 1935–1939 as Božo Banac's mansion; 1950 as exhibition premises and museum; colln of modern and contemporary works of art; library of 2,418 vols; Dir ANTUN MARAĆIC; Curator ROZANA VOJVODA; Curator PETRA GOLUŠIĆ.

Muzej Srpske Pravoslavne Crkve (Museum of the Serbian Orthodox Church): Od Puća 2, HR-20000 Dubrovnik; f. 1953; colln of portraits, and over 170 icons from Serbia, Crete, Corfu, Venice, Russia, Greece, Dubrovnik, Boka-Kotorska; the palace which houses the colln is also of historical interest; library of 25,000 vols.

Rijeka

Muzej Moderne i Suvremene Umjetnosti, Rijeka (Museum of Modern and Contemporary Art, Rijeka): Dolac 1/II, HR-51000 Rijeka; tel. (51) 492-611; fax (51) 492-623; e-mail mmsu-rijeka@ri.t-com.hr; internet www.mmsu.hr; f. 1948; paintings, sculptures, prints, posters, photographs, installations, new media from Croatia and other countries; publs catalogues; colln of over 5,000 artwork, covering periods from the end of the 19th century to present day; 18 mems; library of 30,000 books and catalogues; Dir Dr JERICA ZIHERL.

Prirodoslovni muzej Rijeka (Natural History Museum Rijeka): Lorenzov Prolaz 1, HR-51000 Rijeka; tel. and fax (51) 553-669; fax (51) 553-669; e-mail info@prirodoslovni .com; internet www.prirodoslovni.com; f. 1876; on permanent display: geological history of the Adriatic; inorganic, zoological and botanical collns (90,000 specimens); library of 4,024 vols; Dir MILVANA ARKO PIJEVAC; Sec. TANJA CICAVARIC.

Slavonski Brod

Brlić House (Ivana Brlić-Mažuranić Memorial): Titov trg 8, HR-55000 Slavonski Brod; f. 1933; private family house containing archives, furniture showing the evolution of a Croatian middle-class family over 300 years; Ivana Brlić (1874–1938) was a writer and first woman mem. of the Yugoslav Acad. of Sciences and Arts; library of 8,000 vols; Curator VIKTOR RUŽIĆ.

Split

Arheološki muzej u Splitu (Archaeological Museum Split): Zrinjsko-Frankopanska 25, HR-21000 Split; tel. (21) 329-345; fax (21) 329-360; e-mail info@armus.hr; internet www.mdc.hr/split-arheoloski; f. 1820, present bldg 1914; prehistoric collns, relics from the Greek colonies on the east shore of the Adriatic Sea; Roman and Christian relics from Salonae and Dalmatia; Croatian medieval monuments from 9th to 13th century; numismatic colln; library of 50,000 vols incl. 8 incunabula and 170 16th-century books, spec. colln: Dalmatica; Dir ZRINKA BULJEVIĆ; Museum Consultant MAJA BONACIC MANDINIC (Coin Colln); Museum Consultant BRANKO KIRIGIN (Graeco-Hellenistic Colln); Head of Library ARSEN DUPLANCIC; publ. *Vjesnik za arheologiju i povijest dalmatinsku* (Bulletin of Dalmatian Archaeology and History, 1 a year).

Etnografski muzej Split (Ethnographical Museum of Split): Iza Vestibula 4, HR-21000 Split; tel. (21) 344-164; fax (21) 344-108; e-mail etnografski-muzej-st@st.t-com.hr; internet www.etnografski-muzej-split.hr; f. 1910; 19,500 items; nat. costumes, jewels, weapons, and traditional technological objects from Dalmatia, Dinaric Alps area and other neighbouring regions; illustrations section; library of 3,000 vols; Dir SILVIO BRAICA; Librarian IVA MESTROVIC.

Galerija umjetnina Split (Art Gallery Split): Ul. kralja Tomislava 15, HR-21000 Split; tel. (21) 350-110; fax (21) 350-111; e-mail galerija-umjetnina@galum.hr; internet www.galum.hr; f. 1931; 2,300 paintings and sculptures (ancient and modern); library of 14,000 vols; Dir Prof. BOŽO MAJ-

STOROVIĆ; Sr Curator IRIS SLADE; Sr Curator JASMINKA BABIĆ.

Muzej grada Splita (City Museum of Split): Papalićeva 1, HR-21000 Split; tel. (21) 360-171; fax (21) 344-917; e-mail muzej-grada-st@st.tel.hr; internet www.mdc.hr/splitgr; f. 1946; political and cultural history of Split; library of 8,000 vols; Dir ELVIRA ŠARIĆ KOSTIĆ; Librarian JASNA ĆUBE-LIĆ; publ. *Editions*.

Muzegi Ivana Meštrovića (Ivan Meštrović Museums): Šetalište Ivana Meštrovića 46, HR-21000 Split; tel. (21) 340-800; fax (21) 340-810; e-mail mim@mestrovic.hr; internet www.mdc.hr/mestrovic; f. 1991 as Ivan Meštrović Foundation with admin. HQ in Zagreb, present status 2007; protects and promotes Ivan Meštrović's life and work; permanent exhibition of sculptures of Ivan Meštrović (1883–1962); Dir ANDRO KRSTULOVIĆ OPARA; Sr Curator DANICA PLAZIBAT.

Attached Museums:

Church of the Most Holy Redeemer: HR-22322 Otavice; tel. (22) 872-630; e-mail mim@mestrovic.hr; f. 1952; Ivan Meštrović's family vault and mausoleum; permanent display of stone reliefs carved in the altar and lateral niches and on lateral walls, bas-reliefs of religious themes; spec. wall display: *Annunciation with the Archangel Gabriel and Virgin Mary, Soul of a Dead Man* and *Soul of a Dead Woman*; Curator MAJA ŠEPAROVIĆ PALADA.

Crikvine—Kaštelet: Setaliste Ivana Mestrovica 39, HR-21000 Split; tel. (21) 358-185; e-mail mim@mestrovic.hr; f. 1952; fmr summerhouse of the Capogrosso family built in the early 16th century; bought by Meštrović in 1939; on display in the Holy Crucifix Church: reliefs and artwork inspired by the life of Christ; Curator MAJA ŠEPAROVIĆ PALADA.

Meštrović Atelier: Mletacka 8, HR-10000 Zagreb; tel. (1) 485-1123; fax (1) 485-1126; e-mail mim@mestrovic.hr; f. 1959; works from first four decades of Meštrović's artistic life incl. portraits with the recurring theme of mother and child, female nudes, religious and mythological themes, monuments and historical figures; sculptures in marble, stone, wood and bronze; drawings and graphics; Museum Advisor LJILJANA ČERINA; Sr Curator DANICA PLAZIBAT.

Meštrović Gallery: Setaliste I. Mestrovica 46, HR-21000 Split; tel. (21) 340-800; fax (21) 340-810; e-mail mim@mestrovic.hr; f. 1952; colln of 192 sculptures, 583 drawings, 4 paintings, 291 architectonic plans made by Ivan Meštrovic (1898–1961), 2 furniture sets based on Meštrović's sketches; documentation relating to Meštrović's life and work; Curator MAJA ŠEPAROVIĆ PALADA.

Prirodoslovni muzej i zoološki vrt (Museum of Natural Sciences and Zoo): Kolombatovićevo šetalište 2, HR-21000 Split; tel. (21) 322-988; fax (21) 322-990; e-mail prizoost@st.htnet.hr; internet hvm.mdc.hr/prirodoslovni-muzej-i-zooloski-vr-t,600%3aslt/hr/info; f. 1924; contains more than 100,000 exhibits of mineralogical, palaeontological and zoological specimens from Dalmatia and the Adriatic Sea; collns of coleoptera, shells and birds (mostly Dalmatian); library of 3,500 vols; zoological garden (Vrh Marjana 1); Dir Prof. NEDILJKO ZEVRNJA; Library Man. GOD KOKAN.

Zagreb

Arheološki muzej u Zagrebu (Archaeological Museum of Zagreb): Trg Nikole Šubića Zrinskog 19, POB 13, HR-10000 Zagreb; tel. (1) 4873-101; fax (1) 4873 102; e-mail amz@amz.hr; internet www.amz.hr; f. 1846; museum of archaeological finds from neolithic times to 13th century, incl. prehistoric colln, Egyptian colln, Greek, Roman and medieval collns, numismatic colln; Lapidarium in courtyard, featuring stone monuments from Roman era; colln of nearly 400,000 varied artefacts and monuments; library of 45,000 vols; Dir Prof. ANTE RENDIĆ-MIOČEVIĆ; Head Librarian ROLAND HEIDE; publ. *Vjesnik Arheološkog Muzeja u Zagrebu* (1 a year).

Etnografski muzej Zagreb (Ethnographical Museum Zagreb): Mažuranićev trg 14, HR-10000 Zagreb; tel. (1) 4826-220; fax (1) 4880-320; e-mail emz@emz.hr; internet www.emz.hr; f. 1919; exhibitions, cultural traditions of the 3 ethnographic regions of Croatia: Pannonic, Dinaric, Adriatic; dept of non-European cultures; collns of folks costumes, small decorated wood items, pottery and wickerwork, house inventory items, musical instruments, traditional adornments, textiles, traditional economy and items related with customs and beliefs; library of 15,000 vols; Dir and Sr Curator FRLAN DAMODAR; publ. *Ethnographical Researches* (1 a year).

Glyptothèque HAZU: Medvedgradska 2, HR-10000 Zagreb; tel. (1) 4686-060; fax (1) 4686-052; e-mail gliptoteka@hazu.hr; internet info.hazu.hr/the_glyptotheque; f. 1937; colln of medieval frescos and plaster casts of ancient, medieval and recent sculptures and architecture; originals of Croatian sculptures since 19th century; Hon. Dir IVAN KOŽARIĆ; Dir Prof. ARIANA KRALJ.

Hrvatski muzej naivne umjetnosti (Croatian Museum of Naïve Art): Sv. Cirilometodska 3, Gornji grad, HR-10000 Zagreb; tel. (1) 4851-911; fax (1) 4852-125; e-mail info@hmnu.org; internet hmnu.org; f. 1952 as the Peasant Art Gallery, present name 1994; 1,700 works of art, paintings, sculptures, drawings and prints; permanent display: *Naïve Art as a Segment of Modern Art*; works of ind. Croatian artists and artists from the Hlebine School; Dir Prof. VLADIMIR CRNKOVIĆ; Sr Curator MIRA FRANCETIĆ MALČIĆ; Sec. KSENIJA PAVLINIĆ-TOMAŠEGOVIĆ.

Hrvatski povijesni muzej (Croatian History Museum): Matoševa 9, HR-10000 Zagreb; tel. (1) 4851-900; fax (1) 4851-909; e-mail hismus@hismus.hr; internet www.hismus.hr; f. 1846; history of Croatia; 200,000 artefacts arranged into stone monuments, paintings, prints and sculptures, 20th-century fine art, religious artefacts, objects from everyday life, flags and uniforms, heraldry and sphragistics, decorations, plaques, medals and badges, edged weapons and fire-Arms, maps, first and second documentary, varia and photographs, films and negatives; library of 43,000 vols; Dir Prof. ANKICA PANDŽIĆ; Librarian Prof. ZORA GAJSKY.

Hrvatski prirodoslovni muzej (Croatian Natural History Museum): Demetrova 1, HR-10000 Zagreb; tel. (1) 4851-700; fax (1) 4851-644; e-mail hpm@hpm.hr; internet www.hpm.hr; f. 1846; depts of botany, geology and palaeontology, mineralogy and petrography, zoology; library of 40,000 vols; Dir Dr TATJANA VLAHOVIĆ; Sec. NARCISA ANTONIOLI; publ. *Natura Croatica* (2 a year).

Hrvatski školski muzej (Croatian School Museum): Trg m. Tita 4, HR-10000 Zagreb; tel. (1) 4855-716; fax (1) 4855-825; e-mail hsm@hsmuzej.hr; internet www.hrskolski-muzej.hr; f. 1871 as the Croatian Pedagogic-Literary Society, present name and status 1901; history of the school system and education in Croatia; collns of teaching aids, teaching materials and school equipment, student and teacher writings, text-books and handbooks, school regulations, archival colln of documents, colln of photographs and a record file on schools; library of 37,000 vols on the history of schools and education in general; Dir Prof. BRANKA MANIN; Sr Librarian STEFKA BATINIC; publ. *Anali za povijest odgoja* (Annals of the History of Education, 1 a year).

Kabinet Grafike (Department of Prints and Drawings): Hebrangova 1, HR-10000 Zagreb; tel. and fax (1) 4922-374; e-mail kabgraf@hazu.hr; internet www.kabinet-grafike.hazu.hr; f. 1916 as Arts dept of the fmr Yugoslav Acad. of Sciences and Arts, present status 1951; 17,500 inventory units divided into 4 collns: old colln of drawings and prints (15th–19th century), colln of 20th and 21st centuries (drawings and prints), colln of posters and colln of chalcographic plates; Hon. Dir IGOR FISKOVIĆ; Dir SLAVICA MARKOVIĆ; Sec. TANJA LISEC.

Moderna Galerija (Gallery of Modern Art): Andrije Hebranga 1, HR-10000 Zagreb; tel. (1) 6041-040; fax (1) 6041-044; e-mail moderna-galerija@zg.t-com.hr; internet www.moderna-galerija.hr; f. 1905; Croatian arts since 19th century; collns of painting, sculpture and graphic arts; 1,945 medals; library of 5,922 vols; Dir BISERKA RAUTER PLANČIĆ; Librarian VIŠNJA KOVAČEVIĆ.

Muzej grada Zagreba (Zagreb City Museum): Opatička 20, HR-10000 Zagreb; tel. (1) 4851-361; fax (1) 4851-359; e-mail mgz@mgz.hr; internet www.mgz.hr; f. 1907; exhibits on Zagreb since pre-historic times; 5 collns: pre-historic archaeology, medieval archaeology, colln and flat of the architect Viktor Kovačić, Bela and Miroslav Krleža memorial space, Dr Ivan Ribar and Cata Dujšin-Ribar colln; library of 11,000 vols; Dir Prof. VINKO IVIĆ; Sec. BRANKO BEŠTAK; Librarian SLOBODANKA RADOVČIC; publ. *Iz starog i novog Zagreba* (from Old and New Zagreb, irregular).

Muzej Suvremene Umjetnosti Zagreb (Museum of Contemporary Art Zagreb): Ave Dubrovnik 17, HR-10000 Zagreb; tel. (1) 6052-700; fax (1) 6052-798; e-mail msu@msu.hr; internet www.msu.hr; f. 1954; collns of drawings, graphics, prints and art on paper, 456 films and videocassettes, photographs after the 1950s developed at the Centre for Photography, Film and Television (CEFFT); sculpture colln: 561 artworks, 1,200 works by Croatian and int. artists; Tošo Dabac archive: 200,000 negatives, 2,000 enlargements, photography equipment, newspaper clippings; Seissel Donation: paintings and architectural designs by Josip Seissel; Richter colln: 182 works of art by Vjenceslav Richter dating 1964–2002; Benko Horvat colln: 611 paintings, graphic art dating 15th–18th centuries; library of 12,500 vols; Dir and Sr Curator SNJEŽANA PINTARIĆ.

Muzej za umjetnost i obrt (Museum of Arts and Crafts): Trg maršala Tita 10, HR-10000 Zagreb; tel. (1) 4882-111; fax (1) 4828-088; e-mail muo@muo.hr; internet www.muo.hr; f. 1880; fine and applied arts since 14th century; furniture, textiles, ceramics, glass, metalwork, sculpture, paintings, photography, costumes, clocks and watches, ivory, architecture, design and posters; library: art library of 60,000 vols; Dir Prof. MIROSLAV GAŠPAROVIĆ.

Strossmayerova galerija starih majstora (Strossmayers' Gallery of Old Masters): Trg Nikole Šubića Zrinskog 11, HR-10000 Zagreb; tel. (1) 4813-344; fax (1) 4819-979; e-mail sgallery@hazu.hazu.hr; internet www.mdc.hr/strossmayer; f. 1861, opened to public 1884; art from 14th–19th centuries; library of 10,000 titles in art and cultural history, archeology, ethnology, 400 journals, reference colln; Dir Prof. DURO VANDURA; Curators Prof. BORIVOJ POPOVCAK, SANJA CVETNIC; Librarian Prof. INDIRA CVEK FLASCHAR; publs *Bulletin*, *HAZU*, *Razreda za likovne umjetnosti*.

Tehnički muzej Zagreb (Technical Museum Zagreb): Savska cesta 18, HR-10000 Zagreb; tel. (1) 435-446; fax (1) 428-431; e-mail tehnicki-muzej@zg.tel.hr; internet www.tehnicki-muzej.hr; f. 1954, present bldg 1959; colln of over 5,000 exhibits pertaining to various technical fields; library of 6,000 vols; Dir BOZICA SKULJ; Sr Curator VESNA DAKIC; Sr Curator MIROSLAV MIRKOVIC; Sr Curator NEDA STAKLAREVIC.

Universities

MEDUNARODNO SVEUČILIŠTE U DUBROVNIKU
(Dubrovnik International University)

Sv. 4 Dominika, HR-20000 Dubrovnik

Telephone: (20) 414-111
E-mail: diu@diu.hr
Internet: www.diu.hr
Private control

Pres.: Prof. Dr MIOMIR ŽUŽUL
Provost: Prof. Dr MARGARET MELADYaccepts only 100 students each year

DEANS

School of Arts and Humanities: Prof. Dr PETAR SELEM
School of Economics: Prof. Dr ANTE BABIĆ
School of Diplomacy: Prof. Dr THOMAS P. MELADY

SVEUČILIŠTE JOSIPA JURJA STROSSMAYERA U OSIJEKU
(Josip Jurja Strossmayer University of Osijek)

Trg sv. Trojstva 3, HR-31000 Osijek

Telephone: (31) 224-102
Fax: (31) 207-015
E-mail: rektorat@unios.hr
Internet: www.unios.hr

Founded 1975
State control
Academic year: October to September

Rector: Prof. Dr GORDANA KRALIK
Vice-Rectors: Prof. Dr DRAGO ŽAGAR, Prof. Dr DRAŽEN BARKOVIĆ, Prof. Dr IVAN SAMARDŽIĆ, Prof. Dr RUDOLF EMERT
Sec.-Gen.: ZDENKA BARIŠIĆ
Librarian: DRAGUTIN KATALENAC
Number of teachers: 523
Number of students: 13,214

Publications: *Ekonomski vjesnik* (Economic Courier), *Medicinski vjesnik* (Medical Courier), *Poljoprivreda* (Agriculture), *Pravni vjesnik* (Law Courier), *Sveučilišni Glasnik* (University Newsletter), *Tehnički vjesnik* (Technical Courier)

DEANS

Faculty of Agriculture: VLADO GUBERAC
Faculty of Civil Engineering: DAMIR MARKULAK
Faculty of Economics: ŽELJKO TURKALJ
Faculty of Electrical Engineering: RADOSLAV GALIĆ
Faculty of Food Technology: DRAGO ŠUBARIĆ
Faculty of Law: IGOR BOJANIĆ
Faculty of Mechanical Engineering: DRAŽAN KOZAK
Faculty of Medicine: ALEKSANDAR VČEV
Faculty of Philosophy: VIŠNJA PAVIČIĆ TAKAČ (acting)

Department of Mathematics: RUDOLF SCITOVSKI
Teacher Training College: ANĐELKA PEKO

PROFESSORS

Faculty of Agriculture (tel. (31) 224-200; fax (31) 207-017; e-mail nastava@suncokret.pfos.hr; internet www.pfos.hr):

BERTIĆ, B., Agrochemistry, Fertilizers
BUKVIĆ, Ž., Mechanization in Livestock Farming and Crop Production
EMERT, R., Agricultural Machinery and Maintenance
GUBERAC, V., Plant Breeding, Seed Science
IVEZIĆ, M., Entomology with Phytopharmacy and Plant Protection, Nematology
JOVANOVAC, S., General Livestock, Genetics of Domestic Animals
JURIĆ, I., Principles of Agriculture, Tropical Agriculture
JURKOVIĆ, D., Plant Protection, Phytopharmacy
KALINOVIĆ, I., Storage and Technology of Agricultural Products
KNEŽEVIĆ, I., Cattle Breeding
KNEŽEVIĆ, M., Botany
KOVAČEVIĆ, V., Cereal Crop Production
KRALIK, G., Husbandry of Swine, Poultry and Fur-bearing Animals
KRISTEK, A., Industrial Crops
MADJAR, S., Agricultural Improvement, Irrigation
MILAKOVIĆ, Z., Microbiology
RASTIJA, T., General Cattle and Horse Raising
SENČIĆ, D., Pig Breeding, Livestock Breeding
STEINER, Z., Nutrition of Domestic Animals
STJEPANOVIĆ, M., Forage Crops
VUKADINOVIĆ, V., Plant Physiology, Agricultural Mechanization
ZIMMER, R., Mechanization in Farming, Processing Technology and Storing
ŽUGEC, I., General Crop Production, Alternative Agriculture

Faculty of Civil Engineering (Drinska 16A, HR-31000 Osijek; tel. (31) 274-377; fax (31) 274-444; e-mail dekan@gfos.hr; internet www.gfos.hr):

ANIČIĆ, D., Surveying, Earthquake Engineering
MEDANIĆ, B., Construction Management
SIGMUND, V., Construction Stability and Dynamics, Resistance of Materials
TAKAČ, S., Wooden Buildings, Bricklaying

Faculty of Economics (Gajev trg 7, HR-31000 Osijek; tel. (31) 224-400; fax (31) 211-604; internet www.efos.hr):

BABAN, LJ., Theory of Marketing, International Economics
BARKOVIĆ, D., Operational Research
CRNJAC, M., Mathematics
JELINIĆ, S., Commercial Law
KARIĆ, M., Microeconomics, Cost Management, Accounting
LAMZA-MARONIĆ, M., Management and Information Systems
LAUC, A., Sociology of Management
MELER, M., Introduction to Marketing, Marketing Management
NOVAC, B., Finance Management, Financial Markets
PROKLIN, P., Accounting
SEGETLIJA, Z., Business Logistics, Branch Marketing
SINGER, S., Strategic Management
SRB, V., Finance, Public Finance, Banking
TURKALJ, Ž., Business Organization

Faculty of Electrical Engineering (Knezá Trpimira 2B, HR-31000 Osijek; tel. (31) 224-600; fax (31) 224-605; e-mail etf@etfos.hr; internet www.etfos.hr):

FLEGAR, I., Electronics, Networking Theory, Electrical Compatibility

GODEC, Z., Metrology, Monitoring
JOVIĆ, F., Information and Communications, Computers and Processes, Computer and Terminal Networks, Artificial Intelligence
ŠTEFANKO, S., Fundamentals of Electrical Engineering, Theoretical Electrical Engineering
ŠVEDEK, T., Electronic Components, Microelectronics, High-Frequency Electronics
VALTER, Z., Fundamentals of Electromechanical Engineering

Faculty of Food Technology (F. Kuhača 20, HR-31000 Osijek; tel. (31) 224-300; fax (31) 207-115; e-mail office@ptfos.hr; internet www.ptfos.hr):

MANDIĆ, M., Quality Control, Sensor Analyses, Fundamentals of Food Technology, Food Science
PILIŽOTA, V., Raw Materials in Food Industry, Technology of Fruit and Vegetable Preserving and Processing
ŠERUGA, M., Physical Chemistry, Packing Materials, Methods of Analysis by Instrument
UGARČIĆ-HARDI, Ž, Raw Materials in Food Industry, Flour Production and Processing

Faculty of Law (S. Radića 13, HR-31000 Osijek; tel. (31) 224-500; fax (31) 224-540; e-mail office@pravos.hr; internet www.pravos.hr):

BABAC, B., Administrative Law, Administrative Science
BELAJ, V., Civil Law
JELINIĆ, S., Commercial Law, Social Law, Copyright
KLASIČEK, D., International Law
LAUC, Z., Constitutional Law
LJUBANOVIĆ, V., Criminal Procedural Law
MECANOVIĆ, I., Constitutional Law, Informatics for Lawyers
ROMŠTAJN, I., Transport Law, Insurance Law
SRB, V., Financial Law and Sciences, Banking and Credit

Faculty of Mechanical Engineering (Trg I. B. Mažuranić 18, HR-35000 Slavonski Brod; tel. (35) 446-188; fax (35) 446-446; internet www.sfsb.hr):

BUDIĆ, I., Foundry, Processing Technology, Assembling Technology, Design
GRIZELJ, B., Metal Forming, Technology, Tools
HNATKO, E., Heat Engines and Devices
KATALINIĆ, B., Automation, Flexible Systems
KLJAJIN, M., Machine Elements, Technical Drafting
KRUMES, D., Materials, Heat Processing, Tribology, Surface Engineering, Tools
MAJDANDŽIĆ, N., Computers and Information Systems, Production Process, Artificial Intelligence, Planning Methods
MATEJIČEK, F., Mechanics, Engine Dynamics
RAOS, P., Polymer Processing, Machine Maintenance
VITEZ, I., Materials, New Technologies

Faculty of Medicine (J. Huttlera 4, HR-31000 Osijek; tel. (31) 512-800; fax (31) 512-833; e-mail ured@mefos.hr; internet www.mefos.hr):

BELICZA, B., History of Medicine, Medical Ethics
KOSTOVIĆ-KNEŽEVIĆ, LJ., Histology, Embryology
ŠESTO, M., Internal Medicine
SOLDO, I., Infectious Diseases
TUCAK, A., Urology, Civil War Medicine

Faculty of Philosophy (L. Jägera 9, HR-31000 Osijek; tel. (31) 211-400; fax (31) 212-514):

APARAC-JELUŠIĆ, T., Library Science, Informatics and Communication
BRLENIĆ-VUJIĆ, B., Comparative Literature
JERKOVIĆ, J., Conducting, Choir
MARIJANOVIĆ, S., Croatian Literature
NIKČEVIĆ, M., Methodology of Scientific Work, Methodics of Literature Teaching
OBAD, V., German Literature
ŽIVKOVIĆ, P., Medieval History

Department of Mathematics (Trg Lj. Gaja 6, HR-31000 Osijek; tel. (31) 224-800; fax (31) 224-801; e-mail math@mathos.hr; internet www.mathos.hr):

BUTKOVIĆ, D., Linear Algebra
SCITOVSKI, R., Numerical Mathematics, Computer Exercises II
SVRTAN, D., Theoretical Mechanics, Discrete Mathematics
VOLENEC, V., Geometry Models, Metric Geometry

Teacher Training College (L. Jägera 9, HR-31000 Osijek; tel. (31) 200-602; fax (31) 200-604; e-mail helpdesk@ufos.hr; internet www.ufos.hr):

BABIĆ, N., Pre-School Education, Teaching Methods in Pre-School Education, Education Communication

SVEUČILIŠTE JURJA DOBRILE U PULI
(Juraj Dobrila University of Pula)

Preradovićeva 1/1, HR-52100 Pula
Telephone: (52) 377-000
Fax: (52) 216-416
E-mail: ured@unipu.hr
Internet: www.unipu.hr
Founded 2006
Public control

Rector: ROBERT MATIJAŠIĆ
Vice-Rector for Education and Students: ĐENI DEKLEVA RADAKOVIĆ
Vice-Rector for Finance and Business Relationships: LOVRE BOŽINA
Vice-Rector for Scientific Research: MARLI GONAN BOŽAC
Vice-Rector for International Cooperation: ELVI PIRŠL

Library: see Libraries and Archives
Depts of economics and tourism, education and studies in Italian, humanities, music.

SVEUČILIŠTE U RIJECI
(University of Rijeka)

Trg braće Mažuranića 10, HR-51000 Rijeka
Telephone: (51) 406-500
Fax: (51) 406-588
E-mail: ured@uniri.hr
Internet: www.uniri.hr
Founded 1973
State control
Language of instruction: Croatian (and some courses in Italian)
Academic year: October to July

Rector: Prof. Dr PERO LUČIN (acting)
Vice-Rector: Prof. Dr GORAN KALOGJERA
Vice-Rector: Prof. Dr NEVENKA OŽANIĆ
Vice-Rector: Prof. Dr SNJEŽANA PRIJIĆ-SAMARŽIJA
Sec.-Gen.: ROBERTA HLAČA MLINAR
Librarians: BRUNO DOBRIĆ (Pula), SENKA TOMLJANOVIĆ (Rijeka)

Number of teachers: 928
Number of students: 19,139

Publications: Gaudeamus (irregular), Sveučilišni vodič (guide to curriculums, 1 a year)

DEANS

Academy of Applied Arts: Prof. ANTE VLADISLAVIĆ

Faculty of Civil Engineering in Rijeka: prof. Dr ALEKSANDRA DELUKA-TIBLJAS
Faculty of Economics and Tourism 'Dr Mijo Mirković' in Pula: Prof. Dr HERI BEZIC
Faculty of Economics in Rijeka: Prof. Dr VINKO KANDŽIJA
Faculty of Engineering in Rijeka: Prof. Dr TONČI MIKAC
Faculty of Law in Rijeka: Prof. Dr MIOMIR MATULOVIĆ
Faculty of Maritime Studies: Prof. SERDO KOS
Faculty of Medicine in Rijeka: Prof. Dr ALAN ŠUSTIC
Faculty of Philosophy in Pula: Assoc. Prof. Dr ROBERT MATIJAŠIĆ
Faculty of Philosophy in Rijeka: Prof. Dr PREDRAG ŠUSTAR
Faculty of Teacher Education: Prof. VINKA UZELAC

SVEUČILIŠTE U SPLITU
(University of Split)

Livanjska 5/I, HR-21000 Split
Telephone: (21) 558-200
Fax: (21) 348-163
E-mail: rektorat.office@unist.hr
Internet: www.unist.hr
Founded 1974
State control
Language of instruction: Croatian
Academic year: October to September

Rector: Prof. Dr IVAN PAVIĆ
Vice-Rectors: Prof. Dr IGOR ZANCHI, Prof. Dr ŽELKO DOMAZET, Prof. Dr ROKO ANDRIČEVIĆ, Prof. Dr DRAGAN BOLANČA, Prof. Dr ŠIMUN ANĐELINOVIĆ
Sec.-Gen.: JOSIP ALAJBEG
Library of 369,000 vols
Number of teachers: 1,500
Number of students: 17,000

Publication: Sveučilišni godišnjak

DEANS

Academy of Arts: Dr BRANKO MATULIĆ
Faculty of Catholic Theology: Dr NEDILJKO ANTE ANČIĆ
Faculty of Chemistry and Technology: Dr MLADEN MILOŠ
Faculty of Civil Engineering and Architecture: Dr BERNARDIN PEROŠ
Faculty of Economics: Dr BRANKO GRČIĆ
Faculty of Electrical, Mechanical and Naval Engineering: Dr TOMISLAV KILIĆ
Faculty of Kinesiology: NIKOLA RAUSAVLJEVIĆ
Faculty of Law: Dr BORIS BUKLIJAŠ
Faculty of Medicine: MATKO MARUŠIĆ
Faculty of Natural Sciences, Mathematics and Education: Dr ANKA GOLEMAC
Faculty of Philosophy: MARKO TROGRLIĆ
Faculty of Tourism and Foreign Trade (Dubrovnik): Dr DJURO BENIĆ
Maritime Faculty (Dubrovnik): Dr JOSIP LOVRIĆ

PROFESSORS

Academy of Arts (Glagoljaška bb, HR-21000 Split; tel. (21) 348-622; e-mail office@umas.hr; internet www.umas.hr):

BATOVIĆ, Š., Prehistoric Archaeology
BELOŠEVIĆ, J., Medieval Archaeology
CAMBJ, N., Classical and Old Christian Archaeology
ĆOSIĆ, V., French Language
DUKAT, Z., Greek Language and Literature
FRANIĆ, A., Modern Croatian Literature
GERERSDORFER, V., French Language and Medieval Literature
GRGIN, T., General and Systematic Psychology
JURIĆ, B., Political Economy and National Economic History
KALENIĆ, A. S., Latin Language and Literature

KOLUMBIĆ, N., Old Croatian Literature
MANENICA, I., Systematic Psychology
MIKIĆ, P., German Language
OBAD, S., Modern History
PEDERIN, S., German Literature
PETRICIOLI, I., Art History
SKLEDAR, N., Sociology
ZELIĆ, I., Visual Arts, Teaching Methods
ŽIVKOVIĆ, P., Croatian History up to 1918

Faculty of Chemistry and Technology (Teslina 10/V, HR-21000 Split; tel. (21) 329-420; fax (21) 329-461; e-mail office@ktf-split.hr; internet www.ktf-split.hr):

KOVAČIĆ, T., Polymers
KRSTULOVIĆ, R., Chemistry and Technology of Non-Metals
MEKJAVIĆ, I., Physical Chemistry
PETRIĆ, N., Thermodynamics
RADOŠEVIĆ, J., Electrochemistry
ROJE, U., Organic Industry – Technological Processes; Catalysis; Polymerization
VOJNOVIĆ, I., Materials and Energy Balance
ŽANETIĆ, R., Measuring and Process Operation

Faculty of Civil Engineering and Architecture (Matice Hrvatske 15, HR-21000 Split; tel. (21) 303-333; fax (21) 465-117; e-mail dekan@gradst.hr; internet www.gradst.hr):

BONACCI, O., Hydrology
DAMJANIĆ, F., Technical Mechanics
JOVIĆ, V., Hydromechanics
MARGETA, J., Water Supply
MAROVIĆ, P., Strength of Materials, Testing of Structures
MIHANOVIĆ, A., Mechanics, Stability and Dynamics of Structures
MILIČIĆ, J., Construction and Construction Machines
ŠESTANOVIĆ, S., Geology and Petrology
ŠKOMRLJ, J., Technology and Organization of Construction
STOJIĆ, P., Hydrotechnical Systems
VOJNOVIĆ, J., Building Construction
VRDOLJAK, B., Mathematics

Faculty of Economics (Matice Hrvatske 31, HR-21000 Split; tel. (21) 430-600; fax (21) 430-701; e-mail dekanat@efst.hr; internet www.efst.hr):

ANDRIJIĆ, S., Macroeconomics, Econometrics
BUBLE, M., Organization – Design, Job Evaluation
DOMANČIĆ, P., International Finance
DULČIĆ, A., Economics of Trade and Tourism
JELAVIĆ, A., Business Economics
LUKŠIĆ, B., Business Economics
ŠTAMBUK, D., Regional Economics

Faculty of Electrical, Mechanical and Naval Engineering (Ruđera Boškovića bb, HR-21000 Split; tel. (21) 305-777; fax (21) 463-877; e-mail dekanat@fesb.hr; internet www.fesb.hr):

DEŽELIĆ, R., Materials Technology
GRISOGONO, P., Industrial Furnaces and Fuels, Industrial Transportation
JADRIĆ, M., Electromagnetic Theory and Electrical Machinery
KURTOVIĆ, M., Asynchronous Machines, Electric Motor Plants, General Theory of Electric Machines
PILIĆ, L., Fluid Mechanics
SLAPNIČAR, P., Circuits

Faculty of Law (Domovinskog rata 8, HR-21000 Split; tel. (21) 393-500; fax (21) 393-572; e-mail dekanat@pravst.hr; internet www.pravst.hr):

BILIĆ, I., Political Economy
BORKOVIĆ, I., Administrative Law
BOSNIĆ, P., International Private Law
CARIĆ, A., Criminal Law
CVITAN, O., Administrative Sciences

DUJIĆ, A., Modern Political Systems
GRABOVAC, I., Maritime and Transport Law
PETRIĆ, I., Economic Politics
PETRINOVIĆ, I., History of Political Theories
RUDOLF, D., International Public Law
ŠMID, V., Civil Law
VISKOVIĆ, N., Theory of State and Law

Faculty of Natural Sciences, Mathematics and Education (Teslina 12/III, HR-21000 Split; tel. (21) 385-133; fax (21) 384-086; e-mail dekanat@pmfst.hr; internet www.pmfst.hr):

JAKELIĆ, P., Graphic Design
KALOGJERA, A., Methods of Education
KRSTULOVIĆ, I., Painting
MARASOVIĆ, T., Croatian and European Medieval Art
MIDŽOR, A., Sculpture
MILAT, J., General Pedagogy
OMAŠIĆ, V., History

Faculty of Tourism and Foreign Trade (Dubrovnik):

KONJHODŽIĆ, H., International Finance
MARKOVIĆ, M., Economics and Business Organization
PAPARELA, I., International Finance and Business Finance
REŠETAR, M., Travel Agency Management; Business Analysis
ŽABICA, T., Economic and Tourist Geography

Maritime Faculty (Zrinsko-Frankopanska 38, HR-21000 Split; tel. (21) 380-762; internet www.pfst.hr):

FABRIS, O., Thermodynamics; Ships' Refrigerating Plants
LOVRIĆ, J., Ship Maintenance
SJEKAVICA, I., Terrestrial Navigation

SVEUČILIŠTE U DUBROVNIKU
(University of Dubrovnik)

Branitelja Dubrovnika 29, HR-20000 Dubrovnik
Telephone: (20) 445-744
Fax: (20) 435-590
E-mail: rektorat@unidu.hr
Internet: www.unidu.hr
Founded 2003
Public control
Rector: MATEO MILKOVIĆ
Head Librarian: ANA PUJO

Library of 10,000 monographs, 4,000 projects, Masters and Doctoral dissertations, 43 Croatian magazines and 37 foreign-language magazines
Number of teachers: 160
Number of students: 2,600

Offers undergraduate programmes in art and restoration, aquaculture, economics and business studies, electrical engineering and computing and maritime studies, engineering; graduate programmes in communication technologies, media, public relations.

SVEUČILIŠTE U ZADRU
(University of Zadar)

Mihovila Pavlinovića bb, HR-23000 Zadar
Telephone: (23) 200-501
Fax: (23) 200-605
E-mail: rektorat@unizd.hr
Internet: www.unizd.hr
Founded 2003
State control
Academic year: October to June
Rector: Prof. Dr ANTE UGLEŠIĆ
Pro-Rector: Prof. Dr STIPE BELAK
Pro-Rector: Prof. Dr SREĆKO JELUŠIĆ
Pro-Rector: Prof. Dr VLADIMIR SKRAČIĆ
Pro-Rector: ANA PROROKOVIĆ
Sec.-Gen.: ANTONELLA LOVRIĆ

Librarian: MIRTA MATOŠIĆ
Library of 110,000 vols, 22,000 periodicals, 1,050 MSS
Number of teachers: 365
Number of students: 5,945

Depts of agriculture and Mediterranean aquaculture, archaeology, classical philology, Croatian and Slavic studies, economy, English language and literature, ethnology and cultural antrophology, French language and literature, geography, German language and literature, health studies, history, history of art, information and communication studies, Italian language and literature, linguistics, librarianship and information studies, pedagogy, philosophy, psychology, sociology, teacher and preschool teacher's training, transport and maritime studies.

SVEUČILIŠTE U ZAGREBU
(University of Zagreb)

Trg maršala Tita 14, HR-10000 Zagreb
Telephone: (1) 4564-111
Fax: (1) 4830-602
E-mail: office@unizg.hr
Internet: www.unizg.hr
Founded 1669
Academic year: October to September
Language of instruction: Croatian
Rector: Prof. ALEKSA BJELIŠ
Vice-Rector for Devt and Spatial Planning: Prof. BOJAN BALETIĆ
Vice-Rector for Financing: Prof. TONKO ĆURKO
Vice-Rector for Int. and Inter-institutional Cooperation: Prof. KSENIJA TURKOVIC
Vice-Rector for Science and Technology: Prof. MELITA KOVACEVIC
Vice-Rector for Teaching and Quality Assurance: Prof. LJILJANA PINTER
Chief Admin. Officer: ANA RUŽIČKA

Number of teachers: 4,500
Number of students: 63,000

Publication: Sveučilišni vjesnik (University Herald)

DEANS

Agriculture: Prof. DAVOR ROMIĆ
Architecture: Prof. LENKO PLEŠTINA
Catholic Theology: Dr JOSIP OSLIĆ
Chemical Engineering and Technology: Prof. STANISLAV KURAJICA
Civil Engineering: Prof. MLADEN RADUJKOVIĆ
Defectology: Dr BRANKO RADOVANČIĆ
Dental Medicine: DRAGUTIN KOMAR
Economic Sciences: Dr IVAN LOVRINOVIĆ
Education and Rehabilitation Sciences: DRAŽENKA BLAŽI
Electrical Engineering and Computing: Prof. VEDRAN MORNAR
Food Technology and Biotechnology: Prof. DAMIR JEŽEK
Forestry: Prof. ANDRIJA BOGNER
Geodesy: Prof. STANISLAV FRANGEŠ
Geotechnical Engineering (in Varaždin): Prof. MLADEN BOŽIČEVIĆ
Graduate School of Economics and Business: VLADIMIR ŠIMOVIĆ
Graphic Arts: Prof. DIANA MILČIĆ
Kinesiology: Prof. IGOR JUKIĆ
Law: Prof. ŽELJKO POTOČNJAK
Mechanical Engineering and Naval Architecture: Prof. IZVOR GRUBIŠIĆ
Medicine: Dr DAVOR MILIČIĆ
Metallurgy (in Sisak): Prof. FARUK UNKIĆ
Mining, Geology and Petroleum Engineering: Dr BILJANA KOVAČEVIĆ-ZELIĆ
Natural Sciences and Mathematics: Dr IVAN VICOKOVIĆ
Organization and Informatics (in Varaždin): Dr TIHOMIR HUNJAK
Pharmacy and Biochemistry: Dr NIKOLA KUJUNDŽIĆ

Philosophy: Prof. DAMIR BORAS
Physical Education: Dr MATO BARTOLUCI
Political Sciences: Prof. VLATKO CVRTILA
Science: Prof. MLADEN JURAČIĆ
Stomatology: Dr VLADO CAREK
Teacher Education: Prof. VLADIMIR ŠIMOVIĆ
Textile Technology: Prof. DARKO UJEVIĆ
Transport and Traffic Engineering: Prof. Dr IVAN DADIĆ
Veterinary Medicine: Prof. VELIMIR SUSIC
Academy of Dramatic Arts: Prof. ENES MIDŽIĆ
Academy of Fine Arts: Prof. SLAVOMIR DRINKOVIĆ
Academy of Music: Prof. MLADEN JANJANIN
Graduate School of Economics and Business: Prof. MELITA KOVAČEVIĆ (acting)
Medical School: Prof. DAVOR MILIČIĆ
School of Dental Medicine: Prof. DRAGUTIN KOMAR
University Centre for Croatian Studies: Prof. ZVONIMIR ČULJAK, (Head)

Colleges

Američka visoka škola za management i tehnologiju (American College of Management and Technology): Don Frana Bulića 6, HR-20000 Dubrovnik; tel. (20) 433-000; fax (20) 433-001; e-mail american.college@acmt.hr; internet www.acmt.hr; f. 1997 by the Min. of Science, Education and Sports in collaboration with the Rochester Institute of Technology (USA); Private control; undergraduate programmes in service management and information technology and postgraduate programmes in human resource development and service leadership and innovation; 1,500 students; Pres. and Dean DON HUDSPETH.

Inter-University Centre Dubrovnik: Don Frana Bulića 4, HR-20000 Dubrovnik; tel. (20) 413-626; fax (20) 413-628; e-mail iuc@iuc.hr; internet www.iuc.hr; f. 1972; ind. instn for int. cooperation in teaching and research; courses in crime prevention through criminal law and security studies, organization theory, social philosophy and philosophy of science; library: 10,000 vols; Chair. of Council FRANK LAUBERT (University of Hamburg, Germany); Dir-Gen. Prof. KRUNOSLAV PISK (University of Dubrovnik, Croatia); Deputy Dir-Gen. Prof. PETER KAMPITS (University of Vienna, Austria).

Međunarodna diplomska škola za poslovno upravljanje Zagreb (International Graduate Business School Zagreb): Trg J. F. Kennedya 7, HR-10000 Zagreb; tel. (1) 2314-990; fax (1) 2335-165; e-mail mba@igbs.hr; internet www.igbs.hr; Private control; offers courses in business ethics and law, corporate finance, entrepreneurship and strategic management, European economic policy, financial and managerial accounting, human resources, int. financial strategy and intermediation, int. macroeconomics, investments, managerial economics, marketing strategy, new product management, operations management, quantitative analysis, retailing; Dean ZLATAN FRÖHLICH.

Visoko Gospodarsko Učilište u Križevcima (College of Agriculture at Križevci): Milislava Demerca 1, HR-48260 Križevci; tel. (48) 681-597; fax (48) 682-790; e-mail dekan@vguk.hr; internet www.vguk.hr; f. 1860; graduate and professional programmes in farm management, plant production and zoology; library: 10,000 vols; Dean Dr VINKO PINTIĆ; Head of Library SANDRA KANTAR.

Polytechnics

Tehničko veleučilište u Zagrebu (Technical Polytechnic in Zagreb): Vrbik 8, HR-10000 Zagreb; tel. (1) 5603-900; fax (1) 5603-999; e-mail tvz@tvz.hr; internet www.tvz.hr; f. 1998; programmes in computing and mechanical engineering, construction, electrical engineering, informatics; 5,400 students; Dean Dr MLADEN PETRIČEC.

Veleučilište 'Marko Marulić' u Kninu (Marko Marulić Polytechnic in Knin): Petra Krešimira IV 30, HR-22300 Knin; tel. (22) 664-450; fax (22) 661-374; e-mail info@veleknin.hr; internet www.veleknin.hr; f. 2005; Public control.

Veleučilište u Karlovcu (Karlovac University of Applied Sciences): *Campus 1*: Ivana Meštrovića 10, HR-47000 Karlovac; *Campus 2*: Josipa Juraja Strossmayera 9, HR-47000 Karlovac; tel. (47) 843-500; fax (47) 843-579; e-mail dekanat@vuka.hr; internet www.vuka.hr; Public control; depts of business, food technology, hunting and nature production, mechanical engineering, security and protection, textiles; Dean Prof. Dr ANTUN ALEGRO; Sec.-Gen. MILAN VIGNJEVIĆ.

Veleučiliste u Požegi (Požega Polytechnic): Vukovarska 17, HR-34000 Požega; tel. (34) 271-018; fax (34) 271-008; e-mail knjiznica@vup.hr; internet www.vup.hr; Public control; f. 1998; depts of agriculture and social sciences; library: 32,000 books; 2,000 students; Dean IVAN BUDIĆ; Sec. JASMINA SMOLČIĆ; Librarian Prof. ANTONIO VALEŠIĆ.

Veleučilište u Rijeci (Rijeka Polytechnic): Trpimirova 2/V, HR-51000 Rijeka; tel. (51) 321-300; fax (51) 211-270; e-mail ured@veleri.hr; internet www.veleri.hr; Private control; f. 2008; depts of business, traffic, agriculture and security studies; library: 3,600 vols, 14 foreign and 30 domestic periodicals; Dean Prof. Dr DUŠAN RUDIĆ; Sec. BORIS SERGOVIĆ.

Veleučilište u Šibeniku (Šibenik Polytechnic): Trg Andrije Hebranga 11, Šibenik; tel. (22) 311-060; fax (22) 216-716; internet www.vus.hr; Public control; depts of administration, management and traffic studies.

Veleučilište u Varaždinu (Varaždin Polytechnic): Križanićeva 33, HR-42000 Varaždin, Varaždinska; tel. (42) 493-338; fax (42) 493-333; e-mail tajnistvo@velv.hr; internet www.velv.hr; Private control; f. 2001; programmes in automation, construction, design and implementation, electrical engineering, multimedia, nursing, production engineering; Dean Dr MARIN MILKOVIĆ.

Veleučilište Velika Gorica (Velika Gorica University of Applied Sciences): Zagrebačka cesta 5, HR-10410 Velika Gorica; tel. (1) 6222-501; fax (1) 7897-645; e-mail info@vvg.hr; internet www.vvg.hr; Private control; professional programmes in computer systems maintenance, crisis management, aircraft maintenance, motor vehicle maintenance and eye optics; spec. programmes in crisis management and logistics, information systems; 920 students; Dean Prof. IVAN TOTH.

CUBA

The Higher Education System

The oldest university is the Universidad de la Habana, which was founded in 1728 while Cuba was governed by Spain. Control of the island was ceded to the USA in 1898 and independence was gained in 1902. Most universities have been founded since 1959, when guerrilla forces led by Dr Fidel Castro Ruz seized control of government. State education in Cuba is universal and free at all levels. Education is based on Marxist-Leninist principles and combines study with manual work. Higher education institutions include universities, centros universitarios (university centres), institutos superiores politécnicos (higher polytechnic institutes) and institutos superiores (higher institutes). Workers attending university courses receive a state subsidy to provide for their dependants. Courses at intermediate and higher levels lay an emphasis on technology, agriculture and teacher training. In 2008/09 there were an estimated 710,978 students in tertiary education.

Admission to higher education is based on completion of upper secondary education and results of the national competitive entrance examination. The main undergraduate qualification is the Licenciado, which is awarded after five years of study. Courses may also lead to a professional title, such as Ingeniero (Engineer), Contador (Accountant), Estomatólogo (Dentist) or Arquitecto (Architect). Between undergraduate and doctoral-level studies there is a Masters-level qualification, Título de Máster. The first doctoral-level qualification is the Doctor en Ciencias Específicas, which requires three to four years' study. The second (and final) doctoral-level degree is the Doctor en Ciencias, awarded after additional years of research, published and defended before a jury. Technical and vocational education is offered at the secondary level and higher.

The Junta de Acreditación Nacional (JAN) was established in 1999 as the national umbrella organization responsible for quality assurance, accreditation and evaluation of all tertiary institutions and programmes.

Regulatory and Representative Bodies

GOVERNMENT

Ministry of Culture: Calle 2, No 258, entre 11 y 13, Plaza de la Revolución, Vedado, Havana 10400; tel. (7) 55-2260; fax (7) 66-2053; e-mail atencion@min.cult.cu; internet www.min.cult.cu; Minister ABEL ENRIQUE PRIETO JIMÉNEZ.

Ministry of Education: Obispo 160, Havana; tel. (7) 61-4888; internet www .rimed.cu; Minister LUIS IGNACIO GÓMEZ GUTIÉRREZ.

Ministry of Higher Education: Calle 23, No 565 Of, esq. a F, Vedado, Havana; tel. (7) 55-2335; fax (7) 33-4390; e-mail vecino@reduniv.edu.cu; internet www.mes.edu.cu; Minister JUAN VELA VALDÉS.

NATIONAL BODY

Consejo Nacional de Universidades (National University Council): Ministerio de Educación Superior, Ciudad Libertad, Havana 1; f. 1960; coordinating body for educational and scientific activities and for the admin. of the 4 nat. univs; Pres. JOSÉ RAMÓN FERNÁNDEZ; Sec. Ing. MIGUEL MARRERO VALLET.

Learned Societies

GENERAL

Academia de Ciencias de Cuba (Cuban Academy of Sciences): Industria y San José, Capitolio Nacional, Habana Vieja, Havana 12400; tel. (7) 862-6545; fax (7) 867-0599; e-mail alejandro@academiaciencias.cu; internet www.academiaciencias.cu; f. 1861; attached research institutes: see Research Institutes; National Archive: see Libraries and Archives; Pres. Dr ISMAEL CLARK; publs *Boletín del Archivo Nacional* (1 a year), *Estudios de Historia de la Ciencia y la Tecnología* (1 a year), *Estudios de Política Científica y Tecnología* (1 a year), *Boletín Señal* (52 a year), *Boletín de Síntesis*, *Cablegráfica* (12 a year), *Revista Ciencias*

Técnicas, Físicas y Matemáticas (2 a year), *Revista Ciencias Biológicas* (2 a year), *Revista Ciencias de la Tierra y del Espacio* (2 a year), *Actas Botánicas Cubanas* (1 a year), *Poeyana* (1 a year), *Revista Cubana de Ciencias Sociales* (2 a year), *Datos Astronómicos para Cuba* (1 a year), *Datos Astronómicos para el Caribe* (2 a year), *Boletín Climática* (1 a year), *Boletín Meteorológico Marino* (3 a year), *Revista Cubana de Meteorología* (2 a year), *Resumen Climático de Cuba* (1 a year), *Boletín Oficial de la ONIITEM* (1 a year), *Revista Ciencia de la Información* (4 a year), *Directorio Biotec* (1 a year), *Anuario L L. sobre estudios Lingüísticos*, *Anuario L.L. sobre estudios Literarios*, *Tablas de Mareas* (1 a year).

Ateneo de La Habana (Havana Athenaeum): San Martín 258, Havana; f. 1902; Sec. Dr JOSÉ ENRIQUE HEYMANN Y DE LA GÁNDARA.

Casa de las Américas (House of the Americas): Calle 3ra esquina a G, El Vedado, Havana 10400; tel. (7) 838-2706; fax (7) 834-4554; e-mail presidencia@casa.cult.cu; internet www.casa.cult.cu; f. 1959; cultural instn supporting Latin American literature, art and science; organizes festivals, exhibitions, conferences; maintains the 'José Antonio Echeverría' public library; documentary centre; Pres. ROBERTO FERNÁNDEZ RETAMAR; publs *Anales del Caribe* (1 a year), *Boletín de Música* (2 a year), *Casa de las Américas* (3 a year), *Conjunto* (4 a year), *Criterios* (1 a year).

EDUCATION

UNESCO Office Havana and Regional Bureau for Culture in Latin America and the Caribbean: Calzada 551— Esq. a D, Vedado, Havana; tel. (7) 32-2840; fax (7) 33-3144; e-mail habana@unesco.org; internet www.unesco.org.cu; f. 1950; designated Cluster Office for Cuba, Dominican Republic and Haiti; Dir FRANCISCO JOSÉ LACAYO PARAJON.

LANGUAGE AND LITERATURE

Academia Cubana de la Lengua (Cuban Academy of Language): Centro Cultural Dulce María Loynaz, Calle E 502, entre calles 17 y 19, Vedado, 10400 Havana; tel. (7) 835-2732; e-mail acadcuba@cenyai.inf.cu;

f. 1926; corresp. of the Real Academia Española (Madrid); Dir ROBERTO FERNÁNDEZ RETAMAR; Sec. MARLEN DOMÍNGUEZ HERNÁNDEZ.

Alliance Française: Calle J N° 302 esq. a 15 Vedado, Havana; tel. (7) 833-3370; fax (7) 833-1105; e-mail dgafcuba@enet.cu; offers courses and exams in French language and culture and promotes cultural exchange with France; attached office in Santiago; Prin. ANDRE DE UBEDA.

British Council: 7ma Avda, e/ Calle 34 y 36, Miramar, Havana; tel. (7) 207-9605; fax (7) 214-2218; e-mail information@cu .britishcouncil.org; internet www .britishcouncil.org/cuba; offers courses and exams in English language and British culture and promotes cultural exchange with the UK; Dir JENNY WHITE.

Unión de Escritores y Artistas de Cuba (Writers' and Artists' Union of Cuba): Calle 17 No. 351, Vedado, Havana; tel. (7) 53-5081; fax (7) 33-3158; internet www.uneac.com; f. 1961; 4,589 mems; Pres. CARLOS MARTÍ BRENES; Exec. Sec. MARTIZA HERNANDEZ; publs *Ediciones Unión* (12 a year), *La Gaceta de Cuba* (4 a year), *Literatura Cubana* (2 a year).

MEDICINE

Sociedad Cubana de Historia de la Medicina (Cuban Society for the History of Medicine): Calle L No. 406 esq. 23 y 25, Vedado, Havana 4; e-mail amaro@abril.sld .cu; Pres. Dr RUBÉN RODRÍGUEZ GAVALDÁ; Sec. Dra MARÍA DEL CARMEN AMARO CANO; publ. *Cuadernos*.

Sociedad Cubana de Radiología (Cuban Radiology Society): Calle L 406 esq. 23 y 25, Vedado, Havana 10400; tel. (7) 77-6077; fax (7) 33-5036; e-mail jbanasco@infomed.sld.cu; f. 1968; 200 mems; Pres. Prof. Dr CARLOS UGARTE; Sec. Prof. Dr JORGE BANASCO.

Research Institutes

AGRICULTURE, FISHERIES AND VETERINARY SCIENCE

Centro de Investigaciónes para el Mejoramiento Animal (Research Centre for the Improvement of Livestock): Carretera Central Km 21½, Loma de Tierra, Cotorro, Havana 14000; tel. and fax (7) 57-9408; f. 1970; library of 4,600 vols; Dir JOSÉ R. MORALES; publ. *Revista Cubana de Reproducción Animal* (2 a year).

Centro de Investigaciones Pesqueras (Fisheries Research Centre): Barlovento, Santa Fé, Playa, Havana; tel. (2) 09-7875; fax (2) 04-9827; f. 1959; research on fisheries, marine aquaculture, fish-processing technology; training courses; library of 4,230 vols, 1,500 periodicals; Gen. Dir Dr TIZOL CORREA RAFAEL; publs *Ciencia y Tecnología Pesquera* (4 a year), *Revista Cubana de Investigaciones Pesqueras*.

Estación Experimental Apícola (Experimental Station for Beekeeping): Arroyo Arenas, El Cano, La Lisa, Havana 19190; tel. (7) 202-0027; fax (7) 202-0950; e-mail eeapi@ceniai.inf.cu; f. 1982; library of 2,443 vols; Dir MSc ADOLFO M. PÉREZ PIÑEIRO; publs *Apiciencia* (research, 3 a year), *Boletín Apiciencia* (for beekeepers, 4 a year).

Instituto Cubano de Investigaciones de los Derivados de la Caña de Azúcar (ICIDCA) (Cuban Institute for Research on Sugar Cane By-products): Vía Blanca y Carretera Central 804, Apdo 4026, San Miguel del Padrón, Havana; tel. (7) 55-7015; fax (7) 98-8653; e-mail icidca@ceniai.inf.cu; internet www.icidca.cu; f. 1963; library of 7,000 vols; Dir LUIS O. GÁLVEZ TAUPIER; publ. *Sobre los derivados de la Caña de Azúcar* (4 a year).

Instituto de Investigaciones Agropecuarias 'Jorge Dimitrov' (Jorge Dimitrov Livestock Research Institute): Carretera a Manzanillo Km 16½, Gaveta Postal 2140, Bayamo, Granma; tel. (23) 5239; e-mail dimitrov@dimitrov.granma.inf.cu; attached to Cuban Acad. of Sciences; Dir Dr ISMAEL LEONARD ACOSTA.

Instituto de Investigaciones Avícolas (Poultry Research Institute): Gaveta Postal 1, 17200 Santiago de las Vegas, Havana; tel. (7) 683-9040; fax (7) 683-9034; e-mail viiacan@ceniai.inf.cu; internet www.iia.cu; f. 1976; Dir Dr SAÚL AMIGO DELGADO; publ. *Revista Cubana de Ciencia Avícola* (2 a year).

Instituto de Investigaciones de Sanidad Vegetal (Plant Health Research Institute): Calle 110 No. 514 entre 5ta B y 5ta F, Miramar, Playa, Havana CP 11600; tel. (7) 202-2516; fax (7) 202-9366; e-mail administrador@inisav.cu; internet www.inisav.cu; f. 1970; Dir Dr JORGE OVIES DIAZ; publ. *Fitosanidad* (4 a year).

Instituto de Investigaciones en Viandas Tropicales (Research Institute for Tropical Vegetables): Apdo 6, Santo Domingo 53000, Villa Clara; tel. (42) 40-3103; fax (42) 40-3689; e-mail invivit@ip.etecsa.cu; f. 1967; tropical root and tuber crops, bananas and plantains; library of 14,439 vols; Dir Dr SERGIO RODRIGUEZ MORALES; publ. *Agrotecnia de Cuba*.

Instituto de Investigaciones Forestales (Institute of Forestry Research): Calle 174 No. 1723 e/ 17-B y 17-C, Siboney, Playa, Havana; tel. (7) 208-2189; e-mail direccion@forestales.co.cu; f. 1969; attached to Cuban Acad. of Sciences; library of 10,000 vols; Dir HUMBERTO GARCÍA CORRALES; publ. *Revista Forestal Baracoa* (2 a year).

Instituto de Investigaciones Fundamentales en Agricultura Tropical 'Alejandro de Humboldt' (Alexander von Humboldt Institute of Basic Research in Tropical Agriculture): Calle 2, esq. a 1, Santiago de las Vegas, Havana 17200; tel. (7) 57-9010; fax (7) 57-9014; e-mail yamiletrst@inifat.esihabana.cu; f. 1904; library of 2,600 vols; Dir Dr ADOLFO RODRÍGUEZ NODALS; publ. *Agrotecnia de Cuba*.

Instituto de Investigaciones Porcinas (Pig Research Institute): Carretera del Guatao Km 5½, Punta Brava, Bauta, Havana; e-mail iip00@ceniai.inf.cu; internet www.iip.co.cu; f. 1972.

HISTORY, GEOGRAPHY AND ARCHAEOLOGY

Instituto de Geografía Tropical (Institute of Tropical Geography): Calle 13 No. 409 esquina F. Vedado, Plaza de la Revolución, Havana 10400; tel. (7) 832-4295; fax (7) 836-3174; e-mail geotrop@ama.cu; internet www.geotech.cu; f. 1962; attached to Min. of Science, Technology and Environment; 122 mems; Dir Dra MARLEN MARTHA PALET RABAZA.

LANGUAGE AND LITERATURE

Instituto de Literatura y Lingüística 'José Antonio Portuondo Valdor' (José Antonio Portuondo Valdor Institute of Literature and Linguistics): Ave. Salvador Allende 710 e/ Soledad y Castillejo, Centro, Havana 10300; tel. (7) 878-6486; fax (7) 873-5718; e-mail ill@ceniai.inf.cu; internet www.ill.cu; f. 1965; attached to Min. of Science, Technology and Environment; Dir Dra NURIA GREGORI TORADA; publs *Anuario* (linguistics edition, 1 a year), *Anuario* (literature edition, 1 a year).

MEDICINE

Centro Ingeniería Genética y Biotecnología de Cuba (Centre for Genetic Engineering and Biotechnology of Cuba): Ave 31e 160 y 190, Rpto Cubanacán, Playa, Havana; internet www.cigb.edu.cu; f. 1986; research, devt, production and commercial applications of biotechnology; vaccine research; Dir-Gen. Dr LUIS HERRERA MARTINEZ; publ. *Biotecnología Aplicada*.

Centro Nacional de Información de Ciencias Médicas (CNICM) (National Centre for Information on Medical Science): Calle E No. 454 e/ 19 y 21, El Vedado, 10400 Havana; tel. (7) 32-2004; fax (7) 33-3063; e-mail webmaster@infomed.sld.cu; internet www.sld.cu/cnicm.html; Dir Dr JEREMÍAS HERNÁNDEZ OJITO; publ. *Revista Cubana de Medicina*.

Instituto Nacional de Higiene, Epidemiología y Microbiología (National Institute of Hygiene, Epidemiology and Microbiology): Infanta 1158 e/ Llinás y Clavel, Centro, 10300 Havana; tel. (7) 870-5723; fax (7) 33-3063; internet www.sld.cu/webs/epidem; f. 1943; attached to Min. of Public Health; library of 3,000 vols; Dir Dr MARIANO BONET.

Instituto Nacional de Oncología y Radiobiología de La Habana (National Institute of Oncology and Radiobiology in Havana): Calle 29 y F, Vedado, 10400 Havana; tel. (7) 55-2577; fax (7) 55-2587; e-mail dinor@infomed.sld.cu; f. 1961; library of 2,700 vols; Dir Dr ALBERTO CÉSPEDES CARRILLO; publ. *Revista Cubana de Oncología*.

NATURAL SCIENCES

General

Centro Nacional de Investigaciones Científicas (National Centre for Scientific Research): Ave 25 No. 15202 esq. 158, Reparto Cubanacán, Playa, 12100 Havana; tel. (7) 271-4453; fax (7) 208-0497; internet www.cnic.edu.cu; f. 1969; natural, biomedical and technological sciences, development of medicines and medical equipment; postgraduate education; library of 100,000 vols; Dir Dr CARLOS GUTIERREZ CALZADO; publs *Revista CENIC Ciencias Biológicas* (3 a year), *Revista CENIC Ciencias Químicas* (3 a year).

Instituto de Oceanología (Institute of Oceanology): Ave. 1ra. No. 18406 entre 184 y 186, Rpto. Flores, Playa, 12100 Havana; tel. (7) 21-6008; fax (7) 33-9112; e-mail oceano@oceano.inf.cu; f. 1965; attached to Min. of Science, Technology and Environment; Dir Lic. JUAN PÉREZ; publ. *Avicennia*.

Biological Sciences

Centro Nacional de Producción de Animales de Laboratorio (CENPALAB) (National Centre for the Production of Laboratory Animals): Carretera El Cacahual Km 2½ AP 3, Bejucal, La Habana; e-mail ccalidad@cenpalab.inf.cu; f. 1982; attached to Cuban Acad. of Sciences; Dir Dr LEONARDO CABEZAS RODRÍGUEZ.

Mathematical Sciences

Centro de Estudios de Población y Desarrollo (CEPDE) (Centre for Population and Development Studies): Oficina Nacional de Estadísticas, Paseo 60 e/ 3ra y 5ta, Vedado, Plaza de la Revolución, 10400 Havana; tel. (7) 830-0053; e-mail oneweb@one.gov.cu; attached to National Statistical Office; Dir Dr JUAN CARLOS ALFONSO FRAGA.

Physical Sciences

Centro de Investigaciones para la Indústria Minero-Metalúrgica (Research Centre for the Mineral and Metallurgical Industry): Finca la Luisa, Carretera Varona 12028, Boyeros, A. P. 8067, Havana; tel. (7) 44-2313; fax (7) 57-8082; e-mail cipimm@chab.minbas.cu; attached to Min. of Basic Industry; Dir Dr EDUARDO ACEVEDO DEL MONTE.

Centro Nacional de Investigaciones Sismológicas (CENAIS (National Centre for Seismological Research): Ministerio de Ciencia Tecnología y Medio Ambiente, Calle 17 No. 61 e/ 4 y 6, Vista Alegre, 90400 Santiago de Cuba; tel. (226) 4-1623; fax (226) 4-1579; e-mail cenais@cenais.ciges.inf.cu; f. 1992; Dir Ing. LUIS SIERRA QUESADA.

Instituto de Cibernética, Matemática y Física (ICIMAF) (Institute of Cybernetics, Mathematics and Physics): Calle 15 No. 551 e/ C y D, Vedado, Havana; tel. (7) 832-7764; fax (7) 833-3373; e-mail icimaf@icmf.inf.cu; internet www.icmf.inf.cu; f. 1964; attached to Cuban Acad. of Sciences; Dir Ing. RAIMUNDO FRANCO PARELLADA.

Instituto de Geofísica y Astronomía (Institute of Geophysics and Astronomy): Calle 212 No. 2906, Marianao, Havana; tel. (7) 271-4331; e-mail lpalacio@iga.cu; internet www.iga.cu; f. 1974; attached to Min. of Science, Technology and Environment; library of 1,000 vols; Dir Dra LOURDES PALACIO SUÁREZ; publ. *Datos Astronómicos para Cuba* (1 a year).

Instituto de Meteorología (INSMET) (Institute of Meteorology): Apdo 17032, Loma de Casablanca, Regla, 11700 Havana; tel. (7) 61-7500; fax (7) 867-0711; e-mail meteoro@met.inf.cu; internet www.met.inf.cu; attached to Min. of Science, Technology and Environment; Dir Dr TOMÁS GUTIERREZ PÉREZ; publs *Boletín Meteorológico Marino* (2 a year), *Revista Cubana de Meteorología* (2 a year).

PHILOSOPHY AND PSYCHOLOGY

Instituto de Filosofía (Institute of Philosophy): Calzada No. 251 esq. J., Vedado, Havana 10400; tel. (7) 832-1887; e-mail instituto@filosofia.cu; internet www.filosofia .cu; f. 1966; attached to Cuban Acad. of Sciences; library of 3,000 vols; Dir Dra CONCEPCIÓN NIEVES AYÚS; publs *Revista Cubana de Ciencias Sociales* (2 a year), *Revista Cubana de Filosofía* (online, 3 a year).

RELIGION, SOCIOLOGY AND ANTHROPOLOGY

Centro de Antropología (Centre for Anthropology): Calzada de Buenos Aires 111 e/ Agua Dulce y Diana, Cerro, 10600 Havana; tel. (7) 33-5514; fax (7) 33-8054; e-mail antropol@ceniai.inf.cu; attached to Min. of Science, Technology and Environment; Dir Dra LOURDES SERRANO PERALTA.

Centro de Investigaciones Psicológicas y Sociológicas (CIPS) (Centre for Research in Psychology and Sociology): Calle B No. 352 esq. 15, Vedado, Havana; tel. (7) 830-1451; fax (7) 33-4327; internet www.cips.cu; attached to Min. of Science, Technology and Environment; undertakes socio-psychological surveys which relate to social politics in Cuba and the means of ensuring the participation of workers in the different levels of social planning; Dir Lic. ANGELA CASAÑAS MATA.

TECHNOLOGY

Centro de Desarrollo Científico de Montañas (Centre for the Scientific Development of Mountainous Regions): Matazón, Sabaneta, El Salvador, Guantanamo; tel. (21) 9-9230; attached to Cuban Acad. of Sciences; Dir Ing. FRANCISCO VELÁZQUEZ RODRÍGUEZ.

Centro de Desarrollo de Equipos e Instrumentos Científicos (CEDEIC) (Centre for the Development of Scientific Equipment and Instruments): Luz 375 e/ Compostela y Picota, 10100 Havana; tel. (7) 61-2846; fax (7) 33-8707; e-mail cedeic@ ceniai.inf.cu; attached to Cuban Acad. of Sciences; laser technology and its application in medicine, nutrition and electronics; Dir Ing. LUIS EMILIO GARCÍA MAGARINO.

Centro de Diseño de Sistemas Automatizados de Computación (CEDISAC) (Centre for the Design of Automated Computer Systems): Ave. 47 e/ 18A y 20, Aptdo Postal 604, Miramar, 11300 Havana; tel. (7) 23-5153; fax (7) 24-8202; e-mail cdisac@ ceniai.inf.cu; attached to Cuban Acad. of Sciences; Dir Dra BEATRIZ ALONSO BECERRA.

Centro de Investigaciones de Energía Solar (Centre for Research into Solar Energy): Micro 3 Reparto 'Abel Santamaría', Santiago de Cuba 90800; tel. and fax (226) 7-1131; e-mail relinter@cies.ciges.inf.cu; f. 1986; attached to Min. of Science, Technology and Environment; Dir Ing. ORLANDO LASTRES DANGUILLECOURT.

Centro de Investigaciones para la Industria Minero Metalúrgica (Research Centre of the Metal-Mining Industry): Finca 'La Luisa' Km 1½, Carretera Varona No. 12028, Apdo 8067, Boyeros, Havana; tel. and fax (7) 57-8082; internet www.camaracuba .cu; f. 1967; library of 4,000 vols; Dir Dr EDUARDO ACEVEDO; publs *Infomin* (bulletin, 12 a year), *Resenas*, *Revista Tecnológica* (3 a year).

Libraries and Archives

Havana

Archivo Nacional de Cuba (Cuban National Archive): Compostela 906 esq. a San Isidro, Havana 10100; tel. (7) 862-9436; fax (7) 33-8089; e-mail arnac@ceniai.inf.cu; internet www.ceniai.inf.cu/ciencia/citma/aid/ archivo; f. 1840; 25,000 linear metres of archive material; 12,834 vols, 675 periodicals; Dir Dra BERARDA SALABARRÍA ABRAHAM; publ. *Boletín* (1 a year).

Biblioteca Central 'Rubén Martínez Villena' de la Universidad de la Habana (Rubén Martínez Villena Central Library of the University of Havana): Calle San Lázaro y L, Municipio Plaza de la Revolución, Havana; tel. (7) 78-1230; fax (7) 33-5774; e-mail susan@dict.uh.cu; internet www.dict .uh.cu; f. 1728; 945,000 vols; Dir Lic. BÁRBARA SUSANA SÁNCHEZ VIGNAU; publs *Revista Cubana de Educación Superior* (3 a year), *Revista Cubana de Física* (2 a year), *Revista Cubana de Psicología* (3 a year), *Revista Debates Americanos* (2 a year), *Revista de Biología* (1 a year), *Revista de Ciencias Matemáticas* (2 a year), *Revista del Jardín Botánico Nacional* (1 a year), *Revista de Investigaciones Marinas* (3 a year), *Revista Economía y Desarrollo* (2 a year), *Revista Investigación Operacional* (3 a year), *Revista Universidad de la Habana* (2 a year).

Biblioteca del Instituto Pre-universitario de La Habana (Library of the Havana Pre-University Institute of Education): Zuleta y San José, Havana; f. 1894; 32,000 books, newspaper library; Dir JOSÉ MANUEL CASTELLANOS RODILES.

Biblioteca 'Fernando Ortiz' del Instituto de Literatura y Lingüística (Fernando Ortiz Library of the Institute of Literature and Linguistics): Salvador Allende 710 entre Soledad y Castillejo, Havana 10300; tel. (7) 878-5405; fax (7) 873-5718; e-mail ill@ceniai .inf.cu; f. 1793; 1,000,000 items; Librarian Lic. Ma. ELOISA DÍAZ FAURE.

Biblioteca Histórica Cubana y Americana 'Francisco González del Valle' (Francisco González del Valle Library of Cuban and American History): Tacón 1 e/ Obispo y O'Reilly, Havana; tel. (7) 861-5001; e-mail biblioteca@patrimonio.ohch.cu; internet www.ohch.cu; f. 1938.

Biblioteca 'José Antonio Echeverría' (José Antonio Echeverría Library): G y 3ra, Havana; tel. (7) 838-2706; e-mail biblioservicios@casa.cult.cu; internet biblio .casadelasamericas.org; f. 1959; Caribbean and Latin American books; 150,000 vols, 8,500 journals; Dir ERNESTO SIERRA; publ. *Boletín* (12 a year).

Biblioteca 'Manuel Sanguily' (Manuel Sanguily Library): Cuchillo de Zanja 19, Primer Piso, entre Rayo y San Nicolás, Centro Havana; tel. (7) 63-3232; f. 1960; 29,512 vols, 3,200 periodicals; Dir ESTRELLA GARCÍA.

Biblioteca Nacional 'José Martí' (José Martí National Library): Apdo 6670, Avda de Independencia e/20 de Mayo y Aranguren, Plaza de la Revolución José Martí, Havana; tel. (7) 881-2428; e-mail direccion@bnjm.cu; internet www.bnjm.cu; f. 1901; 4,242,936 items; Dir ELIADES ACOSTA MATOS; publs *Bibliografía Cubana* (1 a year), *Bibliotecas: Anales de Investigación*, *Catálogo Cuba en Publicaciones Extranjeras*, *Indice General de Publicaciones Periódicas Cubanas*, *Revista de la Biblioteca Nacional José Martí*.

Biblioteca Provincial 'Rubén Martínez Villena' (Rubén Martínez Villena Provincial Library): Plaza de Armas, Centro Histórico, Havana; tel. (7) 862-9035; e-mail database@

bpvillena.ohc.cu; internet www.bpvillena.ohc .cu; f. 1960; 94,328 vols; spec. braille colln; Dir Lic. IRMINA DAMAS RODRÍGUEZ.

Centro de Información Bancaria y Económica, Banco Central de Cuba (Banking and Economic Information Centre, Central Bank of Cuba): Cuba 410 e/ Amargua y Lamparilla, 10100 Havana; tel. (7) 62-8318; fax (7) 66-6661; e-mail cibe@bc.gov.cu; internet www.bc.gov.cu; f. 1950; 33,000 vols; Man. ARACELIS CEJAS RODRÍGUEZ; Library Dept Chief JORGE FERNÁNDEZ PÉREZ; publs *Cuba: Half Yearly Economic Report*, *Economic Report* (1 a year), *Revista del Banco Central* (Journal of the Central Bank of Cuba).

Centro de Información y Documentación Agropecuario (Livestock Information and Documentation Centre): Gaveta postal 4149, Havana 4; tel. (7) 81-8808; fax (7) 33-5086; f. 1971; 20,000 vols, 1,400 journals; Dir Dr DAVID WILLIAMS CANTERO; publs numerous journals.

Instituto de Información Científica y Tecnológica (IDICT) (Institute of Scientific and Technical Information): Apdo postal 2213, 10200 Havana; Capitolio de La Habana, Prado entre Dragones y San José, La Habana Vieja, Havana; tel. (7) 862-6531; fax (7) 860-8813; e-mail tere@idict.cu; internet www.idict.cu; f. 1963; attached to Min. of Science, Technology and Environment; 150,000 vols, 8,000 journals; Gen. Dir CARMEN SÁNCHEZ ROJAS; publs *Boletín FID/ CLA* (4 a year), *Ciencia, Innovación y Desarrollo* (4 a year), *Ciencias de la Información* (4 a year).

Santiago

Biblioteca Central de la Universidad de Oriente (Central Library of the University of Oriente): Avda Patricio Lumumba s/n, 90500 Santiago de Cuba; tel. (226) 3-1973; f. 1947; 42,000 vols; Librarian Lic. MAURA GONZÁLEZ PÉREZ; publs *Revista Cubana de Química*, *Revista Santiago*.

Biblioteca Provincial 'Elvira Cape' (Elvira Cape Provincial Library): Calle Heredia 258 e/ Pío Rosado y Hartman, 90100 Santiago de Cuba; tel. (22) 65-4836; e-mail bpcape@lib.cultstgo.cult.cu; internet www .cultstgo.cult.cu/biblioteca/index.htm; f. 1899; 169,000 vols, 1,760 periodicals; Dir DAYMA SERPA LÓPEZ; publ. *Boletín Electrónico*.

Museums and Art Galleries

Camagüey

Museo Ignacio Agramonte (Ignacio Agramonte Museum): Camagüey; tel. (32) 28-2425; e-mail cmqcppatrimonia@pprincips .cult.cu; f. 1955; paintings, furniture, textiles and relics from the colonial period; Dir YOLANDA GUTIÉRREZ CAMPOS.

Cárdenas

Museo Municipal 'Oscar M. de Rojas' (Oscar M. de Rojas Muncipal Museum): Calle Calzada 4 e/ Echeverría y Martí, Cárdenas; f. 1903; exhibits relating to Martí and other aspects of Cuban history, malacology, insects, butterflies and colonial weaponry; library; Curator OSCAR M. DE ROJAS Y CRUZAT.

Havana

Acuario Nacional de Cuba (National Aquarium of Cuba): Ave 1ra y Calle 60, Miramar, Playa, Havana 11300; tel. (7) 203-6401; fax (7) 204-1442; e-mail comercial@ acuarionacional.cu; internet www

.acuarionacional.cu; f. 1960; attached to Min. of Science, Technology and Environment; library of 3,000 vols; Dir Lic. GUILLERMO GARCÍA MONTERO.

Archivo Histórico Municipal (Muncipal Historical Archive): Tacón 1 e/ Obispo y O'Reilly, Havana; tel. (7) 861-5001; e-mail archivo@patrimonio.ohch.cu; internet www .ohch.cu; f. 1938; historical items since 1550.

Jardín Botánico Nacional de Cuba (National Botanical Garden of Cuba): Carretera del Rocío Km 3½, CP 19230, Calabazar, Boyeros, Havana; tel. (7) 697-9310; fax (7) 697-9160; f. 1968; administered by Universidad de la Habana; library of 4,700 vols, 1,253 periodicals; herbarium; 100,000 specimens; Cuban flora colln: fungi, pteridophytes, gymnosperms and angiosperms; postgraduate training on vegetal anatomy, morphology and systematics; Masters degree in botany; Dir-Gen. Dra ANGELA LEIVA SÁNCHEZ; publ. *Revista Jardin Botanico Nacional* (1 a year).

Museo Antropológico Montané (Montané Anthropological Museum): Edif. Felipe Poey, Plaza Ignacio Agramonte, Colina Universitaria, Havana; tel. (7) 879-3488; f. 1903; colln of pre-Columbian artefacts; library of 5,000 vols; Dir Dr ANTONIO J. MARTÍNEZ FUENTES.

Museo Casa Natal José Martí (House Museum of José Martí): Calle Leonor Pérez 314 e/ Calles Egido y Picota, Havana; internet www.cnpc.cult.cu/cnpc/museos/ marti; f. 1925; relics of José Martí and his works; Curator MARIA DE LA LUZ RAMIREZ ESTRADA.

Museo de Arte Colonial de la Habana (Havana Museum of Colonial Art): San Ignacio 61, Plaza de la Catedral, Havana; tel. (7) 862-6440; e-mail colonial@bp .patrimonio.ohc.cu; internet www.ohch.cu; f. 1969; housed in mansion built 1720; Dir MARGARITA SUÑAREZ GARCÍA.

Museo de Historia Natural 'Felipe Poey' (Felipe Poey Museum of Natural History): Facultad de Biología, Universidad de La Habana, Calle 25 e/J e I, Vedado, 10400 Havana; tel. (7) 879-3488; fax (7) 832-1321; e-mail museopoey@fbio.uh.cu; internet www .uh.cu/museos/poey/index.html; f. 1842; zoology; library of 80,520 vols; Dir Dr ALEJANDRO BARRO CAÑAMERO.

Museo Ernest Hemingway (Ernest Hemingway Museum): Finca Vigía, San Francisco de Paula, Havana 19180; tel. (7) 91-0809; fax (7) 55-8090; f. 1962; house, library and personal items of Ernest Hemingway who lived at the address 1939–60; Dir DANILO M. ARRATE HERNÁNDEZ.

Museo Municipal de Guanabacoa (Guanabacoa Muncipal Museum): Calle Martí 108 e/ Versalles y San Antonio, Guanabacoa, Havana; tel. (7) 797-9117; e-mail musgbcoa@cubarte.cult.cu; f. 1964; popular Cuban religions of African origin; Dir MARIA CRISTINA PEÑA REIGOSA.

Museo Nacional y Palacio de Bellas Artes (National Museum and Palace of Fine Arts): Trocadero entre Zulueta y Monserrate, Havana Vieja 10200; tel. (7) 63-9042; fax (7) 62-9626; e-mail musna@cubarte.cult .cu; internet www.museonacional.cult.cu; f. 1913; ancient Egyptian, Greek and Roman art, 16th- to 19th-century European art, Cuban art from the colonial period to the present; Dir MORAIMA CLAVIJO COLOM.

Attached Museums:

Castillo de la Real Fuerza de la Havana (Castle of the Royal Garrison of Havana): O'Reilly entre Avda del Puerto y Tacón, Plaza de Armas, Havana Vieja 10100; tel. (7) 61-6130; fax (7) 61-3857; f. 1977; modern ceramic exhibits housed in a 16th-century fortification; Dir ALEJANDRO G. ALONSO.

Museo de Artes Decorativas (Museum of Decorative Arts): Calle 17, No. 502 entre D y E, Vedado, Havana 10100; tel. (7) 32-0924; fax (7) 61-3857; f. 1964; European and Oriental decorative art since 17th century; Dir KATIA VARELA.

Museo Napoleónico (Napoleonic Museum): San Miguel 1159 esq. Ronda, Plaza de la Revolución, Havana; tel. (7) 79-1460; fax (7) 79-1412; e-mail musnap@cubarte.cult.cu; internet www.cnpc.cult.cu; f. 1961; historical objects and works of art of Revolutionary and Imperial France; specialized library.

Museo Numismático (Numismatic Museum): Obispo 305 e/ Aguiar y Habana, Havana 1; tel. (7) 861-5811; e-mail numismatica@cultural.ohch.cu; internet www.ohch.cu; f. 1975; coins, banknotes, medals and decorations; library; Dir INÉS MORALES GARCÍA.

Parque Zoológico Nacional (National Zoological Garden): Carretera de Varona Km 3½, Boyeros, Havana; tel. (7) 44-7616; fax (7) 57-8054; e-mail pzn@ceniai.inf.cu; f. 1984; attached to Ministry of Science, Technology and Environment; library of 1,300 vols; Dir TOMÁS ESCOBAR HERRERA; publ. *Revista Cubazos*.

Matanzas

Museo Provincial de Matanzas (Matanzas Provincial Museum): Palacio de Junco, Calle Milanés e/ Magdalena y Ayllón, Plaza de la Vigía, Matanzas; tel. (52) 24-3195; f. 1959; history, natural history, decorative arts, weaponry, archaeology and ethnology; library of 1,000 vols; Dir Lic. GONZALO DOMÍNGUEZ CABRERA; publ. *Museo* (2 a year).

Remedios

Museo de Remedios 'José Maria Espinosa' (José Maria Espinosa Museum in Remedios): Maceo 32, Remedios; f. 1933; history, science, art; Dir. ALBERTO VIGIL Y COLOMA.

Santiago

Museo Emilio Bacardi Moreau (Emilio Bacardi Moreau Museum): Pío Rosado esq. Aguilera, 90100 Santiago; tel. (7) 62-8402; e-mail cppatrim@cultstgo.cult.cu; f. 1899; history, art; Curators JOSÉ A. AROCHA ROVIRA, FIDELIA PÉREZ GONZÁLEZ.

Universities

UNIVERSIDAD DE CAMAGÜEY

Carretera de Circunvalación Norte Km 5½, 74650 Camagüey

Telephone: (32) 28-1363
Fax: (32) 26-1587
E-mail: dri@reduc.edu.cu
Internet: www.reduc.edu.cu

Founded as a branch of University of Havana 1967; present name 1974
State control
Academic year: September to July

Rector: Dra C. LIANET GOYAS CÉSPEDES
Vice-Rector for Academic Affairs: Dra ANGELA PALACIOS HIDALGO
Vice-Rector for Administration and Services: MSc. FRANCISCO PRÉSTAMO
Vice-Rector for Extension: Ing. PEDRO RODRÍGUEZ
Vice-Rector for Financial Affairs: Dra ANA FERNÁNDEZ
Vice-Rector for Research and Postgraduate Affairs: Dra HILDA OQUENDO
Registrar: Lic. RAÚL GARRIGA CORZO

Librarian: Lic. SARA ARTILES VISBAL
Number of teachers: 450
Number of students: 3,200

Publications: *Revista de Producción Animal, Revista La Nueva Gestión Organizacional, Revista Retos de la Dirección*

DEANS

Faculty of Animal Sciences: Dr JOSÉ BERTOT
Faculty of Communication: MSc. TEL PINO SOSA
Faculty of Computer Science: Dr LUIS CORRALES BARRIOS
Faculty of Construction: Dr ELIO PÉREZ
Faculty of Economics and Business: Dra ANA DE DIOS
Faculty of Electromechanics: Dr LUIS CORRALES BARRIOS
Faculty of Food Chemistry: Dr PABLO GALINDO
Faculty of Languages: MSc. NORMA MOREDO
Faculty of Law: Dra MARÍA ELENA PRADO
Faculty of Social and Humanistic Sciences: Dra FLOR DE MARÍA FERNÁNDEZ FIFONTES

UNIVERSIDAD DE CIEGO DE AVILA

Km 9 Carretera de Ciego de Avila a Morón, Ciego de Avila 69450

Telephone: (33) 22-4544
Fax: (33) 26-6365
E-mail: webmaster@rect.unica.cu
Internet: www.unica.cu

Founded 1978 as Instituto Superior Agrícola de Ciego de Avila; current name and status since 1996

Rector: Dr MARIO ARES SÁNCHEZ
Library Dir: JORGE ANTONIO GÓMEZ CORDERO
Library of 41,963 vols
Number of teachers: 1,451
Number of students: 6,061

Publication: *Fidelia* (4 a year)

Faculties of Agronomy, Economics, Humanities, Computer Science and Engineering.

UNIVERSIDAD DE CIENFUEGOS 'CARLOS RAFAEL RODRÍGUEZ'

Carretera de Rodas Km 4, Cuatro Caminos, Cienfuegos 59430

Telephone: (432) 2-1521
Fax: (432) 2-2762
E-mail: rector@ucfinfo.ucf.edu.cu
Internet: www.ucf.edu.cu

Founded 1979 as Instituto Superior Técnico de Cienfuegos; university status 1994; current name since 1998
State control

Rector: Dr ANDRÉS OLIVERA RANERO
Vice-Rector for Academic Affairs: Dr ABEL QUIÑONEZ URQUIJO
Vice-Rector for Admin.: MAGDIEL E. CHAVIANO DÍAZ
Vice-Rector for Research and Postgraduates: Dra MIRIAN IGLESIAS LEÓN
Vice-Rector for Standardization of Higher Education: LOURDES POMARES CASTELLÓN
Sec.-Gen.: Lic. BLAS JUANES RAMÍREZ
Librarian: Dr LÁSARO S. DIBUT TOLEDO

Library of 50,000 vols
Number of teachers: 363
Number of students: 2,600

Publication: *Anuarios Científico* (1 a year)

DEANS

Faculty of Computer Science: Dr MARIO ALVAREZ GUERRA PLACENCIA
Faculty of Economics and Business: FRANCISCO BECERRA
Faculty of Humanities: Dr MARIANELA MORALES CALATAYUD
Faculty of Mechanics: Dr JUAN B. COGOLLOS MARTÍNEZ

Faculty of Physical Education: OSCAR MUÑOZ HERNÁNDEZ

ATTACHED RESEARCH INSTITUTES

Centro de Estudios y Desarrollo de la Oleohidráulica y la Neumática (CEDON): e-mail lmcglez@fmec.ucd.edu.cu; Dir Dr LUIS M. CASTELLANOS GONZÁLEZ.

Centre de Estudios de Didáctica y Dirección de la Educación Superior (CEDDES): e-mail mcaceres@rectorado.ucf.edu.cu; Dir Dra MARITZA CÁCERES MESA.

Centro de Estudios de Energía y Medio Ambiente (CEEMA): e-mail marmas@fmec.ucf.edu.cu; Dir Dr MARCOS DE ARMAS TEIRA.

Centro de Estudio Socioculturales de Cienfuegos (CESOC): e-mail lmartin@fmec.ucf.edu.cu; Dir Dra LILIAN MARTÍN BRITO.

Centro de Estudio Para la Transformación Agraria Sostenible (CETAS): e-mail asocorro@fmec.ucf.edu.cu; Dir Dr ALEJANDRO RAFAEL SOCORRO CASTRO.

UNIVERSIDAD DE GRANMA

Carretera de Manzanillo Km 17.5, Bayamo, Granma
Telephone: (23) 9-2130
Fax: (23) 9-2131
E-mail: antonia@udg.granma.inf.cu
Internet: www.udg.co.cu
Founded 1967
State control
Rector: Dra ANTONIA MARÍA CASTILLO RUÍZ
Number of teachers: 316
Number of students: 2,300
Faculties of accountancy and finance, agriculture, engineering, social and human sciences and veterinary medicine.

UNIVERSIDAD AGRARIA DE LA HABANA

Autopista Nacional y Carretera de Tapaste San José de las Lajas, La Habana
Telephone: (64) 6-3014
Fax: (64) 6-3395
E-mail: rector@main.isch.edu.cu
Internet: www.isch.edu.cu
Founded 1976
Rector: Dr JULIÁN RODRÍGUEZ RODRÍGUEZ
Number of teachers: 447
Number of students: 2,300
Faculties of agronomy, mechanization of agricultural production and veterinary science; department of Marxism-Leninism; campus on Isla de la Juventud.

UNIVERSIDAD DE LA HABANA

Calle San Lázaro y L, Municipio Plaza de la Revolución, Havana
Telephone: (7) 832-4245; (7) 33-4163
E-mail: webmaster@uh.cu
Internet: www.uh.cu
Founded 1728, reorganized 1976
Rector: Dr RUBÉN ZARDOYA LOUREDA
Gen. Sec.: Lic. NANCY HERNÁNDEZ CONTRERAS
Library: see Libraries and Archives
Number of teachers: 1,635
Number of students: 15,980
Publications: *Boletín Universitario, Universidad de la Habana*, various scientific and technical publs

DEANS

Faculty of Accounting and Finance: Lic. JOSÉ LUIS TOLEDO SANTANDER
Faculty of Arts and Letters: Dr JOSÉ ANTONIO BAUJÍN PÉREZ

Faculty of Biology: Dra ALICIA OTAZO SÁNCHEZ
Faculty of Chemistry: Dr JOSÉ MANUEL NIETO VILLAR
Faculty of Foreign Languages: Dr ROBERTO ESPÍ VALERO
Faculty of Geography: Dra NANCY PÉREZ RODRÍGUEZ
Faculty of Law: Lic. JOSÉ LUIS TOLEDO SANTANDER
Faculty of Mathematics: Dr LUIS RAMIRO PIÑEIRO DIAZ
Faculty of Philosophy and History: Lic. JOSÉ CARLOS VÁZQUEZ LÓPEZ
Faculty of Physics: Dr ERNESTO ALTSHULER ÁLVAREZ
Faculty of Planning for the National Economy: Dra VILMA HIDALGO DE LOS SANTOS
Faculty of Psychology: M.Sc. KARELYN LÓPEZ SÁNCHEZ
Faculty of Tourism: Lic. RAMÓN MARTÍN FERNÁNDEZ

UNIVERSIDAD DE HOLGUÍN 'OSCAR LUCERO MOYA'

Avda 20 Aniversario, Nuevo Holguín, Gaveta Postal 57, 80100 Holguín
Telephone: (24) 48-1302
Fax: (24) 48-1662
E-mail: acristina@ict.uho.edu.cu
Internet: www.uho.edu.cu
Founded 1976 as Centro Universitario de Holguín; became Instituto Superior Técnico de Holguín 1982; current name and status 1995
Rector: Dr SEGUNDO PACHECO TOLEDO
Librarian: MATILDE RIVERON HERNÁNDEZ
Library of 90,980 vols
Number of teachers: 376
Number of students: 3,276
Publications: *Ambito* (4 a year), *Diéresis* (1 a year)

DEANS

Faculty of Engineering: MANUEL VEGA ALMAGUER
Faculty of Economics: MIGUEL TORRES PEREZ

UNIVERSIDAD CENTRAL 'MARTA ABREU' DE LAS VILLAS

Carretera a Camajuaní Km 5½, 54830 Santa Clara, Villa Clara
Telephone: (42) 28-1519
Fax: (42) 28-1449
E-mail: rector@uclv.edu.cu
Internet: www.uclv.edu.cu
Founded 1952
Academic year: September to July
Rector: Dr JOSÉ RAMÓN SABORIDO LOIDI
Vice-Rector for Academic Affairs: Dra MIRIAM NICADO GRACIA
Vice-Rector for Administrative Affairs: Dr OSVALDO FERNÁNDEZ MARTÍNEZ
Vice-Rector for Economic and Financial Management: Dr JOSÉ RAMÓN CASTELLANOS CASTILLO
Vice-Rector for Extension: Dr JUAN JOSÉ HERNÁNDEZ SANTANA
Vice-Rector for Research and Postgraduate Affairs: Dr ÁNGEL RUBIO GONZÁLEZ
Gen. Sec.: Dr SAMUEL RODRÍGUEZ GARCÍA
Librarian: Ing. JOSÉ RIVERO DÍAZ
Library of 386,000 vols
Number of teachers: 1,187
Number of students: 5,132
Publications: *Centro Agrícola, Centro Azúcar, Biotecnología Vegetal* (4 a year), *Islas* (4 a year)

DEANS

Faculty of Agricultural Sciences: Dr ANDRÉS CASTRO ALEGRÍA
Faculty of Building: Dr GILBERTO QUEVEDO SOTOLONGO
Faculty of Chemistry and Pharmacy: Dr RONALDO SANTOS HERRERO
Faculty of Economics: Dr INOCENCIO RAUL SÁNCHEZ
Faculty of Electrical Engineering: Dr FÉLIX ÁLVAREZ PALIZA
Faculty of Humanities: M.Sc. ANA IRIS DÍAZ MARTÍNEZ
Faculty of Industrial Engineering and Tourism: Dr HUGO GRANELA MARTÍN
Faculty of Information Science and Education: M.Sc. ROBERTO VICENTE RODRÍGUEZ
Faculty of Law: Dr YADIRA GARCÍA RODRIGUEZ
Faculty of Mathematics, Computing and Physics: Dra YANET RODRÍGUEZ SARABIA
Faculty of Mechanical Engineering: Dr ANGEL SILVIO MACHADO RODRÍGUEZ
Faculty of Psychology: Dra OSANA MOLERIO PÉREZ
Faculty of Social Sciences: Dra MELY DEL ROSARIO GONZÁLEZ ARÓSTEGUI

UNIVERSIDAD DE MATANZAS 'CAMILO CIENFUEGOS'

Autopista a Veradero Km 3, Matanzas
Telephone: (53) 52-62222
Fax: (53) 52-53101
E-mail: info@umcc.cu
Internet: www.umcc.cu
Founded 1972
Library of 80,000 vols
Number of teachers: 381
Number of students: 3,020
Rector: Ing. JORGE RODRÍGUEZ PÉREZ
Vice-Rector for Admin. and Services: Ing. JOSÉ R. DÍAZ
Vice-Rector for Research and Postgraduate Studies: Dr ROBERTO VIZCÓN TOLEDO
Vice-Rector for Teaching: Ing. MIGUEL SARRAF GONZÁLEZ
Publications: *Revista de Investigaciones Turísticas, Revista Pastos y Forrajes*

DEANS

Faculty of Agronomy: Dr SERGIO RODRÍGUEZ JIMÉNEZ
Faculty of Chemistry and Mechanics: Dr ROBERTO VIZCÓN TOLEDO
Faculty of Computer Science: Dr JULIO TELOT GONZÁLEZ
Faculty of Economics and Industry: Lic. BENITA N. GARCÍA GUTIÉRREZ
Faculty of Physical Education: Lic. FÉLIX MOYA
Faculty of Social Sciences and Humanities: Lic. ZOE DOMINGUEZ GARCÍA

ATTACHED RESEARCH INSTITUTES

Centro de Estudios de Anticorrosión y Tensioactivos (CEAT): Dir CARLOS A. ECHEVERRÍA LAGE.

Centro de Estudios de Combustión y Energía (CECYEN): e-mail barroso@quimec.umcc.cu; Dir JORGE ÁNGEL BARROSO ESTÉBANEZ.

Centro de Estudio y Desarrollo Educacional (CEDE): e-mail gerardo.ramos@umcc.cu; Dir Dr GERARDO RAMOS SERPA.

Centro de Estudios de Medioambiente (CEMAN): Dir Dra JUANA ZOILA JUNCO HORTA.

UNIVERSIDAD DE ORIENTE

Avda Patricio Lumumba s/n, 90500 Santiago de Cuba
Telephone: (22) 63-1860

Fax: (22) 63-2689
E-mail: marcosc@rect.uo.edu.cu
Internet: www.uo.edu.cu
Founded 1947
Academic year: September to July
Rector: Dr MARCOS CORTINA VEGA
Vice-Rectors: MSc ELIO CASTELLANOS, Dra
ZAIDA VALDÉS ESTRADA, Dr SERGIO CANO
ORTIZ, Dr JUAN BORY REYES, Dr PEDRO A.
BEATÓN SOLER
Sec.-Gen.: Arq. SONIA QUESADA
Librarian: Dr BAYARDO DUPOTEY RIBAS
Library: see Libraries and Archives
Number of teachers: 842
Number of students: 24,500 (5,500 under-
graduate, 19,000 postgraduate and con-
tinuing education)
Publications: *Revista Cubana de Química* (3
a year), *Revista Santiago* (2 a year),
Tecnología Química (3 a year)

DEANS

Faculty of Building Construction: MSc ALE-
JANDRO FAJARDO
Faculty of Chemical Engineering: Dra ANA
SÁNCHEZ DEL CAMPO LAFFITA
Faculty of Computing Sciences and Math-
ematics: MSc ALEJANDRO GARCÉS CALVELO
Faculty of Distance Learning: Dra ROSARIO
LEÓN ROBAINA
Faculty of Economics: MSc ULISES PACHECO
FERIA
Faculty of Electrical Engineering: MSc EMI-
LIO SOTO MORLÁ
Faculty of Humanities: Dra ETNA SANZ
Faculty of Law: Dra JOSEFINA MÉNDEZ
Faculty of Mechanical Engineering: Dr
ROBERTO ZAGARÓ ZAMORA
Faculty of Natural Sciences: Dr PEDRO MUNÉ
BANDERA
Faculty of Social Sciences: Dra MARÍA JULIA
JIMÉNEZ FIOL

UNIVERSIDAD DE PINAR DEL RÍO

Calle J. Martí 270 esq. a 27 de Noviembre,
Pinar del Río 20100
Telephone: (82) 77-9353
Fax: (82) 77-9353
E-mail: mfdez@vrect.upr.edu.cu
Internet: www.upr.edu.cu
Founded 1972
State control
Academic year: September to July
Rector: Dr ANDRÉS ERASMO ARES ROJAS
Vice-Rector for Admin.: Ing. RENÉ PLASENCIA
Vice-Rector for Community Relations: Dra
MARTHA ARROYO CARMONA
Vice-Rector for Research: Dra MARISELA
GONZÁLEZ PÉREZ

Vice-Rector for Teaching: Dr ANTONIO DE LA
FLOR SANTALLA
Sec.-Gen.: Lic. MAGALYS GONZÁLEZ HERNÁN-
DEZ
Librarian: Lic. MABEL RODRÍGUEZ
Number of teachers: 370
Number of students: 5,876
Publication: *Anuario Científico*

DEANS

Faculty of Agronomy and Forestry: Lic. YOEL
PACHECO ESCOBAR
Faculty of Economics: Dra MAYRA CARMONA
GONZÁLEZ
Faculty of Geology and Mechanics: Lic.
JORGE SÁNCHEZ
Faculty of Humanities: Dra ALINA MARTÍNEZ
Faculty of Mining: Lic. YORKY MAYOR
Faculty of Telecommunications and Inform-
atics: Dra MAGDALENA MAZÓN HERNÁNDEZ

AFFILIATED INSTITUTES

Centre of Agroecology: Universidad de
Pinar del Río, Facultad de Forestal y Agronomía Pinar del Río; tel. (48) 75-5452; e-mail
mariol@af.upr.edu.cu; Dir Dra MARIOL MOR-
EJÓN.

Centre for Forestry Sciences: e-mail
betancourt@af.upr.edu.cu; Dir Dr YNOCENTE
BETANCOURT FIGUERAS.

Centre for Higher Education Research:
e-mail tdiaz@vrect.upr.edu.cu; Dir Dra TER-
ESA DE LA C. DÍAZ.

**Centre for Management and Tourism
Studies:** e-mail clazo@eco.upr.edu.cu; Dir Dr
CARLOS LAZO VENTO.

**Centre of Natural Resources and the
Environment:** e-mail jaula@vrect.upr.edu
.cu; Dir Dr JOSÉ A. JAULA BOTET.

Centre for the Study of Co-operatives:
e-mail arivera@eco.upr.edu.cu; Dir Dr CLAU-
DIO A. RIVERA.

Colleges

**Instituto Superior de Ciencias Médicas
de Camagüey:** Carretera Central Oeste
esquina a Madame Curie, Camagüey; tel.
(32) 9-2100; e-mail romulo@finlay.cmw.sld
.cu; f. 1981 from medical faculty of Univ. of
Camagüey; schools of dentistry, medicine,
nursing; biomedical, clinical and sociomedi-
cal research; 587 teachers; 3,500 students;
Rector Dr RÓMULO RODRÍGUEZ RAMOS; publ.
Revista de Ciencias Médicas de Camagüey (2
a year).

**Instituto Superior de Relaciones Inter-
nacionales 'Raul Roa García':** Calle Calzada 308 esq. H, Vedado, Havana 10400; tel.
(7) 831-9495; fax (7) 838-1359; e-mail isri@
isri.minrex.gov.cu; internet www.isri.cu; f.
1971; library: 14,000 vols; special collection
containing the personal library of Dr Raúl
Roa García; 61 teachers; Rector Embajadora
Lic. ISABEL ALLENDE KARAM; Gen. Sec. Dr
RENÉ OCHOA FÚNEZ.

**Instituto Superior Politécnico 'José
Antonio Echeverría':** Calle 114 No. 11901
entre 119 y 127, CUJAE, Marianao, CP
19390, Havana; tel. (7) 261-4932; fax (7)
267-2694; e-mail rosy@tesla.cujae.edu.cu;
internet www.cujae.edu.cu; f. 1976, fmrly
Faculty of Technology of University of
Havana; faculties of architecture, chemical
engineering, civil engineering, electrical
engineering, industrial engineering, information engineering, mechanical engineering;
advanced education centre, biomedical
engineering centre, hydraulic research
centre, innovation and maintenance study
centre, management techniques study
centre, microelectronic research centre,
renewable energy technology study centre,
process engineering centre, systems engineering study centre, tropical architecture and
construction centre; library: 157,370 vols;
1,012 teachers; 5,299 students; Rector Dr
GUSTAVO COBREIRO SUÁREZ; Sec. Ing. RAÚL
CAPETILLO ALVAREZ; publs *Arquitectura y
Urbanismo* (3 a year), *Ingeniería Electrónica,
Automática y Telecomunicaciones* (3 a year),
Ingeniería Energética (3 a year), *Ingeniería
Hidráulica y Ambiente* (3 a year), *Ingeniería
Industrial* (3 a year), *Ingeniería Mecanica* (3
a year).

Schools of Art and Music

**Academia Nacional de Bellas Artes 'San
Alejandro'** (National Academy of Fine Arts):
Avenida 31 y Calle 100 No. 10006, Obelisco
de Marianao, 11400 Havana; tel. (7) 260-
9234; e-mail sanalejandro@cubarte.cult.cu;
internet www.sanalejandro.cult.cu; f. 1818
as Academia de San Alejandro; formerly
Escuela de Pintura, organized by the French
painter Jean Baptiste Vermay; 800 students;
Dir DOMINGO RAMOS ENRÍQUEZ.

**Conservatorio Alejandro García
Caturla:** Avda 31 y Calle 82, Marianao,
Havana.

**Conservatorio de Música Amadeo Rol-
dán:** Rastro y Lealtad, Havana.

CYPRUS

The Higher Education System

Cyprus was governed by the United Kingdom until it achieved independence in 1960, following a guerrilla campaign by Greek Cypriots seeking unification (Enosis) with Greece. Government was on the basis of a power-sharing agreement between the Greek and Turkish communities, but in 1963 the Turks withdrew from central government. In 1974, after Greek officers of the Cypriot National Guard had staged a coup, the Turkish army occupied the northern third of the island, where Turkish Cypriots subsequently established a de facto Government and, in 1975, declared a Turkish Federated State of Cyprus (TFSC). In 1983 the TFSC unilaterally declared an independent Turkish Republic of Northern Cyprus (TRNC). The Greek Cypriot administration, meanwhile, claims to be the Government of all Cyprus, and is generally recognized as such. Until 1965 each community in Cyprus managed its own schooling through a Communal Chamber. On 31 March of that year, however, the Greek Communal Chamber was dissolved and a Ministry of Education (now Ministry of Education and Culture) was established to take its place. Inter-communal education has been placed under this Ministry.

Cyprus:

The University of Cyprus, in Nicosia, was founded in 1989. There were a total of 38 higher education institutions in 2006/07, including professional institutes and colleges for art, forestry and management. In 2007/08 25,688 students (including 7,752 foreign pupils) were enrolled in tertiary education, while a total of 22,530 students from the Greek Cypriot area were studying at universities abroad, mainly in Greece, the USA and the United Kingdom.

Students must hold the main secondary school qualification (Apolytirion) and sit a competitive entrance examination to gain admission to the University of Cyprus. Cyprus became a signatory to the Bologna Process in 2001, and a two-tier Bachelors and Masters degree system has been implemented. Non-university higher education consists of one to four-year Certificate, Diploma and Higher Diploma programmes, offered by the University of Cyprus and private institutions in professional fields of study. Private higher education institutions are registered and accredited by the Ministry of Education and Culture, in accordance with Law 67(I)96, introduced in September 1997.

The first university degree-level is the undergraduate Bachelors degree, which is awarded after four years' study. Students must accumulate 120–180 credit units in eight semesters. Both the postgraduate degrees, Masters and Doctor of Philosophy (PhD) require 30 credit units.

Post-secondary technical and vocational education is offered by both public and private institutions.

Turkish Republic of North Cyprus:

The international community, including the UN and EU, does not recognize the TRNC as a separate self-governing country. The Republic of Cyprus is recognized as having de jure sovereignty over the whole island. The Greek Cypriot Government, which legally remains the competent authority for all of Cyprus, does not recognize or accredit Turkish Cypriot higher education institutions.

The education system in the TRNC follows the Turkish model, and those institutions recognized by the Turkish Government can be expected to have a comparable standard of education to the Turkish mainland.

Cyprus's first university, the Eastern Mediterranean University, which is located near Gazi Mağusa (Famagusta), was opened in 1979 as the Higher Technological Institute and was elevated to full university status under its current name in 1986. A total of 13,809 students attended the university in 2007/08. The European University of Lefke was founded in 1990. In 2007/08 43,021 students were studying at universities in the TRNC, while 1,815 students were pursuing higher education studies abroad, mainly in Turkey, the USA and the United Kingdom. All schools and educational institutes are administered by the Ministry of Education and Culture (with a few exceptions of professional institutes attached to the appropriate Ministry). Education in the Turkish Cypriot zone is divided into two sections, formal and adult education. Formal education covers nursery, primary, secondary and higher education. Adult (informal) education caters for special training outside the school system. In 1982 an International Institute of Islamic Banking and Economics was opened to provide postgraduate training.

Completion of the Lise Bitirme Diplomasi or equivalent is required for entry to university. The organization of undergraduate degrees is based on the US-style 'credit' and grade-point average (GPA) system. The Bachelors degree lasts eight semesters (four years) and students require at least 120 credits and a GPA of 2.0 to graduate. A two-year Diploma course is also available. Masters programmes like the Master of Arts (MA), Master of Business Administration (MBA) and Master of Science (MSc) take 1–2 years' study following the Bachelors, and require between 21 (MSc) and 42 (MBA) credits. A Masters is required for admission onto the Doctor of Philosophy (PhD) programme, which is a combination of core coursework and original research; candidates for PhD must submit a research thesis.

Technical and vocational education is provided by several colleges and institutes, admission to which is dependent upon the Lise Bitirme Diplomasi.

Regulatory and Representative Bodies

GOVERNMENT

Ministry of Education and Culture: Kimonos and Thoukydidou, Akropolis, 1434 Nicosia; tel. 22800931; fax 22305117; e-mail moec@moec.gov.cy; internet www.moec.gov.cy; Minister ANDREAS DEMETRIOU.

Ministry of Education and Culture: Lefkosa, TRNC, via Mersin 10, Turkey; tel. 2283136; fax 2282344; internet www.moec.gov.cy.

ACCREDITATION

Council of Educational Evaluation—Accreditation (CEEA): POB 12592, 2251 Nicosia; tel. 22402476; fax 22305513; e-mail sekap@cytanet.com.cy; internet www.moec.gov.cy/sekap; Pres. GEORGE PHILOKYPROU.

ENIC/NARIC Cyprus: Cyprus Council for the Recognition of Higher Education Qualifications, POB 12758, 2252 Nicosia; tel. 22402472; fax 22402481; e-mail info@kysats.ac.cy; internet www.kysats.ac.cy; Chair. Prof. CONSTANTINOS CHRISTOU.

Learned Societies

GENERAL

Etaireia Kypriakon Spoudon (Society of Cypriot Studies): POB 21436, Nicosia; tel. 22432578; fax 22343439; e-mail cypriotstudies@gmail.com; internet www.cypriotstudies.org; f. 1936; colln, preservation and study of material concerning all periods of the history, dialect and folklore of Cyprus; maintains Museum of Cypriot Folk Art; 950 mems; library of Kypria, Cypriot studies; library of 4,000 vols; Pres. CHRISTODOULOS HADJICHRISTODOULOU; Sec. Dr CHARALAMPOS CHOTZAKOGLOU; publ. Kypriakai Spoudai (Cypriot Studies, 1 a year).

BIBLIOGRAPHY, LIBRARY SCIENCE AND MUSEOLOGY

Kypriake Enose Vivliothikonomon—Epistemonon Pleroforeses (Cyprus Association of Librarians—Information Scientists): POB 21100, 1501 Nicosia; e-mail kebepcy@gmail.com; internet kebep.blogspot.com; f. 1984; promotes library and information science, professional interests of qualified librarians; provision of professional training; coordination of public and private activities regarding libraries and librarianship; 100 mems; Pres. CHRYSANTHI STAVROU.

HISTORY, GEOGRAPHY AND ARCHAEOLOGY

Cyprus Geographical Association: POB 23656, Nicosia; tel. 22368981; f. 1968; research and study of the geography of Cyprus; aims to improve the teaching of geography, and safeguard professional interests of geographers; 200 mems; library of 500 vols; Pres. Prof. PANAYIOTIS ARGYRIDES; publ. *The Geographical Chronicles* (1 a year).

LANGUAGE AND LITERATURE

Alliance Française: 10 Panagi Lappa, POB 56681, 3309 Limassol; tel. 25877784; fax 25662633; e-mail aflima@spidernet.com.cy; internet www.aflimassol.eu; offers courses and exams in French language and culture and promotes cultural exchange with France; Pres. NIKI PAPA.

British Council: POB 21175, 1503 Nicosia; 1–3 Aristotelous St, 1011 Nicosia; tel. 22585000; fax 22585129; e-mail enquiries@cy.britishcouncil.org; internet www.britishcouncil.org/cyprus.htm; offers courses and exams in English language and British culture and promotes cultural exchange with the UK; Dir PETER SKELTON.

Research Institutes
GENERAL

Cyprus Research and Publishing Centre: 3B Abdi Cavus, Lefkosa, TRNC, via Mersin 10, Turkey; tel. 2272592; f. 1984; research in the fields of ethnography, history, language and literature, society; publ. *New Cyprus* (12 a year).

Kentron Epistemonikōn Erevnōn (Cyprus Research Centre): POB 22687, 1523 Nicosia; tel. 22668848; fax 22667816; e-mail kykem@cytanet.com.cy; under the jurisdiction of the Ministry of Education and Culture; f. 1967; aims: the promotion of scientific research in Cyprus with spec. reference to the historico-philological disciplines and the social sciences; research library; sections: (a) Historical Section: editing and publ. of the sources of the history of Cyprus; (b) Ethnographic Section: colln, preservation, and publ. of materials relating to the local culture of the island; (c) Philological and Linguistic Section: colln of lexicographic materials, the preparation of a historical dictionary of the Cypriot dialect, and the editing of literary and dialect texts; (d) Oriental Section: promotion of oriental studies in Cyprus, with spec. reference to Ottoman studies; (e) Archives Section: colln and preservation of MSS. and documents relating to all aspects of the society of Cyprus; Dir CHRISTOS LACOVOU; publs *Epeteris* (1 a year), *Texts and Studies of the History of Cyprus*.

HISTORY, GEOGRAPHY AND ARCHAEOLOGY

Cyprus American Archaeological Research Institute: 11 Andreas Demetriou St, 1066 Nicosia; tel. 22456414; fax 22671147; e-mail librarian@caari.org.cy;

internet caari.org; f. 1978; one of the American Schools of Oriental Research; promotes the study of archaeology and related disciplines in Cyprus; encourages communication among scholars interested in Cyprus and provides residence facilities; library of 8,300 books, 110 current periodicals; representative ceramic, geological, lithic, archaeometallurgical and faunal reference collections, slide archive; Dir Dr THOMAS W. DAVIS; Librarian EVI KARYDA.

Libraries and Archives
Famagusta

Municipal Library: POB 41, Famagusta; f. 1954; reference and lending sections, incl. many books on Cyprus and in several languages; the Famagusta Municipal Art Gallery, with a historical maps section, is attached; 18,000 vols; Librarian and Curator CH. CHRISTOFIDES.

Limassol

Municipal Library: 352 St Andrew St, 3035 Limassol; tel. 25362155; f. 1945; 12,000 vols; Librarian A. KYRIAKIDES.

Nicosia

Cyprus Library: Eleftheria Sq., 1011 Nicosia; tel. 22303180; fax 22304532; e-mail cypruslibrary@cytanet.com.cy; internet www.cypruslibrary.gov.cy; f. 1987; 120,000 vols, 1723 CDs and DVDs, 285 video cassettes, 1007 microforms; spec. colln: Cypriot studies; Librarian Dr ANTONIS MARATHEFTIS; publ. *Bulletin of the Cyprus Bibliography*.

Cyprus Museum Library: POB 2024, Nicosia; tel. 22865848; fax 22303148; e-mail antiquitiesdept@da.mcw.gov.cy; f. 1883; inc. in Dept of Antiquities 1934; 18,328 vols (excl. bound periodicals), 220 periodicals, Pierides colln of 1,400 vols; Librarian MARIA DEMETRIOU-ECONOMIDOU.

Cyprus Turkish National Library: Kizilay Ave, Lefkoşa, TRNC, via Mersin 10, Turkey; tel. 22283257; f. 1961; 56,000 vols; Chief Librarian FATMA ÖNEN.

Library of the Archbishop Makarios III Foundation: POB 21269, 1505 Nicosia; tel. 22430008; fax 22346753; internet www.makariosfoundation.org.cy; f. 1983; research library of 65,000 vols relating mostly to Greek, Byzantine and post-Byzantine studies, Christian theology and recent political history of Cyprus; incorporates the library of Phaneromeni, the library of the Holy Archbishopric of Cyprus, the library of the Society of Cypriot Studies, and the Foundation library; Dir Dr M. STAVROU.

Library of the Institute of Education: Macedonia Avenue, Latsia, 2250 Nicosia; tel. 22402300; fax 22480505; e-mail papandreou@cyearn.pi.ac.cy; internet athena.pi.ac.cy; f. 1972; 60,000 vols, mainly on education; Dir ANDREAS PAPANDREOU.

State Archives of the Republic of Cyprus: Min. of Justice and Public Order, 1461 Nicosia; tel. 22451045; fax 22667680; e-mail statearchives@sa.mjpo.gov.cy; internet www.mjpo.gov.cy; f. 1978; place of deposit for public records received from govt depts and other bodies, subject to the State Archives Law; makes these records publicly available for research; 12,985 vols; 159,000 Secretariat Archives files, 8.462 km of linear shelving of archival holdings; State Archivist EFFY PARPARINOU.

Museums and Art Galleries
Ayia Napa

Marine Life Museum: 25 Ayias Mavris St, Ayia Napa; tel. 23723409; fax 23722607; f. 1922.

Gazimagosa

Icon Museum: Gazimagosa, TRNC, via Mersin 10, Turkey; St Barnabas monastery dating from 5th century; colln of icons from 18th century; works of art from Neolithic to Roman periods; bronze and marble pieces.

Larnaca

Larnaca Municipal Museum of Natural History: Leoforos Grigori Afxentiou, Larnaca; collns of local reptiles, insects, birds, animals, fossils and rock formations; marine life and plants from Cyprus and neighbouring countries; colln of insects and endemic plants.

Lefkosa

Dervish Pasha Mansion: Belig Pasha St, Lefkosa, TRNC, via Mersin 10, Turkey; tel. 2281922; fax 2281934; colln of Ottoman artefacts.

National Struggle Museum: Old Bishopric, Lefkosa, TRNC, via Mersin 10, Turkey; f. 1989; documents, photographs and other memorabilia of the 1955–1959 National Liberation Struggle and from the 1974 Turkish invasion.

Limassol

Cyprus Medieval Museum: Kolossi Castle, Limassol; tel. 25305419; f. 1987; rich colln of local and imported pottery from the Early Christian, Byzantine and medieval periods; unique collns of medieval tombstones, coats of arms and architectural exhibits from palaces, castles and churches; coins, arms, cannons, etc.

Cyprus Wine Museum: Pafos St, Erimi, Limassol; tel. 25873808; fax 25821718; e-mail cypruswinemuseum@cytanet.com.cy; internet www.cypruswinemuseum.com; Dir ANASTASIA GUY.

Municipal Folk Art Museum: 253 Agiou Andreou St, Limassol; tel. 25362303; f. 1985; exhibits of national costumes, tapestry, embroidery, wooden chests, waistcoats, men's jackets, necklaces, a variety of light clothes, town costumes, country tools.

Nicosia

Archbishop Makarios III Foundation Art Galleries: Plateia Archiepiskopou Kyprianou, Nicosia; tel. 22430008; internet www.makariosfoundation.org.cy.

Cyprus Folk Art Museum: POB 21436, 1508 Nicosia; tel. 22432578; fax 22343439; e-mail cypriotstudies@gmail.com; internet www.cypriotstudies.org; f. 1937 by mems of the Society of Cypriot Studies; Cyprus arts and crafts from early to recent times; mainly Cypriot Greek items; 950 mems; Dir Dr CHARALAMPOS CHOTZAKOGLOU; publ. *Cypriot Studies* (1 a year).

Cyprus Historical Museum and Archives: Pentelis 50, Strovolos, Nicosia; f. 1975; a private enterprise to create a cultural centre; aims to tape-record accounts of historical events in Cyprus, to photocopy all existing historical material about Cyprus, to liaise with the Ministry of Education and Culture and Greek historians, to find and publicize historical treasures in private collns; library of 3,000 vols; Pres. PETROS STYLIANOU; Gen. Sec. CLEITOS SYMEONIDES.

Cyprus Museum: POB 22024, Nicosia; tel. 22865888; fax 22303148; f. 1882; incorporated in Dept of Antiquities 1934; collns: (1) pottery from the Neolithic and Chalcolithic periods to the Graeco-Roman Age; (2) terracotta figures of the Neolithic Age to Graeco-Roman times, including the Ayia Irini group; (3) limestone and marble sculpture from the Archaic to the Graeco-Roman Age; (4) jewellery from the Neolithic period, especially Mycenaean (1400–1200 BC), to early Byzantine times, and coins from the 6th century BC to Roman times; (5) misc. collns, incl. inscriptions (Cypro-Minoan, Phoenician, Cypro-syllabic, Latin, Greek), bronzes, glass, alabaster, bone, etc.; exhibitions of jewellery, seals, coins; reconstructed tombs; extensive reserve collns are available for students; an archaeological library (see above) is housed in the Cyprus Museum bldg and is open to all; Dir Dr MARIA HADJICOSTI.

Universities
GREEK CYPRIOT UNIVERSITIES

CYPRUS UNIVERSITY OF TECHNOLOGY

POB 50329, Lemesos
Telephone: 25002500
Fax: 25002450
E-mail: administration@cut.edu.tr
Internet: www.cut.ac.cy
Public control
Accredited by Cyprus Council of Educational Evaluation–Accreditation (CEEA)
Pres.: ELPIDA KERAVNOU
Vice-Pres.: GEORGIOS CHARALAMBIDES
Vice-Pres: IOANNIS MANTAS
Faculties of applied arts and communication, engineering and technology, geotechnical sciences and environmental management, management and economics.

OPEN UNIVERSITY OF CYPRUS

Adamantio Bldg, 13–15 Digeni Akrita, 1500 Nicosia
Telephone: 22411600
Fax: 22411601
Internet: www.ouc.ac.cy
Founded 2004
Public control
Accredited by Cyprus Council of Educational Evaluation–Accreditation (CEEA)
Pres.: Prof. PANOS RAZES
Vice-Pres.: Prof. GEORGIOS PHILOKIPROU
Dir of Admin. and Finance: CHRISTOPHOROS CHRISTODOULIDES
Librarian: PANAGIOTIS THEMISTOCLEOUS.

UNIVERSITY OF CYPRUS

Univ. House 'Anastasios G. Leventis', POB 20537, 1678 Nicosia
Telephone: 22894000
E-mail: info@ucy.ac.cy
Internet: www.ucy.ac.cy
Founded 1989
State control
Languages of instruction: Greek, Turkish
Academic year: September to June
Rector: Prof. STAVROS ZENIOS
Vice-Rector of Academic Affairs: CONSTANTINOS CHRISTOFIDES
Vice-Rector of Int. Affairs, Finance and Admin.: ANTONIS O. KAKAS
Dir of Admin. and Finance: ANDREAS CHRISTOFIDES
Librarian: STEFANOS STAVRIDIS
Number of teachers: 336

Number of students: 6,046

DEANS

Faculty of Economics and Management: Prof. LOUIS N. CHRISTOFIDES
Faculty of Engineering: Prof. PANOS PAPANASTASIOU
Faculty of Humanities: Prof. ANDREAS PAPAPAVLOU
Faculty of Letters: Prof. MICHALIS PIERIS
Faculty of Pure and Applied Sciences: Prof. CONSTANTINOS PATTICHIS
Faculty of Social Sciences and Education: ATHANASIOS GAGATSIS

PROFESSORS

Faculty of Economics and Management:
CHARALAMBOUS, C., Public and Business Administration
CHARITOU, A., Public and Business Administration
CHRISTOFIDES, L., Economics
LEONIDOU, L., Public and Business Administration
MAMUNEAS, T., Economics
MICHAEL, M., Economics
MICHAELIDES, A., Public and Business Administration
PASHARDES, P., Economics
TRIGEORGIS, L., Public and Business Administration
TSOUKAS, H., Public and Business Administration
VAFEAS, N., Public and Business Administration
ZENIOS, S., Public and Business Administration

Faculty of Engineering:
ALEXANDROU, A., Mechanical and Manufacturing Engineering
CHARALAMBOUS, C., Electrical and Computer Engineering
DOUMANIDIS, C., Mechanical and Manufacturing Engineering
PAPANASTASIOU, P., Civil and Environmental Engineering
POLYCARPOU, M., Electrical and Computer Engineering

Faculty of Humanities:
AGAPITOS, P., Byzantine and Modern Greek Studies
ANGELATOS, D., Byzantine and Modern Greek Studies
IACOVOU, M., History and Archaeology
MICHAELIDES, D., History and Archaeology
PANAYOTOU-TRIANTAPHYLLOPOULOU, A., Classics and Philosophy
PIERIS, M., Byzantine and Modern Greek Studies
RIZOPOULOU-EGOUMENIDOU, E., History and Archaeology
TAIFACOS, I., Classics and Philosophy
VOUTOURIS, P., Byzantine and Modern Greek Studies

Faculty of Letters:
AGAPITOS, P., Byzantine and Modern Greek Studies
ANGELATOS, D., Byzantine and Modern Greek Studies
IACOVOU, M., History and Archaeology
MICHAELIDES, D., History and Archaeology
PANAYOTOU-TRIANTAPHYLLOPOULOU, A., Classics and Philosophy
PIERIS, M., Byzantine and Modern Greek Studies
RIZOPOULOU-EGOUMENIDOU, E., History and Archaeology
TAIFACOS, I., Classics and Philosophy
VOUTOURIS, P., Byzantine and Modern Greek Studies

Faculty of Pure and Applied Sciences:
ALEXANDROU, C., Physics
CHRISTOFIDES, C., Physics

CHRISTOFIDES, T., Mathematics
CONSTANTINOU, A., Biology
DAMIANOU, P., Mathematics
DELTAS, C., Biology
EFSTATHIOU, A., Chemistry
EVRIPIDOU, P., Computer Science
GEORGIOU, G., Mathematics
KAKAS, A., Computer Science
KARAGEORGHIS, A., Mathematics
KERAVNOU-PAPAILIOU, E., Computer Science
KOUMANDOS, S., Mathematics
MAVRONICOLAS, M., Computer Science
PANAGOPOULOS, C., Physics
PAPADOPOULOS, G., Computer Science
PAPARODITIS, E., Mathematics
PATRICKIOS, C., Chemistry
PATTICHIS, C., Computer Science
PITSILLIDES, A., Computer Science
RAZIS, P., Physics
SAMARAS, G., Computer Science
SCHIZAS, C., Computer Science
THEOCHARIS, C., Chemistry
TSERTOS, H., Physics
VIDRAS, A., Mathematics

Faculty of Social Sciences and Education:
CHRISTOU, C., Education
DEMETRIOU, A., Psychology
GAGATSIS, A., Education
IOANNIDES KOUTSELINI, M., Education
JOSEPH, J., Social and Political Sciences
KAPARDIS, A., Law
KATSIKIDES, S., Social and Political Sciences

UNIVERSITY OF NICOSIA

46 Makedonitissas Ave, 1700 Nicosia
Telephone: 22841500
Fax: 22357481
E-mail: info@gau.edu.tr
Internet: www.unic.ac.cy
Founded 1980 as Intercollege; univ. status 2007
Private control
Accredited by Cyprus Council of Educational Evaluation–Accreditation (CEEA) for Private Universities
Number of students: 4,000 in Nicosia, 500 on Limassol and Larnaca campuses
Publication: *Cyrpus Review* (2 a year)
Schools of business, education, humanities, social sciences and law.

TURKISH CYPRIOT UNIVERSITIES

CYPRUS INTERNATIONAL UNIVERSITY

Haspolat, Nicosia, TRNC, via Mersin 10, Turkey
Telephone: 26711111
Fax: 26711122
E-mail: info@ciu.edu.tr
Internet: www.ciu.edu.tr
Founded 1997
Private control
Accredited by Turkish Higher Educational Board
Pres.: Prof. Dr MEHMET ALI YÜKSELEN
Vice-Pres.: Prof. Dr NÜKET SARACEL

DEANS

Faculty of Arts and Sciences: Prof. Dr METIN KARADAĞ
Faculty of Communications: Prof. Dr HIKMET SEÇIM
Faculty of Economics and Administrative Sciences: Prof. Dr NÜKET SARACEL
Faculty of Education: Assoc. Prof. Dr AHMET NAZMY
Faculty of Engineering: Prof. Dr METE TAYANÇ
Faculty of Fine Arts: Prof. Dr GÜNKUT AKIN

DIRECTORS

Institute of Sciences: Asst Prof. Dr MEHMEDI
EGEMEN
Institute of Social Sciences: Prof. Dr HIKMET
SEÇIM
School of Applied Sciences: Asst Prof. Dr
SALIH KARANFIL
School of Foreign Languages: Assoc. Prof. Dr
MEHMET ALI YAVUZ
School of Tourism and Hotel Management:
Asst Prof. Dr EBRU GÜNEREN
Vocational School: Asst Prof. Dr ERTAN AKÜN

EASTERN MEDITERRANEAN UNIVERSITY

POB 95, Gazi Mağusa, TRNC, via Mersin 10,
Turkey
Telephone: 26301111
Fax: 23654479
E-mail: info@emu.edu.tr
Internet: www.emu.edu.tr

Founded 1979 as Higher Technological Insti-
tute; univ. status 1986
Language of instruction: English
State control
Academic year: September to June (two
semesters)

Pres.: Prof. Dr UFUK TANERI
Vice-Rector for Academic Affairs: Prof. Dr
DERVIŞ Z. DENIZ
Vice-Rector for Student Affairs: Asst Prof. Dr
KADIR ATLANSOY
Vice-Rector for Financial and Technical
Affairs: Asst Prof. Dr ERALP BEKTAŞ
Vice-Rector for Int. Affairs: Asst Prof. Dr
BAHIR E. ÖZAD
Sec.-Gen.: GÜROL ÖZKAYA
Registrar: HÜSEYIN ÜNSAL YETINER
Librarian: OSMAN SOYKAN

Library of 125,000 vols, 600 periodical sub-
scriptions and 25 electronic networks
Number of teachers: 641 full-time,
Number of teachers: 141 part-time
Number of students: 14,256

Publications: EMU Tourism Research Journal (in English), Journal of Cyprus Studies
(in English), Review of Social, Economic
and Business Studies (in English), Woman
2000 (in English)

DEANS

Faculty of Architecture: Prof. Dr IBRAHIM
NUMAN
Faculty of Arts and Sciences: Prof. Dr OSMAN
YILMAZ
Faculty of Business and Economics: Prof. Dr
ÖZAY MEHMET
Faculty of Communication and Media Stud-
ies: Assoc. Prof. Dr TUGRUL ILTER
Faculty of Education: Assoc. Prof. Dr NECDET
OSAM
Faculty of Engineering: Prof. Dr HASAN AMCA
Faculty of Law: Prof. Dr ESIN KOPNANC

DIRECTORS

Institute of Advanced Technology Research
and Development: Prof. Dr SENER UYSAL
Institute for Graduate Studies and Research:
Prof. Dr ELVAN YILMIZ
Distance Education Institute: Asst Prof. Dr
ISIK AYBAY
School of Foreign Languages: HUSEYIN
DEMIREL
School of Computing and Technology: Asst
Prof. Dr MUSTAFA ILKAN
School of Tourism and Hospitality Manage-
ment: Asst Prof. Dr ILKAY YORGANCI MAL-
ONEY

EUROPEAN UNIVERSITY OF LEFKE

Gemıkonağı, Lefke, TRNC, via Mersin 10,
Turkey
Telephone: 26602000
Fax: 27277528
E-mail: international@lefke.edu.tr
Internet: www.lefke.edu.tr
Founded 1990 by Cyprus Science Founda-
tion; accredited by Higher Education
Council of Turkey
Languages of instruction: English, Turkish
Academic year: October to June
Rector: Prof. Dr M. TURGAY ERGUN
Gen. Sec.: METIN BAYTEKIN
Registrar: MEHMET YALÇIN
Librarian: ELIF BILOKÇUOĞLU

Library of 30,000 vols, 70 periodicals
Number of teachers: 120
Number of students: 2,800

Publication: Laü'nün Sesi Journal (6 a year)

DEANS

Faculty of Agricultural Sciences: Assoc. Prof.
Dr ULRICH KERSTING
Faculty of Architecture and Engineering:
Prof. Dr K. BALASUBRAMANIAN
Faculty of Arts and Sciences: Prof. Dr GÜNAY
KARAAĞAÇ
Faculty of Communication Sciences: Prof. Dr
FARUK KALKAN
Faculty of Economics and Administrative
Sciences: Assoc. Prof. Dr FIKRET KUTSAL
(acting)

PROFESSORS

Faculty of Agricultural Sciences (tel. (392)
7146781; fax (392) 7146783):
  Horticultural Production and Marketing:
  Asst Prof. Dr İLHAMI TOZLU
Faculty of Architecture and Engineering:
  Architecture and Interior Architecture:
  Prof. Dr BOZOK ÖZERDIM
  Civil Engineering: Asst Prof. Dr KONSTAN-
  TIN SOBOLEV
  Computer Sciences: Prof. Dr K. BALASU-
  BRAMANIAN (acting)
  Electrical and Electronic Engineering:
  (vacant)
Faculty of Arts and Sciences:
  English Language Teaching: Asst Prof. Dr
  SÜLEYMAN GÖKER
  History: Asst Prof. Dr MEHMET DEMIR-
  YÜREK
  Turkish Language and Literature: Prof. Dr
  GÜNAY KARAAĞAÇ (acting)
Faculty of Communication Sciences:
  Journalism: Assoc. Prof. Dr FILIZ SEÇIM
  Public Relations and Advertising: Asst
  Prof. Dr FAIK KARTELLI
  Radio, Television and Cinema: Prof. Dr
  FARUK KALKAN (acting)
Faculty of Economics and Administrative
Sciences:
  Business: Asst Prof. Dr SERDAR SAYDAM
  Economics: Assoc. Prof. Dr FIKRET KUTSAL
  International Relations: Asst Prof. Dr
  SUPHI GALIP

GIRNE AMERICAN UNIVERSITY

University Dr., Girne, TRNC, via Mersin 10,
Turkey
Telephone: 26502000
Fax: 26502062
E-mail: info@gau.edu.tr
Internet: www.gau.edu.tr
Founded 1985
Private control
Rector: Prof. Dr YILDIRIM ONER
Chancellor: SERHAT AKPINAR

Vice Rector for Academic Affairs: SADIK
ULKER
Publication: GAU Journal of Social and
Applied Science

DEANS

Faculty of Architecture: Asst Prof. Dr SERDAR
SAYDAM (acting)
Faculty of Business and Economics: Asst
Prof. Dr OSMAN ALTAY (acting)
Faculty of Communication: Prof. Dr ALPAY
ATAOL
Faculty of Educational Science: Prof. Dr
TANJU GÜRKAN
Faculty of Engineering: Asst Prof. Dr ZAFER
AĞDELEN
Faculty of Humanities: Prof. Dr NESRIN KALE

MIDDLE EAST TECHNICAL UNIVERSITY, NORTH CYPRUS CAMPUS

Kalkanlı, Güzelyurt, TRNC, via Mersin 10,
Turkey
Telephone: 26612000
Fax: 26612009
E-mail: ncc@metu.edu.tr
Internet: www.ncc.metu.edu.tr
Founded 2000
Private control
Pres.: Prof. Dr AHMET ACAR
Vice-Pres: Prof. Dr AYSE ÇIĞDEM ERÇELEBI,
Prof. Dr HASAN NEVZAT ÖZGÜVEN, Prof. Dr
MEHMET TUNCAY BIRAND
Number of students: 1,280

DEANS

Faculty of Architecture: HALUK PAMIR
Faculty of Arts And Sciences: CÜNEYT CAN
Faculty of Economic and Administrative Sci-
ences: YASAR EYÜP ÖZVEREN
Faculty of Education: MERAL AKSU
Faculty of Engineering: ZAFER DURSUNKAYA

PROFESSORS

ABDULLAH, O.
ABDURRAHIM, Y.
ADNAN, Y.
AĞACIK, Z.
AHMET, G.
AHMET, I.
AHMET, R.
AHMET, S.
AHMET, G.
AHMET BÜLENT, D.
AHMET CAN, B.
AHMET CEVDET, Y.
AHMET DEMIR, B.
AHMET HALIS, A.
AHMET NEDIM, E.
AHMET NURI, Y.
AHMET ORHAN, E.
AHMET ORHAN, Y.
AHMET RAŞIT, K.
AHMETŞ Ş., U.
AHMETŞ ŞINASI, A.
ALAEDDİN, T.
ALEV, B.
ALI, C.
ALI, E.
ALI, G.
ALI, K.
ALI, K.
ALI, U.
ALI, U.
ALI, T.
ALI, Y.
ALI, T.
ALI BÜLENT, E.
ALI DURSUN, K.
ALI İHSAN, U.
ALI NEZIH, G.
ALI SADI, G.
ALI SAHIR, A.
ALI TAYFUN, A.

ALI TUĞRUL, T.
ALI ÜNAL, S.
ALPAY, A.
ALTAN, B.
ALTUNKAN, H.
AMDULLA, M.
ARİI, D.
ARIF, E.
ASUMAN, T.
ASUMAN, D.
ATALAY, K.
ATİLA, E.
AYDA, E.
AYDAN, E.
AYDIN, E.
AYHAN, I.
AYKUT, C.
AYKUT, K.
AYMELEK, O.
AYŞE, A.
AYŞE, G.
AYŞE, K.
AYŞE, K.
AYŞE ÇIĞDEM, E.
AYŞE FERIDE, A.
AYŞE GÜNIZ, G.
AYŞE NURHAN, S.
AYŞE TÜLAY, O.
AYSEL, A.
AYŞEN, A.
AYŞEN, E.
AYŞEN, Y.
AYŞIL, Y.
AYSIT, T.
BAYRAM, K.
BEAR AYTEN, C.
BEGÜM, O.
BEHÇET MURAT, E.
BILGEHAN, O.
BILGIN, K.
BILGIN, K.
BIROL, D.
BÜLENT, C.
BÜLENT, K.
BÜLENT EMRE, P.
BÜLENT GÜLTEKIN, A.
BÜLENT HULUSİ, E.
BUYURMAN, B.
ÇAĞLAR, G.
ÇAHIT, C.
CAHT, E.
CANAN, T.
CANAN, O.
CARNOT EDWARD, N.
CELAL, G.
CELAL, K.
CELAL FERDI, G.
CEM, T.
CENGIZ, O.
CENGIZ, B.
CENGIZ, E.
ÇETIN, Y.
ÇETN, H.
ÇEVDET, K.
CİHAN, E.
CIHANGIR, T.
CÜNEYT, C.
DEAN WALLACE, O.
DEMET, G.
DEMIR, A.
DENIZ, U.
DENIZ, Z.
DOĞAN, T.
DOĞAN H., A.
DURAN IHSAN, D.
DUYGU, K.
EDUARD, E.
EKREM, S.
EMEL, A.
EMIN, O.
EMINE NEVIN, S.
ENDER, O.
ENGİN, S.
ENGIN, K.
ENGIN SADIK, K.
ENGIN UMUT, A.

ERDAL, C.
ERDAL, B.
ERDAL, O.
ERDIN, B.
ERES, S.
ERGIN, A.
ERHAN ONUR, I.
ERKAN AHMET, K.
ERKUT, G.
EROL, T.
EROL, K.
EROL HASAN, C.
ERSAN, A.
ERSIN, T.
ESIN, T.
ESRA M., Y.
FAIKA DILEK, S.
FARUK, G.
FARUK, P.
FARUK, A.
FARUK ESEN, O.
FARUK TAHSIN, B.
FATIH, C.
FATIH, Y.
FATMA CANAN, C.
FATOŞ TÜNAY, V.
FERAL, E.
FERHUNDE, O.
FERIDE, S.
FERİT, B.
FERRUH, O.
FERSUN AYŞE, P.
FETHI PAYIDAR, G.
FEVZI, G.
FEVZİ SUAT, K.
FEZA, K.
FIKRET, S.
FILIZ BENGÜ, D.
GENCAY, S.
GERHARD, R.
GERHARD WILHELM, W.
GIRAY, B.
GÖKSEL NIYAZII, D.
GÖKTÜRK, U.
GÖNÜL, E.
GÖNÜL, S.
GÖTZ JOCHEN, R.
GÖZDE, A.
GÜLAY, O.
GÜLAY, O.
GÜLBİN, D.
GÜLERMAN, S.
GÜLHAN, O.
GÜLİN, G.
GÜLIN AYŞE, B.
GÜLSER, G.
GÜLSER, K.
GÜLSÜN, G.
GÜNERI, A.
GÜNERI NEVZAT, G.
GÜNEY, O.
GÜNGÖR, G.
GÜRBÜZ, D.
GÜRDAL, T.
GÜRKAN, K.
GÜRKAN HASAN, T.
GÜRSEVIL, T.
GÜZIN, E.
HACER CEYHAN, K.
HAFIT, Y.
HAKAN, G.
HAKKI POLAT, G.
HALE, G.
HALIL, K.
HALIL, O.
HALIM, D.
HALUK, G.
HALUK, P.
HALUK, A.
HALUK, A.
HALUK, D.
HALUK, E.
HALUK, H.
HALUK, S.
HAMIDE, E.
HAMIT, Y.

HASAN, T.
HASAN, S.
HASAN, Y.
HASAN CENGIZ, G.
HASAN NEVZAT, O.
HASAN ÜNAL, N.
HAYRETTIN, Y.
HAYRI, O.
HAYRIYE CANAN, S.
HİLMI ÖNDER, O.
HÜROL, F.
HURŞIIT, O.
HÜSEYIN, I.
HÜSEYIN, B.
HÜSEYIN, V.
HÜSEYIN AVNI, O.
HÜSEYIN KAMIL, B.
HÜSEYIN ÖZTAŞ, A.
HÜSNÜ, O.
HÜSNÜ, E.
İBRAHIM, G.
İBRAHIM SINAN, A.
İBRAHIM YURDAHAN, G.
İHSAN, A.
İLHAN, T.
İLKER, O.
İNCİ, E.
İNCI, T.
İSHAK, K.
IŞIK, O.
İSMAIL, T.
İSMAIL HAKKI, T.
İSMAIL HAKKI, T.
İSMAIL ŞUAYIP, G.
İSMET, E.
İSMİHAN, A.
JALE, H.
JALE ADILE, E.
KADRI FATIH, I.
KADRI SINAN, B.
KAHRAMAN, U.
KAHRAMAN, A.
KEMAL, A.
KEMAL, P.
KEMAL, I.
KEMAL, O.
KERIM, D.
LEMI, T.
LEVENT, Y.
LEVENT, P.
LEVENT A., B.
LEVENT KAMIL, T.
LEYLA, A.
MACIT, O.
MAHINUR, A.
MAHMUT, K.
MAHMUT, P.
MAHMUT VEDAT, A.
MARAT, A.
MARGARETA, O.
MEHMET, Y.
MEHMET, Z.
MEHMET, A.
MEHMET, C.
MEHMET, K.
MEHMET, P.
MEHMET, T.
MEHMET, U.
MEHMET CEMAL, G.
MEHMET CEVDET, C.
MEHMET KADRI, A.
MEHMET KAYHAN, M.
MEHMET KAZIM, A.
MEHMET KEMAL, L.
MEHMET POLAT, S.
MEHMET TUNCAY, B.
MEHMET UFUK, E.
MEHMET ZEKI, C.
MEHMET ZÜLFÜ, A.
MEHPARE, B.
MELIH, E.
MELIH ALI, Y.
MELIHA, A.
MELTEM, S.
MERAL, Y.
MERAL, A.

MERAL, C.
MERAL, A.
MESUDE, I.
METE, S.
METIN, D.
METIN, G.
METIN, G.
METIN, B.
METIN, Z.
METIN, A.
MEYDA, M.
MIRZAHAN, H.
MOTI LAL, T.
MUAMMER, E.
MÜBECCEL, D.
MUHAMMET YAŞAR, O.
MUHARREM, T.
MUHITTIN CEM, S.
MUHTAR, O.
MÜNEVVER, T.
MURAT, T.
MURAT, B.
MURAT, A.
MURAT, D.
MURAT, K.
MÜRVET, V.
MUSA, D.
MÜSLİM, B.
MUSTAFA, K.
MUSTAFA, T.
MUSTAFA, D.
MUSTAFA, S.
MUSTAFA, T.
MUSTAFA, G.
MUSTAFA, K.
MUSTAFA İLHAN, G.
MUSTAFA TURGUT, O.
MUSTAFA VERŞAN, K.
NACI, S.
NACI, B.
NACIYE CAN, M.
NAFI GÜRDAL, A.
NAFIZ, A.
NAIL, B.
NAZIFE, B.
NAZIFE SUZAN, K.
NAZIM KADRI, E.
NAZIYET, G.
NEBI, S.
NECATI, P.
NEŞE, Y.
NESRIN, H.
NEVIN, S.
NEVZAT, O.
NEVZAT, Y.
NEZIHE NILGÜN, K.
NIGAR, A.
NIHAD BEKIR, P.
NILGÜN, G.
NILGÜN, K.
NILGÜN, G.
NIZAMI, H.
NUMAN, T.
NUR EVIN, O.
NURAY AYŞE, K.
NURKAN, K.
NURSEL, I.
OĞUZ, O.
OKAY, C.
OLCAY, O.
OLCAY, I.
ÖMER, G.
ÖMER, A.
ÖMER, T.
ÖMER, G.
ÖMER, K.
ÖMÜR, B.
ORHAN, A.
OSMAN, S.
OSMAN, S.
OSMAN, Y.
OSMAN YAVUZ, A.
OZAN, T.
ÖZDEMIR, A.
ÖZDEMIR, D.
ÖZKAN BENGI, O.

PINAR, C.
PULAT, O.
RAIF ORHAN, Y.
RAMAZAN, A.
RAMAZAN, S.
RAŞIT, T.
REHA, A.
REŞAT, U.
REŞİT, S.
RIKKAT, C.
RIZA, G.
RÜKNETTIN, O.
RUŞEN, K.
RUŞEN, G.
RÜVEYDE SEZER, A.
RÜYAL, E.
SABRI KURTULUŞŞ, K.
SADIK, K.
ŞAFAK, A.
ŞAHİNDE, D.
ŞAIM, O.
ŞAKIR, E.
ŞAKIR, B.
SAVAŞ, K.
ŞAZIYE, G.
SEÇIL, A.
SELAHATTIN, O.
SELMIN, T.
SEMIH, Y.
SEMIH, B.
SEMRA, K.
SEMRA, T.
ŞENAY, K.
ŞENCER, A.
SERGEY, F.
SERHAT, A.
SERPIL, S.
SERVET GÜLÜM, S.
SEVGI, A.
SIBEL, B.
SINAN, K.
ŞINASİ, E.
ŞITKI, D.
SONER, G.
SUAT, U.
SÜHA, B.
SÜHA, O.
ŞÜKRİYE, R.
ŞÜKRÜ, K.
ŞÜKRÜ SELÇUK, B.
SÜLEYMAN, T.
SÜLEYMAN, O.
SYEDA NAZLI, W.
TAKHMASSIB, A.
TALAT MUSTAFA, B.
TAMER, T.
TANJU, M.
TANSEL, T.
TANSI, S.
TARIK, O.
TAYFUN, A.
TAYFUR, O.
TEMEL, O.
TEMEL ENGİN, T.
TEO, G.
TEOMAN, T.
TEOMAN NURIDDIN, N.
TEVFIK, G.
TIMUR, D.
TUĞRUL, A.
TÜLAY, Y.
TÜLIN, G.
TÜLIN, G.
TUNA, B.
TURGUT, T.
TURGUT SAMI, T.
TURHAN Y., E.
TÜRKER, M.
TÜRKER, A.
UFUK, B.
UFUK, G.
UĞUR, H.
UĞURLU NURAY, S.
ÜLKÜ, Y.
ÜLKÜ, Y.
ÜMIT, K.

ÜMIT MUSTAFA, A.
ÜNSAL, Y.
URAL, A.
UYGUR, S.
VACIT, I.
VASIF NEJAT, H.
VEDAT, T.
VEDAT, D.
VOLKAN, A.
WOLF KURT, K.
YAHYA ÖNDER, Y.
YAKIN, E.
YAKUP, K.
YAKUP CEVDET, A.
YALÇIN, M.
YALÇIN, T.
YAŞAR EYÜP, O.
YASEMİN, Y.
YASIN, C.
YAVUZ, Y.
YAVUZ ALI, T.
YAVUZ SAMIM, U.
YENER, O.
YERLI MERYEM, B.
YILDIRAY, O.
YILDIRIM, Y.
YILDIZ, W.
YILDIZ, E.
YILMAZ, A.
YURDANUR, T.
YUSUF, O.
YUSUF ZIYA, O.
ZAFER, E.
ZAFER, N.
ZAFER, U.
ZAFER, D.
ZEKI, K.
ZUHAL, K.

NEAR EAST UNIVERSITY

Near East Ave, Nicosia, TRNC, via Mersin 10, Turkey

Telephone: 22236464
Fax: 22236461
E-mail: info@neu.edu.tr
Internet: www.neu.edu.tr

Founded 1988
Private control

Rector: Prof. Dr UMIT HASSAN
Pres.: Dr SUAT İ. GÜNSEL
Dir of Public Relations: ERDOGAN SARACOGLU

Faculties of Architecture, Arts and Sciences, Ataturk Education, Communication, Dentistry, Economics and Admin. Sciences, Engineering, Fine Arts and Design, Health Sciences, Law, Maritime Studies, Medicine, Performing Arts, Pharmacy; Schools of Physical Education and Sports, Tourism and Hotel Management; Graduate School of Applied Sciences; Institutes of Educational Sciences, Health Sciences, Social Sciences.

Colleges

Americanos College: POB 22425, 1521 Nicosia; tel. 22661122; fax 22664118; e-mail college@ac.ac.cy; internet www.ac.ac.cy; f. 1975; private control; accredited by Cyprus Council of Educational Evaluation–Accreditation (CEEA); Diplomas, Bachelors and Masters degrees.

Arte Music Academy: POB 21207, 1504 Nicosia; tel. 22676823; fax 22665695; internet www.artemusic.org; f. 2002; private control; accredited by Cyprus Council of Educational Evaluation–Accreditation (CEEA); Bachelors degree in Music; Dir PITSA SPYRIDAKI; Artistic Dir MARTINO TIRIMO; Academic Registrar KLERI AGGELIDOU; Librarian ANTRI SPYRIDAKI.

CDA College: POB 21972, 1515 Nicosia; tel. 22661104; fax 22671387; e-mail cdaadm@ spidernet.com.cy; internet www.cdacollege .ac.cy; private control; accredited by Cyprus Council of Educational Evaluation–Accreditation (CEEA); brs in Limassol and Larnaca; Bachelors degree in business studies; programmes in information and communication technology, interior design and drchitectural drawing, travel and tourism admin. secretarial studies; 800 students; Principal D. A. CHRISTOFOROU.

College of Tourism and Hotel Management: POB 20281, 2150 Nicosia; tel. 22462846; fax 22336295; e-mail cothm@ spidernet.com.cy; internet www.cothm.ac.cy; private control; accredited by Cyprus Council of Educational Evaluation–Accreditation (CEEA); Pres. ANTONIS CHARALAMBIDES; Dir SAVVAS ADAMIDES.

CTL Eurocollege: POB 51938, 3509 Limassol; tel. 25736501; fax 25736629; e-mail college@ctleuro.ac.cy; internet www.ctleuro .ac.cy; private control; accredited by Cyprus Council of Educational Evaluation–Accreditation (CEEA); Bachelors degree and Diploma programmes in business, computing, hospitality and tourism, law.

Cyprus College: POB 22006, 1516 Nicosia; tel. 22713000; fax 22662051; internet www .cycollege.ac.cy; f. 1961; 2-year assoc. degree courses, 3- and 4-year bachelors degree courses in Social Sciences, Business Admin., Computer Science, MBA programme; 51 teachers; 1,020 students; library: 35,000 vols; Dir NICOS ANASTASIOU; publ. *Journal of Business and Society.*

Cyprus College of Art: 23 Mehmet Ali St, 6026 Larnaca; tel. 25341387 *UK Office* (all enquiries): 27 Holywell Row, London, EC2A 4JB, UK; e-mail enquiries@artcyprus.org; internet www.artcyprus.org; f. 1969; one-year foundation courses in art and design; undergraduate degree programmes in asscn with partner orgs in the UK; postgraduate courses in fine art; 8 teachers; 40 students; Dir STASS PARASKOS.

Cyprus Forestry College: Prodromos, 4841 Limassol; tel. 25813606; fax 25462646; e-mail forcollege@fc.moa.gov.cy; internet www.moa.gov.cy/fc; f. 1951; technical-level and advanced training in forestry; library: 2,000 vols, 7 periodicals; 7 teachers; 20 students; Prin. CHR. ALEXANDROU.

Cyprus International Institute of Management: 21 Akademias Ave, Aglandjia, POB 20378, Nicosia; tel. 22462246; fax 22331121; e-mail ciim@ciim.ac.cy; internet www.ciim.ac.cy; f. 1990; 1-year full-time and 2-year part-time courses leading to MBA and MPSM degrees and Advanced Diploma; MSc in Science; Executive education; library: 3,000 vols; Dir Dr JIM LEONTIADES.

Frederick Institute of Technology: 7 Frederickou St, Palouriotisa, 0136 Nicosia; tel. 22431355; fax 22438234; e-mail info@fit .ac.cy; internet www.fit.ac.cy; f. 1966; private control; accredited by Cyprus Council of Educational Evaluation–Accreditation (CEEA); campus in Limassol; Bachelors degrees and Diploma programmes in business, engineering, computers, technology, design, education and human sciences.

Global College: 245 Eleonon St, Strovolos, 2048 Nicosia; tel. 22814555; fax 22814580; e-mail gic@cytanet.com.cy; internet www .globalcollege.com.cy; f. 1972; private control; accredited by Cyprus Council of Educational Evaluation–Accreditation (CEEA); secretarial studies, business admin., computer studies; Gen. Dir GEORGE KRITICOS.

Intercollege (International College): 46 Makedonitissa Ave, POB 24005, 1700 Nicosia; tel. 22841500; fax 22352067; e-mail nicosia@intercollege.ac.cy; internet www .intercollege.ac.cy; f. 1980; private control; instruction in English; undergraduate and postgraduate courses lead to qualifying examinations for local, British and US degrees; also centres at Limassol and Larnaca; library: 70,000 vols; 203 teachers (112 full-time, 91 part-time); 5,000 students (incl. 613 at Limassol and 566 at Larnaca); Rector Dr VAN COUFOUDAKIS; publ. *Cyprus Review* (2 a year).

KES College: 5 Kallipolis Ave, 1055 Nicosia; tel. 22875737; fax 22756562; internet www .kes.ac.cy; f. 1971; private control; accredited by Cyprus Council of Educational Evaluation–Accreditation (CEEA); programmes in office admin. and secretarial studies, beauty therapy, medical representatives Courses; Dir THEO P. STYLIANOU.

Mediterranean Institute of Management: POB 20536, 1679 Nicosia; tel. 22806000; fax 22376872; e-mail info@kepa .mlsi.com.cy; internet www.kepa.gov.cy; f. 1976; int. component of Cyprus Productivity Centre (a dept of Min. of Social and Labour Insurance) postgraduate management diploma course; research and management consultancy projects; library: 8,000 vols; 30 teachers; 90 students; Dir Dr IOANNIS MODITIS.

PA College: Larnaca; tel. 24021555; fax 24628860; e-mail information@pacollege.ac .cy; internet www.pacollege.ac.cy; private control; accredited by Cyprus Council of Educational Evaluation–Accreditation (CEEA); BA degree in business admin.; BSc in business computing; Dir Dr ANDREAS Z. PATSALIDES.

Philips College: POB 28008, Strovolos, 2090 Nicosia; 4–6 Lamias St, 2001 Nicosia; tel. 22441860; fax 22315222; e-mail admissions@philips.ac.cy; internet www .philips.ac.cy; private control; accredited by Cyprus Council of Educational Evaluation–Accreditation (CEEA); accounting and finance, business studies, computing and information systems, public relations, social studies; Pres. Prof. PHILIPPOS CONSTANTINOU.

REA College: POB 50625, 3608 Nicosia; 2 Pasikratous St, 3085 Nicosia; tel. 25381095; fax 25383360; internet www.reacollege.ac.cy; f. 1986; private control; accredited by Cyprus Council of Educational Evaluation–Accreditation (CEEA); BSc degrees in aesthetics, dietetics, nutrition.

Susini College: POB 3502, 3502 Limassol; 10 Tagmatarchou Pouliou St, 3020 Limassol; tel. 25366196; fax 25369702; e-mail susini@ spidernet.com.cy; internet www.susini.ac.cy; f. 1982; private control; accredited by Cyprus Council of Educational Evaluation–Accreditation (CEEA); beauty therapy; Dir of Studies PHANIE ANTONIADOU-POUPOUTSI.

Vladimiros Kafkarides School of Drama: Nicosia; tel. 2421609; fax 2493450; private control; accredited by Cyprus Council of Educational Evaluation–Accreditation (CEEA); Dir DEMETRIOS LAZARIDES.

CZECH REPUBLIC

The Higher Education System

Higher education institutions predate the foundation of the former Czechoslovakia in 1918, with the oldest being Univerzita Karlova, which was founded in 1348. In 1990, following the removal of the communist Government, which had been in power since 1948, Czechoslovakia was replaced by the Czech and Slovak Federative Republic (CzSFR). In turn, the CzSFR was dissolved in 1993 and the Czech Republic and Slovakia became independent, sovereign states. Higher education reforms in both states were initiated under Act 172, passed in 1990; the Higher Education Act of 1998 (amended 2001) and a new education law in 2005 have also come into force. In 2007/08 some 344,180 students attended 70 universities. Higher education is financed by the Ministry of Education, Youth and Sport.

The secondary school leaving certificate (Maturita) is the main requirement for admission to higher education. Precise entry requirements vary among institutions, and students may have to sit an entrance examination. Legislation passed in 1998, and amended in 2001, brought the Czech Republic into line with the Bologna Process. The Bakalár is the main undergraduate degree, and lasts for three to four years. The first postgraduate degree, Magistr, is awarded after two to three years' study following the Bakalár. Some disciplines involve integrated undergraduate and postgraduate programmes lasting five to six years, leading to professional qualifications; these include engineering, architecture and medicine. Finally, following Magistr, doctoral studies take three to four years and result in the award of the title Doktor.

Post-secondary technical and vocational education dates from the establishment of vyšší odborná škola (tertiary technical schools) in 1992. There are now about 150 such establishments offering education and training in vocational fields. The period of study is between two to three-and-a-half years, and students are awarded the Diplomovaný Specialista.

The quality of higher education is overseen by the Accreditation Commission.

Regulatory and Representative Bodies

GOVERNMENT

Ministry of Culture: Maltéské nám. 471/1, 118 11 Prague 1; tel. 257085111; fax 224318155; e-mail posta@mkcr.cz; internet www.mkcr.cz; Minister VÁCLAV JEHLIČKA.

Ministry of Education, Youth and Sport: Karmelitská 8, 118 12 Prague 1; tel. 257193111; fax 257193790; e-mail info@msmt.cz; internet www.msmt.cz; Minister ONDŘEJ LIŠKA.

ACCREDITATION

Akreditační komise (Accreditation Commission): Ministry of Education, Youth and Sports, Higher Education Dept, Karmelitská 7, 118 12 Prague 1; tel. 257193488; fax 257193351; e-mail smrckaj@msmt.cz; internet www.msmt.cz/vzdelavani/akreditacni-komise; f. 1990; 21 mems (academic and professional experts); Chair. Prof. Dr VLADIMÍRA DVOŘÁKOVÁ; Sec. Dr JIŘÍ SMRČKA.

ENIC/NARIC Czech Republic: CSVS NARIC, U Luzického Seminári 13, 11 800 Prague 1; tel. 257011335; fax 257531672; e-mail skuhrova@csvs.cz; internet www.naric.cz; Head ŠTEPÁNKA SKUHROVÁ.

NATIONAL BODIES

Česká konference rektorů (Czech Rectors' Conference): Masarykova univerzita, Žerotínovo nám. 9, 601 77 Brno; tel. 549491121; fax 549491122; e-mail crc@muni.cz; internet crc.muni.cz; Pres. Prof. Ing. JAN HRON; Gen. Sec. Dr MARIE FOJTÍKOVÁ.

Rada vysokých škol (Council of Higher Education Institutions): José Martího 31, 162 52 Prague 6; tel. (2) 20560221; fax (2) 20560221; e-mail arvs@ftvs.cuni.cz; internet www.radavs.cz.

Learned Societies

GENERAL

Akademie věd České republiky AV ČR (Academy of Sciences of the Czech Republic): Národní tř. 3, 117 20 Prague 1; tel. 221403111; fax 224240512; e-mail kavcr@kav.cas.cz; internet www.avcr.cz; f. 1992; the Academy is a network of 60 autonomous research institutes which conduct theoretical and applied research in three broad sections: chemical and life sciences (Dir Prof. HELENA ILLNEROVÁ), humanities and social sciences (Dir Dr VILÉM HEROLD), mathematics, physics and earth sciences (Dir Dr KAREL JUNGWIRTH); attached research institutes: see Research Institutes; library and archive: see Libraries and Archives; Pres. Prof. JIŘÍ DRAHOŠ; Pres. of Scientific Council Prof. Dr FRANTIŠEK ŠMAHEL; publ. *Akademický bulletin* (newsletter, 12 a year).

Rada vědeckých společností České republiky (Council of Scientific Societies of the Czech Republic): Středisko společných činností Akademie věd ČR, Národní tř. 3, 117 20 Prague; tel. and fax 221403478; e-mail rvs@kav.cas.cz; internet www.cas.cz/rvs; coordinates 70 scientific socs, representing natural science, medicine and the social, and technical sciences; 34,000 mems; Pres. Prof. Dr IVO HÁNA.

AGRICULTURE, FISHERIES AND VETERINARY SCIENCE

Česká Akademie Zemědělských Věd (Czech Academy of Agricultural Sciences): Těšnov 65/17, 117 05 Prague 1; tel. 222320582; fax 222328898; e-mail cazv@cazv.cz; internet www.cazv.cz; f. 1924; sections of agricultural engineering, energy and devt (Chair. Ing. JAROSLAV KÁRA), animal production (Chair. Doc. Ing. VĚRA SKŘIVANOVÁ), economics, management, sociology and information technology (Chair. Doc. Ing. JAN HRON), food technology and technique (Chair. Ing. JAN DRBOHLAV), forestry (Chair. Ing. VILÉM PODRÁZSKÝ), human nutrition and food quality (Chair. Ing. SLAVOMÍRA VAVRERINOVÁ), plant production (Chair. Dr SLAVOJ PALÍK), plant protection (Chair. Dr JAN NEDĚLNÍK), soil science (Chair. Ing. RADIM VÁCHA), veterinary medicine (Chair. Prof. Dr MIROSLAV TOMAN), water management (Chair. Doc. Ing. MILOSLAV JANEČEK; 699 mems; Pres. Mgr JAN LIPAVSKÝ; Vice-Pres. Prof. Ing. JAN HRON; Sec. VACLAV HRUBY; publs *Genetika a šlechtění* (Czech Journal of Genetics and Plant Breeding, 4 a year), *Journal of Forest Science* (12 a year), *Ochrana rostlin* (Plant Protection Science, 4 a year), *Potravinářské vědy* (Czech Journal of Food Sciences, 6 a year), *Rostlinná výroba* (Plant Production, 12 a year), *Veterinární medicína* (Veterinary Medicine, 12 a year), *Zahradnictví* (Horticultural Science, 4 a year), *Zemědělská ekonomika* (Agricultural Economics, 12 a year), *Zemědělská technika* (Research in Agricultural Engineering, 4 a year), *Živočišná výroba* (Czech Journal of Animal Science, 12 a year).

ARCHITECTURE AND TOWN PLANNING

Obec architektů (Society of Architects): Revoluční 23, 110 00 Prague 1; tel. (2) 57535025; fax (2) 57535033; e-mail obecarch@architekt.cz; internet www.architekt.cz; f. 1989; 1,000 mems; Pres. JIŘÍ MOJŽÍŠ; publ. *Architekt* (12 a year).

ECONOMICS, LAW AND POLITICS

Česká společnost ekonomická (Czech Economic Association): Czech Economics, Politických vězňů 7, 110 00 Prague 1; e-mail c-s-e@volny.cz; internet www.cse.cz; f. 1962; 650 mems; Pres. Dr TOMÁŠ HOLUB; publ. *Bulletin* (3 a year).

Česká společnost pro mezinárodní právo (Czech Society for International Law): Národní tř. 18, 116 91 Prague 1; tel. 224933494; e-mail sturma@prf.cuni.cz; f. 1969 as Czechoslovak Society of International Law, present status 1993; attached to Acad. of Sciences of the Czech Republic; non-profit org. of academics and professionals in the field of int. law; cooperates with the Czech br. of the Int. Law Asscn and with foreign societies of int. law; represents, through its mems, the Czech doctrine of int. law in int. scientific orgs; organizes lectures and discussions, research conferences and publishes non-periodical books and periodicals; 96 mems; Pres. Prof. Dr PAVEL ŠTURMA;

Scientific Sec. Dr VERONIKA BÍLKOVÁ; First Vice-Pres. Prof. Dr DALIBOR JÍLEK.

Česká společnost pro politické vědy (Czech Association for Political Sciences): Nám. W. Churchilla 4, 130 67 Prague 3; tel. (2) 24095204; fax (2) 24220657; e-mail cabada@kap.zcu.cz; internet www.cspv.cz; f. 1964; 160 mems; Pres. Assoc. Prof. LADISLAV CABADA; Sec. Dr HELENA HRICOVÁ; publ. *Politologická Revue* (2 a year).

EDUCATION

Česká komise pro UNESCO (Czech Commission for UNESCO): Rutirska 31, 110 00 Prague 1; tel. 221610126; fax 221610122; e-mail unesco@mzv.cz; internet www.mzv.cz/unesco; f. 1994 as part of Ministry of Foreign Affairs; subsidiary advisory body of govt; Sec.-Gen. Ing. PAVEL SKODA.

Česká pedagogická společnost (Czech Pedagogical Association): Poříčí 31, 603 00 Brno; tel. 549493645; fax 543232722; e-mail sekretar@cpds.cz; internet www.cpds.cz; f. 1964; 240 mems; Pres. Doc. Dr TOMAS CECH; Sec. Dr MARTA RYBIČKOVÁ; publ. *Pedagogická orientace* (4 a year).

FINE AND PERFORMING ARTS

Asociace hudebních umělců a vědců (Association of Musicians and Musicologists): Maltézské nám. 1, 118 01 Prague 1; tel. 251553996; e-mail ahuv@seznam.cz; internet www.ahuv.cz; f. 1990; 1,200 mems; Pres. Prof. JIŘÍ HLAVÁČ; Exec. Sec. MARCELA POSEJPALOVÁ; publ. *Hudební rozhledy* (12 a year).

Česká hudební společnost (Czech Music Society): Radlická 99, 150 00 Prague 5; tel. and fax 251552453; e-mail mila.smetackova@volny.cz; f. 1973; 5,000 mems; Pres. MÍLA SMETÁČKOVÁ; Sec.-Gen. EVA ŠTRAUSOVÁ; publs *CHS News* (2 a year), *Josef Suk Society News* (2 a year), *Vítězslav Novák Society News* (1 a year).

Český filmový a televizní svaz (FITES) (Czech Film and Television Association): Pod Nuselskými schody 1721/3, 120 00 Prague 2; tel. 222562331; fax 222562331; e-mail info@fites.cz; internet www.fites.cz; f. 1966; 720 mems; Pres. MARTIN SKYBA; publ. *Synchron* (6 a year).

Český spolek pro komorní hudbu (Czech Chamber Music Society): c/o Česká filharmonie Rudolfinum, 1, Alšovo nábřeží 12, 110 00 Prague; tel. 227059343; fax 227059226; e-mail cskh@cfmail.cz; internet www.ceskafilharmonie.cz; f. 1894; 3,500 mems; Chair. Ing. IVAN ENGLICH.

Divadelní ústav (Theatre Institute): Celetná 17, 110 00 Prague 1; tel. 224809132; fax 224810278; internet www.divadlo.cz; f. 1956; research and documentation on Czech theatre; Czech centre of the International Theatre Institute (ITI); library of 100,000 vols; Dir ONDŘEJ ČERNÝ; publs *Divadelní noviny* (24 a year), *Divadelní revue* (4 a year), *Informační servis Divadelního ústavu* (12 a year), *Loutkář* (10 a year), *Ročenka českých divadel* (1 a year), *Theatre Czech* (1 a year).

Společnost pro estetiku (Society for Aesthetics): Department of Aesthetics, Faculty of Philosophy, Charles University, Celetná 20, 110 00 Prague 1; tel. 224491384; e-mail vlastimil.zuska@ff.cuni.cz; internet www.cas.cz/rvs/index_gb.html; f. 1969; 85 mems; Pres. Dr ROMAN DYKAST; Sec. K. NOVOTNÁ.

Unie výtvarných umělců (Union of Creative Artists): Masarykovo nábř. 250, 110 00 Prague 1; tel. and fax 541213555; e-mail uvucr@uvucr.cz; internet www.uvucr.cz; f. 1990; supports the professional interests of visual artists; acts as an information centre and coordinates the activities of its members;

keeps a register of professional visual artists working in the Czech Republic; 3,000 mems; Pres. VÁCLAV KUBÁT; Exec. Vice-Pres. VÍT WEBER; publs *Art Folia* (1 a year), *Atelier* (26 a year), *Technologia Artis* (1 a year), *Výtvarné umění* (4 a year).

HISTORY, GEOGRAPHY AND ARCHAEOLOGY

Česká archeologická společnost (Czech Archaeological Society): Letenská 4, 118 01 Prague 1; tel. 224317913; fax 221619730; e-mail zuzana.blahova@ff.cuni.cz; internet www.archaeology.cz/cas; f. 1919; 550 mems; Pres. Dr KAREL SKLENÁŘ; Sec. Dr ONDŘEJ CHVOJKA; publs *Archeologie Moravy a Slezska* (Archaeology of Moravia and Silesia, 1 a year), *Studia Hercynia* (1 a year), *Zprávy* (Bulletin, irregular).

Česká demografická společnost (Czech Demographic Society): Albertov 6, 128 43 Prague 2; tel. 221951418; fax 224920657; e-mail demodept@natur.cuni.cz; internet www.natur.cuni.cz/~demodept/cds; f. 1964; 450 mems; Pres. JITKA RYCHTAŘÍKOVÁ; Sec. FELIX KOSCHIN.

Česká geografická společnost (Czech Geographical Society): Albertov 6, 128 43 Prague 2; tel. 221951383; fax 224920657; e-mail perlin@natur.cuni.cz; internet www.geography.cz; f. 1894; 600 mems; Pres. Prof. TADEUSZ SIWEK; Scientific Sec. Dr RADIM PERLÍN; Sec. Dr DANA FIALOVÁ; publs *Geografické rozhledy* (Geographical perspective, 12 a year), *Geography* (scientific journal, 4 a year), *Informace České geografické společnosti* (2 a year).

Matice moravská (Moravian Society of History and Literature): Arne Nováka 1, 602 00 Brno; tel. 549493552; fax 549491520; e-mail matice@phil.muni.cz; internet www.matice-moravska.cz; f. 1849; 560 mems; Pres. Prof. Dr JIŘÍ MALÍŘ; Sec. Dr BRONISLAV CHOCHOLÁČ; publ. *Časopis Matice moravské* (2 a year).

LANGUAGE AND LITERATURE

Alliance Française: c/o French Embassy in the Czech Republic, Štěpánská 35, 111 21 Prague 1; tel. 221401063; fax 222230576; e-mail michel.wattremez@diplomatie.gouv.fr; internet www.alliancefrancaise.cz; offers courses and exams in French language and culture and promotes cultural exchange with France; attached offices in Brno, České Budějovice, Hradec Králové, Kladno, Kroměříž, Liberec, Louny, Ostrava, Pardubice, Plzeň, Pribram, Ústí nad Labem and Zlín; General Coordinator MICHEL WATTREMEZ.

British Council: Bredovský dvůr, Politických vězňů 13, 110 00 Prague 1; tel. 221991160; fax 224933847; e-mail info.praha@britishcouncil.cz; internet www.britishcouncil.cz; teaching centre; offers courses and exams in English language and British culture and promotes cultural exchange with the UK; attached teaching centre in Pilsen; Dir and Cultural Counsellor MANDY JOHNSON; Asst Dir, Teaching Centre DUNCAN LAMBE.

Český esperantský svaz (Czech Union of Esperantists): c/o Pavel Polnicky, Na Vinici 110/10, 290 01 Podebrady; e-mail cea.polnicky@quick.cz; internet www.esperanto.cz; tel. 325615651; f. 1969; 1,100 mems; Pres. VĚRA PODHRADSKÁ; publ. *Starto* (4 a year).

Czech Centre of International PEN: POB 123, 110 00 Prague 1; Klementinum 190 (Nat. Library Bldg), 5 Fl., 110 00 Prague; tel. and fax (2) 24234343; e-mail centrum@pen.cz; internet www.pen.cz; f. 1924; Writers in Prison Cttee; regular authors' readings,

exhibitions, spring and autumn literary festivals, discussions with writers in schools, clubs and civic facilities; awards Karel Čapek Prize and PEN Club Lifetime Achievement Prize every 2 years; 197 mems, incl. 13 hon. mems; Pres. Mgr JIRI DĚDEČEK; Dir Ing. LIBUŠE LUDVÍKOVÁ; Sec. DANA MOJŽÍŠOVÁ.

Goethe-Institut: Masarykovo nábřeží 32, 110 00 Prague 1; tel. 221962111; fax 221962250; e-mail info@prag.goethe.org; internet www.goethe.de/ins/cz/pra/; offers courses and exams in German language and culture and promotes cultural exchange with Germany; library of 14,000 vols; Dir Dr STEPHAN NOBBE.

Literárněvědná společnost (Literary Society): Katedra slavistiky PF Univerzity Hradec Králové, Rokitanského 62, 500 03 Hradec Králové; tel. 493331360; e-mail oldřich.richterek@uhk.cz; f. 1934; 285 mems; Pres. Prof. Dr OLDŘICH RICHTEREK.

Obec spisovatelů (Society of Czech Writers): Železná 18, 110 00 Prague 1; tel. 224234060; fax 224234060; e-mail obecspis@volny.cz; internet www.obecspisovatelu.cz; f. 1989; seminars, debates and conferences; 700 mems; Hon. Pres. VÁCLAV HAVEL; Pres. VLADIMÍR KŘIVÁNEK; publ. *Dokořán* (4 a year).

MEDICINE

Česká imunologická společnost (Czech Society for Immunology): Vídeňská 1083, 142 20 Prague 4; e-mail cis@biomed.cas.cz; internet www.biomed.cas.cz/cis/; f. 1986; 600 mems; Pres. Prof. Dr ALEŠ MACELA; Sec. Dr MARTIN BILEJ; publ. *Imunologický zpravodaj* (3 a year).

Česká lékařská společnost J. E. Purkyně (J. E. Purkyně Czech Medical Association): Sokolská 31, 120 26 Prague 2; tel. 224266201; fax 224266212; e-mail cls@cls.cz; internet www.cls.cz; f. 1947; 34,500 mems; Pres. Prof. Dr JAROSLAV BLAHOŠ; Scientific Sec. Prof. Dr JIŘÍ HOMOLKA; publs *Acta Chirurgiae Plasticae* (in English, 4 a year), *Anesteziologie a intenzivní medicína* (Anaesthesiology and Intensive Critical Care Medicine, 6 a year), *Časopis lékařů českých* (Journal of Czech Physicians, 12 a year), *Česká a slovenská farmacie* (Czech and Slovak Pharmacy, 6 a year), *Česká a slovenská gastroenterologie a hepatologie* (Czech and Slovak Gastroenterology and Hepatology, 6 a year), *Česká a slovenská neurologie a neurochirurgie* (Czech and Slovak Neurology and Neurosurgery, 6 a year), *Česká a slovenská oftalmologie* (Czech and Slovak Ophthalmology, 6 a year), *Česká a slovenská psychiatrie* (Czech and Slovak Psychiatry, 8 a year), *Česká gynekologie* (Czech Gynaecology, 6 a year), *Česká radiologie* (Czech Radiology, 6 a year), *Česká revmatologie* (Czech Rheumatology, 4 a year), *Česká stomatologie a Praktické zubní lékařství* (Czech Stomatology and Practical Dentistry, 6 a year), *Česko-slovenská dermatologie* (Czech-Slovak Dermatology, 6 a year), *Česko-slovenská patologie a Soudní lékařství* (Czech-Slovak Pathology and Forensic Medicine, 4 a year), *Česko-slovenská pediatrie* (Czech-Slovak Paediatrics, 12 a year), *Česko-slovenská fyziologie* (Czechoslovak Physiology, 4 a year), *Epidemiologie, mikrobiologie, imunologie* (Epidemiology, Microbiology, Immunology, 4 a year), *Hygiena* (Hygiene, 4 a year), *Klinická biochemie a metabolismus* (Clinical Biochemistry and Metabolism, 4 a year), *Klinická onkologie* (Clinical Oncology, 6 a year), *Lékař a technika* (Physician and Technology, 6 a year), *Otorinolaryngologie a foniatrie* (Otorhinolaryngology and Phoniatrics, 4 a year), *Pracovní lékařství* (Occupational Medicine, 4 a year), *Praktický lékař* (The Generalist, 12 a year), *Rehabilitace a fyzikální lékařství*

(Rehabilitation and Physical Medicine, 4 a year), *Rozhledy v chirurgii* (Surgical Review, 12 a year), *Vnitřní lékařství* (Internal Medicine, 12 a year), *Revizní a posudkové lékařství* (Health Insurance and Medical Revision, 4 a year), *Endoskopie* (Endoscopy, 4 a year), *Transfuze a hematologie dnes* (Transfusion and Haematology Today, 4 a year).

NATURAL SCIENCES

General

Český svaz vědeckotechnických společností (Czech Association of Scientific and Technical Societies): Novotného lávka 5, 116 68 Prague 1; tel. 221082294; fax 222221780; e-mail poriz@csvts.cz; internet www.csvts.cz; f. 1990; 136,000 mems; Pres. Ing. DANIEL HANUS; Sec. Ing. VLADIMÍR PORIZ; publs *Bio Prospect* (irregular), *Chemical Papers (Prague)* (6 a year), *Glass Paper* (irregular), *Plant Physician* (4 a year), *Reporter* (4 a year), *Silicate Reporter* (irregular).

Společnost pro dějiny věd a techniky (Society of the History of Sciences and Technology): Kostelní 42, 170 78 Prague 7; tel. 220399208; fax 233371801; e-mail barvikova@archiv.cas.cz; internet dvt .hyperlink.cz; f. 1965; 300 mems; Pres. Prof. PETR SVOBODNY; Sec. Dr MILADA SEKYRKOVÁ; publs *Acta historiae rerum naturalium necnon technicarum* (1 a year), *Dějiny věd a techniky* (4 a year), *Práce z dějin techniky a přívodních věd* (Treatise on the History of Technology and Sciences, irregular).

Biological Sciences

Česká botanická společnost (Czech Botanical Society): Benátská 2, 128 01 Prague 2; tel. 221951664; e-mail botspol@natur .cuni.cz; internet www.natur.cuni.cz/cbs; f. 1912; 787 mems; library of 3,000 vols, 1,400 periodicals; Chair. Dr LUBOMÍR HROUDA; Sec. Dr J. ŠTĚPÁNEK; publs *Preslia* (4 a year), *Zprávy ČBS* (irregular).

Česká parazitologická společnost (Czech Society for Parasitology): c/o Institute of Postgraduate Medical Education, 10, Ruská 85, 100 05 Prague; tel. 271019254; fax 272740458; e-mail fajfrlik@fnplzen.cz; internet www.parazitologie.cz; f. 1993; 199 mems; Pres. Dr LIBUSE KOLÁŘOVÁ; Sec. Dr KAREL FAJFRLÍK; publ. *Zprávy České parazitologické společnosti* (4 a year).

Česká společnost bioklimatologická (Czech Society for Bioclimatology): Boční II 1401, 141 31 Prague 4; tel. 267103321; fax 272761549; e-mail jstr@ig.cas.cz; internet www.cbks.cz; f. 1965; 75 mems; Pres. Dr J. ROŽNOVSKÝ; Sec. J. STŘEŠTIK; publ. *Digests of Science Reports* (1 a year).

Česká společnost entomologická (Czech Entomological Society): Vinicna 7, 128 00 Prague 2; tel. 224923535; e-mail klapagenda@centrum.cz; internet www .entospol.cz; f. 1904; 750 mems; library of 20,500 vols; Pres. Dr JOSEF JELINEK; Sec. Dr KLARA FARKACOVA; publ. *Klapalekiana* (2 a year).

Česká společnost histo- a cytochemická (Czech Society for Histo- and Cytochemistry): Kamenice 3, 625 00 Brno; tel. 549493701; fax 549491320; e-mail pdubovy@med.muni.cz; internet www.med.muni.cz/hcspol; f. 1962; associated with the International Federation of Societies for Histochemistry and Cytochemistry; 120 mems; Pres. Prof. Dr PETR DUBOVÝ; Sec. Prof. Dr SVATOPLUK ČECH.

Česká společnost pro biomechaniku (Czech Society for Biomechanics): FTVS–Katedra anatomie a biomechaniky, J. Martiho 31, 160 00 Prague 6; tel. and fax 220560225; e-mail otahal@ftvs.cuni.cz;

internet biomech.ftvs.cuni.cz/csb; f. 1990; 168 mems; Pres. Prof. STANISLAV OTÁHAL; Sec. Asst Prof. MIROSLAV SOCHOR; publ. *Bulletin* (2 a year).

Česká společnost zoologická (Czech Zoological Society): Viničná 7, 128 44 Prague; tel. 221951860; e-mail chalupsk@natur.cuni.cz; internet www.natur.cuni.cz/zoospol; f. 1927; 230 mems; library of 17,900 vols; Pres. Dr VÁCLAV PIŽL; Sec. Dr M. SVÁTORA; publ. *Acta Societatis Zoologicae Bohemicae* (4 a year).

Česká vědecká společnost pro mykologii (Czech Scientific Society for Mycology): POB 106, 111 21 Prague 1; tel. 533435238; e-mail cvsm@natur.cuni.cz; internet www .natur.cuni.cz/cvsm; f. 1946; voluntary org. for professional and amateur mycologists; organizes mycological lectures for the public, mycological excursions (mushroom-picking, micromycetes), seminar meetings; 200 mems; library of 900 vols, 135 journals; Pres. Dr VLADIMÍR ANTONÍN; Sec. Dr ALENA KUBÁTOVÁ; publs *Czech Mycology* (in English, 2 a year), *Mykologické Listy* (in Czech with English summary, 4 a year).

Československá biologická společnost (Czechoslovak Biological Society): Tomešova 12, 602 00 Brno; tel. and fax 549492394; e-mail rjanisch@med.muni.cz; internet www .med.muni.cz/biolspol; f. 1922; 1,902 vols; Pres. Prof. Dr V. MORNSTEIN; Sec. Prof. Dr R. JANISCH; publ. *Zpravodaj Čs. Biologické společnosti* (Bulletin of the Czechoslovak Biological Society, in Czech, 2 a year).

Československá společnost mikrobiologická (Czechoslovak Society for Microbiology): Vídeňská 1083, 142 20 Prague 4; tel. 296442494; fax 296442396; e-mail gabriel@ biomed.cas.cz; internet www.cssm.info; f. 1928; organizes int. and nat. conferences in the field of basic and applied microbiology, molecular biology and genetics; courses for both undergraduate and postgraduate students; 1,000 mems from Czech Republic and Slovakia; Pres. Prof. IVAN ČIŽNÁR; Sec.-Gen. Dr JIRI GABRIEL; publs *Bulletin* (Czech, Slovak, 4 a year), *Folia microbiologica* (English, 6 a year).

Mathematical Sciences

Jednota českých matematiků a fyziků (Union of Czech Mathematicians and Physicists): Žitná 25, 117 10 Prague 1; tel. 222211100; e-mail predseda@jcmf.cz; internet www.jcmf.cz; f. 1862; 2,300 mems; Pres. S. ZAJAC; publs *Matematika-Fyzika-Informatika* (12 a year), *Pokroky matematiky, fyziky a astronomie* (4 a year), *Rozhledy matematicko-fyzikální* (4 a year), *Učitel matematiky* (4 a year).

Physical Sciences

Česká astronomická společnost (Czech Astronomical Society): Královská obora 233, 170 21 Prague 7; tel. (2) 33377204; e-mail info@astro.cz; internet www.astro.cz; f. 1917; 700 mems; Pres. Dr JIŘÍ BOROVIČKA; Sec. Dr MILOSLAV ZEJDA; publ. *Kosmické rozhledy* (irregular).

Česká geologická společnost (Czech Geological Society): V Holešovičkách 41, 182 09 Prague 8; tel. 266009323; fax 266410649; e-mail budil@cgu.cz; internet www .geologickaspolecnost.cz; f. 1923; 500 mems; Pres. Dr PETR BUDIL; Sec. BLANKA ČIZKOVÁ; publ. *Journal* (4 a year).

Česká meteorologická společnost (Czech Meteorological Society): Na Šabatce 17, 143 06 Prague; tel. 221912548; fax 221912533; e-mail kmop@mff.cuni.cz; internet www .chmi.cz/poboc/br/metspol; f. 1958; provides information on meteorology and climatology, history of meteorology, and meteorological bibliography and terminology; 200 mems;

Pres. Prof. Dr JAN BEDNÁŘ; Sec. Doc. Dr TOMÁŠ HALENKA.

Česká společnost chemická (Czech Chemical Society): Novotneho lavka 5, 116 68 Prague 1; tel. 221082383; fax 222220184; e-mail csch@csch.cz; internet www.csch.cz; f. 1866; 3,480 mems; Pres. Prof. Dr JITKA ULRICHOVÁ; publs *Bulletin* (4 a year), *Chemické Listy* (12 a year).

Spektroskopická společnost J. Marca Marci (J. Marcus Marci Spectroscopic Society): Thákurova 7, 166 29 Prague 6; Masarykova univerzita, Přírodovědecká fakulta, Kotlářská 2, 611 37 Brno; tel. (54) 9491436; fax (54) 9492494; e-mail immss@ spektroskopie.cz; internet www .spektroskopie.cz; f. 1949; 970 mems; Chair. Prof. Dr VIKTOR KANICKÝ; Scientific Sec. Prof. Dr JAN HÁLA.

Vědecká společnost pro nauku o kovech (Metals Society): Ke Karlovu 5, 121 16 Prague 2; tel. 221911362; fax 221911490; e-mail vsnk@met.mff.cuni.cz; f. 1966; 170 mems; Pres. Prof. VLADIMÍR ČÍHAL; Sec. Prof. VLADIMÍR SÍMA.

PHILOSOPHY AND PSYCHOLOGY

Filozofický ústav Akademie věd České republiky (Institute of Philosophy of the Czech Academy of Sciences): Jilská 1, 110 00 Prague 1; tel. 222220099; fax 222220108; e-mail flusekr@site.cas.cz; internet www.flu .cas.cz; f. 1990; 250 mems; Dir Dr PAVEL BARAN; publs *Acta Comeniana* (in English, French and German), *Filosofický časopis* (Philosophical Journal, summaries in English and German; 6 a year), *Teorie vedy* (Theory of Science, in Czech and English; 4 a year).

RELIGION, SOCIOLOGY AND ANTHROPOLOGY

Česká společnost antropologická (Czech Anthropological Society): Viničná 7, 128 44 Prague 2; internet anthropology.cz; f. 1964; 180 mems; Pres. Dr J. JELÍNEK; Sec. Doc. Dr V. NOVOTNÝ; publ. *Zprávy* (4 a year).

Masarykova česká sociologická společnost (Masaryk Czech Sociological Association): Husova 4, 110 00 Prague 1; tel. 222220631; fax 222220631; e-mail mcss@ seznam.cz; internet www.ceskasociologicka .org; f. 1964; 300 mems; Pres. Dr MICHAL ILNER.

Národopisná společnost (Ethnographical Society): Národní třída 3, 117 20 Prague 1; e-mail valka@phil.muni.cz; f. 1893; 280 mems; Pres. Dr MIROSLAV VÁLKA; publs *Národopisný věstník* (1 a year), *Zpravodaj Národopisné Společnosti* (3 a year).

TECHNOLOGY

Česká společnost pro kybernetiku a informatiku (Czech Society for Cybernetics and Informatics): Pod Vodárenskou věží 2, 182 07 Prague 8; tel. 266053901; fax 286585789; e-mail cski@utia.cas.cz; internet www.cski.cz; f. 1966; 350 mems; Pres. OLGA ŠTĚPÁNKOVÁ; Sec. DAGMAR HARMANCOVÁ; publs *Kybernetika* (in English, 6 a year), *Zpravodaj* (12 a year).

Česká společnost pro mechaniku (Czech Society for Mechanics): Dolejškova 5, 182 00 Prague 8; tel. 266053045; e-mail csm@it.cas .cz; internet www.csm.cz; f. 1966; 580 individual mems, 18 organizational mems; Pres. Prof. Ing. MILOSLAV OKROUHLÍK; Sec. Ing. JITKA HAVLÍNOVÁ; publ. *Bulletin* (3 a year).

Česká společnost pro vědeckou kinematografii (Czech Society for Scientific Cinematography): Zemědělská 1665/1, 613 00 Brno-Černá Pole; tel. 545135021; fax 545135013; e-mail rygl@mendelu.cz; f. 1923;

150 mems; Pres. Ing. V. Bouček; Sec. Ing. L. Rygl; publ. *Bulletin* (1 a year).

Research Institutes

ARCHITECTURE AND TOWN PLANNING

ABF—Nadace pro rozvoj architektury a stavitelství (Architecture and Building Foundation): Václavské nám. 833/31, 110 00 Prague 1; tel. 224225001; fax 224233136; e-mail fibiger@abf-nadace.cz; internet www .abf-nadace.cz; f. 1991; includes Česká stavební akademie (Czech Building Academy); organises 2 evaluative competions: Stavba roku (Building of the year) and Vyrok-technologie roku (Product- technology of the year); organises spec. exibitions; library of 10,000 vols; Dir Dr Jan Fibiger; Sec. Petra Prokopova; publs *ABF Forum* (4 a year), *Building Products Review* (1 a year), *Forum of Architecture and Building* (12 a year).

ECONOMICS, LAW AND POLITICS

CERGE-EI: POB 882, Politických vězňů 7, 111 21 Prague 1; tel. 224005123; fax 224227143; e-mail office@cerge-ei.cz; internet www.cerge-ei.cz; f. 1991; attached to Acad. of Sciences of the Czech Republic and to Charles University; conducts American-style PhD program in Economics; library of 80,000 vols; depository for World Bank publs; Dir Dr Lubomír Lízal; publs *Czech Republic* (1 a year), *Working Papers* (12 a year).

Ústav státu práva AV ČR (Institute of State and Law AS CR): Národní 18, 116 91 Prague 1; tel. 221990711; fax 224933056; e-mail ilaw@ilaw.cas.cz; internet www.ilaw .cas.cz; attached to Acad. of Sciences of the Czech Republic; library of 40,000 vols, 100 periodicals; Dir Dr Jaroslav Zachariáš; publ. *Právnik* (12 a year).

FINE AND PERFORMING ARTS

Ústav dějin umění AV ČR, v.v.i. (Institute of Art History AS CR, v. v. i.): Husova 4, 110 00 Prague 1; tel. 222222144; fax 222221654; e-mail arthist@site.cas.cz; internet www.udu .cas.cz; f. 1953; attached to Acad. of Sciences of the Czech Republic; Dir Dr Lubomír Konečný; publs *Estetika: The Central European Journal of Aesthetics* (2 a year), *Fontes Historiae Artium* (book series, irregular), *Studia Rudolphina* (1 a year), *Umění* (6 a year).

HISTORY, GEOGRAPHY AND ARCHAEOLOGY

Archeologický ústav AV ČR, Brno (Archaeological Institute AS CR, Brno): Královopolská 147, 612 64 Brno; tel. 541514101; fax 541514123; e-mail archeo@iabrno.cz; internet www.iabrno.cz; attached to Acad. of Sciences of the Czech Republic; Dir Dr Pavel Kouřil; publs *Fontes Archeologicae Moravicae* (irregular), *Studie Archeologického ústavu* (2 a year).

Archeologický ústav AV ČR, Praha (Archaeological Institute AS CR, Prague): Letenská 4, 118 01 Prague 1; tel. 257530922; fax 257532288; e-mail jiran@arup.cas.cz; internet www.arup.cas.cz; f. 1919; attached to Acad. of Sciences of the Czech Republic; Dir Dr Luboš Jiráň; publs *Archeologické rozhledy* (4 a year), *Památky archeologické* (2 a year).

Historický ústav AV ČR (Institute of History AS CR): Prosecká 76, 190 00 Prague 9; tel. 286887513; fax 286887513; e-mail bucharova@hiu.cas.cz; internet www.hiu.cas .cz; f. 1921; attached to Acad. of Sciences of the Czech Republic; Dir Dr Miloslav

Polívka; publs *Český časopis historický* (4 a year), *Folia Historica Bohemica* (irregular), *Historia Europae Centralis* (1 a year), *Historica* (Historical Sciences in the Czech Republic, annual), *Historická geografie* (every 2 years), *Mediaevalia Historica Bohemica* (1 a year), *Moderní dějiny* (1 a year), *Slovanské historické studie* (1 a year), *Slovanský přehled* (4 a year).

Kabinet pro klasická studia FLÚ AV ČR (Institute for Classical Studies AS CR): Na Florenci 3, 110 00 Prague 1; tel. 222828303; fax 222828305; e-mail uks@ics.cas.cz; internet www.ics.cas.cz; f. 1953; attached to Acad. of Sciences of the Czech Republic; Head Dr Jiří Beneš; publs *Eirene* (on classical studies, 1 a year), *Listy filologické* (Folia Philologica, 2 a year).

Orientální ústav AV ČR (Oriental Institute AS CR): Pod vodárenskou věží 4, 182 08 Prague 8; tel. 266053111; fax 286581897; e-mail orient@orient.cas.cz; internet www .orient.cas.cz; f. 1922; attached to Acad. of Sciences of the Czech Republic; research in history, religious and philosophical systems, languages, literatures and cultures of Asia and Africa; 16 mems; library of 210,000 vols; Dir Dr Stanislava Vavrouškova; Sec. Pavel Hons; publ. *Archiv orientální* (4 a year).

Slovanský ústav AV ČR (Institute of Slavonic Studies AS CR): Valentinská 1, 110 00 Prague 1; tel. 224800251; fax 224800252; e-mail slu@slu.cas.cz; internet www.slu.cas .cz; f. 1922; attached to Acad. of Sciences of the Czech Republic; Dir Prof. Vladimír Vavřínek; publs *Byzantinoslavica* (2 a year), *Germanoslavica* (2 a year), *Slavia* (4 a year).

Ústav pro soudobé dějiny AV ČR v.v.i. (Institute of Contemporary History AS CR v.v.i.): Vlašská 9, 118 40 Prague 1; tel. 257286362; fax 257531121; e-mail usd@usd .cas.cz; internet www.usd.cas.cz; f. 1990; attached to Acad. of Sciences of the Czech Republic; Czech and Slovak history from 1938–2000; library of 35,000 vols; Dir Dr Oldřich Tůma; publ. *Soudobé dějiny*.

Výzkumný ústav geodetický, topografický a kartografický (VUGTK) (Research Institute of Geodesy, Topography and Cartography): 250 66 Zdiby 98; tel. 284890351; fax 284890056; e-mail vugtk@vugtk.cz; internet www.vugtk.cz; f. 1954; library of 70,000 vols; Dir Dr Ing. Václav Slaboch; publ. *Proceedings of Research Works* (every 2 years).

LANGUAGE AND LITERATURE

Ústav pro českou literaturu AV ČR (Institute of Czech Literature AS CR): Na Florenci 3/1420, 110 00 Prague 1; tel. 234612111; fax 224818437; e-mail literatura@ucl.cas.cz; internet www.ucl.cas .cz; f. 1947; attached to Acad. of Sciences of the Czech Republic; library of 130,000 vols; Dir Dr Pavel Janoušek; publ. *Česká literatura* (6 a year).

Ústav pro jazyk český AV ČR (Czech Language Institute AS CR): Letenská 4, 118 51 Prague 1; tel. 257533756; fax 257531761; e-mail ujc@ujc.cas.cz; internet www.ujc.cas .cz; f. 1911; attached to Acad. of Sciences of the Czech Republic; Dir Dr Karel Oliva; publs *Acta Onomastica* (1 a year), *Bibliografie české lingvistiky* (1 a year), *Časopis pro moderní filologii* (2 a year), *Linguistica Pragensia* (2 a year), *Naše řeč* (5 a year), *Slovo a slovestnost* (4 a year).

MEDICINE

Farmakologický ústav AV ČR (Institute of Pharmacology AS CR): 4–Krč, Vídeňská 1083, 142 20 Prague; tel. 261710024; e-mail

fkuavcr@biomed.cas.cz; internet www.cas.cz; attached to Acad. of Sciences of the Czech Republic; Dir Dr Evžen Buchar.

Ústav experimentální medicíny AV ČR (Institute of Experimental Medicine AS CR): Vídeňská 1083, 142 20 Prague 4; tel. 241062230; fax 241062782; e-mail uemavcr@biomed.cas.cz; internet uemweb .biomed.cas.cz; f. 1975; attached to Acad. of Sciences of the Czech Republic; Dir Prof. Eva Syková.

NATURAL SCIENCES

General

Ústav geoniky AV ČR (Institute of Geonics AS CR): Poruba, Studentská 1768, 708 00 Ostrava; tel. 596979352; fax 596919452; e-mail geonics@ugn.cas.cz; internet www .ugn.cas.cz; f. 1982; attached to Acad. of Sciences of the Czech Republic; Dir Prof. Radim Blaheta; publ. *Moravian Geographical Report* (4 a year).

Biological Sciences

Biofyzikální ústav AV ČR (Institute of Biophysics AS CR): Královopolská 135, 612 65 Brno; tel. 541517111; fax 541211293; e-mail ibp@ibp.cz; internet www.ibp.cz; f. 1955; attached to Acad. of Sciences of the Czech Republic; Dir Dr Stanislav Kozubek.

Botanický ústav AV ČR (Institute of Botany AS CR): Zámek 1, 252 43 Průhonice; tel. 271015233; fax 271015105; e-mail ibot@ibot .cas.cz; internet www.ibot.cas.cz; attached to Acad. of Sciences of the Czech Republic; Dir Dr František Krahulec; publs *Folia Geobotanica* (4 a year), *Index Seminum et Plantarum* (1 a year).

Biologické centrum AV ČR, v.v.i., Entomologický ústav (Biology Centre AS CR v.v.i., Institute of Entomology): Branišovská 1160/31, 370 05 České Budějovice; tel. 385310350; fax 385310354; e-mail entu@ entu.cas.cz; internet www.entu.cas.cz; f. 1962, part of Biology Centre AS CR since 2006; attached to Acad. of Sciences of the Czech Republic; basic and applied research on insects as models for biological research or as pests or species important for environment monitoring; Dir Prof. Dr František Sehnal; Head Jan Šula; publ. *European Journal of Entomology* (4 a year).

Fyziologický ústav AV ČR, v.v.i. (Institute of Physiology AS CR): Vídeňská 1083, 142 20 Prague 4; tel. 241062424; fax 241062488; e-mail fgu@biomed.cas.cz; internet www.biomed.cas.cz; f. 1954; attached to Acad. of Sciences of the Czech Republic; Dir Dr Jaroslav Kuneš; publ. *Physiological Research* (6 a year).

Hydrobiologický ústav AV ČR (Hydrobiological Institute AS CR): Na sádkách 7, 370 05 České Budějovice; tel. 387775881; fax 385310248; e-mail hbu@hbu.cas.cz; internet www.hbu.cas.cz; attached to Acad. of Sciences of the Czech Republic; Dir Dr Josef Matěna.

Mikrobiologický ústav AV ČR (Institute of Microbiology AS CR): Vídeňská 1083, 142 20 Prague 4; tel. 244472272; fax 244471286; e-mail mbu@biomed.cas.cz; internet www .biomed.cas.cz/mbu; f. 1962; attached to Acad. of Sciences of the Czech Republic; Dir Prof. RNDr Blanka Říhová; publ. *Folia Microbiologica* (6 a year).

Parazitologický ústav AV ČR (Institute of Parasitology AS CR): Branišovská 31, 370 05 České Budějovice; tel. 387775403; fax 385310388; e-mail paru@paru.cas.cz; internet www.paru.cas.cz; f. 1962; attached to Acad. of Sciences of the Czech Republic; Dir Dr Tomáš Scholz; publ. *Folia Parasitologica* (4 a year).

Ústav biologie obratlorců AV ČR, v.v.i (Institute of Vertebrate Biology AS CR, v.v.i): Květná 8, 603 65 Brno; tel. 543422538; fax 543211346; e-mail ubo@ivb.cz; internet www .ivb.cz; f. 1954; 50 mems; attached to Acad. of Sciences of the Czech Republic; library of 36,371 vols of zoology; Dir Dr Ing. MARCEL HONZA; publs *Biennial Report IVB, Folia Zoologica* (4 a year).

Ústav experimentální botaniky AV ČR (Institute of Experimental Botany AS CR): Rozvojová 263, 165 02 Prague 6; tel. 225106453; fax 225106456; e-mail zazimalova@ueb.cas.cz; internet www.ueb .cas.cz; f. 1962; attached to Acad. of Sciences of the Czech Republic; Dir Asst Prof. Doc. EVA ZAŽÍMALOVÁ; publs *Biologia Plantarum* (irregular), *Photosynthetica* (irregular).

Ústav fyziky plazmatu AV ČR (Institute of Plasma Physics AS CR): Za Slovankou 3, 182 21 Prague 8; tel. 266052052; fax 286586389; e-mail ipp@ipp.cas.cz; internet www.ipp.cas .cz; f. 1959; attached to Acad. of Sciences of the Czech Republic; Dir Prof. Dr Ing. PAVEL CHRÁSKA.

Ústav molekulární biologie rostlin AV ČR, v.v.i. (Institute of Plant Molecular Biology AS CR, v.v.i.): Branišovská 31, 370 05 České Budějovice; tel. 385310357; fax 385310356; e-mail umbr@umbr.cas.cz; internet www.umbr.cas.cz; f. 1991; attached to Biology Centre, Acad. of Sciences of the Czech Republic; Dir Prof. Dr J. ŠPAK.

Ústav molekulární genetiky AV ČR, v.v.i. (Institute of Molecular Genetics AS CR, v.v.i.): Vídeňská 1083, 142 20 Prague 4; tel. 241063215; fax 224310955; e-mail office@ img.cas.cz; internet www.img.cas.cz; f. 1961 as Institute of Experimental Biology and Genetics; joined with several biochemical laboratories of the Institute of Organic Chemistry and Biochemistry and renamed Institute of Molecular Genetics 1977; public research instn 2007; attached to Acad. of Sciences of the Czech Republic; basic and applied research in molecular biology and genetics and in cell biology, incl. molecular and cellular immunology, functional genomics and bioinformatics, virology, oncogene biology, apoptosis, molecular biology of development, mechanisms of receptor signalling and cell differentiation, biology of cytoskeleton, epigenetic mechanisms, genome stability, and structural biology; Dir Prof. VÁCLAV HOŘEJŠÍ.

Ústav organické chemie a biochemie AV ČR (Institute of Organic Chemistry and Biochemistry AS CR): Flemingovo nám. 2, 166 10 Prague 6; tel. 220183333; fax 220183578; e-mail uochb@uochb.cas.cz; internet www.uochb.cas.cz; f. 1950; attached to Acad. of Sciences of the Czech Republic; Dir Dr ZDENĚK HAVLAS; publ. *Collection of Czechoslovak Chemical Communications* (12 a year).

Ústav půdní biologie AV ČR (Institute of Soil Biology AS CR): Na sádkách 7, České Budějovice; tel. 385310134; fax 385300133; e-mail upb@upb.cas.cz; internet www.upb .cas.cz; f. 1979; attached to Acad. of Sciences of the Czech Republic; Dir Dr VÁCLAV PIŽL.

Ústav živočišné fyziologie a genetiky AV ČR (Institute of Animal Physiology and Genetics AS CR): Rumburská 89, 277 21 Liběchov; tel. 206639511; fax 206697186; e-mail uzfg@iapg.cas.cz; internet www.iapg .cas.cz/uzfg; attached to Acad. of Sciences of the Czech Republic; Dir Prof. Dr IVAN MÍŠEK.

Mathematical Sciences

Český statistický úřad (Czech Statistical Office): Na padesátém 81, 100 82 Prague 10; tel. and fax 274054070; internet www.czso .cz; f. 1899; library of 27,500 vols; Pres. JAN FISCHER; publs *CZSO Monthly Statistics, Selected Economic and Social Indicators of the Czech Republic* (4 a year), *Statistical Bulletin* (4 a year).

Matematický ústav AV ČR (Mathematical Institute AS CR): Žitná 25, 115 67 Prague 1; tel. 222090711; fax 222211638; e-mail mathinst@math.cas.cz; internet www.math .cas.cz; f. 1947; attached to Acad. of Sciences of the Czech Republic; Dir Prof. ANTONIN SOCHOR; publs *Applications of Mathematics* (6 a year), *Czechoslovak Mathematical Journal* (4 a year), *Mathematica Bohemica* (4 a year).

Physical Sciences

Astronomický ústav AV ČR (Astronomical Institute AS CR): Fricova 298, 251 65 Ondřejov; tel. 323620113; fax 323620117; e-mail sekretariat@asu.cas.cz; internet www .asu.cas.cz; f. 1950; attached to Acad. of Sciences of the Czech Republic; Dir Dr PETR HEINZEL; publs *Scripta Astronomica* (irregular), *Time and Latitude* (4 a year).

Česká geologická služba (Czech Geological Survey): 118 21 Prague 1, Klárov 3; tel. 257089500; fax 257531376; e-mail secretar@cgu.cz; internet www.geology.cz; f. 1919; library: see Libraries and Archives; Dir Mgr. ZDENĚK VENERA; publs *Bulletin of Geosciences* (4 a year), *Geological Bibliography of the Czech Republic* (1 a year), *Geoscience Research Reports* (1 a year), *Journal of Geological Sciences* (1 a year), *Special Papers* (1 a year).

Fyzikální ústav AV ČR (Institute of Physics AS CR): Na Slovance 2, 182 21 Prague 8; tel. 266053111; fax 286890527; e-mail secretary@fzu.cz; internet www.fzu.cz; f. 1954; attached to Acad. of Sciences of the Czech Republic; Dir Dr KAREL JUNGWIRTH; publs *Československý časopis pro fyziku* (6 a year), *Czechoslovak Journal of Physics* (12 a year), *Jemná mechanika a optika* (Fine Mechanics and Optics, 12 a year).

Geofyzikální ústav AV ČR (Geophysical Institute AS CR): Boční II/1401, 141 31 Prague 4; tel. 267103111; fax 272761549; e-mail gfu@ig.cas.cz; internet www.ig.cas.cz; f. 1953; attached to Acad. of Sciences of the Czech Republic; Dir Dr ALEŠ ŠPIČÁK; publs *Bulletin of the Czechoslovak Seismological Stations* (1 a year), *Studia Geophysica et Geodaetica* (4 a year), *Travaux Géophysiques* (1 a year).

Geologický ústav AV ČR, v.v.i. (Institute of Geology AS CR, v.v.i.): 6–Lysolaje, Rozvojová 269, 165 00 Prague; tel. 233087111; fax 220922670; e-mail inst@gli.cas.cz; internet www.gli.cas.cz; f. 1957; attached to Acad. of Sciences of the Czech Republic; library of 10,000 vols; geology, especially petrology, mineralogy, basin analysis and tectonics, palaeontology, environmental geology and geochemistry, karstology, pedology; Dir Dr VACLAV CILEK; publs *Geolines* (2 a year), *Institute Research Reports* (1 a year).

Společná laboratoř chemie pevných látek AV ČR a Univerzity Pardubice (Joint Laboratory of Solid State Chemistry of the Institute of Macromolecular Chemistry of AS CR and Pardubice University): Studentská 84, 532 10 Pardubice; tel. 406036150; fax 406036011; e-mail slchpl@ upce.cz; internet slchpl.upce.cz; f. 1986; attached to Acad. of Sciences of the Czech Republic; Head Dr LADISLAV TICHÝ.

Státní úřad pro jadernou bezpečnost (State Office for Nuclear Safety): Senovážné nám. 9, 110 00 Prague 1; tel. 221624111; fax 221624704; e-mail podatelna@sujb.cz; internet www.sujb.cz; f. 1993; regulatory activities in nuclear safety, radiation protection, inspection of materials and technologies of dual use for nuclear, biological and chemical weapons; Chair. DANA DRÁBOVÁ.

Ústav analytické chemie AV ČR (Institute of Analytical Chemistry AS CR): Veveří 97, 602 00 Brno; tel. 532290182; fax 541212113; e-mail uiach@iach.cz; internet www.iach.cz/uiach; f. 1956; attached to Acad. of Sciences of the Czech Republic; research in analytical chemistry, devt of theory, methodology, and instrumentation for analytical chemistry; Head Prof. LUDMILA KRIVANKOVA; publ. *Research Activities and Future Trends* (irregular).

Ústav anorganické chemie AV ČR, v.v.i. (Institute of Inorganic Chemistry AS CR, v.v.i.): 250 68 Husinec-Řež; tel. 220940158; fax 220941502; e-mail sekretar@iic.cas.cz; internet www.iic.cas.cz; f. 1959; attached to Acad. of Sciences of the Czech Republic; basic and applied research, preparation of inorganic compounds and materials and their applications in the field of inorganic chemistry; branches of inorganic chemistry, incl. physical chemistry, solid state physics, polymer chemistry, and ecology; bio-inorganic chemistry; attached laboratories of inorganic materials and low temperatures located in Prague; Dir Ing. JANA BLUDSKÁ; publs *Bulletin* (1 a year), *Ceramics–Silikáty* (6 a year).

Ústav chemických procesů AV ČR (Institute of Chemical Process Fundamentals AS CR): Rozvojová 135, 165 02 Prague 6; tel. 220390111; fax 220920661; e-mail icecas@ icpf.cas.cz; internet www.icpf.cas.cz; f. 1960; attached to Acad. of Sciences of the Czech Republic; Dir Prof. JIŘÍ DRAHOŠ.

Ústav fyzikální chemie J. Heyrovského AV ČR, v.v.i. (J. Heyrovský Institute of Physical Chemistry AS CR, v.v.i.): Dolejškova 3, 182 23 Prague 8; tel. 286583014; fax 286582307; e-mail director@jh-inst.cas.cz; internet www.jh-inst.cas.cz; f. 1972; attached to Acad. of Sciences of the Czech Republic; library of 18,000 books and periodicals, 200 current periodical titles; research in physical chemistry, electrochemistry and chemical physics; Dir Prof. Dr ZDENĚK SAMEC; publs *J. Am. Chem. Soc., J. Chem. Phys, J. Phys. Chem.*

Ústav fyziky atmosféry AV ČR, v.v.i. (Institute of Atmospheric Physics AS CR, v.v.i.): 4, Boční II/1401, 141 31 Prague; tel. 272016011; fax 272763745; e-mail iap@ufa .cas.cz; internet www.ufa.cas.cz; f. 1964; attached to Acad. of Sciences of the Czech Republic; monitors atmospheric pollution; carries out research in meteorology, climatology, and ionospheric and magnetospheric physics, space physics, wind energy; library of 8,210 books, 39 periodicals; Dir Dr RADAN HUTH.

Ústav fyziky materiálů AV ČR (Institute of the Physics of Materials AS CR): Žižkova 22, 616 62 Brno; tel. 541212286; fax 541212301; e-mail secretar@ipm.cz; internet www.ipm.cz; f. 1956; attached to Acad. of Sciences of the Czech Republic; Dir Assoc. Prof. Dr PETR LUKÁŠ; publs *Engineering Mechanics* (6 a year), *Metallic Materials* (6 a year).

Ústav jaderné fyziky AV ČR (Nuclear Physics Institute AS CR): 250 68 Řež; tel. 220941147; fax 220941130; e-mail ujf@ujf.cas .cz; internet www.ujf.cas.cz; f. 1955; attached to Acad. of Sciences of the Czech Republic; Dir Dr JAN DOBEŠ.

Ústav jaderného výzkumu Řež a.s. (Nuclear Research Institute Řež plc): Husinec-Řež 130, 250 68 Řež; tel. 266172000; fax 220940840; e-mail paz@ujv.cz; internet www .ujv.cz; f. 1955; nuclear power and safety; fuel cycle chemistry; radiopharmaceuticals; library of 101,200 vols, 21,000 reports; Chair. FRANTIŠEK PAZDERA; publ. *Nucleon* (4 a year).

Ústav makromolekulární chemie AV ČR (Institute of Macromolecular Chemistry AS CR): Heyrovský nám. 2, 162 06 Prague 6; tel. 296809111; fax 296809410; e-mail office@imc .cas.cz; internet www.imc.cas.cz; f. 1959; attached to Acad. of Sciences of the Czech Republic; Dir FRANTIŠEK RYPÁČEK.

Ústav pro hydrodynamiku AV ČR, v.v.i. (Institute of Hydrodynamics AS CR, v.v.i.): Pod Patankou 30/5, 166 12 Prague 6; tel. 233109011; fax 233324361; e-mail ih@ih.cas .cz; internet www.ih.cas.cz; f. 1953; attached to Acad. of Sciences of the Czech Republic; research in hydromechanics, rheology and hydrology; Dir Dr ZDENEK CHARA; publs *Engineering Mechanics* (6 a year), *Journal of Hydrology and Hydromechanics* (6 a year).

Ústav struktury a mechaniky hornin AV ČR (Institute of Rock Structure and Mechanics AS CR): V Holešovičkách 41, 182 09 Prague 8; tel. 266009111; fax 284680105; e-mail irsm@irsm.cas.cz; internet www.irsm .cas.cz; f. 1958; attached to Acad. of Sciences of the Czech Republic; library of 28,000 vols; Dir Ing. KAREL BALIK; publs *Acta Montana, Series A: Geodynamics* (in English, irregular), *Acta Montana, Series B: Fuel, Carbon, Mineral Processing* (in English, irregular), *Acta Montana, Series AB: Geodynamics, Fuel, Carbon, Mineral Processing* (in English and Czech, irregular).

Ústav termomechaniky AV ČR (Institute of Thermomechanics AS CR): Dolejškova 5, 182 00 Prague 8; tel. 286890383; fax 286584695; e-mail secr@it.cas.cz; internet www.it.cas.cz; f. 1954; attached to Acad. of Sciences of the Czech Republic; library of 12,000 vols; Dir Prof. ZBYNEK JANOUR; publs *Acta Technica CSAV* (4 a year), *Engineering Mechanics* (6 a year).

PHILOSOPHY AND PSYCHOLOGY

Centrum pro teoretická studia Univerzity Karlovy (Centre for Theoretical Study at Charles University): Jilská 1, 110 00 Prague 1; tel. 222220671; fax 222220653; e-mail office@cts.cuni.cz; internet www.cts.cuni.cz; attached to Acad. of Sciences of the Czech Republic; Dir Dr IVAN M. HAVEL.

Filozofický ústav AV ČR (Institute of Philosophy AS CR): Jilská 1, 110 00 Prague; tel. 222220124; fax 222220108; e-mail flusekr@site.cas.cz; internet www.flu.cas.cz; f. 1990; attached to Acad. of Sciences of the Czech Republic; Dir Dr PAVEL BARAN; publs *Acta Comeniana* (irregular), *Filosofický časopis* (Philosophical Review, 6 a year), *Teorie vědy* (4 a year).

Psychologický ústav AV ČR (Institute of Psychology AS CR): Veveří 97, 602 00 Brno; tel. 532290270; e-mail cermak@psu.cas.cz; internet www.psu.cas.cz; f. 1967; attached to Acad. of Sciences of the Czech Republic; Dir Doc. Dr IVO ČERMÁK; publs *Bulletin Psychologického ústavu* (irregular), *Československá psychologie* (6 a year), *Zprávy* (irregular).

RELIGION, SOCIOLOGY AND ANTHROPOLOGY

Etnologický ústav AV ČR, v.v.i. (Institute of Ethnology AS CR, v.v.i.): Na Florenci 3, 110 00 Prague; tel. 222828503; fax 222828503; e-mail office@eu.cas.cz; internet www.eu.cas.cz; f. 1954; attached to Acad. of Sciences of the Czech Republic; library of 80,000 ; Dir Dr ZDENĚK UHEREK; publs *Český lid: Etnologický časopis / Český lid Ethnological* (4 a year), *Hudební věda* (4 a year).

Sociologický ústav AV ČR (Institute of Sociology AS CR): Jilská 1, 110 00 Prague; tel. 222221753; e-mail socmail@soc.cas.cz; internet www.soc.cas.cz; f. 1990; attached to

Acad. of Sciences of the Czech Republic; Dir Dr MARIE ČERMÁKOVÁ; publs *Historická demografie* (1 a year), *Sociologický časopis* (Czech Sociological Review, 6 a year).

TECHNOLOGY

Laboratoř anorganických materiálů (Laboratory of Inorganic Materials): Institute of Rock Structure and Mechanics V, Holešovičkách 41, 182 09 Prague 8; tel. 220445191; fax 266009421; e-mail lubomir .nemec@vscht.cz; internet www.vscht.cz/sls; f. 1961; attached to Acad. of Sciences of the Czech Republic and Institute of Chemical Technology; Dir Prof. LUBOMÍR NĚMEC.

SVUSS Praha, s. r. o.: Na Harfě 336/9, 190 00 Prague 9–Vysočany; tel. (2) 66035661; fax (2) 66034712; e-mail suchanek@svuss.cz; internet www.svuss.cz; f. 1998; technical studies in engineering, heat transfer and the power industry; carries out tests and research in the field of thermodynamics; library of 10,000 vols; Dir Ing. MIROSLAV SUCHANEK (acting).

Ústav fotoniky a elektroniky AV ČR (Institute of Photonics and Electronics AS CR): Chaberská 57, 182 51 Prague 8; tel. 284681804; fax 284680222; e-mail ufe@ufe .cz; internet www.ure.cas.cz; f. 1955 as Ústav radiotechniky a elektroniky AV ČR, present name 2007; attached to Acad. of Sciences of the Czech Republic; research and devt in photonics, optoelectronics, and signals and systems; library of 16,500 vols, 390 periodicals; Dir Dr Ing. VLASTIMIL MATĚJEC.

Ústav informatiky AV ČR, v.v.i. (Institute of Computer Science AS CR, v.v.i.): Pod Vodárenskou věží 2, 182 07 Prague 8; tel. 266052083; fax 286585789; e-mail ics@cs.cas .cz; internet www.cs.cas.cz; attached to Acad. of Sciences of the Czech Republic; f. 1975; library of 8,000 vols; Dir Prof. Dr JIRI WIEDERMANN; publ. *Neural Network Word* (int. journal on neural and mass-parallel computing and information systems).

Ústav přístrojové techniky AV ČR, v.v.i. (Institute of Scientific Instruments AS CR, v.v.i.): Královopolská 147, 612 64 Brno; tel. 541514111; fax 541514402; e-mail institute@ isibrno.cz; internet www.isibrno.cz; f. 1957; attached to Acad. of Sciences of the Czech Republic; methodology in selected areas of physics, chemistry, technology, main programs: electron optics and microscopy, vacuum technologies, coherence optics, magnetic resonance, bioinformatics; Dir Dr LUDĚK FRANK.

Ústav teoretické a aplikované mechaniky AV ČR (Institute of Theoretical and Applied Mechanics AS CR): Prosecká 76, 190 00 Prague 9; tel. 286882121; fax 286884634; e-mail itam@itam.cas.cz; internet www.itam .cas.cz; attached to Acad. of Sciences of the Czech Republic; Dir Dr MILOŠ DRDÁCKÝ; publ. *Engineering Mechanics* (6 a year).

Ústav teorie informace a automatizace AV ČR (Institute of Information Theory and Automation AS CR): POB 18, 182 08 Prague 8; Pod Vodárenskou věží 4, 182 08 Prague 8; tel. 266053111; fax 286890378; e-mail utia@ utia.cas.cz; internet www.utia.cas.cz; f. 1959; attached to Acad. of Sciences of the Czech Republic; Dir Prof. Dr JAN FLUSSER; publ. *Kybernetica* (6 a year).

Ústav termomechaniky AV ČR, v.v.i. (Institute of Thermomechanics AS CR, v.v.i.): Dolejškova 1402/5, 182 00 Praha 8; tel. 266052021; fax 286584695; e-mail secr@it .cas.cz; internet www.it.cas.cz; f. 1953; merged with the Institute of Electrical Engineering in 2006; attached to Acad. of Sciences of the Czech Republic; basic research in fluid dynamics, thermodynamics,

dynamics of mechanical systems, solid mechanics, interactions of fluids and solids, environmental aerodynamics, biomechanics, mechatronics, electrophysics, electrical machines, drives and electronics and material diagnostics.; Dir Prof. ZBYNĚK JAŇOUR; Deputy Dir Dr. JIŘÍ PLEŠEK; publs *Acta Technica* (4 a year), *Engineering Mechanics* (6 a year).

VÚTS Liberec a.s. (Research Institute for Textile Machines, Liberec Co.): U jezu 4, 461 19 Liberec 4; tel. 485301111; fax 485302402; e-mail vuts@vuts.cz; internet www.vuts.cz; f. 1951; library of 10,000 vols; 154 mems; Gen. Dir Prof. Ing. MIROSLAV VÁCLAVÍK.

Libraries and Archives

Brno

Knihovna Moravské galerie v Brně (Library of the Moravian Gallery in Brno): Husova 18, 662 26 Brno; tel. 532169127; fax 532169180; e-mail knihovna@ moravska-galerie.cz; internet www .moravska-galerie.cz; f. 1873; 110,000 vols; Dir Dr HANA KARKANOVÁ.

Moravská zemská knihovna (Moravian Library): Kounicova 65A, 601 87 Brno; tel. 541646111; fax 541646100; e-mail mzk@mzk .cz; internet www.mzk.cz; f. 1808; 3,850,000 vols, 4,300 periodicals; Dir Dr J. KUBÍČEK.

Ústřední knihovna a informační středisko Veterinární a farmaceutické univerzity (Central Library and Information Centre of the University of Veterinary and Pharmaceutical Sciences): Palackého 1–3, 612 42 Brno; tel. 541562080; e-mail gect@ vfu.cz; internet sis.vfu.cz; f. 1919; 174,126 vols; Chief Librarian TOMÁŠ GEC; publ. *Acta veterinaria Brno* (4 a year).

České Budějovice

Státní vědecká knihovna (State Research Library): Na Sadech 26-27, Lidická 1, 370 59 České Budějovice; tel. 386111211; fax 386351901; e-mail library@cbvk.cz; internet www.cbvk.cz; f. 1885; 1,500,000 vols; Dir Dr KVETA CEMPIRKOVA.

Hradec Králové

Studijní a vědecká knihovna (Research Library): Pospíšilova 395, POB 7, 500 03 Hradec Králové; tel. 495514871; fax 495511781; e-mail knihovna@svkhk.cz; internet www.svkhk.cz; f. 1949; 1,189,172 vols; Dir Mgr EVA SVOBODOVÁ.

Liberec

Krajská vědecká knihovna v Liberci (Research Library in Liberec): Rumjancevova 1362/1, 460 53 Liberec; tel. 482412111; fax 482412122; e-mail library@kvkli.cz; internet www.kvkli.cz; f. 1945; 760,000 books, 1,600 periodicals, 29,000 vols of standards, 380,000 vols of patents, 27,000 vols of printed music, 9,000 sound recordings, 3,500 vols of maps, 600 CD-ROMs; Dir PAVEL HARVÁNEK; publ. *Světlík* (World of the Liberec Region Libraries, 6 a year).

Olomouc

Vědecká knihovna v Olomouci (Research Library in Olomouc): Bezručova 3, 779 11 Olomouc; tel. 585223441; fax 585225774; e-mail info@vkol.cz; internet www.vkol.cz/ cs; f. 1566; 1,660,000 vols, 1,448 MSS, 1,800 incunabula, 70,000 old prints; Dir Dr MARIE NÁDVORNÍKOVÁ; publ. *Knihovní obzor* (4 a year).

Ostrava

Moravskoslezská vědecká knihovna v Ostravě (Moravian-Silesian Research

Library in Ostrava): Prokešovo nám. 9, 728 00 Ostrava; tel. 596118881; fax 596138322; e-mail msvk@svkos.cz; internet www.svkos .cz; f. 1951; 987,604 vols; Dir Ing. LEA PRCHALOVÁ.

Ústřední knihovna Vysoké školy báňské-Technické univerzity Ostrava (Central Library of the VSB-Technical University of Ostrava): 17 listopadu 15, 708 33 Ostrava-Poruba; tel. 596991278; fax 596994598; e-mail knihovna@vsb.cz; internet www.knihovna.vsb.cz; f. 1849; 380,000 vols; Dir DANIELA TKAČÍKOVÁ; publ. *Sborník vědeckých prací Vysoké školy báňské—Technické univerzity Ostrava* (Transactions, irregular).

Plzeň

Studijní a vědecká knihovna Plzeňského kraje (Education and Research Library of Pilsener Region): Smetanovy sady 2, 305 48 Plzeň; tel. 377224249; fax 377325478; e-mail svk@svkpl.cz; internet www.svkpl.cz; f. 1950; 791,000 books, 1,700 current periodicals, 793,000 documents; Dir Dr JAROSLAV VYČICHLO; publs *Přírůstky zahraniční literatury* (foreign accessions, 4 a year), *Západní Čechy v tisku* (West Bohemia in Print).

Prague

Archiv AV ČR, vědecký útvar Masarykova ústavu a Archivu AVČR, v.v.i. (Archives AS CR, a scientific division of the Masaryk Institute and Archives ASCR, v.v.i.): Gabčíkova 2362/10, 182 00 Prague 8; tel. 286010110; fax 284680150; e-mail sekretariat@mua.cas.cz; internet www.mua .cas.cz; f. 1953; attached to Acad. of Sciences of the Czech Republic; 60,000 vols; Dir Dr LUCIE KOSTRBOVÁ; publs *Práce z Archivu Akademie věd* (Studies of the Archives of the Acad. of Sciences, 1 a year), *Práce z dějin Akademie věd* (Studies on the History of the Academy of Sciences, 2 a year), *Práce z dějin věd* (Studies on the History of Sciences and the Humanities, 2 a year), *Studia historiae academiae scientiarum—Práce z dějin akademie věd* (Studies on the History of the Academy of Sciences, 1 a year), *Studie o rukopisech* (Codicological Studies, 1 a year).

Knihovna Akademie Věd Česky republiky (Library of the Academy of Sciences of the Czech Republic): Národní 3, 115 22 Prague 1; tel. 224240524; fax 224240611; e-mail infoknav@lib.cas.cz; internet www.lib .cas.cz; f. 1952; 1,000,000 vols, 2,102 periodicals; headquarters of the network of information centres and special libraries of academic institutes; Dir IVANA KADLECOVÁ.

Knihovna Archeologického ústavu AV ČR (Library of the Archaeological Institute of the Academy of Sciences of the Czech Republic): Letenská 4, 118 01 Prague; tel. (2) 57014318; fax (2) 57532288; e-mail knihovna@arup.cas.cz; internet www.arup .cas.cz; f. 1919; 12,426 vols; colln severely affected by flooding in 2002, previously 67,200 vols; Chief Librarian EVA SOUFKOVÁ; publs *Archeologické rozhledy* (4 a year), *Castellologica bohemica* (irregular), *Castrum Pragense* (irregular), *Mediaevalia archaeologica* (irregular), *Památky archeologické* (1 a year), *Památky Archeologické-Supplementum* (irregular), *Výzkumy v Čechách* (irregular).

Knihovna České geologické služby (Library of the Czech Geological Survey): Klárov 3, 118 21 Prague 1; tel. 257089411; fax 257320438; e-mail breit@cgu.cz; internet www.cgu.cz; f. 1924; archive of 60,000 vols; 173,010 vols; Dir RNDr HANA BREITEROVÁ; publs *Geological Bibliography of the Czech Republic* (1 a year), *Library of the Geological Survey* (irregular).

Knihovna Evangelické teologické fakulty Univerzity Karlovy (Library of the Protestant Theological Faculty of the Charles University): Černá 9, 115 55 Prague 1; tel. 221988104; fax 221988215; e-mail library@etf.cuni.cz; internet www.etf.cuni.cz/ ~library; f. 1919; 190,000 vols, 185 current periodicals; Dir BARBORA DROBÍKOVÁ; publs *Communio Viatorum* (3 a year), *Teologická reflexe* (2 a year).

Knihovna Národní galerie (Library of the National Gallery): Národní galerie v Praze, Staroměstské nám. 12, 110 15 Prague; located at: Hradčanské nám. 15, 119 04 Prague 1; tel. 220515458; fax 220513180; e-mail library@ngprague.cz; internet www .ngprague.cz; f. 1880; 98,000 vols; Dir Dr MARTINA HORÁKOVÁ.

Knihovna Národního muzea (Library of the National Museum): Václavské nám. 68, 115 79 Prague 1; tel. 224497111; fax 224224914; internet www.nm.cz; f. 1818; 3,600,000 vols; Dir Mgr MARTIN SEKERA; publ. *Sborník Národního muzea, řada C–Literární Historie*.

Knihovna Národního technického muzea (Library of the National Technical Museum): Kostelní 42, 170 78 Prague 7; tel. 220399233; fax 220399200; e-mail knihovna@ntm.cz; internet www.ntm.cz; f. 1833; 6 mems; 200,000 vols; Chief Librarian RICHARDA SVOBODOVÁ.

Knihovna Orientálního ústavu Akademie věd České republiky (Library of the Oriental Institute of the Academy of Sciences of the Czech Republic): Pod vodárenskou věží 2, 182 08 Prague; tel. 266053950; fax 286581835; e-mail jan.luffer@orient.cas.cz; internet www.orient.cas.cz; f. 1929; 5 mems; general library of 210,000 vols; 'Lu Xun' Chinese library of 67,000 vols; Korean library of 3,500 vols; Tibetan colln; Librarian Mgr JAN LUFFER; publs *Archiv orientální* (4 a year), *Nový Orient* (4 a year).

Knihovna Uměleckoprůmyslového musea (Museum of Decorative Arts Library): 17 listopadu 2, 110 01 Prague 1; tel. 251093135; fax 251093296; e-mail knihovna@upm.cz; internet www.knihovna .upm.cz; f. 1885; 175,000 vols; Dir Dr JARMILA OKROUHLÍKOVÁ; publ. *Acta UPM* (irregular).

Městská knihovna v Praze (Municipal Library of Prague): Mariánské nám. 1, 115 72 Prague 1; tel. 222113306; fax 222328230; e-mail knihovna@mlp.cz; internet www.mlp .cz; f. 1891; 167,520 mems; 2,333,963 vols incl. books, journals, maps, CDs, DVDs, MP3s, reproductions; Central Library, 43 brs and 3 mobile libraries; Dir Dr TOMÁŠ ŘEHÁK.

Národní knihovna České republiky (National Library of the Czech Republic): Klementinum 190, 110 00 Prague 1; tel. 221663111; fax 221663277; e-mail sekret .ur@nkp.cz; internet www.nkp.cz; f. 1366; 6,197,320 vols, 14,905 MSS, 3,500 incunabula, 200,000 early printed books; Dir Dr VLASTIMIL JEŽEK; publs *Česká národní bibliografie ČR* (Czech National Bibliography, 12 a year), *Miscellanea oddělení rukopisů a starých tisků* (1 a year), *Národní knihovna* (4 a year).

Branch Library:

    Slovanská knihovna (Slavonic Library): Klementinum 190, 110 00 Prague; tel. 221663356; fax 221663176; e-mail sluzby .sk@nkp.cz; internet www.nkp.cz/slk; f. 1924; 775,000 vols; Dir Dr LUKÁŠ BABKA.

Národní lékařská knihovna (National Medical Library): Nové Město, Sokolská 54, 121 32 Prague 2; tel. 296335911; fax 296335959; e-mail nml@nlk.cz; internet www.nlk.cz; f. 1949; 335,000 vols, 1,500 current periodicals, 6,000 doctoral theses; WHO documentation centre; oversees translation of MeSH into Czech; operates union catalogue of medical literature; Dir HELENA BOUZKOVA; publs *Bibliographia medica čechoslovaca* (12 a year), *Referátový výběr* (series of 4 abstracts journals, 4 or 6 a year).

Národní pedagogická knihovna Komenského (Comenius National Library of Education): Mikulandská 5, 116 74 Prague 1; tel. 221966402; fax 224930550; e-mail library@npkk.cz; internet www.npkk.cz; f. 1919; 471,000 vols; youth br. (Suk Library) of 58,000 vols (since 1790); Dir ALICE KOŠKOVÁ.

Státní technická knihovna (State Technical Library): Mariánské nám. 5, POB 206, 110 01 Prague 1; tel. 2221663111; fax 222221340; e-mail informace@stk.cz; internet www.stk.cz; f. 1718; 1,501,632 vols, 1,524 periodicals, 31 databases; Dir Ing. MARTIN SVOBODA.

Univerzita Karlova, Pedagogická fakulta, Ústřední knihovna (Charles University Faculty of Education, Central Library): Rettigova 4, 116 39 Prague 1; tel. and fax 296242420; e-mail knihovna@pedf .cuni.cz; internet beta.pedf.cuni.cz; f. 1948; 190,859 vols, 239 periodicals; Dir Mgr JITKA BÍLKOVÁ.

Úřad Průmyslového Vlastnictví (Industrial Property Office): Antonína Čermáka 2A, 160 68 Prague 6-Bubeneč; tel. 220383111; fax 224324718; e-mail objednavky@upv.cz; internet www.upv.cz; 30,000,000 documents; Dir of Patent Information Dept Ing. MIROSLAV PACLÍK.

Ústav dějin Univerzity Karlovy a Archiv Univerzity Karlovy Library (Institute of the History of Charles University and Archive of Charles University): Ovocný trh 5, 116 36 Prague 1; tel. 224491463; fax 224491670; e-mail udauk@ruk.cuni.cz; internet udauk .cuni.cz; focuses on history of education and schooling in Czech lands (spec. focus on Charles University); 47,000 vols, 55 km of archival material; Librarian Dr JIŘINA URBANOVÁ; Archivist Dr MAREK ĎURČANSKÝ; publ. *Acta Universitatis Carolinae—Historia Universitatis Carolinae Pragensis*.

Ústav vědeckých informací 1. lékařské fakulty, Univerzita Karlova (Institute of Scientific Information, First Medical Faculty, Charles University): U Nemocnice 4, 121 08 Prague 2; tel. 224965600; fax 224965601; e-mail knihovna@lf1.cuni.cz; internet uvi.lf1 .cuni.cz; f. 1949; 450,512 vols, 712 current periodicals; Dir Dr HANA SKÁLOVÁ; Sec. BĚLA ČERNÁ; publs *Acta Universitatis Carolinae Medica, Folia Biologica, Prague Medical Report, Proceedings of the Scientific Conferences, Sborník lékařský*.

Ústav zemědělských a potravinářských informací (Institute of Agricultural and Food Information): Londýnská 55, 120 21 Prague 2; tel. 224256387; fax 224253938; e-mail knihovna@uzpi.cz; internet www .knihovna.uzpi.cz; f. 1993; 1,200,000 vols; Dir Ing. C. PERLÍN; publs *Genetika a šlechtění* (Genetics and Plant Breeding, 4 a year), *Lesnictví* (Forest Science, 12 a year), *Ochrana rostlin* (Plant Protection Science, 4 a year), *Potravinářské vědy* (Food Science, 6 a year), *Rostlinná výroba* (Plant Production, 12 a year), *Veterinární medicina* (Veterinary Medicine, 12 a year), *Zahradnictví* (Horticulture, 4 a year), *Zemědělská ekonomika* (Agricultural Economics, 12 a year), *Zemědělská technika* (Agricultural Engineering, 4 a year), *Živočišná výroba* (Journal of Animal Science, 12 a year).

Ústřední tělovýchovná knihovna (Central Library of Physical Training): José Martiho 31, 162 52 Prague 6; tel.

220172158; fax 220172018; e-mail utk@ftvs
.cuni.cz; internet www.ftvs.cuni.cz/knihovna;
f. 1927; 300,000 vols; Dir Dr JANA BĚLÍKOVÁ;
publ. *Acta Universitatis Carolinae Kinan-
thropologica.*

Ústřední zemědělská knihovna (Central
Agricultural Library): Slezská 7, POB 39,
120 56 Prague 2; tel. 227010111; fax
227010114; e-mail uzpi@uzpi.cz; internet
www.uzpi.cz; f. 1926; a section of the Institute of Agricultural and Food Information;
1,100,000 vols; Dir Dr BAŠEK VÁCLAV; publ.
Seznam časopisů (List of Periodicals, 1 a
year).

Ústí nad Labem

Severočeská vědecká knihovna (North
Bohemian Research Library): POB 134, W.
Churchilla 3, 401 34 Ústí nad Labem; tel.
475209126; fax 475200045; e-mail library@
svkul.cz; internet www.svkul.cz; f. 1945;
inter library loan; 12,000 mems; 776,000
vols; Dir ALEŠ BROŽEK; publ. *Výběr kultur-
ních výročí* (online at www.svkul.cz/kni-
hovna/dokumenty).

Museums and Art Galleries

Brno

Moravská galerie v Brně (Moravian Gallery in Brno): Husova 18, 662 26 Brno; tel.
532169111; fax 532169180; e-mail m-gal@
moravska-galerie.cz; internet www
.moravska-galerie.cz; f. 1873; mostly European fine and applied art of all periods;
library of 120,000 vols; Dir MAREK POKORNÝ;
publ. *Bulletin* (1 a year).

Moravské zemské muzeum (Moravian
Provincial Museum): Zelný trh 6, 659 37
Brno; tel. 542321205; fax 542212792; e-mail
mzm@mzm.cz; internet www.mzm.cz; f.
1817; history, natural history, geology, arts,
anthropology, horticulture; library of 260,000
vols; Dir Dr PETR ŠULEŘ; publs *Acta Musei
Moraviae–Scientiae Biologicae* (1 a year),
Acta Musei Moraviae–Scientiae Geologicae
(1 a year), *Acta Musei Moraviae–Scientiae
Sociales* (1 a year), *Anthropologie* (3 a year),
Folia Ethnografica (1 a year), *Folia Mendeli-
ana* (1 a year), *Folia Numismatica* (1 a year),
Krystalinikum (1 a year).

Muzeum města Brna (Brno Municipal
Museum): Špilberk 1, 662 24 Brno; tel.
542123611; fax 542123613; e-mail muzeum
.brno@spilberk.cz; internet www.spilberk.cz;
f. 1904; history of Brno and Špilberk Castle;
art gallery; Dir Dr PAVEL CIPRIAN.

Technické muzeum v Brně (Technical
Museum in Brno): Purkyňova 105, 612 00
Brno; tel. 541421411; fax 541214418; e-mail
info@technicalmuseum.cz; internet www
.technicalmuseum.cz; f. 1961; library of
42,000 vols; Dir VLASTIMIL VYKYDAL; publs
Archeologia technica (1 a year), *Muzejní
noviny*, *Nožířské listy* (1 a year), *Sborník z
konzervátorského a restaurátorského semi-
náře* (1 a year).

České Budějovice

**Jihočeské muzeum v Českých Budějovi-
cích** (South Bohemian Museum in České
Budějovice): Dukelská 1, 370 51 České
Budějovice; tel. 387929311; fax 386356447;
e-mail muzeumcb@muzeumcb.cz; internet
www.muzeumcb.cz; f. 1877; history, archaeology, natural history, arts; Dir PAVEL ŠAFR;
publs *Archeologické výzkumy v jižních
Čechách* (archaeology, 1 a year), *Jihočeský
sborník historický* (history, 1 a year), *Sborník
Přírodní vědy* (nature, 1 a year), *Výběr
Časopis pro historii a vlastivědu jižních*

Čech (regional and cultural History, 4 a
year).

Cheb

Krajské muzeum Cheb (Cheb Regional
Museum): nám. Krále Jiřího z Poděbrad
493/4, 350 11 Cheb; tel. 354400620; fax
354422292; e-mail sekretariat@muzeumcheb
.cz; internet www.muzeumcheb.cz; f. 1874;
history, local ceramics; library of 15,000 vols;
spec. colln: library of Franciscan order; Dir
Dr EVA DITTERTOVÁ; publ. *Sborník chebského
muzea* (1 a year).

Chrudim

Muzeum loutkářských kultur (Museum of
Puppets): Břetislavova 74, 537 60 Chrudim;
tel. 469620310; fax 469620650; e-mail
puppets@puppets.cz; internet www.puppets
.cz; f. 1972; Dir Mgr ALENA EXNAROVÁ.

Harrachov

Muzeum skla (Glass Museum): Harrachov
95, 512 46 Harrachov; tel. 481528141; fax
481528148; e-mail obchod@sklarnaharrachov
.cz; internet www.sklarnaharrachov.cz; f.
1972; Dir K. PIPEK.

Hluboká nad Vltavou

Alšova jihočeská galerie (Aleš South
Bohemian Gallery): Zámak è. 144, 373 41
Hluboká nad Vltavou; tel. 387967041; fax
387965436; e-mail ajg@ajg.cz; internet www
.ajg.cz; f. 1953; Czech art since 13th century,
16th–18th century European art, Czech and
world ceramics since early 20th century;
library of 12,950 vols; Dir Dr HYNEK RULÍŠEK.

Hradec Králové

**Muzeum východních Čech, Hradec Krá-
lové** (Museum of East Bohemia, Hradec
Králové): Eliščino nábřeží 465, 500 01 Hradec Králové; tel. 495512462; fax 495512899;
e-mail info@muzeumhk.cz; internet www
.muzeumhk.cz; f. 1879; natural sciences,
history, archeology, education; 1866 War
Memorial; library of 70,000 vols; Dir Dr
ZDENĚK ZAHRADNÍK; publs *Acta* (irregular),
Fontes (irregular), *Historická fotografie*
(irregular), *Královéhradecko* (irregular),
Zpravodaj muzea v Hradci Králové (irregular).

Hukvaldy

Památník Leoše Janáčka (Leos Janacek
Museum): Smetanova 14, Brno; tel.
541212811; e-mail vvejvodova@mzm.cz;
internet www.mzm.cz; f. 1933; renovated
original house of Leos Janacek; exhibits life
and work of Leos Janacek; audiovisual hall;
Dir B. VOLNÝ.

Jablonec nad Nisou

Muzeum skla a bižuterie (Museum of
Glass and Jewellery): Muzea 398/4, 466 01
Jablonec nad Nisou; tel. 483369011; fax
483369012; e-mail msbjbc@quick.cz;
internet www.msb-jablonec.cz; f. 1961; Bohemian glass, Jablonec jewellery; library of
15,000 vols; Dir Ing. JAROSLAVA SLABÁ.

Karlovy Vary

Galerie umění Karlovy Vary (Karlovy
Vary Art Gallery): Goethova stezka 6, 360
01 Karlovy Vary; tel. 353224387; fax
353224388; e-mail info@galeriekvary.cz;
internet www.galeriekvary.cz; f. 1953; 20th-
century Czech art; Dir JAN SAMEC.

Karlovarské muzeum (Karlovy Vary
Museum): Nová louka 23, 360 01 Karlovy
Vary; e-mail sekretariat@kvmuz.cz; internet
www.kvmuz.cz; f. 1870; history, natural history, arts; Dir JAN BATÍK.

Zlatý klíč muzeum (Golden Key Museum):
Lázeňská 3, 360 01 Karlovy Vary; tel.

353223888; f. 1960; art nouveau paintings;
Dir MARIE GULGOVÁ.

Kolín

Regionální muzeum v Kolíně (Kolín
Regional Museum): Brandlova 35, 280 02
Kolín; tel. 321723841; fax 321719018; e-mail
muzeum@kolin.cz; internet www.kolin.cz/
muzeum; f. 1895; local history; open-air
museum at Kouřim; library of 49,500 vols;
Dir JARMILA VALENTOVÁ.

Kopřivnice

Technické muzeum Tatra (Tatra Cars
Museum): Záhumenní 367/1, 742 21 Kopřiv-
nice; tel. 556871106; fax 556821415; e-mail
direktor@tatramuseum.cz; internet www
.tatramuseum.cz; f. 1947; Tatra cars, trucks,
railway carriages, aircraft, engines and chas-
sis, history of Tatra production; Dir LUMÍR
KAVÁLEK.

Kutná Hora

České muzeum stříba (Czech Silver
Museum): Hrádek, Barborská 28, 284 01
Kutná Hora; tel. 327512159; fax 327513813;
e-mail muzeum@kutnohorsko.cz; internet
muzeum.kutnohorsko.cz; f. 1877; medieval
castle, medieval silver mine, Gothic town
house, town life in 17th–19th centuries; Dir
S. HRABÁNKOVÁ.

Liberec

Oblastní galerie v Liberci (Liberec
Regional Art Gallery): U Tiskárny 1, 460 01
Liberec 5; tel. 485106325; fax 485106321;
e-mail oblgal@ogl.cz; internet www.ogl.cz; f.
1873; 16th to 18th century Dutch and
Flemish painting, 19th century French land-
scapes, 20th century Czech art; Dir Dr VĚRA
LAŠTOVKOVÁ.

Severočeské muzeum v Liberci (North
Bohemian Museum in Liberec): Masarykova
tř. 11, 460 01 Liberec; tel. 485246111; fax
485108319; e-mail muzeumlb@muzeumlb.cz;
internet www.muzeumlb.cz; f. 1873; European and Bohemian applied arts, regional
history, natural history; collections of glass,
ceramics, porcelain, textiles, tapestries, jewellery, metal objects, furniture, posters, archaeological artefacts; library of 35,000 vols;
Dir ALOIS ČVANČARA; publ. *Sborník Severo-
českého musea* (one issue each on history and
natural history, every 2 years).

Lidice

Památník Lidice (Lidice Memorial
Museum): Kladno district, 273 54 Lidice;
tel. and fax 312253063; e-mail lidice@
lidice-memorial.cz; internet www
.lidice-memorial.cz; f. 1948; attached to Ministry of Culture of the Czech Republic;
history of the destruction of the village of
Lidice in the Second World War; gallery of
painting and sculptures devoted to Lidice;
Dir MARIE TELUPILOVA.

Litoměřice

**Severočeská galerie výtvarného umění
v Litoměřicích** (North Bohemian Gallery of
Fine Art in Litoměřice): Michalská 7, 412 01
Litoměřice; tel. 416732192; fax 416732383;
e-mail reditel@galerie-ltm.cz; internet www
.galerie-ltm.cz; f. 1958; European art since
the 12th century, spec. collns of naive art,
Czech Gothic art, Czech to present time;
library of 13,000 vols; Dir Dr JAN ŠTÍBR.

Mariánské Lázně

Městské muzeum Mariánské Lázně
(Mariánské Lázně Municipal Museum):
Goethovo nám. 11, 353 01 Mariánské Lázně;
tel. 354622740; e-mail muzeum@goethe-haus
.cz; f. 1887; history, geology; open-air geological park; Dir Ing. JAROMÍR BARTOŠ.

Mladá Boleslav

Škoda Auto Museum (Škoda Auto Museum): Tř. Václava Klementa 294, 293 60 Mladá Boleslav; tel. 326831134; fax 326832039; e-mail museum@skoda-auto.cz; internet www.skoda-auto.com/cze/company/museum; f. 1974; Dir MARGIT ČERNÁ.

Opava

Slezské zemské muzeum (Silesian Provincial Museum): Tyršova 1, 746 01 Opava; tel. and fax 553622999; e-mail szmred@szmo.cz; internet www.szmo.cz; f. 1814; history, natural history, arts; arboretum at Nový Dvůr; library of 200,000 vols; Dir Dr JAROMÍR KALUS; publs *Časopis Slezského zemského muzea* (natural sciences and historical sciences series, each 3 a year), *Index Seminum* (1 a year), *Vlastivědné listy Slezska a severní Moravy* (2 a year).

Pardubice

Východočeské muzeum v Pardubicich (Museum of Eastern Bohemia): Zámek č. 2, 530 02 Pardubice; tel. 466799240; fax 466513056; e-mail vcm@vcm.cz; internet www.vcm.cz; f. 1880; history, natural history, arts; library of 40,000 vols; Dir Dr FRANTISEK ŠEBEK; publs *Panurus* (1 a year), *Východočeský sborník historický* (1 a year), *Východočeský sborník přírodovědný* (1 a year).

Plzeň

Západočeská galerie v Plzni (West Bohemian Gallery in Plzeň): Pražská 13, 301 00 Plzeň; tel. 377223759; fax 377322970; e-mail info@zpc-galerie.cz; internet www.zpc-galerie.cz; f. 1954; Czech art from the 14th century to the contemporary period; Dir Dr JANA POTUŽÁKOVÁ.

Západočeské muzeum v Plzni (West Bohemian Museum in Plzeň): Kopeckého sady 2, 301 00 Plzeň; tel. (378) 370110; fax (378) 370113; e-mail info@zcm.cz; internet www.zcm.cz; f. 1878; history, natural history, arts; Dir Dr FRANTIŠEK FRÝDA; publs *Folia Musei Rerum Naturalium Bohemiae Occidentalis* (separate series for zoology, geology and botany, each 2 a year), *Sborník* (*Příroda*, 5 a year; *Historie*, 1 a year).

Prace u Brna

Mohyla míru (Peace Monument): 664 58 Prace u Brna; tel. 544244724; fax 544244724; f. 1910; battle of Slavkov (Austerlitz); Dir Mgr ANTONÍN REČEK.

Prague

České muzeum výtvarných umění v Praze (Czech Museum of Fine Arts in Prague): Husova 19/21, 110 00 Prague 1; tel. 222220218; fax 222221190; e-mail muzeum@cmvu.cz; internet www.cmvu.cz; f. 1963; temporary exhibitions of modern and contemporary art; Dir Dr IVAN NEUMANN.

Galerie hlavního města Prahy (City Gallery Prague): Staroměstské Náměstí 13, 110 00 Prague; tel. and fax (2) 33325330; fax (2) 33323664; e-mail office@ghmp.cz; internet www.ghmp.cz; f. 1963; Pragensia, works by Czech artists since 19th century; library of 2,000 vols; Dir MILAN BUFKA.

Muzeum hlavního města Prahy (Central Museum of the City of Prague): Na Poříčí 52, 110 00 Prague 1; tel. 224223696; fax 224214306; e-mail muzeum@muzeumprahy.cz; internet www.muzeumprahy.cz; f. 1881; history of Prague, archaeology, fine art; library of 17,000 vols; Dir ZUZANA STRNADOVÁ; publ. *Archeologica pragensia* (1 a year).

Národní galerie v Praze (National Gallery in Prague): Staroměstské nám. 12, 110 15 Prague 1; tel. and fax 222329331; e-mail genreditel@ngprague.cz; internet www.ngprague.cz; f. 1796; art of all periods; library of 71,000 vols; Dir Prof. MILAN KNÍŽÁK; publ. *Bulletin* (irregular).

Národní muzeum (National Museum): Central Bldg, Václavské nám. 68, 115 79 Prague 1; tel. 224497111; fax 224226488; e-mail nm@nm.cz; internet www.nm.cz; f. 1818; expositions, spec. exhibitions, lecturing and teaching, pubs; collns of natural history, prehistory, history of Czech and foreign provenance, especially in the field of anthropology, ancient history of the Near E and Africa, Asian culture, bibliologybotanics, classical archeology, Czech history, entomology, ethnography, geology, history of physical education and sport, history of theatre, hydrobiology, medieval archeology, micology, mineralogy, musicology, non-European ethnography, numismatics, paleontology, prehistory, petrology, zoology; library: see Libraries and Archives; Dir-Gen. Dr MICHAL LUKEŠ; publs *Časopis Národního muzea* (Journal of the National Museum, 2 a year), *Museum* (2 a year), *Numismatické listy* (Numismatic Papers, 4 a year), *Sborník Národního muzea v Praze* (Acta Musei Nationalis Pragae, 2 a year).

Constituent Museums:

České muzeum hudby (Museum of Czech Music): Karmeliská 2, 118 00 Prague 1; tel. 257257757; fax 257322216; e-mail c_muzeum_hudby@nm.cz; internet www.nm.cz; f. 1936; incl. Dvořák (Prague 2, Ke Karlovu 20), Smetana (Prague 1, Novotného lávka 1), musical instruments (Prague 1, Karmeliská 2); library, sound archives; Dir Dr DAGMAR FIALOVÁ.

Historické muzeum (Historical Museum): Václavské nám. 68, 115 79 Prague 1; tel. 224497276; fax 224497246; e-mail pavel_dousa@nm.cz; internet www.nm.cz; f. 1964; history of Czech Republic, history of money, ethnography of the Czech Republic, sport, Czech theatre; Dir Dr PAVEL DOUŠA; publs *Časopis Národního muzea. Řada historická* (2 a year), *Fontes archaeologici Pragenses* (irregular), *Muzeum: Muzejní a vlastivědná práce* (2 a year), *Numismatické listy* (4 a year), *Shornik Národního Muzea v Praze, řada A - Historie* (2 a year).

Náprstkovo muzeum asijských, afrických a amerických kultur (Náprstek Museum of Asian, African and American Cultures): Betlémské nám. 1, 110 01 Prague 1; tel. 222221416; fax 222221418; internet www.nm.cz; f. 1862; research into Asian, African, Australian and Oceanian cultural heritage; permanent and temporary exhibitions, public lectures and cultural events; library of 250,000 vols; Dir Dr JANA SOUČKOVÁ; publ. *Annals* (1 a year).

Přírodovědecké muzeum (Natural History Museum): Václavské nám. 68, 115 79 Prague; tel. 224497111; fax 224222550; e-mail jiri.litochleb@nm.cz; internet www.nm.cz; f. 1964; Dir Dr JIŘÍ LITOCHLEB; publs *Acta Entomologica* (irregular), *Journal of the National Museum, Natural History Series* (1 a year), *Lynx* (1 a year), *Sborník Národního muzea, řada B* (Acta Musei Nationalis Pragae, Series B).

Národní technické muzeum (National Technical Museum): Kostelní 42, 170 78 Prague 7; tel. 220399111; fax 2203399200; e-mail info@ntm.cz; internet www.ntm.cz; f. 1908; library: see Libraries and Archives; Dir Mgr HORYMÍR KUBÍČEK; publs *Bibliografie a prameny Národního technického muzea, Rozpravy Národního technického muzea, Sborník Národního technického muzea v Praze*.

Národní zemědělské muzeum (National Museum of Agriculture): Kostelní 44, 170 00 Prague 7; tel. 233379025; fax 233372561; e-mail nzm.praha@nzm.cz; internet www.nzm.cz; f. 1891; exhibition of agriculture and food industry located in Kačina Castle near Kutná Hora; exhibition of agricultural machinery located in Cáslav; exhibition of forestry, hunting and fisheries in Ohrada Castle nr České Budějovice; exhibition of horticulture in Valtice near Břeclav; library of 120,000 vols, photographic archive; Dir Mgr PŘEMSYL REIBL; publs *Acta Museorum agriculturae, Prameny a studie* (Sources and Studies), *Vědecké práce ZM.* (Scientific Studies).

Památník národního písemnictví (Museum of Czech Literature): Strahovské nádvoří 1/132, 118 38 Prague 1; tel. 220516695; fax 220517277; e-mail post@pamatniknarodnihopisemnictvi.cz; internet www.pamatniknarodnihopisemnictvi.cz; f. 1953; literary archives containing 6m. objects; library of 600,000 vols; Dir EVA WOLFOVÁ; publ. *Literární archiv* (1 a year).

Pedagogické muzeum J. A. Komenského v Praze (Pedagogical Museum of J. A. Comenius in Prague): Valdštejnská 20, 118 00 Prague 1; tel. 257533455; fax 257530661; e-mail pedagog@pmjak.cz; internet www.pmjak.cz; f. 1892; documents illustrating the devt of nat. education and the life and work of Comenius; library of 25,000 vols; Dir Dr MARKÉTA PÁNKOVÁ.

Poštovní muzeum (Postal Museum): Nové mlýny 2, 110 00 Prague 1; tel. 222312006; fax 222311930; internet www.cpost.cz; f. 1918; Dir Dr PAVEL ČTVRTNÍK.

Uměleckoprůmyslové museum v Praze (Museum of Decorative Arts): 17 listopadu 2, 110 00 Prague 1; tel. 251093111; fax 251093296; e-mail info@upm.cz; internet www.upm.cz; f. 1885; applied art from ancient times to the present; library of 150,000 vols; Dir Dr HELENA KOENIGSMARKOVÁ.

Vojenský historický ústav Prahay/Military History Institute, Prague: U. Památníku 2, 130 05 Prague-Žižkov 3; tel. 973204900; fax 222541308; e-mail museum@army.cz; internet www.vhu.cz; f. 1919; library of 250,000 vols books, magazines, historical maps; Dir Mgr ALEŠ KNÍŽEK.

Constituent Museums:

Armádní muzeum Žižkov (Army Museum): U. Památníku 2, 130 05 Prague 3; tel. 220204924.

Letecké muzeum Kbely (Aviation Museum, Kbely): Kbely, Mladoboleslavská ul., 197 00 Prague 3; tel. 220207513; e-mail info@militarymuseum.cz.

Vojenské technické muzeum (Museum of Military Technology): Krhanice, Prague; tel. 317702130; fax 317702123.

Židovské muzeum v Praze (Jewish Museum in Prague): Staré školy 1, 3, 110 00 Prague 1; tel. 221711511; fax 221711584; e-mail office@jewishmuseum.cz; internet www.jewishmuseum.cz; f. 1906; consists of the Maisel Synagogue, the Spanish Synagogue, the Pinkas Synagogue, the Old Jewish Cemetery, the Klausen Synagogue and the Ceremonial Hall; provides detailed commentary on Judaism and Jewish history, as well as the history of the Jews in Bohemia and Moravia; Dir Dr LEO PAVLÁT; publ. *Judaica Bohemiae* (1 a year).

Rožnov pod Radhoštěm

Valašské muzeum v přírodě (Wallachian Open-Air Museum): Palackého 147, 756 61 Rožnov pod Radhoštěm; tel. 571757111; fax 571654494; e-mail muzeum@vmp.cz;

internet www.vmp.cz; f. 1925; open-air museum consisting of a wooden town, Wallachian village and mill valley; methodological centre for open-air museums; library of 15,000 vols; Dir Ing. VÍTĚZSLAV KOUKAL.

Slavkov u Brna

Zámek Slavkov—Austerlitz (Chateau Slavkov—Austerlitz): Palackého nám. 1, 684 01 Slavkov u Brna; tel. 544221204; fax 544227305; e-mail info@zamek-slavkov.cz; internet www.zamek-slavkov.cz; f. 1949; Napoleonic wars (particularly the Battle of Austerlitz), 17th- and 18th-century paintings, chapel of the Holy Cross; library colln on Napoleon; Dir Ing. ALEŠ ŠILHÁNEK.

Tábor

Husitské Muzeum (Hussite Museum): Nám. Mikuláše z Husi 44, 390 01 Tábor; tel. 381252242; fax 381252245; e-mail tabor@husmuzeum.cz; internet www.husmuzeum.cz; f. 1878; Hussite movement; library of 40,000 vols; Dir MILOŠ DRDA; publ. *Husitský Tábor* (1 a year).

Teplice

Regionální muzeum v Teplicích (Teplice Regional Museum): Zámecké nám. 14, 415 01 Teplice; tel. 417537869; fax 417572300; e-mail info@muzeum-teplice.cz; internet www.muzeum-teplice.cz; f. 1897; history, natural history, arts; library of 75,000 vols; Dir Dr DUŠAN ŠPIČKA; publs *Archeologický výzkum* (archaeological research, irregular), *Zprávy a studie* (local history and natural history, every 2 years).

Terezín

Památník Terezín (Terezín Memorial): Principova Alej 304, 411 55 Terezín; tel. 416782225; fax 416782245; e-mail pamatnik@pamatnik-terezin.cz; internet www.pamatnik-terezin.cz; f. 1947; museums of the Small Fortress (resistance and political persecution 1940–45) and the wartime Jewish ghetto of Terezín; Art Exhibition of the Terezín Memorial; Terezín 1780–1939; the Litoměřice concentration camp; library of 11,000 vols; Dir Dr JAN MUNK; publs *Newsletter* (4 a year), *Terezínské listy* (1 a year).

Uherské Hradiště

Slovácké muzeum v Uherském Hradišti (Slovácko Museum in Uherské Hradiště): Smetanovy sady 179, 686 01 Uherské Hradiště; tel. 572556556; fax 572554077; e-mail info@slovackemuzeum.cz; internet www.slovackemuzeum.cz; f. 1914; history, art; library of 30,000 vols; Dir Dr IVO FROLEC; publ. *Slovácko* (1 a year).

Uherský Brod

Muzeum J. A. Komenského v Uherském Brodě (Uherský Brod J. A. Comenius Museum): Ul. Přemysla Otakara II 37, 688 12 Uherský Brod; tel. 572632288; fax 572634078; e-mail muzeum@mjakub.cz; internet www.mjakub.cz; f. 1898; life, work and heritage of Protestant bishop and educational reformer, J. A. Comenius (1592–1670); history and ethnology of the Uherskobrodsko region; library of 40,000 vols; Dir Dr PAVEL POPELKA; publ. *Studia Comeniana et historica* (2 a year).

Zlín

Muzeum jihovýchodní Moravy (Museum of South-Eastern Moravia): Soudní 1, 762 57 Zlín; tel. 577004633; fax 577004632; e-mail info@muzeum.zlin.cz; internet www.muzeum.zlin.cz; f. 1953; social science (archaeology, history, ethnography), natural history (botany, entomology, geology), shoe museum; library of 24,650 vols; Dir Dr IVAN PLÁNKA; publ. *Acta Musealia*.

Obuvnické muzeum (Footwear Museum): Tř. Tomáše Bati 1970, POB 175, 762 57 Zlín; tel. 577213978; fax 577213978; e-mail m.stybrova@seznam.cz; internet www.muzeum.zlin.cz/obuvmuz.htm; f. 1959; library of 3,000 vols; Dir MIROSLAVA ŠTÝBROVÁ.

Universities

ČESKÉ VYSOKÉ UČENÍ TECHNICKÉ V PRAZE
(Czech Technical University in Prague)

Zikova 4, 166 36 Prague 6
Telephone: 224351111
Fax: 224310783
Internet: www.cvut.cz
Founded 1707; reorganized 1806, 1863, 1920, 1960
State control
Languages of instruction: Czech, English
Academic year: October to June

Rector: Prof. Ing. J. WITZANY
Vice-Rector for Construction: Prof. Ing. A. NAVRÁTIL
Vice-Rector for Devt: Prof. Ing. J. MACHÁČEK
Vice-Rector for Education: Prof. Ing. V. STEJSKAL
Vice-Rector for External Relations: Prof. Ing. F. VEJRAŽKA
Vice-Rector for Int. Relations: Prof. Dr M. VLČEK
Vice-Rector for Science and Research: Prof. Ing. L. MUSÍLEK
Chief Admin. Officer: Doc. Ing. Z. VOSPĚL

Number of teachers: 1,468
Number of students: 21,282

Publications: *Acta Polytechnica* (in English, 6 a year), *Pražská Technika* (in Czech, 6 a year)

DEANS

Faculty of Architecture: Prof. Ing. V. ŠLAPETA
Faculty of Civil Engineering: Prof. Ing. Z. BITTNAR
Faculty of Electrical Engineering: Prof. Ing. VLADIMÍR KUČERA
Faculty of Mechanical Engineering: Prof. Ing. PETR ZUNA
Faculty of Nuclear Science and Physical Engineering: Prof. Ing. MIROSLAV HAVLÍČEK
Faculty of Transportation Sciences: Doc. Ing. JOSEF JÍRA

ATTACHED INSTITUTES

Centre for Radiochemistry and Radiation Chemistry: Dir Doc. Ing. J. JOHN.
Computing and Information Centre: Dir Doc. Ing. L. OHERA.
Institute of Biomedical Engineering: Dir Prof. Ing. M. VRBOVÁ.
Institute of Experimental and Applied Physics: Dir Ing. S. POSPÍŠIL.
Klokner (Building) Institute: Dir Ing. T. KLEČKA.
Masaryk Institute of Advanced Studies: Dir Doc. Ing. J. PETR.
Research Institute for Industrial Heritage: Dir Dr B. FRAGNER.
Technology Innovation Centre: Plzeňská 130/221, 15000 Prague 5; tel. 257199913; fax 257212340; e-mail office@tic.cvut.cz; internet www.tic.cvut.cz/l=en; Dir Dr MILAN PRESS.

ČESKÁ ZEMĚDĚLSKÁ UNIVERZITA V PRAZE
(Czech University of Life Sciences, Prague)

Kamýcká 129, 165 21 Prague 6–Suchdol
Telephone: 224381111
Internet: www.czu.cz
Founded 1906
State control
Language of instruction: Czech
Academic year: September to August

Rector: Prof. Dr JOSEF KOZÁK
Pro-Rectors: Prof. Dr JIŘÍ BALÍK, Prof. Dr PAVEL KOVÁŘ, Prof. Dr VÁCLAV SLAVÍK, Prof. Dr MIROSLAV SVATOŠ
Registrar: Dr MILOŠ FRÝBORT
Librarian: Dr IVAN HAUZNER

Library of 225,000 vols
Number of teachers: 429
Number of students: 5,000

Publications: *Agricultura tropica et subtropica* (1 or 2 a year), *Scientia Agriculturae Bohemica* (4 a year), *Scientific Papers*

DEANS

Faculty of Agricultural Economics and Management: Prof. Dr JAN HRON
Faculty of Agronomy: Prof. Dr KAREL VOŘÍŠEK
Faculty of Forestry: Prof. Dr JOSEF GROSS
Technical Faculty: Prof. Dr KAREL POKORNÝ
Institute of Applied Ecology: RNDr ZDENĚK LIPSKÝ (Vice-Dean)
Institute of Tropical and Subtropical Agriculture: Prof. Dr BOHUMIL HAVRLAND

UNIVERZITA HRADEC KRÁLOVÉ
(University of Hradec Králové)

Rokitanského 62, 500 03 Hradec Králové
Telephone: 493331111
Fax: 495545911
Internet: www.uhk.cz
Founded 1959 as Institute of Education; university status 2000
State control

Rector: Dr JAROSLAVA MIKULECKÁ
Vice-Rector for Admin. and External Relations: Dr IVA JEDLIČKOVÁ
Vice-Rectors for Humanities: Prof. Ing. BOHUMIL VYBÍRAL
Vice-Rector for Internal Affairs: Dr ANTONÍN SLABÝ
Vice-Rector for Strategy and Devt: Dr MARTIN BÍLEK
Librarian: Mgr ZDENKA JEŽKOVÁ

Number of teachers: 355
Number of students: 5,600

DEANS

Faculty of Education: Ing. MARKÉTA BEDNÁŘOVÁ
Faculty of Humanities: Ing. IVANA SVOBODOVÁ
Faculty of Informatics and Management: JOSEF HYNEK

UNIVERZITA JANA EVANGELISTY PURKYNĚ V ÚSTÍ NAD LABEM
(Jan Evangelista Purkyně University in Ústí nad Labem)

Hoření 13, 400 96 Ústí nad Labem
Telephone: 475282111
Fax: 472772781
E-mail: rektor@rek.ujep.cz
Internet: www.ujep.cz
Founded as Pedagogical Faculty in Ústí nad Labem; university status 1991
State control

Rector: Dr Dr STANISLAV NOVÁK
Librarian: Dr IVO BROŽEK

Library of 250,000 vols
Number of teachers: 375
Number of students: 6,000

DEANS

Faculty of Art and Design: Dr VLADIMÍR ŠVEC
Faculty of Education: Dr ZDENĚK RADVA-
NOVSKÝ
Faculty of Environmental Studies: Dr Ing.
JOSEF SEJÁK
Faculty of Science: Dr Dr STANISLAV NOVÁK
Faculty of Social and Economic Studies: Prof.
Ing. PAVLIK

JIHOČESKÁ UNIVERZITA V ČESKÝCH BUDĚJOVICÍCH
(University of South Bohemia in České Budějovice)

Branišovská 31, 370 05 České Budějovice
Telephone: 389031111
Fax: 385310348
E-mail: rektorat@jcu.cz
Internet: www.jcu.cz

Founded 1991
State control
Academic year: September to June

Rector: Prof. Ing. FRANTIŠEK STŘELEČEK
Vice-Rector for Foreign Relations: Doc. Dr
MILAN STRAŠKRABA
Vice-Rector for Science: Doc. Ing. MARTIN
KŘÍŽEK
Vice-Rector for Study Programmes: Doc. Dr
JIŘÍ DIVÍŠEK
Vice-Rector for University Devt: Prof. Ing.
VÁCLAV ŘEHOUT

Number of teachers: 418
Number of students: 5,500

Publications: Memorial Volume of the Faculty of Agriculture–Economics (2 a year),
Memorial Volume of the Faculty of Agriculture–Phytotechnics (2 a year), Memorial
Volume of the Faculty of Agriculture–
Zootechnics (2 a year), Opera historica (1
a year)

DEANS

Faculty of Agriculture: Prof. Ing. JAN FRE-
LICH
Faculty of Biological Sciences: Doc. Dr ZDE-
NĚK BRANDL
Faculty of Education: Doc. Dr FRANTIŠEK
MRÁZ
Faculty of Health and Social Studies: Doc. Dr
VLADIMÍR VURM
Faculty of Theology: Prof. Dr KAREL SKALICKÝ

UNIVERZITA KARLOVA
(Charles University)

Ovocný trh 5, 116 36 Prague 1
Telephone: 224491111
Fax: 224210695
E-mail: sekretariat@ruk.cuni.cz
Internet: www.cuni.cz

Founded 1348
State control
Language of instruction: Czech
Academic year: September to June

Rector: Prof. Ing. IVAN WILHELM
Vice-Rectors: Prof. Dr PAVEL KLENER, Doc. Dr
EVA KVASNIČKOVA, Doc. Dr MICHAL SOBR,
Doc. Dr STANISLAV STECH, Prof. Dr JOSEF
STINGL, Doc. Dr JAROSLAVA SVOBODOVÁ
Quaestor: Ing. JOSEF KUBÍČEK
Chancellor: RNDr TOMÁŠ JELÍNEK

Library: see Libraries and Archives
Number of teachers: 4,048
Number of students: 42,475

Publications: Acta Universitatis Carolinae—
series: Mathematica et Physica, Biologica
(4 a year), Environmentalica (1 a year),
Folia Pharmaceutica Universitatis Carolinae, Geographica (2 a year), Geologica (4 a
year), Historia Universitatis Carolinae
Pragensis, Iuridica (4 a year), Kinanthro-
pologica (2 a year), Medica (1 a year),
Novitates Botanicae Universitatis Carolinae (1 a year), Oeconomica (2 a year),
Philologica (10 a year), Philosophica et
Historica (10 a year), Prague Bulletin of
Mathematical Linguistics, Psychologie v
ekonomické praxi (2 a year), Sborník
lékařský (4 a year)

DEANS

Faculty of Catholic Theology: Prof. Dr LUD-
WIG ARMBRUSTER
Faculty of Education: Prof. Dr PAVEL BENEŠ
Faculty of Evangelical Theology: Prof. Dr.
PAVEL FILIPI
Faculty of Humanities: Prof. Dr JAN SOKOL
Faculty of Hussite Theology: Prof. Dr JÁN
LIGUŠ
Faculty of Law: Doc. Dr VLADIMÍR KINDL
Faculty of Mathematics and Physics: Prof. Dr
IVAN NETUKA
1st Faculty of Medicine: Doc. Dr ŠTĚPÁN
SVAČINA
2nd Faculty of Medicine: Prof. Dr JOSEF
KOUTECKÝ
3rd Faculty of Medicine: Doc. Dr BOHUSLAV
SVOBODA
Faculty of Medicine in Hradec Králové: Prof.
Dr VLADIMÍR PALIČKA
Faculty of Medicine in Plzeň: Doc. Dr
JAROSLAV KOUTENSKÝ
Faculty of Pharmacy in Hradec Králové: Doc.
Dr JAROSLAV DUŠEK
Faculty of Philosophy: Prof. Dr JAROSLAV
VACEK
Faculty of Physical Education and Sport:
Prof. Ing. VÁCLAV BUNC
Faculty of Sciences: Prof. Dr PAVEL KOVÁŘ
Faculty of Social Sciences: Doc. Dr JAN AMOS
VÍŠEK

PROFESSORS

Faculty of Catholic Theology (6, Thákurova
3, 160 00 Prague; tel. 220181600; fax
220181215; e-mail dekan@kft.cuni.cz;
internet www.ktf.cuni.cz):

MATĚJKA, J., Practical Theology
POLC, J., Church History
SLABÝ, A., Pastoral Medicine
SOUSEDÍK, S., History of Philosophy
WOLF, V., Systematic Theology
ZEDNÍČEK, M., Canon Law

Faculty of Education (M. D. Rettigové 4,
Prague; tel. 221900111; fax 224947156;
e-mail pavel.vasak@pedf.cuni.cz; internet
www.pedf.cuni.cz):

BENEŠ, P., Chemistry
BRABCOVÁ, R., Czech Language
CORNES, P., History
HEJNÝ, M., Mathematics
HELUS, Z., Pedagogical Psychology
HERDEN, J., Music Education
JELÍNEK, S., Russian Language
KOMAN, M., Mathematics
KOTÁSEK, J., Education
PARIZEK, V., Education
PEŠKOVÁ, J., Philosophy
PIŤHA, P., Philosophy
POLEDŇÁK, K., Music Education
VULTERIN, J., Analytical Chemistry

Faculty of Evangelical Theology (1, Černá 9,
115 55 Prague; tel. 221988216; fax
221988200; e-mail filipi@ftf.cuni.cz; internet
www.ftf.cuni.cz):

FILIPI, P., Practical Theology
POKORNÝ, P., New Testament
REJCHRTOVÁ, N., Church History
TROJAN, J., Social Ethics

Faculty of Humanities (5, V. Kříže 10, 150 00
Prague; tel. 251080111; e-mail sokol@fhs
.cuni.cz; internet www.fhs.cuni.cz):

BENYOVSZKY, L., Philosophy
BOUZEK, J., Archaeology, Classical Phil-
ology
BYSTŘICKÝ, J., Philosophy, Media
ČEŠKA, J., Philosophy, Literature
DOHNALOVÁ, M., Economics
GABRIŠKOVÁ, L., Languages
HALBICH, M., Anthropology
HAVELKA, M., Sociology, Social History
HAVELKOVÁ, H., Gender Studies
HAVLÍČEK, Anthropology, Ethnology
HAVRDOVÁ, Z., Social Psychology
HORSKÝ, J., History, Historical Anthropol-
ogy
HOZÁKOVÁ, J., Sociology
HROCH, M., History
KAČÍREK, M., Law
KRUŽÍK, J., Philosophy
MATOUŠEK, V., Anthropology, Archaeology
MORAVCOVÁ, M., Ethnology
MULLER, K., Sociology
NOVÁK, A., Philosophy
PINC, Z., Philosophy
PRUDKÝ, L., Sociology
RYNDA, I., Human Ecology
SELIGOVÁ, M., History
SHANAHAN, D., Languages, Film
ŠKOVAJSA, M., Political Philosophy
ŠKVAŘILOVÁ, B., Anthropology
SOKOL, J., Anthropology, Philosophy
SOUKUPOVÁ, B., Social History
SVATOŇ, O., Sociology
SVOBODA, A., Art, Design
TURKOVÁ, M., Ethnology
VANČÁT, J., Theory of Art
VANČATOVÁ, M., Ethnology
VOPĚNKA, P., Logic, Mathematics
ZIMA, P., Languages, Sociolinguistics

Faculty of Hussite Theology (4, Pacovská
350/4, 140 21 Prague; tel. 241733131; e-mail
jligus@htf.cuni.cz; internet www.htf.cuni.cz):

HAŠKOVCOVÁ, H., Medical Ethics
HOLETON, D. R., Liturgics
KUČERA, Z., Systematic Theology
LIGUŠ, J., Philosophy of Communication
SÁZAVA, Z., Biblical Theology

Faculty of Law (1, nám. Curieových 7, 116 40
Prague; tel. 221005111; e-mail dekan@ius.prf
.cuni.cz; internet www.prf.cuni.cz):

BAKEŠ, M., Financial Law
BELINA, M., Labour Law
BOGUSZAK, J., Theory of State and Law
CÍSAŘOVÁ, D., Criminal Law
GERLOCH, A., Theory, Philosophy and Soci-
ology of Law
HENDRYCH, D., Administrative Law
KŘIŽ, J., Civil Law
KUČERA, Z., International Law
MALÝ, K., History of State and Law
NOVOTNÝ, O., Criminal Law
PAVLÍČEK, V., Constitutional Law and Civic
Sciences
ŠVESTKA, J., Civil Law
TICHÝ, L., European Law
WINTEROVÁ, A., Civil Law
ZOULÍK, FR., Civil Law

Faculty of Mathematics and Physics (2, K.
Karlovu 3, 121 16 Prague; tel. 221951111; fax
221911292; e-mail dekan@dekanat.mff.cuni
.cz; internet www.mff.cuni.cz):

ANDĚL, J., Mathematics and Statistics
BARVÍK, I., Physics
BEDNÁŘ, J., Physics
BENEŠ, V., Mathematics
BIČÁK, J., Theoretical Physics
BICAN, L., Mathematics
BIEDERMAN, H., Macromolecular Physics
ČÁPEK, V., Theoretical Physics
CIPRA, T., Mathematics
DUPAČOVÁ, J., Mathematics and Statistics
FEISTAUER, M., Mathematics
FORMÁNEK, J., Theoretical Physics
HAJČOVÁ, E., Information Science
HÁLA, J., Physics

HASLINGER, J., Physics
HORÁČEK, J., Theoretical Physics
HOŘEJŠÍ, J., Nuclear Physics
HÖSCHL, P., Physics
HRACH, R., Electronic Physics
HUŠEK, M., Mathematics
HUŠKOVÁ, M., Mathematics
ILAVSKÝ, M., Macromolecular Physics
JUREČKOVÁ, J., Probability and Statistics
KAKGER, A., Mathematics
KEPKA, T., Mathematics
KOWALSKI, O., Mathematics
KVASIL, J., Experimental Physics
LUKEŠ, J., Mathematical Analysis
MARTINEC, Z., Physics and Geophysics
MATOLÍN, V., Electronic Physics
MATOUŠEK, J., Informatics
NEŠETŘIL, J., Mathematics
NETUKA, I., Mathematics
NOVÁK, B., Mathematics
PANEVOVÁ, J., Information Science
PLÁSIL, F., Informatics
POKORNÝ, J., Informatics
PULTR, A., Mathematics
ROHN, J., Mathematics
SECHOVSKÝ, V., Physics
SIMON, P., Mathematics
SKÁLA, L., Physics
SOUČEK, V., Mathematics
ŠTĚPÁN, J., Mathematics
ŠTĚPÁNEK, H., Mathematics
SVOBODA, E., Theoretical Physics
TICHÝ, M., Physics
TROJANOVÁ, Z., Electronic Physics
VALVODA, V., Physics
VELICKÝ, B., Physics
VIŠŇOVSKÝ, Š., Physics
ZAJÍČEK, L., Mathematics
ZIMMERMANN, K., Information Science

1st Faculty of Medicine (2, Kateřinská 32, 121 08 Prague; tel. 224961111; fax 224915413; e-mail stepan.svacina@lf1.cuni.cz; internet www.lf1.cuni.cz):

ASCHERMANN, M., Internal Medicine
BENCKO, V., Hygiene
BETKA, J., Otorhinolaryngology
BROULÍK, P., Internal Medicine
DVOŘÁČEK, J., Urology
ELIŠKA, O., Anatomy
ELLEDER, M., Pathology
FARGHALL, H. M., Pharmacology
FUČÍKOVÁ, T., Immunology and Allergology
HÁJEK, Z., Gynaecology
HORKÝ, K., Internal Medicine
HYNIE, S., Pharmacology
KLENER, P., Oncology
KRAML, J., Biochemistry
LAŠTOVKA, M., Otorhinolaryngology
MAREČEK, Z., Internal Medicine
MAREK, J., Internal Medicine
MARTÍNEK, J., Histology and Embryology
NEČAS, E., Normal and Pathological Physiology
NEVŠÍMALOVÁ, S., Neurology
PAFKO, P., Surgery
PETROVICKÝ, P., Anatomy
POKORNY, J., Physiology
POVÝŠIL, C., Pathological Anatomy
RABOCH, J., Psychiatry
RACEK, J., Stomatology
RYBKA, V., Orthopaedic Surgery
ŠKRHA, J., Internal Medicine
ŠOSNA, A., Surgery
ŠTĚPÁN, J., Biochemistry
ŠTÍPEK, S., Biochemistry
STREJC, P., Forensic Medicine
TERŠÍP, K., Surgery
TESAŘ, V., Internal Medicine
TOPINKOVÁ, E., Social Medicine
TROJAN, S., Medical Physiology
VANĚK, J., Surgery
VÍTEK, F., Biophysics
VYMĚTAL, J., Clinical Psychology
ZEMAN, J., Paediatrics
ZEMAN, M., Surgery

ZIMA, T., Medical Chemistry
ŽIVNÝ, J., Gynaecology and Obstetrics

2nd Faculty of Medicine (5, Vúvalu 84, 150 06 Prague; tel. 224431111; fax 224435820; e-mail josef.koutecky@lfmotol.cuni.cz; internet www.lf2.cuni.cz):

BOUŠKA, I., Forensic Medicine
BROŽEK, G., Physiology
DRUGA, R., Anatomy
GOETZ, P., Biology
HERGET, J., Pathological Physiology
HOŘEJŠÍ, J., Gynaecology and Obstetrics
KODET, R., Pathological Anatomy
KONRÁDOVÁ, V., Histology and Embryology
KOUTECKY, J., Oncology
MATOUŠOVIC, K., Internal Medicine
PELOUCH, V., Medical Chemistry and Biochemistry
ŠEEMANOVÁ, E., Genetics
ŠNAJDAUF, J., Surgery
SVIHOVEC, J., Pharmacology
VÍZEK, M., Pathological Physiology
VOJÁČEK, J., Internal Medicine

3rd Faculty of Medicine (10, Ruská 87, 100 00 Prague; tel. 267102111; e-mail michal .andel@lf3.cuni.cz; internet www.lf3.cuni.cz):

ANDĚL, M., Internal Medicine
CIKRT, M., Hygiene
GREGOR, P., Internal Medicine
HORÁK, J., Internal Medicine
HÖSCHL, C., Psychiatry
JELÍNEK, R., Histology and Embryology, Anatomy
KRŠIAK, M., Pharmacology
KUCHYNKA, P., Ophthalmology
LENER, J., Hygiene
MALINA, L., Dermatology
PROVAZNÍK, K., Hygiene
RAŠKA, I., Medical Biology
ROKYTA, R., Pathological Physiology
SCHINDLER, J., Microbiology
STEFAN, J., Forensic Medicine
STINGL, J., Anatomy

Faculty of Medicine in Hradec Králové (Šimkova 870, 500 38 Hradec Králové; tel. 495816111; fax 495513597; e-mail dekan@ lfhk.cuni.cz; internet www.lfhk.cuni.cz):

DOMINIK, J., Surgery
FIXA, B., Internal Medicine
HEJZLAR, M., Microbiology
HRNČÍŘ, Z., Internal Medicine
HYBÁŠEK, I., Otorhinolaryngology
KRÁL, B., Internal Medicine
KVASNIČKA, J., Internal Medicine
MALÝ, J., Internal Medicine
MARTÍNKOVÁ, J., Pharmacology
NĚMEČEK, S., Histology and Embryology
PIDRMAN, V., Internal Medicine
ROZSÍVAL, P., Ophthalmology
ŠPAČEK, J., Pathological Anatomy
ŠRB, V., Hygiene
ŠTEINER, I., Pathological Anatomy
STRANSKY, P., Biophysics
VOBOŘIL, Z., Surgery
VODIČKA, I., Biophysics
ZADÁK, Z., Internal Medicine

Faculty of Medicine in Plzeň (Husova 13, 306 05 Plzeň; tel. 377593400; fax 197221460; e-mail dekan@lfp.cuni.cz; internet www.lfp .cuni.cz):

AMBLER, Z., Neurology
FAKAN, F., Pathological Anatomy
MICHAL, M., Pathological Anatomy
OPATRNÝ, K., Internal Medicine
RACEK, J., Biochemistry
RESL, V., Dermatovenereology
SKÁLOVÁ, A., Pathology
TĚŠÍNSKÝ, P., Ophthalmology
TOPOLČAN, O., Internal Medicine
TŘEŠKA, V., Surgery

Faculty of Pharmacy in Hradec Králové (Heyrovskiho tř. 1203, 501 65 Hradec Králové; tel. 495067111; fax 495512656; e-mail dusek@faf.cuni.cz; internet www.faf.cuni.cz):

DRŠATA, J., Biochemistry
FENDRICH, Z., Pharmacology
JAHODÁŘ, L., Pharmacognosy
KARLÍČEK, R., Analytical Chemistry
KYASNIČKOVÁ, E., Biochemistry
LÁZNÍČEK, M., Radiopharmacy
VIŠŇOVSKÝ, P., Pharmacology
WAISSER, K., Organic Chemistry

Faculty of Philosophy (1, nám. J. Palacha 2, 116 38 Prague; tel. 221619111; e-mail dekan@ff.cuni.cz; internet www.ff.cuni.cz):

BLÁHOVÁ, M., Auxiliary Historical Sciences
BOUZEK, J., Classical Archaeology
ČERMÁK, F., Czech Language
DOHALSKÁ, M., Phonetics
HALÍK, T., Sociology
HILSKY, M., English Literature
HLEDÍKOVÁ, Z., Auxiliary Historical Sciences
HORYNA, M., History of Art
KÖNIGOVÁ, M., Information and Librarianship
KROPÁČEK, L., History and Culture of Africa and Asia
KUČERA, K., Czech Language
KUKLÍK, J., Czech History
MACUROVÁ, A., Czech Language
MAUR, E., Czech History
OPATRNÝ, J., General History
PALEK, B., General Linguistics
PALKOVÁ, Z., Phonetics and Phonology
SKŘIVAN, A., General History
SLÁMA, J., Archaeology
SLAVICKÝ, M., Music Studies
STEHLÍKOVÁ, E., History and Theory of Theatre
ULIČNÝ, O., Czech Language
VACEK, J., Sanskrit and Tamil Philosophy
VERNER, M., Egyptology

Faculty of Physical Education and Sport (6, José Martiho 31, 162 52 Prague; tel. 220562459; fax 220172370; e-mail karger@ ftvs.cuni.cz; internet www.ftvs.cuni.cz):

BLAHUŠ, P., Kinanthropology
BUNC, V., Kinanthropology
DYLEVSKÝ, I., Anatomy
HOUDEK, V., Theory of Physical Culture
KOVÁŘ, R., Kinanthropology
OTAHAL, S., Biomechanics and Bionics
RYCHTECKÝ, A., Kinanthropology
SLEPIČKA, P., Kinanthropology
SVOBODA, B., Sports Education
TEPLÝ, Z., Human Movement

Faculty of Sciences (2, Albertov 6, 128 43 Prague; tel. 222112111; e-mail stulik@prfdec .natur.cuni.cz; internet www.natur.cuni.cz):

BOUBLÍK, T., Physical and Macromolecular Chemistry
BOUŠKA, V., Geological Mineralogy
BUCHAR, J., Zoology
ČEPEK, P., Geology
ČERNÝ, M., Organic Chemistry
CHLUPÁČ, I., Geology
DROBNÍK, J., Biotechnology
FELTL, L., Analytical Chemistry
GARDAVSKÝ, V., Regional Geography
HAMPL, M., Regional Geography
HŮRKA, K., Zoology
KALVODA, J., Physical Geography
KLINOT, J., Organic Chemistry
KOŘÍNEK, V., Biology
MAREK, F., Geology
MAREŠ, S., Geophysics
MATOLÍN, M., Geophysics
MEJSNAR, J., Biology
NÁTR, M., Plant Physiology
NEUBAUER, Z., Philosophy of Natural Sciences
NOVOTNÝ, I., Biology and Physiology of Animals

PAVLÍK, Z., Demography
PERTOLD, Z., Geology
PEŠEK, J., Geology
PODLAHA, J., Inorganic Chemistry
RIEDER, M., Geology
SMOLÍKOVÁ, L., Physical and Macromolecular Chemistry
ŠTEHLÍK, E., Mathematics
ŠTEMPROK, M., Geology
ŠTRUNECKÁ, A., Biology
ŠTULIK, A., Analytical Chemistry
STYS, P., Entomology
TICHÁ, M., Biochemistry
VÁŇA, J., Botany
VÁVRA, J., Parasitology
ZADRAŽIL, S., Genetics and Microbiology

Faculty of Social Sciences (1, Smetanavo nábřezí 6, 110 00 Prague; tel. 222112111; fax 224235644; e-mail mlcoch@mbox.fsv.cuni .cz; internet www.fsv.cuni.cz):

HLAVÁČEK, Economics
KOUBA, K., Political Economy
KRAUS, J., Mass Communication
KŘEN, J., Czechoslovak History
MESSTŘÍK, M., Economics
MLČOCH, L., Economics
PEŠEK, J., Modern History
PETRUSEK, M., Sociology
POTŮČEK, M., Sociology
REIMAN, M., History and Politics of Russia and Eastern Europe
SOJKA, M., Economic Theory
TURNOVEC, F., Economics
URBAN, L., Political Economy

MASARYKOVA UNIVERZITA V BRNĚ
(Masaryk University in Brno)

Žerotínovo nám. 9, 601 77 Brno
Telephone: 549491011
Fax: 549491070
E-mail: info@muni.cz
Internet: www.muni.cz
Founded 1919
State control
Language of instruction: Czech
Academic year: September to August

Rector: Prof. Dr PETER FIALA
Vice-Rector for Academic Affairs: Prof. Dr ZUZANA BRÁZDOVÁ
Vice-Rector for Research and Devt: Prof. Dr JANA MUSILOVÁ
Vice-Rector for Social Affairs of Students and External Relations: Assoc. Prof. Ing. ANTONÍN SLANÝ

Library of 1,544,000 vols
Number of teachers: 3,072
Number of students: 26,681

Publications: *Universitas* (4 a year), *Scripta Medica* (6 a year), *Archivum mathematicum* (8 a year), *MUNI.CZ* (10 a year, except July and August)

DEANS

Faculty of Arts: Dr JAN PAVLÍK
Faculty of Economics and Administration: Assoc. Prof. Dr IVAN MALÝ
Faculty of Education: Assoc. Prof. Dr VLADISLAV MUŽÍK
Faculty of Informatics: Prof. Dr JIŘI ZLATUŠKA
Faculty of Law: Assoc. Prof. Dr JAN SVATOŇ
Faculty of Medicine: Assoc. Prof. Dr JAN ŽALOUDÍK
Faculty of Science: Assoc. Prof. Dr MILAN GELNAR
Faculty of Sports Studies: Dr MICHAL CHARVÁT
School of Social Studies: Assoc. Prof. Dr LADISLAV RABUŠIC

PROFESSORS

Faculty of Arts (Arna Nováka 1, 660 80 Brno; tel. 549491511; fax 549491520; e-mail dekan@phil.muni.cz; internet www.phil .muni.cz):

BÁTORA, J., Archaeology
BLAŽEK, V., Comparative Indo-European Linguistics
CEJPEK, J., Library Studies
FIALA, J., Czech Literature
GAJDOŠ, J., Theory and History of Theatre
HORÁK, P., Philosophy
HORYNA, B., Study of Religion
HROCH, J., Philosophy
KARLÍK, P., Czech Language
KRČMOVÁ, M., Czech Language
KROUPA, J., History of Arts
KURFÜRST, P., Musicology
MALÍŘ, J., Czech History
MĚŘÍNSKÝ, Z., Archaeology
MUNZAR, J., German Literature
NECHUTOVÁ, J., Classics
NEKUDA, V., Slavonic Archaeology
OSLZLÝ, P., Theatre and Film Studies
PLESKALOVÁ, J., Czech Language
POSPÍŠIL, I., History of Russian Literature
RUSÍNOVÁ, Z., Czech Language
SLAVÍČEK, L., History of Art
SMAJS, J., Philosophy
ŠTEHLÍKOVÁ, E., Theatre and Film Studies
ŠTĚDROŇ, M., Musicology
STŘÍTECKÝ, J., Philosophy
SVOBODA, M., Psychology
ZOUHAR, J., Philosophy

Faculty of Economics and Administration (Lipová 41A, 659 79 Brno; tel. 549491710; fax 549491720; e-mail dekan@econ.muni.cz; internet www.econ.muni.cz):

BLAZEK, L., Theory of Management
IVÁNEK, L., Economics
LANČA, J., Economics and Corporate Management
MÁŠA, M., Management
ONDRČKA, P., Finance
ŠEJBAL, J., Finance
ŽÁK, M., Economics

Faculty of Education (Poříčí 7, 603 00 Brno; tel. 549493050; fax 549491620; e-mail dekan@ped.muni.cz; internet www.ped.muni .cz):

CHALUPA, P., Geography
CHVALINA, J., Mathematics
HLADKÝ, J., English Language
HOROVÁ, I., Mathematics
KOŠUT, M., Teaching of Music
MAŇÁK, J., Education
MAREČKOVÁ, M., History
NOVÁK, V., Mathematics
ŠVEC, V., Education
VÍTKOVÁ, M., Special Education

Faculty of Informatics (Botanická 68A, Brno; tel. 549491810; fax 549491820; e-mail dekan@fi.muni.cz; internet www.fi.muni.cz):

BUZEK, V., Informatics
DOKULIL, M., Philosophy
GRUSKA, J., Informatics
HŘEBÍČEK, J., Company Information Systems
MATERNA, P., Logic
NOVOTNÝ, M., Mathematics and Informatics
SERBA, I., Informatics
ZEZULA, P., Informatics
ZLATUŠKA, J., Informatics

Faculty of Law (Veveří 70, 611 80 Brno; tel. 549491211; fax 541213162; e-mail dekan@ law.muni.cz; internet www.law.muni.cz):

BEJČEK, J., Economic Law
FILIP, J., Constitutional Law and Political Science
HAJN, P., Economic Law
HRUŠÁKOVÁ, M., Civil Law
HURDÍK, J., Civil Law
JÍLEK, D., International Public Law
MALENOVSKÝ, J., International Public Law

ROZEHNALOVÁ, N., International Private Law
TELEC, I., Civil Law
VÁGNER, I., Economics
VLČEK, E., History of State and Law

Faculty of Medicine (Komenského nám. 2, 662 43 Brno; tel. 549491111; fax 542213996; e-mail dekan@med.muni.cz; internet www .med.muni.cz):

ADAM, Z., Internal Medicine
BEDNAŘÍK, J., Neurology
BENDA, K., Radiology
BRÁZDOVÁ, Z., Social Medicine
BRHEL, P., Occupational Medicine
BRYCHTA, P., Surgery
BUČEK, J., Pathology
ČECH, S., Histology
ČEŠKOVÁ, E., Psychiatry
DAPECI, A., Stomatology
DÍTĚ, P., Internal Medicine
DRTÍLKOVÁ, I., Psychiatry
DUBOVÝ, P., Anatomy
DVOŘÁK, K., Pathology
FAKAN, F., Anatomy
FIŠER, B., Pathology and Physiology
GÁL, P., Surgery
HADAŠOVÁ, E., Pharmacology
HEP, A., Internal Medicine
HOLČÍK, J., Social Medicine
HONZÍKOVÁ, N., Pathology and Physiology
HORKÝ, D., Histology
HRUBÁ, D., Social Medicine
JANISCH, R., Biology
KADAŇKA, Z., Neurology
KOSTŘICA, R., Otorhynolaryngology
KUBEŠOVÁ, H., Internal Medicine
KUKLETA, M., Medical Physiology
KUKLETOVA, M., Stomatology
LITZMAN, J., Immunology
LOKAJ, J., Immunology
LUKÁŠ, Z., Anatomy
MALÝ, Z., Gynaecology and Obstetrics
MAYER, J., Internal Medicine
MELUZÍN, J., Internal Medicine
MUNZAROVÁ, M., Internal Medicine
PÁČ, L., Anatomy
PAČÍK, D., Surgery
PENKA, M., Internal Medicine
PETŘEK, M., Immunology
ŘEHŮŘEK, J., Ophthalmology
REJTHAR, A., Pathology
REKTOR, I., Neurology
ROZTOČIL, A., Gynaecology and Obstetrics
SEMRÁD, B., Internal Medicine
SEMRÁDOVÁ, V., Dermatovenereology
ŠEVČÍK, P., Anaesthesiology
SIEGLOVÁ, J., Functional Diagnostics and Rehabilitation
ŠMRČKA, V., Surgery
ŠPINAR, J., Internal Medicine
ŠULCOVÁ, A., Pharmacology
ŠVESTKA, J., Psychiatry
SVOBODA, A., Biology
TOMAN, J., Internal Medicine
VÁCHA, J., Pathological Physiology
VÁLEK, V., Radiology
VANĚK, J., Stomatology
VAŠKŮ, A., Pathological Physiology
VENTRUBA, P., Gynaecology and Obstetrics
VESELÝ, J., Surgery
VÍTOVEC, J., Internal Medicine
VLKOVÁ, E., Ophthalmology
VOMELA, J., Surgery
VORLÍČEK, J., Internal Medicine
WECHSLER, J., Surgery
WENDSCHE, P., Surgery
ZÁHEJSKÝ, J., Dermatovenereology
ŽALOUDÍK, J., Surgery
ZEMAN, K., Internal Medicine

Faculty of Science (Kotlářská 2, 611 37 Brno; tel. 549491411; fax 541211214; e-mail dekan@sci.muni.cz; internet www.sci.muni .cz):

BARTŮSEK, M., Analytical Chemistry
BRÁZDIL, R., Physical Geography

BRZOBOHATÝ, R., Palaeontology
DOŠKAŘ, J., Molecular Biology and Genetics
DOŠLÁ, Z., Mathematics
DOŠLÝ, O., Mathematical Analysis
GAISLER, J., Zoology
GLOSER, J., Plant Physiology
HÁLA, J., Inorganic Chemistry
HAVEL, J., Analytical Chemistry
HOLÍK, M., Physical Chemistry
HOLOUBEK, I., Environmental Chemistry
HOLÝ, V., Physics of Condensed Materials
HORSKÝ, J., Theoretical Physics
HUMLÍČEK, J., Physics
JANČA, J., Physics
JONAS, J., Organic Chemistry
KANICKÝ, V., Analytical Chemistry
KAPIČKA, V., Physics
KNOZ, J., Biology
KOČA, J., Organic Chemistry
KOLÁŘ, I., Algebra and Geometry
KOMÁREK, J., Analytical Chemistry
KOTYK, A., Biochemistry
KUČERA, I., Biochemistry
LENC, M., General Physics and Mathematical Physics
MALINA, J., Archaeology
MUSILOVÁ, J., Physics
NOVÁK, M., Geology
NOVÁK, V., Mathematics
NOVOTNÝ, J., Physics
OHLÍDAL, I., Quantum Electronics and Optics
POTÁČEK, M., Organic Chemistry
PŘICHYSTAL, A., Geology
PROŠEK, P., Physical Geography
RELICHOVÁ, J., Genetics
ROSICKÝ, J., Mathematics
ROZKOŠNÝ, R., Entomology
SCHMIDT, E., Physics
SKLENÁŘ, V., Physical Chemistry
ŠIMEK, M., Animal Physiology
SKULA, L., Mathematics
SLOVÁK, J., Geometry
STANĚK, J., Mineralogy and Petrography
UNGER, J., Anthropology
VAŇHARA, J., Zoology
VELICKÝ, B., Theoretical Physics
VETTERL, J., Physical Electronics
VICHEREK, J., Botany
VŘEŠŤÁL, J., Physical Chemistry
ŽÁK, J., Inorganic Chemistry
ZIMA, J., Zoology

School of Social Studies (Gorkého 7, 602 00 Brno; tel. 549491911; fax 549491920; e-mail dekan@fss.muni.cz; internet www.fss.muni.cz):

FIALA, P., Politology
KELLER, J., Sociology
LIBROVÁ, H., Sociology
MACEK, P., Social Psychology
MAREŠ, P., Sociology
MOŽNÝ, I., Sociology
RABUŠIC, L., Sociology
SIROVÁTKA, T., Social Policy and Social Work
ŠMAUSOVÁ, G., Sociology
SMÉKAL, V., Psychology
STRMISKA, M., Political Science

MENDELOVA ZEMĚDĚLSKÁ A LESNICKÁ UNIVERZITA V BRNĚ
(Mendel University of Agriculture and Forestry, Brno)

Zemědělská 1, 613 00 Brno
Telephone: 545131111
Fax: 545211128
E-mail: info@mendelu.cz
Internet: www.mendelu.cz

Founded by State Law in 1919
State control
Language of instruction: Czech
Academic year: September to January, February to June

Rector: J. HLUŠEK
Pro-Rectors: L. GREGA, M. HAVLÍČEK J. NERUDA R. POKLUDA
Chief Administrative Officer: V. SEDLÁŘOVÁ
Chief Librarian: V. SVOBODOVÁ
Library of 400,000 vols
Number of teachers: 450
Number of students: 10,621 full-time, 1,200 part-time
Publication: *Acta Universitatis Agriculturae et Silviculturae Mendelianae Brunensis* (6 a year)

DEANS

Faculty of Agronomy: L. ZEMAN
Faculty of Business and Economics: J. STÁVKOVÁ
Faculty of Forestry and Wood Technology: P. HORÁČEK
Faculty of Horticulture: P. KUČERA

OSTRAVSKÁ UNIVERZITA V OSTRAVĚ
(Ostrava University)

Dvořákova 7, 701 03 Ostrava
Telephone: 597091111
Fax: 596118219
Internet: www.osu.cz

Founded 1991
State control

Rector: Dr JIŘÍ MOČKOŘ
Vice-Rector for Devt and Information Management: Dr Ing CYRIL KLIMEŠ
Vice-Rector for Research and External Relations: Mgr IGOR FOJTÍK
Vice-Rector for Study: Dr JARMILA KRKOŠKOVÁ
Library of 230,000 vols
Number of teachers: 583
Number of students: 9,470

DEANS

Faculty of Arts: Dr EVA MRHAČOVÁ
Faculty of Fine Arts: Dr ZBYNĚK JANÁČEK
Faculty of Science: Dr DANA KRIČFALUŠI
Faculty of Social Studies: Dr OLDŘICH CHYTIL
Medico-Social Faculty: Dr ARNOŠT MARTÍNEK
Pedagogical Faculty: Dr JOSEF MALACH

UNIVERZITA PALACKÉHO V OLOMOUCI
(Palacký University)

Křížkovského 8, 771 47 Olomouc
Telephone: 585631001
Fax: 585631012
E-mail: rektor@upol.cz
Internet: www.upol.cz

Founded 1573; reopened 1946
State control
Languages of instruction: Czech, English, German
Academic year: September to August

Rector: Prof. Dr LUBOMÍR DVOŘÁK
Vice-Rector for Devt: Prof. Dr EVŽEN WEIGL
Vice-Rector for Int. and Public Relations: Mgr JAKUB DÜRR
Vice-Rector for Organization: Dr LUDMILA LOCHMANOVÁ
Vice-Rector for Scientific and Research Activities: Prof. Dr JITKA ULRICHOVÁ
Vice-Rector for Student Affairs: Doc. Dr MIROSLAV CHRÁSKA
Registrar: Ing. JIŘÍ JIRKA
Librarian: Dr DANA LOŠŤÁKOVÁ

Library of 521,000
Number of teachers: 1,800
Number of students: 20,000
Publication: *Acta Universitatis Palackianae* (4 a year)

DEANS

Faculty of Education: Prof. Dr LIBUŠE LUDÍKOVÁ
Faculty of Law: Dr MICHAL MALACKA
Faculty of Medicine: Prof. Dr ZDERNĚK KOLÁŘ
Faculty of Philosophy: Prof. Dr IVO BARTEČEK
Faculty of Physical Culture: Doc. Dr DUŠAN TOMAJKO
Faculty of Science: Prof. Dr JURAJ ŠEVČÍK
Sts Cyril and Methodius Faculty of Theology: Dr IVANA GABRIELA VLKOVÁ

PROFESSORS

Faculty of Education (Žižkovo nám. 5, 771 40 Olomouc; tel. 585635088; fax 585231400; e-mail libuse.ludikova@upol.cz):

CHRÁSKA, M., Theory of Education
HLÚZA, B., Botany
KLAPIL, P., Music Theory and Pedagogy
KOVAŘÍČEK, V., Theory of Education
LUDÍKOVÁ, L., Pedagogy of Special Needs Education
MEZIHORÁK, F., Czechoslovak History
NELEŠOVSKÁ, A., Theory of Elementary School
SLÁMA, O., Forest Ergonomics
STEINMETZ, K., Music Theory and Pedagogy
STOFFA, J., Electrical Engineering

Faculty of Law (17 Listopadu 8, 771 00 Olomouc; tel. 585637509; fax 585223537; e-mail michal.malacka@upol.cz):

DAVID, V., International Law
MAREČKOVÁ, M., History
MEČL, J., Theory of Law
TELEC, I., Civic Law

Faculty of Medicine (Tř. Svobody 8, 771 26 Olomouc; tel. 585632010; fax 585223907; e-mail zdenek.kolar@upol.cz):

BOUČEK, J., Psychiatry
DLOUHÝ, M., Surgery
DUDA, M., Surgery
EBER, M., Stomatology
EHRMANN, J., Internal Diseases
GLADKIJ, J., Social Medicine
HÁLEK, J., Electronics and Medical Procedures
HOLIBKA, V., General Anatomy
HOUDEK, M., Neurosurgery
HŘEBÍČEK, J., Pathological Physiology
HUŠÁK, V., Applied Physics
INDRÁK, K., Internal Diseases
JANOUT, V., Epidemiology
JAROŠOVÁ, M., Medical Genetics
JEZDINSKÝ, J., Pharmacology
JIRAVA, E., Stomatology
KAMÍNEK, M., Stomatology
KLAČANSKÝ, J., Otorhinolaryngology
KOD'OUSEK, R., Pathological Anatomy
KOLÁŘ, Z., Pathology
KOLEK, V., Internal Diseases
KOMENDA, S., Education
KRÁL, V., Surgery
KRČ, I., Internal Medicine
KUDELA, M., Gynaecology
LENHART, K., General Biology
LICHNOVSKÝ, V., Histology and Embryology
LUKL, J., Internal Diseases
MAČÁK, J., Pathology
MAČÁKOVÁ, J., Pathological Physiology
MACHÁČEK, J., Radiology
MALÍNSKÝ, J., Histology and Embryology
MIHÁL, V., Paediatrics
NEKULA, J., Radiology
PAZDERA, J., Stomatology
PEŠÁK, J., Medical Biophysics
PETŘEK, J., Physiology
ŠANTAVÝ, J., Medical Genetics
ŠČUDLA, V., Internal Diseases
ŠIMÁNEK, V., Medical Chemistry
STAŘEK, I., Otorhinolaryngology
ULRICHKOVÁ, J., Medical Chemistry and Biochemistry
URBÁNEK, K., Neurology
VAVERKOVÁ, H., Internal Diseases

VESELÝ, J., Pathological Physiology

Faculty of Philosophy (Křížkovského 10, 771 80 Olomouc; tel. 585633036; fax 585229162; e-mail ivo.bartecek@upol.cz):

ANDERS, J., Slavonic Studies
BARTEČEK, I., History
BARTONĚK, A., Classical Philology
BLECHA, I., Philosophy
ČERNÝ, J., General Linguistics
DANIEL, L., History of Visual Art
FIALA, J., History of Czech Literature
FIALOVÁ, I., History of German Literature
FLÍDROVÁ, H., Russian Language
FLOSS, P., History of Philosophy
HLOBIL, I., Theory and History of Visual Art
HRABOVÁ, L., General History
JAŘAB, J., American Studies and American Literature
KOMÁREK, M., Slavonic Studies and Czech Language
KOŘENSKÝ, J., Slavonic Studies and Czech Language
KRATOCHVÍL, S., Clinical Psychology
LOTKO, E., Czech Language
MACHÁČEK, J., English Studies and English Language
MAREK, P., Czech History
PEPRNÍK, J., English Language
POLEDŇÁK, I., Theory and History of Music
ŠMAUSOVÁ, G., Sociology
SOBOTKOVÁ, M., History of Czech Literature
ŠPÁČILOVÁ, L., German Language
ŠRÁMEK, J., French Literature
ŠTĚPÁN, J., Philosophy
ŠTĚPÁNEK, P., History of Visual Arts
ŠVARNY, O., General Linguistics
SVOBODA, M., Psychology
TÁRNYIKOVÁ, J., English Studies and English Language
TOGNER, M., History of Fine Art
TRAPL, M., Czech and Slovak History
VÁCLAVEK, L., History of German Literature
VIČAR, J., Theory and History of Music
ZAHRÁDKA, M., Russian Literature

Faculty of Physical Culture (Tř. Míru 115, 771 11 Olomouc; tel. 585636009; fax 585412899; e-mail dusan.tomajko@upol.cz):

FRÖMEL, K., Kinanthropology
HODAŇ, B., Theory of Physical Culture
MĚKOTA, K., Anthropomotory
OPAVSKÝ, J., Neurology
OŠŤÁDAL, O., Internal Diseases
RIEGEROVÁ, J., Kinanthropology
VÁLKOVÁ, H., Kinanthropology
VAVERKA, F., Kinanthropology
VYKOPALOVÁ, H., Security Services

Faculty of Science (Tř. Svobody 26, 771 46 Olomouc; tel. 585634060; fax 585225737; e-mail juraj.sevcik@upol.cz):

ANDRES, J., Mathematical Analysis
BAJER, J., Optics and Optoelectronics
BIČÍK, V., Zoology
BĚLOHLÁVEL, Z., Information Science
BOUCHAL, Z., Optics and Optoelectronics
BUREŠ, S., Zoology
CHAJDA, I., Algebra and Geometry
DUŠEK, M., Quantum Optics
DVOŘÁK, L., Biophysics
FRÉBORT, I., Biochemistry
HOBZA, P., Physical Chemistry
HRADIL, Z., Optics and Optoelectronics
KAMENÍČEK, J., Inorganic Chemistry
KRUPKA, D., Mathematics
KRUPKOVA, O., General Physics and Mathematical Physics
KUBÁČEK, L., Mathematical Statistics
LASOVSKÝ, J., Physical Chemistry
LEBEDA, A., Botany
LEMR, K., Analytical Chemistry
MAJERNÍKOVÁ, E., Physics of Condensed Matter and Acoustics

MAŠLÁŇ, M., Applied Physics
MIKEŠ, J., Geometry and Topology
NAUŠ, J., Biophysics
NEZVALOVA, D., Pedagogy
OPATRNÝ, T., General and Mathematical Physics
PASTOREK, R., Inorganic Chemistry
PEŘINA, J., Optoelectronics
PEŘINOVÁ, V., General Physics and Mathematical Physics
POSPÍŠIL, J., Experimental Physics
RACHŮNEK, J., Algebra
RACHŮNKOVÁ, I., Mathematical Analysis
RYCHNOVSKÁ, M., Ecology
ŠARAPATKA, B., Landscape Engineering
ŠEVČÍK, J., Analytical Chemistry
SLOUKA, J., Organic Chemistry
STANĚK, S., Mathematical Analysis
ŠTĚRBA, O., Ecology
STRNAD, M., Plant Physiology
TKADLEC, E., Ecology
TRÁVNÍČEK, Z., Inorganic Chemistry
ZAPLETAL, J., Geology

Sts Cyril and Methodius Faculty of Theology (Univerzitní 22, 771 11 Olomouc; tel. 585637111; fax 585224174; e-mail petr .chalupa@upol.cz):

AMBROS, P., Theology
GÓRECKI, E., Religious Law
HALAS, F. X., History
KARFÍKOVÁ, L., Evangelical Theory
MUSIL, J., Clinical Psychology
POJSL, M., History of Christian Art
POSPÍŠIL, C. V., Systematic Theology
TICHÝ, L., Theology

UNIVERZITA PARDUBICE
(University of Pardubice)

Studentská 95, 532 10 Pardubice
Telephone: 466036111
Fax: 466036361
E-mail: promotion@upce.cz
Internet: www.upce.cz
Founded 1950 as Vysoká Škola Chemicko-Technologická v Pardubicích; present name and status 1994
State control
Languages of instruction: Czech, English
Academic year: September to August
Rector: Prof. Ing. MIROSLAV LUDWIG
Vice-Rectors: Doc. Ing. JIŘÍ CAKL, Doc. Ing. JAROSLAV JANDA, Doc. Ing. JIŘÍ MÁLEK
Bursar: Ing. MILAN BUKAČ
Librarian: IVA PROCHÁSKOVÁ
Library of 180,000 vols
Number of teachers: 381
Number of students: 4,794
Publications: *Scientific Papers* (1 a year), *Zpravodaj Univerzity Pardubice* (4 a year)

DEANS

Faculty of Chemical Technology: Doc. Ing. PETR MIKULÁŠEK
Faculty of Economics and Administration: Doc. Ing. JAN ČAPEK
Faculty of Humanities: Prof. MILENA LENDEROVÁ
Jan Perner Faculty of Transport: Prof. Dr Ing. KAREL ŠOTEK

ATTACHED RESEARCH INSTITUTES

Institute of Health Studies: Průmyslová 395, 530 03 Pardubice; Dir Prof. Dr. ARNOŠT PELLANT.

Institute of Informatics: Studenská 95, 532 10 Pardubice; Dir Doc. Ing. SIMEON KARAMAZOV.

SLEZSKÁ UNIVERZITA V OPAVÉ
(Silesian University of Opava)

Na Rybníčku 626/1, 746 01 Opava
Telephone: 553684621

Fax: 553718019
E-mail: rektorat@slu.cz
Internet: www.slu.cz
Founded 1991
State control
Rector: Doc. Dr RUDOLF ŽÁČEK
Quaestor: Ing. JAROSLAV KANIA
Library of 77,000 vols, 256 periodicals
Number of teachers: 550
Number of students: 4,000

DEANS

Faculty of Business Administration: Dr BOHUMIL FIALA
Faculty of Philosophy and Science: Prof. Dr ZDENĚK JIRÁSEK

TECHNICKÁ UNIVERZITA V LIBERCI
(Technical University of Liberec)

Hálkova 6, 461 17 Liberec
Telephone: 485351111
Fax: 485105882
E-mail: rektor@vslib.cz
Internet: www.vslib.cz
Founded 1953
State control
Languages of instruction: Czech, English
Academic year: September to June
Rector: Prof. VOJTĚCH KONOPA
Pro-Rectors: Prof. OLDŘICH JIRSÁK, Assoc. Prof. JIŘÍ KRAFT, Assoc. Prof. ZDENĚK KÜS
Registrar: VLADIMÍR STACH
Librarian: ADAM KRETSCHMER
Library of 162,000
Number of teachers: 489
Number of students: 7,600
Publications: *Economics and Management* (7 a year), *Sborník vědeckých prací Technické univerzity* (Annals of Scientific Research)

DEANS

Faculty of Architecture: Prof. BOŘEK ŠIPEK
Faculty of Economics and Business Administration: Assoc. Prof. OLGA HASPROVA
Faculty of Education: Prof. MILOŠ RABAN
Faculty of Mechanical Engineering: Assoc. Prof. PETR LOUDA
Faculty of Mechatronics: Assoc. Prof. JIŘÍ MARYŠKA
Faculty of Textile Engineering: Prof. JIŘÍ MILITKÝ

PROFESSORS

BAKULE, V., Finance and Credit
BENEŠ, S., Construction of Machines and Appliances
BEROUN, S., Transport Machines
CYHELSKÝ, L., Statistics
DUCHOŇ, B., Management Technology in Transport
EHLEMAN, J., Information Management
EXNER, J., Mechanical Engineering Technology
FOUSEK, J., Electromechanical Properties of Dielectrics
HAJNIŠ, K., Physical Education
HANUŠ, B., Control Engineering
HES, L., Textile Valuation
HINDLS, R., Insurance, Statistics
HONCŮ, J., Machine Design
HÝČA, M., Applied Mechanics
IBRAHIM, S., Textile Technology
JANOVEC, V., Electromechanical Properties of Dielectrics
JIRSÁK, O., Textile Technology
KAŇOKOVÁ, J., Statistics
KARGER, A., Mathematics, Economics, Topology
KONOPA, V., Technical Cybernetics
KOPKA, J., Teaching of Mathematics
KOŠEK, M., Technical Cybernetics
KOVÁŘ, R., Textile Technology
KOVÁŘ, Z., Combustion Engines

KRAFT, J., Enterprise Economics, Management
KRATOCHVÍL, P., Materials Engineering
KRYŠTŮFEK, J., Textile Technology
KVAČEK, R., Czech History
LANDOROVÁ, A., Financing
LUKÁŠ, D., Textile Technology
MILITKÝ, J., Textile Technology
NECKÁŘ, B., Structure of Textiles
NOSEK, J., Physics
NOSEK, S., Textile Machines
NOUZA, J., Technical Cybernetics
NOVÁ, I., Engineering Metallurgy
NOVÁK, O., Technical Cybernetics
OLEHLA, J., Machines and Devices Construction
OLEHLA, M., Production Systems and Processes
PŘIVRATSKÁ, J., Physics
SKALLA, J., Servodrivers and Automation
SODOMKA, L., Applied Physics
STIBOR, I., Organic Chemistry
STRAKOŠ, Z., Technical Cybernetics
STŘÍŽ, B., Elasticity and Strength
SUCHOMEL, J., Architecture and Design
ŠKALOUD, M., Mechanics
ŠKLÍBA, J., Applied Mechanics
ŠPATENKA, P., Mechanical Engineering Technology
ULIČNÝ, O., Czech Language
URSÍNY, P., Textile Technology
VÁGNEROVÁ, M., Psychology
VAVERKA, J., Building Engineering
VĚCHET, V., Technical Cybernetics
VOKURKA, K., Applied Physics
VOSTATEK, J., Finance
ZELINKA, B., Mathematical Informatics and Theoretical Cybernetics

UNIVERZITA TOMÁŠE BATI VE ZLÍNĚ
(Tomas Bata University in Zlín)

Mostní 5139, 760 01 Zlín
Telephone: 576031111
Fax: 576032121
E-mail: kancler@utb.cz
Internet: www.utb.cz
Founded 2000
State control
Academic year: September to June
Rector: Prof. IGNAC HOZA
Vice-Rector for Int. Relations: Doc. ALEŠ GREGAR
Vice-Rector for Pedagogical Activities: Prof. ROMAN PROKOPA
Vice-Rector for Research and Devt: Doc. VOJTĚCH KŘESÁLEK
Vice-Rector for Social and Economic Devt: Doc. LUBOMÍR ODEHNAL
Vice-Rector for Strategic Devt: Prof. PETR SÁHA
Number of teachers: 430
Number of students: 12,000

DEANS

Faculty of Applied Informatics: Prof. VLADIMÍR VAŠEK
Faculty of Humanities: Prof. VLASTIMIL ŠVEC
Faculty of Management and Economics: Doc. DRAHOMÍRA PAVELKOVÁ
Faculty of Multimedia Communications: Doc. JANA JANÍKOVÁ
Faculty of Technology: Doc. PETR HLAVÁČEK

ATTACHED RESEARCH INSTITUTE

University Institute: e-mail ondrackova@uni.utb.cz; internet www.uni.utb.cz; Dir Ing. JINDŘIŠKA ONDRÁČKOVÁ.

VETERINÁRNÍ A FARMACEUTICKÁ UNIVERZITA BRNO
(University of Veterinary and Pharmaceutical Sciences Brno)

Palackého 1–3, 612 42 Brno
Telephone: 541562000

Fax: 549250478
E-mail: rektor@vfu.cz
Internet: www.vfu.cz
Founded 1918
State control
Languages of instruction: Czech, English
Academic year: September to August
Rector: Prof. Dr VLADIMIR VEČEREK
Pro-Rector for Education and Vice-Rector: Prof. Dr IVA STEINHAUSEROVÁ
Pro-Rector for Scientific Research and Foreign Relations: Doc. MILOSLAVA LOPATAŘOVÁ
Pro-Rector for Univ. Devt: Prof. Dr Ing. PAVEL SUCHÝ
Registrar: Mgr DANIELA NĚMCOVÁ
Librarian: Mgr JANA SLÁMOVÁ
Library: see Libraries and Archives
Number of teachers: 301
Number of students: 2,951
Publication: *Acta Veterinaria Brno* (4 a year)

DEANS

Faculty of Pharmacy: Doc. Dr MILAN ŽEMLIČKA
Faculty of Veterinary Hygiene and Ecology: Doc. Dr LADISLAV ŠTEINHAUSER
Faculty of Veterinary Medicine: Doc. Dr ALOIS NEČAS

PROFESSORS

Faculty of Pharmacy (tel. 541562801; fax 541219751; e-mail dekanfaf@vfu.cz; internet faf.vfu.cz):

CSÖLLEI, J., Pharmaceutical Chemistry
KVĚTINA, J., Pharmacology and Toxicology
SUCHÝ, J., Pharmacognosy
VÍTOVEC, J., Pharmacology and Toxicology

Faculty of Veterinary Hygiene and Ecology (tel. 541562795; fax 549243020; e-mail fvhe@vfu.cz; internet ww.vfu.cz):

BARANYIOVÁ, E., Behaviour Problems in Animals, Methodology of Scientific Work
BEKLOVÁ, M., Ecology
DVORÁK, P., Physics, Veterinary Biophysics, Radiobiology of Food
LITERÁK, I., Biology and Genetics
PAVLÍK, I., Tuberculosis, Paratuberculosis and Mycobacterioses
PIKULA, J., Ecology, Game Animal Diseases
STRAKOVÁ, E., Farm Animal Nutrition
SUCHÝ, P., Animal Nutrition and Dietetics
SUCMAN, E., Veterinary Chemistry and Biochemistry
SVOBODOVÁ, Z., Veterinary Toxicology and Ecotoxicology
VÁVROVÁ, M., Chemistry and Technology of Environment Protection
VEČEREK, V. A., Veterinary Public Health
VORLOVÁ, L., Food Chemistry, Hygiene and Technology

Faculty of Veterinary Medicine (tel. 541562440; fax 549248841; e-mail dekanfvl@vfu.cz; internet www.vfu.cz):

ČELER, V., Veterinary Microbiology
ČÍŽEK, A., Veterinary Microbiology
DVOŘÁK, R., Diseases of Farm Animals
HALOUZKA, R., Veterinary Morphology
HANÁK, J., Equine Diseases
HERA, A., Veterinary Pharmacology
HOŘÍN, P., Animal Genetics
KNOTEK, Z., Diseases of Small Animals
KOUDELA, B., Veterinary Parasitology
KOVÁŘŮ, F., Physiology
MÍŠEK, I., Veterinary Morphology
NEČAS, A., Veterinary Surgery and Orthopaedics
POSPÍŠIL, Z., Epizootiology
SMOLA, J., Microbiology
SVOBODA, M., Diseases of Small Animals
SVOBODOVÁ, V., Veterinary Parasitology
TICHÝ, F., Histology and Embryology
TOMAN, M., Veterinary Immunology

TREML, F., Epizootiology

VYSOKÁ ŠKOLA BÁŇSKÁ – TECHNICKÁ UNIVERZITA OSTRAVA
(Technical University of Ostrava)

17 Listopadu 15, 708 33 Ostrava-Poruba
Telephone: 596991111
Fax: 596918507
E-mail: vaclav.roubicek@vsb.cz
Internet: www.vsb.cz
Founded 1716
State control
Academic year: September to August
Rector: Prof. Ing. VÁCLAV ROUBÍČEK
Vice-Rector for Devt: Prof. Ing. PETR WYSLYCH
Vice-Rector for Education: Prof. Ing. JAROMÍR POLÁK
Vice-Rector for Finance and Organization: Prof. Ing. MIROSLAV NEJEZCHLEBA
Vice-Rector for Research and Devt and Int. Affairs: Prof. Ing. TOMÁŠ ČERMÁK
Registrar: Ing. STANISLAV DZIOB
Librarian: Mgr DANIELA TKAČÍKOVÁ
Number of teachers: 812
Number of students: 14,579
Publications: *Akademik* (6 a year), *Sborník vědeckých prací VSB-TU Ostrava* (irregular)

DEANS

Faculty of Civil Engineering: Prof. Ing. JINDŘICH CIGÁNEK
Faculty of Economics: Prof. Ing. JIŘÍ KERN
Faculty of Electrical Engineering and Informatics: Doc. Ing. KAREL CHMELÍK
Faculty of Mechanical Engineering: Prof. Ing. PETR HORYL
Faculty of Metallurgy and Material Engineering: Prof. Ing. LUDOVIT DOBROVSKÝ
Faculty of Mining and Geology: Prof. Ing. JAROSLAV DVOŘÁČEK

PROFESSORS

Faculty of Civil Engineering (tel. 596991316; fax 596991356; e-mail dekan.fast@vsb.cz):

ALDORF, J., Mine Construction and Geotechnics
CIGANEK, J., Mine Construction and Geotechnics

Faculty of Economics (1, Sokolská tř. 33, 701 21 Ostrava; fax 596110026):

HALÁSEK, D., Macroeconomics
JUREČKA, V., General Economics
KALUŽA, J., Informatics in Economics
KERN, J., Macroeconomics
NEJEZCHLEBA, M., Finance
POLÁCH, J., Finance
SMOLÍK, D., Environmental Protection and Reclamation
ŠNAPKA, P., Mining Economics and Management

Faculty of Electrical Engineering and Informatics (tel. 596995252; fax 596919597):

BLAHETA, R., Applied Mathematics
BLUNÁR, K., Communications Technology
BRANDŠTETTER, P., Electrical Machines, Apparatus and Drives
ČERMÁK, T., Electrical Drives
DIVIŠ, Z., Transport and Infrastructure
DOSTÁL, Z., Applied Mathematics
HASLINGER, J., Applied Mathematics
HRADÍLEK, Z., Electrical Power Engineering
LITSCHMANN, J., Engineering Cybernetics
NEVŘIVA, P., Technical Cybernetics
PALEČEK, J., Electrical Power Engineering
POKORNÝ, M., Measurement and Control Technology
RUSEK, S., Electrical Power Engineering
SANTARIUS, Electrical Power Engineering

SOKANSKÝ, K., Electrical Power Engineering
VONDRÁK, I., Computer Science

Faculty of Mechanical Engineering (tel. 597321216; fax 596916490):
ANTONICKÝ, S., Transportation and Technology
BAILOTTI, K., Transportation and Preparation Equipment
DANĚK, A., Transportation and Technology
DANĚK, J., Transportation and Technology
DEJL, Z., Machine Parts and Mechanisms
FUXA, J., Applied Mechanics
GONDEK, H., Mining Machinery
JANALÍK, J., Hydraulic Machines and Mechanisms
KOLAT, P., Thermal and Nuclear Power Engineering
KOUKAL, J., Engineering Technology
LENERT, J., Mechanics
MAKURA, P., Applied Mechanics
NOSKIEVIČ, P., Power Engineering
ONDROUCH, J., Technical Mechanics
PETRUŽELKA, M., Mechanical Technology
POLÁK, J., Transportation and Manipulation Technology
TŮMA, J., Automation of Machines and Technological Processes
VÍTEČEK, A., Automation of Machines and Technological Processes

Faculty of Metallurgy and Material Engineering (tel. 596995374; fax 596918592; e-mail jiri.kliber@vsb.cz):
ADOLF, Z., Steel-making
BAŽAN, J., Steel-making
DOBROVSKÝ, L., Chemical Metallurgy
FILIP, P., Materials Engineering
HAŠEK, P., Thermal Engineering in Industry
HYSPECKÁ, L., Physical Metallurgy
JELÍNEK, P., Casting
JONŠTA, Z., Physical Metallurgy
KALOČ, M., Technology of Fuels
KLIBER, J., Materials Forming
KLIKA, Z., Geochemistry, Mineralogy and Technology
KRAUSOVÁ, E., Economics and Management of Metallurgy
KURSA, M., Metallurgical Technology
LEŠKO, J., Chemical Metallurgy
MICHALEK, K., Metallurgical Technology
NENADÁL, J., Quality Management
OBROUČKA, K., Thermal Engineering
PETŘÍKOVÁ, R., Quality and Safety of Technical Systems
PŘÍHODA, M., Thermal Engineering
ROUBÍČEK, V., Technology of Fuels
SCHINDLER, J., Metallurgical Technology
SOMMER, B., Metal Forming
STRNADEL, B., Materials Engineering
TOŠENOVSKÝ, J., Industrial Process
TVRDÝ, M., Materials Engineering
VROŽINA, M., Automation of Metallurgical Processes
WICHTERLE, K., Chemical Engineering

Faculty of Mining and Geology (tel. 596995456; fax 596918589):
DIRNER, V., Environmental Protection and Reclamation
DVOŘÁČEK, J., Economics of Mining
FIGALA, J., General Ecology, Chronobiology
GRYGÁREK, J., Underground Mining
KRYL, V., Mining
LÁNÍČEK, J., Mathematics
LEMBÁK, M., Geotechnics and Underground Civil Engineering
MÁDR, V., Physics
NOVÁČEK, J., Mineral Processing and Ecotechnology
PALAS, M., Economic Geology
PETROŠ, V., Underground Mining
PIŠTORA, J., Applied Physics
PROKOP, P., Mine Ventilation
SCHEJBAL, C., Economic Geology

SCHENK, J., Geodesy and Mine Surveying
SIVEK, M., Economic Geology
STRAKOŠ, V., Automation in Mining
VAŠÍČEK, Z., Geology
VIDLÁŘ, J., Mineral Processing
WYSLYCH, P., Applied Physics
ZAMARSKÝ, V., Geology and Mineralogy

VYSOKÁ ŠKOLA CHEMICKO-TECHNOLOGICKÁ V PRAZE
(Institute of Chemical Technology, Prague)

Technická 5, 166 28 Prague 6
Telephone: 220444144
Fax: 220445018
E-mail: rektorat@vscht.cz
Internet: www.ict-prague.eu
Founded 1807
State control
Language of instruction: Czech
Academic year: September to June

Rector: Assoc. Prof. JOSEF KOUBEK
Vice-Rector for Devt and Building: Assoc. Prof. JAN STANĚK
Vice-Rector for Education: Prof. PAVEL HASAL
Vice-Rector for Research and Devt: Prof. MILAN POSPÍŠIL
Registrar: Ing. IVANA CHVÁLNÁ
Librarian: Dr ANNA SOUČKOVÁ

Library of 225,000 vols
Number of teachers: 470
Number of students: 3,500

DEANS

Faculty of Chemical Engineering: Assoc. Prof. DANIEL TURZÍK
Faculty of Chemical Technology: Assoc. Prof. ALEŠ HELEBRANT
Faculty of Environmental Engineering: Prof. GUSTAV ŠEBOR
Faculty of Food and Biochemical Technology: Assoc. Prof. KAREL MELZOCH

PROFESSORS

BASAŘOVÁ, G., Fermentation Chemistry and Biotechnology
BENDA, V., Biochemistry and Microbiology
BENEŠ, P., Social Sciences
BUBNÍK, Z., Cereal Chemistry and Technology
BURYAN, P., Gas, Coke and Air Protection
ČERVENÝ, L., Organic Technology
ČURDA, D., Food Preservation
DAVÍDEK, J., Food Chemistry and Technology
DEMNEROVÁ, K., Biochemistry and Microbiology
DEYL, Z., Analytical Chemistry
DOHÁNYOS, M., Water Technology and Environmental Engineering
DUCHÁČEK, V., Polymers
ECKERT, E., Chemical Engineering
GROS, J., Economics and Management of the Chemical Industry
HAJŠLOVÁ, J., Food Chemistry and Analysis
HANIKA, J., Organic Technology
HLAVÁČ, J., Silicate Technology
HORÁK, J., Organic Technology
HUDEC, L., Technology of Materials for Electronics
JANDA, V., Water Technology and Environmental Engineering
JIRKŮ, V., Fermentation Chemistry and Biotechnology
JURSÍK, F., Inorganic Chemistry
KADLEC, P., Sugar Technology
KÁŠ, J., Biochemistry
KLÍČ, A., Mathematics
KODÍČEK, M., Biochemistry and Microbiology
KRÁLOVÁ, B., Biochemistry and Microbiology
KRATOCHVÍL, B., Solid-state Chemistry
KUBÍČEK, M., Mathematics
KURAŠ, M., Environmental Engineering
LABÍK, S., Physical Chemistry
LIŠKA, F., Organic Chemistry

MALIJEVSKÝ, A., Physical Chemistry
MAREK, M., Chemical Engineering
MATĚJKA, Z., Power Engine
MATOUŠEK, J., Silicate Technology
NĚMEC, L., Inorganic Materials Laboratory
NOVÁK, J., Physical Chemistry
NOVÁK, P., Chemical Metallurgy and Corrosion Engineering
PÁCA, J., Fermentation Chemistry and Biotechnology
PALEČEK, J., Organic Chemistry
PALETA, O., Organic Chemistry
PAŠEK, J., Organic Technology
PECKA, K., Petroleum Technology and Petrochemistry
PITTER, P., Water Technology and Environmental Engineering
POKORNÝ, J., Food Chemistry and Technology
PORUBSKÝ, Š., Mathematics
PROCHÁZKA, A., Computing and Control Engineering
RAUCH, P., Biochemistry
RODA, J., Polymers
RUML, T., Biochemistry and Microbiology
RŮŽIČKA, V., Physical Chemistry
RYCHTERA, M., Fermentation Chemistry and Biotechnology
SCHMIDT, O., Automated Control Systems
ŠEBOR, G., Petroleum Technology and Petrochemistry
SLÁDEČKOVÁ, A., Water Technology and Environmental Engineering
STIBOR, I., Organic Chemistry
SUCHANEK, M., Analytical Chemistry
ŠVOBODA, J., Organic Chemistry
ŠVORČÍK, V., Materials Science
VELÍŠEK, J., Food Chemistry and Technology
VOLKA, K., Analytical Chemistry
WANNER, J., Water Technology and Environmental Engineering
ZÁBRANSKÁ, J., Water Technology and Environmental Engineering

VYSOKÁ ŠKOLA EKONOMICKÁ V PRAZE
(University of Economics, Prague)

Nám. W. Churchilla 4, 130 67 Prague 3
Telephone: 224095799
Fax: 224095695
E-mail: brazdova@vse.cz
Internet: www.vse.cz
Founded 1919
State control
Languages of instruction: Czech, English
Academic year: September to May

Rector: Prof. JAROSLAVA DURČÁKOVÁ
Vice-Rectors: Prof. IGOR ČERMÁK, Prof. BRONISLAVA HOŘEJŠÍ, Prof. VOJTĚCH KREBS, Prof. JIŘÍ PATOČKA, Prof. ZBYNĚK REVENDA
Bursar: JIŘÍ KŘÍŽ
Number of students: 14,000
Publications: Acta Economica Pragensia (2 a year), Politická Ekonomie (6 a year), Prague Economic Papers (4 a year)

DEANS

Business Administration: Prof. JIŘÍ KLEIBL
Economics and Public Administration: Prof. JIŘÍ SCHWARZ
Finance and Accounting: Prof. BOJKA HAMERNÍKOVÁ
Informatics and Statistics: Prof. RICHARD HINDLS
International Relations: Prof. DANA ZADRAŽILOVÁ
Management: Prof. PAVEL PUDIL

VYSOKÉ UČENÍ TECHNICKÉ V BRNĚ
(Brno University of Technology)

Antonínská 1, 601 90 Brno
Telephone: 541145111
Fax: 541211309
E-mail: rektor@ro.vutbr.cz

Internet: www.vutbr.cz
Founded 1899
State control
Language of instruction: Czech
Academic year: September to July

Rector: Prof. Dr Ing. JAN VRBKA
Pro-Rectors: Asst Prof. PETR DUB, Prof. Dr JOSEF JANČÁŘ, Prof. Ing. JIŘÍ KAZELLE, Asst Prof. LADISLAV ŠTĚPÁNEK
Registrar: JAROMÍR PĚNČÍK
Dir of Public Relations and Admin.: Mgr JITKA VANÝSKOVÁ
Librarian: NATAŠA JURSOVÁ

Number of teachers: 1,026
Number of students: 15,090

Publication: *Události na VUT v Brně* (12 a year)

DEANS

Faculty of Architecture: Asst Prof. Ing. JOSEF CHYBÍK
Faculty of Business and Management: Asst Prof. Ing. KAREL RAIS
Faculty of Chemistry: Prof. Ing. MILAN DRDÁK
Faculty of Civil Engineering: Asst Prof. Ing. JAROSLAV PUCHRÍK
Faculty of Electrical Engineering and Communication: Prof. Ing. RADIMÍR VRBA
Faculty of Fine Arts: Prof. Dr JAN SEDLÁK
Faculty of Information Technology: Prof. Ing. TOMÁŠ HRUŠKA
Faculty of Mechanical Engineering: Prof. Ing. JOSEF VAČKÁŘ

PROFESSORS

Faculty of Architecture (Poříčí 5, 639 00 Brno; tel. 541146600; fax 542142125; e-mail chybik@ucit.fa.vutbr.cz; internet www.fa.vutbr.cz):

DVOŘÁK, J., Economy and Management
KONEČNÝ, M., Economy and Management
MEZNÍK, I., Mathematics
NĚMEČEK, P., Economy and Management

Faculty of Chemistry (Purkyňova 118, 612 00 Brno; tel. 541149111; fax 541211697; e-mail drdak@fch.vutbr.cz; internet www.fch.vutbr.cz):

BRANDŠTETR, J., Chemistry of Materials
DRDÁK, M., Food Science and Biotechnology
FRIEDL, Z., Chemistry and Technology of Environmental Protection
JANČA, J., Chemistry
JANČÁŘ, J., Chemistry of Materials
KUČERA, M., Chemistry of Materials
NEŠPŮREK, S., Chemistry
OMELKA, L., Chemistry
PELIKÁN, P., Chemistry
RYCHTERA, M., Food Science and Biotechnology
SCHAUER, F., Environmental Chemistry and Technology
SOMMER, L., Chemistry and Technology of Environmental Protection
WEIN, O., Chemistry

Faculty of Civil Engineering (Veveří 95, 662 37 Brno; tel. 541147111; fax 5745147; e-mail dekan@fce.vutbr.cz; internet www.fce.vutbr.cz):

ADÁMEK, J., Structural Materials and Testing Methods
DROCHYTKA, R., Technology of Building Materials and Components
FIXEL, J., Geodesy

KOČÍ, J., Building Construction
KOKTAVÝ, B., Physics
MELCHER, J., Metal and Timber Structures
MYSLÍN, J., Building Construction
NEVOSÁD, Z., Geodesy
ŠÁLEK, J., Water Resources Management
STRÁSKÝ, J., Concrete and Masonry Structures

Faculty of Electrical Engineering and Communication (Údolní 53, 602 00 Brno; tel. 541141111; fax 541146100; e-mail dekan@feec.vutbr.cz; internet www.feec.vutbr.cz):

AUTRATA, R., Electrical and Electronic Technology
BIOLEK, D., Telecommunications
BRZOBOHATÝ, J., Microelectronics
CHVALINA, J., Mathematics
DIBLÍK, J., Mathematics
DOSTÁL, T., Radioelectronics
HAVEL, V., Mathematics
HONZÍKOVÁ, N., Biomedical Engineering
HRUŠKA, K., Physics
JAN, J., Biomedical Engineering
KAZELLE, J., Electrical and Electronic Technology
MELKES, F., Mathematics
MUSIL, V., Microelectronics
PIVOŇKA, P., Automation
POSPÍŠIL, J., Radioelectronics
PROCHÁZKA, P., Electrical Engineering
ŘÍČNÝ, V., Radioelectronics
ŠEBESTA, V., Radioelectronics
ŠIKULA, J., Physics
SKALICKÝ, J., Power Electrical and Electronic Engineering
SMÉKAL, Z., Telecommunications
SVAČINA, J., Radioelectronics
TOMÁNEK, P., Physics
VALSA, J., Electrical Engineering
VAVŘÍN, P., Automation and Measurement Engineering
VOMELA, J., Biomedical Engineering
VRBA, K., Telecommunications
VRBA, R., Microelectronics

Faculty of Fine Arts (Rybářská 13, 603 00 Brno; tel. 543146850; fax 543212670; e-mail dekan@ffa.vutbr.cz; internet www.ffa.vutbr.cz):

NAČERADSKÝ, J., Painting
RONAI, P., Figure Painting
SEDLÁK, J., History of Art

Faculty of Information Technology (Božetěchova 2, 612 66 Brno; tel. 541141139; fax 541141270; e-mail info@fit.vutbr.cz; internet www.fit.vutbr.cz):

ČEŠKA, M., Intelligent Systems
DVOŘÁK, V., Computer Systems
HONZÍK, J., Information Systems
HRUŠKA, T., Information Systems
SERBA, I., Computer Graphics and Multimedia

Faculty of Mechanical Engineering (Technická 2, 616 00 Brno; tel. 541141111; fax 541142222; e-mail dekan@fme.vutbr.cz; internet www.fme.vutbr.cz):

BABINEC, F., Process Engineering
BOHÁČEK, F., Machine Design
BUMBÁLEK, B., Technology
CHMELA, P., Optics and Fine Mechanics
CIHLÁŘ, J., Ceramics
DRUCKMÜLLER, M., Stochastics, Teaching of Mathematics
FILAKOVSKÝ, K., Aircraft Design
FOREJT, M., Snagging Technology
HLAVENKA, B., Production Engineering
JANÍČEK, P., Mechanics of Solids
JÍCHA, M., Heat and Nuclear Power
KAČUR, J., Mathematics
KADRNOŽKA, J., Heat and Nuclear Power
KAVIČKA, F., Heat and Nuclear Power
KOCMAN, K., Production Engineering
KOHOUTEK, J., Process Engineering
KOMRSKÁ, J., Physics
KRATOCHVÍL, O., Mechanics of Solids

KULČÁK, L., Aerospace Engineering
LIŠKA, M., Physics
MATAL, O., Heat and Nuclear Power
MEDEK, J., Process Engineering
NOVÁK, V., Mathematics
PÍŠTĚK, A., Aerospace Engineering
PÍŠTĚK, V., Combustion Engines and Motor Vehicles
POCHYLÝ, F., Heat and Nuclear Power
POKLUDA, J., Physics
PTÁČEK, L., Materials Engineering
RUSÍN, K., Foundry Engineering
SCHNEIDER, P., Process Engineering
ŠEDLÁČEK, B., Aerospace Engineering
ŠLAPAL, J., Mathematics, Teaching of Mathematics
SLAVÍK, J., Mechanics of Solids
ŠTEHLÍK, P., Process Engineering
ŠTĚPÁNEK, M., Automation and Computer Science
ŠTRÁNSKÝ, K., Materials Engineering
ŠVEJCAR, J., Materials Engineering
VAČKÁŘ, J., Quality and Metrology
VLK, F., Combustion Engines and Motor Vehicles
VRBKA, J., Mechanics of Solids
ŽENÍŠEK, A., Mathematics

ZÁPADOČESKÁ UNIVERZITA
(University of West Bohemia)

Univerzitní 8, 306 14 Plzeň
Telephone: 377631111
Fax: 377631112
E-mail: rektor@rek.zcu.cz
Internet: www.zcu.cz

Founded 1949 as Plzeň Institute of Technology, present name 1991
State control
Language of instruction: Czech
Academic year: September to June

Rector: Doc. Ing. JOSEF PRŮSA
Vice-Rectors: Doc. Dr FRANTIŠEK JEŽEK, Dr EVA PASÁČKOVÁ, Dr Ing. JAN RYCHLÍK, Doc. Ing. JAN HOREJC
Chancellor: Dr HELENA HEJDOVÁ
Registrar: Ing. ANTONÍN BULÍN
Librarians: Dr MILOSLAVA FAITOVÁ, Mgr ALENA SCHOŘOVSKÁ

Library of 437,342 vols
Number of teachers: 1,218
Number of students: 18,898

Publications: *Stady* (univ. papers, 12 a year), *Trojúhelník* (univ. journal, 4 a year)

DEANS

Faculty of Applied Sciences: Prof. Ing. JIŘÍ KŘEN
Faculty of Economics: Doc. Dr MIROSLAV PLEVNÝ
Faculty of Education: Doc. Dr JANA COUFALOVÁ
Faculty of Electrical Engineering: Doc. Ing. JIŘÍ HAMMERBAUER
Faculty of Health Care Studies: Dr ILONA MAURITZOVÁ
Faculty of Law: Dr JIŘÍ POSPÍŠIL
Faculty of Mechanical Engineering: Doc. Ing. JIŘÍ STANĚK
Faculty of Philosophy and Arts: Doc. Dr PAVEL VAŘEKA

PROFESSORS

Faculty of Applied Sciences (Univerzitní 22, 306 14 Plzeň; tel. 377632000; fax 377632002; internet www.fav.zcu.cz):

DRÁBEK, P., Mathematics
KŘEN, J., Continuum Mechanics, Biomechanics
KUČERA, M., Mathematics
KUFNER, A., Mathematics
KUNEŠ, J., Applied Physics
LAŠ, V., Mechanics
MAREK, P., Mechanics

MATOUŠEK, V., Man–Machine Communication
MÍKA, S., Mathematics
MUSIL, J., Applied Physics
NOVÁK, P., Geodesy
PLÁNIČKA, F., Mechanics
PŘIKRYL, P., Mathematics
PSUTKA, J., Cybernetics
ROSENBERG, J., Mechanics
RYJÁČEK, Z., Mathematics
ŠAFAŘÍK, J., Informatics and Computing
SCHLEGEL, M., Cybernetics
ŠKALA, V., Computer Graphics
ŠESTÁK, J., Mechanics
ŠIMANDL, M., Cybernetics
ŠŤASTNÝ, M., Mechanics
VLČEK, J., Applied Physics
ZEMAN, V., Mechanics

Faculty of Economics (Husova 11, 306 14 Plzeň; tel. 377633000; fax 377633002; internet www.fek.zcu.cz):

KŘIKAČ, K., Organization and Management of Engineering Production
MACEK, J., Statistics in Economics
MACH, M., Business Economics
SEMENIUK, P., Marketing, Trade and Services

Faculty of Education (Sedláčkova 38, 306 14 Plzeň; tel. 377636000; fax 377636002; internet www.fpe.zcu.cz):

HÖPPNEROVÁ, V., German Language
JÍLEK, T., Teaching of History
KRAITR, M., Teaching of Chemistry
KUMPERA, J., Teaching of History
MEHNERT, E., Teaching of German Language
NOVÁK, J., Teaching of Chemistry
PILOUS, V., Materials Engineering
RYCHTECKÝ, A., Physical Training
SCHUPPENER, G., German Language
VIKTORA, V., Czech Language

Faculty of Electrical Engineering (Univerzitní 26, 306 14 Plzeň; tel. 377634000; fax 377634002; internet www.fel.zcu.cz):

BARTOŠ, V., Electrical Machines and Apparatus
BENEŠOVÁ, Z., Theory of Electrical Engineering
DOLEŽEL, I., Theory of Electrical Engineering
HALLER, R., Electric Power Engineering
JERHOT, J., Electronics and Vacuum Technology
KOŽENÝ, J., Electric Power Engineering
KŮS, V., Electrical Drives and Power Electronics
MAYER, D., Theory of Electrical Engineering
MENTLÍK, V., Electrical Technology
MÜHLBACHER, J., Electric Power Engineering
PINKER, J., Electronic Systems
ŠKORPIL, J., Eniginering Ecology
ŠTORK, M., Analog and Digital Circuitry
VONDRÁŠEK, F., Electrical Drives and Power Electronics
VOSTRACKÝ, Z., Electric Power Engineering

Faculty of Law (Sady Pětatřicátníků 14, 306 14 Plzeň; tel. 377637000; fax 377637002; internet www.fpr.zcu.cz):

ADAMOVÁ, S., History of the State and Law
BALÍK, S., History of the State and Law
ELIÁŠ, K., Commercial Law
GERLOCH, A., Theory of Law
HRDINA, A., History of Law
HRONCOVÁ, J., Social Pathology
KOPAL, V., International Law
KUČERA, Z., International Law
PAUKNEROVÁ, M., International Law
RŮŽIČKA, K., International Law
RYBÁŘ, M., Criminology
ŠÁMAL, P., Criminal Law
VÁLKOVÁ, H., Criminal Law
WOKOUN, R., Public Service

Faculty of Mechanical Engineering (Univerzitní 22, 306 14 Plzeň; tel. 377638000; fax 377638002; internet www.fst.zcu.cz):

BASL, J., Computer Integrated Production Systems
DVOŘÁKOVÁ, L., Financial and Management Accounting
FIALA, J., Physics of Solids
HOSNEDL, S., Machine Design
JANDEČKA, K., Technology of Metal Cutting
KOTT, J., Design of Power Machines and Equipment
LEEDER, E., Computer Integrated Production Systems
LINHART, J., Power System Engineering
MAREŠ, R., Thermomechanics
MAŠEK, B., Materials Science and Metallography
PFROGNER, F., Materials Science and Metallography
ZRNÍK, J., Materials Science and Metallography

Faculty of Philosophy and Arts (Sedláčkova 38, 306 14 Plzeň; tel. 377635000; fax 377635002; internet www.ff.zcu.cz):

BLAŽEK, V., Anthropology
BUDIL, I., Anthropology
DOUBRAVOVÁ, J., Philosophy
FUNDA, O., Philosophy
JEŘÁBEK, H., Sociology
NEÚSTUPNÝ, E., Archaeology
SKŘIVAN, A., History
VOPĚNKA, P., Philosophy

Institute of Art and Design:

BARTA, J., Animation
BERÁNEK, J., Sculpture
GAJDOŠ, J., Drama Theory and Criticism
JIRKŮ, B., Drawing and Art of Painting
MATASOVÁ-TEISINGEROVÁ, A., Intermediary Production
NOVÁK, ., Jewellery Craft
ŠERÁK, V., Ceramic Design
ZIEGLER, Z., Graphic Design

ATTACHED RESEARCH INSTITUTES

Institute of Art and Design: tel. 377636700; fax 377636702; e-mail mistera@uud.zcu.cz; internet www.uud.zcu.cz; Dir Doc., Akad. mal. JOSEF MIŠTERA.

New Technologies Research Centre: tel. 377634700; fax 377634702; e-mail rosen@ntc.zcu.cz; internet www.ntc.zcu.cz; Dir Prof. Ing. JOSEF ROSENBERG.

Schools of Art and Music

Akademie múzických umění v Praze (Prague Academy of Performing Arts): Malostranské nám. 12, 118 00 Prague 1; tel. 234344514; fax 234244515; e-mail info@amu.cz; internet www.amu.cz; f. 1945; languages of instruction: Czech, English; academic year October to June; Rector IVO MATHÉ; Vice-Rectors ZDENĚK KIRSCHNER, MIROSLAV KLÍMA; Registrar TAMARA ČUŘÍKOVÁ; library: 161,374 vols; 338 teachers; 1,178 students; publs *Acta Academica Informatorium* (10 a year), *Disk* (4 a year).

Akademie výtvarných umění v Praze (Prague Academy of Fine Arts): U Akademie 4, 170 22 Prague 7; tel. 220408200; fax 233381662; e-mail avu@avu.cz; internet www.avu.cz; f. 1799; languages of instruction: Czech, English; academic year October to July; Rector Prof. JIŘÍ SOPKO; Pro-Rectors Prof. EMIL PŘIKRYL, Doc. JIŘÍ LINDOVSKÝ; Registrar Ing. VLADIMÍR KALUGIN; library: 75,000 vols; 58 teachers; 265 students; publs *Almanach, Exhibition Catalogues*.

Janáčkova Akademie Múzických Umění v Brnì (Janáček Academy of Music and Performing Art in Brno): Beethovenova 2, 662 15 Brno; tel. 542591111; fax 542591140; e-mail rektor@jamu.cz; internet www.jamu.cz; f. 1947; languages of instruction: Czech, English; academic year September to June; Rector Prof. VÁCLAV CEJPEK; Vice-Rector Dr LEOŠ FALTUS; Vice-Rector Doc. Dr MIROSLAV PLEŠÁK; Registrar Dr LENKA VALOVÁ; library: 100,000 vols; special collns of printed music and records; 118 teachers; 580 students.

Janáčkova konzervatoř a Gymnázium v Ostravě: Českobratrská 40, 702 00 Ostrava-Moravská; tel. 596112007; fax 596111443; e-mail info@jko.cz; internet www.jko.cz; f. 1953; 145 teachers; 376 students; library: 23,000 vols, 7,000 records; Dir MILAN BÁCHOREK.

Konzervatoř, Brno (Conservatoire in Brno): třída Kpt. Jaroše 45, 662 54 Brno; tel. 545215568; e-mail reditel@konzervatorbrno.cz; internet www.konzervatorbrno.eu; f. 1919; music and drama departments; 124 teachers; 360 students; library: 7,000 vols, 29,900 scores, 1,600 records; Dir Mgr E. ZÁMEČNÍK.

Konzervatoř P. J. Vejvanovského, Kroměříž: Pilařova 7, 767 01 Kroměříž; tel. 573339501; fax 573343270; e-mail konzervator@konzkm.cz; internet www.konzkm.cz; f. 1949; 55 teachers; 190 students; library: 16,000 vols, 4,600 records; Dir M. ŠIŠKA.

Konzervatoř, Pardubice: Sukova třída 1260, 530 02 Pardubice; tel. 466513503; fax 466513503; e-mail reditelstvi@konzervatorpardubice.cz; internet www.konzervatorpardubice.cz; f. 1978; 79 teachers; 172 students; library: 2,200 books, 7,500 vols of music, 1,100 records; Dir Mgr JAROMÍR HÖNIG.

Konzervatoř, Plzeň: Kopeckého sady 10, 301 00 Plzeň; tel. 377226325; fax 377226387; e-mail sekretariat@konzervatorplzen.cz; internet www.konzervatorplzen.cz; f. 1961; 78 teachers; 158 students; library: 1,500 books, 1,400 records and CDs, 7,000 scores; Dir MIROSLAV BREJCHA.

Konzervatoř, Teplice: Hudba a Zpěv, Českobratrská 15, 415 01 Teplice; tel. 417538425; fax 417532645; e-mail studijni@konzervatorteplice.cz; internet www.konzervatorteplice.cz; f. 1971; 80 teachers; 200 students; library: 10,000 vols, 800 records; Dir Mgr MILAN KUBÍK.

Pražská konzervatoř: Na Rejdišti 1, 110 00 Prague 1; tel. 222319102; fax 222326406; e-mail conserv@prgcons.cz; internet www.prgcons.cz; f. 1808; 254 professors; 600 students; library: 85,000 vols, 19,000 records; Dir Mgr PAVEL TROJAN; Chief of Library (Archives) MILOSLAV RICHTER.

Taneční konzervatoř Praha (Prague Conservatory of Dance): Křižovnická 7, 110 00 Prague 1; tel. 222319145; fax 222324977; e-mail taneckonzpr@volny.cz; internet www.balet.cz/tkpraha; f. 1945; small library; languages of instruction: Czech, English; 60 teachers; 200 students; Dir Mgr JAROSLAV SLAVICKÝ; publ. *Taneční listy* (Dance Review).

Vysoká Škola Uměleckoprůmyslová (Academy of Art, Architecture and Design): nám. Jana Palacha 80, 116 93 Prague 2; tel. 251098111; fax 251098289; e-mail pr@vsup.cz; internet www.vsup.cz; f. 1885; 55 teachers; 400 students; Rector Dr JIŘÍ PELCL; Vice-Rector for International and Public Relations Dr MARTINA PACHMANOVÁ; Vice-Rector for Study Dr PAVLA PEČINKOVÁ; Registrar Ing. LUBOŠ KVAPIL.

DENMARK

The Higher Education System

Københavns Universitet (founded 1479) is the oldest university in Denmark. There are 12 universities and technical universities and many other university-level institutions, such as professional schools and polytechnics, which offer short- and medium-cycle programmes. These university-level institutions are to be merged into supra-institutions under legislation enacted in 1998 and 2001. Short-cycle vocational colleges are being reorganized as erhvervsakademier (vocational academies) and medium-cycle colleges are being merged into Centres for Higher Education. There is also a university in the Faroe Islands, as well as colleges there and in Greenland.

The higher education system is financed by the State; since 2001 the Ministry of Science, Technology and Innovation has been responsible for higher education. (However, the Ministry of Cultural Affairs oversees arts and cultural education programmes, and the Ministry of Education is responsible for short- and medium-cycle higher education.) The Act on the Universities (1992) extended the traditional academic freedom and autonomy enjoyed by the universities, but the Ministries still dictate regulations on inter alia admissions, curricula, quality assurance and appointments of academic staff. Quality assurance in the public universities is overseen by the Danish Evaluation Institute, which incorporated the former Centre for Quality Assurance and Evaluation of Higher Education. Private universities must submit to an accreditation process run by the Danish Educational Support Agency, a body of the Ministry of Education. The quality assurance system was supplemented by the establishment of a national accreditation system for higher education in the autumn of 2007 and an accreditation body called ACE Denmark (Akkrediteringsinstitutionen)

To attend university, students must possess one of the secondary school leaving certificates (or equivalent qualification), namely studentereksamen (Upper Secondary School Leaving Examination), højere forberedelseseksamen (Higher Preparatory Examination), højere handelseksamen eksamen (Higher Business Examination) or højere teknisk eksamen (Higher Technical Examination). The number of available places each year is stipulated by the Minister of Education. Since legislation of 1993, reform of the higher education system of qualifications has broadly brought Denmark into line with the Bologna Process, and the standard degree system consists of Bachelors, Masters (candidatus) and Doctorate. Since 2003 only European Bologna-style degrees have been offered. The Bachelors undergraduate degree takes three to three-and-a-half years, or longer for professional programmes such as engineering or medicine. The Masters degree (candidatus) requires two years of study following the Bachelors, and a Doctorate is awarded following at least eight years of higher education. In 2006 some 119,013 students were enrolled in universities, with many more in other centres of higher education.

There are 15 short-cycle, professionally orientated programmes (erhvervsakademiuddannelser) offered by the erhvervsakademier (vocational academies), which last two years, and 20 medium-cycle programmes offered by Centres for Higher Education, leading to the award of the title of professionsbachelor (Professional Bachelors). Adult and continuing education was reformed under Act No. 488 (2000), which created three levels of qualifications: Videregående voksenuddannelse (advanced adult education), Diplomuddannelse (Diploma programmes) and Masteruddannelse (Masters programmes). Programmes of study last two years (part-time).

Technical and vocational education consist of erhvervsuddannelser (training programmes), grundlæggende social- og sundhedsuddannelser (basic social and health education) and other programmes in different fields. These courses are offered by tekniske skoler (technical colleges), handelsskoler (business colleges), landbrugsskoler (agricultural colleges) and social- og sundhedsskoler (social and healthcare colleges). There are a total of 85 programmes of vocational education.

Regulatory and Representative Bodies

GOVERNMENT

Ministry of Cultural Affairs: Nybrogade 2, 1203 Copenhagen K; tel. 33-92-33-70; fax 33-91-33-88; e-mail kum@kum.dk; internet www.kum.dk; Minister CARINA CHRISTENSEN.

Ministry of Education: Frederiksholms Kanal 21, 1220 Copenhagen K; tel. 33-92-50-00; fax 33-92-55-67; e-mail uvm@uvm.dk; internet www.uvm.dk; Minister BERTEL HAARDER.

Ministry of Science, Technology and Innovation: Bredgade 43, 1260 Copenhagen K; tel. 33-92-97-00; fax 33-32-35-01; e-mail vtu@vtu.dk; internet www.vtu.dk; the Min. has the political responsibility for research, univs, information technology and telecommunications; cooperates with the int. research policy organizations of EC, OECD, Ccl of Europe, UNESCO and UN; provides comprehensive research and design statistics, planning and forecasts; Permanent Sec. UFFE TOUDAL PEDERSEN; Min. HELGE SANDER.

Attached Bodies:

Danmarks Forskningspolitiske Råd (The Danish Council for Research Policy): Bredgade 40, 1260 Copenhagen K; tel. 35-44-62-00; fax 35-44-62-01; e-mail dasti@dasti.dk; internet www.fi.dk/raad-og-udvalg/danmarks-forskningspolitiske-raad; f. 1996; 9 mems appointed by the Minister for Science, Technology and Innovation; advisory body to government in research policy matters, incl. framework conditions for research, funding for research, nat. and int. research infrastructures, devt of national research strategies; makes proposals on resources, structures, etc. required for the development and exploitation of Danish research; research training and recruitment of researchers; Chair. and Man. Dir Dr ASBJØRN BØRSTING; Head of Secretariat KARIN KJÆR MADSEN.

Det Frie Forskningsråd—Samfund og Erhverv (The Danish Council for Independent Research—Social Sciences): c/o The Danish Agency for Science, Technology and Innovation, Bredgade 40, 1260 Copenhagen K; tel. 35-44-62-00; fax 35-44-62-01; e-mail dasti@dasti.dk; f. 1968; 15 mems appointed by the Min. of Research and Information Technology; advisory body to public authorities and instns in the social sciences; initiates and supports nat. and int. research; awards grants and fellowships for scientific research; Chair. Prof. CHRISTIAN LUND.

Det Frie Forskningsråd—Sundhed og Sygdom (The Danish Research Council for Independent Research—Medical Sciences): c/o The Danish Agency for Science, Technology and Innovation, Bredgade 40, 1260 Copenhagen; tel. 35-44-62-00; fax 35-44-62-01; e-mail dasti@dasti.dk; internet www.dasti.dk; f. 1968; 20 mems appointed by the Min. for Science, Technology and Innovation; advisory body to public authorities and instns in medical sciences, incl. odontology and pharmacy; supports research, coordinates research, nat. and int.; awards grants and fellowships for scientific research; Chair. Prof. Dr LARS FUGGER.

Forsknings–og Innovationsstyrelsen (Danish Agency for Science, Technology and Innovation): Bredgade 40, 1260 Copenhagen; tel. 35-44-62-00; fax 35-44-62-01; e-mail fi@fi.dk; internet www.fi.dk; f. 1968; 15 mems appointed by the Min. of Science, Technology and Innovation; advisory body to public authorities and instns in the natural sciences; initiates, supports and coordinates research, nat. and int.; awards grants and fellowships for scientific research; Dir INGE MÆRKEDAHL.

Forskningsråd for Kultur og Kommunikation (Danish Research Council for Culture and Communication): c/o Centre for Independent Research and Research Training, Bredgade 40, 1260 Copenhagen; tel. 35-44-62-76; fax 35-44-62-01; e-mail lgr@fi.dk; internet www.fist.dk; f. 1968; 15 mems appointed by the Min. of Research and Information Technology; advisory body to public authorities and instns in the humanities; initiates and supports nat. and int. research; awards grants and fellowships for scientific research.

Forskningsråd for Teknologi og Produktion (Danish Research Council for Technology and Production): Copenhagen; f. 1973 to replace Danmarks teknisk-videnskabelige Forskningsråd and Statens Teknisk-Videnskabelige Forskningsråd; 15 mems appointed by the Min. of Education; advisory body to public authorities in the technical sciences; initiates and supports nat. and int. research; awards grants and fellowships for scientific research; Chair. Prof. Dr STEEN URECK.

ACCREDITATION

Danmarks Evalueringsinstitut (EVA) (Danish Evaluation Institute): Østbanegade 55, 3. sal, 2100 Copenhagen; tel. 35-55-01-01; fax 35-55-10-11; e-mail eva@eva.dk; internet www.eva.dk; f. 1999; initiates and conducts evaluations of teaching and learning, evaluations cover public educational establishments and private instns in receipt of state subsidy; acts as centre of knowledge for educational evaluation: compiles, produces and communicates nat. and int. experiences in the field of educational evaluation; may initiate evaluations on request, these evaluations are conducted as revenue-generating activities and may be requested by the govt, mins and advisory boards, local authorities and educational establishments; offers courses in methods of self-evaluation, gives presentations on quality issues, and acts as sparring partner should the need arise among e.g. educational instns and local authorities; conducts accreditation of several courses and instns incl. Univ. Colleges and private courses, determining whether students at private teaching establishments should receive the Danish state grant; organized in 3 educational units: nursery and pre-school, basic teaching and education, higher education; unit specialized in methodology focusing on internal and external quality assurance; unit specialized in communication and information work; admin. unit; Exec. Dir AGI CSONKA.

ENIC/NARIC Denmark: CIRIUS, Fiolstræde 44, 1171 Copenhagen K; tel. 33-95-70-00; fax 33-95-70-01; e-mail anerkendelse@ciriusmail.dk; internet www.ciriusonline.dk/recognition; Head of Division BENTE OLSEN.

FUNDING

Styrelsen for Statens Uddannelsesstøtte (Danish Educational Support Agency): Danasvej 30, 1780 Copenhagen V; tel. 33-26-86-00; fax 33-26-86-11; e-mail sustyrelsen@su.dk; internet www.sustyrelsen.dk; attached to Min. of Education; administers the Statens Uddannelsesstøtte (State Education Grant and Loan Scheme); prepares amendments of the scheme, registers applications, pays out grants and loans, offers guidance and information to the educational institutions, deals with complaints and appeals (which are decided by a Board of Appeal), draws up budgets and collects statistics for the use of the Min.; Dir HANNA DAM.

NATIONAL BODIES

CIRIUS: Fiolstræde 44, 1171 Copenhagen K; tel. 33-95-70-00; fax 33-95-70-01; e-mail cirius@ciriusmail.dk; internet www.ciriusonline.dk; attached to Min. of Science, Technology and Innovation; helps to extend and strengthen internationalization of education and training at all levels and to promote mobility; handles the nat. admin. of int. education programmes for school education, vocational education and training, higher education and adult learning as well as the youth sector; is responsible for the assessment and recognition of foreign degrees and qualifications; Dir-Gen. ANDERS GEERTSEN.

Danske Universiteter (Universities Denmark): Fiolstraede 44, 1. th, 1171 Copenhagen K; tel. 33-92-54-05; fax 33-92-50-75; e-mail dkuni@dkuni.dk; internet www.dkuni.dk; f. 1967; asscn of 8 Danish research univs; promotes interests of the univ. sector in dealings with the Min. of Science, Technology and Innovation; Sec.-Gen. SUSANNE BJERREGAARD.

Folkeuniversitetet (University Extension Services in Denmark): c/o Syddansk Universitet, Campusvej 55, 5230 Odense M; tel. 65-50-27-27; e-mail sekr@fu.dk; internet www.folkeuniversitet.dk; f. 1898 to promote education among the Danish population, in particular those unable to gain access to univs; Chair. EVA MØLLER; Man. Dir Dr SØREN EIGAARD.

Learned Societies

GENERAL

Kongelige Danske Videnskabernes Selskab (Royal Danish Academy of Science and Letters): H. C. Andersens Blvd 35, 1553 Copenhagen V; tel. 33-43-53-00; fax 33-43-53-01; e-mail kdvs@royalacademy.dk; internet www.royalacademy.dk; f. 1742; arranges meetings, public lectures, publishes journals; seminars, symposia, sections of History and Philosophy (Chair. CARL HENRIK KOCH), Mathematics and Natural Sciences (Chair. CHRISTIAN BERG); 494 mems (252 Danish, 242 foreign); Pres. Prof. Dr KIRSTEN HASTRUP; Gen. Sec. and Treasurer Prof. Dr SØREN-PETER FUCHS OLESEN; Head of Secretariat PIA GRÜNER; publs *Biologiske Skrifter* (botany, zoology, palaeontology, general biology, irregular), *Historisk-filosofiske Meddelelser* (history, philosophy, philology, archaeology, art history, irregular), *Historisk-filosofiske Skrifter* (history, philosophy, philology, archaeology, art history, irregular), *Matematisk-fysiske Meddelelser* (mathematics, physics, chemistry, astronomy, geology, irregular), *Oversigt/Yearbook* (1 a year).

AGRICULTURE, FISHERIES AND VETERINARY SCIENCE

Dansk Skovforening (Danish Forestry Society): Amalievej 20, 1875 Frederiksberg C; tel. 33-24-42-66; fax 33-24-02-42; e-mail info@skovforeningen.dk; internet www.skovforeningen.dk; f. 1888; attends to the commercial and professional interests of Danish forestry; Chair. NIELS IUEL REVENTLOW; Dir JAN SØNDERGAARD; publ. *Skoven* (12 a year).

Dansk Veterinærhistorisk Samfund (Danish Veterinary History Society): Ejgaardsparken 6, st. th., 2920 Charlottenlund; tel. 97-97-10-01; e-mail anton-rosenbom@post.tele.dk; f. 1934; 320 mems; annual European tour and seminar on the history of veterinary medicine; Pres. Dr ANTON ROSENBOM; publ. *Dansk Veterinærhistorisk Årbog* (every 2 years).

Foreningen af Mejeriledere og Funktionærer (Association of Dairy Managers): Det gamle Mejeri, Landbrugsvej 65, 5260 Odense S; tel. 66-12-40-25; fax 66-14-40-26; e-mail fmf@maelkeritidende.dk; internet www.maelkeritidende.dk; f. 1887; 823 mems; Technical Dir SØREN STEEN JENSEN; publ. *Maelkeritidende* (26 a year).

Jordbrugsakademikernes Forbund (JA) (Danish Federation of Graduates in Agriculture, Horticulture, Forestry and Landscape Architecture): Emdrupvej 28A, 2100 Copenhagen Ø; tel. 33-21-28-00; fax 38-71-03-22; e-mail post@ja.dk; internet www.ja.dk; f. 1976; 5,500 mems; Dir ANN-MARGARET DUUS JENSEN; publs *Jord og Viden*, *moMentum*.

Kongelige Danske Landhusholdningsselskab (Royal Danish Agricultural Society): c/o Landbrug and Fødevarer, Axelborg, Axeltorv 3, 1, 1609 København V; tel. 33-39-42-20; fax 33-39-41-50; e-mail 1769@1769.dk; internet www.1769.dk; f. 1769; Pres. FREDERIK LÜTTICHAU.

ARCHITECTURE AND TOWN PLANNING

Akademisk Arkitektforening (Architects' Association of Denmark): Arkitekternes Hus, Strandgade 27A, 1401 Copenhagen K; tel. 30-85-90-00; fax 32-83-69-01; e-mail aa@aa-dk.dk; internet www.arkitektforeningen.dk; f. 1951; 6,700 mems; Exec. Sec. ELSE MARIE MANDØE; publs *Arkitekten*, *Arkitektur*.

Dansk Byplanlaboratorium (Danish Town Planning Institute): Nørregade 36, 1 1165 Copenhagen K; tel. 33-13-72-81; fax 33-14-34-35; e-mail db@byplanlab.dk; internet www.byplanlab.dk; f. 1921; educational services and seminars; library of 17,000 vols; complete colln of public documents and reports concerning urban and regional planning in Denmark; Chair. FREDDY AVNBY; Sec. (vacant) ELLEN HØJGAARD JENSEN; publ. *Dansk Byplanlaboratorium*.

BIBLIOGRAPHY, LIBRARY SCIENCE AND MUSEOLOGY

Danmarks Biblioteksforening (Danish Library Association): Vesterbrogade 20/5, 1620 Copenhagen V; tel. 33-25-09-35; fax 33-25-79-00; e-mail dbf@dbf.dk; internet www.dbf.dk; f. 1905 to advance the devt of the public library system; Pres. FINN VESTER; Dir WINNIE VITZANSKY; publs *Biblioteksvejviser* (Directory, 1 a year), *Danmarks Biblioteker* (Newsletter, 10 a year).

Danmarks Forskningsbiblioteksforening (Danish Research Library Association): DF Secretariat, Statsbiblioteket, Tangen 2, 8200 Århus N; tel. 89-46-22-07; fax 89-46-22-20; e-mail df@statsbiblioteket.dk; f. 1978; 700 personal, 145 institutional mems; Pres. PER STEEN HANSEN; Office Man. HANNE DAHL; publ. *DF-REVY* (6 a year).

Dansk Biblioteks Center AS: Tempovej 7–11, 2750 Ballerup; tel. 44-86-77-77; fax 44-86-76-93; e-mail dbc@dbc.dk; internet www.dbc.dk; f. 1991; provides Danish libraries with bibliographic data, a union catalogue, databases and online products; Man. Dir MOGENS BRABAND; publ. *DBC Avisen*.

Organisationen Danske Museer: Gl. Strandvej 2, 2990 Nivå; tel. 49-14-39-66; fax 49-14-39-67; internet www.dkm-mus.dk; f. 2005 by merger of Foreningen af Danske Kunstmuseer and Dansk Kulturhistorisk Museums Forening; annual assemblies and study meetings; 200 institutional mems; Chair. LENE FLORIS; Sec. KIRSTEN REX ANDERSEN.

Styrelsen for Bibliotek og Medier (Danish Agency for Libraries and Media): H. C. Andersens Blvd 2, 1553 Copenhagen V; tel. 33-73-33-73; fax 33-73-33-72; e-mail post@

bibliotekogmedier.dk; internet www .bibliotekogmedier.dk; f. 1990 by merger of Mediesekretariatet and Biblioteksstyrelsen; adviser to govt on matters concerning academic and spec. libraries, public libraries, and information and documentation problems; admin. of devt pools and grants, and of nat. Electronic Research Library; media section carries out the daily admin. of broadcasting regulation and assists govt in matters concerning radio and television; Nat. Librarian JENS THORHAUGE; publ. *Bibliotek og Medier* (4 a year).

ECONOMICS, LAW AND POLITICS

Danmarks Jurist- og Økonomforbund (Danish Lawyers and Economists Association): Gothersgade 133, POB 2126, 1015 Copenhagen K; tel. 33-95-97-00; fax 33-95-99-99; e-mail djoef@djoef.dk; internet www .djoef.dk; f. 1972; 47,503 mems; Pres. FINN BORCH ANDERSEN; Dir-Gen. MOGENS KRING RASMUSSEN; publs *DJØF Efteruddannelse* (2 a year), *Juristen* (law, 6 a year), *Samfundsøkonomen* (societal economics, 6 a year).

Dansk Selskab for Europaforskning (Danish Society for European Studies): c/o Centre for European Studies, University of Southern Denmark, Campusvej 55, 5230 Odense M; tel. 65-50-22-17; fax 65-50-22-80; e-mail ecsa-dk@sam.sdu.dk; internet www .ecsa.dk; f. 1975; aims to promote Danish academic study and teaching of the legal, economic, political and social aspects of European integration, by means of seminars and publications; 100 mems; Pres. Prof. FINN LAURSEN; Sec. STEN RYNNING.

International Law Association—Danish Branch: c/o Advocat Jan Erlund, Gorissen Federspiel Kierkegaard, H. C. Andersen Blvd 12, 1553 Copenhagen; fax 33-41-41-33; e-mail al@gfklaw.dk; f. 1925; Pres. ALEX LAUDRUP.

Nationaløkonomisk Forening (Danish Economic Association): Danmarks Nationalbank, Havnegade 5, 1093 Copenhagen K; tel. 33-63-63-63; fax 33-63-71-15; internet www .econ.ku.dk/nf; f. 1873; 1,000 mems; Chair. Prof. MICHAEL MØLLER; Sec. SØREN STORMINGER-DALGAARD; publ. *Nationaloekonomisk Tidsskrift* (3 a year).

Udenrigspolitiske Selskab (Foreign Policy Society): Amaliegade 40A, 1256 Copenhagen K; tel. 33-14-88-86; fax 33-14-85-20; e-mail udenrigs@udenrigs.dk; internet www .udenrigs.dk; f. 1946; studies, debates, publs and confs on int. affairs; library of 100 periodicals; 1,000 individual mems, 200 corporate mems; Chair. UFFE ELLEMANN-JENSEN; Dir KLAUS CARSTEN PEDERSEN; Sec. BRITA V. ANDERSEN; publs *Lande i Lommeformat* (country descriptions: 144 booklets covering 190 countries), occasional monographs, *Udenrigs* (4 a year).

EDUCATION

Mellemfolkeligt Samvirke (Danish Association for International Cooperation): Borgergade 14, 1300 Copenhagen K; tel. 77-31-00-00; fax 77-31-01-01; e-mail ms@ms.dk; internet www.ms.dk; f. 1944; administration of Danish development workers and International Work Camps; public information service on the problems of developing countries and international cooperation; 6,300 mems; library of 40,000 vols on third world issues, immigrants and refugees in Denmark, 600 periodicals, 1,300 films; Gen. Sec. LARS UDSHOLT; publs *Etcetera* (8 a year), *FOCUS Kontakt* (6 a year), *Kontakt Globalt Magasin* (6 a year), *ZAPP Jorden Rundt* (6 a year).

FINE AND PERFORMING ARTS

Billedkunstnernes Forbund (Danish Association of Visual Artists): Vingårdstræde 2, 1, 1070 Copenhagen K; tel. 33-12-81-70; e-mail bkf@bkf.dk; internet www.bkf.dk; 1,250 mems; Chair. NANNA GRO HENNINGSEN; Dir KLAUS PEDERSEN; publ. *Billedkunstneren*.

Dansk Billedhuggersamfund (Danish Sculptors' Society): c/o Mogens Lund 'Sundhuset', Clarasvej 2, 8700 Horsens; tel. 76-28-20-10; fax 75-65-76-60; e-mail mnl@ billedhuggersamfundet.dk; internet www .skulptur.dk; f. 1905; 120 mems; Chair. KIT KJÆRBYE.

Dansk Komponistforening (Danish Composers' Society): Gråbrødretorv 16, 1, 1154 Copenhagen K; tel. 33-13-54-05; fax 33-14-32-19; e-mail dkf@komponistforeningen.dk; internet www.komponistforeningen.dk; f. 1913; 210 mems; Chair. NIELS ROSING-SCHOW; Secs KIRSTEN WREM, TINA SCHELLE.

Dansk Korforening (Danish Choral Society): Absalonsgade 3, 4180 Sorø; f. 1911; mems: 27 choirs; Pres. ASGER LARSEN.

Danske Kunsthåndværkere (Danish Arts and Crafts Association): Bredgade 66, 1260 Copenhagen K; tel. 33-15-29-40; fax 33-15-26-76; e-mail mail@dkkh.dk; internet www .dkkh.dk; f. 1976; arranges exhibitions; professional advice for schools, museums; 8 regional groups of artist-craftsmen; 500 mems; Exec. Sec. NICOLAI STEN GJESSING; publ. *KUNSTUFF–Danish Crafts and Design* (4 a year).

Kunstforeningen GL STRAND (GL STRAND Gallery of Modern and Contemporary Art): Gl. Strand 48, 1202 Copenhagen K; tel. 33-36-02-60; fax 33-36-02-66; e-mail info@glstrand.dk; internet www.glstrand.dk; f. 1825; exhibitions of modern and contemporary art; Dir HELLE BEHRNDT; publs *Nyhedsbrev* (newsletter, 1 or 2 a month), *Medlemsnyt* (4 a year).

Kunstnerforeningen af 18. November (Artists' Association of the 18th November): Frederiksgade 8, 1265 Copenhagen K; tel. 33-15-96-14; f. 1842; workshop, lectures, concerts, exhibitions, art collection; library of 300 vols; 165 mems; Pres. NIELS WAMBERG; Vice-Pres. POUL JENSEN.

Ny Carlsbergfondet (New Carlsberg Foundation): Brolæggerstræde 5, 1211 Copenhagen K; tel. 33-11-37-65; fax 33-14-36-46; internet www.ny-carlsbergfondet.dk; f. 1902; supports the New Carlsberg Glyptotek (see Museums and Art Galleries, Copenhagen), and other Danish art museums; promotes the study of art and art history and develops and fulfils the appreciation of and need for art in Denmark; annual awards; Chair. H. E. NØRREGÅRD-NIELSEN; publ. *Årsskrift* (yearbook).

Samfundet til Udgivelse af Dansk Musik (Society for the Publication of Danish Music): Gråbrødrestræde 18, 1156 Copenhagen K; tel. 33-13-54-45; fax 33-93-30-44; e-mail sales@samfundet.dk; internet www .samfundet.dk; f. 1871; Chair. KLAUS IB JØRGENSEN.

Sammenslutningen af Danske Kunstforeninger (Association of Danish Art Societies): c/o Søren C. Olesen, Søbakkevej 4, 9500 Hobro Copenhagen K; tel. 98-52-20-32; internet www.sdkunst.dk; f. 1942; arranges touring art exhibitions with govt support; 15,000 mems; Dir SØREN C. OLESEN; Sec. FINN MIKELSEN; publ. *Nyhedsbrev* (newsletter, 12 a year).

HISTORY, GEOGRAPHY AND ARCHAEOLOGY

Arktisk Institut (Danish Arctic Institute): Strandgade 102, 1401 Copenhagen K; tel. 32-31-50-50; fax 32-88-01-51; e-mail arktisk@ arktisk.dk; internet www.arktiskinstitut.dk; f. 1954; information, scientific and historic activities related to the Arctic; library of 16,000 vols, archives of Arctic expeditions, diaries, and more than 50,000 photographs, mainly of Greenland; Chair. PETER AUGUSTINUS; Dir BENT NIELSEN.

Dansk Selskab for Oldtids- og Middelalderforskning (Danish Society for Research of Ancient and Medieval Times): Nationalmuseet, 1220 Copenhagen K; e-mail else .rasmussen@natmus.dk; f. 1934; 130 mems; Pres. MICHAEL ANDERSEN; Sec. ELSE MATHORNE RASMUSSEN.

Danske Historiske Forening (Danish Historical Association): Njalsgade 80, 2300 Copenhagen S; tel. 35-32-82-44; e-mail histtid@hum.ku.dk; internet www .historisktidsskrift.dk; f. 1839; 1,500 mems; Chair. Mag. CARSTEN DUE-NIELSEN; Secs Dr JAN PEDERSEN, Dr REGIN SCHMIDT; publ. *Historisk Tidsskrift* (2 a year).

Jysk Arkaeologisk Selskab (Jutland Archaeological Society): Moesgård, 8270 Højbjerg; tel. 89-42-45-04; fax 86-27-23-78; e-mail moesgaard@hum.au.dk; f. 1951; lectures and publication of primary archaeological and ethnological investigations; 1,500 mems; Pres. STEEN HVASS; Sec.-Gen. JAN SKARMBY MADSEN; publs *Handbooks* (irregular), *Jysk Arkaeologisk Selskabs Skrifter* (monographs, irregular), *KUML* (1 a year).

Jysk Selskab for Historie (Jutland Historical Society): Historisk Institut, Århus Universitet, 8000 Århus C; tel. 89-42-20-23; fax 89-42-20-47; f. 1866; 500 mems; Pres. HENRIK FODE; publs *Historie* (2 a year), *Nyt fra Historien* (2 a year).

Kongelige Danske Geografiske Selskab (Royal Danish Geographical Society): Øster Voldgade 10, 1350 Copenhagen K; tel. 35-32-25-00; fax 35-32-25-01; e-mail rdgs@geogr.ku .dk; internet rdgs.dk; f. 1876; 450 mems; library of 100,000 vols; Protector HM Queen MARGRETHE II; Pres. HRH Crown Prince FREDERIK; Sec. OLE MERTZ; Head of Library PREBEN SONNE JØRGENSEN; publs *Atlas of Denmark, Folia Geographica Danica, Geografisk Tidsskrift* (Danish Journal of Geography), *Kulturgeografiske Skrifter*.

Kongelige Danske Selskab for Fædrelandets Historie (Royal Danish Society for National History): c/o Erik Goebel, Kingosvej 16, 4600 Koege; tel. 56-65-90-50; e-mail eg@ sa.dk; internet www.danskemagazin.dk; f. 1745; 65 mems, 20 foreign corresps; Chair. NIELS-KNUD LIEBGOTT; Sec. ERIK GOEBEL; publ. *Danske Magazin*.

Kongelige Nordiske Oldskriftselskab (Royal Society of Northern Antiquaries): Prinsens Palais, Frederiksholms Kanal 12, 1220 Copenhagen K; f. 1825; 750 mems; library: library in the National Museum; Dir NIELS-KNUD LIEBGOTT; Sec. PETER VANG PETERSEN; publs *Aarbøger for Nordisk Oldkyndighed og Historie, Nordiske Fortidsminder*.

Samfundet for Dansk Genealogi og Personalhistorie (Danish Genealogical and Biographical Society): Grysgårdsvej 2, 2400 Copenhagen NV; e-mail info@genealogi.dk; internet www.genealogi.dk; f. 1879; 1,100 mems; Chair. FINN ANDERSEN; Sec. POUL STEEN; publs *Hvem forsker Hvad* (1 a year), *Personalhistorisk Tidsskrift* (2 a year).

Selskabet for Dansk Kulturhistorie (Society for the History of Danish Culture): Rosenborg Castle, Øster Voldgade 4A, 1350 Copenhagen K; tel. 33-15-32-86; fax 33-15-20-46; e-mail jh@dkks.dk; f. 1936; 50 mems; Pres. STEFFEN HEIBERG; Sec. JØRGEN HEIN.

LANGUAGE AND LITERATURE

Alliance Française: Christiansholms Tværvej 19, 2930 Klampenborg, Copenhagen; tel. 39-64-04-28; internet www .alliancefrancaise.dk; offers courses and exams in French language and culture and promotes cultural exchange with France; attached offices in Aarhus and Abyhoj; Dir PETER PREBEN HANSEN.

British Council: Gammel Mønt, 12.3, 1117 Copenhagen K; tel. 33-36-94-00; fax 33-36-94-06; e-mail british.council@britishcouncil .dk; internet www.britishcouncil.org/ denmark; no longer runs educational activities, exams or language courses; activities in 3 regional programme strands: climate change, intercultural dialogue and creative cities; Country Man. HANS MEIER ANDERSEN.

Dansk Forfatterforening (Danish Authors Society): Tordenskjolds Gård, Strandgade 6 st., 1401 Copenhagen K; tel. 32-95-51-00; fax 32-54-01-15; e-mail danskforfatterforening@ danskforfatterforening.dk; internet www .danskforfatterforening.dk; f. 1894; professional org. representing fiction writers, nonfiction writers, poets, translators, writers and illustrators of books for children and young people; 1,300 mems; Pres. LOTTE GARBERS; publ. *Forfatteren* (8 a year).

Danske Sprog- og Litteraturselskab (Society for Danish Language and Literature): Christians Brygge 1, 1219 Copenhagen; tel. 33-13-06-60; fax 33-14-06-08; e-mail sekretariat@dsl.dk; internet www.dsl.dk; f. 1911; 85 mems; Dir Prof. JØRN LUND; Sec. MARIA KROGH LANGNER.

Goethe-Institut: Frederiksborggade 1, 1360 Copenhagen K; tel. 33-36-64-64; fax 33-36-64-61; e-mail bibliotek@kopenhagen.goethe .org; internet www.goethe.de/ne/kop; offers exams in German language and culture and promotes cultural exchange with Germany; Dir MATTHIAS MÜLLER-WIERFERIG.

MEDICINE

Danmarks Farmaceutiske Selskab (Danish Pharmaceutical Society): Rygårds Allé 1, 2900 Hellerup; tel. 39-46-36-00; fax 39-46-36-39; e-mail alt@pharmadanmark.dk; internet www.farmaceutisk-selskab.dk; f. 1912 to encourage the scientific and practical development of Danish pharmacy; 765 mems; Chair. Dr ALEJANDRA MØRK; Sec. Prof. Dr BENT HALLING-SØRENSEN.

Dansk Farmaceutforening (Association of Danish Pharmacists): Rygårds Alle 1, 2900 Hellerup; tel. 39-46-36-00; fax 39-46-36-39; e-mail df@pharmaceut.dk; internet www .farmaceutforeningen.dk; f. 1873; library of 16,000 vols; 3,205 mems; Pres. ARNE KURDAHL; publs *Farmaceuten* (26 a year), *Fredag Formiddag* (52 a year).

Dansk Medicinsk Selskab (Danish Medical Society): Trondhjemsgade 9, 2100 Copenhagen Ø; tel. 35-44-84-01; fax 35-44-84-05; e-mail bda@dadl.dk; internet www.dms.dk; f. 1919; an asscn of 100 socs and 18,000 individual mems, working in all aspects of medical science; awards the August Krogh Prize to a leading Danish scientist, annually; Chair. Prof. Dr JENS CHRISTIAN DJURHUUS; Sec. Prof. Dr J. MICHAEL HASENKAM.

Lægeforeningen (Danish Medical Association): Kristianiagade 12, 2100 Copenhagen Ø; tel. 35-44-85-00; fax 35-44-85-05; e-mail dadl@dadl.dk; internet www.laeger.dk; f. 1857 to unite Danish doctors, to protect and promote the interests of the medical profession, and to serve as the body through which the influence of the medical profession may be exercised; 21,860 mems; Man. Dir BENTE HYLDAHL FOGH; publs *Bibliotek for Læger* (history of medicine, 4 a year), *Danish Med-*

ical Bulletin (English, 6 a year), *DMA Directory (Vejviser)*, *Lægeforeningens Medicinfortegnelse (Physicians Desk Reference)* (every 2 years), *Ugeskrift for Læger* (52 a year).

Tandlægeforeningen (Danish Dental Association): Amaliegade 17, Postboks 143, 1004 Copenhagen K; tel. 70-25-77-11; fax 70-25-16-37; e-mail info@tandlægeforeningen .dk; internet www.tandlægeforeningen.dk; f. 1873; 6,345 mems; Pres. SUSANNE ANDERSEN; publ. *Tandlaegebladet* (15 a year).

NATURAL SCIENCES

General

Selskabet for Naturlærens Udbredelse (Society for the Promotion of Natural Science): UNI-C, Vermundsgade 5, 2100 Copenhagen Ø; tel. 35-87-88-04; fax 35-82-40-76; e-mail snu@naturvidenskab.net; internet www.naturvidenskab.net; f. 1824; 200 mems; Pres. Prof. DORTE OLESEN; Sec. Dr JØRN JOHS. CHRISTIANSEN; publ. *KVANT/Fysisk Tidsskrift* (4 a year).

Biological Sciences

Danmarks Naturfredningsforening (Danish Society for the Conservation of Nature): Masnedøgade 20, 2100 Copenhagen Ø; tel. 39-17-40-00; fax 39-17-41-41; e-mail dn@dn.dk; internet www.dn.dk; f. 1911; 140,000 mems, 216 local cttees; Pres. ELLA MARIA BISSCHOP-LARSEN; Dir GUNVER BENNEKOU; publ. *Tidsskriftet natur og miljø* (4 a year).

Dansk Botanisk Forening (Danish Botanical Society): Sølvgade 83, 1307 Copenhagen K; tel. 33-14-17-03; e-mail dbotf@mail.tele .dk; internet www.botaniskforening.dk; f. 1840; 1,400 mems; Pres. WINNIE DANIELSEN; publ. *Urt* (popular botanical journal).

Dansk Naturhistorisk Forening (Danish Natural History Society): Universitetsparken 15, 2100 Copenhagen Ø; tel. 35-32-11-20; fax 35-32-10-10; e-mail dnf@zmuc.ku.dk; internet www.aki.ku.dk/dnf; f. 1833; 525 mems; Pres. DANNY EIBYE-JACOBSEN; publs *Arsskrift for Dansk Naturhistorisk Forening* (1 a year), *Danmarks Fauna* (irregular).

Dansk Ornithologisk Forening (Danish Ornithological Society): Vesterbrogade 138–140, 1620 Copenhagen V; tel. 33-28-38-00; e-mail dof@dof.dk; internet www.dof.dk; f. 1906; 15,000 mems; Dir JAN EJLSTED; publs *Dansk Ornitologisk Forenings Tidsskrift* (4 a year), *DOF-Nyt* (4 a year), *Fugle i Felten*, *Fugle og Natur* (4 a year).

Entomologisk Forening (Entomological Society): Zoological Museum, Universitetsparken 15, 2100 Copenhagen Ø; internet www.zmuc.dk/entoweb/entomologiskforening/; f. 1868; 360 mems; Pres. MICHAEL FIBIGER; Sec. JAN PEDERSEN; publ. *Entomologiske Meddelelser* (4 a year).

Physical Sciences

Astronomisk Selskab (Astronomical Society): Astronomisk Selskab, Hviddingvej 48, 2610 Rødovre; tel. 36-72-36-34; e-mail mq@ astronomisk.dk; internet www.astronomisk .dk; f. 1916; 600 mems; Chair. MICHAEL QUAADE; publs *Knudepunktet* (4 a year), *Kvant* (jtly with Danish Physical Soc., 4 a year).

Dansk Fysisk Selskab (Danish Physical Society): c/o Jørgen Schou, Afdelingen for Optik og Plasmaforskning, Forskningscenter Risø, 4000 Roskilde; tel. 46-77-47-55; fax 46-77-45-65; e-mail dorthe@ruc.dk; internet www.dfs.nbi.dk; f. 1972; arranges conferences; 700 mems; Pres. JØRGEN SCHOU; publ. *Kvant* (jtly with Astronomical Soc., quarterly).

Dansk Geologisk Forening (Geological Society of Denmark): c/o Geologisk Musem, Øster Voldgade 5-7, 1350 Copenhagen K; tel. 35-32-23-54; fax 35-32-23-25; internet www .2dgf.dk; f. 1893; promotes interest in geology and establishes a forum for geologists; lectures, discussions; excursions; administers 2 prizes; 600 mems; Chair. PETER FRYKMAN; Sec. GUNVER KRARUP PEDERSEN; publs *Bulletin* (2 a year), *Geologisk Tidsskrift* (2 a year).

Kemisk Forening (Danish Chemical Society): H. C. Ørsted Institutet, Universitetsparken 5, 2100 Copenhagen Ø; tel. 35-32-01-55; fax 35-32-02-12; e-mail secretary@ chemsoc.dk; internet www.chemsoc.dk; f. 1879; 870 mems; Pres. PETER WESTH; Sec. MICHAEL PITTELKOW; publ. *Dansk Kemi* (12 a year).

PHILOSOPHY AND PSYCHOLOGY

Dansk Psykolog Forening (Danish Psychological Association): Stockholmsgade 27, 2100 Copenhagen Ø; tel. 35-26-99-55; fax 35-26-97-37; e-mail dp@dp.dk; internet www.dp .dk; f. 1947 for graduate psychologists and students; deals with questions of education and professional matters; works as a trade union to safeguard psychologists' interests; 7,800 mems; Dir MARIE ZELANDER; publ. *Psykolog Nyt* (26 a year).

RELIGION, SOCIOLOGY AND ANTHROPOLOGY

Danske Bibelselskab (Danish Bible Society): Frederiksborggade 50, 1360 Copenhagen K; tel. 33-12-78-35; fax 33-93-21-50; e-mail bibelselskabet@bibelselskabet.dk; internet www.bibelselskabet.dk; f. 1814; editing and distributing Bibles and other biblical scriptures; Chair. CAI FRIMODT-MØLLER; Gen. Sec. Rev. TINE LINDHARDT; publ. *News* (4 a year).

Grønlandske Selskab (Greenland Society): Kraemer Hus, L. E. Bruunsvej 10, 2920 Charlottenlund; tel. 39-63-57-33; fax 39-63-55-43; e-mail dgs@groenlandselskab.dk; internet www.groenlandselskab.dk; f. 1905; 1,500 mems with interest in Greenland and its people; Chair. MARTIN APPELT; publ. *Grønland* (4 a year).

TECHNOLOGY

Akademiet for de Tekniske Videnskaber (Danish Academy of Technical Sciences): 266 Lundtoftevej, 2800 Kgs. Lyngby; tel. 45-88-13-11; fax 45-88-13-51; e-mail atvmail@atv .dk; internet www.atv.dk; f. 1937; 4 divs, covering fundamental and ancillary sciences, chemical science and engineering, mechanical engineering, civil engineering, electrical engineering, information technology, agricultural and food, industrial organization and economics, environmental issues, biology and technical hygiene; thematic professional group on construction and town planning; undertakes professional meetings and projects within these fields; 640 mems; Chair. TORBEN GREVE; Man. Dir LASSE SKOVBY; publ. *ATV NYT* (electronic newsletter, ad hoc, in Danish).

Byggecentrum (Building Centre): Hindsgavl Allé 2, 5500 Middelfart; tel. 70-12-36-00; fax 70-12-38-00; e-mail info@byggecentrum .dk; internet www.byggecentrum.dk; f. 1956; acts as centre for construction information; bookshop, database services, postgraduate training, exhibitions, training centre; Man. Dir JOERN VIBE ANDREASEN.

Dansk Husflidsselskab (Danish Society of Domestic Crafts): Tyrebakken 11, 5300 Kerteminde; tel. 63-32-20-96; fax 63-32-20-97; e-mail dansk@husflid.dk; internet www

.husflid.dk; f. 1873; promotes domestic crafts-manship; 4,800 individual mems, 140 local orgs; Sec. BENTE SKOV MACHHOLM; publ. *Husflid* (6 a year).

Elektroteknisk Forening (Society of Danish Electrotechnicians): Kronprinsensgade 28, 5000 Odense C; tel. 40-56-01-48; e-mail info@dkef.dk; internet www.dkef.dk; f. 1903; 1,400 mems; Sec.-Gen. ANDERS EBBESEN JENSEN; publ. *Elteknik* (10 a year).

Ingeniørforeningen i Danmark (IDA) (Society of Engineers of Denmark): Kalvebod Brygge 31–33, 1780 Copenhagen V; tel. 33-18-48-48; fax 33-18-48-99; e-mail ida@ida.dk; internet www.ida.dk; f. 1937; 61,000 mems; Pres. LARS BYTOFT OLSEN; Chief Exec. IB OUSTRUP; publ. *Ingeniøren* (52 a year).

Research Institutes

GENERAL

Carlsberg Laboratory: Gl. Carlsberg Vej 10, 2500 Copenhagen Valby; e-mail carlslab@crc.dk; internet www.crc.dk; f. 1875; attached to Carlsberg Foundation; research in biochemistry, biotechnology and chemistry; library of 15,000 vols, 300 periodicals; Dir Dr JENS Ø. DUUS; Sec. ANNETTE PETTERSSON; Head of Research Laboratory Dr KLAUS BREDDAM.

AGRICULTURE, FISHERIES AND VETERINARY SCIENCE

Det Jordbrugsvidenskabelige Fakultet (Faculty of Agricultural Sciences): Blichers Allé 20, POB 50, 8830 Tjele; tel. 89-99-19-00; fax 89-99-19-19; e-mail djf@agrsci.dk; internet www.agrsci.dk; f. 1928; research in agriculture and connected subjects; centres in Foulum, Aarslev, Flakkebjerg; 4 experimental stations; 375 scientific staff; attached to Aarhus Univ.; Chair. JENS KAMPMANN; Dean JUST JENSEN.

Hedeselskabet (Danish Land Development Service): Klostermarken 12, POB 110, 8800 Viborg; tel. 87-28-11-33; fax 87-28-10-01; e-mail hedeselskabet@hedeselskabet.dk; internet www.hedeselskabet.dk; f. 1866; forestry, forest nurseries, shelter belts, soil improvement, environmental protection, environmental engineering, land reclamation, drainage, irrigation, hydrology and research; specialists carry out practical assignments and research; technical projects designed and administered for farmers, foresters, industry, government authorities in Denmark and abroad; Man. Dir OVE KOCH; publ. *Vækst* (6 a year).

ECONOMICS, LAW AND POLITICS

Danmarks Statistik (Statistics Denmark): Sejrøgade 11, 2100 Copenhagen Ø; tel. 39-17-39-17; fax 39-17-39-99; e-mail dst@dst.dk; internet www.dst.dk; f. 1849; central institution for all Danish statistics; library: see Libraries and Archives; Dir JAN PLOVSING; publs *Nyt fra Danmarks Statistik* (daily bulletin for media), *Statistisk Årbog* (1 a year), *Statistiske Efterretninger* (daily bulletin for professional users), *Statistisk Månedsoversigt* (12 a year), *Statistisk Tiårsoversigt* (statistical 10-year survey, 1 a year).

Dansk Center for Internationale Studier og Menneskerettigheder (Danish Centre for International Studies and Human Rights): Strandgade 56, 1401 Copenhagen K; tel. 32-69-86-86; fax 32-69-86-00; e-mail dcism@dcism.dk; internet www.dcism.dk; f. 2003; undertakes research and analysis concerning foreign security and development policy; conflict and genocide and human

rights in Denmark and abroad; Head of the Board UFFE ELLEMANN-JENSEN.

Constituent Institutes:

Dansk Institut for Internationale Studier (DIIS) (Danish Institute for International Studies (DIIS)): Strandgade 56, 1401 Copenhagen K; tel. 32-69-87-87; fax 32-69-87-00; e-mail diis@diis.dk; internet www.diis.dk; f. 2003 by act of Parliament (Act no. 411 as of 6 June 2002); research departments: conflict and security studies, cold war studies, European studies, development research, globalization and governance research, holocaust and genocide studies; library of 110,000 vols; Dir NANNA HVIDT; publ. *Den Ny Verden* (The New World, Danish).

Institut for Menneskerettigheder (Institute for Human Rights): Strandgade 56, 1401 Copenhagen K; tel. 32-69-88-88; fax 32-69-88-00; e-mail center@humanrights.dk; internet www.humanrights.dk; f. 2003; programmes incl.: access to justice, civil society and networking, human rights and business, European masters programme, reform of law and state institutions, universities and research partnership programme; Dir MORTEN KJÆRUM.

HISTORY, GEOGRAPHY AND ARCHAEOLOGY

Danske Komité for Historikernes Internationale Samarbejde (Danish Committee for International Historical Cooperation): Copenhagen University, 2300 Copenhagen S; f. 1926; 43 mems; Chair. Prof. NIELS STEENSGAARD.

MEDICINE

Finsen Center–Rigshospitalet: Blegdamsvej 9, 2100 Copenhagen; tel. 35-45-56-15; fax 35-38-54-50; e-mail finsenlab@finsenlab.dk; internet www.finsenlab.dk; f. 1896; cancer research; 24 scientific staff; Head of Laboratory Prof. Dr KELD DANO.

Institute of Cancer Biology: Strandboulevarden 49, 2100 Copenhagen; tel. 35-25-75-00; fax 35-25-77-21; e-mail bio@cancer.dk; internet www.cancer.dk/bio+research; f. 1949; experimental cancer research; Scientific Dir Prof. JULIO E. CELIS; Sec. LAILA FISCHER; publ. *Report* (every 2 years, in English).

NATURAL SCIENCES

General

De Økonomiske Råd (Danish Economic Council): Amaliegade 44, 1256 Copenhagen K; tel. 33-44-58-00; fax 33-32-90-29; e-mail dors@dors.dk; internet www.dors.dk; consists of the Economic Council and the Environmental Economic Council; Chair. HANS JØRGEN WHITTA-JACOBSEN; Chairs MICHAEL ROSHOLM, EIRIK SCHRØDER AMUNDSEN; Sec. LARS HAAGEN PEDERSEN; publ. *Vismandsrapporterne* (2 a year).

Biological Sciences

Arctic Station, University of Copenhagen: Naturvidenskabelige Fakultet, Københavns Univ., Tagensvej 16, 2200 Copenhagen N; tel. 35-32-42-56; fax 35-32-42-20 Arctic Station, POB 504, 3953 Qeqertarsuaq, Greenland; tel. (299) 92-13-84; fax (299) 92-13-85; e-mail as-science@greennet.gl; internet www.arktiskstation.ku.dk; f. 1906, research facility at Univ. of Copenhagen 1953; study of Arctic nature; laboratory; library; research ship 'Porsild'; library of 3,000 books, colln of journals; Head of Board Prof. REINHARDT MØBJERG KRISTENSEN; Chief

Scientist Dr OUTI M. TERVO; Sec. GITTE HENRIKSEN.

DTU Aqua (National Institute of Aquatic Resources): Jægersborg All 1, 2920 Charlottenlund; tel. 33-96-33-00; e-mail aqua@aqua.dtu.dk; internet www.aqua.dtu.dk; f. 1995; fisheries, aquaculture, marine, freshwater and seafood research; large specialist library of fisheries and biology texts; Dir FRITZ W. KÖSTER (acting); publ. *Fisk og Hav*.

Statens Seruminstitut (State Serum Institute): Artillerivej 5, 2300 Copenhagen; tel. and fax 32-68-32-68; e-mail serum@ssi.dk; internet www.ssi.dk; f. 1902; microbiological and immunological research institute and centre for the prevention and control of infectious diseases and congenital disorders; 110 scientists; library of 19,000 vols; Pres. and Chief Exec. NILS STRANDBERG PEDERSEN; Dir of Research ERIK JUHL.

Zoologisk Have (Copenhagen Zoo): Sdr. Fasanvej 79, 2000 Frederiksberg; tel. 72-20-02-00; fax 72-20-02-19; e-mail zoo@zoo.dk; internet www.zoo.dk; f. 1859; 3,300 animals of 264 species; participation in nature conservation projects worldwide; Man. Dir LARS LUNDING ANDERSEN; publ. *Zoo Nyt* (Zoo News, 4 a year).

Physical Sciences

Danmarks Meteorologiske Institut (Danish Meteorological Institute): Lyngbyvej 100, 2100 Copenhagen Ø; tel. 39-15-75-00; fax 39-27-10-80; e-mail epost@dmi.dk; internet www.dmi.dk; f. 1872; attached to Min. of Climate and Energy; meteorology and geophysics; meteorological service for Denmark, Faroe Islands and Greenland; library of 40,000 vols; 400 mems; Dir PETER AAKJÆR; publs *Danmarks Klima* (1 a year), *Magnetic Results* (Godhavn and Thule, Greenland).

De Nationale Geologiske Undersøgelser for Danmark og Grønland (Geological Survey of Denmark and Greenland): Ø. Voldgade 10, 1350 Copenhagen; tel. 38-14-20-00; fax 38-14-20-50; e-mail geus@geus.dk; internet www.geus.dk; f. 1995; library of 30,000 vols; Man. Dir JOHNNY FREDERICIA; publs *Geological Survey of Denmark and Greenland Bulletin*, *Geological Survey of Denmark and Greenland Map Series*.

Kort & Matrikelstyrelsen (National Survey and Cadastre): Rentemestervej 8, 2400 Copenhagen NV; tel. 35-87-50-50; fax 35-87-50-51; e-mail kms@kms.dk; internet www.kms.dk; f. 1989, by amalgamation of former Geodetic Institute, Danish Cadastral Department and Hydrographic Division; responsible for geodetic survey of Denmark, Faroe Islands and Greenland; topographic survey and mapping of those areas, also nautical charting and issue of nautical publs; cadastral survey, registration, and mapping of Denmark; seismographic service in Denmark, Faroe Islands and Greenland; research and development within geodesy and seismology; development of digital maps and charts; Dir JESPER JARMBÆK.

Niels Bohr Institutet: Astronomisk Observatorium, Københavns Universitet, Juliane Maries Vej 30, 2100 Copenhagen Ø; tel. 35-32-59-99; fax 35-32-59-89; e-mail library@astro.ku.dk; internet www.nbi.dk; f. 1642; astronomy, physics and geophysics; library of 12,000 vols, 100 periodicals; Dir Prof. J. R. HANSEN.

RELIGION, SOCIOLOGY AND ANTHROPOLOGY

Instytut Polsko–Skandynawski/Polsk-Skandinavisk Forskningsinstitut (Polish–Scandinavian Research Institute): POB 2584, 2100 Copenhagen Ø; tel. 39-29-98-26; f. 1985; ind. research institute for Polish–

Scandinavian studies; provides support for research in the field of history and biographical science; organizes lectures; 25 mems; library of 1,000 vols; 20m. of archives; Pres. Prof. Dr Hab. E. S. KRUSZEWSKI; Dir Prof. Dr Hab. BOLESLAW HAJDUK; Dir Prof. Dr BARBARA TÖRNQUIST-PLEWA.

SFI—Det Nationale Forskningscenter for Velfærd (Danish National Centre for Social Research): Herluf Trolles Gade 11, 1052 Copenhagen K; tel. 33-48-08-00; fax 38-48-08-33; e-mail sfi@sfi.dk; internet www.sfi .dk; f. 1958; ind. nat. research centre operating under Min. of Social Affairs; library of 32,500 vols; Man. Dir JØRGEN SØNDERGAARD; publ. *Social Forskning* (4 a year).

TECHNOLOGY

Risø Nationallaboratoriet for Bæredygtig Energi (Risø National Laboratory for Sustainable Energy): POB 49, Frederiksborgvej 399, 4000 Roskilde; tel. 46-77-46-77; fax 46-77-56-88; e-mail risoe@risoe.dk; internet www.risoe.dtu.dk; f. 1958; attached to Danmarks Tekniske Universitet; research and devt in fields of industrial materials, new functional materials, energy systems analysis, renewable energy, and nuclear safety; Dir HENRIK BINDSLEV; publ. *Risø Report.*

Libraries and Archives

Ålborg

Aalborg Bibliotekerne (Central Library for the County of North Jutland): Rendsburggade 2, Postboks 839, 9100 Ålborg; tel. 99-31-43-00; fax 99-31-43-90; e-mail bibliotek@ aalborg.dk; internet www .aalborgbibliotekerne.dk; f. 1895; 830,000 vols, 1,300 current periodicals; 15 brs and 3 mobile libraries; Chief Librarian BODIL HAVE.

Aalborg Universitetsbibliotek (Aalborg University Library): Langagervej 2, POB 8200, 9220 Ålborg; tel. 99-40-94-00; fax 98-15-55-31; e-mail aub@aub.aau.dk; internet www.aub.aau.dk; f. 1973; open to the public; 650,000 vols; Chief Librarian NIELS-HENRIK GYLSTORFF.

Århus

Århus Kommunes Biblioteker (Århus Public Library): Møllegade 1, 8000 Århus C; tel. 89-40-92-00; fax 89-40-93-93; e-mail aakb@bib.aarhus.dk; internet www.aakb.dk; f. 1934; 1,124,228 vols (including audiovisual materials); Chief Librarian ROLF HAPEL.

Erhvervsarkivet Statens Erhvervshistoriske Arkiv (Danish National Business History Archives): Vester Allé 12, 8000 Århus C; tel. 86-12-85-33; fax 86-12-85-60; e-mail mailbox@ea.sa.dk; internet www.sa .dk/ea; f. 1948; also a research institute for economic and social history; Chief Archivist CHR. R. JANSEN; publ. *Erhvervshistorisk Årbog* (Business History Yearbook).

Handelshøjskolens Bibliotek (Library of the Århus School of Business): Fuglesangs Allé 4, 8210 Århus V; tel. 89-48-66-88; fax 86-15-96-27; e-mail bibliotek@asb.dk; internet www.lib.asb.dk; f. 1939; 172,000 vols, 18,000 periodicals and electronic serials; spec. colln: European documentation centre for EU; Library Dir TOVE BANG.

Statsbiblioteket (State and University Library): Universitetsparken, 8000 Århus C; tel. 89-46-20-22; fax 89-46-22-20; e-mail sb@statsbiblioteket.dk; internet www .statsbiblioteket.dk; f. 1902; Legal Deposit Library, National Newspaper Collection, National Media Archive, Loan Centre for Public Libraries; 4,850,022 vols; Chief Exec. SVEND LARSEN.

Copenhagen

Administrative Bibliotek: Slotsholmsgade 12, 1216 Copenhagen K; tel. 72-26-98-95; fax 72-26-98-99; e-mail dab@dab.dk; internet www.dab.dk; f. 1924; attached to Min. of Science, Technology and Innovation; central library and documentation centre for civil servants in central govt; 160,000 vols; spec. colln: Danish governmental publs; Head of Library NIELS H. JENSENIUS; publ. *Prima Vista* (4 a year).

CBS Bibliotek (CBS Library): Solbjerg Plads 3, 2000 Frederiksberg; tel. 38-15-38-15; fax 38-15-36-63; e-mail cbs.lib@cbs.dk; internet www.cbs.dk/library; f. 1922; 400,000 vols, 1,000 current print periodicals, 33,000 electronic periodicals; Dir RENÉ STEFFENSEN.

Danmarks Biblioteksskoles Bibliotek (Library of the Royal School of Library and Information Science): Birketinget 6, 2300 Copenhagen S; tel. 32-58-60-66; fax 32-84-02-01; e-mail dbilaan@db.dk; internet www .db.dk/dbi/home_uk.htm; f. 1956; 180,000 vols; Librarian K. M. ØRNSTRUP.

Danmarks Kunstbibliotek (Royal Danish Academy of Fine Arts Library): Kgs Nytorv 1, Postboks 1053, 1007 Copenhagen K; tel. 33-74-48-00; fax 33-74-48-88; e-mail dkb@ kunstbib.dk; internet www.kunstbib.dk; f. 1754; 150,000 vols on history of art and architecture, 205,000 architectural drawings, 364,000 photographs, 164,000 slides; Dir Dr PATRICK KRAGELUND.

Danmarks Paedagogiske Bibliotek (National Library of Education): Tuborgvej 164, POB 840, 2400 Copenhagen NV; tel. 88-88-93-00; fax 88-88-93-90; e-mail dpb@dpu .dk; internet www.dpb.dpu.dk; f. 1887; 895,000 vols, 3,057 current periodicals, 600,000 microfiches; Dir JENS BENNEDSEN.

Danmarks Statistiks Bibliotek og Information (Statistics Denmark Library and Information): Sejrøgade 11, 2100 Copenhagen Ø; tel. 39-17-30-30; fax 39-17-30-03; e-mail bib@dst.dk; internet www.dst.dk/ omds/bib.aspx; f. 1849; attached to Danmarks Statistik (see Research Institutes: Economics, Law and Politics); 235,000 vols; Head of Div. PER KNUDSEN.

Det Biovidenskabelige Fakultetsbibliotek (Faculty of Life Sciences Library): Dyrlægevej 10, 1870 Frederiksberg C; tel. 35-33-21-45; fax 35-34-28-24; e-mail bvfb@kvl.dk; internet www.bvfb.life.ku.dk; f. 1783; 586,000 vols; Chief Librarian FREDE MØRCH.

Det Farmaceutiske Fakultetsbibliotek, Københavns Universitet (Pharmaceutical Sciences Faculty Library, Copenhagen University): Universitetsparken 4, 3rd fl, 2100 Copenhagen; tel. 35-30-63-19; fax 35-30-60-60; e-mail bibliotek@farma.ku.dk; internet www.farma.ku.dk/bibliotek; f. 1892; 65,000 vols; Head of Library Service ALICE NØRHEDE.

Frederiksberg Bibliotek (Frederiksberg Public Library): Falkoner Plads 3, 2000 Frederiksberg; tel. 38-21-18-00; fax 38-21-17-99; e-mail bib@fkb.dk; internet www.fkb .dk; f. 1887; 547,634 vols; 3 brs; also a music library and a special genealogy section; Chief Librarian ANNE MØLLER-RASMUSSEN.

Københavns Biblioteker (Copenhagen Public Libraries): Fælles Service, Islands Brygge 37, 5, 2300 Copenhagen S; tel. 33-66-46-50; fax 33-66-71-20; e-mail bibliotek@ kff.kk.dk; internet www.bibliotek.kk.dk; f. 1885; 2,240,881 vols; Library Dir JENS INGE-MANN.

Københavns Stadsarkiv (Copenhagen City Archives): Rådhuset, 1599 Copenhagen V; tel. 33-66-23-70; fax 33-66-70-39; e-mail stadsarkiv@kff.kk.dk; f. before 1563; 37 linear km of archive material, 150,000 maps and drawings; Dir HENRIK GAUTIER; publ.

Historiske Meddelelser om København (1 a year).

Kongelige Bibliotek, Nationalbibliotek og Københavns Universitetsbibliotek (Royal Library, National Library of Denmark and Copenhagen University Library): POB 2149, 1016 Copenhagen K; tel. 33-47-47-47; fax 33-93-22-18; e-mail kb@kb.dk; internet www.kb.dk; f. 1482 as university library, 1648 as the King's Library, merged 1989; acts as the Danish National Library; principal research and university library for theology, the humanities, law and the social sciences, the natural and health sciences; nat. archive for MSS and archives of prominent Danes; incl. Danish Museum of Books and Printing, National Museum of Photography, Museum of Danish Cartoon Art; open to the public; 5,966,000 vols, 4,500 incunabula, 169,000 manuscripts and archives, 16,000,000 graphic documents, 296,000 maps and prints, 287,000 musical items; Dir-Gen. ERLAND KOLDING NIELSEN; publs *Fund og Forskning i Det Kongelige Biblioteks Samlinger* (1 a year), *Magasin fra Det Kongelige Bibliotek* (4 a year).

Kongelige Garnisonsbibliotek (Royal Danish Military Library): Kastellet 46, 2100 Copenhagen Ø; tel. 33-47-95-25; fax 33-47-95-36; e-mail is-kgb@fak.dk; internet www .kgbmil.dk; f. 1785; Army central research library; 130,000 vols on military development since medieval times; military strategy, operations, tactics, logistics and intelligence; regimental history, uniforms, weaponry and technology; military bibliographies; international relations, defence and security policy, international engagements and peacekeeping operations; 150 periodicals; 5,500 maps since 16th century; access to research databases; Historian SIMON KAREL BERING PAPOUSEK.

Kunstindustrimuseets Bibliotek (National Art and Design Library): Bredgade 68, 1260 Copenhagen K; tel. 33-18-56-56; fax 33-18-56-66; e-mail bib@ kunstindustrimuseet.dk; internet www .kunstindustrimuseet.dk/bibliotek; f. 1890; 180,000 books and leaflets, 3,000 magazines, 30,000 posters, 50,000 graphics, prints and sketches; Chief Librarian LARS DYBDAHL.

Marinens Bibliotek (Royal Danish Naval Library): Henrik Gerners Plads 3, 1433 Copenhagen K; tel. 32-66-40-21; fax 32-66-40-29; e-mail is-mab@fak.dk; internet www .mab.dk; f. 1765; naval affairs and Greenland literature; 40,000 vols; Librarian PIA SØRENSEN.

Patent- og Varemærkestyrelsens bibliotek (Library of the Danish Patent and Trademark Office): Helgeshoj Allé 81, 2630 Taastrup; tel. 43-50-80-00; fax 43-50-80-01; e-mail bibliotek@dkpto.dk; internet www .dkpto.dk/bibliotek; f. 1894; 28,860 vols; 35m. patent specifications; Heads of Library JON FINSEN, LIZZI VESTER; publs *Dansk Brugsmodeltidende* (Danish Utility Models Gazette, 26 a year), *Dansk Mønstertidende* (Danish Design Gazette, 26 a year), *Dansk Patenttidende* (Danish Patent Gazette, 52 a year), *Dansk Varemarketidende* (Danish Trademark Gazette, 52 a year).

Rigsarkivet (Danish National Archives): Rigsdagsgården 9, 1218 Copenhagen K; tel. 33-92-33-10; fax 33-15-32-39; e-mail mailbox@ra.sa.dk; internet www.sa.dk; f. 1582; the Danish Nat. Archives in Copenhagen, together with 4 Provincial Archives (*Landsarkiver*), situated in Copenhagen, Odense, Viborg and Aabenraa, the Nat. Business Archives in Århus and the Danish Data Archives in Odense make up the Danish State Archives; the Danish Nat. Archives' central record office contains most of the medieval documents (1200–1559), the archives of the Central Admin., and the armed forces, and the papers of the Royal family and of famous statesmen; Dir JOHAN PETER NOACK; publs *Arkiv*, *Siden Saxo*.

Esbjerg

Esbjerg Kommunes Biblioteker (Esbjerg Public Library): Nørregade 19, 6700 Esbjerg; tel. 76-16-20-00; fax 76-16-20-01; e-mail biblio@esbjergkommune.dk; internet www .esbbib.dk; f. 1897; 535,171 vols, 71,987 other items, incl. electronic resources, CDs; Chief Librarian ANNETTE BRØCHNER LINDGAARD.

Hellerup

Gentofte Bibliotekerne (Public Library): Ahlmanns Allé 6, 2900 Hellerup; tel. 39-98-58-00; fax 39-98-58-25; e-mail bibliotek@ gentofte.dk; internet www.genbib.dk; f. 1918; 546,808 vols; 5 brs; Chief Librarian PIA HANSEN.

Lyngby

Danmarks Tekniske Informationscenter (Technical Information Centre of Denmark): PO 777, Bldg 101D, Anker Engelunds Vej 1, 2800 Kgs. Lyngby; tel. 45-25-72-00; fax 45-88-30-40; e-mail dtub@dtic.dtu.dk; internet www.dtic.dtu.dk; f. 1942; centre for scientific information and library for the Technical Univ. of Denmark; 700,000 vols, 4,000 current periodicals, 11,000 e-journals; Dir MOGENS SANDFÆR.

Odense

Landsarkivet for Fyn (Provincial Archives of Funen): Jernbanegade 36A, 5000 Odense C; tel. 66-12-58-85; fax 66-14-70-71; e-mail mailbox@lao.sa.dk; internet www.sa.dk/lao; f. 1893; the archives include records of local administration of Funen and neighbouring islands, and collections of private papers; The Karen Brahe Library, the only nearly-complete private Danish library dating from the 17th century, with about 3,400 printed books and 1,153 MSS, is deposited in the Archives; Dir STEEN OUSAGER.

Odense Centralbibliotek (Odense Central Library): Østre Stationsvej 15, 5000 Odense C; tel. 65-51-43-01; fax 66-75-55-09; e-mail teleservice-bib@odense.dk; internet www .odensebib.dk; f. 1924; 865,000 vols, 145,000 CDs, audiobooks, video cassettes and DVDs; Library Dir LENE BYRIALSEN; Chief Librarians JYTTE CHRISTENSEN, KENT SKOV ANDREASEN.

Syddansk Universitetsbibliotek (University Library of Southern Denmark): Campusvej 55, 5230 Odense M; tel. 65-50-10-00; fax 65-15-00-95; e-mail sdub@bib.sdu.dk; internet www.sdu.dk/bibliotek; f. 1965; languages, literature, philosophy, religion, history, music, econ., social sciences, natural sciences, medicine, engineering; 1,500,000 vols, 54,500 periodicals (incl. 51,500 electronic); Dir AASE LINDAHL.

Roskilde

Roskilde Universitetsbibliotek (Roskilde University Library): Universitetsvej 1, POB 258, 4000 Roskilde; tel. 46-74-20-07; fax 46-74-30-90; e-mail rub@ruc.dk; internet www .rub.ruc.dk; f. 1971; open to general public; humanities, social sciences and natural sciences; 625,000 vols, 215,000 units of non-book material, 12,000 electronic books; Dir NIELS SENIUS CLAUSEN; Deputy Dir CLAUS VESTERAGER PEDERSEN.

Silkeborg

Silkeborg Bibliotek (Public Library): Hostrupsgade 41A, 8600 Silkeborg; tel. 87-22-19-00; fax 87-22-19-01; e-mail biblioteket@ silkeborg.bib.dk; internet www .silkeborg-bibliotek.dk; f. 1900; 216,000 vols, plus 128,000 in the Children's Dept, 50,000 records and cassettes; Chief Librarian PETER BIRK.

Vejle

Vejle Bibliotekerne (Vejle Public Libraries): Willy Sørensens Plads 1, 7100 Vejle; tel. 75-82-32-00; fax 75-82-32-13; e-mail vejlebib@vejlebib.dk; internet www.vejlebib .dk; f. 1895; 487,388 vols (incl. audiobooks, CDs and DVDs), 3,922 periodicals; Chief Librarian LONE KNAKKERGAARD.

Viborg

Landsarkivet for Nørrejylland (Provincial Archives of Northern Jutland): 8800 Viborg; tel. 86-62-17-88; fax 86-60-10-06; e-mail mailbox@lav.sa.dk; internet www.sa .dk/lav; f. 1889, opened 1891; 55 km of shelving; Dir C. R. JANSEN.

Museums and Art Galleries

Ålborg

Ålborg Historiske Museum: Algade 48, 9000 Ålborg; tel. 99-31-74-00; fax 98-16-11-31; e-mail historiskmuseum@aalborg.dk; internet www.nordjyllandshistoriske museum.dk; f. 1863; archaeology, history, ethnology, glass, silver, tobacco industry; Dir LARS CHRISTIAN NØRBACH.

Kunsten Museum of Contemporary Art: Kong Christians Allé 50, 9000 Ålborg; tel. 99-82-41-00; fax 98-16-28-20; e-mail kunsten@ aalborg.dk; internet www.kunsten.dk; f. 1877, building inaugurated 1972; Fine Art Dept: Danish art since 1900 (painting, sculpture, graphics, sculpture park); Anna and Kresten Krestensen Colln: Danish and int. art 1920–1950; Kirsten and Axel P. Nielsen Colln (art of 1960s and 1970s); Erik Veistrup Colln (art 1906–2006); library of 13,000 vols; Dir GITTE ØRSKOU.

Århus

ARoS Århus Kunstmuseum (Århus Art Museum): Aros Allé 2, 8000 Århus C; tel. 87-30-66-00; fax 87-30-66-01; e-mail info@aros .dk; internet www.aros.dk; f. 1859; Danish art since the 18th century and modern international art; library of 21,000 vols; Dir JENS ERIK SØRENSEN.

Naturhistorisk Museum (Natural History Museum): Universitetsparken, Bygning 210, 8000 Århus C; tel. 86-12-97-77; fax 86-13-08-82; internet www.naturhistoriskmuseum.dk; f. 1921; Denmark exhibition: natural history of Danish landscapes; Danish Animals exhibition; Animals of the World exhibition; African Savannah exhibition; permanent field laboratory: 'Molslaboratoriet', Femmöller, 8400 Ebeltoft; the museum laboratories are open to scientists, and specialize in terrestrial ecology, limnology, entomology, acarology, mammalogy, ornithology and bioacoustics; the library contains 15,000 vols; Dir THOMAS SECHER JENSEN; publs *Natura Jutlandica* (in English), *Natur og Museum* (in Danish).

Auning

Dansk Landbrugsmuseum (Danish Agricultural Museum): Gl. Estrup, 8963 Auning, Jutland; tel. 86-48-34-44; fax 86-48-41-82; e-mail dansklandbrugsmuseum@gl-estrup .dk; internet www.gl-estrup.dk; f. 1889; exhibitions on the history of country life, agricultural technology and beekeeping; Dir PETER BAVNSHØJ.

Charlottenlund

Ordrupgaard: Vilvordevej 110, 2920 Charlottenlund; tel. 39-64-11-83; fax 39-64-10-05; e-mail ordrupgaard@ordrupgaard.dk; internet www.ordrupgaard.dk; f. 1918; French and Danish 19th- and early 20th-century paintings, including works by Degas, Delacroix, Gauguin, Hammershøi, Manet, Pissarro and Renoir; Danish arts and crafts of the 19th century; Dir ANNE-BIRGITTE FONSMARK.

Copenhagen

Botanisk Have (Botanic Garden): Øster Farimagsgade 2B, 1353 Copenhagen K; tel. 35-32-22-22; fax 35-32-22-21; e-mail snm@ snm.ku.dk; internet botanik.snm.ku.dk; f. 1874; 25 acres of landscape garden, palmhouse and greenhouses; rare trees, plants (13,000 species); Head FLEMMING LARSEN.

Danske Filminstitut—Museum og Cinematek (Danish Film Institute—Archive and Cinematheque): Gothersgade 55, 1123 Copenhagen K; tel. 33-74-34-00; fax 33-74-34-01; e-mail cinematek@dfi.dk; internet www.dfi.dk; f. 1941; collns of films, books, posters, documentation; cinemas with daily screenings; library of 65,000 vols, 13,500 scripts, 370 periodicals; Dir DAN NISSEN; publ. *Kosmorama* (2 a year).

Geologisk Museum (Geological Museum): University of Copenhagen, Øster Voldgade 5–7, 1350 Copenhagen K; tel. 35-32-23-45; fax 35-32-23-25; e-mail rcp@savik.geomus.ku .dk; internet www.nathimus.ku.dk/geomus; f. 1772; minerals, rocks, meteorites and fossils; geology of Denmark and Greenland; Origin of Man; plate tectonics; volcanoes; salt in the subsoil; library; attached to University of Copenhagen; Chair. Prof. MINIK ROSING.

Københavns Museum (Museum of Copenhagen): Absalonsgade 3, 1658 Copenhagen V; located at: Vesterbrogade 59, 1620 Copenhagen V; tel. 33-21-07-72; fax 33-25-07-72; e-mail sekr@bymuseum.dk; internet www .copenhagen.dk; f. 1901; history of Copenhagen incl. pictures, architecture, models; houses the colln of Kierkegaard relics; Dir JETTE SANDAHL.

Kunstindustrimuseet (Danish Museum of Art and Design): Bredgade 68, 1260 Copenhagen K; tel. 33-18-56-56; fax 33-18-56-66; e-mail info@kunstindustrimuseet.dk; internet www.kunstindustrimuseet.dk; f. 1890; European applied art from the Middle Ages to modern times, Chinese and Japanese art; library of 63,000 vols on applied art; Dir BODIL BUSK LAURSEN; Curators ULLA HOUKJAER, CHRISTIAN HOLMSTED OLESEN.

Nationalmuseet (National Museum): Frederiksholms Kanal 12, 1220 Copenhagen K; tel. 33-13-44-11; fax 33-47-33-33; e-mail direktoeren@natmus.dk; internet www .natmus.dk; f. 1807 on basis of the older Royal Collns; consists of 5 divs; Dir CARSTEN U. LARSEN; Keepers of divs: Classical Antiquities BODIL BUNDGAARD RASMUSSEN, Danish Prehistory POUL OTTO NIELSEN, Denmark since 1660 ANNETTE VASSTRÖM, Ethnographic Colln PER KRISTIAN MADSEN, Middle Ages and Renaissance MICHAEL ANDERSEN; publs *Nationalmuseets Arbejdsmark* (1 a year), *Nyt fra Nationalmuseet* (4 a year), *Skrifter* (in 3 series), catalogues.

Attached Museums:

Frihedsmuseet (Museum of Danish Resistance): Churchillparken, 1263 Copenhagen K; tel. 33-47-39-21; fax 33-14-03-14; e-mail frihedsmuseet@natmus.dk; f. 1957; chronological devt of Danish resistance during the Nazi occupation 1940–45; Dir ESBEN KJELDBÆK.

Frilandsmuseet (Open-Air Museum): Kongevejen 100, 2800 Lyngby; tel. 33-47-34-81; fax 33-47-33-97; e-mail frilandsmuseet@natmus.dk; f. 1897; examples of more than 50 farms, mills and houses from 1650 to 1950, representing virtually every region in Denmark and the Faroe Islands as well as the fmr Danish provinces of southern Sweden and northern Germany; displays of rural crafts; incorporates Brede Works factory community with workmen's and foremen's houses, eating house, orphanage and nursery garden; Dir INGER TOLSTRUP.

Musikmuseet—Musikhistorisk Museum og Carl Claudius' Samling (Music Museum—Musical History Museum and Carl Claudius Collection): Åbenrå 30, 1124 Copenhagen K; tel. 33-11-27-26; fax 33-11-60-44; e-mail musik@natmus.dk; f. 1898; extensive colln of musical instruments from all over the world with spec. emphasis on European instruments from the Renaissance onwards; concerts, library, archives; Dir Dr LISBET TORP.

Ny Carlsberg Glyptotek: Dantes Plads 7, 1556 Copenhagen V; tel. 33-41-81-41; fax 33-91-20-58; internet www.glyptoteket.dk; f. 1888; Danish and French sculpture and painting since 19th century, Egyptian, Greek, Roman and Etruscan art, mainly sculpture; Pres. HANS EDVARD NORREGAARD-NIELSEN; Dir FLEMMING FRIBORG; publ. *Meddelelser* (1 a year).

Orlogsmuseet (Royal Danish Naval Museum): Overgaden oven Vandet 58, 1415 Copenhagen K; tel. 33-11-60-37; fax 33-93-71-52; e-mail thm@thm.dk; internet www.orlogsmuseet.dk; f. 1957; 400 items depicting the Danish navy since the early 18th century, including models of ships, weapons, ships' decorations and maritime art; Curators STEEN SCHØN, JAKOB SEERUP.

Rosenborg Slot (Rosenborg Castle): Øster Voldgade 4A, 1350 Copenhagen K; tel. 33-15-76-19; fax 33-15-20-46; e-mail museum@dkks.dk; internet www.rosenborgslot.dk; f. 1833; contains 'The Chronological Collns of the Danish Kings'; the colln was founded by Frederik III in about 1660, and depicts the history of Danish kings from Frederik II in the mid-16th century to Frederik VII in the 19th century; consists of arms, apparel, jewellery, and furniture from 1470–1863; also houses the Royal Regalia and the Crown Jewels; Dir Chamberlain NIELS EILSCHOU HOLM; Museum Dir NIELS-KNUD LIEBGOTT.

Attached Museum:

Amalienborgmuseet (Amalienborg Museum): Christian VIII's Palace, 1257 Copenhagen K; tel. 33-12-32-86; fax 33-93-32-03; e-mail amalienborgmuseet@dkks.dk; internet www.amalienborgmuseet.dk; f. 1994; exhibitions cover the reigns of Danish kings, from 1863–1972 (Christian IX, Frederik VIII, Christian X and Frederik IX); Curator GERDA PETRI.

Statens Museum for Kunst (Danish National Gallery): Sølvgade 48–50, 1307 Copenhagen K; tel. 33-74-84-94; fax 33-74-84-04; e-mail smk@smk.dk; internet www.smk.dk; contains the main collection of Danish paintings and sculpture; a number of works by other Scandinavian artists since 19th century; J. Rump collection of modern French art; about 1,000 paintings by old masters of the Italian, Flemish, Dutch and German Schools (chiefly derived from the old royal collection, which was established as an art gallery in the 1760s); The Print Room includes about 300,000 Danish and foreign prints and drawings; library: about 130,000 vols; Dir ALLIS HELLELAND; publ. *Statens Museum for Kunst Journal*.

Teatermuseet: Christiansborg, Ridebane 10–18, 1218 Copenhagen K; tel. 33-11-51-76; fax 33-12-50-22; internet www.teatermuseet.dk; f. 1912; situated in the old Court theatre, built in 1767; illustrates the development of the Danish theatre since 18th century; Dir ULLA STRØMBERG.

Thorvaldsens Museum: Bertel Thorvaldsens Plads 2, 1213 Copenhagen K; tel. 33-32-15-32; fax 33-32-17-71; e-mail thm@thorvaldsensmuseum.dk; internet www.thorvaldsensmuseum.dk; f. 1839; sculptures and drawings by the Danish sculptor Bertel Thorvaldsen (1770–1844), his collns of contemporary European paintings, drawings and prints and classical antiquities; and his library, archives relating to Thorvaldsen's studies and the museum's history; library of 8,000 vols; Dir STIG MISS.

Tøjhusmuseet (Royal Danish Arsenal Museum): Frederiksholms Kanal 29, 1220 Copenhagen K; Tøjhusgade 3, Copenhagen; tel. 33-11-60-37; fax 33-93-71-52; e-mail thm@thm.dk; internet www.thm.dk; f. 1838; central state museum for the history of the Danish defence forces and for arms and armour; history of arms in Europe, since the introduction of gunpowder; history and development of international military materials; Dir OLE LOUIS FRANTZEN.

Zoologisk Museum (University of Copenhagen Zoological Museum): Universitetsparken 15, 2100 Copenhagen Ø; tel. 35-32-10-00; fax 35-32-10-10; e-mail tpape@zmuc.ku.dk; internet www.zmuc.dk; f. 1770; research is organized in 3 scientific departments: Vertebrates and Quaternary Zoology; Invertebrates (excl. insects, myriapods and arachnids); and Entomology; public education programmes and school service; attached to Faculty of Science, University of Copenhagen; Dir THOMAS PAPE; publ. *Steenstrupia* (2 a year).

Dronningmølle

Rudolph Tegners Museum og Statuepark (Rudolph Tegners Museum and Statue Park): Museumsvej 19, 3120 Dronningmølle; tel. 49-71-91-77; e-mail luise@rudolphtegner.dk; internet www.rudolphtegner.dk; f. 1938; devoted to the works and collections of the sculptor Rudolph Tegner (1873–1950); 200 works in plaster, clay, bronze and marble; Dir LUISE GOMARD.

Elsinore

Danmarks Tekniske Museum (Danish Museum of Science and Technology): Fabriksvej 25, 3000 Elsinore; tel. 49-22-26-11; fax 49-22-62-11; e-mail info@tekniskmuseum.dk; internet www.tekniskmuseum.dk; f. 1911; steam engines, electric appliances (including Valdemar Poulsen's telegraphone, the forerunner of modern tape recording), bicycles, cars and aircraft; authentic pewter workshop; library of 18,000 vols; Dir JENS BREINEGAARD; publ. *Arbog* (Yearbook).

Handels- og Søfartsmuseet (Danish Maritime Museum): Kronborg, 3000 Elsinore; tel. 49-21-06-85; fax 49-21-34-40; internet maritime-museum.pro.dir.dk; f. 1914; Danish shipping since 1400, including the Sound Dues, the Napoleonic Wars, trade with China and the former Danish colonies in India, navigation and the Lifeboat Service; maritime objects, model ships, paintings, photographs and text boards; depiction of the Danish sailor's life since 16th century; regular temporary exhibitions; store rooms containing several thousand paintings and objects; administrative building in the castle grounds containing the museum's records; library of 28,000 vols; spec. colln of logbooks and photographs; Dir HANS JEPPESEN; Sec. ULLA-BRITTA HANSEN.

Kronborg: Kronborg 2C, 3000 Elsinore; tel. 49-21-30-78; fax 49-21-30-52; e-mail kronborg@ses.dk; internet www.ses.dk/kronborg; f. 1425; fortified royal castle dating from the late 16th century; contains the Royal Apartments (furniture, tapestry, regalia), banqueting hall, chapel; known as 'Hamlet's castle'; Dir LARS HOLST.

Hillerød

Nationalhistoriske Museum paa Frederiksborg Slot (Museum of National History at Frederiksborg Castle): Frederiksborg Slot, 3400 Hillerød; tel. 48-26-04-39; fax 48-24-09-66; e-mail frederiksborgmuseet@frederiksborgmuseet.dk; internet www.frederiksborgmuseet.dk; castle built in 1560s, extended 1600–20, and established as museum in 1878; contains a chronological collection of portraits and paintings illustrating the history of Denmark, each era in a separate room, the furniture and appointments in keeping with the period of the paintings; 10,000 exhibits; library of 15,000 vols; Pres. NIELS EILSCHOU HOLM (Chamberlain); Dir METTE SKOUGAARD.

Højbjerg

Moesgård Museum: Moesgård, 8270 Højbjerg; tel. 89-42-11-00; fax 86-27-23-78; e-mail moesgaard@hum.au.dk; internet www.moesmus.dk; f. 1861; collections of Danish prehistoric antiquities; research organization in environmental, Danish and Oriental archaeology and ethnology; Dir JAN SKAMBY MADSEN.

Hørsholm

Jagt- og Skovbrugsmuseet (Danish Museum of Hunting and Forestry): Folehavevej 15–17, 2970 Hørsholm; tel. 45-86-05-72; fax 45-76-20-02; e-mail museum@jagtskov.dk; internet www.jagtskov.dk; f. 1942; Curator JETTE BAAGØE.

Humlebæk

Louisiana Museum of Modern Art: Gl. Strandvej 13, 3050 Humlebæk; tel. 49-19-07-19; fax 49-19-35-05; e-mail curator@louisiana.dk; internet www.louisiana.dk; f. 1958; neoclassic villa and estate transformed into a modern museum of art; colln of int. art, incl. works by Arp, Francis Bacon, Calder, Dubuffet, Ernst, Sam Francis, Kiefer, Henry Moore, Picasso, Rauschenberg and Warhol; exhibitions of contemporary artists; cinema, concerts, theatre; Dir POUL ERIK TOEJNER; publs *Louisiana Magasin* (2 a year), *Louisiana Revy* (2 a year).

Odense

Odense Bys Museer (Odense City Museums): Overgade 48, 5000 Odense C; tel. 65-51-46-01; fax 65-90-86-00; e-mail museum@odense.dk; internet www.odmus.dk; f. 1860; Dir TORBEN GRØNGAARD JEPPESEN; publs *Anderseniana* (1 a year), *Fynske Fortællinger* (1 a year), *Fynske Minder* (1 a year), *Fynske Studier* (1 a year).

Selected Museums:

Carl Nielsen Museet (Carl Nielsen Museum): Claus Bergs Gade, 5000 Odense C; tel. 65-51-46-01; fax 65-90-86-00; e-mail museum@odense.dk; internet www.museum.odense.dk/carl_nielsen.aspx; f. 1980; devoted to the composer's life (1865–1931) and work; Curator EJNAR ASKGAARD.

Fyns Kunstmuseum (Funen Art Museum): Jernbanegade 13, 5000 Odense C; e-mail museum@odense.dk; internet www.museum.odense.dk/fyens_kunstmuseum.aspx; f. 1880 as a smaller version of the Statens Museum for Kunst; art gallery; collection contains works since 1750; Curator ANNE CHRISTIANSEN.

Fynske Landsby (Funen Village): Sejerskovvej 20, 5260 Odense S; tel. 65-51-46-01; fax 65-90-86-00; e-mail museum@odense .dk; internet www.museum.odense.dk/ den_fynske_landsby.aspx; open-air museum recreating the time of the era of Hans Christian Andersen (1805–1875); Curator MYRTUE ANDERS.

Hans Christian Andersens Hus (Hans Christian Andersen Museum): Bangs Boder 29, 5000 Odense C; e-mail museum@odense.dk; internet www .museum.odense.dk/h_c_andersen.aspx; f. 1905; devoted to the writer's life (1805–1875) and work; Curator EJNAR ASKGAARD.

Odense City Museum—Møntergården: Overgade 48, 5000 Odense C; tel. 65-51-46-01; fax 65-90-86-00; e-mail museum@ odense.dk; internet www.museum.odense .dk/bymuseet_moentergaarden.aspx; local cultural history, coins and medals, archaeology; Curators KARSTEN KJER MICHAELSEN, ANDERS MYRTUE.

Roskilde

Vikingeskibsmuseet i Roskilde (Viking Ship Museum): Vindeboder 12, 4000 Roskilde; tel. 46-30-02-00; fax 46-30-02-01; e-mail museum@vikingeskibsmuseet.dk; internet www.vikingeskibsmuseet.dk; f. 1969; exhibits the 5 Viking ships found at Skuldelev in 1962, and aims to promote research in ship-building history in general; research on maritime subjects is carried out in cooperation with the Nat. Museum of Denmark and other nat. and int. research instns; Dir TINNA DAMGÅRD-SØRENSEN.

Universities and Technical Universities

AALBORG UNIVERSITET

POB 159, Fredrik Bajers Vej 5, 9100 Ålborg

Telephone: 96-35-40-99-40
Fax: 98-15-22-01
E-mail: aau@aau.dk
Internet: www.aau.dk

Founded 1974
State control
Academic year: September to July

Rector: FINN KJAERSDAM
Vice-Rector: INGER ASKEHAVE
Dir: PETER PLENGE
Admin. Officer: PETER PLENGE
Librarian: NIELS-HENRIK GYLSTORFF

Number of teachers: 2,500
Number of students: 15,000

Publications: *Studieguiden* (1 a year), *Uglen* (10 a year), *Videnskabet* (2 a year)

DEANS

Faculty of Engineering: FREDE BLAABJERG
Faculty of Humanities: LONE DIRCKINCK-HOLMFELD
Faculty of Social Sciences: MARIANNE ROST-GAARD

AARHUS UNIVERSITET

Nordre Ringgade 1, 8000 Aarhus C

Telephone: 89-42-11-11
Fax: 89-42-11-09
E-mail: au@au.dk
Internet: www.au.dk

Founded 1928
State controlled

Languages of instruction: Danish, English
Academic year: September to June

Rector: NIELS CHRISTIAN SIDENIUS
Pro-Rector: KATHERINE RICHARDSON
Dir: STIG MØLLER

Number of teachers: 2,200
Number of students: 31,000

Publications: *AU-gustus* (4 a year), *CAMPUS* (22 a year)

DEANS

Faculty of Agricultural Sciences: JUST JENSEN
Faculty of Arts: BODIL DUE
Faculty of Health Services: SØREN MOGENSEN
Faculty of Science: ERIK MEINECHE SCHMIDT
Faculty of Social Sciences: TOM LATRUP-PEDERSEN
Faculty of Theology: CARSTEN RIIS
National Environmental Research Institute: HENRIK SANDBECH (Dir-Gen.)
School of Business: BØRGE OBEL
School of Education: LARS-HENRIK SCHMIDT

PROFESSORS

Faculty of Arts (Nordre Ringgade, Bygning 328, 8000 Aarhus C; tel. 89-42-11-11; fax 89-42-12-00; e-mail hum@au.dk; internet www .au.dk/hum):

ANDERSEN, P. B., Media Science
BACH, S., Latin Languages
BOHN, O.-S., English
BRANDT, P. A., Semiotics
DAY, A., English
ENGBERG, J., History
HANNESTAD, N., Classical Archaeology
JUUL JENSEN, U., Philosophy
KYNDRUP, M., Aesthetics and Culture
LANGSTED, J., Drama
LARSEN, S. E., History of Literature
McGREGOR, W. B., Linguistics
MARSCHNER, B., Music
MØLLER, P. U., Slavonic Languages
MORTENSEN, F., Media Science
NØLKE, H., Latin Languages
OTTO, T., Ethnography
PADE, M., Classical Studies
POULSEN, B., History
ROESDAHL, E., Medieval Archaeology
SCHANZ, H.-J., History of Ideas
SØRENSEN, P. E., Scandinavian Studies
TOGEBY, O., Scandinavian Studies
VANDKILDE, H., Prehistoric Archaeology
WAMBERG, N. J., Art History
WEDELL-WEDELLSBORG, A., Chinese

Faculty of Health Sciences (Vennelyst Boulevard 9, 8000 Aarhus C; tel. 89-42-11-22; fax 86-12-83-16; e-mail sun@au.dk; internet www.au.dk.sun):

AALKJAER, C., General Physiology
ANDERSEN, J. P., Molecular Physiology
ASTRUP, J., Neurosurgery
AUTRUP, H. N., Environment and Occupational Medicine
BEK, T., Ophthalmology
BLACK, F. T., Medicine
BOLUND, L., Clinical Genetics
BONDE, J. P., Clinical Occupational Medicine
BÜNGER, C., Experimental Orthopaedic Surgery
CHRISTENSEN, B., General Medicine
CHRISTENSEN, E. I., Structural Cell Biology
CHRISTIANSEN, G., Medical Molecular Biology
CLAUSEN, T., Physiology
DAHL, R., Lung Diseases and Allergology
DANSCHER, G., Neurobiology
DJURHUUS, J. C., Surgery
EHLERS, N., Ophthalmology
ESMANN, M., Biophysics
FALK, E., Ischaemic Heart Disease
FOLDSPANG, A., Health Service Research

FRØKIER, J., Clinical Psychology and Nuclear Medicine
FUGLSANG-FREDERIKSEN, A., Neurophysiology
GJEDDE, A., Positron Tomography
GLIEMANN, J., Biochemistry
GREGERSEN, H., Gastrointestinal Sensory Motor Function
GREGERSEN, M., Forensic Medicine
GREGERSEN, N., Medical Molecular Biology
GUNDERSEN, H. J., Stereology
GYLDENSTED, C., X-ray Diagnostics
HAMILTON-DUTOIT, S., Pathology
HASENKAM, J. M., Heart Surgery
HOKLAND, P., Experimental Clinical Research
HÖLLSBERG, P., Virology
HVID, I., Experimental Orthopaedics
ISIDOR, F., Prosthetics
JAKOBSEN, J. K., Neurology
JENSEN, P. H., Medical Biochemistry
JENSEN, T. S., Pain Research
JENSENIUS, J. C. T., Immunology
JØRGENSEN, T. M., Urology
KARRING, T., Periodontology
KILIAN, M., Microbiology and Immunology
KIRKEVOLD, M., Clinical Nursing Science
KØLVRAA, S., Clinical Genetics
LAMBERT, J. D. C., Physiology
LARSEN, M. J., Endodontics
LAURBERG, P., Endocrinology
LAURITZEN, T., General Practice
LEDET, T., Biochemical Pathology
MAASE, H. VON DER, Oncology
MAUNSBACH, A., Anatomy
MELSEN, B., Orthodontics
MOESTRUP, S. K., Medical Biochemistry
MOGENSEN, C. E. S., Medicine
MOGENSEN, S. C., Virology and Immunology
MORS, N. P. O., Experimental Clinical Research
MOSEKILDE, L., Bone Diseases
MULVANY, M., Cardiovascular Pharmacology
MUNK-JØRGENSEN, P., Psychiatry
MØLLER, J. V., Biophysics
NEXOE, E., Clinical Biochemistry
NIELSEN, S., Structural Cell Biology and Pathophysiology
NIELSEN, T. T., Cardiology
NYGAARD, H., Biomedical Engineering
OLSEN, J., Social Medicine
ØRNTOFT, T. F., Molecular Cancer Diagnostics
OVERGAARD, J., Experimental Cancer Research
OVESEN, T., Experimental Clinical Research
PAASKE, W., Cardiovascular Surgery
PAKKENBERG, B., Neurostereology
PAULSEN, P. K., Surgery
PEDERSEN, F. S., Molecular Oncology
PEDERSEN, J. C. M., Microbiology and Immunology
POULSEN, S., Paediatric Dentistry
RICHELSEN, B., Clinical Nutrition
ROSENBERG, R., Psychiatry
SABROE, S., Health Sciences
SCHIØTZ, P. O., Paediatrics
SCHMITZ, O., Clinical Pharmacology
SCHØNHEYDER, H., Clinical Microbiology
SIGSGAARD, T., Occupational Medicine
SØBALLE, K., Experimental Orthopaedic Surgery
SØRENSEN, F. B., Pathology
SØRENSEN, H. T., Clinical Epidemiology
STENGARD-PEDERSEN, K., Rheumatology
SVENSSON, P., Oral Physiology
THOMSEN, P. H., Psychiatry for Children and Adolescents
TOENNESEN, E., Anaesthesiology
VESTERBY, C. A., Forensic Medicine
VESTERGAARD, P., Psychiatry
VÆTH, M., Biostatistics
VILSTRUP, H., Hepatology

WEEKE, J., Medical Endocrinology
WENZEL, A., Oral Radiology

Faculty of Science (Ny Munkegade, Bygning 520, 8000 Aarhus C; tel. 89-42-31-88; fax 89-42-35-96; e-mail nat@au.dk; internet au.dk/nat):

ANDERSEN, H. H., Mathematics
ANDERSEN, J. U., Experimental Physics
ASMUSSEN, S., Mathematics
BALSLEV, H., Biology
BESENBACHER, F., Experimental Solid State Physics
BOLS, M., Chemistry
BØDKER, S., Computer Science
BØTTIGER, J., Materials Science
CHRISTENSEN, K. R., Biological Oceanography
CHRISTENSEN, N. E., Theoretical Solid State Physics
CHRISTENSEN-DALSGAARD, J., Astronomy
CHRISTIANSEN, F. V. B., Population Biology
CLARK, B., Chemistry
FIELD, D., Experimental Molecular Physics
GRONBAK, K. G., Computer Science
HANSEN, T. I., Sports Medicine
IVERSEN, B., Materials Chemistry
JACOBSEN, H. J., Chemistry
JANTZEN, J. C., Mathematics
JENSEN, J. L., Mathematical Statistics
JENSEN, K., Computer Science
JØRGENSEN, K. A., Organic Chemistry
JØRGENSEN, P., Theoretical Chemistry
KJEMS, J., Molecular Biology
KORSTGÅRD, J. A., Structural Geology and Basin Tectonics
KRAGH, H., History of Science
KRISTENSEN, M., Nanophotonics
LOESCHKE, V., Biology
MACINTOSH, D. J., Biology
MADSEN, I. H., Mathematics
MADSEN, O. L., Computer Science
MØLMER, K., Physics
NIELSEN, J. A., Mathematical Finance
NIELSEN, M., Theoretical Computer Science
NIELSEN, N. C., Solid State NMR
ODGAARD, B. V., Palynology
OGILBY, P. R., Chemistry
PETERSEN, J. S., Chemistry
PIETROWSKI, J., Quaternary Geology
RATTAN, S. I. S., Molecular Biology
REVSBECH, N. P., Microbial Ecology
SKRYDSTRUP, T., Chemistry
STENSGAARD, I., Experimental Solid State Physics
VEDEL, E. B., Mathematical Statistics
WEBER, R. E., Zoophysiology

Faculty of Social Sciences (Bartholins Allé, Bygning 350 Universitetsparken, 8000 Aarhus C; tel. 89-42-11-33; fax 89-42-15-40; e-mail samfundsvidenskab@au.dk; internet www.socialsciences.au.dk):

AGERVOLD, M., Psychology
ANDERSEN, T. M., Economic Planning
BASSE, E. M., Jurisprudence
BLOM-HANSON, J., Political Science
CHRISTENSEN, B. J., Economic Planning
CHRISTENSEN, J. G., Political Science
CHRISTENSEN, J. P., Jurisprudence
DALBERG-LARSEN, J. V., Jurisprudence
DAMGAARD, E., Political Science
DANIELSEN, J. H., Jurisprudence
ELKLIT, A., Psychology
ELKLIT, J., Political Science
EVALD, J., Jurisprudence
GENEFKE, J., Economic Planning
GERMER, P., Jurisprudence
HALDRUP, N., National Economy
HOEGH-OLESEN, H., Psychology
HYLLEBERG, S. A. F., National Economy
IVERSEN, B. O., Jurisprudence
IVERSEN, T., Jurisprudence
JØRGENSEN, P. L., Economics
KRISTENSEN, L. H., Jurisprudence
KVALE, S., Psychology
MADSEN, O. Ø., Economic Planning

MADSEN, P. B., Jurisprudence
MAMMEN, J., Psychology
MOLS, N. P., Management
MORTENSEN, P. B., Register-based Research
NANNESTAD, P., Political Science
NIELSEN, G. T., Jurisprudence
NØRGAARD, I. M., Jurisprudence
NØRGAARD, O., Political Science
NYBORG, H., Psychology
OVERGAARD, P. B., Economic Planning
PALDAM, N. M., Economic Planning
PEDERSEN, J., Jurisprudence
PEDERSEN, P. J., Economics
REVSBECH, K., Jurisprudence
RISBJERG THOMSEN, S., Political Science
ROSHOLM, M., National Economy
SOERENSEN, G., Political Science
SOMMER, D., Psychology
SVENDSEN, G. T., Political Science
SVENSSON, P., Political Science
THOMSEN, H. H. B., Jurisprudence
TOGEBY, L., Political Science
VASTRUP, C., Economics
VEDSTED-HANSEN, J., Jurisprudence
ZACHARIAS, B., Psychology

Faculty of Theology (Tåsingegade 3, 8000 Aarhus C; tel. 89-42-10-24; fax 86-13-04-90; e-mail teo@au.dk; internet www.au.dk/teo):

ANDERSEN, S., Ethics and Philosophy of Religion
BILDE, P., History of Religions
DAVIDSEN, O., Biblical Studies
GEERTZ, A., History of Religions
HVIDBERG-HANSEN, F. O., Semitic Philology
INGESMAN, P., Cultural History of Christianity
JENSEN, H. J. L., Study of Religions
MORTENSEN, V., Missiology and Ecumenical Theology
NIELSEN, K., Old Testament Exegesis
SCHJØRRING, J. H., Church History
WIDMANN, P., Dogmatics

CONSTITUENT INSTITUTIONS

Danmarks Miljøundersøgelser (National Environmental Research Institute): Box 358, Frederiksbergvej 399, 4000 Roskilde; tel. 46-30-12-00; fax 46-30-11-14; e-mail dmu@dmu.dk; internet www.dmu.dk; f. 1989; 295 research and consultancy staff; depts of Arctic environment, atmospheric environment, environmental chemistry and microbiology, feshwater ecology, mrine ecology, policy analysis, trrestrial ecology, wildlife ecology and biodiversity.

Danmarks Pædagogiske Universitetsskole (Danish School of Education): Tuborgvej 164, 2400 Copenhagen NV; tel. 88-88-90-00; fax 88-88-90-01; e-mail dpu@dpu.dk; internet www.dpu.dk; f. 2000; library: see Libraries and Archives; 148 teachers; 4,000 students; depts of curriculum research, eucational anthropology, educational philosophy, educational psychology, educational sociology, learning lab Denmark.

Handelshøjskolen i Aarhus (Aarhus School of Business): Fuglesangs Allé 4, 8210 Aarhus V; tel. 89-48-66-88; fax 86-15-01-88; e-mail asb@asb.dk; internet www.asb.dk; f. 1939; 7,000 students; depts of business studies, economics, language and business communication, law, management, marketing and statistics.

Jordbrugsvidenskabelige Fakultet (Faculty of Agricultural Sciences): Blichers Allé 20, POB 50, 8830 Tjele; tel. 89-99-19-00; e-mail djf@agrsci.dk; internet www.agrsci.org; 375 research scientists; research depts of agricultural engineering, agroecology and environment, animal health, welfare and nutrition, food science, genetics and biotechnology, horticulture, integrated pest management.

DANMARKS TEKNISKE UNIVERSITET (Technical University of Denmark)

Bygning 101A, 2800 Lyngby
Telephone: 45-25-25-25
Fax: 45-88-17-99
E-mail: dtu@adm.dtu.dk
Internet: www.dtu.dk

Founded 1829

Pres.: LARS PALLESEN
Vice-Pres.: Prof. KNUT CONRADSEN
Univ. Dir: JØRGEN HONORÉ

Number of teachers: 1,491
Number of students: 5,949

DEANS OF FACULTY COMMITTEES

Chemistry, Chemical Engineering and Biotechnology: Prof. JOHN VILLADSEN
Civil and Environmental Engineering: Assoc. Prof. KNUD CHRISTENSEN
Electrical Engineering and Physics: Prof. STEEN MØRUP
Information Technology, Electronics and Mathematics: Prof. ERIK BRUUN
Mechanical Engineering, Energy and Production: Prof. P. TERNDRUP PEDERSEN

PROFESSORS

ADLER-NISSEN, J. L., Biotechnology
AHRING, B. K., Biotechnology
ALTING, L., Mechanical Engineering
ANDERSEN, M. A. E., Power Electronics
ANDRAESEN, M. M., Product Development
ANDREANI, P., Analogue Integrated Systems
ARVIN, E., Water Supply Engineering
BAY, N., Materials Processing
BENDSØE, M., Applied Functional Analysis
BJARKLEV, A. O., Optical Communication
BJERG, P. L., Environmental Geochemistry
BJERRUM, N., Chemical Engineering
BJØRNER, D., Computer Science
BLANKE, M.
BOHR, H., Biomolecular Structure and Function
BOHR, J., Physics
BOHR, T., Theoretical Physics
BRUNAK, S., Bio-informatics
BRUUN, K. E., Analogue Electronics
BRUUN, P., Industrial Management
BRØNS, M., Mathmematics
BUCHHAVE, P., Optics
CARLSEN, H., Energy Engineering
CHIFFRE, DE, L., Process Technology, Geometrical Metrology
CHORKENDORFF, I., Heterogeneous Catalysis
CHRISTENSEN, C. J. H., Heterogeneous Catalysis
CHRISTENSEN, E. L., Microwave Systems
CHRISTENSEN, TH. H., Environmental Engineering
CHRISTIANSEN, P. L., Non-linear Dynamics
CLAUSEN, J., Mathematic Optimization
CONRADSEN, K., Statistical Image Analysis
DAM-JOHANSEN, K., Combustion and Chemical Reaction Engineering
DAU, T., Hearing Aid Audiology and Acoustics
DITLEVSEN, O. D., Actions on Structures and Structural Reliability
EMMITT, S., Innovation and Management in Building
FANGER, P. O., Heating and Air Conditioning
FOGED, N., Geotechnical Engineering
FREDSØE, J., Marine Hydraulics
GAARSLEV, A., Construction Management
GANI, R., Systems Design
GIMSING, N. J., Structural Engineering
HAMMER, K., Microbiology
HANSEN, E. H., Analytical Chemistry
HANSEN, H. N., Microtechnical Production
HANSEN, L. K., Digital Signal Processing
HANSEN, P. C., Scientific Computing
HANSEN, P. F., Safety Assessment of Marine Systems
HANSEN, V. L., Mathematics

HASSAGER, O.
HEIN, L., Engineering Design Methodology
HENZE, M., Waste-water Engineering
HVAM, J. M., Optoelectronics
HVILSTED, S.
JACOBI, O. I., Geoinformatics and Photogrammetry
JACOBSEN, K. W., Physics
JAUHO, A.-P., Theoretical Nanotechnology
JENSEN, J. A., Biomedical Signal Processing
JENSEN, J. J., Marine Structures
JENSEN, O. M., Building Materials
JENSEN, P. L., Technology and Working Life, Working Environment
JEPPESEN, P., Optical Communication
JOHNSSON, J. E., Chemical Reaction Engineering
JØRGENSEN, S. B., Technical Chemistry
JUSTESEN, J., Error-Correcting Codes, Information Theory
KLEMM, P., Applied Microbiology
KLIT, P., Machine Elements and Lubrication Theory
KNUDSEN, L. R., Cryptology
KNUDSEN, S., Experimental and Computational Gene Expression Analysis
KRENK, S., Structural Mechanics
KRISTENSEN, M., Glass Components
KROZER, V., Microwave Electronics
LARSEN, P. S., Fluid Mechanics
LELEUR, S., Decision Support Systems and Planning
LIND, M., Control Systems
LUNDT, I.
LYNGAAE-JOERGENSEN, J., Polymer Technology
MADSEN, H.
MADSEN, J., Computer Systems
MADSEN, K., Numerical Analysis
MADSEN, O. G., Transport Optimization
MADSEN, P., Hydrodynamics
MADSEN, S. N.
MARKVORSEN, S., Differential Geometry
MENON, A., Microsystems Technology
MOLIN, S., Applied Microbiogenetics
MOLLERUP, J., Chromatography and Thermodynamics
MØLLER, P., Corrosion and Surface Technology
MØLTOFT, J., Reliability Engineering
MØRK, J., Active Semiconductor Components for Optical Communication Systems
MØRUP, S., Physics of Nanostructures
NIELSEN, J. B., Fermentation Physiology
NIELSEN, M. P., Structural Analysis
NIELSEN, O. A., Transport Planning
NIELSON, F., Computer Science
NIELSON, H. R., Programming Language Technology and Secure IT Systems
NILSSON, J. F., Computer Science
NØRSKOV, J. K., Theoretical Physics
OLESEN, B. W., Indoor Environment and Energy
PAUL, J., Refrigeration
PEDERSEN, N. F.
PEDERSEN, P., Structural Mechanics
PEDERSEN, P. T., Strength of Materials
POLACK, J., Acoustics
QVALE, B., Mechanical Engineering
REITZEL, E., Form-finding of Minimal Structures
ROENNE-HANSEN, J., Electric Power Engineering
SKOU, N., Radar and Radiometer Systems
SKOUBY, K. E., Economy and Regulation of Telecommunication
SKRIVER, H. L.
SOMERS, M. A., Physical Metallurgy
SPLIID, H., Applied Statistics: Statistical Practice and Consulting
STENBY, H. E., Applied Thermodynamics and Separation Processes
STUBKJAER, K. E.
SUNDELL, J.
SVENDSEN, SV. AA. HØJGAARD, Energy Technology in Buildings

SVENSSON, B., Food Protein Biochemistry
TANNER, D., Organic Chemistry
TELLEMAN, P., Biochemical Microsystems
THOMASSEN, C., Mathematics
TØNNESEN, O., Experimental High Voltage Technique
TROMBORG, B., Optoelectronics
TVERGAARD, V., Mechanics of Materials
ULSTRUP, J., Inorganic Chemistry
VESTERAGER, J., Product Development
VILLADSEN, J., Biotechnology
VILLUMSEN, A., Geology
WANHEIM, T., Machine Engineering

DET FARMACEUTISKE FAKULTET/ FACULTY OF PHARMACEUTICAL SCIENCES

Telephone: 35-33-60-00
Fax: 35-33-60-01
E-mail: farma@farma.ku.dk
Internet: www.farma.ku.dk

Founded 1892
Academic year: September to July
Depts of medicinal chemistry, pharmacology and pharmacotherapy, pharmaceutics and analytical chemistry

Dean: Prof. SVEN FRØKJAER
Head of Administration: JUDITH CHRISTIANSEN

Number of teachers: 150
Number of students: 1,400

Publication: *Lægemiddelforskning* (Drug Research, 1 a year).

HANDELSHØJSKOLEN I KØBENHAVN (Copenhagen Business School)

Solbjerg Plads 3, 2000 Frederiksberg
Telephone: 38-15-38-15
Fax: 38-15-20-15
E-mail: cbs@cbs.dk
Internet: www.cbs.dk

Founded 1917
State control
Academic year: September to July
Pres.: FINN JUNGE-JENSEN
Univ. Dir: GERT BECHLUND
Exec. Sec.: PERNILLE RISEGAARD

Library: see under Libraries and Archives
Number of teachers: 378
Number of students: 14,823

Publications: *ARK*, *CEBAL*, *SPRINT*, *Yearbook*

DEANS

Faculty of Economics and Business Administration: JENS AARIS THISTED
Faculty of Languages, Communication and Cultural Studies: SØREN BARLEBO RASMUSSEN

KØBENHAVNS UNIVERSITET (University of Copenhagen)

Frue Plads/Noerregade 10, POB 2177, 1017 Copenhagen K
Telephone: 35-32-26-26
Fax: 35-32-26-28
E-mail: ku@ku.dk
Internet: www.ku.dk

Founded 1479
State control
Language of instruction: Danish
Academic year: September to August (2 terms)

Rector: RALF HEMMINGSEN
Pro-Rector: LYKKE FRIIS
Univ. Dir: ELSE SOMMER
Librarian: MICHAEL COTTA-SCHØNBERG
Number of teachers: 3,583

Number of students: 37,000

DEANS

Faculty of Health Sciences: ULLA WEWER
Faculty of Humanities: JOHN KUHLMANN MADSEN
Faculty of Law: VAGN GREVE
Faculty of Life Sciences: PER HOLTEN-ANDERSEN
Faculty of Science: NIELS O. ANDERSEN
Faculty of Social Sciences: TROELS OESTERGAARD SØRENSEN
Faculty of Theology: STEFFEN KJELDGAARD-PEDERSEN

PROFESSORS

Faculty of Health Sciences (Panum Instituttet, Blegdamsvej 3, 2200 Copenhagen N; tel. 35-32-79-00; fax 35-32-70-70; e-mail sund-fak@adm.ku.dk; internet www.sund.ku.dk):

ASMUSSEN, E., Dental Materials
BENDIXEN, G., Internal Medicine
BOCK, E. M., Cellular Biology
BOCK, J. E., Obstetrics and Gynaecology
BOLWIG, T. G., Psychiatry
BOYSEN, G., Neurology
BRETLAU, P., Otorhinolaryngology
BUUS, S., Basic Immunology
CHRISTENSEN, N. J., Internal Medicine
CHRISTOFFERSEN, P., Pathological Anatomy
DABELSTEEN, S. E., Oral Diagnosis
DEURS, B. G., Structural Cell Biology
DIRKSEN, A., Internal Medicine
GALBO, H., Physiopathology
GJERRIS, F. O., Neurosurgery
GYNTELBERG, F., Occupational Medicine
HALD, T., Surgery
HAUNSØ, S., Internal Medicine
HEMMINGSEN, R. P., Psychiatry
HENRIKSEN, J. H., Clinical Physiology
HJØRTING-HANSEN, E., Oral and Maxillofacial Surgery
HOLLNAGEL, H., General Practice
HOLMSTRUP, P., Periodontology
HØIBY, N., Microbiology
HOLST, J. J., Medical Physiology
HORNSLET, A., Virology
HULTBORN, H., Neurophysiology
KEHLET, N., Surgery
KEIDING, N., Statistics
KRASILNIKOFF, P. A., Paediatrics
KRASNIK, A., Social Medicine
KREIBORG, S., Paedodontics
LARSEN, J. F., Obstetrics and Gynaecology
LARSEN, S., Pathological Anatomy
LORENZEN, I., Internal Medicine
LUND, B., Surgery
LUND-ANDERSEN, H., Eye Diseases
MELLERGÅRD, M. J., Psychiatry
MENNÉ, T., Dermatology
MICHELSEN, N., Clinical Social Medicine
MOGENSEN, J. V., Anaesthesiology
MORLING, N., Forensic Genetics
NIELSEN, J. O., Epidemic Diseases
NORÉN, O., Biochemistry
OLESEN, J., Neurology
ØLGAARD, K., Internal Medicine
OTTESEN, B., Obstetrics and Gynaecology
ÖWALL, B., Prosthodontics
PAULSON, O. B., Neurology
PETERSEN, P. E., Community Dentistry and Postgraduate Education
PETTERSON, G., Thorax Surgery
PHILIP, J., Obstetrics and Gynaecology
POULSEN, H. E., Clinical Pharmacology
PRAUSE, J. U., Eye Diseases
QUISTOR, F. F., Biochemistry
REHFELD, J. F., Clinical Chemistry
REIBEL, J., Oral Pathology and Oral Medicine
RØRTH, M., Clinical Oncology
ROSTGAARD, J., Normal Anatomy
ROVSING, H. C., Radiology
SCHOU, J., Pharmacology

SCHROEDER, T. V., Surgery
SCHROLL, M., Geriatrics
SCHWARTZ, T. W., Molecular Pharmacology
SIGGAARD-ANDERSEN, O., Clinical Chemistry and Laboratory Technique
SIMONSEN, J., Forensic Pathology
SJÖSTRÖM, H., Biochemistry
SKAKKEBÆK, N., Paediatrics
SKINHØJ, P., Epidemic Diseases
SKOUBY, F., Paediatrics
SOLOW, B., Orthodontics
SØRENSEN, T. I. A., Clinical Epidemiology
STADIL, F. W., Surgery
SVEJGAARD, A., Clinical Immunology
THYLSTRUP, A., Cardiology
TOMMERUP, N., Medical Genetics
TOS, M., Otorhinolaryngology
VEJLSGAARD, G., Dermato-venereology
WULF, H. C., Dermato-venereology
WULFF, H. R., Clinical Decision Theory and Ethics

Faculty of Humanities (Njalsgade 80, 2300 Copenhagen S; tel. 35-32-80-60; fax 35-32-80-52; e-mail hum-fak@fak.hum.ku.dk; internet www.hum.ku.dk):

BOLVIG, A., History
BONDEBJERG, I., Film Studies
COLLIN, F., Philosophy
DUNCAN, R., American Studies
EKSELL, K., Semitic Philosophy
ELBRO, C., Linguistics
FLOTO, I., History
FORTESQUE, M., Linguistics
GABRIELSEN, V., Ancient History
HARDER, P., English Literature
HJARVARD, S., Film Studies
HØJRUP, T., Ethnology
HOV, L., Theatre
JENSEN, K. B., Media Studies
JØRGENSEN, J. N., Danish Language
LIND, G., History
LUND, N., History
RANDSBORG, K., Archaeology
RUUS, H., Danish Language
SCHWAB, H., Music
VILLAUME, P., History
ZERLANG, M., Comparative Literature

Faculty of Law (Kannikestraede 11, 1169 Copenhagen K; tel. 35-32-26-26; fax 35-32-35-86; e-mail jurfak@jur.ku.dk; internet www.jur.ku.dk):

BALVIG, F., Legal Sociology and Sociology of Law
BLUME, P., Legal Informatics
BONDESON, U., Criminology
BRYDE ANDERSEN, M., Private Law, Computer Law
DUE, O., European Union Law
FOIGEL, I., Law of Taxation
GREVE, V., Criminal Law
KETSCHER, K., Social Law
KOKTVEDGAARD, M., Law of Competition, Intellectual Property Law
KRARUP, O., Public Law
LOOKOFSKY, J., Law of Contracts and Torts, Private International Law
NIELSEN, L., Family Law
RASMUSSEN, H., International Law and European Union Law
RØNSHOLDT, S., Administrative Law
SMITH, E., Legal Procedure
TAKSØE-JENSEN, F., Family Law, Law of Wills and Succession
TAMM, D., History of Law
VON EYBEN, B., Law of Property
ZAHLE, H., Jurisprudence

Faculty of Life Sciences (Bülowsvej 17, 1870 Frederiksberg C; tel. 35-28-28-28; fax 35-28-26-64; e-mail life@life.dk; internet www.life.ku.dk):

AASTED, B., Veterinary Microbiology
ANKER, H., Economics and Natural Resources
ASTRUP, A., Human Nutrition

BAUER, R., Mathematics and Physics
BISGAARD, M., Veterinary Microbiology
BJERRUM, M., Chemistry
BLIXENKRONE-MØLLER, M., Veterinary Microbiology
BOGETOFT, P., Economics and Natural Resources
BORGGÅRD, O., Chemistry
CHRISTENSEN, L. P. G., Animal Sciences and Animal Health
CHWALIBOG, A., Animal Science and Animal Health
COLLINGE, D., Plant Biology
ERIKSEN, E. N., Agricultural Sciences
ESBJERG, P., Ecology and Molecular Biology
FLAGSTAD, A., Clinical Sciences
FLENSTED-JENSEN, M., Mathematics and Physics
FRANDSEN, F., Ecology and Molecular Biology
FREDHOLM, M., Animal Sciences and Animal Health
FRIIS, C., Pharmacology and Pathobiology
GIESE, H., Ecology and Molecular Biology
GREVE, T., Clinical Sciences
HANSEN, A. K., Pharmacology and Pathobiology
HANSEN, H. C. B., Chemistry
HAVE, H., Agricultural Sciences
HELLES, F., Economics and Natural Resources
HOVE, H., Animal Sciences and Animal Health
HYLDGAARD-JENSEN, J., Anatomy and Physiology
HYTTEL, P., Anatomy and Physiology
JACOBSEN, N., Botany and Forest Genetics
JAKOBSEN, M., Agricultural Sciences
JENSEN, A. L., Clinical Sciences
JENSEN, H. E., Agricultural Sciences
KÆRGAARD, N., Economics and Natural Resources
KJELDSEN-KRAGH, S., Economics and Natural Sciences
LADEWIG, J., Animal Sciences and Animal Health
LARSEN, J. B., Economics and Natural Resources
LARSEN, J. L., Veterinary Microbiology
LARSEN, L. E., General and Inorganic Chemistry
LARSSON, L., Anatomy and Physiology
MADSEN, J., Animal Sciences and Animal Health
MARTENS, M., Dairy and Food Science
MØLLER, B. LINDBERG, Plant Biology
MUNCK, L., Dairy and Food Sciences
NIELSEN, J., Chemistry
NIELSEN, J. P., Clinical Sciences
NIELSEN, N. E., Agricultural Sciences
OLESEN, P. O., Agricultural Sciences
OLSEN, I. A., Economics and Natural Resources
OLSEN, J. E., Veterinary Microbiology
PALMGREN, M., Plant Biology
PORTER, J. R., Agricultural Sciences
PRIMDAHL, J., Economics and Natural Resources
QVIST, K. B., Dairy and Food Sciences
RUDEMO, M., Mathematics and Physics
SANDOE, P., Animal Sciences and Animal Health
SANDSTRÖM, B., Human Nutrition
SEBEK, M., Agricultural Sciences
SKADHAUGE, E., Anatomy and Physiology
SKIBSTED, L. H., Dairy and Food Sciences
SKOVGAARD, I. M., Mathematics and Physics
SØRENSEN, J., Ecology and Molecular Biology
STAUN, H., Animal Sciences and Animal Health
STREIBIG, J. C., Agricultural Sciences
SVALASTOGA, E., Clinical Sciences

SVENDSEN, O., Pharmacology and Pathobiology
THAMSBORG, S. M., Veterinary Microbiology
WEINER, J., Ecology and Molecular Biology

Faculty of Science (Øster Voldgade 3, 1350, Copenhagen K; tel. 35-32-42-12; fax 35-32-80-52; e-mail nat-fak@adm.ku.dk; internet www.nat.ku.dk):

ALS-NIELSEN, J., Experimental Condensed-Matter Physics
AMBJØRN, J., Physics
ANDERSEN, H. H., Physics
ANDERSEN, J. E. B., Human Physiology
ANDERSEN, N. O., Physics
ARCTANDER, P., Zoology
BATES, J. R., Meteorology
BERCHTOLD, M., Molecular Cell Biology
BERG, C., Mathematics
BJØRNHOLM, T., Chemistry
BONDE, H., Human Physiology
BOOMSMA, J., Zoology
BREUNING-MADSEN, H., Geography
CHRISTENSEN, S., Zoology
CHRISTIANSEN, C., Geography, Geomorphology
DAHL-JENSEN, D., Physics
EGEL, R., Genetics
ENGHOFF, H., Zoological Systematics and Zoological Geography
FENCHEL, T. M., Marine Biology
FJELDSÅ, J., Biodiversity
FREI, R. E., Geology
FRIIS, I., Systematic Botany and Plant Geography
GARRETT, R., Biology
GRIMMELIKHUIJZEN CORNELIS, J. P., Zoology
GRUBB, G., Mathematics
HAMANN, O., Botany
HAMMER, C. U., Geophysics
HANSEN, J., Physics
HANSEN, J. R., Physics
HARPER, D. A. T., Geology
HENGLEIN, F., Computer Science
JACKSON, A. O., Theoretical Nuclear Physics
JENSEN, K. H., Geology
JENSEN, K. S., Zoology
JENSEN, M. H., Physics
JOHANSEN, P., Computer Science
JOHANSEN, S., Mathematical Statistics
JONASSON, S. E., Ecological Botany
JONES, N. D., Computer Science
JØRGENSEN, H. E., Astronomy
JUL, E., Computer Science
KIMING, I., Mathematics
KRARUP, J. F., Computer Science
KRISTENSEN, N. P., Systematic Entomology
KRISTENSEN, R. M., Invertebrate Zoology
KROGH, A. S., Bioinformatics
KRÜGER, J., Geography
KÜHL, M., Zoology
LARSEN, E. H., Zoophysiological Laboratory
LARSEN, S. Y., Chemistry
LAURITSEN, F. R., Chemistry
LETH-JØRGENSEN, P., Cell Biology
McGREGOR, P. K., Zoology
MAKOVICKY, E., Geology
MATTHIESSEN, C. W., Geography
MIKKELSEN, K. V., Chemistry
MIKOSCH, T., Mathematics
MOESTRUP, Ø., Spore Plants
MUNDY, J., Plant Physiology
NIELSEN, H. B., Theoretical Physics
NIELSEN, M. S., Freshwater Biology
NIELSEN, O. H., Molecular Biology
NIELSEN, O. J., Chemistry
NOVIKOV, I., Astronomy
ØDUM, N. F., Molecular Biology
OLESEN, P., Physics
PEDERSEN, G. K., Mathematics
PEDERSEN, P. A., Cell Biology
PEJRUP, M., Geography
PFISTER, G. U., Human Physiology
POLZIK, E., Physics

POULSEN, F. M., Molecular Biology
RAHBEK, C., Zoology
RICHTER, E. A., Exercise Physiology, Human Physiology
ROSENDAHL, S., Botany
ROSING, M. T., Geology
SCHMIDLI, H. P., Mathematics
SHAFFER, G., Geophysics
SKELBOE, S., Computer Science
SMITH, H., Physics
SOLOVEJ, J. P., Mathematics
SØRENSEN, M., Mathematics
SURLYK, F., Geology
THYBO, H., Geology
TIND, J., Mathematical Economics
TSCHERNING, C., Geophysics
WILLUMSEN, B. M., Molecular Biology
WINSLØW, C. E. B., Science Education

Faculty of Social Sciences (Kannikestraede 13, 1169 Copenhagen K; tel. 35-32-26-26; fax 35-32-35-32; e-mail samf-fak@samf.ku.dk; internet www.samf.ku.dk):

ANDERSEN, E., Economics
ANDERSEN, E. B., Theoretical Statistics
BERTILSSON, M., Sociology
ESTRUP, H., Economics
GRODAL, B. K., Economics
GØRTZ, E., Social Description
GUNDELACH, P., Sociology
HASTRUP, K., Anthropology
HEURLIN, B., Political Science
HJORTH-ANDERSEN, C., Economics
JØRGENSEN, T. B., Political Science
JUSELIUS, K., Economics
KEIDING, H., Economics
KNUDSEN, T., Political Science
PEDERSEN, O. K., International Politics
PEDERSEN, O. K., Political Science
SCHULTZ, C., Economics
SJØBLOM, B. G., Political Science
SØRENSEN, P. B., Economics
THYGESEN, N. C., Economics
VIND, K., Economic

Faculty of Theology (Købmagergade 44–46, ST, 1150 Copenhagen K; tel. 35-32-26-26; fax 35-32-26-26; e-mail dtf@fak.teol.ku.dk; internet www.teol.ku.dk):

GLEBE-MØLLER, J., Dogmatics
GRANE, L., Church History
GRØN, A., Ethics and Philosophy of Religion
HANSEN, H. B., Church History
HYLDAHL, N. C., New Testament Exegesis
JØRGENSEN, T., Dogmatics
KJELDGAARD-PEDERSEN, S., Church History, History of Dogma
LAUSTEN, M. S., Theology, Danish Church History
LEMCHE, N. P., Old Testament Exegesis
MÜLLER, M., New Testament Exegesis
THOMPSON, T. L., Old Testament Exegesis

ROSKILDE UNIVERSITETSCENTER

POB 260, Universitetsvej 1, 4000 Roskilde
Telephone: 46-74-20-00
Fax: 46-74-30-00
E-mail: ruc@ruc.dk
Internet: www.ruc.dk
Founded 1972
State control
Academic year: September to June (2 semesters)

Rector: HENRIK TOFT JENSEN
Pro-Rector: INGER JENSEN
Admin. Officer: ERIK EBBE
Librarian: NIELS SENIUS CLAUSEN

Library of 500,000 vols
Number of teachers: 500
Number of students: 8,000

PROFESSORS

Humanities:
BRASK, P., Science of Texts, Theory and Methodology of Literary Analysis
BRYLD, C., History
DENCIK, L., Social Psychology
ELLE, B., Educational Psychology
HELTOFT, L., Danish
ILLERIS, K., Educational Research
KAMPMANN, J., Educational Research
KJØRUP, S., Philosophy and Communication
McGUIRE, B. P., History
MORTENSEN, A. T., Philosophy and Communication
NISSEN, G., History
OLESEN, H. S., Educational Psychology
PEDERSEN, S., Philosophy
POULSEN, IB., Danish
POULSEN, J., Journalism
PREISLER, B., English
SCHRØDER, K. CHR., Communication
SIMONSEN, B., Educational Research
WEBER, K., Educational Research
WUCHERPHENNIG, W. P., German

Natural Sciences:
AGGER, P., Environmental Planning
ANDERSEN, O., Environmental Science
BRANDT, J., Geography
DYRE, J. C., Physics
FORBES, V. E., Environmental Biology
GALLAGHER, J. P., Computer Science
HANSEN, P. E., Chemistry
ILLERIS, S., Geography
LØBNER-OLESEN, A., Molecular Biology
NIELSEN, L. K., Transport and Environment
NISS, M., Mathematics
PRÆSTGAARD, E., Chemistry
SCHROLL, H., Environmental Assessment
SIMONSEN, K. F., Geography
SØRENSEN, B. E., Physics
THULSTRUP, E., Chemistry
WESTH-ANDERSEN, P., Chemistry

Social Sciences:
AAGE, H., Political Economy
ANDERSEN, J., Social Sciences
BOGASON, P., Public Administration
BOJE, TH. P., Social Sciences
DAVIS, J. D., Political Economy
FRAMKE, W., Tourism Planning
GREVE, B., Public Administration
JESPERSEN, J., Welfare State Studies
LAURIDSEN, L. S., International Development
MARCUSSEN, H. S., Institutional Aspect of Natural Resource Management
MATTSON, J., Business Administration
NIELSEN, K., Industrial Theory
NIELSEN, K. A., Technological and Organizational Development of Enterprises
OLSEN, O. J., Planning
SCHEUER, S., Social Sciences
SUNDBO, J., Business Administration
TORFING, J., Social Sciences
WHISTON, TH. G., Environmental Regulation

SYDDANSK UNIVERSITET
(University of Southern Denmark)

Campusvej 55, 5230 Odense M
Telephone: 65-50-10-00
Fax: 65-50-10-90
E-mail: sdu@sdu.dk
Internet: www.sdu.dk
Founded 1964 as Odense Univ.; present name 1998, following merger with Handelshøjskole Syd–Ingeniørhøjskole Syd and several other instns of higher education
State control
Languages of instruction: Danish, English
Academic year: September to June (2 semesters)

Rector: JENS ODDERSHEDE
Pro-Rectors: FLEMMING JUST, JØRN HENRIK PETERSEN
Chief Admin. Officer: PER OVERGAARD NIELSEN

Library: see under Libraries and Archives
Number of teachers: 747
Number of students: 16,500
Publication: *Ny Viden* (12 a year)

DEANS

Faculty of Arts: FLEMMING G. ANDERSEN
Faculty of Health Sciences: MOGENS HØRDER
Faculty of Natural and Engineering Sciences: HENRIK PEDERSEN
Faculty of Social Sciences: BJARNE G. SØRENSEN

PROFESSORS

Faculty of Arts (tel. 65-50-29-31; fax 65-93-20-55; internet www.hum.sdu.dk):

BACHE, C., English Language and Literature
BASBØLL, H., Scandinavian Language
BORGNAKKE, K., General Pedagogy
DROTNER, K., Media Studies and Media Culture
HAMMER, O., Religious Studies and Comparative Religion
HOLM, P., Maritime and Regional History
JAKOBSEN, H. G., Scandinavian Language
JENSEN, B., Slavic Studies
JESPERSEN, K. J. V., History
JOHANSEN, J. D., Comparative Literature
JUST, F., History
KLAWONN, E. G., Philosophy
MAI, A.-M., Danish Literature
MORTENSEN, F. H., Scandinavian Language and Literature
NIELSEN, H. F., Historical and Comparative Germanic Linguistics
NYE, D., American Studies
QVORTRUP, L., Multimedia
ROBERING, K., Humanistic Information Science
SAUERBERG, L. O., English Language and Literature
SINHA, C. G., Language and Cognitive Linguistics

Faculty of Health Sciences (Winsløwparken 17/1, 5230 Odense; tel. 65-50-29-32; fax 65-91-89-14; e-mail fac@health-sci.sdu.dk; internet www.sdu.dk/health):

ANDERSEN, K. E., Dermato-venereology
BAKKETEIG, L., Epidemiology
BARINGTON, T., Clinical Immunology
BECK-NIELSEN, H., Medical Endocrinology
BENDIX, T., Biomechanics
BIE, P., Physiology
BINDSLEV-JENSEN, C., Dermatological Allergology
BRO, F., General Practice
BRØSEN, K., Clinical Pharmacology
CHRISTENSEN, K., Ageing and Longevity
DITZEL, H., Biomedicine
DOBBELSTEIN, M., Biomedicine
FENGER, C., Pathology
FINSEN, B., Biomedicine
GRANDJEAN, P. A., Environmental Medicine
GREEN, A., Clinical Epidemiology
HAGHFELT, T., Cardiology
HALLAS, J., Clinical Pharmacology
HØILUND-CARLSEN, P., Clinical Physiology
HOLMSKOV, U., Biomedicine
HØRDER, M., Clinical Chemistry
HUSBY, S., Paediatrics
JAKOBSON, A., Cancer Therapy
JENSEN, W. A., Biomedicine
JUNKER, P., Rheumatology
KASSEM, M., Biomedicine
KOLMOS, H. J., Microbiology
KRAGH-SØRENSEN, P., Psychiatry
LOUS, J., General Practice
MANNICHE, C., Biomechanics

OWENS, T., Biomedicine
PEDERSEN, C., Infectious Medicine
PETERSEN, S., Asthma and Allergy in Childhood
RASMUSSEN, J. Z., Anatomy
RITSKES-HOITINGA, M., Comparative Medicine and Laboratory Animal Science
SAHLIN, K., Exercise Physiology
SCHAFFALITZKY DE MUCKADELL, O. B., Medical Gastroenterology
SCHRØDER, H. D., Neuropathology and Neuromuscular Biology
SJØLIE, A. K., Ophthalmology
SKØTT, O., Physiology
SØRENSEN, T., Psychiatry
THOMSEN, J., Forensic Medicine
TOFT, P., Anaesthesiology
VACH, W., Medical Statistics
VAUPEL, J. W., Demographic Studies
WALTER, S., Surgery
WESTERGAARD, J. G., Obstetrics

Faculty of Natural and Engineering Sciences (tel. 65-50-20-82; fax 65-93-38-05; e-mail natfak@adm.sdu.dk; internet www.sdu.dk/nat):

ANGELOV, C. K., Software Engineering
BERNSEN, N. O., Natural Interactive Systems
BJERREGAARD, P., Biology
BUUR, J., User-oriented Product Development
CANFIELD, D., Biology
DOUTHWAITE, S. R., Molecular Biology
DYBKJÆR, L., Natural Interactive Systems
GERDES, K., Molecular Microbiology
HAAGERUP, U., Mathematics
ISSINGER, O., Biochemistry
JENSEN, J. B., Computer Science
JENSEN, O. N., Protein Mass Spectrometry
JØRGENSEN, B., Statistics
KNUDSEN, J., Biochemistry
KORNERUP, P., Computer Science
KRISTENSEN, B. B., Software Engineering
KRISTIANSEN, K., Eukaryotic Molecular Biology
LARSEN, K. S., Computer Science
LUND, H. H., Information Technology
McKENZIE, C. J., Nanobioscience
MANN, M., Molecular Biology
MICHELSEN, A., Biology
MOURITSEN, O. G., Physics
NIELSEN, H. T., Chemistry
ØSTERGARD, J. E., Physics and Technology
PEDERSEN, H., Mathematics
PERRAM, J. W., Applied Mathematics
PETERSEN, H. G., Applied Mathematics
ROEPSTORFF, P., Molecular Biology
RUBAHN, H.-G., Physics and Technology
RØRDAM, M., Mathematics
SIGMUND, H. P., Physics
TOWN, R. M., Chemistry
VALENTIN-HANSEN, P., Molecular Biology
WENGEL, J., Chemistry
WIIL, U. K., Software Engineering
WILLATZEN, H., Mathematical Modelling

Faculty of Social Sciences (tel. 65-50-29-03; fax 65-93-56-92; e-mail office@sam.sdu.dk; internet www.sam.sdu.dk):

ASKEGAARD, S., Business Studies
BAGER, T., Business Studies
BOUCHET, D., Business Studies
CHRISTENSEN, J. A., Business Studies
CHRISTENSEN, L. T., Business Studies
CHRISTENSEN, P. M., Political Sciences
CHRISTENSEN, P. O., Business Studies
CHRISTENSEN, P. R., Business Studies
CHRISTIANSEN, T., Health Economics
CLAUSEN, N. J., Law
DAHLER-LARSEN, P., Political Sciences
ERIKSEN, B., Business Studies
FREYTAG, P. V., Business Studies
FRIMOR, H., Business Studies
GYRD-HANSEN, D., Health Economics
HANSEN, J. D., Business Studies
HANSEN, S. F., Law

JENSEN, S. E. H., National Economics
JØRGENSEN, N., Business Studies
JØRGENSEN, S., Business Studies
KAISER, V., National Economics
KLAUSEN, K. K., Public Organization Theory
KNUDSEN, T., Business Studies
LARSEN, P., Journalism
LAURSEN, F., Political Science
LUND, A., Journalism
MADSEN, T. K., Business Studies
MORTENSEN, B. O., Law
MOURITZEN, P. E., Political Sciences
MUNK, C., Business Studies
OBEL, B., Business Studies
PEDERSEN, K. M., Health Economics
PEDERSEN, M. N., Political Sciences
PETERSEN, H., Law
PETERSEN, J. H., Social Science
PETERSEN, N. C., Business Studies
SKYRUM-NIELSEN, P., Journalism
SLOTH, B., National Economics
SØRENSEN, C. J., National Economics
STEINICKE, M., Law
TETZSCHNER, H., Business Economics
VESTERGAARD, N., Business Economics

University-level Institutions

Arkitektskolen i Århus (Århus School of Architecture): Nørreport 20, 8000 Århus C; tel. 89-36-00-00; fax 86-13-06-45; e-mail a@aarch.dk; internet www.aarch.dk; f. 1965; architectural design, planning, furniture and industrial design; 100 teachers; 900 students; library: 44,000 vols; Rector PETER KRARUP KJÆR; publs *Skolehåndbogen* (1 a year), *Virksomhedsregnskab* (1 a year).

Danmarks Biblioteksskole (Royal School of Library and Information Science): Birketinget 6, 2300 Copenhagen S; tel. 32-58-60-66; fax 32-84-02-01; e-mail db@db.dk; internet www.db.dk; f. 1956; library: 182,000 vols; 65 teachers; 1,000 students; Rector LEIF LØRRING.

Attached Institute:

Danmarks Biblioteksskole Aalborg (Royal School of Library and Information Science, Aalborg): Sohngårdsholmsvej 2, 9000 Aalborg; tel. 98-15-79-22; fax 98-15-10-42; e-mail dbaa@db.dk; internet www.db.dk; f. 1973; Head LEIF EMEREK.

Danmarks Designskole (Danish School of Design): Strandboulevarden 47, 2100 Copenhagen Ø; tel. 35-27-75-00; fax 35-27-76-00; e-mail mail@dkds.dk; internet www.dkds.dk; f. 1875 as Tegne- og Kunstindustriskolen (School of Drawing and Art Industry); part of Danish National Centre for Design Research; fashion, furniture, graphic communication and digital design, glass, industrial design, pottery, scenography, space, textiles; 650 students; Pres. GØSTA KNUDSEN.

Designskolen Kolding (Kolding Design School): Ågade 10, 6000 Kolding; tel. 76-30-11-00; fax 76-30-11-12; e-mail dk@designskolenkolding.dk; internet www.designskolenkolding.dk; f. 1967; institute for form and theory, fashion and textiles, visual communication, industrial design and interactive media; department of ceramics; temporary exhibitions; 380 students; Rector BIRTE SANDORFF.

Fynske Musikkonservatorium (Carl Nielsen Academy of Music): Islandsgade 2, 5000 Odense C; tel. 66-11-06-63; fax 66-17-77-63; e-mail dfm@adm.dfm.dk; internet www.dfm.dk; f. 1929; 75 teachers; 150 students; library: 35,000 books and scores; Pres. BERTEL KRARUP.

Ingeniørhøjskolen i Århus (Engineering College of Århus): Dalgas Ave 2, 8000 Århus C; tel. 87-30-22-00; fax 87-30-22-01; e-mail iha@iha.dk; internet www.iha.dk; f. 1903; library: 18,000 vols; 110 teachers; 1,400 students; Rector OVE POULSEN.

Ingeniørhøjskolen i København (Engineering College of Copenhagen): Lautrupvang 15, 2750 Ballerup; tel. 44-80-50-88; fax 44-80-50-44; e-mail rector@ihk.dk; internet www.ihk.dk; f. 1879; applied sciences; awards BSc in engineering; library: 32,900 vols; 186 teachers; 2,100 students; Rector FLEMMING KROGH.

Ingeniørhøjskolen Odense Teknikum: Niels Bohrs Alle 1, 5230 Odense M; tel. 63-14-03-00; fax 63-14-03-04; e-mail iot@iot.dk; internet www.iot.dk; f. 1905; library: 30,000 vols; 130 teachers; 1,300 students; Rector HENNING ANDERSEN; Registrar KRISTINE LYNGBO.

Jyske Musikkonservatorium (Royal Academy of Music, Århus): Fuglesangs Allé 26, 8210 Århus V; tel. 89-48-33-88; fax 89-48-33-22; e-mail info@musik-kons.dk; internet www.musik-kons.dk; f. 1927; 150 teachers; 350 students; Principal FINN SCHUMACKER; Administrator KNUD AARUP.

Københavns Tekniske Skole (Copenhagen Technical Academy and Copenhagen Polytechnic): Lygten 16, 2400 Copenhagen NV; tel. 35-86-35-86; fax 35-86-35-87; e-mail kts@kts.dk; internet www.kts.dk; 500 staff; 6,000 students; Dir MOGENS NIELSEN.

Kongelige Danske Kunstakademi, Konservatorskolen (Royal Danish Academy of Fine Arts, School of Conservation): Esplanaden 34, 1263 Copenhagen K; tel. 33-74-47-00; fax 33-74-47-77; e-mail kons@kons.dk; internet www.kons.dk; f. 1973; library: 7,000 vols, 150 periodicals; 20 teachers; 100 students; Rector RENÉ LARSEN.

Kongelige Danske Kunstakademis Arkitektskole (School of Architecture of the Royal Danish Academy of Fine Arts): Philip de Langes Allé 10, 1435 Copenhagen K; tel. 32-68-60-00; fax 32-68-61-11; e-mail arkitektskolen@karch.dk; internet www.karch.dk; f. 1754; library: see Libraries and Archives; 1,100 students; Rector SVEN FELDING.

Kongelige Danske Kunstakademis Billedkunstskoler (School of Visual Arts of the Royal Danish Academy of Fine Arts): Kgs. Nytorv 1, Postboks 3014, 1021 Copenhagen K; tel. 33-74-46-00; fax 33-74-46-66; e-mail bk@kunstakademiet.dk; internet www.kunstakademiet.dk; f. 1754; library: see Libraries and Archives; Rector ELSE MARIE BUKDAHL.

Kongelige Danske Musikkonservatorium (Royal Danish Academy of Music): Rosenørns Allé 22, 1970 Frederiksberg C; tel. 72-26-72-26; fax 72-26-72-72; e-mail dkdm@dkdm.dk; internet www.dkdm.dk; f. 1867; library: 50,000 vols; 170 teachers; 400 students; Principal STEEN PADE; Administrator BJARNE BACH ØSTERGAARD; Librarian TOVE KRAG.

Nordjysk Musikkonservatorium (Academy of Music, Ålborg): Ryesgade 52, 9000 Ålborg; tel. 98-12-77-44; fax 98-11-37-63; e-mail nordkons@nordkons.dk; internet www.nordkons.dk; f. 1930; 60 teachers; 115 students; Rector JENS-OLE BLAK.

Rytmisk Musikkonservatorium (Rhythmic Music Conservatory): Leo Mathisens Vej 1, Holmen, 1437 Copenhagen K; tel. 32-68-67-00; fax 32-68-67-66; e-mail rmc@rmc.dk; internet www.rmc.dk; f. 1986; state control; attached to Ministry of Cultural Affairs; music teaching, music and movement, music performance, sound engineering, music management; 80 teachers; 200 students; Rector HENRIK SVEIDAHL.

Teknologisk Institut (Technological Institute): Gregersensvej, 2630 Tåstrup; tel. 72-20-20-00; fax 72-20-20-19; e-mail info@ teknologisk.dk; internet www.teknologisk .dk; f. 1906; building technology, energy, environment, industry, industrial and business development; 10,000 course partici-

pants; maintains br. in Århus; Pres. SØREN STJERNQVIST.

Vestjysk Musikkonservatorium (Academy of Music, Esbjerg): Kirkegade 61–63, 6700 Esbjerg; tel. 76-10-43-00; fax 76-10-43-10; e-mail info@vmk.dk; internet www.vmk .dk; f. 1946; 70 teachers; 120 students; Dir AXEL MOMME.

Vitus Bering Center for Videregående Uddannelse (Vitus Bering Centre for Higher Education): Strandpromenaden 4C, 8700 Horsens; tel. 76-25-50-00; fax 76-25-51-00; e-mail cvu@vitusbering.dk; internet www .vitusbering.dk; f. 1915; library: 27,000 vols; 260 teachers; 2,000 students; Dir SVEND TRØST; Pro-Rectors SUSAN DALUM, GUNNAR ERIKSEN, BENT BRUUN PEDERSEN; Dir of Studies HANS JØRN HANSEN.

FAROE ISLANDS

Learned Societies

GENERAL

Føroya Fróðskaparfelag/Societas Scientiarum Faeroensis (Faroese Society of Science and Letters): POB 209, FO110 Tórshavn; tel. and fax 322074; e-mail fff@ frodskaparfelag.fo; internet www .frodskaparfelag.fo; f. 1952; procures scientific and scholarly literature and promotes research work; 170 mems; Pres. Dr ANDRAS MORTENSEN; publs *Fróðskaparrit* (Annals), *Supplementa*.

HISTORY, GEOGRAPHY AND ARCHAEOLOGY

Føroya Forngripafelag (Faroese Archaeological Society): POB 1173, FO110 Tórshavn; tel. 312259; f. 1898; attached to Føroya Fornminnissavn (Historical Museum); works in conjunction with the Nat. Museum of Antiquities; 325 mems; Pres. MORTAN WINTHER POULSEN.

LANGUAGE AND LITERATURE

Rithøvundafelag Føroya (Faroese Writers' Association): POB 1124, FO100 Tórshavn; e-mail rit@rit.fo; internet www .rit.fo; f. 1957; promotes the growth of Faroese literature and protects authors' rights; 102 mems; Pres. RAKEL HELMSDAL.

Research Institutes

AGRICULTURE, FISHERIES AND VETERINARY SCIENCE

Havstovan (Faroe Marine Research Institute): Nóatún 1, POB 3051, FO110 Tórshavn; tel. 353900; fax 353901; e-mail hav@hav.fo; internet www.frs.fo; f. 1951; attached to govt of the Faroe Islands; depts of environment, fisheries and technology; Dir EILIF GAARD; publ. *Fiskirannsóknir* (1 or 2 a year).

Heilsufrøðiliga starvsstovan (Faroese Food and Veterinary Agency): Falkavegur 6, 2 hædd, FO100 Tórshavn; tel. 556400; fax 556401; e-mail hfs@hfs.fo; internet www.hfs .fo; f. 1975; research, services, quality control and inspection in the fish and food industry and in the environment; govt dept; Dir BARÐUR ENNI.

Libraries and Archives

Tórshavn

Býarbókasavnid (Public Library): Mánadag fríggjadag kl. 10–18, Leygardag kl. 10–14 Niels Finsens gøtu 7, FO100 Tórshavn; tel. 302020; fax 302031; e-mail bbs@bbs.fo; internet www.byarbok.fo; f. 1969; 73,000 vols; City Librarian ANNA BRIMNES; Librarian HANNE MAGNUSSEN.

Føroya Landsbókasavn (National Library of the Faroe Islands): J. C. Svabosgøtu 16, POB 61, FO110 Tórshavn; tel. (298) 356500; fax (298) 318895; e-mail utlan@flb.fo; internet www.flb.fo; f. 1828; attached to govt of the Faroe Islands; open to the public; responsible for 15 public and 11 school libraries; 168,083 vols (20,000 scientific vols); Dir MARJUN PATURSSON; Librarian ARNBJØRN O. DALSGARÐ; publ. *Føroyskur Bókalisti* (list of Faeroese publs, 1 a year).

Landsskjalasavnið (National Archives of the Faroe Islands): V. U. Hammershaimbsgøta 24, FO100 Tórshavn; tel. 316677; fax 318677; e-mail fararch@lss.fo; internet www .lss.fo; f. 1932; medieval documents (1298–1599), archives of parliament and central and local admin. (1615–1980); Dir SÁMAL T. F. JOHANSEN; Archivist JOHN KJÆR.

Museums and Art Galleries

Tórshavn

Føroya Fornminnissavn (National Museum of Archaeology and Cultural History): Kúrdalsvegur 2, POB 1155, FO110 Tórshavn; tel. 310700; fax 312259; e-mail fornminni@fornminni.fo; internet www .fornminni.fo; f. 1898, taken over by State 1952; archaeology, ethnology, inspection of ancient monuments; Dir ANDRAS MORTENSEN; Museum Curator ERLAND VIBERG JOENSEN.

Føroya Náttúrugripasavn (Natural History Museum): V. U. Hammershaimbsgøta 13, FO100 Tórshavn; tel. 352300; fax 352301; e-mail ngs@ngs.fo; internet www.ngs.fo; f. 1955; depts of botany, zoology; Dir DORETE BLOCH.

Savnið 1940-45 (Faroe-British Museum): POB 362, FO110 Tórshavn; tel. 312074; f. 1983; military and civilian artefacts from British occupation during Second World War (1939–1945).

University

FRÓÐSKAPARSETUR FØROYA/ UNIVERSITAS FÆROENSIS (University of the Faroe Islands)

J. C. Svabos gøta 14, POB 272, FO110 Tórshavn

Telephone: 352500
Fax: 352501
E-mail: setur@setur.fo
Internet: www.setur.fo

Founded 1965
Language of instruction: Faroese
Academic year: September to June

Rector: JÓAN PAULI JOENSEN
Vice-Rector: SÚSANNA M. MORTENSEN
Univ. Dir: RÚNA HJELM
Chair.: HERÁLVUR JOENSEN
Sec. Gen.: RÚNA HJELM

Number of teachers: 63
Number of students: 530

DEANS

Faculty of Language and Literature: TURIÐ SIGURÐARDÓTTIR
Faculty of History and Social Sciences: KÁRI Á RÓGVI
Faculty of Natural Sciences and Technology: HANS PAULI JOENSEN
Nursing College: SÚSANNA M. MORTENSEN
Teachers College: JÓANNES HANSEN

PROFESSORS

ANDREASSEN, E., Oral Literature
BLOCH, D., Zoology
BROWN, R. J., Geophysics
HANSEN, B., Oceanography
JOENSEN, J. P., History and Ethnology
MARNERSDÓTTIR, M., Literature
SIGURDARDÓTTIR, T., Literature
SPARRE ANDERSEN, M., Geophysics

GREENLAND

Regulatory Body
GOVERNMENT
Ministry of Culture, Education, Research and The Church: Indaleeqqap Aqq. 3, POB 1029, 3900 Nuuk; tel. (299) 345000; fax (299) 322073; e-mail kiiip@nanoq.gl; internet uk.nanoq.gl/emner/government/departments.aspx; Min. MIMI KARLSEN.

Learned Societies
GENERAL
Grønlandske Selskab (The Greenland Society): see under Denmark.

Nunani Avannarlerni Piorsarsimassutsikkut Attaveqaat (NAPA)/Nordens Institut i Grønland (The Nordic Institute of Greenland): Imaneq 21, POB 770, 3900 Nuuk; tel. (299) 324733; fax (299) 325733; e-mail napa@napa.gl; internet www.napa.gl; f. 1987; cultural instn: financed by the Nordic Ccl of Mins, 5 Nordic countries and 3 home rule areas within them; develops, supports and stimulates Greenlandic cultural life, prioritizing youth and children; advances inter-Nordic cultural relations; Dir (vacant); Chair. VIVIAN MOEN; Deputy Chair. CLAUS NIELSEN; Institute Man. ANDERS BERNDTSSON; Project Man. BOAZ MILLER.

BIBLIOGRAPHY, LIBRARY SCIENCE AND MUSEOLOGY
NUKAKA–Nunatsinni Katersugaasiviit Kattuffiat/Sammenslutningen af museer i Grønland (Association of Museums in Greenland): c/o Nunatta Katersugaasivia Allagaateqarfialu, POB 145, 3900 Nuuk; tel. (299) 322611; fax (299) 642833; e-mail hans.lange@natmus.gl; internet www.nukaka.gl; f. 1993; supports the interests and devt of archives, local and spec. museums; Chair. HANS LANGE; Vice-Chair. TEA DAHL CHRISTENSEN; Treas. OLE G. JENSEN.

FINE AND PERFORMING ARTS
'Simerneq' (Artists' Society): POB 1009, 3900 Nuuk; f. 1979; arranges exhibitions of works of mems and others; Sec. INGER HAUGE.

LANGUAGE AND LITERATURE
Kalaallit Atuakkiortut/Den Grønlandske Forfatterforening (Greenlandic Authors' Society): c/o ICC, Dronning Ingridsvej 1, POB 25, 3900 Nuuk; tel. (299) 323632; fax (299) 323001; e-mail kalatu@greennet.gl; internet forfatternet.katak.gl; f. 1975; copyrights for authors and translators; writing workshops and poetry festivals fostering interest in poetry among the youth; 80 mems; Pres. HANS A. LYNGE; Chair. AQQALUK LYNGE; Secs RIIKKI GRONVOLD, KARL ELIAS OLSEN; Treas ANE MARIE B. PEDERSEN, T. P. POULSEN; publ. *Kalaaleq* (magazine).

Research Institutes
AGRICULTURE, FISHERIES AND VETERINARY SCIENCE
Forsøgsstationen 'Upernaviarsuk' (Upernaviarsuk Agricultural Research Station): POB 152, 3920 Qaqortoq; tel. (299) 649303; e-mail forsupv@greennet.gl; govt instn carrying out experiments in sheep rearing, fodder crops, tree planting and gardening in a polar environment.

MEDICINE
Greenland Institute for Circumpolar Health Research: Peqqissaannermik Ilinniarfik, POB 1499, 3900 Nuuk; e-mail gihr@peqqik.gl; internet www.pi.gl/content/dk/greenland_institute_f_circumpolar_health_research; f. 2008; attached to Peqqissaannermik Ilinniarfik; enhances cooperation between researchers from other countries and health professionals in Greenland; develops, exchanges, disseminates and applies scientific knowledge; creates nat. and int. networks; Chair. KARIN LADEFOGED; Vice-Chair. and Sec. GERT MULVAD; Research Dir Prof. PETER BJERREGAARD; Treas. SUZANNE MØLLER.

NATURAL SCIENCES
General
Dansk Polarcenter (Danish Polar Center): Strandgade 102, 1401 Copenhagen K, Denmark; tel. 32-88-01-00; fax 32-88-01-01; e-mail dpc@dpc.dk; internet www.dpc.dk; f. 1989; attached to Danish Agency for Science, Technology and Innovation; supports and coordinates Arctic and Antarctic research in Denmark and Greenland; provides information on polar issues; library of 35,000 vols incl. 26,000 books, 9,000 pamphlets, 3,000 theses, 700 periodicals (300 current); Dir HANNE PETERSEN; Librarian VIBEKE SLOTH JAKOBSEN.

Kommissionen for Videnskabelige Undersøgelser i Grønland (Commission for Scientific Research in Greenland): Forsknings- og Innovationsstyrelsen, Forskningspolitisk Center, Bredgade 40, 1260 Copenhagen K, Denmark; tel. and fax 35-44-63-66; e-mail kec@fi.dk; internet www.kvug.dk; f. 1878; attached to Danish Agency for Science, Technology and Innovation; Greenlandic-Danish comm.; proposes jt strategies for polar research; Chair. Prof. MINIK ROSING; Deputy Chair. DANIEL THORLEIFSEN; Spec. Consultant KIRSTEN CANING; publ. *Grønlandsforskning historie og perspektiver*.

Biological Sciences
Arctic Station, University of Copenhagen: see under Denmark.

Danmarks Miljøundersøgelser, Afdeling for Arktisk Miljø (National Environmental Research Institute): Frederiksborgvej 399, POB 358, 4000 Roskilde, Denmark; tel. 46-30-12-00; fax 46-30-19-14; e-mail dmu@dmu.dk; internet www.dmu.dk; f. 1989; attached to Aarhus Univ.; monitors esp. effects of mineral exploitation, climate change ecology in the Arctic, contaminants in Arctic ecosystems; marine mammal research and monitoring; coordinates the Greenland Ecosystem Monitoring programme; 3 research sections: applied arctic environmental research, climate effects and systems modelling, marine mammals and toxicology; 420 staff; Research Dir JESPER MADSEN.

Grønlands Naturinstitut/Pinngortitaleriffik (Greenland Institute of Natural Resources): POB 570, 3900 Nuuk; tel. (299) 361200; fax (299) 361212; e-mail info@natur.gl; internet www.natur.gl; applied research in natural resources, environmental protection and biodiversity; depts of birds and mammals, fish and shrimp, marine ecology and climate impact; Dir KLAUS HOYER NYGAARD; Chair. LENE KIELSEN HOLM.

Physical Sciences
Danmarks Meteorologiske Institut (Danish Meteorological Institute): see under Denmark.

Libraries
Nuuk
Groenlandica (Greenlandic National Library): Manutooq 1, POB 1074, 3900 Nuuk; tel. (299) 362380; fax (299) 362381; e-mail groenlandica@katak.gl; internet www.groenlandica.gl; f. 2008; attached to Nunatta Atuagaateqarfia (Nat. Library of Greenland); harvests, records and stores all Greenlandic literature and publs; colln of foreign literature and information about Inuit and the Arctic area; nat. colln; spec. collns: Samuel Petrus Kleinschmidts Reference Library and Archive, The Oldendow Colln, Svend Frederiksen's Archive, The Jonathan Petersen Colln, The Frederik Nielsen (Faré) Colln; 16,000 vols in nat. colln, 23,724 in study colln; Head CHARLOTTE D. ANDERSON.

Nunatta Atuagaateqarfia/Grønlandske Landsbibliotek (National Library of Greenland): Imaneq 26, POB 1011, 3900 Nuuk; tel. (299) 321156; fax (299) 348949; e-mail nalib@katak.gl; internet www.katak.gl; 70,426 vols; Dir ELISA JEREMIASSEN; Librarian KIRSTEN BIRKEFOSS; Librarian KIRSTEN HEILMANN; Librarian SØREN JENSEN; Librarian STEEN JEPPSON; Librarian VIVI MOTZFELDT.

Museums
Ilulissat
Ilulissat Museum: Nuisariannguaq 9, POB 99, 3952 Ilulissat; tel. (299) 943643; e-mail ilumus@ilulissat.gl; internet www.ilumus.gl; f. 1979; local, cultural and natural history; cultural history of the North Greenlandic sledgedog and the Sermermiut settlement; library and archive of photographs and materials on Knud Rasmussen; Curator and Head of Museum Mag. KIRSTEN STRANDGAARD.

Kangilinnguit
Ivittuut Mine- og Mineralmuseum (Ivittuut Mining and Mineral Museum): 3930 Kangilinnguit; tel. (299) 691077; fax (299) 691073; e-mail museum.ivittuut@sermersooq.gl; internet www.ivittuut.dk/museum; f. 2006; minerals and industrial history and the use of Greenland's raw materials; Pres. PER NUKAARAQ HANSEN; Curator HELLE B. PETERSEN.

Nuuk

Nunatta Katersugaasivia Allagaateqar-fialu/Grønlands Nationalmuseum og Arkiv (Greenland National Museum and Archive): Hans Egedesvej 8, POB 145, DK-3900 Nuuk; tel. (299) 322611; fax (299) 322622; e-mail nka@natmus.gl; internet www.natmus.gl; f. 1966; advises the Home Rule Government in matters concerning archaeological excavations and the final deposition of the excavated material; maintains the central files about preserved ruins, graveyards, buildings and participates in nature conservation and town planning; collns cover the 4,500 years of history in Greenland; collns: Inuit Archaeological Collns, Norse Collns, Gustav Holm Colln (Ammassalik c. 1880), Inughuit and Polar-eskimos (c. 1900), Kayaks; arts, handicrafts and photo colln; Dir DANIEL THORLEIFSEN; Deputy Dir PAULINE KNUDSEN; Curator MIKKEL MYRUP.

Nuuk Kunstmuseum/Nuup Katersugaa-sivii (Nuuk Artmuseum): Kissarneqqor-tuunnguaq 5, POB 1005, 3900 Nuuk; tel. (299) 327733; e-mail kunstmuseum@greennet.gl; internet www .nuukkunstmuseum.gl; f. 2005 by Svend and Helen Junge; displays Svend and Helen Junge's 45-year colln of 300 pictures, paintings, drawings and graphics, 400 sculptures made of soapstone, tooth and wood, colln of 150 paintings by Emanuel A. Petersen (1894–1948).

Qaqortoq

Qaqortoq Museum: Torvevej B-29, POB 154, 3920 Qaqortoq; tel. (299) 641080; fax (299) 642833; e-mail geny@qaqortoq.gl; Dir OLE G. JENSEN.

Qasigiannguit

Qasigiannguit Katersugaasiviat/Qasi-giannguit lokalmuseum (Qasigiannguit Museum): Poul Egedesvej 24, POB 130, 3951 Qasigiannguit; tel. and fax (299) 911477; e-mail qasmus@qaasuitsup.gl; internet www.museum.gl/qasigiannguit; 5

bldgs with separate exhibitions; displays a permanent exhibition of costumes and fishing equipment, colln of stuffed Arctic birds, unique items from the 4,500-year-old Saqqaq culture (first human settlement in West Greenland); provisions for overnight stay at museum cottage for visitors; Dir LAILA MIKAELSEN.

Upernavik

Upernaviup Katersugaasivia (Upernavik Museum): Niuertup Ottup Aqq. B-12, POB 93, 3962 Upernavik; tel. (299) 961085; e-mail inussuk@greennet.gl; internet www .upernivik.gl; f. c. 1950; historical objects, items representing Greenland's hunting culture; colln of photographs; Upernavik Retreat: artist's residence.

University

ILISIMATUSARFIK/GRØNLANDS UNIVERSITET
(University of Greenland)

Manutooq 1, POB 1061, 3900 Nuuk

Telephone: (299) 362300

Fax: (299) 362301

E-mail: mail@uni.gl

Internet: www.ilisimatusarfik.gl

Founded 1984

Public control

Vice-Chancellor (Rector and Pres.): OLE MARQUARDT

Pro-Vice-Chancellor: KAREN LANGGÅRD

Univ. Librarian: BOLETHE OLSEN

Library of 25,000 vols, 125 journals

Number of teachers: 14

Number of students: 150

Publication: *Grønlandsk Kultur- og Samfundsforskning* (1 a year)

3 Univ. instns: Ilimmarfik Institute (depts of cultural and social history, journalism, language, literature and media, management and economics, social work, theology and

religion); institutes of learning (Arctic education and teacher training), nursing and health sciences.

Colleges

Eqqumiitsuliornermik Ilinniarfik/Kunstskolen (School of Arts): c/o KIIIP, POB 286, 3900 Nuuk; tel. (299) 322640; fax (299) 322644; e-mail kunst@greennet.gl; f. 1973; Dir ARNANNGUAQ HØEGH.

Ilinniarfissuaq/Grønlands Seminarium (Greenlands Teacher Training College): C. E. Jansensvej 2, POB 1026, 3900 Nuuk; tel. (299) 321191; fax (299) 322099; e-mail ilinnia@teachnet.gl; internet www .ilinniarfissuaq.gl; f. 1845; attached to Univ. of Greenland; pedagogical, social and administrative education and in-service training; 25 teachers; 163 students; Rector DORTHE KORNELIUSSEN; Librarian LIDA LORENTZEN.

Niuernermik Ilinniarfik/Grønlands Handelsskole (Greenland Business College): Aqqusinersuaq 18, POB 1038, 3900 Nuuk; tel. (299) 323099; fax (299) 323255; e-mail ninuuk@ninuuk.gl; internet www .ninuuk.gl; f. 1979; courses and in-service training in journalism, interpreting and mercantile matters, also technical mercantile training; library: 8,000 vols, 27 journal titles on finance, IT, management, marketing, personnel and sales; 15 full-time teachers; 250 full-time students; Dir BO NÓRRESLET; Librarian CHRISTIAN KIRKEGAARD.

Peqqissaanermik Ilinniarfik (Centre for Health Studies): Centre for Sundhedsuddannelser, POB 1499, 3900 Nuuk; tel. (299) 349950; fax (299) 323985; e-mail cfspost@nanoq.gl; internet www.pi.gl; f. 1993; attached to Dept of Culture, Education, Research and the Church; nurse training, health care and health education; 40 students; Superintendent LISA EZEKIASSEN; Librarian HANNE KRISTOFFERSEN.

DJIBOUTI

The Higher Education System

Higher education in Djibouti is modelled after the French system. The sole university in Djibouti, the Université de Djibouti, was founded in 2006 to replace the Pôle Universitaire de Djibouti, which was founded in 2000 and had 1,928 students in 2005/06. Higher education is the responsibility of the Ministry of National and Higher Education.

The University offers undergraduate and postgraduate courses, and admission is on the basis of secondary school qualifications including the Baccalauréat de l'Enseignement Secondaire, the Baccalauréat Technologique or the Baccalauréat Professionnel. Higher education degrees are divided into three cycles: the Diplôme d'Etudes Universitaires Générales (DEUG) or Diplôme Universitaire de Technologie (DUT) is awarded after two years; the Licence requires one further year of study and the Maîtrise two; and finally the Diplôme Universitaire d'études Approfondies (DEA) is awarded after a further two years of study.

Regulatory Bodies

GOVERNMENT

Ministry of Communication and Culture: BP 32, 1 rue de Moscou, Djibouti; tel. 355672; fax 353957; e-mail mccpt@intnet.dj; internet www.mccpt.dj; Minister ALI ABDI FARAH.

Ministry of National and Higher Education: BP 16, Cité Ministérielle, Djibouti; tel. 350997; fax 354234; e-mail education.gov@intnet.dj; internet www.education.gov.dj; Minister ABDI IBRAHIM ABSIEH.

Learned Society

LANGUAGE AND LITERATURE

Alliance Française: BP 56, Djibouti; tel. 353091; fax 355957; e-mail alliance-francaise@intnet.dj; offers courses and examinations in French language and culture and promotes cultural exchange with France.

Research Institute

GENERAL

Institut Supérieur d'Etudes et de Recherches Scientifiques et Techniques (ISERT): BP 486, Djibouti; tel. 352795; fax 354812; Dir NABIL MOHAMED.

Library

Djibouti

Assemblée Nationale, Service de la Bibliothèque: BP 138, Djibouti; tel. 350172; fax 355503; f. 1977; 2,000 vols; Librarian ILTIREH DJAMA GUIREH.

University

UNIVERSITÉ DE DJIBOUTI

Ave Georges Clemenceau, BP 1904, Djibouti
Telephone: 250459
Fax: 250474
E-mail: ud@univ.edu.dj
Internet: www.univ.edu.dj

Founded 2000 as Pôle Universitaire de Djibouti, present name adopted 2006
Rector: AIDID ADEN GUEDI
Sec.-Gen.: PHILIPPE RIBIERE
Librarian: SAFIA ALI SAID
Number of teachers: 96
Number of students: 1,749

DIRECTORS
Faculty of Languages, Literature and Human Sciences: ABDOULMALIK IBRAHIM ZEID
Faculty of Law, Economics, Management and Tertiary Technological Procedures: Mag. TEEREY IBRAHIM
Faculty of Sciences and Industrial Technological Procedures: IBRAHIM SOULEIMAN GUILLEM

DOMINICA

The Higher Education System

Higher education is provided by a centre of the University of the West Indies, and the Ross University School of Medicine in Dominica (affiliated to Ross University School of Medicine, NJ, in the USA). There is also a teacher-training college and nursing school. In 1995/96 there were 461 students in higher education.

Admission to higher education is based on the Caribbean Examinations Council Secondary Education Certificate or GCE A-levels and O-levels. Students may also be required to sit an entrance examination. The University of the West Indies offers undergraduate Bachelors and postgraduate Masters degrees.

Regulatory Body

GOVERNMENT

Ministry of Education, Sports, and Youth Affairs: Kennedy Ave, Roseau; tel. 4482401; fax 4480644; e-mail minedu@cwdom.dm; Minister VINCE HENDERSON.

Learned Society

LANGUAGE AND LITERATURE

Alliance Française: Elmshall Rd, Bath Estate Bridge, POB 251, Roseau; tel. 4484557; fax 4486008; offers courses and examinations in French language and culture and promotes cultural exchange with France.

Library

Roseau

Library of the House of Assembly: Victoria St, Roseau; tel. 4482401; fax 4498353; f.

1968; 300 vols of parliamentary reports, Proceedings of the House, speeches, ministerial statements, debates, legislation.

Museum

Roseau

Dominica Museum: Bay Front, Roseau; tel. 4488923; exhibits on Dominica's geology, history, archaeology, economy and culture, including its pre-Columbian population and the slave trade.

University

ROSS UNIVERSITY SCHOOL OF MEDICINE IN DOMINICA

POB 266, Portsmouth
Telephone: 4455355
Fax: 4455383

New York office: 460 West 34th St, 12th Floor, New York, NY 10001, USA
Telephone: (212) 279-5500 (New York)
Fax: (212) 629-3147 (New York)
Internet: www.rossmed.edu.dm; attached to Ross University School of Medicine, NJ (USA)
Library of 5,000 books, 190 current journals, 100 audiovisual items, 30 multimedia programmes.

College

University of the West Indies, Dominica Centre: Univ. Centre, POB 82, Roseau; tel. 4483182; fax 4488706; e-mail uwi@cwdom.dm; internet www.cavehill.uwi.edu/bnccde/dominica.

The Higher Education System

The Universidad Autónoma de Santo Domingo, founded by Papal Bull in 1538, claims to be the oldest university in the Americas. Other universities in the Republic were all founded during the 20th century. There are 16 public and private universities under the supervision of the Consejo Nacional de Educación Superior. In 2003/04 there were 293,565 students enrolled in universities. There are also 31 other institutions recognised by the Ministry of Higher Education, Science and Technology. In 2007/08 there were 41,314 students enrolled in vocational studies.

The secondary school qualification (Bachillerato) is the main requirement for admission to higher education. Undergraduate students are awarded the Licenciado or professional title after four years of study, and postgraduate students receive the Maestría after one- to three-years' study following the Licenciado. In some disciplines (law, medicine, dentistry, veterinary medicine) the Doctorado degree may be awarded. Both universities and technological institutes offer technical and vocational education. Courses last for two to three years and students gain the title Técnico.

In 2010 the Government agreed a US $100m. loan with the Inter-American Development Bank for school improvements as part of its 10-year plan for education.

Regulatory and Representative Bodies

GOVERNMENT

Secretaría de Estado de Cultura (Secretariat of State for Culture): Avda George Washington, esq. Pte. Vicini Burgos, 11903 Santo Domingo; tel. 221-4141; fax 555-5555; e-mail contacto@cultura.gov.do; internet www.cultura.gov.do; Sec. of State for Culture José Rafael Lantigua.

Ministry of Education: Secretaría de Estado de Educación, Avda Máximo Gómez 10, esq. Santiago No. 02, Gazcue, 10205 Santo Domingo; tel. 688-9700; fax 689-8688; e-mail libreacceso@see.gov.do; internet www.see.gov.do; Min. of Education Melanio Paredes.

Ministry of Higher Education, Science and Technology: Avda Máximo Gómez 31, esq. Pedro Henríquez Ureña, 11903 Santo Domingo, DN; tel. 731-1100; fax 535-4694; e-mail info@seescyt.gov.do; internet www.seescyt.gov.do; Min. of Education, Science and Technology Ligia Amada de Melo.

NATIONAL BODY

Asociación Dominicana de Rectores de Universidades (Dominican Association of University Presidents): Apdo 2465, Santo Domingo, DN; Calle Juan Paradas Bonilla 5, Apto 3, tercer Nivel, Ensanche Naco, 11093 Santo Domingo; tel. 683-0003; fax 565-4933; e-mail adru@verizon.net.do; internet www.adru.org; f. 1980, present status 1981; 18 mem. univs and higher education institutes; Exec. Dir Ing. José Jorge Goico Germosén.

Learned Societies

GENERAL

Instituto de Cultura Dominicana: Biblioteca Nacional, César Nicolás Penson, 11903 Santo Domingo; f. 1971; promotes cultural tradition of the country, encourages artistic creation and the expression of the spirit of the Dominican people; Pres. Enrique Apolinar Henríquez; Sec. Pedro Gil Iturbides.

BIBLIOGRAPHY, LIBRARY SCIENCE AND MUSEOLOGY

Asociación Dominicana de Bibliotecarios, Inc. (Librarians' Association): c/o Biblioteca Nacional, Plaza de la Cultura, César Nicolás Penson 91, 11903 Santo Domingo; tel. 688-4086; f. 1974; develops library services in the Republic; increases the standing of the profession and encourages the training of its mems; 90 mems; Pres. Próspero J. Mella Chavier; Sec.-Gen. V. Regús; publ. El Papiro (4 a year).

Sociedad Dominicana de Bibliófilos: Calle Las Damas 106, 11903 Santo Domingo; internet bibliofilos.org.do; f. 1973; promotes culture and dissemination of works and productions; library of 13,951 vols; Pres. Mariano Mella; Sec. Octavio Amiama; Treas. Tomás W. Fernández.

HISTORY, GEOGRAPHY AND ARCHAEOLOGY

Academia Dominicana de la Historia (Dominican Academy of History): Casa de las Academias, Calle Mercedes 204, Ciudad Colonial, 10210 Santo Domingo; tel. 689-7907; fax 221-8430; e-mail academiahis@codetel.net.do; internet www.academiahistoria.org.do; f. 1931; promotes knowledge and study of the past in gen. and esp. of the Dominican nation; 24 mems, 36 nat. corresp. mems, 210 foreign corresp. mems; Pres. Dr Emilio Cordero Michel; Admin. Man. Veronica Cass; Exec. Sec. Tessie Brens; publ. Clio (2 a year).

LANGUAGE AND LITERATURE

Academia Dominicana de la Lengua (Dominican Academy): Casa de las Academias, Calle Mercedes 204, 11903 Santo Domingo; tel. and fax 687-9197; e-mail info@academia.org.do; internet www.academia.org.do; f. 1927; Corresp. of the Real Academia Española (Madrid); studies and encourages the devt of the culture and language of Dominican Republic; 24 mems, 32 corresp. mems, 9 partner mems; library of 50,000 vols; Pres. Mariano Lebrón Saviñón; Dir Dr Bruno Rosario Candelier; Sec. Manuel Goico Castro.

Alliance Française: Horacio Vicioso 103, Centro De los Heroes, 11903 Santo Domingo; tel. 532-2935; fax 535-0533; e-mail alianza.francesa@afsd.net; internet www.afsd.net; f. 1914; offers courses and examinations in French language and culture; promotes cultural exchange with France; attached offices in Higuey, Mao, Monte Cristi, San Francisco de Macoris and Santiago de los Caballeros; Hon. Pres. Pozzo Di Borgo S.E. Cécile; Pres. Mario Tolentino Dipp; Vice-Pres. Josefina Pimentel Boves; Treas. Santiago Collado Chastel.

MEDICINE

Asociación Médica de Santiago (Santiago Medical Association): Apdo 445, Santiago de los Caballeros; f. 1941; library of 1,500 vols; 65 mems; Pres. Dr Rafael Fernández Lazala; Sec. Dr José Corominas P.; publ. Boletín Médico (4 a year).

Asociación Médica Dominicana (Dominican Medical Association): Apdo 1237, 11903 Santo Domingo; f. 1941; 1,551 mems; Pres. Dr Angel S. Chan Aquino; Sec. Dr Carlos Lamarche Rey; publ. Revista Médica Dominicana.

Research Institutes

AGRICULTURE, FISHERIES AND VETERINARY SCIENCE

Instituto Azucarero Dominicano (Dominican Sugar Institute): Av. Jiménez Moya, Apdo 667, 11903 Santo Domingo; tel. 532-5571; fax 533-2402; e-mail inst.azucar2@verizon.net.do; internet www.inazucar.gov.do; f. 1965; promotes enhancement and improvement of products derived from the sugar industry; market studies; assists in promotion and removing trade barriers; domestic marketing by setting formalities; supervizes policies; Exec. Dir. Faustino Jimenez.

HISTORY, GEOGRAPHY AND ARCHAEOLOGY

Instituto Cartográfico Militar de las Fuerzas Armadas (Military Cartographic Institute): Base Naval 27 de Febrero, 11903 Santo Domingo; tel. 686-2954; f. 1950; photogrammetry, cartography, geodesy, hydrography, photographic laboratory; sells all kinds of speciality maps of the country; Dir Capt. Domingo Gómez.

Libraries and Archives

Baní

Biblioteca 'Padre Billini': Calle Baní 6, 31000 Duarte; f. 1926; 38,000 vols; Dir Lic. Fernando Herrera.

Moca

Biblioteca Municipal 'Gabriel Morillo': Calle Antonio de la Maza esq. Independencia, 83000 Moca; f. 1942; 6,422 vols; Dir Lic. ADRIANO MIGUEL TEJADA.

San Pedro de Macorís

Biblioteca del Ateneo de Macorís (Library of the Athenaeum of Macorís): 21000 San Pedro de Macorís; f. 1890; 6,274 vols; Pres. Lic. JOSÉ A. CHEVALIER.

Santiago de los Caballeros

Biblioteca de la Sociedad Amantes de la Luz: España esq. Avda Central, Santiago de los Caballeros; f. 1874; public library of cultural society; 18,000 vols; Dir Lic. BERENI ESTRELLA DE INOA.

Santo Domingo

Archivo General de la Nación: Calle Modesto Diaz 2, Zona Universitaria, 10103 Santo Domingo; f. 1935, present status 2000; attached to Min. of Culture; documents dating from the founding of the Republic and others that were inherited from the colonial era; documents of public and private interest; 16,000 vols; Dir-Gen. Dr ROBERTO CASSÁ; Sub-Dir Dr LUÍS MANUEL PUCHEU; publs *Boletín AGN* (4 a year), *Proceedings of Quisqueya* (4 a year).

Cámara de Comercio y Producción de Santo Domingo, Centro de Información y Documentación Comercial (Commercial Information and Documentation Centre of the Chamber of Commerce and Production of Santo Domingo): Arzobispo Nouel 206, Zona Colonial, 10210 Santo Domingo; tel. 682-2688; fax 685-2228; e-mail ccpsd@camarasantodomingo.org.do; internet www.camarasantodomingo.org.do; f. 1848; provides specialized economic, business and trade information; focuses on topics such as trade regulations and Dominican labour, int. economics, nat. and regional trade regulations, foreign trade, economic and fiscal policy and many other related topics; 13,500 vols, incl. books, journals, video cassettes and CD-ROMs; Technician FRANCISCO A. DE LA ROSA; publs *Boletín Digital Camar@cción* (via email), *Camar@cción* (irregular).

Centro Nacional De Conservación De Documentos, Secretaría de Estado de Cultura (Library and Documentation Section): Archivo General de la Nación, calle Modesto Díaz No.2, Zona 10210 Universitaria, Santo Domingo; tel. 532-2508; f. 1976, present name 2000; offers services in environmental health; restoration; digital restoration; consultancy; workshops (technical training); Dir Lic. ELIDA JIMÉNEZ.

Biblioteca de la Secretaría de Estado de Relaciones Exteriores (Library of the Secretariat of Foreign Affairs): Estancia Ramfis, Santo Domingo; spec. collns relating to int. law; Dir Dr PRÓSPERO J. MELLA CHAVIER.

Biblioteca de la Universidad Autónoma de Santo Domingo (Library of Santo Domingo University): Ciudad Universitaria, Apdo 1355, Santo Domingo; 104,441 vols (Dominicana, historical archives, prints, maps, microfilms, etc.), 782,795 reviews (chiefly foreign, relating to the different faculties), gramophone records; Dir Dra MARTHA MARÍA DE CASTRO COTES; publ. *Boletín de Adquisiciones.*

Biblioteca República Dominicana: Dr Delgado esq. Av. Francia, Santo Domingo; tel. 686-0028; fax 688-2009; e-mail biblioteca_rd@yahoo.com; f. 1989, present bldg a chapel of the Dominican Order dating from 1729; promotes culture; collns of periodicals; also contains a students' reading room, textbooks, maps; over 30,000 vols, of which Dominican authors comprise 700; Dir JOSÉ RIJO.

Biblioteca Municipal de Santo Domingo (Municipal Library of Santo Domingo): Padre Billini 18, Santo Domingo; f. 1922; Librarian LUZ DEL CARMEN RAPOZO.

Biblioteca Nacional Pedro Henríquez Ureña: César Nicolás Penson 91, 20711 Santo Domingo; tel. 688-4086; fax 685-8941; f. 1971; collects government publs; houses Nat. Bibliography; exhibits, confs, research and documentation; 153,955 vols; Dir Lic. ROBERTO DE SOTO.

Museums and Art Galleries

Santo Domingo

Amber World Museum: Arz. Mariño 452, Esq. Restauración, Zona Colonial, 10210 Santo Domingo; tel. 682-3309; fax 688-1142; internet www.ambermuseum.com; f. 1996; historical and scientific data of the creation of amber; exhibitions and workshops; Pres. JORGE CARIDAD.

Galería Nacional de Bellas Artes (National Fine Arts Gallery): Santo Domingo; f. 1943; contains the later paintings and sculptures previously exhibited in the Museo Nacional; controlled by the Dirección Gen. de Bellas Artes (Fine Arts Ccl); Dir Dr JOSÉ DE J. ALVAREZ VALVERDE.

Museo Alcázar de Colón: la Plaza España, Zona Colonial, 10210 Santo Domingo; tel. 682-4750; historical colln of over 800 pieces of furniture, carpets, ceramics, sculptures and paintings dating from the 12th century; research and conservation; Dir VICKY JAQUEZ.

Museo Bellapart: Av. JF Kennedy esq. Dr. Lembert Peguero, Edif. Honda 5to Nivel, Santo Doninigo; tel. 541-7721; fax 542-5913; e-mail info@museobellapart.com; internet www.museobellapart.com; f. 1999; devoted solely to Dominican art; paintings from the 1890s; covers all styles and artistic movements of the 20th century to the present; incl. paintings, sculptures, prints and drawings; Pres. JUAN JOSE BELLAPART; Dir PAULA GOMEZ JORGE.

Museo Casa de Tostado: Calle Arzobispo Meriño, esq. Padre Billini, Ciudad Colonial, 10210 Santo Doninigo; tel. and fax 689-5000; e-mail casadetostado@cultura.gov.do; f. 1973; museum of the Dominican family; preserves information of nat. and foreign history; traditions and customs since mid-19th century; exhibits major colln of decorative arts; Dir EVA CAMILO.

Museo de Arte Moderno (Museum of Modern Art): Avda Pedro Henríquez Ureña, Plaza de la Cultura 'Juan Pablo Duarte' 10204 Santo Domingo; tel. 685-2153; fax 685-8280; e-mail museo_de_arte_moderno@yahoo.com; f. 1976 as Gallery of Modern Art, present name 1992; attached to Secretaria de Estado de Cultura; state controlled; modern art of nat. and foreign artists; permanent and exchange exhibitions; organizes lectures, confs, films and children's workshops; library: art library of 2,047 vols, children's library of 2,050 vols; Dir Lic. MARÍA ELENA DITRÉN; publs *Boletín mensual de actividades* (12 a year), *Revista especializada.*

Larimar Museum: Meriño No. 452, esq. Restauración Zona Colonial, Santo Domingo; tel. 686-5700; fax 688-1142; e-mail info@larimarfactory.com; internet www.larimarmuseum.com; f. 1996; educational unit of Amabar Nacional; facts and scientific explanations about blue pectolite or larimar;

Pres. JORGE CARIDAD; Pres. ARELIS DE CARIDAD.

Museo de las Atarazanas Reales: Calle Colón, No. 4, Ciudad Colonial, 10210 Santo Domingo; tel. 682-5834; conserves, exhibits and distributes underwater archaeological heritage on nat. art.

Museo de las Casas Reales (Museum of the Royal Houses): Calle Las Mercedes esq Damas, Ciudad Colonial, Apdo 2664, 10210 Santo Domingo; tel. 682-4202; fax 688-6918; e-mail museodelacasar@verizon.net.do; f. 1511, present status 1973, officially opened 1976; bldgs used to be the headquarters of the colonial government (houses both the Palace of the Governor General and the Royal Court and Accounts); exhibition of items from that period (1492–1821); arms and armour, ceramics and items from shipwrecks; library of 17,700 vols; Dir ANNA YEE; publ. *Casas Reales* (3 a year).

Museo del Hombre Dominicano (Museum of Dominican Man): Plaza de la Cultura Juan Pablo Duarte, Calle Pedro Henríquez Ureña, Santo Domingo; tel. 687-3622; fax 682-9112; e-mail info@museodelhombredominicano.org.do; internet www.museodelhombredominicano.org.do; f. 1973 as Museo Nacional; 19,000 exhibits: *Pre-Columbian* (Indian archaeological, anthropological and ethnographical exhibits; ceramics, wooden objects, idols, amulets, charms, weapons and tools, pots, osseous remains); *Colonial* (weapons and armour, parts of ships, Spanish religious objects, ceramics, bells); educational confs. and workshops; offers specialized courses in social science with emphasis on social research, archeology and socio-cultural anthropology; library of 4,000 vols; Dir Dr CARLOS HERNÁNDEZ SOTO; publs *Boletín, Serie Investigaciones Antropológicas.*

Museo Faro a Colón: Avda Bulv. del Faro, Villa Duarte, 11602 Santo Domingo; tel. 591-1492; dedicated to the memory and houses the remains of Admiral Don Cristobal Colon; researches, exhibits, preserves and disseminates the history and the int. heritage related to the discovery, colonization and evangelization of the Americas.

Museo Nacional de Historia Natural (National Museum of Natural History): Calle Pedro Henriquez Urena, Plaza de la Cultura, 10204 Santo Domingo; tel. 689-0106; fax 689-0100; e-mail jaragua@tricom.net; f. 1974; conserves, researches, exhibits and disseminates nat. natural heritage; geology, palaeontology, zoology; library of 3,000 vols, 10 periodicals; Dir Dr CARLOS ML. RODRÍGUEZ; publs *Boletín Informativo* (4 a year), *Hispaniolana* (journal, irregular).

Museo Nacional de Historia y Geografía (National Museum of History and Geography): Calle Pedro Henríquez Ureña, Plaza de la Cultura Juan Pablo Duarte, Santo Domingo; tel. 686-6668; fax 686-4943; e-mail museohistoriard@yahoo.com; f. 1982; history, geographical features and phenomena of the island of Santo Domingo; Dir HECTOR LUIS MARTINEZ; publ. *Revista de Historia y Geografía.*

Oficina de Patrimonio Cultural: Las Atarazanas 2, Santo Domingo; tel. 682-4750; f. 1967; Dir Arq. MANUEL E. DEL MONTE URRACA.

Controls:

Alcázar de Colón (Columbus Palace): Plaza Spain, Ciudad Colonial, 10210 Santo Domingo; tel. 682-4750; f. museum 1957; the castle, built in 1510, was the residence of Don Diego Columbus, son of Christopher Columbus, and Viceroy of the island; period furniture and objects, paintings, musical instruments, ceramics, and the most important colln of tapestries in the Caribbean.

Casa-Fuerte de Ponce de León (Ponce de León's Fort): San Rafael del, Yuma, Higüey; tel. 551-0118; museum; conservation, exhibition and dissemination of the life of Juan Ponce de Leon; f. 1972; the residence of Ponce de León who discovered Florida and Puerto Rico; authentic furniture and household items from a 16th-century house.

Fortaleza de San Felipe (St Philip's Fortress): West End Malecon, 57000 Puerto Plata; tel. 261-6043; museum; disseminates the military life of the 18th and 19th centuries; f. 1972; 16th-century fort; archaeological objects found during restoration.

Museo de la Familia Dominicana Siglo XIX (Museum of the Dominican Family): Casa de Tostado, Calle Arzobispo Meriño, Santo Domingo; f. 1973, built in 1503; a 16th-century house displaying household items for a noble family of the 19th century.

Sala de Arte Prehispánico: Avda San Martín 279, POB 723, Santo Domingo; tel. 540-7777; fax 541-0201; e-mail saladearte@ embodom.com; f. 1973; run by the García Arévalo Foundation; studies and exhibits culture of pre-Hispanic times; library of 6,000 vols on anthropology and the history of Santo Domingo and the Caribbean; Dir MANUEL ANTONIO GARCÍA ARÉVALO; publs *Caney*, *Salida Semestral*.

Universities

PONTIFICIA UNIVERSIDAD CATÓLICA MADRE Y MAESTRA

Autopista Duarte, Santiago de los Caballeros

Telephone: 580-1962

Fax: 581-7750

E-mail: anunez@pucmmsti.edu.do

Internet: www.pucmmsti.edu.do

Founded 1962, present bldg 1967

Private control

Academic year: August to May (2 semesters) and a session May to July

Rector: Mgr AGRIPINO NÚÑEZ COLLADO

Acad. Vice-Rector: Ing. NELSON GIL

Exec. Vice-Rector: Lic. SONIA GUZMÁN DE HERNÁNDEZ

Registrar: Lic. DULCE RODRÍGUEZ DE GRULLÓN

Librarian: Lic. ALTAGRACIA PEÑA

Number of teachers: 755

Number of students: 9,918

Publications: *Boletín de Noticias*, *Revista de Ciencias Jurídicas*

DEANS

Faculty of Engineering: Ing. VICTOR COLLADO

Faculty of Health Sciences: Dr RAFAEL FERNANDEZ LAZALA

Faculty of Humanities and Sciences: Lic. DAVID ALVAREZ MARTÍN

Campuses in Santo Domingo, Puerto Plata, Bonao

UNIVERSIDAD ABIERTA PARA ADULTOS

Apdo postal 1238, Avda Hispanoamérica, Urb. Thomén, Santiago de los Caballeros

Telephone: 724-0266

Fax: 724-0329

E-mail: univ.adultos@uniabierta.edu.do

Internet: www.uapa.edu.do

Founded 1991, present status 1995

Academic year: January to December

Rector: Dr ÁNGEL HERNÁNDEZ

Vice-Chancellor for Academics: RAFAEL ESPINAL

Vice-Chancellor for Finance: Dr MIRIAN ACOSTA

Vice-Rector for International Relations: MAGDALENA CRUZ

Pres.: Lic. RUBEN HERNANDEZ

Treas.: CORINA MONTERO

Sec.: FRANCISCO SANTOS

Publications: *Boletin UAPA Informa* (newsletter), *Revista Educación Superior*.

UNIVERSIDAD ADVENTISTA DOMINICANA

Au. Duarte km 74 1/2, Monsignor Nouel, Bonao, Sonador

Telephone: 525-7533

Fax: 525-4048

E-mail: info@unad.edu.do

Internet: www.unad.edu.do

Founded 1947, present bldg 1976

Private Control

Faculties of administrative sciences, engineering and technology, humanities, theology.

UNIVERSIDAD APEC

Avda Máximo Gómez 72, El Vergel, Apdo 2867, Santo Domingo

Telephone: 686-0021

Fax: 685-5581

E-mail: univ.apec@codetel.net.do

Internet: www.unapec.edu.do

Founded 1965

Academic year: July to June

Pres.: Dr LUIS HEREDIA BONETTI

Rector: Lic. DENNIS R. SIMÓ

Vice-Rector for Academics: Lic. JUSTO PEDRO CASTELLANOS KHOURI

Vice-Rector for Admin.: Lic. CÉSAR REYNOSO

Vice-Rector for International Affairs: Lic. INMACULADA MADERA

Librarian: Lic. RAMÓN CEDANO

Library of 37,525 vols

Number of teachers: 658

Number of students: 9,000

Publications: *Boletín Trimestral* (4 a year), *Coloquios Jurídicos*, *Investigación y Ciencia*.

UNIVERSIDAD AUTÓNOMA DE SANTO DOMINGO

Ciudad Universitaria, Apdo 1355, Santo Domingo

Telephone: 535-8273

Fax: 535-8273

E-mail: info@uasd.edu.do

Internet: www.uasd.edu.do

Founded 1538 by Papal Bull of Paul III, closed 1801–15; reopened as a lay institution in 1815, reorganized in 1914, present status 1961; oldest university in the Americas

Academic year: January to December

Rector: Dr JULIO RAVELO ASTACIO

Vice-Rector for Academic Affairs: Lic. RAMÓN CAMACHO JIMÉNEZ

Vice-Rector for Admin. Affairs: Lic. JULIO URBÁEZ

Sec.-Gen.: MARIO SURIEL

Personnel Dir.: Lic. JULIO CÉSAR RODRÍGUEZ

Number of teachers: 1,665

Number of students: 26,040

Publications: *Ciencia, Derecho y Política*

DEANS

Faculty of Agronomy and Veterinary Science: Ing. Agr. FRANK M. VALDÉZ

Faculty of Economic and Social Sciences: Dr EDILBERTO CABRAL

Faculty of Engineering and Architecture: Ing. MIGUEL ROSADO MONTES DE OCA

Faculty of Humanities: Lic. ANA DOLORES GUZMÁN DE CAMACHO

Faculty of Law and Politics: Lic. ROBERTO SANTANA

Faculty of Medicine: Dr CÉSAR MELLA MEJÍAS

Faculty of Sciences: Lic. PLÁCIDO CABRERA

UNIVERSIDAD CATÓLICA NORDESTANA

Los Arroyo, Apdo 239, San Francisco de Macorís

Telephone: 588-3505

Fax: 244-1647

E-mail: rectoria@ucne.edu

Internet: www.ucne.edu

Founded 1978

Academic year: January to December (three semesters)

Rector: Rev. Fr Dr RAMÓN DE LA CRUZ BALDERA ALFREDRO

Chancellor: Mgr JESÚS MARÍA DE JESÚS MOYA

Vice-Rector: Lic. PEDRO MANUEL LORA

Vice-Rector: Lic. JULIO CÉSAR PINEDA

Vice-Rector for Academics: ZAMIRA ASILIS ESTÉVEZ

Vice Pres. for Projects: Dr FREDDY ARTURO MARTINEZ

Admin. Vice Chancellor-Financial: Dr YANY ALTAGRACIA ALMANZAR

Librarian: Lic. EMELDA RAMOS

Number of teachers: 210

Number of students: 4,300

Publications: *Ciencia y Humanismo* (every 2 years), *Gaceta Jurídica* (every 2 years)

DEANS

Faculty of Architecture: Arq. ZAMIRA ESTEVEZ

Faculty of Education: Lic. JOSEFINA PANTALEON

Faculty of Engineering: Ing. MARTIN PANTALEON

Faculty of Health Sciences: Dr FEDERICO ANGEL GARABOT

Faculty of Legal Sciences: Dr MARTIN ORTEGA

Faculty of Modern Languages: Lic. RAFAEL SANZ

Faculty of Social Sciences and Economics: Lic. JUAN CASTILLO

Faculty of Tourism: Lic. JAYME LÓPEZ

School of Computing and Systems: Ing. EVELYN VERAS (Dir)

School of Dentistry: DIGNA MARTE (Dir)

School of Medicine: Dr VINICIO BONILLA (Dir)

UNIVERSIDAD CATÓLICA SANTO DOMINGO

Calle Santo Domingo No.3, Ens. La Julia, POB 2733, Santo Domingo

Telephone: 544-2812

Fax: 472-0999

Internet: www.ucsd.edu.do

Founded 1982

Private control

Pres.: NICOLÁS DE JESÚS CARDENAL LÓPEZ RODRÍGUEZ

Sec.: Lic. ALLAN RAMOS

Deputy Sec.: Lic. LUÍS GARCÍA DUBUS

Treas.: Sr DON ANTONIO NAJRI

Vice Treas.: Dr JUAN J. GASSÓ PEREYRA

Rector: Rev. Fr Dr P. RAMÓN ALONSO

Vicer-Rector for Academics: Licda ROSA KRANWINKEL

Vice-Rector for Admin.: Ing. ANGEL MENA

Vice-Rector for Planning: Lic. FRANCISCO CRUZ PASCUAL

Number of teachers: 250

Number of students: 5,000

DEANS

Faculty of Health Sciences: Dr JESÚS ANT. FIALLO

Faculty of Humanities and Education: Licda CARMEN MILDRED LÓPEZ

Faculty of Legal and Political Sciences: Dr MANUEL RAMÓN PEÑA CONCE

Faculty of Science and Technology: Ing. ROBERTO MOREL

Faculty of Religious Science: SOCORRO ALVÁREZ

UNIVERSIDAD CATÓLICA TECNOLÓGICA DEL CIBAO

Avda Universitaria, esq. Pedro A. Rivera, Apdo 401, La Vega

Telephone: 573-1020

Fax: 573-6194

E-mail: uteci@codetel.net.do

Internet: www.ucateci.edu.do

Founded 1983, present name 2002, present status 2006

Academic year: January to December

Rector: Rev. Dr FAUSTO RAMON MEJIA VALLEJO

Pres.: HUGO ALVAREZ VALENCIA

Vice-Pres.: JESUS RUBEN GOMEZ

Sec.: HILDA PEREZ PICHARDO

Treas.: PEDRO ANT RIVERA TORRES

DEANS

Faculty of Health Sciences: Dr JOSE N. PIMENTEL

Faculty of Humanities: JOSE RAFAEL ABREU

UNIVERSIDAD CENTRAL DEL ESTE

Ave. Francisco, Alberto Caamaño Deñó, San Pedro de Macorís

Telephone: 529-3562

Fax: 529-5146

E-mail: info@uce.edu.do

Internet: www.uce.edu.do

Founded 1970

Private control

Academic year: January to December (3 terms)

Pres. and Rector: Dr JOSÉ E. HAZIM FRAPPIER

Vice-Pres.: Dr JOSÉ A. HAZIM AZAR

Exec.-Rector: Lic. VILMA TORRES DE HAZIM

Vice-Rector for Academics: Lic. ISMENIA JIMÉNEZ ABUD

Vice-Rector for Admin.: Lic. DOLORES MONTALVO

Sec.-Gen.: Lic. PIEDAD L. NOBOA MEJÍA

Registrar: Lic. OLGA CHALAS

Librarian: Lic. ROSA DORIVAL

Library of 150,000 vols

Number of teachers: 677

Number of students: 6,700

Publications: *Anuario Científico, Publicaciones Periódicas, UCE*

DEANS

Faculty of Administration and Systems: Lic. SENCIÓN IVELISSE ZOROB

Faculty of Engineering and Natural Resources: Ing. OLGA BASORA

Faculty of Law: Dr ANTONIO LEÓN SASSO

Faculty of Medicine: Dr JUAN A. SILVA SANTOS

Faculty of Science and Technology: Dr FERMÍN MERCEDES

Faculty of Sciences and Humanities: Dr JOSÉ A. HAZIM AZAR

UNIVERSIDAD CENTRAL DOMINICANA DE ESTUDIOS PROFESIONALES

Avda Independencia, km 9, Colegio San Gabriel, Apdo Postal 1263, Santo Domingo

Telephone: 508-3279

Fax: 699-2675

E-mail: info@ucdep.edu.do

Internet: 66.98.64.31

Founded 1975

Private control

Rector: Dr DULCÍLIDO VÁSQUEZ

Vice-Rector for Admin.: Lic. XIOMARA PÉREZ

Vice-Rector for Planning and Devt: Lic. CARLOS HERNÁNDEZ

Exec. Vice-Rector: Ing. MARIO BONILLA M.

Sec.-Gen.: Lic. JUDITH J. VÁZQUEZ

DEANS

Faculty of Health Sciences: CHARLOTTE KING

Faculty of Humanities and Social Sciences: FÉLIX SÁNCHEZ

Faculty of Technology and Natural Resources: RAFAEL LEBRON

UNIVERSIDAD DE LA TERCERA EDAD

Calle Camila Henríquez Ureña, esq. Jesús Maestro, Mirador Norte, Santo Domingo

Telephone: 482-7093

Fax: 482-0109

E-mail: tercera.edad@codetel.net.do

Internet: www.ute.edu.do

Founded 1989, present status 1992

State control

Academic year: January to December (2 semesters)

Rector: Dr JOSÉ NICOLÁS ALMÁNZAR GARCÍA

Vice-Rector for Academics: Lic. ALTAGRACIA NÚÑEZ

Vice-Rector for Admin. and Devt: Dra FANNY POLANCO JORGE

SUBJECT COORDINATORS

Design: Lic. ALICIA ARBAJE

Economics and Administration: Lic. RAFAEL OVIEDO JIMÉNEZ

Education: Lic. CARMEN PEÑA

Law: Lic. RHINA DE LOS SANTOS

Psychology: Lic. GERMANIA MORALES

Public Relations and Social Communication: Lic. RAFAEL PARADELL DÍAZ

UNIVERSIDAD DEL CARIBE

Autopista 30 de Mayo km 7½, POB 67-2, Santo Domingo

Telephone: 616-1616

Fax: 535-0489

E-mail: univ.delcaribe@codetel.net.do

Internet: www.unicaribe.edu.do

Founded 1995

Rector: MIGUEL ROSADO

Vice-Rector for Admin.: ARTURO MENDÉZ.

UNIVERSIDAD DOMINICANA O&M

Apdo postal 509, Ave Independencia 200, Santo Domingo

Telephone: 533-7733

Fax: 535-0084

E-mail: info@udoym.edu.do

Internet: www.udoym.edu.do

Founded 1966

Academic year: January to December

Rector: Dr JOSÉ RAFAEL ABINADER

Number of students: 28,000

Faculties of economics and administration, engineering and technology, humanities and social science, law, and continuing education;

campuses in La Romana, Moca, Puerto Plata, San José de Ocoa, and Santiago.

UNIVERSIDAD EUGENIO MARÍA DE HOSTOS

Apdo Postal 2694, Santo Domingo

Telephone: 532-2495

Fax: 535-4636

Internet: www.uniremhos.edu.do

Founded 1981

Private control

Rector: Lic. CARMEN MARÍA CASTILLO SILVA

Vice-Rector for Academics: Lic. CARMEN ROSA MARTÍNEZ V.

Vice-Rector for Admin.: Rev. RAFAEL MARCIAL SILVA

Gen. Admin.: Dr JORGE DÍAZ VARGAS

DIRECTORS

Faculty of Health Sciences: Dr JOSÉ RODRÍGUEZ SOLDEVILLA

School of Computer Studies: Lic. SANDY SANTOS

School of Law: Lic. CECILIO GÓMEZ PÉREZ

School of Marketing Studies: Lic. PEDRO MELO

School of Medicine: Dr RAÚL ALVAREZ STURLA

School of Nursing: Lic. AMANDA PEÑA DE SANTANA

School of Oral Medicine: Dr CÉSAR LINARES IMBERT

School of Public Health: Dr MANUEL TEJADA BEATO

School of Veterinary Medicine: Dr TULIO S. CASTAÑOS VÉLEZ

Campus in Ozama: Lic. GUILLERMO DÍAZ

Campus in San Cristóbal: Lic. EMILIANO DE LA ROSA

UNIVERSIDAD EXPERIMENTAL 'FELIX ADAM'

Calle Plaza de la Cultura 151, El Millón, Santo Domingo

Telephone: 683-3121

Fax: 683-3425

E-mail: universidadunefa@unefa.edu.do

Internet: www.unefa.edu.do

Founded 1996

Chair.: Dr ANDRÉS MATOS SENA

Rector: Dr BRITO JOSE RAMON HOLGUIN

Number of teachers: 36

UNIVERSIDAD FEDERICO HENRÍQUEZ Y CARVAJAL

Isabel Aguiar No. 100 casi esq. Guarocuya, Herrera, Santo Domingo Oeste

Telephone: 531-1000

Fax: 539-8168

E-mail: info@ufhec.edu.do

Internet: www.ufhec.edu.do

Depts of dentistry, nursing, sciences and humanities.

UNIVERSIDAD IBEROAMERICANA

Apdo Postal 22-333, Avda Francia 129, Gazcue, 10205 Santo Domingo

Telephone: 689-4111

Fax: 687-9384

E-mail: unibe@codetel.net.do

Internet: www.unibe.edu.do

Founded 1982

Academic year: September to August

Rector: Dr JULIO AMADO CASTAÑOS

Academic Dean: NEY ARIAS SCHEKER

Library of 20,000 vols

Publications: *Aretha* (journal of social sciences and economics), *Baka, Revista UNIBE de Ciencia y Cultura* (3 a year),

Scientia (science magazine), *UNIBE Informa*

DEANS

Faculty of Health Sciences: Dr JULIO CASTAÑOS

Faculty of Law and Politics: Dr GUILLERMO MORENO

DIRECTORS

Faculty of Economics and Social Sciences:
School of Business Administration: Lic. MIGUELINA FRANCO
School of Hotel Management and Tourism: Lic. PILAR CONSTANZO
School of Marketing: Lic. ZAYENKA MARTÍNEZ ROA

Faculty of Health Sciences:
School of Dentistry: Dr JACQUELINE RODRIGUEZ RAMIREZ

Faculty of Human Sciences:
School of Advertising and Communication: Lic. RAFAEL RINCÓN M.
School of Architecture: Arq. VENCIAN BEN
School of Design: SANDRA GÓMEZ
School of Education: LAURA SARTORI
School of Psychology: Lic. FRANCESCA HERNÁNDEZ

UNIVERSIDAD INTERAMERICANA

Apdo postal 20687, C/ Dr. Baez 2 y 4, Gazcue, 10205 Santo Domingo

Telephone: 685-6562
Fax: 689-8581
E-mail: unica@codetel.net.do
Internet: www.unica.edu.do

Founded 1977
Private Control
Rector: Lic. GABRIEL READ
Pres.: Dr ZORAIDA HALL VDA. SUNCAR
Vice-Chancellor for Academics: PARMENIO RAUL DIAZ
Vice-Chancellor of Planning and Devt: MIGUEL CIPRIAN
Dean of Faculty and Students: NESTOR MELENCIANO

DEANS

Faculty of Science and Technology: MAX MENDEZ

Faculty of Social Sciences and Humanities: MARY FRANCES CARABALLO

DIRECTORS

Experimental College: Licda JUAN CACERES
School of Accountancy and Business Administration: HENRY JEROME
School of Advertising: FEDERICO SANCHEZ
School of Dental Technology: Dr WALTER SUERO MENDEZ
School of Education: Licda ALTAGRACIA CABRERA
School of LawSchool of Marketing: RODOLFO JIMENEZ
School of Informatics: NARCISO RAMIREZ
School of Social Communication and Public Relations: ADRIANO DE LA CRUZ

UNIVERSIDAD NACIONAL EVANGÉLICA

San Carlos, calle Libertador No. 18, esq. Emilio Prud'Homme, Santo Dominigo

Telephone: 221-6786
Fax: 686-1001
E-mail: rectoria@unev.edu.do
Internet: www.unev-rd.edu.do

Founded 1986
Private control
Pres: Dr PETER GOMEZ
Vice-Pres: Rev. JUAN CARLOS INFANTE, Dr ANA INES POLANCO

Sec.: PABLO VENTURA
Treas.: HOMER BERG
Rector: Lic. SALUSTIANO BOLIVAR MOJICA RIJO
Vice-Rector for Academics: Lic. FÉLIX MIGUEL URENA
Vice-Rector for Admin.: Ing. EPIFANIO GONZALEZ MINAYA

DEANS

Faculty of Health Sciences: Dr WILFREDO MANON ROSSI
Faculty of Humanities: SANTOS GUZMAN
Faculty Rural Development: Dr CESAR LOPEZ

UNIVERSIDAD NACIONAL 'PEDRO HENRÍQUEZ UREÑA'

John F. Kennedy km 6 ½, Santo Domingo

Telephone: 562-6601
Fax: 540-0425
E-mail: info@unphu.edu.do
Internet: www.unphu.edu.do

Founded 1966, present status 1967
Private control
Languages of instruction: Spanish, English
Academic year: September to August (3 semesters)

Rector: Arq. MICHAEL R FIALLOS
Vice-Rector for Academic Affairs: Lic. DANIELA FRANCO DE GUZMÁN
Vice-Rector for Admin. Affairs: Lic. JOSE RAFAEL ESPAILLAT
Vice-Rector for Devt Affairs: Ing. VICTOR BERAS
Registrar: Dra SARI DUVERGÉ MEJÍA
Librarian: Dra CARMEN IRIS OLIVO

Library of 80,000 vols
Number of teachers: 759
Number of students: 8,000

Publications: *Aula, Biblionotas, Cuadernos de Filosofía, Cuadernos Jurídicos*

DEANS

Faculty of Agronomy and Veterinary Science: Dr MIGUEL GONZALEZ
Faculty of Architecture and Arts: Arq. DIANA LAPAIX
Faculty of Economics and Social Sciences: Lic. LUIS MARTINEZ SILFA
Faculty of Engineering and Technology: Ing. CARLOS TRONCOSO
Faculty of Health Science: Dr CARLOS MONTERO
Faculty of Humanities: Lic. DIANA FRANCO DE GUZMAN
Faculty of Law and Politics: Dr MANUEL BERGÉS CHUPANI
Faculty of Postgraduate Studies: Dr VICTOR BERAS
Faculty of Science: Ing. CARLOS TRONCOSO

UNIVERSIDAD NACIONAL TECNOLÓGICA

Calle Dr. Delgado 103, Gazcue, 10205

Telephone: 731-3200
Fax: 221-7907
E-mail: info@unnatec.edu.do
Internet: www.insutec.edu.do

Founded 2003
Private control
Academic year: January to December (3 trimesters)

Pres.: CIELO REYNOSO DE REYES
Dir of Business Admin.: MAESTRA YSAMNA M. MONTERO T.

UNIVERSIDAD ODONTOLÓGICA DOMINICANA

Ave. 27 de Febrero esq. Calle ira. Las Caobas, 10905 Santo Domingo

Telephone: 338-7461
Fax: 560-7524

Internet: www.uod.edu.do
Founded 1983
Rector: DESCHAMPS VILMA BAEZ.

UNIVERSIDAD PSICOLOGÍA INDUSTRIAL DOMINICANA

Calle 1era. No. 27 Urb. KG, km. 6½, Carretera Sánchez, Linea

Telephone: 533-7141
Fax: 274-7827
E-mail: psicologiadom@codetel.net.do
Internet: www.upid.edu.do

Founded 1976 as Industrial Psychology Dominicana, present status 2001
Private Control
Rector: Lic. MILDRED DÍAZ ÁLVAREZ
Vice-Rector for Academics: Lic. MILDRED DÍAZ ÁLVAREZ
Vice-Rector for Admin.: Lic. SORAIMA E. REYES GÓMEZ.

UNIVERSIDAD TECNOLÓGICA DE SANTIAGO (UTESA)

Avda Estrella Sadhalá, esq. Av. Circunvalación, Apdo 685, Santiago de los Caballeros

Telephone: 582-7156
Fax: 582-7644
E-mail: utesa@codetel.net.do
Internet: www.utesa.edu

Founded 1974
Private control
Academic year: January to December

Rector: Dr PRIAMO RODRÍGUEZ CASTILLO
Assist Rector: JOSELINA TAVAREZ
Vice-Rector for Academics: Mag. ARNALDO PEÑA VENTURA
Vice-Rector for Admin.: MARÍA ESTHER U.
Vice-Rector for Campus Premises: Mag. RAMÓN ANÍBAL CASTRO
Sec.-Gen.: Mag. JOSEFINA CRUZ
Registrar: Lic. ANDRÉS VIVAS
Librarian: Mag. ILUMINADA DE LA HOZ

Library of 157,976 vols
Number of teachers: 1,027
Number of students: 35,742

Publications: *Ciencias y Tecnología, Revista Universitas*

Faculties of architecture and engineering, health sciences, sciences and humanities, secretarial sciences, social and economic sciences.

UNIVERSIDAD TECNOLÓGICA DEL SUR

Av. Enriquillo 1, Mejoramiento Social, Azua de Compostela

Telephone: 521-3785
Fax: 521-4164
E-mail: info@utesur.edu.do.
Internet: www.utesur.edu.do

Founded 1978
Rector: ALTAGRACIA MILAGROS GARRIDO DE SÁNCHEZ
Pres.: JUAN VALERIO SÁNCHEZ.

Colleges

Barna Business School: Av. John F. Kennedy no. 34, Ens. Naco; tel. 683-4461; fax 683-4873; e-mail barna@barna.edu.do; internet www.barna.edu.do; offers MBA and MBA intensive; programmes in general management, management development, executive development, marketing management, financial management, credit risk management.

Centros APEC de Educación a Distancia: Ave San Martin No. 147, Villa Juana, 10412 Santo Domingo; tel. 472-1155; fax 472-1189; e-mail cenapec@cenapec.edu.do; internet www.cenapec.edu.do; f. 1972; offers low-cost educational programmes by means of distance education system; 525 teachers; 31,800 students; Pres. LUIS TAVERAS AZAR; Exec. Dir JUAN MIGUEL PEREZ; Admin. Dir Lic BELKIS SANTANA; Academic Dir ANA BELKIS AVILA; Treas. JAIME R. FERNANDEZ; Sec. SONIA VILLANUEVA DE BROUWER.

El Domínico–Americano: Ave. Abraham Lincoln 21, Santo Domingo; tel. 535-0665; fax 533-8809; internet www.icda.edu.do; f. 1947; promotes English as a foreign language; broadening relationships between the Dominican Republic and the USA; conducts exchange programmes; library: 13,300 vols; Dir Lic. ELIZABETH DE WINDT; Gen. Academic Dir Lic. THELMA CAMARENA; Pres. ENGRACIA FRANJUL DE ABATE; Sec. ELLEN DUCY DE PÉREZ; Treas. ERNESTO L. BETANCOURT.

Instituto Politécnico Loyola: Calle Padre Angel Arias 1, 91000 San Cristóbal; tel. 528-4010; fax 528-9229; internet www.ipl.edu.do; f. 1966; offers industrial engineering, network and telecommunications engineering, professional devt and training; library: 20,000 vols; Rector P. FRANCISCO ESCOLÁSTICO H.; Vice-Rector for Academics Lic. MARINO BRITO GUILLÉN.

Instituto Superior de Agricultura (Higher Institute of Agriculture): Apdo 166, Av. Antonio Guzmán Fdez, km 5 1/2, La Herradura, 51000 Santiago; tel. 247-2000; fax 247-2626; internet www.isa.edu.do; f. 1962; independent instn but operates joint programme in agriculture with the Universidad Católica Madre y Maestra; training in agricultural sciences at high school and undergraduate level; offers courses in admin., agrarian reform, agricultural economics, agricultural engineering, animal production, aquaculture, biotechnology, epidemiology, food technology, forestry, horticulture, irrigation, veterinary medicine and animal husbandry; library: 15,000 vols; Rector BENITO FERREIRAS; Pres. ACHILLES BERMDEZ; Treas. FLIX GARCA.

Instituto Tecnológico de Santo Domingo: Avda de los Próceres, Galá, Apdo 342-9, Santo Domingo; tel. 567-9271; fax 566-3200; e-mail desarrollo@mail.intec.edu.do; internet www.intec.edu.do; f. 1972, present status 1973; depts of basic sciences and environment, business, engineering, health, social sciences and humanities; library: 44,000 books, 1,400 periodicals; 2,300 students; Rector Dr MICHAEL J. SCALE; Acad. Vice-Rector Lic. ALTAGRACIA LÓPEZ; Man. EMIL PELLETIER; Librarian Lic. LUCERO ARBOLEDA DE ROA; publs *Ciencia y Sociedad* (4 a year), *Documentos Intec* (1 a year), *Indice de Publicaciones de Universidades* (1 a year).

Instituto Tecnológico del Cibao Oriental: Av Universitaria No. 100, Sanchez Ramirez, Cotuí; tel. 585-2291; fax 240-0603; e-mail iteco@verizon.net.do; internet www.iteco.edu.do; f. 1982, present status 1983; courses in agricultural engineering, bioanalysis, business, law, civil engineering, education, geology and mines; Rector Lic. ESCLARECIDA NÚÑEZ DE ALMONTE; Pres. Lic. JULIO TEJEDA; Vice-Pres. Dr LUIS GARCÍA SANTOS; Sec. Dr MANUEL DE JESÚS BRITO O.

Schools of Art and Music

Dirección General de Bellas Artes (Fine Arts Council): Máximo Gómez esq. Avda Independencia, Santo Domingo; tel. 687-0504; fax 687-2707; e-mail dgba.do@hotmail.com; internet www.bellasartes.gov.do; f. 1940; Dir-Gen. FRANKLIN DOMINGUEZ.

Controls:

Academias de Música (Academies of Music): Villa Consuelo and Villa Francisca, Santo Domingo; also 19 provincial towns.

Conservatorio Nacional de Música (National Conservatoire of Music and Elocution): Santo Domingo.

Escuela de Arte Escénico (School of Scenic Art): Santo Domingo.

Escuela de Artes Plásticas (School of Plastic Arts): Santiago.

Escuela de Bellas Artes (School of Fine Arts): San Francisco de Macorís.

Escuela de Bellas Artes (School of Fine Arts): San Juan de la Maguana.

Escuela Nacional de Bellas Artes (National Fine Arts School): Santo Domingo.

ECUADOR

The Higher Education System

The Universidad Central del Ecuador, founded in 1586 as Universidad de San Fulgencio, is among the oldest universities in the Americas. Several universities were established in the 1860s, but most were founded during the 20th century. In 1990/91 there were 206,500 students in higher education. Higher education is administered by the Consejo Nacional de Educación Superior (National Council for Higher Education), and is governed by the Ley de Educación Superior (number 16 RO/77 of 15 May 2000).

Admission to higher education is on the basis of the Bachillerato, the main secondary school qualification; some universities also set entrance examinations. The main undergraduate degree is the Licenciado, which requires four years of study (a professional title can also be awarded). Following the Licenciado, the Masterado/Magister is a postgraduate degree that is awarded after two years of study. Finally, the Doctorado requires two to three years of study following the Licenciado. Not all institutions offer doctorate programmes. The Tecnólogo is the main qualification for technical and vocational education and is awarded after three-year 'short-cycle' courses.

Regulatory and Representative Bodies

GOVERNMENT

Ministry of Culture: Quito; Min. ANTONIO PRECIADO BEDOYA.

Ministry of Education: San Salvador E 6-49 y Eloy Alfaro, Quito; tel. (2) 255-5014; e-mail info@mec.gov.ec; internet www.mec.gov.ec; Min. RAÚL VALLEJO CORRAL.

ACCREDITATION

Consejo Nacional de Educación Superior (CONESUP): Whymper E7-37 y Alpallana, Quito; tel. (2) 2221-147; fax (2) 2229-576; e-mail gvega@conesup.edu.ec; internet www.conesup.net; f. 1982; responsible for coordination, regulation of univs, technological institutes and academic programmes; Pres. Dr GUSTAVO VEGA; Exec. Dir Ing. TONNY GONZÁLEZ; publs *Boletín Bimensual* (6 a year), *Planinformativo*, *Investigación Universitaria* (2 a year).

Learned Societies

GENERAL

Casa de la Cultura Ecuatoriana 'Benjamín Carrión': Apdo 67, Avda 6 de Diciembre 794, Quito; tel. 223-391; fax 223-391; f. 1944; covers all aspects of Ecuadorian culture; attached museums: see Museums and Art Galleries; library: see Libraries and Archives; 673 mems; Pres. Dr STALIN ALVEAR; Sec.-Gen. Dr MARCO PLACENCIA; publs *Letras de Ecuador* (2 a year), *Línea Imaginaria* (1 a year).

UNESCO Office Quito and Regional Bureau for Communication and Information: Juan León Mera y Av. Patria, Edificio CFN 6to piso, Quito; tel. (2) 2529085; fax (2) 2504435; e-mail lospina@unesco.org.ec; designated Cluster Office for Bolivia, Colombia, Ecuador, Peru and Venezuela; Dir GUSTAVO LÓPEZ OSPINA.

LANGUAGE AND LITERATURE

Academia Ecuatoriana de la Lengua (Academy of Ecuador): Apdo 17-07-9699, Quito; tel. (2) 543-234; fax (2) 901-518; f. 1875; 20 mems; Corresp. of the Real Academia Española (Madrid); library of 3,000 vols; Dir CARLOS JOAQUÍN CÓRDOVA; Sec. Emb. FILOTEO SAMANIÉGO; publs *Memorias* (1 a year), *Horizonte Cultural* (12 a year).

Alliance Française: Eloy Alfaro 32–468, Casilla 17-11-6275, Quito; tel. (2) 245-2017; fax (2) 244-2293; internet www.afquito.org.ec; offers courses and examinations in French language and culture and promotes cultural exchange with France; attached teaching offices in Cuenca, Guayaquil, Loja and Portoviejo; Dir MARCEL TAILLEFER.

MEDICINE

Academia Ecuatoriana de Medicina (Ecuadorian Academy of Medicine): Abel Gilbert N34-13 y Antonio Flores Jijon, Bellavista, Quito; tel. (2) 244-7356; fax (2) 246-5557; e-mail jmalvear@uio.satnet.net; internet www.sg61.org/profjma.htm; f. 1958; 120 mems; Pres. JOSÉ M. ALVEAR.

Federación Médica Ecuatoriana (Medical Federation of Ecuador): Avda Naciones Unidas E2-17 e Iñaquito, Quito; tel. (2) 245-6812; fax (2) 245-2660; f. 1942; 1,435 mems; Pres. Dr EDUARDO CAMACHO; Gen. Sec. Dr JENNY AGUIRRE H.

Sociedad Ecuatoriana de Pediatría (Paediatrics Society of Ecuador): Av. Naciones Unidas E2-17 e Iñaquito, Quito; tel. (2) 226-2881; e-mail secretaria@pediatria.org.ec; f. 1945; scientific extension courses and lectures; Pres. Dr PATRÍCIO PROCEL; Sec. Dr MÓNICA CEVALLOS NOROÑA; publ. *Revista Ecuatoriana de Pediatría*.

Research Institutes

GENERAL

Institut de Recherche pour le Développement (IRD): Apdo 17-12-857, Quito; Whymper 442 y Coruña, Quito; tel. (2) 2504856; fax (2) 2504020; internet www.arqueo-ecuatoriana.ec; f. 1974; geology, pedology, hydrology, botany and vegetal biology, agronomy, geography, human sciences, economics; library of 550 vols, 400 periodicals, 80 extracts; Dir FRANCISCO VALDEZ; (see main entry under France).

AGRICULTURE, FISHERIES AND VETERINARY SCIENCE

Instituto Nacional Autónomo de Investigaciones Agropecuarias (Autonomous National Institute of Agricultural Research): Apartado Postal 17-17-1362, Quito; Avs Amazonas y Eloy Alfaro 30-350, Edif. MAG (4° piso), Quito; tel. (2) 252-8650; fax (2) 240-4240; e-mail iniap@iniap-ecuador.gov.ec; internet www.iniap-ecuador.gov.ec; f. 1959;

Gen. Dir JULIO CÉSAR DELGADO ARCE; publ. *Revista* (4 a year).

Instituto Nacional de Pesca (National Fishery Institute): Letamendi 102 y La Ría, Guayaquil; tel. (4) 401773; fax (4) 401776; internet www.inp.gov.ec; f. 1960; fishing research and development; library of 20,000 vols; Dir Dr ROBERTO JIMÉNEZ S.; publs *Boletín Científico y Técnico*, *Revista Científica de Ciencias Marinas y Limnología*, *Boletín Informativo*.

ECONOMICS, LAW AND POLITICS

Instituto Latinoamericano de Investigaciones Sociales (ILDIS) (Latin American Social Sciences Research Institute): Casilla 17-03-367, Quito; Av República 500 y Diego de Almagro, Edif. Pucará, 4to. Piso, Of. 404, Quito; tel. (2) 2562103; fax (2) 2504337; e-mail ildis@fes.ec; internet www.fes.ec/public/ildis.do; f. 1974; affiliated to the Friedrich-Ebert Foundation; research in economics, sociology, political science and education; library of 15,000 vols; Dir Dr REINHART WETTMANN.

Instituto Nacional de Estadística y Censos (National Statistics and Census Institute): Juan Larrea N15-36 y José Riofrío, Quito; tel. (2) 255-6124; fax (2) 250-9836; e-mail inec1@ecnet.ec; internet www.inec.gov.ec; f. 1976; library of 6,500 vols; Dir-Gen. Ing. VÍCTOR MANUEL ESCOBAR BENAVIDES; publs *Indice de Precios al Consumidor Urbano* (12 a year), *Indice de Precios de Materiales, Equipo y Maquinaria de la Construcción* (12 a year), *Indice de Precios al Productor* (12 a year).

HISTORY, GEOGRAPHY AND ARCHAEOLOGY

Instituto Geográfico Militar (Military Geographical Institute): Senierges y Gral Paz y Miño, Sector El Dorado, Pichincha, Quito; tel. (2) 3975100; fax (2) 3975194; e-mail igm1@igm.mil.ec; internet www.igm.gov.ec; f. 1928; part of Ministry of Defence; main activity is preparation of national map series; undertakes projects for public and private organizations; provides cartographic and geographic documentation for national development and security; formulates disaster and land information systems; library of 10,500 vols; Dir Col IVAN F. ACOSTA A.; publs *Revista Geográfica* (2 a year), *Indices Toponímicos*.

MEDICINE

Instituto Nacional de Higiene y Medicina Tropical 'Leopoldo Izquieta Pérez'

(National Institute of Hygiene): Julian Coronel 905 y Esmeraldas, Guayaquil; tel. (4) 281-542; fax (4) 394-189; f. 1941; 120 departments and sections; library of 5,600 vols; Dir Dr FRANCISCO HERNÁNDEZ MANRÍQUEZ; publ. *Revista Ecuatoriana de Higiene y Medicina Tropical*.

NATURAL SCIENCES
General
Instituto Oceanográfico de la Armada (Naval Oceanographic Institute): Avda 25 de Julio, Apdo 5940, Guayaquil; tel. (4) 248-4723; fax (4) 248-5166; e-mail inocar@inocar.mil.ec; internet www.inocar.mil.ec; f. 1972 to study oceanography and hydrography; library of 2,500 vols; Dir BYRON SANMIGUEL MARÍN (acting); publ. *Acta Oceanográfica del Pacífico* (1 a year).

Biological Sciences
Charles Darwin Research Station: Casilla 17-01-3891, Quito; Puerto Ayora, Isla Santa Cruz, Galapagos; tel. (5) 2526147; fax (5) 2526146; e-mail cdrs@fcdarwin.org.ec; internet www.darwinfoundation.org; f. 1964 under the auspices of the Ecuadorian Government, UNESCO and the Charles Darwin Foundation to study and preserve the flora and fauna of the archipelago; maintains meteorological stations, a herbarium, a zoological museum and a marine laboratory; breeding programme for endangered reptiles; library of 4,000 vols, 12,000 separates, 105 current periodicals, slides, aerial photographs, maps; Dir Dr J. GABRIEL LÓPEZ; publ. *Noticias de Galápagos* (2 a year).

Physical Sciences
Instituto Nacional de Meteorología e Hidrología (Hydrometeorological Office): Iñaquito 36-14 y Corea, Quito; tel. (2) 3971100; fax (2) 2241874; e-mail cpaez@inamhi.gov.ec; internet www.inamhi.gov.ec; f. 1961; library of 6,500 vols; Exec. Dir Ing. CARLOS PÁEZ PÉREZ; publs. *Anuario Meteorológico, Anuario Hidrológico, Boletín Climatológico* 12 a year.

Observatorio Astronómico de Quito (Quito Astronomical Observatory): Apdo 17-01-165, Quito; Av. Gran Colombia s/n, Interior del parque 'La Alameda', Quito; tel. (2) 2570765; fax (2) 2583451; e-mail observaquito@gmail.com; internet oaq.epn.edu.ec; f. 1873; astronomy, astrophysics, seismology, meteorology and archaeoastronomy; library of 5,000 vols; Dir Dr ERICSON LÓPEZ IZURIETA; publs *Boletín Astronómico* (Series A, B), *Boletín Meteorológico*.

RELIGION, SOCIOLOGY AND ANTHROPOLOGY
Instituto Ecuatoriano de Antropología y Geografía (Ecuadorian Institute of Anthropology and Geography): Apdo 17-01-2258, Quito; Avda Orellana 557 y Coruña, Quito; tel. (2) 506-324; fax (2) 509-436; f. 1950; research in anthropology, folklore, history, social psychology and national questions; library of 5,000 vols; Dir Lcdo RODRIGO GRANIZO R.; publ. *Llacta* (review, 2 a year).

TECHNOLOGY
Comisión Ecuatoriana de Energía Atómica (Atomic Energy Commission of Ecuador): Juan Larrea N15-36 y Riofrío, Quito; tel. (2) 2225166; fax (2) 2563336; e-mail comecen1@comecenat.gov.ec; f. 1958; 40 mems; research in nuclear physics, radioisotopes, radiobiology, chemistry, medicine; library of 5,000 vols; Exec. Dir Dr MARCOS BRAVO SALVADOR; publ. *Noticias Trimestrales*.

Dirección General de Hidrocarburos (General Directorate of Hydrocarbons): Avda 10 de Agosto 321, Quito; f. 1969; supervises enforcement of laws relating to petroleum exploration and devt, and sets standards for mining-petroleum industry; 210 mems; Dir-Gen. GUILLERMO BIXBY; Sec. ERNESTO CORRAL; publs *Estadística Petrolera, Indice de Leyes y Decretos de la Industria Petrolera, Reporte Geológico de la Costa Ecuatoriana*.

Instituto de Ciencias Nucleares (Institute of Nuclear Science): Escuela Politécnica Nacional, Apdo 17-01-2759, Quito; tel. (2) 250-7126; fax (2) 256-7848; e-mail rmunoz@server.epn.edu.ec; f. 1957; library with department of microcards and microfilms; equipment for application of radioisotopes to chemistry, agriculture, medicine and radiation control; cobalt-60 pilot irradiator, batch type 40-10 kilocuries, linear electron accelerator 8 MeV with conveyor; 4 departments: Department of Applied Research, Head Prof. RICARDO MUÑOZ BURGOS; Department of Biomedical Applications, Dir RODRIGO FIERRO B.; Department of Industrial Applications, Head Ing. TRAJANO RAMÍREZ; Department of Radiation Control, Dir Ing. FREDDIE ORBE M.; Dir Dr FLORINELLA MUÑOZ BISESTI; publ. *Politécnica* (4 a year).

Libraries and Archives
Cuenca
Biblioteca Panamericana (Pan-American Library): Apdo 57, Cuenca; tel. (7) 826130; f. 1912; 64,000 vols; Dir LADY LISSETH MONAR CADENA.

Biblioteca Pública Municipal (Public Municipal Library): Apdo 202, Cuenca; f. 1927; 50,000 vols; Dir JUAN TAMA MÁRQUEZ.

Centro de Documentación Regional 'Juan Bautista Vázquez' de la Universidad de Cuenca (Juan Bautista Vázquez Regional Documentation Centre): Av. 12 de Abril y Agustín Cueva, Cuenca; f. 1882; 250,000 vols; Dir MICHURÍN AUGUSTO VÉLEZ VALAREZO.

Guayaquil
Biblioteca 'Angel Andrés García' de la Universidad 'Vicente Rocafuerte': Avenida de las Américas frente al Cuartel Modelo, Apartado Postal 1133, Guayaquil; f. 1847; 13,000 vols; Dir SONIA MORETA; publ. *Revista de la Universidad 'Vicente Rocafuerte'*.

Biblioteca de Autores Nacionales 'Carlos A. Rolando' (Library of Ecuadorian Writers): Apartado 6069, Guayaquil; 10 de Agosto entre Chile y Pedro Carbo Palacio Municipal, Guayaquil; tel. (4) 515-738; f. 1913; 12,000 vols, 15,000 pamphlets, 17,000 leaflets, 3,000 MSS relating to Ecuadorian authors and foreign works about Ecuador; Dir (vacant).

Biblioteca General, Universidad de Guayaquil: Ciudadela Universitaria Salvador Allende, Malecón del Salado entre Av. Fortunato Safadi y Av. Kennedy, Guayaquil; tel. (4) 28-24-40; f. 1901; 50,000 vols; Dir Lic. LEONOR VILLAO DE SANTANDER; publs *Revista, El Universitario*.

Biblioteca Histórica y Archivo Colonial (Historical Library and Colonial Archives): Palacio de la Municipalidad, Apdo 75, Guayaquil; f. 1930; Dir Dr CARLOS A. ROLANDO; Sec. Prof. GUSTAVO MONROY GARAICOA.

Biblioteca Municipal 'Pedro Carbo' (Public Library): Avda 10 de Agosto entre Pedro Carbo y Chile, Guayaquil; tel. (4) 524-100 ext, 2105; fax (4) 524-100 ext, 2140;

e-mail dcpc_bib@hotmail.com; f. 1862; 550,000 vols; Dir NANCY PALACIOS DE MEDINA; (see also under Museums).

Quito
Archivo-Biblioteca de la Función Legislativa: Av. 10 de Agosto y Briceño, Quito; f. 1886; scientific and cultural; 27,000 vols; Dir Lic. RAFAEL A. PIEDRA SOLÍS; publs *Clave de la Legislación Ecuatoriana, Diario de Debates de la Legislatura*.

Archivo Nacional de Historia (National Historical Archives): Av. Santa Prisca y Av. 10 de Agosto, Quito; f. 1938; 2,500 vols; colonial documents of the 16th to 19th centuries; Dir JORGE A. GARCÉS Y GARCÉS; Sec. JUAN R. FREKE-GRANIZO; publ. *Arnahis*.

Biblioteca de la Universidad Central del Ecuador (Central University Library): Av. América s/n, Ciudadela Universitaria, Hall del Teatro Universitario, Quito; tel. (2) 250-5859; e-mail bgeneral@ac.uce.edu.ec; f. 1826; 170,000 vols; Dir ALONSO ALTAMIRANO; publs *Anales, Bibliografía Ecuatoriana, Anuario Bibliográfico*.

Biblioteca del Banco Central del Ecuador: Av. 10 de Agosto N11-409 y Briceño, Casilla Postal 339, Quito; tel. 568957; fax 568973; f. 1938; 100,000 vols, 2,000 periodicals; specializes in economics, administration, banking and finance, social sciences; open to the public; Dir CARLOS LANDAZURI; publ. *Boletín Bibliográfico* (irregular).

Has Attached:

Hemeroteca: Calle Arenas y 10 de Agosto Apdo 17-15-0029-C, Quito; tel. 561521; 5,000 periodicals; Dir JULIO OLEAS.

Musicoteca: Calles García Moreno y Sucre, Apdo 339, Quito; tel. 572784; music and video library; Dir ADRIANA ORTIZ.

Biblioteca Ecuatoriana 'Aurelio Espinosa Pólit': José Nogales y Francisco Arcos, Cotocollao, Apdo 17-01-160, Quito; tel. (2) 249-1157; fax (2) 249-3928; e-mail director@beaep.org.ec; internet www.beaep.org.ec; f. 1928; Ecuadorian library, archive, Ecuadorian art and history museum; 300,000 vols; Librarian JULIAN G. BRAVO.

Biblioteca Municipal (Municipal Library): García Moreno 882 y Sucre, Quito; tel. (2) 222-8418; e-mail bibmuni@yahoo.com; internet www.centrocultural-quito.com; f. 1886; 12,500 vols, 300 MSS, 4 incunabula.

Biblioteca Nacional del Ecuador (National Library): 12 de Octubre 555, Apdo 67, Quito; tel. (20 290-2272; f. 1792; 70,000 vols of which 7,000 date from the 16th to 18th centuries; shares legal deposit with municipal libraries; Dir LAURA DE CRESPO.

Attached Library:

Biblioteca de la Casa de la Cultura Ecuatoriana (Library of Ecuadorian Culture): Apdo 67, Avda Colombia, Quito; tel. (2) 222-3391; e-mail biblioteca@cce.org.ec; f. 1944; 12,000 vols and over 20,000 periodicals; incl. the 'Laura de Crespo' Room of Nat. Authors; Dir LUCY MALDONADO.

Museums and Art Galleries
Guayaquil
Museo Antropológico del Banco Central: Av. de las Américas 1100 y Av. Juan Tanca Marengo, Guayaquil; tel. (4) 285-800; internet www.bce.fin.ec/contenido.php?cnt=arb0000393; f. 1974; archaeology of the Ecuadorian coast; gallery of contemporary Latin American art; research; library

of 7,500 vols; Dir FREDDY OLMEDO R.; publ. *Miscelánea Antropológica Ecuatoriana*.

Museo Municipal (Municipal Museum): Calle Sucre entre Chile y Pedro Carbo, Guayaquil; tel. (4) 259-9100 ext. 7404; e-mail info@mumg.info; internet www .mumg.info; f. 1862; historical, ethnographical, palaeontological, geological exhibits; colonial period and modern paintings and numismatics (see also Libraries).

Quito

Museo Antropológico 'António Santiana': Universidad Central del Ecuador, Quito; f. 1925; sections of anthropology, archaeology, ethnography; library of 2,000 vols; Dir Dr HOLGUER JARA; publs *Humanitas, Boletín Ecuatoriano de Antropología* (irregular).

Museo de Arte Colonial: Cuenca St and Mejía St, Quito; tel. 2212-297; f. 1914; attached to Casa de la Cultura Ecuatoriana 'Benjamín Carrión'; many examples of art from the Escuela Quiteña of the colonial epoch (17th and 18th centuries); Dir JUAN CARLOS FERNÁNDEZ-CATALÁN.

Museo de Artes Visuales e Instrumentos Musicales: Avda 12 de Octubre 555 y Patria, Quito; tel. (2) 2223-392; internet www .cultura.com.ec/martemoderno.htm; attached to Casa de la Cultura Ecuatoriana 'Benjamín Carrión'; art from Ecuador and Latin America since 19th century.

Museo de Ciencias Naturales de la Escuela Militar 'Eloy Alfaro': Av. Orellana y Amazonas, Quito; f. 1937; geological specimens and fauna from the Galapagos Islands; taxidermy and anatomy illustrated, especially of mammals and birds; Taxidermist LUIS ALFREDO PÉREZ VACA; publ. *Revista Anual del Plantel*.

Museo Jacinto Jijón y Caamaño (Jacinto Jijón y Caamaño Museum): Edificio de la Biblioteca General de la PUCE 3er piso, Avda 12 de Octubre 1076 y Roca, Quito; tel. (2) 299-1242; e-mail jmjaramillo@puce.edu.ec; internet www.puce.edu.ec/index .php?pagina=museojjc; f. 1969; archaeology, art, ethnography; library of 2,000 vols; Dir ERNESTO SALAZAR.

Museo Municipal de Arte e Historia 'Alberto Mena Caamaño' (Civic Museum of Arts and History): Espejo 1147 y Benalcázar, Pichincha, Quito; tel. (2) 214-018; f. 1959; archaeology, colonial art, 19th-century art, items of historical interest; history archive (1583–1980), information library; Dir ALFONSO ORTIZ CRESPO.

Museo Nacional de la Dirección Cultural del Banco Central del Ecuador: Reina Victoria y Jorge Washington (esquina), Edificio Aranjuez, Apdo 339, Quito; tel. 220547; fax 568972; e-mail jortiz@uio.bce.fin .ec; f. 1969; prehistorical archaeological exhibits; colonial and modern art (sculpture, paintings, etc.); library of 6,000 vols; Dir JUAN ORTIZ GARCÍA.

Universities and Technical Universities

ESCUELA POLITÉCNICA DEL EJERCITO

Campus Politécnico, Avda El Progreso s/n, POB 171-5-231B, Sangolquí

Telephone: (2) 2334950
Fax: (2) 2334952
E-mail: espe@espe.edu.ec
Internet: www.espe.edu.ec

Founded 1922; current name since 1977

State control
Academic year: March to February (two semesters)

Rector: Brig. Gen. RUBÉN NAVIA LOOR
Vice-Rector (Academic): Ing. Col CARLOS RODRÍGUEZ ARRIETA
Vice-Rector (Research): Ing. Lt Col JOSÉ AGUIAR VILLAGÓMEZ
Admin. Man.: Col FERNANDO PROAÑO CADENA.

ESCUELA POLITÉCNICA NACIONAL (National Polytechnic School)

Ladrón de Guevara s/n, Apdo 17-01-2759, Quito

Telephone: (2) 256-2400
Fax: (2) 567-848
E-mail: postmaster@server.epn.edu.ec
Internet: www.epn.edu.ec

Founded 1869
Autonomous control
Academic year: October to February,March

Rector: MARCELO JARAMILLO
Vice-Rector: STALIN SUÁREZ
Sec. Atty: PATRICIO ESTUPIÑÁN
Librarian: GERMANIA MERIZALDE

Number of teachers: 800
Number of students: 8,000

Publication: *Politécnica* (4 a year)

DIRECTORS

School of Engineering: JORGE MOLINA
School of Science: CARLOS ECHEVERRÍA
School of Technology: RODRIGO RUIZ

ESCUELA SUPERIOR POLITÉCNICA AGROPECUARIA DE MANABÍ

10 de Agosto 82 y Granda Centeno, Calceta

Telephone: (5) 2685134
Fax: (5) 2685156
E-mail: espam@espam.edu.ec
Internet: www.espam.edu.ec

Founded 1999
State control
Academic year: June to May (two semesters)

Rector: LEONARDO FÉLIX LÒPEZ
Sec.-Gen.: LYA VILLAFUERTE VÈLEZ

Library of 800 vols

DIRECTORS

Agricultural Industry: SUSANA DUEÑAS DE LA TORRE
Agriculture: KLÉBER PALACIOS SALTOS
Cattle: KLÉBER PALACIOS SALTOS
Computer Science: VICENTE AVEIGA DE SANTANA
Environmental Science: Dr RONALDO MENDOZA VÉLEZ

ESCUELA SUPERIOR POLITÉCNICA DE CHIMBORAZO

Panamericana Sur km 1½, Riobamba

Telephone: (3) 2998200
Internet: www.espoch.edu.ec

Founded 1972
Autonomous control
Language of instruction: Spanish

Rector: Dr SILVIO ALVAREZ LUNA
Vice-Rector for Academic Affairs: EDGAR CEVALLOS ACOSTA
Vice-Rector for Research and Devt: JORGE GONZALO BERMEO RODAS
Gen.-Sec.: Dr JULIO FALCONÍ MEJÍA
Librarian: CARLOS RODRÍGUEZ C.

Library of 35,000 vols, 80,000 periodicals
Number of teachers: 264
Number of students: 4,500 (excluding students from the Dept of Languages)

Publication: *GACETA* (4 a year)

DEANS

Faculty of Animal Husbandry: JOSÉ M. PAZMIÑO
Faculty of Business Administration: VÍCTOR CEVALLOS V.
Faculty of Computer and Electronic Engineering: Dr ROMEO RODRÍGUEZ
Faculty of Mechanical Engineering: GEOVANNY GUILLERMO NOVILLO ANDRADE
Faculty of Natural Resources: FEDERICO ROSERO
Faculty of Public Health: Dr SILVIA VELOZ M.
Faculty of Sciences: Dr EDMUNDO CALUÑA

ESCUELA SUPERIOR POLITÉCNICA DEL LITORAL

Apartado 09-01-5863, Guayaquil
Km 30½ Vía Perimetral, Guayaquil

Telephone: (4) 2851095
Fax: (4) 2854629
E-mail: correo@espol.edu.ec
Internet: www.espol.edu.ec

Founded 1958
State control
Language of instruction: Spanish
Academic year: May to February

Rector: Dr MOISÉS TACLE
Gen. Vice-Rector: ARMANDO ALTAMIRANO
Vice-Rector for Welfare and Student Affairs: MIGUEL FIERRO
Sec.-Gen.: JAIME VÉLIZ LITARDO
Librarian: ELOÍSA PATIÑO LARA

Library of 47,000 vols
Number of teachers: 550
Number of students: 12,005

Publications: *Boletín Informativo Polipesca, Informes de Actividades, Tecnológica*

DIRECTORS

Agriculture School: HAYDÉE TORRES
Centre for the Study of Foreign Languages: DENNIS MALONEY S.
Computer Science School: ALEXANDRA PALADINES
Department of Electrical Engineering and Computer Science: CARLOS VILLAFUERTE
Department of Geology, Mines and Petroleum Engineering: MIGUEL A. CHÁVEZ
Department of Maritime Engineering: EDUARDO CERVANTES
Department of Mechanical Engineering: EDUARDO RIVADENEIRA
Electrical and Electronics School: CAMILO ARELLANO
Fisheries School: FRANCISCO PACHECO
Food Science School: MA. FERNANDA MORALES
Furniture and Cabinet School: VÍCTOR FERNÁNDEZ
Graduate School of Business: MOISÉS TACLE
Institute of Chemistry: JUSTO HUAYAMAVE
Institute of Humanities: OMAR MALUK
Institute of Mathematics: JORGE MEDINA
Institute of Physics: JAIME VÁSQUEZ
Mechanics School: MIGUEL PISCO

UNIVERSIDAD AGRARIA DEL ECUADOR

Apdo 09-01-1248, Avda 25 de Julio y Avda Juan Pio Jaramillo, Via Puerto Maritimo, Guayaquil

Telephone: (4) 493441
Fax: (4) 493441
E-mail: info@uagraria.edu.ec
Internet: www.uagraria.edu.ec

Founded 1992

Rector: JACOBO BUCARAM ORTÍZ
Vice-Rector: GUILLERMO ROLANDO.

UNIVERSIDAD ANDINA SIMÓN BOLÍVAR ECUADOR

POB 17-12-569, Toledo N22-80 (Plaza Brasilia), Quito
Telephone: (2) 3228031
Fax: (2) 3228426
E-mail: uasb@uasb.edu.ec
Internet: www.uasb.edu.ec
Founded 1992
State control

Rector: ENRIQUE AYALA MORA
Sec.-Gen.: VIRGINIA ALTA PERUGACHI
Librarian: ENRIQUE ABAD ROA

Publications: *Comentario Internacional: Revista del Centro Andino de Estudios Internacionales, Foro: Revista de Derecho, Kipus: Revista Andina de Letras, Procesos: Revista Ecuatoriana de Historia*

Campuses in Sucre (Bolivia) and Caracas (Venezuela); offices in Bogotá (Colombia) and La Paz (Bolivia)

DIRECTORS OF SUBJECT AREAS

Arts: FERNANDO BALSECA
Business: ALFONSO TROYA
Communication: JOSÉ LASO
Education: MARIO CIFUENTES
Health Studies: PLUTARCO NARANJO
History: GUILLERMO BUSTOS
Law: JOSÉ VICENTE TROYA
Social and Global Studies: CÉSAR MONTÚFAR

ATTACHED RESEARCH INSTITUTES

Centro Andino de Estudios Internacionales: tel. (4) 2560945; e-mail dctena@hoy.net; Pres. DIEGO CORDOVEZ.

Programa Andino de Derechos Humanos: tel. (4) 2556403; e-mail roque@uasb.edu.ec; Regional Coordinator ROQUE ESPINOSA.

UNIVERSIDAD CENTRAL DEL ECUADOR

Avda América y A. Pérez Guerrero, Casilla 1456, Quito
Telephone: (2) 226080
Fax: (2) 505860
E-mail: rectorado@ucentral.edu.ec
Internet: www.ucentral.edu.ec
Founded 1586 as Univ. de San Fulgencio; became Real y Pontificia Univ. de San Gregorio in 1622, Univ. de Santo Tomás de Aquino in 1688, then Univ. Central del Sur de la Gran Colombia; present name 1826.
State control
Language of instruction: Spanish
Academic year: September to July

Rector: VICTOR HUGO OLALLA PROAÑO
Vice-Rector: CARLOS ARROYO ALVAREZ
Registrar: Dr LIDA FLORES CHACÓN
Librarian: JANETH CORNEJO

Number of teachers: 2,137
Number of students: 31,663

Publication: *Anales*

DEANS

Faculty of Administrative Sciences: Dr JOSÉ VILLAVICENCIO
Faculty of Agricultural Sciences: MIGUEL ARAQUE
Faculty of Architecture and Urbanism: PATRICIO AGUILAR VEINTIMILLA
Faculty of Arts: Prof. VICTORIA CARRASCO
Faculty of Chemistry: Dr ARTURO BASTIDAS
Faculty of Dentistry: Dr GUSTAVO RON
Faculty of Economics: JOSÉ VILLACÍS PAZ Y MIÑO
Faculty of Engineering, Physics and Mathematics: MARCO AYABACA CAZAR
Faculty of Geology, Mines, Petroleum and Environmental Studies: GUSTAVO PINTO ARTEAGA

Faculty of Law and Political and Social Sciences: Dr HOLGER CÓRDOVA
Faculty of Medical Sciences: Dr RICARDO CARRASCO
Faculty of Philosophy and Education: Mgr GUILLERMO PÉREZ
Faculty of Psychology: Dr OSWALDO MONTENEGRO JIMÉNEZ
Faculty of Social Communication: PATRICIO MONCAYO
Faculty of Veterinary Medicine: Dr OSWALDO ALBORNÓZ

Campus at Riobamba offers courses in education, literature and philosophy

UNIVERSIDAD DE CUENCA

Av. 12 de Abril y Agustín Cueva, Cuenca
Telephone: (7) 831556
Fax: (7) 835197
Internet: www.ucuenca.edu.ec
Founded 1867
Academic year: October to July

Rector: Dr JAIME ASTUDILLO ROMERO
Vice-Rector: FABIÁN CARRASCO CASTRO
Sec.-Gen.: Dr WILSON ANDRADE R.
Admin. Dir: MARGARITA GUTIERREZ
Librarian: CELIANO A. VINTIMILLA V.

Number of teachers: 613
Number of students: 8,500

Publications: *Anales de la Universidad de Cuenca, Informe de Coyuntura-Facultad de Ciencias Económicas, IURIS—Revista de la Facultad de Jurisprudencia, Revista de la Facultad de Ciencias Agropecuarias, Revista de la Facultad de Ciencias Médicas, Revista del IDICSA, Revista del IDIS, Revista del IICT*

DEANS

Faculty of Agriculture: Dr MANUEL SORIA PARRA
Faculty of Architecture: ALCIBÍADES VEGA MALO
Faculty of Arts: Dr JULIO MOSQUERA
Faculty of Chemistry: SILVANA LARRIVA GONZÁLEZ
Faculty of Dentistry: Dr OSWALDO VÁSQUEZ CORDERO
Faculty of Economics: MARCO VALENCIA ORELLANA
Faculty of Engineering: BOLÍVAR PEÑAFIEL GONZÁLEZ (acting)
Faculty of Jurisprudence: Dr JORGE MORALES ALVAREZ
Faculty of Medical Sciences: Dr ARTURO QUIZHPE PERALTA
Faculty of Philosophy: MARÍA EUGENIA MALDONADO

DIRECTORS

Institute of Computing and Information Science (ICEI): SALVADOR MONSALVE R.
Institute of Physical Education: JULIO ABAD
Research Institute: Dr ALBERTO QUEZADA R.
Planning Unit: RAFAEL ESTRELLA A.

UNIVERSIDAD DE GUAYAQUIL

Ciudadela Universitaria Salvador Allende, Av. Kennedy y Av. Delta, Guayaquil
Telephone: (4) 2293598
E-mail: webmaster@ug.edu.ec
Internet: www.ug.edu.ec
Founded 1867
Private control
Language of instruction: Spanish
Academic year: April to February (2 semesters)

Rector: Dr CARLOS CEDENO NAVARRETE
Gen. Vice-Rector: Dr SALOMON HITLER QUINTERO ESTRADA
Vice-Rector for Academic Affairs: Dr JOSÉ LIZARDO APOLO PINEDA

Vice-Rector for Admin. Affairs: Dr CÉSAR ROMERO VILLAGRÁN
Librarian: LEONOR V. DE SANTANDER

Number of teachers: 2,848
Number of students: 60,000

Publication: *Revista*

DEANS

Faculty of Administrative Sciences: CARLOS SAN ANDRÉS RIVADENEIRA
Faculty of Agriculture: CÉSAR PACHECO MONROY (acting)
Faculty of Architecture and Town Planning: JORGE CABELLO FARAH
Faculty of Chemical Engineering: FERNANDO QUIROZ PÉREZ
Faculty of Chemistry: Dr CARLOS SILVA HUILCAPI
Faculty of Economics: WASHINGTON AGUIRRE GARCÍA
Faculty of Industrial Engineering: ALFREDO BUCARAM ORTIZ
Faculty of Law, Social Sciences and Politics: ALFREDO RUIZ GUZMÁN
Faculty of Mathematics and Physics: FERNANDO ABAD MONTERO (acting)
Faculty of Medicine: Dr WILSON MAITTA MENDOZA
Faculty of Natural Sciences: JOSÉ CUENCA VARGAS
Faculty of Odontology: Dr ÁNGELA CHONG LÓPEZ
Faculty of Philosophy, Literature and Education: Dr FRANCISCO MORÁN MÁRQUEZ
Faculty of Physical Education, Sport and Recreation: ENRIQUE N. GAMBOA ABRIL
Faculty of Psychology: GONZALO FLORES PAVÓN
Faculty of Social Communication: HÉCTOR CHÁVEZ VILLAO
Faculty of Veterinary Medicine: MARÍO COBO CEDEÑO (acting)

UNIVERSIDAD DEL AZUAY

Avda 24 de Mayo 7-77 y Hernán Malo, Cuenca, Azuay
Telephone: (7) 2881333
Fax: (7) 2815997
E-mail: webmaster@uazuay.edu.ec
Internet: www.uazuay.edu.ec
Founded 1968; present status 1990
Academic year: October to July

Rector: Dr MARIO JARAMILLO PAREDES
Vice-Rector: FRANCISCO SALGADO ARTEGA
Dean (Admin. and Finance): CARLOS CORDERO DÍAZ
Dean (Research): JACINTO GUILLÉN GARCÍA

Library of 40,000 vols

Publication: *Marginalia* (2 a year)

DEANS

Faculty of Administration: MIGUEL MOSCOSO COBOS
Faculty of Design: PATRICIO LEÓN BUSTOS
Faculty of Law: Dr PATRICIO CORDERO ORDOÑEZ
Faculty of Medicine: Dr EDGAR RODAS ANDRADE
Faculty of Philosophy: JORGE QUINTUÑA ALVAREZ
Faculty of Science and Technology: MIRIAM BRIONES GARCÍA
Faculty of Theology: Fr ANTONIO ALONSO MARTÍNEZ

UNIVERSIDAD ESTATAL DE BOLÍVAR

km 3½ sector Alpachaca, Guaranda
Telephone: (3) 2980121
Fax: (3) 2980123
Internet: www.ueb.edu.ec
Founded 1989
State control

Rector: GABRIEL GALARZA LÓPEZ
Vice-Rector for Academic Affairs: PEDRO PABLO LUCIO GAIBOR
Vice-Rector for Finance: DIÓMEDES NÚÑEZ MINAYA
Registrar: GONZALO LOPEZ RIVADENEIRA
Librarian: RODRIGO SALTOS CHAVES
Number of teachers: 182
Number of students: 5,801 (3,063 full-time, 2,738 part-time)
Publication: *Enlace Universitario*

DEANS

Faculty of Administrative Sciences, Business Management and Informatics: ANGEL GARCÍA
Faculty of Agriculture, Natural Resources and the Environment: HUGO VÁZQUEZ COLOMA
Faculty of Education, Social Sciences, Philosophy and Humanistic Sciences: MARCO LARA OLALLA
Faculty of Health Sciences and of the Human Being: CECILIA VILLAVICENCIO
Faculty of Jurisprudence and Politics: CECILIA VILLAVICENCIO

UNIVERSIDAD ESTATAL DE MILAGRO

Km 1½, Vía Milagro Km 26, Los Rios, Milagro
Telephone: (4) 2970881
Fax: (4) 2974319
E-mail: unemi@hotmail.com
Founded 2001
Rector: Dr RÓMULO MINCHALA MURILLO
Sec.-Gen.: AGUSTIN ARELLANO QUIROZ.

UNIVERSIDAD ESTATAL DEL SUR DE MANABÍ

Complejo Universitario, Ciudadela 10 de Agosto, Vía a Noboa, Jipijapa
Telephone: (5) 2600229
E-mail: unesum@hotmail.com
Founded 2001
State control
Rector: JORGE CLIMACO CAÑARTE MURILLO.

UNIVERSIDAD ESTATAL PENÍNSULA DE SANTA ELENA

Avda 9 de Octubre 515, Edificio Ching, 2 Piso, La Libertad
Telephone: (4) 2780018
Fax: (4) 2785398
E-mail: unipen@interactive.net.ec
Founded 1998
Academic year: September to April
Rector: XAVIER TOMALÁ
Vice-Rector: GEORGE CLEMENTE.

UNIVERSIDAD NACIONAL DE CHIMBORAZO

Avda Eloy Alfaro y 10 de Agosto, Riobamba
Telephone: (3) 2962-611
Fax: (3) 2962-611
E-mail: rector@unach.edu.ec
Internet: www.unach.edu.ec
Founded 1995
State control
Academic year: October to July (two semesters)
Rector: EDISON RIERA RODRÍGUEZ
Vice-Rector: ENRIQUE CRESPO
Faculties of education, engineering, humanities and technology, physical education and health sciences, political science and administration.

UNIVERSIDAD NACIONAL DE LOJA

Casilla letra 'S', Loja
Ciudad Universitaria Guillermo Falconí Espinosa 'La Argelia', Loja
Telephone: (7) 2547252
Fax: (7) 2546075
E-mail: rector@unl.edu.ec
Internet: www.unl.edu.ec
Founded 1859 as the Junta Universitaria; univ. status 1943
State control
Language of instruction: Spanish
Academic year: October to July
Rector: Dr GUSTAVO ENRIQUE VILLACÍS RIVAS
Vice-Rector: Dr ERNESTO RAFAEL GONZÁLEZ PESANTES
Librarian: Dr ENITH COSTA MUÑOZ
Library of 3,500 vols
Number of teachers: 720
Number of students: 13,280
Publications: *Estudios Universitarios, Revista Científica,* and various faculty bulletins

DIRECTORS

Agriculture and Renewable Natural Resources: Dr EDGAR BENÍTEZ GONZÁLEZ
Education, Art and Communication: Dr YOVANY SALAZAR ESTRADA
Energy, Industry and Non-Renewable Natural Resources: JOSÉ OCHOA ALFARO
Health Sciences: Dr AMABLE BERMEO FLORES
Law and Social and Politicalciences: Dr ROGELIO CASTILLO BERMEO

UNIVERSIDAD TÉCNICA DE AMBATO

Casilla 18-01-334, Ambato
Telephone: (3) 85-39-05
Fax: (3) 84-91-64
Internet: www.uta.edu.ec
Founded 1969
Rector: VÍCTOR HUGO JARAMILLO
Vice-Rector: ANÍBAL SALTOS SALTOS
Sec.-Gen.: Dr PATRICIO POAQUIZA
Librarian: ELSA NARANJO
Number of teachers: 332
Number of students: 7,200

DEANS

Faculty of Accountancy: SANTIAGO BARRIGA
Faculty of Administration: JOSÉ SILVA
Faculty of Agricultural Engineering: NELLY CHERREZ
Faculty of Civil Engineering: MIGUEL MORA
Faculty of Education: Dr JULIO SALTOS
Faculty of Food Technology: ROMEL RIVERA
Faculty of Systems Engineering: VÍCTOR GUACHIMBOZA
Centro de Estudios a Distancia: GALO JARAMILLO
Centro de Estudios de Postgrado: FRANCISCO FERNÁNDEZ B.

UNIVERSIDAD TÉCNICA DE BABAHOYO

Apdo 66, Babahoyo, Los Ríos
Via Flores, Babahoyo, Los Ríos
Telephone: (5) 730646
Fax: (5) 730647
E-mail: blupera@utb.edu.ec
Internet: www.utb.edu.ec
Founded 1971
Rector: BOLÍVAR LUPERA YCAZA
Vice-Rector for Academic Affairs: Dr RAFAEL FALCONI MONTALVAN
Vice-Rector for Admin. Affairs: Dr ZOILA SÁNCHEZ ANCHUNDIA
Sec.-Gen.: ALBERTO BRAVO MEDINA
Librarian: MIGUEL BASTIDAS
Number of teachers: 450

Number of students: 5,000

DEANS

Faculty of Administration, Finance and Informatics: AUSBERTO COLINA GONZALVO
Faculty of Agriculture: OTTO ORDEÑANA BURNHAN
Faculty of Health Sciences: Dr CÉSAR NOBOA AQUINO
Faculty of Social Sciences and Education: Dr JACINTO MUÑOZ MUÑOZ

UNIVERSIDAD TÉCNICA DE COTOPAXI

Campus Universitario, Av. Simón Rodríguez s/n, Barrio El Ejido, Latacunga, Cotopaxi
Telephone: (3) 2810296
Fax: (3) 2810295
E-mail: webmaster@utc.edu.ec
Internet: www.utc.edu.ec
Founded 1995
Rector: FRANCISCO RAMIRO ULLOA ENRÍQUEZ
Vice-Rector: HERNÁN YÁNEZ
Sec.-Gen.: WILLIAM ESPINOZA
Publication: *Alma Mater.*

UNIVERSIDAD TÉCNICA DE ESMERALDAS 'LUIS VARGAS TORRES'

Av. Kennedy 704 entre Hilda Padilla y Calle H, Esmeraldas
Telephone: (6) 2723700
E-mail: utelvt@utelvt.edu.ec
Internet: www.utelvt.edu.ec
Founded 1970
Rector: Dr BENITO REYES PAZMIÑO
Vice-Rector for Academic Affairs: BETTO VERNAZA CASTILLO
Vice-Rector for Admin. Affairs: LUIS FELIPE PACHECO
Sec.-Gen.: MARCO REINOSO CAÑOTE
Librarian: SOLANDA GOBEA
Number of teachers: 180
Number of students: 800

DEANS

Faculty of Administration and Economics: ARMENGOL PINEDA CUERO
Faculty of Education and Health Sciences: Dr ERMEL TAPIA S.
Faculty of Engineering and Technology: GUILLERMO MOSQUERA Q.
Faculty of Social Sciences and Development Studies: Dr GIRARD VERNAZA A.
Faculty of Stockbreeding and Environmental Science: Dr JEFFERSON QUIÑONEZ B.

UNIVERSIDAD TÉCNICA DE MACHALA

Avda Panamerica Km 5 1/2 via a Pasaje, Machala
Telephone: (72) 992-687
E-mail: utmachala@utmachala.edu.ec
Internet: www.utmachala.edu.ec
Founded 1969
State control
Language of instruction: Spanish
Academic year: March to January
Rector: VÍCTOR HERNÁN CABRERA JARAMILLO
Vice-Rector: ALCIDES ESPINOZA RAMIREZ
Sec.-Gen.: JOSÉ ANTONIO ROMERO TANDAZO
Librarian: MARÍA UNDA SERRANA DE BARREZUETA
Library of 5,000 vols
Number of teachers: 600
Number of students: 9,636
Publication: *Revista de la Facultad de Agronomía y Veterinaria*

DEANS

Faculty of Agronomy and Veterinary Science: MAX IÑIGUEZ
Faculty of Business Administration and Accountancy: DANILO PICO
Faculty of Chemical Sciences: ALBERTO GAME
Faculty of Civil Engineering: LUIS ORDÓÑEZ JARAMILLO
Faculty of Sociology: RAMIRO ORDOÑEZ
Institute of Languages: LAURA LEÓN DE ASTUDILLO
School of Nursing: DAYSI ESPINOZA DE RA-MÍREZ

UNIVERSIDAD TÉCNICA DE MANABÍ

Apdo 82, Portoviejo, Manabí
Avenida Universitaria, Portoviejo, Manabí
Telephone: (5) 2632677
Fax: (5) 2651569
Internet: www.utm.edu.ec
Founded 1954
State control
Academic year: May to January (two semesters)

Rector: JOSÉ FÉLIX VÉLIZ BRIONES
Sec.: Dr PLUTARCO GARCÍA SALTOS
Librarian: MARÍA ANGELA DE CORONEL

Number of teachers: 489
Number of students: 8,000

Publication: *Revista*

DEANS

Faculty of Administration and Economics: GUILLERMO HINOSTROZA
Faculty of Agricultural Engineering: CÉSAR JARRE
Faculty of Agronomy: JULIO TORO GARCÍA
Faculty of Arts and Education: JOSÉ COBEÑA
Faculty of Chemistry, Mathematics and Physics: HERNÁN NIETO
Faculty of Health Sciences: Dr BOSCO BARBERÁN
Faculty of Humanistic Sciences: CLORIS CEVALLOS DE ORMAZA
Faculty of Information Science: CARLOS INTRIAGO
Faculty of Veterinary Sciences: Dr BOLÍVAR ORTEGA
Faculty of Zootechnology: Dr MARIO MATA MOREIRA

UNIVERSIDAD TÉCNICA DEL NORTE

Ciudadela Universitaria 'El Olivo', Avda 17 de Julio, Ibarra
Telephone: (6) 2953461
Fax: (6) 2955833
Internet: www.utn.edu.ec
Founded 1986

Rector: Dr MARCO L. MUÑOZ HERRERIA

Faculties of administration, animal husbandry and environment, applied sciences, educational sciences, health sciences.

UNIVERSIDAD TÉCNICA ESTATAL DE QUEVEDO

Km 1 Vía a Quito, Casilla 73, Quevedo, Los Ríos
Telephone: (5) 751430
Fax: (5) 753300
E-mail: info@uteq.edu.ec
Internet: www.uteq.edu.ec
Founded 1984
State control

Rector: MANUEL HAZ ALVAREZ
Vice-Rector: Dr TITO CABRERA VICUÑA
Librarian: CARMEN VELASCO LÓPEZ

Number of teachers: 144
Number of students: 2,900

DEANS

Faculty of Agrarian Science: GLEN MERA HALLÓN
Faculty of Cattle Science: ROQUE VIVAS MOREIRA
Faculty of Enterprise Science: Dr IGNACIO FUENTES CORNEJO
Faculty of Environmental Science: ANTONIO VÉLIZ MENDOZA
International Relations: Dr JOFFRE RADA PERALTA

Private Universities

PONTIFICIA UNIVERSIDAD CATÓLICA DEL ECUADOR

Avda 12 de Octubre 1076 y Roca, Apdo 17-01-2184, Quito
Telephone: (2) 2991700
Fax: (2) 2567117
E-mail: webmaster@puce.edu.ec
Internet: www.puce.edu.ec
Founded 1946
Private control
Language of instruction: Spanish
Academic year: August to May

Grand Chancellor: Mons. RAÚL VELA CHIRIBOGA
Vice-Grand Chancellor: Rev. FEDERICO MARÍA SANFELÍU VILAR
Rector: Dr JOSÉ RIBADENEIRA ESPINOSA
Vice-Rector: Dr MANUEL CORRALES PASCUAL
Librarian: OSWALDO ORBE CORTEZ

Number of teachers: 1,837
Number of students: 12,931

Publications: *Economía y Humanismo* (4 a year), *Nuestra Ciencia*, *Revista PUCE* (2 a year)

DEANS

Faculty of Accounting and Administrative Sciences: PAULINA RAZA VINUEZA
Faculty of Architecture, Design and Arts: ALEXIS MOSQUERA RIVERA
Faculty of Communication, Linguistics and Literature: Dr LUCÍA LEMOS SILVA
Faculty of Ecclesiastical Philosophical-Theological Sciences: Rev. FERNANDO BARREDO HEINERT
Faculty of Economics: LUCAS PACHECO PRADO
Faculty of Education Sciences: Dra MYRIAM AGUIRRE MONTERO
Faculty of Engineering: ESTUARDO PÁEZ ESPINOSA
Faculty of Exact and Natural Sciences: Dr LAURA ARCOS TERÁN
Faculty of Human Sciences: NELSON REASCOS VALLEJO
Faculty of Jurisprudence: Rev. ERNESTO VÁSCONEZ RIBADENEIRA
Faculty of Medicine: Dr CARLOS ACURIO VELASCO
Faculty of Nursing: LOURDES CARRERA SOSA
Faculty of Psychology: Dr CARLOS QUIROZ PALACIOS

DIRECTORS

School of Medical Technology: Dr JOSEFINA EGAS BENAVIDES
School of Social Work: GABRIEL CUESTA MOSCOSO SEDES

REGIONAL CAMPUSES

Ambato Campus: Rocafuerte y Lalama (Esq.), Apdo. 18-01-662, Ambato; tel. (3) 2416722; fax (3) 2411868; e-mail pucesa@puce.edu.ec; internet www.pucesa.edu.ec; courses in computer technology and English; Pro-Rector Dr CÉSAR GONZÁLEZ LOOR.

Esmeraldas Campus: Calle Espejo y Santa Cruz S/n, Apdo. 08-01-0065, Esmeraldas; tel.

(6) 2726613; fax (6) 2726509 ext. 114; e-mail prorrector@pucese.net; internet www.pucese.net; 391 students; courses in education, accountancy, nursing, English; Pro-Rector AITOR URBINA GARCÍA DE VICUÑA.

Ibarra Campus: Ave Aurelio Espinosa Pólit, Cdla. 'La Victoria', Apdo. 10-10-34, Ibarra; tel. (2) 2641786; fax (2) 2641786; e-mail prorect@pucei.edu.ec; internet www.pucei.edu.ec; 741 students; courses in administration and accountancy, tourism and hotel management, design, civil engineering; Pro-Rector Dr SANTIAGO ACOSTA AIDE.

PUCE—Manabí: Campus Portoviejo, Ciudadela 1° de Mayo, Calle Eudoro Loor s/n y 25 de Diciembre, Portoviejo;Campus Chone, Vía Chone-El Carmen, Km 11, Chone;Campus Bahía de Caráquez, Vía Bahía-Chone, Km 8; tel. and fax (5) 263-7300 (Portoviejo); tel. and fax (5) 295-7269 (Chone); tel. and fax (5) 2399030 (Bahía de Caráquez); fax (5) 2637305; e-mail pucemanabi@hotmail.com; Pro-Rector Rev. HOMERO FUENTES VERA.

PUCE—Santo Domingo de los Colorados: Vía Chone Km. 2 y San Cristóbal, Apdo. 17-24-539, Santo Domingo de los Tsáchila; tel. and fax (2) 3702860; e-mail sprorrectorado@pucesd.edu.ec; Pro-Rector Dr JULIO MARRERO GIRÁLDEZ.

UNIVERSIDAD CATÓLICA DE CUENCA

Apdo 01-01-1937, Cuenca
Telephone: (7) 842606
Fax: (7) 831040
E-mail: uccsis@etapa.com.ec
Founded 1970
Private control
Academic year: October to July (3 terms)

Rector: Dr CÉSAR CORDERO MOSCOSO
Assoc. Rector: Dr CARLOS DARQUEA LÓPEZ
Pro-Rector: Dr MARCO VICUÑA DOMÍNGUEZ
Academic Vice-Rector: Dr EDUARDO DÍAZ
Administrative Vice-Rector: Dr NELSON CÓRDOVA ALVAREZ
Extension Vice-Rector: Dr HUGO ORTIZ SEGARRA
Academic Dir: PABLO CISNEROS QUINTANILLA
Finance Dir: ESTUARDO RUBIO AUQUILLA
Chief Admin. Officer: Dr ENRIQUE CAMPOVERDE CAJAS
Sec.-Gen.: Dr RODRIGO CISNEROS AGUIRRE
Librarian: Prof. CÉSAR RIVERA OCHOA

Library of 7,000 vols
Number of teachers: 650
Number of students: 8,000

Publications: *Diálogo, Estudios, Panoramas, Presencia, Retama*

DEANS

Faculty of Agricultural Engineering, Mines and Veterinary Science: Dr EDUARDO CORONEL DIAZ
Faculty of Chemical and Industrial Engineering: Dr ALEJANDRO VÁSQUEZ CHICA
Faculty of Civil Engineering and Architecture: GERARDO AREVALO IDROVO
Faculty of Commercial Engineering: JULIO HERNÁNDEZ VINTIMILLA
Faculty of Distance Learning: Dr HUGO ORTIZ SEGARRA
Faculty of Economics: Dr HUGO ORTIZ SEGARRA
Faculty of Education and Psychology: Dr JOSÉ ESCANDÓN MEJÍA
Faculty of Electrical Engineering: Dr EDUARDO CORONEL DÍAZ
Faculty of Enterprise Engineering: MARCELO MENDIETA MÉNDEZ
Faculty of Informatics Systems: Dr EDUARDO CORONEL DIAZ
Faculty of Law and Social Sciences: Dr FRANCISCO PIEDRA LOJA

Faculty of Medicine and Health Sciences: Dr CARLOS DARQUEA LOPEZ

Faculty of Odontology: Dr OSWALDO VINTI-MILLA MARCHÁN

Bilingual Secretarial School: Dra GLADIS LEMARIE CAICEDO

Communications, Radio and Television Channel 2: Dr HUGO ORTIZ SEGARRA

Delegation in Europe: Prof. Dr FRANZ KANEHL (Germany)

Extension University at Azogues: Dr MARCO VICUÑA DOMÍNGUEZ

Extension University at Cañar: Dr HERNÁN CRESPO VERDUGO

Extension University at Macas: JOSÉ MERINO V.

Extension University at Méndez: Dr JORGE CÁRDENAS ESPINOZA

Extension University at San Pablo, Troncal: REMIGIO VÁZQUEZ LÓPEZ

Institute of Languages: Dr JOSÉ ESCANDÓN MEJÍA

Institute of Nursing: Dr OSWALDO VINTIMILLA MARCHÁN

Postgraduate Committee: Dr MARCO VICUNA DOMÍNGUEZ

School of Drama and Aerobics: Dr CARLOS EFRAÍN CRESPO

School of Journalism and Communications: Dr PRISCILA TAMAYO DE PALACIOS

School of Physical Education: TARQUINO SUQUINAGUA PATIÑO

School of Social Service: Dr CLAUDIO PEÑA-HERRERA M.

University Hospital: Dr CARLOS DARQUEA LÓPEZ

UNIVERSIDAD CATÓLICA DE SANTIAGO DE GUAYAQUIL

Av. Carlos Julio Arosemena Km $1\frac{1}{2}$ Vía Daule, Guayaquil

Telephone: (4) 2206950

Internet: www.ucsg.edu.ec

Founded 1962

Private control

Academic year: May to April

Rector: Dr MICHEL DOUMET ANTÓN

Vice-Rector: MAURO TOSCANINI SEGALE

Vice-Rector for Academic Affairs: ELIZABETH LARREA DE GRANADOS

Librarian: CLEMENCIA MITE DE SANTILLÁN

Library of 32,974 vols

Number of teachers: 612

Number of students: 6,249

Publications: *Revista Cuadernos*, *Revista Universidad*

DEANS

Faculty of Architecture: ROSA EDITH RADA ALPRECH

Faculty of Arts and Humanities: Dr MARÍA DE LOURDES ESTRADA RUIZ

Faculty of Business: LUIS FERNANDO HIDALGO PROAÑO

Faculty of Economics: KLEBER ALBERTO CORONEL LÓPEZ

Faculty of Engineering: WALTER VICENTE MERA ORTIZ

Faculty of Law: JOSÉ MIGUEL GARCÍA BAQUERIZO

Faculty of Medicine: Dr ALFREDO JOSÉ ESCALA MACCAFERRI

Faculty of Philosophy, Literature and Education: MARÍA CECILIA LOOR DUEÑAS

Faculty of Technical Education for Development: Dr KLEVER GUIDO LÓPEZ PARRALES

UNIVERSIDAD LAICA 'VICENTE ROCAFUERTE' DE GUAYAQUIL

Apartado Postal 1133, Guayaquil

Avda de las Américas frente al Cuartel Modelo, Guayaquil

Telephone: (4) 2287200

E-mail: laicared@gye.satnet.net

Internet: www.ulaicavr.edu.ec

Founded 1847; univ. status 1966

Private control

Language of instruction: Spanish

Academic year: April to January

Rector: Dr ELSA ALARCÓN SOTO

Gen. Vice-Rector: ALFREDO AGUILAR ALAVA

Vice-Rector for Academic Affairs: ALFONSO SÁNCHEZ GUERRERO

Gen.–Sec.: ALFONSO AGUILAR ALAVA

Librarian: CECILIA RODRÍGUEZ GRANDA

Library of 8,000 vols

Number of teachers: 307

Number of students: 9,317

Publications: *Boletín el Contador Laico*, *Boletín de Información Académica* (1 a year)

Faculties of administration, architecture, civil engineering, economics, education, journalism, jurisprudence and social sciences; Schools of accountancy, child education, design, foreign trade, languages, marketing, publicity, secretarial administration.

UNIVERSIDAD TÉCNICA PARTICULAR DE LOJA

Apartado postal 11-01-608, Loja

San Cayetano Alto, Loja

Telephone: (7) 2570275

Fax: (7) 2584893

E-mail: utpl_ects@utpl.edu.ec

Internet: www.utpl.edu.ec

Founded 1971

Private control

Language of instruction: Spanish

Academic year: October to March, April to August

Rector-Chancellor: Pe Dr LUIS MIGUEL ROMERO FERNÁNDEZ

Vice-Chancellor: Dr JOSÉ BARBOSA CORBACHO

Sec.-Gen.: Ing. GABRIEL GARCÍA TORRES

Dir of Open and Distance Education: Dra MARÍA JOSÉ RUBIO GÓMEZ

Librarian: Lic. AMADA JARAMILLO LOJÁN

Library of 25,000 vols

Number of teachers: 190 full-time, 121 distance education

Number of students: 2,200 full-time, 7,218 distance education

Publications: *El Reloj* (12 a year), *Universidad* (12 a year), *Universidad Técnica Particular de Loja* (1 a year)

DIRECTORS

School of Accounting and Auditing: Dr LUPE ESPEJO

School of Agricultural Engineering: HERNÁN LUCERO MOSQUERA

School of Agro-Industry Engineering: RUTH MARTÍNEZ ESPINOZA

School of Architecture: KARINA MONTEROS

School of Arts and Design: ELENA MALO

Banking and Financial Administration Programme: RAMIRO ARMIJOS

School of Biochemistry and Pharmacy: Dr PAULA TORRES BAILÓN

School of Biology: ESTEBAN TORRACHI

School of Business Administration: ANDREA LOAIZA

School of Chemical Engineering: Dr OMAR MALAGÓN AVILÉS

School of Civil Engineering: VINICIO SUÁREZ

School of Economics: JUAN MANUEL GARCÍA

Electronics and Telecommunications Programme: JORGE JARAMILLO

School of English: ANNA GATES TAPIA

Environmental Management Programme: FAUSTO LÓPEZ

School of Geology and Mining: JHON SOTO

School of Hotel and Tourism Administration: MARTHA RUIZ RODRÍGUEZ

School of Information Systems and Computing Engineering: NELSON PIEDRA

School of Law: Dr SILVANA ERAZO

School of Management Assistance and Public Relations: MÓNICA ABENDAÑO

School of Medicine: Dr JUAN VALDIVIESO ARIAS

School of Psychology: SILVIA VACA

School of Social Communication: ABEL SUING RUIZ

College

Centro Internacional de Estudios Superiores de Comunicación para América Latina (International Centre for Advanced Studies in Communications for Latin America): Diego de Almagro N32-113 y Andrade Marín, Apdo 17-01-584, Quito; tel. (2) 544-624; fax (2) 502487; e-mail ejaramillo@ciespal.net; internet www.ciespal.net; f. 1959 with UNESCO aid; training, documentation and research in fields of information science, radio and television; library: 2,000 vols, 20,700 documents; Dir-Gen. EDGAR JARAMILLO SALAS; publ. *Chasqui* (4 a year).

Schools of Art and Music

Conservatorio de Música 'José María Rodríguez': Cuenca; f. 1938; Dir Prof. RAFAEL SOJOS JARAMILLO.

Conservatorio Superior Nacional de Música: Casilla 17-01-3358, Quito; Cochapata E12-56 y Manuel Abascal, Quito; tel. (2) 248666; fax (2) 248666 ext. 128; e-mail conamusidireccion@uio.satnet.net; internet www.conservatorionacional.com.ec; f. 1900; library: 14,000 vols; 120 teachers; 800 students; Dir LUCIANO CARRERA GALARZA; publ. *Conservatorio*.

EGYPT

The Higher Education System

The higher education system in Egypt consists of Islamic and secular sectors. The Islamic sector is based upon Al-Azhar University in Cairo, founded in AD 970 as an adjunct to Al-Azhar mosque. Cairo University, the first secular university, was founded in 1908, and in 1925 it became a public institution. The Ministry of Higher Education and Scientific Research governs secular higher education through the aegis of the Supreme Council of Universities, while the Central Administration of Al-Azhar Institutes, a department of the Supreme Council of Al-Azhar Institutes, controls Islamic higher education. The Government is constitutionally required to provide free higher education to all, but students also pay enrolment fees. In 2004/05 there were an estimated 2,594,186 students enrolled in higher education. By 2009 there were 17 public universities, 51 public non-university institutions, 16 private universities and 89 private higher institutions. Out of the 51 non-university institutions, 47 were two-year middle technical institutes and four were four- to five-year higher technical institutes.

Students intending to attend university must hold the General Secondary School Certificate (or the Technical Secondary School Certificate); exact entry requirements vary between institutions. Islamic or Al-Azhar higher education requires the student to successfully complete Al-Azhar secondary school, otherwise applicants must take one year of Arabic and Koranic studies. The American University of Cairo, founded in 1919, is independent of the Egyptian higher education system but its degrees are recognized as equivalent to those awarded by Egyptian universities.

The main undergraduate degree is the Bachelors, which is usually awarded after four years, but in some disciplines may take five (architecture, dentistry, engineering, pharmacy, veterinary medicine) or six years (medicine). Instruction is in Arabic, except in dentistry, engineering, medicine, pharmacy, science and veterinary medicine, for which it is in English. The first postgraduate degree is the Diploma, which lasts for one year and leads to the award of the Diploma in Higher Studies, Diploma of Graduate Studies or simply the Diploma. The next postgraduate degree, the Masters, requires two years of study. Finally, the Doctor of Philosophy (PhD) is a three- to four-year course, based entirely on research.

Technical and vocational training is available at intermediate vocational institutes, higher technical institutes and as non-formal education. Intermediate technical institutes specialize in post-secondary, two-year diploma courses in the fields of commerce, health and industry; higher technical institutes focus on advanced courses in technical education across a wide range of subjects, leading to either the Diploma (two years) or Bachelors degree (four to five years). Non-formal education consists of refresher courses, evening classes and on-the-job training.

In 2007 a National Authority for Quality Assurance and Accreditation of Education (NAQAAE) was established to oversee the 50,000 educational institutes and prepare them for accreditation. It is the accrediting body for all Egyptian educational society (higher education, pre-university and Al-Azhar education).

Regulatory and Representative Bodies

GOVERNMENT

Ministry of Culture: 2 Sharia Shagaret ed-Dor, Cairo (Zamalek); tel. (2) 37486957; fax (2) 33461417; e-mail mculture@idsc.gov.eg; Minister FAROUK ABD AL-AZIZ HOSNI.

Ministry of Education: 12 Sharia el-Falaky, Cairo; tel. (2) 27959939; fax (2) 27942700; e-mail info@mail.emoe.org; internet www.emoe.org; Minister Dr YOUSRI SABER HUSSEIN EL-GAMAL.

Ministry of Higher Education and Scientific Research: 101 Sharia Qasr el-Eini, Cairo; tel. (2) 27924189; fax (2) 27941005; e-mail info@egy-mhe.gov.eg; internet www.egy-mhe.gov.eg; Minister Dr HANY MAHFOUZ HELAL.

ACCREDITATION

National Authority for Quality Assurance and Accreditation of Education (NAQAAE): Building of the Telecom Institute, 5 Mahmoud Elmeligy St, 6th District, Nasr City; tel. (2) 22630672; fax (2) 22636802; e-mail nagdy@naqaae.org; internet www.naqaae.org; f. 2007; board of 15 mems; Chair. Dr MAGDY KASSEM.

NATIONAL BODY

Supreme Council of Universities: 96 Ahmed Orabi, Mohandsen, Giza; tel. (2) 33029271; e-mail scu@mailer.eun.eg; internet www.scu.eun.eg; f. 1950; delineates gen. policy of univ. education and scientific research in order to attain nat. objectives in social, economic, cultural and scientific devt plans; determines admission numbers, fields of specialization and equivalences; the Egyptian Universities Network links univ. computer centres and research institutes throughout Egypt, and is the Egyptian gateway to the internet, and provides information services and online learning facilities; 33 mem. univs and private institutes; library of 3,300 vols (English and Arabic); Pres. THE MINISTER OF HIGHER EDUCATION AND MINISTER OF STATE FOR SCIENTIFIC RESEARCH; Sec.-Gen. Prof. SALWA EL-GHARIB.

Learned Societies

GENERAL

Academy of the Arabic Language: 15 Aziz Abaza St, Zamalek, Cairo; tel. (2) 27362002; fax (2) 27362002; e-mail acc@idsc.net.eg; internet www.arabicacademy.org.eg; f. 1932; 40 Egyptian active mems, also corresp. mems, hon. mems and foreign active mems; library of 60,000 vols; Pres. Prof. AHMED SHAWKY DHEIF; Sec.-Gen. IBRAHIM ABDEL MEGEED; publ. *Review* (2 a year).

African Society: 5 Ahmed Hishmat St, Zamalik, Cairo; f. 1972 to promote knowledge about Africa and nat. liberation movements in the Afro-Arab world and encourage research on Africa; organizes lectures, debates, seminars, symposia and conferences; participates in celebration of African nat. occasions; arranges cultural and scientific exchange with similar African societies; publishes bulletins and books in Arabic and English; 500 mems; library of 1,500 vols in Arabic; library of 2,000 vols in other languages; Sec.-Gen. M. FOUAD EL BIDEWY; publs *Africa Newsletter* (in Arabic), *African Studies* (irregular).

Institut d'Égypte (Egyptian Institute): 13 Sharia Sheikh Rihane, Cairo; f. 1798 by Napoleon Bonaparte; literature, arts and science relating to Egypt and neighbouring countries; 60 mems; 50 assoc. mems; 50 corresp. mems; library of 160,000 vols; Pres. Dr SILEMAN HAZIEN; Sec.-Gen. P. GHALIOUN-GUI; publs *Bulletin* (1 a year), *Mémoires*.

AGRICULTURE, FISHERIES AND VETERINARY SCIENCE

Egyptian Society of Dairy Science: 1 Ouziris St, Garden City, Cairo; f. 1972; Pres. Dr ISMAEL YOUSRY; publ. *Egyptian Journal of Dairy Science*.

BIBLIOGRAPHY, LIBRARY SCIENCE AND MUSEOLOGY

Egyptian Association for Library and Information Science: c/o Dept of Archives, Librarianship and Information Science, Faculty of Arts, Univ. of Cairo, Cairo; tel. (2) 35676365; fax (2) 35729659; f. 1956; 4,000 mems; Pres. Dr S. KHALIFA; Sec. M. HOSAN EL DIN.

Supreme Council of Antiquities: 3 Al-Adel Abou Bakr St, Zamalek, Cairo; tel. (2) 27365645; fax (2) 27357239; e-mail hawass@sca.gov.eg; internet www.sca.gov.eg; f. 1859 to oversee the preservation of Egyptian cultural heritage; attached to Ministry of Culture of Egypt; Dir Dr GABBALLAH ALI GABBALLAH; Sec.-Gen. Dr ZAHI HAWASS.

ECONOMICS, LAW AND POLITICS

Egyptian Society of International Law: 16 Sharia Ramses, Cairo; tel. and fax (2)

25743162; f. 1945; to promote the study of int. law and to work for the establishment of int. relations, based on law and justice; lectures; Pres. Dr MOUFEED CHEHAB; Sec.-Gen. Dr SALAH AMER; Admin. Dir A. EL MAHROUKY; 800 mems; library of 4,100 books, 120 periodicals, 100,000 documents; publ. *Revue Egyptienne de Droit International* (1 a year).

Egyptian Society of Political Economy, Statistics and Legislation: 16 Sharia Ramses, BP 732, Cairo; tel. (2) 25750797; fax (2) 25743491; e-mail espesl@hotmail.com; internet www.espesl.org.eg; f. 1909; 3,018 mems; library of 45,000 vols; Pres. Prof. AHMAD FATHI SOROOR; Gen.-Sec. Dr MUSTAFA EL SAID; publ. *L'Egypte Contemporaine* (in Arabic, English and French, 4 a year).

FINE AND PERFORMING ARTS

Armenian Artistic Union: 3 Sharia Soliman, el-Halaby, BP 1060, Cairo; tel. (2) 25742282; f. 1920; promotion of Armenian and Arabic culture; 120 mems; Pres. VAHAG DEPOYAN.

L'Atelier: 6 Victor Bassili St, al Pharaana, Azarita, Alexandria; tel. and fax (3) 24860526; e-mail info@atelieralex.com; internet www.atelieralex.com; f. 1935; soc. of artists and writers; 350 mems; library of 5,500 vols; Pres. Dr MOHAMED RAFIK KHALI; Vice-Pres. Dr MOHAMED SALEM; publ. *Bulletin*.

High Council of Arts and Literature: 9 Sharia Hassan Sabri, Zamalek, Cairo; f. 1956; publishes books on literature, arts and social sciences.

Institute of Arab Music: 22 Sharia Ramses, Cairo; tel. (2) 22750702; f. 1924; promotion and teaching of Arab music; libraries of records, tapes and scores of Arab music; Chair. of Board HASSAN TAKER MOK; Sec.-Gen. FARZY RASHAD.

HISTORY, GEOGRAPHY AND ARCHAEOLOGY

Egyptian Geographical Society: 109 Qasr Al-Aini St, BP 422 Mohamed Farid, Cairo; tel. (2) 27945450; fax (2) 27956771; e-mail geoegypt@hotmail.com; internet www-egs-online.com; f. 1875, reorganized 1917; cartography section incl. 15,000 maps; 1,500 mems; library of 50,000 vols; Pres. Prof. M. S. ABULEZZ; Sec.-Gen. Prof. S. AL-HOSEINY; Library Dir H. LOTFY; publs *Al-Majallah Al-Jugrafiyah Al-'Arabiyah* (2 a year), *Bulletin of the Egyptian Geographical Society (Bulletin de la Soeiété de Géographie d'Egypte)* (1 a year), *Geographical research series* (24 occasional issues), proceedings of symposia, conferences workshops dealing with current geographical issues.

Hellenic Society of Ptolemaic Egypt: 20 Sharia Fouad I, Alexandria; f. 1908; Pres. Dr G. PARTHENIADIS; Sec. COSTA A. SANDI.

Société Archéologique d'Alexandrie: 6 Mahmoud, Moukhtar St, BP 815, Alexandria 21111; tel. and fax (3) 24820650; e-mail asalex@yahoo.col; f. 1893; 248 mems; Pres. Prof. M. EL ABBADI; Sec.-Gen. Prof. M HAGGAG.

Society for Coptic Archaeology: 222 Sharia Ramses, Cairo; tel. (2) 24824252; e-mail bgwassif@yahoo.com; f. 1934, for the study of Coptic archaeology, linguistics, papyrology, church history, liturgy and art; 360 mems; library of 16,000 vols; Pres. WASSIF BOUTROS-GHALI; Vice-Pres. Dr PETER GROSSMANN; Librarian Dr AWAD WADI; publ. *Bulletin de la Société Copte d'Archéologie (BSAC)* (1 a year).

LANGUAGE AND LITERATURE

Alliance Française: 4 Aboul Feda St, Port Saïd; tel. and fax (66) 3227431; fax (66) 3227431; e-mail allianceportsaid@suezcanal .net; offers courses and examinations in French language and culture and promotes cultural exchange with France; library of 4,000 vols; Dir BERNARD CHAUMONT-GAIL-LAIRD.

British Council: 192 el Nil St, Agouza, Cairo; tel. (2) 33031514; fax (2) 33443076; e-mail information@britishcouncil.org.eg; internet www.britishcouncil.org/egypt; teaching centre; offers courses and examinations in English language and British culture and promotes cultural exchange with the UK; attached offices in Alexandria and Heliopolis (teaching centre); Dir Dr JOHN GROTE; Dir, English Language Services STEVEN MURRELL.

Goethe-Institut: 5 Sharia el-Bustan, Cairo 11518; tel. (2) 25759877; fax (2) 25771140; e-mail info@cairo.goethe.org; internet www .goethe.de/ins/eg/kai; offers courses and examinations in German language and culture and promotes cultural exchange with Germany; attached centre in Alexandria; Dir and Regional Man. HEIKO SIEVERS.

Instituto Cervantes: 20 Boulos Hann St, Dokki, Cairo; tel. (2) 37601746; fax (2) 37601743; e-mail cencai@cervantes.es; internet elcairo.cervantes.es; offers courses and examinations in Spanish language and culture and promotes cultural exchange with Spain and Spanish-speaking Latin and Central America; library of 18,500 vols; Dir LUIS JAVIER RUIZ SIERRA.

MEDICINE

Alexandria Medical Association: 4 G. Carducci St, Alexandria; f. 1921; 1,200 mems; Pres. Prof. H. S. EL BADAWI; Sec.-Gen. Prof. TOUSSOUN ABOUL AZI; publ. *Alexandria Medical Journal* (English, French and Arabic, 4 a year).

Egyptian Dental Association: 84A Mat'haf el-Manial St, el-Manial, Cairo; tel. (2) 23658568; fax (2) 25319143; internet www .eda-egypt.org; f. 1937; 1960 separated from Egyptian Medical Asscn; Pres. Prof. HATEM ABDEL RAHMAN; Gen. Sec. Dr AHMED FARID SHEHAB; publ. *Egyptian Dental Journal* (4 a year).

Egyptian Medical Association: 42 Sharia Kasr el-Aini, Cairo; tel. (2) 33543406; f. 1919; 2,142 mems; Pres. Prof. A. EL KATEB; Sec.-Gen. Prof. A. H. SHAABAN; Vice-Pres. Prof. M. IBRAHIM; publ. *Journal* (in Arabic and English, 1 a year).

Egyptian Medical Association for the Study of Obesity: 14 el Khalil St, el Mohandessin, Giza, Cairo; tel. (2) 33023642; fax (2) 33027672; e-mail info@emaso-eg.org; internet www.emaso-eg.org; f. 2003; Pres. SHERIF HAFEZ; Gen. Sec. MOHAMED ABOUL-GHATE.

Egyptian Orthopaedic Association: 16 Sharia Houda Shaarawi, Cairo 11111; tel. (2) 23930013; fax (2) 23930054; e-mail eoa@ eoa.org.eg; internet www.eoa.org.eg; f. 1948; scientific and social activities in the field of orthopaedic surgery and traumatology; holds bi-annual scientific meetings, monthly clinical meetings; 1,700 mems; Pres. Prof. KHAMIS H. EL DEEB; Sec.-Gen. Prof. ABDEL MOHSEN ARAFA; publ. *Egyptian Orthopaedic Journal* (4 a year).

Ophthalmological Society of Egypt: Dar el Hekma, 42 Sharia Kasr el-Aini, Cairo; e-mail eos@eyegypt.com; f. 1902; Pres. Prof. KHALIL ABOU SHOUSA EL SAID; Hon. Sec. Dr AHMAD Ez EL DIN NAIM; 480 mems.

NATURAL SCIENCES

Biological Sciences

Egyptian Botanical Society: 1 Ozoris St, Tager Bldg, Garden City, Cairo; f. 1956 to encourage students of botany and links between workers in botany; organizes confs, seminars, lectures, and field trips for collecting, preserving and identifying plants; 230 mems; Pres. Prof. A. M. SALAMA; Sec. Dr MOHAMED FAWZY; publ. *Egyptian Journal of Botany* (3 a year).

Egyptian Entomological Society: 14 Sharia Ramses, BP 430, Cairo; tel. (2) 25750979; fax (2) 25766683; e-mail ees@ees .eg.net; internet www.ees.eg.net; f. 1907; 502 mems; library: publishes bulletins and economic series, library of 28,000 vols; Pres. Prof. MAHMOUD HAFEZ; Vice-Pres. Prof. MOHAMMAD ALI MOHAMMAD; Sec.-Gen. Prof. IBRAHIM MOHAMED.

Egyptian Society of Parasitology: 1 Ozoris St, Tager Bldg, Garden City, Cairo; fax (2) 24036497; f. 1967; holds scientific meetings, annual conf.; covers subjects in the fields of helminthology, medical entomology, protozoology, molluscs, insect control, immuno-diagnosis of parasitic diseases, treatment, etc.; 350 mems; Pres. Prof. MAHMOUD HAFEZ; Sec.-Gen. Prof. TOSSON A. MORSY; publ. *Journal* (2 a year).

Zoological Society of Egypt: Giza Zoo, Giza; f. 1927; aims to promote zoological studies and to foster good relations between zoologists in Egypt and abroad; field courses, lectures, etc.; library of 2,500 vols; 260 mems; Pres. Dr HASSAN A. HAFEZ; Sec. MOHAMED H. AMER; publ. *Bulletin*.

PHILOSOPHY AND PSYCHOLOGY

Egyptian Association for Mental Health: 1 Sharia 'Ilhami, Qasr al-Doubara, Cairo; internet www.arabpsynet.com/associations/ eamh.ass.htm; f. 1948; 630 mems; Pres. Dr JAMEL ABOU ELAZAYEM.

Egyptian Association for Psychological Studies: 1 Osiris St, Tager Bldg, Garden City, Cairo; tel. (2) 33541857; internet www .arabpsynet.com/homepage/psy-ass.htm; f. 1948; 1,200 mems; Pres. Dr ATEF KAMEL; publ. *Yearbook of Psychology*.

RELIGION, SOCIOLOGY AND ANTHROPOLOGY

Institut Dominicain d'Etudes Orientales: Priory of the Dominican Fathers, 1 Sharia Masna al-Tarabish, BP 18, Abbassiah, Cairo 11381; tel. (2) 24825509; fax (2) 26820682; e-mail ideo@link.com.eg; internet www.ideo-cairo.org; f. 1952; library of 100,000 vols; Dir Fr R. MORELON; publ. *Mélanges* (every 2 years).

Social Sciences Association of Egypt: Cairo; f. 1957; 1,234 mems.

TECHNOLOGY

Egyptian Materials Research Society: 33 Abdel-Khalik Tharwat St, Cairo; tel. (2) 23925997; e-mail contact@egmrs.org; internet www.egmrs.org; f. 1978 as Egyptian Soc. of Solid State Science and Applications (ESSA); present name 2003; 500 mems; Chair Prof. KAMEL ABD EL-HADY; publ. *Egyptian Journal of Solids*.

Egyptian Society of Engineers: 28 Sharia Ramses, Cairo; e-mail ese@rusys.eg.net; internet www.ese.eg.net; f. 1920; Pres. Prof. IBRAHIM ADHAM EL DEMIRDASH; Sec. Dr MOHAMED M. EL HASHIMY.

Research Institutes

GENERAL

Academy of Scientific Research and Technology: 101 Kasr el-Eini St, Cairo 11516; tel. (2) 27921267; fax (2) 27921270; e-mail info@asrt.sci.eg; internet www.asrt.sci.eg; f. 1972; nat. body responsible for science and technology; promotes the creation of an integrated system of scientific research; encourages female and youth participation in scientific leadership; affiliated instns: Central Metallurgical Research and Devt Institute, Egyptian Nat. Scientific and Technological Information Network, Gen. Directorate of Statistics on Science and Technology, Institute of Astronomy and Geophysics, Institute of Oceanography and Fisheries, Nat. Information and Documentation Centre, Nat. Institute for Standards, Nat. Network for Technology and Devt (UNTD), Nat. Research Centre, Petroleum Research Institute, Remote Sensing Centre, Scientific Instruments Centre, Science Museum; library of 34,000 vols, 50,000 periodicals; Pres. Prof. MOHAMMAD TAREK HUSSEIN.

National Research Centre: Al-Tahrir St, Dokki, Cairo; tel. (2) 33337615; fax (2) 33370931; e-mail info@nrc.sci.eg; internet www.nrc.sci.eg; f. 1956; began functioning in 1947 and laboratory work started in 1956; fosters and carries out research in both pure and applied sciences; the 54 laboratories are divided into 13 sections: Textile Industries, Food Industries and Nutrition, Pharmaceutical Industries, Chemical Industries, Engineering, Agriculture and Biology, Medical, Applied Organic and Inorganic Chemistry, Physics, Basic Sciences, Environment, Genetic Engineering and Biotechnology; library of 12,000 vols; Pres. Dr HANY EL NAZER; publs *Bulletin*, *NRC News*.

AGRICULTURE, FISHERIES AND VETERINARY SCIENCE

Agricultural Research Centre, Ministry of Agriculture: 9 Gamaa St, Giza; tel. (2) 35720944; fax (2) 35722069; e-mail abouhadid@arc.sci.eg; internet www.arc.sci.eg; Pres. Prof. AYMAN FARID ABOU HADID; Vice-Pres. Prof. MOHAMMED MOSTAFA EL GHARY.

Attached Research Institutes:

Agricultural Economics Research Institute: 7 Nadi El Said St, Dokki, Giza; tel. (2) 33354549; fax (2) 37607651; e-mail aeri84@hotmail.com; f. 1973; Dir Prof. FAUZY ABD ELAZIZ EL SHAZLY; publ. *Classification of the Agricultural Land Resources according to the Yield of the Most Important Field Crops* (every 5 years).

Agricultural Engineering Research Institute: Nadi El Said St, Dokki, Giza; tel. (2) 37487212; fax (2) 33356867; e-mail aenri@aenri.org; internet www.aenri.org; Dir Prof. GAMAL HASSAN EL SAYED; publs *Egyptian Journal of Agricultural Research* (4 a year), *Misr Journal of Agricultural Engineering* (4 a year).

Agricultural Extension and Rural Development Research Institute: tel. (2) 25716301; fax (2) 25716303; e-mail aerdri@hotmail.com; f. 1977; Dir Prof. A. G. EL DEIN SAYED MAHMOUD WAHBA.

Agricultural Genetic Engineering Research Institute: e-mail taymourm@ageri.sci.eg; Dir Prof. TAYMOUR MOHAMED NASR EL DIN IBRAHIM.

Animal Health Research Institute: Nadi El Said St, Dokki; tel. (2) 33374856; fax (2) 33350030; e-mail ahriegypt@gawab.com; internet www.ahri.gov.eg; f. 1928;

Nat. Veterinary Laboratory of the Egyptian Veterinary Services; animal health and safety of food from animal origin; centre of excellence and the point of reference in animal disease diagnosis; Dir Prof. MONA MEHREZ ALY.

Animal Production Research Institute: Nadi El Said St, Dokki, Cairo; tel. (2) 33372934; fax (2) 33372934; e-mail apri_arc@hotmail.com; internet apri.arc.sci.eg; f. 1938; Dir Prof. Dr FATEN FAHMY MOHAMED ABOU-AMMO.

Animal Reproduction Research Institute: 5 Hadek el Ahram, Giza; tel. (2) 33764325; fax (2) 33770822; e-mail arri2002@arabia.com; Dir Prof. ATEF ABEELMONSEF AHMED.

Cotton Research Institute: tel. (2) 35725035; fax (2) 35725035; e-mail cri_egypt@yahoo.com; internet arc.claes.sci.eg; f. 1919; Dir Prof. MOHAMED ABD EL MAGEED ABD EL AZIZ.

Field Crops Research Institute: Cairo University St, Giza; tel. (2) 35738425; fax (2) 35738425; internet www.fcri-egypt.com; f. 1971; Dir Prof. MOHAMED ABOU ZEID EL NAHRAWY.

Food Technology Research Institute: tel. (2) 35735090; fax (2) 35684669; e-mail nlftri@ie-eg.com; f. 1991; Dir Dr SAEB ABDEL-MONEIM HAFEZ.

Horticultural Research Institute: 9 Cairo University St, Giza; tel. (2) 35720617; fax (2) 35721628; e-mail hortinst@yahoo.com; f. 1948; produces new high-yielding early-maturing horticulture crop cultivars; maintains horticulture crop genetic resources; introduces new cultivars and germplasm of certain promising horticulture species; conducts research for optimizing the best cultural practices; implements extension and training programmes to transfer new technologies to farmers nationwide; 695 mems; Dir Prof. SALAMA EID SALEM SHREIF; publ. *Egyptian Journal of Horticulture* (2 a year).

Plant Pathology Research Institute: tel. (2) 35724893; fax (2) 35723146; e-mail nagiabouzeid@link.net; internet www.plant pathology.com; f. 1919; research in various aspects of disease survey: ecology, biology, epidemiology and control measures; 170 research staff; library of 1,098 vols; Dir Prof. NAGI MOHAMED ABOU ZEID; publs *Agricultural Research Review*, *Egyptian Phytopathology*, *Journal of Applied Microbiology*.

Plant Protection Research Institute: 7 Nadi El Said St, Dokki, Giza 12311; tel. (2) 37486163; fax (2) 33372193; e-mail ppri@arc.sci.eg; f. 1912; Dir Prof. NAGI MOHAMED ABOU ZEID.

Soil, Water and Environment Research Institute: Cairo University St, Giza; tel. (2) 35720608; fax (2) 35720608; e-mail swerisweri@hotmail.com; f. 1969; Dir Prof. HAMDY EL HOUSSANY KHALIFA.

Sugar Crops Research Institute: 9 Cairo University St, Giza; tel. (2) 35735699; fax (2) 35697052; e-mail scriare@yahoo.com; Dir Prof. SAMIA SAAD EL SAYED EL MAGHRABY.

Veterinary Serum and Vaccine Research Institute: Abbasia, Cairo; tel. (2) 23421009; fax (2) 23428321; e-mail svri@idsc.gov.eg; internet www.vsvri-eg.com; Dir Prof. FEKRIA ABD ELHAFEZ EL BORDENY.

Institute of Freshwater Fishery Biology: 10 Hassan Sabry St (Fish Garden), BP Zamalik, Cairo; f. 1954; undertakes research in fish biology and culture; 7 scientists; Dir Prof. A. R. EL BOLOCK.

Institute of Oceanography and Fisheries: 101 Kasr El-Aini St, Cairo; tel. (2) 27921342; fax (2) 27921339; e-mail soliman@niof.sci.eg; internet www.niof.sci.eg; f. 1931 in connection with the Faculty of Science, Cairo; undertakes oceanographical, environmental and fisheries research at Alexandria, the Red Sea, the Aqaba and Suez Gulfs at Attaka, inland waters and at Kanater (aquaculture); attached to the Academy of Scientific Research; Dir Prof. SOLIMAN HAMED; publ. *Journal of Aquatic Research*.

Attached Institute:

National Oceanographic Data Center: e-mail ahmedmoustafaelnemr@yahoo.com; internet www.nodc-egypt.org; Dir Dr AHMAD EL NEMR.

ARCHITECTURE AND TOWN PLANNING

Housing and Building National Research Centre: BP 1770, Cairo 12311; tel. (2) 33356853; fax (2) 33351564; e-mail hbrc@hbrc.edu.eg; internet www.hbrc.edu.eg; attached to the Min. of Housing, Utilities and Urban Devt; carries out basic and applied research work on building materials and means of construction; also provides technical information and acts as consultant to the different authorities concerned with bldg and construction materials; 8 specialized laboratories; Chair. Prof. MOSTAFA EL DEMERDASH.

ECONOMICS, LAW AND POLITICS

Centre d'Etudes et de Documentation Economique, Juridique et Sociale: 2 Sikkat al-Fadl, BP 392, Muhammad Farid, Cairo; tel. (2) 23928711; fax (2) 23928791; e-mail cedej@cedej.org.eg; internet www.cedej.org.eg; f. 1969; attached to Sous-direction des Sciences Sociales et Humaines (MAE) and Centre National de la Recherche Scientifique (CNRS), Paris; co-operation, documentation and research on an exchange basis between Egypt and France; research on Egypt (19th and 20th century) and the Arab world; univ. exchanges in co-operation with Egyptian Govt; library of 30,000 vols; 8 documentalists scan and classify 40 Egyptian periodicals; Dir MARC LAVERGNE; publs *Egypte – Monde Arabe* (2 a year), *Mutun* (in Arabic, 2 a year).

Institute of Arab Research and Studies: BP 229, 1 Tolombat St, Garden City, Cairo; tel. (2) 33551648; fax (2) 33562543; f. 1953; affiliated to the Arab League Educational, Cultural and Scientific Organization (ALECSO); library of 77,000 vols, 1,068 periodicals; studies in contemporary Arab affairs, economics, sociology, history, geography, law, literature, linguistics; Dir Prof. AHMED YOUSSEF AHMED; publ. *Bulletin of Arab Research and Studies* (1 a year).

Institute of National Planning: Salah Salem St, Nasr City, Cairo; tel. (2) 22629225; fax (2) 22621151; e-mail inplanning@idsc.net.eg; internet www.inplanning.gov.eg; f. 1960; research, training, documentation and information; organized in 11 scientific and technical centres; library of 70,000 vols; Dir Dr OLA SULEIMAN KHALIL YUSUF AL HAKIM; publs *Egyptian Review of Development and Planning*, *Issues in Planning and Development* (irregular).

EDUCATION

National Centre for Educational Research: Central Ministry of Education, 33 Sharia Falaky, Cairo; f. 1972; coordinates current educational policy with that of the National Specialized Councils; exchanges information with like instns throughout the world; provides local and foreign documents

on education; Dir Dr YOUSSEF KHALIL YOUS-
SEF; publs *Contemporary Trends in Education* (2 a year), *Educational Information
Bulletin* (12 a year); and various works on
education in Egypt and the Arab world.

HISTORY, GEOGRAPHY AND ARCHAEOLOGY

Deutsches Archäologisches Institut
(German Archaeological Institute): 31 Sharia
Abu El-Feda, Cairo-Zamalek 11211; tel. (2)
27351460; fax (2) 27370770; e-mail
sekretariat@kairo.dainst.org; internet www
.dainst.org; Dir Prof. Dr STEPHAN J. SEIDL-
MAYER; Sec. IRENE EL KHORAZATY.

**Institut Français d'Archéologie Orien-
tale** (French Institute of Oriental Archaeology): 37 rue al Cheikh Ali Youssef, BP
11562 Qasr al-Aïny, Cairo 11562; tel. (2)
27971600; fax (2) 27950869; e-mail
direction@ifao.egnet.net; internet www.ifao
.egnet.net; f. 1880; excavations, research,
seminars and publs intended to widen knowledge of Egyptian history from the Pharaohs
to the Islamic period; library of 80,000 books;
Dir LAURE PANTALACCI; publs *Annales Islamologiques* (1 a year), *Bulletin Critique des
Annales Islamologiques, Bulletin de l'Institut
Français d'Archéologie Orientale* (1 a year),
*Cahiers des Annales Islamologiques, Cahiers
de la Céramique Égyptienne.*

MEDICINE

Central Health Laboratories: Ministry of
Health, 19 Sheikh Rehan, Cairo; f. 1885; Dir-
Gen. Dr ABDEL MONEIM EL BEHAIRY; Bacteri-
ology: Dr GUERGIS EL MALEEH; Clinical Path-
ology: Dr NADIR MOHARRAM; Sanitary
Chemistry: MOUNIR AYAD; Toxicology: DALAL
ABDEL REHIM; Food Microbiology: Dr MAGDA
RAKHA; library of 2,000 vols; publs *Bacteri-
ology, Virology, Sera and Vaccines Produc-
tion.*

**National Hepatology and Tropical Medi-
cine Research Institute:** 10 Sharia Kasr
el-Aini, Cairo; tel. (2) 23642494; fax (2)
23683723; e-mail info@nhtmri.org; internet
www.nhtmri.org; f. 1932; depts of Biochemistry, Clinical Pharmacy, Dermatology and
Andrology, Haematology, Microbiology,
Paediatrics, Parasitology, Pathology, Public
Health Epidemiology, Radiology, Tropical
and Liver Surgery, Tropical Medicine;
library of 4,000 vols; Dir-Gen. Prof. Dr
WAHEED DOSS.

**Memorial Institute for Ophthalmic
Research:** Sharia Al-Ahram, Giza, Cairo; f.
1925; library of 2,800 vols; Dir Dr ABDEL
MEGID ABDEL RAHMAN.

National Nutrition Institute: Min. of
Health, 16 Kasr El-Aini St, Cairo; tel. (2)
23646413; fax (2) 23647476; e-mail admin@
nni.org.eg; internet www.nni.org.eg; f. 1955;
research, analysis, training and education in
nutrition science; 469 staff; Dir Dr AZZA
GOHAR; publ. *Bulletin.*

**National Organization for Drug Control
and Research:** 6 Abou Hazem St, Giza; tel.
(2) 27480472; fax (2) 27480478; f. 1976; 300
staff; Chair. Dr ALI HIGAZI.

**VACSERA Holding Company for Bio-
logical Products and Vaccines:** 51 Sharia
Wezarat El-Zeraa, Agouza, Giza 22311; tel.
(2) 37611111; fax (2) 37609177; e-mail ceo@
vacsera.com; internet www.vacsera.com;
Chair. Dr MOHAMED RABIE.

Theodor Bilharz Research Institute:
Warak el Hadar, Embaba, BP 30, Giza
12411; tel. (2) 35401019; fax (2) 35408125;
e-mail info@tbri.sci.eg; internet www.tbri.sci
.eg; f. 1979; for the control, diagnosis and
treatment of endemic diseases, especially
urinary and hepatic schistosomiasis; Dir

Prof. JEHAN G. EL FENDI; publs *Egyptian
Journal of Shistosomiasis, TBRI Biomedical
Bulletin, TBRI Today.*

NATURAL SCIENCES
General

**UNESCO Office Cairo and Regional Bur-
eau for Science and Technology in the
Arab States:** 8 Abdel Rahman Fahmy St,
Garden City, Cairo 11511; tel. (2) 27945599;
fax (2) 27945296; e-mail cairo@unesco.org;
internet www.unesco.org/en/cairo; f. 1947;
designated Cluster Office for Egypt, Sudan
and Yemen; Dir TAREK SHAWKI.

Physical Sciences

Egyptian Mineral Resources Authority:
BP 11511 Ataba, Cairo; fax (2) 24820128;
e-mail info@egsma.gov.eg; internet www
.egsma.gov.eg; f. 1896; regional geological
mapping, mineral prospecting, evaluation of
mineral deposits, and granting mineral
exploration and exploitation rights; cartography laboratory; 763 research workers;
library of 82,000 vols; Chair. HUSSEIN
HAMOUDA.

**National Authority for Remote Sensing
and Space Sciences:** BP 1564, Alf Maskan,
Cairo; tel. (2) 26225801; fax (2) 26225800;
e-mail info@narss.sci.eg; internet www.narss
.sci.eg; f. 1972; covers geology, mineral and
energy resources, hydrogeology, agriculture,
soils, geophysics, photogrammetry, engineering, physics and environment; operates
advanced digital data processing facility for
satellite and aircraft data, also Beechcraft
King-Air aeroplane with most advanced
remote sensing equipment; design and implementation of nat. space scientific and technical activities; library of 2,500 books; Chair.
Prof. AYMAN EL DESSOUKI IBRAHIM; publ.
Journal (1 a year).

**National Research Institute of Astron-
omy and Geophysics:** BP 11421, Helwan,
Cairo; tel. (2) 25549780; fax (2) 25548020;
e-mail astro@nriag.sci.eg; internet www
.nriag.sci.eg; f. 1903; comprises the Helwan
Observatory, the Kottamyia Observatory,
the Misallat geomagnetic observatory, seismic stations at Helwan, Aswan, Matrouh,
and satellite tracking stations at Helwan and
Abu Simbel; attached to the Academy of
Scientific Research and Technology; library
of 10,594 vols; Pres. Prof. ANAS MOHAMED
IBRAHIM OSMAN; publs *Journal of Astronomy
and Astrophysics, Journal of Geophysics.*

RELIGION, SOCIOLOGY AND ANTHROPOLOGY

**Ibn Khaldun Centre for Development
Studies:** BP 13, Mokatim, Cairo; tel. (2)
25081617; fax (2) 26670973; e-mail info@
eicds.org; internet www.eicds.org; f. 1988;
advancement of applied social sciences with
special emphasis on Egypt and the Arab and
Third Worlds; the Centre is an associated
centre of the Arab Social Science Research
network of the Arab Institute for Studies and
Communication (ASSR–AISC); Dir Dr SAAD
EDDIN IBRAHIM; publ. *Civil Society* (12 a
year).

TECHNOLOGY

**Central Metallurgical Research and
Development Institute:** 1 Elfelezat St,
Helwan, Cairo 11421; tel. (2) 25010642; fax
(2) 25010639; e-mail rucmrdi@rusys.eg.net;
internet www.cmrdi.sci.eg; f. 1972; attached
to the Ministry of Scientific Research; extractive metallurgy, ore dressing, technical services, metal-forming and working, welding
research; library of 4,000 vols; Chair. Prof.
Dr BAHAA ZAGHLOUL.

Egyptian Atomic Energy Authority: 8
Ahmad Elzomor St, Nasr City, Children
Village BP, Cairo 11787; tel. (2) 22876033;
fax (2) 22876031; e-mail hisham_f@frcu.eun
.eg; internet www.eaea.org.eg; f. 1957; maintains 22-MW open pool multipurpose reactor
at the Inshas site for production of radioisotopes for industrial and medical applications, research on neutron physics and
personnel training; employs 850 academic
scientists supported by 650 technical staff;
Pres. Prof. ALY ISLAM METWALLY ALY.

Attached Research Centres:

**National Centre for Radiation
Research and Technology
(NCRRT):**tel. (2) 22746791; fax (2)
22749298; internet www.eaea.org.eg/ncrrt
.html; f. 1972; main facilities incl. a
400,000 Ci, Co-60 unit and an electron
accelerator (under construction); organized
in 3 divs: radiation research, industrial
irradiation, biotechnology; Chair. Prof.
AMIN EL BAHY.

Nuclear Research Centre (NRC): BP
13975, Abu Zabal; tel. (4) 620810; fax (4)
620812; internet www.eaea.org.eg/nrc
.html; main facilities incl. a 2-MW ET-
RR-1 research reactor, a 2.5 Van de Graaff
accelerator, a radioisotope production
laboratory, nuclear fuel research and devt
laboratory, laboratories for application of
radioisotopes, electronic instrumentation
laboratory and radiation protection laboratory; organized in 4 divs: basic nuclear
sciences, reactors, material and nuclear
industry, radioisotope applications; Chair.
Prof. NASF CAMSAN.

**The Hot Laboratories and Waste Man-
agement Centre (HLWMC):** BP 13975,
Abu Zabal; tel. (2) 44620784; fax (2)
44620806; internet www.eaea.org.eg/
hlwmc.html; f. 1980; main facilities incl.
low and intermediate level liquid waste
station, radioisotope production laboratories, radwaste disposal site; organized in 3
divs: radioisotopes, fuel treatment, radwaste treatment.

**The National Centre for Nuclear
Safety and Radiation Control
(NCNSRC):**tel. (2) 22728793; fax (2)
22740308; internet www.eaea.org.eg/
ncnsrc.html; f. 1982; organized in 3 divs:
nuclear regulations and emergencies, radiation control, safety of nuclear installations.

Egyptian Petroleum Research Institute:
1 Ahmed el Zomor St, Nasr City, Cairo
11727; tel. (2) 22747847; fax (2) 22747433;
e-mail research@epri.sci.eg; internet www
.epri.sci.eg; f. 1976; organ of the Min. for
Scientific Research; joint Board with Egyptian Gen. Petroleum Corporation; 7 research
sections, dealing with all aspects of petroleum and energy-related problems; contract
research and commercial services to local oil
companies; library of over 5,000 books and
periodicals; 850 staff; Dir Prof. AHMED
MOHAMMAD AHMED AL SABAGH; publ. *Egyptian Journal of Petroleum.*

Hydraulics Research Institute: POB
13621, Police Station St, Delta Barrage,
Cairo; tel. (2) 42188268; fax (2) 42189539;
e-mail info@hri-egypt.org; internet www
.hri-egypt.org; f. 1949; depts of Calibration
and Instrumentation, Numerical Modelling,
Physical Modelling, Sedimentation and Field
Measurements; Dir Prof. FATTHY SAAD HASA-
NAIN AL-GAMAL.

National Institute for Standards: Tersa
St, el-Matbaa, el Haram, POB 136, Giza
12211; fax (2) 33867451; internet www.nis
.sci.eg; f. 1963; attached to the Min. of Higher
Education and Scientific Research; 197 staff;
responsible for maintenance of nat. stand-

ards for physical units and their use for purposes of calibration; research on scientific metrology, to develop new techniques for measurements, calibrations, and devt of new standards; constituent laboratories: electricity, photometry, frequency, thermometry, radiation, acoustics, mass, length metrology, engineering metrology, testing of materials, safety tests and textile testing, ultrasonics, polymer testing, and reference materials; Dir Prof. ALI ABUELEZZ; publ. *Egyptian Journal of Measurement Science and Technology*.

Textile Consolidation Fund: 7 el-Taher St, Abdin, Cairo; tel. (2) 23925521; fax (2) 23928013; e-mail tcf_textiles@tcfegypt.org.eg; internet www.tcfegypt.org.eg; f. 1953; incl. textiles quality control centre and textiles devt centre; library of 5,000 vols; Gen. Man. MAGDI EL AREF.

Libraries and Archives

Alexandria

Alexandria Municipal Library: 18 Sharia Menasha Moharrem Bey, BP 138 el Shatby, Alexandria 21526; tel. (3) 24839999; fax (3) 24820461; e-mail secretariat@bibalex.org; f. 1892; under control of the Bibliotheca Alexandrina; 22,390 Arabic vols, 35,399 European vols, 4,086 MSS; Chief Librarian BESHIR BESHIR EL SHINDI.

Alexandria University Central Library: 136 Horiyah Rd, Shatby, Alexandria; tel. (3) 24282928; fax (3) 24282927; e-mail auclib@auclib.edu.eg; f. 1942; 45,000 books, 1m. microfiches and roll films, 1,200 periodicals, 2,500 MSS, 17,500 dissertations; Supervisor Prof. SHAWKY SALEM.

Bibliotheca Alexandrina: El Shatby, BP 138, Alexandria 21526; tel. (3) 24839999; fax (3) 24820460; e-mail infobib@bibalex.org; internet www.bibalex.org; f. 2001, built as successor to ancient Alexandria library; 4,000,000 vols, 100,000 MSS, 50,000 maps, 250,000 audio and audiovisual items; incl. collns from the Sidi Mursi Abul Abbas Mosque and the Al Azhar Religious Institute in Smouha; deposit library for UNESCO, WTO, Red Cross and Council of Europe; Dir-Gen. Dr ISMAIL SERAGELDIN.

Library of the Greek Orthodox Patriarchate of Alexandria: BP 2006, Alexandria; tel. (3) 24868595; fax (3) 24875684; e-mail patriarchate@greekorthodox-alexandria.org; internet www.greekorthodox-alexandria.org; f. AD 43; 41,000 vols, 542 MSS, contains 2,241 rare editions; Librarian NICOLAS ALEXOPOULOS.

Assiut

Assiut University Library: Assiut; tel. (88) 2412526; e-mail auslibrarynquiries@yahoo.com; internet www.aun.edu.eg/library/index.htm; 250,000 vols; Dir S. M. SAYED.

Cairo

Al-Azhar University Library: Nasr City, Cairo; 80,000 vols, including 20,000 MSS; Librarian M. E. A. HADY.

American University in Cairo Library: AUC Ave, POB 74, New Cairo 11835; tel. (2) 6153648; fax (2) 27974903; e-mail library@aucegypt.edu; internet library.aucegypt.edu; f. 1919; 403,722 vols; Dean of Libraries and Learning Technologies SHAHIRA EL-SAWY.

Arab League Information Centre (Library): Midan al-Tahir, Cairo 11642; tel. (2) 25750511; fax (2) 25740331; f. 1945; Sec.-Gen. Dr SAUD ABD AL AZIZ EL ZABIDI; 30,000 vols, 250 periodicals.

Cairo University Library: Orman, Giza; tel. (2) 37759743; fax (2) 35726747; e-mail sherifshn@cu.edu.eg; internet www.cl.cu.edu.eg; f. 1932; 1,407,000 vols, 10,000 periodicals; Gen. Dir Dr SHERIF SHAHEEN.

Centre of Documentation and Studies on Ancient Egypt: 3 Sharia el-Adel Abou Bakr, Zamalek, Cairo; f. 1956; scientific and documentary reference centre for all Egyptian Pharaonic monuments; 4,500 vols, 33,000 photographs; Dir-Gen. Dr MAHMOUD MAHER TAHA.

Egypt National Agricultural Library: 7 Nadi el Said St, Dokki, Giza; tel. (2) 33351313; fax (2) 33351302; e-mail magdy@nile.enal.sci.eg; internet nile.enal.sci.eg; f. 1920; 25,000 vols; Dir Dr MAGDY ABD EL RAHMAN; publ. *Egyptian Journal of Agricultural Research*.

Egyptian National Library and Archives: Sharia Corniche el-Nil, Bulaq, Cairo; internet www.darelkotob.gov.eg; f. 1870; 1,500,000 vols (400,000 European); 11 brs with 250,000 vols, incl. fine arts library; deposit library; Dir Gen. ALI ABDUL MOHSEN.

Egyptian Library: Abdin Palace, Cairo; over 20,000 vols; Dir ABDEL HAMID HOSNI.

Library of the Central Bank of Egypt: 153 Mohamed Farid St, Cairo; tel. (2) 23905427; fax (2) 23904232; e-mail info@cbe.org.eg; f. 1961; 15,430 vols; publ. *Economic Review* (4 a year).

Library of the Ministry of Education: 16 Sharia el-Falaki, Cairo; tel. (2) 38544805; f. 1927; 55,966 vols (European and Arabic); Dir HASSAN ABDEL SHAFI.

Library of the Ministry of Health: Sharia Magles el Shaab, Cairo 11467; fax (2) 27953966; over 27,000 vols.

Library of the Ministry of Justice: Midan Lazoghli, Cairo; f. 1929; over 90,000 vols and periodicals in Arabic, French and English (law and social science); private library for the use of judges and members of the Parquet (public prosecution and criminal investigation authority); a centre attached to the library contains the latest texts of local and comparative legislature on Personal Status; Dir F. ABOU EL KHEIR.

Library of the Ministry of Supply and Internal Trade: 99 Sharia Kasr el-Aini, Cairo; internet msht.tripod.com; over 20,000 vols.

Library of the Ministry of Waqfs: Sharia Sabri Alu Alam, Ean el-Luk, Cairo; f. 1942; 20,219 vols.

Library of the Monastery of St Catherine: 18 Midan El Daher, Cairo; f. 6th century; over 4,000 Greek, Oriental and Slavonic MSS; contains the Codex Sinaiticus Syriacus; Librarians Monk DANIEL, Monk SYMEON.

Library of the National Research Institute of Astronomy and Geophysics: Helwan, Cairo; internet www.nriag.sci.eg; f. 1903; 11,000 vols; Dir Prof. R. M. KEBEASY.

National Assembly Library: Palace of the National Assembly, Cairo; internet www.parliament.gov.eg/english/publicsec/library; f. 1924; over 61,000 vols; Dir ANTOUN MATTA.

National Research Centre: El Buhoth St, Dokki Cairo; tel. (2) 33371362; fax (2) 33370931; e-mail info@nrc.sci.eg; internet www.nrc.sci.eg; f. 1955; accumulates and disseminates information in all languages and in all branches of science and technology; 35,600 vols, 2,500 periodicals, UNESCO and WHO special collns; Dir WAGLAA MAHMOUD FAHMY.

Damanhour

Damanhour Municipal Library: Damanhour; 13,431 vols.

Mansoura

Mansoura Municipal Library: Mansoura; contains 17,984 vols (Arabic 13,036, European 4,948).

Zagazig

Sharkia Provincial Council Library: Zagazig; contains 12,238 vols (Arabic 7,861, European 4,377).

Museums and Art Galleries

Alexandria

Greco-Roman Museum: Museum St, Alexandria; tel. (3) 24865820; fax (3) 24876434; internet www.grm.gov.eg; f. 1892; exhibits from the Greek, Roman and Byzantine eras; library of 15,500 vols, Omar Tousson colln of 4,000 vols; Dir DOREYA SAID; publs *Annuaire du Musée Gréco-Romain*, *Guide to the Alexandrian Monuments*.

National Maritime Museum: Alexandria; Dir Dr MEHREZ EL HUSSEINI.

Aswan

Nubia Museum: el Fanadek St, Aswan; tel. (97) 319333; fax (97) 317998; e-mail nubiamuseum@numibia.net; internet www.numibia.net/nubia; f. 1997; history of Nubia since prehistoric times; Dir OSSAMA A. W. ABDEL MAGUID.

Cairo

Agricultural Museum: Al Sawra St, Dokki, Cairo; tel. (2) 33608682; f. 1938; exhibits of ancient and modern Egyptian agriculture and rural life, horticulture, irrigation; botanical and zoological sections; library of 8,885 vols; Dir SAMIR M. SULTAN.

Al-Gawhara Palace Museum: The Citadel, Cairo; tel. (2) 25116187; f. 1954, refurnished 1956; built in 1811 in the Ottoman style, the Palace retains much of its original interior; contains Oriental and French furniture, including gilded throne, Turkish paintings, exhibitions of clocks, glass, 19th-century costumes.

Cairo Geological Museum: BP Dawawin, Cairo 11521; Cornish el-Nil, Maadi Rd, Cairo; tel. (2) 23187056; fax (2) 33820128; e-mail info@egsma.gov.eg; internet www.egsma.gov.eg/default2.htm; a general dept of the Egyptian Geological Survey; f. 1904; 50,000 specimens, mostly Egyptian; depts: vertebrates, invertebrates, rocks and minerals; library of 4,200 vols and 6,000 periodicals; Dir-Gen. MOHAMMED AHMED EL BEDAWI.

Cairo Museum of Hygiene: Midan-el-Sakakini, Daher, Cairo; Dir Dr FAWZI SWEHA.

Coptic Museum: Fakhry Abd el Nour St, Abbassia, Cairo; tel. (2) 23639742; f. 1910; sculpture and frescoes, MSS, textiles, icons, ivory and bone, carved wood, metalwork, pottery and glass; library of 6,587 vols; Dir Dr MAHAR SALIB.

Cotton Museum: Gezira, Cairo; tel. (2) 33608682; f. 1923; established by the Egyptian Agricultural Society; all aspects of cotton growing, diseases, pests, and methods of spinning and weaving are shown; Dir M. EL BAHTIMI.

Egyptian (National) Museum: Midan-el-Tahrir, Cairo; tel. (2) 25796948; fax (2) 25794596; e-mail egymu1@idsc.net.eg; f. 1902; exhibits from prehistoric times until the 3rd century AD; excludes Coptic and

Islamic periods; established by decree in 1835 to conserve antiquities; the Antiquities Dept administers the archaeological museums and controls excavations; library of 40,000 vols; Dir MAMDOUH MOHAMED ELDAMATY; publ. *Annals of the Antiquities Service of Egypt.*

Egyptian National Railways Museum: Cairo Station Bldgs, Ramses Sq., Cairo 11669; tel. (2) 25763793; fax (2) 25740000; f. 1933; contains models of foreign and Egyptian railways, and technical information and statistics on the evolution and devt of the Egyptian railway services; library of 5,595 vols (Arabic 2,694, European 2,901); Curator IBRAHIM SALEH ALY.

Gayer-Anderson Museum: Beit el-Kretlia, Cairo; f. 1936; private collns of Oriental art objects bequeathed to Egypt by R. G. Gayer-Anderson Pasha in 1936; Curator YOUNES MAHRAN.

Museum of Islamic Art: Ahmed Maher Sq., Bab al-Khalq, Cairo 11638; tel. (2) 23901520; e-mail islam_mus_director@hotmail.com; internet www.islamicmuseum.gov.eg; f. 1881; colln of 86,000 items representing the evolution of Islamic art from the first quarter of the 7th century to 1900; library of 15,000 vols; Dir-Gen. Dr NIMAT M. ABU-BAKR; publs *Islamic Archaeological Studies* (1 a year), catalogues on Islamic decorative arts.

Museum of Modern Art: 4 Sharia Kasr el-Nil, Cairo; internet www.modernartmuseum .gov.eg; f. 1920; Chair. AHMED NAWAR.

War Museum: The Citadel, Cairo; library of 6,000 vols.

Universities

AIN SHAMS UNIVERSITY

Elkhalifa Elmaamoon St, Abbassia, Cairo 11566

Telephone: (2) 26831231

Fax: (2) 26847824

E-mail: pres@asunet.shams.edu.eg

Internet: net.shams.edu.eg

Founded 1950

Languages of instruction: Arabic, English, French

Academic year: October to June

Pres.: Prof. MAGED MOHAMMED ALI KHALIL EL-DEEB

Vice-Pres. for Community and Environment: Prof. GAMAL SAMY ALI MAHMOUD

Vice-Pres. for Education and Student Affairs: Prof. ATEF MOHAMMED AWAD EL AWAM

Vice-Pres. for Postgraduate Studies and Research: Prof. MOHAMMED SAID SALAMA ALI

Sec.-Gen.: Prof. HASSAN ABD EL AZEEZ AMMAR

Chief Librarian: SOHAIR HASSAN SOMIDA

Library of 15,786 vols (3,318 Arabic, 12,468 English), 63 periodicals, 133,000 theses (30,000 Arabic, 103,000 English)

Number of teachers: 7,297

Number of students: 185,000

DEANS

Faculty of Agriculture: Prof. ESAM OSMAN FAYED

Faculty of Al-Alsun: Prof. ABDEL KADER ATTIA MOHAMMED ABO EL-ANIN

Faculty of Arts: Prof. MAMDOUH MOHAMMED GAD EL-DMATY

Faculty of Commerce: Prof. HUSSEIN MOHAMMED AHMED EID

Faculty of Computer and Information Sciences: Prof. MOHAMED ESAAM KHALIFA

Faculty of Dentistry: Prof. TAREK SALAH EL-DIN HUSSEIN

Faculty of Education: Prof. SUZAN MOHAMMED SALAH EL-DIN FOUAD

Faculty of Engineering: Prof. HADIA MOHAMMED SAID EL-HANAWY

Faculty of Law: Prof. EL SAID EID NAIL

Faculty of Medicine: Prof. AHMED IBRAHIM NASAR

Faculty of Nursing: Prof. SABAH SAAD EL SAID EL SHARKAWY

Faculty of Pharmacy: Prof. NAHED DAWOOD MORTADA

Faculty of Science: Prof. ADEL RAMDAN MOSTFA EL SAYED AHMED

Faculty of Specific Education: Prof. NADIA EL SAYED EL HOSENY

Faculty of Women: Prof. WAFAA MOHAMMED AHMED IBRAHIM

Institute of Environmental Studies and Research: Prof. AHMED MUSTAFA HUSSIEN EL ATIK

Institute of Childhood Studies: Prof. KHALID HUSSEIN MOSTAFA TAMAN

ALEXANDRIA UNIVERSITY

22 el Geish Ave, el Shatby, Alexandria

Telephone: (3) 5960720

Fax: (3) 5960720

E-mail: info@alexeng.edu.eg

Internet: www.alex.edu.eg

Founded 1942

State control

Languages of instruction: Arabic, English, French

Academic year: October to June

Pres.: Prof. HASSAN NADIR KHAIRALLAH

Vice-Pres. for Community Services and Environmental Affairs: Prof. EZAT KHAMES AMIN MOSTAFA

Vice-Pres. for Damanhour Br.: Prof. MOHAMED AHMED BAUOMY

Vice-Pres. for Postgraduate Studies and Research: Prof. GOAD GOAD HAMADA

Vice-Pres. for Undergraduate Studies: Prof. OKASHA MOHAMED ABDEL AAL

Sec.-Gen.: MOHAMED ROSHDY ABDEL GHANI

Chief Librarian: SOHER GAMAL

Library: see Libraries and Archives

Number of teachers: 3,979

Number of students: 144,707

DEANS

Faculty of Agriculture: Prof. TAREK MAHMOUD ELKIEY

Faculty of Agriculture (in Damanhour): Prof. ABDEL SALAM HELMY MOHAMED BELAL

Faculty of Agriculture (in Saba Basha): Prof. ALY IBRAHIM ALY EBEDA

Faculty of Arts: Prof. FATHY ABDEL AZIZ ABORADY

Faculty of Arts (in Damanhour): Prof. MOHAMED ALY BAHGAT EL FADLY

Faculty of Commerce: Prof. MOHAMED ELFAUOMY MOHAMED IBRAHIM

Faculty of Commerce (in Damanhour): Prof. KAMAL ELDIN MOSTAFA ELDAHRAWY

Faculty of Dentistry: Prof. MOSTAFA MOHAMED EL DEBANY

Faculty of Education (in Damanhour): Prof. ANTAR LOTFY

Faculty of Education (in Marsa Matrouh): Prof. SHEBL BADRAN MOHAMED EL GHAREEB

Faculty of Engineering: Prof. ABDEL LOTFY MOHAMADEEN

Faculty of Fine Arts: Prof. MAGDY MOHAMED MOUSSA

Faculty of Kindergartens: Prof. ELHAM MOSTAFA MOHAMED EBED

Faculty of Law: Prof. Dr MAGDY MAHMOUD MOHAMED SHEHAB

Faculty of Medicine: Prof. ABDEL AZIZ BELAL

Faculty of Nursing: Prof. NADIA TAHA MOHAMED AHMED

Faculty of Pharmacy: Prof. NABIL AHMED MOHAMED ABDEL SALAM

Faculty of Physical Education (Females): Prof. SADIA ABDEL GOAD MOHAMED SHEHA

Faculty of Physical Education (Males): Prof. ABDEL MONIEM BADEER ELKOSIER

Faculty of Science: Prof. MOSTAFA HUSSIEN FAHMY

Faculty of Specific Education: Prof. ABDEL RAZEK MOHAMED ELSAYED

Faculty of Tourism and Hotels: Prof. MAHER ABDEL KADER MOHAMED ALY

Faculty of Veterinary Medicine: Prof. Dr MOHAMED ALY EKELA TORKY

Higher Institute of Public Health: Prof. HASSAN KAMEL BASSOUNY MOHAMED (see also under Colleges)

Institute of Medical Research: Prof. AASSER ABDEL HAMIED HAFEZ (Dir)

Institute of Postgraduate Studies and Research: Prof. MOHAMED EZZ ELDIN ELRAIE

AL AZHAR UNIVERSITY

Cairo 11751

Telephone: (2) 22623278

Fax: (2) 22623284

E-mail: azhar@azhar.eun.eg

Internet: www.azhar.edu.eg

Founded AD 970; modernized and expanded 1961

Academic year: September to June

Rector: AHMAD AL TAYIB

Vice-Rectors: Prof. SAMA GAD, Prof. TAHA ABU KREISHA

Library: see Libraries and Archives

Number of teachers: 9,000

Number of students: 185,000 (on several campuses)

DEANS

Faculty of Agriculture: Prof. AMIN YOUSSEF

Faculty of Arabic and Islamic Studies: Prof. MAHMOUD EL SAIED SHAIKHOON

Faculty of Arabic Studies: Prof. ABDULLAH HELLAL

Faculty of Commerce: Prof. ABDEL-HAMID RABEE

Faculty of Education: MUHAMMAD ABDEL SAMEE OTHMAN

Faculty of Engineering: Prof. ABDEL-WAHID AHMAD

Faculty of Islamic Jurisprudence and Law: Prof. MOHAMMAD RAFAT OTHMAN

Faculty of Islamic Theology: Prof. ABDEL-MOUTI MOHAMMAD BAYOMI

Faculty of Language and Translation: Prof. AHMAD BASEM ABDEL-GHAFFAR

Faculty of Medicine: Prof. ISMAEEL KHALAF

Faculty of Science: Prof. ABDEL-WAHAB AL SHARKAWI

Islamic Women's College: Prof. KAWTHAR KAMEL

AMERICAN UNIVERSITY IN CAIRO

Tahrir Sq. Campus, BP 2511, 113 Sharia Kasr el Aini, Cairo 11511

New Cairo Campus, BP 74, Cairo 11835

American Office: 3rd Fl., 420 Fifth Ave, New York, NY 10018-2729, USA

Telephone: (2) 27942964

Fax: (2) 27957565

Internet: www.aucegypt.edu

Founded 1919

Private control

Language of instruction: English

Academic year: September to June

Pres.: DAVID A. ARNOLD

Provost: LISA ANDERSON

Vice-Provost: ALI HADI

Vice-Pres. and Exec. Sec. of Board of Trustees: MARY CORRARINO

Vice-Pres. for Continuing Education: EDWARD SIMPSON

Vice-Pres. for Finance: ANDREW SNAITH

Vice-Pres. for Institutional Advancement: JAMES L. BULLOCK

Vice-Pres. for Planning and Admin.: PAUL DONOGHUE

Vice-Pres. for Student Affairs: ASHRAF EL FIQI

Dean of Libraries: SHAHIRA EL SAWY

Library: see Libraries and Archives

Number of teachers: 303

Number of students: 5,577

Publications: *Alif* (English and Arabic poetry), *Cairo Papers in Social Science*

DEANS

School of Business, Economics and Communications: D. O'CONNOR

School of Humanities and Social Sciences: A. M. LESCH

School of Sciences and Engineering: M. HAROUN

ATTACHED UNITS

Centre for Adult and Continuing Education: non-credit study programme for 30,000 students a year; offers courses and post-secondary and postgraduate career programmes in Arabic/English, Arabic/French translation, English language, business and secretarial skills, and computing; Dean Dr HARRY MILLER.

Desert Development Centre: research to improve the social and economic well-being of new desert settlers, integrating agriculture, renewable energy and community research; Dir Dr RICHARD TUTWILER.

Social Research Centre: current research projects on demography and human resettlement; Dir Dr HODA RASHAD.

ASSIUT UNIVERSITY

Assiut Governorate, Assiut Univ. POB, Assiut 71515

Telephone: (88) 2357007

Fax: (88) 2354130

E-mail: info@aun.eun.eg

Internet: www.aun.edu.eg

Founded 1957

Languages of instruction: Arabic, English

Academic year: September to June

State

Rector: Prof. MOSTAFA MOHAMAD KAMAL

Deputy-Rector for Community Services and Environmental Devt: Prof. MOHAMED AHMED SHANAWANY

Deputy-Rector for Postgraduate Studies and Research Affairs: Prof. MOHAMED RAGAB BAYOUMI

Deputy-Rector for Student Affairs and Education: Prof. SAID AHMED IBRAHIM

Sec.-Gen.: MOHAMED MAHMOUD OMAR

Chief Librarian: SAMIA ALI ISMAIL

Accredited by the Nat. Authority of Education Accreditation and Quality Assurance, Min. of Higher Education

Library of 40,000 vols, abstracts covering all educational and research fields, 35,000 full text periodicals, 28,000 e-books; 28 br. libraries

Number of teachers: 3,975

Number of students: 79,140

Publications: *Assiut Journal of Agricultural Sciences, Assiut Medical Journal, Assiut University Bulletin for Environmental Researches, Assiut University Journal of Computer Science, Assiut University Journal of Geology, Assiut University Journal of Mathematics, Assiut University Journal of Zoology, Assiut Veterinary Medical Journal, Bulletin of Faculty of Physical Education, Bulletin of Pharmaceutical Sci-* ences, *Egyptian Sugar Journal, Journal of Engineering Sciences, Journal of Faculty of Education, Journal of Law Studies* (Arabic)

DEANS

Faculty of Agriculture: Prof. MOHAMED ABD EL WAHAB ABO NOHOUL

Faculty of Arts: Prof. NASEEF SHAKER SAYED

Faculty of Commerce: Prof. ADEL RAYAN MOHAMED RAYAN

Faculty of Education: Prof. SALAH EL DEEN HUSSIEN EL SHARIEF

Faculty of Education (New Valley Branch): Prof. AHMED SAYED MOHAMED IBRAHIM

Faculty of Engineering: Prof. IBRAHIM M. ISMAIL SALEH

Faculty of Information and Computer and Information Sciences: Prof. HOSSNI MOHAMED IBRAHIM (acting)

Faculty of Law: Prof. ESSAM MOHAMED AHMED ZANNATI

Faculty of Medicine: Prof. MAHER ABDEL SALAM EL ASSAL

Faculty of Nursing: Prof. IKRAM ALI HASHIM SOLIMAN

Faculty of Pharmacy: Prof. GAMAL AHMED S. ABD-ELAAL

Faculty of Physical Education: Prof. TAREQ MOHAMED MOHAMED ABDEL AZIZ

Faculty of Science: Prof. AHMED YEHYA ABDEL-MALEK

Faculty of Social Service: Prof. NABIEL IBRAHIM AHMED

Faculty of Specific Education: Prof. MOHAMED SALAH EL-DIN YOUSSEF (acting)

Faculty of Veterinary Medicine: Prof. MOSTAFA KHALIL MOSTAFA

ATTACHED RESEARCH INSTITUTES

South Egypt Cancer Institute: El-Methaq St, Mansheit El-Omara sq., POB 171516, Assiut; tel. (88) 2337670; fax (88) 2348609; e-mail seci@seci.info; f. 1997 as part of the Faculty of Medicine, present status 1999; depts of Surgical Oncology, Anesthesia, ICU and Pain Relief, Radiology, Radiotherapy and Nuclear Medicine, Medical Oncology, Pediatric Oncology, Clinical Pathology, Cancer Biology, Biostatistics and Cancer Epidemiology; Dean Prof. MAHMOUD MOHAMED MOSTAFA.

Sugar Technology Research Institute: Assiut Univ. Old Bldg; tel. (88) 2313713; fax (88) 2313713; e-mail sugar@acc.aun.edu.eg; internet www.aun.edu.eg/suger/general.html; language of instruction: English; teaching, training, devt and research in the Egyptian sugar industry; offers postgraduate diplomas; depts of sugar industry, industrial engineering and management, chemical and pharmaceutical industries, materials and applications, advanced agricultural technology, environmental sciences and pollution treatment; Dean Prof. ABDEL AZIZ AHMED SAID.

There are 46 attached university centres and special units

CAIRO UNIVERSITY

BP 12611, Orman, Giza, Cairo

Telephone: (2) 35729584

Fax: (2) 35688884

E-mail: info@main-scc.cairo.edu.eg

Internet: www.cu.edu.eg

Founded 1908

State control

Languages of instruction: Arabic, English and French

Academic year: October to June

Pres.: Prof. HOSSAM KAMEL

Vice-Pres. for Beni-Suef Br.: Prof. MOHAMED ANAS KASEM GAFAR

Vice-Pres. for Community Services and Environmental Affairs: Prof. ABDALLA ABDEL FATTAH ELTATAWY

Vice-Pres. for Fayoum Branch: Prof. GALAL MOSTAFA SAEED

Vice-Pres. for Postgraduate Studies and Research: Prof. MOTAZ MOHAMED HOSNY KHORSHED

Vice-Pres. for Undergraduate Studies: Prof. HAMED TAHER HASSANEEN FOAD

Sec.-Gen.: FAYZA MEGAHED

Librarian: AHMED SHOAB

Library: see Libraries and Archives

Number of teachers: 7,066

Number of students: 202,167

DEANS

Faculty of Agriculture: Prof. SALWA BAYOUMY MOHAMED EL MAGHOULY

Faculty of Agriculture (in Fayoum): Prof. ABDALLA MOHAMED ABDEL RAHMAN MOUSA

Faculty of Arabic and Islamic Studies (in Fayoum): Prof. MOHAMED SALAH EL DEEN MOSTAFA

Faculty of Archaeology: Prof. OLA MOHAMED ABD EL AZIZ ELAGEZY

Faculty of Archaeology (in Fayoum): Prof. MOHAMED ABDEL HALIM NOUR ELDIN (acting)

Faculty of Arts: Prof. AHMED MAGDY HEGAZY

Faculty of Arts (in Beni-Suef): Prof. MOHAMED MAHRAN RASHWAN (acting)

Faculty of Commerce: Prof. AHMED FARGHALY MOHAMED HASSAN

Faculty of Commerce (in Beni-Suef): Prof. KAWSSAR ABDEL FATTAH MAHAMED AL-ABAGY

Faculty of Computer and Information Science: Prof. Dr ALY ALY MOHAMED FAHMY

Faculty of Dar el Oloum: Prof. AHMED MOHAMED ABD EL AZIZ KESHK

Faculty of Dar el Olum (in Fayoum): Prof. IBRAHIM MOHAMED IBRAHIM SAKR

Faculty of Dentistry: Prof. MAHMOUD IBRAHIM FAHMY EL REFAAY

Faculty of Economics and Political Science: Prof. KAMAL MAHMOUD EL MENOUFY

Faculty of Education (in Beni-Suef): Prof. MOSTAFA HASSAN MOHAMED EL NASHAR

Faculty of Education (in Fayoum): Prof. MOHAMED ABD EL RAHMAN EL SHARNOBY

Faculty of Engineering: Prof. ALY ABDEL RAHMAN YOUSEF

Faculty of Engineering (in Fayoum): Prof. SAMY EL BADAWY YEHYA

Faculty of Kindergartens: Prof. MONA MOHAMED ALY GAD

Faculty of Law: Prof. AHMED ELSAYED SAWY

Faculty of Law (in Beni-Suef): Prof. Dr REDA IBRAHIM EBEID

Faculty of Mass Communication: Prof. MAGY EL HALAWANY

Faculty of Medicine: Prof. MADIHA MOAHMOUD KHATAB

Faculty of Medicine (in Beni-Suef): Prof. MOHAMED ELSAYED EL BATANOUNY

Faculty of Medicine (in Fayoum): Prof. KAMAL ELBASYOUNY

Faculty of Nursing: Prof. BASAMAT OMAR AHMED

Faculty of Pharmacy: Prof. AHMED ATTEIA MOHAMED SEADA

Faculty of Pharmacy (in Beni-Suef): Prof. AHMED ABDEL BARY ABDEL RAHMAN

Faculty of Physiotherapy: Prof. KAMAL EL SAYED MOHAMED SHOKRY

Faculty of Science: Prof. HAMDY MAHMOUD HASSANEN ELSAYED

Faculty of Science (in Beni-Suef): Prof. AHMED HAFEZ HUSSEIN EL GHANDOUR

Faculty of Science (in Fayoum): Prof. KAMAL AHMED MOHAMED HASSAN DEEB

Faculty of Social Service (in Fayoum): Prof. AHMED MAGDY HEGAZY MAHMOUD (acting)

Faculty of Specific Education: Prof. ALY MOHAMED ALY ELMELEGY

Faculty of Specific Education (in Fayoum): Prof. AHMED GALAL EWIES ELAWA

Faculty of Tourism and Hotels (in Fayoum): Prof. AWAD ABBAS RAGAB

Faculty of Urban Planning: Prof. MAHER MOHEB ISTENO AFANDY

Faculty of Veterinary Medicine: Prof. MOHAMED IBRAHIM MOHAMED DESOUKY

Faculty of Veterinary Medicine (in Beni-Suef): Prof. SHAWKY SOLIMAN IBRAHIM SOLIMAN

Institute of African Studies and Research: Prof. EL SAYED ALY FLEEFEL

Institute of Educational Studies and Research: Prof. MOSTAFA ABDEL SAMIAA

Institute of Statistical Studies and Research: Prof. ABDEL GHANI MOHAMED ABDEL GHANI IBRAHIM

National Institute of Laser Science: Prof. HUSSIEN MOSTAFA MUSA KHALED

National Institute of Tumours: Prof. MOHAMED ABDEL HARETH MOHAMED ABDELRAHMAN

HELWAN UNIVERSITY

Ain Helwan, Helwan, Cairo

Telephone: (2) 25590000

Fax: (2) 25555023

E-mail: info@helwan.edu.eg

Internet: www.helwan.edu.eg

Founded 1975, incorporating existing institutes of higher education

State control

Languages of instruction: Arabic, English

Academic year: September to June

Pres.: Prof. ABD ALLAH BARAKAT

Vice-Pres. for Community Service and Environmental Devt: ABLA HANAFY

Vice-Pres. for Postgraduate Studies and Research: Prof. AHMAD ABD EL KAREEM SALAMA

Vice-Pres. for Undergraduate Studies and Student Affairs: MOHAMMAD HAZEM FATHALLAH

Sec.-Gen.: SEKINA HANAFY MAHMOUD MOHAMED

Librarian: MAHMOUD QATR

Library of 34,795 vols, 425 journals, 9,379 theses

Number of teachers: 2,179

Number of students: 95,567

Publications: *Journal of Economic and Legal Studies* (2 a year), *Journal of Educational and Social Studies*, *Journal of Engineering Research* (6 a year), *Journal of the Faculty of Arts* (2 a year), *Journal of Research on Art Education* (3 a year), *Journal of the Science and Art of Sport* (2 a year), *Journal of Studies on Social Work and Humanities*, *Science and Art of Music* (2 a year), *Scientific Journal of Commercial Studies and Research* (4 a year), *Scientific Journal of Physical Studies* (4 a year)

DEANS

Faculty of Applied Arts: Prof. ADEL HEFNAWY

Faculty of Art Education: Prof. MOHAMMAD LABEEB NADA

Faculty of Arts: Prof. MOHAMED YEHIA MOHAMED

Faculty of Commerce and Business Administration: Prof. MOHAMED AMIN ABDALLA AMIN KAED

Faculty of Education: Prof. ABD EL EL-MOTTELEB AL KORETY

Faculty of Engineering (Mataria): Prof. TAHANY YOUSSEF

Faculty of Engineering and Technology (Helwan): Prof. OMAR HANAFY

Faculty of Fine Arts: Prof. MOHAMMAD TAWFEEK

Faculty of Home Economics: Prof. ABD EL RAHMAN ATIA

Faculty of Information and Computer Sciences: Prof. YEHIA KAMAL HELMY

Faculty of Law: Prof. MOHAMED ELSHAHAT ELGENDY

Faculty of Music Education: Prof. AMERA FARAG

Faculty of Pharmacy: Prof. MOHAMED MOHY ELDIN ELMAZAR

Faculty of Physical Education (Men): Prof. SOBHY HASANEIN

Faculty of Physical Education (Women): Prof. HANAN ROSHDY

Faculty of Science: Prof. MOHAMMAD EL SAYYED

Faculty of Social Work: Prof. MOHAMED REFAAT KASSEM ABDEL RAHMAN

Faculty of Tourism and Hotel Management: Prof. DOHA MOUSTAFA

MANSOURA UNIVERSITY

60 Elgomhoria St, Mansoura

Telephone and fax (50) 347900

E-mail: info@mans.edu.eg

Internet: www.mans.eun.eg

Founded 1973 from the Mansoura br. of Cairo Univ.

State control

Languages of instruction: Arabic, English

Academic year: October to June

Pres.: Prof. AHMED GAMAL ELDIN ABDEL FATTAH MOUSA

Vice-Pres. for Community Services and Environmental Affairs: Prof. MOHAMED AHMED GABALLA YOSSEF

Vice-Pres. for Postgraduate Studies and Research: Prof. MAGDY MOHAMED ABOU RAYAAN

Vice-Pres. for Undergraduate Studies: Prof. MOHAMED SUIELM MOHAMED ELBASUONY

Sec.-Gen.: MAGDY AHMED MAHMOUD SALEH

Chief Librarian: ABDALLA HUSSIEN

Number of teachers: 2,230

Number of students: 107,022

Publications: *Egyptian Journal for Commercial Studies* (4 a year), *Journal of the Faculty of Arts* (2 a year), *Journal of Veterinary Medical Research* (1 a year), *Mansoura Dental Journal* (4 a year), *Mansoura Engineering Journal* (4 a year), *Mansoura Faculty of Education Journal* (3 a year), *Mansoura Journal of Forensic Medicine and Clinical Toxicology* (2 a year), *Mansoura Journal of Pharmaceutical Sciences* (2 a year), *Mansoura Medical Journal* (2 a year), *Mansoura Science Bulletin* (2 a year), *Mansoura University Journal of Agriculture* (12 a year), *Revue des Recherches Juridiques et Economiques* (2 a year)

DEANS

Faculty of Agriculture: Prof. HESHAM NAGY ABDEL MAGEED

Faculty of Commerce: Prof. NABIL AL HUSSINI AL NAGGAR

Faculty of Computer and Information Science: Prof. FATMA ABOU-CHADI

Faculty of Medicine: Prof. AMR SARHAN

Faculty of Nursing: Prof. FARDOS RAMADAN

Faculty of Science: Prof. TAHA ZAKI NABAWY SOKKAR

Faculty of Science (in Damiatta): Prof. MOHAMED R. MOSTAFA

Faculty of Veterinary Medicine: Prof. MOHAMED MOHAMED FOUDA

MENIA UNIVERSITY

Menia Governorate, Menia

Telephone: (86) 361443

Fax: (86) 342601

E-mail: info@minia.edu.eg

Internet: www.minia.edu.eg

Founded 1976, incorporating existing faculties of Assiut Univ.

Languages of instruction: Arabic, English

Academic year: October to June

Pres.: Prof. ABD EL MONIEM ABD EL HAMID EL BASSIOUNY

Vice-Pres. for Community Services and Environmental Affairs: Prof. ABD EL GHAFAR FARIED ABD EL GHAFAR

Vice-Pres. for Postgraduate Studies and Research: Prof. MOHAMED SAIED MOHAMED ALY

Vice-Pres. for Undergraduate Studies: Prof. MAHER GABER MOHAMED AHMED

Sec.-Gen.: LAILA AHMED IBRAHIM SOROOR

Chief Librarian: NABELA EL SAWY

Number of teachers: 1,288

Number of students: 36,906

DEANS

Faculty of Agriculture: Prof. MOHAMED ATEF FAHMY AHMED KESHK

Faculty of al Alsun (Languages): Prof. AMAL MOSTAFA KAMAL MOHAMED

Faculty of Arts: Prof. MOHAMED NAGEEB AHMED MOHAMED

Faculty of Computer and Information Science: (vacant)

Faculty of Dar al Olum: Prof. MOHY ELDIN OTHMAN RASHDAN

Faculty of Dentistry: Prof. HANY HUSSIEN MOHAMED AMIN

Faculty of Education: Prof. ATTA TAHA ZEDAN SHEHATA

Faculty of Engineering: Prof. MOHAMED MONESS ALY AHMED

Faculty of Fine Arts: Prof. WAFAA OMAR ABD ELHALEEM

Faculty of Medicine: Prof. MOHAMED IBRAHIM BASUONY

Faculty of Nursing: Prof. GALAL MOHAMED SHAWKY HAMED

Faculty of Pharmacy: Prof. MOHAMED MONTASER ABD ELHAKIM

Faculty of Physical Education (Female): (vacant)

Faculty of Physical Education (Male): Prof. BAHY ELDIN IBRAHIM SALAMA

Faculty of Science: Prof. ABD ELRAHMAN ABD ELAZIZ AHMED

Faculty of Specific Education: Prof. ABD ELAZEEM ABD ELSALAM ELFERGANY

Faculty of Tourism and Hotel Management: Prof. ABD ELBARY AHMED ALY DAWOOD

MINUFIYA UNIVERSITY

Gamal Abd el Nasser St, BP 32511, Shebeen el Kam

Telephone: (48) 222170

Fax: (2) 5752777

E-mail: menofia@menofia.edu.eg

Internet: www.menofia.edu.eg

Founded 1976

State control

Languages of instruction: Arabic, English

Academic year: September to July

Pres.: Prof. MOHAMED A. IZZULARAB

Vice-Pres. for Community and Environmental Devt: Prof. ABD EL ALEEM MOHAMMED ABD EL KHALIK EL DERAEE

Vice-Pres. for Graduate Studies and Research: Prof. THABET ABD EL RAHAMAN EDRESE

Vice-Pres. for Undergraduate Education: Prof. MOSTAFA ABD EL RAHMAN

Vice-Pres. for Sadat Br.: Prof. AHMED HAMED ZAGHLOL

Sec.-Gen.: MOSTAFA SADAK KHALIL

Librarian: HAMDY EL SHAMY

Number of teachers: 2,928

Number of students: 71,225

Publications: *Minoufiya Journal of Electronic Engineering Research* (2 a year), *Minoufiya Medical Journal* (2 a year), *Scientific Journal of the Faculty of Science* (1 a year)

DEANS

Faculty of Agriculture: Prof. ALI IBRAHIM FARAG

Faculty of Arts: Prof. AHMED ABD EL KADER EL SHATHLY

Faculty of Commerce: Prof. GAMAL EL DIN MOHAMED EL MORSEY

Faculty of Commerce (Sadat Br.): Prof. HASANIEN SAYED TAHA

Faculty of Computers and Information: Prof. MOHIEY MOHAMED HADHOUD

Faculty of Education: Prof. ALI MOHAMED SHUAIB

Faculty of Education (Sadat Br.): Prof. ABD EL AAL AGWA

Faculty of Electroni Engineering: Prof. ATEF EL SAYED ABOU EL AZM

Faculty of Engineering: Prof. ADEL ALI ABOU EL ALA

Faculty of Home Economics: Prof. FATMA EL ZAHRAA EL SHERIEF

Faculty of Hotels and Tourism: (vacant)

Faculty of Law: Prof. MOHAMED SAMY EL SHAWA

Faculty of Law (Sadat Br.): Prof. ABD EL HADEY MOHAMED EL ASHREY

Faculty of Medicine: Prof. SAID SHALABY IBRAHIM

Faculty of Science: Prof. GAMALAT YOUSEF OSMAN

Faculty of Special Education: Prof. ALI BADAWI MAHROUS

Faculty of Physical Education: Prof. ESAM EL DIN METWALY ALI

Faculty of Veterinary Medicine: Prof. SALAH EL SAYED IBRAHIM

Institute of Desert Environment Research: Prof. MUBARAK HASSANY ALI

Genetic Engineering and Biotechnology Research Institute: (vacant)

Faculty of Nursing: Prof. MAGDA MOAWAD

National Liver Research Institute: Prof. EMAM ABD EL LATIEF EMAM

MISR UNIVERSITY FOR SCIENCE AND TECHNOLOGY (MUST)

BP 77, Sixth of October City

Telephone: (2) 38354686

E-mail: must@must.edu

Internet: www.must.edu

Founded 1996

Private control

Language of instruction: English

Academic year: October to July

Chancellor: KHALED M. EL-TOUKHY

Pres.: Prof. MOHAMED RAAFAT MAHMOUD

Vice-Pres. for Community Service: Prof. FAROUK ABU-ZAID

Vice-Pres. for Int. Cooperation and Quality Assurance: Prof. MOSTAFA M. KAMEL

Registrar: ASHRAF ABDULLAH

Librarian: Prof. KAMAL ARAFAT

Library of 70,000 vols

Number of teachers: 533

Number of students: 12,348

DEANS

College of Applied Medical Sciences: FATIMA AL-SHARQAWI

College of Archaeology and Tourist Guidance: MOHAMMED IBRAHIM BAKR

College of Biotechnology: Prof. ALI Z. ABDUL-SALAM

College of Business: Prof. MOHAMMED H. AZZAZI

College of Dental Medicine: Prof. TAREK M. AL-SHARKAWI

College of Engineering: Prof. MOHAMMED K. BEDEEWI

College of Foreign Languages and Translation: Prof. MOHSEN ABU-SEDA

College of Information Technology: MOHAMED S. ABDUL-WAHHAB

College of Mass Media: Prof. FAROUK ABU-ZIED

College of Medicine: Prof. MAJED GAMAL ZAYED

College of Pharmacy: Prof. MOHAMMED F. AL-MELEEGI

College of Physical Therapy: Prof. BASEM AL-NAHHAS

SOUTH VALLEY UNIVERSITY

Qena Governorate, Qena

Telephone: (96) 5211277

Fax: (96) 5211279

E-mail: info@svu.edu.eg

Internet: www.svu.edu.eg

Founded 1995

State control

Languages of instruction: Arabic, English

Academic year: September to June

Campuses in Luxor, Hurghada, Aswan

Pres.: Prof. ABBAS MOHAMED MOHAMED MANSOUR

Vice-Pres. for Aswan Campus: Prof. FAWI MOHAMED ASSUGHAYER

Vice-Pres. for Community Services and Environmental Affairs: Prof. MAHMOUD KHODARI MA'LA

Vice-Pres. for Undergraduate Studies: Prof. MOHAMED THARWAT ABD EL RAHMAN

Vice-Pres. for Post-Graduate Studies and Research: Prof. ABDEL-FATAH M. HASHEM

Chief Librarian: AWATEF YASSIEN ALQADI

Number of teachers: 795 assts, 691 PhDs

Number of students: 55,100

DEANS

Faculty of Agriculture: Prof. MOHAMMAD ALI

Faculty of Archaeology: Prof. ABDULLAH K. MOUSA

Faculty of Arts: Prof. ABUELFADL M. M. BADRAN

Faculty of Commerce: Prof. JAMAL IBRAHIM

Faculty of Education: Prof. SAMEH A. M. JAFAR

Faculty of Education (Hurghada): Prof. KAREEMA KHATAAB

Faculty of Engineering: Prof. AREF M. SULAIMAN

Faculty of Fine Arts (Luxor): Prof. SALEH MOHAMED ABDELMU'TI

Faculty of Hotel and Tourism: Prof. MANSOUR ELNOUBI

Faculty of Law: Prof. THARWAT M. ABDEL-'AAL

Faculty of Medicine: Prof. MANSOUR KABBASH

Faculty of Nursing: Prof. SAYED TAHA

Faculty of Physical Education: Prof. EMAD ABU-ELQASEM

Faculty of Science: Prof. SAYED O. AL-KHATEEB

Faculty of Social Work: Prof. ALI A. DANDARAWI

Faculty of Specific Education: Prof. HUFNI ISMAIEL

Faculty of Veterinary Medicine: Prof. ABDEL-LATIF S. SHAKER

DEANS (ASWAN CAMPUS)

Faculty of Arts: Prof. AHAMD SUKRANO ABDEL-HAFEZ (acting)

Faculty of Education: Prof. NADY K. AZIZ

Faculty of Engineering: Prof. ABD-ALLAH IBRAHIM

Faculty of Science: Prof. ALI K. KHALAF-ALLAH

High Institute of Energy: Prof. JABER SHABIB

SUEZ CANAL UNIVERSITY

el Shikh Zayed, Ismailia

Telephone: (64) 3297020

Fax: (64) 325208

E-mail: info@suez.edu.eg

Internet: scuegypt.edu.eg

Founded 1976

State control

Languages of instruction: Arabic, English

Academic year: October to June

Pres.: Prof. FAROUK MAHMOUD ABD EL KADER

Vice-Pres. for Community Services and Environmental Affairs: Prof. ALY IBRAHIM ELSAYED IBRAHIM BADR

Vice-Pres. for Port Said: MOHAMED ELSAYED ALY RAHEEM

Vice-Pres. for Postgraduate Studies and Research: Prof. MOSTAFA KAMEL MOHAMED MOSBAH

Vice-Pres. for Undergraduate Studies: Prof. IBRAHIM ASHOUR IBRAHIM BADR

Sec.-Gen.: NAINAA MOHAMED MOHAMED KHALIFA

Librarian: KAMILIA ALHOSARY

Number of teachers: 1,466

Number of students: 47,488

DEANS

El Arish:

Faculty of Agricultural and Environmental Sciences: Prof. MOHAMED RAGAB ABDO HUMOS

Faculty of Education: Prof. NASSEF BEDEER IBRAHIM ELAASY

Ismailia:

Faculty of Agriculture: Prof. MOHAMED SAMIR MOHAMED ATTEYA ELSHAZLY

Faculty of Commerce: Prof. MOSTAFA ALY MAHMOUD ELBAZ

Faculty of Computers and Information Science: Prof. MOHAMED HELMY MAHRAN

Faculty of Dentistry: Prof. MOHAMED ELHUSSEINY MOHAMED MEKY

Faculty of Education: Prof. MAHMOUD ABBASS MAHMOUD ABDEIN

Faculty of Medicine: Prof. SOLIMAN HAMED SOLIMAN ELKAMASH

Faculty of Pharmacy: Prof. SALAH ELDIN MOHAMED ABDALLA

Faculty of Science: Prof. ELSAYED HUSSEIN MOSTAFA ELTAMNY

Faculty of Tourism and Hotels: Prof. ABD EL RAHMAN ABD EL FATTAH MOHAMED

Faculty of Veterinary Medicine: Prof. MOHAMED ELSAYED ANANY

Port Said:

Faculty of Commerce: Prof. MOHAMED ABD EL RAHMAN ELAADY

Faculty of Education: FAKRY IBRAHIM KHALIL KHALAF

Faculty of Engineering: Prof. AHMAD KAMAL ABD-EL KHALEK

Faculty of Nursing: Prof. HODA WADEEA TAWFEK

Faculty of Physical Education (Male): Prof. SAYED ABDEL GAWAD ELSAYED AHMED

Faculty of Specific Education: Prof. MOHAMED SAYED AHMED SALEH

Suez:

Faculty of Commerce: Prof. MAHMOUD SAYED AHMED SALEM

Faculty of Education: Prof. BELAL AHMED SOLIMAN AHMED

Faculty of Industrial Education: Prof. AHMED ESSA GAMEA ELNEKHILY

Faculty of Petroleum and Mining Engineering: Prof. SHUHDY EL MAGHRABY ELALFY SHALABY

TANTA UNIVERSITY

El Geish St, Tanta
Telephone: (40) 3317928
Fax: (40) 3302785
E-mail: president@tainta.edu.eg
Internet: www.tanta.edu.eg

Founded 1972
State control
Languages of instruction: Arabic, English
Academic year: October to June

Pres.: Prof. ABDELFATTAH A. SADAKAH
Vice-Pres. for Community Service and Environment Devt: Prof. MOHAMED MOSAAD NASSAR
Vice-Pres. for Graduate Studies and Research: Prof. MOHAMED ADEL KHALIFAA
Vice-Pres. for Education and Student Affairs: Prof. AZIZ MAHFOUZ KAFAFY
Sec.-Gen.: RAWIA SOLIMAN GAD
Chief Librarian: ADEL YASSIEN

Number of teachers: 2,042
Number of students: 109,037

DEANS

Faculty of Agriculture: Prof. HELMY ALI ANBAR
Faculty of Arts: Prof. ZAIN EL DEIN MOSTAFA
Faculty of Commerce: Prof. SAID LEBDA
Faculty of Dentistry: Prof. SHWKRIA MOHAMMED ESMAIL
Faculty of Education: Prof. MOHAMMED AMIN ATWA
Faculty of Engineering: Prof. ABDEL-WAHED ASAR
Faculty of Law: Prof. HUSIEN MOHAMMED FATHY
Faculty of Medicine: Prof. SHAWKI ABD-ELAZIZ EL ABD
Faculty of Nursing: Prof. Dr HELMY HAMAD AHMED SHALABY
Faculty of Pharmacy: Prof. MOKHTAR MOHAMMED MABROUK
Faculty of Physical Education: Prof. REYAD ZAKRIA EL MENSHAWY
Faculty of Science: Prof. EBRAHIM KAMEL EL SHORBAGY
Faculty of Specific Education: Prof. HUSIEN MOHAMMED FATHY (acting)

ZAGAZIG UNIVERSITY

Sharkia Governorate, Zagazig
Telephone and fax (55) 238470
E-mail: info@zu.edu.eg
Internet: www.zu.edu.eg

Founded 1974, incorporating existing faculties of Ain-Shams Univ.
State control
Languages of instruction: Arabic, English
Academic year: October to June

Pres.: Prof. MAHER MOHAMED ALI EL DOMIATY
Vice-Pres. for Education and Student Affairs: Prof. AHMED ELREFAAY BAHGAT EL AZIZY
Vice-Pres. for Environmental Affairs: Prof. TAREK YOUSSEF GAAFAR
Vice-Pres. for Postgraduate Studies: Prof. MOHAMED BAHGAT AWAD
Sec.-Gen.: MOHAMMED MOHAMMED HASHEM
Chief Librarian: RAMADAN ALY OTHMAN

Number of teachers: 4,250
Number of students: 151,091

DEANS

Faculty of Agriculture: Prof. MOHAMMED BASSEM ASHOUR
Faculty of Arts: Prof. HASSAN MOHAMMED HAMMAD
Faculty of Commerce: Prof. IBRAHIM MOUSSA ABD ELFATAH
Faculty of Computer and Information Science: Prof. D MOHAMMED ABBAS SHOUMAN
Faculty of Education: Prof. HAMDY HASSAN ELMAHROUKY

Faculty of Engineering: Prof. ASHRAF MOHAMMED ELSHEIHY
Faculty of Law: Prof. ATEF HASSAN MAHMOUD ELNOKALY
Faculty of Medicine: Prof. SAAD SABRY ELOSH
Faculty of Nursing: Prof. NAGWA AHMED ELSHAFEEY
Faculty of Pharmacy: Prof. MOHAMMED NAGUIB MOHAMMED ZAKARIA
Faculty of Physical Education (Female): Prof. NABILA ABDALLA MOHAMED OMRAN
Faculty of Physical Education (Male): Prof. ABD ELAZEEM ABD ELHAMID ELSAYED
Faculty of Science: Prof. MOHAMMED GAMAL HELMY ABD ELWAHED
Faculty of Specific Education: Prof. ADEL EBRAHIM ELBAZ
Faculty of Veterinary Medicine: Prof. ALAA ELDEEN MOHAMMED MORSHEDY
Higher Institute of Ancient Near East Civilizations: Prof. MAHMOUD OMAR MOHAMED
Higher Institute of Asian Research and Studies: Prof. BAYOUMI AWAD ALLAH TARTOUR
Higher Institute of Productive Efficiency: Prof. MOHAMMED NAGY ELGAAFRY

University-Level Institute

BENHA HIGHER INSTITUTE OF TECHNOLOGY

New Benha, el Kaludia, Benha City 13512
Telephone: (13) 3229263
Fax: (13) 3230297
E-mail: ahuzayyin@gmx.net
Internet: www.bhit-buni.edu.eg

Founded 1988
State control

Dean: AHMED SOLIMAN HUZAYYIN
Vice-Dean for Postgraduates: ADEL ALAM EL DIN
Vice-Dean for Students: MAHMOUD FATHY M. HASSAN

Library of 8,100 vols
Number of teachers: 275
Number of students: 1,530

Depts of basic sciences, civil engineering, electrical engineering and mechanical engineering.

Colleges

Arab Academy for Science and Technology and Maritime Transport: Gamal Abdel Naser St, BP 1029, Miami, Alexandria; tel. (3) 5622366; fax (3) 5622525; internet www.aast.edu; f. 1972; Colleges of Engineering and Technology, Management and Technology and Maritime Transport; library: 36,000 vols, 350 periodicals; 490 teachers; 4,000 students; Pres. Dr GAMAL MOKHTAR.

Cairo Polytechnic Institute: 108 Shoubra St, Shoubra, Cairo; f. 1961; Engineering, Agriculture, Commerce; Dir H. H. MOHAMED.

Higher Industrial Institute: Aswan; f. 1962; State control; courses in mechanical, electrical and chemical engineering, mining and natural sciences.

Higher Institute of Public Health: 165 el Horreya Ave, el Hadra, Alexandria; tel. (3) 4285575; fax (3) 4288436; e-mail hiph.adv@gmail.com; internet www.hiph-egypt.net; an autonomous unit of the Univ. of Alexandria; f. 1956; undertakes fundamental teaching and applied public health research; 81 staff mems and 50 instructors; depts of public health administration, biostatistics, nutrition, epidemiology, tropical health, microbiology, occupational and environmental health,

family health; library: 10,000 vols; Dean Prof. MOUSRAFA I. MOURAD; Vice-Dean for Postgraduate Studies and Research Prof. NIHAD I. DABBOUS; Vice-Dean for Community Service and Environmental Affairs Prof. MOHAMED A. EL BARRAWY.

Mansoura Polytechnic Institute: Mit-Khamis St, Mansoura; f. 1957; 147 teachers; 2,290 students; library: 21,400 vols; Dir Dr ESAYED SELIM ELMOLLA.

Regional Centre for Adult Education (ASFEC): Sirs el Layyan, Menoufia; tel. (48) 351596; f. 1952 by UNESCO; training of specialists in fields of literacy, adult education and education for rural devt; production of prototype educational material, research in community devt problems; advisory service; Chair. F. A. GHONEIM; Dir SALAH SHARAKAM.

Sadat Academy for Management Sciences: Kernish el Nile el Maadi, BP 2222, Cairo; tel. (2) 23787628; fax (2) 27530043; e-mail info@sadatacademy.edu.eg; internet www.sadatacademy.edu.eg; f. 1981; principal governmental org. for management devt in Egypt; activities carried out through 10 academic depts: business admin., public admin., economics, production, admin. law, personnel and organizational behaviour, accountancy, insurance and quantitative analysis, computer and information systems, languages; also consists of 4 professional centres: Training, Consultation, Research and Local Administration; and Faculty of Management (undergraduate) and National Institute of Management Development (postgraduate); library: 32,000 vols, 250 periodicals; 124 teachers; 4,948 students; Pres. Prof. AHMED MAHMOUD YOUSSEF; Vice-Pres. for Education and Research Prof. SHERIEF HASSAN; Vice-Pres. for Training and Consultation Prof. ABDELHAMED MOSTAFA ABO NAAM; Vice-Pres. for Postgraduate Studies and Research Prof. MOHAMED ZAKY EID; publ. *Magalet Al-Behouth Al Edaria* (Administrative Research Review, 4 a year, in Arabic and English).

Branches:

Alexandria Branch: 59 Menshya Moharram Bak St, Alexandria; tel. (3) 3931515; fax (3) 3935887; e-mail alex-sams@sadatacademy.edu.eg; Dir Dr BADEAA ELDIN RESHO.

Assyot Branch: Mogamaa al Masaleh, Assyot; tel. and fax (88) 2310499; e-mail asiut-sams@sadatacademy.edu.eg; Dir Dr ABDEL MOHAMMED.

Dekkernes: Korneish el Bahr St, Dekernes; tel. (50) 7472521; fax (50) 7472520; e-mail dekernes-sams@sadatacademy.edu.eg; Dir SALAH ABD EL HAY.

Port Said Branch: Abdel-Salam Arif St, Port Said; tel. (66) 3351396; fax (66) 3352396; e-mail portsaid-sams@sadatacademy.edu.eg; Dir Prof. SAFWAT ALI HMEDA.

Ramsis Branch (Faculty of Management): 14 Ramsis St, Cairo; tel. (2) 225764337; fax (2) 225753350; e-mail ramsis-sams@sadatacademy.edu.eg; Dir MOHAMMED MOUSSA.

Tanta Branch: Sedkee St, Tanta; tel. (40) 3302083; fax (40) 3302017; e-mail tanta-sams@sadatacademy.edu.eg; Dir Prof. SAYED ABD EL MOULA.

Schools of Art and Music

Academy of Arts: el Afghany St, off Alharam Ave, Giza; tel. (2) 35850727; fax

(2) 35611230; e-mail aoarts@idsc.gov.eg; f. 1959; comprises 8 institutes of univ. status; Pres. Prof. FAWZY FAHMY AHMED; Dir of Public Relations AWAD KAMEL FAHMI; publ. *Alfann Almuasir* (4 a year).

Constituent Institutes:

Higher Institute of Arab Music: Cairo; tel. (2) 24851561; f. 1967; depts of instrumentation, singing, theory of composition; Postgraduate Studies; library of 11,000 vols; 125 teachers; 280 students; Dean Dr SAID HAIKUL.

Higher Institute of Art Criticism: Cairo; library of 2,500 vols; 8 teachers; 90 students; Dean Dr NAHIL RACHAB.

Higher Institute of Ballet: Cairo; tel. (2) 35853999; f. 1958; 2 brs in Alexandria and Ismailia; depts of classical ballet, choreography, postgraduate studies; library of 3,500 vols; 21 teachers; 21 students; Dean Dr MAGDA EZZ.

Higher Institute of Child Arts: Cairo; tel. (2) 35850727; f. 1990; postgraduate studies.

Higher Institute of Cinema: Cairo; tel. (2) 35850291; f. 1959; depts of scriptwriting, directing, editing, photography and camerawork, scenery design, sound production, animation, cartoons; postgraduate studies; library of 5,000 vols; 90 teachers; 450 students; Dean Dr SHAWKY ALY MOHAMED.

Higher Institute of Folklore: Cairo; tel. (2) 35851230; f. 1981; dept of postgraduate studies; library of 6,000 vols; 25 teachers; 60 students; Dean Dr ALYAA SHOUKRY.

Higher Institute of Music (Conservatoire): Cairo; tel. (2) 35853451; f. 1959; depts of composition and theory, piano, string instruments, wind instruments, percussion, singing, solfa and music education, musicology; postgraduate studies; library of 24,000 vols, 3,000 records; 90 teachers; 78 students; Dean Prof. NIBAL MOUNIB.

Higher Institute of Theatre Arts: Cairo; tel. (2) 35853233; f. 1944; depts of acting and directing, drama and criticism, scenic and stage design; postgraduate studies; library of 15,500 vols; 90 teachers; 330 students; Dean Dr SANAA SHAFIE.

EL SALVADOR

The Higher Education System

The state-controlled Universidad de El Salvador, founded in 1841, was the only university until the mid-1960s, since when several private universities have been established. The Ministry of Education oversees higher education. Other institutions of higher education include colleges and technical institutes. In 2006/07 there were 132,200 students enrolled in tertiary education.

Entrance to higher education is achieved on the basis of obtaining the main secondary school qualification, the Bachillerato, and success in an entrance examination. The first undergraduate degree is the Diplomado, awarded after two to three years' study. Following this, the Licenciado can last from four to seven years and may also lead to a professional title. The Maestría is awarded after a further two years, and the Doctorado is available in some subjects.

Both universities and non-university institutions (colleges and technical institutes) offer technical and vocational qualifications. Courses last for two to three years, and qualifications include Técnico (two years), Perito, Auxiliar and Técnico Superior (three-and-a-half years).

Regulatory and Representative Bodies

GOVERNMENT

Ministry of Education: Edif. A, Centro de Gobierno, Alameda Juan Pablo II y Calle Guadalupe, San Salvador; tel. 2281-0044; fax 2281-0077; e-mail educacion@mined.gob.sv; internet www.mined.gob.sv; Minister DARLYN MEZA.

ACCREDITATION

Comisión de Acreditación de la Calidad de la Educación Superior (Commission for the Accreditation of Quality in Higher Education): Alameda Juan Pablo II y Calle Guadalupe, Plan Maestro, Centro de Gobierno, Edificio A2, San Salvador; tel. 2281-0282; e-mail cda_dnes@mined.gob.sv; internet www.mined.gob.sv/cda; autonomous body attached to the Min. of Education; awards accredited status to univs and other higher education instns proving their commitment to continuing improvement in academic standards; 7 mems; Pres. Dr HÉCTOR LINDO FUENTES; Exec. Dir Lic. MARÍA DE LOS ÁNGELES DE SALGUERO.

Learned Societies

GENERAL

Academia Salvadoreña (El Salvador Academy): Casa de las Academias, 9a Avda Norte y Alameda Juan Pablo II, San Salvador; fax 2222-9721; e-mail denysfuentesmyk@hotmail.com; f. 1876; corresp. of the Real Academia Española (Madrid); 22 mems; Dir ALFREDO MARTÍNEZ MORENO; Sec. RENÉ FORTÍN MAGAÑA.

HISTORY, GEOGRAPHY AND ARCHAEOLOGY

Academia Salvadoreña de la Historia (El Salvador Academy of History): Km 10 Planes de Renderoz, Col. Los Angeles, Villa Lilia 13, San Salvador; f. 1925; Corresp. of the Real Academia de la Historia (Madrid); 18 mems; library of 9,000 vols; Dir JORGE LARDÉ Y LARÍN; Sec. PEDRO ESCALANTE MENA; publ. *Boletín* (irregular).

LANGUAGE AND LITERATURE

Alliance Française: 51 Avda Norte 152, Col. Escalon, Apdo 0175, San Salvador; tel. 2260-5807; fax 2260-5762; e-mail alliafrance@navegante.com.sv; offers courses and examinations in French language and culture and promotes cultural exchange with France.

MEDICINE

Colegio Médico de El Salvador: Final Pasaje 10, Col. Miramonte, San Salvador; tel. 2260-1111; fax 2260-0324; f. 1943; 1,710 mems; promotes medical research and cooperation; Pres. Dr J. ASCENCIÓN MARINERO CÁCERES; publs *Archivos* (3 a year), *Revista Lealo* (6 a year).

Sociedad de Ginecología y Obstetricia de El Salvador: Colegio Médico de El Salvador, Final Pasaje 10, Col. Miramonte, San Salvador; tel. 2235-3432; fax 2235-3432; f. 1947; 150 mems; library of 2,000 vols; Pres. Dr JORGE CRUZ GONZALEZ; Sec. Dr HENRY AGREDA RODRIGUEZ.

Research Institutes

AGRICULTURE, FISHERIES AND VETERINARY SCIENCE

Centro Nacional de Tecnología Agropecuaria y Forestal: Km 33½, Carretera a Santa Ana, La Libertad; tel. 2302-0200; e-mail info@centa.gob.sv; internet www.centa.gob.sv; f. 1942; research and devt of seeds; library of 11,000 vols, 134 current periodicals; Exec. Dir ERNESTO DAGLIO VAN SEVEREN; publs *Agricultura en El Salvador* (irregular), *Boletín Técnico* (irregular), *Circular* (irregular).

Instituto Salvadoreño de Investigaciones del Café: Ministerio de Agricultura, 23 Avda Norte No. 114, San Salvador; f. 1956; administered by the Ministry of Agriculture; publs monographs, *Boletín Informativo* (6 a year).

ECONOMICS, LAW AND POLITICS

Dirección General de Estadística y Censos (Statistical Office): Avda Juan Bertis 79, Ciudad Delgado, Apdo postal 2670, San Salvador; tel. 2276-5900; fax 2286-2505; f. 1881; Dir-Gen. SALVADOR ARMANDO MELGAR; publs *Anuario Estadístico* (1 a year), *Encuesta de Hogares de Propósitos Múltiples* (1 a year), *Encuesta Económica* (1 a year), *IPC* (12 a year).

NATURAL SCIENCES

Physical Sciences

Centro de Investigaciones Geotécnicas: Apdo 109, San Salvador; tel. 2293-1442; fax 2293-1462; reorganized 1964; departments of seismology, soil mechanics, building materials, geological surveys; 250 mems; library of 1,000 vols; Dir DOUGLAS HERNANDEZ; publs *Investigaciones Geológicas*, reports.

Servicio Meteorológico Nacional: Kilómetro 5½ Carretera a Nueva San Salvador, Calle las Mercedes frente a Círculo Militar y contiguo a Parque de Pelota, San Salvador; tel. 2223-7797; fax 2283-2269; internet www.snet.gob.sv; f. 1889; library of 2,000 vols; Dir LUIS GARCÍA GUIROLA; publs *Almanaque Marino Costero*, *Almanaque Climatológico*, *Boletines Agroclimáticos* (online), *Boletines Climatológicos* (online), *Boletines El Niño* (online), *Weather Forecast, 24 hrs, 48 hrs, 7 days* (online).

TECHNOLOGY

Comisión Salvadoreña de Energía Nuclear (COSEN): c/o Ministerio de Economía, 1A Calle Poniente y 73 Avda Norte, San Salvador; f. 1961; to consider the applications in medicine, agriculture and industry of radioisotopes and nuclear energy.

Libraries and Archives

San Salvador

Archivo General de la Nación: Palacio Nacional, San Salvador; tel. 2222-9418; f. 1948; 2,000 vols; Dir ALBERTO ATILIO SALAZAR; publ. *Repositorio*.

Biblioteca del Ministerio de Relaciones Exteriores (Library of the Ministry of Foreign Affairs): Carretera a Santa Tecla, San Salvador; 10,000 vols; Librarian MANUEL ANTONIO LÓPEZ.

Biblioteca Nacional (National Library): 4ta Calle Oriente y Avda Mons. Oscar A. Romero # 124, San Salvador; tel. 2221-2099; fax 2221-8847; internet www.binaes.gob.sv; f. 1870; 150,000 vols; special collections: old books, titles on int. organizations, Braille room; Dir Dr H. C. MANLIO ARGUETA.

Sistema Bibliotecario de la Universidad de El Salvador: Final 25 Avda Norte, Ciudad Universitaria, Apdo 2923, San Salvador; tel. 2225-0278; fax 2225-0278; e-mail sb@biblio.ues.edu.sv; internet www.ues.edu.sv/biblio.html; f. 1847; 44,000 vols; Dir MLIS CARLOS R. COLINDRES.

Museums and Art Galleries

San Salvador

Museo de Historia Natural de El Salvador: Final Calle Los Viveros, Col. Nicaragua, San Salvador; tel. 2270-9228; fax 2221-4419; f. 1976; Dir DANIEL AGUILAR.

Museo Nacional 'David J. Guzmán' (National Museum): Avda la Revolución, Col. San Benito, San Salvador; f. 1883; specializes in history, archaeology, ethnology, library science and restoration; travelling exhibits programme; Dir MANUEL R. LÓPEZ; publs *Anales, Colección Antropología e Historia, El Xipe, La Cofradía*.

Attached Museums:

  Museo de sitio San Andrés: Parque Arqueológico San Andrés, Km. 32, Carretera Panamericana, Ciudad Arce, Dpto de La Libertad; tel. 2221-4419; fax 2221-4419; e-mail direcciondepatrimonio@concultura .gob.sv; internet www.cultura.gob.sv; f. 1996; museum at major archaeological site of San Andrés, occupation of which spans c. 2,000 years; its apogee was during the Late Classic period (AD 600–900), when it became the capital of a Mayan realm; Head of Cultural Heritage Dr SONIA BAIRES.

  Museo Tazumal: Chalchuapa, Dpto de Santa Ana; f. 1951; archaeological site museum.

Parque Zoológico Nacional: Final Calle Modelo, San Salvador; tel. 270-0828; fax 2274-3950; f. 1953; recreation, environmental education and research, conservation; library of 1,800 vols; Dir Arq. ELIZABETH DE QUANT.

Universities

UNIVERSIDAD CATÓLICA DE OCCIDENTE

25 Calle Oriente y 25 Avda Sur, Santa Ana
Telephone: 2447-8785
Fax: 2441-2655
E-mail: catolica@unico.edu.sv
Internet: www.unico.edu.sv
Founded 1983
Private control
Language of instruction: Spanish
Academic year: February to December
Rector: ROMEO TOVAR ASTORGA
Vice-Rector: MOISÉS ANTONIO MARTINÉZ ZALDIVÁR LACALLE
Sec.-Gen.: CÁSTULO AFRANIO HERNÁNDEZ ROBLES
Dir of Admin.: ROBERTO CHACÓN
Dir of Communications: KAREN MÉNDEZ
Dir of Public Relations: JOSÉ JAIME DELEÓN
Dir of Univ. Welfare: Lic JOSÉ ARÍSTIDES MÉNDEZ
Dirof Library: MAURICIO EDGARDO MENENDÉZ LEMUS
Number of teachers: 200
Number of students: 3,200

DEANS

Faculty of Economic Sciences: JOSÉ RICARDO RIVAS
Faculty of Engineering and Architecture: JULIO ENRIQUE NÁJERA
Faculty of Law and Social Sciences: ROBERTO ANTONIO SAYES
Faculty of Science and Humanities: JAIME OSMÍN TRIGUEROS FLORES

DIRECTORS
Department of Languages: JUAN FRANCISCO LINARES LINARES
Research Unit: NERY FRANCISCO HERRERA

ATTACHED INSTITUTES
Departamento de Educación a Distancia: promotes teacher training courses.
Instituto de Desarrollo Rural: promotes extra-curricular activities in the rural sphere, projects on agricultural devt, training courses for the rural population, technical analysis for agricultural cooperatives and environmental health and hygiene projects.
Instituto de Promoción Humana: promotes courses in administration, administration for rural cooperatives, nutrition, administration for small businesses.

UNIVERSIDAD CENTROAMERICANA 'JOSÉ SIMEÓN CAÑAS'

Apdo 01-168, San Salvador
Blvd Los Próceres, San Salvador
Telephone: 2210-6600
Fax: 2210-6655
E-mail: correo@www.uca.edu.sv
Internet: www.uca.edu.sv
Founded 1965
Private control (Society of Jesus)
Language of instruction: Spanish
Academic year: March to December
Rector: P. JOSE MARIA TOJERIA
Vice-Rector (Academic): Ing. CELINA PEREZ RIVERA
Vice-Rector (Finance): Ing. AXEL SODERBERG
Registrar: Lic. RENÉ ALBERTO ZELAYA
Librarian: JACQUELINE MORALES DE COLOCHO
Library of 286,496 vols
Number of teachers: 440
Number of students: 10,413
Publications: *Boletín Economía Hoy* (12 a year), *Comunica* (online, 15 a year), *De Legibus* (2 a year), *El Salvador en la Mira* (online, 24 a year), *En Plural* (2 a year), *Estudios Centroamericanos ECA* (2 or 3 a year), *La Casa de Todos: Revista de Arquitectura y Urbanismo* (3 a year), *Realidad: Revista de Ciencias Sociales y Humanidades* (4 a year), *Revista Carta a las Iglesias* (12 a year), *Revista Contabilidad y Empresa* (3 a year), *Revista de Administración y Empresas* (2 a year), *Revista Latinoamericana de Teología* (3 a year)

DEANS

Faculty Of Economics: REYNALDO MARTINEZ PLATERO
Faculty Of Engineering: EMILIO MORALES
Faculty Of Human And Natural Sciences: Dr SILVIA ELINOR AZUCENA DE FERNÁNDEZ
Faculty Of Post-grade: LIDIA SALAMANCA

UNIVERSIDAD DE EL SALVADOR

Final 25 Avda, Ciudad Universitaria, Apdo 3110, San Salvador
Telephone: 2225-8826
Fax: 2225-8826
E-mail: mirsalva@navegante.com.sv
Internet: www.ues.edu.sv
Founded 1841
State control
Academic year: February to December
Brs in the Western, Eastern and Paracentral regions of El Salvador
Rector: Dr MARÍA ISABEL RODRÍGUEZ
Vice-Rector for Academics: JOAQUÍN ORLANDO MACHUCA
Vice-Rector for Admin.: Dr CARMEN RODRÍGUEZ DE RIVAS

Registrar: ALICIA MARGARITA RIVAS
Library Dir: JOSEFINA ROQUE
Number of teachers: 1,877
Number of students: 28,306
Publications: *Aquí Odontología* (odontology, 12 a year), *Boletín Informativo de la Facultad de Ciencias Económicas* (12 a year), *Búho Dilecto* (science and humanities, 6 a year), *Contacto Universitario* (bulletin of the Secretariat for National and International Relations,12 a year), *El Quehacer Científico* (natural sciences and mathematics, 1 a year), *El Salvador: Coyuntura Económica* (economics, 4 a year), *El Universitario* (academic review, 4 a year), *Enfoque Tecnológico* (nuclear research, 2 a year), *Revista Electrónica de la Facultad de Medicina* (2 a year), *Ventana Informativa* (bulletin of the Multidisciplinary Faculty of the Western Region, 12 a year)

DEANS

Faculty of Agriculture: JORGE ALBERTO ULLOA
Faculty of Chemistry and Pharmacy: SALVADOR CASTILLO ARÉVALO
Faculty of Dentistry: Dr OSCAR RUBÉN COTO DIMAS
Faculty of Economics: EMILIO RECINOS FUENTES
Faculty of Engineering and Architecture: Ing. MARIO ROBERTO NIETO
Faculty of Humanities: ANA MARÍA GLOWER DE ALVARADO
Faculty of Jurisprudence and Social Sciences: MORENA ELIZABETH NOCHEZ DE ALDANA
Faculty of Medicine: Dr ANA LETICIA ZAVALETA DE AMAYA
Faculty of Natural and Mathematical Sciences: LETICIA NOEMÍ PÁUL DE FLORES
Multidisciplinary Faculty of the Eastern Region: JUAN FRANCISCO MÁRMOL CANJURA
Multidisciplinary Faculty of the Paracentral Region: JOSÉ NOEL ARGUETA
Multidisciplinary Faculty of the Western Region: JORGE MAURICIO RIVERA

UNIVERSIDAD 'DR JOSÉ MATÍAS DELGADO'

Km 8½ carretera a Santa Tecla, Ciudad Merliot
Telephone: 2212-9400
Fax: 2289-5314
E-mail: informacion@umjd.edu.sv
Internet: www.ujmd.edu.sv
Founded 1977
Private control
Language of instruction: Spanish
Academic year: January to June, July to December
Rector: Dr DAVID ESCOBAR GALINDO
Vice-Rector: CARLOS QUINTANILLA SCHMIDT
Academic Vice-Rector: Dr FERNANDO BASILIO CASTELLANOS
Registrar: Dr FERNANDO BASILIO CASTELLANOS
Library Dir: SARA ESCOBAR DE GONZÁLEZ
Library of 25,000 vols
Number of teachers: 380
Number of students: 4,000

DEANS AND DIRECTORS

Faculty of Agriculture and Agricultural Research: MARÍA GEORGIA GÓMEZ DE REYES
Faculty of Economics: ROBERTO ALEJANDRO SORTO FLETES
Faculty of Health Sciences: Dr JUAN JOSÉ FERNÁNDEZ
Faculty of Jurisprudence and Social Sciences: Dr HUMBERTO GUILLERMO CUESTAS
Faculty of Sciences and Arts: LUIS SALAZAR RETANA

School of Applied Arts: LUIS SALAZAR RETANA
School of Architecture: LUIS SALAZAR RETANA
School of Business Administration and Marketing: PATRICIA LINARES DE HERNÁNDEZ
School of Communications: RICARDO CHACÓN
School of Industrial Engineering: SILVIA BARRIOS DE FERREIRO
School of Psychology: ROXANA VIDES

UNIVERSIDAD DE ORIENTE

4a Calle Poniente 705, San Miguel
Telephone: 2661-1180
Fax: 2660-0879
E-mail: info@univo.edu.sv
Internet: www.univo.edu.sv
Founded 1981
Private control

Rector: Dr JOAQUÍN APARICIO ZELAYA
Pres.: Prof. GREGORIO BALMORE IRAHETA
Sec.-Gen.: ROGELIO CISNEROZ LAZO

DEANS

Faculty of Agriculture: ALVARO ARMANDO HERRERA COELLO
Faculty of Economics: LUIS ALONSO SILVA
Faculty of Engineering and Architecture: DAVID ARNOLDO FLORES GARAY
Faculty of Law: Dr GODOFREDO LAHUD
Faculty of Science and Humanities: JOSÉ DAVID DÍAZ REYES

UNIVERSIDAD PANAMERICANA DE EL SALVADOR

Calle El Progreso 214, a 60m de Avda Bernal Colonia Miramonte Poniente, San Salvador
Telephone: 2260-1906
Fax: 2260-1859
E-mail: upaninfo@upan.edu.sv
Internet: www.upan.edu.sv
Founded 1989
Private control

Rector: OSCAR ARMANDO MORÁN FOLGAR
Vice-Rector: NUBIA ADALILA MENDOZA FIGUEROA
Sec.-Gen.: CELINA DEL CARMEN LÓPEZ URÍAS
Registrar: ALMA ARACELY POZAS DE IBARRA
Librarian: RAQUEL HERNÁNDEZ

DEANS

Faculty of Economics: JOSUÉ ELÍAS MONTOYA

Faculty of Jurisprudence: ALEJANDRO GARCÍA GARAY
Faculty of Science and Humanities: NUBIA ADAILILA MENDOZA FIGUEROA

DIRECTORS

Institute of Research, Guidance and Assessment: VIRGINIA QUINTANA ESTRADA
School of Legal Sciences: MARGORI CAROLINA JUSTO
School of Library Science and Information Science: CARLOS FERRER

UNIVERSIDAD SALVADOREÑA ALBERTO MASFERRER

19 Avda Norte, entre 3a Calle Poniente y Alameda Juan Pablo II, Apdo 2053, San Salvador
Telephone: 2221-1136
Fax: 2222-8006
E-mail: informacion@mail.usam.edu.sv
Internet: www.usam.edu.sv
Founded 1979
State control
Language of instruction: Spanish
Academic year: January to December

Rector: Dr CÉSAR AUGUSTO CALDERÓN
ViceRector: Dr MIGUEL ANTONIO BARRIOS
Sec.-Gen.: DAYSI C. M. DE GOMEZ
Registrar: ANA LORENA DE MELÉNDEZ
Librarian: XIMENA TIZNADO

Number of teachers: 283
Number of students: 2,000

Publication: *Revista Somos* (4 a year)

DEANS

Faculty of Dentistry: Dr ARMANDO RAFAEL MARTÍNEZ
Faculty of Law and Social Sciences: DELMER EDMUNDO CRUZ RODRÍGUEZ
Faculty of Medicine: Dra CARMEN J. CABEZAS DE SÁNCHEZ
Faculty of Pharmacy: SOCORRO VALDEZ
Faculty of Veterinary Medicine: Dr ANA EUGENIA VÉZQUEZ LIÉVANO

UNIVERSIDAD TECNOLÓGICA DE EL SALVADOR

Calle Arce 1120, San Salvador
Telephone: 2275-8888
Fax: 2275-8813
E-mail: infoutec@utec.edu.sv

Internet: www.utec.edu.sv
Founded 1981
Private control
Academic year: January to December

Pres. and Rector: JOSÉ MAURICIO LOUCEL
Asst Rector: CARLOS REYNALDO LÓPEZ NUILA
Vice-Rector for Academic Affairs and Strategic Devt: NELSON ZÁRATE SÁNCHEZ
Vice-Rector for Admin.: DANILO DÍAZ
Vice-Rector for Finance: MARÍA DE LOS ANGELES LOUCEL
Vice-Rector for Research and Extramural Studies: RAFAEL RODRÍGUEZ LOUCEL
Registrar: Dr JOSÉ ENRIQUE BURGOS
Librarian: MARÍA ELSA LÉMUS FLORES

Library of 16,000 vols
Number of teachers: 349
Number of students: 14,618

Publications: *Boletín Comunica, Revista de Aniversario, Revista Entorno, Revista Redes*

DIRECTORS

School of Architecture and Design: (vacant)
School of Art and Culture: Dr RAMÓN RIVAS
School of Business: VILMA FLORES DE ÁVILA
School of Communications: (vacant)
School of Languages: (vacant)
School of Law: RENE ALFREDO PORTILLO CUADRA
School of Oceanography: SUSAN LYN DE GUZMÁN
School of Science and Technology: RICARDO NAVARRETE

Colleges

Central American Technical Institute: Apdo 133, Santa Tecla, La Libertad; tel. 2228-0845; fax 2228-1277; f. 1969; courses in agricultural, civil and construction engineering, architecture, electronics, mechanical engineering; library: 6,000 vols; Dir ROLANDO MARÍN COTO.

Escuela Nacional de Agricultura 'Roberto Quiñónez': Km 33½ Carr. a Sta Ana, Apdo 2139, San Salvador; tel. 2228-2735; f. 1956; 350 students; 60 teachers; library: 7,000 vols; Dir Ing. MAURICIO ARÉVALO.

EQUATORIAL GUINEA

The Higher Education System

Equatorial Guinea has been independent for just over three decades, of which two were dominated by a brutal dictatorship. Its intellectual and cultural traditions were determined by colonial values rather than by its own cultural values, although it is slowly redressing this situation. The condition of general education (Equatorial Guinea has very limited resources) has an adverse affect on higher education, with students arriving having had very little access to books, and with an education based almost entirely on recitation. This naturally limits the level and type of coursework that may be offered. That the language of instruction is mainly Spanish while the majority of good jobs require English also presents difficulties. Many students elect to study abroad; this is supported by scholarships from foreign countries or agencies, administered by the Government. Equatorial Guinea has no national programme of scholarship for foreign study. In 1999/2000 there were 1,003 pupils in higher education. Since 1979, assistance in the development of the educational system has been provided by Spain. The Universidad Nacional de Guinea Ecuatorial (UNGE), founded in 1995, is Equatorial Guinea's only university. Two higher education centres, at Bata and Malabo, are administered by the Spanish Universidad Nacional de Educación a Distancia.

Regulatory Bodies

GOVERNMENT

Ministry of Education, Science and Sports: Malabo; Min. CRISTOBAL MEÑANA ELA.

Ministry of Information, Culture and Tourism: Malabo; Min. SANTIAGO NSOBEYA EFUMAN NCHAMA.

Learned Societies

LANGUAGE AND LITERATURE

Centro Cultural Hispano-Guineano: Malabo; f. 1982; maintains library; organizes cultural events; publs *Africa 2000* (3 a year), *Ediciones del Centro Cultural Hispano-Guineano*, series dedicated to Ecuatoguinean writers.

Institut Culturel d'Expression Française (ICEF): BP 936, Malabo; tel. 92660; fax 92985; internet www.chez.com/icefmalabo; f. 1984; offers courses and examinations in French language and culture and promotes cultural exchange with France; Dir VINCENT BRACK.

Research Institute

NATURAL SCIENCES

Biological Sciences

Bioko Biodiversity Protection Program: c/o Universidad Nacional de Guinea Ecuatorial, Carretera Luba s/n, Malabo; tel. 286768; e-mail butynski@bioko.org; internet www.bioko.org; part of academic partnership between Arcadia University (USA, *q.v.*) and Universidad Nacional de Guinea Ecuatorial (*q.v.*); conservation of Bioko Island's biodiversity, especially its critically endangered primates and nesting sea turtles, through devt of economically sustainable educational programmes, research programmes and conservation activities; maintains wildlife research centre at Moka; Co-Dirs GAIL HEARN, WAYNE MORRA; Project Dir JOSE MANUEL ESARA ECHUBE; Research Dir CLAUDIO POSA BOHOME.

Universities

UNIVERSIDAD NACIONAL DE EDUCACIÓN A DISTANCIA (UNED), EQUATORIAL GUINEA BRANCH

Edificio Poveda, C/ Amanecer de África s/n, Barrio de Ela Nguema, Malabo
Telephone: 92911
Fax: 92932
E-mail: unedmalabo@yahoo.es
Founded 1993
Language of instruction: Spanish
Dir: PILAR MONTES PALOMINO
Dir of Studies: Dr ANDRÉS ESONO ONDÓ
Library of 10,000 vols
Part of Universidad Nacional de Educación a Distancia (Spain); br. in Bata (tel. 82277).

UNIVERSIDAD NACIONAL DE GUINEA ECUATORIAL (UNGE)

Carretera Luba s/n, Malabo
Telephone: 91644
Fax: 94361
Founded 1995
State control
Languages of instruction: Spanish, French, English
Rector: CARLOS NSE NSUGA
Library of 7,500 vols
Number of teachers: 100
Number of students: 1,200
Schools of administration (Malabo), agriculture, arts and social science (Malabo), engineering and technology (Bata), fisheries and forestry, medicine (Bata), nursing (Bata) teacher training (Malabo, with br. in Bata).

ERITREA

The Higher Education System

From 1962 to 1993 Eritrea was a *de facto* province of Ethiopia. Independence was achieved in 1993 following a 33-year war of secession. Since independence Eritrea has begun to rebuild its infrastructure, economy and government. The University of Asmara (the only university) was founded by the Camboni Sisters Missionary Institute in 1958 and was originally known as the Holy Family University Institute. In 1960 the Institute was accredited by the Superior Council of the Institute of Italian Universities and in 1968 it achieved university status under its current name; an English section was opened in the same year. In 2004/05 there were some 5,500 students enrolled on Bachelors degree courses at the University of Asmara, which was under the control of the Ministry of Education. Masters degrees were offered from autumn 2004.

The University of Asmara closed in September 2006. Higher education was then provided by six newly established technical institutes, each associated with a relevant Government ministry. The institutes provide education in the fields of science, technology, business and economics, social sciences, agriculture and marine training. The university administration remains on the site and it is thought that the university will start again with postgraduate and research programmes.

Regulatory Body

GOVERNMENT

Ministry of Education: POB 5610, Asmara; tel. (1) 113044; fax (1) 113866; internet www.erimoe.gov.er; Min. SEMERE RUSOM.

Learned Societies

LANGUAGE AND LITERATURE

Alliance Française: POB 209, Asmara; tel. (1) 126599; fax (1) 121036; internet www.afasmara.org.er; offers courses and examinations in French language and culture and promotes cultural exchange with France.

British Council: 175-11, St No. 23, POB 997, Asmara; tel. (1) 123415; fax (1) 127230; e-mail information@britishcouncil.org.er; internet www.britishcouncil.org/africa; offers courses and examinations in English language and British culture and promotes cultural exchange with the UK; Information and Knowledge Centre Man. MICHAEL TEKIE; publs *Economist, New Scientist*.

Libraries and Archives

Asmara

Asmara Public Library: 82 Felket Ave 173, Asmara; tel. (1) 127044; f. 1959; 32,400 vols; branch library with 11,000 vols in north Asmara; Dir EFREM MATHEWOS KAHSAY.

Massawa

Massawa Municipal Library: POB 17, Massawa; tel. (1) 552407; fax (1) 552249; f. 1997; 10,000 vols; Chief Librarian MUHAMMED NUR SAID.

Museum

Asmara

National Museum of Eritrea: St Mariam Ghimbi H., Asmara; tel. and fax (1) 122389; e-mail yozuky@gmail.com; internet www.mrieka.com; f. 1992; archaeology, ethnography, medieval period, natural history and militaria, paleontology; oversees excavations and preservation of the national archaeological heritage; Dir-Gen. Dr YOSIEF LIBSE-QAL.

University

UNIVERSITY OF ASMARA

POB 1220, Asmara
Telephone: (1) 161926
Fax: (1) 162236
E-mail: prcuoa@asmara.uoa.edu.er
Internet: www.uoa.edu.er
Founded 1958 (Italian section); 1968 (English section)
State control
Language of instruction: English
Academic year: September to June (2 semesters)
Chancellor: ISAYAS AFEWERKI
Pres.: Dr WOLDE-AB YISAK
Dir of Admin.: TEWELDE ZEROM
Dir of Academic Affairs: Dr TADESSE MEHARI
Dir of Research and Human Resource Devt: Dr ZEMENFES TSIGHE
Dir of Student Affairs: Dr TEKIE ASEHUN
Librarian: ASSEFAW ABRAHA
Library of 60,000 vols
Number of teachers: 261
Number of students: 4,086
Publication: *Journal of Eritrean Studies* (2 a year)

DEANS AND DIRECTORS

College of Agriculture: Dr WOLDESELASSIE OGABZGHI
College of Arts: Prof. TEJ DHAR
College of Business and Economics: Dr STIFANOS HAILEMARIAM
College of Education: LETTEDENGHIL OGBAMI-CAEL
College of Engineering: KAHSAI NEGUSSE
College of Health Sciences: Dr HIBRENEGUSS TEREFE
Faculty of Law: Dr MENGISTEAB NEGASH
College of Science: Dr TESFAMICAEL HAILE
College of Social Sciences: Dr GEBREMARIAM WOLDEMICHAEL
College of Social and Management Sciences: (vacant)
School of Graduate Studies: Dr BERAKI WOLDEHAIMANOT

ESTONIA

The Higher Education System

From 1940 until 1991 Estonia was a Soviet Socialist Republic within the USSR. Higher education was based on the Soviet system, but following independence the Estonian Education Act of 1992 identified the development of Estonian language and culture as one of the main aims of education. Estonia implemented the Bologna Process at undergraduate level in 2002 and at postgraduate level in 2005; this has led to the establishment of a two-tier Bachelors and Masters degree system (with exceptions in certain subjects). Institutions of higher education are either universities or applied higher education institutes. Universities provide academic education and applied higher education institutes provide vocational education. In 2007/08 there were 34 higher education institutions, including the University of Tartu (founded in 1632) and Tallinn University, with a total of 68,399 students enrolled. The Ministry of Education is responsible for higher education, and up to 2008 several organizations were also involved in administrative and academic oversight; these included the Higher Education Advisory Chamber (HEAC), the Research and Development Council, the Estonian Science Council, the Estonian Innovation Fund and the Higher Education Quality Assessment Council QAC). In January 2009 the Higher Education Quality Agency (HEQA) took over from the HEAC and QAC as an autonomous and independent quality assessment agency. From 2009 to 2011 all higher education institutions will be required to go through the external quality assessment organized by the HEQA. By 2012 no institute will be able to operate without being accredited by the HEQA.

The Ministry of Education sets requirements for admission to higher education, which generally consists of the Secondary Education Leaving Certificate (Gümnaasiumi lõputunnistus) and performance in national entrance examinations (Riigieksamitunnistus). Public university admissions are determined by the State, which sets enrolment quotas, although universities may take additional paying students once the quotas have been met. Specialist institutions may also set specific admissions criteria. Under the Bologna Process, higher education qualifications consist of Bachelors, Masters and Doctoral degrees. The Bakalaureusekraad (Bachelors) is the main undergraduate degree, consisting of three years of study. However, some degrees leading to professional qualifications require five years of study; this is particularly the case in medicine, veterinary medicine, pharmacy, architecture, engineering and teacher training. The first postgraduate degree is the Magistrikaad (Masters), which lasts two years and is dependent on attainment of the Bakalaureusekraad. The second level of postgraduate qualification (and final university degree) is the Doktorikraad; studies at this level last four years. Both the Magistrikaad and Doktorikraad may be either academic or professional qualifications. Since their introduction in 1999, the main institutions of post-secondary vocational and technical education are the rakenduskõrgkool (applied higher education institutes), which offer three- to four-year Diplom degrees.

Regulatory and Representative Bodies

GOVERNMENT

Ministry of Culture: Suur Karja 23, Tallinn 15076; tel. 628-2222; fax 628-2200; e-mail min@kul.ee; internet www.kul.ee; Minister LAINE JÄNES.

Ministry of Education and Research: Munga 18, Tartu 50088; tel. 735-02-22; fax 735-02-50; e-mail hm@hm.ee; internet www.hm.ee; Minister TÕNIS LUKAS.

ACCREDITATION

Eesti Kõrghariduse Kvaliteediagentuur (Estonian Higher Education Quality Agency): Koidula 13A, 10125 Tallinn; tel. 696-24-24; fax 696-24-27; e-mail ekka@archimedes.ee; internet www.ekak.archimedes.ee; Head TIIT LAASBERG.

ENIC/NARIC Estonia: Academic Recognition Information Centre, Foundation 'Archimedes', L. Koidula 13A, 10125 Tallinn; tel. 696-24-15; fax 696-24-19; e-mail enic-naric@archimedes.ee; internet www.archimedes.ee/enic; Head GUNNAR VAHT.

NATIONAL BODY

Rektorite Nõukogu (Estonian Rectors' Conference): Ülikooli 18, 50090 Tartu; tel. and fax 736-68-67; e-mail mart.laidmets@ern.ee; internet www.ern.ee; f. 2000; 6 public univs as mems; Chair. Prof. ALAR KARIS; Sec. Gen. MART LAIDMETS.

Learned Societies

GENERAL

Estonian Academy of Sciences: Kohtu 6, 10130 Tallinn; tel. 644-21-29; fax 645-18-05; e-mail foreign@akadeemia.ee; internet www.akadeemia.ee; f. 1938 to advance scientific research and represent Estonian science nationally and internationally; promotes the adaptation of new knowledge for economic growth and improvement of the quality of life in Estonia; promotes the public appreciation of science and scientific methods of thought; encourages research co-operation at nat. and int. levels; divs of astronomy and physics (Head P. SAARI), biology, geology and chemistry (Head I. KOPPEL), humanities and social sciences (Head P. TULVISTE), informatics and technical Sciences (Head R. KÜTTNER); 75 mems (60 ordinary, 15 foreign); Pres. Prof. Dr RICHARD VILLEMS; Sec.-Gen. Prof. Dr LEO MÕTUS; publs *Acta Historica Tallinnensia, Linguistica Uralica, Oil Shale, Toimetised* (Proceedings: physics and mathematics, engineering, chemistry, Estonian Journal of Earth Sciences; biology/ecology), *Trames*.

HISTORY, GEOGRAPHY AND ARCHAEOLOGY

Estonian Geographical Society: Kohtu 6, 10130 Tallinn; Pres. JAAN-MATI PUNNING; Scientific Sec. LAINE MERIKALJU.

LANGUAGE AND LITERATURE

Alliance Française: Liivaluite 5, 11214 Tallinn; tel. 672-20-13; fax 672-11-98; e-mail hellemichelson@hot.ee; offers courses and examinations in French language and culture and promotes cultural exchange with France.

British Council: Vana-Posti 7, 10146 Tallinn; tel. 625-77-88; fax 625-77-99; e-mail british.council@britishcouncil.ee; internet www.britishcouncil.org/estonia; offers examinations in English; introduces British culture and promotes cultural exchange with the UK; library of 6,000 vols; Dir KYLLIKE TOHVER.

Estonian Mother Tongue Society: Roosikrantsi 6, 10119 Tallinn; tel. 644-93-31; e-mail es@eki.ee; internet www.emakeeleselts.ee; f. 1920; promotes and maintains interest in the Estonian language; coordinates language research and development; systematic research into Estonian dialects; language-planning and modern literary language research; arranges language days outside Estonia; also focuses on the modern literary language, loan-words in Estonian and the Estonian dialectal landscape; 360 mems (350 ordinary, 10 hon.); library of 6,125 vols; Chair. Prof. HELLE METSLANG; Academic Sec. ANNIKA HUSSAR; publs *Emakeele Seltsi aastaraamat* (1 a year), *Oma Keel* (2 a year).

Goethe-Institut: Suurtüki 4B, 10133 Tallinn; tel. 627-69-60; fax 627-69-62; e-mail goethe@goethe.ee; internet www.goethe.de/ne/tal/deindex.htm; offers courses and examinations in German language and culture and promotes cultural exchange with Germany; library of 9,000 vols, 25 periodicals; Dir MIKKO FRITZE.

NATURAL SCIENCES
General

Estonian Union of the History and Philosophy of Science: Ülikooli 18, 50090 Tartu; tel. 742-1514; f. 1967; attached to Estonian Academy of Sciences; 93 mems;

Chair. JAAK AAVIKSOO; Scientific Sec. ERKI TAMMIKSAAR.

Biological Sciences

Estonian Naturalists' Society: Struve 2, 51003 Tartu; tel. 734-19-35; fax 742-70-11; e-mail elus@elus.ee; internet www.elus.ee; f. 1853; 21 scientific and environmental sub-divs; library of 158,453 vols; Pres. Dr TÕNU VIIK; Sec. KATRIN ALEKAND.

Research Institutes

GENERAL

Institute for Islands Development: Lossipargi 1, 93811 Kuressaare; tel. and fax 453-91-45; e-mail kaia@si.edu.ee; attached to Tallinn Technical University; f. 1991; socio-economic and technological devt of the Estonian islands; Dir MARET PANK.

AGRICULTURE, FISHERIES AND VETERINARY SCIENCE

EAU Plant Biotechnological Research Centre EVIKA: Harjumaa, Teaduse 6A, 75501 Saku; tel. 604-14-84; fax 604-11-36; e-mail hilja.pihl@mail.ee; attached to Min. of Education, and Estonian Agricultural Univ.; Dir KATRIN KOTKAS.

Estonian Agrobiocentre: Rõõmu tee 10, 51013 Tartu; tel. and fax 733-97-17; attached to Min. of Agriculture; veterinary research; Dir JÜRI KUMAR.

Estonian Institute of Agricultural Engineering: Harjumaa, Teaduse 13, 76609 Saku; tel. 272-18-54; fax 272-19-61; e-mail ergo@peak.edu.ee; attached to Min. of Agriculture; Dir ARVI KALLAS.

Estonian Research Institute of Agriculture: Teaduse 13, 75501 Saku; tel. 671-15-42; fax 671-15-40; e-mail info@eria.ee; internet www.eria.ee; Dir HINDREK OLDER.

Jõgeva Plant Breeding Institute: Aamisepa 1, 48309 Jõgeva; tel. and fax 776-01-26; e-mail jogeva@jpbi.ee; attached to Min. of Agriculture; f. 1920; Dir MATI KOPPELL.

ARCHITECTURE AND TOWN PLANNING

OÜ ETUI BetonTEST —Ehitusinstituut (ETUI BetonTEST Ltd—Building Institute): Estonia pst. 7, 10143 Tallinn; tel. 645-41-58; fax 644-23-25; e-mail etui@betontest.ee; internet www.betontest.ee; Dir OLAV SAMMAL.

ECONOMICS, LAW AND POLITICS

Estonian Institute for Futures Studies: Lai 34, 10133 Tallinn; tel. 641-11-65; fax 641-17-59; future scenarios for the development of Estonia and its neighbouring areas; Dir ERIK TERK.

Estonian Institute of Economic Research: Rävala puiestee 6, 19080 Tallinn; tel. 681-46-50; fax 667-83-99; e-mail eki@ki .ee; internet www.ki.ee; f. 1934; Dir MARJE JOSING; publs *Economic Indicators of Estonia* (10 a year), *Economic Survey of Baltic States* (4 a year), *Konjunktuur* (4 a year), *Baltic Facts* (1 a year).

Estonian Institute of Economics at Tallinn University of Technology: Estonia tee 7, 10143 Tallinn; tel. 644-45-70; fax 699-88-51; e-mail mail@tami.ee; internet www .tami.ee; f. 1947; attached to Tallinn University of Technology; 19 mems; Dir TIIA PÜSS; Research Dir ÜLO ENNUSTE.

HISTORY, GEOGRAPHY AND ARCHAEOLOGY

Institute of History: Rüütli 6, 10130 Tallinn; tel. 644-65-94; fax 644-37-14; e-mail ai@teleport.ee; f. 1947; Dir PRIIT RAUDKIVI; publs *Acta Historica Tallinnensia* (1 a year), *Eesti Arheoloogia Ajakiri* (1 a year).

LANGUAGE AND LITERATURE

Institute of the Estonian Language: Roosikrantsi 6, 10119 Tallinn; tel. and fax 641-14-43; e-mail eki@eki.ee; internet www .eki.ee; f. 1947; Dir Dr URMAS SUTROP; *Eesti Keele Instituudi Toimetised* (irregular).

Under and Tuglas Literature Centre: Roosikrantsi 6, 10119 Tallinn; tel. 644-31-47; fax 644-01-77; e-mail utkk@utkk.ee; internet www.utkk.ee; f. 1993; attached to Estonian Acad. of Sciences; Dir Dr JAAN UNDUSK.

MEDICINE

Cardiology Centre: Ravi 18, 10138 Tallinn; tel. 620-72-50; fax 620-70-02; e-mail jyri .kaik@mail.ee; f. 1984 as Estonian Institute of Cardiology; present name 2007; attached to Tallinn Univ. of Technology; research areas incl. cardiac arrhythmias, electrophysiology, clinical and preventative cardiology; Dir JÜRI KAIK.

National Institute for Health Development: Hiiu 42, 11619 Tallinn; tel. 659-39-00; fax 659-39-01; e-mail tai@tai.ee; internet www.tai.ee; f. 1947 as Estonian Institute of Experimental and Clinical Medicine; attached to Min. of Social Affairs; Dir MAARIKE HARRO.

Pärnu Institute of Health Resort Treatment and Medical Rehabilitation: Kuuse 4, 40012 Pärnu; tel. 442-59-00; Dir ENDEL VEINPALU.

NATURAL SCIENCES

General

Estonian Marine Institute: Mäealuse 14, 12618 Tallinn; tel. 671-89-01; fax 671-89-00; e-mail meri@sea.ee; internet www.sea.ee; f. 1992; biology and ecology of freshwater and marine fish, population and community dynamics; long-term dynamics of Baltic Sea ecosystem and basic mechanisms behind it; effect of temporal and spatial variability of coastal processes on the biological and functional diversity; optics and remote sensing of coastal and inland waters; investigations on dynamics and regularities of devt of ecological subsystems in the NE Baltic, Gulfs of Finland and Rīga; modelling of the Baltic Sea and Estonian large lakes ecosystems and composing of the operational forecasting models; effect of aquatic invasive species on ecosystems; effect of human induced eutrophication processes on coastal ecosystems of the Baltic Sea; Dir Prof. TOOMAS SAAT; publ. *Estonian Marine Institute Report Series* (irregular).

Biological Sciences

Estonian Biocentre: Riia 23B, 51010 Tartu; tel. 737-50-64; fax 742-01-94; e-mail rvillems@ebc.ee; Dir RICHARD VILLEMS.

Institute of Ecology: Kevade 2, 10137 Tallinn; tel. 662-18-53; fax 662-22-83; e-mail eco@eco.edu.ee; internet www.eco.edu.ee; f. 1992; Dir J.-M. PUNNING.

Institute of Experimental Biology: Instituudi tee 11, 76902 Harku; tel. 656-06-05; fax 650-60-91; e-mail ebi@ebi.ee; f. 1957; attached to Estonian Agricultural Univ.; Dir. Prof. A. AAVIKSAAR.

Institute of Zoology and Botany: Riia 181, 51014 Tartu; tel. 742-80-21; fax 738-30-

13; internet www.zbi.ee; f. 1947; Dir URMAS TARTES.

International Centre for Environmental Biology: Mustamäe tee 4, 10621 Tallinn; tel. 611-58-04; fax 611-58-05; Dir JÜRI MARTIN.

Physical Sciences

Estonian Meteorological and Hydrological Institute: Rävala puiestee 8, 10143 Tallinn; tel. 646-15-63; e-mail jaan.saar@ emhi.ee; internet www.emhi.ee; weather forecasts; environmental protection; collation, treatment and storage of results of meteorological and hydrological measurements; climatological survey of Estonia; attached to Min. of the Environment; Dir-Gen. JAAN SAAR.

Geological Survey of Estonia: Kadaka tee 80–82, 12618 Tallinn; tel. 672-00-94; fax 672-00-91; e-mail egk@egk.ee; internet www.egk .ee; attached to Min. of the Environment; Dir. VELLO KLEIN.

Institute of Geology: Ehitajate tee 5, 19086 Tallinn; tel. 620-30-10; fax 620-30-11; e-mail inst@gi.ee; internet www.gi.ee; f. 1947; attached to Tallinn Univ. of Technology; Dir Dr ALVAR SOESOO; Sec. HELLE POHL-RAIDLA; publ. *Proceedings* (4 a year).

Institute of Physics: Riia 142, 51014 Tartu; tel. 737-46-02; fax 738-30-33; e-mail dir@fi .tartu.ee; internet www.fi.ut.ee; f. 1973; attached to Univ. of Tartu; research and higher education in physics, materials science and nanotechnology; library of 30,000 vols, 50 periodicals; Dir Dr MARCO KIRM.

National Institute of Chemical Physics and Biophysics: Akadeemia tee 23, 12618 Tallinn; tel. 639-83-00; fax 670-36-62; e-mail kbfi@kbfi.ee; internet www.kbfi.ee; f. 1979; Dir AGO SAMOSON.

Oil Shale Research Institute: Järveküla tee 12, 30328 Kohtla-Järve; tel. 334-45-50; fax 334-47-82; f. 1958; library of 100,000 vols; Dir RICHARD JOONAS.

Tartu Observatory: Tõravere, 61602 Tartu Maakond; tel. 741-02-65; fax 741-02-05; e-mail aai@aai.ee; internet www.aai.ee; f. 1808 present status 1947; research in astrophysics and cosmology, atmospheric physics and remote sensing of the earth; library of 100,000 vols; Dir LAURITS LEEDJÄRV; publ. *Tartu Tähetorni Kalender* (1 a year, in Estonian).

RELIGION, SOCIOLOGY AND ANTHROPOLOGY

Estonian Interuniversity Population Research Centre: POB 3012, 10504 Tallinn; tel. 645-41-25; fax 660-41-98; e-mail asta@ekdk.estnet.ee; Dir KALEV KATUS; publ. *EKDK RY* (series A, B, C and D, all irregular).

Institute of International and Social Studies: Estonia puiestee 7, 10143 Tallinn; tel. and fax 645-49-27; e-mail rasi@iiss.ee; internet www.iiss.ee; f. 1988; 25 mems; Dir RAIVO VETIK (acting).

TECHNOLOGY

Estonian Energy Research Institute: Paldiski maantee 1, 10137 Tallinn; tel. 662-20-28; fax 661-36-55; e-mail eeri@eeri.ee; internet www.eeri.ee; Dir ÜLO RUDI.

Institute of Cybernetics: Akadeemia tee 21, 12618 Tallinn; tel. 620-41-50; fax 620-41-51; e-mail dir@ioc.ee; internet www.ioc.ee; f. 1960; attached to Tallinn Technical Univ.; 70 mems; library of 8,000 vols; Dir ANDRUS SALUPERE.

Libraries and Archives

Tallinn

Academic Library of Tallinn University: Rävala Ave 10, 15042 Tallinn; tel. 665-94-01; fax 665-94-00; e-mail tlulib@tlulib.ee; internet www.tlulib.ee; f. 1946; 2,445,165 vols, incunabula; Dir ANDRES KOLLIST.

Eesti Rahvusraamatukogu (National Library of Estonia): Tõnismägi 2, 15189 Tallinn; tel. 630-76-11; fax 631-14-10; e-mail nlib@nlib.ee; internet www.nlib.ee; f. 1918; nat. library status 1988; parliamentary library 1989; nat. and parliamentary library with public access; national ISBN, ISSN and ISMN agency; research library for the humanities and social sciences; professional development centre; cultural centre for book and art exhibitions, concerts, conferences; 34m. vols; Dir-Gen. JANNE ANDRESOO; publs *Eesti Rahvusraamatukogu Toimetised* (Acta Bibliothecae Nationalis Estoniae), *Raamatukogu* (The Library, 6 a year).

Tartu

Tartu University Library: W. Struve 1, 50091 Tartu; tel. 737-57-02; fax 737-57-01; e-mail library@utlib.ee; internet www.utlib.ee; f. 1802; 3,800,000 vols, 505,000 theses, 28,000 MSS; Dir Dr MARTIN HALLIK; Sec. KERSTI KUUSEMÄE.

Museums and Art Galleries

Tallinn

Art Museum of Estonia: Weizenbergi 34, Valge 1, 10127 Tallinn; tel. 602-60-01; fax 602-60-02; e-mail muuseum@ekm.ee; internet www.ekm.ee; f. 1919; colln of fine and applied art; art exhibitions; 55,135 items; Dir SIRJE HELME.

Estonian History Museum: Pirita tee 56, 10127 Tallinn; tel. 641-16-30; fax 644-34-46; e-mail post@eam.ee; internet www.eam.ee; f. 1842; archeology, medieval and near history, numismatics and cultural history; research work of the museum is based mostly on rich museum collns comprising 282,669 artefacts; temporary exhibits, concerts, lectures, publs; closed for renovation until May 2011; library of 11,000 vols; Dir SIRJE KARIS.

Estonian Open Air Museum: Vabaõhumuuseumi tee 12, 13521 Tallinn; tel. 654-91-17; fax 654-91-27; e-mail evm@evm.ee; internet www.evm.ee; f. 1957; architectural and ethnographical objects from 18th–20th centuries; Dir M. LANG.

Estonian Theatre and Music Museum: Müürivahe 12, 10146 Tallinn; tel. 644-21-32; fax 641-81-66; e-mail info@tmm.ee; internet www.tmm.ee; f. 1924; library of 50,000 vols; Dir ÜLLE REIMETS; publ. *AegiKiri* (1 a year).

Tallinn City Museum: Vene 17, 10123 Tallinn; tel. 644-18-29; fax 644-15-74; e-mail info@linnamuuseum.ee; internet www.linnamuuseum.ee; f. 1937; library of 6,300 vols; Dir MARUTA VARRAK.

Tartu

Estonian Literary Museum: Vanemuise 42, POB 368, 50002 Tartu; tel. 737-77-00; fax 737-77-06; e-mail kirmus@kirmus.ee; internet www.kirmus.ee; f. 1909; comprises Archival Library (incl. bibliography dept), Estonian Folklore Archives, Estonian Cultural History Archives, folklore dept and ethnomusicology dept; Dir Mag. JANIKA KRONBERG; publs *Folklore/Electronic Journal of Folklore* (print and electronic, 4 a year), *Maetagused* (print and electronic, 4 a

year), *Paar sammukest* (Some Small Steps, 1 a year), *Pro Folkloristika: Estonian Folklore Archives* (1 a year).

Estonian National Museum: Veski 32, 51014 Tartu; tel. 735-04-00; fax 742-22-54; e-mail erm@erm.ee; internet www.erm.ee; f. 1909; ethnology and culture of the Estonian and Finno-Ugric people; 100 mems; library of 34,482 vols; Dir KRISTA ARU; publs *Eesti Rahva Muuseumi Aastaraamat* (1 a year), *Journal of Ethnology and Folkloristics* (2 a year), *Eesti Rahva Muuseumi Sari* (1 a year).

Tartu Art Museum: Vallikraavi 14, 51003 Tartu; tel. and fax 734-10-50; e-mail tartmus@tartmus.ee; internet www.tartmus.ee; f. 1940; Estonian and European art since 19th century; library of 20,000 vols; Dir REET MARK.

University of Tartu Art Museum: Ülikooli 18, 50090 Tartu; tel. 737-53-84; fax 737-54-40; e-mail kmm@ut.ee; internet www.ut.ee/artmuseum; f. 1803; mainly plaster casts of ancient sculpture, gems and coins, graphic art from 15th–19th centuries, Russian icons, applied art, Greek and Roman antiquities; Dir INGE KUKK.

Universities

EESTI MAAÜLIKOOL
(Estonian University of Life Sciences)

Kreutzwaldi 1A, 51014 Tartu

Telephone: 731-30-01
Fax: 731-30-63
E-mail: info@emu.ee
Internet: www.emu.ee

Founded 1951 as Estonian Agricultural Univ., present name 2005

Rector: Prof. MAIT KLAASSEN
Vice-Rector for Research: Prof. ANNE LUIK
Vice-Rector for Students: Dr JÜRI LEHTSAAR

Number of teachers: 380
Number of students: 4,700

Library of 600,000 vols

Publication: *Eesti Maaülikooli Teaduslike Tööde Kogumik*

Specialized areas: agronomy, horticulture, animal husbandry, veterinary medicine, meat and dairy technology, forestry, food production and marketing, agricultural engineering and energetics, agricultural economics and entrepreneurship, finance, land surveying, landscape architecture and management, water management, agricultural buildings, sustainable use of natural resources, renewable energy resources, nature tourism, aquaculture and applied hydrobiology, management of biodiversity and multifunctional landscapes.

TALLINN TECHNICAL UNIVERSITY

Ehitajate tee 5, 19086 Tallinn

Telephone: 620-20-02
Fax: 620-20-20
E-mail: ttu@ttu.ee
Internet: www.ttu.ee

Founded 1918
Languages of instruction: Estonian, Russian, English
Academic year: September to June

Rector: Prof. PEEP SÜRJE
Vice-Rector for Academic Affairs: Prof. JAKOB KÜBARSEPP
Vice-Rector for Devt: ANDRES KEEVALIK
Vice-Rector for Research: Prof. REIN VEIKMÄE
Librarian: JÜRI JÄRS

Library of 750,000 vols, 730 periodicals
Number of teachers: 1,600 (incl. affiliated institutions)

Number of students: 10,000
Publication: *Mente et Manu* (newsletter, 52 a year)

DEANS

Faculty of Chemistry and Materials Technology: Prof. ANDRES ÖPIK
Faculty of Civil Engineering: Prof. ROODE LIIAS
School of Economics and Business Administration: Prof. ENN LISTRA
Faculty of Humanities: Prof. SULEV MÄELTSEMEES
Faculty of Information Technology: Prof. ENNU RÜSTERN
Faculty of Mechanical Engineering: Prof. PRIIT KULU
Faculty of Power Engineering: Prof. TÕNU LEHTLA
Faculty of Science: Prof. MARGUS LOPP

PROFESSORS

Faculty of Chemistry and Materials Technology (tel. 620-27-96; fax 620-27-96; e-mail k@ttu.ee):

CHRISTJANSON, P., Polymer Technology
KALLAVUS, U., Materials Research
KAPS, T., Woodworking
MELLIKOV, E., Semiconductor Materials Technology
MUNTER, R., Environmental Technology
OJA, V., Chemical Engineering
ÖPIK, A., Physical Chemistry
PAALME, T., Food Science and Technology
SOONE, J., Environmental Technology
TRIKKEL, A., Physical Chemistry
VIIKNA, A., Textile Technology
VOKK, R., Food Science

Faculty of Civil Engineering (tel. 620-25-00; e-mail e@ttu.ee):

AAVIK, A., Road Construction
ENGELBRECHT, J., Applied Mechanics
IDNURM, S., Steel Structures
KLAUSON, A., Structural Mechanics
KÕIV, T. A., Heating and Ventilation
KOPPEL, T., Hydrodynamics
LAVING, J., Traffic and Transportation Engineering
LIIAS, R., Construction Economics and Management
LILL, I., Building Technology
RAADO, L.-M., Building Materials
RANDLEPP, A., Geodesy
SALUPERE, A., Solid Mechanics
SOOMERE, T., Hydrodynamics
SUTT, J., Construction Economics and Management

School of Economics and Business Administration (Kopli tn. 101, 11712 Tallinn; tel. 620-41-01; fax 620-39-46; e-mail t@ttu.ee):

AASMA, A., Economic Mathematics
ALVER, J., Accounting
ALVER, L., Financial Accounting
KEREM, K., Economic Theory
KILVITS, K., Economic Policy
KOLBRE, E., Management Economics
KUKRUS, A., Economic Law and Regulation
LEIMANN, J., Organization and Management
LISTRA, E., Finance and Banking
SAAT, M., Business Administration
TEDER, J., Small Businesses
TINT, P., Working Environment and Safety

Faculty of Humanities (tel. and fax 646-71-48; e-mail h@ttu.ee):

DRECHSLER, W., Governance
KAEVATS, Ü., Philosophy
KATTEL, R., Public Administration and European Studies
MÄELTSEMEES, S., Regional Policy
RAJANGU, V., Educational Policy
TEICHMANN, M., Psychology

Faculty of Information Technology (Raja tn. 15, 12618 Tallinn; tel. 620-22-51; fax 620-22-46; e-mail i@ttu.ee):

BULDAS, A., Information Security
KALJA, A., Systems Programming
KUKK, V., Circuit and Systems Theory
KUUSIK, R., Informatics
LOSSMANN, E., Telecommunications
MIN, M., Electronic Measurement
MÕTUS, L., Real Time Systems
ÕUNAPUU, E., IT Systems
PENJAM, J., Theoretical Computer Science
RANG, T., Electronics Design
RÜSTERN, E., Automatic Control and Systems Analysis
TAKLAJA, A., Microwave Engineering
TAMMET, T., Network Software
TEPANDI, J., Applied Artificial Intelligence
UBAR, R.-J., Computer Engineering and Diagnostics
VAIN, J., Formal Methods

Faculty of Mechanical Engineering (tel. 620-33-50; fax 620-31-96; e-mail m@ttu.ee):

AJAOTS, M., Fine Mechanics
EERME, M., Computer-aided Design and Manufacturing
KIITAM, A., Quality Engineering
KULU, P., Materials Science
KÜTTNER, R., Computer-aided Design and Manufacturing
LAANEOTS, R., Metrology and Measurement Techniques
LAVRENTJEV, J., Automotive Engineering
MELLIKOV, E., Semiconductor Materials Technology
PAIST, A., Thermal Power Engineering
PAPPEL, T., Machine Mechanics
PAPSTEL, J., Production Engineering
ROOSIMÖLDER, L., Product Development
SIIRDE, A., Thermal Power Equipment
TAMRE, M., Mechatronics

Faculty of Power Engineering (Ehitajate tee 5, 19086 Tallinn; tel. 620-35-48; fax 620-36-96; e-mail a@ttu.ee):

JARVIK, J., Electrical Machines
LAUGIS, J., Electrical Drives and Electricity Supply
LEHTLA, T., Robotics
MELDORF, M., Transfer in Power Systems
TAMMOJA, H., Electrical Power Engineering
VALGMA, I., Rock Engineering

Faculty of Science (tel. 620-29-95; fax 620-26-45; e-mail y@ttu.ee):

ELKEN, J., Oceanography
JÄRVEKÜLG, L., Molecular Diagnostics
KALJURAND, M., Analytical Chemistry
KARELSON, M., Molecular Technology
KRUSTOK, J., Applied Physics
LIPPING, T., Radiophysics
LOPP, M., Organic Chemistry
MEIGAS, K., Biomedical Technology
PAAL, E., Algebra and Geometry
PALUMAA, P., Genomics and Proteomics
PUUSEMP, P., Algebra and Geometry
SAMEL, N., Bio-organic and Natural Products Chemistry
TAMM, T., Inorganic and Gen. Chemistry
TAMMERAID, L., Mathematical Analysis
TIMMUSK, T., Molecular Biology
TRUVE, E., Gene Technology
VILU, R., Biochemistry

TALLINN UNIVERSITY

Narva mnt 25, 10120 Tallinn
Telephone: 640-91-01
Fax: 640-91-16
E-mail: tlu@tlu.ee
Internet: www.tlu.ee

Founded 2005; through amalgamation of Tallinn Pedagogical Univ., Estonian Academic Library, Estonian Institute of Humanities and Institute of History
Language of instruction: Estonian

Rector: MATI HEIDMETS
Vice-Rector for Academic Affairs: HELI MATTISEN
Vice-Rector for Open Univ.: MADIS LEPIK
Vice-Rector for Research and Devt: PEETER NORMAK

Number of teachers: 844
Number of students: 7,421

DEANS

Faculty of Educational Sciences: Assoc. Prof. PRIIT REISKA
Faculty of Fine Arts: Prof. EHA RÜÜTEL
Faculty of Mathematics and Natural Sciences: Prof. ANDI KIVINUKK
Faculty of Philology: Prof. SULIKO LIIV
Faculty of Physical Education: Assoc. Prof. KRISTJAN PORT
Faculty of Social Sciences: Prof. ALEKSANDER PULVER

UNIVERSITY OF TARTU

Ülikooli 18, 50090 Tartu
Telephone: 737-51-00
Fax: 737-54-40
E-mail: info@ut.ee
Internet: www.ut.ee

Founded 1632
State control
Language of instruction: Estonian
Academic year: September to June

Rector: ALAR KARIS (acting)
Pro-Rector for Academic Affairs: Prof. BIRUTE KLAAS
Pro-Rector for Research: Prof. KRISTJAN HALLER
Acad. Sec.: IVAR-IGOR SAARNIIT
Library Dir: MARTIN HALLIK

Library: see Libraries and Archives
Number of teachers: 942
Number of students: 16,944

Publications: *Acta et Commentationes Universitatis Tartuensis* (44 series), *Universitas Tartuensis* (12 a year)

DEANS

Faculty of Biology and Geography: Prof. T. MEIDLA
Faculty of Economics and Business Administration: Prof. J. SEPP
Faculty of Education: Prof. HASSO KUKEMELK
Faculty of Law: Prof. K. MERUSK
Faculty of Mathematics: Prof T. LEIGER
Faculty of Medicine: Prof. JOEL STARKOPF
Faculty of Philosophy: Prof. VALTER LANG
Faculty of Physical Education and Sports Sciences: Prof. V. ÖÖPIK
Faculty of Physics and Chemistry: Prof. J. JÄRV
Faculty of Science and Technology: PEETER BURK
Faculty of Social Sciences: Prof. J. HARRO
Faculty of Theology: Prof. R. ALTNURME

PROFESSORS

Faculty of Theology:

ALTNURME, R., Church History
KULL, A., Systematic Theology
KULMAR, T., Comparative Religion
KÄMMERER, T., Ancient Near-Eastern Languages
LEHTSAAR, T., Psychology of Religion

Faculty of Law:

BACHMANN, T., Cognitive Psychology and Psychology of Law
GINTER, J., Criminology
KULL, I., Civil Law
LUTS-SOOTAK, M., Legal History

MERUSK, K., Constitutional and Administrative Law
NARITS, R., Comparative Jurisprudence
PISUKE, H., Intellectual Property Law
SAAR, J., Criminology
SOOTAK, J., Criminal Law
TRUUVÄLI, E., Theory of Law
VARUL, P., Civil Law

Faculty of Medicine:

ALTRAJA, A., Pulmonology
AREND, A., Histology and Embryology
ASSER, T., Neurosurgery
EHA, J., Cardiology
EVERAUS, H., Haematology and Oncology
KAASIK, A., Molecular Toxicology
KARRO, H., Obstetrics and Gynaecology
KIIVET, R., Health Care Management
KÕKS, S., Ship of Physiological Genomics
LEMBER, M., Propaedeutics of Internal Medicine
LUTSAR, I., Medical Microbiology and Virology
MAAROOS, H., Polyclinic and Family Medicine
MAAROOS, J., Sports Medicine and Rehabilitation
MIKELSAAR, A., Human Biology and Genetics
MIKELSAAR, M., Medical Biotechnology
PEETSALU, A., Surgical Diseases
SEPPET, E., Pathological Physiology
SILM, H., Dermatology and Venerology
STARKOPF, J., Anaesthesiology and Intensive Care
ZILMER, M., Medical Biochemistry
ŽARKOVSKI, A., Pharmacology and Toxicology
TAMM, A., Laboratory Medicine
TEESALU, P., Ophthalmology
TILLMANN, V., Paediatrics
UIBO, R., Immunology
UUSKÜLA, A., Epidemiology
VASAR, E., Physiology
VASAR, V., Psychiatry
VESKI, P., Pharmaceutical Technology and Biopharmaceutics
VÄLI, M., Forensic Medicine

Faculty of Philosophy:

COHNITZ, D., Theoretical Philosophy
DULITŠENKO, A., Slavic Languages and Literature
EHALA, M., Didactics of Estonian and Applied Linguistics
ELKEN, J., Painting
HUUMO, T., Finnish Language and Culture
KIRSS, T., Estonian Literature
KISSELJOVA, L., Russian Literature
KRIISKA, A., Laboratory Archaeology
KULL, K., Biosemiotics
KUUTMA, K., Cultural Research
KÜLMOJA, I., Russian Language
LANG, V., Archaeology
LAUR, M., Modern History
LEETE, A., Ethnology
LILL, A., Classical Philology
MAISTE, J., Art History
MATJUS, Ü., History of Estonian Philosophy
MEDIJAINEN, E., Contemporary History
METSLANG, H., Modern Estonian
MUST, A., Archival Studies
PAJUSALU, K., History and Dialects of Estonian Language
PAJUSALU, R., General Linguistics
ROSENBERG, T., Estonian History
SUTROP, M., Practical Philosophy
SUTROP, U., Anthropological and Ethnolinguistics
TALVET, J., Comparative Literature
TOROP, P., Semiotics of Culture
VALK, Ü., Estonian and Comparative Folklore
VALLIKIVI, A., Liberal Arts
VIHALEMM, R., the Philosophy of Science

VOGELBERG, K., English Language and Literature

Faculty of Education:
KIKAS, E., Initial and Primary Education
KRULL, E., General Paedagogy
TOOMELA, A.

Faculty of Exercise and Sport Sciences:
JÜRIMÄE, J., Coaching
JÜRIMÄE, T., Sport Pedagogy
PÄÄSUKE, M., Kinesiology and Biomechanics
RAUDSEPP, L., Sport Psychology
ÖÖPIK, V., Exercise Physiology

Faculty of Science and Technology:
AABLOO, A., the Technology of Polymeric Materials
AHAS, R., Human Geography
BURK, P., Chemical Physics
FREIBERG, A., Biophysics and Plant Physiology
HEINARU, A., Genetics
HÕRAK, P., Animal Physiological Ecology
JAAGUS, J., Climatology
JÄRV, J., Organic Chemistry
KALM, V., Applied Geology
KARELSON, M., Molecular Technology
KIKAS, J., Disordered Systems Physics
KIRSIMÄE, K., Geology and Mineralogy
KIVISAAR, M., Bacterial/microbial genetics
KURG, A., Molecular Biotechnology
KÕLJALG, U., Mycology
KÄRNER, J., General Zoology
LAAN, M., Biotechnology
LANGEL, Ü., Molecular Biotechnology
LEITO, I., Analytical Chemistry
LUST, E., Physical Chemistry
LUŠTŠIK, A., Solid State Physics
LÕHMUS, K., Applied Ecology
MAIMETS, T., Cell Biology
MANDER, Ü., Physical Geography and Landscape Ecology
MEIDLA, T., Palaeontology and Stratigraphy
MERISTE, M., the Technology of Proactive Systems
MERITS, A., Applied Virology
METSPALU, A., Biotechnology
MÄND, R., Animal Ecology
NOOLANDI, J., Polymer Physics
OJA, T., Geoinformatics and Cartography
PAAL, J., Plant Ecology
POOGA, M., Chemical Biology
PÄRTEL, M., Botany
RANNIKMÄE, M., Science Education
REMM, M., Bioinformatics
REMME, J., Molecular Biology

RINKEN, A., Bio-organic Chemistry
RÕÕM, R., Meteorology
SAARI, P., Wave Optics
SAMMELSELG, V., Inorganic Chemistry
SARAPUU, T., Educational Technology in Science
SEDMAN, J., General and Microbial Biochemistry
ZOBEL, K., Ecological Plant Ecology
ZOBEL, M., Plant Ecology
TAMMARU, T., Integrative Zoology
TAMMELO, R., Field Theory
TENSON, T., the Technology of Anti-microscopic Substances
USTAV, M., Biomedical Technology
VILLEMS, R., Archaegenetics

Faculty of Economics and Business Administration:
EAMETS, R., Macroeconomics
HALDMA, T., Accounting
KALDARU, H., Microeconomics
METS, T., Entrepreneurship
PAAS, T., Econometrics
RAJU, O., Economic Theory
REILJAN, J., International Economics
SEPP, J., Economic Policy
VADI, M., Management
VARBLANE, U., International Business

Faculty of Mathematics and Computer Science:
ABEL, M., Geometry and Topology
BULDAS, A., Cryptography
DUMAS MENJIVAR, M., Software Equipment
KAARLI, K., Universal Algebra
KILP, M., Algebra
KOIT, M., Speech Technology
KOLLO, T., Mathematical Statistics
LEIGER, T., Mathematical Analysis
LELLEP, J., Theoretical Mechanics
OJA, E., Functional Analysis
PEDAS, A., Differential and Integral Equations
PÄRNA, K., Probability Theory
VAINIKKO, E., Distributed Systems
VENE, V., Programming Languages Semantics
VILO, J., Bioinformatics

Faculty of Social Sciences:
ALLIK, J., Experimental Psychology
BERG, E., International Relations Theory
HARRO, J., Psychophysiology
KASEKAMP, A., Baltic Politics
LAUK, E., Journalism
LAURISTIN, M., Social Communication
NÄÄTÄNEN, R., Cognitive Neuroscience
PETTAI, V., Comparative Politics

TULVISTE, P., Cultural Psychology
TULVISTE, T., Developmental Psychology
VIHALEMM, P., Media Studies

Viljandi Culture Academy:
AGAN, A.
KOMISSAROV, K., Dramatic Arts
NOORMETS, M.
PEDASTSAAR, T.
RATTUS, K.
VESKI, V.

ATTACHED RESEARCH INSTITUTES

Centre of Excellence in Chemical Biology: Nooruse St 1, Tartu 50411; tel. 737-48-44; e-mail tanel.tenson@ut.ee; Head Prof. TANEL TENSON.

Centre of Excellence in Cultural Theory: tel. 737-56-54; e-mail monika.tasa@ut.ee.

Centre of Excellence for Translational Medicine: Ravila 19, Tartu 50411; tel. 737-53-25; e-mail eero.vasar@ut.ee; Head Prof. EERO VASAR.

Frontiers in Biodiversity Research (FIBIR): Centre of Excellence Lai 40, Tartu 51005; tel. 737-62-23; e-mail martin.zobel@ut.ee; Head Prof. MARTIN ZOBEL.

Other Higher Educational Institutes

Estonian Academy of Arts: Tartu Maantee 1, 10145 Tallinn; tel. 626-73-09; fax 626-73-50; e-mail public@artun.ee; internet www.artun.ee; f. 1914; faculties of fine arts (painting, stage design, sculpture, graphics), applied art (textiles, fashion design, leather work, ceramics, glass and metal work), architecture (interior design, architecture), design (product design, graphic design), art history; 160 teachers; 523 students; library: 54,427 vols; Rector Prof. SIGNE KIVI.

Estonian Academy of Music: Rävala pst. 16, 10143 Tallinn; tel. 667-57-00; fax 667-58-00; e-mail ema@ema.edu.ee; internet www.ema.edu; f. 1919; departments: piano, strings, brass and woodwind, vocal, chamber music, conducting, composition, musicology; institute of music education; institute of teaching training in vocal and instrumental music; higher school of drama; 120 teachers; 560 students; library: 245,000 vols; Rector P. LASSMANN; publ. *Scripta Musicalia* (4 a year).

ETHIOPIA

The Higher Education System

Addis Ababa University is the oldest university in the country. It was originally founded in 1950 as University College of Addis Ababa, became known as Haile Selassie University in 1961 and adopted its current name in 1975. There have been efforts to establish higher education institutions in outlying areas of Ethiopia; however, most institutions are located in the central, north and north-western parts of the country (mostly Addis Ababa, Bahir Dar, Mekelle, Alemaya, Awassa and Jimma). A total of 91,655 students were enrolled in higher education in 2004/05, according to government statistics. By 2007 there were 15,000 students enrolled in Addis Ababa university alone. The private higher education sector in Ethiopia has grown at an impressive rate. From practically zero in 1998, enrolment in privately owned higher education institutions had grown to 39,691 in 2005/2006. In 2008/09 there were 20 universities, all state-controlled.

Higher education is financed by the Government, and the budget of each university is supervised by its Board. The University Senate is the managerial body of a University; the Academic Commission is the main academic body. The Academic Commission controls all aspects regarding the structure of degree programmes, certification and student issues. Heads of Department chair Department Councils, which are subordinate to the Academic Commission, and which make recommendations on matters of study, research, staff recruitment, pedagogy and examinations. The Ministry of Education appoints senior university officers, such as the President and Vice-Presidents. Heads of Department are either appointed by Deans of Faculty or elected by Department Councils.

The Ethiopian School Leaving Certificate Examination is the main requirement for admission to higher education. The primary undergraduate degree is the Bachelors, which takes four years, although some subjects require longer (five years for engineering, law and pharmacy; six years for medicine and veterinary medicine). The first postgraduate degree is the Masters, which lasts for two to three years, and the second postgraduate degree is the Doctor of Philosophy (PhD), which is awarded three years after the Masters.

A formal system of qualifications for technical and vocational education is still evolving, with the aim of creating a uniform structure based on courses of one to three years. Certificates are awarded following completion of Levels I (one year) and II (two years), and a Diploma is awarded after completion of Level III (three years).

In an effort to improve the quality of higher education in Ethiopia a new bill was approved in June 2009 that built upon the 2003 Higher Education proclamation to oversee both state run and private higher educational institutions. The Higher Education Proclamation 351 (Ethiopian Federal Ministry of Education, 2003) made provision for the creation of the Higher Education Relevance and Quality Agency and this was established in 2003 with the aim of safeguarding and enhancing the quality and relevance of higher education. Its mission includes ensuring that accredited higher education institutions are of an appropriate standard and establishing that programmes of study offered are of appropriate quality and relevance to employment and the development needs of the country.

Regulatory Bodies

GOVERNMENT

Ministry of Culture and Tourism: POB 2183, Addis Ababa; tel. (11) 5512310; fax (11) 5512889; e-mail tourismethiopia@ethionet.et; internet www.tourismethiopia.org; Minister MAHMUD DIRIR.

Ministry of Education: POB 1367, Addis Ababa; tel. (11) 1553133; fax (11) 1550877; e-mail heardmoe@telecom.net.et; Minister Dr SINTAVEHU WOLDEMIKAEL.

Learned Societies

GENERAL

UNESCO Office Addis Ababa: POB 1177, Addis Ababa; ECA Bldg, Menelik Ave, POB 1177 Addis Ababa; tel. (11) 5513953; fax (11) 5511414; e-mail addis@unesco.org; designated Cluster Office for Djibouti, Eritrea and Ethiopia; Dir NURELDIN SATTI.

AGRICULTURE, FISHERIES AND VETERINARY SCIENCE

Association for the Advancement of Agricultural Sciences in Africa: POB 30087, Addis Ababa; tel. (11) 5443536; f. 1968; aims to promote the devt and application of agricultural sciences and the exchange of ideas, to encourage Africans to enter training, and to hold seminars annually in different African countries; crop production and protection, animal health and production, soil and water management, agricultural mechanization, agricultural economics, agricultural education, extension and rural sociology, food science and technology; 1,200 mems (individual and institutional); library of 5,000 items; Admin. Sec.-Gen. Prof. M. EL-FOULY (acting); publs *AAASA Newsletter*, *African Journal of Agricultural Sciences*, *Conferences*, *Proceedings of workshops*.

BIBLIOGRAPHY, LIBRARY SCIENCE AND MUSEOLOGY

Ethiopian Library and Information Association: POB 30530, Addis Ababa; tel. (11) 5518020; f. 1961; to promote the interests of libraries, archives, documentation centres, etc., and to serve those working in them; 200 mems; Pres. TAMIRAT MOTA; Sec. ZINABIE MEKONNEN; publs *Bulletin* (2 a year), *Directory of Ethiopian Libraries*, *Newsletter* (2 a year).

LANGUAGE AND LITERATURE

Alliance Française: Wavel St, POB 1733, Addis Ababa; tel. (11) 1550213; fax (11) 1553681; e-mail aef@allianceaddis.org; internet www.allianceaddis.org; offers courses and examinations in French language and culture and promotes cultural exchange with France; attached teaching centre in Dire Dawa.

British Council: POB 1043, Comoros St, Addis Ababa; tel. (11) 6620388; fax (11) 6623315; e-mail information@et.britishcouncil.org; internet www.britishcouncil.org/africa; offers courses and examinations in English language and British culture and promotes cultural exchange with the UK; library of 25,000 vols; Dir BARBARA WICKHAM.

Goethe-Institut: POB 1193, Addis Ababa; tel. (11) 1552888; fax (11) 1551299; e-mail vl@telecom.net.et; internet www.goethe.de/af/add/enindex.htm; offers courses and examinations in German language and culture and promotes cultural exchange with Germany; library of 1,500 vols, 24 periodicals; Dir Dr DIETER WERNER KLUCKE.

MEDICINE

Ethiopian Medical Association: POB 2179, Addis Ababa; e-mail ema.emj@telecom.net.et; tel. (11) 5533742; f. 1961; Pres. Dr TELAHUM TEKA; publ. *Ethiopian Medical Journal* (4 a year).

Ethiopian Public Health Association: Dembel City Centre, POB 7117 Addis Ababa; tel. (1) 5540391; fax (1) 5514870; e-mail epha@ethionet.et; internet www.epha.org.et; f. 1989; for the promotion of public health, prevention of diseases, timely treatment of the sick and rehabilitation of the disabled; Pres. Dr DAMEN HAILEMARIAM; Exec. Sec. Dr GETNET MITIKE; publ. *Ethiopian Journal of Health Development*.

NATURAL SCIENCES

Physical Sciences

Geophysical Observatory: Faculty of Science, Addis Ababa University, POB 1176, Addis Ababa; tel. (11) 1239477; fax (11) 1551863; internet www.sc.aau.edu.et/geophysical; f. 1958; research in seismology, gravity, tectonics, crustal deformation, geomagnetic observation and geodesy; library of 100 vols and 10 periodicals; Sec. Assoc. Prof. LAIKE M. ASFAW; publ. *Seismological Bulletin* (2 a year).

Research Institutes

AGRICULTURE, FISHERIES AND VETERINARY SCIENCE

Awasa Agriculture Research Centre: c/o Awasa Agricultural College, POB 6, Awasa; tel. (46) 2200224; fax (46) 2204521; e-mail arc@padis.gn.apc.org; f. 1967; soil and water management, crop protection, horticulture, field crops, agronomy and crop physiology, agricultural economics and farming systems, livestock, forestry; library of 2,300 vols, 28 journals; Man. DANIEL DAURO.

Ethiopian Institute of Agricultural Research: POB 2003, Addis Ababa; tel. (11) 6460137; fax (11) 6461294; e-mail infocom@eiar.gov.et; internet www.eiar.gov.et; f. 1966; agronomy and crop physiology, crop protection, animal production, animal feeds and nutrition, animal health, agricultural mechanization, horticulture, soil and water management, field crops, forestry, post-harvest technologies, biotechnology; financial aid provided by the Ethiopian govt and other sources; 50 research centres and stations nationally; 2,915 mems; library of 150,000 vols; Deputy Dir-Gen. Dr SOLOMON ASEFA; publs *Ethiopian Journal of Agricultural Economics, Ethiopian Journal of Agricultural Science, Ethiopian Journal of Animal Production, Pest Management Journal of Ethiopia*.

HISTORY, GEOGRAPHY AND ARCHAEOLOGY

Archaeological Institute: POB 76, Addis Ababa; Dir Dr BERHANOU ABBÉBÉ; publ. *Annales d'Ethiopie*.

Ethiopian Mapping Agency: POB 597, Addis Ababa; tel. (11) 5518445; fax (11) 5515189; e-mail ema@ethionet.net.et; internet www.ema.gov.net; f. 1955; under Min. of Economic Development and Co-operation; conducts land surveying, mapping, remote sensing and geographical research; 350 mems; library of 3,000 vols; Dir-Gen. SULTAN MOHAMMED; publ. *Geo-Information Bulletin of Ethiopia* (2 a year).

NATURAL SCIENCES

Biological Sciences

Desert Locust Control Organization for Eastern Africa (DLCO EA): POB 4255, Addis Ababa; tel. (11) 6461477; fax (11) 6460296; e-mail dlc@telecom.net.et; f. 1962; mems: Djibouti, Eritrea, Ethiopia, Kenya, Somalia, Sudan, Tanzania, Uganda; research into and control of desert locust and other pests, incl. armyworm, quelea, tsetse fly and mosquito; library of 2,000 vols; Dir PETER ONYANGO ODIYO.

Institute of Biodiversity Conservation and Research: POB 30726, Addis Ababa; tel. (1) 6612244; fax (1) 6613722; e-mail bioresearch@telecom.net.et; internet www.telecom.net.et/~ibcr; f. 1998; promotes and carries out research into the development and sustainable use of the country's biodiversity; Gen. Man. Dr ABEBE DEMISSIE.

National Herbarium: Biology Dept, Addis Ababa University, POB 3434, Addis Ababa; tel. (11) 1236760; fax (11) 1236769; e-mail info@bio.aau.edu.et; f. 1959; Keeper Prof. SEBSEBE DEMISSEW; Curator Dr ENSERMU KELBESSA; publ. *Flora of Ethiopia and Eritrea* (10 a year).

Physical Sciences

Geological Survey of Ethiopia: POB 2302, Addis Ababa; tel. (11) 6464482; fax (11) 6463326; internet www.geology.gov.et; f. 1968 as a Department within the Ministry of Mines; as Ethiopian Institute of Geological Surveys 1984; 778 mems; library of 66,877 vols; Gen. Man. KETEMA TADESSE; Chief Geologist AMENTI ABRAHAM; Head of Geoscience Information Centre SISAY TESFAY.

RELIGION, SOCIOLOGY AND ANTHROPOLOGY

Institute of Ethiopian Studies: Addis Ababa University, POB 1176, Addis Ababa; tel. (11) 1119469; fax (11) 1552688; e-mail ies.aau@ttelecom.net.et; internet www.ies-ethiopia.org; f. 1963; conducts, promotes and coordinates research and publication on Ethiopian Studies with special emphasis on the humanities and cultural studies; operates an advanced study and documentation centre and an ethnological-historical museum: see Museums and Art Galleries; library: see Libraries and Archives; Dir ELIZABETH W. GIORGIS (acting); publs *IES Bulletin* (4 a year), *Journal of Ethiopian Studies* (2 a year).

Libraries and Archives

Addis Ababa

Addis Ababa University Libraries: POB 1176, Addis Ababa; tel. (11) 1239720; e-mail infolib@lib.aau.edu.et; internet www.aau.edu.et/libraries; f. 1950; 500,000 vols, 632 microfiches, 3,000 serial titles and an electronic journals database; colln includes; 90,000 vols on Ethiopia; consists of the main University library and six branch libraries: the Science Library, Technology North Library (Amist Kilo campus), Technology South Library (Lideta Campus), Faculty of Business and Economics Library, Central Medical Library and Law Library; Librarian Dr TAYE TADESSE.

British Council Knowledge and Learning Services: POB 1043, Artistic Bldg, Adwa Ave, Addis Ababa; tel. (11) 1550022; fax (11) 1552544; e-mail kls@et.britishcouncil.org; f. 1959; 51,000 vols, 137 periodicals; Librarian Ato MULUGETA HUNDE.

Ethiopia National Archives and Library Agency: POB 717, Addis Ababa; tel. (11) 5516532; fax (11) 5526411; e-mail nale@ethionet.et; internet www.nale.gov.et; f. 1944; 164,000 vols; consists of: Reference, Documentation and Periodical Division; Legal Deposit and Copyright Registration; Archives Repository and Research; Microfilm and Microfiche Library; Ethiopian Studies and MSS Division; Dir-Gen. ATIKILT ASSEFA.

Institute of Ethiopian Studies Library: Addis Ababa University, POB 1176, Addis Ababa; tel. (11) 1550844; fax (11) 1123456; e-mail girmajem@ies.aau.edu.et; internet www.ies-ethiopia.org/indexf.htm; f. 1963; colln of printed and non-printed materials on Ethiopia, Somalia, Djibouti, Red Sea, Indian Ocean, Sudan; also materials on Middle East; 110,000 vols, 9,000 MSS; Librarian GIRMA JEMANEH.

Museums and Art Galleries

Addis Ababa

Museum of the Institute of Ethiopian Studies: University of Addis Ababa, POB 1176, Addis Ababa; tel. (11) 1550844; fax (11) 1552688; e-mail ies.aau@telecom.net.et; internet www.ies-ethiopia.org; f. 1963; sections: exhibit of Haile Selassie's bedroom, material culture (household artefacts, clothing, handicrafts, etc.); ethno-musicology (all types of Ethiopian musical instruments, religious music and poetry, record archive of oral tradition and folklore); traditional art (church paintings and furnishings, icons, etc., Islamic calligraphy); stamps, coins and banknotes of Ethiopia; Curator AHMED ZEKARIA.

National Museum of Ethiopia: POB 76, Addis Ababa; tel. (11) 1119113; fax (11) 1553188; collns of early hominid fossils, incl. 'Lucy', a nearly complete skeleton of *Australopithecus afarensis*; Dir MAMITU YILMA.

Universities

ADDIS ABABA UNIVERSITY

POB 1176, Addis Ababa

Telephone: (11) 1239800

Internet: www.aau.edu.et

Founded 1950 as Univ. College of Addis Ababa; became Haile Selassie Univ. 1961; present name 1975

State control

Language of instruction: English

Academic year: September to July

Pres.: Prof. ANDREAS ESHETÉ

Vice-Pres. for Business and Devt: Ato MOHAMMED HABIB

Assoc. Vice-Pres. for Academic Affairs and External Relations Officer: Dr BUTTE GOTU

Assoc. Vice-Pres. for Continuing and Distance Education Programmes: Dr MEKONEN DISASA

Assoc. Vice-Pres. for Research and Graduate Programmes: Prof. ENDASHAW BEKELE

Registrar: Dr ZEMEDE ASFAW

Librarian: Dr TAYE TADESSE

Library of 493,000 vols

Number of teachers: 948

Number of students: 15,364

Publications: *Ethiopian Journal of Development Research, Ethiopian Journal of Education, Register of Current Research on Ethiopia and the Horn of Africa, SINET: An Ethiopian Journal of Science*

DEANS

Faculty of Business and Economics: Dr MULAT DEMEKE

Faculty of Education: Ato AKALU GETANEH

Faculty of Informatics: Ato GETACHEW JEMANEH

Faculty of Law: Ato GETACHEW ABERA

Faculty of Medicine: Dr ZUFAN LAKEW

Faculty of Science: Prof. GEZAHEGN YIRGU

Faculty of Technology: Dr ABEBE DINKU

Faculty of Veterinary Medicine: Dr MERGA BEKANA

College of Social Sciences: Dr BEKELE GUTEMA

School of Pharmacy: Dr TSIGE GEBREMARIAM

Institute of Language Studies: Dr GEREMEW LEMU

DIRECTORS

School of Fine Arts and Design: Dr MELAKU AYELE

School of Music: AKILU ZEWDIE

Institute of Development Research: Asst Prof. MULUGETA FISSEHA

Institute of Education: Ato DANIEL DESTA

Institute of Ethiopian Studies: ELIZABETH GEBREGIORGIS

Institute of Pathobiology: Prof. MOGESSIE ASHENAFI

BAHIR DAR UNIVERSITY

POB 79, Bahir Dar

Telephone: (58) 2205943

Fax: (58) 2202025

Internet: www.ethionet.et/~bdu

Founded 2001 through merger of Bahir Dar Teachers' College and Bahir Dar Polytechnic Institute

Pres.: Asst Prof. TSEHAY JEMBERU

Vice-Pres. for Academic and Research: YALEW ENDEWOKE

Vice-Pres. for Admins. and Devt: ZERIHUN MEKONNEN

Registrar: HAILEEYESUS WORKINEH

Faculties: Education, Engineering, Business and Economics, Law, Institute of Garment and Textile Support; due to open soon: Faculty of Agriculture and Environment, Faculty of Applied Science

Number of teachers: 250

Number of students: 17,000

Publication: *The Ethiopian Journal of Education, Science and Technology*

DEANS

Faculty of Business and Economics: Asst Prof. ABEBE WALLE

Faculty of Education: Asst Prof. MULUGETA KIBRET

Faculty of Engineering: Asst Prof. MESFIN BELACHEW

Faculty of Law: Asst Prof. TADESSE KASSA

HARAMAYA UNIVERSITY

POB 138, Dire Dawa

Telephone: (25) 5530319

Fax: (25) 5530325

E-mail: talamirew@haramaya.edu.et

Internet: www.haramaya.edu.et

Founded 1952; university status 1985

State control

Language of instruction: English

Academic year: September to June

Pres.: Prof. BELAY KASSA

Vice-Pres. for Academic Affairs: Dr TENA ALAMIREW

Vice-Pres. for Admin.: Dr BELAYNEH LEGESSE

Vice-Pres. for Research and Development: (vacant)

Registrar: Dr FEKADU LEMESSA

Librarian: YARED MAMO

Number of teachers: 355

Number of students: 15,863 (9,790 full-time, 3,153 evening, 1,035 distance-education, 1,855 summer in-service)

Publications: *The Alemayan, Alemaya Annual Research Report*

DEANS

Faculty of Agriculture: Dr WAGAYEHU BEKELE

Faculty of Economics and Business: WORKENEH KASSA

Faculty of Education: Dr TESFAHUN KEBEDE

Faculty of Health Sciences: MELAKE DAMENA

Faculty of Law: ABDULMALIK ABUBEKER

Faculty of Technology: Dr KETEMA TILAHUN

Faculty of Veterinary Medicine: Dr MOHAMMED ABDELLA

Continuing Education Programme: Dr KEBEDE W/TSADIK

School of Graduate Studies: Dr CHEMEDA FININSSA

HAWASSA UNIVERSITY

POB 5, Hawassa

Telephone: (46) 2200221

Fax: (46) 2205421

E-mail: info@hu.edu.et

Internet: hu.edu.et

Founded 2000 as Debub Univ. by merger of Hawassa College of Agriculture, Dilla College of Teachers' Education and Health Science and Wondo Genet College of Forestry; present name 2006

State control

Pres.: Dr ADMASU TSEGAYE

Library of 200,000 vols

Number of teachers: 963

Number of students: 20,000

Faculties of Business and Economics, Hotel Management and Tourism, Law, Medicine, Natural Sciences, Public Health, Social Sciences, Technology, Veterinary Medicine; Colleges of Agriculture, Forestry, Health Sciences, Teachers' Education.

JIMMA UNIVERSITY

POB 378, Jimma

Telephone: (47) 1112202

Fax: (47) 1111450

Internet: www.ju.edu.et

Founded 1999 through merger of Jimma College of Agriculture (f. 1952) and Jimma Institute of Health Sciences (f. 1983)

Pres.: Asst Prof. DAMTEW MARIAM

Vice-Pres. for Academics and Research: Asst Prof. SOLOMON MOGUS

Vice-Pres. for Admin. and Devt: KORA TUSHUNE

Vice-Pres. for Training and Health Services: ABRAHAM AMLAK

Registrar: Dr SOLOMON GENET

Dean of Students: EWNETU SEID

Head of External Relations Office: Assoc. Prof. CHALLI JIRA

Head of Library and Documentation Service: GETACHEW BAYISA

Number of teachers: 370

Number of students: 16,279

DEANS

Faculty of Business: Asst Prof. SOLOMON ALEMU

Faculty of Education: ZELALEM TESHOME

Faculty of Medical Sciences: Asst Prof. MINAS TSADIK

Faculty of Public Health: Asst Prof. KIFLE MIKAEL

Faculty of Science and Liberal Arts: TAREKEGN BIRHANU

Faculty of Technology: ADMASSU SHIMELES

College of Agriculture, Ambo: EYLACHEW ZEWDIE

College of Agriculture, Jimma: BERHANU BELAY

School of Graduate Studies: Prof. MEKONNEN ASSEFA

UNIVERSITY OF MEKELLE

POB 231, Mekelle, Tigray Region

Telephone: (34) 4407500

Fax: (34) 4409304

E-mail: mekelle.university@telecom.net.et

Internet: www.mu.edu.et *Adi-Haqi Campus*: POB 451, Mekelle, Tigray Region

Telephone: (34) 4407600

Fax: (34) 4407610

Aider Campus: POB 1871 Mekelle, Tigray Region

Telephone: (34) 4416690

Fax: (34) 4416681

E-mail: mbc@telecom.net.et

State control

Founded 2000

Library of 200,000 vols, 18 periodical titles

Number of teachers: 1,119

Number of students: 16,470

Pres.: Prof. MITUKU HAILE

Vice-Pres. for Academics: Dr KINDEYA GEBREHIWOT

Vice-Pres. for Research and Community Service: Dr ABDELKADIR KEDIR

Vice-Pres. for Support Services: Dr YASIN IBRAHIM

Librarian: Dr HAGOS

Faculties of agriculture, business and commerce, engineering

Publications: *Journal of Drylands* (2 a year), *Momona Ethiopian Journal of Science* (2 a year)

DEANS

College of Business and Economics: Dr ZAID NEGASH

College of Dry Land Agriculture and Natural Resources: Dr GIRMAY TESFAY

College of Engineering: Dr GEBREMESKEL KAHSAY

College of Law and Governance: FANA HAGOS

College of Medicine: Dr ABDELKADIR M.SEID

College of Natural and Computational Sciences: Dr ALEM ABREHA

College of Social Science and Languages: Dr ASSEFA ABEGAZ

College of Veterinary Science: Dr GEBREHIWOT TADESSE

College

Yared Music School: POB 30097, Addis Ababa; tel. (11) 1550166; f. 1967; attached to Addis Ababa University; 130 students; Head TEKLE YOHANES ZIKE.

FIJI

The Higher Education System

The supra-national University of the South Pacific maintains one of its 12 campuses in Fiji. In 2004 there were 16,444 students at the University and its extension centres, of whom 200 held scholarships from the Fijian Government. Other institutes include the Fiji School of Medicine, the Fiji Institute of Technology, both based in Suva, and the Teachers College based in Lautoka on the western side of Viti Levu. In 2008 there were 66 vocational and technical institutions (with 3,162 enrolled students). In the same year Fiji had four teacher-training colleges (with 824 students).

The Fiji School Leaving Certificate and Form Seven Examination are the main criteria for admission to higher education. The undergraduate Bachelors degree lasts for three years, the postgraduate Masters degree for one to two years and the Doctorate for two years following award of the Masters. Post-secondary vocational and technical training is offered by the University and colleges and institutes of professional training and vocational education. The main qualifications are the Certificate and Diploma.

In August 2007 plans were agreed to establish a Higher Education Advisory Commission to develop the higher education sector, which would be referred to as the Higher Education Advisory Board. In 2008 the Higher Education Promulgation law came into effect, which meant that all higher education institutions providing post-secondary education had to register with the Higher Education Commission at the start of the new year. After January 2010 any new institution must apply to the Commission for approval.

Regulatory Body

GOVERNMENT

Ministry of Education: Marela House, Thurston St, PMB, Suva; tel. 3314477; fax 3303511; internet www.education.gov.fj; Min. FILIPE BOLE.

Learned Societies

ECONOMICS, LAW AND POLITICS

Fiji Law Society: 100 Gordon St, POB 2389, Govt Bldgs, Suva; tel. 3315690; fax 3314334; e-mail vanita@fls.org.fj; internet www.fls.org.fj; f. 1956; Pres. DORSAMI NAIDU; Sec. and CEO VANITA SINGH (acting).

LANGUAGE AND LITERATURE

Alliance Française: 14 MacGregor Rd, POB 14548, Suva; tel. 3313802; fax 3313803; e-mail allifra@is.com.fj; offers courses and exams in French language and culture and promotes cultural exchange with France.

MEDICINE

Fiji Medical Association: Ellery St, POB 1116, Suva; tel. and fax 3315388; e-mail fijimedassoc@connect.com.fj; f. 1953; 215 mems; Pres. Dr MARY SCHRAMM; publ. *Fiji Medical Journal* (4 a year).

Libraries and Archives

Lautoka

Western Regional Library: POB 150, Lautoka; tel. 6660091; f. 1964; books, periodicals, audio visual cassette tapes.

Suva

Library Service of Fiji: Ministry of Education, POB 2526, Govt Bldgs, Suva; tel. 3315344; fax 3314994; f. 1964; public spec. and school library service; 12 e-Community Learning Centres, 1 mobile library, 28 school media centres, 40 govt dept libraries; 1.5m. vols; Prin. Librarian SOKOVETI TUIMOALA; publ. *Fiji National Bibliography* (publ. suspended until 2009).

National Archives of Fiji: POB 2125, Govt Bldgs, Suva; 25 Carnarvon St, Suva; tel. 3304144; fax 3307006; e-mail salesia.ikaniwai@govnet.gov.fj; f. 1954 as the Central Archives of Fiji and the Western Pacific High Comm.; govt records since 1871, Anglican and Methodist church records since 1835; 15,000 vols of monographs on the South Pacific, files on local newspapers since 1869, Fiji official publs since 1874, 3,800 reels of microfilm; Prin. Archivist SETAREKI TALE; Librarian SALESIA IKANIWAI.

Suva City Library: POB 176, Suva; tel. 3313433; fax 3302158; f. 1909, known as Carnegie Library, until 1953; public lending library; 77,000 vols (48,000 in children's library, 29,000 in adults' library), 25 periodicals; special collection: Fiji and the Pacific; mobile library service for schools; Chief Librarian HUMESH PRASAD.

Museums and Art Galleries

Suva

Fiji Museum: POB 2023, Government Buildings, Suva; tel. 3315944; fax 3305143; e-mail information@fijimuseum.org.fj; internet www.fijimuseum.org.fj; f. 1904; contains archaeological, ethnological and historical collections relating to Fiji; archives of Fijian oral traditions; photographic archives; Dir SAGALE BUADROMO; publs *Bulletin* (irregular), *Domodomo* (2 a year).

University

FIJI NATIONAL UNIVERSITY

POB 7222, Nasinu
Telephone: 3393245
Fax: 3370915
E-mail: vc@fnu.ac.fj
Internet: www.fnu.ac.fj
Founded 2009
State control
Vice-Chancellor: Dr GANESH CHAND

DEANS

College of Agriculture, Fisheries and Forestry: ASINATE MOROCA (acting)
College of Business, Hospitality and Tourism Studies: (vacant):
College of Engineering, Science and Technology: Dr SURENDRA B. PRASAD
College of Humanities and Education: ALIFERETI CAWANIBUKA
College of Medicine, Nursing and Health Sciences: IAN ROUSE

UNIVERSITY OF THE SOUTH PACIFIC

Private Mail Bag, Suva
Telephone: 3313900
Fax: 3301305
Internet: www.usp.ac.fj
Founded 1968
State control; regional univ. with 12 island state mems
Language of instruction: English
Academic year: February to November (two semesters)

Extension centres in the Cook Islands, Fiji, Kiribati, Marshall Islands, Nauru, Niue, Samoa, Solomon Islands, Tonga, Tuvalu, Vanuatu; link arrangements with Tokelau; the university's second campus is in Alafua, Samoa; third campus is in Vanuatu

Chancellor: FIAME NAOMI MATA'AFA
Vice-Chancellor: (vacant)
Deputy Vice-Chancellor: Dr KONAIHOLEVA THAMAN (acting)
Pro-Vice Chancellors: Prof. ALBERT EBENEBE, Prof. JOHN LYNCH MERE PULEA
Registrar: WALTER FRASER
Librarian: ESTHER WININAMAORI WILLIAMS
Library of 830,000 vols
Number of teachers: 1,159
Number of students: 6,204 on campus, 9,109 extension students
Publications: *Alafua Agricultural Bulletin*, *Journal of Pacific Studies*, *Pacific Islands Communications Journal*, *South Pacific Agricultural News* (26 a year), *SSED Review* (4 a year)

HEADS OF SCHOOLS

School of Agriculture: Prof. ALBERT EBENEBE (acting)
School of Humanities: Dr AKINISI KEDRAYATE
School of Law: Prof. ROBERT HUGHES

School of Pure and Applied Sciences: Dr ANJEELA JOKHAN
School of Social and Economic Development: Dr ROPATE QALO

PROFESSORS

BHASKARA, R., Economics
CAMPBELL, I., History and Politics
GASKELL, I., Literature and Language
HASSALL, G., Governance
HUGHES, R., Law
MEAKINS, R., Biology
NUNN, P., Oceanic Geoscience
OMLIN, C., Computer Science
ONWOBOLU, G., Engineering
PATHAK, R., Management
PETERSON, R., Banking
SHARMA, M. D., Banking
SOTHEESWARAN, S., Organic Chemistry
SUBRAMANI, Literature and Language
THAMAN, R., Pacific Island Biogeography
WHITE, M., Accounting and Financial Management

ZANN, L., Marine Studies

Colleges

Fiji College of Agriculture: POB 1544, Koronivia, Nausori; tel. 3479200; fax 3400275; e-mail elenibai@is.com.fj; f. 1954, reorganized 1962; 3-year diploma course in tropical agriculture; library: library of 9,000 books, 450 periodicals; 10 teachers; 150 students; Prin. FIUWAKI WAQALALA; publs *Annual Research Report*, *Fiji Agricultural Journal* (2 a year), *Fiji Farmer*, *MAFF Technical Bulletin* (12 a year).

Fiji Institute of Technology: POB 3722, Samabula, Suva; tel. 3381044; fax 3370375; e-mail webmaster@fit.ac.fj; internet www.fit.ac.fj; f. 1964 as Derrick Technical Institute; offers courses in building and civil engineering, business studies, electrical and electronic engineering, mechanical engineering, aeronautical engineering, maritime studies, printing, graphic design, hospitality and tourism, automobile engineering, applied computing, applied science, secretarial studies, agricultural engineering, environmental science, occupational health and safety, general studies; 210 full-time teachers; 6,000 students; library: 50,000 vols; Dir GANESH CHAND.

Fiji School of Medicine: Private Mail Bag, Hoodless House, CWM Hospital Campus, Suva; tel. 3311700; fax 3303469; internet www.fsm.ac.fj; f. 1885 as Suva Medical School, reorganized as Central Medical School 1928; present name 1961; courses in medicine, dentistry, physiotherapy, environmental health, radiography, medical laboratory technology, dietetics and nutrition and pharmacy; 780 students; library: 16,000 vols; Dean Dr WAME BARAVILALA.

FINLAND

The Higher Education System

The higher education system consists of two parallel systems, universities and polytechnics: universities focus on academic teaching and research while polytechnics specialize in professional and vocational training. The structure of the degree system is the same in both sectors. There are 20 universities and 31 polytechnics. The oldest university is the Kuvataideakatemia (Academy of Fine Arts), which was founded in 1848. In 2007 student enrolments were as follows: Vocational and professional institutions 266,479; Polytechnics 133,284; Universities 176,304.

All universities are state-owned and are administered by the Ministry of Education's Department for Education and Science Policy. University-level education is currently free but students may be required to pay extraneous services, such as health care and compulsory membership of the Student's Union. Under the Universities Act, universities are obliged to promote free research and provide free education. However. the Organisation for Economic Cooperation and Development suggested in 2010 that students be charged to study as part of a number of reforms to help Finland out of recession. This might encourage them to finish their degrees more quickly. Other suggestions include replacing grants with repayable loans and speeding up the admissions system by standardizing university entrance requirements. Universities have enjoyed relative autonomy in decision-making, based on three-year performance agreements with the Ministry of Education. Government funding used to account for about 64% of university budgets, with the rest coming from the Academy of Finland, the Technology Development Centre Tekes, business enterprises, the European Union and other public bodies. The new Universities Bill of June 2009 further extended the autonomy of universities by giving them an independent legal personality, either as a public corporation or as a foundation under private law, with university staff no longer being employed by the State. The Government continued to provide core funding with the universities responsible for acquiring additional finance.

The current polytechnic system emerged during the 1990s and was in place by 2000. Like the universities, the polytechnics are controlled by the Division for Higher Education and Science within the Ministry of Education. The polytechnics are a mix of municipal and private ownership. Funding of public polytechnics is shared between central government and local government. Polytechnics follow performance agreements made with the Ministry of Education.

Admission to both universities and polytechnics is on the basis of completed secondary education and entrance examinations. University admissions are subjected to the Universities Decree (115/1998), and admission to polytechnics is governed by the Polytechnic Studies Act (351/2003). In 2005 a two-tier Bachelors and Masters degree system was implemented in both universities and polytechnics, in accordance with the Bologna Process. The award of degrees is based on a US-style academic 'credit' system. The university Bachelors degree lasts for three years and students must accrue 120 credits; the university Masters degree is a two-year course requiring 40–60 credits. The polytechnic Bachelors requires 120–160 credits over three-and-a-half to four years, and the polytechnic Masters 40–60 credits in one-and-a-half years. (Admission to the polytechnic Masters requires a polytechnic Bachelors and three years' professional experience.)

In some subject areas the old-style degree system remains in place. For dentistry, medicine and veterinary medicine, the first degree is the Lisensiaatti or Licentiate, which requires 200–250 credits and takes five to six years. The Lisensiaatti/Licentiate is a doctoral-level degree. Students who have received the Masters may take the Tohtori or Doctorate, which lasts four years. In addition to the technical and vocational education offered by polytechnics there is also an apprenticeship scheme combining workplace and classroom learning.

Regulatory and Representative Bodies

GOVERNMENT

Ministry of Education: POB 29, 00023 Helsinki; Meritullinkatu 10, 00171 Helsinki; tel. (9) 16004; fax (9) 1359335; e-mail opmkirjaamo@minedu.fi; internet www.minedu.fi; Min. HENNA VIRKKUNEN.

Opetusministeriö Koulutus-ja tiedepolitiikan osasto (Ministry of Education, Department for Education and Science Policy): POB 29, 00023 Helsinki; tel. (9) 16077415; fax (9) 16077150; e-mail nergis.samaletdin@minedu.fi; internet www.minedu.fi; f. 1809; prepares and implements legislation relating to basic education, upper secondary education and basic education in the arts, vocational education and training, adult education and training, polytechnics and univs, student financial aid, scientific research, and examination boards for tests in Finnish and Swedish; Dir-Gen. Dr SAKARI KARJALAINEN.

ACCREDITATION

ENIC/NARIC Finland: Opetushallitus/Utbildningsstyrelsen, Finnish Nat. Board of Education, POB 380, 00531 Helsinki; tel. (40) 3487555; fax (9) 77477201; e-mail recognition@oph.fi; internet www.oph.fi/info/ recognition; Counsellor of Education, Head of Unit CARITA BLOMQVIST.

FUNDING

Suomen Akatemia (Academy of Finland): Vilhonvuorenkatu 6, POB 99, 00501 Helsinki; tel. (9) 774881; fax (9) 77488299; e-mail kirjaamo@aka.fi; internet www.aka.fi; funding org. for scientific research; works to advance the renewal and diversity of research, and supports the extensive application of research results for the benefit of welfare, culture, the economy and the environment; promotes equal opportunities in research; has wide range of funding instruments tailored to different purposes; funded research projects account for 3,000 researcher FTEs at univs and research institutes; operates within the admin. sector of Min. of Education and receives its funding through the state budget; Pres. Prof. MARKKU MATTILA; Vice-Pres RIITTA MUSTONEN, OSSI MALMBERG.

Tekes/Teknologian ja Innovaatioiden Kehittämiskeskus (Finnish Funding Agency for Technology and Innovation): POB 69, Kyllikinportti 2, 00101 Helsinki; tel. (0) 106055000; fax (9) 6949196; e-mail tekes@tekes.fi; internet www.tekes.fi; f. 1983; funding org. for research and devt projects run by private enterprise, research institutes and univs; invested 465m. in research and innovation activity during 2006; encourages cooperation between differing fields of technology; assists companies to conduct meaningful and valuable research; does not derive any financial profit from its endeavours, nor does it claim any intellectual proprietary rights; has technology devt depts at 14 regional Employment and Economic Devt Centres (known as the T&E Centres); maintains offices in Beijing, Brussels, Tokyo, San Jose, Silicon Valley, Shanghai and Washington, DC; Dir-Gen. Dr VELI-PEKKA SAARNIVAARA.

NATIONAL BODIES

Arene ry/Ammattikorkeoulujen rehtorineuvosto (Finnish Conference of Polytechnic Rectors): Pohjoinen Makasiinikatu 7A, 00130 Helsinki; tel. (9) 6129920; fax (9) 61299230; e-mail timo.luopajarvi@arene.fi; internet www.arene.fi; Sec.-Gen. Dr TIMO LUOPAJÄRVI.

CIMO Kansainvälisen liikkuvuuden ja yhteistyön keskus (Centre for International Mobility): POB 343 (Hakaniemenranta 6), 00531 Helsinki; tel. (0) 207868500; fax (0) 207868601; e-mail cimoinfo@cimo.fi; internet www.cimo.fi; f. 1991; attached to Min. of Education; administers scholarship and exchange programmes and is responsible for implementing EU education, training, culture and youth programmes in Finland;

offers training, information, advisory services and publs; promotes and organizes int. trainee exchanges; Dir PASI SAHLBERG.

Korkeakoulujen arviointineuvosto (KKA) (Finnish Higher Education Evaluation Council): POB 133, Meritullinkatu 1, 00171 Helsinki; tel. (9) 16076913; fax (9) 16077608; e-mail finheec@minedu.fi; internet www.finheec.fi; f. 1995; ind. body assisting higher education instns and the Min. of Education in evaluation; carries out audits of higher education systems of higher education instns and other evaluations; Sec.-Gen. Dr HELKA KEKÄLÄINEN.

Opetushallitus (Finnish National Board of Education): POB 380, 00531 Helsinki; located at: Kumpulantie 3, 00520 Helsinki; tel. (9) 774775; fax (9) 77477865; e-mail opetushallitus@oph.fi; internet www.oph.fi; f. 1991; is the agency responsible for the devt of education in Finland; draws up core curricula for basic and upper secondary education, and the framework for vocational qualifications and competence-based qualifications; evaluates learning results and improves the efficiency of training; Dir-Gen. TIMO LANKINEN.

Suomen yliopistot Unifi (Universities Finland Unifi): Pohjoinen Makasiinikatu 7 A 2, 00130 Helsinki; tel. (50) 5229421; e-mail rectors-council@helsinki.fi; internet www.rectors-council.helsinki.fi; f. 1969 as Finnish Council of University Rectors, present name 2010; promotes and contributes to cooperation between univs and helps them to achieve their common strategic goals; works with political decision-makers, nat. authorities, ministries and central interest groups to advance research and higher education in Finland; strengthens the role of univs as key partners in social and political discussion; promotes int. cooperation between univs, esp. in the Nordic countries, Europe and Asia; 17 mems; Sec.-Gen. Dr LIISA SAVUNEN.

Learned Societies

GENERAL

Finska Vetenskaps-Societeten/Suomen Tiedeseura (Finnish Society of Sciences and Letters): Hallituskatu 2B, 00170 Helsinki; tel. (9) 633005; fax (9) 661065; e-mail societas@scientiarum.fi; internet www.scientiarum.fi; f. 1838; promotes science and the humanities by arranging public lectures, seminars and symposia; publishing scientific literature; awarding grants and prizes; promoting contacts within the scientific community; offering mems possibilities for interdisciplinary contacts; 338 mems; Chair. Prof. LEIF C. ANDERSSON; Permanent Sec. Prof. CARL G. GAHMBERG; publs *Bidrag till kännedom av Finlands natur och folk, Commentationes Humanarum Litterarum, Commentationes Scientiarum Socialium, Sphinx-Årsbok-Vuosikirja* (1 a year).

Suomalainen Tiedeakatemia (Finnish Academy of Science and Letters): Mariankatu 5, 00170 Helsinki; tel. (9) 636800; fax (9) 660117; e-mail acadsci@acadsci.fi; internet www.acadsci.fi; f. 1908; 636 ordinary mems, 206 foreign mems; Pres. ARTO MUSTAJOKI; Sec.-Gen. OLLI MARTIO; publs *Annales Academiae Scientiarum Fennicae* (Mathematica, Geologica-Geographica and Humaniora), *Folklore Fellows' Communications, Yearbook.*

Tieteellisten seurain valtuuskunta/ Vetenskapliga samfundens delegation (Federation of Finnish Learned Societies): Mariankatu 5, 00170 Helsinki; tel. (9)

228691; fax (9) 22869291; e-mail tsv@tsv.fi; internet www.tsv.fi; f. 1899 to promote scholarly publishing, scientific information, scientific cooperation and science policy; houses the Exchange Centre for Scientific Literature and a meeting and conf. centre; 251 mem. socs; Pres. Prof. ILKKA NIINILUOTO; Dir Dr AURA KORPPI-TOMMOLA; publs *Catalogue* (every 5 years), *Tieteessä tapahtuu* (journal, 8 a year).

AGRICULTURE, FISHERIES AND VETERINARY SCIENCE

Meijeritieteellinen Seura r.y. (Finnish Society for Dairy Science): Dept of Food Technology, POB 30, 00039 Valio; f. 1938 to promote research work and cooperation in the field of dairy science; 200 mems; Chair. Prof. TAPANI ALATOSSAVA; Sec. JANNE UUSI-RAUVA; publ. *Meijeritieteellinen Aikakauskirja* (Finnish Journal of Dairy Science).

Suomen Eläinlääkäriliitto (Finnish Veterinary Association): Aleksis Kiven katu 52–54, 00510 Helsinki; tel. (9) 77454810; fax (9) 77454818; internet www.sell.fi; f. 1892 to promote veterinary science and the practice of veterinary medicine; 2,108 mems; Chair. SANNA HELLSTROM; Chief Exec. MIKA LEPPINEN; Sec ELJA PIETILÄ; publ. *Suomen Eläinlääkärilehti* (Finnish Veterinary Journal, 12 a year).

Suomen Maataloustieteellinen Seura r.y. (Scientific Agricultural Society of Finland): c/o MTT Agrifood Research Finland Economic Research, Luutnantintie 13, 00410 Jokioinen; tel. (9) 56080; fax (9) 5631164; e-mail maataloustieteenpaivat@smts.fi; internet www.smts.fi; f. 1909; 504 mems; Pres. Prof. JARI VALKONEN; Sec. KIRSI PARTANEN; publ. *Agricultural and Food Science* (4–6 a year).

Suomen Metsätieteellinen Seura (Finnish Society of Forestry Science): POB 18, 01301 Vantaa; tel. (10) 2112144; fax (10) 2112101; e-mail sms@helsinki.fi; internet www.metsatieteellinenseura.fi; f. 1909 to encourage forest research and wood science in Finland; composed of persons devoting themselves to the study of forestry and its underlying theory; colln of vols held within the Viikki Science Library (see Libraries and Archives); 550 mems; Pres. Prof. ANNIKA KANGAS; Sec.-Gen. Dr RIITTA VÄÄNÄNEN; publs *Dissertationes Forestales* (irregular), *Metsätieteen aikakauskirja* (4 a year), *Silva Fennica* (5 a year).

BIBLIOGRAPHY, LIBRARY SCIENCE AND MUSEOLOGY

Suomen Kirjastoseura/Finlands biblioteksförening (Finnish Library Association): Runeberginkatu 15 A 23, 00100 Helsinki; tel. (40) 659363; e-mail fla@fla.fi; internet kirjastoseura.kaapeli.fi; f. 1910; 2,000 mems; Pres. JUKKA RELANDER; Sec.-Gen. SINIKKA SIPILÄ; publ. *Kirjastolehti* (Bulletin, 6 a year).

Suomen museoliitto/Finlands museiförbund (Finnish Museums Association): Annankatu 16 B 50, 00120 Helsinki; tel. (9) 58411700; fax (9) 58411750; e-mail museoliitto@museoliitto.fi; internet www.museoliitto.fi; f. 1923; 194 mem. museums; devt of museum sector; dissemination of information on museums; training and spec. information for mems; library of 2,000 vols; Sec.-Gen. ANJA-TUULIKKI HUOVINEN; publ. *Museo* (4 a year).

Suomen Tieteellinen Kirjastoseura (Finnish Research Library Association): POB 217, Kirkkokatu 6 (Tieteiden talo), Helsinki 00171; tel. (9) 61299240; fax (9) 61299230; e-mail meri.kuula-bruun@finlit.fi; internet pro.tsv.fi/stks; f. 1929; 696 mems; Chair.

PIRJO VATANEN; Sec. MERI KUULA-BRUUN; publ. *Signum* (Bulletin, 8 a year).

ECONOMICS, LAW AND POLITICS

Ekonomiska Samfundet i Finland (Economic Society of Finland): Swedish School of Economics and Business Admin., POB 479, 00101 Helsinki; tel. (9) 431331; fax (9) 43133333; internet www.ekonomiskasamfundet.fi; f. 1894; 780 mems; Pres. HENRIK WINBERG; Sec. JUTTA HEINO (acting); publ. *Ekonomiska Samfundets Tidskrift* (Journal, 3 a year).

Finnish Legal Society: Advokatbyrå Borenius & Kemppinen Ab, Georgsgatan 13A, 00120 Helsinki; tel. (9) 61533489; fax (9) 61533499; f. 1862; 794 mems; Pres. GUSTAF MÖLLER; Sec. JOHAN ROMAN; publ. *Tidskrift utgiven av Juridiska Föreningen i Finland.*

Hallinnon Tutkimuksen Seura r.y./Sällskapet för Förvaltningsforskning (Finnish Association for Administrative Studies): Dept of Political Science, POB 54, 00014 Univ. of Helsinki; tel. (9) 19124826; e-mail anna-liisa.heusala@helsinki.fi; internet pro.tsv.fi/hts; f. 1981; aims to function as a common link for depts and researchers studying admin. questions, to coordinate the planning and surveillance of training in admin. sciences, to hold lectures and discussions, to take part in int. scientific cooperation; a mem. of the European Group of Public Admin.; 660 individual mems, 4 organizational mems; Pres. TURO VIRTANEN; Sec. ANNA-LIISA HEUSALA; publ. *Hallinnon Tutkimus* (4 a year).

International Law Association, Finnish Branch: Regissorsvagen 22 A7, 00400 Helsingfors; e-mail finnish-ila@helsinki.fi; f. 1946; 105 mems; Pres. Prof. BENGT BROMS; Hon. Sec. MATTI TUPAMÄKI.

Ius Gentium (Finnish International Law Association): POB 208, 00171 Helsinki; tel. (9) 19122468; fax (9) 19123076; e-mail ius-gentium@helsinki.fi; internet www.helsinki.fi/jarj/iusgentium; f. 1983; research on int. law and legal theory; organizes seminars and lectures on topics relating to int. law and legal theory; 100 mems; Chair. ANJA LINDROOS; publs *Acta Societatis Fennicae Iuris Gentium, Finnish Yearbook of International Law, Kansainoikeus/Ius Gentium,* A, B and C series.

Kansantaloudellinen Yhdistys (Finnish Economic Association): c/o Merja Kauhanen, Labour Institute for Economic Research, Pitkänsillanreta 3A, 00530 Helsinki; tel. (9) 25357345; e-mail yhdistys@ktyhdistys.net; internet www.ktyhdistys.net; f. 1884; 1,012 mems; Pres. JUHA TARKKA; Sec. and Treas. MERJA KAUHANEN; publs *Kansantaloudellinen Aikakauskirja* (Finnish Economic Journal), *Kansantaloudellisia Tutkimuksia* (Economic Studies).

Suomalainen Lakimiesyhdistys ry (Finnish Lawyers' Society): Kasarmikatu 23 A 17, 00130 Helsinki; tel. (9) 6120300; fax (9) 604668; e-mail sly@lakimies.org; internet www.lakimies.org; f. 1898; 2,700 mems; Pres. MIKA HEMMO; Sec. HANNELE KLEMETTINEN; publs *Lakimies-aikakauskirja* (8 a year), *Oikeustiede-Jurisprudentia* (1 a year), *Suomalaisen Lakimiesyhdistyksen Julkaisuja* (series A, B, C, D and E).

Suomen Taloushistoriallinen Yhdistys/ Ekonomisk-Historiska föreningen i Finland (Finnish Economic History Association): Dept of History and Ethnology, Univ. of Jyväskylä, POB 35 (H), 40014 Jyväskylä; tel. (14) 2601284; e-mail juhamart@jyu.fi; internet groups.jyu.fi/taloushistoria/en.shtml; f. 1952; studies economic and social history; 100 mems; Chair.

Prof. Dr ILKKA NUMMELA; Hon. Sec. Prof. JARI OJALA; Exec. Dir JUUSO MARTTILA; publs *Scandinavian Economic History Review* (in cooperation with other Scandinavian socs for the advancement of the study of economic history), *Suomen talouselämän vaikuttajat* (in cooperation with Finnish Literature Soc.).

Suomen Tilastoseura/Statistiska Samfundet i Finland (Finnish Statistical Society): c/o Statistics Finland, POB 4A, 00022; tel. (9) 173412628; internet www.stat.fi/sts; f. 1920; aims to promote the development of theoretical and applied statistics, to unite statisticians working in various fields, to promote statistical education and research; 500 mems; Pres. LAURI TARKKONEN; Sec. MARIA VALASTE.

Suomen Väestötieteen Yhdistys (Finnish Demographic Society): c/o Hanna Remes, Dept of Sociology, POB 18, 00014 Univ. of Helsinki; fax (9) 19123967; internet blogit .helsinki.fi/svy; f. 1973; fosters research and promotes interaction between scholars in the field of population studies; 101 mems; Chair. Prof. Dr PEKKA MARTIKAINEN; Sec. HANNA REMES.

Suomen Ympäristöoikeustieteen Seura/ Miljörättsliga Sällskapet i Finland (Finnish Society of Environmental Law): POB 1225, 00101 Helsinki; tel. (9) 27091890; fax (9) 6222293; e-mail sys@pro.tsv.fi; internet pro.tsv.fi/sys; f. 1980 to support and promote legal and admin. research of environmental problems, and to promote cooperation between researchers and authorities; 360 mems; Chair. Prof. ERKKI J. HOLLO; Sec. ROBERT UTTER; publ. *Ympäristöjuridiikka-Miljöjuridik* (Journal of Environmental Law).

FINE AND PERFORMING ARTS

Suomen Musiikkitieteellinen Seura r.y./ Musikvetenskapliga Sällskapet i Finland r.f. (Finnish Musicological Society): Musikin laitos, PL 35, 40014 Jyväskylän yliopisto; tel. (14) 2601397; fax (14) 2601331; e-mail jokavuos@campus.jyu.fi; internet www.musiikkilehti.fi; f. 1917; aims to encourage musicological research, develop int. exchanges, and to function for the good of Finnish musical life by broadening knowledge of music and musical culture; 200 mems; Chair. Dr TUOMAS EEROLA; Sec.-Gen. Prof. JONNA VUOSKOSKI; publs *Acta Musicologica Fennica*, *Musiikki* (4 a year).

Suomen Näytelmäkirjailijaliitto (Finnish Dramatists' Society): Vironkatu 12B, 00170 Helsinki 17; f. 1921; Pres. ESKO SALERVO; Sec. PIRJO WESTMAN.

Suomen Säveltäjät rf (Society of Finnish Composers): Runeberginkatu 15A 11, 00100 Helsinki; tel. (9) 445589; fax (9) 440181; e-mail saveltajat@composers.fi; internet www.composers.fi; f. 1945; 174 mems; Pres. Prof. MIKKO HEINIÖ; Exec. Dir ANNU MIKKONEN.

Suomen Taideyhdistys (Finnish Art Society): Helsingin Taidehalli, Nervanderinkatu 3, 00100 Helsinki; tel. (9) 4577314315; fax (9) 45420610; e-mail info@suomentaideyhdistys .fi; internet www.suomentaideyhdistys.fi; f. 1846; arranges exhibitions, presents awards and scholarships; 1,600 mems; Pres. VEIKKO KASURINEN; Sec. ANNA KINNUNEN.

Suomen Taiteilijaseura/Konstnärsgillet i Finland (Artists' Association of Finland): Nilsiänkatu 11–13 F 5, 00510 Helsinki; tel. (9) 61292120; fax (9) 61292160; internet www .artists.fi; f. 1864; 2,300 mems; mem. socs consist of the Painters' Union of Finland, the Sculptors' Union of Finland, the Association of Graphic Artists in Finland, the Finnish Association of Artists in Photography and the

Federation of the Fine Arts Associations in Finland; promotes professional interests of artists and holds an annual exhibition; Chair. KARI JYLHÄ; Sec.-Gen. PIIA RANTALA; publs *Taide* (Art), *Taiteilija-lenti* (4 a year).

Taidehistorian seura/Föreningen för konsthistoria r.y. (Society for Art History in Finland): PL 3, 00014 University of Helsinki; Unioninkatu 34, 00014 University of Helsinki; fax (9) 19122961; e-mail sihteeri@taidehistorianseura.fi; internet www.taidehistorianseura.fi; f. 1974 to promote research in art history in Finland; 483 mems; Pres. RENJA SUOMINEN-KOKKONEN; publ. *Taidehistoriallisia tutkimuksia/ Konsthistoriska studier (Studies in Art History)*.

Turun Soitannollinen Seura (Musical Society of Turku): Sibelius Museum, Piispankatu 17, Turku; tel. (2) 2313789; fax (2) 518528; internet www.musisoi.net/yhteys .html; f. 1790; 655 mems; Pres. ALARIK REPO.

HISTORY, GEOGRAPHY AND ARCHAEOLOGY

Historian Ystäväin Liitto (Society of the Friends of History): Tieteiden talo, Kirkkokatu 6, 00170 Helsinki; tel. (9) 22869351; e-mail shs@histseura.fi; internet pro.tsv.fi/ hyl; f. 1926; 1,500 mems; Sec. JULIA BURMAN; publs *Historiallinen Aikakauskirja* (Finnish Historical Review, 4 a year), *Historiallinen Kirjasto* (irregular), *Historian Aitta* (irregular).

Suomen Historiallinen Seura/Finska Historiska Samfundet (Finnish Historical Society): Tieteiden talo, Kirkkokatu 6, 00170 Helsinki; tel. (9) 22869351; e-mail shs@ histseura.fi; internet www.histseura.fi; f. 1875; 900 mems; Chair. Dr MARJAANA NIEMI; Exec. Dir JULIA BURMAN; publs *Bibliotheca Historica* (historical studies in Finnish, English and German), *Historiallinen Arkisto* (Historical Archives), *Historiallisia Tutkimuksia* (Historical Researches), *Suomen historian lähteitä* (Sources of the History of Finland), *Studia Fennica: Historica*, *Studia Historica* (historical studies in German, French and English).

Suomen Kirkkohistoriallinen Seura/ Finska Kyrkohistoriska Samfundet (Finnish Society of Church History): Dept of Church History, POB 33 (Aleksanterinkatu 7), 00014 Univ. of Helsinki; tel. (9) 400941723; fax (9) 19123033; e-mail jenni .krapu@helsinki.fi; internet www.skhs.fi; f. 1891; 700 mems; Chair. Assoc. Prof. MIKKO KETOLA; Sec. JENNI KRAPU; publs *Toimituksia-Handlingar* (research papers, 3–6 a year), *Vuosikirja-Årsskrift* (1 a year).

Suomen Maantieteellinen Seura/Geografiska Sällskapet i Finland (Geographical Society of Finland): c/o Dept of Geography, POB 64 (Kumpula campus), 00014 University of Helsinki; tel. (9) 19150763; fax (9) 19150760; internet www .helsinki.fi/ml/maant/geofi; f. 1888; 1,300 mems; library of 56,000 vols; Pres. Dr KATARIINA KOSONEN; Sec. P. HELLEMAA; publs *Fennia* (2 a year), *Terra* (4 a year).

Suomen Muinaismuistoyhdistys/Finska Fornminnesföreningen (Finnish Antiquarian Society): POB 913, 00101 Helsinki; tel. (9) 40501; fax (9) 40509400; e-mail sihteeri@muinaismuistoyhdistys.fi; internet www.muinaismuistoyhdistys.fi; f. 1870; 600 mems; Pres. HELENA EDGREN; Sec. HANNA FORSSELL; publs *Finskt Museum*, *Iskos*, *Kansatieteellinen Arkisto*, *Suomen Muinaismuistoyhdistyksen Aikakauskirja—Finska Fornminnesföreningens Tidskrift*, *Suomen Museo*.

Suomen Sukututkimusseura/Genealogiska Samfundet i Finland (Genealogical Society of Finland): Liisankatu 16A, 00170 Helsinki; tel. (10) 3877901; e-mail seura@ genealogia.fi; internet www.genealogia.fi; f. 1917; 5,600 mems; library of 45,000 vols; Pres. ANU LAHTINEN; Gen. Man. P. T. KUUSILUOMA; publs *Genos* (4 a year), *Sukutieto* (4 a year), *Vuosikirja—Årsskrift* (1 a year).

LANGUAGE AND LITERATURE

British Council: Urho Kekkosen katu 2C, 00100 Helsinki; tel. (9) 7743330; fax (9) 7018725; e-mail office@britishcouncil.fi; internet www.britishcouncil.fi; provides information about study opportunities in the UK; promotes cultural exchange with the UK; Dir TUIJA TALVITIE.

Finlands svenska författareförening (Society of Swedish Authors in Finland): Urho Kekkonens gata 8 B 14, 00100 Helsinki; tel. (9) 446266; e-mail forfattarna@ kaapeli.fi; internet www.forfattarna.fi; f. 1919; 191 mems; Pres. MIKAELA SUNDSTRÖM; Sec.-Gen. MERETE JENSEN.

Goethe-Institut: Mannerheimintie 20A, 00100 Helsinki; tel. (9) 6803550; fax (9) 604377; e-mail info@helsinki.goethe.org; internet www.goethe.de/ne/hel/deindex.htm; offers courses and exams in German language and culture and promotes cultural exchange with Germany; library of 2,800 vols, 30 periodicals; Dir EIKE FUHRMANN.

Klassillis-filologinen yhdistys (Society for Classical Philology): c/o Dept of World Cultures, POB 24, 00014 Univ. of Helsinki; fax (9) 19122161; internet www.helsinki.fi/hum/ kla/kfy; f. 1882; promotes the study of classical philology and classical antiquity in gen.; 91 mems; Pres. Prof. OLLI SALOMIES; Sec. LAURA BUCHHOLZ; publ. *Arctos: Acta Philologica Fennica* (1 a year).

Kotikielen Seura (Society for the Study of Finnish): Castrenianum, PL 3, 00014 Univ. of Helsinki; fax (9) 19123329; e-mail seura@ kotikielenseura.fi; internet www .kotikielenseura.fi; f. 1876; Finnish linguistics; 792 mems; Pres. Prof. MARJA-LEENA SORJONEN; Sec. JOHANNA KOMPPA; publ. *Virittäjä* (4 a year).

Suomalais-Ugrilainen Seura (Finno-Ugrian Society): POB 320, Mariankatu 7, 00171 Helsinki; tel. (9) 662149; fax (9) 6988249; internet www.sgr.fi; f. 1883; Northern Eurasian linguistics and ethnography; 800 mems; Pres. Prof. Dr ULLA-MAIJA KULONEN; Sec. PAULA KOKKONEN; publs *Finnisch-Ugrische Forschungen* (every 2 years), *Journal* (every 2 years), *Mémoires* (2–5 a year).

Suomalaisen Kirjallisuuden Seura/ Finska Litteratursällskapet (Finnish Literature Society): Hallituskatu 1, POB 259, 00171 Helsinki; tel. (20) 1131231; fax (9) 13123220; e-mail sks@finlit.fi; internet www .finlit.fi; f. 1831 to promote study of folklore, ethnology, literature and Finnish language; 3,700 mems; Chair. Prof. PENTTI LEINO; Dir-Gen. and Sec. TUOMAS LEHTONEN; library: see Libraries and Archives; publs *Studia Fennica: Ethnologica*, *Studia Fennica: Folkloristica*, *Studia Fennica: Historica*, *Studia Fennica: Linguistica* (1 a year), *Studia Fennica: Litteraria*.

Suomen englanninopettajat r.y. (Association of Teachers of English in Finland): Rautatieläisenkatu 6A, 00520 Helsinki; tel. (9) 145414; fax (9) 2788100; e-mail english@ suomenenglanninopettajat.fi; internet www .suomenenglanninopettajat.fi; f. 1948; 2,900 mems; Pres. ANNE ONTERO; publ. *Tempus* (8 a year).

Suomen Kirjailijaliitto (The Union of Finnish Writers): Runeberginkatu 32, C28,

00100 Helsinki; tel. (9) 449752; e-mail info@
suomenkirjailijaliitto.fi; internet www
.suomenkirjailijailiitto.fi; f. 1897; allied to the
Scandinavian Authors' Council and European Writers' Congress; 520 mems; Gen.
Sec. PÄIVI LIEDES; publs Suomalaiset kertojat, Suomen Runotar.

Svenska litteratursällskapet i Finland
(Society of Swedish Literature in Finland):
Riddareg. 5, 00170 Helsinki; tel. (9) 618777;
fax (9) 61877377; e-mail info@sls.fi; internet
www.sls.fi; f. 1885; 1,100 mems; library: see
Libraries and Archives; Pres. Prof. HÅKAN
ANDERSSON; Sec. Prof. ANN-MARIE IVARS;
publ. Skrifter (10–15 a year).

Uusfilologinen Yhdistys (Modern Language Society): POB 24, 00014 Univ. of
Helsinki; tel. (9) 19123502; fax (9)
19122384; e-mail marianna.hintikka@
helsinki.fi; internet www.helsinki.fi/jarj/ufy;
f. 1887; 244 mems; Pres. Prof. JUHANI HÄRMÄ;
Hon. Sec. MARIANNA HINTIKKA; publs Mémoires (irregular), Neuphilologische Mitteilungen (Bulletin, 4 a year).

MEDICINE

Cancer Society of Finland: Pieni Roobertinkatu 9, 00130 Helsinki; tel. (9) 135331; fax
(9) 1351093; e-mail society@cancer.fi;
internet www.cancer.fi; f. 1936; 140,000
mems; Pres. Prof. SEPPO PYRHÖNEN; Sec.-
Gen. HARRI VERTIO; publs Focus Oncologie (1
a year), Syöpä – Cancer (6 a year).

Finska Läkaresällskapet (Medical Society
of Finland): Johannesbergsvägen 8, POB 82,
00251 Helsinki; tel. (9) 47768090; fax (9)
4362055; e-mail fls@fls.pp.fi; internet www
.kulturfonden.fi/fls; f. 1835; 1,000 mems;
library of 35,000 vols; Pres. Prof. LEIF
ANDERSON; Sec. Dr MARIANNE GRIPENBERG;
publ. Finska Läkaresällskapets Handlingar.

Suomalainen Lääkäriseura Duodecim
(Finnish Medical Society Duodecim): Kalevankatu 11A, 00100 Helsinki; tel. (9) 618851;
fax (9) 61885200; internet www.duodecim.fi;
f. 1881; 20,000 mems; library of 22,500 vols;
Pres. Dr SEPPO JUNNILA; Sec. Dr ILKKA
RAURAMO; publ. Duodecim (26 a year).

**Suomen Farmaseuttinen Yhdistys/
Farmaceutiska Föreningen i Finland**
(Finnish Pharmaceutical Society): Fredrikinkatu 61, 00100 Helsinki; internet pro.tsv.fi/
finpharmsociety; f. 1887; 290 mems; Pres.
TOM WIKBERG; Sec. LEENA PELTONEN.

Suomen Hammaslääkäriseura Apollonia (Finnish Dental Society Apollonia):
Bulevardi 30 B 5, 00120 Helsinki; tel. (9)
6803120; fax (9) 646263; e-mail toimisto@
apollonia.fi; internet www.apollonia.fi; f.
1892; 6,000 mems; Pres. Dr PEKKA LAINE;
Gen. Sec. Dr MAIJA T. LAINE-ALAVA.

NATURAL SCIENCES

Biological Sciences

Birdlife Finland: POB 1285, 00101 Helsinki; Annankatu 29A, 00101 Helsinki; tel.
(9) 41353300; fax (9) 41353322; e-mail office@
birdlife.fi; internet www.birdlife.fi; f. 1973;
promotes bird-watching, research and protection of birds, their habitats and biological
diversity; 30 nat. assoc. orgs; affiliated to
BirdLife International; 9,000 mems; Dir
MIKA ASIKAINEN; publs Linnut (Birds, 4 a
year), Ornis Fennica (4 a year).

Kasvinsuojeluseura ry (Plant Protection
Society): Araitamaantie 8A (Kannelmäki),
00420 Helsinki; tel. (9) 4770790; fax (9)
47707920; internet www.kasvinsuojeluseura
.fi; f. 1931; research on, and protection from,
diseases, pests and weeds; arranges meetings
and excursions, awards grants to researchers; 1,500 mems; Chair. HANNU SEPPANEN;

Sec. MINNA-MARIA LINNA; publ. Kasvinsuojelulehti.

**Societas Amicorum Naturae Ouluensis/
Oulun Luonnonystäväin Yhdistys r.y.:**
Dept of Biology (Botany), University of Oulu,
90570 Oulu; tel. (8) 5531546; fax (8) 5531500;
f. 1925; 436 mems; Pres. Prof. P. LAHDESMAKI;
Sec. S. KONTUNEN-SOPPELA; publs Aquilo,
Ser. Botanica, Ser. Zoologica.

**Societas Biochemica, Biophysica et
Microbiologica Fenniae** (Biochemical,
Biophysical and Microbiological Society of
Finland): c/o Dr Laura Seppä-Fagerhed,
Viikki Biocenter, POB 56, 00014 University
of Helsinki; tel. (9) 19159428; fax (9)
19159570; internet www.biobio.org; f. 1945;
900 mems; Pres. Dr MARC BAUMANN; Sec. Dr
LAURA SEPPÄ-FAGERHED.

**Societas Biologica Fennica Vanamo/
Suomen Biologian Seura Vanamo:** POB
7, Latokartanonkaari 7, University of Helsinki, 00014 Helsinki; internet www.vanamo
.fi; f. 1896; Pres. SEPPO TURUNEN; Sec. MARIA
PIETILÄINEN; publs Atlas Florae Europaeae,
Luonnon Tutkija (The Naturalist, 5 a year).

**Societas Entomologica Fennica/Suomen
Hyönteistieteellinen Seura** (Entomological Society of Finland): Finnish Museum of
Natural History, 00014 University of Helsinki; tel. (9) 19158662; fax (9) 19158663;
internet www.fmnh.helsinki.fi/users/shs; f.
1935; library; Pres. Dr ILKKA TERÄS; Sec. Dr
NINA LAURENNE; publ. Entomologica Fennica
(4 a year).

Societas pro Fauna et Flora Fennica: c/o
F. Högnabba, Finnish Museum of Natural
History, Mycology Division, POB 7, Unionsgatan 44, 00014 Univ. of Helsinki; tel. (9)
19124495; fax (9) 19124456; e-mail filip
.hognabba@helsinki.fi; internet www
.societasfff.fi; f. 1821; discussion and research
on all aspects of animals and plants in
Finland; 1,026 mems; library of 44,000 vols;
Pres. Prof. C.-A. HÆGGSTRÖM; Hon. Sec. F.
HÖGNABBA; publ. Memoranda Societatis pro
Fauna et Flora Fennica (3 a year).

Physical Sciences

Geofysiikan Seura/Geofysiska Sällskapet (Geophysical Society of Finland): c/o
Taija Huotari, Geological Survey of Finland,
POB 96, 02151 Espoo; internet pro.tsv.fi/
geofysiikanseura; f. 1926; aims to promote
geophysical research and provide links
between researchers; 230 mems; Pres. Prof.
MIKKO ALESTALO; Sec. TAIJA HUOTARI; publ.
Geophysica (2 a year).

**Suomen Geologinen Seura/Geologiska
Sällskapet i Finland** (Geological Society
of Finland): POB 64, 00014 Helsinki; tel. (9)
19150805; e-mail sihteeri@geologinenseura
.fi; internet www.geologinenseura.fi; f. 1886;
1,000 mems; Pres. Dr JAANA HALLA; Sec.
JUSSI HEINONEN; publs Bulletin (2 a year),
Geologi (6 a year).

Suomen Kemian Seura/Kemiska Sällskapet i Finland (Association of Finnish
Chemical Societies): Urho Kekkosen katu 8 C
31, 00100 Helsinki; tel. (9) 4542040; fax (9)
45420440; internet www.kemianseura.fi; f.
1970 to promote research in chemistry,
chemical education, chemical industry; to
organize the annual Finnish Chemical Congress; to act as a link between the three mem.
socs, and to support and coordinate their
activities; represents the mem. socs in common matters; 14 sections: wood and polymer
chemistry, biotechnology, mass spectrometry, NMR spectroscopy, metal analysis, chromatography, chemometrics, explosives,
optical spectroscopy, computational chemistry, catalysis, EURACHEM—Finland, synthetic chemistry, and NBC protection, rescue
and safety; library of 800 vols; Chair. LEIF

RAMM-SCHMIDT; publs Acta Chemica Scandinavica, Kemia-Kemi.
Constituent Societies:

**Finska Kemistsamfundet/Suomen
Kemistiseura** (Chemical Society of Finland): Hietaniemenkatu 2, 00100 Helsinki;
f. 1891; 564 mems; Pres. PEKKA PYYKKÖ;
Sec. URBAN WIIK.

Kemiallisteknillinen Yhdistys (Society
of Chemical Engineers): Hietaniemenkatu
2, 00100 Helsinki; f. 1970; 816 mems; Pres.
JAAKKO E. LAINE; Sec. JUHA VIRTANEN.

Suomalaisten Kemistien Seura (Finnish Chemical Society): Hietaniemenkatu
2, 00100 Helsinki; f. 1919; 3,480 mems;
Pres. Dr TIMO NURMI; Sec. HELEENA KAR
RUS.

PHILOSOPHY AND PSYCHOLOGY

Suomen Filosofinen Yhdistys (Philosophical Society of Finland): Dept of Philosophy,
POB 24 (Unioninkatu 20A), 00014 Univ. of
Helsinki, Helsinki; tel. (9) 77488232; fax (9)
19128060; e-mail risto.vilkko@helsinki.fi;
internet www.helsinki.fi/jarj/sfy; f. 1873; promotes the study of philosophy and related
disciplines in Finland; 420 mems; Pres. Prof.
ILKKA NIINILUOTO; Sec. Dr RISTO VILKKO;
publs Acta Philosophica Fennica (1–3 a
year), Ajatus (1 a year).

Suomen Psykologinen Seura ry (Finnish
Psychological Society): Liisankatu 16A,
00170 Helsinki; tel. (9) 2782122; fax (9)
2781300; e-mail psykologia@genealogia.fi;
internet www.psykologienkustannus.fi/sps;
f. 1952; 1,500 mems; small library; Pres.
Prof. JARKKO HAUTAMÄKI; Sec. TAINA SCHAKIR;
publs Acta Psychologica Fennica (series A,
irregular, and series B, irregular), Psykologia
(6 a year).

RELIGION, SOCIOLOGY AND ANTHROPOLOGY

Suomalainen Teologinen Kirjallisuusseura (Finnish Theological Literature Society): POB 33 (Aleksanterinkatu 7), 00014
University of Helsinki, Helsinki; tel. (9)
19122076; fax (9) 19123033; e-mail stksj@
pro.tsv.fi; internet pro.tsv.fi/stksj; f. 1891;
850 mems; Chair. Prof. SIMO KNUUTTILA.

Suomen Antropologinen Seura/Antropologiska Sällskapet i Finland (Finnish
Anthropological Society): PL 59, 00014 Univ.
of Helsinki; tel. (9) 19123094; fax (9)
19123006; e-mail info@
suomenantropologinenseura.fi; internet
www.antropologinenseura.fi; f. 1975 to promote research in the fields of anthropology
and disciplines closely related to anthropology; organizes meetings and conferences; 300
mems; Pres. MINNA RUCKENSTEIN; Sec. ANNA
AUTIO; publ. Suomen Antropologi/Antropologi i Finland (Journal of the Finnish
Anthropological Society).

Suomen Itämainen Seura (Finnish Oriental Society): c/o Dept of Asian and African
Studies, POB 59 (Unioninkatu 38B), 00014
Univ. of Helsinki; fax (9) 19122094; e-mail
saana.svard@helsinki.fi; internet www
.suomenitamainenseura.org; f. 1917; 192
mems; Pres. Prof. TAPANI HARVIAINEN; Sec.
SAANA SVÄRD; publ. Studia Orientalia.

TECHNOLOGY

Maanmittaustieteiden seura r.y. (Finnish
Society of Surveying Sciences): Kellosilta 10,
00520 Helsinki; tel. (9) 1481900; fax (9)
1483580; internet mts.fgi.fi; f. 1926; 710
mems; Pres. PEKKA RAHKILA; Sec. MIKKO
TAKALO; publ. Nordic Journal of Surveying
and Real Estate Research (2 a year).

Rakenteiden Mekaniikan Seura (Finnish Association for Structural Mechanics): Dept of Civil and Environmental Engineering, Helsinki University of Technology, POB 2100, 02015 Helsinki University of Technology; tel. (9) 4513751; fax (9) 4513826; e-mail juha.paavola@hut.fi; internet rmseura.tkk.fi; f. 1970 for promoting research and exchange of knowledge on engineering materials, structural mechanics and design; 222 individual mems, 10 collective mems; Chair. JUHA PAAVOLA; Sec. SAMI PAJUNEN; publ. *Rakenteiden Mekaniikka* (Journal of Structural Mechanics, 4 a year).

Suomen Atomiteknillinen Seura/Atomtekniska Sällskapet i Finland (Finnish Nuclear Society): c/o VTT, Tietotie 3A, POB 1000, 02044 VTT; tel. (20) 722-5047; fax (20) 722-5000; e-mail sihteeri@ats-fns.fi; internet www.ats-fns.fi; f. 1966 to promote knowledge and devt of nuclear technology in Finland, and exchange information on an int. level; seminars and member meetings; 600 individual mems, 19 institutional mems; Chair. EIJA-KARITA PUSKA; Sec. MALLA SEPPÄLÄ; publ. *ATS Ydintekniikka* (4 a year).

Svenska Tekniska Vetenskapsakademien i Finland (Swedish Academy of Engineering Sciences in Finland): Fredriksgatan 25 B 26, 00120 Helsingfors; tel. (40) 7225711; fax (9) 6818095; e-mail stv@stvif.fi; internet www.stvif.fi; f. 1921; to promote research in engineering sciences; 175 mems; Pres. HENRIK WOLFF; Sec. Dr NIKLAS MEINANDER; publ. *Forhandlingar* (Proceedings).

Tekniikan Akateemisten Liitto TEK r.y. (Finnish Association of Graduate Engineers TEK): Ratavartijankatu 2, 00520 Helsinki; tel. (9) 229121; fax (9) 22912911; e-mail webmaster@tek.fi; internet www.tek.fi; f. 1896; serves as a link between engineers and architects, promotes technical sciences and industry, fosters Finnish economic life; regional offices in Espoo, Tampere, Oulu, Lappeenranta and Turku; 67,000 mems; Sec.-Gen. HEIKKI KAUPPI; publ. *TEK Member Magazine* (9 a year).

Tekniikan edistämissäätiö (Technological Foundation): c/o Kauppa-ja teollisuusministeriö, POB 32 (Aleksanterinkatu 4), 00023 Helsinki 17; internet www.kolumbus.fi/tes; f. 1949 to provide yearly fellowships for the advancement of technology; Pres. YRJÖ NEUVO; Sec. KARI MÄKINEN.

Teknillisten Tieteiden Akatemia/Akademin för Tekniska Vetenskaper r.y. (Finnish Academy of Technology): Mariankatu 8 B 11, 00170 Helsinki; tel. (9) 2782400; fax (9) 2782177; e-mail facte@facte.com; internet www.facte.com; f. 1957 to promote technical-scientific research; 440 mems; Pres. ASKO SAARELA; Sec. ANNELI ROSSI.

Tekniska Föreningen i Finland (Engineering Society in Finland—TFiF): Banvaktsg. 2, 00520 Helsinki; tel. (9) 4767718; fax (9) 4767333; e-mail helpdesk@tfif.fi; internet www.tfif.fi; f. 1880; 3,940 mems; Pres. UFFE CEDERQVIST; Man. Dir LARS ENGSTRÖM; publ. *Forum för ekonomi och teknik*.

Research Institutes

GENERAL

Suomen Akatemia (Academy of Finland): Vilhonvuorenkatu 6, POB 99, 00501 Helsinki; tel. (9) 774881; fax (9) 77488299; e-mail keskus@aka.fi; internet www.aka.fi/eng; f. 1969; promotes and provides funding for research in Finland; 37 acad. professorships; library of 25,000 vols; Pres. RAIMO VÄYRYNEN;

Dir of Admin. JUHA SARKIO; Dir of Research ANNELI PAULI.

AGRICULTURE, FISHERIES AND VETERINARY SCIENCE

Maa-ja elintarviketalouden tutkimuskeskus (MTT Agrifood Research Finland): 31600 Jokioinen; tel. (3) 41881; fax (3) 41882222; internet www.mtt.fi; f. 1898; consists of 4 research units, 2 research programmes; Dir-Gen. Prof. ERKKI KEMPPAINEN; publ. *Agricultural and Food Science* (Journal).

Research Units:

Kasvintuotannon tutkimus (Plant Production Research): 31600 Jokioinen; Dir Prof. AARNE KURPPA.

Kotieläintuotannon tutkimus (Animal Production Research): 31600 Jokioinen; Dir Prof. ASKO MÄKI-TANILA.

Maatalousteknologian tutkimus (Agricultural Engineering Research): Vakolantie 55, 03400 Vihti; tel. (9) 224251; fax (9) 2246210; Dir Prof. HANNU HAAPALA.

MTT Biotekniikka-ja elintarviketutkimus (MTT Agrifood Research Finland, Biotechnology and Food Research): 31600 Jokioinen; Dir EEVA-LIISA RYHÄNEN.

Taloustutkimus (Economic Research): Luutnantintie 13, 00411 Helsinki; tel. (9) 56080; fax (9) 5631164; Dir Prof. KYÖSTI PIETOLA.

Ympäristöntutkimus (Environmental Research): 31600 Jokioinen; Dir Prof. SIRPA KURPPA.

Metsäntutkimuslaitos (Metla) (Finnish Forest Research Institute): Jokiniemenkuja 1, POB 18, 01301 Vantaa; tel. (10) 2111; fax (10) 2112101; e-mail info@metla.fi; internet www.metla.fi; f. 1917; maintains 9 research units; library of 45,000 vols; Dir-Gen. HANNU RAITIO; publs *Metla Bulletin* (online), *Metsätieteellinen aikakauskirja* (4 a year), *Metsätieteen aikakauskirja*, *Silva Fennica* (4 a year), *Working Papers of Metla* (online).

BIBLIOGRAPHY, LIBRARY SCIENCE AND MUSEOLOGY

Museovirasto (National Board of Antiquities): POB 913, 00101 Helsinki; tel. (9) 40501; fax (9) 40509300; internet www.nba.fi; f. 1884; directs and supervises Finland's admin. of antiquities, researches its cultural heritage, preserves artefacts, buildings and sites of cultural and historical value; maintains the Nat. Museum and other museums; library of 180,000 vols with the Finnish Antiquarian Soc.; Dir-Gen. JUHANI KOSTET; Chief Librarian TUIJA SIIMES.

ECONOMICS, LAW AND POLITICS

Elinkeinoelämän Tutkimuslaitos (ETLA) (Research Institute of the Finnish Economy): Lönnrotinkatu 4B, 00120 Helsinki; tel. (9) 609900; fax (9) 601753; e-mail info@etla.fi; internet www.etla.fi; f. 1946; research in economics, business economics and social policy; Man. Dir Dr SIXTEN KORKMAN.

LTT Tutkimus (LTT Research Ltd): Unioninkatu 18, 00130 Helsinki; tel. (9) 43138570; fax (9) 408417; e-mail ltt@hse.fi; internet www.ltt.fi; Chief Exec. TONI RIIPINEN; Dir MIKKO VALTAKARI.

Tilastokeskus (Statistics Finland): 00022 Statistics Finland; tel. (9) 17341; fax (9) 17342279; e-mail kirjaamo@stat.fi; internet www.stat.fi; f. 1865; library: see Libraries and Archives; Dir-Gen. HELI JESKANEN-SUNDSTRÖM; publs *Bulletin of Statistics* (4 a year), *Official Statistics of Finland* (statistical

publs on 26 subjects), *Statistical Yearbook of Finland* (1 a year).

EDUCATION

Suomen Kasvatustieteellinen Seura/Samfundet för Pedagogisk Forskning (Finnish Educational Research Association): Jyväskylän yliopisto/OKL, Seminaarinkatu 15, 40100 Jyväskylä; e-mail kt.paivat@oulu.fi; internet www.kasvatus.net; f. 1967; 245 mems; publ. *Kasvatus*.

MEDICINE

Minerva Foundation Institute for Medical Research: Biomedicum Helsinki, Haartmaninkatu 8, 00290 Helsinki; tel. (9) 4770040; fax (9) 47700425; e-mail dan.lindholm@helsinki.fi; internet www.helsinki.fi/minerva; f. 1959; non-profit organization owned by Minerva Foundation; basic and experimental biomedical, genetic and nutritional research; library of 4,000 vols; Chair. Prof. JIM SCHRÖDER; Head of Inst. Prof. DAN LINDHOLM.

NATURAL SCIENCES

Physical Sciences

Geodeettinen Laitos/Geodetiska institutet (Finnish Geodetic Institute): POB 15, 02431 Masala; tel. (9) 295550; fax (9) 29555200; e-mail kirjasto@fgi.fi; internet www.fgi.fi; f. 1918; 45 mems; library of 23,000 vols; Dir Prof. Dr RISTO KUITTINEN; publs *Suomen geodeettisen laitoksen julkaisuja* (Publications of the Finnish Geodetic Institute), *Suomen geodeettisen laitoksen tiedonantoja* (Reports of the Finnish Geodetic Institute), *Tiedote*.

Geologian Tutkimuskeskus/Geologiska Forskningscentralen (Geological Survey of Finland): POB 96, 02151 Espoo; Betonimiehenkuja 4, 02151 Espoo; tel. 2055011; fax 2055012; e-mail gtk@gtk.fi; internet www.gtk.fi; f. 1885; library of 152,000 vols; Dir-Gen. Dr ELIAS EKDAHL.

Ilmatieteen laitos/Meteorologiska institutet (Finnish Meteorological Institute): POB 503, Erik Palménin aukio 1, 00101 Helsinki; tel. (9) 19291; fax (9) 179581; internet www.fmi.fi; f. 1838; library of 37,000 vols; 10,000 offprints; Pres. Dr PEKKA PLATHAN; publ. *Suomen meteorologinen vuosikirja* (Meteorological Yearbook of Finland, in Finnish and English).

Merentutkimuslaitos (Finnish Institute of Marine Research): Erik Palmenin aukio 1, 00560 Helsinki; tel. (9) 613941; fax (9) 3236728; e-mail info@fimr.fi; internet www.fimr.fi; f. 1918; physical, chemical and biological oceanography, polar studies, Baltic Sea research; library of 55,000 vols; Dir-Gen. Prof. EEVA-LIISA POUTANEN (acting); publs *Contributions* (dissertations), *Meri* (report series).

Säteilyturvakeskus (STUK)/Strålsäkerhetscentralen (Radiation and Nuclear Safety Authority): POB 14, 00881 Helsinki; tel. (9) 759881; fax (9) 75988500; e-mail palaute@stuk.fi; internet www.stuk.fi; f. 1958; govt authority for radiation protection and nuclear safety, incl. inspection and research in the field; library of 30,000 vols; Dir-Gen. Prof. JUKKA LAAKSONEN; publs *Alara* (4 a year), *STUK-A Reports* (irregular).

RELIGION, SOCIOLOGY AND ANTHROPOLOGY

Donnerska institutet för religionshistorisk- och kulturhistoriskforskning/Steinerbiblioteket (Donner Institute for Research in Religious and Cultural History/Steiner Memorial Library): POB 70, Biskopsgatan 13, 20501 Åbo; tel. (2) 2154313; fax (2)

2311290; e-mail donner.institute@abo.fi; internet www.abo.fi/instut/di; f. 1959 to promote research in comparative religion; organizes Nordic conference on comparative religion every three years; library of 80,000 vols; Chair. Prof. NILS G. HOLM; Sec. Dr TORE AHLBÄCK; publ. *Scripta Instituti Donneriani Aboensis* (conference papers, 5 a year).

TECHNOLOGY

VTT Technical Research Centre of Finland: Vuorimiehentie 5, POB 1000, 02044 VTT Espoo; tel. (20) 722111; fax (20) 7227001; e-mail kirjaamo@vtt.fi; internet www.vtt.fi; f. 1942; provides research, development, testing and information services to the public sector, companies and int. orgs; technological focus areas are applied materials, biotechnology and chemistry processes, energy, information and communication technologies, industrial systems management, microtechnologies and electronics, and technology in the community; Chair. (vacant); publs *VTT Review, VTT Symposium, VTT Tiedotteita—Research Notes* (technology magazine), *VTT Impulse* (technology magazine).

Libraries and Archives

Aalto

Aalto University Library, Töölö: Mechelininkatu 3 D E, 00076 Aalto; tel. (9) 43138425; fax (9) 43138539; e-mail library@hse.fi; internet lib.hse.fi; f. 1911; 80,000 vols, several online databases; Chief Librarian Dr EEVA-LIISA LEHTONEN.

Aalto-yliopiston kirjasto, Otaniemi (Aalto University Library, Otaniemi): POB 17000, 00076 Aalto; Otaniementie 9, Espoo; tel. (9) 47024112; fax (9) 47024132; e-mail infolib@tkk.fi; internet lib.tkk.fi; f. 1849; nat. resource library for technology; 1m. vols, 5,000 periodicals on engineering and allied sciences, mathematics, environmental sciences, architecture, urban planning and industrial economy; online databases: index to Finnish technical periodical articles, Masters' theses in engineering and architecture, TKK Research Register, TKK Publs Register, TKK Expert Register; Dir Lic. Tech. ARI MUHONEN.

Åbo

Åbo Akademis Bibliotek (Åbo Akademi University Library): Domkyrkogatan 2–4, 20500 Åbo; tel. (2) 21531; fax (2) 2154795; e-mail anders.ekberg@abo.fi; internet www.abo.fi/library; f. 1918; 2m. vols (excluding pamphlets and MSS); Chief Librarian Dr PIA SÖDERGÅRD; publ. *Skrifter utgivna av Åbo Akademi bibliotek*.

Espoo

Espoon kaupunginkirjasto/maakuntakirjasto (Espoo City Library/Regional Central Library): Vanha maantie 11, 02600 Espoo; tel. (9) 517022; fax (9) 513036; f. 1869; 1m. vols; spec. collns Uusimaa-Nylandica (provincial colln), Norwegian colln; 14 br. libraries, 2 in hospitals and instns, 2 mobile units; Chief Librarian ULLA PACKALÉN.

Helsinki

Eduskunnan kirjasto (Library of Parliament): Aurorankatu 6, 00102 Helsinki; tel. (9) 4323423; fax (9) 4323495; e-mail library@parliament.fi; internet www.parliament.fi/library; f. 1872; 500,000 vols on parliamentary information, legal information, social and political information, admin.; the library is open to the public; reference and archival services, information service, interlibrary loans service, e-services, electronic resources, the Finnish parliamentary glossary, archive of parliament, parliamentary photographic archive, information management training; Dir SARI PAJULA; publs *Bibliographia Iuridica Fennica 1982–1993, Eduskunnan kirjaston tutkimuksia ja selvityksiä* (Library of Parliament Studies and Reports), *Valtion virallisjulkaisut* (Govt Publs in Finland, 1961–1996).

Helsingin Kaupunginkirjasto (Helsinki City Library): POB 4100, 0099 Helsinki; Rautatieläisenkatu 8, 00520 Helsinki; tel. (9) 3108511; fax (9) 31085517; e-mail city.library@hel.fi; internet www.lib.hel.fi; f. 1860; 35 br. libraries, 2 mobile libraries; total 1.9m. vols (1.3m. Finnish, 157,397 Swedish, 191,416 foreign), 208,961 sound recordings, 1,035 newspaper and journal titles; Dir MAIJA BERNDTSON.

Helsingin Yliopiston Kirjasto (Helsinki University Library): POB 53 (Fabianinkatu 32), 00014 University of Helsinki; tel. (9) 19123955; fax (9) 19122700; e-mail library@helsinki.fi; internet www.helsinki.fi/library; 4 brs: City Centre campus, Kumpula campus, Viikki campus, Meilahti campus Library Terkko; 2.3m. vols, 17,000 e-journals; University Librarian KAISA SINIKARA.

Helsingin Yliopiston Kirjasto, Slaavilainen Kirjasto (Helsinki University Library, Slavonic Library): POB 15 (Unioninkatu 36), 00014 University of Helsinki; tel. (9) 19123196; fax (9) 19124067; e-mail hyk-slav@helsinki.fi; internet www.lib.helsinki.fi/hyk/hul; the library held a legal deposit right to all publications printed in Russia from 1828–1917; now acquires available literature in arts and humanities in Slavonic languages; 400,000 vols; Librarian JARMO SUONSYRJÄ.

Kansallisarkisto (National Archives of Finland): POB 258, 00171 Helsinki; tel. (9) 228521; fax (9) 176302; e-mail kansallisarkisto@narc.fi; internet www.arkisto.fi; f. 1869; 87,203 vols, 105,772 m of shelvable archival material, 985,908 cartographical items, 26,474 reels of reading copies, 226,157 microfiches; central office for public archives; controls seven Provincial Archives at Turku, Hämeenlinna, Mikkeli, Vaasa, Oulu, Jyväskylä and Joensuu; holds historical documents and archives of the Govt, Supreme Court and other court records, and private papers of statesmen and politicians; the Provincial Archives contain documents relating to regional and local admin.; Dir-Gen. Dr JUSSI NUORTEVA.

Attached Archive:

> **Helsingin Kaupunginarkisto** (Helsinki City Archives): 53 Eläintarhantie, 3rd Fl., 00530 Helsinki; internet www.hel.fi/tietokeskus; f. 1945; central archive repository for City Admin.; private archives; Dir EEVA MIETTINEN.

Kansalliskirjasto (National Library of Finland): POB 15 (Unioninkatu 36), 00014 University of Helsinki; tel. (9) 19122709; fax (9) 19122719; e-mail kk-palvelu@helsinki.fi; internet www.nationallibrary.fi; f. 1640 in Turku (Åbo), moved to Helsinki 1828; nat. library of Finland and research library of arts and humanities; comprehensive colln of books printed in Finland, large foreign colln, incl. the Slavonic library and the American resource center; Nordenskiöld colln (cartography), Finnish historical newspaper library, spec. collns; web archive, nat. electronic library; 3m. vols, 670,000 MSS, and 410 incunabula, 108,000 m of shelving; Dir Prof. KAI EKHOLM; publ. *The National Library of Finland Bulletin*.

Sibelius-Akatemian Kirjasto/Sibelius-Akademins bibliotek (Sibelius Academy Library): POB 86, 00251 Helsinki; Töölönkatu 28, 00260 Helsinki; tel. (40) 7104224; e-mail sibakirjasto@siba.fi; internet lib.siba.fi/eng; f. 1882; 73,300 scores, 34,000 records, 18,800 books, 186 periodicals, 1020 video cassettes; Head Librarian IRMELI KOSKIMIES.

Sota-arkisto (Military Archives): POB 54, 00581 Helsinki; Työpajankatu 6A, 00580 Helsinki; tel. (9) 18126544; fax (9) 18126505; e-mail sark@sota-arkisto.fi; internet www.sota-arkisto.fi; f. 1918; central archive repository of the Defence Forces; Dir JAANA KILKKI.

Suomalaisen Kirjallisuuden Seuran Kirjasto (Library of the Finnish Literature Society): Hallituskatu 1, POB 259, 00171 Helsinki; tel. 201131272; fax (9) 13123220; e-mail kirjasto@finlit.fi; internet www.finlit.fi; f. 1831; 235,000 vols on folklore, ethnology, cultural anthropology and Finnish literature; Chief Librarian Dr Phil. CECILIA AF FORSELLES.

Attached Libraries:

> **Suomalaisen Kirjallisuuden Seuran Kansanrunousarkisto** (Folklore Archives of the Finnish Literature Society): Hallituskatu 1, POB 259, 00171 Helsinki; fax (9) 13123220; e-mail kansanrunousarkisto@finlit.fi; internet www.finlit.fi; f. 1934; 600 shelf m of MSS, audio recordings, video cassettes and photographs on Finnish folklore and oral history; Dir LAURI HARVILAHTI.

> **Suomalaisen Kirjallisuuden Seuran Kirjallisuusarkisto** (Literary Archives of the Finnish Literature Society): Hallituskatu 1, POB 259, 00171 Helsinki; tel. (201) 131260; fax (9) 13123268; e-mail kirjallisuusarkisto@finlit.fi; internet www.finlit.fi; f. 1831; 1,300 shelf m of MSS, correspondence, recordings and photographs on Finnish literature, history and language; Chief Archivist ULLA-MAIJA PELTONEN.

Hanken Svenska Handelshögskolans Bibliotek (Library of the Swedish School of Economics): Arkadiagatan 22, POB 479, 00101 Helsinki; tel. (40) 3521265; fax (9) 43133425; e-mail lanedisk@hanken.fi; internet www.hanken.fi/library; f. 1909; 100,000 vols; Library Dir TUA HINDERSSON-SÖDERHOLM.

Svenska litteratursällskapet i Finland Folkkultursarkivet (Folk Culture Archives): Riddaregatan 5, 00170 Helsinki; tel. (9) 618777; fax (9) 61877477; e-mail info@sls.fi; internet www.sls.fi; f. 1937; 2,200 collns, 300,000 photographs; publs *Folklivsstudier, Meddelanden från Folkkultursarkivet, Källan.*

Tilastokirjasto (Library of Statistics): POB 2B, Statistics Finland, 00022 Helsinki; Työpajankatu 13B, 2nd Fl., Helsinki; tel. (9) 17342220; fax (9) 17342279; e-mail library@stat.fi; internet www.stat.fi/library; f. 1865; 330,000 vols, 2,790 periodicals, 35,000 microfiches, 726 electronic publs; Head, Information Services MARJA HIRVIKALLIO, SARI PALÉN.

Joensuu

Joensuun seutukirjasto–Pohjois-Karjalan maakuntakirjasto (Joensuu Regional Library–Central Library of North Karelia): POB 114, Koskikatu 25, 80101 Joensuu; tel. (50) 3020563; fax (13) 2676210; e-mail kirjasto@jns.fi; internet seutukirjasto.jns.fi; f. 1862; spec. colln of N Karelia; 500,000 vols; Dir of Libraries REBEKKA PILPPULA.

Joensuun yliopiston kirjasto (Joensuu University Library): Yliopistokatu 4, POB 107, 80100 Joensuu; tel. (13) 2512690; fax

(13) 2512691; e-mail joyk@joensuu.fi; internet www.joensuu.fi/library/english; f. 1970 to become the Univ. of E Finland Library in 2010 by merger of Joensuu Campus Library, Kuopio Campus Library, Savonlinna Campus Library; deposit library; European Documentation Centre; 800,000 vols, 9,000 electronic journals; spec. colln on Kalevala; Library Dir JARMO SAARTI.

Jokioinen

MTT (Maa- ja elintarviketalouden tutkimuskeskus) kirjasto (MTT Agrifood Research Finland Library): 31600 Jokioinen; tel. (3) 41881; fax (3) 41882339; e-mail kirjasto@mtt.fi; internet www.mtt.fi; f. 1935; 80,000 vols, 600 periodicals; Information Specialist SIRPA SUONPÄÄ.

Jyväskylä

Jyväskylän Yliopiston Kirjasto (Jyväskylä University Library): POB 35 (Seminaarinkatu 15), 40014 Jyväskylä Univ.; tel. (14) 2601211; fax (14) 2603371; e-mail jyk@library.jyu.fi; internet kirjasto.jyu.fi; f. 1912; deposit library for Finnish prints and audiovisual material; nat. resource library for education, physical education and psychology; 1.7m. vols; Dir Dr PIRJO VATANEN.

Kuopio

Kuopion kaupunginkirjasto–Pohjois-Savon maakuntakirjasto (Kuopio City Library—Northern Savo Regional Library): Maaherrankatu 12, POB 157, 70101 Kuopio; tel. (17) 182111; fax (17) 182340; internet www.kuopio.fi/kirjasto; f. 1872; 700,000 vols; collns: letters of the author Minna Canth, Kuopio Lyceum colln, Iceland colln, North Saivo region colln; Chief Librarian HILKKA KOTILAINEN.

Kuopion yliopiston kirjasto (Kuopio University Library): POB 1627, 70211 Kuopio; tel. 207872001; fax (17) 163410; e-mail kirjasto@uku.fi; internet www.uku.fi/kirjasto; f. 1972; 200,000 vols; Dir JARMO SAARTI.

Oulu

Oulun yliopiston kirjasto (Oulu University Library): POB 7500, 90014 Univ. of Oulu; tel. (8) 5531011; fax (8) 5533572; e-mail kirjasto@oulu.fi; internet www.library.oulu.fi; f. 1959; 1.7m. vols; depository library; European Documentation Centre; spec. collns incl. material concerning N and Arctic research; Library Dir PÄIVI KYTÖMÄKI; publ. *Acta Universitatis Ouluensis*.

Pori

Porin kaupunginkirjasto–Satakunnan maakuntakirjasto (Pori City Library–Satakunta County Library): Gallen-Kallelankatu 12, POB 200, 28101 Pori; tel. (2) 6215800; fax (2) 6332582; e-mail kirjasto@pori.fi; internet www.pori.fi/kirjasto; f. 1858; 623,000 vols; centre of Hungarian literature; Librarian ASKO HURSTI.

Tampere

Tampereen kaupunginkirjasto–Pirkanmaan maakuntakirjasto (Tampere City Library–Pirkanmaa Regional Library): Pirkankatu 2, PL 152, 33101 Tampere; tel. (3) 314614; fax (3) 31464100; e-mail tampereen.kaupunginkirjasto@tt.tampere.fi; internet www.tampere.fi/kirjasto; f. 1861; 1.1m. vols, 300 newspapers, 2,700 periodicals, 120,000 items of audiovisual material, 20,000 microfilms; spec. collns: Poland, Pirkanmaa region; Dir of Libraries TUULA HAAVISTO.

Tampereen teknillisen yliopiston kirjasto (Tampere University of Technology Library): POB 537, 33101 Tampere; Korkeakoulunkatu 10, 33101 Tampere; tel. (3) 31153155; fax (3) 31152907; e-mail kirjasto@tut.fi; internet www.tut.fi/library; f. 1956; 210,000 vols, 500 printed periodicals, 15,500 electronic journals, 122,000 e-books; Planning Officer SOILE HARJALA.

Tampereen yliopistollisen sairaalan lääketieteellinen kirjasto (Medical Library of Tampere University Hospital): Box 2000, 33521 Tampere; fax (3) 2474364; e-mail kirjasto@pshp.fi; internet www.pshp.fi/kirjasto; f. 1962; 70,000 vols, 900 periodicals, 3,000 electronic journals; Librarian MERVI AHOLA.

Tampereen yliopiston kirjasto (Tampere University Library): Kalevantie 5, 33014 Tampere Univ.; tel. (358) 401909696; fax (3) 35517493; e-mail kirjasto@uta.fi; internet www.uta.fi/laitokset/kirjasto; f. 1925; 504,130 vols, 339, 771 e-books, 28,516 e-journals; Chief Librarian Dr MIRJA IIVONEN; publ. *Bulletiini*.

Turku

Turun kauppakorkeakoulun kirjasto-tietopalvelu (Turku School of Economics, Library and Information Services): Rehtorinpellonkatu 3, 20500 Turku; tel. (2) 481481; fax (2) 4814640; e-mail kirjasto@tse.fi; internet www.tse.fi/kirjasto; f. 1950; 110,000 vols; Dir ULLA NYGRÉN.

Turun yliopiston Kirjasto (Turku University Library): 20014 Turun yliopisto; tel. (2) 3336177; fax (2) 3335050; e-mail library@utu.fi; internet kirjasto.utu.fi; f. 1922; 2.8m. vols; large colln of old Finnish literature; European Documentation Centre; Chief Librarian ULLA NYGRÉN; publ. *Annales Universitatis Turkuensis*.

Museums and Art Galleries

Helsinki

Designmuseo/Designmuseet (Design Museum): Korkeavuorenkatu 23, 00130 Helsinki; tel. (9) 6220540; fax (9) 62205455; e-mail ebba.brannback@designmuseum.fi; internet www.designmuseum.fi; f. 1873; exhibits of industrial design and handicrafts; library of 10,000 vols; Dir MARIANNE AAV.

Helsingin Kaupunginmuseoon/Helsingfors Stadsmuseum (Helsinki City Museum): Sofiankatu 4, 00170 Helsinki; tel. (9) 31036630; fax (9) 31036664; e-mail kaupunginmuseo@hel.fi; internet www.helsinkicitymuseum.fi; f. 1911; cultural history museum; main exhibition on the history of Helsinki; spec. exhibitions to highlight various features of the city's past; colln of 200,000 objects; documentation and inventory pertaining to different eras; Helsinki landscape paintings and graphics; library of 15,000 vols; photo archive with photographs from 1860s to the present; Dir TIINA MERISALO; publs *Memoria, Narinkka*.

Kiasma–Museum of Contemporary Art: Mannerheiminaukio 2, 00100 Helsinki; tel. (9) 17336501; fax (9) 17336503; e-mail info@kiasma.fi; internet www.kiasma.fi; f. 1990; Finnish and international art since 1960s; Dir BERNDT ARELL.

Luonnontieteellinen Keskusmuseo/Naturhistoriska Centralmuseet (Finnish Museum of Natural History): P. Rautatiekatu 13, POB 17, 00014 University of Helsinki; tel. (9) 1911; fax (9) 1911; e-mail luonnontieteellinenmuseo@helsinki.fi; internet www.fmnh.helsinki.fi/english; Dir J. LOKKI.

Constituent Museums:

Eläinmuseo/Zoologiska Museet (Zoological Museum): P. Rautatiekatu 13, POB 17, 00014 University of Helsinki; tel. (9) 1917430; fax (9) 1917443; e-mail luonnontieteellinenmuseo@helsinki.fi; Dir OLAF BISTRÖM.

Geologian Museo/Geologiska Museet (Geological Museum): Snellmaninkatu 3, POB 11, 00014 University of Helsinki; tel. (9) 19123424; fax (9) 19123466; e-mail luonnontieteellinenmuseo@helsinki.fi; Dir MARTTI LEHTINEN.

Kasvimuseo/Botaniska Museet (Botanical Museum): Unioninkatu 44, POB 7, 00014 University of Helsinki; tel. (9) 19124420; fax (9) 19124456; e-mail luonnontieteellinenmuseo@helsinki.fi; Dir PERTTI UOTILA.

Suomen kansallismuseo/Finlands nationalmuseum (National Museum of Finland): POB 913, 00101 Helsinki; Mannerheimintie 34, 00100 Helsinki; tel. (9) 40501; fax (9) 40509400; e-mail kansallismuseo@nba.fi; internet www.kansallismuseo.fi; f. 1893; archaeology, history, ethnography, ethnology, numismatics; open-air museum at Seurasaari; Cygnaeus Gallery at Kaivopuisto, and several historical bldgs throughout Finland; Dir-Gen. HELENA EDGREN.

Valtion Taidemuseo/Statens Konstmuseum (Finnish National Gallery): Kaivokatu 2, 00100 Helsinki; tel. (9) 173361; fax (9) 17336248; e-mail info@fng.fi; internet www.fng.fi; f. 1887 as the Ateneum, re-organized as the Finnish National Gallery in 1990; comprises Ateneum Art Museum, Museum of Contemporary Art Kiasma, Sinebrychoff Art Museum, Central Art Archives; library of 34,000 vols, 80 periodicals, 13,000 catalogues; Dir-Gen. TUULA ARKIO; Dir, Ateneum Art Museum SOILI SINISALO; Dir, Central Art Archives ULLA VIHANTA; Dir, Kiasma Museum of Contemporary Art TUULA KARJALAINEN; Dir, Sinebrychoff Art Museum ULLA HUHTAMÄKI; Librarian IRMELI ISOMÄKI.

Oulu

Pohjois-Pohjanmaan Museo (Northern Ostrobothnia Museum): PL 26, 90015 Oulun Kaupunki; tel. (8) 55847161; fax (8) 55847199; e-mail ppm@ouka.fi; internet www.ouka.fi/ppm; f. 1896; specializes in historical-ethnological research on northern Ostrobothnia; Dir ILSE JUNTIKKA.

Pori

Satakunta Museo (Satakunta Museum): Hallituskatu 11, 28100 Pori; tel. (2) 6211078; fax (2) 6211061; e-mail satakunnanmuseo@pori.fi; internet www.pori.fi/smu; f. 1888; more than 80,000 archaeological and historical exhibits and more than 220,000 photographs relating to the history of the province of Satakunta; library of 13,115 vols in reference library and 9,228 old books; Dir JUHANI RUOHONEN; publ. *Sarka* (1 a year).

Tampere

Sara Hildénin Taidemuseo (Sara Hildén Art Museum): Särkänniemi, 33230 Tampere; tel. (3) 7143500; e-mail sara.hilden@tampere.fi; internet www.tampere.fi/sarahilden; f. 1979; exhibition centre for the works of the Sara Hildén Foundation collection (Foundation f. 1962 when Sara Hildén donated all her art works to it); modern art, with emphasis on Finnish and foreign art of the 1960s and 1970s; library of 9,000 vols; Dir RIITTA VALORINTA.

Tampereen Museot (Tampere Museums): POB 487, 33101 Tampere; tel. (3) 31466966;

e-mail vapriikki@tampere.fi; internet www .tampere.fi/vapriikki; Dir TOIMI JAATINEN.

Component Museums:

Amurin Työläismuseokortteli (Amuri Museum of Workers' Housing): Satakunnankatu 49, 33210 Tampere; f. 1974; the devt of workers' housing 1880–1970, with authentic buildings; Dir TOIMI JAATINEN.

Hämeen Museo (Häme Museum): POB 487, 33101 Tampere; tel. (3) 31465306; f. 1904; prehistory and folk art of the cultural district of Tampere and the old Häme province.

Turku

Sibeliusmuseum/Sibelius-museo (Sibelius Museum): Biskopsgatan 17, 20500 Turku; tel. (2) 2154494; fax (2) 2518528; e-mail sibeliusmuseum@abo.fi; internet www .sibeliusmuseum.abo.fi; f. 1926; archive and library, instrument colln and an exhibition section; archives and library contain material related to Jean Sibelius and to Finnish music; instrument colln includes 1,800 musical instruments; associated with the musicological research department of Åbo Akademi University; Dir and Curator Dr JOHANNES BRUSILA.

Turun Maakuntamuseo/Åbo Landskapsmuseum (Turku Provincial Museum): POB 286, 20101 Turku; tel. (2) 2620111; fax (2) 2620444; e-mail maakuntamuseo@turku.fi; internet www.turku.fi/museo; f. 1881; consists of the Castle of Turku with the collns of Turku Historical Museum, Luostarinmäki Handicrafts Museum, Pharmacy Museum and the Qwensel House, Kylämäki Village of living history, Turku Biological Museum, furniture, paintings, costumes, textiles, porcelain, glass, silver, copper, firearms, uniforms, weapons, coins and medals, etc.; Dir Dr JUHANI KOSTET; publs *Aboa* (yearbook), *Raportteja* (Studies).

Turun Taidemuseo/Åbo Konstmuseum (Turku Art Museum): Aurakatu 26, 20100 Turku; tel. (2) 2627100; fax (2) 2627090; e-mail info@turuntaidemuseo.fi; internet www.turuntaidemuseo.fi; f. 1891; paintings, sculpture, prints and drawings, mainly of Finnish and Scandinavian art since early 19th century; Pres. ROGER BROO; Dir MAIJA KOSKINEN.

Universities

ÅBO AKADEMI
(Åbo Akademi University)

Domkyrkotorget 3, 20500 Turku

Telephone: (2) 21531
Fax: (2) 2517553
Internet: www.abo.fi

Founded 1918
Language of instruction: Swedish
State control
Academic year: September to May

Chancellor: JARL-THURE ERIKSSON
Rector: JORMA MATTINEN
Vice-Rector: CHRISTINA NYGREN-LANDGÄRDS
Vice-Rector: KAISA SERE
Vice-Rector: MALIN BRÄNNBACK
Head of Admin.: ULLA ACHRÉN
Chief Librarian: PIA SÖDERGÅRD

Number of teachers: 360
Number of students: 7,000

Publications: *Årsberättelse* (Annual Review), *Acta Academiae Aboensis*

DEANS

Faculty of Arts: Prof. ULRIKA WOLF-KNUTS
Faculty of Chemical Engineering: Prof. TAPIO SALMI

Faculty of Economics and Social Sciences: Prof. MARIAM GINMAN
Faculty of Education: Prof. ANNA-LENA ØSTERN
Faculty of Mathematics and Natural Sciences: Prof. J. MATTINEN
Faculty of Social and Caring Sciences: Prof. GUNBORG JAKOBSSON
Faculty of Theology: Prof. I. DAHLBACKA

PROFESSORS

Department of Biosciences:

BONSDORFF, E., Marine Ecology
ERIKSSON, J., Cell Biology
JOHNSON, M., Biochemistry
LINDSTRÖM, K., Ecology and Environmental Biology
SISTONEN, L., Cell and Molecular Biology
SLOTTE, J. P., Biochemistry
TÖRNQUIST, K., Biology
VUORELA, P., Pharmacy

Department of Chemical Engineering:

FARDIM, P., Fibre and Cellulose Technology
FAGERVIK, K., Chemical Engineering
HUPA, M., Inorganic Chemistry
IVASKA, A., Analytical Chemistry
LEWENSTAM, A., Analytical Chemistry
MIKKOLA, J-P, Industrial Chemistry and Reaction Engineering
MURZIN, D., Industrial Chemistry and Reaction Engineering
PELTONEN, J., Papper Coating and Converting
SALMI, T., Industrial Chemistry and Reaction Engineering
SAXÉN, H., Thermal and Flow Engineering
TOIVAKKA, M., Papper Coating and Converting
WÄRNÅ, J., Industrial Chemistry and Reaction Engineering
WESTERLUND, T., Process Design and Systems Engineering
WIKSTRÖM, K., Industrial Management
WILÉN, C.-E., Polymer Technology
WILLFÖR, S., Wood and Paper Chemistry
ZEVENHOVEN, R., Thermal and Flow Engineering

Department of Information Technologies:

BACK, B., Information Systems
BACK, R-J, Computer Science
CARLSSON, C., Information Systems
LILIUS, J., Computer Engineering
PETRE, I., Computer Science
PORRES PALTOR, I., Computer Engineering
SERE, K., Computer Science
TOIVONEN, H., Computer Engineering
WALDEN, P., Information Systems
WESTERHOLM, J., Computer Engineering

Department of Natural Sciences:

CORANDER, J., Mathematics and Statistics
EHLERS, C., Geology and Mineralogy
HÖGNÄS, G., Mathematics
HOTOKKA, M., Physical Chemistry
LEINO, R., Organic Chemistry
LINDBERG, M., Physics
SALMINEN, P., Mathematics
SJÖHOLM, R., Organic Chemistry
STAFFANS, O., Mathematics
ÖSTERBACKA, R., Physics

Department of Law:

HONKA, H., Commercial Law
PIRJATANNIEMI, E., Public International Law
SUKSI, M., Public Law
WETTERSTEIN, P., Private Law

Department of Political Science:

ANCKAR, C., Political Science
DJUPSUND, G., Political Science
JOAS, M., Public Administration
KARVONEN, L., Political Science

Department of Psychology and Logopedics:

LAINE, M., Psychology

SANDNABBA, K., Psychology
SANTTILA, P., Psychology
TUOMAINEN, J., Logopedics

Department of Social Sciences:

BJÖRKQVIST, K., Developmental Psychology
EKLUND, E., Rural Studies
ERIKSSON, K., Caring Science
FINNÄS, F., Demograhy
HURME, H., Developmental Psychology
JAKOBSSON, G., Social Policy
LINDSTRÖM, U., Caring Science
LAGERSPETZ, M., Sociology
SILIUS, H., Women's Studies
SUNDBACK, P., Sociology

Faculty of Arts:

AHLUND, C., Comparative Literature
ANDERSSON, E., Swedish Language
ÅSTROM, A.-M., Nordic Ethnology
BERGGREN, L., Art History
BRUSILA, J., Musicology
GUSTAFSSON, M., Philosophy
HAAPAMÄKI, S., Swedish Language
LARJAVAARA, M., French Language and Literature
LÖNNQVIST, B., Russian Language and Literature
NIKANNE, U., Finnish Language and Literature
NEUENDORFF, D., German Language
NYNÄS, P., Comparative Religion
RINGBOM, A., Art History
SELL, R., English Language and Literature
VILLSTRAND, N. E., Nordic History
VIRTANEN-ULFHIELM, T., English Language
WOLF-KNUTS, U., Nordic Folklore

Faculty of Education:

BJÖRKQVIST, O., Didactics of Mathematics and Sciences
GRÖNHOLM, M., Didactics of Languages and the Humanities
ITKONEN, T., Special Education
LINDAHL, M., Early Childhood Education
NYGREN-LANDGÄRDS, C., Pedagogics in Sloyd Education
SALO, P., Adult Education
SJÖHOLM, K., Didactics of Languages and the Humanities
ULJENS, N., General Education

Faculty of Theology:

AF HÄLLSTRÖM, G., Dogmatics
DAHLBACKA, I., Church History
KURTÉN, T., Theological Ethics
LAATO, A., Old Testament Exegesis and Jewish Studies
SUNDKVIST, B., Practical Theology
SYREENI, K., New Testament Exegetics

School of Business and Economics:

BRÄNNBACK, M., International Marketing
HASSEL, L., Accounting
JÄNTTI, M., Economics
KRISTENSSON UGGLA, B., Organization and Management
ÖSTERMARK, R., Accounting
REHN, A., Business Administration
TÖRNROOS, J.-Å., Management Science
WIDÉN, G., Information Studies
WILLNER, J., Economics

HELSINGIN KAUPPAKORKEAKOULU
(Helsinki School of Economics)

Runeberginkatu 14–16, 00100 Helsinki

Telephone: (9) 43131
Fax: (9) 43138707
E-mail: tiedotus@hkkk.fi
Internet: www.hse.fi

Founded 1911
State control
Language of instruction: Finnish
Academic year: September to May

Chancellor: AATTO PRIHTI
Rector: EERO KASANEN

Vice-Rectors: OLLI AHTOLA, JYRKI WALLENIUS
Head of Admin.: ESA AHONEN
Librarian: EEVA-LIISA LEHTONEN

Number of teachers: 156
Number of students: 4,170

Publication: *Acta Academiae Oeconomicae Helsingiensis* (Series B, C, D, F, M)

PROFESSORS

AHTOLA, O., Marketing
ANTTILA, M., Marketing
CHARLES, M., Applied Linguistics
ERONEN, J., Economic Geography
HAAPARANTA, P., International Economics
ILMAKUNNAS, P., Industrial and Labour Economics
KALLIO, M., Management Systems
KANGASHARJU, H., Languages and Communication
KANTO, A., Statistics
KASANEN, E., Finance
KELOHARJU, M., Finance
KINNUNEN, J., Financial Accounting
KIVIJÄRVI, H., Information Systems
KORHONEN, P., Management Science
KYLÄKOSKI, K., Management Accounting
LAHTI, A., Entrepreneurship
LEPPINIEMI, J., Finance and Capital Markets
LILJA, K., Business Administration
LOVIO, R., Organization and Management
MIETTINEN, K., Mathematics
MÖLLER, K., Business Economics
NISKAKANGAS, H., Law
POHJOLA, M., Economics
PUTTONEN, V., Finance
RÄSÄNEN, K., Organization and Management
RUDANKO, M., Law
SÄÄKSJÄRVI, M., Business Information Systems
SAARINEN, T., Information Systems
SERISTÖ, H., European Union Affairs
SUOMINEN, M., Finance
TAINIO, R., Business Administration
TOIVANEN, O., Technology Management
TROBERG, P., International Management Accounting
UUSITALO, L., Marketing Communications and Consumer Theory
VÄLIMÄKI, J., Economics
VEPSÄLÄINEN, A., Logistics
VIRTANEN, K., Management Accounting
WALLENIUS, J., Decision Making and Planning

HELSINGIN YLIOPISTO/ HELSINGFORS UNIVERSITET (University of Helsinki)

POB 33 (Yliopistonkatu 4), 00014 Univ. of Helsinki

Telephone: (9) 1911
Fax: (9) 19123008
E-mail: tiedotus@helsinki.fi
Internet: www.helsinki.fi/university

Founded 1640 Turku (Åbo), 1828 Helsinki
Languages of instruction: Finnish, Swedish
State control
Academic year: September to May (2 terms)

Chancellor: Prof. ILKKA NIINILUOTO
Rector: Prof. T. J. K. WILHELMSSON
Vice-Rectors: Prof. J. BJÖRKROTH, Prof. M. LÖYTÖNEN, Prof. H. M. NIEMI, Prof. M. J. TIKKANEN
Dir of Admin.: K. J. SUOKKO
Librarian: K. R. EKHOLM

Number of teachers: 1,694
Number of students: 37,852

DEANS

Faculty of Agriculture and Forestry: Prof. J. T. S. KOLA
Faculty of Arts: Prof. A. A. NENOLA
Faculty of Behavioural Sciences: Prof. J. J. HAUTAMÄKI

Faculty of Biosciences: Prof. J. K. NIEMELÄ
Faculty of Law: Prof. J. K. KEKKONEN
Faculty of Medicine: Assoc. Prof. M. J. TIKKANEN
Faculty of Pharmacy: Prof. R. V. K. HILTUNEN
Faculty of Science: Prof. H. S. S. SAARINEN
Faculty of Social Sciences: Prof. H. O. NIEMI
Faculty of Theology: Prof. A. M. LAUHA
Faculty of Veterinary Medicine: Prof. H. SALONIEMI

PROFESSORS

Faculty of Agriculture and Forestry (POB 62 (Viikinkaari 11), 00014 Univ. of Helsinki; tel. (9) 19158247; fax (9) 19158575; e-mail mmtdk-international@helsinki.fi; internet www.honeybee.helsinki.fi):

AHOKAS, J. M., Agricultural Engineering
ALATOSSAVA, J. T., Dairy Technology
DAHLIN, S. B., Logistics
HARI, P. K. J., Forest Ecology
HARTIKAINEN, H. H., Soil and Environment Chemistry
HATAKKA, A., Environmental Biotechnology
HEINONEN, I. M., Functional Food
HELENIUS, J. P., Agroecology
HELIÖVAARA, K. T., Forest Zoology
HOKKANEN, H. M. T., Agricultural Zoology
HYVÖNEN, L. E. T., Food Technology
HYVÖNEN, S. M., Marketing
JAAKKOLA, A. O., Agricultural Chemistry and Physics
JUSLIN, H. J., Forest Products Marketing
KANGAS, A., Forest Mensuration and Management
KOLA, J. T. S., Agricultural Politics
KOSKELA, M. O., Food Economics
KUULUVAINEN, J. T. M., Social Economics of Forestry
LAASASENAHO, J. E., Forest Mensuration and Management
LUUKKANEN, M. O., Silviculture in Developing Countries
MAKAROW, M. T., Applied Biochemistry
MÄKELÄ, P. S. A., Crop Production
MÄKINEN, V.-P. J., Agricultural Entrepreneurship
MIKKONEN, E. U. A., Logging and Utilization of Forest Products
MUTANEN, M. L., Nutrition Physiology
NÄSI, J. M., Animal Nutrition
OJALA, M. J., Animal Breeding
OLLIKAINEN, M. M. O., Environmental Economics
PEHKONEN, A. I., Agricultural Engineering
PIIRONEN, V. I., Food Chemistry
PUOLANNE, T. E. J., Meat Technology
PUTTONEN, P. K., Silviculture
RÄSÄNEN, L. K., Nutrition
SALKINOSA-SALONEN, M. S., Microbiology
SALOVAARA, H. O., Cereal Technology
SARIS, P.-E. J., Food Microbiology
SIPI, M. H., Forest Technology
SJÖBERG, A.-M. K., Technology of Households and Institutions
SUMELIUS, J. H., Agricultural Economics
TEERI, T. H., Plant Production
TENKANEN, T. M., Chemistry of Bioproduction
TERVO, M. J., Forest Product Marketing
TOKOLA, T. E., Geoinformatics
TUORILA, H. M., Food Technology
VALKONEN, P. T., Plant Pathology
VALSTA, L., Business Economics of Forestry
VANHATALO, A. O., Animal Science
WESTERMARCK, H. E., Extension Education
WESTMAN, C. J. V., Forest Soil Science
YLÄTALO, E. M. O., Agricultural Economics

Faculty of Arts (POB 3 (Fabianinkatu 33), 00014 Univ. of Helsinki; fax (9) 19123100; internet www.hum.helsinki.fi):

APO, S.-K., Folklore
BACON, G. H. A., Film and Television Research

BREUER, U. M., German Philology
CARLSON, L. H., Language Theory and Translation
CHESTERMAN, A. P. C., Multilingual Communication
CLARK, P. A., Urban History
GOTHONI, R. R., Study of Religions
HAAPALA, A. K., Aesthetics
HAKULINEN, A. T., Finnish Language
HÄMEEN-ANTTILA, J. M., Arabic Language and Islamic Research
HÄRMÄ, J., Romance Philology
HARVIAINEN, J. M. T., Semitic Languages
HELKKULA, M., French Language
HENRIKSSON, M. J., American Studies
HIETARANTA, P. S., English Language
HURSKAINEN, A. J., African Languages and Cultures
HYVÄRINEN, I. K., German Philology
JANHUNEN, J.-A., East Asian Languages and Cultures
KALLIOKOSKI, J. T., Finnish Language
KARLSSON, F. G., General Linguistics
KONTTINEN, K. P. R., Art History
KORHONEN, J. A., German Philology
KOSKENNIEMI, K. M., Computer Linguistics
KOSKI, P. K. M., Theatre Science and Drama Literature
KOURI, E. I., General History
KULONEN, U.-M., Finno-Ugrian Philology
LAITINEN, L. M., Finnish Language
LARJAVAARA, M. E. T., Finnish Philology
LAVENTO, M. T., Archaeology
LEHTINEN, A. T., Finnish Philology
LEHTONEN, J. U. E., Finno-Ugrian Ethnology
LEINO, P. A., Finnish Language
LINDSTEDT, J. S., Slavonic Philology
LYYTIKÄINEN, P. R., Finnish Literature
MAZZARELLA, S. M., Scandinavian Literature
MEINANDER, C. H., History
MUSTAJOKI, A. S., Russian Language and Literature
NENOLA, A. A., Women's Studies
NEVALAINEN, T. T. A., English Philology
NIINILUOTO, I. M. O., Theoretical Philosophy
NIKULA, R. K., Arts History
NUMMI, J. T., Finnish Literature
ÖSTMAN, J.-O. I., English Philology
PARPOLA, S. K. A., Assyriology
PEKKILÄ, E. O., Musicology
PESONEN, P. J., Russian Literature
PETTERSSON, B. J. O., American Literature
PLATO, J. VON, Philosophy
PYRHÖNEN, H. M., General Literature and Aesthetics
RAUD, R., Japanese Languages and Culture
RIIHO, T. T., Iberian Languages and Romanian
RIIKONEN, H. K., General Literature
SAARI, M. H., Scandinavian Languages
SAARINEN, H. K., General History
SALOMIES, O. I., Latin Language and Roman Literature
SANDU, N.-G., Theoretical Philosophy
SIIKALA, A. A.-L., Folklore
SILTALA, J. H., Finnish History
SUOMELA-HÄRMÄ, M. E., Italian Philology
TAAVITSAINEN, I. A. J., English Philology
TARASTI, E. A. P., Musicology
VEHMAS-LEHTO, R. L. I., Russian Language
VENTOLA, E. M., English Philology
VIHAVAINEN, T. J., Russian Studies

Faculty of Behavioural Sciences (POB 9 (Siltavuorenpenger 20R), 00014 Univ. of Helsinki; tel. (9) 1911; fax (9) 19120616; e-mail kaytt-tdk@helsinki; internet www.helsinki.fi/behav):

ÅHLBERG, M. A., Biology Pedagogics
ALHO, K. A., Psychology
BUCHBERGER, A.-I. V., Pedagogics of Mother Tongue Teaching

ENGESTRÖM, Y. H. M., Adult Education
HAUTAMÄKI, J. J., Special Pedagogics
HYTÖNEN, J. M. K., Pedagogics
IIVONEN, A. K., Phonetics
KALLIONIEMI, A. J. V., Theological Pedagogy
KAUKINEN, L. K., Crafts
KELTIKANGAS-JÄRVINEN, A.-L., Applied Psychology
KLIPPI, A. M. K., Logopaedics
KRAUSE, M. C., Cognitive Science
KROKFORS, L. M., Pedagogics
LAVONEN, J. M. J., Pedagogy of Physics and Chemistry
NIEMI, H. M., Pedagogics
NYMAN, G. S., Psychology
OJALA, M. O., Pre-school and Early Childhood Education
PEHKONEN, E. K., Pedagogy of Mathematics and Computer Science
SCHEININ, P. M., Pedagogics
SIMOLA, H. J., Pedagogics
SUMMALA, K. H. I., Psychology
TANI, S. H., Pedagogy of Geography and the Environment
TELLA, S. K., Pedagogics
TUOMI-GRÖHN, T. T., Home Economics
TURKKI, K. M., Home Economics
UUSIKYLÄ, K. T., Pedagogics
VIRKKUNEN, R. J. T., Developmental Work Research
VIRSU, V. V. E., Neuropsychology
VUORINEN, R. H. E., Applied Psychology

Faculty of Biosciences (POB 56 (Viikinkaari 9), 00014 Univ. of Helsinki; tel. (9) 1911; fax (9) 19157561; e-mail bio-sci@helsinki.fi; internet www.helsinki.fi/bio):

BAMFORD, D. H., General Microbiology
DONNER, K. K., Zoology
ELORANTA, P. V., Limnology
GAHMBERG, C.-G., Biochemistry
HÄNNINEN, H. J. P., Zoology
HANSKI, I. A., Morphology and Ecology
HOLM, L. U. T., Bioinformatics
HYVÖNEN, J. T., Botany
KAILA, K. K., Physiological Zoology
KAIRESALO, T. A., Freshwater Ecology
KANGASJÄRVI, J. S., Plant Biology
KAUPPI, P. E., Environmental Protection
KEINÄNEN, K. P., Molecular Biology
KOKKO, H. M., Veterinary Ecology
KORHOLA, A. A., Arctic Global Change
KORHONEN, T. K., General Microbiology
KUIKKA, O. S., Fisheries Biology
KUOSA, H. J., Baltic Sea Research
KUPARINEN, J. S., Marine Biology
LEHTONEN, H. V. T., Fisheries Science
MERILÄ, J. K. K., Population Biology
NIEMELÄ, J. K., Urban Ecology
PALVA, E. T., Genetics
RANTA, E. J., Zoology
RIKKINEN, J. K., Zoology
ROMANTSCHUK, M. L., Environmental Biotechnology
SCHRÖDER, J. P., Genetics
STRÖMMER, R. H., Soil Ecology
SUNDSTRÖM, L. B., Evolution Biology
VIHKO, P., Biochemistry
VOIPIO, J. T. I., Electrophysiology

Faculty of Law (POB 4 (Yliopistonkatu 5), 00014 Univ. of Helsinki; tel. (9) 1911; fax (9) 19122152; internet www.helsinki.fi/oik/tdk):

AUREJÄRVI, E. I., Civil Law
FRÄNDE, D. G., Criminal Law and Judicial Procedure
HALILA, H. J., Sports Law
HAVANSI, E. E. T., Judicial Procedure
HEIMONEN, M. O., Economics
HEMMO, M. A., Insurance and Tort Law
HOLLO, E. J., Environmental Law
KALIMA, K.-E. K., Financial Law
KANGAS, U. P. A., Civil Law
KEKKONEN, J. T., Judicial History and Roman Law
KONSTARI, T. T., Administrative Law

KOSKENNIEMI, M. A., International Law
KOSKINEN, P. T., Criminal Law
LAHTI, R. O. K., Criminal Law
LAPPALAINEN, J. A., Judicial Procedure
MAJAMAA, V. V., Environmental Law
MÄENPÄÄ, O. I., Administrative Law
MAJANEN, M. I., Criminal Law
MIKKOLA, M. L. A., Labour Law
RISSANEN, K. K., Commercial Law
RYYNÄNEN, O. J., Public Law
SISULA-TULOKAS, L. M., Civil Law
TEPORA, J. K., Civil Law
TIITINEN, K.-P., Labour Law
TIKKA, K. S., Financial Law
TUORI, K. H., Administrative Law
WILHELMSSON, T. K. J., Private and Commercial Law

Faculty of Medicine (POB 20 (Tukholmankatu 8), 00014 Univ. of Helsinki; tel. (9) 1911; fax (9) 19126629; e-mail med-studentaffairs@helsinki.fi; internet www.med.helsinki.fi):

ALALUUSUA, A. S. K., Dentistry
ALMQVIST, S. F., Child Psychiatry
ANDERSSON, L. C. L., Pathological Anatomy
BROMMELS, M. H., Health Care Administration
HAAHTELA, T. M. K., Clinical Allergology
HARJULA, A. L. J., Surgery
HÄYRY, P. J., Transplantation Surgery and Immunology
HERNESNIEMI, J. A., Neurosurgery
HIETANEN, J. H. P., Dentistry
HÖCKERSTEDT, K. A. V., Surgery
HOLMBERG, P. E., Physics
HUUSKONEN, M. S., Occupational Health
IKONEN, E. M., Cell and Tissue Biology
JÄNNE, O. A., Physiology
JOENSUU, H. T., Radiotherapy and Oncology
KALIMO, H. O., Applied Neuropathology
KALSO, E. A., Internal Medicine
KAPRIO, J. A., Public Health Service
KARLSSON, H. E., Psychiatry
KARMA, P. H., Otorhinolaryngology
KARPPANEN, H. O., Pharmacology
KARVONEN, J. M., Applied Dermatology and Venereology
KASTE, K. A. M., Neurology
KEKKI, P. V., General Practice and Primary Health Care
KESKI-OJA, J. K., Cell Biology
KINNULA, V. L., Pulmonary Medicine
KINNUNEN, P. K. J., Chemistry
KIVILAAKSO, E. O., Surgery
KIVISAARI, M. L., Diagnostic Radiology
KLOCKARS, M. L. G., General Practice
KNIP, J. M., Paediatrics
KÖNÖNEN, M. H. O., Stomatognatic Physiology and Prosthetic Dentistry
KONTTINEN, Y. T., Oral Medicine
KONTULA, K. K., Molecular Medicine
KORPI, E. R., Pharmacology
KORTTILA, K. T., Anaesthesiology and Intensive Care
LAHELMA, E. T., Public Health Science
LAITINEN, L. A. I., Tuberculosis and Pulmonary Medicine
LEHTO, V. P., Pathological Anatomy
LEIRISALO-REPO, T. K. M., Rheumatology
LEPÄNTALO, M. J. A., Vascular Surgery
LINDQVIST, J. C., Oral and Maxillofacial Surgery
LÖNNQVIST, J. K., Psychiatry
MÄKELÄ, T. P., Biochemistry and Cell Biology
MAURY, C. P. J., Internal Medicine
MERI, S. K., Immunology
MEURMAN, J. H., Dentistry
MURTOMAA, H. T., Oral Public Health
NEUVONEN, P. J., Clinical Pharmacology
NIEMINEN, M. S., Cardiology
NILSSON, C.-G. D., Obstetrics and Gynaecology
PAAKKARI, A. T. I., Pharmacology

PAAVONEN, J. A., Obstetrics and Gynaecology
PANULA, P. A. J., Biomedicine
PELTOLA, H. O., Infectious Diseases
PELTOMÄKI, P. T., Medical Genetics
PELTONEN-PALOTIE, L. P. M., Medical Genetics
PERTOVAARA, A. Y., Physiology
RANKI, P. A., Dermatology and Venereology
REPO, H., Internal Medicine
RINTALA, R. J., Child Surgery
ROSENBERG, P. H., Anaesthesiology
RUUTU, M. L., Urology
SAJANTILA, A. J., Genetic Forensic Medicine
SALASPURO, M. P. J., Alcohol and Narcotics Medicine
SANTAVIRTA, S. S., Orthopaedics and Traumatology
SARNA, S. J., Biometry
SIIMES, M. A., Paediatrics
SINTONEN, H. P., Health Economics
SKURNIK, M., Bacteriology
SOVIJÄRVI, A. R. A., Clinical Physiology
STENMAN, U.-H. E., Clinical Chemistry
TASKINEN, M.-R., Internal Medicine
TERVO, T. M. T., Applied Ophthalmology
TIKKANEN, M. J., Internal Medicine
TILVIS, R. S., Geriatrics
TUOMILEHTO, J. O. J., Public Health Science
UITTO, V. V.-J., Oral Biology
VIRKKUNEN, M. E., Forensic Psychiatry
VIRTANEN, I. T., Anatomy
VON WENDT, L. O. W., Child Neurology
VUORI, E. O., Forensic Chemistry
WAHLBECK, K. L. R., Psychiatry
YKI-JÄRVINEN, H., Internal Medicine
YLIKORKALA, R. O., Obstetrics and Gynaecology

Faculty of Pharmacy (POB 56 (Viikinkaari 9), 00014 Univ. of Helsinki; tel. (9) 1911; fax (9) 19159138; e-mail ftdk-hallinto@helsinki.fi; internet www.helsinki.fi/farmasia):

AIRAKSINEN, M. S. A., Social Pharmacy
ELO, H. O., Pharmacological Chemistry
HILTUNEN, R. V. K., Pharmacognosy
HIRVONEN, J. T., Pharmaceutical Technology
KOSTIAINEN, R. K., Pharmaceutical Chemistry
MÄNNISTÖ, P. T., Pharmacology and Drug Development
MARVOLA, M. L. A., Biopharmacy
TASKINEN, J. A. A., Pharmaceutical Chemistry
TUOMINEN, R. K., Pharmacology and Toxicology
VUORELA, H. J., Pharmacognosy
YLIRUUSI, J. K., Pharmaceutical Technology

Faculty of Science (POB 44 (Jyrängöntie 2), 00014 Univ. of Helsinki; tel. (9) 19150058; fax (9) 19150039; e-mail sci-info@helsinki.fi; internet www.helsinki.fi/facultyofscience):

AHLGREN, T. J., Physics
AHONEN-MYKA, A. H., Computer Science
ANNILA, A. J., Biophysics
ARJAS, A., Biometry
ASTALA, K. O., Mathematics
BECKMANN, A. H.-T., Geophysics
CHAICHIAN, M., High Energy Physics
ENQVIST, K.-P., Cosmogony
ERONEN, M. J., Geology and Palaeontology
FORTELIUS, H. L. M., Evolution Palaeontology
GYLLENBERG, M. A. G., Applied Mathematics
HALONEN, L. O., Physical Chemistry
HÄMERI, K. J., Aerosol Physics
HÄMÄLÄINEN, K. J., Physics
HOYER, P. G., Elementary Particle Physics
ILLMAN, S. A., Mathematics
KAJANTIE, K. O., Theoretical Physics
KARHU, J. A., Geology and Mineralogy

KASKI, S. J. I., Computer Science
KEINONEN, J., Applied Physics
KILPELÄINEN, I. A., Organic Chemistry
KIVINEN, J. T., Computer Science
KOSKINEN, H. E. J., Space Physics
KOSONEN, M. E., Planning Geography
KOTIAHO, A. A. T., Environmental Chemistry and Analytics
KULMALA, M. T., Physics
KUPIAINEN, A. J., Mathematics
LAHTINEN, O. A., Applied Mathematics
LEPPÄRANTA, M. J., Geophysics
LESKELÄ, M. A., Inorganic Chemistry
LÖYTÖNEN, M. K., Cultural Geography
LUMME, K. A., Astronomy
MARTIO, O. T., Mathematics
MATTILA, P. E. J., Mathematics
MATTILA, V. A. K., Astronomy
MAUNU, S.-L., Polymer Chemistry
MICHELSSON, J. A., Mathematics
NORDLUND, K. H., Aerosol Physics
NUMMELIN, E., Applied Mathematics
OIVANEN, M. T., Organic Chemistry
ORAVA, R. O., Experimental Particle Physics
PAAKKI, J. P., Computer Science
PÄIVÄRINTA, L. J., Applied Mathematics
PELLIKKA, P. K. E., Geoinformatics
PESONEN, L. J., Geophysics
PYYKKÖ, V. P., Chemistry
RAATIKAINEN, K. E. E., Computer Science
RÄISÄNEN, J. A., Physics
RÄMØ, O. T., Geology and Mineralogy
RÄSÄNEN, M. O., Physical Chemistry
RIEKKOLA, M.-L., Analytical Chemistry
RISKA, D.-O. W., Physics
RITALA, M. K., Inorganic Chemistry
SAARIKKO, H. M. T., Physics
SAARINEN, H. S. S., Chemistry
SALONEN, V.-P., Environmental Geology
SAVIJÄRVI, H. I., Meteorology
SEPPÄLÄ, M. K., Computer-applied Mathematics
SEPPÄLÄ, M. K., Geography
SERIMAA, R. E., Physics
SIPPU, S. S., Computer Science
SUOMINEN, J. K., Mathematics
TALMAN, P. K., Geography
TENHU, H. J., Polymer Chemistry
TIKKANEN, M. J., Geography
TIRRI, H. R., Computer Science
TOIVONEN, H. T. T., Computer Science
TOPPILA, O. S., Mathematics
TÖRNROOS, R. F., Geology and Mineralogy
TUKIA, P. P., Mathematics
UKKONEN, E. J., Computer Science
VÄÄNÄNEN, J. A., Mathematics
VERKAMO, A. I., Software Engineering
VESALA, T. V., Meteorology
VIITALA, P. J., Planning Geography
WESTERHOLM, J. O., Geography
WÄHÄLÄ-HASE, K., Organic Chemistry

Faculty of Social Sciences (POB 54 (Unioninkatu 37), 00014 Univ. of Helsinki; tel. (9) 1911; fax (9) 19124835; e-mail soc-sci@helsinki.fi; internet www.valt.helsinki.fi):

ÅBERG, L. E. G., Communication
AIRAKSINEN, T., Practical Philosophy
ALAPURO, R. S., Sociology
ARMSTRONG, K. V., Cultural Anthropology
AULA, P. S., Communication
BLOMBERG-KROLL, H. K., Social Policy
ERÄSAARI, R. O., Social Policy
GYLLING, H. A., Applied Ethics
HAILA, A.-K. E., Social Policy
HAUTAMÄKI, A. A., Social Psychology and Psychology
HÄYRINEN-ALESTALO, M. G., Science and Technology and Research
HELKAMA, K. E., Social Psychology
HENTILÄ, S. J., Political History
HJERPPE, R. T., Economic History
HONKAPOHJA, S. M. S., Economics
HUOTARI, K. H., Social Work
JALLINOJA, R. I., Family Sociology

KANNIAINEN, V. L., Economics
KARISTO, A. O., Social Policy
KARVINEN-NIINIKOSKI, S. M. E., Social Policy
KETTUNEN, P. T., Political History
KIVIKURU, U., Journalism
KOPONEN, M. J., Development Studies
KOSKELA, E. A., Economics
KULTTI, K. K., Economics
LIEBKIND-ORMALA, K. R., Social Psychology
MASSA, J. K., Environmental Politics
MORING, T. A., Communication
NIEMI, H. O., Statistics
NYLUND, M., Social Work
PALOKANGAS, T. K., Economics
PATOMÄKI, H. O., Political Science
PEKONEN, K. J., Political Science
PELTONEN, M. T., Social History
PERÄKYLÄ, A. M., Sociology
PIRTTILÄ-BACKMAN, A.-M., Social Psychology
RISKA, E. K., Sociology
ROOS, J. P., Social Policy
SAIKKONEN, P. J., Statistics
SASSI, S. S., Communication
SATKA, M. E. A., Social Policy
SIIKALA, J. J. T., Sociology
SJÖBLOM, S. M., Municipal Administration
SULKUNEN, P. J., Sociology
SUNDBERG, J. H., Political Science
TARKKONEN, L. J., Statistics
TÖRRÖNEN, L. M., Social Work
TUOMELA, R. H., Practical Philosophy
VÄLIVERRONEN, E. T., Mass Communication
VALKONEN, Y. T., Sociology
VARTIA, Y. O., Economics
VIRTANEN, T. I., Political Science

Faculty of Theology (POB 33 (Aleksanterinkatu 7), 00014 Univ. of Helsinki; tel. (09) 1911; fax (9) 19122106; internet www.helsinki.fi/teol):

AEJMELAEUS, L. J. T., Exegetics
HALLAMAA, J. I., Social Ethics
HEIKKILÄ, M. K. J., Practical Theology
HEININEN, S. K. M., General Church History
HELANDER, E. M., Church Sociology
KNUUTTILA, S. J. I., Theological Ethics and Philosophy of Religion
KOTILA, H. T., Practical Theology
LAUHA, A. M., Church History
PENTIKÄINEN, J. Y., Study of Religions
RÄISÄNEN, H. M., New Testament Exegetics
RUOKANEN, M. M., Doctrinal Theology
SAARINEN, R. T., Ecumenics
SOLLAMO, R. T., Biblical Languages
TIRRI, K. A. H., Theological Pedagogy
TYÖRINOJA, R. J., Systematic Theology
VEIJOLA, T. K., Old Testament Exegetics

Faculty of Veterinary Medicine (POB 66 (Agnes Sjöbergin katu 2), 00014 Univ. of Helsinki; tel. (9) 1911; fax (9) 19157161; internet www.vetmed.helsinki.fi):

ANDERSSON, C. M., Animal Breeding
BJÖRKROTH, K. J., Food Hygiene
HÄNNINEN, M. L., Veterinary Environmental Hygiene
JÄRVINEN, A.-K., Pet Diseases
KATILA, M. T. H., Animal Breeding
KORKEALA, H. J., Food Hygiene
LINDBERG, L.-A., Anatomy
PALVA, A., Veterinary Microbiology
POHJANVIRTA, R. K., Toxicology
PÖSÖ, A. R., Veterinary Physiology
PYÖRÄLÄ, S. H. K., Veterinary Medicine
SALONIEMI, H., Animal Hygiene
SNELLMAN, P. M., Diagnostic Radiology
SPILLMANN, T., Veterinary Internal Medicine
SUKUNA, A. K. K., Veterinary Pathology
TULAMO, R.-M., Veterinary Surgery
VAINIO-KIVINEN, O. M., Pharmacology
VAPAATALO, O. P., Virology

JOENSUUN YLIOPISTO
(University of Joensuu)

POB 111, 80101 Joensuu

Telephone: (13) 251111
Fax: (13) 2512050
E-mail: intnl@joensuu.fi
Internet: www.joensuu.fi

Founded 1969
Languages of instruction: Finnish, English
State control
Academic year: September to May (2 semesters)

Rector: Prof. PERTTU VARTIAINEN
Vice-Rector: Prof. TEUVO POHJOLAINEN
Dir of Admin.: PETRI LINTUNEN
Dir of Communications: KARI HIPPI
Dir of Int. Relations: OUTI SAVONLAHTI
Librarian: HELENA HÄMYNEN
Number of students: 8,500

DEANS

Faculty of Biosciences: RITTA JULKUNEN-TIITTO
Faculty of Education: PERTTI VÄISÄNEN
Faculty of Forestry: SEPPO KELLOMÄKI
Faculty of Humanities: MARKKU FILPPULA
Faculty of Law: MATTI TOLVANEN
Faculty of Science: JUHA ROUVINEN
Faculty of Social Sciences: HARRI SIISKONEN
Faculty of Theology: LAURI THURÉN

PROFESSORS

AHLGREN, M., Chemistry
AHPONEN, PL., Social Sciences
ALHO, J., Statistics
ANTIKAINEN, A., Sociology of Education
ATJONEN, P., Education
AULASKARI, R., Mathematics
BASCHMAKOFF, N., Russian Language
COLPAERT, A., Geography
ENKENBERG, J., Education
ERKAMA, T., Mathematics
FILPPULA, M., English Language
FRÄNTI, P., Computer Science
HAAPASALO, L., Education
HALL, C., German Language
HARSTELA, P., Forest Technology
HEIKKINEN, K., Women's Studies
HIRVONEN, P., English Language
HOLOPAINEN, I., Biology
HOLOPAINEN, L., Special Education
HUSA, J., Constitutional Law
HÄLLSTRÖM, G. AF, Theology
HÄMYNEN, T., History of Finland
JULKUNEN, M.- L., Didactics
JULKUNEN-TIITTO, R., Plant Ecology
JÄÄSKELÄINEN, R., English Language
JÄÄSKELÄINEN, T., Physics
KALASNIEMI, M., Russian Language
KELLOMÄKI, S., Forestry
KETTUNEN, P., Practical Theology
KNUUTTILA, H., Materials Science
KNUUTTILA, S., Folklore
KOLEHMAINEN, O., Statistics
KORPELA, J., General History
KOSKI, L., Sociology
KOTIRANTA, M., Church History
KOUKI, J., Forest Ecology and Biodiversity
KUITTINEN, M., Physics
KUKKONEN, J., Biology
KÄRENLAMPI, P., Wood Technology
KÄRKKÄINEN, M., Wood Utilization and Industry
LAINE, I., Mathematics
LEHTINEN, A., Geography
LINDEN, M., Economics
MANNERKOSKI, H., Forest Soil Science
MARTIKAINEN, E., Systematic Theology
MUIKKU-WERNER, P., Finnish Language
MUSTAKALLIO, H., Church History
MYRSKY, M., Tax Law
MÄÄTTÄ, K., Law and Economics
MÄÄTTÄ, T., Environmental Law

NIEMELÄ, P., Forest Ecology
NIEMI, E.- J., Language
NIEMI, S., Swedish Language
NIIKKO, A., Education
NUUTINEN, P., Education
NYBLOM, J., Statistics
OKSANEN, E., Botany
PAKKANEN, T., Chemistry
PAKKANEN, T., Materials Science
PALANDER, M., Finnish Language
PARKKINEN, J., Computer Science
PEIPONEN, K.-E, Physics
PELKONEN, P., Production of Wood and Peat for Energy
PERHO, H., Psychology
PIIROINEN, P., Practical Theology
POHJOLAINEN, T., Public Law
PUKKALA, T., Forest Management Planning
PYYSIÄANEN, M., Pedagogy of Religion
PÄIVINEN, R., Forestry
RANNIKKO, P., Environmental Policy
RAUMA, A., Home Economics
ROININEN, H., Animal Ecology
ROUVINEN, J., Chemistry
RÄTY, H., Psychology
SAASTAMOINEN, O., Forestry
SABOUR, M., Sociology
SAJAMA, S., Philosophy
SAJANIEMI, J., Statistics
SAVOLAINEN, T., Management and Leadership
SEITAMAA-HAKKARAINEN, P., Craft Science
SEPPÄLÄ, H., Church Music
SEPÄNMAA, Y., Literature
SEVÄNEN, E., Literature
SIISKONEN, H., History
SINISALO, P., Psychology
SORVALI, T., Mathematics
SUORANTA, J., Adult Education
SUTINEN, E., Computer Science
SVIRKO, Y., Physics
SYVÄOJA, J., Biochemistry
THURÉN, L., Exegetics
TIRKKONEN-CONDIT, S., Linguistic Theory and Translation
TOLONEN, Y., Economics
TUOMELA, J., Mathematics
TURUNEN, J., Electronics
TYKKYLÄINEN, M., Rural Research
VAINIOTALO, P., Chemistry
VANHALA-ANISZEWSKI, Russian Language
VANHALAKKA-RUOHO, M., Education
VARTIAINEN, P., Human Geography
VORNANEN, M., Animal PhysiologyVÄISÄNEN, P., Education

JYVÄSKYLÄN YLIOPISTO
(University of Jyväskylä)

POB 35, 40014 Univ. of Jyväskylä
Telephone: (14) 2601211
Fax: (14) 2601021
E-mail: tiedotus@jyu.fi
Internet: www.jyu.fi

Founded as Teacher Training School 1863, became College of Education 1934, and Univ. 1966

Languages of instruction: Finnish, English
State control
Academic year: September to July (3 terms)

Rector: Prof. AINO SALLINEN
Vice-Rectors: Prof. TIMO TIIHONEN, Prof. MATTI LEINO
Admin. Dir: ERKKI TUUNANEN
Chief Librarian: PIRJO VATANEN
Number of teachers: 900
Number of students: 16,500

Publications: Jyväskylä Studies in the Arts, Jyväskylä Studies in Biological and Environmental Science, Jyväskylä Studies in Business and Economics, Jyväskylä Studies in Communication, Jyväskylä Studies in Computing, Jyväskylä Studies in Education, Psychology and Social Research,

Jyväskylä Studies in Humanities, Jyväskylä Studies in Languages, Jyväskylä Studies in Sport, Physical Education and Health, Kasvatus (Finnish Journal of Education), Studia Historica Jyväskyläensia, Studia Philologica Jyväskyläensia

DEANS

Faculty of Education (incl. Dept of Teacher Training): Prof. MARJATTA LAIRIO
Faculty of Humanities: Prof. PETRI KARONEN
Faculty of Information Technology: Prof. TOMMI KÄRKKÄINEN
Faculty of Mathematics and Science: Prof. MATTI MANNINEN
Faculty of Social Sciences: Prof. ANITA KANGAS
Faculty of Sport and Health Sciences: Prof. LASSE KANNAS
School of Business and Economics: Prof. JUKKA PELLINEN

PROFESSORS

Faculty of Education (fax (14) 2601601; e-mail ktk.tdk@edu.jyu.fi; internet www.jyu.fi/tdk/kastdk):

ALANEN, L., Early Childhood Education
HAKALA, J., Education
HÄNNIKÄINEN, M., Early Childhood Education
KAIKKONEN, P., Foreign Language Education
KAUPPINEN, A., Finnish Language Education
KORPINEN, E., Education
LAURINEN, L., Education
MÄÄTTÄ, P., Special Education
POIKKEUS, A.-M., Early Childhood Education
PUOLIMATKA, T., Education
RASKU-PUTTONEN, H., Educational Psychology
SALOVIITA, T., Special Education
VIIRI, J., Pedagogy of Mathematics and Science

Faculty of Humanities (fax (14) 2601201; e-mail humtdk@campus.jyu.fi; internet www.jyu.fi/tdk/hum):

ERKKILÄ, J., Music Therapy
HANKA, H., Art History
KALAJA, P., English Language
KARONEN, P., History
KIRSTINÄ, L., Literature
KOSKIMAA, R., Digital Culture
KUNNAS, T., Literature
LAHDELMA, T., Hungarology
LEPPÄNEN, S., English Language
LOUHIVUORI, J., Musicology
LUUKKA, M.-R., Finnish Language
MARTIN, M., Finnish Language
MERISALO, O., Romance Philology
MIELIKÄINEN, A., Finnish Language
MUITTARI, V., Scandinavian Philology
NUMMELA, I., History
PIIRAINEN-MARSH, A., English Philology
RAHKONEN, M., Scandinavian Philology
SALLINEN, A., Speech Communication
SALOKANGAS, R., Journalism
SALO-LEE, L., Intercultural Communication
SIHVOLA, J., History
STARK, L., Ethnology
TOIVIAINEN, P., Musicology
VAINIO, M., Musicology
VALO, M., Speech Communication
VANHALA-ANISZEWSKI, M., Russian Language and Literature
VESTERINEN, I., Cultural Anthropology
VON BONSDORFF, P., Art Education
WAENERBERG, A., Art History
ZETTERBERG, S., History

Faculty of Information Technology (fax (14) 2602209; internet www.infotech.jyu.fi):

HÄMÄLÄINEN, T., Information Technology: Telecommunications
HEIKKILÄ, J., Information Systems and Electronic Business
JOUTSENSALO, J., Information Technology: Telecommunications
KÄRKKÄINEN, T., Software Engineering
LYYTINEN, K., Information Systems
MÄKINEN, R. A. E., Applied Mathematics
NEITTAANMÄKI, P., Mathematical Information Technology
PUURONEN, S., Information Systems
ROSSI, T., Software Technology
SAARILUOMA, P., Cognitive Science
SAKKINEN, M., Software Production
SALMINEN, A., Information Technology
TIIHONEN, T., Mathematical Information Technology
TYRVÄINEN, P., Digital Media
VEIJALAINEN, J., Software Production

Faculty of Mathematics and Science (fax (14) 2602201; e-mail pylvanai@jyu.fi; internet www.science.jyu.fi):

AHLSKOG, M., Physics
ALATALO, R., Ecology
ALÉN, R., Applied Chemistry
ÄYSTÖ, J., Physics
BAMFORD, J., Molecular Biology
GEISS, S., Stochastics
HOIKKALA, A., Evolutionary Genetics
JÄRVENPÄÄ, E., Mathematics
JONES, R. I., Limnology
JULIN, R., Physics
KARJALAINEN, J., Fish Biology and Fisheries
KATAJA, M., Physics
KILPELÄINEN, T., Mathematics
KNUUTINEN, J., Applied Chemistry
KOLEHMAINEN, E., Organic Chemistry
KORPPI-TOMMOLA, J., Chemistry
KOSKELA, P., Mathematics
KUITUNEN, M., Environmental Sciences
KUNTTU, H., Physical Chemistry
KUUSALO, T., Mathematics
LEINO, M., Physics
LESKINEN, E., Statistics
MAALAMPI, J., Physics
MANNINEN, M., Physics
MAPPES, J., Ecology and Environmental Management
MÖNKKÖNEN, M., Applied Ecology
NÄKKI, R., Mathematics
NYBLOM, J., Statistics
OIKARI, A., Environmental Sciences
OKER-BLOM, C., Biotechnology
PENTTINEN, A., Statistics
RINTALA, J., Environmental Sciences
RISSANEN, K., Chemistry
SAKSMAN, E., Mathematics
SILLANPÄÄ, R., Chemistry
TIMONEN, J., Applied Physics
TÖRMÄ, P., Physics
VALKONEN, J., Chemistry
VIRTANEN, J., Nanoscience
VUENTO, M., Biochemistry
WHITLOW, H., Physics
YLÄNNE, J., Cell Biology

Faculty of Social Sciences (fax (14) 2602801; internet www.jyu.fi/tdk/yht):

AHONEN, T., Psychology
HEISKALA, R., Social Policy
JÄRVELÄ, M., Social Policy
JYRKÄMÄ, J., Social Gerontology
KANGAS, A., Cultural Policy
KORHONEN, T., Psychology
LYYTINEN, H., Developmental Neuropsychology
MÄNTYSAARI, M., Social Work
NURMI, J.-E., Psychology
PALONEN, K., Political Science
PULKKINEN, T., Political Science and Women's Studies

SIISIÄINEN, M., Sociology
WAHLSTRÖM, J., Psychology

Faculty of Sport and Health Sciences (fax (14) 2602001; internet www.jyu.fi/liikunta):

HÄKKINEN, K., Sport Coaching and Fitness Testing
HEIKINARO-JOHANSSON, P., Physical Education
HEINONEN, A., Physiotherapy
ITKONEN, H., Sport Sociology
KAINULAINEN, H., Sport Physiology
KANNAS, L., Health Education
KUJALA, U., Sport Medicine
LAAKSO, L., Physical Education
LINTUNEN, T., Sports Psychology
MÄLKIÄ, E., Physiotherapy
RANTANEN, T., Gerontology and Public Health
RINTALA, P., Applied Physical Education
SILVENNOINEN, M., Physical Education
SUOMINEN, H., Sports Gerontology

School of Business and Economics (fax (14) 2603331; e-mail econ-webmaster@econ.jyu.fi; internet www.jyu.fi/economics):

AALTIO, J., Management and Leadership
KOIRANEN, M., Entrepreneurship
NIITTYKANGAS, H., Entrepreneurship
PEHKONEN, J., Economics
PELLINEN, J., Accounting
PESONEN, H.-L., Corporate Environmental Management
TAKALA, T., Management and Leadership
TERVO, H., Economics
UUSITALO, O., Marketing
VIRTANEN, A., Accounting

KUOPION YLIOPISTO
(University of Kuopio)

POB 1627, 70211 Kuopio
Telephone: (17) 162211
Fax: (17) 162131
Internet: www.uku.fi

Founded 1966
State control
Language of instruction: Finnish
Academic year: August to June

Rector: M. I. J. UUSITUPA
Vice-Rectors: P. J. KALLIOKOSKI, S. R. T. SUNTIOINEN
Admin. Dir: P. NERG
Librarian: J. K. K. SAARTI

Number of teachers: 400
Number of students: 6,000 incl. 1,000 postgraduate

DEANS

Business and Information Technology: J. T. NISKANEN
Medicine: J. L. T. PELKONEN
Natural and Environmental Sciences: A. A. RUUSKANEN
Pharmacy: J. T. MÖNKKÖNEN
Social Sciences: J. LAURINKARI
A. I. Virtanen Institute: J. E. KOISTINAHO

PROFESSORS

Faculty of Business and Information Technology (fax (17) 162595; internet www.uku.fi/itka):

AHONEN, J. J., Computer Science
EEROLA, A. E., Computer Science
ERICKSSON, P. M., Small Business Management
KILPELÄINEN, P. T., Computer Science
LITTUNEN, H. T., Business Economics
NIHTILÄ, M. T., Applied Mathematics
NISKANEN, J. T., Accounting and Finance
NYKÄNEN, M. J., Computer Science
TOIVANEN, P. J., Computer Science

Faculty of Medicine (fax (17) 162139; internet www.uku.fi/laake):

ALHAVA, E., Surgery

DUNKEL, L., Paediatrics
ESKELINEN, M. J., Surgery
GYLLING, H. K., Clinical Nutrition
HANNONEN, P. J., Rheumatology
HARVIMA, I. T., Dermatology and Venereology
HEINONEN, S. T., Gynaecology and Obstetrics
HELMINEN, H., Anatomy
HUSMAN, K. R. H., Occupational Medicine
ILONEN, J. S., Clinical Microbiology
JÄÄSKELÄINEN, J. E., Neurosurgery
JOHANSSON, R. T., Radiotherapy and Oncology
KARHU, J. J. T., Physiology
KAUHANEN, J. H., Public Health
KOPONEN, H. G., Psychiatry
KOSMA, V. M., Pathology
KRÖGER, H. P. J., Orthopaedics and Traumatology
KUMPUSALO, E. A., General Practice
LAAKSO, M. H. S., Internal Medicine
LEHTONEN, P. O. J. B., Psychiatry
LÖPPÖNEN, H. J., Otorhinolaryngology
LOUHEVAARA, V. A., Ergonomics
MANNINEN, H. I., Clinical Radiology
MARTTUNEN, M. J., Adolescent Psychiatry
MYKKÄNEN, H. M., Nutrition
NISKANEN, L. K., Internal Medicine
NUUTINEN, V. J., Otorhinolaryngology
PALVIMO, J. J., Medical Biochemistry
PEKKANEN, J. R., Environmental Health
PELKONEN, J. L. T., Clinical Microbiology
PEUHKURINEN, K. J., Molecular Cardiology
PIRTILLÄ, T. A., Neurology
RAUNIO, H. A., Pharmacology
RYYNÄNEN, O. P., Primary Health Care and Gen. Practice
SALONEN, J. T., Community Health (Epidemiology)
SIVENIUS, J., Neurology (Epilepsy and Rehabilitation)
SOININEN, H. S., Neurology
SULKAVA, R., Geriatrics
TAMMI, M. I., Anatomy
TIIHONEN, A. J. T., Forensic Psychiatry
TUKIAINEN, H. O., Pulmonary Diseases
VANNINEN, E. J., Clinical Physiology and Nuclear Medicine
VIINAMÄKI, H. T., Psychiatry
VOUTILAINEN, R. J., Paediatrics
WASKILAMPI, T. M., Sociology

Faculty of Natural and Environmental Sciences (fax (17) 162139; internet www.uku.fi/lyt):

BANIAHMAD, A., Biochemistry
CARLBERG, C., Biochemistry
HÄMÄLÄINEN, J. P. I., Modelling in Paper Making
HIRVONEN, M. R., Environmental Toxicology (Indoor Air)
HOLOPAINEN, T. H., Ecology and Environmental Science
HYNYNEN, K. H., Medical Physics
JOKINIEMI, J., Fine Particle Technology
JURVELIN, J. S., Medical Physics and Engineering
JUUTILAINEN, J. P., Radiation Biology and Radiation Epidemiology
KAIPIO, J. P., Computational Physics
KALLIOKOSKI, P. J., Environmental Sciences (Industrial Hygiene)
KAMCHILINE, A., Optical Sensor Technology
KÄRENLAMPI, S. O., Biotechnology
KARJALAINEN, P. A., Biosignal Analysis and Medical Imaging
KILPINEN, P. T., Environmental Technology (Control of Combustion Processes)
KOLEHMAINEN, M. T., Environmental Informatics
LAAKSONEN, A. J., Environmental Physics
LAATIKAINEN, R., Chemistry
LAPPALAINEN, R. T., Biomedical Technology
MARTIKAINEN, P., Environmental Microbiology

MONONEN, J. J. O., Applied Zoology
NEVALAINEN, T. O., Laboratory Animal Science
OLKKONEN, H. O., Physics (Electronics)
RUUSKANEN, J., Environmental Health (Air Protection)
VEPSÄLÄINEN, J. J., Chemistry
VON WRIGHT, A. J., Nutritional Biotechnology
WONG, G., Bioinformatics

Faculty of Pharmacy (fax (17) 162456; internet www.uku.fi/farmasia):

AHONEN, S. R., Pharmacy Practice
AZHAYEV, A., Pharmaceutical Bio-organic Chemistry
ENLUND, K. H., Social Pharmacy
HONKAKOSKI, P. I., Biopharmacy
JÄRVINEN, P. K., Pharmaceutical Technology
KETOLAINEN, J. A. J., Pharmaceutical Technology
LAPINJOKI, S. P., Pharmaceutical Chemistry
MERVAALA, E. M. A., Pharmacology
MÖNKKÖNEN, J. T., Biopharmacy
PASANEN, M. J., Medical Toxicology
VÄHÄKANGAS, K. H., Toxicology

Faculty of Social Sciences (fax (17) 162523; internet www.uku.fi/yhttdk):

HÄMÄLÄINEN, J. E. A., Social Work and Social Pedagogy
HÄNNINEN, V. I., Social Psychology
JUNTTO, M. A., Housing Research
KINNUNEN, J. E., Health Care Admin.
LAURINKARI, J., Social Policy
NIEMELÄ, P., Social Policy
NIIRANEN, V. A. A., Social Admin. and Management
PIETILÄ, A. M. K., Nursing Science (Preventive)
PÖLKKI, P. L., Child Welfare (Psychological Basis)
SAARI, J., Sociology
SARANTO, K. K., Health and Human Services Informatics
SUOMINEN, T. M., Nursing Science
TOSSAVAINEN, K. A., Nursing Science (Didactics)
TÖTTÖ, P. S., Methods in Social Study
VALTONEN, H. J., Health Economics
VEHVILÄINEN-JULKUNEN, K. M., Nursing Science
VOHLONEN, I. J., Health Politics
VUORI, J. J., Health Care Admin.

A. I. Virtanen Institute for Molecular Sciences (fax (17) 163030; e-mail aivi@uku.fi; internet www.uku.fi/aivi):

ALHONEN, L. I., Animal Biotechnology
JÄNNE, J. E., Biotechnology
KOISTINAHO, J. E., Molecular Brain Research
PITKÄNEN, A. S. L., Neurobiology
TANILA, H. J., Molecular Neurobiology
YLÄ-HERTTUALA, S., Molecular Medicine

KUVATAIDEAKATEMIA
(Academy of Fine Arts)

Kaikukatu 4, 00530 Helsinki
Telephone: 680-3320
Fax: 680-33260
E-mail: kanslia@kuva.fi
Internet: www.kuva.fi

Founded 1848

Rector: MARKUS KONTTINEN

Number of teachers: 16
Number of students: 270

Degree courses in painting, sculpture, graphics, time and space arts (incl. moving image, photography, site and situation specific arts).

LAPIN YLIOPISTO
(University of Lapland)

POB 122, 96101 Rovaniemi
Telephone: (16) 341341
Fax: (16) 3414222
E-mail: tiedotus@ulapland.fi
Internet: www.ulapland.fi

Founded 1979
Languages of instruction: Finnish, English
State funded
Academic year: August to July

Rector: Prof. MAURI YLÄ-KOTOLA
Vice-Rectors: Prof. PAULA KANKAANPÄÄ, Dir
JUKKA MÄKELÄ
Dir of Admin.: JUHANI LILLBERG
Dir of Int. Relations: HARRI MALINEN
Dir of Planning and Financing: TARJA SÄRKKÄ
Dir of Human Resources: MIRJA VÄYRYNEN
Community Dir: MARKUS AARTO
Library Dir: REINO LIPPONEN

Library of 210,000 vols
Number of teachers: 300
Number of students: 4,700

Publication: *KIDE* (12 a year)

DEANS

Faculty of Arts and Design: Prof. TIMO
JOKELA
Faculty of Business and Tourism: Prof. JARI
STENVALL
Faculty of Education: Prof. Dr KYÖSTI KUR-
TAKKO
Faculty of Law: Prof. Dr MATTI NIEMIVUO
Faculty of Social Sciences: Prof. Dr JUHA
PERTTULA

PROFESSORS

Faculty of Art and Design (tel. (16) 3412350;
fax (16) 3412361):

BRUSILA-RÄSÄNEN, R., Media Communica-
tion
GRANÖ, P., Art Education
HAUTALA-HIRVIOJA, T., Art History
HEIKKILÄ-RASTAS, M., Fashion and Textile
Design
HÄNNINEN, K., Textile Design
JOKELA, T., Art Education
KETTUNEN, I., Industrial Design
TUOMINEN, J., Fine Art
UOTILA, M., Design Research
YLÄ-KOTOLA, M., Media Studies

Faculty of Business and Tourism:

HAAHTI, A., Tourism Studies
PANULA, J., Marketing
TYRVAINEN, L., Nature-based Tourism

Faculty of Education (tel. (16) 3412420; fax
(16) 3412401):

KURTAKKO, K., Adult Education, Continu-
ing Education
LAURIALA, A., Teacher Education
MÄÄTTÄ, K., Educational Psychology
NASKALI, P., Women's Studies
POIKELA, E., Education
RAJALA, R., Education
RUOKAMO, H., Media Education

Faculty of Law (tel. (16) 3412520; fax (16)
3412500):

HALTTUNEN, R., , Legal Systems and Legal
History, Legal Theory
JUANTO, J., Tax Law
KARHU, J., Civil Law, Law of Obligations
KOKKO, K., Environmental Law
KORHONEN, R, Legal Informatics
KOSKINEN, S., Labour and Social Welfare
Law
KUUSIKKO, K., Administrative Law
MIKKOLA, T., Private International Law
and Comparative Law
NIEMIVUO, M., Administrative Law
SAARENPÄÄ, A., Family and Inheritance
Law, Privacy Law
TAMMI-SALMINEN, E., Property Law

UTRIAINEN, T., Criminal Law
VIIKARI, L, Public International Law
VIROLAINEN, J., Procedural Law
VIRTANEN, P., Commercial Law

Faculty of Social Sciences (tel. (16) 3412620;
fax (16) 3412600):

HAAHTI, A., Tourism Studies
JÄRVIKOSKI, A., Rehabilitation Science
KINNUNEN, M., Sociology
MERILÄINEN, S., Management
PERTTULA, J., Psychology
POHJOLA, A., Social Work
STENVALL, J., Public Admin.
SUIKKANEN, A., Sociology
TUOMINEN, M., Cultural History
TYRVÄINEN, L., Nature-Based Tourism
VEIJOLA, S., Cultural Studies of Tourism
VIERU, M., Accounting

Arctic Centre Research:

FORBES, B., Global Change
KOIVUROVA, T., Environmental and Minor-
ity Law
MOORE, J., Climate Change
TENNBERG, M., Sustainable Development

ATTACHED RESEARCH INSTITUTES

Arctic Centre: POB 122, 96101 Rovaniemi;
tel. (16) 341341; fax (16) 362934; internet
www.arcticcentre.org; Dir Prof. Dr PAULA
KANKAANPÄÄ.

Centre for Continuing Education: Dir Dr
HELKA URPONEN.

Language Centre: Dir Dr HEIDI STRENGELL.

Meri-Lappi Institute: Dir AARO TIILIKAI-
NEN.

Teacher Training School: POB 122, 96101
Rovaniemi; tel. (16) 341341; Rector EIJA
VALANNE.

Lapland University Consortium: Jokiväylä 11C, 96300 Rovaniemi; Dir Lic.
MARKKU TARVAINEN.

LAPPEENRANNAN TEKNILLINEN KORKEAKOULU
(Lappeenranta University of Technology)

Box 20, 53851 Lappeenranta
Telephone: (5) 62111
Fax: (5) 6212350
Internet: www.lut.fi

Founded 1969
Languages of instruction: Finnish, English
State control
Academic year: August to July (two terms)

Rector: Prof. MARKKU LUKKA
Vice-Rector for Research: Prof. JARMO PARTA-
NEN
Vice-Rector for Studies: Prof. ILKKA PÖYHÖ-
NEN
Admin. Officer: ARTO OIKKONEN
Librarian: ANJA UKKOLA

Library of 145,000 vols
Number of teachers: 200
Number of students: 4,500

PROFESSORS

AALTIO, I., Management and Organization
HANDROOS, H., Machine Automation
KÄLVIÄINEN, H., Information Processing
KÄSSI, T., Industrial Economics
KERTTULA, E., Telematics
KOSKELAINEN, L., Power Plant Engineering
KYLÄHEIKO, K., Economics
LARJOLA, J., Heat Transfer and Fluid Dynam-
ics
LEHTOMAA, A., Entrepreneurship in Technol-
ogy
LINDSTRÖM, M., Physical Chemistry
LIUHTO, J., International Operations
LUKKA, A., Logistics (esp. Transport), Inven-
tories, Purchasing

LUKKA, M., Applied Mathematics
LUUKKO, A., Physics
MANNER, H., Paper Technology
MARQUIS, G., Steel Structures
MARTIKAINEN, J., Welding Technology
MARTIKKA, H., Design of Machine Elements
MARTTILA, E., Environmental Engineering
MIKKOLA, A., Virtual Engineering
MINKKINEN, P., Inorganic and Analytical
Chemistry
NAOUMOV, V., Data Communications
NIEMI, M., Civil Law
NYSTRÖM, L., Process Technology
NYSTRÖM, M., Membrane Technology
PAATERO, E., Chemical Technology
PARTANEN, J., Electrical Systems
PIRTTILÄ, T., Industrial Engineering and
Management (esp. Logistics)
PITKÄNEN, S., Engineering and Technology
Management
PORRAS, J., Data Communications
PÖYHÖNEN, I., Wood Technology
PYRHÖNEN, J., Electrical Machines and
Drives
PYRHÖNEN, O., Control Engineering
RANTANEN, H., Industrial Engineering
SARKOMAA, P., Technical Thermodynamics
TARJANNE, R., Energy Management and Eco-
nomics
TIUSANEN, T., International Operations of
Industrial Firms
TOIVANEN, P., Information Processing
TUOMINEN, M., Industrial Engineering and
Management
TURUNEN, I., Process Systems Engineering
VERHO, A., Structural Design of Machinery
VORACEK, J., Information Processing
ZAMANKHAN, P., Computational Heat and
Fluid Dynamics

OULUN YLIOPISTO
(University of Oulu)

Pentti Kaiteran Katu 1, POB 8000, 90014
University of Oulu
Telephone: (8) 5531011
Fax: (8) 5534551
E-mail: kirjaamo@oulu.fi
Internet: www.oulu.fi

Founded 1958
Language of instruction: Finnish
State control
Academic year: September to May (two
terms)

Rector: Prof. L. LAJUNEN
Vice-Rectors: Prof. L. HUHTALA, Prof. J.
KOISO-KANTTILA, Prof. V. MYLLYLÄ
Admin. Dir: H. PIETILÄ
Librarian: P. KYTÖMÄKI

Number of teachers: 962
Number of students: 16,500

DEANS

Faculty of Economics and Business Admin-
istration: Prof. R. SVENTO
Faculty of Education: Prof. P. SILJANDER
Faculty of Humanities: Prof. M. LEHTIHALMES
Faculty of Medicine: Prof. H. RUSKOAHO
Faculty of Science: Prof. V. MUSTONEN
Faculty of Technology: Prof. V. LANTTO

PROFESSORS

Faculty of Economics and Business Administration (POB 4600, 90014 University of
Oulu; tel. (8) 5532905; fax (8) 5532906;
internet www.taloustieteet.oulu.fi):

ALAJOUTSIJÄRVI, K., Marketing
JUGA, J., Logistics
KALLUNKI, J. P., Accounting
KOIVUMÄKI, T., Electronic Commerce
PELTONEN, T., Management and Organiza-
tion
PERTTUNEN, J., Finance
PUHAKKA, M., Economics

RAHIALA, M., Econometrics
SVENTO, R., Economics

Faculty of Education (POB 2000, 90014 University of Oulu; fax (8) 5533600; e-mail ktk-opintoasiat@oulu.fi; internet www.edu.oulu.fi):

FREDRIKSON, M., Music Education
HAKKARAINEN, P., Early Childhood Education
JÄRVELÄ, S., Education
JÄRVIKOSKI, T., Social Science
JÄRVILEHTO, T., Psychology
KALAOJA, E., Didactics
KERANTO, T., Mathematics and Science Education
KORKEAMÄKI, R.-L., Education
LUUKKONEN, J., Education
MÄKINEN, K., Didactics of Foreign Languages
RUISMÄKI, H., Music Education
SILJANDER, P., Education
SOINI, H., Educational Psychology
SUORTTI, J., Education
SYRJÄLÄ, L., Education
VARIS, M., Didactics of Finnish Language and Literature
YLI-LUOMA, P., Education

Faculty of Humanities (POB 1000, 90014 University of Oulu; fax (8) 5533230; internet www.oulu.fi/hutk/index.html):

BLUHM, L., German Language and Literature
FÄLT, O. K., History
HUHTALA, L., Literature
JOHNSON, A., English
KORPILAHTI, P., Logopaedics
LAUTTAMUS, T., English
LEHTIHALMES, M., Logopaedics
LEHTOLA, V.-P., Saami Culture
MANNINEN, J., History of Science and Ideas
MANTILA, H., Finnish
NUÑES GARCES, M., Archaeology
PENNANEN, J., Cultural Anthropology
ROSSI, P., Scandinavian Languages
SAMMALLAHTI, P., Saami (Lapp) Language and Culture
SORVALI, I., Scandinavian Languages
SULKALA, H., Finnish
SUOMI, K., Phonetics
VAHTOLA, J., Finnish and Scandinavian History

Faculty of Medicine (POB 5000, 90014 University of Oulu; tel. (8) 5375011; fax (8) 5375111; internet www.medicine.oulu.fi):

AIRAKSINEN, P. J., Ophthalmology
ALAHUHTA, S., Anaesthesiology
ALA-KOKKO, L., Medical Biochemistry
HALLMAN, H., Paediatrics
HAUSEN, H., Dentistry
HILLBOM, M., Neurology
HUIKURI, H., Internal Medicine
ISOHANNI, M., Psychiatry
ISOLA, A., Nursing Science
JAAKKOLA, M., Pulmonary Disease
JALOVAARA, P., Surgery
JÄMSÄ, T., Medical Technology
JANHONEN, S., Nursing Didactics
JÄRVELIN, M.-R., Public Health Science
JOUKAMAA, M., Psychiatry
JUVONEN, T., Surgery
KAPRIO, J., Public Health Science
KEINÄNEN-KIUKAANNIEMI, S., General Practice
KESÄNIEMI, A., Internal Medicine
KNUUTTILA, M., Dentistry
KOIVUKANGAS, J., Neurosurgery
KOPONEN, H., Psychiatry
KORTELAINEN, M., Forensic Medicine
LARMAS, M., Dentistry
MÄKELÄ, J., Gastroenterological Surgery
MOILANEN, I., Child Psychiatry
MYLLYLÄ, V., Neurology
NIKKILÄ, J., Health Administration

OIKARINEN, A., Dermatology and Venereology
OIKARINEN, K., Dentistry
PAAVONEN, T., Pathological Anatomy
PELKONEN, O., Pharmacology
PELTONEN, J., Anatomy
PIHLAJANIEMI, T., Medical Biochemistry
PYHTINEN, J., Diagnostic Radiology
RAJANIEMI, H., Anatomy
RÄSÄNEN, P., Psychiatry
RAUSTIA, A., Dentistry
RISTELI, J., Clinical Chemistry
RUOKONEN, A., Clinical Chemistry
RUSKOAHO, H., Molecular Pharmacology
RYYNÄNEN, M., Obstetrics and Gynaecology
SALO, T., Oral Pathology
SAVOLAINEN, M., Internal Medicine
SORRI, M., Otorhinolaryngology
STENBÄCK, F., Pathology
SURAMO, I., Diagnostic Radiology
TAPANAINEN, J., Obstetrics and Gynaecology
TUULONEN, A., Ophthalmology
UHARI, M., Paediatrics
VAINIO, O., Clinical Microbiology
VAINIO, S., Developmental Biochemistry
VIROKANNAS, H., Occupational Health
VUOLTEENAHO, O., Physiology

Faculty of Science (POB 3000, 90014 University of Oulu; fax (8) 5531060; internet www.oulu.fi/science/index.html):

AKSELA, H., Physics
AKSELA, S., Physics
ALAPIETI, T., Geology and Mineralogy
HÄGGMAN, H., Plant Physiology
HANSKI, E., Geochemistry
HEIKKINEN, O., Geography
HEISKANEN, A., Information Processing Science
HILTUNEN, K., Biochemistry
HOHTOLA, A., Plant Physiology
HOHTOLA, E., Zoology
HOLMSTRÖM, L., Applied Mathematics
HORMI, O., Chemistry
HUTTUNEN, S., Botany
IIVARI, J., Information Processing Science
JÄRVILEHTO, M., Animal Physiology
JAUHIAINEN, J., Applied Geography and Regional Planning
JOKISAARI, J., Physics
KAIKKONEN, P., Geophysics
KAITALA, A., Zoology
KARJALAINEN, P. T., Geography
KINNUNEN, J., Mathematics
KUUTTI, K., Information Processing Science
LAAJOKI, K., Geology and Mineralogy
LÄÄRÄ, E., Statistics
LAASONEN, K., Chemistry
LAITINEN, R., Chemistry
LAJUNEN, L., Inorganic Chemistry
LUNKKA, J. P., Surficial Geology
MUOTKA, T., Zoology
MURSULA, K., Physics
MUSTONEN, V., Mathematics
MYLLYLÄ, R., Biochemistry
NORDSTRÖM, K., Statistics
NYGRÉN, T., Physics
OINAS-KUKKONEN, H., Information Processing Science
OIVO, M., Information Processing Science
OKSANEN, J., Plant Ecology
ORELL, M., Zoology
PAASI, A., Geography
PAMILO, P., Genetics
PERÄMÄKI, P., Inorganic Chemistry
PEURANIEMI, V., Surficial Geology
POUTANEN, J., Astronomy
PULLI, P., Information Processing Science
PURSIAINEN, J., Chemistry
RAHIALA, M., Econometrics
RUDDOCK, K., Protein Science
RUMMUKAINEN, K., Theoretical Physics
RUSANEN, J., Geoinformatics
SAARINEN, J., Geography
SARANEN, J., Applied Mathematics

SAUKKONEN, S., Information Processing Science
SAVOLAINEN, O., Genetics
SEPPÄNEN, V., Information Processing Science
SIMILÄ, J., Information Processing Science
TERVONEN, I., Information Processing Science
THUNEBERG, E., Theoretical Physics
TUOMI, J., Botany
VÄÄNÄNEN, K., Mathematics
WECKSTRÖM, M., Biophysics
WIERENGA, R., Biochemistry

Faculty of Technology (POB 4000, 90014 University of Oulu; fax (8) 5532006; internet www.ttk.oulu.fi):

BRONER-BAUER, K., Architecture
GLISIC, S., Telecommunication
HAAPASALO, H., Industrial Engineering and Management
HÄRKKI, J., Metallurgy
HENTILÄ, H., Planning and Urban Design
HEUSALA, H., Electronics
IINATTI, J., Telecommunications
JUNTTI, M., Telecommunications
KARHU, S., Radio Technology
KARHUNEN, J., Machine Design
KARJALAINEN, J., Production Engineering
KARJALAINEN, P., Physical Metallurgy
KEISKI, R., Mass and Heat Transfer Processes
KESS, P., Industrial Engineering and Management
KLØVE, B., Water Management
KOISO-KANTTILA, J., Architecture
KORTELA, U., Control and Systems Engineering
KOSTAMOVAARA, J., Electronics
LAHDELMA, S., Machine Condition Diagnostics
LAKSO, E., Environment Engineering
LANTTO, V., Material Physics
LAPPALAINEN, K., Production Engineering
LATVA-AHO, M., Telecommunications
LEIVISKÄ, K., Process Engineering
LEPPÄNEN, P., Telecommunications
MÄÄTTÄ, K., Electronics
MAHLAMÄKI, R., Architecture
MÄNTYLÄ, P., Mechanical Metallurgy
MYLLYLÄ, R., Optoelectronics and Electronic Measurement Technology
NEUBAUER, P., Bioprocess Engineering
NEVALA, K., Mechatronics
NIINIMÄKI, J., Mechanical Process Engineering
NISKANEN, J., Machine Construction
OJALA, T., Computer Engineering
PIETIKÄINEN, M., Computer Technics
PRAMILA, A., Technical Mechanics
RAHKONEN, T., Electronics
RIEKKI, J., Software Architecture for Embedded Systems
RÖNING, J., Embedded Systems
RUOTSALAINEN, K., Mathematics
SALONEN, E., Radio Technology
SAUVOLA, J., Multimedia Systems
SEIKKALA, S., Applied Mathematics
SEPPÄNEN, T., Biomedical Technology
SILVÉN, O., Signal Processing
SJÖLIND, S., Engineering Mechanics
TARUMAA, A., Planning and Urban Design
TASA, J., Architecture
TUPPURAINEN, Y., Architecture
VÄHÄKANGAS, J., Electronics Production Technology
VÄYRYNEN, S., Work Science

ATTACHED INSTITUTES

Institute of Electron Optics: POB 7100, 90014 University of Oulu; Dir S. SIVONEN.

Kajaani University Consortium: POB 51, 87100 Kajaani; Dir J. SUORTTI.

Laboratory Animal Centre: POB 5000, 90014 University of Oulu; Dir H.-M. VOIPIO.

Language Centre: POB 7200, 90014 University of Oulu; Dir H. ANTTILA.

Learning and Research Services: POB 7910, 90014 University of Oulu; Dir A.-M. YLIMAULA.

Meri-Lappi Institute: 94600 Kemi; Dir A. TIILIKAINEN.

Sodankylä Geophysical Observatory: 99600 Sodankylä; Dir T. TURUNEN.

Thule Institute: POB 7300, 90014 University of Oulu; Dir K. LAINE.

SIBELIUS-AKATEMIA
(Sibelius Academy)

POB 86, 00251 Helsinki
Telephone: (0) 2075390
Fax: (0) 207539600
E-mail: info@siba.fi
Internet: www.siba.fi
Founded 1882
Languages of instruction: Finnish, Swedish
State control
Academic year: September to May
Univ. status
Rector: GUSTAV DJUPSJÖBACKA
Vice-Rector: HANNU APAJALAHTI
Admin. Dir: SEPPO SUIHKO
Library: see Libraries and Archives
Number of teachers: 240
Number of students: 1,700

DEANS

Church Music: PETER PEITSALO
Church Music (in Kuopio): OLAVI HAUTSALO
Composition and Music Theory: RIITTA VALKEILA
Folk Music: HEIKKI LAITINEN
Jazz Music: JARI PERKIÖMÄKI
Music Education: SOILI PERKIÖ
Music Technology: ROBERT DE GODZINSKY
Orchestral Instruments: MERIT PALAS
Piano Music: HUI-YING TAWASTSTJERNA
Vocal Music: OUTI KÄHKÖNEN

PROFESSORS

CANTELL, T., Arts Management
CASTRÉN, M., Music Research
GOTHONI, R., Chamber Music
HELASVUO, M., Wind Instrument Music
JOKINEN, E., Composition
JUSSILA, K., Organ Music
KURKELA, K., Music Performance and Research
KURKELA, V., Popular Music
LAITINEN, H., Folk Music
LAITINEN, M., Music Education
LEE, M.-K., Violin
LEHTINEN, M., Operatic Training
MURTOMÄKI, V., History of Music
NORAS, A., Cello Music
ORAMO, I., Music Theory
PORTHAN, O., Organ Music
PUUMALA, V.-M., Composition
RAEKALLIO, M., Piano Music
ROUSI, M., Cello Music
RUOHONEN, S., Opera
SAARIKETTU, K., Violin Music
SALOMAA, P., Vocal Music
SEGERSTAM, L., Orchestral Conducting
SIVUOJA-GUNARATNAM, A., Music Performance and Research
SUURPÄÄ, L., Music Theory
SZILVAY, R., Violin Music
TAITTO, I., Church Music
TAWASTSTJERNA, E. T., Piano Music
TUPPURAINEN, E., Church Music
UOTILA, J., Jazz Music
WESTERLUND, H., Music Education

HANKEN SVENSKA HANDELSHÖGSKOLAN
(Hanken School of Economics)

Helsinki Campus, POB 479, Arkadiankatu 22 00101 Helsinki
Telephone: (9) 431331
Fax: (9) 431333
Vasa Branch Campus, POB 287, Handelsesplanaden 2, 65101 Vasa
Telephone: (6) 3533700
E-mail: info@hanken.fi
Internet: www.hanken.fi
Founded 1909
Languages of instruction: Swedish, English
State control
Academic year: September to May
Founded 1909
Rector: M. STENIUS
Vice-Rectors: VERONICA LILJANDER, SÖREN KOCK
Admin. Dir: M. LINDROOS
Librarian: TUA HINDERSSON-SÖDERHOLM
Library of 96,300 vols; 140 periodicals
Number of teachers: 101
Number of students: 1,649

PROFESSORS

Accounting:
EKHOLM, B.
TALLBERG, A.
VIITANEN, J.
WALLIN, J.
VEST, T.
Commercial Law:
BRUUN, N.
KUKKONEN, M.
MÄNTYSAARI, P.
Economics and Statistics:
BERGLUND, T.
BLOMQVIST, H. C.
ROSENQVIST, G., Statistics
STENBACKA, R.
Finance:
HANSSON, M.
HÖGHOLM, K.
KNIF, J.
KORKEAMÄKI, T.
LILJEBLOM, E.
LÖFLUND, A.
Management and Organization:
BJÖRKMAN, I.
HEARN, J.
MANTERE, S.
SVEIBY, K.
VAARA, E.
Informatics:
BJÖRK, B.
Entrepreneurship, Management and Organisation:
KOCK, S.
LINDELL, M.
Supply Chain Management and Corporate Geography:
SPENS, K.
Marketing:
BJÖRK, P.
GRÖNROOS, C.
HOLMLUND-RYTKÖNEN, M.
LILJANDER, V.
LINDQVIST, L.
STORBACKA, K.
STRANDVIK, T.

TAIDETEOLLINEN KORKEAKOULU
(University of Art and Design Helsinki)

Hämeentie 135c, 00560 Helsinki
Telephone: (9) 75631
Fax: (9) 75630223

E-mail: info@uiah.fi
Internet: www.uiah.fi
Founded 1871
State control
Languages of instruction: Finnish, English, Swedish
Academic year: September to May
Rector: YRJÖ SOTAMAA
Vice-Rectors: MERJA SALO, YRJÄNÄ LEVANTO
Dir of Admin.: PEKKA SAARELA
Librarian: MARITA TURPEINEN
Library of 65,000 vols
Number of teachers: 695 (106 full-time, 589 part-time)
Number of students: 1,792
Publication: *Arttu* (bulletin, 4 a year)

HEADS OF SCHOOLS

School of Art Education: Prof. JUHA VARTO
School of Design: Prof. HELENA HYVÖNEN
School of Motion Picture, Television and Production Design: Prof. LAURI TÖRHÖNEN
School of Visual Culture: Prof. JAN-KENNETH WECKMAN
Medialab: Prof. PHILIP DEAN

TAMPEREEN TEKNILLINEN YLIOPISTO
(Tampere University of Technology)

Box 527, 33101 Tampere
Telephone: (3) 3652111
Fax: (3) 3652170
Internet: www.tut.fi
Founded 1965
Language of instruction: Finnish
State control
Academic year: September to May
Rector: Prof. JARL-THURE ERIKSSON
Vice-Rectors: Prof. MARKKU KIVIKOSKI, Prof. TUOMO TIAINEN
Dir of Admin.: TIINA ÄIJÄLÄ
Librarian: ARJA-RIITTA HAARALA
Number of teachers: 1,906
Number of students: 12,000

DEANS

Dept of Architecture: Prof. JUHANI KATAINEN
Dept of Automation: Assoc. Prof. PENTTI LAUTALA
Dept of Civil Engineering: Prof. RALF LINDBERG
Dept of Electrical Engineering: Prof. LAURI KETTUNEN
Dept of Environment: Assoc. Prof. HELGE LEMMETYINEN
Dept of Industrial Engineering and Management: Prof. MARKKU PIRJETÄ
Dept of Information Technology: Prof. HANNU-MATTI JÄRVINEN
Dept of Materials Science: Prof. TUOMO TIAINEN
Dept of Mechanical Engineering: Prof. PAUL H. ANDERSSON
Dept of Science and Engineering: Prof. ROLF HERNBERG

PROFESSORS

AITTOMÄKI, A., Refrigeration Technology
ASTOLA, J., Digital Signals Processing
AUMALA, O., Metrology
ERIKSSON, J.-T., Electrodynamics and Magnetism
GABBOUJ, M., Information Technology
HAIKALA, I., Computer Science
HARJU, J., Telecommunications
HARTIKAINEN, J., Soil Mechanics and Foundation Engineering
JAAKKOLA, H., Information Technology
JALLINOJA, R., Architectural Theory
JARSKE, P., Telecommunications
KALLBERG, H., Transport
KALLI, S., Information Technology
KÄRNÄ, J., Electrical Power Engineering

KARVINEN, R., Fluid Dynamics and Heat Transfer
KATAINEN, J., Architectural Design
KAUNONEN, A., Control Engineering
KIVIKOSKI, M., Industrial Electronics
KORPINEN, L., Electrical Power Engineering
KOSKI, J., Structural Mechanics
KURKI-SUONIO, R., Computer Science and Engineering
LAKSO, T., Production Engineering
LAUTALA, P., Control Engineering
LEMMITYINEN, H., Chemistry
LEPISTÖ, T., Mathematics
LINDBERG, R., Structural Engineering
MÄKILÄ, P., Automation Technology
MALMIVUO, J., Bioelectronics
MATTILA, M., Occupational Safety Engineering
MAULA, J., Urban Planning
NOUSIAINEN, P., Textile Technology
NYBERG, T., Paper Machine Automation
OTALA, M., Industrial Management
PESSA, M., Semiconductor Technology
PUHALKA, J., Environmental Biotechnology
RENFORS, M., Telecommunications Engineering
RIIHELÄ, S., Construction Economics and Management
RIITAHUHTA, A., Machine Design
RISTALAINEN, E., Electronics
SAARIKORPI, J., Industrial Management and Engineering
SAARINEN, J., Signal Processing Laboratory
SARAMAKI, T., Signal Processing
SAVOLAINEN, A., Process Engineering
SIEKKINEN, V., Maintenance Technology
SIIKANEN, U., Architectural Construction
TALLQVIST, T., History of Architecture
TIANEN, T., Materials Engineering
TOMBERG, J., Information Technology
TÖRMÄLÄ, P., Plastics Technology
TORVINEN, S., Production Automation
TUHKANEN, T., Environmental Engineering
TUOKKO, R., Automation Technology
TUOMALA, M., Structural Mechanics
UUSI-RAUVA, E., Industrial Management and Engineering
VANHARANTA, H., Industrial Management and Engineering
VILENIUS, M., Hydraulic Machines

ATTACHED INSTITUTES

Institute of Digital Media: POB 553, 33101 Tampere; f. 1994; Dir Prof. PAULI KUOSMANEN.

Optoelectronics Research Centre: POB 692, 33101 Tampere; f. 1999; Dir Prof. MARCUS PESSA.

TAMPEREEN YLIOPISTO
(University of Tampere)

Kalevantie 4, 33014 University of Tampere
Telephone: (3) 355111
Fax: (3) 2134473
E-mail: kirjaamo@uta.fi
Internet: www.uta.fi
Founded 1925
Languages of instruction: Finnish, English
State control
Academic year: September to May
Chancellor: Dr J. SIPILÄ
Rector: Prof. K. VARANTOLA
Vice-Rectors: Prof. J. LEHTO, Prof. A. ROPO
Admin. Dir: T. LAHTI
Librarian: M. IIVONEN

Number of teachers: 698
Number of students: 15,360

Publication: *Acta Universitatis Tamperensis*

DEANS

Faculty of Economics and Administration: Prof. A. HAVERI
Faculty of Education: Prof. T. TAKALA

Faculty of Humanities: Prof. M.-L. PIITULAINEN
Faculty of Information Sciences: Prof. M. JUHOLA
Faculty of Medicine: Prof. P. KIRKINEN
Faculty of Social Sciences: Prof. P. SUHONEN

PROFESSORS

Faculty of Economics and Administration (Kanslerinrinne 1, 33014 University of Tampere; tel. (3) 35516506; fax (3) 35516905; e-mail talhall.tiedekunta@uta.fi; internet www.uta.fi/tiedekunnat/talh):

AHONEN, P., Financial Administration and Public Sector Accounting
HAILA, Y., Environmental Policy
HARISALO, R., Public Administration
HAVERI, A., Local Government
HIRVONEN, M., Economics
HUHTANEN, R., Public Law
HÄKLI, J., Regional Studies
JÄRVINEN, R., Insurance
KULTALAHTI, J., Public Law
KULTALAHTI, O., Regional Studies
KUUSELA, H., Marketing
LAAKSO, S., Public Law
LUMIJÄRVI, I., Security Administration
MEKLIN, P., Local Public Economics
MYLLYMÄKI, A., Public Law
NÄSI, S., Accounting and Finance
NUOLIMAA, R., Business
OULASVIRTA, L., Local Public Economics
PENTTILÄ, S., Tax Law
ROPO, A., Management and Organization
RYYNÄNEN, A., Local Public Law
SOTARAUTA, M., Regional Studies
TUOMALA, M., Economics
VAINIOMÄKI, J., Economics
VARTOLA, J., Public Administration
VEHMANEN, P., Accounting and Finance
YLÄ-LIEDENPOHJA, J., Economics

Faculty of Education (Ratapihankatu 55, 33014 University of Tampere; tel. (3) 35516297; fax (3) 35516620; internet www.uta.fi/tiedekunnat/kasv):

KOHONEN, V., Foreign Language Education
NUMMENMAA, A. R., Early Childhood Education
ROPO, E., Education
RUOHOTIE, P., Education (Vocational)
SYRJÄLÄINEN, E., Education
TAKALA, T., Education (Comparative)
TUOMISTO, J., Adult Education
VARIS, T., Media Education
VÄRRI, V.-M., Education

Faculty of Humanities (Kanslerinrinne 1, 33014 University of Tampere; tel. (3) 35516520; fax (3) 35517240; e-mail humanistinen.tiedekunta@uta.fi; internet www.uta.fi/tiedekunnat/hum):

HAAPALA, P., Finnish History
HARLING-KRANCK, G., Scandinavian Languages
HAVU, J., French Language
HIETALA, M., General History
KLEMOLA, J., English Philology
LAALO, K., Finnish Language
LAUKKANEN, A.-M., Speech Communication and Voice Research
LEHTONEN, M., Media Culture
LEINONEN, M., Slavonic Philology
LEISIÖ, T., Ethnomusicology
LUKKARINEN, V., Art History
MAURANEN, A., English Philology
NIEMI, J., Finnish Literature
NIKULA, K., Scandinavian Languages
PAJUNEN, A., Finnish Language
PIITULAINEN, M.-L., German Language and Culture
RENVALL, Y. J., Actor Training
REUTER, E., German Language and Culture
ROSENHOLM, A., Slavonic Philology
RUDANKO, J., English Philology

SULKUNEN, I., Finnish History
TAMMI, P., Comparative Literature
TIITTULA, L., Translation Studies (German)
TOMMOLA, H., Translation Studies (Russian)
VARANTOLA, K., Translation Studies (English)

Faculty of Information Sciences (Kanslerinrinne 1, 33014 University of Tampere; tel. (3) 35517078; fax (3) 35514002; e-mail informaatiotieteiden.tiedekunta@uta.fi; internet www.uta.fi/tiedekunnat/inf):

HAAPARANTA, L., Philosophy
HELLA, L., Mathematics
JUHOLA, M., Computer Science
JÄRVELIN, K., Information Studies
KANGASSALO, H., Computer Science
KEKÄLÄINEN, J., Information Studies
LISKI, E., Statistics
MÄKINEN, E., Computer Science
MANNINEN, P., Statistics
MERIKOSKI, J., Mathematics
NUMMENMAA, J., Computer Science
RAISAMO, R., Computer Science
RUOHONEN, M., Computer Science
RÄIHÄ, K., Computer Science
RAISAMO, R., Computer Science
SAVOLAINEN, R., Information Studies
SINTONEN, M., Philosophy
SORMUNEN, E., Information Studies
VAKKARI, P., Information Studies
VITELI, J., Hypermedia

Faculty of Medicine (Medisiinarinkatu 3, 33014 University of Tampere; tel. (3) 35516653; fax (3) 35517385; internet www.uta.fi/tiedekunnat/laak):

ÅSTEDT-KURKI, P., Nursing
ELOVAARA, I., Neurology
HEINONEN, P., Obstetrics and Gynaecology
HOLLI, K., Palliative Medicine
HURME, M., Microbiology and Immunology
HYÖTY, H., Virology
JÄRVINEN, M., Surgery
KANNUS, P., Injury Prevention
KARHUNEN, P., Forensic Medicine
KELLOKUMPU-LEHTINEN, P., Radiotherapy and Oncology
KIRKINEN, P., Obstetrics and Gynaecology
KOSMA, V., Pathology
LAASONEN, E. M., Radiology
LEINONEN, E., Psychiatry
LINDGEN, L., Anaesthesiology
MATTILA, K., General Practice
MOILANEN, E., Pharmacology
MUSTONEN, J., Internal Medicine
MÄKI, M., Paediatrics
NIEMELÄ, O., Laboratory Medicine
PAAVILAINEN, E., Nursing
PELTO-HUIKKO, M., Developmental Biology
PUKANDER, J., Otorhinolaryngology
PYYKKÖ, J., Otorhinolaryngology
REUNALA, T., Dermatology and Venereology
SALMINEN, L., Ophthalmology
SARANSAARI, P., Physiology
SEPPÄ, K., General Practice
TAMMELA, T., Urology
TAMMINEN, T., Child Psychiatry
TUOHIMAA, P., Anatomy
TURJANMAA, V., Clinical Physiology
VESIKARI, T., Virology
VIRJO, J., General Practice
YLIKOMI, T., Cell Biology
YLITALO, P., Clinical Pharmacology and Toxicology

Faculty of Social Sciences (Yliopistonkatu 38, 33014 University of Tampere; tel. (3) 35516224; fax (3) 35517386; internet www.uta.fi/tiedekunnat/yht):

ALASUUTARI, P., Sociology
ALESTALO, M., Sociology
ANTTONEN, A., Social Policy
BLOM, R., Sociology
ERÄSAARI, L., Social Work

HARLE, V., International Politics
HIETANEN, J., Psychology
HUJANEN, T., Journalism and Mass Communication
JOKINEN, A., Social Work
JUHILA, K., Social Work
KOISTINEN, P., Social Policy
KORVAJÄRVI, P., Women's Studies
KOSKI-JÄNNES, A., Social Psychology
KUNELIUS, R., Journalism
KÄKÖNEN, J., Jean Monnet Professor
LAHIKAINEN, A. R., Social Psychology
LEHTONEN, H., Social Policy
NORDENSTRENG, K., Journalism and Mass Communication
OJANEN, M., Psychology
PAASTELA, J., Political Science
PALOHEIMO, H., Political Science
PUNAMÄKI, R.-L., Psychology
PÖSÖ, T., Social Work
RAUNIO, K., Social Work
RAUNIO, T., Political Science
ROSTILA, I., Social and Health Services
RYTÖVUORI-APUNEN, H., International Politics
SCHIENSTOCK, G., Work Research
SIPILÄ, J., Social Work
SUHONEN, P., Journalism and Mass Communication
VUORELA, U., Social Anthropology

AFFILIATED INSTITUTES

International School of Social Sciences (ISSS): Tampere; f. 1990; language of instruction: English; Dir K. NORDENSTRENG.

Kielikeskus (Language Centre): Tampere; internet kielikeskus.utu.fi; f. 1975; Dir U.-K. TUOMI.

Lääketieteellisen teknologian instituutti (Institute of Medical Technology): Tampere; f. 1995; Dir O. SILVENNOINEN.

Solu- and kudosteknologiakeskus Regea (Regea Institute for Regenerative Medicine): Tampere; f. 2005; Dir R. SURONEN.

Täydennyskoulutuskeskus (Institute for Extension Studies): Tampere; f. 1970; Dir M. LEPPÄALHO.

Terveystieteen laitos (Tampere School of Public Health): Tampere; f. 1995; Dir P. RISSANEN.

Tietokonekeskus (Computer Centre): Tampere; f. 1966; Dir S. VISALA.

Yhteiskuntatieteellinen tietoarkisto (Finnish Social Science Data Archive): f. 1999; Dir S. BORG.

Yhteiskuntatieteiden tutkimuslaitos (Research Institute for Social Sciences): Tampere; f. 1945; Dir P. ALASUUTARI.

TEATTRIKORKEAKOULU
(Theatre Academy Helsinki)

POB 163, 00531 Helsinki
Haapaniemenkatu 6, 00530 Helsinki

Telephone: (9) 431361
Fax: (9) 43136200
E-mail: international@teak.fi
Internet: www.teak.fi

Founded 1979
State control
Languages of instruction: Finnish, Swedish

Rector: PAULA TUOVINEN
Vice-Rector: ERIK SÖDERBLOM
Head of Admin.: ESA HAMALAINEN
Librarian: H. HAKALA

Library of 40,000 vols, 200 periodicals
Number of teachers: 41
Number of students: 380

PROFESSORS

ARLANDER, A., Performance and Theory
KIRKKOPELTO, E., Artistic Research
LIIMATAINEN, J., Sound Design

MONNI, K., Choreography
OUTINEN, K., Acting (Finnish)
RUIKKA, M., Directing
RUOHONEN, L., Dramaturgy
SÖDERBLOM, E., Acting (Swedish)
TENHULA, N., Contemporary Dance
UIMONEN, M., Lighting Design
VIERIKKO, V., Acting (Finnish)

TEKNILLINEN KORKEAKOULU
(Helsinki University of Technology)

POB 1000, 02015 Helsinki University of Technology

Telephone: (9) 4511
Fax: (9) 4512017
Internet: www.hut.fi

Founded 1908
State control
Language of instruction: Finnish (with some lectures in Swedish and English)
Academic year: September to May

Rector: Prof. MATTI PURSULA
Vice-Rectors: Prof. M. AIRILA, Prof. O. NEVANLINNA
Admin. Dir: E. LUOMALA

Number of teachers: 528 (full-time)
Number of students: 13,500

DEANS

Department of Architecture: Prof. SIMO PAAVILAINEN
Department of Automation and Systems Technology: Prof. AARNE HALME
Department of Chemical Technology: Prof. MATTI LEISOLA
Department of Civil and Environmental Engineering: Prof. PERTTI VAKKILAINEN
Department of Computer Science and Engineering: Prof. OLLI SIMULA
Department of Electrical and Communications Engineering: Prof. PEKKA WALLIN
Department of Engineering, Physics and Mathematics: Prof. PEKKA HAUTOJÄRVI
Department of Forest Products Technology: Prof. TERO PAAJANEN
Department of Industrial Management: Prof. PAUL LILLRANK
Department of Materials Science and Rock Engineering: Prof. KARI HEISKANEN
Department of Mechanical Engineering: Prof. MAURI MÄÄTTÄNEN
Department of Surveying: Prof. KAUKO VIITANEN

PROFESSORS

AALTO, J., Structural Engineering
AALTONEN, K., Production Engineering
AHTILA, P., Industrial Energy Technology
AIRILA, M., Machine Design
AITTAMAA, J., Chemical Engineering
ALA-NISSILÄ, T., Physics
ALKU, P., Speech Communication Technology
ARKKIO, A., Electrical Engineering
ARTTO, K., Industrial Management
AUTIO, E., Industrial Management
BENGS, C., Urban and Rural Planning
BOEHM, J., Physics
DAHL, O., Industrial Environmental Technology
EHROLA, E., Road Engineering
EHTAMO, H., Systems Analysis
EIROLA, T., Mathematics
EKMAN, K., Machine Design
EKROOS, A., Law
ELORANTA, E., Industrial Management
ERNVALL, T., Transport Engineering
ESKELINEN, P., Radio Engineering
FOGELHOLM, C.-J., Energy Engineering
FORSEN, O., Corrosion Science and Hydrometallurgy
GASIK, M., Materials Processing
GRIPENBERG, G., Mathematics
HÄGGMAN, S.-G., Communications
HAGGREN, H., Photogrammetry

HÄKKINEN, P., Naval Architecture and Marine Engineering
HALLIKAINEN, M., Space Technology
HALME, A., Automation Engineering
HALONEN, K., Integrated Circuit Design, Microelectronics Design
HALONEN, L., Power Systems and Illumination Engineering
HÄMÄLÄINEN, R., Applied Mathematics
HÄNNINEN, H., Engineering Materials
HANNULA, S., Material Science
HARRIS, T., Urban Design
HARTIMO, I., Computer Technology
HAUTOJÄRVI, P., Physics
HEISKANEN, K., Mechanical Process Engineering and Recycling
HELANDER, V., History of Architecture
HOFFREN, J., Aeronautical Engineering
HOLAPPA, L., Metallurgy, Theoretical Process Metallurgy
HUKKINEN, J., Environmental Management
HUOVINEN, S., Structural Design of Building and Rehabilitation of Structures
HURME, M., Plant Design
HYÖTYNIEMI, H., Automation Technology
IKKALA, O., Technical Physics
IKONEN, E., Quantitative Science and Technology
JALKANEN, H., Metallurgy
JÄÄSKELÄINEN, I., Cognitive Technology
JÄMSÄ-JOUNELA, S.-L., Process Control and Automation
JÄRVENPÄÄ, E., Work Psychology
JOKELA, R., Chemistry
JOLMA, A., Geoinformatics
JORMAKKA, J., Communications Engineering
JUHALA, M., Automotive Engineering
JUTILA, A., Bridge Engineering
KAIVOLA, M., Engineering Physics
KANERVA, P., Structural Engineering and Building Physics
KANKAINEN, J., Construction Economics and Management
KANTOLA, R., Communications Engineering
KARHUNEN, J., Information Science
KARI, H., Computer Science
KARJALAINEN, M., Acoustics, Audio and Speech Processing
KARVONEN, T., Hydraulic Engineering
KASKI, K., Computational Engineering
KATILA, T., Biomedical Engineering
KAUPPINEN, V., Production Technology
KAURANEN, I., Development and Management in Industry
KIIRAS, J., Construction Economy and Management
KIURU, H., Water and Waste Water Engineering
KIVILAHTI, J., Materials and Manufacturing Technology for Electronics
KIVIVUORI, S., Physical Metallurgy and Materials Science
KOIVO, H., Control Engineering
KOIVUNEN, V., Signal Processing
KOMONEN, M., Architecture
KONTIO, J., Software Business and Engineering
KONTTURI, K., Physical Chemistry
KORHONEN, A., Processing and Heat Treatment of Materials
KOSKINEN, A., Organic Chemistry
KOSKINEN, K., Information Technology in Automation
KRAUSE, O., Industrial Chemistry
KUIVALAINEN, P., Microelectronics
KULMALA, S., Analytical Chemistry
KUOSMANEN, P., Machine Design
KYYRÄ, J., Power Electronics
LAAKSO, S., Biochemistry
LAAKSO, T., Telecommunications
LAAMANEN, T., Technology Strategy
LAINE, J. E., Paper Technology
LAINE, J. K., Digital Economy
LAINE, U., Speech Technology
LAKERVI, E., Power Systems
LAMPINEN, J., Computational Engineering

LAMPINEN, M., Applied Thermodynamics
LAPINTIE, K., Urban and Regional Planning
LARMI, M., Internal Combustion Engine Technology
LASSAS, M., Mathematics
LEHTONEN, M., Information Technology in Electric Energy Automation
LEISOLA, M., Bioprocess Engineering
LEVÄINEN, K., Real Estate Management
LILLRANK, P., Quality Management
LINDELL, I., Electromagnetics
LIPSANEN, H, Nanotechnology
LONDÉN, S.-O., Computational Mathematics
LOUKOLA-RUSKEENIEMI, K., Geology
LUND, P., Engineering Physics
MÄÄTTANEN, M.
LUOMI, J.
MÄKELÄINEN, P.
MALMI, L., Computer Science, Basic Programming Methodology
MANNILA, H., Computer and Information Sciences
MÄNTYLÄ, M., Information Technology
MATUSIAK, J., Naval Architecture and Marine Engineering
MERILÄINEN, P., Engineering Physics
NEVANLINNA, O., Mathematics
NIEMELÄ, I., Computer and Information Sciences
NIEMINEN, R., Physics
NIINISTÖ, L., Inorganic Chemistry
NIKOSKINEN, K., Electromagnetics
NORDSTRÖM, K., Biochemistry
OITTINEN, P., Graphic Arts
OJA, E., Computer and Information Sciences
ORKAS, J., Foundry Technology
ORPONEN, P., Theoretical Computer Science
ÖSTERGÅRD, P., Information Theory
OVASKA, S., Industrial Electronics
PAAVILAINEN, S., Architecture
PAAVOLA, J., Structural Mechanics
PAKANEN, J., Electrical Installations in Buildings
PAULAPURO, H., Paper Technology
PELTONIEMI, M., Geophysics
PENTTALA, V., Building Materials Technology
PIETOLA, M., Machine Design
PIRILÄ, P., Energy Economics
PITKÄRANTA, J., Mathematics
PULLIAINEN, V., Space Technology
PURSULA, M., Transport Engineering
PUSKA, M., Physics
RÄISÄNEN, A., Radio Engineering
RAUTAMÄKI, M., Landscape Architecture
RAVASKA, O., Foundation Engineering and Soil Mechanics
RISKA, K., Arctic Technology
SAARELA, O., Aeronautical Engineering
SAARINEN, E., Systems Thinking
SAARINEN, K., Physics
SAIKKONEN, H., Information Processing Science
SALO, A., Systems Analysis
SALOMAA, M., Engineering Physics
SALOMAA, R., Technical Physics
SAMS, M., Cognitive Technology
SÄRKKÄ, P., Rock Engineering
SARVAS, J., Electromagnetics
SAVIOJA, L., Virtual Technology
SEGERCRANTZ, J., Mathematics
SEPPÄLÄ, J., Polymer Technology
SEPPÄNEN, O., Heating, Ventilation and Air Conditioning Technology
SEPPONEN, R., Applied Electronics
SHARMA, A., Communications Systems
SIHVOLA, A., Electromagnetics
SIIKALA, A.-M., Building Technology
SIIKONEN, T., Applied Thermodynamics
SIITONEN, T., Housing Design
SIMULA, O., Computer and Information Sciences
SINKKONEN, J., Electron Physics
SIRÉN, K., Design of Heating, Ventilating and Air Conditioning Systems
SKYTTÄ, J., Computer Technology
SMEDS, R., Information Networks

SOISALON-SOININEN, E., Information Processing Science
SOMERSALO, E., Mathematics
STENBERG, R., Mechanics
SULONEN, R., Information Processing
SUTTON, A., Computational Engineering
SYRJÄNEN, M., Knowledge Engineering
TAKALA, T., Interactive Digital Media
TANSKANEN, K., Logistics in Industrial Enterprises
TARHIO, J., Computer and Information Sciences
TEIKARI, V., Industrial Psychology
TIKKA, P., Pulping Technology
TIKKANEN, T., Marketing
TITTONEN, I., Physics in Microtechnologies
TRETYAKOV, S., Radio Engineering
TUHKURI, J., Mechanics of Materials
TULKKI, J., Computational Engineering
TUOMINEN, J., Information Technology in Industry
VAINIKAINEN, P., Radio Engineering
VAKKILAINEN, P., Hydrology and Water Resources Management
VÄLIMÄKI, V., Audio Signal Processing
VALTONEN, M., Circuit Theory
VARSTA, P., Naval Architecture and Marine Engineering
VARTIAINEN, M., Work Psychology
VEPSÄLÄINEN, P., Foundation Engineering and Soil Mechanics
VERMEER, P., Geodesy
VIITANEN, K., Real Estate Economics and Valuation
VILJANEN, M., Structural Design of Buildings
VIRRANTAUS, K., Cartography and Geoinformatics
VIRTAMO, J., Telecommunications Technology
VISALA, A., Automation Technology
VUORIMAA, P., Multimedia Technology
VUORINEN, T., Forest Products Chemistry
WALLENIUS, H., Economics
WALLIN, P., Electrical Engineering
WECK, T.-U., Structural Engineering
WICHMAN, R., Signal Processing
YLÄ-JÄÄSKI, A., Telecommunications Software

TURUN KAUPPAKORKEAKOULU
(Turku School of Economics and Business Administration)

Rehtorinpellonkatu 3, 20500 Turku

Telephone: (2) 481481
Fax: (2) 4814299
E-mail: international@tukkk.fi
Internet: www.tukkk.fi

Founded 1950
Languages of instruction: Finnish, English
State control
Academic year: August to July

Rector: TAPIO REPONEN
Vice-Rector: PAAVO OKKO
Chief Admin. Officer: TUULA LIND
Librarian: ULLA NYGRÉN

Number of teachers: 100
Number of students: 2,000

PROFESSORS

ALVAREZ, L., Economic Mathematics and Statistics
GRANLUND, M., Accounting and Finance
HALINEN-KAILA, A., Marketing
HELMINEN, M., Commercial Law
LÄHTEENMÄKI, S., Management and Organization
LIUHTO, K., International Economics
LUKKA, K., Accounting and Finance
MÄKINEN, E. H., Marketing
MARJANEN, H., Economic Geography
NUMMELA, N., International Marketing
NURMI, R. W., Management and Organization
OJALA, L., Logistics
OKKO, P., Economics

PAASIO, A., Business Administration (Entrepreneurship)
SALMELA, H., Information Systems Science
SCHADÉWITZ, H. (acting), Accounting and Finance
SILLANPÄÄ, M., Commercial Law
SUOMI, R. V., Information Systems Science
TAINA, J., Shipping Economics
TOIVONEN, T., Economic Sociology
WIDGREN, M., Economics

TURUN YLIOPISTO
(University of Turku)

20014 Turku

Telephone: (2) 33351
Fax: (2) 3336363
E-mail: international@utu.fi
Internet: www.utu.fi

Founded 1920
State control
Languages of instruction: Finnish, English
Academic year: August to July (2 semesters)

Chancellor: Prof. EERO VUORIO
Rector: Prof. KEIJO VIRTANEN
Vice-Rectors: Prof. HARRI ANDERSSON, Prof. ERNO LEHTINEN, Prof. MATTI K. VILJANEN
Dir of Admin.: KARI HYPPÖNEN
Chief Librarian: TUULIKKI NURMINEN

Library: 2.8m. vols
Number of teachers: 810
Number of students: 17,925

Publication: *Annales Universitatis Turkuensis*

DEANS

Faculty of Education: Prof. MARJA VAURAS
Faculty of Humanities: Prof. KAISA HÄKKINEN
Faculty of Law: Prof. HEIKKI KULLA
Faculty of Mathematics and Natural Sciences: Prof. JARMO HIETARINTA
Faculty of Medicine: Prof. TAPANI RÖNNEMAA
Faculty of Social Sciences: Prof. VELI-MATTI RITAKALLIO

PROFESSORS

Faculty of Education (tel. (2) 3338803; fax (2) 3338500; e-mail education@utu.fi; internet www.edu.utu.fi):

HELENIUS, A., Early Education
KESKINEN, S., Education
KIVIRAUMA, J., Education
KOSKENSALO, A., Teaching of Foreign Languages
LAINE, K., Early Education
LEHTINEN, E., Teacher Training
LEHTONEN, K., Open Univ. Education
NIEMI, P., Education
NIINISTÖ, K., Education (Teacher Training)
NUPPONEN, H., Physical Education
OLKINUORA, E., Education
PELTONEN, J., Education (Teaching of Handicrafts)
RINNE, R., Adult Education
SARMAVUORI, K., Teaching of Mother Tongue
SOININEN, M., Didactics
VAURAS, M., Education (Learning and Teaching)
VIRTA, A., Teaching of History and Social Sciences

Faculty of Humanities (tel. (2) 333 5202; fax (2) 333 5200; e-mail kv-hum@utu.fi; internet www.utu.fi/hum/tdk):

AHOKAS, P., Comparative Literature
ANTTONEN, V., Comparative Religion
CARCEDO, A., Spanish Language, Culture and Translation
DE ANNA, L., Italian Language, Culture and Translation
GAMBIER, Y., French Translation Studies
GRANÖ, P., Cultural Production and Landscape Studies
HAKAMIES, P., Folkloristics

HÄKKINEN, K., Finnish Language
HÄYRYNEN, M., Landscape Studies
HELASVUO, M.-L., Finnish Language
HILTUNEN, R., Finnish Language
HIRVONEN, I., Scandinavian Philology
HOVI, K., General History
HUUMO, T., Cultural History
IMMONEN, K., French Language and Culture
ITÄLÄ, M.-L., German Translation Studies
ITKONEN, E., General Linguistics
JOHANSSON, M., Art History
KEINÄSTÖ, K., Finnish Literature
KORPILAHTI, P., Logopaedics
KOSTIAINEN, A., Ethnology
KUUSAMO, A., Art History
LAPPALAINEN, P., German Language
LEIMU, P., Russian Language and Culture
LILJESTRÖM, M., Women's Studies
MOISALA, P., Musicology
MYLLYNTAUS, T., Finnish History
MYLLYNTAUS, T., Media Studies
NIKULA, H., Finnish Literature
PIETILÄ, P., English
PYYKKÖ, R., Comparative Literature and Drama
RIDELL, S., Media Studies
ROJOLA, L., Finnish Literature
SAARILUOMA, L., English Philology
SAARINEN, S., Scandinavian Philology
SIHVONEN, J., French Language
SUNDMAN, M., English Translation Studies
SUOMELA-SALMI, E., French Language and Culture
TAAVITSAINEN, J.-P., Archaeology
TOMMOLA, J., English Translation Studies
VAAHTERA, J., Classical Languages and Culture
VIRTANEN, K., Cultural History

Faculty of Law (tel. (2) 333 6307; fax (2) 333 6570; e-mail tls@utu.fi; internet www.law.utu.fi):

ÄMMÄLÄ, T., Procedural Law
BACKMAN, E. V., Criminal Law
BJÖRNE, L., Roman, Law and Legal History
HANNIKAINEN, L., Int. Law
HELIN, M., Private Law
JOKELA, A. T., Procedural Law
KAIRINEN, M., Labour Law
KULLA, H., Admin. Law
LAITINEN, A., Criminology and Sociology of Law
MÄHÖNEN, J., Civil Law
OJANEN, T., European Law
OSSA, J., Financial Law
SAARNILEHTO, A., Civil Law
TALA, J., Legislative Studies
TOMMOLA, J., International Commercial Law
TUOMISTO, J., Civil Law
VILJANEN, P., Criminal and Procedural Law
WIKSTRÖM, K., Financial Law

Faculty of Mathematics and Natural Sciences (tel. (2) 3336275; fax (2) 3336575; e-mail intsci@utu.fi; internet www.sci.utu.fi):

ANDERSSON, H., Human Geography
ARO, E.-M., Plant Physiology
ÄYRÄS, P., Organic Chemistry
EKLUND, O., Geology and Mineralology
GLOOS, K., Physics
HAAPAKKA, K., Analytical Chemistry
HARJU, T., Mathematics
HEINO, J., Biochemistry
HIETARINTA, J., Theoretical Physics
HÖLSÄ, J., Inorganic Chemistry
HONKALA, I., Mathematics
HUOPALAHTI, R., Food Chemistry
ISOAHO, J., Electronics and Information Technology
JORMALAINEN, V., Ecology
KALLIO, H., Food Chemistry
KANKARE, J., Analytical Chemistry
KARHUMÄKI, J., Mathematics
KARI, J., Mathematics

KARSTÉN, E., Information Systems Science
KÄYHKÖ, J., Geography
KNUUTILA, T., Computer Science
KORPIMÄKI, E., Ecology
KUKK, E., Physics
LAHDELMA, R., Information Systems Science
LAHTI, R., Biochemistry
LAIHO, R., Physics
LEIPÄLÄ, T., Applied Mathematics
LÖNNBERG, H., Organic Chemistry
LÖVGREN, T., Biotechnology
LUKKARI, J., Physical Chemistry
MÄKELÄ, M., Applied Mathematics
NEVALAINEN, O., Computer Science
NIKINMAA, M., Animal Physiology
NORRDAHL, K., Ecology
NURMINEN, M., Information Systems Science
OKSANEN, LAURI, Plant Ecology
PAASIO, A., Microelectronics
PETTERSSON, K., Biotechnology
PIHLAJA, K., Physical Chemistry
PRIMMER, C., Genetics
RÄSÄNEN, M., Quaternary Geology
RINTAMÄKI, E., Genetics
SAARINEN, T., Geology and Mineralogy
SALAKOSKI, T., Computer Science
SALMINEN, S., Food Devt
SALO, J., Biodiversity Research
SARVALA, J., Ecology
SAVILAHTI, H., Genetics
SOLIN, O., Radiochemistry
SUNDBLAD, K., Geology and Mineralogy
SUOMINEN, K.-A., Physics
TAPANINEN, U., Logistic Systems of Maritime Transport
TENHUNEN, H., Nanoelectronics
TORSTI, J., Space Research
TUOMINEN, A., Electronics
VALTAOJA, E., Astronomy
VALTONEN, M., Astronomy
VÄYRYNEN, J., Physics
YLI-JOKIPII, P., Human Geography
YLINEN, K., Mathematics

Faculty of Medicine (Sirkkalankatu 1, 20520 Turku; tel. (2) 333 8408; fax (2) 333 8413; e-mail intmedi@utu.fi; internet www.med.utu.fi):

AARNIO, P., Surgery
AHOTUPA, M., Physiology
ARO, H., Orthopaedics and Traumatology
ARONEN, P., Diagnostic Radiology
CARPÉN, O., Pathology
COLLAN, Y., Pathology
DEAN, P., Diagnostic Radiology
ELENIUS, K., Medical Biochemistry
ERKKOLA, R., Obstetrics and Gynaecology
FINNE, J., Medical Biochemistry
GRÉNMAN, R., Otorhinolaryngology
HÄNNINEN, P., Medical Physics
HAPPONEN, R.-P., Oral Surgery
HARTIALA, J., Clinical Physiology and Nuclear Medicine
HIETALA, J., Psychiatry
HONKALA, E., Dentistry
HUHTANIEMI, I., Physiology
HUUPPONEN, R., Pharmacology
HYYPIÄ, T., Virology
ISOLAURI, E., Paediatrics
JALKANEN, S., Immunology
JALONEN, J., Anaesthesiology
KÄÄPÄ, P., Paediatrics
KÄHÄRI, V.-M., Dermatology and Venereal Diseases
KANERVA, L., Synthetic Drug Chemistry
KEMPPAINEN, P., Stomatognathic Physiology
KIVELÄ, S.-L., General Practice
KÖNÖNEN, E., Dentistry
KORPI, E., Pharmacology
KOSKENVUO, M., Public Health
KOTILAINEN, P., Infectious Diseases
KOULU, M., Drug Devt
LASSILA, O., Immunobiology

LAUNIS, V., Medical Ethics
LEINO-KILPI, H., Nursing Science
MAJAMAA, K., Neurology
MÄKELA, S., Drug Devt
MÄKINEN, J., Obstetrics and Gynaecology
MARTTILA, R., Neurology
MERTSOLA, J., Paediatrics
MONONEN, I., Clinical Chemistry
MÖTTÖNEN, T., Rheumatology
NÄRHI, T., Dental Prosthetics
NIINIKOSKI, J. H. A., Surgery
NIKOSKELAINEN, E., Ophthalmology
NIKOSKELAINEN, J., Internal Medicine
NUUTILA, P., Internal Medicine
OLKKOLA, K., Anaesthesiology
PARVINEN, M., Anatomy
PELLINIEMI, L., Electron Microscopy
PELTONEN, J., Anatomy
PENTTINEN, R., Medical Biochemistry
PERTOVAARA, A., Physiology
PIHA, J., Child Psychiatry
POUTANEN, M., Physiology
PUOLAKKAINEN, P., Surgery
PYRHÖNEN, S., Oncology and Radiotherapy
RINNE, J., Brain Research
RÖNNEMAA, T., Internal Medicine
ROBERTS, P. J., Surgery
RUUSKANEN, O., Infectious Diseases
SALMINEN, E., Palliative Medicine
SALOKANGAS, R., Psychiatry
SAUKKO, P., Forensic Medicine
SCHEININ, M., Biomaterial Technology
SCHEININ, M., Clinical Pharmacology
SERLO, W., Child Surgery
SIMELL, O. G., Paediatrics
SYRJÄNEN, S., Oral Pathology and Radiology
TENOVUO, J. O., Cardiology
TERHO, E. O., Pulmonary Diseases and Clinical Allergology
TOPPARI, J., Physiology
TUOMINEN, R., Public Health
VÄÄNÄNEN, K., Cell Biology
VÄLIMÄKI, M., Nursing Science
VALLITTU, P., Prosthetic Dentistry and Biomaterials Science
VARRELA, J., Oral Devt and Orthodontics
VIIKARI, J., Internal Medicine
VIITANEN, M., Geriatrics
WICKSTRÖM, G., Occupational Health

Faculty of Social Sciences (tel. (2) 3335362; fax (2) 3336270; e-mail intsoc@utu.fi; internet www.soc.utu.fi):

AINAMO, A., Innovation, Technology and Science Policy
FORSSÉN, K., Social Work
HAKOVIRTA, H., Political Science, International Politics
HÄMÄLÄINEN, H., Psychology
KESKINEN, E., Psychology
KIVINEN, O., Sociology of Education
KOISTINEN, O., Theoretical Philosophy
LAGERSPETZ, E., Practical Philosophy
MELIN, H., Sociology
NIEMI, P., Psychology
NURMI, H., Political Science
PÖNTINEN, S., Sociology
RÄIHÄ, H., Psychology
RENTOLA, K., Contemporary History
RITAKALLIO, V.-M., Social Policy
SALMIVALLI, C., Psychology
SALONEN, H., Economics
SOIKKANEN, T., Contemporary History
UUSIPAIKKA, E., Statistics
VIRÉN, M., Economics
WIBERG, M., Political Science

VAASAN YLIOPISTO (University of Vaasa)

POB 700, 65101 Vaasa
Puuvillakuja 8, 65200 Vaasa

Telephone: (6) 3248111
Fax: (6) 3248208
E-mail: kirjaamo@uwasa.fi

Internet: www.uwasa.fi
Founded 1966
Languages of instruction: Finnish, Swedish, English
State control
Academic year: September to May
Rector: MATTI JAKOBSSON
Vice-Rectors: MERJA KOSKELA JUKKA VESALAINEN
Admin. Dir: ANITA NIEMI-IILAHTI
Librarian: VUOKKO PALONEN
Library of 120,000 vols; also see entry for the Tritonia Academic Library
Number of teachers: 250
Number of students: 5,000
Publication: *Acta Wasaensia*

DEANS

Faculty of Business Studies: Prof. VESA SUUTARI
Faculty of Humanities: Prof. MARIANN SKOG-SÖDERSVED
Faculty of Philosophy: Prof. MERJA KOSKELA
Faculty of Public Admin.: Prof. ARI SALMINEN
Faculty of Technology: Prof. ERKKI ANTILA

PROFESSORS

Faculty of Business Studies (tel. (6) 3248111; fax (6) 3248171; internet www.uwasa.fi/kauppatieteet):

ÄIJÖ, J., Accounting and Business financeANNOLA, V., Business Law
GABRIELSSON, P., Management and Organization
GAHMBERG, H., Marketing
LAAKSONEN, M.,
LAAKSONEN, P., Marketing
LAITINEN, E. K., Accounting and Business Finance
LAITINEN, T., Accounting and Business Finance
LARIMO, J., Int. Marketing
LEHTONEN, A., Law
LINDMAN, M., Marketing
LUOMALA, H., Marketing
NIKKINEN, J., Accounting and Business Finance
PIEKKOLA, H., Economics
ROTHOVIUS, T., Accounting and Business Finance
ROUTAMAA, V., Management and Organization
SALMI, T., Accounting and Business Finance
SUUTARI, V., Management and Organization
VATAJA, J., Economics
VESALAINEN, J., Management and Organization
VIITALA, R., Management and Organization

Faculty of Humanities (tel. (6) 3248111; fax (6) 3248131; internet www.uwasa.fi/hmanistinen):

AALTONEN, S., English Language, Literature and Culture
BJÖRKLUND, S., Language Immersion
KOSKELA, M., Applied Linguistics
LAURÉN, CH., Swedish
LEHTINEN, E., Modern Finnish
NORDMAN, M., Swedish
PIEKKOLA, H., Economics

Faculty of Philosophy (tel. (6) 3248111; fax (6) 3248465; internet www.uwasa.fi/filosofinen):

AALTONEN, S., English Language, Literature and Culture
BJÖRKLUND, S., Language Immersion
LEHTINEN, E., Modern Finnish
MALMBERG, T., Communications
MÅRD-MIETTINEN, K., Swedish Language
NUOPPONEN, A., Applied Linguistics
PARRY, C., German Language

PORTER, G., English Language
SALMINEN, A., Public Admin.
SKOG-SÖDERSVED, M., German Language
VIRKKALA, S., Regional Studies

Faculty of Public Administration (tel. (6) 3248111; fax (6) 3248465; internet www.uwasa.fi/hallintotieteet):

HYYRYLÄINEN, E., Public Admin
KATAJAMÄKI, H., Regional Studies
SALMINEN, A., Public Admin.
VARTIAINEN, P., Public Admin.

Faculty of Technology (tel. (6) 32481111; fax (6) 3248344; internet www.uwasa.fi/trkniikka):

ALANDER, J., Production Automation
ELMUSRATI,, M., Telecommunication Engineering
HASSI, S., Mathematics
HELO, P., Logistics
KAUHANIEMI, K., Electrical Engineering
PYNNÖNEN, S., Statistics
SOTTINEN, T., Business Mathematics
TAKALA, J., Production Economics
VEKARA, T., Electrical Engineering
WANNE, M., Information Technology

Polytechnics

Diakonia-ammattikorkeakoulu (Diaconia University of Applied Sciences): Maistraatinportti 2A, 00240 Helsinki; tel. (20) 1606220; fax (20) 1606222; internet www.diak.fi; f. 1996; education, nursing, social welfare, sign language interpretation and media; library: 140,000 vols, periodicals and audiovisual items; 3,000 students; Rector Dr JORMA NIEMALÄ.

Etelä-Karjalan ammattikorkeakoulu (South Karelia Polytechnic): Pohjolankatu 23, 53101 Lappeenranta; tel. (20) 49600; fax (20) 4966688; e-mail info@scp.fi; internet www.scp.fi; faculties of business administration, fine arts and design, health care and social services, technology and tourism and hospitality; 260 teachers; 2,700 students; Rector ANNELI PIRTTILÄ.

EVTEK-ammattikorkeakoulu (Espoon-Vantaan teknillinen ammattikorkeakoulu) (Espoo-Vantaa Institute of Technology): Vanha maantie 6, 02650 Espoo; tel. (20) 7553500; fax (20) 7553929; e-mail education@evtek.fi; internet www.evtek.fi; three divisions: EVTEK Institute of Technology, EVTEK Mercuria Business School, EVTEK Institute of Art and Design; library: 30,600 vols, 320 periodicals; Pres. Dr PERTTI TÖRMÄLÄ.

Haaga ammattikorkeakoulu (Haaga Polytechnic): POB 8, 00321 Helsinki; tel. (9) 58078214; fax (9) 58078489; e-mail hakutoimisto@haaga.fi; internet www.haaga.fi; Haaga Institute School of Hotel, Restaurant and Tourism Management; Helsinki School of Business; Malmi School of Business and Vierumäki Sports Institute; Pres. ANTTI HALLI.

Hämeen Ammattikorkeakoulu (Häme Polytechnic): Visamäentie 35, 13100 Hämeenlinna; tel. (3) 6461; fax (3) 6464200; e-mail hamk@hamk.fi; internet www.hamk.fi; f. 1996; culture, natural resources and the environment, natural sciences, social sciences, business and administration, social services, health and sports technology, communication and transport tourism, catering and domestic services and vocational teacher education; library: 120,000 vols, 450 periodicals in Finnish, 350 in other languages; 7,500 teachers; 400 students; Rector VEIJO HINTSANEN.

Helsingin Ammattikorkeakoulu Stadia (Helsinki Polytechnic Stadia): POB 4010, Bulevardi 31, 00099 Helsinki; tel. (9) 3108611; fax (9) 31080599; e-mail info@stadia.fi; internet www.stadia.fi; f. 2000; library: 120,000 vols; 551 teachers; 7,284 students; Rector TIMO LUOPAJÄRVI.

Helsingin Liiketalouden Ammattikorkeakoulu (Helsinki Business Polytechnic): Ratapihantie 13, 00520 Helsinki; tel. (9) 148901; fax (9) 14890453; internet www.helia.fi; business management, information technology, journalism, tourism, management assistant training; vocational teacher education programmes; 230 teachers; 5,500 students; Rector RITVA LAAKSO-MANNINEN.

HUMAK (Hakutoimistoon) (Humanities Polytechnic): Kivirannantie 13–15, 95410 Kiviranta; internet www.humak.edu; f. 1998; programmes in civic activities and youth work, cultural management and production, and sign language interpreting; 120 teachers; 1,300 students; Pres. EEVA-LIISA ANTIKAINEN.

Jyväskylän Ammattikorkeakoulu (Jyväskylä Polytechnic): Rajakatu 35, 40200 Jyväskylä; tel. (14) 4446611; fax (14) 4446600; internet www.jypoly.fi; School of Cultural Studies, School of Business, School of Engineering and Technology, School of Information Technology, School of Health and Social Care, School of Tourism and Services Management; Institute of Natural Resources; Vocational Teacher Education College; 600 teachers; 7,500 students; Rector MAURI PANHELAINEN.

Kajaanin Ammattikorkeakoulu (Kajaani Polytechnic): POB 52, Ketunpolku 3, 87101 Kajaani; tel. (8) 618991; fax (8) 61899603; e-mail kajaanin.amk@kajak.fi; internet www.kajak.fi; f. 1992; business and administration, tourism and hospitality management, health and sports and engineering; library: 27,000 vols, 350 periodicals; 130 teachers; 1,500 students; Rector ARTO KARJALAINEN.

Kemi-Tornion Ammattikorkeakoulu (Kemi-Tornio Polytechnic): POB 505, 94101 Kemi; tel. (16) 258400; fax (16) 258401; internet www.tokem.fi; f. 1992; business administration, business and data-processing, cultural and media arts, health care, social services, technology; library: 90,000 vols, 600 periodicals; 195 teachers; 2,400 students; Dean LEENA ALALÄÄKKÖLÄ.

Kymenlaakso Ammattikorkeakoulu (Kymenlaakso Polytechnic): POB 13, Pääskysentie 1, 48231 Kotka; tel. (5) 2208111; fax (5) 2208209; internet www.kyamk.fi; f. 1992; business and administration, culture, forestry and wood technology, maritime studies, social and health care and technology; library: 100,000 vols, 500 periodicals; 500 teachers; 3,500 students; Rector RAGNAR LUNDQVIST.

Lahden Ammattikorkeakoulu (Lahti Polytechnic): POB 214, Paasikivenkatu 7, 15101 Lahti; tel. (3) 82818; fax (3) 8282066; internet www.lamk.fi; f. 1991; business studies, design, fine arts, music, hospitality management, social and health care, sports, technology and engineering, and visual communication; 200 teachers; 5,000 students; Dr RISTO ILOMÄKI.

Laurea Ammattikorkeakoulu (Laurea Polytechnic): Lummetie 2B, 01300 Vantaa; tel. (9) 205787150; fax (9) 205787200; internet www.laurea.fi; culture, natural resources and the environment, natural sciences, social sciences, business and administration, social services, health and sports, tourism, catering and domestic services, hotel and restaurant studies, and correctional services; 8,000 students; Rector PENTTI RAUHALA.

Mikkelin Ammattikorkeakoulu (Mikkeli Polytechnic): Patteristonkatu 3, 50101 Mikkeli; tel. (15) 3556407; fax (15) 3556377; internet www.mikkeliamk.fi; Business School, School of Engineering, School of Social Work and Health Care, School of Culture and Youth Work, School of Hospitality Management, School of Forestry (Pieksämäki), School of Health Care, Tourism and Culture (Savonlinna); 200 teachers; 4,000 students; Rector ERKKI KARPPANEN.

Österbottens Yrkeshögskola (Central Ostrobothnia Polytechnic): Talonpojankatu 4, 67100 Kokkola; tel. (6) 8252012; fax (6) 8252075; internet www.cop.fi; f. 1998; languages of instruction: Finnish, Swedish, English; technology, communication and transport, social sciences, business and administration, social services, health and sports, natural sciences, culture, humanities and education, tourism, catering and domestic services; post graduate programmes in business administration and technology; 246 teachers; 3,300 students; Rector MARJA-LIISA TENHUNEN.

Oulun Seudun ammattikorkeakoulu (Oulu Polytechnic): Albertinkuja 20, POB 222, 90101 Oulu; tel. (8) 3126011; fax (8) 3126009; e-mail international@oamk.fi; internet www.oamk.fi; f. 1992; culture, natural resources and the environment, natural sciences, social sciences, business and administration, social services, health and sports, and technology, communication and transport; 7,700 students; Rector LAURI LANTTO.

Pirkanmaa Ammattikorkeakoulu (Pirkanmaa Polytechnic): Kuntokatu 4, 33520 Tampere; tel. (3) 2452111; fax (3) 2452351; e-mail piramk@piramk.fi; internet www.piramk.fi; f. 1992; social services, health and sports, social sciences, business and administration, natural sciences, tourism, catering and domestic services, culture, technology, communication and transport; 4,000 students; Rector OLLI MIKKILÄ; publ. *Spirit.*

Pohjois-Karjalan ammattikorkeakoulu (North Karelia Polytechnic): Tikkarinne 9, 80200 Joensuu; tel. (13) 2606404; fax (13) 2606401; e-mail info@ncp.fi; internet www.ncp.fi; f. 1992; culture, social sciences, business and administration, natural sciences,

natural resources and the environment, tourism, catering and domestic services, social services, health and sports, technology, communication and transport; adult education; 400 teachers; 4,000 students; Pres. PENTTI MALJOJOKI.

Rovaniemen Ammattikorkeakoulu (Rovaniemi Polytechnic): Jokiväylä 13, 96300; tel. (16) 3313366; fax (16) 3313328; e-mail polytechnic@ramk.fi; internet www.ramk.fi; f. 1996; business and administration, forestry and rural industries, health care and social services, sports and leisure, technology, tourism and hospitality management; 3,000 students; Pres. PENTTI TIERANTA.

Satakunnan Ammattikorkeakoulu (Satakunta Polytechnic): Tiedepuisto 3, 28600 Pori; tel. (2) 6203000; fax (2) 6203030; e-mail int.kesy@samk.fi; internet www.spt.fi; f. 1997; business, fine art and media studies, social services and healthcare, technology, and maritime management and tourism; 530 teachers; 6,417 students.

Savonia-Ammattikorkeakoulu (Pohjois-Savo Polytechnic): POB 6, 70201 Kuopio; tel. (17) 2555062; internet www.savonia-amk.fi; f. 1992; social sciences, business and administration, culture, natural resources and the environment, tourism, catering and domestic services, social services, health and sports technology, communication and transport, and natural sciences; 350 teachers; 7,000 students.

Seinäjoen Ammattikorkeakoulu (Seinäjoki Polytechnic): Keskuskatu 34, 60100 Seinäjoki; tel. (20) 1245000; fax (20) 1245001; e-mail seamk.toimisto@seamk.fi; internet www.seamk.fi; f. 1996; natural resources and the environment, natural sciences, social sciences, business and administration, technology and communication and transport, social services, health and sports, tourism, catering and domestic services and culture; 350 teachers; 4,600 students; Rector TAPIO VARMOLA.

Svenska yrkeshögskolan (Swedish Polytechnic, Finland): Fabriksgatan 1, POB 6, 65200 Vaasa; tel. (6) 3285000; fax (6) 3285110; internet www.syh.fi; language of instruction: Swedish; culture, health care

and social welfare and technology, and communications; Rector ÖRJAN ANDERSSON.

Tampereen Ammattikorkeakoulu (Tampere Polytechnic): Teiskontie 33, PL 21 33521 Tampere; tel. (3) 20711011; e-mail international.office@tamk.fi; internet www.tpu.fi; f. 1996; languages of instruction: Finnish, English; Bachelors-level degrees in art and media, business economics and technology, international business, environmental engineering; teacher education centre; 400 full-time teachers, 700 part-time; 5,000 students; Rector MARKKU LAHTINEN.

Turun Ammattikorkeakoulu (Turku Polytechnic): Sepänkatu 3, 20700 Turku; tel. (10) 55350; fax (10) 5535791; internet www.turkuamk.fi; f. 1992; 460 teachers; 9,000 students; Rector Dr JUHA KETTUNEN.

Vaasa Ammattikorkeakoulu (Vaasa Polytechnic): Raastuvankatu 29, 65100 Vaasa; tel. (6) 3263111; fax (6) 3263002; e-mail info@puv.fi; internet www.puv.fi; f. 1996; languages of instruction: Finnish, Swedish, English; faculties of business economics, tourism, health care and social services, and technology and communication; 240 teachers; 3,500 students; Rector PENTTI RUOTSALA; publ. *Scenario* (1 or 2 a year).

Yrkeshögskolan Arcada (Arcada Polytechnic): Jan-Magnus Janssons plats 1, 00550 Helsingfors; tel. (7) 699699; fax (7) 699622; internet www.arcada.fi; f. 1996; courses in culture, health care and social work, rehabilitation, business administration and tourism, technology; library: 23,500 vols; 90 teachers; 1,900 students; Rector HENRIK WOLFF.

Yrkeshögskolan Sydväst (Sydväst Polytechnic): Raseborgsvägen 9, 10600 Ekenäs; tel. (19) 2227200; fax (19) 2227499; e-mail office@sydvast.fi; internet www.sydvast.fi; language of instruction: Swedish; agriculture, business administration, church community work, culture production, design, engineering, forestry, health care, horticulture, landscape planning and environmental instruction, maritime studies, sports and health promotion, social care, tourism management; 1,350 students; Rector JAN NYBOM.

ÅLAND ISLANDS

Learned Society
GENERAL

Ålands kulturstiftelse r.s. (Åland Cultural Foundation): POB 172, AX- 22101 Mariehamn; tel. (18) 19535; internet www.kultur.aland.fi/kulturstiftelsen; f. 1950; promotes scientific research of Åland history and cultural life in the islands; engages and supports publishing; Pres. and Chair. HENRIK GUSTAFSSON; Vice-Pres. PETER WAHLBERG; Sec. THÉRÈSE KÄHRE; Treas. BEN-ERIK ALM; publs *Det åländska folkets historia* (The History of the Åland People), *Internationella avtal och dokument rörande Åland, läs dem direkt på internet, Meddelanden från Ålands kulturstiftelse* (Communications), *Skrifter*

utgivna av Ålands kulturstiftelse (Papers), *Urkundssamlingen* (The Tract Collection).

Research Institutes
ECONOMICS, LAW AND POLITICS

Ålands Emigrantinstitut (Åland Islands' Emigrant Institute): Norra Esplanadgatan 5, AX- 22100 Mariehamn; tel. (18) 13325; e-mail emi.inst@aland.net; internet www.eminst.net; f. 1996, admin. by the Åland Islands Emigrant Institute Society; promotes research into Ålandic emigration; collects, catalogues and distributes material connected with Ålandic emigration; Chair. ERIK

LINDHOLM; Vice-Chair. BERTIL LINDQVIST; Treas. MAJVOR SÖDERBERG.

Ålands Fredsinstitut (Ålands Islands Peace Institute): Hamngatan 4, POB 85 AX-22101 Mariehamn; tel. (18) 15570; fax (18) 21026; e-mail peace@peace.ax; internet www.peace.ax; f. 1992; conducts projects and research into peace and conflict issues with regard to Ålands and spec. status of Ålands under int. law; library: holds material on peace and conflict issues, minorities, autonomy and human rights; Dir SIA SPILIOPOULOU AKERMARK; Head, Library and Archive JOHN KNIGHT.

Nordens Institut på Åland (Nordic Institute on Åland): Köpmansgatan 4, AX- 22100 Mariehamn; tel. (18) 25000; fax (18) 13301; e-mail asa.juslin@nipa.ax; internet www

.nipa.ax; f. 1985; attached to Nordic Council of Ministers; cultural institution; strengthens cultural life through contacts with other Nordic countries; Dir ÅSA JUSLIN; Sec. HARRIET LUNDELL.

Libraries and Archives

Mariehamn

Mariehamns Stadsbibliotek–Central-Bibliotek för Åland (Mariehamn City Library–Central Library of Åland): POB 76, Strandgatan 29, AX- 22101 Mariehamn; tel. (18) 531411; fax (18) 531619; e-mail biblioteket@mariehamn.ax; internet www .bibliotek.ax; f. 1890 as Åland lending library, present bldg 1939, present name 1987; Alandica colln (works relating to the islands); 135,277 vols, incl. 122,715 books, 7,502 CDs and cassettes, 1,454 DVDs and VHS, 231 magazine subscriptions and 19 newspapers; Library Dir EVA GUSTAFSSON-LINDVALL; Chief Librarian TOM ECKERMAN.

Sund

Sunds Bibliotek: Sundsvägen 1158, Finby, AX- 22530 Sund; tel. and fax (18) 45978; e-mail sundsbibliotek@aland.net; internet www.sund.ax/bibliotek.pbs; Librarian SONJA BERGLUND.

Museums and Art Galleries

Kastelholm

Ålands Fotografiska Museum i Kastelholm (Åland's Camera Museum in Kastelholm): Källbacksvägen 19, AX- 22520 Kastelholm; tel. and fax (18) 43964; e-mail alands.fotografiska.museum@aland.net;

internet www.aland.com/se/ fotografiskamuseum; colln of cameras, accessories and photographic equipment; spec. exhibitions.

Lappo

Skärgårdsmuseet (Archipelago Museum): AX- 22840 Lappo; tel. (18) 56689; fax (18) 56657; e-mail anneli.forsberg@pp1.inet.fi; internet www.skargardsmuseet.net; traditional island and fishing culture; blacksmith's workshop with colln of old utensils; colln of 10 traditional rural boats; photographic exhibition.

Mariehamn

Museibyrån (Åland Board of Antiquities): POB 1060, AX- 22111 Mariehamn; tel. (18) 25000; fax (18) 17440; e-mail museum.info@ regeringen.ax; internet www.museum.ax; administers Åland's antiquities, researches its cultural heritage, preserves artefacts, bldgs and sites of cultural and historical value; maintains Ålands museum and Konstmuseum; responsibile for other museums located on the islands; Dir and Curator VIVEKA LÖNDAHL.

Ålands Konstmuseum (Åland Art Museum): Storagatan 1, 22100 Mariehamn; tel. (18) 25426; fax (18) 17440; e-mail konst .info@regeringen.ax; internet www.museum .ax/museum/konstmuseum.pbs; f. 1963; attached to Museibyrån; local artists since 19th century; promotes artistic activity and disseminates knowledge about art; Curator SUSANNE PROCOPÉ ILMONEN.

Ålands Museum: POB 1060, AX- 22111 Mariehamn; tel. (18) 25000; fax (18) 17440; e-mail museum.info@regeringen.ax; internet www.museum.aland.fi/museum/alandsmuseum/alandsmuseum.pbs; f. 1934; attached to Museibyrån; prehistoric, historic and ethnological material; permanent exhibition of cultural history; spec. exhibitions; free

entry October–April; library of 10,000 vols; Curator ANNIKA DAHLBLOM; publs Åländsk Odling (1 a year), Sevärt (series).

Ålandssjöfartsmuseum (Åland Maritime Museum): Hamngatan 2, POB 98, 22101 Mariehamn; tel. (18) 19930; fax (18) 19936; e-mail info@sjofartsmuseum.ax; internet www.sjofartsmuseum.ax; f. 1935, opened to public 1954; ships' documents, model ships and figureheads; closed for renovation 2010–11; library: collns of Alandica nautical literature, archives incl. muster rolls, log books, colln of clippings, photographs, drawings and charts; Pres. JAN LIMNELL; Dir Dr HANNA HAGMARK-COOPER; publ. Sjöhistorisk Årsskrift för Åland (1 a year).

University

HÖGSKOLAN PÅ ÅLAND
(Åland University of Applied Sciences)

POB 1010, AX- 22111 Mariehamn

Telephone: (18) 537000

Fax: (18) 16913

E-mail: info@ha.ax

Internet: www.ha.ax

Founded 1997, fmrly Åland Polytechnic, present name 2003 after merger with Åland Open Univ.

Public control

Language of instruction: Swedish

Rector: AGNETA ERIKSSON-GRANSKOG

Vice-Rector: HENRIK KARLSSON

Number of teachers: 32

Number of students: 400

Faculties of business administration, electrical engineering, health and caring sciences, hospitality management, information technology, marine engineering, navigation.

FRANCE

The Higher Education System

The French higher education system was restructured following the student-led unrest of 1968. The Loi de l'Orientation d'Education was enacted (it was reconfirmed 1989) and greater autonomy was granted to institutions. However, ultimate responsibility for determining the curricula and teaching methods remains with the Ministries of Education. France and the French Overseas Posssessions are divided into 35 educational districts, called Académies, each responsible for the administration of education, from primary to higher levels, in its area. There are 91 universities (a term that includes instituts universitaires de technologie—university institutes of technology) under the Ministries of Education, including universities in French Overseas Possessions; these institutions are: Université des Antilles et de la Guyane (French Guiana, Guadeloupe, Martinique), Université de la Polynésie Française (French Polynesia), Université de Nouvelle Calédonie (New Caledonia) and Université de la Réunion (Réunion).

Students must have achieved the baccalauréat, the main secondary school qualification, to gain admission to higher education. Some institutions may set additional entrance examinations, and the grandes écoles require students to undertake two to three years' additional study at a lycée. Since 2002 France has gradually implemented the Bologna Process and established a two-tier Bachelors and Masters degree system, completed by Doctoral studies. Some institutions may still offer professional qualifications or non-standard degrees. The standard undergraduate degree is now the three-year Licence (equivalent to Bachelors). Following the Licence, students may take the Masters, which is awarded after two years and replaces the range of pre-Bologna five-year degrees. There are two Masters tracks, Research or Professional. The Research Masters is required for entry to Doctoral studies, and the Doctorate is awarded after three years of study. Alternatively, medical students are required to study for a total of seven years for the Doctoral degree of Diplôme d'état de Docteur en Médecine.

In addition to universities and instituts universitaires de technologie, other public institutions offering higher education include instituts universitaires professionnalisés, grandes écoles and écoles normales supérieures. There are also professional schools for engineering, business and management, political sciences and veterinary sciences. Instituts universitaires de technologie were first established in 1966 and offer specialist two-year programmes leading to the award of Diplôme Universitaire de Technologie. Instituts universitaires professionnalisés have been established since 1992 and train senior executives for engineering, business and management, general administration, information and communication. Courses last for six years, including a six-month work placement, and culminate in the award of the Maîtrise degree. Grandes écoles are regarded as the most prestigious establishments for graduates wishing to enter high public service or business. The most prominent grandes écoles are the écoles normales supérieures; courses last for four years and students are awarded the Diplôme d'études Appronfondies. In 2006/07 2,254,400 students were enrolled in higher education, including universities and university institutes of technology and schools of engineering.

Technical and vocational education is broken down into five levels, Niveau V to Niveau I, and is offered by secondary and post-secondary institutions. Broadly speaking, Niveaux III–I cover the post-secondary level, and lead to the award of a title such as Brevet de Technicien Supérieur, Diplôme d'Etat de Technicien, or Diplôme Universitaire de Technologie.

In August 2007 under the new Nicolas Sarkozy administration the Higher Education Minister, Valerie Pécresse, proposed a law concerning the 'freedom and responsibilities of the universities'. Under the law universities were to be reformed within a year, and were all to become fully autonomous by 2012. University Presidents, elected by an Administrative Council including representatives of industry, were to have more control over how research staff divided their time between research and teaching, and how students were recruited. Publication quotas were to be imposed on researchers and faculties were to become more competitive and productive in terms of the professional market, and were to be free to gain funding by working more closely with industry. The intention was for universities to function much like successful commercial enterprises.

However, the reform project met with considerable resistance amongst the student and researcher populations who saw it as an attack on the traditional republican value of freedom to education, and as undermining fundamental research in favour of applied research. A growing social movement of protest within the academic world began at the end of 2008 and was still in evidence in summer 2009. Strikes at a number of universities that year endangered the end of year examinations and the government eventually sent in security forces to evict students. However, by 2010 51 universities were autonomous as were six higher education schools. By 2012 another 19 universities and six engineering schools are expected to be autonomous.

Regulatory and Representative Bodies

GOVERNMENT

Ministry of Culture and Communication: 3 rue de Valois, 75001 Paris; tel. 1-40-15-80-00; fax 1-40-15-81-72; e-mail point .culture@culture.fr; internet www.culture .gouv.fr; Minister CHRISTINE ALBANEL.

Ministry of Higher Education and Research: 1 rue Descartes, 75231 Paris Cedex 05; tel. 1-55-55-90-90; e-mail secretariat-communication@recherche.gouv .fr; internet www .enseignementsup-recherche.gouv.fr; Minister VALÉRIE PÉCRESSE.

Ministry of National Education: 110 rue de Grenelle, 75357 Paris Cedex 07; tel. 1-55-55-10-10; fax 1-45-51-53-63; internet www .education.gouv.fr; Minister XAVIER DARCOS.

ACCREDITATION

Comité national d'évaluation (CNE): 43 rue de la Procession, 61–65 Street pedestrian entrance Dutot, 75015 Paris; tel. 1-55-55-60-97; fax 1-55-55-63-94; e-mail sgcne@ cne-evaluation.fr; internet www .cne-evaluation.fr; f. 1984; govt org. with authority over all instns of higher education in France; evaluation of quality of main 'missions of public service' of each such instn; First Vice-Pres. MICHEL HOFFERT.

Commission des Titres d'Ingénieur (CTI): Greffe de la CTI, Direction Générale de l'Enseignement Supérieur, 110 rue de Grenelle, 75357 Paris 07 SP; tel. 1-55-55-67-25; e-mail greffe-cti@education.gouv.fr; internet www.cti-commission.fr; f. 1934; quality assurance and accreditation for engineers; Pres. BERNARD REMAUD.

ENIC/NARIC France: Centre international d'études pédagogiques (CIEP), 1 rue Descartes, 75231 Paris Cedex 05; tel. (1) 55-55-04-28; fax (1) 55-55-00-39; e-mail enic-naric@ ciep.fr; internet www.ciep.fr/enic-naricfr; Dir FRANÇOISE PROFIT.

NATIONAL BODIES

Conférence des Directeurs des Ecoles Françaises d'Ingénieurs (CDEFI): 151 blvd de l'Hôpital, 75013 Paris; tel. 1-44-24-64-49; fax 1-44-24-64-51; e-mail cdefi@cdefi .fr; internet www.cdefi.fr; f. 1976; Exec. Dir ALEXANDRE RIGAL.

Conférence des Présidents d'Université: 103 blvd Saint-Michel, 75005 Paris; tel. 1-44-32-90-00; fax 1-44-32-91-02; e-mail contact@cpu.fr; internet www.cpu.fr; f. 1971; consultative body at the disposition of the Min. of Nat. Education; also studies questions of interest to all univs and co-ordinates the activities of various commissions on all aspects of education; mems: 103 pres of univs and state instns; 109 mems; Pres. LIONEL COLLET.

Conférence des Recteurs Français (French Rectors' Conference): Chancellerie des universités de Paris, 47 rue des Ecoles, 75005 Paris; f. 1987; establishes personal and permanent links between mems; encourages the discussion of professional problems; establishes relations with nat. and int. bodies concerned with education, science and culture; the Rectors are Chancellors of the state univs in their admin. area; Pres. Rector MICHEL LEROY (Acad. de Nancy-Metz); Sec.-Gen./Treas. Rector WILLIAM MAROIS (Acad. de Bordeaux).

Fédération Interuniversitaire de l'Enseignement à Distance (FIED): Domaine universitaire de la Bouloie, Bât. TD2, 25030 Besançon Cedex; tel. 3-81-66-58-65; fax 3-81-66-58-71; e-mail info@fied-univ.fr; internet www.fied-univ.fr; f. 1987; promotes distance learning by encouraging co-operation between French and int. univs and instns; 36 mems; Pres. RONAN CHABAUTY; Sec. CHANTAL ACHERÉ.

Office national d'information sur les enseignements et les professions (ONISEP) (National Office for Information on Study and the Professions): 12 mail Barthélémy Thimonnier, 77437 Marne la Vallée Cedex 2; tel. 1-64-80-35-00; internet www.onisep.fr; attached to Min. of Nat. Education; produces careers information for schools, colleges and careers centres; website helps students to search for a course by field, level of study and instn; Dir HERVÉ DE MONTS DE SAVASSE.

Union des Établissements d'Enseignement Supérieur Catholique (UDESCA) (Union of Catholic Higher Education Establishments): 21 rue d'Assas, 75720 Paris Cedex 06; tel. 1-44-39-52-02; comprises the 5 Catholic institutes and univs at Angers, Lille, Lyon, Paris and Toulouse, and represents them in dealings with state instns; Pres. Prof. MICHEL QUESNEL.

Union des Professeurs de Spéciales (Mathématiques et Sciences Physiques): 3 rue de l'Ecole Polytechnique, 75005 Paris; tel. and fax 1-43-26-97-92; fax 9-79-94-36-97; e-mail ups@prepas.org; internet www.prepas.org/ups; f. 1927; 2,500 mems; Pres. BRUNO JEAUFFROY; Sec. ERIC MERLE; publ. *Bulletin* (4 a year).

Learned Societies

GENERAL

Académie des Jeux Floraux: Hotel d'Assézat, 31000 Toulouse; tel. 5-61-21-22-85; e-mail jeux.floraux@free.fr; internet jeux.floraux.free.fr; f. 1323; human sciences; composed of 40 'mainteneurs' and 25 'Maîtres ès Jeux Floraux'; Permanent Sec. JEAN NAYRAL DE PUYBUSQUE; publ. *Recueil* (1 a year).

Académie des Sciences, Agriculture, Arts et Belles-Lettres d'Aix: 2A rue du 4 Septembre, 13100 Aix-en-Provence; tel. 4-42-38-38-95; e-mail musee.arbaud@free.fr; f. 1829; collns of ceramics, paintings, sculptures; library of 60,000 journals and plates, 10,000 books, 5,000 biographical MSS, 2,000 MSS related to local history, 1,200 portraits and 60 paintings of the Aix-en-Provence region; 40 fellows, 50 assoc. mems; Pres. XAVIER LAVAGNE D'ORTIGUE; Perm. Sec. GEORGES SOUVILLE; publ. *Bulletin*.

Académie des Sciences, Arts et Belles-Lettres de Dijon: 5 rue de l'Ecole-de-Droit, 21000 Dijon; tel. 3-80-54-22-93; e-mail acascia@orange.fr; internet www.acascia-dijon.fr; f. 1740; library, symposiums, communications; 550 mems; Pres. PIERRE BODINEAU; Sec. MARTINE CHAUNEY-BOUILLOT; publs *Mémoires de l'Académie* (every 2 years), *Mémoires de la Commission des Antiquités de la Côte d'Or* (every 2 years).

Académie des Sciences, Belles-Lettres et Arts de Lyon: Palais Saint-Jean, 4 ave Adolphe Max, 69005 Lyons; tel. 4-78-38-26-54; fax 4-72-77-90-56; e-mail secretariat@academie-sbla-lyon.fr; internet www.academie-sbla-lyon.fr; f. 1700; weekly meetings, annual grant for researchers in nuclear physics, medicine (oncology), literature, poetry; 52 elected mems; library of 60,000 vols; Pres. Prof. GÉRARD PAJONK; Chancellor Prof. JACQUES R. FAYETTE; publ. *Mémoires* (1 a year).

Académie des Sciences d'Outre-mer: 15 rue Lapérouse, 75116 Paris; tel. 1-47-20-87-93; fax 1-47-20-89-72; e-mail chefdecab@academiedoutremer.fr; internet www.academiedoutremer.fr; f. 1922; sections on economics and sociology, education, geography, law, politics and administration, science and medicine; 275 mems (incl. 100 corresp., 50 assoc., 25 free mems); library of 80,000 vols and 3,000 periodicals; Permanent Sec. PIERRE GENY; publ. *Mondes et Cultures* (1 a year).

Académie Goncourt: Société de Gens de Lettres, c/o Drouant, Place Gaillon, 75002 Paris; internet www.academie-goncourt.fr; f. 1896 by Edmond de Goncourt; comprises 10 writers in the French language; each year they compile a shortlist of the most noteworthy fiction written in French and award 'le prix Goncourt' to the author of the work judged the best; Pres. FRANÇOIS NOURISSIER; Sec.-Gen. DIDIER DECOIN.

Agence de la Francophonie: 28 rue de Bourgogne, 75007 Paris; tel. 1-44-11-12-50; fax 1-44-11-12-76; e-mail oif@francophonie.org; internet www.francophonie.org; f. 1970; an intergovernmental organization of French-speaking countries for co-operation in the fields of education, culture, science, technology, and in any other ways to bring the peoples of those countries closer together; 47 mems; Dir CHRISTIAN VALANTIN.

Alliance Française de Paris: 101 blvd Raspail, 75270 Paris Cedex 06; tel. 1-42-84-90-00; fax 1-42-84-90-91; e-mail info@alliancefr.org; internet www.alliancefr.org; f. 1883; French language school for foreigners; independent institution; 20,000 students; Pres. JACQUES VIOT; Sec.-Gen. JEAN HARZIC; Dir of the School ANNIE MONNERIE-GOARIN.

Comité des Travaux Historiques et Scientifiques: 1 rue Descartes, 75357 Paris Cedex 7; tel. 1-55-95-89-10; fax 1-55-95-89-60; e-mail catherine.gros@cths.fr; internet www.cths.fr; f. 1834; attached to Min. of Higher Education and Research; research and publs in the fields of history, archaeology, geography, human sciences, natural sciences, life sciences; organizes annual nat. congress of learned socs; 255 mems; Vice-Pres. M. J.-R. GABORIT; Gen.–Sec. CATHERINE GROS; publ. *Actes du Congrès national des Sociétés savantes*.

Euskaltzaindia/Académie de la Langue Basque: Plaza Barria 15, 48005 Bilbao; tel. 9-44-155-81-55; fax 9-44-15-81-44; e-mail webmaster@euskaltzaindia.net; internet www.euskaltzaindia.net; See also Spain chapter, Learned Societies.

Institut de France: 23 quai de Conti, 75270 Paris Cedex 06; tel. 1-44-41-44-41; fax 1-44-41-43-41; e-mail com@institut-de-france.fr; internet www.institut-de-france.fr; f. 1795; 623 mems; Chancellor PIERRE MESSMER; Dir of Services ERIC PEUCHOT.

Constituent Academies:

Académie des Beaux-Arts: 23 quai Conti, 75270 Paris Cedex 06; tel. 1-44-41-43-20; fax 1-44-41-44-99; internet academie-des-beaux-arts.fr; f. 1648; sections of painting, sculpture, architecture, engraving, musical composition, free members, artistic creation (cinema and audiovisual arts); 126 mems (55 ordinary, 55 corresp., 16 foreign assocs); Pres. JEAN PRODROMIDRÈS; Permanent Sec. ARNAUD D'HAUTERIVES; publ. *La Lettre de l'Académie des Beaux-Arts* (4 a year).

Académie des Inscriptions et Belles-Lettres: 23 quai Conti, 75270 Paris Cedex 06; tel. 1-44-41-43-10; fax 1-44-41-43-11; e-mail j.leclant.aibl@dial.oleane.com; internet www.aibl.fr; f. 1663; 195 mems (55 academicians, 40 foreign assocs, 50 French and 50 foreign corresp.); Pres. JACQUES JOUANNA; Permanent Sec. JEAN LECLANT; publs *Comptes Rendus des Séances* (4 a year), *Journal des Savants* (2 a year), *Monuments et Mémoires de la Fondation Eugène Piot* (1 a year).

Académie des Sciences: 23 quai Conti, 75270 Paris Cedex 06; tel. 1-44-41-44-41; fax 1-44-41-43-63; internet www.academie-sciences.fr; f. 1666; sections of the first div.: mathematics, mechanical engineering and informatics, physics, sciences of the universe; sections of the second div.: chemistry, genomics, human biology and medical sciences, integrative biology, molecular and cellular biology; inter-section; 250 mems, at most 150 foreign assocs and 143 corresp. mems; Pres. JULES HOFFMANN; Vice-Pres. JEAN SALENÇON; Permanent Secs JEAN DERCOURT (Sciences of the Universe and their Applications), JEAN-FRANÇOIS BACH (Chemical, Biological and Medical Sciences and their Applications); publs *Comptes Rendus Mathématique* (24 a year), *Comptes Rendus Mécanique* (12 a year), *Comptes Rendus Physique* (10 a year), *Comptes Rendus Geoscience* (16 a year), *Comptes Rendus Palevol* (palaeontology and evolution, 8 a year), *Comptes Rendus Chimie* (12 a year), *Comptes Rendus Biologies* (12 a year).

Académie des Technologies (Academy of Technology): Grand Palais des Champs Elysees, Gate C, Franklin D. Roosevelt, 75008 Paris; tel. 1-53-85-44-44; fax 1-53-85-44-45; e-mail secretariat@academie-technologies.fr; internet www.academie-technologies.fr; f. 2000; analyses and publicizes academic studies on technology and its impact on society; ensures that society benefits from technological progress; 218 mems; Pres. ALAIN POMPIDOU; Dir ALAN RODNEY.

Académie des Sciences Morales et Politiques: 23 quai Conti, 75270 Paris Cedex 06; tel. 1-44-41-43-26; fax 1-44-41-43-27; e-mail kerbrat@asmp.fr; internet www.asmp.fr; f. 1795; sections of philosophy, moral and sociological sciences, legislation, public law and jurisprudence, political economy, statistics and finance, history and geography, general interest; 122 mems (50 ordinary, 60 corresp., 12 foreign assocs); Pres. JEAN MESNARD; Permanent Sec. MICHEL ALBERT; publs *Notices* *biographiques et bibliographiques, Cahiers des sciences morales et politiques.*

Académie Française: 23 quai Conti, 75270 Paris Cedex 06; tel. 1-44-41-43-00; fax 1-43-29-47-45; e-mail contact@academie-francaise.fr; internet www.academie-francaise.fr; f. 1635; 40 mems; Permanent Sec. HÉLÈNE CARRÈRE D'ENCAUSSE.

AGRICULTURE, FISHERIES AND VETERINARY SCIENCE

Académie d'Agriculture de France: 18 rue de Bellechasse, 75007 Paris; tel. 1-47-05-10-37; fax 1-45-55-09-78; e-mail aaf@paris.inra.fr; internet www.academie-agriculture.fr; f. 1761; 120 mems; 60 foreign mems; 180 corresp. mems; 60 foreign corresp. mems; Pres. ANDRÉ FROUIN; Perm. Sec. GEORGES PÉDRO; library of 80,000 vols, 500 periodicals; publ. *Comptes rendus* (4 a year).

Académie Vétérinaire de France: 34 rue Bréguet, 75011 Paris; tel. 1-53-36-16-19; e-mail academie@veterinaire.fr; internet www.academie-veterinaire-france.fr; f. 1844; 44 mems; Pres. PIERRE LARVOR; Sec.-Gen. CLAUDE MILHAUD.

Association Centrale des Vétérinaires: 10 place Léon Blum, 75011 Paris; tel. 1-43-56-21-02; fax 1-64-46-54-42; e-mail acveto@orange.fr; internet asso-acv.veterinaire.fr; f. 1889; 1,700 mems; Pres. Dr B. WILMET.

Association Française pour l'Etude du Sol (French Association of Soil Science): INRA, CS40001, 2163 ave de la Pomme de Pin, Ardon 45075 Orléans Cedex 2; tel. 2-38-41-48-23; fax 2-38-41-78-69; e-mail afretsol@orleans.inra.fr; internet www.afes.fr; f. 1934; pedology, agronomy; 800 mems; Pres. Dr JEAN-PAUL LEGROS; publ. *Etude et Gestion des Sols* (4 a year).

Société Française d'Economie Rurale: INA-PG, 16 rue Claude Bernard, 75231 Paris Cedex 05; tel. 1-47-07-47-86; fax 1-44-08-18-42; e-mail sfer@inapg.inra.fr; internet www.sfer.asso.fr/sfer; f. 1949; 2 study sessions a year; 400 mems; Pres. LUCIEN BOURGEOIS; Sec.-Gen. DENIS HAIRY; publ. *Economie Rurale* (6 a year).

Société Nationale d'Horticulture de France (SNHF): 84 rue de Grenelle, 75007 Paris; tel. 1-44-39-78-78; fax 1-45-44-76-57; e-mail info@snhf.org; internet www.snhf.asso.fr; f. 1827; 8,000 mems, 120,000 affiliated mems; library of 16,000 vols; Pres. JEAN PUECH; Gen. Sec. (vacant); publ. *Jardins de France* (10 a year).

Société Vétérinaire Pratique de France: 10 Pl. Léon Blum, 75011 Paris; f. 1879; 750 mems; Pres. JEAN-YVES KERUELLA; Sec.-Gen. MICHEL BERNADOC; publ. *Bulletin* (4 a year).

ARCHITECTURE AND TOWN PLANNING

Académie d'Architecture: 9 place des Vosges, 75004 Paris; tel. 1-48-87-83-10; internet www.archi.fr/aa; f. 1840 as Société Centrale des Architectes, name changed 1953; 100 elected mems; Pres. AYMERIC ZUBLENA; Gen. Sec. JEAN-MARIE VALENTIN.

Association Nationale pour la Protection des Villes d'Art: 39 ave de La Motte-Picquet, 75007 Paris; tel. 1-47-05-37-71; fax 1-45-50-32-95; e-mail florence.rouxcourtois@orange.fr; f. 1963; an association of local societies in 45 cities for the protection and restoration of historic and artistic buildings; Pres. PAULE ALBRECHT.

Cité de l'Architecture et du Patrimoine: Palais de Chaillot, 1 pl. du Trocadéro, 75116 Paris; tel. 1-58-51-52-00; fax 1-58-51-52-50; e-mail info@citechaillot.org; internet www.citechaillot.org; f. 1980; funded by Min. of Culture and Communication; contemporary French architecture and architectural heritage; library of 10,000 vols, 70 periodicals; Pres. FRANÇOIS DE MAZIÈRES; publs *Archiscopie* (12 a year), *Colonnes* (2 a year).

Compagnie des Experts-Architectes près la Cour d'Appel de Paris: 24 rue Bezout, 75014 Paris; tel. 1-43-27-59-69; fax 1-43-20-47-96; e-mail info@ceacap.org; internet www.ceacap.org; f. 1928; 125 mems; Pres. MICHEL AUSTRY; Gen. Sec. ROBERT LEGRAS.

Conseil National de l'Ordre des Architectes: Tour Maine Montparnasse, 33 ave du Maine, BP 154, 75755 Paris Cedex 15; tel. 1-56-58-67-00; fax 1-56-58-67-01; e-mail info@cnoa.com; internet www.architectes.org; f. 1977; official regulating body for the architectural profession; Pres. of Conseil YVES MAGNAN; Sec. ALAIN FABREGA; publ. *d'Architectures* (12 a year).

Office Général du Bâtiment et des Travaux Publics: 55 ave Kléber, 75784 Paris Cedex 16; tel. 1-40-69-51-00; internet www.ogbtp.com; f. 1918; combines the majority of societies, unions and federations of architects and contractors; Pres. YVES TOULET.

Société Française des Architectes: 247 rue St Jacques, 75005 Paris; tel. 1-56-81-10-25; fax 1-56-81-10-26; e-mail contact@sfarchi.org; internet www.sfarchi.org; f. 1877; cultural association; 1,000 mems; Pres. LAURENT SALOMON; publs *Tribune d'Histoire et d'Actualité de l'Architecture* (20 a year), *Le Visiteur* (2 a year).

Société pour la Protection des Paysages, et de l'Esthétique de la France: 39 ave de la Motte-Picquet, 75007 Paris; e-mail sppef@wanadoo.fr; internet sppef.free.fr; f. 1901; 4,000 mems; Pres. P. ALBRECHT; publ. *Sites et Monuments* (4 a year).

BIBLIOGRAPHY, LIBRARY SCIENCE AND MUSEOLOGY

Association des Archivistes Français: 9 rue Montcalm, 75018 Paris Cedex 03; tel. 1-46-06-39-44; fax 1-46-06-39-52; e-mail secretariat@archivistes.org; internet www.archivistes.org; f. 1904; 700 mems; Pres. HENRI ZUBER; Sec. AGNÈS DEJOB; publ. *La Gazette des Archives* (4 a year).

Association des Bibliothécaires Français: 31 rue de Chabrol, 75010 Paris; tel. 1-55-33-10-30; fax 1-55-33-10-31; e-mail abf@abf.asso.fr; internet www.abf.asso.fr; f. 1906; 2,500 mems; Pres. GILLES EBOLI; Gen. Sec. DANIEL LE GOFF; publ. *ABF Bulletin d'Informations* (4 a year).

Association des Professionnels de l'Information et de la Documentation (ADBS): 25 rue Claude Tillier, 75012 Paris; tel. 1-43-72-25-25; fax 1-43-72-30-41; e-mail adbs@adbs.fr; internet www.adbs.fr; f. 1963; 5,000 mems; organizes annual congress with Groupement français de l'industrie de l'information; Pres. CAROLINE WIEGANDT; publ. *Documentaliste–sciences de l'information* (6 a year).

Association Générale des Conservateurs des Collections Publiques de France: 6 ave du Mahatma Gandhi, 75116 Paris; tel. 1-44-17-60-00; fax 1-44-17-60-60; internet www.agccpf.com; f. 1922; promotes and improve museums and museums' curatorship; 1,000 mems; Pres. JACQUES MAIGRET; publ. *Musées et Collections Publiques de France* (4 a year).

Centre d'Archives et de Documentation Politiques et Sociales: 86 blvd Haussmann, 75008 Paris; f. 1949; Dir Dr G. ALBERTINI; publs *Est et Ouest* (12 a year), *Informations Politiques et Sociales* (52 a year in France, Africa and Asia), *Le Monde des Conflits* (12 a year).

Association d'Etudes et d'Informations Politiques Internationales: 86 blvd Haussmann, 75008 Paris; f. 1949; Dir G. ALBERTINI; publs *Documenti sul Comunismo* (Rome), *Est & Ouest* (Paris, 26 a year), *Este y Oeste* (Caracas).

Fondation Nationale des Sciences Politiques: 27 rue Saint Guillaume, 75337 Paris Cedex 07; tel. 1-45-49-50-50; fax 1-42-22-31-26; internet www.sciences-po.fr; f. 1945; administers the Institut d'Etudes Politiques de Paris (*q.v.*); promotes research centres and social science studies, documentation service; library of 620,000 vols; Pres. RENÉ RÉMOND; Admin. R. DESCOINGS; publs *Critique Internationale*, *Mots* (4 a year), *Revue de l'OFCE* (4 a yeary), *Revue Economique* (6 a year), *Revue Française de Science Politique* (6 a year), *Vingtième Siècle*.

Institut des Actuaires Français: 4 rue Chauveau-Lagarde, 75008 Paris; tel. 1-44-51-72-72; fax 1-44-51-72-73; e-mail info@actuaires-paris.com; internet www.institutdesactuaires.com; f. 1890; 600 mems; library of 5,000 vols; Pres. DANIEL BLANCHARD; publ. *Bulletin* (4 a year).

Institut d'Histoire Sociale: 4 ave Benoît-Frachon, 92023 Nanterre Cedex; tel. 1-46-14-09-29; fax 1-46-14-09-25; e-mail bibliotheque@souvarine.fr; internet www.souvarine.fr; f. 1935; study of Communist and Soviet activities; library of 40,000 vols specializing in political sciences and history of workers' movements since beginning of 19th century, trade union periodicals and political reviews; Pres. EMMANUEL LE ROY LADURIE; Librarian VIRGINIE HÉBRARD; publ. *Histoire & Liberté* (4 a year).

Institut Français des Relations Internationales: 27 rue de la Procession, 75740 Paris Cedex 15; tel. 1-40-61-60-00; fax 1-40-61-60-60; e-mail ifri@ifri.org; internet www.ifri.org; f. 1979; studies foreign policy, economy, defence and strategy; 560 mems; library of 32,000 vols; Dir-Gen. THIERRY DE MONTBRIAL; Sec.-Gen. VALÉRINE GENIN; publs *Cahiers d'Asie*, *Etudes de l'Ifri*, *Notes du Cerfa* (12 a year), *Notes du CFE*, *Notes de l'IFRI*, *Nouvelles de Chine* (12 a year), *Policy Papers*, *Politique Etrangère* (4 a year), *RAMSES (Rapport Annuel sur le Système Economique et les Stratégies)* (1 a year), *Travaux et Recherches*.

Société d'Economie et de Science Sociales: 20 rue Notre-Dame-de-Nazareth, 75003 Paris; tel. 1-40-29-96-29; e-mail socsciencesociale@free.fr; internet www.science-sociale.org; f. 1856; concerned with social reforms and sociology; 300 mems; library of 3,000 vols, including collection 'La Réforme Sociale'; Pres. EDOUARD SECRETAN; Sec. Prof. ANTOINE SAVOYE; publ. *Les Etudes Sociales* (2 a year).

Société de Législation Comparée: 28 rue St Guillaume, 75007 Paris; tel. 1-44-39-86-23; fax 1-44-39-86-28; e-mail slc@legiscompare.com; internet www.legiscompare.com; f. 1869; comparative law; publishes books on comparative and foreign law; library of 100,000 vols; 600 mems (400 French, 200 overseas); Pres. JEAN-LOUIS DEWOST; Gen. Sec. DAVID CAPITANT; publ. *Revue Internationale de Droit Comparé* (4 a year).

Société d'Etudes Jaurésiennes: 21 blvd Lefebvre, 75015 Paris; tel. 1-48-28-25-89; fax 1-48-28-25-89; internet www.jaures.info/welcome/index.php; f. 1959; promotes all aspects of the life and works of Jean Jaurès; promotes the publication or re-edition of his speeches and writings; 500 mems; Pres. MADELEINE REBERIOUX; Sec.-Gen. GILLES

HEURÉ; publs *Cahiers Jean Jaurès* (4 a year), *Cahiers Trimestriels* (4 a year).

Société d'Histoire du Droit: Université de Paris II, 12 place du Panthéon, 75005 Paris; f. 1913; 550 mems; Pres. Prof. OLIVIER GUILLOT; Sec. A. LEFEBVRE.

Société Française de Statistique: c/o Institut Henri Poincaré, 11 rue Pierre et Marie Curie, 75231 Paris Cedex 05; tel. 1-44-27-66-60; fax 1-44-07-04-74; e-mail sfds@ihp .jussieu.fr; internet www.sfds.asso.fr; f. 1997; 1,100 mems; library of 60,000 vols; Pres. AVNER BAR-HEN; Gen.-Sec. JEAN-MICHEL MARIN; publs *Journal de la Société Française de Statistique* (4 a year), *Revue de Statistique Appliquée* (4 a year).

EDUCATION

Association Francophone d'Education Comparée (Francophone Association for Comparative Education (AFEC)): c/o Abdel-Rahamane Baba-Moussa, Université de Caen Basse-Normandie, Esplanade de la Paix, 14032 Caen Cedex; e-mail afec-bureau@ hotmail.fr; internet www.afec-info.org; f. 1973; promotes comparative education among francophone teachers and educationalists; organizes one seminar a year and participates in meetings of the Comparative Education Soc. in Europe and the World Ccl of Comparative Educational Socs; 100 mems; Pres. Dr ABDEL RAHAMANE BABA-MOUSSA; Vice-Pres. MOUSSA DAFF; Sec.-Gen. EVE COMANDÉ; publs *Bulletin de liaison et d'information* (3 a year), *Education comparée – nouvelle série* (2 a year).

Centre Culturel Calouste Gulbenkian: 51 ave d'Iéna, 75116 Paris; tel. 1-53-23-93-93; fax 1-53-23-93-99; e-mail calouste@ gulbenkian-paris.org; internet www .gulbenkian-paris.org; f. 1965; attached to Calouste Gulbenkian Foundation in Lisbon (Portugal); non-profit-making; exhibitions, lectures, seminars, concerts; awards grants in the fields of education, art, science and charity; library of 70,000 vols; Dir JOAO PEIRO GARCIA.

Fondation Biermans-Lapôtre: 9A blvd Jourdan, 75014 Paris Cedex 14; tel. 1-40-78-72-00; fax 1-45-89-00-03; e-mail admin@ fbl-paris.org; internet www.ciup.fr/ biermans-lapotre.htm; f. 1924; attached to Fondation Universitaire (see Belgium chapter); house for Belgian and Luxembourg students; promotes academic and scientific exchanges between France and Belgium; offers grants; Dir JOS AELVOET; Dir Adjunct CLAUDE GONFROID.

Office National d'Information sur les Enseignements et les Professions: 12 mail B. Thimonnier, BP 86 Lognes, 77423 Marne la Vallée, Cedex 02; tel. 1-64-80-35-00; fax 1-64-80-35-01; internet www.onisep.fr; f. 1970; Dir MICHEL VALDIGUIÉ; publs *Avenirs*, *Bulletin d'Information* (12 a year), *Les Cahiers de l'ONISEP*, *ONISEP Communiqué* (6 a year), *Réadaptation* (12 a year).

FINE AND PERFORMING ARTS

Association Française d'Action Artistique: 1 bis, ave de Villars, 75007 Paris; tel. 1-53-69-83-00; fax 1-53-69-33-00; e-mail info@ afaa.asso.fr; internet www.afaa.asso.fr; f. 1922; offers international cultural exchanges; assists in the development of the performing arts, visual arts, architecture, heritage and cultural projects in France; Pres. ROBERT LION.

Association du Salon d'Automne: Grand Palais, Porte H, 75008 Paris; tel. 1-43-59-46-07; fax 1-53-76-00-60; e-mail contact@ salon-automne-paris.com; internet www .salon-automne-paris.com; f. 1903; sections: painting, engraving, mural and decorative art, sculpture, photography; Pres. JEAN-FRANÇOIS LARRIEU.

Jeunesses Musicales de France: 20 rue Geoffroy l'Asnier, 75004 Paris; tel. 1-44-61-86-86; fax 1-44-61-86-88; e-mail info@lesjmf .org; internet www.lesjmf.org; f. 1944; encourages young audiences, promotes concerts, festivals; 320 delegates in 450 towns; Pres. J. L. TOURNIER; Dir BRUNO BOUTLEUX.

Société de l'Histoire de l'Art Français: 2 rue Vivienne, 75084 Paris Cedex 02; tel. 1-40-20-50-77; fax 1-40-20-51-17; f. 1873; 1,000 mems; Pres. DANIEL ALCOUFFE; Gen.-Sec. ELIZABETH FOUCART-WALTER; publs *Annuels*, *Archives de l'Art Français*, *Bulletin*.

Société des Amis du Louvre: Palais du Louvre, 75058 Paris Cedex 01; tel. 1-40-20-53-34; fax 1-40-20-53-44; e-mail contact@ amis-du-louvre.org; internet www .amis-du-louvre.org; f. 1897; 70,000 mems; Pres. MARC FUMAROLI; Sec.-Gen. SERGE-ANTOINE TCHEKHOFF; publs *Bulletin Trimestriel* (4 a year), *Chronique*.

Société des Artistes Décorateurs (SAD): Grand Palais, Porte C, Ave Franklin D. Roosevelt, 75008 Paris; tel. 1-43-59-66-10; fax 1-49-53-07-89; e-mail info@sad-expo.com; internet www.sad-expo.com; f. 1901 to promote modern art; 400 mems; Pres. CLAUDE MOLLARD.

Société des Artistes Français: Grand Palais, Porte C, ave Franklin Roosevelt, 75008 Paris; tel. 1-43-59-52-49; fax 1-45-62-85-97; internet www.lesalon-artistesfrancais .com; f. 1882; 5,000 members; organizes the annual Salon des Artistes Français (open to French and foreign artists); Pres. CHRISTIAN BILLET; publ. *Bulletin*.

Société des Artistes Indépendants: Grand Palais, Porte C, Ave Franklin D. Roosevelt, 75008 Paris; tel. 1-45-63-39-15; fax 1-43-59-50-89; e-mail indep@ club-internet.fr; internet www .artistes-independants.fr; f. 1884; 2,500 members; supports modern artists; annual exhibition of paintings, sculpture, tapestry; Salon des Artistes Indépendants since 1884; Pres. ALAIN COLLIARD; Sec.-Gen. FRANÇOISE LE GOFF.

Société des Auteurs, Compositeurs et Editeurs de Musique: 225 ave Charles-de-Gaulle, 92528 Neuilly sur Seine Cedex; tel. 1-47-15-47-15; fax 1-47-45-45-72; e-mail communication@sacem.fr; internet www .sacem.fr/eptic; f. 1851; 120,000 mems; deals with colln and distribution of performing rights; Pres. LAURENT PETITGIRARD; Chair. BERNARD MIYET.

Société d'Histoire du Théâtre: BnF, 58 rue de Richelieu, 75084 Paris Cedex 02; tel. 1-42-60-27-05; fax 1-42-60-27-65; e-mail info@sht.asso.fr; internet www.sht.asso.fr; f. 1948; performing arts library; 600 mems; library of 15,000 books; Pres. ROMAIN MARY-LINE; Sec.-Gen. ROSE MARIE MOUDOUÈS; publ. *Revue d'Histoire du Théâtre* (4 a year).

Société Française de Musicologie: 2 rue Louvois, 75002 Paris; tel. 1-53-79-88-45; e-mail sfmusico@club-internet.fr; internet www.sfm.culture.fr; f. 1917; 650 mems; Pres. DENIS HERLIN; Sec.-Gen. ANNE-SYLVIE BARTHEL-CALVET; publ. *Revue de Musicologie* (2 a year).

Société Française de Photographie: 71 rue de Richelieu, 75002 Paris; tel. 1-42-60-05-98; fax 1-47-03-75-39; internet www.sfp .photographie.com; f. 1854; 430 mems; library of 10,000 vols, and 25,000 old photographs; Pres. MICHEL POIVERT; publs *Bulletin* (4 a year), *Etudes photographiques* (2 a year).

Société Nationale des Beaux-Arts: 11 rue Berryer, 75008 Paris; tel. 1-43-59-47-07; fax 1-43-59-47-07; e-mail snba.berryer@ libertysurf.fr; f. 1890; organizes art exhibitions; 900 mems; Pres. ETIENNE AUDFRAY; Gen. Sec. GUY PERRON.

HISTORY, GEOGRAPHY AND ARCHAEOLOGY

Association de Géographes Français: 191 rue Saint-Jacques, 75005 Paris; tel. 1-44-32-14-00; fax 1-45-29-13-40; e-mail assogeo@wanadoo.fr; internet www .association-de-geographes-francais.fr; f. 1920; 300 mems; Pres. R. POURTIER; Sec. Y. BOQUET; publs *Bulletin de l'Association de Géographes Français* (4 a year), *Bibliographie géographique annuelle* (1 a year).

Association des Amis de la Revue de Géographie de Lyon: 18 rue Chevreul, 69362 Lyons Cedex 07; tel. 4-78-78-75-44; fax 4-78-78-71-58; e-mail buisson@univ-lyon3 .fr; internet www.geocarrefour.org; f. 1923; Pres. NICOLE COMMERÇON; publ. *Revue de Géographie de Lyon* (4 a year).

Centre International d'Etudes Romanes: 7 pl. des Arts, 71700 Tournus; tel. 3-85-32-54-45; fax 3-85-32-18-98; internet www.art-roman.org; f. 1952; 400 mems; Hon. Pres. HUBERT BLANC; Vice-Pres. and Sec.-Gen. MARGUÉRITE THIBERT; publ. *Bulletin* (every 2 or 3 years).

Comité National Français de Géographie: 191 rue Saint-Jacques, 75005 Paris; internet cnfg.univ-paris1.fr; co-ordinates French geographical activity and participates in the work of the International Geographical Union; 400 mems; Pres. ALAIN MIOSSEC; Sec.-Gen. P. ARNOULD; publ. *Bibliographie Géographique Internationale* (published jointly with the International Geographical Union).

Comité Scientifique du Club Alpin Français: 24 ave de Laumière, 75019 Paris; tel. 1-53-72-87-13; fax 1-42-03-55-60; internet www .clubalpin.com; f. 1874; 90,000 mems; Dir J. MALBOS.

Demeure Historique: Hôtel de Nesmond, 57 quai de la Tournelle, 75005 Paris; tel. 1-55-42-60-00; fax 1-43-29-36-44; internet www .demeure-historique.org; f. 1924; study, research and conservation of historic bldgs, châteaux, etc.; 3,000 mems; Pres. JEAN DE LAMBERTYE; publ. *La Demeure Historique* (4 a year).

Fédération Française de Spéléologie: 28 rue Delandine, 75011 Paris; tel. 4-72-56-09-63; fax 4-78-42-15-98; e-mail secretariat@ ffspeleo.fr; internet ffspeleo.fr; f. 1963; speleology; 12,000 mems; library of 2,000 vols, 600 periodicals; Pres. LAURENCE TANGUILLE; Sec.-Gen. HENRY VAUMORON; publs *Bulletin Bibliographique Spéléologique*, *Karstologia* (2 a year), *Karstologia Mémoires*, *Spelunca* (4 a year), *Spelunca Mémoires*.

Institut Français d'Etudes Byzantines: 21 rue d'Assas, 75006 Paris; tel. 1-44-39-52-24; fax 1-44-39-52-36; e-mail bibliotheque .vernon.ifeb@icp.fr; internet www.icp.fr; f. 1897; Byzantine research, particularly on sources of ecclesiastical history; library of 50,000 vols; publ. *Revue des Etudes Byzantines* (1 a year).

Institut Français d'Histoire Sociale: Centre de documentation et de recherche, Archives Nationales, 60 rue des Francs-Bourgeois, 75141 Paris Cedex 03; tel. 1-40-27-64-49; f. 1948; 57 mems; library of 11,000 vols, 50,000 pamphlets, large collection of periodicals, manuscripts and illustrated documents; Pres. JEAN-PIERRE CHALINE; Vice-Pres. ALAIN CORBIN.

Société de Biogéographie: 57 rue Cuvier, 75231 Paris Cedex 05; f. 1924; 350 mems;

Pres. C. SASTRE; Sec.-Gen. M. SALOMON; publs *Biogeographica*, *Mémoires hors série*.

Société de Géographie: 184 blvd St-Germain, 75006 Paris; tel. 1-45-48-54-62; fax 1-42-22-40-93; e-mail socgeo@socgeo.org; internet www.socgeo.org; f. 1821; 850 mems; library of 40,000 vols, 120,000 photographs at Bibliothèque Nationale de France, 58 rue de Richelieu, 75084 Paris Cedex 02 (Librarian JEAN-YVES SARAZIN); Pres. Prof. JEAN-ROBERT PITTE; Sec.-Gen. MICHEL DAGNAUD; publs *Bulletin de liaison des membres de la Société de Géographie*, *La Géographie* (4 a year).

Société de Géographie Humaine de Paris: 8 rue Roquépine, 75008 Paris; f. 1873; Pres. JACQUES AUGARDE; library of 2,000 vols; publ. *Revue Economique Française* (4 a year).

Société de l'Histoire de France: 60 rue des Francs-Bourgeois, 75003 Paris; fax 1-55-42-75-09; internet www.shfrance.org; f. 1834; publishes a series of French historical texts and documents; gives public lectures on French history; 250 mems; Pres. Prof. CLAUDE GAUVARD; Sec. Prof. MARC H. SMITH; publ. *Annuaire-Bulletin* (1 a year).

Société d'Emulation du Bourbonnais: 93 rue de Paris, 03000 Moulins; tel. and fax 4-70-34-08-13; e-mail emulation.bourbonnais@orange.fr; internet www.societedemulationdubourbonnais.com; f. 1845; 400 mems; activities in the fields of history, science, arts and literature; library of 30,000 vols; Pres. SYLVIE VILATTE; publ. *Bulletin* (4 a year).

Société des Océanistes: Musée du Quai Branly, 222 rue de l'Université, 75343 Paris Cedex 7; tel. 1-56-61-71-16; e-mail sdo@projetmuse.net; internet www.mae.u-paris10.fr/oceanistes; f. 1945; 560 mems; Pres. MAURICE GODLIER; Sec.-Gen. CHRISTIAN COIFFIER; publs *Journal* (2 a year), *Publications*.

Société d'Ethnographie de Paris: 6 rue Champfleury, 75007 Paris; f. 1859; 400 mems; Dirs A.-M. D'ANS, R. LACOMBE; publ. *L'Ethnographie* (2 a year).

Société d'Ethnologie Française: 6 ave du Mahatma Gandhi, 75116 Paris; tel. 1-44-17-60-00; 500 mems; holds annual nat. conf. and study sessions; Pres. F. LAUTMAN; Sec.-Gen. F. MAGUET; publ. *Ethnologie Française* (4 a year).

Société d'Etude du XVIIe Siècle: c/o Université de Paris-Sorbonne, Occident Moderne, 1 rue Victor-Cousin, 75230 Paris Cedex 05; f. 1948; 1,250 mems; Pres. JEAN-ROBERT ARMOGATHE; Sec. JEAN-LOUIS QUANTIN; publ. *XVIIe Siècle* (4 a year).

Société d'Histoire Générale et d'Histoire Diplomatique: 13 rue Soufflot, 75005 Paris; tel. 1-43-54-05-97; fax 1-46-34-07-60; f. 1887; history and diplomatic relations; 400 mems; publ. *Revue d'Histoire Diplomatique*.

Société d'Histoire Moderne et Contemporaine: Bureau 110, 56 rue Jacob, 75006 Paris; tel. 1-45-45-11-11; fax 1-58-71-71-96; e-mail rhmc@ens.fr; f. 1901; early modern and modern French and foreign history; 1,100 mems; Presidents PIERRE MILZA, DANIEL ROCHE; Sec.-Gen. PHILIPPE MINARD; publ. *Bulletin-Revue d'Histoire Moderne et Contemporaine* (4 a year, and a supplementary Bulletin 1 a year).

Société Française d'Archéologie: Musée National des Monuments Français, Palais de Chaillot, 1 place du Trocadéro, 75116 Paris; tel. 1-47-04-78-96; fax 1-44-05-94-25; e-mail sfa.sfa@wanadoo.fr; internet www.sfarcheologie.com; f. 1834; mem. of CSSF; 2,800 mems; Pres. JEAN MESQUI; publs *Bulletin Monumental* (4 a year), *Congrès Archéologiques de France* (1 a year).

Société Française d'Egyptologie: Collège de France, pl. Marcelin-Berthelot, 75231 Paris Cedex 05; tel. 1-40-46-94-31; fax 1-40-46-94-31; e-mail s.f.e@orange.fr; internet www.egypt.edu; f. 1923; 850 mems; Pres. D. VALBELLE; Sec. MARIE-CLAIRE CUVILLIER; publs *Bulletin* (3 a year), *Revue d'Egyptologie* (1 a year).

Société Française de Numismatique: Bibliothèque Nationale de France, Département des Monnaies, Médailles et Antiques, 58 rue de Richelieu, 75002 Paris; tel. 1-53-79-86-26; fax 1-53-79-86-26; e-mail secretariat@sfnum.asso.fr; internet www.sfnum.asso.fr; f. 1865; 700 mems; Pres. GEORGES GAUTIER; Gen. Sec. ANDRÉ RONDE; publs *Bulletin de la S. F. N.* (12 a year), *Revue Numismatique* (1 a year).

Société Française d'Histoire d'Outre-Mer: 15 rue Catulienne, 93200 Saint Denis; tel. 6-07-30-04-22; fax 1-45-82-62-99; e-mail sfhom4@yahoo.fr; internet www.sfhom.com; f. 1913; 420 mems; Pres. HÉLÈNE D'ALMEIDA-TOPOR; Sec.-Gen. JOSETTE RIVALLAIN; publ. *Outre-Mers* (history, 2 a year).

Société Historique, Archéologique et Littéraire de Lyon: Archives Municipales de Lyon, 18 rue Dugas Montbel, 69002 Lyon; e-mail shallyon@cegetel.net; f. 1807; 78 mems; Pres. JPIERRE GUTTON; Sec. BRIGITTE BACCONNIER; publ. *Bulletin* (1 a year).

Société Nationale des Antiquaires de France: Palais du Louvre, Pavillon Mollien, 75058 Paris Cedex 01; f. 1804; history, philology and archaeology of Antiquity, Middle Ages and Renaissance; 434 mems, 10 hon. mems, 10 hon. foreign corresps, 45 resident mems; Pres. HERVÉ PINOTEAU; Vice-Pres. JANIC DURAND; Vice-Pres. MICHEL AMANDRY; Sec. Gen. Prof. FRANÇOIS DOLBEAU; publs *Bulletin de la Société nationale des Antiquaires de France* (1 a year), *Mémoires de la Société nationale des Antiquaires de France* (irregular).

Vieilles Maisons Françaises: 93 rue de l'Université, 75007 Paris; tel. 1-40-62-61-71; fax 1-45-51-12-26; internet www.vmf.net; f. 1958; the society seeks to bring together all those who own buildings of historical interest and those who help to preserve them; 16,000 mems; Pres. PHILIPPE TOUSSAINT; publ. *Vieilles Maisons Françaises*.

LANGUAGE AND LITERATURE

Association des Ecrivains de Langue Française (ADELF) (French Language Writers Association): 14 rue Broussais, 75014 Paris; tel. 1-43-21-95-99; e-mail adelf@wanadoo.fr; f. 1926 as 'Société des romanciers et auteurs coloniaux français' to bring together writers of all nationalities whose works are published in French; awards 11 literary prizes; 1,200 mems in 79 countries; library of 2,000 vols; Pres. JACQUES CHEVRIER; Sec.-Gen. SIMONE DREYFUS; publs *Collection des Colloques*, *Lettres et Cultures de langue française* (2 a year).

Association Française des Professeurs de Langues Vivantes: 19 rue de la Glacière, 75013 Paris; f. 1902; 3,000 mems; Pres. SYLVESTRE VANUXEM; Gen. Sec. JEAN-YVES PETITGIRARD; publs *Le Polyglotte* (4 a year), *Les Langues Modernes*.

Association Guillaume Budé: 95 blvd Raspail, 75006 Paris; e-mail info@bude.asso.fr; internet www.bude.asso.fr; f. 1917; 3,000 mems; edits ancient Greek, Latin and Byzantine, classical texts with French translations and studies on history, philology and archaeology, which are published by the Société d'éditions 'Les Belles Lettres' at the same address; Pres. JACQUES JOUANNA; Vice-Pres.

BERNARD DEFORGE, ALAIN MICHEL; publ. *Bulletin* (2 a year).

British Council: 9 rue de Constantine, 75340 Paris Cedex 07; tel. (1) 49-55-73-00; fax (1) 47-05-77-02; e-mail projects@britishcouncil.fr; internet www.britishcouncil.fr; teaching centre; offers courses and exams in English language and British culture and promotes cultural exchange with the UK; Dir JOHN TOD.

Centre National du Livre: 53 rue de Verneuil, 75343 Paris Cedex 07; tel. 1-49-54-68-68; fax 1-45-49-10-21; internet www.centrenationaldulivre.fr; f. 1946, present name 1993, to uphold and encourage the work of French writers; to give financial help to writers, editors and public libraries; to promote translation into French; Pres. BENOIT YVERT; Sec.-Gen. MARC-ANDRE WAGNER; publ. *Lettres*.

Espéranto-Jeunes (JEFO): 4 bis rue de la Cerisaie, 75004 Paris; tel. 1-42-78-68-86; fax 1-42-78-08-47; internet esperanto-jeunes.org; f. 1969; promotes Esperanto among young people; 145 mems; Pres. BERTRAND HUGON; publs *JEFO informas* (4 a year), *Koncize* (4 a year).

Fondation Saint-John Perse: Cité du Livre, 10 rue des Allumettes, 13098 Aix-en-Provence Cedex 2; tel. 4-42-91-98-85; fax 4-42-27-11-86; e-mail fondation.saint.john.perse@wanadoo.fr; internet www.up.univ-mrs.fr/~wperse; f. 1975; collection of 16,000 documents comprising all MSS, books, correspondence, private library and personal belongings of Saint-John Perse (Nobel Prize for literature 1960); organizes annual exhibition and symposium; 500 mems; Pres. YVES-ANDRÉ ISTEL; Dir BEATRICE COIGNET; publs *Cahiers Saint-John Perse* (irregular), *Souffle de Perse* (irregular).

Goethe-Institut: 17 Ave d'Iéna, 75116 Paris; tel. 1-44-43-92-30; fax 1-44-43-92-40; e-mail kallies@paris.goethe.org; internet www.goethe.de/fr/par/deindex.htm; offers courses and exams in German language and culture and promotes cultural exchange with Germany; attached centres in Bordeaux, Lille, Lyons, Nice and Toulouse; library of 25,000 vols; Dir MARION HAASE.

Instituto Cervantes: 7 rue Quentin Bauchart, 75008 Paris; tel. 1-40-70-92-92; fax 1-47-20-27-49; e-mail cenpar@cervantes.es; internet paris.cervantes.es; offers courses and exams in Spanish language and culture and promotes cultural exchange with Spain and Spanish-speaking Latin and Central America; attached centres in Bordeaux and Lyons; library of 42,000 vols, 100 periodicals; Dir AUGSTÍN VERA LUJÁN.

La France Latine: Université de Rennes II, 1 Place du Recteur le Moal, C524307, 35043 Rennes Cedex; e-mail philippe.blanchet@univ-rennes2.fr; internet www.uhb.fr/alc/erellif/credilif/flreo.html; f. 1957 to preserve Latin culture and civilization in all its forms, maintains regional traditions and the 'Langue d'Oc' (Occitan dialect); Scientific Dirs Prof. PHILIPPE BLANCHET, Prof. SUZANNE THIOLIER-MÉJEAN; library of 150 vols; publ. *Revue* (2 a year).

Maison de Poésie (Fondation Emile Blémont): 11 bis rue Ballu, 75009 Paris; tel. 1-40-23-45-99; f. 1928; library of 16,000 vols; annual prizes: Grand Prix de la Maison de Poésie, Prix Paul Verlaine, Prix Edgar Poe, Prix Louis Maudin, Prix Emile Verhaeren, Prix Philippe Chahaneix, Prix Arthur Rimbaud; Pres. JACQUES CHARPENTREAU; Sec. BERNARD PLIN; publ. *Le Coin de Table* (4 a year).

PEN International (Centre français): 6 rue François-Miron, 75004 Paris; tel. 1-42-

77-37-87; fax 1-42-78-64-87; e-mail penfrancais@aol.com; internet www.penclub .fr; f. 1921; 550 mems; Pres. SYLVESTRE CLANCIER; Sec.-Gen. PHILIPPE PUJAS; publ. *La Lettre du PEN Club français* (6 a year).

Société de Linguistique de Paris: Ecole Pratique des Hautes Etudes, 4e section, Sorbonne, 47 rue des Ecoles, 75005 Paris; internet www.slp-paris.com; f. 1864; 800 mems; Pres. A. BORILLO; Sec. M. A. LEMARE-CHAL; publs *Bulletin, Collection Linguistique, Mémoires* (1 a year).

Société des Anciens Textes Français: 19 rue de la Sorbonne, 75005 Paris; f. 1875; 125 mems; Pres. Prof. G. BIANCIOTTO; Dir Prof. G. HASENOHR; Gen. Sec. R. TRACHSLER.

Société des Auteurs et Compositeurs Dramatiques: 11 bis rue Ballu, 75442 Paris Cedex 09; tel. 1-40-23-44-44; fax 1-45-26-74-28; e-mail infosacd@sacd.fr; internet www .sacd.fr; f. 1777; to protect the rights of authors of theatre, radio, cinema, television and multimedia; Pres. CHRISTINE MILLER; publ. *La Revue de la SACD.*

Société des Etudes Latines: 1 rue Victor-Cousin, 75230 Paris Cedex 05; e-mail societe-etudes-latines@paris-sorbonne.fr; internet www.societedesetudeslatines.com; f. 1923; Admin. Prof. JACQUELINE CHAMPEAUX; publ. *Revue des Etudes Latines* (1 a year).

Société des Gens de Lettres: Hôtel de Massa, 38 rue du Faubourg St Jacques, 75014 Paris; tel. 1-53-10-12-00; fax 1-53-10-12-12; e-mail sgdl@sgdl.org; internet www .sgdl.org; f. 1838; defends the moral and social rights of authors and writers; Pres. ALAIN ABSIRE; Gen. Sec. DOMINIQUE LE BRUN; publ. *Lettre.*

Société d'Histoire Littéraire de la France: 112 rue Monge, 75005 Paris; tel. 1-45-87-23-30; fax 1-45-87-23-30; f. 1894; 400 mems; Pres. M. FUMAROLI; Dir S. MENANT; publ. *Revue d'Histoire Littéraire de la France* (6 a year).

MEDICINE

Académie Nationale de Chirurgie: 'Les Cordeliers', 15 rue de l'École de Médecine, 75006 Paris; tel. 1-43-54-02-32; fax 1-43-29-34-44; e-mail ac.chirurgie@bhdc.jussieu.fr; internet www.bium.univ-paris5.fr/ acad-chirurgie; f. 1731; 500 mems; library of 5,000 vols; Pres. Dr JACQUES POILLEUX; Vice-Pres. HENRI BISMUTH; Sec.-Gen. Dr HENRI JUDET; publs *Annales de Chirurgie* (10 a year), *e-Memoires* (online, 4 a year).

Académie Nationale de Médecine: 16 rue Bonaparte, 75272 Paris Cedex 06; tel. 1-42-34-57-70; fax 1-40-46-87-55; internet www .academie-medecine.fr; f. 1820 by Louis XVIII; library of 400,000 vols; 130 mems attached to sections on medicine, surgery, hygiene, biological sciences, social sciences, veterinary medicine, pharmacy; Pres. CLAUDE BOUDÈNE; Perm. Sec. JACQUES-LOUIS BINET; publ. *Bulletin de l'Académie nationale de médecine* (9 a year).

Académie Nationale de Pharmacie: 4 ave de l'Observatoire, 75006 Paris; tel. 1-43-25-54-49; fax 1-43-29-45-85; e-mail info@ acadpharm.org; internet www.acadpharm .org; f. 1803; 440 mems; Pres. FRANÇOIS CHAST; Gen. Sec. J.-P. CHIRON; publ. *Annales Pharmaceutiques Françaises.*

Association des Morphologistes: BP 184, 54505 Vandoeuvre-lès-Nancy; f. 1899; 1,005 mems; Chief Editor Prof. G. GRIGNON; publ. *Morphologie* (4 a year).

Association Française d'Urologie: Colloquium, 12 rue de la Croix Faubin, 75577 Paris Cedex 11; tel. 1-44-64-15-15; fax 1-44-64-15-16; e-mail contact@urofrance.org; internet www.urofrance.org; f. 1896; 1,027

mems; Pres. PASCAL RISCHMANN; Sec. Gen. Dr PATRICK COLOBY; publ. *Progrès en Urologie* (6 a year).

Association Générale des Médecins de France: 34 blvd de Courcelles, 75809 Paris Cedex 17; tel. 1-40-54-54-54; fax 1-40-54-54-40; Pres. P. BAUDOUIN; Sec. Dr TOUCHARD; publ. *Bulletin.*

Association Scientifique des Médecins Acupuncteurs de France (ASMAF): 2 rue du Général de Larminat, 75015 Paris; tel. 1-42-73-37-26; f. 1945 as Société d'Acupuncture; 1,500 mems; Pres. Dr GEORGES CANTONI; Sec.-Gen. Dr H. OLIVO; publ. *Méridiens* (4 a year).

Centre d'Etude de l'Expression: Centre hospitalier Sainte-Anne, 100 rue de la Santé, 75014 Paris; tel. 1-45-89-21-51; e-mail cee@ ch-sainte-anne.fr; internet centre-etude-expression.fr; f. 1973 to develop psychopathological and psychological studies of various forms of expression: plastic, verbal, mimic, body-language, musical, theatrical; exhibitions of artworks from Sainte-Anne's colln and contemporary artists; Pres. PIERRE DAUMARD; Sec.-Gen. Dr ANNE-MARIE DUBOIS.

Comité National contre les Maladies Respiratoires: 66 blvd Saint-Michel, 75006 Paris; tel. 1-46-34-58-80; fax 1-43-29-06-58; e-mail contact@lesouffle.org; internet www .lesouffle.org; f. 1916; research, information, health education, assistance for the handicapped; Pres. FRANÇOIS BONNAUD; publ. *La Lettre du Souffle* (4 a year).

Confédération des Syndicats Médicaux Français: 79 rue de Tocqueville, 75017 Paris; tel. 1-43-18-88-00; fax 1-43-18-88-20; e-mail csmf@csmf.org; internet www.csmf .org; f. 1930; 16,000 mems; Pres. Dr MICHEL CHASSANG; Sec.-Gen. Dr WANNEPAIN.

Fédération des Gynécologues et Obstétriciens de Langue Française: Hôpital St-Antoine, 184 rue du Fg St-Antoine, 75012 Paris; tel. 1-49-28-28-76; fax 1-49-28-27-57; f. 1950; 600 mems; Pres. Prof. ULYSSE GASPARD (Liège); Sec.-Gen. Prof. JACQUES MILLIEZ (Paris); publ. *Journal de Gynécologie Obstétrique et Biologie de la Reproduction* (8 a year).

Fédération Nationale des Médecins Radiologues: 62 blvd de Latour Maubourg, 75007 Paris Cedex 07; tel. 1-53-59-34-00; fax 1-45-51-83-15; e-mail fnmr@fnmr.org; internet www.fnmr.org; f. 1907; 4,800 mems; Pres. Dr DENIS AUCANT; Secs-Gen. Dr JACQUES NINEY, Dr LAURENT VERZAUX.

Société de Médecine de Strasbourg: Faculté de Médecine, 4 rue Kirschleger, 67085 Strasbourg Cedex; tel. 3-88-11-62-59; f. 1919; 450 mems; organizes medical confs; Pres. Prof. E. QUOIX; Sec.-Gen. Prof. E. ANDRÈS; publ. *Journal de Médecine de Strasbourg* (12 a year).

Société de Médecine Légale et de Criminologie de France: 2 place Mazas, 75012 Paris; tel. 1-43-43-42-54; internet www.smlc .asso.fr; f. 1868; Pres. Prof. MICHEL PENNEAU; Sec. DIDIER GOSSET; publ. *Médecine légale-droit médical.*

Société de Neurophysiologie Clinique de Langue Française: Hôpital Sainte Anne, 1 rue Cabanis, 75674 Paris Cedex 14; tel. 1-40-48-82-03; f. 1948; 500 mems; Pres. Dr LUIS GARCIA-LARREA; Sec.-Gen. Dr S. S. LEFAUCHER; publ. *Neurophysiologie Clinique* (6 a year).

Société de Pathologie Exotique: 25 rue du Docteur-Roux, 75724 Paris Cedex 15; tel. 1-45-66-88-69; fax 1-45-66-44-85; e-mail socpatex@pasteur.fr; internet www.pasteur .fr/socpatex; f. 1908; 637 mems; library of 2,000 vols, 125 periodicals; Pres. P. SALIOU;

Sec.-Gen. Y. BUISSON; publ. *Bulletin* (5 a year).

Société de Pneumologie de Langue Française: 66 blvd Saint-Michel, 75006 Paris; tel. 1-46-34-03-87; fax 1-46-34-58-27; e-mail splf@splf.org; internet www.splf.org; Pres. M. FOURNIER; Secs-Gen. J. F. CORDIER, J. P. GRIGNET, B. HOUSSET, E. LEMARIÉ; publ. *Revue des Maladies Respiratoires.*

Société d'Histoire de la Pharmacie: 4 ave de l'Observatoire, 75270 Paris Cedex 06; tel. and fax 1-53-73-97-37; f. 1913; 1,000 mems; Pres. Prof. OLIVIER LAFONT; Sec. B. BONNEMAIN; publ. *Revue d'Histoire de la Pharmacie* (4 a year).

Société d'Ophtalmologie de Paris: 108 rue du Bac, 75007 Paris; f. 1888; Sec.-Gen. Dr JEAN-PAUL BOISSIN; publ. *Bulletin* (12 a year).

Société Française d'Allergologie et d'Immunologie Clinique: Institut Pasteur, 28 rue du Dr Roux, 75724 Paris Cedex 15; tel. 1-45-68-82-41; fax 1-40-61-31-60; internet www.sfaic.com; f. 1947; 860 mems; Pres. Prof. D. VERVLOET; publ. *Revue Française d'Allergologie et d'Immunologie clinique* (5 a year).

Société Française d'Anesthésie et de Réanimation: 74 rue Raynouard, 75016 Paris; tel. 1-45-25-82-25; fax 1-40-50-35-22; e-mail sfar@invivo.edu; internet www.sfar .org; f. 1934; 4,298 mems; Pres. JEAN MARTY; Sec.-Gen. LAURENT JOUFFROY; publ. *Annales françaises d'Anesthésie et de Réanimation* (12 a year).

Société Française d'Angéiologie: 153 ave Berthelot, 69007 Lyons; tel. 4-78-72-38-98; internet www.sfa-online.com; f. 1947; 450 mems; Pres. Dr FRANÇOIS ANDRÉ ALLAERT; Sec.-Gen. Dr MICHÈLE CAZAUBON; publ. *La revue Angéiologie* (4 a year).

Société Française de Biologie Clinique: 194 Ave de Strasbourg, 54000 Nancy Cedex; tel. 3-83-35-36-25; fax 3-83-32-75-13; e-mail sfbc@orange.fr; internet www.sfbc.asso.fr; Pres. ALAIN LEGRAND; Sec.-Gen. NELLY JACOB.

Société Française de Chirurgie Orthopédique et Traumatologique: Secrétariat: 56 rue Boissonade, 75014 Paris; tel. 1-43-22-47-54; fax 1-43-22-46-70; e-mail sofcot@sofcot .com.fr; internet www.sofcot.com.fr; f. 1918; 1,950 mems; Pres. J. M. THOMINE; publs *Revue de Chirurgie Orthopédique, Bulletin des Orthopédistes Francophones* (2 a year).

Société Française de Chirurgie Pédiatrique: 149 rue de Sèvres, 75015 Paris; tel. 4-91-38-66-82; fax 4-91-38-47-14; e-mail webmaster-sfcp@chirpediatric.fr; internet www.chirpediatric.fr; f. 1959; 350 mems; Pres. Prof. PAUL MITROFANOFF; Sec.-Gen. Prof. J. L. CLAVERT; publ. *European Journal of Paediatric Surgery* (6 a year).

Société Française de Chirurgie Plastique, Reconstructive et Esthétique: 26 rue de Belfort, 92400 Courbevoie; tel. 1-46-67-74-85; fax 1-46-67-74-89; e-mail sofcpre@ wanadoo.fr; internet www.plasticiens.fr; f. 1953; 636 mems; Pres. Prof. J. P. CHAVOIN; Sec.-Gen. Prof. M. REVOL; publ. *Annales de Chirurgie Plastique et Esthétique* (6 a year).

Société Française de Chirurgie Thoracique et Cardio-vasculaire (French Society for Thoracic and Cardiovascular Surgery): 56 Blvd Vincent Auriol, 75013 Paris; tel. 1-42-16-42-10; fax 1-42-16-42-09; e-mail sfctcv@sfctcv.net; internet www.fstcvs .org; f. 1948; 643 mems; studies problems linked with thoracic and cardiovascular surgery; Pres. Prof. ALAIN PAVIE; Sec.-Gen. Dr R. NOTTIN; publ. *Journal de Chirurgie Thoracique et Cardiovasculaire* (4 a year).

Société Française de Gynécologie: 36 rue de Toqueville, 75017 Paris; tel. 1-42-27-95-59; e-mail jean.belaisch@wanadoo.fr;

internet www.sfgynecologie.org; 582 mems; Pres. J. P. WOLFF; Sec.-Gen. ANDRÉ GORINS; publ. *Gynécologie* (6 a year).

Société Française de Médecine Aérospatiale: Laboratoire de Médecine Aérospatiale du Centre d'Essais en Vol, 91228 Brétigny sur Orge Cedex; tel. 1-69-88-23-80; fax 1-69-88-27-25; internet www.soframas.asso.fr; f. 1960; publishes papers on experimental and clinical studies; 1,100 mems; Pres. Dr M.-P. CHARETTEUR; Sec.-Gen. Prof. G. SOLIGNAC; publ. *Médecine Aérospatiale* (4 a year).

Société Française de Mycologie Médicale: 191 rue de Vaugirard, 75015 Paris; tel. 1-43-06-68-72; fax 1-42-73-61-10; e-mail sfmm1@orange.fr; internet pagesperso-orange.fr/sfmm; f. 1956; 250 mems; Pres. CLAUDE GUIGUEN; Sec.-Gen. Dr PATRICIA ROUX; publ. *Journal de Mycologie Médicale* (4 a year).

Société Française de Neurologie: Service de Neurologie 1, Clinique Paul Castaigne, Hôpital de la Salpêtrière, 47 blvd de l'Hôpital, 75651 Paris Cedex 13; tel. 1-42-16-18-28; fax 1-44-24-52-47; internet www.sf-neuro .org; f. 1899; 550 mems; library of 22,000 vols; Sec.-Gen. Prof. C. PIERROT-DESEILLIGNY; publ. *Revue Neurologique* (12 a year).

Société Française de Pédiatrie: Hôpital Trousseau, 26 ave du Dr Arnold Netter, 75571 Paris Cedex 12; tel. 1-49-28-92-96; e-mail sfpediatrie@orange.fr; internet www .sfpediatrie.com; f. 1929; 1,500 mems; Pres. Prof. ALAIN CHANTEPIE; Sec.-Gen. Prof. PATRICK TOUNIAN; publ. *Archives de Pédiatrie* (12 a year).

Société Française de Phlébologie: 46 rue Saint-Lambert, 75015 Paris; tel. 1-45-33-02-71; fax 1-42-50-75-18; e-mail sfphlebo@ club-internet.fr; internet www.sf-phlebologie .org; f. 1947; 2,000 mems; Pres. M. PERRIN; Sec.-Gen. F. VIN; publ. *Phlébologie—Annales Vasculaires* (4 a year).

Société Française de Phytiatrie et de Phytopharmacie: CNRA, Route de Saint Cyr, 78000 Versailles; tel. 1-49-50-75-22; f. 1951; 1,000 mems.

Société Française de Radiologie: 20 ave Rapp, 75007 Paris; tel. 1-53-59-59-69; fax 1-53-59-59-60; e-mail sfr@sfradiologie.org; internet www.sfrnet.org; f. 1909; 6,785 mems; Pres. GÉRARD MORVAN; Gen. Sec. PHILIPE GRENIER; publ. *Journal de Radiology* (12 a year).

Société Française de Santé Publique: BP 7, 2 rue Doyen Jacques-Parisot, 54501 Vandoeuvre lès Nancy Cedex; tel. 3-83-44-39-17; fax 3-83-44-37-76; internet www.sfsp.fr; f. 1877; 750 mems; Pres. Dr FRANÇOIS BOURDILLON; publ. *Santé publique* (6 a year).

Société Française d'Endocrinologie: c/o Masson Edit., 120 blvd Saint-Germain, 75280 Paris Cedex 06; e-mail editorial@ santor.net; internet www.sf-endocrino.net; f. 1939; 1,000 mems; Sec.-Gen. Prof. BERNARD CONTE-DEVOLX; publ. *Annales d'Endocrinologie* (6 a year).

Société Française d'Histoire de la Médecine: c/o Dr Jean-Jacques Ferrandis, 6 rue des Impressionnistes, 91210 Draveil; tel. 6-18-46-72-49; e-mail jj.ferrandis@orange.fr; internet www.bium.univ-paris5.fr/sfhm; f. 1902; 700 mems; library; Pres. Prof. GUY PALLARDY; Gen. Sec. Dr JEAN-JACQUES FERRANDIS; publ. *Histoire des Sciences médicales* (4 a year).

Société Française d'Hydrologie et de Climatologie Médicales: 15 ave Charles de Gaulle, 73100 Aix-les-Bains; tel. 4-79-35-14-87; internet www.soc-hydrologie.org; f. 1853; 320 mems; Pres. Prof. MICHEL BOULANGÉ; Sec.-Gen. Dr ROMAIN FORESTIER; publ. *La Presse Thermale et Climatique* (1 a year).

Société Française d'Ophtalmologie: Maison de l'Ophtalmologie, 17 Villa d'Alésia, 75014 Paris; tel. 1-44-12-60-50; fax 1-44-12-23-00; internet www.sfo.asso.fr; f. 1883; annual conference; 7,200 mems; Pres. Dr J. L. ARNÉ; Sec.-Gen. Dr J. P. RENARD; publ. *Journal Français d'Ophtalmologie* (10 a year).

Société Française d'Oto-Rhino-Laryngologie et de Pathologie Cervico-Faciale: 9 rue Villebois-Mareuil, 75017 Paris; internet orl-france.org; f. 1880; 1,500 mems; Pres. Dr R. BATISSE; Sec. Prof. CHARLES FRECHE; publ. *Comptes Rendus and Rapports Discutés au Congrès*.

Société Française du Cancer (French Cancer Society): 14 rue Corvisart, 75013 Paris; tel. 1-45-87-27-62; fax 1-46-33-20-09; e-mail info@sfc.asso.fr; internet www.sfc .asso.fr; f. 1906; 440 mems; offers grants to doctors from abroad or French doctors for work abroad; quarterly meetings, annual symposium; Pres. JACQUES POUYSSEGUR; Sec.-Gen. FRANÇOIS LAVELLE; publ. *Bulletin du Cancer* (12 a year).

Société Médicale des Hôpitaux de Paris: Hôpital Hôtel-Dieu, 1, place du Parvis Notre-Dame, 75181 Paris Cedex 04; e-mail smhp@ wanadoo.fr; internet www.smhp.fr; f. 1849; Sec. Prof. CLAIRE LE JEUNNE; publ. *Annales de Médecine Interne*.

Société Médico-Psychologique: 14/16 ave Robert Schuman, 92100 Boulogne; f. 1852; 675 mems; Pres. Dr BERNARD LAFONT; Sec.-Gen. Prof. JEAN-FRANÇOIS ALLILAIRE; publ. *Annales médico-psychologiques* (12 a year).

Société Nationale Française de Gastro-Entérologie: CHU Reims, rue Serge Kochman, 51092 Reims Cedex; tel. 3-26-35-94-31; fax 3-26-35-95-91; e-mail secretariat.reims@ snfge.org; internet www.snfge.org; f. 1947; 1,800 mems; Pres. Dr ALEX PARIENTE; Sec.-Gen. Prof. GUILLAUME CADIOT; publs *Gastro-entérologie Clinique et Biologique*, *Hepato-Gastro et Oncologie Digestive*.

Société Odontologique de Paris: 6 rue Jean Hugues, 75116 Paris; tel. 1-42-09-29-13; fax 1-42-09-29-08; internet www.sop.asso.fr; 2,500 mems; Pres. PHILIP SAFAR; Man. PHILIPPE CHALANSET; publs *Journal de la Société Odontologique de Paris*, *Revue d'Odonto-Stomatologie* (4 a year).

Société Scientifique d'Hygiène Alimentaire: 16A rue de l'Estrapade, 75005 Paris; tel. 1-43-25-11-85; fax 1-46-34-07-45; e-mail isa@ssha.asso.fr; internet www.ssha.asso.fr; f. 1904; 1,182 mems; Pres. Dr GUY EBRARD.

NATURAL SCIENCES
General

Comité National Français des Recherches Arctiques et Antarctiques: c/o Expéditions Polaires Françaises, 47 ave du Maréchal Fayolle, 75016 Paris; tel. 1-40-79-37-56; fax 1-40-79-37-71; f. 1958; Pres. J.-C. HUREAU.

Fédération Française des Sociétés de Sciences Naturelles: 57 rue Cuvier, 75231 Paris Cedex 05; tel. 1-40-79-34-95; fax 1-40-79-34-88; f. 1919; natural sciences and nature conservation; groups 175 socs; Pres. J. LESCURE; Gen. Sec. J. FRETEY; publ. *Revue de la FFSSN* (1 a year).

Biological Sciences

Les Naturalistes Parisiens: 45 rue de Buffon, 75005 Paris; f. 1904; undertakes research in natural history and deepens the scientific knowledge of its mems; 600 mems; Pres. C. DUPUIS; publs *Bulletin* (4 a year), *Cahiers des Naturalistes*.

Société Botanique de France: rue J. B. Clément, 92296 Châtenay-Malabry Cedex;

tel. 1-46-83-55-20; fax 1-46-83-13-03; internet www.bium.univ-paris5.fr/sbf; f. 1854; 800 mems; President ANDRÉ CHARPIN; Sec. ELISABETH DODINET; publs *Acta Botanica Gallica* (6 or 7 a year), *Le Journal de Botanique* (4 a year).

Société de Biologie: Université Pierre et Marie Curie, CP 2A, 7 quai St Bernard, 75252 Paris Cedex 05; tel. 1-44-27-35-50; e-mail societe.biologie@snv.jussieu.fr; internet www.societedebiologie.com; f. 1848; organizes meetings about innovative biological research; 140 hon. mems; 120 elected mems; Pres. Dr FRANÇOISE DIETERLEN; Sec.-Gen. Dr CLAUDE JACQUEMIN; publ. *Biologie Aujourd'hui* (4 a year, online at www.biologie-journal.org).

Société d'Etudes Ornithologiques de France: Muséum National d'Histoire Naturelle, 55 rue Buffon, CP 51, 75231 Paris Cedex 05; tel. 1-40-79-38-34; fax 1-40-79-30-63; e-mail seof@mnhn.fr; internet www.mnhn .fr/assoc/seof; f. 1993; scientific study of wild birds and their protection; publishes monographs, national and regional ornithological lists, atlases, CDs; 800 mems; library of 23,000 vols; Pres. P. NICOLAU-GUILLAUMET; Sec.-Gen. J. PH. SIBLET; Librarian E. BREMOND-HOSLET; publ. *Alauda* (4 a year).

Société Entomologique de France: 45 rue Buffon, 75005 Paris; tel. 1-40-79-33-84; fax 1-40-79-36-99; e-mail secretaire-general@lasef .org; internet www.lasef.org; f. 1832; 650 mems; library of 12,000 vols, 80 periodicals; Gen. Sec. H. PIGUET; publs *Annales* (4 a year), *Bulletin* (5 a year), *L'Entomologiste* (6 a year).

Société Française de Biologie Végétale: 4 place Jussieu, 75252 Paris Cedex 05; tel. 1-44-27-59-18; fax 1-44-27-61-51; e-mail marie-france.laforge@snv.jussieu.fr; internet www.sfbv.org; f. 1955; 600 mems; Pres. P. MOREAU; Sec.-Gen. A. ZACHOWSKI; publ. *Plant Physiology and Biochemistry* (12 a year).

Société Française d'Ichtyologie: 43 rue Cuvier, 75231 Paris Cedex 05; tel. 1-40-79-37-49; fax 1-40-79-37-71; e-mail keith@mnhn .fr; internet www.mnhn.fr/sfi; f. 1976; fish culture, biology and systematics of fish, sea and freshwater fisheries; 320 mems; library of 5,000 vols, 800 periodicals; Pres. M. GAYET; Sec. P. KEITH; publ. *Cybium* (4 a year).

Société Mycologique de France: 20 rue Rottembourg, 75012 Paris; tel. and fax 1-44-67-96-90; e-mail smf@mycofrance.org; internet mycofrance.org; f. 1884; 1,800 mems; Pres. M. BUYCK; Sec.-Gen. M. CHALANGE; publ. *Bulletin Trimestriel*.

Société Nationale de Protection de la Nature: 9 rue Cels, 75014 Paris; tel. 1-43-20-15-39; fax 1-43-20-15-71; e-mail snpn@ wanadoo.fr; internet www.snpn.com; f. 1854; 4,000 mems; Pres. FRANÇOIS RAMADE; Gen. Sec. MICHEL ECHAUBARD; publs *La Terre et la Vie* (4 a year), *Le Courrier de la Nature* (7 a year), *Zones Humides Infos* (4 a year).

Société Zoologique de France: 195 rue St Jacques, 75005 Paris; tel. 1-40-79-31-10; fax 1-40-79-57-35; e-mail dhondt@mnhn.fr; internet www.snv.jussieu.fr/zoologie; f. 1876; zoology, evolution; 600 mems; Pres. Prof. J. DAGUZAN; Gen. Sec. Dr J. L. D'HONDT; publs *Bulletin* (4 a year), *Mémoires* (irregular).

Mathematical Sciences

Comité National Français de Mathématiciens: c/o S. Ferenczi, Institut de Mathématiques de Luminy, 163 ave de Luminy, Case 907, 13288 Marseilles Cedex 9; fax 4-91-26-96-55; e-mail ferenczi@iml.univ-mrs.fr; f. 1951; Pres. P. ARNOUX; Sec. S. FERENCZI.

Société Mathématique de France: Institut Henri Poincaré, 11 rue Pierre et Marie Curie, 75231 Paris Cedex 05; tel. 1-44-27-67-96; fax 1-40-46-90-96; e-mail smf@dma.ens.fr; internet smf.emath.fr; f. 1872; 2,000 mems; Pres. STEPHANE JAFFARD; Gen.-Sec. CLAIRE ROPARTZ; publs *Annales Scientifiques de l'Ecole Normale Superiere* (6 a year), *Astérisque* (12 a year), *Bulletin* (4 a year), *Cours Spécialisés* (2 a year), *Gazette des Mathématiciens* (4 a year), *Mémoires* (4 a year), *Panoramas et Synthèses* (2 a year), *Revue d'Histoire des Mathématiques* (2 a year).

Physical Sciences

Association Française d'Observateurs d'Etoiles Variables: Observatoire Astronomique, 11 rue de l'Université, 67000 Strasbourg; tel. 3-85-89-09-78; e-mail afoev@astro.u-strasbg.fr; internet www.astro.u-strasbg.fr/afoev; f. 1921; observations (visual, photographic, PEP, CCD) of variable stars; 110 mems; Pres. M. VERDENET; Sec.-Gens J. GUNTHER, D. PROUST; publ. *Bulletin de l'AFOEV* (4 a year).

Association Française pour l'Etude du Quaternaire: Maison de la Géologie, 79 rue Claude Bernard, 75005 Paris; e-mail pierre.antoine@cnrs-bellevue.fr; internet www.afeq.cnrs-bellevue.fr; f. 1962 to prepare scientific publications and exchange information on the Quaternary; 600 mems; Pres. Dr D. LEFÈVRE; Sec. Dr C. FERRIER; publ. *Quaternaire* (4 a year).

Association Scientifique et Technique pour l'Exploitation des Océans: Immeuble Ile de France, La Défense 9, 4 place de la Pyramide, 92070 Paris La Défense Cedex 33; tel. 1-47-67-25-32; f. 1967; oil technology and allied activities, pollution control, polymetallic nodules, sand and gravel workings, fishing technology and fish farming; 80 mem. industries; Chair. PIERRE JACQUARD; Man. Dir B. E. DIMONT; publ. *Annuaire Technique et Industriel*.

Fédération Française pour les sciences de la Chimie: 28 rue Saint-Dominique, 75007 Paris; tel. 1-53-59-02-10; fax 1-45-55-40-33; e-mail pascale.bridou@wanadoo.fr; internet www.ffc-asso.fr; f. 2005; 4,000 mems.

Société Astronomique de France: 3 rue Beethoven, 75016 Paris; tel. 1-42-24-13-74; fax 1-42-30-75-47; e-mail ste.astro.france@wanadoo.fr; internet www.saf-lastronomie.com; f. 1887; 2,200 mems; Pres. PHILIPPE MOREL; Sec.-Gen. FRANCIS OGER; publs *L'Astronomie* (12 a year), *Les Éphémérides* (1 a year), *Observations et Travaux* (3 a year).

Société des Experts-Chimistes de France: 23 rue Saint-Dominique, 75007 Paris; tel. 1-53-59-02-16; fax 1-45-55-40-33; e-mail contact@chimie-experts.org; internet www.chimie-experts.org; f. 1912; 300 mems; Pres. JEAN-PIERRE DAL PONT; Sec.-Gen. THÉRÈSE GIBERT; publ. *Annales des Falsifications de l'Expertise Chimique et Toxicologique*.

Société Française de Biochimie et Biologie Moléculaire: 45 Rue des Saints-Pères, 75270 Paris Cedex 06; tel. 1-42-86-33-77; fax 1-42-86-33-73; e-mail sfbbm@cep.u-psud.fr; internet coli.polytechnique.fr/sfbbm; f. 1914; 1,320 mems; Pres. E. WESTHOF; Gen. Sec. P. DESSEN; publs *Biochimie, Regard sur la Biochimie*.

Société Française de Chimie: 250 rue St Jacques, 75005 Paris; tel. 1-40-46-71-60; fax 1-40-46-71-61; e-mail sfc@sfc.fr; internet www.sfc.fr; f. 1857; 4,600 mems; Pres. ARMAND LATTES; Sec.-Gen. JEAN-CLAUDE BRUNIE; publs *Analusis* (10 a year), *Journal de Chimie physique* (10 a year), *L'Actualité chimique* (12 a year).

Société Française de Minéralogie et de Cristallographie: 4 place Jussieu, casier 83, 75252 Paris Cedex 05; tel. 1-44-27-60-24; fax 1-44-27-60-24; e-mail sfmc@ccr.jussieu.fr; internet www.sfmc-fr.org; f. 1878; 600 mems; Pres. JEAN-ROBERT KIENAST; Gen.-Sec. DANIEL NEUVILLE; publs *Bulletin de Liaison, European Journal of Mineralogy*.

Société Française de Physique: 33 rue Croulebarbe, 75013 Paris; tel. 1-44-08-67-10; fax 1-44-08-67-19; e-mail sfp@sfpnet.org; internet sfp.in2p3.fr; f. 1873; 2,500 mems; Pres. EDOUARD BREZIN; Gen. Sec. JEAN VAN-NIMENUS; publs *Annales de Physique, Bulletin, Catalogue de l'Exposition de Physique, Colloques, Journal de Physique*.

Société Géologique de France: 77 rue Claude-Bernard, 75005 Paris; tel. 1-43-31-77-35; fax 1-45-35-79-10; e-mail accueil@sgfr.org; internet www.sgfr.org; f. 1830; 1,200 mems; library of 65,000 vols, 500 periodicals; Pres. ANDRÉ SCHAAF; Vice-Pres. ISABELLE COJAN; Exec. Dir FRANCOISE PEIFFER-RANGIN; Sec. BERNADETTE TESSIER; publs *Bulletin* (6 a year), *Géochronique* (co-edited with BRGM, 4 a year), *Géologie de la France* (co-edited with BRGM, online), *Mémoires* (irregular), *Terra Nova* (co-edited with EUG and Sociétés Géologiques Européennes).

Union des Professeurs de Physique et de Chimie: 44 blvd Saint-Michel, 76270 Paris Cedex 06; tel. 1-43-25-61-53; fax 1-43-25-28-83; e-mail secretariat.national@udppc.asso.fr; internet www.udp-bup.org; f. 1906; 4,000 mems; Pres J. MAUREL, JEAN-CHARLES JACQUEMIN; publ. *Le BUP* (12 a year).

PHILOSOPHY AND PSYCHOLOGY

Association pour la Diffusion de la Pensée Français: 6 rue Ferrus, 75683 Paris Cedex 14; tel. 1-43-13-11-00; fax 1-43-13-11-25; f. 1946; aims to promote the French language and Francophone culture worldwide; 600 overseas mems; Pres. JACQUES BLOT.

Société Française de Philosophie: c/o 45 rue d'Ulm, 75320 Paris Cedex 005; f. 1901; 180 mems; Pres. BERNARD BOURGEOIS; Sec.-Gen. CHRISTIANE MENASSEYRE; publs *Bulletin, Revue de Métaphysique et de Morale* (4 a year).

Société Française de Psychologie: 71 ave Edouard-Vaillant, 92774 Boulogne Cedex; tel. 1-55-20-58-32; fax 1-55-20-58-34; e-mail sfp@psycho.univ-paris5.fr; internet www.sfpsy.org; f. 1901; 1,000 mems; Pres. JACQUES PY; Sec.-Gen. ALAIN PAINEAU; publs *La Lettre de SFP, Pratiques Psychologiques, Psychologie Française*.

RELIGION, SOCIOLOGY AND ANTHROPOLOGY

Association Française des Arabisants: Collège de France, 52 rue du Cardinal Lemoine, 75005 Paris; e-mail afda@afda.asso.fr; internet www.afda.asso.fr; f. 1973; promotes Arabic studies; studies questions of doctrine and practice relative to teaching and research in Arabic; keeps its members informed of ideas and activities of interest to teachers, researchers and students of Arabic; 450 mems; Pres. JEAN-YVES L'HOPITAL; Sec. ABDELLATIF IDRISSI; publs *Actes des journées d'études arabes* (irregular), *Annuaire des Arabisants* (every 2 years), *L'Arabisant* (every 2 years), *Lettre d'Information* (2 a year).

Société Asiatique: Palais de l'Institut, 23 quai de Conti, 75006 Paris; tel. 1-44-41-43-14; fax 1-44-41-43-14; internet www.aibl.fr/fr/asie/home.html; f. 1822; library of 90,000 vols; 725 mems; Pres. JEAN-PIERRE MAHÉ; publs *Cahiers, Journal Asiatique* (2 a year).

Société d'Anthropologie de Paris: Musée de l'Homme, 17 place du Trocadéro, 75116 Paris; tel. 1-45-59-53-31; fax 1-45-59-53-31; e-mail secretairegeneral@sapweb.fr; internet www.sapweb.fr; f. 1859; biological anthropology; 310 mems; Pres. OLIVIER DUTOUR; Sec.-Gen. ALAIN FROMENT; publ. *Bulletins et Mémoires* (4 a year).

Société de l'Histoire du Protestantisme Français: 54 rue des Saints-Pères, 75007 Paris; tel. 1-45-48-62-07; fax 1-45-44-94-87; e-mail shpf@libertysurf.fr; f. 1852; library of 150,000 vols, 12,000 MSS, 2,000 periodical titles; Pres. THERRY DU PASQUIER; Sec.-Gen. JEAN-HUGUES CARBONNIER; publs *Bulletin, Cahiers de Généalogie Protestante* (4 a year).

Société de Mythologie Française: 3 rue St-Laurent, 75010 Paris; tel. 1-42-05-30-57; e-mail phparrain@mythofrancaise.asso.fr; internet www.mythofrancaise.asso.fr; f. 1950; 200 mems; Pres. BERNARD SERGENT; publ. *Mythologie Française* (4 a year).

Société des Africanistes: Musée de l'Homme, 17 Place du Trocadéro, 75116 Paris; tel. 1-47-27-72-55; fax 1-47-04-63-40; e-mail africanistes@wanadoo.fr; internet www.mae.u-paris10.fr/africanistes; f. 1931; 400 mems; Pres. PHILIPPE LABURTHE-TOLRA; Sec. FRANÇOIS GAULME; publ. *Journal des Africanistes* (2 a year).

Société des Américanistes: Maison René Ginouvès, 21 allée de l'Université, 92023 Nanterre Cedex; tel. 1-46-69-26-34; e-mail jsa@mae.u-paris10.fr; f. 1895; 500 mems; Pres. PHILIPPE DESCOLA; Gen. Sec. DOMINIQUE MICHELET; publ. *Journal* (2 a year).

Société d'Histoire Religieuse de la France: 26 rue d'Assas, 75006 Paris; internet www.enc.sorbonne.fr/shrf; f. 1910; 600 mems; Pres. BERNARD BARBICHE; Sec.-Gen. OLIVIER PONCET; publ. *Revue d'Histoire de l'Eglise de France* (2 a year).

Société Française de Sociologie: 59/61 rue Pouchet, 75849 Paris Cedex 17; tel. 1-40-25-12-63; fax 1-42-28-95-44; e-mail afs@iresco.fr; internet www.iresco.fr/societes/afs; f. 1962; Pres. DANIEL BERTAUX; Sec. MICHÈLE VINAUGER.

TECHNOLOGY

Académie de marine: CC 11, 75398, Paris Cedex 08; 21 pl. Joffre, 75007 Paris; tel. 1-44-42-82-02; fax 1-44-42-82-04; e-mail academiedemarine@wanadoo.fr; internet www.academiedemarine.com; f. 1752; 109 mems; attached to sections on history, literature and arts, law and economics, mercantile marine, military affairs, naval equipment, navigation and oceanic sciences, yachting and fishing; Pres. BERTRAND VIEILLARD-BARON; Vice-Pres. JEAN-PIERRE QUÉNEUDEC; Sec.-Gen. VERONIQUE DE LONGEVIALLE; publ. *Communications et Mémoires* (3 a year).

Association Aéronautique et Astronautique de France (AAAF): 61 Ave du Château, 78480 Verneuil-sur-Seine; tel. 1-39-79-75-15; fax 1-39-79-75-27; internet www.aaafasso.fr; f. 1972; 1,800 mems; formed by merger of Asscn Française des Ingénieurs de l'Aéronautique et de l'Espace and Société Française d'Astronautique; Pres. MICHEL SCHELLER; Sec.-Gen. ROBERT DUBOST; publ. *La Nouvelle Revue d'Aéronautique et d'Astronautique* (4 a year).

Association des Anciens Elèves de l'Ecole Nationale Supérieure des Industries Agricoles et Alimentaires: 9–11 ave Franklin D. Roosevelt, 75008 Paris; tel. 1-42-25-92-48; fax 1-45-62-77-13; internet www.uniagro.fr/gene/main.php?base=1141&url_assoc=y; 1,500 mems; Pres. JEAN-LOUIS TIX-

IER; Sec.-Gen. MICHEL MERY; publ. *Industries Alimentaires et Agricoles* (12 a year).

Association Française des Sciences et Technologies de l'Information: 4 place Jussieu, 75252 Paris Cedex 05; tel. 3-83-59-20-51; e-mail asti.asso@lri.fr; internet www.asti.asso.fr; f. 1998; 25 mem. orgs; Pres. JEAN-PAUL HATON; Sec.-Gen. CLAUDE GIRAULT; publ. *Hebdo*.

Association Française du Froid: 17 rue Guillaume Apollinaire, 75006 Paris; tel. 1-45-44-52-52; fax 1-42-22-00-42; e-mail a.f.f@wanadoo.fr; internet www.aff.asso.fr; f. 1908; 1,000 mems; Pres. LOUIS LUCAS; Sec.-Gen. JEAN LETEINTURIER-LAPRISE; publs *Bulletin: Kryos, Revue Générale du Froid* (10 a year).

Association Nationale de la Recherche Technique: 41 Blvd des Capucines, 75002 Paris; tel. 1-55-35-25-50; fax 1-55-35-25-55; internet www.anrt.asso.fr; f. 1953 to promote technical research and organizations, and to foster contact with technical research institutions abroad; Pres. JEAN-FRANÇOIS DEHECQ; publ. *La lettre Européenne du Progrès Technique* (10 a year).

Conseil National des Ingénieurs et des Scientifiques de France: 7 rue Lamennais, 75008 Paris; tel. 1-44-13-66-88; fax 1-42-89-82-50; internet www.cnisf.org; f. 1848; Pres. NOËL CLAVELLOUX; Sec. MONIQUE MONIN; publ. *I.D.*

Société de l'Electricité, de l'Electronique, et des Technologies de l'Information et de la Communication (SEE): 17 rue de l'Amiral Hamelin, 75783 Paris Cedex 16; tel. 1-56-90-37-00; fax 1-56-90-37-19; e-mail see@see.asso.fr; internet www.see.asso.fr; f. 1883; Pres. ALAIN BRAVO; Sec. PATRICK MORO; publs *e-STA—Revue des Sciences et Technologies de l'Automatique* (online), *Revue de l'Electricité et de l'Electronique* (10 a year), *3EI—Enseigner l'Electrotechnique et l' Electronique Industriel* (4 a year).

Société d'Encouragement pour l'Industrie Nationale: 4 place Saint-Germain-des-Prés, 75006 Paris; e-mail adm@industrienationale.fr; internet www.industrienationale.fr; f. 1801; Dir BERNARD MOUSSON; publ. *L'Industrie Nationale.*

Société Française de Métallurgie et de Matériaux (SF2M): 250 rue Saint Jacques, 75005 Paris; tel. 1-46-33-08-00; fax 1-46-33-08-80; internet www.sf2m.asso.fr; f. 1945; 1,200 mems; Pres. ANNICK PERCHERON-GUEGAN; Sec. PAUL V. RIBOUD.

Société Française de Photogrammétrie et de Télédétection: 2 ave Pasteur, 94165 St Mandé Cedex; tel. 1-64-15-32-86; fax 1-64-15-32-85; e-mail sfpt@ensg.ign.fr; internet www.ign.fr/sfpt; f. 1959; photogrammetry and remote sensing; 615 mems; Pres. G. BEGNI; Sec.-Gen. I. VEILLET; publ. *Bulletin* (4 a year).

Société Française des Microscopies: Case 243, Université Pierre et Marie Curie, 4 pl. Jussieu, 75252 Paris Cedex 05; tel. 1-44-27-26-21; fax 1-44-27-26-22; e-mail sfmu@sfmu.fr; internet www.sfmu.fr; f. 1959; all types of microscopy, electronic optics and electronic diffraction, optical, spectroscopy, microprobe, x-ray; physics, chemistry, biology; 470 mems; Pres. VIRGINIE SERIN; publs *Biology of the Cell* (9 a year), *European Physical Journal: Applied Physics* (6 a year).

Société Hydrotechnique de France: 25 rue des Favorites, 75015 Paris; tel. 1-42-50-91-03; fax 1-42-50-59-83; e-mail shf@shf.asso.fr; internet www.shf.asso.fr; f. 1912; fluid mechanics, applied hydraulics, geophysical hydraulics and water conservation; 600 mems; Pres. DANIEL LOUDIERE; Pres. for Scientific Cttee PIERRE-LOUIS VIOLLET; Gen.

Dir JEAN-GEORGES PHILIPPS; publs *La Houille Blanche Revue Internationale de l'Eau* (6 a year), *Proceedings, Journées de l'Hydraulique* (1 a year), guides on hydroelectricity and flood forecasts, research documents.

Research Institutes
GENERAL

Centre National de la Recherche Scientifique (CNRS): 3 rue Michel-Ange, 75794 Paris Cedex 16; tel. 1-44-96-40-00; fax 1-44-96-49-65; internet www.cnrs.fr; f. 1939; coordinates and promotes scientific research, and proposes to the Govt means of doing research and how to allocate funds; makes grants-in-aid to scientific bodies and to individuals to enable them to carry out research work; subsidizes or sets up laboratories for scientific research; is split into 40 sections, covering all scientific fields; funds 11,600 researchers, 14,400 engineers and 4,000 technicians and admin. staff; depts of Mathematics, Physics, Planet and Universe (Scientific Dir MICHEL LANOO), Chemistry (Scientific Dir GILBERT CHAMBAUD), Life Sciences (Scientific Dir MICHEL VAN DER REST), Human and Social Sciences (Scientific Dir MARIE-FRANÇOISE COUREL), Environment and Sustainable Development (Scientific Dir BERNARD DELAY), Engineering (Scientific Dir PIERRE GUILLON); Pres. CATHÉRINE BRÉCHIGNAC; Dir-Gen. ARNOLD MIGUS; Sec.-Gen. JACQUES BERNARD.

AGRICULTURE, FISHERIES AND VETERINARY SCIENCE

Centre de Co-opération Internationale en Recherche Agronomique pour le Développement (CIRAD): 42 rue Scheffer, 75116 Paris; tel. 1-53-70-20-00; fax 1-47-55-15-30; internet www.cirad.fr; (laboratories: BP 5035, 34032 Montpellier Cedex 1; tel. 4-67-61-58-00); f. 1970, present name 1986; state-owned; research and devt within the framework of French scientific and technical cooperation with developing countries; stations in over 50 countries; library of 134,000 vols, 3,300 scientific periodicals; Dir-Gen. GÉRARD MATHERON; Sec.-Gen. HERVÉ DEPERROIS.

Research Departments:

Département d'Amélioration des Méthodes pour l'Innovation Scientifique (CIRAD-AMIS): 2477 ave Agropolis, TA 40/02, 34398 Montpellier Cedex 5; tel. 4-67-61-58-00; fax 4-67-61-44-55; e-mail amis@cirad.fr; plant modelling, food production, agronomy, crop protection, biotechnology and plant genetic research, economics, policy and marketing; Dir JACQUES MEUNIER; publ. *Sésame bulletin.*

Département d'Élevage et de Médecine Vétérinaire (CIRAD-EMVT): Campus international de Baillarguet, BP 5035, 34398 Montpellier Cedex 5; tel. 4-67-59-37-10; fax 4-67-59-37-95; e-mail valo.emvt@cirad.fr; f. 1948; research and missions to countries of Africa, Asia and South America; Dir EMMANUEL CAMUS; publ. *Revue d'Elevage et de Médecine Vétérinaire des Pays Tropicaux* (4 a year).

Département des Cultures Annuelles (CIRAD-CA): 2477 ave Agropolis, BP 5035, 34398 Montpellier Cedex 5; tel. 4-67-61-58-00; fax 4-67-61-59-88; e-mail dirpersyst@cirad.fr; f. 1992; experts stationed in Benin, Brazil, Burkina Faso, Burundi, Cameroon, Central African Republic, Chad, Colombia, Costa Rica, Côte d'Ivoire, Dominica, Gabon, Ghana, Guinea, Honduras, Laos, Madagascar,

Mali, Niger, Paraguay, Philippines, Senegal, Thailand, Togo, Turkey, Viet Nam; Dir MARCO WOPEREIS; publ. *Agriculture et développement* (4 a year, abstracts in French, English and Spanish).

Département des Cultures Pérennes (CIRAD-CP): Boulevard de la Lirondem, TA 80/PS3, 34398 Montpellier Cedex 5; tel. 4-67-61-58-00; fax 4-67-61-56-59; e-mail dircp@cirad.fr; f. 1992; research and technical assistance relating to cocoa, coconuts, coffee, oil palm and rubber; Dir DOMINIQUE BERRY; publ. *Plantations, recherche, développement* (in French and English or Spanish).

Département des Productions Fruitières et Horticoles (CIRAD-FLHOR): Blvd de la Lironde, TA 50/PS4, 34398 Montpellier Cedex 5; tel. 4-67-61-58-00; fax 4-67-61-58-71; e-mail flhor@cirad.fr; f. 1945; activities in the technical, scientific and economic aspects of horticulture (from product research to distribution) in tropical and Mediterranean zones and with respect to related agro-industries; many overseas brs; Dir HUBERT DE BON; publs *Fruits, FruiTrop.*

Département des Territoires, Environonnement et Acteurs (CIRAD-TERA): 73 rue Jean-François Breton, TA 60/15, 34398 Montpellier Cedex 5; tel. 4-67-61-58-00; fax 4-67-61-12-23; e-mail tera@cirad.fr; smallholder farming, land and resources, savannah and irrigated systems, humid tropics; Dir ROLLAND GUIS.

Département Forestier (CIRAD-Forêt): Campus international de Baillarguet, BP 5035, 34398 Montpellier Cedex 5; tel. 4-67-59-37-10; fax 4-67-59-37-55; e-mail forets@cirad.fr; forestry; Dir BERNARD MALLET; publ. *Bois et forêts des tropiques.*

Centre de Recherches de Jouy: Domaine de Vilvert, 78352 Jouy-en-Josas Cedex; tel. 1-34-65-21-21; fax 1-34-65-20-51; e-mail communication@jouy.inra.fr; internet www.jouy.inra.fr; f. 1950; linked to Institut National de la Recherche Agronomique (*q.v.*); scientific research on livestock production and health, human nutrition, animal biology, microbiology, applied mathematics and bioinformatics, animal models for human and animal health; library of 6,000 vols, 2,200 periodicals; Pres. Dr EMMANUEL JOLIVET.

Institut d'Immunologie Animale et Comparée (Institute of Animal and Comparative Immunology): Ecole Nationale Vétérinaire d'Alfort, 7 ave du Général de Gaulle, 94704 Maisons-Alfort Cedex; tel. 1-43-68-98-82; f. 1981; organizes courses; research in immunostimulation, clinical immunology, immunopathology; Dir Prof. CH. PILET.

Institut National de la Recherche Agronomique (INRA): 147 rue de l'Université, 75338 Paris Cedex 07; tel. 1-42-75-90-00; fax 1-47-05-99-66; internet www.inra.fr; f. 1946; agricultural research, incl. agricultural and food industries, rural economics and sociology, plant and animal production and forestry; administers and subsidizes a large number of centres, laboratories and experimental farms in France; Pres. and Dir-Gen. MARION GUILLOU; publs *Agronomy for Sustainable Development* (10 a year), *Animal Research* (6 a year), *Annales des Sciences Forestières* (6 a year), *Apidologie* (6 a year), *Archorales: Les Métiers de la Recherche* (online), *Bulletin des Technologies* (1 a year), *Cahiers d'Economie et Sociologie rurales* (4 a year), *Courrier de l'Environnement* (online), *Genetics Selection Evolution* (6 a year), *INRA Sciences Sociales* (6 a year), *Le Lait* (6 a year), *Production Animales* (3 a year), *Reproduction Nutrition Development* (6 a year), *Veterinary Research* (6 a year).

Laboratoire Central de Recherches Vétérinaires: BP 67, 22 rue Pierre Curie, 94703 Maisons-Alfort Cedex; tel. 1-49-77-13-00; fax 1-43-68-97-62; f. 1901; 140 mems; study of contagious diseases in domestic and wild animals; supervises sanitary regulations for import and export of livestock; Dir Dr ERIC PLATEAU.

ECONOMICS, LAW AND POLITICS

Centre d'Etudes de l'Emploi: Le Descartes I, 29 promenade Michel Simon, 93166 Noisy-le-Grand Cedex; tel. 1-45-92-68-00; fax 1-49-31-02-44; internet www.cee-recherche.fr; attached to Min. of Employment and Min. of Education; for the study and research of changes in the field of employment; research units: age and work, employment and social security, employment markets and instns, workers and orgs; Dir PIERRE RALLE; publs *CEE.INFO* (3 a year), *Connaisance de l'Emploi* (12 a year).

Centre d'Etudes Prospectives et d'Informations Internationales (Centre for International Prospective Studies and Information): 9 rue Georges Pitard, 75015 Paris; tel. 1-53-68-55-00; fax 1-53-68-55-03; e-mail postmaster@cepii.fr; internet www .cepii.fr; f. 1978 by the govt, under the aegis of Commissariat Général du Plan; aids public and private decision-makers in the int. economic field by conducting synthetic studies of the global economic environment in the midterm (5–10 years), constructing economic models and databases, and by providing a coherent statistical information system of the world economy and its major participants; 50 mems; library of 30,000 vols, 500 periodicals; Dir AGNÈS BÉNASSY-QUÉRÉ; publs *CEPII Working Papers* (12 a year), *CHELEM Data Bank: bilingual CD-ROM* (1 a year), *Economie Internationale* (4 a year), *La Lettre du CEPII* (11 a year), *L'Economie mondiale* (1 a year), *Rapport d'activité* (1 a year).

Institut de Recherches Economiques et Sociales: 16 blvd du Mont d'Est, 93192 Noisy-Le-Grand, Cedex; tel. (1) 48-15-18-93; fax (1) 48-15-19-18; e-mail contact@ires-fr .org; internet www.ires-fr.org; f. 1982 by the main French trade unions in association with the French Govt to meet the economic and social research needs of trade unions; central research areas: employment patterns, industrial relations, wage patterns, work patterns; Pres. PIERRETTE CROSEMARIE; Dir JACKY FAYOLLE; publs *La Chronique Internationale* (6 a year), *La Lettre de l'IRES* (4 a year), *La Revue de L'IRES* (3 a year).

Institut de Sciences Mathématiques et Economiques Appliquées: 1 rue Maurice Arnoux, 92120 Montrouge; tel. 1-55-48-90-70; fax 1-55-48-90-71; e-mail perroux@ univ-mlv.fr; internet www.ismea.org; f. 1944; int. cooperation and links with Third World univs; library of 14,500 vols; Chair. Prof. G. DESTANNE DE BERNIS; publs *Economie Appliquée* (4 a year), *Economies et Sociétés* (12 a year).

Institut National de la Statistique et des Etudes Economiques: 18 blvd Adolphe Pinard, 75675 Paris Cedex 14; tel. 1-41-17-50-50; fax 1-41-17-66-66; e-mail insee-contact@insee.fr; internet www.insee .fr; f. 1946; statistical research: population census, economic indices and forecasts, economic and social studies; library: see Libraries; Dir-Gen. JEAN-PHILIPPE COTIS; publs *Annuaire Statistique de la France* (1 a year, free online), *Bulletin Statistique* (online), *Economie et Statistique* (12 a year, free online), *Insee Méthodes, Insee Première* (60 a year), *Informations Rapides* (370 a year),

Insee Résultats, La Commerce en France (Collection Références), *La France des Services* (Collection Références), *La France et ses Régions, Les salaires en France* (Collection Références), *L'industrie en France* (Collection Références), *Note de Conjoncture* (4 a year), *Tableaux de l'économie Française* (1 a year).

Institut National d'Etudes Démographiques: 133 Blvd Davout, 75980 Paris Cedex 20; tel. 1-56-06-20-00; fax 1-56-06-21-99; internet www.ined.fr; f. 1945; library of 40,000 vols; Dir FRANÇOIS HÉRAN; publs *Classiques de l'Économie et de la Population* (2 or 3 a year), *Les Cahiers de l'INED* (4–6 a year), *Population* (4 a year), *Population et Sociétés* (12 a year).

EDUCATION

Centre International d'Etudes Pédagogiques de Sèvres: 1 ave Léon Journault, BP 75, 92318 Sèvres Cedex; tel. 1-45-07-60-00; fax 1-45-07-60-01; internet www.ciep.fr; f. 1945; research and studies in comparative education; training overseas teachers in French as a foreign language; 170 mems; Dir M. LÉOUTRE; publ. *Revue Internationale d'Education.*

Institut National de Recherche Pédagogique: 19 Mail de Fontenay, BP 17424, 69347 Lyons Cedex 07; tel. 4-72-76-61-71; fax 4-72-76-61-42; e-mail contact@inrp.fr; internet www.inrp.fr; f. 1879; develops and promotes research into teaching and education; 280 staff, 1652 assoc. mems; library: see Libraries and Archives; Dir EMMANUEL FRAISSE; publs *Aster* (2 a year), *Didaskalia* (2 a year), *Etapes de la Recherche, Histoire de l'Education* (4 a year), *Perspectives Documentaires* (3 a year), *Recherche et Formation* (3 a year), *Repères* (2 a year), *Revue Française de Pédagogie* (4 a year).

FINE AND PERFORMING ARTS

Institut de Recherche et Co-ordination Acoustique et de la Musique: Centre National d'Art et de Culture Georges-Pompidou, 1 pl. Igor-Stravinsky, 75004 Paris Cedex 04; tel. 1-44-78-48-43; fax 1-44-78-15-40; internet www.ircam.fr; attached to Centre National d'Art et de Culture Georges-Pompidou; interdisciplinary research centre for musicians and scientists; data processing, electroacoustics, instrumental and vocal research; Dir FRANK MADLENER.

Institut National d'Histoire de l'Art (INHA): 2 rue Vivienne, 75002 Paris; tel. 1-47-03-86-04; fax 1-47-03-86-36; e-mail inha@ inha.fr; internet www.inha.fr; f. 2001; library: Bibliothèque d'art et d'archéologie Jacques Doucet; Dir-Gen. ANTOINETTE LE NORMAND-ROMAIN.

HISTORY, GEOGRAPHY AND ARCHAEOLOGY

Centre de Recherches Historiques: Ecole des Hautes Etudes en Sciences Sociales, UMR 8558, 54 blvd Raspail, 75006 Paris; tel. 1-49-54-24-42; fax 1-49-54-23-99; e-mail crh@msh-paris.fr; internet www.ehess.fr; f. 1950; joint research in economic, social, cultural and political history; 126 mems; Dirs GÉRARD BÉAUR PAUL-ANDRÉ ROSENTAL JUDITH LYON-CAEN; publs *Annales* (history, social sciences, 6 a year), *Cahiers* (2 a year), *Entreprises et Histoire* (4 a year), *Histoire et Mesure* (4 a year), *1900* (1 a year).

Centre d'Études Supérieures de la Renaissance: 59 rue Néricault-Destouches, BP 11328, 37013 Tours Cedex 1; tel. 2-47-36-77-60; fax 2-47-36-77-62; e-mail cesr@ univ-tours.fr; internet www.cesr.univ-tours .fr; f. 1956; library of 45,000 vols; Dir Prof. G. CHAIX; Sec. M. ANCELIN.

Fondation et Institut Charles de Gaulle: 5 rue de Solférino, 75007 Paris; tel. 1-44-18-66-77; fax 1-44-18-66-99; e-mail contact@ charles-de-gaulle.org; internet www .charles-de-gaulle.org; f. Institute 1971, Foundation f. 1992; assembles material related to the life and work of Charles de Gaulle for the purpose of scholarship; library of 4,500 vols, periodicals, documents, cuttings, 4,000 photographs, recorded interviews, audiovisual material; Pres. YVES GUÉNA.

Institut Géographique National: 136 bis rue de Grenelle, 75700 Paris; tel. 1-43-98-80-00; fax 1-43-98-84-00; internet www.ign.fr; f. 1940; satellite-image, aerial and ground surveys, map printing; nat. map and aerial photograph library, scientific library; administers Ecole Nat. des Sciences Géographiques (q.v.); Pres. MICHEL FRANC; Dir-Gen. JEAN POULIT; publ. *Bulletin d'Information* (4 a year).

Sous-Direction de l'Archéologie: 4 rue d'Aboukir, 75002 Paris; tel. 1-40-15-77-81; fax 1-40-15-77-00; e-mail jean-francois .texier@culture.gouv.fr; f. 1964; library of 4,500 vols, 47 periodicals; Dir JEAN-FRANÇOIS TEXIER.

MEDICINE

Institut Alfred-Fournier: 25 blvd Saint-Jacques, 75014 Paris; internet www .institutfournier.org; research into sexually transmitted diseases; f. 1923; Dir Dr P. BARBIER.

Institut Arthur-Vernes: 36 rue d'Assas, 75006 Paris; tel. 1-44-39-53-00; fax 1-42-84-26-09; internet www.institut-vernes.fr; f. 1981; Pres. J. C. SERVAN-SCHREIBER; Gen. Man. CATHERINE RAUCHE.

Institut Gustave-Roussy: 39 rue Camille Desmoulins, 94805 Villejuif Cedex; tel. 1-42-11-42-11; fax 1-42-11-53-00; e-mail roussy@ igr.fr; internet www.igr.fr; f. 1921; diagnosis and treatment of cancer, research, and training in oncology (affiliated with Univ. Paris-Sud for teaching purposes); library of 11,000 vols, with spec. colln on cancerology; Dir Prof. GILBERT LENOIR.

Institut National de la Santé et de la Recherche Médicale (INSERM): 101 rue de Tolbiac, 75654 Paris Cedex 13; tel. 1-44-23-60-00; fax 1-44-23-60-99; internet www .inserm.fr; f. 1941 as Institut National d'Hygiène, renamed 1964; assisted by scientific commissions and the Scientific Council; 270 research units throughout France; Pres. MONIQUE CAPRON; Dir-Gen. Prof. CHRISTIAN BRÉCHOT; publs *Annuaire des laboratoires, rapport d'activité, INSERM Actualités,* Collections, etc.

Institut Pasteur: 25–28 rue du Dr Roux, 75015 Paris; tel. 1-45-68-80-00; e-mail info@ pasteur.fr; internet www.pasteur.fr; f. 1887; Pres. ALICE DAUTRY; Sec. AGNÈS LABIGNE; publs *Annales: Actualités, Annales Research in Virology, Bulletin* (4 a year), *Immunology and Microbiology* (16 a year).

NATURAL SCIENCES

General

Institut de Recherche pour le Développement (IRD): 44 blvdd de Dunkerque 13002 Marseille; tel. 4-91-99-92-00; e-mail dic@paris.ird.fr; internet www.ird.fr; f. 1944; public corpn charged to aid developing countries by means of research, both fundamental and applied, in the non-temperate regions, with spec. application to human environment problems, food production and tropical diseases; 35 centres in Africa, Asia, the Pacific, South America and French overseas territories; library and documentation centre; Pres.

JEAN FRANÇOIS GIRARD; Dir-Gen. SERGE CALA-BRE; Gen.-Sec. CHRISTINE D'ARGOUGES; publ. *Sciences au Sud* (6 a year).

Maintains the Following Services:

Antenne IRD de Bouaké: BP 1434, Bouaké, Côte d'Ivoire; tel. 31-63-95-43; fax 31-63-27-38; e-mail bouake@ird.ci; internet www.ird.ci/ird/bouake.html; f. 1976; jt research project with l'Institut des Savanes; studies of dams for agricultural irrigation, social mobility and sexually transmitted diseases, production and distribution of foodstuffs in the central region of Côte d'Ivoire.

Centre IRD de Bondy: 32 ave Henri Varagnat, 93143 Bondy Cedex; tel. 1-48-02-55-00; fax 1-48-47-30-88; e-mail bondy@ird.fr; internet www.bondy.ird.fr; f. 1945; geophysics, geodynamics, social sciences, entomology, applied computer science, scientific information (cartography, documentation, audiovisual); Dir GEORGES DE NONI.

Centre IRD de Bretagne: BP 70, 29280 Plouzané Cedex; tel. 2-98-22-45-01; fax 2-98-22-45-14; e-mail brest@ird.fr; internet www.brest.ird.fr; f. 1975; oceanography; Dir CLAUDE ROY.

Centre IRD de Montpellier: BP 64501, 34394 Montpellier Cedex 5; tel. 4-67-41-61-00; fax 4-67-41-63-30; e-mail montpellier@ird.fr; internet www.mpl.ird.fr; hydrology, hydrobiology and oceanography, soil biology, agrarian research, phytopathology, phytovirology, applied zoology, medical entomology, nutrition, geology, genetics; Dir YVES DUVAL.

Centre IRD d'Orléans: Technoparc, 5 rue du Carbone, 45072 Orléans Cedex 2; tel. 2-38-49-95-00; fax 2-38-49-95-10; e-mail orleans@ird.fr; internet www.orleans.ird.fr; human adaptation to tropical environments, environmental dynamics between forests, agriculture and biodiversity, valorization of vegetal biodiversity; Dir YVELINE PONCET.

Centre IRD de Sète: CRHMT, Ave Jean Monnet, BP 171, 34203 Sète Cedex; tel. 4-99-57-32-34; fax 4-99-57-32-95; e-mail philippe.cury@ird.fr; Dir Gen. MICHEL LAURENT.

Institut Français de l'Environnement: 5, route d'Olivet, BP 16105 45061 Orléans Cedex 2; tel. 2-38-79-78-78; fax 2-38-79-78-70; e-mail cgdd-soes-orleans@developpement-durable.gouv.fr; internet www.ifen.fr; f. 1991; attached to Min. of Town and Country Planning and the Environment; collects and disseminates statistical information about the environment; focal point in France for European Environment Agency.

Biological Sciences

Institut de Biologie Physico-chimique: 13 rue Pierre et Marie Curie, 75005 Paris; tel. 1-58-41-50-00; fax 1-58-41-50-20; e-mail ifr550@ibpc.fr; internet www.ibpc.fr; f. 1927; Dir Dr J.-P. HENRY; Dirs of Laboratories R. LAVERY (Theoretical Biochemistry), J.-L. POPOT (Molecular Physical Chemistry of Biological Membranes), M. SPRINGER (Regulation of Microbial Gene Expression), J.-P. HENRY (Molecular and Cell Biology of Secretion), F.-A. WOLLMAN (Molecular and Membrane Physiology of the Chloroplast).

Institut de Biologie Structurale (IBS): 41 rue Jules Horowitz, 38027 Grenoble Cedex 1; tel. 4-38-78-95-50; fax 4-38-78-54-94; internet www.ibs.fr; jointly financed by the Commissariat à l'Energie Atomique (CEA) and the Centre National de la Recherche Scientifique (CNRS); Dir Prof. EVA PEBAY-PEYROULA.

Station Biologique de Roscoff: Place Georges-Teissier, BP 74, 29682 Roscoff Cedex; tel. 2-98-29-23-23; fax 2-98-29-23-24; e-mail guyard@sb-roscoff.fr; internet www.sb-roscoff.fr; f. 1872; attached to Univ. Paris VI and CNRS; chemical and biological oceanography, plankton research, microbiology, biology of hydrothermal vent fauna, cell cycle and developmental biology, cell and molecular biology on macroalgae, population genetics, marine genomics; library of 5,000 vols, 1,000 periodicals; Dir Prof. BERNARD KLOAREG; Librarian GUYARD NICOLE; publs *CBM-Cahiers de Biologie marine* (4 a year), *Travaux* (1 a year).

Physical Sciences

Association Nationale pour l'Etude de la Neige et des Avalanches (ANENA): 15 rue Ernest Calvat, 38000 Grenoble; tel. 4-76-51-39-39; fax 4-76-42-81-66; internet www.anena.org; f. 1971; to promote knowledge and give advice about avalanches and safety in snowy, mountainous terrain; 700 mems; library of 2,000 vols; publ. *Neige et Avalanches* (4 a year).

Bureau de Recherches Géologiques et Minières (BRGM): 3 ave Claude Guillemin, BP 6009, 45060 Orléans Cedex 2; tel. 2-38-64-34-34; fax 2-38-64-35-18; internet www.brgm.fr; f. 1959; publicly owned industrial and trading org.; study and devt of underground resources in France and abroad; library of 22,000 vols, 4,000 scientific journals, 55,000 maps; Dir-Gen. Y. LE BARS; publs *Chronique de la Recherche minière* (4 a year), *Géochronique* (published with Société géologique de France, 4 a year), *Géologie de la France* (4 a year), *Hydrogéologie* (4 a year), geological maps, bibliographies, SDI and retrospective searches.

Bureau des Longitudes: Palais de l'Institut, 3 Quai de Conti, 75006 Paris; tel. 1-43-26-59-02; fax 1-43-26-80-90; e-mail contact@bureau-des-longitudes.fr; internet www.bureau-des-longitudes.fr; f. 1795 by Convention Nationale; 50 mems and corresp.; Pres. NICOLE CAPITAINE; Vice-Pres. PIERRE BAÜER; Sec. PASCAL WILLIS; publs *Ephémérides Astronomiques*, *Connaissance des Temps*, *Ephémérides Nautiques*, *Cahier des Sciences de l'Univers*, and supplements to *Connaissance des Temps* (1 a year).

Centre de Recherches Atmosphériques: 8 route de Lannemezan, 65300 Campistrous; tel. 5-62-40-61-00; fax 5-62-40-61-01; e-mail campistrous@free.fr; internet campistrous.free.fr; f. 1960; cloud physics, atmospheric chemistry, planetary boundary layer; library of 2,000 vols; Dir R. DELMAS; publ. *Atmospheric Research* (4 a year).

Centre d'Etudes Marines Avancées: c/o Équipe Cousteau, 7 rue Amiral d'Estaing, 75116 Paris; tel. 1-53-67-77-77; fax 1-53-67-77-71; f. 1953; underwater exploration, study and research; Pres. (vacant); Sec. Gen. HENRI JACQUIER; publ. *Calypso Log* (12 a year).

Centre International pour la Formation et les Echanges en Géosciences (CIFEG): 3 ave Claude Guillemin, BP 36517, 45065 Orléans Cedex 2; tel. 2-38-64-33-67; fax 2-38-64-34-72; e-mail m.laval@cifeg.org; internet www.cifeg.org; f. 1981; geoscientific information networking; documentation centre on earth sciences of Africa and South-East Asia; exchanges between developed and developing countries; library of 3,500 vols, 65 periodicals, 400 maps; Pres. J. GIRI; Dir M. LAVAL; publ. *PANGEA* (2 a year).

Centre National de Recherches Météorologiques: 42 ave G. Coriolis, 31057 Toulouse Cedex; tel. 5-61-07-93-70; fax 5-61-07-96-00; internet www.cnrm.

.meteo.fr; f. 1946; meteorological research; 250 staff; Dir ERIC BRUN.

Commissariat à l'Energie Atomique (CEA): Centre d'Etudes de Saclay, 91191 Gif sur Yvette Cedex 15; tel. 1-64-50-10-00; internet www.cea.fr; f. 1945; basic and applied nuclear research, energy generator studies; 5 affiliated civil research centres; Pres. of Atomic Energy Cttee the Prime Minister; library; Man. Dir YANNICK D'ESCATHA; publs *CEA-Technologies*, *Clefs CEA*, *Les Défis du CEA*.

Attached Research Centres:

Centre CEA de Cadarache (Bouches-du-Rhone): 13108 St-Paul-lez-Durance Cedex; tel. 4-42-25-70-00; fax 4-42-25-45-45; e-mail wwwcad@dircad.cea.fr; internet www-cadarache.cea.fr; f. 1960; nuclear reactor devt (fission and fusion); R&D on new energies: biofuels, hydrogen or solar, nuclear safety and environmental protection; fundamental research; industrial innovation; Dir SERGE DURAND.

Centre CEA de Fontenay-aux-Roses (Hauts-de-Seine): BP 6, 92265 Fontenay-aux-Roses Cedex; tel. 1-46-54-70-80; fax 1-42-53-98-51; f. 1945; first French reactor; Zoé natural uranium, heavy water moderated; work in life sciences; research in: radiobiology, environmental toxicology, neurovirology and emerging diseases; research and development in biomedical imaging and health technologies; cognitics, robotics for nuclear, industrial and medical needs; Dir MALGORYATA TKATCHENKO.

Centre CEA de Grenoble (Isère): 17 rue des Martyrs, 38054 Grenoble Cedex 9; tel. 4-76-78-44-00; fax 4-76-88-34-32; f. 1957; applied nuclear research on heat transfer studies and on behaviour of nuclear fuels; fundamental research on physics, chemistry, biology, materials science; advanced technologies: microelectronics, optronics, instrumentation, materials, heat exchangers, life sciences and tracer studies; library of 31,000 vols; Dir GEORGES CAROLA.

Centre CEA de Saclay (Essonne): 91191 Gif-sur-Yvette Cedex; tel. 1-69-08-90-32; e-mail internet.saclay@cea.fr; internet www-centre-saclay.cea.fr; f. 1949; equipped with 2 high-flux experimental reactors, 6 particle accelerators and special laboratories: spent fuel study facility, isotope and labelled molecule production laboratories, activation analysis centre, ionizing radiations applications centre; laboratories specializing in research on reactors, nuclear metallurgy and chemistry, elementary particle physics, nuclear physics, astrophysics, condensed-matter physics, earth sciences, biology, radioactivity measurement and electronics; library of 48,000 vols, 400,000 reports; Dir ELIANE LOQUET.

Centre CEA de la Marcoule (Gard): BP 171, 30207 Bagnols-sur-Cèze Cedex; tel. 4-66-79-60-00; fax 4-66-90-14-35; internet www-marcoule.cea.fr; f. 1982; fuel cycle research and devt: uranium isotopic enrichment, spent fuel processing, waste conditioning, dismantling; fast reactors; Dir JEAN-YVES GUILLAMOT.

Centre CEA de Valduc (Gold Coast): 21120 Is-sur-Tille; tel. 3-80-23-40-00; e-mail webdam@cea.fr; internet www-dam.cea.fr; f. 1996; nuclear materials used in arms production.

Centre CEA/Cesta (Gironde): BP 2, 33114 Le Barp; tel. 5-57-04-40-00; internet www-dam.cea.fr; production of nuclear arms.

Centre CEA/DAM Ile de France (Essonne): Bruyères-le-Châtel, 91297

Arpajon Cedex; tel. 1-69-26-40-00; internet www-dam.cea.fr; computerized research into nuclear explosions; monitoring of global seismic activity.

Institut Curie: 26 rue d'Ulm, 75248 Paris Cedex 05; tel. 1-44-32-40-00; fax 1-43-29-02-03; internet www.curie.fr; f. 1978 (fmrly Fondation Curie–Inst. du Radium); treatment, research and teaching in cancer; library of 7,000 vols; two sections: Research (Dir M. BORNENS), Medicine (Dir P. BEY); Pres. CLAUDE HURIET; Dir PHILIPPE KOUR-ILSKY.

Institut Français de Recherche pour l'Exploitation de la Mer (IFREMER): 155 rue J. Jacques Rousseau, 92138 Issy-les-Moulineaux Cedex; tel. 1-46-48-21-00; fax 1-46-48-21-21; internet www.ifremer.fr; f. 1984; research in all fields of oceanography and ocean technology; Pres./Dir-Gen. JEAN-FRANÇOIS MINSTER; publs *Aquatic Living Resources* (6 a year), *Oceanologica Acta* (6 a year).

Attached Institutes:

Centre IFREMER de Brest: BP 70, 29280 Plouzane; tel. 2-98-22-40-40; fax 2-98-22-45-45; e-mail egiordma@ifremer.fr; internet www.ifremer.fr/brest; f. 1968; Dir FRANÇOIS LE VERGE.

Centre IFREMER de Nantes: BP 21105, 44311 Nantes Cedex 03; tel. 2-40-37-40-43; fax 2-40-37-40-01; internet www.ifremer.fr/nantes; Dir ROBERT POGGI.

Centre IFREMER de Toulon: BP 330, 83507 La Seyne sur Mer; tel. 4-94-30-48-00; internet www.ifremer.fr/toulon; Dir GUY HERROUIN.

Centre IFREMER Océanologique du Pacifique: BP 7004, 98719 Taravao, Tahiti; tel. 54-60-00; fax 54-60-99; internet www.ifremer.fr/cop/tahiti.htm; f. 1972; development of ocean resources: minerals, fishing and aquaculture in French South Pacific territories; 70 staff; library of 200 vols; Dir DOMINIQUE BUES-TEL.

Institut Polaire Français Paul Emile: Technopôle Brest-Iroise, BP 75, 29280 Plouzané; tel. 2-98-05-65-00; fax 2-98-05-65-55; e-mail infoipev@ipev.fr; internet www.ipev.fr; f. 1992 by merger of Mission de Recherche des Terres Australes et Antarctiques Françaises and Expéditions Polaires Françaises; Dir GÉRARD JUGIE.

Laboratoire d'Astronomie de Lille 1: 1 impasse de l'Observatoire, 59000 Lille; tel. 3-20-52-44-24; internet lal.univ-lille1.fr; f. 1934; astronomy, celestial mechanics; Dir ALAIN VIENNE.

Météo-France: 1 quai Branly, 75340 Paris Cedex 07; tel. 1-45-56-71-71; fax 1-45-56-70-05; internet www.meteofrance.com; f. 1945; Dir JEAN-PIERRE BEYSSON; publs *Atmospheriques* (3 a year), *Bibliographies*, *Bulletin Climatique* (12 a year), *Cours et Manuels* (irregular), *Données et Statistiques*, *La Météorologie* (3 a year), *METEO-HEBDO* (52 a year), *Met Mar* (3 a year), *Monographies*, *Notes techniques*, *Phénomènes Remarquables* (irregular).

Observatoire de Bordeaux: Université de Bordeaux I, CNRS, 2 rue de l'Observatoire, BP 89, 33270 Floirac; tel. 5-57-77-61-00; fax 5-57-77-61-10; internet www.obs.u-bordeaux1.fr; f. 1879; astrometry, astrodynamics, solar physics, radioastronomy, helioseismology, planetary atmosphere, radio aeronomy; library of 3,700 vols; Dir A. CASTETS.

Observatoire de la Côte d'Azur: Boulevard de l'Observatoire, BP 4229, 06304 Nice Cedex 4; tel. 4-92-00-30-11; fax 4-92-00-30-33; internet www.oca.eu; f. 1881; astronomy

and astrophysics; library of 12,000 vols, 250 periodicals; Dir JACQUES COLIN.

Observatoire de Lyon: 9 ave Charles-André, 69561 Saint-Genis-Laval Cedex; tel. 4-78-86-85-34; fax 4-78-86-83-86; e-mail accueil@obs.univ-lyon1.fr; internet www-obs.univ-lyon1.fr; f. 1880; specializes in two-dimensional photometry and infra-red imagery; library of 20,000 vols; Dir BRUNO GUIDERDONI.

Observatoire Astronomique de Marseille–Provence: 38 rue Frédéric Joliot-Curie , 13388 Marseilles Cedex 13; tel. 4-95-04-41-00; fax 4-91-62-11-90; e-mail oampdirection@oamp.fr; internet www.oamp.fr; library of 5,000 vols; Dir OLIVIER LE FÈVRE.

Observatoire de Paris: 61 ave de l'Observatoire, 75014 Paris; tel. 1-40-51-22-21; fax 1-43-54-18-04; internet www.obspm.fr; f. 1667; library of 60,000 vols; Pres. D. EGRET.

Attached Stations:

Observatoire de Paris, Site de Meudon: 5 place Jules Janssen, 92195 Meudon Principal Cedex; tel. 1-45-07-75-30; fax 1-45-07-74-69; administered by the Observatoire de Paris; f. 1875; astrophysics; Dir M. COMBES.

Station de Radioastronomie de Nançay: 18330 Nançay; tel. 2-48-51-82-41; fax 2-48-51-83-18; administered by the Observatoire de Paris; f. 1953; study of the sun, comets, planets and radio sources; radio telescopes; Dir M. COMBES.

Observatoire de Physique du Globe de Clermont-Ferrand: 24 ave des Landais, 63177 Aubière Cedex; tel. 4-73-40-73-80; fax 4-73-40-73-82; e-mail a*flossmann@opgc.univ-bpclermont.fr; internet www.obs.univ-bpclermont.fr; f. 1871; atmospheric physics, cloud systems, earth sciences, and geophysical surveillance; Dir Prof. ANDRÉA FLOSSMANN.

Observatoire Astronomique de Strasbourg: 11 rue de l'Université, 67000 Strasbourg; tel. 3-90-24-24-10; fax 90-24-24-32; internet astro.u-strasbg.fr; f. 1882; specializes in astronomical data and information, galactic evolution, cosmology, high-energy astrophysics; houses the Strasbourg Astronomical Data Centre (CDS); library of 16,000 vols; Dir JEAN-MARIE HAMEURY; publ. *Publications de l'Observatoire* (irregular).

Observatoire des Sciences de l'Univers de Besançon: BP 1615, 41 bis ave de l'Observatoire, 25010 Besançon Cedex; tel. 3-81-66-69-00; fax 3-81-66-69-44; e-mail direction@obs-besancon.fr; internet www.obs-besancon.fr; f. 1882; a research unit of the Université de Franche-Comté; library of 15,000 vols; Dir Prof. FRANÇOIS VERNOTTE.

Observatoire Midi-Pyrénées: Headquarters: 14 ave E. Belin, 31400 Toulouse; tel. 5-61-33-29-29; fax 5-61-33-28-88; internet www.omp.obs-mip.fr; library of 50,000 vols; solar, planetary, stellar, galactic and extragalactic astrophysics, atmospheric physics and chemistry, physical oceanography, surface sciences, earth sciences; Dir DOMINIQUE LE QUEAU.

RELIGION, SOCIOLOGY AND ANTHROPOLOGY

Centre Européen de Recherches sur les Congrégations et Ordres Religieux (CERCOR): 35 rue du 11 Novembre, Bâtiment M, 42023 Saint-Etienne Cedex 2; tel. 4-77-42-16-70; fax 4-77-42-16-84; e-mail cercor@univ-st-etienne.fr; internet cercor.univ-st-etienne.fr; f. 1982; a research group of CNRS (*q.v.*); studies the history of the monastic and religious institutions in Western and Eastern Christianity of Christian

antiquity to the 20th century; coordinates and promotes research (conferences, etc.), runs a specialized documentation service, publishes texts; 1,400 researchers in 35 countries; library of 6,500 vols; Dir DANIEL-ODON HUREL; publ. *Bulletin du CERCOR* (1 a year).

Fondation Maison des Sciences de l'Homme: 54 blvd Raspail, 75270 Paris Cedex 06; tel. 1-49-54-20-00; fax 1-49-54-21-33; internet www.msh-paris.fr; f. 1963; supports research and int. co-operation in the social sciences; library of 155,000 vols, 2,000 current periodicals; Administrator ALAINE D'IRIBARNE; publ. *Lettre d'informations* (4 a year).

Institut d'Ethnologie du Muséum National d'Histoire Naturelle: Musée de l'Homme, Palais de Chaillot, Place du Trocadéro, 75116 Paris; tel. 1-44-05-73-45; fax 1-44-05-73-44; f. 1925; social anthropology, archaeology, linguistics; Dir M. PANOFF; publs *Collections Travaux et Mémoires*, *Mémoires*.

Institut d'Etudes Augustiniennes: 3 rue de l'Abbaye, 75006 Paris; tel. 1-43-54-80-25; fax 1-43-54-39-55; e-mail iea@wanadoo.fr; f. 1943; research into life, thought and times of St Augustine; library of 53,000 vols, 2,000 early printed books, 19 incunabula; Dir J.-C. FREDOUILLE; publs *Recherches Augustiniennes* (irregular), *Revue des Etudes Augustiniennes* (2 a year).

Institut du Monde Arabe: 1 rue des Fossés Saint Bernard, Place Mohammed-V, 75236 Paris Cedex 05; tel. 1-40-51-38-38; fax 1-43-54-76-45; e-mail ahull@imarabe.org; internet www.imarabe.org; f. 1980 by France and 21 Arab countries to promote knowledge of Arab culture and civilization; aims to encourage cultural exchanges, communication and co-operation between France and the Arab world, particularly in the fields of science and technology; international library and documentation centre of 60,000 vols, 1,200 periodicals; museum of Arab-Islamic civilization from 7th–19th century; exhibitions of Arab contemporary art; audio visual centre; Pres. YVES GUÉNA; Dir MOKHTAR TALEB-BENDIAB; publs *Qantara* (4 a year), *Al-Moukhtarat*.

Institut International d'Anthropologie: 1 place d'Iéna, 75116 Paris; tel. 1-47-93-09-73; fax 1-47-93-09-73; internet www.multimania.com/anthropa; f. 1920; 400 mems; affiliated to Ecole d'Anthropologie (*q.v.*); incorporates intercultural documentation centre; Pres. Dr A. PAJAULT; Sec.-Gen. Dr B. HUET; publ. *Nouvelle Revue Anthropologique* (irregular).

Institut Kurde de Paris (Kurdish Institute): 106 rue La Fayette, 75010 Paris; tel. 1-48-24-64-64; fax 1-48-24-64-66; internet www.institutkurde.org; f. 1983; research into Kurdish language, culture and history; Kurdish language teaching and publication of textbooks, maps, music cassettes, video films in Kurdish; library of 10,000 vols (accessible to the public); Pres. KENDAL NEZAN; publs *Etudes Kurdes* (2 a year), *Information Bulletin* (12 a year), *Kurmancî* (2 a year).

Maison Rhône-Alpes de Sciences de l'Homme (MRASH): 14 ave Berthelot, 69363 Lyons Cedex 07; tel. 4-72-72-64-64; fax 4-72-80-00-08; f. 1988; supports research in the social sciences; Dir ALAIN BONNAFOUS.

TECHNOLOGY

Association Française pour la Protection des Eaux: 67 rue de Seine, 94140 Alfortville; tel. 1-43-75-84-84; fax 1-45-18-92-90; e-mail president@anpertos.org;

internet www.anpertos.org; f. 1960; brings to public notice the necessity of protecting and preserving the quality and quantity of water-supplies, studies problems of water pollution and its prevention; 800 mems; Pres. P. L. TENAILLON; publ. *TOS*.

Centre National d'Etudes Spatiales (CNES): 2 place Maurice Quentin, 75001 Paris; internet www.cnes.fr; f. 1961; prepares national programmes of space research, provides information, promotes international co-operation; Pres. YANNICK D'ESCATHA; Dir-Gen. MICHEL LEFÈVRE.

France Telecom R & D: 38–40 rue du Général Leclerc, 92131 Issy les Moulineaux; tel. 1-45-29-44-44; internet www.rd .francetelecom.com; f. 1944; engaged in the devt of future communications systems; responsible for according official approval for telecommunications equipment; 3,700 staff; library of 2,500 vols, 1,000 periodicals; CEO THIERRY BRETON; publs *Annales des Télécommunications* (6 a year), *Annual Report*, *Bulletin Signalétique des Télécommunications* (12 a year), *Innovation Telecom* (12 a year), *L'Echo des Recherches* (4 a year), *Networks*.

Institut d'Hydrologie et de Climatologie: Faculté de Médecine, Pitié-Salpétrière, 91 blvd de l'Hôpital, 75013 Paris; tel. 1-45-33-69-92; 5 main laboratories in Paris, and further laboratories at the principal spas; Gen. Sec. Prof. G. OLIVE.

Institut Français du Pétrole: 1 et 4 ave de Bois-Préau, 92852 Rueil-Malmaison Cedex; tel. 1-47-52-60-00; fax 1-47-52-70-00; internet www.ifp.fr; f. 1945; scientific and technical organization for the purpose of research, development and industrialization, training specialists at the Ecole Nationale Supérieure du Pétrole et des Moteurs, information and documentation, international technical assistance in the different fields of the oil, gas and automotive engineering industries; library of 275,000 vols; Chair. and CEO O. APPERT; publ. *Oil and Gas Science and Technology*.

Institut Laue-Langevin (ILL): BP 156, 38042 Grenoble Cedex 9; tel. 4-76-20-71-11; fax 4-76-48-39-06; e-mail welcome@ill.fr; internet www.ill.fr; f. 1967 by France and Fed. Repub. of Germany, UK became third equal partner in 1973; associated scientific members are Spain (1987), Switzerland (1988), Austria (1990), Russia (1996), Italy (1997) and Czech Republic (1999); research on fundamental and nuclear physics, solid state physics, metallurgy, chemistry and biology by using reactor neutrons; receives 1,500 guest scientists a year and carries out experiments on 25 ILL-funded instruments and several instruments funded by collaborating research groups; central facility is high flux beam reactor producing maximum flux of 1.5×10^{15}n/cm^2/s; library of 11,000 vols, 250 periodicals; Dir Dr C. CARLILE.

Institut National de l'Audiovisuel: 4 ave de l'Europe, 94366 Bry-sur-Marne Cedex; tel. 1-49-83-23-67; fax 1-49-83-21-23; internet www.ina.fr; f. 1975; two research depts: *Recherche Prospective* (research combining telecommunications, computer science and audiovisual science); *Groupe de Recherches Musicales* (numerical development of synthesis and treatment of sound psychoacoustics and musical perception, technology of electroacoustical instruments); library of 3,000 vols; Pres. EMMANUEL HOOG; publ. *Dossiers Audiovisuels* (6 a year).

Institut National de l'Environnement Industriel et des Risques (INERIS) (National Institute for Environmental Technology and Hazards): Parc Technologique ALATA, BP 2, 60550 Verneuil-en-Halatte;

tel. 3-44-55-66-77; fax 3-44-55-66-99; e-mail ineris@ineris.fr; internet www.ineris.fr; f. 1990; library of 28,000 vols; Dir-Gen. GEORGES LABROYE; publ. *INERIS Magazine* (5 a year).

Institut National de Recherche en Informatique et en Automatique (INRIA): Domaine de Voluceau, Rocquencourt, BP 105, 78153 Le Chesnay Cedex; tel. 1-39-63-55-11; fax 1-39-63-53-30; e-mail communication@inria.fr; internet www.inria .fr; f. 1967; eight research units; library of 45,000 vols; Pres. and Dir-Gen. MICHEL COSNARD; publs *ERCIM News*, *Les conférences et supports de cours INRIA*, *Rapports d'activités scientifiques*, *Rapports de recherche et thèses*.

Institut National des Sciences et Techniques Nucléaires (INSTN) (National Institute of Nuclear Science and Technology): CEA-Saclay, 91191 Gif-sur-Yvette Cedex; internet www-instn.cea.fr; f. 1956; provides courses in nuclear engineering, robotics and computer-integrated manufacturing (CIM) and, in co-operation with the univs, post-graduate courses in reactor physics, dynamics of structures, analytical chemistry, radiochemistry, metallurgy, data processing, robotics, radiobiology, energy management, the use of radioisotopes in medicine and pharmacy; Dir JEAN-PIERRE LE ROUX; Pres. BERNARD BIGOT.

Laboratoire de Biotechnologie de l'Environnement: Ave des Etangs, 11100 Narbonne; tel. 4-68-42-51-51; fax 4-68-42-51-60; internet www.montpellier.inra.fr/ narbonne; f. 1895; attached to INRA; research in microbiological wastewater treatment; library of 5,000 vols; Dir JEAN-PHILIPPE DELGENÈS; publ. *Water Research*.

Office International de l'Eau (International Office for Water—IOW): 21 rue de Madrid, 75008 Paris; tel. 1-44-90-88-60; fax 1-40-08-01-45; e-mail cnide@oieau.fr; internet www.oieau.fr; f. 1991; documentation centre on water problems and management; library of 37,000 vols and 180,000 articles; Pres. M. ROUSSEL; Dir D. PREUX; publs *AquaVeille* (52 a year, e-newsletter), *Information Eaux* (24 a year).

Office National d'Etudes et de Recherches Aérospatiales (ONERA): 29 ave de la Division-Leclerc, 92322 Châtillon; tel. 1-46-73-40-40; fax 1-46-73-41-41; internet www.onera.fr; f. 1946 to develop, direct, and coordinate scientific and technical research in the field of aeronautics and space; library of 40,000 vols, 150,000 reports, 11,000 micro-fiches, 850 periodicals; Pres. MICHEL DE GLINIASTY; publ. *Aerospace Science and Technology* (English, 8 a year).

Libraries and Archives

Abbeville

Bibliothèque Municipale: Hôtel d'Emonville, place Clemenceau, BP 20010, 80101 Abbeville Cedex; tel. 3-22-24-95-16; fax 3-22-19-16-93; internet www.ville-abbeville.fr/ equipculturels.htm; f. 1643; 140,000 vols; Librarian P. HAZEBROUCK.

Aix-en-Provence

Bibliothèque Méjanes: 8–10 rue des Allumettes, 13090 Aix-en-Provence; tel. 4-42-91-98-88; fax 4-42-91-98-64; internet www .citedulivre-aix.com; f. 1810; 590,000 vols; Dir GILLES EBOLI.

Bibliothèque de l'Université d'Aix-Marseille III: 3 ave Robert-Schuman, 13626 Aix-en-Provence Cedex 1; tel. 4-42-17-24-40; fax 4-42-17-24-67; internet infobu.u-3mrs.fr;

156,000 vols, 273,000 periodicals, 86,000 theses; Librarian J. C. RODA.

Albi

Mediathèque Pierre Amalric: Ave Charles de Gaulle, 81000 Albi; tel. 5-63-38-56-10; fax 5-63-38-56-15; e-mail mediatheque@albi.fr; internet www .mairie-albi.fr/vivre/mediatheque.html; f. during the French Revolution; 300,000 vols; Librarian MATTHIEU DESACHY.

Amiens

Bibliothèque d'Amiens Métropole: 50 rue de la République, BP 542, 80005 Amiens Cedex 1; tel. 3-22-97-10-10; fax 3-22-97-10-70; internet www.bm-amiens.fr; f. 1826; 800,000 vols, 2,500 MSS, 300 incunabula; Chief Librarian JACQUELINE AYRAULT.

Bibliothèque de l'Université de Picardie Jules Verne: 15 placette Lafleur, BP 446, 80004 Amiens Cedex 01; tel. 3-22-82-71-65; fax 3-22-82-71-66; internet www.bu .u-picardie.fr; f. 1966; 330,000 vols, 3,900 periodicals; Dirs F. MONTBRUN, B. LOCHER.

Angers

Bibliothèque Municipale: 49 rue Toussaint, 49100 Angers; tel. 2-41-24-25-50; fax 2-41-81-05-72; internet www.bm.angers.fr; f. during the French Revolution; 400,000 vols, 2,120 MSS, 111 incunabula; Librarian CLAUDINE BELAYCHE.

Bibliothèque Universitaire d'Angers: 5 rue Le Nôtre, 49045 Angers Cedex; tel. 2-41-22-64-00; fax 2-41-22-64-05; e-mail bu@ univ-angers.fr; internet bu.univ-angers.fr; f. 1970; Dir OLIVIER TACHEAU.

Avignon

Bibliothèque Universitaire: 74 rue Louis Pasteur, 84018 Avignon Cedex 1; tel. 4-90-16-27-60; fax 4-90-16-27-70; e-mail bu@ univ-avignon.fr; internet www.bu .univ-avignon.fr; f. 1968; 100,000 books, 1,200 periodicals, 3,000 electronic periodicals; Dir FRANÇOISE FEBVRE.

Médiathèque Ceccano: 2 bis rue Laboureur, BP 349, 84025 Avignon Cedex 1; tel. 4-90-85-15-59; fax 4-90-14-65-61; e-mail bibliotheque.ceccano@wanadoo.fr; internet www.avignon.fr/fr/pratique/biblio/ceccano .php; f. 1810; 300,000 vols, 7,000 MSS, 700 incunabula, 2,700 musical scores, 40,000 engravings and maps, 30,000 coins; Chief Librarian CÉCILE FRANC.

Besançon

Bibliothèques Municipales: 1 rue de la Bibliothèque, BP 09, 25012 Besançon Cedex; tel. 3-81-87-81-40; fax 3-81-61-98-77; internet www.besancon.com/biblio/francais/bm1.htm; f. 1694; 350,000 vols, 3,800 MSS, 1,000 incunabula, etc.; Dir MARIE-CLAIRE WAILLE.

Bibliothèque de l'Université de Franche-Comté: 32 rue Mégevand, BP 1057, 25001 Besançon Cedex; tel. 3-81-66-53-50; fax 3-81-66-53-00; internet scd .univ-fcomte.fr; f. 1880; Dir SOPHIE DESSEIGNE.

Bordeaux

Bibliothèque Municipale: 85 cours du Maréchal Juin, 33075 Bordeaux Cedex; tel. 5-56-10-30-00; fax 5-56-10-30-90; e-mail bibli@mairie-bordeaux.fr; internet www .mairie-bordeaux.fr/bibliotheque/bibintro .htm; f. 1736; 900,000 vols, 4,200 MSS, 333 incunbula, 1,000 current periodicals; Chief Librarian PIERRE BOTINEAU.

Service Interétablissements de Co-opération Documentaire des Universités de Bordeaux: 4 ave des Arts, 33607 Pessac Cedex; tel. 5-56-84-86-86; fax 5-56-84-86-96;

e-mail sicod@bu.u-bordeaux.fr; internet www
.montesquieu.u-bordeaux.fr/presentation/
sicod.html; 3.2m. vols; Dir GÉRARD BRIAND.

Brest

Service Commun de Documentation:;
tel. 2-98-01-64-04; fax 2-98-47-75-25; e-mail
scd@univ-brest.fr; internet www.univ-brest
.fr; f. 1968; Dir ALAIN SAINSOT.

Caen

Bibliothèque de Caen: Place Louis-Guil-
louard, 14053 Caen Cedex; tel. 2-31-30-47-00;
fax 2-31-30-47-01; e-mail bibliotheque.caen@
agglo-caen.fr; internet www.caenlamer.fr/
bibliothequecaen; f. 1809; 693,000 vols, 6,055
periodicals, 12,000 pre-1800 printed items,
6,000 slides, 5,700 video cassettes, 70,000
CDs, 7,500 talking books for the visually
impaired, 1,900 software disks for micro-
computer and CD-ROMs; spec. Normandy
colln; Librarian NOËLLA DU PLESSIS.

Bibliothèque de l'Université de Caen:
Esplanade de la Paix, BP 5186, 14032 Caen
Cédex; tel. 2-31-56-58-70; fax 2-31-56-56-13;
e-mail bibliotheque@unicaen.fr; internet scd
.unicaen.fr; f. 1955; Dir BERNARD VOUILLOT.

Cambrai

Bibliothèque Municipale Classée: 37 rue
St Georges, BP 179, 59403 Cambrai Cedex;
tel. 3-27-82-93-93; fax 3-27-82-93-94; e-mail
admin@media-cambrai.com; f. 1791; 130,000
vols, 1,400 MSS, 600 incunabula; Librarian
BÉNÉDICTE TÉROUANNE.

Carpentras

**Bibliothèque Inguimbertine et Musées
de Carpentras:** 234 blvd Albin-Durand,
84200 Carpentras; tel. 4-90-63-04-92; fax 4-
90-63-19-11; e-mail jf.delmas@carpentras.fr;
f. 1745; 265,000 vols, 3,126 MSS; Librarian
JEAN-FRANÇOIS DELMAS.

Châlons-sur-Marne

**Bibliothèque Municipale à Vocation
Régionale Georges Pompidou:** 68 rue
Léon-Bourgeois, 51038 Châlons-en-Cham-
pagne Cedex; tel. 3-26-26-94-30; fax 3-26-
26-94-32; e-mail bibliotheque.mairie@
chalons-en-champagne.net; internet www
.chalons-en-champagne.net/bmvr; f. 1803;
330,000 vols, 2,000 MSS, 120 incunabula;
Librarian RÉGIS DUTRÉMÉE.

Chambéry

**Bibliothèque de l'Université de Savoie
(SCD, Service commun de la documentation):** Direction et Service centraux,
Domaine universitaire de Jacob-Bellecomb-
ette, Bât. 15, BP 1104, 73011 Chambéry
Cedex; tel. 4-79-75-91-13; fax 4-79-75-84-90;
e-mail contact-scd@univ-savoie.fr; internet
www.scd.univ-savoie.fr; f. 1962; 197,000 vols,
1,984 periodicals 32,000 e-periodicals; Dir
ALAIN CARACO.

Clermont-Ferrand

**Bibliothèque Municipale et Interuniver-
sitaire:** 1 blvd Lafayette, BP 27, 63001
Clermont-Ferrand Cedex 01; tel. 4-73-40-62-
40; fax 4-73-40-62-19; e-mail bmiu@
univ-bpclermont.fr; internet bmiu
.univ-bpclermont.fr; f. 1902; 682,437 vols,
2,587 current periodicals; Dir LIVIA RAPATEL.

Colmar

Bibliothèque de la Ville de Colmar: 1
place des Martyrs de la Résistance, BP 509,
68021 Colmar Cedex; tel. 3-89-24-48-18; fax
3-89-23-33-80; e-mail bibliotheque@
ville-colmar.com; f. 1803; 400,000 vols, 1,300
MSS, 2,500 incunabula; Chief Librarian
FRANCIS GUETH.

Dijon

Bibliothèque Municipale: 3–7 rue de
l'Ecole-de-Droit, 21000 Dijon; tel. 3-80-44-
94-14; fax 3-80-44-94-34; e-mail bmdijon@
ville-dijon.fr; internet bm-dijon.fr; f. 1701;
460,000 vols; Chief Librarian ANDRÉ-PIERRE
SYREN.

**Bibliothèque de l'Université de Bour-
gogne:** 7 blvd du Docteur Petitjean, 21078
Dijon; tel. 3-80-39-64-63; e-mail emmanuelle
.ashta@u-bourgogne.fr; internet scd
.u-bourgogne.fr; Dir F. HAGENE.

Douai

Bibliothèque Municipale: rue de la Fonderie, 59500 Douai; tel. 3-27-97-88-51; fax 3-
27-99-71-80; e-mail bibliotheque@biblio
.ville-douai.fr; internet www.ville-douai.fr/
culture/bibliot/accueil.htm; f. 1770; 250,000
vols, 2,000 MSS, 300 incunabula, 200 periodicals; Librarian MICHELE DEMARCY.

Grenoble

**Bibliothèque Municipale d'Etude et
d'Information:** 12 blvd Maréchal Lyautey,
BP 1095, 38021 Grenoble Cedex 1; tel. 4-76-
86-21-00; fax 4-76-86-21-19; e-mail info@
bm-grenoble.fr; internet www.bm-grenoble
.fr; f. 1772; 600,000 vols, 654 incunabula,
20,980 MSS, 81,000 prints, 2,575 maps;
special collection: local history; Dir CATHE-
RINE POUYET.

**Service de Co-opération Documentaire
Sciences-Médecine:** BP 66, 38402 St Martin d'Hères; tel. 4-76-51-42-84; fax 4-76-51-
98-51; internet www.ujf-grenoble.fr/bus;
linked with university science and medical
libraries; Dir MARIE-FRANCE ROCHARD.

**Service Interétablissements de Co-opér-
ation Documentaire:** Domaine universitaire BP 85, 38402 St Martin d'Hères
Cedex; tel. 4-76-82-61-61; fax 4-76-82-61-68;
e-mail sicod2admin@upmf-grenoble.fr;
internet odyssee.upmf-grenoble.fr; f. 1880;
Dir MARIE-NOËLLE ICARDO.

Haguenau

**Musée Historique et Archives Munici-
pales:** 9 rue du Maréchal Foch, BP 40 261,
67504 Haguenau Cedex; tel. 3-88-90-29-39;
fax 3-88-90-29-49; e-mail musees-archives@
ville-haguenau.fr; f. 1899; 8,000 vols; Dir PIA
WENDLING; publ. *Etudes Haguenoviennes* (1 a
year).

La Rochelle

Médiathèque Michel Crépeau: Communauté de Villes, Ave Marillac, 17042 La
Rochelle Cedex 1; tel. 5-46-45-71-71; fax 5-
46-45-03-22; e-mail mediatheque@
agglo-larochelle.fr; f. 1750; 360,000 vols;
Librarian BRUNO CARBONE.

Le Havre

Bibliothèque Municipale: 17 rue Jules
Lecesne, 76600 Le Havre; tel. 2-32-74-07-40;
fax 2-32-74-07-50; e-mail biblio@ville-lehavre
.fr; internet www.ville-lehavre.fr/quotidien/
culture/bibliotheque/cadre.htm; f. 1796; public borrowing, reference, record library;
389,237 vols, 1,449 periodicals, 1,020 MSS;
Librarian PATRICIA DOULERS.

Le Mans

Bibliothèque de l'Université du Maine:
Avenue Olivier Messiaen, 72085 Le Mans
Cedex 09; tel. 2-43-83-30-48; fax 2-43-83-35-
37; e-mail bu@univ-lemans.fr; internet scd
.univ-lemans.fr; 140,000 vols, 800 periodicals; Dir C. MENIL.

Lille

Bibliothèque Municipale: 34 rue Edouard
Delesalle, 59043 Lille Cedex; tel. 3-20-15-97-
20; fax 3-20-63-94-59; e-mail bmlille@

mairie-lille.fr; internet www.bm-lille.fr; f.
1726; 650,000 vols; Librarian ISABELLE DUQU-
ENNE; Librarian CAILLIER THIERRY.

**Bibliothèque de l'Université des Sci-
ences et Technologies de Lille: Service
commun de la documentation de Lille I:**
Ave Henri Poincaré, BP 155, 59653 Villeneuve d'Ascq Cedex; tel. 3-20-43-44-10; fax 3-
20-33-71-04; e-mail jean-bernard.marino@
univ-lille1.fr; internet www.univ-lille1.fr/
bustl; 160,000 books, 60,000 theses; economics, humanities, technology, science; Chief
Librarian JEAN-BERNARD MARINO.

**Service Commun de la Documentation
de Lille II:** (Secteur Médecine/Pharmacie
and Secteur Droit/Gestion): 1 place Déliot,
BP 179, 59017 Lille Cedex; tel. 3-20-90-76-50;
fax 3-20-90-76-54; internet www.scd
.univ-lille2.fr; f. 1993; Chief Librarian BRI-
GITTE MULETTE.

**Service Commun de la Documentation
de l'Université de Lille III – Charles de
Gaulle:** Domaine universitaire du Pont-de-
bois, BP 99, 59652 Villeneuve d'Ascq Cedex;
tel. 3-20-41-70-00; fax 3-20-91-46-50; internet
www.univ-lille3.fr/portail/index.php?pa-
ge=scd; Dir JEAN-PAUL CHADOURNE.

Limoges

Bibliothèque Francophone Multimédia:
2 rue Louis Longequeue, 87032 Limoges
Cedex; tel. 5-55-45-96-00; fax 5-55-45-96-96;
e-mail francophonie@bm-limoges.fr; internet
www.francophonie-limoges.com; f. 1804;
530,000 vols, 900 periodicals, 14,000 video
cassettes, 32,000 records; spec. collns incl.
enamels, ceramics, porcelain; Librarian
FRANÇOISE DIET-ESCARFAIL.

**Bibliothèque de l'Université de
Limoges:** 39c rue Camille-Guérin, 87031
Limoges Cedex; tel. 5-55-43-57-00; fax 5-55-
43-57-01; internet www-scd.unilim.fr; f.
1965; 100,000 vols; Dir ODILE ROHOU.

Lyons

**Bibliothèque Interuniversitaire de Let-
tres et Sciences Humaines:** 5 parvis René-
Descartes, BP 7000, 69342 Lyons; tel. 4-37-
37-65-00; internet biu.ens-lsh.fr/biu; Dir
CHARLES MICOL.

Bibliothèque Municipale: 30 blvd Vivier-
Merle, 69431 Lyons Cedex 03; tel. 4-78-62-
18-00; fax 4-78-62-19-49; e-mail bm@bm-lyon
.fr; internet www.bm-lyon.fr; f. 1565; 2.4m.
vols, 12,449 MSS, 1,157 incunabula, 130,000
prints, 12,399 periodicals, 172,000 records,
59,883 photographs; Dir PATRICK BAZIN.

Marseilles

**Bibliothèque et Archives, Chambre de
Commerce et d'Industrie Marseille-
Provence:** La Canebière, Palais de la
Bourse, BP 21856, 13221 Marseilles; tel. 4-
91-39-33-21; fax 4-91-39-56-15; e-mail sylvie
.drago@ccimp.com; internet www
.marseille-provence.cci.fr; f. 1872; economics,
law, business, industry, commerce, agriculture, marine, Provence, overseas, history,
geography; online information service;
60,000 vols, 60,000 brochures, 3,000 periodicals; Dir PATRICK BOULANGER; Librarian
SYLVIE DRAGO.

Bibliothèque Municipale: 23 rue de la
providence, 13001 Marseilles; tel. 4-91-55-90-
00; fax 4-91-55-23-44; internet www.bmvr
.mairie-marseille.fr; f. 1800; 750,000 vols; Dir
FRANÇOIS LARBRE.

**Bibliothèque de l'Université de la Méd-
iterranée (Aix-Marseille II):** Campus
Timone, 27 blvd Jean Moulin, 13385 Marseille Cedex 05; tel. 4-91-32-45-37; fax 4-91-
25-60-22; e-mail anne.dujol@univmed.fr;
internet bu.univmed; f. 1987; 7 academic
libraries in Marseilles, Aix en Provence and

Gap; medicine, pharmacy, dental sciences, sports economics; rare books on medicine; Dir ANNE DUJOL.

Metz

Bibliothèque Municipale: 1 cour Elie Fleur, 57000 Metz; tel. 3-87-55-53-33; fax 3-87-30-42-88; internet bm.mairie-metz.fr/metz; f. 1811; 400,000 vols, 1,195 MSS, 5,000 engravings, 463 incunabula; video cassettes, slides; Chief Librarian PIERRE LOUIS.

Service Commun de Documentation de l'Université Paul Verlaine–Metz: Ile du Saulcy, 57045 Metz Cedex 1; tel. 3-87-31-50-80; fax 3-87-33-22-90; e-mail colinmaire@scd .univ-metz.fr; internet www.scd.univ-metz .fr; f. 1972; 250,000 vols, 1,100 periodicals; Dir HERVÉ COLINMAIRE.

Montpellier

Bibliothèque Interuniversitaire: Administration: 60 rue des Etats généraux, 34965 Montpellier Cedex 2; tel. 4-67-13-43-50; fax 4-67-13-43-51; internet www.biu .univ-montp1.fr; f. 1890; Chief Librarian PIERRE GAILLARD.

Médiathèque Centrale d'Agglomération Emile Zola: 240 rue de l'Acropole, 34000 Montpellier; tel. 4-67-34-87-00; fax 4-67-34-87-01; e-mail accueil.mca@montpellier-agglo .com; internet sbib.bm.montpellier-agglo .com; f. during the French Revolution; 720,000 vols; Dir M. G. GUDIN DE VALLERIN.

Mulhouse

Bibliothèque de l'Université et de la Société Industrielle de Mulhouse (Section Histoire des Sciences): 12 rue de la Bourse, 68100 Mulhouse; tel. 3-89-56-12-74; fax 3-89-33-63-79; e-mail f.pascal@uha.fr; internet www.scd.uha.fr; f. 1826; 30,000 vols, 700 (and 150 current) periodicals; Dir PHILIPPE RUSSELL.

Université de Haute Alsace, Service Commun de Documentation: 8 rue des Frères Lumière, 68093 Mulhouse; tel. 3-89-33-63-60; fax 3-89-33-63-79; e-mail scdmulhouse@uha.fr; internet www.scd.uha .fr; f. 1977; Dir PHILIPPE RUSSELL.

Nancy

Bibliothèque Municipale: 43 rue Stanislas, CS 64230, 54042 Nancy Cedex; tel. 3-83-37-38-83; fax 3-83-37-91-82; e-mail bmnancy@mairie-nancy.fr; f. 1750; 500,000 vols; Chief Librarian ANDRÉ MARKIEWICZ.

Service Commun de Documentation: 30 rue Lionnois, 54000 Nancy; tel. 3-83-68-22-00; fax 3-83-68-22-03; internet scd.uhp-nancy .fr; 356,000 vols, 4,100 periodicals; Chief Librarian SEBASTIEN BOGAERT.

Nantes

Bibliothèque Municipale: 15 rue de l'Heronnière, BP 44113, 44041 Nantes Cedex 01; tel. 2-40-41-95-95; fax 2-40-41-42-00; e-mail bm@mairie-nantes.fr; internet www.bm .nantes.fr; f. 1753; 900,000 vols; Chief Librarian AGNÈS MARCETTEAU.

Bibliothèque Universitaire de Nantes: Chemin de la Censive du Tertre, BP 32211, 44322 Nantes Cedex 03; tel. 2-40-14-12-30; internet www.bu.univ-nantes.fr; f. 1962; 260,000 vols, 5,000 periodicals; Chief Librarian MICHELLE GUIOT.

Nice

Bibliothèque Municipale à Vocation Régionale de Nice: 1 ave Saint-Jean-Baptiste, 06364 Nice Cedex 4; tel. 4-97-13-48-00; fax 4-97-13-48-05; internet www.bmvr-nice .com.fr; f. 1802; network of 15 br. libraries; spec. colln on Michel Butor; 1m. vols, 208,700 compact discs, records and cassettes, 17,002

video cassettes, 519 CD-ROMs; Chief Librarian FRANÇOISE MICHELIZZA.

Bibliothèque de l'Université de Nice–Sophia Antipolis: Parc Valrose, BP 2053, 06101 Nice Cedex 02; tel. 4-92-07-60-00; fax 4-92-07-60-10; internet www.unice.fr/bu; f. 1963; 260,000 vols, 4,400 periodicals; Dir LOUIS KLEE.

Nîmes

Carré d'Art Bibliothèques: Mairie, Place de l'Hôtel de Ville, 30033 Nîmes Cedex 9; tel. 4-66-76-70-01; e-mail webmaster@ ville-nimes.fr; internet bibliotheque.nimes.fr; f. 1803; 323,000 vols, 590 periodicals, 800 MSS, 40,000 ancient books, 19,000 CDs; Chief Librarian J.-M. MASSADAU; publ. *Journal Carré d'Art* (3 a year).

Orléans

Médiathèque d'Orléans: 1 place Gambetta, 45043 Orléans Cedex 1; tel. 2-38-65-45-45; fax 2-38-65-45-40; e-mail bibliotheques@ville-orleans.fr; internet www .bm-orleans.fr; f. 1714; 420,000 vols, 2,550 MSS; Librarian AGNÈS CHEVALIER.

Service Commun de la Documentation de l'Université d'Orléans: Domaine de la Source, 6 rue de Tours, 45072 Orléans Cedex 02; tel. 2-38-41-71-84; fax 2-38-41-71-87; e-mail secretariat.scd@univ-orleans.fr; internet scd.univ-orleans.fr; f. 1965; 290,301 vols and theses, 3,300 periodicals; Dir CATHERINE MOREAU.

Paris

American Library in Paris: 10 rue du Général Camou, 75007 Paris; tel. 1-53-59-12-60; fax 1-45-50-25-83; e-mail alparis@ americanlibraryinparis.org; internet americanlibraryinparis.org; f. 1920; private English-language lending and reference library open to all nationalities (subject to payment of fees); 120,000 vols, 250 periodicals, 2,500 online periodicals; Chair. WILLIAM TORCHIANA; Dir CHARLES TRUEHEART.

Archives de France: 56 rue des Francs-Bourgeois, 75141 Paris Cedex 03; tel. 1-40-27-60-00; fax 1-40-27-66-06; internet www .archivesdefrance.culture.gouv.fr; f. 1790; 480 km documents; Dir-Gen. MARTINE DE BOISDEFFRE.

Attached Units:

Archives Nationales du Monde du Travail: 78 blvd du Général Leclerc, BP 405, 59057 Roubaix, Cedex 1; tel. 3-20-65-38-00; fax 3-20-65-38-01; f. 1993; Chief Curator FRANÇOISE BOSMAN.

Centre des Archives Contemporaines: 2 rue des Archives, 77300 Fontainebleau; tel. 1-64-31-73-00; fax 1-64-31-73-03; Chief Curator CHRISTINE PETILLAT.

Centre des Archives d'Outre-Mer: 29 chemin du Moulin-Detesta, 13090 Aix-en-Provence; tel. 4-42-93-38-50; fax 4-42-93-38-89; f. 1962; Chief Curator MARTINE CORNEDE.

Centre Historique des Archives Nationales: 60 rue des Francs-Bourgeois, 75003 Paris; Chief Curator GÉRARD ERMISSE.

Centre National du Microfilm: Domaine d'Espeyran, 30800 St-Gilles-du-Gard; tel. 4-66-87-30-09; fax 4-66-87-03-44; Chief Curator ANNE DEBANT.

Bibliothèque Administrative de la Ville de Paris: Hôtel de Ville, 75196 Paris Cedex 04; tel. 1-42-76-48-87; fax 1-42-76-63-78; e-mail bavp@paris.frr; f. 1872; 550,000 vols (reports, studies, statistics, official texts, budgets, etc.); 3,200 periodicals, 8,000 photographs, 2,700 MSS, 12,000 architectural designs, 40,000 microfiches, 2,000 microfilms covering areas of French and foreign local

admin., French legislation, economic, political and social history, ex-French colonies and gen. biography; Chief Librarian PIERRE CASSELLE.

Bibliothèque Centrale et Archives des Musées Nationaux: 6 rue des Pyramides, 75041 Paris Cedex 01; tel. 1-40-20-52-66; fax 1-40-20-51-69; e-mail sbadg.dmf@culture .gouv.fr; internet www.inha.fr/bibliotheque/ bcmn.html; f. 1871; 180,000 vols, 1,800 periodicals; books and MSS connected with the Louvre and the National Museums (Egyptology colln, Oriental antiquities, Graeco-Roman antiquities, drawings, paintings and sculptures); open only to curators and authorized persons; Conservateur Général and Librarian FRANÇOISE PETITOU.

Bibliothèque Centrale de l'Ecole Polytechnique: Plateau de Saclay, 91128 Palaiseau Cedex; tel. 1-69-33-40-76; fax 1-69-33-28-33; internet www.bibliotheque .polytechnique.fr; f. 1794; 300,000 vols, 1,700 periodicals; Chief Librarian MADELEINE DE FUENTES.

Bibliothèque Centrale du Muséum National d'Histoire Naturelle: 38 rue Geoffroy-Saint-Hilaire, 75005 Paris; tel. 1-40-79-36-27; fax 1-40-79-36-56; e-mail milenoir@mnhn.fr; internet mussi.mnhn.fr; f. 1635; 405,000 books, 7,050 MSS, 12,000 periodicals; Chief Librarian MICHELLE LENOIR.

Bibliothèque de Documentation Internationale Contemporaine: Centre Universitaire, 6 allée de l'Université, 92001 Nanterre Cedex; tel. 1-40-97-79-00; fax 1-40-97-79-40; e-mail courrier@bdic.fr; internet www.bdic.fr; f. 1914; over 1m. vols, 90,000 series of periodicals, history of the two World Wars and int. relations since beginning of 20th century, social and revolutionary movements, political emigrations; Dir GENEVIÈVE DREYFUS-ARMAND; publs *Journal* (irregular), *Matériaux pour l'Histoire de Notre Temps* (3 a year).

Bibliothèque de Géographie- Sorbonne Institut de Géographie: 191 rue Saint-Jacques, 75005 Paris; tel. 1-44-32-14-63; fax 1-44-32-14-67; e-mail bibgeo@univ-paris1.fr; internet www.univ-paris1.fr; f. 1927; geography; 92,000 vols, 4,600 periodicals, 100,000 maps, 40,000 photographs, 500 other media; Librarian RACHEL CREPPY.

Bibliothèque de la Cour des Comptes: 13 rue Cambon, 75100 Paris Cedex; tel. 1-42-98-97-12; fax 1-42-60-01-59; f. 1807 by Napoleon I; 50,000 vols on finance, law and economy; Librarian (vacant).

Bibliothèque de l'Institut National de la Statistique et des Etudes Economiques: 18 blvd Adolphe Pinard, 75675 Paris Cedex 14; tel. 1-41-17-67-18; fax 1-41-17-50-69; e-mail dg75-bibliotheque-service-public@ insee.fr; internet www.insee.fr/fr/ insee-statistique-publique/default.asp?pa ge=bibliotheque/bibliotheque.htm; f. 1946; 100,000 vols, 5,000 periodicals; current and historical publs on french statistics and economics; regional publs; official publs on int. statistics and economics and publs of statistical offices around the world; Chief Librarian PIERRE-YVES RENARD; Head of Doumentation BERNARD LANCELOT.

Bibliothèque de la Sorbonne: 13 rue de la Sorbonne, 75257 Paris Cedex 05; tel. 1-40-46-30-27; fax 1-40-46-30-44; e-mail info@biu .sorbonne.fr; internet www.bibliotheque .sorbonne.fr/biu; f. 1762; over 22m. vols, 13,000 periodicals; Chief Librarian PHILIPPE MARCEROU; publ. *Mélanges de la Bibliothèque de la Sorbonne.*

Bibliothèque de l'Académie Nationale de Médecine: 16 rue Bonaparte, 75272

Paris Cedex 06; tel. 1-46-34-60-70; fax 1-43-25-84-14; e-mail bibliotheque@academie-medecine.fr; f. 1820; 450,000 vols, 113 incunabula, 4,000 periodicals (500 current); 7,000 biographical dossiers; Archives of the Académie Royale de Chirurgie (1731–93), Société Royale de Médecine (1776–93), Société de l'Ecole de Médecine (1800–21), Comité Central de Vaccine (1803–23) and Académie de Médecine (since 1820); also portraits, medals and sculptures; Librarian LAURENCE CAMOUS; publ. *Bulletin de l'Académie nationale de Médecine* (9 a year).

Bibliothèque de l'Arsenal: 1 rue de Sully, 75004 Paris; tel. 1-42-77-44-21; fax 1-42-77-01-63; internet www.bnf.fr/pages/connaitr/ars_site.htm; f. 1756 by the Marquess of Paulmy, public library in 1797; inc. with Bibliothèque Nationale 1934; specializes in literature; open to scholars; contains 100,000 vols; 15,000 MSS, many autographs; includes archives of the Bastille; 100,000 prints, 18th-century maps; houses the performing arts collection of the Bibliothèque Nationale (2.5m. vols and other items); Dir (vacant).

Service de la Bibliothèque et des archives de l'Assemblée Nationale: Palais Bourbon, 126 rue de l'Université, 75007 Paris; tel. 1-40-63-64-74 (library); 1-40-63-85-77 (archives); fax 1-40-63-52-53; e-mail archives@assemblee-nationale.fr; internet www.assemblee-nationale.fr; f. 1796; open to deputies, staff members, secretaries of political groups, civil servants of the Assembly; 700,000 vols, 1,870 MSS, and 80 incunabula, 3,000 periodicals, 50,000 microfiches, 2,500 microfilms, mainly on history, political science, law, economy; Dir ELIANE FIGHIERA; publs *Sélection d'articles de périodiques*, *Sélection d'ouvrages récemment acquis* (8 a year).

Bibliothèque de l'Ecole Nationale Supérieure des Mines: 60 blvd Saint-Michel, 75272 Paris Cedex 06; tel. 1-40-51-90-56; fax 1-43-25-53-58; e-mail bib@bib.ensmp.fr; internet bib.ensmp.fr; f. 1783; 300,000 vols, 3,820 periodicals, 30,000 maps; Chief Librarian Mme F. MASSON.

Bibliothèque de l'Ecole Normale Supérieure: 45 rue d'Ulm, 75230 Paris Cedex 05; internet halley.ens.fr; f. 1810; 500,000 vols; Chief Librarian LAURE LÉVEILLÉ.

Bibliothèque de l'Institut de France: 23 quai Conti, 75006 Paris; tel. 1-44-41-44-10; fax 1-44-41-44-11; e-mail mireille.pastoureau@bif.univ-paris5.fr; internet www.bibliotheque-institutdefrance.fr; f. 1795; comprises five acads: Académie française, Académie des Inscriptions et Belles-Lettres, Académie des Sciences, Académie des Beaux-Arts, Académie des Sciences morales et politiques; 1m. vols, 8,000 periodicals, 10,000 MSS; Chief Curator Dr MIREILLE PASTOUREAU.

Bibliothèque de l'Institut National de Recherche Pédagogique: 5 parvis René Descartes, 69342 Lyons Cedex 07; tel. 1-37-37-66-10; fax 1-37-37-66-06; e-mail soula@inrp.fr; internet www.inrp.fr; f. 1879; 550,000 vols, 5,000 periodicals, 100,000 textbooks; educational research; Chief Librarian MARIE-LOUISE SOULA.

Bibliothèque de l'Institut National d'Histoire de l'Art–Collections Jacques Doucet: 2 rue Vivienne, 75002 Paris; 58 rue de Richelieu, 75083 Paris Cedex 02; tel. 1-47-03-76-23; fax 1-47-03-76-30; e-mail bibliotheque@inha.fr; internet www.inha.fr; f. 1918; 450,000 vols, 6,674 periodicals; Chief Librarian MARTINE POULAIN.

Bibliothèque des Avocats à la Cour d'Appel: Palais de Justice, 75001 Paris; f. 1708; confiscated during the Revolution, but refounded in 1810; 160,000 vols; not open to the public; Librarian MICHEL BRICHARD.

Bibliothèque Centrale du Conservatoire National des Arts et Métiers: 292 rue St-Martin, 75141 Paris Cedex 03; tel. 1-40-27-27-03; fax 1-40-27-29-87; e-mail mireille.le_van_ho@cnam.fr; internet bibliotheque.cnam.fr; f. 1794; 150,000 vols, 3,600 periodicals on science, technology, political economy; spec. collns: exhibition catalogues, Bartholdi, Organum; Dir MIREILLE LE VAN HO.

Bibliothèque du Ministère des Affaires Etrangères: 3 rue Suzanne Masson, La Courneuve, 93126 Paris; tel. 1-43-17-42-61; fax 1-43-17-51-48; e-mail biblio.archives@diplomatie.gouv.fr; internet www.diplomatie.gouv.fr; f. 1680; 500,000 vols; Head Librarian ISABELLE LEFORT; Librarian LIONEL CHENÉDÉ.

Bibliothèque du Sénat: Palais du Luxembourg, 15 rue de Vaugirard, 75291 Paris Cedex 06; tel. 1-42-34-35-39; fax 1-42-34-27-05; f. 1818; 450,000 vols, chiefly on history and law, 1,343 MSS and 45,000 prints; open to members of Parliament; Dir PHILIPPE MARTIAL.

Bibliothèque du Service Historique de la Marine: Château de Vincennes, BP 122, 00481 Armées; tel. 1-43-28-81-50; fax 1-43-28-31-60; e-mail contact@servicehistorique.marine.defense.gouv.fr; internet www.servicehistorique.marine.defense.gouv.fr; f. 1919; 300,000 vols on naval history; Chief Curator ALAIN MORGAT.

Bibliothèque du Service Historique de l'Armée de Terre: Château de Vincennes, BP 107, 00481 Armées; tel. 1-41-93-34-62; f. c.1800; over 600,000 vols; 16th- to 20th-century science and military history, French history, cartography; Librarian RAPHAËL MASSON.

Bibliothèque et Archives du Conseil d'Etat: Place du Palais-Royal, 75100 Paris 01 SP; tel. 1-40-20-81-31; fax 1-42-61-69-95; internet www.conseil-etat.fr; f. 1871; 100,000 vols on jurisprudence, administrative science, political science and legislation; Librarian SERGE BOUFFANGE.

Bibliothèque Forney: 1 rue du Figuier, 75004 Paris; tel. 1-42-78-14-60; fax 1-42-78-22-59; e-mail bibliotheque.forney@paris.fr; f. 1886; art library; reference library; wallpapers, posters, ephemera; 250,000 vols, 20,000 periodicals (chiefly on arts and crafts), 38,000 posters, 5,000 wallpapers, 1.5m. postcards; Librarian Conservateur général FRÉDÉRIC CASIOT.

Bibliothèque Georges-Duhamel: 44 ave de Paris, 95290 L'Isle-Adam; tel. 1-34-69-41-99; f. 1797; encyclopaedic library; 88,882 vols; record library: 6,400 records, 1,500 compact discs; permanent exhibitions in Georges Duhamel picture gallery; Dir PAUL JOLAS; publ. *Rencontres Artistiques et Littéraires*.

Bibliothèque Gustav Mahler: 11 bis rue Vézelay, 75008 Paris; tel. 1-53-89-09-10; fax 1-43-59-70-22; internet www.bgm.org; f. 1986; reference colln for musicians, students, researchers; 30,000 vols, 35,000 musical scores, 6,000 reviews, 70,000 records; archives: MSS, letters, photos, etc. on Mahler's life and works; also 16,000 dossiers on contemporary composers, autographs and MSS of 19th- and 20th-centuries musicians; Pres. PIERRE BERGÉ; Librarian ALAIN GALLIARI; publ. *Bulletin d'information de la BMGM* (1 a year).

Bibliothèque Historique de la Ville de Paris: 24 rue Pavée, 75004 Paris; tel. 1-44-59-29-40; fax 1-42-74-03-16; f. 1871; 650,000 vols, 15,000 MSS on history of Paris; Curator JEAN DERENS.

Bibliothèque Interuniversitaire Cujas de Droit et Sciences Économiques: 2 rue Cujas, 75005 Paris; tel. 1-44-07-79-87; fax 1-44-07-78-32; e-mail cujasdir@univ-paris1.fr; internet www-cujas.univ-paris1.fr; f. 1876; 1m. vols; Chief Librarian DOMINIQUE ROCHE.

Bibliothèque Interuniversitaire de Médecine: 12 rue de l'Ecole-de-Médecine, 75270 Paris Cedex 06; tel. 1-40-46-19-51; fax 1-44-41-10-20; e-mail bium@bium.univ-paris5.fr; internet www.bium.univ-paris5.fr; f. 1733; 1m. vols, 30,000 pre-1800 books and theses, 109 incunabula, 20,000 periodicals (2,300 current); Chief Librarian GUY COBOLET.

Bibliothèque Interuniversitaire de Pharmacie: 4 ave de l'Observatoire, 75270 Paris Cedex 06; tel. 1-53-73-95-23; fax 1-53-73-95-05; internet www.biup.parisdescartes.fr; f. 1570; centre for the acquisition and dispersion of scientific and technical information (CADIST) on beauty care; 280,000 vols, 945 periodicals, archives of Parisian apothecaries; Dir FRANÇOISE BOUCHERON.

Bibliothèque Mazarine: 23 quai de Conti, 75006 Paris; tel. 1-44-41-44-06; fax 1-44-41-44-07; e-mail webmaster@bibliotheque-mazarine.fr; internet www.bibliotheque-mazarine.fr; f. 1643 by Cardinal Mazarin, present status 1945; attached to Institut de France; 600,000 vols, 4,642 MSS, 2,370 incunabula; Dir CHRISTIAN PÉLIGRY.

Bibliothèque-Musée de l'Opéra: 8 rue Scribe, 75009 Paris; tel. 1-53-79-37-40; fax 1-53-79-39-59; internet www.bnf.fr; f. 1875; a service of Bibliothèque Nationale, music dept; 200,000 vols, 30,000 scores, 80,000 libretti, 100,000 drawings, 40,000 lithographs, 100,000 photographs, 2,000 periodicals; Dir ODILE DUPONT; Curator ROMAIN FEIST.

Bibliothèque Nationale de France: quai François Mauriac, 75013 Paris; tel. 1-53-79-53-79; internet www.bnf.fr; f. 14th century; specialized depts: printed books (11m. vols), periodicals (350,000 titles), maps and plans (890,000), prints and photographs (11m.), MSS (350,000 bound vols), coins, medals and antiques (580,000 items), music (incl. Bibliothèque-Musée de l'Opéra (q.v.)), sound archive and audiovisual aids (1m. discs and tape recordings, 20,000 films, 40,000 video materials), performing arts (3m. items), Bibliothèque de l'Arsenal (q.v.); Pres. JEAN-NOËL JEANNENEY; Dir-Gen. AGNÈS SAAL; publs *Bibliographie nationale Française* (52 a year), *Chronique de la Bibliothèque Nationale de France* (6 a year).

Bibliothèque Polonaise de Paris: 6 quai d'Orléans, 75004 Paris; tel. 1-55-42-83-83; fax 1-46-33-36-31; e-mail b.skrzypek@bplp.fr; internet www.bibliotheque-polonaise-paris-shlp.fr; f. 1854; 200,000 vols, 25,000 drawings and engravings, sculptures, paintings, 8,000 maps (16th–20th centuries), 5,000 photographs, archives of 19th- and 20th-centuries Polish emigration to France; Chopin memorabilia; also posters, medals and periodicals; Mickiewicz museum; specializes in 19th- and 20th-centuries history, literature and art; admin. by Société Historique et Littéraire Polonaise; Dir D. DUBOIS.

Bibliothèque Publique d'Information: Centre Georges-Pompidou, 75197 Paris Cedex 04; tel. 1-44-78-12-33; fax 1-44-78-12-15; e-mail bpi-info@bpi.fr; internet www.bpi.fr; f. 1977; 400,000 books, 2,722 periodicals, 2,425 films, 10,000 music records; Dir PATRICK BAZIN.

Bibliothèque Sainte-Geneviève: 10 pl. du Panthéon, 75005 Paris; tel. 1-44-41-97-97; fax 1-44-41-97-96; e-mail bsgmail@

univ-paris1.fr; internet www-bsg.univ-paris1 .fr; f. 1624 by Cardinal F. de La Rochefoucauld as library of the Abbaye Sainte-Geneviève; collns on computer science, information, general works, philosophy and psychology, religion, social sciences, languages, science and mathematics, technology and applied science, arts and recreation, literature, history and geography; interlibrary loan; guided tours; online databases; 45,000 mems; 1.3m. vols, 14,000 periodicals, 120,000 early printed books, 1,500 incunabula and 4,200 MSS, 50,000 prints; encyclopaedic library; spec. colln: Bibliothèque Nordique (160,000 vols, 3,500 periodicals), Estonian colln (1,000 vols), 3,800 current serial titles; Dir YVES PEYRÉ.

Bibliothèque Thiers: 27 place Saint-Georges, 75009 Paris; tel. 1-48-78-14-33; fax 1-48-78-92-92; e-mail bibliotheque.thiers@ free.fr; internet www.institut-de-france.fr; f. 1905; attached to Institut de France; 130,000 vols, 3,000 MSS and 30,000 engravings on 19th century history; Dir DANUTA MONACHON.

Bibliothèque Universitaire des Langues et Civilisations: 4 rue de Lille, 75007 Paris; tel. 1-44-77-87-20; fax 1-44-77-87-30; e-mail webmaster@bulac.sorbonne.fr; internet www .bulac.fr; f. 1868; languages and cultures of countries in Asia, Africa, Central and Eastern Europe, and Middle Eastern, Oceanian and Amerindian languages; 660,000 vols, 8,695 periodicals; Dir MARIE-LISE TSAGOURIA.

Bibliothèques de l'Institut Catholique de Paris: c/o Bibliothèque de Fels, 21 rue d'Assas, 75270 Paris Cedex 06; tel. 1-44-39-52-30; fax 1-44-39-52-98; e-mail bibliotheque .de.fels@icp.fr; internet www.icp.fr; f. 1875; philosophy, theology, history, literature, psychology, pedagogy; 600,000 vols, incl. 450,000 books, 623 current periodicals, 6,000 other periodicals; Dir of Libraries ODILE DUPONT.

Attached Library:

Bibliothèque Jean de Vernon: 21 rue d'Assas, 75006 Paris; tel. 44-39-52-32; e-mail bibliotheque.de.vernon@icp.fr; internet ipac.icp.fr; 100,000 vols, 400 periodicals; biblical exegesis, archaeology and languages of the ancient near E, orthodox church instns, history of the byzantine empire; Dir. of Library MARIE-FRANÇOISE PAPE.

CÉDIAS—Musée Social: 5 rue Las-Cases, 75007 Paris; tel. 1-45-51-66-10; fax 1-44-18-01-81; e-mail bibliotheque@cedias.org; internet www.cedias.org; f. 1894; social information and documentation; public library; 100,000 vols; Dir JEAN-YVES BARREYRE; publ. *Vie Sociale* (4 a year).

Centre de Documentation Economique de la Chambre de Commerce et d'Industrie de Paris: 16 rue de Châteaubriand, 75008 Paris; tel. 1-55-65-72-72; fax 1-55-65-72-86; f. 1821; economics, business information, management, market surveys, companies; 300,000 vols, 750 periodicals; economic data bank (DELPHES); Dir GÉRARD FALCO.

Centre de Documentation et d'Information Scientifique pour le Développement (CEDID): 209 rue La Fayette, 75010 Paris; tel. 1-48-03-75-95; fax 1-48-03-08-29; f. 1985 by ORSTOM; 70,000 documents on development and North-South co-operation, world environment, tropical agriculture, health, evolving societies, and women in third world countries; 200 general and scientific reviews, press cuttings, database, etc.; open to the public.

Direction des Services d'Archives de Paris: 18 blvd Sérurier, 75019 Paris; tel. 1-53-72-41-23; fax 1-53-72-41-34; f. 1872; collns

of various kinds of documents relating to the history of Paris, urbanization and architecture; 34,000 vols specializing in history of Paris and admin. publs, 1,200 periodicals; Dir AGNÈS MASSON.

Institut François-Mitterrand: 10 rue Charlot, 75003 Paris; tel. 1-44-54-53-93; fax 1-44-54-53-99; e-mail ifm@mitterrand.org; internet www.mitterrand.org; f. 1996; archives documents relevant to the history of the second half of the 20th century.

Service de Documentaire de l'Ecole Ponts et ParisTech: 6 et 8 ave Blaise Pascal, Cité Descartes, Champs sur Marne, 77455 Marne-la-Vallée Cedex 2; tel. 1-64-15-36-90; fax 1-64-15-34-79; e-mail bibliotheque@enpc.fr; internet www.enpc.fr; f. 1747; over 200,000 vols on bldg, civil engineering, urban and regional planning, and transport, 3,200 MSS, 3,000 maps, 10,000 photographs 1850–1900, 10 libraries; Dir ISABELLE GAUTHERON.

UNESCO Library: UNESCO, 7 pl. de Fontenoy, 75007 Paris; tel. 1-45-68-03-56; fax 1-45-68-56-98; e-mail library@unesco.org; internet www.unesco.org/library; f. 1946; reference and information services, incl. online searches, for the org. as a whole, as well as for the gen. public with an interest in UNESCO's fields of competence; manages multilingual UNESCO Thesaurus; 150,000 vols, 800 periodicals; Chief Librarian JOHN MILLER; Reference Librarian PETRA VAN DEN BORN.

Pau

Bibliothèque Square Paul Lafond: Rue Mathieu Lalanne, 64000 Pau; tel. 5-59-27-15-72; fax 5-59-83-94-47; e-mail accueil.bipp@ agglo-pau.fr; internet mediatheque .agglo-pau.fr; f. 1803; 350,000 vols; includes municipal archives; spec. collns on Henri IV and Béarn; Librarian OLIVIER CAUDRON.

Bibliothèque de l'Université de Pau et des Pays de l'Adour: Campus universitaire, 64000 Pau; tel. 5-59-92-33-60; fax 5-59-92-33-62; internet www.univ-pau.fr/scd; f. 1962; 142,000 vols, 2,067 periodicals; Dir SYLVAINE FREULON.

Périgueux

Bibliothèque Municipale: 12 ave Georges Pompidou, 24000 Périgueux; tel. 5-53-45-65-45; fax 5-53-45-65-49; e-mail bibliotheque@ perigueux.fr; f. 1809; 170,000 vols; Librarian J. L. GLÉNISSON.

Perpignan

Bibliothèque Universitaire: BP 59939, Moulin à Vent, 52 ave Paul Alduy, 66962 Perpignan Cedex 9; tel. 4-68-66-22-99; fax 4-68-50-37-72; internet www.univ-perp.fr/ scms/bu/buweb.htm; f. 1962; 155,000 vols and 100,000 theses; spec. collns: Catalan, Mexican studies, history of Languedoc-Roussillon, renewable energy, materials science, geology of North Africa; Dir JOËL MARTRES.

Poitiers

Bibliothèque Universitaire de Poitiers: BP 605, 86022 Poitiers Cedex; tel. 5-49-45-33-11; fax 5-49-45-33-56; e-mail bu@ univ-poitiers.fr; internet www.scd .univ-poitiers.fr; f. 1879; 452,000 vols, 5,830 periodicals; spec. collns: 30,000 early printed vols, Fonds Dubois (16th–19th centuries, economics, politics, social history), Argenson family archives; Dir STÉPHANE BASSINET.

Médiathèque François-Mitterrand: 4 rue de l'Université, BP 619, 86022 Poitiers Cedex; tel. 5-49-52-31-51; fax 5-49-52-31-60; e-mail mediatheque@mairie-poitiers.fr; internet www.bm-poitiers.fr; f. 1803; 750,000 books, 550 current periodicals; Dir

SERGE BOUFFANGE; publ. *Programme* (5 a year).

Reims

Bibliothèque Municipale: 2 rue des Fuseliers, 51095 Reims Cedex; tel. 3-26-35-68-00; fax 3-26-35-68-34; e-mail cathedrale@ bm-reims.fr; internet www.bm-reims.fr; f. 1809; 800,000 vols, 3,000 MSS; Librarian DELPHINE QUÉREUX-SBAÏ; publ. *Ouvrez les guillemets* (12 a year).

Bibliothèque de l'Université de Reims: Ave François Mauriac, 51095 Reims Cedex; tel. 3-26-91-39-28; fax 3-26-91-39-30; e-mail carine.elbekri@univ-reims.fr; internet www .univ-reims.fr/bu; f. 1970; 400,000 vols, 4,278 periodicals; Dir CARINE EL BEKRI.

Rennes

Bibliothèque Municipale: 1 rue de La Borderie, 35042 Rennes Cedex; tel. 2-23-62-26-42; fax 2-23-62-26-45; e-mail bm@ bm-rennes.fr; internet www.bm-rennes.fr; f. 1803; 650,000 vols; Chief Librarian MARINE BEDEL.

Bibliothèque de l'Université de Rennes I:; tel. 2-23-23-34-18; fax 2-23-23-34-19; internet www.scd.univ-rennes1.fr; f. 1855; 550,000 vols; Dir GHYSLAINE DUONG-VINH.

Bibliothèque de l'Université de Rennes II: Place du Recteur Henri Le Moal, 35043 Rennes Cedex; tel. 2-99-14-12-55; fax 2-99-14-12-85; internet www.uhb.fr/scd; Librarian E. LEMAU.

Rouen

Bibliothèque Municipale: 3 rue Jacques-Villon, 76043 Rouen Cedex 1; tel. 2-35-71-28-82; fax 2-35-70-01-56; e-mail bibliotheque@ rouen.fr; f. 1791; 500,000 vols incl. 600 incunabula, 6,000 MSS; Chief Librarian F. LEGENDRE.

Bibliothèque de l'Université de Rouen: Anneau central, rue Lavoisier, 76821 Mont-Saint-Aignan Cedex; tel. 2-35-14-81-75; fax 2-35-76-93-77; internet www.univ-rouen.fr; 400,000 vols; Dir YANNICK VALIN.

St-Etienne

Bibliothèque de l'Université Jean-Monnet: 1 rue Tréfilerie, 42023 St-Etienne Cedex 2; tel. 4-77-42-16-99; fax 4-77-42-16-20; e-mail achard@univ-st-etienne.fr; internet www.univ-st-etienne.fr/scdoc; Dir MARIE-CLAUDE ACHARD.

Strasbourg

Bibliothèque Nationale et Universitaire de Strasbourg: 5 rue du Maréchal Joffre, BP 51029, 67070 Strasbourg Cedex; tel. 3-88-25-28-00; fax 3-88-25-28-03; e-mail contact@ bnu.fr; internet www.bnu.fr; f. 1871; 3.5m. vols; books, newspapers, reviews, MSS; Admin. ALBERT POIROT.

Toulon

Bibliothèque de l'Université de Toulon et du Var: BP 10122, 83957 La Garde Cedex; tel. 4-94-14-23-26; fax 4-94-14-21-38; e-mail scd@univ-tln.fr; internet bu.univ-tln.fr; f. 1971; general library; Dir J. KERIGUY.

Toulouse

Bibliothèque de Toulouse: 1 rue de Périgord, BP 7092, 31070 Toulouse Cedex 7; tel. 5-61-22-21-78; fax 5-61-22-34-30; internet www.bibliothequedetoulouse.fr; f. 1782; 20 brs; 914,000 vols, 3,700 periodicals; Chief Librarian PIERRE JULLIEN (acting).

Bibliothèque Universitaire de l'Arsenal (Toulouse 1): 11 rue des Puits-Creusés, BP 7093, 31070 Toulouse Cedex 7; tel. 5-34-45-61-11; fax 5-34-45-61-30; internet www .univ-tlse1.fr/scd; f. 1879; 900,000 vols; spec.

collns: Fonds Pifteau (books printed in Toulouse, books on regional history and geography), Fonds Chabaneau (18th-century books), Fonds Liguge (Spanish history), Fonds Claude Perroud (French Revolution), Fonds Montauban (History of Protestantism); Dir Marcel Marty; Chief Librarian M. van Dooren.

Tours

Bibliothèque Municipale: 2 bis, ave André Malraux, 37042 Tours Cedex; tel. 2-47-05-47-33; fax 2-47-31-07-33; e-mail contact@bm-tours.fr; internet www.bm-tours.fr; f. 1791; original library destroyed in 1940; 142 mems; 552,000 vols, 3,400 periodicals, 1,632 MSS; Dir Régis Rech.

Service Commun de la Documentation de l'Université de Tours: 5 rue des Tanneurs, 37041 Tours Cedex (Letters); tel. 2-47-36-64-86; fax 2-47-36-67-99 Parc de Grandmont, 37200 Tours (Sciences and Pharmacy); 2 bis blvd Tonnellé, 37032 Tours Cedex (Medicine); 50 ave Portalis, 37206 Tours Cedex 3 (Law); tel. 2-47-36-11-24 6 place Jean-Jaurès, 41000 Blois (Blois section); internet www.scd.univ-tours.fr; Dir Gil-François Euvrard.

Troyes

Médiathèque de l'Agglomération Troyenne: 7 rue des Filles-Dieu, BP 602, 10088 Troyes Cedex; tel. 3-25-43-56-20; fax 3-25-43-56-21; e-mail contact@mediatheque-agglo-troyes.fr; internet www.mediatheque-agglo-troyes.fr; f. 1651; 400,000 vols; Librarian Thierry Delcourt.

Valence

Médiathèque Publique et Universitaire: Place Charles Huguenel, 26000 Valence; tel. 4-75-79-23-70; fax 4-75-79-23-82; e-mail medieval@wanadoo.fr; internet sicd2.upmf-grenoble.fr/bu/valence; f. 1775; 100,000 vols, 650 periodicals; Librarian Johann Berti.

Valenciennes

Bibliothèque Municipale: 2–6 rue Ferrand, BP 282, 59300 Valenciennes Cedex; tel. 3-27-22-57-00; fax 3-27-22-57-01; e-mail mpdion@ville-valenciennes.fr; internet www.valenciennes.fr; f. 1598; 400,000 vols, also incl. 80,000 prints, photographs, maps; Dir Marie-Pierre Dion-Turkovics.

Vandoeuvre-lès-Nancy

Institut de l'Information Scientifique et Technique (INIST-CNRS): 2 allée du Parc de Brabois, 54514 Vandoeuvre-lès-Nancy Cedex; tel. 3-83-50-46-00; fax 3-83-50-46-50; e-mail infoclient@inist.fr; internet www.inist.fr; f. 1988; collects, processes and distributes international research findings; produces two databases: PASCAL (Sciences, Technology, Medicine) and FRANCIS (Humanities, Social Sciences, Economics); 10,000 vols, 26,000 serial titles, 60,000 scientific reports, 62,000 conference proceedings, 110,000 doctoral theses; Dir-Gen. Raymond Duval.

Versailles

Bibliothèque Municipale: 5 rue de l'Indépendance Américaine, 78000 Versailles; tel. 1-39-07-13-20; fax 1-39-07-13-22; e-mail bibliotheque@versailles.fr; internet www.bibliotheques.versailles.fr/statique; f. 1803; 800,000 vols, 900 periodicals; Chief Librarian Marie-Françoise Rose.

Museums and Art Galleries

Agen

Musée des Beaux-Arts: Place du Docteur Esquirol, 47916 Agen Cedex 9; tel. 5-53-69-47-23; fax 5-53-69-47-77; e-mail musee@ville-agen.fr; internet www.ville-agen.fr/musee; f. 1876; local, Roman and medieval archaeology; paintings by Corneille de Lyon, de Troy, Drouais, Nattier, Goya, the Impressionists, Roger Bissière and François-Xavier Lalanne; ceramics; Chinese art; Curator Marie-Dominique Nivière.

Aix-en-Provence

Musée Granet: Place Saint Jean de Malte, 13100 Aix-en-Provence; tel. 4-42-52-88-32; fax 4-42-26-84-55; internet www.museegranet-aixenprovence.fr; f. 1765; Egyptian, Greek, Celto-Ligurian, Roman and Gallo-Roman archaeology; pictures of Cézanne and the French Schools, with special emphasis on Provence; Italian, Spanish, Flemish, Dutch and German Schools; modern painting; sculpture; furniture of 16th, 17th and 18th centuries; Curator Denis Coutagne.

Alençon

Musée des Beaux-Arts et de la Dentelle: Cour Carrée de la Dentelle, 61000 Alençon; tel. 2-33-32-40-07; fax 2-33-26-51-66; e-mail musee@mairie-calais.fr; internet www.musee.calais.fr; f. 1857; French, Dutch and Flemish paintings from 17th–19th centuries; French, Italian and Dutch drawings from 16th–19th centuries; French, Flemish, Italian and Eastern European lace since 16th century; French and British prints from 16th–19th centuries; ethnological items from Cambodia; Curator Aude Pessey-Lux.

Amboise

Musée de l'Hôtel de Ville: rue François I, BP 247, 37402 Amboise; tel. 2-47-23-47-42; fax 2-47-23-19-80; colln incl. tapestries, statues and paintings relating to the history of Amboise; Curator Agathe Guenand.

Amiens

Musée de Picardie: 48 rue de la République, 80000 Amiens; tel. 3-22-97-14-00; fax 3-22-97-14-26; e-mail musees-amiens@amiens-metropole.com; internet w2.amiens.com/museedepicardie; f. 1854; fine colln of paintings of Northern and French Schools; murals by Puvis de Chavannes and Sol Le Witt; Egyptian, Greek and Roman antiquities; prehistoric, Iron and Bronze age collns; objets d'art of Middle Ages and Renaissance; 19th-century sculpture; 20th-century paintings; Chief Curator Sabine Cazenave.

Angers

Musée des Beaux-Arts: 14 rue du Musée, 49100 Angers; tel. 2-41-05-38-00; fax 2-41-86-06-38; e-mail musees@ville.angers.fr; internet www.angers.fr/mba; f. 1797; housed in 15th-century 'logis Barrault'; paintings of 18th-century French School and 17th-century Dutch and Flemish Schools; sculpture, including busts by Houdon; Dir Patrick Le Nouëne.

Affiliated Museums:

Galerie David d'Angers: 33 bis rue Toussaint, 49100 Angers; tel. 2-41-05-38-90; fax 2-41-05-38-09; e-mail musees@ville.angers.fr; internet www.angers.fr/musees; f. 1984; sited in restored gothic church; almost all the sculptor's work; Dir and Curator Patrick Le Nouëne.

Musée Jean Lurçat et de la Tapisserie Contemporaine: 4 blvd Arago, 49100 Angers; tel. 2-41-24-18-45 (Musée Jean Lurçat); tel. 2-41-24-18-48 (Musée de la Tapisserie Contemporaine); fax 2-41-86-06-38; occupies 12th-century Hôpital Saint-Jean; paintings of Jean Lurçat and tapestry.

Musée Pincé: 32 bis rue Lenepveu, 49100 Angers; tel. 2-41-88-94-27; fax 2-41-86-06-38; f. 1889; Greek, Roman, Etruscan and Egyptian antiquities; Chinese and Japanese art.

Antibes

Musée Picasso: Château Grimaldi, 06600 Antibes; tel. 4-92-90-54-20; fax 4-92-90-54-21; e-mail musee.picasso@ville-antibes.fr; internet www.antibes-juanlespins.com/fr/culture; f. 1948; 230 works by Picasso; collection of modern and contemporary art: Atlan, Miró, Calder, Richier, Ernst, Hartung and others; Nicolas de Staël room with works from Antibes period; sculpture garden; Dir Maurice Fréchuret; publ. catalogues.

Arras

Musée des Beaux-Arts d'Arras: Ancienne Abbaye Saint-Vaast, 22 rue Paul Doumer, 62000 Arras; tel. 3-21-71-26-43; fax 3-21-23-19-26; e-mail musee.arras@ville-arras.fr; internet www.musenor.com/gm/gmarras.htm; f. 1825; medieval sculpture, 17th- and 19th-century paintings, porcelain, Gallo-Roman archaeology; Chief Curator Stephanie Deschamps.

Arromanches

Exposition Permanente du Débarquement (Permanent Exhibition of the Landings): Place du 6 Juin, 14117 Arromanches; tel. 2-31-22-34-31; fax 2-31-92-68-83; e-mail info.arromanches@normandy1944.com; internet www.normandy1944.com; f. 1954; exhibition of the Normandy landings of D-Day, 6th June 1944; comprises artificial port and museum of relief maps, working models, photographs, diorama and films.

Avignon

Musée Calvet: 65 rue Joseph Vernet, 84000 Avignon; tel. 4-90-86-33-84; fax 4-90-14-62-45; e-mail musee.calvet@wanadoo.fr; internet www.musee-calvet-avignon.com; f. 1810; fine art since 16th century; Dir Sylvain Boyer; Curator for Archaeology Odile Cavalier.

Musée Lapidaire: 27 rue de la République, 84000 Avignon; tel. 4-90-85-75-38; internet www.avignon.fr/fr/culture/musees/lapidaire.php; f. 1933; ancient Egyptian, Greek and Gallo-Roman sculpture; Curator Odile Cavalier.

Musée du Petit Palais: Place du Palais des papes, 84000 Avignon; tel. 4-90-86-44-58; fax 4-90-82-18-72; internet www.avignon.fr/fr/culture/musees/petipal.php; f. 1976; in the old archbishop's palace (14th–15th century); medieval and Renaissance paintings of the Avignon and Italian Schools, medieval sculpture from Avignon; Curator Dominique Vingtain.

Bayonne

Musée Basque et de l'histoire Bayonne: 37 quai des Corsaires, 64100 Bayonne; tel. 5-59-59-08-98; fax 5-59-25-73-38; internet www.musee-basque.com; f. 1922; 4 sections covering the history and folklore of the town of Bayonne, the French Basque country, the Spanish Basque country, and the Basques in the New World; library of 30,000 vols; Dir Rafael Zulaika; Curator Olivier Ribeton; publ. *Bulletin* (2 a year).

Besançon

Musée des Beaux-Arts et d'Archéologie: 1 place de la Révolution–place du Marché, 25000 Besançon; tel. 3-81-87-80-49; fax 3-81-80-06-53; e-mail musee-beaux-arts-archeologie@besancon.fr; internet www.musee-arts-besancon.org; f. 1694, moved to present bldgs 1843; Danish (pre- and protohistoric), Egyptian, Greek, Etruscan and Roman antiquities; regional (pre- and protohistoric, Gallo-Roman, early medieval) antiquities; medieval objets d'art; 15th- to 20th-centuries European paintings (especially French 18th–19th century), sculpture, ceramics and objets d'art; 15th- to 20th-centuries drawings in temporary exhibitions; Curators F. SOULIER-FRANÇOIS, P. LAGRANGE, F. THOMAS-MAURIN.

Biot

Musée National Fernand Léger: Chemin du Val de Pome, 06410 Biot; tel. 4-92-91-50-30; fax 4-92-91-50-31; internet www.musee-fernandleger.fr; permanent exhibition of paintings, drawings, ceramics.

Blérancourt

Musée National de la Coopération Franco-Américaine: Château de Blérancourt, 33 place du Général Leclerc, 02300 Blérancourt; tel. 3-23-39-60-16; fax 3-23-39-62-85; e-mail musee.blerancourt@culture.gouv.fr; internet www.museefrancoamericain.fr; f. 1924 to contain collections presented to the State by Mrs Anna Murray Dike, Miss Anne Morgan, and other French and American benefactors, relating to the history of Franco-American relations; the castle, formerly the ancestral home of the Ducs de Gesvres, is classed as an historical monument; library of 3,500 vols; Curator PHILIPPE GRUNCHEC.

Bordeaux

Musée d'Aquitaine: 20 cours Pasteur, 33000 Bordeaux; tel. 5-56-01-51-00; fax 5-56-44-24-36; e-mail musaq@mairie-bordeaux.fr; internet www.mairie-bordeaux.fr; f. 1987; regional prehistory, history and ethnology; ethnographical collection of pieces from Africa and Oceania; library of 20,000 vols; Curator HÉLÈNE LAFONT-COUTURIER.

Musée d'Art Contemporain de Bordeaux: Entrepôt Lainé, 7 rue Ferrère, 33000 Bordeaux; tel. 5-56-00-81-50; fax 5-56-44-12-07; e-mail capc@mairie-bordeaux.fr; internet www.mairie-bordeaux.fr/musees/capc/capc.htm; f. 1984 by 'Capc' asscn (f. 1974), financed by Direction des Musées de France and Bordeaux town; temporary exhibitions; permanent colln; photos, slides, video cassettes; education service for schools; library of 25,000 vols, mostly catalogues; publs *Calendrier* (5 a year), *Catalogue* (4 a year).

Musée des Beaux-Arts: Jardin de la Mairie, 20 cours d'Albret, 33000 Bordeaux; tel. 5-56-10-20-56; fax 5-56-10-25-13; e-mail musbxa@mairie-bordeaux.fr; internet www.culture.fr/culture/bordeaux; f. 1801; 2,300 paintings, 504 sculptures, 2,370 drawings; Curator FRANÇOISE GARCIA.

Caen

Musée de Normandie: Château de Caen, 14000 Caen; tel. 2-31-30-47-60; fax 2-31-30-47-69; e-mail mdn@ville-caen.fr; internet www.musee-de-normandie.caen.fr; f. 1946; history, archaeology and ethnology of Normandy; Dir J.-Y. MARIN; publs *Annales de Normandie* (4 a year), *Publications* (irregular).

Carnac

Musée de Préhistoire: 10 pl. de la Chapelle, 56340 Carnac; tel. 2-97-52-22-04; fax 2-97-52-64-04; e-mail contact@museedecarnac.fr; internet www.museedecarnac.com; municipal museum; f. 1881; local prehistory and archaeology; most important museum in the world for collns from megalithic period; research library; photographic archive (3,000 items); Dir ANNE-ELISABETH RISKINE.

Chantilly

Musée et Château de Chantilly (Musée Condé): Château de Chantilly, 60500 Chantilly; tel. 3-44-27-31-80; fax 3-44-54-90-73; e-mail daniele.clergeot@fondationdechantilly.org; internet www.chateaudechantilly.com; f. 1898; paintings, miniatures, furniture, drawings, 70,000 books, 3,000 MSS, etc.; Curator OLIVIER BOSC; publ. *Le Musée Condé* (1 a year).

Compiègne

Musée National du Château de Compiègne: 60200 Compiègne; tel. 3-44-38-47-02; fax 3-44-38-47-01; e-mail chateau.compiegne@culture.gouv.fr; internet www.musee-chateau-compiegne.fr; royal palace of the first kings of France, reconstructed under Louis XV and Louis XVI and partly redecorated under the 1st Empire; furniture of 18th and 19th centuries, mostly 1st Empire period; tapestries of 18th century; collns from the 2nd Empire period; souvenirs of the Empress Eugénie; Chief Curator EMMANUEL STARCKY.

Affiliated Museum:

Musée National de la Voiture et du Tourisme: Château de Compiègne, 60200 Compiègne; tel. 3-44-38-47-00; fax 3-44-38-47-01; e-mail chateau.compiegne@culture.gouv.fr; internet www.musee-chateau-compiegne.fr; f. 1927 with the cooperation of the Touring Club de France; old carriages, sedan chairs, survey of devt of the bicycle and the automobile; 180 vehicles; Chief Curator JACQUES PEROT.

Dijon

Musée des Beaux-Arts: Palais des Etats, Cour de Bar, 21000 Dijon; tel. 3-80-74-52-70; fax 3-80-74-53-44; e-mail museedesbeauxarts@ville-dijon.fr; internet www.ville-dijon.fr; f. 1787 and housed in the Palace of the Dukes of Burgundy and the Palace of the States of Burgundy; Swiss primitives; paintings of Franco-Flemish School of 15th century and of other French and foreign schools; prints and drawings; sculptures from tombs of the Dukes of Burgundy; marble, ivory, armour; modern art; Granville colln; Chief Curator EMMANUEL STARCKY.

Musée Magnin: 4 rue des Bons-Enfants, 21000 Dijon; tel. 3-80-67-11-10; fax 3-80-66-43-75; internet www.musee-magnin.fr; Italian and French paintings from 16th–19th centuries; Curator RÉMI CARIEL.

Fontainebleau

Musée National du Château de Fontainebleau: 77300 Château de Fontainebleau; tel. 1-60-71-50-70; fax 1-60-71-50-71; e-mail contact.chateau-de-fontainebleau@culture.fr; internet www.musee-chateau-fontainebleau.fr; bldgs from 12th–19th centuries; paintings, interior decoration and furniture of the Renaissance, 17th and 18th centuries, 1st and 2nd Empires and 19th century; Dir BERNARD NOTARI.

Giverny

Claude Monet Foundation: 84 rue Claude Monet, 27620 Giverny; tel. 2-32-51-28-21; fax 2-32-51-54-18; e-mail contact@fondation-monet.com; internet www.fondation-monet.com; f. 1980 after restoration; consists of Monet's house and garden where he lived from 1883 to 1926; it was left by his son in 1966 to the Académie des Beaux-Arts; the house contains Monet's collection of Japanese engravings; Curator GERALD VAN DER KEMP; Sec.-Gen. Mme C. LINDSEY.

Grenoble

Musée de Grenoble: 5 pl. Lavalette, BP 326, 38010 Grenoble Cedex 01; tel. 4-76-63-44-44; fax 4-76-63-44-10; internet www.museedegrenoble.fr; f. 1796; art and antiquities; library of 50,000 vols; Dir GUY TOSATTO.

Langeais

Château de Langeais: 37130 Langeais; tel. 2-47-96-72-60; fax 2-47-96-54-44; e-mail contact@chateau-de-langeais.com; internet www.chateau-de-langeais.com; built in 15th century by Louis XI, given to the Institut de France in 1904; furniture and tapestries from the 13th–15th centuries and 15th-century architecture; Admin. SANDRINE DURAND.

Le Havre

Musée des Beaux-Arts 'André Malraux': Blvd J. F. Kennedy, 76600 Le Havre; tel. 2-35-19-62-62; fax 2-35-19-93-01; internet www.ville-lehavre.fr; f. 1845; permanent colln from 14th to 20th century (Boudin, Impressionists, Dufy); Dir ANNETTE HAUDIQUET.

Affiliated Museums:

Espace Maritime et Portuaire du Havre: Quai Frissard, 76600 Le Havre; tel. 2-35-24-51-00; fax 2-35-26-76-69; e-mail musées.histoire@city lehavre.fr; internet www.ville-lehavre.fr; Le Havre maritime and port history since 1830; Dir C. MAUBANT.

Musée de l'Hôtel Dubocage de Bléville: Rue Jérôme Bellarmato, 76600 Le Havre; tel. 2-35-42-27-90; fax 2-35-26-76-69; e-mail musees.histoire@ville-lehavre.fr; internet www.musees-haute-normandie.fr; f. 2010 fmrly Musée de l'Ancien Havre; drawings and documents on the history of Le Havre from 1517 to the present; reserves colln; Dir ELISABETH LEPRÊTRE.

Musée du Prieuré de Graville: Rue Elisée Reclus, 76600 Le Havre; tel. 2-35-24-51-00; fax 2-35-26-76-69; e-mail musees.histoire@ville-lehavre.fr; internet www.ville-lehavre.fr; f. 1926; sculpture from the 12th to 18th century; models of old houses; Dir ELIZABETH LEPRÊTRE.

Le Mans

Musée Automobile de la Sarthe: Circuit des 24 Heures du Mans, BP 29254, 72009 Le Mans Cedex 1; tel. 2-43-72-72-24; fax 2-43-85-38-96; e-mail musee.automobile.lemans@wanadoo.fr; internet www.sarthe.com/sport/museeauto.htm; f. 1961; cars, cycles and motorcycles; Dir FRANCIS PIQUERA.

Musée de la Reine Bérengère: 9–13 rue de la Reine Bérengère, 72000 Le Mans; tel. 2-43-47-38-51; fax 2-43-47-49-93; e-mail musees@ville-lemans.fr; 16th-century architecture, folklore, ceramics, local history; Curator FRANÇOISE CHASERANT.

Musée de Tessé: 2 ave de Paderborn, 72000 Le Mans; tel. 2-43-47-38-51; fax 2-43-47-49-93; fine arts, paintings and sculpture, archaeology, Egyptology; Curator FRANÇOISE CHASERANT.

Les Eyzies de Tayac

Musée National de Préhistoire: 1 rue du Musee, BP 7, 24620 Les Eyzies de Tayac; tel. (5) 53-06-45-45; fax (5) 53-06-45-55; e-mail reservation.prehistorie@culture.gouv.fr; internet www.musee-prehistoire-eyzies.fr; f. 2004; 18,000 exhibited objects, incl. prehistoric carvings; permanent exhibitions on human evolution and the prehistoric people of the Périgord region; Dir JEAN-JACQUES CLEYET-MERLE.

Lille

Musée des Beaux-Arts: 18 bis rue de Valmy, 59000 Lille; tel. 3-20-06-78-00; fax 3-20-06-78-15; e-mail cvilliers@mairie-lille.fr; internet www.pba-lille.fr; f. 1801; paintings of Flemish, Italian, Spanish, German, French and Dutch Schools; exceptional colln of drawings; sculpture, ceramics and archaeological exhibits; Chief Curator ALAIN TAPIÉ.

Limoges

Musée Municipal de l'Evêché: Place de la Cathédrale, 87000 Limoges; tel. 5-55-45-98-10; fax 5-55-34-44-14; e-mail museveche@ville-limoges.fr; internet www.ville-limoges.fr; f. 1912; paintings, drawings, engravings, sculptures, Limoges enamels, metalwork; Egyptian colln; archaeological and lapidary colln; enamels research centre; library of 7,000 vols; Curator VÉRONIQUE NOTIN.

Musée National Adrien Dubouché: Place Winston Churchill, 87000 Limoges; tel. 5-55-33-08-50; fax 5-55-33-08-55; e-mail contact.musee-adriendubouche@culture.gouv.fr; internet www.musee-adriendubouche.fr; f. 1900; ceramics and glass; Curator CHANTAL MESLIN-PERRIER.

Lyons

Musée des Beaux-Arts: 20 place des Terreaux, 69001 Lyons; tel. 4-72-10-17-40; fax 4-78-28-12-45; internet www.mba-lyon.fr; f. 1801 and housed in the former Benedictine Abbey of the Dames de Saint-Pierre, built in 1659; the important collection contains paintings of French, Flemish, Dutch, Italian and Spanish Schools, and sections devoted to local painters, modern art, and murals by Puvis de Chavannes; ancient, medieval and modern sculpture; French, Italian, Oriental and Hispano-Moorish ceramics; drawings, prints, furniture, numismatic collection; Egyptian, Greek, Roman and Near and Middle Eastern antiquities; library of 50,000 vols; Chief Curator SYLVIE RAMOND; publs *Cahiers du Musée des Beaux-Arts de Lyon* (1 a year), illustrated guides.

Magny-les-Hameaux

Musée National de Port-Royal: Route des Granges, 78114 Magny-les-Hameaux; tel. 1-39-30-72-72; fax 1-30-64-79-55; e-mail musee.port-royal@culture.gouv.fr; internet www.port-royal-des-champs.eu; f. 1952; history of Port-Royal and Jansenism; ruins of the Abbey of Port-Royale; presented in the house of 'Petites Ecoles' where Racine studied; Curator PHILIPPE LUEZ.

Maisons-Laffitte

Château de Maisons-Laffitte: 78600 Maisons-Laffitte; tel. 1-39-62-01-49; fax 1-39-12-34-37; internet www.maisonslaffitte.net; château dates from 1642; contains paintings, sculptures, tapestries; Curator FLORENCE DE LA RONCIÈRE.

Marseilles

Musée d'Archéologie Méditerranéenne: 2 rue de la Charité, 13002 Marseilles; tel. 4-91-14-58-80; fax 4-91-14-58-81; internet www.mairie-marseille.fr/vivre/culture/musees/archeo.htm; f. 1863; Egyptian, Greek, Cypriot, Celto-Ligurian, Etruscan, Roman and Gallo-Roman antiquities; library of

4,500 vols; Curators ANNIE PHILIPPON, BRIGITTE LESCURE.

Affiliated Museum:

Musée des Docks Romains: 28 place Vivaux, 13002 Marseilles; tel. 4-91-91-24-62; internet www.culture.gouv.fr/culture/archeosm/fr/fr-act-mus4.htm; f. 1963; ancient commerce; exhibits include amphorae, ingots and marine archaeology; Curator AGNÈS DURAND.

Musée des Beaux-Arts: Palais Longchamp, Aile Gauche, 7 rue Edouard Stephan, 13004 Marseilles; tel. 4-91-14-59-30; fax 4-91-14-59-31; e-mail dgac-musee-beauxarts@mairie-marseille.fr; internet www.mairie-marseille.fr/vivre/culture/musees/boart.htm; f. 1802; paintings (French, Italian, Flemish and German schools); murals by French artists, including Courbet, Corot, Daubigny, Millet, Daumier and Puvis de Chavannes; collection of paintings and sculptures by Puget; sculptures by Daumier and Rodin; Curator MARIE-PAULE VIAL.

Musée Cantini: 19 rue Grignan, 13006 Marseilles; tel. 4-91-54-77-75; fax 4-91-55-03-61; internet www.mairie-marseille.fr/vivre/culture/musees/cantini.htm; f. 1936; modern art (1900–60); library of 20,000 vols on 20th-century art; Curators NICOLAS CENDO, OLIVIER COUSINOU.

Musée de la Marine et de l'Economie de Marseille: Chambre de Commerce et d'Industrie Marseille-Provence, Palais de la Bourse, La Canebière, BP 21856, 13221 Marseilles Cedex 1; tel. 4-91-39-33-21; fax 4-91-39-56-15; e-mail patrick.boulanger@ccimp.com; internet www.ccimp.com/patrimoine; f. 1932; history of Marseilles and Mediterranean shipping; models of ships, paintings, drawings, plans; 25,000 tape recordings; Nossof, Cantelar and Grimard collns (history of steam ships); Archivist, Chief of Cultural Heritage Dept PATRICK BOULANGER.

Metz

Metz, Musées de La Cour d'Or: 2 rue du Haut Poirier, 57000 Metz; tel. 3-87-68-25-00; fax 3-87-36-51-14; e-mail musees@ca2m.com; internet www.mairie-metz.fr:8080; f. 1839; prehistory, protohistory, arts and popular traditions of northern Lorraine, and natural history collections (not open to public); architecture; fine arts (since 15th century); archaeology and history; military collns (not open to public); library of 5,000 vols, 100 periodicals; Dir CLAUDE VALENTIN.

Montpellier

Musée Atger: Faculté de Médecine, 2 rue de l'Ecole de Médecine, 34000 Montpellier; tel. 4-67-41-76-30; fax 4-67-41-76-39; internet www.biu-montpellier.fr; f. 1813; drawings and paintings of French, Italian and Flemish schools, 16th–18th centuries (Fragonard, Natoire, Tiepolo); Curator H. LORBLANCHET.

Musée Fabre: 13 rue Montpelliéret, 34000 Montpellier; tel. 4-67-14-83-00; fax 4-67-66-09-20; e-mail musee.fabre@montpellier-agglo.com; internet museefabre.montpellier-agglo.com; f. 1825 by the painter François-Xavier Fabre; paintings of French (Greuze, Delacroix, Courbet, Bazille, Géricault), Italian, Spanish, Dutch and Flemish Schools; drawings, sculpture (Houdon), furniture, tapestries, porcelain, silver; Dir MICHEL HILAIRE.

Mulhouse

Cité de l'Automobile–Musée National, Collection Schlumpf: 192 ave de Colmar, BP 1096, 68051 Mulhouse; tel. 3-89-33-23-23; fax 3-89-32-08-09; internet www.collection-schlumpf.com/schlumpf; f. 1982; history of the motor car since 1878; 424

vehicles on display, incl. an important colln of Bugattis; library of 4,500 vols; Dir EMANUEL BACQUET.

Musée de l'Impression sur Etoffes: 14 rue Jean-Jacques Henner, BP 1468, 68072 Mulhouse; tel. 3-89-46-83-00; fax 3-89-46-83-10; e-mail accueil@musee-impression.com; internet www.musee-impression.com; f. 1955; 18th–20th century printed textiles; Curator JAQUELINE JACQUÉ; publ. *L'Imprimé* (2 a year).

Nancray

Musée de Plein Air des Maisons Comtoises: 25360 Nancray; tel. 3-81-55-29-77; fax 3-81-55-23-97; e-mail musee@maisons-comtoises.org; internet www.maisons-comtoises.org; f. 1984; folklore of Franche-Comté; 60,000 illustrations of rural architecture; Dir CATHERINE LOUVRIER; publs *Barbizier, Revue Régionale d'Ethnologie Comtoise* (1 a year).

Nancy

Musée des Beaux-Arts: Place Stanislas, 54000 Nancy; tel. 3-83-85-30-72; fax 3-83-85-30-76; e-mail mbanancy@mairie-nancy.fr; internet www.mairie-nancy.fr; f. 1793; paintings, sculpture, drawings, prints and glass from 15th–20th century; temporary exhibitions; Curator BLANDINE CHAVANNE.

Nantes

Musée des Beaux-Arts: 10 rue Georges-Clemenceau, 44000 Nantes; tel. 2-51-17-45-00; fax 2-51-17-45-16; e-mail contact@nantes.fr; internet www.nantes.fr/culture/musees-nantais/musee-des-beaux-arts.html; f. 1800; 2,200 paintings; library of 10,000 vols; Curator JEAN AUBERT.

Nice

Direction des Musées de Nice: Palais Masséna, 65 rue de France, 06050 Nice Cedex 1; tel. 4-93-88-11-34; fax 4-93-82-39-79; f. 1935; Dir JEAN FRANÇOIS MOZZICONACCI.

Comprises:

Galerie de la Marine: 59 quai des Etats-Unis, 06300 Nice; tel. 4-93-62-37-11; Curator ANNE-MARIE VILLERI.

Galerie des Ponchettes: 77 quai des Etats-Unis, 06300 Nice; tel. 4-93-62-31-24; Curator ANNE-MARIE VILLERI.

Musée d'Archéologie: 160 Ave des Arènes de Cimiez, 06000 Nice; tel. 4-93-81-59-57; fax 4-93-81-08-00; f. 1989; Curator Mlle D. MOUCHOT.

Musée d'Art et d'Histoire: Palais Masséna, 65 rue de France, 06050 Nice Cedex 1; tel. 4-93-88-11-34; fax 4-93-82-39-79; f. 1921; art and history; Dir LUC THEVENON.

Musée d'Art Moderne et d'Art Contemporain: Promenade des Arts, 06300 Nice; tel. 4-93-62-61-62; fax 4-93-13-09-01; e-mail mamac@ville-nice.fr; internet www.mamac-nice.org; f. 1990; colln 'Nice à partir des années 60'; nouveaux réalistes, pop art, fluxus, colour field painting; Dir GILBERT PERLEIN.

Musée des Beaux-Arts: 33 ave des Baumettes, 06000 Nice; tel. 4-93-44-50-72; fax 4-93-97-67-07; internet www.musee-beaux-arts-nice.org; f. 1928; painting and sculpture 18th- and 19th-century, (Impressionists, Van Dongen); works of Jules Chéret; Dir BÉATRICE DEBRABANDÈRE-DESCAMPS.

Muséum d'Histoire Naturelle: 60 bis blvd Risso, 06300 Nice; tel. 4-97-13-46-80; fax 4-97-13-46-85; f. 1823; Curator ALAIN BIDAR.

Musée International d'Art Naïf Anatole Jakovsky: Château Ste Hélène-ave Val-Marie, 06200 Nice; tel. 4-93-71-78-33; fax 4-93-72-34-10; f. 1982; Dir ANNE DEV-ROYE-STILZ.

Musée Matisse: 164 ave des Arènes de Cimiez, 06000 Nice; tel. 4-93-81-08-08; fax 4-93-53-00-22; e-mail matisse@ nice-coteazur.org; internet www .musee-matisse-nice.org; f. 1963; collns of paintings and sculptures by Henri Matisse; Curator MARIE-THÉRÈSE PULVÉNIS DE SÉLIGNY.

Musée Naval: Tour Bellanda, Colline du Château, 06300 Nice; tel. 4-93-80-47-61; Curator JEAN WURSTHORN.

Musée de Paléontologie–Terra Amata: 25 blvd Carnot, 06300 Nice; tel. 4-93-55-59-93; fax 4-93-89-91-31; f. 1976; Curator Mme M. GOUDET.

Musée du Vieux-Logis: 59 ave Saint Barthélémy, 06100 Nice; tel. 4-93-84-44-74; f. 1937; medieval furniture and sculpture; Curator LUC THEVENON.

Palais Lascaris: 15 rue Droite, 06300 Nice; tel. 4-93-62-72-40; fax 4-93-92-04-19; f. 1970; 17th- and 18th-century frescoes, furniture and art; Curator CH. ASTRO.

Musée National Message Biblique Marc Chagall: Ave du Dr Ménard, 06000 Nice; tel. 4-93-53-87-20; fax 4-93-53-87-39; e-mail museecie@rmn.fr; internet www .musee-chagall.fr; f. 1973; permanent collection of the artist's biblical works; temporary exhibitions; library of 3,000 vols; Curator JEAN LACAMBRE.

Nîmes

Musée Archéologique: 13 blvd Amiral-Courbet, 30000 Nîmes; tel. 4-66-76-74-80; fax 4-66-76-74-94; internet musees.nimes.fr; f. 1823; protohistoric and Gallic and Roman archaeology; library of 6,000 vols; Curator DOMINIQUE DARDE.

Musée d'Art Contemporain: Carré d'Art, 16 pl. de la Maison Carree, 30000 Nîmes Cedex 1; tel. 4-66-76-35-70; fax 4-66-76-35-85; e-mail info@carreartmusee.com; internet carreartmusee.nimes.fr; f. 1993; Dir FRANÇOISE COHEN.

Musée d'Histoire Naturelle: 13 blvd Amiral-Courbet, 30033 Nîmes Cedex 9; tel. 4-66-76-73-45; fax 4-66-76-73-46; e-mail museum@ville-nimes.fr; internet musees .nimes.fr; f. 1892; library of 3,000 vols; Dir LUC GOMEL.

Musée du Vieux Nîmes: Place aux Herbes, 30000 Nîmes Cedex; tel. 4-66-76-73-70; fax 4-66-76-73-71; e-mail musee.vieux-nimes@ ville-nimes.fr; internet musees.nimes.fr; f. 1921; local history, folklore and traditional crafts; Curator MARTINE NOUGARÈDE.

Orléans

Musée des Beaux-Arts: 1 rue Fernand Rabier, 45000 Orléans; tel. 2-38-79-21-55; fax 2-38-79-20-08; e-mail vgalliot-rateau@ ville-orleans.fr; internet www.ville-orleans .fr; f. 1823; sculpture since 16th century; French, Flemish, Italian, Dutch, German and Spanish paintings and pastels (especially of 18th century); Max Jacob and Gaudier-Brzeska room; Curator and Dir ISABELLE KLINKA-BALLESTEROS.

Attached Museum:

Musée Historique et Archéologique de l'Orléanais: Hôtel Cabu, Place Abbé Desnoyers, 45000 Orléans; tel. (2) 38-79-21-55; fax (2) 38-79-20-08; e-mail vgalliot-rateau@ ville-orleans.fr; internet www.ville-orleans .fr; f. 1855; Gallo-Roman bronzes from Neuvy-en-Sullias; 17th- to 19th-century Orléans arts and crafts; the old port and

river traffic; glassware and ceramics; Curator ISABELLE KLINKA; Muséum Asst CATHERINE GORGET.

Paris

Centre des Monuments Nationaux (Monum): Hôtel Béthune-Sully, 62 rue Saint-Antoine, 75004 Paris; tel. 1-44-61-21-54; fax 1-44-61-20-36; e-mail courrier@ monuments-nat.fr; internet www.monum.fr; Dir CHRISTOPHE VALLET.

Cité des Sciences et de l'Industrie: 30 ave Corentin Cariou, 75930 Paris Cedex 19; tel. 1-40-05-70-00; fax 1-40-05-73-44; internet www.cite-sciences.fr; f. 1986; located in La Villette complex; permanent exhibitions: the universe, the earth, the environment, space, life, communication, etc.; multimedia public library (300,000 vols, 2,700 periodicals, 4,000 films, 1,300 educational software discs), history of science multimedia library, the Louis Braille room for the visually handicapped, Science Newsroom; Pres. GÉRARD THÉRY.

Galerie Nationale du Jeu de Paume: 1 place de la Concorde, 75008 Paris; tel. 1-47-03-12-50; fax 1-47-03-12-51; internet www .jeudepaume.org; re-f. 1991; devoted to temporary exhibitions of contemporary art; Dir DANIEL ABADIE.

Galeries Nationales du Panthéon Bouddhique: 19 ave d'Iéna, 75116 Paris; tel. 1-40-73-88-00; Chinese and Japanese art; Curator JEAN-FRANÇOIS JARRIGE.

Les Arts Décoratifs: 107 rue de Rivoli, 75001 Paris; tel. 1-44-55-57-50; fax 1-44-55-57-84; e-mail webmaster@lesartsdecoratifs .fr; internet www.lesartsdecoratifs.fr; f. 1864; library of 120,000 vols, 2,000 periodicals, 40,000 sale catalogues since 18th century; Pres. HÉLÈNE DAVID-WEILL; Gen. Man. SOPHIE DURRLEMAN; Dir of Museums BÉATRICE SALMON.

Affiliated Museums:

Musée des Arts Décoratifs: Les Arts Décoratifs, 107 rue de Rivoli, 75001 Paris; tel. 1-44-55-57-50; fax 1-44-55-57-84; e-mail webmaster@lesartsdecoratifs.fr; internet www.lesartsdecoratifs.fr; f. 1883; colln from Middle Ages to the present: woodwork, sculpture, tapestries, textiles, jewels, ceramics, furniture, painting, gold and silver work, glass; library of 100,000 vols, 1,500 periodicals; Dir BÉATRICE SALMON.

Musée de la Mode et du Textile: Les Arts Décoratifs, 107 rue de Rivoli, 75001 Paris; tel. 1-44-55-57-50; fax 1-44-55-57-84; e-mail webmaster@lesartsdecoratifs.fr; internet www.lesartsdecoratifs.fr; f. 1985; fashion, textiles and accessories; Dir BÉATRICE SALMON.

Musée Nissim de Camondo: Les Arts Décoratifs, 63 rue de Monceau, 75008 Paris; tel. 1-53-89-06-40; fax 1-53-89-06-42; e-mail webmaster@lesartsdecoratifs.fr; internet www.lesartsdecoratifs.fr; bequeathed by Count Moïse de Camondo, who collected unique 18th-century objects in his Hôtel Parc Monceau; Dir BÉATRICE SALMON; Chief Curator SYLVIE LEGRAND-ROSSI.

Musée de la Publicité: Les Arts Décoratifs, 107 rue de Rivoli, 75001 Paris; tel. 1-44-55-57-50; fax 1-44-55-57-84; e-mail webmaster@lesartsdecoratifs.fr; internet www.lesartsdecoratifs.fr; non-permanent exhibitions of posters, television, film and radio commercials; interactive multimedia library; Dir BÉATRICE SALMON.

Maison de Balzac: 47 rue Raynouard, 75016 Paris; tel. 1-55-74-41-80; fax 1-45-25-19-22; internet www.balzac.paris.fr; f. 1960; museum and library of 15,000 books and

periodicals; documents relating to life and work of Honoré de Balzac; first edns and autographed letters; comprehensive range of work from the romantic period; Curator YVES GAGNEUX.

Maison de Victor Hugo: 6 place des Vosges, 75004 Paris; tel. 1-42-72-10-16; fax 1-42-72-06-64; e-mail maisonsvictorhugo@ paris.fr; internet www.musee.hugo.paris.fr; f. 1903; personal belongings, correspondence, first editions, drawings by Victor Hugo; library of 10,000 vols, 6,000 pamphlets; Curator DANIELLE MOLINARI.

Musée Astronomique de l'Observatoire de Paris: 61 ave de l'Observatoire, 75014 Paris; f. 1667; astronomical instruments of the 16th, 17th, 18th and 19th centuries; statues and pictures of celebrated astronomers.

Musée Carnavalet—Histoire de Paris: 23 rue de Sévigné, 75003 Paris; tel. 1-44-59-58-58; fax 1-44-59-58-11; internet www .carnavalet.paris.fr; f. 1880; Paris and its history from prehistoric times; depts of archaeology, graphic arts, furniture, numismatics, painting, architectural models, sculpture; Chief Curator JEAN-MARC LÉRI.

Musée Cernuschi: 7 ave Vélasquez, 75008 Paris; tel. 1-53-96-21-50; fax 1-53-96-21-96; internet www.paris.fr/musees/cernuschi; f. 1896; Chinese art; Dir GILLES BÉGUIN.

Musée Cognacq-Jay: 8 rue Elzévir, 75003 Paris; tel. 1-40-27-07-21; fax 1-40-27-89-44; internet www.paris.fr/musees/cognacq_jay; f. 1929; 18th-century works of art, French and English paintings, pastels, sculptures, porcelain, furniture, etc.; Curator JOSE DE LOS LLANOS.

Musée d'Art Moderne de la Ville de Paris: 9 rue Gaston de Saint-Paul, 75116 Paris; located at: 11 ave du Président Wilson, 75116 Paris; tel. 1-53-67-40-00; fax 1-47-23-35-98; internet www.mam.paris.fr; f. 1961; modern and contemporary art; Curator FABRICE HERGOTT.

Musée de la Marine: Palais de Chaillot, 17 place du Trocadéro, 75116 Paris; tel. 1-53-65-69-69 ext. 120; fax 1-53-65-69-42; internet www.musee-marine.fr; f. 1827; colln of models and paintings of the navy; oceanographic research; library: 50,000 documents, 190,000 photographs; Dir Rear-Adm. GEORGES PRUD'HOMME; publs Neptunia (4 a year), catalogues.

Musée de la Monnaie: Monnaie de Paris, 11 quai de Conti, 75270 Paris Cedex 06; tel. 1-40-46-55-35; fax 1-40-46-57-09; e-mail musee@monnaiedeparis.fr; internet www .monnaiedeparis.fr; f. 1771; collections of coins, medals, drawings, paintings, old machines, engravings and stained glass windows; Dir BENOIT MONTARIOL.

Musée de l'Air et de l'Espace: BP 173, Aéroport du Bourget, 4 93352 Le Bourget Cedex; tel. 1-49-92-71-99; fax 1-49-92-70-95; internet www.mae.org; f. 1919; aeronautics, representative colln of aircraft; library of 40,000 vols; Dir-Gen. GERARD FELDZER; publ. Pégase (4 a year).

Musée de l'Armée: Hôtel des Invalides, 129 rue de Grenelle, 75007 Paris; tel. 1-44-42-38-77; fax 1-44-42-38-44; e-mail accueil-ma@ invalides.org; internet www.invalides.org; f. 1905; collections of artillery, arms, armour, uniforms, flags; history of French Army from its origin to present day; Napoleon's tomb; Second World War; library of 50,000 vols, 60,000 prints, 74,400 photographs; Dir B. DEVAUX; publ. Revue de la Société des Amis du Musée de l'Armée (2 a year).

Musée de l'Histoire de France: Centre historique des Archives nationales, 60 rue des Francs-Bourgeois, 75141 Paris Cedex 03;

tel. 1-40-27-60-96; fax 1-40-27-66-45; e-mail infomusee.archivesnationales@culture.gouv .fr; f. 1867; frequent exhibitions showing original documents from the Nat. Archives tracing the principal events in the history of France; also historical objects and iconography; Dir ISABELLE NEUSCHWANDER; Curator PIERRE FOURNIÉ.

Musée de l'Homme: Palais de Chaillot, place du Trocadéro, 75116 Paris; tel. 1-44-05-72-03; fax 1-44-05-72-12; e-mail bmhweb@ mnhn.fr; internet www.mnhn.fr/mnhn/bmh; f. 1878; library of 400,000 vols, 5,000 periodicals, 1,000 microfiches; ethnography, anthropology, prehistory; attached to the Muséum National d'Histoire Naturelle (*q.v.*); also a research and education centre; Profs BERNARD DUPAIGNE, ANDRÉ LANGANEY, HENRY DE LUMLEY.

Musée de l'Orangerie: Jardin des Tuileries, 75001 Paris; tel. 1-44-50-43-00; fax 1-44-50-43-30; e-mail musee.orangerie@culture .gouv.fr; internet www.musee-orangerie.fr; f. 1927; permanent exhibition of the 'Nymphéas' (Water Lilies) murals by Claude Monet, and Jean Walter et Paul Guillaume colln (Cézanne, Renoir, Rousseau, Picasso, Matisse, Derain, Modigliani, Soutine, Utrillo); Dir EMMANUEL BRÉON.

Musée d'Ennery: 59 ave Foch, 75116 Paris; tel. 1-45-53-57-96; fax 1-45-05-02-66; f. 1903; 17th- to 19th-century Far East decorative arts; closed for renovation; Curator JEAN-FRANÇOIS JARRIGE.

Musée des Arts et Métiers: 60 rue Réaumur, 75003 Paris; 292 rue St Martin, 75141 Paris Cedex 03; tel. 1-53-01-82-00; fax 1-53-01-82-01; e-mail musee@cnam.fr; internet www.arts-et-metiers.net; f. 1794; evolution of industrial technology from 16th century to the present; Dir DANIEL THOULOUZE.

Musée des Monuments Français: Palais de Chaillot, 1 place du Trocadéro, 75116 Paris; tel. 1-44-05-39-10; fax 1-47-55-40-13; internet www.citechaillot.fr/musee.php; f. 1882; casts of portions of monuments and sculptures from beginning of Christianity to 20th century; architectural models; library of 10,000 works on history of art, 200,000 photographs, colln of scale reproductions of murals of the Middle Ages and materials connected with building and decoration; Dir GUY COGEVAL; publ. *Guides*.

Musée des Plans-Reliefs: Hôtel National des Invalides, 75007 Paris; tel. 1-45-51-95-05; fax 1-47-05-11-07; internet www .museedesplansreliefs.culture.fr; f. 1668; Dir MAX POLONOVSKI.

Musée d'Histoire Contemporaine: Hôtel National des Invalides, 129 rue de Grenelle, 75007 Paris; tel. 1-44-42-42-44; fax 1-44-18-93-84; e-mail mhc@bdic.fr; internet www .bdic.fr/page.php?id_page=125; f. 1914; attached to Bibliothèque de Documentation Internationale Contemporaine (*q.v.*); 400,000 documents (paintings, engravings, posters, cartoons, etc.); 800,000 photographs and postcards; Curator LAURENT GERVEREAU.

Musée d'Orsay: 62 rue de Lille, 75343 Paris; tel. 1-40-49-48-00; fax 1-45-44-96-82; internet www.musee-orsay.fr; f. 1986; works from the second half of the 19th century and early 20th century: paintings and pastels, sculptures, art objects, photographs, also plans, sketches, etc.; audiovisual information, database, cultural service, exhibitions and dossier-exhibitions, cinema, lectures, concerts; Pres. SERGE LEMOINE.

Musée du Louvre: 75058 Paris Cedex 01; tel. 1-40-20-50-50; fax 1-40-20-54-42; e-mail info@louvre.fr; internet www.louvre.fr; f. 1793; Gen.-Dir HENRI LOYRETTE; depts and curators: Oriental Antiquities (ANNIE CAU-

BET), Egyptian Antiquities (CHRISTIANE ZIEGLER), Greek, Etruscan and Roman Antiquities (ALAIN PASQUIER), Islamic Art (FRANÇIS RICHARD), Sculpture (JEAN-RENÉ GABORIT), Objets d'art (DANIEL ALCOUFFE), Paintings (VINCENT POMAREDE), Drawings and Prints (FRANÇOISE VIATTE).

Musée du Luxembourg: 19 rue de Vaugirard, 75006 Paris; tel. 1-43-54-87-71; fax 1-43-25-20-33; e-mail info@museeduluxembourg .fr; internet www.museeduluxembourg.fr; f. 1750; hosts temporary exhibitions, according to a programme decided by the Min. of Culture and Communications and the Senate; Pres. of Senate CHRISTIAN PONCELET.

Musée du Petit Palais: 5 ave Dutuit, 75008 Paris; Ave Winston Churchill, 75008 Paris; tel. 1-53-43-40-00; fax 1-42-65-24-60; municipal museum, f. 1900; paintings, sculptures and works of art from antiquity to 1925; Dir Mlle THÉRÈSE BUROLLET.

Musée Galliera Musée de la Mode de la Ville de Paris: 10 ave Pierre Ier de Serbie, 75116 Paris; tel. 1-56-52-86-46; fax 1-47-23-38-37; e-mail bibliodoc.galliera@paris.fr; internet www.galliera.paris.fr; f. 1977; temporary exhibitions of French costumes and accessories from 1725 to the present day; library of 9,000 vols; Dir CATHERINE JOIN-DIETERLE; Librarian DOMINIQUE REVELLINO.

Musée Gustave Moreau: 14 rue de la Rochefoucauld, 75009 Paris; tel. 1-48-74-38-50; fax 1-48-74-18-71; e-mail info@ musee-moreau.fr; internet www .musee-moreau.fr; f. 1903 from a bequest by the painter Gustave Moreau of his house and contents, including paintings, watercolours, sketches, wax sculptures and designs; Curator GENEVIÈVE LACAMBRE.

Musée Jacquemart-André: 158 blvd Haussmann, 75008 Paris; tel. 1-45-62-11-59; fax 1-45-62-16-36; e-mail message@ musee-jacquemart-andre.com; internet www .musee-jacquemart-andre.com; f. 1912; painting, sculpture, ceramics, tapestry and furniture from Renaissance to 18th century; Dir ALAIN SCHIEDÉ.

Musée Marmottan: 2 rue Louis Boilly, 75016 Paris; tel. 1-44-96-50-33; fax 1-40-50-65-84; e-mail marmottan@marmottan.com; internet www.marmottan.com; f. 1932; Primitives, Renaissance, Empire and Impressionists; Wildenstein Colln of medieval miniatures; permanent exhibition 'Monet et ses Amis'; affiliated to the Académie des Beaux-Arts-Fondation Rouart; Dir JEAN-MARIE GRANIER.

Musée National d'Art Moderne: 75191 Paris Cedex 04; tel. 1-44-78-12-33; internet www.centrepompidou.fr; attached to Centre National d'Art et de Culture Georges-Pompidou; painting since beginning of 20th century, sculpture, architecture, design, new media, drawings, photographs, art films; Dir ALFRED PACQUEMENT.

Musée National de la Légion d'Honneur et des Ordres de Chevalerie: Hôtel de Salm, 2 rue de la Légion d'Honneur, 75007 Paris; tel. 1-40-62-84-25; e-mail musee.gclh@ free.fr; internet www.legiondhonneur.fr; f. 1925; contains histories of National Orders from the Middle Ages until the present and Awards of all countries: unique collection of decorations, costumes, arms, documents, etc.; also collection and documents relating to Napoleon I; Centre de Documentation International de l'Histoire des Ordres et des Décorations; Dir-Curator ANNE DE CHEFDEBIEN.

Musée National des Arts Asiatiques Guimet: 6 place d'Iéna, 75116 Paris; tel. 1-56-52-53-00; fax 1-56-52-53-54; internet www .guimet.fr; f. 1889; Asiatic Dept of Nat.

Museums; library of 100,000 vols; art, archaeology, religions, history and music of India, Central Asia, Tibet, Afghanistan, China, Korea and Japan, Khmer, Thailand and Indonesia; Chief Curator JACQUES GIES; Librarian FRANCIS MACOUIN; publs *Annales, Arts Asiatiques*.

Musée National des Arts d'Afrique et d'Océanie: 293 ave Daumesnil, 75012 Paris; tel. 1-44-74-84-80; f. 1931 as Musée des Colonies, 1935 Musée de la France d'Outre-Mer, present name 1960; exhibits from Maghreb, Africa and the Pacific Islands; tropical aquarium; temporary exhibitions; library: c. 5,000 vols, 160 periodicals; Dir GERMAIN VIATTE.

Musée National des Arts et Traditions Populaires: 6 ave du Mahatma Gandhi, 75116 Paris; tel. 1-44-17-60-00; fax 1-44-17-60-60; f. 1937; 142,000 objects; library: 90,000 books, 2,000 periodicals, 281,000 photographic documents, 70,000 tape records; Curator MICHEL COLARDELLE; publs *Architecture rurale française, Mobilier traditionnel français, Récits et contes populaires, Archives d'Ethnologie Française, Guides Ethnologiques, Catalogues des Expositions, Ethnologie française* (4 a year).

Musée National du Moyen Âge/Musée de Cluny: 6 pl. Paul Painlevé, 75005 Paris; tel. 1-53-73-78-00; fax 1-43-25-85-27; e-mail contact.musee-moyenage@culture.gouv.fr; internet www.musee-moyenage.fr; f. 1843; everyday life and fine and decorative arts of the Middle Ages; medieval art; sculptures, illuminated MSS, stained-glass panels, goldsmith work, furniture and tapestries; Lady and the Unicorn tapestries set; Dir ELISABETH DELAHAYE.

Musée Picasso: 5 rue de Thorigny, 75003 Paris; tel. 1-42-71-25-21; fax 1-48-04-75-46; internet www.musee-picasso.fr; f. 1985 from a colln begun in 1979; traces the evolution of Picasso's art; 251 paintings, 160 sculptures, 107 ceramics, 1,500 drawings and engravings; library: c. 2,000 vols on Picasso and his world; Dir ANNE BALDASSARI; Chief Curator GÉRARD RÉGNIER; publs catalogues, guides.

Musée Rodin: Hôtel Biron, 79 rue de Varenne, 75007 Paris; tel. 1-44-18-61-10; fax 1-45-51-17-52; internet www .musee-rodin.fr; f. 1919; sculpture and drawings by Rodin and objects from his collns; annexe in Meudon; Dir DOMINIQUE VIÉVILLE.

Muséum National d'Histoire Naturelle: see under State Colleges and Institutes.

Palais du Cinéma: Palais de Tokyo, 24 rue Hamelin, 75116 Paris; tel. 1-45-53-74-74; fax 1-45-53-74-76; exhibitions concerning motion pictures; motion picture theatres; library and film archive; Dir XAVIER NORTH.

Palais de la Découverte: Ave Franklin D. Roosevelt, 75008 Paris; tel. 1-56-43-20-21; fax 1-56-43-20-29; internet www .palais-decouverte.fr; f. 1937 as a scientific centre for the popularization of science; experiments explained to the public; depts of mathematics, astronomy, physics, chemistry, biology, medicine, earth sciences; also includes a Planetarium and cinema; library of 7,000 vols; Dir JACK GUICHARD; publs *Revue, Monographies*.

Pavillon de l'Arsenal: 21 blvd Morland, 75004 Paris; tel. 1-42-76-33-97; fax 1-42-76-26-32; internet www.pavillon-arsenal.com; f. 1988; information and documentation centre on urban planning and architecture; permanent exhibition on Paris; temporary exhibitions, photo library, educational facilities, etc.; Dir Mme DOMINIQUE ALBA; publ. catalogues.

Pavillon des Arts: Les Halles—Porte Rambuteau—Terrasse Lautréamont, 101 rue

Rambuteau, 75001 Paris; tel. 1-42-33-82-50; fax 1-40-28-93-22; f. 1983; municipal art gallery for temporary exhibitions; Dir BÉATRICE RIOTTOT EL-HABIB.

Musée de la Poste: 34 boulevard de Vaugirard, 75015 Amboise; tel. 1-42-79-24-24; fax 1-42-79-24-00; e-mail reservation.dnmp @ laposte.fr; f. 1971; colln incl. material on historic postal services and transport; Curator CHAPPE.

Pau

Musée Bernadotte: 8 rue Tran, 64000 Pau; tel. 5-59-27-48-42; internet musee.ville-pau .fr/infospratiques/liens/bernadotte; f. 1935; pictures and documents tracing the career of Jean Baptiste Bernadotte, Marshal under Napoleon, later King of Sweden; Swedish pictures; Curator PH. COMTE; publ. *Bulletin* (1 a year).

Musée des Beaux-Arts: rue Mathieu Lalanne, 64000 Pau; tel. 5-59-27-33-02; fax 5-59-98-70-10; e-mail museedesbeauxarts .pau@laposte.net; internet musee.ville-pau .fr; f. 1864; pictures from French, Flemish, Dutch, English, Italian and Spanish schools; contemporary artists; sculptures, engravings and drawings; numismatic collections; Curator GUILLAUME AMBROISE.

Musée National du Château de Pau: 64000 Pau; tel. 5-59-82-38-02; fax 5-59-82-38-18; e-mail olivier.pouvreau@culture.gouv .fr; internet www.musee-chateau-pau.fr; f. 1927; 16th- and 17th-century colln of tapestries; state apartments of Louis-Philippe I and Napoleon III; exhibition on the reign of King Henry IV; engravings, drawings; library and research facility (Centre Jacques de Laprade) for students of history, literature and history of art; Curator PAUL MIRONNEAU; publ. *Bulletin* (4 a year).

Musée Régional Béarnais: 64000 Pau; tel. 5-59-27-07-36; a colln relating to the Bearnese country.

Perpignan

Casa Pairal, Musée Catalan des Arts et Traditions Populaires: Mairie de Perpignan, BP 931, 66931 Perpignan Cedex; located at: Le Castillet, Place de Verdun, 66000 Perpignan; tel. 4-68-35-42-05; fax 4-68-66-32-80; internet www.mairie-perpignan .fr; f. 1963; ethnography, folklore and anthropology of the Catalan region; Curator JACQUES-GASPARD DELONCLE.

Poitiers

Conservation des Musées de Poitiers: 3 bis rue Jean-Jaurès, 86000 Poitiers; tel. 5-49-41-07-53; fax 5-49-88-61-63; e-mail musees .poitiers@alienor.org; internet www .musees-poitiers.org; f. 1794; library of 10,000 vols, 50 periodicals; Curators MICHEL REROLLE, MARIE-CHRISTINE PLANCHARD, MARYSE REDIEN, PHILIPPE BATA.

Attached Museums:

Baptistère Saint-Jean: Rue Jean-Jaurès, 86000 Poitiers; c/o Office de Tourisme de Poitiers, 45 pl. Charles De Gaulle, 86009 Poitiers; tel. 5-49-41-21-24; e-mail accueil@ot-poitiers.fr; internet www .ot-poitiers.fr; f. 1836; Merovingian archaeology.

Hypogée des Dunes: 101 rue du Père de la Croix, 86000 Poitiers; f. 1909; 7th–8th-century Merovingian archaeology.

Musée Rupert de Chièvres: 9 rue Victor Hugo, 86000 Poitiers; tel. 5-49-41-07-53; f. 1887; reconstruction of a 19th-century collector's private house; pre-1800 paintings, furniture, objets d'art.

Musée Sainte-Croix: 3 bis rue Jean-Jaurès, 86000 Poitiers; tel. 5-49-41-07-53;

f. 1974; fine arts, history of Poitou (archaeological, ethnographical collections, sculpture and paintings post 1800).

Reims

Musée des Beaux-Arts: 8 rue Chanzy, 51100 Reims; tel. 3-26-35-36-00; fax 3-26-86-87-75; e-mail sylvie.leibel@mairie-reims .fr; internet www.ville-reims.fr/fr/culture/ a-visiter/musee-des-beaux-arts; f. 1795; paintings (especially French School, 17th-century Le Nain, and 19th-century Corot–Delacroix), and Cranach drawings; 15th- and 16th-century 'Toiles Peintes'; colln of ceramics; Curator DAVID LIOT.

Musée Saint-Remi: 53 rue Simon, 51100 Reims; tel. 3-26-35-36-30; fax 3-26-82-07-99; internet www.ville-reims.fr/fr/culture/ a-visiter/musee-saint-remi; the old Abbey of St Remi (12th to 18th centuries); Prehistoric, Celtic, Gallo-Roman, Romanesque and Gothic antiquities and sculptures; tapestries of St-Remi life (1530); old weapons; Chief Curator MARC BOUXIN.

Rennes

Musée des Beaux-Arts: 20 quai Emile Zola, 35000 Rennes; tel. 2-99-28-55-85; fax 2-99-28-55-99; e-mail museebeauxarts@ ville-rennes.fr; internet www.mbar.org; f. 1799; paintings, drawings, engravings, sculpture of French and foreign Schools from the 15th century; archaeology; library of 35,000 vols; Curator FRANCIS RIBEMONT.

Musée de Bretagne: 46 blvd Magenta, CS 51138, 35011 Rennes Cedex; tel. 2-23-40-66-70; fax 2-23-40-66-94; internet www .musee-bretagne.fr; f. 1960; geology, prehistory, Armorica at the Roman period, medieval art, historical documents, popular art, furniture, 19th-century costumes, contemporary regional art and history; Dir PASCAL AUMASSON.

Rouen

Musées de la Ville de Rouen: 1 pl. Restout, 76000 Rouen; tel. 2-35-71-28-40; fax 2-35-15-43-23; internet www.rouen-musees.com.

Attached Museums:

Musée des Beaux-Arts: Esplanade Marcel Duchamp, 76000 Rouen; tel. 2-35-71-28-40; fax 2-35-15-43-23; f. 1801; paintings, drawings, sculpture, decorative art; Dir LAURENT SALOMÉ.

Musée de la Céramique: 1 rue Faucon, 76000 Rouen; tel. 2-35-07-31-74; fax 2-35-15-43-23; f. 1983; 16th–19th century– ceramics.

Musée de la Ferronnerie: Rue Jacques Villon, 76000 Rouen; tel. 2-35-88-42-92; fax 2-35-15-43-23; f. 1922; 3rd to 19th-century ironwork; Curator MARIE PESSIOT.

Rueil-Malmaison

Musée National des Châteaux de Malmaison et de Bois-Préau: 92500 Rueil-Malmaison; tel. 1-41-29-05-55; fax 1-41-29-05-56; internet www.chateau-malmaison.fr; f. 1906; historical colln of Napoleon I and Joséphine; Dir AMAURY LEFEBURE.

St-Denis

Musée d'art et d'histoire: 22 bis rue Gabriel Péri, 93200 St-Denis; tel. 1-42-43-05-10; fax 1-48-20-07-60; e-mail musee@ ville-saint-denis.fr; internet www .musee-saint-denis.fr; f. 1901; located in a disused 17th-century Carmelite monastery; collns: medieval archaeology and ceramics; history and memorabilia from the monastery and Madame Louise; the Paris Commune; paintings by Albert André; Paul Eluard and Francis Jourdain collns; remains of the old

hospital; documentation room for researchers and students; Curator SYLVIE GONZALEZ.

St-Etienne

Musée d'Art et d'Industrie: Place Louis Comte, 42000 St-Etienne; tel. 4-77-49-73-00; fax 4-77-49-73-05; e-mail museemai@ mairie-st-etienne.fr; internet www .mairie-st-etienne.fr; f. 1833, at Palais des Arts since 1850; armaments, fabrics, bicycles; Curator NADINE BESSE.

Attached Museums:

Musée d'Art Moderne de Saint-Etienne Métropole: La Terrasse, BP 80241 42006 St-Etienne, Cedex 1; tel. 4-77-79-52-52; fax 4-77-79-52-50; e-mail mam@ agglo-st-etienne.fr; internet www .mam-st-etienne.fr; f. 1987; colln of modern and contemporary art; temporary exhibitions; Gen. Dir Dr LORAND HEGYI.

Musée de la Mine: 3 blvd Franchet d'Esperey, 42000 St-Etienne; tel. 4-77-43-83-23; fax 4-77-43-83-29; e-mail museemin@mairie-st-etienne.fr; mining and industrial museum on the site of a former working mine.

St-Germain-en-Laye

Musée des Antiquités Nationales: Château, BP 3030, 78103 St-Germain-en-Laye Cedex; tel. 1-39-10-13-00; fax 1-34-51-73-93; internet www.musee-antiquitesnationales.fr; f. 1862; prehistoric, Bronze Age, Celtic, Gallo-Roman and Merovingian antiquities, comparative archaeology; library of 25,000 vols; Dir PATRICK PÉRIN; publ. *Antiquités nationales* (1 a year).

St-Malo

Musée de St-Malo: Château de St-Malo, 35400 St-Malo; tel. 2-99-40-71-57; fax 2-99-40-71-56; e-mail musee@ville-saint-malo.fr; f. 1950; history of Saint-Malo and temporary exhibitions; Curator PH. PETOUT.

Attached Museum:

Musée International du Long Cours Cap-Hornier: Tour Solidor, St-Servan, 35400 St-Malo; tel. 2-99-40-71-58; e-mail musee@ville-saint-malo.fr; f. 1969; int. history of sailing around the world since 16th century; Curator PH. PETOUT.

St-Paul-de-Vence

Fondation Maeght: 06570 St-Paul-de-Vence; tel. 4-93-32-81-63; fax 4-93-32-53-22; e-mail contact@fondation-maeght.com; internet www.fondation-maeght.com; f. 1964; modern paintings and sculpture incl. Bonnard, Braque, Giacometti, Miró and Calder; work by contemporary artists; library of 40,000 vols on modern arts and daily films on art and artists; Dir ISABELLE MAEGHT.

St-Tropez

Annonciade, Musée de St-Tropez: Place Georges Grammont, 83990 St-Tropez; tel. 4-94-17-84-10; fax 4-94-97-87-24; e-mail annonciade@ville-sainttropez.fr; internet www.saint-tropez.fr; f. 1955; French paintings 1890–1950; Curator JEAN-PAUL MONERY.

Saumur

Château Musée: Le Château, 49400 Saumur; tel. 2-41-40-24-40; fax 2-41-40-24-49; e-mail chateau.musee@ville-saumur.fr; internet www.ville-saumur.fr; f. 1829 and reorganized 1960; local archaeology, the Comte Charles Lair colln of decorative arts, including tapestries, furniture, wood carvings, liturgical ornaments; fine porcelain of 16th–18th centuries; Curator JACQUELINE MONGELLAZ.

Sceaux

Parc et musée de l'Ile de France: Château de Sceaux, Domaine de Sceaux, 92330 Sceaux; tel. 1-41-87-29-50; fax 1-41-87-29-51; e-mail museeidf@cg92.fr; internet www .chateau-sceaux.fr; f. 1935; old and modern paintings, sculpture, engravings, furniture, decorative art, tapestries, history and drawings of the environs of Paris; documentation centre on the Paris region; educational services; multimedia centre; annexes: Orangerie and Pavillon de l'Aurore, les Ecuries (Parc de Sceaux); Dir DOMINQUE BREME.

Sèvres

Musée National de Céramique: Place de la Manufacture, 92310 Sèvres; tel. 1-41-14-04-20; fax 1-45-34-67-88; e-mail musee .sevres@culture.gouv.fr; f. 1824; ancient and modern ceramic art; Curator ANTOINETTE HALLÉ; publ. *Revue de la Société des Amis du Musée National de Céramique* (1 a year).

Soissons

Musée Municipal: 2 rue de la Congrégation, 02200 Soissons; tel. 3-23-93-30-50; fax 3-23-93-30-51; e-mail musee@ville-soissons .fr; internet www.musee-soissons.org; f. 1857; antiquities, medieval sculpture, paintings since 17th century, local history and protohistory; archaeology of the Aisne Valley from Neolithic to Middle Ages; Curator DOMINIQUE ROUSSEL.

Attached Museum:

Musée Arsenal: Site de l'abbaye Saint-Jean-des-Vignes, rue Saint Jean, 02200 Soissons; tel. 3-23-53-42-40; fax 3-23-93-30-51; internet www.musee-soissons.org; temporary exhibition space in the Arsenal; Dir DOMINIQUE ROUSSEL.

Strasbourg

Palais Rohan: 2 place du Château, 67076 Strasbourg Cedex; tel. 3-88-52-50-00; fax 3-88-52-50-09; internet www .musees-strasbourg.org.

Attached Museums:

Musée Archéologique: c/o Palais Rohan, 2 place du Château, 67000 Strasbourg; tel. 3-88-52-50-00; fax 3-88-52-50-09; f. 1856; prehistoric, Celtic, Gallo-Roman and Merovingian collns; results of excavations in Alsace; Curator BERNADETTE SCHNITZLER.

Musée des Arts Décoratifs et Appartements Historiques: c/o Palais Rohan, 2 place du Château, 67076 Strasbourg Cedex; tel. 3-88-52-50-00; fax 3-88-52-50-46; f. 1883; furniture from 18th and 19th centuries; French paintings; ceramics; silver objects; musical instruments; wrought-iron and tin; Curator ETIENNE MARTIN.

Musée des Beaux-Arts: c/o Palais Rohan, 2 place du Château, 67000 Strasbourg; tel. 3-88-52-50-00; fax 3-88-52-50-09; f. 1801; French and foreign paintings: Old Masters, art from 14th–19th centuries, Italian, Spanish, Flemish, Dutch and French schools; Chief Curator DOMINIQUE JACQUOT.

Toulouse

Musée des Augustins: 21 rue de Metz, 31000 Toulouse; tel. 5-61-22-21-82; fax 5-61-22-34-69; e-mail augustins@mairie-toulouse .fr; internet www.augustins.org; f. 1793 and housed in the former Augustine Convent, of which parts date from the 14th and 15th centuries; Roman and Gothic sculptures, 16th–19th-century local and foreign paintings; Curator ALAIN DAGUERRE DE HUREAUX.

Tours

Musée des Beaux-Arts: 18 place François-Sicard, 37000 Tours; tel. 2-47-05-68-73; fax 2-47-05-38-91; e-mail musee-beauxarts@ ville-tours.fr; internet www.musees .regioncentre.fr; f. 1793 and moved in 1910 to the fmr Archbishop's palace; paintings by Mantegna, Rembrandt, Rubens, Vignon, Lancret, Boucher, Delacroix, Degas, Debré; sculpture by Le Moyne, Houdon, Bourdelle, Davidson, Calder; furniture, tapestries and objets d'art; library of 15,000 vols; Curator PHILIPPE LE LEYZOUR.

Affiliated Museums:

Château d'Azay-le-Ferron: 36290 Azay-le-Ferron; tel. 2-54-39-20-06; bldgs, objets d'art and furniture of the 15th to 19th centuries; Curator PHILIPPE LE LEYZOUR.

Musée Saint-Martin: 3 rue Rapin, 37000 Tours; tel. 2-47-64-48-87; fax 2-47-05-38-91; f. 1990; contains collection of souvenirs of St Martin; Curator PHILIPPE LE LEYZOUR.

Musée du Compagnonnage: 8 rue Nationale, 37000 Tours; tel. 2-47-61-07-93; fax 2-47-21-68-90; e-mail museecompagnonnage@ ville-tours.fr; f. 1968; archives and historical masterpieces; Curator LAURENT BASTARD.

Musée de la Société Archéologique de Touraine: Hôtel Gouin, 25 rue du Commerce, 37000 Tours; tel. 2-47-66-22-32; Gallic and Roman archaeology, medieval and 16th century sculptures, prehistoric artefacts; iconography of Tours, 18th–19th century pottery; closed for renovation until 2012.

Musée des Vins de Touraine: 16 rue Nationale (parvis Saint-Julien), 37000 Tours; tel. 2-47-61-07-93; fax 2-47-21-68-90; f. 1975; Curator LAURENT BASTARD.

Ungersheim

Ecomusée d'Alsace: BP 71, 68190 Ungersheim; tel. 3-89-74-44-74; fax 3-89-74-44-65; e-mail contact@ecoparcs.com; internet www .ecomusee-alsace.com; f. 1984 by the Asscn Maisons Paysannes d'Alsace to safeguard the rural architecture of Alsace; an open-air museum comprising a reconstituted village of 70 cottages, showing life in olden days with a baker, an oil-mill, a blacksmith, a clog-maker, and a sawmill working on site; nature walks, seminars; library of 950 vols, 4,000 drawings and reliefs, 25,000 photographs, video cassettes; Pres. MARC GRODWOHL.

Vaison-la-Romaine

Musée Archéologique Théo Desplans: Colline de Puymin, 84110 Vaison-la-Romaine; tel. 4-90-36-50-48; fax 4-90-35-66-17; e-mail reservegroupe@vaison-la-romaine .com; internet www.vaison-la-romaine.com; f. 1920, present site 1975; archaeological colln from excavations at Vaison; Curator CHRISTINE BEZIN.

Valenciennes

Musée des Beaux-Arts: blvd Watteau, 59300 Valenciennes; tel. 3-27-22-57-20; fax 3-27-22-57-22; e-mail mba@ ville-valenciennes.fr; internet www .valenciennes.fr; painting, sculpture, archaeology, etc.; Dir P. RAMADE.

Vallauris

Musée National Picasso 'La Guerre et la Paix': Place de la Libération, 06220 Vallauris; tel. 4-93-64-71-83; fax 4-93-64-50-32; internet www.musee-picasso-vallauris.fr; f. 1959; works by Picasso incl. *La Guerre et la Paix* in 12th-century chapel; Curator JEAN-MICHEL FORAY.

Verdun

Centre Mondial de la Paix, des Libertés et des Droits de l'Homme: Palais Episcopal, BP 183, 55100 Verdun; tel. 3-29-86-55-00; fax 3-29-86-15-14; e-mail cmpaix@ wanadoo.fr; f. 1994; exhibition on the First World War; and 'From War to Peace', an interactive exhibition, which depicts the origins of war in Europe, attempts at peace-keeping and punishment of war crimes, the history of European cooperation and the EU, the UN, and the nature and application of human rights; meetings, confs and roleplay situations for students; Dir JEAN-LUC DEMANDRE.

Versailles

Musée et Domaine National du Château de Versailles: Château de Versailles, Place d'Armes, RP 834, 78000 Versailles; tel. 1-30-83-78-00; e-mail direction.public@ chateauversailles.fr; internet www .chateauversailles.fr; f. 1623 by Louis XIII; historical painting and sculpture, furniture of the 17th to 19th centuries; Grand Trianon, Petit Trianon châteaux, Hameau de la Reine, park; Pres. JEAN-JACQUES AILLAGON.

Vizille

Musée de la Révolution Française: Château de Vizille, 38220 Vizille; tel. 4-76-68-07-35; fax 4-76-68-08-53; e-mail musee .revolution@cg38.fr; internet www .musee-revolution-francaise.fr; f. 1984; relics, art and library connected with the French Revolution of 1789; library of 20,000 vols, 25,000 microfiches; Dir ALAIN CHEVALIER.

State Universities

UNIVERSITÉ BLAISE PASCAL

34 ave Carnot, BP 185, 63006 Clermont-Ferrand Cedex 1

Telephone: 4-73-40-63-63
Fax: 4-73-40-64-31
E-mail: president@univ-bpclermont.fr
Internet: www.univ-bpclermont.fr

Founded 1810, present status 1984 as Université de Clermont-Ferrand II–Université Blaise Pascal

Pres.: NADINE LAVIGNOTTE
Vice-Pres: BETTINA ABOAB, MARIE-JOSEPH BIACHE, PAUL FORCE
Sec.-Gen.: XAVIER FAUVEAU
Librarian: L. RAPATEL

Number of teachers: 800
Number of students: 16,000

Publications: *Journal de l'Université Blaise Pascal* (3 a year), *Programme des Colloques* (1 a year).

TEACHING AND RESEARCH UNITS

Applied Language and Communication: 34 ave Carnot, 63037 Clermont-Ferrand Cedex; tel. 4-73-40-64-05; fax 4-73-40-64-24; internet www.lacc.univ-bpclermont.fr; Dir SUZAN GOUTET.

Centre Universitaire de Sciences et Techniques (CUST): Rue des Meuniers, BP 206, 63174 Aubière Cedex; tel. 4-73-40-75-00; fax 4-73-40-75-10; internet www.cust .univ-bpclermont.fr; Dir CLAUDE-GILLES DUSSAP.

Computer Engineering (ISIMA): Complexe des Cézeaux, BP 125, 63173 Aubière Cedex; tel. 4-73-40-50-00; fax 4-73-40-50-01; internet www.isima.fr; Head A. QUILLIOT.

Exact and Natural Sciences (Teaching): 24 ave des Landais, 63177 Aubière Cedex; tel. 4-73-40-70-02; fax 4-73-40-70-12; internet www.sciences.univ-bpclermont.fr; Dir G. BOURDIER.

Literature, Languages and Human Sciences: 29 blvd Gergovia, 63037 Clermont-Ferrand Cedex; tel. 4-73-34-65-04; fax 4-73-34-65-44; internet www.lettres .univ-bpclermont.fr; Dir MICHELINE DECORPS.

National Higher School of Chemistry: Ensemble scientifique des Cézeaux, BP 187, 63174 Aubière Cedex; tel. 4-73-40-71-45; fax 4-73-40-70-95; internet ensccf .univ-bpclermont.fr; Dir JACQUES LACOSTE.

Observatoire de Physique du Globe (OPGC): 24 ave des Landais, 63001 Clermont-Ferrand Cedex; tel. 4-73-40-73-80; fax 4-73-40-73-82; internet www.opgc .univ-bpclermont.fr; Dir ANDRÉA FLOSSMANN.

Physical Education and Sport: Complexe Scientifique des Cézeaux, BP 104, 63172 Aubière Cedex; tel. 4-73-40-75-40; fax 4-73-40-74-46; Dir HUGUETTE GONZALEZ.

Psychology, Social Sciences and Educational Science: 34 ave Carnot, 63037 Clermont-Ferrand Cedex; tel. 4-73-40-64-63; fax 4-73-40-64-82; internet www.psycho .univ-bpclermont.fr; Dir P. CHAMBRES.

Scientific and Technical Research: 24 ave des Landais, 63177 Aubière Cedex; tel. 4-73-40-70-03; fax 4-73-40-70-12; internet www .rst.univ-bpclermont.fr; Dir GILLES PETEL.

University Institute of Technology (Montluçon): Ave Aristide Briand, BP 408, 03107 Montluçon Cedex; tel. 4-70-02-20-00; fax 4-70-02-20-78; internet www.moniut .univ-bpclermont.fr; Dir BERNARD GUILLE-MET.

UNIVERSITÉ D'ANGERS

40 rue de Rennes, BP 73532, 49035 Angers Cedex

Telephone: 2-41-96-23-23
Fax: 2-41-96-23-00
E-mail: presidence@univ-angers.fr
Internet: www.univ-angers.fr

Founded 1971; fmrly Centre Universitaire d'Angers

President: ALAIN BARREAU
Vice-President: PHILIPPE VIOLIER
Secretary-General: HENRI-MARC PAPAVOINE
Librarian: OLIVIER TACHEAU

Number of teachers: 861
Number of students: 16,000

Publications: *Plantes médicinales et phytothérapie, Journal of the Short Story in English, Publications du Centre de Recherche en Littérature et Linguistique de l'Anjou et des Bocages*

DEANS

Faculty of Law, Economic Sciences and Business Sciences: D. MARTINA
Faculty of Letters and Human Sciences: D. LE GALL
Faculty of Medicine: J.-P. ANDRE
Faculty of Pharmacy: H. GUINAUDEAU
Faculty of Science: G. MOGUEDET

ATTACHED INSTITUTES

Etudes Supérieures de Tourisme et Hôtellerie d'Angers (ESTHUA): 7 allée François Mitterrand, BP 40455, 49004 Angers; tel. 2-41-96-21-99; fax 2-41-96-22-00; Dir M. BONNEAU.

Institut des Sciences et Techniques de l'Ingénieur d'Angers (ISTIA): 62 ave Notre-Dame du Lac, 49000 Angers; tel. 2-41-22-65-00; fax 2-41-22-65-01; Dir C. ROBLEDO.

Institut Universitaire de Technologie (IUT): 4 blvd Lavoisier, BP 42018, 49016 Angers Cedex; tel. 2-41-73-52-52; fax 2-41-73-53-30; Dir Y. MEIGNEN.

UNIVERSITÉ D'ARTOIS

9 rue du Temple, BP 665, 62030 Arras Cedex
Telephone: 3-21-60-37-00
Fax: 3-21-60-37-37
Internet: www.univ-artois.fr

Founded 1991
Pres.: JEAN-JACQUES POLLET (acting)
Sec.-Gen.: MARIE-PAULE DEJONGHE
Vice-Pres.: MANUEL GROS
Librarians: CORINNE LEBLOND (Arras), ALEXANDRE ALLAIN (Béthune), FRÉDÉRIC WATRELOT (Douai), GHISLAINE HEYER (Lens), JULIE ROUSSEL (Liévin)

Number of teachers: 432 (incl. univ. institutes of technology)
Number of students: 12,000 (incl. univ. institutes of technology)

Publication: *Interpôles Artois* (8 a year)

TEACHING AND RESEARCH UNITS
Arras:

Centre de Recherche en Histoire Ancienne: Dir: JEAN-NICOLAS CORVISIER
Centres de Recherche Histoire Economique Contemporaine: Dir: DENIS VARASCHIN
CERACI (Centre d'Etudes et de Recherches de l'Artois sur les Cultures et les Intertextualités): Dir: JEAN-JACQUES POLLET
CERTA (Centre d'Etudes et de Recherche en Traductologie de l'Artois): Dir: MICHEL BALLARD
CERTEL (Centre d'Etudes et de Recherches sur les Textes Electroniques Littéraires)
CRELID (Centre de Recherches Littéraires 'Imaginaire et Didactique'): Dir: FRANCIS MARCOIN
Faculty of Arts: Dir: JEAN-MARC VERCRUYSSE
Faculty of Economic and Social Administration: Dir: GILLES FIEVET
Faculty of History and Geography: Dir: GILLES DEREGNAUCOURT
Faculty of Languages: Dir: JACQUES SYS
Grammatica (French Linguistics)
Laboratoire Des Anciens Pays-Bas à l'Eurorégion: Dir: GILLES DEREGNAUCOURT
Laboratoire 'Dynamique des réseaux et territoires': Dir: JEAN-PIERRE RENARD
Professional University Institute of Heritage and Tourism: Dir: CHARLES GIRY-DELOISON
Béthune:

EREIA (Equipe de recherche en économie internationale de l'Artois): Dir: THIERRY GRANGER
Faculty of Applied Sciences: Dir: FRANCIS NOTELET
Faculty of Economic Sciences: Dir: AHMED HENNI
Laboratoire de Chimie Physique Appliquée: Dir: RODOLPHE MINETTI
LGI2A (Laboratoire de Génie Informatique et d'Automatique de l'Artois): Dir: DANIEL JOLLY
LSEE (Laboratoire des Systèmes Electrotechniques et Environnement): Dir: JEAN-FRANÇOIS BRUDNY
Douai:

Faculty of Law: Dir: ALEXIS DE TOCQUEVILLE
Legal Research: Dir: MANUEL GROS
Lens:

Centre IT Research: Dir: ERIC GRÉGOIRE
Faculty of Science: Dir: BRAHIM KHELIFA
LBHE (Laboratoire de la barrière hémato-encéphalique): Dir: ROMÉO CECCHELLI
LPCIA (Laboratoire de Physico-Chimie des Interfaces et Applications): Dir: MARC WARENGHEM
Mathematics Laboratory: Dir: DANIEL LI
Liévin:

Faculty of Sports Science
LAMAPS (Laboratoire d'Analyse Multidisciplinaire des Pratiques Sportives): Dirs: OLIVIER CHOVAUX, VALÉRIE FAYT

UNIVERSITÉ D'AUVERGNE (CLERMONT-FERRAND I)

49 blvd F. Mitterrand, 63001 Clermont-Ferrand Cedex

Telephone: 4-73-34-77-77
Internet: www.u-clermont1.fr

Founded 1976; present status 1985

Pres.: ANNIE VEYRE
Sec.-Gen.: MICHÈLE MOSNIER
Librarian: Mlle SART

Number of teachers: 600
Number of students: 12,000.

TEACHING AND RESEARCH UNITS

Medicine: 28 place Henri Dunant, BP 38, 63001 Clermont-Ferrand; tel. 4-73-17-79-79; fax 4-73-17-79-13; internet medecine .u-clermont1.fr; Dean Prof. PATRICE DETEIX.

Pharmacy: 28 place Henri Dunant, BP 38, 63001 Clermont-Ferrand; tel. 4-73-17-79-79; fax 4-73-17-79-14; Dean Prof. M. MADESCLAIRE.

Law and Politics: 41 blvd F. Mitterrand, BP 38, 63002 Clermont-Ferrand; tel. 4-73-17-76-00; fax 4-73-17-75-75; e-mail ufr-droit@ droit.u-clermont1.fr; internet www-droit .u-clermont1.fr; Dean Prof. J.-P. MASSIAS.

Economic and Social Sciences: 41 blvd F. Mitterrand, BP 54, 63002 Clermont-Ferrand; tel. 4-73-43-42-00; fax 4-73-17-75-75; Dir CLAIRE GRELET.

University Institute of Technology (Clermont-Ferrand): Ensemble universitaire des Cézeaux, BP 86, 63172 Aubière; tel. 4-73-17-70-00; fax 4-73-17-70-20; internet iutweb.u-clermont1.fr; Dir Prof. D. RICHARD.

Dentistry: 11 blvd Charles de Gaulle, 63000 Clermont-Ferrand Cedex; tel. 4-73-17-73-00; fax 4-73-17-73-09; internet webodonto .u-clermont1.fr; Dean Prof. THIERRY ORLIAGUET.

University Professional Institute of Business Management: Pôle Tertiaire et Technologique 26, Ave Léon-Blum, 63000 Clermont-Ferrand; tel. 4-73-17-77-00; fax 4-73-17-77-01; internet iup-management.net; Dir Prof. M. CHENEVOY.

IPAG: 26, Ave Léon-Blum, 63000 Clermont-Ferrand; tel. 4-73-17-77-50; fax 4-73-17-77-55; Dir Prof. M. DEYRA.

UNIVERSITÉ D'ÉVRY-VAL D'ESSONNE

Boulevard des Coquibus, 91025 Évry Cedex
Telephone: 1-69-47-70-10
Fax: 1-64-97-27-34
Internet: www.univ-evry.fr

Pres.: DANIEL ANDRÉ
Sec.-Gen.: CHRISTOPHE MARMIN

Number of teachers: 462 , incl. 127 at IUT
Number of students: 9,963 , incl. 1,652 at IUT.

UNIVERSITY INSTITUTE

Institut Universitaire de Technologie (IUT): 22 allée Jean Rostand, 91025 Évry Cedex; Dir PAUL DEMAREZ.

UNIVERSITÉ D'ORLÉANS

Château de la Source, BP 6749, 45067 Orléans Cedex 2
Telephone: 2-38-41-71-71
Fax: 2-38-41-70-69
Internet: www.univ-orleans.fr

Founded 1961
Language of instruction: French
Academic year: September to June

Pres.: GÉRARD BESSON

Vice-Pres: MICHEL PERTUÉ, JACQUES CHAR-
VET, JEAN-MARIE GINESTA
Sec.-Gen.: GÉRARD GASQUET
Librarian: Mme DESBORDES
Number of teachers: 832
Number of students: 17,500

Publications: *Bulletin d'informations de
l'Université* (5 a year), *Internships* (1 a
year), *Plaquette en direction des entreprises* (1 a year), *1er contact* (1 a year),
research catalogue

TEACHING AND RESEARCH UNITS

Ecole Polytechnique: Dir: JEAN-LOUIS BIL-
LOËT
Law, Economics and Management: Dir: JAC-
QUES LEROY
Letters, Languages and Human Sciences:
Dir: JEAN-MARIE GINESTA
Sciences: Dir: RENÉ ERRE
Sciences and Sports Sciences: Dir: RÉGIS DE
REYKE
University Institute of Technology (Orléans):
Dir: GÉRARD BAILLARGUET
University Institute of Technology (Bourges):
Dir: JACQUES GUILLY
University Institute of Technology (Char-
tres): Dir: LEVI ALLAM
University Institute of Technology (Indre):
Dir: CHRISTIAN ETIENNE

UNIVERSITÉ D'AVIGNON ET DES PAYS DE VAUCLUSE

74 rue Louis Pasteur, 84029 Avignon Cedex 9
Telephone: 4-90-16-25-11
Fax: 4-90-16-25-20
E-mail: presidence@univ-avignon.fr
Internet: www.univ-avignon.fr

Founded 1303 closed in 1793 after French
revolution; reopened in 1963; univ. status
since 1984
State control
Language of instruction: French
Academic year: September to June

Pres.: Prof. EMMANUEL ETHIS
Dir. Gen.: LUÇAY SAUTRON
Librarian: ISABELLE DIMONDO

Library of 155,600 vols, 73 online databases,
8,311 periodical titles
Number of teachers: 330
Number of students: 7,000

Publications: *Culture et Musée, Etudes Vau-
clusiennes, Ecologia Mediterranea*

TEACHING AND RESEARCH UNITS

Exact and Natural Sciences: Dir: YVAN COTTA
Arts and Humanities: Dir: JACQUES MABY
Applied Sciences: Dir: ANDRÉ ULPAT
Law, Politics and Economics: Dir: MARTINE
LE FRIANT

ATTACHED RESEARCH INSTITUTES

**Institut Universitaire de Technologie
(IUT):** 337 Chemin des Meinajaries, BP
1207, 84911 Avignon Cedex 9; tel. 4-90-84-
14-00; fax 4-90-84-00-77; internet www.iut
.univ-avignon.fr; Dir J. SOUMILLE.

**Institut Universitaire Professionnalisé
(IUP) en Génie Informatique et Mathématique:** Technopôle d'Agroparc, BP 1228,
84911 Mont Favet; tel. 4-90-84-35-00; fax 4-
90-84-35-01; e-mail secretariat@iup
.univ-avignon.fr; internet www.iup
.univ-avignon.fr; Dir PATRICK ISOARDI.

UNIVERSITÉ DE BORDEAUX I

351 cours de la Libération, 33405 Talence
Cedex
Telephone: 5-40-00-60-00
Fax: 5-56-80-08-37
Internet: www.u-bordeaux1.fr

Pres.: FRANCIS HARDOUIN
Vice-Pres.: ROBERT CORI (Admin.), YVES LER-
OYER (Curriculum and Univ. Life), PATRICK
BUAT-MENARD (Science)
Sec.-Gen.: ANNE-MARIE BOISLIVEAU
Number of students: 14,000

TEACHING AND RESEARCH UNITS

Biology: Dir: DANIEL GALEY
Biosciences: Dir: PATRICK COTTIN
Chemistry: Dir: JEAN-BAPTISTE VERLHAC
Continued Professional Training: Dir: GÉR-
ARD DEMAZEAU
Earth and Marine Sciences: Dir: GÉRARD
BLANC
Geology and Oceanology: Dir: JEAN-PIERRE
PEYPOUQUET
Mathematics and Informatics: Dir: J. BOA-
SEREZ
Physics: Dir: JEAN LABARSOUQUE
Sciences: Dir: MARIE-LISE SANTUCCI
Technology: Dir: PIERRE LAFON

CONSTITUENT INSTITUTES AND SCHOOLS

**Ecole Doctorale de Mathématiques et
Informatique:** tel. 5-40-00-69-39; fax 5-40-
00-69-55; e-mail ecole@math.u-bordeaux1.fr;
internet www.math.u-bordeaux.fr/
ecole_doctorale; Dir THIERRY COLIN.

**Ecole Doctorale du Vivant, Géosciences,
Sciences de l'Environnement:** tel. 5-40-
00-33-01; fax 5-40-00-33-86; internet www
.disvu.u-bordeaux1.fr/ecoles/edsvgse; Dirs
ROBERT JAFFARD, JEAN-PIERRE PEYPOUQUET.

**Ecole Doctorale des Sciences Chimi-
ques:** tel. 5-40-00-65-61; internet www.edsc
.u-bordeaux.fr; Dir FRANÇOIS CARMONA.

**Ecole Doctorale des Sciences Physiques
et de l'Ingénieur:** tel. 5-40-00-65-26; fax 5-
40-00-65-25; e-mail edoc@ufr-phys
.u-bordeaux.fr; internet www.disvu
.u-bordeaux1.fr/ecoles/edsp; Dir NATHALIE
LABAT.

Ecole Matmeca: tel. 5-40-00-60-53; fax 5-
40-00-38-56; internet www.matmeca
.u-bordeaux.fr; Dir PIERRE FABRIE.

**Institut de Chimie de la Matière Con-
densée de Bordeaux (ICMCB):** tel. 5-40-
00-62-96; fax 5-40-00-66-34; internet www
.icmcb-bordeaux.cnrs.fr; Dir CLAUDE DELMAS.

**Institut de Mathématiques de Bordeaux
(IMCB):** tel. 5-40-00-60-70; fax 5-40-00-21-
23; e-mail institut@math.u-bordeaux1.fr;
internet www.math.u-bordeaux.fr/maths;
Dir PHILIPPE CASSOU-NOGUES.

**Institut de Physique Fondamentale
(IPF):** tel. 5-40-00-83-13; internet www
.u-bordeaux1.fr/ipf; Dir ERIC FREYS.

**Institut de Recherche pour l'Enseigne-
ment des Mathématiques (IREM):** tel. 5-
40-00-89-74; Dir PIERRE DAMEY.

**Institut des Sciences et Techniques
d'Alimentation de Bordeaux (ISTAB):**
tel. 5-40-00-87-53; fax 5-56-37-03-36; e-mail
scolarite@istab.u-bordeaux1.fr; internet
www.u-bordeaux1.fr/istab; Dir FRANÇOIS
RIBOULET.

Institut du Pin (IP): tel. 5-40-00-64-20; fax
5-40-00-64-22; e-mail ipin@ipin.u-bordeaux1
.fr; internet www.u-bordeaux1.fr/ipin; Dir
JEAN BARANGER.

**Institut Européen de Chimie et Biologie
(IECB):** tel. 5-40-00-22-16; internet www
.iecb-polytechnique.u-bordeaux.fr; Dir JEAN-
JACQUES TOULME.

Institut Universitaire de Technologie:
Domaine Universitaire, 33405 Talence
Cedex; tel. 5-56-84-57-02; internet www.iut
.u-bordeaux1.fr; Dir PIERRE LAFON.

Observatoire: 2 rue de l'Observatoire,
33270 Floirac; tel. 5-57-77-61-63; fax 5-57-

77-61-10; internet www.obs.u-bordeaux1.fr;
Dir THIERRY JACQ.

UNIVERSITY PROFESSIONAL INSTITUTES

**University Professional Institute of
Computer-Assisted Management:** tel. 5-
40-00-89-49; internet miage.u-bordeaux.fr;
Dir NICOLE BIDOIT.

**University Professional Institute of
Electrical Engineering and Industrial
Informatics:** tel. 5-40-00-28-30; internet
www.creea.u-bordeaux.fr; Dir YVES DANTO.

**University Professional Institute of
Industrial Systems Engineering—Aircraft Maintenance:** tel. 5-56-13-31-58;
internet www.u-bordeaux1.fr/ima; Dir CHRIS-
TIAN BOUILLE.

**University Professional Institute of
Mechanical Engineering:** tel. 5-40-00-65-
15; internet www.u-bordeaux1.fr/iup_gm;
Dir MICHEL NOUILLANT.

ATTACHED INSTITUTES; (SEE UNDER COLLEGES
AND INSTITUTES)

**École Nationale Supérieure de Chimie
et de Physique de Bordeaux (ENSCPB):**
16 ave Pey Berland, 33607 Pessac Cedex; tel.
5-40-00-65-65; fax 5-40-00-66-33; e-mail
admin@enscpb.fr; internet www.enscpb.fr;
Dir BERNARD CLIN.

**École Nationale Supérieure d'Électroni-
que et de Radiocommunication de Bordeaux (ENSERB):** 1 ave du Dr Albert
Schweitzer 33402 Talence Cedex; tel. 5-56-
84-65-00; fax 5-56-37-20-23; internet www
.enserb.u-bordeaux.fr; Dir PHILIPPE MARCHE-
GAY.

UNIVERSITÉ DE BOURGOGNE

Maison de l'Université, Esplanade Erasme,
BP 138, 21004 Dijon Cedex
Telephone: 3-80-39-50-11
Fax: 3-80-39-50-69
Internet: www.u-bourgogne.fr

Founded 1722 as Dijon Faculty of Law

Pres.: JEAN-CLAUDE FORTIER
Sec.-Gen.: PATRICE SERNICLAY
Librarian: F. HAGENE
Number of students: 24,879

Publications: *Annuaire, Journal d'Information, Livret de la recherche, Publications de
l'Université* (irregular series of monographs)

TEACHING AND RESEARCH UNITS

Earth Sciences: Dir: JEAN-PIERRE GARCIA
Economics and Business Studies: Dir: MARIE-
CLAUDE PICHERY
Higher Institute of Transport and the Car:
Dir: GEORGES VERCHERY
Higher National School of Applied Biology:
Dir: JEAN-PIERRE GRENOUILLET
Human Sciences: Dir: MICHÈLE DION
Languages and Communication: Dir: ANN
PIROELLE
Law and Political Science: Dir: FRANCOISE
FORTUNET
Life Sciences: Dir: YVES JASSEY
Literature and Philosophy: Dir: NICOLE FICK
Medicine: Dir: MAURICE GIROUD
Pharmacy: Dir: SYLVETTE HUICHARD
Physical Education and Sport: Dir: BERNARD
MEURGEY
Preparatory Institute for General Adminis-
tration: Dir: ALAIN WERNER
Science and Technology: Dir: JEAN-PAUL
DUFOUR
Training of Research Engineers in Materials
Science and Technology: Dir: ALEXIS STEIN-
BRUNN
University Institute of Technology (Chalon-
sur-Saône): Dir: FRANCK HENDEL

University Institute of Technology (Dijon): Dir: ANDRÉ BERNARD
University Institute of Technology (Le Creusot): Dir: J.-L. GISCLON
University Professional Institute in Burgundy for Industrial Engineering: Dir: B. BOBIN
Viticulture and Oenology Experimental Centre: Dir: JEAN-CLAUDE FOURNIOUX

PROFESSORS

Arts Faculties:

ABDI, Psychology
ALI BOUACHA, French Linguistics
BASTIT, Philosophy
BAVOUX, Geography
BENONY, Psychology
Mme BERCOT, Modern Literature
CHAPUIS, Geography
CHARRIER, Geography
CHARUE, German
Mme CHARUE, German
CHEVIGNARD, American English
CHIFFRE, Geography
COMANZO, English
Mme COURTOIS, Comparative Literature
Mme DOBIAS, Classical Literature
DUCHENE, History
Mme DUCOS, Classical Literature
DURIX, English
Mme DURU, Education
Mme FAYARD, Modern History
FAYOL, Psychology
FERRARI, Philosophy
FOYARD, French Philology
GARNOT, Modern History
Mme HAAS, French Linguistics
IMBERTY, Italian
JACOBI, Information and Communication Science
Mlle JOLY, Latin
LAMARRE, Geography
LARRAZ, Romance Languages
Mme LAVAUD, Spanish
LAVAUD, Spanish
McCARTHY, English
MORDANT, Protohistory
NOUHAUD, Spanish
Mlle PELLAN, English
Mme PERARD, Geography
Mme PERROT, Philosophy
Mme PIROELLE, English
PITAVY, English
Mme PITAVY, English
Mme POURKIER, Greek
QUILLIOT, Philosophy
RATIE, English
REFFET, German
RONSIN, Modern History
Mme SADRIN, English
SADRIN, French Literature
SAINT-DENIS, Medieval History
SAURON, Audiology
SOUILLER, Comparative Literature
SOUTET, Linguistics, Phonetics
TABBAGH, Medieval Archaeology
TAVERDET, French Philology
TUROWSLI, History of Art
Mme VINTER, Psychology
WOLIKOW, History and Civilization
WUNENBURGER, Philosophy
ZAGAR, Psychology

Faculties of Law and Economic Science:

BALESTRA, Economic Sciences
BART, Law, Roman Law
Mme BAUMONT, Economics
BODINEAU, History of Law
BOLARD, Private Law
BROUSSOLLE, Public Law
CASIMIR, Management
CHADEFAUX, Management
CHAPPEZ, Public Law
CHARREAUX, Management
CLERE, History of Law
COURVOISIER, Political Sciences

DE MESNARD, Economics
DESBRIÈRES, Economics
DOCKES, Private Law
DUBOIS, Public Law
FILSER, Management Sciences
Mme FORTUNET, History of Law
FRITZ, Political Sciences
Mme GADREAU, Economics
HURIOT, Economic Sciences
JACQUEMONT, Management
JOBERT, History of Law
KORNPROBST, Public Law
LOQUIN, Private Law
Mme MARTIN-SERF, Private Law
MATHIEU, Public Law
MICHELOT, Economics, Mathematics
PAUL, Economics of Education
PERREUR, Economic Sciences
PICHERY, M. C., Economics
PIERI, History of Law
Mme PIERI, Private Law
PIZZIO, Private Law
ROUGET, Economics
SALMON, Political Economy
SIMON, Public Law

Faculties of Medicine and Pharmacy:

ARTUR, Physical Biochemistry
AUTISSIER, Anatomy
Mme AUTISSIER, Physical Chemistry
BEDENNE, Gastroenterology
BELON, Pharmacology
BESANCENOT, Internal Medicine
BINNERT, Radiology
BLETTERY, Resuscitation
BONNIN, Parasitology
BRALET, Physiology
BRENOT, Vascular Surgery
BRON, Ophthalmology
BROSSIER, Physical Chemistry
BRUN, Endocrinology
BRUNOTTE, Biophysics
CAMUS, Pneumology
Mme CARLI, Haematology
CASILLAS, Rehabilitation
CHAILLOT, Pharmacy
CHAVANET, Infectious Diseases
COUGARD, Surgery
CUISENIER, Surgery
DAVID, Thoracic and Cardiac Surgery
DELCOURT, Pharmacy
DIDIER, Rehabilitation
Mme DUBOIS-LACAILLE, Pharmacognosy
DUMAS, Neurology
Mme DUMAS, Pharmacology
DUSSERRE, Biostatistics
ESCOUSSE, Clinical Pharmacology
FAIVRE, Gastroenterology
FANTINO, Physiology
FAVRE, General Surgery
FELDMAN, Gynaecology and Obstetrics
FREYSZ, Anaesthesiology
GAMBERT, Biochemistry
GIRARD, Anaesthesiology
GIROUD, Neurology
GISSELMANN, Epidemiology
GOUYON, Paediatrics
GRAMMONT, Orthopaedic Surgery and Traumatology
GUERRIN, Oncology
HILLON, Hepatology, Gastroenterology
HORIOT, Radiotheraphy
Mme HUICHARD, Pharmaceutical Law
JEANNIN, Pneumology
Mlle JUSTRABO, Pathological Anatomy
KAZMIERCZAK, Bacteriology, Virology
KRAUSE, Radiology
LAMBERT, Dermatology
LORCERIE, Internal Medicine
LOUIS, Cardiology
MABILLE, S. P., Radiology
MACK, Biochemistry
MALKA, Stomatology and Maxillofacial Surgery
MARTIN, F., Immunology
MOURIER, Neurosurgery

NEEL, Biochemistry
NIVELON, Paediatrics
PADIEU, Biological Chemistry
PFITZEMEYER, Internal Medicine
Mme PIARD, Pathological Anatomy
PORTIER, Infectious and Tropical Diseases
POTHIER, Bacteriology
Mme POURCELOT, Pharmacy
RAT, General Surgery
RIFLE, Nephrology
Mme ROCHAT, Pharmacy
ROCHETTE, Pharmacy
ROMANET, Otorhinolaryngology
ROUSSET, Bacteriology
SAGOT, Gynaecology
SAUTREAUX, Neurosurgery
SCHREIBER, Pharmacy
SMOLIK, Occupational Medicine
SOLARY, Haematology
TAVERNIER, Rheumatology
TEYSSIER, Cytogenetic Histology
THEVENIN, Pharmacy
THIERRY, Neurosurgery
TRAPET, Adult Psychiatry
TROUILLOUD, Orthopaedic Surgery and Anatomy
VERGES, Endocrinology of Metabolic Diseases
WEILLER, Radiology
WILKENING, Anaesthesiology
WOLF, Cardiology
ZAHND, Embryology

Higher Institute of Transport and the Car:

AIVAZZADEH, S., Mechanics
LESUEUR, Mechanics
VERCHERY, Mechanics

Higher National School of Applied Biology:

BELIN, Alimentary Biotermology
BESNARD, Physiology of Nutrition
DIVIES, Microbiology
GERVAIS, Process Engineering
LE MESTE, Physical Chemistry of Food
L'HUGUENOT, Biochemistry
MOLIN, Mathematics
TAINTURIER, Organic Chemistry
Mme VOILLEY, Biology, Biochemistry

Physical Education and Sport:

MORLON, B., Biophysics
VANHOECKE, J., Physical Education and Sport

Science Faculties:

ANDREUX, Geochemistry
BELLEVILLE, J., Animal Physiology
BERGER, Physics
BERTRAND, Chemistry
BESANÇON, Chemistry
BOBIN, Physics
BONNARD, Mathematics
BOQUILLON, Physics
CAMPY, Geology
CEZILLY, Ecology
CHABRIER, Computer Sciences
CHAMPION, Physics
CLOUET, Animal Physiology
COLSON, Chemistry
CONNAT, Animal Biology
COQUET, Physics
CORTET, Mathematics
DEMARQUOY, Animal Physiology
DEREUX, Physics
DOLECKI, Mathematics
DORMOND, Chemistry
DULIEU, Animal Physiology
FANG, Mathematics
FLATO, Mathematics
FRANGE, Chemistry
FROCHOT, B., Ecology
GAUTHERON, B., Chemistry
GOUDONNET, Physics
GUILARD, R., Mathematics
GUIRAUD, Geology
JANNIN, Physics
JANNOT, Physics
JAUSLIN, Physics

JOUBERT, Mathematics
KUBICKI, Chemistry
LALLEMANT, Chemistry
LANG, J., Geology
LANGEVIN, Mathematics
LARPIN, Physical Chemistry
LASSALE, Mathematics
LATRUFFE, Biochemistry
LAURIN, Geology
LENOIR-ROUSSEAU, Zoology
LINES, Mathematics
LOETE, Physics
LOREAU, Geology
MARCUARD, Statistical Probability
MARNIER, Physics
MARTY, Plant Biology
MATVEEV, Mathematics
MAUME, B., Biochemistry
MEUNIER, Chemistry
Mme MICHELOT, Physics
MICHON, Mathematics
MILAN, Electronics
MILLOT, Physics
MOÏSE, C., Chemistry
MOUSSU, Mathematics
MUGNIER, Chemistry
NIEPCE, J.-CL., Chemistry
PAINDAVOINE, Automatics
PALLO, Informatics
PAUL, Plant Biology
PAUTY, Physics
PERRON, Mathematics
PIERRE, Physics
PINCZON, Mathematics
PRIBETICH, Electronics
PUGIN, Biochemistry
RACLIN, Mechanics
REMOISSENET, Physics
ROUSSARIE, Mathematics
SCHMITT, Mathematics
SEMENOV, Mathematics
SIEROFF, Neurophysiology
SIMON, Mathematics
STEINBRUNN, Chemistry
THIERRY, Geology
Mme TOURNEFIER, Biology
VALLADE, Plant Biology
WABNITZ, Physics
YETONGNON, Informatics

University Institute of Technology:

BELEY, Biology, Applied Biochemistry
BERLIÈRE, Contemporary History
BERNARD, Physiology and Nutrition
BESSIS, Botany
BIZOUARD, M., Thermodynamics
BUGAUT, Biochemistry
CHANUSSOT, Physics
DIOU, Industrial Computer Science
GORRIA, Computer Engineering
GREVEY, Materials
POISSON, Biochemistry
SACILOTTI, Physics
TRUCHETET, Computer Engineering

University Professional Institute of Management in Education, Training and Culture:

JAROUSSE, J.-P., Education
PATRIAT, C., Informatics and Communication
SOLAUX, A., Education

Viticulture and Oenology Experimental Centre:

CHARPENTIER, O., Oenology
FEUILLAT, M., Oenology

UNIVERSITÉ DE BRETAGNE OCCIDENTALE

Site 1–3, Rue des Archives, BP 808, 29285 Brest Cedex
Telephone: 2-98-01-60-20
Fax: 2-98-01-60-01
Internet: www.univ-brest.fr

Pres.: JEAN-CLAUDE BODÉRÉ
Sec.-Gen.: RENÉ FIRMIN

Librarian: ALAIN SAINSOT
Number of teaching staff: 820
Number of students: 19,090

TEACHING AND RESEARCH UNITS

Ecole Supérieure de Microbiologie et Sécurité Alimentaire de Brest (ESMISAB): Dir: YVES TIRILLY
Euro-Institut d'Actuariat (EURIA): Dir: HERVÉ LE BORGNE
Institut d'Administration des Entreprises: Dir: CHRISTIAN CADIOU
Institut de Préparation à l'Administration Générale: Dir: THIERRY SELLIN
Institut Universitaire Génie Mécanique et Productique: Dir: BERNARD GINESTE
Institut Universitaire Ingénierie Informatique: Dir: YVON AUTRET
Institut Universitaire Professionnalisé Innovation en Industrie Alimentaire: Dir: FABIENNE GUERARD
Institut Universitaire Professionnalisé Métiers des Arts et de la Culture
Institut Universitaire Télécommunications et Réseaux: Dir: PIERRE VILBE
Law, Economics and Management: Dean: VÉRONIQUE LABROT
Letters and Social Sciences: Dean: JEAN-CLAUDE GARDE
Medicine: Dean: YVES BIZAIS
Odontology: Dean: ALAIN ZERILLI
Science and Technology: Dean: PASCAL OLIVARD
University Institute of Technology (Brest): Dir: JOËL LE GUEN
University Institute of Technology (Quimper): Dir: ROGER PRAT

ATTACHED RESEARCH INSTITUTES

École Supérieure de Microbiologie et Sécurité Alimentaire de Brest (ESMISAB): Technopôle Brest-Iroise, 29280 Plouzané; tel. 2-98-05-61-00; fax 2-98-05-61-01; e-mail esmisab@univ-brest.fr; internet www.univ-brest.fr/esmisab; Dir YVES TIRILLY.

Institut de Recherche sur l'Enseignement des Mathématiques (IREM): 6 Ave Victor Le Gorgeu, 29238 Brest Cedex 3; tel. 2-98-01-65-44; fax 2-98-01-64-41; e-mail irem@univ-brest.fr; Dir (vacant).

Institut des Sciences Agro-alimentaires et du Monde Rural: 2 rue de l'université, 29334 Quimper Cedex; tel. 2-98-90-85-48; Dir ADRIEN BINET.

Institut de Synergie des Sciences de la Santé: Site CHU Morvan, 29609 Brest Cedex; tel. 2-98-01-81-30; fax 2-98-01-81-24; internet www.univ-brest.fr/i3s; Dir CLAUDE FEREC.

Institut Universitaire Européen de la Mer (IUEM): place Nicolas Copernic, 29280 Plouzané; tel. 2-98-49-86-00; fax 2-98-49-86-09; e-mail direction.iuem@univ-brest.fr; internet www.univ-brest.fr/iuem; Dir PAUL TREGUER.

UNIVERSITÉ DE CAEN BASSE-NORMANDIE

Esplanade de la Paix, 14032 Caen Cedex
Telephone: 2-31-56-55-00
Fax: 2-31-56-56-00
Internet: www.unicaen.fr

Founded 1432; reorganized 1985

Rector: JEAN-BAPTISTE CARPENTIER
Pres.: NICOLE LE QUERLER
Vice-Pres.: PATRICK DALLEMAGNE ROBERT FERRANDIER CÉLINE LECONTE
Sec.-Gen.: FRANÇOIS RIOU
Librarian: FRANÇOISE BERMANN

Library: see Libraries
Number of teachers: 1,154
Number of students: 26,667

TEACHING AND RESEARCH UNITS

Law and Political Science: Dir: ANNICK BATTEUR
Geography: Dir: ANNE-MARIE FIXOT
Economics and Management Science: Dir: CÉCILE LE CORROLLER
Medicine: Dir: JEAN-LOUIS GERARD
Psychology: Dir: JOËLLE LEBREUILLY
Pharmaceutical Sciences: Dir: P. DALLEMAGNE
Science of Man: Dir: BERNARD DEFORGE
Modern Languages: Dir: ERIC GILBERT
History: Dir: JEAN QUELLIEN
Sciences: Dir: CHRISTIAN DUBUC
Sciences et Techniques des Activités Physiques et Sportives (STAPS): Dir: FRANCIS LESTIENNE
Institute of Fundamental and Applied Biology: Dir: ANDRÉ NOUVELOT
Business Administration: Dir: FABRICE LEVI-GOUREUX
General Administration: Dir: FRANÇOISE EPINETTE
Institut universitaire professionnalisé Banque-Assurance: Dir: R. FERRANDIER
Institut universitaire professionnalisé: Agroalimentaire: Dir: JEAN-PAUL VERNOUX
Institut universitaire professionnalisé: Management du social et de la santé: Dir: DOMINIQUE BEYNIER
Institut universitaire de technologie de Cherbourg–Manche: Dir: PHILIPPE MAKANY
Institut universitaire de technologie d'Alencon: Dir: MOHAMED AYACHI
Institut universitaire de technologie de Caen: Dir: DENIS BLANCHON
Ecole d'Ingénieurs de Cherbourg: Dir: DOMINIQUE KERVADEC

ATTACHED INSTITUTES

Ecole Nationale Supérieure d'Ingénieurs de Caen: 6 Blvd Maréchal Juin, 14050 Caen Cedex; tel. 2-31-45-27-50; fax 2-31-45-27-60; internet www.ensicaen.fr; Dir D. GUERREAU.

Institut Universitaire de Formation des Maîtres: 186 rue de la Délivrande, 14053 Caen Cedex 04; tel. 2-31-46-70-80; fax 2-31-93-31-27; internet www.caen.iufm.fr; Dir JEAN MARC GUEGUENIAT.

UNIVERSITÉ DE CERGY-PONTOISE

8 Le Campus, 95033 Cergy-Pontoise Cedex
Telephone: 1-34-25-49-49
Fax: 1-34-25-49-04
Internet: www.u-cergy.fr

Pres.: THIERRY COULHON
Sec.-Gen.: ERIC FRANÇOIS
Number of students: 11,225

UNIVERSITÉ DE CORSE PASQUALE PAOLI/UNIVERSITÀ DI CORSICA

BP 52, 7 ave Jean-Nicoli, 20250 Corti
Telephone: 4-95-45-00-00
Internet: www.univ-corse.fr

Founded 1976; opened 1981

Pres.: ANTOINE AIELLO
Sec.-Gen.: FABIENNE PALMARO
Chief Librarian: ROLAND RINALDI

DEANS

Faculty of Law and Economics: JEAN-YVES COPPOLANI
Faculty of Literature, Languages, Arts and Human Sciences: JEAN-MARIE COMITI
Faculty of Sciences: VANINA PASQUALINI
University Institute of Technology: CHRISTIAN CRISTOFARI

ATTACHED RESEARCH INSTITUTES

'Sciences pour l'environnement': SPE UMA 6134, Quartier Grossetti, BP 52,

20250 Corte; tel. 4-95-45-01-65; fax 4-95-45-01-62; e-mail spe@univ-corse.fr; internet spe.univ-corse.fr; Dir PAUL BISGAMBIGLIA.

Centre de Recherche Corse Méditerranée (CRCM): tel. 4-95-45-00-77; Dir PHILIPPE PESTEIL.

Institut de Développement des Iles Mediterranéennes (IDIM): tel. 4-95-45-00-18; Dir JEAN YVES COPPOLANI.

Institut d'Études Scientifiques de Cargèse: 20130 Cargèse; fax 4-95-26-80-45; internet cargese.univ-corse.fr; Dir ÉLISABETH DUBOIS-VIOLETTE.

'Lieux, Identités, eSpaces et Acitvités': tel. 4-95-45-01-78; fax 4-95-45-01-66; Dir MARIE-ANTOINETTE MAUPERTUIS.

UNIVERSITÉ DE FRANCHE-COMTÉ

1 rue Claude Goudimel, 25030 Besançon Cedex

Telephone: 3-81-66-50-34
Fax: 3-81-66-50-36
E-mail: dri@univ-fcomte.fr
Internet: www.univ-fcomte.fr

Founded 1423 at Dôle, 1691 at Besançon

Pres.: FRANÇOISE BÉVALOT
Vice-Pres.: DANIEL RONDOT, FRANCIS FARRUGIA, PIERRE-MARIE BADOT, ERIC PRÉDINE, NICOLAS CLERE
Sec.-Gen.: LOUIS BÉRION
Library: see Libraries
Number of teachers: 1,244
Number of students: 20,718

Publications: *En Direct*, *Tout l'U*

TEACHING AND RESEARCH UNITS

Besançon Observatory: Dir: FRANÇOIS VERNOTTE
Centre of Applied Linguistics: Dir: SERGE BORG
Higher Institute of Engineering: Dir: PHILIPPE PICART
Industrial Science, Management and Technology: Dir: GABRIÈLE PADBERG
Institute of Business Administration: Dir: BENOÎT PIGÉ
Law, Economics and Politics: Dir: BERNARD LIME
Literature and Human Sciences: Dir: CLAUDE CONDÉ
Medicine and Pharmacy: Dir: HUGUES BITTARD
Physical Education and Sport: Dir: JACQUELINE CALLIER
Science and Technology: Dir: JOËL BERGER
University Institute of Technology (Besançon-Vesoul): Dir: MICHEL TACHEZ
University Institute of Technology (Belfort-Montbéliard): Dir: PHILIPPE PRACHT

UNIVERSITÉ DE GRENOBLE I (UNIVERSITÉ JOSEPH FOURIER)

BP 53, 38041 Grenoble Cedex 9

Telephone: 4-76-51-46-00
Fax: 4-76-51-48-48
E-mail: secretariat.general@ujf-grenoble.fr
Internet: www.ujf-grenoble.fr

Founded 1339
Academic year: September to June

Pres.: FARID OUABDESSELAM
Vice-Pres: ARTHUR SOUCEMARIANADIN, LAURENT DAUDEVILLE, JACQUES GASQUI ERIC BEAUGNON CATHERINE BERRUT, PIERRE BACONNIER, BERNARD SELE, JEAN-GABRIEL VALAY, GEOFFROY CARRIER
Sec.-Gen.: JEAN-LUC ARGENTIER

Number of teachers: 1,300
Number of students: 18,000

Publications: *Info-Hebdo* (52 a year), *La Pie* (12 a year), *Le Gluon* (12 a year), *Les*

Dépêches de l'UJF (12 a year), *Papyrus* (2 a year)

TEACHING AND RESEARCH UNITS

Applied Mathematics and Computer Sciences: Dir: JEAN-CLAUDE FERNANDEZ
Biology: Dir: MICHEL ROBERT-NICOUD
Chemistry: Dir: GUY SERRATRICE
Geography: Dir: MARIE-CHRISTINE FOURNY
Mathematics: Dir: CHRISTINE LAURENT
Mechanical Engineering: Dir: HENRI PARIS
Medicine: Dir: BERNARD SÈLE
Pharmacy: Dir: RENÉE GRILLOT
Physical Education and Sport: Dir: YVES ÉBERHARD
Physics: Dir: KONSTANTIN PROTASSOV

ATTACHED INSTITUTES

Centre Scientifique Joseph Fourier Drôme-Ardèche: BP 2, 26901 Valence Cedex 9; tel. 4-56-52-11-11; fax 4-75-56-16-20; e-mail contact.valence@ujf-grenoble.fr; internet www-valence.ujf-grenoble.fr; Dir ISABELLE COLOMB.

Collège des Ecoles Doctorales: tel. 4-76-51-45-08; fax 4-76-51-44-22; Dir PATRICK WITOMSKI.

Département Licence Sciences et Technologies: 480 ave centrale, 38400 St Martin d'Hères; tel. 4-76-51-45-63; fax 4-76-51-42-68; internet dlst.ujf-grenoble.fr; Dir BERNARD YCART.

Ecole de Physique des Houches: La Côte des Chavants, 74310 Les Houches; tel. 4-50-54-40-69; fax 4-50-55-53-25; e-mail secretariat.houches@ujf-grenoble.fr; internet houches.ujf-grenoble.fr; Dir LETICIA CUGLIANDOLO.

Ecole Polytechnique—Polytech'Grenoble: 28 ave Benoît Frachon, 38400 St Martin d'Hères; tel. 4-76-82-79-02; fax 4-76-82-79-01; e-mail polytech@ujf-grenoble.fr; internet www.polytech-grenoble.fr; Dir RENE-LOUIS INGLEBERT.

Floralis–Filiale de la Valorisation de la Recherche de l'UJF: 6 allée de Bethléem, 38610 Gières; tel. 4-76-00-70-30; fax 4-76-00-70-28; e-mail contact@floralis.fr; internet www.floralis.fr; Dir ERIC LARREY.

Formation Continue: 2 ave de Vignate, 38610 Gières; tel. 4-56-52-03-29; fax 4-56-52-03-32; e-mail formation-continue@ujf-grenoble.fr; Dir JEAN-GABRIEL VALAY.

Institut Universitaire de Formation des Maîtres: 30 ave Marcelin Berthelot, 38100 Grenoble; tel. 4-56-52-07-00; fax 4-76-87-19-47; internet iufm.ujf-grenoble.fr; Dir PATRICK MENDELSON.

Institut Universitaire de Technologie: 151 rue de la Papeterie, 38402 St Martin d'Hères; tel. 4-76-82-53-00; fax 4-76-82-53-26; e-mail administration.iut@ujf-grenoble.fr; internet www-iut.ujf-grenoble.fr; Dir JEAN-MICHEL TERRIEZ.

Observatoire des Sciences de l'Univers Grenoble: 414 rue de la Piscine, 38400 St Martin d'Hères; tel. 4-76-51-49-81; fax 4-76-63-55-35; e-mail obs-dir@ujf-grenoble.fr; internet www.obs.ujf-grenoble.fr/osug; Dir HENRI-CLAUDE NATAF.

Service Commun des Enseignements Transversaux: Dir JEAN-PIERRE HENRY.

UNIVERSITÉ DE GRENOBLE II (UNIVERSITÉ PIERRE MENDÈS-FRANCE)

BP 47X, 38040 Grenoble Cedex

Telephone: 4-76-82-54-00
Fax: 4-76-82-56-54
Internet: www.upmf-grenoble.fr

Founded 1970
Academic year: September to June

Pres.: CLAUDE COURLET
Vice-Pres.: ALAIN PESSIN (Education, Documentation and Culture), ALAIN SPALANZANI (Exec. Board), JACQUES FONTANEL (Int. Relations), THÉOPHILE OHLMANN (Scientific Ccl), DAMIEN REUMAUX (Student Body)
Sec.-Gen.: FRANCK LENOIR
Library: see Libraries
Number of teachers: 718
Number of students: 19,531

Publications: *Guide de l'Etudiant, Intercours*

TEACHING AND RESEARCH UNITS

Institute for Political Studies: Dir: PIERRE BRÉCHON
Institute of Urban Studies: Dir: GILLES NOVARINA
School of Economics: Dir: ALBAN RICHARD
School of Economy, Strategy and Enterprise: Dir: BERNARD GERBIER
School of Higher Business Studies: Dir: DIDIER RETOUR
School of Human and Social Sciences: Dir: JACQUES BAILLE
School of Humanities: Dir: JEAN-LUC LAMBOLEY
School of Law: Dean: MARCEL-RENÉ TERCINET
Médiat Rhône-Alpes: Dir: MARIE-MADELEINE SABY
Plate-forme Multimédia à Vigny Musset: Dir: GUY ROMIER
Professional Institute of Business and Sales
Professional Institute of Economic Engineering: Dir: BERNARD DRUGMAN
Professional Institute of Arts and Culture: Dir: JEAN-MARC FRANCONY
University Technical Institute–Grenoble II: Dir: CLAUDE BENOÎT
University Technical Institute–Valence: Dir: GÉRARD JOUVE

PROFESSORS

ALBOUY, M., Management
ANTONIADIS, A., Mathematics
ARNAUD, P., Sociology
BAILLE, J., Education
BARREYRE, P.-Y., Management
BELLISSANT, C., Computer Science
BERNARD, J.-P., Political Science
BIAYS, J. P., Political Science
BILLAUDOT, B., Economics
BORRELLY, R., Economics
BOUTOT, A., Philosophy
BRECHON, P., Political Science
CHATELUS, M., Economics
CHIANEA, G., History of Law
COURTIN, J., Informatics
COVIAUX, C., Private Law
CROISAT, M., Political Science
D'ARCY, F., Political Science
DESTANNE DE BERNIS, G., Economics
DIDIER, P., History of Law
DROUET D'AUBIGNY, G., Mathematics
EUZEBY, A., Economics and Management
EUZEBY, C., Economics
FOUCHARD, A., History
FRANCILLON, J., Private Law
GIROD, P., Management
GLEIZAL, J.-J., Public Law
GOUTAL, J.-L., Private Law
GRANGE, D., History
GRELLIERE, V., Law
GROC, B., Computer Science
GUILHAUDIS, M., Public Law
HOLLARD, M., Economics
JOLIBERT, A., Management
LARGUIER, J., Private Law
LESCA, H., Management
LE STANC, C., Law
MAISONNEUVE, B., Mathematics
MARIGNY, J., History
MARTIN, C., Management
N'GUYEN XUAN DANG, M.
OHLMANN, T., Psychology
PAGE, A., Management

PARAVY, P., History
PASCAL, G., Philosophy
PATUREL, R., Management
PECCOUD, F., Computer Science
PETIT, B., Private Law
PIETRA, R., Philosophy
POUSSIN, G., Psychology
POUYET, B., Public Law
RENARD, D., Political Science
RICHARD, A., Economics
ROMIER, G., Applied Mathematics
ROUSSET, M., Public Law
SALVAGE, PASCALE, Law
SALVAGE, PHILIPPE, Law
SCHNEIDER, C., Public Law
SEGRESTIN, D., Industrial Engineering
SIRONNEAU, J.-P., Sociology
SOLE, J., History
SOULAGE, B., Political Science
TERCINET, M., Public Law
TESTON, G.
TIBERGHIEN, G., Psychology
TRAHAND, J., Management
VALETTE-FLORENCE, P.
VERNANT, D., Philosophy

UNIVERSITÉ DE GRENOBLE III (UNIVERSITÉ STENDHAL)

BP 25, 38040 Grenoble Cedex 9
1180 ave Centrale, 38400
Telephone: 4-76-82-43-00
Fax: 4-76-82-41-85
Internet: www.u-grenoble3.fr
Founded 1970
Pres.: PATRICK CHÉZAUD
Vice-Pres.: ODILE LAGOACHERIE, FRANÇOISE PAPA, MICHEL LAFON
Sec.-Gen.: GERARD LANCIAN
Number of teachers: 330
Number of students: 7,500
Publication: *La Gazette de l'Université*

TEACHING AND RESEARCH UNITS

Communication Sciences: Dir: LUIZ BUSATO
English: Dir: SUSAN BLATTES
Languages: (vacant)
Linguistic Science: Dir: CHRISTIAN ABRY
Literature: Dir: ROGER BELLON

DIRECTORS OF DEPARTMENTS

Languages, Literature and Foreign Civilizations:
  Applied Foreign Languages: (vacant)
  German and Dutch Studies: JEAN-FRANÇOIS MARILLIER
  Iberian and Spanish-American Studies: ANNE CAYUELA
  Italian and Romanian Studies: ENZO NEPPI
  Oriental Studies: RITA MAZEN
  Russian and Slav Studies: ISABELLE DESPRES
  Trilingual Law and Economics: SUZAN BERTHIER
Modern and Classical Literature:
  Classical Studies: BENOÎT GOIN
  Comparative Literature: FLORENCE GOYET
  Languages, Literatures and French Civilization: BRIGITTE COMBE
Sciences of Language:
  French as a Foreign Language: VIOLAINE DE NUCHÈZE, JEAN EMMANUEL LE BRAY

UNIVERSITÉ DE HAUTE-ALSACE

2 rue des Frères Lumière, 68093 Mulhouse Cedex
Telephone: 3-89-33-60-00
Fax: 3-89-33-63-19
Internet: www.univ-mulhouse.fr
Founded 1975
Pres.: GUY SCHULTZ
Sec.-Gen.: ALAIN COLLANGE

Librarian: PHILIPPE RUSSELL
Number of teachers: 473
Number of students: 8,000

TEACHING AND RESEARCH UNITS

Applied Mathematics: Dir: MICHEL GOZE
Biology: Dir: BERNARD WALTER
European Centre for Accident Law: Dir: CLAUDE LIENHARD
Faculty of Economic and Social Sciences: Dir: DANIEL CHASSIGNET
General Photochemistry: Dir: DANIEL JOSEPH LOUGNOT
Geometric Modelling and Algorithms: Dir: JEAN-CLAUDE SPEHNER
Group Security and Chemical Ecology: Dir: SERGE WALTER
High Energy Physics: Dir: RENE BLAES
Institute of Chemistry: Dir: JACQUES SCHULTZ
Institute of European Languages and Literature: Dir: ERIC LYSOE
Institute of Technology Colmar: Dir: REINER BLAES
Institute of Technology Mulhouse: Dir: FRANCOIS OTT
Intelligent Processing Systems: Dir: PIERRE AMBS
Letters and Humanities: Dir: YANN KERDILES
Mineralogy: Dir: JOËL PATARIN
Organic and Bio-organic Chemistry: Dir: JACQUES EUSTACHE
Organizational Research: Dir: CLAUDE NOSOL
Pluridisciplinaire d'Enseignement Professionnalisé Supérieur (PEPS): Dir: SALOUA BENNAGHMOUCH
Physics and Electronic Spectroscopy: Dir: JOËL PATARIN
Risk Assessment: Dir: PIERRE EHRBURGER
Sciences: Dir: ALAIN BRILLARD
Roman and Christian Antiquity: Dir: MARIE-LAURE FREYBURGER
Science, Arts and Technology Research: Dir: PIERRE FLUCK
Technology: Dir: MARIE-HÉLÈNE TUILIER
Textile Research: Dir: JEAN-YVES DREAN

UNIVERSITÉ DE LA MÉDITERRANÉE AIX-MARSEILLE II

58 blvd Charles Livon, 13284 Marseilles Cedex 07
Telephone: 4-91-39-65-00
Fax: 4-91-31-31-36
Internet: www.univmed.fr
Founded 1973
Language of instruction: French
Academic year: October to June

Univs of Aix en Provence consist of three univs in Aix en Provence; economic science and information technology are the principal subjects of instruction here

Pres.: YVON BERLAND
Vice-Pres. for Admin. Council: DIDIER LAUSSEL
Vice-Pres. for Science Council: PIERRE CHIAPPETTA
Vice-Pres. for Education and Student Life: THIERRY PAUL
Vice-Pres. for Communication: PATRICE VANELLE
Vice-Pres. for Int. Relations: ROGER GIUDICHELLI
Sec.-Gen.: DAMIEN VERHAEGHE
Number of teachers: 660
Number of students: 24,186.

TEACHING AND RESEARCH UNITS

Faculty of Economic Science and Management: 14 rue Puvis de Chavannes, 13001 Marseilles; tel. 4-91-13-96-00; fax 4-91-90-58-29; Dean THIERRY PAUL.

Faculty of Medicine: 27 blvd Jean Moulin, 13385 Marseilles Cedex 5; tel. 4-91-32-43-00; fax 4-91-32-44-96; internet www.timone

.univ-mrs.fr/medecine; Dean GEORGES LEONETTI.

Faculty of Pharmacy: 27 blvd Jean Moulin, 13385 Marseilles Cedex 5; tel. 4-91-83-55-00; fax 4-91-80-26-12; internet www.pharmacie.univ-mrs.fr; Dean PATRICE VANELLE.

Faculty of Odontology: 27 blvd Jean Moulin, 13385 Marseilles Cedex 5; tel. 4-91-78-46-70; fax 4-91-78-23-43; Dean JACQUES DEJOU.

Faculty of Sciences at Luminy: 163 ave de Luminy, 13288 Marseilles Cedex 09; tel. 4-91-82-90-00; fax 4-91-26-92-00; internet www.sciences.univmed.fr; Dean CHENG-CAI ZHANG.

Faculty of Sports Sciences: 163 ave de Luminy, Case 910, 13288 Marseilles Cedex 9; tel. 4-91-17-04-12; fax 4-91-17-04-15; internet www.staps.univ-mrs.fr; Dean ERIC BERTON.

Institute of Labour: 12 traverse St Pierre, 13100 Aix en Provence; tel. 4-42-17-43-11; fax 4-42-21-20-12; e-mail irt@romarin.univ-aix.fr; Dir PATRICK BARRAU.

Institute of Mechanics: 60 rue Joliot Curie, 13453 Marseilles; tel. 4-91-11-38-02; fax 4-91-11-38-38; Dir PATRICK VIGLIANO.

Institut Universitaire de Technologie d'Aix-en-Provence: 413 Ave Gaston Berger, 13625 Aix en Provence Cedex 1; tel. 4-42-93-90-00; fax 4-42-93-90-90; internet www.iut.univ-aix.fr; Dir CLAUDE FIORE.

Centre d'Océanologie de Marseille: Campus de Luminy, 163 ave de Luminy, 13288 Marseilles Cedex 9; tel. 4-91-82-93-00; fax 4-91-82-93-03; internet www.com.univ-mrs.fr; Dean M. IVAN DEKEYSER.

Ecole Supérieure d'Ingénieurs de Luminy (ESIL): 163 ave de Luminy, Case 925, 13288 Marseilles Cedex 9; tel. 4-91-82-85-00; fax 4-91-82-85-91; e-mail contact@esil.univmed.fr; internet www.esil.univ-mrs.fr; Dir HENRI KANOUI.

School of Journalism and Communication: 21 rue Virgile Marron, 13392 Marseilles Cedex 05; tel. 4-91-24-32-00; fax 4-91-24-32-10; e-mail ejcm@ejcm.univmed.fr; internet www.ejcm.univ-mrs.fr; Dir LIONEL FLEURY.

ATTACHED INSTITUTES

Centre de Recherche pour l'Enseignement des Mathématiques (IRÉM): Faculté des Sciences de Luminy, 163 ave de Luminy, 13288 Marseilles Cedex 9; tel. 4-91-26-90-91; fax 4-91-26-93-43; research into the teaching of mathematics; Dir ROBERT ROLLAND.

Centre International de Formation et de Recherche en Didactique (CIFORD): Faculté des Sciences de Luminy, 163 ave de Luminy, 13288 Marseilles Cedex 9; tel. 4-91-26-90-30; fax 4-91-26-93-55; Dir PAUL ALLARD.

Centre Universitaire Régional d'Etudes Municipales (CURET): 191 rue Breteuil, 13006 Marseilles; tel. 4-91-37-61-62; fax 4-91-37-61-63; courses in local government administration; Dir M. FOUCHET.

Institut Universitaire Professionnalisé (IUP) Affaires et Finances: Faculté des Sciences Economiques, 14 ave Jules Ferry, 13621 Aix-en-Provence Cedex; tel. 4-42-33-48-70; fax 4-42-33-48-72; course on business and finance.

UNIVERSITÉ DE LILLE I (UNIVERSITÉ DES SCIENCES ET TECHNOLOGIES DE LILLE)

59655 Villeneuve d'Ascq Cedex
Telephone: 3-20-43-43-43

Fax: 3-20-43-49-95
Internet: www.univ-lille1.fr

Founded 1855 as Faculty of Sciences, present status 1971

Pres.: HERVÉ BAUSSART
Vice-Pres: JEAN-MICHEL ROBBE, LUCIEN LECLERCQ, PATRICK CARON, PIERRE BEHAGUE, BRUNO BOGAERT, JACQUES BROCARD, MARTINE CARETTE, BERTIN DE BETTIGNIES, VALÉRIE DELDEVRE, JACQUES DUFRESNE, NABI EL HAGGAR, MICHEL FEUTRIE, LUDOVIC LEGRAND, MARTINE SWITEK, BERNARD TOURSEL
Sec.-Gen.: YVES CHAIMBAULT

Number of teachers: 1,310
Number of students: 20,058

TEACHING AND RESEARCH UNITS

Agricultural Institute: Dir: BRUNO DELBREIL
Biology: Dir: JEAN-CLAUDE ANDRIES
Chemistry: Dir: ROBERT HUBAUT
Computer Science, Electronics; Electrical Engineering and Automation: Dir: MAOUCHE SALAH
Earth Sciences: Dir: Mme DELCAMBRE
Economics and Social Sciences: Dir: PHILIPPE ROLLET
Geography and Spatial Development: Dir: JEAN-PIERRE BONDUE
Higher National School of Chemistry in Lille: Dir: JEAN-CLAUDE BOIVIN
Institute of Business Studies: Dir: PIERRE LOUART
Pure and Applied Mathematics: Dir: MOSTAFA MBEKHTA
Physics: Dir: MICHEL FOULON
Polytech'Lille: Dir: JEAN-LOUIS BON
Telecom Lille: Dir: GUY MARMET
University Centre for the Economics of Permanent Education: Dir: JACQUES CLAUDEL
University Institute of Technology (Lille): Dir: HENRI BOCQUET

PROFESSORS

BOILLY, B., Biology
BONNELLE, J.-P., Chemistry
BREZINSKI, C., Computer Sciences
BRUYELLE, P., Geography
CHAMLEY, H., Geotechnics
CONSTANT, E., Electronics
CORDONNIER, V., Calculus and Information Science
DAUCHET, M., Theoretical Computing
DEBOURSE, J.-P., Management Science
DEBRABANT, P., Engineering
DEGAUQUE, P., Electronics
DHAINAUT, A., Biology
DORMARD, S., Economics
DOUKHAN, J.-C., Engineering
DUPOUY, J.-P., Biology
DYMENT, A., Mathematics
ESCAIG, B., Solid State Physics
FOCT, J., Chemistry
FOURET, R., Physics
FRONTIER, S., Biology
GLORIEUX, P., Physics
GOSSELIN, G., Sociology
GOUDMAND, P., Energy Generation
GRUSON, L., Pure and Applied Mathematics
GUILBAULT, Biology
LABLACHE-COMBIER, A., Organic Chemistry
LAVEINE, J.-P., Palaeobotany
LEHMANN, D., Geometry
Mme LENOBLE, Atmospheric Optics
LOMBARD, J., Sociology
LOUCHEUX, C., Macromolecular Chemistry
MACKE, B., Physics
MAILLET, P., Economic and Social Sciences
MICHEAUX, P., Mechanical Engineering
PAQUET, J., Applied Geology
PORCHET, M., Biology
PROUVOST, J., Mineralogy
RACZY, L., Computer Sciences
SALMER, G., Electronics
SCHAMPS, J., Physics

SEGUIER, G., Electro-Technology
SIMON, M., Economic and Social Sciences
SLIWA, H., Chemistry
SPIK, G., Biology
STANKIEWICZ, F., Economic Sciences
TOULOTTE, J.-M., Computer Sciences
TURREL, G., Chemistry
VERNET, P., Biology of Populations and Ecosystems
VIDAL, P., Automation
ZEYTOUNIAN, R., Mechanics

UNIVERSITÉ DE LILLE II (DROIT ET SANTÉ)

42 rue Paul Duez, 59800 Lille
Telephone: 3-20-96-43-43
Fax: 3-20-88-24-32
E-mail: ri@hp-sc.univ_lille2.fr
Internet: www.univ-lille2.fr

Founded 1969
State control
Language of instruction: French
Academic year: October to June

Pres.: Prof. CHRISTIAN SERGHERAERT
Vice-Pres: Prof. XAVIER VANDENDRIESSCHE, Prof. PIERRE MATHIOT, Prof. JEAN-PIERRE AUBERT, Prof. SALEM KACET, CLAIRE DAVAL, IRENE LAUTIER, Prof. PAUL FRIMAT, ROBIN SEMAL
Sec.-Gen.: GUY BAILLIEUL

Number of teachers: 1,000
Number of students: 22,000

DEANS

Faculty of Biological and Pharmaceutical Sciences: Prof. LUC DUBREUIL
Faculty of Dentistry: Prof. PIERRE LAFFORGUE
Faculty of Legal, Political and Social Sciences: Prof. CHRISTIAN MARIE WALLON LEDUCQ
Faculty of Medical Sciences: Prof. DIDIER GOSSET
Physical Education and Sport: Dir: IRENE LAUTIER

UNIVERSITÉ DE LILLE III, CHARLES DE GAULLE (SCIENCES HUMAINES, LETTRES ET ARTS)

rue du Barreau, BP 149, 59653 Villeneuve d'Ascq Cedex
Telephone: 3-20-41-60-00
Fax: 3-20-91-91-71
Internet: www.univ-lille3.fr

Founded 1560, present status 1985
Pres.: PHILIPPE ROUSSEAU
Sec.-Gen.: DANIÈLE SAVAGE
Librarian: JEAN-PAUL CHADOURNE

Number of teachers: 821
Number of students: 22,000

Publications: *Bien dire, bien apprendre, Cahiers de Recherches de l'institut de Papyrologie et d'Egyptologie, Etudes Irlandaises* (2 a year), *Germanica* (1 or 2 a year), *Graphé, Lexique* (1 a year), *Revue des Sciences Humaines* (4 a year), *Revue du Nord* (history, 5 a year), *Roman 20–50* (2 a year), *Uranie*

TEACHING AND RESEARCH UNITS

Applied Foreign Languages: Dir: BERNARD BACH
Arts and Culture: Dir: CHRISTIAN HAUER
Classical Languages and Culture: Dir: ALAIN DEREMETZ
Education: Dir: ALAIN DUBUS
English Language, Literature and Civilization: Dir: THOMAS FRASER
German and Scandinavian Studies: Dir: MARTINE-SOPHIE BENOÎT-ROUBINOWITZ
History, Art and Politics: Dir: STÉPHANE LEBECQ
INFOCOM: Dir: BERNARD DELFORCE

Information, Documentation and Scientific and Technical Information: Dir: MARIE DESPRES-LONNET
IUP–Artistic and Cultural Professions: Dir: PIERRE DELCAMBRE
IUP–Information Communication: Dir: OLIVIER CHANTRAINE
Mathematics, Economics and Social Sciences: Dir: PIERRE COURONNE
Modern Literature: Dir: MARIE-MADELEINE CASTELLANI
Romance, Slav and Oriental Studies: Dir: NORAH DEI CAS
Philosophy: Dir: MICHEL CRUBELLIER
Psychology: Dir: DANIEL BEAUNE
Training Centre for Accompanying Musicians: Dir: PASCAL HAMEAUX
University Institute of Technology B: Dir: MICHEL BUGHIN

PROFESSORS (1ST CLASS AND EXCEPTIONAL)

Classics:

BOULOGNE, J., Greek Language and Literature
DUMONT, J.-CHR., Social History of the Roman Republic

English Studies:

BECQUEMONT, D., History of Ideas, Phonetics and Phonology
DUPAS, J. C., Anglo-Saxon Language and Literature
DURAND, R., North American Literature and Civilization
ESCARBELT, B., Anglo-Saxon Language and Literature
GOURNAY, J.-F., 19th-century Literature and Civilization
SYS, J., British Civilization, History of Ideas

French Linguistics and Literature:

ALLUIN, B., Modern and Contemporary Language and Literature
BONNEFIS, PH., 19th-century Literature
BRASSEUR, A., Medieval Language and Literature
BUISIRE, A., French Language and Literature
CORBIN, D., French Language
GARY-PRIEUR, M. N., French Language
GUILLERM, J.-P., 19th-century Literature
GUILLERM-CURUTCHET, L., French Language and Literature
HORVILLE, R., 17th-century Literature
LESTRINGANT, FR., 16th-century Literature
MALANDAIN, P., Modern and Contemporary Language and Literature

German Studies:

COLONGE, P., 19th- and 20th-century Literature and Civilization
ROUSSEAU, A., Dutch Linguistics
VAN DE LOUW, G., Dutch
VAYDAT, P., Anglo-German Relations: 1870–1914

History, Art and Politics:

CHADEAU, E., Contemporary History
DELMAIRE, B., Medieval History
DELMAIRE, R., Ancient Roman History
GUIGNET, PH., Modern History
ROSSELLE, D., Modern Economic and Social History
VALBELLE, D., Egyptology

Mathematics, Economics, Social Sciences:

CELEYRETTE, J., Mathematics

Philosophy:

KINTZLER, C., General Philosophy and Aesthetics
KIRSCHER, G., Modern and Contemporary Philosophy
MACHEREY, P., Aesthetics and History of Philosophy

Psychology:

LECONTE, P., Experimental Psychology

Verquerre, R., Psychology
Romance, Slav, Semitic and Hungarian Studies:
  Allain, A., Russian
Other Professors:
  Losfeld, G., Information Science
  Reuter, Y., Teaching of French

UNIVERSITÉ DE LIMOGES

33 rue François Mitterrand, BP 23204, 87032 Limoges Cedex 01
Telephone: 5-55-14-91-00
Fax: 5-55-14-91-01
Internet: www.unilim.fr
Founded 1968
Academic year: September to June
Pres.: Jacques Fontanille
Sec.-Gen.: Daniel Poumérouly
Librarian: Joëlle Cartigny
Library: see Libraries
Number of teachers: 925
Number of students: 14,528

DEANS

Faculty of Arts and Humanities: Jacques Migozzi
Faculty of Law and Economic Sciences: Hélène Pauliat
Faculty of Medicine: Jean-Claude Vandroux
Faculty of Pharmacy: Francis Comby
Faculty of Science and Technology: Alain Celerier

PROFESSORS

Faculty of Arts and Humanities (39e rue Camille Guérin, 87036 Limoges Cedex; tel. 5-55-43-56-00; fax 5-55-43-56-03; e-mail jacques.migozzi@unilim.fr; internet www.flsh.unilim.fr):
  Balabanian, O., Geography and Development
  Barrière, B., Medieval Archaeological History
  Bedon, R., Ancient Language and Literature
  Behar, P., Germanic and Scandinavian Language and Literature
  Capdeboscq, A. M., Romance Language and Literature
  Caron, P., Modern and Contemporary French Language and Literature
  Chandes, G., Middle Age to Renaissance French Language and Literature
  Dumont, J., Ancient World Archaeological History
  El Gammal, J. M., World Medieval Archaeological History
  Filteau, C., Modern and Contemporary French Language and Literature
  Fontanille, J., Language Sciences
  Gendreau-Massaloux, Romance Language and Literature
  Grassin, J.-M., Comparative Literature
  Grassin, M., Anglo-Saxon English Language and Literature
  Leclanche, J.-L., Middle Age to Renaissance French Language and Literature
  Lemoine, B., Anglo-Saxon English Language and Literature
  Levet, J.-P., Ancient Language and Literature
  Moreau, J.-P., Anglo-Saxon English Language and Literature
  Nouhaud, M., Ancient Language and Literature
  Rambaux, C., Ancient Language and Literature
  Valadas, B., Economic and Regional Geography
  Verdon, J., World Medieval Archaeological History

Faculty of Law and Economic Sciences (5 rue Félix Eboué, BP 3127, 87031 Limoges Cedex 1; tel. 5-55-34-97-03; fax 5-55-34-97-11; e-mail helene.pauliat@unilim.fr; internet www.fdse.unilim.fr):
  Alaphilippe, F., Private Law and Criminology
  Archer, R., Economics
  Cavagnac, M., Economics
  Darreau, P., Economics
  Flandin-Blety, P., Legal and Institutional History
  Karaquillo, J.-P., Private Law and Criminology
  Lenclos, J.-L., Public Law
  Marguenaud, J.-P., Private Law
  Mouly, J., Private Law
  Pauliat, H., Public Law
  Prieur, M., Public Law
  Sauviat, A., Economics
  Tarazi, A., Economics
  Texier, P., Legal and Institutional History
  Vareille, B., Private Law

Faculty of Medicine (2 rue du docteur Marcland, 87025 Limoges Cedex; tel. 5-55-43-58-00; fax 5-55-43-58-01; e-mail doyen.medecine@unilim.fr; internet www.unilim.fr/medecine):
  Adenis, J.-P., Ophthalmology
  Alain, L., Infantile Surgery
  Aldigier, J.-C., Cardiology
  Archambeaud, F., Clinical Medicine
  Arnaud, J. P., Orthopaedics, Traumatology, Plastic Surgery
  Barthe, D., Histology, Embryology
  Baudet, J., Obstetrics and Gynaecology
  Bensaid, J., Clinical Cardiology
  Bertin, P., Therapeutics
  Bessede, J.-P., Otorhinolaryngology
  Bonnaud, F., Pneumo-Phthisiology
  Bonnetblanc, J.-M., Dermatology, Venereology
  Boulesteix, J., Paediatrics and Medical Genetics
  Bouquier, J.-J., Clinical Paediatrics
  Boutros, T. F., Epidemiology
  Breton, J.-C., Biochemistry
  Catanzano, G., Pathological Anatomy
  Colombeau, P., Urology
  Cubertafond, P., Digestive Surgery
  Darde, M. L., Parasitology
  De Lumley-Woodyear, L., Paediatrics
  Denis, F., Bacteriology, Virology
  Denizot, N., Anaesthesiology
  Descottes, B., Anatomy
  Dudognon, P., Occupational Therapy
  Dumas, J. Ph., Urology
  Dumas, M., Neurology
  Dumont, D., Occupational Medicines
  Dupuy, J.-P., Radiology
  Feiss, P., Anaesthesiology
  Gainant, A., Digestive Surgery
  Garoux, R., Child Psychiatry
  Gastinne, H., Resuscitation
  Hugon, J., Histology, Embryology
  Labrousse, C., Occupational Therapy
  Laskar, M., Thoracic and Cardiovascular Surgery
  Laubie, B., Endocrinology, Metabolism, Nutrition
  Leger, J.-M., Adult Psychiatry
  Leroux-Robert, C., Nephrology
  Menier, R., Physiology
  Merle, L., Pharmacology
  Moreau, J.-J., Neurosurgery
  Moulies, D., Infantile Surgery
  Pecout, C., Orthopaedics, Traumatology, Plastic Surgery
  Pichon Bourdessoule, D., Haematology
  Pillegand, B., Hepatogastroenterology
  Piva, C., Forensic Medicine and Toxicology
  Pra Loran, V., Haematology
  Ravon, R., Neurosurgery
  Rigaud, M., Biochemistry
  Rousseau, J., Radiology

  Sauvage, J.-P., Otorhinolaryngology
  Tabaste, J.-L., Gynaecology, Obstetrics
  Treves, R., Rheumatology
  Vallat, J.-M., Neurology
  Valleix, D., Anatomy
  Vandroux, J.-C., Biophysics
  Weinbreck, P., Tropical Medicine

Faculty of Pharmacy (2 rue du docteur Marcland, 87025 Limoges Cedex; tel. 5-55-43-58-00; fax 5-55-43-58-01; e-mail doyen.pharmacie@unilim.fr; internet www.facpharmacie.unilim.fr):
  Bernard, M., Physical Chemistry and Pharmaceutical Technology
  Bosgiraud, C., Biology
  Brossard, C., Physical Chemistry and Pharmaceutical Technology
  Buxeraud, J., Pharmacology
  Cardot, Ph., Physical Chemistry and Pharmaceutical Technology
  Chulia, A., Pharmacology
  Clement-Chulia, D., Physical Chemistry and Pharmaceutical Technology
  Delage, C., Physical and Mineral Chemistry
  Ghestem, A., Botany
  Habrioux, G., Biochemistry
  Oudart, N., Pharmacology

Faculty of Science and Technology (123 ave Albert Thomas, 87060 Limoges Cedex; tel. 5-55-45-72-00; fax 5-55-45-72-01; e-mail directeur.sciences@unilim.fr; internet www.sciences.unilim.fr):
  Baronnet, J.-M., Energetics
  Berland, R., Electronics, Electrotechnology and Automatics
  Besson, J.-L., Dense Media and Materials
  Caperaa, S., Civil Engineering
  Caron, A., Information Processing
  Catherinot, A., Energetics
  Colombeau, B., Optics
  Coudert, J. F., Methodology, Plasma and Automation
  Decossas, J. L., E.E.A.
  Deschaux, P., Physiology
  Desmaison, J., Mineral Chemistry
  Duval, D., Mathematics
  Fauchais, P., Energetics
  Fray, C., Electronics, Electrotechnology and Automatics
  Frit, B., Mineral Chemistry
  Gaudreau, B., Mineral Chemistry
  Glandus, J.-C., Mechanics, Mechanical Engineering and Civil Engineering
  Goursat, P., Mineral Chemistry
  Guillon, P., Electronics, Electrotechnology and Automation
  Jecko, B., Electronics, Electrotechnology and Automatics
  Jecko, F., Electronics, Electrotechnology and Automatics
  Julien, R., Biochemistry
  Krausz, P., Organic, Analytical and Industrial Chemistry
  Labbe, J.-C., Chemistry of Materials
  Laubie, F., Mathematics
  Malaise, M., Mechanics, Mechanical Engineering and Civil Engineering
  Marcou, J., Electronics, Electrotechnology and Automation
  Martin, C., Energetics
  Mazet, M., Organic, Analytical and Industrial Chemistry
  Mercurio, D., Mineral Chemistry
  Mercurio, J.-P., Mineral Chemistry
  Moliton, A., Optics
  Moliton, J. P., E.E.A.
  Morvan, H., Biology
  Nardou, F., Physical Chemistry
  Obregon, J., Electronics, Electrotechnology and Automatics
  Platon, F., Mechanics, Mechanical Engineering and Civil Engineering
  Quere, R., Electronics, Electrotechnology and Automation

QUINTARD, P., Dense Media and Materials
RATINAUD, M. M., Biochemistry and Biology
SABOURDY, G., Geology
THERA, M., Mathematics

AFFILIATED INSTITUTES

ENSIL (Limoges Engineering School):
16, Rue d'Atlantis, parc ESTER, 87068 Limoges Cedex; tel. 5-55-42-36-70; fax 5-55-42-36-80; e-mail direction@ensil.unilim.fr; internet www.ensil.unilim.fr; Dir PATRICK LEPRAT.

GEIST Institute ('Genetics, Environment, Immunity, Health and Therapy'):
Faculty of Medecine, 2 rue du Docteur Marcland, 87000 Limoges; tel. 5-55-43-58-48; e-mail michel.cogne@unilim.fr; Dir MICHEL COGNÉ.

Higher National School of Industrial Ceramics: 47–73 ave Albert Thomas, 87065 Limoges Cedex; tel. 5-55-45-22-22; fax 5-55-79-09-98; e-mail directin@ensci.fr; internet www.ensci.fr; Dir CHRISTIAN GAULT.

IAE (Institute of Business Administration): 3 rue François Mitterrand, 87031 Limoges; tel. 5-55-14-90-32; e-mail alain.rivet@unilim.fr; internet www.iae.unilim.fr; Dir ALAIN RIVET.

Institute of Life and Health Sciences: 123 ave Albert Thomas, 87060 Limoges Cedex; tel. 5-55-45-76-76; fax 5-55-45-72-01; Dir RAYMOND JULIEN.

Institute of the Environment and Water: 123 ave Albert Thomas, 87060 Limoges Cedex; tel. 5-55-45-74-69; fax 5-55-45-74-59; Dir JEAN-CLAUDE BOLLINGER.

IPAG (Institute of Preparation for General Administration/ Institut de Préparation à l'Administration Générale): 32 rue Turgot, 87000 Limoges; tel. 5-55-34-97-44; e-mail ipag@unilim.fr; internet www.ipag.unilim.fr; Dir CHRISTIAN MOULINARD.

IPAM 'Processes Applied to Materials' Research Institute: Faculty of Sciences and Technology, 123 ave Albert Thomas, 87060 Limoges Cedex; tel. 5-55-45-76-70; fax 5-55-45-72-70; e-mail armelle.vardelle@unilim.fr; Dir ARMELLE VARDELLE.

IUFM (Institute for Teacher Training): 209 boulevard de Vanteaux, 87000 Limoges; tel. 5-55-01-76-86; fax 5-55-01-76-99; internet www.limousin.iufm.fr; Dir VALÉRIE LEGROS.

IUT (University Institute of Technology (Limousin)): Allée Andrés Maurois, 87065 Limoges Cedex; tel. 5-55-43-43-55; fax 5-55-43-43-56; e-mail dir.iut@unilim.fr; internet www.iut.unilim.fr; Dir GILLES BROUSSAUD.

Science, Technology, Health: 13 Rue de Genève, 87065 Limoges Cedex; tel. 5-55-45-76-74; fax 5-55-45-76-73; e-mail ed-sts@unilim.fr; internet www.unilim.fr/edsts; Dir ABBAS CHAZAD MOVAHHEDI.

SHS Institute of Human and Social Sciences: Faculty of Law and Economics, 5 rue Félix Eboué, BP 3127, 87031 Limoges Cedex; tel. 5-55-14-92-10; e-mail alain.sauviat@unilim.fr; Dir ALAIN SAUVIAT.

University Professional Institute: 2 Rue du Docteur Marcland, 87025 Limoges Cedex; tel. 5-55-43-59-15; fax 5-55-43-59-36; e-mail iup@unilim.fr; Dir JEAN-FRANÇOIS NYS.

XLIM Mixed Research Unit: Faculty of Sciences and Technology, 123 ave Albert Thomas, 87060 Limoges Cedex; tel. 5-55-45-72-50; fax 5-55-45-72-01; e-mail dominique.cros@unilim.fr; internet www.xlim.fr; Dir DOMINIQUE CROS.

UNIVERSITÉ DE LYON

Caserne Sergent Blandan, 37 rue du Repos, 69365 Lyon

Telephone: 4-37-37-26-70
Fax: 4-37-37-26-71
Internet: www.universite-lyon.fr

Founded 2007 by merger of 9 founding mems and 11 assoc. mems
State control

Pres.: MICHEL LUSSAULT

Number of teachers: 9,500
Number of students: 120,000.

FOUNDING MEMBER INSTITUTIONS

Université Lyon I (Université Claude-Bernard)

43 blvd du 11 Novembre 1918, 69622 Villeurbanne Cedex

Telephone: 4-72-44-80-00
Fax: 4-72-43-10-20
Internet: www.univ-lyon1.fr

Founded 1970
State control
Language of instruction: French
Academic year: October to June

Pres.: DOMITIEN DEBOUZIE
Vice-Pres: ROBERT GARRONE (Administration), JEAN-FRANÇOIS MORNEX (Sciences), GUY ANNAT (Studies)
Secr.-Gen.: JEAN-PASCAL BONHOTAL

Number of teachers: 1,900
Number of students: 27,000

Publications: *Annuaire sur la Recherche* (1 a year), *Lettre FLASH/INFO* (4 a year), *Livret de l'Etudiant* (1 a year)

DIRECTORS OF TEACHING AND RESEARCH UNITS

Medicine:

Dentistry: J. OLIVIER ROBIN
Human Biology: PIERRE FARGE
Medicine 'Grange-Blanche': XAVIER MARTIN
Medicine 'Lyon-Nord': FRANÇOIS MAUGUIÈRE
Medicine 'Rth Laennec': DENIS VITAL-DURAND
Medicine 'Sud': FRANÇOIS-NOËL GILLY
Pharmaceutical and Biological Sciences: FRANÇOIS LOCHER
Rehabilitation: LIONEL COLLET

Sciences:

Biology: HUBERT PINON
Chemistry and Biochemistry: JEAN-PIERRE SCHARFF
Computer Science: MARCEL EGEA
Earth Sciences: PIERRE HANTZPERGUE
Electrical Engineering: ANDRÉ BRIGUET
Institute of Financial and Actuarial Sciences: JEAN-CLAUDE AUGROS
Lyon Institute of Science and Engineering Technology: JEAN-PIERRE PUAUX
Mathematics: MARC CHAMARIE
Mechanical Engineering: HAMDA BEN HADID
Observatory: ROLAND BACON
Physics: JEAN-LOUIS VIALLE
Science and Technology of Physical Education and Sport: RAPHAEL MASSAREL
University Institute of Technology 'A': MICHEL ODIN
University Institute of Technology 'B': GILBERT MAREST

Université Lyon 2 (Université Louis Lumière)

86 rue Pasteur, 69365 Lyons Cedex 07

Telephone: 4-78-69-70-00
Fax: 4-78-69-56-01
Internet: www.univ-lyon2.fr

Pres.: GILBERT PUECH

Vice-Pres. for Communication: ALEXANDRE BONUCCI
Vice-Pres. for Int. Relations: ISABELLE GUINAMARD
First Vice-Pres. for Human Resources and Admin.: HENRI BÉJOINT
Vice-Pres. for Research: YVES GRAFMEYER
Vice-Pres. for Resources and Budget: YVES CROZET
Vice-Pres. for Studies: FRANÇOISE DURIEUX
Vice-Pres. for Training: ISABELLE BON-GARÇIN
Vice-Pres. for Univ. Life, Culture and Sport: ALEXIS CHVETZOFF
Sec.-Gen.: BERNARD FRADIN

Number of teachers: 567
Number of students: 27,197

Publication: *Le Rayon Vert* (10 a year)

DEANS

Faculty of Anthropology and Sociology: JACQUES BONNIEL
Faculty of Economics and Business Studies: ANDRÉ TIRAN
Faculty of Geography, History, History of Art and Tourism: JEAN-MICHEL DEWAILLY
Faculty of Law and Political Science: CLAUDE JOURNÈS
Faculty of Literature, Science of Language and Arts: DENIS REYNAUD
Faculty of Modern Languages: FABRICE MALKANI

DIRECTORS

Institute of Communication: DOMINIQUE BOURGAIN
Institute of Labour: ALAIN BOUILLOUX
Institute of Political Studies: DANIEL DUFOURT
Institute of Psychology: JEAN-MARIE BESSE
Institute of Teacher Training: CHARLES GARDOU
Institute of Trade Union Training: FLORENCE DEBORD
Institut Universitaire de Technologie Lumière: MICHEL LE NIR

Université Lyon 3 (Université Jean Moulin)

1 rue de l'Université, BP 0638, 69239 Lyons Cedex 02

Telephone: 4-78-78-78-78
Fax: 4-78-78-79-79
Internet: www.univ-lyon3.fr

Founded 1973

President: GUY LAVOREL
Vice-Pres: IONNA SCHMIDT, JEAN-JACQUES WUNENBURGER, JACQUES BONNET, LAID BOUZIDI
Sec.-Gen.: CLAUDE MARSOT

Number of teachers: 500
Number of students: 20,000

Publication: *Lyon 3 Infos* (12 a year)

DEANS

Faculty of Languages: JEAN-LOUIS CHAUZIT
Faculty of Law: J. SAID
Faculty of Letters and Civilizations: NICOLE GONTHIER
Faculty of Philosophy: JEAN-JACQUES WUNENBURGER
Institute of Business Administration and Management: GILLES GUYOT
Institut Universitaire de Technologie

Université Jean Monnet de Saint-Etienne

34 rue Francis Baulier, 42023 Saint-Etienne Cedex

Telephone: 4-77-42-17-00
Fax: 4-77-42-17-99
Internet: www.univ-st-etienne.fr

Founded 1969 as Université de Saint-Étienne; present name 1991

State control
Language of instruction: French
Academic year: October to June
Pres.: MAURICE VINCENT
Vice-Pres: YVES BOUVERET, JEAN-BAPTISTE ORSINI, ANDRÉ GEYSSANT
Sec.-Gen.: P. BESSENAY
Librarian: Mme ACHARD

Number of teachers: 592
Number of students: 13,684

Publications: *L'Université communique* (52 a year), and various institute bulletins

TEACHING AND RESEARCH UNITS

Arts, Communication, Pedagogy: Dir: CHRISTIANE LAUVERGNAT (acting)
Institute of Advanced Science and Technology (ISTA): Dir: ROBERT ROUGNY
Institute of Industrial Management: Dir: GÉRARD LABAURE
Law and Economics: Dir: P. ANCEL
Letters and Human Sciences: Dir: G. ARGOUD
Medicine: Dir: P. QUENEAU
Sciences: Dir: B. BUISSON
University Institute of Technology: Dir: J. MAZERAN

Ecole Normale Supérieure de Lyon

46 allée d'Italie, 69364 Lyons Cedex 07

Telephone: 4-72-72-80-00
Fax: 4-72-72-80-80
E-mail: webmaster@ens-lyon.fr
Internet: www.ens-lyon.fr

Founded 1987
Library of 48,400 vols, 830 periodicals
Number of teachers: 225 teachers and researchers
Number of students: 915

Dir: BERNARD BIGOT
Sec.-Gen.: FRANÇOISE GRANGER
Dean of Teaching Departments: MARIE-CHRISTINE ARTRU
Librarian: JACQUELINE DE CONDAPPA.

Ecole Normale Supérieure Lettres et Sciences Humaines

15 parvis René Descartes, BP 7000, 69342 Lyon Cedex 07

Telephone: 4-37-37-60-00
Fax: 4-37-37-60-60
Internet: www.ens-lsh.fr

Number of teachers: 372
Number of students: 1,078

Ecole Centrale de Lyon

36 ave Guy de Collongue, 69134 Ecully Cedex

Telephone: 4-72-18-60-00
Fax: 4-78-43-39-62
Internet: www.ec-lyon.fr

Pres.: PRÉSIDENT CHRISTIAN MARI
Vice-Pres.: FRANÇOIS VIDAL
Dir: PATRICK BOURGIN
Deputy Dir: JEAN-PIERRE ROGNON
Dir of Studies: MARIE-ANNICK GALLAND
Dir of Research: JEAN-PIERRE BERTOGLIO
Sec.-Gen.: YVES GLORION.

Institut National des Sciences Appliquées de Lyon

20 ave Albert Einstein, 69621 Villeurbanne Cedex

Telephone: 4-72-43-83-83
Fax: 4-72-43-85-00
E-mail: dir@insa-lyon.fr

Founded 1957
Library of 80,000 vols
Number of teachers: 450
Number of students: 4,500

Biochemistry, computer science, civil, electrical, energetics, production and mechanical engineering, material science

Dir: JOËL ROCHAT.

Ecole Nationale des Mines de Saint-Etienne

158 cours Fauriel, 42023 Saint-Étienne Cedex 2

Telephone: 4-77-42-01-23
Fax: 4-77-42-00-00
Internet: www.emse.fr.

UNIVERSITÉ DE MARNE-LA-VALLÉE

5 blvd Descartes, Champs/Marne, 77454 Marne la Vallée Cedex 2

Telephone: 1-60-95-75-00
Fax: 1-60-95-75-75
Internet: www.univ-mlv.fr

Founded 1991
Pres.: YVES LICHTENBERGER
Sec.-Gen.: DENIS GUILLAUMIN
Librarian: EDWIGE ARCHIER
Number of teachers: 400
Number of students: 11,000

TEACHING AND RESEARCH UNITS

Arts and Technologies: GISÈLE SEGINGER
Economic Sciences: MANON DOS SANTOS
Engineering: DOMINIQUE PERRIN
Geosciences Engineering Institute: MICHEL MADON
Human and Social Sciences: FRÉDÉRIC MORET
Institute of Computing and Electronics: JACQUES DÉSARMÉNIEN
Institute of Engineering Services: DANIEL LAURENT
Languages and Civilization: GILLES ROBEL
Letters, Arts and Communication: GISÈLE SEGINGER
Mathematics: MATHIEU MEYER
Material Sciences: ROBERTO MARQUARDT
Science and Technology: PATRICK FAUCONNIER
Sports Science: ERIC LEVET-LABRY
University Institute of Technology: DOMINIQUE PRÉSENT

UNIVERSITÉ DE MONTPELLIER II (SCIENCES ET TECHNIQUES DU LANGUEDOC)

Place Eugène Bataillon, 34095 Montpellier Cedex 5

Telephone: 4-67-14-30-30
Fax: 4-67-14-30-31
E-mail: presidence@univ-montp2.fr
Internet: www.univ-montp2.fr

Pres.: JACQUES BONNAFE
Vice-Pres. for Ccl of Admin.: ALAIN SZAFARCZYK
Vice-Pres. for Ccl of Studies and Univ. Life: PIERRE MERLE
Vice-Pres. for Scientific Ccl: JEAN-LOUIS CUQ
Sec.-Gen.: NOELLE AVARD-CARDONA
Librarian: MIREILLE GALCERAN
Number of teachers: 745
Number of students: 13,450

Publications: *Cahiers de Mathématiques*, *Naturalia Monspelianesia*, *Paléobiologie Continentale—Paléovertebrata*.

TEACHING AND RESEARCH UNITS

Centre de Formation d'Apprentis: 8 Rue Jules Raimu, 30907 Nîmes Cedex; tel. 4-66-62-85-92; fax 4-66-62-85-91; e-mail cfaum2@univ-montp2.fr; internet www.cfa.iut-nimes.fr; Dir DANIEL MIGLIORINI.

Continued Professional Training: 99 ave d'Occitanie, 34096 Montpellier Cedex 5; tel. 4-99-58-52-72; fax 4-99-58-52-81; e-mail formperm@univ-montp2.fr; Dir JOSEPH CALAS.

Faculty of Sciences: Place Eugène Bataillon, 34095 Montpellier Cedex 5; tel. 4-67-14-

30-34; fax 4-67-14-47-00; internet www.ufr.univ-montp2.fr; Dir JEAN-LOUIS VIDAL.

Institute of Business Management: tel. 4-67-14-38-65; fax 4-67-14-42-42; e-mail courrier@iae.univ-montp2.fr; internet www.iae.univ-montp2.fr; Dir ALAIN BRIOLE.

Polytech' Montpellier: tel. 4-67-14-31-60; fax 4-67-14-45-14; e-mail scola@polytech.univ-montp2.fr; internet www.polytech.univ-montp2.fr; Dir MICHEL DESBORDES.

University Institute of Technology of Montpellier: 99 ave d'Occitanie, 34296 Montpellier Cedex 5; tel. 4-67-14-40-40; fax 4-99-58-50-41; Dir ALAIN ROUSSET.

University Institute of Technology of Nîmes: 8 Rue Jules Raimu, 30907 Nîmes Cedex; tel. 4-66-62-85-00; fax 4-66-62-85-01; internet www.iut-nimes.fr; Dir SALAM CHARAR.

UNIVERSITÉ DE MONTPELLIER III (UNIVERSITÉ PAUL VALÉRY)

Route de Mende, BP 5043, 34199 Montpellier Cedex 5

Telephone: 4-67-14-20-00
Fax: 4-67-14-20-52
Internet: www.univ-montp3.fr

Founded 1970
State control
Language of instruction: French
Academic year: September to July

Pres.: ANNE FRAÏSSE
Vice-Pres. for Admin.: YANN BISIOU
Vice-Pres. for Int. Relations: BURGHART SCHMIDT
Vice-Pres. for Science: PATRICK GILLI
Vice-Pres. for Studies and Univ. Life: CÉCILE POUSSARD
Sec.-Gen.: YVES CHAIMBAULT
Librarian: JEAN-FRANCOIS FOUCAUD
Number of teachers: 486
Number of students: 15,117

Publication: 68 research periodicals

TEACHING AND RESEARCH UNITS

Letters, Arts, Philosophy and Psychoanalysis: Dir: CHRISTIAN BELIN
Languages and Foreign and Regional Cultures: Dir: MARIE-PAULE MASSON
Human and Environmental Sciences: Dir: DAVID LEFÈVRE
Economic, Mathematical and Social Sciences: Dir: PATRICE SÉÉBOLD
Science of Society: Dir: RENÉ PRY

UNIVERSITÉ DE NANCY I (HENRI POINCARÉ)

24 rue Lionnois, BP 60120, 54003 Nancy Cedex

Telephone: 3-83-68-20-00
Fax: 3-83-68-21-00
E-mail: claire.bergerot@uhp.u-nancy.fr
Internet: www.uhp-nancy.fr

Founded 1970

Pres.: JEAN-PIERRE FINANCE
Vice-Pres. (Admin.): HENRY COUDANE
Vice-Pres. (Scientific): PATRICK ALNOT
Vice-Pres. (Studies and Univ. Life): CHRISTINE ATKINSON
Sec.-Gen.: JEAN DÉROCHE
Number of teachers: 1,434
Number of students: 16,764

Publications: *Bulletin d'Information* (10 a year), *Transversales* (3 a year)

TEACHING AND RESEARCH UNITS

Biological Sciences: Dir: CHRISTIAN DOURNON
Dental Surgery: Dir: JEAN-PAUL LOUIS
Higher School of Computing and its Applications: Dir: ANDRÉ SCHAFF

Higher School of the Science and Technology of Engineering: Dir: MICHEL ROBERT
Higher School of the Science and Technology of the Wood Industry: Dir: PASCAL TRIBOULOT
Materials Science and Processes: Dir: PIERRE GUILMIN
Mathematics, Computing and Automation: Dir: MARIE-CHRISTINE HATON
Medicine: Dir: PATRICK NETTER
Pharmacy: Dir: FRANCINE PAULUS
Sciences: Dir: PIERRE GUILMIN
Sport and Physical Education: Dir: JEAN HUOT
University Institute of Technology (Longwy): Dir: PHILIPPE PIERROT
University Institute of Technology (Nancy-Brabois): Dir: JEAN-MARIE HORNUT
University Institute of Technology (Saint Dié): Dir: THIERRY CECCHIN

UNIVERSITÉ DE NANCY II

25 rue Baron Louis, BP 454, 54001 Nancy Cedex

Telephone: 3-83-34-46-00
Fax: 3-83-30-05-65
Internet: www.univ-nancy2.fr

Founded 1970
State control
Language of instruction: French
Academic year: October to May

President: HERBERT NERY
Vice-President, Administration Council: CHRISTIAN DUGAS DE LA BOISONNY
Vice-President, Scientific Council: BRUNO DEFFAINS
Vice-President, Council for Study and University Life: PASCALE FADE
Secretary-General: ODILE THIBIER
Librarian: J. B. MARINO

Library: see Libraries
Number of teachers: 531
Number of students: 22,000

Publications: Les Annales de l'Est, Verbum, Revue Géographique de l'Est, Autrement dire, Etudes d'archéologie classique, La Revue française d'études américaines

TEACHING AND RESEARCH UNITS

Business Management (Lorraine): Dir: CHRISTIAN BOURION
European University Centre: Dir: JEAN DENIS MOUTON
Foreign Languages and Literature: Dir: NICOLE FOURTANE
Historical and Geographical Sciences and Musicology: Dir: PATRICK CORBET
Human Sciences: Dir: NICOLE DUBOIS
Institute of Cinematographic Studies: Dir: RÉGIS LATOUCHE
Law, Economic Sciences and Management: Dir: ETIENNE CRIQUI
Literature: Dir: MARCEL PAUL-CAVALLIER
Regional Institute of Labour: Dir: DANIEL BOULMIER
Science of Languages: Dir: RICHARD DUDA
Social and Economic Administration: Dir: MARTIAL DELIGNON
Training Institute in General Administration: Dir: HUBERT GERARDIN, University Institute of Technology (at Nancy): Dir: HERVÉ COILLAND
University Institute of Technology (at Épinal): Dir: JEAN LEPAGE (acting)

UNIVERSITÉ DE NANTES

1 quai de Tourville, BP 13522, 44035 Nantes Cedex 01

Telephone: 2-40-99-83-83
Fax: 2-40-93-83-00
E-mail: president@president.univ-nantes.fr
Internet: www.univ-nantes.fr

Founded 1962
State control
Pres.: FRANÇOIS RESCHE
Vice-Pres.: SOPHIE VAN GOETHEM (Admin.), YVON LE GALL (Culture), OLGA GALATANU (Int. Relations), JOSEPH SAILLARD (Scientific Ccl), SOPHIE BINET (Students), JACQUES MARCHAND (Studies and Univ. Life)
Librarian: MICHÈLE GUIOT

Number of teachers: 1,354
Number of students: 33,278

Publication: Prisme (6 a year)

TEACHING AND RESEARCH UNITS

Dentistry: BERNARD GIUMELLI
Economic Science and Business Studies: BRUNO HENRIET
Higher Institute of Electronics: M. REMAUD
History, Art History and Archaeology: JACQUES WEBER
Human Sciences: Mme GANGLER
Institute of Business Administration: BERNARD FIOLEAU
Institute of Geography: MARC ROBIN
Institute of Preparatory Administrative Studies: LIONEL PROUTEAU
Institute of Technology (Nantes): G. COEURDEUIL
Institute of Technology (Roche-sur-Yon): ALAIN DUBOUX
Institute of Technology (St-Nazaire): M. LEFEVRE
Institute of Thermodynamics and Materials: M. SCHLEICH
International Language Centre
Law and Political Sciences: M. HELIN
Letters and Languages: DOMINIQUE GANGLER
Medicine: M. GROLLEAU
Pharmacology: ALAIN PINEAU
Polytech' Nantes: l'Ecole d'ingénieurs de l'Université: BERNARD REMAUD
Psychology: MOHAMMED BERNOUSSI
Sociology: CHARLES SUAUD
Science and Technology: DANIEL ARDOUIN
Sports Science: ARNAUD GUEVEL

UNIVERSITÉ DE NICE SOPHIA ANTIPOLIS

Grand Château, 28 parc Valrose, BP 2135, 06103 Nice Cedex 2

Telephone: 4-92-07-60-60
Fax: 4-92-07-66-00
Internet: www.unice.fr

Founded 1965
State control
Language of instruction: French

President: ALBERT MAROUANI
Vice-Presidents: J. MAGNÉ A. CHIAVELLI, P. FERRAN, Y. HERVIER
Secretary-General: P. R. VERNISSE
Librarian: LOUIS KLEE

Number of teachers: 1,200
Number of students: 27,500

Publications: Annuaire, Guide des formations de Recherche.

TEACHING AND RESEARCH UNITS

Culture and Space: Dir P. CARREGA.
Higher School of Engineering: 1645 route des Lucioles, 06410 Biot; tel. 4-92-38-85-00; fax 4-92-38-85-02; internet www.esinsa.unice.fr; Dir A. CHAVE.
Higher School of Information Sciences: 930 route des Colles, 06903 Sophia Antipolis Cedex; tel. 4-92-96-50-50; fax 4-92-96-50-55; e-mail essi@essi.fr; Dir A. GIULIERI.
Institute of Business Administration: Dir N. TOURNOIS.
Institute of Law, Peace and Development: 39 Ave Emile Henriot, 06050 Nice Cedex 1; tel. 4-92-15-71-94; fax 4-92-15-71-97; Dir L. BALMOND.

Medicine: Dir M. BENCHIMOL.
Odontology: Dir Prof. JASMIN.
Law, Politics, Economics and Management: Dir R. BERNARDINI.
Letters, Arts and Human Sciences: Dir A. ARNAUD.
Physical Education and Sports Sciences: 261 route de Grenoble, 06205 Nice Cedex 3; tel. 4-92-29-65-00; Dir I. MARGARITIS.
Sciences: Parc Valrose, 06108 Nice Cedex 2; tel. 4-92-07-60-60; Dir R. NÉGREL.
University Institute of Technology: internet www.iut.unice.fr; Dir R. CHIGNOLI

PROFESSORS

Law, Politics, Economics and Management (7 ave Robert Schuman, 06050 Nice Cedex 1; tel. 4-92-15-70-00; fax 4-92-15-71-01):

Economics:
ARENA, R.
BERTHOMIEU, C.
BOMEL, P.
GAFFARD, J.-L.
GUICHARD, J.-P.
JOB, L.
MAROUANI, A.
RAINELLI, M.
RAVIX, J.
ROMANI, P.-M.
SPINDLER, J.
TORRE, D.

History of Law:
BOTTIN, M.
CARLIN, M.-L.
ORTOLANI, M.
VERNIER, O.

Management:
BARTHE, N.
BARTOLI, J. A.
BOYER, A.
CHIAVELLI, A.
GIORDANO, Y.
GUYON, C.
MARTIN, M.
MARTORY, B.
NOBRE, T.
TELLER, R.
TOURNOIS, N.
WEISL, R.

Private Law:
AMBROISE CASTEROT, C.
ARRIGHI, J. P.
BERNARDINI, N.
BERNARDINI, R.
BOY, L.
COLLOMB, P.
LUCAS, F. X.
MARTIN, G.
RENUCCI, J. F.
VIDAL, D.

Politics:
BASSO, J.
BIDEGARAY, C.
BOUVET, L.
DABENE, O.
HEURTIN, J. P.

Public Law:
ASSO, B.
AUVRET-FINOK, J.
CHARVIN, R.
CRISTINI, R.
FERRARI, P.
LINOTTE, D.
NOËL, G.
PIQUEMAL, A.
QUIOT, G.
RAINAUD, J.-M.
RIDEAU, J.
SAUNIER, P.
TOUSCOZ, J.

VALLAR, CH.
WAGNER, F.
WECKEL, P.

Letters, Arts and Human Sciences (98 blvd E. Henriot, BP 3209, 06204 Nice Cedex 3; tel. 4-93-37-53-53; fax 4-93-37-55-36):

Comparative Literature:
CHEMAIN, A.
PUECH, S.

English:
BONIFAS, G.
GALLAGHER, M.
JUILLARD, M.
LAPRAZ, F.
LEMOSSE, M.
LLASERA, M.
MORGAN, G.
REMY, M.
SOUESME, J.-C.
TERREL, D.
VIOLA, A.
ZEENDER, M.

French Literature:
BONHOMME, B.
DOMENECH, J.
MARTINEAU, C.
PERIGOT, B.
RIEU, J.
SEILLAN, J. M
TASSEL, A.

French Philosophy:
GUEDJ, C.

Geography:
CARREGA, P.
DAUPHINE, A.
ESCALLIER, R.
LABORDE, J.-P.
ROGNANT, L.
VOIRON, C.

German:
DARMAUN, J.
FAURE, A.
VUILLAUME, M.
ZINGLE, H.

History:
ARNAUD, P.
BOURSIER, J. Y.
CANDAU, J.
DEVEAU, J. M.
EL MECHAT, S.
JANSEN, P.
LAUWERS, M.
REBUFFAT, F.
SCHOR, R.

Information Science:
HILLAIRE, N.
RASSE, P.

Latin:
BIRAUD, M.
DELBEY, E.
GUELFUCCI, M. R.
KIRCHER, C.
MUSTAPHA, M.

Linguistics and Phonetics:
BOUCHET, R.
DALBERA, J.-PH.
GASIGLIA, R.
KOTLER, E.
MOLLO, E.
NICOLAI, R.
ZINGLE, H.

Music:
BONNET, A.
CARDUCCI, M.
LELEU, J.-L.

Philosophy:
DASTUR, F.
LARTHOMAS, J.-P.
MATTEÏ, J.-F.

ROBELIN, J.
TOSEL, A.

Psychology:
BACCINO, T.
CARIOU, M.
FAURE, S.
GEFFROY, Y.
JURANVILLE, A.
LÉONARD, F.
MIOLLAN, C.
SCHADRON, G.
STEINER, D.

Romance Languages:
BARRACHINA, M. L.
BRAU, J.-L., Spanish
CASSAC, M.
FRESINA, C.
JAUBERT, A., French
MARTI, M.
MUSTAPHA, M.
SPIZZO, J., Italian

Sociology and Ethnology:
DE VOS, C.
MANN, P.
ZIROTTI, J P.

Medicine (Ave de Valombrose, 06107 Nice Cedex 2; tel. 4-93-37-77-77; fax 4-93-53-15-15):

ALBERTINI, M., Paediatrics
AMIEL, J., Urology
AYRAUD, N., Genetics
BALAS, D., Histology
BATT, M., Surgery
BAUDOUY, M., Cardiology
BENCHIMOL, D.
BERNARD, A., Immunology
BERNARD, E., Paediatrics
BERNARDIN, G., Resuscitation
BLAIVE, B., Pneumology
BOCQUET, J.-P., Hygiene
BOILEAU, P., Orthopaedic Surgery
BONGAIN, A., Obstetrics
BOQUET, P., Bacteriology
BOURGEON, A., Anatomy
BOUTTE, P., Paediatrics
BRUNETON, J.-N., Radiology
BUSSIÈRE, F., Biophysics
CAMOUS, J.-P., Therapeutics
CANIVET, B., Internal Medicine
CAREL, C., Histology
CASSUTO, J.-P., Haematology
CHATEL, M., Neurology
COUSSEMENT, A., Radiology
DARCOURT, G., Psychiatry
DELLAMONICA, P., Infectious Diseases
DEMARD, F., Otorhinolaryngology
DE PERETTI, F., Anatomy
DESNUELLE, C., Cellular Biology
FENICHEL, P.
FERRARI, E., Cardiology
FUZIBET, J.-G., Internal Medicine
GASTAUD, P., Ophthalmology
GIBELIN, P., Cardiology
GILLET, J.-Y., Gynaecology
GRELLIER, P., Neurosurgery
GRIMAUD, D., Anaesthesiology
GUGENHEIM, J., Digestive Surgery
HASSEN KHOOJA, R., Vascular Surgery
HERUTERNE, X., Nutrition
JAECHER, P., Nephrology
JCHAI, C., Anaesthesiology and Resuscitation
JOURDAN, J., Thoracic Surgery
LACOUR, J.-P., Dermatology
LAMBERT, J.-CL., Genetics
LAZOUNSKI, M., Molecular Biochemistry and Biology
LEBRETON, E., Surgery
LEFEBVRE, J.-C., Bacteriology
LE FICHOUX, Y., Parasitology
MATTEI, M., Resuscitation
MICHIELS, J.-F., Pathological Anatomy
MOUIEL, J., Digestive Surgery

MOUROUX, J., Cardiac and Thoracic Surgery
MYQUEL, M., Child Psychiatry
ORTONNE, J.-P., Dermatology
PADOVANI, B., Medical Radiological Imagery
PAQUIS, P., Neurosurgery
PAQUIS, V., Genetics
PESCE, A., Geriatric Internal Medicine
PRINGUEY, D., Psychiatry
QUATREHOMME, G., Regional Medicine and Health Law
RAMPAL, P., Hepatology
RAUCOULES, A. M., Anaesthesiology and Resuscitation
RAUNAUDNÉE CHINCHILLA, D., Blood Transfusion
ROBERT, P., Adult Psychiatry
SADOUL, J.-L., Metabolic Medicine
SANTINI, J., Otorhinolaryngology
TOUBOL, J., Urology
TRAN, D. K., Gynaecology
VAN OBBERGHEN, E., Molecular Biochemistry and Biology
ZIEGLER, L., Rheumatology

Non-Linear Institute of Nice:
COULLET, P.
DEMAY, Y.
EHRENSTEIN, U.
IOOSS, G.
LE BELLAC, M.
ROCCA, F.

Odontology (24 ave des Diables Bleus, 06357 Nice Cedex 4; tel. 4-92-00-11-11; fax 4-92-00-12-63):
BOLLA, M.
BOLLA, M.
JASMIN, J.
MALHER, P.
MONTEIL, R.
ROCCA, J.-P.

Physical Education and Sports Sciences (261 route de Grenoble, BP 3259, 06205 Nice Cedex 3; tel. 4-92-29-65-00; fax 4-92-29-65-49):
BRUANT, G.
LEGROS, P.
MARINI, J. F.

Sciences (Parc Valrose, 06108 Nice Cedex 2; tel. 4-92-07-69-96; fax 4-92-07-69-76):

General:
PETIT, L.

Mathematics:
AUBERT, G.
BEAUVILLE, A.
BERNHARD, P.
BLUM, J.
BRIANCON, J.
CATHELINEAU, J.-L.
CHENAIS, D.
DIENER, F.
DIENER, M.
ELENCWAJG, G.
FABRE, S.
GALLIGO, A.
GIULIERI, A.
HIRSCHOWITZ, A.
LE BARZ, P.
LEBEAU, G.
LEMAIRE, J.
LEMAIRE, J.-M.
LE ROUX, J.
LOBRY, C.
MAISONOBE, P.
MARLIN, R.
MERLE, M.
MICHEL, O.
POPESCU, S.
POUPAUD, F.
RASCLE, M.
RIX, H.
ROUSSELET, B.
ROUVIÈRE, F.

SIMPSON, N.
THIELIGEN, A.
WALTER, C.
WOJTKOWIAK, Z.
XIOA, G.

Information Sciences:
BOND, I.
CAROMEL, D.
CAVARERO, A.
CAVARERO, J.-L.
COLLARD, P.
COSNARD, M.
FEDOU, J. M.
KOUNALIS, E.
LAFON, J. C.
LE CARME, O.
LE THANH, N.
LITOVSKY, I.
MIRANDA, S.
PEYRAT, CL.
PIERRE, L.
RUEHER, M.
SANDER, P.
RIGAULT, J.-P.

Physics:
AZEMA, A.
BATROUNI, G.
BROCH, H.
FARGES, J. P.
FEMENIAS, J. L.
GILLI, J. M.
JACQUEMOD, G.
KOFMAN, R.
KOSSIAVAS, G.
LAHEURTE, J.-P.
LAPRAZ, D.
LEGRAND, O.
LÉVY-LEBLOND, J.-M.
LEYCURAS, C.
LIPPI, G. L.
MALLET, G.
MEUNIER, J.-L.
OSTROWSKY, D.
OSTROWSKY, N.
PROVOST, J.-P.
ROMAGNON, J.-P.

Electronics and Industrial Computer
Science:
ALENGRIN, G.
ANDRÉ, C.
BARCI, G.
CAMBIAGGIO, E.
CHAVE, A.
CHAZE, A. M.
CONDOM, R.
CUVELIER, L.
DUVAL, D.
GERIBALDI, S.
GINGRAS, M.
IACCONI, P.
LEGENDRE, J. J.
MARMIER, N.
MENEZ, J.
SBIRRAZZUOLI, N.

Astrophysics:
AIME, C.
BORGNINO, J.
LANTERI, H.
RICORT, G.
SCHOLL, M.

Geology:
BLANCHET, R.
CARUBA, R.
CHEMANDA, A.
DELTEIL, J.
LARDEAUX, J. M.
POPOFF, M.
PUPIN, J. P.
SCHARER, U.
STEPHAN, J.-F.
VIRIEUX, J.

General Chemistry:
CABROL BASS, D.

GUION, J.
Organic, Mineral and Analytical Chemistry:
GAL, F.
GAYMARD, F.
GUEDJ, R.
PASTOR, R.
ROUILLARD, M.

Biochemistry:
AILHAUD, G.
CHRISTEN, R.
CLERTANT, P.
COUSIN, J. L.
CUPPO, A.
CUZIN, F.
GLAICHENHAUS, N.
NEGREL, R.
VINCENT, J.-P.

Physiology and Biology:
ALLEMAND, D.
DELAUNAY, F.
EHRENFELD, J., Cellular and Comparative
Physiology
FRANCOUR, P.
GARCIA, R.
GIRARD, J.-P., Cellular and Comparative
Physiology
GOTTESMANN, C., Psychophysiology
HEROUART, D.
LE RUDULIER, D., Plant Biology and
Microbiology
MARSAULT, R.
MEINESZ, A., Marine Ecology and Biology
MIENVILLE, J. M.
NICAISE, G., Applied Microscopy
PAYAN, P., Cellular and Comparative
Physiology
PUPPO, A., Plant Biology and Microbiology
VIANI, R., Biophysics

Higher School of Information Sciences:
FRANCHI-ZANNETTACCI, P.
GIULIERI, A.
LAFON, J.-C.
University Institute of Technology (41 blvd
Napoleon III, 06141 Nice Cedex; tel. 4-97-25-
82-00; fax 4-97-25-83-30):
BARLAUD, M.
DEMARTINI, J.
POMPEI, D.
TREDDICE, J.
TSCHAEGLE, A.

UNIVERSITÉ DE PARIS II
(UNIVERSITÉ PANTHÉON-ASSAS)

12 place du Panthéon, 75231 Paris Cedex 05
Telephone: 1-44-41-57-00
Fax: 1-44-41-55-13
Internet: www.u-paris2.fr
Founded 1970
Pres.: JACQUELINE DUTHEIL DE LA ROCHÈRE
Sec.-Gen.: THIÉRRY CRÉDEVILLE
Librarian: GENEVIÈVE SONNEVILLE

Number of teachers: 300
Number of students: 18,109

TEACHING AND RESEARCH UNITS
Centre for Human Resources Training: F.
BOURNOIS
Centre for Studies and Research in Con-
struction and Housing: Dir: Prof. P. MAL-
INVAUD
Law (First cycle): PIERRE CROCQ
Law (Second cycle) and Political Science: M.
COMBACAU
Law (Third cycle) and Political Science:
LAURENT LEVENEUR
Economics: ANTOINE BILLOT
Economic and Social Administration (First
and Second cycles): MARTINE PELE
Higher Institute for Defence Studies: Dir:
Prof. YVES CARO

Information Sciences (French Press Insti-
tute): Dir: Prof. NADINE TOUSSAINT-DES-
MOULINS
Image and Communication Institute: Dir:
Prof. C. TUAL
Institute for Administration Training: Dir:
JEAN-MICHEL DE FORGES
Institute of Advanced International Studies:
Dirs: C. LEBEN, P.-MARIE DUPUY
Institute of Business Law: Dir: Prof. MICHEL
GERMAIN
Institute of Comparative Law: Dir: Prof.
LOUIS VOGEL
Institute of Criminology: Dir: Prof. JACQUES-
HENRI ROBERT
Institute of Judicial Studies: Dir: Prof. S.
GUINCHARD
IUP–Management: Dir: Prof. RAYMOND TRÉ-
MOLIÈRES

PROFESSORS
ALLAND, D., Public Law
ALPHANDERY, E., Economic Sciences
AMSELEK, P., Public Law
ANCEL, D., Private Law
AUBY, J. B., Public Law
AUDIT, B., Private Law
AVRIL, P., Political Science
BALLE, F., Political Science
BALLOT, G., Economic Sciences
BARRAT, J., Information Sciences
BÉAUD, O., Public Law
BENZONI, L., Economic Sciences
BERNARD, M., Education Sciences
BETBEZE, J.-P., Economic Sciences
BETTATI, M., Public Law
BIENVENU, J. J., Public Law
BILLOT, A., Economic Sciences
BLAISE, J.-B., Private Law
BLUMANN, C., Public Law
BOISIVON, J.-P., Management Science
BONET, G., Private Law
BONNEAU, T., Private Law
BOURNOIS, F., Management Science
BRESSON, G., Economic Sciences
BURDEAU, F., History of Law
BUREAU, D., Private Law
CARBASSE, J. M., History of Law
CARO, J.-Y., Economic Sciences
CARTIER, M.-E., Private Law
CASTALDO, A., History of Law
Mme CATALA, N., Private Law
CAZENAVE, P., Economic Sciences
CHAGNOLLAUD, D., Political Science
CHAMPENOIS, G., Private Law
CHARPIN, F., Economic Sciences
CHEVALLIER, J., Public Law
CHRISTIN, Y., Economic Sciences
COCATRE-ZILGIEN, P., History of Law
COHEN-JONATHAN, G., Public Law
COMBACAU, J., Public Law
CROCQ, P., Private Law
DECOCQ, A., Private Law
DELVOLVE, P., Public Law
DERIEUX, E., Information Sciences
DESNEUF, P., Economic Sciences
DESPLAS, M., Economic Sciences
DIBOUT, P., Public Law
DIDIER, P., Private Law
DISCHAMPS, J. C., Management Science
DONIO, J., Computing
DRAGO, G., Public Law
DUBOIS, P.-M., Public Law
DUPUY, G., Public Law
DURRY, G., Private Law
DUTHEIL DE LA ROCHÈRE, J., Public Law
FACCARELLO, G., Economic Sciences
FEYEL, G., History
FOUCHARD, P., Private Law
FOYER, J., Private Law
GAUDEMET, Y., Public Law
GAUDEMET-TALLON, H., Private Law
GAUTIER, P. Y., Private Law
GERMAIN, M., Private Law
GHOZI, A., Private Law
GJIDARA, M., Public Law

GOYARD, C., Public Law
GRIMALDI, M., Private Law
GUINCHARD, S., Private Law
HAROUEL, J.-L., History of Law
HUET, J., Private Law
HUMBERT, M., History of Law
JAHEL, S., Private Law
JARROSON, C., Private Law
JAUFFRET-SPINOSI, C., Private Law
JAVILLIER, J.-C., Private Law
JOUET, J., Information Sciences
LABROUSSE, C., Economic Sciences
LAFAY, G., Economic Sciences
LAINGUI, A., History of Law
LAMARQUE, J., Public Law
LARROUMET, C., Private Law
LEBEN, C., Public Law
LEFEBVRE-TEILLARD, A., History of Law
LE GALL, J.-P., Private Law
LEMENNICIER-BUCQUET, B., Economic Sciences
LEMOYNE DE FORGES, J. M., Public Law
LEQUETTE, Y., Private Law
LEVENEUR, L., Private Law
LOMBARD, M., Public Law
LOMBOIS, C., Private Law
LUBOCHINSKY, C., Economic Sciences
MALINVAUD, P., Private Law
MARTINEZ, J. C., Public Law
MAYAUD, Y., Private Law
MAZEAU, D., Private Law
MERLE, P., Private Law
MOLFESSIS, N., Private Law
MONCONDUIT, F., Political Science
MORANGE, J., Public Law
MOREAU, J., Public Law
Mme MOURGUES, M. DE, Economic Sciences
Mme NÊME, C., Economic Sciences
OLIVIER, J. M., Private Law
OTTAYJ, L., Private Law
PELÉ, M., Management Science
PERINET-MARQUET, H., Private Law
PONDAVEN, C., Economic Sciences
PORTELLI, H., Political Science
QUENET, M., History of Law
RAYNAUD, P., Political Science
REDSLOB, A., Economic Sciences
RIALS, S., Public Law
RIEFFEL, R., Information Sciences
RIGAUDIERE, A., History of Law
ROBERT, J.-H., Private Law
ROUGEMONT, M. DE, Computing
SCANNAVINO, A., Economic Sciences
SCHWARTZENBERG, R. G., Public Law
SUR, S., Public Law
SYNVET, H., Private Law
TERRÉ, F., Private Law
TEYSSIÉ, B., Private Law
THERY, P., Private Law
TOUSSAINT-DESMOULINS, N., Information Sciences
TREMOLIÈRES, R., Management Science
TRUCHET, D., Public Law
TUAL, C., English
VEDEL, C., Economic Sciences
VERPEAUX, M., Public Law
VITRY, D., Economic Sciences
VOGEL, L., Private Law
ZOLLER, E., Public Law

UNIVERSITÉ DE PARIS III (SORBONNE-NOUVELLE)

17 rue de la Sorbonne, 75230 Paris Cedex 05
Telephone: 1-40-46-28-84
Fax: 1-43-46-29-36
Internet: www.univ-paris3.fr
Founded 1970
State control
Language of instruction: French
Academic year: October to June
Pres.: Prof. MARIE-CHRISTINE LEMARDELEY
Vice-Pres.: DANIEL MOUCHARD (Admin.), PHILIPPE DUBOIS (Int. Relations), PIERRE CIVIL

(Science and Research), ANNE SALAZAR ORVIG (Studies and Univ. Life)
Sec.-Gen.: VINCENT GAILLOT

Number of teachers: 493
Number of students: 17,800

TEACHING AND RESEARCH UNITS

Cinema and Audiovisual Studies: Dir: CHONTAL DUCHET
Communication: Dir: ERIC MAIGRET
Cultural Mediation: Dir: BRUNO PEQUIGNOT
Department of Applied Foreign Languages: Dir: VALERIE PYRONEL
Department of Studies of Contemporary Society: Dir: VIOLAINE DELTEIL
English-speaking World: Dir: ANDRÉ TOPIA
French and Latin Literature and Linguistics: Dir: MICHEL MAGNIEN
French as a Foreign Language: Dir: JEAN-LOUIS CHISS
Theatre Studies: Dir: CHRISTINE HAMON-SIRÉJOLS
General and Applied Linguistics and Phonetics: Dir: MARTINE VERTALIER
General and Comparative Literature: Dir: ALEXANDRE STROEV
German: Dir: ALAIN LATTARD
Higher School of Interpreters and Translators (ESIT): Dir: CATHERINE TUELE-MARTIN
Iberian and Latin American Studies: Dir: JEAN-PIERRE JARDIN
Institute of Latin-American Studies (IHEAL): Dir: GEORGES COUFFIGNAL
Italian and Romanian Studies: Dir: VERONIQUE ABBRUZZETTI
Interuniversity Centre of Hungarian Studies (CIEH): Dir: PATRICK RENAUD
The East and the Arab World: Dir: JEAN FEZAS

UNIVERSITÉ DE PARIS IV (PARIS-SORBONNE)

1 rue Victor-Cousin, 75230 Paris Cedex 05
Telephone: 1-40-46-22-11
Fax: 1-40-46-25-88
Internet: www.paris-sorbonne.fr
Founded 1970
State control
Language of instruction: French
Academic year: October to June
Pres.: GEORGES MOLINIE
Vice-Pres.: DENIS LABOURET, BARTHÉLÉMY JOBERT, MAXIME LONLAS
Sec.-Gen.: SYLVIE N'GUYEN
Librarian: PHILIPPE MARCEROU
Number of teachers: 1,132
Number of students: 22,688

TEACHING AND RESEARCH UNITS

Applied Foreign Languages: Dir: Prof. LILIANE GALLET-BLANCHARD
Art and Archaeology: Dir: Prof. ALEXANDRE FARNOUX
English: Dir: Prof. PIERRE COTTE
French and Comparative Literature: Dir: Prof. DIDIER ALEXANDRE
French Language: Dir: Prof. OLIVIER SOUTET
Geography: Dir: Prof. GUY CHEMLA
Germanic Studies: Dir: Prof. MARTINE DALMAS
Greek: Dir: Prof. PAUL DEMONT
History: Dir: Prof. JEAN-PIERRE CHALINE
Iberian and Latin-American Studies: Dir: Prof. SADI LAKHDARI
Italian and Romanian: Dir: Prof. FRANÇOIS LIVI
Latin Language and Literature: Dir: Prof. GÉRARD CAPDEVILLE
Music and Musicology: Dir: Prof. FRÉDÉRIC BILLIET
Philosophy and Sociology: Dir: Prof. MICHEL FICHANT
Slavonic Studies: Dir: Prof. JEAN BREUILLARD

Institute of Applied Humanities: Dir: Prof. CLAUDE MONTACIE
Institute of Information and Communication: Dir: Prof. VÉRONIQUE RICHARD
Institute of Eastern Studies: Dir: Prof. JEAN-PIERRE POUSSOU

DIRECTORS OF GRADUATE SCHOOLS

Ancient and Medieval Worlds: Prof. O. PICARD
Civilization, Cultures, Literature and Societies: M. M. MARTINET
Classical World and its Legacy: Prof. J. JOUANNA
Concepts and Languages: Prof. O. SOUTET
Contemporary Societies: Prof. G. H. SOUTOU
French and Comparative Literatures: Prof. B. MARCHAL
Foreign Literatures and Cultures: Prof. J. M. VALENTIN
Geography and Urban Studies: Prof. L. TISSIER
History of Art and Archaeology: Prof. A MEROT
History of Modern Civilizations: Prof. J. P. POUSSOU
Medieval Studies: Prof. PH. MÉNARD
Modern and Contemporary History: Prof. D. BARJOT
Music and Musicology: Prof. L. JAMBOU
Philosophy and Social Sciences: Prof. R. BOUDON
Sciences of Language and Communication: Prof. P. VALENTIN
Sciences of Religion and Religious Anthropology: Prof. J. C. FREDOUILLE

UNIVERSITÉ DE PARIS VI (PIERRE ET MARIE CURIE)

4 place Jussieu, 75252 Paris Cedex 05
Telephone: 1-44-27-44-27
Fax: 1-44-27-38-66
E-mail: secretariat.general@upmc.fr
Internet: www.upmc.fr
Founded 1971
Pres.: GILBERT BÉRÉZIAT
Sec.-Gen.: JEAN-YVES GACON
Number of teachers: 2,685
Number of students: 28,558

TEACHING AND RESEARCH UNIT DIRECTORS

Chemistry: JEAN-MARC VALERY
Computer Sciences: ANNE DERIEUX
Earth Sciences and the Evolution of Natural Environments: PHILIPPE D'ARCO
Electrical, Electronic and Automation, Applied Physics: PIERRE ENCRENAZ
Fundamental and Applied Physics: FRANÇOIS GENDRON
Life Sciences: DOMINIQUE DUNON
Mathematics: SYLVIE DELABRIERE
Mechanical and Robotic Engineering and Energy: PASCAL CHALLANDE
Medicine, Pitié-Salpétrière: GÉRARD SAILLANT
Medicine, Saint-Antoine: SERGE UZAN
Pure and Applied Mathematics: M. GAVEAU
Stomatology and Maxillofacial Surgery: JACQUES-CHARLES BERTRAND
Henri Poincaré Institute: MICHEL BROUE
Institute of Science and Technology: JEAN-MARIE CHESNEAUX
Oceanological Observatory, Banyuls: GILLES BOEUF
Oceanological Observatory, Roscoff: BERNARD KLOAREG
Oceanological Observatory, Villefranche-sur-Mer: MICHEL GLASS

UNIVERSITÉ DE PARIS VII (DENIS DIDEROT)

2 place Jussieu, 75251 Paris Cedex 05
Telephone: 1-44-27-44-27
Fax: 1-44-27-69-64

E-mail: mmtx@sigu7.jussieu.fr
Internet: www.diderotp7.jussieu.fr

Founded 1970

Pres.: BENOÎT EURIN
Sec.-Gen.: GEORGES ROQUEPLAN
Dirs: PATRICE PERRIN (Admin.), MARIE-JEANNE ROSSIGNOL (Academic and Univ. Life), LUCIENNE GERMAIN (Int. Relations), ANNE JANIN (Science)

Number of teachers: 1,800
Number of students: 26,000

TEACHING AND RESEARCH UNITS

Anthropology, Ethnology and Religious Studies: Dir: P. DESHAYES
Biochemistry: Dir: PATRICK VICART
Biology and Natural Sciences: Dir: CLAUDE LAMOUR-ISNARD
Chemistry: Dir: JEAN AUBARD
Clinical Human Sciences: Dir: PAUL-LAURENT ASSOUN
Computer Studies: Dir: GUY COUSINEAU
Dental Surgery: Dir: MARIE-LAURE BOY-LEFEVRE
Earth and Physical Sciences: Dir: YVES GAUDEMER
Eastern Asian Languages and Literature: Dir: CÉCILE SAKAI
Film, Communication and Information Studies: Dir: BAUDOIN JURDANT
Geography, History and Social Sciences: Dir: JEAN-PIERRE VALLAT
Institute of English: Dir: PHILIPPE JAWORSKI
Institute of Haematology: Dir: FRANÇOIS SIGAUX
Intercultural Studies in Applied Languages: Dir: JOHN HUMBLEY
Linguistic Research: Dir: ALAIN ROUVERET
Mathematics: Dir: PIERRE VOGEL
Medicine (Lariboisière-Saint-Louis): Dir: ALAIN LE DUC
Medicine (Xavier-Bichat): Dir: J. M. DESMONTS
Physics: Dir: LUC VALENTIN
Sciences of Texts and Documents: Dir: PIERRE CHARTIER
Social Sciences: Dir: ETIENNE TASSIN
University Institute of Technology: Dir: ALAIN JUNGMAN

UNIVERSITÉ DE PARIS VIII—VINCENNES À ST-DENIS

2 rue de la Liberté, 93526 St Denis Cedex 02
Telephone: 1-49-40-67-89
Fax: 1-48-21-04-46
Internet: www.univ-paris8.fr

Founded 1969
State control
Language of instruction: French

Pres.: RENAUD FABRE
Vice-Pres: DANIEL LEPAGE (Academic Studies and Univ. Life), DANIÈLE BUSSY-GENEVOIS (Admin.), FRANÇOISE DECROISETTE (Scientific)
Sec.-Gen.: ALEXIS NAVROCORDATO
Librarian: MADELEINE JULLIEN

Number of teachers: 739
Number of students: 24,825

Publications: Enseignement, Epistémologie, Extrême-Occident, Extrême-Orient, Histoire, Humoresques, Langage, Littérature, Médiévales, Pratiques de Formation, Recherches linguistiques de Vincennes, Théorie

TEACHING AND RESEARCH UNITS

Arts, Philosophy and Aesthetics: Dir: S. VENDEVILLE
Communication, Animation, Teaching: Dir: L. COLIN
History, Literature, Society: Dir: D. JEAN
Languages, Societies, Foreign Cultures: Dir: A. SARRABAYROOSE

Linguistics, Computer Studies, Technology: Dir: J. LOPEZ-KRAHE
Power, Administration, Trade: Dir: F. ARPIN-GONNET
Psychology, Clinical and Social Practices: Dir: T. NATHAN
Territory, Economics and Society: Dir: D. GAZAGNADOU

UNIVERSITÉ DE PARIS IX (PARIS-DAUPHINE)/UNIVERSITÉ PARIS DAUPHINE

Place du Maréchal de Lattre de Tassigny, 75775 Paris Cedex 16
Telephone: 1-44-05-44-05
Fax: 1-44-05-49-49
Internet: www.dauphine.fr

Founded 1968
State control
Language of instruction: French

Pres.: BERNARD DE MONTMORILLON
Vice-Pres. of the Admin. Ccl: MICHEL POIX (Financial Affairs and Logistics), ALAIN-SERGE MESCHERIAKOFF (Legal Affairs)
Vice-Pres. of the Scientific Ccl: VANGELIS PASCHOS
Vice-Pres. of Studies and Univ. Life: FRANÇOISE PICQ, JULIEN JACOB (Students)
Head of Secretariat: LILIANE BEGAT
Library: General library of 150,000 vols, 2,000 current periodicals
Number of teachers: 1,446 (incl. 1000 part-time)
Number of students: 7,988

DIRECTORS

Teaching and Research Units:
    Applied Economics: RÉGIS BOURBONNAIS
    Business (I) and Applied Economics: PIERRE BEZBAKH
    Business (II): JAQUELINE DE LA BRUSLERIE
    Business Informatics: BERNARD GOLDFARB
    Decision Mathematics: (vacant)
    Science of Organizations: MARIE-EVE JOEL
University Professional Institutes:
    Applied Methods of Informatics and Business Enterprise: DANIÈLE MAILLES
    Mathematics and Informatics: GENEVIÈVE JOMIER
    Traditional Business (Banking, Finance and Insurance): LAURENT BATSCH

PROFESSORS

ALTER, N., Sociology
ARNOLD, V., Mathematics
AUBIN, J.-P., Mathematics
BENSOUSSAN, A., Applied Mathematics
BERLIOZ-HOUIN, B., Business Law
BERTHET, CH., Computer Studies
BIENAYME, A., Industrial Economics
BLONDEL, D., Economics
BOUQUIN, H., Finance
BRUNET, A., Civil Law
CAREY-ABRIOUX, C.
CAZES, P., Statistics
CHAITIN-CHATELIN, F., Mathematics
CHAVENT, G., Mathematics
CHEDIN, G., English Languages
CHEVALIER, J.-M., Economics
CLAASSEN, E., Economics
COHEN, F., Finance
COLASSE, B., Finance
COTTA, A., Business Organization
COUSOT, P., Computer Studies
DANA, R.
DE MONTMORILLON, B., Finance
DESMET, P.
DIDAY, E., Computer Studies
DOSS, H., Mathematics
EKELAND, I., Mathematics
ETNER, F., Economics
FLORENS, D., Mathematics
FRISON-ROCHE, M. A., Civil Law

GAUVIN, C., English Language
GEMAN, H., Finance
GHOZI, A., Civil Law
GIOVANNANGELI, J.-L., English Language and Literature
GOURIEROUX, C., Mathematics
GRELON, B., Civil Law
GUILLAUME, M., Economics
GUILLOCHON, B., Economics
HADDAD, S., Computer Studies
HAMON, J., Finance
HESS, C., Mathematics
JOMIER, G., Computer Studies
LARNAC, P.-M., Economics
LENA, H., Public Law
LE PEN, C., Economics
LE TALLEC, P., Mathematics
LEVY, E., Economics
LEVY, G., Computer Studies
LIONS, P.-L., Mathematics
LIU, M., Sociology
LOMBARD, M., Public Law
LORENZI, J.-H., Economics
MAILLES, D., Computer Studies
MANIN, A., Public Law
MARIET, F., Education
MATHIS, J., Finance
METAIS, J., Economics
MEYER, Y., Mathematics
MICHALET, C., Economics
MOREL, J.-M., Mathematics
NUSSENBAUM, M., Finance
PALMADE, J., Sociology
PARLY, J.-M., Economics
PASCHOS, V., Computer Studies
PIGANIOL, B., Management
PILISI, D., Economics
PINSON, S., Computer Studies
PIQUET, M., English Language and Literature
PRAS, B., Finance
RICHARD, J., Finance
RIGAL, J.-L., Computer Studies
RIVES-LANGE, J. L., Civil Law
ROMELAER, P., Finance
ROUX, D., Business Economics
ROY, B., Scientific Methods of Management
SALIN, P., Monetary Economics
SCHMIDT, C., Sociology
SIMON, Y., Finance
SIROEN, J.-M., Economics
SULZER, J.-R., Finance
TERNY, G., Public Economics
THIETART, R., Finance
TOLLA, P., Computer Studies
TRINH-HEBREARD, S., Sociology
VALLEE, C., Public Law

UNIVERSITÉ DE PARIS X (PARIS-NANTERRE)

200 ave de la République, 92001 Nanterre Cedex
Telephone: 1-40-97-72-00
Fax: 1-40-97-75-71
E-mail: service.communication@u-paris10.fr
Internet: www.u-paris10.fr

Pres.: BERNADETTE MADEUF
Sec.-Gen.: DIDIER RAMOND
Librarian: JEAN MALLET

Number of teachers: 1,500
Number of students: 34,000

TEACHING AND RESEARCH UNITS

Anglo-American Studies: Dir: Mme FRISON
Economic Sciences: Dir: M. GIBERT
German, Romance Languages, Slav and Applied Foreign Languages: Dir: M. PHILLIPENKO
History, Geography and Sociology: Dir: M. LEVILLAIN
Institute of Technology (Ville d'Avray): Dir: M. PRIOU
Juridical Sciences: Dir: Mme TALLINEAU

Letters, Linguistics and Philosophy: Dir: Mme DELAVEAU

Psychology and Education Sciences: Dir: M. SIROTA

Science and Techniques of Physical and Sporting Activities: Dir: M. PINARD

UNIVERSITÉ DE PARIS XI (PARIS-SUD)

15 rue G. Clémenceau, 91405 Orsay Cedex
Telephone: 1-69-41-67-50
Fax: 1-69-41-61-35
E-mail: secretariat@presidence.u-psud.fr
Internet: www.u-psud.fr
Founded 1970
State control
Language of instruction: French
Academic year: September to June

Pres.: ANITA BERSELLINI
Sec.-Gen.: DANIEL PERAULT
Librarian: ANNE-MARIE MOTAIS DE NARBONNE

Number of teachers: 1,720
Number of students: 28,000

Publications: *Aspects de la recherche* (1 a year), *Plein-Sud* (6 a year).

TEACHING AND RESEARCH UNITS

Law and Economic Science (Sceaux): 54 blvd Desgranges, 92331 Sceaux Cedex; tel. 1-40-91-17-00; fax 1-46-60-92-62; Dean PIERRE SIRINELLI.

Medicine (Kremlin-Bicêtre): 63 rue Gabriel Péri, 94276 Le Kremlin-Bicêtre Cedex; tel. 1-49-59-67-67; fax 1-49-59-67-00; Dean BERNARD CHARPENTIER.

Pharmacy (Châtenay-Malabry): 5 rue Jean Baptiste Clément, 92290 Châtenay-Malabry; tel. 1-46-83-57-89; fax 1-46-83-57-35; Dean ANNE-MARIE QUERDO.

Sciences (Orsay): 15 rue Georges Clémenceau, 91405 Orsay Cedex; tel. 1-69-41-67-50; fax 1-69-15-63-64; Dean JEAN-CLAUDE ROYNETTE.

UNIVERSITY INSTITUTES

University Institute of Technology at Cachan: 9 ave de la Division Leclerc, 94230 Cachan; tel. 1-41-24-11-00; fax 1-46-64-62-18; Dir PIERRE DAUMEZON.

University Institute of Technology at Orsay: BP 127, 91403, Orsay Cedex; tel. 1-69-33-60-00; fax 1-60-19-33-18; Dir MICHEL PEDOUSSAUT.

University Institute of Technology at Sceaux: 8 ave Cauchy, 92330 Sceaux; tel. 1-40-91-24-99; fax 1-46-60-64-79; Dir RICHARD MILKOFF.

UNIVERSITÉ DE PARIS XII (PARIS-VAL-DE-MARNE)

61 ave du Général de Gaulle, 94010 Créteil Cedex
Telephone: 1-45-17-10-00
Fax: 1-42-07-70-12
Internet: www.univ-paris12.fr
Founded 1970
Academic year: October to July

Pres.: PAUL MENGAL
Vice-Pres: MARCEL PARIAT, FRANÇOISE BARTHELEMY, PHILIPPE GUERIN, J. F. DUFEU PATRICIA POL, VALERIO MOTTA
Sec.-Gen.: GUY CAMUS
Librarian: PIERRE CARBONE

Number of teachers: 1,200
Number of students: 26,000

UNIVERSITÉ DE PARIS XIII (PARIS-NORD)

99 ave Jean-Baptiste Clément, 93430 Villetaneuse
Telephone: 1-49-40-30-00
Fax: 1-49-40-33-33
E-mail: cab-pres@upn.univ-paris13.fr
Internet: www.univ-paris13.fr
Founded 1970
Academic year: September to June

Pres.: JEAN-LOUP SALZMANN
Vice-Pres.: A. NEUMAN
Sec.-Gen.: RÉMY GICQUEL
Librarian: A. TANE

Number of teachers: 1,000
Number of students: 21,500

Publications: *Psychologie clinique, Annales du CESER, Cahiers de Linguistique Hispanique Médiévale*

TEACHING AND RESEARCH UNITS

Economic Sciences and Business Administration: Dir: P. GEOFFRON

Expression and Communications Sciences: Dir: D. CARRÉ

Institute of Town and Health: Dir: P. CORNILLOT

Law and Political Science: Dir: P. SUEUR

Letters and Humanities: Dir: J. BIARNES

Medicine and Human Biology Experimental Centre: Dir: D. BLADIER

Scientific and Polytechnic Centre: Dir: N. LEBLANC

University Institute of Technology (Saint-Denis): Dir: J. P. BERTHIER

University Institute of Technology (Villetaneuse): Dir: G. VICARD

UNIVERSITÉ DE PAU ET DES PAYS DE L'ADOUR

Ave de l'Université, BP 576, 64012 Pau Cedex
Telephone: 5-59-40-70-00
Fax: 5-59-40-70-01
E-mail: communication@univ-pau.fr
Internet: www.univ-pau.fr
Founded 1970
State control

Pres.: JEAN-LOUIS GOUT
Vice-Pres.: J.-C. DOUENCE, J.-P. GACON, C. POUCHAN, J. P. MONTFORT, C. FIÉVET, M. UHALDEBORDE, E. POQUET, M. PARSONS
Sec.-Gen.: JEAN RAVON
Librarian: SYLVAINE FREULON

Number of teachers: 600
Number of students: 14,100

TEACHING AND RESEARCH UNITS

Faculty of Exact Sciences: Dean: ALAIN GRACIA

Faculty of Law, Economics and Management: Dean: GÉRARD DENIS

Faculty of Literature, Languages and Human Sciences: Dean: CHRISTIAN MANSO

Higher National School of Industrial Engineering: Dean: M. ROQUES

Institute of Business Administration: Dean: J.-J. RIGAL

Multidisciplinary Faculty (in Bayonne): Dean: HENRI LABAYLE

University Institute of Scientific Research: Dir: JEAN PEYRELASSE

University Institute of Technology (in Bayonne): Dir: BERNARD CAUSSE

University Institute of Technology (in Pau): Dir: ROBERT HOO-PARIS

UNIVERSITÉ DE PERPIGNAN

52 ave Paul Alduy, 66860 Perpignan Cedex
Telephone: 4-68-66-20-00
Fax: 4-68-66-20-19

E-mail: webmaster@univ-perp.fr
Internet: www.univ-perp.fr
Founded 1971

Pres.: JEAN-MICHEL HOERNER
Sec.-Gen.: JEAN-POL ISAMBERT
Librarian: FERNAND BELLEDENT

Number of teachers: 230
Number of students: 4,500

TEACHING AND RESEARCH UNITS

Exact and Experimental Sciences: Dir: NAGUI EL GHANDOUR

Humanities, Juridical, Economic and Social Sciences: Dir: JACQUELINE AMIEL DONAT

University Institute of Technology: Dir: CATHERINE SABATE

PROFESSORS

Exact and Experimental Sciences:

AMOUROUX, M., Applied Physics and Computer Science
BAILLY, J. R., Biochemistry
BERÇOT, P., Applied Organic Synthesis
BLAISE, P., Chemistry
BODIOT, D., Mineral Chemistry and Thermochemistry
BOMBRE, F., Solid State Physics
BONNARD, M., Algebraic Topology
BOURGAT, R., General Biology
BRUNET, S., Applied Physics and Computer Science
BRUSLE, J., Marine Biology
CAUVET, A. M., Plant Biology and Physiology
CHOU, C. C., Functional Analysis
CODOMIER, L., Biology and Chemistry of Marine Plants (Research)
COMBES, C., Animal Biology
CROZAT, G., Physics
DAGUENET, M., Thermodynamics and Energetics
DUPOUY, J., General Biology
EL JAÏ, A., Computer Science
FABRE, B., Thermology
FOUGERES, A., Mathematics
GIRESSE, P., Marine Sedimentology Research Centre
GONZALEZ, E., Organic Chemistry
GOT, H., Sedimentology and Marine Geochemistry
HENRI-ROUSSEAU, O., Theoretical Chemistry
HILLEL, R., Chemistry
HORVATH, C., Mathematics
HUYNH, V. C., Atomic and Molecular Physics
JUPIN, H., Plant Biology
MARTY, R., Mathematics applied to Human Sciences
MEYNADIER, CHR., Thermodynamics and Energetics
PENON, P., Plant Physiology
SOULIER, J., Organic Chemistry
SOURNIA, A., Atomic and Molecular Physics
SPINNER, B., Mineral Chemistry and Thermochemistry
VIALLET, P., Physical Chemistry

Humanities, Juridical, Economic and Social Sciences

Humanities:

ANDIOC, R., Romance Languages and Literature
AUBAILLY, J.-C., French
BELOT, A., Romance Languages and Literature
BROC, N., Geography
DAUGE, Y., Classics
DELEDALLE, G., Philosophy
DENJEAN, A., English Language and Anglo-Saxon Literature
HOLZ, J. M., Geography
HUGUET, L., Germanic and Scandinavian Languages and Literature
ISSOREL, J., Spanish

LEBLON, B., Romance Languages and Literature
MEYER, J., Contemporary History
RETHORE, J., Literature
SAGNES, J., History

Law and Economics:
BLANC, F. P., History of Law
BREJON DE LAVERGNEE, N., Economic Dynamics
CONSTANS, L., Public Law
Mme DONAT, J., Private Law and Criminology
DOUCHEZ, M.-H., Administrative Law
HUNTZINGER, J., International Law
PEROCHON, F., Law
RUDLOFF, M., Economics
SAINT-JOURS, Y., Private Law and Criminology
SERRA, Y., Private Law

University Institute of Technology:
AZE, D., Mathematics
BARRIOL, R., Mechanical Engineering
BARUSSEAU, J. P., Marine Sedimentology
COMBAUT, G., Marine Chemistry
COSTE, C., Industrial Chemistry
FARINES, M., Organic Chemistry
GRELLET, P., Biochemistry, Applied Biology
MASSE, J., Organic Chemistry
MASSON, PH., Animal Husbandry

UNIVERSITÉ DE PICARDIE JULES VERNE

Chemin du Thil, 80025 Amiens Cedex 01
Telephone: 3-22-82-72-72
Fax: 3-22-82-75-00
E-mail: dany.gryson@ca.u-picardie.fr
Internet: www.u-picardie.fr

Founded 1965
Academic year: October to June

Pres.: GILLES DEMAILLY
Sec.-Gen.: MICHEL DAUMIN
Librarian: FRANÇOISE MONTBRUN
Number of teachers: 800
Number of students: 23,000.

TEACHING AND RESEARCH UNITS

Economics: Dir Prof. P. MAURISSON.
Law: Dir Prof. N. DECOOPMAN.
Literature: Dir Prof. P. BERTHIER.
History and Geography: Dir Prof. N. CHALINE.
Mathematics: 33 rue Saint Leu, 80039 Amiens Cedex; Dir M. MYOUPO.
Medicine: 12 rue des Louvels, Amiens; Dir Prof. B. NEMITZ.
Modern Languages: Dir Prof. P. SICARD.
Pharmacy: 3 rue des Louvels, 80037 Amiens Cedex; Dir M. BRAZIER.
Philosophy and Human Sciences: Dir Prof. F. ROPEZ.
Sciences: 33 rue Saint-Leu, Amiens; Dir Prof. D. BEAUPÈRE.
UER (Saint-Quentin): 48 rue Raspail, 02109 Saint-Quentin Cedex; Dir A. LEBRUN.
University Institute of Technology: Ave des Facultés, Le Bailly, Amiens; Administrator M. LANGLET.

UNIVERSITÉ DE POITIERS

15 rue de l'Hôtel-Dieu, 86034 Poitiers Cedex
Telephone: 5-49-45-30-00
Fax: 5-49-45-30-50
E-mail: webmaster@univ-poitiers.fr
Internet: www.univ-poitiers.fr

Founded 1431

Pres.: JEAN-PIERRE GESSON
Sec.-Gen.: BERNARD CONTAL
Librarian: GENEVIÈVE FIROUZ-ABADIE

Number of teachers: 1,300
Number of students: 25,000
Publications: *Les Cahiers de Civilisation Médiévale, Les Cahiers Forell, La Licorne, Migrinter, Revue Norois*

TEACHING AND RESEARCH UNITS

Centre for Aerodynamic and Thermic Studies: Dir: MICHEL GUILBAUD
Economics: Dir: JACQUES LÉONARD
Establishment for Research in Human Sciences and Society: Dir: CLAIRE GIRARD
Fundamental and Applied Sciences: Dir: GILLES RABY
Human Sciences: Dir: JEAN-MICHEL PASSERAULT
Institute of Communication and New Technologies: Dir: JACQUES DEBORD
Languages and Literatures: Dir: JOËL DALANÇON
Law and Social Sciences: Dir: CHRISTIAN CHÊNE
Medicine and Pharmacy: Dir: ROGER GIL
National Higher School of Mechanical and Aero-engineering: Dir: FRANÇOIS ARMANET
Physical Education and Sport: Dir: PATRICK LEGROS
Poitiers Higher School for Engineering (ESIP): Dir: JEAN-HUGUES THOMASSIN
Preparatory Institute of General Administration: Dir: JEAN-LOUIS GOUSSEAU
University Institute of Business Administration: Dir: SERGE PERCHERON
University Institute of Technology in Angoulême: Dir: MICHEL PINÇON
University Institute of Technology in Poitiers: Dir: CHRISTIAN BERRIER

UNIVERSITÉ DE PROVENCE (AIX-MARSEILLE I)

3 pl. Victor Hugo, 13331 Marseilles Cedex 3
Telephone: 4-91-10-60-00
Fax: 4-91-10-60-06
E-mail: webup@up.univ-mrs.fr
Internet: www.univ-provence.fr

Founded 1970; attached to PRES Aix-Marseille Université

University restructured in 2009 into 9 research units, an engineering school, an institute of technology, and a Masters institute based on campuses in Aix, Marseille, Aubagne, Lambesc, Salon de Provence, Arles, Digne, and Avignon

Pres.: YVES MATHIEU
Vice-Pres. for Admin.: JEAN-CLAUDE LORAUD
Vice-Pres. for Science: DENIS BERTIN
Vice-Pres. for Studies and Univ. Life: CATHERINE VIRLOUVET
Sec. Gen.: GÉRARD BARBERAN
Librarian: Mme GACHON
Library: see Libraries
Number of students: 23,000.

TEACHING AND RESEARCH UNITS

Centre de Formation des Musiciens Intervenants (CFMI): tel. 4-42-96-32-40; fax 4-42-65-32-60; e-mail cfmi@univ-provence.fr; Dir PHILIPPE BOIVIN.
Centre Interuniversitaire de Mécanique (UNIMECA): 60 rue Joliot-Curie, 13453 Marseilles Cedex 13; tel. 4-91-11-38-00; fax 4-91-11-38-38; internet artemmis.univ-mrs.fr/im2; Dir PATRICK VIGLIANO.
Département Environnement Technologie et Société (DENTES): tel. 4-91-10-63-28; fax 4-91-10-62-85; Dir RÉMI CHAPPAZ.
Département Métiers de l'Image et du Son (SATIS): 9 blvd Lakanal, 13400 Aubagne; tel. 4-42-82-41-91; fax 4-42-82-41-90; e-mail satis@univ-provence.fr; internet sites.univ-provence.fr/satis; Dir JACQUES SAPIEGA.

École Polytechnique Universitaire de Marseille: 60 rue Joliot-Curie, 13453 Marseilles Cedex 13; tel. 4-91-11-26-56; e-mail direction@polytech.univ-mrs.fr; internet www.polytech-marseille.com; Dir DAVID E. ZEITOUN.
Institut de la Francophonie: tel. 4-42-95-35-53; internet sites.univ-provence.fr/francophonie; Dir ROBERT CHAUDENSON.
Institut Universitaire de Formation des Maîtres (IUFM) de l'Académie d'Aix-Marseille: 33 rue Eugène Cas, 13248 Marseilles Cedex 04; tel. 4-91-10-75-75; fax 4-91-08-40-67; internet www.aix-mrs.iufm.fr; Dir JACQUES GINESTIÉ.
IUT de Provence (Arles): BP 90178, 13637 Arles Cedex; tel. 4-90-52-24-10; fax 4-90-52-24-15; e-mail contact-iut-arles@liste.univ-provence.fr; Dir ROBERT PUJADE.
IUT de Provence (Digne les Bains): 19 Blvd Saint-Jean Chrysostome, 04000 Digne les Bains; tel. 4-92-30-23-70; fax 4-92-30-23-71; internet sites.univ-provence.fr/iutdigne; Dir YVES ALPE.
Maison Méditerranéenne des Sciences de l'Homme (MMSH): 5 rue du Château de l'Horloge, BP 647, 13094 Aix en Provence Cedex 2; tel. 4-42-52-40-44; internet www.mmsh.univ-aix.fr; Dir BERNARD MOREL.
Observatoire Astronomique de Marseille-Provence (OAMP): see Research Institutes.
UFR Civilisations et Humanités: 29 Ave Robert Schuman, 13090 Aix en Provence; tel. 4-42-95-32-51; fax 4-42-95-33-03; e-mail direction.civhum@univ-provence.fr; Dir XAVIER LAFON.
UFR de Psychologie, Sciences de l'Éducation: 29 Ave Robert Schuman, 13621 Aix en Provence Cedex 1; tel. 4-42-95-37-01; internet sites.univ-provence.fr/wpse; Dir THIERRY RIPOLL.
UFR Études Romanes, Latino-américaines, Orientales et Slaves (ERLAOS): internet www.univ-provence.fr/erlaos; Dir PASCAL GANDOULPHE.
UFR Langue Anglo-saxonnes et Germaniques–Langues Etrangères Appliquées (LAG–LEA): internet sites.univ-provence.fr/ufrlaglea; Dir DOMINIQUE BATOUX.
UFR Lettres, Arts, Communications et Sciences du langage (LACS): internet sites.univ-provence.fr/lacs; Dir DENIS COLLOMP.
UFR Mathématiques, Informatique, Mécanique (MIM): 39 rue Frédéric Joliot-Curie, 13453 Marseille Cedex 13; tel. 4-91-11-35-15; fax 4-91-11-35-02; e-mail direction@cmi.univ-mrs.fr; internet www.cmi.univ-mrs.fr; Dir DENIS LUGIEZ.
UFR Sciences de la Matière (SM): Ave Escadrille Normandie Niemen, 13397 Marseille Cedex 20; tel. 4-91-28-90-40; fax 4-91-28-90-48; e-mail ufrsm@up.univ-mrs.fr; internet sites.univ-provence.fr/~ufrsm; Dir ANDRÉ THEVAND.
UFR Sciences de la Vie, de la Terre et de l'Environnement (SVTE): Dir JEAN-PIERRE ROLL.
UFR Sciences Géographiques et de l'Aménagement: 29 Ave Robert Schuman, 13621 Aix en Provence Cedex 1; tel. 4-42-95-38-44; fax 4-42-95-38-80; internet sites.univ-provence.fr/wgeo; Dir JEAN-LUC BONNEFOY.

UNIVERSITÉ DE REIMS CHAMPAGNE-ARDENNE

9 blvd de la Paix, 51097 Reims Cedex
Telephone: 3-26-05-30-00
Fax: 3-26-05-30-98

Internet: www.univ-reims.fr

Founded 1548

Pres.: RICHARD VISTELLE

Vice-Pres: JEAN-JACQUES ABNET, JACQUES BUR, MARCEL BAZIN

Sec.-Gen.: MARTINE BEURTON

Library: see Libraries

Number of teachers: 1,000

Number of students: 26,000

Publications: *Cahiers de l'Institut du Territoire et de l'Environnement de l'Université de Reims* (1 a year), *Cahiers du Centre de Recherches sur la Décentralisation Territoriale* (1 a year), *Etudes Champenoises* (1 a year), *Flash-Infos* (52 a year), *Imaginaires, Jurisprudence Cour d'appel* (4 a year), *Livret de l'Université, Revue de l'Institut de Géographie* (irregular)

TEACHING AND RESEARCH UNITS

Economic Sciences and Management: Dir: GILLES RASSELET

Exact and Natural Sciences: Dir: JACQUES PERRIN

Higher School of Packaging: Dir: JEAN-CLAUDE PRUDHOMME

Law and Political Sciences: Dir: GÉRARD CLÉMENT

Letters and Human Sciences: Dir: GÉRARD DUFOUR

Medicine: Dir: FRANÇOIS-XAVIER MAQUART

Odontology: Dir: MICHEL MAQUIN

Pharmacy: Dir: JEAN LÉVY

University Institute of Technical Training in Charleville: Dir: JACQUES MALICET

University Institute of Technology in Reims: Dir: GUY DELABRE

University Institute of Technology in Troyes: Dir: JOËL HAZOUARD

UNIVERSITÉ DE RENNES I

2 rue du Thabor, 35065 Rennes Cedex

Telephone: 2-23-23-36-36

Fax: 2-23-23-36-00

E-mail: sai@listes.univ-rennes1.fr

Internet: www.univ-rennes1.fr

Academic year: September to May

Pres.: GUY CATHELINEAU

Sec.-Gen.: MARTINE RUOUD

Number of teachers: 1,601

Number of students: 23,303.

TEACHING AND RESEARCH UNITS

Faculté de Droit et Science Politique: 9 rue Jean-Macé, CS 54203 Rennes Cedex; tel. 2-23-23-76-76; fax 2-23-23-76-55; Dean Prof. DAVID GADBIN.

Faculté de Médecine: 2 rue du Professeur Léon Bernard, CS 34317 Rennes Cedex; tel. 2-23-23-44-20; fax 2-23-23-49-75; Dean Prof. PHILIPPE DE LAVAL.

Faculté d'Odontologie: 2 rue du Professeur Léon Bernard, CS 34317 Rennes Cedex; tel. 2-23-23-43-41; fax 2-23-23-43-93; Dean Prof. GILBERT DE MELLO.

Faculté des Sciences Economiques: 7 place Hoche, CS 86514 Rennes Cedex; tel. 2-23-23-35-45; fax 2-99-38-80-84; Dean Prof. ISABELLE CADORET.

Faculté des Sciences Pharmaceutiques et Biologiques: 2 rue du Professeur Léon Bernard, CS 34317 Rennes Cedex; tel. 2-23-23-44-30; fax 2-23-23-49-75; Dean Prof. JEAN DEUFF.

Faculté des Sciences de la Vie et de l'Environnement: Bât. 13, Campus Scientifique de Beaulieu, 263 rue du Général Leclerc, 35042 Rennes Cedex; tel. 2-23-23-61-12; fax 2-23-23-67-69; Prof. MARIE-ANNICK RICHARD.

UFR Mathématiques: 263 rue du Général Leclerc, CS 74205 Rennes Cedex; tel. 2-23-23-66-67; fax 2-23-23-67-90; Dir BERNARD DELYON.

UFR Philosophie: 263 rue du Général Leclerc, CS 74205 Rennes Cedex; tel. 2-23-23-63-02; fax 2-23-23-51-51; Dir PIERRE SORAY.

UFR Structure et Propriétés de la Matière: 263 rue du Général Leclerc, CS 74205 Rennes Cedex; tel. 2-23-23-62-44; fax 2-23-23-69-85; Dir ALAIN BOURDILLON.

Ecole Nationale Supérieure des Sciences Appliquées et de Technologie: 6 rue de Kérampont, BP 80518, 22305 Lannion Cedex; tel. 2-96-46-90-00; fax 2-96-37-01-99; Dir JOËL CRESTEL.

Institut de Formation Supérieure en Informatique et Communication: Campus de Beaulieu, 35042 Rennes Cedex; tel. 2-99-84-74-02; fax 2-99-84-71-71; Dir GILLES LESVENTES.

Institut de Gestion de Rennes: 11 rue Jean-Mace, CS 70803, 35708 Rennes Cedex 7; tel. 2-23-23-77-77; fax 2-23-23-78-00; Dir LAURENT BIRONNEAU.

Institut de Préparation à l'Administration Générale: 106 blvd de la Duchesse Anne, 35700 Rennes; tel. 2-23-23-78-93; fax 2-23-23-78-92; Dir GILLES GUIHEUX.

Institut Universitaire de Technologie de Lannion: Rue Edouard Branly, BP 30219, 22302 Lannion Cedex; tel. 2-96-46-93-00; fax 2-96-48-13-20; Dir DIDIEU DEMIGNY.

Institut Universitaire de Technologie de Rennes: 3 Rue du Clos-Courtel, BP 90422, 35704 Rennes Cedex 7; tel. 2-23-23-40-00; fax 2-23-23-40-01; Dir JACQUES MIRIEL.

Institut Universitaire de Technologie de St Brieuc: 18 rue Henri Wallon, BP 40, 22004 St Brieuc Cedex 1; tel. 2-96-60-96-60; fax 2-96-60-96-12; Dir JACQUES BERTHOUN.

Institut Universitaire de Technologie de St Malo: rue de la Croix Desilles, BP 195, 35403 St Malo Cedex 1; tel. 2-99-21-95-00; fax 2-99-21-95-01; Dir JEAN-JACQUES MONTOIS.

UNIVERSITÉ DE ROUEN

1 rue Thomas Becket, Secrétariat-Général, 76821 Mont-Saint-Aignan Cedex

Telephone: 2-35-14-60-00

Fax: 2-35-14-63-48

Internet: www.univ-rouen.fr

Founded 1966

Academic year: September to June

Pres.: ERNEST GIBERT

Vice-Pres.: MOHAMED KETATA, BERNARD PROUST

Sec.-Gen.: (vacant)

Librarian: YANNICK VALIN

Number of teachers: 778

Number of students: 30,000.

TEACHING AND RESEARCH UNITS

Behavioural and Educational Sciences: Rue Lavoisier, 76821 Mont-Saint-Aignan; Dir R. WEIL.

Law and Economics: Blvd Siegfried, 76821 Mont-Saint-Aignan Cedex; Dir Y. SASSIER.

Letters and Humanities: Rue Lavoisier, 76821 Mont-Saint-Aignan Cedex; Dir J. MAURICE.

Medicine and Pharmacy: BP 97, 76800 Saint-Etienne-du-Rouvray; Dir P. LAURET.

Sciences and Technology: Place Emile Blondel, 76821 Mont-Saint-Aignan Cedex; Dir M. LEREST.

Sport: Blvd Siegfried, 76821 Mont-Saint-Aignan Cedex; Dir J. P. LEFEVRE.

University Institute of Technology: Place Emile Blondel, 76821 Mont-Saint-Aignan; Dir P. MICHE

PROFESSORS

Behavioural and Educational Sciences:

ABALLERA, F., Sociology

ASTOLFI, J. P., Educational Sciences

DURAND, J., Sociology

GATEAUX, J., Educational Sciences

HOUSSAYE, J., Educational Sciences

KOKOSOWSKI, A., Educational Sciences

LEMOINE, CL., Psychology

MALANDAIN, CL., Psychology

MARBEAUX-CLEIRENS, B., Psychology

MELLIER, D., Psychology

Law and Economics:

BADEVANT, B., Law

BRAS, J. P., Public Law

CAYLA, O., Public Law

CHRÉTIEN, P., Public Law

COURBE, P., Private Law

DAMMAME, D., Political Science

EPAULARD, A., Economics

GOY, R., Public Law

KULLMANN, J., Private Law

LEHMANN, P., Economics

MONNIER, L., Economics

PORTIER, F., Economics

RENOUX, M. F., Law

SASSIER, Y., Law

TAVERNIER, P., Public Law

TEBOUL, G., Public Law

TONNEL, M., Economics

VATTEVILLE, E., Administration and Management

VESPERINI, J.-P., Economics

Letters and Humanities:

ARNAUD, J. C., Geography

BALAN, B., Epistemology

BENAY, J., German

BERGER, PH., Spanish

CAITUCOLI, C., Linguistics

CAPET, A., English

COIT, K., English

CORTES, J., Linguistics

CYMERMAN, C., Spanish

DELAMOTTE, R., Linguistics

GARDIN, B., Linguistics

GRANIER, J., Philosophy

GUERMOND, Y., Geography

HUSSON, G., Greek

LE BOHEC, S., Ancient History

LECLAIRE, J., English

LECLERC, Y., French

LEGUAY, J.-P., Medieval History

LEMARCHAND, G., Modern History

LESOURD, M., Geography

MAQUERLOT, J. P., English

MAURICE, J., French

MAZAURIC, C., Modern History

MERVAUD, C., French

MERVAUD, M., Russian

MILHOU, A., Spanish

MORTIER, D., Comparative Literature

NIDERST, A., French

NOISETTE DE CRAUZAT, CL., Musical History

PASTRE, J. M., German

PHILONENKO, A., Philosophy

PICHARDIE, J. P., English

PIERROT, J., Modern French Literature and Language

PIGENET, M., Contemporary History

POINSOTE, J. L., Classics

PUEL, M., English

RAVY, G., German

RETAILLE, B., Geography

ROUDAUT, F., French

SALAZAR, B., Spanish

SOHNA, R., Modern History

THELAMON, F., Ancient History

TREDE, M., Classics

VAN DER LYNDEN, A. M., Spanish

WALLE, M., German

WILLEMS, M., English
ZYLBERBER, G. M., Modern History

Medicine and Pharmacy:
ANDRIEU-GUTTRANCOURT, J., Otorhinolaryngology
AUGUSTIN, P., Neurology
BACHY, B., Infantile Surgery
BENOZIO, E., Radiology
BERCOFF, E., Internal Medicine
BESANÇON, P., Chemistry
BESSOU, J. P., Surgery
BEURET, F., Rehabilitation
BIGA, N., Orthopaedics
BLANQUART, F., Rehabilitation
BONMARCHAND, G., Resuscitation
BONNET, J. J., Pharmacology
BRASSEUR, G., Ophthalmology
BRASSEUR, P. H., Bacteriology
CAILLARD, J.-F., Industrial Medicine
CAPRON, R., Biophysics
COLIN, R., Gastroenterology
COLONNA, L., Psychiatry
COMOY, D., Biochemistry
COSTENTIN, J., Pharmacology
COURTOIS, H., Internal Medicine
CRIBIER, A., Cardiology
CZERNICHOW, P., Epidemiology
DEHESDIN, D., Otorhinolaryngology
DENIS, P., Physiology
DUCROTTE, P., Hepatology
DUVAL, C., Clinical Obstetrics
FESSARD, C., Paediatrics
FILLASTRE, J. P., Nephrology
FREGER, P., Anatomy
GARNIER, J., Botany and Cryptogam
GODIN, M., Nephrology
GRISE, PH., Urology
HECKETSWEILER, P., Hepatology
HEMET, J., Pathological Anatomy
HUMBERT, G., Tropical and Infectious Diseases
JANVRESSE, C., Hygiene
JOLY, P., Dermatology
JOUANY, M., Toxicology
KUHN, J. M., Endocrinology
LAFONT, O., Organic Chemistry
LAURET, P., Dermatology
LAVOINNE, D., Biochemistry
LECHEVALLIER, J., Infantile Surgery
LEDOSSEUR, P., Radiology
LEFUR, R., Cancerology
LELOET, X., Rheumatology
LEMELAND, J. F., Hygiene
LEMOINE, J. P., Gynaecology
LEREBOURS, E., Nutrition
LEROY, J., Therapeutics
LETAC, B., Cardiology
MACE, B., Histology
MAITROT, B., Biochemistry
MALLET, E., Biology
MARCHAND, J., Chemical Pharmacology
MATRAY, F., Medical Biochemistry
METAYER, J., Anatomy
MICHOT, F., Digestive Tract Surgery
MIHOUT, B., Neurology
MITROFANOFF, P., Infantile Surgery
MONCONDUIT, M., Haematology
MUIR, J. F., Pneumology
NOUVET, G., Pneumology
ORECCHIONI, A.-M., Pharmacology
PASQUIS, P., Physiology
PEILLON, C., Orthopaedic and Traumatological Surgery
PERON, J. M., Stomatology
PETIT, M., Psychiatry
PIGUET, H., Immuno-haematology
PROTAIS, P., Physiology
PROUST, B., Forensic Medicine
SAOUDI, N., Cardiology
SORIA, C., Pharmaceutical Biochemistry
SOYER, R., Thoracic Surgery
TADIE, M., Neurosurgery
TENIÈRE, P., General Surgery
TESTART, J., Clinical Surgery
THIEBOT, J., Radiology

THOMINE, M., Orthopaedic and Traumatological Surgery
THUILLIEZ, C., Therapeutics
TILLY, H., Haematology
TRON, F., Immunology
TRON, P., Paediatrics
VANNIER, J. P., Paediatrics
WATELET, J., General Surgery
WINCKLER, C., Anaesthesiology
WOLF, L., Therapeutic Internal Medicine

Sciences and Technology:
ANTHORE, R., Physics
ATTIAS, J., Biochemistry
AUGER, P., Physics
BALANGE, P., Biochemistry
BANEGE, A., Physics
BARBEY, G., Chemistry
BLANCHARD, D., Mechanics
BLAVETTE, D., Physics
BOISARD, J., Vegetal Biology
BORGHI, R., Mechanics
BOUAZIZ, R., Chemistry
BRISSET, J. L., Chemistry
CAGNON, M., Physics
CALBRIX, J., Mathematics
CARLES, D., Electronics
CARPENTIER, J. M., Chemistry
CASTON, J., Biology
CAZIN, L., Biology
CHAMPRANAUD, J. M., Computer Sciences
CHARPENTIER, J., Physiology
CHERON, B., Thermodynamics
COMBRET, C., Chemistry
COTTEREAU, M. J., Thermodynamics
DAVOUST, D., Chemistry
DEBRUCQ, D., Electronics
DERRIDJ, M., Mathematics
DE SAM LAZARO, J., Mathematics
DESBENE, A., Chemistry
DESBENE, P., Chemistry
DONATO, P., Mathematics
DOSS, H., Mathematics
DUHAMEL, P., Chemistry
DUVAL, J.-P., Computer Sciences
DUVAL, P., Physics
FOUCHER, B., Biochemistry
FRILEUX, P. N., Biology
GALLOT, J., Physics
GAYOSO, J., Chemistry
GORALCIK, P., Computer Sciences
GRENET, J., Physics
GUESPIN, J., Microbiology
HANNOYER, B., Physics
HANSEL, G., Mathematics
HUSSON, A., Biology
LAMBOY, M., Geology
LANERY, E., Mathematics
LANGE, C., Chemistry
LECOURTIER, Y., Electronics
LEDOUX, M., Thermodynamics
LENGLET, M., Chemistry
LOPITAUX, J., Chemistry
MAHEU, B., Thermodynamics
MENAND, A., Physics
METAYER, M., Chemistry
MEYER, R., Geology
MICHON, J. F., Computer Sciences
OZKUL, C., Physics
PAULMIER, C., Chemistry
PEREZ, G., Chemistry
PETIPAS, C., Physics
POIRIER, J. M., Chemistry
QUEGUINNER, G., Chemistry
RIPOLL, C., Biochemistry
SELEGNY, E., Chemistry
STRELCYN, J. M., Mathematics
SURIN, A., Mathematics
TEILLET, J., Physics
UNANUE, A., Chemistry
VAILLANT, R., Animal Physiology
VAUTIER, C., Physics
VERCHERE, J. F., Chemistry
VIGER, C., Electronics
VIGIER, P., Physics
WEILL, M., Thermodynamics

UNIVERSITÉ DE SAVOIE (CHAMBÉRY)

BP 1104, 73011 Chambéry Cedex
27 rue Marcoz, 73000 Chambéry

Telephone: 4-79-75-85-85
Fax: 4-79-75-84-44
Internet: www.univ-savoie.fr

Founded 1970
Academic year: October to July

Pres.: CLAUDE JAMEUX
Vice-Pres.: GILBERT ANGENIEUX (Admin. Ccl), MYRIAM DONSIMONI (Ccl of Studies and Univ. Life), JAMES SHEPHERD (Int.l Relations), ROMAN KOSSAKOWSKI (Scientific Ccl)
Sec.-Gen.: JEAN-JACQUES PELLEGRIN
Dir of Libraries: SIMONE LAMARCHE

Number of teachers: 600
Number of students: 12,368

Publications: *Annales* (1 a year), *Présences* (12 a year)

TEACHING AND RESEARCH UNITS

Faculty of Fundamental and Applied Sciences: Dir: PIERRE BARAS
Faculty of Language, Literature and Social Science: Dir: MICHÈLE PACHTER
Faculty of Law and Economics: Dir: GENEVIÈVE GONDOUIN
Interdisciplinary Centre for Mountain Sciences: Dir: PIERRE FAIVRE
Tertiary Management Studies: Dir: RENÉ THIEBLEMONT

ATTACHED INSTITUTES

Annecy National College of Engineering: BP 806, 74016 Annecy Cedex;5 chemin de Bellevue, 74016 Annecy-Le-Vieux; tel. 4-50-09-66-00; fax 4-50-09-66-49; e-mail etudes@esia.univ-savoie.fr; internet www.esia.univ-savoie.fr; Dir LAURENT FOULLOY.

Chambéry National College of Engineering: 73376 Le Bourget du Lac; tel. 4-79-75-88-06; fax 4-79-75-87-72; internet www.esigec.univ-savoie.fr; Dir PIERRE BATTISTI.

Institute of Technology Annecy: 9 rue de l'Arc-en-ciel, BP 240, 74942 Annecy-Le-Vieux; tel. 4-50-09-22-22; fax 4-79-75-87-72; internet www.iut.univ-savoie.fr; Dir GILLES HEIDSIECK.

Institute of Technology Chambéry: Savoie Technolac, 73376 Le-Bourget-du-Lac Cedex; tel. 4-79-75-81-75; fax 4-79-75-81-64; internet src-serveur2.univ-savoie.fr; Dir NICOLE ALBEROLA.

UNIVERSITÉ DE STRASBOURG

4 rue Blaise Pascal, CS 90032, 67081 Strasbourg Cedex

Telephone: 3-68-85-00-00
E-mail: president@unistra.fr
Internet: www.unistra.fr

Founded 2009 by merger of Universités de Strasbourg I (Université Louis Pasteur), II (Université Marc Bloch, Sciences Humaines) and III (Université Robert Schuman)
State control

Pres.: ALAIN BERETZ
Sr Vice-Pres.: MICHEL DENEKEN
Vice-Pres. for Continuing Education: FRÉDÉRIQUE GRANET
Vice-Pres. for Research and Doctoral Studies: ÉRIC WESTHOF
Vice-Pres. for University Affairs: JOANNIE CRINON
Vice-Pres. for Social Sciences: BERNARD ANCORI
Vice-Pres. for Human Resources and Social Policy: HUGUES DREYSSÉ
Vice-Pres. for Business Partnerships: JEAN-MARC JELTSCH

Vice-Pres. for International Relations: ANNE KLEBES-PÉLISSIER
Vice-Pres. for Heritage: YVES LARMET
Vice-Pres. for Digital Policy and Information Systems: CATHERINE MONGENET
Library: 1.2m.vols
Number of teachers: 5,200
Number of students: 42,000

UNIVERSITÉ DE TECHNOLOGIE DE BELFORT-MONTBÉLIARD

90010 Belfort Cedex
Telephone: 3-84-58-30-00
Fax: 3-84-58-30-30
E-mail: contact@utbm.fr
Internet: www.utbm.fr
Founded 1999 as a result of merger of Ecole Nationale d'Ingénieurs de Belfort and Institut Polytechnique de Sévenans
State control
Dir: Dr PASCAL FOURNIER.

UNIVERSITÉ DE TECHNOLOGIE DE COMPIÈGNE

Centre B. Franklin, BP 60319, Rue Roger Couttolenc, 60206 Compiègne Cedex
Telephone: 3-44-23-44-23
Fax: 3-44-23-43-00
E-mail: utc@utc.fr
Internet: www.utc.fr
Founded 1972
Academic year: September to August (2 semesters)
Pres.: FRANÇOIS PECCOUD
Sec.-Gen.: LUC ZIEGLER
Dir of Int. Relations: P. WAGSTAFF
Librarian: ANNIE BERTRAND
Number of teachers: 313
Number of students: 3,200
Publication: UTC-Infos (6 a year)

DIRECTORS

Department of Biological Engineering: N. COCHET
Department of Chemical Engineering: E. BRUNIER
Department of Computer Science: P. SIMARD
Department of Mechanical Engineering: M. SIDAHMED
Department of Mechanical Engineering Systems: P. RAMOND
Department of Technology and Human Sciences: F. SEITZ
Department of Urban Engineering Systems: P. ORSERO

UNIVERSITÉ DE TECHNOLOGIE DE TROYES

12 rue Marie Curie, BP 2060, 10010 Troyes Cedex
Telephone: 3-25-71-76-00
Fax: 3-25-71-76-76
E-mail: infos@utt.fr
Internet: www.utt.fr
Founded 1994
State control
Academic year: September to June
Pres.: Prof. PAUL GAILLARD
Dir of Studies: Prof. PIERRE BAE
Head of Library: SABINE BARRAL
Library of 10,000 vols
Number of teachers: 90
Number of students: 1,150 (1,080 undergraduate, 70 postgraduate)

UNIVERSITÉ DE TOULON ET DU VAR

ave de l'Université, BP 20132, 83957 La Garde Cedex
Telephone: 4-94-14-20-00

Fax: 4-94-14-21-57
Internet: www.univ-tln.fr
Founded 1970
Academic year: September to July
Pres.: (vacant)
Vice-Pres.: (vacant)
Sec.-Gen.: FATIHA BASTIANI
Librarian: M. DANIEL EYMARD
Number of teachers: 380
Number of students: 10,000

TEACHING AND RESEARCH UNITS

Adult Education: DENIS DUMOULIN
Economic Sciences: PHILIPPE GILLES
Humanities: GILLES LEYDIER
Law: JEAN JACQUES PARDINI
Sciences and Technology: SERGE DESPIAU
Sports: JACQUES CRÉMIEUX
School of Engineering: OLIVIER LE CALVE
Media and Information Technology Institute: FRANCK RENUCCI
University Institute of Technology: ROBERT CHANU

UNIVERSITÉ DE TOULOUSE I (SCIENCES SOCIALES)

2 rue du Doyen-Gabriel-Marty, 31042 Toulouse Cedex 9
Telephone: 5-61-63-35-00
Fax: 5-61-63-37-98
Internet: www.univ-tlse1.fr
Founded 1229
State control
Pres.: BERNARD SAINT-GIRONS
Vice-Pres.: JACQUES IGALENS
Sec.-Gen.: DANIELE ROULLAND
Librarians: GERMAINE ROGÉ, MONIQUE PUZZO
Number of teachers: 411
Number of students: 19,027
Publications: Livret de l'Etudiant, Annales, Livre de la Recherche, UT1 Magazine

TEACHING AND RESEARCH UNITS

Economic and Social Administration: Dir: S. REGOURD
Economics: Dir: B. BELLOC
Information Science: Dir: C. ERNST
Law: Dir: H. ROUSSILLON

ATTACHED INSTITUTES

Centre Universitaire d'Albi: 2 ave Franchet d'Espérey, 81011 Albi Cedex 09; tel. 5-63-48-19-79; fax 5-63-48-19-71; Dir O. DEVAUX.

Centre Universitaire de Montauban: 116 blvd Montauriol, 82017 Montauban Cedex; tel. 5-63-63-32-71; fax 5-63-66-34-07; Dir B. MARIZ.

Ecole Supérieure Universitaire de Gestion: 2 rue Albert Lautmann, 31042 Toulouse Cedex; tel. 5-61-21-55-18; fax 5-61-23-84-33; Dir P. SPITERI.

Institut d'Etudes Politiques: 2 ter rue des Puits Creusés, 31042 Toulouse Cedex; tel. 5-61-11-02-60; fax 5-61-22-94-80; Dir C. HEN.

Institut Universitaire Technologique de Rodez: 33 ave du 8 mai 1945, 12000 Rodez; tel. 5-65-77-10-80; fax 5-65-77-10-81; Dir B. ALLAUX.

UNIVERSITÉ DE TOULOUSE II (LE MIRAIL)

5 allées Antonio Machado, 31058 Toulouse Cedex 9
Telephone: 5-61-50-42-50
Fax: 5-61-50-42-09
Internet: www.univ-tlse2.fr
Pres.: M. DANIEL FILATRE

Vice-Pres.: M. PIERRE-YVES BOISSAU NADINE CASCINO, MARLE CHRISTINE JAILLET, M. PATRICK M'PONDO-DICKA
Number of teachers: 781
Number of students: 26,504
Publications: Anglophonia (2 a year), Caravelle (2 a year), Cinémas d'Amérique Latine (1 a year), Clio (2 a year), Criticón (3 a year), Homo (1 a year), Kairos (2 a year), Littératures (2 a year), Pallas (2 a year), Science de la Société (3 a year), Sud/Ouest Européen

TEACHING AND RESEARCH UNITS

Ancient Literature and Languages: Dir: J.-P. MAUREL
Audio-visual Studies: Dir: G. CHAPOUILLIE
Behavioural Sciences, Education: Dir: S. ALAVA
Continuing Education: Dir: M. FOURNET
French Literature, Languages and Music: Dir: F. GEVREY
Geography: Dir: D. WEISSBERG
Hispanic and Hispano-American Studies: Dir: C. CHAUCHADIS
History, Archaeology and History of Art: Dir: P. VAYSSIÈRE
Institut Universitaire de Formation de Musiciens Intervenant à l'Ecole Elémentaire et Pré-Élémentaire (IFMI): Dir: J. BROUSSAU-DIER
Latin-American Studies (IPEALT): Dir: J. GILARD
Mathematics, Computer Science Statistics, Economics and Business Studies: Dir: P. CARBONNE
Modern Languages, Foreign Literatures and Civilizations and General Linguistics: Dir: H. HOMBOURG
Philosophy and Politics: Dir: L. SALA-MOLINS
Psychology: Dir: J.-R. HAÏT (acting)
Social Sciences: Dir: M. PERVANCHON (acting)
Studies of the English-Speaking World: Dir: J. L. BRETEAU
University Institute of Technology: Dir: J. J. MERCIER

UNIVERSITÉ DE TOURS (UNIVERSITÉ FRANÇOIS-RABELAIS)

3 rue des Tanneurs, BP 4103, 37041 Tours Cedex 1
Telephone: 2-47-36-66-00
Fax: 2-47-36-64-10
E-mail: suio@univ-tours.fr
Internet: www.univ-tours.fr
Founded 1970
State control
Accredited by Min. of Higher Education and Research
Language of instruction: French
Academic year: September to June
Pres.: LOÏC VAILLANT
Vice-Pres. for Research, Doctoral Studies and Promotion: MICHEL ISINGRINI
Vice-Pres. for Means and Resources: ALAIN RONCIN
Vice-Pres. for Studies, Univ. Life and Culture: NADINE IMBAULT
Vice-Pres. for European and Int. Affairs: SÉBASTIEN SALBAYRE
Vice-Pres. for Students: WILFRIED SCHWARTZ
Registrar: CHRISTINE POIRIER
Communications Man.: LAURENCE LECOMTE
Librarian: CORINNE TOUCHELAY
Library of 600,000 vols, 5,600 periodical titles
Number of teachers: 1,250
Number of students: 20,400

DEANS

Academic Institute of Technology (Blois): ISABELLE LAFFEZ

Academic Institute of Technology (Tours): DANIELLE PODER

Center for Higher Renaissance Studies: PHILIPPE VENDRIX

Engineer School: CHRISTIAN PROUST

Faculty of Arts and Human Sciences: BERNARD BURON

Faculty of Humanities and Languages: HEINZ RASCHEL

Faculty of Law, Economics and Social Sciences: CLAUDE OPHELE

Faculty of Medicine: DOMINIQUE PERROTIN

Faculty of Pharmaceutical Sciences: ALAIN GUEIFFIER

Faculty of Sciences and Technologies: ALAIN VERGER

Health, Sciences, Technologies Doctoral College: GILLES VENTURINI

Human and Social Sciences Doctoral College: JEAN ROSSETTO

UNIVERSITÉ DE VALENCIENNES ET DU HAINAUT-CAMBRESIS

Le Mont Houy, BP 311, 59304 Valenciennes Cedex

Telephone: 3-27-14-12-34

Fax: 3-27-14-11-00

E-mail: uvhc@univ-valenciennes.fr

Internet: www.univ-valenciennes.fr

Founded 1964

State control

Language of instruction: French

Academic year: September to June

Pres.: PASCAL LEVEL

Sec.-Gen.: JEAN-PIERRE DARRAS

Librarian: A. STEINER

Library of 73,000 vols

Number of teachers: 485

Number of students: 12,000

Publications: *16 Lez Valenciennes* (1 a year), *Guide d'étudiant* (1 a year), *Lettre de l'Université* (12 a year), *Rapport d'activité des laboratoires de recherche* (1 a year)

TEACHING AND RESEARCH UNITS

Department of Administrative Studies: Dir: X. MOREAU

Institute of Science and Technology: Dir: P. LEVEL

Institute of Technology: Dir: J. M. DESRUMAUX

Law, Economics and Management: Dir: M. DEFOSSEZ

Literature, Modern Languages and Art: Dir: J. VAILLANT

School of Data Processing and Production Technology: Dir: D. WILLAEYS

School of Mechanics: Dir: J. P. BRICOUT

School of Mechanics and Energetics: Dir: YVES RAVALARD

UNIVERSITÉ DE VERSAILLES SAINT-QUENTIN-EN-YVELINES

55 ave de Paris, 78035 Versailles Cedex

Telephone: 1-39-25-78-00

Fax: 1-39-25-78-01

Internet: www2.uvsq.fr

Founded 1991

Pres.: DOMINIQUE GENTILE

Number of students: 9,300.

TEACHING AND RESEARCH UNITS

Unité de Formation et de Recherche St-Quentin-en-Yvelines: 47 blvd Vauban, 78280 Guyancourt; tel. 1-39-25-50-00; fax 1-39-25-53-55; courses in law, economics, social sciences, humanities; Dir JEAN-FRANÇOIS LEMETTRE.

Unité de Formation et de Recherche Versailles: 45 ave des Etats-Unis, 78000 Versailles; tel. 1-39-25-40-00; fax 1-39-25-40-

19; courses in science; Dir JACQUES LAVERGNAT.

UNIVERSITÉ DU HAVRE

25 rue Philippe Lebon, BP 1123, 76063 Le Havre Cedex

Telephone: 2-32-74-40-00

Fax: 2-35-21-49-59

E-mail: presidence@univ-lehavre.fr

Internet: www.univ-lehavre.fr

Founded 1984

State control

Academic year: September to July

Pres.: PIERRE-BRUNO RUFFINI

Vice-Pres.: THIERRY DERREY, PASCAL PAREIGE, MADELEINE BROCARD, CAMILLE GALAP

Sec.-Gen.: FRANÇOIS BEAUCARNE

Librarian: PIERRETTE PORTRON

Number of teachers: 460

Number of students: 6,977

TEACHING AND RESEARCH UNITS

Faculty of International Affairs: Dean: JEAN-PAUL BARBICHE

Faculty of Letters and Human and Social Sciences: Dean: BENJAMIN STECK

Faculty of Science and Technology: Dir: ALAIN PIEL

Higher Institute of Logistics and Engineering: Dir: ALAIN PORTRON

University Institute of Technology: Dir: JEAN-PIERRE SCEAUX

UNIVERSITÉ DU LITTORAL CÔTE D'OPALE

Services Centraux, 1 place de l'Yser, BP 1022, Général-De-Gaulle, 59375 Dunkerque Cedex 1

Telephone: 3-28-23-73-73

Fax: 3-28-23-73-13

Internet: www.univ-littoral.fr

Founded 1991

Campuses in Boulogne, Calais, Dunkerque and St-Omer

Pres.: DANIEL BOUCHER

Director of Library Services: MIREILLE CHAZAL

Library of 100,000 vols, 900 periodical subscriptions; CD-ROM databases; spec. colln: Centre de Documentation Européenne, Relais INSEE (statistics), science fiction, cartoons, theses

Number of students: 11,000

Areas of study: law, economics, management, literature, languages, fine and performing arts, humanities, social sciences, natural sciences, technology, sport.

UNIVERSITÉ DU MAINE

Ave Olivier Messiaen, 72085 Le Mans Cedex 9

Telephone: 2-43-83-30-00

Fax: 2-43-83-30-77

Internet: www.univ-lemans.fr

Founded 1977

Pres.: MAURICE HENRY

Sec.-Gen.: PHILIPPE WISLER

Number of teachers: 395

Number of students: 10,308

Publication: *Livret de l'Etudiant* (1 a year)

DEANS

Faculty of Law and Social Sciences: O. BIENCOURT

Faculty of Letters and Human Sciences: ABDELOUAHADE MOUBARIK

Faculty of Sciences: MICHEL PEZERIL

ATTACHED INSTITUTES

Higher National School of Engineering: Rue Aristote, 72085 Le Mans Cedex 09; tel. 2-43-83-35-93; fax 2-43-83-37-94; e-mail ensim@univ-lemans.fr; internet ensim.univ-lemans.fr.

University Institute of Technology (Laval): 52 rue des docteurs Calmette et Guérin, BP 2045, 53000 Laval Cedex 09; tel. 2-43-59-49-05; fax 2-43-59-49-08; internet www.iut-laval.univ-lemans.fr.

University Institute of Technology (Le Mans): Ave Olivier Messiaen, 72085 Le Mans Cedex 09; tel. 2-43-83-34-01; fax 2-43-83-30-88; internet iut.univ-lemans.fr.

UNIVERSITÉ MICHEL DE MONTAIGNE (BORDEAUX III)

Domaine Universitaire, 33607 Pessac Cedex

Telephone: 5-57-12-44-44

Fax: 5-57-12-44-90

E-mail: accueil@u-bordeaux3.fr

Internet: www.u-bordeaux3.fr; attached to PRES Université de Bordeaux

Pres.: PATRICE BRUN

Vice-Pres. for Admin. Ccl: JEAN-PAUL JOURDAN

Vice-Pres. for Education and Student Life: JEAN-YVES COQUELIN

Vice-Pres. for Science Ccl: PATRICK BAUDRY

Sec.-Gen.: THOMAS RAMBAUD

Chief Librarian: M. GUERIN

Number of teachers: 646

Number of students: 15,200

Publications: *Annales du Midi, Aquitania, Bulletin hispanique, Cahier d'outre-mer, Communication et organisation, Revue des études anciennes, Sud-Ouest européen*

TEACHING AND RESEARCH UNITS

Faculty of Anglophone Countries: Dir: JEAN-PAUL REVAUGER

Faculty of Arts: Dir: MARIE-BERNADETTE DUFOURCET-HAKIM

Faculty of Foreign and Applied Languages: Dir: RENÉE-PAULE DEBAISIEUX-ZEMOUR

Faculty of Germanic and Scandinavian Studies: Dir: STÉPHAN MARTENS

Faculty of Geography and Development: Dir: JOSÉ-MANUEL LAZCANO

Faculty of History: Dir: JEAN-PAUL JOURDAN

Faculty of History of Art and Archaeology: Dir: FRANÇOISE BECHTEL

Faculty of Iberian and Ibero-American Studies: Dir: JEAN-MARC BUIGUÈS

Faculty of Letters: Dir: ARMELLE DESCHAUD

Faculty of Philosophy: Dir: LAYLA LAÏD

Institute of Environment, Geo-Engineering and Development (EGID): Dir: JEAN-MARIE MALEZIEUX

Institute of Information Sciences and Information: Dir: PHILIPPE LOQUAY

Institute of Journalism Bordeaux Aquitaine: Dir: MARIA SANTOS-SAINZ

Institut Universitaire de Technologie: Dir: CLOTILDE DE MONTGOLFIER

PROFESSORS

ABECASSIS, A., Philosophy

AGOSTINO, M., Contemporary History

AGUILA, Y., Spanish

AUGUSTIN, J.-P., Geography

BARAT, J.-C., English

BART, F., Geography

BAUDRY, P., Sociology

BECHTEL, F., Physics applied to Archaeology

BERIAC, F., Medieval History

BERTIN-MAGHIT, J.-P., Cinema

BESSE, M. G., Portuguese Literature

BOHLER, D., Medieval Languages and Literature

BOST, J.-P., Ancient History

BOUCARUT, M., Petrography

BRAVO, F., Spanish
BRESSON, A., Medieval History
CABANES, J.-L., Contemporary French Literature
CAMBRONNE, P., Latin
CHAMPEAU, G., Spanish
CHARRIE, J.-P., Geography
COCULA, A.-M., Modern History
COCULA, B., French Language
CORZANI, J., Contemporary French Literature
COSTE, D., Comparative Literature
DEBORD, P., Ancient History
DE CARVALHO, P., Latin
DECOUDRAS, P. M., Land and Society in Tropical Environments
DEPRETTO, C., Russian
DESCAT, R., Greek History
DESCHAMPS, L., Latin
DES COURTILS, J., History of Art
DESVOIS, J.-M., Spanish
DI MÉO, G., Geography
DOTTIN ORSINI, M., Comparative Literature
DUBOIS, C., French
DUCASSE, R., Information Science
DURRUTY, S., English
DUTHEIL, F., Italian
DUVAL, G., English
FONDIN, H., Information and Communication Science
FOURTINA, H., English
FRANCHET D'ESPEREY, H., Latin
GARMENDIA, V., Spanish
GAUTHIER, M., American English
GILBERT, B., English
GORCEIX, P., German
GOZE, M., Urban Planning
GRANDJEAT, Y., North American Civilization
GUILLAUME, P., Modern History
GUILLAUME, S., Modern History
HOTIER, H., Information and Communication Science
HUMBERT, L., Geology
JARASSE, D., History of Modern Art
JOLY, M., Image Analysis
JOUVE, M., English
LACHAISE, B., Modern History
LACOSTE, J., History of Art
LAMORE, J., Spanish
LANGHADE, J., Arabic
LARRERE, C., Philosophy
LAVAUD, C., Philosophy
LAVEAU, P., German
LEBIGRE, J.-M., Physical Geography, Biogeography
LEPRUN-PIÉTON, S., Art, Plastic Arts
LERAT, C., English
LOPEZ, F., Spanish
LOUISE, G., Medieval History
LOUPES, P., History
LY, A., Spanish
MAILLARD, J.-C., Geography
MALEZIEUX, J.-M., Geology
MALLET, D., Arabic
MANTION, J.-R., 18th-century French Literature
MARIEU, J., Urban Planning and Projects
MARQUETTE, J.-B., History
MARTIN, D., French Language and Literature
MATHIEU, M., Contemporary Francophone Literature
MAZOUER, C., Contemporary French Literature
MONDOT, J., German
MORIN, S., Tropical Geography
MOULINE, L., Theatre
MULLER, C., General Linguistics
NAVARRI, R., French Language and Literature
NOTZ, M.-F., Medieval Language and Literature
OLLIER, N., English
ORPUSTAN, J.-B., Basque
PAILHE, J., Geography
PELLETIER, N., German

PERRIN-NAFFAKH, A.-M., Contemporary Language and Literature
PERROT, M., Information and Communications Science
PEYLET, G., Contemporary Language and Literature
PICCIONE, M.-L., Contemporary Language and Literature
PONCEAU, J.-P., Medieval Language and Literature
PONTET, J., Modern History
PORTINE, H., Teaching French as a Foreign Language
POUCHAN, P., Geology
RABATE, D., Contemporary French Literature
RAMOND, C., Philosophy
REYNIER-GIRARDIN, C., English
RIBEIRO, M., Portuguese
RICARD, M., Tropical Pacific Phytoplankton
RIGAL-CELLARD, B., English
RITZ, R., English
ROCHER, A., Japanese
RODDAZ, J.-M., Ancient History
ROSSI, G., Geography
ROUCH, M., Italian
ROUDIE, P., Geography
ROUYER, M.-C., English
ROUYER, P., Plastic Art
RUIZ, A., German
SALOMON, J.-N., Geography
SCHVOERER, M., Physics applied to Archaeology
SENTAURENS, J., Spanish
SEVESTRE, N., Music and History of Music
SHEN, J., Applied Mathematics
SHUSTERMAN, R., English
SINGARAVELOU, Geography
TAILLARD, C., History of Modern Art
TERREL, J., Philosophy
VADE, Y., Contemporary Language and Literature
VAGNE-LEBAS, M., Social Communication
VIGNE, M.-P., English
VITALIS, A., Information and Communication Science
VLES, V., Urban Planning
ZAVIALOFF, N., Russian

TEACHING AND RESEARCH UNITS

Faculty of Anglophone Countries: tel. 5-57-12-44-62; fax 5-57-12-46-01; e-mail anglais@u-bordeaux3.fr.

Faculty of Arts: tel. 5-57-12-44-57; fax 5-57-12-46-69; e-mail arts@u-bordeaux3.fr.

Faculty of Foreign and Applied Languages (LE-LEA): tel. 5-57-12-46-44; fax 5-57-12-46-14; e-mail le.lea@u-bordeaux3.fr.

Faculty of Geography and Development: tel. 5-57-12-44-41; fax 5-57-12-45-33; e-mail geographie@u-bordeaux3.fr.

Faculty of Germanic and Scandinavian Studies: tel. 5-57-12-21-07; fax 5-57-12-44-78; e-mail allemand.scandinave@u-bordeaux3.fr.

Faculty of History: tel. 5-57-12-44-51; fax 5-57-12-46-33; e-mail histoire@u-bordeaux3.fr.

Faculty of History of Art and Archaeology: tel. 5-57-12-44-77; fax 5-57-12-21-12; e-mail histoire.art@u-bordeaux3.fr.

Faculty of Iberian and Ibero-American Studies: tel. 5-57-12-47-97; fax 5-57-12-45-74; e-mail etudes.iberiques@u-bordeaux3.fr.

Faculty of Letters: tel. 5-57-12-15-26; fax 5-57-12-45-29; e-mail lettres@u-bordeaux3.fr.

Faculty of Philosophy: tel. 5-57-12-44-79; fax 5-57-12-46-09; e-mail philosophie@u-bordeaux3.fr.

Institute of Environment, Geo-Engineering and Development (EGID): tel. 5-57-12-10-00; fax 5-57-12-10-01; e-mail administration@egid.u-bordeaux.fr; internet www.egid.u-bordeaux3.fr.

Institute of Information Sciences and Information (ISIC): tel. 5-57-12-45-71; fax 5-57-12-45-28; e-mail isic@u-bordeaux3.fr; internet isic.u-bordeaux3.fr.

Institute of Journalism Bordeaux Aquitaine (IJBA): 1 Rue Jacques Ellul, 33080 Bordeaux Cedex; tel. 5-57-12-20-20; fax 5-57-12-20-81; e-mail journalisme@ijba.u-bordeaux3.fr; internet www.ijba.u-bordeaux3.fr.

Institut Universitaire de Technologie Michel de Montaigne: 1 Rue Jacques Ellul, 33080 Bordeaux Cedex; tel. 5-57-12-21-20; fax 5-57-12-20-09; e-mail direction@iut.u-bordeaux3.fr; internet www.iut.u-bordeaux3.fr.

UNIVERSITÉ MONTESQUIEU (BORDEAUX IV)

Ave Léon-Duguit, 33608 Pessac

Telephone: 5-56-84-85-86
Fax: 5-56-37-00-25
E-mail: umb4@montesquieu.u-bordeaux.fr
Internet: www.u-bordeaux4.fr

Founded 1995 from units fmrly within the Univ. of Bordeaux I

State control; attached to PRES Bordeaux

7 Establishments at Bordeaux, Agen and Périgueux; 3 doctoral schools, 12 research units, 2 technology institutes, 1 business management institute, 1 political science institute

Pres.: JEAN-PIERRE LABORDE
Vice-Pres. for Admin. and Finance: GÉRARD AUBIN
Vice-Pres. for Education: MICHEL DUPUY
Vice-Pres. for Int. Relations: CHRISTIAN GRELLOIS
Vice-Pres. for Lifelong Learning: PIERRE BONFILS
Vice-Pres. for Research: LOÏC GRARD
Sec.-Gen.: MARLÈNE BARBOTIN
Librarian: D. MONTBRUN-ISRAËL

Number of teachers: 600 incl. researchers
Number of students: 17,500

TEACHING AND RESEARCH UNITS

Faculty of Economics, Management and Social Institutions: Dir: BERTRAND BLANCHETON
Faculty of Public Law and Political Science: Dir: JEAN-FRANÇOIS BRISSON
Institute of Business Administration: Dir: SERGE EVRAERT
IUT Bordeaux Montesquieu: Dir: JEAN-FRANÇOIS BRISSON
IUT Périgueux Bordeaux IV: Dir: JEAN-LUC GIRAUDEL
IUFM d'Aquitaine: Dir: PHILIPPE GIRARD

TEACHING AND RESEARCH UNITS

Institut d'Administration des Entreprises (IAE): 35 Ave Abadie, 33100 Bordeaux Cedex; tel. 5-56-00-45-67; internet www.iae-bordeaux.fr.

Institut Universitaire de Formation des Maîtres d'Aquitaine (IUFM): 160 Ave de Verdun, 33705 Mérignac; tel. 5-56-12-67-00; fax 5-56-12-67-99; internet iufm.u-bordeaux4.fr; f. 1991; in 2008 became Univ. School.

Institut Universitaire de Technologie Bordeaux Montesquieu: tel. 5-56-00-96-05; e-mail directeur-iutbxm@u-bordeaux4.fr; internet www.iut.u-bordeaux4.fr.

Institut Universitaire de Technologie Périgueux Bordeaux IV: 35 Rue Paul Mazy, 24019 Périgueux Cedex; tel. 5-53-02-58-58; fax 5-53-02-58-71; e-mail iutpxbx4@u-bordeaux4.fr; internet www.perigueux.u-bordeaux4.fr.

ATTACHED INSTITUTE

Institut d'Etudes Politiques: 11 Ave Ausone, 33607 Pessac Cedex; tel. 5-56-84-42-52; fax 5-56-37-45-37; e-mail direction@sciencespobordeaux.fr; internet www.sciencespobordeaux.fr; Dir VINCENT HOFFMANN-MARTINOT.

UNIVERSITÉ MONTPELLIER I

Service Communication, 5 blvd Henri IV, 34967 Montpellier Cedex 2

Telephone: 4-67-41-74-00
Fax: 4-67-41-02-46
Internet: www.univ-montp1.fr
Founded 1970
State control
Language of instruction: French
Academic year: September to June

Pres.: YVES LOUBATIÈRES
Gen. Sec.: SYLVAIN SALTIEL
Librarian: BENOÎT LECOQ

Number of teachers: 829
Number of students: 18,538

Publications: *Cadran, Journal de Médecine, L'Economie Méridionale, Le Ligament, Revue de la Société d'Histoire du Droit*

TEACHING AND RESEARCH UNITS

Alimentary, Oenological and Environmental Studies: Dir: J. C. CABANIS
Economic and Social Administration: Dir: YVES CHIROUZE
Industrial Pharmacy: Dir: H. DELONCA
Law: Dir: O. DUGRIP
Medicine: Dir: C. SOLASSOL
Odontology: Dir: P. PARGUEL
Pharmacy: Dir: J.-L. CHANAL
Physical Education and Sport: Dir: L. BELEN
Science and Economics: Dir: J. PERCEBOIS

UNIVERSITÉ PARIS DESCARTES (PARIS V)

12 rue de l'École de Médecine, 75270 Paris Cedex 06

Telephone: 1-40-46-16-16
Fax: 1-40-46-16-15
E-mail: secretaire.general@parisdescartes.fr
Internet: www.parisdescartes.fr
Founded 1970
Academic year: October to July

Pres.: A. KAHN
Vice-Pres.: A. DUCRUIX B. VARET S. IONESCU M. H. JEANMERET-CRETTEZ
Sec.-Gen.: F. PAQUIS
Librarian: J. KALFON

Number of teachers: 1,890
Number of students: 33,500

Publication: *Diologues de Descartes* (4 a year)

TEACHING AND RESEARCH UNITS

Biomedicine: Dir: D. JORE
Dentistry: Dean: G. LEVY
Faculty of Law: Dean: J. MACHELON
Human and Social Sciences: Dean: S. MAURY
Institute of Psychology: Dir: F. MARTY
Mathematics and Data Processing: Dir: D. SERET
Medicine: Dean: PATRICK BERCHE
Pharmaceutical and Biological Sciences: Dean: M. AIACH
Physical Education and Sports: Dir: B. DURING RILHAC
University Institute of Technology: Dir: DOMINIQUE GASCON

UNIVERSITÉ PARIS I (PANTHÉON-SORBONNE)

12 place du Panthéon, 75231 Paris Cedex 05
Telephone: 1-44-07-77-04
Fax: 1-46-34-20-56

E-mail: cabpresi@univ-paris1.fr
Internet: www.univ-paris1.fr
Founded 1971
State control
Language of instruction: French
Academic year: September to June

Pres.: JEAN-CLAUDE COLLIARD
Vice-Pres. for Admin. Council: JEAN DA SILVA
Vice-Pres. for Science Council: YVONNE FLOUR
Vice-Pres. for Education and Univ. Life: GRÉGOIRE LOISEAU
Vice-Pres. for Int. Affairs: CHRISTINE MENGIN
Vice-Pres. for Industrial Partnerships and Professionalisation: PIERRE PECH
Sec.-Gen.: FRANÇOIS RIOU
Librarian: GENEVIÈVE SIMONOT

Number of teachers: 1,024
Number of students: 43,256

TEACHING AND RESEARCH UNITS

Business Law: Dir: YVONNE FLOUR (acting)
Economic and Social Administration, Labour and Social Studies: Dir: Prof. R. LENOIR
Economics: Dir: A. HERVIER
General Economics, Business Administration: Dir: HUBERT DE LA BRUSLERIE
Geography: Dir: Prof. P. BEKOUCHE (acting)
History: Dir: Prof. JEAN-MARIE BERTRAND (acting)
History of Art and Archaeology: Dir: Prof. CHR. PRIGENT
International and European Studies: Dir: JEAN-CLAUDE MASCLET
Legal Studies: Dir: Prof. FRANÇOIS GAUDU (acting)
Mathematics and Informatics: Dir: Prof. J. BLOT (acting)
Philosophy: Dir: ANNICK JAULIN
Plastic Arts and Science of Art: Dir: JEAN DA SILVA (acting)
Political Science: Dir: Prof. FR. DREYFUS (acting)
Public Administration and Public Law: Dir: Prof. B. CASTAGNEDE (acting)

INSTITUTES

Institute of Business Administration: Dir: PIERRE-LOUIS DUBOIS
Institute of Demography: Dir: MARLÈNE LAMY (acting)
Institute of Economic and Social Development: Dir: Prof. BR. LAUTIER (acting)
Institute of Labour Social Sciences: Dir: JEAN-MARIE MONNIER

DEPARTMENTS

Applied Modern Languages, Economics and Law: Dir: L. THOMPSON (acting)
Applied Modern Languages, Humanities: Dir: A. HAKKAK (acting)
Social Sciences: Dir: Mme YOTTE

PROFESSORS

Applied Modern Languages, Economics and Law (12 place du Panthéon, 75005 Paris; tel. 1-44-07-78-33; fax 1-44-07-78-33; e-mail seglas@univ-paris1.fr):

BULLIER, A.-J., Legal English Studies
KERSAUDY, F., English for Economists

Business Administration (21 rue Broca, 75005 Paris; tel. 1-53-55-28-00; fax 1-53-55-27-01; e-mail iae@univ-paris1.fr):

ALLOUCHE, J., Human Resources Management
GIARD, V., Operations Management
HELFER, J.-P., Marketing and Strategy
HOARAU, C., Finance and Control
LE FLOCH, P., Business Law
MAILLET, P., Finance
PAUCELLE, J. L., Information Systems
TRIOLAIRE, G., Management

Business Law (tel. 1-44-07-77-36; fax 1-43-54-97-54; e-mail ufr05@univ-paris1.fr):

AYNES, L., Private and Civil Law
BOULOC, B., Criminal Law
CADIET, L., Civil Procedure
CHAPUT, Y., Commercial Law – Insolvency
DAIGRE, J. J., Business Law
DAVID, C., Tax Law
DELEBECQUE, P., Civil Law
FLOUR, Y., Civil Law
GAUDU, F., Labour Law
GIUDICELLI, G., Criminal Law
GUTMANN, D., Insurance Law
HEUZE, V., Insurance Law
JOURDAIN, P., Civil Law
LABRUSSE, C., Civil Law
LE CANNU, P., Business Law
LE NABASQUE, H., Business Law
LIBCHABER, R., Civil Law
LUCAS DE LEYSSAC, C., Commercial Law
MENJUCQ, M., International Corporate Law
MUIR-WATT, H., Civil Law and International Civil Law
PARLEANI, G., Business Law
POLLAUD-DULIAN, F., Artistic and Literary Copyright Law
THIREAU, J. L., History of Law
VINEY, G., Civil Law

Demography (i DUP, Centre PMF, 90 rue de Tolbiac, 75634 Paris Cedex 13; tel. 1-44-07-86-46; fax 1-44-07-86-47; e-mail cridup@univ-paris1.fr):

DITTGEN, A., Socio-Demography
GROSSAT, B., Socio-Demography
LAMY-FESTY, M., Social Demography
NORVEZ, A., Socio-Demography

Development, International, European and Comparative Studies (tel. 1-44-07-77-33; fax 1-44-07-08-33; e-mail ufr07@univ-paris1.fr):

BARAV, A., European Community Law
BERLIN, D., European Community Law
BURDEAU, G., International Public Law
CARREAU, D., Economic Public Law
DAUDET, Y., International Public Law
DELMAS-MARTY, M., Penal Law
EISEMAN, P. M., International Public Law
HUDAULT, J., History of Law
IDOT, L., European Community Law
JUILLARD, P., International Economic Law
LAGARDE, P., International Private Law
LEGRAND, P., Comparative Law
LE ROY, E., Legal Anthropology
LOVISI, C., History of Law
MANIN, P., European Community Law
MASCLET, J. C., European Community Law
MAYER, P., International Private Law
RENOUX-ZAGAMÉ, M. F., History of Law
RUIZ FABRI, H., Constitutional Law
SIRINELLI, P., Private Law
SOREL, J. M., International Public Law
STERN, B., International Public Law

Economic Analysis and Politics, Econometrics, Labour and Human Resources (Centre P.M.F., 90 rue de Tolbiac, 75013 Paris; tel. 1-44-07-88-88; fax 1-44-07-86-15; e-mail ufr02@univ-paris1.fr):

ANDREFF, W., Economy of the Transition
ARCHAMBAULT, E., Accountancy and Social Economics
BERTHELEMY, J. C., International Economics
BORDES, C., Money and Macroeconomics
CHAUVEAU, TH., Money and Finance
DE BOISSIEU, C., Monetary Economics
ENCAOUA, D., Industrial Economics
FARDEAU, M., Health Economics, Social Economics
FAU, J., Economic Analysis
FONTAGNE, L., International Economics
GARDES, J., Econometrics
GREFFE, X., Political Economy
HAIRAULT, J. O., Macroeconomics
HENIN, P., Macroeconomics
KEMPF, H., Macroeconomics

KOPP, P., Microeconomics
LAFAY, J. D., Public Economy
LAFFARGUE, J. P., International Economics
LANTNER, R., Economics and Industrial Politics
LAPIDUS, A., History of Economic Thought
LEVY-GARBOUA, L., Microeconomics
MASSON-D'AUTUME, A., Macroeconomics
MEIDINGER, C., Microeconomics
MENARD, C., Theory of Organization
PRADEL, J., Statistics
SCHUBERT, K., Macroeconomics
SOFER, C., Microeconomics
SOLLOGOUB, M., Microeconomics
VERNIÈRES, M., Economic Analysis
WIGNIOLLE, B., Macroeconomics
ZAGAME, P., Macroeconomics

Economic and Social Development (45 bis avenue de la Belle-Gabrielle, 94736 Nogent sur Marne Cedex; tel. 1-43-94-72-22; fax 1-43-94-72-44; e-mail iedes@univ.-paris1.fr):

GRELLET, G., Economic Development
HAUBERT, M., Social Development
LAUTIER, B., Economic and Social Development

Economic and Social Administration, Labour and Social Studies (tel. 1-44-07-79-08; fax 1-44-07-79-08; e-mail raufr12@univ-paris.fr):

CHAPOULIE, Sociology
COUTURIER, G., Labour Law
GAZIER, B., Labour Economy
LENOIR, R., Sociology
PIGENET, Sociology
RODIÈRE, P., Labour Law
TSIKOUNAS, History

Geography (191 rue St Jacques, 75005 Paris; tel. 1-44-32-14-03; fax 1-44-32-14-54; e-mail raufr08@univ-paris1.fr):

BECKOUCHE, P., Economic Geography
BOUINOT, J., Planning and Economic Geography
BRUN, J., Social Geography
CAZES, G., Geography of Tourism
CHALÉARD, J. L., Geography of Developing Countries
FRUIT, J. P., Rural Geography
KAISER, B., Geomorphology
LE COEUR, C., Natural Resources, Geomorphology
MALEZIEUX, J., Regional Geography, Land Use
MERLIN, P., Urban Geography
PECH, P., Environment
POURTIER, R., Tropical Geography
PREVELAKIS, G., Geopolitics
PUMAIN, D., Urban Geography
SAINT-JULIEN, TH., Human Geography, Statistics
SOPPELSA, J., Geopolitics
TABEAUD, M., Climatology

History (17 rue de la Sorbonne, 75231 Paris Cedex 05; tel. 1-40-46-27-88; fax 1-40-46-31-80; e-mail millot9@univ-paris1.fr):

BALARD, M., Mediterranean Medieval History
BENOÎT, P., Modern History
BERTRAND, J. M., Ancient History
BOULÈGUE, J.-M., History of Black Africa
BOURIN, M., Medieval History
CABANTOUS, A., Modern History
CHARLE, C., Contemporary History
CHARPIN, D., Near Eastern History
CHRISTOL, M., Roman History
CORBIN, A., Contemporary History
CORSI, P., Modern History
D'ALMEIDA-TOPOR, H., Contemporary History
DAVID, J. M., Ancient History
FRANK, R., Contemporary History
GAUVARD, C., Medieval History
GENET, J. P., Medieval History
GUERRA, F., History of Latin America
KAPLAN, M., Byzantine Medieval History
KASPI, A., History of North America

LEMAITRE, N., Modern History
MARSEILLE, J., Economic and Social History
MARTIN, J. C., Modern History
MICHAUD, C., Modern History
MICHEAU, F., Medieval History
MICHEL, B., History of Eastern Europe
ORY, P., Contemporary History
PARISSE, M., Medieval History
REY, M. P., Contemporary History
RIVET, D., Contemporary History
ROBERT, J. L., Contemporary History
SCHMITT, P., Ancient History
WORONOFF, D., Economic and Social History
ZYLBERBERG, M., Modern History

History of Art and Archaeology (3 rue Michelet, 75006 Paris; tel. 1-53-73-71-00; fax 1-53-73-71-13; e-mail ufr03sec@univ-paris1.fr):

BURNOUF, J., Medieval Archaeology
CROISSANT, F., Greek Archaeology
DAGEN, P., Contemporary Art
DARRAGON, E., Contemporary Art
DEMOULE, J.-P., Protohistory
DENTZER, J. M., Oriental Archaeology
DUMASY, F., Classical Archaeology
GILI, J., Cinema
HUOT, J. L., Oriental Archaeology
LICHARDUS, M., Protohistory
MONNIER, G., History of Contemporary Art
MOREL, P., Modern Art
PIGEOT, N., Archaeology and Protohistory
POLET, J., African Art and Archaeology
PRESSOUYRE, L., Medieval Art and Archaeology
PRIGENT, C., Medieval Art
RABREAU, D., Modern Art
SCHNAPP, A., Greek Archaeology
SODINI, J. P., Byzantine Archaeology
TALADOIRE, E., Meso-American Archaeology
TREUIL, R. A., Archaeology and Protohistory
VANCI, M., Contemporary Art
VAN DER LEEUW, S., Archaeology and Protohistory
VOLFOVSKY, C., Preservation of Cultural Heritage

Institute of Social Sciences (tel. 1-45-36-16-40; fax 1-46-65-70-80; e-mail patrick.diez@univ-paris1.fr):

FREYSSINET, J., Economics
OFFERLE, M., Political Science
PAULRE, B., Economics
PIOTEL, F., Sociology

Managerial Economics and Business (17 rue de la Sorbonne, 75231 Paris Cedex 05; tel. 1-40-46-27-78; fax 1-40-46-31-77; e-mail raufr06@univ-paris1.fr):

AMADIEU, J. F., Human Resources Management
BAETCHE, A., Scientific Methods Applied to Marketing
CHIROLEU-ASSOULINE, M., Macroeconomics
COT, A., Economics
COURET, A., Business Law
DE LA BRUSLERIE, H., Finance
DESAIGUES, B., Environmental Economics
GOFFIN, R., Finance
GREGORY, P., Marketing
IPSOMER, I., Marketing
LAURENT, P., Business Law
MUCHIELLI, J.-L., Industrial Economics
PEYRARD, M., International and European Business
PONCET, P., Finance
RAIMBOURG, P., Finance
RAY, J.-E., Labour Law
ROJOT, J., Organization Theory and Human Resources Management
ROLLAND, C., Computer Science
ROURE, F., Finance

STEYER, A., Speculative Methods in Marketing

Mathematics, Statistics and Computer Science:

ABDOU, J., Game Theory
AUSLENDER, A., Optimization
BALASKO, Y., Mathematical Economics
BONNISSEAU, J.-M., Mathematics and Economics
CORNET, B., Mathematics and Economics
COTTRELL, M., Probability, Statistics and Neural Networks
GIRE, F., Computer Science
GUYON, X., Probability and Statistics
HADDAD, G., Differential Equations and Functional Analysis
JOUINI, E., Mathematics and Economics

Philosophy (UFR Philosophie—Université Paris 1 Panthéon Sorbonne, 17 rue de la Sorbonne 75005 Paris; tel. 1-40-46-31-68; fax 1-40-46-31-57; e-mail philosec@univ-paris1.fr):

BLONDEL, E., Moral and Political Philosophy
BONARDEL, F., Philosophy of Religion
BRAGUE, R., History of Philosophy
CHAUVIRÉ, C., American Philosophy and Anthropology
CHEDIN, O., History of Philosophy
GRAS, A., Social Philosophy
KAMBOUCHNER, D., History of Philosophy
KERVEGAN, J. F., Philosophy of Law
MICHAUD, Y., Political Philosophy
MOEGLIN-DELCROIX, A., Aesthetics
MOSCONI, J., Philosophy of Mathematics
PINTO, E., Aesthetics
POLITIS, H., History of Philosophy
RIVENC, F., Philosophy of Logic
SALEM, J., History of Philosophy

Plastic Arts (162 rue St Charles, 75015 Paris; tel. 1-44-25-04-01; fax 1-45-58-30-47; e-mail raufr04@univ-paris1.fr):

BAQUE, P., Visual Arts
CHATEAU, D., Aesthetics
CHIRON, E., Visual Arts
CLANCY, G., Aesthetics
CONTE, R., Visual Arts
DARRAS, B., Culture and Communication
DUGUET, A. N., Video and Media
FRENAULT-DERUELLE, P., Semiotics
HUYGHE, P. D., Visual Arts and Aesthetics
JIMENEZ, M., Aesthetics
LANCRI, J., Visual Arts
LEBENSZTEJN, J. C., History of Art
MIEREANU, C., Musicology
NOGUEZ, D., Cinema and Audiovisual Arts
SERCEAU, D., Cinema and Audiovisual Arts
SICARD, N., Visual Arts

Political Science (17 rue de la Sorbonne, 75231 Paris Cedex 05; tel. 1-40-46-28-04; fax 1-40-46-31-65; e-mail depscpo2@univ-paris1.fr):

BIRNBAUM, P., Political Sociology
BRAUD, P., Political Sociology
COLLIARD, J. C., Comparative Government
COTTERET, J.-M., Political Communication
FRANÇOIS, B., Constitutional Law
GAXIE, D., Political Sociology
GRESLE, F., Sociology
KLEIN, J., International Relations
LAGROYE, J., Political Ideology
LESAGE, M., Theory of Organizations
SFEZ, L., Communication
ZORGBIBE, C., International Relations

Public Administration and Public Internal Law (tel. 1-44-07-77-38; fax 1-44-07-17-75; e-mail ufr01@univ-paris1.fr):

BRECHON-MOULÈNES, C., Public Economic Law
CASTAGNEDE, B., Public Finance
DURUPTY, M., Public Law
FATOME, E., Administrative Law
FRIER, P., Public Law

GICQUEL, J., Public Law
JEGOUZO, Y., Administrative Law
LE MIRE, P., Public Law
MAISL, H., Administrative Law
MARCOU, G., Administrative Law
MATHIEU, B., Constitutional Law
MODERNE, F., Administrative Law
MORABITO, M., History of Law
MORAND-DEVILLER, J., Administrative Law
PFERS MANN, O., Comparative Public Law
PICARD, E., Administrative Law
RICHER, L., Administrative Law
TIMSIT, G., Public Law

UNIVERSITÉ PAUL CEZANNE–AIX-MARSEILLE III

3 ave Robert Schuman, 13628 Aix-en-Provence Cedex 1

Telephone: 4-42-17-28-00
Internet: www.univ-cezanne.fr

Founded 1973 as Univ. d'Aix-Marseille III (Univ. de Droit, d'Economie et des Sciences)
Academic year: September to June

Univs of Aix en Provence consist of 3 univs in Aix and Provence; law, economics and foundation science are the principal subjects of instruction here

Pres.: MARC PENA
Vice-Pres. for Admin. Council: BRUNO HAMELIN
Vice-Pres. for Education and Student Life: DOMINIQUE VIRIOT-BARRIAL
Vice-Pres. for Int. Relations: PAUL DJONDANG
Vice-Pres. for Science Ccl: MICHEL LANNOO
Sec.-Gen.: THÉRÈSE CHETAIL
Librarian: J.-C. RODA

Number of teachers: 760
Number of students: 22,500

Publications: Interface (12 a year), L'Inter Cours (12 a year), annual research reports

DEANS
Faculty of Applied Economics: J.-P. CENTI
Faculty of Law and Political Science: G. ORSONI
Faculty of Science and Technology: J.-M. PONS

TEACHING AND RESEARCH UNITS
Faculty of Applied Economics: tel. 4-42-17-29-85; internet www.fea-upcam.fr.
Faculty of Law and Political Science: 3 Ave Robert Schuman, 13628 Aix en Provence; tel. 4-42-17-29-15; fax 4-42-20-46-51; e-mail secretariat.sridroit@univ-cezanne.fr; internet www.facdedroit.univ-cezanne.fr.
Faculty of Science and Technology: tel. 4-91-28-89-46; e-mail sec-doyen.fst@univ-cezanne.fr; internet www.fst.univ-cezanne.fr.
Institute of Business Administration: Blvd des Camus, 13540 Puyricard; tel. 4-42-28-08-08; fax 4-42-28-08-00; internet www.iae-aix.com; Dir A. GED.
Institute of French Studies for Foreign Students: 23 rue Gaston de Saporta, 13628 Aix en Provence; tel. 4-42-21-70-90; fax 4-42-23-02-64; internet www.iefee.com; Dir R. GHEVONTIAN.
Institute of Public Management and Regional Government: 23 rue Gaston de Saporta, 13100 Aix en Provence; tel. 4-42-17-05-54; fax 4-42-17-05-56; internet www.managementpublic.univ-cezanne.fr; Dir R. FOUCHET.
Institut Universitaire de Technologie: 142 Traverse Charles Susini, 13388 Marseilles Cedex 13; tel. 4-91-28-93-00; fax 4-91-28-94-94; internet iutmrs.univ-cezanne.fr; Dir MICHEL GAUCH.

UNIVERSITÉ PAUL SABATIER (TOULOUSE III)

118 route de Narbonne, 31062 Toulouse Cedex 9

Telephone: 5-61-55-66-11
Fax: 5-61-55-64-70
Internet: www.ups-tlse.fr

Founded 1969
State control
Academic year: September to June

Number of teachers and researchers: 1,650

Pres.: RAYMOND BASTIDE
Vice-Pres: R. CAUBET (Scientific Council), G. SOUM (Council of Studies and University Life)
Sec.-Gen.: Mme A. VERDAGUER
Librarian: Mme HEUSSE

Number of students: 28,000

Publication: Campus CONTACT Actualité (12 a year)

DEANS
Faculty of Dental Surgery: J. PH. LODTER
Faculty of Medicine (Purpan): B. GUIRAUD CHAUMEIL
Faculty of Medicine (Rangueil): G. LAZORTHES
Faculty of Pharmacy: P. COURRIÈRE

TEACHING AND RESEARCH UNITS
Earth and Life Sciences: Dir: Prof. J. DERAMOND
Mathematics, Information Science, Management: Dir: Prof. H. SENATEUR
Modern Languages: Dir: R. FAURE
Physics, Chemistry and Automation: Dir: Y. SALAMERO
Scientific Study of Physical and Sporting Activities: Dir: G. AUNEAU
University Institute of Technology: Dir: M. EYCHENE

UNIVERSITÉ PAUL VERLAINE–METZ

Ile du Saulcy, BP 80794, 57012 Metz Cedex 1

Telephone: 3-87-31-50-50
Fax: 3-87-31-50-55
E-mail: com@univ-metz.fr
Internet: www.univ-metz.fr

Founded 1970

Pres.: RICHARD LIOGER
Vice-Pres.: G. RHIN, M. POTIER-FERRY, G. GINTER
Sec.-Gen.: MICHEL CLEMENS
Librarian: SIMONE LAMARCHE

Number of teachers: 623
Number of students: 15,729

DEANS
Arts and Human Sciences: ERIC PEDON
Fundamental and Applied Sciences: JEAN-GEORGES GASSER
Higher Franco-German Institute of Technology, Economy and Sciences: GABRIEL MICHEL
Higher Management Studies: ETIENNE BAUMGARTNER
Law, Economics and Administration: YAHN MANGEMATIN
Letters and Languages: ALAIN CULLIERE
Mathematics, Computer Science, Mechanics: ABDERRAHIM ZEGHLOUL
University Institute of Technology: BERNARD HEULLUY
University Institute of Technology at Thionville/Yutz: FRANÇOIS-XAVIER ROYER

UNIVERSITÉ RENNES 2—HAUTE BRETAGNE

Place du Recteur Henri Le Moal, CS 24307, 35043 Rennes Cedex

Telephone: 2-99-14-10-00

Internet: www.uhb.fr

Founded 1969

Pres.: FRANÇOIS MOURET
First Vice-Pres.: MARC GONTARD
Sec.-Gen.: PHILIPPE GUY
Librarian: ELISABETH LEMAU

Number of teachers: 629
Number of students: 21,475.

TEACHING AND RESEARCH UNITS
Arts, Literature, Communications: Dir PIERRE BAZANTAY.
Humanities: Dir GÉRARD GUINGOUAIN.
Languages: Dir FRANÇOISE DUBOSQUET.
Physical Education and Sport: Dir PAUL DELAMARCHE.
Social Sciences: Dir MARC DAVID.
CIREFE (Teaching French to Foreign Students): Dir MARIE-FRANÇOISE BERTHU-COURTIVRON.

UNIVERSITÉ VICTOR SEGALEN (BORDEAUX 2)

146 rue Léo-Saignat, 33076 Bordeaux Cedex

Telephone: 5-57-57-10-10
Fax: 5-56-99-03-80
E-mail: info@u-bordeaux2.fr
Internet: www.u-bordeaux2.fr

Founded 1970
Academic year: September to July

Pres.: BERNARD BÉGAUD
Sec.-Gen.: CORINNE DUFFAU

Number of teachers: 1,012
Number of students: 17,005

Publication: Anima (4 a year)

TEACHING AND RESEARCH UNITS
Biochemistry and Cellular Biology: Dir: C. SCHLICK
Bordeaux Higher Technical School of Biomolecular Science: Dir: C. CASSAGNE
Hydrothermal Therapy: Dir: C. NGUYEN BA
Institute of Cognitive Science: Dir: B. CLAVERIE
Institute of Oenology: Dir: Y. GLORIES
Medical Sciences I Paul Broca: Dir: A. DURANDEAU
Medical Sciences II Hyacinthe Vincent: Dir: C. BÉBÉAR
Medical Sciences III Victor Pachon: Dir: P. MORLAT
Odontology: Dir: G. DORIGNAC
Pharmacy: Dir: J. CAMBAR
Public Health and Epidemiology: Dir: R. SALAMON
Sciences and Model Theory: Dir: C. SCHLICK
Social and Psychological Sciences: Dir: P. CLANCHÉ
Sports Science and Physical Education: Dir: S. FAUCHÉ

Polytechnic Institutes

GROUPE GRENOBLE INP

46 ave Félix Viallet, 38031 Grenoble Cedex 1

Telephone: 4-76-57-45-00
Fax: 4-76-57-45-01
E-mail: contact@grenoble-inp.fr
Internet: www.grenoble-inp.fr

Founded 1907

29 Research laboratories, 6 constituent schools

Pres.: PAUL JACQUET
Vice-Pres. for Admin. Ccl: NADINE GUILLEMOT
Vice-Pres. for Science Ccl: DIDIER GEORGES
Vice-Pres. for Education Ccl and Univ. Life: CHRISTIAN SCHAEFFER

Vice-Pres. for Int. Relations: JEAN-LUC KON-ING

Vice-Pres. for Industry Partnerships: CHRISTIAN VOILLOT

Vice-Pres. for Students: GUILLAUME PERRIN

Number of teachers: 350

Number of students: 5,076

Publication: *Ingénieurs INPG* (52 a year).

CONSTITUENT SCHOOLS

Ecole Nationale Supérieure d'Ingénieurs pour l'Energie, l'Eau et l'Environnement (ENSE3): BP 46, Rue de la Houille Blanche, 38402 Saint Martin d'Hères Cedex; tel. 4-76-82-62-00; e-mail direction .ense3@grenoble-inp.fr; internet ense3 .grenoble-inp.fr; f. 2008 by merger of Ecole Nationale Supérieure d'Ingénieurs Electriciens de Grenoble (ENSIEG) and Ecole Nationale Supérieure d'Hydraulique et de Mécanique de Grenoble (ENSHMG).

Ecole Nationale Supérieure d'Informatique, de Mathématiques Appliquées et de Télécommunications (ENSIMAG): 681 rue de la Passerelle, 38402 Saint-Martin-d'Hères Cedex; tel. 4-76-82-72-00; internet ensimag.grenoble-inp.fr; f. 2008 by merger of Ecole Nationale Supérieure d'Informatique et de Mathématiques Appliquées de Grenoble (ENSIMAG) and INP Grenoble TELECOM; Dir JACQUES MOSSIÈRE.

Ecole Nationale Supérieure des Systèmes Avancés et Réseaux (ESISAR): 50 rue Barthélémy de Laffemas, BP 54, 26902 Valence Cedex 9; tel. 4-75-75-94-00; fax 4-75-43-56-42; e-mail direction@esisar .grenoble-inp.fr; internet esisar.grenoble-inp .fr; Dir CHANTAL ROBACH.

École Internationale du Papier de la Communication Imprimée et des Biomatériaux (PAGORA): 461 rue de la Papeterie, BP 65, 38402 Saint-Martin-d'Hères Cedex; tel. 4-76-82-69-00; fax 4-76-82-69-33; e-mail contact.pagora@grenoble-inp.fr; internet pagora.grenoble-inp.fr; f. 2008, fmrly l'Ecole Française de Papeterie et des Industries Graphiques (EFPG); Dir BERNARD PINEAUX.

Ecole Nationale Supérieure de Physique, Electronique, Matériaux (PHELMA): 3 Parvis Louis Neel, BP 257, 38016 Grenoble Cedex; tel. 4-56-52-91-00; fax 4-56-52-91-03; internet phelma.grenoble-inp .fr; f. 2008 by merger of Ecole Nationale Supérieure de Physique de Grenoble (ENSPG), Ecole Nationale Supérieure d'Electricité et de Radioelectricité (ENSERG) and Ecole Nationale Supérieure d'Electrochimie et d'Electrométallurgie de Grenoble (ENSEEG).

Génie Industriel: tel. 4-76-57-46-01; internet genie-industriel.grenoble-inp.fr; f. 2008 by merger of Ecole Nationale Supérieure de Génie Industriel (ENSGI) and part of the Ecole Nationale Supérieure d'Hydraulique et de Mécanique de Grenoble (ENSHMG); Dir JEANNE DUVALLET.

INSTITUT NATIONAL POLYTECHNIQUE DE LORRAINE

2 ave de la Forêt de Haye, BP 3, 54501 Vandoeuvre

Telephone: 3-83-59-59-59

Fax: 3-83-59-59-55

E-mail: inpl@inpl-nancy.fr

Internet: www.inpl-nancy.fr

Founded 1970

Language of instruction: French

28 Research laboratories, 7 constituent schools

Pres.: FRANÇOIS LAURENT

Sec.-Gen.: JEAN-YVES RIVIÈRE.

CONSTITUENT SCHOOLS

Ecole Européenne d'Ingénieurs en Génie des Matériaux (EEIGM): 6 rue B. Lepage, 54010 Nancy Cedex; tel. 3-83-36-83-00; fax 3-83-36-83-36; e-mail eeigm@eeigm .inpl-nancy.fr; internet www.eeigm .inpl-nancy.fr; f. 1991; 191 students; Dir BRIGITTE JAMART.

Ecole Nationale Supérieure d'Agronomie et des Industries Alimentaires (ENSAIA): 2 ave de la Forêt de Haye, BP 172, 54505 Vandoeuvre Cedex; tel. 3-83-59-58-51; fax 3-83-59-58-04; e-mail ensaia@ ensaia.inpl-nancy.fr; internet www.ensaia .inpl-nancy.fr; f. 1970; 58 teachers; 436 students; library of 7,500 vols; Dir MICHEL FICK; publ. *Bulletin Scientifique* (1 a year).

Ecole Nationale Supérieure d'Electricité et de Mécanique (ENSEM): 2 ave de la Forêt de Haye, 54500 Vandoeuvre; tel. 3-83-59-55-43; fax 3-83-44-07-63; e-mail ensem@ensem.inpl-nancy.fr; internet www .ensem.inpl-nancy.fr; f. 1990; 50 teachers; 379 students; Dir YVES GRANJON.

Ecole Nationale Supérieure en Génie des Systèmes Industriels (ENSGSI): 8 rue Bastien Lepage, BP 647, 54010 Nancy; tel. 3-83-19-32-32; fax 3-83-19-32-00; e-mail ensgsi@ensgsi.inpl-nancy.fr; internet www .ensgsi.inpl-nancy.fr; f. 1993; 20 teachers; 315 students; Dir PASCAL L. HOSTE.

Ecole Nationale Supérieure de Géologie (ENSG): Rue du Doyen Marcel Roubault, BP 40, 54501 Vandoeuvre lès Nancy; tel. 3-83-59-59-59; fax 3-83-59-64-64; e-mail accueil@ ensg.inpl-nancy.fr; internet www.ensg .inpl-nancy.fr; f. 1908; 36 teachers; 300 students; Dir JEAN-MARC MONTEL.

Ecole Nationale Supérieure des Industries Chimiques (ENSIC): 1 rue Grandville, 54001 Nancy; tel. 3-83-17-50-00; fax 3-83-35-08-11; e-mail ensic@ensic.inpl-nancy .fr; internet www.ensic.inpl-nancy.fr; f. 1887; 63 teachers; 420 students; Dir MICHAEL MATLOSZ.

Ecole Nationale Supérieure des Mines de Nancy (ENSMN): Parc de Saurupt, 54042 Nancy; tel. 3-83-58-42-32; fax 3-83-58-43-44; e-mail ensmn@mines.inpl-nancy.fr; internet www.mines.inpl-nancy.fr; f. 1919; 803 students; library of 37,500 vols, 180 periodicals; Dir JACK-PIERRE PIGUET.

INSTITUT NATIONAL POLYTECHNIQUE DE TOULOUSE

6 allée Emile Monso, BP 34038, 31029 Toulouse Cedex 4

Telephone: 5-34-32-30-00

Fax: 5-34-32-31-00

E-mail: inp@inp-toulouse.fr

Internet: www.inp-toulouse.fr

Founded 1970

4 Constituent schools and 17 research laboratories

Pres.: GILBERT CASAMATTA

Vice-Pres. for Science Ccl: OLIVIER SIMONIN

Vice-Pres. for Education and Univ. Life: GRÉGORY DECHAP-GUILLAUME

Vice-Pres. for Int. Relations: HENRI DELMAS

Sec.-Gen.: GILLES BOUCHER.

CONSTITUENT SCHOOLS

Ecole Nationale Supérieure Agronomique de Toulouse (ENSAT): Ave de l'Agrobiopole, BP 32607, Auzeville-Tolosane, 31326 Castanet-Tolosan Cedex; tel. 5-62-19-39-00; fax 5-62-19-39-01; internet www.ensat.fr; f. 1909 as Institut Agricole de Toulouse; Dir AHMED LEBRIHI.

Ecole Nationale Supérieure d'Electrotechnique, d'Electronique, d'Informatique et d'Hydraulique et des

Télécommunications (ENSEEIHT): 2 rue Camichel, BP 7122, 31071 Toulouse Cedex 7; tel. 5-61-58-82-00; fax 5-61-62-09-76; internet www.enseeiht.fr; Dir ALAIN AYACHE.

Ecole Nationale Supérieure des Arts Chimiques et Technologiques (ENSIACET): tel. 5-34-32-33-00; fax 5-34-32-33-99; internet www.ensiacet.fr; f. 2001; 106 teachers; 700 students; Dir JEAN-MARC LE LANN.

Ecole Nationale d'Ingénieurs de Tarbes (ENIT): 47 ave d'Azereix, BP 1629, 65016 Tarbes Cedex; tel. 5-62-44-27-00; fax 5-62-44-27-27; internet www.enit.fr; f. 1963; Dir JACQUES-ALAIN PETIT.

State Colleges and Institutes

Due to space limitations, we are restricted to giving a selection of colleges. Almost every one is a 'Grande Ecole' and awards a national degree.

GENERAL

Collège de France: 11 place Marcelin-Berthelot, 75231 Paris Cedex 05; tel. 1-44-27-12-11; fax 1-44-27-11-09; internet www .college-de-france.fr; f. 1530 by François I; library: 85,000 vols; 54 professors; Administrator JACQUES GLOWINSKI.

Ecole des Hautes Etudes en Sciences Sociales: 54 blvd Raspail, 75006 Paris; tel. 1-49-54-25-25; fax 1-45-44-93-11; internet www.ehess.fr; f. 1947; 270 teachers; 2,800 students; Pres. DANIÈLE HERVIEU-LÉGER.

Ecole Pratique des Hautes Etudes: 45–47 rue des Ecoles, 75005 Paris; tel. 1-40-46-33-97; fax 1-40-46-33-98; e-mail valerie.laffitte@ ephe.sorbonne.fr; internet www.ephe .sorbonne.fr; f. 1868; library: 50,000 vols; 300 teachers; 4,000 students; Pres. JEAN BAU-BÉROT; Chief Administrative Officer JEAN-CHARLES LINET.

Divisions:

Department of History and Philology: 45–47 rue des Ecoles, 75005 Paris; tel. 1-40-46-31-25; fax 1-40-46-31-39; f. 1868; Pres. LAURENT DUBOIS; publ. *Annuaire*.

Department of Life and Earth Science: 46 rue Saint-Jacques, 75005 Paris; tel. 1-40-46-31-30; fax 1-40-46-47-08; e-mail fbeauve@ephe.sorbonne.fr; f. 1868; Pres. JACQUES MICHAUX; publ. *Annuaire*.

Department of Religious Studies: 45–47 rue des Ecoles, 75005 Paris; tel. 1-40-46-31-37; fax 1-40-46-31-46; f. 1886; Pres. CLAUDE LANGLOIS; publ. *Annuaire*.

Pôle Universitaire Léonard de Vinci: 92916 Paris La Défense Cedex; located at: 12 ave Léonard de Vinci, 92400 Courbevoie, Hauts-de-Seine; tel. 1-41-16-70-00; fax 1-41-16-70-99; e-mail contact@devinci.fr; internet www.devinci.fr; f. 1995 by the Gen. Ccl of the Hauts-de-Seine Département; depts: economics and social sciences, languages, gen. culture, personal devt, sport; library: 40,000 books, reports, memoirs, market research reports, 800 journals, 800 CD-ROM titles, 600 int. databases.

ADMINISTRATION

Ecole Nationale d'Administration: 13 rue de l'Université, 75007 Paris; tel. 1-49-26-45-45; fax 1-42-60-26-95; f. 1945 to provide training for the higher ranks of the civil service; 600 teachers; 400 students; library: 25,000 vols; Dir ANTOINE DURRLEMAN.

Groupe ESC Clermont: 4 blvd Trudaine, 63037 Clermont-Ferrand Cedex; tel. 4-73-98-24-24; fax 4-73-98-24-49; e-mail info@esc-clermont.fr; internet www.esc-clermont.fr; f. 1919; dependent on the Direction de l'Enseignement Supérieur du Ministre de l'Education; 200 teachers; 600 students; library: 9,000 vols, Chamber of Commerce library of 12,000 vols; Dir L. HUA; publs *Développements* (3 a year), *Point Zéro* (6 a year).

AGRICULTURE, FORESTRY, VETERINARY SCIENCE

AgroParisTech: 16 rue Claude Bernard, 75231 Paris Cedex 05; tel. 1-44-08-16-61; fax 1-44-08-16-00; internet www.agroparistech.fr; f. 1972 with present title; teaching personnel 129; library: 50,000 vols and 1,700 periodicals; Dir (vacant).

Attached Institute:

AgroParisTech—Centre de Grignon: Avenue Lucien Brétignières, 78850 Thiverval-Grignon; tel. 1-30-81-53-53; fax 1-30-81-53-27; f. 1979; library: c. 1,000 vols; publ. *Sols* (3 or 4 a year).

Centre National d'Etudes Agronomiques des Régions Chaudes: 1101 ave Agropolis, BP 5098, 34033 Montpellier Cedex 1; tel. 4-67-61-70-00; fax 4-67-41-02-32; e-mail sauboa@cnearc.fr; internet www.cnearc.fr; f. 1902; 4 sections: Cycle d'Etudes Supérieures d'Agronomie Tropicale, Département de la Formation Continue, Master Professionnel Natura 'Vulgarisation et Organisations Professionnelles Agricoles', Master of Science 'Développement Agricole Tropical'; library: 22,000 vols, 350 periodicals; 20 teachers; 150 students; Dir M. LATHAM.

Ecole Nationale d'Ingénieurs des Travaux Agricoles de Clermont-Ferrand: Marmilhat, 63370 Lempdes; tel. 4-73-98-13-15; fax 4-73-98-13-98; e-mail gosset@gentiane.enitac.fr; internet www.enitac.fr; f. 1984; 45 teachers; 300 students; library: 10,000 vols; Dir GEORGES GOSSET.

Ecole Nationale du Génie Rural des Eaux et des Forêts: Centre de Nancy, 14 rue Girardet, 54042 Nancy Cedex; tel. 3-83-39-68-00; fax 3-83-30-22-54; internet www.engref.fr; f. 1965 by merger of the Ecole Nationale du Génie Rural and the Ecole Nationale des Eaux et Forêts; 15 teachers; 200 students; library: 50,000 vols, 1,600 periodicals; Dir DOMINIQUE DANGUY DES DÉSERTS; publ. *Revue Forestière Française* (6 a year).

Ecole Nationale Supérieure Agronomique de Montpellier: Place Viala, 34060 Montpellier Cedex 1; tel. 4-99-61-24-44; fax 4-99-61-29-00; e-mail dep@ensam.inra.fr; internet www:agro-montpellier.fr; f. 1872; 70 teachers; 620 students; library: 100,000 vols, 1,400 periodicals; Dir ETIENNE LANDAIS.

Ecole Nationale Supérieure Agronomique de Rennes (ENSAR): 65 rue de Saint-Brieuc, 35042 Rennes Cedex; tel. 2-23-48-56-97; fax 2-23-48-56-80; e-mail dep@agrorennes.educagri.fr; internet www.agrorennes.educagri.fr; f. 1830; library: 10,000 vols; 90 teachers; 550 students; Dir P. THIVEND.

Ecole Nationale Supérieure des Industries Agricoles et Alimentaires (ENSIA): 1 ave des Olympiades, 91744 Massy Cedex; tel. 1-69-93-50-50; fax 1-69-20-02-30; e-mail ensia@ensia.fr; internet www.ensia.fr; f. 1893; library: 10,000 vols; 45 teachers; 450 students; Dir YVES DEMARNE; publs *Compte Rendu d'Activités* (1 a year), *Industries Alimentaires* (12 a year), *Livret de l'Etudiant* (1 a year).

Ecole Nationale Supérieure du Paysage: 10 rue du Maréchal Joffre, 78000 Versailles; tel. 1-39-24-62-00; fax 1-39-24-62-01; internet www.versailles.ecole-paysage.fr; f. 1975; rural development, ecology, humanities, plastic arts, architecture, landscaping, town planning; library: 6,000 vols, 75 periodicals; Dir J. B. CUISINIER; publ. *Les Carnets du Paysage* (4 a year).

Ecole Nationale Vétérinaire d'Alfort: 7 ave Général de Gaulle, 94700 Maisons-Alfort; tel. 1-43-96-71-00; fax 1-43-96-71-25; e-mail direction@vet-alfort.fr; internet www.vet-alfort.fr; f. 1765; 72 teachers; library: 150,000 vols; Dean Prof. ANDRÉ-LAURENT PARODI; publ. *Le Recueil de Médecine Vétérinaire.*

Ecole Nationale Vétérinaire de Lyon: 1 ave Bourgelat, BP 83, 69280 Marcy L'Etoile; tel. 4-78-87-25-00; fax 4-78-87-82-62; internet www.vet-lyon.fr; f. 1762; library: 10,000 vols; 73 teachers; Dir S. MARTINOT; publ. *Revue de Médecine Vétérinaire* (12 a year).

Ecole Nationale Vétérinaire de Nantes: Atlanpole-La Chantrerie, BP 40706, 44307 Nantes Cedex 03; tel. 2-40-68-77-77; fax 2-40-68-77-78; e-mail direction@vet-nantes.fr; internet www.vet-nantes.fr; f. 1979; 73 teachers; 634 students; Dir (vacant).

Ecole Nationale Vétérinaire de Toulouse: 23 chemin des Capelles, BP 87614, 31076 Toulouse Cedex 3; tel. 5-61-19-38-00; fax 5-61-19-39-93; e-mail direction@envt.fr; internet www.envt.fr; f. 1828; library: 50,000 vols; 69 teachers; Dir Prof. P. BÉNARD; Sec.-Gen. J. G. McCOOK; Librarian Prof. J. EUZEBY; publ. *Revue de Médecine Vétérinaire* (12 a year).

Institut National d'Horticulture: 2 rue Le Notre, 49045 Angers Cedex 01; tel. 2-41-22-54-54; fax 2-41-73-15-57; e-mail inh@inh.fr; internet www.inh.fr; f. 1874; library: 19,000 vols; 50 teachers; 450 students; Dir F. COLSON.

Institut National Supérieur de Formation Agro-Alimentaire (INSFA): 65 rue de Saint-Brieuc, CS 84215, 35042 Rennes Cedex; tel. 2-23-48-50-00; fax 2-23-48-54-90; e-mail insfa@agrorennes.educagri.fr; internet www.agrorennes.educagri.fr; f. 1990; quality management, production management, marketing, research and devt; library: 10,000 vols; 90 teachers; 238 students; Dir P. THIVEND.

ARCHITECTURE

Ecole d'Architecture de Lille et des Régions Nord: 2 rue Verte, quartier de l'Hôtel de Ville, 59650 Villeneuve d'Ascq; tel. 3-20-61-95-50; fax 3-20-61-95-51; internet www.lille.archi.fr; f. 1755 as Ecole d'Architecture, reorganized 1968; library: 15,000 vols; 100 teachers; 750 students; Dir BERNARD WELCOMME.

Ecole Nationale Supérieure d'Architecture de Paris-La Villette: 144 ave de Flandre, 75019 Paris; tel. 1-44-65-23-00; fax 1-44-65-23-01; e-mail directeur@paris-lavillette.archi.fr; internet www.paris-lavillette.archi.fr; f. 1969, present name 1982; attached to Min. of Culture and Communications; 80 teachers; 2,300 students; library: 25,000 vols; Dir GERARD CATTALANO.

Ecole Spéciale d'Architecture: 254 blvd Raspail, 75014 Paris; tel. 1-40-47-40-47; fax 1-43-22-81-16; e-mail info@esa-paris.fr; internet www.esa-paris.fr; f. 1865; library: 7,000 vols; 60 teachers; 450 students; Dir OLIVIER LEBLOIS.

ECONOMICS, LAW AND POLITICS

Centre Français de Droit Comparé: 28 rue Saint-Guillaume, 75007 Paris; tel. 1-44-39-86-23; fax 1-44-39-86-28; e-mail cfdc@legiscompare.com; f. 1951; library: 100,000 vols; Pres. JACQUES ROBERT; Sec.-Gen. DIDIER LAMÈTHE; publ. *Revue Internationale de Droit Comparé* (4 a year).

Ecole Nationale de la Magistrature: 10 rue des Frères Bonie, 33080 Bordeaux Cedex; tel. 5-56-00-10-10; fax 5-56-00-10-99; e-mail initiale@enm_magistrature.fr; internet www.enm.justice.fr; f. 1958; 450 students; library: 50,000 vols; Dir DOMINIQUE MAIN; publs *Instruction actualité* (6 a year), *Mémento de l'Instruction* (2 a year), *Revue* (1 a year).

Ecole Nationale de la Statistique et de l'Administration Economique (ENSAE): 3 ave Pierre Larousse, 92245 Malakoff Cedex; tel. 1-41-17-65-25; fax 1-41-17-38-52; e-mail info@ensae.fr; internet www.ensae.fr; f. 1942; attached to the Institut National de la Statistique et des Etudes Economiques (see Research Institutes); economics, statistics, finance; 330 students; Chair. A. TROGNON.

Ecole Nationale de la Statistique et de l'Analyse de l'Information (ENSAI): Campus de Ker Lann, rue Blaise Pascal, 35170 Bruz; tel. 2-99-05-32-32; fax 2-99-05-32-05; e-mail accueil@ensai.fr; internet www.ensai.com; f. 1942; attached to the Institut National de la Statistique et des Etudes Economiques (see Research Institutes); statistics and information processing at Masters level; 20 teachers; 310 students; Dir P. JOLY.

Institut d'Etudes Politiques: Ave Ausone, Domaine Universitaire, 33607 Pessac; tel. 5-56-84-42-52; fax 5-56-37-45-37; f. 1948; affiliated with Univ. Bordeaux IV; politics and admin., economics, management; library: 80,000 vols; 200 teachers and researchers; 1,200 students; Dir ROBERT LAFORVE.

Institut d'Etudes Politiques de Paris: 27 rue Saint-Guillaume, 75007 Paris; tel. 1-45-49-50-50; fax 1-42-22-31-26; internet www.sciences-po.fr; f. 1945 as successor to l'Ecole Libre des Sciences Politiques; attached to Fondation Nationale des Sciences Politiques; library: 700,000 vols; 4,000 students; Dir R. DESCOINGS.

EDUCATION

Ecole Normale Supérieure: 45 rue d'Ulm, 75230 Paris Cedex 05; tel. 1-44-32-30-00; fax 1-44-32-20-99; e-mail communication@ens.fr; internet www.ens.fr; f. 1794 by the National Convention; library: see Libraries; 2,000 students; graduate and postgraduate studies in humanities, social sciences and science; Dir ETIENNE GUYON; Sec.-Gen. JEAN PASCAL BONHOTAL; Librarian PIERRE PETITMENGIN; publ. *Annales Scientifiques de l'Ecole Normale Supérieure.*

Ecole Normale Supérieure: 31 ave Lombart, 92260 Fontenay aux Roses; tel. 1-41-13-24-00; fax 1-41-13-24-09; f. 1880; library: 200,000 vols, 700 periodicals; 120 teachers; 450 students; Dir SYLVAIN AUROUX; Sec.-Gen. A. COURDAVAULT; Dir of Studies F. MAZIÈRE; publ. *Collections des Presses de l'ENS.*

Ecole Normale Supérieure de Cachan: 61 ave du Président Wilson, 94235 Cachan Cedex; tel. 1-47-40-20-00; fax 1-47-40-20-74; e-mail webmaster@ens-cachan.fr; internet www.ens-cachan.fr; f. 1912; library: 55,000 vols; 145 teachers; 1,150 students; Dir BERNARD DECOMPS.

GEOGRAPHY

Ecole Nationale des Sciences Géographiques: 6 et 8 ave Blaise Pascal, Cité Descartes, Champs-sur-Marne, 77455 Marne-la-Vallée Cedex 2; tel. 1-64-15-30-01; fax 1-64-15-31-07; e-mail info@ensg.ign.fr; internet www.ensg.ign.fr; f. 1941; administered by Institut Géographique National; library: specialized library of 36,000 books, 950,000 maps, 1.1m. aerial photographs; 30 teachers; 300 students, 2,000 trainees; Dir M. DENÈGRE.

HISTORY

Ecole Nationale des Chartes: 19 rue de la Sorbonne, 75005 Paris; tel. 1-55-42-75-00; fax 1-55-42-75-09; internet www.enc.sorbonne .fr; f. 1821, reorganized 1846; library: 150,000 vols; 170 students; Dir A. GUERREAU; Sec. J. BELMON; Chief Librarian I. DIU; publs *Bibliothèque de l'Ecole des Chartes, Etudes et Rencontres, Matériaux pour l'Histoire, Mémoires et Documents, Positions des thèses* (1 a year).

Institut National du Patrimoine: Galerie Colbert, 2 rue Vivienne, 75002 Paris; tel. 1-44-41-16-41; fax 1-44-41-16-76; e-mail webmaster@inp.fr; internet www.inp.fr; f. 1990; trains curators of museums, archives and historical monuments; Dir JEAN-PIERRE BADY.

LANGUAGE AND LITERATURE

Institut National des Langues et Civilisations Orientales (INALCO): 2 rue de Lille, 75343 Paris Cedex 07; tel. 1-49-26-42-00; fax 1-49-26-42-99; e-mail secretariat .general@inalco.fr; internet www.inalco.fr; f. 1669; 228 teachers; 10,500 students; Pres. JACQUES LEGRAND; Sec.-Gen. JOSETTE LE CALVEZ.

Research Centres:

Centre d'Etudes Balkaniques: INALCO, 73 rue Broca, 75013 Paris; tel. (1) 44-08-89-67; fax (1) 44-08-89-79; internet www.inalco.fr; Dir ODILE DANIEL.

Centre d'Etudes Chinoises: INALCO, 73 rue Broca, 75013 Paris; tel. (1) 44-08-89-72; fax (1) 44-08-89-79; internet www .inalco.fr; Dir ISABELLE RABOT.

Centre d'Etudes de l'Europe Médiane: INALCO, 104–106 quai de Clichy, 92110 Clichy-La Garenne; tel. 1-41-40-89-51; fax 1-41-40-89-21; Dir MARIA DE LA PERRIÈRE.

Centre d'Etudes Japonaises: INALCO, 73 rue Broca, 75013 Paris; tel. (1) 44-08-89-55; fax (1) 44-08-89-79; internet www .inalco.fr; Dir F. MACÉ.

Centre Georges Dumézil d'Etudes sur le Caucase: INALCO, 73 rue Broca, 75013 Paris Cedex 07; tel. (1) 44-08-89-57; fax (1) 44-08-89-79; internet www.inalco.fr; Dir ANAÏD DONABEDIAN.

Centre de Recherche Berbère: INALCO, 10 rue Riquet, 75019 Paris Cedex 07; tel. (1) 55-26-81-22; fax (1) 55-26-81-29; internet www.inalco.fr; Dir SALEM CHAKER.

Centre de Recherche sur l'Océan Indien Occidental: INALCO, 2 rue de Lille, 75343 Paris Cedex 07; tel. (1) 49-26-42-15; fax (1) 49-26-42-99; internet www .inalco.fr; Dir CLAUDE ALLIBERT.

Centre de Recherche sur l'Oralité: INALCO, 2 rue de Lille, 75343 Paris Cedex 07; tel. (1) 49-26-99-25; fax (1) 49-26-42-99; internet www.inalco.fr; Dir MICHÈLE THERRIEN.

Centre de Recherche Russe et Euro-Asiatique: INALCO, 104–106 quai de Clichy, 92110 Clichy-La Garenne; tel. 1-41-40-89-50; fax 1-41-40-89-21; Dir J. RADVANYI.

Cercle de Linguistique de L'INALCO: INALCO, 2 rue de Lille, 75343 Paris Cedex 07; tel. 1-49-26-42-31; fax 1-49-26-42-99; internet www.inalco.fr; Dir ANAÏD DONABEDIAN.

LIBRARIANSHIP

Ecole Nationale Supérieure des Sciences de l'Information et des Bibliothèques (ENSSIB): 17/21 blvd du 11 Novembre 1918, 69623 Villeurbanne Cedex; tel. 4-72-44-43-43; fax 4-72-44-43-44; e-mail enssib@ enssib.fr; internet www.enssib.fr; f. 1963; 26 teachers; 300 students; library: 17,000 vols and 585 periodicals, also audio-visual items; Dir FRANÇOIS DUPUIGRENET DESROUSSILLES; publ. *Bulletin des Bibliothèques de France* (6 a year).

MEDICINE

Ecole d'Application du Service de Santé des Armées: 1 place Alphonse Laveran, 75230 Paris Cedex 05; tel. 1-40-51-47-33; fax 1-40-51-47-74; f. 1850; mainly two-year graduate courses; library: 40,000 vols and 2,067 periodicals; Dir MGI DE SAINT-JULIEN; publ. *Médecine et Armées*.

Ecole des Hautes Études en Santé Publique (EHESP): Ave du Professeur Léon Bernard, 35043 Rennes Cedex; tel. 2-99-02-22-00; fax 2-99-02-26-25; internet www.ehesp .fr; f. 1945; post-university courses; 60 full-time teachers; 500 full-time students; 4,000 part-time students; library: 15,000 vols; Dir PASCAL CHEVIT.

SCIENCES

Ecole Nationale de la Météorologie: 42 ave G. Coriolis, 31057 Toulouse Cedex 1; tel. 5-61-07-80-80; fax 5-61-07-96-30; e-mail enm .fr@meteo.fr; internet www.enm.meteo.fr; f. 1948; library: 4,000 vols; 35 teachers; 230 students; Dir JEAN-PIERRE CHALON.

Institut National des Sciences Appliquées de Rennes (INSA Rennes): 20 ave des Buttes de Coësmes, 35043 Rennes Cedex; tel. 2-23-23-82-00; fax 2-23-23-83-96; internet www.insa-rennes.fr; f. 1961; physical and materials science, electronic engineering, civil engineering and town planning, computer science, communications systems, mechanical engineering and control; 130 teachers; 1,200 students; Dir DÉSIRÉ AMOROS.

Institut National des Sciences Appliquées de Rouen (INSA Rouen): Place Émile Blondel, BP 08, 76131 Mont-Saint-Aignan Cedex; tel. 2-35-52-83-00; fax 2-35-52-83-69; e-mail insa@insa-rouen.fr; internet www.insa-rouen.fr; f. 1985; chemistry, mathematics, energy, mechanical engineering, technology and applied sciences; 109 teachers; 985 students; library: 15,000 vols, 200 periodicals; Dir Prof. GILBERT TOUZOT.

Muséum National d'Histoire Naturelle: Jardin des Plantes, 57 rue Cuvier, 75005 Paris Cedex 05; tel. 1-40-79-56-01; fax 1-40-79-54-48; e-mail webaccueil@mnhn.fr; internet www.mnhn.fr; f. 1635; teaching and research in natural history; administers the Zoological Garden, the Musée de l'Homme and several other natural history depts and institutions; Dir Prof. BERTRAND-PIERRE GALEY; Librarian MONIQUE DUCREUX.

TECHNOLOGY

Conservatoire National des Arts et Métiers: 292 rue St Martin, 75141 Paris Cedex 03; tel. 1-40-27-20-00; internet www.cnam.fr;

f. 1794; 55 regional centres, diploma and doctorate courses; library: see Libraries and Archives; 470 teachers; 75,000 students (full-and part-time); Administrator LAURENCE PAYE-JEANNENEY.

Ecole Centrale de Lille: Cité Scientifique, BP 48, 59651 Villeneuve d'Ascq Cedex; tel. 3-20-33-53-53; fax 3-20-33-54-99; e-mail renseignements@ec-lille.fr; internet www .ec-lille.fr; f. 1872; 7 research laboratories; library: 10,000 vols; 82 teachers; 1,040 students; Dir Prof. JEAN-CLAUDE GENTINA.

Ecole Centrale des Arts et Manufactures: Grande Voie des Vignes, 92295 Châtenay-Malabry Cedex; tel. 1-41-13-10-00; fax 1-41-13-10-10; e-mail webmaster@ads.ecp.fr; internet www.ecp.fr; f. 1829; higher degrees in multiple disciplines of engineering; library: 60,000 vols and 340 periodicals; 1,400 students; Dir HERVÉ BIAUSSER; publ. *Centraliens* (12 a year).

Ecole des Mines de Douai: 941 rue Charles Bourseul, BP 838, 59508 Douai Cedex; tel. 3-27-71-22-22; fax 3-27-71-25-25; f. 1878; library: 15,000 vols; 250 teachers; 650 students; Dir PIERRE FRANCK CHEVET.

Ecole Nationale de l'Aviation Civile: 7 ave Edouard-Belin, BP 54005, 31055 Toulouse Cedex 4; tel. 5-62-17-40-00; fax 5-62-17-40-23; internet www.enac.fr; f. 1948; training of civil aviation personnel; advanced studies in engineering; library: 30,000 vols; 408 teachers and researchers; Dir M. SOUCHELEAU.

Ecole Nationale d'Ingénieurs de Metz (ENIM): Ile du Saulcy, 57045 Metz Cedex 1; tel. 3-87-34-69-03; fax 3-87-34-69-35; e-mail padilla@enim.fr; f. 1962; 1,000 students; Dir PIERRE PADILLA.

Ecole Nationale d'Ingénieurs de Tarbes (ENIT): 47 ave d'Azereix, BP 1629, 65016 Tarbes Cedex; tel. 5-62-44-27-00; fax 5-62-44-27-27; e-mail mugniery@enit.fr; internet www.enit.fr; f. 1963; mechanical, industrial and production engineering; 60 teachers; 850 students; library: 4,000 vols; Dir BERNARD MUGNIERY.

Ecole Nationale de la Photographie: 16 rue des Arènes, BP 149, 13631 Arles Cedex; tel. 4-90-99-33-33; fax 4-90-99-33-59; e-mail communication@enp-arles.com; internet www.enp-arles.com; f. 1982; under auspices of Ministry of Culture and Communications; 3-year course; 7 teachers; 75 students; library: 10,000 vols; Dir ALAIN LELOUP.

Ecole Nationale des Ponts et Chaussées: 6–8 ave Blaise Pascal, Cité Descartes, Champs-sur-Marne, 77455 Marne-la-Vallée Cedex 2; tel. 1-64-15-30-30; internet www .enpc.fr; f. 1747; civil and mechanical engineering, town and country planning, transport; library: 85,000 vols, 2,500 periodicals, 37,000 18th century MSS, 900 maps, 30,000 photographs; 300 teachers; 1,300 students; Dir PHILIPPE CORTIER; Dep. Dir ALAIN NEVEU.

Ecole Nationale des Travaux Publics de l'Etat: Rue Maurice Audin, 69518 Vaulx en Velin Cedex; tel. 4-72-04-70-70; fax 4-72-04-62-54; e-mail webmaster@entpe.fr; internet www.entpe.fr; f. 1953 in Paris, moved 1975; 700 teachers (100 full-time, 600 part-time); 600 students; library: 14,000 vols; Dir PHILIPPE DHÉNEIN.

Ecole Nationale du Génie de l'Eau et de l'Environnement de Strasbourg: 1 quai Koch, BP 1039F, 67070 Strasbourg Cedex; tel. 3-88-24-82-82; fax 3-88-37-04-97; e-mail engees@engees.u-strasbg.fr; internet www-engees.u-strasbg.fr; f. 1960; 164 teachers (14 full-time, 150 part-time); 242 students; Dir D. LOUDIÈRE.

Ecole Nationale Supérieure d'Electronique, Informatique et Radiocommunica-

tions de Bordeaux (ENSEIRB): 1 ave du Dr Albert Schweitzer, BP 99, 33402 Talence Cedex; tel. 5-56-84-65-00; fax 5-56-37-20-23; e-mail com@enseirb.fr; internet www.enseirb .fr; f. 1920; affiliated with Univ. Bordeaux I; 62 teachers; 716 students; Dir RICHARD CASTANET.

Ecole Nationale Supérieure de Chimie et de Physique de Bordeaux (ENSCPB): 16 Ave Pey Berland, 33607 Pessac Cedex; tel. 5-40-00-65-65; fax 5-40-00-66-33; e-mail admin@enscpb.fr; internet www.enscpb.fr; f. 1891; affiliated with Université de Bordeaux I; 400 students; Dir BERNARD CLIN.

Ecole Nationale Supérieure des Arts et Industries Textiles (ENSAIT): 9 rue de l'Ermitage, BP 30329, 59056 Roubaix Cedex 01; tel. 3-20-25-64-64; fax 3-20-24-84-06; e-mail jean-marie.castelain@ensait.fr; internet www.ensait.fr; f. 1883; library: 4,000 vols, 70 periodicals; 50 teachers; 210 students; Dir JEAN-MARIE CASTELAIN.

Ecole Nationale Supérieure d'Arts et Métiers: 8 blvd Louis XIV, 59046 Lille Cedex; tel. 3-20-62-22-10; fax 3-20-53-55-93; internet www.lille.ensam.fr; university-level courses with emphasis on mechanical engineering; f. 1881; 340 students; Dir Prof. J.-P. FRACHET; Librarian MICHÈLE DECORTE.

Ecole Nationale Supérieure d'Arts et Métiers (ENSAM): 151 blvd de l'Hôpital, 75013 Paris; tel. 1-44-24-62-99; fax 1-44-24-63-26; internet www.paris.ensam.fr; f. 1780; mechanical, computer, engineering and industrial sciences; 3,500 students; library: 20,000 vols; Dir-Gen. GUY GAUTHERIN; Librarian C. OLLENDORF.

Ecole Nationale Supérieure d'Ingénieurs de Constructions Aéronautiques: 1 place Emile Blouin, 31056 Toulouse Cedex 5; tel. 5-61-61-85-00; fax 5-61-61-85-85; e-mail mcastel@ensica.fr; f. 1946; aeronautics and space; library: 10,000 vols; 410 students; Dir JEAN-LOUIS FRESON.

Ecole Nationale Supérieure de Céramique Industrielle: 47–73 ave Albert Thomas, 87065 Limoges Cedex; tel. 5-55-45-22-22; fax 5-55-79-09-98; e-mail direction@ensci.fr; internet www.ensci.fr; f. 1893; library: 4,000 vols; 25 teachers; 150 students; Dir CHRISTIAN GAULT; publ. Annuaire.

Ecole Nationale Supérieure de l'Electronique et de ses Applications (ENSEA): 6 ave du Ponceau, 95014 Cergy Pontoise Cedex; tel. 1-30-73-66-66; fax 1-30-73-66-67; e-mail directeur@ensea.fr; internet www .ensea.fr; f. 1952; postgraduate courses in electrical engineering, computing and telecommunications; library: 6,000 vols, 150 periodicals; 80 teachers and researchers; 650 students; Dir PIERRE POUVIL.

Ecole Nationale Supérieure de Mécanique: see under University of Nantes.

Établissement Public Local d'Enseignement et de Formation Professionnelle Agricoles (EPLEFPA): ave François Mitterrand, BP 49, 17700 Surgères; tel. 5-46-27-69-00; fax 5-46-07-31-49; e-mail enil .surgeres@educagri.fr; internet www .enilia-ensmic.educagri.fr; f. 1924; courses in milling, baking, cereal food industry and feed technology; affiliated with UPMC-Univ. Paris VI (training of engineers); 260 students; Dir CHRISTIANE MAZEL; publs Industries des Céréales (6 a year), Les Journées de l'ENSMIC (1 a year).

Ecole Nationale Supérieure des Mines de Paris: 60 blvd St Michel, 75272 Paris Cedex 06; tel. 1-40-51-90-00; fax 1-43-25-94-95; e-mail webmaster@paris.ensmp.fr; internet www.ensmp.fr; f. 1783; library: 500,000 vols and 2,500 periodicals; 290 teachers; 1,100 students; Pres. D. RANQUE;

Dir B. LEGAIT; Sec.-Gen. PHILIPPE TOGNAZZONI; Librarian MASSON.

Ecole Nationale Supérieure des Mines de Saint-Etienne: 158 cours Fauriel, 42023 Saint-Etienne Cedex 2; tel. 4-77-42-01-23; fax 4-77-42-00-00; e-mail tor@emse.fr; internet www.emse.fr; f. 1816; chemical process engineering, computer science, materials science, international project management, environmental science; library: 10,000 vols; 250 teachers and researchers; 600 students; Dir M. HIRTZMAN.

Ecole Nationale Supérieure du Pétrole et des Moteurs: 228–232 ave Napoléon Bonaparte, 92852 Rueil-Malmaison Cedex; tel. 1-47-52-64-57; fax 1-47-52-67-65; e-mail info-ifpschool@ifp.fr; internet www.ifp-school .com; f. 1954; 400 students; five centres: geological or geophysical exploration; petroleum engineering and project management; refining, petrochemicals, gas; internal combustion engines; economics and management; Dir J. L. KARNIK.

Ecole Nationale Supérieure de Techniques Avancées: 32 blvd Victor, 75015 Paris; tel. 1-45-52-44-08; fax 1-45-52-55-87; e-mail hoffmann@ensta.fr; internet www .ensta.fr; f. 1741, refounded 1970; systems engineering, naval architecture, oceanology, mechanics, nuclear techniques, chemical engineering, electronics, information technology; 3-year curriculum; 78 permanent teachers, 800 visiting; 170 students a year; undergraduate and postgraduate studies; library: 10,000 vols; Dir H. PASTEAU.

Ecole Polytechnique: 91128 Palaiseau Cedex; tel. 1-69-33-33-33; internet www .polytechnique.fr; f. 1794; 362 teachers; 859 students; library: 300,000 vols; Dir-Gen. JEAN NOVACQ; Librarian MADELEINE DE FUENTES.

Ecole Supérieure de Physique et de Chimie Industrielles de la Ville de Paris: 10 rue Vauquelin, 75005 Paris; tel. 1-40-79-44-00; fax 1-40-79-44-25; internet www.espci .fr; f. 1882; training of research engineers; 20 research laboratories; library: 5,000 vols; 65 teachers; 300 students; Dir JACQUES PROST.

Institut des Hautes Études Scientifiques: 35 route de Chartres, 91440 Bures-sur-Yvette; tel. 1-60-92-66-00; fax 1-60-92-66-69; internet www.ihes.fr; f. 1958; advanced research in mathematics, theoretical physics; library: 4,000 vols, 125 periodicals; Dir J.-P. BOURGUIGNON; publ. Publications Mathématiques (2 a year).

Institut Nationaldes Sciences Appliquées (INSA Strasbourg): 24 blvd de la Victoire, 67084 Strasbourg Cedex; tel. 3-88-14-47-00; fax 3-88-24-14-90; internet www .insa-strasbourg.fr; f. 1875; 5-year diploma courses in mechanical, electrical, civil, building services and energetics, land surveying, polymer and composite materials, mechatronics and architecture; 948 students; Dir MARIE-CHRISTINE CRETON.

Institut Supérieur de l'Aéronautique et de l'Espace (ISAE): 10 ave Edouard Belin, BP 54032, 31055 Toulouse Cedex 4; tel. 5-61-33-80-80; fax 5-61-33-83-30; e-mail communication@isae.fr; internet www.isae .fr; f. 1909; 700 students; library: 15,000 vols; Dir J. KERBRAT.

TELECOM & Management SudParis – Institut National des Télécommunications: 9 rue Charles Fourier, 91011 Evry Cedex; tel. 1-60-76-40-40; fax 1-60-76-43-25; e-mail webmaster@it-sudparis .eu; internet www.it-sudparis.eu; f. 1979; attached to Min. of Finance, Industry and the Economy; mem. of Conférence des Grandes Ecoles; engineering and business

schools; 150 full-time teachers; 1,000 students; Dir MICHEL LARTAIL.

Supméca Paris—Institut Supérieur de Mécanique de Paris: 3 rue Fernand Hainaut, 93407 St Ouen Cedex; tel. 1-49-45-29-00; fax 1-49-45-29-91; e-mail informations@ supmeca.fr; internet www.supmeca.fr; f. 1948; 400 students; library: 3,000 vols; Dir JEAN-JACQUES MAILLARD; publ. La Lettre de l'ISMCM-CESTI (2 a year).

Supméca Toulon: Maison des Technologies, Place Georges Pompidou, 83000 Toulon; tel. 4-94-03-88-00; fax 4-94-03-88-04; e-mail informations@toulon.supmeca.fr; internet www.supmeca.fr; f. 1994; training of engineers, applied research in automation and industrial engineering; 30 teachers; 150 students; Dir PASCALE AZOU-BRIARD.

Télécom Bretagne – Ecole Nationale Supérieure des Télécommunications de Bretagne: Technopôle Brest-Iroise, 29238 Brest Cedex 3; tel. 2-29-00-11-11; fax 2-29-00-10-00; internet www.enst-bretagne.fr; f. 1977; attached to Min. of Technology, Information and Posts; 108 full-time teachers; 764 students (207 postgraduate); Dir ANDRÉ CHOMETTE.

TELECOM & Management SudParis – Institut National des Télécommunications: 9 rue Charles Fourier, 91011 Evry Cedex; tel. 1-60-76-40-40; fax 1-60-76-43-25; e-mail webmaster@it-sudparis .eu; internet www.it-sudparis.eu; f. 1979; attached to Min. of Finance, Industry and the Economy; mem. of Conférence des Grandes Ecoles; engineering and business schools; 150 full-time teachers; 1,000 students; Dir MICHEL LARTAIL.

TELECOM ParisTech – Ecole Nationale Supérieure des Télécommunications: 46 rue Barrault, 75634 Paris Cedex 13; tel. 1-45-81-77-77; fax 1-45-89-79-06; internet www .telecom-paristech.fr; f. 1878; attached to France Telecom; Dir JEAN HERR.

Catholic Colleges and Institutes

INSTITUT CATHOLIQUE DE PARIS

21 rue d'Assas, 75270 Paris Cedex 06

Telephone: 1-44-39-52-00

Fax: 1-45-44-27-14

E-mail: contact@icp.fr

Internet: www.icp.fr

Founded 1875

Academic year: October to June

Chancellor: Mgr ANDRÉ VINGT-TROIS

Rector: JOSEPH MAÏLA

Vice-Rector: Sr GENEVIÈVE MEDEVIELLE

Gen. Sec.: FRANÇOIS ARDONCEAU

Dir of Communication: FRANÇOISE GARDERE-CREAC'H

Librarian: ODILE DUPONT

Library: see Libraries

Number of teaching staff: 847, including 96 professors

Number of students: 15,000 (excluding affiliated schools)

Publications: Guide des Études (1 a year), Transversalités: Revue de l'Institut Catholique de Paris (4 a year)

DEANS AND DIRECTORS

Faculty of Canon Law: Père JEAN-PAUL DURAND

Faculty of Letters: NATHALIE NABERT

Faculty of Philosophy: Abbé P. CAPELLE

Faculty of Theology: Abbé HENRI-JÉRÔME GAGEY

Higher Institute of Ecumenical Studies: Abbé YVES-MARIE BLANCHARD

Higher Institute of Liturgy: Frère PATRICK PRÉTOT

Higher Institute of Pastoral Catechetics and University Extension: DENIS VILLEPELET

Higher Institute of Pedagogy: FRANÇOISE CHEBAUX

Institute for French Language and Culture and University Summer School: MURIEL CORDIER

Institute of Music and Liturgical Music: E. BELLANGER

Institute of Sacred Art: GENEVIÈVE HEBERT

Institute of Science and Theology of Religions: R. P. PAUL COULON

Institute of Social Sciences and Economics: JOSEPH MAÏLA

Biblical and Systematic Theology: Abbé JESUS ASURMENDI

Doctoral Studies: P. HERVÉ LEGRAND

School of Ancient Oriental Languages: FLORENCE MALBRAN-LABAT

University for Retired People: Dir: J. MENU

AFFILIATED SCHOOLS AND INSTITUTES

Centre de Formation Pédagogique Emmanuel Mounier: 78A rue de Sèvres, 75341 Paris Cedex 07; Dir R. MOREAU.

Ecole de Bibliothécaires-Documentalistes: Paris; Dir D. VIGNAUD.

Ecole de Formation Psycho-Pédagogique: Paris; Dir M. C. DAVID.

Ecole de Psychologues-Praticiens: Paris; Dir J. P. CHARTIER.

Ecole Supérieure de Chimie Organique et Minérale: 95000 Cergy; Dir G. SANTINI.

Ecole Supérieure des Sciences Economiques et Commerciales: 95000 Cergy; Dir P. TAPIE.

Institut Géologique Albert-de-Lapparent: 95000 Cergy; Dir C. CHOMAT.

Institut Libre d'Education Physique Supérieure: 95000 Cergy; Dir F. HELAINE.

Institut Polytechnique Saint-Louis: 95000 Cergy.

Constituent Schools:

Ecole de Biologie Industrielle: 95000 Cergy; Dir F. DUFOUR.

Ecole d'Electricité, de Production et des Méthodes Industrielles: 95000 Cergy; Dir M. DARCHERIF.

Institut d'Agro-Développement International: 95000 Cergy; Dir S. LAMY.

Institut Supérieur Agricole de Beauvais: Rue Pierre Waguet, 60000 Beauvais and 95000 Cergy; f. 1855; Dir M. P. CHOQUET.

Institut Supérieur d'Electronique de Paris: Dir M. CIAZYNSKI.

Institut Supérieur d'Interprétation et de Traduction: Paris; Dir M. MERIAUD.

INSTITUT CATHOLIQUE DE TOULOUSE

31 rue de la Fonderie, BP 7012, 31068 Toulouse Cedex 7

Telephone: 5-61-36-81-00

Fax: 5-61-36-81-08

E-mail: documentation@ict-toulouse.asso.fr

Internet: www.ict-toulouse.asso.fr

Founded 1877 and administered by a Ccl of Bishops of the region

Academic year: October to June

Chancellor: HE Mgr ROBERT LE GALL (Archbishop of Toulouse)

Rector: Père PIERRE DEBERGÉ

Registrar: MONIQUE DELCROIX

Librarian: MAGALI HURTREL-PIZARRO (acting)

Library of 250,000

Number of teachers: 238

Number of students: 6,334

Publications: *Bulletin de Littérature ecclésiastique* (4 a year), *Revue Purpan* (4 a year)

DEANS

Faculty of Canon Law: B. DU PUY-MONTBRUN

Faculty of Law: A. MASSART

Faculty of Letters: B. BILLEREY

Faculty of Philosophy: B. HUBERT

Faculty of Theology: P. MOLAC

INSTITUT DE SCIENCES ET THÉOLOGIE DES RELIGIONS

11 Impasse Flammarion, 13001 Marseilles

Telephone: 4-91-50-35-50

Fax: 4-91-50-35-55

E-mail: istr@cathomed.cef.fr

Internet: cathomed.cef.fr

Founded 1991 by the Diocese of Marseilles

Rector: CHRISTIAN SALENSON

Library of 500 vols

Number of teachers: 30

Number of students: 250

Publication: *Chemins de Dialogue* (every 2 years).

UNIVERSITÉ CATHOLIQUE DE LILLE

60 blvd Vauban, BP 109, 59016 Lille Cedex

Telephone: 3-20-13-40-00

Fax: 3-20-13-40-01

E-mail: saio@icl-lille.fr

Internet: www.univ-catholille.fr

Founded 1875 as Faculty of Law, became univ. instn in 1877

Private (Roman Catholic) control

Rector: ME TH. LEBRUN

Vice-Rectors: PÈRE B. CAZIN, O. TRANCHANT, J. C. CAILLIEZ

Admin. Officer: B. MAELFAIT

Librarian: D. PENEZ

Library: nearly 500,000 vols

Number of teachers: 3,284

Number of students: 20,186

Publications: *Catho Actualités, Encyclopédie Catholicisme, La Lettre de la Catho, Mélanges de Science Religieuse* (3 a year), *Mémoires et Travaux, Repères, Vie et Foi, Vues d'ensemble*

DEANS

Faculty of Economic Sciences: D. VANPETEGHEM

Faculty of Law: A. MASSART

Faculty of Letters and Human Sciences: J. HEUCLIN

Faculty of Medicine: G. FORZY

Faculty of Science: J. C. CAILLIEZ

Faculty of Theology: J. Y. BAZIOU

FEDERATED INSTITUTES

Centre de Recherches Economiques, Sociologiques et de Gestion (CRESGE): Rue du Port, 59000 Lille; tel. 3-20-54-58-92; f. 1964; Dir L. AUBREE.

Ecole de Hautes Etudes Commerciales du Nord (EDHEC): 58 rue du Port, 59046 Lille Cedex; tel. 3-20-15-45-00; f. 1920; 1,886 students; Dirs-Gén. O. OGER, J.-L. TURRIÈRE.

Branch:

EDHEC Nice: 393 Promenade des Anglais, BP 116, 06202 Nice Cedex; tel. 4-93-18-99-66; 736 students; EDHEC Paris; 131 students.

Ecole des Hautes Etudes Industrielles (HEI): 13 rue de Toul, 59046 Lille Cedex; tel. 3-28-38-48-58; f. 1885; civil engineering, chemistry and electrical engineering; 1,676 students; Dir J. M. IDOUX.

Ecole de Sages-Femmes (ESF): Campus Saint Raphaël, 59000 Lille; tel. 3-20-13-47-36; f. 1882; 109 students; Dir CHRISTIANE ROUX.

Ecole Supérieure de Traducteurs, Interprètes, et de Cadres du Commerce Extérieur (ESTICE): 83 blvd Vauban, BP 109, 59016 Lille Cedex; tel. 3-20-54-90-90; f. 1961; 113 students; Dir O. TRANCHANT.

Ecole Supérieure de Management et l'Entreprise (ESPEME): 23 rue Delphin Petit, 59046 Lille Cedex; tel. 3-20-15-45-00; f. 1988; 912 students; Dir A. F. MALVACHE.

Branch:

ESPEME Nice: 393 Promenade des Anglais, BP 116, 06202 Nice Cedex; tel. 4-93-18-99-66; 912 students; Dir BERNARD BOTTERO.

Ecole Supérieure Privée d'Application des Sciences (ESPAS): 83 blvd Vauban, 59800 Lille; tel. 3-20-57-58-71; f. 1988; 88 students; Dir O. TRANCHANT.

IFsanté (Ecole d'aides soignants IFAS + école de puéricultrices ECPUER + école de formation aux soins infirmiers IFSI): Campus Saint Raphaël, 59000 Lille; tel. 3-28-36-10-10; f. 1927; 499 students; Dir BERNADETTE MIROUX.

Institut Catholique d'Arts et Métiers (ICAM): 6 rue Auber, 59046 Lille Cedex; tel. 3-20-22-61-61; f. 1898; 850 students; Dir-Gen. G. CARPIER; Dir PH. CARPENTIER.

Institut de Communication Médicale: 83 blvd Vauban, 59000 Lille Cedex; tel. 3-20-57-58-71; f. 1988; 20 students; Dir MARC DENEUCHE.

Institut d'Economie Scientifique et de Gestion (IESEG): 3 rue de la Digue, 59800 Lille; tel. 3-20-54-58-92; f. 1964; 1,702 students; Dir J. P. AMMEUX.

Institut de Formation d'Animateurs de Catéchèse pour Adultes (IFAC): 60 blvd Vauban, 59016 Lille Cedex; tel. 3-20-57-69-33; f. 1980; 113 students; Dir J.M. BEAURENT.

Institut de Formation en Kinésithérapie, Pédicurie et Podologie: 10 rue J. B. de la Salle, 59000 Lille; tel. 3-20-92-06-99; f. 1964; 798 students; Dirs M. PAPAREMBORDE, D. VENNIN.

Institut de Formation Pedagogique (IFP): 236 rue du Fg de Roubaix, 59041 Lille Cedex; tel. 3-20-13-41-20; f. 1962; 584 students; Dir E. THEVENIN.

Institut des Stratégies et Techniques de Communication (ISTC): 83 blvd Vauban, 59800 Lille; tel. 3-20-54-32-32; f. 1991; 262 students; Dir CLAUDE DOGNIN.

Institut Social Lille (ISL): 83 blvd Vauban, BP 12, 59004 Lille Cedex; tel. 3-20-21-93-93; f. 1932; 527 students; Dir E. PRIEUR.

Institut Supérieur d'Agriculture (ISA): Blvd Vauban, , 59046 Lille Cedex; tel. 3-28-38-48-48; f. 1963; agricultural, agro-engineering; five-year course; 952 students; Dir P. CODRON.

Institut Supérieur d'Electronique du Nord (ISEN): 41 blvd Vauban, 59046 Lille Cedex; tel. 3-20-30-40-50; f. 1956; electronics engineering; 107 teachers; 614 students; Dir-Gen. PAUL ASTIER; Dir P. GIORGINI.

Institution Saint Jude: 18/22 rue Larmartine, 59820 Cambria; tel. 3-20-77-10-49; 82 students; Dir N. CARLIER.

Lycée privé commercial 'De la Salle': 2 rue Jean Le Vasseur, 59046 Lille Cedex; tel. 3-20-93-50-11; 267 students; Dir GUY MICHEL MAHIEU.

Lycée privé La Sagesse: 7 rue du temple, 59400 Cambria; tel. 3-27-82-28-28; 188 students; Dir B. DUMORTIER.

Lycée privé Notre-Dame de Grâce: Quai des Nerviens, BP 127, 59602 Maubeuge Cedex; tel. 3-27-53-00-66; 82 students; Dir JEAN-PIERRE LAMQUET.

Lycée privé Saint-Joseph: 26 route de Calais, 62200 Saint-Martin-lez-Boulogne; tel. 3-21-99-06-99; 274 students; Dir MICHEL DUFAY.

Lycée privé Saint Paul: 25bis rue Colbert, 59000 Lille Cedex; tel. 3-20-55-10-20; 168 students; Dir JEAN-CLAUDE PONTHIER.

Lycée Technologique OZANAM: 50 rue Saint Gabriel, 59000 Lille; tel. 3-20-21-96-50; 384 students; Dir R. PRIESTER.

UNIVERSITÉ CATHOLIQUE DE L'OUEST

3 place André Leroy, BP 808, 49008 Angers Cedex 01

Telephone: 2-41-81-67-55
Fax: 2-41-81-66-45
E-mail: relint@uco.fr
Internet: www.uco.fr

Founded 1875, under the patronage of the Bishops of the western region of France
Academic year: September to June

Rector: Dr ROBERT ROUDDEAU
Vice-Rectors: LUC PASQUIER PATRICK GILLET
Sec.-Gen.: BERNARD FLOURIOT
Librarian: Y. LE GALL
Library of 200,000 vols and periodicals
Number of students: 12,500

Publications: *Annuaire, Impacts* (4 a year)

DEANS

Applied Ecology Institute: P. GILLET
Applied Mathematics Institute: J. M. MARION
Basic and Applied Research Institute: J. P. BOUTINET
Education and Communication Institute: CATHERINE NAFTI-MALHERBE
Faculty of Theology: LOUIS MICHEL RENIER
Institute of Applied Psychology and Sociology: PATRICK MARTIN
International Centre for French Studies (for Foreign Students): MARC RELIN
Literature and History Institute: B. HAM
Modern Languages Institute: D. STAQUET
Teacher Training Institute: R. MARTIN

AFFILIATED SCHOOLS

Ecole Supérieure d'Electronique de l'Ouest: 4 rue Merlet de la Boulaye, 49000 Angers; f. 1956; Dir M. V. HAMON.

Ecole Supérieure des Sciences Commerciales d'Angers: 1 rue Lakanal, 49000 Angers; Dir M. POTE.

Ecole Technique Supérieure de Chimie de l'Ouest: 50 rue Michelet, 49000 Angers; Dir B. DAVID.

Institut de Formation et de Recherche pour les Acteurs du Développement et de l'Entreprise: 1 place A. Leroy, 49008 Angers Cedex 01; Dir FASICURE LEBLOND.

Institut Supérieur d'Action Internationale et de Production: 18 rue du 8 Mai 1945, 49124 St Barthélemy; Dir J. Y. BIGNONET.

Institut Supérieur des Métiers: 91 rue Haute Follio, 53000 Laval; Dir EMMANUEL ROUSSEAU.

Maison de L'Initiative: Campus de la Tour, d'Auvergne, 37 rue du Maréchal Foch, 22204 Guingamp Cedex; Dir C. NAFTI-MALHERBE.

Université Catholique de l'Ouest Bretagne Nord: Campus de la Tour, d'Auvergne, 37 rue du Maréchal Foch, 22204 Guingamp Cedex; Dir MICHEL DORVEAUX.

Université Catholique de l'Ouest Bretagne Sud: Le Vincin, BP 17, 56610 Arradon; Dir SYLVIE MURZEAU.

UNIVERSITÉ CATHOLIQUE DE LYON

25 rue du Plat, 69288 Lyons Cedex 02

Telephone: 4-72-32-50-12
Fax: 4-72-32-50-19
Internet: www.univ-catholyon.fr

Founded 1875

Rector: MICHEL QUESNEL
Vice-Rector: DENISE LE LOUP
Sec.-Gen.: PATRICK BORDET
Librarian: Mlle BEHR
Library of 240,000 vols
Number of teachers: 300
Number of students: 7,422

Publications: *Bulletin, Cahiers*

DEANS

Faculty of Law: PASCALE BOUCAUD
Faculty of Letters: HENRI BRENDERS
Faculty of Philosophy: PIERRE GIRE
Faculty of Science: J. M. EXBRAYAT
Faculty of Theology: JEAN-PIERRE LEMONON

Independent Institutes

GENERAL

American University of Paris: 31 ave Bosquet, 75007 Paris; tel. 1-40-62-06-00; fax 1-47-05-34-32; e-mail admissions@aup.edu; internet www.aup.edu; f. 1962; language of instruction: English; mem. of Middle States Asscn of Colleges and Schools; 4-year arts and sciences undergraduate courses; two summer sessions; adult education programmes; large computer science laboratory; technical writing programme; library: over 100,000 vols; 100 teachers; 800 students; Pres. Dr MICHAEL K. SIMPSON.

Groupe IPAC:; e-mail info@ipac-france .com; internet www.ipac-france.com; private control; accredited by the state for studies up to Masters level; courses in management, consulting, design, health, social and environmental studies, business; attached institute IFALPES offers French as a foreign language for adults; Pres. JEAN-MICHEL DELAPLAGNE.

Campuses:

IPAC Albertville: 542 rue Louis Armand Za du Chiriac, 73200 Albertville; tel. 4-79-37-14-01; fax 4-79-37-17-29; Dir JÉRÔME BAPTENDIER.

IPAC Annecy: 42 chemin de la Prairie, 74000 Annecy; tel. 4-50-45-13-91; fax 4-50-45-84-81; Dir PAUL TARDIVEL.

IPAC Chambéry: L'Axiome, 44 rue Charles Montreuil, 73000 Chambéry; tel. 4-79-69-65-91; fax 4-79-62-94-79; Dir ISABELLE DELIÈGE.

IPAC Geneva: 58 Rue du Grand pré, 1201 Geneva, Switzerland; tel. 22-340-42-00; fax 22-344-62-36.

IPAC Genvois–Léman: 15 rue Montréal, 74100 Ville la Grand; tel. 4-50-37-14-32; fax 4-50-87-22-93; Dir GÉRARD PONT.

IPAC Thonon: 5F ave du Général de Gaulle, Centre commercial de l'Etoile, 74200 Thonon les Bains; tel. 4-50-70-72-43; fax 4-50-70-68-78.

IPAC Vallée de l'Arve: Espace Scionzier, Bâtiment 3, 560 ave des Lacs, 74950 Scionzier; tel. 4-50-96-13-00; fax 4-50-96-14-50; Dir RÉGIS DUVAL.

Schiller International University— France: (For general information, see entry for Schiller International University in Germany chapter).

Campuses:

Schiller International University— Paris Campus: 32 blvd de Vaugirard, 75015 Paris; tel. 1-45-38-56-01; fax 1-45-38-54-30; e-mail info-schiller@schillerparis .com; internet www.paris-schiller.com; Dir SOUHA AKIKI.

Schiller International University— Strasbourg Campus: Château du Pourtalès, 161 rue Mélanie, 67000 Strasbourg; tel. 3-88-45-84-64; fax 3-88-45-84-60; e-mail blasiush@aol.com; internet www .schillerstrasbourg.com.

AGRICULTURE

Ecole Supérieure d'Agriculture de Purpan: 75 voie du Toec, 31076 Toulouse Cedex 3; tel. 5-61-15-30-30; fax 5-61-15-30-00; e-mail malummer@esa_purpan.fr; internet www.esa_purpan.fr; f. 1919; 5-year diploma course; master's degrees in agriculture, management and technology in the food industry, agricultural economics and management, environment and regional devt; library: 20,000 vols, 1,100 periodicals; 100 teachers (37 full-time); 700 students; Dir MICHEL ROUX; publ. *Purpan* (4 a year).

Esitpa – Ecole d'Ingénieurs en Agriculture: 3 rue du Tronquet, BP 40118, 76134 Mont-Saint-Aignan Cedex; tel. 2-32-82-92-00; fax 2-35-05-27-40; e-mail webmaster@ esitpa.org; internet www.esitpa.org; f. 1919; 5-year diploma courses for agricultural engineers; Dir P. DENIEUL.

Groupe ESA – Ecole Supérieure d'Agriculture d'Angers: 55 rue Rabelais, BP 30748, 49007 Angers Cedex 01; tel. 2-41-23-55-55; fax 2-41-23-55-00; e-mail webmaster@ groupe-esa.com; internet www.groupe-esa .com; f. 1898; library: 45,000 vols, 520 periodicals; 600 students; Dir AYMARD HONORÉ; publs *Bibliographie Agricole et Rurale* (5 a year), *Cahiers Agriscope* (3 a year).

COMMERCE, BUSINESS ADMINISTRATION AND STATISTICS

Audencia Nantes Ecole de Management: 8 route de la Jonelière, BP 31222, 44312 Nantes Cedex 3; tel. 2-40-37-34-34; fax 2-40-37-34-07; internet www.audencia.com; f. 1900; library: 13,000 vols, 450 periodicals; 343 teachers (43 full-time, 300 part-time); 1,200 students; Pres. JEAN-FRANÇOIS MOULIN; Dir-Gen. and Dean AÏSSA DERMOUCHE.

Centre Européen d'Education Permanente (CEDEP) (European Centre for Executive Development): Blvd de Constance, 77305 Fontainebleau Cedex; f. 1971; management development courses in business administration for member companies (6 French, 2 Danish, 3 British, 1 Swedish, 2 Belgian, 1 Indian, 2 Dutch, 5 European); associated with the Institut Européen d'Administration des Affaires; Gen. Dir MITCHELL KOZA.

CERAM Business School: Rue Dostoïevski, BP 085, 06902 Sophia Antipolis Cedex; tel. 4-89-88-98-24; fax 4-93-65-45-24; e-mail info@ceram.fr; internet www.ceram .edu; f. 1978 by Nice Chamber of Commerce; library: 16,000 vols; 100 full-time; 120 part-time teachers; 750 students, plus 100 on Master's course; Dir MAXIME CRENER.

Ecole de Management de Normandie: 30 rue de Richelieu, 76087 Le Havre Cedex; tel. 2-32-92-59-99; e-mail info@ ecole-management-normandie.fr; internet www.ecole-management-normandie.fr; f. 1871; campuses in Caen, Cherbourg and Deauville; courses in business administration, tourism and leisure management; library: 37,050 vols, 39 databases; 37 teachers; 1,302 students; Dir–Gen. JEAN GUY BERNARD.

Ecole du Chef d'Entreprise (ECE): 24–26 rue Hamelin, 75116 Paris; f. 1944; business administration; 50 teachers; Pres. M. Y. CHOTARD; Dir C. GOURDAIN; Sec.-Gen. Mlle M. JANNOR.

Ecole Nouvelle d'Organisation Economique et Sociale – Groupe ENOES: 62 rue de Miromesnil, 75008 Paris; internet www.enoes.com; f. 1937; courses in transport and logistics, business administration and accountancy; Pres. GILLES DE COURCEL; Gen. Sec. MICHEL OHAYON.

Ecole Supérieure de Commerce de Montpellier: 2300 ave des Moulins, 34185 Montpellier Cedex 4; tel. 4-67-10-25-00; fax 4-67-45-13-56; e-mail info@supco-montpellier.fr; internet www.supdeco-montpellier.com; f. 1897; 250 teachers; 1,750 students; three-year courses in business administration and management sciences; Dir Dr DIDIER JOURDAN.

Ecole Supérieure des Sciences Economiques et Commerciales (ESSEC Business School – Paris): Ave Bernard Hirsch, BP 50105, 95021 Cergy-Pontoise Cedex; tel. 1-34-43-30-00; fax 1-34-43-30-01; e-mail indigo@essec.fr; internet www.essec.com; f. 1907; 4-year, 3-year, 2-year and 1-year degree courses; Master's degree in business administration and management; MSc in marketing, finance, logistics, information and decision systems, international law and management, agribusiness management, international supply management, urban management, and strategy and management of international business; MBA programmes in hospitality, luxury-brand management; Exec. MBA and other executive education courses; doctoral and BBA programmes; library: 49,000 vols, 1,500 periodicals; 370 teachers (100 full-time, 270 part-time); 3,700 students; Pres. PIERRE TAPIE.

EDHEC Business School: 58 rue du Port, 59046 Lille Cedex; tel. 3-20-15-45-00; fax 3-20-15-45-01; internet www.edhec.com; f. 1906; MBA programmes; Dir–Gen. OLIVIER OGER.

EMLYON Business School: 23 ave Guy de Collongue, 69134 Ecully Cedex; tel. 4-78-33-78-00; fax 4-78-33-61-69; e-mail info@em-lyon.com; internet www.em-lyon.com; f. 1872; library: 12,927 vols; 80 teachers; 1,250 students; Dir–Gen. PATRICK MOLLE.

ESC Bretagne Brest: 2 ave de Provence, CS23812, 29238 Brest Cedex 3; tel. 2-98-34-44-44; fax 2-98-34-44-69; e-mail info@esc-bretagne-brest.com; internet www.esc-brest.fr; f. 1962; library: 5,000 vols, 150 periodicals; 110 teachers; 533 students; Dir C. MONIQUE.

ESC Pau – Groupe Ecole Supérieure de Commerce de Pau: 3 rue Saint John Perse, Campus Universitaire BP 7512, 64075 Pau Cedex; tel. 5-59-92-64-64; fax 5-59-92-64-55; e-mail info@esc-pau.fr; internet www.esc-pau.fr; f. 1970 by the Chamber of Commerce; library: 5,000 vols; 16 full-time; 120 part-time teachers; 500 students; Dir LAURENT HUA.

ESCP-EAP European School of Management: 79 ave de la République, 75543 Paris Cedex 11; tel. 1-49-23-20-00; fax 1-49-23-22-12; e-mail info@escp-eap.net; internet www.escp-eap.net; f. 1999 by merger of Groupe ESCP and Ecole Européenne des Affaires (EAP); 120 teachers in five countries; 3,000 students in five countries; campuses in Paris (France), London (UK), Berlin (Germany), Madrid (Spain) and Turin (Italy); postgradu-

ate degree programmes, executive education; 5 research centres; Dean JEAN-LOUIS SCARINGELLA.

Groupe CPA – Centre de Perfectionnement aux Affaires: 14 ave de la Porte de Champerret, 75017 Paris; tel. 1-44-09-34-00; fax 1-44-09-34-99; f. 1930 by the Paris Chamber of Commerce and Industry; gen. management courses for top executives; establishing close links with Groupe HEC (Hautes Etudes Commerciales); Dir JEAN-LOUIS SCARINGELLA.

Branches; see entry for HEC School of Management for details of branch institutions:

CPA Paris.

CPA Lyon.

CPA Nord.

CPA Grand Sud-Ouest.

CPA Méditerranée.

CPA Madrid.

ESC Bordeaux: 680 cours de la Libération, 33405 Talence Cedex; tel. 5-56-84-55-55; fax 5-56-84-55-00; e-mail info@bem.edu; internet www.bem.edu; f. 1874 by Chamber of Commerce; library: 17,000 vols; 74 teachers; 1,800 students; Dir GEORGES VIALA.

ESCEM – Groupe Ecole Supérieure de Commerce et de Management: 1 rue Léo Delibes, BP 0535, 37205 Tours Cedex 3; tel. 2-47-71-71-71; fax 2-47-71-72-10; e-mail com@escem.fr; internet www.escem.fr; f. 1961; graduate management degree programme, Master's and int. MBA. degree programmes, continuing education and distance learning in management; courses in economics, marketing, finance, accountancy, management information systems, international business; Master's degrees in business admin. and information systems; 405 teachers (55 full-time, 350 part-time); 1,600 students; library: 13,000 vols; Dir GUY LE BOUCHER; publ. *Les Cahiers de Recherche de l'ESCEM* (2 a year).

Branch campus:

Groupe ESCEM Campus Poitiers: 11 rue de l'Ancienne Comédie, BP 5, 86001 Poitiers Cedex; tel. 5-49-60-58-00; fax 5-49-60-58-30; internet www.escem.fr.

ESIDEC – Ecole Supérieure Internationale de Commerce de Metz: 3 place Edouard Branly, BP 95090, 57073 Metz Cedex 3; tel. 3-87-56-37-37; fax 3-87-56-37-99; e-mail gregory.marongio@icn-groupe.fr; internet www.esidec.fr; f. 1988; run by the Moselle Chamber of Commerce and Industry; courses in management, logistics, marketing, finance, law, trade, purchasing; 40 teachers; 210 students; Dir THIERRY JEAN.

Groupe ESC Lille – Ecole Supérieure de Commerce de Lille: Ave Willy Brandt, 59777 Euralille; tel. 3-20-21-59-62; fax 3-20-21-59-59; internet www.esc-lille.fr; f. 1892; library: 3,700 vols, 270 periodicals; 1,000 students; Dir JEAN-PIERRE DEBOURSE.

Groupe EAC – Ecole Supérieure d'Economie, d'Art et de Communication: 33 rue de La Boétie, 75008 Paris; tel. 1-47-70-23-83; fax 1-47-70-17-83; e-mail paris@groupeeac.com; internet www.groupeeac.com; f. 1987; library: 500 vols; 70 teachers; 350 students; Dir CLAUDE VIVIER.

HEC School of Management: 78351 Jouy-en-Josas Cedex; tel. 1-39-67-70-00; fax 1-39-67-74-40; e-mail hec@hec.fr; internet www.hec.edu; f. 1881; sponsored by the Paris Chamber of Commerce and Industry; incorporates CPA (Centre de Perfectionnement aux affaires); degree courses in fields of management; executive development programmes; library: 60,000 vols; 589 teachers (104 full-time, 450 part-time, 35 visiting); 2,500 stu-

dents; Dean BERNARD RAMANANTSOA; Dir of CPA DEAN-MARC DE LEERSNYDER.

CPA Sites:

CPA Grand Sud-Ouest: 20 blvd Lascrosses, 31000 Toulouse; tel. 5-61-29-49-91; fax 5-61-13-98-31; Dir ALAIN MAINGUY.

CPA Lyon: 93 chemin des Mouilles, 69130 Ecully Cedex; tel. 4-78-33-52-12; fax 4-78-33-37-06; Dir CHARLES AB-DER-HALDEN.

CPA Madrid: Calle Serrano 208, 28012 Madrid, Spain; tel. 91-538-37-59; fax 91-538-37-58; Dir TEODORO AGUADO DE LOS RÍOS.

CPA Méditerranée: c/o CERAM II, 60 rue Dostoïevski, 06902 Sophia Antipolis; tel. 4-92-96-96-95; fax 4-93-95-44-21; Dir ADRIEN CORBIÈRE-MÉDECIN.

CPA Nord: 551 rue Albert Bailly, 59700 Marcq-en-Baroeul; tel. 3-20-25-97-53; fax 3-20-27-12-94; Dir JEAN-CLAUDE VACHER.

CPA Paris: 14 ave de la Porte de Champerret, 75017 Paris; tel. 1-44-09-34-00; fax 1-44-09-34-99.

INSEAD: Blvd de Constance, 77305 Fontainebleau; tel. 1-60-72-40-00; fax 1-60-74-55-00; internet www.insead.fr; f. 1958; postgraduate MBA programme; PhD programme; executive development programmes; 100 professors; library: 40,000 vols; Chair. Board of Govs CLAUDE JANSSEN; Dean Prof. GABRIEL HAWAWINI.

Reims Management School: 59 rue Pierre-Taittinger, 51100 Reims Cedex; tel. 3-26-77-47-47; fax 3-26-04-69-63; e-mail service.com@reims-ms.fr; internet www.reims-ms.fr; f. 1928; schools and subject areas: Sup de Co (new economy), Cesem (International School of Management), Tema (management school with emphasis on technology), Sup TG (sales and administration), MBA (part- and full-time); 62 full-time teachers; 2,600 students; Dir DOMINIQUE WAQUET.

LAW AND POLITICAL SCIENCE

American Graduate School of International Relations and Diplomacy: 6 rue de Lubeck, 75116 Paris; tel. 1-47-20-00-94; fax 1-47-20-81-89; e-mail info@agsird.edu; internet www.agsird.edu; f. 1994; MA and PhD programmes; 11 teachers; 90 students (50 full-time, 40 part-time); Dir Dr MARCIA A. GRANT.

Ecole des Hautes Etudes Internationales: 107 rue de Tolbiac, 75013 Paris; tel. 1-45-70-73-37; fax 1-45-70-99-33; e-mail contact@hep-hei-esj.net; internet www.hep-hei-esj.net; f. 1904; Pres. M. SCHUMANN; Dir P. CHAIGNEAU.

Ecole de Notariat d'Amiens: 44 square des 4 Chênes, 80000 Amiens; tel. 3-22-92-61-26; fax 3-22-92-90-84; e-mail ecolenotariat-amiens@wanadoo.fr; internet www.cr-picardie.notaires.fr/front/actualites/ecolenotariat.asp; f. 1942; Dir ALAIN DORÉ.

Ecole de Notariat de Paris: 9 rue Villaret-de-Joyeuse, 75017 Paris; tel. 1-43-80-87-62; fax 1-46-22-01-46; f. 1896; Dir M. P. MATHIEU.

Ecole Supérieure de Journalisme: 107 rue Tolbiac, 75013 Paris; tel. 1-45-70-73-37; fax 1-45-70-99-33; e-mail contact@hep-hei-esj.net; internet www.hep-hei-esj.net; f. 1899; Pres. M. CAZENEUVE; Dir P. CHAIGNEAU.

Institut International des Droits de l'Homme (International Institute of Human Rights): 2 Allée René Cassin, 67000 Strasbourg; tel. 3-88-45-84-45; fax 3-88-45-84-50; e-mail administration@iidh.org; internet www.iidh.org; f. 1969 by René Cassin; postgraduate teaching in international and comparative law of human rights; annual study session during July; annual two-week course in June on refugee law, organized in collaboration with the United Nations High Commissioner for Refugees (in French); 50 teachers; 350 students; Pres. GÉRARD COHEN-JONATHAN; Sec.-Gen. JEAN-FRANÇOIS FLAUSS.

Attached Centre:

International Centre for University Human Rights Teaching: Strasbourg; f. 1973 at the request of UNESCO; two-week courses for university teachers; 2 teachers; 40 students; Sec.-Gen. Prof. JEAN-FRANÇOIS FLAUSS.

MEDICINE

Ecole Dentaire Française: 1 bis 3 rue de l'Est, 75020 Paris; tel. 1-47-97-77-81; fax 1-47-97-46-64; e-mail edf@lesmetiersdelasante .com; internet www.ecole-dentaire.fr; f. 1886; Dir R. J. CACHIA.

Institut et Centre d'Optométrie: 134 route de Chartres, 91440 Bures-sur-Yvette; tel. 1-64-86-12-13; fax 1-69-28-49-99; e-mail ico.direction@wanadoo.fr; internet www .ecole-optometrie.fr; f. 1917; 40 teachers; 350 students; Dir JEAN-PAUL ROOSEN.

RELIGION

Faculté Libre de Théologie Protestante de Paris: 83 blvd Arago, 75014 Paris; tel. 1-43-31-61-64; fax 1-43-31-62-67; e-mail secretariat@iptheologie.fr; internet www .iptheologie.fr; f. 1877; religious history, Old and New Testament, ecclesiastical history, systematic theology, philosophy, practical theology, Hebrew, Greek, German, English; library: 60,000 vols; 12 professors, 180 students; Dean JACQUES-NOËL PÉRÈS.

Institut de Théologie Orthodoxe Saint-Serge: 93 rue de Crimée, 75019 Paris; tel. 1-42-01-96-10; fax 1-42-08-00-09; e-mail ito@ saint-serge.net; internet www.saint-serge .net; f. 1925; 15 professors and 50 students; library: 30,000 vols; Dean Rev. Fr BORIS BOBRINSKOY; publ. *Pensée Orthodoxe* (every 2 years).

Institut Européen des Sciences Humaines: Centre de Bouteloin, 58120 Saint-Léger-de-Fougeret; tel. 3-86-79-40-62; fax 3-86-85-01-19; internet www.iesh.org; f. 1990; Muslim theology; library: 5,000 vols; 8 teachers; capacity for 200 students; Dir ZUHAIR MAHMOOD.

Institut Orthodoxe Français de Paris Saint-Denys: 96 blvd Auguste-Blanqui, 75013 Paris; tel. 6-89-32-25-38; e-mail institut.saintdenys@club-internet.fr; internet institutdetheologie.free.fr; f. 1944; 20 professors and 125 students; library: 5,000 vols; faculties of theology and philosophy; Rector BERTRAND-HARDY (Bishop Germain of Saint Denis); publ. *Présence Orthodoxe*.

Séminaire Israélite de France (Ecole Rabbinique): 9 rue Vauquelin, 75005 Paris; tel. 1-47-07-21-22; fax 1-43-37-75-92; f. 1829; Talmud, Bible, Jewish history and philosophy, Hebrew language and literature studies, rabbinical law; 6 teachers; 15 students; library: 60,000 vols; Dir Chief Rabbi MICHEL GUGENHEIM.

SCIENCES

Ecole d'Anthropologie: 1 place d'Iéna, 75116 Paris; tel. 1-47-93-09-73; fax 1-47-93-09-73; e-mail institutanthropologie@hotmail .fr; internet www.multimania.com/anthropa; f. 1876 by Prof. Broca; prehistory, physical anthropology, ethnology, biology, genetics, immunology, ethnography, demography, third world–problems, psychology, criminology, anthropotechnics, biometeorology; Dir

Prof. BERNARD J. HUET; publ. *Nouvelle revue anthropologique* (irregular).

Institut de Paléontologie Humaine: 1 rue René Panhard, 75013 Paris; tel. 1-43-31-62-91; fax 1-43-31-22-79; e-mail iph@mnhn.fr; f. 1910 by Prince Albert I of Monaco; vertebrate palaeontology, palynology, palaeo-anthropology, prehistory, quaternary geology, sedimentology, geochronology; library: 25,000 vols; 107 students; Dir HENRY DE LUMLEY; publs *Archives*, *L'Anthropologie*, *Etudes Quaternaires*.

Institut Edouard Toulouse: 1 rue Cabanis, 75014 Paris; tel. 1-45-65-81-36; f. 1983; teaching, training and research in psychiatry, seminars on psychoanalysis; Pres. Dr JEAN AYME; Sec. Dr MARCEL CZERMAK; publ. *Cahiers de l'Hôpital Henri Rousselle.*

Institut Océanographique: 195 rue Saint Jacques, 75005 Paris; tel. 1-44-32-10-70; fax 1-40-51-73-16; e-mail institut@oceano.org; internet www.oceano.org; education, scientific research, museology, publishing; f. 1906 by Prince Albert I of Monaco; library: 30,000 vols; Pres. JEAN CHAPON; Dir LUCIEN LAUBIEN; Sec. C. BEAUVERGER; publ. *Oceanis* (4 a year).

Attached Museum:

Musée Océanographique: see under Monaco.

SOCIAL AND ECONOMIC SCIENCES

Collège Libre des Sciences Sociales et Economiques: 184 blvd Saint-Germain, 75006 Paris; f. 1895; composed of six sections: social, economic, international and public relations; evening and correspondence courses; diplomas conferred after two or three years' study, and submission of theses on some aspect of applied economics; Pres. J. RUEFF; Dir L. DE SAINTE-LORETTE.

Ecole de Hautes Etudes Sociales: 107 rue Tolbiac, 75013 Paris; tel. 1-45-70-73-37; fax 1-45-70-99-33; e-mail contact@hep-hei-esj .net; internet www.hep-hei-esj.net; f. 1899; Pres. M. SCHUMANN; Dir P. CHAIGNEAU.

Faculté des Lettres et Sciences Sociales: BP 800, 29200 Brest; tel. 2-98-80-19-87; f. 1960; library: 18,000 vols; 105 teachers; 2,752 students; President and Dean Prof. MICHEL QUESNEL.

IFG-CNOF: 37 quai de Grenelle, 75015 Paris; tel. 1-40-59-30-30; internet www .ifgcnof.com; f. 1926; provides executive, managerial and administrative training.

Institut Européen des Hautes Etudes Internationales (IEHEI): 10 ave des Fleurs, 06000 Nice; tel. 4-93-97-93-70; fax 4-93-97-93-71; e-mail iehei@wanadoo.fr; internet www.iehei.org; f. 1964; library: 4,000 vols; 20 teachers; 35 students; Pres. VLAD CONSTANTINESCO; Dir CLAUDE NIGOUL.

TECHNOLOGY

Ecole Catholique d'Arts et Métiers (ECAM): 40 montée Saint-Barthélemy, 69321 Lyons Cedex 05; tel. 4-72-77-06-00; fax 4-72-77-06-11; e-mail info@ecam.fr; internet www.ecam.fr; f. 1900; courses in mechanical engineering, materials science, electrical and electronic engineering, automation, information technology, production engineering; library: 5,000 vols; 525 students; Dir BERNARD PINATEL; publ. *Bulletin* (4 a year).

Ecole Centrale de Lyon: BP 163, 36 ave Guy de Collongue, 69131 Ecully Cedex; tel. 4-72-18-60-00; fax 4-78-43-39-62; f. 1857; cultural, scientific and technical training for engineers in all branches of industry; library:

15,000 vols; 900 students; Dir E. PASCAUD; Sec.-Gen. C. LACROIX.

Ecole de Thermique: 3 rue Henri Heine, 75016 Paris; tel. 1-44-30-41-00; fax 1-40-50-07-54; teaching centre for the Institut Français de l'Energie (IFE); Dir (vacant).

Ecole Généraliste d'Ingénieurs de Marseille (EGIM): Technopôle de Château-Gombert, 38 rue Joliot Curie, 13451 Marseilles Cedex 20; tel. and fax 4-91-05-45-45; e-mail sdei@egim-mrs.fr; internet www .egim-mrs.fr; f. 1891; specialist courses in information and communications technology, mechatronics, systems engineering, marine engineering, thermal systems engineering, mechanical and materials engineering, microelectronics design, civil engineering; 70 teachers; 778 students; Dir JEAN-PAUL FABRE.

Ecole Spéciale des Travaux Publics, du Bâtiment et de l'Industrie: 57 blvd Saint-Germain, 75005 Paris; tel. 1-44-41-11-18; fax 1-44-41-11-12; e-mail information@adm.estp .fr; internet www.estp.fr; f. 1891; civil engineering training programmes at undergraduate and graduate levels; continuing education courses; 700 teachers; 2,000 students; library: 10,000 vols; Dir S. EYROLLES.

Ecole Supérieure d'Optique et Institut d'Optique: Centre Scientifique d'Orsay, Bât. 503, 91403 Orsay Cedex; tel. 1-69-35-88-88; fax 1-69-35-87-00; e-mail international@iota .u-psud.fr; internet www.institutoptique.fr; attached to Univ. Paris XI; f. 1920; optical engineering, optics and photonics at postgraduate level; 60 teachers (20 full-time, 40 assoc.); 240 students; Dir Prof. ANDRÉ DUCASSE.

Ecole Supérieure de Fonderie et de Forge: 44 ave de la division Leclerc, 92310 Sèvres; tel. 1-55-64-04-40; fax 1-55-64-04-45; e-mail contact@esff.fr; internet www.esff.fr; f. 1923; library: 2,150 vols; Dir G. CHAPPUIS.

Ecole Supérieure des Industries du Vêtement: 73 blvd Saint-Marcel, 75013 Paris; tel. 1-40-79-92-60; fax 1-40-79-92-91; e-mail info@esiv.fr; internet www.esiv.fr; f. 1946; 14 teachers; 70 students; Dir ANNE STEFANINI.

Ecole Supérieure des Industries Textiles d'Epinal: 85 rue d'Alsace, 88025 Epinal Cedex; tel. 3-29-35-50-52; fax 3-29-35-39-21; e-mail esite@wanadoo.fr; f. 1905; training of industrial textile engineers; library: 1,500 vols; Dir J. TIERCET.

Ecole Supérieure des Techniques Aéronautiques et de Construction Automobile: 34 rue Victor Hugo, 92300 Levallois-Perret; tel. 1-41-27-37-00; fax 1-47-37-50-83; e-mail infos@estaca.fr; internet www.estaca .fr; f. 1925; private school offering 5-year courses in aeronautical, automotive, railway and space engineering; Master's course in safety of transportation systems (taught in English); EUROMIND, European Master's in design and technology of advanced vehicle systems (taught in English); 1,000 students; Dir ERIC PARLEBAS.

Ecole Supérieure du Bois: rue Christian Pauc, BP 10605, 44306 Nantes Cedex 3; tel. 2-40-18-12-12; fax 2-40-18-12-00; e-mail contact@ecolesuperieuredubois.com; internet www.ecolesuperieuredubois.com; f. 1934; training of engineers and management for wood industry; 13 full-time, 20 external; 250 students; Dir X. MARTIN.

Ecole Supérieure du Soudage et de ses Applications (Advanced Postgraduate Welding Engineering School): BP 50362, 95942 Roissy CDG Cedex; tel. 1-49-90-36-27; fax 1-49-90-36-50; e-mail m.d.jols@ institutdesoudure.com; internet www

.institutdesoudure.com; f. 1930; 55 teachers; 30 students; Dir MICHEL DIJOLS.

Ecole Technique Supérieure du Laboratoire: 95 rue du Dessous-des Berges, 75013 Paris; tel. 1-45-83-76-34; fax 1-45-83-58-85; e-mail mail@etsl.fr; internet www.etsl.fr; f. 1934; Pres. J. CHOMIENNE; Dir. F. LAISSUS.

EFREI – Ecole Française d'Electronique et d'Informatique: 30–32 ave de la République, 94815 Villejuif; tel. 1-46-77-64-67; fax 1-46-77-65-77; e-mail admission@efrei.fr; internet www.efrei.fr; f. 1936; courses in telecommunications, electronic engineering and computer science; 50 teachers; 1,170 students; Dir ERIC PARLEBAS.

ESIEE Paris: Cité Descartes, BP 99, 93162 Noisy-le-Grand Cedex; tel. 1-45-92-65-00; fax 1-45-92-66-99; e-mail admissions@esiee.fr; internet www.esiee.fr; f. 1962; computer science, automation, telecommunications, signal processing, microelectronics; 100 teachers; 1,000 students; library: 18,000 vols; Dir ALAIN CADIX.

ESME Sudria: 38 rue Molière, 94200 Ivry-sur-Seine; 51 blvd de Brandenbourg, 94200 Ivry-sur-Seine; tel. 1-56-20-62-00; fax 1-56-20-62-62; e-mail contact@esme.fr; internet www.esme.fr; f. 1905; training in electrical engineering, electronics, telecommunications and computer engineering; Dir-Gen. HERVÉ LABORNE.

EPF – Ecole d'Ingénieurs: 3 bis rue Lakanal, 92330 Sceaux; tel. 1-41-13-01-51; fax 1-46-60-39-94; internet www.epf.fr; f. 1925; engineering training; Pres. Dr ALAIN JENEVEAU.

European Institute of Technology: 8 rue Saint Florentin, 75001 Paris; tel. 1-40-15-05-69; fax 1-49-27-98-11; f. 1988 to strengthen industrial research and development, and to increase the contribution of technological innovation to economic growth in Europe; Sec.-Gen. JOHN M. MARCUM.

IFOCA – Institut National de Formation et d'Enseignement Professionnel du Caoutchouc: 60 rue Auber, 94408 Vitry-sur-Seine Cedex; tel. 1-49-60-57-57; fax 1-49-60-70-66; e-mail info@ifoca.com; internet www.ifoca.com; f. 1941; 8 teachers; 35 students; Dir GÉRARD GALLAS.

Institut Français Textile–Habillement: Ave Guy de Collongue, 69134 Ecully Cedex; tel. 4-72-86-16-00; fax 4-72-86-16-50; e-mail information@ifth.org; internet www.ifth.org; f. 1946; library: 255 vols and documents; Dir M. BEDEAU.

Institut Textile et Chimique de Lyon (ITECH): 87 chemin des Mouilles, 69134 Ecully Cedex; tel. 4-72-18-04-80; fax 4-72-18-95-45; e-mail info@itech.fr; internet www.itech.fr; f. 1899; diploma courses in leather technology, painting and adhesives technology; plastics; textiles; 120 teachers; 360 students; Dir JEAN-PIERRE GALLET; Dean CHRISTIANE BASSET.

International Space University: Parc d'Innovation, 1 rue Jean Dominique Cassini, 67400 Illkirch-Graffenstaden; tel. 3-88-65-54-30; fax 3-88-65-54-47; e-mail info@isu.isunet.edu; internet www.isunet.edu; f. 1987; offers Master of Space Studies and Master of Space Management degree programmes, introductory space course and a summer session programme; 6 full-time, 6 part-time and 100 visiting teachers; 150 students; Pres. Dr MICHAEL SIMPSON.

Supélec – Ecole Supérieure d'Electricité: Plateau du Moulon, 3 rue Joliot-Curie, 91192 Gif-sur-Yvette Cedex; tel. 1-69-85-12-12; fax 1-69-85-12-34; internet www.supelec.fr; campuses at Gif, Metz and Rennes; f. 1894; two- or three-year courses in electrical engineering, radio engineering, information science, electronics and computer science; 120 permanent teachers; 1,200 students; attached to Univ. Paris XI; Dir–Gen. J. J. DUBY; Dir of Studies F. MESA; Gen.-Sec. A. POTONNIER.

SUPINFO – Ecole Supérieure d'Informatique: 23 rue du Château Landon, 75010 Paris; tel. 1-53-35-97-00; e-mail paris@supinfo.com; internet www.supinfo.com; f. 1965; 90 teachers; 1,000 students; Dir LEO ROZENTALIS; publ. *Dossiers de l'Association pour la Promotion de l'Ecole Supérieure d'Informatique.*

Schools of Art and Music

Conservatoire National de Région de Musique et de Danse de Lyon: 4 montée Cardinal Decourtray, 69321 Lyons; tel. 4-78-25-91-39; fax 4-78-15-09-60; e-mail communication@conservatoire-lyon.fr; internet www.conservatoire-lyon.fr; f. 1872; 190 teachers; 2,900 students; library: 2,600 vols, 40,000 scores, 4,500 records, 2,000 orchestral scores; Dir ALAIN JACQUON.

Conservatoire à Rayonnement Régional de Boulogne-Billancourt—Centre Georges-Gorse: 22 rue de la Belle-Feuille, 92100 Boulogne-Billancourt; tel. 1-55-18-45-85; fax 1-55-18-45-86; internet www.bb-cnr.com; f. 1959 as Conservatoire de Boulogne-Billancourt; achieved national school status as Conservatoire National de Région de Musique et de Danse de Boulogne-Billancourt in 1979; present name and status 2007; library: 7,000 books, 40 periodicals, 20,000 scores, 6,000 records, 600 audiovisual and multimedia items.; 90 teachers; 1,650 students; Dir ALAIN LOUVIER.

Conservatoire National Supérieur d'Art Dramatique: 2 bis rue du Conservatoire, 75009 Paris; tel. 1-42-46-12-91; fax 1-48-00-94-02; e-mail communication@cnsad.fr; internet www.cnsad.fr; f. 1786; 55 teachers; 100 students; library: 23,500 vols; Dir DANIEL MESGUICH.

Conservatoire National Supérieur de Musique et de Danse de Paris: 209 ave Jean Jaurès, 75019 Paris; tel. 1-40-40-45-45; fax 1-40-40-45-00; e-mail cnsmdp@cnsmdp.fr; internet www.cnsmdp.fr; f. 1795; 386 teachers; 1,413 students; Dir ALAIN POIRIER.

Conservatoire National Supérieur Musique et Danse de Lyon: 3 quai Chauveau, CP 120, 69266 Lyons Cedex 09; tel. 4-72-19-26-26; fax 4-72-19-26-00; e-mail cnsmd@cnsmd-lyon.fr; internet www.cnsmd-lyon.fr; f. 1980; library: 42,000 vols; 170 teachers; 550 students; Dir HENRY FOURÈS.

Ecole supérieure des beaux-arts de Marseille: 184 ave de Luminy, 13288 Marseilles Cedex 9; tel. 4-91-82-83-10; fax 4-91-82-83-11; e-mail fballongue@mairie-marseille.fr; internet www.esbam.fr; f. 1710; 420 students; library: 15,000 vols; Dir NORBERT DUFFORT; publs *Verba Volant* (2 a year), *Recherche et Création Artistiques* (monographs, 5 a year).

Ecole du Louvre: Palais du Louvre, Porte Jaujard, Place du Carrousel, 75038 Paris Cedex 01; tel. 1-55-35-18-00; fax 1-42-60-40-36; internet www.ecoledulouvre.fr; f. 1882; library: 40,000 vols; 1,700 students; Principal PH. DUREY; Sec.-Gen. M. C. DEVEVEY.

Ecole Nationale Supérieure des Arts Décoratifs (ENSAD): 31 rue d'Ulm, 75240 Paris Cedex 05; tel. 1-42-34-97-00; fax 1-42-34-97-85; e-mail info@ensad.fr; internet www.ensad.fr; f. 1766; visual arts and design; library: 15,000 vols and spec. colln; 164 teachers; 600 students; Dirs ELIZABETH FLEURY PATRICK RAYNAUD; publs *Catalogue des Projets de Fin d'Etudes* (2 a year), *Journal des Arts-Déco* (3 a year).

Ecole Nationale Supérieure des Beaux-Arts: 14 rue Bonaparte, 75272 Paris Cedex 06; tel. 1-47-03-50-00; fax 1-47-03-50-80; f. 1648 as Académie Royale de Peinture et de Sculpture, and in 1671 as Académie Royale d'Architecture; library: 120,000 vols; 75 teachers; 650 students; Dir (vacant); publs *Beaux-Arts Histoire*, *Ecrits d'Artistes*, *Espaces de l'art.*

Ecole Supérieure d'Art Clermont Communauté: 142 ave Jean Mermoz, 63100 Clermont-Ferrand; tel. 4-73-91-43-86; fax 4-73-90-27-80; e-mail erba@ville-clermont-ferrand.fr; internet www.ecoledart.ville-clermont-ferrand.fr; f. 1882; library: 7,000 vols and spec. colln; 17 teachers; 130 students; Dir SYLVAIN LIZON.

Schola Cantorum: 269 rue St Jacques, 75005 Paris; tel. 1-43-54-15-39; fax 1-43-29-78-70; e-mail info@schola-cantorum.com; internet www.schola-cantorum.com; f. 1896 by Vincent d'Indy; music, dance and dramatic art; Dir MICHEL DENIS.

FRENCH GUIANA

Regulatory Body

GOVERNMENT

Commission for Higher Education, Research, Science and Technology of Information and Communication: 66 ave du Général de Gaulle, 97300 Cayenne; tel. 5-94-25-66-84; fax 5-94-37-94-24; e-mail ccee@cr-guyane.fr; internet www.cr-guyane.fr; Pres. JOSEPHINE EGALGI; Vice-Pres. LYDIA CARISTAN.

Research Institutes

GENERAL

Institut de Recherche pour le Développement: 0,275 km Route de Montabo, BP 165, 97323 Cayenne Cedex; tel. 5-94-29-92-92; fax 5-94-31-98-55; e-mail guyane@ird.fr; internet www.cayenne.ird.fr; f. 1949; teledetection, pedology, hydrology, sedimentology, botany and vegetal biology, medical and agricultural entomology, ornithology, phytopharmacology, oceanography, sociology; library of 7,000 vols; Rep. JEAN-MARIE FOTSING; publ. *L'Homme et la Nature en Guyane*; (see main entry under France).

ECONOMICS, LAW AND POLITICS

Institut d'Etudes Judiciaires (Institute of Judicial Studies): Cayenne; tel. 5-96-72-73-80; fax 5-96-72-73-73; internet www.univ-ag.fr/fr/institution/instituts/iej.html; attached to Univ. des Antilles et de la Guyane; offers programmes for training of legal professionals; organizes seminars, conferences and courses.

EDUCATION

Institut d'enseignement supérieur de la Guyane (Institute of Higher Education of Guyana): Campus Saint-Denis, ave d'Estree; tel. 5-94-29-62-00; fax 5-94-29-62-10; internet www.univ-ag.fr/fr/institution/instituts/iesg.html; f. 1991; attached to Univ. des Antilles et de la Guyane; depts of arts, languages and humanities, legal science and economics, science, technology and health; 1,500 students.

Institut de Recherche sur l'Enseignement en Mathématiques (Institute for Research in Mathematics Education): Cayenne; tel. 5-90-48-30-43; e-mail irem.antilles-guyana@univ-ag.fr; internet www.univ-ag.fr/fr/institution/instituts/irem.html; research in mathematics education; training; Dir ALEX MERIL.

MEDICINE

Institut Pasteur de la Guyane: 23 ave Pasteur, BP 6010, 97306 Cayenne Cedex; tel. 5-94-29-26-00; fax 5-94-30-94-16; e-mail reseau@pasteur.fr; internet www.pasteur-cayenne.fr; f. 1940, fmrly Institute of Hygiene and Prophylaxis; medical and biological research; Dir Dr ANDRÉ SPIEGEL.

TECHNOLOGY

Institut Universitaire de Technologie (University Institute of Technology): ave Bois Chaudat, BP 725, Cayenne; tel. 5-94-32-80-00; fax 5-94-32-22-63; internet www.univ-ag.fr/fr/institution/instituts/iut.html; f. 1986, opened 1988; attached to Univ. des Antilles et de la Guyane; depts of biological engineering, business management and administration, electrical engineering and computer industrial, health safety and environment, logistics and transport management, marketing techniques, networking and telecommunications; 200 students.

Libraries and Archives

Cayenne

Archives Départementales: Pl. Léopold Héder, BP 5021, 97397 Cayenne Cedex; tel. 5-94-29-52-70; fax 5-94-29-52-89; internet www.cg973.fr/archives-departementales; f. 1796, present status 1983; history of French Guiana; classification; storage; research; Dir FRANÇOISE LEMAIRE-THABOUILLOT.

Bibliothèque Alexandre Franconie: 1 ave du Général de Gaulle, 97300 Cayenne; tel. 5-94-29-59-16; fax 5-94-29-59-12; e-mail bibliotheque.franconie@cg973.fr; internet biblioweb.cg973.fr; f. 1885; attached to Bibliothèques du Conseil Général de la Guyane (Library of the Gen. Council of Guiana); gen. lending library; 35,000 vols; Dir MARIE-ANNICK ATTICOT.

Service Commun de la Documentation (Bibliothèques de la Guyane): Campus St-Denis, BP 1179, 97346 Cayenne Cedex; tel. 5-94-29-40-46; fax 5-94-29-40-17; e-mail nicole.clementmartin@guyane.univ-ag.fr; internet www.univ-ag.fr/fr/documentation.html; f. 1984; attached to Université des Antilles et de la Guyane; 36,000 vols, 240 periodicals; Dir of French Guiana Branch NICOLE CLÉMENT-MARTIN.

Museum

Cayenne

Musée Départemental: 1 ave Général de Gaulle, 97300 Cayenne; tel. 5-94-29-59-13; fax 5-94-29-59-11; e-mail musee@cg973.fr; internet www.cg973.fr/-musee-franconie; f. 1901; flora and fauna of Guiana; historical documents; Dir JEAN-PASCAL STERVINOU.

University

UNIVERSITÉ DES ANTILLES ET DE LA GUYANE

Campus de Saint-Denis, BP 1179, 97346 Cayenne Cedex

Telephone: 5-94-29-40-16
Fax: 5-94-29-40-17
E-mail: charge.communication@guyane.univ-ag.fr
Internet: www.univ-ag.fr

Founded 1880, present status 1982
State control

(See also under Guadeloupe and Martinique)

Pres.: PASCAL SAFFACHE
Vice-Pres. (French Guiana): ANTOINE PRIMEROSE

Library: see Libraries and Archives
Number of students: 1,692

FRENCH POLYNESIA

Regulatory Bodies

GOVERNMENT

Ministry of Culture and Handicrafts: tel. 47-22-80; fax 47-22-90; e-mail ambroise.colombani@presidence.pf; internet www.culture.gov.pf; Min. MITA TERIIPAIA.

Ministry of Education, Higher Education and Research: Pirae, Près Ecole Tuterai Tane; tel. 54-49-00; fax 54-49-10; Min. MOANA GREIG.

Learned Societies

GENERAL

Te Fare Tauhiti Nui–Maison de la Culture: 646 Blvd Pomaré, BP 1709, 98713 Papeete; tel. 54-45-44; fax 42-85-69; e-mail secretariat@maisondelaculture.pf; internet www.maisondelaculture.pf; f. 1971 as Maison des Jeunes–Maison de la Culture, change in admin. 1980, present name and status 1998; promotes culture locally and abroad; sponsors many public and private cultural events; library of 13,000 vols, children's library of 7,000 vols; Dir HEREMOANA MAA-MAATUAIATAPU (acting); Sec. CHRISTIANE BROTHERSON BALDERANIS.

NATURAL SCIENCES
General
Société des Etudes Océaniennes: BP 110, 98713 Papeete Tahiti; tel. 41-96-03; fax 41-96-04; e-mail seo@archives.gov.pf; internet www.seo.pf; f. 1917; study of archeology, anthropology, ethnography, natural sciences, philosophy, history, customs and traditions of Polynesia; attached library; 450 mems; library of 7,000 vols; Pres. SIMONE GRAND; Vice-Pres. FASAN CHONG DIT JEAN KAPE; Sec. MICHEL BAILLEUL; Treas. YVES BABIN; publ. *Bulletin de la Société des Etudes Océaniennes* (4 a year).

Research Institutes
GENERAL
Institut de Recherche pour le Développement (IRD) Centre de Tahiti: BP 529, 98713 Papeete Tahiti; tel. 50-62-00; fax 42-95-55; e-mail dirpapet@ird.pf; f. 1963; medical entomology, anthropology, oceanography; library of 7,000 vols; Rep. JACQUES ILTIS; (see main entry under France).

AGRICULTURE, FISHERIES AND VETERINARY SCIENCE
Centre Océanologique du Pacifique: BP 7004, 98719 Taravao Tahiti; tel. 54-60-00; fax 54-60-99; e-mail communication@ifremer.fr; internet www.ifremer.fr/cop; f. 1972; part of IFREMER (*q.v.*); research in aquaculture (crustacea, fish, shellfish); spec. library; 49 mems; Dir MARC TAQUET.

FINE AND PERFORMING ARTS
Institut de la Communication Audiovisuelle: BP 4469, 98713 Papeete Tahiti; tel. 50-67-50; fax 50-67-57; internet www.ica.pf; attached to Min. of Culture and Handicrafts; collects, preserves and restores audiovisual heritage of Polynesia; produces television programmes and documentaries; collns incl. video recordings, local television broadcasts and feature films; colln of images and sounds on the archipelagos of French Polynesia (Australes, Tuamotu, Gambier, Marquises, Société); library of 34,000 vols in reference colln.

MEDICINE
Institut Louis Malardé: BP 30, 98713 Papeete Tahiti; tel. 41-64-65; fax 43-15-90; internet www.ilm.pf; f. 1947, present bldg 1950, present name and status 2001; parasitology (particularly lymphatic filariasis), virology (dengue), microbiology, immunology, serology, biochemistry, pharmacotoxicology, bio-ecology and marine biochemistry, medical entomology; library of 1,000 vols, 9,185 periodicals; Dir Dr PATRICK HOWELL; Exec. Sec. MARIE-CLAUDE RENARD.

RELIGION, SOCIOLOGY AND ANTHROPOLOGY
Département des Traditions Orales, du Centre Polynésien des Sciences Humaines 'Te Anavaharau': Pk 15, Pointe de Pêcheurs, Punaauia Tahiti; tel. 58-34-76; fax 58-43-00; study of Polynesian oral tradition.

Archive
Papeete
Service des Archives Territoriales: BP 9063, 98715 Papeete Tahiti; tel. 41-96-01; fax 41-96-04; e-mail service.archives@archives.gov.pf; Head of Service PIERRE MORILLON.

Museums and Art Galleries
Papeari
Musée Paul Gauguin: BP 7029, 98727 Papeari Tahiti; tel. 57-10-58; fax 57-10-42; e-mail museegauguin@mail.pf; f. 1964; 1,000 documents on the life and work of the artist Paul Gauguin (1848–1903), who spent the last part of his life in Tahiti and other parts of the South Pacific; library of unpublished documents; colln of paintings by Buffet, R. Delaunay, S. Delaunay and others; 20 original works by Gauguin (paintings, sculptures, watercolours); Curator G. ARTUR.

Tamanu
Te Fare Manaha–Musée de Tahiti et des Iles: Pointe des pêcheurs 'Nu'uroa, Punaauia, BP 380 354, 98718 Tamanu; tel. 58-34-76; fax 58-43-00; e-mail secretariat@museetahiti.pf; internet www.museetahiti.pf; f. 1974, fmrly as Musée de Tahiti et des Iles–Te Fare Iamanaha, present name 2005; collects, conserves and appreciates Polynesian cultural heritage; Dir HIRIATA MILLAUD.

University
UNIVERSITÉ DE LA POLYNÉSIE FRANÇAISE
(University of French Polynesia)

BP 6570, 98702 Faa'a Tahiti

Telephone: 80-38-94
Fax: 80-38-04
E-mail: courrier@upf.pf
Internet: www.upf.pf

Founded 1999 from the French Polynesia centre of the fmr Université Française du Pacifique (f. 1987)
State control
Academic year: September to June
Library of 50,000 books, 260 periodicals, 700 audiovisual items
Number of teachers: 62
Number of students: 2,664

Rector: LOUISE PELTZER

Depts of arts and humanities, law, economics and management, physical activities and sport, and science, medicine and technology.

College
Conservatoire artistique de Polynésie française 'Te Fare Upa Rau': BP 463, 98713 Papeete Tahiti; tel. 50-14-14; fax 43-71-29; e-mail conserv.artist@mail.pf; internet www.conservatoire.pf; f. 1979; attached to Min. of Culture and Handicrafts; conserves and promotes Polynesian culture; provides theoretical and practical training in fine and performing arts; 1,693 students; Dir FABIEN DINARD.

GUADELOUPE

Research Institutes
AGRICULTURE, FISHERIES AND VETERINARY SCIENCE
CIRAD Guadeloupe: Station de Neufchâteau, Sainte-Marie, 97130 Capesterre-Belle-Eau; tel. 5-90-86-30-21; fax 5-90-86-80-77; e-mail cecile.gaume@cirad.fr; internet www.cirad.fr/guadeloupe; cultivation of bananas and other fruits, sugar cane, flowers; animal parasitology and control; biodiversity management; 31 research staff; Regional Dir PHILIPPE GODON; Head of Caribbean Regional Cooperation DOMINIQUE POLTI; (see main entry under France).

INRA Antilles-Guyane: Domaine Duclos, Prise d'Eau, 97170 Petit Bourg; tel. 5-90-25-59-00; fax 5-90-25-59-98; e-mail xande@antilles.inra.fr; internet www.antilles.inra.fr; f. 1949 as Centre de Recherches des Antilles et de la Guyane; attached to Min. of Higher Education and Research and Min. of Agriculture and Fisheries; (see main entry under France); soil science, animal science, forestry, plant science, rural economy and sociology, zoology and biological control, technology transfer; controls 5 research units, 3 experimental farms and a documentation service; Pres. DANIELLE CÉLESTINE-MYRTIL-MARLIN.

MEDICINE
Institut Pasteur de la Guadeloupe: BP 484, 97183 Abymes Cedex; tel. 5-90-89-69-40; fax 5-90-89-69-41; internet www.pasteur-guadeloupe.fr; f. 1948; medical and microbiological analysis laboratories; int. vaccination centre; Public Health Dept certified laboratories for water and food analysis

(chemical and microbiological); mycobacteria research centre; small library; Dir Dr ANTOINE TALARMIN; Exec. Sec. Dr HENRIETTA DESIREE; publ. *Archives* (1 a year).

Libraries and Archives
Basse-Terre

Département de la Guadeloupe Archives Départementales: BP 74, 97102 Basse-Terre Cedex; tel. 5-90-81-13-02; fax 5-90-81-97-15; e-mail info@cg971.fr; internet www.cg971.fr/archives; f. 1951; holds records that date back to 1661; 10,000 vols; Dir ANNE LEBEL; publ. *Bulletin de la Société d'Histoire de la Guadeloupe* (3 a year).

Pointe-à-Pitre

Bibliothèque Universitaire Antilles-Guyane: Campus de Fouillole, BP 32, 97159 Pointe-à-Pitre Cedex; tel. 5-96-48-90-01; fax 5-96-48-90-89; e-mail jacques.faule@univ-ag.fr; internet www.univ-ag.fr/buag; f. 1972; 65,000 vols, 750 periodicals, 2,200 electronic journals; Dir, Guadeloupe Br. JACQUES FAULE.

Museums and Art Galleries
Basse-Terre

Historical Museum of Guadeloupe: Fort Delgrès, 97100 Basse-Terre; tel. 5-90-81-37-48.

Pointe-à-Pitre

Musée Municipal Saint John Perse: 9 Rue Noziéres, 97110 Pointe-à-Pitre; tel. 5-90-90-01-92; fax 5-90-83-98-31; e-mail musee

.st-john-perse@wanadoo.fr; f. 1987; 2-storey 19th-century colonial house: colln of accounts from life of poet St John Perse; exhibits incl. MSS and personal items; attached library and videotheque.

Musée Victor Schoelcher: 24 rue Peynier, 97110 Pointe-à-Pitre; tel. 5-90-82-08-04; fax 5-90-83-78-39; e-mail musee.schoelcher@cg971.fr; internet www.cg971.fr/musees/schoelcher/index_schoecher.htm; f. 1883; colln assembled by Victor Schoelcher (1804–1893), local politician and campaigner against slavery; pictures of European monuments and historic sites, reproductions of antique sculptures from the Musée du Louvre, Paris; Egyptian antiquities, Senegalese ritual bell, Aztec and Greek pottery fragments; writing on travel and slavery by Schoelcher; Dir H. PETITJEAN ROGET.

Affiliated Museums:

Musée Edgar Clerc: La Rosette, 97160 Le Moule; tel. 5-90-23-57-57; fax 5-90-23-57-43; internet www.cg971.fr/musees/clerc/index_edgar.htm; f. 1984; archaeological museum; library of 800 vols.

Ecomusée de Marie-Galante: Habitation Murat, 97112 Grand Bourg, Marie Galante; tel. 5-90-97-94-41; internet www.cg971.fr/musees/ecomusee/index_ecomuse.htm; f. 1980; local arts, history and traditions and history of sugar cane; medicinal herb garden in the fmr animal enclosure; library of 400 vols; Dir C. MOMBRUN.

Musée Fort Fleur d'Epée: Bas du Fort, 97190 Gosier; tel. 5-90-90-94-61; internet www.cg971.fr/musees/fleurdepee/index_e-pee.htm; f. 1759; military history; art gallery; coin colln.

Parc Archéologique des Roches Gravées: Bord de mer, 97114 Trois-Rivières; tel. 5-90-92-91-88; internet www.cg971.fr/musees/parc/index_roche.htm; f.

1970; 1 ha, containing tropical vegetation, volcanic rocks and stones bearing marks made by Arawak Indians, the original inhabitants of the island.

Vieux-Habitants

Musée du Café: Le Bouchu, 97119 Vieux-Habitants; tel. 5-90-98-54-96; fax 5-90-98-54-59; e-mail cafe.chaulet@wanadoo.fr; internet www.in-west-indies.com/site-museums-mu-see-du-cafe–cafe-chaulet-909.htm; history of coffee from 1721 to present day Guadeloupe; production and processing techniques of picking, roasting and converting coffee beans into a beverage.

University
UNIVERSITÉ DES ANTILLES ET DE LA GUYANE

Fouillole, BP 250, 97157 Pointe-à-Pitre Cedex

Telephone: 5-90-48-30-30
Fax: 5-90-91-06-57
Internet: www.univ-ag.fr

Founded 1982
Public control

Pres.: PASCAL SAFFACHE
Vice-Pres. for Guadeloupe: EUSTASE JANKY
Library: see Libraries and Archives
Number of teachers: 233
Number of students: 5,728

TEACHING AND RESEARCH UNITS

Exact and Natural Sciences: Dean: ALEX MERIL
Law and Economics: Dir: CHRISTIAN THERESINE
Medicine: Dir: Dr GEORGES JEAN-BAPTISTE
Sports: Dir: CHRISTIAN ALIN

MARTINIQUE

Learned Society
AGRICULTURE, FISHERIES AND VETERINARY SCIENCE

Martinique Billfish Association: Chevalier de Ste-Marthe, 97200 Fort-de-France; tel. 5-96-55-26-73; fax 5-96-63-94-48; e-mail referencement@pixellweb.com; internet www.martinique-billfish.org; f. 1993; devt and practice of fishing; study of ecosystems, wildlife and underwater biological balance; Pres. JOSÉ ZÉCLER.

Research Institutes
AGRICULTURE, FISHERIES AND VETERINARY SCIENCE

Institut de Recherche pour le Développement (IRD) – Centre IRD Martinique-Caraïbe: BP 8006, 97259 Fort de France Cedex; tel. 5-96-39-77-39; fax 5-96-50-32-61; e-mail martinique@ird.fr; internet www.mq.ird.fr; f. 1958, fmrly ORSTOM; soil science, nematology; library of 1,700 vols; Dir and

Rep. MARC MORELL; (see main entry under France).

Martinique Agricultural Research Pole: BP 214, 97285 Le Lementin; tel. 5-90-42-30-00; fax 5-90-42-31-00; e-mail dir-reg.martinique@cirad.fr; internet www.cirad.fr; attached to CIRAD Agricultural Research for Devt; cultivation of bananas, pineapples, fruit-producing trees and intensive farming; Rep. CHRISTIAN CHABRIER.

MEDICINE

Laboratoire Départemental d'Analyses: 35 blvd Pasteur, BP 628, 97261 Fort de France Cedex; tel. 5-96-71-34-52; fax 5-96-70-61-23; e-mail lda@cg972.fr; internet lda97.com; f. 1977; attached to Le Conseil Général de la Martinique; hygiene research and analysis of human blood and food and water; entomology; immunology of parasitic diseases; Pres. of Gen. Ccl CLAUDE LISE; Dir Dr J. M. P. LAFAYE.

Libraries and Archives
Fort-de-France

Archives Départementales de la Martinique: 19 ave Saint-John-Perse, BP 649, 97263 Fort-de-France Cedex; tel. 5-96-63-88-46; fax 5-96-70-04-50; e-mail archives@cg972.fr; f. 1949; 12,000 vols; Dir DOMINIQUE TAFFIN.

Bibliothèque Schoelcher: 1 rue de la Liberté, BP 640, 97264 Fort-de-France Cedex; tel. 5-96-70-26-67; fax 5-96-72-45-55; e-mail bibliothèque.schoelcher@cg972.fr; internet www.cg972.fr/biblio_schoelcher/html/default.htm; f. 1883; attached to Le Conseil Général de la Martinique; promotes study and research in heritage and modernity, literary and scientific culture of the city; 226,000 vols; Dir ANIQUE SYLVESTRE; Adjoint Dir LUCIEN PAVILLA.

Schoelcher

Bibliothèque Universitaire Antilles Guyane, Service Commun de la Documentation: BP 7210, 97275 Schoelcher Cedex; tel. 5-96-72-75-30; fax 5-96-72-75-27;

e-mail sylvain.houdebert@univ-ag.fr; internet www.univ-ag.fr/buag/main.php; f. 1972; admin. HQ for the 3 brs of the univ. library (see also French Guiana and Guadeloupe); 100,000 vols, 738 periodicals; Dir of SCDUAG SYLVAIN HOUDEBER; Dir of Martinique Br. MARIE-FRANCE GROUVEL.

Museums and Art Galleries

Anse-Turin

Gauguin Art Centre and Museum: Anse-Turin; tel. 5-96-78-22-66; historical site; art and history museum; art of famous painter Gaugin.

Fort-de-France

Musée Départemental d'Archéologie Précolombienne et de Préhistoire de la Martinique: 9 rue de la Liberté, 97200 Fort-de-France; tel. 5-96-71-57-05; fax 5-96-73-03-80; e-mail musarc@cg972.fr; f. 1971; prehistory of Martinique; archaeological colls; Dir CÉCILE CELMA.

Musée Régional d'Histoire et d'Ethnographie: 10 blvd du Général de Gaulle, 97200 Fort-de-France; tel. 5-96-72-81-87; fax 5-96-63-74-11; e-mail cr.972.musées@wanadoo.fr; internet www.cr-martinique.fr; f. 1999; attached to Conseil Régional Martinique; displays furnishings, antiques, a gallery of traditional costumes and jewellery, as well as numerous paintings and engravings (18th and 19th centuries) retracing briefly the historical milestones of the island and the history of Saint-Pierre and Fort-de-France; attached library specializing in works on slavery; Curator LYNE-ROSE BEUZE.

Riviere-Pilote

L'Ecomusée (The Living Museum): Anse Figuier, 97211 Riviere-Pilote; tel. 5-96-62-79-14; fax 5-96-62-73-77; internet www.cr-martinique.fr; f. 1993 by Asscn Martiniquaise de Promotion et de Protection des Arts et Traditions Populaires; attached to Conseil Régional Martinique; displays prehistory to present-day Native America; beginnings of French colonialism; economy-oriented cultures of cotton, tobacco and indigo; slave-period crops of sugar cane, coffee, and cocoa; central factories; advent of the banana economy; Conservateur LYNE-ROSE BEUZE.

Trois-Ilets

La Savane des Esclaves: Quartier La Ferme, 97229 Trois-Ilets; tel. 5-96-68-33-91; e-mail lasavanedesesclaves@wanadoo.fr; restored habitat that displays the way of life of slaves who fled the plantations to seek refuge in nature.

Maison De La Canne (House of Cane): Quartier Valable, 97229 Trois-Ilets; tel. 5-96-68-31-68; fax 5-96-68-42-69; internet www.cr-martinique.fr; f. 1987; attached to Conseil Régional Martinique; history and devt of sugar cane products; Conservator LYNE-ROSE BEUZE; Documentalist MARIE-JOSÉ SYLVESTRE.

University

UNIVERSITÉ DES ANTILLES ET DE LA GUYANE

Campus de Shoelcher, BP 7209, 97275 Schoelcher Cedex

Telephone: 5-90-48-91-98

Fax: 5-90-48-92-78

E-mail: vp-cur-gpe@univ-ag.fr

Internet: www.univ-ag.fr

Public control

(See also under French Guiana and Guadeloupe)

Pres.: PASCAL SAFFACHE

Vice-Pres. for Martinique: PHILIPPE SAINT CYR

Library: see Libraries and Archives
Number of teachers: 158
Number of students: 5,607

TEACHING AND RESEARCH UNITS

Arts and Humanities: Dean: CORINNE MENCE-CASTER

Law and Economics: Dean: JUSTIN DANIEL

NEW CALEDONIA

Regulatory Bodies

GOVERNMENT

Department of Cultural and Customary Affairs: 8 rue de Sébastopol, BP T5, 98852 Nouméa; tel. 26-97-66; fax 26-97-67; e-mail secretariat.dacc@gouv.nc; internet www.gouv.nc/portal/page/portal/gouv/annuair-e_administration/administration/daccnc; Min. EPÉRI 'DÉWÉ' GORODEY; Dir RÉGIS VENDEGOU.

Department of Education: 19 ave du Maréchal Foch, Immeuble Foch, BP 8244, 98807 Nouméa; tel. 23-96-00; fax 27-29-21; e-mail denc@gouv.nc; internet www.denc.gouv.nc; Dir JACQUES BRIAND; Sec. SANDRA SERCAN.

Department of Vocational Training: 19 ave du Maréchal Foch, BP 110, 98845 Nouméa; tel. 24-66-22; fax 28-16-61; e-mail dfpc@gouv.nc; internet www.dfpc.gouv.nc; Min. PIERRE NGAIHONI.

Learned Societies

GENERAL

Groupe de Recherche en Histoire Océanienne Contemporaine (GRHOC) (Research Group for the Modern History of Oceania): BP R4, 98845 Nouméa; tel. 26-58-58; e-mail angleviel@univ-nc.nc; f. 1996; historical and anthropological research; devt of regional research; 10 mems; Pres. (vacant); publs *101 Mots pour Comprendre* (1 a year), *Annales d'Histoire Calédonienne* (1 a year).

HISTORY, GEOGRAPHY AND ARCHAEOLOGY

Société d'Etudes Historiques de la Nouvelle-Calédonie (New Caledonia Society for Historical Studies): BP 63, 98845 Nouméa; tel. 76-71-55; e-mail seh_nc@lagoon.nc; f. 1968; research and study of the past; heritage conservation; publishes books and periodicals on history, prehistory, Melanesian society; close contact with the univs of the Pacific area; 200 mems; archives; Pres. GABRIEL VALET; publ. *Bulletin* (4 a year).

LANGUAGE AND LITERATURE

Association des Ecrivains de Nouvelle-Calédonie (Writers' Association of New Caledonia): 8 rue Paul Monchovet, Pointe Brunelet, BP 712, 98800 Nouméa; e-mail contact@ecrivains-nc.net; internet www.ecrivains-nc.net; f. 1996; exchanges ideas and promotes writing in all its forms; 27 mems; Pres. JEAN VANMAI; Vice-Pres. NICOLAS KURTOVITCH; Treas. MARC BOUAN; Sec. CLAUDE MAILLAUD.

Research Institutes

GENERAL

Institut de Recherche pour le Développement (IRD) (Institute of Research for Development): Centre de Nouméa, 101 Promenade Roger Laroque, Anse Vata, BP A5, 98848 Nouméa Cedex; tel. 26-10-00; fax 26-43-26; internet www.ird.nc; f. 1946; agropedology, archaeology, botany and plant ecology, geology, geophysics, hydrology, microbiology, pharmacology, phytopathology and applied zoology, physical and biological oceanography; library of 12,500 vols, 150 periodicals; Dir FABRICE COLIN; Commr and Dir of the Centre for South Pacific CATHERINE HARTMANN (acting); Asst Dir ANNE-SOPHIE IHOPU; publs *Earth Sciences, Life Sciences, Sea Sciences, Social Sciences*; (see main entry under France).

EDUCATION

Centre de documentation pédagogique de Nouvelle-Calédonie (New Caledonia Centre for Pedagogic Documentation): Immeuble Flize, 6 rue Carcopino, BP 215, 98845 Nouméa Cedex; tel. 24-28-34; fax 28-31-13; e-mail librairie@cdp.nc; internet www.cdp.nc; f. 1978 fmrly Centre Territorial de Recherche et de Documentation Pédagogiques de Nouvelle-Calédonie; research in education; library of 12,000 vols, 800 video tapes, 2,200 slide serials; Pres. IVES MELET; Dir CHRISTIAN LUCIEN; Sec.-Gen. HENRI TOURNACHE.

MEDICINE

Institut Pasteur de Nouvelle Calédonie (Pasteur Institute of New Caledonia): 9–11 ave Paul Doumer, BP 61, 98845 Nouméa Cedex; tel. 27-26-66; fax 27-33-90; e-mail direction@pasteur.nc; internet www.institutpasteur.nc; f. 1913 as Institut de Microbiologie de Nouvelle-Calédonie, name changed to Institut Pasteur de Nouméa 1954, present name 1990; medical analysis laboratory; research laboratory: dengue fever, leptospirosis, tuberculosis; library of 1,080 vols; Dir Prof. SUZANNE CHANTEAU; Exec. Sec. SIDAVY SABOT; publ. *Rapport technique* (1 a year).

RELIGION, SOCIOLOGY AND ANTHROPOLOGY

Coordination pour l'Océanie des Recherches sur les Arts, les Idées et les Littératures (CORAIL): BP 2448, 98846 Nouméa Cedex; fax 25-95-27; f. 1987; studies francophone and anglophone literatures and civilizations of the South Pacific; annual themed conference; Pres. VÉRONIQUE FILLIOL; Sec. JACQUES VERNAUDON; publ. *Actes du Colloque* (1 a year).

Libraries and Archives
Nouméa

Bibliothèque Bernheim (Bernheim Library): BP G1, 98848 Nouméa Cedex; tel. 24-20-90; fax 27-65-88; e-mail contact@bernheim.nc; internet www.bernheim.nc; f. 1901; public library (adults and children); record library; historical, ethnological collns of 2,500 vols dealing with New Caledonia and the Pacific Islands; associated with the Bibliotheque Nationale de France for the colln of legal deposit; 141,000 vols, 28,500 vols of children's books, 85 periodicals; Librarian J. F. CARREZ-CORRAL.

Secretariat of the Pacific Community Library: 95 Promenade Roger Laroque, Anse Vata, BP D5, 98848 Nouméa Cedex; tel. 26-20-00; fax 26-38-18; e-mail library@spc.int; internet www.spc.int/library; f. 1947; SPC Nouméa reference library: collns on health, women, youth, statistics, demography, cultural policy, agriculture, forestry, fisheries, and economic and social devt in the Pacific Islands; br. library in Suva, Fiji: holds six collns serving the forestry regional office,

maritime programme, community education centre, regional media centre, agriculture and adolescent reproductive health; 40,000 regional and int. publs in French, English and other Pacific languages; Librarian ELEANOR KLEIBER; Archivist ROBERT APPEL; publs *New Additions to the Library* (4 a year), *Select List of Publications* (1 a year).

Service des Archives de Nouvelle Calédonie (New Caledonia Archive Service): 3 rue Félix Raoul Thomas, Nouville, BP 525, 98845 Nouméa Cedex; tel. 26-60-20; fax 27-12-92; e-mail archives@gouv.nc; internet www.archives.gouv.nc; f. 1987; manages the historical and administrative archives of the territory; 7,000 vols, 5,196 linear m of archives; Dir JACQUES ANCEY (acting).

Museums
Nouméa

Musée de l'Histoire Maritime (Museum of Maritime History): 11 ave James Cook, BP 1755, 98845 Nouméa Cedex; tel. 26-34-43; fax 28-68-21; e-mail mdhm@canl.nc; internet www.patrimoine-maritime.asso.nc; f. 1999; attached to Patrimoine Maritime de Nouvelle Calédonie; preserves and displays collns from archaeological underwater excavations carried out by the Fortunes de Mer Calédoniennes and Assn Salomon.

Musée de Nouvelle-Calédonie (Museum of New Caledonia): BP 2393, 98846 Nouméa Cedex; 45 ave du Maréchal Foch, Nouméa; tel. 27-23-42; fax 28-41-43; e-mail smp@gouv.nc; f. 1971; colln of 4,500 items; emblematic wooden sculptures, masks, ritual dance costumes, jewellery, pottery and other objects reflecting cultural practices and religious beliefs; Dir MARIE-SOLANGE NEAOUTYINE.

University

UNIVERSITÉ DE LA NOUVELLE-CALÉDONIE
(University of New Caledonia)

BPR 4, 98851 Nouméa Cedex
Telephone: 26-58-00

Fax: 25-48-29
E-mail: president@univ-nc.nc
Internet: www.univ-nc.nc

Founded 1999 from the New Caledonia centre of the fmr Université Française du Pacifique
State control
Academic year: February to November

Pres.: JEAN-MARC BOYER
First Vice-Pres.: YANNICK LERRANT
Second Vice-Pres.: JÉRÔME AUPLAT
Sec.-Gen.: ODILE BOYER
Registrar: THIERRY MABRU
Library Dir: PHILIPPE BESNIE

Library of 34,000 books, 350 periodicals
Number of teachers: 70
Number of students: 2,300

Publication: *UNC-Info* (12 a year)

Depts of arts, economics and management, languages and humanities, law, science and technology.

Colleges

Conservatoire National des Arts et Métiers (National Conservatory of the Arts and Crafts): 15 rue de Verdun, Immeuble CCI, 2ième étage, BP 3562, 98846 Nouméa Cedex; tel. 28-37-07; fax 27-79-96; e-mail noucnam@offratel.nc; internet cnam.nc; f. 1794; attached to the Conservatoire National des Arts et Métiers in Paris; higher technical education; 12 staff; 500 students; Pres. JEAN BEGAUD; Dir BERNARD SCHALL; Dir-Gen. CHRISTIAN FOREST; Dir for Teaching HENRI CHARLES.

Institut de Formation des Maîtres de Nouvelle-Calédonie (Institute of Teacher Training of New Caledonia): 14 rue Pierre Sauvan, BP 8036, 98807 Nouméa; tel. 26-45-41; fax 26-28-50; e-mail cp@ifmnc.nc; internet www.ifmnc.nc; f. 1990, present status 2001; continuing education for teachers; Dir CHANTAL MANDAOUÉ; Sec.-Gen. MICHEL PIOT.

RÉUNION

Learned Societies
GENERAL

Académie de la Réunion: 24 ave Georges Brassens, Le Moufia, 97702 St-Denis Messag. Cedex 9; tel. 2-62-48-10-10; fax 2-62-28-69-48; e-mail communication.secretariat@ac-reunion.fr; internet www.ac-reunion.fr; f. 1913; 25 mems; Rector MOSTAFA FOURAR; Deputy Rector BERNARD ZIER; Sec.-Gen. EUGÈNE KRANTZ; publ. *Bulletin*.

HISTORY, GEOGRAPHY AND ARCHAEOLOGY

Association Historique Internationale de l'Océan Indien: c/o Archives Départe-

mentales de la Réunion, 4 rue Marcel Regnol, 97490 St-Denis; f. 1960; 86 mems; Pres. CL. WANQUET; Sec.-Gen. B. JULLIEN; publ. *Bulletin de Liaison et d'Information* (2 a year).

Research Institutes
AGRICULTURE, FISHERIES AND VETERINARY SCIENCE

CIRAD la Réunion: Station de la Bretagne, BP 20, 97408 St-Denis Messag. Cedex 9; tel. 2-62-52-80-00; fax 2-62-52-80-01; e-mail dir-reg.reunion@cirad.fr; internet www.cirad.fr/reunion; f. 1962; attached to CIRAD Agricultural Research for Devt (France); agro-

nomic research, mainly on sugar cane, fruit, vegetables, maize and fodder crops; water management and prevention of soil erosion; 181 staff, 55 researchers; 6 research stations; 1,180 publs; library of 5,000 vols; Regional Dir GILLES MANDRET; Dir for Environmental Risk, Agriculture and Integrated Management of Resources PAUL FALLAVIER; Dir for Plant Protection BERNARD REYNAUD; Dir for Quality of Agricultural and Tropical Food Productions ERIC CARDINALE.

ECONOMICS, LAW AND POLITICS

Institut National de la Statistique et des Études Économiques–Direction Régionale de la Réunion (National Institute of

Statistics and Economic Studies–Regional Directorate of Réunion): 10 rue Demarne, BP 13, 97408 St-Denis Cedex 9; tel. 2-62-48-89-63; fax 2-62-48-89-89; internet www.insee.fr/fr/insee_regions/reunion/home/home_page.asp; f. 1966; attached to INSEE, Paris (see main entry in chapter on France); produces statistical data, economic studies; database with 10,000 bibliographical references on the region, data bank with 2,000 chronological series; Dir JEAN GAILLARD; publs *L'Economie de la Réunion* (4 a year), *Tableau Economique de la Réunion* (1 a year).

HISTORY, GEOGRAPHY AND ARCHAEOLOGY

CRESOI Centre d'Histoire de l'Université de la Réunion Histoire, Politique et Patrimoine (CRESOI Centre of History University of Reunion Island History, Politics and Heritage): Univ. of Reunion, Rue René Cassin, 97400 St-Denis; e-mail cresoi@centre-histoire-ocean-indien.fr; internet www.centre-histoire-ocean-indien.fr; f. 2001; attached to Univ. de La Réunion; researches colonization, decolonization, heritage, history of slavery, industrial tourism, political and cultural history, tourism; Dir Prof. YVAN COMBEAU; publ. *Revue Historique de l'Océan Indien*.

NATURAL SCIENCES

Association Réunionnaise de Développement de l'Aquaculture: Z. I. Les Sables, BP 16, 97427 Etang-Salé; tel. 2-62-26-50-82; fax 2-62-26-50-01; e-mail arda.reunion@wanadoo.fr; internet www.arda.fr; f. 1991 by the Conseil Régional de La Réunion; inland and marine aquaculture; study and devt of aquatic environments.

Libraries and Archives

St-Denis

Bibliothèque Centrale de Prêt de la Réunion: 1 pl. Joffre, 97400 St-Denis; tel. 2-62-21-03-24; fax 2-62-21-41-30; e-mail bdp@cg974.fr; f. 1956; 100,000 vols; Dir ELISABETH DÉGON.

Bibliothèque Départementale de la Réunion: 52 rue Roland Garros, 97400 St-Denis; tel. 2-62-21-13-96; fax 2-62-21-54-63; e-mail bdr@cg974.fr; f. 1855; 95,000 vols; Dir ALAIN VAUTHIER.

Service Commun de la Documentation (Bibliothèque Universitaire): Université de la Réunion, 15 ave René Cassin, BP 7152, 97715 St-Denis Cedex 9; tel. 2-62-93-83-79; fax 2-62-93-83-64; e-mail scd@univ-reunion.fr; internet bu.univ-reunion.fr; f. 1971; attached to Univ. de la Réunion; arts, economics, human sciences, law, management, medicine, politics, social sciences, science; 171,252 vols, 1,495 current periodicals, 3,000 online periodicals; special collns on the Indian Ocean islands; Library Dir ANNE-MARIE BLANC.

St-Pierre

Mediathèque Raphaël Barquissau: Rue du Collège Arthur, BP 396, 97458 St-Pierre Cedex; tel. 2-62-96-71-96; fax 2-62-25-74-10; e-mail ksl@mediatheque-saintpierre.fr; internet www.mediatheque-saintpierre.fr; f. 1967; 130,000 vols, 190 periodicals, more than 530 ancient books, 12,000 CDs, 2,500 videotapes; Dir and Chief Librarian LINDA KOO SEEN LIN.

Ste-Clotilde

Archives Départementales de La Réunion: 4 rue Marcel Pagnol, Champ-Fleuri, 97490 St-Clotilde; tel. 2-62-94-04-14; fax 2-62-94-04-21; internet www.cg974.fr/culture/index.php/archives/présentation-archives/archives-departementales.html; f. 1946; public and private sources of history on Bourbon Island and Réunion French dept; some Mauritius island archives on microfilms for French period; 5,000 vols, 150,000 items in public and private archives; Dir NADINE ROUAYROUX.

Museums and Art Galleries

St-Denis

Muséum d'Histoire Naturelle: Jardin de l'Etat, 97400 St-Denis; tel. 2-62-20-02-19; fax 2-62-21-33-93; e-mail museum@cg974.fr; internet www.cg974.fr; f. 1855, fmrly the Legislative Palace built by the East India Co; zoology and mineralogy; permanent colln of rocks, minerals, wildlife from the Indian Ocean region; library of 7,000 vols; Dir S. RIBES.

Musée Léon-Dierx: 28 rue de Paris, 97400 St-Denis; tel. 2-62-20-24-82; fax 2-62-21-82-87; e-mail musee.dierx@cg974.fr; internet www.cg974.fr/culture; f. 1911, old bldg destroyed 1963, museum reopened to the public 1965, colln and reserves reinstated 1970; fine arts; colln of contemporary art, installations and videos; library: literature on featured artists, history of art, catalogues, monographs, essays and articles; Curator LAURENCE LECIEUX.

St-Gilles-les-Hauts

Musée Historique de Villèle:; e-mail valerie.sinama@cg974.fr Domaine Panon-Desbassyns, 97435 St-Gilles-les-Hauts; tel. 2-62-55-64-10; fax 2-62-55-51-91; e-mail musee.villele@cg974.fr; internet www.cg974.fr/index.php/culture-et-sport/les-musees/musee-historique-de-villele.html; f. 1974; 18th-century plantation house and adjoining properties; French East India Co furniture and china, prints, models, weapons, documents; Curator JEAN BARBIER.

St-Leu

Musée Stella Matutina: 6 allée des Flamboyants, 97424 St Leu; tel. 2-62-34-16-24; e-mail com.seml@wanadoo.fr; f. 1991 as museum, fmr sugar cane factory built 1855, closed 1978, bought and restored by Réunion Island dept 1986; dedicated to sugar cane production and other agricultural products like coffee, spices and vanilla; a laboratory that teaches the art of smelling and creating fragrances.

University

UNIVERSITÉ DE LA RÉUNION

15 ave René Cassin, BP 7151, 97715 St-Denis Messag. Cedex 9

Telephone: 2-62-93-80-80

Fax: 2-62-93-80-13
E-mail: ur.com@univ-reunion.fr
Internet: www.univ-reunion.fr
Founded 1970, present status 1982
Pres.: Prof. SERGE SVIZZERO
Vice-Pres.: Prof. GWENHAËL PONNAU
Vice-Pres. for Admin.: Prof. MOHAMED ROCHDI
Vice-Pres. for Int. Relations: Prof. LAURENT SERMET
Vice-Pres. for Research Devt: Prof. PATRICK BACHELERY
Vice-Pres. for Science: Prof. SERGE SVIZZERO
Vice-Pres. for Students: BRUNO RASSABY
Vice-Pres. for Studies and Univ. Life: Dr GILLES LAJOIE
Dir of South Campus: Prof. JEAN-CLAUDE GATINA
Librarian: ANNE-MARIE BLANC
Library: see Service Commun de la Documentation, Réunion
Number of teachers: 370
Number of students: 12,000

DEANS

Faculty of Arts and Humanities: Prof. GUY FONTAINE
Faculty of Law and Economics: Prof. JEAN-BAPTISTE SEUBE
Faculty of Science and Technology: Prof. JEAN-PIERRE CHABRIAT

Colleges

Ecole Supérieure d'Ingénieurs Réunion Océan Indien: ESIROI-IDAI, Parc Technologique Universitaire, 2 rue Joseph Wetzell, 97490 St Clotilde; tel. 2-62-48-33-44; fax 2-62-48-33-48 ESIROI-CODE, 117 rue du Général Ailleret, 97430 Le Tampon; tel. 2-62-57-91-60; fax 2-62-57-95-51 ESIROI-STIM, 15, ave René Cassin, BP 7151, 97715 St-Denis Messag. Cedex 9; tel. 2-62-52-89-06; fax 2-62-52-89-05; e-mail secretariat.stim@univ-reunion.fr; internet esiroi.univ-reunion.fr; attached to Univ. de la Réunion; depts of integrated agri-food innovation and development (IDAI), sustainable construction and environment (CODE), telecommunications services, computer and multimedia (STIM); Dir for Integrated Agri-Food Innovation and Development (ESIROI-IDAI) Dr MIREILLE FOUILLAUD.

Institut d'Administration des Entreprises de La Réunion: 24–26 ave de la victoire, BP 7151, 97715 St-Denis Messag. Cedex 9; tel. 2-62-21-16-26; fax 2-62-21-48-56; e-mail iae@univ-reunion.fr; internet www.iae-reunion.fr; f. 1998; attached to Univ. de la Réunion; industry research; devt of science and management techniques; Dir Prof. MICHEL BOYER; Exec. Sec. VERONIQUE ROCHE.

Institut Universitaire de Technologie: 40 ave de Soweto, Terre Ste, BP 373, 97410 St-Pierre; tel. 2-62-96-28-70; fax 2-62-96-28-79; e-mail iut.contact@univ-reunion.fr; internet www.univ-reunion.fr/universite/composantes/iut.html; attached to Univ. de la Réunion; depts of biological engineering, business management and administration, civil engineering, network telecommunications; Dir FRANCK LUCAS.

GABON

The Higher Education System

Gabon gained its independence from France in 1960, and the higher education system still reflects its French heritage; many students also go to France to attend university or receive technical training. The first institutions of higher education were a polytechnic institute and law school associated with the Central African Higher Education Foundation, created in 1961 by the heads of state of the former French Equatorial Africa. Université Omar Bongo, the first university, was founded in 1970 and adopted its current name in 1978. The other two universities are Université des Sciences et Techniques de Masuku (founded 1986) and Université des Sciences de la Santé (founded 2002). Higher education is highly centralized and controlled mostly by the State, which subsidizes each student for about 95% of the cost of education and provides financial aid equivalent to 40% of the total budget allocation for higher education. Student fees represent only 3% of income. In 1998/99 there were some 7,473 people enrolled in tertiary education.

Admission to higher education is dependent upon award of the Baccalauréat, the main secondary school qualification. University-level degrees are divided into three cycles. The first cycle lasts for two years and leads to the award of Diplôme Universitaire d'Etudes Littéraires, Diplôme Universitaire d'Etudes Scientifiques, Diplôme Universitaire d'Etudes Juridiques, or Diplôme Universitaire d'Etudes Economicas. A further year of study (three in total) leads to the award of the Licence; alternatively, a further two years (four in total) leads to the Maîtrise; these degrees comprise the second cycle. Some professional titles, such as Diplôme d'Ingénieur and the Doctorat en Médecine, are awarded after five to six years of study. Finally, the third cycle consists of diploma programmes offered by professional institutions, admission to which is conditional on the Maîtrise. Higher vocational education is offered by professional schools and institutes.

Higher education has contributed significantly to Gabon's development. Graduates operate effectively at all levels of public and private administration. However, the recent increase in student numbers and the lack of sufficient funds are likely to have an adverse affect on the quality of both teaching and research. Despite this, higher education is still viewed as an investment that benefits all levels of society.

Regulatory Bodies

GOVERNMENT

Ministry of Culture: BP 1007, Libreville; tel. 76-32-33; Minister PAUL MBA ABBESOLE.

Ministry of National and Higher Education: BP 6, Libreville; tel. 72-44-61; fax 72-19-74; Minister of National Education MICHEL MENGA M'ESSONE; Minister of Higher Education DIEUDONNÉ PAMBOU.

Learned Societies

GENERAL

UNESCO Office Libreville: BP 2183, Libreville; Cité de la Démocratie, Bâtiment 6, Libreville; tel. (1) 762879; fax (1) 762814; designated Cluster Office for Republic of Congo, Democratic Republic of Congo, Equatorial Guinea, Gabon, São Tomé e Príncipe; Dir MAKHILY GASSAMA.

LANGUAGE AND LITERATURE

Alliance Française: BP 1371, Port Gentil; tel. and fax (2) 565941; offers courses and exams in French language and culture and promotes cultural exchange with France.

Research Institutes

GENERAL

Centre National de la Recherche Scientifique et Technologique (CENAREST): BP 13354, Libreville; tel. (1) 732578; internet www.cenarest.org; f. 1976; principal research body; designs and operates research programmes into human sciences, tropical ecology, agronomy, medicinal plants and plant biotechnology; consists of 5 research institutes: l'Institut de Pharmacopée et de Médecine Traditionnelles; l'Institut de Recherches Agronomiques et Forestières; l'Institut de Recherches en Ecologie Tropicale; l'Institut de Recherches en Sciences Humaines; and l'Institut des Recherches Technologiques; Dir SAMUEL MBADIGA.

AGRICULTURE, FISHERIES AND VETERINARY SCIENCE

Centre Technique Forestier Tropical, Section Gabon: BP 149, Libreville; f. 1958; silviculture, technology, genetic improvement; library of 500 vols; Dir J. LEROY DEVAL.

Institut de Recherches Agronomiques et Forestières (IRAF): BP 2246, Libreville; tel. (1) 732375; fax (1) 732378; e-mail angoye@assala.com; internet www.cenarest .org/instituts/iraf; f. 1977; attached to Centre National de la Recherche Scientifique et Technologique (CENAREST); research into agronomy, silviculture and forestry; Dir ALFRED NGOYE.

MEDICINE

Centre International de Recherches Médicales de Franceville: BP 769, Franceville; tel. (2) 677096; fax (2) 677295; e-mail faxcirmf@cirmf.sci.ga; f. 1979; undertakes basic and applied research in medical parasitology (e.g. malaria, filariosis, trypanosomiasis) and viral diseases (incl. HIV/AIDS, Ebola); library of 1,800 vols, 72 periodicals, 20,000 microfiches; Dir-Gen. Prof. PHILIPPE BLOT.

Institut de Pharmacopée et de Médecine Traditionnelle (IPHAMETRA): BP 1935, Libreville; tel. (1) 734786; fax (1) 732578; internet www.cenarest.org/instituts/ iphametra; f. 1976; attached to Centre National de la Recherche Scientifique et Technologique (CENAREST); Dir Dr HENRI PAUL BOUROBOU.

NATURAL SCIENCES

Biological Sciences

Institut de Recherche en Ecologie Tropicale (IRET): BP 13354, Makokou; tel. (1) 443319; internet www.cenarest.org/instituts/ iret; f. 1979; attached to Centre National de la Recherche Scientifique et Technologique (CENAREST); Dir PAUL POSSO.

RELIGION, SOCIOLOGY AND ANTHROPOLOGY

Institut de Recherches en Sciences Humaines (IRSH): BP 846, Libreville; tel. (1) 734719; internet www.cenarest.org/ instituts/irsh; f. 1976; attached to Centre National de la Recherche Scientifique et Technologique (CENAREST); Dir Dr MAGLOIRE MOUNGANGAI.

TECHNOLOGY

Bureau de Recherches Géologiques et Minières (BRGM): BP 175, Libreville; f. 1960; Dir M. BERTUCAT; (See main entry under France).

Institut de Recherches Technologiques (IRT): BP 14070, Libreville; tel. (1) 733089; internet www.cenarest.org/instituts/irt; f. 1976; attached to Centre National de la Recherche Scientifique et Technologique (CENAREST); Dir Dr JEAN DANIEL MBEGAI.

Libraries and Archives

Libreville

Bibliothèque du Centre d'Information: BP 750, Libreville; f. 1960; 6,000 vols; 80 current periodicals.

Direction Générale des Archives Nationales, de la Bibliothèque Nationale et de la Documentation Gabonaise (DGABD): BP 1188, Libreville; tel. (1) 736310 (Archives Nationales); tel. (1) 730972 (Bibliothèque Nationale); tel. (1) 737247 (Documentation Gabonaise); f. 1969 (Nat. Archives and Nat. Library), 1980 (Gabonese Documentation); 36 mems; 29,000 vols, 2,000 periodical titles; 2 linear km archives, 639 microfilms, 666 maps and plans, 1,712 archive photographs; Archives Dir JÉRÔME ANGOUME-NGOGHE; Nat. Library Dir JEAN MICHEL NOUDODO; Documentation Dir JEAN PAUL MIFOUNA; Dir-Gen. RENÉ GEORGES SONNET-AZIZE.

Museum

Libreville

Musée National des Arts et Traditions du Gabon: BP 4018, Libreville; tel. (1) 761456; national museum; thematic exhibition on Gabonese masks; public library on arts from Gabon; Dir Prof. PAUL ABA'A NDONG.

Universities

UNIVERSITÉ OMAR BONGO

BP 13 131, Blvd Léon M'Ba, Libreville
Telephone: (1) 732045
E-mail: uob@internetgabon.com
Internet: www.uob.ga
Founded 1970, renamed 1978
State control
Language of instruction: French
Academic year: October to July
Rector: JEAN-ÉMILE MBOT
Vice-Rector for Academic Affairs and Research: JÉRÔME KWENZI-MAKALA
Vice-Rector for Admin. and Inter-University Cooperation: JÉRÔME NDZOUNGOU
Sec.-Gen.: GUY ROSSATANGA-RIGNAULT
Librarian: FERDINAND NGOUNGOULOU
Library of 12,000 vols
Number of teachers: 300
Number of students: 4,800
Publications: *Cahiers Gabonais d'Anthropologie, Cahiers d'Histoire et d'Archéologie, Exchorésis, Gabonica, Kilombo, Psychologie et Culture, Revue Gabonaise des Sciences de l'Homme, Revue Gabonaise des Sciences du Langage, Waves*

DEANS

Faculty of Law and Economics: Prof. JEAN JACQUES EKOMIE

Faculty of Letters and Sciences: GUY SERGE BIGNOUMBA

ATTACHED RESEARCH INSTITUTES

Centre d'Etudes en Littérature Gabonaise: Dir HÉMERY-HERVAIS SIMA EYI.

Centre d'Etudes et de Recherches d'Histoire Économique, Administrative et Financière (CERHEAF): Dir Prof. PIERRE NDOMBI.

Centre d'Etudes et de Recherches du Monde Anglophone (CERMA): Dir DANIEL RENÉ AKENDENGUE.

Centre d'Etudes et de Recherches Philosophiques (CERP): Dir GILBERT ZUE NGUEMA.

Centre de Recherches Afro-Hispaniques (CRAHI): Dir GISÈLE AVOME MBA.

Centre de Recherches et d'Etudes en Psychologie (CREP): Dir THÉODORE KOUMBA.

Groupe de Recherches en Langues et Cultures Orales (GRELACO): Dir Prof. JAMES DUPLESSIS EMEJULU.

Institut Cheikh Anta Diop (ICAD): Dir GRÉGOIRE BIYOGO NANG.

Laboratoire d'Analyse Spatiale et des Environnements Tropicaux (LANASPET): Dir GALLEY YAWO.

Laboratoire de Graphique et de Cartographie (LAGRAC): Dir Dr JULES DJEKI.

Laboratoire National d'Archéologie (LANA): Dir MICHEL ATHANASE LOCKO.

Laboratoire Universitaire de la Tradition Orale (LUTO): Dir Prof. FABIEN OKOUE-METOGO.

Politiques et Développement des Espaces et Sociétés de l'Afrique Subsaharienne (CERGEP): Dir MARC LOUIS ROPIVIA.

UNIVERSITÉ DES SCIENCES DE LA SANTÉ

BP 18231, Owendo, Libreville
Telephone: (1) 702028

Fax: (1) 702919
E-mail: rectorat@uss-univ.com
Founded 2002
State Control
Rector: ANDRÉ MOUSSAVOU-MOUYAMA
Courses in health sciences.

UNIVERSITÉ DES SCIENCES ET TECHNIQUES DE MASUKU

BP 901, Franceville
Telephone: (2) 677449
Fax: (2) 677520
Founded 1986
State control
Language of instruction: French
Rector: JACQUES LEBIBI
Vice-Rector for Academic Affairs and Research: BERTRAND M'BATCHI
Vice-Rector for Admin. Affairs and Inter-university Cooperation: Prof. AMBROISE EDOU MINKO
Sec.-Gen.: Dr GEORGES AZZIBROUCK
Librarian: YVES NTOUTOUME
Library of 11,000 vols
Number of teachers and researchers: 110
Number of students: 800

DEAN

Faculty of Sciences: Dr LÉON NGADI

Colleges

Ecole Interprovinciale de Santé: BP 530, Mouila; tel. (2) 861177; f. 1981; 18 teachers; 76 students; Dir PIERRE FRANKLIN NGUEMA ONDO.

Institut Africain d'Informatique: BP 2263, Libreville; tel. (1) 720005; fax (1) 720011; e-mail info@iai.ga; internet www.iai.ga; f. 1971 by member states of OCAM to train computer programmers, computer science engineers and analysts; small library; 8 permanent teachers; 281 students; Dir FABIEN MBALLA.

GAMBIA

The Higher Education System

Higher education, in the sense of an institution offering Bachelors, Masters and Doctorate degrees, did not exist in Gambia until 1995. Prior to this, Gambians wishing to pursue higher education could either study abroad or enrol at a post-secondary institution, the main such institutions being the Gambia College and the Gambia Technical Training Institute. A University Extension Programme was established in 1995 as a collaborative effort between the Government and the Nova Scotia Gambia Association (NSGA), a Canadian NGO, and Saint Mary's University (located in Halifax, Nova Scotia). The first university, the University of The Gambia, Banjul, was opened in 1999, with the assistance of Saint Mary's University. The higher education sector in Gambia is administered and funded by the Government. Some 1,591 students were enrolled at tertiary establishments in 1994/95 but by 2007 the number was 8,373. In addition to the tertiary institutions, there are about 103 registered Skills Training Centres providing courses towards local and external certificates and diplomas in a variety of professional fields. These are mainly privately operated centres.

Admission to university is on the basis of the West African Secondary School Certificate or equivalent qualification. The University of The Gambia offers Bachelors degrees, which are awarded following four years. Until recently, there were no postgraduate degree courses, but in 2007 a Master of Arts degree programme in history was introduced. Technical and vocation education is offered by the Gambia Technical Training Institute and Gambia College. The main qualifications are the Diploma and Certificate.

A higher education policy is being developed following the establishment of the new Department of State for Higher Education, Research and Science in early 2007. In the interim, the tertiary and higher education component of the Education Policy 2004–2015, prepared by the Department of State for Education, is being used to guide the activities of the new Department of State.

Regulatory Bodies
GOVERNMENT

Department of State for Education: Willy Thorpe Bldg, Banjul; tel. 4227236; fax 4224180; internet www.edugambia.gm; Sec. of State FATOU L. FAYE.

Department of State for Higher Education, Research and Science: Banjul; Sec. of State ABDOULIE SALLAH.

Department of State for Tourism and Culture: New Administrative Bldg, The Quadrangle, Banjul; tel. 4227593; fax 4227753; e-mail masterplan@gamtel.gm; Sec. of State ANGELA COLLEY.

Learned Society
LANGUAGE AND LITERATURE

Alliance Franco-Gambienne: Kairaba Ave, Kanifing, POB 2930, Serrekunda, Banjul; tel. 4375418; fax 4374172; e-mail alliancefg@hotmail.com; internet www .alliancefranco.gm; offers courses and exams in French language and culture and promotes cultural exchange with France.

Research Institutes
MEDICINE

Medical Research Council: POB 273, Banjul; Atlantic Blvd, Fajara; tel. 4496715; fax 4494154; e-mail aoffong@mrc.gm; internet www.mrc.gm; f. 1947; laboratory research, field research and clinical studies aimed at reducing illness and death from tropical infectious diseases; research on viral diseases, bacterial diseases and malaria; a nutrition research group is based at the MRC Keneba Field Site; Unit Dir and Chair. Prof. TUMANI CORRAH.

Medical Research Council Dunn Nutrition Unit, Keneba: Keneba, West Kiang; f. 1974; field station of the Dunn Nutrition Unit laboratory in Cambridge, UK; research on maternal undernutrition, including work on paediatric gastroenterology and nutrition, and the physiological adaptation of mothers to pregnancy and lactation; maternal vitamin and mineral requirements; research into long-term effects of antenatal and early postnatal nutrition; research on growth deficiency and the role of economic status on malnutrition; calorimetry research on comparisons of energy expenditure between Gambians and Europeans; Supervisor Dr ELIZABETH POSKITT.

Library
Banjul

Gambia National Library: Department Mail Bag, Reg Pye Lane, Banjul; tel. 4228312; fax 4223776; f. 1946 by British Ccl, taken over by Govt 1962, autonomous 1985; serves as a public and nat. library; nat. deposit library; 115,400 vols, 85 periodicals; spec. colln of Gambiana; Dir ABDOU WALLY MBYE; publs *National Bibliography*, *Wax Taani Xalel Yi* (children's magazine).

Museum
Banjul

Gambia National Museum: PMB 151, Independence Drive, Banjul; tel. 4226244; fax 4227461; e-mail musmon@qanet.gm; library of 645 vols; f. 1982; Curator HASSOUM CESSAY.

University
UNIVERSITY OF THE GAMBIA

Administration Bldg, Kanifing, POB 3530, Serrekunda
Telephone: 4372213
Fax: 4395064
E-mail: unigambia@qanet.gm
Internet: www.unigambia.gm
Founded 1999
State control
Academic year: October to July (two semesters)
Vice-Chancellor: Prof. DONALD E. U. EKONG
Registrar: E. J. AKPAN
Student Affairs: LAMIN S. JAITEH
Senate: LANG SAJO MUSTAPHA JADAMA
Council: MOMODOU LAMIN TARRO
Number of teachers: 99 (78 full-time, 21 part-time)
Number of students: 1,356

DEANS

Faculty of Economics and Management Sciences: SULAYMAN M. B. FYE
Faculty of Humanities and Social Sciences: Prof. EDRIS MAKWARD
Faculty of Medicine and Allied Health Sciences: Prof. ETIM M. ESSIEN
Faculty of Science and Agriculture: Prof. FELIXTINA JONSYN-ELLIS (acting)

College

Gambia College: Brikama Campus, POB 144, Banjul; tel. 4484812; fax 4483224; e-mail gcollege@qanet.gm; f. 1978; library: 23,000 vols; 57 teachers; 400 students; Pres. A. B. SENGHORE; Registrar N. S. MANNEH

HEADS OF SCHOOLS

Agriculture: EBRIMA CHAM (acting)
Education: W. A. COLE
Nursing and Midwifery: F. SARR
Public Health: B. A. PHALL

GEORGIA

The Higher Education System

Georgia was formerly a constituent republic of the USSR, from which it gained its independence in 1999. Most institutions were founded during the Soviet period and consequently reflected Soviet practices, but since independence there have been numerous reforms and ongoing projects. The Law of Education (2004) laid out further plans for the reform of secondary and higher education, including implementation of the Bologna Process. In addition to state institutions, many private institutions of higher education were opened after 1991; there were 109 in 2008/09. In 2008/09 there were 93,637 students enrolled at institutions of higher education (including universities). Higher education is administered by the Ministry of Education and Science.

Higher education admissions are determined on the basis of performance in the Unified National University Entry Examinations, administered by the National Assessment and Examinations Centre. Students take a range of compulsory and voluntary subjects relevant to their intended path of study. In

May 2005 Georgia signed up to the Bologna Process. It is intended that Georgia will have a new degree structure in place by 2007/08 consisting of Bachelors, Masters and Doctorate degrees, and that the European Credit Transfer System (ECTS) will be adopted to facilitate student transfers. The Bakalavris Diplomi (Bachelors) is the main undergraduate degree and is awarded after three to fours years' study. The older, Soviet-style Certified Specialist degree is still awarded in some (mainly) professional fields. A Masters degree is awarded after the Bachelors following two years of study. A new doctoral degree is being developed to replace the old-style Candidate of Science and Doctor of Science degrees.

Since 2004 the accreditation of institutes of higher education has been the responsibility of the State Accreditation Service (SAS). Full institutional accreditation is only granted when institutions have completed a full self-evaluation and have satisfied the standards of the SAS with regard to the quality of their programmes, the quality of their teaching and the quality of their physical environment.

Regulatory and Representative Bodies

GOVERNMENT

Ministry of Culture: 0108 Tbilisi, Pr. Rustaveli 37; tel. (32) 93-22-55; fax (32) 99-90-37; e-mail info@mcs.gov.ge; internet www.mcs.gov.ge; Minister NIKA VACHEISHVILI.

Ministry of Education and Science: 0102 Tbilisi, D. Uznadze 52; tel. (32) 95-70-10; fax (32) 91-04-47; e-mail pr@mes.gov.ge; internet www.mes.gov.ge; Minister GIA NODIA.

ACCREDITATION

ENIC/NARIC Georgia: Div. of Academic Recognition and Mobility, Min. of Education and Science, 0102 Tbilisi, D. Uznadze 52; tel. (32) 95-75-23; fax (32) 96-98-21; e-mail mobility_division@yahoo.com; Head Dr IRAKLI MACHABELI.

Learned Societies

GENERAL

Georgian Academy of Sciences: 0108 Tbilisi, Pr. Rustaveli 52; tel. (32) 99-88-91; fax (32) 99-88-23; e-mail frg@gw.acnet.ge; internet www.acnet.ge; f. 1941; depts of Agricultural Science Problems (Academ-ician-Sec. O. G. NATISHVILI), Applied Mech-anics, Machine Building and Control Processes (Academician-Sec. M. E. SALIK-VADZE), Biology (Academician-Sec. G. KVESI-TADZE), Chemistry and Chemical Technology (Academician-Sec. G. G. GVELESIANI), Earth Sciences (Academician-Sec. E. P. GAMKRE-LIDZE), Linguistics and Literature (Academ-ician-Sec. T. GAMKRELIDZE), Mathematics and Physics (Academician-Sec. J. LOMINADZE), Physiology and Experimental Medicine (Academician-Sec. T. N. ONIANI), Social Sci-ences (Academician-Sec. G. B. TEVZADZE); 135 mems (66 academicians, 69 corresp.); attached research institutes: see Research Institutes; library: see Libraries and Arch-ives; Pres. Acad. Prof. Dr THOMAS V. GAMK-RELIDZE; publs *Metsnierba da Technika* (12 a

year), *Moambe* (Bulletin, in Georgian and English, 12 a year).

HISTORY, GEOGRAPHY AND ARCHAEOLOGY

Georgian Geographical Society: 0107 Tbilisi, Ketskhoveli 11; attached to Georgian Acad. of Sciences; Chair. V. SH. DZHAOSHVILI.

Georgian History Society: 0108 Tbilisi, Pr. Rustaveli 52; attached to Georgian Acad. of Sciences; Vice-Chair. A. M. APAKIDZE.

LANGUAGE AND LITERATURE

Amateur Society of Basque Language and Culture: 0108 Tbilisi, Pr. Rustaveli 52; attached to Georgian Acad. of Sciences; Chair. SH. V. DZIDZIGURI.

British Council: 0108 Tbilisi, Pr. Rustaveli 34; tel. (32) 25-04-07; fax (32) 98-95-91; e-mail office@ge.britishcouncil.org; internet www.britishcouncil.org.ge; offers courses and examinations in English language and Brit-ish culture and promotes cultural exchange with the UK; Dir JO BAKOWSKI; Librarian TAMUNA KVACHADZE.

Goethe-Institut: 0108 Tbilisi, ul. Sandukeli 16; tel. (32) 93-89-45; fax (32) 93-45-68; internet www.goethe.de/ins/ge/tif/deindex .htm; offers courses and examinations in German language and culture and promotes cultural exchange with Germany; library of 3,500 vols; Dir UWE RIEKEN.

MEDICINE

Georgian Bio-Medico-Technical Society: 0103 Tbilisi, Telavi 51; attached to Georgian Acad. of Sciences; Chair. K. SH. NADAREISH-VILI.

Georgian Neuroscience Association: c/o Beritashvili Institute of Physiology, 0160 Tbilisi, Gotua St 14; tel. (32) 37-21-50; fax (32) 37-12-31; e-mail nodmit@biphysiol.ge; internet www.itic.org.ge/gena; f. 1996; 105 mems; Pres. Prof. SIMON KHECHINASHVILI; Exec. Sec. Prof. Dr NODAR MITAGVARIA.

Georgian Society of Patho-Anatomists: 0103 Tbilisi, V. Pshavela 27в; attached to

Georgian Acad. of Sciences; Chair. T. I. DEKANOSIDZE.

NATURAL SCIENCES

Biological Sciences

Georgian Botanical Society: 0107 Tbilisi, Kodzhorskoe shosse; attached to Georgian Acad. of Sciences; Chair. G. SH. NAKHUTS-RISHVILI.

Georgian Society of Biochemists: 0177 Tbilisi, Universitetis 2; tel. (32) 30-39-97; fax (32) 22-11-03; f. 1958; attached to Georgian Acad. of Sciences; 850 mems; Pres. Prof. NOUGZAR ALEKSIDZE; Sec. NANA ABASHIDZE.

Georgian Society of Geneticists and Selectionists: 0160 Tbilisi, ul. L. Gotua 3; tel. (32) 37-42-27; attached to Georgian Acad. of Sciences; Chair. T. G. CHANISHVILI.

Georgian Society of Parasitologists: 0179 Tbilisi, Pr. Chavchavadze 31; tel. (32) 22-33-53; fax (32) 22-01-64; attached to Geor-gian Acad. of Sciences; f. 1958; 83 mems; Pres. Prof. B. E. KURASHVILI; Sec. K. G. NIKOLAISHVILI; publ. *Actual Problems of Parasitology in Georgia*.

Physical Sciences

Georgian Geological Society: 0108 Tbilisi, Pr. Rustaveli 52; tel. (32) 99-64-45; fax (32) 99-88-23; f. 1933; attached to Georgian Acad. of Sciences; 500 mems; Chair. IRAKLI P. GAMKRELIDZE.

Georgian National Speleological Soci-ety: 0193 Tbilisi, M. Aleksidze (Bl. 8); tel. (32) 33-74-49; fax (32) 33-14-17; f. 1980; attached to Georgian Acad. of Sciences; 75 mems; Chair. Z. K. TATASHIDZE; publ. *Caves of Georgia* (irregular).

PHILOSOPHY AND PSYCHOLOGY

Georgian Philosophy Society: 0108 Tbi-lisi, Pr. Rustaveli 29; attached to Georgian Acad. of Sciences; Chair. N. Z. CHAVCHA-VADZE.

Georgian Society of Psychologists: 0179 Tbilisi, Janashvili 22; attached to Georgian Acad. of Sciences; Chair. N. Z. NADIRASHVILI.

Research Institutes

GENERAL

Kutaisi Scientific Centre: 4600 Kutaisi, Abashidze 22; tel. (331) 7-77-77; attached to Georgian Acad. of Sciences; Dir R. ADAMAI.

AGRICULTURE, FISHERIES AND VETERINARY SCIENCE

Gulisashvili, V. Z., Institute of Mountain Forestry: 0186 Tbilisi, E. Mindeli 9; tel. (32) 30-34-66; e-mail postmaster@forest.acnet.ge; f. 1945; attached to Georgian Acad. of Sciences; Dir G. N. GIGAURI.

Institute of Water Management and Engineering Ecology: 0162 Tbilisi, Pr. Chavchavadze 60; tel. (32) 22-72-00; fax (32) 22-74-01; e-mail tsotnem@rambler.ru; f. 1929; attached to Georgian Acad. of Sciences; Dir T. MIRTSHOULAVA; publs *Proceedings, Recent Problems of Water Management, Transactions of International Conferences.*

Scientific Research Centre of the Biological Basis of Cattle-Breeding: 0162 Tbilisi, Paliashvili 87; tel. (32) 29-40-03; f. 1991; attached to Georgian Acad. of Sciences; Dir A. DOLMAZASHVILI.

ARCHITECTURE AND TOWN PLANNING

Kiriak Zavriev Institute of Structural Mechanics and Earthquake Engineering: 0193 Tbilisi, M. Aleksidze 8; tel. (32) 33-59-28; fax (32) 33-27-52; e-mail info@ismee.ge; internet ismee.ge; f. 1947; attached to Georgian Acad. of Sciences; Dir Prof. P. REKVAVA.

BIBLIOGRAPHY, LIBRARY SCIENCE AND MUSEOLOGY

Kekelidze, K. S., Institute of Manuscripts: 0193 Tbilisi, Merab Aleksidze St, Korp. 3; tel. (32) 36-24-54; fax (32) 94-25-18; e-mail manuscript@iatp.org.ge; internet www.acnet.ge/manuscr.htm; f. 1958; attached to Georgian Acad. of Sciences; Dir Z. ALEKSIDZE; publ. *Mravaltavi* (philology and history, 1 a year).

ECONOMICS, LAW AND POLITICS

Gugushvili, P. V., Institute of Economics: 0105 Tbilisi, ul. Kikodze 22; tel. (32) 99-68-53; fax (32) 99-83-89; e-mail root@econom.acnet.ge; f. 1944; attached to Georgian Acad. of Sciences; Dir G. TSERETELI.

Institute of Political Science: 0162 Tbilisi, Paliashvili 87; tel. (32) 22-41-04; e-mail politic@gw.acnet.ge; f. 2000; attached to Georgian Acad. of Sciences; Dir V. KESHELAVA.

Institute of State and Law: 0105 Tbilisi, ul. Kikodze 14; tel. (32) 98-32-45; e-mail root@stlow.acnet.ge; f. 1957; attached to Georgian Acad. of Sciences; Dir (vacant).

FINE AND PERFORMING ARTS

Chubinashvili, G. N., Institute of History of Georgian Art: 0108 Tbilisi, Pr. Rustaveli 52; tel. (32) 99-05-88; f. 1941; attached to Georgian Acad. of Sciences; Dir T. SAKVARELIDZE; publ. *Ars Georgica.*

HISTORY, GEOGRAPHY AND ARCHAEOLOGY

Ivane Javakhishvili Institute of History and Ethnology: 0179 Tbilisi, ul. Melikishvili 10; tel. (32) 99-06-82; e-mail histend55@yahoo.com; f. 1941; attached to Georgian Acad. of Sciences; scientific researches in ancient and modern history; confs, seminars; library of 55,000 vols; Dir Prof. Dr VAZHA I. KIKNADZE; publ. *Proceedings of the Institute of History and Ethnology* (1 a year).

Lordkipanidze Centre for Archaeological Studies: 0102 Tbilisi, D. Uznadze 14; tel. (32) 95-97-65; attached to Georgian Acad. of Sciences.

Mtskheta Institute of Archaeology: 3300 Mtskheta; f. 1994; attached to Georgian Acad. of Sciences; Dir A. APAKIDZE; publ. *Mtskheta.*

Vakhushti Bagrationi Institute of Geography: 0193 Tbilisi, M. Aleksidze 1 (Bl. 8); tel. (32) 33-74-49; fax (32) 33-14-07; e-mail geograf@gw.acnet.ge; f. 1933; attached to Georgian Acad. of Sciences; library of 68,000 vols; Dir ZURAB TATASHISZE; publ. *Caves of Georgia* (irregular).

LANGUAGE AND LITERATURE

Chikobava, A. S., Institute of Linguistics: 380002 Tbilisi, P. Ingorokva St 8; tel. (32) 93-29-21; internet www.acnet.ge/ike .htm; e-mail root@ike.acnet.ge; f. 1941; attached to Georgian Acad. of Sciences; Dir G. KVARATSKHELIA; publs *Dialectological Studies, Etymological Studies, Iberian-Caucasian Linguistics, Problems of Georgian Language Structure, Problems of Georgian Literary Norms, Problems of Modern General Linguistics.*

Shota Rustaveli Institute of Georgian Literature: 0108 Tbilisi, Kostava St 5; tel. (32) 99-53-00; fax (32) 99-53-00; e-mail litinst@litinstituti.ge; internet www .litinstituti.ge; f. 1932; attached to Georgian Acad. of Sciences; Georgian literature; literature theory and folklore; Dir Prof. IRMA RATIANI; Deputy Dir Prof. MAKA ELBAKIDZE; publs *Literary Researches* (1 a year), *Litinfo* (electronic), *Sjani* (peer-reveiwed int. journal of literary theory and comparative literature, 1 a year).

Tsereteli, G. V., Institute of Oriental Studies: 0103 Tbilisi, ul. G. Tsereteli 3; tel. (32) 23-23-72; fax (32) 23-30-08; e-mail root@orient.acnet.ge; f. 1960; attached to Georgian Acad. of Sciences; Dir T. GAMKRELIDZE.

MEDICINE

Beritashvili Institute of Physiology: 0160 Tbilisi, ul. Gotua 14; tel. (32) 37-12-31; fax (32) 37-34-11; e-mail info@biphysiol.ge; internet www.biphysiol.ge; f. 1935 as Academic Research Institute; attached to Min. of Education and Science; 100 mems; library of 48,000 vols; Dir Dr M. G. TSAGARELI; Sec N. EMUKHVARI.

Eliyava Institute of Bacteriophage, Microbiology and Virology: 0160 Tbilisi, ul. L. Gotua 3; tel. (32) 37-42-27; fax (32) 99-91-53; e-mail chanish@kheta.ge; f. 1923; attached to Georgian Acad. of Sciences; Dir T. CHANISHVILI.

Georgian Scientific Research Institute of Industrial Hygiene and Occupational Diseases: 0102 Tbilisi, D. Agmashenebeli 60; tel. (32) 95-65-94; f. 1927; library of 24,000 vols; Dir RUSUDAN DJAVAKHADZE; publ. periodicals on occupational hygiene and industrial diseases.

Institute of Medical Biotechnology: 0159 Tbilisi, Chiaureli 2; tel. and fax (32) 54-07-25; e-mail imb_admin@caucasus.net; internet www.imb.org.ge; f. 1991; attached to Min. of Education and Science of Georgia; 63 mems; Dir TEIMURAZ TOPURIA; Head of Scientific Board Assoc. Prof. IA PANTSULAIA.

Institute of Pharmaceutical Chemistry: 0159 Tbilisi, P. Sarajishvili 36; tel. (32) 52-98-50; fax (32) 25-00-26; e-mail root@pharmac.acnet.ge; f. 1932; attached to Georgian Acad. of Sciences; library of 3,500 vols, 40 periodicals; Dir Prof. ETHER P. KEMERTELIDZE; publ. *Transactions.*

Natishvili, A. N., Institute of Experimental Morphology: 0159 Tbilisi, Chiaureli 2; tel. (32) 52-09-06; f. 1946; attached to Georgian Acad. of Sciences; Dir N. A. JAVAKHISHVILI; publ. *Proceedings.*

Research and Teaching Clinical and Experimental Centre of Traumatology and Orthopaedics: 0102 Tbilisi, ul. Kalinina 51; tel. (32) 95-53-81; Dir B. TSERETELI.

Research Institute of Clinical Medicine: 0112 Tbilisi, ul. Tevdore Mgvdeli 13; tel. (32) 94-02-89; fax (32) 34-49-23; f. 1991; Dir Prof. FRIDON TODUA; publ. *Georgian Journal of Radiology* (4 a year).

Research Institute of Psychiatry: 0177 Tbilisi, ul. M. Asatiani 10; tel. (32) 39-47-65; fax (32) 94-36-73; f. 1925; library of 8,000 vols, 7,000 periodicals.

Research Institute of Skin and Venereal Diseases: 0112 Tbilisi, ul. Ninoshvili 55; tel. (32) 95-35-64; fax (32) 96-48-02; f. 1935; library of 23,800 vols; Dir Dr BADZI CHLAIDZE; publ. *Trudy* (Proceedings, 1 a year).

Scientific Research Centre for Radiobiology and Radiation Ecology: 0103 Tbilisi, Telavi 51; tel. (32) 94-20-17; fax (32) 93-61-26; e-mail kiazo@gw.acnet.ge; internet www.acnet.ge/radiobio; f. 1990; attached to Georgian Acad. of Sciences; Dir K. SH. NADAREISHVILI; publs *Biomedical Techniques* (2 a year), *Problems of Ecology* (2 a year), *Radiation Studies* (2 a year).

Virsaladze Institute of Medical Parasitology and Tropical Medicine: 0112 Tbilisi, D. Agmashenebeli 139; tel. (32) 95-92-26; e-mail medpari@yahoo.com; internet geoparasitology.dsl.ge; f. 1924; parasitic and tropical diseases; Dir GIA CHUBABRIA; Deputy Dir NINO IASHVILI.

Zhordania Institute of Human Reproduction: 0109 Tbilisi, Kostava 43; tel. (32) 99-61-97; fax (32) 99-81-08; e-mail archil@list .ru; Dir Prof A. KHOMASSURIDZE.

NATURAL SCIENCES

Biological Sciences

Batumi Botanical Gardens: 6400 Makhinjauri; f. 1912; attached to Georgian Acad. of Sciences; Dir V. PAPUNIDZE; publ. *Bulletin.*

Central Botanical Gardens: 0105 Tbilisi, Botanikuri 1; tel. and fax (32) 72-34-09; f. 1636; attached to Georgian Acad. of Sciences; Dir J. KERESELIDZE; publ. *Proceedings.*

Davitashvili, L. Sh., Institute of Palaeobiology: 0108 Tbilisi, Niagvris 4; tel. (32) 93-12-82; e-mail guram@paleobi.acnet.ge; f. 1957; attached to Georgian Acad. of Sciences; Dir G. A. MCHEDLIDZE.

Durmishidze Institute of Plant Biochemistry: 0102 Tbilisi, D. Agmashenebeli 10; tel. (32) 95-81-45; fax (32) 25-06-04; e-mail postmaster@biochem.acnet.ge; f. 1971; attached to Georgian Acad. of Sciences; library of 72,000 vols; Dir Prof. Dr G. I. KVESITADZE.

Institute of Molecular Biology and Biological Physics: 0160 Tbilisi, ul. L. Gotua 14; tel. (32) 37-17-33; fax (32) 93-91-57; e-mail admin@biophys.org.ge; f. 1986; attached to Georgian Acad. of Sciences; Dir Dr M. M. ZAALISHVILI.

Institute of Zoology: 0179 Tbilisi, Pr. Chavchavadze 31; tel. (32) 22-01-64; f. 1941; attached to Georgian Acad. of Sciences; Dir I. ELIYAVA.

Ketskhoveli, N., Institute of Botany: 0105 Tbilisi, Kojori 1; tel. (32) 99-74-48; fax (32) 00-10-77; e-mail nakhutsrishvili@yahoo .com; f. 1933; attached to Georgian Acad. of Sciences; Dir G. NAKHUTSRISHVILI.

Mathematical Sciences

Muskhelishvili Institute of Computational Mathematics: 0171 Tbilisi, Akuri 8; tel. (32) 33-24-38; e-mail root@compmath.acnet.ge; f. 1956; attached to Georgian Acad. of Sciences; Dir Prof. N. VAKHANIYA; publs *Computational Mathematics and Programming*, *Mathematical and Technical Cybernetics*.

Razmadze, A., Mathematical Institute: 0193 Tbilisi, M. Aleksidze 1; tel. (32) 33-45-95; fax (32) 36-40-86; e-mail ninopa@rmi.acnet.ge; internet www.rmi.acnet.ge; f. 1935; attached to Min. of Education and Science; 70 mems; library of 95,690 vols; Dir Prof. NINO PARTSVANIA; publs *Georgian Mathematical Journal* (in English, 4 a year), *Memoirs on Differential Equations and Mathematical Physics* (in English, 3 a year), *Proceedings* (in English, 3 a year).

Physical Sciences

Abastumani Astrophysical Observatory: 0301 Abastumani, Kanobili Mountain; tel. (32) 95-53-67 0179 Tbilisi, ul. Kazbegi 2A; tel. (32) 37-63-03; e-mail roki@gw.acnet.ge; f. 1941; attached to Georgian Acad. of Sciences; Dir R. KILADZE; publ. *Bulletin*.

Andronikashvili Institute of Physics: 0162 Tbilisi, ul. Tamarashvili 6; f. 1950; attached to Georgian Acad. of Sciences; Dir G. A. KHARADZE.

Dzanelidze, A. I., Geological Institute: 0193 Tbilisi, M. Aleksidze 1 bldg 9; tel. (32) 29-39-41; e-mail geolog@gw.acnet.ge; f. 1925; attached to Georgian Acad. of Sciences; incorporates Scientific and Technical Centre of Physical Crystallography; Dir Prof. MIRIAN TOPCHISHVILI; publ. *Proceedings* (irregular).

Ferdinand Tavadze Institute of Metallurgy and Materials Science: 1060 Tbilisi, Al. Kazbegi Ave 15; tel. (32) 37-02-67; fax (32) 37-02-67; e-mail info@mmi.ge; internet mmi.ge; f. 1945; attached to Georgian Acad. of Sciences; main fields of research: metallurgical processes, new materials and technologies, materials science and powder metallurgy; 136 mems; library of 152,953 vols; Dir Prof. Dr GIORGI F. TAVADZE.

Institute of Geophysics: 0193 Tbilisi, M. Aleksidze 1; tel. (32) 36-37-93; fax (32) 33-28-67; e-mail seismo@ig.acnet.ge; f. 1933; attached to Georgian Acad. of Sciences; incorporates National Service of Seismic Defence; Dir T. L. CHELIDZE.

Institute of Hydrometeorology: 0112 Tbilisi, D. Agmashenebeli 150A; tel. (32) 95-10-47; fax (32) 95-11-60; e-mail root@hydmet.acnet.ge; f. 1953; attached to Georgian Acad. of Sciences; Dir G. G. SVANIDZE; publ. *Transactions*.

Institute of Inorganic Chemistry and Electrochemistry: 0186 Tbilisi, Mindeli 11; tel. (32) 54-15-59; fax (32) 30-14-30; e-mail iice@caucasus.net; internet www.iice-eng.myweb.ge; f. 1956 to explore research opportunities in hydrogen and solar power generation, corrosion-resistant coatings and using uranium filters for water purification; attached to Georgian Acad. of Sciences; main fields of research: electrochemistry, inorganic chemistry, physical chemistry, chemical physics; Dir GRIGOR TATISHVILI.

Ferdinand Tavadze Institute of Metallurgy and Materials Science: 1060 Tbilisi, Al. Kazbegi Ave 15; tel. (32) 37-02-67; fax (32) 37-02-67; e-mail info@mmi.ge; internet mmi.ge; f. 1945; attached to Georgian Acad. of Sciences; main fields of research: metallurgical processes, new materials and technologies, materials science and powder

metallurgy; 136 mems; library of 152,953 vols; Dir Prof. Dr GIORGI F. TAVADZE.

Melikishvili, P. G., Institute of Physical and Organic Chemistry: 0186 Tbilisi, V. Jikia 5; tel. (32) 99-88-23; f. 1929; attached to Georgian Acad. of Sciences; Dir T. ANDRONIKASHVILI.

Transcaucasian Hydrometeorological Research Institute: 0112 Tbilisi, D. Agmashenebeli 150A; tel. (32) 63-74-01; fax (32) 23-22-93.

PHILOSOPHY AND PSYCHOLOGY

Tsereteli Institute of Philosophy: 0108 Tbilisi, Pr. Rustaveli 29; tel. (32) 99-52-62; e-mail root@philos.acnet.ge; attached to Georgian Acad. of Sciences; f. 1946; Dir T. BUACHIDZE.

Uznadze, D. N., Institute of Psychology: 0105 Tbilisi, ul. Iashvili 22; tel. (32) 93-24-54; e-mail root@psycho.acnet.ge; f. 1943; attached to Georgian Acad. of Sciences; Dir SH. NADIRASHVILI.

RELIGION, SOCIOLOGY AND ANTHROPOLOGY

Abuserisdze Tbeli Batumi Scientific Research Institute: 6016 Batumi, Ninoshvili 23; tel. (222) 3-29-01; fax (222) 7-58-17; e-mail isac@batumi.net; f. 1958; attached to Georgian Acad. of Sciences; Dir Dr IURI BIBILEISHVILI; publs *Culture and Life in South-Western Georgia* (1 a year), *Economic Problems in South-Western Georgia* (1 a year), *Folklore of South-Western Georgia* (1 a year), *Monuments of South-Western Georgia* (1 a year).

Institute of Demography and Sociological Studies: 0105 Tbilisi, ul. Pushkina 5; tel. (32) 93-36-93; fax (32) 98-65-88; internet www.acnet.ge/demograph; f. 1990; attached to Georgian Acad. of Sciences; Dir Dr L. L. CHIKAVA; publ. *Demography* (4 a year).

TECHNOLOGY

Eliashvili Institute of Control Systems: 0160 Tbilisi, K. Gamsakhurdia 34; tel. (32) 37-20-44; e-mail postmaster@contsys.acnet.ge; f. 1956; attached to Georgian Acad. of Sciences; library of 10,000 vols; Dir M. SALUKVADZE; publs *Language Processors and Speech Recognition* (1 a year), *Theory and Devices of Automatic Control* (1 a year).

Institute of Cybernetics: 0186 Tbilisi, ul. S. Euli 5; tel. (32) 30-30-49; e-mail inst@cybern.acnet.ge; f. 1960; attached to Georgian Acad. of Sciences; Dir G. KHARATISHVILI.

Institute of Hydrogeology and Engineering Geology: 0188 Tbilisi, Rustaveli Ave 31; tel. (32) 52-72-19; fax (32) 00-11-53; e-mail bguram@gw.acnet.ge; internet www.acnet.ge/hydrogeology_eng.htm; f. 1958; attached to Georgian Acad. of Sciences; Dir G. BUACHIDZE; publ. *Problems of Hydrogeology and Engineering Geology*.

Institute of Machine Mechanics: 0186 Tbilisi, Mindeli 10; tel. (32) 32-39-56; fax (32) 31-52-05; e-mail imm@posta.ge; internet www.argosoft.com/imm; f. 1960; attached to Georgian Acad. of Sciences; Dir ROBERT ADAMIA.

Sukhumi I. N. Vekua Institute of Physics and Technology: 0108 Tbilisi, Pr. Rustaveli 52; tel. and fax (32) 99-69-13; e-mail sipt@myoffice.ge; internet www.sipt.org.ge; f. 1945; attached to Georgian Acad. of Sciences; relocated from Sukhumi due to conflict in Abkhazia; Dir V. KASHIA.

Tbilisi Scientific-Industrial Institute 'Analizkhelsatsko': 0190 Tbilisi, Georgia Kakheti 36; tel. and fax (32) 77-68-22;

e-mail ninodzagania@yahoo.com; f. 1956; attached to Georgian Acad. of Sciences; Dir-Gen. TAMAZ DZAGANIA.

Tsulukidze, G. A., Institute of Mining Mechanics: 0186 Tbilisi, Mindelli 7; tel. (32) 31-91-16; e-mail root@minig.acnet.ge; f. 1957; attached to Georgian Acad. of Sciences; Dir L. A. JAPARIDZE.

Libraries and Archives

Tbilisi

Central Library of the Georgian Academy of Sciences: 0193 Tbilisi, M. Aleksidze 1–4; tel. (32) 36-34-13; fax (32) 33-01-35; e-mail acadlibrary@gw.acnet.ge; f. 1941; 3,200,000 vols; Dir M. ZAALISHVILI.

Mikeladze, G. S., Scientific and Technical Library of Georgia: 0100 Tbilisi, ul. Dzneladze 27; 10,100,000 vols (without patents); Dir R. D. GORGILADZE.

National Library of Georgia: 0107 Tbilisi, Gulisashvili 5; tel. and fax (32) 99-80-95; f. 1846; 6,000,000 vols, 24,000 periodicals; Dir LEVAN BERDZENISHVILI.

Tbilisi 'Javakhishvili' State University Library: 0128 Tbilisi, Pr. Chavchavadze 1; tel. (32) 22-10-32; internet www.tsu.edu.ge; f. 1918; 3,000,000 vols; Dir S. APAKIDZE.

Museums and Art Galleries

Kutaisi

Berdzenishvili, N. A., Kutaisi State Museum of History and Ethnography: 4600 Kutaisi, ul. Tbilisi 1; tel. (331) 5-56-76; f. 1912; attached to Georgian Acad. of Sciences; library of 25,000 vols; Dir Dr M. V. NIKOLEISHVILI.

Sokhumi

Sokhumi Botanical Garden: 6600 Sokhumi, ul. Chavchavadze 20; tel. (122) 2-44-58; attached to Georgian Acad. of Sciences; Dir (vacant).

State Museum of the Abkhazian Autonomous Republic: 6600 Sokhumi, ul. Lenina 22; f. 1915; history of the Abkhazian people; Dir A. A. ARGUN.

Tbilisi

Georgian National Museum: 0105 Tbilisi, 3 Rustaveli Ave; tel. (32) 99-80-22; fax (32) 98-21-33; e-mail info@museum.ge; internet www.museum.ge; f. 1852; history, natural history; attached to Georgian Acad. of Sciences; library of 250,000 vols; Gen. Dir Acad. DAVID LORDKIPANIDZE.

Georgian National Museum—National Gallery of Art: 0108 Tbilisi, Rustaveli Ave 11; tel. (32) 98-48-14; fax (32) 98 21 33; e-mail lanakaraia@yahoo.com; internet www.museum.ge; f. 1920, merged with Georgian National Museum in 2007; Collns of Modern Georgian Art (painting, drawing, sculpture, applied art); Dir-Gen. DAVID LORDKIPANIDZE; Admin. Man. LANA KARAIA.

Georgian State Art Museum: 0107 Tbilisi, Ul. Gulisashvili 1; tel. (32) 99-66-35; f. 1920; Dir NODAR LOMOURI.

Georgian State Museum of Oriental Art: 0100 Tbilisi, ul. Azizbekova 3; Georgian fine and applied art; Dir G. M. GVISHIANI.

State Museum of Georgian Literature: 0108 Tbilisi, Giorgi Chanturia 10; tel. (32) 99-86-67; f. 1930; Georgian literature since 19th century; library of 11,893 vols; Dir I. A. ORDZHONIKIDZE; publ. *Literary Chronicle*.

Tbilisi State Museum of Anthropology and Ethnography: 0100 Tbilisi, Pr. Komsomolskii 11; history and ethnography of Georgia; library of 150,000 vols; Dir A. V. TKESHELASHVILI.

Universities

ABKHAZIAN 'A. M. GORKII' STATE UNIVERSITY

6600 Sokhumi, ul. Tsereteli 9

Telephone: (122) 2-25-98

Founded 1985

State control

Number of students: 3,800

Faculties of biology and geography, economics, history and law, philology, physics and mathematics, teacher training.

AKAKI TSERETELI STATE UNIVERSITY

4600 Kutaisi, Tamar Mepe St 59

Telephone: (331) 4-57-84

Fax: (331) 4-38-33

E-mail: atsu@atsu.edu.ge

Internet: atsu.edu.ge

Founded 1933

State control

Rector: GIORGI ONIANI

Number of teachers: 437

Number of students: 5,987

DEANS

Faculty of Arts: Prof. NINO CHIKHLADZE

Faculty of Exact and Natural Sciences: Assoc. Prof. EREKLE JAPARIDZE

Faculty of Maritime Transport: Prof. ZURAB ARKANIA

Faculty of Medicine: Prof. BORIS CHAKVE-TADZE

Faculty of Pedagogics: Prof. GOGI BERDZU-LISHVILI

Faculty of Social Science: Assoc. Prof. GODERDZI VACHRIDZE

Faculty of Technical Engineering: Prof. AVTANDIL TVALCHRELIDZE

Faculty of Technological Engineering: Prof. MERAB SHALAMBERIDZE

BATUMI 'M. ABASHIDZE' STATE INSTITUTE OF CULTURE

6000 Batumi, Tamaris Dasaheba

Telephone: (222) 5-02-64

Founded 1992

State control

Rector: GAIOZ JORDANIA (acting)

Vice-Rector for Academic Affairs: NODAR VARSHANIDZE

Faculties of art research, ballet, cinema, drama, fine arts, musical disciplines, television and radio journalism.

BATUMI 'RUSTAVELI' STATE UNIVERSITY

6010 Batumi, Ninoshvili 35

Telephone: (222) 7-17-80

Fax: (222) 7-17-86

E-mail: info@bsu.edu.ge

Internet: bsu.edu.ge

Founded 1935

State control

Rector: NUGZAR MGELADZE

Faculties of biology, economics, education, foreign languages, geography, history, initial military education and physical culture, medicine, philology, physics and mathematics.

GEORGIAN ACADEMY OF PHYSICAL EDUCATION

0179 Tbilisi, Pr. Chavchadze 49

Telephone: (32) 22-31-60

Fax: (32) 29-37-59

Founded 1938

State control

Rector: OMAR GOGIASHVILI.

GEORGIAN STATE ACADEMY OF ANIMAL HUSBANDRY AND VETERINARY MEDICINE

0114 Tbilisi, Krtsanisi

Telephone: (32) 72-04-49

Fax: (32) 99-50-91

Founded 1932

State control

Rector: JEMAL GUGUSHVILI

Vice-Rector: ROMAN TSAGAREISHVILI.

GEORGIAN TECHNICAL UNIVERSITY

0171 Tbilisi, ul. M. Kostava 77

Telephone: (32) 44-11-66

Fax: (32) 44-11-66

E-mail: intrelgu@yahoo.com

Internet: www.gtu.edu.ge

Founded 1990 (1922 as Georgia Polytechnic Institute)

State control

Languages of instruction: Georgian, Russian, English

Academic year: September to June

Rector: Prof. R. KHURODZE

Vice-Rector: Prof. ARCHIE PRANGISHVILI

Head of Foreign Affairs: TARIEL TAKTAKISH-VILI

Head of Teaching and Methodology: O. ZUMBURIDZE

Librarian: V. PAPASKIRI

Number of teachers: 2,050

Number of students: 28,000

Publication: *Agmshenebeli* (newspaper)

DEANS

Faculty of Architecture: G. MIKIASHVILI

Faculty of Aviation: S. TEPNADZE

Faculty of Basic Sciences: T. DADIANI

Faculty of Chemical Engineering: N. KUTSLAVA

Faculty of Civil Engineering: C. LAGUNDAR-IDZE

Faculty of Communication: A. ROBITACHVILI

Faculty of Humanities: K. KOKRASHVILI

Faculty of Hydraulic Engineering: L. GOGELIANI

Faculty of Information Technology: Z. TSVERAIDZE

Faculty of Mechanics and Machine-Building: A. TAVKHELIDZE

Faculty of Metallurgy: N. TSERETELI

Faculty of Mining and Geology: A. ABSHILAVA

Faculty of Power Engineering: G. ARABIDZE

Faculty of Transport: O. GEBASHVILI

GORI STATE UNIVERSITY

1400 Gori, Chavchavadze 53

Telephone: (370) 7-29-97

Fax: (370) 7-32-13

E-mail: gori@ip.osgf.ge

Founded 1935

State control

Rector: GEDEVAN KHELAIA

Vice-Rector for Admin.: JEMALI DZIDZIGURI

Library of 200,000 vols

Depts of auditing, accountancy and statistics, correspondence learning, finance and commerce, foreign languages, history and law, international economic relations, business and management, nature and philology, pedagogics and medicine.

'ILIA CHAVCHAVADZE' STATE UNIVERSITY

0179 Tbilisi, Pr. I. Chavchavadze 32

Telephone: (32) 29-41-97

Fax: (32) 22-00-09

E-mail: uni@iliauni.edu.ge

Internet: www.iliauni.edu.ge

Founded 2006 by merger of Tbilisi 'Ilia Chavchavadze' State Univ. of Language and Culture and Tbilisi 'Sulkhan-Saba Orbeliani' State Pedagogical Univ.

State control

Rector: Prof. GIGI TEVZADZE

Admin. Dir: SERGO RATIANI

DEANS

Faculty of Education: IVANE KALADZE

Faculty of Humanities and Cultural Studies: SHUKIA APRIDONIDZE

Faculty of Life Sciences: GIORGI NAKHUTS-RISHVILI

Faculty of Philology of Foreign Languages: MZIA BAKRADZE

Faculty of Philosophy and Social Sciences: Prof. GIGI TEVZADZE

Faculty of Physics and Mathematics: JUANSHER CHKAREULI

PROFESSORS

Faculty of Education (depts of Correctional Pedagogy and Pre-School Pedagogy, Education Economics and Management, Education Psychology, General Pedagogy, Specific Methods):

IMEDADZE, NATELA

KALADZE, IVANE

KORINTELI, REVAZ

MALAZONIA, DAVID

MAQASHVILI, KETEVAN

SHAVERDASHVILI, EKATERINE

Faculty of Humanities and Cultural Studies (depts of Culture, History, Linguistics, Literary Studies):

APRIDONIDZE, SHUKIA

GHAGHANIDZE, MERAB

KOBALAVA, IZABELA

KOCHLAMAZASHVILI, TAMAZ

LADARIA, NODAR

PITSKHELAURI, KONSTANTINE

Faculty of Life Sciences (dept of Biology):

BADRIDZE, IASON, Ecology of Behaviour

GEGELASHVILI, GIORGI, Molecular and Cellular Biochemistry

KOPALIANI, NATIA, Zoology, Conservative Biology

NAKHUTSRISHVILI, GIORGI, Botany, Ecology

SHATIRISHVILI, AIVENGO, Genetics, Evolutionary Biology

SOLOMONIA, REVAZ, Biochemistry, Physiology

TARKHNISHVILI, DAVID, Ecology, Evolutionary Biology

Faculty of Philology of Foreign Languages (depts of American/English Studies, Comparative Literary Studies, Germanic Studies, Linguoculturology, Oriental Studies, Romance Studies, Slavic Studies):

BAKRADZE, MZIA

DOKHTURISHVILI, MZAGHO

GAJIEV, VALEKH

GOGOLADZE, TEIMURAZ

GVENTSADZE, MZIA

JASHI, KETEVAN

LEBANIDZE, GURAM VAKHTANG

MARSAGISHVILI, REZO

MIKADZE, MZIA

PIRTSKHALAVA, NINO

Faculty of Philosophy and Social Sciences (depts of Economics, International Relations and Security Studies, Journalism, Philosophy, Politology, Psychology, Sociology and Demography):

BERIASHVILI, MAMUKA
DARCHIASHVILI, DAVID
IMEDADZE, IRAKLI
NODIA, GIORGI
SURGULADZE, REVAZ
TEVZADZE, GIGI
TEVZADZE, GURAM
TSULADZE, GIOGI

Faculty of Physics and Mathematics (depts of Mathematics, Physics):

CHKAREULI, JUANSHER
JANGVELADZE, TEMUR
KHARAZISHVILI, ALEXANDRE
KHIMSHIASHVILI, GIORGI
MURUSIDZE, IVANE
SVANADZE, MERAB
TSIBAKHASHVILI, NELI

TBILISI 'JAVAKHISHVILI' STATE UNIVERSITY

0179 Tbilisi, Pr. Chavchavadze 1
Telephone: (32) 22-56-79
Fax: (32) 22-56-79
E-mail: international@tsu.ge
Internet: www.tsu.edu.ge
Founded 1918
State control
Language of instruction: Georgian
Academic year: September to June
Chancellor: ROMAN KHARBEDIA
Rector: Prof. GIORGI KHUBUA
Vice-Rector: Dr IRINE DARCHIA
Head of the Scientific Library: TAMAR NEMSITSVERIDZE
Library: see Libraries and Archives
Number of teachers: 1,340
Number of students: 18,000
Publications: *Proceedings* (4 a year, in 2 series), *Tbilisi University* (52 a year)

DEANS

Faculty Economics and Business: ELENE KHARABADZE
Faculty of Exact and Natural Sciences: RAMAZ BOTCHORISHVILI
Faculty of Humanities: GOCHA JAPARIDZE
Faculty of Law: IRAKLI BURDULI
Faculty of Medicine: ALEXANDER TSISKARIDZE
Faculty of Social and Political Sciences: NODAR BELKANIA

TBILISI STATE INSTITUTE OF CULTURE

0102 Tbilisi, D. Agmashenebeli 40
Telephone: (32) 95-10-50
Fax: (32) 94-37-28
Founded 1992
State control
Rector: TEMUR ZHGENTI
Vice-Rector: VLADIMER KIRVALISHVILI
Faculties of choreography, fine and applied arts, humanities and musicology.

TBILISI STATE MEDICAL UNIVERSITY

0177 Tbilisi, Vazha-Pshavela 33
Telephone: (32) 39-18-79
Fax: (32) 94-25-19
E-mail: iad@tsmu.edu
Internet: www.tsmu.edu
Founded 1918
State control
Academic year: September to June
Rector: Prof. ALEXANDER TELIA

Library of 500,000 vols
Number of teachers: 700
Number of students: 4,000
Publications: *Annals of Biomedical Research and Education* (4 a year), *Georgian Medical News* (12 a year), *Research* (1 a year)

DEANS

Faculty of General Medicine: Prof. RAMAZ SHENGELIA
Faculty of Paediatrics: Prof. GURAM DAVITAIA
Faculty of Pharmacy: Prof. NIKOLOZ GONGADZE
Faculty of Psychotherapy and Psychosomatic Medicine: Prof. RAMZ SAKVARELIDZE
Faculty of Social Care and Management: Prof. BIDZINA ZURASHVILI
Faculty of Stomatology: Prof. GEORGE KIPIANI

TBILISI STATE UNIVERSITY OF ECONOMIC RELATIONS

0144 Tbilisi, Ketevan Tsamebuli 55
Telephone: (32) 94-28-83
Fax: (32) 94-31-60
E-mail: rectori@internet.ge
Founded 1992
State control
Rector: AVTANDIL CHUTLASVILI
Vice-Rector: GURAM TAVARTKILADZE
Library of 29,000
Number of students: 1,811

DEANS

Business Administration: Prof. GELA ALADASHVILI
Law: Prof. VENEDI BENIDZE

TELAVI 'I. GOGEBASHVILI' STATE UNIVERSITY

2200 Telavi, Universitetis 1
Telephone: (350) 7-15-33
Fax: (350) 7-32-64
E-mail: office_teasu@grena.ge
Internet: www.tesau.edu.ge
Founded 1939
State control
Academic year: September to June
Rector: GEORGE GOTSIRIDZE
Head of Admin.: HAMLET RAZMADZE
Head of Quality Assurance Office: TINATIN ZURABISHVILI
Head of Library: NANA KARAULASHVILI
Library of 148,000 vols; 3 periodical titles
Number of teachers: 212
Number of students: 1,652

DEANS

Faculty of Actuarial and Natural Sciences: TEA MCHEDLURI
Faculty of Agriculture and Food Processing: NIKO SULKHANISHVILI
Faculty of Humanities: MALKHAZ TCIRIKIDZE
Faculty of Medicine: LALI MEKOKISHVILI
Faculty of Pedagogical Sciences: NINO NAKHUTSRISHVILI
Faculty of Social Sciences, Business and Law: IRMA SHIOSHVILI

PROFESSORS

BERTLANI, A., Russian Philology
BOKHASHVILI, I., Law
BURDULI, M., Medicine
CHACHANIDZE, G., Informatics
CHANTURIA, E., Law
CHIBURDANIDZE, L., Economics
CHICHIASHVILI, E., Foreign Languages
CHIKADZE, R., Georgian Philology
CHKHARTISHVILI, N., Viti Culture
DOGONADZE, N., Pedagogical Sciences
ELANIDZE, V., History of Georgia
ELIZBARASHVILI, E., Geography

FARSADANISHVILI, A., History of Diplomacy
GELDIASHVILI, N., Georgian Philology
GIGASHVILI, K., Georgian Philology
GIORGADZE, G., Law
GOGOCHURI, N., Georgian Philology
GOTSIRIDZE, G., World History
IANVARASHVILI, L., Philosophy and Social Sciences
JACHVADZE, E., World History
JANASHIA, L., Pedagogical Sciences
JANGULASHVILI, E., Pedagogical Sciences
JAVAKHISHVILI, A., Economics
JAVAKHISHVILI, G., Georgian Philology
JAVAKHISHVILI, M., Chemistry and Technology
KATSITADZE, N., Physical Culture
KHOSITASHVILI, M., Wine Making
KOKILASHVILI, V., Physics and Mathematics
KURATASHVILI, A., Economics
KVASHILAVA, A., Law
MALATSIDZE, V., Medicine
MAMUKELASHVILI, E., Political Studies
MCHEDLISHVILI, D., Physics and Mathematics
MIKELADZE, M., Georgian Philology
MODEBADZE, N., Physics and Mathematics
NADIRADZE, T., Biology and Ecology
NANOBASHVILI, K., Informatics
RAINAULI, Z., Medicine
RCHEULISHVILI, G., History of Georgia
ROSTOMASHVILI, N., Physics and Mathematics
SHALVASHVILI, L., Georgian Philology
SHIOSHVILI, I., Philosophy and Social Sciences
VAKHTANGISHVILI, T., History of Georgia
ZURABISHVILI, T., Philosophy and Social Sciences
ZUROSHVILI, L., Biology and Ecology

TSKHINVALI PEDAGOGICAL INSTITUTE–GEORGIAN SECTOR

Shida Qartli, 1400 Gori, Chavchavadze 57
Telephone: (370) 2-19-35
Founded 1932
State control
Rector: VAHTANG AHALAIA
Vice-Rector: V. BURCHULADZE
Faculties of biology, chemistry and physical training, education, teaching and methods, foreign languages, Georgian language and literature, history and philology, mathematics and physics, natural sciences.

Other Higher Educational Institutes

Georgian 'S. Rustaveli' State Institute of Theatre and Cinematography: 0108 Tbilisi, Pr. Rustaveli 17; tel. (32) 99-94-11; fax (32) 98-30-97; e-mail eliso@geo.net.ge; f. 1939; drama, film, television, stage management, archive management, art history; library: 50,000 vols; 150 teachers; 800 students; Rector Prof. GIGA LORDKIPHANIDZE.

Georgian State Agrarian University: 0131 Tbilisi, D. Agmashenebeli 13-km, Dighomi; tel. (32) 95-71-47; fax (32) 52-00-47; e-mail agrdig@geointer.net.ge; f. 1929 as Georgian Agricultural Institute; present name and status 1991; faculties of agricultural electrification and automation, agricultural mechanization, agronomy, economics and humanities, forestry, hydromelioration and engineering ecology, technology and viticulture; library: 747,600 vols; 583 teachers; 7,500 students; Rector Prof. Dr NAPOLEON KARKASHADZE.

Georgian State Institute of Subtropical Agriculture: 4600 Kutaisi, Pr. Chavchavadze 13; tel. (331) 7-06-14; e-mail ssmsi@sanet.net.ge; faculties of agri-business, agricultural engineering, agriculture and food technology, economics; library: 90,000 vols; Rector GURAM KILASONIA.

Kutaisi 'N. I. Muskhelishvili' Technical University: 4614 Kutaisi, Akhalgazrdobis Gamziri 98; tel. and fax (331) 2-06-90; e-mail vg@posta.ge; f. 1973; institutes of automobile and transport, cybernetics, electrical engineering, food and chemical industry, humanities and economics, mechanical engineering,

technology and design; library: 250,000 vols, 300 periodicals; 360 teachers; 5,600 students; Rector AMIRAN HVADAGIANI.

Tbilisi State Academy of Arts: 0108 Tbilisi, ul. Griboedova 2; tel. and fax (32) 93-69-59; e-mail nanniashuili@posta.ge; f. 1922; faculties of architecture, art history and theory, design, fine arts; library: 42,000 vols; 355 teachers; 1,600 students; Rector Prof. IOSEB KOIAVA; publ. *Works* (1 a year).

Tbilisi 'V. Saradzhishvili' State Conservatoire: 0108 Tbilisi, 8 ul. Griboedova; tel. and fax (32) 99-91-44; e-mail tbil_conservatory@hotmail.com; f. 1917; courses in choral conducting, composition, musicology, orchestral instruments, piano, singing; library: 100,000 vols; 205 teachers; 700 students; Rector Prof. MANANA DOIJASHVILI.

GERMANY

The Higher Education System

During 1949–90 Germany was divided between the sovereign states of the Federal Republic of Germany (FRG) and the German Democratic Republic (GDR). Both states developed their own higher education systems. In the FRG, the Grundgesetz (Basic Law) of 1949 stated that the majority of aspects of the administration and legislation of the education system were the responsibility of the Länder (States). Following reunification in 1990, the former GDR was incorporated into the Federal structure, and adopted the higher education standards already implemented in the former FRG. Higher education thus remains the responsibility of the 16 Länder, and is overseen by the national Kultusministerkonferenz (Standing Conference of the Ministers of Education and Cultural Affairs of the Länder). Higher education is divided between Hochschulen and Fachhochschulen. Hochschulen encompass classical universities (Universität), technical universities (Technische Hochschulen/Universität), combined Hochschulen-Fachhochschulen (Universität-Gesamthochschulen), teacher-training institutes (Pädagogische Hochschulen), theological universities (Theologische Hochschulen), art universities (Kunsthochschulen) and music universities (Musikhochschulen). Fachhochschulen are universities of applied science specializing in technical vocation education and training. In 2005/06 335,961 students were enrolled in higher education (non-university) institutions and 1,953,504 were enrolled in universities and equivalent institutions.

Admission to Hochschulen is based on performance in Zeugnis der Allgemeinen Hochschulreife or Fachgebundene Hochschulreife, and admission to Fachhochschulen depends on Fachhochschulreife, Zeugnis der Allgemeinen Hochschulreife or Fachgebundene Hochschulreife. Germany has implemented the Bologna Process and introduced a two-tier Bachelors and Masters degree system to replace the traditional German degrees in Hochschulen. The Bachelors lasts three to four years and the Masters a further one to two years. Doctoral studies follow the Masters. In Fachhochschulen, the traditional Fachhochschuldiplom (four years) has been retained as, unlike the Bachelors, it involves a large element of practical training; however, both the Bachelors and Masters degrees have been introduced in Fachhochschulen.

Mixed academic and vocational training is also offered by Berufsakademien or Studienakademien, which were first established in Baden-Württemberg in 1974; they are not present in every Land. Students are awarded the Berufsakademien Diplom after a three-year course. Technical and vocational education is offered by different types of institution in addition to the degree-level programmes offered by the Fachhochschulen. An estimated two-thirds of German students of the relevant age attend Berufsschulen, which combine classroom-based instruction and practical experience in a three-year course. Berufsfachschulen specialize in two- to three-year occupational training courses, leading to the award of the titles Facharbeiterbrief (Skilled Worker Certificate), Kaufmannsgehilfenbrief (Clerical Assistant Certificate) and Gesellenbrief (Craftsman Certificate). Berufsoberschulen are only available in some Länder and allow those who have completed secondary education and have acquired at least five years of professional experience to study for the Fachgebundende Hochschulreife, which confers eligibility to enter Hochschulen and Fachhochschulen. Fachschulen provide one- to three-year courses for those who already have previous vocational education and professional experience.

Regulatory and Representative Bodies

GOVERNMENT

Federal Ministry of Education and Research: Hannoversche Str. 28–30, 10115 Berlin; tel. (30) 18570; fax (30) 185783601; e-mail bmbf@bmbf.bund.de; internet www.bmbf.de; Federal Minister ANNETTE SCHAVAN.

Gemeinsame Wissenschaftskonferenz: Friedrich-Ebert-Allee 38, 53113 Bonn; tel. (228) 5402-0; fax (228) 5402-150; e-mail gwk@gwk-bonn.de; internet www.gwk-bonn.de; f. 1970 as Bund-Länder Commission for Educational Planning (Bund-Länder-Kommission für Bildungsplanung) by agreement between the Federal and Länder govts; granted additional functions in 1975 by the Skeleton Agreement on Research Promotion; adopted present name 2008; intergovernmental commission; permanent forum for discussion of all questions of education and research promotion that are of common interest to the Federal and Länder govts; makes recommendations to the Heads of the Federal and Länder govts on educational planning and research promotion; cooperates closely with the various Conferences of Länder Ministers; Chair. Prof. Dr ANNETTE SCHAVAN; Dir JÜRGEN SCHLEGEL.

Kultusministerkonferenz/Die Ständige Konferenz der Kultusminister der Länder in der Bundesrepublik Deutschland (Standing Conference of the Ministers of Education and Cultural Affairs of the Länder): Postfach 2240, 53012 Bonn; Lennéstr. 6, 53113 Bonn; tel. (228) 5010; fax (228) 501777; e-mail poststelle@kmk.org; internet www.kmk.org; f. 1948; conference of ministers and senators of the 16 Länder whose portfolios encompass culture, education, research and training; maintains offices in Berlin; Pres. Dr LUDWIG SPAENLE; Gen. Sec. Prof. Dr ERICH THIES.

ACCREDITATION

Akkreditierungs-, Certifizierungs- und Qualitätssicherungs-Instituts (ACQUIN) (Accreditation, Certification and Quality Assurance Institute): c/o Universität Bayreuth, 95440 Bayreuth; Prieserstr. 2, 95444 Bayreuth; tel. (921) 55-4841; fax (921) 55-4842; e-mail sekr@acquin.org; internet www.acquin.org; f. 2001 as a consequence of the Bologna process and the need for assuring the quality of newly introduced undergraduate and postgraduate degrees in Germany; member-based, non-profit org.; licensed by the Akkreditierungsrat (q.v.) to award its quality seal to study programmes that have successfully undergone accreditation; accreditation of German Bachelors and Masters study programmes in all subject fields based on the expertise of Standing Expert Cttee mems; evaluation and accreditation of selected int. study programmes; int. cooperation and networking; organizes projects and workshops with nat. and int. partners; develops new quality assurance methods; pilot project: 'Process Quality in Teaching and Learning'; Dir Prof. Dr GERD ZIMMERMANN.

Akkreditierungsagentur für Studiengänge der Ingenieurwissenschaften, der Informatik, der Naturwissenschaften und der Mathematik—ASIIN eV: Postfach 10 11 39, 40002 Düsseldorf; Robert-Stolz-Str. 5, 40470 Düsseldorf; tel. (211) 900977-0; fax (211) 900977-99; e-mail info@asiin.de; internet www.asiin.de; f. 1999 as ASII, merged with Akkreditierungsagentur für die Studiengänge Chemie, Biochemie und Chemieingenieurwesen an Universitäten und Fachhochschulen (A-CBC) and adopted present name in 2002; accredited by Akkreditierungsrat since 2002, full member of ENQA since 2007, accepted into EQAR since 2009; not-for-profit branch of ASIIN; official accreditation in Germany since 2002; the only German accreditation agency to be explicitly specialized in accrediting degree programmes in engineering, informatics, natural sciences and mathematics; non-profit, registered asscn; accredited by Akkreditierungsrat (q.v.); represents competence in mechanical engineering, process engineering, civil engineering, surveying, architecture, city and spatial planning, physical technologies, materials and processes, agronomy, nutritional science, landscape architecture, life sciences, physics, electrical engineering, IT, informatics, computer science, business informatics, information systems, industrial engineering, chemistry, geosciences, mathematics as well as in quality management and quality assurance in higher education; also incl. system accreditation and institutional reviews/accreditation; 40 mems; Man. Dir Dr IRING WASSER.

Akkreditierungsagentur für Studiengänge im Bereich Heilpädagogik, Pflege, Gesundheit und Soziale Arbeit eV (AHPGS) (Accreditation Agency for Study Programmes in Special Education, Care, Health Sciences and Social Work): Hebelstr. 29, 79104 Freiburg; tel. (761) 203-5529; fax (761) 203-5516; e-mail sekretariat@ahpgs.de; internet www.ahpgs.de; promotes quality and transparency of German univ. study courses for health and social professionals; works to guarantee uniform and internationally comparable quality standards in the new Bachelors and Masters degrees through accreditation procedures; operates continual information exchange with other nat. and int. accreditation agencies as well as univ. representatives, practicioners' orgs and asscns; mems incl. the dean conference nursing science (33 univs), the assemblies of the depts of social work (73 univs) and remedial education (8 univs) as well as the German Coordinating Agency for Public Health; accredited by the Akkreditierungsrat (q.v.); Dir Prof. Dr JÜRGEN VON TROSCHKE.

Akkreditierungsrat (Accreditation Council): Adenauer Allee 73, 53113 Bonn; tel. (228) 338306-0; fax (228) 338306-79; e-mail akr@akkreditierungsrat.de; internet www.akkreditierungsrat.de; f. 1999 by Kultusministerkonferenz (q.v.) and Hochschulrektorenkonferenz (q.v.); attached to Stiftung zur Akkreditierung von Studiengängen in Deutschland (Foundation for the Accreditation of Study Programmes in Germany); acts on behalf of Länder to accredit accreditation agencies and degree programmes leading to Bakkalaureus/Bachelors and Magister/Masters degrees; financed by Stifterverband für die Deutsche Wissenschaft (q.v.); Man. Dir Dr ACHIM HOPBACH.

AQAS eV/Agentur für Qualitätssicherung durch Akkreditierung von Studiengängen: In der Sürst 1, 53111 Bonn; tel. (228) 90960-10; fax (228) 90960-19; e-mail info@aqas.de; internet www.aqas.de; f. 2002; accredited by Akkreditierungsrat (q.v.); Chair. Prof. Dr DIETER TIMMERMANN; Man. EDNA HABEL.

ENIC/NARIC Germany: Central Office for Foreign Education, Secretariat of the Standing Conference of the Ministers of Education and Cultural Affairs, POB 2240, 53012 Bonn; tel. (228) 501-264; fax (228) 501-229; e-mail zab@kmk.org; internet www.kmk.org/zab; f. 1905; attached to Kultusministerkonferenz (q.v.); Head of Dept BARBARA BUCHAL-HÖVER.

Foundation for International Business Administration Accreditation (FIBAA): Berliner Freiheit 20–24, 53111 Bonn; tel. (228) 280-3560; fax (228) 280-3569; e-mail info@fibaa.org; internet www.fibaa.org; f. 1995; accredits Bachelors, Masters and Diploma courses in fields such as economics, business computing, engineering and business admin., business psychology, business law, etc., in Germany, Austria and Switzerland; provides information and advice on Bachelors and Masters courses to univs, students and private enterprises; maintains offices in Zürich (Switzerland); Man. Dirs HANS-JÜRGEN BRACKMANN, Dr HEINZ-ULRICH SCHMIDT.

FUNDING

Deutscher Akademischer Austauschdienst e V (DAAD) (German Academic Exchange Service): Postfach 200404, 53134 Bonn; Kennedyallee 50, 53175 Bonn; tel.

(228) 882-0; fax (228) 882-444; e-mail postmaster@daad.de; internet www.daad.de; br. office in Berlin; foreign brs in Beijing, Brussels, Cairo, Hanoi, Jakarta, London, Mexico City, Moscow, Nairobi, New Delhi, New York, Paris, Rio de Janeiro, Tokyo, Warsaw; f. 1925; awards scholarships and grants, largely funded from Federal budget, to promote academic and cultural exchange between German and foreign students and thereby encourage closer relations between Germany and other countries; exchange of professors, lecturers in German for foreign universities, IAESTE—student-trainees, scholarships for German and foreign students and graduates; 232 mem. univs; Vice-Pres. Prof. Dr MAX G. HUBER; Gen. Sec. Dr CHRISTIAN BODE; publ. *Change by Exchange* (image brochure and flyers).

NATIONAL BODIES

Deutsche Hochschulverband (DHV) (German Association of University Professors and Lecturers): Rheinallee 18, 53173 Bonn; tel. (228) 90266-66; fax (228) 90266-80; e-mail dhv@hochschulverband.de; internet www.hochschulverband.de/cms; 22,990 mems; Pres. Prof. Dr BERNHARD KEMPEN; Man. Dr MICHAEL HARTMER.

Deutscher Volkshochschul-Verband eV (German Adult Education Association): Obere Wilhelmstr. 32, 53225 Bonn; tel. (228) 97569-20; fax (228) 97569-30; e-mail info@dvv-vhs.de; internet www.dvv-vhs.de; f. 1953; 16 regional asscns of 1,000 Volkshochschulen with 4,000 brs; Pres. Prof. Dr RITA SÜSSMUTH; Chair. Dr ERNST-DIETER ROSSMANN; Dir ULRICH AENGENVOORT; publs *Adult Education and Development* (2 a year, in English, French and Spanish), *DVV magazin dis.kurs* (4 a year).

Hochschulrektorenkonferenz (German Rectors' and Presidents' Conference): Ahrstr. 39, 53175 Bonn; tel. (228) 887-0; fax (228) 887110; e-mail sekr@hrk.de; internet www.hrk.de; f. 1949; central voluntary body representing the univs and higher education instns; 261 mems; Pres. Prof. Dr MARGRET WINTERMANTEL; Sec.-Gen. Dr CHRISTIANE GAEHTGENS.

Katholischer Akademischer Ausländer-Dienst: Hausdorffstr. 151, 53129 Bonn; tel. (228) 91758-0; fax (228) 9175858; e-mail zentrale@kaad.de; internet www.kaad.de; f. 1958; coordinates activities of Catholic orgs concerned with foreign students in Germany and grants scholarships; Pres. Prof. Dr JOSEF REITER; Dirs Dr HEINRICH GEIGER, Dr HERMANN WEBER; publ. *Jahresakademie* (1 a year).

Learned Societies

GENERAL

Akademie der Künste (Academy of Arts): Pariser Pl. 4, 10117 Berlin-Mitte; tel. (30) 20057-1000; e-mail info@adk.de; internet www.adk.de; f. 1696; sections of fine art, architecture, music, literature, performing arts, film and media arts; 385 mems; Pres. Prof. KLAUS STAECK; publ. *Sinn und Form* (6 a year).

Akademie der Wissenschaften in Göttingen (Göttingen Academy of Sciences and Humanities): Theaterstr. 7, 37073 Göttingen; tel. (551) 395362; fax (551) 395365; e-mail udeppe@gwdg.de; internet www.adw-goe.de; f. 1751; sections of Philology and History, Mathematics and Physics; 381 mems and corresp. mems; Pres. Prof. Dr CHRISTIAN STARCK; Gen. Sec. Dr ANGELIKA SCHADE;

publs *Abhandlungen, Neue Folge, Göttingische Gelehrte Anzeigen, Jahrbüch.*

Akademie der Wissenschaften und der Literatur Mainz (Mainz Academy of Sciences, Humanities and Literature): Geschwister Scholl-Str. 2, 55131 Mainz; tel. (6131) 577-0; fax (6131) 577-111; e-mail generalsekretariat@adwmainz.de; internet www.adwmainz.de; f. 1949; 200 mems; Pres. Prof. Dr ELKE LÜTJEN-DRECOLL; Sec.-Gen. Prof. Dr CLAUDIUS GEISLER; Vice-Pres. for Literature Prof. Dr NORBERT MILLER; Vice-Pres. for Mathematics and Natural Sciences Prof. Dr GERHARD WEGNER; Vice-Pres. for Philosophy and Social Sciences Prof. Dr GERNOT WILHELM; publs *Abhandlungen, Forschungsreihen.*

Bayerische Akademie der Wissenschaften (Bavarian Academy of Sciences and Humanities): Alfons-Goppel-Str. 11, 80539 Munich; tel. (89) 23031-0; fax (89) 23031-1100; e-mail info@badw.de; internet www.badw.de; f. 1759; sections of mathematics and natural sciences (Secs Prof. Dr GOTTFRIED SACHS, Prof. Dr HORST KESSLER) and Philosophy and History (Secs Prof. Dr ARNOLD PICOT, Prof. Dr THOMAS O. HÖLLMANN); 172 mems; Pres. Prof. Dr DIETMAR WILLOWEIT; Gen. Sec. EVA REGENSCHEIDT-SPIES.

Berlin-Brandenburgische Akademie der Wissenschaften (Berlin-Brandenburg Academy of Sciences and Humanities): Jaegerstr. 22/23, 10117 Berlin; tel. (30) 20370-0; fax (30) 20370-600; e-mail bbaw@bbaw.de; internet www.bbaw.de; f. 1700, refounded 1992/93; sections of Humanities, of Social Sciences, of Mathematics and Natural Sciences, of Biological and Medical Sciences, of Engineering Sciences; 307 mems (166 ordinary, 69 extraordinary, 70 emeriti, 2 hon.); Pres. Prof. Dr GÜNTER STOCK; publs *Berichte und Abhandlungen* (irregular), *Gegenworte—Zeitschrift für den Disput über Wissen, Jahrbuch* (1 a year).

Deutsche Akademie der Naturforscher Leopoldina—Nationale Akademie der Wissenschaften (German Academy of Sciences Leopoldina): Emil-Abderhalden-Str. 37, 06108 Halle (Saale); tel. (345) 47239-0; fax (345) 47239-19; e-mail leopoldina@leopoldina.org; internet www.leopoldina.org; f. 1652; attached to Nationale Akademie der Wissenschaften; 1,300 mems; library: see Libraries and Archives; Pres. Prof. Dr JÖRG HACKER; Sec.-Gen. Prof. Dr JUTTA SCHNITZER-UNGEFUG; Sec., Medicine Prof. Dr INGO HANSMANN; publs *Acta Historica Leopoldina, Jahrbuch* (1 a year), *Nova Acta Leopoldina*.

Branch Office:

Deutsche Akademie der Naturforscher Leopoldina, Berliner Büro: Reinhardtstr. 14, 10117 Berlin; tel. (345) 47239-801; e-mail presse@leopoldina.org; Press Contact CAROLINE WICHMANN.

Goethe-Gesellschaft in Weimar eV: Burgpl. 4 99423 Weimar; Postfach 2251, 99403 Weimar; tel. (3643) 202050; fax (3643) 202061; internet www.goethe-gesellschaft.de; e-mail goetheges@aol.com; f. 1885; literature, art and history of Goethe's time; 3,000 mems; Pres. Dr JOCHEN GOLZ; Dir Dr PETRA OBERHAUSER; publs *Goethe-Jahrbuch, Schriften der G.G.* (irregular).

Goethe-Institut: Dachauer Str. 122, 80637 Munich; tel. (89) 15921-0; fax (89) 15921-450; e-mail zv@goethe.de; internet www.goethe.de; f. 1951 to promote a wider knowledge abroad of the German language and to foster cultural cooperation with other countries; 147 institutes globally, 13 in Germany; Pres. Prof. Dr KLAUS-DIETER LEHMANN; Sec.-Gen. Dr HANS-GEORG KNOPP; publs *Fikrun* *wa fann* (2 a year), *Goethe-Institut aktuell* (4 a year), *Humboldt* (2 a year), *Willkommen, Yearbook* (1 a year).

Heidelberger Akademie der Wissenschaften (Heidelberg Academy of Sciences and Humanities): Karlstr. 4, 69117 Heidelberg; tel. (6221) 543265; fax (6221) 543355; e-mail haw@urz.uni-heidelberg.de; internet www.haw.baden-wuerttemberg.de; f. 1909; sections of Mathematics and Natural Sciences (Sec. Prof. Dr HANS GÜNTER DOSCH), Philosophy and History (Sec. Prof. Dr VOLKER SELLIN); Pres. Prof. Dr PETER GRAF KIELMANSEGG; Man. Dir GUNTHER JOST.

Institut für Auslandsbeziehungen (Institute for Foreign Cultural Relations): Postfach 102463, 70020 Stuttgart; Charlottenpl. 17, 70173 Stuttgart; tel. (711) 2225-0; fax (711) 2264346; e-mail info@ifa.de; internet www.ifa.de; f. 1917; library of 450,000 vols; Pres. URSULA SEILER-ALBRING; Gen. Sec. RONALD GRAETZ; Librarian GUDRUN CZEKALLA; publs *Ifa//dokumente*, *Ifa//literaturrecherchen*, *Kulturaustausch*, *Reihe Dokumentation*.

Nordrhein-Westfälische Akademie der Wissenschaften (Northrhine-Westphalia Academy of Sciences and Humanities): Palmenstr. 16, 40217 Düsseldorf; tel. (211) 61734-0; fax (211) 341475; e-mail akdw@akdw.nrw.de; internet www.akdw.nrw.de; f. 1950; sections of Natural, Engineering and Economic Sciences, Philosophy; 166 mems; Pres. Prof. Dr MANFRED J. M. NEUMANN; publs *Abhandlungen*, *Sitzungsberichte*.

Prinz-Albert-Gesellschaft eV (Prince Albert Society): c/o Silvia Böcking, Alte Schlossstr. 9, 96253 Untersiemau; tel. (921) 554190; fax (921) 55844188; e-mail prinz-albert-gesellschaft@uni-bayreuth.de; internet www.prinz-albert-gesellschaft.uni-bayreuth.de; f. 1981; encourages research into Anglo-German relations in spheres of scholarship, culture and politics; Chair. Prof. Dr DIETER WEISS; Sec. SILVIA BÖCKING; publ. *Prince Albert Studies* (Series).

Sächsische Akademie der Wissenschaften zu Leipzig (Saxon Academy of Sciences and Humanities in Leipzig): Postfach 100440, 04004 Leipzig; tel. (341) 7115350; fax (341) 7115344; e-mail sekretariat@saw-leipzig.de; internet www.saw-leipzig.de; f. 1846; about 30 research projects; 221 mems (142 ordinary, 79 corresp.); Pres. Prof. Dr PIRMIN STEKELER-WEITHOFER; Sec.-Gen. Dr UTE ECKER; Head of Mathematics and Natural Sciences Section Prof. Dr DIETER MICHEL; Head of Philology and History Section Prof. Dr HEINER LÜCK; Head of Technical Sciences Section Prof. Dr HARTMUT WORCH; publs *Abhandlungen*, *Denkströme* (www.denkstroeme.de), *Jahrbuch* (every 2 years), *Sitzungsberichte*.

Union der Deutschen Akademien der Wissenschaften (Union of the German Academies of Sciences and Humanities): Geschwister-Scholl-Str. 2, 55131 Mainz; tel. (6131) 218528-0; fax (6131) 218528-11; e-mail info@akademienunion.de; internet www.akademienunion.de; f. 1973; consists of academies of sciences and humanities in Berlin, Düsseldorf, Göttingen, Heidelberg, Leipzig, Mainz and Munich; deals with research projects common to the academies and co-ordinates the work of their mems; Pres. Prof. Dr GERHARD GOTTSCHALK; Gen. Sec. Dr DIETER HERRMANN.

AGRICULTURE, FISHERIES AND VETERINARY SCIENCE

Agrarsoziale Gesellschaft eV (ASG): Postfach 1144, 37001 Göttingen; Kurze Geismarstr. 33, 37073 Göttingen; tel. (551) 497090; fax (551) 49709-16; e-mail info@asg-goe.de; internet www.asg-goe.de; f. 1947;

389 mems, plus 168 corporate mems; library of 6,000 vols; Chair. Dr HANS-HERMAN BENTRUP; Pres. HEINZ CHRISTIAN BÄR; publs *Arbeitsbericht der ASG*, *Kleine Reihe der ASG*, *Ländlicher Raum* (6 a year), *Materialsammlung der ASG*, *Schriftenreihe für ländliche Sozialfragen*.

Dachverband Wissenschaftlicher Gesellschaften der Agrar-, Forst-, Ernährungs-, Veterinär- und Umweltforschung eV: Eschbormer Landstr. 122, 60489 Frankfurt am Main; tel. (69) 24788306; fax (69) 24788114; internet daf.zadi.de; f. 1973; advancement and co-ordination of research; information; contacts; representation; 29 mems; Pres. Prof. Dr FOLKHARD ISERMEYER; Man. Dir LOTHAR HÖVELMANN.

Deutsche Landwirtschafts-Gesellschaft eV (German Agricultural Society): Eschborner Landstr. 122, 60489 Frankfurt; tel. (69) 24788-0; fax (69) 24788110; e-mail info@dlg-frankfurt.de; internet www.dlg.org; f. originally 1885, re-founded 1947; 16,000 mems; Pres. PHILIP VON DEM BUSSCHE; Dir Dr REINHARD GRANDKE; publs *Agrifuture* (for European farmers, in English, 4 a year), *Entwicklung und ländlicher Raum* (monthly, in German, English and French), *Journal of International Agriculture* (4 a year), *Mitteilungen* (1 a year), *Zeitschrift für Agrargeschichte und Agrarsoziologie* (4 a year).

Deutsche Veterinärmedizinische Gesellschaft: Frankfurter Str. 89, 35392 Gießen; tel. (641) 24466; fax (641) 25375; e-mail media@dvg.net; internet www.dvg.net; f. 1949; 4,800 mems; Pres. Prof. Dr HOLGER MARTENS; Sec. Prof. Dr KARSTEN FEHLHABER; publ. *Kongressbericht* (every 2 years).

Deutscher Forstwirtschaftsrat eV (German Forestry Council): Flerzheimer Allee 13, 53125 Bonn; tel. (228) 61963-0; fax (228) 61963-21; e-mail dfwr-rheinbach@t-online.de; internet www.dfwr.de; f. 1950; promotion of forestry; 67 mems; Pres. Bürgermeister HERMANN ILAENDER; Man. Dir STEPHAN SCHÜTTE.

Verband Deutscher Landwirtschaftlicher Untersuchungs- und Forschungsanstalten eV (VDLUFA) (Association of German Agricultural, Analytical and Research Institutes): c/o LUFA Speyer, Obere Langgasse 40, 67346 Speyer; tel. (6232) 136-121; fax (6232) 136-122; e-mail info@vdlufa.de; internet www.vdlufa.de; f. 1888; devt of methods and quality assurance in agricultural analytical sector; provides bases for a standardised evaluation of test results; initiates and advances applied agricultural research; 550 mems; Pres. Prof. Dr FRANZ WIESLER; Vice-Pres. for Animals Prof. Dr HANS SCHENKEL; Vice-Pres. for Plants Prof. Dr THOMAS EBERTSEDER; Exec. Sec. Dr HANS-GEORG BROD; publs *Handbuch der landwirtschaftlichen Versuchs- und Untersuchungsmethodik (VDLUFA-Methodenbuch)*, *VDLUFA-Mitteilungen*, *VDLUFA-Schriftenreihe*.

ARCHITECTURE AND TOWN PLANNING

Bauhaus Dessau Foundation: Gropiusallee 38, 06846 Dessau; tel. (340) 6508-0; fax (340) 6508-226; e-mail service@bauhaus-dessau.de; internet www.bauhaus-dessau.de; f. 1994 to preserve and convey the historic heritage of Bauhaus and contribute ideas and solutions to the problems of design in the contemporary environment; library: public research and reference library with particular reference to urban design, architecture and living; archive of 25,000 items from collections and legacies of Bauhaus teachers and students.

Attached College:

Bauhaus Kolleg: Gropiusallee 38, 06846 Dessau; tel. (340) 6508-403; fax (340) 6508-404; e-mail goegel@bauhaus-dessau.de; f. 1999; 1-year postgraduate programme; language of instruction: English; Dir OMAR AKBAR; Man. INA GOEGEL.

DAI–Verband Deutscher Architekten- und Ingenieurvereine eV: Keithstr. 2–4, 10787 Berlin; tel. (30) 21473174; fax (30) 21473182; e-mail dai@architekt.de; internet www.architekt.de; f. 1871; 5,500 mems; Chair. Prof. Dr-Ing. JÜRGEN FISSLER; publ. *DAI-Verbandszeitschrift BAUKULTUR*.

Deutscher Verband für Wohnungswesen, Städtebau und Raumordnung eV (German Federation for Housing and Planning): Georgenstr. 21, 10117 Berlin; tel. (30) 20613250; fax (30) 20613251; e-mail info@deutscher-verband.org; internet www.deutscher-verband.org; f. 1946; independent research in housing; urban and country planning; 700 mems; Chair. Dr IRENE WIESE-VON OFEN; Sec.-Gen. Dr HANS-MICHAEL BREY.

BIBLIOGRAPHY, LIBRARY SCIENCE AND MUSEOLOGY

Arbeitsgemeinschaft der Spezialbibliotheken eV: Geschaeftsstelle, c/o Ms Jadwiga Warmbrunn, Herder Institut eV Bibliothek, Gisonenweg 5–7, 35037 Marburg; tel. (6421) 184150; fax (6421) 184139; e-mail geschaeftsstelle@aspb.de; internet www.aspb.de; f. 1946; asscn of specialized libraries in the German-speaking countries; organizes conferences; acts as Section 5 (Spec. Libraries) of the German Libraries Asscn; 600 mems; Pres. Dr JÜRGEN WARMBRUNN; publ. *Conference proceedings (Tagungsband der Arbeits- und Fortbildungstagung)* (every 2 years).

Berufsverband Information Bibliothek eV (Association of Information and Library Professionals): Postfach 13 24, Gartenstr. 18, 72703 Reutlingen; tel. (7121) 3491-0; fax (7121) 300433; e-mail mail@bib-info.de; internet www.bib-info.de; f. 1949 as Verein der Bibliothekare und Assistentenen, present name 2000; represents the interests of librarians; maintains professional standards; stresses the importance of professional training and salaries that correspond to the level of training; increases public awareness of the social and educational importance of libraries and professional standards; 6,300 mems; Pres. SUSANNE RIEDEL; Sec. MICHAEL REISSER; publs *BuB (Buch und Bibliothek)—Forum Bibliothek und Information* (10 a year), *OPL-Checklisten*.

Deutsche Gesellschaft für Informationswissenschaft und Informationspraxis eV: Hanauer Landstr. 151–153, 60314 Frankfurt; tel. (69) 430313; fax (69) 4909096; e-mail mail@dgi-info.de; internet www.dgi-info.de; f. 1948 as Deutsche Gesellschaft für Dokumentation, present name 1999; promotion of information and documentation, information science and practice; 1,100 mems; Pres. Prof. Dr STEFAN GRADMANN; publs *Information–Wissenschaft & Praxis-IWP* (8 a year), *Nachrichten für Dokumentation* (6 a year), *Proceedings DGI-Online-Conference/DGI-Connference* (1 a year), *Proceedings Oberhofer Kolloquium* (every 2 years).

Deutscher Museumsbund eV (German Museums Association): In der Halde 1, 14195 Berlin; tel. ((30) 84109517; fax ((30) 84109519; e-mail office@museumsbund.de; internet www.museumsbund.de; f. 1917 to promote museums, their development and museology; 2,000 mems; Pres. Dr VOLKER RODEKAMP; Vice-Pres. Prof. Dr REINHOLD

LEINFELDER; Dir ANJA SCHALUSCHKE; publs *Bulletin* (4 a year), *Einkaufsführer für Museen* (1 a year), *Museumskunde* (2 a year).

Internationale Vereinigung der Musik-bibliotheken, Musikarchive und Musik-dokumentationszentren (IVMB) Gruppe Deutschland eV (International Association of Music Libraries, Archives and Documentation Centres—IAML): c/o Universitäts-und Landesbibliothek, 64283 Darmstadt; tel. (6151) 16-5807; fax 9(3212) 1011715; e-mail sekretaerin@aibm.info; internet www.aibm.info; f. 1951; 210 mems; Pres. Dr BARBARA WIERMANN; Vice-Pres. Dr ANDREAS ODENKIRCHEN; Sec. Dr SILVIA UHLEMANN; Treas. PETRA WAGENKNECHT; publs *Fontes Artis Musicae* (4 a year), *Forum Musikbibliothek* (4 a year).

Verein Deutscher Bibliothekare eV (Association of German Academic Librarians): Universitätsbibliothek Augsburg, Universitätsstr 22, 86159 Augsburg; tel. (821) 5985300; fax (821) 5985354; internet www.vdb-online.org; f. 1900, refounded 1948; annual librarians' congress, workshops, seminars; 1,650 mems; Pres. Dr ULRICH HOHOFF; Sec. Dr THOMAS STÖBER; publs *Jahrbuch der Deutschen Bibliotheken* (every 2 years), *VDB-Mitteilungen* (2 a year).

Württembergische Bibliotheksge-sellschaft (Society of Friends of the Württemberg State Library): Postfach 105441, 70047 Stuttgart; tel. (711) 212-4428; fax (711) 212-4422; e-mail wbg@wlb-stuttgart.de; internet www.wlb-stuttgart.de/die-wlb/freunde-der-bibliothek; f. 1946; supports the reconstruction of the Württemberg State Library, holds lectures, meetings, exhibitions, etc.; 400 mems; Pres. (vacant); Chair. Dr WULF D. VON LUCIUS; Sec. CHRISTINE DEMMLER.

ECONOMICS, LAW AND POLITICS

AFW Wirtschaftsakademie Bad Harz-burg GmbH (Academy for Distance Study of Economics in Bad Harzburg): An den Weiden 15, 38667 Bad Harzburg; tel. (5322) 902034; fax (5322) 902040; e-mail bildung@afwbadharzburg.de; internet www.afwbadharzburg.de; until 1999 Akademie für Fernstudium (AfF); Dir DIETMAR BORSCH.

Deutsche Aktuarvereinigung eV: Hohenstaufenring 47–51, 50674 Cologne; tel. (221) 912554-0; fax (221) 912554-44; e-mail info@aktuar.de; internet www.aktuar.de; f. 1948; society for promotion of actuarial theory in collaboration with the universities; 838 mems; Pres. NORBERT HEINEN; Man. Dir MICHAEL STEINMETZ; publ. *Blätter* (2 a year).

Deutsche Gesellschaft für Auswärtige Politik eV (German Council on Foreign Relations): Rauchstr. 17–18, 10787 Berlin; tel. (30) 2542310; fax (30) 25423116; e-mail info@dgap.org; internet www.dgap.org; f. 1955; discusses and promotes research on problems of int. politics; operates one of the oldest specialized libraries on German foreign policy (open to the public); library of 75,000 vols, 270 periodicals; 1,800 mems; Pres. Dr AREND OETKER; Exec. Vice-Pres. FRITJOF VON NORDENSKJÖLD; Otto Wolff-Dir of the Research Institute EBERHARD SANDSCHNEIDER; publs *Die Internationale Politik* (1 a year), *Internationale Politik* (6 a year, supplement 'Global Edition').

Deutsche Gesellschaft für Osteuropa-kunde eV (German Association for Eastern European Studies): Schaperstr. 30, 10719 Berlin; tel. (30) 21478412; fax (30) 21478414; e-mail info@dgo-online.org; internet www.dgo-online.org; f. 1913; 850 mems; Pres. Prof. Dr RITA SÜSSMUTH; Exec. Dir Dr GABRIELE FREITAG; publs *Osteuropa*

(12 a year), *Osteuropa-Recht* (6 a year), *Osteuropa-Wirtschaft* (4 a year).

Deutsche Statistische Gesellschaft: Albertus-Magnus-Pl., 50923 Cologne; tel. (221) 4704130; fax (221) 4705084; e-mail post@dstatg.de; internet www.dstatg.de; f. 1911; 800 mems; Pres. Prof. Dr KARL MOSLER; Man. Dir NANA DYCKERHOFF; publ. *Allgemeines Statistisches Archiv* (4 a year).

Deutsche Vereinigung für Politische Wissenschaft (German Political Science Association): c/o Osnabrück University FB1-Sozialwissenschaften, 49069 Osnabrück; tel. (541) 969-6264; fax (541) 969-6266; e-mail dvpw@dvpw.de; internet www.dvpw.de; f. 1951; 1,552 mems; Pres. Prof. Dr SUZANNE SCHÜTTEMEYER; Dir FELIX W. WURM; publ. *Politische Vierteljahresschrift* (4 a year).

Deutscher Juristentag eV: Postfach 1169, 53001 Bonn; tel. (228) 9839185; fax (228) 9839140; e-mail info@djt.de; internet www.djt.de; f. 1860; furthers discussion among jurists; 6,000 mems; Pres. Prof. Dr MARTIN HENSSLER.

Gesellschaft für Öffentliche Wirtschaft (Society for Public Economy): Sponholzstr. 11, 12159 Berlin; tel. (30) 8521045; fax (30) 8525111; e-mail goew.dsceep@t-online.de; internet www.goew.de; f. 1951; 70 mems; research and information service and providers of public services; Pres. MICHAEL SCHÖNEICH; Dir WOLF LEETZ; publ. *Zeitschrift für öffentliche und gemeinwirtschaftliche Unternehmen* (4 a year).

Gesellschaft für Rechtsvergleichung e.V. (Society for Comparative Law e.V.): Belfortstr. 16, 79098 Freiburg; tel. (761) 2032126; fax (761) 2032127; e-mail gfr@uni-freiburg.de; internet www.jura.uni-freiburg.de/gfr; f. 1894; 1,000 mems; Chair. Prof. Dr JÜRGEN SCHWARZE; Sec.-Gen. Prof. Dr MARTIN SCHMIDT-KESSEL; publs *Ausländische Aktiengesetze, Rechtsvergleichung und Rechtsvereinheitlichung*.

Gesellschaft für Sozial- und Wirtschafts-geschichte (Society for Social and Economic History): Friedrich-Wilhelms-Universität Bonn, Konviktstr. 11, 53113 Bonn; tel. (228) 735172; fax (228) 735171; internet www.gswg.net; f. 1961; 220 mems; Pres. Prof. Dr GÜNTHER SCHULZ; Sec. Prof. Dr RAINER METZ.

Kommission für Geschichte des Parla-mentarismus und der politischen Par-teien (Commission for History of Parliamentarism and Political Parties): Colmantstr. 39, 53115 Bonn; tel. (228) 604830; fax (228) 6048323; e-mail info@kgparl.de; internet www.kgparl.de; f. 1951; 21 mems; Pres. Prof. Dr K. HILDEBRAND; Gen. Sec. Dr M. SCHUMACHER; publs *Beiträge zur Geschichte des Parlamentarismus und der politischen Parteien, Quellen zur Geschichte des Parlamentarismus und der politischen Parteien*.

EDUCATION

Humboldt Gesellschaft für Wis-senschaft, Kunst und Bildung eV (Humboldt Society for Science, Art and Education): Finkenstr. 14, 37154 Northeim; tel. (5551) 8278; f. 1962; 650 mems; Pres. Dr MARIA VON NEREE-LOEBNITZ; publs *Abhandlungen* (every 2 years), *Mitteilungen* (every 2 years).

FINE AND PERFORMING ARTS

Bayerische Akademie der Schönen Künste: Max-Joseph-Pl. 3, 80539 Munich; tel. (89) 290077-0; fax (89) 290077-23; e-mail info@badsk.de; internet www.badsk.de; f. 1948; 242 mems; Pres. Prof. Dr DIETER BORCHMEYER; Gen. Sec. Dr KATJA SCHAEFER; publ. *Jahrbuch*.

Deutsche Gesellschaft für Photographie eV (German Society for Photography): Rheingasse 8–12, 50676 Cologne; tel. (221) 9232069; fax (221) 9232070; e-mail dgph@dgph.de; internet www.dgph.de; f. 1951; 1,000 mems; Chair. Prof. Dr ULRICH NICKEL; publ. *DGPh-Intern* (4 a year).

Deutsche Mozart-Gesellschaft eV (German Mozart Society): Frauentorstr. 30, 86152 Augsburg; tel. (821) 518588; fax (821) 157228; e-mail deutsche-mozart-gesellschaft@t-online.de; internet www.deutsche-mozart-gesellschaft.de; f. 1951; 3,000 mems; Pres. Dr DIRK HEWIG; publ. *Acta Mozartiana* (1 a year).

Deutscher Komponistenverband eV (German Composers' Association): Kadettenweg 80B, 12205 Berlin; tel. (30) 84310580; fax (30) 84310582; e-mail info@komponistenverband.org; internet www.komponistenverband.de; f. 1954; 1,200 mems; Pres. JÖRG EVERS.

Deutscher Verein für Kunstwis-senschaft eV (German Society for Studies in Art History): Jebensstr. 2, 10623 Berlin; tel. (30) 3139932; fax (30) 75632108; e-mail dvfk@aol.com; internet www.dvfk-berlin.de; f. 1908; support, promotion and publication of research in German art history; 1,000 mems; Chair. Prof. Dr RAINER KAHSNITZ; Sec. Dr JOSEF RIEDMAIER; publ. *Zeitschrift des Deutschen Vereins für Kunstwissenschaft*.

IWF Wissen und Medien GmbH (IWF Knowledge and Media Ltd): Nonnenstieg 72, 37075 Göttingen; tel. (551) 5024-0; fax (551) 5024-400; e-mail iwf-goe@iwf.de; internet www.iwf.de; f. 1956; supports science and education through the development and transfer of audiovisual media, which it collects and customizes for use in teaching and research; offers media training and special courses, ranging from basic film-training to web design and video applications; 60 mems; library of 8,000 media items for higher education; Dir Dr H. U. FRHR VON SPIEGEL.

Kestnergesellschaft: Goseriede 11, 30159 Hanover; tel. (511) 70120-0; fax (511) 70120-20; e-mail kestner@kestner.org; internet www.kestner.org; f. 1916; activities concerned with the promotion of modern art; 4,300 mems; Dir Dr VEIT GOERNER.

Stiftung Preussischer Kulturbesitz (Prussian Cultural Foundation): Von-der-Heydt-Str. 16–18, 10785 Berlin; tel. (30) 25463-0; fax (30) 25463-268; e-mail info@hv.spk-berlin.de; internet www.preussischer-kulturbesitz.de; f. 1961 to preserve, augment and reunite the Prussian cultural heritage; comprises 16 State Museums, the State Library, the State Privy Archives, the Iberian-American Institute and the State Institute for Research in Music with the Museum for Musical Instruments; Pres. Prof. Dr phil. h.c. KLAUS-DIETER LEHMANN; publ. *Jahrbuch* (1 a year).

Verband Deutscher Kunsthistoriker eV (Association of German Art Historians): c/o Zentralinstitut für Kunstgeschichte, Meiserstr. 10, 80333 Munich; tel. (89) 553488; fax (89) 54505221; e-mail info@kunsthistoriker.org; internet www.kunsthistoriker.org; f. 1948; 1,750 mems; Pres. Prof. Dr GEORG SATZINGER; Sec. Dr KATHARINA CORSEPINS; publ. *Kunstchronik* (12 a year).

HISTORY, GEOGRAPHY AND ARCHAEOLOGY

Arbeitsgemeinschaft Historischer Kom-missionen und Landesgeschichtlicher Institute (Association of Historic Councils and Regional History Institutes): Schückingstr. 36, 35037 Marburg; tel. (6421) 1840; f. 1898; controls 51 societies and institutes; Pres. Prof. Dr RODERICH SCHMIDT; Man. Dir Dr WINFRIED IRGANG.

Deutsche Akademie für Landeskunde eV (German Academy for Regional Geography of Germany): c/o Institut für Länderkunde, Schongauerstr. 9, 04329 Leipzig; tel. (341) 2556510; fax (341) 2556598; internet www.deutsche-landeskunde.de; f. 1882, refounded 1946; study of regional geography of Germany and German-speaking Central Europe; Chair. (Bochum) Prof. Dr HARALD ZEPP; Chair. (Bonn) Prof. Dr WINFRIED SCHENK; publs *Berichte zur deutschen Landeskunde* (4 a year), *Forschungen zur deutschen Landeskunde* (series, 1 or 2 a year).

Deutsche Gesellschaft für Geographie: c/o Geographisches Institut der Humboldt-Universität Berlin, Unter den Linden 6, 10099 Berlin; tel. (30) 20936814; fax (30) 20936856; internet www.geographie.de; Pres. Prof. Dr ELMAR KULKE; Sec. Dr SEBASTIAN KINDER.

Deutsche Gesellschaft für Kartographie eV: c/o Steffen Hild, Stadtweg 9A, 01169 Dresden; tel. (511) 4505136; fax (511) 4505140; e-mail sekretaer@dgfk.net; internet www.dgfk.net; f. 1950; promotes scientific and practical cartography; 1,700 mems; Pres. Dr PETER ASCHENBERNER; Sec. STEFFEN HILD; publ. *Kartographische Nachrichten* (6 a year).

Deutsche Gesellschaft für Ortung und Navigation eV (German Institute of Navigation): Kölnstr. 70, 53111 Bonn; tel. (228) 20197-0; fax (228) 20197-19; e-mail dgon .bonn@t-online.de; internet www.dgon.de; f. 1951 as Ausschuss für Funkortung, present name 1961; promotes research and devt of methods and systems used for navigation; Pres. Prof. Dr PETER VÖRSMANN; publ. *European Journal of Navigation* (jt publ. of various European navigation instns, 4 a year).

Deutscher Nautischer Verein von 1868 eV (German Nautical Association of 1868): Striepenweg 31, 21147 Hamburg; tel. (40) 79713401; fax (40) 79713402; e-mail info@ dnvev.de; internet www.dnvev.de; f. 1868; 4,598 mems in 20 local nautical asscns, 47 corporate mems; Pres. Prof. Dr PETER EHLERS; Sec. NICOLAI WOELKI; publ. *Kalendar* (1 a year).

Fränkische Geographische Gesellschaft: Kochstr. 4/4, 91054 Erlangen; tel. (9131) 8522633; fax (9131) 8522013; e-mail fgg@geographie.uni-erlangen.de; internet www.fgg.uni-erlangen.de; f. 1954; 830 mems; library of 10,300 vols; Dir Prof. Dr HORST KOPP; Jt Gen. Secs Dr SONJA HOCK, Dr MANFRED SCHNEIDER; publs *Erlanger Geographische Arbeiten* (1 a year), *Erlanger Geographische Arbeiten, Sonderband* (irregular), *Mitteilungen* (1 a year).

Gesamtverein der Deutschen Geschichts- und Altertumsvereine (Union of German Historical and Archaeological Societies): MPZ-Infanteriestr. 1, 80797 Munich; tel. (89) 1213-2300; fax (89) 1213-2302; e-mail treml@mpz.bayern.de; f. 1852; 238 affiliated asscns; Pres. Prof. Dr M. TREML; Treas. Dr KLAUS NEITMANN; publ. *Blätter für deutsche Landesgeschichte*.

Gesellschaft für Erdkunde zu Berlin (Geographical Society of Berlin): Arno-Holz-Str. 14, 12165 Berlin; tel. (30) 790066-0; fax (30) 790066-12; e-mail mail@gfe-berlin.de; internet www.die-erde.de; f. 1828 by Heinrich Berghaus, Carl Ritter and other eminent Prussian scientists of the early 19th century, with the support of Alexander von Humboldt; study of geography, geosciences and related disciplines; lectures, seminars, confs and

excursions; 350 mems; library of 100,000 vols; Pres. Dr HARTMUT ASCHE; Sec. Dr CHRISTOF ELLGER; publs *DIE ERDE—Zeitschrift der Gesellschaft für Erdkunde zu Berlin (Journal of the Geographical Society of Berlin)* (4 a year), *Verhandlungen der Gesellschaft für Erdkunde zu Berlin* (1 a year).

Monumenta Germaniae Historica: Ludwigstr. 16, Postfach 34 02 23, 80099 Munich; tel. (89) 286382384; fax (89) 281419; e-mail sekretariat@mgh.de; internet www.mgh.de; f. 1819; library of 130,000 vols; Pres. Prof. Dr RUDOLF SCHIEFFER; Sec. Prof. Dr GERHARD SCHMITZ; Exec. Sec. Dr HORST ZIMMERHACKL; Librarian Prof. Dr ARNO MENTZEL-REUTERS; publ. *Deutsches Archiv für Erforschung des Mittelalters*.

Verband der Historiker und Historikerinnen Deutschlands (Union of German Historians): c/o Prof. Dr Simone Lässig, Georg-Eckert-Institut Celler Str. 3, 38114 Braunschweig; tel. (531) 123103217; fax (531) 5909999; e-mail vhd@gei.de; internet www.vhd.gwdg.de; f. 1893, refounded 1949; 2,300 mems; Pres. Prof. Dr PETER FUNKE; Sec. Prof. Dr SIMONE LÄSSIG.

LANGUAGE AND LITERATURE

British Council: Alexanderpl., 10178 Berlin; tel. (30) 3110990; fax (30) 31109920; e-mail info@britishcouncil.de; internet www .britishcouncil.de/e; teaching centre; offers courses and exams in English language and British culture and promotes cultural exchange with the UK; attached offices in Düsseldorf, Leipzig and Munich; Dir JOHN WHITEHEAD; IELTS Man. CAROLINE MURDOCH.

Deutsche Gesellschaft für Sprachwissenschaft (German Society for Linguistics): c/o Nicole Dehé, Institut für Englische Philologie, Freie Universität Berlin, Habelschwerdter Allee 45, 14195 Berlin; tel. (30) 83872311; fax (30) 83872300; e-mail ndehe@ zedat.fu-berlin.de; internet www.dgfs.de; f. 1978; supports advancement of the scientific investigation of language, and the linguists engaged in this; 1,100 mems; Pres. Prof. Dr JÜRGEN LENERZ; Sec. Dr NICOLE DEHÉ; publ. *Zeitschrift für Sprachwissenschaft* (2 a year).

Gesellschaft für deutsche Sprache eV (Society for the German Language): Spiegelgasse 13, 65183 Wiesbaden; tel. (611) 99955-0; fax (611) 99955-30; e-mail sekr@gfds.de; internet www.gfds.de; f. 1947; 3,000 mems; library of 20,000 vols; Chair. Prof. Dr RUDOLF HOBERG; publs *Der Sprachdienst* (6 a year), *Muttersprache* (4 a year).

Hölderlin-Gesellschaft eV: Hölderlinhaus, 72070 Tübingen; tel. (7071) 22040; fax (7071) 22948; e-mail info@hoelderlin-gesellschaft .de; internet www.hoelderlin-gesellschaft .info; f. 1943, reconstituted 1946; 1,300 mems; Pres. Dr ULRICH GAIER; Dir VALÉRIE LAWITSCHKA; publs *Hölderlin-Jahrbuch* (every 2 years), *Lyrik im Hölderlinturm*, *Schriften der Hölderlin-Gesellschaft* (irregular), *Turm-Vorträge*.

Instituto Cervantes: Rosenstr. 18–19, 10178 Berlin; tel. (30) 257618-0; fax (30) 257618-19; e-mail berlin@cervantes.de; internet www.cervantes.de; offers courses and exams in Spanish language and culture and promotes cultural exchange with Spain and Spanish-speaking Latin and Central America; attached centres in Bremen and Munich; library of 4,500 vols; Dir JOSÉ IGNACIO OLMOS SERRANO.

Mommsen-Gesellschaft e.V.: Geschäftsstelle Jacob-Burckhardt-Str. 5, 79098 Freiburg i.Br.; internet www .mommsen-gesellschaft.de; f. 1950; 620

mems; association of university teachers of classics, ancient history and archaeology, named after the classicist Theodor Mommsen (1817–1903); Pres. Prof. Dr WULF RAECK; Second Pres. Prof. Dr CHRISTIANE REITZ.

PEN Zentrum Bundesrepublik Deutschland (German PEN Centre): Kasinostr. 3, 64293 Darmstadt; tel. (6151) 23120; fax (6151) 293414; e-mail pen-germany@t-online .de; f. 1951; 682 mems; Pres. JOHANN STRASSER; Sec.-Gen. WILFRIED F. SCHOELLER.

MEDICINE

Anatomische Gesellschaft (Anatomical Society): Institut für Anatomie und Zellbiologie, Martin-Luther-Universität Halle Wittenberg, Grosse Steinstr. 52, 06097 Halle (Saale); tel. (345) 557-1701; fax (345) 557-1700; e-mail friedrich.paulsen@medizin .uni-halle.de; internet www .anatomische-gesellschaft.de; f. 1886; 850 mems; Sec. Prof. Dr FRIEDRICH PAULSEN; publs *Annals of Anatomy* (6 a year), Congress abstracts.

Deutsche Dermatologische Gesellschaft: Robert-Koch-Pl. 7, 10115 Berlin; tel. (30) 246253-0; fax (30) 246253-29; e-mail ddg@ derma.de; internet www.derma.de; f. 1888; 3,500 mems; Pres. Prof. Dr THOMAS LUGER; Sec.-Gen. Prof. Dr RUDOLF STADLER; Sec. S. SCHÖNLAU; publ *Hautarzt* (12 a year), *JDDG (Journal of the German Society of Dermatology)*.

Deutsche Gesellschaft für Anästhesiologie und Intensivmedizin: Roritzerstr. 27, 90419 Nuremberg; tel. (911) 933780; fax (911) 3938195; e-mail dgai@dgai-ev.de; internet www.dgai.de; f. 1953; 10,000 mems; Dir HOLGER SORGATZ; Pres. Prof. Dr JOACHIM RADKE; Sec. Prof. Dr K. VAN ACKERN; publ. *Anästhesiologie, Intensivmedizin, Notfallmedizin und Schmerztherapie (AINS)*.

Deutsche Gesellschaft für Angewandte Optik eV (German Society for Applied Optics): Str. 12 14, 15827 Dahlewitz; tel. (3641) 807440; fax (3641) 807600; internet www.dgao.de; f. 1923; 680 mems; Pres. Dr F. MERKLE; Sec. Dr CHRISTEL BUDZINSKI; publ. *Optik* (12 a year).

Deutsche Gesellschaft für Chirurgie (German Surgical Society): Luisenstrasse 58/59, 01117 Berlin; tel. (30) 28876290; fax (30) 28876299; e-mail dgchirurgie@t-online .de; internet www.dgch.de; f. 1872; 3,444 mems; Pres. H. D. SAEGER; Sec. H. BAUER; publ. *Langenbecks Archiv für Chirurgie*.

Deutsche Gesellschaft für Endokrinologie: c/o EndoScience, Endokrinologie Service GmbH, Thalkirchner Str. 1, 80337 Munich; tel. (89) 23237571; fax (89) 23237579; e-mail dge@endokrinologie.net; internet www .endokrinologie.net; f. 1953; 1,300 mems; Pres. Prof. Dr THOMAS GUDERMANN; Sec. Prof. Dr MARTIN GRUBENDORF; publ. *Endokrinologie-Informationen* (6 a year).

Deutsche Gesellschaft für Gynäkologie und Geburtshilfe (German Society for Gynaecology and Birth Support): Robert-Koch-Pl. 7, 10115 Berlin; tel. (30) 5148333; fax (30) 51488344; internet www.dggg.de; f. 1885; Pres. Prof. Dr K. DIEDRICH.

Deutsche Gesellschaft für Hals-Nasen-Ohren-Heilkunde, Kopf- und Hals-Chirurgie (German Society for Otorhinolaryngology and Head and Neck Surgery): Hittorfstr. 7, 53129 Bonn; tel. (228) 231770; fax (228) 239385; internet www.hno.org; f. 1921; 10 European archives of Otorhinolaryngology; 3,675 mems; Pres. Prof. Dr KARL HÖRMANN; Sec. Prof. Dr KARL-BERND HÜTTENBRINK; publ. *Laryngo-Rhino-Otologie*.

Deutsche Gesellschaft für Hygiene und Mikrobiologie: Institut für Hygiene und

Mikrobiologie, Josef-Schneiderstr. 2, 97080 Würzburg; tel. (931) 20146936; fax (931) 20146445; internet www.dghm.org; f. 1906; 1,850 mems; Chair. Prof. Dr M. FROSCH; Sec. Prof. Dr S. SUERBAUM.

Deutsche Gesellschaft für Innere Medizin (Internal Medicine): Schöne Aussicht 1, 65193 Wiesbaden; tel. (611) 2058040-0; fax (611) 2058040-46; e-mail info@dgim.de; internet www.dgim.de; f. 1882; 7,000 mems; Chair. Prof. Dr WERNER SEEGER; Gen. Sec. Prof. Dr HANS-PETER SCHUSTER; publ. *Supplementum of Abstracts* (1 a year).

Deutsche Gesellschaft für Kinderheilkunde und Jugendmedizin (Paediatrics and Adolescent Medicine): Eichendorffstr. 13, 10115 Berlin; tel. (30) 3087779-0; fax (30) 3087779-99; e-mail info@dgkj.de; internet www.dgkj.de; f. 1883; 8,500 mems; Pres. Prof. Dr HANSJOSEF BÖHLES; Dir Dr GABRIELE OLBRISCH.

Deutsche Gesellschaft für Neurochirurgie: c/o Porstmann Kongresse GmbH, Alte Jakobstr. 77, 10179 Berlin; tel. (30) 284499-22; fax (30) 284499-11; e-mail gs@dgnc.de; internet www.dgnc.de; f. 1950; 244 mems; Pres. Prof. Dr med. DIETMAR STOLKE; Sec. Prof. Dr med. DIETER-KARSTEN BÖKER; publ. *Zentralblatt für Neurochirurgie* (4 a year).

Deutsche Gesellschaft für Orthopädie und Orthopädische Chirurgie eV: Kronprinzendamm 15, 10711 Berlin; tel. (30) 79744444; fax (30) 79744445; e-mail dgooc@bvonet.de; internet www.dgooc.de; f. 1901; Pres. Prof. Dr JOCHEN EULERT; Gen. Sec. Prof. Dr FRITZ UWE NIETHARD; publ. *Orthopädie Mitteilungen* (6 a year).

Deutsche Gesellschaft für Physikalische Medizin und Rehabilitation: c/o Prof. Dr Lothar Beyer, Westbahnhofstr. 2, 07745 Jena; tel. and fax (3641) 622178; internet www.dgpmr.de; f. 1886; physical medicine and rehabilitation; 550 mems; Pres. Prof. Dr PETER KRÖLING; publs *Kurortmedizin* (6 a year), *Physikalische Medizin*, *Rehabilitationsmedizin*.

Deutsche Gesellschaft für Plastische und Wiederherstellungschirurgie eV (German Society for Plastic and Reconstructive Surgery): Diakoniekrakenhaus, Elise-Averdieck-Str. 17, 27356 Rotenburg/Wümme; tel. (4261) 77-2126/7; fax (4261) 77-2128; e-mail info@dgpw.de; internet www.dgpw.de; f. 1962; 680 mems; Dir Dr V. STUDTMANN; Gen. Sec. Prof. Dr E. E. SCHELLER; publ. *Journal* (2 a year).

Deutsche Gesellschaft für Psychiatrie, Psychotherapie und Nervenheilkunde (Psychiatry, Psychotherapy and Neurosciences): Reinhardtstr. 14, 10117 Berlin; tel. (30) 28096601; fax (30) 28093816; internet www.dgppn.de; f. 1842; 2,000 mems; Pres. Prof. Dr WOLFGANG GAEBEL; Chief Exec. Dr THOMAS NESSELER; Sec. Dr JÜRGEN ZIELASEK; publs *Nervenarzt*, *Spektrum*.

Deutsche Gesellschaft für Psychoanalyse, Psychotherapie, Psychosomatik und Tiefenpsychologie (DGPT) eV: Johannisbollwerk 20 III, 20459 Hamburg; tel. (40) 319-26-19; fax (40) 319-43-00; e-mail psa@dgpt.de; internet www.dgpt.de; f. 1949 to train psychotherapists; 3,400 mems; Pres. Dipl.-Psych. ANNE SPRINGER.

Deutsche Gesellschaft für Rechtsmedizin (German Society of Legal Medicine): Alberstr. 9, 79104 Freiburg; tel. (761) 2036854; fax (761) 2036858; e-mail legalmed@uniklinik-freiburg.de; internet www.dgrm.de; Pres. Prof. Dr STEFAN POLLAK.

Deutsche Gesellschaft für Sozialmedizin und Prävention (German Society for Social Medicine and Prevention): c/o Institut für Sozialmedizin und Gesundheitsökono-

mie, Leipziger Str. 44, 39120 Magdeburg; tel. (391) 6724300; fax (391) 6724310; internet www.dgsmp.de; f. 1964; 500 mems; Pres. Prof. Dr BERNT-PETER ROBRA; publ. *Das Gesundheitswesen* (12 a year).

Deutsche Gesellschaft für Tropenmedizin und Internationale Gesundheit eV: Bernhard-Nocht-Str. 74, 20359 Hamburg; tel. (40) 42818-478; fax (40) 42818-512; e-mail dtg@bni-hamburg.de; internet www.dtg.org; f. 1907 to bring together persons interested in medical questions related to the tropics; 870 mems; Pres. Prof. E. REISINGER; Sec. Prof. Dr G. D. BURCHARD.

Deutsche Gesellschaft für Zahn-, Mund- und Kieferheilkunde (German Society for Dental, Oral and Craniomandibular Sciences): Liesegangstr. 17A, 40211 Düsseldorf; tel. (211) 610198-0; fax (211) 610198-11; e-mail dgzmk@dgzmk.de; internet www.dgzmk.de; f. 1859; 10,500 mems; Pres. Prof. Dr THOMAS HOFFMAN; Sec. Dr ULRICH GAA; publs *APW DVD Journal*, *Clinical Oral Investigations*, *Deutsche Zahnärztliche Zeitung* (12 a year), *Oralprophylaxe*, *Zeitschrift für Zahnärztliche Implantologie*.

Deutsche Ophthalmologische Gesellschaft eV: Platenstr. 1, 80336 Munich; tel. (89) 55057680; fax (89) 550576811; e-mail geschaeftsstelle@dog.org; internet www.dog.org; f. 1857; 5,800 mems; Pres. Prof. Dr GERHARD K. LANG; Sec. Prof. Dr ANSELM KAMPIK; publs *Der Ophthalmologe* (12 a year), *Graefe's Archive for Clinical Research* (12 a year), *Klinische Monatsblätter für Augenheilkunde* (12 a year).

Deutsche Physiologische Gesellschaft eV: Physiologisches Institut der Universität zu Kiel, Olshausenstr. 40, 24098 Kiel; tel. (431) 8802032; fax (431) 8804580; internet www.physiologische-gesellschaft.de; f. 1904; 890 mems; Pres. Prof. Dr GERHARD BURCKHARDT; Sec. Prof. Dr med. MICHAEL ILLERT; publ. *Zeitschrift: Physiologie* (2 a year).

Deutsche Psychoanalytische Gesellschaft: Arnimallee 12, 14195 Berlin; tel. (30) 84316152; fax (30) 84316153; e-mail geschaeftsstelle@dpg-psa.de; internet www.dpg-psa.de; f. 1910; psychoanalytic training, education and research; 500 mems; Pres. Prof. Dr FRANZ WELLENDORF; Dir Dr THILO EITH; publs *Forum der Psychoanalyse*, *Praxis der Kinderpsychologie und Kinderpsychiatrie*, *Zeitschrift für Psychosomatische Medizin und Psychoanalyse*.

Deutsche Psychoanalytische Vereinigung eV: Körnerstr. 11, 10785 Berlin; tel. (30) 26552504; fax (30) 26552505; e-mail geschaeftsstelle@dpv-psa.de; internet www.dpv-psa.de; br. of the International Psychoanalytical Association; Pres. Dr GERHARD SCHNEIDER; Sec. Dr HELGA KREMP-OTTENHEYM.

NATURAL SCIENCES

General

Georg-Agricola Gesellschaft zur Förderung der Geschichte der Naturwissenschaften und der Technik eV: Institut für Wissenschafts- und Technikgeschichte, TU Bergakademie Freiberg, 09596 Freiberg; tel. (3731) 3934-91; fax (3731) 3928-32; internet www.georg-agricola-gesellschaft.de; f. 1926; promotes study of the history of science and technology, organizes annual meetings; 190 mems; 23 mem. asscns; Pres. Prof. REINHARD SCHMIDT; Sec. Dr NORMAN POHL; Chair. of the Scientific Bd Prof. Dr HANS-JOACHIM BRAUN; publ. *Die Technikgechichte als Vorbild der Modernen Technik*.

Gesellschaft Deutscher Naturforscher und Ärzte eV (Association of German Nat-

ural Scientists and Physicians): Hauptstr. 5, 53604 Bad Honnef; tel. (2224) 980713; fax (2224) 980789; e-mail gdnae@gdnae.de; internet www.gdnae.de; f. 1822; 5,000 mems; Pres. Prof. Dr HARALD FRITZSCH; Gen. Sec. Dr WOLFGANG T. DONNER; publ. *Verhandlungen der GDNAe* (every 2 years).

Görres-Gesellschaft zur Pflege der Wissenschaft: Adenauerallee 19, 53111 Bonn; tel. (228) 2674371; f. 1876; 3,000 mems; Pres. Prof. Dr h.c. mult. PAUL MIKAT; Gen. Sec. Prof. Dr RUDOLF SCHIEFFER.

Joachim Jungius-Gesellschaft der Wissenschaften eV: Edmund-Siemers-Allee 1, 20146 Hamburg; tel. (40) 417444; fax (40) 4480752; e-mail jungiusges@uni-hamburg.de; internet www.jungius-gesellschaft.de; f. 1947; 145 mems (107 ordinary, 38 corresp.); Vice-Pres. Prof. Dr JÖRN HENNING WOLF; publs *Berichte aus den Sitzungen* (4 a year), *Veröffentlichungen* (1 a year).

Naturwissenschaftlicher Verein für Bielefeld und Umgegend eV (Natural History Society for Bielefeld and the Region): Kreuzstr. 38, 33602 Bielefeld; tel. (521) 172434; fax (521) 5218810; e-mail info@nwv-bielefeld.de; internet www.nwv-bielefeld.de; f. 1908; 14 working groups, incl. astronomy, entomology and experimental archaeology; 600 mems; Pres. CLAUDIA QUIRINI; publ. *ILEX* (2 a year).

Wissenschaftsrat (Science Council): Brohlerstr. 11, 50968 Cologne; tel. (221) 3776-0; internet www.wissenschaftsrat.de; f. 1957 through cooperation of Länder and Federal Governments; advisory and coordinating body for science policy; makes recommendations on the structural and curricular development of the universities and on the organization and promotion of science and research; 54 nominated mems in two commissions (Scientific and Administrative); Chair. Prof. Dr KARL-MAX EINHÄUPL; Sec.-Gen. WEDIG VON HEYDEN; publ. *Empfehlungen und Stellungnahmen* (1 a year).

Biological Sciences

Bayerische Botanische Gesellschaft (Bavarian Botanical Society): Menzinger Str. 67, 80638 Munich; tel. (89) 17861-267; fax (89) 172638; e-mail bbg@lrz.uni-muenchen.de; internet www.bbgev.de; f. 1890; research into the flora of Bavaria and adjacent countries; preservation of species and plant communities; 750 mems; library of 20,000 vols; Pres. Prof. Dr JÖRG PFADENHAUER; publ. *Berichte der Bayerischen Botanischen Gesellschaft*.

Botanischer Informationsknoten Bayern (BIB) (Botanical Information Agency of Bavaria): Am Galgenberg 7, 93109 Wiesent; internet www.bayernflora.de; collects information and data on flora from regional research institutes; Pres. WOLFGANG AHLMER.

Deutsche Botanische Gesellschaft: Institut für Biologie, Humboldt-Universität zu Berlin, Invalidenstr. 42, 10115 Berlin; tel. (30) 20938816; fax (30) 20938445; e-mail info@deutsche-botanische-gesellschaft.de; internet www.deutsche-botanische-gesellschaft.de; f. 1882; 1,050 mems; Pres. Prof. Dr U.-I. FLÜGGE; publ. *Plant Biology*.

Deutsche Gesellschaft für Allgemeine und Angewandte Entomologie eV (German Society for General and Applied Entomology): Eberswalder Str. 84, 15374 Müncheberg; tel. (333432) 824730; fax (333432) 824760; e-mail dgaae@dgaae.de; internet www.dgaae.de; f. 1976; 870 mems; Pres. Prof. Dr GERALD BERND MORITZ; Sec.-Gen. Dr P. LÖSEL; publs *DGaaE Nachrichten* (3–4 a year), *Mitteilungen* (every 2 years).

Deutsche Gesellschaft für Züchtungskunde e.V. (DGfZ): Adenauerallee 174, 53113 Bonn; tel. (228) 9144761; fax (228) 9144766; e-mail info@dgfz-bonn.de; internet www.dgfz-bonn.de; f. 1905; livestock breeding, animal housing, reproduction, hygiene, nutrition; 650 mems; Pres. Dr ERNST-JÜRGEN LODE; Man. Dir Dr BETTINA BONGARTZ; publ. *Züchtungskunde* (6 a year).

Deutsche Malakozoologische Gesellschaft: Senckenberganlage 25, 60325 Frankfurt am Main; internet www.hausdernatur.de; f. 1868; study of Mollusca; 270 mems; library of 30,000 vols; Pres. Dr VOLLRATH WIESE; Sec. Dr RONALD JANSSEN; publs *Archiv für Molluskenkunde* (2 a year), *Mitteilungen* (1–2 a year).

Deutsche Ornithologen-Gesellschaft eV: c/o Institut f. Vogelforschung, An der Vogelwarte 21, 26386 Wilhelmshaven; tel. (44) 23914148; fax (44) 21968955; e-mail geschaeftsstelle@do-g.de; internet www.do-g.de; f. 1850; 22,500 mems; Pres. Prof. Dr FRANZ BAIRLEIN; publs *Journal of Ornithology* (4 a year), *Vogelwarte* (4 a year).

Deutsche Phytomedizinische Gesellschaft eV (German Phytomedical Society): Messeweg 11–12, 38104 Brunswick; tel. (531) 2993213; fax (531) 2993019; e-mail geschaeftsstelle@dpg.phytomedizin.org; internet www.phytomedizin.org; f. 1949; 1,800 mems; Pres. Prof. Dr ANDREAS VON TIEDEMANN.

Deutsche Zoologische Gesellschaft eV (German Zoological Society): Corneliusstr. 12, 80469 München; tel. (89) 54806960; fax (89) 26024574; e-mail dzg@zi.biologie.uni-muenchen.de; internet www.dzg-ev.de; f. 1890; represents zoological sciences in Germany, Austria and Switzerland; promotes zoology as a modern, multi-disciplinary and integrating science and enables the exchange of recent scientific findings; 1,700 mems; Pres. Prof. Dr WOLF-MICHAEL WEBER (Münster); Sec. Dr THOMAS KEIL (Martinsried/München); publs *Frontiers in Zoology* (online only), *Zoologie—Mitteilungen der Deutschen Zoologischen Gesellschaft*.

Gesellschaft für Biochemie und Molekularbiologie: Mörfelder Landstr. 125, 60598 Frankfurt; tel. (69) 660567-0; fax (69) 660567-22; e-mail info@gbm-online.de; internet www.gbm-online.de; f. 1947; 5,500 mems; Chair. Prof. Dr FRANZ-ULRICH HARTL; Sec. Prof. Dr U. BRANDT; Treasurer WOLFGANG E. TROMMER; publs *Biological Chemistry* (12 a year), *BIOspektrum* (7 a year).

Gesellschaft für Naturkunde in Württemberg: Rosenstein 1, 70191 Stuttgart; tel. (711) 8936-201; fax (711) 8936-100; internet www.ges-naturkde-wuertt.de; f. 1844; 691 mems; Pres. Prof. Dr MARTIN BLUM; publ. *Jahreshefte*.

Münchner Entomologische Gesellschaft eV (Munich Entomological Society): Münchhausenstr. 21, 81247 Munich; tel. (89) 81070; fax (89) 8107300; e-mail megmail@zsm.mwn.de; internet www.zsm.mwn.de; f. 1904; 550 mems; library of 13,406 vols, 383 running journals, 6,800 separata; attached to library of the Zoological State Collection; Pres. Prof. Dr ERNST-GERHARD BURMEISTER; Chief Librarian Dr JULIANE DILLER; publs *Mitteilungen* (1 a year), *Nachrichtenblatt der Bayerischen Entomologen* (2 a year).

Naturhistorische Gesellschaft Hannover (Hanover Society of Natural History): Willy-Brandt-Allee 5, 30169 Hanover; tel. (511) 9807871; fax (511) 9807879; internet www.n-g-h.org; f. 1797; 501 mems; Pres. Dr D. SCHULZ; publs *Beihefte*, *Berichte*.

Naturkundeverein Schwäbisch Gmünd eV (Natural History Society of Schwäbisch Gmünd): Im Prediger, Johannispl. 3, 73525 Schwäbisch Gmünd; tel. (7171) 6034130; e-mail vorstand@nkv-gd.de; internet www.nkv-gd.de; f. 1890; works to promote public awareness of and protection of the natural environment; oversees protected sites; Pres. WERNER K. MAYER; publ. *Unicornis*.

Naturwissenschaftlicher und Historischer Verein für das Land Lippe eV (Natural History and Historical Society for the Lippe Region): Willi-Hofmann-Str. 2, 32756 Detmold; tel. (5231) 766213; fax (5231) 766114; e-mail info@nhv-lippe.de; internet www.nhv-lippe.de; f. 1835; 4 groups in Detmold, Bad Salzuflen, Lage and Lemgo; research into natural sciences, prehistory and local folk and art history; 800 mems; Pres. Prof. Dr JÜRGEN DÖHL; publs *Lippische Mitteilungen aus Geschichte und Landeskunde* (1 a year), *Lippischen Geschichtsquellen*.

Naturwissenschaftlicher Verein der Niederlausitz eV (Natural History Society of Lower Lusatia): Postfach 101005, 03010 Cottbus; e-mail info@nvn-cottbus.de; internet www.nvn-cottbus.de; f. 1990; research into local natural sciences and protection of nature and the environment; 90 mems; Pres. URSULA STRIEGLER.

Naturwissenschaftlicher Verein in Hamburg (Natural History Society of Hamburg): c/o Zoologisches Museum, Martin-Luther-King-Pl. 3, 20146 Hamburg; tel. (40) 428385635; fax (40) 428383937; e-mail nwv.zoologie@uni-hamburg.de; internet www.naturwissenschaftlicher-verein.de; f. 1837; 460 mems; Chair. Prof. Dr HARALD SCHLIEMANN.

Naturwissenschaftlicher Verein zu Bremen (Bremen Natural Science Association): c/o Übersee-Museum, Bahnhofspl. 13, 28195 Bremen; tel. (421) 16038153; fax (421) 1603899; e-mail info@nwv-bremen.de; internet www.bremen.de/info/nwv; f. 1864; 500 mems; Chair. HEINRICH KUHBIER; publ. *Abhandlungen* (1 a year).

Verein Naturschutzpark eV (Nature Reserves Federation): Niederhaverbeck 7, 29646 Bispingen; tel. (5198) 987030; fax (5198) 987039; e-mail vnp-info@t-online.de; internet www.verein-naturschutzpark.de; f. 1909; 4,500 mems; Dir Dr MATHIAS ZIMMERMANN; publ. *Naturschutz- und Naturparke*.

Vereinigung für Angewandte Botanik eV (Association for Applied Botany): Ohnhorststr. 18, 22609 Hamburg; tel. (40) 42816-349; fax (40)42816-565; e-mail helmut.kassner@botanik.uni-hamburg.de; f. 1902; 150 mems; Pres. Prof. Dr R. LIEBEREI; Sec. Prof. Dr H.-J. JÄGER; Treas. Dr HELMUT KASSNER; publ. *Angewandte Botanik* (Journal of Applied Botany and Food Quality, 2 a year).

Mathematical Sciences

Berliner Mathematische Gesellschaft eV (Berlin Mathematical Society): c/o Freie Universität Berlin, Institut für Mathematik, Arnimallee 3, 14195 Berlin; e-mail bmg.ev@berlin.de; internet www.w-volk.de/bmg; f. 1901; Sec. Prof. Dr WOLFGANG VOLK; publ. *Sitzungsberichte*.

Deutsche Mathematiker Vereinigung eV (German Mathematical Society): c/o WIAS, Mohrenstr. 39, 10117 Berlin; tel. (30) 20372306; fax (30) 20372307; e-mail dmv@wias-berlin.de; internet dmv.mathematik.de; f. 1890; 4,000 mems; Pres. Prof. Dr WOLFGANG LÜCK; Sec. Prof. Dr GÜNTER TÖRNER.

Gesellschaft für Angewandte Mathematik und Mechanik (Society for Applied Mathematics and Mechanics): GAMM–Geschäftsstelle, Technische Universität Dresden, c/o Prof. Dr V. Ulbricht, Institut für Festkörpermechanik, 01062 Dresden; tel. (351) 463-34285; fax (351) 463-37061; e-mail gamm@mailbox.tu-dresden.de; internet gamm.ev.de; f. 1922; advancement of scientific work and international cooperation in applied mathematics, mechanics and physics; 2,300 mems; Pres. Prof. Dr R. JELTSCH; Sec. Prof. Dr V. ULBRICHT.

Gesellschaft für Operations Research eV (GOR) (German Society for Operations Research): Joseph-Sommer-Str. 34, 41812 Erkelenz; tel. (2431) 9026710; fax (2431) 9026711; e-mail geschaeftsstelle@gor-ev.de; internet www.gor-online.de; f. 1998 by merger of Deutsche Gesellschaft für Operations Research and Gesellschaft für Mathematik, Ökonometrie und Operations Research; promotes development of operations research and encourages coordination of theoretical and practical advances in the area; 1,060 mems; Pres. Prof. Dr HORST W. HAMACHER; publs *Mathematical Methods of Operations Research* (6 a year), *OR News* (3 a year), *OR Spectrum* (4 a year).

Physical Sciences

Astronomische Gesellschaft: c/o Regina von Berlepsch, Astrophysikalisches Institut Potsdam, An der Sternwarte 16, 14482 Potsdam; tel. (331) 7499-348; fax (331) 7499-216; e-mail schriftfuehrerin@astronomische-gesellschaft.de; internet www.astronomische-gesellschaft.org; f. 1863; 800 mems; Pres. Prof. Dr RALF-JUERGEN DETTMAR; Sec. REGINA VON BERLEPSCH; publs *Mitteilungen der Astronomischen Gesellschaft* (1 a year), *Reviews in Modern Astronomy* (1 a year).

Deutsche Bunsen-Gesellschaft für Physikalische Chemie eV: Theodor-Heuss Allee 25, 60486 Frankfurt; tel. (69) 7564525; fax (69) 7564622; e-mail foerster@bunsen.de; internet www.bunsen.de; f. 1894; 1,500 mems; Chair. Prof. Dr WOLFGANG VON RYBINSKI; Dir Dr ANDREAS FÖRSTER; publs *Bunsen-Magazin* (6 a year), *Physical Chemistry Chemical Physics* (jtly with other learned socs, 52 a year).

Deutsche Geophysikalische Gesellschaft eV (German Geophysical Society): c/o GFZ German Research Centre for Geosciences, Telegrafenberg, 14473 Potsdam; tel. (331) 288-1206; fax (331) 288-1204; internet www.dgg-online.de; f. 1922; 1,050 mems; supports committees, working groups and student activities; Pres. Prof. Dr UGUR YARAMANCI; Exec. Man. Dr BIRGER LUEHR; Treasurer ALEXANDER RUDLOFF; publs *DGG Mitteilungen (Red Pages)* (3 or 4 a year), *Geophysical Journal International* (12 a year), *GMIT* (2 a year).

Deutsche Gesellschaft für Biophysik eV: c/o Prof. Dr Ulrike Alexiev, Fachbereich Physik, Freie Universität Berlin, Arnimallee 14, 14195 Berlin; tel. (30) 83855157; fax (30) 83856510; e-mail ulrike.alexiev@physik.fu-berlin.de; internet www.dgfb.org; f. 1943; 450 mems; Chair. Prof. Dr GERD ULRICH NIENHAUS; Sec. Dr ULRIKE ALEXIEV.

Deutsche Gesellschaft für experimentelle und klinische Pharmakologie und Toxikologie eV: Institut für Pharmakologie und Toxikologie, Universität Bonn, Reuterstr. 2B, 53113 Bonn; tel. (228) 739558; fax (228) 735404; e-mail dgpt-online@uni-bonn.de; internet www.dgpt-online.de; f. 1920; 2,500 mems; Pres. Prof. Dr W. SCHMITZ.

Deutsche Gesellschaft für Geowissenschaften (DGG) (German Geological Society): Stilleweg 2, 30651 Hanover; tel. (511) 643-2507; fax (511) 643-2695; e-mail dgg@bgr.de; internet www.dgg.de; f. 1848; scientific and technical congresses, confs and meetings, several spec. sections (Fachsektionen); 3,000 mems; library of 130,000 vols; Chair. Prof. Dr STEFAN WOHNLICH, Prof. Dr MARTIN MESCHEDE; Treas. Dr HEINZ-GERD RÖHLING; Librarian ANDREAS NIKOLAUS KÜPPERS; publs *Exkursionsführer & Tagungspublikationen (EDGG)* (irregular), *Geowissenschaftliche Mitteilungen* (4 a year), *Schriftenreihe der Deutschen Gesellschaft für Geowissenschaften (SDGG)* (irregular), *Zeitschrift der Deutschen Gesellschaft für Geowissenschaften (ZDGG)* (4 a year).

Deutsche Meteorologische Gesellschaft eV (German Meteorological Society): c/o Freie Universität Berlin, Carl-Heinrich-Becker-Weg 6-10, 12165 Berlin; tel. (30) 79708324; fax (30) 7919002; e-mail sekretariat@dmg-ev.de; internet www .dmg-ev.de; f. 1883; 1,750 mems; Pres. Prof. Dr ULRICH LUBASCH; Sec. Dr PETRA JANKIEWICZ; publs *Meteorologische Zeitschrift* (6 a year), *Mitteilungen DMG* (4 a year).

Deutsche Mineralogische Gesellschaft (German Mineralogical Society): Institut für Geologie, Mineralogie und Petrologie der Universität Tübingen, Wilhelmstr. 56, 72074 Tübingen; tel. (7071) 2972930; fax (7071) 293060; e-mail info@dmg-home.de; internet www.dmg-home.de; f. 1908; crystallography, petrology, geochemistry, ore minerals, applied mineralogy; 1,700 mems; Pres. Prof. Dr GREGOR MARKL; publs *Beihefte* (1 a year), *European Journal of Mineralogy (EJM)* (6 a year).

Deutsche Physikalische Gesellschaft eV: Hauptstr. 5, 53604 Bad Honnef; tel. (2224) 9232-0; fax (2224) 9232-50; e-mail dpg@ dpg-physik.de; internet www.dpg-physik.de; f. 1845; 58,000 mems; Pres. Prof. Dr WOLF-GANG SANDNER; Sec. Dr BERNHARD NUNNER; publs *Physik Journal* (12 a year), *Verhandlungen der DPG* (3 or 6 a year).

Deutscher Zentralausschuss für Chemie: Postfach 90 04 40, 60444 Frankfurt am Main; located at: Carl Bosch-Haus, Varrentrappstr. 40–42, 60486 Frankfurt am Main; tel. (69) 7917323; fax (69) 79171323; e-mail b.koehler@gdch.de; f. 1952; 7 mems; Sec. Prof. Dr WOLFRAM KOCH.

Deutsches Atomforum eV (German Forum on Nuclear Energy): Robert-Koch-Pl. 4, 10115 Berlin; tel. (30) 498555-0; fax (30) 498555-19; internet www.kernenergie.de; f. 1959; promotes the peaceful uses of atomic energy; Pres. Dr RALF GÜLDNER; Dir DIETER H. MARX.

Geologische Vereinigung e.V. (Geological Association): Vulkanstr. 23, 56743 Mendig; tel. (2652) 989360; fax (2652) 989361; e-mail info@g-v.de; internet www.g-v.de; f. 1910; 1,700 mems; Chair. Prof. Dr GEROLD WEFER; Sec. RITA SPITZLEI; publ. *Geologische Rundschau* (International Journal of Earth Sciences, 8 a year).

Gesellschaft Deutscher Chemiker: Postfach 90 04 40, 60444 Frankfurt am Main; Carl Bosch-Haus, Varrentrappstr. 40–42, 60486 Frankfurt am Main; tel. (69) 7917320; fax (69) 7917307; e-mail gdch@ gdch.de; internet www.gdch.de; f. 1946; 29,000 mems; Pres. Prof. Dr MICHAEL DRÖSCHER; Exec. Dir Prof. Dr WOLFRAM KOCH; publs *Analytical and Bioanalytical Chemistry* (24 a year), *Angewandte Chemie* (int. edn in English, 52 a year), *ChemBioChem* (12 a year), *Chemie-Ingenieur-Technik* (12 a year), *Chemie in unserer Zeit* (6 a year), *Chemischer Informationsdienst* (52 a year), *Chemistry—A European Journal* (24 a year), *ChemPhysChem* (12 a year), *European Journal of Inorganic Chemistry* (24 a year), *European Journal of Organic Chemistry* (24 a year), *Nachrichten aus der Chemie* (12 a year).

Paläontologische Gesellschaft (Palaentological Society): Department für Geo- und Umweltwissenschaften (Sektion Paläontologie), Richard-Wagner-Str. 10, 80333 Munich; tel. (89) 2180-6603; e-mail b.reichenbacher@ lrz.uni-muenchen.de; internet www .palaeontologische-gesellschaft.de; f. 1912; Pres. Prof. Dr BETTINA REICHENBACHER; publ. *Paläontologische Zeitschrift* (4 a year).

PHILOSOPHY AND PSYCHOLOGY

Deutsche Gesellschaft für Philosophie eV: c/o Prof. Dr Michael Quante, Philosophisches Seminar, Univ. zu Köln, Albertus-Magnus-Pl., 50923 Cologne; tel. (221) 4706360; fax (221) 4705006; internet www .dgphil.de; f. 1948 as Allgemeine Gesellschaft für Philosophie in Deutschland eV; 1,261 mems; Pres. Prof. Dr JULIAN NIDA-RUMELIN; Dir Prof. Dr MICHAEL QUANTE.

Deutsche Gesellschaft für Psychologie eV (German Psychology Society): Geschäftsstelle, Postfach 08 04 50, 10004 Berlin; tel. (2533) 2811520; fax (2533) 281144; e-mail geschaeftsstelle@dgps.de; internet www.dgps .de; f. 1904; 2,800 mems; Pres. Prof. Dr URSULA M. STAUDINGER; Sec. Prof. Dr CHRISTOPH STEINEBACH; publ. *Psychologische Rundschau* (4 a year).

Gesellschaft für Antike Philosophie eV: c/o Prof. Dr Christoph Horn, Institut für Philosophie, Universität Bonn, Am Hof 1, 53113 Bonn; internet www.ganph.de; f. 1999 to advance research into ancient philosophy; Pres. Prof. Dr MICHAEL ERLER.

Gesellschaft für Geistesgeschichte eV (Society for the History of Ideas): c/o Moses Mendelssohn Zentrum für Europäisch-Jüdische Studien, Am Neuen Markt 8, 14467 Potsdam; tel. (331) 280940; fax (331) 2809450; e-mail aludewig@rz.uni-potsdam .de; internet www.geistesgeschichte.net; f. 1958; 80 mems; Pres. Prof. Dr JULIUS H. SCHOEPS; Sec. Dr ANNA-DOROTHEA LUDEWIG; publ. *Zeitschrift für Religions- und Geistesgeschichte.*

Gesellschaft für Wissenschaftliche Gerichts- und Rechtpsychologie (Society for Forensic and Legal Science): Rablstr. 45, 81669 Munich; tel. (89) 4481282; fax (89) 44718018; e-mail info@gwg.info; internet www.gwg-institut.com; f. 1982; community of psychologists and doctors specializing in forensics; Dir Dr JOSEPH SALZGEBER.

Gottfried-Wilhelm-Leibniz-Gesellschaft eV: Waterloostr. 8 (Gottfried Wilhelm Leibniz Bibliothek — Niedersächsische Landesbibliothek), 30169 Hanover; tel. (511) 1267331; fax (511) 1267202; internet www .gwlb.de/leibniz/gesellschaft; f. 1966; 395 mems; Pres. Prof. ROLF WERNSTEDT; Gen. Sec. Dr WOLFGANG DITTRICH; publs *Studia Leibnitiana, Studia Leibnitiana Supplementa / Sonderhefte.*

RELIGION, SOCIOLOGY AND ANTHROPOLOGY

Albertus-Magnus-Institut: Adenauerallee 17, 53111 Bonn; tel. (228) 20146-0; fax (228) 20146-30; e-mail ami@ albertus-magnus-institut.de; internet www .albertus-magnus-institut.de; f. 1931; critical publishing of the works of Albertus Magnus; 8 mems; Dir Prof. Dr L. HONNEFELDER; publs *Editio Coloniensis, Lectio Albertina, Subsidia Albertina.*

Berliner Gesellschaft für Anthropologie, Ethnologie und Urgeschichte (Berlin Society for Anthropology, Ethnology and Prehistory): Alix Hänsel Museum für Vor- und Frühgeschichte, Schloss Charlottenburg, Langhansbau Spandauer Damm 22, 14059 Berlin; tel. (30) 32674817; fax (30)

32674812; internet www.bgaeu.de; f. 1869; 350 mems; Pres. CARSTEN NIEMITZ; publ. *Mitteilungen.*

Deutsche Gesellschaft für Asienkunde eV (German Association for Asian Studies): Rothenbaumchaussee 32, 20148 Hamburg; tel. (40) 445891; fax (40) 4107945; e-mail post@asienkunde.de; internet www .asienkunde.de; f. 1967; promotes and coordinates contemporary Asian research; 800 mems; Pres. Dr PETER CHRISTIAN HAUS-WEDELL; Sec. JÖRG JOSWIAK; publ. *Asien—The German Journal on Contemporary Asia* (4 a year).

Deutsche Gesellschaft für Soziologie: c/o Institut für Soziologie, Chemnitzer Str. 46A, 01062 Dresden; tel. (351) 46337404; fax (351) 46337113; e-mail dgs@mailbox.tu-dresden .de; internet www.soziologie.de; f. 1909; 1,350 mems; Pres. Prof. Dr KARL-SIEGBERT REHBERG; publ. *Soziologie–Forum der DGS.*

Deutsche Gesellschaft für Volkskunde eV (German Society for European Ethnology): Universität Hamburg, Institut für Volkskunde, Bogenallee 11, 24098 Kiel; tel. (40) 428385949; fax (40) 428386346; e-mail dgv@uni-hamburg.de; internet www.d-g-v .de; f. 1904; 1,200 mems; Pres. Prof. Dr THOMAS HENGARTNER; publs *Internationale Volkskundliche Bibliographie* (1 a year), *Mitteilungen der Deutschen Gesellschaft für Volkskunde* (4 a year), *Zeitschrift für Volkskunde* (2 a year).

Deutsche Morgenländische Gesellschaft (German Oriental Society): Centrum fur Nah- uns Mittelost- Studien, Universitat Marburg, Deutschhausstr. 12, 35032 Marburg; tel. (6421) 2824946; e-mail dmg@staff .uni-marburg.de; internet www.dmg-web.de; f. 1845; 698 mems; attached research institutes (Orient-Institut) in Beirut and Istanbul: see chapters on Lebanon and Turkey; library of 50,000 vols; Sec. Prof. Dr LESLIE TRAMONTINI; publs *Abhandlungen für die Kunde des Morgenlandes, Beiruter Texte und Studien, Bibliotheca Islamica, Journal of the Nepal Research Centre, Verzeichnis der orientalischen Handschriften in Deutschland, Zeitschrift der Deutschen Morgenländischen Gesellschaft.*

Deutsche Orient-Gesellschaft eV (German Oriental Society): Hüttenweg 7, Geschäftsstelle Altorientalisches Seminar der FU Berlin, 14195 Berlin; tel. (30) 83853601; fax (30) 83853600; e-mail dogva@ mail.zedat.fu-berlin.de; internet www .orient-gesellschaft.de; f. 1898; 976 mems; Pres. Prof. Dr HANS NEUMANN; Sec. Prof. Dr FELIX BLOCHER; publs *Abhandlungen, Alter Orient aktuell* (1 a year), *Mitteilungen der DOG* (1 a year), *Wissenschaftliche Veröffentlichungen.*

Deutsches Orient-Institut: Neuer Jungernfernstieg 21, 20354 Hamburg; tel. (40) 42825-514; fax (40) 42825-509; e-mail doi@doi.duei .de; internet www.duei.de; f. 1960 to study contemporary political, economic, and social developments in the countries of North Africa, the Middle East and Central Asia; 20 mems; library of 33,000 vols, 230 periodicals; Dir Prof. Dr UDO STEINBACH; Deputy Dir Dr HANSPETER MATTES; publs *Hamburger Beiträge: Medien und politische Kommunikation — Naher Osten und islamische Welt* (irregular), *Jahrbuch Nahost* (1 a year), *Mitteilungen* (irregular), *Orient* (4 a year), *Schriften des Deutschen Orient-Instituts* (irregular).

Gesellschaft für Anthropologie (Society for Anthropology): c/o Dr Mike Schweissing, Dept für Biologie der LMU München, Biodiversitätforschung/Anthropologie, Richard-Wagner-Str. 10, 8033 Munich; tel. (89) 21806716; e-mail m.schweissing@lmu.de;

internet www.gfanet.de; f. 1992 by merger of Deutsche Anthropologische Gesellschaft und Gesellschaft für Anthropologie und Humangenetik; Chair. Prof. Dr GISELA GRUPE; Sec. Dr MIKE SCHWEISSING.

GIGA—German Institute of Global and Area Studies (Leibniz-Institut für Globale und Regionale Studien): Neuer Jungfernstieg 21, 20354 Hamburg; tel. (40) 42825-516; fax (40) 42825-547; e-mail info@giga-hamburg.de; internet www.giga-hamburg.de; f. 1956 as Institut für Asienkunde; research into political, economic and social aspects of contemporary South, South-East and East Asia; 125 mems; library of 160,000 books, 750 journals; Pres. Prof. Dr ROBERT KAPPEL; Vice-Pres. Prof. Dr DETLEF NOLTE; publs *Africa Spectrum* (online), *GIGA Working Papers* (online), *Journal of Current Chinese Affairs—China aktuell* (4 a year), *Journal of Current Southeast Asian Affairs* (4 a year), *Journal of Politics in Latin America* (online), *Korea Yearbook—Politics, Economy and Society* (1 a year).

Rheinische Vereinigung für Volkskunde: Am Hofgarten 22, 53113 Bonn; tel. (228) 737618; fax (228) 739440; internet www.rvvb.uni-bonn.de; f. 1947; regional ethnology of the Rhineland; 300 mems; Pres. Prof. Dr H. FISCHER; publs *Bonner kleine Reihe zur Alltagskultur, Rheinisches Jahrbuch für Volkskunde.*

Wissenschaftliche Gesellschaft für Theologie eV: Paulsenstr. 55-56, 121063 Berlin; tel. (30) 82097223; fax (30) 82097105; e-mail wgth.berlin@gmx.de; internet www.wgth.de; f. 1973; 629 mems in Germany, Switzerland, Austria, UK, Netherlands, Romania, Czech Republic, Hungary and Scandinavia; 6 sections: Old Testament, New Testament, Church History, Systematic Theology, Practical Theology, Missions and Religion; Pres. Prof. Dr FRIEDRICH SCHWEITZER.

TECHNOLOGY

DECHEMA (Gesellschaft für Chemische Technik und Biotechnologie eV): Theodor-Heuss-Allee 25, 60486 Frankfurt am Main; tel. (69) 7564-0; fax (69) 7564-201; e-mail info@dechema.de; internet www.dechema.de; f. 1926; promotes and supports research and technological progress in chemical technology and biotechnology; an interface between science, economy, state and public; organizes ACHEMA summit for chemical technology, environmental protection and biotechnology; 5,000 mems; library of 25,000 vols; Chair. Dr HANS JÜRGEN WERNICKE; Exec. Dir Dr KURT WAGEMANN; publs *Chemie — Ingenieur — Technik* (12 a year), *Materialwissenschaft und Werkstofftechnik* (12 a year), *Materials and Corrosion* (1 a year).

Deutsche Gemmologische Gesellschaft eV (German Gemmological Association): Prof. Schlossmacher Str. 1, 55743 Idar-Oberstein; tel. (6781) 50840; fax (6781) 508419; e-mail info@dgemg.com; internet www.dgemg.com; f. 1932; administers the German Gemmological Training Centre; 2,000 mems; library of 2,500 vols; Dir Dr ULRICH HENN; publ. *Gemmologie* (4 a year, currently as 2 double issues).

Deutsche Gesellschaft für Luft- und Raumfahrt—Lilienthal-Oberth eV (DGLR) (German Society for Aeronautics and Astronautics): Godesberger Allee 70, 53175 Bonn; tel. (228) 30805-0; fax (228) 30805-24; e-mail peter.brandt@dglr.de; internet www.dglr.de; f. 1912; support of aeronautics and astronautics for all scientific and technical purposes; 3,000 mems; Pres. Prof. Dr-Ing. JOACHIM SZODRUCH; Vice-Pres

Dr-Ing. DETLEF MÜLLER-WIESNER, Dipl.-Ing. FRIEDER BEYER; Sec.-Gen. PETER BRANDT; publs *Luft- und Raumfahrt* (6 a year), *Mitteilungen* (6 a year).

Deutsche Gesellschaft für Materialkunde eV (Materials Science and Engineering): Senckenberganlage 10, 60325 Frankfurt; tel. (69) 75306-750; fax (69) 75306-733; e-mail dgm@dgm.de; internet www.dgm.de; f. 1919; 2,700 mems; Pres. Prof. Dr GÜNTER GOTTSTEIN; Dir Dr P. P. SCHEPP; publs *Advanced Engineering Materials, Zeitschrift für Metallkunde.*

Deutsche Gesellschaft für Photogrammetrie, Fernerkundung und Geoinformation (DGPF) eV: c/o EFTAS GmbH, Oststr. 2–18, 48145 Münster; tel. (0251) 133070; fax (0251) 1330733; f. 1909; 850 mems; Pres. Prof. Dr CORNELIA GLÄSSER; Sec. Dr Ing. MANFRED WIGGENHAGEN; publ. *Photogrammetrie-Fernerkundung-Geoinformation* (6 a year).

Deutsche Gesellschaft für Zerstörungsfreie Prüfung eV (DGZfP) (German Association for Non-Destructive Testing): Max-Planck-Str. 6, 13489 Berlin; tel. (30) 67807-0; fax (30) 67807-109; e-mail mail@dgzfp.de; internet www.dgzfp.de; f. 1933; conferences, training courses and personnel certification; 1,450 mems; Pres. JÖRG VÖLKER; Dir Dr RAINER LINK; publ. *ZfP-Zeitung* (12 a year).

Deutsche Glastechnische Gesellschaft eV (German Society of Glass Technology):; tel. (69) 975861-0; fax (69) 975861-99; e-mail info@hvg-dgg.de; internet www.hvg-dgg.de; f. 1922; 1,200 mems; online retrieval service; library of 21,500 vols; Dir Dr ULRICH ROGER; publ. *dgg journal* (for mems).

Deutsche Keramische Gesellschaft eV (German Ceramic Society): Am Grott 7, 51147 Cologne; tel. (2203) 96648-0; fax (2203) 69301; e-mail info@dkg.de; internet www.dkg.de; f. 1919; 1,400 mems; Chair. Prof. Dr RAINER TELLE; Dir Dr MARKUS BLUMENBERG; publ. *cfi-ceramic forum international/Berichte der DKG* (12 a year).

Deutsche Lichttechnische Gesellschaft eV: Burggrafenstr. 6, 10787 Berlin; tel. (30) 2601-2439; fax (30) 2601-1255; e-mail litg@din.de; internet www.litg.de; f. 1912; 2,500 mems; Sec. REGINA VOIGT; publ. *Licht* (12 a year).

Deutscher Beton- und Bautechnik-Verein eV (German Concrete Association): Kurfürstenstr. 129, 10785 Berlin; tel. (30) 236096-20; fax (30) 236096-23; internet www.betonverein.de; f. 1898; quality control, research, standardization and construction advice; 750 mems; Pres. Dr-Ing. HANS-ULRICH LITZNER; publs *Bemessungsbeispiele, Beton-Handbuch, Vorträge Betontag.*

Deutscher Kälte- und Klimatechnischer Verein eV (German Refrigeration Association): Pfaffenwaldring 10, 70569 Stuttgart; tel. (711) 6856-3200; fax (711) 6856-3242; e-mail info@dkv.org; internet www.dkv.org; f. 1909; 5 sections for production and industrial application of refrigeration, food science and technology, storage, transport and air conditioning; 1,300 mems; Pres. Dr-Ing. FRANK RINNE; Sec. IRENE REICHERT; publs *DKV-Aktuell* (4 a year), *DKV-Forschungsberichte* (irregular), *DKV-Statusberichte* (irregular), *DKV-Tagungsbericht* (1 a year).

Deutscher Markscheider Verein eV (Mining Surveyors): Shamrockring 1, 44623 Herne; tel. (2323) 154660; fax (2323) 154611; e-mail geschaeftsstelle@dmv-ev.de; internet www.dmv-ev.de; Pres. Dr-Ing. PETER GOERKE-MALLET.

Deutscher Verband für Materialforschung und -prüfung eV (DVM) (German Association for Materials Research and

Testing): Unter den Eichen 87, 12205 Berlin; tel. (30) 811-30-66; fax (30) 811-93-59; e-mail office@dvm-berlin.de; internet www.dvm-berlin.de; f. 1896; organizes conferences, seminars and workshops; 350 mems; Pres. Dr Ing. MANFRED BACHER-HOECHST; Sec. KATHRIN LEERS; publs *DVM-Nachrichten* (news, 3–4 a year), *Materialprüfung* (12 a year).

Deutscher Verband für Schweissen und verwandte Verfahren eV (German Welding Society): Postfach 101965, 40010 Düsseldorf; Aachener Str. 172, 40223 Düsseldorf; tel. (0211) 1591-0; fax (0211) 1591-200; e-mail verwaltung@dvs-hg.de; internet www.die-verbindungs-spezialisten.de; f. 1947; welding and allied processes; 20,000 mems; Pres. Dr-Ing. A. GÄRTNER; Chair. Dr-Ing. H. GEIS; publs *Aufbau und Verbindungstechnik in der Elektronic* (also English edn), *Der Praktiker, Die Schweisstechnische Praxis, DVS-Berichte, DVS-Merkblätter, DVS-Richtlinien, DVS-Videos, Fachbibliographie Schweisstechnik, Fachbuchreihe Schweisstechnik, Fachwörterbücher, Forschungsberichte Humanisierung des Arbeitslebens der Schweisser, Referateorgan Schweissen und verwandte Verfahren, Schweissen und Schneiden* (also English edn), *Schweisstechnische Forschungsberichte, Schweisstechnische Software.*

Deutscher Verband Technisch-wissenschaftlicher Vereine (Federation of Technical and Scientific Associations): Steinpl. 1, 10623 Berlin; tel. (30) 310078386; fax (30) 310078216; e-mail info@dvt-net.de; internet www.dvt-net.de; f. 1916; natural science and technology and represents the interests of engineers in relation to science, economics, society, politics, and administration; comprises 45 technical and scientific asscns; 45 mems; Chair. Prof. Dr HUBERTUS CHRIST; Vice-Chair. Dr Ing. WALTER THIELEN; Dir JÖRG MAAS.

Deutscher Verein des Gas- und Wasserfaches eV (DVGW) (German Technical and Scientific Association on Gas and Water): Josef-Wirmer Str. 1–3, 53123 Bonn; tel. (228) 9188-5; fax (228) 9188-990; e-mail info@dvgw.de; internet www.dvgw.de; f. 1859; specifications and standardization, testing and certification, research and development, training, providing consultancy services and information; 6,700 mems; Pres. Prof. Dr-Ing. KLAUS HOMANN; publs *DVGW—Informationen, DVGW—Nachrichten, DVGW—Regelwerk, DVGW—Schriftenreihen.*

DIN Deutsches Institut für Normung eV (German Institute for Standardization): Burggrafenstr. 6, 10787 Berlin; tel. (4930) 2601-0; fax (4930) 2601-1231; e-mail info@din.de; internet www.din.de; f. 1917; 1,796 mems; Pres. Prof. Dr-Ing. KLAUS HOMANN; Dir Dr-Ing. TORSTEN BAHKE; publs *DIN-Catalogue* (1 a year), *DIN Management Letter* (6 a year), *DIN-Mitteilungen* (12 a year).

Fachgebiet Wasserwirtschaft und Hydrosystemmodellierung: Institut für Bauingenieurwesen, Technische Univ., Sekr. TIB1-B14, Gustav-Meyer-Allee 25, 13355 Berlin; tel. (30) 314-23961; fax (30) 313-72430; e-mail reinhard.hinkelmann@wahyd.tu-berlin.de; internet www.tu-berlin.de; f. 1891, fmrly Deutscher Verband für Wasserwirtschaft und Kulturbau; hydromechanics, hydrology, hydraulic engineering, hydrosystems, modelling, water resources management; 118 mems; Dir Prof. Dr-Ing. REINHARD HINKELMANN.

Gesellschaft für Informatik eV: Wissenschaftszentrum, Ahrstr. 45, 53175 Bonn; tel. (228) 302-145; fax (228) 302-167; e-mail gs@gi-ev.de; internet www.gi-ev.de; f. 1969; promotes informatics in research, education, applications; 24,500 mems; Pres. Prof. Dr STEFAN JAEHNICHEN; Man. Dir Dr PETER FEDERER; Exec. Dir CORNELIA WINTER; publs *Informatik Spektrum, Künstliche Intelligenz, Wirtschaftsinformatik.*

Informationstechnische Gesellschaft im VDE (ITG) (Information Technology Society within VDE): Stresemannallee 15, 60596 Frankfurt; tel. (69) 6308360; fax (69) 6315233; e-mail itg@vde.com; internet www .vde.com; f. 1954; 33,000 mems; Chair. Prof. Dr-Ing. ALEXANDER RÖDER; Dir Dr-Ing. V. SCHANZ; publs *AEU International Journal of Electronics, Nachrichtentechnische Zeitschrift (NTZ)* (12 a year).

Institut für gewerbliche Wasser- wirtschaft und Luftreinhaltung GmbH (IWL) (Institute for Commercial Water Supply and the Prevention of Air Pollution): Chemiepark Knapsack, Industriestr., 50354 Hürth; tel. (2233) 482100; fax (2233) 482099; e-mail iwl-umweltinstitut@knapsack.de; internet www.iwl-umweltinstitut.de; f. 1956; Prof. Dr HORST-DIETER SCHÜDDEMAGE; publ. *IWL-Umweltbrief* (12 a year).

Rationalisierungs-Kuratorium der Deutschen Wirtschaft eV (RKW) (German Centre for Productivity and Innovation): Düsseldorfer Str. 40, 65760 Eschborn; tel. (6196) 4952812; fax (6196) 4954801; e-mail heitzer@rkw.de; internet www.rkw.de; f. 1921; 4,000 mems; Dirs Dr INGRID VOIGT, W. AXEL ZEHRFELD; publ. *RKW-Magazin* (4 a year).

Stahlinstitut VDEh: Sohnstr. 65, 40237 Düsseldorf; tel. (211) 6707-0; fax (211) 6707-310; e-mail vdeh@vdeh.de; internet www .stahl-online.de; f. 1860 as Verein Deutscher Eisenhüttenleute; present name 2003; promotion of research, literature, documentation and information, education and training; 9,000 mems; library of 120,000 vols; Pres. and Exec. Dir Prof. Dr Ing. D. AMELING; publs *Literaturschau Stahl und Eisen* (26 a year), *MPT Metallurgical Plant and Technology International* (6 a year), *Stahl* (6 a year), *Stahl und Eisen* (12 a year), *Stahlmarkt* (12 a year), *Steel Research (Archiv für das Eisenhüttenwesen)* (12 a year).

VDE Verband Deutscher Elektrotechni- ker eV (German Association of Electrical Engineers): Stresemannallee 15, 60596 Frankfurt am Main; tel. (69) 6308-0; fax (69) 6312925; e-mail service@vde.com; internet www.vde.com; f. 1893; 34,000 mems; Chair. ENNO LIESS; publs *Dialog VDE-Mitglieder-Information, Elektrotech- nische Zeitschrift, Nachrichtentechnische Zeitschrift, VDE-Buchreihe, VDE-Fachber- ichte, VDE-Schriftenreihe, VDE-Vorschrif- ten.*

Verein der Zellstoff- und Papier-Chemi- ker und -Ingenieure eV (Association of Pulp and Paper Chemists and Engineers): Emilestrasse 21, 64293 Darmstadt; tel. (6151) 33264; fax (6151) 311076; e-mail info@zellcheming.de; internet www .zellcheming.com; f. 1905; 2,050 mems; Exec. Dir Dr Ing. WILHELM BUSSE; Chair. Dr CLEMENS BÜLOW; publ. *ipw-Das Papier.*

Verein Deutscher Giessereifachleute (VDG) (German Foundrymen's Association): Postfach 105144, 40042 Düsseldorf; tel. (211) 6871-0; fax (211) 6871-364; e-mail info@vdg .de; internet www.vdg.de; f. 1909; 3,100 mems; library of 35,000 vols; Chair. Dr-Ing. GOTTHARD WOLF; publs *Casting Plant Tech- nology International* (4 a year), *Giesserei* (12 a year), *Giessereiforschung* (4 a year), seminars and courses.

Verein Deutscher Ingenieure (VDI) (Association of German Engineers): Postfach 101139, 40002 Düsseldorf; Graf-Recke-Str. 84, 40239 Düsseldorf; tel. (211) 6214-0; fax (211) 6214-175; e-mail kundencenter@vdi.de; internet www.vdi.de; f. 1856; technical and scientific cooperation in 21 engineering sections concerning all fields of technology; training courses for professional engineers; documentation in various branches of engineering and prevention of air pollution and noise; 130,000 individual mems, 2,000 corporate mems; Dir Prof. Dr-Ing. EIKE LEHMANN; publs *VDI-Verlag: Program: VDI-Nachrichten* (weekly newspaper), technical journals, books, etc.

Research Institutes
GENERAL

Max-Planck-Gesellschaft zur Förderung der Wissenschaften eV (Max Planck Society for the Advancement of Science): Postfach 101062, 80084 Munich; tel. (89) 2108-0; fax (89) 2108-1111; e-mail webmaster@gv.mpg .de; internet www.mpg.de; f. 1948; Pres. Prof. Dr PETER GRUSS; Sec.-Gen. Dr BARBARA BLUDAU; publ. *MaxPlanckResearch* (4 a year).

Attached Research Institutes:

Bibliotheca Hertziana–Max-Planck- Institut für Kunstgeschichte (Bibliotheca Hertziana—Max Planck Institute for Art History): Via Gregoriana 28, 00187 Rome, Italy; tel. 06-699931; fax 06-69993333; e-mail institut@biblhertz.it; internet www.biblhertz.it; f. 1913; library of 277,500 vols; Man. Dir Prof. Dr SYBILLE EBERT-SCHIFFERER; publs *Römische For- schungen der Bibliotheca Hertziana, Römisches Jahrbuch der Bibliotheca Hertziana, Römische Studien der Bib- liotheca Hertziana, Studi della Bibliotheca Hertziana.*

Friedrich-Miescher-Laboratorium für Biologische Arbeitsgruppen in der Max-Planck-Gesellschaft (Biological Research Groups of the Max Planck Institute Society): Postfach 2109, 72011 Tübingen; Spemannstr. 37–39, 72076 Tübingen; tel. (7071) 601-460; fax (7071) 601-455; internet www.fml.tuebingen.mpg.de; f. 1969; Man. of Spang Laboratory of Yeast and Worms Dr ANNE SPANG.

Fritz-Haber-Institut der Max-Planck- Gesellschaft: Faradayweg 4–6, 14195 Berlin; tel. (30) 8413-30; fax (30) 8413-3155; e-mail ertl@fhi-berlin.mpg.de; internet www.fhi-berlin.mpg.de; f. 1911; physical chemistry; Man. Dir Prof. Dr HANS-JOACHIM FREUND.

Kunsthistorisches Institut in Flor- enz—Max-Planck-Institut (Art History Institute in Florence—Max Planck Institute): Via Giuseppe Guisti 44, 50121 Florence, Italy; tel. 055-24911-1; fax 055-24911-55; internet www.khi.fi.it; f. 2002; Man. Dir Prof. Dr GERHARD WOLF; Dir Prof. Dr ALESSANDRO NOVA.

Max-Planck-Arbeitsgruppen für strukturelle Molekularbiologie am DESY (Max Planck Working Group for Structural Molecular Biology): c/o DESY, Notkestr. 85, Geb. 25B, 22607 Hamburg; tel. (40) 89-982801; fax (40) 89-716810; e-mail office@mpasmb.desy.de; internet www.mpasmb-hamburg.mpg.de; f. 1985; Heads Dr HANS-DIETER BARTUNIK, Prof. Dr ADA YONATH, Prof. Dr ECKHARD MANDELKOW.

Max-Planck-Forschungsstelle für Enzymologie der Proteinfaltung (Max Planck Research Institute for Enzymology of Protein Folding): Weinbergweg 22, 06120 Halle (Saale); tel. (345) 5522801; fax (345) 5511972; e-mail user@ enzyme-halle.mpg.de; internet www .enzyme-halle.mpg.de; f. 1997; Dir Prof. Dr GUNTER S. FISCHER.

Max-Planck-Forschungsstelle für Ornithologie (Max Planck Research Institute for Ornithology): Schlossallee 2, 78315 Radolfzell; tel. (7732) 1501-0; fax (7732) 1501-69; e-mail berthold@vowa .ornithol.mpg.de; internet erl.ornithol.mpg .de; f. 1998; Man. Dir Prof. Dr PETER BERTHOLD.

Max-Planck-Institut für Astronomie (Max Planck Institute for Astronomy): Königstuhl 17, 69117 Heidelberg; tel. (6221) 5280; fax (6221) 528246; e-mail user@mpia.de; internet www.mpia.de; f. 1967; Man. Dir Prof. Dr THOMAS HENNING; publ. *Sterne und Weltraum* (12 a year).

Max-Planck-Institut für Astrophysik (Max Planck Institute for Astrophysics): Karl-Schwarzschild-Str. 1, 85748 Garching; tel. (89) 30000-0; fax (89) 30000-2235; e-mail info@mpa-garching.mpg.de; internet www.mpa-garching.mpg.de; f. 1958; Man. Dir Prof. Dr RASHID SUNYAEV.

Max-Planck-Institut für Auslän- disches und Internationales Priva- trecht (Max Planck Institute for Foreign and International Criminal Law): Mittel- weg 187, 20148 Hamburg; tel. (40) 41900-0; fax (40) 41900-288; e-mail mpicc @mpicc .de; internet www.mpicc.de; f. 1926; Dirs Prof. Dr REINHARD ZIMMERMANN, ULRICH SIEBER; publ. *Rabels Zeitschrift für auslän- disches und internationales Privatrecht* (4 a year).

Max-Planck-Institut für Auslän- disches und Internationales Sozial- recht (Max Planck Institute for Foreign and International Social Law): Amalienstr. 33, 80799 Munich; tel. (89) 386020; fax (89) 38602490; e-mail user@mpipf-muenchen .mpg.de; internet www.mpipf-muenchen .mpg.de/mpisr; f. 1980; Man. Dir Prof. Dr ULRICH BECKER; publ. *Zeitschrift für aus- ländisches und internationales Arbeits- und Sozialrecht* (4 a year).

Max-Planck-Institut für Auslän- disches und Internationales Stra- frecht (Max Planck Institute for Foreign and International Criminal Law): Günter- stalstr. 73, 79100 Freiburg im Breisgau; tel. (761) 70811; fax (761) 7081-294; e-mail webmaster@iuscrim.mpg.de; internet www .iuscrim.mpg.de; f. 1938; library of 64,000 vols; Man. Dir Prof. Dr HANS-JÖRG ALBRECHT; publs *Auslandsrundschau der Zeitschrift für die gesamte Strafrechtswis- senschaft, European Journal of Crime, Criminal Law and Criminal Justice* (4 a year).

Max-Planck-Institut für Auslän- disches Öffentliches Recht und Völk- errecht (Max Planck Institute for Comparative Public Law and International Law): Im Neuenheimer Feld 535, 69120 Heidelberg; tel. (6221) 482-1; fax (6221) 482-288; e-mail information@mpil.de; internet www.mpil.de; f. 1924; Man. Dir Prof. Dr ARMIN VON BOGDANDY; publ. *Zeitschrift für ausländisches öffentliches Recht und Völkerrecht.*

Max-Planck-Institut für Bildungs- forschung (Max Planck Institute for Human Development): Lentzeallee 94, 14195 Berlin; tel. (30) 82406-0; fax (30) 8249939; e-mail sekmaydell@mpib-berlin .mpg.de; internet www.mpib-berlin.mpg .de; f. 1963; Man. Dir Prof. Dr UTE FREVERT.

Max-Planck-Institut für Bioanorga- nische Chemie (Max Planck Institute for Bioinorganic Chemistry): Stiftstr. 34–

36, 45470 Mülheim/Ruhr; tel. (208) 306-4; fax (208) 306-3951; e-mail mpibac@ mpi-muelheim.mpg.de; internet www .mpibac.mpg.de; f. 1958, fmrly Institute for Radiation Chemistry; Man. Dir Prof. Dr WOLFGANG LUBITZ.

Max-Planck-Institut für Biochemie (Max Planck Institute for Biochemistry): Am Klopferspitz 18A, 82152 Martinsried bei München; tel. (89) 85781; fax (89) 85783777; e-mail user@biochem.mpg.de; internet www.biochem.mpg.de; f. 1973; Man. Dir Prof. Dr DIETER OESTERHELT.

Max-Planck-Institut für Biogeochemie (Max Planck Institute for Biogeochemistry): Hans-Knöll-Str. 10, 07745 Jena; tel. (3641) 57-60; fax (3641) 57-70; e-mail info@bgc-jena.mpg.de; internet www.bgc-jena.mpg.de; f. 1997; Man. Dir Prof. Dr MARTIN HEIMANN.

Max-Planck-Institut für Biologische Kybernetik (Max Planck Institute for Biological Cybernetics): Spemannstr. 38, 72076 Tübingen; tel. (7071) 601510; fax (7071) 601520; e-mail info.kyb@tuebingen .mpg.de; internet www.kyb.tuebingen.mpg .de; f. 1968; works in the elucidation of cognitive processes; 350 mems; Man. Dir Prof. Dr NIKOS K. LOGOTHETIS.

Max-Planck-Institut für Biophysik (Max Planck Institute for Biophysics): Max-von-Laue-Str. 3, 60438 Frankfurt am Main; tel. (69) 6303-0; fax (69) 6303-4502; e-mail info@mpibp-frankfurt.mpg.de; internet www.mpibp-frankfurt.mpg.de; f. 1937; Man. Dir Prof. Dr WERNER KÜHL-BRANDT.

Max-Planck-Institut für Biophysikalische Chemie (Karl-Friedrich-Bonhoeffer-Institut) (Max Planck Institute for Biophysical Chemistry): Am Fassberg 11, 37077 Göttingen; tel. (551) 201-0; fax (551) 201-1222; e-mail ehoelsc@gwdg.de; internet www.mpibpc.gwdg.de; f. 1971; Man. Dir Prof. Dr REINHARD LÜHRMANN.

Max-Planck-Institut für Chemie (Otto-Hahn-Institut) (Max Planck Institute for Chemistry): Joh.-Joachim-Becher-Weg 27, 55128 Mainz; tel. (6131) 3050; fax (6131) 305388; e-mail gfd@mpch-mainz.mpg.de; internet www.mpch-mainz.mpg.de; f. 1912; Man. Dir Prof. Dr JOHANNES LELIE-VELD.

Max-Planck-Institut für Chemische Ökologie (Max Planck Institute for Chemical Ecology): Winzerlaer Str. 10, 07745 Jena; tel. (3641) 57-0; fax (3641) 57-2011; internet www.ice.mpg.de; f. 1996; Man. Dir Prof. Dr IAN BALDWIN.

Max-Planck-Institut für Chemische Physik fester Stoffe (Max Planck Institute for Chemical Physics of Solids): Nöthnitzer Str. 40, 01187 Dresden; tel. (351) 46460; fax (351) 464610; e-mail cpfs@cpfs .mpg.de; internet www.cpfs.mpg.de; f. 1995; Man. Dir Prof. JURI GRIN.

Max-Planck-Institut für Demografische Forschung (Max Planck Institute for Demographic Research): Konrad-Zuse-Str. 1, 18057 Rostock; tel. (381) 2081-0; fax (381) 2081-202; e-mail webmaster@demogr .mpg.de; internet www.demogr.mpg.de; f. 1996; Man. Dir Prof. Dr JAMES W. VAUPEL.

Max-Planck-Institut für Dynamik Komplexer Technischer Systeme (Max Planck Institute for Dynamics of Complex Technical Systems): Sandtorstr. 1, 39106 Magdeburg; tel. (391) 61100; fax (391) 6110500; e-mail presse@mpi-magdeburg .mpg.de; internet www.mpi-magdeburg .mpg.de; f. 1996; Man. Dir Prof. Dr Ing. KAI SUNDMACHER.

Max-Planck-Institut für Eisenforschung GmbH (Max Planck Institute for Iron Research): Postfach 140 444, 40074 Düsseldorf; Max-Planck-Str. 1, 40237 Düsseldorf; tel. (211) 67920; fax (211) 6792440; e-mail mpi@mpie.de; internet www.mpie.mpg.de; f. 1917; Man. Dir Prof. Dr MARTIN STRATMANN.

Max-Planck-Institut für Entwicklungsbiologie (Max Planck Institute for Developmental Biology): Spemannstr. 35, 72076 Tübingen; tel. (7071) 601350; fax (7071) 601300; e-mail mpi .entwicklungsbiologie@tuebingen.mpg.de; internet www.eb.tuebingen.mpg.de; f. 1937; Man. Dir Prof. Dr ANDREI N. LUPAS.

Max-Planck-Institut für Ethnologische Forschung (Max Planck Institute for Social Anthropology): Advokatenweg 36, 06114 Halle (Saale); tel. (345) 2927-0; fax (345) 2927-502; e-mail hann@eth.mpg .de; internet www.eth.mpg.de; f. 1998; Man. Dir Prof. Dr GÜNTHER SCHLEE.

Max-Planck-Institut für Europäische Rechtsgeschichte (European Legal History): Hausener Weg 120, 60489 Frankfurt am Main; tel. (69) 78978-0; fax (69) 78978169; e-mail user@mpier .uni-frankfurt.de; internet www.mpier .uni-frankfurt.de; f. 1964; Man. Dir Prof. Dr MARIE THERES FÖGEN; publ. *Jus Commune.*

Max-Planck-Institut für Evolutionäre Anthropologie (Max Planck Institute for Evolutionary Anthropology): Deutscher Pl. 6, 04103 Leipzig; tel. (341) 3550-0; fax (341) 3550-119; e-mail info@eva.mpg.de; internet www.eva.mpg.de; f. 1997; Man. Dir Prof. Dr CHRISTOPHE BOESCH.

Max-Planck-Institut für Evolutionsbiologie (Max Planck Institute for Evolutionary Biology): August-Thienemann-Str. 2, 24306 Plön; tel. (4522) 763-0; fax (4522) 763-351; e-mail tautz@evolbio.mpg.de; internet www.evolbio.mpg.de; f. 1891; library of 10,600 vols; Man. Dir Prof. Dr DIETHARD TAUTZ; Librarian BRIGITTE LECHNER.

Max-Planck-Institut für Experimentelle Endokrinologie (Max Planck Institute for Experimental Endocrinology): Feodor-Lynen-Str. 7, 30625 Hanover; tel. (511) 5359-0; fax (511) 5359-148; e-mail gottschalk@vw.endo.mpg.de; internet www.endo.mpg.de; f. 1979; Man. Dir Prof. Dr GREGOR EICHELE.

Max-Planck-Institut für Experimentelle Medizin (Max Planck Institute for Experimental Medicine): Hermann-Rein-Str. 3, 37075 Göttingen; tel. (551) 3899-0; fax (551) 3899-389; e-mail kraemer@em .mpg.de; internet www.em.mpg.de; f. 1947; molecular biology, neurosciences; library of 80,000 vols; Man. Dir Prof. Dr NILS BROSE; Librarian INGEBORG KRAEMER.

Max-Planck-Institut für Extraterrestrische Physik (Max Planck Institute for Extraterrestrial Physics): Giessenbachstr., 85748 Garching; tel. (89) 30000-0; fax (89) 30000-3569; e-mail mpe@mpe .mpg.de; internet www.mpe.mpg.de; f. 1963; Man. Dir Prof. Dr GÜNTHER HASINGER.

Max-Planck-Institut für Festkörperforschung (Max Planck Institute for Solid State Research): Heisenbergstr. 1, 70569 Stuttgart; tel. (711) 6890; fax (711) 689-1010; e-mail gs@fkf.mpg.de; internet www .fkf.mpg.de; f. 1969; Man. Dir Prof. Dr JOACHIM MAIER; Man. Dr MICHAEL EPPARD.

Max-Planck-Institut für Geistiges Eigentum, Wettbewerbs- und Steuerrecht (Max Planck Institute for Intellec-tual Property, Competition and Tax Law): Marstallpl. 1, 80539 Munich; tel. (89) 24246-0; fax (89) 24246-501; internet www.ip.mpg.de; f. 1966; Man. Dir Prof. Dr RETO M. HILTY.

Max-Planck-Institut für Gesellschaftsforschung (Max Planck Institute for the Study of Societies): Paulstr. 3, 50676 Cologne; tel. (221) 2767-0; fax (221) 2767-555; e-mail info@mpifg.de; internet www .mpifg.de; f. 1984; library of 60,000 vols; researches on sociology of markets, institutional change in contemporary capitalism, European liberalization policies, institution building across borders, economic patriotism, science, technology and innovation, governance of global structures, theories and methods; Man. Dir Prof. Dr JENS BECKERT; Man. Dir Prof. Dr WOLFGANG STREECK; publs *MPIfG Discussion Papers, MPIfG Journal Article, MPIfG Working Papers.*

Max-Planck-Institut für Gravitationsphysik (Albert-Einstein-Institut) (Max Planck Institute for Gravitational Physics): Am Mühlenberg 1, 14476 Potsdam; tel. (331) 567-70; fax (331) 567-7298; e-mail office@aei.mpg.de; internet www.aei .mpg.de; f. 1994; Man. Dir Prof. Dr GERHARD HUISKEN.

Max-Planck-Institut für Herz- und Lungenforschung (W. G. Kerckhoff-Institut) (Max Planck Institute for Heart and Lung Research): Ludwigstr. 43, 61231 Bad Nauheim; tel. (6032) 7050; fax (6032) 705211; e-mail info@mpi-bn.mpg.de; internet www.mpi-bn.mpg.de; f. 1931; Man. Dir Prof. Dr THOMAS BRAUN.

Max-Planck-Institut für Hirnforschung (Max Planck Institute for Brain Research): Postfach 710 662, 60496 Frankfurt am Main; Deutschordenstr. 46, 60528 Frankfurt am Main; tel. (69) 96769-0; fax (69) 96769-440; e-mail betz@ mpih-frankfurt.mpg.de; internet www .mpih-frankfurt.mpg.de; f. 1914; Man. Dir Prof. Dr HEINRICH BETZ.

Max-Planck-Institut für Immunbiologie (Max Planck Institute for Immunobiology): Stübeweg 51, 79108 Freiburg; tel. (761) 5108-100; fax (761) 5108-1358; internet www.immunbio.mpg.de; f. 1961.

Max-Planck-Institut für Infektionsbiologie (Max Planck Institute for Infection Biology): Schumannstr. 21–22, 10117 Berlin; tel. (30) 28460-0; fax (30) 28460-111; e-mail sek@mpiib-berlin.mpg.de; internet www.mpiib-berlin.mpg.de; f. 1993; Man. Dir Prof. Dr THOMAS F. MEYER.

Max-Planck-Institut für Informatik (Max Planck Institute for Informatics): Campus E1 4, 66123 Saarbrücken; tel. (681) 9325-0; fax (681) 9325-999; e-mail mpi@mpi-inf.mpg.de; internet www .mpi-inf.mpg.de; f. 1988; Man. Dir Prof. Dr KURT MEHLHORN.

Max-Planck-Institut für Kernphysik (Max Planck Institute for Nuclear Physics): Saupfercheckweg 1, 69117 Heidelberg; tel. (6221) 516-0; fax (6221) 516-601; e-mail mpik@mpi-hd.mpg.de; internet www .mpi-hd.mpg.de; f. 1958; Man. Dir Prof. Dr JOACHIM ULLRICH.

Max-Planck-Institut für Kohlenforschung (Max Planck Institute of Coal Research): Kaiser-Wilhelm-Platz 1, D-45470 Mülheim an der Ruhr; tel. (208) 306-1; fax (208) 306-2980; e-mail contact@ mpi-muelheim.mpg.de; internet www .mpi-muelheim.mpg.de; f. 1912; library of 17,000 vols; research in the catalytic transformation of compounds and materials with the highest degree of chemo-, regio-

and stereoselectivity under mild conditions and with an economical use of energy and resources in the following 5 areas: synthetic organic chemistry, homogeneous catalysis, heterogeneous catalysis, organometallic chemistry and theory; Man. Dir Prof. Dr ALOIS FÜRSTNER.

Max-Planck-Institut für Kolloid- und Grenzflächenforschung (Max Planck Institute for Colloid and Interface Research): Am Mühlenberg 1, 14476 Golm; tel. (331) 5679-0; fax (331) 5679-102; e-mail info@mpikg-golm.mpg.de; internet www.mpikg-golm.mpg.de; f. 1992; Man. Dir Prof. Dr HELMUTH MÖHWALD.

Max-Planck-Institut für Marine Mikrobiologie (Max Planck Institute for Marine Microbiology): Celsiusstr. 1, 28359 Bremen; tel. (421) 2028-50; fax (421) 2028-580; e-mail contact@mpi-bremen.de; internet www.mpi-bremen.de; f. 1992; Man. Dir Prof. Dr FRIEDRICH WIDDEL.

Max-Planck-Institut für Mathematik (Max Planck Institute for Mathematics): Vivatsgasse 7, 53111 Bonn; tel. (228) 402-0; fax (228) 402-277; e-mail director@mpim-bonn.mpg.de; internet www.mpim-bonn.mpg.de; f. 1981; Man. Dir Prof. Dr DON ZAGIER; Sec. ANDREA KOHLHUBER.

Max-Planck-Institut für Mathematik in den Naturwissenschaften (Max Planck Institute for Mathematics in the Sciences): Inselstr. 22–26, 04103 Leipzig; tel. (341) 9959-50; fax (341) 9959-658; e-mail ezeidler@mis.mpg.de; internet www.mis.mpg.de; f. 1996; Man. Dir Prof. Dr EBERHARD ZEIDLER.

Max-Planck-Institut für Medizinische Forschung (Max Planck Institute for Medical Research): Jahnstr. 29, 69120 Heidelberg; tel. (6221) 4860; fax (6221) 486-351; e-mail sekr@mpimf-heidelberg.mpg.de; internet www.mpimf-heidelberg.mpg.de; f. 1927; Man. Dir Dr WINFRIED DENK.

Max-Planck-Institut für Metallforschung (Max Planck Institute for Metals Research): Heisenbergstr. 3, 70569 Stuttgart; tel. (711) 689-3094; fax (711) 689-1931; e-mail info@mf.mpg.de; internet www.mf.mpg.de; f. 1921; Condensed Matter Science Fluctuations, Self organization and Structure Formation in Nanoconfinement Synchrotron Radiation, Neutrons, Microscopy Nano-Oxidation, Solid–Liquid Interfaces; Dir Prof. Dr JOACHIM SPATZ.

Max-Planck-Institut für Meteorologie (Max Planck Institute for Meteorology): Bundesstr. 53, 20146 Hamburg; tel. (40) 41173-0; fax (40) 41173-298; e-mail annette.kirk@zmaw.de; internet www.mpimet.mpg.de; f. 1975; Man. Dir Prof. Dr JOCHEM MAROTZKE.

Max-Planck-Institut für Mikrostrukturphysik (Max Planck Institute for Microstructure Physics): Weinberg 2, 06120 Halle am Saale; tel. (345) 558250; fax (345) 5511223; e-mail bruno@mpi-halle.de; internet www.mpi-halle.mpg.de; f. 1991; Man. Dir Prof. Dr JÜRGEN KIRSCHNER.

Max-Planck-Institut für Molekulare Biomedizin (Max Planck Institute for Molecular Biomedicine): Röntgenstr. 20, 48149 Münster; tel. (251) 70-3650; e-mail presse@mpi-muenster.mpg.de; internet www.mpi-muenster.mpg.de; f. 2001; Man. Dir Prof. Dr DIETMAR VESTWEBER.

Max-Planck-Institut für Molekulare Genetik (Max Planck Institute for Molecular Genetics): Ihnestr. 63–73, 14195 Berlin; tel. (30) 8413-0; fax (30) 8413-1388; e-mail info@molgen.mpg.de; internet www.molgen.mpg.de; f. 1964; analysis of human genes, their function and evolution; bioinformatics, devt and implementation of new methods for functional genome analysis; library of 50,000 vols; Man. Dir Prof. Dr MARTIN VINGRON.

Max-Planck-Institut für Molekulare Pflanzenphysiologie (Max Planck Institute for Molecular Plant Physiology): Am Mühlenberg 1, 14476 Golm Potsdam; tel. (331) 56780; fax (331) 5678408; e-mail contact@mpimp-golm.mpg.de; internet www.mpimp-golm.mpg.de; f. 1994; Man. Dir Prof. Dr RALPH BOCK.

Max-Planck-Institut für Molekulare Physiologie (Max Planck Institute for Molecular Physiology): Otto-Hahn-Str. 11, 44227 Dortmund; tel. (231) 133-0; fax (231) 133-2699; e-mail acting.director@mpi-dortmund.mpg.de; internet www.mpi-dortmund.mpg.de; f. 1993; Man. Dir Prof. Dr HERBERT WALDMANN.

Max-Planck-Institut für Molekulare Zellbiologie und Genetik (Max Planck Institute for Molecular Cell Biology and Genetics): Pfotenhauerstr. 108, 01307 Dresden; tel. (351) 210-0; fax (351) 210-2000; e-mail info@mpi-cbg.de; internet www.mpi-cbg.de; f. 1998; Man. Dir Prof. Dr MARINO ZERIAL.

Max-Planck-Institut für Neurobiologie (Max Planck Institute for Neurobiology): Am Klopferspitz 18, 82152 Martinsried; tel. (89) (89) 8578-1; fax (89) (89) 8578-3541; e-mail merker@neuro.mpg.de; internet www.neuro.mpg.de; f. 1917, present name 1998; research on the devt, functions, and diseases of the nervous system; molecular developmental biology, cellular and systems studies of neural plasticity, pathology and immunology of the central and peripheral nervous system, information processing in the invertebrate visual system; incl. 8 independent research groups; Man. Dir Prof. Dr HARTMUT WEKERLE; Public Relations Officer Dr STEFANIE MERKER.

Max-Planck-Institut für Neurologische Forschung (Max Planck Institute for Neurological Research): Gleueler Str. 50, 50931 Cologne; tel. (221) 4726-0; fax (221) 4726-298; e-mail wdh@pet.mpin-koeln.mpg.de; internet www.mpin-koeln.mpg.de; f. 1982; Man. Dir Prof. Dr WOLF-DIETER HEISS.

Max-Planck-Institut für Neuropsychologische Forschung (Max Planck Institute for Cognitive Neuroscience): Stephanstr. 1A, 04103 Leipzig; tel. (341) 9940-00; fax (341) 9940-104; e-mail orendi@cns.mpg.de; internet www.cns.mpg.de; f. 1994; Dirs Prof. Dr ANGELA D. FRIEDERICI, Prof. Dr DETLEV YVES VON CRAMON.

Max-Planck-Institut für Ökonomik (Max Planck Institute for Economics): Kahlaische Str. 10, 07745 Jena; tel. (3641) 686-5; fax (3641) 686-990; e-mail witt@econ.mpg.de; internet www.econ.mpg.de; f. 1993; Dir Prof. Dr WERNER GÜTH.

Max-Planck-Institut für Physik (Werner-Heisenberg-Institut) (Max Planck Institute for Physics): Föhringer Ring 6, 80805 Munich; tel. (89) 32354-0; fax (89) 3226704; e-mail bethke@mppmu.mpg.de; internet www.mppmu.mpg.de; f. 1917; Man. Dir Prof. Dr SIEGFRIED BETHKE.

Max-Planck-Institut für Physik komplexer Systeme (Max Planck Institute for Physics of Complex Systems): Nöthnitzer Str. 38, 01187 Dresden; tel. (351) 871-0; fax (351) 8711999; e-mail gneisse@mpipks-dresden.mpg.de; internet www.mpipks-dresden.mpg.de; f. 1992; Dir Prof. Dr PETER FULDE.

Max-Planck-Institut für Plasmaphysik (Max Planck Institute for Plasma Physics): Boltzmannstr. 2, 85748 Garching; tel. (89) 3299-01; e-mail info@ipp.mpg.de; internet www.ipp.mpg.de; f. 1960; Scientific Dir Prof. Dr GUNTHER HASINGER.

Max-Planck-Institut für Polymerforschung (Max Planck Institute for Polymer Research): Ackermannweg 10, 55128 Mainz; tel. (6131) 379-0; fax (06131) 379-100; e-mail schwiesow@mpip-mainz.mpg.de; internet www.mpip-mainz.mpg.de; f. 1983; Man. Dir Prof. Dr KLAUS MÜLLEN.

Max-Planck-Institut für Psychiatrie (Deutsche Forschungsanstalt für Psychiatrie) (Max Planck Institute for Psychiatry): Kraepelinstr. 2–10, 80804 Munich; tel. (89) 30622-1; fax (89) 30622605; e-mail holsboer@mpipsykl.mpg.de; internet www.mpipsykl.mpg.de; f. 1917; basic and clinical research, clinical services in psychiatry and neurology; main topics incl. depression, anxiety disorders, multiple sclerosis; Man. Dir Prof. Dr FLORIAN HOLSBOER.

Max-Planck-Institut für Psycholinguistik (Max Planck Institute for Psycholinguistics): Wundtlaan 1, 6525 XD Nijmegen, Netherlands; tel. (Netherlands) (24) 3521911; fax (Netherlands) (24) 3521213; e-mail general@mpi.nl; internet www.mpi.nl; f. 1976; Man. Dir Prof. Dr ANNE CUTLER.

Max-Planck-Institut für Psychologische Forschung (Max Planck Institute for Psychological Research): Postfach 340 121, 80098 Munich; Amalienstr. 33, 80799 Munich; tel. (89) 386020; fax (89) 38602199; internet www.mpipf-muenchen.mpg.de; f. 1981; Man. Dir Prof. Dr WOLFGANG PRINZ.

Max-Planck-Institut für Quantenoptik (Max Planck Institute for Quantum Optics): Hans-Kopfermann-Str. 1, 85748 Garching; tel. (89) 32 905-0; fax (89) 32905-200; e-mail gerhard.rempe@mpq.mpg.de; internet www.mpq.mpg.de; f. 1981; Man. Dir Prof. Dr GERHARD REMPE.

Max-Planck-Institut für Radioastronomie (Max Planck Institute for Radio Astronomy): Auf dem Hügel 69, 53121 Bonn; tel. (228) 525-0; fax (228) 525-229; e-mail postmaster@mpifr-bonn.mpg.de; internet www.mpifr-bonn.mpg.de; f. 1966; Man. Dir Dr KARL M. MENTEN.

Max-Planck-Institut für Sonnensystemforschung (Max Planck Institute for Solar System Research): Max-Planck-Str. 2, 37191 Katlenburg-Lindau; tel. (5556) 979-0; fax (5556) 979-240; e-mail user@mps.mpg.de; internet www.mps.mpg.de; f. 1955; Man. Dir Prof. Dr SAMI K. SOLANKI.

Max-Planck-Institut für Strömungsforschung (Max Planck Institute for Flow Research): Bunsenstr. 10, 37073 Göttingen; tel. (551) 5176-0; fax (551) 5176-669; e-mail gwdg@gwdg.de; internet www.mpisf.mpg.de; f. 1925; Head Prof. Dr HERBERT WALTHER.

Max-Planck-Institut für Terrestrische Mikrobiologie (Max Planck Institute for Terrestrial Microbiology): Karl-von-Frisch-Str., 35043 Marburg; tel. (6421) 178-0; fax (6421) 178-999; e-mail mpi@mailer.uni-marburg.de; internet www.uni-marburg.de/mpi; f. 1990; Man. Dir Prof. Dr REGINE KAHMANN.

Max-Planck-Institut für Wissenschaftsgeschichte (Max Planck Institute for History of Science): Boltzmannstr. 22, 14195 Berlin; tel. (30) 22667-0; fax (30) 22667-299; e-mail public@mpiwg-berlin .mpg.de; internet www.mpiwg-berlin.mpg .de; f. 1994; library of 60,000 vols; Exec. Dir Prof. Dr Jürgen Renn; Dir Prof. Dr Lorraine Daston.

Max-Planck-Institut für Züchtungsforschung (Max Planck Institute for Plant Breeding Research): Carl-von-Linné-Weg 10, 50829 Cologne; tel. (221) 5062-0; fax (221) 5062-513; e-mail user@ mpiz-koeln.mpg.de; internet www .mpiz-koeln.mpg.de; f. 1927; Man. Dir Dr Paul Schulze-Lefert.

Max Planck-Institut zur Erforschung Multireligiöser und Multiethnischer Gesellschaften (Max Planck Institute for The Study of Religious and Ethnic Diversity): Hermann-Föge-Weg 11, 37073 Göttingen; tel. (551) 4956-0; fax (551) 4956-170; e-mail info@mmg.mpg.de; internet www.mmg.mpg.de; f. 2007, fmrly Max-Planck-Institut für Geschichte; library of 115,000 vols; Man. Dir Prof. Dr Steven Vertovec; Librarian Heidemarie Oltmann.

Max-Planck-Institut zur Erforschung von Gemeinschaftsgütern (Max Planck Institute for Research into Collective Property): Kurt-Schumacher-Str. 10, 53113 Bonn; tel. (228) 91416-0; fax (228) 91416-55; internet www.mpp-rdg.mpg.de; f. 2003; Head Prof. Dr Christoph Engel.

AGRICULTURE, FISHERIES AND VETERINARY SCIENCE

Bundesforschungsanstalt für Landwirtschaft (FAL) (Federal Agricultural Research Centre): Bundesallee 50, 38116 Braunschweig; tel. (531) 596-0; fax (531) 596-1099; internet www.fal.de; f. 1947; 12 institutes for specialized agricultural research; library of 133,000 vols; Pres. Prof. Dr Klaus-Dieter Vorlop; publs Landbauforschung Völkenrode (3 or 4 a year), Wissenschaft Erleben (2 a year).

Deutsche Gesellschaft für Holzforschung eV (German Society for Wood Research): Bayerstr. 57–59, 5 Stock, 80335 Munich; tel. (89) 5161700; fax (89) 531657; e-mail mail@dgfh.de; internet www.dgfh.de; f. 1942; Pres. Dipl.-Ing. X. Haas; Man. Dipl.-Ing. Axel Yeutsch; publ. DGfH aktuell (3 a year).

Forschungsgesellschaft für Agrarpolitik und Agrarsoziologie: Meckenheimer Allee 125, 53115 Bonn; tel. (531) 5965165; fax (531) 5965299; internet www.faa-bonn.de; f. 1952; study and scientific investigation of economic and social problems of agriculture and rural areas; 65 mems; Pres. Prof. Dr W. Henrichs-Meyer; Dir Dr Heinrich Becker.

Gesellschaft für Hopfenforschung (Society of Hops Research): 85283 Wolnzach-Hüll; tel. (8442) 3597; fax (8442) 2871; e-mail gfh@ hopfenforschung.de; internet www .hopfenforschung.de; f. 1926; Pres. Dipl.-Ing. Michael Möller; Dir Dr Fritz Ludwig Schmucker.

Johänn Heinrich von Thünen Institute/ Federal Research Institute for Rural Areas, Forestry and Fisheries: Bundesalle 50, 38116 Braunscweig; tel. (531) 596-0; fax (531) 596-1099; e-mail info@vti.bund.de; internet www.vti.bund.de; f. 2008, by merger of Federal Research Centre for Fisheries (f. 1948), the Federal Research Centre for Forestry and Forestry Products and divs of the Federal Agricultural Research Centre; library of 68,500 vols; Pres. Prof. Dr Folkhard Isermeyer.

Attached Research Institutes:

Institut für Fischereiökologie: Palmaille 9, 22589 Hamburg; tel. (40) 38905-290; fax (40) 38905-261; e-mail info@ifo .bfa-fisch.de; Dir Prof. Dr Hans-Stephan Jenke.

Institut für Fischereitechnik und Fischereiökonomie: 22767 Hamburg; tel. (40) 38905-185; fax (40) 38905-264; e-mail info@ifh.bfa-fisch.de; internet www .bfa-fisch.de/iff; Dir Prof. Dr Erdmann Dahm.

Institut für Ostseefischerei: Alter Hafen Süd 2, 18069 Rostock; tel. (381) 81161-00; fax (381) 81161-99; e-mail info@ ior.bfa-fisch.de; Dir Dr Cornelius Hammer.

Institut für Seefischerei: 22767 Hamburg; tel. (40) 38905-178; fax (40) 38905-263; e-mail info@ish.bfa-fisch.de; Dir Dr Siegfried Ehrich.

ARCHITECTURE AND TOWN PLANNING

Akademie für Raumforschung und Landesplanung (Academy for Spatial Research and Planning): Hohenzollernstr. 11, 30161 Hanover; tel. (511) 34842-0; fax (511) 34842-41; e-mail arl@arl-net.de; internet www.arl-net.de; f. 1946; 550 mems (125 full, 425 corresp.); library of 20,000 vols; Pres. Prof. Dr Hans Heinrich Blotevogel; Gen. Sec. Prof. Dr-Ing. Dietmar Scholich; publ. Raumforschung und Raumordnung (Spatial Research and Planning, 6 a year, in German with summaries in English).

Deutsche Akademie für Städtebau und Landesplanung (Town and Country Planning Academy of Germany): Gubenerstr. 49, 10243 Berlin; tel. (30) 29362825; fax (30) 29362826; e-mail dasl-berlin@t-online.de; internet www.dasl.de; f. 1922; 600 mems; library of 5,000 vols; Pres. Prof. Dr-Ing. Christiane Thalgott; publs Almanach (1 a year), Vorbereitende Bericht (1 or 2 a year).

BIBLIOGRAPHY, LIBRARY SCIENCE AND MUSEOLOGY

Gutenberg-Gesellschaft (Gutenberg Society): Liebfrauenpl. 5, 55116 Mainz; tel. (6131) 226420; fax (6131) 233530; e-mail gutenberg-gesellschaft@freenet.de; internet www.gutenberg-gesellschaft.uni-mainz.de; f. 1901 for the publication of research work on the art of printing and books from Gutenberg until the present day; 2,000 mems; Pres. The Mayor of the City of Mainz; Dir Dr Cornelia Fischer; Sec. Karl Delorme; publ. Gutenberg-Jahrbuch (1 a year).

ECONOMICS, LAW AND POLITICS

Arbeitsgemeinschaft Deutscher Wirtschaftswissenschaftlicher Forschungsinstitut eV (Assn of German Economic Science Research Institutes): Königin-Luise-Str. 5, 14195 Berlin; f. 1949; 31 mem. institutes; coordinates programmes of the institutes and provides a permanent base for research exchange and cooperation; Chair. Prof. Dr Klaus F. Zimmermann; Sec.-Gen. Ralf Messer; publ. Gemeinschaftsdiagnose (2 a year).

Member Institutes:

Abteilung Wirtschaftswissenschaft im Osteuropa Institut an der Freien Universität Berlin (Economics Department of the East European Institute at the Free University, Berlin): Garystr. 55, 14195 Berlin; tel. (30) 83854008; fax (30) 83852072; e-mail schrettl@wiwiss .fu-berlin.de; internet web.fu-berlin.de/ wipol; f. 1950; economic research on East European countries; 10 mems; library of 85,000 vols and 95 periodicals; Dir Prof. Dr Wolfram Schrettl; publs Berichte des Osteuropa Instituts/Reihe Wirtschaft und Recht, Wirtschaftswissenschaftliche Veröffentlichungen.

BAW Institut für Wirtschaftsforschung GmbH (BAW Economic Research Institute Ltd): Wilhelm-Herbst-Str. 5, 28359 Bremen; tel. (421) 20699-0; fax (421) 20699-99; e-mail info@ baw-bremen.de; internet www.baw .uni-bremen.de; f. 1947; library of 20,000 vols; Dir Prof. Dr Frank Haller; publs BAW-Monatsbericht (12 a year), Regionalwirtschaftliche Studien (irregular).

Deutsches Institut für Wirtschaftsforschung (German Institute for Economic Research): Königin-Luise-Str. 5, 14195 Berlin; tel. (30) 897890; fax (30) 89789200; e-mail postmaster@diw.de; internet www.diw.de; f. 1925; Pres. Prof. Dr Klaus F. Zimmermann; publs Economic Bulletin (12 a year), Vierteljahrshefte zur Wirtschaftsforschung (4 a year), Wochenbericht (52 a year).

Deutsches Wirtschaftswissenschaftliches Institut für Fremdenverkehr an der Universität München (German Institute for Economic Research in Tourism and Travel, University of Munich): Sonnenstr. 27, 80331 Munich; tel. (89) 267091; fax (89) 267613; e-mail info@dwif .de; internet www.dwif.de; f. 1950; 6 staff; library of 8,000 vols; Dir Dr J. Maschke; publ. Jahrbuch für Fremdenverkehr (1 a year).

Energiewirtschaftliches Institut an der Universität zu Köln: Alte Wagenfabrik, Vogelsanger Str. 321, 50827 Cologne; tel. (221) 27729100; fax (221) 27729400; internet www.ewi.uni-koeln.de; f. 1943; energy economics, environmental economics; 30 mems; library of 12,000 vols, 90 periodicals; Dir Prof. Dr Marc O. Bettzüge; publ. Zeitschrift für Energiewirtschaft (4 a year).

Forschunginstitut für Wirtschaftspolitik an der Universität Mainz: see under Johannes Gutenberg-Universität.

Forschungsstelle für Allgemeine und Textile Marktwirtschaft an der Universität Münster (Research Institute for General and Textile Economics): Fliednerstr. 21, 48149 Münster; tel. (0251) 22939; fax (0251) 83-31438; e-mail 22fatm@wiwi.uni-muenster.de; internet www.wiwi.uni-muenster.de; f. 1941; 25 mems; library of 15,000 vols; Dirs Prof. Dr Dieter Ahlert, Prof. Dr Gustav Dieckheuer.

GfK-Nürnberg, Gesellschaft für Konsum-, Markt- und Absatzforschung eV (GfK Association): Nordwestring 101, 90319 Nuremberg; tel. (911) 395-0; fax (911) 395-2209; e-mail gfk_verein@gfk .com; internet www.gfk-verein.de; f. 1934; the not-for-profit section of the GfK Group for the Promotion of Market Research; carries out research and maintains close co-operation with scientific institutions, particularly Friedrich-Alexander University at Erlangen-Nuremberg; supports the education of market researchers, the ongoing training of leadership personnel and participation in commercial ventures; 600 mems; Pres. Hajo Riesenbeck; publ. Yearbook of Marketing and Consumer Research.

Historisches Forschungszentrum der Friedrich-Ebert-Stiftung (Centre for Historical Research of the Friedrich-Ebert-Foundation): Godesberger Allee 149, 53175 Bonn; tel. (228) 883-0; fax (228) 883-9204; e-mail michael .schneider@fes.de; internet www.fes.de; f.

1925; Dir Prof. Dr MICHAEL SCHNEIDER; publ. *Archiv für Sozialgeschichte.*

ifo-Institut für Wirtschaftsforschung (ifo-Institute for Economic Research): Poschingerstr. 5, 81679 Munich; tel. (89) 9224-0; fax (89) 985369; e-mail ifo@ifo.de; internet www.ifo.de; f. 1949; empirical economic research; library of 90,000 vols; Pres. Dr HANS-WERNER SINN; publs *CESifo DICE* (in English, 4 a year), *CESifo Economic Studies* (in English), *CESifo Forum* (in English, 4 a year), *ifo Dresden berichtet* (6 a year), *ifo Schnelldienst* (36 a year), *ifo Wirtschaftskonjunktur* (12 a year).

Institut der Deutschen Wirtschaft eV: Gustav-Heinemann-Ufer 84–88, 50968 Cologne; tel. (221) 4981-1; fax (221) 4981-533; e-mail welcome@iwkoeln.de; internet www.iwkoeln.de; f. 1951; education and labour market; economic and social policy; library of 200,000 vols; Pres. Dr HANS-DIETRICH WINKHAUS; Dir Prof. Dr MICHAEL HÜTHER; publ. *iw-trends* (4 a year).

Institut für Angewandte Wirtschaftsforschung Tübingen (Institute for Applied Economic Research): Ob dem Himmelreich 1, 72074 Tübingen; tel. (7071) 9896-0; fax (7071) 9896-99; e-mail iaw@iaw.edu; internet www.iaw.edu; f. 1957; international integration and regional development, labour markets and social security, public finance and environmental economics; library of 1,250 vols; Dir Prof. Dr CLAUDIA M. BUCH; publ. *IAW-News* (4 a year).

Institut für Arbeitsmarkt- und Berufsforschung der Bundesanstalt für Arbeit (Institute for Employment Research): Regensburger Str. 104, 90478 Nürnberg; tel. (911) 179-0; fax (911) 179-3258; e-mail info@iab.de; internet www.iab.de; f. 1967; researches the labour market to advise policy-makers at all levels; library of 70,000 vols; Dir Prof. Dr JOACHIM MÖLLER; publ. *Zeitschrift für Arbeitsmarkt-Forschung (ZAF)* (4 a year).

Institut für Handelsforschung an der Universität zu Köln: Säckinger Str. 5, 50935 Cologne; tel. (221) 943607-0; fax (221) 943607-99; e-mail info@ifhkoeln.de; internet www.ifhkoeln.de; Dir Prof. Dr L. MÜLLER-HAGEDORN.

Institut für Marktanalyse und Agrarhandelspolitik der Bundesforschungsanstalt für Landwirtschaft Braunschweig-Völkenrode (FAL) (Institute for Market Analysis and Agricultural Trade Policy): Bundesallee 50, 38116 Brunswick; tel. (531) 596-5301; fax (531) 596-5399; e-mail ma@fal.de; internet www.ma.fal.de; f. 1948; Dir Prof. Dr M. BROCKMEIER (acting); publ. *Agrarwirtschaft* (11 a year).

Institut für Seeverkehrswirtschaft und Logistik (Institute of Shipping Economics and Logistics): Universitätsallee 11–13, 28359 Bremen; tel. (421) 22096-0; fax (421) 22096-55; e-mail info@isl.org; internet www.isl.org; f. 1954; applied research and development projects in logistics systems, maritime economics and transport, information logistics/planning and simulation systems; library of 125,000 vols, 230 periodicals and newspapers; Exec. Dir Prof. Dr HANS-DIETRICH HAASIS; publs *ISL Book Series, ISL Lectures, Contributions and Presentations, Shipping Statistics and Market Review* (figures of shipping, shipbuilding, sea ports and seaborne trade, 10 a year and online at www.infoline.de), *Shipping Statistics Yearbook* (and online at www.infoline.de).

Institut für Weltwirtschaft an der Universität Kiel: see under Christian-Albrechts Universität.

Institut für Wirtschaft und Gesellschaft Bonn eV (IWG BONN) (Bonn Institute for Economic and Social Research): Wissenschaftszentrum, Ahrstr. 45, 53175 Bonn; tel. (228) 372044; fax (228) 375869; e-mail kontakt@iwg-bonn.de; internet www.iwg-bonn.de; f. 1977; Dir STEFANIE WAHL; Scientific Dir MEINHARD MIEGEL.

Institut für Wirtschaftspolitik an der Universität zu Köln: Pohligstr. 1, 50969 Cologne; tel. (221) 470-5347; fax (221) 470-5350; e-mail iwp@wiso.uni-koeln.de; internet www.iwp.uni-koeln.de; economic policy, foreign trade policy, EU research; Dirs Prof. Dr JÜRGEN B. DONGES, Prof. Dr JOHANN EEKHOFF; publs *Untersuchungen zur Wirtschaftspolitik, Zeitschrift für Wirtschaftspolitik* (3 a year).

Osteuropa-Institut München: Scheinerstr. 11, 81679 Munich; tel. (89) 998396-0; fax (89) 9810110; e-mail oei@oei-muenchen.de; internet www.oei-muenchen.de; f. 1952; research into the history and economics of Eastern Europe and fmr USSR; library of 168,000 vols; Dir Prof. Dr JOACHIM MÖLLER; publs *Economic Systems* (4 a year), *Jahrbücher für Geschichte Osteuropas* (4 a year).

Rheinisch-Westfälisches Institut für Wirtschaftsforschung (Rhine-Westphalia Institute for Economic Research): Hohenzollernstr. 1–3, 45128 Essen; tel. (201) 8149-0; fax (201) 8149-200; e-mail rwi@rwi-essen.de; internet www.rwi-essen.de; f. 1943; study of the structure and devt of the German (and int.) economy; spec. research facilities, advice on admin. and economics for firms and students; 80 mems; library of 110,000 vols; Pres. Prof. Dr CHRISTOPH M. SCHMIDT; Vice-Pres. Prof. Dr THOMAS K. BAUER; Dir Prof. Dr WIM KÖSTERS; publs *Konjunkturberichte* (Economic Report, 2 a year), *Materialien* (surveys and extensive articles, irregular), *Ruhr Economic Papers* (irregular), *Schriften* (articles on aspects of economic policy, irregular).

Schmalenbach-Gesellschaft für Betriebswirtschaft eV: Bunzlauer Str. 1, 50858 Cologne; tel. (2234) 480097; fax (2234) 480005; e-mail sg@schmalenbach.org; internet www.schmalenbach.org; f. 1978; economic research; 1,500 mems; Pres. Prof. Dr CLEMENS BÖRSIG; Man. Dr MARIA ENGELS; publ. *Schmalenbachs Zeitschrift für betriebswirtschaftliche Forschung (ZfbF)* (12 a year).

Statistisches Bundesamt (Federal Statistical Office): Gustav-Stresemann-Ring 11, 65189 Wiesbaden; tel. (611) 75-2405; fax (611) 75-3330; e-mail poststelle@destatis.de; internet www.destatis.de; f. 1950; library of 500,000 vols; Pres. RODERICH EGELER; publs *Datenreport* (2 a year), *Die Bundesländer: Strukturen und Entwicklungen* (2 a year), *Glossar statistischer Fachbegriffe* (irregular), *Kreiszahlen* (1 a year), *Statistik lokal—Daten für die Gemeinden, kreisfreien Städte und Kreise Deutschlands* (1 a year), *Statistik regional—Daten für die Kreise und kreisfreien Städte Deutschlands* (database, published in English as *Regional Statistics*, 1 a year), *Statistisches Jahrbuch für das Ausland* (Statistical Yearbook for Foreign Countries, 1 a year), *Statistisches Jahrbuch für die Bundesrepublik Deutschland* (Statistical Yearbook for the Federal Republic of Germany, 1 a year), *Wirtschaft und Statistik* (12 a year), *Zahlenkom-*

pass—Statistisches Taschenbuch für Deutschland (published in English as *Key Data on Germany*, 1 a year).

Wirtschafts- und Sozialwissenschaftliches Institut in der Hans-Böckler-Stiftung (Economic Research Institute of the Hans Böckler Foundation): Hans-Böckler-Str. 39, 40476 Düsseldorf; tel. (211) 7778-0; fax (211) 7778-120; e-mail zentrale@boeckler.de; internet www.boeckler.de; Dir Prof. Dr HEIDE PFARR; publ. *Mitteilungen* (12 a year).

Arnold Bergstraesser Institut für kulturwissenschaftliche Forschung (ABI): Windausstr. 16, 79110 Freiburg im Breisgau; tel. (761) 88878-0; fax (761) 88878-78; e-mail abifr@arnold-bergstraesser.de; internet www.arnold-bergstraesser.de; f. 1960; socio-political research particularly on education, administration, political development and ethnic conflicts in Africa, Asia, Middle East and Latin America; depts of overseas education and overseas admin.; 4 regional depts: Africa, Asia, Latin America, Middle East/North Africa; 20 mems; library of 72,000 vols; Dir Prof. Dr HERIBERT WEILAND; publ. *International Quarterly for Asian Studies* (2 a year).

Frobenius-Institut an der Johann Wolfgang Goethe-Universität: Grüneburgpl. 1, 60323 Frankfurt; tel. (69) 79833050; fax (69) 79833101; internet www.frobenius-institut.de; f. 1898; African, Indonesian and Melanesian cultures and history; library of 96,000 vols; Dir Prof. Dr KARL-HEINZ KOHL; publ. *Paideuma* (1 a year).

Gesellschaft für Deutschlandforschung eV (Society for Research on Germany): c/o Prof. Dr Karl Eckart, Horster Str. 51, 46236 Bottrop; tel. (2041) 61716; fax (2041) 24016; e-mail info@gfd-berlin.de; internet www.gfd-berlin.de; f. 1978; contemporary research on Germany; seminars and conferences; Pres. Prof. Dr KARL ECKART; Vice-Pres. Prof. Dr HANS-JÖRG BÜCKING (Berlin).

GIGA Informationszentrum (GIGA Information Centre): Neuer Jungfernstieg 21, 20354 Hamburg; tel. (40) 42825-598; fax (40) 42825-512; e-mail iz@giga-hamburg.de; internet www.giga-hamburg.de/iz; f. 1966; sections on Africa, Asia and South Pacific, Latin America, Near and Middle East; database of 6,665,000 documentary units (references to research literature) available online from the database of the 'Fachinformationsverbund Internationale Beziehungen und Länderkunde'; library of 160,000 vols, 750 current journals, online documents, press cuttings, archives and databases; Head Dipl. Bibl. GERDA HANSEN; publs *Ausgewählte neuere Literatur* (selected bibliographies of recent literature, by regions, 4 a year), *Kompendium der deutsch-[ausländischen] Beziehungen* (directory on German relations with foreign countries, irregular), *Kurzbibliographien* (working/introductory bibliographies, irregular), *Spezialbibliographien* (specialized bibliographies, irregular), also online bibliographies (irregular) and new acquisitions lists (6 a year).

Herder-Institut eV: Gisonenweg 5–7, 35037 Marburg/Lahn; tel. (6421) 1840; fax (6421) 184139; e-mail herder@herder-institut.de; internet www.herder-institut.de; f. 1950; historical research on countries and peoples of Eastern Central Europe; library: see Libraries and Archives; Dir Prof. Dr PETER HASLINGER; publ. *Zeitschrift für Ostmitteleuropa-Forschung* (4 a year).

Institut Finanzen und Steuern eV (Finance and Taxation Institute): Postfach 7269, 53072 Bonn; Markt 14, 53111 Bonn; tel. (228) 982210; fax (228) 9822150; e-mail info@ifst.de; internet www.ifst.de; f. 1949; Dir HANS-JÜRGEN MÜLLER-SEILS.

Leibniz Institut für Globale und Regionale Studien (German Institute of Global and Area Studies (GIGA)): Neuer Jungfernstieg 21, 20354 Hamburg; tel. (40) 42825-593; fax (40) 42825-547; e-mail info@ giga-hamburg.de; internet www .giga-hamburg.de; f. 1963; basic and applied research on political, economic and social developments in Africa, Asia, Latin America, and the Near and Middle East; policy advice to political instns, the business community and the media; networking within the area studies and comparative area studies community; 4 constituent orgs: Institute of African Affairs (IAA), Institute of Asian Studies (IAS), Institute of Latin American Studies (ILAS), Institute of Middle East Studies (IMES); library of 46,000 vols and 400 periodicals; Dir Prof. Dr ROBERT KAPPEL; publs *Comparative Perspectives* (Journal of Transnational and Area Studies, 3 a year), *GIGA Focus, GIGA Journal Family, NORD-SÜD aktuell* (4 a year).

Stiftung Wissenschaft und Politik (SWP) (German Institute for International and Security Affairs): Ludwigkirchpl. 3–4, 10719 Berlin; tel. (30) 88007-0; fax (30) 88007-100; e-mail swp@swp-berlin.org; internet www .swp-berlin.org; f. 1962; interdisciplinary research in int. affairs and security, computerized information system for the fields of int. relations and area studies (660,000 references), publicly available database 'World Affairs On-line'; library of 94,000 vols, 360 periodicals; Pres. U. HARTMANN; Dir Prof. Dr V. PERTHES; publs *SWP Comments, SWP Research Papers*.

Wissenschaftszentrum Berlin für Sozialforschung: Reichpietschufer 50, 10785 Berlin; tel. (30) 25491-0; fax (30) 25491684; e-mail wzb@wzb.eu; internet www.wzb.eu; f. 1969; a non-profit organization; conducts int. and interdisciplinary, empirical social science research on 4 research areas: education, work and life chances, markets and politics, society and economic dynamics, civil society, conflicts and democracy; library of 150,000 vols, 450 periodicals (printed), 8,500 periodicals (online access), 75 databases; Pres. Prof. Dr JUTTA ALLMENDINGER; publs *WZB Abstracts* (1 a year), *WZBrief Arbeit, WZBrief Bildung, WZB-Forschung* (4 a year), *WZB-Mitteilungen* (4 a year).

EDUCATION

Deutsches Institut für Internationale Pädagogische Forschung (German Institute for International Educational Research): Schloss-Str. 29, 60486 Frankfurt am Main; tel. (69) 24708-0; fax (69) 24708-444; e-mail dipf@dipf.de; internet www.dipf.de; f. 1951; educational information and research; library of 920,000 vols; libraries in Berlin and Frankfurt; Dir Prof. Dr MARC RITTBERGER; Deputy Dir Prof. Dr MARCUS HASSELHORN; publ. *DIPF informiert* (2 a year).

Gesellschaft für Pädagogik und Information eV: Pädagogisches Büro, Rathenaustr. 16, Postfach 2228, 33052 Paderborn; tel. (5251) 34024; f. 1964 to promote research and development in the field of educational technology and information science; 400 mems; Chair. Prof. Dr U. LEHNERT, Prof. Dr G. E. ORTNER; publs *Pädagogik und Information, Schul Praxis—Wirtschaft und Weiterbildung*.

Gesellschaft zur Förderung Pädagogischer Forschung eV (Society for the Promotion of Educational Research): Postfach 900280, 60442 Frankfurt am Main; Schloss-Str. 29, 60486 Frankfurt am Main; tel. (69) 247080; fax (69) 24708444; f. 1950;

dissemination of research results, organization of communication processes between educational research and school practice; 300 mems; Pres. BERND FROMMELT; Sec. P. DOEBRICH; publ. *Materialen zur Bildungsforschung* (book series, 2–3 a year).

FINE AND PERFORMING ARTS

Gesellschaft für Musikforschung: Heinrich-Schütz-Allee 35, 34131 Kassel-Wilhelmshöhe; tel. (561) 3105-255; fax (561) 3105-254; e-mail g.f.musikforschung@t-online.de; internet www.musikforschung.de; f. 1946; 1,800 mems; Pres. Prof. Dr WOLFGANG AÜHAGEN; Treas. Dr GABRIELE BUSCHMEIER; publ. *Die Musikforschung* (4 a year).

Staatliches Institut für Musikforschung Preussischer Kulturbesitz mit Musikinstrumenten-Museum: Tiergartenstr. 1, 10785 Berlin; tel. (30) 25481-0; fax (30) 25481-172; e-mail sim@sim.spk-berlin.de; internet www.sim-berlin.de; f. 1888 as Königliche akademische Hochschule, present name and status 1945; collects musicological material, instruments, records, phonograms and tape recordings; conducts research into the devt and history of musicology, incl. acoustics, musical instruments and the style and practice of executing music of the past; archival and documentary research and comparative musicological research; open to the public; lectures, concerts and exhibitions; library of 67,000 vols; Dir Dr THOMAS ERTELT; Dir of Museum Prof. Dr CONNY RESTLE; publs *Bibliographie des Musikschrifttums* (1 a year, online), *BMS online* (digital successor of the printed Bibliography), *Briefwechsel der Wiener Schule, Geschichte der Musiktheorie, Jahrbuch* (1 a year), *Klang und Begriff: Perspektiven musikalischer Theorie und Praxis, Studien zur Geschichte der Musiktheorie*.

Zentralinstitut für Kunstgeschichte (History of Art): Meiserstr. 10, 80333 Munich; tel. (89) 289-27556; fax (89) 289-27607; e-mail direktion@zikg.eu; internet www.zikg.eu; f. 1947; library of 480,000 vols; 800,000 photographs in image colln; Dir Prof. Dr WOLF TEGETHOFF; publs *Kunstchronik* (12 a year), *Reallexikon zur Deutschen Kunstgeschichte, RIHA Journal*.

HISTORY, GEOGRAPHY AND ARCHAEOLOGY

Deutsches Archäologisches Institut (German Archaeological Institute): Podbielskiallee 69–71, 14195 Berlin; tel. (1888) 7711-0; fax (1888) 7711-191; e-mail info@dainst.de; internet www.dainst.org; f. 1829; brs in Rome (Prof. Dr DIETER MERTENS), Athens (Prof. Dr WOLF-DIETRICH NIEMEIER), Cairo (Prof. Dr GÜNTER DREYER), Istanbul (Prof. Dr ADOLF HOFFMANN), Madrid (Prof. Dr DIRCE MARZOLI), Middle East (Prof. Dr RICARDO EICHMANN), Sana'a (Dr IRIS GERLACH), Damascus (Dr KARIN BARTL), Eurasia (Prof. Dr SVEND HANSEN) and Tehran; also Römisch-Germanische Kommission, Frankfurt am Main (Prof. Dr SIEGMAR FREIHERR VON SCHNURBEIN), Kommission für Alte Geschichte und Epigraphik, München (Prof. Dr CHRISTOF SCHULER) and Kommission für Allgemeine und Vergleichende Archäologie, Bonn (Dr BURKHARDT VOGT); Pres. Prof. Dr HERMANN PARZINGER; Dir ORTWIN DALLY; publs *Archäologischer Anzeiger, Archäologische Berichte aus dem Yemen, Athenische Mitteilungen, Baghdader Mitteilungen, Berichte der Römisch-Germanischen-Kommission, Chiron, Damaszener Mitteilungen, Germania, Istanbuler Mitteilungen, Jahrbuch, Madrider Mitteilungen, Mitteilungen des DAI Kairo, Römische Mitteilungen, Teheraner Mitteilungen*.

Institut für Europäische Geschichte (Institute of European History): Alte Universitätsstr. 19, 55116 Mainz; tel. (6131) 3939350; fax (6131) 3935326; e-mail ieg4@ ieg-mainz.de; internet www.ieg-mainz.de; f. 1950; conducts and promotes research on the historical foundations of Europe; cross-cultural projects on European communication and transfer processes; projects on concepts and perceptions of Europe since 1450; research fellowship programme (research, training and int. networking); library of 220,000 vols; Dir for History of Religion Prof. Dr IRENE DINGEL; Dir for Universal History Prof. Dr HEINZ DUCHHARDT; Research Coordinator Dr JOACHIM BERGER; publs *Archiv für Reformationsgeschichte–Literaturbericht* (1 a year), *IEG-MAPS* (online), *Jahrbuch für Europäische Geschichte* (1 a year), *Veröffentlichungen des Instituts für Europäische Geschichte* (monographs and conf. documentation), *Veröffentlichungen des Instituts für Europäische Geschichte, Beihefte online* (conf. documentation, online).

Institut für Zeitgeschichte München–Berlin (Institute of Contemporary History Munich and Berlin): Leonrodstr. 46B, 80636 Munich; tel. (89) 126880; fax (89) 12688-191; e-mail ifz@ifz-muenchen.de; internet www .ifz-muenchen.de; f. 1949; German and European history research since 1918, particularly Weimar Republic, National Socialism and post-1945 history; library of 200,500 vols; Dir Prof. Dr Dr h.c. HORST MOELLER; publs *Biographische Quellen zur Zeitgeschichte, Quellen und Darstellungen zur Zeitgeschichte, Schriftenreihe der Vierteljahrshefte für Zeitgeschichte* (2 a year), *Studien zur Zeitgeschichte, Texte und Materialien zur Zeitgeschichte, Vierteljahrshefte für Zeitgeschichte* (4 a year), *Zeitgeschichte im Gespräch*.

Vereinigung zur Erforschung der Neueren Geschichte eV (Modern History Research Association): Argelanderstr. 59, 53115 Bonn; tel. (228) 216205; fax (228) 2426044; e-mail apw@uni-bonn.de; internet www.pax-westphalica.de; f. 1957; history from 17th century to present day; library of 8,000 vols; Dir Prof. Dr MAXIMILIAN LANZINNER; Vice Dir Prof. Dr KONRAD REPGEN; publ. *Acta Pacis Westphalicae* (Sources of the Westphalian Peace Conf.).

LANGUAGE AND LITERATURE

Arbeitsstelle für Osterreichische Literatur und Kultur Robert-Musil-Forschung: Universität des Saarlandes, Gebäude 53/3 or, OG/323, Postfach 151150, 66041 Saarbrücken; tel. (681) 302-3334; fax (681) 302-3034; e-mail fzoelk@mx .uni-saarland.de; internet www.uni-saarland .de/fak4/fr41/afoelk; f. 1970; archives; study programmes, publications, symposia, bibliography; library of 5,000 vols; Dirs Prof. Dr PIERRE BÉHAR, Prof. Dr MARIE-LOUISE ROTH; publ. research reports.

Institut für Deutsche Sprache: POB 101621, 68016 Mannheim; R5 6–13, 68161 Mannheim; tel. (621) 1581-0; fax (621) 1581-200; e-mail webmaster@ids-mannheim.de; internet www.ids-mannheim.de; f. 1964; scientific study of present-day and historical German; library of 80,000 vols, 300 journals; Dir Prof. Dr LUDWIG M. EICHINGER; publs *Amades-Arbeitspapiere und Materialien zur deutschen Sprache, Deutsch im Kontrast, Deutsche Sprache* (4 a year), *Jahrbuch, Phonai, Schriften, Sprachreport* (4 a year), *Studienbibliographien Sprachwissenschaft, Studien zur deutschen Sprache*.

MEDICINE

Bernhard-Nocht-Institut für Tropenmedizin (Tropical Medicine): Bernhard-Nocht-Str. 74, 20359 Hamburg; tel. (40) 42818-0; fax (40) 42818400; e-mail bni@bni-hamburg .de; internet www.bni-hamburg.de; f. 1900; tropical medicine and parasitology; Nat. Reference Centre for Tropical Infections; library of 44,000 vols and 47,500 reprints; Dir Prof. Dr ROLF HORSTMANN; publ. *Scientific Report* (1 a year).

C. & O. Vogt-Institut für Hirnforschung, Universität Düsseldorf (Brain Research): Postfach 101007, 40001 Düsseldorf; tel. (211) 8112777; fax (211) 8112336; f. 1937; morphometry, neuroanatomy, immunohistochemistry, psychopharmacology; neurochemistry; Dir Prof. Dr KARL ZILLES.

Chemotherapeutisches Forschungsinstitut Georg-Speyer-Haus: Paul-Ehrlich-Str. 42/44, 60596 Frankfurt am Main; tel. (69) 63395-0; fax (69) 63395297; e-mail kost@ em.uni-frankfurt.de; internet www .georg-speyer-haus.de; f. 1904; research into HIV/AIDS, tumours and allergies; library of 27,664 vols; Dir Prof. Dr BERND GRONER.

Deutsche Gesellschaft für Kardiologie, Herz- und Kreislaufforschung (German Cardiac Society): Achenbachstr. 43, 40237 Düsseldorf; tel. (211) 600692-0; fax (211) 600692-10; e-mail info@dgk.org; internet www.dgk.org; f. 1927; 5,140 mems; Dir and Gen. Sec. Prof. Dr GUNTHER ARNOLD; publs *Basic Research in Cardiology* (6 a year), *Clinical Research in Cardiology, Herzschrittmachertherapie und Elektrophysiologie, Intensiv- und Notfallmedizin.*

Deutsche Gesellschaft für Sexualforschung eV (German Association for Research on Sexuality): Universitätsklinikum Hamburg-Eppendorf, Zentrum für Psychosoziale Medizin, Institut und Poliklinik für Sexualforschung und Forensische Psychiatrie, Martinistr. 52, 20246 Hamburg; tel. (40) 42803-2225; fax (40) 42803-6406; e-mail briken@uke.uni-hamburg.de; internet www .dgfs.info; f. 1950; 300 mems; Pres. Prof. Dr ULRIKE BRANDENBURG; Dir Dr PEER BRIKEN; publ. *Zeitschrift für Sexualforschung.*

Deutsche Krebsgesellschaft eV (German Cancer Society): Steinlestr. 6, 60596 Frankfurt am Main; tel. (69) 630096-0; fax (69) 630096-66; e-mail service@krebsgesellschaft .de; internet www .deutsche-krebsgesellschaft.de; f. 1900; promoting research, treatment and prevention of cancer; Pres. Prof. Dr M. BAMBERG; Sec.-Gen. Dr S. VON OESTERREICH; publs *Der Onkologe, Forum* (German Cancer Society news, 8 a year), *Journal of Cancer Research and Clinical Oncology* (6 a year).

Geomedizinische Forschungsstelle der Heidelberger Akademie der Wissenschaften (Geomedical Research Office of the Heidelberg Academy of Sciences): Karlstr. 4, 69117 Heidelberg; tel. (6221) 543265; fax (6221) 543355; e-mail haw@urz .uni-heidelberg.de; internet www.haw .baden-wuerttemberg.de; f. 1952; epidemiology of atherosclerotic diseases in Europe and Asia; 50 mems; library of 3,000 vols; Dir Prof. Dr G. SCHETTLER; publs *Geomedical Monographs Series* (6 vols), *World Atlas of Epidemic Diseases* (3 vols 1952–1961), *World Maps of Climatology*, geomedical studies.

GSF–Forschungszentrum für Umwelt und Gesundheit GmbH (National Research Centre for Environment and Health): Ingolstädter Landstr. 1, 85764 Neuherberg; tel. (89) 31870; internet www.gsf.de; f. 1964; controls 20 institutes; 1,500 mems; library: central library of 120,000 vols, 350 journals; Scientific and Technical Dir Prof.

Dr E.-G. AFTING; Administrative Dir Dr HANS JAHREISS.

Herz- und Diabeteszentrum NRW: Georgstr. 11, 32545 Bad Oeynhausen; tel. (5731) 97-0; fax (5731) 97-2300; e-mail info@ hdz-nrw.de; internet www.hdz-nrw.de; f. 1985; cardiology, thoracic and cardiovascular surgery, paediatric cardiology, diabetology, gastroenterology, nuclear medicine, anaesthesiology, radiology, molecular biophysics, radiopharmacy, laboratory and transfusion medicine; library of 3,000 vols and 180 periodicals; Dir Dr O. FOIT.

Institut für Umweltmedizinische Forschung an der Heinrich-Heine-Universität Düsseldorf (Environmental Health Research Institute): Auf'm Hennekamp 50, 40225 Düsseldorf; tel. (211) 33890; fax (211) 3190910; internet www.iuf.uni-duesseldorf .de; f. 2001; molecular preventive medical research in the field of environmental health; evaluation of risks to human health that result from environmental factors, in order to develop preventive and therapeutic strategies; 110 mems; library of 15,000 vols; Dir Prof. Dr med. JEAN KRUTMANN.

Institut für Wasser-, Boden- und Lufthygiene, Forschungsstelle Bad Elster (Institute for Water, Soil and Air Purity, Bad Elster Research Unit): Heinrich-Heine-Str. 12, 08645 Bad Elster; tel. (37437) 760; fax (37437) 76219; f. 1962; fed. govt instn; research in drinking water and bathing water, microbiology, toxicology, chemical analysis and ecology; library of 17,000 vols; Dir (Berlin) Prof. Dr H. LANGE-ASSCHENFELDT.

Institut für Wasserchemie und Chemische Balneologie der Technischen Universität München (Institute for Hydrochemistry and Chemical Balneology at the Technical University of Munich): Marchionistr. 17, 81377 Munich; tel. (89) 2180-78231; fax (89) 2180-78255; internet www.ws .chemie.tu-muenchen.de; f. 1951; water chemistry, hydrogeology, environmental analytical chemistry; Dir Prof. Dr R. NIESSNER.

Max von Pettenkofer-Institut für Hygiene und Medizinische Mikrobiologie (Max von Pettenkofer Institute of Hygiene and Medical Microbiology): Pettenkoferstr. 9A, 80336 Munich; tel. (89) 5160-5201; fax (89) 5160-5202; internet www.mvp .uni-muenchen.de; Dirs Prof. Dr JÜRGEN HEESEMANN, Prof. Dr ULRICH KOSZINOWSKI.

Paul-Ehrlich-Institut, Bundesamt für Impfstoffe und biomedizinische Arzneimittel: Paul-Ehrlich-Str. 51–59, 63225 Langen; tel. (6103) 77-0; fax (6103) 77-1234; e-mail pei@pei.de; internet www.pei.de; f. 1896 as Institute for Serum Testing and Serum Research; German and European medicinal product legislation; approval of clinical trials; marketing authorisation of biological medicinal products, vaccines for humans and animals, medicinal products containing antibodies, allergens for therapy and diagnostics, blood and blood products, tissue and medicinal products for gene therapy, somatic cell therapy and xenogenic cell therapy; research in the field of life sciences; depts of bacteriology, virology, immunology, veterinary medicine, allergology, medicinal biotechnology, haematology and transfusion medicine; research into safety of medicinal products and devices; c. 770 mems; library of 55,000 vols; Pres. Prof. Dr KLAUS CICHUTEK; publ. *Arbeiten aus dem Paul-Ehrlich-Institut.*

Verein für Wasser-, Boden- und Lufthygiene eV (Society for Water, Soil and Air Purity): Rotthauser Str. 19, 45879 Gelsenkirchen; tel. (209) 9242-190; fax (209) 9242-

199; e-mail verein@wabolu.de; internet www .wabolu.de; f. 1902; researches and subsidizes international studies into environmental water and air issues; Dir Prof. Dr LOTHAR DUNEMANN.

NATURAL SCIENCES
General

Forschungsinstitut und Naturmuseum Senckenberg (Research Institute and Natural History Museum): Senckenberganlage 25, 60325 Frankfurt am Main; tel. (69) 7542-0; fax (69) 746238; internet www .senckenberg.de; f. 1817; systematics, anatomy, distribution, ecology, evolution in zoology, botany, palaeozoology, palaeobotany, marine biology and geology, palaeoanthropology; Dir Prof. Dr V. MOSBRUGGER; publs *Abhandlungen der Senckenbergischen Naturforschenden Gesellschaft, Archiv für Molluskenkunde, Courier Forschungsinstitut Senckenberg, Natur und Museum* (6 a year), *Senckenbergiana biologica, Senckenbergiana lethaea, Senckenbergiana maritima.*

Biological Sciences

Alfred-Wegener-Institut für Polar- und Meeresforschung (Alfred Wegener Institute for Polar and Marine Research): Postfach 120161, 27515 Bremerhaven; tel. (471) 4831-0; fax (471) 4831-1149; e-mail info@awi .de; internet www.awi.de; f. 1980; Dir Prof. Dr KARIN LOCHTE; Admin. Dir Dr HEIKE WOLKE; Sec. J. MARTIN; publ. *Berichte zur Polar- und Meeresforschung* (Reports of Polar and Marine Research, irregular).

Constituent Research Units:

Biologische Anstalt Helgoland (Biological Institution Heligoland): Postfach 180, 27483 Heligoland; tel. (4725) 819-0; fax (4725) 819-283; internet www .awi-bremerhaven.de/bah/index-d.html; f. 1892; research in marine ecology, esp. in the N Sea; library of 63,000 vols; Head Prof. Dr FRIEDRICH BUCHHOLZ; publ. *Helgoländer Meeresuntersuchungen* (Heligoland Marine Research, 4 a year).

Forschungsstelle Potsdam des Alfred-Wegener-Instituts für Polar und Meeresforschung (Potsdam Research Unit of the Alfred Wegener Institute for Polar and Marine Research): Postfach 600149, 14401 Potsdam; tel. (331) 288-2100; fax (331) 288-2137; internet www.awi-potsdam.de; f. 1992; terrestrial geoscientific research in the periglacial regions; research into atmospheric processes; Head Prof. Dr HANS-WOLFGANG HUBBERTEN.

Wadden Sea Station, List/Sylt: Hafenstr. 43, 25992 List/Sylt; tel. (4651) 956-0; fax (4651) 956-200; internet www .awi-bremerhaven.de/bah/sylt-d.html; f. 1924; studies of coastal biological processes and ecosystems and monitoring of coastal changes and their long-term impact; Head Prof. Dr KARSTEN REISE.

Biozentrum Klein Flottbek: Ohnhorststr. 18, 22609 Hamburg; tel. (40) 42816-0; fax (40) 42816-254; e-mail sekretariat@botanik .uni-hamburg.de; internet www.biologie .uni-hamburg.de/bzf; f. 1821; research in plant physiology, cell biology, plant systematics, genetics and microbiology, applied plant molecular biology; botanical garden and herbarium comprising 800,000 specimens; 250 mems; library of 45,000 vols and 49,000 reprints; Man. Dir Prof. Dr MICHAEL BÖTTGER; publs *Institut für Allgemeine Botanik Hamburg, Mitteilungen.*

Deutsche Gesellschaft für Moor- und Torfkunde (German Peat Society): Stilleweg 2, 30655 Hanover; tel. (511) 643-3612; fax (511) 643-3612; e-mail gerfried.caspers@

lbeg.niedersachsen.de; internet www.dgmtev.de; f. 1970; 350 mems; Pres. Dr G. CASPERS; publ. *TELMA* (1 a year).

Forschungszentrum Borstel Leibniz–Zentrum für Medizin und Biowissenschaften (Borstel Research Centre for Medicine and Biological Sciences): Parkallee 1–40, 23845 Borstel; tel. (4537) 188-0; fax (4537) 188-721; internet www.fz-borstel.de; f. 1947; research in fields of pneumology, infection biology, allergology and inflammation medicine; library of 50,000 vols; Dirs Prof. Dr SILVIA BULFONE-PAUS, Prof. Dr PETER ZABEL, Prof. Dr ULRICH SCHAIBLE; Admin. Man. SUSANN SCHRADER.

Institut für Angewandte Botanik (Institute of Applied Botany at Hamburg University): Biozentrum Klein Flottbek und Botanischer Garten der Universität Hamburg, Ohnhorststr. 18, 22609 Hamburg; tel. (40) 428160; fax (40) 428162-48; e-mail secretariat@botanik.uni-hamburg.de; internet www.biologie.uni-hamburg.de/bzf; f. 1885; library of 130,000 vols; 140 mems; research on plant products, agriculture and horticulture; Dir Prof. Dr GÜNTER ADAM.

Institut für Vogelforschung 'Vogelwarte Helgoland' (Institute of Avian Research): An der Vogelwarte 21, 26386 Wilhelmshaven; tel. (4421) 96890; fax (4421) 968955; e-mail ifv@ifv-vogelwarte.de; internet www.vogelwarte-helgoland.de; f. 1910; research in the fields of bird migration, bird population dynamics, climate change and applied aspects; Dir Prof. Dr FRANZ BAIRLEIN; publ. *Vogelwarte* (4 a year).

Naturforschende Gesellschaft Bamberg eV: Litzendorferstr. 17, 96129 Strullendorf; tel. (9505) 6356; fax (9505) 8305; internet www.stadt.bamberg.de; f. 1834; 250 mems; library of 18,000 vols; Dir Dipl.-Biol. K. WEBER; publ. *Berichte*.

Naturforschende Gesellschaft Freiburg i. Br.: Albertstr. 23B, 79104 Freiburg; tel. (761) 2036484; fax (761) 2036483; e-mail naturforschende@geologie.uni-freiburg.de; internet www.naturforschende-gesellschaft.uni-freiburg.de; f. 1821; 300 mems; Pres. Prof. Dr R. MAECKEL.

Mathematical Sciences

Mathematisches Forschungsinstitut Oberwolfach GmbH (Mathematical Research Institute): Schwarzwaldstr. 9–11, 77709 Oberwolfach; tel. (7834) 979-0; fax (7834) 979-55; e-mail admin@mfo.de; internet www.mfo.de; f. 1944; library of 75,000 vols; Dir Prof. Dr GERT-MARTIN GREUEL; Librarian VERENA FRANKE; publ. *Oberwolfach Reports* (4 a year).

Physical Sciences

Astronomisches Institut der Universität Würzburg: Am Hubland, 97074 Würzburg; tel. (931) 888-5031; fax (931) 888-4603; internet www.astro.uni-wuerzburg.de; f. 1967; astronomy, theoretical astrophysics; library of 5,000 vols, 50 journals; Dir Prof. Dr KARL MANNHEIM.

Astronomisches Rechen-Institut (Astronomical Institute): Mönchhofstr. 12–14, 69120 Heidelberg; tel. (6221) 54-1845; fax (6221) 54-1888; internet www.ari.uni-heidelberg.de; f. 1700; attached to Zentrum für Astronomie der Universität Heidelberg; theoretical astronomy; 50 mems; library of 26,000 vols; Dir Prof. Dr JOACHIM WAMBSGANß; Dir Prof. Dr EVA GREBEL; publs *Apparent Places of Fundamental Stars, Astronomische Grundlagen für den Kalender, Veröffentlichungen*.

Astrophysikalisches Institut und Universitäts-Sternwarte: Schillergässchen 2, 07745 Jena; tel. (3641) 947501; fax (3641)

947502; e-mail moni@astro.uni-jena.de; internet www.astro.uni-jena.de; f. 1813; Dir Prof. Dr RALPH NEUHÄUSER.

Bundesamt für Seeschiffahrt und Hydrographie (Federal Maritime and Hydrographic Agency): Bernhard-Nocht-Str. 78, 20359 Hamburg; tel. (40) 3190-0; fax (40) 3019-5000; e-mail posteingang@bsh.de; internet www.bsh.de; f. 1945; under the Federal Ministry of Transport; oceanography, tides and currents, geomagnetism, gravimetry, nautical technics, navigating methods, tonnage measurement, hydrographic surveying and nautical geodesy, bathymetry, seabed geology, pollution control, ice information service, nautical charts and publications; library of 153,000 vols; hydrographic information service; 900 mems; Pres. Prof. Dr PETER EHLERS; publs *Deutsche Hydrographische Zeitschrift* (4 a year), *Nachrichten für Seefahrer* (52 a year).

Bundesanstalt für Geowissenschaften und Rohstoffe (BGR) (Federal Institute for Geosciences and Natural Resources): Stilleweg 2, 30655 Hanover; tel. (511) 643-0; fax (511) 643-2304; e-mail poststelle@bgr.de; internet www.bgr.bund.de; f. 1958; geoscientific investigation, evaluation of mineral resources, environmental protection, geotechnology, seismology, marine and polar research; library of 296,000 vols; Pres. Prof. Dr HANS-JOACHIM KÜMPEL; publs *Geologisches Jahrbuch, Zeitschrift fur angewandte Geologie*.

Deutscher Wetterdienst (German Meteorological Service): Postfach 100465, 63004 Offenbach am Main; Frankfurter Str. 135, 63067 Offenbach am Main; tel. (69) 8062-0; fax (69) 8062-4484; e-mail info@dwd.de; internet www.dwd.de; f. 1952; central office for the Federal Republic; library of 178,000 vols; Pres. WOLFGANG KUSCH; Head of Operations Vis. Prof. Dr G. R. HOFFMANN; Chief Librarian BRITTA BOLZMANN; publs *Annalen der Meteorologie, Berichte des Deutschen Wetterdienstes, Deutsches Meteorologisches Jahrbuch* (1 a year), *Die Grosswetterlagen Europas* (12 a year, online), *Europäischer Wetterbericht* (online), *Geschichte der Meteorologie, Klimastatusbericht* (1 a year), *promet-Meteorologische Fortbildung* (4 a year), *Witterungsreport*.

Forschungszentrum Jülich GmbH (Jülich Research Centre): Wilhelm-Johnen-Str., 52425 Jülich; tel. (2461) 61-0; fax (2461) 61-8100; e-mail info@fz-juelich.de; internet www.fz-juelich.de; f. 1956; operated jointly by German federal Govt (90%) and state of North Rhine-Westphalia (10%); research in information technology and physical basic research, energy (materials and technology), environmental life sciences; library of 600,000 vols, 250,000 microforms, 2,000 journal titles; CEO Prof. Dr JOACHIM TREUSCH.

Forschungszentrum Karlsruhe GmbH (Karlsruhe Research Centre): Hermann-von-Helmholtz-Pl. 1, 76344 Eggenstein-Leopoldshafen; tel. (7247) 82-0; fax (7247) 82-5070; e-mail info@kit.edu; internet www.kit.edu; f. 1956; energy, nano, micro science and technology, elementary particle and astroparticle physics, climate and environment, computation, mobility systems, optics and photonics, humans and technology, new and applied materials; 7,000 mems; library of 500,000 vols, 1,600 periodical titles, 587,000 reports; Pres. Prof. Dr EBERHARD UMBACH, Prof. Dr HORST HIPPLER; publs *FZKA-Berichte, KIT dialog, Nachrichten*.

Fraunhofer-Institut für Bauphysik: POB 800469, Nobelstr. 12, 70504 Stuttgart; tel. (711) 970-00; fax (711) 970-3395; e-mail info@ibp.fraunhofer.de; internet www.ibp.fraunhofer.de; f. 1929; research, develop-

ment, testing, demonstration and consulting in the field of building physics; noise control, sound insulation, optimization of audibility conditions in lecture halls, measures for energy economy, lighting technology, new building materials, indoor climate, weathering protection, hygrothermics; Dirs Prof. Dr GERD HAUSER, Prof. Dr KLAUS SEDLBAUER; publ. *IBP Report* (building physics research results).

Geologisch-Paläontologisches Institut und Museum, Universität Hamburg (Geological and Palaeontological Institute and Museum): Bundesstr. 55, 20146 Hamburg; tel. (40) 428384999; fax (40) 428384007; internet www.geowiss.uni-hamburg.de/i-geolo/start.html; f. 1907; 12 scientific mems; library of 80,000 vols; Dir Prof. Dr CHRISTIAN BETZLER; publ. *Mitteilungen aus dem Geologisch-Paläontologischen Institut der Universität Hamburg* (1 a year).

Hamburger Sternwarte (Hamburg Observatory): Gojenbergsweg 112, 21029 Hamburg; tel. (40) 42838-8512; fax (40) 42838-8598; e-mail sternwarte@hs.uni-hamburg.de; internet www.hs.uni-hamburg.de; f. 1833; cosmology, quasars, stellar physics, interstellar medium; library of 65,000 vols; Dir Prof. J. H. M. M. SCHMITT.

Helmholtz-Zentrum Berlin für Materialien und Energie GmbH: Glienicker Str. 100, 14109 Berlin; tel. (30) 80620; fax (30) 80622181; e-mail info@helmholtz-berlin.de; internet www.helmholtz-berlin.de; f. 1959 as Hahn-Meitner-Institut Berlin GmbH, merged with BESSY GmbH in 2008; solid state physics, atomic and molecular structures, solar energy (photovoltaic); library of 61,000 vols, 420,000 reports; Dirs Prof. Dr ANKE PYZALLA, Prof. Dr WOLFGANG EBERHARDT, Dr ULRICH BREUER; Librarian WOLFGANG FRITSCH.

Institut für Astronomie und Astrophysik Tübingen: Sand 1, 72076 Tübingen; tel. (7071) 2972486; fax (7071) 293458; internet astro.uni-tuebingen.de; f. 1949; attached to Dept of Mathematics and Physics of Eberhard-Karls Univ. Tübingen; UV- and X-ray astronomy, optical astronomy, stellar atmospheres; library of 13,995 vols; Head Prof. KLAUS WERNER; Sec. and Librarian HEIDRUN OBERNDÖRFFER.

Institut für Astrophysik Göttingen (Institute of Astrophysics, Göttingen): Friedrich-Hund-Pl. 1, 37077 Göttingen; tel. (551) 394037; fax (551) 395043; e-mail sekr@astro.physik.uni-goettingen.de; internet www.uni-sw.gwdg.de; f. 1750; galactic and extragalactic astrophysics, high-energy astrophysics, solar physics, stellar spectroscopy and theoretical astrophysics; houses a modern Cassegrain reflecting telescope with 50 cm mirror diameter and 5 m focal length; Exec. Dir Prof. Dr W. KOLLATSCHNY.

Institut für Umwelt- und Zukunftsforschung (IUZ) an der Sternwarte Bochum: Blankensteiner Str. 200A, 44797 Bochum; tel. (234) 47711; fax (234) 5798958; e-mail info@iuz-bochum.de; internet www.sternwarte-bochum.de; development and testing of electronic equipment for tracking and reception of satellite data, development of display and reproduction systems for satellite imagery, photo-interpretation of satellite imagery for geo-scientific and environmental studies; remote sensing; Dir THILO ELSNER.

Attached Institution:

Sternwarte Bochum-Grossplanetarium: 44791 Bochum, Castroper Str. 67; tel. (234) 9103691.

Kiepenheuer-Institut für Sonnenphysik: Schöneckstr. 6, 79104 Freiburg im

Breisgau; tel. (761) 3198-0; fax (761) 3198-111; e-mail secr@kis.uni-freiburg.de; internet www.kis.uni-freiburg.de; f. 1942; optical investigation of the solar atmosphere, observatory at Tenerife (Canary Islands); 57 mems; Dir Prof. Dr OSKAR VON DER LÜHE.

Landessternwarte auf dem Königstuhl bei Heidelberg: Königstuhl, 69117 Heidelberg; tel. (6221) 5417-00; fax (6221) 5417-02; e-mail postmaster@lsw.uni-heidelberg.de; internet www.lsw.uni-heidelberg.de; f. 1897; astronomical scientific research; 50 mems; library of 25,000 vols; Dir Prof. Dr A. QUIRRENBACH.

Leibniz-Institut für Analytische Wissenschaften —ISAS—e.V. (Institute for Analytical Sciences): Bunsen-Kirchhoff-Str. 11, 44139 Dortmund; tel. (231) 1392-0; fax (231) 1392-120; e-mail info@isas.de; internet www.isas.de; f. 1952 as Institute of Spectrochemistry and Applied Spectroscopy; focuses on analytical and spectroscopical methods in material sciences and life sciences; Dir Prof. Dr ALBERT SICKMANN; Dir Prof. Dr NORBERT ESSER.

Remeis-Sternwarte (Remeis Observatory): Sternwartstr. 7, 96049 Bamberg; tel. (951) 952220; fax (951) 952222; internet www.sternwarte.uni-erlangen.de; f. 1889; stellar astrophysics; attached to Erlangen–Nürnberg Univ.; Chairs Prof. Dr JÖRN WILMS, Prof. Dr ULRICH HEBER.

Universitäts-Sternwarte–Institut für Astronomie und Astrophysik und Observatorium Wendelstein: Scheinerstr. 1, 81679 Munich; tel. (89) 21806001; fax (89) 21806003; internet www.usm.uni-muenchen.de; f. 1816; extragalactic astronomy, plasma astrophysics, stellar atmospheres, stellar evolution, cosmochemistry; library of 18,000 vols; Dir Prof. Dr MANFRED HIRT.

UWG Gesellschaft für Umwelt- und Wirtschaftsgeologie GmbH: Wolfener 36, Aufg. K, 12681 Berlin; tel. (30) 23144-684; fax (30) 23144-700; geoscientific and environmental library (books, data, photographs (remote sensing), maps; Dir Dr KLAUS ERLER.

PHILOSOPHY AND PSYCHOLOGY

Institut für Forensische Psychiatrie: Charité–Universitätsmedizin Berlin, Campus Benjamin Franklin, Limonenstr. 27, 12203 Berlin; tel. (30) 8445-1411; fax (30) 8445-1440; e-mail info@forensik-berlin.de; internet www.forensik-berlin.de; f. 1970; studies and research in forensic psychiatry and psychology; weekly interdisciplinary colloquium; annual forensic science conference; library of 21,257 vols, 61 current periodicals, 1,476 special prints, 104 video cassettes; Dir Prof. Dr HANS-LUDWIG KRÖBER.

Institut für Gerichtspsychologie (IfG) (Institute of Forensic Psychology): Gilsingstr. 5, 44789 Bochum; tel. (234) 34091; internet www.gerichtspsychologie-bochum.de; f. 1951; carries out reports on behalf of the courts and solicitors; 41 mems; Dir Dr FRIEDRICH ARNTZEN.

Institut für Philosophie Humboldt-Universität (Institute of Philosophy at Humboldt University): Unter den Linden 6, 10099 Berlin; tel. (30) 2093-2204; fax (30) 2093-2419; internet www2.hu-berlin.de/phil; offers open lectures; Kant archive; Dir Prof. Dr OLAF MUELLER.

Institut für Philosophie Universität Leipzig (Institute of Philosophy at Leipzig University): Beethovenstr. 15, 04107 Leipzig; tel. (341) 9735820; fax (341) 9735819; internet www.uni-leipzig.de/~philos; organizes conferences and weekly colloquia; Dir

Prof. Dr PIRMIN STEKELER-WEITHOFER; publ. *Leipziger Schriften zur Philosophie.*

Institut für Rechtspsychologie Halle (Institute of Forensic Psychology, Halle): Kleine Marktstr. 5, 06108 Halle/Salle; tel. (345) 2033566; fax (345) 6784703; e-mail institut@rechtspsychologie-halle.de; internet www.rechtspsychologie-halle.de; f. 1997; carries out studies in forensic psychology for law courts; Man. BÄRBEL GOLDHAMMER.

RELIGION, SOCIOLOGY AND ANTHROPOLOGY

Arbeitsgemeinschaft Sozialwissenschaftlicher Institute eV (Association of Social Science Institutes): Dreizehnmorgenweg 42, 53175 Bonn; tel. (228) 2281; fax (228) 2281-550; e-mail asi@asi-ev.org; internet www.asi-ev.org; f. 1949 to promote research in social sciences; 100 mems; Pres. Prof. Dr FRANK FAULBAUM; Man. Dir MATTHIAS STAHL; publ. *Soziale Welt* (4 a year).

Bundesinstitut für Bevölkerungsforschung (Federal Institute for Population Research): Postfach 5528, Friedrich-Ebert-Allee 4, 65180 Wiesbaden; tel. (0611) 752235; fax (0611) 753960; e-mail bib@destatis.de; internet www.bib-demografie.de; f. 1973; attached to Statistisches Bundesamt; promotes all fields of demographic research and coordinates research work undertaken by demographers, incl. those in foreign countries; Dir Prof. Dr NORBERT F. SCHNEIDER; publs *Bevölkerungsforschung Aktuell* (6 a year), *BIB-Mitteilungen* (4 a year), *Comparative Population Studies—CPoS, Demographie: Zeitschrift für Bevölkerungswissenschaft* (4 a year).

Forschungsgruppe für Anthropologie und Religionsgeschichte eV (Research Group for Anthropology and History of Religion): Droste-Hülshoff-Str. 9B, 48341 Altenberge; tel. and fax 2505-1347; e-mail ugarit@uni-muenster.de; internet www.ugarit-verlag.de; f. 1970; research and documentation refer to all fields of religion including interconnections with anthropology, psychology, culture and environment; methodology of research; international cooperation and exchange; Pres. Prof. Dr M. L. G. DIETRICH; publs *Forschungen zur Anthropologie und Religionsgeschichte* (3 a year), *Mitteilungen für Anthropologie und Religionsgeschichte* (1 a year).

Gesellschaft Sozialwissenschaftlicher Infrastruktureinrichtungen eV (German Social Science Infrastructure Services): POB 12 21 55, 68072 Mannheim; tel. (621) 1246-0; fax (621) 1246-100; e-mail info@gesis.org; internet www.gesis.org; f. 1986; infrastructural services on numerical data, information bases and research methods for social scientists; Chair. Prof. Dr OSCAR W. GABRIEL; Chief Exec. Prof. Dr WOLFGANG JAGODZINSKI; Pres. Prof. Dr HANS RATTINGER; publs *HSR Historical Social Research* (3 or 4 a year), *Informationsdienst Soziale Indikatoren* (2 a year), *IZ Telegramm* (4 a year), *Newsletter Sozialwissenschaften in Osteuropa* (4 a year), *ZA Information* (2 a year), *ZUMA Nachrichten* (2 a year), *ZUMA Nachrichten Spezial* (irregular).

Informationszentrum Sozialwissenschaften (Social Sciences Information Centre): Lennéstr. 30, 53113 Bonn; tel. (228) 2281-0; fax (228) 2281-121; e-mail info@gesis.org; internet www.gesis.org/iz; f. 1969; colln and dissemination of information in the social sciences; Scientific Dir Prof. Dr JÜRGEN KRAUSE; publ. *Sozialwissenschaftlicher Fachinformationsdienst* (2 a year).

TECHNOLOGY

Arbeitsgemeinschaft Industrieller Forschungsvereinigungen 'Otto von Guericke' eV (AiF): Bayenthalgürtel 23, 50968 Köln; tel. (221) 376800; fax (221) 3768027; e-mail info@aif.de; internet www.aif.de; f. 1954; promotion of co-operative research for small and medium-sized industry; Pres. JOHANN WILHELM ARNTZ; Dir-Gen. Dr-Ing. MICHAEL MAURER.

Bundesanstalt für Materialforschung und -prüfung (Federal Institute for Materials Research and Testing): Unter den Eichen 87, 12205 Berlin; tel. (30) 8104-0; fax (30) 8112029; e-mail info@bam.de; internet www.bam.de; f. 1871; analytical chemistry; reference materials, chemical safety engineering, containment systems for dangerous goods, materials and the environment, materials engineering, materials protection and surface technologies, safety of structures, nondestructive testing, accreditation, quality in testing; library of 80,000 vols; Pres. Prof. Dr rer. nat. MANFRED HENNECKE; publ. *Amtsblatt* (4 a year).

Clausthaler Umwelttechnik-Institut GmbH (Clausthal Institute of Environmental Technology): Leibnizstr. 21–23, 38678 Clausthal-Zellerfeld; tel. (5323) 933-0; fax (5323) 933-100; e-mail cutec@cutec.de; internet www.cutec.de; f. 1990; wholly owned by state of Lower Saxony; research into waste avoidance, recycling and disposal; Man. Dir Prof. Dr-Ing. OTTO CARLOWITZ.

Deutsche Forschungsanstalt für Lebensmittelchemie (German Research Institute for Food Chemistry): Lise-Meitner Str. 34, 85354 Freising; tel. (8161) 712932; fax (8161) 712970; e-mail dfa lebensmittelchemie@lrz.tum.de; internet dfa.leb.chemie.tu-muenchen.de; f. 1918; library of 3,000 vols; Dir Prof. Dr PETER SCHIEBERLE.

Deutsche Montan Technologie GmbH (DMT): Am Technologiepark 1, 45307 Essen; tel. (201) 172-01; fax (201) 172-1462; e-mail dmt-info@dmt.de; internet www.dmt.de; f. 1990; specialists in mining; Pres. Dr MICHAEL KOPPITZ.

Deutsche Zentrum für Luft- und Raumfahrt eV (DLR) (German Aerospace Centre): Linder Höhe, 51147 Cologne; tel. (2203) 601-0; fax (2203) 67310; e-mail redaktion@dlr.de; internet www.dlr.de; f. 1969; flight mechanics, guidance and control, fluid mechanics, structures and materials, space flight, telecommunication technology and remote sensing, energetics; library of 400,000 vols; Chair. Prof. Dr SIGMAR WITTIG; publs *DLR-Forschungsberichte* (irregular), *DLR-Mitteilungen* (irregular), *DLR-Nachrichten* (4 a year).

Deutsches Textilforschungszentrum Nord-West eV: Öffentliche Prüfstelle (ÖP), Adlerstr. 1, 47798 Krefeld; tel. (2151) 843-0; fax (2151) 843143; e-mail oeffentliche.pruefstelle@dtnw.de; internet www.dtnw.de; f. 1990; 100 mems; Dir Prof. Dr ECKHARD SCHOLLMEYER.

Forschungsinstitut Edelmetalle & Metallchemie (fem) (Research Institute of Precious Metals and Metals Chemistry): Katharinenstr. 17, 73525 Schwäbisch Gmünd; tel. (7171) 10060; fax (7171) 100654; e-mail fem@fem-online.de; internet www.fem-online.de; f. 1922; basic and applied research into precious metals science and technology, electrochemical deposition, corrosion, light metals surface technology, plasma surface technology, physical metallurgy, environmental technology and analyses; Dir Dr A. ZIELONKA.

Forschungsinstitut für Wärmeschutz eV München (Thermal Insulation, Testing,

Research): Lochhamer Schlag 4, 82166 Grä-
felfing; tel. (89) 858000; fax (89) 8580040;
e-mail info@fiw-muenchen.de; internet www
.fiw-muenchen.de; f. 1918; 140 mems; Scientific Dirs Dr ROLAND GELLERT, Dr Ing. MAR-
TIN ZEITLER, Dr Ing. MARTIN SPITZNER; publ.
Mitteilungen aus dem FIW München (irregular).

**Fraunhofer-Institut für Verfahrenstech-
nik und Verpackung** (Process Engineering
and Packaging): Giggenhauser Str. 35, 85354
Freising; tel. (8161) 491-100; fax (8161) 491-
111; internet www.ivv.fraunhofer.de; f. 1942;
food processing, environmental technology,
preservation and packaging, general packaging; library of 6,000 vols; Dir HORST-
CHRISTIAN LANGOWSKI.

**GSI Helmholtzzentrum für Schwerio-
nenforschung GmbH:** Planckstr. 1, 64291
Darmstadt; tel. (6159) 71-0; fax (6159) 71-
2785; e-mail info@gsi.de; internet www.gsi
.de; f. 1969; carries out basic research with
heavy ions in nuclear physics and chemistry,
solid state and atomic physics, radiation
biology, tumour therapy with ion beams,
etc.; heavy ion linear accelerator, synchrotron, storage ring and laboratory; library of
3,000 vols; Scientific Dir CHRISTIANE NEU-
MANN; publ. *GSI-Scientific Report* (1 a year).

Institut für Bauforschung eV (Building
Research): An der Markuskirche 1, 30163
Hanover; tel. (511) 96516-0; fax (511) 96516-
26; e-mail office@bauforschung.de; internet
www.bauforschung.org; f. 1946; Dir Prof. Dr-
Ing. MARTIN PFEIFFER.

Institut für Erdöl- und Erdgasforschung
(German Petroleum Institute): Walther-
Nernst-Str. 7, 38678 Clausthal-Zellerfeld;
tel. (5323) 711100; fax (5323) 711200; f.
1943; oil and gas recovery, reservoir engineering, refinery technology, research in petroleum products, hydrocarbons and
environment; 53 mems; library of 5,000
vols; Dir Prof. Dr D. G. KESSEL; publ.
Research Report (1 a year).

**Institut für Textil- und Verfahrenstech-
nik:** Körschtalstr. 26, 73770 Denkendorf; tel.
(711) 9340-0; fax (711) 9340-297; e-mail itv@
itv-denkendorf.de; internet www
.itv-denkendorf.de; f. 1921; 165 staff; library
of 2,500 vols; Dir Prof. Dr-Ing. HEINRICH
PLANK.

**Landesamt für Natur, Umwelt und Ver-
braucherschutz Nordrhein-Westfalen**
(North Rhine-Westphalia State Agency for
Nature, Environment and Consumer Protection): Leibnizstr. 10, 45659 Recklinghausen;
tel. (2361) 3050; fax (2361) 3053215; e-mail
poststelle@lanuv.nrw.de; internet www
.lanuv.nrw.de; f. 2007; research and advice in
the fields of air pollution and noise control;
prevention of accidental releases; water,
wastewater, groundwater and waste management; engineering, circular economy, veterinary issues, food safety and agricultural
commodity market; Pres. Dr HEINRICH BOT-
TERMANN.

**Lehr- und Forschungsgebiet Inter-
nationale Wirtschaftsbeziehungen**
(Chair of International Economics): Templergraben 64 (Sammelbau, 6th Fl.), 52056
Aachen; tel. and fax (241) 80693931;
internet www.iw.rwth-aachen.de; f. 1957; 36
mems; library of 100,000 vols; Dir Prof. Dr
OLIVER LORZ; publs *Aachener Beiträge zur
Internationalen Zusammenarbeit, Internationale Kooperation, Intertechnik.*

**Max Rubner-Institut, Bundesforschung-
sinstitut für Ernährung und Lebensmit-
tel** (Max Rubner Institute, Federal Research
Centre for Nutrition and Food): Haid-und-
Neustr. 9, 76131 Karlsruhe; tel. (721) 6625-0;
fax (721) 6625-111; e-mail poststelle@mri
.bund.de; internet www.mri.bund.de; f. 2008;

research instn of the Federal Ministry of
Food, Agriculture and Consumer Protection;
focuses on health and consumer protection in
the food sector, incl. determination and
nutritional assessment of food ingredients,
investigation of processing procedures, quality assurance of vegetable and animal food,
investigation of the motivation of nutritional
behaviour, and improvement of nutritional
information; library of 300,000 vols; 470
mems.

Physikalisch-Technische Bundesanstalt
(National Metrology Institute): Bundesallee
100, 38116 Brunswick; tel. (531) 5923006; fax
(531) 5923008; e-mail presse@ptb.de;
internet www.ptb.de; f. 1887; divs for mechanics and acoustics, electricity, thermodynamics and explosion protection, optics,
precision engineering, ionizing radiation,
temperature and synchrotron radiation, and
medical physics and information technology;
library of 125,000 vols; Pres. Prof. Dr E. O.
GÖBEL; publs *Maßstäbe* (1 a year), *PTB-
Mitteilungen* (4 a year), *PTB news* (3 a year).

**Staatliche Materialprüfungsanstalt
Darmstadt–Fachgebiet und Institut für
Werkstoffkunde** (State Material-Testing
Foundation-Faculty and Institute of Material
Science): Grafenstr. 2, 64283 Darmstadt; tel.
(6151) 162351; fax (6151) 166118; internet
www.mpa-ifw.tu-darmstadt.de; f. 1927;
attached to Technical University of Darmstadt; Dir Prof. Dr-Ing. C. BERGER.

Libraries and Archives

Aachen

**Hochschulbibliothek der RWTH
Aachen:** Templergraben 61, 52056 Aachen;
tel. (241) 80-94445; fax (241) 8092273; e-mail
bth@bth.rwth-aachen.de; internet www.bth
.rwth-aachen.de; f. 1870; 2,100,000 vols; Dir
Dr ULRIKE EIKE.

Stadtbibliothek Aachen (Aachen Public
Library): Couvenstr. 15, 52058 Aachen; tel.
(241) 4791-0; fax (241) 408007; e-mail
bibliothek@mail.aachen.de; internet
stadtbibliothek-aachen.de; f. 1831; general
information about Aachen and the region,
regional history; 511,000 vols, spec. collns
incl. folklore, ethnology, archaeology, organ
literature; Dir MANFRED SAWALLICH.

Amberg

Staatsarchiv Amberg: Archivstr. 3, 92224
Amberg; tel. (9621) 307270; fax (9621)
307288; e-mail poststelle@staam.bayern.de;
f. 1437, became state archive in 1921; 2.9m.
items in archives; 33,700 vols; Co-Dir Dr
MARIA RITA SAGSTETTER; Co-Dir R. FRITSCH.

Augsburg

Staats- und Stadtbibliothek: Stadt Augsburg, 86143 Augsburg; Schaezlerstr. 25,
86152 Augsburg; tel. (821) 3242739; fax
(821) 3242732; e-mail bibliothek.stadt@
augsburg.de; internet www.sustb.augsburg
.de; f. 1537; 522,742 vols, 3,662 MSS, 2,798
incunabula, 16,250 drawings and engravings; Dir Dr HELMUT GIER; Librarian IRM-
GARD KRULL.

Staatsarchiv Augsburg: Salomon-Idler-
Str. 2, 86159 Augsburg; tel. (821) 59963-30;
fax (821) 59963-333; e-mail poststelle@staau
.bayern.de; internet www.gda.bayern.de/
augsb00.htm; f. 1830 in Neuburg; 2.4m.
items; Dir Dr PETER FLEISCHMANN.

Universitätsbibliothek: Universitätsstr.
22, 86159 Augsburg; tel. (821) 5985300; fax
(821) 5985354; e-mail dir@bibliothek
.uni-augsburg.de; internet www.bibliothek
.uni-augsburg.de; f. 1970; 2,032,917 vols,

77,431 theses, 59,345 maps, 397,164 items
of audiovisual material and microforms,
1,267 incunabula, 1,544 MSS, 2,295 music
MSS; Dir Dr ULRICH HOHOFF.

Aurich

Niedersächsisches Staatsarchiv Aurich:
Oldersumer Str. 50, 26603 Aurich; tel. (4941)
176660; fax (4941) 176673; e-mail aurich@nla
.niedersachsen.de; internet www
.staatsarchiv-aurich.niedersachsen.de; f.
1872; 20,000 vols; Dir Dr BERNHARD PARISIUS.

Bamberg

Staatsarchiv Bamberg: Hainstr. 39, 96047
Bamberg; tel. (951) 986220; fax (951) 98622-
50; e-mail poststelle@staba.bayern.de;
internet www.gda.bayern.de; f. 13th century,
became Bavarian state archive in 1803;
27,500 vols; spec. colln: Frankish history,
maps, plans, MSS, documents; Dir Dr RAINER
HAMBRECHT.

Staatsbibliothek Bamberg: Neue Residenz, Dompl. 8, 96049 Bamberg; tel. (951)
95503-0; fax (951) 95503-145; e-mail info@
staatsbibliothek-bamberg.de; internet www
.staatsbibliothek-bamberg.de; f. 1803;
496,988 vols, spec. colln of 6,121 MSS, 3,404
incunabula and 80,000 prints and drawings;
Dir Prof. Dr WERNER TAEGERT; Deputy Dir Dr
STEFAN KNOCH.

Universitätsbibliothek: Postfach 2705,
96018 Bamberg; Feldkirchenstr. 21, 96052
Bamberg; tel. (951) 8631501; fax (951)
8631565; e-mail universitaetsbibliothek@
uni-bamberg.de; internet www.uni-bamberg
.de/ub; f. 1973; 1,624,427 vols; Dir Dr FABIAN
FRANKE; publ. *Schriften der Universitätsbibliothek Bamberg.*

Bayreuth

Universitätsbibliothek: Universitätsge-
lände, 95440 Bayreuth; tel. (921) 553420;
fax (921) 553442; e-mail auskunft@ub
.uni-bayreuth.de; internet www.ub
.uni-bayreuth.de; f. 1973 to serve the university and the public; 1,700,000 vols; Dir Dr
RALF BRUGBAUER.

Berlin

**Akademiebibliothek der Berlin-Bran-
denburgischen Akademie der Wissenschaften:** Jägerstr. 22–23, 10117
Berlin; tel. (30) 20370487; fax (30)
20370476; e-mail bibliothek@bbaw.de;
internet bibliothek.bbaw.de; f. 1700; spec.
colln of the publs of academies and learned
socs; 650,000 vols, 730 periodicals; Dir Dr
STEFAN WIEDERKEHR.

**Auswärtiges Amt, Referat 116, Bib-
liothek und Informationsvermittlung:**
Werderscher Markt 1, 10117 Berlin; tel.
(30) 18172208; fax (30) 181752208; e-mail
116-information@auswaertiges-amt.de;
300,000 vols, 2,900 periodicals, 90,000 maps;
Dir Dr GUNDULA FELTEN.

Bibliothek des Deutschen Bundestages:
Pl. der Republik 1, 11011 Berlin; tel. (30)
22733073; fax (30) 22736087; e-mail
bibliothek@bundestag.de; internet www
.bundestag.de/htdocs_e/documents/library/; f.
1949; 1,400,000 vols, 8,000 periodicals; spec.
collns of German and foreign official publs
and parliamentary papers; depository library
of 10 int. orgs; Dir URSULA FREYSCHMIDT;
publs *Literaturtipps* (on topical economic and
political subjects), *Neue Bücher und Aufsätze
in der Bibliothek, Schnellinformationen.*

**Bibliothek für Bildungsgeschichtliche
Forschung:** Postfach 171138, 10203 Berlin;
Warschauer Str. 34–38, 10243 Berlin; tel.
(30) 293360-0; fax (30) 293360-25; e-mail
bbf@bbf.dipf.de; internet www.bbf.dipf.de; f.
1876; holds conferences and exhibitions;

710,000 vols; Dir Dr CHRISTIAN RITZI; publs *Bestandsverzeichnisse zur Bildungsgeschichte* (directory of publications on the history of education, series), *Bibliographie Bildungsgeschichte* (history of education bibliography, 1 a year), *Jahrbuch für Historische Bildungsforschung* (yearbook of education research history, 1 a year), *Neuerwerbungsverzeichnis* (list of new acquisitions, 12 a year), *Quellen und Dokumente zur Alltagsgeschichte der Erziehung* (sources and documents on the everyday history of education, series), *Tagungsbände* (conf. papers).

Geheimes Staatsarchiv Preussischer Kulturbesitz (Secret Central Archives of the Prussian Cultural Possession): Dahlem, Archivstr. 12–14, 14195 Berlin; tel. (30) 26644-7500; fax (30) 26644-3126; e-mail gsta.pk@gsta.spk-berlin.de; internet www.gsta.spk-berlin.de; f. 1598; material and research on history of Prussia and the former Prussian territories since 12th century; 185,000 vols, 2,000 periodicals, 650,000 records and files, 120,000 maps; Dir Prof. Dr JÜRGEN KLOOSTERHUIS; publ. *Veröffentlichungen* (2–3 a year).

Ibero-Amerikanisches Institut Preussischer Kulturbesitz: Potsdamer Str. 37, 10785 Berlin; tel. (30) 266451500; fax (30) 266351550; e-mail iai@iai.spk-berlin.de; internet www.iai.spk-berlin.de; f. 1930; research institute and library dedicated to Latin America, Spain and Portugal; 1,200,000 vols, 4,500 current periodicals; Dir Dr BARBARA GÖBEL; publs *Bibliotheca Ibero-Americana, Biblioteca Luso-Brasileira, Iberoamericana, Indiana, Revista Internacional de Linguistica Iberoamericana.*

Kunstbibliothek Staatliche Museen zu Berlin: Matthäikirchpl. 6, 10785 Berlin; tel. (30) 266424101; fax (30) 266424199; e-mail kb@smb.spk-berlin.de; internet www.smb.spk-berlin.de/kb; f. 1867; 480,000 vols; spec. collns: ornamental and architectural books, Lipperheidesche Kostumbibliothek, artists' books, posters, photographs, graphic design, drawings; Dir Dr MORITZ WULLEN.

Landesarchiv Berlin (Berlin Regional Archive): Eichborndamm 115–121, 13403 Berlin; tel. (30) 90264-0; fax (30) 90264-250; e-mail info@landesarchiv-berlin.de; internet www.landesarchiv-berlin.de; f. 1948; legal documents, etc. for the Berlin area, and important material on the history of Berlin; 76,000 vols and 5,200 film rolls; Dir Prof. Dr UWE SCHAPER; publs *Berlin in Geschichte und Gegenwart, Jahrbuch des Landesarchivs Berlin.*

Politisches Archiv des Auswärtigen Amts (Political Archive of the Foreign Office): Werderscher Markt 1, 10117 Berlin; tel. (30) 1817-2159; fax (30) 1817-3948; e-mail 117-r@diplo.de; internet www.auswaertiges-amt.de/diplo/de/aamt/politischesarchiv2009/uebersicht.html; f. 1920; Foreign Office archives; documents since 1867; archives of former Foreign Ministry of the German Democratic Republic; Dir L. BIEWER; publs *Akten zur auswärtigen Politik der Bundesrepublik Deutschland* (series), *Akten zur deutschen auswärtigen Politik 1918–1945* (series), *Biographisches Handbuch des deutschen Auswärtigen Dienstes 1871–1945* (series).

Senatsbibliothek Berlin: Str. des 17 Juni 112, 10623 Berlin; tel. (30) 39987-324; fax (30) 39987-322; e-mail auskunft@senatsbibliothek.de; internet www.senatsbibliothek.de; f. 1949; central govt library of Berlin and spec. library for urban and land planning and regional research; 501,034 vols, 892 periodicals; Dir MARION HECKER.

Staatsbibliothek zu Berlin–Preußischer Kulturbesitz: Unter den Linden 8, 10117 Berlin; also:Potsdamer Str. 33 (Tiergarten), 10785 Berlin; tel. (30) 266-0; fax (30) 266-331301; internet www.staatsbibliothek-berlin.de; f. 1661; 10,600,000 vols, 25,000 current periodicals and newspapers, 18,400 occidental MSS, 66,500 musical MSS, 458,000 music prints, 1m. maps, 4,400 incunabula, 321,000 autographs, 17,500,000 pictures, 2m. microforms; Mendelssohn archive; Gen. Dir BARBARA SCHNEIDER-KEMPF.

Universitätsbibliothek der Freie Universität Berlin: Garystr. 39, 14195 Berlin; tel. 83851111; fax 83853738; e-mail auskunft@ub.fu-berlin.de; internet www.ub.fu-berlin.de; f. 1952; 2,150,000 vols, 1,800 periodicals, 38,500 e-journals, 362,000 theses, 7.6m. vols in departmental libraries; Dir Prof. Dr rer. pol. ULRICH NAUMANN; publ. *Universitätsbibliographie.*

Universitätsbibliothek der Humboldt-Universität zu Berlin (University Library of Humboldt University, Berlin Branch): Hessische Str. 1–2, 10115 Berlin; tel. (30) 20933212; fax (30) 20933207; e-mail info@ub.hu-berlin.de; internet www.ub.hu-berlin.de; f. 1831; 6,000,000 vols, 10,000 current periodicals; Dir Dr MILAN BULATY; publ. *Schriftenreihe.*

Universitätsbibliothek der Technische Universität Berlin: Universitätsbibliothek, Fasanenstr. 88, (im Volkswagen-Haus), 10623 Berlin; tel. (30) 31476101; fax (30) 31476104; e-mail info@ub.tu-berlin.de; internet www.ub.tu-berlin.de; f. 1884; 2,012,059 vols, 2,778 periodicals, 13,538 e-journals, 86,250 architectural drawings, complete German standards; Dir Dr W. ZICK.

Zentral- und Landesbibliothek Berlin (Berlin Central and Provincial Library): Breite Str. 30–36, 10178 Berlin; tel. (30) 90226-401; fax (30) 90226-163; e-mail info@zlb.de; internet www.zlb.de; f. 1901; central public library of Berlin; 3,200,000 vols, in print and online; Dir Dr CLAUDIA LUX.

Bochum

Stadtbücherei Bochum: Gustav-Heinemann Pl. 2–6 (BVZ), 44777 Bochum; tel. (234) 910-2481; fax (234) 910-2437; e-mail stadtbue@bochum.de; internet www.bochum.de/stadtbuecherei; f. 1905; 406,000 vols; Dir H. ALBRECHT.

Universitätsbibliothek: 44780 Bochum; tel. (234) 3222350; fax (234) 3214736; e-mail direktion@ub.ruhr-uni-bochum.de; internet www.ub.ruhr-uni-bochum.de; f. 1962; 1,942,000 vols, 371,000 theses; Dir Dr E. LAPP.

Bonn

Archiv der sozialen Demokratie (Friedrich-Ebert-Stiftung) (Archive of Social Democracy—Friedrich Ebert Foundation): Godesberger Allee 149, 53175 Bonn; tel. (228) 883-0; fax (228) 883-9204; e-mail archiv.auskunft@fes.de; internet www.fes.de; f. 1969; contains material relating to the Sozialdemokratische Partei Deutschlands (SPD) and the German trade unions; history of German and int. social movement, labour movement, labour problems; 600,000 vols, 3,000 periodicals; Dir for the Archive of Social Democracy Dr ANJA KRUKE; Dir for the Library of the Friedrich-Ebert-Foundation Dr RÜDIGER ZIMMERMANN.

Bibliothek der Hochschulrektorenferenz (Library of the University Rectors' Conference): Ahrstr. 39, 53175 Bonn; tel. (228) 887-159; fax (228) 887-110; e-mail bibliothek@hrk.de; internet www.hrk.de/de/berichte_und_publikationen/130.php; f. 1954

(Westdeutsche Rektorenkonferenz); 68,000 vols, 800 periodicals, 95,000 records and acts; Head Dr ULRICH MEYER-DOERPINGHAUS; Librarian THOMAS LAMPE.

Bundesamts für Bauwesen und Raumordnung, Wissenschaftliche Bibliothek: Postfach 210150, 53156 Bonn; tel. (1888) 4012281; fax (1888) 4012249; e-mail karin.goebel@bbr.bund.de; internet www.bbr.bund.de; f. 1941; 150,000 vols, 450 periodicals; Dir Dr phil. KLAUS SCHLIEBE; publs *Forschungen* (series, irregular), *Informationen zur Raumentwicklung* (12 a year), *Raumforschung und Raumordnung* (5 or 6 issues a year), *Werkstatt: Praxis* (series, irregular).

Stadtarchiv und Stadthistorische Bibliothek Bonn (Bonn City Archive and Historical Library): Berliner Platz 2, 53103 Bonn; tel. (228) 772410; fax (228) 774301; e-mail stadtarchiv@bonn.de; internet www.archive.nrw.de/home.asp?stadta-bonn; f. 1899; 140,000 vols; Archivist and Librarian Dr NORBERT SCHLOSSMACHER; publs *Bonner Geschichtsblätter* (1 a year), *Studien zur Heimatgeschichte des Stadtbezirkes Bonn-Beuel, Veröffentlichungen des Stadtarchivs Bonn.*

Universitäts- und Landesbibliothek: Postfach 2460, 53014 Bonn; located at: Adenauerallee 39–41, 53113 Bonn; tel. (228) 737350; fax (228) 737546; e-mail ulb@ulb.uni-bonn.de; internet www.ulb.uni-bonn.de; f. 1818; 1,975,000 vols, 130,000 micro materials, 6,800 current periodicals; Dir Dr RENATE VOGT.

Bremen

Bibliothek/Informationszentrum des Instituts für Seeverkehrswirtschaft und Logistik (ISL): Universitätsallee GW1 Block A, 28359 Bremen; tel. (421) 22096-44; fax (421) 22096-55; e-mail infocenter@isl.org; internet www.isl.org; f. 1954; centre for maritime information and documentation offering professional services about industries, markets and companies within the areas of maritime industries, transport and logistics; 125,000 vols; Head BRIGITTE OGIOLDA.

Staats- und Universitätsbibliothek: Postfach 330160, 28331 Bremen; tel. (421) 2182601; fax (421) 2182614; e-mail suub@uni-bremen.de; internet www.suub.uni-bremen.de; f. 1660; 3,198,948 vols, 8,257 current print periodicals, 21,003 online periodicals; Dir MARIA ELISABETH MÜLLER; publ. *Jahresbibliographie Massenkommunikation.*

Staatsarchiv: Am Staatsarchiv 1, 28203 Bremen; tel. (421) 361-6221; fax (421) 361-10247; e-mail office@staatsarchiv.bremen.de; internet www.staatsarchiv-bremen.de; f. 1727; Dir Prof. Dr KONRAD ELMSHÄUSER (acting); publs *Bremisches Jahrbuch, Kleine Schriften des Staatsarchivs Bremen, Veröffentlichungen aus dem Staatsarchiv der Freien Hansestadt Bremen.*

Brunswick

Bundesforschungsinstitut für Kulturpflanzen Informationszentrum und Bibliothek (Federal Research Centre for Cultivated Plants Information Centre and Library): Messeweg 11/12, 38104 Braunschweig; tel. (531) 299-3397; fax (531) 299-3018; e-mail bibliothek@bba.de; internet www.bba.de; f. 1950; attached to Julius Kühn-Institut; plant protection and related fields; 59,000 vols, 1,200 periodicals, 44,000 reprints, 2,200 microfilms; Head A. BADKE; publs *Amtliche Pflanzenschutzbestimmungen* (irregular), *Berichte aus der Biologischen Bundesanstalt für Land- und Forstwirtschaft, Nachrichtenblatt des Deutschen Pflanzenschutzdienstes*

(12 a year), *Pflanzenschutzmittel-Verzeichnis* (1 a year).

Stadtarchiv (City Archive): Löwenwall 18B, 38100 Braunschweig; tel. (531) 470-4711; fax (531) 470-4725; e-mail stadtarchiv@ braunschweig.de; internet www .braunschweig.de/rat_verwaltung/verwaltung/fb41_4; f. 1860; 125,000 documents since 1031, municipal records, charters, maps and plans since 1228, special collections on the history of the town; special historical archive on prominent Brunswick women; Dir (vacant).

Stadtbibliothek: Schlosspl. 2, 38100 Braunschweig; tel. (531) 470-6801; fax (531) 470-6899; e-mail stadtbibliothek@ braunschweig.de; internet www .braunschweig.de/stadtbibliothek; f. 1861; 597,646 vols, medieval MSS, 426 incunabula, 2,500 maps and plans up to 1850; special colln on the history of the town; Dir Dr ANETTE HAUCAP-NASS; publs *Braunschweiger Werkstücke*, *Kleine Schriften* (irregular).

Universitätsbibliothek Braunschweig: Pockelsstr. 13, 38106 Braunschweig; tel. (531) 391-5018; fax (531) 391-5836; e-mail ub@tu-bs.de; internet www.biblio.tu-bs.de; f. 1748; exhibitions; various lectures; Digitale Bibliothek Braunschweig with nearly 7,000 documents; archive of the Technische Universität Braunschweig; 21,687 mems; 1,414,708 vols, 2,420 periodicals, 40,500 online journals, about 120,000 standards, 175,000 printed dissertations; 51,000 microfiches; areas of specialization incl. pharmacy (virtual library), DFG-Sondersammelgebiet, 15th–19th century technology and natural history, children's books since 16th century, archive library of 6 publishing houses; Dir Prof. Dr DIETMAR BRANDES; Deputy Dir BEATE NAGEL.

Bückeburg

Niedersächsisches Landesarchiv, Staatsarchiv Bückeburg: Schlosspl. 2, 31675 Bückeburg; tel. (5722) 9677-30; fax (5722) 1289; e-mail bueckeburg@nla.niedersachsen .de; internet www.nla.niedersachsen.de; f. 1961; archives of the old county, later principality, of Schaumburg-Lippe and the district of Schaumburg; central workshops for restoration and security filming for Lower Saxony; 4,000 documents, 35,000 vols, 20,000 maps; Dir Dr STEFAN BRÜDERMANN; publs *Inventare und kleinere Schriften des Staatsarchivs Bückeburg*, *Schaumburger Studien*.

Chemnitz

Stadtbibliothek (City Library): Moritzstr. 20, 09111 Chemnitz; tel. (371) 4884222; fax (371) 4884299; e-mail info@ stadtbibliothek-chemnitz.de; internet www .stadtbibliothek-chemnitz.de; f. 1869; 500,000 vols; special collection of literature on local government; Dir ELKE BEER.

Universitätsbibliothek: Str. der Nationen 62, 09107 Chemnitz; tel. (371) 5311283; fax (371) 5311569; e-mail sekretariat@bibliothek .tu-chemnitz.de; internet www.bibliothek .tu-chemnitz.de; f. 1836; 1,185,000 vols, 97,000 theses, 2,580 periodicals, 12,068,000 patents; Dir INGRID THÜMER.

Clausthal-Zellerfeld

Universitätsbibliothek der Technischen Universität Clausthal (Library of the Technical University of Clausthal): Leibnizstr. 2, 38678 Clausthal-Zellerfeld; tel. (5323) 722301; fax (5323) 723639; e-mail ubclz@tu-clausthal.de; internet bibliothek .tu-clausthal.de; f. 1810; 459,000 vols, 805 periodicals, 5,000 geological maps; Dir Dr J. SCHÜLING.

Coburg

Landesbibliothek (State Library): Schlosspl. 1, 96450 Coburg; tel. (9561) 8538-0; fax (9561) 8538-201; e-mail geschaeftsstelle@landesbibliothek-coburg.de; internet www.landesbibliothek-coburg.de; f. c. 1550, fmr ducal library of the duchy Sachsen-Coburg (until 1918); 410,000 vols, 600 periodicals; Dir Dr SILVIA PFISTER.

Staatsarchiv Coburg (State Archive of Coburg): Herrngasse 11, 96450 Coburg; tel. (9561) 427070; fax (9561) 4270720; e-mail poststelle@staco.bayern.de; internet www .gda.bayern.de/archive/coburg; f. 13th century; present title 1939; archives of the duchy and republic of Saxe-Coburg, since 1920 the rural district of Coburg; 380,000 documents; 8,000 vols; Dir Dipl.-Archivar HORST GEHRINGER.

Cologne

Deutsche Zentralbibliothek für Medizin (German National Library of Medicine): Gleueler Str. 60, 50931 Cologne; tel. (221) 4785600; fax (221) 4785697; e-mail info@ zbmed.de; internet www.zbmed.de; f. 1908; 1,150,000 vols and microforms, 7,300 current periodicals; virtual library of medicine (www.medpilot.de), virtual library of nutrition, environment and agriculture (www.greenpilot.de), open access journals in medicine (www.egms.de); offers document delivery by post, fax and e-mail; Dir ULRICH KORWITZ.

Erzbischöfliche Diözesan- und Dombibliothek mit Bibliothek St Albertus Magnus (Archbishop's Diocesean and Cathedral Library incl. Library St Albertus Magnus): Postfach 10-11-45, 50451 Cologne; Kardinal-Frings-Str. 1–3, 50668 Cologne; tel. (221) 16423781; fax (221) 16423783; e-mail dombibliothek@erzbistum-koeln.de; internet www.dombibliothek-koeln.de; f. 1738; 700,000 vols; Dirs Prof. Dr HEINZ FINGER, Prof. Dr SIEGFRIED SCHMIDT; publ. *Analecta Coloniensia*, *Libelli Rhenani*.

Historisches Archiv der Stadt Köln: Heumarkt 14, 50667 Cologne; tel. (221) 221-22327; fax (221) 221-22480; e-mail historischesarchiv@stadt-koeln.de; internet www.stadt-koeln.de/historisches-archiv; f. 1322; records since AD 875; 140,000 vols; Dir Dr BETTINA SCHMIDT-CZAIA; publ. *Mitteilungen*.

Kunst- und Museumsbibliothek der Stadt Köln: Kattenbug 18–24, 50667 Cologne; tel. (221) 221-22388; fax (221) 221-22210; e-mail kmb@stadt-koeln.de; internet www.museenkoeln.de/kmb; f. 1957; 370,000 vols; Curator Dr E. PURPUS.

LVR-Archivberatungs-und Fortbildungszentrum, Abteilung Archivberatung (Archive and Museums Office of the Rheinland, Department of Archive Services): Ehrenfriedstr. 19, 50259 Pulheim; tel. (2234) 9854300; fax (2234) 9854285; e-mail afz@lvr .de; internet www.archivberatung.lvr.de; f. 1929; archive of the Landschaftsverband Rheinland with sources of the last 200 years; collections relating to local history; 16,500 vols; Dir Dr ARIE NABRINGS; publs *Archivhefte* (archival science in Rheinland), *Inventare nichtstaatlicher Archive* (inventories of non-state archives in Rheinland), *Rheinprovinz* (regional history of Rheinland).

Stiftung Rheinisch-Westfälisches Wirtschaftsarchiv zu Köln: Unter Sachsenhausen 10–26, 50667 Cologne; tel. (221) 1640-800; fax (221) 1640-829; f. 1906; economic records of the region; research and publication of research results; lending and reference library of business documents; 35,000 vols; Dir Dr ULRICH S. SOÉNIUS; publ.

Schriften zur rheinisch-westfälischen Wirtschaftsgeschichte.

Universitäts- und Stadtbibliothek: Universitätsstr. 33, 50931 Cologne; tel. (221) 4702260; fax (221) 4705166; e-mail sekretariat@ub.uni-koeln.de; internet www .ub.uni-koeln.de; f. 1920; 3,200,000 vols; Dir Prof. Dr W. SCHMITZ.

Darmstadt

Hessisches Staatsarchiv (State Archive of Hesse): Karolinenpl. 3, 64289 Darmstadt; tel. (6151) 165900; fax (6151) 165901; e-mail poststelle@stad.hessen.de; internet www .staatsarchiv-darmstadt.hessen.de; f. 1567; Dir Prof. Dr FRIEDRICH BATTENBERG; publs *Darmstädter Archivdokumente für den Unterricht*, *Darmstädter Archivenschriften*, *Geschichte im Archiv*.

Universitäts- und Landesbibliothek Darmstadt: Schloss, 64283 Darmstadt; tel. (6151) 165850; fax (6151) 165897; e-mail info@ulb.tu-darmstadt.de; internet www.ulb .tu-darmstadt.de; f. 1560; 1,900,000 vols, 4,090 MSS, 2,050 incunabula, 15,000 musicalia, 28,000 maps, 4,600,000 German and European patent documents; Dir Dr HANS-GEORG NOLTE-FISCHER.

Dessau

Anhaltische Landesbücherei Dessau: Zerbster Str. 10/35, 06844 Dessau; tel. (340) 2042048; fax (340) 2042948; e-mail bibliothek@dessau-rosslau.de; internet www .bibliothek.dessau.de; f. 1898; 285,195 vols, 133 incunabula, 599 MSS, 342 current periodicals; Dir GABRIELE SCHNEIDER.

Detmold

Landesarchiv Nordrhein-Westfalen-Staats- und Personenstandarchiv Detmold: Willi-Hofmann-Str. 2, 32756 Detmold; tel. (5231) 7660; fax (5231) 766114; e-mail stadt@lav.nrw.de; internet www.archive.nrw .de; f. 1957 (formerly Lippisches Landesarchiv, f. 16th century); archives of former regions of Lippe (12th century to 1947) and Minden (1815–1947), Dominion of Vianen (Netherlands), Detmold (since 1947); spec. collns: genealogy, French Citizens' Registers, Parish Registers, Jewish and Dissenters' Registers of Westphalia (1808–1874); copies of registers of births, deaths and marriages (1874–1938); 72,000 vols; Dir Dr JUTTA PRIEUR-POHL.

Lippische Landesbibliothek Detmold: Hornsche Str. 41, 32756 Detmold; tel. (5231) 926600; fax (5231) 92660-55; e-mail llbmail@llb-detmold.de; internet www .llb-detmold.de; f. 1614; 550,000 vols, 10,000 MSS; Dir DETLEV HELLFAIER.

Dortmund

Stadt- und Landesbibliothek Dortmund: Königswall 18, 44137 Dortmund; tel. (231) 50-23225; fax (231) 50-23199; e-mail stlb@ stadtdo.de; internet www.bibliothek .dortmund.de; f. 1907; 1,200,000 vols; spec. colln of MSS and autographs and material on Westphalia; music dept; Dir ULRICH MOESKE; publs *Autographenausstellungen* (irregular), *Mitteilungen* (irregular), *Mitteilungen aus dem Literaturarchiv Kulturpreis der Stadt Dortmund* (every 2 years).

Stiftung Westfälisches Wirtschaftsarchiv (WWA) (Foundation of the Westphalian Economic Archive): Märkische Str. 120, 44141 Dortmund; tel. (231) 5417296; fax (231) 5417117; e-mail wwado@dortmund.ihk .de; internet www.archive.nrw.de; f. 1941; records of the economic, social and industrial history of Westphalia and the Ruhr; research; 4,000 shelf-metres of records; 50,000 vols; Dir Dr KARL-PETER ELLERBROCK.

Universitätsbibliothek Dortmund: Vogelpothsweg 76, 44227 Dortmund; tel. (231) 755-4001; fax (231) 755-4032; e-mail information@ub.tu-dortmund.de; internet www.ub.tu-dortmund.de; f. 1965; 1,700,000 vols, 7,500,000 patents; Dir MARLENE NAGELSMEIER-LINKE.

Dresden

Sächsische Landesbibliothek–Staats- und Universitätsbibliothek Dresden: Zellescher Weg 18, 01069 Dresden; tel. (351) 4677-123; fax (351) 4677-111; e-mail direktion@slub-dresden.de; internet www .slub-dresden.de; f. 1996; 4,101,000 vols, 147,000 theses, 131,000 maps, 178,000 tapes and records, 2,000,000 photographs, 131,000 standards, 12,850 current periodicals; Dir-Gen. THOMAS BÜRGER; publs *Bibliographie Geschichte der Technik* (1 a year), *Sächsische Bibliographie* (1 a year), *SLUB-Kurier* (4 a year).

Sächsisches Staatsarchiv—Hauptstaatsarchiv Dresden: Postfach 100 444, 01074 Dresden; Archivstr. 14, 01097 Dresden; tel. (351) 80060; fax (351) 8021274; e-mail poststelle-d@sta.smi.sachsen.de; internet www.archiv.sachsen.de; f. 1834; 71,000 vols; Dir Dr GUNTRAM MARTIN; publs *Einzelveröffentlichungen, Schriftenreihe des Sächsischen Hauptstaatsarchivs* (13 vols).

Städtische Bibliotheken Dresden (City Libraries of Dresden): Freibergerstr. 33, 01067 Dresden; tel. (351) 8648101; fax (351) 8648102; e-mail mail@bibo-dresden.de; internet www.bibo-dresden.de; f. 1910; 751,490 vols; Dir Dr AREND FLEMMING.

Duisburg

Stadtarchiv Duisburg (City Archives of Duisburg): Karmelpl. 5 (Am Innenhafen), 47049 Duisburg; tel. (203) 283-2154; fax (203) 283-4330; e-mail stadtarchiv@stadt-duisburg.de; internet www.archive .nrw.de; f. 12th century; admin., research into local and city history; reference library on local history and customs of Duisburg and Lower Rhine; 60,000 vols; Dir Dr HANS GEORG KRAUME; publs *Duisburger Forschungen, Duisburger Geschichtsquellen.*

Stadtbibliothek (City Library): Düsseldorfer Str. 5–7, 47049 Duisburg; tel. (203) 283-4218; fax (203) 283-4294; e-mail stadtbibliothek@stadt-duisburg.de; internet www.stadtbibliothek-duisburg.de; f. 1901; public library of 680,000 vols, 1,177 periodicals; Dir Dr JAN-PIETER BARBIAN; publs *Blickpunkt Bibliothek* (26 a year), *Literary Catalogues* (Amerikanische Literatur, Schiller, Heine, Brecht, Böll, Kafka).

Düsseldorf

Bibliotek und Archiv des Heinrich-Heine-Instituts (Heinrich Heine Institute Library and Archives): Bilker Str. 12–14, 40213 Düsseldorf; tel. (211) 8995574; fax (211) 8929044; e-mail elena.camaiani@ duesseldorf.de; internet www.duesseldorf.de/ heineinstitut; f. 1970; exhibitions, readings, lectures, 55,000 vols, literature by/on Heinrich Heine, documents regarding the revolutionary 'Vormärz' era and the Rhineland as well as music and arts in Düsseldorf; MSS collns from 1600 to the present, more than 130 literary, musical and artistic estates, among them the largest colln of autographs by Heinrich Heine, spec. collns of autographs by Clara and Robert Schumann as well as the Düsseldorf School of Painting; Dir Dr SABINE BRENNER-WILCZEK; Librarian ELENA CAMAIANI; publs *Archiv–Bibliothek–Museum* (irregular), *Heine-Jahrbuch* (1 a year), *Heine-Studien* (irregular).

Landesarchiv Nordrhein-Westfalen: Graf-Adolf-Str. 67, 40210 Düsseldorf; tel.

(211) 159238-0; fax (211) 159238-111; e-mail poststelle@lav.nrw.de; internet www.lav.nrw .de; f. 2004; consists of Zentrale Dienste, Fachbereich Grundsätze, Abteilung Rheinland (f. 1832), Abteilung Westfalen (f. 1829), Abteilung Ostwestfalen-Lippe (f. 1955); Pres. Prof. Dr WILFRIED REININGHAUS; publ. *Archivar. Zeitschrift für Archivwesen* (4 a year).

Universitäts- und Landesbibliothek Düsseldorf (University and State Library of Düsseldorf): Universitätsstr. 1, 40225 Düsseldorf; tel. (211) 81-12030; fax (211) 81-13054; e-mail sekretariat@ub .uni-duesseldorf.de; internet www.ub .uni-duesseldorf.de; f. 1970; 209,305 vols, 13,892 electronic periodicals, 3,744 in print; Dir Dr IRMGARD SIEBERT.

Eichstätt

Universitätsbibliothek Eichstätt-Ingolstadt (University Library of Eichstätt-Ingolstadt): Universitätsallee 1, 85072 Eichstätt; tel. (8421) 93-1330; fax (8421) 93-1791; e-mail ub-direktion@ku-eichstaett.de; internet www.ku-eichstaett.de/bibliothek.de; f. 16th century; developed from former Library of Diocesan Seminary and State Library; spec. collns: theology, archives of Asscn of German Catholic Press and of Asscn of Catholic publishers and booksellers, Schlecht music library and MSS, Glossner Oriental and Judaistic library, archives and library of the Inklings Society; 1,919,064 vols, 432,118 units of non-book materials, 2,844 MSS, 3,001 musical MSS, 1,244 incunabula, 3,378 periodicals; Dir Dr ANGELIKA REICH; publs *Aus den Beständen der Universitätsbibliothek Eichstätt, Bibliographien der Universitätsbibliothek Eichstätt, Kataloge der Universitätsbibliothek Eichstätt, Schriften der Universitätsbibliothek Eichstätt.*

Erfurt

Stadt- und Regionalbibliothek Erfurt: 40.03, 99111 Erfurt; Dompl. 1, 99084 Erfurt; tel. (361) 6551590; fax (361) 6551599; e-mail bibliothek@erfurt.de; internet bibliothek .erfurt.de; f. 1897; 526,712 vols (237,312 vols in scientific spec. collns), 500 periodicals; Dir Dr EBERHARD KUSBER.

Erlangen

Universitätsbibliothek Erlangen-Nürnberg (University Library of Erlangen-Nuremberg): Universitätsstr. 4, 91054 Erlangen; tel. (9131) 8523950; fax (9131) 8529309; e-mail direktion@bib.uni-erlangen.de; internet www.ub.uni-erlangen.de; f. 1743; spec. collns on education, science and philosophy; 4,800,000 vols, 870,000 theses, 2,432 MSS, 140 papyri, 2,136 incunabula; Dir K. SOELLNER.

Frankfurt am Main

Bibliothek des Freies Deutschen Hochstifts (Library of the Free German Literature Institute): Frankfurter Goethe-Museum, Grosser Hirschgraben 23–25, 60311 Frankfurt am Main; tel. (69) 13880-0; fax (69) 13880-222; e-mail info@ goethehaus-frankfurt.de; internet www .goethehaus-frankfurt.de; f. 1859; 120,000 vols, 40,000 MSS and handwritten letters, 500 paintings and 16,000 prints on public display in the graphic art colln; Dir Dr CARL VON BOEHM-BEZING; Librarian NORA SCHWARZ.

Deutsche Nationalbibliothek (German National Library): Adickesallee 1, 60322 Frankfurt am Main; tel. (69) 15250; fax (69) 15251010; e-mail info-f@d-nb.de; internet www.d-nb.de; Deutsche Bibliothek (Frankfurt am Main) and Deutsche Bücherei (Leipzig) unified 1990; central archival library and

nat. bibliographic centre; collects, permanently archives, documents, records and makes available to public all German and German-language publs from 1913 onwards; spec. collns incl. Reichsbibliothek 1848, German exile literature 1933–1945, Anne-Frank-Shoah-Bibliothek; Dir-Gen. Dr ELISABETH NIGGEMANN; publ. *Deutsche Nationalbibliografie* (48 a year, 12 a year and 4 a year, online).

Constituent Libraries:

Deutsche Nationalbibliothek Deutsches Musikarchiv: Gärtnerstr. 25-32, 12207 Berlin; tel. (30) 77002-0; fax (30) 77002-299; e-mail info-b@d-nb.de; internet www.d-nb.de; f. 1970; 1,200,000 vols; Head of Dept Dr INGO KOLASA.

Deutsche Nationalbibliothek Frankfurt am Main: Adickesallee 1, 60322 Frankfurt am Main; tel. (69) 15250; fax (69) 15251010; e-mail info-f@d-nb.de; internet www.d-nb.de; f. 1912; central archival library and nat. bibliographic centre; collects, permanently archives, documents and records German and German-language publs from 1913; foreign publs about Germany, translations of German works, and the works of German-speaking emigrants between 1933–1945; 25,400,000 vols; Dir-Gen. Dr ELISABETH NIGGEMANN.

Deutsche Nationalbibliothek Leipzig: Deutscher Pl. 1, 04103 Leipzig; tel. (341) 22710; fax (341) 2271444; e-mail info-l@ d-nb.de; internet www.d-nb.de; f. 1912; 14,545,826 vols; Dir MICHAEL FERNAU.

Institut für Stadtgeschichte (Stadtarchiv) Frankfurt am Main: Münzgasse 9, 60311 Frankfurt am Main; tel. (69) 21237914; fax (69) 21230753; e-mail helmut .nordmeyer@stadt-frankfurt.de; internet www.stadtgeschichte-ffm.de; f. 1436; municipal records; documents since 9th century, registers since 13th century, deeds since 14th century; records on Frankfurt from other archives; historical records in writings, pictures and sound; 50,000 vols, 750 current periodicals; Dir Dr EVELYN BROCKHOFF.

Universitätsbibliothek Johann Christian Senckenberg: Bockenheimer Landstr. 134–138, 60325 Frankfurt am Main; tel. (69) 798-39-230; fax (69) 798-39-062; e-mail direktion@ub.uni-frankfurt.de; internet www.ub.uni-frankfurt.de; f. 1484; present name 2005 following merger of Stadt- und Universitätsbibliothek Frankfurt am Main (StUB) and the Senckenbergische Bibliothek (SeB) 2005; 4,200,000 vols; Dir BERNDT DUGALL.

Freiberg im Sachsen

Technische Universität Bergakademie Freiberg Universitätsbibliothek 'Georgius Agricola': Agricolastr. 10, 09596 Freiberg in Sachsen; tel. (3731) 392959; fax (3731) 393289; e-mail unibib@ub.tu-freiberg .de; internet tu-freiberg.de/ze/ub; f. 1765; 717,200 vols, 2,820 autographs, 26,000 standards, 4,470 cards, 71,300 univ. publs; spec. collns: mining and metallurgy, geosciences; Dir SABINE ALBANI; Head KATRIN STUMP; publ. *Veröffentlichungen der Bibliothek 'Georgius Agricola' der TU Bergakademie Freiberg* (irregular).

Freiburg im Breisgau

Deutsches Volksliedarchiv, Institut für internationale Popularliedforschung (German Folksong Archive, Research Centre for Song and Popular Culture): Silberbachstr. 13, 79100 Freiburg; tel. (761) 705030; fax (761) 70503-28; e-mail info@dva .uni-freiburg.de; internet www.dva .uni-freiburg.de; f. 1914; 70,000 vols; Head

Dr NILS GROSCH; publs *Deutsche Volkslieder mit ihren Melodien, Historisch-kritisches Liederlexikon 2005ff* (1 a year), *Jahrbuch für Volksliedforschung, Populäre Kultur und Musik. 2010ff, Volksliedstudien 2001ff.*

Stadtarchiv Freiburg im Breisgau (City Archive of Freiburg im Breisgau): Grünwälderstr. 15, 79098 Freiburg im Breisgau; tel. (761) 201-2701; fax (761) 201-2799; e-mail stadtarchiv@stadt.freiburg.de; internet www.freiburg.de; f. 1840; 5 km of records from 12th century to present day; 75,000 vols; Dir Dr ULRICH P. ECKER; publs *Neue Reihe, Schau-ins-Land, Veröffentlichungen aus dem Archiv der Stadt Freiburg.*

Universitätsbibliothek: Rempartstr. 10–16, Schwarzwaldstr. 80, Postfach 1629, 79016 Freiburg im Breisgau; tel. (761) 203-3900; fax (761) 203-3987; e-mail info@ub.uni-freiburg.de; internet www.ub.uni-freiburg.de; f. 1457; 3,556,218 vols, incl. dissertations; Dir Dr ANTJE KELLERSOHN.

Fulda

Hochschul- und Landesbibliothek: Heinrich-von-Bibra-Pl. 12, 36037 Fulda; tel. (661) 9640-970; fax (661) 9640-954; e-mail hlb@hlb.hs-fulda.de; internet www.hs-fulda.de/hlb; f. 1778; 630,000 vols, 840 MSS and 431 incunabula; Dir Dr MARIANNE RIETHMÜLLER.

Gießen

Universitätsbibliothek Gießen: Otto-Behaghel-Str. 8, 35394 Gießen; tel. (641) 9914032; fax (641) 9914009; e-mail auskunft@bibsys.uni-giessen.de; internet www.ub.uni-giessen.de; f. 1612; 3,836,599 vols, 398,554 dissertations, 2,710 MSS, 877 incunabula, 2,841 papyri; Dir Dr PETER REUTER; Librarian CORINA THOMÄ.

Görlitz

Oberlausitzische Bibliothek der Wissenschaften bei den Städtischen Sammlungen für Geschichte und Kultur Görlitz (Upper Lusatian Library of Science, at the City Collection for History and Culture in Görlitz): Neiss Str. 30, Postfach 300131, 02826 Görlitz; tel. (3581) 671350; fax (3581) 671375; e-mail olb@goerlitz.de; internet olb.goerlitz.de; f. 1950 (original library 1779); scientific, historical and gen. library incl. rare book colln; 140,000 vols; Librarian MATTHIAS WENZEL.

Gotha

Universitäts- und Forschungsbibliothek Erfurt/Gotha (University and Research Library of Erfurt/Gotha): Postfach 90 02 22, 99105 Erfurt; tel. (361) 7375800; fax (361) 7375779 Postfach 10 01 30, 99851 Gotha; tel. (361) 7375530; fax (361) 7375539; e-mail bibliothek@uni-erfurt.de; internet www.uni-erfurt.de/bibliothek; f. 1994 at Erfurt; 1,059,529 vols, 1,950 MSS, 639 incunabula; f. 1647 at Gotha; 688,906 vols, 11,338 handwritings 1,052 incunabula; Dir CHRISTIANE SCHMIEDEKNECHT.

Göttingen

Niedersächsische Staats- und Universitätsbibliothek Göttingen: Platz der Göttinger Sieben 1, 37073 Göttingen; tel. (551) 395212; fax (551) 395222; e-mail sekretariat@sub.uni-goettingen.de; internet www.sub.uni-goettingen.de; f. 1734; 4,157,734 vols, 31,631 electronic publs, 13,272 periodicals, 24,949 electronic periodicals, 13,433 MSS, 3,107 incunabula, 308,249 map sheets; Dir Dr NORBERT LOSSAU.

Greifswald

Universitätsbibliothek (University Library): Felix-Hausdorff-Str. 10A, 17489 Greifswald; tel. (3834) 861515; fax (3834) 861501; e-mail ub@uni-greifswald.de; internet www.ub.uni-greifswald.de; f. 1604; 2,990,800 vols, including 4,100 periodicals, 2,081 autographs, 330 incunabula; Dir Dr PETER WOLFF; Librarian PETRA ZEPERNICK.

Halle am Saale

Bibliothek der Deutschen Akademie der Naturforscher Leopoldina: Postfach 110543, 06019 Halle/Saale; August-Bebel-Str. 50A, 06108 Halle/Saale; tel. (345) 4723947; fax (345) 4723949; e-mail biblio@leopoldina-halle.de; internet www.leopoldina-halle.de; f. 1732; 260,000 vols, 20,000 theses; Dir JOCHEN THAMM.

Universitäts- und Landesbibliothek Sachsen-Anhalt: August-Bebel-Str. 13 u. 50, 06098 Halle/Saale; tel. (345) 5522001; fax (345) 5527140; e-mail direktion@bibliothek.uni-halle.de; internet bibliothek.uni-halle.de; f. 1696; 4,916,000 vols, 6,500 print periodicals, 8,600 online journals, 115,200 MSS and autographs; spec. collns incl. Middle East and North Africa, regional studies and history of Saxony-Anhalt; Ponikau's library; Library of the Deutsche Morgenländische Gesellschaft; Dir Dr HEINER SCHNELLING; publs *Hercynia, Regionalbibliographie Sachsen-Anhalt* (online), *Schlechtendalia.*

Hamburg

Bibliothek des Max-Planck-Institut für Ausländisches und Internationales Privatrecht (Max-Planck Institute Library for Foreign and International Private Law): Mittelweg 187, 20148 Hamburg; tel. (40) 41900-0; fax (40) 41900-288; e-mail knudsen@mpipriv.de; internet www.mpipriv.mpg.de; f. 1926; 460,000 vols, 4,000 periodicals, of which 1,950 current; Dir Prof. Dr HOLGER KNUDSEN.

Commerzbibliothek der Handelskammer Hamburg: Adolphspl. 1, 20457 Hamburg; tel. (40) 36138377; fax (40) 36138437; e-mail service@commerzbibliothek.de; internet www.commerzbibliothek.de; f. 1735 by the Commerzdeputation, later Hamburg Chamber of Commerce; historical map series; Hamburg newspapers 1721–1915; 180,000 vols on law, economics and social science; Librarian ULRIKE VERDIECK.

Deutsches Bibel-Archiv (German Bible Archive): Von Melle Park 6, 20146 Hamburg; tel. (40) 428384781; fax (40) 428384785; internet www.sub.uni-hamburg.de; f. 1931; biblical traditions in German literature and art; Bible translations; 8,000 vols; Dir Prof. Dr HEIMO REINITZER; publs *Abhandlungen und Vorträge, Bibel und deutsche Kultur, Naturalis historia bibliae, Vestigia bibliae.*

Staats- und Universitätsbibliothek Hamburg 'Carl von Ossietzky': Von-Melle-Park 3, 20146 Hamburg; tel. (40) 42838-2233; fax (40) 42838-3352; e-mail auskunft@sub.uni-hamburg.de; internet www.sub.uni-hamburg.de; f. 1479; deposit library for literature published in Hamburg; spec. collns: political science, administrative science, literature on American Indians and Eskimos, sea and coastal fishing, literature on Portugal and Spain; 3,408,000 vols, 20,344 MSS (incl. 990 papyri); Dir Prof. Dr GABRIELE BEGER; publs *Kataloge der Handschriften, F. G. Klopstock: Werke und Briefe, Publikationen der Staats-und Universitätsbibliothek Hamburg.*

Staatsarchiv der Freien und Hansestadt Hamburg (State Archive of the Free and Hanseatic City of Hamburg): Kattunbleiche 19, 22041 Hamburg; tel. (40) 42831-3200; fax (40) 42831-3201; e-mail poststelle@staatsarchiv.hamburg.de; internet www.hamburg.de/staatsarchiv; f. 13th century; history of Hamburg; 150,000 books; Dir Dr UDO SCHÄFER; publs *Hamburgisches Urkundenbuch, Veröffentlichungen.*

Hanover

Gottfried Wilhelm Leibniz Bibliothek—Niedersächsische Landesbibliothek (Gottfried Wilhelm Leibniz Library—State Library of Lower Saxony): Waterloostr. 8, 30169 Hanover; tel. (511) 1267-0; fax (511) 1267-202; e-mail information@gwlb.de; internet www.gwlb.de; f. 1665; colln of coats of arms and seals; Leibniz archive; 1,600,000 vols, 5,065 periodicals, 4,424 MSS, 80,000 autographs, 375 incunabula, several thousand maps, etchings, woodcuts; Dir Dr GEORG RUPPELT.

Niedersächsisches Landesarchiv (Regional Archive of Lower Saxony): Am Archiv 1, 30169 Hanover; tel. (511) 120-6601; fax (511) 120-6699; e-mail poststelle@nla.niedersachsen.de; internet www.nla.niedersachsen.de; fmrly Hauptstaatsarchiv Hannover, 32,000 m shelf-space; Dir Dr BERND KAPPELHOFF.

Stadtbibliothek (City Library): Hildesheimer Str. 12, 30169 Hanover; tel. (511) 168-42169; fax (511) 168-46410; e-mail stadtbibliothek-hannover@hannover-stadt.de; internet www.stadtbibliothek-hannover.de; f. 1440; gen. information about the city and region; 680,000 vols, 2,000 periodicals; Dir Dr CAROLA SCHELLE-WOLFF; Divisional Dir UWE NIETIEDT.

Technische Informationsbibliothek und Universitätsbibliothek Hannover (TIB/UB) (German National Library of Science and Technology and University Library Hannover): Welfengarten 1B, 30167 Hanover; tel. (511) 762-2268; fax (511) 762-4075; e-mail auskunft@tib.uni-hannover.de; internet www.tib.uni-hannover.de; f. 1831; German research reports, patent specifications, standards; conf. proceedings; doctoral dissertations and American reports (microforms); spec. emphasis on technical and scientific literature in Eastern and E Asian languages; acts as German Nat. Library of Science and Technology; 8,200,000 vols, 21,000 current periodicals; Dir UWE ROSEMANN.

Heidelberg

Bibliothek des Max-Planck-Instituts für Ausländisches Öffentliches Recht und Völkerrecht (Library of the Max Planck Institute for Comparative Public Law and International Law): Im Neuenheimer Feld 535, 69120 Heidelberg; tel. (6221) 4821; fax (6221) 482288; e-mail library@mpil.de; internet www.mpil.de/ww/de/pub/bibliothek.cfm; f. 1924; 600,000 vols, 2,650 periodicals; Dir Dr HARALD MÜLLER; Deputy Dir RUTH FUGGER.

Universitätsbibliothek (University Library): Plöck 107–109, 69117 Heidelberg; tel. (6221) 542380; fax (6221) 542623; e-mail ub@uni-hd.de; internet www.ub.uni-heidelberg.de; f. 1386; 3,000,000 vols, 6,600 MSS, 1,800 incunabula; Dir Dr VEIT PROBST; publs *Schriften der Universitätsbibliothek, Theke* (online).

Jena

Thüringer Universitäts- und Landesbibliothek: Postfach, 07740 Jena; Bibliothekspl. 2, 07737 Jena; tel. (3641) 940000; fax (3641) 940002; e-mail thulb_auskunft@thulb.uni-jena.de; internet www.thulb.uni-jena.de; f. 1558; 171 mems; 3,927,557 vols; Dir Dr SABINE WEFERS; Deputy Dir GABOR KUHLES; publ. *Thüringen-Bibliographie* (online).

Karlsruhe

Badische Landesbibliothek: Erbprinzenstr. 15, 76133 Karlsruhe; tel. (721) 175-0; fax (721) 175-2333; internet www.blb-karlsruhe.de; f. 1500; 1,798,422 vols; 9,706 MSS; 1,361 incunabula; Dir Dr PETER MICHAEL EHRLE.

Bibliothek des Bundesgerichtshofs (Library of the Federal Court): Herrenstr. 45A, 76133 Karlsruhe; tel. (721) 1595000; fax (721) 1595612; e-mail bibliothek@bgh.bund.de; internet www.bundesgerichtshof.de; f. 1950; law library; 418,000 vols; Dir D. PANNIER.

KIT-Bibliothek: Postfach 6920, 76049 Karlsruhe; tel. (721) 608-3101; fax (721) 608-4886; e-mail direktion@bibliothek.kit.edu; internet www.bibliothek.kit.edu; f. 1840; 1,400,000 vols; Dir FRANK SCHOLZE; Librarian SABINE BENZ.

Landesarchiv Baden-Württemberg—Generallandesarchiv Karlsruhe: Nördliche Hildapromenade 2, 76133 Karlsruhe; tel. (721) 9262206; fax (721) 9262231; e-mail glakarlsruhe@la-bw.de; internet www.landesarchiv-bw.de/glak; f. 1803; 130,000 documents, 42,000 MSS, 3,500,000 report files; 79,000 vols on Baden history; Dir Prof. Dr VOLKER RÖDEL; publ. *Zeitschrift für die Geschichte des Oberrheins* (1 a year).

Kassel

Documenta Archiv: Untere Karlsstr. 4, 34117 Kassel; tel. (561) 787-4022; fax (561) 787-4028; e-mail documentaarchiv@stadt-kassel.de; internet www.documentaarchiv.de; f. 1961; also a research institute and administers the Arnold Bode Estate and the Harry Kramer Estate; 30,000 monographs, 60,000 exhibition catalogues, 150 journals and magazines, 2,000 new acquisitions annually, 2,000 file archives, 250,000 newspaper clippings, 150,000 invitations, 25,000 slides, 3,000 video titles, 450 DVDs, 10,000 photographs, 1,000 Ektachromes, 2,000 artist portraits; Librarians PETRA HINCK, SABINE FRANKE.

Universitätsbibliothek Kassel–Landesbibliothek und Murhardsche Bibliothek der Stadt Kassel: Diagonale 10, 34111 Kassel; tel. (561) 804-2117; fax (561) 804-2125; e-mail direktion@bibliothek.uni-kassel.de; internet www.ub.uni-kassel.de; f. 1580; 1,883,890 vols, 30,234 MSS, 26,228 musical scores, 17,936 maps, 20,047 autographs, 4,162 print and 21,299 electronic periodicals; Dir Dr AXEL HALLE.

Kiel

Deutsche Zentralbibliothek für Wirtschaftswissenschaften (ZBW) (German National Library of Economics): Leibniz-Informationszentrum Wirtschaft, Düsternbrooker Weg 120, 24105 Kiel; tel. (431) 8814-555; fax (431) 8814-520; e-mail info@zbw.eu; internet www.zbw.eu; f. 1919; 4,200,000 vols; Dir EKKEHART SEUSING; publs *Intereconomics—Review of European Economic Policy* (6 a year), *Wirtschaftsdienst—Journal for Economic Policy* (12 a year).

Schleswig-Holsteinische Landesbibliothek: Wall 47–51, 24103 Kiel; tel. (431) 6967733; fax (431) 6967711; e-mail landesbibliothek@shlb.de; internet www.shlb.de; f. 1895; culture, civilization, literature, musical scores and pictorial representations of topics concerning Schleswig-Holstein, editors of Schleswig-Holstein Bibliography and Dictionary of Schleswig-Holstein biography; spec. colln on chess; 280,000 vols and literary bequests of about 100 authors and scholars; Dir J. AHLERS.

Universitätsbibliothek (University Library): Leibnizstr. 9, 24118 Kiel; tel. (431) 880; fax (431) 1596; e-mail sekretariat@ub.uni-kiel.de; internet www.uni-kiel.de/ub; f. 1665; 3 depts and 49 specialist libraries; special colln on Scandinavian languages, history and literature; 4,600,000 vols, 8,240 periodicals; Dir Dr ELSE WISCHERMANN.

Koblenz

Bundesarchiv: Postfach 56064 Koblenz; Potsdamer Str. 1, 56075 Koblenz; tel. (261) 505-0; fax (261) 505-226; e-mail koblenz@bundesarchiv.de; internet www.bundesarchiv.de; f. 1952; central archives of the Federal Republic; 2,157,426 vols; 306,518 m of records of Reich, Federal and GDR Govts, agencies, political parties, private asscns; colln of private papers; 1.0m. documentaries and newsreels (incl. 146,000 feature films), 12.4m. photographs; 87,370 posters, 1.2m. maps and technical drawings, 42,722 audio recordings, 9.3m. files of machine-readable data held at various sites throughout Germany; Pres. Prof. Dr HARTMUT WEBER.

Landesbibliothekszentrum/Rheinische Landesbibliothek: Bahnhofpl. 14, 56068 Koblenz; tel. (261) 91500-400; fax (261) 91500-910; e-mail info.rlb@lbz-rlp.de; internet www.lbz-rlp.de; f. 1987; became part of Landesbibliothekszentrum Rheinland-Pfalz 2004; 591,366 vols, 3,207 periodicals, vols on all subjects, with spec. references to N part of Rhineland-Palatinate; Central Educational Library of Rhineland-Palatinate; Dir Dr HELMUT FRÜHAUF; Man. LARS JENDRAL.

Landeshauptarchiv Koblenz (Central State Archive): Postfach 201047, 56010 Koblenz; tel. (261) 9129-0; fax (261) 9129-112; e-mail post@landeshauptarchiv-ko.de; internet www.landeshauptarchiv.de; f. 1832; 48,260 vols, 47,900 linear m of archives; history of Rhineland Palatinate and fmr territories; Dir Dr ELSBETH ANDRE; publs *Blätter für deutsche Landesgeschichte* (1 a year), *Jahrbuch für westdeutsche Landesgeschichte* (1 a year).

Konstanz

Universitätsbibliothek: Universitätsstr. 10, 78457 Konstanz; tel. (7531) 88-2800; fax (7531) 88-3082; e-mail information.ub@uni-konstanz.de; internet www.ub.uni-konstanz.de; f. 1965; 2,000,000 vols, 110,000 theses; Dir P. HAETSCHER.

Landshut

Staatsarchiv Landshut: Burg Trausnitz, 84036 Landshut; tel. (871) 92328-0; fax (871) 92328-8; e-mail poststelle@stala.bayern.de; internet www.gda.bayern.de; f. 1753; 34,000 vols; Dir Dr M. RÜTH.

Leipzig

Leibniz-Institut für Länderkunde eV Geographische Zentralbibliothek und Archiv für Geographie (Central Library and Archive of the Leibniz Institute for Regional Geography): Schongauer Str. 9, 04329 Leipzig; tel. (341) 2556529; fax (341) 2556598; e-mail bibliothek@ifl-leipzig.de; internet www.ifl-leipzig.de; f. 1896; central geographical library containing 200,000 vols, special collection of maps and atlases of the 16th–18th centuries, geography archives; Dir Dr HEINZ-PETER BROGIATO; publs *Beiträge zur Regionalen Geographie* (2 a year), *Berichte zur Deutschen Landeskunde* (2 a year), *Daten, Fakten, Literatur zur Geographie Europas* (1 a year), *Europa regional* (4 a year), *Forum IfL*.

Stadtarchiv: 04092 Leipzig; Torgauer Str. 74, 04318 Leipzig; tel. (341) 2429-0; fax (341) 2429-121; e-mail stadtarchiv@leipzig.de; internet www.leipzig.de/de/buerger/bildung/archive/stadt; f. c. 1100; Dir Dr BEATE BERGER.

Stadtbibliothek Leipzig: Postfach 100927, 04009 Leipzig; premises at: Wilhelm-Leuschner-Platz 10–11, 04107 Leipzig; tel. (341) 1235343; fax (341) 1235305; e-mail stadtbib@leipzig.de; internet www.leipzig.de/stadtbib.htm; f. 1677; 1,065,182 vols; Dir REINHARD STRIDDE.

Universitätsbibliothek (University Library): Beethovenstr. 6, 04107 Leipzig; tel. (341) 9730500; fax (341) 9730599; e-mail direktion@ub.uni-leipzig.de; internet www.ub.uni-leipzig.de; f. 1543; 5,000,000 vols, 7,200 periodicals; Hirzel colln contains books and material by and about Johann Wolfgang von Goethe (1749–1832); Dir Prof. Dr JOHANNES ULRICH SCHNEIDER.

Lübeck

Archiv der Hansestadt Lübeck: Mühlendamm 1–3, 23552 Lübeck; tel. (451) 1224150; fax (451) 1221517; e-mail archiv@luebeck.de; internet www.luebeck.de/kultur_bilding/archiv; f. 1298; municipal archives and documents of the churches, recognized public bodies, instns and private persons; 40,000 vols; Dir Prof. Dr A. GRASSMANN.

Bibliothek der Hansestadt Lübeck (Library of the Hanseatic City of Lübeck): Hundestr. 5–17, 23552 Lübeck; tel. (451) 1224114; fax (451) 1224112; e-mail stadtbibliothek@luebeck.de; internet www.stadtbibliothek.luebeck.de; f. 1616; 1.1m. vols, 3,667 maps, 43,484 vols of printed music, 11,922 MSS; 18,889 mems; Dir Dr B. HATSCHER.

Ludwigsburg

Landesarchiv Baden-Württemberg—Staatsarchiv Ludwigsburg: Arsenalpl. 3, 71638 Ludwigsburg; tel. (7141) 18-6310; fax (7141) 18-6311; e-mail staludwigsburg@la-bw.de; internet www.landesarchiv-bw.de/stal; f. 1868; archives for the admin. dist. of Stuttgart (Nordwürttemberg); 36,000 m of deeds; 500,000 files from the time of the Third Reich and the time after the Second World War; 43,000 vols; Dir Dr PETER MUELLER.

Magdeburg

Landeshauptarchiv Sachsen-Anhalt (State Archive of Saxony-Anhalt): Hegelstr. 25, 39104 Magdeburg; tel. (391) 56643; fax (391) 5664440; e-mail poststelle@lha.mi.lsa-net.de; f. 1823; 103,000 vols; 48,000 m of records, 158,000 maps; archives of state public record offices; Dir Dr ULRIKE HÖROLDT.

Stadtbibliothek Magdeburg: Breiter Weg 109, 39104 Magdeburg; tel. (391) 5404800; fax (391) 5404803; e-mail stadtbibliothek@magdeburg.de; internet www.magdeburg.de; f. 1525; 404,000 vols; Dir PETER PETSCH.

Mainz

Universitätsbibliothek Mainz (University Library of Mainz): Jakob-Welder-Weg 6, 55128 Mainz; tel. (6131) 3922633; fax (6131) 3923822; e-mail info@ub.uni-mainz.de; internet www.ub.uni-mainz.de; 2,000,000 vols, 814 MSS; Dir Dr A. ANDERHUB.

Wissenschaftliche Stadtbibliothek: Rheinallee 3B, 55116 Mainz; tel. (6131) 12-26-49; fax (6131) 12-35-70; e-mail stb.direktion@stadt.mainz.de; internet www.bibliothek.mainz.de; f. 1477 as University Library, taken over by the City of Mainz in 1805; 638,089 vols, 2,364 incunabula, 1,332 MSS; Dir Dr STEPHAN FLIEDNER (acting); publs *Beiträge zur Geschichte der Stadt Mainz, Mainzer Zeitschrift, Veröffentlichungen der Bibliotheken der Stadt Mainz.*

Mannheim

Universitätsbibliothek (University Library): Schloss, Ostflügel, 68131 Mannheim; tel. (621) 181-2941; fax (621) 181-2939; e-mail ub@bib.uni-mannheim.de; internet www.bib.uni-mannheim.de; 2,100,000 vols; Dir CHRISTIAN BENZ.

Marbach am Neckar

Deutsches Literaturarchiv Marbach: Schillerhöhe 8–10, 71672 Marbach; tel. (7144) 8480; fax (7144) 848299; e-mail info@dla-marbach.de; internet www.dla-marbach.de; f. 1895; German literature since 1750; large collection of autographs and documents, 1,100 legacies, 750,000 vols; Dir Prof. Dr ULRICH RAULFF; publs *Jahrbuch der Deutschen Schillergesellschaft* (1 a year), *Marbacher Bibliothek* (1 a year), *Marbacher Katalog* (1 a year), *Marbacher Magazin* (4 a year).

Marburg

Bibliothek des Herder-Instituts: Gisonenweg 5–7, 35037 Marburg; tel. (6421) 184150; fax (6421) 184139; e-mail bibliothek@herder-institut.de; internet www.herder-institut.de; f. 1950; research library specializing in the history and culture of East Central Europe (Poland, Czech Republic, Slovakia, Estonia, Latvia, and Lithuania); 400,000 vols; Chief Librarian Dr JÜRGEN WARMBRUNN.

Deutsches Adelsarchiv (Germany Archive of the Nobility): Schwanallee 21, 35037 Marburg; tel. (6421) 26162; fax (6421) 27529; e-mail info@adelsarchiv.de; f. 1945; genealogy of German nobility; 20,000 vols; Dir Dr CHRISTOPH FRANKE; publ. *Genealogisches Handbuch des Adels*.

Hessisches Staatsarchiv Marburg: Friedrichspl. 15, 35037 Marburg; tel. (6421) 9250-0; fax (6421) 161125; e-mail poststelle@stama.hessen.de; internet www.staatsarchiv-marburg.hessen.de; f. 1870; 150,097 books, 130,120 charts, 330,004 maps and plans, 66 km of records of the Electorate of Hesse-Kassel, the abbeys of Fulda, Hersfeld, the principality of Waldeck; Dir Dr ANDREAS HEDWIG; publs *Repertorien*, *Schriften*.

Universitätsbibliothek: Postfach 1920, 35008 Marburg; Wilhelm-Röpke-Str. 4, 35039 Marburg; tel. (6421) 2821319; fax (6421) 2826506; e-mail verwaltung@ub.uni-marburg.de; internet www.uni-marburg.de/bis; f. 1527; 2,057,493 vols, 716,860 theses, 3,020 MSS; Dir Dr H. NEUHAUSEN; Librarian ANDREAS SEIBEL.

Mönchengladbach

Bibliothek Wissenschaft und Weisheit (Library of Theology and Philosophy): Franziskanerstr. 30, 41063 Mönchengladbach; tel. (2161) 899135; fax (2161) 899171; f. 1929; attached to Zentralbibliothek der Kölnischen Franziskanerprovinz (fmrly Hochsculbibliothek); 70,000 vols; Dir Father O. GIMMNICH.

Stadtbibliothek (City Library): Blücherstr. 6, 41050 Mönchengladbach; tel. (2161) 256340; fax (2161) 256369; e-mail stadtbibliothek@moenchengladbach.de; internet www.stadtbibliothek-mg.de; f. 1904; 437,000 vols; special collection on social and political questions, library of the 'Volksverein für das katholische Deutschland 1890–1933'; Head GUIDO WEYER.

Munich

Bayerische Staatsbibliothek: 80328 Munich; Ludwigstr. 16, 80539 Munich; tel. (89) 28638-0; fax (89) 28638-2200; e-mail info@bsb-muenchen.de; internet www.bsb-muenchen.de; f. 1558; deposit library for Bavaria; 9,530,000 vols, 1.2m. microforms, 93,000 MSS, 55,000 current periodicals, 400,000 maps, 360,000 scores, 88,000 audiovisual items, 2.2m. single sheets and photographs; Dir Dr ROLF GRIEBEL; publs *Bibliotheksforum Bayern* (4 a year), *Bibliotheksmagazin* (3 a year).

Bayerisches Hauptstaatsarchiv: Postfach 22 11 52, 80501 Munich; Schönfeldstr. 5, 80539 Munich; tel. (89) 28638-2596; fax (89) 28638-2954; e-mail poststelle@bayhsta.bayern.de; internet www.gda.bayern.de; f. 13th century, reorganized 1978; comprises 5 departments: (1) Altere Bestände: 268,500 charters, 589,900 documents and vols, 24,000 maps and plans; (2) Neuere Bestände (since 19th century): 4,100 charters, 1,010,700 documents, 174,900 maps and plans; (3) Geheimes Hausarchiv: 10,500 charters, 27,300 documents and vols, 9,900 pictures; (4) Kriegsarchiv: 477,900 documents and vols, 130,300 maps and plans, 99,700 pictures; (5) Nachlässe und Sammlungen: collections of private papers, publications, posters, pictures, etc.; Dir Dr GERHARD HETZER; publs *Archivalische Zeitschrift*, *Archive in Bayern*, *Bayerische Archivinventare*, *Nachrichten aus den Staatlichen Archiven Bayerns*.

Bibliothek des Deutschen Museums: Museumsinsel 1, 80538 Munich; tel. (89) 2179-224; fax (89) 2179-262; e-mail bibliothek@deutsches-museum.de; internet www.deutsches-museum.de/bibliothek; f. 1903; research library for the history of science and technology; 900,000 vols; Dir Dr HELMUT HILZ.

Deutsches Bucharchiv München (Institut für Buchwissenschaften): Bibliothek und Dokumentationsstelle, Literaturhaus München, Salvatorplatz 1, 80333 Munich; tel. (89) 291951-0; fax (89) 291951-95; e-mail kontakt@bucharchiv.de; internet www.bucharchiv.de; f. 1948; documentation, scientific and technical information about books and periodicals; special library for book research; 30,000 vols, 180 periodicals; Dir Prof. Dr LUDWIG DELP.

Deutsches Patent- und Markenamt (German Patent and Trademark Office): Abt. Informationsdienste (Bibliothek), 80297 Munich; tel. (89) 2195-0; fax (89) 2195-2221; e-mail info@dpma.de; internet www.dpma.de; f. 1877; industrial property; 1,116,000 vols, 37m. patent specifications; Pres. CORNELIA RUDLOFF-SCHÄFFER.

Evangelischer Presseverband für Bayern eV (Evangelical Press Society of Bavaria): Birkerstr. 22, 80636 Munich; tel. (89) 12172-0; fax (89) 12172-138; e-mail redaktion@epv.de; internet www.epv.de; f. 1963; Pres. HARTMUT JOISTEN.

Münchner Stadtbibliothek (City Library of Munich): Rosenheimer Str. 5, 81667 Munich; tel. (89) 48098-3203; fax (89) 48098-3233; e-mail stb.zentraledienste.sekretariat.kult@muenchen.de; internet www.muenchner-stadtbibliothek.de; f. 1843; 3m. vols; Dir Dr WERNER SCHNEIDER.

Staatsarchiv (State Archive): Schönfeldstr. 3, 80539 Munich; tel. (89) 28638-2525; fax (89) 28638-2526; e-mail poststelle@stam.bayern.de; internet www.gda.bayern.de; f. 1814; 11,295,125 files (records), 9,157 documents (charts), 30,455 maps and plans, 25,000 vols (library); Dir RAINER BRAUN.

Stadtarchiv (City Archives): Winzererstr. 68, 80797 Munich; tel. (89) 2330308; fax (89) 23330830; e-mail stadtarchiv@muenchen.de; f. 1520; 65,000 vols, 78,000 documents, 16m. deeds, 22,000 maps and plans, 1,200,000 photos and postcards, 3,050 soundtracks, 1,500 films, 26,629 posters; Dir Dr R. BAUER.

Universitätsbibliothek: Geschwister-Scholl-Pl. 1, 80539 Munich; tel. (89) 21802428; e-mail direktion@ub.uni-muenchen.de; internet www.ub.uni-muenchen.de; f. 1473; 6,800,000 vols, 3.300 MSS, incl. 650 from the Middle Ages, 170 estates, containing about 55,000 autographs, 475,000 old books published before 1900, rare book colln with around 12,000 vols, ex libris colln, broadsheet and handbill collns; Dir Dr KLAUS-RAINER BRINTZINGER.

Universitätsbibliothek der Technischen Universität (Technical University Library): Arcisstr. 21, 80333 Munich; tel. (89) 28928601; fax (89) 28928622; e-mail infocenter@ub.tum.de; internet www.ub.tum.de; f. 1868; 1,834,911 vols; Dir Dr REINER KALLENBORN.

Münster

Landesarchiv Nordrhein-Westfalen, Staatsarchiv Münster: Bohlweg 2, 48147 Münster; tel. (251) 4885-0; fax (251) 4885-100; e-mail stams@lav.nrw.de; internet www.archive.nrw.de; f. 1829 as Provinzialarchiv for Westphalia, present title since 1946; 30,000 metres of documents and 100,000 charters, from 9th century to the present; 150,000 vols; Dir Dr MECHTHILD BLACK-VELTRUP.

LWL-Archivamt für Westfalen Landschaftsverband Westfalen-Lippe: Jahnstr. 26, 48133 Münster; tel. (251) 5913890; fax (251) 591269; e-mail lwl-archivamt@lwl.org; internet www.lwl-archivamt.de; f. 1927; non-state archives; training of archivists; 30,000 vols; Dir Dr MARCUS STUMPF; publs *Inventare der nichtstaatlichen Archive Westfalens*, *Westfälische Quellen und Archivpublikationen*, *Archivpflege in Westfalen-Lippe* (Journal, 2 a year), *Texte und Untersuchungen zur Archivpflege*.

Universitäts- und Landesbibliothek: Postfach 8029, Krummer Timpen 3–5, 48043 Münster; tel. (251) 8324021; fax (251) 8328398; e-mail sekretariat.ulb@uni-muenster.de; internet www.uni-muenster.de/ulb; f. 1588, refounded 1902; 2,334,800 vols incl. 305,660 theses, 821 incunabula, 1,406 MSS, 7,258 print periodicals, 3,214 e-journals; Dir Dr BEATE TRÖGER.

Nuremberg

Bibliothek des Germanischen Nationalmuseums: Postfach 119580, 90105 Nuremberg; Kornmarkt 1, 90402 Nuremberg; tel. (911) 1331-151; fax (911) 1331-351; e-mail bibliothek@gnm.de; internet www.gnm.de; f. 1852; arts, history of civilization, German-speaking regions; special colln of art-history works since AD 800; 650,000 vols, 3,380 MSS, 3,000 16th-century prints, 1,708 current periodicals; Dir Dr EBERHARD SLENCZKA; Librarian Dr JOHANNES POMMERANZ; publs *Anzeiger des Germanischen Nationalmuseums* (1 a year), *Schrifttum zur Deutschen Kunst* (1 a year).

Landeskirchliches Archiv der Evangelisch-Lutherischen Kirche in Bayern: Veilhofstr. 28, 90489 Nuremberg; tel. (911) 588690; fax (911) 5886969; e-mail archiv@elkb.de; internet www.archiv-elkb.de; f. 1931; 12,000 m of documents; 23,000 microfiches; Dir Dr ANDREA SCHWARZ.

Staatsarchiv (State Archive): Archivstr. 17, 90408 Nuremberg; tel. (911) 93519-0; fax (911) 93519-99; e-mail poststelle@stanu.bayern.de; f. 1806; archives of middle Franconia since the Middle Ages; includes Nuremberg trial documents; 49,000 vols; Dir Dr RECHTER.

Stadtarchiv Nürnberg: Marientorgraben 8, 90402 Nuremberg; tel. (911) 231-2770; fax (911) 231-4091; e-mail stadtarchiv@stadt.nuernberg.de; internet www.stadtarchiv.nuernberg.de; f. 1865; reference library of 45,000 vols; Dir Dr MICHAEL DIEFENBACHER; Librarian WALTER GEBHARDT; publs *Ausstellungskataloge, Nürnberger Werkstücke zur Stadt- und Landesgeschichte, Quellen und Forschungen zur Geschichte und Kultur der Stadt Nürnberg.*

Stadtbibliothek Nürnberg: Egidienpl. 23, 90403 Nürnberg; tel. (911) 2312790; fax (911) 2315476; e-mail stadtbibliothek-nuernberg@stadt.nuernberg.de; internet www.stadtbibliothek.nuernberg.de; f. 1370; 90,000 vols, 3,132 MSS, 2,140 incunabula; Dir EVA HOMRIGHAUSEN.

Universitätsbibliothek Erlangen-Nürnberg, Wirtschafts- und Sozialwissenschaftliche Zweigbibliothek (University Library of Erlangen-Nuremberg, Economics and Social Studies Branch): Lange Gasse 20, 90403 Nuremberg; tel. (911) 5302-830; fax (911) 5302-852; e-mail bibliothek@wiso.uni-erlangen.de; internet www.ub.uni-erlangen.de/wisobib; f. 1919; 243,000 vols, 1,390 current periodicals; Dir JOACHIM HENNECKE.

Offenbach am Main

Deutscher Wetterdienst Deutsche Meteorologische Bibliothek (German Meteorological Service National Library for Meteorology): Postfach 100465, Frankfurter Str. 135, 63067 Offenbach am Main; tel. (69) 8062-4273; fax (69) 8062-4123; e-mail bibliothek@dwd.de; internet www.dwd.de/bibliothek; f. 1847; the nat. library for meteorology and climatology, inter-library loans; 178,000 vols, 20 incunabula, 14,000 pre-1900, 800 current periodicals; Chief Librarian BRITTA BOLZMANN.

Oldenburg

Landesbibliothek: Pferdemarkt 15, Postfach 3480, 26024 Oldenburg; tel. (441) 799-2800; fax (441) 799-2865; e-mail lbo@lb-oldenburg.de; internet www.lb-oldenburg.de; f. 1792; regional library; 801,375 vols, 94,553 microforms, 1,113 MSS; Dir C. ROEDER; Librarians Dr R. FIETZ, M. KLINKOW, Dr K.-P. MÜLLER; publ. *Schriften.*

Niedersächsisches Staatsarchiv in Oldenburg (Archive of Lower Saxony in Oldenburg): Damm 43, 26135 Oldenburg; tel. (441) 9244100; fax (441) 9244292; e-mail oldenburg@nla.niedersachsen.de; internet www.staatsarchive.niedersachsen.de; f. before 1615; public record office for the former district of Oldenburg; record repository with 13,000 m of files; contributes to *Veröffentlichungen der Niedersächsischen Archivverwaltung*; 66,000 vols; Dir Prof. Dr GERD STEINWASCHER; Librarian HANNELORE KLÖCKER.

Osnabrück

Niedersächsisches Landesarchiv–Staatsarchiv Osnabrück (State Archive of Lower Saxony): Schloßstr. 29, 49074 Osnabrück; tel. (541) 33162-0; fax (541) 33162-62; e-mail osnabrueck@nla.niedersachsen.de; internet www.staatsarchive.niedersachsen.de; f. 1869; 82,000 vols; Dir Dr KEHNE.

Passau

Staatliche Bibliothek: Michaeligasse 11, 94032 Passau; tel. (851) 7564400; fax (851) 75644027; e-mail sbp_info@staatliche-bibliothek-passau.de; internet www.staatliche-bibliothek-passau.de; f. 1612 as Jesuit library, refounded 1803 as nat. library; special collns: philosophy, theology,

regional history and literature, emblematic, Jesuitica; 326,000 vols, 151 MSS, 322 incunabula; Dir Dr MARKUS WENNERHOLD.

Universitätsbibliothek (University Library): Innstr. 29, 94032 Passau; tel. (851) 509-1630; fax (851) 509-1602; internet www.ub.uni-passau.de; f. 1976; 1,900,000 vols, 88,000 theses; Dir CAROLA RESCH.

Potsdam

Brandenburgisches Landeshauptarchiv Potsdam (Brandenburg State Central Archive, Potsdam): Postfach 60 04 49, 14404 Potsdam; Zum Windmühlenberg, 14469 Potsdam; tel. (331) 5674-0; fax (331) 5674-212; e-mail poststelle@blha.brandenburg.de; internet www.blha.de; f. 1949; brs at Lübben (Spreewald) and Frankfurt an der Oder; 109,000 vols, 46,000 linear m of files; Dir KLAUS NEITMANN; publs *Brandenburgische Archive* (1 a year), *Quellen, Findbücher und Inventare des Brandenburgischen Landeshauptarchivs, Veröffentlichungen des Brandenburgischen Landeshauptarchivs.*

Stadt- und Landesbibliothek Potsdam: Am Kanal 47, 14467 Potsdam; tel. (331) 2896600; fax (331) 2896402; e-mail slb@bibliothek.potsdam.de; internet www.bibliothek.potsdam.de; f. 1969; Brandenburg collection, Gottfried Benn collection; 585,000 vols; Dir MARION MATTEKAT.

Regensburg

Bischöfliche Zentralbibliothek: St Petersweg 11–13, 93047 Regensburg; tel. (941) 597-2513; fax (941) 597-2521; e-mail bibliothek@bistum-regensburg.de; internet www.bistum-regensburg.de; f. 1972; 304,353 vols, 420 journals, with special collns on ascetics and sacred music; includes the library of St Jacob's Irish monastery and Proske's music library; Dir PAUL MAI; Librarian WEINBERGER ROSEMARIE.

Staatliche Bibliothek Regensburg: Gesandtenstr. 13, 93047 Regensburg; tel. (941) 630806-0; fax (941) 630806-28; e-mail sbr@bib-bvb.de; internet www.staatliche-bibliothek-regensburg.de; f. 1816; spec. colln of regional history; 290,000 vols, 13,264 maps, 16,302 microforms; Dir Dr BERNHARD LUEBBERS.

Universitätsbibliothek Regensburg (University Library of Regensburg): 93042 Regensburg; Universitätsstr. 31, 93053 Regensburg; tel. (941) 943-3900; fax (941) 943-3285; e-mail rafael.ball@bibliothek.uni-regensburg.de; internet www.bibliothek.uni-regensburg.de; f. 1964; 3,500,000 vols, 6,824 print periodicals, 21,847 electronic journals, 376 databases; all fields of science except technology and agriculture; spec. holdings: Library of the Regensburg Botanical Soc., Prince Thurn and Taxis Court Library and Central Archive, Regensburg Portrait Gallery, Archive of Historical Radio Commercials; Dir Dr RAFAEL BALL.

Rostock

Universitätsbibliothek: Albert-Einstein-Str. 6, 18059 Rostock; tel. (381) 4988601; fax (381) 4988602; e-mail direktion.ub@uni-rostock.de; internet www.uni-rostock.de/ub; f. 1569; 2,300,000 vols, 330,000 theses, 1,729 print periodicals, 24,039 e-periodicals, 3,350 MSS, 6,085,000 patents, 49,500 standards, 337 databases; Dir RENATE BÄHKER (acting).

Saarbrücken

Landesarchiv Saarbrücken (State Archive of Saarbrücken): Dudweilerstr. 1, 66133 Saarbrücken; tel. (681) 501-00; fax (681) 501-1933; e-mail landesarchiv@landesarchiv.saarland.de; internet www.landesarchiv.saarland.de; f. 1948; 14,000 m of archives

concerning the Saar, 25,000 vols; Dir Dr LUDWIG LINSMAYER; 170 official publs.

Saarländische Universitäts- und Landesbibliothek (University and State Library of the Saarland): Postfach 151141, 66041 Saarbrücken; tel. (681) 302-58026; fax (681) 302-2796; e-mail e-journals@sulb.uni-saarland.de; internet www.sulb.uni-saarland.de; Medical Library in Homburg, Saar; f. 1950; 1,705,000 vols incl. 375,000 theses; Dir Dr BERND HAGENAU; Librarian CHRISTEL BAUER-LANGGUTH; Librarian e-media CORNELIA VINZENT.

Schleswig

Landesarchiv Schleswig-Holstein: Prinzenpalais, 24837 Schleswig; tel. (4621) 86-1800; fax (4621) 86-1801; e-mail landesarchiv@la.landsh.de; internet www.landesarchiv.schleswig-holstein.de; f. 1870; 35,000 m of documents since 1059; 450,000 m of documentary film on Schleswig-Holstein; 137,000 vols; Dir Prof. Dr RAINER HERING.

Schwerin im Meckl

Landesbibliothek Mecklenburg-Vorpommern: Johannes-Stelling-Str. 29, 19053 Schwerin; tel. (385) 558440; fax (385) 5584424; e-mail lb@lbmv.de; internet www.lbmv.de; f. 1779; 650,000 vols; Dir Dr R.-J. WEGENER.

Sigmaringen

Landesarchiv Baden-Württemberg–Abteilung Staatsarchiv Sigmaringen: Postfach 1638, 72486 Sigmaringen; Karlstr. 1–3, 72488 Sigmaringen; tel. (7571) 101551; fax (7571) 101552; e-mail stasigmaringen@la-bw.de; internet www.landesarchiv-bw.de/stas; f. 1865; archives of Regierungsbezirk Tübingen and Sigmaringen municipal archive; family archives of the princes of Hohenzollern, barons of Stauffenberg, etc.; 19,200 m of archives since 11th century; 65,200 vols; Co-Dirs Dr VOLKER TRUGENBERGER, Dr F.-J. ZIWES.

Speyer

Landesarchiv: Otto-Mayer-Str. 9, 67346 Speyer; tel. (6232) 9192-0; fax (6232) 9192-100; e-mail post@landesarchiv-speyer.de; internet www.landeshauptarchiv.de/speyer; f. 1817; historical archives of the Palatinate (878–1798), of the French administration until 1815 and the Bavarian admin. until 1945; current accessions of admins in the Palatinate and Rheinhesse; colln of maps; Dir Dr WALTER RUMMEL; Librarian SCHMIDT.

Landesbibliothekszentrum/Pfälzische Landesbibliothek (Regional Library of Palatinate): Otto-Mayer-Str. 9, 67343 Speyer; tel. (6232) 9006-224; fax (6232) 9006-200; e-mail info.plb@lbz-rlp.de; internet www.lbz-rlp.de; f. 1921, part of the Landesbibliothekszentrum Rheinland-Pfalz 2004; 1,020,967 vols on all subjects, with spec. reference to the Palatinate and the Saar, incl. library of the Historischer Verein der Pfalz; Dir Dr HELMUT FRÜHAUF; Man. UTE BAHRS.

Stuttgart

Bibliothek der Staatlichen Hochschule für Musik und Darstellende Kunst: Urbanstr. 25, 70182 Stuttgart; tel. (711) 212-4664; fax (711) 212-4663; e-mail bibliothek@mh-stuttgart.de; internet www.mh-stuttgart.de; f. 1857; 20,907 vols, 87,155 musical scores, 3,624 records, 8,936 CDs, 243 video cassettes, 561 DVDs; Librarians CATERINA BECKER, CLAUDIA NIEBEL.

Bibliothek des Instituts für Auslandsbeziehungen (Institute for Foreign Relations, Library): Postfach 102463, 70020 Stuttgart; Charlottenpl. 17, 70173 Stuttgart;

tel. (711) 2225147; fax (711) 2225-131; e-mail bibliothek@ifa.de; internet cms.ifa.de/info/ bibliothek; f. 1917; 400,000 vols, 2,300 current periodicals, 11,000 microfilms; Pres. ALOIS VON WALDBURG-ZEIL; publ. *KulturAustausch* (online).

Bibliothek für Zeitgeschichte in der Württembergischen Landesbibliothek: Konrad Adenauer Str. 8, 70173 Stuttgart; tel. (711) 2124516; fax (711) 2124517; e-mail bfz@wlb-stuttgart.de; internet www .wlb-stuttgart.de/sammlungen/bibliothek-- fuer-zeitgeschichte; f. 1915; contemporary history, political sciences, military sciences, esp. concerning World Wars I and II, and other conflicts since the beginning of 20th century; 360,000 vols, 450 current periodicals, and special collns (photographs, maps, leaflets, posters, microfiches, etc.); Dir Prof. Dr GERHARD HIRSCHFELD; Vice-Dir Dr HANS-CHRISTIAN PUST; publs *Schriften der Bibliothek für Zeitgeschichte–Neue Folge, Stuttgarter Vorträge zur Zeitgeschichte.*

Fraunhofer-Informationszentrum Raum und Bau (IRB) (Fraunhofer Information Centre for Regional Planning and Building Construction): POB 800469, 70504 Stuttgart; Nobelstr. 12, 70569 Stuttgart; tel. (711) 970-2500; fax (711) 970-2508; internet www.irb.fraunhofer.de; f. 1941; information centre for architecture and town and regional planning in Germany; 117,200 vols and 5,600 research reports, standards, test certificates and licences; Dir THOMAS H. MORSZECK; publs *ARCONIS Wissen zum Planen und Bauen und zum Baumarkt* (4 a year), *Kurzberichte aus der Bauforschung* (6 a year).

Hauptstaatsarchiv Stuttgart: Konrad-Adenauer-Str. 4, 70173 Stuttgart; tel. (711) 212-4335; fax (711) 212-4360; e-mail hstastuttgart@la-bw.de; internet www .landesarchiv-bw.de/hstas; history and regional studies of south-west Germany, with particular reference to Württemberg and Baden-Württemberg since 9th century; archives of 107,000 charters, 18,000 m of files and vols, 40,000 maps and plans, 100,000 seals and arms; Dir (vacant).

Rathausbücherei der Landeshauptstadt Stuttgart (Town Hall Library of the State Capital of Stuttgart): Marktpl. 1, 70173 Stuttgart; tel. (711) 2163301; fax (711) 2163506; internet www.stuttgart.de/ stadtbuecherei/rathausbuecherei; f. archives 1730; history of Stuttgart and Württemberg, legal history, public administration; 127,383 vols; spec. collns incl. first editions published in Stuttgart during 18th–19th centuries; Dir GABY VOLLMER.

Universitätsbibliothek (University Library): Postfach 104941, 70043 Stuttgart; Holzgartenstr. 16, 70174 Stuttgart; tel. (711) 6858-2222; fax (711) 6858-3502; e-mail sekretariat@ub.uni-stuttgart.de; internet www.ub.uni-stuttgart.de; f. 1829; 1,276,849 books, incl. 215,000 theses, 2,017 print and 25,757 electronic periodicals, 190,000 standards and 110,000 micromaterials, 301,368 electronic documents; Dir WERNER STEPHAN; publs *Dissertationen und Hochschulschriften der Universität Stuttgart* (2 a year), *Reden und Aufsätze der Universität Stuttgart* (irregular).

Universitätsbibliothek Hohenheim: Garbenstr. 15, 70599 Stuttgart; tel. (711) 45922096; fax (711) 45923262; e-mail ubmail@uni-hohenheim.de; internet ub .uni-hohenheim.de; f. 1818; 500,000 vols; agriculture, sciences, economics; Dir KARL-WILHELM HORSTMANN.

Württembergische Landesbibliothek (State Library of Würtemberg): Postfach 105441, 70047 Stuttgart; Konrad Adenauerstr. 8, 70173 Stuttgart; tel. (711) 212-

4424; fax (711) 212-4422; e-mail direktion@ wlb-stuttgart.de; internet www.wlb-stuttgart .de; f. 1765; 3,389,586 vols, 7,062 incunabula; large collection of old Bibles; 15,248 MSS; Hölderlin archive and Stefan George archive; music and ballet collns; Dir Dr JÖRG ENNEN.

Trier

Bibliothek des Priesterseminars Trier: Postfach 1330, 54203 Trier; Jesuitenstr. 13, 54290 Trier; tel. (651) 9484-141; fax (651) 9484-181; e-mail flohr@uni-trier.de; internet www.bps-trier.de; f. 1805; 440,000 vols on philosophy and theology, 542 theological manuscripts, and 122 incunabula; Librarian Dr MICHAEL EMBACH.

Stadtbibliothek und Stadtarchiv Trier (Municipal Library and Archives of Trier): Weberbach 25, 54290 Trier; tel. (651) 718-1429 (library); tel. (651) 718-4420 (archives); fax (651) 718-1428 (library); fax 718-4 4428 (archives); e-mail stadtbibliothek@trier.de (library); e-mail stadtarchiv@trier.de (archives); internet www.trier.de; f. Library 1804; Library: developed from the fmr Jesuit Library (f. 1560) and Univ. Library (f. 1722); contains considerable parts of the libraries of the dissolved religious instns of the region of Trier (since 1802); contains 2,500 MSS and about 3,000 incunabula; 422,000 younger media; scientific library; colln incl. a Gutenberg Bible, and a page of the *Codex Egberti*; UNESCO world heritage site; f. Archive 1894; Archives: inc. into the library; contains royal and papal charters since the 8th century for the above named religious instns and (since 1149) for the town, 5 km of younger archive material (originating from the town, the religious instns and from the Counts of Kesselstatt); collns: portraits, maps, photographs; Chief Librarian Prof. Dr MICHAEL EMBACH; Chief Archivist Dr REINER NOLDEN; publs *Ausstellungskataloge Trierer Bibliotheken, Kurtrierisches Jahrbuch, Landeskundliche Vierteljahrsblätter, Ortschroniken des Trierer Landes, Rheinland-pfälzische Bibliographie.*

Universitätsbibliothek: Universitätsring 15, 54296 Trier; tel. (651) 201-2496; fax (651) 201-3977; e-mail bibliothek@ub .uni-trier.de; internet www.ub.uni-trier.de; f. 1970; open to the public; 1,610,000 vols; Dir Dr HILDEGARD MÜLLER.

Tübingen

Universitätsbibliothek: Wilhelmstr 32, 72016 Tübingen; tel. (7071) 2972577; fax (7071) 293123; e-mail sekretariat@ub .uni-tuebingen.de; internet www.ub .uni-tuebingen.de; f. in the last quarter of 15th century; 3.4m. books, journals, microfilms and microfiches, 2,800,000 vols and journals in faculty libraries, 2,100 incunabula, 8,863 MSS; central library of Tübingen Univ.; archive and lending library; platforms and support for e-Learning and online publs for mems of the univ.; Dir Dr M. DÖRR; publ. *Index theologicus (Ixtheo) Zeitschrifteninhaltsdienst Theologie.*

Ulm

Stadtbibliothek Ulm (City Library of Ulm): Vestgasse 1, 89073 Ulm; tel. (731) 161-4100; fax (731) 161-1633; e-mail stadtbibliothek@ ulm.de; internet www.stadtbibliothek.ulm .de; f. 1516; 491,432 vols, 518 current periodicals; special collections: the arts, regional history; Dir J. LANGE.

Weimar

Herzogin Anna Amalia Bibliothek: Pl. der Demokratie 1, 99423 Weimar; tel. (3643) 545200; fax (3643) 545220; e-mail haab@ klassik-stiftung.de; internet www .klassik-stiftung.de/einrichtungen/herzogi-

n-anna-amalia-bibliothek; f. 1691; history of literature, art and music; special collns: German literature of the Classical Period (1750–1850), Faust, Liszt, Nietzsche, Shakespeare; 50,000 vols destroyed by fire September 2004; reopened in 2007; 62,000 destroyed books to be restored by 2015; 1,000,000 vols; Dir Dr MICHAEL KNOCHE; publ. *Internationale Bibliographie zur deutschen Klassik* (online).

Thüringisches Hauptstaatsarchiv Weimar (Central State Archive of Thuringia in Weimar): Postfach 2726, 99408 Weimar; Marstallstr. 2, 99423 Weimar; tel. (3643) 870-0; fax (3643) 870-100; e-mail weimar@ staatsarchive.thueringen.de; internet www .thueringen.de/de/staatsarchive; f. 1547; Dir Dr BERNHARD POST.

Wiesbaden

Bibliothek des Statistischen Bundesamtes: Gustav-Stresemann-Ring 11, 65180 Wiesbaden; tel. (611) 754573; fax (611) 754433; e-mail bibliothek@destatis.de; internet www.destatis.de/bibliothek; f. 1948; colln of statistical records, esp. on the economic and demographic devt of all countries; 500,000 vols, 1,000 journals; Head of Library HARTMUT RAHM; Librarian GÜNTER HINKES.

Hessische Landesbibliothek Wiesbaden (State Library of Hesse in Wiesbaden): Rheinstr. 55–57, 65185 Wiesbaden; tel. (611) 334-2670; fax (611) 334-2694; e-mail information@hlb-wiesbaden.de; internet www.hlb-wiesbaden.de; f. 1813; 800,000 vols, 4,500 current periodicals, 300 MSS and 400 incunabula; Dir (vacant).

Hessisches Hauptstaatsarchiv Wiesbaden (Central State Archive of Hesse in Wiesbaden): Mosbacher Str. 55, 65187 Wiesbaden; tel. (611) 881-0; fax (611) 881-145; e-mail poststelle@hhstaw.hessen.de; internet www.hauptstaatsarchiv.hessen.de; f. 1963; regional documents since 10th century; Dir Dr KLAUS EILER; publ. *Nassauische Annalen* (1 a year).

Wolfenbüttel

Herzog August Bibliothek: Lessingplatz 1, Postfach 1364, 38299 Wolfenbüttel; tel. (5331) 8080; fax 808134; e-mail direktor@hab .de; internet www.hab.de; f. 1572; cultural history from the Middle Ages to the Enlightenment; 902,711 vols, 12,296 manuscripts, 3,500 incunabula, 3,600 artists' books; Dir Prof. Dr HELWIG SCHMIDT-GLINTZER; publs *Ausstellungskataloge, Kleine Schriften, Repertorien zur Erforschung der frühen Neuzeit, Wolfenbütteler Abhandlugen zur Renaissance-Forschung, Wolfenbütteler Arbeiten zur Barockforschung, Wolfenbütteler Barocknachrichten, Wolfenbütteler Beiträge, Wolfenbütteler Bibliotheks-Informationen, Wolfenbütteler Forschungen, Wolfenbütteler Hefte, Wolfenbütteler Mittelalter-Studien, Wolfenbütteler Notizen zur Buchgeschichte, Wolfenbütteler Renaissance-Mitteilungen, Wolfenbütteler Schriften zur Geschichte des Buchwesens.*

Niedersächsisches Staatsarchiv (State Archive of Lower Saxony): Forstweg 2, 38302 Wolfenbüttel; tel. (5331) 935-0; fax (5331) 935-170; e-mail wolfenbuettel@nla .niedersachsen.de; internet www .staatsarchive.niedersachsen.de; f. 16th century; contains documents and records of the province of Brunswick; 60,000 vols; Dir Dr HORST-RÜDIGER JARCK.

Worms

Stadtarchiv im Raschi Haus: Hintere Judengasse 6, 67547 Worms; tel. (6241) 853-4700; fax (6241) 853-4710; e-mail stadtarchiv@worms.de; internet www .stadtarchiv.worms.de; Judaic museum;

large collection of records, documents and maps; Head Archivist Dr GEROLD BOENNEN.

Stadtbibliothek (City Library): Marktpl. 10, 67547 Worms; tel. (6241) 853-4209; fax (6241) 853-4220; e-mail stadtbibliothek@ worms.de; internet www .stadtbibliothek-worms.de; f. 1881; 324,000 vols, 165 incunabula; spec. collns on Luther, Kant and the Nibelungenlied; Dir Dr BUSSO DIEKAMP; publ. *Der Wormsgau.*

Wuppertal

Stadtbibliothek (City Library): Kolpingstr. 8, 42103 Wuppertal; tel. (202) 563-2302; fax (202) 563-8489; e-mail stadtbibliothek@stadt .wuppertal.de; internet www.wuppertal.de/ stadtbib; f. 1852; central library and 9 brs; special collections: theology, early socialism; Else Lasker-Schüler-Archiv, Armin T. Wegner-Archiv; 750,000 vols; Dir UTE SCHAR-MANN.

Würzburg

Staatsarchiv Würzburg (State Archive of Würzburg): Residenz-Nordflügel, 97070 Würzburg; tel. (931) 35529-0; fax (931) 35529-70; e-mail poststelle@stawu.bayern .de; internet www.gda.bayern.de/staarin .htm; f. in Middle Ages; 36,000 vols, 6,850,000 documents; archives of Lower Franconia since Middle Ages; Dir Dr W. WAGENHÖFER.

Universitätsbibliothek: Am Hubland, 97074 Würzburg; tel. (931) 888-5943; fax (931) 888-5970; e-mail direktion@bibliothek .uni-wuerzburg.de; internet www.bibliothek .uni-wuerzburg.de; f. 1619; 3,324,306 vols, 225,063 theses, 2,949 incunabula, 2,258 manuscripts, 73 papyri; special Franconian collection; Dir Dr KARL SUEDEKUM.

Zweibrücken

Landesbibliothekszentrum/Bibliotheca Bipontina: Bleicherstr. 3, 66482 Zwei-brücken; Bleicherstr. 3, 66482 Zweibrücken; tel. (6332) 16403; fax (6332) 18418; e-mail bipontina@lbz-rlp.de; internet www.lbz-rlp .de; f. 1817, 2004 became part of the Land-esbibliothekszentrum Rheinland-Pfalz; 110,440 113,634 vols, 1254 periodiclesper-iodicals; 12,.000 vols from 16th–18th centur-ies; incl. libraries of Historischer Verein Zweibrücken, Pollichia Zweibrücken, Natur-wissenschaftlicher Verein Zweibrücken and Verein Deutscher Rosenfreunde; Dir Dr HELMUT FRÜHAUF; Man. Dr SIGRID HUBERT-REICHLING.

Museums and Art Galleries

Aachen

Couven-Museum: Hühnermarkt 17, 52062 Aachen; tel. (241) 432-4421; fax (241) 432-4959; e-mail info@couven-museum.de; internet www.couven-museum.de; f. 1958 in a house built in 1662; 20 rooms showing history of interior design during 18th–19th centuries, featuring the rococo, Louis XVI, Napoleon Empire and Biedermeier periods; incl. reconstructed 'Adler-Apotheke', where chocolate was made for the first time in the city; collns of porcelain and silverware; Dir DAGMAR PREISING.

Internationales Zeitungsmuseum der Stadt Aachen (International Newspaper Museum): Markt 39 / Haus Löwenstein, 52062 Aachen; tel. (241) 4324910; fax (241) 4090656; e-mail izm@mail.aachen.de; internet www.izm.de; f. 1886; 200,000 news-papers; spec. library for press history; Dir ANDREAS DÜSPOHL.

Ludwig Forum für Internationale Kunst (Ludwig Forum for International Art): Jüli-cher Str. 97–109, 52070 Aachen; tel. (241) 1807-104; fax (241) 1807-101; e-mail info@ ludwigforum.de; internet www.ludwigforum .de; f. 1969; modern art since the 1960s; library: Modern art library of 35,000 vols, periodicals and video cassettes; spec. collns of graffiti, light sculptures, American pop art and video art; Dir BRIGITTE FRANZEN.

Museum Burg Frankenberg (Burg Museum of Frankenberg): Bismarckstr. 68, 52066 Aachen; tel. (241) 432-4410; fax (241) 37075; e-mail info@ suermondt-ludwig-museum.de; internet www.burgfrankenberg.de; f. 1961; castle dates from 13th century; history of the city from Karl the Great to present; collns of coins, local art; Dir Dr ADAM C. OELLERS.

Suermondt-Ludwig-Museum: Wil-helmstr. 18, 52070 Aachen; tel. (241) 47980-0; fax (241) 37075; e-mail info@ suermondt-ludwig-museum.de; internet www.suermondt-ludwig-museum.de; f. 1882; Gothic art and sculptures; 17th-century paintings (Dutch and Flemish Schools in particular); 10,000 sketches and watercol-ours, incl. some by Dürer, Rembrandt and Goya; local art since 19th century; library: history of art library of 50,000 vols; Dir ADAM C. OELLERS.

Zollmuseum Friedrichs (Customs Museum): Horbacher Str. 497, 52072 Aachen; tel. (241) 99706015; internet www .zollmuseum-friedrichs.de; 20 rooms and 3,000 exhibits documenting customs practice and history; collns of confiscated materials and smugglers' devices; Dir KURT CREMER.

Baden-Baden

Museum Frieder Burda: Lichtentaler Allee 8B, 76530 Baden-Baden; tel. (7221) 39898-0; fax (7221) 39898-30; e-mail office@ museum-frieder-burda.de; internet www .museum-frieder-burda.de; f. 2004; colln of 850 works of modern art with focus on German expressionism, German contempor-ary art, American abstract expressionism and later works by Picasso; colln is shown in alternation with spec. exhibitions of mod-ern art; Man. Dir BERT ANTONIUS KAUFMANN; Man. Dir ANNETTE SMETANIG.

Staatliche Kunsthalle Baden-Baden (State Art Exhibition Hall): Lichtentaler Allee 8A, 76530 Baden-Baden; tel. (7221) 300763; fax (7221) 30076500; e-mail info@ kunsthalle-baden-baden.de; internet hosting .zkm.de/kbb; f. 1909; int. exhibitions of clas-sical and contemporary art; Dir KAROLA KRAUS (acting); Admin. Dir URSULA EBER-HARDT.

Bayreuth

Deutsches Freimaurer Museum in Bayr-euth (German Freemasons' Museum in Bayreuth): Im Hofgarten 1, 95444 Bayreuth; tel. (921) 69824; fax (921) 512850; e-mail museum.bayreuth@freimaurer.org; f. 1902; freemasonry history and practice; library of 25,000 membership records since 1933; incl. sections on Rosicrucians, Illuminati, Tem-plars; Dir THAD PETERSON.

Historisches Museum Bayreuth (Histor-ical Museum of Bayreuth): Kirchpl. 4, 95444 Bayreuth; tel. (921) 764010; fax (921) 7640123; e-mail historischesmuseum@ bayreuth.de; f. 1996; covers 1,200 sq. m, 34 exhibition rooms recording history of Bayr-euth since 15th century; Dir Dr SYLVIA HABERMANN.

Kunst Museum Bayreuth (Art Museum of Bayreuth): Altes Rathaus, Maximilianstr. 33, 95444 Bayreuth; tel. (921) 76453-10; fax (921) 76453-20; e-mail info@

kunstmuseum-bayreuth.de; internet www .kunstmuseum-bayreuth.de; f. 1999; art since beginning of 20th century; collns include Dr Helmut und Constanze Meyer Kunststiftung, fantastic realism of Caspar Walter Rauh, British-American Tobacco colln on the history of the tobacco industry; Dir Dr MARINA VON ASSEL.

Richard-Wagner-Museum mit Nationa-larchiv und Forschungsstätte der Richard-Wagner-Stiftung (Richard Wagner Museum with National Archive and Richard Wagner Foundation Research Centre): Richard-Wagner-Str. 48, 95444 Bayreuth; tel. (921) 757280; fax (921) 7572822; e-mail info@wagnermuseum.de; internet www.wagnermuseum.de; f. 1976; museum and archive of the life and works of Richard Wagner (1813–1883) and of the history of the Bayreuth festival (1876–pre-sent); Dir Dr SVEN FRIEDRICH; Librarian KRISTINA UNGER.

Berlin

Berlinische Galerie: Alte Jakobstr. 124–28, 10969 Berlin; tel. (30) 78902600; fax (30) 78902700; e-mail bg@berlinischegalerie.de; internet www.berlinischegalerie.de; f. 1975; permanent colln of works since beginning of 20th century: paintings and drawings (including works by Dix, Grosz and Kirch-ner), photographs, architectural drawings and models; temporary exhibitions of modern art; library of 65,000 vols, mainly on art since beginning of 20th century; Dir Dr URSULA PRINZ (acting); Librarian SABINE SCHARDT.

Botanischer Garten und Botanisches Museum Berlin-Dahlem (Botanic Garden and Botanical Museum Berlin-Dahlem): Königin-Luise-Str. 6–8, 14191 Berlin; tel. (30) 83850-100; fax (30) 83850-186; e-mail zebgbm@bgbm.org; internet www.bgbm.org; f. 1679, Herbarium (f. 1815), Museum (f. 1879); attached to Freie Universität Berlin; plant taxonomy and phytogeography; library of 160,000 vols, 2,300 current periodicals, 3.5m. specimens; Dir Prof. Dr W. GREUTER; publs *Englera* (irregular), *Willdenowia* (2 a year).

Brücke-Museum: Bussardsteig 9, 14195 Berlin; tel. (30) 8312029; fax (30) 8315961; e-mail bruecke-museum@t-online.de; internet www.bruecke-museum.de; f. 1967; German expressionism, paintings, sculptures and graphic art of the Brücke group; Dir Prof. Dr MAGDALENA MOELLER; publ. *Brücke Archiv* (1 a year).

Deutsches Historisches Museum (Ger-man Historical Museum): Unter den Linden 2, 10117 Berlin; tel. (30) 203040; fax (30) 20304543; internet www.dhm.de; f. 1987; German and modern European history; library of 3,000 vols; Gen. Dir Dr HANS OTTOMEYER.

Haus der Wannsee-Konferenz, Gedenk-und Bildungsstätte (House of the Wannsee Conference, Memorial and Educational Site): Am Grossen Wannsee 56–58, 14109 Berlin; tel. (30) 8050010; fax (30) 80500127; e-mail info@ghwk.de; internet www.ghwk.de; f. 1992; memorial and educational site, with a permanent exhibition documenting the per-secution and murder of Jews in Europe 1933–1945; educational dept; offer of multi-lingual seminars and study days (free of charge) for school classes, youth groups and adults; library of 30,000 vols, 120 journals; Dir Dr NORBER KAMPE; Vice-Dir Dr WOLF KAISER.

Käthe-Kollwitz-Museum Berlin: Fasa-nenstr. 24, 10719 Berlin; tel. (30) 8825210; fax (30) 8811901; e-mail info@ kaethe-kollwitz.de; internet www .kaethe-kollwitz.de; f. 1986; private museum (colln of Prof. Hans Pels-Leusden); permanent exhibition of Käthe Kollwitz's work; temporary exhibitions of artists influenced by Käthe Kollwitz; Dir MARTIN FRITSCH.

Museum für Naturkunde der Humboldt-Universität zu Berlin (Natural History Museum): Invalidenstr. 43, 10115 Berlin; tel. (30) 2093-8591; fax (30) 2093-8814; e-mail info@mfn-berlin.de; internet www.naturkundemuseum-berlin.de; f. 1889; attached to Leibniz Institute for Research on Evolution and Biodiversity, Humboldt Univ.; incl. research institutes of palaeontology, mineralogy and systematic zoology; Dir Prof. REINHOLD LEINFELDER; publs *Deutsche Entomologische Zeitschrift, Fossil Record, Zoosystematics and Evolution.*

Staatliche Museen zu Berlin—Preussischer Kulturbesitz: Stauffenbergstr. 41, 10785 Berlin; tel. (30) 2662610; fax (30) 2662992; internet www.smb.museum; f. 1957; supervises museums and collns at the following sites in Berlin: Berlin–Mitte (Museumsinsel), Tiergarten (Kulturforum), Dahlem, Charlottenburg, Köpenick; Gen. Dir Prof. Dr STEFAN WEBER.

Museums:

Ägyptisches Museum und Papyrussammlung (Egyptian Museum and Papyrus Collection): Bodestr. 1-3, 10178 Berlin; e-mail aemp@smb.spk-berlin.de; internet www.smb.museum; f. 1828 as a section of the former Royal Art Collection, collns united 1991; Dir Dr FRIEDERIKE SEYFRIED.

Alte Nationalgalerie (Old National Gallery): Bodestr. 1-3, 10178 Berlin; tel. (30) 20905801; fax (30) 20905802; e-mail ang@smb.spk-berlin.de; internet www.smb.museum; f. 1861; 19th-century sculpture and painting; Dir Dr BERNHARD MAAZ.

Antikensammlung, Pergamonmuseum und Altes Museum (Collection of Classical Antiquties at the Pergamon Museum and the Old Museum): Berlin; tel. (30) 20905201; fax (30) 20905202; e-mail ant@smb.spk-berlin.de; internet www.smb.museum; f. 1830; colln also presented in Neues Museum; displays Egyptian and prehistoric objects; Dir Prof. Dr ANDREAS SCHOLL (Classical Antiquities).

Berggruen Museum (Berggruen Museum): Schlossstr. 1, 14059 Berlin–Charlottenburg; tel. (30) 32695815; fax (30) 32695819; e-mail museum-berggruen@smb.spk-berlin.de; internet www.smb.museum/mb; f. 1996 by the art dealer and collector Heinz Berggruen; colln focusing on Picasso and his contemporaries, incl. Braque, Matisse, Klee, Laurens, Giacometti.

Ethnologisches Museum (Ethnological Museum): Lansstr. 8, Berlin–Dahlem; tel. (30) 8301-0; fax (30) 8301500; e-mail md@smb.spk-berlin.de; internet www.smb.museum; f. 1829 as the Ethnographic Colln, museum f. 1873; Dir Prof. Dr VIOLA KÖNIG.

Friedrich Christian Flick Collection: Invalidenstr. 50/51, 10557 Berlin; tel. and fax (30) 39783412; e-mail hbf@smb.spk-berlin.de; internet www.smb.museum; 2,000 works, mainly since 1990.

Friedrichswerdersche Kirche (Friedrichswerder Church): Werderscher Markt, Berlin–Mitte; tel. (30) 2081323; e-mail nng@smb.smb.museum; early 19th-century sculpture.

Gemäldegalerie (Old Masters' Gallery): Matthäikirchpl., Berlin–Tiergarten; tel. (30) 2662101; fax (30) 2662103; e-mail gg@smb.spk-berlin.de; internet www.smb

.museum; f. 1830 from collns of The Great Elector (1620–1688) and Frederick the Great (1712–1786); Dir Prof. Dr BERND LINDEMANN.

Gipsformerei: Sophie-Charlotten-Str. 17–18, 14059 Berlin; tel. (30) 3267690; fax (30) 32676912; e-mail gf@smb.spk-berlin.de; internet www.smb.museum; f. 1819; replicas of 6,500 sculptures, from Germany and other European museums.

Hamburger Bahnhof–Museum für Gegenwart—Berlin (Museum of the Present): Invalidenstr. 50–51, Berlin–Tiergarten; tel. (30) 39783412; fax (30) 39783413; e-mail hbf@smb.spk-berlin.de; internet www.smb.museum; f. 1996; art since 1950.

Helmut Newton Stiftung (Helmut Newton Foundation): Jebensstr. 2, 10623 Berlin; tel. (30) 31864856; fax (30) 31864855; e-mail info@helmut-newton-stiftung.org; internet www.helmutnewton.com; f. 2003 by the photographer Helmut Newton (1920–2004); preserves and displays Newton's works and those of his wife, June (Alice Springs); temporary exhibitions of work by other photographers; Curator Dr MATTHIAS HARDER.

Kunstbibliothek: see Libraries and Archives.

Kunstgewerbemuseum (Museum of Decorative Arts): Tiergartenstr. 6, D-10785 Berlin; tel. (30) 266424301; fax (30) 266424311; e-mail kgm@smb.spk-berlin.de; internet www.smb.museum; f. 1867; Dir Dr SABINE THÜMMLER.

Kupferstichkabinett–Sammlung der Zeichnung und Druckgraphik (Museum of Prints and Drawings): Matthäikirchpl. 8, 10785 Berlin–Tiergarten; tel. (30) 266424201; fax (30) 266424214; e-mail kk@smb.spk-berlin.de; internet www.kupferstichkabinett.de; f. 1831; colln covers Europe from the Middle Ages to the present and includes more recent items from the USA; 111,000 drawings, 550,000 prints, illuminated MSS, printed illustrated books, etc.; works by Botticelli, Dürer, Bruegel the Elder, Rembrandt, Schinkel, Menzel, Kirchner, Picasso, Warhol, Hirst; Dir Prof. Dr HEIN-TH. SCHULZE ALTCAPPENBERG.

Münzkabinett der Staatlichen Museen zu Berlin, Stiftung Preussischer Kulturbesitz (Numismatic Collection): Bodestr. 1–3, 10178 Berlin; tel. (30) 20905701; fax (30) 20905702; e-mail mk@smb.spk-berlin.de; internet www.smb.museum/ikmk; f. 1868, fmrly Kunstkammer of Prussian Electors (f. 1649); more than 500,000 coins, medals, paper money, seals, models, dies, minting tools: Greek, Roman, Middle Ages to present European, Oriental and Islamic; 4 permanent and 1 additional temporary exhibition gallery in Bode-Museum, additional permanent exhibits at Pergamonmuseum (antiquity), Altes Museum (antiquity) and Neues Museum (antiquity and Middle Ages); Dir Prof. Dr BERND KLUGE.

Museum Europäischer Kulturen (Museum of European Culture): Arnimallee 25, Berlin–Dahlem; tel. (30) 266426800; fax (30) 266426804; e-mail mek@smb.spk-berlin.de; internet www.smb.museum; f. 1999 following merger of the Museum für Volkskunde (Museum of Folklore) and European holdings from the Museum für Völkerkunde (Museum of Ethnology); Dir Prof. Dr KONRAD VANJA.

Museum für Fotografie (Museum of Photography): Lansstr. 8, Berlin–Dahlem; e-mail mv@smb.spk-berlin.de; internet

www.smb.museum; f. 1829 as the Ethnographic Colln, museum f. 1873; Dir Prof. Dr KLAUS HELFRICH.

Museum für Indische Kunst (Museum of Indian Art): Lansstr. 8, Berlin–Dahlem; tel. (30) 8301361; fax (30) 8301502; e-mail mik@smb.spk-berlin.de; internet www.smb.museum; f. 1963; Dir Prof. Dr MARIANNE YALDIZ.

Museum für Islamische Kunst (Museum of Islamic Art): Pergamonmuseum, am Kupfergraben, Berlin–Mitte; tel. (30) 20905401; fax (30) 20905402; e-mail isl@smb.spk-berlin.de; internet www.smb.museum; f. 1904 as dept of Kaiser Friedrich Museum (now Bodemuseum); Dir Prof. Dr STEFAN WEBER.

Museum für Ostasiatische Kunst (Museum of East Asian Art): Lansstr. 8, Berlin–Dahlem; tel. (30) 8301382; fax (30) 8301501; e-mail oak@smb.spk-berlin.de; internet www.smb.museum; f. 1992 following merger of collns from the Pergamon Museum and the Museum in Dahlem; Dir Prof. Dr WILLIBALD VEIT.

Museum für Vor- und Frügeschichte (Museum of Pre- and Early History): Schloss Charlottenburg (Langhansbau), Berlin–Charlottenburg; tel. (30) 32674811; fax (30) 32674812; e-mail mvf@smb.spk-berlin.de; internet www.smb.museum; f. 1931, colln made independent from the Museum for Ethnology; Dir Prof. Dr WILFRIED MENGHIN.

Neue Nationalgalerie (New National Gallery): Potsdamer Str. 50, Berlin–Tiergarten; tel. (30) 266424510; fax (30) 266424545; e-mail nng@smb.spk-berlin.de; internet www.smb.museum; f. 1968 following merger of collns from the Alte Nationalgalerie and the Gallery of 20th Century Art; painting and sculpture since early 20th century.

Skulpturensammlung und Museum für Byzantische Kunst (Sculpture Collection and Museum of Byzantine Art): Am Kupfergraben, Bodemuseum, Berlin–Mitte; internet www.smb.museum; f. 2000 following unification of the Sculpture Colln and the Museum of Byzantine Art; Head Dr JULIEN CHAPOIS.

Vorderasiatisches Museum (Museum of Ancient Near East): Am Kupfergraben, Berlin–Mitte; e-mail vam@smb.spk-berlin.de; internet www.smb.museum; f. 1899 as Dept of Ancient Near East.

Stiftung Stadtmuseum Berlin, Landesmuseum für Kultur und Geschichte Berlins: Poststr. 13–14, 10178 Berlin; tel. (30) 24002-162; fax (30) 24002-187; e-mail info@stadtmuseum.de; internet www.stadtmuseum.de; f. 1874 as Märkisches Museum; illustrates history of Berlin, its culture and its art; library of 102,000 vols; Dir-Gen. Dr FRANZISKA NENTWIG.

Verwaltung der Staatlichen Schlösser und Gärten, West-Berlin (Administration of State Castles and Gardens): Charlottenburg Luisenpl., 10585 Berlin, Schloss; tel. (30) 32091-1; f. 1927; the admin. controls Charlottenburg Castle, Grunewald Hunting Castle (with colln of paintings), Glienicke Castle and Peacock Island (Castle and Park); library of 5,000 vols; Chief Officers Prof. Dr WINFRIED BAER, Prof. Dr HELMUT BÖRSCH-SUPAN, Prof. Dr JÜRGEN JULIER.

Bonn

Beethoven-Haus: Bonngasse 18–26, 53111 Bonn; tel. (228) 98175-0; fax (228) 98175-31; e-mail info@beethoven-haus-bonn.de; internet www.beethoven-haus-bonn.de; f. 1889; birthplace of Ludwig van Beethoven

(1770–1827); museum and research centre with library; 1,000 mems; library of 30,000 vols, 125 periodicals, 25,000 music scores (6,000 by Beethoven); Dir Dr PHILIPP ADLUNG.

Kunstmuseum Bonn: Friedrich-Ebert-Allee 2, 53113 Bonn; tel. (228) 776260; fax (228) 776220; e-mail kunstmuseum@bonn.de; internet www.bonn.de/kunstmuseum; f. 1882, restored 1948, new building 1992; collection of 20th-century art; German expressionist painting, with important August Macke collection; contemporary international graphic art, contemporary German art, photos and video cassettes; library of 47,000 vols; Dir Prof. Dr DIETER RONTE.

LVR—LandesMuseum Bonn (LVR State Museum Bonn): Colmantstr. 14–16, 53115 Bonn; tel. (228) 2070-0; fax (228) 2070-299; e-mail info.landesmuseum-bonn@lvr.de; internet www.landesmuseum-bonn.lvr.de; f. 1820; prehistoric, Roman and Frankish antiquities of the Rhineland; Rhenish sculpture, painting and applied arts up to the 20th century; Dutch paintings; library of 150,000 vols; Dir Dr GABRIELE UELSBERG; publs *Bonner Jahrbücher des Rheinischen Landesmuseums und des Vereins von Altertumsfreunden im Rheinlande* (1 a year), *Das Rheinische Landesmuseum Bonn* (4 a year).

Zoologisches Forschungsinstitut und Museum 'Alexander Koenig' (Alexander Koenig Zoological Research Institute and Museum): Adenauerallee 160, 53113 Bonn; tel. (228) 9122-0; fax (228) 9122-212; e-mail info.zfmk@uni-bonn.de; internet www.museumkoenig.de; f. 1912; zoology—vertebrates and insects; library of 150,000 vols; Dir Prof. Dr J. W. WÄGELE; publs *Bonner zoologische Beiträge* (4 a year), *Myotis: Mitteilungsblatt für Fledermauskundler* (1 a year).

Bremen

Focke-Museum (District Museum for Art and Culture): Schwachhauser Heerstr. 240, 28213 Bremen; tel. (421) 699600-0; fax (421) 69960066; e-mail post@focke-museum.de; internet www.focke-museum.de; f. 1900; exhibits from Stone Age to 20th century; library of 40,000 vols; Dir Dr FRAUKE VON DER HAAR.

Kunsthalle Bremen – Der Kunstverein in Bremen (Bremen Art Museum): Am Wall 207, 28195 Bremen; tel. (421) 329080; fax (421) 32908470; e-mail office@kunsthalle-bremen.de; internet www.kunsthalle-bremen.de; f. 1823; European paintings since 14th century, prints and drawings; sculpture since 16th century; Japanese drawings and books; 7,000 mems; library of 100,000 vols; Dir Prof. Dr WULF HERZOGENRATH.

Übersee-Museum Bremen (Museum of Overseas Culture, Bremen): Bahnhofsplatz 13, 28195 Bremen; tel. (421) 16038-101; fax (421) 16038-99; e-mail office@uebersee-museum.de; internet www.uebersee-museum.de; f. 1896; ethnology, history of commerce, natural history; library of 70,000 vols; Dir Dr WIEBKE AHRNDT; publ. *TenDenZen* (1 a year).

Brunswick

Herzog Anton Ulrich-Museum: Museumstr. 1, 38100 Braunschweig; tel. (531) 1225-0; fax (531) 1225-2408; e-mail info@museum-braunschweig.de; internet www.museum-braunschweig.de; f. 1754; collection includes old pictures, prints and drawings, medieval art, ceramics, 16th-century French enamels, carvings in ivory, bronzes, collection of lace, old clocks, etc.;

library: art library of 60,000 vols; Dir Prof. Dr J. LUCKHARDT.

Städtisches Museum (City Musuem): Steintorwall 14 (Am Löwenwall), 38100 Brunswick; tel. (531) 4704505; fax (531) 4704555; e-mail staedtisches.museum@braunschweig.de; internet www.braunschweig.de/staedtisches_museum; f. 1861; collections illustrate topography, history and culture of the town; paintings since 19th century; coins and medals (all periods and territories, with about 80,000 pieces); ethnographical collections; closed until 2012; Dir Dr CECILIE HOLLBERG; publs *Arbeitsberichte, Braunschweiger Werkstücke, Miszellen*.

Branch Museum:

Zweigmuseum Altstadtrathaus: Altstadtmarkt 7, 38100 Brunswick; tel. (531) 4704551; fax (531) 4704544; e-mail staedtisches.museum@braunschweig.de; internet www.braunschweig.de/kultur/museen; f. 1991; building dates from late 13th century; history of the city since 9th century.

Cologne

Kölnisches Stadtmuseum: Zeughausstr. 1–3, 50667 Cologne; tel. (221) 221-25789; fax (221) 221-24154; e-mail ksm@museenkoeln.de; internet www.museenkoeln.de; f. 1888; history of Cologne from the Middle Ages to the present day; collns illustrate local culture, economy and everyday life, political history, craftsmen's and merchants' guilds, devotional objects, Judaica, transport, inventions made in the city, paintings by the Berckheyde brothers and Geldorp Gortzius, crafts, early globes, puppet theatre, Eau de Cologne; library of 30,000 vols; Dir Dr MICHAEL EULER-SCHMIDT (acting); Curator for Graph Dept RITA WAGNER; Curator for Middle Ages Dr BETTINA MOSLER.

Museum für Angewandte Kunst (Museum of Applied Art): An der Rechtschule, 50667 Cologne; tel. (221) 221-23860; fax (221) 221-23885; e-mail mfak@stadt-koeln.de; internet www.museenkoeln.de; f. 1888; library: see Libraries; applied art since Middle Ages; design colln since 1900; Dir Dr PETRA HESSE.

Museum für Ostasiatische Kunst (Museum of East Asian Art): Universitätsstr. 100, 50674 Cologne; tel. (221) 22128608; fax (221) 22128610; e-mail mok@mok.museenkoeln.de; internet www.museenkoeln.de/mok; f. 1909; library of 27,000 vols; art from China (religious bronzes and ceramics), Korea (celadon objects of the 10th- to 14th-century Koryo dynasty) and Japan (Buddhist painting and wood sculpture, Japanese screen painting); Dir Dr ADELE SCHLOMBS.

Museum Ludwig: 50667 Cologne; tel. (221) 221-26165; fax (221) 221-24114; e-mail info@museum-ludwig.de; internet www.museum-ludwig.de; f. 1976; paintings, modern sculpture, prints, photos, video cassettes; library; largest colln of Pop Art outside the USA; Russian avant-garde art; several hundred works by Picasso; collns Agfa Foto-Historma: photographs, caricatures and documents; colln of cameras returned to Agfa and Gaevert in Belgium; Dir Prof. KASPER KÖNIG.

Museum Schnütgen: Cäcilienstr. 29–33, 50667 Cologne; tel. (221) 22123620; fax (221) 22128489; e-mail museum.schnutgen@stadt-koeln.de; internet www.museenkoeln.de; f. 1906; library of 20,000 vols; 13,000 works of medieval art; houses 11th-century wooden crucifix; Dir Prof. Dr HILTRUD WESTERMANN-ANGERHAUSEN.

Rautenstrauch-Joest-Museum: Leonhard-Tietz-Str. 10, 50676 Cologne; tel. (221) 221-31356; fax (221) 221-31333; e-mail rjm@stadt-koeln.de; internet www.museenkoeln.de/rautenstrauch-joest-museum; f. 1901; ethnological museum; library of 40,000 vols; Dir Prof. Dr KLAUS SCHNEIDER; publ. *Ethnologica*.

Römisch-Germanisches Museum: Roncallipl. 4, 50667 Cologne; tel. (221) 22122304; fax (221) 22124030; e-mail roemisch-germanisches-museum@stadt-koeln.de; internet www.museenkoeln.de/rgm; f. 1946; library of 14,000 vols; Dir Prof. Dr HANSGERD HELLENKEMPER; publs *Kölner Forschungen, Kölner Jahrbuch* (prehistory and early history, 1 a year).

Wallraf-Richartz-Museum & Fondation Corboud: Obenmarspforten (Am Kölner Rathaus), 50667 Cologne; tel. (221) 221-21119; fax (221) 221-22629; e-mail wallraf@museenkoeln.de; internet www.wallraf.museum; f. 1824; paintings, sculpture, prints, drawings dating from the Middle Ages, Baroque period, and 18th and 19th centuries; library: see Libraries and Archives; Dir Dr ANDREAS BLÜHM; publs *Jahrbuch für Kunstgeschichte, Wallraf-Richartz-Jahrbuch*.

Darmstadt

Grossherzoglich-Hessische Porzellansammlung (Grand-Ducal Porcelain Collection): Schlossgartenstr. 10, Prinz-Georg-Palaïs, 64289 Darmstadt; tel. (6151) 713233; e-mail info@porzellanmuseum-darmstadt.de; internet www.schlossmuseum-darmstadt.de; f. 1908; colln consists of a variety of products manufactured by the European porcelain and faience artists of the 18th and 19th centuries; Head ALEXA-BEATRICE CHRIST (acting).

Hessisches Landesmuseum Darmstadt (State Museum of Hesse in Darmstadt): Friedenspl. 1, 64283 Darmstadt; tel. (6151) 165703; fax (6151) 28942; e-mail info@hlmd.de; internet www.hlmd.de; f. 1820; archaeology, prehistory, zoology, geology, palaeontology, mineralogy; art collns and cultural history since 9th century, incl. crafts, prints and drawings, stained glass, sculptures, paintings, European art since 1945; library of 55,000 vols; Dir Dr INA BUSCH; publs *Kaupia–Darmstädter Beiträge zur Naturgeschichte* (2 a year), *Kunst in Hessen und am Mittelrhein* (1 a yearl).

Jagdmuseum Schloss Kranichstein: Kranichstein, 64289 Darmstadt, Schloss; tel. (6151) 718613; fax (6151) 732332; e-mail hessischer.jaegerhof@t-online.de; internet www.jagdschloss-kranichstein.de; f. 1918; pictures, hunting trophies and weapons, furnished rooms; owned by Stiftung Hessischer Jägerhof; Dir MONIKA KESSLER.

Schlossmuseum (Castle Museum): Residenzschloss, Marktpl. 15, 64283 Darmstadt; tel. (6151) 24035; fax (6151) 997457; e-mail info@schlossmuseum-darmstadt.de; internet www.schlossmuseum-darmstadt.de; f. 1924; furnished rooms with paintings, porcelain, glass, etc.; military colln, ceremonial carriages and harness; Head ALEXA-BEATRICE CHRIST (acting).

Dortmund

Museum für Kunst und Kulturgeschichte Dortmund (Dortmund Museum of Art and Cultural History): Hansastr. 3, 44137 Dortmund; tel. (231) 5025522; fax (231) 5025511; internet www.museendortmund.de/mkk; f. 1883; collns incl. medieval art and sculpture, furniture since 15th century, design, *objets d'art*, paintings, archaeology; library of 18,000 vols; Dir WOLFGANG E. WEICK.

Dresden

Landesamt für Archäologie mit Landesmuseum für Vorgeschichte (State Office of Archaeology and Museum of Prehistory): Japanisches Palais, Zur Wetterwarte 7, 01109 Dresden; tel. (351) 8926-603; fax (351) 8926-604; e-mail info@archsax .smwk.sachsen.de; internet www.archsax .sachsen.de; f. 1993; preservation of ancient monuments, archaeological research and exhibitions; library of 40,000 vols specializing in prehistory; Dir Dr J. OEXLE; publs *Arbeits- und Forschungsberichte* (1 a year), *Archäologie aktuell im Freistaat Sachsen* (1 a year).

Mathematisch-Physikalischer Salon: Zwinger, 01067 Dresden; tel. (351) 4914661; fax (351) 4914666; e-mail simone.koehler@ skd-dresden.de; internet www.skd-dresden .de/en/museum/math_phys_salon/; f. 1560; historical watches and clocks, globes, scientific instruments, etc.; library of 7,000 vols; Dir Dr PETER PLASSMEYER.

Militärhistorisches Museum der Bundeswehr (Military-Historical Museum of the Federal Army): Olbrichtpl. 2, 01099 Dresden; tel. (351) 8232803; fax (351) 8232805; e-mail milhistmuseumbweingang@ bundeswehr.org; internet www.mhm .bundeswehr.de; f. 1990; German military history from the late Middle Ages to the present; exhibits include weapons, equipment, documents, uniforms and combat vehicles; cannons and caissons; also a mid-19th-century submarine, models, dioramas, paintings and sculptures; main focus of collns is post-1945 Germany; open partially due to reconstruction; Dir Oberstleutnant FERDINAND FREIHERR VON RICHTHOFEN.

Museum für Tierkunde Dresden (Dresden Museum of Zoology): Königsbrücker Landstr. 159, 01109 Dresden; tel. (351) 8926326; fax (351) 8926327; e-mail birgit .walker@snsd.smwk.sachsen.de; internet globiz.sachsen.de/snsd/mtd_info.htm; f. 1728; library of 60,000 vols; Dir UWE FRITZ; publs *Entomologische Abhandlungen, Faunistische Abhandlungen, Malakologische Abhandlungen, Reichenbachia Zeitschrift für entomolog. Taxonomie* (1 a year), *Zoologische Abhandlungen.*

Museum Schloss Moritzburg (Museum of Moritzburg Castle): Schloss Moritzburg, 01468 Moritzburg bei Dresden; tel. (35207) 8730; fax (35207) 87311; e-mail schloss .moritzburg@schloesser.smf.sachsen.de; internet www.schloss-moritzburg.de; f. 1947; leather hangings, furniture, paintings, statues, porcelain, glasswork, principally of the 18th century; Dir INGRID MÖBIUS.

Staatliche Ethnographische Sammlungen Sachsens:see Staatliche Ethnographische Sammlungen Sachsen, Leipzig.

Staatliche Kunstsammlungen Dresden: Postfach 120551, 01006 Dresden; Residenzschloss, Taschenberg 2, 01067 Dresden; tel. (351) 49142000; fax (351) 4914616; e-mail info@skd.smwk.sachsen.de; internet www .skd-dresden.de; f. 1560; library of 130,000 vols, housed in the Residenzschloss; Gen. Dir Dr MARTIN ROTH; publs *Dresdener Kunstblätter* (6 a year), *Jahrbuch* (1 a year).

Constituent Institutions:

Gemäldegalerie Alte Meister (Picture Gallery of Old Masters): Semperbau am Zwinger, Theaterpl. 1, 01067 Dresden; tel. (351) 4914679; fax (351) 4914694; e-mail gam@skd.smwk.sachsen.de; internet www .skd-dresden.de; f. 16th century; Italian Renaissance artists Raffael, Giorgione and Titian; 17th-century Flemish art,

Rembrandt, Vermeer, Rubens; old German and Dutch, Jan van Eyck, Dürer, Cranach, Holbein; Spanish and French 17th-century artists Ribera, Murillo, Poussin, Lorrain; Dir Prof. Dr HARALD MARX.

Gemäldegalerie Neue Meister (Picture Gallery of New Masters): Albertinum, Brühlsche Terrasse, 01067 Dresden; tel. (351) 4914731; fax (351) 4914732; e-mail gnm@skd.smwk.sachsen.de; internet www .skd-dresden.de; f. 1960; art since 19th century; collns of German Impressionism and Expressionism; Dir Dr ULRICH BISCHOFF.

Grünes Gewölbe (Green Vault): Residenzschloss, Taschenberg 2, 01067 Dresden; tel. (351) 4914591; fax (351) 4914599; e-mail gg@skd.smwk.sachsen.de; internet www.skd-dresden.de; Renaissance and Baroque artefacts; f. 1723; Dir Dr DIRK SYNDRAM.

Kunstgewerbemuseum (Museum of Decorative Arts): Schloss Pillnitz, August-Böckstiegel-Str. 2, 01326 Dresden; tel. (351) 26130; fax (351) 2613222; e-mail kgm@skd-dresden.de; internet www .skd-dresden.de; f. 1876; courtly items incl. textiles and ceramics; Dir Dr ÁNDRÉ W. A. VAN DER GOES (acting).

Kupferstich-Kabinett (Cabinet of Prints and Drawings): Taschenberg 2, 01067 Dresden; tel. (351) 4914211; fax (351) 4914222; e-mail kk@skd.smwk.sachsen .de; internet www.skd-dresden.de; f. 1720; 50,000 paper works by 11,000 artists since 12th century; Dir Dr WOLFGANG HOLLER.

Münzkabinett (Coin Cabinet): Schlossstr. 25, 01067 Dresden; tel. (351) 4914231; fax (351) 4914233; e-mail mk@skd.smwk .sachsen.de; internet www.skd-dresden.de; f. early 16th century; library of 30,000 specialist vols; 30,000 objects, incl. coins, medals, banknotes; Dir Dr RAINER GRUND (acting).

Museum für Sächsische Volkskunst mit Puppentheatersammlung (Museum of Saxon Folk Art with Puppet Theatre Collection): Jägerhof, Köpckestr. 1, 01097 Dresden; tel. (351) 49144502; fax (351) 49144500; e-mail info@skd.smwk .sachsen.de; internet www.skd-dresden.de; f. 1897; items of folk history; costumes; puppet colln; Dir Dr IGOR A. JENZEN.

Porzellansammlung (Porcelain Collection): Zwinger, Glockenspielpavillon, 01067 Dresden; tel. (351) 49142000; fax (351) 49142001; e-mail besucherservice@ skd-dresden.de; internet www.skd-dresden .de; f. 1717; 20,000 pieces of Meissner, Japanese and Chinese porcelain; Dir Dr ULRICH PIETSCH.

Rüstkammer (Armoury): Semperbau am Zwinger, Theaterpl. 1, 01067 Dresden; tel. (351) 4914611; fax (351) 4914690; e-mail rk@skd.smwk.sachsen.de; internet www .skd-dresden.de; f. 1567; 10,000 chivalric objects, weapons and costumes; Dir Dr HEINZ-WERNER LEWERKEN.

Skulpturensammlung (Sculpture Collection): Albertinum, Brühlsche Terrasse, 01067 Dresden; tel. (351) 4914741; fax (351) 4914350; internet www.skd-dresden .de; sculptures since 3,000 BC; Dir Dr MORITZ WOELK.

Staatliches Museum für Mineralogie und Geologie (State Museum of Mineralogy and Geology): Königsbrücker Landstr. 159, 01109 Dresden; tel. (351) 8926403; fax (351) 8926404; internet globiz.sachsen.de/snsd; f. 1728; library of 35,000 vols; 400,000 minerals and fossils; Dir Dr ULF LINNEMANN; publs *Geologica Saxonica–Abhandlungen* (1 a year), *Schriften* (1–2 a year).

Stadtmuseum Dresden (Dresden City Museum): Wilsdruffer Str. 2, 01067 Dresden; tel. (351) 65648611; fax (351) 4951288; e-mail sekretariat@stmd.de; internet stadtmuseum .dresden.de; f. 1891; Dresden history and culture; library of 7,500 vols, 22,500 pictures, 55,000 photographs; Dir Dr WERNER BARLMEYER.

Attached Museums:

Kraszewski-Museum: Nordstr. 28, 01099 Dresden; tel. and fax (351) 8044450; exhibition on Polish history, in particular Józef Ignacy Kraszewski (1812–1887), who fought for Polish independence in the 19th century; exhibits in German and Polish; Dir JOANNA MAGACZ.

Kügelgenhaus–Museum der Dresdner Romantik (Museum of German Romanticism): Hauptstr. 13, 01097 Dresden; tel. (351) 8044760; fax (351) 8044760; f. 1981; home to the Museum der Dresdner Romantik; Dir MICHAELA HAUSDING.

Schillerhäuschen (The Schiller House): Schillerstr. 19, 01326 Dresden; tel. (351) 65648611; dedicated to the poet Friedrich Schiller (1759–1805).

Weber-Museum: Dresdner Str. 44, 01326 Dresden; tel. (351) 2618234; fax (351) 2618234; dedicated to the works of composer Carl Maria von Weber (1786–1826); concert venue; Dir DOROTHEA RENZ.

Verkehrsmuseum Dresden (Transport Museum Dresden): Augustusstr. 1, 01067 Dresden; tel. (351) 8644-0; fax (351) 8644-110; e-mail info@verkehrsmuseum-dresden .de; internet verkehrsmuseum-dresden.de; f. 1952; collection of automobiles, motorcycles, bicycles, streetcars, aircraft, model ships and railways; library of 59,000 vols (14,156 vols in special collection); Dir Dr MATTHIAS STIER.

Düsseldorf

Aquazoo Löbbecke Museum: Kaiserswertherstr. 380, 40200 Düsseldorf; tel. (211) 899-6198; fax (211) 899-4493; internet www .dusseldorf.de/aquazoo; f. 1904 (museum), 1876 (zoo); zoo and natural science museum; library of 600 vols; Dir Dr W. W. GETTMANN; publs *Aquarius* (2 a year), *Westdeutscher Entomologentag Düsseldorf.*

Kunsthalle Düsseldorf: Grabbeplatz 4, 40213 Düsseldorf; tel. (211) 899-6243; fax (211) 8929168; e-mail mail@ kunsthalle-duesseldorf.de; internet www .kunsthalle-duesseldorf.de; f. 1967; contemporary art; Dir Dr GREGOR JANSEN.

Kunstsammlung Nordrhein-Westfalen (North Rhine-Westphalia Art Collection): Grabbepl. 5, 40213 Düsseldorf; tel. (211) 8381-130; fax (211) 8381-201; e-mail info@ kunstsammlung.de; internet www .kunstsammlung.de; f. 1961; painting and sculpture since beginning of 20th century; Dir Dr MARION ACKERMANN; publs *K20K21 Programmbroschüre* (4 a year), *Quartalsprogramm* (4 a year), *20_21* (2 a year).

Museum Kunst Palast (mit Sammlung Kunstakademie and Glasmuseum Hentrich) (Art Palace Museum (incorporating the Art Academy Collection and Hentrich Glass Museum)): Ehrenhof 4–5, 40479 Düsseldorf; tel. (211) 89242460; fax (211) 8929307; e-mail info@museum-kunst-palast .de; internet www.museum-kunst-palast.de; f. 1913; European art and applied art from the Middle Ages to 1800; colln of 19th-century German painting; early Iranian bronzes and ceramics; 6,500 textiles from late antiquity to the 19th century; glass colln, mainly Art Nouveau, Jugendstil and Art Deco; colln of prints and drawings, incl. extensive colln of Italian Baroque drawings; contemporary art; design; museum for young visitors; library of 80,000 vols; Dir JEAN-HUBERT MARTIN.

Essen

Museum Folkwang: Goethestr. 41, 45128 Essen; tel. (201) 88-45002; fax (201) 88-45001; internet www.museum-folkwang.de; f. 1902; art since 19th century, including drawings, prints, posters and photographs; incl. German Poster Museum (Deutsches Plakat Museum) with 340,000 posters; library of 100,000 vols; Dir Dr HARTWIG FISCHER.

Flensburg

Museumsberg Flensburg: 24937 Flensburg; tel. (461) 852956; fax (461) 852993; e-mail museumsberg@flensburg.de; internet www.museumsberg.flensburg.de; f. 1876; contains about 26,000 exhibits, mainly arts and crafts, peasant art, and prehistory of Schleswig; library of 12,000 vols; Dir Dr ULRICH SCHULTE-WÜLWER; publs *Beiträge zur Kunst- und Kulturgeschichte, Nordelbingen*.

Frankfurt am Main

Archäologisches Museum (Archaeological Museum): Karmelitergasse 1, 60311 Frankfurt am Main; tel. (69) 212-35896; fax (69) 212-30700; e-mail info.archaeolmus@stadt-frankfurt.de; internet www.archaeologisches-museum.frankfurt.de; f. 1937; prehistoric, Roman and early medieval objects from the Frankfurt area; Mediterranean and oriental archaeology; Dir Dr EGON WAMERS.

Deutsches Architekturmuseum (German Architecture Museum): Schaumainkai 43, 60596 Frankfurt am Main; tel. (69) 212-38844; fax (69) 212-36386; e-mail info.dam@stadt-frankfurt.de; internet www.dam-online.de; f. 1979, opened 1984; int. colln of plans, sketches, paintings and models primarily of modern architecture; changing exhibitions, lectures, symposia; library and archive; library of 20,000 vols, 60 current periodicals and yearbooks; Dir PETER CACHOLA SCHMAL; publs *German Architecture* (1 a year), *Jahrbuch Architektur*.

Deutsches Filmmuseum (German Film Museum): Schaumainkai 41, 60596 Frankfurt am Main; tel. (69) 961220220; fax (69) 961220999; e-mail info@deutsches-filmmuseum.de; internet www.deutsches-filmmuseum.de; f. 1984; exhibits relating to the German and int. film industry; library: See library and archives of the Deutsches Filminstitut; Dir CLAUDIA DILLMANN.

Freies Deutsches Hochstift, Frankfurter Goethe-Haus Museum (Free German Literature Institute, Frankfurt Goethe-Museum (Goethe House)): Gr. Hirschgraben 23–25, 60311 Frankfurt am Main; tel. (69) 13880-0; fax (69) 13880-222; e-mail info@goethehaus-frankfurt.de; internet www.goethehaus-frankfurt.de; f. 1859; birthplace of Johann Wolfgang von Goethe (1749–1832); German literature of the Romantic period and of Goethe's time; selected works since 19th century; 30,000 MSS of German poetry principally from Goethe's time; 400 paintings, 16,000 etchings; library: see Libraries and Archives; Dir Prof. Dr ANNE BOHNENKAMP-RENKEN; publs *Jahrbuch, Reihe der Schriften*.

Historisches Museum Frankfurt: Saalgasse 19, 60311 Frankfurt am Main; tel. (69) 212-35599; fax (69) 212-30702; e-mail info.historisches-museum@stadt-frankfurt.de; internet www.historisches-museum.frankfurt.de; f. 1878; history of Frankfurt to the present; spec. colln: documents relating to elections of emperors 1562–1792, to the

Assembly of Paulskirche 1848/49, and to trade fairs in the 16th–18th centuries; Hoechst Porcelain 1746–1796; comic art and caricature; coin colln; children's museum; library of 50,000 vols; Dir Dr JAN GERCHOW.

Museum der Weltkulturen: Schaumainkai 29–37, 60594 Frankfurt am Main; tel. (69) 212-35391; fax (69) 212-30704; e-mail museum.weltkulturen@stadt-frankfurt.de; internet www.mdw.frankfurt.de; f. 1904; collns of art and ethnography from all continents, esp. Oceania, South-East Asia, Africa, North and South America; spec. colln of contemporary art; library of 43,000 vols, 90 periodicals; Dir Dr CLEMENTINE DELISS; publ. *Journal-Ethnologie* (online, www.journal-ethnologie.de).

Museum für Angewandte Kunst (Museum of Applied Art): Schaumainkai 17, 60594 Frankfurt am Main; tel. (69) 212-34037; fax (69) 212-30703; e-mail info.angewandte-kunst@stadt-frankfurt.de; internet www.museumfuerangewandtekunst.frankfurt.de; f. 1877; European applied art, Gothic to art nouveau and 20th-century art; Islamic and Far Eastern art; prints; Russian icons; digital applied art; library of 60,000 vols, 170 current periodicals and yearbooks; Dir Dr ULRICH SCHNEIDER.

Museum für Kommunikation: Schaumainkai 53, 60596 Frankfurt am Main; tel. (49) 696060-0; fax (49) 696060-666; e-mail mk.frankfurt@mspt.de; internet www.mfk-frankfurt.de; f. 1872; items on history of post and telecommunications; library of 35,000 vols; Dir Dr HELMUT GOLD.

Museum für Moderne Kunst (Museum of Contemporary Art): Domstr. 10, 60311 Frankfurt am Main; tel. (69) 212-30447; fax (69) 212-37882; e-mail mmk@stadt-frankfurt.de; internet www.mmk-frankfurt.de; f. 1991; art since the 1960s; library of 40,000 vols; Dir SUSANNE GAENSHEIMER; Chief Curator Dr ANDREAS BEE.

Städelsches Kunstinstitut und Städtische Galerie (Städel Art Museum and City Gallery): Dürerstr. 2, 60596 Frankfurt am Main; tel. (69) 605098-0; fax (69) 610163; e-mail info@staedelmuseum.de; internet www.staedelmuseum.de; f. 1816; 2,700 paintings, 100,000 drawings and prints, 600 sculptures spanning 700 years; library of 50,000 vols; Dir MAX HOLLEIN.

Freiburg im Breisgau

Adelhausermuseum: Gerberau 32, 79098 Freiburg im Breisgau; tel. (761) 2012561; fax (761) 2012563; e-mail adelhausermuseum@stadt.freiburg.de; internet www.museen.freiburg.de; f. 1895; native and exotic fauna; herb collection, mineralogy, precious stones, wood types, beekeeping, traditional arts and crafts from Africa, America, Asia and Oceania; social and cultural anthropology; library: ethnology: 4,700 vols, natural history: 5,000 vols; Dir Dr EVA GERHARDS.

Archäologisches Museum Colombischlössle: Colombischlössle, Rotteckring 5, 79098 Freiburg im Breisgau; tel. (761) 2012574; fax (761) 2012579; e-mail arco-museum@stadt.freiburg.de; internet www.museen.freiburg.de; f. 1936; regional archaeology; library of 5,000 vols; Dir Dr HELENA PASTOR.

Augustinermuseum: Augustinerpl. 1–3, 79098 Freiburg im Breisgau; tel. (761) 2012521; fax (761) 2012597; e-mail augustinermuseum@stadt.freiburg.de; internet www.augustinermuseum.de; f. 1923; art and culture of Upper Rhine area from Middle Ages to the 20th century; library of 50,000 vols; Dir Dr DETLEF ZINKE.

Museum für Neue Kunst (Museum of Modern Art): Marienstr. 10A, 79098 Freiburg

im Breisgau; tel. (761) 2012581; fax (761) 2012589; e-mail mnk@stadt.freiburg.de; internet www.museen.freiburg.de; f. 1985; German art since 1910; Dir Dr JOCHEN LUDWIG.

Museum für Stadtgeschichte (Museum of City History): Münsterpl. 30, 79098 Freiburg im Breisgau; tel. (761) 2012515; fax (761) 2012598; e-mail msg@stadt.freiburg.de; internet www.museen.freiburg.de; city history since 1100; Dir PETER KALCHTHALER.

Gießen

Liebig Museum: Liebigstr. 12, 35390 Giessen; tel. (641) 76392; fax (641) 2502599; internet www.liebig-museum.de; exhibition of the life and work of Liebig through documents and pictures; pharmaceutical laboratory and display of chemical analysis since 19th century; Chair. WOLFGANG BERGENTHUM.

Oberhessisches Museum und Gailsche Sammlungen der Stadt Gießen: Brandpl. 2, 35390 Giessen; tel. (0641) 3062477; fax (0641) 3012005; e-mail museum@giessen.de; internet www.giessen.de; f. 1879; palaeolithic colln, first Middle European flint tools; archaeological collns and treasures of Roman-German and Hessian Franconian culture; oil paintings, watercolours and modern copperplate engravings; Dir Dr FRIEDHELM HÄRING.

Comprises:

Altes Schloss: Brandpl. 2, 35390 Giessen; houses furniture and art in 14th-century bldg; collns of Gothic, Baroque, Renaissance, artefacts since 19th century.

Leib'sches Haus: Georg-Schlosser-Str. 2, 35390 Giessen; f. 1978; originally the seat of the Junkers of Rodenhausen; now museum of local history and culture; exhibits of material culture of Gießen and surrounding area; portraits, pictures, maps, engravings, textile manufacture and handicraft; furniture, farm implements, costumes, pottery; special exhibitions on the political thinkers Georg Büchner and Wilhelm Liebknecht (founder of the German Social Democratic Party).

Wallenfels'sches Haus: Kirchenpl. 6, 35390 Giessen; ethnological museum with artefacts dating from prehistoric times; examples from India, China, Japan, Sri Lanka, Java, East and West Africa, Egypt, New Guinea and Australia.

Gotha

Kommunale Galerien am Hauptmarkt: Hauptmarkt 44, 99867 Gotha; tel. (3621) 401101; fax (3621) 52669; Dir MARLIES MIKOLAJCZAK.

Münzkabinett (Coin Cabinet): Schloss Friedenstein, 99867 Gotha; tel. (3621) 53036; e-mail vorstand@stiftungfriedenstein.de; internet www.gotha.de/schloss_muenzen.htm; 130,000 numismatic objects; Dir UTA WALLENSTEIN.

Museum der Natur: Postfach 100319, 99853 Gotha; Parkallee 15, 99867 Gotha; tel. (3621) 823010; fax (3621) 823020; e-mail mng@stiftungfriedenstein.de; internet www.stiftungfriedenstein.de; f. 1843; animal and fossil exhibitions, insects, local natural history; Dir RAINER SAMIETZ; publ. *Abhandlungen und Berichte*.

Museum für Kartographie (Museum of Cartography): Schloss Friedenstein, 99867 Gotha; tel. (3621) 854016; e-mail vorstand@stiftungfriedenstein.de; maps, atlases and globes; original copper engraving; Curator JUTTA SIEGERT.

Museum für Regionalgeschichte und Volkskunde (Museum of Regional History and Folklore): Schloss Friedenstein, 99867 Gotha; tel. (3621) 823415; fax (3621) 823419; e-mail mrv@stiftungfriedenstein.de; internet www.stiftungfriedenstein.de; f. 1928; exhibition of local history, with *Ekhof-Theater* (baroque theatre); Dir THOMAS HUCK; publ. *Gothaisches Museumsjahrbuch* (1 a year).

Schlossmuseum (Castle Museum): Schloss Friedenstein, 99867 Gotha; tel. (3621) 823415; fax (3621) 823419; e-mail schlossmuseum@stiftungfriedenstein.de; internet www.stiftungfriedenstein.de; art collections, historical rooms, coin collections, Egyptological exhibition; Dir Dr KATHARINA BECHLER.

Göttingen

Städtisches Museum (Municipal Museum): Ritterplan 7/8, 37073 Göttingen; tel. (551) 400-2843; fax (551) 400-2059; internet www .goettingen.de/kultur/museum; f. 1889; prehistory and early history, ecclesiastical art, history of Göttingen and the University, arts and crafts, etc.; library of 20,000 vols; Dir Dr JENS-UWE BRINKMANN.

Halle am Saale

Landesamt für Denkmalpflege und Archäologie Sachsen-Anhalt (Landesmuseum für Vorgeschichte) (State Museum of Prehistory): Richard-Wagner-Str. 9, 06114 Halle Saale; tel. (345) 5247-30; fax (345) 5247-351; e-mail poststelle@lda.mk .sachsen-anhalt.de; internet www.lda-lsa.de; f. 1882; pre- and medieval history; library of 121,000 vols; Dir Dr HARALD MELLER; publs *Archäologie in Sachsen-Anhalt* (1 a year), *Jahresschrift für mitteldeutsche Vorgeschichte* (1 a year), *Veröffentlichungen* (1 a year).

Hamburg

Altonaer Museum in Hamburg/Norddeutsches Landesmuseum (Altona Museum in Hamburg/North German Regional Museum): Postfach 500125, 22701 Hamburg; Museumstr. 23, 22765 Hamburg; tel. (40) 42811-3582; fax (40) 42811-2122; e-mail info@altonaermuseum.de; internet www.altonaer-museum.de; f. 1863; collections on art and cultural history, folk art, shipping and fishing; library of 70,000 vols; Dir Prof. Dr BÄRBEL HEDINGER; publs *Altonaer Museum in Hamburg*, *Jahrbuch* (Yearbook), catalogues of collections and exhibitions.

Hamburger Kunsthalle: Glockengiesserwall, 20095 Hamburg; tel. (40) 42813-1200; fax (40) 42854-2482; e-mail info@ hamburger-kunsthalle.de; internet www .hamburger-kunsthalle.de; f. 1869; paintings since 14th century, sculpture since 19th century, drawings and engravings since 14th century, Greek and Roman coins, medals since 14th century; library of 167,377 vols; Dir Prof. HUBERTUS GASSNER.

Museum für Hamburgische Geschichte: Holstenwall 24, 20355 Hamburg; tel. (40) 428132-2380; fax (40) 428132-3103; e-mail info@hamburgmuseum.de; internet www .hamburgmuseum.de; f. 1839; attached to Stiftung Historische Museen Hamburg; political history of Hamburg, library, coins, handicrafts, models, paintings, history of music, etc.; Dir Prof. Dr LISA KOSOK; publs *Beiträge zur deutschen Volks- und Altertumskunde*, *Hamburger Beiträge zur Numismatik*, *Numismatische Studien*.

Museum für Kunst und Gewerbe Hamburg (Hamburg Museum of Art and Industry): Steintorpl. 1, 20099 Hamburg; tel. (40) 428134-2732; fax (40) 428134-2834; e-mail service@mkg-hamburg.de; internet www .mkg-hamburg.de; f. 1877; European sculpture and art since the Middle Ages, ancient art, art of the Near and Far East, European popular art, graphic, photographic and textile collns, contemporary design, historical keyboard instruments; library of 160,000 vols, 450 current periodicals; Dir Prof. Dr SABINE SCHULZE.

Museum für Völkerkunde Hamburg: Rothenbaumchaussee 64, 20148 Hamburg; tel. (40) 428879-0; fax (40) 428879-242; e-mail marketing@voelkerkundemuseum .com; internet www.voelkerkundemuseum .com; f. 1879; ethnological collns from Africa, America, Australia, Indonesia and the South Seas; library of 130,000 vols; Dir Dr W. KÖPKE; publs *Beiträge zur Mittelamerikanischen Wegweiser zur Völkerkunde* (irregular), *Mitteilungen aus dem Museum für Völkerkunde, N.F.* (1 a year).

Hanover

Historisches Museum am Hohen Ufer (Historical Museum on the High Bank): Pferdestr. 6, 30159 Hanover; tel. (511) 16843052; fax (511) 16845003; e-mail historisches.museum@hannover-stadt.de; internet www.hannover-museum.de; f. 1903 as Vaterländisches Museum, 1937–50 Niedersächsisches Volkstumsmuseum, 1950–66 as Niedersächsisches Heimatmuseum; three sections: Lower Saxon Folklore, History of the City of Hanover, History of the Kingdom of Hanover up to 1866; library of 20,000 vols; Dir Dr T. SCHWARK.

Kestner-Museum: Trammplatz 3, 30159 Hanover; tel. (511) 16842730; fax (511) 16846530; e-mail museum-august-kestner@ hannover-stadt.de; internet www .museum-august-kestner.de; f. 1889; Egyptian, Greek, Etruscan and Roman art; illuminated MSS, incunabula, applied art and design since the Middle Ages; ancient, medieval and modern coins, medals; library of 40,000 vols, 200 current periodicals; Dir Dr WOLFGANG SCHEPERS; Curator for Classical Archaelogy Dr ANNE VIOLA SIEBERT; Curator for Egyptology Dr CHRISTIAN E. LOEBEN; Curator for Numismatics Dr SIMONE VOGT.

Niedersächsisches Landesmuseum Hannover (Hanover State Museum): Willy-Brandt-Allee 5, 30169 Hanover; tel. (511) 9807-686; fax (511) 9807-684; e-mail info@ nlm-h.niedersachsen.de; internet www .landesmuseum-hannover.de; f. 1852; art dating from the Middle Ages to the early 20th century; natural archaeology and ethnology sections; libraries attached to each section; Dir JAAP BRAKKE; Dir (Ethnology) Dr ANNA SCHMID; Dir (Landesgalerie) Dr THOMAS ANDRATSCHKE; Dir (Natural History) ANDREA SPAUTZ; Dir (Prehistory) Prof. Dr DAGMAR-BEATRICE GAEDTKE-ECKARDT (acting); Operational Dir STEFFEN FÄRBER.

Heidelberg

Kurpfälzisches Museum der Stadt Heidelberg: Hauptstr. 97, 69117 Heidelberg; tel. (6221) 5834020; fax (6221) 5834900; e-mail kurpfaelzischesmuseum@heidelberg .de; internet www.museum-heidelberg.de; f. 1879; Dir Prof. Dr FRIEDER HEPP.

Hildesheim

Roemer-und Pelizaeus Museum: Am Steine 1–2, 31134 Hildesheim; tel. (5121) 93690; fax (5121) 35283; e-mail info@ rpmuseum.de; internet www.rpmuseum.de; f. 1845; natural history, applied art, prehistory, ethnography, Egyptian art; library of 35,000 vols; Dir Dr KATJA LEMBKE.

Jena

Goethe-Gedenkstätte (im Inspektorhaus des Botanischen Gartens): Friedrich Schiller Universität Jena, Fürstengraben 26, 07743 Jena; f. 1921; Curator Dr MICHAEL PLATEN.

Optisches Museum der Ernst-Abbe-Stiftung Jena (Optical Museum at the Ernst Abbe Foundation): Carl-Zeiss-Pl. 12, 07743 Jena; tel. (3641) 443165; fax (3641) 443224; e-mail info@optischesmuseum.de; internet www.optischesmuseum.de; f. 1922; history and devt of optical instruments; vision aids and glasses, cameras and magic lanterns, stereoscopes and magic lantern images, historic workshop of Carl Zeiss; library of 4,000 vols.

Romantikerhaus–Museum der deutschen Frühromantik (Romantikerhaus—Museum of Early German Romanticism): Unterm Markt 12A, 07743 Jena; tel. (3641) 443263; fax (3641) 228829; e-mail romantikerhaus@msn.com; internet www .romantikerhaus.jena.de; f. 1981; Dir KLAUS SCHWARZ.

Stadtmuseum Göhre (Göhre City Museum): Markt 7, 07743 Jena; tel. (3641) 498261; fax (3641) 496255; e-mail stadtmuseum@jena.de; internet www .museen.jena.de; f. 1903; library of 30,000 vols; regional historical literature; art colln and town historical colln; Dir MATIAS MIETH.

Karlsruhe

Badisches Landesmuseum: Schloss, 76131 Karlsruhe; tel. (721) 926-6514; fax (721) 926-6537; e-mail info@landesmuseum .de; internet www.landesmuseum.de; f. 1919; colln incl. prehistoric, Egyptian, Greek and Roman antiquities, medieval, renaissance and baroque sculpture, works of art from the Middle Ages to the 20th century, weapons, folklore and coins, colln of Turkish trophies; library of 75,000 vols; Dir Prof. Dr HARALD SIEBENMORGEN.

Museum für Literatur am Oberrhein: Prinz-Max-Palais, Karlstr. 10, 76133 Karlsruhe; tel. (721) 133-4087; fax (721) 133-4089; e-mail info@literaturmuseum.de; internet www.karlsruhe.de/kultur/mlo; f. 1965; exhibition of the works, MSS and pictures of various authors; library of 8,000 vols; Pres. Dr HANSGEORG SCHMIDT-BERGMANN; publs *Jahresgabe*, *Mitteilungen*.

Staatliche Kunsthalle: Hans-Thoma-Str. 2–6, 76133 Karlsruhe; tel. (721) 926-3359; fax (721) 926-6788; e-mail info@ kunsthalle-karlsruhe.de; internet www .kunsthalle-karlsruhe.de; f. 1846; German, Dutch, Flemish, French paintings and sculpture from the 14th–20th centuries; print room; 90,000 prints and drawings; education service; library of 150,000 vols; Dir Dr PIA MÜLLER-TAMM.

Staatliches Museum für Naturkunde Karlsruhe (State Museum of Natural History, Karlsruhe): Erbprinzenstr. 13, 76133 Karlsruhe; tel. (721) 1752111; fax (721) 1752110; e-mail museum@naturkundeka-bw .de; internet www .naturkundemuseum-karlsruhe.de; f. 1789; research and exhibitions in botany, zoology, mineralogy, geology, entomology, palaeontology, vivarium; library of 50,000 vols; Dir Prof. Dr NORBERT LENZ; publs *Andrias*, *Carolinea*, *Exhibition Catalogues* (irregular).

Kassel

Brüder Grimm-Museum Kassel: Brüder Grimm-Pl. 4A, 34117 Kassel; tel. (561) 103235; fax (561) 713299; e-mail grimm-museum@t-online.de; internet www .grimms.de; f. 1960; preservation of works of Jacob, Wilhelm and Ludwig Emil Grimm; colln of works by the brothers; original paintings, autographs, letters, drawings, etchings; Dir Dr BERNHARD LAUER.

Museumslandschaft Hessen Kassel (State Art Museums): Schloss Wilhelmshöhe, 34131 Kassel; tel. (561) 316800; fax (561) 31680111; e-mail info@museum-kassel.de; internet www.museum-kassel.de; f. 18th century; Dir Dr ERNST WEGENER (acting).

Constituent Museums:

Astronomisch-Physikalisches Kabinett: Karlsaue 20C, Kassel; tel. (561) 31680500; fax (561) 31680555; e-mail info@museum-kassel.de; internet www.museum-kassel.de; f. 1992; astronomy and physics collection with history of technology section; planetarium; Dir Dr KARSTEN GAULKE.

Hessisches Landesmuseum: Brüder-Grimm-Pl. 5, Kassel; tel. (561) 31680300; fax (561) 31680333; e-mail info@museum-kassel.de; internet www.museum-kassel.de; f. 1913; pre- and early history; arts-handicraft; folklore; wall papers; closed until 2013; Dir Dr BERND KUSTER.

Museum Schloss Wilhelmshöhe: 34131 Kassel; tel. (561) 316800; fax (561) 31680111; e-mail info@museum-kassel.de; internet www.museum-kassel.de; f. 1800; department of classical antiquities, gallery of old master paintings from 15th–18th centuries, collection of drawings and engravings; library of 70,000 vols; Dir Dr MICHAEL EISSENHAUER.

Neue Galerie: Schöne Aussicht 1, Kassel; tel. (561) 31680400; fax (561) 31680444; e-mail info@museum-kassel.de; internet www.museum-kassel.de; f. 1976; paintings and sculpture from 1750 to present; Dir Dr MICHAEL EISSENHAUER.

Schloss Friedrichstein Museum: Bad Wildungen; tel. (5621) 6577; fax (5621) 3650700; e-mail info@museum-kassel.de; internet www.museum-kassel.de; f. 1980; military and hunting exhibits from 15th–19th centuries; Curator Dr ANTJE SCHERNER.

Konstanz

Archäologisches Landesmuseum (Regional Archaeological Museum): Benediktinerpl. 5, 78467 Konstanz; tel. (7531) 9804-0; fax (7531) 68452; e-mail info@konstanz.alm-bw.de; internet www.konstanz.alm-bw.de; f. 1990; local archaeological artefacts; Dir JÖRG HEILIGMANN.

Bodensee-Naturmuseum (Lake Constance Natural History Museum): SeaLife Centre, Hafenstr. 9, 78462 Konstanz; tel. (7531) 128739-010; fax (7531) 128739-017; e-mail info@sealife.de; internet www.konstanz.de/kultur_freizeit/museen_galerien; f. 1967; geology, palaeontology, zoology and botany of Lake Constance; Curator Dr INGO SCHULZ-WEDDIGEN.

Hus-Museum: Hussenstr. 64, 78462 Konstanz; tel. (7531) 29042; e-mail hus-museum@t-online.de; internet www.konstanz.de/kultur_freizeit/museen_galerien; f. 1965; house of religious thinker, philosopher and reformer, Jan Hus (c. 1369–1415); display by Czech and Slovak artists depicting Hus's life, Council of Constance and the Hussite wars; Dir Dr LIBUSE RÖSCH.

Rosgarten Museum: Rosgartenstr. 3–5, 78462 Konstanz; tel. (7531) 900277; internet www.konstanz.de/kultur_freizeit/museen_galerien; f. 1870; central museum for Lake Constance area; prehistoric, early historic colln; arts and crafts from the Middle Ages to 19th century; library of 6,000 vols; Dir Dr TOBIAS ENGELRING.

Leipzig

Deutsches Buch- und Schriftmuseum der Deutschen Nationalbibliothek Leipzig (German Book Museum): Deutscher Pl. 1, 04103 Leipzig; tel. (341) 2271-324; fax (341) 2271-440; e-mail dbsm@d-nb.de; internet www.d-nb.de; f. 1884; exhibits relate to history of books, writing and paper; closed for refurbishment, scheduled to reopen in 2011; library of 167,618 vols, 1,156 incunabula and MSS, 4,1951 items of graphic art, 402,659 watermarks; Dir Dr STEPHANIE JACOBS.

Museum der Bildenden Künste Leipzig (Leipzig Museum of Fine Arts): Katharinenstr. 10, 04109 Leipzig; tel. (341) 216999-20; fax (341) 216999-99; e-mail mdbk@leipzig.de; internet www.mdbk.de; f. 1837; 3,000 paintings; collns of drawings and sculptures; Dir Dr HANS-WERNER SCHMIDT.

Museum für Kunsthandwerk Leipzig, Grassi-Museum (Museum of Applied Arts): Neumarkt 20, 04109 Leipzig; tel. (341) 2133719; fax (341) 2133715; e-mail grassimuseum@leipzig.de; internet www.grassimuseum.de; f. 1874; textiles, ceramics, glass, wood, and metal objects; prints and patterns relating to design; Dir Dr EVA M. HOYER.

Staatliche Ethnographische Sammlungen Sachsen, Staatlichen Kunstsammlungen Dresden (State Ethnographical Collection of Saxony): Postfach 100 955, 04009 Leipzig; Museum für Völkerkunde zu Leipzig/Grassimuseum, Johannispl. 5–11, 04103 Leipzig; tel. (341) 9731900; fax (341) 9731909; e-mail mvl-grassimuseum@ses.museum; internet www.mvl-grassimuseum.de; f. 2003 by the merger of Museum für Völkerkunde zu Leipzig, Museum für Völkerkunde Dresden and Völkerkundemuseum Herrnhut; Dir Dr CLAUS DEIMEL.

Constituent Museums:

Museum für Völkerkunde Dresden (Ethnographical Museum Dresden): Königsbrücker Landstr. 159, 01109 Dresden; tel. (351) 8926202; fax (351) 8926203; e-mail voelkerkunde.dresden@ses.smwk.sachsen.de; internet www.ses-sachsen.de; f. 1875; ethnography, physical anthropology; library of 60,000 vols; publs *Abhandlungen und Berichte* (Essays and Records), *Bibliographien Africa 1–3, Oceania 1–3* (irregular), *Dresdner Tagungsberichte* (irregular), *Kleine Beiträge* (irregular).

Museum für Völkerkunde zu Leipzig (Ethnographical Museum in Leipzig): GRASSI Museum für Völkerkunde zu Leipzig, Johannispl. 5–11, 04103 Leipzig; Postfach 100 955, 04009 Leipzig; tel. (341) 9731900; fax (341) 9731909; mvl-grassimuseum@ses.museum; internet www.mvl-grassimuseum.de; f. 1869; ethnographical collns from Asia, Australia, Pacific Islands, Africa, America, Europe; library of 170,000 vols; publs *Abhandlungen und Berichte*, *Jahrbuch* (1 a year).

Völkerkundemuseum Herrnhut (Ethnographical Museum Herrnhut): Goethestr. 1, 02747 Herrnhut; tel. (35873) 2403; fax (35873) 2403; e-mail voelkerkunde.herrnhut@ses.museum; internet www.ses-sachsen.de; f. 1878; ethnography; contains collns made by Moravian Church missionaries; Curator STEPHAN AUGUSTIN.

Stadtgeschichtliches Museum Leipzig: Neubau, Böttchergäßchen 3, 04109 Leipzig; tel. (341) 9651-30; fax (341) 9651-352; e-mail stadtmuseum@leipzig.de; internet www.stadtgeschichtliches-museum-leipzig.de; f.

1909; library of 160,000 items; Dir Dr VOLKER RODEKAMP.

Lübeck

Museen für Kunst und Kulturgeschichte (Museums for Art and Cultural History): Düvekenstr. 21, 23552 Lübeck; tel. (451) 122-4134; fax (451) 122-4183; e-mail mkk@luebeck.de; internet www.museen.luebeck.de; library of 30,000 vols; Dir Dr THORSTEN RODIEK; publs *Katalog des Behnhauses*, *Kataloge des St Annen-Museums*.

Branch Museums:

Katharinenkirche: Königstr., Lübeck; tel. (451) 122-4143; fax (451) 122-4183; e-mail mkk@luebeck.de; internet www.luebeck.de/museen; 14th-century bldgs; fmrly Franciscan monasteries church; Dir Dr THORSTEN RODIEK.

Museum Behnhaus/Drägerhaus: Königstr. 9–11, Lübeck; tel. (451) 122-4148; e-mail mkk@luebeck.de; internet www.museen.luebeck.de; f. 1921; museum of 19th-century art located in late 18th-century patrician house; art from Overbeck to Munch; Dir Dr THORSTEN RODIEK.

Museum Holstentor: Holstentorpl., Lübeck; tel. (451) 122-4129; fax (451) 122-4183; e-mail mkk@luebeck.de; internet www.luebeck.de/museen; built 1464–1478; history of the city and the merchant of Lübeck; Dir Dr THORSTEN RODIEK.

St Annen-Museum und Kunsthalle St Annen (St Annen Museum and Art Gallery): St Annenstr. 15, Lübeck; tel. (451) 122-4137; fax (451) 122-4183; e-mail mkk@luebeck.de; internet www.luebeck.de; f. 1915 (Museum), 2003 (Art Gallery); Late Gothic convent, built 1502–1515; medieval ecclesiastical art from Lübeck; domestic art from Lübeck, from Middle Ages to 18th century; modern and contemporary art; Dir Dr THORSTEN RODIEK.

Völkerkundesammlung (Ethnographic Collection): Grosser Bauhof 14, 23522 Lübeck; Parade 10, 23552 Lübeck; tel. (451) 122-4342; fax (451) 122-4348; e-mail vks@luebeck.de; internet www.luebeck.de; f. 1893; Dir BRIGITTE TEMPLIN.

Magdeburg

Magdeburger Museen: Otto-von-Guericke-Str. 68–73, 39104 Magdeburg; tel. (391) 5403501; fax (391) 5403510; e-mail museen@magdeburg.de; internet www.magdeburgermuseen.de; f. 1906; local history collection, art gallery, sculptures, handicrafts, graphics, bibliophilia, costumes, sociology, natural history and prehistory collection; Kulturhistorisches Museum, Kunstmuseum Kloster Unser Lieben Frauen, Museum für Naturkunde, Technikmuseum; library of 50,000 vols; Dir MATTHIAS PUHLE; publs *Abhandlungen und Berichte Naturkunde und Vorgeschichte*, *Magdeburger Museumshefte* (irregular), *Magdeburger Museumsschriften* (irregular).

Mainz

Gutenberg-Museum: Liebfrauenpl. 5, 55116 Mainz; tel. (6131) 122640; fax (6131) 123488; e-mail gutenberg-museum@stadt.mainz.de; internet www.gutenberg-museum.de; f. 1900; world museum of typography; library of 90,000 vols; Dir Dr EVA-MARIA HANEBUTT-BENZ.

Landesmuseum Mainz: Grosse Bleiche 49–51, 55116 Mainz; tel. (6131) 2857-0; fax (6131) 2857-88; internet www.landesmuseum-mainz.de; f. 1803; cultural history and art; Dir Dr ISABELLA FEHLE.

Münzsammlung (Coin Collection): Stadtarchiv Mainz, Rheinallee 3B, 55116 Mainz; tel. (6131) 122178; fax (6131) 123569; e-mail stadtarchiv@stadt.mainz.de; internet www .stadtarchiv.mainz.de; f. 1784; Dir Dr WOLF-GANG DOBRAS.

Naturhistorisches Museum Mainz (Natural History Museum): Reichklarastr./Mitternachtspl., 55116 Mainz; tel. (6131) 122646; fax (6131) 122975; e-mail naturhistorisches.museum@stadt.mainz.de; internet www.uni-mainz.de/~lsnhmmz; f. 1834 (collns); museum f. 1910); mineralogy, geology, palaeontology, zoology and botany of Rheinland-Pfalz and Rwanda; library of 40,000 vols, 60,000 pamphlets; Dir Dr MICHAEL SCHMITZ; publs *Mainzer Naturwissenschaftliches Archiv* (1 a year), *Mainzer Naturwissenschaftliches Archiv, Beihefte, Mitteilungen der Rheinischen Naturforschenden Gesellschaft* (1 a year).

Römisch-Germanisches Zentralmuseum–Forschungsinstitut für Vor- und Frühgeschichte (Central Roman-German Museum–Research Museum for Prehistory and Early History): Ernst-Ludwig-Pl. 2, 55116 Mainz; tel. (6131) 91240; fax (6131) 9124199; e-mail info@rgzm.de; internet web .rgzm.de; f. 1852; studies in Old World archaeology and prehistory, conservation of prehistoric, Roman and early medieval antiquities; library of 80,000 vols; Gen. Dir Dr FALKO DAIM; publs *Arbeitsblätter für Restauratoren, Archäologisches Korrespondenzblatt, Ausstellungskataloge, Corpus Signorum Imperii Romani, Führer durch die Ausstellungen, Jahrbuch, Kataloge, Studien zu den Anfängen der Metallurgie, Vulkanpark-Forschungen*.

Mannheim

Reiss-Engelhorn-Museen Mannheim: 68030 Mannheim, POB 103051; tel. (621) 293-3151; fax (621) 293-3099; e-mail reiss-engelhorn-museen@mannheim.de; internet reiss-engelhorn-museen.mannheim .de; f. 1957 as Reiss-Museum; museum of art, crafts and decorative arts, local theatre history, archaeology and prehistory, ethnology, local history and natural history; collection of historical European musical instruments; Forum Internationale Photgraphie (FIP); library of 120,000 vols; Dir Prof. Dr ALFRIED WIECZOREK.

Städtische Kunsthalle (City Art Museum): Moltkestr. 9, 68165 Mannheim; tel. (621) 293-6413; fax (621) 293-6412; e-mail kunsthalle@mannheim.de; internet www .kunsthalle-mannheim.com; f. 1907; 33,000 drawings, water colours and graphics, 1,700 paintings and 600 sculptures; Dir Dr ROLF LAUTER.

Marburg

Universitätsmuseum für Bildende Kunst: Lahn, Biegenstr. 11, im Ernst von Hülsen-Haus, 35032 Marburg; tel. (6421) 2822355; fax (6421) 2822166; e-mail museum@verwaltung.uni-marburg.de; internet www.uni-marburg.de/zv/news/ uni-museum; f. 1927; Dir Dr JÜRGEN WITTSTOCK.

Universitätsmuseum für Kulturgeschichte: Landgrafenschloss, Wilhelmsbau, 35032 Marburg/Lahn; tel. (6421) 28225871; fax (6421) 2822166; e-mail museum@verwaltung.uni-marburg.de; internet www.uni-marburg.de/zv/news/museum; f. 1875; Dir Dr JÜRGEN WITTSTOCK.

Mettmann

Neanderthal-Museum: Talstr. 300, 40822 Mettmann; tel. (2104) 979797; fax (2104) 979796; e-mail museum@neanderthal.de; internet www.neanderthal.de; f. 1996; human evolution since earliest times; library of 4,000 vols; Dir Prof. Dr GERD-C. WENIGER.

Munich

Archäologische Staatssammlung München (State Archaeological Collection, Munich): Lerchenfeldstr. 2, 80538 Munich; tel. (89) 2112-402; fax (89)2112-4401; e-mail archaeologische.staatssammlung@extern .lrz-muenchen.de; internet www .archaeologie-bayern.de; f. 1885; prehistoric, Roman and early medieval antiquities from Southern Germany, prehistoric archaeology of Mediterranean and Near East; Dir Prof. Dr L. WAMSER; publ. *Kataloge* (irregular).

Bayerische Staatsgemäldesammlungen (Bavarian State Art Galleries): Barerstr. 29, 80799 Munich; tel. (89) 23805-0; fax (89) 23805-251; e-mail info@pinakothek.de; internet www.pinakothek.de; medieval to modern art, painting and sculpture; Gen. Dir Dr KLAUS SCHRENK; Dir Doerner Institute Dr ANDREAS BURMESTER.

Bayerisches Nationalmuseum (National Bavarian Museum): Prinzregentenstr. 3, 80538 Munich; tel. (89) 21124-01; fax (89) 21124-201; e-mail bay.nationalmuseum@ bnm.mwn.de; internet www .bayerisches-nationalmuseum.de; f. 1855; European fine arts, especially sculpture, decorative art and folk art; library of 75,000 vols; Dir Dr RENATE EIKELMANN; publs *Bayerische Blätter für Volkskunde, Bildführer, Forschungshefte, Kataloge*.

Deutsches Museum von Meisterwerken der Naturwissenschaft und Technik (German Museum of Scientific and Technological Masterpieces): 80306 Munich; Museumsinsel 1, 80538 Munich; tel. (89) 2179213; fax (89) 2179262; e-mail information@deutsches-museum.de; internet www.deutsches-museum.de; f. 1903; history of science and technology from its origins to the present day; spec. colln of MSS and autographs, trade literature, plans, pictorial art, films, commemorative medals; research institute for the history of science and technology; 'Kerschensteiner Kolleg' for teacher in-service training; library of 920,000 vols, 3,500 current periodicals; Dir-Gen. Prof. Dr WOLFGANG M. HECKL; publ. *Kultur und Technik* (4 a year).

Affiliated Museums:

Deutsches Museum Bonn (German Museum in Bonn): Ahrstr. 45, 53175 Bonn; tel. (228) 302255; fax (228) 302254; e-mail info@deutsches-museum-bonn.de; internet www.deutsches-museum-bonn .de; f. 1995; science and technology in Germany since 1945; Dir Dr ANDREA NIEHAUS.

Deutsches Museum Flugwerft Schleissheim (German Museum in Flugwerft Schleissheim): Effnerstr. 18, 85764 Oberschleissheim; tel. (89) 3157140; fax (89) 31571450; e-mail fws@deutsches-museum .de; f. 1992; aeronautical collection; Dir-Gen. Prof. Dr WOLF PETER FEHLHAMMER.

Deutsches Museum Verkehrszentrum (German Museum—Transport Centre): Theresienhöhe 14A, 80339 Munich; tel. (89) 2179-529; e-mail fws@ deutsches-museum.de; internet verkehrszentrum.deutsches-museum.de; f. 2003; traffic museum; Dir SYLVIA HLADKY.

Generaldirektion der Staatlichen Naturwissenschaftlichen Sammlungen Bayerns, München (Bavarian Natural History Collections): Menzingerstr. 71, 80638 Munich; tel. (89) 17999240; fax (89) 17999255; internet www .naturalhistorybavaria.de; f. 1827; Gen. Dir Prof. Dr GERHARD HASZPRUNAR.

Subordinate Institutions:

Bayerische Staatssammlung für Paläontologie und Geologie: Richard-Wagner-Str. 10, 80333 Munich; tel. (89) 2180-6630; fax (89) 2180-6601; e-mail pal .sammlung@lrz.uni-muenchen.de; internet www.paleo.de/psm_home.htm; f. 1759; Dir Prof. Dr REINHOLD LEINFELDER; publ. *Zitteliana*.

Botanische Staatssammlung: Menzinger-Str. 67, 80638 Munich; tel. (89) 17861265; fax (89) 17861193; e-mail office@bsm.mwn.de; internet www .botanischestaatssammlung.de; f. 1813; Dir Prof. Dr SUSANNE RENNER; publ. *Arnoldia*.

Botanischer Garten München–Nymphenburg: Menzinger Str. 65, 80638 Munich; tel. (89) 17861310; fax (89) 17861340; e-mail info@botmuc.de; internet www.botmuc.de; f. 1914; Dir Prof. Dr SUSANNE RENNER.

Jura-Museum: Willibaldsburg, 85072 Eichstätt; tel. (8421) 2956; fax (8421) 89609; e-mail jura-museumvf@ altmuehlnet.de; internet www .jura-museum.de; f. 1976; natural history; Man. Dr MARTINA KÖLBL-EBERT; publ. *Archaeopteryx*.

Mineralogische Staatssammlung: Theresienstr. 41, 80333 Munich; tel. (89) 21804312; fax (89) 21804334; e-mail mineralogische.staatssammlung@lrz .uni-muenchen.de; internet www .lrz-muenchen.de/~mineralogische.staats-sammlung; f. 1823; Dir Prof. Dr PETER GILLE.

Museum Mensch und Natur: Schloss Nymphenburg, 80638 Munich; tel. (89) 179589-0; fax (89) 179589-100; e-mail museum@musmn.de; internet www .musmn.de; f. 1990; modern natural history with interactive exhibition design; permanent exhibitions cover range of subjects from geology and mineralogy to neurobiology, genetics, ecology; temporary exhibitions; Dir MICHAEL APEL; Deputy Dir Dr SIMON GILLA.

Naturkunde-Museum Bamberg: Fleischstr. 2, 96047 Bamberg; tel. (951) 8631249; fax (951) 8631250; e-mail info@ naturkundemuseum-bamberg.de; internet www.naturkundemuseum-bamberg.de; f. 1790; Man. Dr MATTHIAS MÄUSER.

Rieskrater-Museum Nördlingen: Eugene-Shoemaker-Pl. 1, 86720 Nördlingen; tel. (9081) 2738220; fax (9081) 27382220; e-mail rieskratermuseum@ noerdlingen.de; internet www .riescrater-museum.de; f. 1990; natural history; Man. Dr MICHAEL SCHIEBER.

Staatssammlung für Anthropologie und Paläoanatomie: Karolinenpl. 2A, 80333 Munich; tel. (89) 5488438-0; fax (89) 5488438-17; e-mail asm.grupe@ extern.lrz-muenchen.de; internet www .naturwissenschaftlichesammlungen-bayerns.de/anthropologie/anthro.html; f. 1886; Dirs Prof. Dr GISELA GRUPE, Prof. Dr JORIS PETERS.

Urwelt-Museum Oberfranken: Kanzleistr. 1, 95444 Bayreuth; tel. (921) 511211; fax (921) 511212; e-mail urwelt-museum-oberfranken@t-online.de; internet www.urwelt-museum.de; f. 1997; natural history; Man. Dr JOACHIM RABOLD.

Zoologische Staatssammlung München: Münchhausenstr. 21, 81247 Munich; tel. (89) 81070; fax (89) 8107300; e-mail zsm@zsm.mwn.de; internet www .zsm.mwn.de; f. 1807; library of 92,664 vols (books and serials), 823 running journals, 129,020 separata; Dir Prof. Dr GERHARD HASZPRUNAR; publs *Journal of Zoology, Spixiana, Spixiana Supplements*.

Neue Sammlung–Staatliches Museum für Angewandte Kunst (State Museum for Applied Arts): Türkenstr. 15 (Pinakothek der Moderne), 80333 Munich; tel. (89) 272725-0; fax (89) 272725-561; e-mail info@ die-neue-sammlung.de; internet www .die-neue-sammlung.de; f. 1925; modern industrial arts and crafts, architecture, urban planning; industrial and graphic design; Dir Prof. Dr FLORIAN HUFNAGL.

Staatliche Antikensammlungen und Glyptothek (State Antique Collections): Königspl. 1, 80333 Munich; tel. (89) 286100; fax (89) 28927516; e-mail info@ antike-am-koenigsplatz.mwn.de; internet www.antike-am-koenigsplatz.mwn.de; Greek and Etruscan vases and bronzes, Greek and Roman sculpture, terracottas and bronzes, glass, jewellery; Conservator Dr MATTHIAS STEINHART.

Staatliche Graphische Sammlung München: Meiserstr. 10, 80333 Munich; tel. (89) 28927650; fax (89) 28927653; e-mail direktion@graphische-sammlung.mwn.de; internet www.sgsm.eu; f. 1758; German, Dutch, French and Italian prints and drawings since 15th century; Dir Dr MICHAEL SEMFF.

Staatliche Münzsammlung (State Coin Collection): Residenzstr. 1, 80333 Munich; tel. (89) 227221; fax (89) 299859; e-mail info@ staatliche-muenzsammlung.de; internet www.staatliche-muenzsammlung.de; f. 16th century; coins from different countries and centuries; special collections: Greek, Roman and Byzantine coins, German and Italian Renaissance medals, Bavarian coins, precious stones from antiquity, Middle Ages and Renaissance, Japanese lacquer cabinets; library of 20,000 vols; Dir Dr KLOSE.

Staatliches Museum Ägyptischer Kunst (State Museum of Egyptian Art): Meiserstr. 10, 80333 Munich; premises at: Hofgartenstr., Munich; tel. (89) 28927-630; fax (89) 28927-638; e-mail info@ aegyptisches-museum-muenchen.com; internet www.aegyptisches-museum-muenchen .de; f. 1966; library: small specialized library; Dir Dr SYLVIA SCHOSKE.

Staatliches Museum für Völkerkunde München (State Museum of Ethnology Munich): Maximilianstr. 42, 80538 Munich; tel. (89) 210136-100; fax (89) 210136-247; e-mail museum.voelkerkunde@mfv.bayern .de; internet www .voelkerkundemuseum-muenchen.de; f. 1868; collns on Asia, America, Africa and the Pacific Islands; library of 50,000 vols, 75 current periodicals; Dir Dr CLAUDIUS MÜLLER.

Städtische Galerie im Lenbachhaus: Luisenstr. 33, 80333 Munich; tel. (89) 233-32000; fax (89) 233-32003; e-mail lenbachhaus@muenchen.de; internet www .lenbachhaus.de; f. 1929; Munich artists including paintings by Kandinsky, Klee and the Blaue Reiter group; int. contemporary art; exhibitions, lectures, performances; Dir Dr HELMUT FRIEDEL.

Münster

Landesmuseum für Kunst und Kulturgeschichte (Westphalian Museum of Art and Cultural History): Dompl. 10, 48143 Münster; tel. (251) 590701; fax (251) 5907210; e-mail landesmuseum@lwl.org; internet www.landesmuseum-muenster.de; f. 1908; sculpture, painting, graphic art, goldsmith work since 9th century; engraved portraits, history, numismatics; library of 121,000 vols; Dir Dr HERMANN ARNHOLD.

Nuremberg

Albrecht-Dürer-Haus: Albrecht-Dürer-Str. 39, D- 90403 Nuremberg; tel. (911) 2312568; fax (911) 2312443; e-mail museen@stadt .nuernberg.de; internet www.museen .nuernberg.de; f. 1828; life and work of the engraver Albrecht Dürer (1471–1528) presented in his home (inhabited 1509–28); Dir Dr THOMAS SCHAUERTE.

Germanisches Nationalmuseum: Kartäusergasse 1, 90402 Nuremberg; tel. (911) 1331-0; fax (911) 1331-200; e-mail info@gnm .de; internet www.gnm.de; f. 1852; German art and culture from prehistoric times to the present, fine art galleries, folk art, public library, archives, print room, musical instruments, arms, toys, etc.; library of 548,000 vols, 1,600 current periodicals; Chief Dir Prof. Dr G. ULRICH GROSSMANN.

Kunsthalle Nürnberg (Nuremberg Art Museum): Lorenzer Str. 32, 90402 Nuremberg; tel. (911) 231-2853; fax (911) 231-3721; e-mail kunsthalle@stadt.nuernberg.de; internet www.kunsthalle.nuernberg.de; f. 1967; changing exhibitions of international contemporary art; Dir ELLEN SEIFERMANN.

Stadtmuseum Fembohaus: Burgstr. 11, 90403 Nuremberg; tel. (911) 2315418; fax (911) 2315422; internet www.museen .nuernberg.de; f. 1958; art and cultural history of Nuremberg; Dir RUDOLF KÄS.

Offenbach am Main

Klingspor-Museum Offenbach: Herrnstr. 80, 63061 Offenbach am Main; tel. (69) 80652954; fax (69) 80652669; e-mail klingspormuseum@offenbach.de; internet www.klingspor-museum.de; f. 1953; colln and exhibition of calligraphy, typography, bookbinding, modern book art and private presses; spec. colln of 20th-century calligraphy; library of 66,000 vols; Dir Dr STEFAN SOLTEK; Librarians MARTINA WEISS STEPHANIE EHRST.

Pforzheim

Schmuckmuseum Pforzheim im Reuchlinhaus: Jahnstr. 33, 75173 Pforzheim; located at: Jahnstr. 42, 75173 Pforzheim; tel. (7231) 392126; fax (7231) 391441; e-mail schmuckmuseum@stadt-pforzheim.de; internet www.schmuckmuseum.de; f. 1938; jewellery; Dir CORNELIE HOLZACH.

Potsdam

Brandenburgisches Landesmuseum für Ur- und Frühgeschichte (Pre- and Early History): Forstweg 1, 14656 Brieselang; tel. (332) 3236940; f. 1953; Dir Prof. Dr J. KUNOW; publs *Forschungen zur Archäologie im Land Brandenburg* (1 a year), *Veröffentlichungen des Brandenburgischen Landesmuseums für Ur- und Frühgeschichte* (1 a year).

Stiftung Preussische Schlösser und Gärten Berlin-Brandenburg (Prussian Palaces and Gardens Foundation of Berlin-Brandenburg): Postfach 601462, 14414 Potsdam; Allee nach Sanssouci 5, 14471 Potsdam; tel. (331) 9694-0; fax (331) 9694-102; e-mail generaldirektion@spsg.de; internet www .spsg.de; f. 1995; administers gardens and 150 palaces and other historic buildings in and around Berlin and Potsdam; Dir-Gen. Prof. Dr HARTMUT DORGERLOH; Admin. Dir Dr HEINZ BERG.

Recklinghausen

Museen der Stadt Recklinghausen (Recklinghausen City Museums): Grosse-Perdekamp-Str. 25–27, 45657 Recklinghausen; tel. (2361) 501935; fax (2361) 501932; e-mail info@kunst-re.de; internet www

.kunst-re.de; f. 1950; Dir Dr FERDINAND ULLRICH.

Attached Museums:

Ikonen-Museum (Icon Museum): Kirchpl. 2A, 45657 Recklinghausen; tel. (2361) 501941; fax (2361) 501942; e-mail ikonen@kunst-re.de; internet www .kunst-re.de; f. 1956; Russian, Byzantine, Greek and Balkan icons, miniatures, metal work, Coptic art and textiles; Dirs Dr FERDINAND ULLRICH, Dr EVA HAUSTEIN-BARTSCH.

Städtische Kunsthalle (City Art Gallery): Recklinghausen; tel. (2361) 501935; fax (2361) 501932; e-mail info@kunst-re .de; internet www.kunst-re.de; f. 1950; paintings, drawings, prints and sculptures by contemporary artists; Dirs Dr FERDINAND ULLRICH, Dr HANS-JUERGEN SCHWALM.

Vestisches Museum: Hohenzollernstr. 12, 45659 Recklinghausen; tel. (2361) 501946; fax (2361) 501932; e-mail info@ kunst-re.de; internet www.kunst-re.de; f. 1987; Westphalian arts and crafts, local history, native art; Dirs Dr FERDINAND ULLRICH, Dr HANS-JUERGEN SCHWALM.

Schleswig

Stiftung Schleswig-Holsteinische Landesmuseen Schloss Gottorf (Foundation of State Museums in Schleswig-Holstein in Schloss Gottorf): Schloss Gottorf, 24837 Schleswig; tel. (4621) 813-0; fax (4621) 813535; e-mail info@schloss-gottorf.de; internet www.schloss-gottorf.de; f. 1835; houses Archaeological and Art and Culture Museums and the Centre for Baltic and Scandinavian Archaeology; library of 40,000 vols; Dirs Prof. Dr CLAUS VON CARNAP-BORNHEIM, Dr RALF BLEILE; publs *Ausgrabungen in Haithabu* (irregular), *Ausgrabungen in Schleswig* (irreggular), *Berichte über die Ausgrabungen in Haithabu* (irreggular), *Die Funde der älteren Bronzezeit des nordischen Kreises* (irreggular), *Offa* (1 a year), *Offa Bücher* (irreggular), *Untersuchungen und Materialien zur Steinzeit in Schleswig-Holstein* (irregular).

Affiliated Museums:

Archäologisches Landesmuseum (Provincial Museum of Archaeology):; f. 1985; archaeological and ethnological exhibits.

Eisenkunstgussmuseum Büdelsdorf (Ironwork Museum): Glück-Auf-Allee 4, 24782 Büdelsdorf; f. 1981; history of ironwork.

Jüdisches Museum Rendsburg (Jewish Museum): Prinzessinstr. 7–8, 24768 Rendsburg; tel. (4331) 25262; e-mail jmuseum@t-online.de; internet www .juedisches-museum-rendsburg.de; f. 1988.

Landesmuseum für Kunst und Kulturgeschichte (Museum of Art and Culture):- artefacts from Middle Ages onwards; colln of 19th-century paintings.

Volkskunde Museum Schleswig (Folklore Museum in Schleswig):tel. (4621) 96760; fax (4621) 967634; e-mail volkskunde@schloss-gottorf.de; f. 1993; history of local arts and crafts; Dir GUNTRAM TURKOWSKI.

Wikinger Museum Haithabu–Stiftung Schleswig-Holsteinische Landesmuseen Schloss Gottorf (Museum of the Viking–age settlement Haithabu):; history of the archaeological dig; restored longship on port.

Schwerin

Archäologisches Landesmuseum und Landesamt für Bodendenkmalpflege Mecklenburg-Vorpommern: Domhof 4/5,

19055 Schwerin; tel. (385) 5214-0; fax (385) 5214-198; e-mail poststelle@kulturerbe-mv .de; internet www.kulturerbe-mv.de; f. 1953; library of 44,000 vols; Dir Dr FRIEDRICH LÜTH; publs *Archäologie in Mecklenburg-Vorpommern*, *Archäologische Berichte aus Mecklenburg-Vorpommern*, *Beiträge zur Ur- und Frühgeschichte Mecklenburg-Vorpommerns*, *Bodendenkmalpflege in Mecklenburg-Vorpommern Jahrbuch*, *Materialhefte*, *Museumskataloge*.

Speyer

Historisches Museum der Pfalz (Historical Museum of the Palatinate): Domplatz, 67324 Speyer; tel. (6232) 13250; fax (6232) 132540; e-mail info@museum.speyer.de; internet www.museum.speyer.de; f. 1869; art and cultural history of the Palatinate, includes wine museum and diocesan museum; library of 20,000 vols; Dir Dr ALEXANDER KOCH; publs *Mitteilungen des Historischen Vereins* (1 a year), *Pfälzer Heimat* (4 a year).

Stralsund

Kulturhistorisches Museum Stralsund (Cultural and Historical Museum of Stralsund): Mönchstr. 25–27, 18439 Stralsund; tel. (3831) 28790; fax (3831) 280060; e-mail khm@gmx.de; internet www.stralsund .abelnet.de/museen; f. 1858; prehistory, ecclesiastical art, folklore, local history, furniture, history of navigation and navy, modern art, handicrafts, 18th-century products; Dir Dr ANDREAS GRÜGER.

Stuttgart

Kunstmuseum Stuttgart (Stuttgart Art Museum): Kleiner Schlosspl. 1, 70173 Stuttgart; tel. (711) 2162188; fax (711) 216-7824; e-mail info@kunstmuseum-stuttgart.de; internet www.kunstmuseum-stuttgart.de; f. 1924; paintings, drawings, graphics and sculptures by artists since 19th century; Otto Dix colln, Adolf Hölzel colln, Willi Baumeister archive; Dir Dr ULRIKE GROOS; Curators Dr SIMONE SCHIMPF, Dr DANIEL SPANKE.

Landesmuseum Württemberg: Altes Schloss, 70173 Stuttgart; tel. (711) 2793498; fax (711) 2793490; e-mail info@ landesmuseum-stuttgart.de; internet www .landesmuseum-stuttgart.de; f. 1862; archaeology from prehistoric to medieval times; 4,000 years of glass-making, Swabian sculpture, Renaissance clocks, musical instruments, Württemberg crown jewels; Roman lapidarium; Dir Prof. Dr CORNELIA EWIGLEBEN; Chief Curator Dr THOMAS BRUNE.

Linden-Museum Stuttgart, Staatliches Museum für Völkerkunde (Linden Museum Stuttgart, State Museum for Ethnography): Hegelpl. 1, 70174 Stuttgart; tel. (711) 2022-3; fax (711) 2022-590; e-mail sekretariat@lindenmuseum.de; internet www.lindenmuseum.de; f. 1882; ethnographical museum, exhibitions; library of 50,000 vols, 270 current periodicals; Dir Dr INÉS DE CASTRO; Librarian GUENTER DARCIS; publ. *Tribus* (1 a year).

Staatliches Museum für Naturkunde Stuttgart: Rosenstein 1, 70191 Stuttgart; tel. (711) 89360; fax (711) 8936-100; e-mail museum.smns@naturkundemuseum-bw.de; internet www.naturkundemuseum-bw.de/ stuttgart/start.html; f. 1791; botany, palaeontology, zoology; library of 75,000 vols; Dir Prof. Dr JOHANNA EDER; publs *Stuttgarter Beiträge zur Naturkunde, Serie A: Biologie* (irregular—up to 25 a year), *Stuttgarter Beiträge zur Naturkunde, Serie B: Geologie/Paläontologie* (irregular—up to 25 a year), *Stuttgarter Beiträge zur Naturkunde, Serie C: Wissen für Alle* (2 a year).

Staatsgalerie Stuttgart: Postfach 104342, 70038 Stuttgart; Konrad-Adenauerstr. 30–32, Stuttgart; tel. (711) 47040-0; fax (711) 2369983; e-mail info@staatsgalerie.de; internet www.staatsgalerie.de; f. 1843; art since the Middle Ages; colln of prints, drawings and photographs; Oskar Schlemmer Archive, Will Grohmann Archive, Sohm Archive, Adolf Hölzel's art-theoretical writings; Dir SEAN RAINBIRD.

Trier

Rheinisches Landesmuseum Trier (Museum of the Rheinland in Trier): Weimarer Allee 1, 54290 Trier; tel. (651) 9774-0; fax (651) 9774-222; e-mail info@ landesmuseum-trier.de; internet www .landesmuseum-trier.de; f. 1877; Roman and early medieval exhibits excavated in Trier and the local area; art history from the Middle Ages to the 19th century; numismatic colln; restoration workshops; dendrochronological and archeobotanical analyses; municipal and regional archaeological research; library of 70,000 vols; Dir Dr ECKHART KOHNE; publs *Funde und Ausgrabungen im Bezirk Trier* (1 a year), *Schriftenreihe des Rheinischen Landesmuseums Trier* (irregular), *Trierer Grabungen und Forschungen* (irregular), *Trierer Zeitschrift für Geschichte und Kunst* (1 a year).

Ulm

Ulmer Museum (Ulm Museum): Marktpl. 9, 89070 Ulm; tel. (731) 1614300; fax (731) 1611626; e-mail info.ulmer-museum@ulm .de; internet www.museum.ulm.de; f. 1924; collections of Ulm and Swabian art from 14th–19th centuries, international art since beginning of 20th century, archaeological collections, archives of the former Ulm School of Design (Hochschule für Gestaltung); Dir Dr BRIGITTE REINHARDT.

Weimar

Stiftung Weimarer Klassik und Kunstsammlungen: Burgplatz 4, 99423 Weimar; tel. (3643) 545-0; fax (3643) 202174; e-mail info@swkk.de; internet www.swkk.de; f. 1953; preserves and researches Weimar's artistic and cultural sites and collns, primarily the classical period in Weimar and modern art in Weimar; administers the Goethe-Nationalmuseum (comprises 23 museums and houses connected with Goethe and Schiller, and other buildings, incl. Liszt's house); also the Nietzsche-Archiv, the Schlossmuseum, the Bauhaus Museum, the Neues Museum, the Goethe- und Schiller-Archiv (800,000 MSS of German writers, artists, composers and scientists) and the Duchess Anna Amalia Bibliothek (850,000 vols); Pres. HELLMUT SEEMANN; Admin. Dir BEATE ALTMEYER.

Thüringisches Landesamt für Denkmalpflege und Archäologie (Thuringian Regional Office for the Preservation of Monuments and Archaeology): Humboldtstr. 11, 99423 Weimar; tel. (3643) 903324; fax (3643) 903328; e-mail post@tlad.de; internet www .tlad.de; f. 1888; library of 28,000 vols; publs *Ausgrabungen und Funde im Freistaat Thüringen, Jahresschrift 'Alt-Thüringen', Restaurierung und Museumstechnik, Weimarer Monographien zur Ur- und Frühgeschichte*.

Attached Museums:

Museum für Ur- und Frühgeschichte Thüringens (Thuringian Museum for Prehistory and Early History): Humboldtstr. 11, 99423 Weimar; tel. (3643) 818300; fax (3643) 818390; local history since 400,000 BC.

Steinsburgmuseum: Waldhaussiedlung 8, 98631 Römhild; tel. (36948) 20561; fax (36948) 82853; Celtic site and artefacts; Dir Dr M. SIEDEL.

Wittenberg

Lutherhaus, Reformationsgeschichtliches Museum (Museum of the History of the Reformation): Collegienstr. 54, 06886 Lutherstadt Wittenberg; tel. (3491) 42030; fax (3491) 4203270; e-mail info@ martinluther.de; internet www.martinluther .de; f. 1883; portraits, MSS, pictures, woodcuts, copperplates, medallions and original works on the history of the Reformation; library of 60,000 vols; Dir Dr STEFAN RHEIN.

Worms

Museum der Stadt Worms im Andreasstift (Worms City Museum): Weckerlingpl. 7, 67547 Worms; tel. (6241) 9463914; fax (6241) 24068; e-mail museum@worms.de; internet www.worms.de/deutsch/tourismus/museen; f. 1881; archaeology, town history of Worms, spec. colln of glassware, Luther Room (diet of 1521); Dir for Admin. Dr GERALD BOENNEN; publs *Der Wormsgau* (1 a year, with supplements), *Zeitschrift der Stadt Worms und des Altertumsvereins Worms*.

Museum Heylshof: Stephansgasse 9, 67547 Worms; tel. and fax (6241) 22000; internet www.heylshof.de; f. 1923; paintings, sculptures, pottery, porcelains and glass from 15th–19th centuries; Curators CORNELIUS ADALBERT, F. V. HEYL.

Universities

ALBERT-LUDWIGS-UNIVERSITÄT FREIBURG

Fahnenbergplatz, 79085 Freiburg im Breisgau

Telephone: (761) 2030
Fax: (761) 203-4369
Internet: www.uni-freiburg.de

Founded 1457
Academic year: October to July

Rector: Prof. Dr Dr WOLFGANG JÄGER
Pro-Rectors: Prof. Dr GERHARD SCHNEIDER, Prof. Dr KARL-REINHARD VOLZ, Prof. Dr MATHIAS LANGER
Director of Admin.: WOLF-ECKHARD WORMSER
Librarian: BÄRBEL SCHUBEL

Number of teachers: 2,400
Number of students: 21,000

DEANS

Faculty of Applied Sciences: Prof. Dr JAN G. KORVINK
Faculty of Arts: Prof. Dr HERMANN SCHWENGEL
Faculty of Biology: Prof. Dr GEORG FUCHS
Faculty of Business and Behavioural Science: Prof. Dr HANS SPADA
Faculty of Chemistry, Pharmacology and Geosciences: Prof. Dr HARALD HILLEBRECHT
Faculty of Forestry and Environmental Sciences: Prof. Dr ERNST E. HILDEBRAND
Faculty of Law: Prof. Dr ANDREAS VOSSKUHLE
Faculty of Mathematics and Physics: Prof. Dr JOSEF HONERKAMP
Faculty of Medicine: Prof. Dr JOSEF ZENTNER
Faculty of Philology: Prof. Dr E. CHEAURÉ
Faculty of Theology: Prof. Dr HELMUT HOPING

PROFESSORS

Faculty of Applied Sciences:
ALBERS, S., Parallel and Distributed Computing
BASIN, D., Informatics
BECKER, B., Informatics
BERGARD, W., Autonomous Intelligent Systems
BURKHARDT, H., Informatics

HAUSSELT, J., Microsystems Technology
KORVINK, J. G., Microsystems Technology
KUNTZ, Information Technology
LAUSEN, G., Informatics
LEUE, S., Computer Networks
MANOLI, Information Technology
MENZ, W., Microsystems Technology
NEBEL, B., Informatics
OTTMANN, TH., Informatics
PAUL, Information Technology
RAEDT, L. DE, Machine Learning
RÜHE, Information Technology
SCHMIDT-THIEME, L., Computer-Based New Media
SCHNEIDER, G., Communication Systems
SCHOLL, C., Operating Systems
THIEMANN, P., Programming Languages
URBAN, G. A., Microsystems Technology
WILDE, Information Technology
WOIAS, Information Technology
ZAPPE, Information Technology
ZENGERLE, Information Technology

Faculty of Biology:

AERTSEN, A., Neurobiology
BAUER, G., Evolutionary Biology
BAUMEISTER, R., Neurogenetics
BECK, C., Biology
BEYER, P., Cell Biology
BOGENRIEDER, A., Geobotany
DEIL, U., Geobotany
DRIEVER, W., Neurobiology
FISCHBACH, K. F., Biology
FUCHS, G., Microbiology
FUKSHANSKY, L., Botany
GÜNTHER, K., Neurobiology
HAEHNEL, W., Biochemistry
HARTMANN, R., Neurobiology
HERTEL, R., Biology
KLEINIG, H., Cell Biology
MÜLLER, J., Chemical Ecology
NEUBÜSER, A., Neurobiology
NEUHAUS, G., Cell Biology
OELZE, J., Microbiology
PESCHKE, K., Zoology
RESKI, R., Biotechnology
RETH, M., Molecular Immunology
ROSSEL, S., Neurobiology
SCHÄFER, E., Botany
SCHRÖDER, J., Biochemistry
VOGT, K., Neurobiology
WAGNER, E., Botany
WECKESSER, J., Microbiology
WELLMANN, E., Botany

Faculty of Business and Behavioural Sciences:

BLÜMLE, G., Mathematical Economics
FUCHS, R., Sport Science
GEHRIG, T., Economic Development
GIEß-STÜBER, P., Sport Science
GOLLHOFER, A., Sport Science
FRANCKE, H. H., Financial Economics
HAUSER, S., Imperial Economics
HILKE, W., Commercial Economics
KESSLER, W., Business Economics
KNIEPS, G., Political Economy
LANDMANN, O., Economic Theory
RAFFELHÜSCHEN, Financial Economics
REHKUGLER, H., Commercial Economics
SCHAUENBERG, B., Management Economics
SCHOBER, F., Computer Science
SCHULTZ, G., Socio-political Economics
STRUBE, G., Cognition Science
TSCHEULIN, D., Health Service Economics
VANBERG, V., Political Economics

Faculty of Chemistry, Pharmacology and Geosciences:

BANNWARTH, W., Organic Chemistry
BECHTHOLD, A., Pharmaceutical Biology
BEHRMANN, J., Geology
BREIT, B., Organic Chemistry
BRÜCKNER, R., Organic Chemistry
BUCHER, K., Mineralogy
EBERBACH, W., Biochemistry
FINKELMANN, H., Molecular Chemistry

FRIEDRICH, K., Organic Chemistry
GLAWION, R., Geography
GOSSMANN, H., Geography
GRAPES, R., Geosciences
GRONSKI, W., Macromolecular Chemistry
HENK, A., Geology
HILLEBRECHT, H., Inorganic Chemistry
JANIAK, CH., Inorganic Chemistry
KELLER, J., Mineralogy
KRAMER, V., Crystallography
LEIBUNDGUT, CH., Hydrology
MÄCKEL, R., Geography
MAYER, H., Meteorology
MERFORT, I., Pharmaceutical Biology
MÜHLHAUPT, R., Macromolecular Chemistry
OTTO, H. H., Pharmaceutical Technology
PLATTNER, D., Organic Chemistry
PRINZBACH, H., Organic Chemistry
RÖHR, C., Inorganic Chemistry
RÜCHARDT, C., Organic Chemistry
SCHULZ, G. E., Biochemistry
SCHWESINGER, R., Organic Chemistry
SEITZ, S., Ethnology
STADELBAUER, J., Geography
TIPPER, J. C., Geology
VAHRENKAMP, H., Inorganic Chemistry
WIMMENAUER, W., Geosciences

Faculty of Forestry and Environmental Sciences:

ABETZ, P., Forest Growth
BAUHAUS, J., Silviculture
BECKER, G., Forest Utilization and Work Science
BECKER, M., Forest Policy
BOPPRÉ, M., Forest Zoology
EISFELD, D., Forest Zoology
ESSMANN, H., Environmental Policy
FINK, S., Forest Botany
HILDEBRAND, E. E., Soil Sciences and Forest Nutrition
JAEGER, L., Meteorology
KOCH, B., Land Information Systems
KONOLD, W., Land Use Planning
KRINGS, T., Cultural Geography
LEWARK, S., Forest Utilization and Work Science
MAYER, H., Meteorology
MEIDINGER, E., Forest Management
MITSCHERLICH, G., Forest Growth
OESTEN, G., Forest Management
PELZ, D. R., Biometrics
REIF, A., Silviculture
RENNENBERG, H., Tree Science
ROEDER, A., Forest Management
SCHMIDT, U., Environmental Policy
SCHRÖDER, E.-J., Cultural Geography
SPIECKER, H., Forest Production
VOLZ, K., Forest Policy

Faculty of Law:

BLAUROCK, U., Economic Law
BLOY, R., Penal Law
ESER, A., Penal Law
FRISCH, W., Penal Law
HAEDICKE, M., Civil Law
HAGER, G., International Civil Law
HOHLOCH, G., International Civil Law
HOLLERBACH, A., History of Law, Church Law, Philosophy of Law
KÖBL, U., Social Insurance Law
LEIPOLD, D., Civil, Labour and Procedural Law
LIEBS, D., History of Modern Law
LÖWISCH, M., Civil, Labour, Social Insurance and Commercial Law
MERKT, H., International Civil Law
MURSWIEK, D., State Law
NEHLSEN-VON STRYCK, K., History of Law
PERRON, W., Penal Law
SCHOCH, F., Public Law
SCHWARZE, J., European and International Law
STÜRNER, R., Civil Law
TIEDEMANN, K., Criminal Law and Procedure

VOßKUHLE, A., History of Law, Philosophy of Law
WAHL, R., Administrative Law
WÜRTENBERGER, T., State Law

Faculty of Mathematics and Physics:

BAMBERGER, A., Experimental Physics
BANGERT, V., Mathematics
BLUMEN, A., Theoretical Physics
BRENN, R., Experimental Physics
BRIGGS, J. ST., Theoretical Physics
DZIUK, G., Applied Mathematics
EBBINGHAUS, H.-D., Mathematical Logic
EBERLEIN, E., Stochastics
FLUM, J., Mathematical Logic
GRABERT, H., Theoretical Physics
GROHE, M., Logic
HABERLAND, H., Experimental Physics
HEINZEL, T., Physics
HELM, H., Experimental Physics
HERMES, H., Logic
HERTEN, G., Physics
HONERKAMP, J., Theoretical Physics
JAKOBS, K., Physics
KLAR, H., Physics
KÖNIGSMANN, K., Physics
KRÖNER, D., Applied Mathematics
KUWERT, E., Analysis
LANDGRAF, U., Physics
LUDWIG, J., Physics
POHLMEYER, K., Theoretical Physics
RÖMER, H., Theoretical Physics
RÖPKE, H., Experimental Physics
RÜSCHENDORF, L., Stochastics
RUZICKA, M., Applied Mathematics
SCHMIDT, V., Physics
SCHMITT, H., Experimental Physics
SCHNEIDER, R., Mathematics
SIEBERT, B., Geometry
SOERGEL, W., Algebra
SPILKER, J., Actuarial Mathematics
STROBL, G., Experimental Physics
VAN DER BIJ, J., Theoretical Physics
WAGNER, F., Logic
WEIDEMÜLLER, M., Physics
WITTING, H., Applied Mathematics
WOLKE, D., Mathematics
ZIEGLER, M., Mathematical Logic

Faculty of Medicine:

AKTORIES, K., Pharmacology and Toxicology
BEHRENDS, J., Physiology
BESSLER, W., Immunology
BEYERSDORF, F., Cardiovascular Surgery
BIRNESSER, H., Sports Traumatology
BLUM, H., Gastroenterology
BODE, C., Cardiology
BOGDAN, CH., Microbiology
BORNER, C., Stem Cell Research
BRAND-SABERI, B., Anatomy and Cell Biology
BRANDIS, M., Paediatrics
BRANDSCH, R., Biochemistry
CHRIST, B., Anatomy
DASCHNER, F., Environmental Medicine
DECKER, K., Biochemistry
DICKHUT, H.-H., Rehabilitation and Sports Medicine
FAKLER, Physiology
FROMMHOLD, H., Radiology
FROTSCHER, M., Anatomy
FUNK, J., Eye Hospital
GEIGER, K., Anaesthesiology
GITSCH, G., Gynaecology
GOEPPERT, S., Medical Psychology
GUTTMAN, J., Anaesthesiology
HASSE, J., Surgery
HELLWIG, E., Dentistry
HOFFMAN, H.-D., Anatomy
HOPT, U., General and Visceral Surgery
HUANG, R., Anatomy
JACKISCH, R., Pharmacology and Toxicology
JONAS, Physiology
JONAS, J., Dentistry
KECECIOGLU, D., Paediatric Cardiology

KIST, M., Microbiology
KLAR, R., Medicine Informatics
KORINTHENBERG, R., Neurology and Muscular Diseases
KURZ, H., Anatomy
LANGER, M., Radiology
LASZIG, R., Otorhinolaryngology
LEVEN, K.-H., History of Medicine
MERTELSMANN, R., Internal Medicine
MEYER, D. K., Pharmacology and Toxicology
MOSER, E., Radiology
MÜLLER-QUERNHEIM, J., Pneumology
NIERNEYER, C., Paediatric Haemotology and Oncology
NIKKHAH, G., Neurosurgery
OSTERTAG, C., Neurosurgery
PAHL, H., Anaesthesiology
PANNEN, B., Anaesthesiology
PETER, H. H., Rheumatology
PETERS, C., Molecular Medicine
PFANNER, N., Biochemistry
PIRCHER, H., Immunology
POLLAK, S., Forensic Medicine
REICHELT, A., Orthopaedics
ROSPERT, S., Biochemistry
SCHEMPP, W., Cytogenetics
SCHMELZEISEN, R., Oral and Maxillofacial Surgery
SCHÖPF, E., Dermatology
SCHUMACHER, M., Medical Statistics
SIEBERT, F., Biophysics
STARK, B., Plastic and Hand Surgery
STARKE, K., Pharmacology and Toxicology
STRUB, J., Dentistry
SÜDKAMP, N. P., Traumatology
SZABO, B., Pharmacology and Toxicology
TRÖHLER, U., History of Medicine
TROPSCHUG, M., Biochemistry
VOLK, B., Neuropathology
VON TROSCHKE, J., Medical Sociology
VOOS, W., Biochemistry
WALZ, G., Nephrology
WERNER, M., Pathology
WETTERAUER, U., Urology
WOLF, U., Human Genetics and Anthropology
ZENTNER, J. F., General Neurosurgery

Faculty of Philology:

ADAMS, J., American Literature
ANZ, H., Scandinavian Studies
ARNHAMMER, A., German Philology
AUER, P., German Philology
BANNERT, R., Scandinavian Studies
BERG, W. B., Literature
BLANK, W., German Philology
BÖNING, T., German Philology
CHEURÉ, E., Slavonics
DANGEL-PELLOQUIN, E., German Philology
DITTMANN, J., German Philology
DREWS, P., Slavonics
FLUDERNIK, M., English Philology
GÜNTHER, H.-C.
HAHN, U., German Philology
HALFORD, B., Oral Language
HAUSMANN, R., Romance Philology
HERRMANN, H.-P., German Philology
HESS, R., Romance Philology
HOCHBRUCK, W., Literature
JURT, J., Literature
KAISER, G., German Philology
KÄSTNER, H.-J., German Philology
KILIAN, E., Literature
KNOOP, U., German Philology
KOCHENDÖRFER, G., German Philology
KOHL, N., English Literature
KORTE, B., Literature
KORTMANN, B., English Philology
KÜHNE, U., German Philology
KUNZE, K., German Philology
LEFÈVRE, E., Classical Philology
LÖNKER, F., German Philology
MAIR, C., Caribbean Language and Literature
MATTHEWS, R., Linguistics

MAUSER, W., German Philology
MICHEL, W., German Philology
MÜRB, F., German Philology
PIETZCKER, C., German Philology
PILCH, H., English Philology
PÖRKSEN, U., German Philology
PÜTZ, M., English Philology
RENNER, R., German Philology
SASSE, G., German Philology
SCHÄFER, E., Latin Philology
SCHMIDT, J., German Philology
SCHOLZ, R., German Philology
SCHWAN, W., German Philology
SIEGERT, R., German Philology
RAIBLE, W., Romance Philology
RIX, H., Indogermanic Languages
THOMAS, C., German Philology
TICHY, E., Indogermanic Languages
TRISTRAM, H., German Philology
WEIHER, E., Slavonics
ZIMMERMAN, B., German Philology
ZUTT, H., German Philology

Faculty of Philosophy:

ASCHE, R., Modern History
BERGER, C., Music
BRÜGGEMEIER, F.-J., Economic and Social History
DEGELE, N., Sociology
ESSBACH, W., Sociology
FIGAL, G., Philosophy
GEHRKE, H.-J., Ancient History
GREINER, P., Sinology
HINÜBER, O., Indology
JÄGER, W., Political Science
JANHSEN, A., History of Art
KUNTZ, A., Ethnology
KÜSTER, K., Music
LAUT, J.-P., Islamic History
MARTIN, J., Ancient History
MATTER, M., Ethnology
MERTENS, D., Medieval History
MEZGER, W., Ethnology
MORDEK, H., Medieval History
NEUTATZ, D., Modern and East European History
NUBER, H. U., Roman Provincial Archaeology
PALETSCHEK, S., Modern History
PRATER, A., History of Art
REBSTOCK, U., Islamic History
RIESCHER, G., Political History
RÜLAND, J., Political History
SCHLEHE, J., Ethnology
SCHLINK, W., History of Art
SCHMIDT, G., Medieval Latin Philology
SCHNITZLER, G., Modern German Literature and Music
SCHWENGEL, H., Sociology
SEITZ, S., Ethnology
SENGER, H., Sinology
STEIBLE, H., Oriental Philology
STEUER, H., Prehistory
STRAHM, C., Prehistory
STROCKA, V., Classical Archaeology
TRÖHLER, U., History of Medicine
WARLAND, R., Christian Archaeology and Byzantine Art
WINDLER, C., Modern History
WINTERLING, A., Ancient History
ZOTZ, T., Medieval History

Faculty of Theology:

ALBUS, M., Pedagogics and Catechism
ENDERS, M., Philosophy
FRANK, S., Old Church History
GLATZEL, N., Christian Society
HOPING, H., Dogmatics and Liturgical History
IRSIGLER, H., Old Testament
NOTHELLE-WILDFEUER, U., Pastoral Theology
OBERLINNER, L., New Testament Literature
POMPEY, H., Caritas Science and Social Work
RAFFELT, A., Dogmatics
SCHOCKENHOFF, E., Moral Theology

SMOLINSKY, H., New Church History
TZSCHEETZSCH, W., Pedagogics and Catechism
UHDE, B., History
VERWEYEN, H. J., Fundamental Theology
WALTER, P., Dogmatics
WARLAND, R., Christian Archaeology and Art History
WINDISCH, H., Pastoral Theology
ZAPP, H., Church Law

BAUHAUS-UNIVERSITÄT WEIMAR

Geschwister-Scholl-Str. 8, 99421 Weimar

Telephone: (3643) 58-0

Fax: (3643) 58-1120

E-mail: rektor@uni-weimar.de

Internet: www.uni-weimar.de

Founded 1860

Academic year: October to June

Chancellor: Dr-Ing. HEIKO SCHULTZ

Rector: Prof. Dr GERD ZIMMERMANN

Vice-Rectors: Prof. Dr KARL BEUCKE, Prof. LORENZ ENGELL, Prof. Dr WOLFGANG SATTLER

Librarian: Dr FRANK SIMON-RITZ

Number of teachers: 83

Number of students: 5,000

Publications: *Der Bogen* (9 a year), *Philosophische Diskurse* (1 a year), *Schriften der Bauhaus-Universität* (2 a year), *Thesis* (6 a year), *VERSO-Architekturtheorie* (1 a year)

DEANS

Faculty of Architecture: Prof. BERND RUDOLF
Faculty of Arts: Prof. HERMANN STAMM
Faculty of Construction Engineering: Prof. Dr-Ing. JOCHEN STARK
Faculty of Media: Prof. Dr MATTHIAS MAIER

PROFESSORS

Faculty of Architecture (tel. (3643) 583113; fax (3643) 583114; e-mail lars-christian .uhlig@archit.uni-weimar.de; internet www .uni-weimar.de/cms/?297):

BARZ-MALFATTI, H., Design and Settlement Planning I
BÜTTNER-HYMAN, H., Principles of Design
CHRIST, W., Design and Town Planning I
DONATH, D., Information Technology in the Architectural Planning Process
GLEITER, J. H., Design and Architectural Theory
GLÜCKLICH, D., Principles of Ecological Construction
GRASHORN, B., Design and Building Construction
GUMPP, R., Design and Structural Engineering
HASSENPFLUG, D., Sociology and Social History of Towns
KÄSTNER, A., Technology of Building Design
KIEßL, K., Building Ecology and Air-conditioning
KLEIN, B., Design and Town Planning II
KOPPÁNDY, J., Landscape Architecture
LOUDON, M., Design and Industrial Buildings
Care of Historic Monuments: (vacant)
NENTWIG, B., Building Industry and Building Management
RIEß, H., Design and Building Construction I
RUDOLF, B., Theory of Building Construction
RUTH, J., Structural Engineering
SCHIRMBECK, E., Design and Interior Design
SCHMITZ, K.-H., Design and Building Construction II
SCHULZ, M., Construction Technology

STAMM-TESKE, W., Design and House-Building
WELCH GUERRA, M., Space Research, Development and Land Planning

Faculty of Arts (tel. (3643) 583206; fax (3643) 583230; e-mail christa.billing@gestaltung .uni-weimar.de; internet www.uni-weimar .de/gestaltung):

BABTIST, G., Product Design
BACHHUBER, L., Free Art
BARTELS, H., Product Design
BOCK, W., Art Science
FRÖHLICH, E., Free Art
GRONERT, S., Art Science
HINTERBERGER, N. W., Free Art
HOLZWARTH, W., Visual Communication
NEMITZ, B., Free Art
PREIß, A., Art Science
RUTHERFORD, J., Visual Communication
SATTLER, W., Product Design
SCHAWELKA, K., Art Science
STAMM, H., Visual Communication
WEBER, O., Art Science
WENTSCHER, H., Visual Communication

Faculty of Construction Engineering (tel. (3643) 584415; fax (3643) 584413; e-mail elke.lindner@bauing.uni-weimar.de; internet www.uni-weimar.de/bauing):

ALFEN, Construction Management
BARGSTÄDT, Construction Site Management
BECKMANN, Waste Management
BERGMANN, Experimental Analysis of Materials and Structures
BEUCKE, Informatics in Construction
BIDLINGMAIER, Waste Management
BRANNOLTE, General Building Materials
BUCHER, Construction Engineering
FREUNDT, Applied Mathematics
GÜRLEBECK, Applied Mathematics
HACK, Preparation of Materials and Recycling
HÜBLER, Information Processing
KAPS, Chemistry for Building
KÖNKE, Building Statistics
KORNADT, Physics of Building
KRANAWETTREISER, Electrical Engineering
LONDONG, Urban Water Management
MÜLLER, Preparation of Materials and Recycling
RAUE, Solid Buildings I
RAUTENSTRAUCH, Wood and Stone Construction
RUTH, Solid Buildings II
SCHANZ, Soil Mechanics
SCHWARZ, Earthquake Centre
SCHWARZ, Surveying
STARK, General Building Materials
TRABERT, Construction Engineering Planning
WERNER, Steel Construction
WITT, Foundation Engineering

Faculty of Media (tel. (3643) 583703; fax (3643) 583701; e-mail medien@uni-weimar .de; internet www.uni-weimar.de/medien):

ENGELL, L., Media Philosophy
FRÖHLICH, B., Virtual Reality Systems
GEELHAAR, J., Interface Design
GROSS, T., Computer Supported Cooperative Work
HENNIG-THURAU, T., Marketing and Media
KISSEL, W., Media Events
LEEKER, M., History and Theory of Artificial Worlds
MAIER, M. (acting), Media Management
MINARD, R., Electronic Sound Production
SIEGERT, B., History and Theory of Cultural Technologies
STEIN, B., Content Management and Web Technology
WÜTHRICH, C., Graphical Data Processing

BAYERISCHE JULIUS-MAXIMILIANS-UNIVERSITÄT WÜRZBURG

Sanderring 2, 97070 Würzburg
Telephone: (931) 310
Fax: (931) 312600
E-mail: universitaet@zv.uni-wuerzburg.de
Internet: www.uni-wuerzburg.de

Founded 1582
State control
Academic year: October to September

President: Prof. Dr rer. nat. A. FORCHEL
Vice-Presidents: Prof. Dr phil. M. GOTZ, Prof. Dr phil. M. LOHSE, Dr rer. nat. E. PACHE, Dr rer. nat. W. RIEDEL
Chancellor: E. KRUSE
Chief Librarian: Dr phil. KARL SÜDEKUM

Library of 3,000,000 vols
Number of teachers: 900
Number of students: 20,500

Publications: *Blick* (2 a year), *Jahresbericht*, *Würzburg Heute* (2 a year)

DEANS

Faculty of Biology: Prof. Dr MARTIN MUELLER
Faculty of Catholic Theology: Prof. Dr HANS-GEORG ZIEBERTZ
Faculty of Chemistry and Pharmacy: Prof. Dr FRANK WUERTHNER
Faculty of Economics: Prof. Dr MARTIN KUKUK
Faculty of Law: Prof. Dr CHRISTOPH WEBER
Faculty of Mathematics and Computer Science: Prof. Dr PHUOC TRAN-GIA
Faculty of Medicine: Prof. Dr MATTHIAS FROSCH
Faculty of Philosophy I (Historical, Philological, Culture- and Geographical Sciences): Prof. Dr WOLFGANG REIDEL
Faculty of Philosophy II (Philosophy, Education Sciences and Social Sciences): Prof. Dr HANS-PETER KRUEGER PAULI
Faculty of Physics and Astronomy: Prof. Dr REINHOLD RUECKL

PROFESSORS

Faculty of Biology (Am Hubland, Biozentrum, 97074 Würzburg; tel. (931) 3184440; e-mail i-tbi@biozentrum.uni-wuerzburg.de):

DANDEKAR, TH., Bioinformatics
GOEBEL, W., Microbiology
HEDRICH, R., Botany
HEISENBERG, M., Genetics
LINSENMAIR, K. E., Zoology
MÜLLER, M., Pharmaceutical Biology
RIEDERER, M., Botany
SCHEER, U., Zoology
ZIMMERMANN, U., Biotechnology

Faculty of Catholic Theology (Sanderring 2, 97070 Würzburg; tel. (931) 3182252; fax (931) 3182673; e-mail thde001@mail .uni-wuerzburg.de):

DROESSER, G., Christian Sociology
DÜNZL, F., Church History
ERNST, S., Moral Theology
GARHAMMER, E., Pastoral Theology
HALLERMANN, H., Theological Law
HEININGER, B., New Testament Exegesis
KLAUSNITZER, W., Basic Theology and Comparative Religion
MEUFFELS, O., Dogmatics
SEIDL, TH., Old Testament Exegesis and Biblical Oriental Languages
WEISS, W., History of the Frankish Church
ZIEBERTZ, H.-G., Religious Instruction

Faculty of Chemistry and Pharmacy (Am Hubland, 97074 Würzburg; tel. (931) 8885364; fax (931) 8884607; e-mail hopf .dekanat@uni-wuerzburg.de):

BRAUNSCHWEIG, H., Inorganic Chemistry
BRINGMANN, G., Organic Chemistry
FISCHER, U., Biochemistry
HOLZGRABE, U., Pharmaceutical Chemistry
TACKE, R., Inorganic Chemistry

WÜRTHNER, F., Organic Chemistry
ZIMMERMANN, I., Pharmaceutical Technology

Faculty of Economics (Sanderring 2, 97070 Würzburg; tel. (931) 312901; fax (931) 312101; e-mail f-wifak@wifak .uni-wuerzburg.de):

BERTHOLD, N., Political Economy
BOFINGER, P., Political Economy
BOGASCHEWSKY, R., Industrial Management
FEHR, J., Economics
FREERICKS, W., Business Management Taxation
KUKUK, M., Econometrics
LENZ, H., Accounting and Consultancy
MEYER, M., Marketing
SCHULZ, N., Political Economy
THOME, R., Economics and Computer Science
WÄLDE, K., Political Economy
WENGER, E., Banking

Faculty of Law (Domerschulstr. 16, 97070 Würzburg; tel. (931) 3182389; fax (931) 3182477; e-mail dekanat@jura .uni-wuerzburg.de):

DREIER, H., Philosophy of Law, Political and Administrative Law
HARKE, J., Civil Law, Roman Law and Historical Comparative Law
HILGENDORF, E., Criminal Law, Criminal Procedural Law
KIENINGER, E.-M., German and European Civil Law, International Civil Law
LAUBENTHAL, K., Criminology and Penal Law
PACHE, E., State Law, International Law, International Economic Law, Economic Administrative Law
REMIEN, O., Civil Law and European Economic Law
SCHERER, I., Civil Law
SCHULZE-FIELITZ, H., Public Law, Environmental Law and Administrative Science
SOSNITZA, O., Civil Law
SUERBAUM, J., Public and Administrative Law
WEBER, C., Civil Law and Labour Law
WEITZEL, J., Civil Law, History of European Law and Procedural Law
ZIESCHANG, F., Criminal Law, Criminal Procedural Law

Faculty of Mathematics and Computer Science (Am Hubland, 97074 Würzburg; tel. (931) 8885021; fax (931) 8884614; e-mail dekan@mathinfo.uni-wuerzburg.de):

ALBERT, J., Computer Science
DOBROWOLSKI, M., Applied Mathematics
FALK, M., Mathematical Statistics
GRUNDHÖFER, TH., Mathematics
HELMKE, U., Mathematics
KANZOW, CH., Applied Mathematics
KOLLA, R., Computer Science
MÜLLER, P., Mathematics and Algebra
NOLTEMEIER, H., Computer Science
PUPPE, F., Computer Science
RUSCHEWEYH, S., Mathematics
SCHILLING, K., Technical Computer Science
TRAN-GIA, P., Computer Science
WAGNER, K. W., Computer Science
WEIGAND, H.-G., Teaching of Mathematics

Faculty of Medicine (Josef-Schneider-Str. 2, Klinikum (Haus D7), 97080 Würzburg; tel. (931) 20155458; fax (931) 20153860; e-mail f-medizin@uni-wuerzburg.de):

BECKMANN, H., Psychiatry
BRÖCKER, E.-B., Dermatology, Venerology and Allergology
DIETL, J., Obstetrics and Gynaecology
DRENCKHAHN, D., Anatomy
EINSELE, H., Internal Medicine
ELERT, O., Thoracic and Cardiovascular Surgery
ERTL, G., Internal Medicine

EULERT, J., Orthopaedics
FLENTJE, M., Radiology
FROSCH, M., Hygiene and Microbiology
GREHN, F., Ophthalmology
HACKER, J., Molecular Biology of Infections
HAGEN, R., Molecular Biology of Infections
HAHN, D., Radiodiagnostics
HELMS, J., Otorhinolaryngology
HÖHN, H., Human Genetics
HÜNIG, T., Virology
KARSCHIN, A., Neurophysiology
KLAIBER, B., Dentistry
KOEPSELL, H., Anatomy
KUHN, M., Physiology
LOHSE, M., Pharmacology
LUTZ, W., Toxicology
MÜLLER-HERMELINK, H. K., Pathology
PATZELT, D., Forensic and Social Medicine
RAPP, U., Medical Radiology
REINERS, CH., Medical Radiology
RETHWILM, A., Virology
REUTHER, J., Dentistry, Maxillofacial Surgery
RICHTER, E.-J., Dental and Facial Medicine
RIEDMILLER, H., Urology
ROEWER, N., Anaesthesiology
ROOSEN, K., Neurosurgery
SCHARTL, M., Physiological Chemistry
SEBALD, W., Physiological Chemistry
SENDTNER, M., Clinical Neurobiology
SPEER, C., Paediatrics
STELLZIG-EISENHAUER, A., Dental and Facial Orthopaedics
STOLBERG, M., History of Medicine
TOYKA, K. V., Neurology
WALTER, U., Clinical Biochemistry and Pathobiochemistry
WARNKE, A., Child Psychiatry

Faculty of Philosophy I and Institute of Geosciences (Residenzplatz 2, 97070 Würzburg; tel. (931) 312879; fax (931) 8887050; e-mail f-philfak1@uni-wuerzburg.de):

BRÜCKNER, H., Indology
BRUSNIAK, F., Music Education, Teaching of Music
ERLER, M., Classical Philology
HANNICK, CH., Slavic Philology
HETTRICH, H., Comparative Linguistics
KONRAD, U., Musicology
KUHN, D., Oriental Philology
SCHIER, W., Prehistoric Archaeology
SCHOLZ, U. W., Classical Philology
SCHÖNBEIN, M., Japanology
SINN, U., Classical Archaeology
WILHELM, G., Oriental Philology

Faculty of Philosophy II (Am Hubland, 97074 Würzburg; tel. (931) 8885221; fax (931) 8884601; e-mail f-philfak2@mail.uni-wuerzburg.de):

ACHILLES, J., American Studies
ALT, P.-A., History of Modern German Literature
ALTGELD, W., Modern and Contemporary History
BRUNNER, H., German Philology
BURGSCHMIDT, E., English Linguistics
DAXELMÜLLER, C., European Ethnology
DIETZ, K., Early History
FLACHENECKER, H., Frankish History
FUCHS, F., Medieval History
KOHL, ST. M., English Literature and British Cultural Studies
KUMMER, S., History of Art
NEUGEBAUER, W., Modern History
PENZKOFER, G., Romance Philology
PFOTENHAUER, H., History of Modern German Literature
PÖTTERS, W., Romance Philology
WOLF, N. R., German Linguistics

Faculty of Physics and Astronomy (Am Hubland, 97074 Würzburg; tel. (931) 8885720; fax (931) 8885508; e-mail f-physik@physik.uni-wuerzburg.de):

CLAESSEN, R., Experimental Physics

DYAKONOV, V., Experimental Physics, Energy Research
FORCHEL, A., Semiconductor Technology and Physics
GERBER, G., Experimental Physics
HANKE, W., Theoretical Physics
HEUER, D., Physics Teaching
JAKOB, P., Biophysics
KINZEL, W., Computational Physics
MANNHEIM, K., Astronomy
MOLENKAMP, L., Experimental Physics
RÜCKL, R., Theoretical Physics
UMBACH, E., Experimental Physics

BERGISCHE UNIVERSITÄT WUPPERTAL

Gaussstr. 20, 42097 Wuppertal

Telephone: (202) 439-1
Fax: (202) 439-2901
Internet: www.uni-wuppertal.de

Founded 1972
State control
Language of instruction: German
Academic year: October to September

Rector: Prof. Dr VOLKER RONGE
Co-Rector for Academic Affairs: Prof. Dr ANNEGRET MAACK
Co-Rector for Planning and Finance: Prof. Dr HEINZ-REINER TREICHEL
Co-Rector for Science and Research: Prof. Dr WOLFGANG SPIEGEL
Chancellor: Dr HANS-JOACHIM VON BUCHKA
Librarian: UWE STADLER

Number of teachers: 298
Number of students: 13,500

DEANS

Faculty of Architecture, Design and Art: Prof. Dr FRANK WERNER
Faculty of Civil, Mechanical and Safety Engineering: Prof. Dr DIETRICH HOEBORN
Faculty of Economics and Social Sciences: Prof. Dr LAMBERT T. KOCH
Faculty of Educational Science: Prof. Dr ANDREAS SCHAARSCHUCH
Faculty of Electrical, Information and Media Engineering: Prof. Dr BERND TIBKEN
Faculty of Humanities: Prof. Dr HANS-JOACHIM LIETZMANN
Faculty of Mathematics and Natural Sciences: Prof. Dr REINT EUJEN

BRANDENBURGISCHE TECHNISCHE UNIVERSITÄT COTTBUS

Postfach 101344, 03013 Cottbus
Konrad-Wachsmann-Allee 1, 03046 Cottbus

Telephone: (355) 69-0
Fax: (355) 69-2108
E-mail: intoff@tu-cottbus.de
Internet: www.tu-cottbus.de

Founded 1991
State control
Academic year: October to July

Chancellor: WOLFGANG SCHRÖDER
Pres.: Prof. Dr WALTHER CH. ZIMMERLI
Vice-Pres. for Academics: MATTHIAS KOZIOL
Vice-Pres. for Research: Prof. Dr-Ing. CHRISTOPH LEYENS
Librarian: MAGDALENE FREWER-SAUVIGNY

Library of 577,000 vols, 2,000 periodicals, 80,000 technical standards
Number of teachers: 637
Number of students: 5,600

Publications: Bodenschutz (4 a year), Bodenschutz und Rekultivierung (10–12 a year), Energie, Forum der Forschung, Wissenschaftsmagazin der BTU Cottbus (1 a year), Lehrstuhl Industriesoziologie (2 a year)

DEANS

Faculty of Architecture and Civil Engineering: Prof. Dipl.-Ing. HEINZ NAGLER
Faculty of Environmental Sciences and Process Engineering: Prof. Dr GERHARD WIEGLEB
Faculty of Mathematics, Physics and Information Sciences: Prof. Dr JÜRGEN REIF
Faculty of Mechanical Engineering, Electrical Engineering and Industrial Engineering: Prof. Dr BERND VIEHWEGER

CHRISTIAN-ALBRECHTS UNIVERSITÄT ZU KIEL

24098 Kiel

Telephone: (431) 88000
Fax: (431) 880-2072
E-mail: mail@uni-kiel.de
Internet: www.uni-kiel.de

Founded 1665
State control
Academic year: October to July (two terms)

Rector: Prof. Dr JÖRN ECKERT
Vice-Rectors: Prof. Dr THOMAS BAUER, Prof. Dr GERHARD FOUQUET
Chancellor: Dr OLIVER HERRMANN
Librarian: Dr ELSE M. WISCHERMANN

Number of teachers: 600
Number of students: 20,000

Publications: Christiana Albertina (2 a year), Unizeit (7 a year)

DEANS

Faculty of Agricultural and Nutritional Sciences: Prof. Dr SIEGFRIED WOLFFRAM
Faculty of Economics and Social Sciences: Prof. Dr ANDREAS DREXL
Faculty of Engineering: Prof. Dr PETER SEEGEBRECHT
Faculty of Law: Prof. Dr jur. JOACHIM JICKELI
Faculty of Mathematics and Natural Sciences: Prof. Dr JÜRGEN GROTEMEYER
Faculty of Medicine: Prof. Dr MICHAEL ILLERT
Faculty of Philosophy: Prof. Dr SIEGFRIED OESCHLE
Faculty of Theology: Prof. Dr theol. ULRICH HÜBNER

PROFESSORS

Faculty of Agricultural and Nutritional Sciences (Hermann-Rodewald-Str. 4, 24098 Kiel; tel. (431) 880-2591; fax (431) 880-7334; e-mail dekanat@agrar.uni-kiel.de; internet www.agrar.uni-kiel.de):

ABDULAI, A., Food Economics and Food Policy
BRUHN, M., Agricultural Marketing
FOHRER, N., Hydrology and Water Resources Management
HENNING, C., Agricultural Policy
HORN, R., Soil Science
JUNG, C., Plant Breeding and Genetics
KAGE, H., Crop Science
KALM, E., Animal Breeding and Genetics
KRIETER, J., Animal Husbandry, Quality of Products
LATACZ-LOHMANN, U., Farm Management and Production Economics
LOY, J.-P., Agricultural Market Theory
MÜLLER, M. J., Internal Medicine, Human Nutrition
MÜLLER, R. A. E., Agricultural Economics, Information, Innovation
RIMBACH, G., Food Science
ROOSEN, J., Health Economics
ROWECK, H., Landscape Ecology
SATTELMACHER, B., Plant Nutrition
SCHALLENBERGER, E., Animal Husbandry, Hygienics
SCHWARZ, K., Food Technology
SUSENBETH, A., Animal Nutrition
TAUBE, F., Grass and Forage Science, Organic Farming

VERREET, J.-A., Phytopathology, Plant Diseases

WOLFFRAM, S., Animal Nutrition and Nutritional Physiology

WYSS, U., Phytopathology, Biotechnology

Faculty of Economics and Social Sciences (Wilhelm-Seelig-Platz 1, 24098 Kiel; tel. (431) 880-2140; fax (431) 880-1691; e-mail dekanat@bwl.uni-kiel.de; internet www.bwl.uni-kiel.de):

ALBERS, S., Innovation, New Media and Marketing

BRÖCKER, J., Regional Science

DREXL, A., Production Management and Logistics

FRIEDL, B., Controlling

HERWARTZ, H., Econometrics

KLAPPER, D., Marketing

KRAUSE, J., Politics

KRUBER, K.-P., Political and Economic Education

LIESENFELD, R., Statistics and Empirical Economics

LUX, T., Monetary Economics and International Financial Markets

NIPPEL, P., Financial Management

RAFF, H., Industrial Economics

REQUATE, T., Economics of Innovation, Competition and Institutions

SEIDL, C., Public Finance and Choice Theory

SNOWER, D., Economics

VEIT, K.-R., Accounting

WALTER, A., Entrepreneurship and Innovation Management

WOHLTMANN, H.-W., Macroeconomics

WOLF, J., Organization

Faculty of Engineering (Kaiserstr. 2, 24143 Kiel; tel. (431) 880-6001; fax (431) 880-6003; e-mail dekanat@tf.uni-kiel.de; internet www.tf.uni-kiel.de):

BERGHAMMER, R., Computer-Aided Program Development

BROCKS, W., Material Mechanics

DIRKS, H., Electromagnetic Field Theory

FAUPEL, F., Multicomponent Materials

FÖLL, H., General Materials Science

FUCHS, F. W., Power Electronics and Electrical Devices

HACKBUSCH, W., Practical Mathematics

HANUS, M., Programming Languages and Compiler Construction

HANXLEDEN, R. VON, Real-time and Embedded Systems

HEUBERGER, A., Semiconductor Technology

HEUTE, U., Circuits and System Theory

HÖHER, P., Information and Coding Theory Laboratory

JÄGER, W., Centre for Microanalysis

JANSEN, K., Theory of Parallelism

KLINKENBUSCH, I., Computational Electromagnetics Group

KNÖCHEL, R., Microwave Group

KOCH, R., Multimedia Information Processing

LUTTENBERGER, N., Communication Systems

RÖCK, H., Automation and Control Engineering

ROEVER, W. P. DE, Software Technology

ROSENKRANZ, W., Communications

SCHIMMLER, M., Computer Engineering

SCHNEIDER, R., Scientific Computing

SEEGEBRECHT, P., Semiconductor Electronics

SOMMER, G., Cognitive Systems

SRIVASTAV, A., Discrete Optimization

THALHEIM, B., Information Systems Engineering

WEPPNER, W., Sensors and Solid State Ionics

WILKE, T., Theoretical Computer Science

Faculty of Law (Leibnizstr. 4, 24098 Kiel; tel. (431) 880-2125; fax (431) 880-1689; e-mail dekanat@law.uni-kiel.de; internet www.uni-kiel.de/fakultas/jura):

ALEXY, R., Public Law and Legal Philosophy

ECKERT, J., History of German and European Law, Civil Law, Commercial Law

EINSELE, D., Civil Law, Commercial Law, Private International Law, Comparative Law

FISCHER, M., Civil, Commercial and Economic Tax Law

FROMMEL, M., Criminology and Criminal Law

HOYER, A., Penal Law and Procedure

IGL, G., Public Law, Social Law

JICKELI, J., Civil Law, Commercial Law

KRACK, R., Penal Law and Procedure

MEYER-PRITZL, R., Civil Law, Roman Law, History of Law in Modern Times, Comparative Law

MUTIUS, A. VON, Public Law and Administration

REUTER, D., Civil, Commercial and Economic Law

SCHACK, H., International Civil Law, Private and Civil Trial Law, Copyright Law

SCHMIDT-JORTZIG, E., Public Law

SMID, S., Civil Law and Procedure

TRUNK, A., Civil and Civil Trial Law, International Private Law and Comparative Law

ZIMMERMANN, A., German and Foreign Public, International, and European Law, and General Theory of the State

Faculty of Mathematics and Natural Sciences (Christian-Albrechts-Platz 4, 24098 Kiel; tel. (431) 880-2128; fax (431) 880-2320; e-mail dekanat@mnf.uni-kiel.de; internet www.uni-kiel.de/fakultas/mathnat):

ALBAN, S., Pharmaceutical Biology

BÄHR, J., Geography

BAUER, T., Ecology

BAYRHUBER, H., Teaching Methods of Biology

BENDER, H., Mathematics

BENSCH, W., Inorganic Chemistry

BERGWEILER, W., Mathematics

BERNDT, R., Solid-State Physics

BETTEN, D., Mathematics

BILGER, W., Ecology

BISCHOF, K., Marine Biology

BLASCHEK, W., Pharmaceutical Biology

BODENDIEK, R., Mathematics

BÖNING, C., Theoretical Oceanography

BONITZ, M., Theoretical Physics

BORK, H.-R., Ecology System Research

BOSCH, T., General Zoology

BRENDELBERGER, H., Zoology and Limnology

CEMIČ, L., Mineralogy and Petrology

CLEMENT, B., Pharmaceutical Chemistry

COLIJN, F., Coastal Ecology

CORVES, C., Geography

DAHMKE, A., Applied Geology

DEMUTH, R., Teaching of Chemistry

DEPMEIER, W., Mineralogy and Crystallography

DEVEY, C., Geology

DIERSSEN, K., Botany

DOMMENGET, D., Meteorology

DULLO, W. C., Palaeo-Oceanography

DUTTMANN, R., Geography

EISENHAUER, A., Marine Ecogeology

EULER, M., Teaching of Physics

FRANK, M., Geology

GÖTZE, H.-J., Geophysics

GROOTES, P., Experimental Physics, Isotope Research

GROTEMEYER, J., Physical Chemistry

HACKNEY, R., Geophysics

HAMANN, M., Teaching Methods of Biology

HANEL, R., Fishery Biology

HÄNSEL, W., Pharmaceutical Chemistry

HARTKE, B., Theoretical Chemistry

HARTL, G. B., Zoology

HASSENPFLUG, W., Geography

HEBER, J., Mathematics

HELBIG, V., Physics

HERGES, R., Organic Chemistry

HERZIG, P., Marine Science

HOERNLE, K., Vulcanology, Magmatic Petrology

HOPPE, H. G., Microbiology

IMHOFF, J., Marine Microbiology

IRLE, A., Probability Theory and Mathematical Statistics

KEMPKEN, F., Botany

KIPP, L., Experimental Physics

KOESTER, D., Astronomy and Astrophysics, Theoretical Physics

KÖNIG, H., Mathematics

KÖRTZINGER, A., Organic Marine Chemistry

KRUPINSKA, K., Cell Biology

KUHNT, W., Geology and Palaeontology

KUNZE, I., Pharmaceutical Chemistry

LATIF, M., Meterology

LEIPPE, M., Zoology

LINDHORST, T., Organic Chemistry

LOCHTE, K., Plankton

LÜNING, U., Organic Chemistry

MACKE, A., Meteorology

MÄDER, H., Physical Chemistry

MAGNUSSEN, O. M., Experimental Physics

MAYERLE, R., Applied Coastal Geology

MIKELSKIS-SEIFERT, S., Teaching Methods of Physics

MÜLLER, B., Pharmaceutical Technology

MÜLLER, D., Mathematics

MÜLLER, M., Physics

NELLE, O. A., Ecology

NERDEL, C., Teaching Methods of Chemistry

NEWIG, J., Geography

PEHLKE, E., Theoretical Physics

PIEL, A., Experimental Physics

PRECHTL, H., Teaching Methods of Biology

RABBEL, W., Geophysics

REISE, K., Biological Oceanography

RESTON, T. J., Marine Geophysics

REVILLA DIEZ, J., Economy of Geography

RIEBESELL, U., Marine Biology

ROEDER, T., Zoology

ROHR, G. VON, Geography

RÖSLER, U., Stochastics

RUPRECHT, E., Meteorology

SAUTER, M., Botany

SCHÄFER, P., Geology

SCHANZE, S., Teaching Methods of Chemistry

SCHENK, V., Petrology and Mineralogy

SCHMIDT, R., Mathematics

SCHMITZ-STREIT, R. A., Microbiology

SCHNACK, D., Ichthyology

SCHNEIDER, R., Geology

SCHÖNHEIT, P., Microbiology

SCHREMPP, B., Theoretical Physics

SCHULZ-FRIEDRICH, R., Botany

SCHUSTER, H. G., Theoretical Physics

SEND, U., Physical Oceanography

SOMMER, U., Sea-Floor Ecology

SPENGLER, U., Teaching Methods of Mathematics

SPINAS, O., Logic

SPINDLER, M., Polar Ecology

STATTEGGER, K., Geology and Palaeontology

STELLMACHER, B., Mathematics

STERR, H., Physical Geography

STOCK, N., Inorganic Chemistry

STOFFERS, P., Geology

SUESS, E., Marine Environmental Geology

TEMPS, F., Physical Chemistry

TUCZEK, F., Inorganic Chemistry

UHLARZ, H., Botany

VISBECK, M., Physical Oceanography

VON KLITZING, R., Physical Chemistry

WAHL, M., Marine Biology and Zoology

WALLACE, D., Marine Chemistry

WALTHER, G., Teaching of Mathematics

WILLEBRAND, J., Oceanography
WIMMER-SCHWEINGRUBER, R., Experimental Physics

Faculty of Medicine (Christian-Albrechts-Platz 4, 24098 Kiel; tel. (431) 880-2126; fax (431) 880-2129; e-mail dekanat@med.uni-kiel.de; internet www.uni-kiel.de/fak/med/med.html):

ALBERS, H.-K., Dentistry
ALDENHOFF, J., Psychiatry, Psychotherapy
ALZHEIMER, C., Psychology
AMBROSCH, P., Otorhinolaryngology
BARON, R., Neurology
BLEICH, M., Physiology
CREMER, J., Surgery
DEUSCHL, G., Neurology and Neurophysiology
FICKENSCHER, H., Medical Microbiology
FISCHER-BRANDIES, H., Dentistry
FÖLSCH, U. R., Internal Medicine
GERBER, W.-D., Clinical Psychology
GIESELER, F., Internal Medicine
GLÜER, C., Medicinal Physics
GROTE, W., Human Genetics
HASSENPFLUG, J., Orthopaedics
HELLER, M., Radiological Diagnosis
HENZE, E., Nuclear Medicine
HERDEGEN, T., Physiology, Molecular Pharmacology
ILLERT, M., Physiology
JANSEN, O., Neuroradiology
JONAT, W., Gynaecology and Obstetrics
JÜNEMANN, K.-P., Urology
JUST, U., Biochemistry
KAATSCH, H.-J., Legal Medicine
KABELITZ, D., Medical Microbiology and Immunology
KALTHOFF, H., Immunology and Cell Biochemistry
KERN, M., Dentistry
KIMMIG, B. N., Clinical Radiology
KLÖPPEL, G., Pathology and Pathological Anatomy
KNEBA, M., Internal Medicine
KOVACS, G., Clinical Radiology
KRAMER, H.-H., Child Medicine, Child Cardiology
KRAWCZAK, M., Human Genetics
KREMER, B., Surgery
KUNZENDORF, U., Internal Medicine, Nephrology
LUCIUS, R., Anatomy
LÜLLMANN-RAUCH, R., Anatomy
MASER, E., Toxicology
MEHDORN, H., Neurosurgery
METTLER, L., Gynaecology
OEHMICHEN, M., Legal Medicine
PARWARESCH, R., Haematopathology
PLAGMANN, H.-CH., Dentistry
PROKSCH, E., Dermatology and Venereology
ROIDER, J., Opthalmology
ROSE-JOHN, S., Biochemistry
SAFTIG, P., Biochemistry
SCHÖCKLMANN, H., Nephrology, Internal Medicine
SCHOLZ, J., Anaesthesiology
SCHRAPPE, M., Paediatrics
SCHREIBER, S., Internal Medicine and Gastroenterology
SCHRÖDER, J. M., Experimental Dermatology
SCHÜNKE, M., Anatomy
SCHÜTZE, G., Child Psychiatry
SCHWARTZ, T., Dermatology
SIEVERS, J., Anatomy
SIMON, R., Cardiology
STEPHANI, U., Paediatrics, Neuropaediatrics
STICK, C., Physiology
TONNER, P., Anaesthesiology
WEILER, N., Anaesthesiology
WILTFANG, J., Dental Surgery

Faculty of Philosophy (Christian-Albrechts-Platz 4, 24098 Kiel; tel. (431) 880-3055; fax (431) 880-7301; e-mail dekan@philfak.uni-kiel.de; internet www.uni-kiel.de/fakultas/philosophie):

BILLER, K.-H., Pedagogics
BLIESENER, T., Medieval and Modern History
BRINKHAUS, H., Indology
BRINKMANN, W., Pedagogics
CARNAP-BORNHEIM, C. VON, Prehistory and Early History
CONZELMANN, A., Sports Psychology
CORNELISSEN, C., Modern and Contemporary History
DORMEIER, H., Medieval and Modern History
ENGEL, A., Slavic Philology
FERSTL, R., Clinical Psychology
FLEISCHMANN, B., English Philology
FOUQUET, G., Economic and Social History
GÓMEZ-MONTERO, J., Romance Philology
GÖTTSCH-ELTEN, S., Folklore
GROSS, K., English Philology
HAAS, R., English Language and Literature
HAMEYER, U., Pedagogics
HANISCH, M., Teaching of History
HARRINGTON, J., Phonetics
HELDMANN, K., Classical Philology
HOEKSTRA, J., Friesian Philology
HOINKES, U., Romance Philology
HORATSCHEK, A. M., English Philology
JAWORSKI, R., East European History
JOBST, C., Art History
JONGEBLOED, H. C., Pedagogics
KAPP, V., Romance Philology
KÄPPEL, L., Classical Philology
KERSTING, W., Philosophy
KLEIN, D., Old German Literature
KÖHNKEN, G., Diagnostic and Differential Psychology
KONERSMANN, R., Teaching of Philosophy
KONRADT, U., Industrial, Marketing and Organizational Psychology
KROPE, P., Pedagogics
KUDER, U., Art History
KÜHNE, U., Ancient History, Medieval Linguistics
LINCK, G., Sinology
MAROLD, E., Old Norse Philology
MAUSFELD, R., Psychology
MEIER, A., History of Modern German Literature
MEYER, M., English Philology
MIETHLING, W.-D., Sports Pedagogics
MOERKE, O., Early Modern and Modern History
MÖLLER, J., Psychology
MOSEL, U., Linguistics
MÜLLER, J., Prehistory and Early History
MÜLLER, W.-U., Prehistory and Early History
NÜBLER, N., Slavic Philology
OECHSLE, M., Music
PALLASCH, W., Pedagogics
PETERSEN, J., Pedagogics
PISTOR-HATAM, A., Oriental Philology
POHL, K.-H., Teaching of History
PRAHL, H.-W., Pedagogics
PRENZEL, M., Pedagogics
RADICKE, J., Classical Philology
REBAS, H., Northern History
RIIS, T., History of Schleswig-Holstein
RÜHLING, L., Modern Scandinavian Literature
SCHMALTZ, B., Classical Archaeology
SCHMIDT, A., Folklore
SIELERT, U., Pedagogics
SIMON, B., Psychology
SOMMER, M., Philosophy
SPONHEUER, B., Music
STEINDORFF, L., East European History
THUN, H., Romance Philology
TUCHOLSKI-DÄKE, B.-C., Art
ULRICH, W., German Philology, Teaching of German Language

WEISS, P., Ancient History
WEISSER, B., Sports Medicine
WIESEHÖFER, J., Ancient History
WULFF, H. J., Theatre and Film Studies
WÜNSCH, M., History of Modern German Literature

Faculty of Theology (Leibnitzstr. 4, 24118 Kiel; tel. (431) 880-2124; fax (431) 880-1735; e-mail dekanattheo@email.uni-kiel.de; internet www.uni-kiel.de/fak/theol):

BARTELMUS, R., Old Testament Studies, Biblical and Middle Eastern Languages
BOBERT, S., Practical Theology
HÜBNER, U., Old Testament Studies and Biblical Archaeology
MECKENSTOCK, G., Systematic Theology
PREUL, R., Practical Theology
ROSENAU, H., Systematic Theology
SÄNGER, D., New Testament Studies
SCHILLING, J., Church History
VON BENDEMANN, R., New Testament Studies

ATTACHED INSTITUTES

Institut für Sicherheitspolitik an der Universität Kiel (ISUK) (Institute for Security Policy at Kiel University): Olshausenstr. 40, 24098 Kiel; Dir Prof. Dr J. KRAUSE.

Institut für Weltwirtschaft an der Universität Kiel (Institute for World Economics at Kiel University): Düsternbrooker Weg 120, 24105 Kiel; Pres. Prof. D. SNOWER.

Leibniz-Institut für Meereswissenschaften (IFM-GEOMAR) (Leibniz Institute of Marine Sciences): Wischhofstr. 1–3, 24148 Kiel; Dir Prof. Dr P. HERZIG.

Leibniz-Institut für die Pädagogik der Naturwissenschaften an der Universität Kiel (Leibniz Institute for Science Education): Olshausenstr. 62, 24098 Kiel; Dir Prof. Dr M. PRENZEL.

Lorenz-von-Stein-Institut für Verwaltungswissenschaften an der Universität Kiel (Lorenz von Stein Institute for Management Sciences at Kiel University): Olshausenstr. 40, 24098 Kiel; Dir Prof. Dr JOACHIM JICKELI.

Schleswig-Holsteinisches Institut für Friedenswissenschaften (Schleswig Holstein Institute for Peace Studies): Kaiserstr. 2, 24143 Kiel; Dir Prof. Dr K. POTTHOFF.

DEUTSCHE HOCHSCHULE FÜR VERWALTUNGSWISSENSCHAFTEN SPEYER

Freiherr-vom-Stein-Str. 2, 67346 Speyer
Telephone: (6232) 654-0
Fax: (6232) 654-208
E-mail: dhv@dhv-speyer.de
Internet: www.dhv-speyer.de

Founded 1947
State control
Languages of instruction: German, English
Academic year: May to January

Rector: Prof. Dr RUDOLF FISCH
Vice-Rector: Prof. Dr KARL-PETER SOMMERMEYER
Admin. Officer: CHRISTIANE MÜLLER
Librarian: Prof. Dr STEFAN FISCH

Library of 270,000 vols
Number of teachers: 90 (incl. 72 part-time)
Number of students: 500

A postgraduate institution offering courses in administrative sciences for senior civil service managers

PROFESSORS

BOHNE, E., Public Administration
FÄRBER, G., Public Finance and Economics
FISCH, R., Empirical Social Sciences
FISCH, S., Modern History

HILL, H., Public Administration, Public Law
JANSEN, D., Sociology of Organizations
KNORR, A., International Economics
KÖNIG, T., Political Science
MAGIERA, S., Public Law, European Law and
  Public International Law
MERTEN, D., Public Law, Social Law
MÜHLENKEMP, H., Public Finance
PITSCHAS, R., Public Administration, Devel-
  opment Policy and Public Law
REINERMANN, H., Public Administration,
  Information Technology
SIEDENTOPF, H., Public Administration, Pub-
  lic Law
SOMMERMANN, K.-P., Public Law, Constitu-
  tional Law, Comparative Law
WIRTZ, B., Information and Communication
  Management
ZIEKOW, J., Public Law and Administrative
  Law

ATTACHED INSTITUTE

**Forschungsinstitut für Öffentliche Ver-
waltung** (Research Institute for Public
Administration): Dir Prof. Dr JAN ZIEKOW.

DEUTSCHE SPORTHOCHSCHULE KÖLN

Am Sportpark Müngersdorf 6, 50933 Cologne
Telephone: (221) 4982-0
Fax: (221) 4982-8330
Internet: www.dshs-koeln.de
Founded 1920 in Berlin, reopened in Cologne
  1947
State control
Academic year: October to March, April to
  September
Rector: Prof. Dr WALTER TOKARSKI
Chancellor: Dr JOHANNES HORST
Librarian: Dr HEIKE SCHIFFER
Number of teachers: 230
Number of students: 5,381

EBERHARD-KARLS-UNIVERSITÄT TÜBINGEN

Wilhelmstr. 7, 72074 Tübingen
Telephone: (7071) 29-0
Fax: (7071) 29-5990
E-mail: registratur@verwaltung
  .uni-tuebingen.de
Internet: www.uni-tuebingen.de
Founded 1477
Academic year: October to July
Pres.: Prof. Dr EBERHARD SCHAICH
Chief Administrative Officer: Dr ANDREAS
  ROTHFUSS
Librarian: Dr ULRICH SCHAPKA
Number of teachers: 1,650
Number of students: 24,000
Publications: *Attempto! Forum der Universi-
tät Tübingen* (2 a year), *Rechenschaftsber-
icht des Rektors* (1 a year), *Tuebinger
Universitätsnachrichten* (6 a year)

PROFESSORS

Department of Biology (Auf der Morgenstelle
28, 72076 Tübingen; tel. (7071) 29-76853; fax
(7071) 295134; e-mail dek-bi@uni-tuebingen
.de; internet www.mikrobio.uni-tuebingen
.de):

BRAUN, V., Microbiology
ENGELS, E.-M., Development Physiology
GÖTZ, F., Microbiological Genetics
HAMPP, R., Botany
HARTER, K., Plant Physiology
JÜRGENS, G., Development Genetics
MAIER, W., Zoology
MALLOT, H., Cognitive Neurosciences
MICHIELS, N., Evolution Ecology of Animals
NORDHEIM, A., Molecular Biology
OBERWINKLER, F., Botany

SCHNITZLER, H.-U., Zoophysiology
SCHÖFFL, F., Genetics
WOHLLEBEN, W., Microbiology, Biotechnol-
  ogy

Department of Catholic Theology (Liebermeisterstr. 18, 72076 Tübingen; tel. (7071)
29-72544; fax (7071) 29-5407; e-mail
u02-info@uni-tuebingen.de; internet www
.uni-tuebingen.de/kath-theologie):

BIESINGER, A., Educational Religion
ECKERT, M., Fundamental Theology
FREYER, T., Dogmatic Theology
FUCHS, O., Practical Theology
GROSS, W., Old Testament
HILBERATH, B. J., Systematics
HOLZEM, A., Medieval and Modern Church
  History
MIETH, D., Moral Theology and Social
  Sciences
PUZA, R., Church Law
SEELIGER, H.-R., Ancient Church History,
  Patrology, Christian Archaeology
THEOBALD, M., New Testament

Department of Chemistry and Pharmacy
(Auf der Morgenstelle 8, 72076 Tübingen;
tel. (7071) 29-72920; fax (7071) 29-5198;
e-mail dekanat-chem-pharm@uni-tuebingen
.de; internet www.uni-tuebingen.de/chemie):

HAMPRECHT, B., Biochemistry
HEIDE, L., Pharmacology
LAUFER, S., Pharmacology
MAIER, M., Organic Chemistry
MEIXNER, A., Physical Chemistry
NÜRNBERGER, T., Organic Biochemistry
OBERHAMMER, H., Physical Chemistry
RUTH, P., Pharmacology
STEHLE, T., Biochemistry
STRÄHLE, J., Inorganic Chemistry
WESEMANN, L., Inorganic Chemistry
ZIEGLER, T., Organic Chemistry

Department of Cultural Sciences (Hölder-
linstr. 19, 72074 Tübingen; tel. (7071) 29-
76858; fax (7071) 551567; e-mail a11-info@
uni-tuebingen.de; internet www
.uni-tuebingen.de/kultur-dekanatl):

ANTONI, K., Japanology
BUTZENBERGER, K., Indology, Comparative
  Religion
EGGERT, M., Pre- and Ancient History
GERÖ, ST., Oriental Christian Philology
  and Culture
HOFMANN, H., Classical Philology
KLEIN, P., Art History
LEITZ, C., Egyptology
LEONHARDT, J., Latin Philology
PERNICKA, E., Archaeometry, Archaeome-
  tallurgy
RICHTER-BERNBURG, L., Oriental Studies
SCHAEFER, T., Classical Archaeology
SCHMID, M. H., Music
SCHUBERT, G., Sinology
STELLRECHT, I., Ethnography
SZLEZÁK, TH., Greek Philology
VOGEL, H.-U., Sinology
VOLK, K., Oriental History

Department of Economics (Nauklerstr. 47,
72074 Tübingen; tel. (7071) 29-72563; fax
(7071) 29-5179; e-mail w04.dekanat@
uni-tuebingen.de; internet www
.uni-tuebingen.de/uni/w04):

BATEN, J., Economic History
BERNDT, R., Commerce
BUCH, C.-M., Economics
CANSIER, D., Economics
GRAMMIG, J., Economics and Statistics
HECKER, R., Commerce
HOFMANN, C., Commerce
JAHNKE, B., Commerce
KOHLER, W., Economics
NEUS, W., Commerce
PULL, K., Commerce
SCHAICH, E., Economics and Statistics
SCHÖBEL, R., Commerce
STADLER, M., Economics

STARBATTY, J., Economics
WAGNER, F. W., Commerce

Department of Geosciences (Sigwartstr. 17,
72076 Tübingen; tel. (7071) 29-76861; fax
(7071) 550744; e-mail e16-info@
uni-tuebingen.de; internet www
.uni-tuebingen.de/geo):

CONARD, N., Palaeohistory and Protohis-
  tory
EBERLE, D., Geography
FÖRSTER, H., Geography
FRISCH, W., Geology
HADERLEIN, S., Environmental Mineralogy
KUCERA, M., Micropalaeontology
MOSBRUGGER, V., Palaeontology
SATIR, M., Geological Chemistry

Department of Information Science and
Computer Science (Sand 13, 72076 Tübingen;
tel. (7071) 29-77046; fax (7071) 29-5919;
e-mail dekanat@informatik.uni-tuebingen
.de; internet www.informatik.uni-tuebingen
.de):

CARLE, G., Computer Science
DIEHL, M., Psychology
HAUCK, P., Computer Science
HAUTZINGER, M., Psychology
HESSE, F., Psychology
HUSON, D., Computer Science
KLAEREN, H., Computer Science
KOHLBACHER, O., Computer Science
LANGE, K.-J., Computer Science
ROSENSTIEL, W., Computer Science
SCHWAN, S., Psychology
STAPF, K.-H., Psychology
STRASSER, W., Computer Science
ULRICH, R., Psychology
ZELL, A., Computer Science

Department of Law (tel. (7071) 29-72545; fax
(7071) 29-5178; e-mail dekanat@jura
.uni-tuebingen.de; internet www.jura
.uni-tuebingen.de):

ASSMANN, H.-D., Civil Law, Trade and
  Commercial Law
GÜNTHER, H.-L., Penal Law
HAFT, F., Penal Law and Procedural Law
KÄSTNER, K.-H., Civil Law, State Church
  Law
KERNER, H.-J., Criminology
KIRCHHOF, F., Public Law
KÜHL, K., Penal Law and Procedural Law
MAROTZKE, W., Civil Law and Procedural
  Law
MÖSCHEL, W., Civil, Trade and Commercial
  Law
NETTESHEIM, M., Public Law, European
  Law, Civil Law
PICKER, E., Civil Law, Labour and Trade
  Law
REICHOLD, H., Public Law, Trade and
  Commercial Law, Labour Law
REMMERT, B., Public Law, European Law
  and Constitution History
RONELLENFITSCH, M., Public Law
SCHIEMANN, G., Civil Law
SCHRÖDER, J., Penal and Private Law,
  History of German Law
VITZTHUM, W. GRAF, Public Law
VOGEL, J., Penal Law, Procedural Law
WEBER, U., Penal Law, Procedural Law
WESTERMANN, H. P., Civil, Trade and Com-
  mercial Law

Department of Mathematics and Physics
(Auf der Morgenstelle 4, 72076 Tübingen;
tel. (7071) 29-72567; fax (7071) 29-5400;
e-mail dekanat.physik@uni-tuebingen.de;
internet www.physik.uni-tuebingen.de/
dekanat):

BATYREV, V., Algebra
FÄSSLER, A., Theoretical Physics
HERING, C., Geometry
JOCHUM, J., Experimental Physics
KAUP, W., Complex Analysis
KERN, D., Basic Physical Computer Science
KLEY, W., Computational Physics

LUBICH, C., Numerical Analysis
PLIES, E., Applied Physics
REINHARDT, H., Theoretical Physics
RUDER, H., Theoretical Astrophysics
SANTANGELO, A., Astronomy, Astrophysics
SCHÄTZLE, R., Analysis
SCHOPOHL, N., Theoretical Physics
SCHREIBER, F., Biophysical Structures
TEUFEL, S., Mathematical Methods in Natural Sciences
WERNER, K., Astronomy and Astrophysics
YSERENTANT, H., Numerical Analysis
ZERNER, M., Stochastics
ZIMMERMANN, C., Experimental Physics

Department of Medicine (Geissweg 5, 72076 Tübingen; tel. (7071) 29-72566; fax (7071) 29-5188; e-mail judith.jovanovic@med.uni-tuebingen.de; internet www.medizin.uni-tuebingen.de/pages/med_fakultaet):

AUTENRIETH, I. B., Medical Microbiology
BAMBERG, M., Radiography
BARES, R., Nuclear Medicine
BARTZ-SCHMIDT, K.-U., Ophthalmology
BECKER, H. D., Surgery
BIRBAUMER, N., Psychology
BUCHKREMER, G., Psychiatry
BÜLTMANN, B., Pathology
CLAUSSEN, C., Radiography
DICHGANS, H., Neurology
DIETZ, K., Medical Biometrics
DREWS, U., Anatomy
FUCHS, J., Child Surgery
GAWAZ, M., Internal Medicine
GOSSER, T., Neurology
GÖZ, G., Dentistry
GREGOR, M., Internal Medicine
HÄRING, H.-U., Internal Medicine
HOFBECK, M., Paediatrics
JAHN, G., Medical Virology
JUCKER, M., Neurology
KANDOLF, R., Molecular Pathology
KANZ, L., Internal Medicine
KLOSINSKI, G., Child and Youth Psychiatry
KNOBLOCH, J., Tropical Medicine
KÖNIGSRAINER, A., Surgery
KRÄGELOH-MANN, J., Paediatrics
LANG, F., Physiology
LÖST, C., Dentistry
MEYERMANN, R., Neuropathology
NIESS, A., Sports Medicine
OSSWALD, H., Pharmacology
POETS, C. F., Paediatrics
RAMMENSEE, H.-G., Immunology
REINERT, S., Maxillofacial Surgery
RIESS, O., Clinical Genetics
RÖCKEN, M., Dermatology
SCHALLER, H.-E., Plastic, Hand and Burns Surgery
SCHWEIZER, P., Child Surgery
SELBMANN, H.-K., Medical Statistics and Data Processing
STENZL, A., Urology
TATAGIBA, M., Neurosurgery
THIER, H. P., Neurology
UNERTL, K., Anaesthesiology
VOIGT, K., Neuroradiology
WAGNER, H.-J., Anatomy
WALLWIENER, D., Gynaecology
WEBER, H., Dentistry
WEHNER, H.-D., Forensic Medicine
WEISE, K., Traumatology
WIESING, U., Medical Ethics
WULKER, N., Orthopaedics
ZENNER, H.-P., Otorhinolaryngology
ZIEMER, G., Thoracic and Cardiovascular Surgery
ZIPFEL, S., Psychosomatic Medicine, Psychotherapy
ZRENNER, E., Ophthalmology

Department of Modern Languages (Wilhelmstr. 50, 72074 Tübingen; tel. (7071) 29-72952; fax (7071) 29-4253; e-mail dek-nphil@uni-tuebingen.de; internet www.uni-tuebingen.de/neuphil-dekanat):

BAUER, M., English Philology

BERGER, T., Slavonic Philology
BRAUNGART, G., German Philology
ENGLER, B., English Philology
FICHTE, J., English Philology
HINRICHS, E., Computing Science of Linguistics
HOTZ-DAVIES, I., English Philology
HUBER, CH., Medieval German Literature
KEMPER, H.-G., German Philology
KILCHER, A., German Philology
KLUGE, R.-D., Slavonic Philology
KOBATEK, J., Romance Philology
KOCH, P., German Philology
KOHN, K., English Philology
MATZAT, W., Romance Philology
MOOG-GRÜNEWALD, M., Romance Philology
REINFANDT, C., English Philology
REIS, M., German Philology
RIDDER, K., Medieval German Literature
SCHAHADAT, S., Slavonic Philology
STECHOW, A. VON, Theoretical Linguistics
UEDING, G., Rhetorics
WERTHEIMER, J., German Philology

Department of Philosophy and History (*Philosophy Section*, Bursagasse 1, 72070 Tübingen; tel. (7071) 29-76852; fax (7071) 29-5295; e-mail dekanat@philosophie.uni-tuebingen.de; internet www.uni-tuebingen.de/philosophie*History Section*, Sigwartstr. 17, 72076 Tübingen; tel. (7071) 29-72568; fax (7071) 29-252897; e-mail stefan.zaunder@uni-tuebingen.de; internet www.uni-tuebingen.de/dekanat-geschichte):

BEYRAU, D., East European History
DOERING-MANTEUFFEL, A., Modern and Contemporary History
FRANK, M., Philosophy
HARTMANN, W., Medieval and Modern History
HEIDELBERGER, M., Philosophy
HÖFFE, O., Philosophy
KOCH, A. F., Philosophy
KOLB, F., Ancient History
LANGEWIESCHE, D., Medieval and Modern History
LORENZ, S., Medieval and Modern History
SCHINDLING, A., Medieval and Modern History

Department of Protestant Theology (Liebermeisterstr. 12, 72076 Tübingen; tel. (7071) 29-72538; fax (7071) 29-3318; e-mail ev.theologie@uni-tuebingen.de; internet www.uni-tuebingen.de/ev-theologie):

BAYER, O., Systematic Theology
BLUM, E., Old Testament
DRECOLL, V., Church History
DREHSEN, V., Practical Theology
ECKSTEIN, H.-J., New Testament
HENNIG, G., Practical Theology
HERMS, E., Systematic Theology
HOFIUS, O., New Testament
JANOWSKI, B., Old Testament
KÖPF, U., Church History
LICHTENBERGER, H., New Testament and Ancient Jewish Culture
SCHWEIZER, F., Practical Theology
SCHWÖBEL, C., Systematic Theology

Department of Social and Behavioural Sciences and Pedagogics (Wächterstr. 67, 72074 Tübingen; tel. (7071) 29-76857; fax (7071) 29-5115; e-mail s08info@uni-tuebingen.de; internet www.uni-tuebingen.de/faksozver):

BOECKH, A., Political Studies
DEUTSCHMANN, CH., Sociology
DIGEL, H., Theory of Physical Education
GILDEMEISTER, R., Sociology
HORN, K.-P., Pedagogics
HRBEK, R., Political Studies
HUBER, G., Pedagogics
JOHLER, R., Cultural Studies
MÜLLER, S., Social Pedagogics
RITTBERGER, V., Political Studies
SCHRADER, J., Pedagogics
THIEL, A., Theory of Physical Education

TREPTOW, R., Pedagogics
WANK, V., Theory of Physical Education

ATTACHED INSTITUTES

Goethe-Wörterbuch: Frischlinstr. 7, 72074 Tübingen; Dir of Commission Prof. Dr W. KÜHLMANN.

Institut für Wissensmedien (Media Institute): Konrad-Adenauer-Str. 40, 72072 Tübingen; Dir Prof. Dr FRIEDRICH W. HESSE.

ERNST-MORITZ-ARNDT-UNIVERSITÄT GREIFSWALD

Baderstr. 1, 17487 Greifswald

Telephone: (3834) 86-1150
Fax: (3834) 86-1151
E-mail: rektor@uni-greifswald.de
Internet: www.uni-greifswald.de

Founded 1456
Academic year: October to September

Chancellor: Dr THOMAS BEHRENS
Rector: Prof. Dr rer.nat. RAINER WESTERMANN
Pro-Rectors: Prof. Dr CLAUS DIETER CLASSEN, Prof. Dr med. OTTO-ANDREAS FESTGE
Librarian: Dr PETER WOLFF

Number of teachers: 235
Number of students: 8,200

Publications: *Greifswalder Universitätsreden* (irregular), *Wissenschaftliche Beiträge* (irregular)

DEANS

Faculty of Law and Economics: Prof. Dr rer. pol. ROLAND ROLLBERG
Faculty of Mathematics and Natural Sciences: Prof. Dr rer. nat. KLAUS FESSER
Faculty of Medicine: Prof. Dr rer. nat. HEYO K. KROEMER
Faculty of Philosophy: Prof. Dr soz. wiss. MANFRED BORNEWASSER
Faculty of Theology: Prof. Dr theol. CHRISTFRIED BÖTTRICH

EUROPA-UNIVERSITÄT VIADRINA
(Viadrina European University)

Grosse Scharrnstr. 59, 15230 Frankfurt an der Oder

Telephone: (335) 5534-0
Fax: (335) 5534-305
E-mail: study@euv-frankfurt-o.de
Internet: www.euv-ffo.de

Founded 1991
Languages of instruction: German, English
Academic year: October to July

President: Dr GUNTER PLEUGER
Chancellor: CHRISTIAN ZENS
Registrar: BEATRIX ECKERT
International Office: PETRA WEBER
Librarian: Dr HANS-GERD HAPPEL

Number of teachers: 190
Number of students: 6,200

DEANS

Faculty of Cultural and Social Studies: Prof. Dr KONSTANZE JUNGBLUTH
Faculty of Economics: Prof. Dr STEVEN HUSMANN
Faculty of Law: Prof. Dr MATTIAS PECHSTEIN

ATTACHED COLLEGE

Collegium Polonicum: (situated in Slubice in Poland, and managed jointly by the Europa-Universität Viadrina and the Adam Mickiewicz University in Poznań).

FERNUNIVERSITÄT IN HAGEN
(Distance-Learning University in Hagen)

58084 Hagen
Telephone: (2331) 9872444

Fax: (2331) 987316
E-mail: info@fernuni-hagen.de
Internet: www.fernuni-hagen.de
Founded 1974
54 Study centres within Germany, Austria, Switzerland, Hungary and Russia
State control
Language of instruction: German
Academic year: October to September
Rector: Prof. Dr-Ing. HELMUT HOYER
Vice-Rectors: Prof. Dr UWE SCHIMANK, Prof. Dr GUNTER SCHLAGETER
Chief Exec. and Chancellor: REGINA ZDEBEL
Librarian: KARIN MICHALKE (acting)
Number of teachers: 942
Number of students: 55,450 (full- and part-time and assoc.)
Publications: *Anleitung zur Belegung, FernUni Perspektive* (newspaper of the univ.), *Forschungsbericht, Informationen zum Studium, Schriftenreihen* (scientific publ.)

DEANS

Faculty of Culture and Social Sciences: Prof. Dr INGRID JOSEPHS
Faculty of Economics and Business: Prof. Dr SABINE FLIEß
Faculty of Electrical Engineering: Prof. Dr HALANG
Faculty of Law: Prof. Dr ULRICH WACKER-BARTH
Faculty of Mathematics and Computer Science: Prof. Dr RUTGER VERBEEK

FREIE UNIVERSITÄT BERLIN

Kaiserswerther Str. 16–18, 14195 Berlin (Dahlem)
Telephone: (30) 838-1
Fax: (30) 838-73217
E-mail: oei@zedat.fu-berlin.de
Internet: www.fu-berlin.de
Founded 1948
Academic year: October to July
Pres.: Prof. Dr DIETER LENZEN
Chancellor: PETER LANGE (acting)
Librarian: Dr ULRICH NAUMANN
Library: see Libraries and Archives
Number of teachers: 2,800
Number of students: 43,000

DIRECTORS OF DEPARTMENTS

Biology, Chemistry and Pharmacy: Prof. Dr HARTMUT H. HILGER
Economics and Business Administration: Prof. Dr MICHAEL KLEINALTENKAMP
Education and Psychology: Prof. Dr GERD R. HOFF
Geo-Sciences: Prof. Dr M. BÖSE
History and Culture: Prof. Dr MICHAEL BONGARDT
Humanities: Prof. Dr MARGOT. BÖSE
Law: Prof. Dr JOCHEM SCHMITT
Mathematics and Informatics: Prof. Dr J. SCHILLER
Medicine: Prof. Dr MARTIN PAUL
Philosophy and Humanities: Prof. Dr WIDU-WOLFGANG EHLERS
Physics: Prof. Dr NIKOLAUS SCHWENTNER
Political and Social Sciences: Prof. Dr UTE LUIG
Veterinary Medicine: Prof. Dr LEO BRUNN-BERG

CENTRAL ATTACHED INSTITUTES

John F. Kennedy-Institut für Nordamerikastudien (J. F. K. Institute of North American Studies): Lanstr. 7, 14195 Berlin; tel. (30) 83852703; fax (30) 83852882; e-mail jfki@zedat.fu-berlin.de; internet web .fu-berlin.de/jfki; Chair. DETLEF BROSE.
Lateinamerika-Institut (Institute of Latin American Studies): Rüdesheimer Str. 54-56,

14197 Berlin; tel. (30) 83853073; fax (30) 83855464; e-mail ai@zedat.fu-berlin.de; internet web.fu-berlin.de/lai; Chair. Prof. Dr MARIANNE BRAIG.
Osteuropa-Institut (Institute of East European Studies): Garystr. 55, 14195 Berlin; tel. (30) 83853380; fax (30) 83853788; e-mail oei@ zedat.fu-berlin.de; internet www.oei .fu-berlin.de; Chair. DETLEF BROSE.

FRIEDRICH-ALEXANDER-UNIVERSITÄT ERLANGEN-NÜRNBERG

Postfach 35 20, 91023 Erlangen
Telephone: (9131) 85-0
Fax: (9131) 8522131
E-mail: presse@zuv.uni-erlangen.de
Internet: www.uni-erlangen.de
Founded 1743, merged with Universität Altdorf 1809
State control
Pres.: Prof. Dr KARL-DIETER GRÜSKE
Vice-Pres.: Prof. JOHANNA HABERER
Vice-Pres.: Prof. Dr HANS-PETER STEINRÜCK
Vice-Pres.: CHRISTOPH KORBMACHER
Chancellor: THOMAS A. H. SCHÖCK
Librarian: Dr KONSTANZE SÖLLNER
Library: 5.4m. vols, 53,516 periodicals
Number of teachers: 550
Number of students: 27,300
Publications: *Erlanger Bausteine zur fränkischen Heimatforschung, Erlanger Forschungen, Geologische Blätter für Nordost-Bayern und angrenzende Gebiete, Jahrbuch für fränkische Landesforschung, Jahresbericht, Jahresbibliographie und Forschungsbericht, Unikurier, Unikurier aktuell*

DEANS

School of Business and Economics and Law School: Prof. Dr HEINRICH DE WALL
School of Engineering: Prof. Dr Ing. REINHARD GERMAN
School of Humanities and Social Sciences and School of Theology: Prof. Dr HEIDRUN STEIN-KECKS
School of Sciences: Prof. Dr FRANK DUZAAR
Medicine School: Prof. Dr JÜRGEN SCHÜTTLER

FRIEDRICH-SCHILLER-UNIVERSITÄT JENA

Fürstengraben 1, 07743 Jena
Telephone: (3641) 9300
Fax: (3641) 931682
E-mail: aaa@uni-jena.de
Internet: www.uni-jena.de
Founded 1558
Languages of instruction: German, English
Academic year: October to September
Rector: Prof. Dr KARL-ULRICH MEYN
Pro-Rectors: Prof. Dr ROLF STEYER, Prof. Dr CHRISTIAN RÜSSEL
Registrar: Dr KLAUS KÜBEL
Librarian: Dr SABINE WEFERS
Number of teachers: 1,974
Number of students: 19,500
Publications: *Forschungsmagazin, Jenaer Reden und Schriften, Mitteilungen der Thüringer Universitäts- und Landesbibliothek, Uni-Journal Jena*

DEANS

Faculty of Biology and Pharmaceutics: Prof. Dr GABRIELE DIEKERT
Faculty of Chemistry and Geosciences: Prof. Dr DIETER KLEMM
Faculty of Economics: Prof. Dr JOHANNES RUHLAND
Faculty of Law: Prof. Dr MICHAEL BRENNER

Faculty of Mathematics and Computer Science: Prof. Dr WERNER ERHARD
Faculty of Medicine: Prof. Dr HEINRICH SAUER
Faculty of Philosophy: Prof. Dr WALTER AMELING
Faculty of Physics and Astronomy: Prof. Dr PAUL SEIDEL
Faculty of Social and Behavioural Sciences: Prof. Dr HOLGER GABRIEL
Faculty of Theology: Prof. Dr JÜRGEN VAN OORSCHOT

GEORG-AUGUST-UNIVERSITÄT GÖTTINGEN

37073 Göttingen
Telephone: (551) 390
Fax: (551) 399612
E-mail: pressestelle@uni-goettingen.de
Internet: www.uni-goettingen.de
Founded 1737
Academic year: October to July
Pres.: Prof. Dr KURT VON FIGURA
Vice-Pres: Prof. Dr REINER KREE, Prof. Dr DORIS LEMMERMÖHLE, Prof. Dr JOACHIM MÜNCH
Librarian: Prof. Dr ELMAR MITTLER
Number of teachers: 800
Number of students: 23,000
Publications: *Georgia-Augusta* (2 a year), *Jahresforschungsbericht* (every 2 years), *Spektrum* (4 a year)

DEANS

Faculty of Agriculture: Prof. Dr RAINER MARGGRAF
Faculty of Biology: Prof. Dr THOMAS RAMMSAYER
Faculty of Chemistry: Prof. Dr ULF DIEDERICHSEN
Faculty of Earth Sciences: Prof. Dr WERNER KREISEL
Faculty of Economics: Prof. Dr LOTHAR SCHRUFF
Faculty of Forestry: Prof. Dr REINER FINKELDEY
Faculty of Law: Prof. Dr VOLKER LIPP
Faculty of Mathematics: Prof. Dr INA KERSTEN
Faculty of Medicine: Prof. Dr CORNELIUS FRÖMMEL
Faculty of Philosophy: Prof. Dr EBERHARD WINKLER
Faculty of Physics: Prof. Dr RAINER G. ULBRICH
Faculty of Social Sciences: Prof. Dr MARGRET KRAUL
Faculty of Theology: Prof. Dr HERMANN SPIEKERMANN

GOETHE-UNIVERSITÄT FRANKFURT AM MAIN

Senckenberganlage 31, Postfach 111932, 60054 Frankfurt am Main
Telephone: (69) 798-0
Fax: (69) 798-28383
E-mail: presse@uni-frankfurt.de
Internet: www.goethe-universitaet.de
Founded 1914
Academic year: October to September (2 semesters)
Pres.: Prof. Dr WERNER MÜLLER-ESTERL
Vice-Pres.: Prof. Dr WOLF ABMUS, Prof. Dr RAINER KLUMP, Prof. Dr MATTHIAS LUTZ-BACHMANN, Prof. Dr MANFRED SCHUBERT-ZSILAVECZ, Prof. Dr ROSER MARIA VALENTI
Chancellor: HANS GEORG MOCKEL
Librarian: BERNDT DUGALL
Number of teachers: 2,600 (641 professors, 821 asst professors/scientific assts)
Number of students: 33,000

Publications: *Forschung Frankfurt* (4 a year), *Forschungsbericht* (1 a year), *Uni-Report* (6 or 7 a year)

DEANS

Department of Biochemistry, Chemistry and Pharmaceutical Sciences: Prof. Dr DIETER STEINHILBER

Department of Biological Sciences: Prof. Dr VOLKER MÜLLER

Department of Catholic Theology: Prof. Dr CLAUS ARNOLD

Department of Computing and Mathematics: Prof. Dr DETLEF KRÖMKER

Department of Economics: Prof. Dr RAINER KLUMP

Department of Education: Prof. Dr BARBARA FRIEBERTSHÄ

Department of Geosciences and Geography: Prof. Dr GERHARD BREY

Department of Law: Prof. Dr ULFRID NEUMANN

Department of Linguistic and Cultural Studies: Prof. Dr THOMAS PAULSEN

Department of Medicine: Prof. Dr JOSEF M. PFEILSCHIFTER

Department of Modern Languages: Prof. Dr ECKHARD LOBSIEN

Department of Philosophy and History: Prof. Dr MATTHIAS LUTZ-BACHMANN

Department of Physics: Prof. Dr DIRK-HERMANN RISCHKE

Department of Protestant Theology: Prof. Dr HANS-GÜNTER HEIMBROCK

Department of Psychology and Sport: Prof. Dr HELFRIED MOOSBRUGGER

Department of Social Sciences: Prof. Dr UTA RUPPERT

PROFESSORS

Department of Biochemistry, Chemistry and Pharmaceutical Sciences (Biozentrum, Marie-Curie-Str. 9, 60439 Frankfurt am Main; tel. (69) 798-29545; fax (69) 798-29546):

AUNER, N., Inorganic Chemistry
BADER, H.-J., Chemistry Teaching
BAMBERG, E., Biophysical Chemistry
BRUTSCHY, B., Physical Chemistry
DINGERMANN, TH., Pharmaceutical Biology
DRESSMAN, J. B., Pharmaceutical Technology
EGERT, E., Organic Chemistry
ENGELS, J., Organic Chemistry
GÖBEL, M., Organic Chemistry
KARAS, M., Analytical Chemistry
KOLBESEN, B., Inorganic Chemistry
KREUTER, J., Pharmaceutical Technology
LAMBRECHT, G., Pharmacology for Natural Scientists
LUDWIG, B., Biochemistry
MARSCHALEK, R., Pharmaceutical Biology
MOSANDL, A., Food Chemistry
MÜLLER, W. E., Pharmacology and Toxicology
PRISNER, TH. F., Physical Chemistry
REHM, D., Physical and Organic Chemistry
RÜTERJANS, H., Physical Biochemistry
SCHUBERT-ZSILAVECZ, M., Pharmaceutical Chemistry
STARK, H., Pharmaceutical Chemistry
STEINHILBER, D., Pharmaceutical Chemistry
STOCK, G., Theoretical Chemistry
WACHTVEITL, J., Physical Chemistry
WAGNER, M., Inorganic Chemistry

Department of Biological Sciences (Feldbergstr. 42, 60323 Frankfurt am Main; tel. (69) 798-23956):

BEREITER-HAHN, J., Cell Research
BRÄNDLE, K., Zoology
BRENDEL, M., Biology for Doctors
BRÜGGEMANN, W., Botany
DROBNIK, O., Architecture and Business Systems

ENTIAN, K.-D., Microbiology
FEIERABEND, F., Botany
FLEISSNER, G., Zoology
GEIHS, K., Practical Informatics
GNATZY, W., Zoology
HAGERUP, T., Theoretical Informatics
KAHL, G., Botany
KEMP, R., Applied Informatics
KOENIGER, N., Apiculture
KROEGER, A., Microbiology
KRÖMKER, D., Graphical Data Processing
KUNZ, W., Drafting Methods
LANGE-BERTALOT, H., Botany
MASCHWITZ, U., Zoology
NOVER, L., Botany
OSIEWACZ, H., Botany
PONS, F., Microbiology
PRINZINGER, R., Zoology
PROTSCH VON ZIETEN, R., Anthropology
SANDMANN, G., Botany
SCHMIDT-SCHAUSS, M., Artificial Intelligence
SCHNITGER, G., Theoretical Informatics
STARZINSKI-POWITZ, A., Human Genetics
STEIGER, H., Microbiology
STREIT, B., Zoology
TROMMER, G., Biology Teaching
WALDSCHMIDT, K., Applied Informatics
WILTSCHKO, W., Zoology
WITTIG, R., Botany
WOTSCHKE, D., Computer Languages
ZICARI, R., Databases
ZIMMERMANN, H., Zoology
ZIZKA, G., Botany

Department of Catholic Theology (Grüneburgplatz 1, 60323 Frankfurt am Main; tel. (69) 798-33344):

DENINGER-POLZER, G., Catholic Theology
HAINZ, J., Exegesis of the New Testament
HOFFMANN, J., Moral Theology, Social Ethics
KESSLER, H., Systematic Theology
RASKE, M., Practical Theology
SCHREIJÄCK, T., Catholic Theology
WIEDENHOFER, S., Systematic Theology

Department of Computing and Mathematics (Robert-Mayer-Str. 6–8, 60325 Frankfurt am Main; tel. (69) 798-28920; e-mail dekanat@ math.uni-frankfurt.de):

BAUMEISTER, J. B., Optimum and Convex Functions
BEHR, H., Pure Mathematics
BIERI, R., Pure Mathematics
BLIEDTNER, J., Pure Mathematics
CONSTANTINESCU, F., Mathematics
DINGES, H., Probability Theory and Statistics
FÜHRER, L., Mathematics Teaching
GROOTE, H. DE, Applied Mathematics
KERSTING, G., Stochastics
KLOEDEN, P. E., Applied Mathematics
KRUMMHEUER, G., Mathematics Teaching
LUCKHARDT, H., Fundamental Mathematics
METZLER, W., Mathematics
MÜLLER, K. H., Applied Mathematics
REICHERT-HAHN, M., Mathematics
SCHNORR, C., Applied Mathematics
SCHWARZ, W., Mathematics
SIEVEKING, M., Applied Mathematics
WAKOLBINGER, A., Probability Theory
WEIDMANN, J., Mathematics
WOLFART, J., Mathematics

Department of Economics (Mertonstr. 17–25, 60054 Frankfurt am Main; tel. (69) 798-22305; fax (69) 798-22678):

BARTELS, H. G., Business Administration, Operational Research
BAUER, T., Economic Systems and Transition
BINDER, M., Macroeconomics
BLONSKI, M., Microeconomics
BÖCKING, H.-J., Corporate Governance
EWERT, R., Controlling and Auditing

FITZENBERGER, B., Labour Economics
GEBHARDT, G., Economic Management
GOMBER, P., e-Finance
HALIASSOS, M., Macroeconomics and Financial Markets
HASSLER, U., Statistics
HOLTEN, R., Business Information Systems
HOMMEL, M., Auditing and Invoicing
HORLEBEIN, M., Economic Pedagogics
HUJER, R., Statistics and Econometrics
ISERMANN, H., Business Administration
KAAS, K. P., Industrial Economics
KLAPPER, D., Marketing
KLUMP, R., Business Development
KÖNIG, W., Economic Management
KRAHNEN, J. P., Financial Management
KRÜGER, D., Macroeconomy
LAUX, H., Theory of Organization
MATHES, H. D., Production Planning
MAURER, R., Investment
MELLWIG, W., Industrial Economics
NATTER, M., Trade
NAUTZ, D., Empirical Macroeconomy
RANNENBERG, K., Business Computing
ROMMELFANGER, H., Mathematics for Economists
SCHEFOLD, B., Political Economics
SCHLAG, CH., Financial Economics
SCHMIDT, R., Economic Management
SKIERA, B., Electronic Commerce
VELTHUIS, L., Organization and Management
WAHRENBURG, M., Business Administration (Banking)
WALZ, U., Industry Economics
WEICHENRIEDER, A., Financial Economics
WIELAND, V., Money Theory and Policy

Department of Education (Senckenberganlage 15, 60054 Frankfurt am Main; tel. (69) 798-22392):

BRAKEMEIER-LISOP, I., Economic Pedagogics
BRUMLIK, M., Pedagogics
CREMER-SCHÄFER, H., Pedagogics and Social Pedagogics
DEPPE-WOLFINGER, H., Special Education
DUDEK, P., Pedagogics
FAUST-SIEHL, G., Primary Education
GRUSCHKA, A., Teacher Training
HESS, H., Social Pedagogics
HOFMANN-MÜLLER, C. H., Pedagogics
JACOBS, K., Special and Remedial Education
KADE, J., Theory and Practice of Adult Education
KALLERT, H., Social Pedagogics
KAMINSKI, W., Pedagogics
KATZENBACH, D., Pedagogics
MARKERT, W., Economic Pedagogics
MEIER, R., Primary Teacher Training
NITTEL, D., Social Pedagogics and Adult Education
NYSSEN, F., Teacher Training
OVERBECK, A., Special Education
RADTKE, F.-O., Pedagogics
RANG, B., History and Pedagogics of Women's Studies
SCHLÖMERKEMPER, J., Pedagogics
SCHOLZ, G., Primary Education
ZANDER, H., Social Pedagogics
ZENZ, G., Social Pedagogics

Department of Geosciences and Geography (Bockenheimer Landstr. 133, 60325 Frankfurt am Main; tel. (69) 798-22691; fax (69) 798-28416; e-mail dekanat-geowiss@em .uni-frankfurt.de):

ALBRECHT, V., Teaching of Geography
ANDRES, W., Physical Geography
BATHELT, H., Economic Geography
BREY, G., Mineralogy
BRINKMANN, W. L. F., Hydrology
HASSE, J., Teaching of Geography
HERBERT, F., Theoretical Meteorology
HUESSNER, H., Geology and Palaeontology
JUNGE, A., Geophysics

KLEINSCHMIDT, G., Geology
KOWALCZYK, G., Regional Geology
MÜLLER, G., Mathematical Geophysics
OSCHMANN, W., Palaeontology
PÜTTMANN, W., Environmental Analysis
RUNGE, J., Physical Geography
SCHAMP, E., Economic Geography
SCHICKHOFF, I., Human Geography
SCHMELING, H., Solid Earth Physics
SCHMIDT, U., Atmospheric Physics
SCHÖNWIESE, C., Meteorological Environmental Research
SCHROEDER, R., Palaeontology
STEIN, N., Physical Geography
STEININGER, F. F., Palaeontology and Historical Geology
THARUN, E., Cultural Geography
THIEMAYER, H., Hydrology
WOLF, K., Cultural Geography

Department of Law (tel. (69) 798-22201; e-mail dekanat.fb01@jur.uni-frankfurt.de):

ALBRECHT, P., Criminology and Criminal Law
BAUMS, TH., Business Law (Banking and Media)
CAHN, A., Law and Finance
CORDES, A., European History of Law
EBSEN, I., Constitutional, Administrative and Social Law
FABRICIUS, D., Criminal Law, Criminology and Psychology of Law
FRANKENBERG, G., Public Law
GILLES, P., Legal Procedure, Civil and Comparative Law
GÜNTHER, K., Theory of Law, Penal Law and Law of Criminal Procedure
HAAR, BRIGITTE, Civil Law
HASSEMER, W., Theory of Law, Social and Criminal Law
HERMES, G., Public Law
HOFMANN, R., Civil Law
KADELBACH, S., Public Law, European Law
KARGL, W., Theory of Law, Philosophy of Law and Criminal Law
KOHL, H., Civil Law
NEUMANN, U., Social, Criminal, and Criminal Adjective Law and Philosophy of Law
OGOREK, R., Roman Law, Civil Law
OSTERLOH, L., Public Law, Tax Law
PRITTWITZ, C., Criminal Law
REHBINDER, E., Business, Environmental and Comparative Law
RÜCKERT, J., History of Law
SACKSOFSKY, U., Public Law and Comparative Law
SIEKMANN, H., Money and Bank Law
SIRKS, B., History of Law and Civil Law
STOLLEIS, M., Public Law, History of Law
TEUBNER, G., Civic Rights, Commercial Law
VESTING, T., Public Law, Media Law
WANDT, M., German and International Civil Law, Commercial and Insurance Law
WEISS, M., Labour Law and Civic Rights
WELLENHOFER, MARINA, Civil and Process Law
WIELAND, J., Public Law, Financial Law and Tax Law
ZEKOLL, J., Civil Law

Department of Linguistic and Cultural Studies (Bockenheimer Landstr. 133, 60325 Frankfurt am Main; tel. (69) 798-22915; fax (69) 798-28474):

BASTIAN, H. G., Teaching of Music
BÜCHSEL, M., History of European Art
DAIBER, Oriental Studies
ERDAL, M., Turkish Studies
FASSLER, M., European Ethnology
FISCHER, J., Art Teaching
FREIDHOF, G., Slavonic Studies
GIPPERT, J., Comparative Linguistics
HERDING, K., Art History
LANGER, G., Slavonic Studies

MEYER, J.-W., Archaeology
NEU, T., Art Teaching
NEUMEISTER, C., Classical Philology
NOTHOFER, B., Southeast Asian Studies
NOVA, A., Art History
NOWAK, A., Musicology
RAECK, W., Classical Archaeology
RICHARD, B., Art Teaching
SCHLÜTER, M., Jewish Studies
SCHMITZ, TH., Greek Philology
SIEVERT, A., Art Teaching
VOSSEN, R., African Languages
WELZ, G., European Ethnology

Department of Medicine (Theodor-Stern-Kai 7, 60596 Frankfurt am Main; tel. (69) 6301-6010; fax (69) 6301-6301; e-mail kersken-nuelens@em.uni-frankfurt.de):

AUBURGER, G., Applied Neurology
BITTER, K., Maxillofacial Surgery
BÖHLES, H. J., Paediatrics
BÖTTCHER, H. D., Radiation Therapy
BRAAK, H., Anatomy
BRADE, V., Hygiene, Microbiology
BRANDT, U., Biochemistry
BRATZKE, H., Forensic Medicine
BRETTEL, H.-F., Forensic Medicine
BUSSE, R., Physiology
CASPARY, W., Internal Medicine and Gastroenterology
CHANDRA, P., Therapeutic Biochemistry
DELLER, T., Anatomy
DEPPE, H.-U., Medical Sociology
DOERR, H. W., Medical Virology
DUDZIAK, R., Anaesthesiology
ELSNER, G., Industrial Medicine
ENCKE, A., General and Abdominal Surgery
FELLBAUM, CH., Pathology and Pathological Anatomy
FIEGUTH, H.-B., Thoracic Surgery
FÖRSTER, H., Applied Biochemistry
GALL, V., Child Audiology
GEIGER, H., Internal Medicine
GEISSLINGER, G., Clinical Pharmacology
GIERE, W., Documentation and Data Processing
GRONER, B., Molecular Infection and Tumour Biology
GROSS, W., Physiological Chemistry
GRÜNWALD, F., Nuclear Medicine
GSTÖTTNER, W., Ear, Nose and Throat Surgery
HANSMANN, M.-L., Pathology
HEIDEMANN, D., Dental and Maxillofacial Medicine
HELLER, K., Surgery
HOELZER, D., Haematology
HOFMANN, D., Child Health
HOFSTETTER, R., Child Cardiology
HOHMANN, W., Materials in Dentistry
JONAS, D., Urology
JORK, K., General Medicine
KAUERT, G., Forensic Toxicology
KAUFMANN, M., Gynaecology
KAUFMANN, R., Dermatology and Venereology
KERSCHBAUMER, F., Orthopaedics and Orthopaedic Surgery
KLINGEBIEL, T., Child Health
KLINKE, R., Physiology
KOCH, F.-H., Ophthalmology
KORF, H.-W., Anatomy
KUHL, H., Experimental Endocrinology
LANGENBECK, U., Human Genetics
LAUER, H.-CHR., Dentistry
LEUSCHNER, U., Gastroenterology
MAURER, K., Psychiatry
MELCHNER VON DYDIOWA, H., Clinical Molecular Biology
MOELLER, M., Medical Psychology
MORITZ, A., Thoracic, Heart and Vessel Surgery
MÜLLER-ESTERL, W., Biological Chemistry
MÜLSCH, A., Physiology

NENTWIG, G.-H., Dental and Maxillofacial Medicine
NÜRNBERGER, F., Anatomy, Neurobiology
OHRLOFF, CH., Ophthalmology and Experimental Ophthalmology
OVERBECK, A., Psychosomatics
PFEILSCHIFTER, J. M., Pharmacology and Toxicology
PFLUG, B., Psychiatry
POUSTKA, F., Child and Adolescent Psychiatry
RÄTZKE, P., Dental and Maxillofacial Medicine
SCHMIDT, H., Paediatric Radiology
SCHMITZ-RIXEN, TH., Vascular Surgery
SCHOPF, P., Maxillofacial Surgery
SCHUBERT, R., Hygiene
SEIFERT, V., Neurosurgery
SIEFERT, H., History of Medicine
SIGUSCH, V., Sexology
STEIN, J., Gastroenterology and Clinical Nutrition
STEINMETZ, H., Neurology
STÜRZEBECHER, E., Medical Acoustics
USADEL, K.-H., Internal Medicine
VOGL, TH., Radiological Diagnosis
VON JAGOW, G., Psychological Chemistry
VON LOEWENICH, V., Child Health
WAGNER, TH., Internal Medicine and Allergistics
WINCKLER, J., Anatomy
ZANELLA, F., Neuroradiology
ZEIHER, A. M., Internal Medicine
ZICHNER, L., Orthopaedics

Department of Modern Languages (Grüneburgplatz 1, 60323 Frankfurt am Main; tel. (69) 798-32742; fax (69) 798-32743):

BOHN, V., Modern German Philology
BROGGINI, G., German Philology
BUSCHENDORF, C., American Studies
ERFURT, J., Romance Philology
EWERS, H., German Philology and Literature (Children's Literature)
FREY, W., German
GARSCHA, K., Romance Philology
GREWENDORF, G., German Linguistics
HAMACHER, W., Modern German Philology
HANSEN, O., American Studies
HELLINGER, M., English Studies
HERRMANN, W., Teaching of German Language and Literature
KELLER, U., English
KLEIN, H. G., Romance Philology
KÜHNEL, W., English and American
LAUERBACH, G., English Studies
LEHMANN, H.-T., Theatre Studies
LEUNINGER, H., German Linguistics
LINDNER, B., German Language and Literature Teaching
LOBSIEN, E., English
METZNER, E., German
MITTENZWEI, I., Modern German
OPFERMANN, S., American Studies
OSSNER, J., Language Science of Modern German
QUETZ, J., English Teaching
RAITZ, W., History of German Literature
REICHERT, K., English/American Language
ROSEBROCK, C., Teaching of Literary Appreciation
RÜTTEN, R., French Language and Literature
SCHARLAU, B., Romance Philology
SCHEIBLE, H., German Language and Literature
SCHLOSSER, H. D., German
SCHLÜPMANN, H., Film Science
SCHNEIDER, G., Romance Philology
SCHRADER, H., Teaching of French
SEITZ, D., German
SOLMECKE, G., Teaching of English Language
STEGMANN, T., Romance Languages and Literature
WEISE, W.-D., English Teaching

WIETHÖLTER, W., Modern German Literature
WOLFZETTEL, F., Romance Philology
ZIMMERMANN, TH., Semantics

Department of Philosophy and History (Grüneburgplatz 1, 60323 Frankfurt am Main; tel. (69) 798-32758):

BREUNIG, P., Archaeology
CLAUSS, M., Ancient History
DETEL, W., Philosophy
ESSLER, W. K., Philosophy, Logic and Educational Theory
FEEST, CHR., Ethnology
FRIED, J., Ancient History
GALL, L., Medieval and Modern History
GREFE, E.-H., Teaching of History
HENNING, J., Prehistory
HONNETH, A., Social Philosophy
KOHL, K.-H., Ethnology
KULENKAMPFF, A., Philosophy
LENTZ, C., Ethnology
LÜNING, J., Prehistory
LUTZ-BACHMANN, M., Medieval Philosophy
MERKER, B., Philosophy
MUHLACK, U., General History
MÜLLER, H., Medieval Philosophy
PLUMPE, W., Economic and Social History
RECKER, M.-L., Recent History
SCHORN-SCHÜTTE, L., The Renaissance
VON KAENEL, H. M., Greek and Roman History

Department of Physics (Gräfstr. 39, 60486 Frankfurt am Main; tel. (69) 798-23313; fax (69) 798-28309):

ASSMUS, W., Experimental Physics
BECKER, R., Applied Physics
DREIZLER, R., Theoretical Physics
ELZE, T., Nuclear Physics
GÖRNITZ, T., Physics Teaching
GREINER, W., Theoretical Physics
HAUG, H., Theoretical Physics
HENNING, W., Experimental Nuclear Physics
JELITTO, R., Theoretical Physics
KEGEL, W., Theoretical Physics
KING, D. A., History of Natural Sciences
KOPIETZ, P., Theoretical Solid State Physics
LACROIX, A., Applied Physics
LANG, M., Experimental Physics
LYNEN, U., Nuclear Physics
MÄNTELE, W., Biophysics
MARUHN, J., Theoretical Physics
MESTER, R., Applied Physics
MOHLER, E., Applied Physics
RATZINGER, U., Applied Physics
RISCHKE, D.-H., Theoretical Heavy Ion Physics
ROSKOS, H., Experimental Physics
SALTZER, W., History of Science
SCHMIDT-BÖCKING, H., Experimental Atomic Physics
SCHUBERT, D., Physics for Doctors
SIEMSEN, F., Physics Teaching
STOCK, R., Experimental Nuclear Physics
STÖCKER, H., Theoretical Physics
STRÖBELE, H., Experimental Nuclear Physics

Department of Protestant Theology (Grüneburgplatz 1, 60323 Frankfurt am Main; tel. (69) 798-33344; fax (69) 798-24992; e-mail stenger@em.uni-frankfurt.de):

DEUSER, H., Protestant Theology
FAILING, W.-E., Protestant Theology
HEIMBROCK, H. G., Protestant Theology
WEBER, E., Protestant Theology

Department of Psychology and Sport (Kettenhofweg 128, 60054 Frankfurt am Main; tel. (69) 798-23267; fax (69) 798-24956):

BALLREICH, A., Training Science
BANZER, W., Prevention and Rehabilitation
BAUER, W., General Psychology
DEGENHARDT-EWERT, A., Diagnostic Psychology

ECKENSBERGER, L. H., Psychology
EMRICH, E., Sport Science
GIESEN, H., Educational Psychology
GOLD, A., Pedagogical Psychology
HAASE, H., Psychology and Sociology of Sport
HODAPP, V., Diagnostic Psychology
KNOPF, M., Psychology
LANGFELDT, H.-P., Pedagogical Psychology
LAUTERBACH, W., Clinical Psychology
MOOSBRUGGER, H., Psychological Methodology, Statistics
PREISER, S., Educational Psychology
PROHL, R., Sports
ROHDE-DACHSER, CH., Psychoanalysis
SARRIS, V., Psychology
SCHMIDTBLEICHER, D., Training Science
SCHWANENBERG, E., Social Psychology
SIRETEANU, R., Physiological Psychology
ZAPF, D., Psychology

Department of Social Sciences (Robert-Mayer-Str. 5, 60054 Frankfurt am Main; tel. (69) 798-22521):

ALLERBECK, K., Sociology
ALLERT, T., Sociology and Social Psychology
APITZSCH, U., Sociology
BOSSE, H., Theory of Socialization
BROCK, L., International Politics
CLEMENZ, M., Sociology of Education
ESSER, J., Study of Politics, Sociology
GERHARD, U., Sociology
GLATZER, W., Social Structures
GRESS, F., Political Science
HELLMANN, G., Foreign Policy
HIRSCH, J., Political Science
HOFMANN, G., Methods of Social Research, Statistics
HONDRICH, K. O., Sociology
KAHSNITZ, D., Polytechnic and Technical Instruction Course
KELLNER, H.-F., Sociology
KRELL, G., Political Science
MANS, D., Methods of Social Research
MAUS, I., History of Political Ideas
MÜLLER, H., Political Science
NEUMANN-BRAUN, K., Sociology
NONNENMACHER, F., Teaching of Social Sciences
OEVERMANN, U., Sociology, Social Psychology
PROKOP, D., Mass Communications Research
PUHLE, H.-J., Political Science
RODENSTEIN, M., Sociology
ROPOHL, G., Polytechnic and Technical Instruction Course
ROTTLEUTHNER-LUTTER, M., Methodology
SCHMID, A., Polytechnic and Technical Instruction Course
SCHUMM, W., Sociology
SIEGEL, T., Sociology of Industrialized Societies
STEINERT, H., Sociology
TATUR, M., Political Science and Political Sociology

HEINRICH-HEINE-UNIVERSITÄT DÜSSELDORF

Universitätsstrasse 1, 40225 Düsseldorf
Telephone: (211) 81-00
Fax: (211) 342229
Internet: www.uni-duesseldorf.de
Founded 1965; formerly Medizinische Akademie, f. 1907
State control
Language of instruction: German
Academic year: October to September

Rector: Prof. Dr ALFONS LABISCH
Chancellor: ULF PALLME KÖNIG
Pro-Rectors: Prof. Dr RAIMUND SCHIRMEISTER, Dr HILDEGARD HAMMER, Prof. Dr VITTORIA BORSÒ, Prof. Dr JÜRGEN SCHRADER

Head of Student Secretariat: K.-H. FEHR
Dir of the International Office: Dr WERNER J. STÜBER
Librarian: Dr IRMGARD SIEBERT
Library: see Libraries and Archives
Number of teachers: 3,200
Number of students: 26,353

DEANS

Faculty of Economics: Prof. Dr HEINZ-DIETER SMEETS
Faculty of Law: Prof. Dr HORST SCHLEHOFER
Faculty of Mathematics and Natural Sciences: Prof. Dr GERD FISCHER
Faculty of Medicine: Prof. Dr WOLFGANG H. M. RAAB
Faculty of Philosophy: Prof. Dr BERND WITTE

PROFESSORS

Faculty of Economics (Universitätsstr. 1, Bld. 23.32.01.64, 40225 Düsseldorf; tel. (211) 81-13820; fax (211) 81-15353; e-mail wiwifak@uni-duesseldorf.de; internet www.uni-duesseldorf.de:7280/hhu/fakultaeten/wiwi):

BORNER, C., Business Administration and Finance
DEGEN, H., Statistics and Econometrics
FRANZ, K. P., Control and Taxation
GÜNTER, B., Business Administration and Marketing
HAMEL, W., Management and Business Administration
SCHIRMEISTER, R., Business Administration and Finance
SMEETS, H.-D., Economics
THIEME, H. J., Economics
WAGNER, G. R., Business Administration, Production Management and Environmental Economics

Faculty of Law (Universitätsstr. 1, Gebäude 24.91 U1 R65, 40225 Düsseldorf; tel. (211) 81-11414; fax (211) 81-11431; e-mail dekanat.jura@uni-duesseldorf.de; internet www.jura.uni-duesseldorf.de):

ALTENHAIN, K., Criminal Law
BUSCHE, J., Civil Law
DIETLEIN, J., Public Law
FEUERBORN, A., Civil Law, Industrial Law and International Civil Law
FRISTER, H., Criminal Law and Law of Criminal Procedure
HEY, J., Entrepreneurial Tax Law
JANSEN, N., German and International Private Law
LOOSSCHELDERS, D., Civil Law and International Law
LORZ, R. A., German and International Public Law
MICHAEL, L., Public Law
MORFOCK, M., Public Law, Sociology of Law and Economic Law
NOACK, U., Civil Law and Commercial Law
OLZEN, D., Civil Law and Law of Civil Procedure
POHLMAN, P., Civil Law and International Commercial Law
PREUSS, NICOLA, Civil Law, Int. Economic Law, Commercial Law
SCHLEHOFER, H., Criminal Law and Law of Criminal Procedure

Faculty of Mathematics and Natural Sciences (Universitätsstr. 1, Bld. 25.32.00.30, 40225 Düsseldorf; tel. (211) 81-12235; fax (211) 81-15191; e-mail dekan.math-nat-fak@uni-duesseldorf.de; internet www.math-nat-fak.uni-duesseldorf.de):

ALFERMANN, A.-W., Botany
AURICH, V., Informatics
BOTT, M., Biochemistry
BRAUN, M., Organic Chemistry
BUCHNER, A., Psychology
BUELDT, G., Biological Structural Research
CONRAD, S., Informatics

DHONT, J.-K., Physics
EGGER, R., Theoretical Physics
ERNST, J. F., Microbiology
FISCHER, G., Mathematics
FRANK, W., Inorganic and Structural Chemistry
GANTER, CH., Inorganic and Structural Chemistry
GETZLAFF, M., Applied Physics
GÖRLITZ, A., Physics
GREVEN, H., Zoology
GRIESHABER, M., Zoophysiology
GRUNEWALD, F., Mathematics
VON HAESELER, A., Bioinformatics
HEGEMANN, J., Microbiology
HEHL, F.-J., Psychology
HEIL, M., Psychology
HEINZEL, THOMAS, Experimental Physics
HOCHBRUCK, M., Applied Mathematics
HOLLENBERG, C., Microbiology
HÖLTJE, H.-D., Pharmacy
HUSTON, J. P., Psychology
JAEGER, K.-E., Molecular Enzyme Technology
JAHNS, H. M., Botany
JANSSEN, A., Statistics and Documentation
JANSSEN, K., Mathematics
JARRE, F., Mathematics
JORDAN, E., Physical Geography
KERNER, O., Mathematics
KIRSCHBAUM, C., Psychology
KISKER, E., Applied Physics
KLÄUI, W., Inorganic Chemistry
KLEINEBUDDE, P., Pharmaceutical Technology
KLEINERMANNS, K., Physical Chemistry
KLÜNERS, JÜRGEN, Mathematics
KNUST, E., Genetics
KÖHLER, K., Mathematics
KÖHNEN, W., Teaching of Mathematics
KORNYSHEV, A., Physics
KOWALLIK, K. V., Botany
KRAUTH, J., Psychology
KUCKLÄNDER, U., Pharmaceutical Chemistry
KUNZ, W., Genetics
LÄER, STEPHANIE, Clinical Pharmacy
LEUSCHEL, MICHAEL, Informatics
LI, SHU-MING, Pharmaceutical Biology and Biotechnology
LIKOS, CH., Theoretical Physics
LÖSCH, R., Botany
LÖWEN, H., Theoretical Physics
LUNAU, K., Neurobiology
MARIAN, CH., Theoretical Chemistry
MARTIN, WILLIAM, Botany
MAURE, M., Informatics
MEHLHORN, H., Zoology
MEISE, R., Mathematics
MEWIS, A., Inorganic and Structural Chemistry
MÜLLER, THOMAS, Organic Chemistry
MUSCH, JOCHEN, Psychology
NÄGELE, GERHARD, Physics
OLBRICH, STEFAN, Informatics
PAUSE, BETTINA, Psychology
PIETROWSKY, R., Psychology
PIETRUSZKA, JÖRG, Bio-organic Chemistry
PRETZLER, G., Experimental Physics
PROKSCH, P., Pharmaceutical Biology
PUKHOV, A., Theoretical Physics
RATSCHEK, H., Mathematics
REITER, D., Laser and Plasma Physics
RIESNER, D., Physical Biology
RITTER, H., Organic Chemistry
ROSE, C. R., Neurobiology
ROTHE, J., Informatics
RUETHER, U., Zoophysiology
SAHM, H., Biotechnology
SAMM, U., Plasma Physics
SCHIERBAUM, K., Raw Materials Science
SCHILLER, S., Experimental Physics
SCHLUE, W.-R., Neurobiology
SCHMITT, LUTZ, Biochemistry
SCHÖTTNER, MICHAEL, Informatics
SCHRÖER, STEFAN, Mathematics

SCHURR, U., Botany
SEIDEL, C., Physical Chemistry
SIMON, R., Genetics
SINGHOF, W., Mathematics
SPATSCHEK, K.-H., Theoretical Physics
STANDT-BICKEL, C., Organic Chemistry
STAUDT, CLAUDIA, Organic Chemistry
STEFFEN, K., Mathematics
STOERIG, P., Psychology
STREHBLOW, H.-H., Physical Chemistry
VOLLMER, G., Teaching of Chemistry
WAGNER, R., Physical Biology
WANKE, E., Informatics
WEBER, H., Pharmacy
WEIN, N., Teaching Geography
WEINKAUF, R., Physical Chemistry
WEISS, H., Biochemistry
WENZENS, G., Geography
WESTHOFF, P., Botany
WILLBOLD, D., Physical Biology
WILLI, O., Experimental Physics
WISBAUER, R., Mathematics
WITSCH, K., Mathematics
WUNDERLICH, F., Parasitology

Faculty of Medicine (Universitätsstr. 1, Bld. 23.11 Ebene 02 Raum 65, 40225 Düsseldorf; tel. (211) 81-12242; fax (211) 81-12285; e-mail nappm@uni-duesseldorf.de; internet www.uni-duesseldorf.de/hhu/fak/newmed):

ABHOLZ, H.-H., General Medicine
ACKERMANN, R., Urology
ALBERTI, L., Psychosocial Disturbances
ANGERSTEIN, W., Phoniatry and Audiology
BARZ, J., Forensic Medicine
BAYER, R., Physiology
BECKER, J., Dentistry
BENDER, H. G., Obstetrics and Gynaecology
BÖCKING, A., General Pathology and Pathological Anatomy
BOEGE, F., Clinical Chemistry and Laboratory Diagnostics
BOJAR, H., Physiological Chemistry
BORNSTEIN, ST., Internal Medicine
BORSCH-GALETKE, E., Industrial Medicine
BUDACH, WILFRIED, Radiology
DAHL, ST. VOM, Industrial Medicine
DALDRUP, T., Forensic Toxicology
DALL, P., Obstetrics and Gynaecology
DRESCHER, D., Dentistry
FISCHER, J. H., Pharmacology and Toxicology
FÖRSTER, IRMGARD, Molecular Immunology
FRANZ, M., Psychiatry, Clinical Psychology
FRITZEMEIER, C. U., Dentistry
FÜRST, G., Radiology
GABBERT, H. E., Pathology
GAEBEL, W., Psychiatry
GAMS, E., Cardiological Surgery
GANZER, U., Otorhinolaryngology
GERAEDTS, M., Health Sciences and Social Medicine
GERHARZ, C.-D., Pathology
GIANI, G., Diabetes Research, Biometry
GÖBEL, U., Paediatrics
GÖDECKER, AXEL, Physiology
GOTTMAN, KURT, Neurophysiology
GRABENSEE, B., Internal Medicine
HAAS, H., Neurophysiology
HAAS, R., Internal Medicine
HÄUSSINGER, D., Internal Medicine
HARTUNG, H.-P., Neurology
HARTWIG, H.-G., Anatomy
HEINZ, H.-P., Medical Microbiology
HENGEL, HARTMUT, Virology
HERFORTH, A., Dentistry
HERING, P., Laser Medicine
HERNER, B., Neurology
HEUCK, C. C., Clinical Chemistry and Biochemistry
HEUGGE, U., Dermatology
HOHLFELD, T., Experimental Pharmacology
HOMEY, BERNHARD, Dermatology
IDEL, H., Hygiene
JANSSEN, ANTONIA, Opthalmology
KAHL, R., Toxicology

KELM, M., Internal Medicine
KNOEFEL, W., Internal Surgery
KRAUSPE, R., Orthopaedics
KRUTMANN, J., Dermatology and Venereology
KÜBLER, N., Dentistry and Plastic Surgery
LABISCH, A., History of Medicine
LINS, E. J. F., Neuroradiology
LUDWIG, S., Molecular Medicine
MAI, J. K., Neuroanatomy
MANNHOLD, R., Investigation of Molecular Active Substances
MAU, J., Statistics and Biomathematics in Medicine
MAYATEPEK, E., General Paediatrics
MEYER, ULRICH, Dentistry
MÖDDER, U., Clinical Radiology
MORGENSTERN, J., Applied Biomedicine
MSCHEN, MARKUS, Immunology
MUELLER, H. W., Neurobiology
MUELLER, H. W., Nuclear Medicine
MÜLLER-WIELAND, D., Clinical Biochemistry
NANENBERG, HELMUT, Paediatrics
NOVOTNY, G. E. K., Anatomy
NÜRNBERG, B., Physiological Chemistry
PFEFFER, K. D., Medical Microbiology
POREMBA, C., Pathology
RAAB, W., Dentistry
REHKAEMPER, G., Brain Research
REIFFENBERGER, G., Neuropathology
RITZ-TIMME, STEFANIE, Forensic Medicine
ROSS, H.-G., Physiology
ROTH, S.
ROYER-POKORA, B., Human Genetics
RUZICKA, T., Dermatology and Venereology
SANDMANN, W., Surgery
SCHARF, R., Haematology
SCHERBAUM, W. A., Internal Medicine
SCHMIDT, K. G., Paediatrics
SCHMITT, G., Radio-oncology
SCHNEIDER, F., Psychiatry
SCHNEIDER, M., Internal Medicine
SCHNITZLER, ALFONS, Neurology
SCHRADER, J., Physiology
SCHRÖR, K., Pharmacology and Toxicology
SCHULZE-OSTHOFF, K., Molecular Medicine
SEITZ, R., Neurology
SIEGRIST, J., Medical Sociology
SIES, H., Physiological Chemistry
STAHL, W. J., Physiological Chemistry
STEIGER, H.-J., Neurology
STEINGRÜBER, H.-J., Medical Psychology
STRAUER, B.-E., Internal Medicine
STÜTTGEN, U., Dentistry
SUNDMACHER, R., Ophthalmology
TARNOW, J., Anaesthesiology
THÄMER, V., Physiology
TRESS, W., Psychiatry
WEHLING, PETER, Molecular Orthopaedics
WENDEL, U., Paediatrics
WINDOLF, JOACHIM, Internal Surgery
WINTERER, GEORG, Neurology, Psychiatry
ZILLES, K., Anatomy

Faculty of Philosophy (Universitätsstr. 1, Bld. 23.21 Ebene 00 Raum 63—Dekanatsbüro, 40225 Düsseldorf; tel. (211) 81-12936; fax (211) 81-12244; e-mail witte@phil-fak.uni-duesseldorf.de; internet www.phil-fak.uni-duesseldorf.de):

VON ALEMANN, U., Politics
APTROOT, M., Yiddish Culture, Language and Literature
BARZ, H., Education
BAURMANN, M., Sociology
BEEH, V., Germanic Philology
BIRNBACHER, D., Philosophy
BLECKMANN, B., Ancient History
BÖHME-DÜRR, K., Media Sciences
BÖRNER-KLEIN, D., Yiddish Studies
BORSÒ, V., Romance Languages and Literature
BRANDES, D., Culture and History of Germans in Eastern Europe
BROCKE, M., Yiddish Studies

BÜHLER, A., Philosophy
BUSSE, D., Germanic Philosophy
BUSSE, W., English
DIETZ, S., Philosophy
FRIEDL, H., English
GEISLER, H., Romance Languages and Literature
GLOGER-TIPPELT, G., Developmental and Educational Psychology
GOMILLE, M., English
GÖRLING, REINHOLD, Media and Cultural Sciences
GÖTZ VON OLENHUSEN, I., Modern History
HARTMANN, P., Sociology
HECKER, H., East European History
HERWIG, H., Germanic Philology
HÜLSEN-ESCH, A., Art History
HUMMEL, H., Politics
KANN, C., Philosophy
KELLER, R., Germanic Philology
KILBURY, J., Computer Linguistics
KÖRNER, H., Art History
KOUTEVA, T., English
KROPP, SABINE, Politics
KRUMEICH, G., Modern History
KÜPPERS, J., Classical Philology
LABISCH, A., History of Medicine
LAHIRI, A., Linguistics
LAUDAGE, J., Medieval History
LEINEN, F., Romance Philology
MAE, M., Modern Japan
MATUSSEK, P., Modern German
MILLER-KIPP, G., Education
MOLITOR, H., Modern History
NOUN, CH., Modern History
POTT, H.-G., Modern German
REICHEL, M., Classical Philology
RETTIG, W., Romance Philology
REUBAND, K. H., Sociology
ROHRBACHER, S., Yiddish Studies
SCHAFROTH, ELMAR, Romance Languages and Literature
SCHURZ, G., Philosophy
SCHWARZER, C., Education
SEIDEL, T., English
SHIMADA, SHINGO, Modern Japan
SIEPE, H., Romance Philology
STEIN, D., English
STEIN, MARKUS, Classical Philology/Latin Sciences
STIERSTORFER, K., English
STOCK, W. G., English
TIEGEL, G., Sport
VOWE, GERHARD, Communication and Media Sciences
WEBER, CH., Modern History
WEISS, RALPH, Communication and Media Sciences
WITTE, B., Modern German
WUNDERLI, P., Romance Philology

ATTACHED INSTITUTES

Arbeitsgemeinschaft Elektrochemischer Forschungsinstitutionen AGEF eV: Universitatsstr. 1, 40225 Düsseldorf; Chair. Prof. Dr J. W. SCHULTZE.

Deutsches Diabetes-Forschungsinstitut an der Heinrich-Heine-Universität Düsseldorf: Auf'm Hennekamp 65, 40225 Düsseldorf; Dir Prof. Dr D. MÜLLER-WIELAND.

Deutsches Krankenhausinstitut: Tersteegenstr. 3, 40474 Düsseldorf; Dir UDO MÜLLER.

Düsseldorfer Institut für Dienstleistungs-Management: Dir Prof. Dr W. HAMEL.

Eichendorff-Institut—Literaturwissenschaftliches Institut der Stiftung Haus Oberschlesien: 6-Hösel, Bahnhofstr. 71, 40883 Ratingen; Dir Prof. Dr B. WITTE.

Institut für Biologische Informationsverarbeitung, Forschungszentrum Jülich GmbH: Dir Prof. Dr G. BÜLDT.

Institut für Biotechnologie, Forschungszentrum Jülich GmbH: 52428 Jülich; Dir Prof. Dr H. SAHM.

Institut für Chemie und Dynamik der Geosphäre: 52428 Jülich; Dir Prof. Dr U. SCHURR.

Institut für die Kultur und Geschichte der Deutschen im ostlichen Europa: Dir Prof. Dr DETLEF BRANDES.

Institut für Internationale Kommunikation: Hildebrandtstr. 4, 40215 Düsseldorf; Man. Dir Dr M. JUNG.

Institut für Medizin, Forschungszentrum Jülich GmbH: 52428 Jülich; Dir Prof. Dr K. ZILLES.

Institut für Umweltmedizinische Forschung an der Heinrich-Heine-Universität Düsseldorf: see under Research Institutes.

Institut 'Moderne im Rheinland': Dir Prof. Dr CEPL-KAUFMANN.

Neurologisches Therapiezentrum (NTC) an der Heinrich-Heine-Universität Düsseldorf: Hohensandweg 37, 40591 Düsseldorf; Dir Prof. Dr V. HÖMBERG.

Ostasien-Institut: Dir Prof. Dr MICHIKO MAE.

Technische Akademie Wuppertal eV: Postfach 100409, 42004 Wuppertal; Man. Dir Dipl. oec. ERICH GIESE.

HELMUT SCHMIDT UNIVERSITÄT— UNIVERSITÄT DER BUNDESWEHR HAMBURG
(University of the Federal Armed Forces, Hamburg)

Postfach 700822, Holstenhofweg 85, 22008 Hamburg

Holstenhofweg, 22043 Hamburg

Telephone: (40) 6541-1

Fax: (40) 6541-2869

Internet: www.hsu-hh.de

Founded 1972

State control

Languages of instruction: German, English

Academic year: October to September

Chancellor: VOLKER STEMPEL

Pres.: Prof. Dr-Ing. HANS-CHRISTOPH ZEIDLER

Vice-Pres.: Prof. Dr KLAUS BECKMANN

Librarian: Dr JOHANNES MARBACH

Library of 750,000 vols

Number of teachers: 100

Number of students: 2,700

Publications: *Uniforum* (1 a year), *Uniforschung* (1 a year)

DEANS

Dept of Economics and Social Sciences: Prof. Dr WILFRIED SEIDEL

Dept of Educational Science: Prof. Dr THOMAS HOPPE

Dept of Electrical Engineering: Prof. Dr-Ing. GERD SCHOLL

Dept of Mechanical Engineering: Prof. Dr-Ing. JOACHIM HORN

HOCHSCHULE WISMAR

Philipp-Müller-Str., Postfach 1210, 23952 Wismar

Telephone: (3841) 753-0

Fax: (3841) 753-400

E-mail: postmaster@hs-wismar.de

Internet: www.hs-wismar.de

Founded 1908 as Ingenieurhochschule Wismar, renamed 1939, 1969, 1988; present name 1992

State control

Academic year: September to August

Rector: Prof. Dr rer. nat. NORBERT GRÜNWALD

Pro-Rectors: Prof. Dr RAIMOND DALLMANN, Prof. Dr GUNNAR PRAUSE

Librarian: UTE KINDLER

Number of teachers: 140

Number of students: 5,100

DEANS

Architecture and Design: Prof. GEORG GIEBELER

Engineering: Prof. Dr WOLF-RAINER BUSCH

Wismar Business School: Prof. Dr JOACHIM WINKLER

HUMBOLDT-UNIVERSITÄT ZU BERLIN

Unter den Linden 6, 10099 Berlin

Telephone: (30) 2093-2946

Fax: (30) 2093-2107

E-mail: pr@hu-berlin.de

Internet: www.hu-berlin.de

Founded 1810

State control

Academic year: October to September

Pres.: Prof. Dr CHRISTOPH MARKSCHIES

Vice-Pres.: Prof. Dr UWE JENS NAGEL, Dr FRANK EVESLAGE, Prof. Dr MICHAEL W. LINSCHEID

Librarian: Dr M. BULATY

Library: see Libraries and Archives

Number of teachers: 2,322 (incl. 384 professorships, no FTEs)

Number of students: 34,072

Publications: *Humboldt-Spektrum* (4 a year), *Humboldt-Zeitung* (12 a year during each semester)

DEANS

Charité—Berlin University Medicine: Prof. Dr MARTIN PAUL

Faculty of Agriculture and Horticulture: Prof. Dr OTTO KAUFMANN

Faculty of Arts and Humanities I: Prof. Dr CHRISTOF RAPP

Faculty of Arts and Humanities II: Prof. Dr MICHAEL KÄMPER-VAN DEN BOOGAART

Faculty of Arts and Humanities III: Prof. Dr BERND WEGENER

Faculty of Arts and Humanities IV: Prof. Dr WILTRUD GIESEKE

Faculty of Economics and Business Administration: Prof. Dr OLIVER GÜNTHER

Faculty of Law: Prof. Dr CHRISTOPH PAULUS

Faculty of Mathematics and Natural Sciences I: Prof. Dr LUTZ-HELMUT SCHÖN

Faculty of Mathematics and Natural Sciences II: Prof. Dr PETER FRENSCH

Faculty of Theology: Prof. Dr ANDREAS FELDTKELLER

INTERNATIONAL UNIVERSITY IN GERMANY

Postfach 1550, 76605 Bruchsal

Telephone: (7251) 700110

Fax: (7251) 700150

E-mail: info@i-u.de

Internet: www.i-u.de

Founded 1998

Language of instruction: English

Academic year: September to July

President: Prof. Dr IAN CLOETE

Chancellor and CFO: MICHAEL SCHEITHAUER

Number of teachers: 35

Number of students: 200

DEANS

School of Business Administration: Prof. Dr FRANK MAIER

School of Information Technology: Prof. Dr KEIICHI NAKATA

JACOBS UNIVERSITY BREMEN GMBH

Campus Ring 1, 28759 Bremen
Telephone: (421) 200-40
Fax: (421) 200-4113
E-mail: info@jacobs-university.de
Internet: www.jacobs-university.de

Founded 1999
Private control
Language of instruction: English
Academic year: September to May

CEO: Prof. Dr JOACHIM TREUSCH
Chair.: KARIN LOCHTE
Dir for Admissions: JON IKRAM
Dir for Campus Activities and College Coordination: MARITA HARTNACK
Dir for Corporate Communications and Media Relations: PETER WIEGAND
Dir for Information Resources and Multimedia (IRC): HANS ROES
Dir for Resource Devt: ULF HANSEN
Dir for Student Marketing: CHRISTINE SOUDERS
Vice-Pres. for Science Park and Business Devt: Dr ALEXANDER ZIEGLER-JOENS
Librarian: HANS ROES
Library of 45,000 vols, 14,500 e-books, 100 journals, 35,000 e-journals
Number of students: 2,082

DEANS

Jacobs Centre for Lifelong Learning and Institutional Development: Prof. Dr URSULA STAUDINGER
School of Engineering and Science: Prof. Dr BERNHARD KRAMER
School of Humanities and Social Sciences: Prof. Dr HENDRIK BIRUS

JOHANNES GUTENBERG-UNIVERSITÄT MAINZ

55099 Mainz
Saarstr. 21, 55128 Mainz
Telephone: (6131) 39-0
Fax: (6131) 39-29-19
Internet: www.uni-mainz.de

Founded 1477, closed 1816; reopened 1946

Pres.: Prof. Dr JÖRG MICHAELIS
Chancellor: GOETZ SCHOLZ
Vice-Pres. for Academic Studies and Teaching: Prof. Dr JÜRGEN OLDENSTEIN
Vice-Pres. for Research: Prof. Dr JOHANNES PREUSS
Librarian: Dr A. ANDERHUB
Library: see Libraries and Archives
Number of teachers: 2,800
Number of students: 34,600

Publications: *Forschungsbericht, Forschungsmagazin*

DEANS

Faculty of Applied Linguistic and Cultural Studies: KARL-HEINZ STOLL
Faculty of Biology: Prof. Dr HARALD PAULSEN
Faculty of Catholic and Evangelical Theology: Prof. Dr LEONHARD HELL
Faculty of Chemistry, Pharmacy and Earth Sciences: Prof. Dr PETER LANGGUTH
Faculty of Evangelical Theology: Prof. Dr FRIEDRICH-WILHELM HORN
Faculty of History and Cultural Studies: Prof. JAN KUSBER
Faculty of Law and Economics: Dr ROLAND EULER
Faculty of Medicine: Prof. Dr med. Dr rer. nat. R. URBAN
Faculty of Philosophy and Pedagogics: Prof. Dr STEPHAN BÜRMAFÜSSEL NN
Faculty of Physics, Mathematics and Computing: Prof. Dr DIETRICH VON HARRACH
Music College and Academy of Art: Prof. Dr phil. JÜRGEN BLUME

PROFESSORS

Faculty of Applied Linguistic and Cultural Studies (06) (An der Hochschule 2, 76711 Germersheim; tel. (7274) 508-0; fax (7274) 508-35429; e-mail dekan06@uni-mainz.de; internet www.fask.uni-mainz.de):

VON BARDELEBEN, R.
FORSTNER, M.
GIPPER, A.
HUBER, D.
KELLETAT, A.
KLENGEL, S.
KUPFER, P.
LOENHOFF, J.
MENZEL, B.
MÜLLER, K. P.
PERL, M.
SCHREIBER, M.
STOLL, K.-H.
WORBS, E.

Faculty of Biology (10) (Gresemundweg 2, 55128 Mainz; tel. (6131) 39-22548; fax (6131) 39-23500; internet www.uni-mainz.de/fb/biologie/biologie.html):

ALT, K. W.
BÖHNING-GAESE, K.
CLAßEN-BOCKHOFF, R.
DECKER, H.
EISENBEIS, G.
HANKELN, T.
HENKE, W.
KADEREIT, J. W.
KAMP, G.
KÖNIG, H.
MARKL, J.
MARTENS, J.
NEUMEYER, C.
PAULSEN, H.
PFLUGFELDER, G.
ROTHE, G.
SCHMIDT, E. R.
SEITZ, A.
STÖCKER, W.
TECHNAU, G.
TROTTER, J.
UNDEN, G.
WEGENER, G.
WERNICKE, W.
WOLFRUM, U.
ZISCHLER, H.

Faculty of Catholic and Evangelical Theology (01) (Forum 6, 55099 Mainz; tel. (6131) 39-22215; fax (6131) 39-23501; e-mail kath-dekanat@uni-mainz.de; internet www.theologie.uni-mainz.de):

BAUMEISTER, T.
DIETZ, W.
DINGEL, I.
FECHTNER, K.
FRANZ, A.
HELL, L.
HORN, F. W.
LANDMESSER, C.
LEHNARDT, A.
MEIER, J.
REISER, M.
REITER, J.
RIEDEL-SPANGENBERGER, I.
SIEVERNICH, M.
SIMON, W.
SLENCZKA, N
WEYER-MENKHOFF, S.
WIßMANN, H.
ZWICKEL, W.

Faculty of Chemistry, Pharmacy and Earth Sciences (09) (Becherweg 14, 55128 Mainz; tel. (6131) 39-22273; fax (6131) 39-23521; e-mail dekan19@uni-mainz.de; internet www.uni-mainz.de/fb/chemie/fbhome):

BANHART, F.
BASCHÉ, T.
DANNHARDT, G.
DOMRÖS, M.
EPE, B.

ESCHER, A.
FAHRENHOLZ, F.
FELSER, C.
FOLEY, S. F.
FREY, H.
GAUß, J.
GRUNERT, J.
HOFFMANN, T.
JANSHOFF, A.
KERSTEN, M.
KLINKHAMMER, K.
KOCH-BRANDT, C.
KRATZ, J. V.
KRÖNER, A.
KUNZ, H.
LANGGUTH, P.
LÖWE, H.
MEIER, H.
MEYER, G.
NUBBEMEYER, U.
PASSCHIER, C. W.
PINDUR, U.
PREUß, J.
RATTER, B. M. W.
REGENAUER-LIEB, K.
REICH, T.
RENTSCHLER, E.
RÖSCH, F.
SCHENK, D.
SCHMIDT, M.
SIROCKO, F.
STÖCKIGT, J.
TREMEL, W.
WILCKE, W.
WILKEN, R.
WITULSKI, B.
ZENTEL, R.

Faculty of History and Cultural Studies (07) (Jakob-Welder-Weg 18, 55128 Mainz; tel. (6131) 39-23346; fax (6131) 39-24619):

ALTHOFF, J.
BEER, A.
BIERSCHENK, T.
BLÜMER, WI.
BRAUN, E. A.
FELTEN, F. J.
GAUDZINSKI-WINDHEUSER, S.
KASTENHOLZ, R.
KIßENER, M.
KREIKENBOM, D.
KUSBER, J.
LENTZ, C.
MATHEUS, M.
MÜLLER, M.
OY-MARRA, E.
PARE, C. F. E.
PESCHLOW, U.
PRECHEL, D.
PRINZING, G.
RÖDDER, A.
SCHUMACHER, L.
VERHOEVEN-VAN ELSBERGEN, U.
WALDE, C.
WIESEND, R.

Faculty of Law and Economics (03) (Jakob-Welder-Weg 9, 55128 Mainz; tel. (6131) 39-22225; fax (6131) 39-23529; e-mail dekanat-fb03@uni-mainz.de; internet www.uni-mainz.de/fachbereiche/1754.php):

BECK, K.
BELLMANN, K.
BOCK, M.
BREUER, K.
BRONNER, R.
DÖRR, D.
DREHER, M.
ERB, V.
EULER, R.
FINK, U.
FRIEDL, G.
GOERKE, L.
GRÖSCHLER, P.
GURLIT, E.
HAAS, U.
HABERSACK, M.

HAIN, K.-E.
HEIL, O. P.
HENTSCHEL, V.
HEPTING, R.
HERGENRÖDER, C. W.
HETTINGER, M.
HUBER, F.
HUBER, P.
HUFEN, F.
KAISER, D.
KOLMAR, M.
KUBE, H.
LEISEN, D.
MÜLBERT, P. O.
OECHSLER, J.
PEFFEKOVEN, R.
RAMMERT, S.
ROTH, A.
RUTHIG, J.
SAUERNHEIMER, K
SCHULZE, P. M.
TRAUTMANN, S.
VOLKMANN, U.
WEDER, B.
ZOPFS, J.

Faculty of Medicine (04) (Obere Zahlbacher Straße 63, 55131 Mainz; tel. (6131) 39-33180; internet dekanat.medizin.uni-mainz.de):

BARTENSTEIN, P.
BEHL, C.
BEHNEKE, N.
BEUTEL, M. E.
BHAKDI, S.
BIRKLEIN, F.
BLETTNER, M.
BORK, K.
BRISENO, B.
BROCKERHOFF, P.
BUHL, R.
D'HOEDT, B.
DICK, B.
DIETERICH, M.
DÜBER, C.
DUSCHNER, H.
FISCHER, T.
FÖRSTERMANN, U.
GALLE, P. R.
HAAF, T.
HEINE, J.
HEINEMANN, M.
HEINRICHS, W.
HIEMKE, C.
HOMMEL, G.
HUBER, C.
JAGE, J.
JANSEN, B.
JUNGINGER, T.
KAINA, B.
KEMPSKI, O.
KIRKPATRICK, C. J.
KLEINERT, H.
KNOP, J.
KÖLBL, H.
KONERDING, M. A.
KRAFT, J.
KÜMMEL, W. F.
LACKNER, K. J.
LETZEL, S.
LEUBE, R.
LOOS, M.
LÜDDENS, H.
LUHMANN, H.
LUTZ, B.
MAEURER, M.
MANN, W.
MICHAELIS, J.
MÜLLER, W. E. G.
MÜLLER-KLIESER, W.
MÜNTEFERING, H.
MÜNZEL, T.
MUSHOLT, T.
NEURATH, M.
NIX, W.
OESCH, F.
OTTO, G.

PAUL, N. W.
PERNECZKY, A.
PFEIFFER, N.
PIETRZIK, C.
PLACHTER, B.
POHLENZ, J.
POLLOW, K.
POMMERENING, K.
REDDEHASE, M. J.
REITTER, B.
RESKE-KUNZ, A. B.
ROMMENS, P. M.
SAHIN, U.
SCHELLER, H.
SCHIER, F.
SCHILD, H.
SCHMIDBERGER, H.
SCHMITT, H. J.
SCHRECKENBERGER, M.
SCHREIBER, W.
SCHULTE, E.
SCHUMACHER, R.
SOMMER, C.
STOETER, P.
STOFFT, E.
STOPFKUCHEN, H.
STREECK, R. E.
THEOBALD, M.
THÜROFF, J. W.
TREEDE, R.-D.
VAUPEL, P.
VON BAUMGARTEN, R.
WAGNER, W.
WEBER, M. M.
WEHRBEIN, H.
WEILEMANN, L. S.
WERNER, C.
WILLERSHAUSEN, B.
WOJNOWSKI, L.
WÖLFEL, T.
ZABEL, B.
ZANDER, R.
ZEPP, F.
ZÖLLNER, E. J.

Faculty of Philosophy and Pedagogics (05) (Jakob-Welder-Weg 18, 55128 Mainz; tel. (6131) 39-20005; fax (6131) 39-20085; e-mail fsb05@uni-mainz.de):

BISANG, W.
BOESCHOTEN, H.
BRENDEL, E.
BREUER, U.
DREYER, M.
ECKEL, W.
EICHLER, K.-D.
ERLEBACH, P.
FISCHER, E.
FÜSSEL, S.
GEISLER, E.
GIRKE, W.
GÖBLER, F.
GRÄTZEL, S.
HORNUNG, A.
KREUDER, F.
KROPP, M.
LAMPING, D.
LEY, K.
MARTIN, A.
MEIBAUER, J.
MEISIG, K.
METZINGER, T.
MÜLLER-WOOD, A.
NÜBLING, D.
PORRA, V.
REITZ, B.
SARHIMAA, A.
SCHEIDING, O.
SCHULTZE, B.
SEELBACH, D.
SIMON, M.
SOLBACH, A.
SPIES, B.
STAIB, B.
STÖRMER-CAYSA, U.
VEITH, W. H.

VON HOFF, D.
WEHR, B.

Faculty of Physics, Mathematics and Computing (08) (Staudingerweg 9, 55128 Mainz; tel. (6131) 39-22267; fax (6131) 39-22994; e-mail info@phmi.uni-mainz.de; internet www.phmi.uni-mainz.de):

ADRIAN, H.
ARENDS, H.-J.
BACH, V.
BINDER, K.
BLOCH, I.
BORRMANN, S.
BROCKMANN, R.
DE JONG, T.
DOLL, T.
ELMERS, H.-J.
GÖTTLER, H.
GRAMSCH, B.
HANKE-BOURGEOIS, M.
HEIL, W.
HÖPFNER, R.
HUBER, G.
JAENICKE, R.
JÜNGEL, A.
KLEINKNECHT, K.
KLENKE, A.
KÖPKE, L.
LEHN, M.
MÜLLER-STACH, S.
OSTRICK, M.
PALBERG, T.
PAPADOPOULOS, N.
PERL, J.
POCHODZALLA, J.
REUTER, M.
ROWE, D. E.
SANDER, H.-G.
SCHILCHER, K.
SCHILLING, R.
SCHLEINKOFER, G.
SCHÖMER, E.
SCHÖNHENSE, G.
SCHUH, H.-J.
TAPPROGGE, S
VAN DONGEN, P. J.
VAN STRATEN, D.
VON HARRACH, D.
WALZ, J.
WERNLI, H.
WIRTH, V.
WITTIG, H.
ZUO, K.

Faculty of Social Sciences, Media and Sport (02) (Colonel-Kleinmann-Weg 2, 55128 Mainz; tel. (6131) 39-22247; fax (6131) 39-23347; e-mail fritsche@mail.uni-mainz.de):

AUFENANGER, S.
AUGUSTIN, D.
BÜRMANN, J.
DITTGEN, H.
DORMANN, C.
DRUWE, U.
FALTER, J. W.
GARZ, D.
GROB, N.
HAMBURGER, F.
HECHT, H.
HEINEMANN, E.
HILLER, W.
HRADIL, S.
HUFNAGEL, E.
JUNG, K.
KEPPLINGER, H. M.
KOEBNER, T.
KOLBE, F.-U.
KROHNE, H. W.
KUNCZIK, M.
KUNZ, V.
MEINHARDT, G.
MESSING, M.
MÜLLER, N.
NIENSTEDT, H.-W.
OCHSMANN, R.
PREISENDÖRFER, P.

RENNER, K.N.
RICKER, R.
ROLLER, E.
SCHELLE, C.
SCHNEIDER, N. F.
SCHWEPPE, C.
SEIFFGE-KRENKE, I.
VON FELDEN, H.
WILKE, J.
WOLFF, V.
ZIMMERLING, R.

Music College and Academy of Art (11) (Binger Str. 26, 55122 Mainz; tel. (6131) 39-35538; fax (6131) 39-30146; e-mail wenkel@ mail.uni-mainz.de; internet www.musik .uni-mainz.de):

BERNING, A., Academy of Art
BLUME, J., Theory of Music
DAUS, J., College of Music
DELNON, G., Stage Theory
DEUTSCH, N., Oboe
DEWALD, T., Singing
DOBNER, M., Double Bass
DREYER, L., Music Theory
EDER, C., Singing
FRANK, B., Piano
GAVRIC, D., Chamber Music
GERMER, K., Piano
GMEINDER, J., Clarinet
GNANN, G., Church Music
HAHN, G., Academy of Art
HELLMANN, U., Academy of Art
KAISER, H.-J., Church Music
KIEFER, P., Modern Music
KIESSLING, D., Academy of Art
KNOCHE-WENDEL, E., Academy of Art
MARX, K., Chamber Music
REICHERT, M., Modern Music
SHIH, A., Violin
SPACEK, V., Academy of Art
STRIEGEL, L., Music Theory
VETRE, O., Piano
VIRNICH, W., Academy of Art
VOGELGESANG, K., Academy of Art
WALLFISCH, R., Violoncello
ZARBOCK, H., Piano
ZIMMERMANN, J., Academy of Art

ATTACHED INSTITUTES

Forschungsinstitut für Wirtschaftspolitik (Institute for Economic Research): Universität, Jakob-Welder-Weg 4, 55099 Mainz; Dirs Prof. Dr HARTWIG BARTLING, Prof. Dr HELMUT DIEDERICH, Prof. Dr WALTER HAMM, Prof. Dr WERNER ZOHLNHÖFER.

Forschungsinstitut Lesen und Medien (Institute for Media Research): Fischtorplatz 23, 55116 Mainz; Dir Prof. Dr STEPHAN FÜSSEL.

Institut für Europäische Geschichte (Institute for European History): see under Research Institutes.

Institut für Geschichtliche Landeskunde (Institute for Historical Regional Studies of Rhineland-Palatinate): Universität, Johann-Friedrich-von-Pfeiffer-Weg 3, 55099 Mainz; Dirs Prof. Dr A. HAVERKAMP, Prof. Dr W. KLEIBER, Prof. Dr M. MATHEUS.

Institut für Internationales Recht des Spar-, Giro- und Kreditwesens (Institute for International Law of Banking): Universität, Saarstrasse 21, Haus Recht und Wirtschaft, 55122 Mainz; Dirs Prof. Dr W. HADDING, Prof. Dr U. H. SCHNEIDER.

Institut für Mikrotechnik GmbH (Institute for Microtechnology): Postfach 421364, 55071 Mainz;Carl-Zeiss-Str. 18–20, 55129 Mainz; Dir Prof. Dr W. EHRFELD.

Tumorzentrum Rheinland-Pfalz eV (Tumour Centre Rhineland-Palatinate): Am Pulverturm 13, 55101 Mainz; Dir Prof. Dr C. HUBER.

JUSTUS-LIEBIG-UNIVERSITÄT GIEßEN

Ludwigstr. 23, 35390 Gießen
Telephone: (641) 99-0
Fax: (641) 99-12259
Internet: www.uni-giessen.de
Founded 1607
State control
Academic year: October to September (two terms)
Pres.: Prof. Dr STEFAN HORMUTH
Vice-Pres: Prof. Dr JÜRGEN JANEK, Prof. Dr JOACHIM STIENSMEIER-PELSTER
Chief Admin. Officer: Dr MICHAEL BREITBACH
Librarian: Dr PETER REUTER
Number of teachers: 380
Number of students: 22,000
Publication: *Spiegel der Forschung* (1 a year)

DEANS

Department of Agrarian Sciences, Nutritional Sciences, Environmental Management: Prof. W. KÖHLER
Department of Biology, Chemistry and Geosciences: Prof. JÜRGEN MAYER
Department of Economics: Prof. Dr WOLFGANG SCHERF
Department of History and Cultural Studies: Prof. Dr HELMUT KRASSER
Department of Human Medicine: Prof. HANS MICHAEL PIPER
Department of Language, Literature and Culture: Prof. Dr HARTMUT STENZEL
Department of Law: Prof. Dr GABRIELE WOLFSLAST
Department of Mathematics and Information Studies, Physics, Geography: Prof. VOLKER METAG
Department of Psychology and Sport: Prof. Dr JOACHIM STIENSMEIER-PELSTER
Department of Social and Cultural Studies: Prof. Dr KLAUS FRITZSCHE
Department of Veterinary Medicine: Prof. MANFRED REINMACHER

PROFESSORS

Department of Agrarian Sciences, Nutritional Sciences, Environmental Management (Bismarckstr. 24, 35390 Gießen; tel. (641) 99-37001; fax (641) 99-37009):

BAUER, S., Project and Regional Planning
BECKER-BRANDENBURG, K., Nutritional Biochemistry
BOLAND, H., Agricultural Extension and Communication
BRÄUNIG, D., Management of Services for Persons
BRÜCKNER, H.-O., Food Science
DZAPO, V., Genetics, Breeding and Husbandry of Pigs and Small Animals
ERHARDT, G., Animal Breeding and Genetics
EVERS, A., Comparative Health and Social Policy
FELIX-HENNINGSEN, P., Soil Science and Soil Conservation
FREDE, H.-G., Resources Management
FRIEDT, W., Plant Breeding
GÄTH, S., Waste Management and Environmental Research
HERRMANN, R., Agricultural and Food Market Analysis
HOFFMANN, I., Nutritional Ecology
HONERMEIER, B., Crop Science
HOY, S., Farm Animal Housing and Biology
HUMMEL, H. E., Biological and Biotechnical Plant Protection
KÄMPFER, P., Recycling Microbiology
KOGEL, K.-H., Molecular Plant Pathology
KÖHLER, W., Biometry and Population Genetics
KRAWINKEL, M., Human Nutrition, International Nutrition

KÜHL, R. W., Food Economics and Marketing Management
KUHLMANN, F., Farm Management
KUNZ, C., Human Nutrition, Evaluation of Food
LEITHOLD, G., Organic Farming
LEONHÄUSER, I.-U., Nutrition Education and Consumer Behaviour
MEIER, U., Economics of Private Households and Family Sciences
MÜHLING, K.-H., Biochemical Aspects of Plant Nutrition
NEUHÄUSER-BERTHOLD, M., Human Nutrition
NUPPENAU, E. A., Agricultural and Environmental Policy
OPITZ VON BOBERFELD, W., Grassland Management and Forage Growing
OTTE, A., Landscape Ecology and Landscape Planning
PALLAUF, J., Animal Nutrition
SCHLICH, E., Home Engineering
SCHMITZ, P. M., Agricultural and Development Economics and Policy Analysis
SCHNELL, S., General and Soil Microbiology
SCHNIEDER, B., Housing and Human Ecology
SCHUBERT, S., Plant Nutrition
SEUFERT, H., Agricultural Engineering
VILCINSKAS, A., Applied Entomology

Department of Biology, Chemistry and Geosciences (Heinrich-Buff-Ring 58, 35392 Gießen; tel. (641) 99-35001; fax (641) 99-35009):

ASKANI, R., Organic Chemistry
BINDEREIF, A., Biochemistry
CLAUß, W., Animal Physiology
DORRESTEIJN, A. W. CH., Zoology
EHRENHOFER-MURRAY, A. E., Cosmetics
EMMERMANN, R., Mineralogy
ESSER, G., Plant Ecology
FORCHHAMMER, K., Microbiology
FRANKE, W., Geology
FRÖBA, M., Inorganic Chemistry
GEBELEIN, H., Chemistry Teaching
HAACK, U., Mineralogy
HUGHES, J., Plant Physiology
IPAKTSCHI, J., Organic Chemistry
JÄGER, H.-J., Experimental Plant Ecology
JANEK, J., Physical Chemistry
KLEE, R., Biology Teaching
KLUG, G., Microbiology
KUNTER, M., Anthropology
KUNZE, C., Botany
LAKES-HARLAN, R., Sensory Physiology
MARTIN, M., Immunology
MAYER, J., Teaching of Biology
OVER, H., Physical Chemistry
PINGOUD, A., Biochemistry
RENKAWITZ, R., Genetics
SCHINDLER, S., Inorganic Chemistry
SCHREINER, P., Organic Chemistry
SCHULTE, E., Zoology
SPENGLER, B., Analytical Chemistry
TRENCZEK, M., Zoology
VAN BEL, A. J. E., Organic Botany
VOLAND, E., Philosophy
WAGNER, G., Botany
WIEKE, T., Zoology and Biodiversity
WOLTERS, V., Animal Ecology

Department of Economics (Licher Str. 74, 35394 Gießen; tel. (641) 99-22001; fax (641) 99-22009; e-mail dekanat@wirtschaft .uni-giessen.de):

ABERLE, G., General Economics, Price Theory, Industrial Organization and Competition Policy, Transport Economics
ALEXANDER, V., General Economics, Money, Credit and Currency
BESSLER, W., General Business Administration, Finance and Banking
ESCH, F.-R., General Business Administration, Marketing

GLAUM, M., Business Administration, International Management, Accounting and Auditing

HEMMER, H.-R., General Economics, Development Economics

KABST, R., General Business Administration, Human Resource Management

KRÜGER, W., General Business Management, Organization, Leadership

MECKL, H., General Economics, International Economics

MORLOCK, M., General Business Management, Risk Management and Insurance

MÜLLER, H., General Economics, Economics for Subsidiary Students, Environmental Economics

RINNE, H., Statistics and Econometrics

SCHERF, W., General Economics, Public Finance

SCHWICKERT, A., General Business Administration, Computer Science in Business

SPENGEL, C., General Business Administration, Company Taxation

WEIßENBERGER, B., Business Administration, Management of Industrial Corporations, Controlling

Department of History and Cultural Studies (Otto-Behaghel-Str. 10, Haus G, 35394 Gießen; tel. (641) 99-28000; fax (641) 99-28009; e-mail dekanat@fb04.uni-giessen.de):

BÄUMER, F.-J., Religious Education Studies and Teaching of Religion

BAUMGARTNER, M., History of Art

CARL, H., Medieval and Modern History

EISEN, U., Bible Studies, Old Testament and New Testament

GOSEPATH, S., Practical Philosophy

GRÄB-SCHMIDT, E., Systematic Theology

HARTMANN, A., Islamic Studies

HAUSER, L., Systematic Theology

KIRCHNER, M., Turcology

KRASSER, H., Classical Philology

KURZ, W., Religion Lessons

LENGER, F., Medieval and Modern History

LEXUTT, A., History of the Church

MARTINI, W., Classical Archaeology

OSWALT, V., History Teaching

PROSTMEIER, F., Bible Studies, New Testament

QUANDT, S., History Teaching

REINELE, C., German Regional History

REULECKE, J., Modern History

RÖSENER, W., Medieval and Modern History

SPEITKAMP, W., Modern History

SPICKERNAGEL, E., History of Art

TAMMEN, S., History of Art

VON MÖLLENDORFF, P., Greek Philology

Department of Human Medicine (Rudolf-Buchheim-Str. 6, 35392 Gießen; tel. (641)-99-48001; fax (641) 99-48009):

ALZEN, G., Paediatric Radiology

BAUER, R., Nuclear Medicine

BAUMGART-VOGT, E., Anatomy and Cellular Biology

BECK, E., Molecular Biology

BECKMANN, D., Medical Psychology

BEIN, G., Clinical Immunology and Transfusion Medicine

BOHLE, R., Pathology

BÖKER, D.-K., Neurosurgery

BRETZEL, R., Internal Medicine

CHAKRABORTY, T., Medical Microbiology

DREYER, F., Pharmacology and Toxicology

EIKMANN, T., Hygiene

ENGELHART-CABILLIC, R., Radiology

FERGER, D., Dentistry

FLEISCHER, G., Auditory Research

FRIEDRICH, R., Molecular Genetics and Virology

GALLHOFER, B., Psychiatry

GERLICH, W., Medical Virology

GEYER, R., Biochemistry

GIELER, U., Psychosomatics and Psychotherapy

GLANZ, H., Otorhinolaryngology

GRIMMINGER, F., Internal Medicine, Pneumology

HEMPELMANN, G., Anaesthesiology and Operative Intensive Medicine

HOWALDT, H.-P., Surgery of the Mouth, Jaws and Face

KAPS, M., Neurology

KATZ, N., Clinical Chemistry

KAUFMANN, H., Ophthalmology

KIESSLING, J., Audiology

KLIMEK, J., Dentistry

KOCKAPAN, C., Endodontics

KRAWINKEL, M., Paediatrics, Nutritional Science

KREUDER, J., Paediatrics

KUMMER, W., Anatomy and Cellular Biology

LINDEMANN, H., Paediatrics

LOHMEYER, J., Internal Medicine

MEINHARDT, A., Anatomy and Cellular Biology

MERSCH-SUNDERMANN, V., Indoor-air Toxicology and Environmental Toxicology

MEYLE, J., Paradontology

MIDDENDORFF, R., Anatomy and Cellular Biology

MÜLLER, U., Human Genetics

NEUBAUER, B., Paediatrics

PADBERG, W., Visceral, Thoracic and Transplantation Surgery

PANCHERZ, H. J., Dental Orthopaedics

PIPER, H. M., Physiology

PRALLE, H., Internal Medicine

PREISSNER, K., Biochemistry

RAU, W. S., Radiological Diagnostics

REIMER, C., Clinical Psychosomatics and Psychotherapy

REITER, A., Paediatric Haematology and Oncology

ROELCKE, V., History of Medicine

SAUER, H., Physiology

SCHACHENMAYR, W., Neuropathology

SCHÄFFER, R., Cytopathology

SCHILL, W.-B., Dermatology and Andrology

SCHLÜTER, K.-D., Physiology

SCHNETTLER, R., Accident Surgery

SCHRANZ, D., Paediatric Cardiology

SCHULZ, A., Pathology

SEEGER, W., Internal Medicine, Pneumology

SKRANDIES, W., Physiology

STÜRZ, H., Orthopaedics

TILLMANNS, H., Internal Medicine, Cardiology

TINNEBERG, H.-R., Gynaecology

TRAUPE, H., Neuroradiology

VOGT, P., Cardiology, Vascular Surgery

WEIDNER, W., Urology

WEILER, G., Forensic Medicine

WETZEL, W.-E., Paediatric Dentistry

WÖSTMANN, B., Gerodontology and Clinical Aspects of Dental Materials

Department of Language, Literature and Culture (Otto-Behaghel-Str. 10, Haus G, 35394 Gießen; tel. (641) 99-31001; fax (641) 99-31009):

BERSCHIN, H., Romance Linguistics

BORGMEIER, R., Modern English and American Literature

EHLER, S., Teaching of German Language and Literature

EHRISMANN, O., German Language, Historical Linguistics

FEIEKE, H., German Linguistics and Teaching of German Language

FINTER, H., Applied Theatre Studies

FLOECK, W., Spanish Literature

FRITZ, G., German Philology

GANSEL, C., Teaching of German Language and Literature

GAST, W., Teaching of German Language and Literature

GOEBBELS, H., Applied Theatre Studies

GRAF, A., Slavonic Literatures

HORSTMANN, U., Modern English and American Literature

KURZ, G., History of Modern German Literature

LEGUTKE, M., Teaching of English Language

LEIBFRIED, E., General Literature and History of Literature

LOBIN, H., Applied Linguistics and Computer Linguistics

MEISSNER, F.-J., Teaching of Romance Languages and Literature

MUKHERJEE, J., English Language

NÜNNING, A., English and American Literature and Cultural Studies

OESTERLE, G., Modern German Literature

PRINZ, M., Teaching of Romance Languages and Literature

RAMGE, H., German Linguistics

RIEGER, D., Romance Literature

RÖSLER, D., German as a Foreign Language

SEEL, M., Philosophy

STENZEL, H., Romance Literature and Cultural Studies

WINGENDER, M., Slavonic Linguistics

WINKELMANN, O., Romance Linguistics

Department of Law (Licher Str. 72, 35394 Gießen; tel. (641) 99-21000; fax (641) 99-21109; e-mail dekanat@fb01.uni-giessen.de):

BEHNICKE, C., Civil Law, Commercial Law, Comparative Law, International Civil Law

BRITZ, G., Public Law, European Law

BRYDE, B.-O., Public Law

EKKENGA, J., Civil Law, Commercial Law

GIESEN, R., Civil Law, Labour and Social Law

GROPP, W., Criminal Law, Criminal Procedural Law

GROSS, T., Public Law, Administrative Science

HAMMEN, H., Civil Law, Commercial Law

HECKER, B., Criminal Law, Criminal Procedural Law

KREUZER, A., Criminology, Juvenile Criminal Law

LANGE, K., Public Law, Administration Teaching

LIPP, M., German Legal History and Civil Law

MARAUHN, T., Public Law, International Public Law, European Law

SCHAPP, J., Civil Law and Philosophy of Law

WALKER, W.-D., Civil Law, Labour Law, Civil Procedural Law

WOLFSLAST, G., Criminal Law, Criminal Procedural Law

Department of Mathematics and Information Studies, Physics, Geography (Heinrich-Buff-Ring 16, 35392 Gießen; tel. (641) 99-33000; fax (641) 99-33009):

BARTSCH, T., Analysis

BAUMANN, B., Mathematics, Algebra

BEUTELSPACHER, A., Mathematics, Geometry

BUHMANN, M., Numerical Mathematics

BUNDE, A., Theoretical Physics

CASSING, W., Theoretical Physics

DÜREN, M., Experimental Physics

FELIX-HENNINGSEN, P., Soil Science, Land Conservation

FENSKE, C., Mathematics

FRANKE, M., Teaching of Mathematics

GIESE, E., Economic Geography

HÄUSLER, E. K., Stochastics

HAVERSATH, J. B., Teaching of Geography

HERMANN, G., Experimental Physics

KANITSCHEIDER, B., Philosophy of Natural Sciences

KING, L., Geography

KOHL, C.-D., Applied Physics

KÜHN, W., Experimental Physics

METAG, V., Experimental Physics

METSCH, K., Mathematics, Geometry
MEYER, B., Experimental Physics
MOSEL, U., Theoretical Physics
MÜLLER, A., Experimental Physics
OVERBECK, L., Mathematics
PROFKE, L., Didactics of Mathematics
SALZBORN, E., Nuclear Physics
SAUER, T., Numerical Mathematics
SCHEID, W., Theoretical Physics
SCHLETTWEIN, D., Applied Physics
SCHOLZ, U., Geography
SCHWARZ, G., Teaching of Physics
SEIFERT, V., Geography
STUTE, W., Mathematical Statistics
TIMMESFELD, F. G., Mathematics, Algebra
WALTHER, H.-O., Mathematics, Analysis
WERLE, O., Didactics of Geography

Department of Psychology and Sport (Otto-Behaghel-Str. 10, Haus F1, 35394 Gießen; tel. (641) 99-26000; fax (641) 99-26009; e-mail dekanat@fb06.uni-giessen.de):

BORG, I., Applied Psychological Methods
BRUNNSTEIN, J., Educational Psychology
ENNEMOSER, M., Special Educational Psychology
FRESE, M., Work and Organizational Psychology
GEGENFURTNER, K., General and Experimental Psychology
GLOWALLA, U., Educational Psychology
HALDER-SINN, P., Psychological Diagnosis
HENNIG, J., Differential Psychology
MUNZERT, J., Sports Psychology
NEUMANN, H., Sport and Training
PROBST, H., Special Educational Psychology
SCHUSTER, C., Psychological Methodology
SCHWARZER, G., Developmental Psychology
SCHWIER, J., Sport and Teaching of Sport
SPORER, S., Social Psychology
STIENSMEIER-PELSTER, J., Educational Psychology

Department of Social and Cultural Studies (Karl-Glöckner-Str. 21, Haus E/B, 35394 Gießen; tel. (641) 99-23001; fax (641) 99-23009; e-mail dekan@fb03.uni-giessen.de; internet www.uni-giessen.de/fb03):

BIRCKENBACH-WELLMANN, H.-M., Political Science, European Studies
BULLERJAHN, C., Political Science, European Studies
CLAUS-BACHMANN, M., Music
DUBIEL, H., Sociology
DUNCKER, L., Educational Science
EBERS, A., Comparative Health and Social Policy
ECARIUS, J., Educational Science
FORNECK, H., Educational Science
FRITZSCHE, K., Political Science
GRONEMEYER, R., Sociology
HOFMANN, C., Educational Science
HOLLAND-CUNZ, B., Political Science, Gender Studies
KREBS, D., Empirical Research in Social Sciences
LEGGEWIE, C., Political Science
LIPPITZ, W., Philosophy of Education, Comparative Studies of Education
MOSER, V., Educational Science
NECKEL, S., Sociology
NITSCHE, P., Music
PHLEPS, T., Music
REIMANN, B., Sociology
RICHTER-REICHENBACH, K.-S., Teaching of Art
SANDER, W., Teaching of Social Sciences
SCHMIDT, P., Empirical Social Research
SCHWANDER, M., Educational Science
SEIDELMANN, R., Political Science, International Relations
SPICKERNAGEL, E., History of Art
STACHOWIAK, F., Educational Science
STANICZEK, J., Art Practice
STÖPPLER, R., Educational Science

WILLEMS, H., Microsociology and Qualitative Methods
WISSINGER, J., Educational Science

Department of Veterinary Medicine (Frankfurter Str. 74, 35392 Gießen; tel. (641) 99-38001; fax (641) 99-38009; e-mail dekanat@vetmed.uni-giessen.de):

BALJER, G., Infectious Diseases and Hygiene
BAUERFEIND, R., Control of Epidemics
BERGMANN, M., Veterinary Anatomy, Histology and Embryology
BOSTEDT, H., Physiology and Pathology of Reproduction
BÜLTE, M., Veterinary Nutrition
CLAUß, W., Animal Physiology
DIENER, M., Veterinary Physiology
DOLL, K., Diseases of Ruminants
EISGRUBER, H., Hygiene of Food of Animal Origin and Consumer Protection
ERHARDT, G., Animal Breeding and Genetics of Domestic Animals
GERSTBERGER, R., Veterinary Physiology
HOFFMANN, B., Physiology and Pathology of Reproduction
KALETA, E., Diseases and Hygiene of Poultry
KÖLLE, S., Veterinary Anatomy, Histology and Embryology
KRAMER, M., Small Animal Surgery
KRESSIN, M., Veterinary Anatomy, Histology and Embryology
LEISER, R., Veterinary Anatomy, Histology and Embryology
LITZKE, L.-F., Equine Surgery
MORITZ, A., Internal Medicine
NEIGER, R., Small Animal Internal Medicine
PETZINGER, E. D., Pharmacology and Toxicology
REINACHER, M., Pathology
REINER, G., Department of Swine Diseases (Internal Medicine and Surgery)
RÜMENAPF, T., Clinical Virology
THIEL, H.-J., Virology
USLEBER, E., Milk Science
WENGLER, G., Virology and Cellular Biology
WÜRBEL, H., Animal Welfare and Ethology
ZAHNER, H., Parasitology

KATHOLISCHE UNIVERSITÄT EICHSTÄTT-INGOLSTADT

Ostenstrasse 26–28, 85072 Eichstätt
Telephone: (8421) 93-0
Fax: (8421) 931796
E-mail: info@ku-eichstaett.de
Internet: www.ku-eichstaett.de
Founded 1972, reviving a foundation of 1564
Academic year: April to February
President: Prof. Dr RUPRECHT WIMMER
Vice-President: Prof. Dr HELMUT FISCHER
Chief Administrative Officer: Dr GOTTFRIED FRHR. VON DER HEYDTE
Librarian: Dr ANGELIKA REICH
Library of 1,600,000 vols
Number of teachers: 460
Number of students: 4,400
Publications: *Agora* (2 a year), *Eichstätter Beiträge* (2 a year), *Eichstätter Materialen* (2 a year), *Eichstätter Studien* (3 a year)

DEANS

Faculty of Economic Sciences: Prof. Dr JOHANNES SCHNEIDER
Faculty of History and Social Sciences: Prof. Dr KARSTEN RUPPERT
Faculty of Languages and Literature: Prof. Dr GERHARD ZIMMER
Faculty of Mathematics and Geography: Prof. Dr HANS-PETER BLATT
Faculty of Philosophy and Education: Prof. Dr PETER BRÜNGER

Faculty of Religious Education: Prof. Dr UTO MEIER
Faculty of Social Studies: Prof. Dr ULRICH BARTOSCH
Faculty of Theology: Prof. Dr ALOIS SCHIFFERLE

PROFESSORS

Faculty of Economic Sciences (Auf den Schanz 49, 85049 Eichstätt; tel. (8421) 937-1801; fax (8421) 937-1950; e-mail elisabeth.batz@ku-eichstaett.de; internet www.ku-eichstaett.de/fakultaeten/wwf):

BURGER, A., General Business Management
BÜSCHKEN, J., Business Administration and Marketing
DJANANI, C., General Business Management
FISCHER, H., Economics
FISCHER, T. M., General Business Management Controlling
FUCHS, M., Law for Economists
GENOSKO, J., Economic and Social Policy
KUHN, H., Business Administration, Production and Operations Management
KÜSTERS, U., Statistics
KUTSCHKER, M., General Business Management, International Management
LUTTERMANN, C., Law for Economists
RINGLSTETTER, M., General Business Management
SCHNEIDER, J., Economics
STAUSS, B., Business Administration and Services Management
WILDE, K., General Business Management and Economic Information Technology
WILKENS, M., General Business Management, Financing

Faculty of History and Social Sciences (Universitätsallee 1, 85072 Eichstätt; tel. (8421) 931286; fax (8421) 931798; e-mail gertraud.reinwald@ku-eichstaett.de; internet www.ku-eichstaett.de/fakultaeten/ggf):

DETJEN, J., Political Science
DICKERHOF, H., Medieval History
GRECA, R., Sociology
KÖNIG, H.-J., Latin American History
LAMNEK, S., Sociology
LUKS, L., Contemporary Eastern European History
MALITZ, J., Ancient History
MÜLLER, R. A., Early Modern History
RUPPERT, K., Modern and Contemporary History
SCHREIBER, W., Theory and Teaching of History
SCHUBERT, K., Political Science
SCHWINN, T., Sociology
TREIBER, A., Folklore
ZSCHALER, F., History of Economics and Social Development

Faculty of Languages and Literature (Universitätsallee 1, 85072 Eichstätt; tel. (8421) 931517; fax (8421) 931797; e-mail monika.bittl@ku-eichstaett.de; internet www.ku-eichstaett.de/fakultaeten/slf):

BAMMESBERGER, A., English Linguistics
DICKE, G., German Literature
GSELL, O., Romance Linguistics
HÖMBERG, W., Journalism
KLÖDEN, H., Romance Linguistics
KRAFFT, P., Classical Philology
MARTIN, F.-P., Teaching of French Language
MUELLER, K., German as a Foreign Language
NATE, R., English Literature
NEUMANN, M., Modern German Literature
PITTROF, T., New German Literature
RENK, H. E., Teaching of German Language and Literature
RONNEBERGER-SIBOLD, E., Historic German Linguistics

SCHNACKERTZ, H.-J., American Literature
TONNEMACHER, J., Journalism
TSCHIEDEL, H.-J., Classical Philology
WEHLE, W., Romance Literature
WEIGAND, R. U., Medieval German Literature
ZIMMER, G., Classical Archaeology

Faculty of Mathematics and Geography (Ostenstr. 28, 85072 Eichstätt; tel. (8421) 931456; fax (8421) 931789; e-mail claudia .banzer@ku-eichstaett.de; internet www .ku-eichstaett.de/fakultaeten/mgf):

BECHT, M., Physical Geography
BISCHOFF, W., Mathematics
BLATT, H.-P., Mathematics
DESEL, J., Informatics
DIEHL, S., Informatics
FELIX, R., Mathematics
FISCHER, H., Mathematics
HEMMER, I., Teaching of Geography
HOPFINGER, H., Geography
KUTSCH, H., Physical Geography
PECHLANER, H., Tourism
RESSEL, P., Mathematics
RICKER, W., Mathematics
ROHLFS, J., Mathematics
SOMMER, M., Mathematics
STEINBACH, J., Geography

Faculty of Philosophy and Education (Ostenstr. 26, 85072 Eichstätt; tel. (8421) 931298; fax (8421) 931799; e-mail dekanat .ppf@ku-eichstaett.de; internet www .ku-eichstaett.de/fakultaeten/ppf):

BRÜNGER, P., Music Education
FELL, M., Adult Education
FETZ, R., Philosophy
GEISER, G., Pedagogics of Work
GRABOWSKI, F., Psychology
HABISCH, A., Central Institute for Marriage and Family in Society
HELLBRÜCK, J., Psychology
JENDROWIAK, H.-W., General Pedagogics
KALS, E., Psychology
KERKHOFF, G., Psychology
KÖCK, M., Pedagogics of Work
KONRAD, F.-M., Historical and Comparative Pedagogy
KÖPPEL, G., Art
LÄMMERMANN, G., Protestant Theology
LOVEN, C., Musicology
LUTTER, K., Sports
SCHMIDT, H.-L., Social Pedagogics
SCHÖNIG, W., Pedagogics of School
SCHULTHEIS, K., Elementary Education
THOMAS, F., Psychology
ZIMMERMANN, M., Art History

Faculty of Religious Education (vocational courses) (Pater-Philipp-Jeningen-Platz 6, 85072 Eichstätt; tel. (8421) 931275; fax (8421) 931784; e-mail dekanat.rpf@ ku-eichstaett.de; internet www.ku-eichstaett .de/fakultaeten/rpf):

EHAM, M., Music and Voice Training
KURTEN, P., Dogmatics
MEIER, U., Religious Education
OBERRÖDER, W., Theory and Practice of Church Work
SCHUSTER, B., Psychology
SILL, B., Moral Theology and Social Ethics
STAUCHIGL, B., Pedagogics
TAGLIACARNE, P., Old Testament
TRAUTMANN, M., New Testament
WILLERS, U., Fundamental Theology and Philosophy

Faculty of Social Studies (vocational courses) (Ostenstr. 26, 85072 Eichstätt; tel. (8421) 931246; fax (8421) 931773; e-mail dekanat .fsw@ku-eichstaett.de; internet www .ku-eichstaett.de/fakultaeten/swf):

BARTOSCH, U., Pedagogics
BECK, C., Social Work
ERATH, P., Social Work
GÖPPNER, H.-J., Psychology
KLUG, W., Social Work

OXENKNECHT-WITZSCH, R., Law
SCHIEREN, S., Political Science

Faculty of Theology (P.-Philipp-Jeningen-Platz 6, 8507 Eichstätt; tel. (8421) 931437; fax (8421) 931779; e-mail karin.lepschy@ ku-eichstaett.de; internet www.ku-eichstaett .de/fakultaeten/thf):

BÄRSCH, F., Liturgy
BÖTTIGHEIMER, C., Fundamental Theology
FISCHER, N., Philosophy and Basic Questions of Theology
GERWING, M., Dogmatics
GROSS, E., Religious Teaching and Teaching of Catholic Religion
HOFMANN, J., Old Church History and Patrology
MAIER, K., Middle and New Church History
MAYER, B., New Testament
MÖDE, E., Homiletics
MÜLLER, S. E., Moral Theology
SCHIFFERLE, A., Pastoral Theology
WEIß, A., Canon Law/History of Church Law
ZAPFF, B., Old Testament

LEUPHANA UNIVERSITÄT LÜNEBURG

Scharnhorststr. 1, 21335 Lüneburg

Telephone: (4131) 677-0
Fax: (4131) 677-1099
E-mail: info@leuphana.de
Internet: www.leuphana.de

Founded 1946
State control

Pres.: Dr SASCHA SPOUN
Vice-Pres: Prof. Dr HEINRICH DEGENHART, HOLM KELLER, Prof. Dr FERDINAND MÜLLER-ROMMEL, Prof. Dr SABINE REMDISCH, Prof. Dr STEFAN SCHALTEGGER
Librarian: TORSTEN AHRENS

Library of 630,000 vols
Number of teachers: 443
Number of students: 7,541

Publication: *Forschungsberichte* (every 3 years)

DEANS

Faculty of Business Administration, Behavioural Sciences and Law: Prof. Dr THOMAS WEIN
Faculty of Education, Cultural and Social Sciences: Prof. Dr PETER PEZ
Faculty of Environmental Sciences and Information Technology: Prof. Dr ULRICH HOFFMAN

PROFESSORS

Faculty of Business Administration, Behavioural Sciences and Law (tel. (4131) 677-2001; fax (4131) 78-2009; e-mail hackbarth@ uni.leuphana.de; internet www.leuphana.de/ fakultaet2):

BAXMANN, U., Banking, Finance and Accounting
HEINEMANN, M., Economics
LOHMANN, M., Experimental Industrial Psychology (LüneLab)
MARTIN, A., Small- and Medium-Sized Enterprises
MERZ, J., Research Institute on Professions
REMDISCH, S., Small- and Medium-Sized Enterprises
WEINRICH, G., Analytical Management
WEISENFELD, U., Corporate Development
ZENZ, E., Business Law

Faculty of Education, Cultural and Social Sciences (tel. (4131) 677-1601; fax (4131) 677-1608; e-mail sartisohn@uni.leuphana.de; internet www.leuphana.de/fakultaet1):

BURKART, G., Sociology

CZERWENKA, K., School and Higher Education Research
FAULSTICH, W., Applied Media Research
GUDER, K., Mathematics and Mathematics Education
KARSTEN, M., Social Work and Social Pedagogy
KIRCHBERG, V., Cultural Research and Arts
KIRSCHNER, U., Urban and Cultural Area Research
MASET, P., Studies in Arts, Music and Mediation
MÜLLER-ROMMEL, F., Political Science
NEIDHARDT, E., Psychology
ÓSULLIVAN, E., English Studies
ROOSE, H., Theology and Pedagogy of Religion
RÖSER, J., Communications and Media Culture
RUWISCH, S., Mathematics and Mathematics Education
STANGE, W., Social Work and Social Pedagogy
STOLTENBERG, U., Integrative Studies
UHLE, R., Educational Science
WEINHOLD, S., German Language and Literature Education
WÖHLER, K., Leisure Science, Play and Physical Education

Faculty of Environmental Sciences and Information Technology (tel. (4131) 677-2801; fax (4131) 677-2803; e-mail dembeck@ uni-lueneburg.de; internet www .uni-lueneburg.de/fakultaet3/):

AßMANN, TH., Ecology and Environmental Chemistry
BAUMGÄRTNER, S., Sustainability Management
BONIN, H., Computer Science
GROß, M., Electronic Business Management
HOFMEISTER, S., Environmental Strategy
MICHELSEN, G., Environmental and Sustainability Communication
RUCK, W., Ecology and Environmental Chemistry
SCHALTEGGER, S., Sustainability Management
SCHLEICH, H., Production Technologies
SCHOMERUS, T., Environmental Strategy
WEINRICH, G., Analytical Management
WELGE, R., Distributed Autonomic Systems and Technologies

LUDWIG-MAXIMILIANS-UNIVERSITÄT MÜNCHEN

Geschwister-Scholl-Pl. 1, 80539 Munich

Telephone: (89) 2180-0
Fax: (89) 2180-2322
Internet: www.lmu.de

Founded 1472
Academic year: October to July

Pres.: Prof. Dr rer. pol. BERND HUBER
Vice-Pres.: Prof. Dr med. Dr h.c. REINHARD PUTZ
Vice-Pres.: Prof. Dr INKA MULDER-BACH
Vice-Pres.: Dr SIGMUND STIUTZING
Vice-Pres.: Prof. Dr THOMAS CARELL
Chief Admin. Officer: CHRISTOPH MUELKE
Dir of Library: Dr KLAUS-RAINER BRINTZINGER

Number of teachers: 3,399
Number of students: 45,539

Publications: *'Einsichten'* (1 a year), *LMU at a glance* (every 2 years), *MUM* (4 a year), *Veranstaltungskalender* (12 a year), *Vorlesungsverzeichnis* (2 a year)

DEANS

Faculty of Biology: Prof. Dr BENEDICT GROTHE
Faculty of Business Administration: Prof. Dr THOMAS HESS

Faculty of Catholic Theology: Prof. Dr KON-
RAD HILPERT
Faculty of Chemistry and Pharmacy: Prof.
Dr MARTIN BEIL
Faculty of Cultural Studies: Prof. Dr KLAUS
VOLLMER
Faculty of Economics: Prof. Dr ANDREAS
HAUFLER
Faculty of Geosciences: Prof. Dr WOLFRAM
MAUSER
Faculty of History and the Arts: Prof. Dr
CHRISTOPHER BALME
Faculty of Languages and Literatures: Prof.
Dr ULRICH SCHWEIER
Faculty of Law: Prof. Dr ALFONS BUERGE
Faculty of Mathematics, Computer Science
and Statistics: Prof. Dr HEINRICH HUSS-
MANN
Faculty of Medicine: Prof. Dr MAXMILIAN
REISER
Faculty of Philosophy, Philosophy of Science
and the Study of Religion: Prof. Dr JULIAN
NIDA-RUEMELIN
Faculty of Physics: Prof. Dr AXEL SCHENZLE
Faculty of Protestant Theology: Prof. Dr
CHRISTOPH LEVIN
Faculty of Psychology and Educational Sci-
ences: Prof. Dr JOACHIM KAHLERT
Faculty of Social Sciences: Prof. Dr HANS-
BERND BROSIUS
Faculty of Veterinary Medicine: Prof. Dr
JOACHIM BRAUN

MARTIN LUTHER-UNIVERSITÄT HALLE-WITTENBERG

Universitätsplatz 10, 06099 Halle (Saale)
Telephone: (345) 552-0
Fax: (345) 552-7077
E-mail: rektor@uni-halle.de
Internet: www.uni-halle.de
Founded 1502 (Wittenberg), 1694 (Halle),
1817 (Halle-Wittenberg)
Academic year: October to September
Rector: Prof. Dr WILFRIED GRECKSCH
Number of teachers: 340
Number of students: 18,500
Publication: *Scientia halensis* (4 a year).

MEDIZINISCHE HOCHSCHULE HANNOVER

Carl-Neuberg-Str. 1, 30625 Hanover
Telephone: (511) 532-0
Fax: (511) 532-5550
E-mail: pressestelle@mh-hannover.de
Internet: www.mh-hannover.de
Founded 1965
Pres.: Prof. Dr DIETER BITTER-SUERMANN
Vice-Pres: HOLGER BAUMANN, Dr ANDREAS
TECKLENBURG
Librarian: Dr ANNAMARIE FELSCH-KLOTZ
Library of 280,000 vols
Number of teachers: 614
Number of students: 3,197

DEANS

Biology: Prof. Dr G. GROS
Dentistry: Prof. Dr H. TSCHERNITSCHEK
Medicine: Prof. Dr HERMANN HALLER

PROFESSORS

Anatomy:
GROTE, C., Neuroanatomy
GRUBE, D., Microscopic Anatomy
PABST, R., Functional and Applied Anat-
omy
UNGEWICKELL, E., Anatomy
Biochemistry:
GAESTEL, M., Physiological Chemistry
GERARDY-SCHAHN, R., Cellular Chemistry
LENZEN, S., Biochemistry
MANSTEIN, D., Biophysical Chemistry

Laboratory Medicine:
BLASCZYK, R., Transfusion Medicine
FÖRSTER, R., Immunology
GOSSLER, A., Molecular Biology
HEDRICH, H.-J., Animal Research
SCHULZ, T., Laboratory Medicine
SUERBAUM, S., Microbiology and Hospital
Hygiene
Medical Technologies:
HECKER, H., Biometry
MATTHIES, H., Medical Computing
Pathology, Genetics and Forensic Medicine:
KREIPE, H.-H., Pathology
SCHLEGELBERGER, B., Pathology, Genetics
and Forensic Medicine
SCHMIDTKE, J., Human Genetics
TRÖGER, H.-D., Medical Law
Pharmacology and Toxicology:
JUST, I., Toxicology
RESCH, K., Pharmacology
STICHTENOTH, O., Clinical Pharmacology
WRBITZKY, R., Occupational Medicine
Physiology:
BRENNER, B., Molecular and Cell Physi-
ology
FAHLKE, C., Neurophysiology
GROS, G., Vegetative Physiology
MAASEEN, N., Sports Physiology/Sports
Medicine
Public Health Care:
GEYER, S., Medical Sociology
HUMMERS-PRADIER, E., General Medicine
LANGE, K., Medical Psychology
LOHFF, B., History, Ethics and Philosophy
of Medicine
SCHWARTZ, F. W., Epidemiology, Social
Medicine and Health Systems Research

MEDIZINISCHE UNIVERSITÄT ZU LÜBECK

Ratzeburger Allee 160, 23538 Lübeck
Telephone: (451) 500-0
Fax: (451) 500-3016
E-mail: presse@uni-luebeck.de
Internet: www.mu-luebeck.de
Founded 1964
Rector: Prof. Dr med. PETER DOMINIAK
Pro-Rectors: Prof. Dr med. THOMAS MARTI-
NETZ, Prof. Dr rer. nat. PETER SCHMUCKER
Chancellor: ASTRID KÜTHER
Number of teachers: 232
Number of students: 2,400
Publications: *Focus MUL* (4 a year), *For-
schungsbericht*

DEANS

Faculty of Medicine: Prof. Dr med. WOLF-
GANG JELKMANN
Faculty of Science and Technology: Prof. Dr
rer. nat. ENNO HARTMANN

DIRECTORS

Directors of Institutes
Medicine:
Anaesthesiology: Prof. Dr PETER
SCHMUCKER
Anatomy: Prof. Dr JÜRGEN WESTERMANN
Biometry and Statistics: Prof. Dr ANDREAS
ZIEGLER
Cardiology: Prof. Dr HANS-HINRICH SIEVERS
Child Psychology: Prof. Dr ULRICH
KNÖLKER
Clinical Chemistry: Prof. Dr MICHAEL
SEYFARTH
Clinical Rheumatology: Prof. Dr WOLFGANG
L. GROSS
Dermatology: Prof. Dr DETLEF ZILLIKENS
Ear, Nose and Throat: Prof. Dr BARBARA
WOLLENBERG

Experimental and Clinical Pharmacology
and Toxicology: Prof. Dr PETER DOMINIAK
Gynaecology and Childbirth: Prof. Dr
KLAUS DIEDRICH
Human Genetics: Prof. Dr GABRIELE GIL-
LESSEN-KAESBACH
Immunology and Transfusion Medicine:
Prof. Dr HOLGER KIRCHNER
Jaw and Facial Surgery: Prof. Dr Dr PETER
SIEG
Medical Clinic: Prof. Dr WERNER SOLBACH
Medical Clinic I: Prof. Dr HORST LORENZ
FEHM
Medical Clinic II: Prof. Dr HERIBERT
SCHUNKERT
Medial Clinic III: Prof. Dr PETER ZABEL
Medical Psychology: Prof. Dr Dr FRITZ
SCHMIELAU
Molecular Medicine: Prof. Dr GEORG SCZA-
KIEL
Neuroendocrinology: Prof. Dr JAN BORN
Neurology: Prof. Dr FRITZ HOHAGEN
Neuroradiology: Prof. Dr DIRK PETERSEN
Neurosurgery: Prof. Dr VOLKER TRONNIER
Occupational Medicine: Prof. Dr Dr
RICHARD KESSEL
Ophthalmology: Prof. Dr HORST LAQUA
Orthopaedics: Dr MARTIN RUSSLIES
Paediatrics: Prof. Dr EGBERT HERTING
Paediatric Surgery: Prof. Dr LUCAS WESSEL
Pathology: Prof. Dr ALFRED CHRISTIAN
FELLER
Physiology: Prof. Dr WOLFGANG JELKMANN
Plastic Surgery: Prof. Dr PETER MAILÄNDER
Psychosomatic Illnesses: Prof. Dr DETLEV-
O. NUTZINGER
Radiology and Nuclear Medicine: Prof. Dr
THOMAS HELMBERGER
Radiotherapy: Prof. Dr JÜRGEN DUNST
Research Centre Borstel: Prof. Dr Dr
SILVIA BULFONE-PAUS
Social Medicine: Prof. Dr Dr HANS-HEIN-
RICH RASPE
Surgery: Prof. Dr HANS-PETER BRUCH
Urology: Prof. Dr DIETER JOCHAM

Science and Technology:

Biochemistry: Prof. Dr ROLF HILGENFELD
Biology: Prof. Dr ENNO HARTMANN
Biomedical Optics: Prof. Dr REGINALD
BIRNGRUBER
Chemistry: Prof. Dr THOMAS PETERS
Information Systems: Prof. Dr VOLKER
LINNEMANN
International School of New Media: Prof.
Dr JOACHIM HASEBROOK
Mathematics: Prof. Dr JÜRGEN PRESTIN
Medical Computing: Prof. Dr SIEGFRIED J.
PÖPPL
Molecular Biology: Prof. Dr PETER KARL
MÜLLER
Multimedia and Interactive Systems: Prof.
Dr MICHAEL HERCZEG
Neuro- and Bioinformatics: Prof. Dr THO-
MAS MARTINETZ
Physics: Prof. Dr ALFRED X. TRAUTWEIN
Robotics and Cognitive Systems: Prof. Dr
ACHIM SCHWEIKARD
Software and Program Languages: Prof.
Dr WALTER DOSCH
Technical Informatics: Prof. Dr ERIK
MAEHLE
Telematics: Prof. Dr STEFAN FISCHER
Theoretical Computing: Prof. Dr RÜDIGER
K. REISCHUK

PROFESSORS

Faculty of Medicine:
ARNOLD, H., Neurosurgery
BRUCH, H.-P., Surgery
DIEDRICH, K., Gynaecology and Obstetrics
DOMARUS, H., Maxillary and Facial Sur-
gery
DOMINIAK, P., Pharmacology, Toxicology
and Clinical Pharmacology
FEHM, H. L., Internal Medicine

FELLER, A. C., Pathology
GROSS, W. L., Rheumatology
HALSBAND, H., Paediatric Surgery
HOHAGEN, F., Psychiatry
JELKMANN, W., Physiology
JOCHAM, D., Urology
KATUS, H. A., Internal Medicine
KESSEL, R., Industrial Medicine
KIRCHNER, H., Immunology and Transfusional Medicine
KNÖLKER, U., Child and Adolescent Psychiatry
KÖMPF, D., Neurology
KRUSE, K., Paediatrics
LAQUA, H., Ophthalmology
LÖHR, J., Orthopaedics
OEHMICHEN, M., Forensic Medicine
RASPE, H.-H., Social Medicine
RICHTER, E., Radiotherapy and Nuclear Medicine
SCHMIELAU, F., Medical Psychology
SCHMUCKER, P., Anaesthesiology
SCHWINGER, E., Human Genetics
SCZAKIEL, G., Molecular Medicine
SEYFARTH, M., Clinical Chemistry
SIEVERS, H. H., Cardiac Surgery
SOLBACH, W., Medical Microbiology and Hygiene
WEERDA, H., Otolaryngology
WEISS, H.-D., Radiology
WESTERMANN, J., Anatomy
WOLFF, H. H., Dermatology and Venereology

Faculty of Science and Technology:

AACH, T., Signal Processing and Process Control
DOSCH, W., Software Engineering
DÜMBGEN, L., Mathematics
ENGELHARDT, D., History of Medicine and Science
FISCHER, B., Mathematics
HARTMANN, E., Biology
HERCZEG, M., Multimedia and Interactive Systems
HOGREFE, D., Telematics
KONECNY, E., Medical Technology
LINNEMANN, V., Practical Informatics
MAEHLE, E., Computer Engineering
MARTINETZ, TH., Neuro- and Bioinformatics
MÜLLER, K.-P., Medical Molecular Biology
PETERS, TH., Chemistry
PÖPPL, S., Medical Informatics and Statistics
PRESTIN, J., Mathematics
REISCHUK, K. R., Theoretical Computer Science
RIETSCHEL, E.-TH., Immunochemistry and Biochemical Microbiology
ROELCKE, V., History of Medicine and Science
SCHÄFER, G., Biochemistry
TRAUTWEIN, A., Physics
VOSWINCKEL, P., History of Medicine and Science
ZEUGMANN, TH., Theoretical Computer Science

OTTO-FRIEDRICH-UNIVERSITÄT BAMBERG

Kapuzinerstr. 16, 96045 Bamberg
Telephone: (951) 863-0
Fax: (951) 863-1005
E-mail: post@uni-bamberg.de
Internet: www.uni-bamberg.de
Founded 1647
State control
Academic year: October to September (2 semesters)
Pres.: Prof. Dr Hab. GODEHARD RUPPERT
Vice-Pres. for Research: Prof. Dr ANNA STEINWEG
Vice-Pres. for Teaching: Prof. Dr SEBASTIAN KEMPGEN

Chancellor: Dr DAGMAR STEUER-FLIESER
Librarian: Dr FABIAN FRANKE
Number of teachers: 138
Number of students: 9,143
Publications: *Bamberger Beiträge zur Englischen Sprachwissenschaft* (1 a year), *Bamberger Editionen*. Hg. v. H. Unger und H. Wentzlaff-Eggebert, *Bamberger Geographische Schriften* (1–2 a year), *Bamberger Universitätszeitung "uni.doc"* (7 a year), *Bericht des Rektors*, *Gratia: Bamberger Schriften zur Renaissanceforschung* (2 a year), *Forschungsforum* (1 a year), *Informationen* (irreggular), *Personal- und Vorlesungsverzeichnis* (1 a term), *Pressemitteilungen*, *Uni.kat*, *uni.vers* (2 a year)

DEANS

Faculty of Humanities: Prof. Dr KLAUS VAN EICKELS
Faculty of Human Sciences and Education: Prof. Dr SIBYLLE RAHM
Faculty of Information Systems and Applied Computer Science: Prof. Dr CHRISTOPH SCHLIEDER
Faculty of Social Sciences, Economics and Business Administration: THOMAS GEHRING

PROFESSORS

Faculty of Humanities:

ABRAHAM, U., German Language and Literature Instruction
ALBRECHT, S., Art History (Medieval Art History)
ALZHEIMER, H., European Ethnology
BARTL, A., Modern German Literature
BECKER, T., German Linguistics
BEHMER, M., Media Studies (Journalism Research)
BEHZADI, L., Arabic Studies
BENNEWITZ, I., Medieval German Philology
BIEBERSTEIN, K., Old Testament
BRANDT, H., Ancient History
BRASSAT, W., History of Art (Early Modern and Modern Art)
BREITLING, S., Building Research
BRUNS, P., Church History and Patrology
DE RENTIIS, D., Romance Philology
DIX, A., Historical Geography
DORNHEIM, A., Modern and Contemporary History
DREWELLO, R., Building Preservation Sciences
ECKER, H., Diffusion Processes of Literature
ENZENSBERGER, H., History (Diplomatics and Palaeography)
ERICSSON, I., Medieval and Post Medieval Archaeology
FÖLLINGER, S., Greek Studies
FRANKE, P., Islamic Studies
FREYBERGER, B., History Instruction
GIER, A., Romance Literature
GLÜCK, H., German Linguistics and German as a Foreign Language
GÖLER, D., Human Geography I (Social and Population Geography)
HAASE, M., Romance Philology
HÄBERLEIN, M., Early Modern History
HEIMBACH-STEINS, M., Christian Social Theory
HERZOG, C., Turkish Studies
HOFFMANN, B., Iranian Studies
HOUSWITSCHKA, C., English Literature
HUBEL, A., Monument Preservation and Restoration
ILLIES, C., Philosophy II
ILYASOV, D., Islamic Art and Archaeology
JANSOHN, C., British Culture
JÜNKE, C., Spanish and Latin American Literature
KEMPGEN, S., Slavic Linguistics
KONRAD, M., Archaeology of the Roman Provinces

KORN, L., Islamic Art and Archaeology
KRUG, M., English Linguistics
KÜGLER, J., New Testament Sciences
MARX, F., Modern German Literature
MÜLLER, M., English and American Studies (American Literatures)
NOEL, P., German Linguistics
RAEV, A., Slavic Art and Cultural History
RAHNER, J., Systematic Theology
SAALFELD, T., Comparative Politics
SCHÄFER, A., Prehistoric Archaelogy
SCHAMBECK, M., Religious Eduaction
SCHELLMANN, G., Geography II (Physical Geography and Landscape History)
SCHINDLER, A., Medieval German Philology
SCHÖTTLER, H., Pastoral Theology
STÖBER, R., Communication Studies
TALABARDON, S., Jewish Studies
THEIS-BERGLMAIR, A., Communication Theory and Journalism
ULRICH, M., Romance Linguistics
VAN EICKELS, K., Medieval History incl. Regional History of the Middle Ages
VON ERDMANN, E., Slavic Literatures
WAGNER-BRAUN, M., Economic and Innovation History

Faculty of Human Sciences and Education:

ARTELT, C., Educational Research
BEDFORD-STROHM, H., Protestant Theology/Systematic Theology and Contemporary Theological Issues
BENDER, W., Andragogy
CARBON, C., General Psychology and Methodology
CARSTENSEN, C., Psychology (Empirical Educational Research)
FAUST, G., Primary School Education
HERAN-DÖRR, E., Primary School Education (Science Education)
HOCK, M., Educational Psychology
HÖRMANN, G., Pedagogics
HÖRMANN, S., Music Pedagogy and Music Didactics
LAUTENBACHER, S., Physiological Psychology
LAUX, L., Psychology
RAHM, S., School Education
REINECKER, H., Clinical Psychology and Psychotherapy
RITTER, W., Protestant Theology/Religious Pedagogy and Didactics
ROßBACH, H., Early Childhood Education
RÜSSELER, J., General Psychology
SCHAAL, S., Science Education
SCHÄFER, CH., Philosophy I
SCHRÖDTER, M., Social Pedagogy
STEINWEG, A., Mathematics Education and Computer Science Education
WEINERT, S., Developmental Psychology
WOLSTEIN, J., Pathopsychology

Faculty of Information Systems and Applied Computer Science:

FERSTL, O., Information Systems (Industrial Application Systems)
HEINRICH, A., Media Informatics
KRIEGER, U., Computer Networks Group
LÜTTGEN, G., Software Engineering and Programming Languages
MENDLER, M., Foundation of Computer Science
SCHLIEDER, C., Computing in the Cultural Sciences
SCHMID, U., Applied Informatics (Cognitive Systems)
SINZ, E. J., Information Systems (Systems Engineering)
WEITZEL, T., Information Systems and Services
WIRTZ, G., Practical Computer Science, Distributed and Mobile Systems

Faculty of Social Sciences, Economics and Business Administration (Feldkirchenstr. 21, 96052 Bamberg; tel. (951) 863-2501; fax (951)

863-1200; e-mail dekanat@sowi.uni-bamberg
.de; internet www.uni-bamberg.de/sowi):

ANDRESEN, M., Human Resource Management
BECKER, W., Business Administration
BIRK, U.-A., Social Security
BLIEN, U., Sociology (Labour Market and Area Studies)
BLOSSFELD, H., Sociology
BRÜCKER, H., Economics (European Markets)
DERLIEN, H., Public Administration
ECKEL, C., International Economics
EGNER, T., Business Administration and Taxation
EIERLE, B., International Accounting and Auditing
ENGELHARD, J., Business Administration (International Management)
ENGELHARDT-WÖLFLER, H., Population Studies
GEHRING, T., International Policy
IVENS, B., Marketing
MUCK, M., Financial Control
MÜNCH, R., Sociology
OEHLER, A., Finance, Management, and Business Administration
PIEPER, R., Town and Social Planning
RÄSSLER, S., Statistics and Econometrics
RIEGER, E., Sociology of Transnational and Global Processes
SCHNEIDER, T., Sociology (Educational Inequality in the Life-Course)
SCHOEN, H., Political Sociology
SCHWARZE, J., Social Policy
SEMBILL, D., Business and Human Resource Education
STOCKÉ, V., Sociology (Longitudinal Educational Research)
STRUCK, O., Ergonomics and Sociology of Work
SUCKY, E., Operations Management and Business Logistics
WALZL, M., Economics (Industrial Economics)
WENZEL, H., Public Economics
WESTERHOFF, F., Economics (Economic Policy)
ZINTL, R., Political Science
ZOHLNHÖFER, R., Comparative Public Policy

OTTO-VON-GUERICKE-UNIVERSITÄT MAGDEBURG

Universitätspl. 2, 39106 Magdeburg
Telephone: (391) 67-01
Fax: (391) 11156
E-mail: rektor@ovgu.de
Internet: www.uni-magdeburg.de
Founded 1953, present status 1993
State control
Academic year: October to September (two semesters)
Chancellor: DIETMAR NIEMANN
Rector: Prof. Dr KLAUS ERICH POLLMANN
Vice-Rector for Planning and Devt: Prof. Dr HELMUT WEISS
Vice-Rector for Research: Prof. Dr BERNHARD SABEL
Vice-Rector for Study: Prof. Dr JENS STRACKELJAN
Librarian: Dr-Ing. ECKHARD BLUME
Library of 1,200,120 vols
Number of teachers: 200
Number of students: 13,770
Publications: *Research-Report* (1 a year), *Science Journal* (2 a year), *Uni-Report* (12 a year)

DEANS

Faculty of Computer Sciences: Prof. Dr GRAHAM HORTON

Faculty of Economics and Management: Prof. Dr BIRGITTA WOLF
Faculty of Electrical and Information Engineering: Prof. Dr ANDREAS LINDEMANN
Faculty of Humanities, Social Sciences and Education: Prof. Dr WINFRIED MAROTZKI
Faculty of Mathematics: Prof. Dr WOLFGANG WILLEMS
Faculty of Mechanical Engineering: Prof. Dr KARL-HEINRICH GROTE
Faculty of Medicine: Prof. Dr H.-J. ROTHKOETTER
Faculty of Natural Sciences: Prof. Dr JUERGEN CHRISTEN
Faculty of Process and Systems Engineering: Prof. Dr JUERGEN TOMAS

PROFESSORS

Faculty of Computer Sciences (Universitätspl. 2, Bldg 29, 39106 Magdeburg; tel. (391) 67-18853):

ARNDT, H.-K., Applied Informatics
DASSOW, J., Theoretical Computer Science
DITTMANN, J., Technical and Business Information Systems
DUMKE, R., Software Engineering
HOHMEIER, R., Continious Simulation
HORTON, G., Simulation and Graphics
KAISER, J., Information Systems
KRUSE, R., Neural and Fuzzy Systems
NETT, E., Distributed Systems
PREIM, B., Computer Graphics
ROESNER, D., Knowledge and Language Engineering
SAAKE, G., Databases and Information Systems
SCHIRRA, S., Algorithmics
SPILIPOULOU, M., Business Informatics
TOENNIS, K.-D., Computer Graphics

Faculty of Economics and Management (Universitätspl. 2, Bldg 22, 39106 Magdeburg; tel. (391) 67-18585):

BURGARD, U., Law and Economics
CHWOLKA, A., Accounting
ERICHSON, B., Marketing
GISCHER, H., Money Credit
INDERFURTH, K., Logistics
KIRSTEIN, R., Economics and Business and Law
PAQUE, K.-H., International Business
RAITH, M., Entrepreneurship
REICHLING, P., Finance and Banking
RUNKEL, M., Finance
SCHOENDUBE-PIRCHEGGER,, B., Accounting and Controlling
SCHWOEDIAUER, G., Political Economy
SPENGLER, T., Business Management
VOGT, B., Business Research
WAESCHER, G., Management Science
WEIMANN, J., Political Economy
WOLFF, B., International Management

Faculty of Electrical and Information Engineering (Universitätspl. 2, Bldg 09, 39106 Magdeburg; tel. (391) 67-18635):

BURTE, E. P., Technology of Semiconductors
KIENLE, A., Automation Engineering
KLEINE, U., Electronics
KORN, U., Control Engineering
LINDEMANN, A., Power Electronics
MICHAELIS, B., Technical Computer Science
OMAR, A. S., Microwave and Communications Engineering
PALIS, F., Power Electronics
ROSE, G., Medical Telematic and Medical-Technics
SCHMIDT, B., Measurement Technology and Microsystems
STYCZYNSKI, Z. A., Electrical Power Networks and Renewable Energy Resources
VICK, R., Electromagnetic Compability
WENDEMUTH, A., Cognitive Systems
WOLLENBERG, G., Theoretical and General Electrical Engineering

Faculty of Humanities, Social Sciences and Education (Zschokkestr. 32, Bldg 40, 39104 Magdeburg; tel. (391) 67-16541):

BELENTSCHIKOW, R., Slavic Linguistics
BERGIEN, A., English Linguistics
BRUCHHÄUSER, H.-P., Administrative Management and New Media
BURKHARDT, A., German Linguistics
DREHER, M., Ancient History
EDELMANN-NUSSER, Sports and Technics
FRITSCHE, K.-P., Comparative Political Systems
FROMMBERGER, D., Vocational Education Studies
FROMME, J., Education Science Media Research
FUHRER, U., Developmental and Educational Psychology
GIRMES, R., General Didactics and School Theory
JENEWEIN, K., Didactic Technical Subject Areas
KAISER, G., Social Psychology
KERSTEN, H., English and American Studies
KNOLLE, N., Music Education
LABOUVIE, E., Contemporary History and Gender Research
LANGE, B. P., English Literary and Cultural Studies
LOHMANN, G., Practical Philosophy
MAROTZKI, W., General Education
MUENTE, T. F., Psychology
PETERS, S., Work-based Education
POLLMANN, K. E., Modern History and History of Science
RENZSCH, W., Political System and Sociology of the Federal Republic of Germany
ROS, A., Theoretical Philosophy
SCHILLING, M., Older German Literature and Linguistics
SCHLICHTE, K., International Relations
SUESS, H.-M., Methology, Psychodiagnostic and Evaluation Research

Faculty of Mathematics (Universitätspl. 2, Bldg 03, 39106 Magdeburg; tel. (391) 67-16519):

CHRISTOPH, G., Mathematical Stochastics
DECKELNICK, K., Analysis
GAFFKE, N., Mathematical Stochastics
GRUNAU, H.-C., Analysis
HENK, M., Geometry
KAIBEL, V., Mathematical Optimization
POTT, A., Discrete Mathematics
SCHWABE, R., Mathematical Stochastics
TOBISKA, L., Numerical Analysis
WARNECKE, G., Numerical Mathematics
WEISMANTEL, R., Mathematical Optimization
WILLEMS, W., Mathematics

Faculty of Mechanical Engineering (Universitätspl. 2, 39106 Magdeburg; tel. (391) 67-18519):

BERTRAM, A., Strength of Materials
DEML, B., Ergonomics and Industrial Engineering
DETERS, L., Machine Elements and Tribology
GABBERT, U., Numerical Mathematics
GROTE, K. H., Product Development and Engineering Design
KARPUSCHEWSKI, B., Metal Cutting and Removal Technology
KASPER, R., Mechatronics
KUEHNLE, H., Factory Operation and Manufacturing Systems
MOLITOR, M., Manufacturing Measurement Technology and Quality Management
SCHENK, M., Logistics Networks
SINAPIUS, M., Adapt Lightweight Construction
STRACKELJAN, J., Technical Dynamics

TSCHOEKE, H., Measurement Technology and Reciprocating Machines
VAJNA, S., Computer Applications in Mechanical Engineering
ZADECK, H., Logistics

Faculty of Medicine (Leipzigerstr. 44, 39120 Magdeburg; tel. (391) 67-15750):

AHRENS, C., Otorhinolaryngology
AMTHAUER, H., Nuclear Medicine
BEHRENS-BAUMANN, W., Clinical Pharmacology
BERNSTEIN, H., Neuroanatomy and Neuromorphology
BOGE-BOEGER, S., Ophthalmology
BOHNEKOH, B., Dermatology
BRUNNER-WINZIERL, M., Experimental Paediatry
FISCHER, K., Biochemistry and Cytology
FISCHER, T., Haematology and Oncology
FLECHTNER, H., Child and Adolescent Psychiatry
FROMMER, J., Psychosomatic Medicine
GRASSHOF, H., Orthopaedics
GREKSCH, G., Pharmacology And Toxicology
GUNZER, M., Molecular Immunology
HEIM, M., Transfusion Medicine And Immunohematology
HOPF, J., Cognitive Neuropsychology
KLEINSTEIN, J., Endrocrinology and Infertility
LENDECKEL, U., Experimental Internal Medicine
LESSMANN, V., Physiology
LEVERKUS, C., Experimental Dermatology
LINKE, R., Anatomy
MAWRIN, C., Neuropathology
MERTENS, P., Nephrology
REINHOLD, D., Immunology
REISER, G., Neurobiochemistry
RICKE, J., Diagnostic Radiology and Nuclear Medicine
SABEL, B., Medical Psychology
SCHMITZ, I., System-Oriented Inflammation Research and Immunology
SCHOENFELD, P., Biochemistry
SCHUBERT, W., Molecular and Neurobiology
SCHWEGLER, H., Neuroanatomy
VOGES, J., Stereotactic Surgery
VOIGT, T., Special Subject of Physiology
WINCKLER, S., Trauma Surgery
ZENCLUSSEN, A., Experimental Gynaecology

Faculty of Natural Sciences (Universitätspl. 2, Bldg 16, 39106 Magdeburg; tel. (391) 67-18678):

BRAUN, A. K., Biology and Zoology
BRAUN, J., Cognitive Biology
CHRISTEN, J., Experimental Physics
CLOS, R., Experimental Physics
HERMANN, CH., Biology Psychology
KASSNER, K., Computational Physics
KROST, A., Experimental Physics
MUENTE, T. F., Neuropsychology
RICHTER, J., Theoretical Physics
STANNARIUS, R., Experimental Physics and Non-linear Phenomena
STORK, O., Molecular Neurobiology
WIERSIG, J., Theoretical Physics

Faculty of Process and Systems Engineering (Universitätspl. 2, Bldg 10, 39106 Magdeburg; tel. (391) 67-11190):

EDELMANN, F., Inorganic Chemistry
HAUPTMANNS, U., Plant Safety
REICHL, U., Biochemical Engineering
SCHEFFLER, F., Chemical Engineering
SCHINZER, D., Organic Chemistry
SCHMIDT, J., Thermodynamics
SEIDEL-MORGENSTEIN, A., Chemical Reaction Engineering
SPECHT, E., Technical Thermodynamics and Combustion
SUNDMACHER, K., Process System Engineering

THÉVENIN, D., Fluid Dynamics
TOMAS, J., Mechanical Process Engineering
TSOTSAS, E., Thermal Process Engineering
WEISS, H., .Physical Chemistry

PHILIPPS-UNIVERSITÄT MARBURG

Biegenstr. 10-12, 35032 Marburg
Telephone: (6421) 2820
Fax: (6421) 2822500
E-mail: grassman@verwaltung.uni-marburg .de
Internet: www.uni-marburg.de
Founded 1527
State control
Academic year: October to July (2 terms)
Pres.: Prof. Dr VOLKER NIENHAUS
Vice-Pres: Prof. Dr GERHARD HELDMAIER, Dr HERBERT CLAAS
Chancellor: Dr FRIEDHELM NONNE
Librarian: Dr DIRK BARTH
Library: see Libraries and Archives
Number of teachers: 650
Number of students: 17,900

Publication: *Journal* (2 a year)

PROFESSORS

Department of Biology (Karl-von-Frisch-Str., 35032 Marburg; tel. (6421) 2822047; fax (6421) 2822057; e-mail pega@mailer .uni-marburg.de):

BATSCHAUER, A., Plant Physiology, Photobiology
BÖLKER, M., Genetics
BRANDL, R., Animal Ecology
BREMER, E., Microbiology
BUCKEL, W., Microbiology
GALLAND, P., Plant Physiology, Photobiology
HASSEL, M., Morphology
HELDMAIER, G., Zoology
HOMBERG, U., Animal Physiology
KAHMANN, R., Genetics
KIRCHNER, C., Zoology
KLEIN, A., Molecular Genetics
KOST, G., Botany, Mycology
LINGELBACH, U., Zoology, Parasitology
MAIER, U., Cell Biology and Botany
MATTHIES, D., Plant Ecology
PLACHTER, H., Nature Conservancy Studies
RENKAWITZ-POHL, R., Molecular Genetics
THAUER, R., Microbiology
WEBER, H. C., Botany
ZIEGENHAGEN, B., Nature Conservancy Biology

Department of Chemistry (Hans-Meerwin-Str., 35032 Marburg; tel. (6421) 2825543; fax (6421) 2828917; e-mail dekanat@chemie .uni-marburg.de):

BRÖRING, M., Inorganic Chemistry
ELSCHENBROICH, CHR., Inorganic Chemistry
ENSINGER, W., Analytical and Nuclear Chemistry
ESSEN, L.-O., Biochemistry
FRENKING, G., Chemistry-Related Computer Studies
GERMANO, G., Physical Chemistry
GREINER, A., Macromolecular Chemistry
HAMPP, N., Physical Chemistry
HARBRECHT, B., Inorganic Chemistry
HILT, G., Organic Chemistry
KOERT, W., Organic Chemistry
MARAHIEL, M., Biochemistry
MÜLLER, U., Inorganic Chemistry
SCHRADER, T., Organic Chemistry
SEUBERT, A., Analytical Chemistry
STUDER, A., Organic Chemistry
SUNDERMEYER, J., Metal-organic Chemistry
UHL, W., Inorganic Chemistry
WEITZEL, K.-M., Physical Chemistry
WENDORFF, J., Physical Chemistry

Department of Economics (Universitätsstr. 25, 35032 Marburg; tel. (6421) 2821722; fax (6421) 2824858; e-mail dekanat@wiwi .uni-marburg.de):

ALPAR, P., Economics, Computer Science
FEHL, U., Economic Theory
FELD, L., Financial Science
FLEISCHER, K., Statistics
GERUM, E., Commerce
GÖPFERT, I., Commerce, Logistics
HASENKAMP, U., Business Management and Economic Information Studies
KERBER, W., Political Economy
KIRK, M., Development Policy, Agricultural Economics and Cooperative Science
KRAG, J., Commerce
LINGENFELDER, M., Marketing
PRIEWASSER, E., Banking
RÖPKE, J., Economic Theory
SCHIMENZ, B., Business Economics
SCHÜLLER, A., Economic Theory
STORZ, C., Japanese Economics
WEHRHEIM, M., Commerce

Department of Education (Wilhelm-Röpke-Str. 6B, 35032 Marburg; tel. (6421) 2824770; fax (6421) 2828946; e-mail dekan21@mailer .uni-marburg.de):

ACKERMANN, H., General Teaching
BECKER, P., Sociology of Sports
BÜCHNER, P., Sociology of Education
HAFENEGER, B., Extracurricular Education
KÖNIGS, F., General Teaching, Applied Linguistics
KUCKARTZ, U., Education
LAGING, R., Sports Science
LERSCH, R., School Education
NUISSL VON REIN, E., Adult Education
PROKOP, U., Socialization Theory
ROHR, E., Education
ROHRMANN, E., Education
SCHNOOR, H., Pedagogics
SEEWALD, J., Educational Kinesiology
SEITTER, W., Education
SOMMER, H.-M., Sports Medicine

Department of Foreign Languages and Philology (Wilhelm-Röpke-Str. 6D, 35032 Marburg; tel. (6421) 2824764; fax (6421) 2824715; e-mail kissling@mailer.uni-marburg.de):

BISCHOFF, V., American Literature
HAHN, M., Indology
HANDKE, J., English Linguistics
HOFER, H., Romance Philology
IBLER, R., Slavic Philology
KÖNSGEN, E., Latin Philology of the Middle and Modern Ages
KUESTER, M., English Studies
LEONHARDT, J., Classic Philology
POPPE, E., General Language and Celtology
RIEKEN, E., Comparative Language
SCHALLER, H., Slavic Philology
SCHMITT, A., Classic Philology
SOMMERFELD, W., Ancient Oriental Studies
STILLERS, R., Romance Philology
UHLIG, C., English and American Philology
WENINGER, S., Semitistics
ZIMMERMANN, R., English Linguistics
ZOLLNA, J., Romance Philology

Department of Geography (Deutschhausstr. 10, 35032 Marburg; tel. (6421) 2825916; fax (6421) 2828950; e-mail jansen@mailer .uni-marburg.de):

BARTHELT, H., Cultural Geography
BENDIX, J., Climatic Geography and Geoecology
BRÜCKNER, H., Morphology and Geoecology
MIEHE, G., Geography of Asia and East Africa
OPP, CH., Physical Geography
PAAL, M., Cultural Geography
PLETSCH, A., Cultural Geography and Geography of North America
STRAMBACH, S., Cultural Geography

Department of Geosciences (Hans-Meerwein-Str., 35032 Marburg; tel. (6421) 2823000; fax

(6421) 2828919; e-mail napieral@mailer
.uni-marburg.de):

BUCK, P., Crystallography
HOFFER, E., Petrology
PRINZ-GRIMM, P., Historical and Regional
Geology
SCHMIDT-EFFING, R., Geology
VOGLER, ST., Structural Geology

Department of German Studies and Art
(Wilhelm-Röpke-Str. 6A, 35032 Marburg;
tel. (6421) 2824542; fax (6421) 2827056;
e-mail dekan09@mailer.uni-marburg.de):

ALBERT, R., German Language
ANZ, TH., Modern German Literature
BERTELSMEIER-KIERST, C., German Phil-
ology
DEDNER, B., Modern German Literature
DOHM, B., Modern German Literature
HEINZLE, J., German Philology
HELLER, H.-B., Modern German Literature
HENZE-DÖHRING, G., Music
HERKLOTZ, I., History of Art
HERRGEN, J., German Linguistics
HEUSINGER, L., Informatics in History of
Art
KRAUSE, K., History of Art
KREMERS, E., Graphics and Painting
KÜNZEL, H., Phonetics
MIX, Y.-G., Modern German Literature
OSINSKI, J., Modern German Literature
PRÜMM, K., Media Teaching
SCHLESEWSKY, M., Neurolinguistics
SCHMIDT, J., Dialect and Linguistics
SCHÜTTE, W., History of Art
WIESE, R., German Linguistics

Department of History and Cultural Sciences
(Wilhelm-Röpke-Str. 6C, 35032 Marburg; tel.
(6421) 2824518; fax (6421) 2826948; e-mail
dekan06@mailer.uni-marburg.de):

BÖHME, H. W., Prehistory
BORSCHEID, P., Social and Economic His-
tory
CONZE, E., Modern History
DREXHAGE, H.-J., Ancient History
ERRINGTON, R. M., Ancient History
FRONING, H., Classical Archaeology
HARDACH, G., Social and Economic History
KAMPMANN, C., Modern History
KRIEGER, W., Modern History
LAUTER, H., Classical Archaeology
MEYER, A., Medieval History
MÜLLER-KARPE, A., Prehistory
PAUER, E., Japanese Studies
PLAGGENBORG, S., East European History
POSTEL, V., Medieval History
ÜBELHÖR, M., Sinology
WINTERHAGER, W. E., Modern History

Department of Law (Universitätsstr. 6,
35032 Marburg; tel. (6421) 2823101; fax
(6421) 2823181; e-mail dekanat01@mailer
.uni-marburg.de):

BACKHAUS, R., Roman and Civil Law
BÖHM, M., Public Law
BUCHHOLZ, ST., German Legal History and
Civil Law
DETTERBECK, S., Public Law
FREUND, G., Criminal and Procedural Law,
Philosophy of Law
FROTSCHER, W., Public Law
GORNIG, G.-H., Public Law
GOUNALAKIS, G., Civil and Comparative
Law
HORN, H.-D., Public Law
LANGENBÜCHER, K., Civil Law
LANGER, W., Criminal and Procedural Law
MENKHAUS, H., Japanese Law
MUMMENHOFF, W., Civil and Labour Law
RADTKE, H., Criminal Law, Procedural Law
RÖSSNER, D., Criminal Law, Procedural
Law
RUPPRECHT, H.-A., Papyrology
SCHANZE, E., Civil Law
VOIT, W., Civil Law
WERTENBRUCH, J., Civil Law

Department of Mathematics (Hans-Meerwein-Str., 35032 Marburg; tel. (6421)
2825463; fax (6421) 2825466; e-mail dekan@
mathematik.uni-marburg.de):

BAUER, T., Geometrical Algebra
DAHLKE, S., Numerics
FREISLEBEN, B., Practical Informatics
GROMES, W., Analysis
GUMM, H.-P., Theoretical Informatics
HESSE, W., Software Engineering
HÜLLERMEIER, E., Informatics
KNÖLLER, F. W., Topology and Geometry
LOOGEN, R., Functional Programmes
MAMMITZSCH, V., Probability Theory and
Mathematical Statistics
PORTENIER, C., Analysis
SCHLICKEWEI, H. P., Algebra
SCHUMACHER, G., Topology and Geometry
SCHWENTICK, T., Theoretical Informatics
SEEGER, B., Databases
SOMMER, M., Practical Informatics
ULTSCH, A., Neuroinformatics
UPMEIER, H., Analysis
WELKER, V., Combinatorics

Department of Medicine (Baldingerstr.,
35032 Marburg; tel. (6421) 2866201; fax
(6421) 2861548; e-mail dekanat@post.med
.uni-marburg.de):

ARNOLD, R., Internal Medicine
AUMÜLLER, G., Anatomy
AUSTERMANN, K.-H., Maxillofacial Surgery
BACK, T., Neurology
BASLER, H.-D., Psychology
BAUER, M., Molecular Biology
BAUM, E., General Medicine
BEHR, T., Nuclear Medicine
BERGER, R., Otorhinolaryngology
BERTALANFFY, H., Neurosurgery
BESEDOVSKY, H., Physiology
BIEN, S., Neurosurgery
CETIN, Y., Anatomy
CZUBAYKO, F., Pharmacology
DAUT, J., Physiology
DIBBETS, J., Dentistry
DONNER-BANZHOFF, N., General Medicine
EILERS, M., Molecular Biology
ENGENHART-CABILLIC, R., Radiotherapy
FEHRENBACH, H.-G., Pneumology
FLORES DE JACOBY, L., Paradontology
GARTEN, W., Virology
GÖKE, R., Internal Medicine
GOTZEN, L., Surgery
GRISS, P., Orthopaedics
GRZESCHIK, K.-H., Human Genetics
GUDERMANN, T., Pharmacology and Toxi-
cology
HAPPLE, R., Dermatology
HASILIK, A., Physiological Chemistry
HEBEBRAND, J., Child Psychiatry
HEEG, K., Microbiology
HOFMANN, R., Urology
JONES, D., Orthopaedics
KANN, P., Internal Medicine
KLENK, H.-D., Virology
KLINGMÜLLER, V., Nuclear Diagnosis
KLOSE, K., Radiology
KRAUSE, W., Andrology
KRETSCHMER, V., Transfusion Medicine
KRIEG, J. C., Psychology
KROLL, P., Ophthalmology
KUHN, K., Medical Informatics
LANG, R. E., Experimental Nuclear Medi-
cine
LILL, R., Cytobiology
LISS, B., Physiology
LOHOFF, M., Microbiology
LOTZMANN, K.-U., Dentistry
MAIER, R., Neonatology
MAISCH, B., Cardiology
MAX, M., Anaesthesiology and Intensive
Therapy
MOLL, R., Pathology
MOOSDORF, R., Cardiac Surgery
MUELLER, U., Medical Sociology
MÜLLER, R., Molecular Biology

NEUBAUER, A., Internal Medicine
OERTEL, W., Neurology
PIEPER, K., Dentistry for Children
RADSAK, K., General Medicine
REMSCHMIDT, H., Child Psychology
RENZ, H., Interdisciplinary Medical Centre
RÖPER, J., Physiology
ROSENOW, F., Neurology
ROTHMUND, M., Surgery
RUPP, H., Cardiology
SCHÄFER, H., Medical Biometry
SCHMIDT, S., Obstetrics
SCHWARZ, R., Parasitology
SEITZ, A., Anatomy
SEYBERTH, H. W., Child Medicine, Clinical
and Theoretical Pharmacology
SOMMER, N., Neurology (Neuroimmunol-
ogy)
STACHNISS, V., Dentistry
STEINIGER, B., Anatomy
STREMPEL, J., Ophthalmology
VOGELMEIER, C., Pneumology
VOIGT, K.-H., Physiology
WAGNER, H.-J., Radiology
WAGNER, W., Obstetrics
WEIHE, E., Anatomy
WERNER, J., Otolaryngology, Head and
Neck Surgery
WULF, H., Anaesthesiology and Intensive
Therapy

Department of Pharmacy (Wilhelm-Roser-
Str. 2, 35032 Marburg; tel. (6421) 2825890;
fax (6421) 2825815; e-mail dekanat
.pharmazie@mailer.uni-marburg.de):

FRIEDRICH, C., History of Pharmacy
HANEFELD, W., Pharmaceutical Chemistry
HARTMANN, R., Pharmaceutical Chemistry
KEUSGEN, M., Pharmaceutical Chemistry
KISSEL, T., Pharmaceutical Technology and
Biopharmacy
KLEBE, G., Pharmaceutical Chemistry
KRIEGLSTEIN, J., Pharmacology and Toxi-
cology
KUSCHINSKY, K., Pharmacology and Toxi-
cology
LINK, A., Pharmaceutical Chemistry
MATERN, U., Pharmaceutical Biology
MATUSCH, R., Pharmaceutical Chemistry
PETERSEN, M., Pharmaceutical Biology

Department of Physics (Renthof 6, 35032
Marburg; tel. (6421) 2821314; fax (6421)
2821309; e-mail dekanat@physik
.uni-marburg.de):

BREMMER, F., Applied Physics
ECKHARDT, B., Theoretical Physics
ECKHORN, R., Applied Physics
GEBHARD, F., Theoretical Physics
HEIMBRODT, W., Experimental Physics
HÖFER, U., Experimental Physics
JAKOB, P., Experimental Physics
KIRA, M., Theoretical Physics
KOCH, S., Theoretical Physics
LENZ, P., Theoretical Physics
NEUMANN, H., Theoretical Physics
PÜHLHOFER, F., Experimental Physics
RIES, H., Experimental Physics
RÜHLE, W., Experimental Physics
STÖCKMANN, H.-J., Experimental Physics
THOMAS, P., Theoretical Physics
WEISER, G., Experimental Physics

Department of Psychology (Gutenbergstr. 18,
35032 Marburg; tel. (6421) 2823674; fax
(6421) 2826949; e-mail dekanpsy@mailer
.uni-marburg.de):

LACHNIT, H., General Psychology
LIEBHART, E., Educational Psychology
LOHAUS, A., Developmental Psychology
RIEF, W., Clinical Psychology
RÖHRLE, B., Clinical Psychology
RÖSLER, F., Cognitive Psychology, Neu-
roscience
ROST, D., Educational Psychology
SCHEIBLECHNER, H., Psychological Method-
ology

SCHMIDT-ATZERT, L., Psychological Diagnostics
SCHULZE, H.-H., Psychological Methodology
SCHWARTING, R., General and Physiological Psychology
SOMMER, G., Clinical Psychology
STELZL, I., Psychological Methodology and Diagnostics
STEMMLER, G., Psychological Diagnostics
WAGNER, U., Social Psychology

Department of Social Science and Philosophy (Wilhelm-Röpke-Str. 6B, 35032 Marburg; tel. (6421) 2824726; fax (6421) 2825467; e-mail ciok@mailer.uni-marburg.de):

BERG-SCHLOSSER, D., Political Science
BIELING, H.-J., Political Science
BORIS, H.-D., Sociology
BRANN, K., European Ethnology
BREDOW, W. VON, Political Science
DEPPE, F., Political Science
FÜLBERTH-SPERLING, G., Political Science
FUNDER, M., Sociology
GUTMANN, M., Philosophy
JANICH, P., Philosophy
KÄSLER, D., Sociology
KISSLER, L., Sociology
KURZ-SCHERF, I., Political Science
LÜDTKE, H., Sociology
MERKEL, I., Ethnology
MÜNZEL, M., Ethnology
NOETZEL, T., Political Science
PYE, M., General Religious Science
RUPP, H.-K., Political Science
SCHILLER, TH., Political Science
ZIMMERMANN, H.-P., European Ethnology

Department of Theology (Alte Universität, Lahntor 3, 35032 Marburg; tel. (6421) 2822441; fax (6421) 2828968; e-mail dekan05@mailer.uni-marburg.de):

AVEMARIE, F., New Testament
BARTH, H.-M., Systematic Theology
BIENERT, W., Church History
DABROCK, P., Social Ethics
DRESSLER, B., Practical Theology
ELSAS, C., Religious History
JEREMIAS, J., Old Testament
KAISER, J.-C., Church History
KESSLER, R., Old Testament
KOCH, G., Christian Archaeology
KORSCH, D., Systematic Theology
MARTIN, G. M., Practical Theology
NETHÖFEL, W., Social Ethics
PINGGERA, K., Church History
SCHNEIDER, H., Church History
SCHWEBEL, H., Religious Communication
STANDHARTINGER, A., New Testament
WAGNER-RAU, H., Practical Theology

RHEINISCH-WESTFÄLISCHE TECHNISCHE HOCHSCHULE AACHEN

52056 Aachen

Telephone: (241) 801
Fax: (241) 8092312
E-mail: international@zhv.rwth-aachen.de
Internet: www.rwth-aachen.de

Founded 1870 as Polytechnikum, attained univ. status 1880
Academic year: October to September
Rector: Prof. Dr BURKHARD RAUHUT
Pro-Rectors: Prof. Dr KONSTANTIN MESKOURIS, Prof. Dr ROLF ROSSAINT, Prof. Dr REINHART POPRAWE
Chancellor: MANFRED NETTEKOVEN
Head of Int. Office: Dr HEIDE NADERER
Head of Public Relations Office: TONI WIMMER
Head of Technology Transfer and Research Funding: Dr REGINA OERTEL
Librarian: Dr ULRIKE EICH

Library: see Libraries and Archives
Number of teachers: 4,248

Number of students: 29,598

DEANS

Faculty of Architecture: Prof. Dr PETER JOHN RUSSELL
Faculty of Arts and Humanities: Prof. Dr PAUL HILL
Faculty of Civil Engineering: Prof. Dr EKKEHARD WENDLER
Faculty of Economics: Prof. Dr MICHAEL BASTIAN
Faculty of Electrical Engineering and Information Technology: Prof. Dr. KAY HAMEYERL
Faculty of Geo-resources and Materials Engineering: Prof. Dr FRANZ MICHAEL MEYER
Faculty of Mathematics, Computer Science and Natural Sciences: Prof. Dr MATTHIAS WUTTIG
Faculty of Mechanical Engineering: Prof. Dr KLAUS HENNING
Faculty of Medicine: Prof. Dr JOHANNES NOTH

PROFESSORS

Faculty of Architecture (Schinkelstr. 1, 52056 Aachen; tel. (241) 8095000809; fax (241) 8092237; e-mail dekan@architektur.rwth-aachen.de; internet arch.rwth-aachen.de):

BAUM, M., Design Construction
BRUCHHAUS, G., District Planning and Design
COERSMEIER, U., Interior Design
HOFFMANN, H., Visual Form
HUMBLÉ, F., Building Planning and Design
JANSEN, M., History of Urban Devt
KADA, K., Building Design and Function
KRAUSE, C., Landscape Ecology and Landscape Design
LAUENSTEIN, H., Open Space and Landscape Planning
MARKSCHIES, A., History of Art
NICOLIC, V., Building Construction and Design
PIEPER, J., History of Architecture and Conservation
RUOFF, J., Environment, Services and Design
RUSSELL, P., Computer-aided Design
SCHMIDT, H., Conservation
SCHNEIDER, H. N., Building Construction and Design
SCHULZE, M., Sculpture
SELLE, K., Planning Theory and Town Planning
TRAUTZ, M., Building Construction (Structural Design)
VAN DEN BERGH, W., Housing and Residential Devt
VINKEN, G., Theory of Architecture
WACHTEN, K., Urban Design and Country Planning

Faculty of Arts and Humanities (Kármánstr. 17–19, 52056 Aachen; tel. (241) 8096002; fax (241) 8092334; e-mail adrian.leipold@fb7.rwth-aachen.de; internet www.rwth-aachen.de/fb7):

BEIER, R., Applied Linguistics
BEIN, T., Medieval German Language and Literature
DERINGER, L., English and American Language and Literature
ERTLER, K., Romance Languages and Literatures
ESSER, A., Philosophy
FICK, M., German Literature
GELLHAUS, A., German Literature
GILLMAYR-BUCHER, S., Biblical Studies
VON HAEHLING, R., History
HAMMERICH, K., Sociology
HEINEN, A., Modern and Contemporary History
HILL, P. B., Sociology

HORCH, H.-O., German and Jewish Literature
HÖRNING, K.-H., Sociology
HORNKE, L., Psychology
JÄGER, L., Linguistics and Media Theory
JAKOBS, E.-M., Communication Science
KEIL, G., Theoretical Philosophy
KELLERWESSEL, W., Philosophy
KERNER, M., Medieval and Modern History
KÖNIG, H., Political Science
LEWATER, D., Education Science
LIEDTKE, F., German Language
LUEKE, U., Theology
MEY, H., Sociology
MEYER, G., Theology
MEYER, P. G., English Linguistics (Synchronic)
MICHELSEN, U. A., Education
MOESSNER, L., English Linguistics and Medieval Studies
MÜSSELER, J., Work Psychology and Cognition
NEUSCHAEFER, A., Romance Languages and Literatures
NIEHR, T., German Language
PANGRITZ, A., Theology
RICHTER, E., Political Science
ROTTE, R., Political Science
SCHERBERICH, K., History
SCHMITZ, S., German Language
SPIJKERS, W., Psychology
STETTER, C., Germanic Linguistics
WENZEL, P., English Literature

Faculty of Civil Engineering (Mies-van-der-Rohe-Str. 1, 52074 Aachen; tel. (241) 8025075; fax (241) 8022201; e-mail dekanat@fb3.rwth-aachen.de; internet www.rwth-aachen.de/fb3):

BECKMANN, K. J., Urban and Transport Planning
BENNING, W., Geodesy
BRAMERSHUBER, W., Building Materials Research
BRUNK, M. F., Construction Management and Building Services
DOETSCH, P., Waste Management
FELDMANN, M., Steel and Light-Metal Construction
GÜLDENPFENNING, J., Mechanics and Building Construction
HEGGER, J., Structural Concrete
KÖNGETER, J., Hydraulic Engineering and Water Resources Management
MESKOURIS, K., Structural Statistics and Dynamics
NACKEN, H., Engineering Hydrology
OSEBOLD, R., Construction Management—Project Management
PINNEKAMP, J., Sanitary and Waste Engineering
RAUPACH, M., Building Materials Research
REICHMUTH, J., Airport and Air-Transportation Research
STEINAUER, B., Road Engineering, Earth Works and Tunnelling
WENDLER, E., Transport Economics, Railway Engineering and Railway Operations
ZIEGLER, M., Geotechnics in Civil Engineering

Faculty of Economics (Kármánstr. 17–19, 52056 Aachen; tel. (241) 8096000; fax (241) 8092166; e-mail dekanat-fb8@rwth-aachen.de; internet www.wiwi.rwth-aachen.de):

BASTIAN, M., Business Information Systems and Operations
BRETTEL, M., Business Admin. and Sciences for Engineers and Scientists (Centre for Entrepreneurship)
BREUER, W., Business Administration (Finance)
DYCKHOFF, H., Business Theory, Environmental Management and Industrial Controlling
FEESS, E., Economics (Microeconomics)

HARMS, P., Macroeconomics
HÖMBURG, R., Business Taxation and Auditing
HUBER, C., Civil Law, Business and Labour Law
LORZ, O., Int. Economics
MÖLLER, H. P., Business Admin., Accounting and Finance
REIMERS, K., Business Information Systems (Electronic Business)
SCHRÖDER, H.-H., Technology and Innovation Management
SEBASTIAN, H.-J., Optimization of Distribution Networks
STEFFENHAGEN, H., Corporate Policy and Marketing
THOMES, P., Economic and Social History
VON NITZSCH, R., Business Management
WOYWODE, M., Int. Management

Faculty of Electrical Engineering and Information Technology (Muffeter Weg 3, 52074 Aachen; tel. (241) 8027572; fax (241) 8022343; e-mail dekanat@fb6.rwth-aachen.de; internet www.fb6.rwth-aachen.de):

AACH, T., Image Processing
ASCHEID, G., Integrated Signal Processing Systems
BEMMERL, T., Operation Systems and Scalable Computing
DE DONCKER, R., Power Electronic and Electrical Drives
HAMEYER, K., Electrical Mechanics
HAUBRICH, H.-J., Power Systems and Power Economics
HEINEN, S., Integrated Analogue Circuits
JANSEN, R., Electromagnetic Theory
KAISER, W., History of Engineering and Technology
KRAISS, K.-F., Technical Informatics and Computer Science
KURZ, H., Semiconductor Technology
LEONHARDT, K. S., Medical Information Technology
LEUPERS, R., Software for Systems on Silicon
MAEHOENEN, P. H., Wireless Networks
MATHAR, R., Information Theory
MEYR, H., Integrated Signal Processing Systems
MOKWA, W., Materials in Electrical Engineering
NOLL, T. G., Electrical Engineering and Computer Systems
OHM, J.-R., Communications Engineering
SAUER, U., Electrochemical Energy Conversion
SCHNETTLER, A., High Voltage Technology
VARY, P., Communication Systems and Data Processing
VESCAN, A., GaN Device Technology
VORLÄNDER, M., Technical Acoustics
WALKE, B., Communications Networks
WASER, R., Materials in Electrical Materials

Faculty of Geo-resources and Materials Engineering (Intzestr. 1, 52056 Aachen; tel. (241) 8095665; fax (241) 8092370; e-mail dekanat-fb5@rwth-aachen.de; internet www.rwth-aachen.de):

Section of Geoscience:

AZZAM, R., Engineering Geology and Hydrogeology
BREUER, H., Geography, Economic and Applied Geography
CLAUSER, C., Applied Geophysics
FLAJS, G., Geology and Palaeontology
GRÄF, P., Geography, Physical Geography and Climatology
HAVLIK, G., Geography, Physical Geography and Climatology
HEGER, G., Crystallography
KRAMM, U., Mineralogy and Geochemistry
KUKLA, P., Geology and Palaeontology

LEHMKUHL, F., Geography, Physical Geography and Geoecology
LITTKE, R., Geology and Geochemistry of Petroleum and Coal
MEYER, M., Mineralogy and Economic Geology
ROTH, G., Applied Crystallography and Mineralogy
STANJEK, H., Clay Mineralogy
URAI, J. L., Structural Geology, Tectonics and Geomechanics

Section of Metallurgy and Materials Technology:

BLECK, W., Materials Science of Steels
BUERIG-POLACZ, A., Foundry Technology
CONRADT, R., Glass and Ceramic Composites
EMMERICH, H., Computational Materials Engineering
EPPLE, U., Process Control Engineering
FRIEDRICH, B., Process Metallurgy and Metal Recycling
GOTTSTEIN, G., Physical Metallurgy and Metal Physics
KAYSSER, W. A., Materials Science of Nonferrous Metals
KÖHNE, H., Heat and Mass Transfer
KOPP, R., Metal Forming
ODOJ, R., Materials Chemistry
PFEIFER, H., High Temperature Engineering
SCHNEIDER, J., Materials Chemistry
SENK, D. G., Metallurgy of Iron and Steel
TELLE, R., Ceramics and Refractories

Section of Mining Engineering:

FRENZ, W., Mining and Environment
HEIL, J., Coking, Briquetting and Thermal Waste Treatment
MARTENS, P. N., Mining Engineering
NIEHAUS, K., Excavation and Mining Equipment
NIEMANN-DELIUS, C., Surface Mining and Drilling
PRETZ, T., Processing and Recycling of Solid Waste Materials
PREUSSE, A., Mine Surveying, Mining Subsidence Engineering and Geophysics in Mining
SEELIGER, A., Mining and Metallurgical Machine Engineering
WOTRUBA, H., Mineral Processing

Faculty of Mathematics, Computer Science and Natural Sciences (Templergraben 64, 52064 Aachen; tel. (241) 8094500; fax (241) 8092124; e-mail dekan@fb1.rwth-aachen.de; internet www.fb1.rwth-aachen.de):

ALBRECHT, M., Organic Chemistry
BALLMANN, J., Mechanics
BAUMANN, H., Chemistry
BEGINN, U., Macromolecular and Supramolecular Chemistry
BEMELMANS, V., Mathematics
BENEKE, M., Theoretical Physics
BERGER, C., Experimental Physics
BERLAGE, T., Computer Science (Life Science Informatics)
BERNREUTNER, W., Theoretical Physics
BISCHOF, C., Computer Science (Scientific Computing)
BLUEMICH, B., Macromolecular Chemistry/NMR
BLÜGEL, S., Theoretical Physics
BOCK, H. H., Applied Statistics
BOEHM, A., Experimental Physics
BOHRMANN, J., Zoology and Human Biology
BOLM, C., Chemistry
BORCHERS, J., Computer Science (Media Computing)
BRAEUNIG, P.-M., Developmental Biology and Morphology of Animals
BRUECKEL, T., Experimental Physics
CAPELLMANN, H., Theoretical Physics
CONRATH, U., Plant Biochemistry
CRAMER, E., Applied Statistics

DAHMEN, W., Mathematics
DEDERICHS, P. H., Theoretical Physics
DOHM, V., Theoretical Physics
DRONSKOWSKI, R., Theoretical and Synthetic Solid-State Chemistry
ELLING, L., Biomaterial Sciences
ENDERS, D., Organic Chemistry
ENGLERT, U., Inorganic Chemistry
ENSS, V., Mathematics
ESSER, K.-H., Applied Mathematics
FELD, L., Experimental Physics
FISCHER, R., Molecular Biotechnology
FLEISCHHAUER, J., Theoretical Chemistry
FLÜGGE, G., Experimental Physics
FRENTZEN, M., Botany
GAIS, H.-J., Organic Chemistry
GÄRTNER, F., Computer Science (Dependable Systems)
GIESL, J., Computer Science
GRAEDEL, E., Mathematical Foundations of Computer Science
GÜNTHERODT, G., Experimental Physics
HARTMEIER, W., Biotechnology
HEINKE, H., Experimental Physics
HERMANN, P., Mathematics
HISS, G., Mathematics
HÖLDERICH, W., Fuel Chemistry
HROMKOVIC, J., Computer Science (Algorithms and Complexity)
IBACH, H., Experimental Physics
INDERMARK, K., Computer Science (Programming Languages)
JANK, G., Engineering Mathematics
JARKE, M., Computer Science (Information Systems)
JONGEN, H. TH., Mathematics
KAMPS, U., Statistics
KLEE, D., Biomaterials
KLEMRADT, U., Experimental Physics
KLINNER, U., Applied Microbiology
KOBBELT, L., Computer Science (Computer Graphics and Multimedia)
KÖLLE, U., Organometallic and Coordination Chemistry of the Transition Metals
KOWALEWSKI, S., Computer Science (Embedded Systems)
KREIBIG, U., Experimental Physics
KREUZALER, F., Botany/Molecular Genetics
KRIEG, A., Mathematics
KULL, H.-J., Theoretical Physics
LAKEMEYER, G., Computer Science (Knowledge-based Systems)
LEITNER, W., Technical Chemistry and Petrochemistry
LENGELER, B., Experimental Physics
LIAUW, M., Technical Chemistry and Reaction Engineering
LICHTER, H., Computer Science (Software Construction)
LÜCHOW, A., Theoretical and Computational Chemistry
LUEKEN, H., Inorganic Chemistry
LUKSCH, P., Computer Science
LÜTH, H., Experimental Physics
MAIER-PAAPE, S., Mathematics
MARTIN, M., Physical Chemistry
MERKE, I., Physical Chemistry
MÖLLER, M., Macromolecular Chemistry
MÜLLER-KRUMBHAAR, H., Theoretical Physics
NAGEL, M., Computer Science (Software Engineering)
NEY, H., Computer Science (Pattern Recognition)
NOELLE, S., Mathematics
OKUDA, J., Organometallic Chemistry
PAHLINGS, H., Mathematics
PLESKEN GEN. WIGGER, W., Mathematics
PRIEFER, U., Biology (Soil Ecology)
PRINZ, W., Computer Science (Cooperation Systems)
RAABE, G., Theoretical Chemistry
RAUHUT, B., Statistics and Mathematics of Economics
RICHTERING, W., Physical Chemistry

ROSSMANITH, P., Computer Science (Theoretical Computer Science)
SALZER, A., Organometallic Chemistry
SCHAEL, S., Experimental Physics
SCHÄFFER, A., Environmental Biology and Chemodynamics
SCHMITZ, D., Experimental Physics
SCHOELLER, H., Theoretical Physics
SCHOLLWOECK, U., Theoretical Physics
SCHROEDER, U., Computer Science (Computer-based Learning)
SCHUPHAN, I., Biology (Ecology, Ecotoxicology, Ecochemistry)
SCHWEIGERT, CH., Theoretical Physics
SEIDEL, T., Computer Science (Data Mining)
SELKE, W., Theoretical Physics
SIELING, D., Physics
SIMON, U., Inorganic Chemistry and Nanomaterials
SLUSARENKO, A., Plant Physiology
SPANIOL, O., Computer Science (Communication Systems)
STAHL, W., Physical Chemistry
STAPF, S., Macromolecular Chemistry
THOMAS, W., Computer Science (Logic and Discrete Systems)
TRIESCH, E., Mathematics
URBAN, K., Experimental Physics
VON DER MOSEL, H., Mathematics
VON PLESSEN, G., Experimental Physics
WAGNER, H., Biology
WALCHER, S., Mathematics
WEINHOLD, E., Bio organic Chemistry
WENZL, H., Experimental Physics
WIEGNER, M., Mathematics
WOLF, K., Microbiology
WUTTIG, M., Experimental Physics
ZEIDLER, M., Physical Chemistry

Faculty of Mechanical Engineering (Eilfschornsteinstr. 18, 52062 Aachen; tel. (241) 8095305; fax (241) 8092144; e-mail dekanat-fb4@rwth-aachen.de; internet www.fb4.rwth-aachen.de):

ABEL, D., Automatic Control
ALLES, W., Flight Dynamics
BEHR, M. A., Computational Analysis of Technical Systems
BEISS, P., Materials Technology
BOBZIN, K., Surface Technology, Materials Science
BOHN, D., Steam and Gas Turbines
BRECHER, C., Machine Tools
BÜCHS, Z., Bioprocess Engineering
CORVES, B., Mechanism Theory and Dynamics of Machines
DELLMANN, T., Rail Vehicles and Materials-Handling Technology
DILTHEY, U., Welding Technology
EL-MAGD, E. A., Engineering Materials
FELDHUSEN, J., Engineering Design
GOLD, P. W., Machine Elements and Design
GRIES, T., Textile Engineering
GRUENEFELD, G., Laser Technology
HABERSTROH, E., Synthetic Rubber Technology
HENNING, K., Methods of Cybernetics in Engineering Sciences
ITSKOV, M., Continuum Machines
KLOCKE, F., Manufacturing Technology
KNEER, R., Heat and Mass Transfer
KUGELER, K., Reactor Safety and Reactor Technology
LOOSEN, P., Technology of Optical Systems
LUCAS, K., Technical Thermodynamics
MAIER, H.-R., Ceramic Components in Mechanical Engineering
MARQUARDT, W., Process Systems Engineering
MELIN, T., Chemical Engineering
MICHAELI, W., Plastics Processing
MODIGELL, M., Mechanical Unit Operations
MURRENHOFF, H., Fluid Power Drives and Control

NIEHUIS, R., Jet Propulsion and Turbo Machinery
OLIVIER, H., High-Temperature Gas Dynamics
PETERS, N., Technical Mechanics
PFENNING, A., Thermal Unit Operations
PISCHINGER, S., Internal Combustion Engines
PITZ-PAAL, R., Solar Technology
POPRAWE, R., Laser Technology
REIMERDES, H.-G., Aerospace and Lightweight Structures
SCHLICK, C., Industrial Engineering and Ergonomics
SCHMACHTENBERG, E., Plastics Materials Technology
SCHMITT, R., Metrology and Quality Management
SCHOMBURG, W. K., Construction and Devt of Microsystems
SCHROEDER, W., Fluid Dynamics
SCHUH, G., Production Engineering
SCHULZ, W., Laser Production Processes
SINGHEISER, L., Materials for Energy Technology
STOLTEN, D., Fuel Cells
WALLENTOWITZ, H., Automotive Engineering
WEICHERT, D., General Mechanics

Faculty of Medicine (Pauwelstr. 30, 52074 Aachen; tel. (241) 8089167; e-mail dekanat@ukaachen.de; internet www.ukaachen.de):

AMUNTS, K., Structural-Functional Brain Mapping
AUTSCHBACH, R., Thoracic and Cardiovascular Surgery
BEIER, H., Anatomy and Reproductive Biology
BERNHAGEN, J., Biochemistry
BÜLL, U., Nuclear Medicine
CONRADS, G., Medical Microbiology
DIEDRICH, P., Orthodontics
DOTT, W., Hygienics and Environmental Medicine
EBLE, M. J., Radiotherapy
ELLING, I., Biomaterial Science
ELLRICH, J., Neurosurgery
FAHLKE, C., Physiology
FINK, G., Cognitive Neurology
FLOEGE, J., Internal Medicine
GAUGGEL, G., Medical Psychology and Medical Sociology
GERZER, R., Aerospace Medicine
GILSBACH, J., Neurosurgery
GRESSNER, A. M., Clinical Chemistry and Pathobiochemistry
GREVEN, J., Pharmacology and Toxicology
GRÜNDER, G., Experimental Neuropsychiatry
GÜNTHER, R., Diagnostic Radiology
HANRATH, P., Internal Medicine
HEIMANN, G., Paediatrics
HEINRICH, P., Biochemistry
HERPERTZ-DAHLMANN, B., Child and Adolescent Psychiatry and Psychotherapy
HILGERS, R.-D., Medical Statistics
HÖRNCHEN, H., Paediatrics
HUBER, W., Neurolinguistics
JAHNEN-DECHENT, W., Cell and Molecular Biology at Interfaces
JAKSE, G., Urology
KAUFMANN, P., Anatomy
KNÜCHEL-CLARKE, C., Pathology
KORR, H., Anatomy
KRAUS, T., Occupational Medicine
KUHLEN, H., Anaesthesiology
KÜPPER, W., Laboratory Animal Science
LAMPERT, F., Conservative Dentistry, Periodontics and Preventive Dentistry
LENDLEIN, A., Technology and Devt of Medical Products
LEONHARDT, S., Medical Informatics Technology
LUECKHOFF, A., Physiology

LUESCHER, B., Biochemistry and Molecular Biology
LUETTICKEN, R., Medical Microbiology
MARX, R., Dental Materials
MATERN, H., Internal Medicine
MATHIAK, K., Behavioural Psychobiology
MERK, H. F., Dermatology
MURKEN, A. H., History of Medicine and Hospitals
NEULEN, J., Gynaecological Endocrinology and Reproductive Medicine
NEUSCHAEFER-RUBE, C., Phoniatrics and Pedaudiology
NIENDORF, T., Experimental MR-Imaging
NIETHARD, F. U., Orthopaedics
NOTH, J., Neurology
OSIEKA, R., Internal Medicine
PAAR, O., Surgery
PALLUA, N., Plastic Surgery, Hand and Reconstructive Surgery
RATH, W., Gynaecology
RIEDIGER, D., Oral, Maxillofacial and Plastic Facial Surgery
RINK, L., Immunology
RITTER, K., Virology
ROSSAINT, R., Anaesthesiology
SCHMALZIG, G., Pharmacology and Toxicology
SCHMITZ-RODE, T., Diagnostic Radiology
SCHNEIDER, F., Psychiatrics and Psychotherapy
SCHUMPELICK, V., Surgery
SEGHAYE, M.-C., Paediatric Cardiology
SPIEKERMANN, H., Prosthodontics
SPITZER, K., Medical Informatics
THRON, A., Neuroradiology
VÁSQUEZ-JIMÉNEZ, J., Paediatric Heart Surgery
WALTER, P., Opthalmology
WEBER, C., Cardiovascular Molecular Biology
WEIS, J., Neuropathology
WELLMANN, A., Pathology (Cytology)
WESTHOFEN, M., Otorhinolaryngology
WILLMES-VON HINCKELDEY, K., Neuropsychology
ZENKE, M., Biomedical Engineering and Cell Biology
ZERRES, K., Human Genetics

AFFILIATED INSTITUTIONS

Aachen Global Academy GmbH: Kármánstr. 17, 52056 Aachen; Dir Dr CHRISTOPH K. HEINEN.

Aachener Demonstrationslabor für integrierte Produktionstechnik GmbH: Seilbachstr. 25, 52062 Aachen; Dir Dr WERNER FISCHER.

ACCES eV—Materials + Processes: Intzestr. 5, 52072 Aachen; Dir ROBERT GUNTLIN.

Deutsches Wollforschungsinstitut eV (German Wool Research Institute): Veltmanplatz 8, 52062 Aachen; Dir Prof. Dr MARTIN MÖLLER.

Forschungsinstitut für Rationalisierung (Institute for Research in Rationalization): Pontdriesch 14–16, 52062 Aachen; Dir Prof. Dr HOLGER LUCZAK.

Forschungsinstitut für Wasser- und Abfallwirtschaft (Research Institute for Water and Waste Management): Mies-van-der-Rohe-Str. 17, 52062 Aachen; Dir FRIEDRICH-WILHELM BOLLE.

Forschungsstelle Technisch-Wirtschaftliche Unternehmensstrukturen der Stahlindustrie (Research Department for Technical and Economic Corporate Structures in the Steel Industry): Intzestr. 1, 52072 Aachen; Dir Prof. Dr WINFRIED DAHL.

Fraunhofer-Institut für Produktionstechnologie (Fraunhofer Institute for Production Technology): Steinbachstr. 17, 52074 Aachen; Dir Prof. Dr G. SCHUH.

Freunde und Förderer der RWTH Aachen: Wüllnerstr. 9, 52062 Aachen; em. Prof. ROLAND WALTER.

Institut für Kunststoffverarbeitung in Industrie und Handwerk (Institute of Plastics Technology): Ponstr. 49–55, 52062 Aachen; Dir Prof. Dr WALTER MICHAELI.

Institut für Prozess- und Anwendungstechnik Keramik (Institute for Process and Application Technology in Ceramics): Dir Prof. Dr HORST R. MAIER.

Prüf- und Entwicklungsinstitut für Abwassertechik: Mies-van-der-Rohe-Str. 1, 52074 Aachen; Dir Dr ELMAR DORGELOH.

Technische Akademie, Wuppertal eV: Hubertusallee 18, 42117 Wuppertal; Dir Dr MARTIN STACHOWSKE.

WZLfoum an der RWTH Aachen: Steinbachstr. 53, 52074 Wuppertal; Dir Dr TORSTEN KURR.

RHEINISCHE FRIEDRICH-WILHELMS-UNIVERSITÄT BONN

Regina-Pacis-Weg 3, 53113 Bonn
Telephone: (228) 73-5950
Fax: (228) 73-7722
E-mail: presse.info@uni-bonn.de
Internet: www.uni-bonn.de

Founded 1786, refounded 1818
State control
Academic year: October to September

Rector: Prof. Dr MATTHIAS WINIGER
Chancellor: Dr REINHARDT LUTZ
Librarian: Dr RENATE VOGT

Number of teachers: 517
Number of students: 28,313

Publications: *Academica Bonnensia, Alma Mater, Bonner Akademische Reden, Bonner Universitäts-Nachrichten "Forsch"* (4 a year), *Bonn University News International* (in English, 1 a year), *Politeia, Studium Universale*

DEANS

Faculty of Agriculture: Prof. Dr KARL SCHELLANDER
Faculty of Catholic Theology: Prof. Dr MICHAEL SCHULZ
Faculty of Evangelical Theology: Prof. Dr GÜNTER RÖHSER
Faculty of Law and Economics: Prof. Dr CHRISTIAN HILLGRUBER
Faculty of Mathematics and Natural Sciences: Prof. Dr ULF-G. MEIßNER
Faculty of Medicine: Prof. Dr THOMAS KLOCKGETHER
Faculty of Philosophy: Prof. Dr GÜNTHER SCHULZ

PROFESSORS

Faculty of Agriculture (Meckenheimer Allee 174, 59115 Bonn; tel. (228) 722867; fax (228) 732140; e-mail landwirtschaftliche .fakultaet@uni-bonn.de; internet www.lwf .uni-bonn.de):

BERG, E., Agricultural Economics
DEHNE, H., Phytopathology
FÖRSTNER, W., Photogrammetry
GALENSA, R., Food Science and Food Chemistry
GOLDBACH, H., Plant Nutrition
HELFRICH, H.-P., Practical Mathematics
ILK, K. H., Satellite-assisted Physical Geodesy
KÖPKE, U., Ecological Agriculture
KÜHBAUCH, W., Plant Breeding
KUNZ, B., Food Technology and Food Biotechnology
KUTSCH, TH., Agricultural and Domestic Sociology
LÉON, J., Plant Production and Breeding
NOGA, G., Fruit and Vegetable Production

SCHELLANDER, K., Animal Breeding
SCHIEFER, G., Agricultural Economy
SCHNABL, H., Botany
STEHLE, P., Nutrition
WEIß, E., House and Town Planning
WITTMANN, D., Agricultural Zoology and Ecology

Faculty of Catholic Theology (Am Hof 1, 53113 Bonn; tel. (228) 73-7344; fax (228) 73-5985):

FABRY, H. J., Old Testament
FINDEIS, H.-J., New Testament
FÜRST, W., Pastoral Theology
GERHARDS, A., Liturgy
HOPPE, R., New Testament Science
HOSSFELD, F.-L., Old Testament Science
HÖVER, G., Moral Theology
LÜDECKE, N., Canon Law
MENKE, K.-H., Dogmatics, Theological Propaedeutics
MUSCHIOL, G., Church History
SCHÖLLGEN, G., Ancient Church History and Patrology
SCHULZ, M., Dogmatics
SONNEMANS, H., Fundamental Theology

Faculty of Evangelical Theology (Am Hof 1, 53113 Bonn; tel. (228) 73-7202):

BADER, G., Systematic Theology
HAUSCHILDT, E., Practical Theology
KINZIG, W., Church History
KREß, H., Systematic Theology, Social Ethics
MEYER-BLANCK, M., Theology Education
PANGRITZ, A., Systematic Theology
RÖHSER, G., New Testament
RÜTERSWÖRDEN, U., Old Testament
SCHMIDT-ROST, R., Practical Theology
STOCK, K., Systematic Theology
WOLTER, M., New Testament

Faculty of Law and Economics (Adenauerallee 24–42, 53113 Bonn; tel. (228) 73-9101; fax (228) 73-9100; e-mail dekanat@jura .uni-bonn.de; internet www.jura.uni-bonn .de):

BÖSE, D., Political Economy
BREITUNG, J., Economics
BREUER, R., Public Law
DI FABIO, U., Public Law
DOLZER, R., German and International Public Law
FLEISCHER, H., Civil Law
VON HAGEN, J., Economics
HERDEGEN, M., Public Law
HILLGRUBER, CHR., Public Law
KINDHÄUSER, U., Criminal Law
KNÜTEL, R., Roman and Civil Law
KÖNDGEN, J., Civil Law
KORTE, B., Operational Research
KRÄKEL, M., Business Administration
LÖWER, W., Public Law
MOLDOVANU, B., Economic Theory, Mathematical Theory of Economics
NEUMANN, M., Economic Policy
PAEFFGEN, H.-U., Criminal Law
PIETZCKER, J., Public Law
ROTH, W.-H., Civil Law, International Private Law, and Comparative Law
SANDMANN, K., Economic Policy
SCHILKEN, E., Civil Law
SCHMIDT-PREUß, M., Public Law
SCHWEIZER, U., Economic Policy
SHAKED, A., Economic Policy
THEISSEN, E., Business Administration
VERREL, T., Criminology
WAGNER, G., Civil Law
WALTERMANN, R., Civil Law
ZACZYK, R., Criminal Law, Philosophy of Law
ZIMMER, D., Commercial Law
ZIMMERMANN, K., Economic Policy

Faculty of Mathematics and Natural Sciences (Wegelerstr. 10, 53113 Bonn; tel. (228) 73-2233; fax (228) 73-3892; e-mail dekan@

iam.uni-bonn.de; internet www .math-nat-fakultaet.uni-bonn.de):

ALBEVERIO, S., Mathematics
ALT, H. W., Mathematics
AUMANN, D., Chemistry
BALLMANN, W., Mathematics
BARGON, J., Physical Chemistry
BARTHLOTT, W., Botanics
BLECKMANN, H., Zoology
BRIESKORN, E., Mathematics
CREMERS, A. B., Informatics
DE BOER, K., Astronomy
DIETZ, K., Theoretical Physics
DIKAU, R., Geography
DÖTZ, K. H., Organic Chemistry
ECKMILLER, R., Informatics
EHLERS, E., Social and Economic Geography
FREHSE, J., Applied Mathematics
GLOMBITZA, K.-W., Pharmaceutical Biology
GRIEBEL, M., Scientific Computing
GROTZ, R., Geography
HAMENSTÄDT, U., Mathematics
HARDER, G., Mathematics
HERZOG, V., Cell Biology
HILDEBRANDT, S., Mathematics
HILGER, E., Experimental Physics
HUBER, M. G., Theoretical Atomic Physics
KARPINSKI, M., Informatics
KELLER, R., Zoology
KILIAN, K., Experimental Atomic Physics
KIRFEL, A., Mineralogy
KLEIN, F., Experimental Physics
KLEMPT, E., Experimental Physics
VON KOENIGSWALD, W., Palaeontology
LEISTNER, E., Pharmaceutical Biology
LIEB, I., Mathematics
MADER, W., Inorganic Chemistry
MAIER, K., Experimental Physics
MASCHUW, R., Atomic Physics
MEBOLD, U., Radio Astronomy
MENZ, G., Geography
MENZEL, D., Botany
MESCHEDE, D., Experimental Physics
MONIEN, H., Theoretical Physics
MÜLLER, W., Mathematics
NAHM, W., Mathematical Physics
NEUGEBAUER, H., Geophysics
NICKEL, P., Pharmaceutical Chemistry
NIECKE, E., Inorganic and Analytical Chemistry
NILLES, H. P., Theoretical Physics
PEYERIMHOFF, S., Theoretical Chemistry
RAITH, M., Geology and Petrology
SANDHAS, W., Theoretical Physics
SANDHOFF, K., Biochemistry
SAUER, K. P., Zoology and Ecological Studies
SCHOCH, B., Physics
SCHÖNHAGE, A., Informatics
SIMMER, C., Meteorology
SPETH, J., Theoretical Physics
STEFFENS, K. J., Pharmaceutical Technology
THEIN, J., Geology
TRÜPER, H. G., Microbiology
VÖGTLE, F., Chemistry
WANDELT, K., Physical Chemistry
WANDREY, CH., Biotechnology
WERMES, N., Experimental Physics
WILLECKE, K., Genetics
WINIGER, M., Geography

Faculty of Medicine (Sigmund-Freud-Str. 25, Haus 23, 53105 Bonn-Venusberg; tel. (228) 28-79201; fax (228) 28-79211; e-mail med-deha@ukb.uni-bonn.de; internet www .med.uni-bonn.de):

BAUR, M. P., Medical Statistics
BIDLINGMAIER, F., Clinical Biochemistry
BIEBER, TH., Dermatology and Venereology
BIERSACK, H.-J., Nuclear Medicine
ELGER, C. E., Epileptology
EXNER, M., Hygiene
FRANZ, TH., Anatomy
GÖTHERT, M., Pharmacology, Toxicology

GROTE, J., Physiology
HANFLAND, P., Experimental Haematology
HANSIS, M. L., Clinical Quality Management
HERBERHOLD, C., Otorhinolaryngology
HIRNER, A., Surgery
HOEFT, A., Anaesthesiology
JÄGER, A., Dentistry
KOECK, B., Dentistry
LENTZE, M. J., Paediatrics
LIEDTKE, R., Psychosomatic Medicine and Psychotherapy
LÜDERITZ, B., Internal Medicine, Cardiology
MADEA, B., Forensic Medicine
MAIER, W., Psychiatry
MÜLLER, ST., Urology
NOLDEN, R., Dentistry
PFEIFER, U., Pathology, Pathological Anatomy
PROPPING, P., Human Genetics
REICH, R., Oral and Maxillofacial Surgery
SAUERBRUCH, T., Internal Medicine
SCHAAL, K. P., Medical Microbiology
SCHILD, H. H., Radiology
SCHILLING, K., Anatomy
SCHMITT, O., Orthopaedics
SCHOTT, H., History of Medicine
SCHRAMM, J., Neurosurgery
SEITZ, H. M., Medical Parasitology
SPITZNAS, M., Ophthalmology
VETTER, H., Internal Medicine
WAHL, G., Oral Surgery
WIESTLER, O., Neuropathology

Faculty of Philosophy (Am Hof 1, 53113 Bonn; tel. (228) 73-7295; fax (228) 73-5986; internet www.philfak.uni-bonn.de):

BONNET, A.-M., History of Art
BREDENKAMP, J., Psychology
BRÜGGEN, E., Germanic Studies
COX, H. L., Folklore
DAHLMANN, D., East European History
DUMKE, D., Psychology
EHLERS, E., Social and Economic Geography
ESSER, J., English Philology
FEHN, K., Historical Geography
FISCHER, E., Musicology
FOHRMANN, J., Germanic Studies
GALSTERER, H., Ancient History
GROTZ, R., Geography
HESS, W., Communication and Phonetics
HILDEBRAND, K., Medieval and Modern History
HILGENHEGER, N., Education
HIRDT, W., Romance Philology
HOGREBE, W., Philosophy
HONNEFELDER, L., Philosophy
HÖNNIGHAUSEN, L., English Philology
KAISER, K., Political Science
KARSTEN, D., Political Science
KEIPERT, H., Slavonic Studies
KELZ, H., Phonetics
KLAUER, K. C., Psychology
KLEIN, TH., Germanic Studies
KLIMKEIT, H.-J., Comparative Religion
KOHRT, M., Germanic Studies
KÖLZER, T., Medieval and Modern History, Archival Science
KREINER, J., Japanology
KUBIN, W., Sinology
KUHN, A., History
KÜHNHARDT, L., Political Science
LADENTHIN, V., Education
LANGE, W. D., Romance Philology
LAUREYS, M., Philology
MECHLING, H., Sports
MIELSCH, H., Archaeology
NEUBAUER, W., Psychology
OEHLER, D., Comparative Science of Literature
PANTZER, P., Japanology
POHL, H., Constitutional History, Economics, Social History
POTTHOFF, W., Slavonic Studies

PREM, H. J., Ethnology
REICHL, K., English Philology
RÖBLER, U., Egyptology
ROSEN, K., Ancient History
SCHALLER, H.-J., Sports
SCHMITT, C., Roman Philology
SCHNEIDER, H., Germanic Studies
SCHOLZ, O. B., Psychology
SCHWARZ, H.-P., Political Science
SIMEK, R., Germanic Studies
STUHLMANN-LAEISZ, R., Logic and Foundations
WEEDE, E., Sociology
WILD, S., Semitic Philology
WINIGER, M., Geography
WOLF, H. J., Romance Philology
ZIMMER, ST., Linguistics
ZWIERLEIN, O., Classical Philology

RUHR-UNIVERSITÄT BOCHUM

Postfach 102148, 44801 Bochum
Universitätsstr. 150, 44780 Bochum
Telephone: (234) 32-25486
Fax: (234) 32-14684
E-mail: monika.sprung@uv.ruhr-uni-bochum.de
Internet: www.ruhr-uni-bochum.de
Founded 1965
State control
Languages of instruction: German, English
Academic year: October to July

Rector: Prof. Dr ELMAR W. WEILER
Pro-Rectors: Prof. Dr-Ing. PETER AQAKOWICZ, Prof. Dr BERNHARD STÖCKHERT, Prof. Dr TIBOR KISS
Chancellor: GERHARD MÖLLER
Librarian: Dr ERDMUTE LAPP
Library of 2,000,000 vols
Number of teachers: 2,376
Number of students: 32,772

DEANS

Faculty of Biology: Prof. Dr STÜTZEL
Faculty of Catholic Theology: Prof. Dr GÖLLNER
Faculty of Chemistry: Prof. Dr FISCHER
Faculty of Civil Engineering: Prof. Dr SCHUMANN
Faculty of East Asian Studies: Prof. Dr FINDEISEN
Faculty of Economics: Prof. Dr PELLENS
Faculty of Electrical Engineering: Prof. Dr BRINKMANN
Faculty of Geosciences: Prof. Dr WOHNLICH
Faculty of History: Prof. Dr ZIEGLER
Faculty of Law: Prof. Dr SEER
Faculty of Mathematics: Prof. Dr DETTE
Faculty of Mechanical Engineering: Prof. Dr SCHERER
Faculty of Medicine: Prof. Dr MUHR
Faculty of Philology: Prof. Dr EIKELMANN
Faculty of Philosophy, Pedagogy and Journalism: Prof. Dr W. JAESCHKE
Faculty of Physics and Astronomy: Prof. Dr MEYER
Faculty of Protestant Theology: Prof. Dr JÄHNICHEN
Faculty of Psychology: Prof. Dr SCHÖLMERICH
Faculty of Social Sciences: Prof. Dr VOSS
Faculty of Sport Science: Prof. Dr A. NEUMAIER

DIRECTORS OF CENTRAL ACADEMIC INSTITUTIONS

Centre for Further Education: Prof. Dr M. MUHLER
Centre for Interdisciplinary Research in the Ruhr Area: Prof. Dr K. P. STROHMEIER
Institute for Development Research and Development Policy: Prof. Dr U. ANDERSEN
Institute for Energy and Natural Resources Law: Prof. Dr C. PIELOW
Institute for German Cultural Studies: Prof. Dr W. VOSS

Institute for Industrial Science: Prof. Dr H. MINSSEN
Institute for International Law of Peace and Human Rights: Prof. Dr J. WOLF
Institute for Neuro-Computing: Prof. Dr G. SCHÖNER
Institute for Social Movements: Prof. Dr K. TENFELDE
Institute for Teacher Training: Prof. Dr R. FISCHER

PROFESSORS

Faculty of Biology (tel. (234) 322-4573; fax (234) 321-4237; internet www.biologie.ruhr-uni-bochum.de):

BENNERT, W., Plant Taxonomy
DENHARDT, G., General Zoology and Neurobiology
DISTLER, C., General Zoology and Neurobiology
FAISSNER, A., Cell Morphology and Molecular Neurobiology
GERWERT, K., Biophysics
HAEUPLER, H., Geobotany
HAPPE, T., Plant Biochemistry, Photobiotechnology
HATT, H., Cell Physiology
HOFFMANN, K.-P., General Zoology and Neurobiology
HOFMANN, E., Protein Crystallography, Biophysics
JANCKE, D., Cognitive Neurobiology, General Zoology and Neurobiology
KIRCHNER, W. H., Behavioural Biology and Teaching of Biology
KÜCK, U., General and Molecular Botany
LINK, G., Plant Cell Physiology and Molecular Biology, Plant Physiology
LÜBBEN, M., Biophysics
LÜBBERT, H., Animal Physiology
NARBERHAUS, F., Biology of Micro-organisms
NECKER, R., Animal Physiology
NICKELSEN, J., Biology of Micro-organisms
ÖTTMAYER, W., Plant Biochemistry
PÖGGELER, S., General and Molecular Botany
RAETHER, W., Special Zoology
RÖGNER, M., Plant Biochemistry
SCHAUB, G., Animal Taxonomy, Parasitology
SCHLITTER, J., Biophysics
SCHMIDT, M., General Zoology and Neurobiology
SCHÜNEMANN, O., General and Molecular Botany
SCHWENN, J.-D., Plant Biochemistry
STÖRTKUHL, K., Cell Physiology, Sensory Physiology
STÜTZEL, T., Plant Taxonomy, Spermatophytes
WAHLE, P., Developmental Neurobiology, General Zoology and Neurobiology
WEILER, E., Plant Physiology
WETZEL, C., Cell Physiology

Faculty of Catholic Theology (tel. (234) 32-22619; fax (234) 3214-410; e-mail kath-theol-fak@ruhr-uni-bochum.de):

DAMBERG, W., Medieval and Modern Church History
DSCHULNIGG, P., New Testament
FREVEL, C., Old Testament Exegesis and Theology
GEERLINGS, W., Church History, Patrology
GÖLLNER, R., Practical Theology
KNAPP, M., Fundamental Theology
KNOCH, W., Dogmatics
REINHARDT, H. J. F., Canon Law
WIEMEYER, J., Christian Social Ethics
ZELINKA, U., Moral Theology

Faculty of Chemistry (tel. (234) 32-24732; fax (234) 32-14108; e-mail chemie-dekanat@ruhr-uni-bochum.de; internet www.ruhr-uni-bochum.de/chemie):

BENNECKE, G., Receptor Biochemistry
DYKER, G., Organic Chemistry
FEIGEL, M., Organic Chemistry
FISCHER, R., Inorganic Chemistry
GRÜNERT, W., Technical Chemistry
HAVENITH-NEWEN, M., Physical Chemistry
HERMANN, C., Physical Chemistry
HEUMANN, R., Molecular Neurobiochemistry
HOLLMANN, M., Receptor Biochemistry
HOVEMANN, B., Molecular Cell Biochemistry
VON KIEDROWSKI, G., Organic Chemistry
MARX, D., Theoretical Chemistry
MUHLER, M., Technical Chemistry
MÜLLER, S., Organic Chemistry
SANDER, W., Organic Chemistry
SCHUHMANN, W., Analytical Chemistry
SHELDRICK, W. S., Analytical Chemistry
SOMMER, K., Didactics of Chemistry
STAEMMLER, V., Theoretical Chemistry
WEINGÄRTNER, H., Physical Chemistry
WÖLL, C., Physical Chemistry

Faculty of Civil Engineering (tel. (234) 322-6124; fax (234) 3214-147; e-mail dekanat-bi@ruhr-uni-bochum.de; internet www.ruhr-uni-bochum.de/fbi):

BREITENBÜCHER, R., Building Materials
BRILON, W., Traffic Engineering
BRUHNS, O. T., Mechanics
HACKL, K., Mechanics
HARTMANN, D., Applied Computer Science
HÖFFER, R., Aerodynamics and Fluid Mechanics
KINDMANN, R., Steel and Composite Constructions
MESCHKE, G., Structural Mechanics
ORTH, H., Environmental Engineering
REESE, S., Computational Mechanics and Simulation
SCHERER, M., Surveying and Geodesy
SCHMID, G., Structural Mechanics and Computer Simulation
SCHUMANN, A., Hydrology, Water Resources Management and Environmental Engineering
STANGENBERG, F., Reinforced and Prestressed Concrete Structures
STOLPE, H., Environmental Technology and Ecology
TRIANTAFYLLIDIS, TH., Soil Mechanics
WILLEMS, W., Structural Design and Building Physics

Faculty of East Asian Studies (tel. (234) 322-6189; e-mail anne.mueller@ruhr-uni-bochum.de; internet www.ruhr-uni-bochum.de/oaw):

EGGERT, M., Korean Studies
FINDEISEN, R., Chinese Language and Literature
GU, X., East Asian Politics
KLENNER, W., East Asian Economics
MATHIAS, R., Japanese History
RICKMEYER, J., Japanese Language and Literature
ROETZ, H., Chinese History and Philosophy

Faculty of Economics (tel. (234) 32-22884; fax (234) 32-14140; e-mail wiwi-dekanat@ruhr-uni-bochum.de; internet www.wiwi.ruhr-uni-bochum.de):

BAUER, T., Empirical Economics
BENDER, D., Int. Economic Relations
DIRRIGL, H., Controlling
FOLKERS, C., Public Finance
GABRIEL, R., Business Informatics
HAMMANN, P., Management and Marketing
HAUCUP, J., Economic Policy
KARL, H., Economic Policy
KÖSTERS, W., Monetary Economics
LÖSCH, M., Statistics and Econometrics
MAG, W., Theoretical Industrial Economics

MANN, T., Law concerning the Economy
NIENHAUS, V., Economic Policy
PAUL, S., Banking and Finance
PELLENS, B., Int. Accounting
SCHIMMELPFENNIG, J., Theoretical and Applied Microeconomics
SMOLNY, W., Applied Economics
STEVEN, M., Production and Operations
STREIM, H., Financial Accounting and Auditing
VOIGT, S., Economic Policy
WERNERS, B., Operations Research and Accounting

Faculty of Electrical Engineering (tel. (234) 32-25666; fax (234) 3214-444; e-mail dekanat-ei@ruhr-uni-bochum.de; internet www.et.ruhr-uni-bochum.de):

AWAKOWICZ, P., General Electrical Engineering/Plasma Technology
BALZERT, H., Software Engineering
BRINKMANN, R. P., Theoretical Electrical Engineering/Plasma Technology
ERMERT, H., High-Frequency Engineering
FISCHER, H. D., Communications Engineering
GÖCKLER, H., Digital Signal Processing
HAUSNER, J., Integrated Systems
HOFMANN, M., Optoelectronic Devices and Materials
HUDDE, H., Sound and Vibration
KUNZE, U., Electronic Materials and Nanoelectronics
LANGMANN, U., Integrated Circuits
LUNZE, J., Automation
MARTIN, R., Information Technology and Communication Acoustics
MELBERT, J., Electronic Circuits and Measurement Techniques
OEHM, J., Circuit Design
PAAR, CH., Communication Security
SADIGHI, A.-R., Applied Data Security
SCHMILZ, G., Medical Engineering
SCHWENK, J., Network and Data Security
SOURKOUNIS, C., Power System Technology
STEIMEL, A., Power Engineering
TÜCHELMANN, Y., Integrated Information Systems

Faculty of Geosciences (tel. (234) 32-23505; fax (234) 3214-535; e-mail geodekanat@ruhr-uni-bochum.de; internet www.ruhr-uni-bochum.de/exogeol/geowiss.html):

ALBER, M., Engineering Geology
BUTZIN, B., Geography
CHAKRABORTY, S., Mineralogy and Petrology
FLEER, H., Climatology and Hydrogeology
FRIEDRICH, W., Geophysics
GIES, H., Mineralogy and Crystallography
HOHN, U., Economic and Social Geography
JÜRGENS, C., Geo-Remote Sensing
LÖTSCHER, L., Geography and Cultural Geography
MARESCH, W. V., Mineralogy
MÜLLER, J.-C., Cartography
MUTTERLOSE, J., Palaeontology and Geology
OTTO, K.-H., Didactics of Geography
RENNER, J., Seismology
SCHMITT, TH., Geography
STÖCKHERT, B., Geology
WOHNLICH, ST., Applied Geology
ZEPP, H., Physical Geography

Faculty of History (tel. (234) 32-22525; fax (234) 32-14240; e-mail dekan-gw@ruhr-uni-bochum.de; internet www.ruhr-uni-bochum.de/geschichtswissenschaft):

ADANIR, F., Southeast European History
BERGEMANN, J., Archaeology
BLEEK, W., Sociology, Political Science
BONWETSCH, B., East European History
BÜSING, H., Archaeology
EBEL-ZEPEZAUER, W., Pre- and Proto-History

EDER, W., Ancient History
ERBEN, D., History of Art
VON GRAEVE, V., Archaeology
GÜNTHER, L.-M., Ancient History
HÖLSCHER, L., Theory of History
HOPPE-SAILER, R., History of Art
MATHIAS, R., East Asian Studies
OBERWEIS, M., Auxiliary Sciences (Diplomacy, Palaeography, Numismatics)
SCHULTE, R., Modern and Contemporary History, Gender Studies
SÖNTGEN, B., History of Art
STEINHAUSER, M., History of Art
TENFELDE, K., Social History and Social Movement
WALA, M., History of North America
WALZ, R., Early Modern History
WEBER, W., Economic and Technical History
ZIEGLER, D., Economic and Business History

Faculty of Law (tel. (234) 32-26566; fax (234) 3214-530; e-mail denise.sablotny@jura.ruhr-uni-bochum.de; internet www.ruhr-uni-bochum.de/jura):

BERNSMANN, K., Criminal Law, Criminal Procedural Law
BORGES, G., Civil Law, Media Law and Law of Information Technology
BURGI, M., Public Law
FELTES, TH., Criminology
GREMER, W., Public Law, European Law
HÖRNLE, T., Criminal Law, Criminal Procedural Law
HUSTER, S., Public Law
KINDLER, P., Civil Law, Commercial Law, Int. Civil Law and Comparative Law
KRAMPE, CHR., Civil Law, Ancient Law and Roman Law
MUSCHELER, K., History of German Law, Civil Law, Church Law
POSCHER, R., Public Law, Sociology of Law
PUTTLER, A., Public Law
SCHILDT, B., History of Law, Civil Law
SCHREIBER, K., Procedural Law, Civil and Labour Law
SEER, R., Tax Law and Administrative Law
SIEKMANN, H., Public Law
WANK, R., Civil Law, Commercial and Labour Law
WINDEL, A., Procedural Law, Civil Law
WOLF, J., Public Law
WOLTERS, G., Criminal Law, Criminal Procedural Law

Faculty of Mathematics (tel. (234) 322-3476; fax (234) 3214-103; e-mail ffm@ruhr-uni-bochum.de; internet www.ruhr-uni-bochum.de/ffm):

ABRESCH, U., Mathematics
AVANZI, R., Mathematics
BARTENWERFER, W., Mathematics
BERTSCH, E., Computer Science
DEHLING, H., Mathematics
DETTE, H., Mathematics
DOBBERTIN, H., Mathematics, Cryptology
EICHELSBACHER, P., Mathematics
FLENNER, H., Mathematics
GERRITZEN, L., Mathematics
HEINZNER, P., Mathematics
HUCKLEBERRY, A. T., Mathematics
KIRSCH, W., Mathematical Physics
KNIEPER, G., Mathematics
KRIECHERBAUER, T., Mathematics
LAURES, G., Mathematics
MATTHIES, G., Mathematics
SIMON, H., Mathematics, Computer Science
STORCH, U., Mathematics
VERFÜRTH, R., Mathematics
WASSERMANN, G., Differential Topology

Faculty of Mechanical Engineering (tel. (234) 32-26191; fax (234) 32-14291; e-mail dekanmb@itm.ruhr-uni-bochum.de; internet www.ruhr-uni-bochum.de/maschinenbau):

ABRAMOVICI, M., Computer Science
EGGELER, G., Materials Science
MEIER, Production Systems
PAPENFUSS, H.-D., Applied Fluid Mechanics
POHL, M., Materials Testing
PREDKI, W., Mechanical Components—Industrial and Automotive Power Transmission
REINIG, G., Control Systems Engineering
ROGG, B., Fluid Mechanics
RÖHM, H.-J., Chemical and Environmental Engineering
SCHERER, V., Energy Plant Technology
SCHWEIGER, G., Applied Laser Technology and Measuring Systems
STOFF, H., Fluid Flow Machines
STÖVER, D. H. H., Materials Processing
STRATMANN, M., Materials Surfaces and Interfaces
SVEJDA, P., Thermodynamics of Mixtures
THEISEN, W., Materials Technology
WAGNER, G., Mechanical Components and Materials Handling
WAGNER, H.-J., Energy Systems and Energy Economics
WAGNER, W., Thermodynamics
WEIDNER, E., Process Engineering
WELP, E. G., Mechanical Components and Methodical Design

Faculty of Medicine (tel. (234) 32-24960; fax (234) 3214-190; e-mail medizin@rub.de; internet www.ruhr-uni-bochum.de/medizin):

ADAMIETZ, J. A., Radiology
ALTMEYER, P., Dermatology and Venereology
BRÜNING, TH., Industrial Medicine
BUFE, A., Paediatrics
BURCHERT, W., Radiology
DAZERT, S., Otorhinolaryngology
DERMIETZEL, R., Anatomy
VON DÜRING, M., Anatomy
ENGERT, J., Paediatric Surgery
EPPLEN, J., Genetics
ERDMANN, R., Biochemistry
EYSEL, U., Physiology
GATERMANN, S., Medical Microbiology
GOODY, R., Physiological Chemistry
GRONEMEYER, U., Ophthalmology
GUZMAN Y ROTAECHE, J., Pathology
HARDERS, A. G., Neurosurgery
HASENBRING, M., Medical Psychology
HERPERTZ, S., Psychosomatic Medicine and Psychotherapy
HEUSER, L., Radiology
HOHLBACH, G.-R., Surgery
HORSTKOTTE, D., Internal Medicine
INOUE, K., Anaesthesiology
JENSEN, A. W. O., Gynaecology and Obstetrics
KLEESIEK, K., Clinical Chemistry and Pathobiochemistry
KLEIN, H. H., Internal Medicine
KOESLING, D., Pharmacology and Toxicology
KÖRFER, R., Thoracic and Cardiovascular Surgery
KÖSTER, O., Radiology
KRÄMER, J., Orthopaedics
KRIEG, M., Clinical Chemistry
LACZKOVICS, A., Surgery, Thoracic and Cardiovascular Surgery
LAUBENTHAL, H., Anaesthesiology
LIERMANN, D., Radiology
MALIN, J.-P., Neurology
MANNHERZ, H. G., Anatomy and Cell Biology
MAYER, H., Paediatric Cardiology
MELLER, K., Experimental Cytology
MORGENROTH, K., Pathology
MÜGGE, A., Internal Medicine

MUHR, G., Surgery
MÜLLER, I., History of Medicine
MÜLLER, K.-M., Pathology
NICOLAS, V., Radiology
NOLDUS, J., Urology
PESKAR, B., Clinical Experimental Medicine
PIENTKA, L., Geriatrics
POTT, L., Cellular Physiology
PRZUNTEK, H., Neurology
PUCHSTEIN, CH., Anaesthesiology
REUSCH, P., Pharmacology and Toxicology
RIEGER, CH., Paediatrics
RUMP, L. C., Nephrology
RUSCHE, H. H., General Medicine
SCHLEGEL, U., Neurology
SCHMIDT, W. E. W., Internal Medicine
SCHMIEGEL, W.-H., Internal Medicine
SCHULTZE-WERNINGHAUS, G., Internal Medicine
STEINAU, H.-U., Surgery
TRAMPISCH, H. J., Medical Informatics and Biomathematics
TRAPPE, H.-J., Internal Medicine
TSCHÖPE, D., Internal Medicine
ÜBERLA, K. T., Virology
UHE, W., Surgery
VIEBAHN, R., Surgery
WERNER, J., Biomedical Engineering
WILHELM, M., Hygiene
WOLFF, K.-D., Maxillofacial Surgery
ZENZ, M., Anaesthesiology

Faculty of Philology (tel. (234) 32-22623; fax (234) 32-14324; internet www.dekphil.ruhr-uni-bochum.de):

BASTERT, B., German Philology
BAUSCH, K.-R., Romance Philology
BEHRENS, R., Romance Philology
BEILENHOFF, W., Cinematography and Television Studies
BERNHARD, G., Romance Philology
BEYER, M., English Philology
BOETTCHER, W., Teaching of German Language and Literature
BOLLACHER, M., Modern German Literature
DEUBER-MANKOWSKI, A., Media Studies
EBEL, E., Scandinavian Studies
EFFE, B., Classical Philology
EIKELMANN, M., German Philology
ENDRESS, G., Arabic and Islamic Studies
FLUCK, H.-R., German Linguistics
FREITAG, K., American Studies
GLEI, R., Classical Philology/Latin
HASS, U., Theatre Studies
HEDIGER, V., Media Studies
HIMMELMANN, N., General Linguistics
HISS, G., Theatre Studies
HOUWEN, L., English Philology
KISS, T., General Linguistics
KLABUNDE, R., General Linguistics
KLODT, C., Classical Philology/Latin
KNAUTH, K. A., Romance Philology
KRENN, H., Romance Philology
LEBSANFT, F., Romance Philology
MENGE, H., German Linguistics
NIEDERHOFF, B., English
PITTNER, K., German Linguistics
PLUMPE, G., Modern German Literature
REICHMUTH, S., Islamic Studies
RUPP, G., Didactics of German Philology
SAPPOK, C., Slavonic Studies
SCHMID, U., Slavonic Studies
SCHMITZ-EMANS, M., General and Comparative Literature
SCHNEIDER, M., Modern German Literature
SCHÖNEFELD, D., English Philology
SIMONIS, L., General and Comparative Literature
SPANGENBERG, P., Media Sciences
STEINBRÜGGE, L., Romance Philology
THOMAS, B., Media Studies
TIETZ, M., Romance Philology
UHLENBRUCH, B., Russian and Soviet Culture

WARTH, E.-M., Cinematography and Television Studies
WEBER, I., English Philology
WEGERA, K.-P., History of German Language
WIEHL, P., Germanic Philology
ZELLE, C., Modern German Literature

Faculty of Philosophy, Pedagogy and Journalism (tel. (234) 32-22712; fax (234) 32-14505; e-mail reinhild.topp@ruhr-uni-bochum.de):

ADICK, C., Comparative Education
BELLENBERG, G., Educational Research Focus on Schools
DRIESCHNER, M., Natural Philosophy
HAARDT, A., Philosophy
HARNEY, K., Vocational Education and Lifelong Learning, Methods of Educational Research
HERZIG, B., Learning and Teaching Research
JAESCHKE, W., Classic German Philosophy
KEINER, E., History of Education
LESSING, H.-U., Philosophical Anthropology and Theory of the Humanities
MEYER-DRAWE, K., General Education
MOJSISCH, B., History of Philosophy
PARDEY, Logic and Philosophy of Language
PULTE, H., History and Philosophy of Science
ROSEMANN, B., Educational Psychology
SCHMIDT, K., Classic German Philosophy, Symbolic and Mathematical Logic
SCHOLTZ, G., History and Theory of the Humanities
SCHWEIDLER, Practical Philosophy
STEIGLEDER, K., Ethics in Medicine and Biosciences
WITTPOTH, J., Adult Education

Faculty of Physics and Astronomy (tel. (234) 322-3445; fax (234) 3214-447; e-mail dekanat@physik.ruhr-uni-bochum.de; internet physik.ruhr-uni-bochum.de):

CHINI, R., Astrophysics
CZARNETZKI, U., Experimental Physics
DETTMAR, R.-J., Astronomy
EFETOV, K., Theoretical Physics
FEUERBACHER, B., Experimental Physics
GERWERT, K., Biophysics
GOEKE, K., Theoretical Physics
GRAUER, R., Theoretical Physics
HERLACH, D., Experimental Physics
VON KEUDELL, A., Experimental Physics
KOCH, H., Experimental Physics
KÖHLER, U., Experimental Physics
KÖNIG, J., Theoretical Physics
VON DER MALSBURG, C., Neuroinformatics
MEYER, W., Experimental Physics
PELZL, J., Experimental Physics
POLYAKOV, U., Theoretical Physics
RITMAN, J., Experimental Physics
ROLFS, C., Experimental Physics
RUHL, H., Theoretical Physics
SCHLICKEISER, R., Theoretical Physics
SCHÖNER, G., Neuroinformatics
SOLTWISCH, H., Experimental Physics
WIECK, A., Experimental Physics
WINTER, J., Experimental Physics
WOLF, R., Experimental Physics
ZABEL, H., Experimental Physics

Faculty of Protestant Theology (tel. (234) 32-2250; fax (234) 3214-722; e-mail ulrike.burgner@ruhr-uni-bochum.de; internet www.ruhr-uni-bochum.de/ev-theol):

BEYER, F.-H., Practical Theology
EBACH, J., Old Testament
GELDBACH, E., Ecumenical and Denominational Studies
JÄHNICHEN, T., Christian Social Science
KARLE, J., Practical Theology
KRECH, V., Religious Science
STROHM, C., Church History (Reformation and Modern)
THIEL, W., Old Testament

THOMAS, G., Systematic Theology
WENGST, K., New Testament Exegesis and Theology
WICK, P., New Testament
WYRWA, D., Church History

Faculty of Psychology (tel. (234) 322-4606; fax (234) 3214-588; e-mail psy-dekanat@ruhr-uni-bochum.de; internet www.ruhr-uni-bochum.de/psy-dekanat):

BIERHOFF, H.-W., Social Psychology
BOCK, M., Psychology of Language and Communication
DAUM, I., Neuropsychology
GÜNTÜRKÜN, O., Biopsychology
GUSKI, R., Cognitive and Environmental Psychology
HASENBRING, M., Medical Psychology
REULECKE, W., Sport Psychology
ROSEMANN, B., Educational Psychology
SCHÖLMERICH, A., Development Psychology
SCHULTE, D., Clinical Psychology and Psychiatry
WOTTAWA, H., Methodology, Diagnostic and Evaluation
ZIMOLONG, B., Industrial and Organizational Psychology

Faculty of Social Sciences (tel. (234) 322-22967; fax (234) 3214-507; e-mail christel.maleszka@ruhr-uni-bochum.de; internet www.ruhr-uni-bochum.de/sowi):

ALTHAMMER, J., Social Politics
ANDERSEN, U., Political Science
BLEEK, W., Political Science
HEINZE, R. G., Sociology
LEHNER, F., Political Science
LENZ, I., Sociology
MINNSSEN, H., Labour Organization
NOLTE, H., Social Psychology
OTT, N., Social Politics
PETZINA, D., Social and Economic History
PRIES, L., Participation and Organization
ROHWER, G., Methodology of Social Science and Social Statistics
SCHMIDT, G., Political Science
STROHMEIER, K. P., Sociology
TIEDE, M., Mathematical and Empirical Procedure in Social Sciences
VOSS, W., Mathematical and Empirical Procedure in Social Sciences
WIDMAIER, Political Science
WOLFF, J., Sociology of Developing Countries

Faculty of Sport Science (Gebäude UHW, Stiepelerstr. 129, 44801 Bochum; tel. (234) 322-7793; fax (234) 3214-246; e-mail sportwiss-dekanat@ruhr-uni-bochum.de; internet www.ruhr-uni-bochum.de/spowiss):

BECKERS, E., Pedagogy of Sport
FERRANTI, A., Applied Training Science
HECK, H. J., Medicine in Sport
KELLMANN, M., Sports Psychology
KLEIN, M. L., Sociology of Sport, Sports Management
NEUMAIER, A., Theory of Movement, Biomechanics

Centre for Further Education (Geb. LOTA, 44780 Bochum; tel. (234) 322-6466; fax (234) 321-4255; e-mail wbz@ruhr-uni-bochum.de; internet www.ruhr-uni-bochum.de/wbz):

MUHLER, M.

Institute for Development Research and Development Policy (tel. (234) 322-2418; fax (234) 321-4294; e-mail ieeoffice@ruhr-uni-bochum.de; internet www.ruhr-uni-bochum.de/iee):

ANDERSEN, U., Society, Politics, Public Admin.
BENDER, D., Int. Economic Relations
DÜRR, H., Social and Economic Geography
NIENHAUS, V., Economic Policy
VOSS, W., Statistics and Econometrics
WOLF, J., Int. Law

WOLFF, J. H., Society, Politics, Public Admin.

Institute for Energy and Natural Resources Law (tel. (234) 322-7333; fax (234) 321-4292; e-mail tbe@ruhr-uni-bochum.de; internet www.ruhr-uni-bochum.de/ibe):

DRESEN, L., Seismology
HÜFFER, U., Civil Law, Commercial Law
IPSEN, K., Public Law
STEIN, D., Pipe Construction and Maintenance
TETTINGER, P. J., Public Law
UNGER, H., Nuclear and Modern Energy Systems
VON DANWITZ, T., Public Law, European Law

Institute for German Cultural Studies (tel. (234) 322-7863; fax (234) 321-4587; e-mail idf@ruhr-uni-bochum.de; internet www.ruhr-uni-bochum.de/deutschlandforschung):

ANDERSEN, U., Political Science
ANWEILER, D., Educational Research, Comparative Educational Research
BLEEK, W., Political Science
FAULENBACH, B., Modern History
KLUSSMANN, P. G., Modern German Literature
KROSS, E., Didactics of Geography
VOSS, W., Mathematical and Empirical Procedure in Social Sciences

Institute for Industrial Engineering (tel. (234) 322-7730; internet www.iaw.ruhr-uni-bochum.de/iaw):

MINNSSEN, H. (Dir)

Institute for Industrial Science (tel. (234) 322-3293; fax (234) 321-4118; internet www.iaw.ruhr-uni-bochum.de):

KAILER, N., Personnel and Qualifications
MINNSSEN, H., Organization of Work
SCHNAUBER, H., Working Systems Design
STAUDT, E., Economics of Work

Institute for International Law of Peace and Human Rights (tel. (234) 322-7366; fax (234) 321-4208; internet www.ruhr-uni-bochum.de/ifhv):

WOLF, J., Int. Law

Institute for Neuro-Computing (tel. (234) 322-7965; fax (234) 321-4209; e-mail institut@neuroinformatik.ruhr-uni-bochum.de; internet www.neuroinformatik.ruhr-uni-bochum.de):

SCHÖNER, G., Theoretical Biology
VON DER MALSBURG, CH., Systems Biophysics

Institute for Social Movements (44789 Bochum, Clemensstr. 17–19; tel. (234) 322-4687; fax (234) 321-4249; internet www.ruhr-uni-bochum.de/isb):

TENFELDE, K., Social History and Social Movements

Institute for Teacher Training (tel. (234) 321-1942; fax (234) 321-4647; e-mail zfl-kontakt@ruhr-uni-bochum.de; internet www.ruhr-uni-bochum.de/zfl):

BAUSCH, K. R., Romance Philology
BELLENBERG, G., Educational Science
KAMMERTÖNS, A., Didactics of Social Sciences
OTT, N., Social Politics
TIETZ, M., Romance Philology
WIECK, A., Experimental Physics

ATTACHED INSTITUTES

Berufsgenossenschaftliches Forschungsinstitut für Arbeitsmedizin (Research Institute for Occupational Medicine): Bürkle-de-la-Camp-Pl. 1, 44789 Bochum; Dir Prof. Dr H. BRÜNING.

Forschungsinstitut Arbeit, Bildung, Partizipation (Research Institute for Labour, Education and Participation): Mün-

sterstr. 13–15, 45657 Recklinghausen; Dir Dr K. DÖRRE.

Institut für Angewandte Innovationsforschung (Institute for Applied Innovation Research): Buscheypl. 13, 44801 Bochum; Chair. Prof. Dr B. KRIEGESMANN.

Institut für Diaspora- und Genozidforschung (Institute of Diaspora and Genocide Studies): Dir Dr M. DABAG.

Institut für Gefährstoff-Forschung (Institute for Research into Dangerous Substances): Waldring 97, 44789 Bochum; e-mail igf@igf-bbg.de; Dir Dr D. DAHMANN.

Institut für Umwelthygiene und Umweltmedizin des Hygiene-Instituts des Ruhrgebiets in Gelsenkirchen (Institute of Environmental Hygiene and Medicine): Rotthauserstr. 19, 45879 Gelsenkirchen; Dir Prof. Dr L. DUNEMANN.

Institut für Wohnungswesen, Immobilienwirtschaft, Stadt- und Regionalentwicklung GmbH (Institute of Housing, Real Estate, Urban and Regional Development Ltd): Springorumallee 20, 44795 Bochum; Dirs Prof. Dr V. EICHENER, M. SCHAUERTE.

KT-Institut für unterirdische Infrastruktur (KT-Institute for Underground Infrastructure): Exterbruch 1, 45886 Gelsenkirchen; Man. Dirs R. W. WANIEK, Dr-Ing. B. BOSSELER.

RUPRECHT-KARLS-UNIVERSITÄT HEIDELBERG

Postfach 105760, 69047 Heidelberg
Telephone: (6221) 54-0
Fax: (6221) 542618
E-mail: gb@zuv.uni-heidelberg.de
Internet: www.uni-heidelberg.de

Founded 1386
Academic year: October to September

Rector: Prof. Dr BERNHARD EITEL
Pro-Rectors: Prof. Dr THOMAS PFEIFFER, Prof. Dr KURT ROTH, Prof. Dr KARLHEINZ SONNTAG, Prof. Dr FRIEDERIKE NÜSSEL
Chancellor: Dr MARINA FROST
Librarian: Dr VEIT PROBST

Number of teachers: 4,259
Number of students: 28,266

Publications: *Alumni Revue* (2 a year), *Heidelberger Jahrbücher*, *Personalia* (12 a year), *Ruperto Carola* (3 a year), *Unispiegel* (5 a year)

DEANS

Faculty of Behavioural and Cultural Studies: Prof. Dr ANDREAS KRUSE
Faculty of Biology: Prof. Dr THOMAS HOLSTEIN
Faculty of Chemistry and Earth Sciences: Prof. Dr HEINZ FRIEDRICH SCHÖLER
Faculty of Clinical Medicine (Mannheim): Prof. Dr KLAUS VAN ACKERN
Faculty of Economics and Social Sciences: Prof. Dr MANFRED G. SCHMIDT
Faculty of Law: Prof. Dr CHRISTIAN BALDUS
Faculty of Mathematics and Computer Sciences: Prof. Dr RAINER WEISSAUER
Faculty of Medicine (Heidelberg): Prof. Dr CLAUS R. BARTRAM
Faculty of Modern Languages: Prof. Dr CHRISTIANE VON STUTTERHEIM
Faculty of Philosophy and History: Prof. Dr HEINZ-DIETRICH LÖWE
Faculty of Physics and Astronomy: Prof. Dr CHRISTIAN ENSS
Faculty of Theology: Prof. Dr JAN CHRISTIAN GERTZ

PROFESSORS (INSTITUTE DIRECTORS)

Faculty of Behavioural and Cultural Sciences (Voßstraße 2, Gebäude 37, I. OG, 69115 Heidelberg; tel. (6221) 542894; fax (6221)

543650; e-mail dekanat@verkult .uni-heidelberg.de):

BOENICKE, R., Education
HAGEMANN, D., Psychology
KRUSE, A., Ethnology
KRUSE, A., Gerontology
ROTH, K., Sports

Faculty of Biology (Im Neuenheimer Feld 234, 69120 Heidelberg; tel. (6221) 545648; fax (6221) 544953; e-mail dekanat-bio@urz .uni-heidelberg.de):

BADING, H., Neurobiology
HELL, R., Heidelberg Plant and Fungal Biology Graduate School
HOLSTEIN, T., Zoology
JÄSCHKE, A., Pharmacy and Molecular Biotechnology

Faculty of Chemistry and Earth Sciences (Im Neuenheimer Feld 234, 69120 Heidelberg; tel. (6221) 544844; fax (6221) 544589; e-mail dcg@urz.uni-heidelberg.de):

BUBENZER, O., Geography
CEDERBAUM, L., Physical Chemistry
HASHMI, S., Organic Chemistry
HIMMEL, H.-J., Inorganic Chemistry
SCHÖLER, F., Earth Sciences

Faculty of Clinical Medicine (Mannheim) (Theodor-Kutzer-Ufer 1-3, 68167 Mannheim; tel. (621) 3839770; fax (621) 3839769; e-mail dekan@medma.uni-heidelberg.de):

FISCHER, J., Public Health
GOERDT, S., Dermatology and Venereal Disease
GRODEN, C., Neuroradiology
HOF, H., Medicine Microbiology and Hygiene
HÖRMANN, K., Oto–Rhino–Laryngology
JONAS, J., Ophthalmology
KLÜTER, H., Transfusions Medicine and Immunology
MARX, A., Pathology
MEYER-LINDENBERG, A., Mental Health
MICHEL, M., Urology
NEUMAIER, M., Clinical Chemistry
POST, S., Surgery
SCHAD, L., Computer-assisted Clinical Medicine
SCHARF, H., Orthopaedics
SCHMIEDER, K., Neurological Surgery
SCHÖNBERG, S., Clinical Radiology
SCHROTEN, A., Paedeatrics
SÜTTERLIN, M., Women's Hospital
VAN ACKERN, K., Anaesthesiology
WEIß, C., Medical Statistics, Biomathematics and Information
WENZ, F., Experimental Radiation Oncology
WESSEL, L., Children's Surgery
WIELAND, T., Pharmacology and Toxicology

Faculty of Economics and Social Sciences (Bergheimer Str. 58, 69115 Heidelberg; tel. (6221) 543445; fax (6221) 543496; e-mail wiso-dekanat@urz.uni-heidelberg.de):

CROISSANT, A., Political Science
GOESCHL, T., Interdisciplinary Institute for Environmental Economics
IRMEN, A., Economics
SCHWINN, T., Sociology

Faculty of Law (Friedrich-Ebert-Anlage 6–10, 69117 Heidelberg; tel. (6221) 547631; fax (6221) 547654; e-mail dekanat@jurs .uni-heidelberg.de):

BALDUS, C., Historical Law
DÖLLING, D., Criminal Law
EBKE, W., German and European Company and Business Law
HESS, B., Foreign and International Private and Business Law
KIRCHHOF, P., Fiscal and Tax Law
MÜLLER-GRAFF, P., Civil, Commercial, Corporate and Commercial Law, European Law and Comparative Law

VON HOYNINGEN-HUENE, G., Civil Law, Labour Law and Insolvency

Faculty of Mathematics and Computer Sciences (Im Neuenheimer Feld 288, 69120 Heidelberg; tel. (6221) 545758; fax (6221) 548312; e-mail dekanat@mathi .uni-heidelberg.de):

DAHLHAUS, R., Applied Mathematics
GERTZ, M., Computer Sciences
WINGBERG, K., Mathematics

Faculty of Medicine (Heidelberg) (Im Neuenheimer Feld 672, 69120 Heidelberg; e-mail dekanat@med.uni-heidelberg.de):

AUFFARTH, G., Ophthalmology
BARTRAM, C., Human Genetics
BÜCHLER, M., Surgery
ECKART, W., History of Medicine
ENK, A., Dermatology
EWERBECK, V., Orthopaedics
GERNER, H., Orthopaedics
HACKE, W., Neurology
HECKER, M., Physiology and Pathophysiology
HERZOG, W., Internal Medicine
HOFFMANN, G., Paediatrics
HOHENFELLNER, M., Urology
KAUCZOR, H., Radiology
KIESER, M., Medical Biometrics and Computer Science in Medicine
KIRSCH, J., Anatomy
KRÄUSSLICH, H., Hygiene
MARTIN, E., Anaesthesiology
MATTERN, R., Forensic Medicine
MEUER, S., Immunology
MÜHLING, J., Dentistry
MUNDT, C., Psychiatry
PLINKERT, P., Oto–Rhino–Laryngology
SCHIRMACHER, P., Pathology
SOHN, C., Women's Hospital
TRIEBIG, G., Social and Industrial Medicine
UNTERBERG, A., Neurosurgery

Faculty of Modern Languages (Voßstraße 2, Gebäude 37, 69115 Heidelberg; tel. (6221) 542891; fax (6221) 543625; e-mail neuphil-fak@uni-hd.de):

WEIAND, C., Romance Philology
FRANK, A., Computer Linguistics
GLAUSER, B., English Philology
GVOZDANOVIC, J., Slavic Philology
HUBER, C., Translating and Interpreting
LICHT, T., Philology of the Middle Ages
RIECKE, J., German Philology
RIECKE, J., Language Laboratory
ROESCH, G., German as a Foreign Language Philology

Faculty of Philosophy and History (Voßstr. 2, Bldg 4370, 69115 Heidelberg; tel. (6221) 542329; fax (6221) 543635; e-mail philosophische-fakultaet@uni-hd.de):

AHN, G., Religious Studies
ENDERWITZ, S., Languages and Cultures of the Near East
HERREN-OESCH, M., History
HESSE, M., European Art History
JÖRDENS, A., Papyrology
KLOSS, G., Classical Studies
LEDDEROSE, L., East Asian Art History
LEOPOLD, S., Musicology
LÖWE, H., History of Eastern Europe
MCLAUGHLIN, P., Philosophy
MARAN, J., Prehistory and Protohistory and Middle Eastern Archaeology
MITTLER, B., Sinology
PANAGIOTOPOULOS, D., Classical Archaeology
QUACK, J., Egyptology
SCHNEIDMÜLLER, B., History of Franconia and the Palatinate
SEIFERT, W., Japanese Studies
STEPHAN-KAISSIS, C., Byzantine Archaeology and Art History
TRAMPEDACH, K., Ancient History and Epigraphics

WEINFURTER, S., History of Franconia and the Palatinate

Faculty of Physics and Astronomy (Albert-Ueberle-Str. 3–5 2OG Ost, 69120 Heidelberg; tel. (6221) 549298; fax (6221) 549347; e-mail dekanat@physik.uni-heidelberg.de):

GREBEL, E., Astronomical Computing Institute
KLESSEN, R., Theoretical Astrophysics
MEIER, K., Kirchhoff-Institute for Physics
PLATT, U., Environmental Physics
QUIRRENBACH, A., National Observatory King Chair
WAMBSGANß, J., Astronomical Computing Institute
WEIDEMÜLLER, M., Physics
WETTERICH, C., Theoretical Physics

Faculty of Theology (Hauptstr. 231, 1 OG, 69117 Heidelberg; tel. (6221) 543334; fax (6221) 543372; e-mail dekanat@theologie .uni-heidelberg.de):

EURICH, J., Study of Christian Social Service
LIENHARD, F., Practical-Theological Seminary
LÖHR, W., Scientific-Theological Seminary
NÜSSEL, F., Ecumenical Institute

ATTACHED INSTITUTES

Biochemie-Zentrum Heidelberg (Heidelberg University Biochemistry Center): Im Neuenheimer Feld 328, 69129 Heidelberg; Dir Prof. Dr M. BRUNNER.

BioQuant: Im Neuenheimer Feld 267, Raum 741, 69120 Heidelberg; Dirs Prof. Dr ROLAND EILS, Prof. Dr HANS-GEORG KRÄUSSLICH, Prof. Dr JÜRGEN WOLFRUM.

Forschungszentrum für Internationale und Interdisziplinäre Theologie (Research Center for International and Interdisciplinary Theology): Hauptstr. 240, 69117 Heidelberg; Dir Prof. MICHAEL WELKER, Prof. Dr PETER LAMPE, Prof. Dr ANDREAS KRUSE.

Heidelberg Center for American Studies (HCA): Curt und Heidemarie Engelhorn Palais, Hauptstraße 120, 69117 Heidelberg; Dir Prof. Dr DETLEF JUNKER.

Institut für Technische Informatik als zentrale Einrichtung der Universität Heidelberg: B6, 26, Bauteil B, 8131 Mannheim; Dir Prof. Dr K.-H. BRENNER.

Interdisziplinäres Zentrum für Neurowissenschaften (Interdisciplinary Centre for Neuroscience): Im Neuenheimer Feld 307, 69120 Heidelberg; Dir Prof. Dr HILMAR BADING.

Interdisziplinäres Zentrum für Wissenschaftliches Rechnen (Interdisciplinary Centre for Scientific Computing): Im Neuenheimer Feld 368, 69120 Heidelberg; Dir Prof. Dr HANS GEORG BOCK.

Südasien-Institut (South Asia Institute): Im Neuenheimer Feld 330, 69120 Heidelberg; Dir Prof. Dr MARCUS NÜSSER.

Zentrum für Astronomie (Centre for Astronomy of Heidelberg University): Mönchhofstr. 12-14, 69120 Heidelberg; Dir Prof. Dr JOACHIM WAMBSGANß.

Zentrum für Molekulare Biologie der Universität Heidelberg (Centre for Molecular Biology of Heidelberg University): Im Neuenheimer Feld 282, 69120 Heidelberg; Dir Prof. Dr BERND BUKAU.

Zentrum für Soziale Investitionen und Innovationen (Centre for Social Investment): Adenauerplatz 1, 69115 Heidelberg; Dir Prof. Dr HELMUT K. ANHEIER.

TECHNISCHE UNIVERSITÄT BERGAKADEMIE FREIBERG

Akademiestr. 6, 09599 Freiberg

Telephone: (3731) 39-0

Fax: (3731) 22195

E-mail: rektorat@zuv.tu-freiberg.de

Internet: tu-freiberg.de

Founded 1765

State control

Academic year: October to August

Rector: Prof. Dr BERND MEYER

Pro-Rectors: Prof. Dr MICHAEL SCHLÖMANN, Prof. Dr RUDOLF KAWALLA, Prof. Dr CHRISTOPH BREITKREUZ

Chancellor: Dr ANDREAS HANDSCHUH

Librarian: KARIN MITTENZWEI

Number of teachers: 383

Number of students: 4,852

Publications: *Fakultät Mathematik und Informatik Preprints, Freiberger Forschungshefte, Wissenschaftliche Mitteilungen des Instituts für Geologie*

DEANS

Faculty of Chemistry and Physics: Prof. Dr MATTHIAS OTTO

Faculty of Economics and Business Administration: Prof. Dr BRUNO SCHÖNFELDER

Faculty of Geosciences, Geotechnology and Mining: Prof. Dr ANTON SROKA

Faculty of Materials Science and Technology: Prof. Dr HORST BIERMANN

Faculty of Mathematics and Computer Science: Prof. Dr WOLFGANG MÖNCH

Faculty of Mechanical, Process and Energy Engineering: Prof. Dr GEORG HÄRTEL

Interdisciplinary Ecological Centre: Prof. Dr JÖRG MATSCHULLAT

TECHNISCHE UNIVERSITÄT BERLIN

Str. des 17 Juni 135, 10623 Berlin

Telephone: (30) 314-0

Fax: (30) 314-23222

Internet: www.tu-berlin.de

The Bauakademie (Building Academy) of Berlin (f. 1799) and the Gewerbeakademie (f. 1821) were merged in 1879 as the Technische Hochschule Berlin, which was opened under its present name in 1946

President: Prof. Dr KURT KUTZLER

Vice-Pres.: Prof. Dr KLAUS PETERMANN, Prof. Dr JÖRG STEINBACH, ULRIKE STRATE

Chancellor: Dr ULRIKE GUTHEIL

Librarian: Dr WOLFGANG ZICK

Library: see Libraries and Archives

Number of students: 31,700

Publications: *Mitteilungsblatt der TUB* (26 a year), *TU intern* (9 a year), *TU International* (4 a year), *Universitätsführer* (every two years), *Vorlesungsverzeichnis* (2 a year)

DEANS

Architecture: Prof. Dr RUDOLF SCHÄFER

Economy and Management: Prof. Dr REINHARD BUSSE

Electrotechnology and Computing: Prof. Dr THOMAS SIKORA

Humanities: Prof. Dr ADRIAN VON BUTTLAR

Mathematics and Natural Sciences: Prof. Dr CHRISTIAN THOMSEN

Process Sciences and Engineering: Prof. Dr ULF STAHL

Transport and Machine Systems: Prof. Dr VOLKER SCHINDLER

TECHNISCHE UNIVERSITÄT CAROLO WILHELMINA ZU BRAUNSCHWEIG

Pockelsstr. 14, 38106 Braunschweig

Telephone: (531) 391-0

Fax: (531) 391-4577

E-mail: president@tu-bs.de

Internet: www.tu-braunschweig.de

Founded 1745 as Collegium Carolinum; became Herzogliche Polytechnische Schule 1862 and Technische Hochschule 1877; present name 1968

State control

Academic year: October to September (two terms)

President: Prof. Dr-Ing. JÜRGEN HESSELBACH

Vice-Pres.: Prof. BERTHOLD BURKHARDT, Fr Prof. BARBARA JÜRGENS, Prof. RAINER KOLSCH

Head of Int. Office: Dr ASTRID SEBASTIAN

Librarian: Prof. Dr rer. nat. habil. DIETMAR BRANDES

Library: see Libraries and Archives

Number of teachers: 230 full-time professors

Number of students: 13,366

Publications: *Forschungsbericht* (every 5 years), *Mitteilungen der Carolo-Wilhelmina* (1 or 2 a year), *Personal- und Vorlesungsverzeichnis* (2 a year), *TU-aktuell* (6 a year), *Veröffentlichung der Technischen Universität Braunschweig* (1 a year)

DEANS

Faculty of Architecture: Prof. Dr WERNER KAAG

Faculty of Biosciences and Psychology: Prof. Dr FRANK EGGERT

Faculty of Chemistry and Pharmacy: Prof. Dr KARL-HEINZ GERICKE

Faculty of Civil Engineering: Prof. Dr-Ing. DIETER DINKLER

Faculty of Economics and Social Sciences: Prof. Dr CHRISTIAN FLOTO

Faculty of Electronics and Information Technology: Prof. Dr-Ing. WOLFGANG KOWALSKY

Faculty of Humanities and Educational Sciences: Prof. Dr HERO JANßEN

Faculty of Mathematics and Computer Science: Prof. Dr LARS WOLF

Faculty of Mechanical Engineering: Prof. Dr-Ing. ROLF RADESPIEL

Faculty of Physics and Geosciences: Prof. Dr ANDREAS HANGLEITER

TECHNISCHE UNIVERSITÄT CHEMNITZ

09107 Chemnitz

Telephone: (371) 531-0

Fax: (371) 531-1684

E-mail: pressestelle@tu-chemnitz.de

Internet: www.tu-chemnitz.de

Founded 1836 as a royal trade school of Chemnitz; became Technische Universtät Chemnitz-Zwickau 1986; present name 1997

State control

Academic year: October to September

Rector: Prof. Dr KLAUS-JÜRGEN MATTHES

Vice-Rectors: Prof. Dr WOLFRAM DÖTZEL, Prof. Dr DIETER HAPPEL, Prof. Dr CORNELIA ZANGER

Chancellor: Dr EBERHARD ALLES

Librarian: ANGELA MALZ

Number of teachers: 158

Number of students: 1,032

Publication: *Spectrum* (4 a year)

DEANS

Faculty of Computer Science: Prof. Dr WOLFRAM HARDT

Faculty of Economics and Business Administration: Prof. Dr UWE GÖTZE

Faculty of Electrical Engineering and Information Technology: Prof. Dr THOMAS GEßNER

Faculty of Engineering: Prof. Dr BERNHARD WIELAGE

Faculty of Mathematics: Prof. Dr BERND HOFFMANN

Faculty of Natural Sciences: Prof. Dr KARL HEINZ HOFFMANN

School of Philosophy: Prof. Dr BERNHARD NAUCK

TECHNISCHE UNIVERSITÄT CLAUSTHAL

Adolph-Roemer-Str. 2A, 38678 Clausthal-Zellerfeld

Telephone: (5323) 72-0

Fax: (5323) 72-3500

E-mail: info@tu-clausthal.de

Internet: www.tu-clausthal.de

Founded 1775 as Bergakademie Clausthal, attained univ. status 1968

State control

Academic year: April to March

Pres.: Prof. Dr. THOMAS HANSCHKE

Vice-Pres.: Dr INES SCHWARZ

Librarian: Dr HELMUT CYNTHA

Number of teachers: 180 , incl. 90 ordinary prof

Number of students: 3,200

Publications: *Lösestunde, Mitteilungsblatt, Vorlesungsverzeichnis* (1 a year)

DEANS

Faculty of Energy and Environment: Prof. Dr OLIVER LANGEFELD

Faculty of Mathematics/Computing and Engineering: Prof. Dr JÜRGEN DIX

Faculty of Natural and Material Sciences: Prof. Dr ALBRECHT WOLTER

TECHNISCHE UNIVERSITÄT DARMSTADT

Karolinenpl. 5, 64289 Darmstadt

Telephone: (6151) 1601

Fax: (6151) 165489

E-mail: praesident@pvw.tu-darmstadt.de

Internet: www.tu-darmstadt.de

Founded 1836 as Höhere Gewerbeschule, acquired univ. status in 1877

Pres.: Prof. Dr-Ing. JOHANN-DIETRICH WÖRNER

Vice-Pres.: Prof. Dr REINER ANDERL, Prof. Dr JOHANNES BUCHMANN

Chancellor: Dr HANNS SEIDLER

Number of teachers: 295

Number of students: 16,000

Publication: *Thema Forschung* (2 a year)

DEANS

Architecture: Dipl.-Ing. JULIAN WÉKEL

Biology: Prof. Dr rer. nat. GERHARD THIEL

Chemistry: Prof. Dr MATTHIAS REHAHN

Computer Science: Prof. Dr ALEJANDRO BUCHMANN

Construction Engineering and Geodesy: Prof. Dr PETER CORNEL

Electrical Engineering and Information Technology: Prof. Dr PETER MEIßNER

History and Social Sciences: Prof. Dr HUBERT HEINELT

Human Sciences: Prof. Dr JOSEF WIEMEYER

Law and Economic Sciences: Prof. Dr AXEL WIRTH

Material Sciences and Geoscience: Prof. Dr HEINZ VON SEGGERN

Mathematics: Prof. Dr MATTHIAS HIEBER

Mechanical Engineering: Prof. Dr rer. nat. RALF LOTH

Mechanics: Prof. Dr-Ing. RICHARD MARKERT

Physics: Prof. Dr phil. nat. THEODOR TSCHUDI

PROFESSORS

ABELE, E., Mechanical Engineering

ABROMEIT, H., History and Social Sciences
ADAMY, J. H., Electrical Engineering and Information Technology
ALBE, K., Material Sciences and Geoscience
ALBER, G., Physics
ALBER, H. D., Mathematics
ALBERT, B., Chemistry
ALEXA, M., Computing
ALFF, L., Material Sciences and Geoscience
ANDERL, R., Mechanical Engineering
ARICH-GERZ, B., History and Social Sciences
ARSLAN, U., Construction Engineering and Geodesy
BÄCHMANN, K., Chemistry
BALD, S., Construction Engineering and Geodesy
BALZER, G., Electrical Engineering and Information Technology
BARENS, I., Law and Economic Science
BAYREUTHER, F., Law and Economic Science
BECKER, M., Construction Engineering and Geodesy
BECKER, W., Mathematics
BERGER, C., Mechanical Engineering
BERGES, J., Physics
BERKING, H., History and Social Sciences
BETSCH, O., Law and Economic Science
BETTE, K. H., Human Sciences: Developmental Sciences, Psychology and Sport Science
BIBEL, W., Computing
BINDER, A., Electrical Engineering and Information Technology
BIRKHOFER, H., Mechanical Engineering
BIRKL, G., Physics
BÖHM, H. R., Construction Engineering and Geodesy
BOKOWSKI, J., Mathematics
BOLTZE, M., Construction Engineering and Geodesy
BORCHERDING, K., Human Sciences: Developmental Sciences, Psychology and Sport Science
BRAUN-MUNZINGER, P., Physics
BREUER, B. J., Mechanical Engineering
BRICKMANN, J., Chemistry
BRUDER, R., Mathematics
BRUDER, R., Mechanical Engineering
BUCHLER, J. W., Chemistry
BUCHMANN, A., Computing
BUCHMANN, J., Computing
BURMEISTER, P., Mathematics
BUSCH, M., Chemistry
BUSCHINGER, A., Biology
BUXMANN, P., Law and Economic Science
CASPARI, V., Law and Economic Science
CLAUS, P., Chemistry
CORNEL, P., Construction Engineering and Geodesy
CREUTZIG, J., Mathematics
DENCHER, N., Chemistry
DENINGER-POLZER, G., History and Social Sciences
DINSE, K. P., Chemistry
DIPPER, C., History and Social Sciences
DOMSCHKE, W., Law and Economic Science
DÖRSAM, E., Mechanical Engineering
DROSSEL, B., Physics
DÜR, M., Mathematics
ECKERT, C., Computing
ECKERT, J., Material Sciences and Geoscience
EGLOFF, G., History and Social Sciences
ELLERMEIER, W., Mathematics
ELSÄBER, W., Physics
ENCARNACAO, J., Computing
ENDERS, J., Physics
ENSINGER, W., Material Sciences and Geoscience
ENTORF, H., Law and Economic Science
EPPLE, B., Mechanical Engineering
EULER, P., Human Sciences: Developmental Sciences, Psychology and Sport Science
EVEKING, H., Electrical Engineering and Information Technology
EXNER, H. E., Material Sciences and Geoscience
FARWIG, R., Mathematics

FÄSSLER, T. F., Chemistry
FEILE, R., Physics
FERREIRO MÄHLMANN, R., Material Sciences and Geoscience
FESSNER, W.-D., Chemistry
FRIEDL, P., Chemistry
FRYDE-STROMER V. REICHENBACH, N., History and Social Sciences
FUEß, H., Material Sciences and Geoscience
FUJARA, F., Physics
FÜRNKRANZ, J., Computing
GALUSKE, R., Biology
GAMM, G., History and Social Sciences
GATERMANN, D., Architecture
GEHRING, P., History and Social Sciences
GERSHMAN, A., Electrical Engineering and Information Technology
GERSTENECKER, C., Construction Engineering and Geodesy
GIERSCH, C., Biology
GIVSAN, H., History and Social Sciences
GLESNER, M., Electrical Engineering and Information Technology
GÖPFERT, W., Construction Engineering and Geodesy
GÖRINGER, U., Biology
GÖTTSCHING, L., Mechanical Engineering
GRAUBNER, C.-A., Construction Engineering and Geodesy
GREWE, N., Physics
GRIEM, J., History and Social Sciences
GROCHE, P., Mechanical Engineering
GROSS, D., Mathematics
GROSSE-BRAUCKMANN, K., Mathematics
GRUBER, E., Chemistry
GRÜBL, P., Construction Engineering and Geodesy
GRUTTMANN, F., Construction Engineering and Geodesy
HAASE, W., Chemistry
HAGEDORN, P., Mathematics
HAHN, H., Material Sciences and Geoscience
HAMPE, M., Mechanical Engineering
HÄNSEL, F., Human Sciences: Developmental Sciences, Psychology and Sport Science
HANSELKA, H., Mechanical Engineering
HÄNSLER, E., Electrical Engineering and Information Technology
HARD, M., History and Social Sciences
HARTKOPF, T., Electrical Engineering and Information Technology
HARTMANN, E., Mathematics
HARTMANN, H., Human Sciences: Developmental Sciences, Psychology and Sport Science
HARTMANN, M. L., History and Social Sciences
HARTNAGEL, H. L., Electrical Engineering and Information Technology
HASSLER, U., Law and Economic Science
HAUSCHILD, M., Architecture
HEGGER, M., Architecture
HEIDER, J., Biology
HEIL, E., Mathematics
HEINELT, H., History and Social Sciences
HELM, C., Law and Economic Science
HERRMANN, C., Mathematics
HIEBER, M., Mathematics
HIMSTEDT, W., Biology
HINDERER, M., Material Sciences and Geoscience
HINRICHSEN, V., Electrical Engineering and Information Technology
HOFFMANN, D. H. H., Physics
HOFFMANN, H. J., Computing
HOFFMANN, R., Computing
HOFMANN, K. H., Mathematics
HOFMANN, T., Computing
HOHENBERG, G., Mechanical Engineering
HOLSTEIN, T. W., Biology
HOPPE, A., Material Sciences and Geoscience
HUSS, S., Computing
HÜTT, M.-T., Biology
IHRINGER, T., Mathematics
ISERMANN, R., Electrical Engineering and Information Technology

JAEGERMANN, W., Material Sciences and Geoscience
JAGER, J., Construction Engineering and Geodesy
JAKOBY, R., Electrical Engineering and Information Technology
JANICH, N., History and Social Sciences
JANICKA, J., Mechanical Engineering
JANNIDIS, F., History and Social Sciences
JOSWIG, M., Mathematics
KAISER, F., Physics
KAISER, W., Biology
KALDENHOFF, R., Biology
KAMMERER, P., Computing
KANGASHARJU, J., Computing
KANKELEIT, E., Physics
KAST, W., Mechanical Engineering
KATZENBACH, R. H., Construction Engineering and Geodesy
KEIMEL, K., Mathematics
KEMPE, S., Material Sciences and Geoscience
KIEHL, M., Mathematics
KINDLER, J., Mathematics
KLEEBE, H.-J., Material Sciences and Geoscience
KLEIN, A., Electrical Engineering and Information Technology
KLEIN, H.-F., Chemistry
KLINGAUF, U., Mechanical Engineering
KNODT, M., History and Social Sciences
KOCH, A., Computing
KOHLENBACH, U., Mathematics
KOLMAR, H., Chemistry
KÖNIG, H. D., Electrical Engineering and Information Technology
KONIGORSKI, U., Electrical Engineering and Information Technology
KOOB, M., Architecture
KÖRDING, A., Physics
KOSTKA, A., Electrical Engineering and Information Technology
KRAIS, B., History and Social Sciences
KRAMER, L., Mathematics
KÜBLER, J., Physics
KÜHNE, T., Computing
KÜMMERER, B., Mathematics
LANDAU, K., Mechanical Engineering
LANG, J., Mathematics
LANGANKE, K., Physics
LANGE, J., Construction Engineering and Geodesy
LANGHEINRICH, W., Electrical Engineering and Information Technology
LANGNER, G., Biology
LAYER, PAUL G., Biology
LEHN, J., Mathematics
LEICHNER, R., Human Sciences: Developmental Sciences, Psychology and Sport Science
LICHTENTHALER, F., Chemistry
LIEBENWEIN, W., Architecture
LINKE, H.-J., Construction Engineering and Geodesy
LORCH, W., Architecture
LOTH, R., Mechanical Engineering
LÖW, M., History and Social Sciences
LUSERKE, M., History and Social Sciences
LÜTTGE, U., Biology
MARKERT, R., Mathematics
MARLY, J., Law and Economic Science
MARTIN, A., Mathematics
MATHÉY, G. K., Architecture
MÄURER, H., Mathematics
MAY, A., Mathematics
MAY, H. D., Material Sciences and Geoscience
MEIßNER, P., Electrical Engineering and Information Technology
MEZINI, M., Computing
MOLEK, H., Material Sciences and Geoscience
MOTZKO, C., Construction Engineering and Geodesy
MÜHLHÄUSER, M. E., Computing
MÜLLER, R., Mathematics
MÜLLER, W. F., Material Sciences and Geoscience

MÜLLER-PLATHE, F., Chemistry
MULSER, P., Physics
MÜNK, H. D., Human Sciences: Developmental Sciences, Psychology and Sport Science
MUTSCHLER, P., Electrical Engineering and Information Technology
NEEB, K.-H., Mathematics
NESTLE, N., Physics
NEUHOLD, E., Computing
NEUNHOEFFER, H., Chemistry
NICKEL, E., Law and Economic Science
NOLTE, W., Mathematics
NORDMANN, A., History and Social Sciences
NORDMANN, R., Mechanical Engineering
OBERLACK, M., Mathematics
ORTNER, E., Law and Economic Science
ORTNER, H., Material Sciences and Geoscience
OSTERMANN, K., Computing
OSTROWSKI, M., Construction Engineering and Geodesy
OTTO, M., Mathematics
PAHL, G., Mechanical Engineering
PAULINYI, A., History and Social Sciences
PAUL-KOHLHOFF, A., Human Sciences: Developmental Sciences, Psychology and Sport Science
PAVLIDIS, D., Electrical Engineering and Information Technology
PETZINKA, K.-H., Architecture
PFEIFER, F., Biology
PFEIFER, G., Architecture
PFEIFFER, W., Electrical Engineering and Information Technology
PFLÜGER, M., Law and Economic Science
PFNÜR, A., Law and Economic Science
PFOHL, H.-C., Law and Economic Science
PINNAU, R., Mathematics
PLENIO, H. H., Chemistry
PONGRATZ, L., Human Sciences: Developmental Sciences, Psychology and Sport Science
PORTO, M., Physics
PUHANI, P., Law and Economic Science
QUICK, R., Law and Economic Science
RAUH, H., Material Sciences and Geoscience
REGGELIN, M., Chemistry
REHAHN, M., Chemistry
REIF, U., Mathematics
REISTER, D., Construction Engineering and Geodesy
RETZKO, H. G., Construction Engineering and Geodesy
RICHTER, A., Physics
RIEDEL, R., Material Sciences and Geoscience
RITTER, K., Mathematics
RÖDEL, J., Material Sciences and Geoscience
ROESNER, K., Mathematics
ROSE, H., Physics
ROTH, R., Physics
RÜPPEL, U., Construction Engineering and Geodesy
RÜRUP, H.-A., Law and Economic Science
RÜTZEL, J., Human Sciences: Developmental Sciences, Psychology and Sport Science
SASS, I., Material Sciences and Geoscience
SCHABEL, S., Mechanical Engineering
SCHÄFER, M., Mechanical Engineering
SCHÄFER, R., Chemistry
SCHÄFER, S. M., Construction Engineering and Geodesy
SCHAPPACHER, N., Mathematics
SCHEBEK, L., Construction Engineering and Geodesy
SCHEFFOLD, E., Mathematics
SCHEU, S., Biology
SCHIELE, B., Computing
SCHIFFER, H.-P., Mechanical Engineering
SCHLAAK, H., Electrical Engineering and Information Technology
SCHLEMMER, H., Construction Engineering and Geodesy
SCHMALZ-BRUNS, R., History and Social Sciences
SCHMID, V., Law and Economic Science
SCHMIDT, B., Chemistry

SCHMIDT, R., Human Sciences: Developmental Sciences, Psychology and Sport Science
SCHMIDT-CLAUSEN, H.-J., Electrical Engineering and Information Technology
SCHMIEDE, R., History and Social Sciences
SCHMITZ, B., Human Sciences: Developmental Sciences, Psychology and Sport Science
SCHNEIDER, J., Chemistry
SCHNEIDER, U. H., Law and Economic Science
SCHNEIDER, W. C., History and Social Sciences
SCHNELLENBACH-HELD, M., Construction Engineering and Geodesy
SCHOTT, D., History and Social Sciences
SCHUBERT, E., Construction Engineering and Geodesy
SCHULZ, H., Mechanical Engineering
SCHÜRMANN, H., Mechanical Engineering
SCHÜRR, A., Electrical Engineering and Information Technology
SCHUSTER, R., Chemistry
SCHÜTH, C., Material Sciences and Geoscience
SCHWABE-KRATOCHWIL, A., Biology
SCHWALKE, U., Electrical Engineering and Information Technology
SEELIG, W., Physics
SEILER, T. B., Human Sciences: Developmental Sciences, Psychology and Sport Science
SESINK, W., Human Sciences: Developmental Sciences, Psychology and Sport Science
SESSELMEIER, W., Law and Economic Science
SESSLER, G., Electrical Engineering and Information Technology
SIEKER, S., Law and Economic Science
SORGATZ, H., Human Sciences: Developmental Sciences, Psychology and Sport Science
SPECHT, G., Law and Economic Science
SPELLUCCI, P., Mathematics
STADTLER, H., Law and Economic Science
STAHL, M., History and Social Sciences
STEINMETZ, R., Electrical Engineering and Information Technology
STENZEL, J., Electrical Engineering and Information Technology
STEPHAN, P. C., Mechanical Engineering
STOFFEL, B., Mechanical Engineering
STREICHER, T., Mathematics
STÜHN, B., Physics
SURI, N., Computing
TEICH, E., History and Social Sciences
THIEL, G., Biology
TREBELS, W., Mathematics
TROPEA, C., Mechanical Engineering
TSAKMAKIS, C., Mathematics
TSCHUDI, T., Physics
ULLRICH-EBERIUS, C., Biology
URBAN, W., Construction Engineering and Geodesy
VIADA, E., Mathematics
VOGEL, H., Chemistry
VOGT, M., History and Social Sciences
VON NEUMANN-COSEL, P., Physics
VON SEGGERN, H., Material Sciences and Geoscience
VON STRYK, O., Computing
VORMWALD, M., Construction Engineering and Geodesy
VOSS, H.-G., Human Sciences: Developmental Sciences, Psychology and Sport Science
WALDSCHMIDT, H., Computing
WALTER, H., Computing
WALTHER, C., Computing
WALTHER, T., Physics
WAMBACH, J., Physics
WEGMANN, H., Mathematics
WEIHE, K., Computing
WEILAND, T., Electrical Engineering and Information Technology
WEINBRUCH, S., Material Sciences and Geoscience
WEISCHEDE, D., Architecture
WEISSMANTEL, H., Electrical Engineering and Information Technology
WÉKÉL, J., Architecture

WERTHSCHÜTZKY, R., Electrical Engineering and Information Technology
WIEMEYER, J., Human Sciences: Developmental Sciences, Psychology and Sport Science
WILHELM, M., Mechanical Engineering
WILLE, R., Mathematics
WINNER, H., Mechanical Engineering
WIPF, H., Physics
WIRTH, A. E. H., Law and Economic Science
WOLF, K.-D., History and Social Sciences
WÖLFEL, H., Mechanical Engineering
WOLLENWEBER, E., Biology
WROBEL, B., Construction Engineering and Geodesy
WURL, H.-J., Law and Economic Science
ZANKE, U., Construction Engineering and Geodesy
ZILGES, A., Physics
ZOUBIR, A. M. D. E., Electrical Engineering and Information Technology

TECHNISCHE UNIVERSITÄT DORTMUND

44221 Dortmund
Eichlinghofen, August-Schmidt-Str., 44227 Dortmund

Telephone: (231) 755-11
Fax: (231) 755-5145
Internet: www.tu-dortmund.de

Founded 1968
State control
Languages of instruction: German, English
Academic year: April to February

Rector: Prof. Dr URSULA GATHER
Vice-Rectors: Prof. Dr WALTER GRÜNZWEIG, Prof. Dr METIN TOLAN, Prof. Dr UWE SCHWIEGELSHOHN
Chancellor: Dr ROLAND KISCHKEL
Librarian: MARLENE NAGELSMEIER-LINKE

Library of 1,720,000 vols
Number of students: 21,540

Publications: *Mundo* (2 a year), *Unizet* (10 a year)

DEANS

Faculty of Architecture and Civil Engineering: Prof. Dr DIETER UNGERMANN
Faculty of Cultural Studies: Prof. Dr HORST PÖTTKER
Faculty of Economics and Social Sciences: Prof. Dr WOLFGANG SCHÜNEMANN
Faculty of Electrical Engineering and Information Technology: Prof. Dr THORSTEN BERTRAM
Faculty of Human Sciences and Theology: Prof. Dr NORBERT METTE
Faculty of Mechanical Engineering: Prof. Dr ANDREAS BRÜMMER
Faculty of Rehabilitation Sciences: Prof. Dr ELISABETH WACKER
Faculty of Spatial Planning: Prof. HANS-PETER TIETZ
Department of Arts and Sports Studies: Prof. Dr GÜNTHER RÖTTER
Department of Biochemical and Chemical Engineering: Prof. Dr GABRIELE SADOWSKI
Department of Chemistry: Prof. Dr NORBERT KRAUSE
Department of Computer Science: Prof. Dr PETER BUCHHOLZ
Department of Education and Sociology: Prof. Dr PETER VOGEL
Department of Mathematics: Prof. Dr STEFAN TUREK
Department of Physics: Prof. Dr BERNHARD SPAAN
Department of Statistics: Prof. Dr WALTER KRÄMER

PROFESSORS

Faculty of Architecture and Civil Engineering (tel. (231) 755-2074; fax (231) 755-5279; e-mail dekanat@busch.bauwesen.tu-dortmund.de; internet www.bauwesen.tu-dortmund.de):

BARTHOLD, F.-J., Numerical Methods and Information Processing
BLECKEN, U., Construction Management and Machines
BOFINGER, H., Design and Building Theory
HASSLER, U., Conservation and Building Research
HETTLER, A., Soil Mechanics and Foundation Engineering
MÄCKLER, C., Urban Design
MAURER, R., Concrete Engineering
MÜLLER, H., Environmental Architecture
NALBACH, G., Design, Spatial Design and the Fundamentals of Presentation
NEISECKE, J., Building Materials
NOEBEL, W., Design and Industrial Building
OBRECHT, H., Structural and Computational Mechanics
ÖTES, A., Structural Design
SCHIFFERS, K.-H., Organization of Building Planning and Site Management (OPS)
STANDKE, G. R., Design and Building Construction
UNGERMANN, D., Steel Construction

Faculty of Cultural Studies (tel. (231) 755-2919; fax (231) 755-2894; e-mail zimmerma@mail.fb15.tu-dortmund.de; internet www.fb15.tu-dortmund.de):

Institute of English and American Studies:
BIMBERG, C.
GRÜNZWEIG, W.
KRAMER, J.
NOLD, G.
PETERS, H.

Institute of German Language and Literature:
BRÜNNER, G.
CONRADY, P.
DENNELER, I.
GERHARD, U.
HOFFMANN, L.
KÜHN, R.
LINK, J.
PARR, R.
QUASTHOFF, U.
RIEMENSCHNEIDER, H.
RISHOLM, E.
STORRER, A.

Institute of History:
HÖMIG, H.
SOLLBACH, G.
ZETTLER, A.

Institute of Journalism:
BOHRMANN, H.
BRANAHL, U.
EURICH, C.
HEINRICH, J.
KOPPER, G.
MACHILL, M.
PÄTZOLD, U.
PÖTTKER, H.
RAGER, G.

Faculty of Economics and Social Sciences (tel. (231) 755-3182; fax (231) 755-4375; e-mail elke.klika@wiso.tu-dortmund.de; internet www.wiso.tu-dortmund.de):

HIRSCH-KREINSEN, H., Technology and Society
HOLLÄNDER, H., Macroeconomic Theory
HOLZMÜLLER, H., Marketing
JEHLE, E., Operations Management and Logistics
KRAFT, K., Economics (Economic Policy)
LACKES, R., Business Information and Management Information Systems

LEININGER, W., Microeconomic Theory
LIENING, A., Teaching of Economics
NEUENDORFF, H., Sociology
RECHT, P., Operations Research and Economic Informatics
REICHMANN, T., Management Accounting
RICHTER, W., Public Economics
SCHÜNEMANN, W., Private Law
TEICHMANN, U., Money and Credit
WAHL, J., Investments and Finance
WELGE, M., Management
WEYER, J., Sociology

Faculty of Electrical Engineering and Information Technology (tel. (231) 755-2123; fax (231) 755-2051; e-mail info@dekanat.e-technik.tu-dortmund.de; internet www.e-technik.tu-dortmund.de):

FIEDLER, H., Integrated Systems
GÖTZE, J., Information Processing
HANDSCHIN, E., Electric Power Supply
KAYS, R., Communication Technology
KULIG, S., Electric Machines, Drive and Power Electronics
NEYER, A., Microstructure Technology
PEIER, D., High Voltage Engineering
SCHEHRER, R., Electronic Systems and Switching
SCHRÖDER, H., Circuits and Systems
SCHUMACHER, K., Microelectronics
SCHWIEGELSHOHN, U., Computer Engineering
VOGES, E., High Frequency Technology

Faculty of Human Sciences and Theology (tel. (231) 755-2886; fax (231) 755-5452; e-mail leschner@fb14.tu-dortmund.de; internet www.fb14.tu-dortmund.de):

Catholic Theology:
DORMEYER, D.
METTE, N.
MÖLLE, H.
RUSTER, T

Home Economics:
EISSING, G.

Organizational Psychology:
KASTNER, M.
KLEINBECK, U.

Philosophy:
FALKENBERG, B.
POST, W.
WINGERT, L.

Politics:
MEYER, T.

Protestant Theology:
BÜTTNER, G.
GREWEL, H.
MAURER, E.
MUNZEL, F.
POLA, T.
RIESNER, R.

Psychology:
GASCH, B.
KASTNER, M.
KLEINBECK, U.
LASOGGA, F.
METZ-GÖCKEL, H.
NEUMANN, R.
ROEDER, B.
ZIMMERMANN, P.

Faculty of Mechanical Engineering (tel. (231) 755-2723; fax (231) 755-2706; e-mail dekan@mb.tu-dortmund.de; internet www.mb.tu-dortmund.de):

CLAUSEN, U., Transport Systems and Logistics
CROSTACK, H.-A., Quality Control
DEUSE, J., Work and Production Systems
HOMPELTEN, M., Transportation and Storage
JANSEN, R., Logistics
KAUDER, K., Fluid Energy Machines

KLEINER, M., Forming Technology and Lightweight Construction
KREIS, W., Machine Elements, Design and Handling Techniques
KUHN, A., Plant Organization
KÜNNE, B., Machine Elements
OTT, B., Technical Didactics
SVENDSEN, B., Mechanics
THERMANN, K., Machine Dynamics
TILLMANN, W., Materials Technology
UHLE, M., Measurement Technology
WEINERT, K., Machining Technology

Faculty of Rehabilitation Sciences (Emil-Figge-Str. 50, 44227 Dortmund; tel. (231) 755-4541; fax (231) 755-4503; e-mail dekanat.fb13@tu-dortmund.de; internet www.tu-dortmund.de/fb13):

Adapted Physical Activity and Movement Therapy:
HÖLTER, G.

Art Education and Art Therapy:
JÁDI, F.

Education for Individuals with Mental Disabilities:
DÖNHOFF, K.
HAVEMAN, M.
MEYER, H.

Gender Research in Special Needs Education:
SCHILDMANN, U.

Music Education and Music Therapy:
MERKT, I.

Rehabilitation for Individuals with Blindness and Visual Impairments:
CSOCSÁN, E.
WALTHES, R.

Rehabilitation for Individuals with Communication Disorders:
DUPUIS, G.
KATZ-BERNSTEIN, N.

Rehabilitation and Education for Individuals with Disabilities:
DEDERICH, M.

Rehabilitation for Individuals with Emotional and Behavioural Disorders:
PETERMANN, U.

Rehabilitation for Individuals with Learning Difficulties:
SCHMETZ, D.
WEMBER, F.

Rehabilitation for Individuals with Physical Disabilities:
LEYENDECKER, C.

Rehabilitation Psychology:
FRANKE, A.
FRÖSTER, H.

Rehabilitation Technology:
BÜHLER, C.

Sociology in Rehabilitation:
WACKER, E.

Vocational Education and Training:
BIERMANN, H.

Faculty of Spatial Planning (August-Schmidt-Str. 10, 44221 Dortmund; tel. (231) 755-2284; fax (231) 755-2620; e-mail dekanat.rp@tu-dortmund.de; internet www.raumplanung.tu-dortmund.de):

BADE, F.-J., Regional Economics
BAUMGART, S., Urban and Regional Planning
BECKER, R., Women's Studies and Housing in Spatial Planning
BLOTEVOGEL, H.-H., Regional and Federal Planning
DAVID, C.-H., Law and Spatial Planning
DAVY, B., Land Policy and Management

FINKE, L., Ecology and Landscape Planning

HENNINGS, G., Industrial and Commercial Development Planning

HOLZ-RAU, C., Transport Planning

KRAUSE, K.-J., Urban and Landscape Design

KREIBICH, V., Spring Centre, Urban and Regional Geography

KROES, G., Spring Centre, Urban and Regional Geography

KUNZMANN, K., Spatial Planning in Europe

REICHER, C., Urban Design and Land Use Planning

RÖDDING, W., Systems Theory and Systems Engineering

SCHMALS, K. M., Sociology and Spatial Planning

TIETZ, H.-P., Supply and Disposal Systems in Spatial Planning

VELSINGER, P., Political Economics, Regional Economics

Department of Arts and Sports Studies (tel. (231) 755-4153; fax (231) 755-4506; e-mail dek16ri@pop.tu-dortmund.de; internet www .tu-dortmund.de/fb16):

Institute of Art and Education:

BERTRAM-MÖBIUS, U.

BUSSE, K.-P.

VAN HAAREN, B.

WELZEL, B.

Institute of Geography and Education:

NUTZ, M.

SCHMIDT-KALLERT, E.

Institute of Music and Education:

ABEGG, W.

HOUBEN, E.

RÖTTER, G.

VON SCHOENEBECK, M.

STEGEMANN, M.

Institute of Sport and Education:

BRÄUTIGAM, M.

STARISCHKA, S.

THIELE, J.

Institute of Textile Design and Education/ Comparative Textile Sciences:

MENTGES, G.

Department of Biochemical and Chemical Engineering (tel. (231) 755-2362; fax (231) 755-2361; e-mail dekanat@ct.tu-dortmund .de; internet www.chemietechnik .tu-dortmund.de):

AGAR, D., Technical Chemistry

BEHR, A., Technical Chemistry

ENGELL, S., Plant Control Technology

FAHLENKAMP, H., Environmental Technology

FRIEDRICH, C., Technical Microbiology

GÓRAK, A., Fluid Separation Processes

KÖSTER, U., Materials Science

SADOWSKI, G., Thermodynamics

SCHMID, A., Chemical Biotechnology

SCHMIDT-TRAUB, H., Plant Technology

STRAUß, K., Energy Processing and Fluid Mechanics

WALZEL, P., Mechanical Process Engineering

WEIß, E., Chemical Plant Technology

WICHMANN, R., Biological Engineering

Department of Chemistry (tel. (231) 755-3720; fax (231) 755-3771; e-mail dekan-chemie@chemie.tu-dortmund.de; internet www.chemie.tu-dortmund.de):

EILBRACHT, P., Organic Chemistry

GEIGER, A., Physical Chemistry

GRAF, D., Biology

HAAG, R., Organic Chemistry

JURKSCHAT, K., Inorganic Chemistry

KELLER, H.-L., Inorganic Chemistry

KRAUSE, N., Organic Chemistry

LIPPERT, B., Inorganic Chemistry

MELLE, I., Chemistry Teaching

MINKWITZ, R., Inorganic Chemistry

MITCHELL, T. N., Organic Chemistry

NIEMEYER, C. M., Biological and Chemical Microstructure Technology

REHAGE, H., Physical Chemistry

SANDMANN, A., Biology

SCHMUTZLER, R.-W., Physical Chemistry

VERBEEK, B., Biology

WALDMANN, H., Organic Chemistry

WINTER, R., Physical Chemistry

Department of Computer Science (tel. (231) 755-2121; fax (231) 755-2130; e-mail kossmann@dekanat.cs.tu-dortmund.de; internet www.informatik.tu-dortmund.de):

BISKUP, J., Information Systems

BUCHHOLZ, P., Modelling and Simulation

DITTRICH, G., Automata and Systems Theory

DOBERKAT, E.-E., Software Technology

KERN-ISBERNER, G., Information Engineering

KRUMM, H., Computer Networks and Distributed Systems

LINDEMANN, C., Computing Systems and Performance Analysis

MARWEDEL, P., Technical Computer Science, Embedded Systems

MORIK, K., Artificial Intelligence

MÜLLER, H., Computer Graphics

MÜTZEL, P., Algorithm Engineering

PADAWITZ, P., Compiler Construction

REUSCH, B., Automata and Sequential Logic Systems Theory

SCHWEFEL, H.-P., Systems Analysis

STEFFEN, B., Programming Systems

WEDDE, H., Operating Systems/Computer Architecture

WEGENER, I., Efficient Algorithms and Complexity Theory

Department of Education and Sociology (tel. (231) 755-2194; fax (231) 755-5285; e-mail dekanat@fb12.tu-dortmund.de; internet www.fb12.tu-dortmund.de):

Institute of General and Vocational Education:

PÄTZOLD, G.

VOGEL, P.

WIGGER, L.

Institute of School Development Research:

BOS, W.

HOLTAPPELS, H.

SCHULZ-ZANDER, R.

Institute of Social and Elementary Education:

BIERFLEITER, C.

FRIED, L.

NOLDA, S.

UHLENDORFF, U.

Sociology:

BÜHRMANN, A. D.

GOLL, T.

HITZLER, R.

HORNBOSTEL, S.

KALBITZ, R.

NAEGELE, G.

REICHERT, M.

STALLBERG, E.

Institute of Teaching Science:

BEUTEL, S.-I.

KOCH-PRIEWE, B.

WIEDERHOLD, K.-A.

WILDT, J.

Department of Mathematics (tel. (231) 755-3051; fax (231) 755-3054; e-mail dekan@ mathematik.tu-dortmund.de; internet www .mathematik.tu-dortmund.de):

ACHTZIGER, W., Applied Mathematics

BECKER, E., Algebra

BLUM, H., Applied Mathematics

HAZOD, W., Analysis and Stochastics

HENN, H.-W., Mathematics Teaching

KABALLO, W., Analysis

KOCH, H., Analysis

KREUZER, M., Algebra

KUZMIN, D., Applied Mathematics and Numerics

MENKE, K., Function Theory

MÖLLER, M., Approximation Theory

MÜLLER, G., Mathematics Teaching

ROSENBERGER, G., Algebra

SCHARLAU, R., Geometry and Algebra

SCHWACHTHÖFER, L., Differential Geometry

SELTER, C., Mathematics Teaching

SIBURG, F., Function Theory

SKUTELLA, M., Discrete Optimization

STEINMETZ, N., Function Theory

STÖCKLER, J., Approximation Theory

TUREK, S., Applied Mathematics and Numerics

VOIT, M., Analysis and Stochastics

ZAMFIRESCU, T., Geometry and Algebra

Department of Physics (tel. (231) 755-3503; fax (231) 755-5027; e-mail dekanat@physik .tu-dortmund.de; internet www.physik .tu-dortmund.de):

BAACKE, J., Theoretical Physics

BAYER, M., Experimental Physics

BÖHMER, R., Experimental Physics

GERLACH, B., Theoretical Physics

GÖSSLING, C., Experimental Physics

KEITER, H., Theoretical Physics

NIEMAX, K., Plasma and Laser Spectrochemistry

PASCHOS, E., Theoretical Physics

PFLUG, A., Physics Teaching

REYA, E., Theoretical Physics

RHODE, W., Experimental Physics

SPAAN, B., Experimental Physics

SUTER, D., Experimental Physics

TOLAN, M., Experimental Physics

WEBER, W., Theoretical Physics

WEISS, T., Acceleration Physics

WESTPHAL, C., Experimental Physics

WILLE, K., Accelerator Physics

WOGGON, U., Experimental Teaching

Department of Statistics (Vogelpothsweg 87, 44227 Dortmund; tel. (231) 755-3113; fax (231) 755-3454; e-mail dekanat@statistik .tu-dortmund.de; internet www.statistik .tu-dortmund.de):

GATHER, U., Mathematical Statistics and Industrial Application

HARTUNG, J., Statistics Applied in Engineering

ICKSTADT, K., Statistics in Biosciences

KRÄMER, W., Economic and Social Statistics

KUNERT, J., Mathematical Statistics and Scientific Application

TRENKLER, G., Statistics and Econometrics

URFER, W., Statistical Methods in Genetics and Ecology

WEIHS, K., Computer-Aided Statistics

ATTACHED INSTITUTES

Fraunhofer Institut für Materialfluss und Logistik: Heads Prof. Dr UWE CLAUSEN, Prof. Dr MICHAEL TEN HOMPEL, Prof. Dr AXEL KUHN.

Fraunhofer Institut für Software- und Systemtechnik (ISST): Joseph-von-Fraunhofer-Str. 20, 44227 Dortmund; Head Prof. Dr HERBERT WEBER.

Institut für Arbeitsphysiologie: Ardeystr. 67, 44139 Dortmund; Dir Prof. Dr HERMANN M. BOLD.

Institut für Gerontologie: Head Prof. Dr GERHARD NAEGELE.

Institut für Landes- und Stadtenwicklungsforschung des Landes NW.

Institut für Roboterforschung: Head Prof. Dr UWE SCHWIEGELSHOHN.

Institut für Spektrochemie und Angewandte Spektroskopie: Heads Prof. Dr KAI NIEMAX, Prof. Dr A. MANZ.

Institut für Umweltschutz: Head Prof. Dr MICHAEL SPITELLER.

Landesinstitut Sozialforschungsstelle Dortmund.

Max-Planck-Institut für Molekulare Physiologie (MPI): Otto-Hahn-Str. 11, 44227 Dortmund; Head Prof. Dr HERBERT WALDMANN.

Technologie Zentrum Dortmund GmbH.

TECHNISCHE UNIVERSITÄT DRESDEN

Mommsenstr. 10, 01062 Dresden
Telephone: (351) 46335358
E-mail: auslandsamt@tu-dresden.de
Internet: www.tu-dresden.de
Founded 1828, University status 1961
State control
Academic year: October to September
Rector: Prof. Dr HERMANN KOKENGE
Vice-Rectors: Prof. MANFRED CURBACH, Prof. JÖRG WEBER, Prof. KARL LENZ
Chancellor: WOLF-ECKHARD WORMSER
Number of teachers: 4,200
Number of students: 35,000, not incl. Faculty of Medicine
Publication: *Wissenschaftliche Zeitschrift* (6 a year)

DEANS

Faculty of Architecture: Prof. WOLFRAM JÄGER
Faculty of Civil Engineering: Prof. Dr RAINER SCHACH
Faculty of Computer Science: Prof. Dr WOLFGANG E. NAGEL
Faculty of Economics and Business Management: Prof. Dr ALEXANDER KARMANN
Faculty of Education: Prof. Dr JOHANN GÄNGLER
Faculty of Electrical Engineering and Information Technology: Prof. Dr PETER SCHEGNER
Faculty of Forestry, Geosciences and Hydrosciences: Prof. Dr PETER WERNER
Faculty of Law: Prof. Dr HORST-PETER GÖTTING
Faculty of Literature, Linguistics and Cultural Studies: Prof. Dr BRIGITTE GEORGI-FINDLAY
Faculty of Mathematics and Natural Sciences: Prof. Dr MICHAEL RUCK
Faculty of Mechanical Engineering: Prof. Dr VOLKER ULBRICHT
'Carl Gustav Carus' Faculty of Medicine: Prof. Dr H. REICHMANN
Faculty of Philosophy: Prof. Dr CHRISTIAN SCHWARKE
'Friedrich List' Faculty of Transportation and Traffic Sciences: Prof. Dr CHRISTIAN LIPPOLD

TECHNISCHE UNIVERSITÄT HAMBURG-HARBURG

21071 Hamburg
Telephone: (40) 42878-0
Fax: (40) 42878-2040
E-mail: pressestelle@tu-harburg.de
Internet: www.tu-harburg.de
Founded 1978
Academic year: October to September
Pres.: Prof. Dr EDWIN KREUZER
Vice-Pres.: Prof. Dr ULRICH KILLAT
Chancellor: KLAUS-JOACHIM SCHEUNERT
Librarian: INKEN FELDSIEN-SUDHAUS
Library of 2,500 vols
Number of teachers: 101
Number of students: 3,800

DEANS

Chemical and Process Engineering: Prof. Dr MÄRKL
Civil Engineering: Prof. Dr WICHMANN
Electrical Engineering: Prof. Dr SINGER
General Engineering Sciences: Prof. Dr BAUHOFER
Mechanical Engineering: Prof. Dr ACKERMANN

TECHNISCHE UNIVERSITÄT ILMENAU

Postfach 100565, 98684 Ilmenau
Premises at: Max-Planck-Ring 14, 98693 Ilmenau
Telephone: (3677) 69-0
Fax: (3677) 69-1701
E-mail: webmaster@tu-ilmenau.de
Internet: www.tu-ilmenau.de
Founded 1953 as Hochschule für Elektrotechnik, present name and status 1992
State control
Academic year: October to September
Rector: Prof. Dr rer. nat. habil. PETER SCHARF
Vice-Rector for Science: Prof. Dr-Ing. KLAUS AUGSBURG
Vice-Rector for Teaching: Prof. Dr-Ing. JÜRGEN PETZOLDT
Chancellor: Dr BERNHARD HAUPT
Librarian: GERHARD VOGT
Number of teachers: 625
Number of students: 7,100
Publications: *'Information / Dokumentation'* (proceedings, every 2 years), *Tagungsberichte des Internationalen Kolloquiums* (1 a year), *Wissenschaftliches Magazin*

DEANS

Faculty of Business Economics: Prof. Dr rer. pol. habil. DIRK STELZER
Faculty of Computer Science and Automation: Prof. Dr-Ing. habil. ANDREAS MITSCHELE-THIEL
Faculty of Electrical Engineering and Information Technology: Prof. Dr-Ing. habil. HEINZ-ULRICH SEIDEL
Faculty of Mathematics and Natural Sciences: Prof. Dr rer. nat. habil. JOCHEN HARANT
Faculty of Mechanical Engineering: Prof. Dr-Ing. habil. PETER KURTZ

TECHNISCHE UNIVERSITÄT KAISERSLAUTERN

Gottlieb-Daimler-Str., 67663 Kaiserslautern
Telephone: (631) 205-0
Fax: (631) 205-3200
E-mail: auslandsamt@uni-kl.de
Internet: www.uni-kl.de
Founded 1970 as Universität Trier Kaiserslautern, separated 1975
State control
Academic year: October to September
Pres.: Prof. Dr H. J. SCHMIDT
Vice-Pres: Prof. Dr H.-D. FESER, Prof. Dr W. FREEDEN
Admin. Officer: STEFAN LORENZ
Librarian: Dipl.-Ing. ROLF WERNER WILDERMUTH
Number of teachers: 583
Number of students: 8,600

DEANS

Faculty of Architecture, Regional Planning and Civil Engineering: Prof. Dr jur. WILLY SPANNOWSKY
Faculty of Biology: Prof. Dr rer. nat. REGINE HAKENBECK
Faculty of Chemistry: Prof. Dr-Ing. STEFAN ERNST

Faculty of Computer Science: Prof. Dr MICHAEL RICHTER
Faculty of Electrical Engineering: Prof. Dr-Ing. NORBERT WEHN
Faculty of Mathematics: Prof. Dr JÜRGEN FRANKE
Faculty of Mechanical Engineering: Prof. Dr-Ing. DIETMAR EIFLER
Faculty of Physics: Prof. Dr BURKHARD HILLEBRANDS
Faculty of Social and Economic Sciences: Prof. Dr Dr JÜRGEN ENSTHALER

PROFESSORS

Faculty of Architecture, Regional Planning and Civil Engineering:
  BAYER, D., Digital and Methodical Modelling
  BECKMANN, R., Ecological Planning and Environmental Compatibility
  BÖHM, W., Theory of Buildings and Design
  CASTORPH, M., Component-orientated Planning Processes
  DENNHARDT, H., Regional Planning
  FILIBECK, R., Construction Management
  GÖPFERT, N., Statics of Rising Structures
  GOTZ, M., Urban Construction and Planning
  HEINRICH, B., Building Physics and Equipment
  HOFRICHTER, H., Architecture, History of Town Planning
  KAHLFED, P., Industrial Construction III and Design
  KLEINE-KRANEBURG, H., Industrial Construction II and Design
  KLOPF, H., Load-bearing Structure Design
  KOEHLER, G., Civil Engineering
  MECHTCHERINE, V., Construction Material Technology
  MEDINA-WARMBURG, H., Construction History
  MERX, L., Representation and Composition
  MEYERSPEER, B., Industrial Construction I and Design
  NADLER, M., Building Development
  SCHMITT, T. G., Water Management in Residential Areas
  SCHNELL, J., Concrete and Building Construction
  SEITZ, E., Room Design
  SPANNOWSKY, W., Public Law
  SPELLENBERG, A., Urban Sociology
  STEITZBACH, G., Urban Planning
  STREICH, B., Computer-assisted Design and Construction
  TOBIAS, K., Ecological Planning and Environmental Compatibility
  TOPP, H. H., Traffic Management
  TROEGER-WEIß, A., Regional Development and Planning
  TRUMPKE, K., Surveying
  VRETTOS, C., Soil Mechanics and Foundation Engineering
  WASSERMANN, K., Civil Engineering
  WITTEK, U., Civil Engineering
  WÜST, H.-S., Landscaping

Faculty of Biology:
  ANKER, T., Biotechnology
  BRÜNE, A., Cell Biology
  BÜDEL, D., Systematic Botany
  CULLUM, J. A., Genetics
  DEITMER, J. W., Zoology
  FRIAUF, A., Animal Physiology
  HAHN, A., Phytopathology
  HAKENBECK, R., Microbiology
  LAKATOS, A., Ecology
  LEITZ, A., Animal Development
  NEUHAUS, A., Physiology of Plants
  SCHMIDT, H., Physiological Ecology
  ZANKL, H., Human Biology and Genetics

Faculty of Chemistry:
  EISENBRAND, G., Food Chemistry and Toxicology

ERNST, S., Technical Chemistry
HARTMANN, M., Chemical Technology
HARTUNG, J., Organic Chemistry
HIMBERT, G., Organic Chemistry
KIETZTMANN, T., Biochemistry
KREITER, C., Inorganic Chemistry
KRÜGER, H. J., Inorganic Chemistry
KUBALL, H.-G., Physical Chemistry
KUBIK, S., Organic Chemistry
MARKO, D., Food Chemistry and Toxicology
MEMMER, R., Physical and Theoretical Chemistry
MEYER, W., Physical and Theoretical Chemistry
NIEDER-SCHATTEBURG, A., Physical and Theoretical Chemistry
REGITZ, M., Organic Chemistry
SCHERER, O. J., Inorganic Chemistry
SCHRENK, D., Food Chemistry and Toxicology
SITZMANN, H., Inorganic Chemistry
THIEL, W., Inorganic Chemistry
TROMMER, W., Organic Chemistry, Biochemistry

Faculty of Computer Science:

BERNS, K., Robotic Systems
BREUEL, T., Pattern Recognition
DENGEL, A., Knowledge-based Systems
DEBLOCK, S., Heterogenous Informations System
EBERT, A., Visualization
GOTZHEIN, R., Networked Systems
HAGEN, H., Graphic Data Processing, Computer Geometry
HÄRDNER, T., Data Management Systems
HEINRICH, S., Numeral Algorithms in Computer Science
LIGGESMEYER, P., Software Engineering Dependability
MADLENER, K., Principles of Computer Science
MAYER, O., Principles of Programming and Computer Languages
MER, P., Shared Algorithms
MÜLLER, P., Integrated Communication Systems
NEHMER, J., Software Technology
POETZSCH-HEFFTER, A., Software Technology
RAUSCH, A., Software Technology
ROMBACH, D., Software Engineering
SCHMITT, J., Shared Systems (DISCO)
SCHNEIDER, K., Reactive Systems
SCHÜRMANN, B., Modelling of Embedded Systems
UMLAUF, G., Algorithms
WIEHAGEN, R., Algorithmic Learning (Theory)

Faculty of Electrical Engineering:

BAIER, P. W., Radio Frequency Communication
BEISTER, J., Circuits
FREY, A., Agent-based Automation
HAUCK, A., Power Electronics (Teaching)
HUTH, H., Mechatronics and Electrical Drives
KOENIG, A., Integrated Sensor Systems
KUNZ, A., Electronic Design Automation
LITZ, L., Automatic Control
LIU, A., Control Systems
POTCHINKOV, M., Digital Signal Processing
TIELERT, R., Principles of Microelectronics
TUTTAS, A., Power Systems-Transmission and Power Plants (Teaching)
URBANSKY, R., Public Telecommunications Engineering
WEHN, N., Microelectronics
WEISS, P., High-voltage Engineering, Principles of Electrical Engineering
ZENGERLE, R., Theory of Electrical and Electronic Engineering, Optical Communications

Faculty of Mathematics:

BECKER, H., Mathematics

BRAKHAGE, H., Applied Mathematics
DEMPWOLFF, U., Mathematics
FRANKE, J., Stochastics
FREEDEN, W., Mathematics
GREUEL, G.-M., Topology
HAMACHER, H., Econometrics
LÜNEBURG, H., Mathematics
NEUNZERT, H., Mathematics
PFISTER, G., Computer Algebra
PRÄTZEL-WOLTERS, D., Mathematics
RADBRUCH, K., Mathematics, Teaching of Mathematics
SCHOCK, E., Applied Mathematics
SCHWEIGERT, D., Mathematics
TRAUTMANN, G., Pure Mathematics
VON WEIZÄCKER, H., Analysis

Faculty of Mechanical Engineering:

AURICH, J. C., Institute of Manufacturing Engineering and Production Management
BART, H.-J., Chemical Engineering
EIFLER, D., Materials Science
EIGNER, M., Product Development
FLIERL, R., Workgroup for Combustion Engines
HABERLAND, R., Precision Engineering
HELLMANN, D., Fluid Mechanics
MAURER, G., Thermodynamics
RENZ, R., Recyclability in Product Design and Disassembly
RIPPERGER, S., Institute for Particle Technology
SAUER, B., Machine Components
SCHINDLER, C., Institute of Design Engineering
ZÜLKE, D., Production Automation

Faculty of Physics:

AESCHLIMANN, M., Experimental Physics
BEIGANG, R., Experimental Physics
BERGMANN, K., Experimental Physics
DILL, R., Experimental Physics
EGGERT, S., Theoretical Physics
FLEISCHHAUER, M., Theoretical Physics
FOUCKHARDT, H., Experimental Physics
HILLEBRANDS, B., Experimental Physics
HOTOP, H., Experimental Physics
HÜBNER, W., Theoretical Physics
JODL, H.-G., Teaching of Physics, Experimental Physics
KORSCH, J., Theoretical Physics
KRÜGER, H., Theoretical Physics
KUPSCH, J., Theoretical Physics
OESTERSCHULZE, E., Experimental Physics
SCHMORANZER, H., Experimental and Applied Physics
SCHNEIDER, H. C., Theoretical Physics
SCHÜNEMANN, V., Experimental Physics
URBASSEK, H. M., Applied Physics
ZIEGELER, C., Technical Physics

Faculty of Social and Economic Sciences:

ARNOLD, R., Education
BLIEMEL, F., Marketing
CORSTEN, H., Production Management
DUTKE, S., Psychology
ENSTHALER, J., Civil and Economic Law
FESER, H.-D., Economics and Economic Policy I
GESMANN-NUISSL, D., Business Law
VON HAUFF, M., Economics and Economic Policy
HÖLSCHER, R., Finance and Investment
JAINTER, T., Sports
LINGNAU, H.V., Management Accounting and Management Control Systems
NEUSER, W., Philosophy
PÄTZOLD, H., Education
RITTBERGER, B., Politics
WENDT, O., Information Systems and Operations Research
WILZEWSKI, J., Politics
ZINK, K. J., Business Management

AFFILIATED INSTITUTES

Deutsches Forschungszentrum für Künstliche Intelligenz GmbH (DFKI) (Research Centre for Artificial Intelligence): Erwin-Schrödinger-Str. (Gebäude 57), Postfach 2080, 67663 Kaiserslautern; Dir (vacant).

Institut für Oberflächen- und Schichtanalytik GmbH (Institute for Surface and Coating Analysis): Erwin-Schrödinger-Str. (Gebäude 56), 67663 Kaiserslautern; Dir Prof. Dr rer. nat. HANS OECHSNER.

Institut für Verbundwerkstoffe GmbH (IVW) (Institute for Composite Materials): Erwin-Schrödinger-Str., 67663 Kaiserslautern; Dir Prof. Dr-Ing. MANFRED NEITZEL.

TECHNISCHE UNIVERSITÄT MÜNCHEN

Arcisstr. 21, 80333 Munich

Telephone: (89) 289-01
Fax: (89) 289-22000
E-mail: praesident@tu-muenchen.de
Internet: www.tu-muenchen.de

Founded 1868
State control
Academic year: October to September
Pres.: Prof. Dr Dr h.c. mult. WOLFGANG A. HERRMANN
Vice-Pres: Prof. Dr rer. nat. Dr-Ing. habil. ARNDT BODE, Dr phil. HANNEMOR KEIDEL, Prof. Dr rer. nat. ERNST RANK, Prof. Dr-Ing. habil. RUDOLF SCHILLING
Chancellor: Dr jur. LUDWIG KRONTHALER
Librarian: Dr REINER KALLENBORN

Number of teachers: 3,357
Number of students: 20,462

Publication: *Jahrbuch* (1 a year)

DEANS

Faculty of Architecture: Prof. Dr THOMAS HERZOG
Faculty of Chemistry: Prof. Dr JOHANNES A. BUCHNER
Faculty of Civil Engineering and Geodesy: Prof. Dr REINER RUMMEL
Faculty of Economics and Social Sciences: Prof. Dr Dr h.c. RALF REICHWALD
Faculty of Electrical Engineering and Information Technology: Univ.-Prof. Dr-Ing. JÖRG EBERSPÄCHER
Faculty of Informatics: Prof. Dr rer. nat. JOHANN SCHLICHTER
Faculty of Life Science: Prof. Dr BERTOLD HOCK
Faculty of Mathematics: Prof. Dr rer. nat. MARTIN BROKATE
Faculty of Mechanical Engineering: Prof. Dr HARTMUT HOFFMANN
Faculty of Medicine: Prof. Dr med. MARKUS SCHWAIGER
Faculty of Physics: Prof. Dr ALFRED LAUBEREAU
Faculty of Sports Science: Prof. Dr Dr h.c. JOSEF HACKFORTH

PROFESSORS

Faculty of Architecture (tel. (89) 289-22351; fax (89) 289-28442; e-mail marga.cervinka@lrz.tu-muenchen.de; internet www.arch.tu-muenchen.de):

BARTHEL, R., Structural Engineering
BOCK, T., Building Implementation and Information Technology
COTELO LÓPEZ, V., Design and the Conservation of Historical Buildings
DEUBZER, H., Design, Spatial Art and Lighting Design
EBNER, P., Housing and Housing Economics
EMMERLING, E., Restoration, Art Technology and Conservation

FINK, D., Integrated Construction

HAUSLADEN, G., Indoor Climate and Mechanical Services

HERZOG, T., Building Technology

HORDEN, R., Architecture and Product Development

HUGUES, T., Building Construction and Materials

HUSE, N., History of Art

KIESSLER, U., Integrated Buildings

KOENIGS, W., History of Building and Building Research

KRAU, I., Town Planning and Urban Development

LATZ, P., Landscape Architecture and Planning

MUSSO, F., Design, Building Construction and Materials Science

OSTERTAG, D., House Technology

REICHENBACH-KLINKE, M., Planning and Construction in Rural Areas

STRACKE, F., Urban Development and Regional Planning

THIERSTEIN, A., Territorial and Spatial Development

WIENANDS, R., Principles of Design and Representation

WITTENBORN, R., Visual Design

WOLFRUM, S., Urban and Regional Planning

ZBINDEN, U., Building Construction and Design Methodology

Faculty of Chemistry (Lichtenbergstr. 4, 85748 Garching; tel. (89) 289-3001; fax (89) 289-4386; e-mail dekanat@ch.tum.de; internet www.chemie.tu-muenchen.de):

BACH, T., Organic Chemistry I

BACHER, A., Organic Chemistry and Biochemistry

BONDYBEY, V. E., Physical Chemistry

BUCHNER, J., Biotechnology

DOMCKE, W., Theoretical Chemistry

FÄSSLER, T., Inorganic Chemistry

HEIZ, U., Physical Chemistry I

HERRMANN, W., Inorganic Chemistry

HINRICHSEN, O., Chemical Technology I

KESSLER, H., Organic Chemistry II

KETTRUP, A., Ecological Chemistry and Environmental Analytics

LANGOSCH, D., Bipolymer Chemistry

LERCHER, J., Chemical Technology II

LIMBERG, C., Inorganic Chemistry

NEUMEIER, D., Clinical Chemistry and Pathobiochemistry

NIEßNER, R., Hydrogeology, Hydrochemistry and Environmental Analytical Chemistry

NITSCH, W., Chemical Engineering

NUYKEN, O., Macromolecular Substances

PLANK, J., Construction Chemistry

SCHIEBERLE, P., Food Chemistry

SCHIEMANN, O., Physical Chemistry II

SCHMIDBAUR, H., Inorganic and Analytical Chemistry

SKERRA, A., Biological Chemistry

TÜRLER, A., Radiochemistry

VEPREK, S., Chemistry of Inorganic Materials

Faculty of Civil Engineering and Geodesy (tel. (89) 289-22400; fax (89) 289-23841; e-mail dekanat@bv.tum.de; internet www.bv.tum.de):

ALBRECHT, G., Steel-girder Construction

BLETZINGER, K., Structural Analysis

BÖSCH, H.-J., Tunnel Construction, Building Management

BUSCH, F., Traffic Engineering and Control

EBNER, H., Photogrammetry

FAULSTICH, M., Water Quality Control and Waste Management

GRUNDMANN, H., Building Mechanics

HAUSER, G., Building Physics

KIRCHHOFF, P., Transport and Town Planning

LEYKAUF, G., Road, Railway and Airfield Construction

MAGEL, H., Ground Preparation and Land Development

MENG, L., Cartography

MÜLLER, G., Building Mechanics

RANK, E., Building Informatics

RUMMEL, R., Astronomical and Physical Geodesy

SCHIESS, R., Building Materials and Materials Testing

SCHIESSL, P., Building Materials and Materials Testing

SCHIKORA, K., Analysis of Civil Engineering Structures

SCHUNCK, E., Building Construction

SPAUN, G., Geology

STROBL, TH., Hydraulic and Water Resources Engineering

THURO, K., Geology

VALENTIN, F., Hydraulics and Hydrography

VOGT, N., Foundations, Soil Mechanics and Rock Mechanics

WILDERER, P., Water Quality and Waste Management

WINTER, S., Building Construction

WUNDERLICH, T., Geodesy

ZILCH, K., Concrete Structures

ZIMMERMANN, J., Building Process Management

Faculty of Economics and Social Sciences (tel. (89) 289-25066; fax (89) 289-25070; e-mail dekanat@wi.tum.de; internet www.wi.tu-muenchen.de):

ACHLEITNER, A., KfW Entrepreneurial Finance

ANN, C., Corporate Law and Intellectual Property

BÄUMLER, G., Physical Education (Psychology)

BELZ, F., Brewing and Food Industry

BLÜMELHUBER, C., Marketing and Distribution

BÜSSING, A., Psychology

ENNEKING, U., Agribusiness and Food Industry

GRANDE, E., Political Science

GROSSER, M., Science of Movement and Training

HACKER, W., Psychology

HEINRITZ, G., Geography

HEISSENHUBER, A., Agricultural Economics and Farm Management

HENKEL, J., Technology and Innovation Management

HOFMANN, W., Political Science

HOLZHEU, F., Economics

KARG, G., Consumer Economics

KASERER, C., Financial Management and Capital Markets

KOLISCH, R., Technical Services and Operational Management

LEIST, K.-H., Physical Education Teaching

LÜCK, W., Business Management, Accounting, Auditing and Consulting

MOOG, M., Forest Management

REICHWALD, R., Information, Organization and Management

SALHOFER, K., Environmental Economics and Agricultural Policy

SCHELTEN, A., Pedagogics

STEINMÜLLER, H., Social Policy and Insurance

SUDA, M., Forest Policy and Forest History

TRINCZEK, R., Sociology

WEINDLMAIER, J., Dairy and Food Industry Management

VON WEIZSÄCKER, R. FRHR., Economics

WENGENROTH, U., History of Engineering

WILDEMANN, H., Management, Logistics and Production

WITT, D., Service Management

ZACHMANN, K., History of Technology

Faculty of Electrical Engineering and Information Technology (tel. (89) 289-28378; fax (89) 289-22559; e-mail dekanat@ei.tum.de; internet www.e-technik.tu-muenchen.de):

AMANN, M., Semiconductor Technology

ANTREICH, K., Computer-aided Design

BIRKHOFER, A., Reactor Dynamics and Reactor Safety

BOECK, W., High Voltage Engineering and Power Plants

BUSS, M., Automatic Control Engineering

DIEPOLD, K., Data Processing

EBERSPÄCHER, J., Communication Networks

FÄRBER, G., Real-time Computer Systems

GÜNTHER, C., Communication and Navigation

HAGENAUER, J., Communications Engineering

HEKERSDORF, A., Integrated Systems

KINDERSBERGER, J., High Voltage Engineering and Electric Power Transmission

KOCH, A., Measurement Systems and Sensor Technology

LANG, M., Man–Machine Communication

LUGLI, P., Nanoelectronics

NOSSEK, J., Circuit Theory and Signal Processing

RIGOLL, G., Man–Machine Communication

RUGE, I., Integrated Circuits

RUSSER, P., High Frequency Engineering

SCHLICHTMANN, U., Electronic Design Automation

SCHMIDT, G., Control Engineering

SCHMITT-LANDSIEDEL, D., Technical Electronics

SCHRÖDER, D., Electrical Drives

SWOBODA, J., Data Processing

WACHUTKA, G., Physics of Electrotechnology

WAGNER, U., Energy Economy and Application Technology

WOLF, B., Medical Electronics

Faculty of Informatics (Boltzmannstr. 3, 85748 Garching; tel. (89) 289-17590; fax (89) 289-17591; e-mail gemkow@in.tum.de; internet www.informatik.tu-muenchen.de):

BAYER, R., Computer Science

BICHLER, M., Internet-based Information Systems

BODE, A., Computer Organization, Parallel Computer Architecture

BRAUER, W., Theoretical Computer Science and Foundations of Artificial Intelligence

BROY, M., Software and Systems Engineering

BRÜGGE, B., Applied Software Engineering

BUNGARTZ, H.-J., Computer Science in Engineering, Numerical Programming

EICKEL, J., Computer Science

FELDMANN, A., Network Architecture

GRUST, T., Database Systems

HEGERING, H.-G., Technical Informatics—Computer Networks

HUBWIESER, P., Didactics of Informatics

JESSEN, E., Computer Science

KNOLL, A., Robotics and Embedded Systems

KRAMER, S., Bioinformatics

KRCMAR, H., Information Systems

MATTHES, F., Software Engineering for Business Applications

MAYR, E. W., Efficient Algorithms

NAVAB, N., Computer-aided Medical Procedures

RADIG, B., Image Understanding and Knowledge-based Systems

SCHLICHTER, J., Applied Informatics/Collaborative Systems

SEIDL, H., Formal Languages, Compiler Construction, Software Construction

SPIES, P., System Architecture

WESTERMANN, R., Computer Graphics and Visualization

ZENGER, C., Computer Science

Faculty of Life Science (Alte Akademie 8, 85354 Freising; tel. (8161) 71-3258; fax (8161) 71-3900; e-mail dekanat@wzw.tum .de; internet www.wzw.tu-muenchen.de):

AUERNHAMMER, H., Agricultural Engineering

BACK, W., Brewing Technology I

BAUER, J., Animal Hygiene

DANIEL, H., Physiology of Nutrition

DELGADO, A., Fluid Mechanics and Process Automation

ENGEL, K.-H., Food and Nutrition

FAULSTICH, M., Technology of Biogenic Products

FORKMANN, G., Floriculture

FRIEDRICH, J., Physics

FRIES, H.-R., Animal Breeding

GIERL, A., Genetics

GRILL, E., Botany

HABE, W., Landscape Ecology

HAUNER, H., Nutritional Medicine

HOCK, B., Cell Biology

HRABÉ DE ANGELIS, M., Experimental Genetics

KETTRUP, A., Ecological Chemistry and Environmental Analytics

KÖGEL-KNABNER, I., Soil Science

KULOZIK, U., Food Process Engineering

LANGOSCH, D., Biopolymer Chemistry

LANGOWSKI, H.-C., Brewery Installations and Food Packaging Technology

LATZ, P., Landscape Architecture and Planning

MANLEY, G. A., Zoology

MATYSSEK, R., Ecophysiology of Plants

MENZEL, A., Ecoclimatology

MEWES, H.-W., Genome-orientated Bioinformatics

MEYER, H., Physiology

MEYER-PITTROFF, R., Energy and Environmental Technologies of the Food Industry

MOOG, M., Forestry

MOSANDL, R., Silviculture and Forest Planning

PARLAR, H., Chemical-Technical Analysis and Chemical Food Technology

PFADENHAUER, J., Vegetation Ecology

PRETZSCH, H., Forest Yield Science

QUEDNAU, H.-D., Work Science and Applied Computer Science

RECHKEMMER, G., Biofunctionality of Food

ROTHENBURGER, W., Horticultural Economics

SCHEMANN, M., Human Biology

SCHLEIFER, K.-H., Microbiology

SCHMIDHALTER, U., Plant Nutrition

SCHNITZLER, W. H., Vegetable Science

SCHNYDER, H., Grassland

SCHÖN, J., Land Engineering

SCHOPF, R., Animal Ecology

SKERRA, A., Biological Chemistry

SOMMER, K., Machinery and Apparatus

SUDA, M., Politics and History of Forestry

VALENTIEN, C., Landscape Architecture and Design

VOGEL, R., Industrial Microbiology

WARKOTSCH, W., Forest Industry and Applied Computer Science

WEGENER, G., Wood Science and Wood Engineering

WEISSER, H., Brewery Construction and Food Packaging Technology

WENZEL, G., Plant Cultivation

WOLF, P. F. J., Phytopathology

WOLFRAM, G., Human Nutrition

WURST, W., Developmental Genetics

ZANDER, J., Land Use Planning and Nature Conservation

Faculty of Mathematics (Boltzmannstr. 3, 85747 Garching; tel. (89) 289-16806; fax (89) 289-17584; e-mail dekanat@ma.tum.de; internet www.ma.tum.de):

BORNEMANN, F., Scientific Computing

BROKATE, M., Mathematical Modelling

BULIRSCH, R., Numerical Analysis

FRIESEKE, G., Global Analysis

GRITZMANN, P., Combinatorial Geometry

HOFFMAN, K.-H., Mathematical Modelling

KEMPER, G., Algorithmic Algebra

KLÜPPELBERG, C., Statistics

LASSER, R., Biomathematics

LOSS, M., Global Analysis

RENTROP, P., Numerical Analysis

RICHTER-GEBERT, J., Geometry and Visualization

RITTER, K., Optimization

SCHEURLE, J., Dynamic Systems

SPOHN, H., Mathematical Physics

ZAGST, R., Mathematical Finance

Faculty of Mechanical Engineering (Boltzmannstr. 15, 85748 Garching; tel. (89) 289-5020; fax (89) 289-5024; e-mail wagner@mw .tum.de; internet www.mw.tu-muenchen.de):

ADAMS, N., Aerodynamics

BAIER, H., Lightweight Structures

BENDER, K., Information Technology

BUBB, H., Ergonomics and Human Factors

GREGORY, J. K., Materials

GÜNTHER, A., Material Flow and Logistics

GÜNTHNER, W., Production Technology

HEIN, D., Thermal Power Plants

HEINZL, J., Precision Mechanics and Microengineering

HEISSING, B., Automotive Engineering

HOFFMANN, H., Metal Forming and Casting

HÖHN, R., Machine Elements

KAU, H. P., Flight Propulsion

LASCHKA, B., Fluid Mechanics

LINDEMANN, U., Product Development

LOHMANN, B., Automatic Control

PEUKERT, W., Chemical Process Engineering

PEUKERT, W., Solid Fuel Process Engineering

REINHART, G., Assembly Systems and Factories

RENIUS, K. T., Agricultural Machinery

SACHS, G., Flight Mechanics and Control

SATTELMAYER, T., Thermodynamics

SCHILLING, R., Fluid Mechanics

SCHMITT, D., Aeronautical Engineering

STICHLMAIR, J., Process Engineering

STROHMEIER, K., Apparatus and Plant Construction

ULBRICH, H., Applied Mechanics

WACHTMEISTER, G., Internal Combustion Engines

WALL, W., Computational Mechanics

WALTER, U., Astronautics

WERNER, E., Materials Science and Mechanics

WEUSTER-BOTZ, D., Biochemical Engineering

WINTERMANTEL, E., Medical Engineering

ZÄH, M., Machine Tools and Industrial Management

Faculty of Medicine (Ismaninger Str. 48, 81675 Munich; tel. (89) 4140-2121; fax (89) 4140-4870; e-mail huebener@nt1.chir.med .tu-muenchen.de; internet www.med .tu-muenchen.de):

ARNOLD, W., Otorhinolaryngology

BURDACH, S., Paediatrics

CLASSEN, M., Internal Medicine

CONRAD, B., Neurology

EISENMENGER, W., Forensic Medicine

EMMRICH, P., Paediatrics

ERFLE, V., Virology

FÖRSTL, H., Psychiatry and Psychotherapy

GÄNSBACHER, B., Experimental Oncology and Therapy Research

GÖTTLICHER, M., Clinic for Industrial and Environmental Medicine

GRADINGER, R., Orthopaedics and Sport Orthopaedics

GREIM, H., Toxicology and Environmental Hygiene

HALLE, M., Preventive and Rehabilitative Sports Medicine

HARTUNG, R., Urology

HAUNER, H., Nutritional Medicine

HESS, J., Paediatric Cardiology

HÖFLER, H., General Pathology and Pathological Anatomy

HOFMANN, F., Molecular Medicine

HOFMANN, F., Pharmacology and Toxicology

HORCH, H.-H., Dentistry

JESCHKE, D., Preventive and Rehabilitative Sports Medicine

KIECHLE, M., Gynaecology

KOCHS, E. F., Anaesthesiology

KUHN, K. A., Medical Statistics and Epidemiology

LANGE, R., Cardiac Surgery

LANZL, I. M., Ophthalmology

MEITINGER, T., Genetics

MERTZ, M., Ophthalmology

MOLLS, M., Radiotherapy and Radiological Oncology

NEISS, A., Medical Statistics and Epidemiology

NEUMEIER, D., Clinical Chemistry and Pathobiochemistry

NOWAK, D., Clinic for Industrial and Environmental Medicine

PESCHEL, C., Internal Medicine III

RING, J., Dermatology and Allergology

RUMMENY, E. J., X-Ray Diagnostics

SCHMID, R., Internal Medicine II

SCHÖMIG, A.-W., Internal Medicine I

SCHWAIGER, M., Nuclear Medicine

SIEWERT, J.-R., Surgery

SPEICHER, M., Genetics

TRAPPE, A. E., Neurosurgery

VON RAD, M., Clinical Psychology and Psychotherapy

WAGNER, H., Clinical Microbiology, Immunology and Hygiene

WILMANNS, J. C., Medical History and Ethics

Faculty of Physics (James Franck Str., 85748 Garching; tel. (89) 289-12492; fax (89) 289-14474; e-mail dekanat@physik.tu-muenchen .de; internet www.physik.tu-muenchen.de):

ABSTREITER, G., Experimental Semiconductor Physics I

BÖNI, P., Experimental Physics

BURAS, A. J., Theoretical Physics IV

DIETRICH, K., Theoretical Physics I

VON FEILITZSCH, F., Experimental Physics and Astro-Particle Physics

FEULNER, P., Physics

FISCHER, S., Theoretical Physics II

FRIEDRICH, H., Theoretical Physics

FRIEDRICH, J., Physics

GROSS, R., Technical Physics

GROß, A., Theoretical Physics

VAN HEMMEN, J. L., Theoretical Physics

KINDER, H., Experimental Physics

KLEBER, M., Theoretical Physics

KOCH, F., Physics

KRÜCKEN, R., Physics

LAUBEREAU, A., Experimental Physics

LINDNER, M., Theoretical Particle and Astro-Particle Physics

NETZ, R., Theoretical Physics II

PARAK, F. G., Physics and Biophysics

PAUL, S., Physics I

PETRY, W., Experimental Physics

RIEF, M., Physics

RING, P., Theoretical Physics

STIMMING, U., Physics

STUTZMANN, M., Experimental Semiconductor Physics II

VOGL, P., Theoretical Physics III

WEISE, W., Theoretical Physics

ZWERGER, W., Theoretical Physics V

Faculty of Sports Science (Connollystr. 32, 80809 Munich; tel. (89) 289-24601; fax (89) 289-24636; e-mail dekanat.sport@sp.tum.de; internet www.sport.tu-muenchen.de):

HACKFORTH, J., Sport, Media and Communication
KELLER, J. A., Sport Psychology
LEIST, K.-H., Sport Pedagogy
MICHNA, H., Sport and Health Promotion
TUSKER, F., Human Movement Science and Training

TIERÄRZTLICHE HOCHSCHULE HANNOVER
(Hanover School of Veterinary Medicine)

Postfach 711180, 30545 Hanover
Bünteweg 2, 30559 Hanover
Telephone: (511) 953-6
Fax: (511) 953-8050
E-mail: presse@tiho-hannover.de
Internet: www.tiho-hannover.de

Founded 1778 as Königliche Rossarzneischule, attained university status 1887
State control
Academic year: October to September

Pres.: Dr GERHARD GREIF
Vice-Pres.: Dr BURKHARD MEINECKE, Dr ANDREA TIPOLD
Number of teachers: 122
Number of students: 2,160

Publications: TiHo-Anzeiger (8 a year), TiHo Forschung fürs Leben (1 a year)

HEADS

Centre for Food Toxicology: Prof. Dr HEINZ NAU
Clinic for Cattle: Prof. Dr HEINRICH BOLLWEIN
Clinic for Horses: Prof. Dr KARSTEN FEIGE
Clinic for Pigs, Small Ruminants, Forensic Medicine and Ambulatory Service: Prof. Dr K.-H. WALDMANN
Clinic for Poultry: Prof. Dr U. NEUMANN
Clinic for Small Domestic Animals: Prof. Dr INGO NOLTE
Department of Analytical Chemistry and Endocrinology: Prof. Dr H.-O. HOPPEN
Department of Biometry, Epidemiology and Data Processing: Prof. Dr L. KREIENBROCK
Department of Fish Pathology and Fish Farming: Prof. Dr WOLFGANG KÖRTING
Department of General Radiology and Medical Physics: Prof. Dr HERMANN SEIFERT
Department of History of Veterinary Medicine and Domestic Animals: Prof. Dr JOHANN SCHÄFFER
Department of Immunology: Prof. Dr WOLFGANG LEIBOLD
Institute of Anatomy: Prof. Dr H. WAIBL
Institute for Animal Behaviour and Protection: Prof. Dr HANSJOACHIM HACKBARTH
Institute of Animal Breeding and Genetics: Prof. Dr OTTMAR DISTL
Institute for Animal Ecology and Cell Biology: Prof. Dr BERND SCHIERWATER
Institute for Animal Hygiene and Protection: Prof. Dr JÖRG HARTUNG
Institute for Animal Nutrition: Prof. Dr J. KAMPHUES
Institute of Epidemics: Prof. Dr THOMAS BLAHA
Institute for Food Quality and Safety: Prof. Dr G. KLEIN
Institute for Microbiology: Prof. Dr JOERCH MERKEL
Institute for Parasitology: Prof. Dr THOMAS SCHNEIDER
Institute for Pathology: Prof. Dr WOLFGANG BAUMGÄRTNER
Institute for Physiology: Prof. Dr GERHARD BREVES
Institute for Physiological Chemistry: Prof. Dr HASSAN Y. NAIM
Institute for Reproductive Medicine: Prof. Dr EDDA TÖPFER-PETERSEN
Institute for Virology: Prof. Dr VOLKER MOENNIG

Institute for Wildlife Research: Prof. Dr KLAUS POHLMEYER
Institute for Zoology: Prof. Dr ELKE ZIMMERMANN

UKRAINISCHE FREIE UNIVERSITÄT

Pienzenauerstr. 15, 81679 Munich
Telephone: (89) 99-738830
Fax: (89) 99-99148914
E-mail: ufu@extern.lrz-muenchen.de
Internet: www .ukrainische-freie-universitaet.mhn.de

Founded 1921
Private, State-approved
Languages of instruction: Ukrainian, English, German
Academic year: October to August (incl. Summer Courses July–August)

Rector: Prof. Dr ALBERT KIPA
Chancellor/Registrar: Prof. Dr NICOLAS SZAFOWAL
Librarian: IVANNA REBET
Number of teachers: 56
Number of students: 110

Publications: Naukovi Zapysky UVU (1 a year), Naukovi Zbirnyky UVU, Specimina dialectorum ucrainorum, Studien zu deutsch–ukrainischen Beziehungen

DEANS

Faculty of Govt and Political Economics: Prof. Dr IVAN MYHUL
Faculty of Philosophy: Prof. Dr FRANK SYSYN
Faculty of Ukrainian Studies: Prof. Dr ANATOLIJ POHRIBNYJ
Pedagogical Institute: (vacant)
Research Institute for German-Ukrainian Relations: Prof. HANSJURGEN DOSS

PROFESSORS

Faculty of Govt and Political Econ. (tel. (89) 99-73-88-42):
  FUTEY, B., Law
  ISAJIW, V., Sociology
  KOSTYCKY, M., Law
  MYHUL, I., Political Economics
  NAGY, L., Geography
  PYNZENYK, V., Political Economics
  SUBTELNY, O., History of Political Ideas
  SZAFOWAL, N., Political Science
Faculty of Philosophy (Humanities):
  ANDRIEWSKY, O., History
  DACKO, I., Theology
  GUDZIAK, B., Church History
  JERABEK, B., Education
  KIPA, A., Comparative Literature
  KOSYK, W., History
  KYSILEWSKA-TKACH, A., Education
  LABUNKA, M., Ukrainian History
  MAKSYMTSCHUK, W., Comparative Literature
  PIETSCH, R., Philosophy
  RUDNYTZKY, L., Comparative Literature
  STEPOWYK, D., Cultural History
  SYSYN, F., History
  ZLEPKO, D., History of Eastern Europe
  ZUK, L., Ukrainian Music
  ŽUK, R., History of Architecture
Faculty of Ukrainian Studies:
  AVVAKUMOV., G., Church Slavonic
  KOPTILOV, V., Ukrainian Language and Literature
  KOZAK, S., Slavonic Literature
  MELNYK, Y., Ukrainian Literature
  MUSHINKA, M., Ukrainian Ethnology
  POHRIBNYJ, A., Ukrainian Language and Literature
  PRYSJAZNIJ, M., Journalism
  SALYHA, T., History of Ukrainian Literature

UNIVERSITÄT-GESAMTHOCHSCHULE-ESSEN

45117 Essen
Telephone: (201) 183-1
Fax: (201) 183-2151
E-mail: universitaet@uni-essen.de
Internet: www.uni-essen.de

Founded 1972
State control
Academic year: October to September

Rector: Prof. Dr URSULA BOOS-NÜNNING
Chancellor: Dr ELMAR LENGERS
Pro-Rector for Development Planning: Prof. Dr KLAUS ECHTLE
Pro-Rector for Information, Communication and Media: Prof. Dr ULRICH SCHREIBER
Pro-Rector for Finance: Prof. Dr STEPHAN ZELEWSKI
Pro-Rector for Quality Management of Research, Teaching and Organization: Prof. Dr KARL-HEINZ JÖCKEL
Librarian: ALBERT BILO
Number of teachers: 1,050
Number of students: 22,000

Publication: Essener Unikate (2 a year)

DEPARTMENTS AND DEANS

Philosophy, History, Religion and Social Studies: Prof. Dr ULRICH BUSSE
Education, Psychology, Sport and Kinesiology: Prof. Dr WOLFGANG STARK
Literature and Linguistics: Prof. Dr RÜDIGER BRANDT
Design and Art Education: Prof. Dr RALPH BRUDER
Economic Sciences: Prof. Dr LUDWIG MOCHTY
Mathematics and Computer Science: Prof. Dr DIETER LUTZ
Physics: Prof. Dr DIETRICH VON DER LINDE
Chemistry: Prof. Dr ECKART HASSELBRINK
Bioscience and Geosciences: Prof. Dr REINHARD HENSEL
Civil Engineering: Prof. Dr-techn. RENATUS WIDMANN
Surveying: Prof. Dr-Ing. HEINZ-JÜRGEN PRZYBILLA
Mechanical Engineering: Prof. Dr-Ing. PAUL WINSKE
Medicine: Prof. Dr HANS GROSSE-WILDE

UNIVERSITÄT AUGSBURG

Universitätsstr. 2, 86159 Augsburg
Telephone: (821) 598-0
Fax: (821) 5985505
Internet: www.uni-augsburg.de

Founded 1970
State control
Language of instruction: German
Academic year: October to July

Rector: Prof. Dr WILFRIED BOTTKE
Vice-Rectors: Prof. Dr BERNHARD FLEISCHMANN, Prof. Dr ALOIS LOIDL, Prof. Dr THOMAS SCHEERER
Chancellor: ALOIS ZIMMERMAN
Registrar: HERMANN GOHL
Dir for Int. Relations: Dr SABINE TAMM
Librarian: Dr ULRICH HOHOFF
Library: see Libraries and Archives
Number of teachers: 458
Number of students: 12,386

Publication: Mitteilungen Institut fur Europaeische Kulturgeschichte

DEANS

Faculty of Applied Computing: Prof. Dr WOLFGANG REIF
Faculty of Catholic Theology: Prof. Dr FRANZ SEDLMEIER
Faculty of Economics: Prof. Dr KLAUS TUROWSKI
Faculty of History and Philology: Prof. Dr HUBERT ZAPF

Faculty of Law: Prof. Dr MICHAEL KORT
Faculty of Mathematics and Natural Sciences: Prof. Dr SIEGFRIED HORN
Faculty of Philosophy and Social Sciences: Prof. Dr RAINER-OLAF SCHULTZE

PROFESSORS

Faculty of Applied Computing (86135 Augsburg; tel. (821) 5982174; fax (821) 5982175; e-mail reif@informatik.uni-augsburg.de; internet www.uni-augsburg.de/fakultaeten/fai):

ANDRÉ, ELISABETH, Multimedia Concepts and Applications
BAUER, BERNHARD, Software and Programming Languages
FRIEDMANN, ARNE, Physical Geography
HAGERUP, TORBEN, Theoretical Computing
HILLENBRAND, HANS, Didactics
HILPERT, MARKUS, Human Geography
JACOBEIT, JUCUNDUS, Physical Geography
KIESSLING, WERNER, Databases and Information Systems
LIENHART, RAINER, Multimedia Computing
MÖLLER, BERNHARD, Databases and Information Systems
PEYKE, GERD, Human Geography
POSCHWATTA, WOLFGANG, Human Geography
REIF, WOLFGANG, Software and Programming Languages
SCHNEIDER, THOMAS, Didactics
THIEME, KARIN, Human Geography
UNGERER, THEO, Information and Communication Systems
VOGLER, WALTER, Software and Programming Languages
WIECZOREK, ULRICH, Didactics

Faculty of Catholic Theology (Universitätsstr. 10, 86159 Augsburg; tel. (821) 5985820; fax (821) 5985503; e-mail dekanat@kthf.uni-augsburg.de; internet www.kthf.uni-augsburg.de):

ARNTZ, KLAUS, Moral Theology
BALMER, H. P., Philosophy
GÜTHOFF, ELMAR, Church Law
HAUSMANNINGER, TH., Christian Ethics
KIENZLER, K., Basic Theology
KÜPPERS, K., Liturgy Science
RIEDL, GERDA, New Testament Exegesis
SCHEULE, RUPERT M. (acting), Christian Ethics
SEDLMEIER, F. (acting), Old Testament Exegesis
WURST, F., Church History

Faculty of Economics (Universitätsstr. 16, 86159 Augsburg; tel. (821) 5984015; fax (821) 5984212; e-mail dekanat@wiwi.uni-augsburg.de; internet www.wiwi.uni-augsburg.de):

BAMBERG, G., Statistics
BOEHLE, F., Socio-economics
BUHL, H. U., Business Administration
COENENBERG, A., Business Administration
FLEISCHMANN, B., Business Administration
GIEGLER, H., Sociology
GIERL, H., Business Administration
HANUSCH, H., Economics
HEINHOLD, M., Business Administration
KIFMANN, M., Sociology
KLEIN, R., Sociology
LAU, C., Sociology
LEHMANN, E., Business Management
MAUSSNER, A., Economics
MEIER, M., Economics
MICHAELIS, D., Economics
NEUBERGER, O., Psychology
PFAFF, A., Economics
SCHITTKO, U., Econometrics
STEINER, M., Business Administration
STENGEL, M., Psychology
TUMA, A., Business Administration
TUROWSKI, K., Business Informatics and Systems Engineering
WELZEL, P., Economics

Faculty of History and Philology (Universitätsstr. 10, 86159 Augsburg; tel. (821) 5982764; fax (821) 5985501; e-mail dekan.phil2@phil.uni-augsburg.de; internet www.philhist.uni-augsburg.de):

BICKENDORF, G., Art History
BUBLITZ, W., English Linguistics
BURKHARDT, J., History of Early Modern Times
DOERING-MANTEUFFEL, S., Folklore
ELSPASS, S., German Language
FÄCKE, C., French Didactics
GEPPERT, H. V., German and Comparative Literature
GÖTZ, D., Applied Linguistics
HERINGER, H.-J., German as a Foreign Language, German Philology
JACOB, J., Modern German
KAUFHOLD, M., Medieval History
KIESSLING, R., Bavarian and Swabian History
KOCKEL, V., Classical Archaeology
KRAUSS, H., Romance Literature
LAUSBERG, M., Classical Philology
LÖSER, F., German Language and Medieval History
MAYER, M., English Literature
MIDDEKE, M., English Literature
SCHEERER, T. M., Hispanic Studies
SCHRÖDER, K., Didactics of English
SCHWARZE, S., Romance Languages
TSCHOPP, S. S., History of European Culture
WEBER, G., Ancient History
WERNER, R., Applied Linguistics
WILLIAMS, W., German Language and Medieval Literature
WIRSCHING, A., Modern and Contemporary History
ZAPF, H., American Studies

Faculty of Law (Universitätsstr. 24, 86159 Augsburg; tel. (821) 598-4500; fax (821) 598-4503; e-mail dekan@jura.uni-augsburg.de; internet www.jura.uni-augsburg.de):

ALBERS, M., Civil Law
APPEL, I. (acting), Constitutional Law
BECKER, C., Civil Law, History of European Law
BEHR, V., Civil Law
BOTTKE, W., Penal Law
BUCHNER, H., Civil Law
GASSNER, U. M., Public Law
GSELL, B., Civil Law
JAKOB, W., Public Law
KORT, M., Civil Law
LEISTNER, M., Civil Law, Trade and Labour Law
MASING, J. (acting), Constitutional and Administrative Law
MÖLLERS, TH., Civil Law, Economic Law, European Law
NEUNER, J., Civil Law, Labour and Trade Law
ROSENAU, H., International Penal Law
ROTSCH, T., Penal Law
VEDDER, CH. (acting), Public Law

Faculty of Mathematics and Natural Sciences (Universitätsstr. 14, 86159 Augsburg; tel. (821) 5982250; fax (821) 5982300; e-mail dekan@mnf.uni-augsburg.de; internet www.uni-augsburg.de/einrichtungen/mnf):

BEHRINGER, K., Experimental Plasma Physics
BRÜTTING, W., Experimental Physics
CLAESSEN, R., Experimental Physics
COLONIUS, F., Applied Mathematics
DORFMEISTER, J., Analysis and Geometry
ECKERN, U. (acting), Theoretical Physics
ESCHENBURG, J., Differential Geometry
GIESL, P., Nonlinear Analysis
HAIDER, F., Experimental Physics
HÄNGGI, P., Theoretical Physics
HARTMANN, L., Chemistry, Physics and Material Sciences

HEINRICH, L., Applied Mathematics
HEINTZE, E., Pure Mathematics
HILSCHER, H., Didactics of Physics
HÖCK, K. H., Theoretical Physics
HOPPE, R. H. W., Applied Mathematics
HORN, S., Experimental Physics
INGOLD, G.-L., Theoretical Physics
JUNGNICKEL, D., Applied Mathematics, Discrete Mathematics, Optimization, Operations Research
KAMPF, A., Theoretical Physics
KIELHÖFER, H.-J., Applied Analysis
KOPP, T., Physics
LOIDL, A., Experimental Physics
MANNHART, J., Experimental Physics
PUKELSHEIM, F., Applied Mathematics
RELLER, A., Solid State Chemistry
RITTER, J., Pure Mathematics
SCHERER, W., Chemistry, Physics and Material Sciences
SCHERTZ, R., Mathematics
SCHNEIDER, E., Didactics
SIEBERT, K. (acting), Applied Analytical Mathematics
STRITZKER, B., Experimental Physics
UNWIN, A., Computer-Oriented Statistics and Data Analysis
VOLLHARDT, D., Theoretical Physics
WIXFORTH, A., Experimental Physics
ZIEGLER, K., Theoretical Physics
ZIMMERMAN, R., Chemistry

Faculty of Philosophy and Social Sciences (Universitätsstr. 10, 86159 Augsburg; tel. (821) 5982605; fax (821) 5985504; e-mail dekan.phil1@phil.uni-augsburg.de; internet www.philso.uni-augsburg.de):

ALTENBERGER, H., Sports Education
ASBACH, O., Protestant Philosophy
ASCHENBRÜCKER, K., Didactics
BOEHLE, F., Sociology
BRUNOLD, A., Social Studies
EILDERS, C., Communications
GIEGLER, H., Sociology and Empirical Social Research
HERWARTZ-EMDEN, L., Pedagogics
HOYER, J., Music
KIRCHNER, C. (acting), Art Education
KRAEMER, R. D., Musical Training
LAEMMERMANN, G., Protestant Theology with Didactics of Religion
LAMES, M., Movement and Training
LAU, C., Sociology
MACHA, H., Pedagogics
MAINZER, K., Philosophy
MATTHES, E., Pedagogics
MÜHLEISEN, H.-O., Political Science
OBENDORFER, B., Protestant Theology
REINMANN, G., Media Education
SCHNEIDER, W., Sociology
SCHRÖER, C., Philosophy
SCHULTZE, R.-O., Political Science
STENGEL, M., Psychology
ULICH, D., Psychology
VON GEMÜNDEN, P., Protestant Theology
WIATER, W., Pedagogics
WÜSTNER, K., Psychology

UNIVERSITÄT BAYREUTH

95440 Bayreuth
Telephone: (921) 55-0
Fax: (921) 55-5290
E-mail: poststelle@uvw.uni-bayreuth.de
Internet: www.uni-bayreuth.de
Founded 1972
Academic year: October to September
Pres.: Prof. Dr HELMUT RUPPERT (acting)
Vice-Pres: Prof. Dr GEORG KRAUSCH, Prof. Dr WIEBKE PUTZ-OSTERLOH
Chancellor: Dr EKKEHARD BECK
Librarian: Dr KARL BABL
Number of teachers: 186
Number of students: 9,530

DEANS

Department of Applied Natural Sciences: Prof. Dr-Ing. ROLF STEINHILPER
Department of Biology, Chemistry and Geosciences: Prof. Dr ORTWIN MEYER
Department of Cultural Studies: Prof. Dr WOLFGANG SCHOBERTH
Department of Language and Literature: Prof. Dr DYMITR IBRISZIMOW
Department of Law and Economics: Prof. Dr PETER OBERENDER
Department of Mathematics and Physics: Prof. LORENZ KRAMER

PROFESSORS

Department of Applied Natural Sciences (tel. (921) 55-7101; fax (921) 55-7106):

AKSEL, N., Applied Mechanics and Fluid Dynamics
ALTSTÄDT, V., Polymerics
BRÜGGEMANN, D., Technical Thermodynamics, Transport Processes
FISCHERAUER, G., Measurement Technology and Control Engineering
FREITAG, R., Bioprocess Technology
GLATZEL, U., Metallic Materials
JESS, A., Chemical Engineering
KRENKEL, W., Ceramic Materials
MOOS, R., Working Materials
RIEG, F., Engineering Design and CAD
STEINHILPER, R., Environmentally Compatible Production Technology
WILLERT-PORADA, M., Material Processing

Department of Biology, Chemistry and Geosciences (tel. (921) 55-2229; fax (921) 55-2351):

BACH, L., Urban and Regional Planning
BALLAUFF, M., Physical Chemistry I
BECK, E., Plant Physiology
BEIERKUHNLEIN, C., Biogeography
BITZER, K., Geology
BOGNER, F. X., Didactics of Biology
BREU, J., Inorganic Chemistry I
DETTNER, K., Animal Ecology II
DRAKE, H. L., Soil Microbiology
FOKEN, T., Micrometeorology
FRANK, H., Environmental Pollution
HAUHS, M., Ecological Modelling
HOFFMANN, K. H., Animal Ecology I
VON HOLST, D., Animal Physiology
HÜSER, K., Geomorphology
HUWE, B., Soil Science
KEMPE, R., Inorganic Chemistry II
KEPPLER, H., Experimental Geophysics
KOMOR, E., Plant Physiology
KRAUSCH, G., Physical Chemistry II
KRAUSS, G., Biochemistry
LEHNER, C., Genetics
LIEDE-SCHUMANN, S., Plant Systematics
LOHNERT, B., Geographical Development Research
MAIER, J., Economic Geography
MATZNER, E., Soil Sciences
MEYER, O., Microbiology
MONHEIM, R., Cultural Geography
MORYS, P., Inorganic Chemistry
MÜLLER, A., Macromolecular Chemistry II
MÜLLER-MAHN, D., Population and Social Geography
OBERMAIER, G., Didactics of Geography
PEIFFER, ST., Hydrology
PLATZ, G., Physical Chemistry I
POPP, H., Urban and Rural Geography
RAMBOLD, G., Plant Systematics
RÖSCH, P., Structure and Chemistry of Biopolymers
RUBIE, D., Structure and Dynamics of Earth Materials
SCHMID, F. X., Biochemistry
SCHMIDT, H.-W., Macromolecular Chemistry I
SCHOBERT, R., Organic Chemistry
SCHUMANN, W., Genetics
SEIFERT, F., Experimental Geosciences
SEIFERT, K., Organic Chemistry I/2
SENKER, J., Organic Chemistry I

SPRINZL, M., Biochemistry
STEUDLE, E., Plant Ecology
TENHUNEN, J., Plant Ecology
ULLMANN, M., Biocomputer Science
UNVERZAGT, C., Bio-organic Chemistry
WESTERMANN, B., Cell Biology
WRACKMEYER, B., Inorganic Chemistry II
ZECH, W., Soil Science and Soil Geography
ZÖLLER, L., Geomorphology

Department of Cultural Studies (tel. (921) 55-4101; fax (921) 55-844101):

BARGATZKY, T., Ethnology
BERNER, U., Religious Studies I
BETZWIESER, T., Musicology
BOCHINGER, CH., Religious Studies II
BORMANN, L., Evangelical Theory III
BOSBACH, F., History
BREHM, W., Sport Science and Physical Education
EBNER, R., Catholic Religious Teaching II
HAAG, L., School Education
HEGSELMANN, R., Philosophy I
HIERY, H., History
KLUTE, G., Ethnology (Africa)
KOCH, L., Education
KÜGLER, J., Catholic Theology I
LANGE, D., History (Africa)
LINDGREN, U., History of Science
NEUBERT, D., Developmental Sociology
PUTZ-OSTERLOH, W., Psychology
RITTER, W., Protestant Theology II
SCHEIT, H., Social Philosophy
SCHMIDT, W., Sports Medicine
SCHOBERTH, W., Evangelical Theology I
SCHORCH, G., Elementary School Education
SCHÜSSLER, R., Philosophy II
SPITTLER, G., Ethnology
UNGERER-RÖHRICH, U., Sports
WEISS, D., Bavarian Regional Geology
ZIESCHANG, K., Sport Science and Physical Education
ZINGERLE, A., Sociology
ZÖLLER, M., Sociology II

Department of Language and Literature (tel. (921) 55-3625; fax (921) 55-3641):

BEGEMANN, C., New German Literature
BENESCH, K., English Literature
BERGER, G., Romance Linguistics
DRESCHER, M., Roman and General Linguistics
HAUSENDORF, H., German Linguistics
IBISZIMOW, D., African Studies II
KHAMIS, S., Literatures in African Languages
KLOTZ, P., German Language and Literature
MIEHE, G., African Linguistics I
MÜLLER, J., Media Studies
MÜLLER-JACQUIER, B., Intercultural German Language and Literature
OSSWALD, R., Islamic Studies
OWENS, J., Arabic Studies
SCHMID, H.-J., English Linguistics
STEPPAT, M., English Literature
VILL, S., Theatre Studies
WOLF, G., Early German Philology

Department of Law and Economics (tel. (921) 55-2894; fax (921) 55-2985):

BERG, W., Public Law
BÖHLER, H., Economics III
BREHM, W., Civil Law
DANNECKER, G., Criminal Law
EMMERICH, V., Civil Law
EYMANN, T., Economics VIII
GÖRGENS, E., Economics II
GUNDEL, J., Public Law
HEERMANN, P., Civil Law
HERZ, B., Economics I
KAHL, W., Public Law
KLIPPEL, D., Civil Law, History of Law
KÜHLMANN, T., Economics IV
LEPSIUS, O., Public Law
LESCHKE, M., Economics V
LORITZ, K.-G., Civil Law II

MECKL, R., Economics IX
MICHALSKI, L., Civil Law
MÖSTL, M., Public Law and Constitutional History
NAGEL, E., Health Service Management and Health Sciences
OBERENDER, P., Economics IV
OHLY, A., Civil Law
REMER, A., Economics VI
SCHLÜCHTERMANN, J., Economics V
SCHMITZ, R., Criminal Law
SIGLOCH, J., Economics II
SPELLENBERG, U., Civil Law
ULRICH, V., Economics III
WORATSCHEK, H., Economics VIII

Department of Mathematics and Physics (tel. (921) 55-3196; fax (921) 55-2999):

BAPTIST, P., Mathematics and Didactics
BRAND, H., Theoretical Physics III
BRAUN, H., Experimental Physics V
BÜTTNER, H., Theoretical Physics I
CATANESE, F., Mathematics VIII
ESKA, G., Experimental Physics V
GRÜNE, L., Applied Mathematics
HENRICH, D., Applied Computer Science III
KERBER, A., Mathematics
KÖHLER, J., Experimental Physics IV
KÖHLER, W., Experimental Physics IV
KRAMER, L., Theoretical Physics II
KRÄMER, M., Mathematics
KÜPPERS, J., Experimental Physics III
LAUE, R., Computer Science
LEMPIO, F., Applied Mathematics
MERTENS, F.-G., Theoretical Physics I
MÜLLER, W., Mathematics
OTT, A., Experimental Physics I
PASCHER, H., Experimental Physics I
PESCH, H. J., Engineering Mathematics
PETERNELL, T., Mathematics
RAUBER, T., Applied Computer Science II
REHBERG, I., Experimental Physics V
REIN, G., Applied Mathematics
RIEDER, H., Applied Mathematics
ROESSLER, E., Experimental Physics II
SCHAMEL, H., Theoretical Physics
SCHITTKOWSKI, K., Computer Science
SCHWOERER, M., Experimental Physics II
SEILMEIER, A., Experimental Physics III
SIMADER, C. G., Mathematics
VAN SMAALEN, S., Crystallography
VON WAHL, W., Applied Mathematics
WESTFECHTEL, B., Applied Computer Science
ZIMMERMANN, W., Applied Computer Science

ATTACHED INSTITUTES

Afrikazentrum (IWALENA-Haus) (Africa Centre): Dir Dr T. WENDL.

Bayerisches Forschungsinstitut für Experimentelle Geochemie und Geophysik (Bayerisches Geoinstitut, IBGI) (Bavarian Research Institute for Experimental Geochemistry and Geophysics): Dir Prof. Dr D. RUBIE.

Bayreuther Institut für Europäisches Recht und Rechts Kultur, insbesondere Rechtsvergleichung und Wirtschaftsrecht (Bayreuth Institute for European Law and Legal Culture, Comparative Law and Economic Law): Dir Prof. Dr Dr h.c. mult. P. HÄBERLE.

Bayreuther Institut für Makromolekülforschung (BIMF) (Bayreuth Institute for Macromolecular Research): Dir Prof. Dr H.-W. SCHMIDT.

Bayreuther Institut für Terrestrische Ökosystemforschung (BITÖK) (Bayreuth Institute for Terrestrial Ecology Research): Dir Prof. Dr E. MATZNER.

Bayreuther Zentrum für Kolloide und Grenzflächen (BZKG) (Bayreuth Centre for Colloide and Border Areas): Dir Prof. Dr M. BALLAUFF.

Bayreuther Zentrum für Molekulare Biowissenschaften (BZMB) (Bayreuth Centre for Molecular Biosciences): Dir Prof. Dr O. MEYER.

Bayreuther Zentrum für Ökologie und Umweltforschung (Bayreuth Centre for Ecology and Environmental Research): Dir Prof. Dr E. MATZNER.

Forschungsinstitut für Musiktheater (FIMT) (Research Institute for Music Theatre): Dir (vacant).

Institut für Afrikastudien (IAS) (Institute for African Studies): Dir Prof. Dr H. POPP.

Institut für Materialforschung (Institute for Materials Research): Dir Prof. Dr G. ZIEGLER.

Zentrum zur Förderung des Mathematisch- Naturwissenschaftlichen Unterrichts (Centre for Mathematical and Scientific Instruction): Dir Prof. Dr F. X. BOGNER.

UNIVERSITÄT BIELEFELD

Universitätsstr. 25, 33615 Bielefeld

Telephone: (521) 106-00
Fax: (521) 106-5844
E-mail: post@uni-bielefeld.de
Internet: www.uni-bielefeld.de

Founded 1969
State control
Academic year: April to March

Rector: Prof. Dr DIETER TIMMERMANN
Pro-Rectors: Prof. Dr CHRISTOPH GUSY, Prof. Dr GERHARD SAGERER, Prof. Dr NORBERT SEEWALD, Prof. Dr ELKE WILD
Chancellor: HANS-JÜRGEN SIMM
Dir. for Int. Relations: Dr WERNER AUFDER-LANDWEHR
Librarian: Dr NORBERT LOSSAU

Number of teachers: 758
Number of students: 17,521

Publications: *Bielefelder Universitätsgespräche* (irregular), *Bielefelder Universitätszeitung* (4 a year), *Forschungsbericht* (online), *Forschungsmagazin* (2 a year), *Jahresbericht des Rektors und Statistisches Jahrbuch* (1 a year), *Personalverzeichnis/Lehrveranstaltungen* (2 a year), *Pressedienst Forschung* (irregular)

DEANS

Faculty of Biology: Prof. Dr KARL-JOSEF DIETZ
Faculty of Chemistry: Prof. Dr GISELA LÜCK
Faculty of Economics: Prof. Dr ROLF KÖNIG
Faculty of Education: Prof. Dr KATHARINA GRÖNING-LIENKER
Faculty of Health Sciences: Prof. Dr KLAUS HURRELMANN
Faculty of History, Philosophy and Theology: Prof. Dr ANGSAR BECKERMANN
Faculty of Law: Prof. Dr DETLEF KLEINDIEK
Faculty of Linguistics and Literature: Prof. Dr LORE BENZ
Faculty of Mathematics: Prof. Dr WOLF-JÜRGEN BEYN
Faculty of Physics: Prof. Dr FRITHJOF KARSCH
Faculty of Psychology and Sport Science: Prof. Dr ULRICH SCHIEFELE
Faculty of Sociology: Prof. Dr LUTZ LEISERING
Faculty of Technology: Prof. Dr HELGE RITTER
Centre for Interdisciplinary Research: Prof. Dr IPKE WACHSMUTH

UNIVERSITÄT BREMEN

Postfach 330440, 28334 Bremen
Bibliothekstr., 28359 Bremen

Telephone: (421) 218-1
Fax: (421) 218-4259
E-mail: presse@uni-bremen.de

Internet: www.uni-bremen.de

Founded 1971
State control
Academic year: October to September (two terms)

Rector: Prof. Dr WILFRIED MÜLLER
Chancellor: GERD-RÜDIGER KÜCK
Pro-Rectors: Prof. Dr ANGELIKA BUNSE-GERST-NER, Prof. Dr ILSE HELBRECHT
Librarian: ANNETTE RATH-BECKMANN

Number of teachers: 366
Number of students: 18,000

Publications: *Bremer Uni Schlüssel* (5 a year), *Impulse aus der Forschung* (2 a year), *Research Report* (every 2 years)

DEANS

Department of Biology and Chemistry: Prof. Dr G.-O. KIRST
Department of Cultural Sciences: Prof. Dr H. G. ARTUS
Department of Economics: Prof. Dr H.-D. HAASIS
Department of Geosciences: Prof. Dr H. VILLINGER
Department of Health and Human Studies: Prof. Dr A. KEIL
Department of Law: Prof. Dr L. BOELLINGER
Department of Literature and Language Studies: Prof. Dr G. PASTERNACK
Department of Mathematics and Computer Science: Prof. Dr B. KRIEG-BRUECKNER
Department of Physics and Electrical Engineering: Prof. Dr JUERGEN GUTOWSKI
Department of Production Engineering, Economics for Engineering, and Commercial and Technical Science: Prof. Dr F.-J. HEEG
Department of Social and Educational Sciences: Prof. Dr A. KRETSCHMANN
Department of Social Sciences: Prof. Dr G. BAHRENBERG

PROFESSORS

Department 1 (Physics; Electrical Engineering)

Electrical Engineering:

ANHEIER, W., Microelectronics, Digital Systems
ARNDT, F., High Frequency Technology
BENECKE, W., Silicon-Micromechanics, Sensors and Actuators
BINDER, J., Micro- and Sensor-Systems, and Space Technology
GRÄSER, A., Automation Engineering
GRONWOLD, D., Electrical Technology
KAMMEYER, K.-D., Communications
LAUR, R., Electronics and Microelectronics
LOHMANN, B., Automatic Control
MARTE, G., Electronics
MEINERZHAGEN, B., Field Theory
MÜLLER, W., Analysis of the Engineering Professions
ORLIK, B., Electrical Drives and Power Electronics
RAUNER, F., Electrical Technology
SILBER, D. H., Power Electronics and Devices

Physics:

VON AUFSCHNAITER, S., Teaching of Physics
AUGSTEIN, E., Meteorology and Physics of the Oceans
BLECK-NEUHAUS, J., Experimental and Environmental Physics
BOSECK, S., Experimental Physics
BURROWS, P., Environmental Physics
CZYCHOLL, G., Theoretical Physics
DIEHL, H., Biophysics
DREYBRODT, W., Experimental Physics, Molecular Spectroscopy
FALTA, J., Surface Science of Semiconductors
GUTOWSKI, J., Semiconductor Optics
HOMMEL, D., Epitaxy of Semiconductors
JÜPTNER, W., Laser Application

KÜNZI, K., Environmental Physics
LANGE, H., Sociology of Labour
NIEDDERER, H., Teaching of Physics
NOACK, C. C., Theoretical Physics
OLBERS, D., Theoretical Physics
PAWELZIK, K., Theoretical Biology
RICHTER, P., Theoretical Physics
ROETHER, W., Physical Oceanography in the Polar Regions
RYDER, P., Physics of Metals
SCHMITZ-FEUERHAKE, I., Experimental Physics
SCHWEDES, H., Teaching of Science
SCHWEGLER, H., Theoretical Physics, Theoretical Biophysics
STAUDE, W., Experimental Physics

Department 2 (Biology; Chemistry)

Biology:

ARNTZ, W., Ocean Ecology
BLOHM, D., Biotechology
ENTRICH, H., Theory and Practice of Education in the Natural Sciences
FAHLE, M., Neurobiology and Human Biology
FISCHER, H., Marine Microbiology
FLOHR, H., Biology
GRIMME, L. H., Biology, Biochemistry
HAGEN, W., Marine Zoology
HEYSER, W., Botany
HILDEBRANDT, A., Biology
KIRST, G.-O., Marine Botany
KOENIG, F., Botany
KREITER, A., Neurobiology
MOSSAKOWSKI, D., Evolutionary Biology
POERTNER, H.-O., Marine Biology
REINHOLD-HUREK, B., Microbiology
ROTH, G., Neurobiology
SAINT-PAUL, U., Marine Ecology
SCHLOOT, W., Genetics, Human Genetics
SMETACEK, V., Marine Biology
VALLBRACHT, A., Virology
WITTE, H., Zoology
WOLFF, M., Marine Ecology

Chemistry:

BALZER, W., Marine Chemistry
BEYERSMANN, D., Biochemistry
BREUNIG, H.-J., Inorganic Chemistry
GABEL, D., Organic Chemistry, Biochemistry
JAEGER, N., Physical Chemistry
JASTORFF, B., Organic Chemistry
JUST, E., Teaching of Chemistry
LEIBFRITZ, D., Organic Chemistry
MEWS, R., Inorganic Chemistry
MONTFORTS, F., Organic Chemistry
PLATH, P., Chemistry
RIEKENS, R., Teaching of Chemistry
RÖSCHENTHALER, G., Inorganic Chemistry
SCHREMS, O., Physical Chemistry
SCHROER, W., Physical Chemistry
SCHULZ-EKLOFF, G., Physical Chemistry
STOHRER, W.-D., Chemistry
THIEMANN, W., Physical Chemistry
WANCZEK, K., Inorganic Chemistry
WÖHRLE, D., Chemistry

Department 3 (Mathematics; Computer Science)

Computer Science:

BORMANN, U., Computer Networks
BRUNS, F.-W., Technology Design
FRIEDRICH, J., Computing and Society
GOGOLLA, M., Database Systems
HAEFNER, K., Education Technologies, Social Impacts and Transport Implications
HERZOG, O., Expert Systems and Foundations of Artificial Intelligence
KREOWSKI, H.-J., Theoretical Computer Science
KRIEG-BRÜCKNER, B., Programming Languages, Compilers and Software Engineering
KUBICEK, H., Information Management and Telecommunications

MAASS, S., Women's Studies and Technology

NAKE, F., Graphic Data Processing and Interactive Systems

PELESKA, J., Operating Systems, Distributed Systems

RÖDIGER, K.-H., Software Engineering and Ergonomics

SZCZERBICKA, H., Computer Architecture and Modelling

Mathematics:

ARNOLD, L., Random Dynamic Systems

BAENSCH, E., Numerical Methods for Partial Differential Equations

BECKER, G., Teacher Education

BOEHM, M., Modelling and Partial Differential Equations

BUNSE-GERSTNER, A., Numerical Linear Algebra

DENNEBERG, D., Non-additive Integration, Risk, Uncertainty and Insurance

DEUTSCH, M., Logic and Foundations of Mathematics

DOMBROWSKI, H.-D., Mathematical Foundations of Physics

FISCHER, H. W., Complex Analysis

GAMST, J., Algorithmic Algebra and Number Theory

HERRLICH, H., Topology, Category Theory

HINRICHSEN, D., Systems and Control Theory

HOFFMANN, R.-E., Topology, Categories and Lattices

HORNEFFER, K., Differential Geometry, Mathematical Foundations of Physics

HUPPERTZ, H., Teacher Education

KRAUSE, U., Positive Dynamic Systems

LINDENAU, V., Teacher Education

MAASS, P., Inverse Problems and Wavelets

MÜNZNER, H.-F., Differential Geometry, Dynamic Systems

OELJEKLAUS, E., Complex Algebraic Geometry

OSIUS, G., Statistics, Biometry

PEITGEN, H.-O., Complex Systems, Computer-aided Radiology

PORST, H.-E., Categorical Algebra

SCHÄFER, R., Numerical Hydrogeology

WISCHNEWSKY, M., Modelling, Neural Networks, Fuzzy Systems

Department 4 (Production Engineering; Economics for Engineering; Commercial and Technical Science):

BAUCKHAGE, K., Chemical and Process Engineering

BRINKSMEIER, E., Manufacturing Technology

GENTHNER, K., Technical Thermodynamics, Heat and Mass Transfer

GOCH, G., Metrology, Automation and Quality Science

GRATHWOHL, G., Ceramic Materials and Components

HARIG, H., Material Technology and Composites

HEEG, F.-J., Work Science

HENNEMANN, O. D., Bonding Technology and Polymers

HIRSCH, B. E., Production Resources, Logistics, Telematics

HOPPE, M., Vocational Teaching of Metal Engineering

KIENZLER, R., Applied Mechanics and Structural Mechanics

KUNZE, H.-D., Near Net Shape Production Technologies

MAYR, P., Material Science

MÜLLER, D. H., Engineering Design, CAE, CAD

RÄBIGER, N., Environmental Process Engineering

RATH, H. J., Technical Mechanics and Fluid Mechanics

SEPOLD, G., Laser and Plasma Technologies for Materials Processing

VISSER, A., Production Facilities

WITTKOWSKY, A., Design and Development of Technology

Department 5 (Geosciences):

BLEIL, U., Marine Geophysics

BROCKAMP, O., Mineralogy, Petrography, Clay Mineralogy

DEVEY, C., Petrology of the Ocean Crust

FISCHER, R. X., Crystallography

FÜTTERER, D., Geology

HENRICH, R., Sedimentology, Palaeo-oceanography

HERTERICH, K., Palaeo-oceanographic Modelling

JÖRGENSEN, B. B., Biogeochemistry

KUSS, H. J., Geology, Stratigraphy, Sedimentology

MILLER, H., Geophysics

OLESCH, M., Geology of the Polar Regions, Petrology

SCHULZ, H., Geochemistry, Hydrogeology

SPIESS, V., Marine Technology, Marine Environmental Geophysics

VILLINGER, H., Marine Technology, Geophysical Sensor Development

WEFER, G., Geology

WILLEMS, H., Historical Geology and Palaeontology

Department 6 (Law):

BÖLLINGER, L., Criminal Law

BRÜGGEMEIER, G., Civil and Economic Law

DAMM, R., Civil Law, Economic Law

DÄUBLER, B., Labour, Commercial and Economic Law

DERLEDER, P., Civil and Banking Law

DUBISCHAR, R., Civil Law

FEEST, J., Criminal Law and Criminology

FRANCKE, R., Legal Didactics

GESSNER, V., Comparative Law and Legal Sociology

HART, D., Economic Law

HINZ, M., Public Law and Political and Legal Sociology

HOFFMANN, R., Public Law, Labour Law and Political Science

JOERGES, C., Civil and Comparative Law

KNIEPER, R., Civil and Economic Law

LICHTENBERG, H., Labour and European Law

REICH, N., Civil and European Law

RINKEN, A., Public Law

RUEHE, U., Public Law

RUST, U., Gender Law

SCHEFOLD, D., Public Law

SCHMIDT, E., Civil Law and Procedure

SCHMINCK-GUSTAVUS, C., History of Law

SCHUMANN, K. F., Criminology

STUBY, G., Public Law and Political Science

THOSS, P., Criminal Law

WASHNER, R., Labour Law

WESSLAU, E., Criminal Law and Procedure

WINTER, G., Public and Environmental Law

Department 7 (Economics):

BAUER, E., Marketing of Research and Management

BIESECKER, A., Economic Theory

BRITSCH, K., Economic Statistics

DWORATSCHEK, S., Project Management

ECKSTEIN, W., Economics of Logistic Systems

ELSNER, W., Economic, Industrial and Regional Policy, Institutional Evolutionary Economics

FRANCKE, R., Economic Theory

GERSTENBERGER, H., Theory of State and Society

GRENZDÖRFFER, K., Economic Statistics, Labour Economics

HAASIS, H.-D., Production Management and Industrial Organization

HEIDE, H., Town and Country Planning

HICKEL, R., Public Finance

HUFFSCHMID, J., Political Economy, Economic Policy

KALMBACH, P., Economics

KOPFER, H., Economics of Logistics Systems

LEITHÄUSER, G., Economic Policy

LEMPER, A., Foreign Trade Theory and Politics

LIONVILLE, J., International Economics

MARX, F. J., Financial Accounting and Business Taxation

PODDIG, TH., Finance

SCHAEFER, H., Theory, Forecasting and Control

SCHMÄHL, W., Economics and Social Policy

SCHWIERING, D., Economics

SELL, A., International Economics

STEIGER, O., General Economic Theory and Monetary Economics

STUCHTEY, R. W., Economics of Marine Transport

VON DER VRING, TH., Political Economy

WOHLMUTH, K., Comparative Economic Systems

ZACHCIAL, M., Transport Science and Transport Planning

Department 8 (Social Sciences)

Cultural History of Eastern Europe:

EICHWEDE, W., History and Politics of Socialist Countries

KRASNODEBSKY, Z., Polish Social and Cultural History

STÄDTKE, K., Cultural History of Eastern Europe

Geography:

BAHRENBERG, G., Social and Economic Geography

SCHRAMKE, W., Geography, Teaching of Geography

TAUBMANN, W., Cultural Geography

TIPPKÖTTER, R., Geography of Soils

VENZKE, J.-F., Physical Geography

History:

BARROW, L., Social and Political History of England

EICHWEDE, W., History and Politics of Socialist Countries

HACHTMANN, R., History of the 19th and 20th Centuries

HÄGERMANN, D., Medieval History

HAHN, M., History of Business, Political Theories

HOEDER, D., Social History of the USA

KLOFT, H., Ancient History

KOPITZSCH, F., History

KRAUSS, M., History of 19th- and 20th-Century Social Economics

RECH, M., Prehistoric and Medieval History

SCHMIDT, J., Curricula in Economic and Social Studies

WAGNER, W., Politics, History of Political Education

Politics:

ALBERS, D., Labour Relations

EICHWEDE, W., History and Politics of Socialist Countries

KOOPMANN, K., Didactics of Social Science Education

LIEBERT, U., Comparative Politics, European Integration

LOTHAR, R., Politics, and Federal and Constitutional Law

PETERS, B., Political Theory and History of Ideas

SCHMIDT, M., Politics, Comparative Social Policies

WAGNER, W., Politics, History of Political Education

WIRTH, M., Parliamentary System of Federal Germany

ZOLL, R., History and Theory of Trade Unions

ZÜRN, M., Politics

Postgraduate Programme Development Policy with Focus on Non-Governmental Organizations:

VON FREYHOLD, M., Development Policy and Sociology of Development

Sociology:

VON FREYHOLD, M., Social Science
KRÄMER-BADONI, T., Town and Regional Planning
KRAUSE, D., Educational Planning
KRÜGER, M., Social Analysis
LAUTMANN, R., General Sociology and Sociology of Law
LUEDEMANN, CHR., Statistics and Empirical Research
PETER, L., Labour and Industrial Sociology
QUENSEL, S., Resocialization and Rehabilitation
REICHELT, H., Theory of Science and Society
SENGHAAS, D., Peace and Conflict Studies
WEYMANN, A., Social Theory, Educational Research

Department 9 (Cultural Sciences)

Art:

BUDDEMEIER, H., Communication, Mass Media
MÜLLER, M., Art History and Cultural Studies
PETERS, M., Art Education
SCHADE-THOLEN, S., Art History, Aesthetics

Cultural Science:

DRÖGE, F., Mass Communication Research
DUERR, H. P., Ethnology and Cultural History
NADIG, M., European Ethnology and Cultural Anthropology
RICHARD, J., Teaching of Drama
RICHTER, D., German Literature

Music:

BRECKOFF, W., Teaching of Music
KLEINEN, G., Teaching of Music, Musicology
RIEGER, E., Musicology

Philosophy:

MOHR, G., Practical Philosophy
SANDKÜHLER, H. J., Theoretical Philosophy
STÖCKLER, M., Philosophy of Natural Sciences

Religious Science:

KIPPENBERG, H.-G., Theory and History of Religions
LOTT, J., Religious Education
SCHULZ, H., Comparative Religion

Sport:

ARTUS, H. G., Teaching of Physical Education
BRAUN, H., History of Sport
FIKUS, M., Psychomotor Behaviour
SCHEELE, K., Sports Medicine

Department 10 (Literature and Language Studies)

Communication:

BACH, G., Teaching of English
BARROW, L., Social and Political History of England
BATEMANN, J. A., Applied Functional Linguistics, Natural Language Processing and Translation Science
DAHLE, W., German Language and Literature
EMMERICH, W., German Literature
FRANZBACH, M., Literature and Social History of Spain and Latin America
GALLAS, H., German Literature
JÄGER, H.-W., History of German Literature
KOCH, H. A., German and Comparative Literature

LIEBE-HARKORT, K., German as a Foreign Language
LIENERT, E., German Literature of the Middle Ages and the Early Modern Period
MENK, A.-K., Linguistics
PASTERNACK, G., Theory of Literature
PAUL, L., Applied Linguistics
SAUTERMEISTER, G., History of German Literature
STOLZ, TH., Linguistics
WAGNER, K.-H., Linguistics
WILDGEN, W., Linguistics
ZIMMERMANN, K., Spanish and Portuguese Linguistics

Department 11 (Health and Human Studies)

Psychology:

BAUMGÄRTL, F., Psychological Diagnosis
BERNDT, J., Physiology
GNIECH, G., Psychology
HEINZ, W.-R., Sociology and Social Psychology
HENNING, H.-J., Psychology
KIESELBACH, TH., Psychology
LEITHÄUSER, T., Development Psychology
PETERMANN, F., Clinical Psychology
REINKE, E., Clinical Psychology
STADLER, M., Psychology
VETTER, G., Theory of Learning
VOGT, R., Psychology
VOLMERG, B., Psychology

Public Health:

FRENTZEL-BEYME, R., Occupational and Environmental Epidemiology
GREISER, E., Occupational Health and Social Medicine
MÜLLER, R., Health Policy, Occupational Health and Social Medicine

Social Education:

AMENDT, G., Sub-Cultures
BAUER, R., Social Pedagogy
BLANDOW, J., Social Education
BROCKMANN, A.-D., Town and Regional Planning
HEINSON, G., Social Pedagogy
KEIL, A., General Education
LEIBFRIED, S., Social Planning
MERKEL, J., Pre-School Education

Teacher Training:

GOERRES, ST., Social Gerontology
HYAMS-PETER, H.-U., Social Education
KRÜGER-MÜLLER, H., Sociology
LITTEK, W., Education and Economics
VAN MAANEN, H., Nursing Sciences
ORTMANN, H., Educational Sciences

Work Study:

MÜLLER, R., Health Policy, Occupational Health and Social Medicine
SENGHASS-KNOBLOCH, E., Humanization of Work
SPITZLEY, H., Technology and Society

Department 12 (Social and Educational Sciences)

Education Diploma:

DIETZE, L., Public Law
ROTH, L., Theory of Teaching
SCHÖNWÄLDER, H. G., Educational Planning and Economics
STRAKA, G., Extracurricular Education
ZIECHMANN, J., Psychology of Learning

Educational Science:

BECK, J., Educational Social Sciences
BOEHM, U., Structure and Development of Education
DRECHSEL, R., Education
DRECHSEL, W., Educational Social History
HUISKEN, F., Educational Political Economy
POLZIN, M., Aesthetic Education
PREUSS, O., Sociology of Education
UBBELOHDE, R., Educational Science
VINNAI, G., Analytical Social Psychology

VOIGT, B., Teacher Training

Further Education:

GERL, H., Adult Education
GÖRS, D., Distance Education
HOLZAPPFEL, G., Curricular Planning
KUHLENKAMP, D., Educational Planning
MADER, W., Adult Education
SCHLUTZ, E., Adult Education
WOLLENBERG, J., Adult Education in Political Science

Primary Education:

MILHOFFER, P., Sociology and Political Education
SCHMITT, R., Developmental Psychology
SPITTA, G., Beginning of German Language

Teaching the Handicapped:

DÖHNER, O., Medicine of Mental Illness
FEUSER, G., Education of Mentally Disturbed Children
HOMBURG, G., Educating People with Speech Defects
JANTZEN, W., History of Educating the Handicapped
KRETSCHMANN, R., Training of Educationally Handicapped
PIXA-KETTNER, U., Educating People with Speech Defects
REINCKE, W., Education for the Mentally Disturbed

Work Experience:

FISCHER, W. C., Consumer Economics
FRÖLEKE, H., Nutrition
HUISKEN, F., Educational Science
SCHRÖDER, A., Textile Technology

UNIVERSITÄT DER BUNDESWEHR MÜNCHEN

Werner-Heisenberg-Weg 39, 85579 Neubiberg

Telephone: (89) 6004-0
Fax: (89) 60042009
E-mail: info@unibw.de
Internet: www.unibw.de

Founded 1973
Academic year: October to September (3 semesters)
President: Prof. Dr MERITH NIEHUSS
Vice-Presidents: Prof. Dr UWE M. BORGHOFF, Prof. Dr THOMAS WÜSTRICH
Chancellor: (vacant)
Registrar: INGO FRITZ
Librarian: Dr HANS-JOACHIM GENGE

Library of 773,000 vols
Number of teachers: 200
Number of students: 2,700

Publications: 'Der Hochschulkurier' (3 a year), *Forschungsbericht*

DEANS

Faculty of Aviation and Space, Aerospace Engineering: Prof. Dr-Ing. K.-J. SCHWENZFEGER
Faculty of Civil Engineering, Surveying and Geodesy: Prof. Dr-Ing. D. KRAUS
Faculty of Computer and Information Sciences: Prof. Dr rer. nat. S. BRAUN
Faculty of Economics and Organizational Sciences: Prof. Dr rer. pol. P. FRIEDRICH
Faculty of Education: Prof. Dr A. KAISER
Faculty of Electrical Engineering: Prof. Dr-Ing. K. HOFFMANN
Faculty of Social Sciences: Prof. Dr Z. VOIGT
Polytechnical College of Business Administration: Prof. Dr jur. W. ROTTMANN
Polytechnical College of Civil and Electrical Engineering: Prof. Dr-Ing. G. STICHLER
Polytechnical College of Mechanical Engineering: Prof. Dipl.-Ing. J. HERRMANN

UNIVERSITÄT DER KÜNSTE BERLIN
(Berlin University of the Arts)

POB 120544, 10595 Berlin
Einsteinufer 43–53, 10587 Berlin
Telephone: (30) 3185-0
Fax: (30) 3185-2870
E-mail: presse@udk-berlin.de
Internet: www.udk-berlin.de

Founded 1975 by amalgamation of the Staatliche Hochschule für Bildende Künste (f. 1696) and the Staatliche Hochschule für Musik und Darstellende Kunst (f. 1869)

Departments of aesthetic education, architecture, art and cultural sciences, art education and art science, design, educational and social sciences, fine arts, music, music education and science, performing arts and drama, publicity and communication, visual communication,

President: Prof. MARTIN RENNERT
Vice-Pres.: Prof. Dr PATRICK DINSLAGE, Prof. KIRSTEN LANGKILDE, Prof. CHRISTIANE MÖBUS, Prof. KARL-LUDWIG OTTO
Librarian: ANDREA ZEYNS

Library of 650,000 vols
Number of students: 4,300

UNIVERSITÄT DES SAARLANDES

Postfach 151150, 66041 Saarbrücken
Telephone: (681) 3020
Fax: (681) 302-3900
E-mail: praesident@uni-saarland.de
Internet: www.uni-saarland.de
Founded 1948
Academic year: October to July

Pres.: Prof. Dr MARGRET WINTERMANTEL
Vice-Pres: Prof. Dr ROLF W. HARTMANN, Prof. Dr MATHIAS HERMANN, Prof. Dr PATRICIA OSTER-STIERLE
Librarian: Prof. Dr BERND HAGENAU

Number of teachers: 1,090
Number of students: 15,500

Publications: *Annales Universitatis Saraviensis* (4 a year), *Campus* (irregular), *Forschungsbericht* (1 a year), *Jahresbibliographie* (1 a year), *Vorlesungsverzeichnis* (2 a year)

DEANS

Faculty of Law and Business: Prof. Dr RUDOLF WENDT
Faculty of Medicine: Prof. Dr MATHIAS MONTENARH
Faculty of Natural Sciences and Technology I: Prof. Dr THORSTEN HERFET
Faculty of Natural Sciences and Technology II: Prof. Dr ANDREAS SCHÜTZE
Faculty of Natural Sciences and Technology III: Prof. Dr KASPAR HEGETSCHWEILER
Faculty of Philosophy I: Prof. Dr MICHAEL HÜTTENHOFF
Faculty of Philosophy II: Prof. Dr ULRIKE DEMSKE
Faculty of Philosophy III: Prof. Dr RAINER KRAUSE

PROFESSORS

Faculty of Law and Business (tel. (681) 302-2003; fax (681) 302-4213; e-mail dekanat@rewi.uni-sb.de; internet www.rewi.uni-sb.de):

ALBERT, M., Economics
AUTEXIER, C., French Public Law
BECKMANN, R., Civil, Commercial, Economic and Labour Law
BIEG, H., Business Economics
CHIUSI, T., Civil Law, Roman Law
FRIEDMANN, R., Statistics
GLASER, H., Business Economics
GRÖPL, C., State and Management Law
GRÖPPEL-KLEIN, A., Business Economics

HERBERGER, M., Civil Law, Theory of Law, Computer Applications in Jurisprudence
JUNG, H., Penal and Procedural Law, Criminal Law, Law of Criminal Procedure, Criminology and Comparative Criminal Jurisprudence
KORIATH, H., Criminal Law, Criminal Procedural Law, Philosophy of Law, Sociology of Law
KUßMAUL, H., Business Economics
KÜTING, K., Business Economics
LOOS, P., Business Economics
MARTINEK, M., Civil, Commercial and Economic Law, International Private Law and Comparative Jurisprudence
MATUSCHE-BECKMANN, A., Civil, Commercial and Economic Law and Labour Law
MENG, W., Public Law, International Law, European Community Law
MOMSEN, C., Penal and Procedural Law
NICKEL, S., Business Economics
PIERZIOCH, C., Economics
RANIERI, F., European Civil Law
RÜSSMANN, H., Civil and Procedural Law, Philosophy of Law
SCHMIDT, G., Business Economics
SCHMIDTCHEN, D., Economics
SCHOLZ, C., Business Economics
STEIN, T., European Law, European Public Law, International Law
STROHMEIER, S., Business Economics
WADLE, E., History of German Law, Civil Law
WASCHBUSCH, G., Business Economics
WENDT, R., Constitutional and Administrative Law, Revenue and Tax Law
WETH, S., German and European Procedural and Industrial Law
WITZ, C., French Public Law
ZENTES, J., Business Economics

Faculty of Medicine (Medizinische Fakultät, Universitätskliniken des Saarlandes, 66421 Homburg; tel. (6841) 16-24737; fax (6841) 16-26003; e-mail mfdekan@med-rz.uni-sb.de):

ABDUL-KHALIQ, H., Paediatrics
BOCK, R., Anatomy
BOHLE, R., Pathology
BÖHM, M., Internal Medicine
BRUNS, D., Physiology
BUCHTER, A., Occupational Medicine
CAVALIÉ, A., Pharmacology and Toxicology
FALKAI, P., Psychiatry and Psychotherapy
FASSBENDER, K., Psychiatry and Psychotherapy
FEIDEN, W., Neuropathology
FLOCKERZI, V., Pharmacology and Toxicology
FREICHEL, M., Pharmacology and Toxicology
FUHR, G., Medical Technology
GORTNER, L., Paediatrics
GRAF, N., Paediatrics
HANNIG, M., Oral and Maxillofacial Medicine
HERRMANN, E., Mathematical Modelling in Molecular Medicine
HERRMANN, M., Microbiology
HERRMANN, W., Clinical Chemistry
HOTH, M., Physiology
HÜTTERMANN, J., Biophysics
KIENECKER, E.-W., Anatomy
KINDERMANN, W., Sports Medicine
KIRSCH, C.-M., Nuclear Medicine
KÖHLER, H., Internal Medicine
KOHN, D., Orthopaedics
LARSEN, R., Anaesthesiology
LIPP, P., Molecular Cell Biology
LISSON, J., Oral and Maxillofacial Medicine
LÖBRICH, M., Biophysics and Physical Basis of Medicine
MAURER, H. H., Pharmacology and Toxicology
MEESE, E., Human Genetics and Molecular Biology

MENGER, M., Institute for Clinical and Experimental Surgery
MESTRES-VENTURA, P., Anatomy
MEYERHANS, A., Virology
MONTENARH, M., Medical Biochemistry
MÜLLER-LANTZSCH, N., Virology
PFREUNDSCHUH, M., Internal Medicine
POHLEMANN, T., Casualty Surgery
POSPIECH, P., Oral and Maxillofacial Medicine
REITH, W., Diagnostic Radiology
RETTIG, J., Physiology
RÖSLER, M., Psychiatry, Neurology
RÜBE, CH., Radiotherapy
SCHÄFERS, H.-J., Surgery
SCHEIDIG, A., Structural Biology
SCHILLING, M., Surgery
SCHMIDT, W., Gynaecology and Obstetrics
SCHMITZ, F., Neuroanatomy
SCHULZ, I., Physiology
SEITZ, B., Occular Medicine
SPITZER, W. C., Maxillofacial Surgery
STAHL, H., Medical Biochemistry
STEUDEL, W.-I., Neurosurgery
STÖCKLE, M., Urology
SYBRECHT, G. W., Internal Medicine
THIEL, G., Medical Biochemistry
TILGEN, W., Dermatology and Venereology
VON GONTARD, A., Child Psychiatry
WALLDORF, U., Developmental Biology
WANKE, K., Neurology, Psychiatry
WILSKE, J., Forensic Medicine
ZEUZEM, S., Internal Medicine
ZIMMERMANN, R., Physiological Chemistry

Faculty of Natural Sciences and Technology I: Mathematics and Computer Science (tel. (681) 302-5070; fax (681) 302-5068; e-mail sekr.fakultaet@mx.uni-saarland.de; internet www.uni-saarland.de/fak6):

ALBRECHT, E., Mathematics
BACKES, M., Computer Science
BLÄSER, M., Computer Science
BROSAMLER, G.-A., Mathematics
DECKER, W., Mathematics
ESCHMEIER, J., Mathematics
FUCHS, M., Mathematics
GEKELER, E.-U., Mathematics
HERFET, T., Computer Science
HERMANNS, H., Computer Science
HISCHER, H., Teaching of Mathematics
JOHN, V., Mathematics
KOCH, C., Computer Science
KOHLER, M., Mathematics
LENHOFF, H., Bioinformatics
LOUIS, A. K., Mathematics
PAUL, W., Information Science
RJASANOW, S., Mathematics
SCHEIDIG, H., Informatics
SCHREYER, F.-O., Mathematics
SCHULZE-PILLOT, R., Mathematics
SEIDEL, R., Theoretical Informatics
SIEKMANN, J., Informatics
SLUSALLEK, P., Informatics
SMOLKA, G., Information Science
WAHLSTER, W., Informatics
WEICKERT, J., Mathematics
ZELLER, A., Software Engineering

Faculty of Natural Sciences and Technology II: Physics and Electrical Engineering (tel. (681) 302-4943; fax (681) 302-4973; e-mail dekan.fak7@mx.uni-saarland.de; internet www.uni-saarland.de/fak7):

BECHER, C., Physical Engineering
BIRRINGER, R., Physical Engineering
DYCZIJ-EDLINGER, R., Electrical Theory
HARTMANN, U., Experimental Physics
JAKOBS, K., Experimental Physics
JANOCHA, H., Process Automation
KLAKOW, D., Speech Processing
KLIEM, H., Electrical Engineering Physics
KNORR, K., Physical Engineering
KÖNIG, K., Microsensor Technology
KRÜGER, J. K., Experimental Physics
KUGI, A., Systems Theory and Control Engineering

LÜCKE, M., Theoretical Physics
MÖLLER, M., Electronics and Circuits
NICOLAY, T., High Frequency Engineering
PELSTER, R. (acting), Experimental Physics
RIEGER, H., Theoretical Physics
SANTEN, L., Theoretical Physics
SCHÜTZE, A., Measurement
SEIDEL, H., Micromechanics
WAGNER, C., Experimental Physics
WICHERT, T., Physical Engineering
XU, CHIHAO, Microelectronics

Faculty of Natural Sciences and Technology III: Chemistry, Pharmacy, Materials Science (tel. (681) 302-2400; fax (681) 302-3421; e-mail dekan.fak8@mx.uni-saarland.de; internet www.uni-saarland.de/fak8):

BAUER, P., Botany
BECK, H. P., Inorganic and Analytical Chemistry, Radiochemistry
BERNHARDT, I., Biophysics
BERNHARDT, R., Biochemistry
BLEY, H., Production Engineering
BUSCH, R., Metallic Materials
CLASEN, R., Materials Science
DIEBELS, S., Applied Mechanics
GIFFHORN, F., Microbiology
HARTMANN, R. W., Pharmaceutical Chemistry
HEGETSCHWEILER, K., Inorganic Chemistry
HEINZLE, E., Technical Bioengineering
HELMS, V., Computational Biology
HUBER, C., Analytical Chemistry
JAUCH, J., Organic Chemistry
KAZMAIER, U., Organic Chemistry
KIEMER, A. K., Pharmaceutical Biology
KRÖNING, M., Non-destructive Materials Testing
LEHR, C.-M., Pharmaceutical Technology
MAIER, W., Technical Chemistry
MÜCKLICH, F., Work Materials
MÜLLER, R., Pharmaceutical Biotechnology
MÜLLER, U., Zoology and Physiology
POSSART, W., Polymers and Surfaces
SCHMIDT, H., New Materials
SCHMITT, M., Microbiology
SPRINGBORG, M., Physical Chemistry
VEHOFF, H., Materials Science, Methodology
VEITH, M., Inorganic Chemistry
WALTER, J., Genetics
WEBER, C., Construction Engineering
WENZ, G., Macromolecular Chemistry

Faculty of Philosophy I: History and Cultural Sciences (tel. (681) 302-2300; fax (681) 302-4234; e-mail u.weisgerber@pfdek.uni-sb.de):

BEHRINGER, W., Early Times
BRANDOLINI, A., Art Education
DE JONG, R., Art Education
DETZLER, B., Art Education
GIRARDET, K. M., Ancient History
GOERTZ, S., Practical Theology and Social Ethics
GRABAS, M., Economic and Social History
GÜTHLEIN, K., History of Art
HAUSIG, D., Art Education
HECKMANN, H., Philosophy
HINSCH, W., Philosophy
HUDEMANN, R., Modern and Contemporary History
HULLMANN, H., Art Education
HÜTTENHOFF, M., Protestant Theology
KASTEN, B., Medieval History
KRAUS, W., New Testament
KUBISCH, C., Art Education
LICHTENSTERN, C., History of Art
MAKSIMOVIC, I., Art Education
NESTLER, W., Art Education
NORTMANN, U., Philosophy
OHLIG, K.-H., Theology
POPP, H., Art Education
REINSBERG, C., Classical Archaeology
RIEMER, P., Classical Philology
ROMPZA, S., Art Education
ROSENBACH, U., Art Education
SACHSSE, R., Art Education

SCHERZBERG, L., Systematic Theology
SCHMITT, R., Comparative Indo-Germanic Languages
SCHNEIDER, H., Medieval History
SCHRÖDER, B., Religious Education
WALICZKY, M., Art Education
WINZEN, A., Art Education
ZIMMERMANN, C., Cultural History and Media History

Faculty of Philosophy II: Language, Literature and Cultural Studies (tel. (681) 302-3360; fax (681) 302-4535; e-mail g.braun@pfdek.uni-sb.de):

ALBERT, M., Romance Philology
BARRY, W. J., Phonetics, Phonology
BÉHAR, P., German for Francophones
BEM, J., Romance Philology
CROCKER, M., Psycholinguistics
DEMSKE, U., German Linguistics
ENGEL, M., German Language and Literature
GERZYMISCH-ARBOGAST, H., English Translation
GHOSH-SCHELLHORN, M., English Philology
GIL ARROYO, A., Translation Studies, Romance Languages
GÖTZE, L., German as a Foreign Language
HALLER, J., Mechanical Transmission
HAUBRICHS, W., Medieval German Literature
KLEINERT, S., Romance Philology
LOHMEIER, A.-M., Modern German Philology and Literature
LÜSEBRINK, H.-J., Romance Civilization, Intercultural Communication
MARTENS, K., English Philology, American Literature
MARTI, R., Slavonic Philology
NORRICK, N., English Philology, Linguistics
OSTER-STIERLE, P., French Literature
PINKAL, M., Computer Languages
SAUDER, G., Modern German Philology and Literature
SCHMELING, M., General and Comparative Literature
SCHWEICKARD, W., Romance Philology
SPRAUL, H., Russian
STEINER, E., English Linguistics and Translation
USZKOREIT, H., Computer Linguistics

Faculty of Philosophy III: Empirical Humanities (tel. (681) 302-3700; fax (681) 302-2953; e-mail s.mersdorf@pfdek.uni-sb.de; internet www.uni-saarland.de/fak5):

ASCHERSLEBEN, G., Developmental Psychology
BRÜCHER, W., Geography
BRÜNKEN, R., Education Science
EMRICH, E., Kinesiology and Exercise Science
HERZMANN, P., Education Science
KERKOFF, G., Clinical Neuropsychology
KRAUSE, R., Psychology
KUBINIOK, J., Physical Geography
LÖFFLER, E. W., Physical Geography
MAXEINER, J., Education
SPINATH, F., Differential Psychology and Diagnostics
STARK, R., Personal Development and Education
STOCKMANN, R., Sociology
WASSMUND, H., Political Science
WENTURA, D., General Psychology and Methodology
WINTERHOFF-SPURK, P., Psychology
WINTERMANTEL, M., Social Psychology
WYDRA, G., Sports Education
ZIMMERMANN, H. H., Information Science

UNIVERSITÄT DUISBURG-ESSEN

Campus Duisburg, Forsthausweg 2, 47057 Duisburg
Telephone: (203) 379-0

Fax: (203) 379-3333
E-mail: pressestelle@uni-due.de*Campus Essen*, Universitätsstr. 2, 45117 Essen
Telephone: (201) 183-1
Fax: (201) 183-2151
E-mail: pressestelle@uni-due.de
Internet: www.uni-duisburg-essen.de

Founded 2003 by merger of Gerhard-Mercator-Universität Duisburg (f. 1972) and Universität-Gesamthochschule-Essen (f. 1972)

Academic year: October to September (two semesters)

Rector: Prof. Dr LOTHAR ZECHLIN
Chancellor: Dr RAINER AMBROSY
Librarians: SIGURD PRAETORIUS (Duisburg), ALBERT BILO (Essen)

Library of 2,600,000 vols
Number of teachers: 2,333
Number of students: 33,166

Publications: *Essener Unikate* (2 a year), *Forschungsbericht* (every 2 years), *Forum Forschung* (1 a year), *Results of Mathematics* (4 a year)

DEANS

Faculty of Art and Design: Prof. Dr KURT MEHNERT
Faculty of Biology and Geography: Prof. Dr ULRICH SCHREIBER
Faculty of Business Economics: Prof. Dr PETER CHAMONI
Faculty of Business Studies: Prof. Dr HENDRIK SCHRÖDER
Faculty of Chemistry: Prof. Dr ELKE SUMFLETH
Faculty of Construction Science: Prof. Dr RENATUS WIDMANN
Faculty of Education Sciences: Prof. Dr HORST BOSSONG
Faculty of Engineering Sciences: Prof. Dr ANDRÉS KECSKEMÉTHY
Faculty of Humanities: Prof. Dr ERHARD RECKWITZ
Faculty of Mathematics: Prof. Dr WERNER HAUßMANN
Faculty of Medicine and University Clinic: Prof. Dr KARL-HEINZ JÖCKEL
Faculty of Physics: Prof. Dr ROLF MÖLLER
Faculty of Social Sciences: Prof. Dr GERHARD BÄCKER

ATTACHED RESEARCH INSTITUTES

Deutsches Textilforschungszentrum Nord-West eV: Dir Prof. Dr ECKHARD SCHOLLMEYER.

Deutsch-Französisches Institut für Automation und Robotik (IAR): Speaker Prof. Dr-Ing. STEVEN X. DING.

Entwicklungszentrum für Schiffstechnik und Transportsysteme eV: Dir Prof. Dr P. ENGELKAMP.

Essener Kolleg für Geschlechterforschung: Dir Prof. Dr DORIS JANSHEN.

Forschungsinstitut für wirtschaftliche Entwicklungen im Pazifikraum eV (FIP): Dir Prof. Dr GÜNTER HEIDUK.

Foundation Centre of Turkish Studies: internet www.zft-online.de; Dir Prof. Dr FARUK SEN.

Institut für Energie- und Umwelttechnik eV (IUTA): internet www.iuta.de; Dir Prof. Dr K. G. SCHMIDT.

Institut für Experimentelle Mathematik (IEM): internet www.exp-math.uni-essen.de; Dir Prof. Dr H. VINCK.

Institut für Mobil- und Satellitenfunktechnik GmbH (IMST GmbH): internet www.imst.de; Dirs Prof. Dr-Ing. INGO WOLFF, Dr-Ing. PETER WALDOW.

Instituts für niederrheinische Kultur-geschichte und Regionalenwicklung: Dir Prof. Dr DIETER GEUENICH.

Institut für Prävention und Gesundheitsförderung: internet www .ipg-uni-essen.de; Dir Dr ALFONS SCHRÖER.

IWW Rheinisch-Westfälisches Institut für Wasserforschung gemeinnützige GmbH: internet www.iww-online.de; Dirs Dr-Ing. WOLF MERKEL, KLAUS-DIETER NEUMANN.

Rhein-Ruhr-Institut für Sozialforschung und Politikberatung eV (RISP): internet www.risp-duisburg.de; applied regional socio-economic research; promotes communication and co-operation between the academic world and public and private sector institutions in the Ruhrgebiet; Dir Prof Dr HERIBERT SCHATZ.

Salomon Ludwig Steinheim Institut für deutsch-jüdische Geschichte eV (StI): internet sti1.uni-duisburg.de; research and adult education on Jewish history in Germany from the Renaissance to the present; Dir Prof. Dr MICHAEL BROCKE.

UNIVERSITÄT HAMBURG

Edmund-Siemers-Allee 1, 20146 Hamburg

Telephone: (40) 42838-0
Fax: (40) 42838-2449
E-mail: presse@rrz.uni-hamburg.de
Internet: www.uni-hamburg.de

Founded 1919
State control
Academic year: October to July

President: Dr Dr h.c. JÜRGEN LUTHJE
Vice-Presidents: Prof. Dr HOLGER FISCHER, Prof. Dr KARL-WERNER HANSMANN
Chief Administrative Officer: MANFRED NETTEKOVEN
Director for International Affairs: Dr JOCHEN HELLMANN
State and University Librarian: Prof. Dr PETER RAU

Number of teachers: 3,172
Number of students: 40,996

DEANS

Department of Biology: Prof. Dr ARNO FRÜHWALD
Department of Chemistry: Prof. Dr JOACHIM THIEM
Department of Computer Science: Prof. Dr H. SIEGFRIED STIEHL
Department of Cultural History and Cultural Science: Prof. Dr BRUNO REUDENBACH
Department of Earth Sciences: Prof. Dr HELMUT SCHLEICHER
Department of Economic Sciences: Prof. Dr LOTHAR STREITFERDT
Department of Education: Prof. Dr KARL-DIETER SCHUCK
Department of History and Philosophy: Prof. Dr JÜRGEN SARNOWSKY
Department of Language, Literature and Media Studies: Prof. Dr KNUT HICKETHIER
Department of Law: Prof. Dr KARL-HEINZ LADEUR
Department of Mathematics: Prof. Dr ALEXANDER KREUZER
Department of Medicine: Prof. Dr CHRISTOPH WAGENER
Department of Oriental Studies and Asia–Africa Institute: Prof. Dr RAINER CARLE
Department of Physical Education: Prof. Dr K. MICHAEL BRAUMANN
Department of Physics: Prof. Dr GÜNTER HUBER
Department of Protestant Theology: Prof. Dr STEFAN TIMM
Department of Psychology: Prof. Dr BERNHARD DAHME

Department of Social Sciences: Prof. Dr MICHAEL GREVEN

PROFESSORS

Department of Biology (Allende-Platz 2, 20146 Hamburg; tel. (40) 42838-0; fax (40) 42838-7025):

ABRAHAM, R., Entomology
ADAM, G., Phytopathology
BAUCH, J., Timber Biology
BEUSMANN, V., Biotechnics, Society and Environment
BOCK, E., General Microbiology
BÖTTGER, M., General Botany
BRANDT, A., Zoology
BRETTING, H., Zoology
BUCHHOLZ, F.
CHOPRA, V., Anthropology
DREYLING, G., Applied Botany
ECKSTEIN, D., Timber Biology
FLEISCHER, A., Work Science
FORTNAGEL, P., Botany
FRÜHWALD, A., Mechanical Processing of Timber
GANZHORN, J., Zoology
GEWECKE, M., Zoology, Animal Physiology
GIERE, O., Zoology
GRIMM, R., Zoology
HAHN, H., Zoology, Ecology
HARTMANN, H., Systematic Botany
HEINZ, E., Botany
HEUVELDOP, J., International Forest Management
JÜRGENS, N., Biological Systems, Plant Evolution
KAUSCH, H., Hydrobiology
KIES, L., General Botany
KRISTEN, U., General Botany
LIEBEREI, R., Phytopathology
LÖRZ, H., Applied Plant Molecular Biology
MANTAU, U., Economics of Forestry
MERGENHAGEN, D., Cell Biology
MÜHLBACH, H.-P., Molecular Genetics
PARZEFALL, J., Zoology
PATT, R., Chemical Timber Technology
PRATJE, E., General Botany
REISE, K., Heligoland Biological Institute
RENWRANTZ, L., Zoology
RESSEL, J., Wood Physics
RODEWALD, A., Anthropology and Human Genetics
SCHÄFER, W., Biology
SCHURIG, V.
STAHL-BISKUP, E., Pharmaceutical Biology
TEMMING, A., Fisheries Sciences
WEBER, A., General Botany
WIENAND, U., General Botany
WIESE, K., Neurophysiology
WILKENS, H., Zoology
ZEISKE, E., Zoology

Department of Chemistry (Martin-Luther-King-Platz 6, 20146 Hamburg; tel. (40) 42838-0; fax (40) 42838-2893):

BASLER, W. D.
BEIER, U., Home Economics
BENNDORF, C., Physical Chemistry
BISPING, B., Food Microbiology and Hygiene
BREDEHORST, R., Biochemistry
DEPPERT, W., Molecular Biochemistry
DUCHSTEIN, H.-J., Pharmaceutical Chemistry
FÖRSTER, S., Physical and Macromolecular Chemistry
FRANCKE, W., Organic Chemistry
GEFFKEN, D., Pharmaceutical Chemistry
HECK, J., Inorganic Chemistry
HEISIG, P., Pharmaceutical Biology, Microbiology
KAMINSKY, W., Inorganic Chemistry
KERSCHER, M., Personal Hygiene
KÖNIG, W., Organic Chemistry
KRAMOLOWSKY, R., Inorganic Chemistry
KRICHELDORF, H., Applied Chemistry
KULICKE, W., Technical Chemistry

LECHERT, H., Physical Chemistry
MARGARETHA, P., Organic Chemistry
MEIER, C., Organic Chemistry
MEYER, B., Organic Chemistry
MIELCK, J., Pharmaceutical Technology
MORITZ, H.-U., Technical and Macromolecular Chemistry
MÜHLHAUSER, I., Health
REHDER, D., Inorganic Chemistry
STAHL-BISKUP, E., Pharmaceutical Biology
STEINHART, J., Food Chemistry
THIEM, J., Organic Chemistry
THORN, E., Technical and Macromolecular Chemistry
WELLER, H., Electrochemistry

Department of Computer Science (Vogt-Kölln-Straße 30, 22527 Hamburg; tel. (40) 42883-0; fax (40) 42838-2206):

BRUNNSTEIN, K., Computer Applications
DRESCHLER-FISCHER, L., Cognitive Systems
FLOYD, C., Software Technics
FREKSA, C.
HABEL, C., Information and Documentation
JANTZEN, M., Computer Theory
KAISER, K., Computer Applications
KUDLEK, M., Computer Theory
LAMERSDORF, W., Technical Basics of Computer Science
MENZEL, W.
MERTSCHING, B.
MÖLLER, D.
NEUMANN, B., Cognitive Systems
OBERQUELLE, H., Computer Theory
PAGE, B., Computer Applications
ROLF, A., Computer Theory
SCHEFE, P., Computer Applications
STIEHL, H.-S., Cognitive Systems
VALK, R., Computer Theory
VON HAHN, W., Natural Language Systems
VON DER HEIDE, K., Technical Basics of Computer Science
WOLFINGER, B., Computer Organization
ZÜLLIGHOVEN, H.

Department of Cultural History and Cultural Science (Rothenbaumchaussee 67/69, 20148 Hamburg; tel. (40) 42838-4051; fax (40) 42838-6530):

ALTENMÜLLER, H., Egyptology
DÖMLING, W., Music
FEHR, B., Classical Archaeology
GREEVE, B., Music
HENGAUTNER, T., Folklore
HIPP, H., History of Art
KEMP, W., Art History
KOKOT, W., Ethnology
KURTH, D., Egyptology
LANG, H., Ethnology
LEHMANN, A., German Archaeology and Folklore
MISCHUNG, B., Ethnology
NIELSEN, I., Classical Archaeology
PETERSEN, P., Musicology
REUDENBACH, B., Art History
ROLLE, R., Prehistory of Europe
RÖSING, H., Systematic Music
SCHNEIDER, A., Systematic Music
SMAILUS, O., Ancient American Languages and Culture
WAGNER, M., Art History
WARNKE, M., History of Art

Department of Earth Sciences (Bundestraße 55, 20146 Hamburg; tel. (40) 42838-5230; fax (40) 42838-5270):

BACKHAUS, J., Oceanography
BANDEL, K., Palaeontology and Historic Geology
BETZLER, C., Geology
BISMAYER, U., Mineralogy, Crystallography
BRÜMMER, B., Meteorology
DAHM, T.
FRAEDRICH, K., Meteorology
GAJEWSKI, D., Geophysics
GRASSL, H., Meteorology

GRIMMEL, E., Geography
GUSE, W., Mineralogy
HILLMER, G., Geology and Palaeontology
JASCHKE, D., Geography
LAFRENZ, J., Geography
LEUPOLT, B., Geography
MAKRIS, J., Geophysics
MEINCKE, J., Regional Oceanography
MICHAELIS, W., Organic Geochemistry
MIEHLICH, G., Soil Science
NAGEL, F. N., Geography
OSSENBRÜGGE, J., Geography
POHL, D., Mineralogy
RASCHKE, E., Meteorology
REUTHER, C.-D., Geology
ROSSMANITH, E., Mineralogy
SCHATZMANN, M., Meteorology
SCHLEICHER, H., Mineralogy, Petrography
SCHWARZ, R., Geography
SPAETH, CH., Geology and Palaeontology
SPIELMANN, H.-O., Geography
SÜNDERMANN, J., Oceanography
TARKIAN, M., Mineralogy
THANNHEISER, D., Geography
TIETZ, G. F., Sedimentary Petrography
TOL, R. S., Sustaining the Environment
VINX, R., Mineralogy
WONG, H. K., Geology
ZAHEL, W., Oceanography

Department of Economic Sciences (Von-Melle-Park 5, 20146 Hamburg; tel. (40) 42838-0; fax (40) 42838-6322):

ADAMS, M., Economic Law
ALTROGGE, G., Business Administration
ARNOLD, B., National Economy
CZERANOWSKY, G., Business Administration
ENGELHARDT, G., National Economy
FREIDANK, C.-C., Business Administration, Auditing Taxation
FUNKE, M., National Economy
GROTHERR, S., Business Administration
HANSEN, K., Business Administration
HANSMANN, K.-W., Business Administration
HASENKAMP, G., National Economy
HAUTAU, H., National Economy
HESBERG, D.
HOFMANN, H., National Economy
HOLLER, M., National Economy
HUMMELTENBERG, W., Business Administration
KRAUSE-JUNG, G., International Finance
KÜPPER, W., Business Administration
LAYER, M., Business Administration
LORENZEN, G., National Economy
LUCKE, B., National Economy
MAENNIG, W., National Economy
NELL, M., Insurance
PFÄHLER, W., National Economy
PRESSMAR, D., Business Administration
REITSPERGER, W. D., Business Administration
RIETER, H., National Economy
RINGLE, G., Business Administration
SATTLER, H., Business Administration
SCHÄFER, H.-B., National Economy
SCHEER, C., Finance
SCHLITTGEN, R., National Economy, Statistics
SCHMIDT, H., Business Administration
SEELBACH, H., Business Administration
STAHLECKER, H.-P., National Economy, Statistics
STOBER, R., Economic Law
STRAUBHAAR, T.
STREITFERDT, L., Business Administration
TIMMERMANN, V., National Economy
TOL, R. (Endowed Chair, Sustaining the Environment)
VON OEHSEN, J. H., Finance
WEGSCHEIDER, K., National Economy, Statistics

Department of Education (Von-Melle-Park 8, 20146 Hamburg; tel. (40) 42838-0; fax (40) 42838-2112):

AUFENANGER, S.
BASTIAN, J.
BECK, I.
BOLLMANN, H.
BOS, W.
BRAND, W.
BRUSCH, W.
BÜRGER, W.
BUTH, M.
CLAUSEN, B.
COMBE, A.
DECKE-CORNILL, H.
DEGENHART, S.
DEHN, M.
DUISMANN, G.
EHNI, H. W.
FAULSTICH, P.
FAULSTICH-WIELAND, H.
FIEDLER, U.
FILIPP, K.
GEBHARD, U.
GOGOLIN, I.
GRAMMES, T.
GRENZ, D.
GUDJONS, H.
GÜNTHER, K.-R.
HARTER-MEYER, R.
HARTMANN, W.
HEMMER, K.
HOFSÄSS, T.
JUNG, H. W.
KAISER, G.
KAISER, H.-J.
KIPP, M.
KLEIN, P.
KOKEMOHR, R.
KOLLER, H.-C.
KRAUTHAUSEN, G.
KRETSCHMER, J.
KÜNNE, W.
LECKE, B.
LEGLER, W.
LOHMANN, I.
MARTENS, E.
MAYER, C.
MEYER, H.
MEYER, M.
MIELKE, R.
MITCHELL, G.
NEUMANN, U.
NEVERS, P.
NOLTE, M.
OPASCHOWSKI, H.
PAZZINI, K.-J.
PETERSEN, J.
RAUER, W.
RENZELBERG, G.
RICHTER, H.
ROTHWEILER, M.
SCARBATH, H.
SCHÄFER, H.-P.
SCHENK, B.
SCHERLER, K.
SCHREIER, H.
SCHUCK, K. D.
SEYD, W.
SPRETH, G.
STRUCK, P.
STRUVE, K.
STÜTZ, G.
TENFELDE, W.
TRAMM, T.
VOLLMER, T.
VON BORRIES, B.
WAGNER, A.
WALLRABENSTEIN, W.
WARZECHA, B.
WEICHERT, W.
WEISSE, W.
WELLING, A.
WILLENBERG, H.
WIMMER, K.-M.

WOCKEN, H.
WUDTKE, H.
ZIMPEL, A.

Department of History and Philosophy (Rothenbaumchaussee 67/69, 20148 Hamburg; tel. (40) 42838-4049; fax (40) 42838-6333):

ANGERMANN, N., Medieval and Modern History
BARTUSCHAT, W., Philosophy
CLEMENS, G., Modern European History (Western European Integration)
DEININGER, J., Ancient History
DIEDERICH, W., Philosophy
DINGEL, J., Classical Philology
EIDENEIER, H., Byzantine and Modern Greek Philology
FINZSCH, N., Modern and North American History
FREDE, D., Philosophy
GÄHDE, U., Philosophy
GALL, D., Classical Philology
GOETZ, H.-W., Medieval and Modern History
GOLCZEWSKI, F., Eastern European History
HALFMANN, H., Ancient History
HARLFINGER, D., Classical Philology
HERGEMÖLLER, B.-U., Medieval History
HERZIG, A., Modern History
KÜNNE, W., Philosophy
MEJCHER, H., Modern History
MOLTHAGEN, J., Ancient History
PIETSCHMANN, H., Modern History
RECKI, B., Philosophy
SARNOWSKY, V., Medieval History
STEINVORTH, U., Philosophy
VOGEL, B., Modern History

Department of Language, Literature and Media Studies (Rothenbaumchaussee 67/69, 20148 Hamburg; tel. (40) 42838-0; fax (40) 42838-5977):

BERG, T., English Linguistics
BLESSIN, S., German Literature, German as a Foreign Language
BÖRNER, W., Linguistics
BRAUNMÜLLER, K., Germanic Philology
BRINKER, K., German Linguistics
BUNGARTEN, T., German Linguistics
CORTHALS, J., Comparative Language Studies
DAMMANN, G., German Literature
DIEWALD, G., German Linguistics
EDMONDSON, W., Language Instruction Research
FISCHER, L., German Literature
FISCHER, R., German Sign Language
FREYTAG, H., German Philology
FREYTAG, W., German Literature
FRIEDL, B., American Studies
GREINER, N., English Literature
GUTJAHR, O., Modern German Literature
GUTKNECHT, C., English Language
HABEL, C., Language Processing
HARTENSTEIN, K., Russian
HASEBRINK, E., Empirical Communications Science
HELIMEKI, E., Finno-Ugrian Philology
HENKEL, N., German Philology
HENNIG, J., German Linguistics
HICKETHIER, K., German Literature
HILL, P., Slavonic Philology
HODEL, R., Slavonic Philology
HOTTENROTH, P.-M., French and Italian Linguistics
HOUSE, J., Language Instruction Research
HÜHN, P., English Philology
IBANEZ, R., Hispanic Linguistics
KÖSTER, U., German Literature
LATOUR, B., German as a Foreign Language
LEHMANN, V., Language Instruction Research
LLEO, C., Hispanic Linguistics
MEIER, J., German Linguistics
MEISEL, J. M., Romance Philology

MEYER, W., Romance Philology
MEYER-ALTHOFF, M.
MEYER-MINNEMANN, K., Romance Philology
MÜLLER, H.-H., German Literature
NEUMANN, M., Romance Philology
PANTHER, K.-U., English Linguistics
PÉTURSSON, M., General Applied Phonetics
PRESCH, G., German Linguistics
PRILLWITZ, S., German Linguistics
REHBEIN, J., German Linguistics, German as a Foreign Language
REICHARDT, D., Romance Philology
REINITZER, H., German Literature
RODENBURG, H.-P., American Studies
SAGER, S., German Linguistics
SCHLUMBOHM, D., Romance Philology
SCHMID, W., Slavonic Literature
SCHMIDT, J., English Philology
SCHMIDT-KNÄBEL, S., German Linguistics
SCHÖBERL, J., German Literature
SCHÖNERT, J., German Literature
SCHÖPP, J. K., American Studies
SCHULLER, M., German Literature
SCHULMEISTER, R., Higher School Didactics
SCHULTZE, B., English Philology
SEGEBERG, H., German Literature
SETTEKORN, W., French
TERNES, E., Phonetics
TRAPP, F., Modern German Literature
VINKEN, B., Romance Philology
VOIGT, B., Spanish
VON HAHN, W., Natural Language Systems
WERGIN, U., Modern German Literature
WINTER, H.-G., German Literature
WITTSCHIER, H. W., Romance Philology

Department of Law (Rothenbaumchaussee 41, 20148 Hamburg; tel. (40) 42838-0; fax (40) 42838-6352):

BEHRENS, P., Civil, Commercial and International Private Law
BORK, R., Civil, Commercial, Economic and International Private Law
BRUHA, T., Public, European and International Law
BULL, H. P., Constitutional and Administrative Law
FELIX, D., Public and Social Law
FEZER, G., Criminal Law
FROTSCHER, G., International Financial and Taxation Law
GIEHRING, H., Criminal Law
HAAG, F., Sociology
HANSEN, U., Criminal Law
HILF, M., Public, European and International Law
HIRTE, H., Public, Commercial and Business Law
HOFFMAN-RIEM, W., Public, Administrative, Revenue and Tax, and Economic Law
JACHMANN, M., Public, Financial and Taxation Law
JOOST, D., Civil and Labour Law
KARPEN, U., Public Law
KELLER, R., Criminal Law
KOCH, H.-J., Public Law, Philosophy of Law
KÖHLER, M., Criminal Law, Philosophy of Law
KRIECHBAUM, M., Roman Law
LADEUR, K.-H., Public Law
LAGONI, R., Public, Maritime, International and Constitutional Law
LUCHTERHANDT, O., Public and Eastern Law
LÜDICKE, J., International Financial and Taxation Law
MAGNUS, U., Civil Law
MANKOWSKI, P., Civil, Comparative and International Private and Procedural Law
MARTENS, K. P., Civil, Labour and Commercial Law
MERKEL, R., Criminal Law, Philosophy of Law

MORITZ, K., Civil and Labour Law, Sociology of Law
OETER, S., Public, International and European Law
OTT, C., Sociology of Law, Civil, Commercial and Company, and Economic Law
PASCHKE, M., Civil, Commercial and Economic Law
PFARR, H., Civil and Labour Law
RAMSAUER, U., Public Law
RANDZIO, R., Civil Law
RITTSTIEG, H., Public Law
SCHÄFER, H.-B., National Economy
SCHEERER, S., Criminology
SCHWABE, J., Public Law
SESSAR, K., Criminology and Juvenile Criminal Law
SONNEN, B.-R., Criminal Law
STOBER, R., Economic Law
STRUCK, G., Civil Law
VILLMOW, B., Criminology
WALZ, R., Commercial, Economic, Civil and Tax Law
WERBER, M., Civil and Insurance Law

Department of Mathematics (Bundesstraße 55, 20146 Hamburg; tel. (40) 42838-4106; fax (40) 42838-4927):

ANDREAE, T.
BANDELT, H.-J.
BÄR, C.
BERNDT, R.
BRÜCKNER, H.
DADUNA, H.
DIESTEL, R.
ECKHARDT, U.
GEIGER, C.
HASS, H.
HOFMANN, W. D.
HÜBNER, G.
HÜNEMÖRDER, C.
KRÄMER, H.
KREMER, E.
KREUZER, A.
LAUTERBACH
MICHALICEK, J.
MÜLLER, H.
NEUHAUS, G.
OBERLE, H. J.
ORTLIEB, C.
REICH, K.
RIEMENSCHNEIDER, O.
SCHRÖDER, E.
SEIER, W.
STRADE, H.
STRUCKMEIER, J.
TAUBERT, K.
WERNER, B.
WOLFSCHMIDT, G.

Department of Medicine (Universitätsklinikum Hamburg-Eppendorf, Martinistr. 52, 20246 Hamburg; tel. (40) 42803-0; fax (40) 42803-6752):

ADAM, G., X-ray Diagnosis
AGARWAL, D., Human Genetics
ALBERTI, W., Radiotherapy
BAISCH, H., Biophysics
BAUR, X., Industrial Medicine
BECK, H., Anaesthesiology
BEIL, F. U., Internal Medicine
BEISIEGEL, U., Biochemistry
BENTELE, K., Paediatrics
BERGER, J., Mathematics and Computer Applications of Medicine
BERGER, M., Child Psychology
BERNER, W., Psychiatry
BÖGER, R., Clinical Pharmacology
BOHUSLAVIZKI, H., Nuclear Medicine
BRAENDLE, L.-W., Gynaecology and Obstetrics
BRAULKE, T., Pathophysiology and Molecular Biological Genetic Health
BRAUMANN, K.-M., Internal-Physiological Sports Medicine
BROMM, B., Physiology
BULLINGER, M., Medical Psychology

BURDELSKI, M., Paediatrics
BUSSCHE, H. VAN DEN, Didactics
CLAUSEN, M., Nuclear Medicine
DALLEK, M., Surgery, Accident Surgery
DAVIDOFF, M., Anatomy
DELLING, G., General Pathology and Pathological Anatomy
DENEKE, F.-W., Psychosomatic Medicine
DÖRING, V., Surgery
DRIESCH, P., Dermatology and Venereology
EHMKE, H., Physiology
EIERMANN, T., Transfusion Medicine
ENGELMANN, K., Ophthalmology
FEUCHT, H.-H., Medical Microbiology and Immunology
FIEDLER, W., Internal Medicine
FLEISCHER, B., Immunology, Virology
GAL, A., Medical Genetics
GÖTZE, P., Psychiatry
GRETEN, H., Internal Medicine
HALATA, Z., Anatomy
HAND, I., Psychiatry
HEGEWISCHE-BECKER, S., Internal Medicine
HELLWEGE, H., Paediatrics
HELMCHEN, U., Pathology
HESS, M., Otorhinolaryngology
HÖHNE, K.-H., Information and Data Processing in Medicine
HÖLTJE, W.-J., Maxillary Surgery
HORSTMANN, R., Internal Medicine
HOSSFELD, D., Internal Medicine
HÜBENER, K.-H., Radiology
HULAND, H., Urology
HUNEKE, A., Gynaecology and Obstetrics
IZBICKI, J., Surgery
JÄNICKE, F. K.-H., Gynaecology and Obstetrics
JANKE-SCHAUB, G., Paediatrics
JENTSCH, T., Cell Biology
JÜDE, H. D., Dental Medicine
JUNG, H., Biophysics and Radiobiology
KAHL-NIEKE, B., Orthodontics
KAULFERS, P.-M., Medical Microbiology
KAUPEN-HAAS, H., Medical Sociology
KOCH, U., Otorhinolaryngology
KOCH-GROMUS, U., Medical Psychology
KOHLSCHÜTTER, A., Paediatrics
KOLLEK, R., Biotechnology
KORTH, M., Pharmacology
KRAUSZ, M., Psychiatry
KREYMANN, K. G., Internal Medicine
KRUPPA, J., Physiological Chemistry
KRUSE, H.-P., Internal Medicine
KÜHNL, P., Transfusions, Immuno-Haematology
LAMBRECHT, W., Surgery
LAUFS, R., Medical Microbiology and Immunology
LEICHTWEISS, H.-P., Physiology
LEUWER, R., Otorhinolaryngology
LOCKEMANN, U., Legal Medicine
LÖNING, T., General Pathology, Pathological Anatomy
MACK, D., Medical Microbiology, Infection Epidemiology and Hospital Hygiene
MANGOLD, U., Anatomy
MARQUARDT, H., General Toxicology
MAYR, G. W., Physiological Chemistry
MEINERTZ, T., Cardiology
MESTER, J., Nuclear Medicine
MOLL, I., Dermatology, Venereology
MÜHLHAUSER, I., Health
MÜLLER, D., Neurosurgery
MÜLLER-WIEFEL, D. E., Internal Medicine
MUNZEL, T., Internal Medicine
NABER, D., Psychiatry
NEUBER, K., Dermatology and Venereology
NEUMAIER, M., Clinical Chemistry
NOLDUS, J., Neurology
PANTEL, K., Molecular Genetics in Gynaecological Ontomology
PAUS, R., Dermatology and Venereology
PFEIFFER, E., Hygiene
PFEIFFER, G., Neurology
PFORTE, A., Internal Medicine
PLATZER, U., Dentistry

PONGS, O., Neurology
PÜSCHEL, U., Forensic Medicine
RICHARD, G., Ophthalmology
RICHTER, D., Physiological Chemistry
RICHTER, R., Medical Psychology, Psychosomatics
RIEDESSER, P., Paediatric Psychology
ROGIERS, X., Surgery
ROTHER, U., Radiological Diagnostics on Dental Medicine
RUDAT, T., Radiotherapy
RUEGER, J. M., Accident Surgery
RUMBERGER, E., Physiology
RUTHER, K., Ophthalmology
RUTHER, W., Orthopaedics
SCHACHNER CAMARTIN, M., Neurobiology
SCHÄFER, H., General Pathology and Pathological Anatomy
SCHALLER, C., Neurobiology
SCHIFFNER, U., Dental Medicine
SCHMALE, H., Biochemistry
SCHMELZLE, R., Dental Medicine
SCHMIDT, G., Sexology
SCHMOLDT, A., Forensic Medicine
SCHNEPPENHEIM, R., Paediatric Haematology and Oncology
SCHOLZ, H., Pharmacology and Toxicology
SCHRÖDER, H. J., Physiology
SCHULTE AM ESCH, J., Anaesthesiology
SCHULTE-MARKWORT, M., Child and Youth Psychiatry
SCHULZE, C., Anatomy
SCHULZE, W., Anatomy
SCHUMACHER, U., Anatomy
SCHWARZ, J., Physiology
SCHWORM, H. D., Ophthalmology
SEITZ, H.-J., Physiological Chemistry
SOEHENDRA, N., Surgery
STAHL, R., Internal Medicine
STANDL, T., Anaesthesiology
STAVROU, D., Neuropathology
STEINER, P., Radiology
STRÄTLING, W., Physiological Chemistry
TANNICH, E., Molecular Parasitology
THAISS, F., Internal Medicine
TROJAN, A., Social Medicine
ULLRICH, K. H. O., Paediatrics
UBMULLER, J., Otorhinolaryngology
VONDERLAGE, M., Physiology
WAGENER, C., Clinical Chemistry
WEIL, J., Paediatric Cardiology
WEILLER, C., Neurology
WESTENDORF, J., Toxicology, Pharmacology
WIEDEMANN, K. B., Biological Psychiatry
WIELAND, T., Pharmacology
WILL, H. K., Microbiology
WILLIG, R. P., Paediatrics
WINDLER, E., Internal Medicine
WINTERPACHT, A., Human Genetics
ZANDER, A., Bone Marrow Transplantation
ZEUMER, H., Neuroradiology
ZYWIETE, F., Biophysics, Radiobiology

Department of Oriental Studies and Asia–Africa Institute (Rothenbaumchaussee 67/69, 20148 Hamburg; tel. (40) 42838-4054; fax (40) 42838-6530; e-mail aai@uni-hamburg.de):

CARLE, R., Indonesian and South Seas Languages
CONRAD, L., Islamic Sciences
EBERSTEIN, B., Sinology
EMMERICK, R., Iranian Studies
FRIEDRICH, M., Sinology
GERHARDT, L., African Languages and Cultures
JACKSON, D., Tibetology
KAPPERT, P., Turkish Studies
ORANSKAIA, T., Indic Studies
POHL, M., Japanese Politics
REH, M., African Languages and Cultures
ROTTER, G., Islamic Studies
SASSE, W., Chinese
SCHMITHAUSEN, L., Indology
SCHNEIDER, R., Japanese
STUMPFELDT, H., Sinology

TERWIEL, B., Thai Language and Culture
UHLIG, S., African Languages and Cultures
WEZLER, A., Indology

Department of Physical Education (Mollerstraße 10, 20148 Hanburg; tel. (40) 42838-2474; fax (40) 42838-5666):

BRAUMANN, K.-M.
EICHLER, G.
FUNKE-WIENEKE, J.
LANGE-AMELSBERG, J.
NIEDLICH, H.-D.
STRIPP, K.
TIEDEMANN, C.
TIWALD, H.
WEINBERG, P.

Department of Physics (Dammtorstraße 12, 2 stock, 20354 Hamburg; tel. (40) 42838-4056; fax (40) 42838-6233):

BARTELS, J., Theoretical Physics
BLOBEL, V., Experimental Physics
BÜSSER, F.-W., Experimental Physics
FAY, D., Theoretical Physics
FREDENHAGEN, K., Theoretical Physics
GERAMB, H. V. VON, Theoretical Physics
HANSEN, W., Experimental Physics
HEINZELMANN, G., Experimental Physics
HEITMANN, D., Applied Physics
HEMMERICH, A., Experimental Physics
HEUER, R.-D., Elementary Particle Physics
HEYSZENAU, H., Theoretical Physics
HUBER, G., Experimental Physics
JOHNSON, R., Experimental Physics
KLANNER, R., Experimental Physics
KÖTZLER, J., Applied Physics
KRAMER, B., Theoretical Physics
MACK, G., Theoretical Physics
MERKT, U., Experimental Physics
NAROSKA, B., Experimental Physics
NEUHAUSER, W., Experimental Physics
OEPEN, H. P., Experimental Physics
PFANNKUCHE, D., Theoretical Physics
REIMERS, D., Astronomy
SCHARNBERG, K., Theoretical Physics
SCHMIDT-PARZEFALL, W., Experimental Physics
SCHMITT, J., Astronomy
SCHMÜSER, P., Experimental Physics
SCOBEL, W., Experimental Physics
SENGSTOCK, K., Experimantal Physics
SONNTAG, B., Experimental Physics
SPITZER, H., Fundamental Physics
WAGNER, A., Elementary Particle Physics
WENDKER, H., Astronomy
WICK, K., Experimental Physics
WIESENDANGER, R., Experimental Physics
WURTH, W., Experimental Physics
ZIMMERER, G., Experimental Physics

Department of Protestant Theology (Sedanstr. 19, 20146 Hamburg; tel. (40) 42838-0; fax (40) 42838-4013):

AHRENS, T., Missions
DIERKEN, J., Systematic Theology
GRÜNBERG, W., Practical Theology
GUTMANN, H.-M., Practical Theology
KOCH, T., Systematic Theology
LINDNER, W. V., Practical Theology
LOHR, W., Church and Dogmatic History
MAGER, I., Church History and Dogma
MOXTER, M., Systematic Theology
SCHRAMM, T., New Testament
SCHRÖTER, J., New Testament
SCHUMANN, O., Religious and Missionary Science
SELLIN, G., New Testament
STEIGER, J. A., Church and Dogmatic History
TIMM, S., Old Testament
WILLI-PLEIN, I,, Old Testament

Department of Psychology (Von-Melle-Park 5, 20146 Hamburg; tel. (40) 42838-5460; fax (40) 42838-5492):

BAMBERG, E.
BERBALK, H.
BURISCH, M.

BUSE, L.
DAHME, B.
ECKERT, J.
HEINZE, B.
LANGER, I.
OETTINGEN, G
ORTH, B.
PAWLIK, K.
PROBST, P.
RHENIUS, D.
SCHMIDTCHEN, S.
SCHULZ VON THUN, F.
SCHWAB, R.
TONNIES, S.
VAGT, G.
WITT, H.
WITTE, E.

Department of Social Sciences (Allende-Platz 1, 20146 Hamburg; tel. (40) 42838-0; fax (40) 42838-4506):

EICHNER, K., Sociology
GOERTZ, H.-J., Social and Economic History
GREVEN, M., Political Science
HEINEMANN, K., Sociology
JAKOBEIT, C., Political Science
KAUPEN-HAAS, H.
KLEINSTEUBER, H. J., Political Science
LANDFRIED, C., Political Science
LÜDE, R. VON, Sociology
MILLER, M., Sociology
NEVERLA, I., Journalism, Communications
PIEPER, M., Sociology
RASCHKE, P., Political Science
RENN, H., Sociology
RUNDE, P., Sociology
SCHEERER, S., Criminology
SEBAR, K., Criminology
TETZLAFF, R., Political Science
TROITZSCH, U., Social Sciences
VILLMOW, B., Criminology
WEISCHENBERG, S., Communications Science, Journalism

UNIVERSITÄT HANNOVER

Welfengarten 1, 30167 Hanover
Telephone: (511) 762-0
Fax: (511) 762-3456
E-mail: info@pressestelle.uni-hannover.de
Internet: www.uni-hannover.de

Founded 1831

Pres.: Prof. Dr ERICH BARKE
Vice-Pres: Prof. Dr KLAUS HULEK, Prof. Dr SABINE E. KUNST, GÜNTER SCHOLZ
Library Director: U. ROSEMANN

Number of teachers: 1,272
Number of students: 31,880

DEANS

Department of Architecture and Landscape: Prof. E. ECKERLE
Department of Civil Engineering: Prof. T. SIEFER
Department of Economics: Prof. S. HOMBURG
Department of Electrical Engineering and Information Technology: Prof. P. PIRSCH
Department of Law: Prof. V. EPPING
Department of Mathematics and Physics: Prof. O. LECHTENFELDL
Department of Mechanical Engineering: Prof. F. W. BACH
Department of Natural Sciences: Prof. W. FISCHER
Department of Philosophy: Prof. F. JOHANNSENS

PROFESSORS

Department of Architecture and Landscape (Schlosswender Str. 1, 30159 Hanover; tel. (511) 762-4276; fax (511) 762-2115; e-mail hobert@dek-arch.uni-hannover.de):

BARTH, H. G., Regional Planning
BRAUM, M., Town Planning

BUCHERT, M., History of Art and Construction

DWORSKY, A., Rural Design

ECKERLE, E., Fine Arts

EHRMANN, W., Work Methods and Processing of Wood and Artificial Materials

FRIEDRICH, J., Design and Building Construction

FURCHE, A., Structural Design and Research

FÜRST, D., Regional Planning

GABRIEL, I., Construction and Design

GANZERT, J., History of Art and Construction

GENENGER, H.-G., Architecture

GERKEN, H., Planning Technology

HAAREN, CHR. V., Conservation

HACKER, E., Conservation

KAPPELER, D., Painting and Graphic Arts

KAUP, P., Construction and Design

KENNEDY, M., Resource-saving in Building

LÉON, H., Building Typology and Design Section

LITTMAN, K., Work Methods and Processing of Wood and Artificial Materials

LÖSKEN, G., Open Space Planning and Garden Architecture

OPPERMANN, B., Open Space Planning

PARAVICINI, U., Theory of Architecture

POHL, W.-H., Building Materials Technology

REICH, M., Plant Ecology

SCHMID-KIRSCH, A., Drawing and Computer-Assisted Design

SCHOMERS, M., Design

SCHULTE, K., Industrial Design

SLAWIK, H., Construction and Design

TESSIN, W., Planning-related Sociology

TROJAN, K., Town Planning

TURKALI, Z., Construction and Design

VON SEGGERN, H., Open Space Planning

WEILACHER, U., Landscape Architecture

WÖBSE, H. H., Landscape Aesthetics and Design

WOLSCHKE-BULMAHN, J., Open Space Planning and Garden Architecture

ZIBELL, B., Theory of Architecture

Department of Civil Engineering (Callinstr. 34, Hanover; tel. (511) 762-2447; fax (511) 762-4783; e-mail dekanat@fb-bauing .uni-hannover.de; internet www.fb-bauing .uni-hannover.de):

ACHMUS, M., Foundations, Dams

BILLIB, M., Hydrology

BLÜMEL, W., Foundations, Dams

DAMRATH, R., Applied Informatics

DOEDENS, H., Water Supply

FRIEDRICH, B., Traffic Economics, Highway System, Town Planning

GRÜNBERG, J., Concrete Construction

HOFFMANN, B., Hydrology

HOTHAN, J., Traffic Economics, Highway Systems, Town Planning

IWAN, G., Construction Management

KONECNY, G., Photogrammetry and Engineering Surveying

KUNST, S., Water Supply

LECHER, K., Hydrology

LIERSE, J., Building Construction

LOHAUS, L., Building Materials Science

MARKOFSKY, M., Flow Mechanics

MULL, R., Hydrology

MÜLLER, U., Graduate Centre for Environmentally Relevant Fluxes in Water and Soil

MÜLLER-KIRCHENBAUER, H., Foundations, Dams

NACKENHORST, U., Mechanics and Computational Mechanics

PELZER, H., General Surveying

ROKAHR, R., Statics and Geomechanics

ROSEMEIER, G., Flow Mechanics

ROSENWINKEL, K.-H., Water Supply

ROTHERT, H., Statics

SCHAUMANN, P., Steel Construction

SCHELLING, W., Building Technology

SEEBER, G., Geodesy

SESTER, M., Cartography

SIEFERT, T., Railways and Roads

SIEKER, F., Hydrology

VERWORN, H.-R., Hydrology

WRIGGERS, P., Mechanics and Computational Mechanics

ZIELKE, W., Flow Mechanics

ZIMMERMANN, C., Hydroengineering

Department of Economics (Königsworther Platz 1, 30167 Hanover; tel. (511) 762-5350; fax (511) 762-5665; e-mail heer@mbox.vul .uni-hannover.de; internet www.wiwi .uni-hannover.de):

BREITNER, M. H., Computer Science

FÖRSTER, G., Business Taxation

GEIGANT, F., Money, Credit, Currency

GERLACH, K., Political Economy and Labour Economics

HANSEN, U., Marketing

HASLINGER, F., Economics

HEINEMANN, H.-J., International Economic Relations

HOFMANN, CH., Controlling

HOMBURG, S., Public Economics

HÜBL, L., Economic Policy

HÜBLER, O., Econometrics

JÖHNK, M.-D., Econometrics and Statistics

KIRSCH, H.-J., Economics

LÖFFLER, A., Economics

MENKHOFF, L., Money, Credit, Currency

MEYER, W., Economic Policy

MÜLLER, U., Economic Systems, Anti-Trust Policy and Stabilization

RIDDER, H.-G., Personnel Management

SCHMIDT, U., Economics

SCHULENBURG, J.-M. GRAF VON DER, Insurance

SCHWARZE, J., Computer Science

STEINLE, C., Management Economics

WAIBEL, H., Horticultural Economics

WIEDMANN, K.-P., Marketing

Department of Electrical Engineering and Information Technology (Appelstr. 9A, 30167 Hanover; tel. (511) 762-19645; fax (511) 762-19646; e-mail fbbuero@et.uni-hannover.de; internet www.et.uni-hannover.de):

BARKE, E., Microelectronic Systems

EUL, H., High Frequency Technology

GARBE, H., Basic Electrical Engineering

GERTH, W., Control Technology

GOCKENBACH, E., High Voltage

GRABINSKI, H., Theoretical Electrical Engineering

GRAUL, J., Semiconductor Technology and Materials of Electrical Engineering

HAASE, H., Electrical Engineering

HOFMANN, K., Semiconductor Technology and Materials of Electrical Engineering

JOBMANN, K., General Communications Technology

KUCHENBECKER, H.-P., General Communications Technology

LIEDTKE, C.-E., Theoretical Communications Technology

MARQUARDT, J., High Frequency Technology

MATHIS, W., Theoretical Electrical Engineering

MUCHA, J., Theoretical Electrical Engineering

MÜLLER-SCHLOER, C., Computing Sciences

MUSMANN, H.-G., Theoretical Communications Technology

NACKE, B., Electrical Process Technology

NEJDL, W., Knowledge-based Systems

NESTLER, J., Power Electronics

OSTEN, J., Technology and Materials of Electrical Engineering

OSWALD, B. R., Electricity Supply

PIRSCH, P., Microelectronical Engineering

PONICK, B., Electrical Machines and Drives

SEINSCH, H. O., Electrical Machines and Drives

STÖLTING, H.-D., Electrical Machines and Drives

WAGNER, B., Electrical Systems and Teaching of Electrical Engineering

Department of Law (Königsworther Platz 1, 30167 Hanover; tel. (511) 762-8104; fax (511) 762-8107; e-mail dekanat@jura.rw .uni-hannover.de; internet www.jura .uni-hannover.de):

ABELTSHAUSER, T., Civil Law

BUCK, P., Civil Law

BUTZER, H., Public Law

CALLIESS, R.-P., Criminal Law

DORNDORF, E., Civil Law

EPPING, V., Public Law

FABER, H., Public Law

FENGE, H., Civil Law

FOLZ, H.-E., Public Law

FORGÓ, N., Civil Law

FRANK, J., Economics

HESSE, H. A., Teaching of Law, Sociology of Law

KILIAN, W., Civil Law

KÜHNE, J.-D., Public Law

MAGOULAS, G., Economics

MASSING, O., Politics

MEDER, S., Civil Law, History of Law

MEIER, B.-D., Criminal Law

NAHAMOWITZ, P., Theory of Organization and Planning

NOCKE, M., Teaching of Law

OPPERMANN, B., Civil Law

PFEIFFER, C., Criminology

RÜPING, H., Criminal Law

SALJE, P., Civil Law

SCHNEIDER, H.-P., Public Law

SCHWARZE, R., Civil Law

SCHWERDTFEGER, G., Public Law

TREIBER, H., Theory of Organization and Planning

WAECHTER, K., Public Law

WALTHER, M., Teaching of Law and Philosophy

WENDELING-SCHRÖDER, U., Civil Law

WOLF, CH., Civil Law

ZIELINSKI, D., Criminal Law

Department of Mathematics and Physics (tel. (511) 762-4466; fax (511) 762-5819; e-mail dekanat@math.uni-hannover.de):

BARINGHAUS, L., Mathematical Stochastics

BARKE, E., Microelectronic Systems

BÄUERLE, N., Mathematical Stochastics

BESSENRODT, CH., Mathematics

BOTHMER, H.-CH. V., Mathematics

BREHM, B., Atomic Processes

DANZMANN, K., Experimental Physics

DEMMIG, F., Plasma Physics

DRAGON, N., Theoretical Physics

EBELING, W., Mathematics

ERNÉ, M., Mathematics

ERTMER, W., Experimental Physics

ESCHER, J., Applied Mathematics

ETLING, D., Theoretical Meteorology

EVERTS, H.-U., Theoretical Physics

FORSTER, P., Applied Mathematics

GROSS, G., Meteorology

GROSSER, J., Atomic Processes

GRÜBEL, R., Probability Theory and Statistics

HAUF, T., Meteorology

HAUG, R., Experimental Physics

HEINE, J., Applied Mathematics

HENZLER, M., Experimental Physics

HOTJE, H., Mathematics

HULEK, K., Mathematics

KOCK, M., Plasma Physics

LECHTENFELD, O., Theoretical Physics

LEWENSTEIN, M., Theoretical Physics

LIPECK, U., Computer Science

MIKESKA, H. J., Theoretical Physics

MÜHLBACH, G., Approximation Theory and Numerical Analysis

MÜLLER, D., Computer Science

NEJDL, W., Computer Science

OESTREICH, M., Experimental Physics

PARCHMANN, R., Computer Science
PFNÜR, H., Experimental Physics
PIRSCH, P., Microelectronic Systems
PRALLE, H., Head of Regional Computer Centre, Lower Saxony
REINEKE, J., Mathematics
SAUER, P. U., Theoretical Physics
SCHMIDT-WESTPHAL, U., Mathematics
SCHNOEGE, K. J., Applied Mathematics
SCHULZ, E., Plasma Physics
SCHULZ, H., Theoretical Physics
SECKMEYER, G., Meteorology
STARKE, G., Applied Mathematics
STEFFENS, K., Mathematics
STEPHAN, E., Applied Mathematics
SZCZERBICKA, H., Systems Engineering
TIEMANN, E., Experimental Physics
VOLLMER, H., Computer Science
WAGNER, B., Systems Engineering
WELLEGEHAUSEN, B., Applied Physics
WOLTER, F.-E., Applied Systems
ZAWISCHA, D., Theoretical Physics

Department of Mechanical Engineering (Im Moore 11B, 30167 Hannover; tel. (511) 762-2779; fax (511) 762-2763; e-mail dekan@ maschinenbau.uni-hannover.de; internet www.maschinenbau.uni-hannover.de):

BACH, F.-W., Materials
BESDO, D., Mechanics
BRAUNE, R., Mechanisms and Machine Elements
DEKENA, B., Production Engineering and Machine Tools
DOEGE, E., Metal Forming and Machines
GATZEN, H.-H., Microtechnology
GERTH, W., Machine Dynamics
GIETZELT, M., Steam and Fuel Engineering
HAFERKAMP, H. D., Materials
HALLENSLEBEN, M. L., Macromolecular Chemistry
HEIMANN, B., Machine Dynamics
KABELAC, S., Thermodynamics
LOUIS, H., Material Testing
MEIER, G. E. A., Fluid Mechanics
MERKER, G. P., Internal Combustion Engine
MEWES, D., Chemical Engineering
NYHUIS, P., Factory Building and Logistics
OVERMEYER, L., Conveying Technology and Mining Machinery
POLL, G., Construction Science
POPP, K., Mechanics
RAUTENBERG, M., Radial Compressors
REDEKER, G., Factory Building
REHFELDT, D., Welding Technology
REITHMEIER, E., Measurement and Control Technology
RIESS, W., Turbo Machinery
ROSEMANN, H., Construction Science
SCHULZE, L., Department Planning, Control of Warehouse and Transport Systems
SCHWERES, M., Labour Science, Ergonomics
SENME, J., Turbo Machinery
STEGEMANN, D., Nuclear Technology
VOSS, G., Railway Machines
WIENDAHL, H.-P., Plant Engineering and Production Control

Department of Natural Sciences (Schneiderbeg 50, 30167 Hannover; tel. (511) 762-3318; fax (511) 762-5874; internet www.unics .uni-hannover.de/geo/index.html):

ANDERS, A., Biophysics
ARNOLD, A., Human Geography
AULING, G., Microbiology
BECKER, J. A., Physical Chemistry
BEHRENS, P., Inorganic Chemistry
BELLGARDT, K.-H., Technical Chemistry
BERGER, R. G., Applied Chemistry
BINNEWIES, M., Inorganic Chemistry
BÖTTCHER, J., Soil Science
BRAKHAGE, A., Microbiology
BUCHHOLZ, H. J., Human Geography
BUHL, J.-CH., Mineralogy

BUTENSCHÖN, H., Organic Chemistry
CARO, J., Physical Chemistry
DUDDECK, H., Organic Chemistry
FENDRIK, I., Biophysics
FISCHER, R., Palaeontology
FISCHER, W. R., Soil Science
HAHN, A., Domestic Technology
HALLENSLEBEN, M. L., Macromolecular Chemistry
HAU, B., Phytopathology
HEITJANS, P., Physical Chemistry
HESSE, D., Technical Chemistry
HITZMANN, B., Technical Chemistry
HOFFMANN, H. M. R., Organic Chemistry
HOLTZ, F., Mineralogy
HÖRMANN, D., Gardening Management
HORST, W., Plant Nutrition
HOTHORN, L., Biology Informatics
HUCHZERMEYER, B., Botany
HÜPPE, J., Palaeoecology
IMBIHL, R., Physical Chemistry
JACOBSEN, H.-J., Molecular Biology
JUG, K., Theoretical Chemistry
KIRSHNING, A., Organic Chemistry
KLOPPSTECH, K., Botany
KOLB, A., Biophysics
KRETZMER, G., Technical Chemistry
KUHLMANN, H., Plant Nutrition
KUHNT, G., Physical Geography
KUSTER, H., Palaeoecology
LIEFNER, I., Economic Geography
MAISS, E., Phytopathology
MARTEN, I., Biophysics
MEYER, H. H., Organic Chemistry
MOSIMANN, T., Physical Geography
NAUMANN, I., Domestic Technology
NIEMEYER, R., Botany
POTT, R., Botany
RATH, T., Horticulture
ROTZOLL, G., Technical Chemistry
SCHÄTZL, L., Economic Geography
SCHENK, E.-W., Gardening Management and Accountancy
SCHENK, M., Plant Nutrition
SCHEPER, T., Technical Chemistry
SCHERER, G., Crop Physiology
SCHMIDT, A., Botany
SCHMIDT, E., Horticultural Economics
SCHMITZ, U. K., Applied Genetics
SCHÖNHERR, J., Fruit Science
SCHÜLKE, I., Geology
SCHÜNGERL, K., Technical Chemistry
SEREK, M., Gardening Management and Accountancy
SPETHMANN, W., Nursery Gardening
STÜTZEL, Vegetable Science
TANTAU, H.-J., Horticultural Engineering
TATLIOGLU, T., Applied Genetics
URLAND, W., Inorganic Chemistry
VAN DER PLOEG, R. VAN DER, Soil Science
VOGT, C., Inorganic Chemistry
VON BLANCKENBURG, F., Mineralogy
WAIBEL, H., Horticultural Economics
WATKINSON, B. M., Food Science
WINSEMANN, J., Geology
WINTERFELDT, E., Organic Chemistry
WÜNSCH, G., Inorganic Chemistry
ZIMMER, K., Ornamental Plants

Department of Philosophy (Königsworther Platz 1, 30167 Hanover; tel. (511) 762-4556; fax (511) 762-8243; e-mail dekanat@fbls .uni-hannover.de; internet www.fbls .uni-hannover.de):

ACHINGER, G., Sociology
AHLERS, I., Human Geography
ANTES, P., Study of Religions
ASCHOFF, H.-G., Modern History and Ecclesiastical History
AVERKORN, R., Medieval History
BARMEYER-HARTLIEB, H., Modern History
BAUSENHART, G., Roman Catholic Religious Education
BAYER, K., German
BECKER-SCHMIDT, R., Psychology
BERG, D., Medieval History

BEUTLER, K., Education
BEZZEL, CH., German Language
BICKES, H., German Language
BILLMANN-MAHECHA, H., Psychology
BINDEL, W.-R., Special Education
BIRKNER, G., English Philology
BLANKE, B., Political Science
BLELL, G., Teaching of English
BLEY, H., Modern History
BOLSCHO, D., Pedagogy
BÖNSCH, M., School Pedagogy
BRODTMANN, D., Sports
BROKMEIER, P., Political Science
BRÜGGEMANN, H., Modern German Literature
BUCKMILLER, M., Political Science
BULTHAUP, P., Philosophy
CALLIES, H., Ancient History
CLAUSSEN, D., Sociology
DAIBER, K.-F., Study of Religions
DIEWALD, G., Modern German Literature
DISCHNER-VOGEL, G., Modern German Literature
DITTRICH, J.-H., Technology of Clothing and Textiles
DORDEL, H. J., Sports
DUDEN, B., Sociology
EBINGHAUS, H., Physics
EGGERT, D., Psychology
EGGS, E., Romance Philology and Language
EHRHARDT, J., Education
EHRHARDT, M. L., German
FELDMANN, K., Sociology
FISCHER, H., German Literature
FRACKMANN, M., Social Education
FRANZKE, R., Social Education
FÜLLBERG-STOLLBERG, O., Modern History
GHOLAMASAD, D., Sociology
GIPSER, D., Special Education
GLAGE, L., English Literature
GLITHO, S., Modern German Literature
GÖRTZ, H.-J., Roman Catholic Religious Education
HAENSCH, D., Political Science
HASEMANN, K., Mathematics
HAUPTMEYER, C.-H., Early Medieval History
HEINEMANN, M., Education
HERWIG, J., Music
HIEBER, L., Sociology
HOECKER, B., Political Science
HOEGES, D., Romance Philology and Literature
HÖLKER, K., Romance Philology and Literature
HORSTER, D., Education
ILIEN, A., Education
JANSSEN, B., School Pedagogy
JETTER, K., Therapy
JOHANNSEN, F., Evangelical Religious Education
JUNGK, D., Vocational Education
KENTLER, H., Social Education
KIESELBACH, T., Psychology
KNAPP, G.-A., Psychology
KOETHEN, E., Art and Visual Media, Teaching of Art and Visual Media
KÖPCKE, K. M., German
KORFF, F.-W., Philosophy
KREUTZER, L., Modern German Literature
KRIWET, I., Education of Mentally Handicapped People
KROVOZA, A., Psychology
KRUIP, G., Roman Catholic Religious Education
KÜHNE, A., Psychology
KUNTZ, K. M., Education
KUPETZ, R., Teaching of English, Applied Linguistics
LAGA, G., Sociology
LEMKE, C., Political Science
LENK, E., German Literature
LOHRER-PAPE, Arts
LUDWIG, O., German Language
MANZ, W., Vocational Education

MAYER, R., English Literature
MENSCHING, G., Philosophy
MESCHKAT, K., Sociology
MICKLER, O., Sociology
MÜHLHAUSEN, K., Education
MÜLLER, R.-W., Political Science
NARR, R., School Pedagogy
NAUMANN, G., Home Technology
NAUMANN, H., German
NEGT, O., Sociology
NOLL, A.-H., Social Studies
NOLTE, H.-H., Medieval History
NOORMANN, J., Teaching of Evangelical Relations
OELSCHLÄGER, H., Educational Planning and Reform
PAEFGEN, E., German
PEIFFER, L., Sports
PERELS, J., Political Science
PETERS, J., Modern German Literature
RAUFUSS, D., Education
RECTOR, M., Modern German Literature
REHKÄMPER, K., Modern German Literature
REISER, H., Special Education
REUMANN, R.-D., Technology of Clothing and Textiles
RIEDEL, M., Modern History
RIEMEN, F., Music
RIES, W., Philosophy
ROHLOFF, H., English Philosophy
RUNTE, A., Modern German Literature
RUST, H., Sociology
RÜTTERS, K., Vocational Education
SANDERS, H., Romance Philology and Literature
SAUER, W., German Language
SCHÄFER, G., Political Science
SCHAEFFNER, L., Adult Education
SCHLOBINSKI, P., German Language
SCHMAUDERER, E., Food Science
SCHMID, H.-D., History and History Teaching
SCHMIDT, M., Adult Education
SCHMITZ, K., Education
SCHÖNBERGER, F., Special Education
SCHREIBER, G., Technology of Clothing and Textile
SCHUCHARDT, E., Education
SCHULZE, R., English Language and Linguistics
SCHWARZ, B., Medieval History
SIEBERT, H., Adult Education
STIMPFLE, A., Roman Catholic Religious Education
SWIENTEK, CH., Special Education
TIEDEMANN, J., Psychology
TILCH, H., Social Education
TREBELS, A. H., Sports
TROCHOLEPCZY, B., Roman Catholic Religious Education
URBAN, A., Psychology
VASSEN, F., Modern German Literature
VESTER, M., Political Science
VON SALDERN, A., Modern History
WACKER, A., Psychology
WAGNER-HASEL, B., Ancient History
WATKINSON, B. M., Food Science
WEBER, H., English Philology
WELLENDORF, F., Psychology
WELZER, H., Psychology
WENZEL, F., Scientific and Technical Russian
WERNER, W., Roman Catholic Religious Education
WERNING, R., Education of Mentally Handicapped People
WILHARM, I., History and History Teaching
WILKEN, E., Special Education
WIPPERMANN, H., Mathematics
WÜNDERICH, V., Latin American History
WÜNDERICH, V., Sociology
ZIEHE, T., Education

UNIVERSITÄT HILDESHEIM

Marienburger Platz 22, 31141 Hildesheim
Telephone: (5121) 883102
Fax: (5121) 883104
E-mail: presse@uni-hildesheim.de
Internet: www.uni-hildesheim.de

Founded 1978
State control
Academic year: October to September

Pres.: Prof. Dr WOLFGANG-UWE FRIEDRICH
Vice-Pres: Prof. Dr KLAUS AMBROSI, Dr MARGITTA RUDOLPH, Dr BARBARA WEINMANN, Prof. Dr CHRISTA WORMSER-HACKER
Librarian: (vacant)

Number of teachers: 157
Number of students: 3,997

Publication: Uni Hildesheim. Das Magazin (2 a year)

DEANS

Faculty I (Education and Sociology): Prof. Dr MARTINA SCHREINER
Faculty II (Cultural Education): Prof. Dr WOLFGANG SCHNEIDER
Faculty III (Information and Communication): Prof. Dr HORST KIERDORF

PROFESSORS

Faculty I (Education and Sociology) (tel. (5121) 883-401; fax (5121) 883-402):

BORSCHE, T., Philosophy
BRÄNDLE, W., Protestant Theology
CLOER, E., General Pedagogy
EBERLE, H.-J., Social Pedagogy
FRIEDRICH, W., Political Science
HELFRICH-HÖLTER, W., Psychology
HOPF, CH., Sociology
JAUMANN-GRAUMANN, O., Education
KECK, R., Education
KÖHNLEIN, W., General Science
KUNERT, H., General Education Studies
MEIER-HILBERT, G., Geography
MÜLLER, B., Social Pedagogy
NICKEL, U., Sport
OVERESCH, M., History
SCHREINER, M., Protestant Theology
SIEBERG, H., Sociology
STRANG, H., Social Education Studies
WALLRAVEN, K., Sociology
WERNER, W., Catholic Theology
WOLFF, ST., Social Education Studies

Faculty II (Cultural Education) (tel. (5121) 883-601; fax (5121) 883-602):

BERG, J., Media Education
FRÜHSORGE, G., Fine Arts
GIFFHORN, H., Media Education
GORNIK, H., German Literature and Linguistics
GROMES, H., Theatre
GÜNZEL, R., Fine Arts and Visual Communication
HÜGEL, H.-O., Popular Culture
KURZENBERGER, H.-J., Theatre
LÖFFLER, W., Music and Aural Communication
MENZEL, W., German Language and Linguistics
NOLTE, J., Fine Arts and Visual Communication
SCHNEIDER, W., Cultural Politics
TESKE, U., Fine Arts
VIETTA, J., Literature
WEBER, R., Music and Aural Communication

Faculty III (Information and Communication) (tel. (5121) 883-801; fax (5121) 883-802):

AMBROSI, K., Computer Science
ARNTZ, R., Romance Languages and Linguistics
BENEKE, J., English, Linguistics and Intercultural Communication
BENTZ, H.-J., Mathematics
DIRKS, U., English Studies

FLECHSIG, E., Chemistry
FRANZBECKER, W., Technical Studies
HAUENSCHILD, CH., Computational Linguistics
KAHLE, D., Mathematics
KIERDORF, H., Biology
KOLB, G., General Economics
KREUTZKAMP, TH., Mathematics
SABBAN, A., Romance Languages and Linguistics
SCHWARZER, E., Physics
STURM, H., Biology
WEGNER, N., Technology
WOMSER-HACKER, CH., Information Science

UNIVERSITÄT HOHENHEIM

70593 Stuttgart
Telephone: (711) 459-0
Fax: (711) 459-3960
E-mail: post@uni-hohenheim.de
Internet: www.uni-hohenheim.de

Founded 1818
Academic year: October to September

Rector: Prof. Dr H.-P. LIEBIG
Pro-Rectors: Prof. Dr A. FANGMEIER, Prof. Dr U. MACKENSTEDT, Prof. Dr E. TROSSMANN
Administrative Dir: A. FUNK
Univ. Librarian: K.-W. HORSTMANN

Number of teachers: 780
Number of students: 5,500

DEANS

Faculty of Agricultural Sciences: Prof. Dr S. DABBERT
Faculty of Economics and Social Sciences: Prof. Dr M. AHLHEIM
Faculty of Natural Sciences: Prof. Dr K. BOSCH

PROFESSORS

Faculty of Agricultural Sciences:

AMSELGRUBER, W., Anatomy and Physiology of Domestic Animals
BECKER, K., Animal Nutrition in Tropical and Subtropical Areas
BECKER, T., Rural Markets and Rural Marketing
BESSEI, W., Animal Breeding
BLAICH, R., Viticulture
BÖCKER, R., Landscape Ecology
BÖHM, R., Veterinary Hygiene
BUCHENAUER, H., Plant Protection
CLAUPEIN, W., Plant Production
CLAUS, R., Stockbreeding
DABBERT, S., Production Theory in Agriculture
DOLUSCHITZ, R., Farm Management
DOPPLER, W., Farm Management in Tropical and Subtropical Areas
DROCHNER, W., Animal Nutrition
FANGMEIER, A., Plant Ecology and Ecotoxicology
GEIGER, H. H., Genetics
GELDERMANN, H., Stockbreeding
GROSSKOPF, W., Agricultural Politics
HAUSSMANN, A., Stockbreeding
HEIDHUES, F., Agricultural Economics in Tropical and Subtropical Areas
HOFFMANN, V., Agricultural Communication
HURLE, K., Plant Protection
JUNGBLUTH, T., Agricultural Technology
KANDELER, E., Soil Biology
KLEISINGER, S., Agricultural Technology
KÖLLER, K., Agricultural Technology in Developing Countries
KORFF, H.-R., Socioeconomics in the Tropics and Subtropics
KROMKA, F., Agricultural Sociology
KRUSE, M., Seed Technology
KUTZBACH, H.-D., Agricultural Technology
LIEBIG, H.-P., Vegetable Cropping

MELCHINGER, A., Genetics and Plant Breeding
MOSENTHIN, R., Animal Nutrition
MÜHLBAUER, W., Agricultural Technology in Tropical and Subtropical Areas
OPPEN, M. VON, Agricultural Economics in Developing Countries
PIEPHO, H.-P., Bioinformatics
RÖMHELD, V., Plant Nutrition
SAUERBORN, J., Ecology of Tropical and Subtropical Areas
SCHULTZE-KRAFT, R., Biodiversity and Land Rehabilitation in Tropical and Subtropical Areas
STAHR, K., Soil Sciences
STÖSSER, R., Applied Botany
STRECK, T., Biogeophysics
VALLE ZÁRATE, A., Stockbreeding in Tropical and Subtropical Areas
WEBER, G., Special Plant Breeding
WIRÉN, N. VON, Plant Nutrition
ZEBITZ, C., Plant Protection
ZEDDIES, J., Agricultural Economics

Faculty of Economics and Social Sciences:

AHLHEIM, M., Environmental Economics
BACKES-HAASE, A., Vocational Training
BAREIS, P., Taxation and Management
BELKE, A., International Economics
BUSS, E., Sociology
CAESAR, R., Financing
DITTMAN, A., Law
ESCHER-WEINGART, C., Law
GERYBADZE, A., International Management
HABENICHT, W., Industrial Economics
HACHMEISTER, B., Accounting and Finance
HAGEMANN, H., Economic Theory
HERDZINA, K., Economics
JUNGKUNZ, D., Vocational Teaching
KIRN, C., Informatics
KUHNLE, H., Business Administration
MACHARZINA, K., Management and Organizational Research
MAST, C., Journalism
MELL, U., Theology and Didactics
MÜHLENKAMP, H., Economics of Social Sciences
MÜLLER, C., Entrepreneurship
PFETSCH, B., Communication Policy
SCHENK, M., Communication and Social Research
SCHRAMM, M, Theology and Didactics
SCHULER, H., Psychology
SCHULZ, W., Environmental Management
SCHWALBE, U., Industrial Economics
SEEL, B., Household Management
SPAHN, P., Economics
STREB, D., Social and Economic History
TROSSMANN, E., Controlling
VOETH, M., Marketing
WAGENHALS, G., Statistics and Econometry

Faculty of Natural Sciences:

BECKER-BENDER, G., Physics
BEIFUSS, U., Bio-organic Chemistry
BIESALSKI, H. K., Biochemistry and Nutrition
BLUM, M., Zoology
BODE, C., Nutrition
BOSCH, K., Mathematics
BREER, H., Zoophysiology
CARLE, R., Food Technology
DEHNHARDT, W., Informatics
DUFNER, J., Mathematics
EHRENSTEIN, W., Applied Physiology
FISCHER, A., Food Technology
FISCHER, L., Biotechnology
GRAEVE, L., Biochemistry and Nutrition
HAMMES, W., Food Technology
HANKE, W., Zoophysiology
HINRICHS, J., Food Technology
ISENGARD, H.-D., Food Analysis
JETTER, K., Applied Mathematics
KOTTKE, V., Food Process Technology
KUHN, A., Microbiology
KUHN, E., Plant Physiology
KÜPPERS, M., Botany

MACKENSTEDT, U., Zoology
MENZEL, P., Chemistry and Ecology
PFITZNER, A., Virology
PREISS, A., Genetics
RASSOW, J., Microbiology
RÖSNER, H., Zoology
SCHALLER, J., Animal Ecology
SCHWACK, W., Food Chemistry
SPRING, O., Botany
STRASDEIT, H., Bio-inorganic Chemistry
VETTER, A., Food Technology
WULFMEYER, V., Physics and Meteorology

UNIVERSITÄT KARLSRUHE

Kaiserstr. 12, 76128 Karlsruhe
Telephone: (721) 608-0
Fax: (721) 6084290
E-mail: post@uni-karlsruhe.de
Internet: www.uni-karlsruhe.de
Founded 1825
State control
Academic year: October to September
First technical institute in Germany and the first to acquire univ. status
Rector: Prof. Dr HORST HIPPLER
Pro-Rectors: Prof. Dr NORBERT HENZE, Prof. Dr Ing. JÜRGEN BECKER, Prof. Dr rer. NORBERT HENZE, Dr DETLET LÖHE
Chief Admin. Officer: (vacant)
Librarian: Dipl.-Ing. CHRISTOPH-HUBERT SCHÜTTE

Number of teachers: 700
Number of students: 17,600

Publication: *Fridericiana* (2 a year)

DEANS

Faculty of Architecture: Prof. Dipl.-Ing. MARKUS NEPPL
Faculty of Business Engineering and Economics: Prof. Dr CLEMES PUPPE
Faculty of Chemical and Process Engineering: Prof. Dr Ing. hab. HERMANN NIRSCHL
Faculty of Chemistry and Biosciences: Prof. Dr STEFAN BRÄSE
Faculty of Civil, Geo- and Environmental Sciences: Prof. Dr FRANZ NESTMANN
Faculty of Computer Science: Prof. Dr Ing. HEINZ WÖRN
Faculty of Electrical Engineering and Information Technology: Prof. Dr-Ing. GERT F. TROMMER
Faculty of Humanities and Social Sciences: Prof. Dr KLAUS BÖS
Faculty of Mathematics: Prof. Dr FRANK HERRLICH
Faculty of Mechanical Engineering: Prof. Dr MARTIN GABI
Faculty of Physics: Prof. Dr HEINZ KALT

PROFESSORS

Faculty of Architecture:

BAVA, H.
BÖKER, H. J.
CRAIG, S.
GOTHE, K.
JANSON, A.
NÄGELI, W.
NEPPL, M.
PFEIFFER, M.
RICHTER, P.
SCHNEIDER, N.
SCHULZE, U.
SEWING, W.
VON BOTH, P.
WAGNER, A.
WALL, A.

Faculty of Chemical and Process Engineering:

BOCKHORN, H.
FRIMMEL, F. H.
HUBBUCH, I.
KASPER, G.

KIND, M.
KOLB, T.
KRAUSHAAR-CZERNETSKI, B.
NIRSCHL, H.
OELLRICH, L.
OLIVEROS, E.
POSTEN, C.
REIMERT, R.
SCHABEL, W.
SCHABER, K.
SCHAUB, G.
SCHUCHMANN, H.
SYLDATK, C.
WETZEL, T.
WILLENBACHER, N.
ZARZALIS, N.

Faculty of Chemistry and Biosciences:

AHLRICHS, R.
BARNER-KOWOLLIK, C.
BASTMEYER, M.
BOCKHORN, H.
BRÄSE, S.
DEUTSCHMANN, O.
FELDMANN, C.
FISCHER, R.
GECKEIS, H.
HIPPLER, H.
KÄMPER, J.
KAPPES, M.
KLOPPER, W.
LAMPARTER, T.
MARKO, D.
METZLER, M.
NICK, P.
OLZMANN, M.
PODLECH, J.
POWELL, A.
PUCHTA, H.
RICHERT, C.
ROESKY, P.
SCHUSTER, R.
SCHWARZ, U.
TARASCHEWSKI, H.
ULRICH, A.
WEDLICH, D.
WILHELM, M.

Faculty of Civil, Geo- and Environmental Sciences:

BLAß, H. J.
BURGER, D.
GEHBAUER, F.
GENTES, S.
GREILING, R.
HECK, B.
HENNES, M.
HINZ, S.
HOHNECKER, E.
JIRKA, G.
KRAMER, C.
LENNERTS, K.
MEURER, M.
MÜLLER, H.
NESTMANN, F.
ROOS, R.
RUCK, B.
SCHILLING, F.
SCHMITT, G.
SCHWEIZERHOF, K.
STEMPNIEWSKI, L.
STOSCH, H.-G.
STÜBERN, D.
TRIANTATYLLIDIS, T.
UHLMANN, M.
UMMENHAFER, T.
VOGT, J.
WAGNER, W.
WINTER, J.
ZUMKELLER, D.

Faculty of Electrical Engineering and Information Technology:

BECKER, J.
BOLZ, A.
BRAUN, M.
DÖSSEL, O.

DOSTERT, K.
FREUDE, W.
IVERS-TIFFÉE, E.
JONDRAL, F.
KREBS, V.
LEIBFRIED, T.
LEMMER, U.
LEUTHOLD, J.
MOREIRA, A.
MÜLLER-GLASER, K.-D.
NOE, M.
PUENTE, F.
SIEGEL, M.
TROMMER, G.
TUUMM, M.
ZWICK, T.

Faculty of Humanities and Social Sciences:
BÖHN, A.
BÖS, K.
FISCHER, M.
FRIES, S.
GIDION, G.
GLEITSMANN-TOPP, R.-J.
GRUNWALD, A.
GUTMANN, M.
JAPP, U.
NOLLMANN, G.
PFADENHAUER, M.
REKUS, J.
SCHÜTT, H.-P.
SCHWAMEDER, H.

Faculty of Mathematics:
ALEFELD, G.
AUMANN, G.
BÄUERLE, N.
DÖRFLER, W.
HENZE, N.
HERRLICH, F.
HEUVELINE, V.
JANNHE, T.
KAUCHER, E.
KIRSCH, A.
LAST, G.
LEUZINGER, E.
PLUM, M.
REICHEL, W.
RIEDER, A.
SCHMIDT, C.-G.
VERAANT, L.
WEIL, W.
WEIß, J.-P.
WEIS, L.
WIENERS, N.

Faculty of Mechanical Engineering:
ALBERS, A.
BAUER, H.-J.
BÖHLKE, T.
BRETTHAUER, G.
CACCUCI, D.
ELSHER, P.
FLEISCHER, J.
FURMANS, K.
GABI, M.
GAUTERIN, F.
GEIMER, M.
GRATZFELD, P.
GUMBSCH, P.
HENNING, F.
HOFFMANN, M. J.
KRAFT, O.
LANZA, G.
LÖHE, D.
MAAS, U.
OERTEL, H.
OVTCHAROVA, J.
PROPPE, C.
SAILE, V.
SEEMANN, W.
SPICHER, U.
STILLER, C.
WANNER, A.
ZÜLCH, G.
ZUM GAHR, K.-H.

Faculty of Physics:
BAUMBACH, T.
BEHENG, K. D.
BLÜMER, H.
BUSCH, K.
DE BOER, W.
DREXLIN, G.
FEINDT, M.
GERTHSEN, D.
GUAST, G.
JONES, S.
KALT, H.
KLINGSHIRN, C.
KOHMEIER, C.
KÜHN, J.
MÜLLER, TH.
NIERSTE, U.
SCHIMMERL, T.
SCHÖN, G.
SHNIRMAN, A.
STEINHAUSER, M.
USTINOV, A.
VON LÖHNEYSEN, H.
WEGENER, M.
WEIß, G.
WENZEL, F.
WÖLFLE, P.
WULFHEKEL, W.
ZEPPENFELD, D.

UNIVERSITÄT KASSEL

Präsidialverwaltung, Mönchebergstr. 19, 34109 Kassel
Telephone: (561) 804-0
Fax: (561) 804-2330
E-mail: poststelle@uni-kassel.de
Internet: www.uni-kassel.de
Founded 1971
State control
Language of instruction: German
Academic year: October to July
Pres.: Prof. Dr ROLF-DIETER POSTLEP
Vice-Pres: Prof. Dr ALEXANDER ROSSNAGEL, Prof. Dr CLAUDIA BRINKER-VON DER HEYDE, Prof. Dr Ing. MARTIN LAWERENZ
Chancellor: Dr ROBERT KUHN
Librarian: Dr AXEL HALLE
Library of 845,512 books, 25,155 periodicals
Number of teachers: 312
Number of students: 19,557

DEANS

Architecture, Urban Planning, Landscape Planning: Prof. Dipl. Ing. MAYA REINER
Business and Economics: Prof. Dr GEORG VAN WANGENHEIM
Civil Engineering: Prof. Dr-Ing. PETER RACKY
Ecological Agriculture: Prof. Dr MICHAEL WACHENDORF
Educational Science, Humanities and Music: Prof. Dr PAUL-GERHARD KLUMBIES
Electrical Engineering, Computer Science: Prof. Dr-Ing. JOSEF BÖRCSÖK
Languages and Literature: Prof. Dr ANDREAS GARDT
Mathematics and Information Science: Prof. Dr REINHARD HOCHMUTH
Mechanical Engineering: Prof. Dr-Ing. OLAF WÜNSCH
Natural Sciences: Prof. Dr FRIEDRICH-W. HERBERG
Social Work: Prof. Dr STEPHAN RIXEN
Social Sciences: Prof. Dr INGRID BAUMGÄRTNER
School of Art: Prof. Dr KARIN STEMPEL

ATTACHED RESEARCH INSTITUTES

Competence Centre for Climate Change Mitigation and Adaptation(CLIMA): Dir Dr MICHAELA SCHALLER.
Centre for Environmental Systems Research (CESR): internet www.usf

.uni-kassel.de/cesr; Dir Prof. Dr ANDREAS ERNST.
Centre for Nanostructure Science and Technology (CINSaT): Dir Prof. Dr KLAUS MASSELI.
International Centre for Development and Decent Work (ICDD): Exec. Dir Prof. Dr CHRISTOPH SCHERRER.
International Centre for Higher Education Research (INCHER-Kassel): Moenchebergstr. 17, 34109 Kassel; tel. (561) 804-2415; fax (561) 804-7415; e-mail mahe@uni-kassel.de; internet www.incher.uni-kassel.de; Dir Prof. Dr BARBARA KEHM.

UNIVERSITÄT KONSTANZ

78567 Konstanz
Telephone: (7531) 88-0
Fax: (7531) 88-3688
Internet: www.uni-konstanz.de
Founded 1966
Academic year: October to September
Rector: Prof. Dr ULRICH RÜDIGER
Pro-Rectors: CARSTEN EULITZ, KATHARINA HOLZINGER, SABINE SONNENTAG
Registrar: JENS APITZ
Librarian: PETRA HÄTSCHER
Number of teachers: 177
Number of students: 9,528
Publication: *Uni'kon*

DEANS

Faculty of Humanities: Prof. Dr ULRICH GOTTER
Faculty of Law, Economics and Politics: Prof. Dr FRIEDRICH BREYER
Faculty of Sciences: Prof. Dr PAUL LEIDERER

PROFESSORS

Faculty of Humanities
Department of History and Sociology:
GEORG, W., Sociology
GIESEN, B., Sociology
GOTTER, U., History
GÖTZ, T., Empirical Educational Research
HAUSER, S., History
HINZ, T., Sociology
KIRSCH, T., Sociology
KLEEBERG, B., History
KNORR, C., Sociology
OSTERHAMMEL, J., History
PIETROW-ENNKER, B., History
RECKWITZ, A., Sociology
REICHHARDT, S., History
RIEHLE, H., Sports Science
SCHLÖGL, K., History
SIGNORI, G., History
WELTECKE, D., History
WISCHERMANN, C., History
WOLL, A., Sport Science

Department of Linguistics:
BAYER, J.
BRAUN, B.
BREU, W.
BUTT, M.
DEHÉ, N.
EULITZ, C.
GRIJZENHOUT, J.
KABAK, B.
KAISER, G.
PLANKE, F.
REMBERGER, E.-M.
ROMERO, M.

Department of Literature:
ASSMANN, A.
BAUDY, G.
FEICHTINGER, B.
JOAN I TOUS, P.
KOSCHORKE, A.
KÜMMEL-SCHNUR, A.
MATALA DE MAZZA, E.

MERGENTAL, S.
MURASOV, J.
NISCHIK, R.
OCHSNER, B.
OTTO, I.
POLASCHEGG, A.
QUAST, B.
SPRENGER, U.
STIEGLER, B.
THÜRLEMANN, F.
VOGEL, J.
WEITIN, T.
ZIMMERMANN, T.

Department of Philosophy:
ROSEFELDT, T.
SEEBASS, G.
SPOHN, W.
STEMMER, P.
WEBER, M.

Faculty of Law, Economics and Politics
Department of Economics:
ALÓS-FERRER, C.
BREYER, F.
BRÜGGEMANN, R.
BRUTTEL, L.
DEISSINGER, T.
FISCHBACHER, U.
FRANKE, G.
FRIEHE, T.
GENSER, B.
GLASER, M.
GRIEBEN, W.
HERTWECK, M.
HOCHHOLDINGER, S.
JACKWERTH, J.
KAAS, L.
LUKAS, C.
POHLMEIER, W.
SANDER, H.
SCHOLL, A.
SEIFRID, J.
STEFANI, U.
URSPRUNG, H.

School of Law:
ALTHAMMER, C.
ARMGARDT, M.
BOECKEN, W.
EISELE, J.
ENNUSCHAT, J.
FEZER, K.
GLÖCKNER, J.
HAILBRONNER, K.
IBLER, M.
KOCH, J.
RENGIER, R.
RÖHL, H.
SCHÖNBERGER, C.
STADLER, A.
THEILE, H.

Department of Politics and Management:
BEHNKE, N.
BOERNER, S.
FREITAG, M.
HOLZINGER, K.
KELLER, B.
KNILL, C.
SCHNEIDER, G.
SCHNEIDER, V.
SEIBEL, W.
SELB, P.

Faculty of Sciences
Department of Biology:
ADAMSKA, J.
APELL, H.
BÜRKLE, A.
COOK, A.
DEUERLING, E.
DIEDRICHS, K.
DIETRICH, D.
ECKMANN, R.
GALIZIA, G.
GRÖTTRUP, M.
HAUCK, C.

KROTH, P.
KÜPPER, H.
LEIST, M.
MAY, E.
MAYER, T.
MENDGEN, K.
MEYER, A.
OHLSCHLÄGER, P.
PEETERS, F.
ROTHAUPT, K.
SCHEFFNER, M.
SCHINK, B.
STÜRMER, C.
WELTE, W.
WIKELSKI, M.

Department of Chemistry:
EXNER, T.
GROTH, U.
HARTIG, J.
HAUSER, K.
MARX, A.
MECKING, S.
MÖLLER, H.
MÜLLER, G.
POLARZ, S.
PRZYBYLSKI, M.
WITTMANN, V.
ZUMBUSCH, A.

Department of Computer and Information Science:
BERTHOLD, M.
BRANDES, U.
DEUSSEN, O.
KEIM, D.
KOCH, M.
KUHLEN, R.
LEUE, S.
MERHOF, D.
REITERER, H.
SAUPE, D.
SCHOLL, M.
WALDVOGEL, M.

Department of Mathematics and Statistics:
BARTHEL, G.
BERAN, J.
DENK, R.
DREHER, H.
FREISTÜHLER, H.
HOFFMANN, D.
JUNK, M.
KOHLMANN, M.
RACKE, R.
SCHEIDERER, C.
SCHNÜRER, O.
SCHROPP, J.
SCHWEIGHOFER, M.

Department of Physics:
BELZIG, W.
BURKARD, G.
DEKORSY, T.
FUCHS, M.
GANTEFÖR, G.
HAHN, G.
LEIDERER, P.
LEITENSTORFER, A.
MARET, G.
NIELABA, P.
NOWAK, U.
RÜDIGER, U.
SCHEER, E.

Department of Psychology:
ELBERT, T.
GOLLWITZER, P.
HÜBNER, R.
KEMPF, W.
KIßLER, J.
KÜTTNER, C.
RENNER, B.
ROCKSTROH, B.
SCHUPP, H.
SONNENTAG, S.

UNIVERSITÄT LEIPZIG
Postfach 100920, 04009 Leipzig
Located at: Ritterstr. 26, 04109 Leipzig
Telephone: (341) 97108
Fax: (341) 9730099
Internet: www.uni-leipzig.de
Founded 1409
State control
Academic year: October to September (two semesters)
Rector: Prof. Dr FRANZ HÄUSER
Vice-Rector for Education: Prof. Dr CHARLOTTE SCHUBERT
Vice-Rector for Research and Promotion of Young Scientists: Prof. Dr MARTIN SCHLEGEL
Vice-Rector for Univ. Devt: Prof. Dr PETER WIEDEMANN
Chancellor: PETER GUTJAHR-LÖSER
Librarian: Dr CHARLOTTE BAUER
Number of students: 31,000

DEANS

Faculty of Biosciences, Pharmacy and Psychology: Prof. Dr KURT EGER
Faculty of Chemistry and Mineralogy: Prof. Dr HARALD MORGNER
Faculty of Economics and Management: Prof. Dr ROLF HASSE
Faculty of Education: Prof. Dr HARALD MARX
Faculty of History, Art and Oriental Studies: Prof. Dr HELMET LOOS
Faculty of Law: Prof. Dr MARTIN OLDIGES
Faculty of Mathematics and Computer Science: Prof. Dr GERHARD HEYER
Faculty of Medicine: Prof. Dr WIELAND KIESS
Faculty of Philology: Prof. Dr ERWIN TSCHIRMER
Faculty of Physics and Earth Science: Prof. Dr GERD TETZLAFF
Faculty of Social Sciences and Philosophy: Prof. Dr WOLFGANG FACH
Faculty of Sports Science: Prof. Dr JÜRGEN KRUG
Faculty of Theology: Prof. Dr WOLFGANG RATZMANN
Faculty of Veterinary Medicine: Prof. Dr GOTTHOLD GÄBEL

PROFESSORS

Faculty of Biosciences, Pharmacy and Psychology (Brüderstr. 35, 04103 Leipzig; tel. (341) 9736700; fax (341) 9736749; e-mail dekanat .bio@uni-leipzig.de):

BECK-SICKINGER, A. G., Biochemistry
BUSOT, F., Terrestrial Ecology
COLLANI, G. VON, Cognitive Social Psychology
EGER, K., Pharmaceutical Chemistry
HARMS, H., Environmental Microbiology
HAUSCHILDT, S., Immunobiology
HOFMANN, H.-J., Biophysical Chemistry
JESCHENIAK, D., Cognitive Psychology
MOHR, G., Industrial and Organizational Psychology
MORAWETZ, W., Special Botany
MÖRL, M., Biochemistry and Molecular Biology
MÜLLER, M., Experimental Psychology and Cognitive Neuroscience
NIEBER, K., Pharmacology
PETERMANN, H., Psychology of Personality and Psychological Intervention
POEGGEL, G., Human Biology
RAUWALD, J.-W., Pharmaceutical Biology
REISSER, W., General and Applied Botany
ROBITZKI, A., Molecular Biological-Biochemical Processing Technology
RÜBSAMEN, R., Neurobiology
SASS, H., Genetics
SCHILDBERGER, K.-M., General Zoology and Animal Behaviour Physiology
SCHLEGEL, M., Molecular Evolution and Systematics of Animals

SCHRÖDER, H., Clinical Psychology

SCHRÖGER, E., Cognitive Psychology and Biological Psychology

WILHELM, CHR., Plant Physiology

WITRUK, E., Educational Rehabilitation Psychology

Faculty of Chemistry and Mineralogy (Johannisallee 29, 04103 Leipzig; tel. (341) 9736000; fax (341) 9736099; e-mail dekanat@ chemie.uni-leipzig.de; internet www .uni-leipzig.de/chemie):

BENTE, K., Mineralogy, Crystallography

BERGER, St., Analytical Chemistry

BREDE, O., Physical Chemistry

GIANNIS, A., Organic Chemistry

HEY-HAWKINS, E., Inorganic Chemistry

HOFFMANN, R., Bioanalytics

KRAUTSCHEID, H., Inorganic Chemistry

MORGNER, H., Physical Chemistry

PAPP, H., Technological Chemistry

REINHOLD, J., Theoretical Chemistry

SCHNEIDER, C., Organic Chemistry

STRÄTER, N., Structural Analysis of Biopolymers

Faculty of Economics and Management (Marschnerstr. 31, 04109 Leipzig; tel. (341) 9733500; fax (341) 9733509; e-mail dekanat@ wifa.uni-leipzig.de; internet www.uni-leipzig .de/wifa):

BRUHNKE, K.-H., Industrial Engineering and Structural Engineering: Technical and Infrastructural Management

DIEDRICH, R., Business Management: Controlling and Management Accounting

EISENECKER, U., Manager Information Systems: Software Development, Business and Administration

FÖHR, S., Business Management: Personnel Management

FRANCZYK, B., Manager Information Systems: Information Management

GRAW, K.-U., Industrial Engineering and Structural Engineering: Laying of Foundations/Hydraulic Engineering

HASSE, R., Economics: Economic Policy

HEILEMANN, U., Empirical Economics and Econometrics

HOLLÄNDER, R., Environmental Management in Small and Medium Enterprises

KALISKE, M., Industrial Engineering and Structural Engineering: Statics and Dynamics of Structures

LANG, S., Economics, Statistics

LENK, T., Economics: Public Finance Theory

LÖBLER, H., Business Management: Marketing

PAHL, B., Industrial Engineering and Structural Engineering: Drafting/Construction Design

PARASKEWOPOULOS, S., Economics: Macroeconomics

PELZL, W., Business Management: Real Estate Management

POSSELT, T., Business Management: Service Management

RAUTENBERG, H.-G., Business Management: Management Accounting and Corporate Taxation

RINGEL, J., Urban Management

SCHMIDT, H., Business Management: Accounting and Auditing

SCHUHMACHER, F., Business Management: Corporate Finance

SINGER, H. J., Business Management: Banking

TUE, V., Industrial Engineering and Structural Engineering: Solid Construction/ Building Material Technology

VOLLMER, U., Economics and Currency

WAGNER, F., Business Management: Insurance Company Management

WANZEK, T., Industrial Engineering and Structural Engineering: Steel-Girder Construction

WIESE, H., Economics: Microeconomics

Faculty of Education (Karl-Heine-Str. 22B, 04229 Leipzig; tel. (341) 9731400; fax (341) 9731499; e-mail dekanat.fakerz@uni-leipzig .de; internet www.uni-leipzig.de/~erzwiss):

DOBSLAFF, O., Special Education, Language and Speech Pathology

HOFSÄSS, T., Special Education, Learning Disabilities

HOPPE-GRAFF, S., Educational Psychology

HÖRNER, W., Comparative Education

KLAUSER, F., Economics, Business Education and Management Training

KNOLL, J., Adult Education

MARX, H., Psychology in School and Instruction

MELZER, M., School Education

MUTZECK, W., Behaviour Problems and Therapy in Special Education

SCHULZ, D., School Education

TOEPELL, M., Teaching Primary School Mathematics

VON WOLFFERSDORFF-EHLERT, C., Social Education

WOLLERSHEIM, H. W., General Education

Faculty of History, Art and Oriental Studies (Burgstr. 21, 04109 Leipzig; tel. (341) 9737000; fax (341) 9737049; e-mail dekgko@ rz.uni-leipzig.de; internet www.uni-leipzig .de/fak/gesch.htm):

BAUMBACH, G., Drama

BAXMANN, J., Drama (Dance)

BÜNZ, E., History of Saxony

CAIN, H.-U., Classical Archaeology

DENZEL, M. A., Social and Economic History

DINER, D., Jewish History and Culture

EBERHARD, W., East and Middle European History

EBERT, H.-G., Islamic Law

FEURICH, H.-J., Teaching of Music

FISCHER-ELFERT, H.-W., Egyptology

FRANCO, E., Indology

VON FRANZ, R., Modern Sinology

GERTEL, J., Economy and Social Geography of the Middle East

GIRSHAUSEN, TH., Drama

HEEG, G., Drama

HEYDEMANN, G., Modern History

HÖPKEN, W., East and South-east European History

JONES, A., African History

KAPPEL, R., African Politics and Economy

KLOTZ, S., Systematic Musical Science

LANGE, B., History of Art

LOOS, H., Historical Music Science

MAREK, M., History of Art

MORITZ, R., Classical Sinology

PREISSLER, H., History of Middle Eastern Religions

RICHTER, S., Japanology

RIECKHOFF-HESSE, S., Prehistory and Early History

RIEKENBERG, M., Comparative History and Ibero-American History

RUDERSDORF, M., History of the Early Modern Era

SCHUBERT, CH., Classical History

SCHULZ, E., Arabic Linguistic and Translation Science

SCHULZ, F., Teaching of Art

SEIWERT, H., General and Comparative Religion

SÖRENSEN, P. K., Central Asian Studies

STRECK, B., Ethnology

STRECK, M., Ancient Near East

TOPFSTEDT, TH., History of Art

VON HEHL, U., Modern History

WOLFF, E., African Studies

ZÖLLNER, F., History of Art

Faculty of Law (Burgstr. 27, 04109 Leipzig; tel. (341) 9735100; fax (341) 9735299; e-mail simue@rz.uni-leipzig.de; internet www .uni-leipzig.de/~jura):

BECKER-EBERHARD, E., Civil Law and Civil Action Law

BERGER, CHR., Civil and Civil Trial Law, Copyright

BOEMKE, B., Civil and Industrial Law, Social Legislation

DEGENHART, C., Commercial, Environmental and Planning Law

DOLEZALEK, G., Civil Law

DRYGALA, T., Civil Law, Commercial, Social and Business Law

ENDERS, CHR., Public Law

GOERLICH, H., Public, Constitutional and Administrative Law

HÄUSER, F., Civil, Industrial and Banking Law

KAHLO, M., Criminal and Criminal Trial Law, Legal Philosophy

KERN, B.-R., Civil and Medical Law, History of Law

KLESCZEWSKI, D., Criminal Trial Law and European Criminal Law

KÖCK, W., Environmental Law

OLDIGES, M., Public Law

RAUSCHER, TH., Private International Law, Comparative and Civil Law

SCHUMANN, H., Criminal and Commercial Law

STADIE, M.-H., Tax Law and Public Law

WELTER, R., Civil Law, German and International Economic Law

Faculty of Mathematics and Computer Science (Augustusplatz 10–11, 04109 Leipzig; tel. (341) 9732100; fax (341) 9732199; e-mail matinf@mathematik.uni-leipzig.de; internet www.uni-leipzig.de/matinf):

BEYER, K., Applied Mathematics

BORNELEIT, P., Teaching of Mathematics

BREWKA, G., Intelligent Systems

FREY, R., Discrete Mathematics

FRITZSCHE, B., Probability Theory

GIRLICH, H.-J., Stochastics

GRUHN, V., Applied Telematics

GÜNTHER, M., Partial Differential Equations

HERRE, H., Formal Concepts of Computer Science

HERZOG, B., Principles of Mathematics, Logic, Theory of Numbers

HEYER, G., Natural Language Processing

HUBER-KLAWITTER, A., Theoretical Mathematics

IRMSCHER, K., Computer Networks and Split Systems

KEBSCHULL, U., Technical Information Technology

KIRSTEIN, B., Mathematical Statistics

KUNKEL, P., Numerical Mathematics and Scientific Computing

KÜRSTEN, K.-D., Operator Algebra

LUCKHAUS, ST., Mathematical Optimization

MIERSEMANN, E., Calculus of Variations

RADEMACHER, H.-B., Differential Geometry

RAHM, E., Databases

SCHMÜDGEN, K., Functional Analysis

SCHUMANN, R., Analysis

SCHWARZ, M., Mathematics in Science

STADLER, P., Bioinformatics

STÜCKRAD, J., Algebra

WOLLENBERG, M., Mathematical Physics

Faculty of Medicine (Liebigstr. 27, 04103 Leipzig; tel. (341) 9715930; fax (341) 9715939; e-mail teichh@medizin.uni-leipzig .de):

ADAM, H., Anaesthesiology and Intensive Therapy

ALEXANDER, H., Obstetrics and Gynaecology

ALLGAIER, C., Pharmacology and Toxicology

ANGERMEYER, M., Psychiatry

ARENDT, T., Neuroanatomy

ARNOLD, K., Medical Physics and Biophysics

ASMUSSEN, G., Physiology
BADER, A., Cell Biology
BAERWALD, C., Internal Medicine, Rheumatology
BAIER, D., Obstetrics and Gynaecology
BLATZ, R., Medical Microbiology
BÖHME, H.-J., Biochemistry
BRÄHLER, E., Medical Psychology
BÜHRDEL, P., Paediatrics
VON CRAMON, Y., Cognitive Neurology
DANNHAUER, K.-H., Orthodontics
DECKERT, F., Diagnostic Radiology
DIETZ, A., Otorhinolaryngology
DONATH, E., Medical Physics and Biophysics
EICHFELD, U., Thorax Surgery
EILERS, J., Physiology
EMMRICH, P., Pathology
ENGELE, J., Anatomy, Embryology
ENGELMANN, L., Internal Medicine, Intensive Medicine
ESCHRICH, K., Biochemistry
ETTRICH, C., Child and Adolescent Psychiatry, Psychotherapy
FROSTER, U., Genetics
GEBHARDT, R., Biochemistry
GERTZ, H.-J., Psychiatry
GEYER, M., Psychosomatic Medicine and Psychotherapy
GLANDER, H.-J., Andrology
GRÄFE, H.-G., Paediatric Surgery
GRÜNDER, W., Medical Physics and Biophysics
GUMMERT, J. F., Cardiac Surgery
HÄNTZSCHEL, H., Internal Medicine, Rheumatology
HAUSS, J. P., Abdominal, Transplantation and Vascular Surgery
HEMPRICH, A., Maxillofacial Surgery
HENGSTLER, J., Molecular Toxicology
HERBARTH, O., Environmental Medicine
HIRSCH, W., Diagnostic Radiology
HÖCKEL, M., Obstetrics and Gynaecology
HORN, F., Molecular Immunology
HUMMELSHEIM, H., Neurology
ILLES, P., Pharmacology and Toxicology
JAKSTAT, H., Dental Prosthetics and Materials
JANOUSÈK, J., Paediatric Cardiology
JASSOY, C., Molecular Virology
JENTSCH, H., Parodontology
JOSTEN, CH., Traumatology
KAHN, TH., Diagnostic Radiology
KÄSTNER, I., History of Medicine
KELLER, E., Paediatrics
KIESS, W., Paediatrics
KLEEMANN, W. J., Forensic Medicine
KLÖTZER, B., Surgery
KÖNIG, F., Anaesthesiology and Intensive Therapy
KÖNIG, H.-H., Health Economy
KÖRHOLZ, D., Paediatrics, Haematology and Oncology
KORTMANN, R.-D., Radiotherapy
KOSTELKA, M., Paediatrics, Cardiac Surgery
LIEBERT, U. G., Virology
LÖFFLER, M., Medical Informatics, Statistics and Epidemiology
MEIXENSBERGER, J., Neurosurgery
MERKENSCHLAGER, A., Paediatrics
MERTE, K., Restorative Dentistry
METZNER, G., Clinical Immunology, Allergology
MOHR, F.-W., Cardiac Surgery
MÖSSNER, J., Internal Medicine, Gastroenterology
MOTHES, TH., Clinical Chemistry
NIEDERWIESER, D., Internal Medicine, Haematology
NÖRENBERG, W., Pharmacology and Toxicology
OLTHOFF, D., Anaesthesiology and Intensive Therapy
PASCHKE, R., Internal Medicine, Endocrinology

PFÄFFLE, R., Paediatrics, Endocrinology, Gastroenterology
PFEIFFER, D., Internal Medicine, Cardiology
PLÖTTNER, G., Psychosomatic Medicine and Psychotherapy
PREISS, R., Clinical Pharmacology
REIBER, TH., Dental Prosthetics and Materials
REICHENBACH, A., Neurophysiology
RICHTER, V., Clinical Chemistry, Metabolic Disorders
RIEDEL-HELLER, S., Public Health
RIHA, O., History of Medicine
RODLOFF, A., Medical Microbiology
SABRI, O., Nuclear Medicine
VON SALIS-SOGLIO, G., Orthopaedics
SANDHOLZER, H., Internal Medicine
SCHELLENBERGER, W., Biochemistry
SCHMIDT, F., Diagnostic Radiology
SCHOBER, R., Neuropathology
SCHÖNEBERG, T., Biochemistry, Molecular Endocrinology
SCHREINICKE, G., Industrial Medicine
SCHUBERT, ST., Internal Medicine
SCHULER, G., Internal Medicine, Cardiology
SCHUSTER, V., Paediatrics
SCHWARZ, J., Neurology
SCHWARZ, R., Social Medicine
SCHWOKOWSKI, CH., Surgical Oncology
SEIBEL, P., Molecular Cell Therapy
SIMON, J.-C., Dermatology
SPANEL-BOROWSKI, K., Anatomy
STICHERLING, M., Dermatology
STUMWOLL, M., Internal Medicine, Gastroenterology, Hepatology
TANNAPFEL, A., Pathology
THIERY, J., Laboratory Medicine
TILLMANN, H.-L., Internal Medicine, Gastroenterology and Hepatology
TREIDE, A., Child Dentistry
WAGNER, A., Neurology
WIEDEMANN, P., Ophthalmology
WILD, H. A., Paediatric Orthopaedics
WINTER, A., Medical Informatics
WIRTZ, H., Internal Medicine, Pulmology
WITTEKIND, C., Pathology, Immunopathology
ZIMMER, H.-G., Physiology

Faculty of Philology (Beethovenstr. 15, 04107 Leipzig; tel. (341) 9737300; fax (341) 9737349; e-mail dekphilo@uni-leipzig.de; internet www.uni-leipzig.de/~philol):

BARZ, I., Contemporary German Linguistics and Lexicology
BAUMANN, K., Applied Linguistics/LSP Communication (English, Russian, German)
BICKEL, B., Linguistic Typology and Diversity
DE TORO, A., Romance Literature
DEUFERT, M., Classical Philology and Latin Literature
EILERT, H., Modern German Literature
FELTEN, U., French and Italian Literature
FIX, U., Contemporary German Linguistics
GÄRTNER, E., Romance Linguistics
GOTTZMANN, C., Old German Literature
HARRESS, B., Slavic Literature and Cultural History
HINRICHS, U., Southern Slavic Linguistics and Translation Science
HOFFMANN-MAXIS, A., General and Comparative Literature and Literary Theory
KEIL, H., North American Cultural History
KOENEN, A., American Literature
LÖRSCHER, W., English Linguistics
MEIER, B., Teaching of German
MÜLLER, G., General Linguistics
NASSEN, U., Children's Literature and Juvenile Literature
ÖHLSCHLÄGER, G., German Linguistics
PECHMANN, TH., Psycholinguistics
POLLNER, C., English Linguistics

RITZER, M., Modern German Literature
RYTEL-KUC, D., West Slavic Linguistics
SCHENKEL, E., English Literature
SCHMITT, A. P., Linguistics and Translation Studies (English)
SCHWARZ, W., Literature and Cultural History of the Western Slavs
SCHWEND, J., Cultural Studies (Great Britain)
SIER, K., Classical Philology and Greek Literature
STOCKINGER, L., Modern German Literature
TSCHIRNER, E., German as a Foreign Language
UDOLPH, J., Onomastic Science
WERNER, E., Sorbian Studies
WIESE, I., Contemporary German Linguistics
WOTJAK, B., German as a Foreign Language, Lexicology of Contemporary German Linguistics
WOTJAK, G., Romance Linguistics and Translation Science (Spanish and French)
ZYBATOW, G., Slavic Linguistics

Faculty of Physics and Earth Science (Linnéstr. 5, 04103 Leipzig; tel. (341) 9732400; fax (341) 9732499; e-mail dekan@physik.uni-leipzig.de):

BUTZ, T., Experimental Physics
EHRMANN, W., Geology
ESQUINAZI, P. D., Experimental Physics
FREUDE, D., Chemical Physics
GLÄSSER, W., Geology, Hydrogeology
GRILL, W., Experimental Physics
GRUNDMANN, M., Experimental Physics
HEINRICH, J., Physical Geography and Landscape-based Environmental Research
HEINTZENBERG, J., Atmospheric Physics
HERRMANN, H., Chemistry of the Atmosphere
IHLE, D., Theoretical Physics
JACOBI, CHR., Meteorology
JACOBS, F., Geophysics
JANKE, W., Theoretical Physics
KÄRGER, J., Experimental Physics
KÄS, J., Experimental Physics
KIRSTEIN, W., Geography and Geoinformatics
KORN, M., Theoretical Geophysics
KREMER, F., Experimental Physics
KROY, K.-D., Theoretical Physics
LENTZ, S., Regional Geography
LÖSCHE, M., Experimental Physics
MELLES, M., Geology
METZ, W., Theoretical Meteorology
OEHME, W., Teaching of Physics
RAUSCHENBACH, B., Applied Physics
RENNER, E., Modelling of Atmospheric Processes
RUDOLPH, G., Theoretical Physics
SALMHOFER, M., Theoretical Physics
SIBOLD, K., Theoretical Physics
TETZLAFF, G., Meteorology
WEILAND, U., Urban Ecology
WIESSNER, R., Anthropogeography, Economic Geography and the Labour Market

Faculty of Social Sciences and Philosophy (Burgstr. 21, 04109 Leipzig; tel. (341) 9735600; fax (341) 9735699; e-mail foerster@rz.uni-leipzig.de):

BARTELBORTH, TH., Philosophy of Science
BENTELE, G., Public Relations
ELSENHANS, H., Political Science and International Politics
FACH, W., Political Theory
FENNER, C., Comparative Politics
FLAM, H., Sociology
FRÜH, W., Empirical Communications and Media Research
GIESEN, K.-G., International Politics
GOTTWALD, S., Logic

HALLER, M., Journalism and Media Science

HUBER, M., International Politics

KALTER, F., Sociology

KÖHNKE, K., Theory and Philosophy of Culture

KUTSCH, A., Historical and Systematic Communication Studies

LÜBBE, W., Philosophy

MACHILL, M., Journalism and Media Science

MEGGLE, G., Philosophy

MEUSCHEL, S., Political Systems

MÜHLER, K., Sociology

SCHORB, B., Teaching of Media Studies, Further Education

SIEGRIST, H., Comparative History of Modern Europe

STEINMETZ, R., Media and Media Culture

STEKELER-WEITHOFER, P., Philosophy

STIEHLER, H.-J., Empirical Communications and Media Research

VOBRUBA, G., Sociology

VOSS, T., Sociology

Faculty of Sports Science (Jahnallee 59, 04109 Leipzig; tel. (341) 9731600; fax (341) 9731699; e-mail spodekan@rz.uni-leipzig.de; internet www.uni-leipzig.de/~sportfak):

ALFERMANN, D., Psychology of Sport

BUSSE, M., Sports Medicine

INNENMOSER, J., Sports Therapy, Sport for Handicapped People

KRUG, J., General Movement and Training Science

Faculty of Theology (Otto-Schill-Str. 2, 04109 Leipzig; tel. (341) 9735400; fax (341) 9735499; e-mail dekanat@theologie .uni-leipzig.de; internet www.uni-leipzig.de/ ~theolweb):

BERLEJUNG, A., Old Testament

FITSCHEN, K., Church History

HANISCH, H., Religious Education

HERZER, J., New Testament

LUX, R., Old Testament

PETZOLDT, M., Principles of Theology, Hermeneutics

PETZOLDT, M., Systematic Theology

RATZMANN, W., Practical Theology

SCHNEIDER, G., Systematic Theology

SCHRÖTER, J., New Testament

WARTENBERG, G., Church History

WOHLRAB-SAHR, M., Religious and Church Sociology

Faculty of Veterinary Medicine (An den Tierkliniken 19, 04103 Leipzig; tel. (341) 9738000; fax (341) 9738099; e-mail dekanat@vetmed.uni-leipzig.de):

ALBER, G., Immunology

BLESSING, M., Molecular Pathogenesis

BRAUN, R., Milk Hygiene

DAUGSCHIES, A., Parasitology

EDINGER, J., Orthopaedics

EINSPANIER, A., Endocrinology

FEHLHABER, K., Food Hygiene and Consumer Protection

FERGUSON, J., Large-Animal Surgery

FUHRMANN, H., Physiological Chemistry

GÄBEL, G., Physiology

GREVEL, V., Small-Animal Surgery

KRAUTWALD-JUNGHANNS, M.-E., Bird Diseases

KRÜGER, M., Bacteriology and Mycology

LÜCKER, E., Meat Hygiene

MÜLLER, H., Virology

OECHTERING, G., Small-Animal Medicine

SALOMON, F.-V., Anatomy

SCHOON, H.-A., Histopathology and Clinical Pathology

SCHUSSER, G., Large-Animal Medicine

SEEGER, J., Histology and Embryology

SOBIRAJ, A., Obstetrics and Gynaecology

TRUYEN, U., Epidemiology

UNGEMACH, F. R., Pharmacology and Pharmacy

Institute of German Literature: Wächterstr. 34, 04107 Leipzig; tel. (341) 9730300; fax (341) 9730319; e-mail kahl@uni-leipzig .de; internet www.uni-leipzig.de/dll

PROFESSORS

HASLINGER, J., Literary Aesthetics

TREICHEL, H.-U., German Literature

UNIVERSITÄT MANNHEIM

Schloss, 68131 Mannheim

Telephone: (621) 181-0

Fax: (621) 181-1050

E-mail: rektorat@verwaltung.uni-mannheim .de

Internet: www.uni-mannheim.de

Founded 1907 as Städtische Handelshochschule, attached to Heidelberg Univ. 1933, reopened as Wirtschaftshochschule 1946, Univ. status 1967

Languages of instruction: German, English

Academic year: April to February

Rector: Prof. Dr HANS-WOLFGANG ARNDT

Pro-Rectors: Prof. Dr KAI BRODERSEN, Prof. Dr MILA MAJSTER-CEDERBAUM, Prof. Dr WALTER OECHSLER

Chancellor: Dr SUSANN-ANNETTE STORM

Librarian: Dipl.-Phys. CHRISTIAN BENZ

Number of teachers: 113

Number of students: 11,500

DEANS

Faculty of Business Administration: (vacant)

Faculty of Law: Prof. Dr KONRAD STAHL

Faculty of Mathematics and Information Sciences: Prof. Dr MATTHIAS KRAUSE

Faculty of Philosophy: Prof. Dr THOMAS KLINKERT

Faculty of Social Sciences: Prof. Dr JOSEF BRÜDERL,

UNIVERSITÄT OLDENBURG

Postfach 2503, 26111 Oldenburg

Located at: Ammerländer Heerstr. 114–118, 26129 Oldenburg

Telephone: (441) 798-0

Fax: (441) 7983000

E-mail: webmaster@uni-oldenburg.de

Internet: www.uni-oldenburg.de

Founded 1974

Academic year: October to September (two terms)

Pres.: (vacant)

Vice-Pres: Dr HEIDE AHRENS, Dr MATHIAS WICKLEDER, HANS-JÜRGEN APPELRATH

Librarian: HANS-JOACHIM WÄTJEN

Number of teachers: 173 professors

Number of students: 9,956

Publications: *Data Work* (computer sciences, 3 a year), *Einblicke* (research at the University, 2 a year), *Monoculus* (biology, 2 a year)

DEANS

Faculty 1 (School of Education): Prof. Dr BERNHARD KITTEL

Faculty 2 (School of Computer Science, Business Administration, Economics and Law): Prof. Dr AXEL HAHN

Faculty 3 (Linguistics and Cultural Studies): Prof. Dr GERD HENTSCHEL

Faculty 4 (Humanities and Social Sciences): Prof. Dr RUDOLF HOLBACH

Faculty 5 (Mathematics and Natural Science): Prof. Dr GEORG KLUMP

PROFESSORS

Faculty 1 (School of Education) (Ammerländer Heerstr. 114–118, 26129 Oldenburg; tel. (441) 798-2002; fax (441) 798-2924; e-mail

dekanat.fk1@uni-oldenburg.de; internet www.uni-oldenburg.de/fk1):

Department of Education:

HANFT, A., Adult Education and Continuing Vocational Education

KAISER, A., Elementary Science, Elementary Social Studies

KIPER, H., Theory and Practice in Secondary Education

MEYER, H., General Education, School Teaching

MOSCHNER, B., Teaching and Learning Research

NITSCH, W., Theory of Knowledge

SCHMIDTKE, H.-P., Intercultural Education

Department of Special Needs Education:

ORTMANN, M., Education for the Physically Handicapped

SCHULZE, G. C., Special Education Needs

WITTROCK, M., Education for People with Disturbed Behaviour

Faculty 2 (School of Computer Science, Business Administration, Economics and Law) (Ammerländer Heerstr. 114–118, 26129 Oldenburg; tel. (441) 798-4140; fax (441) 798-4199; internet www.uni-oldenburg.de/fk2):

Business Administration and Education:

BREISIG, T., Organization and Human Resources

LACHNIT, L., Financial and Management Accounting

MOHE, X., Business Consultancy

MÜLLER, M., Production and Environmental Management

PFRIEM, R., General and Environmental Management

RAABE, T., Marketing

REBMANN, K., Vocational and Business Education

SIEBENHÜNER, Ecological Economics

Computer Science:

APPELRATH, H.-J., Information Systems and Databases

BEST, E., Parallel Systems

DAMM, W., Safety Critical Embedded Systems

FATIKOW, S., Microrobotics, Control Engineering

FRÄNZLE, M., Hybrid Systems

HABEL, A., Formal Languages

HASSELBRING, W., Software Engineering

HEIN, A., Automation and Measurement Engineering

JENSCH, P., Image Processing and Process Control

KOWALK, W., Computer Networks and Telecommunications

MÖBUS, C., Learning Environments and Knowledge-based Systems

NEBEL, W., Embedded Hardware/Software Systems Design

OLDEROG, E.-R., Correct System Design

SONNENSCHEIN, M., Environmental Informatics

STIEGE, G., Graphs and Networks

THEEL, O., System Software and Distributed Systems

Economics:

EBERT, U., Public Finance

LITZ, H.-P., Economic Statistics

SCHEELE, Economic Policy

SCHÜLER, K. W., Econometrics

TRAUTWEIN, H. M., International Economics

WELSCH, H., Economic Theory

Law:

BLANKE, T., Labour Law

FRANK, G., Public Economic Law

SCHIEK, D., European Economic Law

TAEGER, J., Private Law, Business and Economic Law, Legal Informatics

Teaching of Economics and of Technology:
HENSELER, K., Teaching of Technology
KAMINSKI, H., Teaching of Economics
LEWALD, A., Home Economics
REICH, G., Teaching of Technology

Faculty 3 (Linguistics and Cultural Studies) (Ammerländer Heerstr. 114–118, 26129 Oldenburg; tel. (441) 798-2347; fax (441) 798-2115; e-mail fk3@uni-oldenburg.de; internet www.uni-oldenburg.de/fk3):

Dutch Studies:
GRÜTTEMEIER, R., Dutch Literature

English Studies:
GELUYKENS, R., Pragmatics, Discourse Analysis, Social Variation
HAMANN, C., Acquisition of First and Second Languages, Bilingualism, Formal Syntax and Semantics
KOEHRING, K., American Literature and Culture

Fine Arts and Visual Communication:
HOFFMANN, D., History of Fine Arts
SPRINGER, P., Theory and History of Art
THIELE, J., Fine Arts and Visual Communication
WENK, S., History of Art, Gender Studies

German Studies:
BRANDES, H., Literature
DOERING, S., Literature
EICHLER, W., Didactics and Linguistics
GLOY, J., Linguistics
KYORA, S., Literature
MEVES, U., Medieval German Literature and Language
STÖLTING, W., German as a Second or Foreign Language

Music:
DINESCU, V., Applied Composition
HOFFMANN, F., Music Education
SCHLEUNING, P., History of Music, Music Teaching
STROH, W. M., Theory of Music and Music Pedagogics

Slavonic Studies:
GRÜBEL, R., Slavonic Literature
HENTSCHEL, G., Linguistics and Slavonic Languages

Visual and Material Culture:
ELLWANGER, K., History of Culture
MÖRSCH, C., Teaching of Material Culture

Faculty 4 (Humanities and Social Sciences) (Ammerländer Heerstr. 114–118, 26129 Oldenburg; tel. (441) 798-2634; fax (441) 798-2624; e-mail dekanat.fk4@uni-oldenburg.de; internet www.uni-oldenburg.de/fk4):

Geography:
HAGEN, D., Cartography and Physical Geography

History:
BUDDE, G., 19th- and 20th-century German and European History
ETZEMÜLLER, T., Contemporary History
FREIST, D., Early Modern History
GÜNTHER-ARNDT, H., Teaching of History
HAHN, H.-H., Modern and East European History (esp. History of Poland)
HOLBACH, R., Medieval History
REEKEN, D. VON, Teaching of History
SCHEER, T., Ancient History

Philosophy:
GERHARD, M., Philosophy of Nature and of Science, Continental Philosophy
KREUZER, J., Philosophy and History of Philosophy
MÖBUSS, S., Philosophy and Jewish Philosophy
PUSTER, E., Epistemology, Philosophy of Language, Ethics
RUSCHIG, U., Philosophy

SCHULZ, R., Philosophy and History of Science
SUKALE, M., Philosophy and Philosophy of Science

Psychology:
BELSCHNER, W., Psychology
COLONIUS, H., Psychological Methods
HELLMAN, A., Psychological Methods
HÖGE, H., Environmental Psychology and Empirical Aesthetics
LAUCKEN, U., Social Psychology
MEES, U., General Psychology
NACHREINER, F., Applied Psychology
SCHICK, A., Psychological Acoustics and Environmental Psychology
SZAGUN, D., Developmental Psychology
VIEBAHN, P., Educational Psychology
WALCHER, K.-P., Psychology of Personality, Environmental Psychology

Social Sciences:
FLAAKE, K., Women's Studies
GRUNENBERG, A., Political Theory and Political Culture
KRAIKER, G., Social and Political Theory
LOEBER, H.-D., Sociology of Labour and Education
MÜLLER-DOOHM, S., Sociology of the Mass Media
NASSMACHER, K.-H., Comparative Politics
WEISMANN, A., Sociology, Methods of Social Research

Sports Science:
ALKEMEYER, T., Sociology and Philosophy of Sport
LIPPENS, V., Motor Control and Learning
SCHIERZ, M., Sports Science
SCHMÜCKER, B., Sports Science and Sports Medicine

Theology:
GOLKA, F., Jewish Studies, Old Testament
HEUMANN, J., Religious Education
LINK-WIECZOREK, U., Systematic Theology and Religious Education
WEISS, W., New Testament

Faculty 5 (Mathematics and Natural Science) (Ammerländer Heerstr. 114–118, 26129 Oldenburg; tel. (441) 798-3442; fax (441) 798-5601; e-mail fk5@uni-oldenburg.de; internet www.uni-oldenburg.de/fk5):

Biology, Earth and Environmental Sciences:
BRUMSACK, H.-J., Geomicrobiochemistry
CYPIONKA, H., Palaeomicrobiology
EBER, W., Botany, Morphology
GIANI, L., Soil Sciences
HAESELER, V., Terrestrial Ecology
HAGEN, D., Cartography and Physical Geography
HOESSLE, C., Biology, School Teaching
JANIESCH, P., Botany, Physiological Ecology
KLEYER, M., Landscape Ecology
KLUMP, G. M., Zoophysiology
KOCH, K.-W., Biochemistry
KRETZBERG, J.
KUMMERER, K., Regional Planning and Development
RICHTER-LANDSBERG, C., Molecular Neurobiology, Neurochemistry
RINKWITZ, S., Neurogenetics
SCHMINKE, H. K., Zoology, Zoosystematics and Morphology
SIMON, U., Biology of Geological Processes
STABENAU, H., Plant Physiology
VARESCHI, E., Aquatic Ecology
WACKERNAGEL, W., Genetics
WEILER, R., Zoology, Neurobiology
WINDELBERG, J., Infrastructure and Environmental Planning

Chemistry:
AL-SHAMERY, K., Physical Chemistry
BECKHAUS, R., Inorganic Chemistry
GMEHLING, J., Industrial Chemistry

KLEINER, T., Physical Chemistry
KÖLL, P., Organic Chemistry
MARTENS, J., Organic Chemistry
METZGER, J. O., Organic Chemistry
POWCHMANN, J., Chemistry, Theory and Practice of School Teaching
RÖSSNER, F., Industrial Chemistry
WICKLEDER, M., Inorganic Chemistry
WITTSTOCK, G., Physical Chemistry

Mathematics:
DEFANT, A., Mathematics, Functional Analysis
HERZBERGER, J., Applied Mathematics, Instrumental Mathematics
KNAUER, U., Mathematics, Algebraic Methods
LEISSNER, W., Mathematics, Geometry
MÜLLER, CH., Mathematics, Stochastics
PFLUG, P., Mathematics, Complex Variables
PIEPER-SEIER, I., Mathematics, Algebra
QUEBBEMANN, H.-G., Mathematics, Number Theory
SCHMALE, W., Mathematics, Dynamic Systems
SCHMIEDER, G., Mathematics, Complex Analysis
SPÄTH, H., Applied Mathematics
VETTER, U., Mathematics, Commutative Algebra

Physics:
BAUER, G. H., Experimental Physics
ENGEL, A., Theoretical Physics
HINSCH, K., Experimental Physics
HOLTHAUS, M., Theoretical Physics
KOLLMEIER, B., Applied Physics
KOLNY, J., Applied Physics
KUNZ-DROLSHAGEN, J., Theoretical Physics, Field Theory
MAIER, K. H., Experimental Physics
MELLERT, V., Applied Physics
MERTINS, A., Applied Physics
PARISI, J., Experimental Physics
PEINKE, J., Experimental Physics
RIESS, F., Teaching of Physics
VERHEY, J., Applied Physics

UNIVERSITÄT OSNABRÜCK

Neuer Graben/Schloss, 49069 Osnabrück

Telephone: (541) 969-0
Fax: (541) 969-4570
E-mail: aaa@uni-osnabrueck.de
Internet: www.uni-osnabrueck.de

Founded 1973
Languages of instruction: German, English
Academic year: October to September

Pres.: Prof. Dr CLAUS R. ROLLINGER
Vice-Pres.: Prof. Dr PETER HERTEL
Registrar: Dr UWE SIELEMAN
Librarian: FELICITAS HUNDHAUSEN

Number of teachers: 500
Number of students: 10,500

Publication: *Forschungsbericht* (every 2 years).

UNIVERSITÄT PADERBORN

Warburger Str. 100, 33098 Paderborn

Telephone: (5251) 600
Fax: (5251) 602519
E-mail: pressestelle@zv.uni-paderborn.de
Internet: www.uni-paderborn.de

Founded 1972
State control
Language of instruction: German
Academic year: October to July

Rector: Prof. Dr NIKOLAUS RISCH
Chancellor: Dr JÜRGEN PLATO
Librarian: Dr DIETMAR HAUBFLEISCH

Library of 1,700,000 vols, 1.500 periodicals
Number of teachers: 1,350
Number of students: 14,700

Publications: *Forschungsforum* (1 a year), *Paderborner Universitätsreden* (irregular), *Paderborner Universitätszeitung* (2 a year)

DEANS

Faculty of Arts and Humanities: Prof. Dr VOLKER PECKHAUS

Faculty of Business Administration and Economics: Prof. Dr F. E. PETER SLOANE

Faculty of Computer Science, Electrical Engineering and Mathematics: Prof. Dr FRANZ JOSEF RAMMIG

Faculty of Cultural Studies: Prof. Dr FRANZ GÖTTMANN

Faculty of Mechanical Engineering: Prof. Dr DETMAR ZIMMER

Faculty of Science: Prof. Dr HANS-JOACHIM WARNECKE

PROFESSORS

Faculty of Arts and Humanities:

ALLKEMPER, A.
ARNOLD, R.
AUTSCH, S.
BAUER, G.
BEDER, J.
BRAUERHOCH, A.
BUBLITZ, H.
BURRICHTER, R.
CORTIEL, J.
ECKER, G.
ECKHARDT, J.
EHLAND, C.
EKE, N.
ENGLISCH, B.
FELDBUSCH, E.
FREITAG, C.
GEMBRIS, H.
GÖTTMANN, F.
GROTJAHN, R.
HAGENGRUBER, R.
HERZIG, B.
HOFMANN, M.
HORNÄK, S.
JACKE, C.
KAMP, H.
KEIL, W.
KLENKE, D.
KOELLE, L.
KOLHOFF-KAHL, I.
KRETTENAUER, T.
KUHLMANN, H.
KÜRTZ, A.
LANG, B.
LANGENBACHER-LIEBGOTT, J.
LAUBENTHAL, A.
LEMKE, I.
LEUTZSCH, M.
MARX, N.
MEISTER, D.
MÜLLER, S.
MÜLLER-LIETZKOW, J.
ÖHLSCHLÄGER, C.
PECKHAUS, V.
PIENEMANN, M.
RENDTORFF, B.
RIBBAT, C.
SCHAPER, N.
SCHARLAU, I.
SCHMITZ, S.
SCHROETER-WITTKE, H.
SCHUSTER, B.
SENG, E.
SÖLL, F.
STEINECKE, A.
STRÖTER-BENDER, J.
STROTMANN, A.
STRUBE, M.
SÜSSMANN, J.
TÖNNIES, M.
TOPHINKE, D.
VON STOSCH, K.
WILK, N.
WINKLER, H.
ZIELKE, G.

Faculty of Business Administration and Economics:

BARTON, D.
BETZ, S.
BEUTNER, M.
DANGELMAIER, W.
DILLER, M.
EGGERT, A.
EGGERT, W.
FAHR, R.
FENG, Y.
FISCHER, J.
FRICK, B.
GILROY, B.
GRIES, T.
HAAKE, C.
HOGREVE, J.
ISEKE, A.
KLIEWER, N.
KOBERSTEIN, A.
KREMER, H.
KRIEGER, T.
KRIMPHOVE, D.
KUNDISCH, D.
LÖFFLER, A.
MÜLLER, J.
ROSENTHAL, K.
SCHILLER, B.
SCHNEIDER, G.
SCHNEIDER, M.
SLOANE, P.
SUHL, L.
SURETH, C.
WERNER, T.

Faculty of Computer Science, Electrical Engineering and Mathematics:

BELLI, F.
BENDER, P.
BLÖMER, J.
BÖTTCHER, S.
BRINKMANN, A.
BRUNS, M.
BÜRGISSER, P.
DELLNITZ, M.
DIETZ, H.
DOMIK-KIENEGGER, B.
ENGELS, G.
GAUSCH, F.
HÄB-UMBACH, R.
HANSEN, S.
HAUENSCHILD, W.
HENNING, B.
HILLERINGMANN, U.
KASTENS, U.
KEIL, R.
KLEINE, B.
KÖCKLER, N.
MAGENHEIM, J.
MEYER, F.
NOÉ, R.
RAMMIG, F.
RINKENS, H.

Faculty of Mechanical Engineering:

GAUSEMEIER, J.
HOMBERG, W.
KENIG, E.
KOCH, R.
MAHNKEN, R.
MAIER, H.
MORITZER, E.
RICHARD, H.
SCHMID, H.
SCHÖPPNER, V.
SEXTRO, W.
TRÄCHTLER, A.
TRÖSTER, T.
VRABEC, J.
ZIMMER, D.

Faculty of Science:

BECKER, H.
BRANDL-BREDENBECK, H.
BREMSER, W.
FELS, G.
GRUNDMEIER, G.

HENKEL, G.
HESEKER, H.
HUBER, K.
KITZEROW, H.
KUCKLING, D.
LINDNER, J.
LISCHKA, K.
MEIER, C.
MEIER, T.
OLIVIER, N.
REINHOLD, P.
RISCH, N.
SCHINDLMAYR, A.
SCHLEGEL-MATTHIES, K.
SCHMIDT, C.
SCHMIDT, W.
SCHUBERT, V.
SOHLER, W.
WARNECKE, H.
WEISS, M.
ZRENNER, A.

UNIVERSITÄT PASSAU

Innstr. 41, 94032 Passau

Telephone: (851) 509-0
Fax: (851) 509-1005
E-mail: auslandsamt@uni-passau.de
Internet: www.uni-passau.de

Founded 1972
State control
Language of instruction: German
Academic year: October to September

Pres.: Prof. Dr WALTER SCHWEITZER
Vice-Pres.: Prof. Dr ERNST STRUCK
Vice-Pres.: Prof. Dr BURKHARD FEITAG
Vice-Pres.: Prof. Dr WOLFGANG HAU
Admin. Officer: LUDWIG BLOCH
Librarian: Dr STEFFEN WAWRA

Library: 2m. vols
Number of teachers: 115
Number of students: 8,446

DEANS

Faculty of Business Sciences: Prof. Dr FRANZ LEHNER

Faculty of Law: Prof. Dr ULRIKE MÜSSIG

Faculty of Computer Sciences and Mathematics: Prof. Dr HARALD KOSCH

Faculty of Philosophy: Prof. Dr WERNER GAMERITH

Faculty of Theology: Prof. Dr ANTON LANDERSDORFER

PROFESSORS

Faculty of Business Sciences (94030 Passau; tel. (851) 509-2400; fax (851) 509-2603; e-mail dekanat@wiwi.uni-passau.de; internet www.wiwi.uni-passau.de):

BORCK, R., Economic Policy
BÜHNER, R., Organization and Human Resource Management
FIEDLER, M., Management, People And Information
FISCHER, M, Marketing And Services
JUNGWIRTH, C., Economic Policy
KLEINSCHMIDT, P., Business Computing I
LAMBSDORFF, J. G., Economic Theory
LEHNER, F., Business Computing II
MOOSMÜLLER, G., Statistics
PFLÜGNER, M., Foreign Trade and International Economics
SCHWEITZER, W., Statistics
WAGNER, N., Financial Controlling
WILHELM, J., Finance
ZIEGLER, H., Production and Logistics

Faculty of Law (94030 Passau; tel. (851) 509-2201; fax (851) 509-2207; e-mail dekanat .jura@uni-passau.de; internet www.jura .uni-passau.de):

ALTMEPPEN, H., Private Law, Commercial and Business Law I
BAYREUTHER, F., Civil Law and Labour Law

BEULKE, W., Penal Law

BRAUN, J., Civil Law, Civil Procedural Law and Philosophy of Law

DEDERER, H.-G., Constitutional and Administrative Law, Public International Law, European and International Economic Law

ENGLÄNDER, A., Criminal Law and Criminal Procedure

ESSER, R., German, European and International Criminal Law, Criminal Procedure and White-Collar Crime

HAU, W., Private Law, Civil Procedure, Private International Law

HECKMANN, D., Public Law, Security Law and Internet Law

HERRMANN, C., Constitutional and Administrative, European Law, European and International Economic Law

KRAMER, U., Public Law

KUHN, T., Civil Law

MANTHE, U., Civil Law and Roman Law

MÜLLER-TERPITZ, R., State, Administrative, Media and Information Law

MÜSSIG, U., Civil Law, German and European Legal History

PUTZKE, H., Penal Law

SOLOMON, D., Private Law, Private International Law and Comparative Law

WERNSMANN, R., State and Administrative Law, Tax Law

Faculty of Computer Sciences and Mathematics (94030 Passau; tel. (851) 509-3001; fax (851) 509-3002; e-mail dekanat@fim.uni-passau.de; internet www.fim.uni-passau.de):

BEYER, D., Computer Science, Software Systems

BRANDENBURG, F.-J., Computer Science, Theoretical Computer Science

DE MEER, H., Computer Science, Computer Networks/Computer Communications

DONNER, K., Mathematics, Numerical Mathematics (Analysis)

FREITAG, B., Computer Science, Information Management

GRAF, S., Mathematics, Measure and Integration

KAISER, T., Mathematics

KOSCH, H., Computer Science and Distributed Information Systems

KREUZER, M., Mathematics and Symbolic Computation

LENGAUER, CH., Computer Science and Programming

LUKOWICZ, P., Computer Science and Embedded Systems

MÜLLER-GRONBACH, T., Mathematics, Mathematical Stochastics and its Appliances

POLIAN, I., Computer Science and Computer Engineering

POSEGGA, J., Computer Science and IT Security

SCHWARTZ, N., Mathematics and Algebraic Geometry

Faculty of Philosophy (94030 Passau; tel. (851) 509-2600; fax (851) 509-2626; e-mail dekanat.phil@uni-passau.de; internet www.phil.uni-passau.de):

ANHUF, D., Physical Geography

BACH, M., Sociology

BARMEYER, C., Ch. Intercultural Communication

BAUER, L., Didadactics of Teaching Mathematics

BAUMGARTNER, I., Science of Christian Society and Charity

BERNERT, W., Didadactics of Teaching Social Studies

ERKENS, F., Medival History

FITZ, K., American Studies

FONK, P., Moral Theology

FRENZ, T., Medival History and and Historical Science

GAMERITH, W., Regional Geography

GELLNER, W., Political Science II

GLAS, A., Education of Arts

GÖLER, D., European Studies

HARNISCH, R., German Philology

HARTWIG, S., Romanic Literature and Culture

HEINRICH, H., Methods of Empirical Social Research

HIERING, P., Didadactics of Teaching Biology

HINZ, M., Romanic Literature and Applied Geography with Emphasis on Italy

HOHLFELD, R., Media and Communication

KAMM, J., English Literature and Culture

KORFF, R., South-East-Asia Studies II

KRAH, H., Modern German Literature

KRAUS, H.-CH., Modern History

LANDERSDORFER, A., Church History

LISKE, M.-TH., Philosophy

MÄGDEFRAU, J., Education and Didadactis for Secondary School

MENDL, H., Education of Religion and Didaktics of Teaching Religion

MICHLER, A., Didactics of Teaching History

MOGEL, H., Psychology

MÜLLER, K., Didadactics of German Language and Literature

NOLTE, T., Medival German Literature

OBERREUTER, H., Political Science I

POLLAK, G., Science of Education

REUTNER, U., Romanic Linguistics

SCHWANKL, O., Exegesis and biblical Theology

SEIBERT, N., Science of School Education

STAMPFL, I., Education of Music

STINGLHAMMER, H., Dogmatic and History of Dogmata

STOLL, O., Early History

STRUCK, E., Anthropogeography

THIES, C., Philosophy

UFFELMANN, D., Slavic Literature and Culture

WALTER, K., Romanic Literature and Applied Geography with Emphasis on France

WÜNSCH, T., Modern History of Eastern Europe and its Culture

ZECHMEISTER-MACHHART, M., Fundamental Theology

ZEHNPFENNING, B., Political Theory and History

Faculty of Theology (94030 Passau; tel. (851) 509-2001; fax (851) 509-2003; internet www.ktf.uni-passau.de):

BAUMGARTNER, I., Christian Social Studies and Pastoral Theology

FONK, P., Moral Theology

LANDERSDORFER, A., Church History

LISKE, M.-T., Philosophy

MENDL, J., Religious Education and Teaching Methods

SCHWANKL, O., New Testament Exegesis

SCHWIENHORST-SCHÖNBERGER, L., Old Testament Exegesis and Hebrew

STINGLHAMMER, H., Dogmatics

ZECHMEISTER-MACHHART, Basic Theology

UNIVERSITÄT POTSDAM

Postfach 601553, 14415 Potsdam

Am Neuen Palais 10, 14469 Potsdam

Telephone: (331) 977-0

Fax: (331) 977-972163

E-mail: presse@rz.uni-potsdam.de

Internet: www.uni-potsdam.de

Founded 1991

Languages of instruction: German, English

Academic year: October to September

Rector: Prof. Dr WOLFGANG LOSCHELDER

Vice-Rector for Planning and Finance: Prof. Dr JÜRGEN RODE

Vice-Rector for Research and Scientific Development: Prof. Dr FRIEDER SCHELLER

Vice-Rector for Scientific and Technology Transfer and Innovation: Prof. Dr HARALD FUHR

Vice-Rector for Teaching and Study: Prof. Dr GERDA HASSLER

Number of teachers: 226 professors, 923 other academic staff

Number of students: 17,200

DEANS

Faculty of Arts: Prof. Dr BERNHARD KROENER

Faculty of Economic and Social Sciences: Prof. Dr DETLEV HUMMEL

Faculty of Human Sciences: Prof. Dr RIA DE BLESER

Faculty of Law: Prof. Dr HEIDRUN POHL-ZAHN

Faculty of Mathematics and Natural Sciences: Prof. Dr ROBERT SECKLER

UNIVERSITÄT REGENSBURG

Universitätsstr. 31, 93053 Regensburg

Telephone: (941) 943-01

Fax: (941) 943-2305

E-mail: rudolf.dietze@verwaltung.uni-regensburg.de

Internet: www.uni-regensburg.de

Public control

Founded 1962

Academic year: October to September

Rector: Prof. Dr ALF ZIMMER

Pro-Rectors: Prof. Dr REINHARD ANDREESEN, Prof. Dr UDOO HEBEL, Prof. Dr ARMIN KURTZ

Admin. Officer: Dr CHRISTIAN BLOMEYER

Librarian: Dr FRIEDRICH GEISSELMANN

Number of teachers: 1,379

Number of students: 17,277

Publications: Blick in die Wissenschaft, Research Report (online at www.uni-regensburg.de/universitaet/forschungsbericht)

DIRECTORS OF DEPARTMENTS

Biology and Pre-clinical Medical Studies: Prof. Dr R. WITZGALL

Business Management, Economics and Management Information Systems: Prof. Dr H. HRUSCHKA

Catholic Theology: Prof. Dr E. DIRSCHERL

Chemistry and Pharmacy: Prof. Dr A. PFITZNER

History, Social Sciences and Geography: Prof. Dr S. G. BIERLING

Language and Literature: Prof. Dr R. HAMMWÖHNER

Law: Prof. Dr H. ROTH

Mathematics: Prof. Dr K. KÜNNEMANN

Medicine: Prof. Dr B. WEBER

Philosophy, Sport and Arts: Prof. Dr B. HOFMANN

Physics: Prof. Dr C. BACK

Psychology and Pedagogy: Prof. Dr M. W. GREENLEE

PROFESSORS

Department of Biology and Pre-clinical Medical Studies (tel. (941) 943-3110; fax (941) 943-4341; internet www.biologie.uni-regensburg.de):

BAUMANN, R., Physiology

DRESSELHAUS, T., Cell Biology and Plant Physiology

FÖRSTER, C., Zoology

HEINZE, J., Zoology

KALBITZER, H. R., Biophysics

KRAMER, B., Zoology

KUNZELMANN, B., Physiology

KURTZ, A., Physiology

LÄNGST, G., Biochemistry

MINUTH, W., Anatomy

NEUMANN, I., Neurology and Animal Physiology

OBERPRIELER, C., Botany

POSCHLOD, P., Botany
SCHNEUWLY, S., Developmental Biology
SEUFERT, W., Genetics
STERNER, R., Biochemistry
STROM, E., Zoology
TAMM, E., Anatomy
THOMM, M., Microbiology
TSCHOCHNER, H., Biochemistry
WARTH, R., Physiology
WIRTH, R., Microbiology
WITZGALL, R., Molecular and Cellular Anatomy

Department of Business Management, Economics and Management Information Systems (tel. (941) 943-2269; fax (941) 943-4752; internet www.wiwi.uni-regensburg.de):

ARNOLD, L., Economics, Economic Theory
BARTMANN, D., Business Informatics
BUCHHOLZ, W., Public Finance and Environmental Economics
DORFLEITNER, G., Finance
DOWLING, M., Management of Technology and Innovation
FEDERRATH, H., Business
GÖMMEL, R., History of Economics
GRAF, A., Management and Organization Design
HALLER, A., Financial Accounting and Auditing
HAMERLE, A., Statistics
HRUSCHKA, H., Marketing
JERGER, J., International Economy
LEE, G., Real Estate Economics
LEIST, S., Business Informatics
LORY, P., Business Informatics
MEYER-SCHARENBERG, D., Business Taxation
MÖLLER, J., Empirical Macroeconomics and Regional Economics
OTTO, A., Controlling and Logistics
PERNUL, G., Business Informatics
RÖDER, K., Financial Services
SCHÄFERS, W., Real Estate Management
TSCHERNIG, R., Econometry
WIEGARD, W., Economics

Department of Catholic Theology (tel. (941) 943-3746; fax (941) 943-4944; internet www.uni-regensburg.de/fakultaeten/theologie):

DEMEL, S., Canon Law
DIRSCHERL, E., Dogmatics
DOHMEN, C., Exegesis and Hermeneutics of the Old Testament
HAUSBERGER, K., Church History
KNOLL, A., Fundamental Theology
LAUX, B., Theological Anthropology
LEINSLE, U., Philosophical–Theological Propaedeutic
MERKT, A., Old Church History and Patrology
NIKLAS, T., Exegesis and Hermeneutics of the New Testament
PORZELT, B., Didactics of Religious Education
SCHLÖGEL, H., Moral TheologySCHÖTTLER, H.-G., Pastoral Theology

Department of Chemistry and Pharmacy (tel. (941) 943-2556; fax (941) 943-4275; internet www.chemie.uni-regensburg.de):

BUSCHAUER, A., Pharmaceutical Chemistry
DICK, B., Physical Chemistry
ELZ, S., Pharmaceutical Chemistry
GÖPFERICH, A., Pharmaceutical Technology
GSCHWIND, R., Organic Chemistry
HEILMANN, J., Pharmaceutical Biology
KÖNIG, B., Organic Chemistry
KORBER, N., Inorganic Chemistry
KRIENKE, H., Physical Chemistry
KUNZ, W., Physical Chemistry
PFITZNER, A., Inorganic Chemistry
REISER, O., Organic Chemistry
SCHEER, M., Inorganic Chemistry
SCHLOSSMANN, J., Pharmacology and Toxicology
SCHMEER, J., Physical Chemistry

SCHÜTZ, M., Theoretical Chemistry
SEIFERT, R., Pharmacology and Toxicology
WAGENKNECHT, H.-A., Organic Chemistry
WINTER, R., Inorganic Chemistry
WOLFBEIS, O., Analytical Chemistry

Department of History, Social Sciences and Geography (tel. (941) 943-3587; fax (941) 943-3993; internet www.uni-regensburg.de/fakultaeten/phil_fak_iii):

BAUER, F., History
BIERLING, S., Political Science, International Politics
BOHN, T., History of Eastern Europe
DAUM, B., Physical Geography
HERB, K., Political Philosophy and History of Ideas
HERZ, P., Ancient History
KORTÜM, H.-H., Medieval History
LUTTENBERGER, A. P., Early Modern History
MA'CKÓV, D., Comparative Political Science (Middle and Eastern Europe)
OBERSTE, J., Medieval History
SCHAUER, P., Pre- and Early History
SCHMID, P., History of Bavaria
SEBALDT, M., Political Science (Western Europe)

Department of Language and Literature (tel. (941) 943-3592; fax (941) 943-1811; e-mail fachbereich.sl@sprachlit.uni-regensburg.de; internet www.uni-regensburg.de/fakultaeten/phil_fak_iv):

BECK, J.-W., Classical Philology (Latin)
DAIBER, J., German Philology
DEPKAT, V., American Studies
DOTZLER, B., Media Science
DRASCEK, D., Comparative Cultural Studies
FEISTNER, E., Medieval German Literature
FISCHER, R., English Linguistics
GEISENHANSLÜKE, A., Modern German Literature
GELHARD, D., Comparative Literary Studies
GREULE, A., German Linguistics
HAMMWÖHNER, R., Linguistic Computer Science
HANSEN, B., Slavic Linguistics
HEBEL, U., American Studies
HELMBRECHT, J., General and Comparative Linguistics
JUNKERJÜRGEN, R., Romance Cultural Studies
KOSCHMAL, W., Slavonic Literary Studies
MECKE, J., Romance Literary Studies
NEKULA, M., Western Slavic Philology (Bohemian Studies)
NEUMANN-HOLZSCHUH, J., Romance Linguistics
RECHENAUER, G., Classical Philology (Greek)
REGENER, U., German Philology
SCHILCHNER, A., Didactics of the German Language and Literature
SCHNEIDER, E. W., English Linguistics
SCHULZ, M., Medieval German Literature
SELIG, M., Romance Linguistics
THURMAIR, M., German Linguistics (German as a Foreign Language)
TIEFENBACH, H., German Linguistics
WETZEL, H., Romance Literature
WOLFF, C., Media Informatics

Department of Law (tel. (941) 943-2267; fax (941) 943-2013; internet www.uni-regensburg.de/fakultaeten/jura):

ARNOLD, R., Public Law
ECKHOFF, R., Public Law
FRITSCHE, J., Civil Law, Commercial and Economic Law
GOTTWALD, P., Civil Law and Int. Private Law
GRIGOLEIT, H. C., Civil Law, Commercial Law and European Private Law
KINGREEN, T., Public Law and Social Law

KRAPPENBURG, I., Civil Law, History of Law
KÜHLING, J., Public Law, Real Estate Law
MANSSEN, G., Public Law (German and European Admin. Law)
MÜLLER, H. E., Criminal Law
PAWLIK, H., Criminal Law, Philosophy of Law
ROTH, H., Civil Law, Procedural Law
SCHLACHTER, M., Civil Law, Comparative Law
SPICKHOFF, A., Civil Law, Int. Private Law, Comparative Law
UERPMANN-WITTZACK, R., Public Law, Int. Law
ZIMMERMAN, R., Civil Law, Roman Law and Historical Comparative Law

Department of Mathematics (tel. (941) 943-2024; fax (941) 943-4923; internet www.uni-regensburg.de/fakultaeten/nat_fak_i):

AMMANN, B.
BINGENER, J.
BUNKE, U.
DOLZMANN, G.
FINSTER, F.
GARCKE, H.
HEINZE, A.
JANNSSEN, U.
KINGS, G.
KNORR, K.
KÜNNEMANN, K.
SCHMIDT, A.

Department of Medicine (Franz-Josef-Strauß Allee 11, 93053 Regensburg; tel. (941) 944-6082; fax (941) 944-6079; internet www.uni-regensburg.de/fakultaeten/medizin):

AIGNER, L., Experimental Neurology
ANDREESEN, R., Haematology and Oncology
BOGDAHN, U., Neurology
BOẞERHOFF, U., Molecular Pathology
BRAWANSKI, A., Neurosurgery
EICHHAMMER, P., Psychiatry and Psychotherapy
EILLES, C., Nuclear Medicine (Radiotherapy)
FEUERBACH, S., Radiology
FLECK, M., Experimental Internal Medicine
GEISSLER, E., Experimental Surgery
GRIFKA, J., Orthopaedics
HACKI, T., Otorhinolaryngology
HAJAK, G., Psychiatry
HANDEL, G., Prosthodontics
HEHLGANS, T., Molecular Immunology
HELBIG, H., Ophthalmology
HENGSTENBERG, C., Internal Medicine (Molecular Cardiology)
HOBBHAHN, J., Anaesthesiology
HOFMANN, S., Cardiac and Thoracic Surgery
HOFSTÄDTER, F., Pathology
HOHENLEUTNER, U., Dermatology
JILG, W., Medical Microbiology
KLEIN, H. E., Psychiatry
KÖLBL, O., Radiotherapy
KRÄMER, B., Internal Medicine
LANDTHALER, M., Dermatology
LEHN, N., Medical Microbiology
LOEW, T., Psychosomatic Medicine and Psychotherapy
LUCHNER, A., Internal Medicine
MACK, M., Internal Medicine (Nephrology)
MÄNNEL, D., Tumour Immunology (Pathology)
MELTER, M., Paediatrics
NERLICH, M., General Surgery
OEFNER, P., Functional Genomics
ORTMANN, O., Gynaecology
OSTERHEIDER, M., Forensic Psychiatry
PFEIFER, M., Internal Medicine
PISO, P., Surgery (Gastrointestinal Oncology)
REICHERT, T., Oral Surgery
RIEGGER, G., Internal Medicine and Intensive Care
SALZBERGER, B., Internal Medicine

SCHLITT, H. J., Surgery
SCHMALZ, G., Periodontology
SCHMID, C., Cardiac and Thoracic Surgery
SCHMITZ, G., Clinical Chemistry and Laboratory Medicine
SCHÖLMERICH, J., Internal Medicine
SEELBACH-GÖBEL, D., Gynaecology and Obstetrics
SEGERER, H., Neonatology
SPANG, R., Bioinformatics
STRAUB, R., Internal Medicine
STRAUB, O., Experimental Ophthalmology
STRUTZ, J., Otorhinolaryngology
TAEGER, K., Anaesthesiology
VOGT, T., Dermatology
WAGNER, R., Molecular Microbiology
WEBER, B., Human Genetics
WIELAND, F., Urology
WINKLER, J., Neurology
WOERTGEN, C., Neurosurgery
WOLF, H., Medical Microbiology

Department of Philosophy, Sport and Arts (tel. (941) 943-3592; fax (941) 943-3993; e-mail philosophie.sport.kunst@verwaltung.uni-regensburg.de; internet www.uni-regensburg.de/fakultaeten/phil_fak_i):

DIETL, A., History of Art
DITTSCHEID, H.-C., History of Art
HILEY, D., Musicology
HOFMANN, B., Music Education
HORN, W., Musicology
KUNZE, C., Archaeology
MEINEL, C., History of Science
ROTT, H., Theoretical Philosophy
SCHÖLLER, W., History of Art
SCHÖNBERGER, R., History of Philosophy
WAGNER, C., History of Art

Department of Physics (tel. (941) 943-2040; fax (941) 943-2021; internet www.physik.uni-regensburg.de):

BACK, C., Experimental and Applied Physics
BALI, G., Theoretical Physics
BRACK, M., Theoretical Physics
BRAUN, V., Theoretical Physics
FABIAN, J., Theoretical Physics
GANICHEV, S., Experimental and Applied Physics
GIEßIBL, F., Experimental and Applied Physics
GRIFONI, M., Theoretical Physics
MORGENSTERN, I., Theoretical Physics
REPP, J., Experimental and Applied Physics
RICHTER, K., Theoretical Physics
SCHÄFER, A., Theoretical Physics
SCHLIEMANN, J., Theoretical Physics
SCHÜLLER, C., Experimental and Applied Physics
STRUNK, D., Experimental and Applied Physics
WEGSCHEIDER, W., Experimental and Applied Physics
WEISS, D., Experimental and Applied Physics
WETTIG, T., Theoretical Physics
ZWECK, J., Experimental and Applied Physics

Department of Psychology and Pedagogy (tel. (941) 943-3587; fax (941) 943-3993; internet www.uni-regensburg.de/fakultaeten/phil_fak_ii):

BÄUML, K.-H., Psychology
FÖLLING-ALBERS, M., Didactics of the Elementary School
GREENLEE, M. W., Psychology
GRUBER, H., Pedagogy
LANGE, K., Psychology
LUKESCH, H., Psychology
MULDER, R., Pedagogy
RICHTER, S., Didactics of the Elementary School
STÖGER, H., School Education
WILD, K. P., Pedagogy

ZIMMER, A., Psychology

UNIVERSITÄT ROSTOCK

Universitätspl. 1, 18051 Rostock
Telephone: (381) 4980
Fax: (381) 4981015
E-mail: kanzler@uni-rostock.de
Internet: www.uni-rostock.de
Founded 1419
State control
Academic year: October to September
Rector: Prof. Dr JÜRGEN WENDEL
Vice-Rectors: Prof. Dr DETLEF CZYBULKA, Prof. Dr KARL HANTZSCHMANN, Prof. Dr GERD RÖPKE
Chancellor: JOACHIM WITTERN
Library Director: Dr JÜRGEN HEEG
Library: see Libraries and Archives
Number of teachers: 332
Number of students: 9,757

Publications: *Archiv der Freunde der Naturgeschichte in Mecklenburg, Erziehungswissenschaftliche Beiträge, Forschungsbericht der Universität Rostock, Pädagogisches Handeln, Rostocker Agrar- und Umweltwissenschaftliche Beiträge, Rostocker Arbeitspapiere zu Rechnungswesen und Controlling, Rostocker Arbeitspapiere zu Wirtschaftsentwicklung und Human Resource Development, Rostocker Beiträge zur Deutschen und Europäischen Geschichte, Rostocker Beiträge zur Regional- und Strukturforschung, Rostocker Beiträge zur Sprachwissenschaft, Rostocker Beiträge zur Verkehrswissenschaft und Logistik, Rostocker Forum Theologie, Rostocker Informatik-Berichte, Rostocker Informationen zu Politik und Verwaltung, Rostocker Materialen für Landschaftsplanung und Raumentwicklung, Rostocker Mathematisches Kolloquium, Rostocker Medizinische Beiträge, Rostocker Meeresbiologische Beiträge, Rostocker Philosophische Manuskripte, Rostocker Schriften zur Bank und Finanzmarktforschung, Rostocker Schriften zum Bankrecht, Rostocker Studien zur Kulturwissenschaft, Schiffbauforschung, Thunen-Reihe Angewandter Volkswirtschftstheorie,* and various faculty publs

DEANS

Faculty of Agricultural and Environmental Science: Prof. Dr WOLFGANG RIEDEL
Faculty of Economics and Social Sciences: Prof. Dr JAKOB RÖSEL
Faculty of Information Technology and Electroscience: Prof. Dr URSULA VAN RIENEN
Faculty of Law: Prof. Dr RALPH WEBER
Faculty of Mathematics and Natural Sciences: Prof. Dr UDO KRAGL
Faculty of Mechanical Engineering and Shipping Technology: Prof. Dr ALFRED LEDER
Faculty of Medicine: Prof. Dr GABRIELE NÖLDGE-SCHOMBURG
Faculty of Philosophy: Prof. Dr WERNER MÜLLER
Faculty of Theology: Prof. Dr HERMANN MICHAEL NIEMANN

UNIVERSITÄT SIEGEN

Am Herrengarten 3, 57068 Siegen
Telephone: (271) 740-0
Fax: (271) 740-4899
E-mail: buero@rektorat.uni-siegen.de
Internet: www.uni-siegen.de
Founded 1972
State control
Academic year: October to July (2 semesters)
Rector: Prof. Dr RALF SCHNELL

Vice-Rectors: Prof. Dr SABINE HERING, Prof. Dr. PETER HARING BOLIVAR, Prof. Dr MANFRED GRAUER, Prof. Dr CHRISTIAN UEBING
Chancellor: Dr JOHANN PETER SCHÄFER
Librarian: WERNER REINHARDT
Library of 1,191,296 vols
Number of teachers: 558
Number of students: 12,926

Publications: *Diagonal, LiLi—Zeitschrift für Literaturwissenschaft und Linguistik, MuK—Massenmedien und Kommunikation, Navigationen, Reihe Medienwissenschaften, Reihe Siegen, Research Report, Siegen: Sozial (2 a year), Siegener Hochschulzeitung, Siegener Pädagogische Studien, SPIEL (2 a year)*

DEANS

School of Economic Disciplines: Prof. Dr PETER KREBS
Department of Architecture and Town Planning: Prof. Dr-Ing. ULRICH EXNER
Department of Art and Music Education: Prof. Dr ANGELA ZIESCHE
Department of Chemistry, Biology: Prof. Dr HANS-JÖRG DREISEROTH
Department of Civil Engineering: Prof. Dr PETER SCHMIDT
Department of Education Science, Psychology and Physical Education: Prof. Dr RICHARD HUISINGA
Department of Electrical Engineering: Prof. Dr RAINER LOHE
Department of Electrical Engineering and Computer Science: Prof. Dr ELMAR GRIESE
Department of Languages, Literature and Media Sciences: Prof. Dr GEORG STANITEEK
Department of Mathematics: Prof. Dr HANS PETER SCHEFFLER
Department of Mechanical Engineering: Prof. Dr-Ing. BERND ENGEL
Department of Physics: Prof. Dr PETER BUCHHOLZ
Department of Sociology, Philosophy, Theology, History and Geography: Prof. Dr SIGRID BARINGHORST

UNIVERSITÄT STUTTGART

Postfach 106037, 70049 Stuttgart
Telephone: (711) 121-0
Fax: (711) 121-3500
Internet: www.uni-stuttgart.de
Founded 1829 as Gewerbeschule, univ. status 1967
Academic year: October to September
Rector: Prof. Dr-Ing. DIETER FRITSCH
Vice-Rector for Academic: Prof. Dr-Ing. PETER GÖHNER
Vice-Rector for Research and Marketing: Prof. Dr-Ing. KARL-HEINZ WEHKING
Vice-Rector for Structure and Controlling: Prof. Dr-Ing. PETER GÖHNER
Chancellor: J. SCHWARZE
Chief Librarian: W. STEPHAN
Library: see Libraries
Number of teachers: 2,600
Number of students: 18,500

Publications: *Forschung-Entwicklung-Beratung* (in German and English, 1 a year), *News* (newsletter, online), *Science* (newsletter, online), *Stuttgarter Uni-Kurier* (3–4 a year), *Wechselwirkungen- Aus Lehre und Forschung der Universität Stuttgart* (1 a year)

PROFESSORS

Aerospace Engineering and Geodetic Science (Universitätsbereich Vaihingen, Pfaffenwaldring 27, Zi.02, Stuttgart; tel. (711) 685-2400; fax (711) 685-3617; e-mail dekanat@f06.uni-stuttgart.de; internet www.f06.uni-stuttgart.de):

AUWETER-KURTZ, M., Space Transportation Technology
DRECHSLER, K., Aircraft Construction
FRITSCH, D., Photogrammetry and Land Surveying
GRAFAREND, E. W., Geodetic Science
KELLER, W., Physical Geodetic Science
KLEUSBERG, A., Navigation
KRÄMER, E., Aerodynamics
KRÖPLIN, B.-H., Statics and Dynamics of Aerospace Structures
KÜHN, M., Aerodynamics
MÖHLENBRINK, W., Aviation Telemetry
MUNZ, C.-D., Air and Gas Dynamics
REICHEL, R., Aviation Systems
RÖSER, H.-P., Space Systems
STAUDACHER, S., Turbojet Engines
VOIT-NITSCHMANN, R., Aircraft Construction
VON WOLFERSDORF, J., Aerospace Thermodynamics
WAGNER, S., Air and Gas Dynamics
WEIGAND, B., Aerospace Thermodynamics
WELL, K. H., Guidance and Control of Aerospace Vehicles
WOLF, D., Theory and Modelling of Geodetic Systems

Architecture and City Planning (Universitätsbereich Stadtmitte, Keplerstr. 11, 70714 Stuttgart; tel. (711) 121-3223; fax (711) 121-2788; e-mail dekanat@f01.uni-stuttgart.de; internet www.architektur.uni-stuttgart.de):

ADAM, J., Design and Construction
BEHLING, S., Building Construction and Design
BOTT, H., City Planning and Urban Design
CHERET, P., Building Construction and Design
DE BRUYN, G., Theory of Architecture and Design
EISENBIEGLER, G., Structures and Constructional Design
ERTEL, H., Building Materials, Building Physics, Mechanical Equipment
HARLANDER, T., Housing and Design
HERRMANN, D., Building Materials, Building Physics, Mechanical Equipment
HÜBNER, P., Building Constructions and Design
JESSEN, J., City and Regional Planning
JOCHER, T., Housing and Design
KAULE, G., Landscape Planning and Ecology
KIMPEL, D., History of Architecture
KNIPPERS, J., Structures and Constructional Design
KNOLL, W., Drawing, Drafting and Modelling
MORO, J. L., Planning and Construction of High-rise Buildings
PESCH, F., City Planning and Urban Design
PODREKA, B., Interior Design and Architectural Design
RIBBECK, E., Planning and Building Development
SCHÖNWANDT, W., Foundations of Planning
SCHÜRMANN, P., Building Materials, Building Physics, Mechanical Equipment
SOBEK, W., Lightweight Structures and Conceptual Design
TRAUB, H., Drawing, Drafting and Modelling
ULLMANN, F., Interior Design and Architectural Design

Biological and Geosciences (Universitätsbereich Vaihingen, Herdweg 51, 70174 Stuttgart; tel. (711) 121-1334; fax (711) 2237978; e-mail dekanat@g04.uni-stuttgart.de; internet www.uni-stuttgart.de/geowissenschaft):

BLÜMEL, W. D., Geography
GAEBE, W., Cultural Geography
GHOSH, R., Bioenergetics
GOERTZ, H. D., Zoology
HEYER, A., Botany

JESKE, H., Molecular Biology and Virology of Plants
KELLER, P., Mineralogy and Crystal Chemistry
MASSONNE, H.-J., Mineralogy and Crystal Chemistry
MATTES, R., Industrial Genetics
MUTTI, M., Geology and Palaeontology
NUSSBERGER, S., Biophysics
PFIZENMAIER, K., Cell Biology and Immunology
SCHEURICH, P., Molecular Immunology
SCHNEIDER, G., Geophysics
SEUFERT, W., Industrial Genetics
SEYFRIED, H., Geology and Palaeontology
SPRENGER, G., Microbiology
WIELANDT, E., Geophysics
WOLF, D. H., Biochemistry
WOLLNIK, F., Animal Physiology

Chemistry (Universitätsbereich Vaihingen, Pfaffenwaldring 55, 7.OG, Stuttgart; tel. (711) 685-4584; e-mail dekanat@f03.uni-stuttgart.de; internet www.uni-stuttgart.de/chemie):

ALDINGER, F., Non-Metallic Inorganic Materials
ARZT, E., Metallurgy
BECKER, G., Inorganic Chemistry
BERTAGNOLLI, H., Physical Chemistry
CHRISTOFFERS, J., Organic Chemistry
EISENBACH, C., Chemical Engineering
GIESSELMANN, F., Physical Chemistry
GUDAT, D., Inorganic Chemistry
HASHMI, S., Organic Chemistry
JÄGER, V., Organic Chemistry
KAIM, W., Inorganic Chemistry
LASCHAT, S., Organic Chemistry
MITTELMEIJER, E., Metallurgy
RODUNER, E., Physical Chemistry
SCHLEID, T., Inorganic Chemistry
SCHMID, R., Technical Biochemistry
WEITKAMP, J., Chemical Engineering
WERNER, H.-J., Theoretical Chemistry
WOLF, D., Biochemistry
ZABEL, F., Physical Chemistry

Civil Engineering and Surveying (Universitätsbereich Vaihingen, Pfaffenwaldring 7, 2.OG, Stuttgart; tel. (711) 685-6234; e-mail dekanat@fak2.uni-stuttgart.de; internet www.uni-stuttgart.de/bauingenieur):

BÁRDOSSY, A., Water Management
BERNER, F., Construction Industry
EHLERS, W., Engineering Mechanics
ELIGEHAUSEN, R., Materials Science in Structural Engineering
ENGESSER, K.-H., Biological Cleaning of Used Air
FRIEDRICH, M., Transport Planning and Traffic Control
GERTIS, K., Building Physics
HELMIG, R., Hydromechanics and Hydrosystems Modelling
KRANERT, M., Sanitary Engineering, Waste Water and Solid Waste Management
KUHLMANN, U., Design and Construction
MARTIN, U., Railway and Transportation Engineering
METZGER, J., Hydrochemistry and Hydrobiology, Sanitary Engineering, Waste Water and Solid Waste Management
MIEHE, C., Engineering Mechanics
MÖHLENBRINK, W., Applied Geodesy
MORO, J. L., Planning and Construction of High-rise Buildings
NOVÁK, B., Large-scale Construction
PINNEKAMP, J., Waste Water Engineering
RAMM, E., Structural Engineering
REINHARDT, H.-W., Materials Science in Structural Engineering
RESSEL, W., Road and Transport Planning and Engineering
ROTT, U., Water Quality Management, Sanitary Engineering
SEDLBAUER, K., Constructional Physics

SOBEK, W., Interdisciplinary Research, Architecture and Civil Engineering
TREUNER, P., Regional Development Planning
VERMEER, P. A., Geotechnology
WIEPRECHT, S., Water Engineering

Computer Science, Electrical Engineering and Information Technology (Universitätsbereich Vaihingen, Pfaffenwaldring 47, Zi. 4.116, Stuttgart; tel. (711) 685-7234; fax (711) 685-7236; e-mail dekanat@f-iei.uni-stuttgart.de; internet www.f-iei.uni-stuttgart.de):

BERROTH, M., Communications Engineering
BUNGARTZ, H.-J., Simulation of Large Systems
CLAUS, V., Formal Concepts of Computer Science
DIEKERT, V., Theoretical Computer Science
EGGENBERGER, O., Operating Systems
ERTL, T., Dialogue Systems
ESPARZA, J., Secure and Reliable Software Systems
FRÜHAUF, N., Display Technology
GÖHNER, P., Control Engineering and Process Automation
KASPER, E., Semiconductor Engineering
KÜHN, P. J., Communications Switching and Data Techniques
LAGALLY, K., Operating Systems
LANDSTORFER, F., Radio Frequency Technology
LEHMANN, E., Export Systems
LEVI, P., Computer Vision
LUDEWIG, J., Software Engineering
MITSCHANG, B., User Software
PLÖDEREDER, E., Programming Languages
ROLLER, D., Computer Science Fundamentals
ROTH-STIELOW, J., Power Electronics and Control Engineering
ROTHERMEL, K., Distributed Systems
RUCKER, W., Theory of Electrical Engineering
SCHÄFER, Energy Conversion
SPEIDEL, J., Telecommunications
TENBOHLEN, S., High-Voltage Technology
WERNER, J. H., Physical Electronics
WUNDERLICH, H.-J., Computer Architecture
YANG, B., Network and Systems Theory

Mathematics and Physics (Universitätsbereich Vaihingen, Pfaffenwaldring 57, 70550 Stuttgart; tel. (711) 685-2400; fax (711) 685-3617; e-mail dekanat@f08.uni-stuttgart.de; internet www.uni-stuttgart.de/mathephysik):

BECHINGER, C., Experimental Physics
BLIND, G., Mathematics
BRÜDERN, J., Mathematics
DENNINGER, G., Physics
DIETRICH, S., Theoretical Physics
DIPPER, R., Mathematics
DOSCH, H., Experimental Physics
DRESSEL, M., Experimental Physics
GEKELER, E., Mathematics
HÄHL, H., Mathematics
HERRMANN, H., Theoretical Physics
HESSE, C., Mathematics
HÖLLIG, K., Mathematics
KÜHNEL, W., Mathematics
LUNK, A., Plasma Research
MAHLER, G., Theoretical Physics
MICHLER, P., Experimental Physics
MIELKE, A., Mathematics
MURAMATSU, A., Theoretical Physics
PFAU, T., Institute of Physics
PÖSCHEL, J., Mathematics
SANTOS, L., Theoretical Physics
SCHWEITZER, D., Experimental Physics
SEIFERT, U., Theoretical Physics
STRAUSS, W., Mathematics
TREBIN, H.-R., Theoretical and Applied Physics
WALK, H., Mathematics

WEIDL, T., Mathematics
WEISS, U., Theoretical Physics
WOHLMUTH, B., Mathematics
WRACHTRUP, J., Experimental Physics
WUNNER, G., Theoretical Physics

Mechanical Engineering (Universitätsbereich Vaihingen, Pfaffenwaldring 9, 5.OG, 70569 Stuttgart; tel. (711) 685-6470; fax (711) 685-6492; e-mail dekanat@f07.uni-stuttgart.de; internet www.f07.uni-stuttgart.de):

ALLGÖWER, F., Systems Theory in Engineering
BARGENDE, M., Combustion Engines
BERTSCHE, B., Machine Elements (Gear Design, Cab Sealing Technology)
BINZ, H., Machine and Gearing Design
BRUNNER, H., Interface Chemistry
BULLINGER, H.-J., Industrial Science and Technology Management
BUSSE, G., Non-destructive Testing
CASEY, M., Thermal Turbo-Engines
EBERHARD, P., Mechanics
EIGENBERGER, G., Chemical Process Engineering
EYERER, P., Polymer Testing and Polymer Science
FRIEDRICH, H., Vehicle Concepts
FRITZ, H. G., Polymer Processing
GADOW, R., Manufacturing Technologies of Ceramic Compounds and Composites
GAUL, L., Mechanics
GILLES, E. D., System Dynamics and Control Systems
GÖDE, E., Fluid Machines and Hydraulic Pumps
GRAF, T., Network Engineering
HAASE, H., Technical Thermodynamics
HEIN, K. R. G., Process Engineering and Steam Boiler Technology
HEISEL, U., Machine Tools
KISTNER, A., Engineering Mechanics
KLEMM, P., Control Engineering
KÜCK, H., Time Measuring, Precision Engineering and Microengineering
LAURIEN, E., Nuclear Engineering
LOHNERT, G., Nuclear Engineering and Energy Systems
MAIER, T., Technical Design
MERTEN, C., Chemical Engineering
MÜLLER-STEINHAGEN, H., Thermodynamics and Heat Engineering
NAGEL, J., Biomedical Technology
OSTEN, W., Technical Optics
PIESCHE, M., Mechanical Production Engineering
PLANCK, H., Textile Technology and Process Engineering
PRITSCHOW, G., Control Technology of Machine Tools and Production Systems
REUSS, H.-C., Automobile Mechatronics
REUSS, M., Biochemical Engineering
ROOS, E., Materials Testing, Materials Science and Strength of Materials
SANDMAIER, H., Time Measuring, Precision Engineering and Microengineering
SCHINKÖTHE, W., Design and Production in Precision Engineering
SCHMAUDER, S., Process Development
SCHMIDT, M., Heating and Air-conditioning Engineering
SEIFERT, H., Thermal Waste Utilization
SIEGERT, K., Metal Forming
SPATH, D., Technology Management
VOSS, A., Energy Economics
WEHKING, K.-H., Conveyer and Transmission Technology, Gear Technology
WEHLAN, H., Process Control Engineering
WESTKÄMPER, E., Industrial Production and Plant
WIEDEMANN, J., Motor Vehicle Engineering
ZEITZ, M., System Dynamics Control

Philosophy and History (Universitätsbereich Stadtmitte, Keplerstr. 17, KII, 3.OG, 70174 Stuttgart; tel. (711) 121-3089; fax (711) 121-

2803; e-mail dekanat@f09.uni-stuttgart.de; internet www.f09.uni-stuttgart.de):

ALEXIADOU, M., Linguistics and English
BAHLKE, J., Early Modern History
BARK, J., Modern German Literature
CZERWINSKI, P., German Philology
DOGIL, G., Computational Linguistics
GÖBEL, W., American Studies and Modern English Literature
VON HEUSINGER, K., Linguistics and German
HUBIG, C., Theory of Science and Technical Philosophy
KAMP, H., Formal Logic and Philosophy of Language
KRÜGER, R., Roman Studies
MAAG, G., Italian Studies
OLSHAUSEN, E., Ancient History
PAFEL, J., Linguistics and German
PYTA, W., Modern History
QUARTHAL, F., Regional History of Baden-Württemberg
REICHERT, F., History
ROHRER, CH., Computational Linguistics
SEEBER, H. U., Modern English Literature
STEIN, A., Linguistics/Roman Studies
STEINER, R., History of Arts
STÜRNER, W., History
THOMÉ, H., Modern German Literature
WYSS, B., History of Arts

Social Sciences and Economics (Universitätsbereich Stadtmitte, Keplerstr. 17, KII, 10 OG, 70174 Stuttgart; tel. (711) 121-3046; fax (711) 121-2807; e-mail dekanat@wiso.uni-stuttgart.de; internet www.uni-stuttgart.de/wiso):

ACKERMANN, K.-F., Economics
ALT, W., Sports
ARNOLD, U., Economics
BRINKHOFF, K.-P., Sports
ENGLMANN, F., Economics
FRANKE, S. F., Economic Policy and Public Law
FROMM, M., Educational Theory
FUCHS, D., Political Science
GABRIEL, O. W., Political Science
HERZWURM, G., Economics
HORVÁTH, P., Economics
KEMPER, H.-G., Economics
MAJER, H., Economics
NICKOLAUS, R., Vocational and Economic Education
REISS, M., Economics
RENN, O., Sociology of Environment and Technology
SCHÄFER, H., Economics
SCHLICHT, W., Sports
URBAN, D., Sociology
WOECKENER, B., Economics
ZAHN, E., Economics

UNIVERSITÄT TRIER

Universitätsring 15, 54286 Trier
Telephone: (0651) 201-0
Fax: (0651) 201-4299
E-mail: presse@uni-trier.de
Internet: www.uni-trier.de

Founded 1473, reopened 1970
Academic year: October to September

President: Prof. Dr PETER SCHWENKMEZGER
Vice-Presidents: Prof. Dr MICHAEL JÄCKEL, Prof. Dr WOLFGANG KLOOB
Chancellor: Dr KLAUS HEMBACH (acting)
Librarian: Dr HILDEGARD MÜLLER

Number of teachers: 462 full-time
Number of students: 11,046

Publications: *Trierer Beiträge* (1 a year), *UNI-Journal* (4 a year)

DEANS

Faculty I: Pedagogy, Philosophy and Psychology: Prof. Dr BERND DÖRFLINGER

Faculty II: Language and Literature: Prof. Dr FRANZISKA SCHÖßLER
Faculty III: History, Political Science, Classical Archaeology, Egyptology, Art History, Papyrology: Prof. Dr HELGA SCHNABEL-SCHÜLE
Faculty IV: Management Economics, Sociology, Political Economy, Applied Mathematics, Computer Science and Ethnology: Prof. Dr DIETER SADOWSKI
Faculty V: Law: Prof. Dr MICHAEL REINHARDT
Faculty VI: Geography and Geosciences: Prof. Dr REINHARD HOFFMANN
Faculty VII: Theology: Rector REINHOLD BOHLEN

PROFESSORS

Faculty I: Pedagogy, Philosophy and Psychology (Fachbereich I, 54286 Trier; tel. (651) 2012015; fax (651) 2013942; e-mail kohrg@uni-trier.de; internet www.psychologie.uni-trier.de/fbi):

ANTON, F., Psychobiology
BECKER, P., Psychology
BRANDTSTÄDTER, J., Psychology
CONNY, A., Psychology
DÖRFLINGER, B., Philosophy
FILIPP, S.-H., Psychology
HELLHAMMER, D., Psychology
HOMFELDT, H.-C., Pedagogy
HONIG, M. S., Pedagogy
KRAMPEN, G., Psychology
MEYER, J., Psychobiology
MULLER, C., Psychobiology
MÜLLER-FOHRBRODT, G., Pedagogy
PRECKEL, F., Psychology
RUSTEMEYER, D., Pedagogy
SCHÄCHINGER, H., Psychobiology
SCHELLER, R., Psychology
SCHWENKMEZGER, P., Psychology
WALTHER, E., Psychology
WENDER, K. F., Psychology

Faculty II: Language and Literature (Fachbereich II, 54286 Trier; tel. (651) 2012210; fax (651) 2013901; e-mail dienhart@uni-trier.de; internet www.uni-trier.de/uni/fb2/dekanat):

ALTHAUS, H. P., German Linguistics, Yiddish Language
BENDER, K.-H., Romance Literature
BREUER, H., English Literature
BUCHER, H.-J., Media Studies
CHIAO, W., Sinology
EIGLER, U., Classical Philology
GÄRTNER, K., German Philology
GELHAUS, H., German Linguistics
GÖSSMANN, H., Japanese Studies
HASLER, J., English and American Literature
HÖLZ, K., Romance Literature
HURM, G., English Literature
KLOOSS, W., English Philology
KÖHLER, H., Romance Literature
KÖHLER, R., Linguistic Data Processing
KÖSTER, J.-P., Applied Linguistics, Phonetics
KRAMER, J., Romance Philology
KREMER, D., Romance Philology
KRÖNER, H. O., Classical Philology
KÜHLWEIN, W., English Philology
KÜHN, P., German as a Foreign Language
LIANG, Y., Sinology
LOIPERDINGER, M., Media Studies
MOULIN, C., Old German Philology
NEUBERG, S., Yiddish Studies
NIEDEREHE, H.-J., Romance Philology
PIKULIK, L., Modern German Literature
PLATZ, N., English Literature
POHL, K. H., Chinese Studies
REINHARDT, H., Modern German Literature
RESSEL, G., Slavistics
RIEGER, B., Linguistic Data Processing, Computer Languages
RÖLL, W., German Philology, Yiddish Language

SCHOLZ-CIONCA, S., Japanese Studies
SCHÖßLER, F., New German Literature
STAHL, H., Slavic Literature
STRAUSS, J., English Philology
STUBBS, M., English Linguistics
THORAU, H.-E., Portuguese Philology
TIMM, E., Yiddish Language
UERLINGS, H., Modern German Literature
WIMMER, R., German Linguistics
WÖHRLE, G., Classical Philology
ZIRKER, H., English Literature

Faculty III: History, Political Science, Classical Archaeology, Egyptology, Art History, Papyrology (Fachbereich III, 54286 Trier; tel. (651) 2012144; fax (651) 2013936; e-mail merz@uni-trier.de; internet www.uni-trier.de/uni/fb3/dekanat/fb3.html):

ANTON, H. H., Medieval History
CLEMENS, L., History
DORN, F., History
EBELING, D., History
FRANZ, G., History
GERHARDT, C., History
GESTRICH, A., Modern History
HAVERKAMP, A., Medieval History
HEINEN, H., Ancient History
HERRMAN-OTTO, E., Ancient History
HOLTMANN, W., History
IRSIGLER, F., Cultural History
KETTENHOFEN, E., History
KÖNIG, I., History
KRAMER, B., Papyrology
MOLT, P., Political Science
RAPHAEL, L., Modern and Recent History
SCHMID, W., History
SCHNABEL-SCHÜLE, H., Modern History
TACKE, A., Art History
VEEN, H. J., Political Science
VLEEMING, S. P., Egyptology
VOLTMER, E., History
WEBER, W., History
WIELING, H., History
WÖHRLE, G., Greek Philology

Faculty IV: Management Economics, Sociology, Political Economy, Applied Mathematics, Computer Science and Ethnology (Fachbereich IV, 54286 Trier; tel. (651) 2012640; fax (651) 2013927; e-mail dekanfb4@uni-trier.de; internet www.uni-trier.de/uni/fb4/dekanat/index.htm):

AMBROSI, C. M., Political Economy
ANTWEILER, C., Ethnology
BAUM, D., Computer Science
BERGMANN, R., Computer Science
BRAUN, H., Sociology
CZAP, H., Computer Science
DICKERTMANN, D., Political Economy
DIEHL, S., Computer Science
ECKERT, R., Sociology
EL-SHAGI, E. S., Political Economy
FILC, W., Political Economy
FEHR, H. J., Accounting
FERNAU, H., Computer Science
GAWRONSKI, W., Mathematics
HAHN, A., Sociology
HAMM, B., Sociology
HARDES, H.-D., Political Economy
HECHELTJEN, P., Political Economy
JÄCKEL, M., Sociology
KLÄS, F., Accounting
KNAPPE, E., Political Economy
LEHMANN, M., Management Economics
LIEBIG, M., Sociology
MILDE, H., Management Economics
MÜNNICH, R., Economics
NÄHER, S., Computer Science
OFFERMANN-CLAS, CH., European Community
RÜCKLE, D., Management Economics
SACHS, E., Mathematics
SADOWSKI, D., Management Economics
SCHERTLER, W., Strategic Management
SCHMIDT, A., Economics
SPEHL, H., Political Economy
STURM, P., Computer Science

SWOBODA, B., Management Economics
WÄCHTER, H., Management Economics
WALTER, B., Computer Science
WEIBER, R., Management Economics

Faculty V: Law (Fachbereich V—Rechtswissenschaft, 54286 Trier; tel. (651) 2012524; fax (651) 2013911; e-mail dekanatfb5@uni-trier.de; internet www.uni-trier.de/uni/fb5/fachbereich/dekanat.htm):

AXER, P., Public Law
BACHMANN, G., Civil Law, Commercial Law
BIRK, R., Private Law, Labour Law, Conflict of Laws
BURMESTER, G., National and International Finance and Tax Law
DORN, F., Private Law, Legal History, Comparative Law
ECKHARDT, D., Civil Law
HENDLER, R., Constitutional and Administrative Law
HOFFMANN, B. VON, Private Law, Conflict of Laws, Comparative Law
JÄGER, C., Criminal Law
KREY, V., Criminal Law, Criminal Procedure, Legal Methods
KÜHNE, H.-H., Criminal Law, Criminology, Criminal Procedure
RAAB, T., Public Law, Commercial Law, Labour Law
REIFF, P., Private Law, Commercial Law, Corporation Law, Insurance Law
REINHARDT, M., Constitutional and Administrative Law
ROBBERS, G., Public Law, Ecclesiastical Law, Philosophy of Law
RÜFNER, T., Public Law, German and International Civil Law
SCHRÖDER, M., Public, International and EU Law

Faculty VI: Geography and Geosciences (Fachbereich VI, 54286 Trier; tel. (651) 2014530; fax (651) 2013939; e-mail dekanatfb6@uni-trier.de; internet dekanatfb6.uni-trier.de):

ALEXANDER, J., Physical Geography
BECKER, CHR., Applied Geography and Geography of Tourism
BLÖMEKE, B., Ecotoxicology
BOLLMANN, J., Cartography
CALTEUX, G., Geography of Tourism
DIESTER-HAAß, L., Biogeography
EBERLE, I., Economic and Social Geography
FISCHER, K., Inorganic and Analytical Chemistry
HEINEMANN, G., Climatology
HILL, J., Remote Sensing
HOFFMANN, R., Geography and its Teaching
MONHEIM, H., Applied Geography, Urban and Regional Planning and Development
RIES, J. B., Physical Geography
SAILER, U., Cultural and Regional Geography
SYMADER, W., Hydrology
THOMAS, F., Geobotany
VOGEL, H., Communal Science
WAGNER, J.-F., Geology

Faculty VII: Theology (Universitätsring 19, 54296 Trier; tel. (651) 2013520; fax (651) 2013951; e-mail theofak@uni-trier.de; internet www.uni-trier.de/uni/theo):

BOHLEN, Biblical Studies
BRANDSCHEIDT, Old Testament
ECKERT, New Testament
EULER, Fundamental Theology
FIEDROWICZ, Medieval Church History and Christian Archaeology
GÖBEL, Moral Philosophy
HEINZ, Liturgical Studies
KRÄMER, Church Law
KRIEGER, Philosophy I
OCKENFELS, Medieval Church History
SCHNEIDER, Church History
SCHÜßLER, Philosophy II
THEIS, Religious Instruction

VODERHOLZER, Dogma and History of Dogma
WAHL, Pastoral Theology

UNIVERSITÄT ULM

89069 Ulm

Telephone: (731) 502-01
Fax: (731) 502-2038
E-mail: post@uni-ulm.de
Internet: www.uni-ulm.de

Founded 1967 as Medizinische-Naturwissenschaftliche Hochschule, University charter 1967
State control
Language of instruction: German
Academic year: October to September

Rector: Prof. Dr KARL JOACHIM EBELING
Pro-Rectors: Prof. Dr GUIDO ADLER, Prof. Dr PETER DÜRRE, Prof. Dr WERNER KRATZ
Chancellor: DIETER KAUFMANN
Chief Librarian: SIEGFRIED FRANKE

Number of teachers: 480
Number of students: 5,000
Publication: *Uni Ulm Intern* (8 a year)

DEANS

Faculty of Engineering: Prof. Dr HANS-JÖRG PFLEIDERER
Faculty of Information Science: Prof. Dr H. PARTSCH
Faculty of Mathematics and Mathematical Economics: Prof. Dr ULRICH STADTMÜLLER
Faculty of Medicine: Prof. Dr KLAUS-MICHAEL DEBATIN
Faculty of Natural Sciences: Prof. Dr KLAUS-DIETER SPINDLER

UNIVERSITÄT WITTEN/HERDECKE
(Witten/Herdecke University)

Alfred-Herrhausen-Str. 50, 58448 Witten

Telephone: (2302) 926-0
Fax: (2302) 926-407
E-mail: public@uni-wh.de
Internet: www.uni-wh.de

Founded 1982
Private control
Languages of instruction: German, English
Academic year: October to July

Pres.: Prof. Dr WOLFGANG GLATTHAAR
Librarian: IRIS KOCH

Library of 150,000 books, 500 periodicals
Number of teachers: 295
Number of students: 1,327

DEANS

Faculty of Dental Medicine: Prof. Dr PETER GÄNGLER
Faculty of Economics and Business Administration: Prof. Dr BERND FRICK
Faculty of Fundamental Studies: Prof. Dr. MATTHIAS KETTNER
Faculty of Medicine: Prof. Dr MATTHIAS SCHRAPPE
Faculty of Natural Sciences: Prof. Dr WOLFGANG WINTERMEYER

UNIVERSITÄT ZU KÖLN

Albertus-Magnus-Pl., 50923 Cologne

Telephone: (221) 470-0
Fax: (221) 4705151
E-mail: aaa@verw.uni-koeln.de
Internet: www.uni-koeln.de

Founded 1388
Academic year: October to July

Rector Magnificus: Prof. Dr AXEL FREIMUTH
First Vice-Rector: Prof. Dr THOMAS KRIEG
Chancellor: Dr jur. JOHANNES NEYSES
Librarian: Prof. Dr W. SCHMITZ

Number of teachers: 2,132
Number of students: 49,000

DEANS

Faculty of Economics, Business Administration and Social Sciences: Prof. Dr NORBERT HERZIG

Faculty of Education: Prof. Dr KLAUS KÜNZEL

Faculty of Law: Prof. Dr MICHAEL WALTER

Faculty of Mathematics and Natural Sciences: Prof. Dr ULRICH RADTKE

Faculty of Medicine: Prof. Dr med. EDGAR SCHÖMIG

Faculty of Philosophy: Prof. Dr HANS-PETER ULLMANN

Faculty of Special Education: Prof. Dr GERHARD LAUTH

PROFESSORS

Faculty of Economics, Business Administration and Social Sciences (tel. (221) 470-5607; fax (221) 470-5179; e-mail dekanat@wiso.uni-koeln.de; internet www.wiso.uni-koeln.de):

ANDEREGG, R. G., Political Economy
BAUM, H., Economics
BEUERMANN, G., Business Administration
DELFMANN, W., Business Administration
DERIGS, U., Information Systems, Operations Research
DONGES, J., Economics
EEKHOFF, J., Economics
EISENFÜHR, F., Business Administration
FELDERER, B., Economics
FELDSIEPER, M., Economics
FISCHER, L., Business Psychology
FRESE, E., Business Administration
FRIEDRICHS, J., Sociology
FUNK, P., Economics
GLÄSSER, E., Economic Geography
HARTMANN-WENDELS, T., Business Administration
HERZIG, N., Business Administration, Taxation
JÄGER, T., Political Science
JAGODZINSKI, W., Sociology
KEMPF, A., Business Administration, Finance
KITTERER, W., Economics
KÖHLER, R., Marketing
KOPPELMANN, U., Business Administration
KUHNER, C., Business Administration
LEIDHOLD, W., Political Science
LINDNER-BRAUN, C., Sociology
LÖBBECKE, C., Electronic Commerce
MELLIS, W., Business Informatics
MEULEMANN, H., Sociology
MOSLER, K., Statistics, Econometrics
MÜLLER-HAGEDORN, L., Business Administration
PIERENKEMPER, T., Economic History
RETTIG, R., Economics
RÖSNER, H. J., Social Politics
SCHELLHAASS, H. M., Economics
SCHMID, F., Statistics
SCHRADIN, H. R., Business Administration, Insurance
SCHULZ-NIESWANDT, F., Social Policy
SEIBT, D., Information Science, Business Administration
STERNBERG, R., Economic Geography
TEMPELMEIER, H., Business Administration
WAGNER, M., Sociology
WEIZSÄCKER, C. C. VON, Economics
WESSELS, W., Political Science
WIED-NEBBELING, S., Economics
WISWEDE, G., Business Psychology
ZERCHE, J., Social Policy

Faculty of Education (tel. (221) 470-5777; fax (221) 470-5073; e-mail dekanat@ew.uni-koeln.de; internet www.uni-koeln.de/ew-fak):

ADOLPHI, K., Biology
ANACKER, U., General Education
AUERNHEIMER, G., Intercultural Education
BANNWARTH, H., Biology
BARTELS, G., Geography
BECKER-MROTZEK, M., German

BOMBEK, M., Textile Design
BREULL, W.-R., Biology and Human Biology
BROSSEDER, J., Catholic Theology
BUKOW, W.-D., Sociology
BURSCHEID, H. J., Mathematics
BUTTERWEGGE, C., Political Science
DONNERSTAG, J., English
GLÜCK, G., General Education and School Education
GRÜNEWALD, B., Philosophy
GÜNTHER, HARTMUT, German Language and Literature
GÜNTHER, HENNING, General Education and School Education
HAIDER-HASEBRINK, H., Psychology
HURRELMANN, B., German Language and Literature
KLEIN, K., Biology
KOCH-PRIEWE, B., General Education and School Education
KOENEN, K., Protestant Theology
KÜNZEL, K., Adult Education
LAMM, H., Psychology
LLARYORA, R., Sociology
MESSELKEN, H., German Language and Literature
MINSEL, W.-R., Psychology
OTT, T., Music
RECH, P., Art
REICH, K., General Education
SCHÄFER, G., General Education
SCHMIDT, S., Mathematics
SCHNEIDER, R., Music
SCHOLTEN, C., Roman Catholic Theology
SCHÖN, E., German Language and Literature
SCHRÖDER, J., History
SEIBEL, H. D., Sociology
STOCK, A., Theology
STRUVE, H., Mathematics
THIEMANN, F., General Education
THIEME, G., Geography
TIMM, U., Biology
TÖNNIS, G., Art
VOLKENBORN, A., Mathematics
WEGENER-SPÖHRING, G., General Education
WEISER, W., Mathematics
WICHARD, W., Biology
WICKERT, J., Psychology
WIEGERSHAUSEN, H.-W., Art
WILKENDING, G., German Language and Literature
ZILLESSEN, D., Protestant Theology

Faculty of Law (tel. (221) 470-2218; fax (221) 470-5106; e-mail jura-dekanat@uni-koeln.de; internet www.dekanat.de):

BAUR, J. F., Civil Law, Commercial Law, European Law
BÖCKSTIEGEL, K.-H., International and Constitutional Law, German and International Commercial Law
DAUNER-LIEB, B., Civil Law, Commercial Law, Industrial Law
DEPENHEUER, O., Public Law, Philosophy of Law
GRUNEWALD, B., Civil Law, Commercial Law
HENSSLER, M., Civil Law, Commercial Law, Industrial Law
HOBE, S., Public Law, International Law, European Law
HÖFLING, W., Constitutional Law, Administrative Law, Financial Law
HORN, N., Civil Law, German and International Commercial and Banking Law, Philosophy of Law
HÜBNER, U., Insurance Law, Civil Law, Commercial Law, Foreign and International Private Law
LANG, J., Tax Law, Public Law
MANSEL, H.-P., Civil Law, International Private Law, Comparative Law

MITTENZWEI, I., Civil Law, Civil Process Law, Philosophy of Law
MUCKEL, S., Public Law, Canon Law
NESTLER, C., Criminal Law, Criminal Case Law
PRÜTTING, H., Civil Law, Industrial Law
SCHIEDERMAIR, H., Public Law, International Law, Philosophy of Law
SCHMITT-KAMMLER, A., Constitutional and Administrative Law
SEIER, J., Criminal Law, Criminal Case Law
TETTINGER, P. J., Constitutional and Administrative Law
WALTER, M., Criminology, Criminal Law
WALTHER, S., Criminal Law, Criminal Procedural Law, Comparative Law
WEIGEND, T., Criminal Law, Criminal Procedural Law, Comparative Criminal Law, Criminology

Faculty of Mathematics and Natural Sciences (tel. (221) 470-5643; fax (221) 470-5108; e-mail math-nat-fakultaet@uni-koeln.de; internet www.uni-koeln.de/math-nat-fak):

ARMBRUST, M., Mathematics
ARNDT, H., Zoology
BACHEM, A., Applied Mathematics and Informatics
BELOW, R., Micropalaeontology and Palaeoecology
BERKESSEL, A., Organic Chemistry
BERKING, S., Zoology
BESLER, H., Geography
BOHATÝ, L., Crystallography
BOTHE, H., Botany
BRUNOTTE, E., Geography
BUNDSCHUH, P., Mathematics
BÜSCHGES, A., Zoology
CAMPOS-ORTEGA, J. A., Developmental Physiology
COENEN, H. H., Nuclear Chemistry
DEITERS, U., Physical Chemistry
DOHMEN, J., Genetics
DOST, M., Physics
ECKART, A., Experimental Physics
EILENBERGER, G., Theoretical Physics
ERMER, O., Organic Chemistry
FAIGLE, U., Applied Mathematics
FLÜGGE, U.-I., Botany
FREIMUTH, A., Experimental Solid State Physics
GOMPPER, G., Theoretical Physics
GRIESBECK, A. G., Organic Chemistry
HAUSEN, K., Zoology
HEHL, F. W., Theoretical Physics
HENKE, W., Mathematics
HERBIG, H.-G., Palaeontology and Historical Geography
HOHLNEICHER, G., Physical Chemistry
HOWARD, J. C., Genetics
HÜLSKAMP, M., Botany
ILGENFRITZ, G., Physical Chemistry
JOLIE, J., Experimental Physics
JÜNGER, M., Informatics
KAUPP, U. B., Biophysical Chemistry
KAWOHL, B., Mathematics
KEMPER, B., Genetics and Genetic Engineering
KERSCHGENS, M., Meteorology
KLEIN, H. W., Biochemistry
KORSCHING, S., Genetics
KRAAS, F., Anthropogeography
KRAMER, R., Biochemistry
KRUMSIEK, K., Geology
KÜPPER, T., Mathematics
LAMOTKE, K., Mathematics
LANGE, H., Mathematics
LANGER, T., Genetics
LEPTIN, M., Genetics
LESCH, M., Mathematics
LEYTHAEUSER, D., Geology
MELKONIAN, M., Botany
MEYER, G., Inorganic Chemistry
MICKLITZ, H., Experimental Physics
MÜHLBERG, M., Crystallography

MÜLLER-HARTMANN, E., Theoretical Physics
NATTERMANN, T., Theoretical Physics
NAUMANN, D., Inorganic and Analytical Chemistry
NEUBAUER, F. M., Geophysics and Meteorology
NEUMANN, M., Applied Mathematics
NEUWIRTH, W., Physics
NIMTZ, G., Physics
NIPPER, J., Geography
PAETZ GEN. SCHIECK, H., Physics
PALME, H., Mineralogy
PLICKERT, G., Zoology
POHLEY, H.-J., Developmental Biology
RADTKE, U., Geography
RAJEWSKY, K., Molecular Genetics
RAMMENSEE, W., Mineralogy
RAPOPORT, M., Mathematics
RECKZIEGEL, H., Mathematics
RICKEN, W., Geology
ROTH, S., Developmental Biology
RUSCHEWITZ, U., Inorganic Chemistry
SCHIEDER, R., Experimental Physics
SCHIERENBERG, E., Zoology
SCHLICHTER, D., Zoology
SCHMALZ, H.-G., Organic Chemistry
SCHMITZ, K., Botany
SCHNEIDER-POETSCH, HJ., Botany
SCHNETZ, K., Genetics
SCHOMBURG, D., Biochemistry
SCHRADER, R., Informatics
SEIDEL, E., Geochemistry
SEYDEL, R., Mathematics
SOYEZ, D., Anthropogeography
SPECKENMEYER, E., Informatics
SPETH, P., Geophysics and Meteorology
STAUFFER, D., Theoretical Physics
STERNER, R., Biochemistry
STREY, R., Physical Chemistry
STRÖHER, H., Experimental Nuclear Physics
STUTZKI, J., Physics
TAUTZ, D., Genetics
TEZKAN, B., Geophysics
THORBERGSSON, G., Mathematics
TIEKE, B., Physical Chemistry
TOPP, W., Zoology
TROTTENBERG, U., Applied Mathematics
WALKOWIAK, W., Zoology
WEISSENBÖCK, G., Botany
WERR, W., Developmental Biology
WESEMANN, L., Inorganic Chemistry
ZIRNBAUER, M., Theoretical Physics
ZITTARTZ, J., Theoretical Physics

Faculty of Medicine (tel. (221) 478-0; fax (221) 478-4097; e-mail med-dekanat@ medizin.uni-koeln.de; internet www.medizin .uni-koeln.de):

ABKEN, H., Onco-genetics, Cell Biology
ADDICKS, K., Anatomy
BALDAMUS, C., Internal Medicine
BAUMANN, M. A., Dentistry
BERGDOLT, K., History of Medicine, Medical Ethics
BERTHOLD, F., Paediatrics
BÖRNER, U., Anaesthesiology
BRUNKWALL, J. S., Surgery
BUZELLO, W., Anaesthesiology
DECKERT-SCHLÜTER, M., Neuropathology
DIEHL, V., Internal Medicine
DIENES, H. P., Pathology and Pathological Anatomy
DÖPFNER, M., Psychopathology
ENGELMANN, U., Urology
ERDMANN, E., Internal Medicine
FRICKE, U., Pharmacology and Toxicology
FUHR, U., Pharmacology
GOESER, T., Internal Medicine
HACKENBROCH, M. H., Orthopaedics
HAUPT, G., Urology
HEISS, W.-D., Neurology and Psychiatry
HERHOLZ, K., Neurology
HERZIG, S., Pharmacology and Toxicology
HESCHELER, J., Physiology

HÖLSCHER, A. H., Surgery
HÖPP, H.-W., Internal Medicine
KERSCHBAUM, T., Dentistry
KLAUS, W., Pharmacology and Toxicology
KLOSTERKÖTTER, J., Psychiatry
KLUG, N., Neurosurgery
KOEBKE, J., Anatomy
KÖHLE, K., Psychosomatic Medicine and Psychotherapy
KONEN, W., Ophthalmology
KRIEG, T., Dermatology and Venereology
KRIEGLSTEIN, G. K., Ophthalmology
KRONE, W., Internal Medicine
KRÖNKE, M., Hygiene and Microbiology
LACKNER, K., Clinical Radiology
LAUTERBACH, K. W., Health Economics
LECHLER, E., Internal Medicine
LEHMACHER, W., Medical Statistics, Informatics and Epidemiology
LEHMANN, K., Anaesthesiology
LEHMKUHL, G., Child and Adolescent Psychiatry
MAHRLE, G., Dermatology
MALLMANN, P., Gynaecology and Obstetrics
MICHALK, D., Paediatrics
MÖSGES, R., Medical Informatics
MÜLLER, R.-P., Radiology
MÜLLER-WIELAND, D., Internal Medicine
NEISS, W. F., Anatomy
NIEDERMEIER, W., Dental Prosthetics
NOACK, M. J., Dentistry
NOEGEL, A. A., Biochemistry
PAULSSON, M., Biochemistry
PFAFF, H., Medical Sociology
PFEIFFER, P., Dentistry
PFISTER, H., Virology
PFITZER, G., Physiology
PIEKARSKI, C., Industrial Medicine
REHM, K. E., Surgery and Accident Surgery
ROTH, B., Paediatrics
RÜSSMANN, W., Ophthalmology
SCHEFFNER, M., Biochemistry
SCHICHA, H., Nuclear Medicine
SCHIRMACHER, P., Pathology
SCHRÖDER, H., Anatomy
STENNERT, E., Otorhinolaryngology
STURM, V., Neurosurgery
THIELE, J., Pathology
TROIDL, H., Surgery
TSCHUSCHKE, V., Medical Psychology
DE VIVIE, E. R., Thorax- and Cardio-Surgery
WIELCKENS, K., Clinical Chemistry
WIESNER, R. J., Physiology
ZÖLLER, J. E., Dental Surgery

Faculty of Philosophy (tel. (221) 470-2212; fax (221) 470-5133; e-mail dekan.philfak@ uni-koeln.de; internet www.uni-koeln.de/ phil-fak):

AERTSEN, J., Philosophy
ALEXANDER, M., Modern History
ALLEMANN-GHIONDA, C., Intercultural Education
ANTOR, H., English Philology
ARMBRUSTER, C., Romance Philology
AX, W., Classical Philology
BALD, W.-D., Applied Linguistics
BEHREND-ENGELHARDT, H., African Studies
BENTE, G. M., Psychology
BERRESSEM, H., American Studies
BIEG, L., Modern Chinese Literature
BLAMBERGER, G., Modern German Literature
BLATTMANN, M., Medieval History
BLUMENTHAL, P., Romance Philology
BLUMRÖDER, C. VON, Musicology
BOLLIG, M., Cultural Anthropology
BOS, G., Jewish Studies
BOSCHUNG, D., Classical Archaeology
BOSINSKI, G., Prehistory and Early History
BRENNER, P. J., Modern German Literature
BUCK, E., Theatre, Film and Television Studies
CASIMIR, M., Cultural Anthropology
CLAESGES, U., Philosophy

DÄMMER, H.-W., Prehistory and Early History
DANN, O., Modern History
DIEM, W., Islamic Studies
DIMMENDAAL, G. J., African Studies
DRUX, R., Modern German Literature
DÜLFFER, J., Modern History
DÜSING, K., Philosophy
ECK, W., Ancient History
EHMCKE, F., Japanese Studies
ELEY, L., Philosophy
ENGELS, O., Medieval and Modern History
ERICKSON, J., Applied Linguistics
FISCHER, G., Psychology
FISCHER, T., Classical Archaeology
FRISCH, P., Classical Philology
FROST, U., Education
GARCÍA-RAMÓN, J. L., Linguistics
GAUS, J., History of Art
GEYER, P., Romance Philology
GÖRLACH, M., English Philology
GRAEVENITZ, A. VON, Art History
GREIVE, A., Romance Philology
GROEBEN, N., Psychology
GRONEWALD, M., Classical Philology
GÜNTHER, R., Musicology
HEINE, B., African Studies
HESBERG, H. VON, Classical Archaeology
HEUSER, R., Chinese Law
HÖHN, H.-J., Catholic Theology
HOLKESKAMP, K.-J., Early History
HUSSY, W., Psychology
ISENMANN, E., Medieval History
JÄRVENTAUSTA, M., Finnish Studies
JENAL, G., Medieval History
KABLITZ, A., Romance Philology
KAEHLER, K., Philosophy
KÄMPER, D., Musicology
KAPP, D. B., Indology and Tamil Studies
KINDERMANN, U., Medieval Latin
KLEINSCHMIDT, E., Modern German Literature
KREUTZER, G., Nordic Philology
KUNISCH, J., Medieval and Modern History
KWASMAN, T., Jewish Studies
LEBEK, W. D., Classical Philology
LENERZ, J., German Philology
LIEBRAND, C., Modern German Literature and Gender Studies
MANUWALD, B., Classical Philology
MERTENS, G., Education
NEUHAUS, V., Modern German and Comparative Literature
NEUMEIER, B., English Philology
NITSCH, W., Romance Philology
NUSSBAUM, N., Art History and Urban Conservation
OBST, U., Slavonic Philology
OST, H., Art History
PAPE, W., Modern German Philology
PETERS, U., Medieval German Literature
PLÖGER, W., Education
POTTHAST, B., Latin American History
PRIMUS, B., German Linguistics
ROLSHOVEN, J., Philological and Linguistic Computing
RÜPPELL, H., Education
SALBER, W., Psychology
SASSE, H.-J., Comparative Linguistics
SCHARPING, T., Sinology
SCHMIDT, C., East European History
SCHMIDT-DENTER, U., Psychology
SCHNEIDER, I., Theatre, Film and Television Studies
SCHNEIDER, W., Education
SCHUMACHER, R., Musicology
SEIFERT, U., Musicology
STEPHAN, E., Psychology
STRUVE, T., Medieval History
TAUCHMANN, K., Ethnology
THALLER, M., Informatics in Historical and Cultural Studies
THISSEN, H. J., Egyptology
ULLMANN, H.-P., Modern History
WEIHER, E. VON, Ancient Oriental Philology
WIENBRUCH, U., Philosophy

ZAHRNT, M., Early History
ZELINSKY, B., Slavonic Philology
ZEUSKE, M., Iberian and Latin American History
ZICK, G., Art History
ZIEGELER, H. J., Medieval German Literature
ZIMMERMANN, A., Prehistory and Early History

Faculty of Special Education (tel. (221) 470-4640; fax (221) 470-5953; internet www .uni-koeln.de/hp-fak):

BUCHKREMER, H., General Therapy and Social Education
CONINX, F., Education of the Deaf and Hard of Hearing
DREHER, W., Education of the Mentally Handicapped
FENGLER, J., Psychology
FISCHER, K., Physical Education
FORNEFELD, B., Education of the Mentally Handicapped
KIRFEL, B., Sociology of the Handicapped
LAUTH, G., Psychology and Psychotherapy
LIST, G., Psychology
MASENDORF, F., Special Education and Rehabilitation of the Educationally Subnormal
OSKAMP, U., Education of the Physically Handicapped
PIEL, W., Music Therapy
SCHLEIFFER, R., Psychiatry and Psychotherapy
SEIFERT, R., Education of the Physically Handicapped
TSCHERNER, K. W. H., Teaching of the Educationally Subnormal
WEINWURM-KRAUSE, E.-M., Psychology and Psychiatry
WICHELHAUS, B., Art Therapy
WILLAND, H., Special Education and Rehabilitation of the Educationally Subnormal
WISOTZKI, K. H., Education of the Deaf and Hard of Hearing
WÖRNER, G., Arts and Crafts

WESTFÄLISCHE WILHELMS-UNIVERSITÄT MÜNSTER

Schlossplatz 2, 48149 Münster
Telephone: (251) 830
Fax: (251) 8332090
E-mail: verwaltung@uni-muenster.de
Internet: www.uni-muenster.de
Founded 1780, became Academy in 1818; Univ. status again in 1902
State control
Academic year: October to July (two terms)
Rector: Prof. Dr JÜRGEN SCHMIDT
Pro-Rectors: Prof. Dr WOLFGANG BERDEL, Prof. Dr ULRICH MÜLLER-FUNK, Prof. Dr ULRICH PFISTER, Prof. Dr HARALD ZÜCHNER
Chancellor: Dr BETTINA BÖHM
Librarian: Dr BEATE TRÖGER
Number of teachers: 1,217
Number of students: 40,000
Publication: Forschungsjournal (2 a year)

DEANS

Faculty of Biology: Prof. Dr CHRISTIAN KLÄMBT
Faculty of Catholic Theology: Prof. Dr REINHARD HOEPS
Faculty of Chemistry and Pharmacy: Prof. Dr BERNHARD WÜNSCH
Faculty of Earth Sciences: Prof. Dr HANS KERP
Faculty of Economic Sciences: Prof. Dr THERESIA THEURL
Faculty of Education and Social Sciences: Prof. Dr HANSJÖRG SCHEERER
Faculty of History/Philosophy: Prof. Dr MAGDALENE SÖLDNER

Faculty of Languages: Prof. Dr JÜRGEN HEIN
Faculty of Law: Prof. Dr REINER SCHULZE
Faculty of Mathematics and Computing: Prof. Dr KLAUS H. HINRICHS
Faculty of Medicine: Prof. Dr HERIBERT JÜRGENS
Faculty of Physics: Prof. Dr GERNOT MÜNSTER
Faculty of Protestant Theology: Prof. Dr HANS-RICHARD REUTER
Faculty of Psychology and Sports Science: Prof. Dr BERND STRAUß
Music School: Prof. Dr REINBERT EVERS

WISSENSCHAFTLICHE HOCHSCHULE FÜR UNTERNEHMENSFÜHRUNG (WHU)
(Otto Beisheim School of Management)

Burgplatz 2, 56179 Vallendar
Telephone: (261) 6509-0
Fax: (261) 6509-509
E-mail: info@whu.edu
Internet: www.whu.edu
Founded 1984
Private control
Languages of instruction: German, English
Academic year: September to August
Rector: Prof. Dr MICHAEL FRENKEL
Pro-Rector: Prof. Dr MARTIN FASSNACHT
Chancellor: Dr PETER STOMBERG
Librarian: HANNELORE PÖTHIG
Library of 35,000 vols
Number of teachers: 81
Number of students: 536
Publication: Signale (2 a year)

PROFESSORS

FASSNACHT, M., Marketing and Commerce
FENDEL, R., Monetary Economics
FRENKEL, M., Macroeconomics and Int. Economics
FÜLBIER, R. U., Accounting
GRICHNIK, D., Entrepreneurship
HÖFFLER, F., Regulatory Economics
HÖGL, M., Leadership and Human Resource Management
HOLGER, E., Technology and Innovation Management
HUCHZERMEIER, A., Production Management
HUTZSCHENREUTER, T., Corporate Strategy and Electronic Media Management
JENSEN, O., Business-to-Business Marketing
JOHANNING, L., Empirical Capital Market Research
JOST, P.-J., Organization Theory
KAUFMANN, L., Int. Business and Supply Management
KLEINDIENST, I., Strategy Processes
KNIRSCH, C., Corporate Finance
KOZIOL, D., Taxation and Accounting
LAMMERS, C., Corporate Finance
NÖLDEKE, M., Finance
REHM, S.-V., Business Information Science and Information Management
RUDOLF, F., Organization Theory
SCHÄFFER, U., Management Accounting and Control
WAGNER, S., Logistics Management
WEBER, J., Controlling and Telecommunications
WEIGAND, J., Microeconomics and Industrial Organization

Colleges
GENERAL

Schiller International University – Germany: Bergstr. 106, 69121 Heidelberg; tel. (6221) 4581-0; fax (6221) 402703; e-mail campus@siu-heidelberg.de; internet www .siu-heidelberg.de; f. 1964 as independent international university; language of instruc-

tion: English (all campuses); campuses in France, Germany, Spain, Switzerland, UK and USA (for which see respective chapters); depts of commercial art, computer studies, engineering management, international business, international tourism and hospitality management, international relations and diplomacy, literature, para-legal studies, premedicine; degrees at Florida (USA) campus conferred under charter granted by State of Florida; degrees at all other campuses conferred under charter granted by State of Delaware (USA); library: 91,000 vols (total for all campuses); 25 teachers (Heidelberg campus only); 1,519 students (total for all campuses, of which 210 at Heidelberg campus); Pres. Dr WALTER W. LEIBRECHT; Vice-President for Academic Affairs C. F. EBERHART.

Wissenschaftskolleg zu Berlin (Institute for Advanced Study): Wallotstr. 19, 14193 Berlin; tel. (30) 89001-0; fax (30) 89001-300; e-mail wiko@wiko-berlin.de; internet www .wiko-berlin.de; f. 1980; private institution for international and interdisciplinary postdoctoral research; 40 Fellows; library mainly reference collection; Rector Prof. Dr DIETER GRIMM; Sec. Dr JOACHIM NETTELBECK; Librarian Dr GESINE BOTTOMLEY.

ART, ARCHITECTURE

Akademie der Bildenden Künste (Academy of Fine Arts): Akademiestr. 2, 80799 Munich; tel. (89) 3852-0; fax (89) 3852-203; e-mail sekretariat@adbk.mhn.de; internet www.adbk.mhn.de; f. 1770 (Charter conferred 1808 and 1953); languages of instruction: German, English; 35 professors; 630 students; library: 110,000 vols, 100 current periodicals; Rector Prof. NIKOLAUS GERHART; Chancellor BIANCA MARZOCCA; Librarians CHARLOTTE DIEHL, INGE SICKLINGER-SEUß.

Akademie der Bildenden Künste in Nürnberg: Bingstr. 60, 90480 Nuremberg; tel. (911) 94040; fax (911) 9404150; e-mail info@adbk-nuernberg.de; internet www .adbk-nuernberg.de; f. 1662; 27 teachers; 350 students; library: 22,000 vols; President Prof. OTTMAR HÖRL; Vice-Presidents Prof. PETER ANGERMANN, Prof. CLAUS BURY, Prof. PETER ANGERMANN; Chancellor AXEL KLON; Librarian MARTINA KEMMSIES.

Bauhaus Kolleg: see entry for Bauhaus Dessau Foundation.

Deutsche Film- und Fernsehakademie Berlin GmbH (German Film and Television Academy): Potsdamer Straße 2, 10785 Berlin; tel. (30) 257590; fax (30) 25759161; e-mail info@dffb.de; internet www.dffb.de; f. 1966; 40 teachers; 110 students; library: 80,000 vols; Dir Prof. REINHARD HAUFF.

Hochschule für Bildende Künste Braunschweig: Johannes-Selenka-Platz 1, 38118 Brunswick; tel. (531) 391-9122; fax (531) 391-9292; e-mail hbk@hbk-bs.de; internet www.hbk-bs.de; f. 1963; depts of art (painting, graphics, sculpture, film, video, performing arts and photography), design (industrial and graphic), art teaching, art history; institute for media and film studies, institute for art history and visual research; languages of instruction: German, English; library: 26,000 vols; 1,200 students; President BARBARA STRAKA; publs Schriftenreihe (3–5 a year), Vorlesungsverzeichnis/Studienführer (2 a year).

Hochschule für Bildende Künste Dresden: 01288 Dresden; premises at: Güntzstr. 34, 01307 Dresden; tel. (351) 49267-0; fax (351) 4952023; e-mail info@serv1 .hfbk-dresden.de; internet www .hfbk-dresden.de; f. 1764; stage and theatre design, costume design, painting, sculpture, graphics, restoration, art therapy; languages of instruction: German, English; 31 teachers; 566 students; Rector Prof. CHRISTIAN SERY; Chancellor HANS-JÜRGEN SCHÖNEMANN; Librarians KARIN HUß, CHRISTINE POSSEGGA.

Hochschule für Bildende Künste Hamburg: Lerchenfeld 2, 22081 Hamburg; tel. (428) 989205; fax (428) 989206; e-mail presse@hfbk.hamburg.de; internet www .hfbk-hamburg.de; depts of architecture, art, education and technology, industrial design, visual communication,; Pres. MARTIN KÖTTERING; Chancellor HORST-VOLKERT THIEL; Librarian ELISABETH WILKER.

Hochschule für Film und Fernsehen 'Konrad Wolf' Potsdam-Babelsberg (Academy of Film and Television): Marlene-Dietrich-Allee 11, 14482 Potsdam; tel. (331) 6202-0; fax (331) 6202-549; e-mail info@ hff-potsdam.de; internet www.hff-potsdam .de; f. 1954; 100 teachers; 500 students; library: 82,000 vols, 16,000 video cassette titles, 170 film magazines, 1.6m. newspaper cuttings, 2,800 HFF (student) films; President Prof. Dr sc. DIETER WIEDEMANN; publ. *BFF (Beiträge zur Film- und Fernsehwissenschaft)* (irregular).

Hochschule für Grafik und Buchkunst Leipzig (Leipzig State Academy of Graphic Arts and Book Design): Wächterstr. 11, 04107 Leipzig; tel. (341) 2135-0; fax (341) 2135-166; e-mail hgb@hgb-leipzig.de; internet www.hgb-leipzig.de; f. 1764; painting, graphic arts, book art, graphic design, photography, media art; 48 teachers; 350 students; library: 40,000 vols, 100 current periodicals; Rector Prof. JOACHIM BROHM; Chancellor MARIA-CORNELIA ZIESCH; Librarian CLAUDIA-MARIA DARMER.

Hochschule für Künste Bremen: Am Speicher XI 8, 28217 Bremen; tel. (421) 9595-100; fax (421) 9595-2000; e-mail studsek@hfk-bremen.de; internet www .hfk-bremen.de; f. 1988; library: 40,000 vols; 90 teachers; 723 students (623 undergraduate, 100 postgraduate); Rector Prof. Dr PETER RAUTMANN; Chancellor MARKUS WORTMANN; Librarians VERONIKA GREUEL, SIEGFRIED STANGE.

Kunstakademie Düsseldorf, Hochschule für Bildende Künste (Academy of Fine Art, Düsseldorf): Eiskellerstr. 1, 40213 Düsseldorf; tel. (211) 1396-0; fax (211) 1396-225; e-mail postmaster@ kunstakademie-duesseldorf.de; internet www.kunstakademie-duesseldorf.de; f. 1773; 50 teachers; 700 students; library: 110,000 vols; Rector Prof. Dr MARKUS LÜPERTZ; Rector Prof. Dr PETER MICHAEL LYNEN; Librarian HELMUT KLEINENBROICH.

Kunsthochschule Berlin-Weissensee, Hochschule für Gestaltung: Bühringstr. 20, 13086 Berlin; tel. (30) 47705-0; fax (30) 47705-290; e-mail rektor@kh-berlin.de; internet www.kh-berlin.de; f. 1946; fine arts, industrial design, ceramics, fashion design, textile design, communication design, architecture, stage design, sculpture; 550 students, 39 teachers; library: 20,000 vols; Rector Prof. GERHARD STREHL.

Staatliche Akademie der Bildenden Künste: Postfach 6267, 76042 Karlsruhe; Reinhold-Frank-Str. 67, 76133 Karlsruhe; tel. (721) 9265210; fax (721) 9265213; e-mail mail@kunstakademie-karlsruhe.de; www.kunstakademie-karlsruhe.de; f. 1854; library: 30,000 vols; Rector Prof. ERWIN GROSS; Chancellor RÜDIGER WEIS; Librarian RENATE WINKLER-WILDE.

Staatliche Akademie der Bildenden Künste: Am Weissenhof 1, 70191 Stuttgart; tel. (711) 28440-0; fax (711) 28440-225; e-mail info@abk-stuttgart.de; internet www .abk-stuttgart.de; f. 1761; art, graphics,

sculpture, architecture, design, conservation, ceramics, textiles and industrial design; Rector Dr LUDGER HUENHKEUS; Pro-Rectors Prof. PETER LITZLBAUER, Prof. ANDREAS OPIOLKA.

Staatliche Hochschule für Bildende Künste–Städelschule: Dürerstr. 10, 60596 Frankfurt; tel. (69) 605008-0; fax (69) 605008-52; e-mail rektor@staedelschule.de; internet www.staedelschule.de; f. 1817; art, architecture, film, sculpture, painting, drawing, architecture (conceptual design); 9 profs; 150 students; library: 16,000 vols; Rector Prof. Dr DANIEL BIRNBAUM; Exec. Dir JÜRGEN GRUMANN; Librarian HEIKE BELZER.

ECONOMICS, POLITICAL AND SOCIAL SCIENCES, PUBLIC ADMINISTRATION

European Business School: Schloss Reichartshausen, 65375 Oestrich-Winkel; tel. (6723) 69-0; fax (6723) 69-133; e-mail info@ ebs.de; internet www.ebs.de; f. 1971; private, state-recognized diploma courses; 22 teachers; 835 students; library: 22,000 vols, 150 current periodicals; Pres. Prof. Dr HANS TIETMEYER; Rector Prof. ULRICH HOMMEL; Chancellor Dr PETER ADLER; Librarian SILVA SCHELLHAS.

Hochschule für Politik München: Ludwigstr. 8, 80539 Munich; tel. (89) 285018; fax (89) 283705; e-mail hfp-muenchen@hfp.mhn .de; internet www.hfp.mhn.de; f. 1950; 150 teachers; 950 students; library: 35,000 vols; Rector Prof. Dr P. C. MAYER-TASCH; publs *Junge Wissenschaft* (irregular), *Schriftenreihe* (irregular), *Zeitschrift für Politik* (4 a year).

HWP – Hamburger Universität für Wirtschaft und Politik: Von-Melle-Park 9, 20146 Hamburg; tel. (40) 42838-2180; fax (40) 42838-4150; e-mail hildc@hwp-hamburg .de; internet www.hwp-hamburg.de; f. 1948; undergraduate degree courses in business and management, law, economics, sociology; postgraduate degree courses in socio-economics, international business administration, European studies; languages of instruction: German, English; 80 teachers; 2,600 students; Pres. Dr DOROTHEE BITTSCHEIDT; Registrar DIETMAR PLUM.

Stuttgart Institute of Management and Technology: Filderhauptstr. 142, 70599 Stuttgart; tel. (711) 451001-0; fax (711) 451001-45; e-mail info@uni-simt.de; internet www.uni-simt.de; f. 1998; MBA in international management, finance and investment, management information systems, technology and innovation management; international executive MBA; part-time programmes; 68 teachers (8 full-time, 60 part-time); 150 students; Man. Dir Dr BERNHARD SEITZ.

LANGUAGES

Akademie für Fremdsprachen (Academy of Foreign Languages): Postfach 150104, 10663 Berlin; Nürnberger Str. 38, 10777 Berlin; tel. (30) 884302-0; fax 884302-23; e-mail post@akafremd.de; internet www .akafremd.de; f. 1971; translators' and interpreters' courses in German, English, French, Spanish, Italian, Russian, and courses in German as a foreign language; 1,600 students; Sec. NORBERT ZÄNKER.

MEDICINE

Medizinische Akademie Erfurt: Nordhäuser Str. 74, PSF 595, 99089 Erfurt; tel. (361) 790; fax 23697; f. 1954; 121 teachers; 750 students; library: 140,000 vols; Rector Prof. Dr Dr h.c. mult. W. KÜNZEL; Pro-Rector Prof. Dr G. ENDERT; Medical Dir Prof. Dr W. KRAFFT; Librarian Dr B. ADLUNG.

MUSIC AND DRAMA

Hochschule für Musik Saar: Bismarckstr. 1, 66111 Saarbrücken; tel. (681) 96731-0; fax (681) 96731-30; e-mail t.wolter@hfm .saarland.de; internet www.hfm.saarland; f. 1947; 110 teachers; 350 students; library: 82,000 vols; Rector Prof. THOMAS DUIS; Man. Dir ALFONS SIMON; Librarian ILSE HAHN.

Hochschule für Musik: Schwarzwaldstr. 141, 79095 Freiburg im Breisgau; tel. (761) 319150; fax (761) 3191542; e-mail info@ mh-freiburg.de; internet www.mh-freiburg .de; f. 1946; 160 teachers; 540 students; Rector MANFRED KLIMANSKI.

Hochschule für Musik 'Hanns Eisler': Charlottenstr. 55, 10117 Berlin; tel. (30) 90269-700; fax (30) 90269-701; e-mail rektorat@hfm.in-berlin.de; internet www .hfm-berlin.de; f. 1950; departments of voice, music, stage and theatre direction; strings, harp and guitar; brass, woodwind, percussion and conducting; and piano, accordion and composition/harmony; 433 teachers (113 full-time, 320 part-time); 702 students; Dir Prof. CHRISTHARD GÖSSLING.

Hochschule für Musik Detmold: Neustadt 22, 32756 Detmold; tel. (5231) 975-5; fax (5231) 975-972; internet www.hfm-detmold .de; f. 1946; 120 teachers; 580 students; library of 157,800 items; Rector Prof. MARTIN CHRISTIAN VOGEL.

Hochschule für Musik 'Carl Maria von Weber' Dresden: Wettiner Platz 13, Postfach 120039, 01001 Dresden; tel. (351) 4923600; fax (351) 4923657; e-mail rektorat@hfmdd.smwk.sachsen.de; internet www.hfmdd.de; library: 50,000 vols, 7,000 records and CDs, contains Heinrich-Schütz archive; 80 teachers; 631 students; attached institute for musicology (in co-operation with the Heinrich-Schütz Archive), institute for music medicine, studio for voice research, studio for electronic music; Rector Prof. Dr STEFAN GIES; Pro-Rectors Prof. HEIDRUN RICHTER, Prof. GÜNTER SOMMER; publ. *Schriftenreihe der Hochschule für Musik* (irregular).

Hochschule für Musik Köln: Dagobertstr. 38, 50668 Cologne; tel. (221) 912818-0; fax (221) 131204; internet www.mhs-koeln.de; f. 1925; centres in Cologne, Aachen and Wuppertal; instrumental music and musicology; 330 teachers; 1,800 students; library: 136,000 vols, 8,600 records, 400 films; Rector Prof. JOSEF PROTSCHKA; Chancellor URSULA WIRTZ-KNAPSTEIN; publ. *Journal* (2 a year).

Hochschule für Musik und Theater 'Felix Mendelssohn Bartholdy' Leipzig: PSF 100809, 04008 Leipzig; Grassistr. 8, 04107 Leipzig; tel. (341) 214455; fax (341) 2144503; e-mail rektor@hmt-leipzig.de; internet www.hmt-leipzig.de; f. 1843; library: 163,000 vols; 850 students; Rector Prof. KONRAD KÖRNER.

Hochschule für Musik Nürnberg-Augsburg: Veilhofstr. 34, 90489 Nuremberg; tel. (911) 2318443; fax (911) 2317697; e-mail hfm-rektorat@stadt.nuernberg.de; internet www.hfm-n-a.de; f. 1873 as Leopold Mozart Konservatorium; present name 1999; international college of higher education; concerts, productions, International Leopold Mozart Competition for Young Violinists, Studio for Old and New Music; 98 teachers; 200 students; library: 12,500 vols in Nuremberg and Augsburg libraries; Rector SIEGFRIED JERUSALEM; Chancellor HANS-WERNER ITTMANN.

Hochschule für Musik 'Franz Liszt' Weimar: Platz der Demokratie 2/3, 99423 Weimar; tel. (3643) 555-0; fax (3643) 555-117; f. 1872; 840 students; 132 teachers; library: 65,000 vols and 45,000 tapes; Rector Prof.

ROLF-DIETER ARENS; Pro-Rectors Prof. ANNE-KATHRIN LINDIG, Prof. GERO SCHMIDT-OBER-LÄNDER; instruction in: keyboard, string and wind instruments, accordion, guitar, jazz/pop instruments and vocal, composition, conducting, singing and music teaching, church music and musicology.

Hochschule für Musik: Hofstallstr. 6–8, 97070 Würzburg; tel. (931) 321870; fax (931) 321872800; e-mail hochschule@hfm-wuerzburg.de; internet www .hfm-wuerzburg.de; f. 1804; 220 teachers; 650 students; library: 14,200 vols, 45,400 music scores, 47 current periodicals; Rector Prof. SILKE-THORA MATTHIES; Chancellor Dr EVA STUMPF-WIRTHS; Librarian BARBARA KONRAD.

Hochschule für Musik und Darstellende Kunst: Eschersheimer Landstrasse 29–39, 60322 Frankfurt am Main; tel. (69) 154007-0; fax (69) 154007-108; internet www .hfmdk-frankfurt.de; 60 teachers; 850 students; f. 1878 as Konservatorium, Hochschule since 1938; Rector Prof. THOMAS RIETSCHEL.

Hochschule für Musik und Theater Hannover: Emmichpl. 1, 30175 Hanover; tel. (511) 31001; fax (511) 3100200; e-mail pressestelle@hmt-hannover.de; internet www.hmt-hannover.de; f. 1961; 280 teachers; 1,100 students; library: 203,000 vols; Pres. Prof. Dr KLAUS-ERNST BEHNE.

Hochschule für Musik und Theater: Harvestehuder Weg 12, 20148 Hamburg; tel. (40) 428482586; fax (40) 428482666; internet www.hfmt-hamburg.de; f. 1950; 250 teachers; 750 students; library: 20,000 vols; Pres. Prof. ELMAR LAMPSON; Chancellor BERNHARD LANGE; Librarians SILKE BROSE, MELANIE KINTZEL.

Hochschule für Musik und Theater München: Arcisstr. 12, 80333 Munich; tel. (89) 289-03; fax (89) 28927419; e-mail verwaltung@musikhochschule-muenchen.de; internet www.musikhochschule-muenchen .de; f. 1846; 300 teachers; 900 students; Pres. Prof. Dr SIEGFRIED MAUSER.

Internationales Musikinstitut Darmstadt (IMD): Nieder-Ramstäder Str. 190, 64285 Darmstadt; tel. (6151) 132416; fax (6151) 132405; e-mail imd@darmstadt.de; internet www.imd.darmstadt.de; f. 1946; international holiday courses on contemporary music (composition, interpretation); international music lending library (works since beginning of 20th century) of 35,000 scores, 5,000 vols, 4,000 tapes, 1,500 records; Dir SOLF SCHAEFER.

Musikhochschule Lübeck: Gr. Petersgrube 17-29, 23552 Lübeck; tel. (451) 1505-0; fax (451) 1505-300; e-mail info@mh-luebeck.de; internet www.mh-luebeck .de; f. 1933; musical training on all instruments, opera singing and performing, training of music teachers, sacred music (Protestant and Catholic), preparatory training of professional musicians and music teachers; library: 110,000 vols; 130 teachers; 500 students; Rector Prof. INGE-SUSANN RÖM-HILD; Administrator DETLEF BAUDISCH; Librarian TORSTEN SENKBEIL.

Richard-Strauss-Konservatorium: Kellerstr. 6, 81667 Munich; tel. (89) 48098-4415; fax (89) 48098-4417; e-mail sekretariat@rsk.musin.de; internet www.rsk .musin.de; f. 1962; courses in vocal and instrumental studies, conducting, composition, jazz; 120 teachers; 500 students; library: 20,000 vols; Dir MARTIN MARIA KRÜGER; Librarian TOM HOPFINGER.

Robert-Schumann-Hochschule Düsseldorf: Fischerstr. 110, 40476 Düsseldorf; tel. (211) 49180; fax (211) 4911618; e-mail rsh@rsh-duesseldorf.de; internet www .rsh-duesseldorf.de; f. 1935; languages of instruction: German, English; library: 120,000 vols; 191 teachers; 830 students; Rector Prof. RAIMUND WIPPERMANN; Pro-Rector Prof. BARBARA SZCZEPANSKA; Chancellor BARBARA SZCZEPANSKA.

Staatliche Hochschule für Musik Karlsruhe: Postfach 6040, 76040 Karlsruhe; Am Schloss Gottesaue 7, 76131 Karlsruhe; tel. (721) 662950; fax (721) 662966; internet www .hfm-karlsruhe.de; f. 1884; library: 115,000 vols; 150 teachers; 550 students; Rector Prof. WOLFGANG MEYER; Chancellor WOLFRAM SCHERER; Librarian HANNELORE BERNT.

Staatliche Hochschule für Musik und Darstellende Kunst: Urbanstr. 25, 70182 Stuttgart; tel. (711) 2124631; fax (711) 2124632; e-mail rektor@mh-stuttgart.de; internet www.mh-stuttgart.de; f. 1857; 200 teachers; 770 students; library: 10,000 vols; Rector Prof. Dr WERNER HEINRICHS; Chancellor ALBRECHT LANG.

Staatliche Hochschule für Musik und Darstellende Kunst Heidelberg-Mannheim: N7, 18, 68161 Mannheim; fax (621) 2922072; e-mail rektorat@muho-mannheim .de; internet www.muho-mannheim.de; f. 1899; 200 teachers; 550 students; Rector Prof. R. MEISTER; Man. Dir THILO FISCHER; Librarian KATHRIN WINTER.

PHILOSOPHY, THEOLOGY

Augustana Hochschule: Waldstr. 11, 91564 Neuendettelsau; tel. (9874) 509-0; fax (9874) 509-555; e-mail hochschule@augustana.de; internet www.augustana.de; f. 1947; 30 teachers; 200 students; Rector Prof. Dr HELMUT UTZSCHNEIDER; Librarian ARMIN STEPHAN.

Hochschule für Philosophie: Kaulbachstr. 31A, 80539 Munich; tel. (89) 23862300; fax (89) 23862302; e-mail admin@hfph.mwn.de; internet www.hfph .mwn.de; f. 1925; library: 199,000 vols; 20 teachers; 500 students; Rector Prof. Dr MICHAEL BORDT; Chancellor Dr IGNAZ FISCHER-KERLI; Librarian J. OSWALD; publ. *Theologie und Philosophie* (4 a year).

Kirchliche Hochschule Bethel: Postfach 130140, 33544 Bielefeld; premises at: Remterweg 45, 33617 Bielefeld; tel. (521) 144-3948; fax (521) 1443961; e-mail rektorat .kihobethel@uni-bielefeld.de; internet www .kiho-bethel.de; f. 1905; languages of instruction: German, English; library: 125,000 vols; 23 teachers; 200 students; Rector Prof. Dr FRANÇOIS VOUGA; publ. *Jahrbuch—Wort und Dienst* (every 2 years).

Kirchliche Hochschule Wuppertal: Missionstr. 9B, 42285 Wuppertal; tel. (202) 2820-100; fax (202) 2820-101; e-mail rektorat-kiho@uni-wuppertal.de; internet www.kiho.uni-wuppertal.de; f. 1935; Protestant; library: 100,000 vols; 15 teachers; 200 students; Rector Prof. Dr DIETER VIEWEGER.

Lutherische Theologische Hochschule Oberursel: Altkönigstrasse 150, 61440 Oberursel im Taunus; tel. (6171) 9127-0; fax (6171) 9127-70; e-mail lthh@lthh-oberursel .de; internet www.lthh-oberursel.de; f. 1947; library: 35,000 vols; 8 teachers; 30 students; publ. *Lutherische Theologie und Kirche* (4 a year).

Philosophisch-Theologische Hochschule Sankt Georgen: Offenbacher Landstr. 224, 60599 Frankfurt am Main; tel. (69) 60610; fax (69) 6061307; e-mail rektorat@st-georgen.uni-frankfurt.de; internet www.st-georgen.uni-frankfurt.de; f. 1926 (since 1950 combined with Jesuit Theological Faculty, f. 1863); languages of instruction: German, English; library: 390,000 vols;

23 teachers; 460 students; Rector Prof. Dr HELMUT ENGEL; Librarian MARCUS STARK; publs *Frankfurter Theologische Studien* (2–3 a year), *Sankt Georgener Hochschulschriften* (1 a year), *Theologie und Philosophie* (4 a year).

Theologische Fakultät Fulda (Staatlich anerkannte Wissenschaftliche Hochschule): Eduard-Schick-Pl. 2, 36037 Fulda; tel. (661) 87220; fax (661) 87224; e-mail rektorat@thf-fulda.de; internet www .thf-fulda.de; f. 1748; languages of instruction: German, English; 20 teachers; 40 students; Rector Prof. Dr BERND WILLMES; publs *Fuldaer Hochschulschriften*, *Fuldaer Studien*.

Theologische Fakultät Paderborn: Kamp 6, 33098 Paderborn; tel. (5251) 1216; fax (5251) 121700; e-mail theol-fakultaet-paderborn@t-online.de; internet www.theofak-pb.de; f. 1615; 26 teachers; 351 students; Rector Prof. Dr GÜNTHER WILHELM; Pro-Rector Prof. Dr MICHAEL KUNZLER; Librarian Prof. Dr KARL HENGST; publ. *Theologie und Glaube* (4 a year).

Theologische Fakultät Trier: Universitätsring 19, 54296 Trier; tel. (651) 201-3520; fax (651) 201-3951; e-mail theofak@uni-trier .de; internet www.uni-trier.de/uni/theo; f. 1950; library: 400,000 vols; 20 ordinary professors; 315 students; Chancellor Dr REINHARD MARX (Bishop of Trie); Rector Prof. Dr REINHOLD BOHLEN; publ. *Trierer Theologische Zeitschrift* (4 a year).

TECHNOLOGY

Burg Giebichenstein Hochschule für Kunst und Design Halle: 06108 Halle, Neuwerk 7; tel. (345) 7751-50; fax (345) 7751-569; e-mail rektorat@burg-halle.de; internet www.burg-halle.de; f. 1915; language of instruction: German; library: 64,000 vols of various media, 170 journals; 90 teachers; 980 students; Rector Prof. ULRICH KLIEBER; Dean, School of Design Prof. AXEL MÜLLER-SCHÖLL; Dean, School of Fine Arts Prof. THOMAS RUG.

Attached Research Institutes:

Institut Computer Art & Design: tel. (345) 7751-900; fax (345) 7751-907; e-mail ca&d@burg-halle.de; internet cad .burg-halle.de; Dir LEONORE PUNK.

Institut für Software Consulting und Entwicklung: tel. (345) 7751-701; fax (345) 7751-719; e-mail isce@burg-halle.de; internet www.burg-halle.de/~isce; Dir Prof. JOSEF WALCH.

Institut idea (Interior Design, Environment and Architecture): tel. (345) 7751-868; fax (345) 7751-868; e-mail idea@burg-halle.de; internet www .burg-halle.de/~idea.

Hochschule Anhalt (FH): Bernburger Str. 52–57, 06366 Köthen; tel. (3496) 671000; fax (3496) 671099; internet www.hs-anhalt.de; f. 1891, present status 1992; Köthen: mechanical engineering (plant construction), chemical and environmental engineering, biotechnology and food processing, computer science, electrical engineering; Bernburg: business economics, agriculture, landscape architecture and planning, food and health management; Dessau: architecture, civil engineering, surveying, design; President Prof. Dr DIETER ORZESSEK; Vice-Pres Prof. Dr CAROLA GRIEHL, Prof. Dr RUDOLF LÜCKMANN, Prof. Dr NORBERT OTTO.

Hochschule Mittweida (FH)–University of Applied Sciences: Postfach 1457, 09644 Mittweida; tel. (3727) 580; fax (3727) 581379; e-mail info@htwm.de; internet www.htwm .de; f. 1867; electrical engineering, electronics, microelectronics, mechanical engineering, mathematics, physics, economic sciences, social sciences, media technology, media management, microsystems engineering, precision engineering, steel and metal construction, building engineering, physical engineering, environmental engineering, computer sciences; library: 140,000 vols; 298 teachers; 4,824 students; Rector Prof. Dr WERNER TOTZAUER.

Hochschule für Technik, Wirtschaft und Kultur Leipzig (Leipzig University of Applied Sciences): Postfach 301166, 04251 Leipzig; Karl-Liebknecht-Str. 132, 04277 Leipzig; tel. (341) 3076-0; fax (341) 3076-6456; e-mail studinf@k.htwk-leipzig.de; internet www.htwk-leipzig.de; f. 1992; architecture, civil engineering, electrical engineering, mechanical engineering, printing technology, multimedia technology, publishing, computer science, business mathematics, business administration, social work,

library and information science, museology, book trade/publishing, engineering with management (electrical engineering, energy engineering, mechanical engineering, civil engineering), international management; library: 320,000 vols; 180 teachers; 6,000 students; Rector Prof. Dr-Ing. MANFRED NIETNER.

Hochschule Zittau/Görlitz (FH): Postfach 1454, 02754 Zittau; Theodor-Koerner-Allee 16, 02763 Zittau; tel. (3583) 611401; fax (3583) 611402; e-mail info@hs-zigr.de; internet www.hs-zigr.de; f. 1992; architecture, civil engineering, business management, chemistry, electrical engineering, process engineering, power and environmental engineering, real estate and housing management, computer science, mechanical engineering, ecology and environmental protection, mechatronics, tourism, translating English and Czech, social work, social education, special needs education, communica-

tions psychology, business mathematics, marketing, electrical and electronic engineering, business studies, industrial engineering; library: 179,254 vols; 121 teachers; 3,800 students; Rector Prof. Dr-Ing. RAINER HAMPEL; Chancellor Dr-Ing. P. REINHOLD.

Westsächsische Hochschule Zwickau (FH): Dr-Friedrichs-Ring 2A, 08056 Zwickau; tel. (375) 536-0; fax (375) 536-1127; e-mail rektorat@fh-zwickau.de; internet www .fh-zwickau.de; f. 1992; schools of applied arts, applied economics, architecture, electrical engineering, health and healthcare management, languages, mechanical and automotive engineering, physical and computer sciences, textile and leather production engineering,; languages of instruction: German, English; library: 198,000 vols; 191 teachers; 4,700 students; Rector Prof. Dr-Ing. habil. KARL-FRIEDRICH FISCHER; publs *Hochschulforschungsbericht* (1 a year), *Hochschulführer* (1 a year).

GHANA

The Higher Education System

In 1957 the former British dependencies of Togoland and Gold Coast declared the independent state of Ghana, which subsequently became a republic in 1960. The first institution of higher education, Achimota College, was founded in 1924, and the first university-level institution, University College of the Gold Coast, was founded in 1948 in conjunction with the University of London (United Kingdom), and achieved full university status in 1961; it is now known as University of Ghana, and is based in the capital, Accra. Some 82,346 students were enrolled in higher education in 1996/97, with 23,126 students attending the country's five universities. By 1998/99 the number of universities in Ghana had increased to seven. Tertiary institutions also included 38 teacher-training colleges, eight polytechnics and 61 technical colleges. In 2006/07 some 140,000 students were enrolled in tertiary education.

Higher education is administered by the Ministry of Education, Science and Sports. The National Council for Tertiary Education is the body that advises the Government on higher education policy. The National Accreditation Board (NAB) classifies institutions of higher education as universities, university colleges, polytechnics, colleges, schools, institutes, academies, or tutorial colleges. The NAB is responsible for accrediting private and public institutions of higher education, approving programmes of study, ensuring quality assurance, and determining degree equivalency. Institutions of higher education usually have two-tier systems of governance, consisting of a Council, which oversees administrative issues such as finance and personnel, and either a Senate or Academic Board, which deals with academic issues. The Chancellor is the head of the University.

Admission to university is based on suitable scores in either six subjects at SSSCE (Senior Secondary School Certificate Examinations) level or three subjects at A-level. The main undergraduate degree is the three- to four-year Bachelors, though both University of Ghana and Kwame Nkrumah University of Science and Technology offer two-year Diploma programmes. The Bachelors degree is based on the US-style 'credit' and semester scheme, and students are required to accrue a specified number of credits in major and minor subjects in order to graduate. Only the five state-controlled universities offer postgraduate degrees, which include one- to two-year Masters and Postgraduate Diploma programmes and Doctorate programmes lasting a minimum of three years.

The National Coordinating Committee for Technical and Vocational Education and Training is the Government body responsible for technical and vocational education. The leading institutions for technical and vocational education are the polytechnics, which were elevated to higher education-level status in 1993. They offer four main qualifications: Vocational Craft Certificate, Advanced Craft Certificate, Diploma, and Higher National Diploma.

Regulatory and Representative Bodies

GOVERNMENT

Ministry of Culture and Chieftaincy: Accra; Minister of State SAMPSON KWAKU BOAFO.

Ministry of Education, Science and Sports: POB M45, Accra; tel. (21) 666070; fax (21) 664067; Minister Prof. DOMINIC FOBIH.

ACCREDITATION

National Accreditation Board: IPS, Trinity Rd, POB CT 3256, Cantonments, Accra; tel. (21) 518570; fax (21) 518629; e-mail nabsec@nab.gov.gh; internet www.nab.gov.gh; f. 1993; attached to Min. of Education, Science and Sports; accredits public and private tertiary instns with respect to the content and standard of their programmes; determines the equivalences of diplomas, certificates and other qualifications awarded by instns in Ghana or elsewhere; 15 mems; Chair. Prof. D. A. AKYEAMPONG; Exec. Sec. KWAME DATTEY.

NATIONAL BODY

National Council for Tertiary Education: POB M28, Accra; tel. (21) 770198; e-mail info@ncteghana.org; f. 1993; attached to Min. of Education, Science and Sports; advises the Minister on the devt of tertiary education instns in Ghana and on their financial needs; recommends nat. standards on staff, costs, accommodation and time utilization, and monitors the implementation of any approved nat. standards by the instns; Exec. Sec. PAUL EFFAH.

Learned Societies

GENERAL

Centre for National Culture: POB 2738, Accra; tel. (21) 664099; f. 1958; to promote and develop the arts and preserve traditional arts; includes a research section; a regional museum is planned; Chair. NII AYITEY AGBOFU II; Dir M. K. AMOATEY; publ. DAWURO.

Ghana Academy of Arts and Sciences: POB M.32, Accra; tel. (21) 772002; fax (21) 772032; e-mail gaas@ug.edu.gh; internet www.gaas-gh.org; f. 1959; sections of Arts (Chair. Prof. KWAME GYEKYE), Sciences (Chair. Prof. IVAN ADDAE MENSAH); 90 Fellows; Pres. Dr S. K. B. ASANTE; Hon. Sec. Prof. KWESI YANKAH; publ. Proceedings (1 a year).

UNESCO Accra Cluster Office: POB CT 4949, Accra; 8 Mankralo St, East Cantonments, Accra; tel. (21) 740840; fax (21) 765498; e-mail accra@unesco.org; designated Cluster Office for Benin, Côte d'Ivoire, Ghana, Nigeria, Sierra Leone and Togo; Dir ELIZABEH MOUNDO.

ARCHITECTURE AND TOWN PLANNING

Ghana Institute of Architects: POB M.272, Accra; fax (21) 229464; e-mail giarch@internet.com.gh; internet www.internet.com.gh/gia; f. 1962; 300 mems; Pres. KENNETH AMPRATWUM; Hon. Sec. JOSEPH E. HAYFORD; publs Bulletin (12 a year), Ghana Architect, PATO.

BIBLIOGRAPHY, LIBRARY SCIENCE AND MUSEOLOGY

Ghana Library Association: POB 4105, Accra; tel. (21) 763523; f. 1962; Pres. HELENA ASAMOAH-HASSAN; Sec. ANGELINA LILY ARMAH; publ. Ghana Library Journal (1 a year).

ECONOMICS, LAW AND POLITICS

Economic Society of Ghana: c/o Department of Economics, University of Ghana, POB 57, Legon, Accra; f. 1957; 500 mems; publs Economic Bulletin of Ghana, Social and Economic Affairs (4 a year).

Ghana Bar Association: POB 4150, Accra; tel. and fax (21) 226748; 2,500 mems; Nat. Pres. PAUL ADU-GYAMFI; Nat. Sec. BENSON NUTSUKPUI.

EDUCATION

West African Examinations Council: Examination Loop, POB GP 125, Accra; tel. (21) 248967; fax (21) 222905; e-mail waechqrs@africaonline.com.gh; internet www.waecheadquartersgh.org; f. 1952 by the 4 W African Commonwealth countries; nat. offices in Lagos, Nigeria; Accra, Ghana; Freetown, Sierra Leone; Banjul, The Gambia; Monrovia, Liberia; conducts the W African Sr School Certificate Examination (WASSCE) for The Gambia, Sierra Leone, Nigeria and Ghana; Basic Education Certificate Examination for The Gambia, Ghana and Sierra Leone; and 9th and 12th grade examinations for Liberia; also selection examinations for entry into secondary schools and similar instns and the Public Services; entrance and final examinations for teacher training colleges, commercial and technical examinations at the request of the various Ministries of Education; holds examinations on behalf of the UK examining authorities and the Educational Testing Service, Princeton, NJ, USA; 5 mem. countries; Chair. Prof. JONAS A. S. REDWOOD-SAWYERR; Registrar/Chief Exec. Alhaja MULIKAT AYONI BELLO; publ. Research Report (abstracts and findings of research projects conducted by the Ccl).

HISTORY, GEOGRAPHY AND ARCHAEOLOGY

Ghana Geographical Association: University of Ghana; f. 1955; Pres. Prof. E. V. T. ENGMANN; Hon. Sec. Dr L. J. GYAMFI-FENTENG; publ. *Bulletin* (1 a year).

Historical Society of Ghana: POB 12, Legon; f. 1952; formerly Gold Coast and Togoland Historical Soc.; 600 mems; Pres. T. A. OSAE; Sec. R. ADDO-FENING; publ. *Transactions* (1 a year).

LANGUAGE AND LITERATURE

Alliance Française: Liberation Link, Airport Residential Area, POB CT 4904, Accra; tel. (21) 760278; fax (21) 760279; e-mail info@ alliancefrancaiseghana.org; internet www .alliancefrancaiseghana.org; offers courses and examinations in French language and culture and promotes cultural exchange with France; attached teaching centres in Cape Coast, Kumasi, Takoradi and Tema.

British Council: Liberia Rd, POB GP 771, Accra; tel. (21) 683068; fax (21) 683062; e-mail infoaccra@gh.britishcouncil.org; internet www.britishcouncil.org/ghana; f. 1943; conducts British examinations, supports personal and professional development through physical and electronic resources; projects include school and higher education partnership, leadership training; attached centre in Kumasi; library of 4,000 vols, more than 50 periodicals; 1,500 video cassettes and DVDs, electronic resources; Dir MOSES ANIBABA.

Ghana Association of Writers: POB 4414, Accra; tel. (21) 776586; f. 1957; aims at bringing together all the writers of the country, to protect and champion the interests of Ghanaian writers, to encourage contact with foreign writers, and to foster the development of Ghanaian literature; literary evenings, annual congress, etc.; Pres. ATUKWEI OKAI; Gen. Sec. J. E. ALLOTEY-PAPPOE; publ. *Angla* (anthology, 1 a year).

Goethe-Institut: 30 Kakramadu Rd, Cantonments, Accra; tel. (30) 2776764; fax (30) 2779770; e-mail info@accra.goethe.org; internet www.goethe.de/af/acc/deindex.htm; f. 1961; offers courses and examinations in German language and culture and promotes cultural exchange with Germany; library of 2,603 vols; Dir ELEONORE SYLLA.

MEDICINE

Pharmaceutical Society of Ghana: POB 2133, Accra; tel. (21) 228341; fax (21) 239583; f. 1935; aims to advance chemistry and pharmacy and maintain standards of the profession; 8 regional brs; library of 250 vols; 1,200 mems; Pres. ALEXANDER NII OTO DODDO; Executive Sec. DENNIS SENA AWITTY; publ. *The Ghana Pharmaceutical Journal* (4 a year).

NATURAL SCIENCES

General

Ghana Science Association: POB 7, Legon; tel. (21) 500253; f. 1959; Nat. Pres. Dr P. A. KURANCHIE; Nat. Sec. I. J. KWAME ABOH; publ. *The Ghana Journal of Science.*

West African Science Association: c/o Botany Dept, POB 7, University of Ghana, Legon; f. 1953; mems: Ghana, Nigeria, Sierra Leone, Côte d'Ivoire, Senegal, Togo, Niger, Benin; observers: Burkina Faso, Liberia; Pres. Prof. ANDRÉ DOVI KUEVI; Sec. Dr J. K. B. A. ATA; publ. *Journal* (1 a year).

RELIGION, SOCIOLOGY AND ANTHROPOLOGY

Ghana Sociological Association: c/o Dept of Sociology, University of Ghana, Legon; f. 1961; financial aid from the universities and the Academy of Arts and Sciences; academic activities, conferences, etc.; 215 mems; Pres. Prof. J. M. ASSIMENG; Sec. E. H. MENDS; publ. *Ghana Journal of Sociology.*

TECHNOLOGY

Ghana Institution of Engineers: POB 7042, Accra-North; tel. (21) 772005; e-mail ghie@ncs.com.gh; f. 1968; 1,000 mems; Pres. Ing. K. OFORI-KURAGO; Exec. Sec. Ing. LAURI LAWSON; publ. *The Ghana Engineer* (4 a year).

Research Institutes

GENERAL

Council for Scientific and Industrial Research (CSIR): POB M.32, Accra; tel. (21) 777651; fax (21) 777655; internet www .csir.org.gh; f. 1958; functions incl. advice to the Govt, encouragement of scientific and industrial research relevant to nat. devt and commercialization of research results; coordination of research in all its aspects in Ghana, and collation, publ. and dissemination of research results; library: Institute for Scientific and Technological Information: see Libraries and Archives; Dir-Gen. Prof. E. OWUSU-BENNOAH; Sec. E. ODARTEI-LARYEA; publs *CSIR Handbook, Ghana Journal of Agricultural Science, Ghana Journal of Science.*

Attached Research Institutes:

Animal Research Institute: POB AH20, Achimota; tel. (21) 401846; fax (21) 511588; e-mail e-mailari@africaonline.com.gh; f. 1957; Dir Dr K. G. ANING.

Building and Road Research Institute: Univ. POB 40, Knust, Kumasi; tel. (51) 60064; fax (51) 60080; internet www .brri.org; f. 1952; research into bldg and road problems, traffic and transportation, geosciences, material sciences; library of 15,244 vols; Dir EUGENE ATIEMO; publs *Construction Cost Indices* (4 a year), *Journal of Building and Road Research* (2 a year).

Crops Research Institute: POB 3788, Kwadaso, Kumasi; tel. (51) 60389; fax (51) 60396; e-mail cridirector@cropsresearch .org; Dir Rev. Dr J. N. ASAFU-AGYEI.

Food Research Institute: POB M.20, Accra; tel. (21) 519091-5; fax (21) 50031115; e-mail director@fri.csir.org.gh; internet www.csir.org.gh; f. 1964; food processing, preservation, storage, analysis, marketing; Dir Dr W. A. PLAHAR; publ. *Bulletin.*

Forestry Research Institute of Ghana: POB 63, Knust, Kumasi; tel. (51) 60123; fax (51) 60121; e-mail director@forig.org; Dir Dr J. R. COBBINAH; publ. *Ghana Journal of Forestry* (every 2 years).

Oil Palm Research Institute: POB 74, Kade; tel. (803) 610257; fax (803) 610235; f. 1964; Dir Dr T. E. O. ASAMOAH.

Plant Genetic Resources Centre: POB 7, Bunso; tel. (81) 24124; fax (81) 24124; Dir Dr S. O. BENNETT-LARTEY.

Savanna Agricultural Research Institute: POB TL 52, Tamale; tel. (71) 22411; fax (71) 23483; e-mail rokowusu@yahoo .com; internet www.csir.org.gh; f. 1947, formerly known as Nyankpala Agricultural Experimental Station; present status

since 1996; research in food and fibre crops in 3 northern regions of Ghana; plant breeding, agronomy, plant protection, soil fertility improvement, post-harvest, agricultural economics and rural sociology; library of 5,000 vols; Dir Dr STEPHEN NUTSUGAH.

Science and Technology Policy Research Institute: POB CT 519, Cantonments, Accra; tel. (21) 773856; fax (21) 773068; e-mail director@stepri.csir.org.gh; Dir Dr J. O. GOGO.

Soil Research Institute: Academy PO, Kwadaso, Kumasi; tel. (51) 50353; fax (51) 50308; e-mail soil@aol.com.gh; f. 1951; Dir Dr R. D. ASIAMAH.

Water Research Institute: POB AH.38, Achimota; tel. (21) 775357; fax (21) 777170; e-mail wri@ghana.com; Dir Dr C. A. BINEY.

AGRICULTURE, FISHERIES AND VETERINARY SCIENCE

Cocoa Research Institute of Ghana: POB 8, New Tafo-Akim; tel. (27) 7609900; fax (27) 7900029; e-mail crig@crig.org; internet www .crig.org; f. 1938; research on cocoa, cola, coffee, shea nuts and cashews; 3 substations; 3 cocoa plantations for research and development of cocoa by-products; library of 17,700 vols, 8,222 pamphlets, 2,054 journals; Exec. Dir Dr F. M. AMOAH; publ. *Technical Bulletin.*

MEDICINE

Health Laboratory Services: Ministry of Health, POB 300, Accra; f. 1920; laboratory services, public health reference laboratory, reference haematology laboratory, training of laboratory technicians; research on public health microbiology, abnormal haemoglobins and allied subjects; library of 8,000 vols combined with that of the Ghana Medical School; Head E. C. MARBELL.

NATURAL SCIENCES

Physical Sciences

Geological Survey of Ghana: POB M.80, Accra; tel. (21) 228093; fax (21) 228063; e-mail ghgeosur@ghana.com; f. 1913; geological mapping and geophysical surveying of the country, research and evaluation of mineral resources; library of 30,216 vols; Dir CHARLES EDWARD ODURO.

Ghana Meteorological Agency: POB LG 87, Legon; tel. (21) 7012520; fax (21) 511981; e-mail meteo@africaonline.com.gh; internet www.meteo.gov.gh; f. 1937 as Ghana Meteorological Services Dept; present name 2004; provision of meteorological information, advice and warnings for the benefit of agriculture, civil and military aviation, surface and marine transport, operational hydrology and management of energy and water resources to mitigate the effects of natural disasters such as floods, storms, and drought on socio-economic devts and projects; Dir ZINEDEME MINIA.

Libraries and Archives

Accra

Accra Central Library: Thorpe Rd, POB 2362, Accra; tel. (21) 665083; f. 1950; central reference library; central lending library; central children's library; mobile library unit; union catalogues; Regional Librarian SUSANNAH MINYILA.

George Padmore Research Library on African Affairs: POB 663, Accra; tel. (21) 665083; fax (21) 662795; e-mail info@ ghanalibraryboard.org; internet www

.ghanalibraryboard.org; f. 1961; collection, processing and dissemination of recorded literature related to history, culture, anthropology, economics, law and public administration of all Africa; incl. Ghana National Collection; 52,651 vols, 80 periodicals; Librarian OMARI MENSAH TENKORANG; publs *Ghana National Bibliography* (6 a year and 1 a year), *special subject bibliographies* (irregular).

Ghana Library Board: POB 663, Accra; tel. (21) 662795; f. 1950; comprises Accra Central Library, regional libraries at Kumasi, Sekondi, Ho, Tamale, Bolgatanga, Cape Coast, Koforidua, Sunyani, Research Library on African Affairs (*q.v.*); 37 br. libraries, mobile libraries, children's libraries; research library 35,029 vols, adults' libraries 1,167,653 vols, children's libraries 1,383,712 vols; Dir of Library Services DAVID CORNELIUS.

Institute for Scientific and Technological Information (INSTI): POB M.32, Accra; tel. (21) 778808; fax (21) 777655; internet www.csir.org.gh; f. 1964; attached to Council for Scientific and Industrial Research; 21,873 vols, 60 current periodicals; 10 mems; Dir JOEL SAM (acting); publs *Gains News* (4 a year), *Ghana Journal of Agricultural Science* (2 a year), *Ghana Journal of Science* (2 a year), *Ghana Science Abstracts* (1 a year), *Union List of Agricultural Serials in Ghana, Union List of Scientific and Technological Journals in Ghana.*

Public Records and Archives Administration Department: POB GP. 3056, Accra; tel. (21) 221234; fax (21) 220014; e-mail praad@4u.com.gh; internet www.praad.gov.gh; f. 1946 as Nat. Archives of Ghana (legal recognition 1955); preserves Ghana's historical records; regional offices in Kumasi, Cape Coast, Sekondi, Tamale, Sunyani, Koforidua and Ho; 128 staff; provision of Record Centre services for the keeping of semi-current records of Mins, Municipalities, Depts and Agencies of the Govt of Ghana and some other private instns; setting of standards in record management practices for governmental instns; provides search services to the public; certification of archival documents; conservation of archival documents of Ghana; 2,000 documents to provide supplementary services to the searchroom; Dir FELIX NYARKO AMPONG (acting); publs *Brochure, Class Lists of the Holdings of PRAAD.*

Kumasi

Ashanti Regional Library: Bantama Rd, POB 824, Kumasi; tel. (51) 2784; f. 1954; lending, reference and extension services for adults, students and school children; 20,000 vols, incl. local collection on Ghana of 450 vols; Librarian KOFI S. ANTIRI.

Kwame Nkrumah University of Science and Technology Library: University PO, Kumasi; tel. (51) 60133; fax (51) 60358; e-mail library@knust.edu.gh; internet www.knust.edu.gh; f. 1951; 202,810 vols, 340 periodicals, 9,000 e-journals; Librarian H. R. ASAMOAH-HASSAN.

Legon

University of Ghana Library (Balme Library): POB 24, Legon; tel. (21) 512407; fax (21) 502701; e-mail balme@ug.edu.gh; f. 1948; 367,896 vols; comprises Arabic, United Nations, World Bank, Africana, Braille, Volta Basin Research Project collections and Students' Reference libraries; Librarian Prof. A. A. ALEMNA; publ. *Library Bulletin.*

Sekondi

Western Regional Library: Old Axim Rd, POB 174, Sekondi; tel. (31) 46816; f. 1955; 41,480 vols; Librarian S. Y. KWANSA.

Museums and Art Galleries

Accra

Ghana National Museum: Barnes Rd, POB 3343, Accra; tel. (21) 221633; f. 1957; controlled by the Ghana Museums and Monuments Board; archaeological and ethnological finds from all over Ghana and West Africa; modern works by Ghanaian artists; the preservation and conservation of ancient forts and castles and traditional buildings; the achievement of man in Africa; Dir I. N. DEBRAH (acting).

Museum of Science and Technology: POB 3343, Accra; tel. (21) 223963; fax (21) 234843; f. 1965; a temporary exhibition hall with an open-air cinema is used for the display of working models, charts, films and other exhibits on science and technology; collection of exhibits for permanent galleries has begun; temporary exhibitions are taken to the regions, films shown to colleges and schools and regional and national Science Fairs are organized; Asst Dir K. A. ADDISON.

Cape Coast

Cape Coast Castle Museum: POB 281, Cape Coast; tel. (42) 32701; fax (42) 30264; e-mail ghct@ghana.com; f. 1971; cultural history of Ghana's Central region; Senior Curator ALBERT WUDDAH-MARTEY.

Universities

KWAME NKRUMAH UNIVERSITY OF SCIENCE AND TECHNOLOGY

University PO, Kumasi
Telephone: (51) 60351
Fax: (51) 60137
E-mail: ustlib@ust.gn.apc.org
Internet: www.knust.edu.gh
Founded 1951 as College of Technology, University status 1961
Language of instruction: English
State control
Academic year: October to June (2 semesters)
Chancellor: (vacant)
Vice-Chancellor: Prof. JOHN SEFA KWADWO AYIM
Pro-Vice-Chancellor: Prof. E. Y. SAFO
Registrar: SOPHIA QUASHIE-SAM
Librarian: HELENA ASAMOAH-HASSAN
Number of teachers: 487
Number of students: 11,633
Publication: *Journal of the University of Science and Technology*

DEANS

Faculty of Agriculture: Prof. D. B. OKAI
Faculty of Environmental and Development Studies: Prof. K. K. ADARKWA
Faculty of Pharmacy: Prof. A. K. ABAITEY
Faculty of Science: (vacant)
Faculty of Social Sciences: Prof. A. A. SACKEY
Board of Postgraduate Studies: Prof. ANTHONY A. ADIMADO
College of Art: Dr K. EDUSEI
School of Engineering: Prof. K. A. ANDAM
School of Medical Science: Prof. E. TSIRI AGBENYEGA

DIRECTORS

Bureau of Integrated Rural Development: (vacant)
Centre for Cultural Studies: VESTA ADU-GYAMFI
Distance Education: P. ADOLINAMA
Institute of Land Management and Development: Prof. S. O. ASIAMA

Institute of Mining and Mineral Engineering: Dr E. K. ASIAM
Institute of Renewable Natural Resources: Dr FRIMPONG-MENSAH
Institute of Technical Education: P. ADOLINAMA
Technology Consultancy Centre: PETER DONKOR
Western University College, Tarkwa: Prof. MIREKU-GYIMAH (Provost)

PROFESSORS

ANDAM, K. A., Civil Engineering
BROBBY, G. W., Ear, Eye, Nose and Throat Surgery
KASANGA, K., Land Economy
OSEI, S. A., Animal Science
OWUSU-SARPONG, A. K., Languages
SARPONG, K., Pharmacy
TUAH, A. K., Animal Science

UNIVERSITY FOR DEVELOPMENT STUDIES

POB 1350, Tamale
Telephone: (71) 22078
Fax: (71) 22080
Internet: www.uds.edu.gh
Founded 1992
State control
Accredited by Nat. Accreditation Bd, Ghana Medical and Dental Council, Nurses and Midwives Council of Ghana
Academic year: September to July (three semesters)
Language of instruction: English
Vice-Chancellor: Prof. KAKU SAGARY NOKOE (acting)
Pro-Vice-Chancellor: Prof. DAVID MILLAR
Registrar: S. M. KUUIRE (acting)
Librarian: I. K. ANTWI
Library of 31,906 vols
Number of teachers: 271
Number of students: 10,587
Publications: *Academic Calendar* (every 5 years), *Faculties and Departments at a Glance* (every 2 years), *Ghana Journal of Development Studies* (every 2 years), *Strategic Plan* (every 5 years)

DEANS

Faculty of Agriculture: Dr GABRIEL TEYE
Faculty of Applied Sciences: Dr KENNETH PELIG-BA
Faculty of Integrated Development Studies: Rev. Prof. ABRAHAM BERINYUU
Faculty of Planning and Land Management: Dr FRANCIS BACHO
Faculty of Renewable Natural Resources: Dr THOMAS BAYORBOR
Graduate School: Prof. DAVID MILLAR
School of Medicine and Health Sciences: Dr EBENEZER N. GYADER (acting)

UNIVERSITY OF CAPE COAST

University PO, Cape Coast
Telephone: (42) 32480
Fax: (42) 32485
E-mail: vcucc@yahoo.com
Internet: www.ucc.edu.gh
Founded 1962
Language of instruction: English
State control
Academic year: August to June (2 semesters)
Chancellor: Dr SAM ESSON JONAH
Pro-Chancellor: Dr CHARLES MENSA
Vice-Chancellor: Prof. E. A. OBENG
Pro-Vice-Chancellor: Prof. K. YANKSON
Registrar: S. KOFI OHENE
Librarian: ALFRED K. MARTEY
Number of teachers: 300
Number of students: 11,637

Publications: *ASEMKA* (Faculty of Arts, 2 a year), *Journal of Educational Management* (IEPA, 2 a year), *Journal of the Institute of Education* (IEPA, 2 a year), *Journal of Social Sciences* (Faculty of Social Sciences, 2 a year), *Oguaa Educator* (Faculty of Education, 2 a year), *Primary Teacher* (Dept of Primary Education, 2 a year)

DEANS

Faculty of Arts: Prof. D. D. KUUPOLE
Faculty of Education: Dr J. A. OPARE (acting)
Faculty of Science: Prof. V. P. Y. GADZEKPO
Faculty of Social Sciences: Prof. K. AWUSABO-ASARE
School of Agriculture: Prof. P. K. TURKSON
Graduate Studies: Prof. JANE NAANA OPOKU AGYEMANG

DIRECTORS

Centre for Development Studies: Dr S. B. KENDIE (acting)
Centre for Research on Improving the Quality of Primary Education in Ghana: J. M. DZINYELA
Institute of Education: Dr A. K. AKYEMPONG (acting)
Institute for Educational Planning and Administration: Dr A. L. DARE (acting)

UNIVERSITY OF EDUCATION, WINNEBA

POB 25, Winneba
Telephone and fax (432) 22269
Fax: (432) 22269
E-mail: info@uew.edu.gh
Internet: www.uew.edu.gh

Founded 1992 as Univ. College of Education of Winneba by merger of 7 colleges: present name and status 2004
Campuses in Winneba, Kumasi, Mampong-Ashanti, and Ajumako; the Ajumako Campus currently hosts the Ghana Education Service Staff Devt Institute (GESDI)
State Control; attached to Nat. Accreditation Board, Ghana
Academic year: August to May (2 semesters)
Vice-Chancellor: Prof. AKWASI ASABERE-AMEYAW
Pro Vice-Chancellor: Prof. MAWUTOR AVOKE
Registrar: CHRISTOPHER Y. AKWAA-MENSAH
Finance Officer: BENJAMIN K. KPODO
Librarian: VALENTINA BANNERMAN

Library of 102,577 vols, 1,427 periodicals, 2,1000 online journals, 31 online databases, and over 138 CD-ROMs
Number of teachers: 322
Number of students: 25,024

Publications: *African Journal of Special Needs Education, Ghana Educational Media and Technology Association Journal, The Social Educator*

DEANS

Faculty of Agriculture Education, Mampong: Prof. K. T. DJANG-FORDJOUR
Faculty of Business Education, Kumasi: GILBERT O. AGYEDU
Faculty of Educational Studies, Winneba: Prof. GRACE Y. GADAGBUI
Faculty of Languages Education, Winneba: Prof. EMMANUEL N. ABAKAH
Faculty of Science Education, Winneba: (vacant)
Faculty of Social Sciences Education, Winneba: Prof. R. H. K. DARKWAH
Faculty of Vocational and Technical Education, Kumasi: Prof. REYNOLDS OKAI
School of Creative Arts, Winneba: Prof. JAMES E. FLOLU
School of Research and Graduate Studies, Winneba: Prof. THOMAS ESSILFIE (acting)

ATTACHED RESEARCH INSTITUTES

Centre for Educational Policy Studies: Winneba; tel. (432) 20337; e-mail aabroni@uew.edu.gh; Dir Rev. Dr Fr ANTHONY AFFUL-BRONI.

Centre for Hearing and Speech Services: Winneba; tel. (246) 782776; e-mail ynyaduoffei@yahoo.com; Coordinator YAW NYADU OFFEI.

Centre for School and Community Science and Technology Studies: Winneba; tel. (432) 22268; e-mail jophusam@gmail.com; Dir Prof. JOPHUS ANAMUAH-MENSAH (acting).

Institute for Educational Development and Extension: Winneba; tel. (432) 22497; e-mail aboagye@yahoo.com; Dir Prof. JOSEPH K. ABOAGYE (acting).

National Centre for Research into Basic Education: Winneba; tel. (432) 20415; e-mail rofori@gmail.com; Dir Dr RICHARD OFORI.

UNIVERSITY OF GHANA

POB 25, Legon, Accra
Telephone: (21) 501967
Fax: (21) 502701
E-mail: pad@ug.gn.ape.org
Internet: www.ug.edu.gh

Founded 1948 as University College of Gold Coast; University status 1961
Language of instruction: English
Academic year: September to June
State control
Vice-Chancellor: Prof. CLIFFORD N. B. TAGOE (acting)
Pro-Vice-Chancellor: Prof. KWESI YANKAH (acting)
Director of Finance: J. E. MINLAH
Registrar: A. T. KONU
Librarian: Prof. A. ALEMNA

Number of teachers: 766
Number of students: 27,414

Publications: *Basic Statistics, Campus Update, Newsfile, Universitas*

DEANS

Faculty of Arts: Prof. KWESI YANKAH
Faculty of Law: Prof. NII ASHIE KOTEY
Faculty of Science: Prof. GEORGE ODAMTTEN
Faculty of Social Studies: Prof. ATU AYEE
College of Agriculture: ANNA BARNES
School of Administration: Prof. J. K. A. POKU (acting)
Business School: Prof. KOFI NTI
Dental School: Dr N. O. NARTEY (acting)
Medical School: Prof. R. B. BIRITWUM (acting)
Graduate Studies: Prof. JACOB SONGSORE
International Educational Programmes: Prof. S. SEFA-DEDEH

PROFESSORS

ADDAE, S. K., Physiology
ADDAE-MENSAH, I., Chemistry
ADDO, S. T., Geography and Resource Development
ADU-GYAMFI, Y., Anaesthesia
AHENKORAH, Y., Crop Science
AKYEAMPONG, D. A., Mathematics
ALEMNA, A. A., Information Studies
AMOAH, A. G. B., Medicine and Therapeutics
AMUZU, J. K. A., Physics
ANTESON, R. K., Microbiology
ANYIDOHO, K., English
APT, N. A., Sociology
ARCHAMPONG, E. Q., Surgery
ARDAYFIO-SCHANDORF, E., Geography and Resource Development
ASENSO-OKYERE, K., Institute of Statistical, Social and Economic Research
ASHITEY, G. A., Community Health
ASSIMENG, J. M., Sociology

ASSOKU, R. K. G., Animal Science
AYERTEY, J. N., Crop Science
AYETTEY, A. S., Anatomy
AYETTEY, E., Institute of Statistical, Social and Economic Research
AYISI, N. K., Noguchi Institute for Medical Research
BADOE, E. A., Surgery
BAETA, R. D., Physics
BENNEH, G., Geography and Resource Development
BOADI, L. A., Linguistics
BRITWUM, K., French
CLERK, G. C., Botany
COKER, W. Z., Zoology
DANSO, S. K. A., Soil Science
DOKU, E. V., Crop Science
FYNN, J. K., History
GYASI, E. A., Geography and Resource Development
KROPP DAKUBU, M. E., Sociolinguistics
MINGLE, J. A. A., Microbiology
NEEQUAYE, J. E., Child Health
NKRUMAH, F. K., Paediatrics
NUKUNYA, G. K., Sociology
ODURO, K. A., Anaesthesia
OFORI-AMANKWAH, E. H., Law
OFORI-SARPONG, E., Law
OFOSU-AMAAH, S., School of Public Health
OLIVER-COMMEY, J. O., Child Health
OWUSU, S. K., Medicine and Therapeutics
SEFA-DEDEH, S., Nutrition and Food Science
TAGOE, C. N. B., Anatomy
TETTEH, G. K., Physics
YANKAH, K., Linguistics
YANKSON, P. W. K., Geography and Resource Development
YEBOAH, E. D., Surgery

ATTACHED INSTITUTES

Institute of Adult Education: POB 31, Legon, Accra; Dir R. A. AGGOR.

Institute of African Studies: POB 73, Legon, Accra; Dir Prof. T. MANUH (acting).

Institute of Statistical, Social and Economic Research: POB 74, Legon, Accra; Dir Prof. E. ARYEETEY.

Legon Centre for International Affairs: Legon, Accra; Dir Prof. K. KUMADO (acting).

Noguchi Memorial Institute for Medical Research: POB 25, Legon, Accra; f. 1979; international centre for basic and applied research; Dir Prof. D. OFORI-ADJEI; Provost Rev. Prof. A. S. AYETTEY (acting).

Regional Institute for Population Studies: POB 96, Legon, Accra; f. 1972 with UN aid; Dir Dr S. O. KWANKYE (acting).

Regional Training Centre for Archivists: POB 60, Legon, Accra; Head C. O. KISIEDU.

School of Communication Studies: POB 53, Legon, Accra; Dir Prof. K. ANSU-KYER-EMEH.

School of Performing Arts: POB 19, Legon, Accra; Dir Prof. M. OWUSU.

School of Public Health: POB 13, Legon, Accra; Dir Dr I. QUAKYI (acting).

United Nations University Institute for Natural Resources in Africa: Private Mail Bag, Kotoka International Airport, Accra; Dir Dr UZO MOKWUNYE.

Volta Basin Research Project: Legon, Accra; Chair. Prof. S. G. K. ADIKU.

AGRICULTURAL RESEARCH STATIONS

Agricultural Research Station, Accra: POB 38, Legon, Accra; Officer-in-Charge Dr E. A. CANACOO.

Agricultural Research Station, Kade: POB 43, Kade; Officer-in-Charge Dr J. K. OSEI.

Agricultural Research Station, Kpong: POB 9, Kpong; Officer-in-Charge Dr E. O. Darkwa.

Colleges

Accra Polytechnic: POB GP 561, Accra; tel. (21) 662263; fax (21) 664797; f. 1949; technical and vocational education with practical research programmes in manufacturing, commerce, science and technology; from technician to higher national diploma level; library: 15,800 vols; 340 teachers; 6,400 students; Principal Prof. RALPH K. ASABERE.

Accra Technical Training Centre: POB M.177, Accra; f. 1966 to train tradesmen for industry and civil service; attached to Ministry of Education, Science and Sports; library: 10,500 vols; 350 students; Principal T. K. ADZEI.

Ghana Institute of Management and Public Administration: Greenhill, POB 50, Achimota; tel. (21) 405805; fax (21) 405805; f. 1961; research, consultancy, human resource development, strategic studies and policy analysis and postgraduate studies, diploma, certificate and Masters degree programmes; 30 teachers; library: 50,000 vols; Dir-Gen. Dr STEPHEN ADEI; publs *Administrators' Digest, Ghana Economic Outlook* (2 a year), *GIMPA News* (4 a year), *Greenhill Case Studies Book, Greenhill Journal of Administration* (2 a year).

Ho Polytechnic: POB 217, Ho, Volta Region; tel. (91) 26456; fax (91) 28398; e-mail gafeti@africaonline.com.gh; f. 1968; training of middle-level management personnel and technicians to HND standard; library: 13,000 vols; 100 teachers; 2,500 students; Principal Dr G. M. AFETI; Registrar F. K. DZINEKU.

Koforidua Technical Institute: POB 323, Koforidua; f. 1960; 9 teachers; 206 students; library: 2,000 vols; Principal P. C. NOI.

Kpandu Technical Institute: Technical Division, POB 76, Kpandu, Volta Region; tel. Kpandu 22; f. 1956; 70 teachers; 689 students; library: 4,000 vols; Principal J. Y. VODZI.

National Film and Television Institute (NAFTI): PMB, GPO, Accra; tel. (21) 777610; fax (21) 774522; e-mail nafti@ghana.com; f. 1978 by Government decree; 4-year Bachelors of Fine Arts degree courses in film and television production with special emphasis on the production of educational programmes, and feature, informative, animation, documentary and industrial films; mem. of CILECT, Int. Asscn of Film and Television Schools; receives financial help from public funds and technical assistance from NGOs and UNESCO; 2-year diploma courses in film and television production; exchange programmes; 68 students; library: specialized library of 51,000 vols; Dir MARTIN LOH; publ. *NAFTI Concept.*

Sunyani Polytechnic: POB 206, Sunyani; tel. (61) 23278; fax (61) 24921; e-mail spolytec@ghana.com.gh; f. 1967 as Technical Institute; present name and status 1997; technical and business education, electrical and electronic engineering, hotel, catering and institutional management, secretaryship and management studies; accredited by International Professional Managers Association (IPMA—UK) and Charted Institute of Marketing (UK); library: 11,020 vols; 180 teachers; 4,528 students; Principal Dr KWASI NSIAH-GYABAA; Sec. S. A. OBOUR.

Takoradi Polytechnic: POB 256, Takoradi; tel. (31) 22918; fax (31) 25256; f. 1955; 130 teachers; 4,500 students; library: 10,250 vols, 48 periodicals; Principal Dr SAMUEL OBENG APORI; Sec. KOFI MANUKURE-HENAKU.

West Africa Computer Science Institute: POB 1643, Mamprobi, Accra; tel. (21) 229927; fax (21) 229575; e-mail wacsi@internetghana.com; f. 1988; independent college providing training in computers, accounting and related fields; 10 teachers; 300 students; Pres. AIKINS BRIGHT KUMI; Principal LAWRENCE NYARKO.

GREECE

The Higher Education System

The country's first universities were established shortly after Greece secured its independence from Ottoman Turkish rule in 1830. Ethniko Metsovio Polytechneio (National Technical University of Athens) was founded in 1836, and both Anotati Scholi Kalon Technon (Athens School of Fine Art) and Ethnikon Kai Kapodistriakon Panepistimion Athinon (National and Capodistrian University of Athens) were founded in 1837. Institutions of higher education are separated into two categories, Anotera Ekpedeftika Idrimata (AEI) and Technologika Ekpedeftika Idrimata (TEI). AEIs are university-level institutions, which encompass universities, polytechneia (technical universities), and the Athens School of Fine Art. TEIs are technological higher education institutions, which were officially upgraded to university status in 2001 but are still regarded as distinct from AEIs. There are 19 AEIs in Greece. Overall responsibility for higher education lies with the Ministry of Education and Religious Affairs, and the Constitution stipulates that only public institutions may provide higher education. AEIs and TEIs are autonomous institutions.

Admission to higher education is on the basis of the Apolyterio, the leading secondary school certificate, and Vevaiosi Provasis, a certificate of access to higher education, which is calculated according to scores in the Apolyterio. Although Greece is a signatory to the Bologna Process, it has yet to implement the required reforms; however, the traditional degree system does consist of three stages. In both AEIs and TEIs, the main degree is the Ptychio, which is a four-year programme of study in most subjects, but in some subjects lasts five years (engineering, agriculture, veterinary studies, dentistry and architecture) and in medicine lasts six years. To take postgraduate degrees, students holding the Ptychio must undergo a selection process or sit examinations. The first postgraduate degree is the Metaptychiakon Spoudon, which lasts two years and is broadly equivalent to the Masters. Finally, the Didaktor is a doctoral-level degree awarded following a period of research and submission of a thesis.

The establishment of private institutions of higher education is forbidden by Greek law, and qualifications offered by private institutions are not regarded as equivalent to qualifications from public institutions. However, private institutions may operate as laboratories of liberal science, purely with a view to providing education related to the arts and professional studies.

Technical and vocational education is overseen by different government bodies, notably the Ministry of Education and Religious Affairs, the Organization of Vocational Education and the Ministry of Labour, Employment and Manpower Organization. The Organization of Vocational Education runs Institutes of Vocational Training, which offer courses of study leading to the award of diplomas. The Employment and Manpower Organization has a National Council for vocational training, which oversees apprenticeships and on-the-job training.

Figures given for 2005/06 showed that 171,967 students were enrolled in universities (this excludes data from the Medical School of Athens), while 147,715 were enrolled in technical, vocational and ecclesiastical institutions.

Regulatory and Representative Bodies

GOVERNMENT

Ministry of Culture: Odos Bouboulinas 42, 106 82 Athens; tel. 210-8894800; fax 210-8894805; e-mail dpse@hch.culture.gr; internet www.culture.gr; Minister MICHALIS LIAPIS.

Ministry of Education and Religious Affairs: Odos Metropoleos 15, 101 85 Athens; tel. 210-3723000; fax 210-3248264; e-mail webmaster@ypepth.gr; internet www.ypepth.gr; Minister EVRIPIDIS STYLIANIDIS.

ACCREDITATION

ENIC/NARIC Greece: DOATAP, 54, Ag. Konstantinou St, 10437 Athens; tel. (210) 5281000; fax (210) 5239679; e-mail information_dep@doatap.gr; internet www.doatap.gr.

NATIONAL BODIES

Ethniko Kentro Pistopoiisis (EKEPIS) (National Accreditation Centre for Continuing Vocational Training): Konstantinoupoleos 49, 118 55 Athens; tel. 210-3403200; e-mail info@ekepis.gr; internet www.ekepis.gr; f. 1997; autonomous body attached to the Min. of Employment and Social Protection; ensures quality assurance in vocational training; Pres. DIMITRIOS SIAMOPOULOS; Dir Prof. M. GEORGIAKODIS.

Syndesmos Ellinidon Epistimonon (SEE) (Hellenic Association of University Women): 44A Voulis St, 105 58 Athens; tel. 210-3234268; e-mail evibatra@central.tee.gr; f. 1924; NGO with particular interest in matters of higher education, environment, family planning, health care, child rearing, and educational support for the advancement of women; aims to fight discrimination against women; helps university women to influence the improvement of working conditions and labour legislation; Pres. PARASKEVI BATRA; Sec.-Gen. FLORA KAMARI.

Synodos Prytaneon Ellinikon Panepistimion (Greek Rectors' Conference): Synodos Prytaneon Ellinikon, Univ. of Athens, Panepistimiou 30, 106 79 Athens; tel. 210-3631813; fax 210-3647337; internet www.crue.org/eurec/member/gr.html; f. 1977; Secs ALKISTIS DAI, LILIANA NIKOLETOPOULOU.

Learned Societies

GENERAL

Akadimia Athinon (Academy of Athens): Odos Panepistimiou 28, 106 79 Athens; tel. 210-3664700; fax 210-3634806; e-mail info@academyofathens.gr; internet www.academyofathens.gr; f. 1926; sections of Literature and Fine Arts (Pres. TH. VALTINOS), Moral and Political Sciences (Pres. E. SPILIOTOPOULOS) and Positive Sciences (Pres. N. ARTEMIADIS); 219 mems (45 ordinary, 18 foreign, 150 corresp., 6 hon.); attached research institutes: see Research Institutes; library: see Libraries and Archives; Pres. CONSTANTINOS SVOLOPOULOS; Sec.-Gen. NIKOLAOS MATSANIOTIS; publ. *Praktika* (Proceedings, 1 a year).

BIBLIOGRAPHY, LIBRARY SCIENCE AND MUSEOLOGY

Enosi Ellinon Vivliothikonomon kai Epistimon Pliroforisis (EEBEP) (Greek Association of Librarians and Information Scientists): Themistocleus 73, 106 83 Athens; tel. 210-3302128; fax 210-3302128; e-mail info@eeb.gr; internet eeb.gr; f. 1968; 500 mems; Pres. GEORGE YANNAKOPOULOS; Gen. Sec. MARIA MARINOPOULOU; publ. magazine.

EDUCATION

Syllogos pros Diadosin ton Hellenikon Grammaton (Society for the Promotion of Greek Education): Odos Pindarou 15 (136), Athens; f. 1869; 9 mems; Pres. PHILIP DRAGOUMIS; Sec.-Gen. ALEXANDRATOS PANAYIOTIS.

FINE AND PERFORMING ARTS

Enosis Hellinon Mousourgon (Union of Greek Composers): Deinokratous 35, 106 76 Athens; tel. and fax 210-7256607; e-mail gcu@otenet.gr; internet www.gcu.org.gr; f. 1931; 200 mems; Pres. THEODORE ANTONIOU; Sec.-Gen. IOSSIF PAPADATOS.

Epimelitirion Ikastikon Technon Ellados (Chamber of Fine Arts): 14 Koletti St, 106 81 Athens; tel. 210-3301206; fax 210-3301408; e-mail chafartg@otenet.gr; f. 1945; promotion of the fine arts, support for artists, organizes exhibitions in Greece and abroad, organizes conferences, etc.; 3,100 mems; library of 2,000 vols; Pres. MICHALIS PAPADAKIS.

HISTORY, GEOGRAPHY AND ARCHAEOLOGY

Archaeologiki Hetairia (Archaeological Society): Odos Panepistimiou 22, 106 72 Athens; tel. 210-3609689; fax 210-3644996; e-mail archetai@otenet.gr; internet www .archetai.gr; f. 1837; 401 mems; library of 118,500 vols; Pres. EPAMINONDAS SPILIOTO-POULOS; Sec.-Gen. BASIL PETRAKOS; publs *Archaeologiki Ephimeris* (1 a year), *Ergon* (1 a year), *O Mentor* (4 a year), *Praktika* (1 a year).

Hellenic Geographical Society: 11 Voucourestiou St, 106 71 Athens; tel. 210-3631112; f. 1919; 148 mems; Pres. DIMITRIOS DIMITRIADIS; Gen. Sec. GEORGE IVANTCHOS; publ. *Bulletin*.

Historical and Ethnological Society of Greece: Old Parliament, Stadiou St, 105 61 Athens; tel. 210-3237617; fax 210-3213786; internet www.culture.gr; f. 1882; Pres. CONSTANTINOS TSAMADOS; Sec.-Gen. IOANNIS C. MAZARAKIS-AENIAN.

LANGUAGE AND LITERATURE

British Council: 17 Kolonaki Sq., 106 73 Athens; tel. 210-3692333; fax 210-3614658; e-mail customerservices@britishcouncil.gr; internet www.britishcouncil.org/greece; teaching centre; offers courses and exams in English language and British culture and promotes cultural exchange with the UK; attached office in Thessaloniki; f. 1939; Dir DESMOND LAUDER.

Etairia Ellinon Logotechnon (Society of Greek Men of Letters): 8 Gennadiou St and Acadimias, 106 78 Athens; tel. 210-3634559; f. 1934; 700 mems; Pres. PAUL NATHANAIL; Sec. E. ANAGNOSTAKI-TZAVARA.

Etairia Ellinon Theatricon Syngrapheon (Greek Playwrights' Society): Asklipiou St 33, 10 680 Athens; tel. 210-3232472; e-mail eeths@otenet.gr; internet www.eeths .gr; f. 1908; 120 mems; Pres. GIORGOS LAZARIDIS; Sec. GIORGOS CHRISTOFILAKIS.

Goethe-Institut: Omirou 14–16, POB 30383, 100 33 Athens; tel. 210-3661000; fax 210-3643518; e-mail info@athen.goethe.org; internet www.goethe.de/om/ath/deindex .htm; offers courses and exams in German language and culture and promotes cultural exchange with Germany; attached centre in Thessaloniki; library of 15,000 vols; Dir and Regional Head of Operations HORST DEINWALLNER.

Instituto Cervantes: Skoufá 31, 106 73 Athens; tel. 210-3634117; fax 210-3647233; e-mail cenate@cervantes.es; internet atenas .cervantes.es; offers courses and exams in Spanish language and culture and promotes cultural exchange with Spain and Spanish-speaking Latin and Central America; library of 11,000 vols; Dir NATIVIDAD GÁLVEZ GARCÍA.

NATURAL SCIENCES

Mathematical Sciences

Elliniki Mathimatiki Eteria (Greek Mathematical Society): Odos Panepistimiou 34, 106 79 Athens; tel. 210-3616532; fax 210-3641025; e-mail info@hms.gr; internet www .hms.gr; f. 1918; seminars, lectures, summer schools, educational policy; 15,000 mems; library of 2,000 vols; Pres. Prof. NIC ALEXANDRIS; Gen. Sec. JOHN TYRLIS; publs *Astrolavos* (Informatics Review, 2 a year), *Deltion* (Bulletin, 1 a year), *Euclides* (4 a year), *Mathimatiki Epitheorissi* (Review, 2 a year).

Physical Sciences

Enosis Ellinon Chimikon (Association of Greek Chemists): Odos Kanningos 27, 106 82 Athens; tel. 210-3621524; e-mail info@eex.gr; internet www.eex.gr; f. 1924; official adviser to the state on matters relating to chemistry; promotes the chemical science in industry, education and research; protects the benefits and the professional rights of chemists; 14,000 mems; library of 5,000 vols, 100 periodicals; Pres. P. HAMAKIOTIS; Gen. Sec. D. PSOMAS; publs *ChemBioChem*, *Chemistry, A European Journal*, *ChemPhysChem*, *European Journal of Inorganic Chemistry*, *European Journal of Organic Chemistry*.

TECHNOLOGY

Elliniki Epitropi Atomikis Energhias (Greek Atomic Energy Commission): POB 60092, 153 10 Aghia Paraskevi, Athens; tel. 210-6506748; fax 210-6533939; internet www .eeae.gr; independent service, supervised by the General Secretariat of Research and Technology (GSRT), under the Ministry of Development; responsible for nuclear power and technology issues and for the protection of the population, workers and environment from the ionization and artificially produced non-ionizing radiation; f. 1954; Pres. Prof. LEONIDAS CAMARINOPOULOS.

Research Institutes

GENERAL

Ethnikon Idryma Erevnon (National Hellenic Research Foundation): 48 Vassileos Constantinou Ave, 116 35 Athens; tel. 210-7273500; fax 210-7246618; internet www.eie .gr; f. 1958; carries out basic and applied research in its own institutes (humanities, natural sciences); library of 2,000 periodicals; Euronet facilities; specialized libraries attached to the humanities institutes; Nat. Documentation Centre: see Libraries and Archives; Dir Prof. DIMITRIOS A. KYRIAKIDIS.

Attached Research Institutes:

Institute of Biological Research and Biotechnology: 48 Vassileos Constantinou Ave, 116 35 Athens; tel. 210-7273759; fax 210-7273758; e-mail kolisis@eie.gr; internet www.eie.gr/nhrf/institutes/ibrb/ index-en.html; Dir Prof. FRAGISKOS KOLISIS (acting).

Institute for Byzantine Research: 48 Vassileos Constantinou Ave, 116 35 Athens; tel. (210) 7273619; fax (210) 7273629; e-mail ibe@eie.gr; internet www .eie.gr; f. 1960 as Centre for Byzantine Research; uses archival, literary and archaeological sources for Byzantine cultural history and daily life in the Greek Middle Ages, the relations of Byzantium with the peoples of the Balkans, the E Mediterranean and the W, and the historical geography and historical demography of the Greek world; organizes int. symposia and academic meetings; library of 40,000 books, offprints, journals, maps, audiovisual material; Dir Prof. Dr TAXIARCHIS KOLIAS; publ. *Byzantina Symmeikta* (fmrly Symmeikta, 1 a year).

Institute of Greek and Roman Antiquity: 48 Vassileos Constantinou Ave, 116 35 Athens; tel. 210-7273675; fax 210-7234145; e-mail mhatzkop@eie.gr; internet www.eie.gr/nhrf/institutes/igra/ index-en.html; f. 1979; Dir MILTIADES HATZOPOULOS.

Institute for Neohellenic Research: 48 Vassileos Constantinou Ave, 116 35 Athens; tel. 210-7273556; fax 210-7246212; e-mail kne@eie.gr; internet www .eie.gr/nhrf/institutes/inr/index-en.html; f. 1960; Dir Prof. PASCHALIS M. KITROMILIDES; publs *Historical Review* (1 a year), *Tetradia Ergasias* (1 a year).

Institute of Organic and Pharmaceutical Chemistry: 48 Vassileos Constantinou Ave, 116 35 Athens; tel. 210-7273868; fax 210-7273831; e-mail ngo@eie.gr; internet www.eie.gr/nhrf/institutes/iopc/ index-en.html; f. 1979; research in the fields of organic and organometallic chemistry, pharmaceutical chemistry, structural biology and chemistry, computational chemistry and molecular analysis; carries out the rational design, synthesis, and evaluation of molecules against major diseases with an emphasis on type 2 diabetes, cancer, inflammation and neurodegeneration; Sec. MARIA KALATZI.

Institute of Theoretical and Physical Chemistry: 48 Vassileos Constantinou Ave, 116 35 Athens; tel. 210-7273792; fax 210-7273794; e-mail eikam@eie.gr; internet www.eie.gr/nhrf/institutes/tpci/ index-en.html; Dir EFSTRATIOS KAMITSOS.

AGRICULTURE, FISHERIES AND VETERINARY SCIENCE

Benaki Phytopathological Institute: St Delta St 8, 145 61 Kifissia, Athens; tel. 210-8079603; fax 210-8077506; e-mail p .panayotounis@bpi.gr; internet www.bpi.gr; f. 1930; phytopathology, entomology, agricultural zoology, pesticides; 21 laboratories; museum of zoological and entomological specimens, including 22,000 species, and culture collns; library of 11,000 vols, 30,000 pamphlets, 1,400 current periodicals; Dir Dr P. PAPAIOANNOU-SOULIOTIS; publ. *Hellenic Plant Protection Journal* (English edition; irregular).

Hellenic Centre for Marine Research: POB 712, 190 13 Anavissos, Attica; tel. 229-1076466; fax 229-1076323; internet www .hcmr.gr; f. 1965 as National Centre for Marine Research (NCMR); merged with Institute of Marine Biology of Crete (IMBC) 2003; marine and freshwater fisheries and biology, marine chemistry, geology and geophysics; operational oceanography, aquaculture, inland waters, marine biology and genetics; operates 2 research vessels, a hydrobiological research station (with aquarium and museum) on Rhodes, and the Thalassocosmos aquarium in Crete; library of 3,000 vols, 541 periodicals; Dir and Pres. Prof. GEORGIOS TH. CHRONIS; publ. *Mediterranean Marine Science* (2 a year).

Attached Research Institutes:

Institute of Aquaculture: Limani Irakleiou, POB 2214, Heraklion; tel. 2810-346860; fax 2810-241882; Dir Dr PASCAL DIVANACH.

Institute of Inland Waters: POB 712, 190 13 Anavyssos; tel. 22910-76458; fax 22910-76323; Dir Dr ARISTIDIS DIAPOULIS.

Institute of Marine Biological Resources: Agios Kosmas, 166 10 Athens; tel. 210-9821354; fax 210-9811713; Dir Dr K. PAPACONSTANTINOU.

Institute of Marine Biology/Genetics: Gournes Pediados, POB 2214, Heraklion; tel. 2810-337806; fax 2810-337822; Dir Dr A. MAGOULAS.

Institute of Oceanography: POB 17, 190 13 Attica; tel. 22910-76452; fax 22910-76347; Dir Dr EFSTATHIOS BALOPOULOS.

ECONOMICS, LAW AND POLITICS

Centre of International and European Economic Law: POB 14, 55102 Kalamaria, Thessaloniki; tel. 231-0486900; fax 231-0476366; e-mail kdeod@cieel.gr; internet www.cieel.gr; f. 1977; nat. documentation and research centre, specializing in European Union law, protection of human rights in Europe, int. economic law; European Documentation Centre by decision of the EEC (now EU); library of 55,000 vols, 192 periodicals; Dir and Pres. of Board Prof. WASSILIOS SKOURIS; Dir EVANGELIA KOUTOUPA-REGAKOU; Sec. Prof. GEORGIOS TRANTAS; publs *Hellenic Review of European Law* (4 a year in Greek, 1 a year in English), *Public Procurement and State Aid Law Review* (3 a year).

Centre for Planning and Economic Research: Amerikis 11, 106 72 Athens; tel. 210-3676300; fax 210-3611136; e-mail kepe@ kepe.gr; internet www.kepe.gr; f. 1961; scientific study of the economic problems of Greece, the promotion of economic research, and cooperation with other Greek research institutes; library of 29,425 vols, 700 periodical titles, 315 series of statistical bulletins; Chair. and Scientific Dir Prof. KYPRIANOS P. PRODROMIDIS; publ. *Economic Perspectives* (3 a year).

Hellenic Centre for European Studies (EKEM): 4 Xenofontos St, 106 80 Athens; tel. 210-3215549; fax 210-3215096; e-mail ekem@ ekem.gr; internet www.ekem.gr; f. 1988; non-profit-making independent org. under supervision of the Ministry of Foreign Affairs; advises the govt, academic bodies and private companies on matters of European policy and integration; organizes conferences and seminars; library: maintains Depository Library of the European Union, with 7,000 vols; Pres. of Admin. Council and Dir Assoc. Prof. KOSTAS IFANTIS.

Hellenic Institute of International and Foreign Law: 1 Vas. Sofias Ave, 106 71 Athens; tel. 210-3681000; internet www.mfa .gr; f. 1939; library of 40,000 vols; Dir Prof. KONSTANTINOS KERAMEUS; publ. *Revue hellénique de droit international* (in English and French, 2 a year).

Institute of International Public Law and International Relations: Vass. Herakliou St, 546 25 Thessaloniki; tel. 2310-552295; fax 2310-566953; e-mail ipilir@ otenet.gr; internet web.auth.gr/ institute-iplir; f. 1966; research, documentation and education centre; courses run during June to September; library: World Bank and UN depository library; Dir Prof. KALLIOPI K. KOUFA; publ. *Thesaurus Acroasium* (1 a year).

Kentron Ereunes Historias Hellenikou Dikaiou (Centre for Research in the History of Greek Law): Anagnostopoulou 14, 106 73 Athens; tel. 210-3664607; fax 210-3664628; e-mail keied@academyofathens.gr; internet www.academyofathens.gr; f. 1929; attached to Acad. of Athens; conducts research on legal instns from antiquity, Byzantine and post-Byzantine times; library of 12,000 vols; Pres. APOSTOLOS GEORGIADIS; Dirs Dr LYDIA PAPARRIGA-ARTEMIADI, Dr DEMETRA KARABULA, Dr ILIAS ARNAOUTOGLOU, Dr IOANNIS HATZAKIS; publs *Epetiris* (1 a year), *Parartima tes Epetiridos* (supplement to *Epetiris*, 1 a year).

FINE AND PERFORMING ARTS

Kentro Erevnas Byzantinis kai Metabyzantinis Technis (Research Centre for Byzantine and Post-Byzantine Art): Odos Anagnostopoulou 14, 106 73 Athens; tel. 210-3664613; fax 210-3664652; e-mail kevmt@academyofathens.gr; internet academyofathens.gr; f. 1994; attached to Akadimia Athinon (Acad. of Athens); research on Byzantine archaeology and wall-paintings in Greece; library of 6,000 vols; Pres. PANAYOTIS L. VOCOTOPOULOS; Dir IOANNA BITHA (acting).

HISTORY, GEOGRAPHY AND ARCHAEOLOGY

Centre for Asia Minor Studies: Kydathineon 11, 105 58 Athens; tel. 210-3239225; fax 210-3229758; e-mail kms@otenet.gr; internet users.otenet.gr/~kms; f. 1930; ind., private, non-profit organization; research into history and civilization of Greek communities in Asia Minor before 1922; library of 15,000 vols, 501 MSS; oral history archive of 150,000 MS pages; photographic archive of 5,000 photographs; folk music archive of 1,000 records, 700 tapes; spec. collns: Karamanli books, and Greek books, newspapers and periodicals printed in Turkey, maps, MSS; Pres. Prof. M. B. SAKELLARIOU; Dir Dr S. TH. ANESTIDIS (acting); publ. *Deltio K. M. S.* (1 a year).

Foundation of the Hellenic World: 38 Poulopoulou St, 118 51 Athens; tel. 212-2543800; fax 212-2543838; e-mail webmaster@fhw.gr; internet www.fhw.gr/ fhw/en; f. 1993; uses the latest information and computer technology in pursuit of research, awareness and understanding of Hellenic history and culture; Cultural Centre: Hellenic Cosmos located at 254 Pireos St, 177 78 Athens; Pres. LAZAROS D. EFRAIMOGLOU; Man. Dir DIMITRIS EFRAIMOGLOU.

Institute for Balkan Studies: Meg. Alexandrou Ave 31A, 546 41 Thessaloniki; tel. 231-0832143; fax 231-0831429; e-mail imxa_iss@yahoo.gr; internet www.imxa.gr; f. 1953; research centre concerned with the historical, literary, political, economic and social devt of the Balkan peoples since early times; library of 30,000 vols, 260 periodicals; Dir Prof. Dr YANNIS MOURELOS; Chair. Prof. BASIL KONDIS; publs *Balkan Studies* (2 a year), *Valkanika Symmeikta* (1 a year).

International Centre for Classical Research (of the Hellenic Society for Humanistic Studies): 47 Alopekis St, Athens 140; study of and research into ancient Greek culture, scientific research and promotion of popular education through conferences and publications; f. 1959; 700 mems; library of 20,000 vols; Pres. Prof. ARISTOXENOS D. SKIADAS; Sec.-Gen. GEORGE BABINIOTIS; publs *Antiquity and Contemporary Problems, Studies and Research.*

Kentron Erevnis Archaiotitos (Research Centre for Antiquity): Odos Anagnostopoulou 14, 106 73 Athens; tel. 210-3664612; fax 210-3602448; e-mail kea@academyofathens.gr; internet www.academyofathens.gr; f. 1977; attached to Acad. of Athens; Supervisor S. IAKOVIDIS; Dir M. PIPILI.

Kentron Erevnis Messeonikou kai Neou Ellinismou (Centre for Research into Medieval and Modern Hellenism): Anagnostopoulou 14, 106 73 Athens; tel. 210-3664610; fax 210-3664637; e-mail kemne@ academyofathens.gr; internet www .academyofathens.gr; f. 1930; attached to Acad. of Athens; 7 mems; library of 25,000 vols; Dir K. LAPPAS; publ. *Messeonika kai Nea Ellinika* (1 a year).

Kentron Erevnis Neoterou Ellinismou (Research Centre for the History of Modern Hellenism): Anagnostopoulou St 14, 106 73 Athens; tel. 210-3664603; fax 210-3664661; e-mail keine@academyofathens.gr; internet www.keine-academyofathens.gr; f. 1957; attached to Acad. of Athens; Greek history since 1821; 7 research scholars; library of 15,000 vols, 12,000 microfilms; Head, Supervisory Board MICHAEL SAKELLARIOU; Dir HELEN KATSIADAKIS; publ. *Neoellinika Istorika.*

LANGUAGE AND LITERATURE

Kentron Ereunes Hellenikes kai Latinikes Grammateias (Centre for the Research of Greek and Latin Literature): Anagnostopoulou 14, 106 73 Athens; tel. and fax 210-3664630; e-mail keelg@ academyofathens.gr; internet www .academyofathens.gr; f. 1955; attached to Acad. of Athens; Pres. NIKOLAOS KONOMIS; Supervisor ATHANASIOS KAMBYLIS; Librarian ELENI MASTROGEORGIOU.

Research Centre for Modern Greek Dialects: Al. Soutsou 22, 106 71 Athens; tel. 21-12111000; fax 210-3609187; e-mail ksilneg@ academyofathens.gr; internet www .academyofathens.gr/ilne; f. 1914; attached to Acad. of Athens; compiles *Historical Dictionary of Modern Greek Dialects and Local Varieties*; maintains modern Greek dialectal archives (1,469 MSS, 3.8m. cards, 300 hours of sound recordings); linguistic research, especially on modern Greek dialects; research on modern Greek onomastics (incl. relevant archives of place names, proper names, etc.); library of 9,300 vols; Pres. Prof. MICHAEL SAKELLARIOU; Dir CHRISTINA BASSEA-BEZANTAKOU; publ. *Lexicographikon Deltion (Bulletin lexicographique)* (1 a year).

Research Centre for Scientific Terms and Neologisms: Solonos St 84, 106 80 Athens; tel. 210-3664732; e-mail geon@ academyofathens.gr; internet www .academyofathens.gr; f. 2003; attached to Acad. of Athens; Pres. N. KONOMIS; Dir TITOS P. JOCHALAS; publ. *Bulletin of Scientific Terminology and Neologisms.*

MEDICINE

Institut Pasteur Hellénique: 127 Vassilissis Sofias Ave, 115 21 Athens; tel. 210-6478800; fax 210-6423498; internet www .pasteur.gr; f. 1919; study and research of bacteriology, biochemistry, biotechnology, immunology, microbiology, molecular biology, molecular virology, parasitology, virology; library of 3,500 vols and 155 periodicals; Dir A. F. MENTIS.

NATURAL SCIENCES

Physical Sciences

Institouton Geologikon kai Metalleutikon Ereunon (Institute of Geology and Mineral Exploration): 70 Messoghion St, 115 27 Athens; tel. 210-7771438; fax 210-7752211; e-mail dirgen@igme.gr; internet www.igme.gr; f. 1952; operates under the Ministry of Development; consultant to the Government on geoscientific matters and on mine legislation; carries out the geological study of Greece; surveys and evaluates all mineral raw materials, except hydrocarbons, and groundwater resources; 819 mems; library of 9,500 vols, 500 periodicals, 4,000 maps and 6,000 reports; Dir-Gen. ANDREAS N. GEORGAKOPOULOS; publs *Geological and Geophysical Research, Special Research.*

Kentron Erevnis Phissikistis Atmospheras kai Climatologias (Research Centre for Atmospheric Physics and Climatology): Odos Panepistimiou 28, Athens; tel. and fax 210-8832048; e-mail phatmcli@ otenet.gr; internet www.academyofathens .gr; f. 1977; attached to Acad. of Athens; Pres. C. ALEXOPOULOS; Dir CHR. REPAPIS.

National Observatory of Athens: POB 20048, 118 10 Athens; tel. 210-3490101; fax 210-3490140; internet www.noa.gr/indexen .html; f. 1842; library of 60,000 vols; Pres. of the Administration Board Prof. D. P. LALAS; Dir, Institute of Astronomy and Astrophysics Prof. CHRISTOS GOUDIS; Dir, Institute for Astroparticle Physics Prof. LEONIDAS RESVANIS; Dir, Institute for Environmental Research and Sustainable Development Dr PETRAKIS MICHAEL; Dir, Institute of Geodynamics Dr G. STAVRAKAKIS (acting); Dir, Institute for Space Applications and Remote Sensing Dr I. A. DAGLIS; publs *Annals of the National Observatory of Athens, Memoirs, Series I—Astronomy, Series II—Meteorology*, bulletins of the Astronomical, Meteorological, Ionospheric and Geodynamics Institutes.

Research Centre of Pure and Applied Mathematics (RCPAM): Odos Panepistimiou 28, Athens; tel. 210-3664717; fax 210-3664718; e-mail nikartem@academyofathens.gr; internet www.academyofathens.gr; f. 1992; attached to Acad. of Athens; Pres. G. KONTOPOULOS; Supervisor N. K. ARTEMIADIS.

PHILOSOPHY AND PSYCHOLOGY

Kentron Erevnis Ellinikis Philosophias (Centre for Research in Greek Philosophy): Anagnostopoulou St 14, 106 73 Athens; tel. 210-3664626; fax 210-3664624; e-mail emouts@academyofathens.gr; internet www.academyofathens.gr; f. 1971; attached to Acad. of Athens; philosophy research; conferences and monthly seminars on Greek philosophy; bibliographical and consulting services to graduate and postgraduate philosophy students; free use of library for profs, researchers, students; library of 10,000 vols; Pres. Prof. CONSTANTINE DESPOTOPOULOS; Dir Dr MARIA PROTOPAPAS-MARNELI; Supervisor Prof. EVANGHELOS MOUTSOPOULOS (acting); publ. *Philosophia* (1 a year).

RELIGION, SOCIOLOGY AND ANTHROPOLOGY

Athens Center of Ekistics: Strat. Syndesmou St 23, 106 73 Athens; tel. 210-3623216; fax 210-3629337; e-mail ekistics@otenet.gr; internet www.ekistics.org; f. 1963; research, education, collaboration and documentation in the devt of human settlements; secretariat of World Soc. for Ekistics; library of 1,000 vols, 100 periodical titles (historic colln of 20,000 vols largely transferred in 2003 to School of Architecture, Nat. Technical Univ. of Athens, *q.v.*); Dir PANAYOTIS C. PSOMOPOULOS; publ. *Ekistics* (6 a year).

Hellenic Folklore Research Centre of the Academy of Athens: Ipitou St 3, 105 57 Athens; tel. 210-3318042; fax 210-3313418; e-mail keel@academyofathens.gr; internet www.kentrolaografias.gr; f. 1918; folklore, anthropology, ethnology (ethnography), folk music, social, spiritual life, archives of folk material, MSS, tape, video tape, cassette movie, photos, slides; library of 16,000 vols, 5,055 MSS, 28,000 songs, 17,000 folktales and stories, 200,000 proverbs, customs, etc.; Dir Dr AIK. POLYMEROU-KAMILAKI; publ. *Yearbook*.

Kentron Erevnis Ellinikis Kinonias (Research Centre for Greek Society): 8 Chr. Milioni St, 106 73 Athens; tel. 210-3609990; fax 210-369960; e-mail keek@academyofathens.gr; internet www.academyofathens.gr; f. 1978; attached to Acad. of Athens; research into Greek Society, especially the historical development of the Greek family and the social and economic consequences of migration in Greece; library of 4,500 vols; Dirs Prof. M.-G. LILY STYLIANOUDI, Dr ALICE VAXEVANOGLOU, Dr NIKOLAOS KAMBERIS; publs *Elliniki Koinonia* (Yearbook of the Centre), *Epeteiris tou KEEK*.

National Centre of Social Research (EKKE): 14–18 Messogeion Ave, 115 27 Athens; tel. 210-7491600; fax 210-7489127; e-mail president@ekke.gr; internet www.ekke.gr; f. 1960; operates under the Ministry of Research and Technology; promotes the devt of the social sciences in Greece; orga-

nizes and conducts social research and acts as a link between Greek and foreign social scientists; promotes int. cooperation in this field; Dirs THOMAS MALOUTAS, IOANNIS SAKELLIS; publ. *Epitheorissis Koinonikon Erevnon* (Greek Review of Social Research, 4 a year).

Patriarchal Institute for Patristic Studies: 64 Eptapyrgiou St, Moni Vlatadon, 546 34 Thessaloniki; tel. and fax 231-0203620; f. 1968; research centre with depts of patrology, palaeography, history of Byzantine art, history of worship and ecclesiastical history; library of 15,000 vols, 300 periodicals, 115 codex MSS, 450 rare books, 10,000 MSS on microfilm, colour slides of illuminated MSS; Dir Prof. JOHN FOUNTOULIS; publ. *Kleronomia* (2 a year).

TECHNOLOGY

'Demokritos' National Centre for Scientific Research: POB 60228, 153 10 Aghia Paraskevi, Athens; tel. 210-6503285; fax 210-6522965; e-mail info@lib.demokritos.gr; internet www.demokritos.gr; f. 1961; study and research by 8 institutes: nuclear physics, materials science, microelectronics, biology, nuclear technology and radiation protection, informatics and telecommunications, physical chemistry, radioisotopes and radiodiagnostic products; library of 20,000 vols, 300,000 technical reports, 1,500 periodicals; Dir Prof. EMMANUEL G. FLORATOS; Librarian NORIA CHRISTOPHORIDOU; publ. *DEMO Reports*.

Libraries and Archives

Athens

Academy of Athens Library: Anagnostopoulou 14, 106 73 Athens; tel. 210-3664607; fax 210-3364628; e-mail keied@academyofathens.gr; internet www.academyofathens.gr; f. 1926; collects and publishes Greek historical legal documents, incl. those of the Byzantine and post-Byzantine periods; 10,000 vols; Dir Dr LYDIA PAPARRIGA-ARTEMIADI; Research Staff Dr DIMITRA KARAMBULA, Dr ILIAS ARNAOUTOGLOU, Dr YANNIS HATZAKIS; publ. *Epetiris tou Kentrou Ereunes Historias tou Hellenikou Dikaiou* (1 a year).

Athens University of Economics and Business Library: 76 Patission St, 104 34 Athens; tel. 210-8203261; fax 210-8221456; e-mail library@aueb.gr; internet www.lib.aueb.gr; f. 1928; 75,000 vols, 700 serial titles (40,000 vols), 30,000 full-text serial titles, 19 databases; 3 documentation centres: European Documentation Center (EDC) f. 1992, Depository Library of OECD f. 1997, and Depository Library of WTO f. 2004; Dirs Prof. E. J. YANNAKOUDIS, GEORGIA THEOPHANOPOULOU.

Eugenides Foundation Library: Syngrou Ave 387, Paleon Phaleron, 175 64 Athens; tel. 210-9469631; fax 210-9469631; e-mail lib@eugenfound.edu.gr; internet www.eugenfound.edu.gr; f. 1966; 60,000 vols, 441 periodicals (science and technology); Head Librarian HARA BRINDESI.

Gennadius Library: Odos Souidias 61, 106 76 Athens; tel. 210-7210536; fax 210-7237767; e-mail gen_recep@ascsa.edu.gr; internet www.ascsa.edu.gr/index.php/gennadius; f. 1926; rare book and research library attached to American School of Classical Studies; 115,000 vols; spec. colln on Greece, the Near East, the Balkans and travel accounts; first editions of classics; maps; literary and other archives; Dir Dr MARIA GEORGOPOULOU; Librarian IRINI SOLOMONIDI; publs *Exhibition Catalogues, Genna-*

deion Monographs, The New Griffon (1 a year).

Greek Chamber of Deputies Library: Parliament Bldg, 100 21 Athens; tel. 210-3235030; fax 210-3236072; e-mail abadjis@artemis.parl.ariadne-t.gr; f. 1844, damaged by fire 1859, rebuilt 1875; 1.5m. vols; Dir IRENE CON. ELIOPOULOU.

Music Library of Greece 'Lilian Voudouri': Vasilissis Sofias and Kokkali, 115 21 Athens; tel. 210-7282775; fax 210-7259196; e-mail library@megaron.gr; internet www.mmb.org.gr; f. 1994; holds the Greek Music Archives; 20,000 vols, 71 periodicals, 13,000 recordings, microforms, MSS and online databases; Dir STEPHANIA MERAKOU.

National Library of Greece: Odos Panepistimiou 32, 106 79 Athens; tel. 210-3382601; fax 210-3382502; e-mail gzachos@nlg.gr; internet www.nlg.gr; f. 1828; 2.5m. vols; collection of MSS; serves as the national bibliographical centre and as the national centre for ISBN and ISSN; Gen. Dir Dr GEORGE K. ZACHOS.

National Technical University of Athens Central Library: Odos Heroon Polytechniou 9, Zografou Campus, 157 73 Athens; tel. 210-7721570; fax 210-7721565; e-mail library@central.ntua.gr; internet www.lib.ntua.gr; f. 1836; 115,000 vols; Librarian MARIA KALAMPALIKI.

Nordic Library at Athens: Kavalotti 7, 117 42 Athens; tel. 210-9249210; fax 210-9216487; internet www.norlib.gr; 40,000 vols, 450 periodicals; Greek archaeology and ancient Greek religion and history; jt venture by archaeological institutes of Denmark, Finland, Norway and Sweden; Head Librarian CHRISTINA TSAMPAZI-REID.

Technical Chamber of Greece–Documentation and Information Unit: Odos Lekka 23–25, 105 62 Athens; tel. 210-3245180; fax 210-3237525; e-mail tee_lib@tee.gr; internet library.tee.gr; f. 1926; 60,000 vols, 1,400 periodicals, TCG publications; Head of Unit KATERINA TORAKI.

Chios

Koraes Central Public Historical Library of Chios: 2 Korai St, 821 00 Chios; tel. 22710-44246; fax 22710-28251; e-mail bibkor@aegean.gr; internet vivl-chiou.chi.sch.gr; f. 1792; colln of rare and unique Homeric edns; 200,000 vols; Dir ANASTASIOS SARRIS.

Hania

Technical University of Crete Library: 731 00 Hania; tel. 821-037273; fax 821-037576; e-mail maria@library.tuc.gr; internet www.library.tuc.gr; f. 1985; 69,000 vols, 426 current periodicals, maps and dissertations; scientific fields of the institute, arts and history; Library Dir MARIA NTAOUNTAKI.

Patras

University of Patras Library and Information Service: 265 00 Patras; tel. 61-997290; internet www.upatras.gr/services/library/library.php?lang=en; 90,000 vols, 2,400 journals; biology, medicine, theatre, mathematics, computer science, economics, literature, applied sciences, education and general reference.

Piraeus

University of Piraeus Library: 80 Dimitriou and Kalaoli Sts, 185 34 Piraeus; internet www.lib.unipi.gr; economics, business admin., industrial management, finance, and maritime studies; 45,000 vols, 350 periodicals.

Rethymnon

University of Crete Library: Gallos Campus, Knossou Ave, 731 00 Rethymnon; tel. 831-77810; fax 831-77850; e-mail webauthor@lib.uoc.gr; internet www.lib.uoc.gr/english; f. 1978; 3 brs at Heraklion; Dir ELENI DIAMANTAKI.

Thessaloniki

Aristotle University Library: 541 24 Thessaloniki; tel. 231-995378; fax 231-995364; e-mail libraryweb@lib.auth.gr; internet www.lib.auth.gr; f. 1927; attached to Aristotle University of Thessaloniki; 181,500 vols, 122,950 journals, 7,055 dissertations; rare books from the 18th and 19th centuries; Librarians X. AGOROGIANNI, S. ALEXANDRIDOU, EL. KOSEOGLOU.

University of Macedonia, Economic and Social Sciences Library: 156 Egnatia St, 540 06 Thessaloniki; tel. 2310-891752; fax 2310-857794; e-mail maclib@uom.gr; internet www.lib.uom.gr.

Tripolis

Pan Library (Circle of the Friends of Progress): Odos Giorgios 43, Tripolis, Arcadia; vols on all subjects.

Veria

Veria Central Public Library: 8 Ellis St, 591 00 Veria; tel. 2331-24494; fax 2331-24600; e-mail vivlver@libver.gr; internet www.libver.gr; f. 1952; 90,000 vols; Central Library for the Prefecture of Imathia.

Volos

Library of the Three Hierarchs: Demetriados-Ogl, 382 21 Volos; tel. and fax 24210-25641; f. 1907; 23,000 vols; literature, religion, history, philosophy, physical sciences; Asst Dir ACHILLES K. GLAVATOS.

University of Thessaly Central Library: 2 Metamorforseos St, 383 33 Volos; tel. 24210-74891; fax 24210-74851; e-mail clib@uth.gr; internet www.lib.uth.gr; f. 1988; other brs: Veterinary Science in Karditsa; Medicine in Larisa; Physical Education and Sport in Trikala; Humanities, Technological Sciences and Kitsos Makris Folklore Centre in Volos; 112,000 vols, 75,000 books and 37,000 journals; Library Dir Dr IOANNIS CLAPSOPOULOS.

Museums and Art Galleries

Athens

Acropolis Museum: Dionysiou Arepagitou 15, 117 42 Athens; tel. 210-9000900; fax 210-9000902; e-mail info@theacropolismuseum.gr; internet www.theacropolismuseum.gr; f. 1874; contains the sculptures discovered on the Acropolis; illustrates the origins of Attic art, pedimental compositions, archaic horsemen, Korai, sculptures of the Parthenon, Temple of Niké, Erechtheion; Pres. Prof. DIMITRIOS PANDERMALIS.

Benaki Museum: Odos Koumbari 1, 106 74 Athens; tel. 210-3671000; fax 210-3671063; e-mail benaki@benaki.gr; internet www.benaki.gr; f. 1930; Greek art from Neolithic to late Roman period; Byzantine and post-Byzantine; Greek folk art and costumes; historic memorabilia from the War of Independence in 1821 to 1936; 18th- and 19th-century paintings, engravings and drawings; works of art by N. Hadjikyriakos-Ghikas; Coptic and Islamic art; textiles and embroidery from Far East and Western Europe; neolithic to modern Chinese porcelain; children's toys and games from antiquity to the mid-20th century; historical and photographic archives (Documentation Centre for Neo-Hellenic Architecture); library of 50,000 vols, 500 MSS; Dir Prof. Dr ANGELOS DELIVORRIAS.

Byzantine and Christian Museum: 22 Vasilissis Sophias Ave, 106 75 Athens; tel. 210-7211027; fax 210-7231883; e-mail documentation@byzantinemuseum.gr; internet www.byzantinemuseum.gr; f. 1914; more than 25,000 objects since 3rd century AD, incl. sculptures, icons and other works of art; wall paintings, ceramics, textiles, MSS, drawings, anthibola, engravings, incunabula and copies of wall paintings and mosaics of the Byzantine and post-Byzantine eras; Dir Dr DIMITRIOS KONSTANTIOS; Sub-Dir Dr ANASTASIA LAZARIDOU.

National Archaeological Museum: 1 Tositsa St, 106 82 Athens; tel. 210-8217724; fax 210-8213573; e-mail eam@culture.gr; internet www.culture.gr; f. 1889; original Greek sculptures and Roman copies of Greek originals; sculptures of the Archaic, Classical, Hellenistic and Roman periods; Neolithic objects from Thessaly; Bronze Age relics from the mainland and the Aegean Islands; Mycenaean treasures; frescoes and pottery from Thera; rich collns of Greek vases and terracottas; collns of jewels and bronzes; Egyptian antiquities; Dir Dr NIKOLAOS KALTSAS; Head of Bronzes Colln Dr ROZA PROSKYNITOPOULOU; Head of Prehistoric, Egyptian and Anatolian Antiquities Colln Dr ELENI PAPAZOGLOU; Head of Sculpture Colln Dr ELENI KOURINOU; Head of Vases and Minor Art Colln ELISAVET STASINOPOULOU.

National Art Gallery and Alexander Soutzos Museum: 50 Vassileos Konstantinou Ave, 115 28 Athens; tel. 210-7211010; fax 210-7224889; internet www.nationalgallery.gr; f. 1900; Greek paintings since the 17th century, sculptures and prints; European paintings since the 14th century, including El Greco, Caravaggio, Jordaens, Poussin, Tiepolo, Delacroix, Mondrian, Picasso; engravings; drawings; library of 8,000 vols; Dir Prof. MARINA LAMBRAKI-PLAKA.

National Historical Museum of Greece: Old Parliament, Stadiou St, 105 61 Athens; tel. 210-3237617; fax 210-3213786; e-mail info@fhw.gr; internet www.fhw.gr/projects/vouli; f. 1882; chronicles the history of Modern Greece from the 16th to the 20th century; ethnographic colln of traditional regional costumes, jewellery, embroidery and textiles; Dir IOANNIS K. MAZARAKIS-AINIAN.

National Museum of Contemporary Art, Athens (EMST): 14 Amvr. Frantzi St, 117 43 Athens; tel. 210-9242111; fax 210-9245200; e-mail protocol@emst.gr; internet www.emst.gr; f. 2000; paintings, installations, photography, video, new media, architecture and industrial design; Dir ANNA KAFETSI.

Stoa of Attalos: 10 555 Athens; tel. 210-3210185; f. as a museum in 1956; the design of the original building (constructed in the 2nd century BC) was exactly reproduced in the reconstruction carried out 1953–56 by the American School of Classical Studies; collections include all material found in the excavations of the Athenian Agora, illustrating 5,000 years of Athenian history; Dir P. KALLIGAS.

Zoological Museum of the University of Athens: Panepistimiopolis, 157 84 Athens; tel. 210-7274609; fax 210-7274619; e-mail zoolmuse@biol.uoa.gr; internet www.biol.uoa.gr/zoolmuseum; f. 1858; permanent and temporary exhibitions on Greek and world fauna: birds, mammals, shells, insects, etc.; research in ecology and zoogeography; Curator Prof. SOTIRIOS MANOLIS.

Canea

Archaeological Museum of Canea: 731 31 Canea; tel. 28210-90334; fax 28210-94487; internet www.culture.gr; f. 1963; housed in the katholikon of the Venetian monastery of St Francis; artefacts of prehistoric and historical times from the dept of Canea; Dir MARIA VLAZAKI.

Maritime Museum of Crete: Akti Koundourioti , 731 36 Canea; tel. 2821-91875; fax 2821-74484; internet www.greece-museums.com/museum/109; f. 1973; Dir K. MANIOUDAKIS.

Corfu

Archaeological Museum: Armeni Vraila 1, 491 00 Corfu; tel. 2661-30680; fax 2661-43452; internet www.greece-museums.com/museum/116; f. 1967; bronze statues from Archaic to Roman era; funeral offerings from the Archaic, Classical and Hellenistic eras; findings from Prehistoric era and 7th and 6th centuries BC; Menecrates lion, clay pottery, terracotta statuettes from shrines of Corfu; Gorgon-Medusa pediment from the great temple of Artemis, constructed in 585BC.

Museum of Asian Art: St Michael and St George Palace, 491 00 Corfu; tel. 26610-30443; fax 26610-20193; internet www.greece-museums.com/museum/35; f. 1927; Greek-Buddhistic colln of sculptures from Gadara, Pakistan, dating from the 1st–5th century AD.

Corinth

Archaeological Museum in Corinth: Corinth 200 10; tel. and fax 210-741031207; f. 1932; items from the Geometric to Hellenistic periods, Roman and Byzantine eras, from excavations at the Asklepieion of Corinth; sculptures and inscriptions; Dir ALEXANDROS MANTIS.

Delphi

Archaeological Museum: 330 54 Delphi; tel. 2265-082313; fax 2265-082966; e-mail protocol@iepka.culture.gr; internet www.culture.gr; f. 1903; finds from the Delphic excavations; library of 5,200 vols; Dir ATHANASIA PSALTI.

Heraklion

Archaeological Museum: 2 Xanthoudidou St, 712 02 Heraklion, Crete; tel. 281-0224630; fax 281-0332610; e-mail protocol@amh.culture.gr; f. 1904; contains rich collection of Minoan art (pottery, sealstones, frescoes, jewellery); traces the development of Cretan art up to the Roman period; Dir RETHEMIOTAKI PANAGIOTA.

Nafplion

Komboloi Museum: 25 Staikopoulou St, 211 00 Nafplion; tel. 2752-21618; e-mail arisevag@otenet.gr; internet www.komboloi.gr; f. 1987; 400 komboloi (prayer beads) findings from the period 1750–1950; komboloi belonging to Buddhists, Catholics, Hindus, Muslims and Orthodox Monks.

Peloponnesian Folklore Foundation: Vas. Alexandrou 1, 211 00 Nafplion; tel. 2752-028379; fax 2752-027960; e-mail pff@otenet.gr; internet www.pli.gr; f. 1974; research, presentation, study and preservation of the material culture of Greece (costume, music and dance); br. in Stathmos; library of 10,115 vols; Pres. IOANNA PAPANTONIOU; Curator KANELLOS KANELLOPOULOS; publs *Endymatologica, Ethnographica*.

Olympia

Archaeological Museum: 270 65 Olympia; tel. and fax 2624-022529; e-mail protocol@zepka.culture.gr; internet www.culture.gr; f. 1970; Greek geometric and archaic bronzes;

two pediments from Temple of Zeus, Hermes of Praxiteles, Victory of Paionios; finds from Sanctuary of Olympia and Pheidias' workshop; Roman sculpture; Dir GEORGIA CHATZI-SPILIOPOULOU.

Attached Museums:

Museum of the History of Excavations in Ancient Olympia: Olympia; tel. and fax 2624-022529; e-mail zepka@culture.gr; f. 2004; presentation of the history of the 19th-century German excavation and archaeological activity in Ancient Olympia; Dir GEORGIA CHATZI-SPILIOPOULOU.

Museum of the History of the Olympic Games: Olympia; tel. and fax 2624-022529; e-mail protocol@zepka.culture.gr; f. 1888; 463 objects (statues, inscriptions, vases, bronzes, etc.) detailing the history of the Olympic Games from the Mycenean to the Roman periods; Dir GEORGIA CHATZI-SPILIOPOULOU.

Paiania

Vorres Museum of Contemporary Greek Art and Folk Art: 1 Parodos Diad. Konstantinou, 190 02 Paiania, Attica; tel. 210-6642520; fax 210-6645775; e-mail info@vorresmuseum.gr; internet www.vorresmuseum.gr; f. 1983; covers 4,000 years of Greek history; two sections: folk art and architecture (a group of traditional buildings containing artefacts, furniture, etc.) and a museum of contemporary Greek art; Dir IAN VORRES; publ. *Catalogue*.

Rethymnon

Archaeological Museum: 741 00 Rethymnon; tel. 2831-54668; internet www.ellada.net/crete-info/museums/rethymno.php; f. 1991; artefacts from the late Neolithic period, early to late Minoan periods, Geometric and Archaic periods and Hellenistic and Roman periods.

Historical and Folk Art Museum: 30 M. Vernardou St, 741 00 Rethymnon; tel. 2831-23398; fax 2831-23667; internet www.ellada.net/crete-info/museums/rethymno.php; f. 1998; 5,000 items of folk art; history of textiles; Pres. FALY G. VOYATZAKIS.

Rhodes

Archaeological Museum: Medieval City, 85 100 Rhodes; tel. 2241-031048; f. as Hospital of the Knights, built 1440–89; sculpture, vases and other objects from Rhodes, Ialysos, Kamiros and other sites, from Mycenean to late Roman times, funerary stelae and weapons dating from Middle Ages; library of 27,400 vols.

Rhodes Jewish Museum: Dossiadou St, Rhodes; tel. 31047-54779; fax 31047-58144; e-mail info@rhodesjewishmuseum.org; internet www.rhodesjewishmuseum.org; housed in fmr women's prayer rooms at 16th-century Kahal Shalom synagogue; attached to Rhodes Jewish Historical Foundation; Pres. BELLA RESTIS.

Thessaloniki

Archaeological Museum of Thessaloniki: Manolis Andronikos St 6, 546 21 Thessaloniki; tel. 2310-830538; fax 2310-861306; e-mail info.amth@culture.gr; internet www.amth.gr; f. 1912 renovated in 2006; exhibitions on prehistoric Macedonia, the birth of Macedonian cities, Macedonia from the 7th century BC to Late Antiquity, and Thessaloniki; educational activities for children and adults; archaeological and historical lectures; modern theatrical productions of ancient drama; library of 8,000 vols; Dir Dr POLYXENI ADAM-VELENI; publs *Archeologiko Ergo ste Makedonia kai Thrace* (1 a

year), *Crater* (1 a year), *Thessaloniki Philippou Vassilissan*.

Macedonian Museum of Contemporary Art of Thessaloniki: 154 Egnatia St, 546 36 Thessaloniki; tel. 2310-240002; fax 2310-281567; e-mail mmcart@mmca.org.gr; internet www.macedonian-heritage.gr/museums; f. 1979; 2,000 works by Greek and foreign artists; library of 2,500 vols; Dir ANTONIS KOURTIS.

State Museum of Contemporary Art at Thessaloniki: Kolokotroni 21, Moni Lazariston, 564 30 Thessaloniki; tel. 2310-589140; fax 2310-600123; internet www.greekstatemuseum.com/contact_en; f. 1997; Costakis colln of 1,275 works of Russian avant-garde art; also houses Museum of Photography and Centre of Contemporary Art; Dir MILTIADES PAPANIKOLAOU.

Technical Museum at Thessaloniki: 2nd Road, Bldg 47, Industrial Zone of Thessaloniki, 570 22 Thessaloniki; tel. 2310-799773; fax 2310-796816; e-mail info@tmth.edu.gr; internet www.tmth.edu.gr; f. 1978; objects and multimedia information grouped by theme: Ancient Greek Technology, Spinning and Textile Making, Printing, Electricity, Telecommunications, New Telecommunications Technologies, Electronic Computers, Radio and Television, Amateur Radio, Navigational Instruments, Oil, Rubber, Automobiles, the Railway, Aviation, Air Traffic Control Tower Telecommunications, Human Beings in Space, Meteorology, Instruments for Physics Experiments, Photography, Holograms, Audiovisual Media, Traditional Technology, Medical Apparatus and Instruments; Dir CHRIS G. PAPADAKIS.

Thessaloniki Museum of Photography: Warehouse A, Port of Thessaloniki, POB 23, 540 15 Thessaloniki; tel. 2310-566716; fax 2310-566717; e-mail press.thmp@culture.gr; internet www.thmphoto.gr; f. 1997; historical and contemporary Greek and int. photography; collects, preserves and promotes photographic heritage; collns and archives incl. 100,000 photographic objects; library of 17,000 vols; Dir VANGELIS IOAKIMIDIS.

Thessaloniki Olympic Museum: 3rd September & Ag. Dimitriou St, 546 36 Thessaloniki; tel. 2310-968531; fax 2310-968726; e-mail pr@olympicmuseum.org.gr; internet www.olympicmuseum-thessaloniki.org; f. 1998; history of athletics; Dir Arch. KYRIAKI OUDATZI.

Universities

ANOTATI SCHOLI KALON TECHNON
(Athens School of Fine Art)

Odos Patission 42, 106 82 Athens
Telephone: 210-3816930
Fax: 210-3816926
E-mail: info@asfa.gr
Internet: www.asfa.gr
Founded 1837
Rector: YANNIS PAPADAKIS
Library of 29,000 vols
Number of teachers: 38
Number of students: 783

DIRECTORS OF SECTIONS
Painting: Prof. CHR. BOTSOGLOU
Printmaking: Prof. G. MILIOS
Sculpture: Prof. G. LAPPAS
Theoretical Studies: Prof. M. LAMBRAKI

Brs in Delphi, Hydra, Mykonos, Rhodes, Lesbos and Rethymnon.

ARISTOTELEIO PANEPISTIMIO THESSALONIKIS
(Aristotle University of Thessaloniki)

University Campus, 541 24 Thessaloniki
Telephone: 2310-996000
Internet: www.auth.gr
Founded 1925
State Univ., with autonomous function
Language of instruction: Greek
Academic year: September to August

Rector: Prof. ANASTASIOS MANTHOS
Vice-Rector for Academic Affairs and Personnel: Prof. ATHANASIA TSATSAKOU
Vice-Rector for Finance and Devt: Assoc. Prof. ANDREAS GIANNAKOUDAKIS
Vice-Rector and Head of the Special Account of Research Funds: Prof. STAVROS PANNAS
Head of International Relations: HELEN KOTSAKI
Librarian: Prof. CHRISTOS BABATZIMOPOULOS
Library: see Libraries and Archives
Number of teachers: 2,287
Number of students: 92,509
Publications: *Panepistimioupoli* (4 a year), catalogue, scientific annals and faculty periodicals

DEANS

Faculty of Agriculture: NIKOLAOS MISOPOLINOS (Chair.)
Faculty of Dentistry: Prof. ATHANASIOS ATHANASIOU (Chair.)
Faculty of Education: Prof. SOFRONIOS CHATZISAVIDIS
Faculty of Engineering: Prof. NIKOLAOS MOUSIOPOULOS
Faculty of Fine Arts: Prof. G. KATSAGELOS
Faculty of Forestry and the Natural Environment: Prof. ANASTASIOS NASTIS (Chair.)
Faculty of Law, Economics and Political Sciences: Prof. GIANNOULA KARYMBALI-TSIPTSIOU
Faculty of Medicine: Prof. IOANNIS BONDIS (Chair.)
Faculty of Philosophy: Prof. PHOEVUS GIKOPOULOS
Faculty of Science: Prof. IOANNIS PAPADOGIANNIS
Faculty of Theology: Prof. IOANNIS KOGOULIS
Faculty of Veterinary Medicine: Prof. DIMITRIOS RAPTOPOULOS (Chair.)

CHAIRMEN OF SCHOOLS

Faculty of Education (tel. 2310-995062; fax 2310-995061):
    School of Early Childhood Education: Prof. GIORGIOS TSIAKALOS
    School of Primary Education: Prof. DEMETRIOS GERMANOS
Faculty of Engineering (tel. 2310-995601; fax 2310-995611):
    School of Architecture: Prof. NIKOLAOS KALOGIROU
    School of Chemical Engineering: Prof. VASSILIOS PAPAGEORGIOU
    School of Civil Engineering: Prof. DIMOSTHENIS ANGELLIDIS
    School of Electrical and Computer Engineering: Prof. NIKOLAOS MARGARIS
    School of Mathematics, Physics and Computational Sciences: Prof. GERASIMOS KOUROUKLIS
    School of Mechanical Engineering: Prof. NIKOLAOS MOUSIOPOULOS
    School of Rural and Survey Engineering: Prof. PETROS PATIAS
    School of Urban Regional Planning and Development (Veroia): Prof. NIKOLAOS RODOLAKIS
Faculty of Fine Arts (tel. 231-995071; fax 231-995073):
    School of Drama: Prof. NIKIFOROS PAPANDREOU

School of Film Studies: Prof. APOSTOLOS-FOKION VETTAS

School of Musical Studies: Prof. DIMITRIOS GIANNOU

School of Visual and Applied Arts: Prof. GEORGIOS GOLFINOS

Faculty of Law, Economics and Political Sciences (tel. 2310-996539; fax 2310-996526):

School of Economics: C. PAPADOPOULOS

School of Law: K. HATZIKONSTANTINOU

Faculty of Philosophy (tel. 2310-995173; fax 2310-997152):

School of English Language and Literature: Prof. ANGELIKI ATHANASIADOU

School of French Language and Literature: Prof. A. NENOPOULOU-DROSOU

School of German Language and Literature: Prof. IOANNA EKONOMOU-AGORASTOU

School of History and Archaeology: Prof. THEOHARIS PAZARAS

School of Italian Language and Literature: Prof. ANTONIOS TSOMPANOGLOU

School of Philology: Prof. ANTONIOS REGAKOS

School of Philosophy and Education: Prof. NIKOLAOS TERZIS

School of Psychology: Prof. G. KIOSEOGLOU

Faculty of Science (tel. 2310-998020; fax 2310-998022):

School of Biology: Prof. Z. SKOURAS

School of Chemistry: Assoc. Prof. ANDREAS GIANNAKOUDAKIS

School of Geology: Prof. GEORGIOS CHRISTOFIDIS

School of Informatics: A. POMBORTZIS

School of Mathematics: Prof. POLYCHRONIS MOISIADES

School of Physics: Prof. STERGIOS LOGOTHETIDIS

Faculty of Theology:

School of Ecclesiastical and Social Theology: Prof. GEORGIOS THEODOROUDIS

School of Theology: Prof. MILTIADES KONSTANTINOU

Independent Schools:

School of Journalism and Mass Media Studies: Prof. THEODOROS KORRES

School of Pharmacy: Prof. ASTERIOS TSIFTSOGLOU

School of Physical Education and Athletics in Serres: Prof. C. KAMPITSIS

School of Physical Education and Athletics in Thessaloniki: Prof. ASTERIOS DELIGIANNIS

DIMOKRITEIO PANEPISTIMIO THRAKIS
('Demokritos' University of Thrace)

Admin. Bldg, University Campus, 691 00 Komotini

Telephone: 2531-039000
Fax: 2531-039081
E-mail: intrela@duth.gr
Internet: www.duth.gr

Founded 1973
State control
Language of instruction: Greek
Academic year: September to August

Rector: A. KARABINIS
Vice-Rectors: K. SIMOPOULOS, ATH. KARABINIS, G. HADJICONSTANTINOU
Administrative Officer: E. TSITSOPOULOS

Library of 236,656 vols, 4,060 periodicals
Number of teachers: 495
Number of students: 18,627

DEANS

Faculty of Educational Sciences: TH. VOUGIOUKLIS

Faculty of Engineering: I. DIAMANTIS

Faculty of Law: K. KALAVROS

Faculty of Medicine: D. HATSERAS

Faculty of the Science of Physical Education and Sport: G. MAVROMMATIS

Department of Agricultural Development: G. VASSILIOU

Department of Architectural Engineering: C. ATHANASSOPOULOS

Department of Civil Engineering: ATH. KARABINIS

Department of Electrical Engineering and Computer Engineering: D. PAPADOPOULOS

Department of Environmental Engineering: VASS. TSICHRINTZIS

Department of Forestry and Management of the Environment and Natural Resources: K. SIDERIS

Department of Greek Literature: A. CHARALAMBAKIS

Department of History and Ethnology: D. SAMSARIS

Department of International Economic Relations and Development: G. HADJICONSTANTINOU

Department of Languages, Literature and Culture of the Black Sea Countries: I. SCHINAS

Department of Molecular Biology and Genetics: G. BOURIKAS

Department of Pre-School Education Sciences: L. BEZE

Department of Production and Management Engineering: ATH. KARABINAS

Department of Social Administration: K. REMELIS

Pedagogical Department of Primary Education: E. TARATORI

PROFESSORS

Faculty of Law (University Campus, New Law School, 691 00 Komotini; tel. 2531-039890; fax 2531-039897):

ALIPRANDIS, N., Labour Law
CHARALAMBAKIS, A., Penal Law
KALAVROS, K., Civil Procedural Law
KONSTANDINIDIS, A., Penal Procedural Law
MANIOTIS, D., Civil Procedural Law
PARARAS, P., Constitutional Law
PITSAKIS, K., History of Law
POULIS, G., Ecclesiastical Law
REMELIS, K., Administrative Law
SCHINAS, J., Commercial Law

Faculty of Medicine (Ioakim Kavyri 6, 681 00 Alexandroupoli; tel. 25510-30921; fax 25510-30922):

BOUGIOUKAS, Cardiac Surgery
BOURIKAS, G., Pathology
BOUROS, D., Pneumonology
CHATSERAS, D., Cardiology
CHOURDAKIS, K., Toxicology, Forensic Medicine
DIMITRIOU, TH., Anatomy
KARTALIS, G., Pathology
KOUSKOUKIS, K., Dermatology, Venereal Diseases
KTENIDOU-KARTALI, S., Microbiology
MALTEZOS, E., Pathology
MANOLAS, K., Surgery
MAROULIS, G., Obstetrics and Gynaecology
MINOPOULOS, G., Surgery
PAPADOPOULOS, E., Urology
PRASSOPOULOS, P., Radiology
SIMOPOULOS, K., Surgery
SIVRIDIS, E., Pathology
VARGEMEZIS, V., Nephrology

Faculty of the Science of Physical Education and Sport (7 km on National Rd, Komotini–Xanthi, 691 00 Komotini; tel. 2531-039621; fax 2531-039623; e-mail tefaa@phyed.duth.gr):

CHARACHOUSOU-KABITSI, Y., Mass Sports
GODOLIAS, G., Sports Medicine
KABITSIS, CH., Classical Athletics

KIOUMOURTZOGLOU, E., Basketball Coaching
LAIOS, ATH., Basketball Coaching
LAPARIDIS, K., Nutrition in Sports
MANDIS, K., Tennis
MAVROMATIS, G., Statistics
SERBEZIS, V., Teaching of Greek Folk Dancing
TAXILDARIS, K., Basketball
TOKMAKIDIS, S., Exercise Physiology

Department of Agricultural Development (Pantazidou 193, 682 00 Orestiada; tel. 2552-041161; fax 2552-041191; e-mail ezelidou@ores.duth.gr):

ABAS, Z., General and Special Animal Husbandry
BEZIRTZOGLOU, E., Microbiology, Microbe Ecology
GALANOPOULOS, K., Agricultural Economy
KOTOULA-SYKA, EL., Pests, Pesticides, Pest Control
KOUTROUMANIDIS, TH., Applied Economic Statistics
KOUTROUMBAS, SP., General and Special Agriculture
SPARTALIS, ST., Algebra
TOKATLIDIS, I., Genetics and Plant Improvement
VASSILIOU, G., Agricultural Pharmacology and Ecotoxicology

Department of Architectural Engineering (Vasilissis Sofias 1, 671 00 Xanthi; tel. 2541-079350; fax 2541-079349; e-mail info@arch.duth.gr):

AMERICANOU, E., Architectural Design
BARKAS, N., Building Construction and Architectural Acoustics
EXARCHOPOULOS, P.-L., Architectural Design and Compositions
KOKKORIS, P., Architectural Design
KOLOKOTRONIS, I., History of Art, European and American Art of the 20th Century
LIANOS, N., Architectural Design
MANTZOU, P., Architectural Design, Building Compositions
MICHAELIDIS, A., Architectural and Construction Sculpture
PATRIKIOS, G., Architectural Design, Spatial Organization and Microenvironment
POLYCHRONOPOULOS, D., Urban Planning
POTAMIANOS, I., History of Architecture
PREPIS, ALK., History of Art
THEONI, X., Architectural Design and Compositions, Creation of Building Units for Professional and Private Use
THOMAS, N., Architectural and Construction Drawing
TSIOUKAS, VASS., Topography

Department of Civil Engineering (Vasilissis Sofias 1, 671 00 Xanthi; tel. 2541-079031; fax 2541-020275; e-mail info@civil.duth.gr):

ATHANASSOPOULOS, CHR., Building Construction
GALOUSSIS, Ev., Steel Construction
GDOUTOS, EM., Technical Engineering and Applied Mechanics
KARABINIS, ATH., Reinforced Concrete Structures
KARAGIANNIS, CH., Construction of Reinforced Concrete
KARALIS, TH., Soil Mechanics: Foundations
KOTSOVINOS, N., Hydraulics
LABRINOS, P., Higher Mathematics
LIOLIOS, AST., Higher Mathematics
MATSOUKIS, P.-F., Maritime Engineering
PANAGIOTAKOPOULOS, D., Construction Project Management
PANTAZOPOULOU, ST., Construction of Reinforced Concrete
PAPADOPOULOS, V., General Topology
SIDERIS, K., Building Materials
STEPHANIS, VAS., Transport Engineering, Survey Engineering

Department of Electrical Engineering and Computer Engineering (Vasilissis Sofias 1, 671 00 Xanthi; tel. 2541-079035; fax 2541-079037; e-mail info@ee.duth.gr):

BEKAKOS, M., Computers, Hardware
CHAMZAS, CHR., Signal and Image Processing, Coding, MM Communication Systems, Networks
GEORGOULAS, N., Microelectronic and Optoelectronic Materials and Elements
PAPADOPOULOS, D., Electric Engines
PAPAMARKOS, N., Electric Cicuits, Digital Filters, Digital Image Processing
SARRIS, EM., Electromagnetic Theory
SPARIS, P., Special Mechanical Engineering
THANAILAKIS, A., Electrical and Electronic Materials Technology
TSALIDIS, PH., Computer Science
TSANGAS, N., Nuclear Engineering and Technology

Department of Environmental Engineering (University Campus of Xanthi, Kimmeria, 671 00 Xanthi; tel. 2541-079101; fax 2541-079108; e-mail mlekidou@lib.duth.gr):

AIVAZIDIS, AL., Environmental Technology
OUZOUNIS, K., Environmental Chemistry
RAPSOMANIKIS, SP., Air Pollution, Atmospheric Pollutant Control Technology
TSICHRINTZIS, V., Ecological Engineering Technology
VOUDRIAS, E., Solid Waste Management

Department of Forestry and Management of the Environment and Natural Resources (Pantazidou 193, 682 00 Orestiada; tel. 2552-041171; fax 2552-041192; e-mail impatzio@ores.duth.gr):

AVRAMIDIS, ST., Wood Science
ILIADIS, LAZ., Forestry Informatics
KARANIKOLA, P., Forest Wood Entomology
MANOLAS, EV., Sociology and Environmental Science, Forest Education
MILIOS, IL., Silviculture
PAPAGEORGIOU, AT., Forest Genetics
TSACHALIDIS, E., Game Ecology and Management

Department of Greek Literature (University Campus, 691 00 Komotini; tel. 25310-39900; fax 25310-39901):

IOANNIDOU, CH., Ancient Greek Literature
KAMBAKI-VOUGIOUKLI, P., Applied Linguistics
KONTOGIANNI, VASS., Modern Greek Literature
MANAKIDOU, H., Ancient Greek Literature
MANOS, AND., Ancient Greek Philosophy
PANTELIDIS, N., General Linguistics
TSOURIS, K., Byzantine History and Archaeology
TZIATZI-PAPAGIANNI, M., Byzantine Literature

Department of History and Ethnology (Panaghi Tsaldari 1, 691 00 Komotini; tel. 25310-39462; fax 25310-39462):

CHATZOPOULOS, K., History of Modern Hellenism
GALLIS, K., Prehistoric Archaeology
PAPAZOGLOU, G., History (based on sources such as Codices)
SAMSARIS, D., Roman History
XIROTYRIS, N., Physical Anthropology

Department of International Economic Relations and Development (University Campus, 691 00 Komotini; tel. 2531-039826; fax 2531-039830; e-mail ekostant@ierd.duth.gr; internet www.ierd.duth.gr):

CHATZIKONSTANTINOU, G., Economic Theory
CHIONIS, DION., International (Direct) Investments and Multinationals
KONSTANDINIDIS, E., International Economic Law, International and European Business Law
MOURMOURIS, I., Transportation Economics and Management

Department of Languages, Literature and Culture of the Black Sea Countries (Panaghi Tsaldari 1, 691 00 Komotini; tel. 2531-039413; fax 2531-039421; e-mail ddiamant@kom.duth.gr):

FALANGAS, A., History and Civilization of the Western and Northern Black Sea Area
KEKRIDIS, E., Contemporary and Recent Culture of the Black Sea Peoples
THOMADAKI, EV., Theoretical Linguistics

Department of Molecular Biology and Genetics (Dimitras 19, Old Hospital, 681 00 Alexandroupoli; tel. and fax 25510-30610; e-mail secr@mbg.duth.gr):

CHLICHLIA, AIK., Immunobiology
GRIGORIOU, M., Molecular Biology
KOFFA, M., Cell Biology
PHYLAKTAKIDOU, K., Chemistry
SANDALTZOPOULOS, RAF., Molecular Biology

Department of Pre-School Education Sciences (Nea Chili, 681 00 Alexandroupoli; tel. 25510-39623; fax 25510-39624; e-mail secr@psed.duth.gr; internet www.psed.duth.gr):

BEZE, L., Psychology and Sociology of Education
GOGOU-KRITIKOU, L., Sociology of Education
METAXAKI-KOSIONIDOU, CHR., Informatics Applications in Pre-School Education
PETROGIANNIS, KON., Development Psychology

Department of Production and Management Engineering (University Campus of Xanthi, Kimmeria, 671 00 Xanthi; tel. 2541-079345; fax 2541-079361; e-mail secr@pme.duth.gr):

ANAGNOSTOPOULOS, K., Business Economics and Management with Engineering
CHATZOGLOU, P., Information Systems in Administration
SIMINTIRAS, A., Marketing
TOURASSIS, VASS., Industrial Production

Department of Social Administration (Panaghi Tsaldari 1, 691 00 Komitini; tel. 25310-39409; fax 25310-39442; e-mail dgogou@kom.duth.gr):

CHATZOPOULOS, VASS., EU Law and Policies
KALLINIKAKI-MANGRIOTI, TH., Social Work
KANDYLAKI, AG., Social Work and Local Development in Multicultural Societies
KATROUNGALOS, G., Public Law
PAPASTYLIANOU, A., Social Psychology
PAPATHEODOROU, CH., Social Policy
PETMEZIDOU-TSOULOUVI, M., Social Policy
VENIERIS, D., Social Policy
VIDALI, SOF., Criminology, Anti-crime Policy

Pedagogical Department of Primary Education (Nea Chili, 681 00 Alexandroupoli; tel. 25510-30024; fax 25510-39630; e-mail tsesmel@eled.duth.gr):

DAVAZOGLOU, ANG., Education of Children with Special Needs
KARAKATSANIS, P., Educational Philosophy
KEKKERIS, G., Informatics, Multimedia in Aesthetics Education
KEVREKIDIS, TH., Biology and Ecology
MICHAS, P., Teaching of Natural Sciences
PAPAGEORGIOU, G., Teaching of Chemistry, Environmental Chemistry
PETROPOULOS, I., Ancient Greek Literature
ROKKA, ANG., Earth Sciences, Geology, Geography
SAKONIDIS, CHAR., Teaching of Mathematics
TARATORI, EL., Teaching Methodology
VOUGIOUKLIS, TH., Mathematics

ELLINIKO ANOIKTO PANEPISTIMIO (Hellenic Open University)

18 Parodos Aristotelous St, 26 335 Patra
Telephone: 2610-367300
Fax: 2610-367350
E-mail: info@eap.gr
Internet: www.eap.gr

Founded 1992 as a distance-learning university, offering undergraduate and postgraduate courses to adults
State control

Pres.: PANAYIOTIS SIAFARIKAS
Secretary-General: CHARALAMPOS RODOPOULOS

Number of teachers: 1,348
Number of students: 28,068 (8,251 undergraduate, 4,455 postgraduate)

DEANS

Faculty of Applied Arts: DEMETRIOS ZEVGOLIS
Faculty of Humanities: ALEXIOS KOKKOS
Faculty of Sciences and Technology: MARIA CHATIZINIKOLAOU
Faculty of Social Sciences: GEORGE AGIOMIRGIANAKIS

ETHNIKON KAI KAPODISTRIAKON PANEPISTIMION ATHINON (National and Capodistrian University of Athens)

Odos Panepistimiou 30, 106 79 Athens
Telephone: 210-3614301
Fax: 210-3602145
Internet: www.uoa.gr

Founded 1837
State control
Language of instruction: Greek
Academic year: September to June

Rector: Prof. GEORGE DEMETRIUS BABINIOTIS
Vice-Rector for Academic Affairs and Personnel: Prof. CH. KITTAS
Vice Rector for Financial Planning and Development: Prof. M. DERMITZAKIS
Vice Rector for Strategic Planning Works and Student Affairs: Prof. D. ASIMAKOPOULOS

Number of teachers: 1,709
Number of students: 45,000

DEANS

Faculty of Arts: IOANNIS PARASKEVOPOULOS
Faculty of Health Sciences: KONSTANTINOS DIMOPOULOS
Faculty of Law, Economic and Political Sciences: CHRISTOS ROZAKIS
Faculty of Sciences: NIKOLAOS SIMEONIDIS
Faculty of Theology: CONSTANTINE SCOUTERIS

ETHNIKO METSOVIO POLYTECHNEIO (National Technical University of Athens)

Polytechnioupoli, Zografou, 157 80 Athens
Telephone: 210-7722017
Fax: 210-7722028
Internet: www.ntua.gr

Founded 1836
State control
Language of instruction: Greek
Academic year: September to August

Rector: Prof. ANDREAS ANDREOPOULOS
Vice-Rectors: P. KOTTIS, E. DRIS
Chief Admin. Officer: E. RELAKI
Librarian: M. KALABALIKI

Library: see Libraries and Archives
Number of teachers: 700
Number of students: 1,000

Publications: *Pyrphoros* (24 a year), *Scientific Papers*, *Scientific Year Book*

DIRECTORS OF SECTIONS

Applied Mathematics and Physics:

Humanities, Social Science and Law: V. NIKOLAIDOU
Mathematics: K. KYRIAKIS
Physics: P. PISSIS

Architecture:

Architectural Design: AMILIOS KORONAIOS
Design and Technology: ALEKSANDRA MONEMVASITOU
Design, Visual Studies and Communication: IOANNIS TSOUDEROS
Urban and Regional Planning: IOANNIS TERZOGLOU

Chemical Engineering:

Chemical Sciences: A. HARALAMBOUS
Material Science and Engineering: F. ROUBANI-KALANZOPOULOU
Process Analysis and Plant Design: A. BOUDOUVIS
Synthesis and Development of Industrial Processes: A. VLYSSIDIS

Civil Engineering:

Engineering Construction and Management: A. ANAGNOSTOPOULOS
Geotechnical Engineering: (vacant)
Structural Engineering: J. ERMOPOULOS
Transportation Planning and Engineering: J. FRANTSESKAKIS
Water Resources, Hydraulic and Maritime Engineering: A. ADREADAKIS

Electrical and Computing Engineering:

Computer Science: G. STASINOPOULOS
Electrical Power: J. STATHOPOULOS
Electroscience: N. OUZOUNOGLOU

Mechanical Engineering:

Fluid Mechanics Engineering: G. BERGELES
Industrial Management and Operational Research: G. FOKAS-KOSMETATOS
Manufacturing Technology: A. MAMALIS
Mechanical Construction and Automatic Control: P. MAKRIS
Nuclear Engineering: D. LEONIDOU
Thermal Engineering: K. RAKOPOULOS

Mining and Metallurgical Engineering:

Geological Sciences: Prof. Dr E. MPOSKOS
Metallurgy and Materials Technology: Assoc. Prof. K. TSAKALAKIS
Mining Engineering: Prof. ALEXANDROS I. SOFIANOS

PROFESSORS

AFRATI, F., Electrical and Computer Engineering
ANAGNOSTOU, M., Electrical and Computer Engineering
ANASTASSOPOULOU, I., Materials Science and Engineering
ANDREOPOULOS, A., Synthesis and Development of Industrial Processing
ANDROUTSOPOULOS, G., Process Analysis and Plant Design
ANTONOPOULOS, K., Mechanical Engineering
ASSIMAKOPOULO, D., Process Analysis and Plant Design
ASSIMAKOPOULOS, V., Electrical and Computer Engineering
ATHANASOULIS, G., Naval Architecture and Marine Engineering
AVARITSIOTIS, J., Electrical and Computer Engineering
BAFA, G., Process Analysis and Plant Design
BATIS, G., Materials Science and Engineering
BOUDOUVIS, A., Process Analysis and Plant Design
BOURKAS, P., Electrical and Computer Engineering
CAPROS, P., Electrical and Computer Engineering
CAPSALIS, C., Electrical and Computer Engineering

CARAYANNIS, G., Electrical and Computer Engineering
CHRYSSOULAKIS, J., Materials Science and Engineering
CONSTANTINOU, F., Electrical and Computer Engineering
COTTIS, P., Electrical and Computer Engineering
DERVOS, K., Electrical and Computer Engineering
DIALINAS, E., Electrical and Computer Engineering
FRANGOPOULOS, CH., Naval Architecture and Marine Engineering
FRANGOS, P., Electrical and Computer Engineering
FTICOS, CHR., Synthesis and Development of Industrial Processing
GLYTSIS, E., Electrical and Computer Engineering
HATZIARGYRIOU, N., Electrical and Computer Engineering
HIZANIDIS, K., Electrical and Computer Engineering
KAKATSIOS, X., Mechanical Engineering
KAKLIS, P., Naval Architecture and Marine Engineering
KANELLOPOULOS, J., Electrical and Computer Engineering
KASELOURI-RIGOPOULOU, V., Chemical Sciences
KAYAFAS, E., Electrical and Computer Engineering
KOLISIS, FR., Synthesis and Development of Industrial Processing
KOLLIAS, S., Electrical and Computer Engineering
KOUKIOS, E., Synthesis and Development of Industrial Processing
KOULOUMBI, N., Materials Science and Engineering
KOUMANTAKIS, I., Geological Sciences
KOUSSIOURIS, T., Electrical and Computer Engineering
KOUTSOURIS, D., Electrical and Computer Engineering
KRIKELIS, N., Mechanical Engineering
KYRTATOS, N., Naval Architecture and Marine Engineering
LIVADITI, K., Geological Sciences
LOIS, E., Synthesis and Development of Industrial Processing
LOIZIDOU-MALAMIS, M., Chemical Sciences
LOUKAKIS, TH., Naval Architecture and Marine Engineering
MACHIAS, A., Electrical and Computer Engineering
MAGLARIS, V., Electrical and Computer Engineering
MAMALIS, A., Mechanical Engineering
MANIAS, S., Electrical and Computer Engineering
MARAGOS, P., Electrical and Computer Engineering
MARATOS, N., Electrical and Computer Engineering
MARINOS-KOURI, D., Process Analysis and Plant Design
MARKATO, N., Process Analysis and Plant Design
MARKOPOULOU-IGGLESI, O., Chemical Sciences
MAROULI, Z., Process Analysis and Plant Design
MATHIOUDAKIS, K., Mechanical Engineering
MAVRAKOS, S., Naval Architecture and Marine Engineering
MITROU, N., Electrical and Computer Engineering
MOROPOULOU, A., Materials Science and Engineering
MPERGELES, G., Mechanical Engineering
MPOSKOS, E., Geological Sciences
NEOU-SYNGOUNA, P., Metallurgy and Materials Technology

OCHSENKUEHN-PETROPOULOU, M., Chemical Sciences
PANAGIOTOU, G. N., Mining Engineering
PANAGOPOULOS, C., Metallurgy and Materials Technology
PANAGOPOULOS, K. J., Mining Engineering
PAPADIMITRIOU, G., Metallurgy and Materials Technology
PAPAILIOU, K., Mechanical Engineering
PAPAKONSTANTINOU, G., Electrical and Computer Engineering
PAPANIKOLAOU, A., Naval Architecture and Marine Engineering
PAPANTONIS, D., Mechanical Engineering
PAPASPYRIDES, C. D., Synthesis and Development of Industrial Processing
PAPAVASILOPOULOS, G., Electrical and Computer Engineering
PAPAYANNAKI, L., Process Analysis and Plant Design
PAPAYANNAKOS, N., Process Analysis and Plant Design
PAPAZOGLOU, V., Naval Architecture and Marine Engineering
PARASKEVOPOULOS, P., Electrical and Computer Engineering
PASPALIARIS, I., Metallurgy and Materials Technology
PEKMESTZI, K., Electrical and Computer Engineering
PHILIPPOPOULOS, K., Process Analysis and Plant Design
PROTONOTARIOS, E., Electrical and Computer Engineering
PSARAFTIS, CH., Naval Architecture and Marine Engineering
RAKOPOULOS, K., Mechanical Engineering
ROGDAKIS, E., Mechanical Engineering
ROUBANI-KALANZOPOULOU, F., Materials Science and Engineering
ROUMELIOTIS, J., Electrical and Computer Engineering
SAMOUILIDIS, E., Electrical and Computer Engineering
SELLIS, T., Electrical and Computer Engineering
SFANTSIKOPOULOS, M., Mechanical Engineering
SIMITZIS, J., Materials Science and Engineering
SIMOPOULOS, S., Mechanical Engineering
SKORDALAKIS, E., Electrical and Computer Engineering
SPENTZAS, K., Mechanical Engineering
SPYRELLIS, N., Chemical Sciences
STAFYLOPATIS, A. G., Electrical and Computer Engineering
STAMATAKI, S., Mining Engineering
STASSINOPOULOS, G., Electrical and Computer Engineering
STATHOPULOS, I. A., Electrical and Computer Engineering
STOURNAS, S., Synthesis and Development of Industrial Processing
SYKAS, E., Electrical and Computer Engineering
TATSIOPOULOS, I., Mechanical Engineering
THEODOROU, N., Electrical and Computer Engineering
THEODOROU, TH., Materials Science and Engineering
THEOLOGOU, M., Electrical and Computer Engineering
TRIANTAFYLLOU, G., Naval Architecture and Marine Engineering
TSALAMENGAS, J., Electrical and Computer Engineering
TSANAKAS, P., Electrical and Computer Engineering
TSANGARIS, G., Materials Science and Engineering
TSANGARIS, S., Mechanical Engineering
TSEZOS, M., Metallurgy and Materials Technology
TSIMAS, S., Chemical Sciences

TZABIRAS, G., Naval Architecture and Marine Engineering

TZAFESTAS, S., Electrical and Computer Engineering

UZUNOGLOU, N., Electrical and Computer Engineering

VASSILIOU, P., Materials Science and Engineering

VASSILIOU, Y., Electrical and Computer Engineering

VGENOPOULOS, A., Geological Sciences

VLYSSIDIS, A., Synthesis and Development of Industrial Processing

VOMVORIDIS, J., Electrical and Computer Engineering

VOURNAS, C., Electrical and Computer Engineering

XANTHAKIS, J., Electrical and Computer Engineering

YOVA, D., Electrical and Computer Engineering

ZACHOS, S., Electrical and Computer Engineering

ZEVGOLIS, E. N., Metallurgy and Materials Technology

GEOPONIKO PANEPISTIMIO ATHINON
(Athens Agricultural University)

Iera Odos 75, 118 55 Athens

Telephone: 210-5294802

Fax: 210-3460885

E-mail: r@aua.gr

Internet: www.aua.gr

Founded 1920

Rector: Prof. ANDREAS KARAMANOS

Sec.-Gen.: CON. TSAKOUMAKIS

Number of teachers: 177

Number of students: 3,500

Faculties of agricultural biotechnology, animal science, crop science, food science and technology, natural resources management and agricultural engineering, rural economics and development, science.

DIRECTORS

Laboratory of Agribusiness Management: PATSIS PANAGIOTIS

Laboratory of Agricultural Engineering: NICK SIGRIMIS

Laboratory of Agricultural Extension, Agricultural Systems and Rural Sociology: KASIMIS CHARALAMBOS

Laboratory of Agricultural Hydraulics: PETROS G. KERKIDES

Laboratory of Agricultural Zoology and Entomology: NIKOLAOS G. EMMANUEL

Laboratory of Agronomy: ANDREAS KARAMANOS

Laboratory of Anatomy and Physiology of Farm Animals: IOANNIS MENEGATOS

Laboratory of Animal Breeding and Husbandry: ROGDAKIS EMMANUEL

Laboratory of Animal Nutrition: GEORGE ZERVAS

Laboratory of Applied Hydrobiology: SOFRONIOS E. PAPOUTSOGLOU

Laboratory of Botany: GEORGE SARLIS

Laboratory of Dairy Research: IOANNIS KANDARAKIS

Laboratory of Ecology and Environmental Sciences: GERASIMOS ARAPIS

Laboratory of Electron Microscopy: KONSTANTINOS FASSEAS

Laboratory of Enzyme Technology: Y. CLONIS

Laboratory of Floriculture and Landscape Architecture: JOANNIS CHRONOPOULOS

Laboratory of Food Chemistry: M. KOMAITIS

Laboratory of Food Process Engineering, Treatment and Preservation of Agricultural Products: P. RODIS

Laboratory of Food Quality Control and Hygiene: P. ATHANASOPOULOS

Laboratory of General and Agricultural Meteorology: AIKATERINI CHRONOPOULOU-SERELI

Laboratory of General and Agricultural Microbiology: GEORGE AGGELIS

Laboratory of General Chemistry: MOSCHOS POLISSIOU

Laboratory of Genetics: MICHAEL LOUKAS

Laboratory of Informatics: ALEXANDROS SIDERIDIS

Laboratory of Mathematics and Theoretical Mechanics: TAKIS SAKKALIS

Laboratory of Microbiology and Biotechnology of Foods: G. I. NYCHAS

Laboratory of Mineralogy and Geology: GEORGE MIGIROS

Laboratory of Molecular Biology: POLYDEUKIS HATZOPOULOS

Laboratory of Pesticide Science: BASIL ZIOGAS

Laboratory of Physics: ATHANASIOS HOUNTAS

Laboratory of Plant Breeding and Biometry: PANTOUSES J. KALTSIKES

Laboratory of Plant Physiology and Morphology: IOANNIS DROSSOPOULOS

Laboratory of Political Economy and European Integration: MARTINOS NIKOLAOS

Laboratory of Pomology: CONSTANTINE A. PONTIKIS

Laboratory of Rural Economic Development: SOPHIA EFSTRATOGLOU

Laboratory of Rural Policy and Cooperatives: DAMIANOS DIMITRIS

Laboratory of Sericulture and Apiculture: PASCHALIS HARIZANIS

Laboratory of Soil Science and Agricultural Chemistry: KOLLIAS VASSILIKI

Laboratory of Vegetable Crops: CHRISTOS M. OLYMPIOS

Laboratory of Viticulture: MANOLIS N. STAVRAKAKIS

HAROKOPIO PANEPISTIMION
(Harokopio University)

70 El. Venizelou St, 17671 Athens

Telephone: 210-9549100

Fax: 210-9577050

E-mail: haruniv@hua.gr

Internet: www.hua.gr

Founded 1990

State control

Rector: ANDREAS KIRIAKOUSIS

Vice-Rector for Academic Affairs and Staff: KATERINA MARIDAKI-KASSOTAKI

Vice-Rector for Economic Planning and Development: SMARAGDI ANTONOPOULOU

Library of 8,000 vols, 200 journals

Number of teachers: 65

Number of students: 430

IKONOMIKON PANEPISTIMION ATHINON
(Athens University of Economics and Business)

Odos Patission 76, 104 34 Athens

Telephone: 210-8203250

Fax: 210-822841947 Evelpidon Str., 113 62 Athens

Telephone: 210-8203640

Fax: 210-8228655

Internet: www.aueb.gr

Founded 1920

Faculties of business administration, computer science, economics, international and European economic studies, management science, marketing and statistics

Rector: Prof. ANDREAS KINTIS

Sec.-Gen.: S. BENOS

Librarian: G. THEOFANOPOULOU

Library of 100,000 vols, 1,000 periodicals: See Libraries and Archives

Number of teachers: 118

Number of students: 11,800

IONIO PANEPISTIMIO
(Ionian University)

Rizospaston Voulefton 7, 491 00 Corfu

Telephone: 2661-044878

Fax: 2661-022549

E-mail: int_rel@ionio.gr

Internet: www.ionio.gr

Founded 1984

State control

Academic year: October to July

Rector: DIMITRIOS TSOUGARAKIS

Vice-Rector for Academic Management and Human Resources: CHARALAMBOS XANTHOUDAKIS

Vice-Rector for Financial Management: VASILIOS CHRISIKOPOULOS

Departments of archives and library science, audio and visual arts, computer science, foreign languages, history, music studies, translation and interpreting.

PANEPISTIMION AEGAEOU
(University of the Aegean)

University Hill, Admin. Bldg 2, 811 00 Mytilene

Telephone: 2251-036000

Fax: 2251-036009

Internet: www.aegean.gr

Founded 1984

Chios campus: depts of business administration, shipping, transport and trade; Mytilene campus: depts of environmental studies, geography, marine sciences, social anthropology, sociology; Rhodes campus: depts of Mediterranean studies, primary education, secondary education; Samos campus: depts of mathematics, information and communication systems

Rector: Prof. SOKRATIS K. KATSIKAS

Librarian: ELLI VLACHOU

Library of 86,674 vols

Number of teachers: 422

Number of students: 11,828 (7,599 undergraduate, 4,229 postgraduate)

PANEPISTIMION IOANNINON
(University of Ioannina)

University Campus, 451 10 Ioannina

Telephone: 2651-097446

Fax: 2651-097200

E-mail: intlrel@cc.uoi.gr

Internet: www.uoi.gr

Founded 1964 as a dept of the Aristotle Univ. of Thessaloniki;ind. univ. 1970

State control

Language of instruction: Greek

Academic year: September to June

Rector: Prof. GEORGIOS DIMOU

Vice-Rectors: Prof. NIKI J. AGNANTIS, Prof. IOANNIS GEROTHANASIS, Prof. CHRISTOS MASSALAS

Registrar: L.-N. PAPALOUKAS

Librarian: GEORGIOS ZACHOS (acting)

Library of 310,000 vols

Number of teachers: 500

Number of students: 13,000

Publications: *Eperitis 'Dodoni I'* (History and Archaeology, 1 a year), *Eperitis 'Dodoni II'* (Philology, 1 a year), *Eperitis 'Dodoni III'* (Philosophy, Education and Psychology, 1 a year)

DEANS

School of Educational Sciences: Prof. A. PAPAIOANNOU

School of Medicine: Prof. EPAMINONDAS TSIANOS

School of Natural Resources in Agrinio: Prof. GEORGE LEONTARIS (acting)

School of Natural Sciences: Prof. GEORGIOS KARAKOSTAS

School of Philosophy: Prof. ERATOSTHENIS KAPSOMENOS

School of Science and Technology: (vacant)

PROFESSORS

School of Educational Sciences (tel. 2651-097454; fax 2651-097020):

DIMOU, G., Pedagogics and Psychology of Learning Disabilities

KANAVAKIS, M., Pedagogics

KAPSALIS, G.

KARAFYLIS, G., Society Philosophy

KARPOZILOU, M.

KONSTANTINOU, C., School Pedagogics

STAVROU, L., Psychology of Pre-School Education

TZOULIS, CH., Modern Greek Literature

ZAHARIS, D., Evolutionary Psychology in Education

School of Medicine (tel. 2651-097201; fax 2651-097019):

AGNADI-GIRA, N. J., Pathological Anatomy

ANDRONIKOU, S., Neo-Natology

ASIMAKOPOULOS, C., Otorhinolaryngology

BERIS, A., Orthopaedics

BOURANTAS, C., Pathology, Haematology

DROSOS, A., Pathology-Rheumatology

EFRAIMIDIS, S., Radiology

EVANGELOU, A., Physiology

FOTSIS, TH., Biological Chemistry

GEORGATOS, S., Biology

GEROULANOS, ST., History of Medicine

GLAROS, D., Medical Physics

HATZIS, I., Dermatology

IOANNIDIS, I., Hygiene

KALEF-EZRA, J., Medical Physics

KANAVAROS, P., Anatomy-Histology

KAPPAS, A., Surgery

KIRITSIS, A., Neurology

KONSTANTOPOULOS, S., Pathology and Pneumonology

LOLIS, D., Obstetrics and Gynaecology

MALAMOU-MITSI, V., Pathology

MARSELOS, M.-A., Medical Pharmacology

MAVREAS, V., Psychiatry

PAPADOPOULOS, G., Anaesthiology

PARASKEVAIDIS, C., Organic Peptide Chemistry

PAVLIDIS, N., Oncology

PSILAS, C., Ophthalmology

SEFERIADIS, C., Biological Chemistry

SIAMOPOULOS, K., Pathology and Nephrology

SIAMOPOULOU-MAVRIDOU, A., Paediatrics

SKEVAS, A., Otorhinolaryngology

SOFIKITIS, N., Urology

SOUCACOS, P., Orthopaedics

TSIANOS, E., Oncology

TZAFLIDOU, M., Medical Physics

XENAKIS, T., Orthopaedics

School of Natural Resources in Agrinio:

FOTOPOULOS, CH., Administration of Agricultural Enterprises

MATTHOPOULOS, D., Administration of Environment and Natural Resources

School of Natural Sciences (tel. 2651-097190; fax 2651-097005):

AKRIVIS, G., Computer Science

ALBANIS, T., Environmental Protection

ALISSANDRAKIS, C., Physics of the Sun and Space

ASSIMAKOPOULOS, P., Nuclear Physics and Radio Ecology

BAIKOUSIS, CH., Differential Geometry

BATAKIS, N., Physics

BOLIS, TH., Combinatorial Group Theory

BOLOVINOS, AG., Atomic and Molecular Physics

DOUGIAS, S., Mathematical Analysis

DRAINAS, C., Chemistry

EVANGELOU, SP., Physics, Theory of Condensed Matter

EVMIRIDIS, N., Inorganic Chemistry

FERENTINOS, K., Statistics

FILOS, C., Mathematical Analysis

GALATSANOS, N., Computer Science

GEROTHANASIS, I., Organic Chemistry

GRAMMATIKOPOULOS, M., Differential Equations

HADJILIADIS, N., Inorganic and General Chemistry

HASANIS, T., Differential Geometry

KAMARATOS, E., Physical Chemistry

KAMBANOS, T., Inorganic Chemistry

KARAKOSTAS, G., Mathematical Analysis and Applications

KATSARAS, A., Functional Analysis

KATSOULIS, V., Meteorology and Climatology

KONDOMINAS, M., Chemistry

KOSMAS, M., Chemistry

KOSTARAKIS, P., Physics

KOUFOGIORGOS, TH., Differential Geometry

KOVALA-DEMERTZI, D., Inorganic Chemistry

LAGARIS, I., Computer Science

LEONDARIS, G., Physics, Elemental Multiplets

LOUKAS, S., Statistics

MANESIS, E., Physics, High Energy Theory

MARMARIDIS, N., Algebra

MASSALAS, CH., Continuum Physics and Mechanics

PANTIS, G., Theory of Nuclear Physics

PHILOS, C., Differential Equations

POMONIS, F., Industrial Chemistry

SAKARELLO DAITSO, M., Biochemistry

SAKARELLOS, C., Organic Peptide Chemistry

SDOUKOS, A., Industrial Chemistry

SFIKAS, Y. G., Differential Equations

STAVROULAKIS, I., Differential Equations

TAMVAKIS, K., Elementary Particle Theory and Cosmology

TRIANTIS, F., High-Energy Physics and Related Technological Applications

TSAMATOS, P., Mathematical Analysis

TSANGARIS, J., Inorganic and General Chemistry

VAGIONAKIS, C., Physics

VERGADOS, J., Theoretical Physics

School of Philosophy (tel. 2651-097176):

APOSTOLOPOULOU, G., History, Interpretation and Practice of Philosophy

ATHANASIOU, L., Language Teaching and Evaluation

CHADJIDAKI-BAHARA, T., Byzantine Archaeology

GOTOVOS, A., Pedagogics

HADJIDAKI-BACHARA, T., Byzantine Archaeology

KAPSOMENOS, E., Modern Greek Literature and Literary Theory

KARPOZILOS, A.-D., Medieval Greek Literature

KATSOURIS, A., Ancient Greek Philology

KONDORINI, B., History and Archaeology

KONSTANDINIDIS, C., Ancient and Medieval Greek Literature

KORDOSIS, M., Ancient and Medieval Greek Literature

MARAGOU, E., Classical Archaeology

MAVROMATIS, J., Byzantine Philology and Post-Byzantine Philology

MAVROYIORGOS, Y., Pedagogic Educational Policy

NOUTSOS, CH., History of Education

NOUTSOS, P., Philosophy

PALIOURAS, A., Byzantine Archaeology

PAPACONSTANDINOU, P., Pedagogics

PAPADIMITRIOU, E., Philosophy

PAPADOPOULOS, A., Prehistoric Archaeology

PAPAGEORGIOU, G., Modern History

PAPAPOSTOLOU, J., Classical Archaeology

PERISSINAKIS, J., Ancient Greek Literature

PLOUMIDIS, G., Venetian History and Historical Geography

RAIOS, D., Ancient Greek and Latin Philology

SIOROKAS, G., Modern European History

STASINOS, D., Psychology

SYNODINOU, A., Ancient Greek Philology

TRIANTI, A., Archaeology

TSANGALAS, K., Folklore

School of Science and Technology:

CHARALAMBOPOULOS, A., Material Science

DRAINAS, C., Chemistry

KAXIRAS, E., Material Science

MASSALAS, CH., Continuum Physics and Mechanics

PSARROPOULOU, A., Animal Physiology

Independent Department of Economics:

PALYVOS, TH., Economics

PANEPISTIMIO KRITIS
(University of Crete)

741 00 Rethymnon, Crete

Telephone: 2831-077900

Fax: 2831-077909

E-mail: rectsecr@cc.uoc.gr

Internet: www.uoc.gr

Founded 1973

State control

Language of instruction: Greek

Academic year: September to June

Rector: Prof. CHRISTOS NIKOLAOU

Vice-Rectors: Prof. MICHAEL DAMANAKIS, Prof. AGELOS KRANIDIS

Dir for Int. and Public Relations: Dr STELLA PAPADAKI-TZEDAKI

Librarian: MICHALIS TZEKAKIS

Library of 145,000 vols

Number of teachers: 580

Number of students: 10,628

Publications: *Ariadne* (faculty of letters), *Mandatoforos* (Modern Greek studies).

AFFILIATED INSTITUTION

Foundation for Research and Technology–Hellas: POB 1385, 711 10 Heraklion; tel. 281-391500; fax 281-391555; e-mail central@admin.forth.gr; internet www.forth.gr; f. 1983; 254 research and teaching staff; 374 graduate students; Chair. Prof. E. N. ECONOMOU.

Constituent Institutes:

Institute of Applied and Computational Mathematics: internet www.iacm.forth.gr; Dir Prof. VASSILIOS DOUGALIS.

Institute of Chemical Engineering and High Temperature Chemical Processes: internet www.iceht.forth.gr; Dir Prof. A. C. PAYATAKES.

Institute of Chemical Process Engineering Research: internet www.cperi.forth.gr; Dir Prof. C. KIPARISSIDES.

Institute of Computer Science: internet www.ics.forth.gr; Dir Prof. CONSTANTINE STEPHANIDIS.

Institute of Electronic Structure and Lasers: internet www.iesl.forth.gr; Dir Prof. C. FOTAKIS.

Institute of Mediterranean Studies: internet www.ims.forth.gr; Dir Prof. A. KALPAXIS.

Institute of Molecular Biology and Biotechnology: internet www.imbb.forth.gr; Dir Prof. G. THIREOS.

PANEPISTIMION MAKEDONIAS
(University of Macedonia)

Egnatia 156, POB 1591, 540 06 Thessaloniki

Telephone: 231-0844825

Fax: 231-0844536
E-mail: grad@uom.gr
Internet: www.uom.gr
Founded 1957 as Graduate Industrial School
of Thessaloniki
State control
Rector: Prof. KONSTANTINOS VELENZAS
Vice-Rectors: Prof. CONSTANTINOS MARGARI-
TIS, Prof. CONSTANTINOS VELENTZAS
Secretary-General: TSOMOU-FISTA EVAGGELIA
Librarian: ANNA FRANKOU
Number of teachers: 108
Number of students: 8,000

PROFESSORS

ALYGIZAKIS, ANTONIOS, Music Science and Art
BARALEXIS, SPYROS, Accounting and Finance
CHARALAMPOUS, DIMITRIOS, Educational and
Social Studies
GEORGANTA, ZOE, Applied Informatics
IOANNIDIS, DIMITRIOS, Economics
KAPSALIS, ACHILEAS, Educational and Social
Studies
KARAGIANNI, STELLA, Economics
KARFAKIS, COSTAS, Economics
KATOS, ANASTASIOS, Applied Informatics
KATRANIDIS, STELIOS, Economics
KONSTANTOPOULOU, CHRYSSOULA, Applied
Informatics
KOUSKOUVELIS, ILIAS, International, Euro-
pean, Economic and Political Studies
LABRIANIDIS, LOIS, Economics
LAZARIDIS, JOHN, Accounting and Finance
LAZOS, BAIOS, Business Administration
MARGARITIS, KONSTANTINOS, Applied Inform-
atics
MOURMOURAS, IOANNIS, Economics
NOULAS, ATHANASIOS, Accounting and
Finance
PALIVOS, THEODORE, Economics
PAPADIMITRIOU, JOHN, Applied Informatics
PAPADOPOULOS, DIMITRIOS, Accounting and
Finance
PAPAMATTHEOU MATSCHKE, HANS-UWE, Music
Science and Art
PAPARRIZOS, KONSTANTINOS, Applied Inform-
atics
PAULIDIS, GEOGRIOS, Educational and Social
Studies
PEKOS, GEORGE, Applied Informatics
PIPEROPOULOS, GEORGE, Business Adminis-
tration
SKALIDIS, ELEFTHERIOS, Accounting and
Finance
TARABANIS, KONSTANTINOS, Business Admin-
istration
THEMELI, CHRISANTHI, Accounting and
Finance
THEODOSIOU, IOANNIS, Economics
TRIARHOU, LAZAROS, Educational and Social
Studies
TSIOTRAS, GEORGE, Business Administration
TSOPELA, VINIA, Music Science and Art
VELENTZAS, KONSTANTINOS, Economics
XIARHOS, STAVROS, Economics
XIROTIRI-KOUFIDOU, STELLA, Business Admin-
istration
XOURIS, DIMITRIOS, Business Administration

PANEPISTIMION PATRON
(University of Patras)

University Campus, 265 04 Patras
Telephone: (261) 991822
Fax: (261) 991771
E-mail: rectorate@upatras.gr
Internet: www.upatras.gr
Founded 1964
State control
Language of instruction: Greek
Academic year: September to August
Rector: Prof. STAVROS KOUBIAS
Vice-Rector for Academic Affairs and Person-
nel: Prof. DIMITRIOS DOUGENIS

Vice-Rector for Financial Planning and Devt:
Prof. KONSTANTINOS RAVANIS
Vice-Rector for Strategic Research Planning
and Devt: Prof. VASSILIOS ANASTASSOPOU-
LOS
Admin. Officer: CHRISTINA KOLOKITHA
Number of teachers: 925
Number of students: 27,586

DEANS

School of Engineering: Prof. NIKOLAOS
SPYROU
School of Health Sciences: Prof. GEORGIOS
NIKIFORIDIS
School of Humanities and Social Sciences:
Prof. CHRISTOS TEREZIS
School of Natural Sciences: Assoc. Prof.
AVRAAM ZELILIDIS

PROFESSORS

School of Economics and Management Sciences

Department of Business Administration:

PAVLIDES, G.
SYRIPOULOS, K.
VERNARDAKIS, N.
ZAHARATOS, G.

Department of Economics:

DAOULI-DEMOUSI, I.
DEMOUSSIS, M.
DIMARA, E.
SKOURAS, D.
SYPSAS, P.

School of Engineering
Department of Architecture:

POLYDORIDES, N.

Department of Chemical Engineering:

DASSIOS, G.
KENNOU, ST.
KOUTSOUKOS, P.
KRAVARIS, K.
LADAS, S.
LYBERATOS, G.
NIKOLOPOULOS, P.
PANDIS, S.
PAVLOU, S.
PAYATAKES, A.
RAPAKOULIAS, D.
TSAHALIS, D.
TSAMOPOULOS, J.
TSITSILIANIS, K.
VAYENAS, C.
VERYKIOS, X.

Department of Civil Engineering:

ANAGNOSTOPOULOS, S.
ATHANASOPOULOS, G.
ATMATZIDIS, D.
BESKOS, D.
CHRYSIKOPOULOS, K.
DEMETRACOPOULOS, A.
DRITSOS, ST.
FARDIS, M.
KALERIS, V.
KARABALIS, D.
MAKRIS, N.
PAPAGEORGIOU, A.
STEFANIDIS, G.
THEODORAKOPOULOS, D.
TRIANTAFYLLOU, A.

Department of Computer Engineering and
Informatics:

ALEXIOU, G.
BERBERIDIS, K.
BOURAS, CH.
CHRISTODOULAKIS, D.
GALLOPOULOS, E.
KAKLAMANIS, CH.
KIROUSSIS, E.
KOSMADAKIS, S.
LIKOTHANASSIS, S.
NIKOLOS, D.
PAPATHEODOROU, TH.

SPIRAKIS, P.
TRIANTAPHILLOU, P.
TSAKALIDIS, A.
VARVARIGOS, E.
ZAROLIAGKIS, CH.

Department of Electrical and Computer
Engineering:

ALEXANDRIDIS, A.
ANTONAKOPOULOS, TH.
AVOURIS, N.
BIRBAS, A.
BITSORIS, G.
FAKOTAKIS, N.
GALATSANOS, N.
GIANNAKOPOULOS, G.
GOUTIS, C.
GROUMPOS, P.
HOUSSOS, E.
KOTSOPOULOS, ST.
KOUBIAS, S.
KOUFOPAVLOU, O.
KOUSSOULAS, N.
MOURTZOPOULOS, I.
MOUSTAKIDES, G.
PIMENIDIS, T.
SAFACAS, A.
SERPANOS, D.
SPYROU, N.
STOURAITIS, A.
TZES, A.
VOVOS, N.

Department of Engineering Science:

HATZIKONSTANTINOU, P.
IOAKIMIDIS, N.
KOUTROUVELIS, I.
LIANOS, P.
MARKELLOS, V.
PAPADAKIS, K.
PERDIOS, E.
POLITIS, C.
SFETSOS, K.
VELGAKIS, M.

Department of Mechanical Engineering and
Aeronautics:

AIKATERINARIS, I.
ANIFANTIS, N.
ASPRAGATHOS, N.
CHRYSSOLOURIS, G.
FASSOISS, S.
KALLINTERIS, I.
KARAKAPILIDIS, N.
KOSTOPOULOS, V.
MISSIRLIS, I.
PANTELAKIS, S.
PAPANICOLAOU, G.
POLYZOS, D.
SARAVANOS, D.

School of Health Sciences
Faculty of Medicine:

ALEXANDRIDIS, TH.
ALEXOPOULOS, D.
ANASTASIOU, E.
ANDONOPOULOS, A.
ATHANASIADOU-GIKA, A.
BASSIARIS, H.
BERATI, S.
DIMAKOPOULOS, P.
DIMOPOULOS, J.
DOUGENIS, D.
DRAINAS, D.
FLORDELLIS, CH.
GARTAGANIS, S.
GOGOS, C.
GOUMAS, P.
KALFARENTZOS, F.
KALOFONOS, CH.
KALPAKSIS, D.
KARAVIAS, D.
KOSTOPOULOS, G.
KYRIAZOPOULOU, V.
MANTAGOS, S.
MARAZIOTIS, TH.
MOSXONAS, N.

MOUZAKI, A.
NIKIFORIDIS, G.
NIKOLOPOULOU, V.
PALIOGIANNI, PH.
PALLIKARAKIS, N.
PANAGIOTAKIS, G.
PANAGIOTOPOULOS, I.
PAPANASTASIOU, D.
PAPATHANASOPOULOS, P.
PERIMENIS, P.
SIABLIS, D.
SKOPA, CH.
SPYROPOULOS, K.
SYNETOS, D.
TSAMBAOS, D.
TYLLIANAKIS, M.
TZORAKOELETHERAKIS, E.
VASILAKOS, P.
VLACHOJANNIS, J.
ZOUMBOS, N.

Department of Pharmacy:
CORDOPATIS, P.
TZARTOS, S.

School of School of Humanities and Social Sciences

Department of Educational Sciences and Early Childhood Education:
RAVANIS, K.
XIROMERITI, A.
ZOGZA, V.

Department of Philology:
RALLI, A.

Department of Philosophy:
PATELI, I.
TEREZIS, CH.

Department of Primary Education:
BOUZAKIS, J.
DELLIS, I.
GEORGOGIANNIS, P.
KATSILLIS, I.
KOLEZA, E.
KRIVAS, S.
LAMPROPOULOU, V.
PORPODAS, C.
VERGIDIS, D.

Department of Theatre Studies:
STEFANOPOULOS, TH.
XAAS, D.

School of Natural Sciences
Department of Biology:
ALAHIOTIS, ST.
CHRSISTODOULAKIS, D.
DEMOPOULOS, N.
DIMITRIADIS, G.
GEORGIADIS, TH.
GEORGIOU, CH.
ILIOPOULOU, I.
KAMARI-FITOU, G.
KOUTSIKOPOULOS, C.
MANETAS, I.
PSARAS, G.
STEPHANOU, G.
TZANOUDAKIS, D.
YANNOPOULOS, G.
ZACHAROPOULOU, A.
ZAGRIS, N.

Department of Chemistry:
BARLOS, K.
CHRISTOPOULOS, TH.
GLAVAS, S.
IOANNOU, P.
KALLITSIS, I.
KANELLAKI, M.
KARAISKAKIS, G.
KARAMANOS, N.
KLOURAS, N.
KORDOULIS, CH.
KOUTINAS, A.
LYCOURGHIOTIS, A.
MANESI, E.
MAROULIS, G.

MATSOUKAS, J.
MIKROYIANNIDIS, J.
NTALAS, E.
PAPAIOANNOU, D.
PERLEPES, S.
POULOS, C.
TSEGENIDIS, TH.
VYNIOS, D.
ZAFIROPOULOS, TH.

Department of Geology:
CHRISTANIS, K.
CONTOPOULOS, N.
FERENTINOS, G.
FRYDAS, D.
HATZIPANAGIOTOU, K.
KALLERGIS, G.
KATAGAS, C.
KOUKIS, G.
LABRAKIS, N.
PAPAMARINOPOULOS, S.
TSELENTIS, G.
TSOLIS-KATAGAS, P.
VARNAVAS, S.
ZELILIDIS, A.

Department of Material Science:
GALIOTIS, C.
PHOTINOS, D.

Department of Mathematics:
BOUNTIS, A.
COTSIOLIS, A.
DROSSOS, C.
FILIPPOU, A.
KAFOUSSIAS, N.
KONTOLATOU, A.
KOTSIOLIS, A.
KOUROUKLIS, S.
METAKIDES, G.
PAPANTONIOU, V.
PHILIPPOU, A.
PINTELAS, P.
PNEVMATIKOS, S.
SAMARIS, N.
SIAFARIKAS, P.
TSOUBELIS, D.
TZANNES, V.
VRAHATIS, M.
ZAGOURAS, CH.

Department of Physics:
ANASTASOPOULOS, V.
BAKAS, I.
FOTOPOULOS, S.
GEORGAS, A.
GEROGIANNIS, V.
GIANNOULIS, P.
GOUDIS, CHR.
HARITANTIS, I.
KARAHALIOS, G.
KOURIS, ST.
MYTILINEOU, E.
PERSEFONIS, P.
PIZANIAS, M.
SAKKOPOULOS, S.
TOPRAKTSIOGLOU, CH.
YIANOULIS, P.
ZDETSIS, A.
ZIOUTAS, K.

PANEPISTIMIO PELOPONNESOU
(University of the Peloponnese)

28 Erithrou Stayrou and Kariotaki Sts, 221 00 Tripolis
Telephone and fax 2710-230006
E-mail: info@uop.gr
Internet: www.uop.gr
Founded 2002
State control
Chair., Board of Trustees: CONSTANTIN DIMO-POULOS
Vice-Chair., Board of Trustees: IOANNIS PARA-SKEVOPOULOS

PROFESSORS
Department of Social and Education Policy (Damaskinou and Kolokotroni Sts, 201 00 Korinth; tel. 27410-74991; fax 27410-74993; e-mail sep-secr@uop.gr):

KLADIS, D., Education Policy
KOULAIDIS, V., Design of Educational Programmes
KOULOURI, C., History of Modern Greek Education and Society

Department of Telecommunications Science and Technology (End of Karaiskaki St, 221 00 Tripolis; tel. 2710-372163; fax 2710-372160; e-mail ntalagan@uop.gr):

BOUCOUVALAS, A. C.
MARAS, A.

PANEPISTIMION PIREOS
(University of Piraeus)

80 Karaoli and Dimitriou St, 185 34 Piraeus
Telephone: 210-4142000
Fax: 210-4142328
E-mail: publ@unipi.gr
Internet: www.unipi.gr
Founded 1938, univ. status 1958

Depts of business administration, economics, statistics and insurance science, financial management and banking, industrial management, informatics, maritime studies, teachers education and technology

Rector: T. GAMALETSOS
Sec.: A. GOTSIS
Library of 27,000 vols, 200 periodicals
Number of teachers: 90
Number of students: 11,400

Publication: *Spoudai* (4 a year).

PANEPISTIMIO THESALIAS
(University of Thessaly)

Argonafton and Filellinon, 382 21 Volos
Telephone: 2421-074000
E-mail: webmaster@uth.gr
Internet: www.uth.gr
Founded 1984
State control

Rector: Prof. CONSTANTINOS BAGIATIS
Vice-Rectors: Prof. CONSTANTINOS GOURGOU-LIANIS, Prof. NAPOLEON MITSIS
Library of 80,000 books, 828 journals

14 Departments in four schools (Agricultural Sciences, Engineering, Health Sciences and Humanities), and two independent departments (Economic Studies and Physical Education and Sport).

PANTEION PANEPESTIMION IKONOMIKON KAI POLITCON EPISTIMON
('Panteios' University of Social and Political Sciences)

Leoforos A. Syngrou 136, 176 71 Athens
Telephone: 210-9220100
Fax: 210-9223690
E-mail: rector@panteion.gr
Internet: www.panteion.gr
Founded 1930

Rector: D. CONSTAS
Gen. Sec.: M. VARELLA
Number of students: 7,500

POLYTECHNION KRITIS
(Technical University of Crete)

Agiou Markou St, 731 32 Chania
Telephone: 2821-037047
Fax: 2821-028418
E-mail: intoffice@isc.tuc.gr
Internet: www.tuc.gr

Founded 1977, first student intake 1984
State control
Academic year: September to June
Rector: Prof. JOAKIM GRISPOLAKIS
Vice-Rector for Academic Affairs and Personnel: Prof. MICHALIS PATERAKIS
Vice-Rector for Planning and Devt: Prof. NIKOS BAROTSIS
Librarian: MARIA NTAOUNTAKI
Library of 30,000 vols
Number of teachers: 212 (incl. 91 full profs)
Number of students: 2,500

DIRECTORS OF LABORATORIES

Air, Water and Solid Wastes Management: ALEXANDER P. ECONOMOPOULOS
Analytical and Environmental Chemistry: NIKOLAOS KALLITHRAKAS-KONTOS
Applied Geology: ZACHARIAS G. AGIOUTANTIS
Applied Geophysics: ANTONIS VAFIDIS
Applied Mathematics and Computers: YIANNIS SARIDAKIS
Applied Mechanics: CONSTAS P. PROVIDAKIS
Applied Mineralogy: GEORGE KOSTAKIS
Applied Socioeconomic Research: GEORGE LIODAKIS
Atmospheric Aerosol: MIHALIS LAZARIDIS
Automation: MICHALIS ZERVAKIS
Biochemical Engineering and Environmental Biotechnology: NIKOS KALOGERAKIS
Ceramics and Glass Technology: ATHINA TSETSEKOU
Chemical Processes and Wastewater Treatment: DIONYSIOS MANTZAVINOS
Computer-Aided Design and Robotics: NIKOLAOS BILALIS
Computer-Aided Manufacturing: YIANNIS PHILLIS
Data Analysis and Forecasting: CHRISTOS SKIADAS
Decision Support Systems: ATHANASIOS MIGDALAS
Digital Image and Signal Processing: MICHALIS ZERVAKIS
Distributed Multimedia Information Systems and Applications: STAVROS CHRISTODOULAKIS
Drilling Technology and Applied Fluid Mechanics: VASSILIOS KELESSIDIS
Dynamic Systems and Simulation: MARKOS PAPAGEORGIOU
Ecology and Biodiversity: NIKOS KALOGERAKIS
Electric Circuits and Renewable Energy Sources: KOSTAS KALAITZAKIS
Electrical Circuits and Electronics: PAVLOS S. GEORGILAKIS
Electronics: KOSTAS KALAITZAKIS
Environmental Engineering and Management: EVAN DIAMADOPOULOS
Financial Engineering: CONSTANTIN ZOPOUNIDIS
General Geology: EMMANOUEL MANUTSOGLU
Geodesy and Geomatics Enigineering: STELIOS MERTIKAS
Geoenvironmental Engineering: GEORGE KARATZAS
Geostatistics: DIONISSIOS T. HRISTOPOULOS
Hydrogeochemical Engineering and Soil Remediation: NIKOLAOS NIKOLAIDIS
Information and Computer Networks: VASSILIS DIGALAKIS
Inorganic and Organic Geochemistry and Organic Petrography: VASSILIS PERDIKATSIS
Intelligent Systems: EMMANOUEL KOUMBARAKIS
Intelligent Systems and Robotics: NIKOS C. TSOURVELOUDIS
Management Systems: VASSILIS MOUSTAKIS
Materials Structure and Laser Physics: STAVROS MOUSTAIZIS
Microprocessor and Hardware: APOSTOLOS DOLLAS
Mine Design: GEORGE EXADAKTYLOS
Mineral Processing: ELIAS STAMBOLIADIS

Minerals Quality Control — Health and Safety: MICHAEL GALETAKIS
Mining and Metallurgical Waste Management: KOSTAS KOMNITSAS
Petrology and Economic Geology: THEODOROS MARKOPOULOS
Physical Chemistry and Chemical Processes: IOANNIS V. YENTEKAKIS
PVT and Core Analysis: NIKOS VAROTSIS
Robotics: ANASTASIOS POULIEZOS
Rock Mechanics: ZACHARIAS G. AGIOUTANTIS
Safety of Work and Cognitive Ergonomics: TOM KONTOGIANNIS
Software Systems and Network Application: EMMANOUEL KOUMBARAKIS
Solid Fuels Benification and Technology: DESPINA VAMVOUKA
Telecommunications: NIKOS SIDIROPOULOS
Toxic and Hazardous Waste Management: EVANGELOS GIDARAKOS
Transport Phenomena and Applied Thermodynamics: VASSILIS GEKAS
Water Resources Management and Coastal Engineering: IOANNIS K. TSANIS

PROFESSORS

AGIOUTANIS, Z.
ALEVIZOS, G.
AVDELAS, G.
BALAS, K.
BILALIS, N.
CHRISTIDIS, G.
CHRISTODOULAKIS, S.
CHRISTODOULOU, M.
CHRISTOPOULOS, D.
DARRAS, T.
DELLIS, A.
DIAMADOPOULOS, E.
DIGALAKIS, V.
DOLLAS, A.
DOUMPOS, M.
ECONOMOPOULOS, A.
ELLINAS, D.
EXADAKTYLOS, G.
FOSCOLOS, A.
FRAGOMIHELAKIS, M.
GALETAKIS, M.
GEKAS, V.
GEORGILAKIS, P.
GIDARAKOS, E.
GRIGOROUDIS, E.
GRYSPOLAKIS, J.
KALAITZAKIS, K.
KALLITHRAKAS, K. N.
KALOGERAKIS, N.
KANDYLAKIS, D.
KARAKASSIS, I.
KARATZAS, G.
KATSANOS, A.
KAVOURIDIS, K.
KELESIDIS, V.
KOMNITSAS, K.
KONTOGIANNIS, T.
KOSMATOPOULOS, E.
KOSTAKIS, G.
KOUBARAKIS, E.
KOUIKOGLOU, V.
LAZARIDIS, M.
LIODAKIS, G.
MANOUTSOGLOU, E.
MANTZAVINOS, D.
MARIA, E.
MARKOPOULOS, T.
MATHIOUDAKIS, M.
MATSATSINIS, N.
MERTIKAS, S.
MIGDALAS, A.
MONOPOLIS, D.
MOUSTAIZIS, S.
MOUSTAKIS, V.
NIKOLAIDIS, N.
NIKOLOS, I.
PANTINAKIS, A.
PAPADOPOULOU, E.
PAPAGEORGIOU, M.
PASADAKIS, N.

PATELIS, D.
PATERAKIS, M.
PERDIKATSIS, V.
PETRAKIS, E.
PETRAKIS, M.
PHILLIS, Y.
PNEVMATIKATOS, D.
POTAMIANOS, A.
POULIEZOS, A.
PROVIDAKIS, K.
SAMELIS, A.
SAMOLADAS, V.
SARIDAKIS, Y.
SIDIROPOULOS, N.
SINOLAKIS, K.
SKIADAS, C.
STAMPOLIADIS, E.
STAVRAKAKIS, G.
STAVROULAKIS, P.
SYNOLAKIS, C.
TRAFALIS, T.
TSANIS, I.
TSETSEKOU, A.
TSOMPANAKIS, I.
TSOURVELOUDIS, N.
VAFIDIS, A.
VAMVOUKA, D.
VAROTSIS, N.
YENTEKAKIS, Y.
ZERVAKIS, M.
ZOPOUNIDIS, K.

ATTACHED INSTITUTE

Institute of Telecommunications Systems: e-mail tsi@tsinet.gr; internet www.tsinet.gr; Dir Prof. MICHALIS PATERAKIS.

Colleges
ARCHAEOLOGY, GREEK STUDIES

American School of Classical Studies at Athens: Odos Souidias 54, 106 76 Athens; tel. 210-7236313; fax 210-7250584; e-mail ascsa@ascsa.edu.gr; internet www.ascsa.edu.gr; f. 1881; research institute and postgraduate school for students of classical and post-classical literature, history and archaeology; controlled by a committee representing 160 American and Canadian universities; library: Gennadius and Blegen libraries with 195,000 vols; 13 teachers; 60 students; Dir STEPHEN V. TRACY; publ. *Hesperia* (4 a year).

British School at Athens: Odos Souidias 52, 106 76 Athens; tel. 210-7210974; fax 210-7236560 *London office*: Senate House, Malet St, London, WC1E 7HU, United Kingdom; tel. (20) 7862-8732; fax (20) 7862-8733; e-mail admin@bsa.ac.uk; internet www.bsa.gla.ac.uk; f. 1886; archaeology and Hellenic studies; Fitch Laboratory for research and analysis; library: over 60,000 vols (ancient, medieval and post-medieval Greek studies and archaeology of all periods) incl. the Finlay Library (Greek travel and modern Greek studies); Chair. Prof. Lord COLIN RENFREW; Dir Dr JAMES WHITLEY; London Sec. HELEN FIELDS.

Deutsches Archäologisches Institut, Abteilung Athen (German Archaeological Institute in Athens): Odos Fidiou 1, 106 78 Athens; tel. 210-3307400; fax 210-3814762; e-mail sekretariat@athen.dainst.org; internet www.dainst.de; f. 1874; library: 66,000 vols; Dirs Prof. Dr WOLF-DIETRICH NIEMEIER, Dr REINHARD SENFF; publs *Athenische Mitteilungen* (1 a year), *Beihefte*.

Ecole Française d'Athènes (French Archaeological School): Odos Didotou 6, 106 80 Athens; tel. 210-3679900; fax 210-3632101; e-mail efa@efa.gr; internet www.efa.gr; f. 1846; library: 80,000 vols; Dir D. MULLIEZ;

Sec.-Gen. M. BRUNET; publs *Bulletin de correspondance hellénique* (1 a year), *Bulletin des études grecques modernes et contemporaines* (1 a year).

Italian School of Archaeology at Athens/ Scuola Archeologica Italiana di Atene: 14 Parthenonos, 117 42 Athens; tel. 210-9239163; fax 210-9220908; e-mail segretario@scuoladiatene.it; internet www .scuoladiatene.it; f. 1909; postgraduate studies in archaeology, epigraphy and antiquities, ancient architecture; research and excavations in Greece; library: 48,300 vols; Dir Prof. EMANUELE A. GRECO; Library Dir Dr STEFANO GARBIN; publs *Annuario della Scuola Archeologica di Atene e delle Missioni Italiane in Oriente* (1 a year), *Monografie della Scuola Archeologica di Atene e delle Missoni Italiane in Oriente* (irregular), *Notiziario* (2 a year), *Tripodes* (irregular).

Svenska Institutet i Athen (Swedish Institute at Athens): 9 Mitseon St, 117 42 Athens; tel. 210-9232102; fax 210-9220925; e-mail swedinst@sia.gr; internet www.sia.gr; f. 1948; researches into Greek antiquity and archaeology, and cultural exchange between Sweden and Greece; library: 40,000 vols (housed at the Nordic Library, Kavalotti 7, 117 42 Athens); 2 teachers; 15 students; Dir

ANNE-LOUISE SCHALLIN; Librarian JENNY WALLENSTEN; publ. *Skrifter utgivna av Svenska Institutet i Athen* (Acta Instituti Atheniensis Regni Sueciae and *Opuscula Atheniensia*).

ARTS, DRAMA, MUSIC

American College of Greece: 6 Gravias St, Aghia Paraskevi, 153 42 Athens; tel. 210-6009800; fax 210-6009811; e-mail acg@acg .edu; internet www.acg.edu; f. 1875; comprises Deree College (BA courses in dance, economics, English, history, history of art, music, philosophy, psychology, sociology, BSc course in business administration, MBA), Junior College (associate degrees in arts and sciences) and Pierce College (high school); library: 150,000 vols; 250 teachers (incl. Junior College division); 5,000 students (incl. Junior College division); Pres. JOHN S. BAILEY; publ. *Library Series*.

Dramatiki Scholi (Drama School): National Theatre, Odos Menandrou 65, Athens; internet www.n-t.gr; f. 1924; open to actors who desire to improve their art and to young people who desire to take up the stage as a career; the staff comprises the director, 11 professors, and 2 teachers.

Kratiko Odeio Thessaloniki (State Conservatory of Music): Leondos Sofou Str. 16, 546 25 Thessaloniki; tel. 231-0510551; fax 231-0522158; e-mail odiokrat@otenet.gr; internet www.odiokrat.gr; f. 1914; instrumental, vocal and theoretical studies; 60 teachers; 630 students; library: 17,000 vols, scores, records, slides, compact discs, video cassettes, including collection in Braille; exhibition of musical instruments; Chair. Prof. P. I. RENTZEPERIS.

Attached Conservatory:

Odeion Athenon (Odeon of Athens): Odos Rigillis and Vassileos Georgiou 17–19, Athens; f. 1871; comprises a music section, a drama section, a section for military music, and a section for Byzantine Church music; 53 professors, 40 teachers and 1,200 students; Dir A. GAROUFALIS.

Odeion Ethnikon (National Conservatory): 8 Maizonos and 18 Mayer Sts, Athens 104 38; tel. 210-5233175; fax 210-5245291; e-mail ethnodio@otenet.gr; f. 1926; sections for music and opera; 200 teachers; 5,000 students; Dirs HARA KALOMIRI, PERIKLIS KOUKOS; publ. *Deltio* (1 a year).

GRENADA

The Higher Education System

Before 1968 higher education in Grenada was limited to the provision of sponsorship for study abroad. In that year Grenada acquired the Extra-Mural Department of the University of the West Indies (UWI) and the Grenada Teacher Training College was founded, its 2-year programme being monitored and certified by the UWI. In 1974 the Government established a number of other colleges relevant to the country's social and economic needs. During 1979–83 the new People's Revolutionary Government enhanced existing teacher-training programmes and increased scholarships offered for university and technical education abroad. The Institute of Higher Education in Grenada, which approximated the idea of a university, was also established during this period. In 1988 the restored, post-colonial Government amalgamated a number of institutions, including the Grenada Teachers College and the Institute for Further Education, to form the Grenada National College, which was renamed the T. A. Marryshow Community College (TAMCC) in 1996. In the same year the UWI and St George's University expanded their activities. In 1993 there were 651 students in higher education (excluding figures for the Grenada Teachers College). In 2006 there were 2,710 full-time, enrolled students at the T. A. Marryshow Community College. Technical Centres have been established in St Patrick's, St David's and St John's, and the Grenada National College, the Mirabeau Agricultural Training School and the Grenada Teachers College have been incorporated into the Technical and Vocational Institute in St George's.

The Government is responsible for higher education, although both St George's University and the UWI enjoy a greater degree of autonomy than does the TAMCC. The TAMCC is required by law to report directly to the Ministry of Education and Labour, primarily for financial purposes and for powers of jurisdiction. Higher education is governed by the Grenada Education Act, and the St George's University (School of Medicine) Act, 1976. The Ministry of Education and Labour is the main source of funding for the TAMCC. It also provides some support for the UWI, although this is largely funded through the collective contributions of the Caribbean countries to the UWI as a whole. St George's University is funded mainly by student fees. The Australian Agency for International Development is providing opportunities through the Australian Leadership Awards Scholarship to study at Masters or Doctorate level in an Australian university commencing in 2011.

Regulatory Bodies

GOVERNMENT

Ministry of Education and Labour: Ministry of Education Bldg, Ministerial Complex, Botanical Gardens, Tanteen, St George's; tel. 440-2737; fax 440-6650; internet www.grenadaedu.com; Minister CLARIS CHARLES.

Ministry of Tourism, Civil Aviation, Culture and the Performing Arts: Ministerial Complex, 4th Floor, Botanical Gardens, St George's; tel. 440-0366; fax 440-0443; e-mail tourism@gov.gd; internet www.grenada.mot.gd; Minister CLARICE MODESTE-CURWEN.

Learned Society

HISTORY, GEOGRAPHY AND ARCHAEOLOGY

Grenada National Trust: Grenada National Museum, Young St, St George's; tel. 440-3725; f. 1967 to preserve evidence of the history and growth of the island, and to support the Grenada National Museum; 240 mems; Pres. GORDON DE LA MOTHE; Sec. KAY SIMON.

Libraries and Archives

St George's

Founders Library, St George's University: POB 7, St George's; tel. 444-1573; fax 444-2884; e-mail library@sgu.edu; internet www.sgu.edu; f. 1979; 13,000 vols, 350 periodicals; Dir JOHN MCGUIRK.

Grenada Public Library: Carenage, St George's; tel. 440-2506; fax 440-6650; e-mail fedon2000@yahoo.com; f. 1853; 60,000 vols; spec. W Indian and Nat. Archives of Grenada collns; reference, research and lecture facilities; links its activities with other educational agencies; attached to Ministry of Education and Labour; Dir S. LILLIAN SYLVESTER; Librarian DEON DAVID.

Museum

St George's

Grenada National Museum: Young St, St George's; tel. 440-3725; fax 440-9292; f. 1976; history, technology, fauna and flora; Dir JEANNE FISHER; Curator HUGH THOMAS; publs *Art 'y' Facts* (2 a year), *Relics*.

Universities and Colleges

ST GEORGE'S UNIVERSITY

University Centre, POB 7, St George's

Telephone: 444-4175
Fax: 444-4823
E-mail: sguinfo@sgu.edu
Internet: www.sgu.edu

Founded 1977
Language of instruction: English
Academic year: August to June

Chancellor: CHARLES R. MODICA
Registrar: MARGARET LAMBERT
Librarian: JOHN MCGUIRK

Library: see Libraries and Archives

Number of teachers: 776 (76 full-time, 700 part-time)
Number of students: 2,000

DEANS

Arts and Sciences: T. HOLLIS
Basic Sciences: A. PENSICK
Clinical Studies: STEPHEN WEITZMAN
Veterinary Medicine: R. SIS

T. A. Marryshow Community College (TAMCC): Tanteen, St George's; tel. 440-1389; fax 440-3079; e-mail tamcc@caribsurf.com; internet www.tamcc.edu.gd; f. 1988 by a merger of The Grenada Teachers College, The Grenada Technical and Vocational Institute, The Institute for Further Education, The National Institute of Handicraft, The Mirabeau Agricultural Training School, The Domestic Arts Institute, The Continuing Education Programme and The School of Pharmacy; present name and status 1996; offers full-time and part-time programmes leading to Bachelors and Associate Degrees, Certificates and Diplomas; Prin. Dr JEFFERY BRITTON (acting); Registrar C. NIGEL GRAVE-SANDE; Dean of Applied Arts and Technology DESMOND LA TOUCHE; Dean of Arts, Sciences and Professional Studies Dr DUNBAR STEELE.

University of the West Indies School of Continuing Studies: Marryshow House, H. A. Blaize St, POB 439, St George's; tel. 440-2451; fax 440-4985; e-mail rtscsuwi@caribsurf.com; internet www.uwichill.edu.bb/bnccde/grenada; f. 1956; 1st-year univ. courses and general courses; library: 10,000 vols; folk theatre, telecommunications distance teaching centre; 27 teachers; 150 students; Resident Tutor BEVERLEY A. STEELE.

GUATEMALA

The Higher Education System

Under Spanish colonial rule, Guatemala was part of the Viceroyalty of New Spain. Independence was obtained from Spain in 1821, from Mexico in 1824 and from the Federation of Central American States in 1838. The oldest university is the Universidad de San Carlos de Guatemala, which was founded by King Carlos II of Spain in 1676. In total, there are 12 universities, of which 11 are privately run. Figures for 2005/06 showed that some 112,215 students were enrolled in further and higher education.

The main requirement for admission to university is the Bachiller or Bachillerato, the secondary school qualification. The Licenciado is the undergraduate degree and is awarded after four years, though some subjects (such as medicine) require longer periods of study. In professional fields of study, a professional title is awarded. Following the Licenciado, the first postgraduate degree is the Maestría, which is awarded after two years of study. However, the Doctorado can also be awarded following two years of study after the Licenciado, although some doctoral programmes require a Maestría.

Technical and vocational education is offered by the universities and specialized post-secondary institutions. The Instituto Técnico de Capitación y Productividad provides apprenticeships and courses. The main vocational qualification is the Diplomado, awarded after two-and-a-half to three years of study.

The responsibility for higher education in Guatemala, by constitutional mandate, is shared by the University of San Carlos, which is exclusively in charge of state-owned higher and professional university education, and by the private universities. The first is an autonomous institution, with legal status, which regulates and governs itself, while the latter are authorized and controlled by the Council of Private Higher Education. The University of San Carlos has also undertaken the task of tackling the problems in higher education including the creation of the Central American Accreditation Council, within the framework of the Central American Higher University Council.

Regulatory and Representative Bodies

GOVERNMENT

Ministry of Culture and Sport: 12 Avda 11-11, Zona 1, Guatemala City; tel. 2253-0543; fax 2253-0540; internet www.mcd.gob .gt; Minister JERÓNIMO LANCERIO CHINGO.

Ministry of Education: 6a Calle 1-87, Zona 10, Guatemala City; tel. 2360-0911; fax 2361-0350; e-mail info@mineduc.gob.gt; internet www.mineduc.gob.gt; Minister ANA ORDÓÑEZ DE MOLINA.

NATIONAL BODIES

Consejo de la Enseñanza Privada Superior (Council of Private Higher Education): Edif. Colegios Profesionales, Segundo Nivel, 0 Calle 15-46 Zona 15, Colonia El Maestro, Guatemala City; tel. 2369-6344; internet www.ceps.edu.gt; f. 1966.

Learned Societies

GENERAL

Academia de Ciencias Médicas, Físicas y Naturales de Guatemala (Academy of Medical, Physical and Natural Sciences): 13 Calle 1–25, Zona 1, Apdo Postal 569, 01001 Guatemala City; tel. (2) 2238-1251; fax (2) 2232-7291; e-mail manuelgonzalez@yahoo .com; f. 1945; 80 mems; library of 4,000 vols; Pres. MANUEL GONZÁLEZ AVILA; Sec. Dr CARLOS ROLZ ASTURIAS; publs *Annals* (irregular), research summaries.

FINE AND PERFORMING ARTS

Sociedad Pro-Arte Musical (Musical Society): 12 Calle 2–09, Zona 3, Apdo 980, Guatemala City; f. 1945; 200 mems; Pres. LULÚ C. DE HERRARTE; Exec. Sec. DORA G. DE MENDIZÁBAL.

HISTORY, GEOGRAPHY AND ARCHAEOLOGY

Academia de Geografía e Historia de Guatemala (Geographical and Historical Academy of Guatemala): 3 Avda 8–35, Zona 1, Guatemala City; tel. 2253-5141; fax 2232-3544; e-mail acgeohis@gmail.com; f. 1923; 45 mems; library of 30,000 vols; Pres. GUILLERMO DÍAZ ROMEU; Sec. BARBARA KNOKE DE ARATHOON; publs *Anales* (1 a year), *Biblioteca Goathemala, Viajeros*.

LANGUAGE AND LITERATURE

Academia Guatemalteca de la Lengua (Guatemala Academy of Letters): 12 Calle 6–40, Zona 9, Oficina 403–404, Edificio Plazuela, Guatemala City; tel. 2332-2824; fax 2332-2824; e-mail aglesp@correo.terra.com .gt; f. 1887; corresp. of the Real Academia Española (Madrid, Spain); library of 5,000 vols; Dir MARIO ANTONIO SANDOVAL SAMAYOA; Sec.-Gen. FRANCISCO MORALES SANTOS.

Alliance Française: 5ta Calle 10–55, Zona 13, Finca la Aurora; tel. 2440-2102; e-mail info@alianzafrancesa.org.gt; internet www .alianzafrancesa.org.gt; offers courses and exams in French language and culture and promotes cultural exchange with France; attached teaching offices in La Antigua and Quetzaltenango.

NATURAL SCIENCES

Biological Sciences

Asociación Guatemalteca de Historia Natural: Jardín Botánico, Universidad de San Carlos, Mariscal Cruz 1–56, Zona 10, Guatemala City; f. 1960; 86 mems; Pres. Dr MARIO DARY RIVERA.

TECHNOLOGY

Colegio de Ingenieros de Guatemala: 7A Avda 39–60, Zona 8, 01008 Guatemala City; tel. 2471-7544; fax 2472-4224; e-mail juntadirectiva@cig.org.gt; internet www.cig .org.gt; f. 1947; 1,965 mems; Pres. Ing. CARLOS GERARDO BRAN GUZMÁN; publ. *Revista Ingeniería* (4 a year).

Research Institutes

ECONOMICS, LAW AND POLITICS

Centro de Investigaciones Económicas Nacionales (Centre for National Economic Studies): 12 Calle 1–25, Zona 10, Edif. Géminis 10, Torre Norte, Nivel 17, Oficina 1702, Guatemala City; tel. 2335-3415; fax 2335-3416; internet www.cien.org.at; f. 1982; study of economic and social problems; Dir JORGE LAVARREDA; publ. *Carta Económica* (12 a year).

Instituto Nacional de Estadística (National Statistical Institute): 8a Calle 9–55, Zona 1, Guatemala City; tel. 2232-3188; fax 2232-4790; e-mail fhernandez@ine.gob .gt; internet www.ine.gob.gt; f. 1879 as Sección de Estadística, present name 1985; compiles and publishes nat. statistics; Dir SIEGFRIDO LEE LEIVA; publs *Censo Nacional Agropecuario* (national agricultural census, online), *Censo Nacional de Población y de Habitación* (national population and dwellings census, online), *Índice de Precios al Consumidor* (retail price index; online, 12 a year).

HISTORY, GEOGRAPHY AND ARCHAEOLOGY

Instituto de Antropología e Historia: 12 Avda 11–11, Zona 1, 01001 Guatemala City; tel. 2232-5956; fax 2232-5956; e-mail guatepazidaeh@yahoo.com; f. 1946; research on Middle-American history, Mayan archaeology, ethnology, philology, and Spanish Colonial history; supervises archaeological sites, monuments and museums; library of 12,000 vols; Dir-Gen. Arq. ARTURO PAZ; publs *Revista Anual de Antropología e Historia de Guatemala* (1 a year), books and special publs.

Instituto Geográfico Nacional 'Ing. Alfredo Obiols Gómez': Avda Las Américas 5-76, Zona 13, Guatemala City; tel. 2332-2611; fax 2331-3548; e-mail ign@ign.gob.gt; internet www.ign.gob.gt; f. 1945; Dir Ing. FERNANDO AMILCAR BOITON VELÁSQUEZ.

MEDICINE

Instituto de Nutrición de Centro América y Panamá (INCAP) (Institute of Nutrition of Central America and Panama): Calzada Roosevelt 6–25, Zona 11, Apdo Postal 1188-01901, Guatemala City; tel. 2472-3762; fax 2473-6529; internet www.incap.org .gt; f. 1949; member countries: Belize, Costa Rica, El Salvador, Guatemala, Honduras, Nicaragua, Panama; administered by Pan American Health Bureau Organization (PAHO)/World Health Organization (WHO); Food and Nutrition Security Program considers food systems, nutrition education and communication, and health and nutrition with an emphasis on mother and child; Masters programme and short training courses; well-documented library publishes scientific articles in Spanish and English, information bulletins, periodic compilations of scientific publs for member govts, annual reports, monographs, various other documents; Dir Dr HERNÁN DELGADO.

NATURAL SCIENCES

Biological Sciences

Centro de Estudios Conservacionistas: Avda La Reforma 0–63, Zona 10, Guatemala City; tel. 2331-0904; fax 2334-7664; e-mail direccioncecon@yahoo.com; internet www .usac.edu.gt/cecon; f. 1981; management and admin. of protected areas; investigation and studies of biodiversity and sustainable management of natural resources; management of nat. botanical garden and nat. biodiversity database; 142 mems; Exec. Dir JORGE ALBERTO RUIZ ORDOÑEZ.

Physical Sciences

Instituto Nacional de Sismología, Vulcanología, Meteorología e Hidrología (National Institute of Seismology, Vulcanology, Meteorology and Hydrology): 7ta Avda 14–57, Zona 13, Guatemala City; tel. 2331-5944; fax 2331-5005; e-mail direccion@ insivumeh.gob.gt; internet www.insivumeh .gob.gt; f. 1976; Dir EDDY HARDIE SÁNCHEZ; publs *Boletín Anual Hidrológico* (electronic, hydrology, 1 a year), *Boletín de Tsunamis* (electronic, catalogue of tsunamis), *Boletín Estacional* (electronic, quarterly forecast), *Boletín Mensual* (electronic, monthly forecast), *Boletín Meteorológico Diario* (electronic, daily weather forecast), *Boletín Sismológico* (electronic, monthly catalogue of earthquakes), *Boletín Sismológico Especial* (electronic, catalogue of significant earthquakes), *Boletín Vulcanológico Diario* (electronic, catalogue of current eruptions), *Boletín Vulcanológico Especial* (electronic, catalogue of significant eruptions), *Mareas Oceánicas* (electronic, monthly tidal forecast), *Normales Climáticas* (electronic, climate statistics), *Pronóstico de Fin de Semana* (electronic, weekend forecast), *Pronóstico de 1 a 3 Días* (electronic, four-day forecast), *Tiempo Presente* (electronic, current forecast).

TECHNOLOGY

Dirección General de Energía Nuclear: 24 Calle 21-12, Zona 12, Apdo Postal 1421, Guatemala City; tel. 2477-0746; fax 2476-2007; f. 1978; work concerns peaceful application of nuclear energy in medicine, industry, agriculture, etc.; 50 mems; library of 1,200 vols; Dir Ing. RAÚL EDUARDO PINEDA GONZÁLEZ.

Instituto Centroamericano de Investigación y Tecnología Industrial (ICAITI) (Central American Research Institute for Industry): Apdo Postal 1552-01901, Guatemala City; Avda La Reforma 4–47, Zona 10, Guatemala City; tel. 2331-0631; fax 2331-

7470; internet www.icaiti.org.gt; f. 1956; research on marketing, development of new industries and manufacturing techniques, establishment of Central American standards, information services to industry, and professional advice; library of 36,000 vols; Dir Lic. LUIS FIDEL CIFUENTES ECHEVERRIA (acting).

Libraries and Archives

Guatemala City

Archivo General de Centro América (National Archives): 4 Avda 7–16, Zona 1, Guatemala City; tel. 2232-3037; f. 1846; comprises two sections: La Colonia, archive with 8,427 files of 99,157 documents relating to Guatemala, Chiapas, El Salvador, Honduras, Nicaragua and Costa Rica; library contains ancient and modern historical volumes; periodicals pertaining to the colonial epoch and the period of independence; microfilm and photocopying service for researchers; Dir ARTURO VALDÉS OLIVA; publ. *Boletín.*

Biblioteca Central de la Universidad de San Carlos de Guatemala: Ciudad Universitaria, Zona 12, Guatemala City; tel. 2476-7217; fax 2476-9652; internet biblioteca.usac.edu.gt; f. 1965; economics, humanities and multidisciplinary collections; thesis collection; newspaper and magazine collection; Guatemalan collection, Carlos Mérida collection; 82,881 vols, 756 periodical titles; Dir Licda OFELIA AGUILAR (acting).

Biblioteca del Banco de Guatemala: 7a Avda 22–01, Zona 1, Apdo 365, Guatemala City; tel. 2429-6000; internet www.banguat .gob.gt/biblio; f. 1955; 38,000 vols; Librarian JULIO C. MARISCAL.

Biblioteca del Congreso Nacional: 9 Avda 9–42, Guatemala City; f. 1823; 7,000 vols; Dir CARLOS H. GODOY Z.

Biblioteca del Organismo Judicial: 21 Calle 7–70, Zona 1, Guatemala City; tel. 2248-7000; e-mail biblioteca@oj.gob.gt; f. 1881; 10,000 vols; Dir DORA CRISTINA GODOY LÓPEZ; publs *Informador Bibliotecario* (electronic, 52 a year), *Informador Bibliotecario Mensual* (electronic, 12 a year).

Biblioteca Nacional de Guatemala: 5A Avda 7–26, Zona 1, Guatemala City; tel. 2232-2443; fax 2253-9071; e-mail biblioguatemala@intelnett.com; internet www.biblionet.edu.gt; f. 1879; 350,000 vols; Dir Lic. VICTOR CASTILLO LÓPEZ.

Quezaltenango

Biblioteca Pública de Quezaltenango: a/ c Casa Cultura Occidente 7a, Calle 11–35, Zona 1, Quezaltenango; reopened 1958; 25,000 vols; Dir JULIO CÉSAR ALVAREZ.

Museums and Art Galleries

Chichicastenango

Museo Regional de Chichicastenango: 5a Avda 4-47, Zona 1, Chichicastenango; f. 1950; articles of the Maya-Quiché culture; Dir RAÚL PÉREZ MALDONADO.

Guatemala City

Museo Nacional de Arqueología y Etnología de Guatemala (Archaeological and Ethnographical Museum): Edif. No. 5, La Aurora, Zona 13, Guatemala City; tel. 2472-0489; fax 2472-0489; f. 1948; collection of some 3,000 archaeological pieces, mainly Mayan art, and 1,000 ethnological exhibits,

all from Guatemala; Dir Licda DORA GUERRA DE GONZÁLEZ; publ. *Revista* (2 a year).

Museo Nacional de Arte Moderno: Edif. No. 6, Finca La Aurora, Zona 13, Guatemala City; tel. 2472-0467; fax 2471-1422; f. 1975; paintings, sculpture, engravings, drawings, etc.; Dir J. OSCAR BARRIENTOS.

Museo Nacional de Historia (National Museum of History): 9 Calle 9–70, Zona 1, Guatemala City; tel. 2253-6149; fax 2253-6149; f. 1975; 19th- and 20th-century paintings, sculpture, documents, furniture and tools, all from Guatemala; Dir ITALO MORALES HIDALGO.

Museo Nacional de Historia Natural 'Jorge A. Ibarra': 6A Calle 7–30, Zona 13, Apdo 987, Guatemala City; tel. and fax 2472-0468; f. 1950; colln of geological, botanical and zoological specimens; library of 2,600 vols; Dir and Founder JORGE A. IBARRA.

Universities

UNIVERSIDAD DE SAN CARLOS DE GUATEMALA

Ciudad Universitaria, Zona 12, 01012 Guatemala City

Telephone: 2443-9672
Fax: 2476-7221
E-mail: webmaster@usac.edu.gt
Internet: www.usac.edu.gt

Founded 1676 by King Carlos II, est. in its present form 1927, autonomous status 1944
Private control
Language of instruction: Spanish
Academic year: January to November

Rector: Dr M. V. LUIS ALFONSO LEAL MONTERROSO
Sec.-Gen.: Dr CARLOS ENRIQUE MAZARIEGOS MORALES
Dir-Gen. for Admin.: Lic. CARLOS SIERRA ROMERO
Dir-Gen. for Planning: Lic. JOSÉ H. CALDERÓN DÍAZ
Dir-Gen. for Research: Dr RODOLFO ESPINOZA SMITH
Dir-Gen. for Teaching: Lic. JUAN ALBERTO MARTINEZ
Dir-Gen. for Univ. Devt: Arq. BYRON RABÉ
Registrar: Ing. ROLANDO GRAJEDA
Librarian: Licda MERCEDES DE BEECK

Library: see Libraries
Number of teachers: 2,600
Number of students: 114,000

Publications: *Revista de la Universidad de San Carlos de Guatemala* (4 a year), *Universidad* (12 a year), *USAC al Día* (26 a year)

DEANS

Faculty of Agronomy: Dr ARIEL ABDERRAMAN ORTIZ
Faculty of Architecture: Arq. CARLOS VALLADARES
Faculty of Chemistry and Pharmacy: Lic. GERARDO ARROYO
Faculty of Dentistry: Dr CARLOS ALVARADO CEREZO
Faculty of Economics: Lic. EDUARDO VELASQUEZ
Faculty of Engineering: Ing. SYDNEY SAMUELS
Faculty of Humanities: Lic. MARIO CALDERON
Faculty of Law and Social Sciences: Lic. BONERGE MEJÍA ORELLANA
Faculty of Medicine: Dr CARLOS ALVARADO DUMAS
Faculty of Veterinary Medicine: Dr MARIO LLERENA

DIRECTORS

School of Communications Science: Lic. GUSTAVO ADOLFO BRACAMONTE CERÓN
School of History: Lic. GABRIEL MORALES
School of Political Science: Lic. FERNANDO MOLINA
School of Psychology: Lic. RIQUELMI GASPARICO
School of Social Work: Lic. RUDY RAMÍREZ
School of Teacher-Training: Ing. FRANCISCO ROSALES CEREZO

UNIVERSIDAD DEL VALLE DE GUATEMALA

Apdo Postal No. 82, 01901 Guatemala City
located at: 18 Avda 11-95, Zona 15, Vista Hermosa III, Guatemala City
Telephone: 2364-0336
Fax: 2364-0212
E-mail: info@uvg.edu.gt
Internet: www.uvg.edu.gt
Founded 1966
Language of instruction: Spanish
Private control
Academic year: February to November
Rector: Lic. ROBERTO MORENO GODOY
Vice-Rector and Dir of Studies: MARÍA LUISA DURANDO DE BOEHM
Registrar: Lda. VICTORIA EUGENIA ROSALES
Librarian: Dra MARÍA EMILIA LÓPEZ
Library of 68,000 vols, 130 current periodicals
Number of teachers: 250
Number of students: 2,000

DEANS

Faculty of Education: JACQUELINE GARCÍA DE DE LEÓN
Faculty of Engineering: Ing. CARLOS PAREDES
Faculty of Science and Humanities: EDUARDO ÁLVAREZ MASSIS
Faculty of Social Sciences: MARÍA DEL PILAR DE RODRÍGUEZ
Research Institute: Ing. CARLOS ROLZ
University College: EDUARDO ÁLVAREZ MASSIS

UNIVERSIDAD FRANCISCO MARROQUIN

6 Calle Final, Zona 10, Guatemala City
Telephone: 2338-7700
Fax: 2334-6896
E-mail: info@ufm.edu.gt
Internet: www.ufm.edu.gt
Founded 1971
Language of instruction: Spanish
Private control
Academic year: January to November
Rector: Ing. GIANCARLO IBÁRGÜEN D.
Sec.-Gen.: Lic. RICARDO CASTILLO
Librarian: Dr JULIO H. COLE
Library of 75,000 vols
Number of teachers: 450
Number of students: 7,379
Publications: *Laissez-Faire* (2 a year), *Revista de la Facultad de Derecho* (2 a year)

DEANS

School of Architecture: Arq. ERNESTO PORRAS
School of Dentistry: Dr RAMIRO ALFARO
School of Economics: Dr WENCESLAO GIMÉNEZ
School of Law: Dr MILTON ARGUETA
School of Medicine: Dr RODOLFO HERRERA-LLERANDI
Graduate School of Economics and Business Administration: Dr JUAN CARLOS CACHANOSKY

UNIVERSIDAD GALILEO

Calle Dr Eduardo Suger Cofiño (7a Avda Final), Zona 10, 01010 Guatemala City
Telephone: 2423-8000
Fax: 2362-2731
Internet: www.galileo.edu
Founded 2000
Private control
Rector: Dr JOSÉ EDUARDO SUGER COFIÑO
Vice-Rector: Dr JOSÉ CYRANO RUIZ CABARRÚS
Vice-Rector for Academics: Lic. MYRA ROLDAN DE RAMÍREZ
Sec.-Gen.: Lic. JORGE FRANCISCO RETOLAZA

DEANS

Faculty of Education: Dr BERNARDO RENÉ MORALES FIGUEROA
Faculty of Science, Technology and Industry: Ing. JORGE IVÁN ECHEVERRÍA PERMOUT
Faculty of Systems Engineering: Ing. JOSÉ EDUARDO SUGER CASTILLO

DIRECTORS

Institute of Open Education: Ing. STEPHANY OROZCO
School of Graduate Studies: Ing. CARLOS ARNADI-KLEE
School of Professional Development and Training: Lic. LUIS MANUEL ALVAREZ ALVAREZ

UNIVERSIDAD MARIANO GÁLVEZ DE GUATEMALA

Apdo Postal 1811, Guatemala City
Telephone: 2288-7592
Internet: www.umg.edu.gt
Founded 1966
Language of instruction: Spanish
Private control
Academic year: February to November
Rector: Lic. ALVARO R. TORRES MOSS
Vice-Rectors: Lic. HUGO C. MORALES Y MORALES, Dr ALFREDO SAN JOSÉ
Sec.: Licda RUBY SANTIZO DE HERNÁNDEZ
Registrar: Lic. JOSÉ CLODOVEO TORRES MOSS
Librarian: GLORIA MARINA ARROYO
Library of 9,000 vols
Number of teachers: 400
Number of students: 10,000
Publication: *Boletín Mensual* (12 a year)

DIRECTORS

School of Architecture: Arq. VÍCTOR HUGO HERNÁNDEZ ORDÓÑEZ
School of Business Administration: Lic. CARLOS F. CÁRDENAS C.
School of Civil Engineering: Ing. HANS JOAQUÍN LOTTMANN
Schools of Economics, Public Auditing and Accounting: Lic. OSCAR EUGENIO DUBÓN PALMA
School of Education: Lic. VÍCTOR EGIDIO AGREDA GODÍNEZ
School of Humanities: Lic. VÍCTOR EGIDIO AGREDA GODÍNEZ
School of Information Systems: Ing. JORGE A. ARIAS TOBAR
School of Languages: Dr NEVILLE STILES
School of Law: Lic. RODERIGO SEGURA TRUJILLO
School of Linguistics: Dr DAVID OLTROGGE
School of Nursing: Licda DELIA LUCILA CHANG CHANG
School of Odontology: Dr ROLANDO DÍAZ LOZZA
School of Theology: Lic. ADALBERTO SANTIZO ROMÁN

UNIVERSIDAD RAFAEL LANDÍVAR

Vista Hermosa III, Zona 16, Apdo Postal 39 'C', Guatemala City
Telephone: 2369-2751
Fax: 2369-2756
E-mail: info@url.edu.gt
Internet: www.url.edu.gt
Founded 1961
Language of instruction: Spanish
Private control
Academic year: January to November
Rector: GONZALO DE VILLA
Gen. Vice-Rector: GUILLERMINA HERRERA
Vice-Rectors: RENÉ POITEVIN (Academic), Arq. CARLOS HAUESLER (Administrative)
Gen. Sec.: LUIS QUAN
Librarian: REGINA ROMERO DE LA VEGA
Number of teachers: 1,008
Number of students: 20,000
Publications: *Aprapalabra*, *Boletín de Lingüística* (6 a year), *Cultura de Guatemala* (3 a year), *Estudios Sociales* (4 a year), *Vida Universitaria* (12 a year), *Revista de Literatura*

DEANS

Faculty of Agriculture and Environmental Sciences: Ing. JAIME CARRERA
Faculty of Architecture: Arq. SERGIO TULIO CASTANEDA
Faculty of Economic Sciences: JOSÉ ALEJANDRO AREVADO
Faculty of Engineering: EDWIN ESCOBAR
Faculty of Health Sciences: MIGUEL GARCÉS
Faculty of Humanities: MA. EUGENIA SANDOVAL
Faculty of Political and Social Sciences: RENZO ROSAL
Faculty of Theology: DENIS LEDER

ATTACHED INSTITUTES

Institute of Agriculture, Natural Resources and the Environment: Dir Ing. JUVENTINO GÁLVEZ.

Institute of Dance: Dir Dr SABRINA CASTILLO.

Institute of Economic and Social Research: Dir TOMAS ROSADA.

Institute of Linguistics: Dir Dr LUCIA VERDUGO.

Institute of Musicology: Dir Dr DIETER LEHNHOFF.

Institute of Psychology: Dir Dr FIDELIO SWANA.

Institute of Science and Technology: Dir LYS CIFUENTES.

Schools of Art and Music

Conservatorio Nacional de Música (National Academy of Music): 3a Avda 4-61, Zona 1, 01001 Guatemala City; f. 1875; 40 teachers; 900 students; Dir LUIS A. LIMA Y LIMA.

Escuela Nacional de Artes Plásticas 'Rafael Rodríguez Padilla': 6 Avda 22-00, Zona 1, Guatemala City; f. 1920; library: 2,500 vols; Dir ZIPACNÁ DE LEÓN; publ. *Revista de la Escuela Nacional de Artes Plásticas 'Rafael Rodríguez Padilla'.*

GUINEA-BISSAU

The Higher Education System

Guinea-Bissau was formerly Portuguese Guinea (Guiné), during which time education as a whole was geared to serve a narrow élite, consisting mainly of the colonial rulers' children. The country gained its independence in 1974 following a military coup in Portugal. The first institution of higher education, a school of law, was established in 1979, followed by centres for medicine, education, nursing and sports. In 1999 a Government decree placed all these institutions under the authority of the Ministry of National and Higher Education (formerly Ministry of Education), with a view to establishing a university at the National Institute of Studies and Research.

In 2000/2001, 473 students were enrolled in tertiary education. Some 200 students completed their studies in Havana, Cuba, in 2002, while a further 186 had scholarships to study in Paris, France, and Dakar, Senegal. To counter this trend, in 2003 the Universidade Amílcar Cabral, Guinea-Bissau's first university, was founded. In the same year a private university, the Universidade Colinas de Boé, also opened. In 2004, after three years of a feasibility study, the Universidade Lusófona de Humanidades e Tecnologias based in Lisbon, Portugal, opened its own subsidiary, the Universidade Lusófona de Guiné. By the end of 2008 internal financial problems had caused Amílcar Cabral University to lose its autonomous status and it was subsumed into the Universidade Lusófona de Guiné.

Technical and vocational education is available at two institutions, the Centre of Administrative Training and the Centre of Experimental Training.

Regulatory Bodies

GOVERNMENT

Ministry of Culture, Youth and Sports: Bissau; Minister ADIA DJALÓ NANDINGA.

Ministry of National and Higher Education: Rua Areolino Cruz, Bissau; tel. 202244; Minister ALFREDO GOMES.

Research Institutes

GENERAL

Centro de Estudos da Guiné-Bissau (Study Centre of Guinea-Bissau): CP 37, Bissau; f. 1945.

Instituto Nacional de Estudos e Pesquisa (INEP) (National Institute of Studies and Research): CP 112, Bairro Cobornel, Bissau; Complexo Escolar 14 de Novembro, Bissau; tel. 251867; fax 251125; f. 1987; damaged during conflict between govt forces and rebels in 1999; restoration, with the support of int. scholars, began in 2000; library of 40,000 vols, incl. archives and museum; also holds periodicals, photographs, plays, press cuttings; fees for using facility and for exhibitions.

Libraries and Archives

Bissau

Biblioteca Nacional da Guiné-Bissau (National Library of Guinea-Bissau): Praça do Império, CP 37, Bissau; f. 1970.

Museums and Galleries

Bissau

Museu da Guiné-Bissau (Museum of Guinea Bissau): Praca do Império, CP 37, Bissau; f. 1945; library of 14,000 vols; collns of economics, ethnography, history, natural science.

Museu Etnografico Nacional (National Ethnographical Museum): Complexo Escolar 14 de Novembro, CP 338, Bissau; tel. 215600; fax 204400; photographic archive depicting former colln of African masks and statues (largely destroyed during military conflict in 1998).

University and Colleges

UNIVERSIDADE AMÍLCAR CABRAL

Endereço Bairro da Ajuda, 2a Fase, CP 659, Bissau

Telephone: 255970

Fax: 202244

E-mail: geral@uac.com

Founded 2003

State control

Rector: Prof. Dr TCHERNO DJALÓ

Faculties of agricultural and veterinary science, economics, letters and communications, science, technology; school of physical education and sport.

Faculdade de Direito da Guiné-Bissau: Complexo Escolar 14 de Novembro, CP 595, Bissau Codex; tel. 252770; fax 204304; e-mail geral@fdbissau.com; internet www.fdbissau.com; f. 1990; Dir FODÉ ADULAI MANÉ.

Instituto Nacional para o Desenvolvimento da Educação (INDE): Rua Dr Herman Gmeiner, Bairro 7, 2a Fase, CP 132, Bissau; tel. 204534; fax 202054; e-mail indebissau@hotmail.com; Pres. ALFREDO GOMES; Dir-Gen. AUGUSTO PEREIRA.

GUINEA

The Higher Education System

Guinea (formerly French Guinea) was part of French West Africa until it gained its independence in 1958, and the education system is still based on the French system. There are two state-controlled universities, Université Gamal Abdel Nasser de Conakry (founded in 1962) and Université Julius Nyéréré de Kankan (founded in 1963, current name and status since 1987). Additional institutions of higher education include professional institutes and schools attached to the universities. The Ministry of Higher Education and Scientific Research is the main controlling body, through the aegis of the Department for Scientific and Technical Research and the Department for Higher Education, but higher education institutions enjoy significant autonomy. Higher education is wholly financed by the Government (except for private institutions).

In 2005/06 42,700 students were enrolled in further and higher education.

Students must hold the secondary school qualification, Baccalauréat Deuxième Partie, and sit a competitive entrance examination in order to be admitted to university. There are two undergraduate degrees: the Diplôme d'Etudes Universitaires Générales, which is awarded after two years, and the Licence, which is awarded after four years. Undergraduates may also receive a professional diploma (Diplôme), depending on the subject. After the Licence, the Maîtrise or the Diplôme d'Etudes Supérieures are the first postgraduate qualifications, both awarded after one year of study. Finally, the third stage of university-level qualifications is the Doctorat, which is a research-based, two-year course leading to submission of a thesis.

Regulatory Bodies

GOVERNMENT

Ministry of National Education and Scientific Research: face à la Cathédrale Sainte-Marie, BP 964, Conakry; tel. 30-45-12-17; fax 30-41-20-12; Minister Dr OUSMANE SOUARÉ.

Ministry of Youth, Sports and Culture: ave du Port Secrétariat, BP 262, Conakry; tel. 30-41-19-59; fax 30-41-19-26; Minister BAIDI ARIBOT.

Learned Society

LANGUAGE AND LITERATURE

PEN Centre de Guinée: BP 107, Labé; tel. 30-44-14-75; f. 1989; 32 mems; library of 92 vols; Sec. ZEINAB KOUMANTHIO DIALLO; publ. *Pour Mémoire*.

Research Institutes

GENERAL

Direction Nationale de la Recherche Scientifique et Technique: Conakry, BP 561; f. 1958; 60 mems; 2 libraries; Dir Dr FODE SOUMAH; publ. *Bulletin*.

AGRICULTURE, FISHERIES AND VETERINARY SCIENCE

Centre de Recherche Agronomique de Foulaya: BP 156, Kindia; tel. 30-61-01-48; e-mail iragdq@irag.org.gn; f. 1946; Dir Dr MAHMOUD CAMARA.

Institut de Recherche Agronomique de Guinée: Blvd du Commerce, BP 1523, Conakry; tel. 30-21-19-57; e-mail iragdg@biasy.net.gn.

Institut de Recherche en Animalculture Pastoria: BP 146, Kindia; tel. 30-61-08-11; f. 1923; fmr *Institut Pasteur*, nationalized 1965; research on infectious animal diseases; production of various vaccines; 18 staff; library of 362 vols; Dir Dr ALHASSANE DIALLO.

Libraries and Archives

Conakry

Archives Nationales: BP 1005, Conakry; tel. 30-44-42-97; f. 1960; Dir ALMANY STELL CONTE.

Bibliothèque Nationale: BP 561, Conakry; tel. 30-46-10-10; f. 1958; 40,000 vols, also spec. colln on slavery (500 books, pamphlets and MSS); 225 current periodicals; courses in librarianship; Dir LANSANA SYLLA.

Museum

Conakry

Musée National: BP 139, Conakry; tel. 30-45-10-66; f. 1960; Dir SORY KABA.

Universities

UNIVERSITÉ GAMAL ABDEL NASSER DE CONAKRY

BP 1147, Conakry
Telephone: 30-46-46-89
Fax: 30-46-48-08
E-mail: uganc@mirinet.net.gn
Founded 1962
State control

Rector: OUSMANE SYLLA
Vice-Rector for Academics: JEAN-MARIE TOURÉ
Vice-Rector for Research: Dr M. KODJOUGOU DIALLO
Sec.-Gen.: GALEMA GUILAVOGUI
Dir of Library: MANSA KANTÉ
Library of 4,000 vols
Number of teachers: 824
Number of students: 5,000
Publications: *Guinée Médicale*, *Horizons*

DEANS
Faculty of Arts and Humanities: GOUDOUSSY DIALLO
Faculty of Law, Economics and Management: HAWA FOFANA
Faculty of Medicine and Pharmacy: (vacant)
Faculty of Science: Dr DJELIMANDJAN CONDÉ
Polytechnic Institute: Prof. NANAMOUDOU MAGASSOUBA (Director-General)

UNIVERSITÉ JULIUS NYÉRÉRÉ DE KANKAN

Ministère de l'Enseignement Supérieur et de la Recherche Scientifique, Kankan
Telephone: 30-71-20-93
Founded 1963; univ. status 1987
State control

Academic year: October to June
Rector: Dr SEYDOUBA CAMARA
Vice-Rector for Academics: Dr MAWIATOU BAH
Vice-Rector for Research: Dr SIDAFA CAMARA
Sec.-Gen.: DOMINIQUE KOLY
Dir of Financial and Administrative Affairs: ELHADJ ALPHA OUSMANE DIALLO
Dir of International Relations and Cooperation: MARTIN KOIVOGUI
Dir of Univ. Publs: ELHADJ NAMANDIAN DOUMBOUYA
Library Dir: JOSEPH KOKOLY DRAMOU
Library of 12,160 vols
Number of teachers: 95
Number of students: 3,012
Publication: *Revue Scientifique de l'Université de Kankan* (2 a year)

DEANS
Faculty of Natural Sciences: Dr BAKARY KAMANO
Faculty of Social Sciences: Dr AMADOU BAÏLO BARRY
Ecole Supérieure des Sciences de l'Information: SIBA BILIVOGUI

Colleges

Ecole Nationale des Arts et Métiers: POB 240, Conakry; tel. 30-46-25-62; fax 30-46-25-62; f. 1962; industrial automation, electro-mechanical engineering, electronics, refrigeration and air-conditioning, diesel mechanics, industrial maintenance; Dir MAHMOUDOU BARRY.

Ecole Nationale de la Santé: Conakry; tel. 30-29-52-49; fax 30-46-50-09; Dir BARRY YAYA.

Ecole Supérieure d'Administration: Conakry; f. 1964.

Institut Supérieur Agronomique et Vétérinaire 'Valéry Giscard d'Estaing' de Faranah: BP 131, Faranah; tel. 30-81-02-15; fax 30-81-08-18; e-mail isav1@mirinet.net.gn; f. 1978; library: 3,629 vols, 207 periodicals; 110 teachers; 2,515 students; faculties of agriculture, agricultural engineering, rural economics, stockbreeding and veterinary medicine, waters and forestry; common-core syllabus; Dir-Gen. Dr YAZORA SOROPOGUI.

GUYANA

The Higher Education System

Guyana, formerly British Guiana, a colony of the United Kingdom, achieved independence in 1966. The Free Education Act of 1976 guaranteed the right to free education at all levels from pre-school to higher education. The Ministry of Education is the supreme body for higher education. The state-controlled University of Guyana (founded in 1963) is the only university, but higher education is also available at professional schools, technical institutes and colleges. In 1999/200 some 7,496 students were enrolled in the University.

The Caribbean Examinations Council Secondary Education Certificate is the standard requirement for admission to higher education, though GCE O-levels and A-levels are also accepted. The main degrees are the undergraduate Bachelors, which is awarded after four years of study, and the postgraduate Masters, which is awarded after one further year of study. There are also undergraduate and graduate Diploma programmes in mainly professional fields of study. Masters programmes are not offered in all subjects.

The University of Guyana has an Institute of Distance and Continuing Education, which runs extramural courses; the Adult Education Association offers similar programmes. Post-secondary vocational and technical qualifications include Craft Certificate, Technician Certificate and Technician Diploma.

In 2006 Guyanese students were offered 365 scholarships by the Cuban Government to conduct their further education in Cuba, while an additional 150 scholarships would be offered each year until 2010.

Regulatory Bodies

GOVERNMENT

Ministry of Culture, Youth and Sport: 71–72 Main St, South Cummingsburg, Georgetown; tel. 227-7860; fax 225-5067; e-mail mincys@guyana.net.gy; Minister Dr FRANK ANTHONY.

Ministry of Education: 21 Brickdam, Stabroek, POB 1014, Georgetown; tel. 223-7900; fax 225-8511; e-mail moegyweb@yahoo.com; internet www.sdnp.org.gy/minedu; Minister SHAIK K. Z. BAKSH.

Learned Societies

BIBLIOGRAPHY, LIBRARY SCIENCE AND MUSEOLOGY

Guyana Library Association: c/o National Library, 76–77 Main St, POB 10240, Georgetown; tel. 226-2690; fax 227-4052; f. 1968; 35 personal mems, 13 institutional mems; Pres. IVOR RODRIGUES; Sec. GWYNETH GEORGE; publ. *Bulletin*.

ECONOMICS, LAW AND POLITICS

Guyana Institute of International Affairs: POB 101176, Georgetown; tel. 227-7768; fax 227-7768; f. 1965; 100 mems; library of 5,000 vols; Pres. DONALD A. B. TROTMAN; publs *Annual Journal of International Affairs*, occasional papers.

EDUCATION

Adult Education Association of Guyana Inc. M.S.: 88 Carmichael St, POB 101111, Georgetown; tel. 225-0758; fax 227-2273; e-mail aea@guyana.net.gy; f. 1957; 1,000 mems; NGO that aims to provide opportunities for Guyanese to improve their skills, raise the level of awareness of their culture, acquire a critical understanding of major contemporary issues; programmes: academic, technical, scientific, creative art, commercial and professional devt; operates remedial school for people who have dropped out of school and slow learners; runs adult literacy classes; Pres. HANSEL BARROW; Exec. Dir PATRICIA DAVID.

LANGUAGE AND LITERATURE

Alliance Française: The Hive, 27/28 Queen St, Kitty, Georgetown; offers courses and exams in French language and culture and promotes cultural exchange with France.

Research Institutes

AGRICULTURE, FISHERIES AND VETERINARY SCIENCE

Inter-American Institute for Cooperation on Agriculture (IICA)– Cooperation Agency in Guyana: Lot 18, Brickdam, Stabroek, POB 10-1089, Georgetown; tel. 226-8347; fax 225-8358; e-mail iica@networksgy.com; internet www.iica.int; f. 1974; Guyana branch of the specialized agency of the OAS for the agricultural sector; promotes food safety and the prosperity of the rural sector in the Americas; library of 1,550 vols, 25 periodicals; Rep. IGNATIUS JEAN; publs *Agriview* (4 a year), *Caribbean News* (4 a year), *COMUNIICA* (4 a year), *Tropical Fruits Newsletter* (4 a year).

MEDICINE

Pan-American Health Organization, Guyana Office: Lot 8, Brickdam, Stabroek, POB 10969, Georgetown; tel. 225-5150; fax 226-6654; e-mail moemark@guy.paho.org; internet www.guy.paho.org; f. 1902; maternal and child health, environmental health, health services development, human resource development, communicable diseases, management programmes for national development; library of 3,500 vols; Rep. Dr BERNADETTE THEODORE-GANDI.

Libraries and Archives

Georgetown

Bank of Guyana Library: POB 1003, Georgetown; tel. 226-3261; fax 227-2965; e-mail boglib@guyana.net.gy; internet www.bankofguyana.org.gy; f. 1966; provides support for the information needs of the staff; 15,000 vols, 150 periodicals; special collections: staff publs, conference papers, IMF documents, World Bank publs; Librarian BEVERLY BAKER.

Documentation Centre, Caribbean Community Secretariat: Turkeyen, Greater Georgetown, POB 10827, Georgetown; tel. 222-0001; fax 222-0170; e-mail doccentre@caricom.org; internet www.caricom.org; f. 1980; 18,700 vols, 24,167 books and pamphlets, 18,048 official documents, 16,067 monographic titles, 5,039 microfiches, 229 CD-ROMs; collns (documents): CARICOM, UN, UN agencies; Deputy Programme Man. MAUREEN C. NEWTON.

Guyana Medical Science Library: Georgetown Hospital Compound, Georgetown; f. 1966; attached to the Ministry of Health; provides medical information to doctors, nurses, and health personnel; 9,914 vols, 300 journals, 1,000 pamphlets; Librarian JENNIFER WILSON; publ. *Bulletin* (4 a year).

National Library: 76–77 Church and Main St, POB 10240, Georgetown; tel. 226-2699; fax 226-4053; internet www.natlib.gov.gy; f. 1909; combines the functions of a nat. library and public library; legal depository for material printed in Guyana; 197,355 vols; special collections: Caribbeana, library science, A. J. Seymour, UNESCO deposit; Chief Librarian GWYNETH BROWMAN (acting); publ. *Guyanese National Bibliography* (4 a year).

University of Guyana Library: POB 101110, Georgetown; fax 225-4885; internet fss.uog.edu.gy/university_library.htm; f. 1963; 200,000 vols, 3,000 periodicals; special collections: UN deposit collection, Caribbean Research Library, Law Collection; Librarian YVONNE LANCASTER; publs *Additions in the Humanities* (6 a year), *Additions in Science and Technology* (6 a year), *Caribbean Additions* (6 a year).

Museums and Art Galleries

Georgetown

Guyana Museum: Company Path, North St, Georgetown; f. 1853 by the Royal Agricultural and Commercial Society; subjects covered incl. industry, art, history, anthropology, zoology; Curator CLAYTON RODNEY; publ. *Journal* (1 a year).

Incorporates:

Guyana Zoo: Company Path, North St, Georgetown; specializes in the display, care and management of South American fauna; Dir GEORGE E. BURNHAM.

University

UNIVERSITY OF GUYANA

POB 101110, Turkeyen, Greater Georgetown
Telephone: 222-4184
Fax: 222-3596
E-mail: ug_pro@telsnetgy.net
Internet: www.uog.edu.gy
Founded 1963
State control
Language of instruction: English
Academic year: two terms, beginning September and January
Chancellor: (vacant)
Vice-Chancellor: Dr LAWRENCE CARRINGTON
Deputy Vice-Chancellor: TOTA MANGAR
Registrar: Dr VINCENT ALEXANDER
Librarian: GWYNETH GEORGE
Library: See Libraries and Archives
Number of teachers: 206
Number of students: 5,750
Publication: *University of Guyana Bulletin* (1 a year)

DEANS

Faculty of Agriculture and Forestry: Dr THEODOSIUS VELLOZA
Faculty of Health Sciences: Dr EMANUEL CUMMINGS
Faculty of Natural Sciences: Dr BRIJ BHUSHAN TEWARI
Faculty of Social Sciences: Dr MICHAEL SCOTT
Faculty of Technology: Dr SHERWOOD LOWE
School of Education and Humanities: AL CREIGHTON

PROFESSORS

BISHOP, A., Law
BRITTON, P., Law
EVERSELY, C., Law

LONCKE, J., French, Literature and Music
MASSIAH, K., Law
PERSICO, A., Spanish
SAMAD, D., English
TEWARI, B. B., Chemistry
THOMAS, C. Y., Economics and Business Administration
VERMA, V. N., Chemistry

Colleges

American International School of Medicine: Oceanview Campus, POB 101728, Georgetown; e-mail info@aism.edu; internet www.aism.edu; tel. 222-3437; fax 225-1646; f. 1997; library: 2,500 vols; 30 teachers; 50 students; Pres. COLIN A. WILKINSON.

Critchlow Labour College: Woolford Ave, Non Pareil Park, Georgetown; tel. 226-2481; f. 1970; library: 2,000 vols; 40 teachers; 600 students; industrial and social studies; Principal T. ANSON SANCHO.

E. R. Burrowes School of Art: 96 Carmichael St, Georgetown; tel. 226-3649; f. 1975; 4-year diploma course; library: 750 vols; 13 teachers; 52 students; Administrator AGNES JONES.

Government Technical Institute: Woolford Ave, Georgetown; tel. 226-2468; f. 1951; library: 3,500 vols; 37 teachers; 2,000 students; Principal LENNOX B. WILLIAMS.

Guyana Industrial Training Centre: Woolford Ave and Albert St, Non Pareil Park, Georgetown; tel. 226-6196; f. 1966; library: 1,600 vols; 6 teachers; 120 full-time, 90 part-time students; Dir SYDNEY R. WALTERS.

Guyana School of Agriculture Corporation: Mon Repos, East Coast Demerara; tel. and fax 220-2297; e-mail gsa@sdnp.org.gy; internet www.sdnp.org.gy/minagro/; f. 1963; library: 7,000 vols; Principal LYNETTE P. CUNHA.

Kuru-Kuru Cooperative College: 128 D'Urban St, D'Urban Backlands, Lodge, Georgetown; tel. 225-8433; e-mail kurukuruguy@netscape.net; f. 1973; library: 5,800 vols; 26 teachers; 270 students; Principal AVRIL BACCHUS (acting); Librarian LINDA CALDER.

Linden Technical Institute: Lot 1, New Rd, Constabulary Compound, Mackenzie, Linden; tel. 444-3333; fax 444-6719; internet www.sdnp.org.gy/geap/lti/; f. 1958; Guyana technical education examination courses in carpentry and joinery, driver training, electrical installation, internal combustion engines, instrumentation, mechanical fitting, metal machining, motor vehicle work, , , welding; 10 instructors; 86 full-time students; Principal ISAAC LAMAZON (acting).

New Amsterdam Technical Institute: POB 50, Garrison Rd, Fort Ordnance, New Amsterdam, Berbice; tel. 333-2702; f. 1971; Guyana technical education examination; courses in agricultural mechanics, automotive engineering, electrical trades, fitting, masonry, radio and electronic servicing, plumbing, welding, wood trades; agricultural engineering technician course; architectural and building construction technician course; ordinary technician diploma, mechanical engineering technician course; secretarial and business studies; library: 2,186 vols; 32 teachers; 1,000 students; Principal RONALD L. SIMON.

HAITI

The Higher Education System

Haiti (formerly Saint-Domingue) was under French sovereignty until 1804, when it gained its independence, but later came under US supervision from 1915 until 1934. The traditional education system has strong French influences, though some private institutions follow the American system. French and Creole are the official languages of instruction. The Ministry of Education and Vocational Training has responsibility for education. There are three universities, the state-controlled Université d'État d'Haiti (founded in 1920) and the private Université Quisqueya (founded in 1988) and Université Roi Henri Christophe (founded in 1980). Before the January 2010 earthquake, the Haitian system of higher education comprised at least 159 institutions, divided into disparate public and private sectors. The former consisted of a small network of 14 public, government-run institutions of higher education (Instituts d'enseignement superieur, IESs) including the State University of Haiti (Université d'État d'Haïti, or UEH). Besides the UEH, the public university sector also included 13 IESs either affiliated with or independent of UEH. In contrast, the private higher education sector consisted of a vast array of 145 institutions of varying quality. Of the 145 private universities, 10 provided high-quality, accredited education; of the remaining 135 (often religious-based institutions), 97 did not have permission to operate from the governmental Agency of Higher Education and Scientific Research. In 2007, the Ministry of National Education and Professional Formation reported the university population of Haiti was approximately 40,000 students. Of these 28,000 were in public universities and 12,000 in private ones

The main secondary school qualification, the Baccalauréat, is the leading requirement for admission to higher education. Undergraduates study for three to four years for the Diplôme d'Etudes Supérieures, Certificat d'Etudes Supérieures or a professional title. The first postgraduate degree is the Maîtrise, received after one year of study following the undergraduate degree. The second postgraduate degree is the Doctorat, but is only available in the fields of ethnology and development sciences.

Many addresses in Port-au-Prince and surrounding areas were destroyed in the earthquake of January 2010. At least 28 of the major universities were completely destroyed and the rest seriously damaged, and 2,599 to 6,000 students may have perished.

Regulatory Bodies

GOVERNMENT

Ministry of Culture: 31 rue Roy, Port-au-Prince; tel. 2223-7357; e-mail dg1@haiticulture.org; likely to have been destroyed in the earthquake of January 2010; Minister DANIEL ELIE.

Ministry of Education and Vocational Training: rue Dr Audain, Port-au-Prince; tel. 2222-1036; fax 2223-7887; likely to have been destroyed in the earthquake of January 2010; Minister GABRIEL BIEN-AIMÉ.

Learned Societies

GENERAL

UNESCO Office Port-au-Prince: 19, Delmas 60, Musseau par Bourdon, Petion Ville, Port-au-Prince; tel. 2511-0460; fax 2244-9366; e-mail unescohaiti@hainet.net; likely to have been destroyed in the earthquake of January 2010; Dir JORGE ESPINAL.

BIBLIOGRAPHY, LIBRARY SCIENCE AND MUSEOLOGY

Le Bibliophile: Cap Haïtien; f. 1923 to promote knowledge and readership of world literature; 28 mems; Pres. SILVIO FASCHI; Sec. LOUIS TOUSSAINT; publs *La Citadelle* (52 a year), *Stella* (12 a year).

LANGUAGE AND LITERATURE

Alliance Française: 99 rue Lamartinière, BP 131, Port-au-Prince; tel. 2244-0016; fax 2244-0017; e-mail dgalliancefr_haiti@yahoo.fr; offers courses and examinations in French language and culture and promotes cultural exchange with France; attached offices in Cap-Haïtien, Gonaïves, Jacmel, Jeremies, Les Cayes, Port-de-Paix; likely to have been destroyed in the earthquake of January 2010.

NATURAL SCIENCES

General

Conseil National des Recherches Scientifiques (National Council for Scientific Research): Département de la Santé Publique et de la Population, Port-au-Prince; f. 1963; to coordinate scientific development and research, particularly in the field of public health; likely to have been destroyed in the earthquake of January 2010; Pres. Prof. VICTOR NOËL; Sec. M. DOUYON.

Research Institute

RELIGION, SOCIOLOGY AND ANTHROPOLOGY

Bureau National d'Ethnologie: Angle rue St Honoré and ave Magloire Ambroise, Place des Héros de l'Indépendance, BP 915, Port-au-Prince; tel. 2222-5232; f. 1941; departments of African and Haitian ethnography, pre-Columbian archaeology; likely to have been destroyed in the earthquake of January 2010; Dir Dr MAX PAUL; publ. *Bulletin* (2 a year).

Libraries and Archives

Port-au-Prince

Archives Nationales d'Haiti: Angle rues Geffrard et Borgella, BP 1299, Port-au-Prince; tel. 2222-8566; fax 2222-6280; internet www.anhhaiti.org; f. 1860; likely to have been destroyed in the earthquake of January 2010; Dir-Gen. JEAN WILFRID BERTRAND.

Bibliothèque Haitienne des F. I. C.: 180 rue du Centre, BP 1758, Port-au-Prince 6110; tel. 2223-2148; fax 2223-2029; f. 1920; 13,000 vols; Haitian literature, newspapers since the 19th century, history of St Domingue and Haiti, Haitian legislation; likely to have been destroyed in the earthquake of January 2010; Dir ERNEST EVEN.

Bibliothèque Nationale d'Haïti: 193 rue du Centre, Port-au-Prince; tel. 2222-1198; fax 2223-8773; f. 1940; 23,000 vols, 419 periodicals; 12 brs; likely to have been destroyed in the earthquake of January 2010; Dir FRANÇOISE BEAULIEU THYBULLE.

Museums and Art Galleries

Port-au-Prince

Centre d'Art: 58 rue Roy, Port-au-Prince; tel. 2222-2018; f. 1944; arranges representative exhibitions of Haitian art in the Americas and Western Europe; likely to have been destroyed in the earthquake of January 2010; Dir FRANCINE MURAT.

Musée du Panthéon National Haitien: Place des Héros de l'Indépendance, Champ de Mars, Port-au-Prince Ouest; tel. 2222-3167; fax 2221-8838; e-mail mupanah@yahoo.fr; f. 1983; historical artefacts, arts and crafts; likely to have been destroyed in the earthquake of January 2010; Dir-Gen. MARIE-LUCIE VENDRYES.

Universities

UNIVERSITÉ D'ÉTAT D'HAITI

21 rue de Houx, BP 2279, Port-au-Prince

Telephone: 2244-2943
Fax: 2244-2940
E-mail: recteur@ueh.edu.ht
Internet: www.ueh.edu.ht

Founded 1920
State control
Language of instruction: French
Academic year: October to July

Rector: JEAN VERNET HENRY

Vice-Rector for Academic Affairs: MICHEL HECTOR

Vice-Rector for Admin.: MARIE CARMEL AUSTIN

Secretary-General: LESLIE DUCHATELLIER

Librarian: (vacant)

Library of 7,000 vols

Number of teachers: 664

Number of students: 10,446

Likely to have been destroyed in the earthquake of January 2010

DEANS AND COORDINATORS

Faculty of Agronomy and Veterinary Medicine: JEAN VERNET HENRY

Faculty of Applied Linguistics: PIERRE VERNET

Faculty of Ethnology: JEAN YVES BLOT, PATRICIA MICHEL FOUCAULT

Faculty of Humanities: JEAN RENOL ELIE

Faculty of Law and Economics: JUSTIN CASTEL

Faculty of Medicine and Pharmacy: Dr MARIO ALVAREZ

Faculty of Odontology: Dr ALIX CHATEIGNE

Faculty of Science: GUICHARD BEAULIEU (Academic: CHRISTIAN ROUSSEAU (Admin.)

Ecole Normale Supérieure: BERARD CENATUS, ROGER PETIT-FRÈRE

Institut d'Etudes et de Recherches Africaines d'Haiti: ERNST BERNADIN

Institut National d'Administration de Gestion et des Hautes Etudes Internationales (INAGHEI): EDDY CARRÉ

UNIVERSITÉ QUISQUEYA

Angle rue Chareron et boulevard Harry Truman, BP 796, Port-au-Prince

Telephone: 2222-9002

Fax: 2221-4211

E-mail: recteur@uniq.edu

Internet: www.uniq.edu.ht

Founded 1988

Private control

Language of instruction: French

Academic year: September to July

Rector: JACKY LUMARQUE

Vice-Rector for Academic Affairs: EDGARD PRÉVILON

Vice-Rector for Admin.: LIONEL RICHARD

Gen.-Sec.: MARIE GISÈLE PIERRE

Librarian: CARLO DUPUY

Library of 22,000 vols

Number of teachers: 256

Number of students: 2,036

Publication: *Revue Juridique de l'UniQ* (4 a year)

Destroyed in the earthquake of January 2010

DEANS

Faculty of Agriculture and the Environment: EDGARD JEANNITON

Faculty of Economics and Management: NARCISSE FIÈVRE

Faculty of Education: ROLAND MATHIEU

Faculty of Health Sciences: KYSS JEAN-MARY

Faculty of Law: MIRLANDE MANIGAT

Faculty of Science and Engineering: GÉRARD-LUC JEAN-BAPTISTE

UNIVERSITÉ ROI HENRI CHRISTOPHE

BP 98, rues 17–18, H-1, Cap-Haïtien

Telephone: 2262-1316

Fax: 2262-0802

Internet: www.urhchaiti.org

Founded 1980

Private control

Rector: JOSEPH YVON

Administrator: EDGARD BERNARDIN

Librarian: MARIE-MERCIE PREDESTIN

Number of students: 100

DEANS

Faculty of Agriculture: BRUNEL GARÇON

Faculty of Engineering: (vacant)

Faculty of Medicine: Dr GUY DUGUÉ

Colleges

Ecole Nationale des Arts et Métiers: 266 rue Monseigneur Guilloux, Port-au-Prince; tel. 2222-9686; f. 1983; likely to have been destroyed in the earthquake of January 2010; Dirs EMERANTE DE PRADINES MORSE, ROBERT BAU DUY.

Ecole Nationale de Technologie Médicale: Faculty of Medicine and Pharmacy, Université d'Etat d'Haiti, 89 rue Oswald Durand, POB 2599, Port-au-Prince 6110; tel. 2222-0487; e-mail fmp@ueh.edu.ht; likely to have been destroyed in the earthquake of January 2010; Dir PAULETTE A. CHAMPAGNE.

Institut International d'Etudes Universitaires: c/o Fondation Haitienne de Développement, 106 ave Christophe, Port-au-Prince; likely to have been destroyed in the earthquake of January 2010; Dir Y. ARMAND.

HONDURAS

The Higher Education System

The oldest institution of higher education is the Universidad Nacional Autónoma de Honduras, which was founded in 1847. There are two further state universities and seven private ones. The Ministry of Public Education is responsible for the provision of higher education. In 2005/06 145,171 students were enrolled in university-level education.

The secondary school qualification Bachillerato (Académico) is the main requirement for admission to higher education. The primary undergraduate degrees are the Licenciado or profes-sional title, awarded after four years of study, and the Bachillerato Universitario, a technological qualification also awarded after four years. Following the Licenciado, the first postgraduate degree is the Maestría, awarded after two to three years of study. The Bachillerato Universitario does not always guarantee admission to postgraduate studies.

Higher technical and vocational education is offered by professional colleges and schools. The leading qualification is the Técnico or Técnico Universitario, which requires one-and-a-half years of study.

Regulatory Bodies

GOVERNMENT

Ministry of Culture, Art and Sports: Avda La Paz, Apdo 328, Tegucigalpa; tel. 236-9643; fax 236-9532; e-mail binah@ sdnhon.org.hn; Minister Dr RODOLFO PASTOR FASQUELLE.

Ministry of Education: 1a Avda, 2a y 3a Calle 201, Comayagüela, Tegucigalpa; tel. 222-8571; fax 237-4312; e-mail info@se.gob .hn; internet www.se.gob.hn; Minister of State MARLÓN BREVÉ REYES.

Learned Societies

GENERAL

Academia Hondureña (Honduran Academy): Apdo 4003, Tegucigalpa; located at: Avda Tiburcio Carías Andino 811, Col. Alameda, Tegucigalpa; tel. 232-1322; fax 232-1322; e-mail ahlengua@hotmail.com; f. 1949; corresp. of the Real Academia Española (Madrid); 28 mems; Dir ÓSCAR ACOSTA; Sec. MARÍA ELBA NIETO SEGOVIA; publ. *Boletín*.

ARCHITECTURE AND TOWN PLANNING

Colegio de Arquitectos de Honduras (College of Honduran Architects): Apdo 1974, Tegucigalpa; tel. 235-8828; fax 235-7965; e-mail cah1@e-cah.org; internet www .e-cah.org; f. 1979; 727 mems; library; publ. *Arquitectura y Contexto* (4 a year).

BIBLIOGRAPHY, LIBRARY SCIENCE AND MUSEOLOGY

Asociación de Bibliotecarios y Archivistas de Honduras: 11a Calle, 1a y 2a Avdas No. 105, Comayagüela, Tegucigalpa; f. 1951; 53 mems; library of 3,000 vols; Pres. FRANCISCA DE ESCOTO ESPINOZA; Sec.-Gen. JUAN ANGEL AYES R.; publ. *Catálogo de Préstamo* (12 a year).

HISTORY, GEOGRAPHY AND ARCHAEOLOGY

Academia Hondureña de Geografía e Historia: Apdo 619, Tegucigalpa; f. 1968; 21 mems; library of 1,535 vols; Pres. Dr RAMÓN E. CRUZ; Sec. PM FERNANDO FERRARI BUSTILLO; publ. *Revista*.

LANGUAGE AND LITERATURE

Alliance Française: Col. Lomas Del Guijarro, Apdo Postal 3445, Tegucigalpa; tel. 239-6164; fax 239-6163; offers courses and examinations in French language and cul-ture and promotes cultural exchange with France; attached teaching offices in La Ceiba, San Pedro Sula, Tegucigalpa and Tela.

Research Institutes

GENERAL

Instituto Hondureño de Cultura Interamericana (IHCI): Apdo 201, Tegucigalpa; 2da Avda entre 5 y 6, Calle No. 520, Comayagüela; tel. 220-1393; fax 238-0064; f. 1939; courses in English, bilingual secretarial studies; art gallery; library of 8,000 vols (English and Spanish); Dir ROSARIO ELENA CÓRDOVA.

AGRICULTURE, FISHERIES AND VETERINARY SCIENCE

Instituto Hondureño del Café (Honduran Coffee Institute): Apdo Postal 3147, Tegucigalpa; located at: Col. Las Minitas, Edif. El Faro Contiguo a Embajada de Guatemala, Tegucigalpa; tel. 232-2544; fax 232-2768; internet www.cafedehonduras.hn/ ihcafe2005/ihcafe/quienessomos.html; f. 1970; CEO JUAN JOSÉ OSORTO.

Instituto Nacional Agrario (National Agrarian Institute): Col. Alameda, Calle Principal, 4a Avda entre 10 y 11 Calle, No. 1009, Tegucigalpa; tel. 232-4893; fax 239-7398; Dir ERASMO PORTILLO.

HISTORY, GEOGRAPHY AND ARCHAEOLOGY

Instituto Geográfico Nacional (IGN) (National Geographic Institute): Apdo Postal 3177, Tegucigalpa; Barrio La Bolsa, Tegucigalpa; tel. 225-2759; fax 225-2753; f. 1946; delineates natural and mineral resources, their evaluation and their exploitation; 130 staff; library of 8,000 vols; Dir-Gen. Ing. ANGEL PORFIRIO SANCHEZ SANCHEZ; publs *Boletín de la Dirección General de Cartografía*, *Boletín de la Dirección General de Cartografía del Ministerio de Obras Públicas, Transporte y Vivienda*, *Boletín del Instituto Geográfico Nacional*.

Instituto Hondureño de Antropología e Historia: Apdo 1518, Villa Roy, Barrio Buenos Aires, Tegucigalpa; tel. 222-3470; fax 222-2552; e-mail ihah2003@yahoo.com; internet www.ihah.hn; f. 1952; library of 12,000 vols; research and conservation of cultural property, archaeology, history, ethnography, linguistics, museology; Dir MARGARITA DURÓN DE GÁLVEZ; publ. *Yaxkin* (1 a year).

Libraries and Archives

Tegucigalpa

Archivo Nacional de Honduras: Avda Cristóbal Colón, Calle Salvador Mendieta 1117, Tegucigalpa; tel. 222-8338; fax 236-9532; internet www.secad.gob.hn/archi.htm; f. 1880; 700 linear m of documents; 2,700 vols and 100 periodicals; Dir CARLOS WILFREDO MALDONADO.

Biblioteca Nacional de Honduras: Apdo Postal 4563, Tegucigalpa; located at: Ave Cristobal Colón, Calle 'Salvador Mendieta', POB 1117, Tegucigalpa; tel. 228-0241; fax 222-8577; e-mail binah@sdnhon.org.hn; internet www.binah.gob.hn; f. 1880; 70,000 vols; co-ordinates national and international exchange; shares legal deposit with other centres; Dir HECTOR ROBERTO LUNA; publ. *Anuario Bibliográfico*.

Biblioteca 'Wilson Popenoe': Escuela Agrícola Panamericana, Apdo 93, Tegucigalpa; tel. 776-6140; fax 776-6113; e-mail hgallo@zamorano.edu; internet www .zamorano.edu/biblioteca; f. 1946; tropical agriculture; 19,000 vols, 950 periodicals, 1,200 DVDs; Librarian HUGO ALBERTO GALLO M.; publ. *Ceiba* (2 a year).

Sistema Bibliotecario Universidad Nacional Autónoma de Honduras: Edif. de Biblioteca, 3er piso, Carretera a Suyapa, Ciudad Universitaria, Tegucigalpa; tel. 232-2204; fax 232-2204; internet www.biblio .unah.hn; f. 1847; 200,000 vols; Librarian ORFYLIA PINEL; publ. *Boletín del Sistema Bibliotecario* (4 a year).

Museums and Art Galleries

Comayagua

Museo Arqueológico de Comayagua: Frente a Plaza San Francisco, Ciudad de Comayagua; tel. 772-03-86; f. 1946; archaeological collection from the Comayagua Valley; some contemporary items; Dir SALVADOR TURCIOS.

Copán

Museo Regional de Arqueología Maya: Ciudad de Copán; f. 1939; objects relate exclusively to Maya culture; Dir Prof. OSMIN RIVERA.

Cortés

Museo de la Fortaleza de San Fernando de Omoa: Omoa, Cortés; tel. 658-9167;

e-mail ihah2003@yahoo.com; internet www
.ihah.hn; attached to Honduran Institute of
Anthropology and History; f. 1959 in former
prison; colonial and historical items; Dir
GERARDO JOHNSON.

Universities

UNIVERSIDAD NACIONAL AUTÓNOMA DE HONDURAS

POB 3560, Tegucigalpa, DC

Telephone: 235-3361

Fax: 235-3361

Internet: www.unah.hn

Founded 1847

Autonomous control

Language of instruction: Spanish

Academic year: February to December

Rector: GUILLERMO PÉREZ-CADALSO ARIAS
Vice-Rector: OCTAVIO SÁNCHEZ MIDENCE
Admin.-Sec.: RAÚL FLORES
Gen.-Sec.: AFREDO HAWIT
Librarian: ORFYLIA PINEL

Library: see Libraries and Archives

Number of teachers: 3,486

Number of students: 56,077

Publications: *Catálogo de Estudios, Memoria
Anual, Presencia Universitaria, Revista de
la Universidad,* and various faculty publs

DEANS

Faculty of Law and Social Sciences: JESÚS
MARTINEZ
Faculty of Economics, Business Administra-
tion and Accountancy: GABRIEL ORDOÑEZ
Faculty of Medicine and Nursing: GUSTAVO
VALLEJO
Faculty of Chemistry and Pharmacy: GOD-
OFREDO CRUZ
Faculty of Dentistry: RAÚL SANTOS

Faculty of Engineering: ADOLFO RACHEL
QUAN

DIRECTORS

Atlantic Coast University Centre (La Ceiba):
Ing. JORGE SOTO MONICO
General Studies Centre: RAQUEL ANGULO
Regional Studies Centre: MARTÍN CASTRO
University Centre of the North (San Pedro
Sula): DARIO E. TURCOS

UNIVERSIDAD PEDAGÓGICA NACIONAL 'FRANCISCO MORAZÁN'

POB 3394, Calle El Dorado, Blvd Miraflores,
Tegucigalpa

Telephone: 239-8037

E-mail: webmaster@upnfm.edu.hn

Internet: www.upnfm.edu.hn

Founded 1957 as Escuela Superior del Pro-
fesorado, in co-operation with UNESCO;
current name and status since 1989

State control

Academic year: February to November (two
semesters)

Rector: RAMÓN ULISES SALGADO
Vice-Rector for Academic Affairs: LEA AZU-
CENA CRUZ
Vice-Rector for Admin.: DAVID ORLANDO
MARÍN
Vice-Rector for University Centre for Dis-
tance Learning: MARCIO BULNES
Sec.-Gen.: GUSTAVO ZELAYA
Librarian: ADÁN BRITO

Library of 35,000 vols

Number of teachers: 520

Number of students: 9,000

Publications: *Codice* (12 a year), *Revista
Paradigma* (4 a year)

Faculties of humanities, science and technology.

UNIVERSIDAD TECNOLÓGICA DE HONDURAS

Carretera a Armenta, Frente a Rio Blanco,
San Pedro Sula

Telephone: 551-2236

Fax: 551-6108

E-mail: mirna.rivera@uth.hn

Internet: www.uth.hn

Founded 1986 as Instituto Superior Tecnológico; current name and status since 1996

State control

Pres.: Lic. ROGER D. VALLADARES
Rector: RICARDO ANTILLÓN
Vice-Rector: Ing. FERNANDO FERRERA
Academic Dir: Lic. CELESTINO PADILLA

Number of students: 4,100

DIRECTORS

El Progreso Campus: Ing. ROBERTO CÁCERES
La Ceiba Campus: Lic. LUIS RIETTI
Puerto Cortés Campus: Dr MOHAM MERZKANI

College

**Escuela Agrícola Panamericana Zamor-
ano:** Apdo 93, Tegucigalpa; tel. 776-6140; fax
776-6240; e-mail gerencia_mercadeo@
zamorano.edu; internet www.zamorano.edu;
f. 1942; private, non-profit pan-American
instn of higher education; offers 4-year
undergraduate degree, with programmes in
Agricultural Science and Production, Agroin-
dustry, Agribusiness, and Socioeconomic
Development and Environment; 70 teachers;
800 students; library: 14,000 vols, 500 periodicals; Rector Dr KENNETH L. HOADLEY;
publ. *CEIBA* (3 a year).

HUNGARY

The Higher Education System

Higher education in Hungary dates back to the 14th century, with the establishment in 1367 of Pécsi Tudományegyetem (University of Pécs). Other long-established universities include Debreceni Egyetem (University of Debrecen; founded in 1538), Debreceni Református Hittudományi Egyetem (University of Reformed Theology of Debrecen; founded in 1538) and Evangélikus Hittudományi Egyetem (Evangelical–Lutheran Theological University; founded in 1557). In 1999–2000 the system of higher education underwent a major reorganization, as a result of which from 1 January 2000 there were 30 state-run universities and colleges, 26 church universities and colleges and six colleges run by foundations. In 2005 a new Act on Higher Education legislated the creation of a new system of university degrees (see below), and introduced financial and managerial reforms. In 2008/09 the figure for student enrolments in further and higher education was 381,033.

The Ministry of Education and Culture is responsible for establishing and recognizing institutions of higher education, which must gain accreditation from the Hungarian Accreditation Committee and Higher Education and Academic Council. The Act on Higher Education (2005) established an Economic Council to take responsibility for all decisions regarding the financing and management of the higher education sector. Universities and colleges are autonomous institutions and set their own curricula and courses.

Since 2004 admission to higher education has been based purely on results in the Erettsegi or Matura, the main secondary school qualifications. (Previously, admission had been based on a combination of the Erettsegi/Matura and competitive entrance examination.) In September 2006 a Bachelors-Masters-Doctorate degree system was introduced, based on the principles of the Bologna Process. The new courses are based on a 'credit semester' system, with students accruing a specified number of credits each semester in order to graduate. The main undergraduate degree is the Bachelors, which lasts six to eight semesters (three to four years) for which students must accumulate 180–240 credits. Following the Bachelors, the Masters is the first postgraduate degree, lasting two to four semesters (one to two years) during which students must accrue 60–120 credits (teacher training lasts five semesters or two-and-a-half years and requires 150 credits). In total, combined Bachelors and Masters studies must not last less than 10 nor more than 12 semesters. Finally, the Doctoral degree (PhD) is a six-semester programme (three years) requiring 180 credits.

Technical and vocational education has been integrated into the mainstream education system and the old system of apprenticeships has been phased out. Courses are offered by post-secondary vocational schools and last two years. Students are awarded the Technikusi Oklevel qualification and the title of Technikus (Technician).

Regulatory and Representative Bodies

GOVERNMENT

Ministry of Education and Culture: 1055 Budapest, Szalay u. 10-14; tel. (1) 302-0600; fax (1) 302-2002; e-mail info@okm.gov.hu; internet www.okm.gov.hu; Minister ISTVÁN HILLER.

ACCREDITATION

ENIC/NARIC Hungary: Educational Authority, Hungarian Equivalence and Information Centre, 1054 Budapest, Bathory u. 10; tel. (1) 374-2200; fax (1) 374-2492; e-mail ekvivalencia@oh.gov.hu; internet www.naric.hu; Head GABOR MESZAROS.

Magyar Felsőoktatási Akkreditációs Bizottság (Hungarian Accreditation Committee): 1061 Budapest, Király u. 16; tel. (1) 344-0314; fax (1) 344-0313; e-mail titkarsag@mab.hu; internet www.mab.hu; f. 1993; ind. body accrediting higher education instns and study programmes in disciplinary groups, in 5-year cycles; evaluates applications to set up new higher education instns and new study programs (framework requirements on national and program applications on institutional level); 19 mems; Pres. Prof. Dr GYÖRGY BAZSA.

NATIONAL BODIES

Felsőoktatási és Tudományos Tanács (Higher Education and Research Council): 1055 Budapest, Szalay u. 10-14, Room 105; tel. (1) 302-8603; fax (1) 269-5559; e-mail ftt@om.hu; internet www.ftt.hu; advisory body assisting the Min. of Education; reports on plans regarding the devt and modernization of instns and education systems; gives its opinion on preferred professions based on labour-market forecasts and employment statistics; 21 mems; Pres. Prof. Dr GYÖRGY BAZSA; Sec. Dr ANDRÁS VÁRKONYI.

Felsőoktatási Konferenciák Szövetsége (Confederation of Hungarian Conferences on Higher Education): 1146 Budapest, Ajtósi Dürer sor 19-21; tel. (1) 344-0310; fax (1)-251 3003; e-mail bilik@fksz.huninet.hu; Sec. Gen. Dr ISTVÁN BILIK.

Magyar Rektori Konferencia (Hungarian Rectors' Conference): 1064 Bp, Benczúr, u. 43. IV/3.; tel. (70) 932-4203; fax (1) 322-9679; e-mail mrk@mail.mrk.hu; internet www.mrk.hu; f. 2006; represents higher education instns and works to protect their interests; mems are 72 heads of higher education instns; Pres. Dr GÁBOR SZABÓ; Co-Pres. Dr ÉVA SÁNDORNÉ KRISZT, Dr IMRE RUDAS.

Learned Societies

GENERAL

Magyar Tudományos Akadémia (Hungarian Academy of Sciences): 1051 Budapest, Roosevelt tér 9; tel. (1) 411-6100; e-mail priroda@office.mta.hu; internet www.mta.hu; f. 1825; sections of 1. Linguistic and Literary Sciences (Chair. MIKLÓS MARÓTH), 2. Philosophy and Historical Sciences (Chair. MIKLÓS SZABÓ), 3. Mathematical Sciences (Chair. DOMOKOS SZÁSZ), 4. Agricultural Sciences (Chair. PÉTER HORN), 5. Medical Sciences (Chair. LÁSZLÓ ROMICS), 6. Technical Sciences (Chair. JÓZSEF GYULAI), 7. Chemical Sciences (Chair. KÁLMÁN MEDZIHRADSZKY), 8. Biological Sciences (Chair. SÁNDOR DAMJANO-VICH), 9. Economics and Law (Chair. ÁDÁM TÖRÖK), 10. Earth Sciences (Chair. JÓZSEF ÁDÁM), 11. Physical Sciences (Chair. ZALÁN HORVÁTH); 707 mems (203 hon., 250 ordinary, 92 corresp., 162 external); attached research institutes: see Research Institutes; library: see Libraries and Archives; Pres. E. SYLVE-STER VIZI; Gen. Sec. ATTILA MESKÓ; publs Acta Agronomica, Acta Alimentaria, Acta Antiqua, Acta Archaeologica, Acta Biologica, Acta Botanica, Acta Chirurgica, Acta Ethnographica, Acta Geodaetica et Geophysica, Acta Historiae Artium, Acta Historica, Acta Juridica, Acta Linguistica, Acta Mathematica, Acta Medica, Acta Microbiologica et Immunologica, Acta Oeconomica, Acta Orientalia, Acta Physica, Acta Physiologica, Acta Phytopathologica, Acta Technica, Acta Veterinaria, Acta Zoologica, Analysis Mathematica, Studia Musicologica, Studia Scientiarium Mathematicarum Hungarica, Studia Slavica, Bulletins of the Sections of the Academy, in five series.

Műszaki és Természettudományi Egyesületek Szövetsége (Federation of Technical and Scientific Societies): 1055 Budapest, Kossuth L. tér 6–8; tel. (1) 353-2808; fax (1) 353-0317; e-mail mtesz@mtesz.hu; internet www.mtesz.hu; f. 1948; 42 mem. socs; Pres. Dr GÁBOR SZÉLES; Sec.-Gen. ÁGOTA KÓSZ.

Széchenyi Irodalmi és Művészeti Akadémia (Széchenyi Academy of Letters and Arts): 1051 Budapest, Roosevelt tér 9; tel. (1) 331-4117; fax (1) 331-4117; e-mail szima@office.mta.hu; internet www.mta.hu; f. 1825 as an independent section of Hungarian Acad. of Sciences, ind. 1992; sections of Fine Arts, of Letters, of Music, of Theatre and Film; 98 mems, 86 full mems, 12 hon. mems; Pres. LÁSZLÓ DOBSZAY; Exec. Pres. GYŐZŐ FERENCZ; Exec. Sec. MAGDA FERCH.

AGRICULTURE, FISHERIES AND VETERINARY SCIENCE

Magyar Agrártudományi Egyesület (Hungarian Society of Agricultural Sciences): 1055 Budapest, Kossuth Lajos tér 6–8; tel. (1) 353-1950; fax (1) 353-0651; f. 1951; 8,500 mems; 17 affiliated socs; Sec.-Gen. Dr KÁROLY NESZMÉLYI; Pres. Dr KÁROLY TAMÁS; publ. *Magyar Mezőgazdaság* (Hungarian Agriculture, 12 a year).

Magyar Élelmezésipari Tudományos Egyesület (MÉTE) (Hungarian Scientific Society for Food Industry): 1027 Budapest, Fő u. 68; tel. (1) 214-6691; fax (1) 214-6692; e-mail mail.mete@mtesz.hu; internet www .mete.mtesz.hu; f. 1949; poultry breeding and processing, viticulture, sugar industry, confectionery, grain processing, meat industry, cold storage, canning, paprika, tobacco, oil, soap, cosmetics, brewery, bakery, distillery; 3,800 mems; Pres. Dr PETER BIACS; Exec. Dir Dr LÁSZLÓ CSERHÁTI; publs *A Hús* (Meat, 4 a year), *Ásványvíz-Üdítőital-Gyümölcslé* (Mineral Water-Softdrink-Juice, 4 a year), *Cukoripar* (Sugar Industry, 4 a year), *Édesipar* (Confectionery Industry, 4 a year), *Élelmezési Ipar* (Food Industry, 12 a year), *Hűtőipar* (Frozen Food Industry, 4 a year), *Konzervújság* (Canning News, 4 a year), *Molnárok Lapja* (Millers' Journal, 6 a year), *Olaj, Szappan, Kozmetika* (Oil, Soap, Cosmetics, 6 a year), *Sütőipar* (Baking Industry, 4 a year), *Szeszipar* (Distilling Industry, 4 a year), *Tejgazdaság* (Dairy Industry, 2 a year).

Országos Erdészeti Egyesület (Hungarian Forestry Association): 1027 Budapest, Fő u. 68; tel. (1) 201-6293; fax (1) 201-7737; e-mail oee@mtesz.hu; internet quercus.emk .nyme.hu/oee; f. 1866; forestry, forest industries, environment protection; 5,000 mems; library of 20,000 vols; Pres. JÓZSEF KÁLDY; Sec.-Gen. GÁBOR BARÁTOSSY; publ. *Erdészeti Lapok* (Forestry Bulletin).

ARCHITECTURE AND TOWN PLANNING

Építéstudományi Egyesület (Scientific Society for Building): 1027 Budapest, Fő u. 68; tel. and fax (1) 201-8416; e-mail info@ eptud.org; internet www.eptud.org; f. 1949; 3,500 mems; Pres. Dr CELESZTIN MESZLÉRY; Sec.-Gen. PÁL SEENGER; publs *Magyar Építőipar* (Hungarian Building Industry), *Magyar Épületgépészet* (Hungarian Sanitary and Installation Engineering).

BIBLIOGRAPHY, LIBRARY SCIENCE AND MUSEOLOGY

Magyar Könyvtárosok Egyesülete (Association of Hungarian Librarians): 1827 Budapest, Budavári Palota F.ép. 439 sz; tel. and fax (1) 311-8634; e-mail mke@oszk.hu; internet www.mke.oszk.hu; f. 1935; decision-making, library education and training; promotes librarianship and information sharing between libraries and librarians; 2,200 mems (incl. institutional mems); Pres. KLÁRA BAKOS; Sec.-Gen. ANIKÓ NAGY; Vice-Pres. Prof. ÁGNES HAJDU BARÁT; Vice-Pres. Dr ÉVA BARTOS; Vice-Pres. GÁBOR KISS.

Magyar Levéltárosok Egyesülete (Association of Hungarian Archivists): 1014 Budapest, Hess András tér 5; tel. and fax (20) 234-4822; e-mail mle.titkarsag@gmail.com; internet www.leveltaros.hu; f. 1986; 850 mems; Pres. ÁRPÁD TYEKVICSKA; Sec. ANITA KISS.

EDUCATION

Magyar Művelődési Intézet (Hungarian Institute of Culture): 1011 Budapest, Corvin tér 8; tel. (1) 201-5053; fax (1) 201-5764; e-mail mmi@mmi.hu; internet www.mmi.hu; f. 1951; analyses the social impact of cultural values, the changes in the content and organization of community education and the activities of cultural communities; organizes training for professionals in community education; centre for life-long education, folk art, minority cultures, amateur artistic and leisure pursuits, community devt, arts and crafts; 80 mems; library of 60,000 vols; special colln on past and present Hungarian folk high schools; Dir ANDRÁS FÖLDIÁK; publ. *SZIN* (6 a year).

FINE AND PERFORMING ARTS

Ferenc Liszt Academy of Music: 1391 Budapest, POB 206; 1061 Budapest, Liszt Ferenc tér 8; tel. (1) 462-4600; fax (1) 462-4648; internet www.lisztacademy.hu; f. 1875 to promote the work of the composer Franz Liszt (1811–1886), and to further the interest of audiences in live music; concerts, competitions, annual Liszt Record Grand Prix; establishment of Liszt memorials; 2 attached institutes: Béla Bartók Conservatory of Music and Secondary School, Zoltán Kodály Pedagogical Institute of Music; academic year September to June; 400 mems; library of 500,000 vols; 230 teachers (146 full-time, 84 part-time); 755 students (full-time); Rector Dr ANDRÁS BATTA; Vice-Rector JÁNOS DEVICH; Librarian ÁGNES GÁDOR.

Magyar Zenei Tanács (Hungarian Music Council): BMC Hungarian Music Information Centre, Lónyay u. 54, 1093 Budapest; tel. (1) 476-1097; fax (1) 210-6908; internet www.bmc.hu; f. 1996 to replace Magyar Zeneművészek Szövetsége; library of 7,400 vols, 13,600 scores, 1,700 CDs, 5,600 records, 800 tapes with 1,400 Hungarian compositions; Dir ADRIENNE MANKOVITS; Exec. Sec. ÁGNES PÁLDY; Head of the Music Information Centre ESZTER VIDA; publs *Polifónia* (irregular), *Magyar Zene* (Hungarian Music, 4 a year).

Magyar Zeneművészeti Társaság (Hungarian Music Society): 1111 Budapest, Bertalan u. 15; tel. (30) 351-8383; e-mail emzete@gmail.com; internet www.mzt008 .hu; f. 1987; 60 mems; aims to foster cultivation of Hungarian music, to promote the interests of musical artists, to educate young people's musical taste, to preserve Hungarian music past and present and performs only Hungarian contemporary pieces in the concerts of the Mini-Festival, held on the last weekend of every January; Pres. KLÁRA KÖRMENDI.

Országos Színháztörténeti Múzeum és Intézet (Hungarian Theatre Museum and Institute): 1013 Budapest, Krisztina-krt. 57; tel. (1) 375-1184; fax (1) 375-1184; e-mail oszmi@ella.hu; internet www.oszmi.hu; f. 1952; to research into theatre history and theory, information on Hungarian drama and theatre for abroad and on world drama and theatre for Hungarian professionals; controls the theatrical memorial places, and the Bajor Gizi Actors' Museum; 40 mems; Dir. Dr ANDRÁS NAGY; publs *Világszínház* (World Theatre, 6 a year), *Színháztudományi szemle* (Theatre Studies, 1 a year), *Évkönyv* (Yearbook).

HISTORY, GEOGRAPHY AND ARCHAEOLOGY

Magyar Földmérési, Térképészeti és Távérzékelési Társaság (Hungarian Society for Surveying, Mapping and Remote Sensing): 1371 Budapest, POB 433; 1149 Budapest, Bosnyák tér 5; tel. (1) 201-8642; fax (1) 460-4163; e-mail mfttt@freemail.hu; internet www.mfttt.hu; f. 1956; 1,000 mems; Pres. Dr SZABOLCS MIHÁLY; Sec.-Gen. ZOLTÁN UZSOKI; publ. *Geodézia és Kartográfia* (Geodesy and Cartography).

Magyar Irodalomtörténeti Társaság (Society of Hungarian Literary History): 1052 Budapest, Piarista köz 1; tel. (1) 337-7819; f. 1912; Pres. SÁNDOR IVÁN KOVÁCS; Gen. Sec. MIHÁLY PRAZNOVSZKY; publ. *Irodalomtörténet* (Literary History, 4 a year).

Magyar Történelmi Társulat (Hungarian Historical Society): 1014 Budapest, Uri u. 53; tel. (1) 375-9011; f. 1867; Pres. DOMOKOS KOSÁRY; Gen. Sec. IGNÁC ROMSICS; publ. *Századok* (6 a year).

LANGUAGE AND LITERATURE

Alliance Française: 6722 Szeged, Petofi Sandor SGT. 36, POB 1240; tel. and fax (62) 420-427; e-mail szeged@af.org.hu; internet www.af.org.hu; offers courses and examinations in French language and culture and promotes cultural exchange with France; attached offices in Debrecen, Gyor, Miskolc and Pécs; Dir SÜMEGI ISTVÁN.

British Council: 1068 Budapest, Benczúr u. 26; tel. (1) 478-4700; fax (1) 342-5728; e-mail information@britishcouncil.hu; internet www.britishcouncil.hu; teaching centre; offers courses and examinations in English language and British culture and promotes cultural exchange with the UK; Dir JIM McGRATH; Teaching Centre and Examinations Man. JOHN PARE.

Goethe-Institut: 1092 Budapest, Ráday utca 58, Ungarn; tel. (1) 374-4070; fax (1) 374-4080; e-mail info@budapest.goethe.org; internet www.goethe.de/budapest; offers courses and examinations in German language and culture and promotes cultural exchange with Germany; library of 13,000 vols; Dir Dr BRIGITTE KAISER-DERENTHAL.

Hungarian PEN Centre: 1053 Budapest, Károlyi Mihály u. 16; tel. (1) 411-0270; fax (1) 411-0270; e-mail hungary@penclub.t-online .hu; f. 1926; 325 mems; Pres. GÁBOR GÖRGEY.

Instituto Cervantes: 1064 Budapest, Vörösmarty u. 32; tel. (1) 354-3670; fax (1) 302-2954; e-mail cenbud@cervantes.es; internet budapest.cervantes.es; offers courses and exams in Spanish language and culture and promotes cultural exchange with Spain and Spanish-speaking Latin and Central America; Dir JOSEP MARIA DE SAGARRA ÁNGEL.

Magyar Írószövetség (Union of Hungarian Writers): 1062 Budapest, Bajza u. 18; tel. (1) 322-8840; fax (1) 321-3419; f. 1945; 1,100 mems; Pres. MÁRTON KALÁSZ.

Magyar Nyelvtudományi Társaság (Hungarian Linguistic Society): 1052 Budapest, Piarista köz 1; tel. (1) 137-6819; f. 1904; 660 mems; Pres. LORÁND BENKŐ; Gen.-Sec. JENŐ KISS; Sec. ANDRÁS ZOLTÁN; publ. *Magyar Nyelv* (The Hungarian Language, 4 a year).

Magyar Ujságirók Országos Szövetsége (National Federation of Hungarian Journalists): 1062 Budapest, Andrássy u. 101; tel. (1) 478-9071; fax (1) 343-4599; e-mail szakoszt@ muosz.hu; internet www.muosz.hu; 5,000 mems; Pres. ANDRÁS KERESZTY; Gen. Sec. GÁBOR BENCSIK.

MEDICINE

Magyar Gyógyszerészeti Társaság (Hungarian Pharmaceutical Society): 1085 Budapest, Gyulai Pál u. 16; tel. (1) 266-9395; fax (1) 483-1465; e-mail titkarsag@mgyt.hu; internet www.mgyt.hu; f. 1924; 1,200 mems; Pres. Dr I. ERŐS; Gen. Sec. L. BOTZ; publs *Acta Pharmaceutica Hungarica*, *Gyógyszerészet*.

Magyar Orvostársaságok és Egyesületek Szövetsége (MOTESZ) (Association of Hungarian Medical Societies): POB 145,

1443 Budapest; 1051 Budapest, Nádor u. 36; tel. (1) 311-6687; fax (1) 383-7918; e-mail szalma@motesz.hu; internet www.motesz .hu; f. 1966; 30,000 mems, 115 mem. socs; Pres. Prof. Dr PÉTER SÓTONYI; Dir-Gen. Dr BÉLA SZALMA; publ. *MOTESZ Magazine* (8 a year).

NATURAL SCIENCES
General

Tudományos Ismeretterjesztő Társulat (Society for the Dissemination of Scientific Knowledge): 1088 Budapest, Bródy Sándor u. 16; tel. (1) 338-2496; fax (1) 338-3320; e-mail eszter@fok.hu; f. 1841; library of 20,000 vols; 17,000 mems; Gen. Dir ESZTER PIRÓTH (acting); publs *Élet és Tudomány* (Life and Science, 52 a year), *Természet Világa* (World of Nature, 12 a year), *Valóság* (Reality, 12 a year).

Biological Sciences

Magyar Biofizikai Társaság (Hungarian Biophysical Society): 1371 Budapest, POB 433;; tel. (1) 202-1216; fax (1) 202-1216; e-mail mmt@mtesz.hu; internet www.mbft .hu; f. 1961; medical physics, ultrasound, radiation biophysics, photo-biophysics; 450 mems; Pres. Dr LAJOS KESZTHELYI; Sec.-Gen. Dr SÁNDOR GYÖRGYI; publ. *Magyar Biofizikai Társaság Értesítője* (every 3 years).

Magyar Biokémiai Egyesület (Hungarian Biochemical Society): 1518 Budapest, POB 7; 1113 Budapest, Karolina u. 29; tel. (1) 466-5856; fax (1) 466-5856; e-mail biro@enzim .hu; f. 1949; 1,015 mems; Pres. Dr PETER FRIEDRICH; Sec.-Gen. Dr PETER CSERMELY; publ. *Biokémia*.

Magyar Biológiai Társaság (Hungarian Biological Society): 1027 Budapest, Fő u. 68; tel. (1) 224-1423; fax (1) 201-7456; e-mail mbt@mtesz.hu; internet www.mbt.mtesz.hu; f. 1952; 1,500 mems; Pres. Dr TAMÁS PÓCS; Sec.-Gen. Dr ERNŐ BÁCSY; publs *Allattani Közlemények* (1 a year), *Antropológiai Közlemények* (1 a year), *Botanikai Közlemények* (1 a year), *Természetvédelmi Közlemények* (1 a year).

Magyar Biomassza Társaság (Hungarian Biomass Association): 9400 Sopron, Ady Endre u. 5; tel. (99) 518-188; fax (99) 357-480; e-mail mbmt@asys.hu; internet www .mbmt.hu; f. 1991; Pres. Prof. Dr JENŐ KOVÁCS; Gen. Sec. Prof. Dr BÉLA MAROSVÖLGYI.

Magyar Rovartani Társaság (Hungarian Entomological Society): 1088 Budapest, Baross u. 13; tel. (1) 267-7100; fax (1) 267-3462; internet www.magyarrovartanitarsasag.hu; f. 1910; 400 mems; Pres. Dr K. VIG; Sec. G. PUSKÁS; publ. *Folia Entomologica Hungarica / Rovartani Közlemények* (1 a year).

Mathematical Sciences

Bolyai János Matematikai Társulat (János Bolyai Mathematical Society): 1027 Budapest, Fő u. 68; tel. (1) 225-8410; fax (1) 201-6974; e-mail bjmt@renyi.hu; internet www.bolyai.hu; f. 1891; 2,000 mems; Pres. GYULA KATONA; Gen. Sec. ANDR'AS RECSKI; publs *Abacus* (9 a year), *Alkalmazott Matematikai Lapok* (Gazette for Applied Mathematics, 2 a year), *Combinatorica* (combinatorics and the theory of computing, 6 a year), *Középiskolai Matematikai Lapok* (Mathematical Gazette for Secondary Schools, 9 a year), *Matematikai Lapok* (Mathematical Gazette, 2 a year), *Periodica Mathematica Hungarica* (2 a year).

Physical Sciences

Eötvös Loránd Fizikai Társulat (Roland Eötvös Physical Society): 1027 Budapest, Fő u. 68; tel. (1) 201-8682; fax (1) 201-8682; e-mail mail.elft@mtesz.hu; internet www .kfki.hu/~elfthp; f. 1891; physics and astronomy; 1,800 mems; Pres. JUDIT NÉMETH; Gen. Sec. GÁBOR SZABÓ; publ. *Fizikai Szemle* (Physics Review, 12 a year).

Hungarian Association for Geo-Information (HUNAGI): 1122 Budapest, Pethényi ú. 11B; tel. (30) 415 8276; fax (1) 356-8003; e-mail hunagi@hunagi.hu; internet www.fomi.hu/hunagi; f. 1994; non-profit, interdisciplinary umbrella asscn promoting and supporting the devt and use of geo-information and its associated technologies; 66 governmental and non-governmental mem. orgs; Pres. and Chair. ZSOLT BARKÓCZI; Sec.-Gen. Dr GÁBOR REMETEY-FÜLÖPP; publs *Geodézia és Kartográfia, Geomatika*.

Magyar Asztronautikai Társaság (Hungarian Astronautical Society): 1027 Budapest, Fő u. 68; tel. (1) 201-8443; e-mail mant@ freemail.hu; internet www.mant.hu; f. 1956; 400 mems; Pres. Dr IVÁN ALMÁR; Gen. Sec. ANDRÁS VARGA.

Magyar Geofizikusok Egyesülete (Association of Hungarian Geophysicists): 1027 Budapest, Fő u. 68 I/113; tel. and fax (1) 201-9815; e-mail geophysic@mtesz.hu; internet www.elgi.hu/mge; f. 1954; 650 mems; Pres. Dr FERENC ABELE; Sec. ANDRÁS PÁLYI; publ. *Magyar Geofizika* (Hungarian Geophysics, 4 a year).

Magyar Hidrológiai Társaság (Hungarian Hydrological Society): POB 433, 1371 Budapest; tel. (1) 201-7655; fax (1) 202-7244; e-mail mail.mht@mtesz.hu; internet www .mtesz.hu/tagegyesuletek/mht; f. 1917; 5,000 mems; Pres. Dr ÖDÖN STAROSOLSZKY; Sec.-Gen. ZOLTÁN SZÖLLŐSI; publs *Hidrológiai Közlöny* (Hydrological Journal, every 2 months), *Hidrológiai Tájékoztató* (Circular on Hydrology, 1 a year).

Magyar Karszt-és Barlangkutató Társulat (Hungarian Speleological Society): 1025 Budapest, Pusztaszeri u. 35; tel. (1) 346-0494; fax (1) 346-0495; internet www.barlang .hu; f. 1910; 1,000 mems; library of 5,000 vols; Pres. Dr LÁSZLÓ KORPÁS; Sec.-Gen. PÉTER BÖRCSÖK; publ. *Karszt és Barlang* (with summaries in English, 1 a year).

Magyar Kémikusok Egyesülete (Hungarian Chemical Society): 1027 Budapest, Fő u. 68; tel. (1) 201-6883; fax (1) 201-8056; e-mail androsits@mke.org.hu; internet www.mke .org.hu; f. 1907; 6,000 mems; Pres. Dr PÉTER MÁTYUS; Sec.-Gen. Dr ATTILA KOVÁCS; publs *Középiskolai Kémiai Lapok* (Secondary School Chemical Papers, 5 a year), *Magyar Kémiai Folyóirat* (Hungarian Journal of Chemistry, 12 a year), *Magyar Kémikusok Lapja* (Hungarian Chemical Journal, 12 a year).

Magyar Meteorológiai Társaság (Hungarian Meteorological Society): 1371 Budapest, Fő u. 68, POB 433; tel. (1) 201-7525; fax (1) 202-1216; e-mail mmt@mtesz.hu; f. 1925; 360 mems; Pres. Dr PÁL AMBRÓZY; Gen. Sec. Dr GYÖRGY GYURÓ.

Magyarhoni Földtani Társulat (Hungarian Geological Society): 1051 Budapest, Csalogány u. 12. I/1; tel. and fax (1) 201-9129; e-mail mft@mft.t-online.hu; internet www .foldtan.hu; f. 1848; 900 mems; Pres. Dr JÁNOS HAAS; Sec.-Gen. Dr ZOLTÁN UNGER; publ. *Földtani Közlöny* (Bulletin, 4 a year).

Optikai, Akusztikai és Filmtechnikai Tudományos Egyesület (Scientific Society for Optics, Acoustics, Motion Pictures and Theatre Technology): 1027 Budapest, Fő u. 68; tel. (1) 202-0452; internet www.opakfi.hu; f. 1933; 1,800 mems; Pres. Dr LUPKOVICS GÁBOR; Sec.-Gen. Dr BALOGH GÉZA; publs *Elektrónikai Technológia-Mikrotechnika* (Electronic Technology-Microtechnics, 12 a year), *Kép és Hangtechnika* (Picture and Audio Techniques, every 2 months), *Szinháztechnikai Fórum* (Forum of the Technical Theatre, 4 a year).

PHILOSOPHY AND PSYCHOLOGY

Magyar Filozófiai Társaság (Hungarian Philosophical Association): 1364 Budapest, Pf. 107; tel. and fax (1) 266-4195; f. 1987; 400 mems; Pres. KRISTÓF NYÍRI; Gen. Sec. ISTVÁN M. BODNÁR.

Magyar Pszichológiai Társaság (Hungarian Psychological Association): 1132 Budapest, Victor Hugo 18–22; tel. (1) 350-0555; fax (1) 350-0555; f. 1928; 1,293 mems; Pres. MAGDA RITOÓK; Scientific Sec. KATALIN VARGA; publ. *Magyar Pszichológiai Szemle* (Hungarian Psychological Review).

RELIGION, SOCIOLOGY AND ANTHROPOLOGY

Magyar Néprajzi Társaság (Hungarian Ethnographical Society): 1055 Budapest, Kossuth Lajos tér 12; tel. and fax (1) 269-1272; e-mail mnt@neprajz.hu; f. 1889; 1,340 mems; Pres. LÁSZLÓ KÓSA; Sec.-Gen. IMRE GRÁFIK; publ. *Ethnographia* (4 a year).

Magyar Szociológiai Társaság (Hungarian Sociological Association): 1014 Budapest, Országház u. 30; tel. (1) 224-0786; fax (1) 224-0790; e-mail mszt@socio.mta.hu; internet www.szociologia.hu; f. 1978; conferences, debates, discussions for domestic and int. researchers in order to facilitate and maintain int. sociological partnerships; follows nat. and int. sociological research and its results; cooperates with the instns of science and education to discuss the training of sociologists; 682 mems; Pres. GYÖRGY CSEPELI; Sec. Gen. VERONIKA PAKSI; publs *Szociológiai Szemle* (4 a year), *Review of Sociology* (2 a year).

TECHNOLOGY

Bőr-, Cipő-, és Bőrfeldolgozóipari Tudományos Egyesület (Scientific Society of the Leather, Shoe and Allied Industries): 1325 Budapest, POB 155; 1047 Budapest, Attila u. 64; tel. (1) 272-0011; fax (1) 369-1058; e-mail bimeo@bimeo.hu; internet www.bimeo.hu/ bor-cipo/bcbte.htm; f. 1930; Pres. Dr TAMÁS KARNITSCHER; publ. *Bőr és Cipőtechnika* (Leather and Shoe News, 6 a year).

Energiagazdálkodási Tudományos Egyesület (Scientific Society of Energy Economics): 1372 Budapest, POB 451; 1055 Budapest, Kossuth Lajos tér 6–8; tel. (1) 153-2751; fax (1) 153-3894; e-mail mail.ete@ mtesz.hu; internet www.ete.mtesz.hu; f. 1949; 3,000 mems; Pres. Dr TAMÁS ZETTNER; Vice-Pres. GYŐZŐ WIEGAND; publ. *Energiagazdálkodás (Energetrics)* (12 a year).

Faipari Tudományos Egyesület (Scientific Society of the Timber Industry): 1027 Budapest, Fő u. 68; tel. (1) 201-9929; e-mail fate.bp@freemail.hu; f. 1950; 1,800 mems; Pres. Dr SÁNDOR MOLNÁR; Sec.-Gen. DEZSŐ LELE; publ. *Faipar* (Timber Industry).

Gépipari Tudományos Egyesület (GTE) (Scientific Society of Mechanical Engineers): 1371 Budapest, Fő u. 68, POB 433; tel. (1) 202-0582; fax (1) 202-0252; e-mail mail.gte@ mtesz.hu; internet www.mtesz.hu/gtagegy/ gte; f. 1949; sciences of mechanical engineering, dissemination of technical culture, assisting the technical and economic development of Hungary; 4,800 mems; library of 1,500 vols; Pres. Prof. Dr JÁNOS TAKÁCS; Sec.-Gen. Dr TAMÁS BÁNKY; publs *Gép* (Machine, 12 a year), *Jármüvek* (Vehicles, 12 a year), *Gépgyártás* (Production Engineering, 12 a year), *Műanyag és Gumi* (Plastics and Rubber, 12 a year), *Gépipar* (Machinery, 12 a year).

Hírközlési és Informatikai Tudományos Egyesület (Scientific Association for Info-communication): 1055 Budapest, Pf. 451, Kossuth Lajos tér 6–8; tel. (1) 353-1027; fax (1) 353-0451; e-mail info@hte.hu; internet www.hte.hu; f. 1949; organization of conferences, discussions, seminars, technical exhibitions, postgraduate courses, study trips, expert advice for official organs and enterprises, recommendations for official organs, public discussion and criticism of technical, economic, scientific and educational matters, engineering activities; 2,500 mems; Pres. Prof. Dr GYULA SALLAI; Sec.-Gen. PÁL HORVÁTH; publs *Híradástechnika*, *Hírlevél*.

Közlekedéstudományi Egyesület (Scientific Association for Transport): 1055 Budapest, Kossuth Lajos tér 6–8; tel. (1) 153-2005; fax (1) 153-2005; e-mail info.kte@mtesz.hu; internet www.mtesz.hu/kte; f. 1949; 6,723 mems; Pres. Dr SÁNDOR GYURKOVICS; Sec.-Gen. Dr ANDRÁS KATONA; publs *Közlekedéstudományi Szemle* (Communications Review), *Közúti és Mélyépítési Szemle* (Civil Engineering Review), *Városi Közlekedés* (Urban Transport).

Magyar Elektrotechnikai Egyesület (Hungarian Electrotechnical Association): 1055 Budapest, Kossuth Lajos tér 6–8; tel. (1) 353-0117; fax (1) 353-4069; e-mail mee@mee.hu; internet www.mee.hu; f. 1900; 6,500 mems; Pres. Dr ISTVÁN KRÓMER; Dir PÉTER LERNYEI; publ. *Elektrotechnika* (Electrical Engineering, 12 a year).

Magyar Iparjogvédelmi és Szerzői Jogi Egyesület (Hungarian Association for the Protection of Industrial Property and Copyright): 1055 Budapest, Kossuth Lajos tér 6–8; tel. (1) 153-1661; fax (1) 153-1780; e-mail mie@axelero.hu; internet www.mie.org.hu; f. 1962; 2,250 mems; Pres. Dr BACHER VILMOS; Sec.-Gen. Dr GÖDÖLLE ISTVÁN.

Méréstechnikai és Automatizálási Tudományos Egyesület (Scientific Society for Measurement, Automation and Informatics): 1055 Budapest V, Kossuth tér 6–8; tel. (1) 332-9571; fax (1) 353-1406; e-mail mate@mtesz.hu; internet www.mate.mtesz.hu; f. 1952; 1,075 mems; Pres. ISTVÁN KOCSIS; Man. Gen. Sec. Dr ZSUZSANNA PINTÉR; publ. *Mérés és Automatika* (Measurement and Automation).

Neumann János Számítógéptudományi Társaság (John von Neumann Computer Society): 1054 Budapest, Báthori u. 16; tel. (1) 472-2730; fax (1) 472-2728; e-mail titkarsag@njszt.hu; internet www.njszt.hu; f. 1968 to promote the study, development and application of computer sciences; 2,400 mems; library of 3,000 vols; Pres. Prof. GÁBOR PÉCELI; Man. Dir ISTVÁN ALFÖLDI.

Országos Magyar Bányászati és Kohászati Egyesület (Hungarian Mining and Metallurgical Society): 1027 Budapest, Fő u. 68; tel. (1) 201-7337; fax (1) 201-7337; e-mail ombke@mtesz.hu; internet www.ombkenet.hu; f. 1892; 4,000 mems; library of 1,500 vols; Pres. Dr LAJOS TOLNAY; Gen. Sec. ÁRPÁD KOVACSICS; publs *Bányászat* (Mining, 6 a year), *Kohászat* (Metallurgy, 6 a year), *Kőolaj és Földgáz* (Oil and Gas, 12 a year).

Papír- és Nyomdaipari Műszaki Egyesület (Technical Association of the Paper and Printing Industry): 1371 Budapest, Pf. 433; 1027 Budapest, Fő u. 68; tel. (1) 457-0633; fax (1) 202-0256; e-mail mail.pnyme@mtesz.hu; internet www.pnyme.hu; f. 1948; 1,800 individual mems, 130 corporate mems; Pres. Dr ZOLTAN SZIKLA; Sec.-Gen. ENDRE FÁBIAN; publs *Magyar Grafika* (Hungarian Printers and Graphic Designers), *Papíripar* (Paper Industry).

Szervezési és Vezetési Tudományos Társaság (Society for Organization and Management Science): 1027 Budapest, Fő u. 68; tel. (1) 202-1083; fax (1) 202-0856; e-mail szvt@szvt.hu; internet www.szvt.hu; f. 1970; 5,000 mems; Pres. Dr FERENC TRETHON; Sec.-Gen. Dr JÁNOS PAKUCS; publ. *Ipar-Gazdaság* (Industrial Economy, 12 a year).

Szilikátipari Tudományos Egyesület (Scientific Society of the Silicate Industry): 1027 Budapest, Fő u. 68; tel. (1) 201-9360; e-mail mail.szte@mtesz.hu; internet www.szte.org.hu; f. 1949; 2,300 mems; library of 2,500 vols; Pres. JENŐ VIG; Sec.-Gen. Dr MÁRTA FODOR; publ. *Építőanyag* (Building Materials).

Textilipari Műszaki és Tudományos Egyesület (Hungarian Society of Textile Technology and Science): 1027 Budapest, Fő u. 68; tel. (1) 201-8782; fax (1) 224-1454; e-mail info.tmte@mtesz.hu; internet www.tmte.hu; f. 1948; 1,300 mems; Pres. Dr FERENC CSÁSZI; Gen. Sec. Dr KATALIN MÁTHÉ; publs *Magyar Textiltechnika* (Hungarian Textile Engineering), *Textiltisztitás* (Textile Cleaning).

Research Institutes

AGRICULTURE, FISHERIES AND VETERINARY SCIENCE

Állattenyésztési és Takarmányozási Kutatóintézet (Research Institute for Animal Breeding and Nutrition): 2053 Herceghalom, Gesztenyés u. 1; tel. (23) 319-133; fax (23) 319-120; e-mail atk@atk.hu; internet www.atk.hu; research into large animal breeding, nutrition, reproductive biology, genetics, nutrition biology and microbiology; library of 4,800 vols; Gen. Dir Dr JÓZSEF RÁTKY; publ. *Állattenyésztés és Takarmányozás* (Animal Production, 6 a year, with English summaries).

Gabonakutató Nonprofit Közhasznú Kft. (Cereal Research Non-Profit Ltd.): 6701 Szeged, POB 391; tel. (62) 435-235; fax (62) 434-163; e-mail info@gabonakutato.hu; internet www.gabonakutato.hu; f. 1924; research into the cultivation of wheat, barley, oats, maize, triticale, sunflower, linseed, winter rapeseed, red clover, soybean, sorghum, Sudan grass, millet; breeding, agronomy, seed trading, dietetic food; library of 12,000 vols; Dir Dr J. MATUZ; publ. *Cereal Research Communications* (4 a year).

Magyar Tejgazdasági Kisérleti Intézet (Hungarian Dairy Research Institute): 9200 Mosonmagyaróvár, Lucsony u. 24; tel. (96) 215-711; fax (96) 215-789; e-mail mtki@mtki.hu; internet www.mtki.hu; f. 1903; brs in Budapest and Pécs; scientific research of raw materials, technology, engineering, chemistry, microbiology, economics; library of 5,700 vols; Dir Dr ANDRÁS UNGER.

Magyar Tudományos Akadémia Állatorvos-tudományi Kutatóintézete (Veterinary Medical Research Institute, Hungarian Academy of Sciences): 1143 Budapest, Hungária krt. 21; tel. (1) 252-2455; fax (1) 252-1069; e-mail harrach@vmri.hu; internet www.vmri.hu; f. 1949; research in infectious and parasitic diseases of domestic and wild animals (virology, bacteriology, fish parasitology); library of 6,750 vols; Dir Dr TIBOR MAGYAR (acting); Vice-Dir Dr. ISTVAN TOTH; publ. *Acta Veterinaria Hungarica* (4 a year).

Magyar Tudományos Akadémia Mezőgazdasági Kutatóintézete (Agricultural Research Institute of the Hungarian Academy of Sciences): 2462 Martonvásár; tel. (22) 569-500; fax (22) 460-213; internet www.mgki.hu; f. 1949; research in plant genetics, plant physiology, plant breeding and plant cultivation of maize and wheat; library of 16,000 vols; Dir ZOLTÁN BEDŐ; publ. *Martonvásár* (2 a year).

Magyar Tudományos Akadémia Növényvédelmi Kutatóintézete (Plant Protection Institute, Hungarian Academy of Sciences): 1525 Budapest II, Herman Ottó u. 15, Box 102; tel. (1) 487-7500; fax (1) 487-7555; e-mail bbar@nki.hu; internet www.nki.hu; f. 1880, reorganized 1950; research on plant diseases, insect pests, pesticide chemistry and plant biochemistry, biotechnology, virology; 100 mems; library of 20,000 vols; Dir Dr BALÁZS BARNA.

Magyar Tudományos Akadémia Talajtani és Agrokémiai Kutató Intézete (Research Institute for Soil Science and Agricultural Chemistry of the Hungarian Academy of Sciences): 1022 Budapest, Herman Ottó u. 15; tel. and fax (1) 356-4682; e-mail rissac@rissac.hu; internet www.taki.iif.hu; f. 1949; research in soil physics, chemistry, geography and cartography, reclamation of salt-affected and sandy soils, irrigation, conservation, fertilization, soil mineralogy, soil microbiology, soil ecology, recultivation; library of 27,000 vols; Dir Prof. Dr T. NÉMETH; publ. *Agrokémia és Talajtan* (Agrochemistry and Soil Science, 2 a year).

Országos Állategészségügyi Intézet (Central Veterinary Institute): 1149 Budapest, Tábornok u. 2; tel. (1) 252-8444; fax (1) 252-5177; e-mail web@oai.hu; internet sgicenter.oai.hu/oai; f. 1928; diagnostic examinations and research work on the infectious, parasitic and metabolic diseases of animals, also veterinary toxicology and diseases of wild animals; 95 mems; library of 5,966 vols; Dir L. TEKES.

Országos Mezőgazdasági Minősitő Intézet (National Institute for Agricultural Quality Control): 1024 Budapest, Keleti Károly u. 24; tel. (1) 336-9114; fax (1) 336-9011; e-mail novenytermesztesi.ig@ommi.hu; internet www.ommi.hu; f. 1988 by amalgamation of four orgs; 606 mems; library of 20,000 vols; Dir Dr KATALIN ERTSEY; publ. National List of Varieties, Descriptive List of Varieties, List of approved grape and fruit varieties, selections and foreign varieties permitted for propagation (1 a year), *Yearbook* of cattle, pig, sheep, horse, water fowl, fish breeding and beekeeping.

Szőlészeti és Borászati Kutató Intézet (Research Institute for Viticulture and Oenology): 6000 Kecskemét-Miklóstelep, Urihegy 5/A, POB 25; tel. (76) 494-888; fax (76) 494-924; e-mail titkarsag@szbkik.hu; f. 1898; viticulture, oenology, economy; library of 7,200 vols; Dir Dr ERNŐ PÉTER BOTOS; publ. *Bor és Piac* (12 a year).

VITUKI Környezetvédelmi és Vízgazdálkodási Kutató Intézet nonprofit Kft (VITUKI Environmental and Water Management Research Institute nonprofit Ltd.): 1095 Budapest, Kvassay Jenő u. 1; tel. (1) 215-6140; fax (1) 216-1514; e-mail vituki@vituki.hu; internet www.vituki.hu; f. 1952; basic and applied research associated with hydrological data colln, processing, storage, information; hydrology of groundwater, karst water, regional soil moisture control; hydromechanics of hydraulic structures; pollution and quality control of water; hydrological and hydraulic problems in agricultural water management (drainage, irrigation); air pollution control; odour and noise control; remediation; waste management; library of 13,000 vols; Man. Dir ATTILA KARI; publs *Hydrological Yearbook of Hungary* (1 a year), *VITUKI Proceedings* (1 a year).

ECONOMICS, LAW AND POLITICS

Magyar Tudományos Akadémia Jogtudományi Intézete (Institute for Legal Studies of the Hungarian Academy of Sciences): 1014 Budapest, Országház u. 30; tel. (1) 355-7384; fax (1) 375-7858; e-mail lamm@jog.mta.hu; f. 1949; departments of legal theory, international law, constitutional and administrative law, civil law, criminal law, comparative law, human rights; library of 52,000 vols; Dir Prof. Dr VANDA LAMM; publs *Állam- és Jogtudomány* (2 a year), *Acta Juridica Hungarica* (2 a year).

Magyar Tudományos Akadémia Közgazdaságtudományi Intézet (Institute of Economics of the Hungarian Academy of Sciences): 1112 Budapest, Budaörsi u. 45; tel. (1) 309-2651; fax (1) 309-2650; e-mail titkarsag@econ.core.hu; internet econ.core.hu; f. 1954; research in macroeconomics, growth and economic policy, labour economics and human resources, public and institutional economics, microeconomics and sectoral economics, international economics, mathematical economics, history of economic thought, agricultural economics and rural devt, economics of technological change; empirical industrial organization; globalization, EU-integration and convergence; public economics and public policies; economics of education; library of 45,000 vols, 124 periodicals; Deputy Dir for Scientific Issues Prof. LÁSZLÓ HALPERN; Scientific Sec. Dr ZSUZSA BALABÁN; publs *Budapesti Munkagazdaságtani Füzetek* (Budapest Working Papers on the Labour Market, in English and Hungarian, 9 or 10 a year), *Műhelytanulmányok* (Discussion Papers, in English and Hungarian, 9 or 10 a year), *Munkatudományi Kutatások* (Labour Research Volumes, 1 a year), *Munkaerőpiaci tükör* (Labour Market Yearbook, with chapters in English), *Verseny és Szabályozás* (Competition and Regulation, in Hungarian, 12 a year).

Magyar Tudományos Akadémia Politikai Tudományok Intézete (Institute for Political Science of the Hungarian Academy of Sciences): 1014 Budapest, Országház u. 30; tel. (1) 224-6724; fax (1) 224-6727; e-mail ipshas@mtapti.hu; internet www.mtapti.hu; f. 1991; study of political systems, party politics, nat. and local govt, political culture, elections, problems of integration with the EU, migration, security policy and NATO; library of 43,000 vols; Research Dir Dr ANDRÁS KÖRÖSÉNYI; publ. *Hungarian Political Science Review* (in Hugarian, 4 a year).

Magyar Tudományos Akadémia Világgazdasági Kutató Intézete (Institute for World Economics of the Hungarian Academy of Sciences): 1014 Budapest, Országház u. 30; tel. (1) 224-6760; fax (1) 224-6761; e-mail vki@vki3.vki.hu; internet www.vki.hu; f. 1965; research in world economics; library of 102,000 vols; Dir Prof. ANDRÁS INOTAI; publs *Kihívások* (Challenges, irregular), *Műhelytanulmányok* (Workshop Studies, irregular), *Trends in World Economy*, *Working Papers* (in English, irregular).

Teleki László Intézet (László Teleki Institute): 1125 Budapest, Szilágyi Erzsébet fasor 22/c; tel. (1) 391-5721; fax (1) 391-5745; e-mail mki@tla.hu; internet www.telekialapitvany.hu; f. 1999; prepares analytical material and information for foreign policy instns; research on theoretical issues of international relations; organizes round-table conferences, seminars, lectures; reference library; Dir Prof. GYÖRGY GRANASZTÓI; publs *Külügyi Szemec* (foreign policy; in Hungarian 4 a year, in English 2 a year), *Reyio* (minorities, soc., politics; in Hungarian 4 a year, in English 1 a year).

EDUCATION

Felsőoktatási Kutatóintézet (Hungarian Institute for Higher Educational Research): 1146 Budapest, Ajtósi Dürer sor 19–21; tel. (1) 221-0365; fax (1) 208-056; e-mail oktataskutato@ella.hu; internet www.hier.iif.hu; f. 1981; applied social research and postgraduate training in school education, higher education and vocational education; library of 23,000 vols; Dir Dr LISKO ILONA; publs *Educatio* (review, 4 a year), *Kutatás Közben* (Research Papers, 6 a year).

FINE AND PERFORMING ARTS

Magyar Tudományos Akadémia Művészettörténeti Kutatóintézet (Research Institute for Art History of the Hungarian Academy of Sciences): 1014 Budapest, Uri u. 49; tel. (1) 224-6700; fax (1) 375-0493; e-mail arthist@arthist.mta.hu; internet www.arthist.mta.hu; f. 1969; research on Hungarian art since 10th century; library of 40,000 vols; Dir LÁSZLO BEKE; publ. *Ars Hungarica* (2 a year).

Magyar Tudományos Akadémia Zenetudományi Intézet (Institute for Musicology of the Hungarian Academy of Sciences): 1014 Budapest, Táncsics Mihály u. 7; tel. (1) 356 6858; fax (1) 375-9282; e-mail info@zti.hu; internet www.zti.hu; f. 1961; incorporates the Bartók Archives, the Museum of History of Music, and depts of Folk Dances, Folk Music, History of Early Music, History of Hungarian Music; library of 150,000 vols; 100,000 recorded melodies; Dir Prof. Dr TIBOR TALLIÁN; publ. *Studia Musicologica* (4 a year).

HISTORY, GEOGRAPHY AND ARCHAEOLOGY

Magyar Tudományos Akadémia Földrajztudományi Kutatóintézet (Geographical Research Institute, Hungarian Academy of Sciences): 1112 Budapest, Budaörsi u. 45; tel. (1) 309-2600; fax (1) 309-2690; e-mail kocsisk@mtafki.hu; internet www.mtafki.hu; f. 1950, reorg. 1952; research in physical and human geography; library of 71,967 vols; Dir Dr KÁROLY KOCSIS; publs *Földrajzi Értesítő* (Hungarian Geographical Bulletin, 4 a year), *Földrajzi Tanulmányok*, *Studies in Geography in Hungary*, *Geographical Abstracts from Hungary*.

Magyar Tudományos Akadémia Régészeti Intézete (Archaeological Institute of the Hungarian Academy of Sciences): 1250 Budapest, Uri u. 49; tel. (1) 356-4567; fax (1) 224-6719; e-mail konyvtar@archeo.mta.hu; internet www.archeo.mta.hu; f. 1958; research in archaeology and associated sciences; 58 mems; library of 70,281 vols; Dir Prof. CSANÁD BÁLINT; publs *Magyarország Régészeti Topográfiája* (Archaeological Topography of Hungary), *Antaeus* (yearbook, in German and English), *Varia Archaeologica Hungarica* (in foreign languages, irregular).

Magyar Tudományos Akadémia Regionális Kutatások Központja (Research Centre for Regional Studies of the Hungarian Academy of Sciences): 7621 Pécs, Papnövelde u. 22; tel. (72) 523-800; fax (72) 523-803; e-mail postmaster@rkk.hu; internet www.rkk.hu; f. 1943; research into regional planning, geography, economics, government, sociology, ethnography, and history; 60 mems; library of 40,000 vols; Dir-Gen. Prof. GYULA HORVÁTH; publs *Tér és Társadalom* (4 a year), *Alföldi Tanulmányok* (irregular).

Magyar Tudományos Akadémia Történettudományi Intézete (Institute of Historical Science of the Hungarian Academy of Sciences): 1014 Budapest, Uri u. 53; tel. (1) 224-6755; fax (1) 224-6756; e-mail apok@tti .hu; internet www.tti.hu; f. 1949; five depts of Hungarian history and comparative European history, one dept of documentation and bibliography, historiography; library of 100,000 vols; Dir Prof. FERENC GLATZ; publs *Történelmi Szemle* (4 a year), annual bibliography of historical works published in Hungary.

LANGUAGE AND LITERATURE

Magyar Tudományos Akadémia Irodalomtudományi Intézete (Institute of Literary Studies of the Hungarian Academy of Sciences): 1118 Budapest, Ménesi u. 11–13; tel. (1) 385-8790; fax (1) 185-3876; internet www.iti.mta.hu; f. 1956; research in Hungarian and world literature; library of 170,000 vols; Dir Prof. LÁSZLÓ SZÖRÉNYI; publs *Irodalomtörténeti Közlemények* (6 a year), *Helikon* (4 a year), *Literatura* (4 a year), *Irodalomtörténeti Füzetek* (studies, irregular), *Neohelicon* (2 a year).

Magyar Tudományos Akadémia Nyelvtudományi Intézete (Research Institute of Linguistics of the Hungarian Academy of Sciences): 1399 Budapest, POB 701/518; 1068 Budapest, Benczúr u. 33; tel. (1) 351-0413; fax (1) 322-9297; e-mail kiefer@nytud.hu; internet www.nytud.hu; f. 1949; research in theoretical linguistics, phonetics, neuro- and sociolinguistics, historical linguistics, lexicography, corpus linguistics; library of 40,000 vols; Dir Dr ISTVÁN KENESEI; publs *Magyar Fonetikai Füzetek* (Hungarian Papers in Phonetics, 2 a year), *Műhelymunkák a nyelvészet és társtudományai köréből* (Working Papers on Linguistics and Related Sciences, irregular), *Nyelvtudományi Közlemények* (Linguistic Publications, 2 a year).

MEDICINE

Magyar Tudományos Akadémia Kísérleti Orvostudományi Kutatóintézete (Institute of Experimental Medicine of the Hungarian Academy of Sciences): 1083 Budapest, Szigony u. 43; tel. (1) 210-9400; fax (1) 210-9423; e-mail info@koki.hu; internet www.koki.hu; f. 1952; conducts basic biomedical research, primarily in the field of neuroscience, incl. studies on neurotransmission, learning and memory, behaviour, ischaemic and epileptic brain damage, and the central and peripheral control of hormone secretion; library of 18,500 vols; Dir Prof. Dr TAMAS F. FREUND.

Mozgássérültek Pető András Nevelőképző és Nevelőintézete (András Pető Institute of Conductive Education and Conductor Training College): 1125 Budapest, Kutvölgyi u. 6; tel. (1) 224-1500; fax (1) 224-1531; e-mail info@peto.hu; internet www.peto.hu; f. 1945; library of 35,000 vols; conductive education for 1,200 children and adults with motor disabilities due to damage to the central nervous system; undergraduate conductor training with specialization in preschool or primary school teaching; conductor-helper postgraduate specialist training; higher-level vocational training in youth protection; Rector Dr FRANZ SCHAFFHAUSER; publ. *Conductive Education Occasional Papers* (2 a year).

Országos Epidemiológiai Központ (National Centre for Epidemiology): 1097 Budapest, Gyáli u. 2–6; tel. and fax (1) 476-1369; e-mail konyvtar@oek.antsz.hu; internet www.antsz.hu/oek; f. 1927; research in epidemiology, microbiology, virology, bacteriology, parasitology, mycology, vaccines; library of 30,000 vols; Dir-Gen. Dr MÁRTA MELLES; publ. *EPINFO* (48 a year).

Országos Epidemiológiai Központ, Mikrobiológiai Kutatócsoport (Microbiological Research Group of the National Centre for Epidemiology): 1529 Budapest, Pihenő u. 1; tel. (1) 394-5044; fax (1) 394-5409; e-mail mini@microbi.hu; f. 1963; research into oncogenic viruses, virus tumours, HIV/AIDS, interferon, DNA methylation; library of 2,000 vols; Dir Dr JÁNOS MINÁROVITS.

Országos 'Fréderic Joliot-Curie' Sugárbiológiai és Sugáregészségügyi Kutató Intézet (National Research Institute for Radiobiology and Radiohygiene): 1775 Budapest, POB 101; tel. (1) 482-2001; fax (1) 482-2003; e-mail radbiol@hp.osski.hu; f. 1957; under Min. of Health; radiohygiene, including protection of workers from radiation; radiobiology research on effects of external ionizing radiation and incorporated radioisotopes; radiation and radioisotope applications; medical preparedness for response to radio-nuclear emergencies; teaching within the Semmelweis Medical School, Budapest; library of 7,000 vols; Dir Prof. Dr ISTVAN TURAI.

Országos Haematológiai és Immunológiai Intézet (National Institute of Haematology and Immunology): 1519 Budapest, POB 424; 1113 Budapest, Daróczi u. 24; tel. (1) 466-5877; fax (1) 372-4352; internet www.c3.hu/~haemat; f. 1948; research and clinical activities in haematology and immunology, including bone-marrow transplantation; library of 10,000 vols, 91 periodicals; Dir Prof. Dr GYŐZŐ PETRÁNYI; publs *Haematologia* (in English, 4 a year), *Transzfúzió* (in Hungarian, 4 a year).

Országos Onkológiai Intézet (National Institute of Oncology): 1122 Budapest, Ráth György u. 7/9; tel. (1) 224-8600; fax (1) 224-8620; f. 1952; experimental and clinical activities; library of 15,973 vols, 164 periodicals, service for reprints of all publs available; Dir Dr M. KASLER; publ. *Magyar Onkológia* (4 a year).

NATURAL SCIENCES

Biological Sciences

Magyar Tudományos Akadémia Balatoni Limnológiai Kutatóintézete (Balaton Limnological Research Institute of the Hungarian Academy of Sciences): 8237 Tihany, POB 35; tel. (87) 448-244; fax (87) 448-006; e-mail intezet@tres.blki.hu; internet www.blki.hu; f. 1927; research particularly in hydrobiology, and experimental zoology; library of 16,000 vols; Dir Dr SÁNDOR HERODEK; publ. collected reprints, progress report.

Magyar Tudományos Akadémia Ökológiai és Botanikai Kutatóintézete (Institute of Ecology and Botany of the Hungarian Academy of Sciences): 2163 Vácrátót, Alkotmány ut. 2–4; tel. (28) 360-122; fax (28) 360-110; e-mail obki@botanika.hu; internet www.obki.hu; f. 1952; theoretical and experimental research in the field of botany, flora, plant, taxonomy, dendrology, aquatic ecology, plant ecology, vegetation and community ecology, functional ecology, forest ecology, landscape ecology, grassland ecology, nature conservation, conservation biology, vegetation mapping, climate change, lichenology, land-use history, botanical gardens, gardening, river restoration, shallow lakes; library of 10,000 vols; Dir Dr KATALIN TÖRÖK.

Magyar Tudományos Akadémia Szegedi Biológiai Központja (Biological Research Centre of the Hungarian Academy of Sciences): 6701 Szeged, Temesvári krt. 62, POB 521; tel. (62) 599-600; fax (62) 432-576; e-mail kulugy@brc.hu; internet www.brc.hu; f. 1971; library of 30,000 vols; Dir-Gen. Prof. PÁL ORMOS.

Attached Institutes:

Biofizikai Intézet (Institute of Biophysics): c/o Magyar Tudományos Akadémia Szegedi Biológiai Központja, 6701 Szeged, Temesvári krt. 62, POB 521; tel. (62) 433-465; f. 1971; Dir PAL ORMOS.

Biokémiai Intézet (Institute of Biochemistry): c/o Magyar Tudományos Akadémia Szegedi Biológiai Központja, 6701 Szeged, Temesvári krt. 62, POB 521; tel. (62) 433-506; f. 1971; Dir LÁSZLÓ VIGH.

Enzimológiai Intézet (Institute of Enzymology): 1113 Budapest, Karolina u. 29; tel. (1) 279-3100; fax (1) 466-5465; f. 1950; Dir PETER ZAVODSKY.

Genetikai Intézet (Institute of Genetics): c/o Magyar Tudományos Akadémia Szegedi Biológiai Központja, 6701 Szeged, Temesvári krt. 62, POB 521; tel. (62) 599-657; fax (62) 433-503; f. 1971; Dir ISTVÁN RASKÓ.

Növénybiológiai Intézet (Institute of Plant Biology): c/o Magyar Tudományos Akadémia Szegedi Biológiai Központja, 6701 Szeged, Temesvári krt. 62, POB 521; tel. (62) 433-434; fax (62) 433-434; f. 1970; Dir DÉNES DUDITS.

Természetvédelmi Hivatal, Madártani Intézet (Authority for Nature Conservation, Institute for Ornithology): 1121 Budapest, Költő u. 21; tel. (1) 391-1759; e-mail buki@mail.kvvm.hu; internet www.termeszetvedelem.hu; f. 1893; library of 8,000 vols, 1,000 periodicals; Librarian JÓZSEF BÜKI; publ. *Aquila* (1 a year).

Mathematical Sciences

Magyar Tudományos Akadémia Rényi Alfréd Matematikai Kutatóintézet (Alfréd Rényi Institute of Mathematics, Hungarian Academy of Sciences): 1364 Budapest, POB 127; 1053 Budapest, Reáltanoda u. 13–15; tel. (1) 483-8300; fax (1) 483-8333; e-mail math@renyi.hu; internet www.renyi.hu; f. 1950; research in fields of pure and applied mathematics; 80 mems; library of 60,000 vols; Dir G. O. H. KATONA; publ. *Studia Scientiarum Mathematicarum Hungarica*.

Physical Sciences

Magyar Állami Eötvös Loránd Geofizikai Intézet (Eötvös Loránd Geophysical Institute of Hungary): 1145 Budapest, Columbus u. 17–23; tel. (1) 252-4999; fax (1) 363-7256; e-mail elgi@elgi.hu; internet www.elgi.hu; f. 1907; geophysical exploration for hydrocarbons, coal, bauxite, water, ores; engineering geophysics; geophysical research, gravity, magnetics, lithosphere, ionosphere; library of 30,000 vols; Dir Dr TAMÁS FANCSIK; publ. *Geophysical Transactions* (4 a year).

Attached Institute:

Geophysical Observatory: 8237 Tihany; tel. (87) 448-501; fax (87) 538-001; e-mail csontos@elgi.hu; f. 1954; Head LÁSZLÓ HEGYMEGI.

Magyar Tudományos Akadémia Atommagkutató Intézete (Institute of Nuclear Research of the Hungarian Academy of Sciences): 4026 Debrecen, Bem tér 18C; tel. (52) 509-200; fax (52) 416-181; e-mail fulop@atomki.hu; internet www.atomki.hu; f. 1954; nuclear physics, atomic physics, particle physics, materials science and analysis, earth and cosmic sciences, environmental research, biological and medical research, devt of methods and instruments; 200 mems; library of 55,000 vols; Dir Dr ZSOLT FÜLÖP; Sec. ERZSÉBET LEITER.

Magyar Tudományos Akadémia Csillagászati Kutatóintézete (Konkoly Observatory of the Hungarian Academy of Sciences): 1525 Budapest, POB 67; 1121 Budapest, Konkoly Thege Miklós u. 15–17; tel. (1) 391-9322; fax (1) 275-4668; internet www.konkoly.hu; f. 1871; 52 staff; library of 32,000 vols; Mountain Station: Piszkéstető, Galyatető (f. 1962), with Schmidt telescope, Cassegrain-reflector and 100 cm Ritchey-Chretien telescope; Dir LAJOS G. BALÁZS; publs *Information Bulletin on Variable Stars of Commission 27 of the IAU*, *Mitteilungen der Sternwarte der Ungarischen Akademie der Wissenschaften* (Communications from the Konkoly Observatory of the Hungarian Academy of Sciences).

Magyar Tudományos Akadémia Csillagászati Kutatóintézetének Napfizikai Obszervatóriuma (Heliophysical Observatory of the Hungarian Academy of Sciences): 4010 Debrecen, Egyetem tér 1, POB 30; 4010 Debrecen, Egyetem tér 1; tel. (52) 311-015; internet fenyi.sci.klte.hu; f. 1958; studies of solar activity: sunspots, solar flares, prominences; library of 10,000 vols, 20 periodicals, 5,500 sunspot drawings (1872–1919), 100,000 full-disc solar photographs; Dir B. KÁLMÁN.

Magyar Tudományos Akadémia Geodéziai és Geofizikai Kutató Intézete (Geodetical and Geophysical Research Institute of the Hungarian Academy of Sciences): 9400 Sopron, Csatkai E. u. 6–8; tel. (99) 508-340; fax (99) 508-355; internet www.ggki.hu; f. 1955 as 2 separate laboratories, merged as 1 institute 1972; research in advanced problems of geodesy and geophysics including seismology; library of 34,000 vols; Dir Prof. J. ZAVOTI; publs *Rapport Microséismique de Hongrie* (1 a year), *Geophysical Observatory Reports* (1 a year), *Publications in Geomatics* (1 a year).

Magyar Tudományos Akadémia, Kémiai Kutatóközpont (Chemical Research Centre of the Hungarian Academy of Sciences): 1025 Budapest, Pusztaszeri u. 59-67; tel. (1) 325-7900; fax (1) 325-7554; e-mail palg@chemres.hu; internet www.chemres.hu; f. 1954; fundamental research in organic, medicinal, biomolecular and bio-organic chemistry, surface reactions and heterogeneous catalysis, nanochemistry, kinetics and mechanism of chemical reactions, theoretical chemistry, electrochemistry and corrosion, polymer chemistry and polymer physics, environmental and analytical chemistry, materials chemistry and molecular structure, spectroscopy and diffraction, nuclear and isotope chemistry, photochemistry; library of 60,000 vols; Dir-Gen. Prof. Dr GÁBOR PÁLINKÁS.

Magyar Tudományos Akadémia Kémiai Kutatóközpont Izotóp- és Felületkémiai Intézet (Institute of Isotope and Surface Chemistry Chemical Research Centre of the Hungarian Academy of Sciences): 1525 Budapest, POB 77; 1121 Budapest, Konkoly Thege M. u. 29–33; tel. (1) 392-2222; fax (1) 392-2533; e-mail wojn@alpha0.iki.kfki.hu; internet www.iki.kfki.hu; f. 1959; research in the fields of catalysis, surface chemistry, adsorption, radiation chemistry, photochemistry, molecular spectroscopy, nuclear spectroscopy, nuclear safety, radioactive tracer technique; library of 14,000 vols; Dir Dr LÁSZLÓ WOJNÁROVITS.

Magyar Tudományos Akadémia, Műszaki Fizikai és Anyagtudományi Kutatóintézet (Research Institute for Technical Physics and Materials Science of the Hungarian Academy of Sciences): 1525 Budapest, POB 49; 1121 Budapest, Konkoly Thege Miklós u. 29–33; tel. (1) 392-2224; fax (1) 392-2226; e-mail info@mfa.kfki.hu; internet www.mfa.kfki.hu; f. 1992; library: shares library of 120,000 vols; Dir Prof. ISTVÁN BÁRSONY.

Magyar Tudományos Akadémia, KFKI Atomenergia Kutató Intézet (KFKI Atomic Energy Research Institute of the Hungarian Academy of Sciences): 1525 Budapest, POB 49;; tel. (1) 395-9293; fax (1) 392-2222; internet www.kfki.hu/~aekihp; f. 1992; library: shares library of 120,000 vols; Dir JÁNOS GADÓ.

Műszaki Kémiai Kutató Intézet (Research Institute of Chemical and Process Engineering): 8200 Veszprém, Egyetem u. 10; tel. (88) 624-023; fax (88) 624-025; e-mail ujvari@dcs.vein.hu; f. 1960; attached to University of Veszprem; fundamental and applied research in traditional chemical engineering, bioengineering and systems engineering; library of 8,500 vols; Dir Dr ENDRE NAGY; publ. *Hungarian Journal of Industrial Chemistry*.

Uránia Csillagvizsgáló (Urania Public Observatory): 1016 Budapest, Sánc u. 3B; tel. (1) 186-9233; fax (1) 267-1391; f. 1947; centre of the Hungarian amateur astronomy movement; 8-inch Heyde refractor, 6-inch Zeiss reflector; library of 1,700 vols; Dir OTTO ZOMBORI; publ. *Uránia Füzetek* (Urania Letters, 1 a year).

PHILOSOPHY AND PSYCHOLOGY

Magyar Tudományos Akadémia Filozófiai Kutatóintézete (Research Institute for Philosophy of the Hungarian Academy of Sciences): 1398 Budapest 62, POB 594; tel. and fax (1) 312-0243; internet www.phil-inst.hu; f. 1957 for research into problems of epistemology, philosophy of science, social philosophy, methodological problems of social sciences, philosophy of religion, political philosophy, history of philosophical thought; library: institute library of 26,000 vols; Dir Prof. Dr KRISTÓF NYÍRI.

Magyar Tudományos Akadémia Pszichológiai Kutatóintézet (Institute for Psychology of the Hungarian Academy of Sciences): 1394 Budapest, POB 398; tel. (1) 239-6726; fax (1) 239-6727; e-mail czigler@cogpsyphy.hu; internet www.mtapi.hu; f. 1902; basic research on cognitive psychophysiology and neuropsychology, devtl psychology, social psychology and personality, research on educational psychology, psychology of decision-making, cross-cultural psychology; library of 20,000 vols; Dir Dr ISTVÁN CZIGLER; publ. *Pszichológia* (4 a year).

RELIGION, SOCIOLOGY AND ANTHROPOLOGY

Magyar Tudományos Akadémia Néprajzi Kutatóintézete (Institute of Ethnology of the Hungarian Academy of Sciences): 1250 Budapest, POB 29; tel. (1) 224-6700; fax (1) 356-8058; internet www.etnologia.mta.hu; f. 1967; research in ethnology of the Hungarian people, general anthropology, folklore and traditions, study of gypsies; library of 68,000 vols; Dir BALÁZS BALOGH; publs *Népi Kultura—Népi Társadalom, Magyar Néprajz, Folklór Archivum, Documentatio Ethnographica, Életmód és Tradició, Folklór és Tradició, Néprajzi tanulmányok, Ethnolore*.

Magyar Tudományos Akadémia Szociológiai Kutatóintézet (Institute of Sociology of the Hungarian Academy of Sciences): 1014 Budapest, Uri u. 49; tel. (1) 224-0786; fax (1) 224-0790; e-mail tiborit@socio.mta.hu; internet www.socio.mta.hu; f. 1963; climate change; research of values (European Social Survey); equal opportunities, poverty; environmental policy, sociology; cultures, policies, lifestyle; political cultures, institute systems, European integration; sociology of work and

orgs; gender and social minorities; social structure, welfare policy; urban devt policy; knowledge and innovation; ageing; library of 8,000 vols; Dir TIBORI TIMEA; Scientific Sec. VERONIKA PAKSI; publs *Társadalomkutatás* (Research in the Social Sciences, 4 a year), *INFO—Társadalomtudomány* (INFO—Social Science, 4 a year).

TECHNOLOGY

Magyar Tudományos Akadémia Számítástechnikai és Automatizálási Kutató Intézete (Computer and Automation Research Institute of the Hungarian Academy of Sciences): 1518 Budapest, POB 63; tel. (1) 279-6000; fax (1) 466-7503; e-mail pr@sztaki.hu; internet www.sztaki.hu; f. 1964; conducts research in intelligent computing, control and information systems, new computation structures, and computer applications for engineering, production and administration systems; library of 45,600 vols; Dir Dr PÉTER INZELT; publ. *Transactions* (irregular).

Szilikátipari Központi Kutató és Tervező Intézet (Central Research and Design Institute for the Silicate Industry): 1034 Budapest, Bécsi u. 122–124; tel. (1) 188-2360; fax (1) 168-7626; f. 1953; research and technological design in the silicate sciences and building materials industry; library of 25,000 vols, 7,000 periodicals; Dir CSABA ÁRPÁD RÉTI; publs *Transactions* (irregular, in English, German, French, Russian), *Tudományos Közlemények* (irregular, summaries in English, German, French, Russian).

Villamosenergiaipari Kutató Intézet (Institute for Electric Power Research): 1251 Budapest, POB 80; 1016 Budapest, Gellérthegy u. 17; tel. (1) 457-8273; fax (1) 457-8274; e-mail i.kromer@veiki.hu; internet www.veiki.hu; f. 1949; research and development on safety assessment of nuclear power plants, combustion technology and environmental management, mechanical and power engineering technology, equipment of the electricity networks, high voltage and high power laboratory testing, systems of control engineering and telemechanics; library: technical library of 25,000 vols; Gen. Man. Dr ISTVÁN KRÓMER; publ. *VEIKI Publications* (Hungarian, with abstracts in English, 1 a year).

Libraries and Archives

Budapest

Budapest Főváros Levéltára (Budapest City Archives): 1052 Budapest, Városház u. 9-11; tel. (1) 317-7306; fax (1) 318-3319; e-mail bfl@bparchiv.hu; internet www.bparchiv.hu; f. 1901; 23,000 m of bookshelves; Dir Dr LÁSZLÓ A. VARGA; publ. *Budapesti Negyed* (4 a year).

Budapesti Corvinus Egyetem Központi Könyvtár (Corvinus University of Budapest Central Library): 1093 Budapest, Közraktaru. 4–6; tel. (1) 482-7075; fax (1) 482-7072; e-mail konyvtar@uni-corvinus.hu; internet www.lib.uni-corvinus.hu; f. 1850; economic sciences, world economy, management sciences, public admin., business and finance, sociology, political science, social sciences, environment protection, agriculture; 17,150 mems; 470,920 vols; Dir-Gen. GABRIELLA ALFÖLDI.

Budapesti Corvinus Egyetem Entz Ferenc Könyvtár és Levéltár (Corvinus University of Budapest, Entz Ferenc Library and Archives): 1118 Budapest, Villányi u. 29–43; tel. (1) 482-6300; fax (1) 482-6334; internet helix.uni-corvinus.hu; f. 1860; horticulture,

floriculture, nursery, medicinal plants, fruit-growing, landscape and garden architecture, urban planning, environmental protection; food industry, canning technology, food fermentation, processing of animal products, processing of cereals and industrial plants, oenology, brewing; 320,000 vols, 365 current periodicals; Dir Dr ÉVA ZALAI-KOVÁCS; publ. *'Lippay János' Tudományos Ülésszak Előadásai* (every 2 years).

Budapesti Műszaki és Gazdaságtudományi Egyetem Országos Műszaki Információs Központ és Könyvtár (BME OMIKK) (Budapest University of Technology and Economics National Technical Information Centre and Library): 1502 Budapest, POB 91; 1111 Budapest XI, Muegyetem rkp. 3; tel. (1) 463-2441; fax (1) 463-2440; e-mail pvasarhelyi@omikk.bme.hu; internet www.omikk.bme.hu; f. 1848; 2,084,352 vols, 340,000 periodicals; Dir-Gen. ILONA FONYO; publ. *Tudományos és Műszaki Tajekoztatas* (Scientific and Technical Information, 12 a year).

Egészségügyi Stratégiai Kutatóintézet Egészségpolitikai Szakkönyvtár (National Institute for Strategic Health Research Health Policy Library): 1051 Budapest, Arany János u. 6-8; tel. (1) 354-5377; fax (1) 354-5370; e-mail konyvtar@eski.hu; internet www.eski.hu; f. 1949; library for Ministry of Health staff, health policy makers, health professionals, health care managers, health workers; colln includes Hungarian publications on health policy and related fields, statistics, social and family affairs; selected publs from foreign literature; deposit library of the European regional office of the World Health Org.; 40,000 vols; Dir-Gen. Dr GYULA KINCSES; Head of Library Dr MARIA PALOTAI; publs *Magyar Orvosi Bibliográfia* (Hungarian Medical Bibliography, 4 a year), *Nővér* (Nurse, 4 a year), *Országtanulmányok* (Country Profiles).

Eötvös Loránd Tudományegyetem Egyetemi Könyvtára (Eötvös Loránd University Library): 1053 Budapest, Ferenciek tere 6; tel. (1) 411-6738; fax (1) 411-6737; e-mail info@lib.elte.hu; internet www.konyvtar.elte.hu; f. 1635; central library of the Univ. and national scientific library for philosophy, psychology, medieval history and history of Christianity; 1,500,000 vols, 1,339 periodicals, 60,000 MSS, 185 codices, 1,150 incunabula, 2,600 old Hungarian printed works (to 1711), 9,600 old and rare books; Dir-Gen. Dr LÁSZLÓ SZÖGI; publ. Egyetemi Könyvtár Évkönyve (University Library Annals, irregular).

Fővárosi Szabó Ervin Könyvtár (Metropolitan Ervin Szabó Library): VIII Szabó Ervin tér 1, Pf. 487, 1371 Budapest; tel. (1) 411-5000; fax (1) 411-5002; e-mail titkar@fszek.hu; internet www.fszek.hu; f. 1904; sociology, humanities, literature, history of Budapest; 3,356,420 vols (1,541,997 vols in central library); 78 brs; Dir PÉTER FODOR; publs *Databases* (CD-ROM), *Yearbook*.

Hadtörténeti Könyvtár és Térképtár (Library of Military History and Cartographic Collection): 1014 Budapest, Kapisztrán tér 2; tel. (1) 325-1672; fax (1) 212-0286; e-mail terkeptar@mail.militaria.hu; internet www.hm-him.hu; f. 1920; 190,000 vols, 500,000 maps; Dir LÁSZLÓ VESZPRÉMY; publs *Bibliography* (1 a year), *Hadtörténelmi Közlemények* (Review of Military History, 4 a year).

Iparművészeti Múzeum Könyvtára (Library of the Museum of Applied Arts): 1091 Budapest, Üllői u. 33–37; tel. (1) 456-5177; fax (1) 217-5838; e-mail konyvtar@imm.hu; internet www.imm.hu; f. 1874; scientific research library for the decorative arts;

60,000 vols, 20,000 periodicals; Dir ESTHER TISZAVÁRI; publ. *Ars Decorativa* (1 a year).

Keve András Madártani és Természetvédelmi Szakkönyvtár (Andras Keve Library for Ornithology and Nature Conservation): 1121 Budapest, Költő u. 21; tel. (1) 202-2530; e-mail buki@mail.kvvm.hu; internet aotk.hunteka.ikron.hu/keve; f. 1893; 9,000 vols 20,000 periodicals, 1,500 scientific reports; Librarian JÓZSEF BÜKI; publ. *Aquila* (1 a year).

Központi Statisztikai Hivatal Könyvtár (Library of the Central Statistical Office): 1024 Budapest, 1525 Pf. 10, II, Keleti Károly u. 5; tel. (1) 345-6105; fax (1) 345-6112; e-mail kodosz@ksh.hu; internet konyvtar.ksh.hu; f. 1867; 800,000 books, periodicals, maps and electronic documents; nat. and research library of statistics and demography; Dir-Gen. Dr ERZSÉBET NEMES; publ. *Magyarország Történeti Helységnévtára* (Historical Gazetteer of Hungary).

Liszt Ferenc Zeneművészeti Egyetem Könyvtára (Library of the Ferenc Liszt Academy of Music): 1391 Budapest, Liszt Ferenc tér 8, POB 206; tel. (1) 462-4673; fax (1) 462-4672; e-mail agnes.gador@lisztakademia.hu; internet www.zeneakademia.hu; f. 1875; 450,000 musical scores plus 90,000 vols and periodicals, 40,000 records; research library for music history; Dir AGNES GÁDOR.

Magyar Nemzeti Galéria Könyvtára (Library of the Hungarian National Gallery): 1250 Budapest, POB 31; 1014 Budapest, Szent György tér 2; tel. (2) 439-7453; fax (1) 212-7356; e-mail library@mng.hu; internet www.mng.hu; f. 1957; books on art from all over the world, specializing in Hungarian sculpture, wood carvings, panel paintings, Baroque art, art since the 12th century; 80,000 vols, 27,000 catalogues, 8,800 periodicals, 15,000 slides; Dir Mrs FERENC BERÉNYI; Head of Library ANELIA TÚŰ; publ. *A Magyar Nemzeti Galéria Évkönyve* (Annals).

Magyar Nemzeti Múzeum Régészeti Könyvtára (Archaeological Library of the Hungarian National Museum): 1088 Budapest, Múzeum-körút 14–16; tel. (1) 113-4400; e-mail konyvtar@hnm.hu; internet www.hnm.hu; f. 1952; 104,000 vols of Hungarian and foreign archaeology, numismatics and history; Dir Dr ENDRE TÓTH; Librarian ÉVA HOPPÁL; publs *Folia Archaeologica*, *Folia Historica*, *Inventaria Praehistorica Hungariae*.

Magyar Országos Levéltár (National Archives of Hungary): 1250 Budapest, POB 3; 1014 Budapest, Bécsikapu tér 2–4; tel. (1) 225-2800; fax (1) 225-2817; e-mail info@mol.gov.hu; internet www.mol.gov.hu; f. 1756; 70,500 m of shelving; records from the 12th century to 1989; Gen. Dir Dr LAJOS GECSÉNYI; publs *Levéltári Közlemények* (journal), *Levéltári Szemle* (journal).

Magyar Tudományos Akadémia Földrajztudományi Kutató Intézet Könyvtára (Library of the Geographical Research Institute of the Hungarian Academy of Sciences): 1388 Budapest, POB 64; 1112 Budapest, Budaörsi u. 45; tel. (1) 319-3119; fax (1) 309-2690; e-mail magyar@sparc.core.hu; internet www.mtafki.hu; f. 1952; 70,580 vols, 17,905 maps, 8,128 MSS, 8,088 periodicals; Librarians ARPÁD MAGYAR, GABRIELLA PETZ; publs *Elmélet-módszer-gyakorlat* (Theory-Methods-Practice), *Földrajzi Értesítő*, *Studies in Geography in Hungary*.

Magyar Tudományos Akadémia Könyvtára (Library of the Hungarian Academy of Sciences): 1245 Budapest, Arany János ut. 1, POB 1002; tel. (1) 411-6100; fax (1) 331-6954; e-mail mtak@mtak.hu; internet www.mtak.hu; f. 1826; colln incl. oriental MSS, old prints and incunabula; depository library for Academy's dissertations; Academy's archives; 1,525,785 vols, 362,608 periodicals, 718,450 MSS, 32,588 microfilms, 685 electronic documents, 69 audio-visual titles; Dir-Gen. Prof. GABOR NARAY-SZABO.

Politikatörténeti Intézet Könyvtára (Library of the Institute of Political History): 1054 Budapest, Alkotmány u. 2; tel. (1) 301-2024; e-mail konyvtar@phistory.hu; internet www.polhist.hu; f. 1948; 175,000 vols; Chief Librarian ÉVA TÓTH.

Oktatási és Kulturális Minisztérium, Levéltári Osztály (Ministry of Education and Culture, Archives Department): 1055 Budapest, Szalay u. 10–14; tel. (1) 473-7450; fax (1) 473-7018; e-mail radojka .gorjanac@okm.gov.hu; internet www.okm .gov.hu; f. 1950; functions as supervising board of all archives in Hungary; Head RADOJKA GORJANAC.

Országgyűlési Könyvtár (Library of the Hungarian Parliament): 1357 Budapest, Pf. 4, Kossuth Lajos-tér 1–3; tel. (1) 441-4686; fax (1) 441-4853; e-mail ambrusj@ogyk.hu; internet www.ogyk.hu; f. 1870; 820,000 vols; parliamentary papers (Hungarian and foreign), contemporary history, administrative and legal sciences, politics; UN depository library, EU depository library; Librarian JÁNOS AMBRUS; publs *INFO-Társadalomtudomány* (4 a year), *Pressdok* (review on floppy disk and CD-ROM of Hungarian newspapers and periodicals), *Hundok* (review on floppy disk and CD-ROM of foreign newspapers and weekly periodicals dealing with Hungarian issues).

Országos Idegennyelvü Könyvtár (National Library of Foreign Literature): 1056 Budapest, Molnár u. 11; tel. (1) 318-3688; fax (1) 318-0147; e-mail tajekoztato@oik.hu; internet www.oik.hu; f. 1956; fmrly the Gorky State Library; specializing in foreign literature, the theory of literature, linguistics, language teaching materials, musicology, music scores and records, literature concerning national minorities and ethnics; 370,000 vols; Dir IBOLYA MENDER; publs *Database of minorities-related articles*, *Ethnic Minority Bibliography* (1 a year), *Literary translations database*, *New Books for Nationalities* (irregular).

Országos Mezőgazdasági Könyvtár és Dokumentációs Központ (National Agricultural Library and Documentation Centre): 1012 Budapest, Attila u. 93; tel. (1) 489-4900; fax (1) 489-4939; e-mail omgkref@omgk.hu; internet www.omgk.hu; f. 1951; 292,820 vols, 443 periodicals; Gen. Dir GABRIELLA LÜKŐ-ÖRSI; publs *Az Európai Unió Agrárgazdasága* (12 a year), *Agrárkönyvtári Hírvilág* (online, 4 a year), *Magyar Mezőgazdasági Bibliográfia* (on disk, 4 a year).

Országos Pedagógiai Könyvtár és Múzeum (National Educational Library and Museum): 1089 Budapest, Könyves Kálmán u. 40; tel. (1) 323-5508; fax (1) 323-5508; internet www.opkm.hu; f. 1877, reorganized 1958; methodological library for education; pedagogical museum; 550,000 vols; Dir (vacant); publs *Külföldi Pedagógiai Információ* (International Educational Information, on CD-ROM), *Magyar Pedagógiai Irodalom* (Hungarian Educational Literature, on CD-ROM), *Könyv és Nevelés* (Books and Education, 4 a year).

Országos Rabbiképző – Zsidó Egyetem Könyvtára (Library of the Jewish Theological Seminary—University of Jewish Studies): 1428 Budapest, POB 21; located at: 1085 Budapest, Bérkocsis u. 2; tel. (1) 267-5415 ext. 103; fax (1) 318-7049 ext. 150; internet www.rabbi.hu; f. 1877; 100,000 vols; Dir BERTA BIRÓ BÉRI.

Országos Széchényi Könyvtár (National Széchényi Library): 1827 Budapest, Budavári Palota F-épület; tel. (1) 224-3700; fax (1) 202-0804; internet www.oszk.hu; f. 1802; 2,634,000 books and periodicals, 4,750,000 manuscripts, maps, prints, microfilms, etc.; Dir-Gen. ISTVÁN MONOK; publs include *Magyar Nemzeti Bibliográfia, Könyvek bibliográfiája* (Hungarian National Bibliography, Monographs, 26 a year), *Magyar Nemzeti Bibliográfia. Időszaki kiadványok repertóriuma* (Hungarian National Bibliography, Repertory of Periodicals, 12 a year), *Magyar Nemzeti Bibliográfia, Időszaki kiadványok bibliográfiája* (Hungarian National Bibliography, Periodicals, 1 a year), *Magyar Nemzeti Bibliográfia* (Hungarian National Bibliography, Books and Periodicals CD-ROM, 2 a year); *Hungarika Információ* (Hungarica Information, 3 current indexes, 1 cumulative index a year), *Mikrofilmek cimjegyzéke* (lists of microfilms, irregular), *Az Országos Széchényi Könyvtár Füzetei* (Studies of the National Széchényi Library, irregular), *Magyarországi egyházi könyvtárak kéziratkatalógusai* (Catalogues of the Manuscript Collections in Hungarian Church Libraries, irregular), *Libri de Libris* (irregular), National Collection (irregular), *Margarithe Bibliothecae Nalis Hungariae* (irregular), *A Kárpát-medence koraújkori könyvtáraj* (Libraries of the Early Modern Age in the Carpathian Basin, irregular).

Affiliated Libraries:

Könyvtártudományi és Módszertani Központ (Centre for Library and Information Science): 1827 Budapest, Budavári Palota F-épület; tel. (1) 224-3788; f. 1959; research and development, promotion of inter-library co-operation, literature propaganda, public relations, training and library documentation services; library science; 107,000 vols; Dir ERZSÉBET GYŐRI (acting); publs *Könyvtári Figyelő* (Library Review), *A Magyar Könyvtári Szakirodalom Bibliográfiája* (Bibliography of Hungarian Library Literature), *Hungarian Library and Information Science Abstracts* (in English), *Uj Könyvek* (New Books), *Uj Periodikumok* (New Periodicals), *MANCI* (database of library science periodical articles with quarterly updates on floppy disk).

Reguly Antal Historic Library: 8420 Zirc, Rákóczi-tér 1; tel. and fax (88) 593-800; f. 1720; 68,618 vols; Librarian KATALIN URBÁN.

Pázmány Péter Katolikus Egyetem, Hittudományi Kar Könyvtára (Library of the Péter Pázmány Catholic University's Faculty of Theology): 1053 Budapest, Veres Pálné u. 24; tel. (1) 318-1643; fax (1) 484-3054; e-mail ppke_htk@ella.hu; internet www.htk.ppke .hu; f. 1635; history, theology and linguistics; 63,500 vols (books from c. 1880, older material kept in the Library of the University); also houses the Collection of the Brothers of St Paul (f. 1775; 12,000 vols; incunabula and MSS from the 15th and 16th centuries), and the Library of the Central Catholic Seminary (Központi Papnevelő Intézet Könyvtára) (f. 1805; 17,300 vols; Dir Dr HUBA RÓZSA.

Semmelweis Egyetem Egészségtudományi Kar Könyvtár (Semmelweis University Faculty of Health Sciences Library): 1428 Budapest, POB 229; 1088 Budapest, Vas u. 17; tel. (1) 486-5955; fax (1) 486-5951; e-mail lib@se-etk.hu; internet www.se-etk.hu; f. 1975; 45,000 vols; Chief Librarian IMOLA JEHODA.

Semmelweis Egyetem Központi Könyvtára (Central Library of Semmelweis University): 1085 Budapest, Ullői u. 26; tel. (1) 317-0948; fax (1) 317-1048; e-mail lvasas@lib

.sote.hu; internet www.lib.sote.hu; f. 1828; 537,127 vols; Dir Dr LÍVIA VASAS.

Semmelweis Egyetem Testnevelési és Sporttudományi Kar Könyvtára (Library of the Faculty of Physical Education and Sport Sciences, Semmelweis University): 1123 Budapest, Alkotás u. 44; tel. (1) 487-9200 ext. 12-34; fax (1) 356-6337; e-mail linda@mail.hupe.hu; internet www.hupe.hu; f. 1925; collection covers physical education, sport, human kinesiology, management, mental health, recreation and allied domains, also literature by Hungarian and foreign authors; 98,500 vols, 77 domestic and 4 foreign trade papers; Dir FERENC KRASOVEC.

Szent István Egyetem Állatorvostudományi Könyvtár, Levéltár és Múzeum (Veterinary Science Library, Archives and Museum—Szent István University): 1400 Budapest, Pf. 2; 1078 Budapest, István u. 2; tel. (1) 478-4226; fax (1) 478-4227; e-mail library.univet@aotk.szie.hu; internet library .univet.hu; f. 1787; 85,000 vols, 161 current periodicals; spec. collns: ancient veterinary literature, historical archives; museum of veterinary history; distance education for veterinarians; Dir JUDIT SZABÓNÉ SZÁVAY; Head of services ÉVA ORBÁN; publs *Bibliography of Hungarian Veterinary Literature* (online), *Noctua* (newsletter, online).

Debrecen

Debreceni Egyetem Egyetemi és Nemzeti Könyvtár (University of Debrecen University and National Library): 4010 Debrecen, Egyetem tér 1, Pf. 39; tel. (52) 410-443; fax (52) 410-443; e-mail marta@lib .unideb.hu; internet www.lib.unideb.hu; f. 1912; 2,178,050 vols and periodicals, 2,618,085 MSS, prints, microfilms, etc.; Dir-Gen. Dr MÁRTA VIRÁGOS; publ. *Könyv és Könyvtár* (1 a year).

Debreceni Egyetem Orvos- és Egészségtudományi Centrum Kenézy Elettudományi Könyvtár (Life Sciences Library of the Medical and Health Sciences Centre of the University of Debrecen): 4032 Debrecen, Egyetem tér 1; tel. (52) 518-610; fax (52) 413-847; e-mail kenezy@lib.unideb.hu; internet kenezy.lib.unideb.hu; f. 1947; 190,000 vols; Librarian GYONGYI KARACSONY.

Tiszántúli Református Egyházkerületi és Kollégiumi Nagykönyvtár (Library of the Reformed College and of the Transtibiscan Church District): 4044 Debrecen, Kálvint tér 16, POB 201; tel. (52) 516-856; fax (52) 516-919; e-mail theca@silver.drk.hu; internet silver.drk.hu; f. 1538; 570,000 vols; Dir Dr GÁBORJÁNI SZABÓ BOTOND.

Esztergom

Főszékesegyházi Könyvtár (Library of Esztergom Cathedral): 2500 Esztergom, Pázmány Péter u. 2; tel. (33) 510-130; e-mail bibliotheca@invitel.hu; internet www.ehf.hu/~bibliotheca; f. 11th century; 250,000 items, incl. Fugger, Batthyany and Mayer collns; Dir BÉLA CZÉKLI.

Gödöllő

Szent István Egyetem Gödöllői Tudományos Könyvtár (St Stephen's University Gödöllő Campus Library): 2103 Gödöllő, Páter Károly u. 1; tel. (28) 522-004; fax (28) 410-804; f. 1945; 370,000 vols, 535 current periodicals; Dir Dr TIBOR KOLTAY; publ. *Bibliográfia* (every 2 or 3 years).

Keszthely

Veszprémi Egyetem Georgikon Mezőgazdaságtudományi Kar, Keszthely Központi Könyvtár és Levéltár (Georgikon Faculty of Agriculture, University of Veszprém, Keszthely Central Library and Arch-ives): 8360 Keszthely, Deák F. u. 16, POB 66; tel. (83) 312-330; fax (83) 315-105; e-mail lib@ georgikon.hu; f. 1797, reorganized 1954; 150,000 vols; Dir CSILLA PÓR; publ. *Georgikon for Agriculture* (2 a year).

Miskolc

Miskolci Egyetem Könyvtár, Levéltár, Múzeum (Library, Archives and Museum of the University of Miskolc): 3515 Miskolc-Egyetemváros; tel. (46) 565-324; fax (46) 563-489; e-mail konzsamb@gold.uni-miskolc.hu; internet www.lib.uni-miskolc.hu; f. 1735; 612,000 vols, 113,000 periodicals; Dir-Gen. Dr LÁSZLÓ ZSÁMBOKI.

Pannonhalma

Főapátsági Könyvtár Pannonhalma (Benedictine Abbey Library): 9090 Pannonhalma, Vár 1; tel. (96) 570-142; fax (96) 470-011; e-mail fokonyvtar@osb.hu; internet www.osb.hu; f. 1802; collection of early records, MSS, codices, source material for the Hungarian language; 350,000 vols; Dir P. MIKSA BÁNHEGYI.

Pécs

Pécsi Tudományegyetem Egyetemi Könyvtára (University Library of Pécs): 7601 Pécs, Pf. 227; 7621 Pécs, Szepesy I. u. 1–3; tel. (72) 501-600; fax (72) 325-552; e-mail webmaster@lib.pte.hu; internet www.lib.pte .hu; f. 1774; 1,165,000 vols; Gen. Dir. Dr ÁGNES FISCHER-DÁRDAI.

Pécsi Tudományegyetem Orvostudományi és Egészségtudományi Centrum Könyvtára (Medical Centre Library, Pécs University): 7643 Pécs, Szigeti u. 12; tel. (72) 536-000; fax (72) 536-293; e-mail konkozi@ aok.pte.hu; internet www.aok.pte.hu; f. 1926; collection covers medicine, health sciences, chemistry, physics and biology; 472,413 vols; Dir TÜNDE GRACZA.

Sárospatak

Sárospataki Református Kollégium Tudományos Gyűjteményei Nagykönyvtára (Scholarly Collection of the Reformed College of Sárospatak): 3950 Sárospatak, Rákóczi u. 1; tel. and fax (47) 311-057; e-mail reftud@iif.hu; internet www .patakarchiv.hu; f. 1531; 404,974 vols; Dir DÉNES DIENES; publ. *Egyháztörténeti Szemle* (www.egyhtortszemle.hu, 4 a year).

Sopron

Nyugat-Magyarországi Egyetem Központi Könyvtár es Leveltar (Central Library and Archives of the University of West Hungary): 9400 Sopron, Bajcsy-Zsilinszky ul. 4; tel. (99) 518-223; fax (99) 518-267; e-mail library@nyme.hu; internet ilex .efe.hu; f. 1735; 303,000 vols; Dir SÁNDOR SARKADY.

Szeged

Somogyi-könyvtár (Somogyi Library): 6720 Szeged, Dóm tér 1–4; tel. (62) 425-525; fax (62) 426-521; e-mail library@sk-szeged .hu; internet www.sk-szeged.hu; f. 1881; 914,000 vols; Dir ERZSÉBET SZŐKEFALVINAGY; publs *Szegedi Műhely* (Workshop of Szeged), *Csongrád Megyei Könyvtáros* (Librarian of Csongrád County).

Szegedi Tudományegyetem Egyetemi Könyvtár (Main Library of the University of Szeged): 6722 Szeged, Ady tér 13; tel. (62) 546-665; fax (62) 546-665; e-mail mader@bibl .u-szeged.hu; internet www.bibl.u-szeged.hu; f. 1921; 1,500,000 vols; Dir Dr BÉLA MADER; publs *Acta Bibliothecaria, Dissertationes ex Bibliotheca Universitatis de Attila József nominatae.*

Veszprém

Pannon Egyetem, Egyetemi Könyvtár és Levéltár (University of Pannonia, Library and Archive): 8200 Veszprém, Wartha V. u. 1; tel. (88) 624-534; fax (88) 624-531; e-mail hazitibo@almos.uni-pannon.hu; internet library.uni-pannon.hu; f. 1949; 255,516 vols; Dir Dr MÁRTA EGYHÁZY; publs *Hungarian Journal of Industrial Chemistry* (4 a year), *Studia Germanica Universitatis Vesprimensis* (4 a year).

Museums and Art Galleries

Badacsony

Egry József Emlékmúzeum (József Egry Memorial Museum): 8261 Badacsony, Egry József Sétány 12; tel. (87) 431-044; e-mail egry.badacsony@museum.hu; f. 1973; art gallery of works by Lake Balaton landscape painter Egry.

Baja

Türr István Múzeum: 6501 Baja, Deák Ferenc u. 1, POB 55; tel. (79) 324-173; fax (79) 324-173; f. 1937; archaeological and ethnographic collections, modern Hungarian painters, local history; library of 10,000 vols; Dir ZSUZSA MERK; publs *Türr István Múzeum Kiadványai, Bajai Dolgozatok.*

Balassagyarmat

Palóc Múzeum: 2660 Balassagyarmat, Palóc liget 1; tel. (35) 300-168; fax (35) 300-168; e-mail paloc.balassagyarmat@museum .hu; f. 1891; ethnography, local folk art and shepherds' art; collns of Nógrád costumes, embroidery, folk religion and folk instruments; library of 12,000 vols; Dir GABOR LIMBACHER.

Békéscsaba

Munkácsy Mihály Múzeum: 5600 Békéscsaba, Széchenyi u. 9; tel. and fax (66) 323-377; e-mail mmm@bmmi.hu; internet www.munkacsy.hu; f. 1899; archaeological, historical and regional ethnographic collns, modern Hungarian paintings, ornithology, natural science; paintings and legacies of the painter Mihály Munkácsy (1844–1900); library of 19,000 vols; Dir Dr IMRE SZATMÁRI.

Budapest

Bartók Béla Emlékház (Béla Bartók Memorial House): 1025 Budapest, Csalán u. 29; tel. (1) 394-2100; fax (1) 394-4472; e-mail bartok-1981@axelero.hu; internet www .bartokmuseum.hu; f. 1981; organizes musical programmes and concerts; Dir JÁNOS SZIRÁNYI.

Budapesti Történeti Múzeum (Budapest History Museum): 1014 Budapest, Szent György tér 2; tel. (1) 487-8801; fax (1) 487-8872; internet www.btm.hu; f. 1887; medieval antiquities, medieval royal castle, Gothic statues; library of 45,700 vols; Dir-Gen. Dr SÁNDOR BODÓ; publs *Budapest Régiségei* (Antiquities of Budapest), *Monumenta Historica Budapestinensia* (irregular), *Tanulmányok Budapest Múltjából* (Studies on the History of Budapest).

Attached Museums:

Aquincum Múzeum: 1033 Budapest, Záhony u. 3; 1033 Budapest, Szentendrei út 139; tel. (1) 430-1081; fax (1) 430-1083; e-mail h7442tot@iif.hu; internet www .aquincum.hu; f. 1894; prehistory and Roman history of Budapest; Dir Dr PAULA ZSIDI; publ. *Aquincumi Füzetek* (excavations and rescue work at the Aquincum Museum).

Fővárosi Képtár (Municipal Picture Gallery): 1037 Budapest, Kiscelli u. 108; tel. (1) 388-8560; fax (1) 368-7917; e-mail fovarosikeptar@mail.btm.hu; internet www.btmfk.iif.hu; fine arts since the 19th century; Dir PÉTER FITZ.

Kiscelli Múzeum: 1037 Budapest, Kiscelli u. 108; tel. (1) 388-7817; fax (1) 368-7917; e-mail fovarosikeptar@mail.btm.hu; internet www.btmfk.iif.hu; f. 1899; history of Budapest since 1686; fine art colln; Dir Dr PÉTER FARBAKY.

Budavári Mátyás-templom Egyházmüvészeti Gyüjteménye (Matthias Church of Buda Castle Ecclesiastical Art Collection): 1014 Budapest, Szentháromság tér 2; tel. (1) 488-7716; fax (1) 488-7717; e-mail muzeum@matyas-templom.hu; internet www.matyas-templom.hu; f. 1964; permanent collection of Roman Catholic religious objects in the gallery of Matthias Church; Dir MÁTÉFFY BALÁZS.

HM HIM Hadtörténeti Múzeum és Könyvtár (Military History Museum and Library): located at: Tóth Árpád sétány 40, 1014 Budapest; POB 7, 1250 Budapest; tel. and fax (1) 356-1575; e-mail him.muzeum@hm-him.hu; internet www.hm-him.hu; f. 1918; Hungarian and Hungarian-related militaria incl. arms, medals, flags, uniforms, art, books, documents, photographs, posters, prints, maps; 39 mems; library of 300,025 vols; Dir Colonel Dr JÓZSEF LUGOSI; publ. *A Hadtörténeti Múzeum Értesítője/Acta Musei Militaris in Hungaria* (Yearbook of the Hungarian Military Museum, with summaries in English and German, 1 a year).

Holocaust Memorial Centre: 1094 Budapest, Páva u. 39; tel. (1) 455-3333; fax (1) 455-3399; e-mail info@hdke.hu; internet www.hdke.org; f. 2004; Exec. Dir LASZLO HARSANYI.

Iparművészeti Múzeum (Museum of Applied Arts): 1091 Budapest, Üllői u. 33–37; tel. (1) 456-5100; fax (1) 217-5838; internet www.imm.hu; f. 1872; European and Hungarian decorative arts; library: see Libraries; Gen. Dir Dr KÁROLY SIMON; publs catalogues, *Ars Decorativa* (1 a year).

Component Museums:

Hopp Ferenc Kelet-Ázsiai Művészeti Múzeum (Ferenc Hopp Museum of Eastern Asiatic Arts): 1062 Budapest, Andrássy u. 103; tel. (1) 322-8476; fax (1) 217-5838; f. 1919; collns of Asiatic arts; library of 29,000 vols; Chief Curator Dr GYÖRGYI FAJCSÁK.

Nagytétényi Kastélymúzeum (Castle Museum of Nagytétény): 1225 Budapest, Kastélypark u. 9–11; tel. (1) 207-0005; fax (1) 207-4680; internet www.nagytetenyi.hu; f. 1948; European furniture of the 15th to the 19th centuries; Manager ELUIRA KIRÁLY.

Ráth György Múzeum: 1068 Budapest, Városligeti-fasor 12; tel. (1) 342-3916; f. 1906; Chief Curator Dr GYÖRGYI FAJCSÁK.

Közlekedési Múzeum (Transport Museum): 1146 Budapest, Városligeti krt 11; tel. (1) 273-3840; fax (1) 363-7822; e-mail km@ella.hu; internet www.km.iif.hu; f. 1896; models of railway locomotives and rolling stock, old vehicles, railway, nautical, aeronautic, road and urban transport collns, road- and bridge-building, etc.; 4 br. museums incl. aviation and railway exhibitions with open-air displays; library of 140,000 vols; Dir Dr LÁSZLÓ EPERJESI; publ. *A Közlekedési Múzeum Évkönyve.*

Liszt Ferenc Emlékmúzeum és Kutatóközpont (Ferenc Liszt Memorial Museum and Research Centre): 1064 Budapest VI, Vörösmarty u. 35; tel. (1) 342-7320; fax (1)

413-1526; e-mail lisztmuzeum@lisztakademia.hu; internet www.lisztmuseum.hu; f. 1986; reconstruction of the composer Franz Liszt's (1811–1886) residence in the bldg of the Old Acad. of Music, with his instruments, furniture, library and other memorabilia; permanent and temporary exhibitions; colln of Liszt's music MSS, letters and other documentation, in collaboration with the Research Library for Music History; Dir Dr ZSUZSANNA DOMOKOS.

Magyar Bélyegmúzeum (Stamp Museum): 1400 Budapest, Pf. 86, 1074 Hársfa u. 47; tel. (1) 341-5526; fax (1) 342-3757; e-mail belyegmuzeum@axelero.hu; f. 1930; collections of 12 million Hungarian and foreign stamps; philatelic history; exhibitions locally and abroad; library of 5,000 vols; Dir ROSALIE SOLYMOSI; publ. *Yearbook.*

Magyar Építészeti Múzeum (Hungarian Museum of Architecture): 1036 Budapest, Mókus u. 20; tel. (1) 388-6170; fax (1) 367-2686; f. 1968; architecture and history of architecture; library of 7,000 vols; Dir KÁROLY BUGAR-MÉSZÁROS; publ. *Pavilon* (1 a year).

Magyar Kereskedelmi és Vendéglátóipari Múzeum (Hungarian Museum of Trade and Tourism): 1051 Budapest, Szent István tér 15; tel. (1) 212-1245; fax (1) 269-5428; e-mail mkvm@iif.hu; internet www.mkvm.hu; catering trade colln f. 1966, covers the subjects of sales and services, particularly in tourism, hotels and hostelry, cuisine, coffee houses, confectionery, shop fittings; commerce colln f. 1970, contains shop fittings, samples, storage pots, packing material, measuring instruments and coins; the 2 depts also contain documents, photos, posters; Dir IMPRE KISS.

Magyar Mezőgazdasági Múzeum (Museum of Hungarian Agriculture): 1146 Budapest, Városliget, Vajdahunyadvár; tel. (1) 363-1117; fax (1) 364-0076; e-mail museum@mmgm.hu; internet www.mmgm.hu; f. 1896; library of 85,000 vols; collection, preservation and presentation of objects and documents related to the history of agriculture and agro-industries in Hungary; conferences; provincial brs; Dir-Gen. Dr GYÖRGY FEHÉR; publs *Agrártörténeti Szemle* (Agricultural History Review, 2 a year), *Bibliographia Historiae Rerum Rusticarum Internationalis* (International Bibliography of Agrarian History, every 4 years), *Magyar Mezőgazdasági Múzeum Közleményei* (Proceedings, every 2 years).

Magyar Nemzeti Galéria (Hungarian National Gallery): 1250 Budapest, Budavári Palota, Pf. 31; tel. (1) 375-7533; fax (1) 375-8898; e-mail mng@mng.hu; internet www.mng.hu; f. 1957; collns incl. Hungarian art since the 11th century,; paintings, sculptures, drawings, engravings, medals; library of 76,000 vols; Dir Dr LÓRÁND BERECZKY; publ. *A Magyar Nemzeti Galéria Évkönyve* (Annals).

Magyar Nemzeti Múzeum (Hungarian National Museum): 1088 Budapest, Múzeum krt 14–16; tel. (1) 338-2122; fax (1) 317-7806; e-mail info@hnm.hu; internet www.hnm.hu; f. 1802; history, archaeology, numismatics; library of 240,000 vols; Dir-Gen. Dr TIBOR KOVÁCS; publs *Folia Archaeologica* (1 a year), *Folia Historica* (1 a year), *Régészeti Füzetek* (Fasciculi Archaeologici), *Communicationes Archaeologicae Hungariae* (1 a year), *Múzeumi Műtárgyvédelem* (Protection of Museum Art Objects, 1 a year), *A magyar múzeumok kiadványainak bibliográfiája* (Bibliography of the Hungarian Museum's publications), *Bibliotheca Humanitatis Historica, Inventaria Praehistorica Hungariae.*

Magyar Sportmúzeum (Hungarian Museum of Sport): 1146 Budapest, Dózsa György u. 3; tel. (1) 252-1696; fax (1) 469-5012; internet www.sportmuzeum.hu; f. 1963; documents and photos of history of sport in Hungary and abroad; 7,000 books, 35,000 plaques and medals, 4,000 trophies, etc., 500,000 photos, films; Dir Dr LAJOS SZABÓ.

Magyar Természettudományi Múzeum (Hungarian Natural History Museum): 1088 Budapest, Baross u. 13; tel. (1) 267-7101; fax (1) 317-1669; internet www.nhmus.hu; f. 1802; depts of mineralogy and petrography, geology and palaeontology, botany, zoology, anthropology; library of 250,000 vols; Chief Dir Dr ISTVÁN MATSKÁSI; publs *Acta zoologica Academiae Scientiarum Hungaricae* (4 a year), *Annales Historico-Naturales Musei Nationalis Hungarici* (1 a year), *Folia Entomologica Hungarica* (1 a year), *Fragmenta Palaeontologica Hungarica* (1 a year), *Studia Botanica Hungarica* (1 a year).

Magyar Zsidó Múzeum és Levéltár (Hungarian Jewish Museum and Archives): 1077 Budapest, Dohány u. 2; tel. (1) 343-6756; fax (1) 343-6756; e-mail info@bpjewmus.hu; f. 1916; Jewish pieces of archaeology and art history, religious objects; Dir ROBERT B. TURÁN.

Műcsarnok (Palace of Art): 1406 Budapest, POB 35; tel. (1) 460-7000; fax (1) 363-7205; e-mail info@mucsarnok.hu; internet www.mucsarnok.hu; f. 1896; temporary exhibitions of Hungarian and foreign contemporary art; library of 15,000 vols; Dir Dr JULIA FABÉNYI.

Néprajzi Múzeum (Museum of Ethnography): 1055 Budapest, Kossuth Lajos tér 12; tel. (1) 473-2410; fax (1) 473-2411; e-mail info@neprajz.hu; internet www.neprajz.hu; f. 1872; collections and research activities cover peasant and tribal folk cultures; library of 169,000 vols; Ethnographic Archive with 28,000 MSS and 318,000 photographs, 252 films; Folk Music Archive with 62,000 entries; Gen. Dir Dr ZOLTÁN FEJŐS; publs *Néprajzi Értesítő* (Yearbook), *Hungarian Folklore Bibliography* (1 a year), *Fontes Musei Ethnographiae, Tabula* (2 a year), *MaDok-füzetek.*

Öntödei Múzeum (Foundry Museum): 1027 Budapest, Bem József u. 20; tel. (1) 201-4370; e-mail ontode@omm.hu; f. 1969; attached to the Hungarian Museum of Science and Technology; used by Ábrahám Ganz and others until 1964; original foundry equipment; history of technological devt of foundry trade, old mouldings; library of 1,483 vols; Curator KATALIN LENGYEL-KISS.

OMM Elektrotechnikai Múzeuma (Museum of Electrical Engineering): 1075 Budapest, Kazinczy u. 21; tel. and fax (1) 342-5750; e-mail emuzeum@qwertynet.hu; f. 1970; historic colln of electrical engineering; library of 10,000 vols; Dir Dr SÁNDOR JESZENSZKY.

Magyar Műszaki és Közlekedési Múzeum (Hungarian Museum for Technology and Transport): 1426 Budapest, Pf. 37; 1146 Budapest, Városligeti krt 11; tel. (1) 273-3840; fax (1) 363-7822; e-mail info@mmkm.hu; internet www.km.iif.hu; f. 2003 merger of Transport museum (f. 1896) and the Nat. museum for Science and Technology (f. 1973); collection covers inventions and prototypes with reference to natural science and technology, historic exhibits from the early days of industry and its development to the present; colln of locomotives and wagons on a 1:5 scale; railway technology; history of road traffic, the history of sailing and the history of flight and space flight; library of 150,000 vols, 2,889 m of written material; Dir

Dr ERZSEBET KOCZIAN-SZENTPETERI; publs *A Közlekedési Múzeum Évkönyve* (Yearbook of the Transport Museum), *Technikatörténeti Szemle* (Review of History of Technology).

Petőfi Irodalmi Múzeum és Kortárs Irodalmi Központ (Petőfi Museum of Hungarian Literature and Centre for Contemporary Literature): 1053 Budapest, Károlyi M. u. 16; tel. (1) 317-3611; fax (1) 317-1722; e-mail muzeuminf@pim.hu; internet www.pim.hu; f. 1954; literature since the 19th century; library of 400,000 vols; archive of 950,000 MSS, 30,000 photographs, 4,900 sound recordings; art colln of 20,000 items; Dir Dr RITA RATZKY.

Postamúzeum (Postal Museum): 1061 Budapest, Andrássy u. 3; tel. (1) 268-1997; fax (1) 268-1958; e-mail info@postamuzeum.hu; internet www.postamuzeum.hu; f. 1955; permanent exhibition of the history of post and telecommunications; library of 11,000 vols; Dir MAKKAI VÁRKONYI ILDIKÓ; publs *Postai és Távközlési Múzeumi Alapítvány Évkönyve* (1 a year), *Hírközlési Múzeumi Alapítvány*.

Semmelweis Orvostörténeti Múzeum, Könyvtár és Levéltár (Semmelweis Medical Historical Museum, Library and Archives): 1013 Budapest, Apród. u. 1–3 (Museum); 1023 Budapest, Török u. 12 (Library and Archives); tel. (1) 201-1577 (Museum), (1) 212-5421 (Library and Archives); fax (1) 375-3936; e-mail semmelweis@museum.hu; internet www.semmelweis.museum.hu; f. 1951 (Library), 1965 (Museum), 1972 (Archives); administers 12 attached medical museums; library of 112,000 vols, 20,000 periodicals; Gen. Dir BENEDEK VARGA; Man. Dir (vacant); publ. *Orvostörténeti Közlemények / Communicationes de Historia Artis Medicinae* (1 a year).

Szépművészeti Múzeum (Museum of Fine Arts): 1146 Budapest, Dózsa György u. 41; tel. (1) 469-7100; fax (1) 469-7172; e-mail titkarsag@szepmuveszeti.hu; internet www.szepmuveszeti.hu; f. 1896, opened 1906; collns and galleries incl. Egyptian and Greco-Roman antiquities, foreign paintings, sculptures, drawings and engravings; library of 150,000 vols; Dir-Gen. Dr LÁSZLÓ BAÁN; publs *Bulletin du Musée Hongrois des Beaux-Arts*, *MúzeumCafé* (24 a year).

Attached Museum:

Vasarely Múzeum: 1033 Budapest, Szentlélek tér 1; tel. (1) 388-7551; fax (1) 250-1540; e-mail vasarely.budapest@museum.hr; internet www.muzeum.hu/budapest/vasarely; Dir LILLA SZABÓ.

Textil és Textilruházati Ipartörténeti Múzeum (Museum of the Textile and Clothing Industry): 1036 Budapest III, Lajos u. 138; tel. (1) 430-1387; fax (1) 367-5910; e-mail vajk.eva@axelero.hu; internet www.museum.hu/budapest/textilmuzeum; f. 1972; exhibits from Hungary and Central Europe; library of 3,690 vols; Dir ÉVA VAJK; publ. *Évkönyv* (Year Book).

Tűzoltó Múzeum (Fire Brigade Museum): 1105 Budapest, Martinovics tér 12; tel. (1) 261-3586; e-mail okf.tuzoltomuzeum@katved.hu; internet www.katasztrofavedelem.hu/muzeum; f. 1955; includes old fire-fighting equipment, carts, pumps and hoses; universal and Hungarian history of fire protection, its means and organization; library of 15,000 vols; Curator GYULA CSICSMANN; Librarian ESZTER BEREC; publ. *Tűzoltó Múzeum Évkönyve* (Yearbook).

Zenetörténeti Múzeum (Museum of History of Music): H-1014 Budapest, Táncsics M. u. 7; tel. (1) 214-6770; fax (1) 375-9282; e-mail director@zti.hu; internet www.zti.hu; f. 1969; library of 1,200 vols; colln of instruments,

MSS, personal objects used by great musicians; Dir Prof. Dr TIBOR TALLIAN.

Cegléd

Kossuth Lajos Múzeum: 2700 Cegléd, Múzeum u. 5; tel. (53) 310-637; fax (53) 310-637; e-mail kossuthmuzeum@pmmi.hu; f. 1917; relics of Lajos Kossuth; ethnography, archaeology, arts, numismatics; library of 14,000 vols; Dir GYULA KOCSIS; publ. *Ceglédi Füzetek* (1 a year).

Debrecen

Déri Múzeum: 4001 Debrecen, Déri tér 1, Pf. 61; tel. (52) 417-577; fax (52) 417-560; e-mail derimuzeum@freemail.hu; internet www.derimuz.hu; f. 1902; archaeological, ethnographic, fine and applied art, natural history, literary and local history collections and exhibitions; library of 50,000 vols, photographic archive of 100,500 negatives and slides; Dir Dr IBOLYA SZATHMÁRI; publs *A Déri Múzeum Évkönyve* (Yearbook), *Múzeumi Kurir* (Review).

Dunaújváros

Fejér Megyei Múzeumok Igazgatósága—Intercisa Múzeum: 2400 Dunaújváros, Városháza tér 4; tel. (25) 408-970; fax (25) 411-315; e-mail intercisamuz@gmail.com; f. 1951; prehistoric, Roman and medieval collns; regional history, archaeology and ethnography; library of 5,900 vols; Curator Dr MÁRTA MATUSSNÉ LENDVAI.

Eger

Dobó István Vármúzeum: 3301 Eger, Vár 1; tel. (36) 312-744; fax (36) 312-450; e-mail varmuzeum@div.iif.hu; f. 1872; originally archiepiscopal picture gallery and museum; enlarged by Fort Eger excavation material 1949; local remains of archaeology, ethnography, history of literature and of arts; relics of the Turkish occupation; library of 30,000 vols; Dir Dr TIVADAR PETERCSÁK; publs *Agria* (Yearbook), *Studia Agriensia*.

Esztergom

Balassa Bálint Múzeum: 2500 Esztergom, Mindszenty tér 3; tel. (33) 412-185; e-mail balassa.esztergom@museum.hu; f. 1894; history, archaeology, numismatics, applied arts; library of 12,000 vols; Curator Dr ISTVÁN HORVÁTH.

Keresztény Múzeum (Christian Museum): 2501 Esztergom, Mindszenty tér 2; tel. (33) 413-880; fax (33) 413-880; e-mail keresztenymuzeum@vnet.hu; internet www.christianmuseum.hu; f. 1875; Hungarian, Italian, Dutch, Austrian and German late medieval and Renaissance paintings and sculpture; collns of baroque and modern art, decorative arts, prints and drawings; library of 11,000 vols; Dir PÁL CSÉFALVAY.

Magyar Környezetvédelmi és Vízügyi Múzeum (Hungarian Environmental and Water Management Museum): 2500 Esztergom, Kölcsey u. 2; tel. (33) 500-250; fax (33) 500-251; internet www.dunamuzeum.org.hu; f. 1973; history of water management; library of 9,700 vols; Curator IMRE KAJÁN; publ. *Vizgazdálkodás* (Water Management).

Vármúzeum: 2500 Esztergom, Szent István tér 1; tel. (33) 415-986; fax (33) 500-095; e-mail varmegom@invitel.hu; internet www.mnmvarmuzeuma.hu; f. 1967; excavated and reconstructed royal palace from the times of the Hungarian House of the Árpáds; municipal history of Esztergom as royal seat in the Middle Ages; Curator BÉLA HORVÁTH.

Fertőd

Esterházy Castle Museum: 9431 Fertőd, Joseph Haydn u. 2; tel. (99) 537-640; e-mail kastelymuzeum.fertod@museum.hu; f. 1959;

historic castle of Esterházy family; local documents, furnishings, applied art, memorabilia of composer Haydn; Dir JOLÁN BAK.

Gyöngyös

Mátra Múzeum (Museum Historico-Naturale Matraense): 3200 Gyöngyös, Kossuth u. 40; tel. (37) 505-530; fax (37) 505-531; internet www.matramuzeum.hu; f. 1957; natural history: palaeontology, zoology and botany of Hungary and Europe; history of hunting; library of 12,000 vols; Curator Dr LEVENTE FÜKÖH; publs *Folia Historico-naturalia Musei Matraensis* (1 a year), *Malacological Newsletter* (1 a year).

Győr

Xántus János Múzeum: 9022 Győr, Széchenyi tér 5; tel. (96) 310-588; fax (96) 310-731; e-mail xantus@gymsmuzeum.hu; f. 1854; archaeological collection containing relics of the ancient town of Arrabona (now Győr); history, art, anthropology, Roman lapidarium; picture gallery; library of 38,000 vols; Dir Dr ESZTER SZŐNYI; publ. *Arrabona* (1 a year).

Gyula

Erkel Ferenc Múzeum (Ferenc Erkel Museum): 5700 Gyula, Kossuth u. 17; tel. (66) 361-236; e-mail erkel.gyula@museum.hu; f. 1868; archaeology, art, local history, musicological and ethnographic collns; library of 9,052 vols; Curator Dr PÉTER HAVASSY.

Hajdúböszörmény

Hajdúsági Múzeum: 4220 Hajdúböszörmény, Kossuth L. u. 1; tel. (52) 371-038; fax (52) 371-038; e-mail hajdusagi.hajduboszormeny@museum.hu; f. 1924; sections: archaeology, ethnography, history and fine arts; library of 15,000 vols; Curator Dr MIKLÓS NYAKAS; publs *Évkönyv* (in Hungarian and German, every 2 years), *Közlemények* (in Hungarian, German, English and Russian, 1 a year).

Herend

Porcelán Múzeum: 8440 Herend, Kossuth u. 140; tel. (88) 523-197; fax (88) 261-801; e-mail porcelanmuveszeti.herend@museum.hu; f. 1964; exhibits from the famous china factory, est. 1826; library of 4,500 vols; Dir MAGDOLNA SIMON.

Hódmezővásárhely

Tornyai János Múzeum és Közművelődési Központ (Tornyai Janos Museum and Cultural Centre): 6800 Hódmezővásárhely, Dr Rapcsák András u. 16–18; tel. (62) 242-224; e-mail tornyai.hodmezovasarhely@museum.hu; f. 1905; archaeological, ethnographic and folk-art collns, Tornyai paintings and Medgyessy sculptures; pottery and farm museum; library of 5,500 vols; Dir Dr IMRE NAGY.

Jászberény

Jász Múzeum: 5100 Jászberény, Táncsics u. 5; tel. (57) 412-753; e-mail jasz.jaszbereny@museum.hu; f. 1873; collns from the late Stone, Copper, Bronze and Iron Ages; ethnography, local history; library of 6,593 vols; Curator JÁNOS TÓTH.

Kalocsa

Viski Károly Múzeum: 6300 Kalocsa, Szent István Király u. 25, POB 82; tel. (78) 462-351; fax (78) 462-351; e-mail viski.kalocsa@museum.hu; f. 1932; regional museum, folk art; library of 9,000 vols; Dir IMRE ROMSICS.

Kaposvár

Somogy Megyei Múzeumok Igazgatósága (Somogy County Museums Authority):

7400 Kaposvár, Fő u. 10; tel. (82) 314-011; fax (82) 312-822; e-mail titkarsag@smmi.hu; internet www.smmi.hu; f. 1909; archaeological and ethnographic collns, contemporary history, fine arts, natural history; library of 13,000 vols; Dir Dr László Költő; publs *Múzeumi Tájékoztató, Somogyi Múzeumok Füzetei, Somogyi Múzeumok Közleményei*.

Karcag

Györffy István Nagykun Múzeum: 5300 Karcag, Kálvin u. 4; tel. (59) 312-087; fax (59) 503-164; e-mail karcagimuzeum@gmail.com; f. 1906; regional museum, ethnography; library of 8,000 vols; Curator Miklós Nagy Molnár.

Kecskemét

Bozsó Collection: 6000 Kecskemet, Klapka u. 34; tel. and fax (76) 324-625; e-mail bozsoal@mail.datanet.hu; internet www.bozso.net; Dir Klára Lóránd.

Katona József Memorial House: 6000 Kecskemét, Katona József u. 5; tel. (76) 328-420; fax (76) 328-420; e-mail klio.ilona@axelero.hu; f. 1894; life and work of 18th-century writer József Katona; library of 16,600 vols; Dir Dávid Mária Kriskóné.

Magyar Naiv Művészek Múzeuma (Museum of Hungarian Naive Art): 6000 Kecskemét, Gáspár A. u. 11; tel. (76) 324-767; fax (76) 481-122; e-mail naivmuzeum@freemail.hu; f. 1976; exhibitions of works of Hungarian primitive painters and sculptors; Dir Dr Bárt János igazgató; publ. *Magyar Naiv Művészek Múzeuma*.

Szórakaténusz Játékmúzeum (Toy Museum): 6000 Kecskemet, Gáspár A. u. 11; tel. and fax (76) 481-469; e-mail muzeumesmuhely@szorakatenusz.hu; internet www.szorakatenusz.hu; f. 1981; library of 3,000 vols; Dir Mária Váczi; publ. *Studies of the History of Play*.

Keszthely

Balatoni Múzeum: 8360 Keszthely, Múzeum-u. 2; tel. (83) 312-351; fax (83) 312-351; e-mail balatonimuz@georgikon.hu; internet www.zmmi.hu; f. 1898; prehistoric and historic collections relating to Lake Balaton; library of 29,000 vols; Director Dr Bálint Havasi.

Helikon Kastélymúzeum (Helikon Castle Museum): 8360 Keszthely, Kastély u. 1; tel. (83) 312-190; fax (83) 315-039; e-mail khelikon@freemail.hu; internet www.helikonkastely.hu; f. 1974; 18th-century castle built by the Festetics family; exhibitions: aristocratic lifestyle, arts of the Islamic world, Helikon library; coach museum, hunting museum and historical model railway exhibit; library of 94,000 vols; Dir Dr László Czoma.

Kiskunfélegyháza

Kiskun Múzeum: 6100 Kiskunfélegyháza, Dr Holló L. u. 9; tel. (76) 461-468; fax (76) 462-542; e-mail kiskun.kiskunfelegyhaza@museum.hu; f. 1902; ethnography; library of 20,000 vols; Curator Dr Erzsébet Molnár.

Kiskunhalas

Thorma János Múzeum: 6400 Kiskunhalas, Köztársaság u. 2; tel. (77) 422-864; fax (77) 422-864; e-mail muzeum@halas.hu; f. 1874; ethnography, archaeology and history; library of 7,000 vols; Curator Aurél Szakál.

Kőszeg

Városi Múzeum (Municipal Museum): 9730 Kőszeg, Jurisics tér 6; tel. and fax (94) 360-156; e-mail museum.koszeg@axelerod.hu; f. 1932; collection of castle and town history; library of 9,300 vols; Dir Prof. Dr Kornél Bakay.

Mátészalka

Szatmári Múzeum: 4700 Mátészalka, Kossuth-ut. 5; tel. and fax (44) 502-646; e-mail szatmari.mateszalka@museum.hu; internet www.museum.hu/mateszalka/szatmari; f. 1972; local history and ethnographic collections; Dir Dr László Cservenyák.

Miskolc

Herman Ottó Múzeum: 3529 Miskolc, Görgey Artúr u. 28; tel. (46) 560-172; fax (46) 555-397; e-mail hermuz@axelero.hu; internet www.hermuz.hu; f. 1899; collections of archaeology, regional ethnography, fine arts and applied arts, natural science, minerals of Hungary, local history, literary history, history of photography; library of 44,000 vols; Dir Dr László Veres; publs *A Herman Ottó Múzeum Évkönyve* (Yearbook), *Officina Musei, A Miskolci Herman Ottó Múzeum Közleményei* (Communications), *Néprajzi Kiadványok* (Ethnographical Studies), *Documentatio Borsodiensis, Natura Borsodiensis*.

Kohászati Múzeum (Foundry Museum): 3517 Miskolc-Felsőhámor, Palota-u. 22; tel. (46) 379-375; e-mail kohmuz@kohmuz.t-online.hu; internet www.kohmuz.t-online.hu; f. 1949; history of the foundry, science and technology; archaeological foundry of the 9th to 12th centuries; technical monument from the 18th century, the Fazola foundry; Dir László Porkoláb.

Mohács

Kanizsan Dorottya Múzeum: 7700 Mohács, Városház u. 1; tel. (69) 311-536; e-mail kanizsai.mohacs@museum.hu; f. 1923; ethnography of the Serbs, Croats and Slavs; library of 2,300 vols; Curator Jakab Ferkov.

Mosonmagyaróvár

Hansági Múzeum: 9200 Mosonmagyaróvár, Szent István u. 1; tel. (96) 213-834; fax (96) 212-094; e-mail hansagi.mosonmagyarovar@museum.hu; f. 1882; regional museum; archaeology, ethnography, lapidarium, local history, paintings by János Szale, Gyurkovits colln; library of 7,216 vols; Dir Károly Szentkuti.

Nagycenk

Széchenyi István Emlékmúzeum (Széchenyi Memorial Museum): 9485 Nagycenk, Kiscenki u. 3; tel. (99) 360-023; fax (99) 360-260; e-mail szechenyi.nagycenk@museum.hu; f. 1973; history of the Széchenyi family and life (iconography, bibliography) of 19th-century statesman Count István Széchenyi; library of 5,000 vols; Curator Dr Attila Környei.

Nagykanizsa

Thury György Múzeum: 8800 Nagykanizsa, Zrínyi u. 62; tel. (93) 317-233; fax (93) 317-233; e-mail tgym@zmmi.hu; f. 1919; archaeological and ethnographical collections, local history displays, numismatics; library of 5,000 vols; Curator Dr László Horváth.

Nagykőrös

Arany János Múzeum: 2751 Nagykőrös, Ceglédi-u. 19; tel. (53) 350-810; fax (53) 350-770; e-mail ajmpmi@freemail.hu; f. 1928; regional museum; archaeology, ethnography, local history, literary documents of poet J. Arany; library of 20,019 vols; Dir Dr László Novák; publs *Acta Musei, Archivum Musei*.

Nyirbátor

Báthory István Múzeum: 4300 Nyirbátor, Károlyi-u. 15; tel. (42) 510-218; fax (42) 510-218; e-mail bathori.nyirbator@museum.hu; f.

1955; archaeology, local history and art; library of 2,900 vols; Curator Pilipkó Erzsébet.

Nyiregyháza

Jósa András Múzeum: 4400 Nyíregyháza, Benczúr tér 21, Pf. 57; tel. (42) 315-722; fax (42) 315-722; e-mail jam@jam.nyirbone.hu; internet jam.nyirbone.hu; f. 1868; collections of archaeology, ethnography and local history; fine and applied arts, numismatics; library of 20,000 vols; Dir Dr Péter Németh; publ. *A nyíregyházi Jósa András Múzeum Évkönyve* (1 a year).

Pannonhalma

Pannonhalmi Főapátság Gyűjteménye (Abbey of Pannonhalma Collection): 9090 Pannonhalma, Vár 1; tel. (96) 570-191; fax (96) 470-011; e-mail foapatsag.pannonhalma@museum.hu; f. 1802; paintings, sculptures, applied arts in an ancient Benedictine Abbey.

Pápa

Gróf Esterházy Károly Kastély- és Tájmúzeum (Count Charles Esterházy Castle and Regional Museum): 8500 Pápa, Fő tér 1, Várkastély; 8501 Pápa, POB 208; tel. (89) 313-584; e-mail kastely.papa@museum.hu; f. 1960; ethnographical, archaeological and industrial collns from the town and environment; library of 10,000 vols; Dir Dr Péter László; publ. *Acta Musei Papensis* (1 a year).

Pécs

Csontváry Múzeum: 7621 Pécs, Janus Pannonius u. 11; tel. (72) 310-544; fax (72) 315-694; e-mail jpm@jpm.hu; f. 1973; administered by the Baranya County Museums' Directorate; art gallery comprising selected works by the Expressionist painter Tivadar Csontváry Kosztka; Man. Gábor Tillai.

Janus Pannonius Múzeum: 7601 Pécs, POB 158; 7621 Pécs, Káptalan u. 5; tel. (72) 310-172; fax (72) 315-694; e-mail jpm@jpm.hu; f. 1904; natural sciences, archaeology, ethnography, modern Hungarian art, local history; library of 25,000 vols; Dir Zoltán Huszár; publ. *Dunántuli Dolgozatok* (Trans-Danubian Studies).

Modern Magyar Képtár I (Modern Hungarian Gallery I, 1890–1950): 7621 Pécs, Káptalan u. 4; tel. (72) 324-822; e-mail keptar.pecs@museum.hu; f. 1957; administered by the Baranya County Museums' Directorate; examples of the Nagybánya school (Hollósy, Ferenczy), pre-war art (Rippl-Rónai, Gulácsy), the Eight (Pór, Kernstok, Berény, Tihanyi), Activism (Nemes Lampért, Uitz, Mattis-Teutsch), the Avantgarde (Breuer, Molnár, Moholy-Nagy), artists with social sensitivity (Dési Huber, Derkovits, Goldman, Bokros Birman), the school of Rome and artists of Szentendre (Vajda, Ámos, Barcsay, Czóbel, Kmetty), the European school (Korniss, Gyarmathy, Anna Margit).

Modern Magyar Képtár II (Modern Hungarian Gallery II, 1955–2001): 7621 Pécs, Papnövelde u. 5; tel. (72) 324-822; f. 1957; administered by the Baranya County Museums' Directorate; Contemporary Colln: paintings by Barcsay, Bizse, Korniss, Lantos, Orosz.

Vasarely Múzeum: 7621 Pécs, Káptalan-u. 3; tel. (72) 324-822; fax (72) 315-694; e-mail jpm@jpm.hu; f. 1976; administered by the Baranya County Museums' Directorate; art gallery comprising works by Hungarian-born French artist Victor Vasarely; Man. Gábor Tillai.

Rudabánya

Alapítvány Érc- és Ásványbányászati Múzeum (Museum of Mining of Metals and Minerals): 3733 Rudabánya, Petöfi u. 24; tel. (48) 353-151; e-mail eabmuz@axelero.hu; f. 1956; history of the industry, exhibitions; Curator BÉLA SZUROMI.

Salgótarján

Nógrádi Történeti Múzeum (Nógrád Historical Museum): 3100 Salgótarján, Múzeum tér 2, Pf. 3; tel. (32) 314-169; fax (32) 512-335; e-mail nograditmuzeum@nogradi-muzeumok.hu; internet www.museum.hu; f. 1959; social history since the 19th century, history of art, literary history, numismatics, industrial history, esp. mining; library of 16,000 vols; Dir Dr ANNA KOVÁCS; publ. *Yearbook of the Museums of Nógrád County*.

Sárospatak

Rákóczi Múzeum: 3950 Sárospatak, Szent Erzsébet u. 19; tel. (47) 311-083; fax (47) 511-135; internet www.spatak.hu; f. 1950; housed in the Castle of Sárospatak; historical, ethnographic, archaeological and applied art collections; library of 18,000 vols; Curator Dr DANKÓ KATALIN JÓSVAINÉ.

Sárvár

Nádasdy Ferenc Múzeum: 9600 Sárvár, Vár-u. 1; tel. (95) 320-158; e-mail nadasdy.sarvar@museum.hu; f. 1951; late Renaissance and Baroque Hungarian milieu reconstructed in state rooms of 16th-century castle; library of 3,900 vols; Dir ISTVÁN SÖPTEI.

Sopron

Központi Bányászati Múzeum (Central Mining Museum): 9400 Sopron, Templom u. 2; tel. (99) 312-667; fax (99) 338-902; e-mail info@kbm.hu; internet www.kbm.hu; f. 1957; science and technology; history of mining in the Carpathian basin since prehistoric age; Dir Dr KOVÁCSNÉ BIRCHER ERZSÉBET.

Soproni Múzeum: 9400 Sopron, Fő tér 8; tel. (99) 311-327; fax (99) 311-347; e-mail soproni@gymsmuzeum.hu; f. 1867; archaeology, folk art, pharmacy, medieval synagogue, local Baroque art and Storno Collns in 11 exhibition halls; library of 29,000 vols; Dir Dr ATTILA KÖRNYEI.

Szarvas

Tessedik Sámuel Múzeum: 5540 Szarvas, Vajda P. u. 1; tel. (66) 312-960; f. 1951; archaeology, ethnography and local history collns; Dir Dr JÓZSEF PALOV.

Szécsény

Kubinyi Ferenc Múzeum: 3170 Szécsény, Ady Endre-u. 7; tel. (32) 370-143; e-mail kubinyi.szecseny@museum.hu; f. 1973; archaeology and local history; library of 8,400 vols; Curator Dr KATALIN SIMÁN.

Szeged

Móra Ferenc Múzeum: 6701 Szeged, POB 474; 6720 Szeged, Roosevelt tér 1–3; tel. (62) 549-040; fax (62) 549-061; e-mail info@mfm.u-szeged.hu; internet www.mfm.u-szeged.hu; f. 1883; archaeological, ethnographic and biological collections, history of arts and regional collections; library of 50,000 vols; spec. colln include: Sándor Bálint bequest of 5,500 vols on archaic religions and beliefs, old books of prayers and liturgies, Győző Csongor Bequest of 5,500 vols on local history; Dir Dr GABRIELLA VÖRÖS; publs *Studia Archaeologica* (1 a year), *Studia Ethnographica* (1 a year), *Studia Historica* (1 a year), *Studia Naturalia* (1 a year), *Studia Historiae Literarum et Artium* (1 a year), *Monographia Archaeologica* (1 a year).

Székesfehérvár

Szent István Király Múzeum: 8002 Székesfehérvár, Fő u. 6, P4. 78; tel. (22) 315-583; fax (22) 311-734; e-mail fmmuz@mail.iif.hu; f. 1873; prehistoric, Roman and medieval collections, anthropological collection, regional ethnography, art gallery, musical collection, numismatic collection, stones of the Basilica of King St Stephen; library of 80,000 vols; Dir GYULA FÜLÖP; publs *Bulletin*, *Alba Regia* (Scientific Almanac).

Szekszárd

Wosinsky Mór Megyei Múzeum: 7101 Szekszárd, Szent István tér 26; tel. (74) 316-222; fax (74) 316-222; e-mail wmmm@terrasoft.hu; f. 1896; collections of folk art, archaeology, history, fine arts and applied arts; library of 11,300 vols; Dir Dr ATTILA GAÁL; publ. *Yearbook*.

Szentendre

Ferenczy Múzeum: 2001 Szentendre, Fő tér 6, pf. 49; tel. (26) 310-244; fax (26) 310-790; e-mail pmmikozmuvelodes@freemail.hu; internet www.pmmi.hu; f. 1951; paintings, drawings, sculptures and Gobelin tapestries; centre for 30 museums in Pest County; library of 24,000 vols, 210 periodicals; Dir Dr LÁSZLÓ SIMON; publ. *Studia Comitatensia* (yearbook of papers published by the Museums of Pest County).

Szabadtéri Néprajzi Múzeum (Hungarian Open-Air Museum): 2001 Szentendre, Sztaravodai u., POB 63; tel. (26) 502-500; fax (26) 502-502; e-mail sznm@sznm.hu; internet www.skanzen.hu; f. 1967; vernacular architecture and furniture; library of 50,000 vols; archive of 110,000 photographs, 20,000 ethnographical, historical, architectural documents, films, maps, drawings, etc.; Dir Dr MIKLÓS CSERI; publs *Téka* (4 a year), *Ház és Ember* (1 a year).

Szentes

Koszta József Múzeum: 6600 Szentes, Szechenyi Liget 1; tel. (63) 313-352; fax (63) 313-352; e-mail muzeum@szentesinfo.hu; f. 1894; archaeological and ethnographical collection and paintings by Koszta; Dir JÁNOS SZABÓ.

Szigetvár

Zrínyi Miklós Vármúzeum: 7900 Szigetvár, Vár u. 1; tel. (73) 311-442; f. 1917; local history colln, relating particularly to the period of Turkish occupation (16th to 17th centuries).

Szolnok

Damjanich János Múzeum: 5000 Szolnok, Templom u. 2; tel. (56) 513-640; fax (56) 341-204; e-mail titkarsag@djm.hu; internet www.djm.hu; f. 1933; archaeology, ethnography, palaeontology, fine arts, applied art and local history collns; library of 50,000 vols; Dir Dr RÓBERT KERTÉSZ; publ. *Tisicum* (1 a year).

Szombathely

Savaria Múzeum: 9701 Szombathely, Kisfaludy Sándor u. 9; tel. (94) 312-554; fax (94) 313-736; e-mail info@savariamuseum.hu; internet www.savariamuseum.hu; f. 1872; natural history, archaeology, local cultural history, ethnography; library of 32,000 vols; Dir Dr SÁNDOR HORVÁTH; publs *Savaria* (Journal, 1 a year), *Praenorica – Folia Historico-Naturalia* (irregular).

Tác

Gorsium Szabadtéri Múzeum (Gorsium Open-Air Museum): 8121 Tác, Fövenypuszta Ady E. u. 56; tel. (22) 362-443; e-mail lak5706@mail.iif.hu; f. 1963; excavations of a Roman city, the ruins showing the original shape; Dir Prof. Dr JENŐ FITZ.

Tata

Kuny Domokos Megyei Múzeum: 2892 Tata, Néppark, Kiskastély, POB 224; tel. (34) 487-888; fax (34) 487-888; e-mail muzeum@kunymuzeum.hu; internet www.kunymuzeum.hu; f. 1954; history, archaeology, ethnology, art, palaeobotany; library of 27,000 vols; Dir Dr ÉVA MÁRIA FÜLÖP.

Vác

Tragor Ignác Múzeum: 2600 Vác, Zrínyi u. 41A; tel. (27) 500-750; fax (27) 500-758; e-mail muzeum@dunaweb.hu; internet www.muzeum.vac.hu; f. 1895; archaeology, ethnography, local history and fine arts exhibits; library of 10,565 vols, 4,760 periodicals and newsletters; Dir KŐVÁRI KLÁRA; publ. *Váci Könyvek* (Bulletin).

Várpalota

Magyar Vegyészeti Múzeum (Hungarian Chemical Museum): 8100 Várpalota, Szabadság tér 1; tel. (88) 575-670; fax (88) 471-702; e-mail vegymuz@vegyeszetimuzeum.hu; internet www.vegyeszetimuzeum.hu; f. 1963; history of the chemical industry; library of 18,618 vols; Dir ISTVÁN PRÓDER.

Vértesszőllős

Magyar Nemzeti Múzeum Vértesszőllősi Bemutatóhelye: 2837 Vértesszőllős; tel. (1) 327-7744; e-mail hnm@hnm.hu; internet www.hnm.hu; f. 1975; permanent open-air exhibition; dwelling-place and remains of early man; part of Archaeology Dept of Nat. Museum; Curator Dr VIOLA DOBOSI.

Veszprém

Laczkó Dezső Múzeum: 8201 Veszprém, Erzsébet sétány 1; tel. (88) 564-310; fax (88) 426-081; e-mail titkar@vmmuzeum.hu; internet www.c3.hu/~vmmuzeum; f. 1903; ethnographic, archaeological, historical, fine and industrial arts, history of literature, numismatic exhibits from Veszprém County; library of 36,000 vols; Dir Dr ZSUZSA FODOR; publs *Veszprém Megyei Múzeumok Közleményei, Publicationes Museorum Comitatus Vesprimiensis* (Communications of the Museums of Veszprém County).

Visegrád

Mátyás Király Múzeum (King Matthias Museum): 2025 Visegrád, Fő u. 23–25; tel. (26) 398-026; fax (26) 398-252; f. 1933; managed by Magyar Nemzeti Múzeum of Budapest; 13th-century upper and lower castle with Roman and medieval archaeological remains; partially restored 15th-century royal palace; library of 10,000 vols; Dir MÁTYÁS SZŐKE.

Zalaegerszeg

Göcseji Falumúzeum: 8900 Zalaegerszeg, Falumúzeum u. 18., POB 176; tel. (92) 703-295; fax (92) 511-972; e-mail muzeum@zmmi.hu; internet www.zmmi.hu; f. 1968; collections of regional history, archaeology, ethnography, paintings and sculpture; exhibition of sculptures by Zs. Kisfaludi-Strobl; exhibition on the history of County Zala; library of 20,658 vols; Dir Dr LÁSZLÓ VÁNDOR; publ. *Zalai Múzeum* (1 a year).

Magyar Olajipari Múzeum (Museum of the Hungarian Petroleum Industry): 8900 Zalaegerszeg, Wlassics Gyula. u. 13; tel. (92) 313-632; fax (92) 311-081; e-mail moim@olajmuzeum.hu; internet www.olajmuzeum.hu; f. 1969; exhibitions of the history of the professional and technical devt of the oil industry; equipment, documents, photographs, etc.; library of 9,000 vols; Dir JÁNOS TÓTH.

Zirc

Bakonyi Természettudományi Múzeum (Bakony Mountains Natural History Museum): 8420 Zirc, Rákóczi tér 3–5; tel. (88) 575-300; fax (88) 575-301; e-mail btmz@ bakonymuseum.koznet.hu; internet www .bakonymuseum.koznet.hu; f. 1972; natural history exhibits from Bakony Mountains, minerals from the Carpathian Basin; library of 25,000 vols, incl. 17,000 journals; Curator ÁGOTA KASPER; publs *A Bakony természettudományi kutatásának eredményei* (Results of Research into the Natural History of Bakony, 1 a year), *Folia Musei Historico-naturalis Bakonyiensis* (A Bakonyi Természettudományi Múzeum Közleményei, Communications of the Bakony Mountains Natural History Museum, 1 a year).

State Universities

BUDAPESTI CORVINUS EGYETEM
(Corvinus University of Budapest)

1093 Budapest, Fövám tér 8
Telephone: (1) 482-5000
Fax: (1) 482-5019
E-mail: intoffice@uni-corvinus.hu
Internet: www.uni-corvinus.hu

Founded 1920 as Budapesti Közgazdaságtudományi és Államigazgatási Egyetem
State control
Languages of instruction: Hungarian, English, French, German
Academic year: September to June
Rector: Prof. Dr TAMÁS MÉSZÁROS
Vice-Rector for Academic Affairs: Prof. Dr SÁNDOR KEREKES
Vice-Rector for Int. Affairs: Dr NORBERT KIS
Vice-Rector for Strategy and Devt: Prof. Dr IMRE JÁMBOR
Librarian: ISTVÁNNÉ ALFÖLDI

Number of teachers: 867
Number of students: 17,897

Publications: *Társadalom és Gazdaság* (Society and Economy, in Hungarian, 2 a year; in English, 3 a year), *Applied Ecology and Environmental Research* (2 a year)

DEANS

Faculty of Business Administration: Prof. ÁGNES HOFMEISTER
Faculty of Economics.: LÁSZLÓ TRAUTMANN
Faculty of Food Science: CSABA BALLA
Faculty of Horticultural Science: Prof. MAGDOLNA TÓTH
Faculty of Landscape Architecture: Prof. ATTILA CSEMEZ
Faculty of Public Administration.: Prof. MIKLÓS IMRE
Faculty of Social Sciences: Prof. ZSOLT ROSTOVÁNYI

PROFESSORS

ÁGH, A., Politics
ANGYAL, Á, Management and Organization
BALATON, K., Management and Organization
BALÁZS, P., European Studies
BÁNFI, T., Finance
BARICZ, R., Accountancy
BÉKÁSSY-MOLNÁR, E., Food Engineering
BEKKER, ZS., Economic Theory
BENCZÚR, E., Floriculture and Dendrology
BERÁCS, J., Marketing
BERNÁTH, J., Herb and Aroma Products
BLAHO, A., World Economics
BOD, P. Á., Economic Policy
BÚZA, J., Economic History
CHIKÁN, A., Logistics
CSÁKI, CS., Agriculture

CSEMEZ, A., Landscape Planning and Development
CSER, L., Computer Science
CSIMA, P., Landscape Protection
CSIZMADIA, S., Philosophy
DEÁK, D., Economic Law
DOBÁK, M., Management and Organization
FARAGÓ, T., Economic History
FEKETE, A., Physics Control
FODOR, P., Applied Chemistry
FORGÓ, F., Operations Research
GÁBOR, R. I., Human Resources
GÁL, P., World Economics
GALASI, P., Human Resources
GÁLIK, M., Media Economics
GEDEON, P., Comparative Economics
HAJDU, I., Food Economy
HÁMORI, B., Comparative Economics
HOÓS, J., Public Administration
HORÁNYI, Ö., Communication
HROTKÓ, K., Pomology
HRUBOS, I., Sociology
JÁMBOR, I., Landscape Technology and Garden Techniques
JENEI, GY., Public Administration
KÁLLAY, H., Oenology
KEREKES, S., Environmental Management
KERÉKGYÁRTÓ, GY., Statistics
KISS, J. L., International Relations
KONCZ, K., Human Resources
KOSÁRY, J., Applied Chemistry
KUCZI, T., Sociology
LADÁNYI, J., Sociology
LÁNG, Z., Technology
LENGYEL, GY., Sociology
LIGETI, S., Finance
LŐRINC ISTVÁNFFY, H., European Studies
MAGYAR, M., Language Centre
MAGYARI-BECK, I., Psychology and Pedagogy
MARÁZ, A., Microbiology
MÉSZÁROS, T., Strategy and Project Management
MÓCZÁR, J., Mathematics
MOKSONY, F., Sociology
NOVÁKY, E., Futurology
PALÁNKAI, T., World Economics
PAPP, J., Pomology
QUITTNER, P., Information Systems
RADICS, L., Ecology and Sustainable Economic Systems
RIMÓCZI, I., Botanics
ROSTOVÁNYI, Zs., International Relations
SCHMIDT, G., Floriculture and Dendrology
SURÁNYI, S., World Economics
SZABÓ, K., Comparative Economics
SZAKÁCS, S., Economic History
SZÁZ, J., Finance
TALLOS, P., Mathematics
TARI, E., Management and Organization
TEMESI, J., Operations Research
TÖRÖK, G., Business Law
TÓTH, G. M., Pomology
VATAI, G., Food Engineering
VERMES, L., Soil Science and Water Management
VITA, L., Statistics
ZALAI, E., Econometrics
ZÁMBORINÉ, N. E., Medicinal and Aromatic Plants
ZELKÓ, L., Finance
ZSOLNAI, L., Business Ethics

ATTACHED INSTITUTES

Institute for Postgraduate Studies in Economics: 1093 Budapest, Lónyay u. 12; tel. (1) 216-4441; fax (1) 216-2809; Dir ZITA ZOLTAY PAPRIKA.

International Studies Centre (ISC): 1093 Budapest, Fővám tér 8; tel. (1) 482-5443; fax (1) 482-5449; 351 students; Dir JÓZSEF BERÁCS.

BUDAPESTI MŰSZAKI ÉS GAZDASÁGTUDOMÁNYI EGYETEM
(Budapest University of Technology and Economics)

1111 Budapest, Műegyetem rkp. 3

Telephone: (1) 463-1111
Fax: (1) 463-1110
E-mail: rektor@mail.bme.hu
Internet: www.bme.hu

Founded 1782 as Institutum Geometricum Hydrotechnicum and reorganized as Hungarian Palatine Joseph Technical Univ. in 1871. Építőipari és Közlekedési Műszaki Egyetem (Technical Univ. of Building and Transport Engineering) was incorporated with the univ. in 1967. Present name 2000
State control
Languages of instruction: Hungarian, English, German, French, Russian
Academic year: September to June

Rector: Prof. Dr KÁROLY MOLNÁR
Vice-Rectors: Prof. Dr JÁNOS KÖVESI, Dr GYULA SALLAI, Dr MIKLÓS ZRÍNYI
Librarian: ISTVÁNNÉ FONYÓ

Number of teachers: 1,190
Number of students: 22,567

Publication: *A Budapesti Műszaki Egyetem Évkönyve* (1 a year)

DEANS

Faculty of Architecture: Dr GÁBOR BECKER
Faculty of Chemical Technology and Biotechnology.: Dr GYÖRGY POKOL
Faculty of Civil Engineering: Dr ANTAL LOVAS
Faculty of Economic and Social Sciences: Dr JÁNOS KÖVESI
Faculty of Electrical Engineering and Informatics: Dr LÁSZLÓ VAJTA
Faculty of Mechanical Engineering: Dr GÁBOR STÉPÁN
Faculty of Natural Sciences: Dr PÉTER MOSON
Faculty of Transportation Engineering: Dr BÉLA KULCSÁR

PROFESSORS

Faculty of Architecture (tel. (1) 463-3521; fax (1) 463-3520; e-mail dekanihivatal@eszk.bme .hu; internet www.epitesz.bme.hu):

BALOGH, B., Design
BITÓ, J., Housing Design
CSÁGOLY, F., Design of Public Buildings
DOMOKOS, G., Structural Mechanics
ISTVÁNFI, GY., History of Architecture
KASZÁS, K., Design of Public Buildings
KLAFSZKY, E., Building Management and Organization
LÁZÁR, A., Industrial and Agricultural Architecture
MAJOROS, A., Sanitary Engineering
MEGGYESI, T., Urban Studies
NAGY, L., Sanitary Engineering
PETRÓ, B., Building Constructions
TÖRÖK, F., Design of Public Buildings
VÖRÖS, F., Building Construction
ZÖLD, A., Sanitary Engineering

Faculty of Chemical Technology and Biotechnology (tel. (1) 463-3571; fax (1) 463-3570; e-mail dekan@mail.bme.hu; internet www.ch .bme.hu):

BITTER, I., Organic Chemical Technology
BORSA, J., Plastics and Rubber Industries
FAIGL, F., Organic Chemical Technology
FEKETE, J., General and Analytical Chemistry
FONYÓ, ZS., Chemical Unit Operations
GÁL, S., General and Analytical Chemistry
GROFCSIK, A., Physical Chemistry
HARGITTAI, I., General and Analytical Chemistry
HENCSEI, P., Inorganic Chemistry
HORVAI, GY., Chemical Informatics

KALAUS, GY., Organic Chemistry
KEGLEVICH, GY., Organic Chemical Technology
KEMÉNY, S., Chemical Unit Operations
KUBINYI, M., Physical Chemistry
MIHÁLTZ, P., Chemical Unit Operations
NOVÁK, B., Agricultural Chemical Technology
NOVÁK, L., Organic Chemistry
NYITRAI, J., Organic Chemistry
NYULÁSZI, L., Inorganic Chemistry
ÖRSI, F., Biochemistry and Food Technology
POKOL, GY., General and Analytical Chemistry
PUKÁNSZKY, B., Plastics and Rubber Industries
RÉFFY, J., Inorganic Chemistry
SALGÓ, A., Biochemistry and Food Technology
SEVELLA, B., Agricultural Chemical Technology
SZÉCHY, G., Chemical Technology
SZEPESVÁRI TOTH, K., General and Analytical Chemistry
TÖKE, L., Organic Chemical Technology
TUNGLER, A., Chemical Technology
VESZPRÉMI, T., Inorganic Chemistry
ZRINYI, M., Physical Chemistry

Faculty of Civil Engineering (tel. (1) 463-3531; fax (1) 463-3530; e-mail titkarsag@epito.bme.hu; internet www.epito.bme.hu/hivatal):

ADAM, J., Geodesy and Surveying
BALÁZS, GY., Building Materials and Engineering Geology
BOJTÁR, I., Structural Mechanics
DETREKŐI, Á., Photogrammetry and Geoinformatics
FARKAS, GY., Reinforced Concrete Structures
FARKAS, J., Geotechnics
FI, I., Road and Railway Engineering
GÁLOS, M., Building Materials and Engineering Geology
GÁSPÁR, ZS., Structural Mechanics
HEGEDÜS, I., Reinforced Concrete Structures
IJJAS, I., Hydraulic and Water Resources Engineering
IVÁNYI, M., Steel Structures
KISS PAPP, L., Geodesy and Surveying
KURUTZ KOVÁCS, M., Structural Mechanics
MEGYERI, J., Road and Railway Engineering
PATONAI, D., Building Construction
SÁRKÖZY, F., Geodesy and Surveying
SOMLYODY, L., Sanitary and Environmental Engineering
SZALAY, K., Reinforced Concrete Structures
SZÉLL, M., Building Construction
TARNAI, T., Structural Mechanics

Faculty of Economic and Social Sciences (tel. (1) 463-3591; fax (1) 463-3590; e-mail gtk-dekani@gtdh.bme.hu; internet www.gtk.bme.hu):

ANTALOVITS, M., Ergonomics and Psychology
BÁNDI, GY., Environmental Economics and Law
BENEDEK, A., Technical Education
BISZTERSZKY, E., Technical Education
DINYA, L., Industrial Management and Business Economics
FARKAS, J., Sociology
FEHÉR, M., Philosophy and History of Science
HORÁNYI, Ö., Sociology
HRONSZKY, I., Innovation Studies and History of Technology
KERÉKGYÁRTÓ, GY., Economics
KÖVESI, J., Industrial Business and Management
MARGITAY, T., Philosophy and History of Science

PLÉH, CS., Information Management
SÁRKÖZY, T., Law and Business Organization
S. NAGY, K., Sociology
SZLÁVIK, J., Environmental Economics and Technical Law
TÖRÖK, Á., Industrial Business and Management
VERESS, J., Economic and Business Policy
VINCZE, P., Physical Education

Faculty of Electrical Engineering and Informatics (1111 Budapest, Egry F. u. 18; tel. (1) 463-3581; fax (1) 463-3580; ; fax vikdhvez@vik-dh.bme.hu; internet www.vik.bme.hu):

ARATÓ, P., Process Control
BENYÓ, Z., Process Control
BERTA, I., High-Voltage Engineering
FRIGYES, I., Microwave Telecommunications
GORDOS, G., Telecommunications and Telematics
GYŐRFI, L., Mathematics
HALÁSZ, S., Electrical Machines
ILLYEFALVI-VITÉZ, ZS., Electronic Technology
KEVICZKY, L., Automation
KÓCZY, T. L., Telecommunications and Telematics
KOLLÁR, I., Measurement and Instrument Engineering
LANTOS, B., Process Control
LEVENDOVSZKY, J., Telecommunications
MOJZES, I., Electronic Technology
PAPP, L., Telecommunications
PÉCELI, G., Measurement and Instrument Engineering
RECSKI, A., Mathematics
RÓNYAI, L., Mathematics
ROSKA, T., Measurement and Instrument Engineering
SALLAI, GY., Telecommunications and Telematics
SCHMIDT, I., Electrical Machines
SELÉNYI, E., Measurement and Instrument Engineering
SZABÓ, CS., Telecommunications
SZÉKELY, V., Electronic Devices
SZIRMAY-KALOS, L., Process Control
TARNAY, K., Electronic Devices
VAJDA, I., Telecommunications
VAJK, I., Automation
VARJU, GY., Electric Power Plants and Networks
VESZELY, GY., Automation
ZOMBORY, L., Microwave Telecommunications

Faculty of Mechanical Engineering (tel. (1) 463-3541; fax (1) 463-3540; e-mail gepeszd@mail.bme.hu; internet www.gepesz.bme.hu):

ARTINGER, I., Mechanical Technology
BÉDA, GY., Technical Mechanics
BÜKI, G., Energetics
CZVIKOVSZKY, T., Polymer Engineering and Textile Technology
GARBAI, L., Sanitary Engineering
GINSZTLER, J., Electrical Materials Technology
HALÁSZ, G., Hydraulic Machines
HALMAI, A., Precision Mechanics – Optics
HORVÁTH, M., Machine Production
JÓRI, J. I., Agricultural Machine Design
KOVÁCS, L., Hydraulic Machines
KOZMA, M., Machine Elements
LAJOS, T., Fluid Mechanics
MEGGYES, A., Heat Engines
MOLNÁR, K., Process Engineering
PARTI, M., Fluid Mechanics
PENNINGER, A., Heat Engines
REMÉNYI, K., Energetics
STÉPÁN, G., Technical Mechanics
VÁRADI, K., Agricultural Machine Design
VARGA, L., Machine Elements
ZIAJA, GY., Mechanical Technology

Faculty of Natural Sciences (tel. (1) 463-3561; fax (1) 463-3560; e-mail ttk-dekani@ttdh.bme.hu; internet www.ttk.bme.hu):

CSISZÁR, I., Stochastics
CSOM, GY., Nuclear Technology
DEÁK, P., Atomic Physics
FRITZ, J., Differential Equations
GYULAI, J., Experimental Physics
JÁNOSSY, A., Experimental Physics
KERTÉSZ, J., Physics
MIHÁLY, GY., Quantum Theory
MOLNÁR, E., Geometry
NAGY, B., Analysis
NOSZTICZIUS, Z., Chemical Physics
PETZ, D., Analysis
RICHTER, P., Atomic Physics
RÓNYAI, L., Algebra
SCHMIDT, T., Algebra
SZÁSZ, D., Stochastics
SZATMÁRY, Z., Nuclear Technology
TÓTH, B., Stochastics
VERHÁS, J., Chemical Physics
VIROSZTEK, A., Quantum Theory
ZAWADOWSKI, A., Physics

Faculty of Transportation Engineering (1111 Budapest, Bertalan L. u. 2; tel. (1) 463-3551; fax (1) 463-3550; e-mail felv@kma.bme.hu; internet www.kozlek.bme.hu):

BOKOR, J., Transport Automatics
ELEÖD, A., Machine Elements
KÖVES GILICZE, É., Transport Operation
KULCSÁR, B., Building and Materials-Handling Machines
MÁRIALIGETI, J., Machine Elements
PALKOVICS, L., Motor Vehicles
ROHÁCS, J., Aircraft and Ships
TAKÁCS, J., Machine Production Technology
TÁNCZOS, LNÉ., Transport Economics
TARNAI, G., Transport Automatics
VÁRLAKI, P., Motor Vehicles
ZOBORY, I., Railway Vehicles

Centre for Learning Innovation and Adult Learning (1111 Budapest, Egry J. u. 1; tel. (1) 463-3866; fax (1) 463-2561; e-mail info@edu-inno.bme.hu; internet www.bme-tk.bme.hu):

SZŰCS, A.

Institute for Continuing Engineering Education (1111 Budapest, Műegyetem rkp. 9; tel. (1) 463-2471; fax (1) 463-2470; e-mail info@mti.bme.hu; internet www.mti.bme.hu):

GINSZTLER, J.

International Education Centre (1111 Budapest, Bertalan L. u. 2; tel. (1) 463-2461; fax (1) 463-2460; e-mail admission@tanok.bme.hu; internet www.tanok.bme.hu):

Dr MÉSZÁROS, P.

DEBRECENI EGYETEM
(University of Debrecen)

4032 Debrecen, Egyetem tér 1,(52)412-060
Fax: (52) 416-490
E-mail: rector@admin.unideb.hu
Internet: www.unideb.hu

Founded 1538; became Kossuth Lajos Tudományegyetem (Lajos Kossuth Univ.) 1912; present name 2000 upon integration with Debreceni Agrártudományi Egyetem (Debrecen Univ. of Agricultural Sciences), Debreceni Orvostudományi Egyetem (Univ. Medical School of Debrecen) and Wargha István Pedagógiai Főiskola (István Wargha College of Education)
State control
Languages of instruction: Hungarian, English
Academic year: September to June
Rector: Prof. Dr LÁSZLÓ FÉSÜS
Vice-Rector for Academic Affairs: Prof. Dr ATTILA DEBRECZENI

Vice-Rector for Educational Affairs: Prof. Dr
ANDRÁS JÁVOR
Vice-Rector for Strategic Affairs: Prof. Dr
ZOLTÁN SZILVÁSSY
Registrar: Dr MÓNIKA RÓFI
Dir of Finance: ZOLTÁN MAG
Dir of Human Resources Management: Dr
NOÉMI BÍRÓ SIPOS
Dir of the Univ. and Nat. Library: Dr MÁRTA
VIRÁGOS

Library: Libraries with a total of 5,300,000
vols
Number of teachers: 1,500
Number of students: 33,000

Publications: *Acta Andragogiae* (1 a year),
Acta Classica (1 a year), *Acta Debrecina* (1
a year), *Acta geographica ac geologica et
meteorologica Debrecina* (1 a year), *Acta
Neerlandica* (1 a year), *Acta pericemonolo-
gica rerum ambientum Debrecina* (irregu-
lar), *Acta Physica et Chimica* (1 a year), *A
Debreceni Egyetem évkönyve* (1 a year), *A
Debreceni Egyetem Magyar Nyelvtudomá-
nyi Intézetének kiadványai* (1 a year),
Agrártudományi közlemények (irregular),
Annual Report (1 a year), *Collectio iuridica
Universitatis Debreceniensis* (irregular),
Competitio (4 a year), *Debreceni szemle* (4
a year), *Ethnica* (irregular), *English Programme Bulletin Dentistry* (1 a year),
*English Programme Bulletin Faculty of
Medicine* (1 a year), *Ethnographica Fol-
cloristica Carpatica* (1 a year), *Folia
Uralica Debreceniensia* (1 a year), *Gond*
(4 a year), *Hungarian Journal of English
and American Studies* (2 a year), *Italia-
nistica Debreceniensis* (1 a year), *Journal
of Agricultural Sciences* (irregular), *Kitai-
belia* (2 a year), *Könyv és Könyvtár* (1 a
year), *Magyar Nyelvjárások* (1 a year),
Módszerek és eljárások (1 a year), *Ókortu-
dományi Értesítő* (1 a year), *Posztbizánci
Közlemények* (every 2 years), *Publ. Math-
ematicae* (2 a year), *Sprachteorie und
Germanistiche Linguistik* (2 a year), *Studia Litteraria* (1 a year), *Studia Romanica*
(linguistics, 1 a year), *Studies in Linguistics* (1 a year), *Teaching Mathematics and
Computer Science* (2 a year), *Történeti
Tanulmányok* (irregular)

DEANS

Faculty of Agriculture: Dr JÁNOS KÁTAI
Faculty of Agronomics and Rural Develop-
ment: Dr ANDRÁS NÁBRÁDI
Faculty of Arts: Dr TIBOR LACZKÓ
Faculty of Child and Adult Education: Dr
ÉVA BAKOSI
Faculty of Dentistry: Dr ILDIKÓ MÁRTON
Faculty of Economics and Business Admin-
istration: Dr JÁNOS KORMOS
Faculty of Engineering
Faculty of Health: Dr ISTVÁN KALAPOS
Faculty of Informatics: Dr ATTILA PETHŐ
Faculty of Law: Dr BÉLA SZABÓ
Faculty of Medicine: Dr LÁSZLÓ CSERNOCH
Faculty of Music: Dr MIHÁLY DUFFEK
Faculty of Pharmacy: Dr ÁRPÁD TÓSAKI
Faculty of Public Health: Dr RÓZA ÁDÁNY
Faculty of Sciences and Technology: Dr
KORNÉL SAILER

DIRECTORS

Hajdúböszörményi College Faculty of Educa-
tion: Dr T. TALLÓDI (Dir-Gen.)
College Faculty of Engineering: Dr L. FARKAS
(Dir-Gen.)
Faculty of Health College: Dr MIKLÓS OROSZ-
TÓTH
Centre of Agricultural Sciences: Dr I. ERTSEY
Conservatory of Debrecen: M. DUFFEK
Experimental Farm and Regional Research
Institute: GY. SZABÓ
Institute of Information Technology: Dr A.
PETHŐ

Institute of Public Health: Dr R. ÁDÁNY
Medical and Health Science Centre: Dr L.
FÉSÜS
Debrecen Farm and Regional Research Insti-
tute: Dr T. KONCZ
Research Institute of Karcag: Dr L. BLASKÓ
Research Institute of Nyíregyháza: Dr S.
TŐGYI

PROFESSORS

Faculty of Agriculture (4032 Debrecen, POB
36; tel. (52) 508-412; fax (52) 486-292):

BARDÓCZ, Z.
BLASKÓ, L.
CSAPÓ, J.
FÁRI, M.
GONDA, I.
GYŐRI, Z., Food Processing and Quality
Control
JÁVOR, A.
KÁTAI, J., Soil Science and Microbiology
KOVÁCS, A.
MIHÓK, S., Animal Husbandry, Breeding
and Nutrition
NAGY, J., Land Cultivation
PEPÓ, PÁL, Genetics and Plant Breeding
PEPÓ, PÉTER, Crop Production and Applied
Ecology
SINÓROS SZABÓ, B., Land Cultivation
TAMÁS, J.

Faculty of Agroeconomics and Rural Development (4015 Debrecen, POB 36; tel. (52)
508-304; fax (52) 413-385; e-mail csapone@
helios.date.hu):

ERTSEY, I., Economic Analysis and Statis-
tics
LAZÁNYI, J., Rural Development
NÁBRÁDI, A., Farm Business Management
NAGY, G., Rural Development
NEMESSÁLYI, ZS., Farm Business Manage-
ment
REKE, B.
SZABÓ, G., Agricultural and General Eco-
nomics
SZABÓ, Z.

Faculty of Arts (4010 Debrecen, POB 38; tel.
(52) 316-210; fax (52) 412-336; e-mail
nemesne@tigris.klte.hu):

ABÁDI-NAGY, Z., North American Studies
AGYAGÁSI, K.
BARTA, J., Medieval and Early Modern
World History
BARTHA, E., Ethnography
BITSKEY, I., Old Hungarian Literature
CZIEGLER, I., General Psychology
DEBRECZENI, A.
DOBOS, I.
GÖRÖMBEI, A., Modern Hungarian Lan-
guage
HAJNÁDY, Z.
HUNYADI, L., Applied Linguistics
IMRE, L., 19th-century Hungarian Litera-
ture
IMRE, M.
KERTÉSZ, A., German Linguistics
KLEIN, S., Psychology
NÉMETH, GY., Ancient History
NOVÁK RÓZSA, E., History of Philosophy
PAPP, I.
SOLYMOSI, L., History
SZABÓ, L., Ethnography
VARGA, P.
VIRÁGOS, ZS., North American Studies

Faculty of Child and Adult Education (4220
Hajdúböszörmény, Désány I. u. 1–9; tel. (52)
229-433; fax (52) 229-559):

BÁLINT, P.
KOVÁCSNÉ, E. B.
VARGA, G.

Faculty of Dentistry (4012 Debrecen, POB
13; tel. (52) 413-545; fax (52) 342-224; e-mail
angyal@fogaszat.dote.hu):

MAJOR, P.

PAP, G.
PETH, A.
STOYAN, G.
SZTRIK, J.
TERDIK, G.
VÉGH, J.
VERTSE, T.

Faculty of Economics and Business Administration (4010 Debrecen, POB 82; tel. (52)
416-580; fax (52) 419-728; e-mail mura@
tigris.klte.hu):

CSABA, L., Economics
KORMOS, J.
LOSONCZI, L.
MAKÓ, C.
POLÓNYI, I., Management and Marketing

Faculty of Engineering (4011 Debrecen, POB
40; tel. (52) 417-979; fax (52) 415-155; e-mail
kati@infosrv.tech.klte.hu):

CSANÁDY, G.
FERNEZELYI, S.
GULYÁS, L.
HAJDU, M.
HALÁSZ, G.
HORVÁTH, R., Chemical Engineering
JOLÁNKAI, G.
KALMÁR, F.
KOCSIS, I.
KŐSZEGHY, A., Settlement Engineering
KOVÁCS, I.
KULCSÁR, A., Construction Industry
MAJOR, J.
POKRÁDI, L., General Machinery
TELEKES, G.
TIBA, ZS., General Machinery
TÓTH, L.
VARGA, S. E.

Faculty of Health (4400 Nyíregyháza, Sóstói
u. 2; tel. (42) 404-403; fax (42) 408-656; e-mail
sztunde@creative.doteefk.hu):

CSERI, J.
FÁBIÁN, G.
GÓTH, L., Labour Analysis and Clinical
Diagnostics
HAJNAL, B.
KALAPOS, I., Preventive Medicine for Dis-
trict Nurses
LUKÁCSKÓ, ZS., Social Work
PUNYICZKI, M.

Faculty of Informatics (4010 Debrecen, POB
12; tel. (52) 512-900; fax (52) 416-857):

DÖMÖSI, P., Computer Science
PAP, G., Applied Mathematics and Probab-
lity Theory
SZTRIK, J., Informatics Systems and Net-
works
TERDIK, G., Information Technology

Faculty of Law (4010 Debrecen, POB 81; tel.
(52) 438-033; fax (52) 446-919; e-mail
volosine@delfin.klte.hu; internet www.law
.klte.hu):

DÉNES, I. Z., Social Sciences
FARKAS, A.
HORVÁTH M., T.
SZABADFALVI, J., Philosophy and Sociology
of Law
SZABÓ, B., History of Law
VÁRNAY, E.

Faculty of Medicine (4012 Debrecen, POB 15;
tel. (52) 410-006; fax (52) 410-006; e-mail
mfux@jaguar.dote.hu):

ANTAL, M., Anatomy, Histology and
Embryology
BAKÓ, GY., Internal Medicine
BALLA, GY., Neonatology
BALLA, J.
BERTA, A., Ophthalmology
BODA, Z., Internal Medicine
BODOLAY, E.
BOGNÁR, L.
BORSOS, A., Obstetrics and Gynaecology
CSERNOCH, L.
CSIBA, L., Neurology

DAMJANOVICH, S., Biophysics and Cell Biology
DOMBRÁDI, V., Medical Chemistry
ÉDES, I., Cardiology
ERDŐDI, F.
FEKETE, I.
FEKETE, K.
FÉSÜS, L., Biochemistry and Molecular Biology
FÜLESDI, B.
GALUSKA, L.
GÁSPÁR, R., Biophysics and Cell Biology
GERGELY, L., Medical Microbiology
GERGELY, P., Medical Chemistry
GÓTH, J.-P.
HERNÁDI, Z., Obstetrics and Gynaecology
HUNYADI, J., Dermatology and Venereology
KAPPELMAYER, J.
KISS, A.
KISS, C.
KOVÁCS, L., Physiology
KOVÁCS, P.
LUKÁCS, G., Surgery
MARÓDI, L., Paediatrics
MATESZ, K., Anatomy, Histology and Embryology
MÁTYUS, L.
MIKÓ, I.
MOLNÁR, P.
MUSZBEK, L., Clinical Biochemistry and Molecular Pathology
NAGY, E.
NAGY, L.
NÁNÁSI, P., Physiology
NEMES, Z., Pathology
OLÁH, É., Paediatrics
PARAGH, GY., Internal Medicine
RAJNAVÖLGYI, S., Immunology
REMENYIK, E.
SÁPY, P., Surgery
SIPKA, S., Internal Medicine
SZABÓ, B.
SZABÓ, G., Biophysics and Cell Biology
SZÁNTÓ, J.
SZEKANECZ, Z.
SZIKLAI, I., Otolaryngology
SZILVÁSSY, Z., Pharmacology
SZÖLLŐSI, J., Biophysics and Cell Biology
SZONDY, Z.
SZŰCS, G., Physiology
TÓTH, CS., Urology
TÓTH, Z., Obstetrics and Gynaecology
TŐZSÉR, J.
TRÓN, L., Positron Emission Tomography Centre
UDVARDY, M., Internal Medicine
VARGA, S., Central Service Laboratory
VIRÁG, L.
ZEHER, M., Internal Medicine

Faculty of Music (4032 Debrecen, Egyetem tér 2; tel. (52) 319-466; fax (52) 411-226):
DUFFEK, M.
KAMMERER, A.
KARASSZON, D.
MOHAY, M.
NEMES, F.
MATUZ, I.
MOHOS NAGY, E.
SZABÓ, J.

Faculty of Pharmacy (4012 Debrecen, Nagyerdei krt. 98.; tel. and fax (52) 453-586; e-mail tosaki@king.pharmacol.dote.hu):
BLASKÓ, G.
GUNDA, T.
HALMOS, G.
HERCZEGH, P.
TÓSAKI, A., Pharmacological Effects

Faculty of Public Health (4028 Debrecen, Kassai u. 26/B; tel. (52) 460-194; fax (52) 460-195; e-mail bardos@jaguar.dote.hu):
ÁDÁNY, R., Hygiene and Epidemiology
BALÁZS, M.
ILYÉS, I.
MOLNÁR, P.

Faculty of Science and Technology (4010 Debrecen, POB 18; tel. (52) 316-012; fax (52) 533-677; e-mail labalogh@kltesrv.klte.hu):
ANTUS, S.
BÁNYAI, I.
BATTA, B.
BAZSA, G.
BEKE, D.
ERDŐDINÉ, K.
FÁBIÁN, I.
FARKAS, E.
GAÁL, I.
GÁSPÁR, V.
GYŐRY, K.
JOÓ, F.
JOÓ, P.
KERÉNYI, A.
LÓKI, J.
MAKSA, G.
MOLNÁR, L.
NAGY, A.
NAGY, P.
PÁLES, Z.
PÁLINKÁS, J.
PATONAY, T.
POSTA, J.
RÁBAI, G.
SAILER, K.
SIPICZKI, M.
SOMSÁK, L.
SÓVÁGÓ, I.
SÜLI-ZAKAR, I.
SZÉKELYHIDI, L.
TÓTH, I.
TÓTHMÉRÉSZ, B.
TRÓCSÁNYI, Z.
VARGA, Z.
VIBÓK, A.
ZSUGA, M.

Conservatory (4032 Debrecen, Egyetem tér 2; tel. (52) 411-226; fax (52) 411-226; e-mail adamk@dragon.klte.hu):
ÁDÁM, K., Stringed Instruments
KAMMERER, A., Brass and Percussion
KEDVES, T., Stringed Instruments
KISS, V. P., Stringed Instruments
KÖKÉNYESSY, M., Stringed Instruments
MATÚZ, I., Woodwind
SZESZTAY, ZS., Music Theory, Choir Conducting

Hajdúböszörményi College Faculty of Education (4220 Hajdúböszörmény, Désány I u. 1–9; tel. (52) 229-433; fax (52) 229-559; e-mail tit8003@helka.iif.hu):
BAKOSI, É., Children's Education
FRÁTER, K., Children's Education
KÖVÉR, I., Children's Education
VARGA, GY., Social Studies

Farm and Regional Research Institute (4032 Debrecen, Böszörményi u. 138; tel. (52) 508-334; fax (52) 413-385; e-mail csapone@helios.date.hu):
KONCZ, T., Dir

Institute of Information Technology:
GISPERT, S.
MAJOR, P.
PAP, G.
PETHŐ, A.

EÖTVÖS LORÁND TUDOMÁNYEGYETEM
(Loránd Eötvös University)

1056 Budapest, POB 109
1053 Budapest, Egyetem tér 1–3
Telephone: (1) 411-6500
Fax: (1) 411-6712
Internet: www.elte.hu
Founded 1635
State control
Academic year: September to June (two terms)

Rector: Dr ISTVÁN KLINGHAMMER
Pro-Rector: Dr LAJOS IZSÁK
Pro-Rector for Education and Scientific Affairs: Dr FERENC HUDECZ
Pro-Rector for International Affairs: Dr LÁSZLÓ BOROS
Sec.-Gen.: Dr GYÖRGY RÁK
Head Librarian: Dr LÁSZLÓ SZÖGI
Library: see Libraries and Archives
Number of teachers: 1,090
Number of students: 31,882
Publications: Acta Facultatis Politico-iuridicae Universitatis Scientiarum Budapestinensis, Annales (geological, juridical and geological series, 1 a year)

DEANS

Faculty of Arts: Dr KÁROLY MANHERZ
Faculty of Elementary and Nursery Teachers' Training: Dr ISTVÁN HORTOBÁGYI
Faculty of Informatics: Dr LÁSZLÓ KOZMA
Faculty of Law and Political Science: Dr BARNA MEZEY
Faculty of Pedagogy and Psychology: Dr GYÖRGY HUNYADY
Faculty of Science: Dr FERENC LÁNG
Faculty of Social Sciences: Dr TAMÁS RUDAS
Faculty of Special Education: Dr GYÖRGY KÖNCZEI

PROFESSORS

Faculty of Arts (1088 Budapest, Múzeum körút 4/a):
ADAMIK, T., Latin Language and Literature
BALÁZS, G., Linguistics
BALOGH, A., Modern World History
BANCZEROWSKI, J., Polish Language and Literature
BÁRDOSI, V., Romance Studies
BENCE, GY., Ethics and Social Philosophy
BERTÉNYI, I., Medieval and Early Modern Hungarian History
BÍRÓ, F., 18th- and 19th-century Hungarian Literature
DÁVID, G., Oriental Studies
DOMOKOS, P., Finno-Ugric Linguistics
ERDÉLYI, Á., Philosophy
FODOR, S., Semitic Philology and Arabic Studies
GAÁL, E., Egyptology
GÉHER, I., English
GERGELY, A., History
GERGELY, J., Modern and Contemporary Hungarian History
GERŐ, A., Economic and Social History
GIAMPAOLO, S., Romance Studies
GLATZ, F., Historical Auxiliary Sciences
GÓSY, M., Linguistics
GRANASZTÓI, G., Romance Studies
GYIVICSÁN, A., Slavonic Studies
HESSKY, P., German Linguistics
HORVÁTH, I., Old Hungarian Literature
JEREMIÁS, É., Oriental Studies
KARA, GY., Central Asian Studies
KARDOS, J., History
KARDOS, J., Historical Auxiliary Sciences
KELEMEN, J., Ethics and Social Philosophy
KÉLÉNYI, G., History of Art
KENYERES, Z., Modern Hungarian Literature
KESZLER, B., Contemporary Hungarian Linguistics
KISS, J., Hungarian Historical Linguistics and Dialectology
KLAUDY, K., Linguistics
KNIPF, E., German
KOMORÓCZY, G., Assyriology and Hebrew Studies
KÓSA, L., Cultural History
KOVÁCS, A., Slavonic Studies
KOVÁCS, S. I., Old Hungarian Literature
KÖVECSES, Z., English
KRAUSZ, T., History
KULCSÁR SZABÓ, É., Comparative Literature

LUDASSY, M., Ethics and Social Philosophy
LUFT, U., Egyptology
MANHERZ, K., Germanic Linguistics
MAROSI, E., Art History
MASÁT, A., Scandinavian Languages and Literature.
MEDGYES, P., English Teacher Training
MISKOLCZY, A., Romance Studies
NÉMETH, G., History
NYOMÁRKAY, I., Slavic Philology
OROSZ, M., German
PALÁDI-KOVÁCS, A., Ethnography
PALOTÁS, E., East European History
PASSUTH, K., Art History
PÉTER, M., Eastern Slavonic and Baltic Philology
PROKOPP, M., History of Art
PUSKÁS, I., History
RACZKY, P., Archaeology
RADNÓTI, S., Aesthetics
ROMSICS, I., Modern and Contemporary Hungarian History
RÓNAY, L., Modern Hungarian Literature
SIPOS, L., Literary History
SOLYMOSI, L., History
STEIGER, K., Philosophy
SZABICS, I., French Language and Literature
SZABÓ, K., Medieval World History
SZABÓ, M., Classical Archaeology
SZÁVAI, J., Comparative and World Literature
SZEGEDY-MASZÁK, M., Comparative Literature
SZÉKELY, G., History
SZVÁK, G., History
TOLCSVAI, N. G., Linguistics
TÓTH, B., Romance Studies
TVERDOTA, G., Literary History
VARGA, L., English
VARGYAI, GY., Historical Auxiliary Sciences
VÁSÁRI, I., Turkish Studies
VOIGT, V., Folklore
VÖRÖS, I., French Language and Literature

Faculty of Law (1053 Budapest, Egyetem tér 1–3):

BIHARI, M., Political Science
BÖHM, A., Political Science
BURJÁN, L., International Law
ERDEI, A., Criminal Procedural Law
FICZERE, L., Public Administration Law
FÖLDESI, T., Philosophy
FÖLDI, A., Roman Law
GÖNCZÖL, K., Criminology
HAMZA, G., Roman Law
HARMATHY, A., Civil Law
HORVÁTH, P., Universal Legal and Political History
KARÁCSONY, A., Philosophy
KÖRÖSNYI, A., Political Science
KUKORELLI, I., Constitutional Law
LENKOVITS, B., Civil Law
LÉVAY, M., Criminology
LÓRINCZ, L., Public Administration Law
MEZEI, B., Universal Legal and Political History
PACSOLAY, P., Political Science
PÁNDI, G., Public Administration Law
POKOL, B., Political Science
SÁJO, A., Civil Law
SÁRI, J., Constitutional Law
SCHLETT, I., Political Science
STUMPF, I., Political Science
SZABÓ, MÁRTON, Political Science
SZABÓ, MÁTÉ, Political Science
SZILÁGYI, P., Theory of Law
TAMÁS, A., Theory of Law
VALKI, L., International Law
VÉKÁS, L., Civil Law

Faculty of Science (1088 Budapest, Rákoczi út 5):

BERCZIK, Á., Systematic Zoology and Ecology
BÖDDI, B., Biology
BODZSÁR, É., Biology

CSÁNYI, V., Behaviour Genetics
CSIKOR, F., Theoretical Physics
DEMETROVICS, J., Information Systems
DÉTÁRI, L., Biology
DÓZSA-FARKAS, K., Biology
ERDEI, A., Immunology
FARSANG, GY., Inorganic and Analytical Chemistry
FODOR, Z., Theoretical Physics
FRANK, A., Operational Research
GALÁCZ, A., Palaeontology
GERE, G., Biology
GESZTI, T., Physics of Complex Systems
GRÁF, L., Biochemistry
GYENIS, G., Biology
GYURJÁN, I., Plant Anatomy
HEGYI, G., Biology
HORVÁTH, Z., Theoretical Physics
KISS, Á., Atomic Physics
KISS, E., Mathematics
KOMJÁTH, P., Computer Science
KONDOR, I., Physics of Complex Systems
KOVÁCS, J., Biology
KÜRTI, J., Physics
LACZKOVICH, M., Analysis
LÁNG, F., Biology
LENDVAI, J., General Physics
LOVÁSZ, L., Computer Science
NAGY, D. L., Atomic Physics
ORMOS, P., Physics
OROSZ, L., Biology
PÁLFY, P., Algebra and Number Theory
PALLA, L., Theoretical Physics
PATKÓS, A., Atomic Physics
PODANI, J., Biology
POLONYI, J., Atomic Physics
SÁRMAY, G., Immunology
SASS, M., General Zoology
SZABÓ, K., Physical Chemistry
SZALAY, S., Atomic Physics
SZATHMÁRI, E., Plant Taxonomy and Ecology
SZIGETI, Z., Biology
TÉL, T., Theoretical Physics
TICHY, G., Solid State Physics
UNGÁR, T., General Physics
VESZTERGOMBI, G., Physics
VICSEK, T., Biological Physics
VINCZE, I., Physics
ZÁVODSZKÝ, P., Biological Physics

Institute and Postgraduate Centre for Sociology and Social Policy (1088 Budapest, Pollack Mihály tér 10):

ANGELUSZ, R., Sociology
CSEPELI, GY., Social Psychology
FERGE, ZS., Social Policy
HUSZÁR, T., Historical Sociology
NÉMEDI, D., Social Theory
PATAKI, F., Social Psychology
SOMLAI, P., Social Theory

Teacher-Training Faculty (1075 Budapest, Kazinczy u. 23–27):

CS. VARGA, I., Hungarian Language and Literature
DEMETER, J., Hungarian Language and Literature
DRUZSIN, F., Hungarian Language and Literature
DUKKON, Á., Hungarian Language and Literature
ESTÓK, J., History
FRIED, I., Italian Language and Literature
GAIZER, F., Chemistry
GÖDÉNY, E., Hungarian Language and Literature
GRÉTSY, L., Hungarian Linguistics
HAJDU, P., Social Theory
HEGYVÁRI, N., Mathematics
HELTAI, P., English
HORVÁTH, G., Geography
JÁSZÓ, A., Hungarian Linguistics
MADARÁSZ, I., Hungarian Linguistics
MILKOVITS, I., Biology
NÉMETH, A., Educational Science
SALAMON, K., History

SAPSZON, F., Music
SIPOSNÉ-JÁGER, K., Biology
UZONYI, P., German
ZÁVODSKY, G., History
ZIRKULI, P., French Language and Literature

KAPOSVÁRI EGYETEM
(University of Kaposvár)

7401 Kaposvár, Guba Sándor u. 40

Telephone: (82) 505-910
Fax: (82) 505-896
E-mail: kszi@mail.atk.u-kaposvar.hu
Internet: www.u-kaposvar.hu

Founded 2000 from Faculty of Animal Husbandry of Pannon Agrártudományi Egyetem (Pannon Univ. of Agricultural Sciences) and Csokonai Vitéz Mihály Teacher-Training College
Incl. College Faculty of Art, not yet acccredited by the HAC (2009)
State control
Language of instruction: Hungarian
Academic year: September to June

Rector: Prof. Dr László BABINSZKY

Number of teachers: 250
Number of students: 4,800

Publication: Acta Agraria Kaposváriensis (quarterly4 a year)

DEANS

Faculty of Animal Science: Prof. ISTVÁN HOLLÓ
Faculty of Economic Science: Prof. GYULA VARGA
Faculty of Pedagogy: Prof. ISTVÁN ROSTA

PROFESSORS

Faculty of Animal Science (fax (82) 320-757; e-mail hollo@mail.atk.u-kaposvar.hu; internet www.atk.u-kaposvar.hu):

BABINSZKY, L., Animal Nutrition
BOGENFÜRST, F., Poultry Breeding
CSAPÓ, J., Biochemistry
DÉR, F., Plant Production
GYENIS, J., Process Engineering
HECKER, W., Academy of Equitation
HORN, P., Pig Production
HORVÁTH, GY., Social Sciences
KOVÁCS, M., Physiology and Animal Hygiene
PAÁL, J., Mathematics and Computer Science
REPA, I., Digital Imaging, Radiology
SARUDI, J., Chemistry and Biochemistry
STEFLER, J., Cattle Production
SZAKÁLY, S., Food Science
SZÉLES, GY., Farm Economics
SZENDRŐ, ZS., Animal Breeding
TAKÁTSY, T., Agricultural Engineering

Faculty of Economic Science (fax (82) 320-175; e-mail szekeres@mail.atk.u-kaposvar .hu; internet www.gtk.u-kaposvar.hu):
,

Faculty of Pedagogy (fax (82) 505-899; e-mail leva@csoki.csvmtkf.hu; internet www.pfk .u-kaposvar.hu):
,

ATTACHED INSTITUTE

Feed Crops Research Centre: 7095 Iregszemcse, Napraforgo u. 1; tel. (74) 481-127; fax (74) 481-253; e-mail tki.ireg@axelero.hu; Dir-Gen. Dr László TAKÁCS.

LISZT FERENC ZENEMŰVÉSZETI EGYETEM
(Ferenc Liszt Academy of Music)

1391 Budapest, POB 206, Liszt Ferenc tér 8

Telephone: (1) 462-4600
Fax: (1) 462-4648

Internet: www.liszt.hu
Founded 1875
State control
Academic year: September to June
Rector: Dr ANDRÁS BATTA
Vice-Rector: Prof. LÁSZLO TIHANYI
Librarian: Dr. J. KÁRPÁTI

Library of 187,000 vols
Number of teachers: 158
Number of students: 767.

ATTACHED INSTITUTES

Bartók Béla Zeneművészeti Szakközépiskola és Gimnázium (Béla Bartók Conservatory of Music and Secondary School):
1065 Budapest, Nagymező u.1; Dir T. SZABÓ.

Budapesti Tanárképző Intézet (Teacher Training Institute in Budapest): 1052 Budapest, Semmelweiss u. 12; Dir Prof. LEHEL BOTH.

MOHOLY-NAGY MŰVÉSZETI EGYETEM
(Moholy-Nagy University of Arts)

1121 Budapest, Zugligeti ú. 9–25
Telephone: (1) 392-1193
Fax: (1) 392-1190
E-mail: international@mome.hu
Internet: w2.mome.hu
Founded 1880; fmrly Magyar Iparművészeti Egyetem; present name 2006
State control
Academic year: September to June
Rector: GÁBOR KOPEK
Vice-Rector: LÁSZLÓ ZSÓTÉR
Chancellor: Dr PÁL HATOS
Dir of Finance: BALÁZS KOHUT
Dir of Int. and Public Relations: ZSOLT PETRI
Librarian: KLÁRA LÉVAI

Library of 42,000 vols
Number of teachers: 98
Number of students: 570

Publications: *Kék Ég* (4 a year), *Diploma* (1 a year)

DIRECTORS OF INSTITUTES

Institute of Foundation Studies: Prof. JÓZSEF SCHERER
Institute of Humanities: Prof. GYULA ERNYEY
Institute for Manager Training: Prof. Dr ÁGNES KAPITÁNY

MAGYAR KÉPZŐMŰVÉSZETI EGYETEM
(University of Fine Arts)

1062 Budapest, Andrássy u. 69–71
Telephone: (1) 342-1738
Fax: (1) 342-1563
E-mail: rektor@mke.hu
Internet: www.mke.hu
Founded 1871
State control
Rector: FRIGYES KŐNIG
Vice-Rector: KÁROLY HANTOS
Int. Affairs: ZSÓFIA RUDNAY
Registrar: ISTVÁN PONGÓ
Librarian: KATALIN BLASKÓ MAJKÓ

Library of 60,000 vols, 90 periodicals
Number of teachers: 134
Number of students: 552

PROFESSORS

FARKAS, Á., Sculpture
KOCSIS, I., Graphic Art
MENRÁTH, P., Restoration
MOLNÁR, K., Applied Graphic Art
NAGY, G., Painting
PETERNÁK, M., Multimedia Studies
SZABADI, J., Art History
SZÉKELY, L., Stage and Costume Design
TÖLG-MOLNÁR, Z., Painting

MISKOLCI EGYETEM
(University of Miskolc)

3515 Miskolc-Egyetemváros
Telephone: (46) 565-111
Fax: (46) 565-014
E-mail: stbes@uni-miskolc.hu
Internet: www.uni-miskolc.hu
Founded 1735 in Selmecbánya, Academy status 1770; moved 1919 to Sopron; reorganized 1949 in Miskolc
State control
Languages of instruction: Hungarian, English for foreign students
Academic year: September to June
Rector: Dr GYULA PATKÓ
Vice-Rector for Educational Affairs: Prof. ISTVÁN STIPTA
Vice-Rector for Gen. Affairs: Prof. ISTVÁN SZŰCS
Vice-Rector for Int. Relations: Prof. MIHÁLY DOBRÓKA
Vice-Rector for Scientific Affairs: Prof. MIHÁLY DOBRÓKA
Sec.-Gen.: VIKTOR KOVÁCS
Librarian: Dr L. ZSÁMBOKI

Number of teachers: 920
Number of students: 13,571

Publications: *Miskolc Journal of International Law*, *Miskolci Egyetem Közleményei* (papers in Hungarian, irreg.), *Publications of the University of Miskolc* (papers in German, English and Russian, irreg.)

DEANS

Faculty of Arts: Dr C. FAZEKAS
Faculty of Earth Science and Engineering: Dr J. BŐHM
Faculty of Economics: Dr G. KOCZISZKY
Faculty of Law: Dr M. SZABÓ
Faculty of Materials Science and Engineering: Dr Z. GÁCSI
Faculty of Mechanical Engineering and Information Science: Dr A. DÖBRÖCZÖNI

PROFESSORS

Faculty of Arts (tel. (46) 565-211; fax (46) 563-459; e-mail boldek@uni-miskolc.hu; internet www.bolcsweb.hu):

ANDRIK-HELL, J., Philosophy
BAÁN, I., Medieval and Early Modern Hungarian History and Associated Sciences of History
BESSENYEI, J., Medieval and Early Modern Hungarian History and Associated Sciences of History
CZÖVEK, I., World History
DOMÁNSZKY, G., Comparative Literature and Cultural History
FERENCZI, L., Literature of the Enlightenment, Romanticism and Regional History
FORRAI, G., History of Philosophy
FÜLÖP, Zs., English Literature
FURMAN-PANKUCSI, M., Sociology
GYAPAY, L., Literature of the Enlightenment, Romanticism and Regional History
GYULAI, É., Cultural History and Museology
HELTAI, J., Old Hungarian Literature
HORVÁTH, E., World History
ILLÉS-KOVÁCS, M., Hungarian Linguistics
KABDEBÓ, L., Contemporary Hungarian Literature
KLAUDY, K., Applied Linguistics
KOTICS, J., Cultural and Visual Anthropology
KOVÁCS, J. Ö., Modern Hungarian History
MOLNÁR, J., German Literature
PETHŐ, S., Classical Philology and Religion
PETNEKI, Á., Central European Literature and Culture
RINGER, Á., Prehistory and Antiquity

SALÁNKI, Á., German Linguistics
SIMIG-FENYŐ, S., Applied Linguistics
SIMON, J., Political Science
SZIGETI, J., Central European Literature and Culture
SZILI-JUHÁSZ, E., Contemporary Hungarian Literature
VÁRADI, T., English Linguistics

Faculty of Earth Science and Engineering (tel. (46) 565-051; fax (46) 563-465; e-mail rekbdhiv@uni-miskolc.hu; internet www.uni-miskolc.hu/~mfk):

BOBOK, E., Natural Gas Engineering
BŐHM, J., Environmental Management
BUÓCZ, Z., Mining and Geotechnology
CSETE, J., Natural Gas Engineering
CSŐKE, B., Process Engineering
DOBRÓKA, M., Geophysics
FÖLDESSY, J., Geology and Mineral Resources
GYULAI, Á., Geophysics
HAHN, GY., Human Geography
HAVASI, I., Geodesy and Mine Surveying
HEVESI, A., Geography and Environmental Sciences
KOCSIS, K., Human Geography
KOVÁCS, F., Mining and Geotechnology
LAKATOS, I., Mining Chemistry
PÁPAY, I., Petroleum Engineering
SOMOSVÁRI, Zs., Mining and Geotechnology
SZABÓ, I., Hydrogeology and Engineering Geology
SZAKÁLL, S., Mineralogy
TAKÁCS, G., Petroleum Engineering
TIHANYI, L., Natural Gas Engineering
VŐNEKI, GY., Equipment for Geotechnology

Faculty of Economics (tel. (46) 565-190; fax (46) 563-471; e-mail gazddek@uni-miskolc.hu; internet www.gtk.uni-miskolc.hu):

BESENYEI, L., Business Statistics and Forecasting
BOZSIK, S., Finance
CZABÁN, J., Business Economics
DANKÓ, L., International Marketing
FEKETE, I., Human Resources
ILLÉS, M., Business Economics
KOCZISZKY, GY., Regional Economics
NAGY, A., Economic Theory
PÁL, T., Accounting
PELCZ-GÁLL, I., Entrepreneurship
PISKÓTI, I., Marketing Strategy and Communication
SZAKÁLY, D., Innovation and Technology Management
SZILÁGYI, D., World Economy and Comparative Economics
SZINTAY, I., Management
VERES-SOMOSI, M., Organizational Behaviour

Faculty of Law (tel. (46) 565-170; fax (46) 367-933; e-mail rekrat@uni-miskolc.hu; internet www.jogikar.uni-miskolc.hu):

BIRÓ, GY., Civil Law
BRAGYOVA, A., Constitutional Law
CSÁK, Cs., Labour Law and Agricultural Law
FARKAS, Á., Criminal Procedural Law and Law Enforcement
FEHÉR, L., Criminal Law and Criminology
GÖRGÉNYI, I., Criminal Law and Criminology
KALAS, T., Administrative Law
KOVÁCS, P., International Law
LÉVAY, M., Criminal Law and Criminology
LÉVAY-FAZEKAS, J., European and International Private Law
MISKOLCZI BODNÁR, P., Commercial Law
PÁSZTOR-ERDŐS, É., Financial Law
PÉTER, O., Roman Law
PETROVICH-WOPERA, Zs., Civil Procedural Law
PRUGBERGER, T., Labour Law and Agricultural Law
STIPTA, I., Legal History

SZABADFALVI, J., Legal Theory and Legal Sociology
SZABÓ, B., Roman Law
SZABÓ, M., Legal Theory and Legal Sociology
TORMA, A., Administrative Law

Faculty of Materials Science and Engineering (tel. (46) 565-091; fax (46) 565-408; e-mail rekkdhpg@uni-miskolc.hu; internet www .mak.uni-miskolc.hu):

BÁRÁNY, S., Chemistry
BÁRCZY, P., Polymer Engineering
GÖMZE, A. L., Ceramics and Silicate Engineering
KAPROS, T., Energy Utilization
KAPTAY, GY., Chemistry
KÁROLY, GY., Metallurgical and Foundry Engineering
KOVÁCS, K., Quality Assurance
KOVÁCS, K., Chemistry
PALOTÁS, Á. B., Combustion Technology and Thermal Energy
ROÓSZ, A., Physical Metallurgy

Faculty of Mechanical Engineering and Information Science (tel. (46) 565-131; fax (46) 563-453; e-mail gkdh3@uni-miskolc.hu; internet www.gepesz.uni-miskolc.hu):

ÁDÁM, T., Automation
AJTONYI, I., Automation
BALLA, K., Mathematical Analysis
CSELÉNYI, J., Materials Handling and Logistics
CSER, L., Information Engineering
DÖBRÖCZÖNI, Á., Machine Elements
DUDÁS, I., Production Engineering
FEGYVERNEKI, S., Applied Mathematics
GALÁNTAI, A., Applied Mathematics
ILLÉS, B., Materials Handling and Logistics
JÁRMAI, K., Materials Handling and Logistics
JUHÁSZ, I., Descriptive Geometry
KACSUK, P., Automation
KOVÁCS, E., Electrotechnology and Electronics
KUNDRÁK, J., Production Engineering
LUKÁCS, J., Mechanical Technology
ORTUTAY, M., Chemical Machinery
PÁCZELT, I., Mechanics
PARIPÁS, B., Physics
PATKÓ, GY., Machine Tools
RONTÓ, M., Mathematical Analysis
SZABÓ, SZ., Heat and Fluid Engineering
SZEIDL, GY., Mechanics
SZIGETI, J., Mathematical Analysis
TISZA, M., Mechanical Technology
TÓTH, L., Mechanical Technology
TÓTH, T., Information Engineering
VADÁSZ, D., Information Technology

ASSOCIATE INSTITUTES

Bela Bartók Music Institute: 3530 Miskolc, Bartók tér 1; Dir Dr SÁNDOR KOVÁCS.

Comenius Teacher-Training College: 3950 Sárospatak, Eötvös u. 7; tel. (47) 513-000; internet www.ctif.hu; Dir S. KOMÁROMY.

Institute of Health Care Studies: 3508 Miskolc, Mész u. 1; tel. (46) 366-560; fax (46) 366-961; e-mail rekefk@uni-miskolc.hu; internet www.uni-miskolc.hu/~wwweti; Dir Dr BARKAI LÁSZLÓ.

NYUGAT-MAGYARORSZÁGI EGYETEM (University of West Hungary)

9400 Sopron, Bajcsy-Zs. u. 4
Telephone: (99) 518-100
Fax: (99) 311-103
E-mail: rectoro@nyme.hu
Internet: www.nyme.hu

Founded 2000 on merger of Soproni Egyetem (University of Sopron, f. 1762 as Academy of Mining and Forestry), Mosonmagyaró-vár Faculty of Agriculture (f. 1818) of Pannon Agrártudományi Egyetem (Pan-non University of Agricultural Sciences), Apáczai Csere János Teacher-Training College (f. 1778), and Benedek Elek College of Education (f. 1959)

State control
Language of instruction: Hungarian
Academic year: September to June

Rector: Prof. Dr SÁNDOR FARAGÓ
Pro-Rectors: Prof. Dr KÁROLY MÉSZÁROS, Prof. Dr RESZŐ SCHMIDT, Prof. Dr PÉTER TAKÁTS
Economic Dir: LÁSZLÓ HERCZEG
Admin. Officer: Dr MÁRIA MERÉNYI
Librarian: SÁNDOR SARKADY, Jr

Library of 380,000 vols
Number of teachers: 562
Number of students: 12,500

Publications: *Acta Agronomica Ovariensis* (in German and English, 2 a year), *Acta Facultatis Forestalis* (in German and English), *Acta Facultatis Ligniensis* (in German and English), *Apáczai Csere János Tanítóképző Főiskolai Kar Tanulmánykötet* (in Hungarian, 1 a year), *Benedek Elek Pedagógiai Főiskolai Kar Tudomány napja* (in Hungarian, 1 a year), *Erdészeti Tallózó* (in Hungarian, 12 a year), *Faipar* (Wood Science, in Hungarian with English summary, 5 a year), *Magyar Apróvad Közlemények* (Hungarian Small Game Bulletin, in Hungarian and English, 1 or 2 a year), *Magyar Vízivad Közlemények* (Hungarian Waterfowl Publication, in Hungarian and English, 1 or 2 a year), *Tilia* (in Hungarian, 1 or 2 a year)

DEANS AND DIRECTORS

Faculty of Agricultural Sciences: Dr VINCE ÖRDÖG
Faculty of Economic Sciences: Prof. Dr ERZSÉBET GIDAI
Faculty of Forestry: Prof. Dr KÁROLY MÉSZÁROS
Faculty of Wood Sciences: Prof. Dr SÁNDOR MOLNÁR
Benedek Elek College of Education: Dr ERZSÉBET ALPÁRNÉ SZÁLA
College of Geoinformatics: Dr BÉLA MÁRKUS
Apáczai Csere János Teacher-Training College: Dr SÁNDOR CSEH

DIRECTORS OF INSTITUTES

Faculty of Agricultural and Food Sciences (9200 Mosonmagyaróvár, Vár 2; tel. (96) 566-637; fax (96) 566-620; e-mail ordogvin@mtk .nyme.hu; internet www.mtk.nyme.hu):

Institute of Agricultural Economics and Social Sciences:

Agricultural Economics and Marketing: Dr TAMÁS SÁNTHA
Social Sciences: Prof. Dr ISTVÁN SZABÓ

Institute of Agricultural, Food and Environmental Engineering:

Biological and Environmental Engineering: Prof. Dr KÁROLY KACZ
Food Process Engineering and Environmental Techniques: Prof. Dr MIKLÓS NEMÉNYI

Institute of Animal Breeding Husbandry:

Cattle- and Sheep-breeding: Dr ERNŐ BÁDER
General Animal Husbandry: Dr LÁSZLÓ GULYÁS
Poultry- and Pig-breeding: Prof. Dr KATALIN GAÁL

Institute of Biological and Environmental Sciences:

Animal Health: Prof. Dr BORISZ EGRI
Botany: Prof. Dr ÁKOS MÁTHÉ
Soil Science and Water Management: Prof. Dr MIHÁLY SZŰCS
Zoology: Prof. Dr PÁL BENEDEK

Institute of Crop Sciences:

Crop Production: Prof. Dr KÁROLY POCSAI
Genetics and Plant Breeding: Dr JÓZSEF KISS
Plant Physiology and Plant Biotechnology: Prof. Dr VINCE ÖRDÖG
Soil Management: Prof. Dr RESZŐ SCHMIDT

Institute of Farm Business Management:

Farm Management: Prof. Dr LAJOS SALAMON
Accountancy and Financial Management: Prof. Dr BARNABÁS REKE
Statistics and Economic Information Management: Dr RÓZSA CSATAI

Institute of Food Sciences:

Food Technology and Microbiology: Prof. Dr JENŐ SZIGETI
Food Quality Assurance: Dr ZSOLT AJTONY
Dairying Science: Dr LÁSZLÓ VARGA

Institute of Management and Labour Sciences:

Labour Organization and Production Techniques: Dr JÓZSEF ORBÁN
Management and Organizational Development: Dr LEONA MORVAY

Departments not within an Institute:

Animal Nutrition: B. KISS, Dr GERTRÚD KELEMEN
Animal Physiology and Biotechnology: Dr ELEMÉR GERGÁCZ
Chemistry: Prof. Dr PÁL SZAKÁL
EU Educational Centre: Prof. Dr FRIGYES NAGY
Foreign Languages: JÓZSEF OLÁH
Horticulture: Dr JÓZSEF IVÁNCSICS
Mathematics and Physics: Dr OTTÓ DÓKA
Physical Training: MIHÁLY MÉSZÁROS
Plant Protection: Prof. Dr PÉTER REISINGER

Faculty of Economic Sciences (9400 Sopron, Ady E. u. 5; tel. (99) 518-257; fax (99) 518-257; e-mail ecoman@ktk.nyme.hu; internet ktk.nyme.hu):

Institute of Applied Economics:

Business Economics: Dr FERENC TÓTH
Business Studies: Dr CHAUDHURI SUJIT
Sectoral Economics: Dr LAJOS JUHÁSZ

Institute of Applied Mathematics and Statistics:

Applied Mathematics: Dr JÓZSEF ZÁVOTI
Statistics: Dr LASZLÓ SZALAY

Institute of Business Informatics:

Applied Business Informatics: Dr ISTVÁN SZŰTS
Theoretical Business Informatics: Dr ATTILA KOVÁCS

Institute of Economics:

Economic Policy and Collective Management: Dr EMESE EGETŐ
Economics: Prof. Dr ERZSÉBET GIDAI
International and Comparative Economics: Dr ATTILA FÁBIÁN

Institute of Finance and Accounting:

Accounting: Dr LÁSZLÓ NYIKOS
Finance: Dr CSABA LENTNER

Institute of Management:

Management: Dr JÁNOS HERCZEG
Marketing: Dr ESZTER PATAKI SZABÓNÉ
Service Organization and Tourism: Dr MÁTYÁS FEKETE

Institute of Social Economics and Law:

Human Resource Economics: Dr GYULA LAKATOS
Law: Dr ATTILANÉ TÓTH
Social Economics: Dr ATTILANÉ TÓTH

Institute of Social Geography and World Economics:

Foreign Economics and European Integration: Dr EMESE FAYNÉ PÉTER
Social Geography: Prof. Dr JUDIT BALÁZS

World Economics: Prof. Dr JUDIT BALÁZS
Departments not within an Institute:
Centre for European Studies: Dr EMESE FÁYNÉ PÉTER
Regional Economy Research Institute: Prof. Dr ERZSÉBET GIDAI

Faculty of Forestry (9400 Sopron, Ady E. u. 5; tel. (99) 518-207; fax (99) 329-808; e-mail fdoffice@emk.nyme.hu):

Institute of Botany Forest Site:
Botany: Prof. Dr DÉNES BARTHA
Forest Site: Dr GÁBOR KOVÁCS

Institute of Environmental Sciences:
Ecology and Genetics: Prof. Dr CSABA MÁTYÁS
Environmental Biology: Dr ERNŐ FÜHRER
Environmental and Nature Protection: Dr JÓZSEF PÁJER
Landscape and Regional Planning: Dr ÉVA KONKOLYNÉ GYÚRÓ

Institute of Forest Resource Management:
Forestry Management: Dr GÁBOR VEPERDI
Forestry Policy and Economics: Prof. Dr KÁROLY MÉSZÁROS
Practical Training Centre: Dr GÁBOR HALÁSZ

Institute of Forestry and Environmental Engineering:
Energetics: Prof. Dr BÉLA MAROSVÖLGYI
Forestry Mechanics: Prof. Dr BÉLA HORVÁTH
Forest Utilization: Prof. Dr JÁNOS RUMPF

Institute of Geomatics and Civil Engineering:
Forest Development and Water Management: Prof. Dr MIKLÓS KOSZTKA
Geodesy and Remote Sensing: Prof. Dr LÁSZLÓ BÁCSATYAI

Departments not within an Institute:
Foreign Language Centre: IMRE KRISCH
Silviculture: Prof. Dr JÓZSEF KOLOSZÁR

Faculty of Wood Sciences (9400 Sopron, Ady E. u. 5; tel. (99) 518-101; fax (99) 518-259; e-mail fadek@fmk.nyme.hu; internet www .nyme.hu):

Institute of Applied Arts: GYÖRGY MÉSZÁROS
Institute of Applied Mechanics and Structures: Dr JÓZSEF SZALAI
Institute of Informatics: Dr LÁSZLÓ JEREB
Institute of Physics: Dr GYÖRGY PAPP
Institute of Product Development and Technology: Dr ZSOLT KOVÁCS
Institute of Wood and Paper Technology: Prof. Dr ANDRÁS WINKLER
Institute of Wood Sciences: Dr SÁNDOR MOLNÁR
Institute of Woodworking Machinery: Dr MIKLÓS LANG
Teacher-Training Institute: Dr ISTVÁN LÜKŐ

PANNON EGYETEM
(University of Pannonia)

8200 Veszprém, Egyetem u. 10, POB 158
Telephone: (88) 422-022
Fax: (88) 423-866
E-mail: pr@uni-pannon.hu
Internet: www.uni-pannon.hu
Founded 1949; absorbed Georgikon Faculty of Agriculture of the former Pannon Agrártudományi Egyetem (Pannon University of Agricultural Sciences) 2000
State controlled
Languages of instruction: Hungarian, English
Academic year: September to June
Rector: Prof. Dr ÁKOS RÉDEY
Pro-Rector for Education and Accreditation: Prof. Dr JÁNOS KRISTÓF

Pro-Rector for Int. Affairs: Prof. Dr ÁRPÁD MIHALOVICS
Dir-Gen. of Economic Affairs: MÁRIA ZSIBORÁCS PETRÓ
Pro-Rector for Scientific Affairs: Prof. Dr FERENC HUSVÉTH
Librarian: Dr M. EGYHÁZY
Library: see Libraries
Number of teachers: 435
Number of students: 6,794 (6,313 full-time, 481 part-time)
Publication: *Hungarian Journal of Industrial Chemistry* (4 a year)

DEANS

Georgikon Faculty of Agriculture: Prof. KÁROLY DUBLECZ
Faculty of Economics: Dr ANDRÁS JANCSIK
Faculty of Engineering: Dr OTTÓ HORVÁTH
Faculty of Humanities: Prof. Dr ISTVÁN SZILÁGYI
Faculty of Information Technology: Prof. Dr FERENC FRIEDLER
Faculty of Teacher Training: Prof. CSABA FÖLDES

PROFESSORS

ALMÁDI, L., Botany
ANDA, A., Water Management
BAKOS, J., Organic Chemistry
BÁRDOS, J., English Language
BENCZE, L., Organic Chemistry
BÉRES, I., Botany
BUDAI, L., English Language
BUZÁS, GY., Economics
FISCHL, G., Plant Pathology
FÖLDES, CS., German Language
FRIEDLER, F., Systems Engineering in Computer Science
GAÁL, Z., Management and Economy
GÁBORJÁNYI, R., Plant Pathology
GYŐRI, I., Mathematics
HANGOS, K., Systems Engineering in Computer Science
HLAVAY, J., Analytical Chemistry
HORVÁTH, A., Inorganic Chemistry
HORVÁTH, GY., Pedagogy and Psychology
HORVÁTH, J., Plant Pathology
HORVÁTH, O., Inorganic Chemistry
HUSVÉTH, F., Zoology
KANYÁR, B., Radiochemistry
KARDOS, Z., Economics
KARDOS, Z., Social Sciences
KISMÁNYOKI, T., Agronomy
KOCSONDI, J., Management and Economy
KOVÁCS, Z., Management and Economy
KOZMANN, GY., Informatics
KRISTÓF, J., Analytical Chemistry
LENGYEL, ZS., Applied Linguistics
LISZI, J., Physical Chemistry
LŐRINCZ, A., International Economics
MAJOR, I., Economics
MARTON, GY., Chemical Process Engineering
MÉSZÁROS, E., Environmental Sciences
MIHALOVICS, Á., French Language
MIHÁLYI, P., Economics
MINK, J., Analytical Chemistry
NAGY, I., Theatre Studies
PADISÁK, F., Limnology
PALKOVICS, M., Agricultural Economics
PAPP, S., Inorganic Chemistry
PUPOS, T., Economics
RÉDEY, A., Chemical Technology, Environmental Engineering
SOMOGYI, S., Management and Economics
SPEIER, G., Organic Chemistry
SUGÁR, L., Zoology
SZABÓ, F., Animal Husbandry
SZABÓ, F., Hungarian Linguistics
SZABÓ, I., Botany
SZABÓ T, A., Biology
SZILÁGYI, I., Social Sciences
SZIRDNYI, T., Image Processing and Neurocomputing

SZOLGAY, P., Display Optics, Colour Image Sensing
TÖRÖK, Á., Economics
TUZA, ZS., Mathematics
UNGVÁRY, F., Organic Chemistry
VARGA, K., Radiochemistry
VÁRNAGY, L., Agricultural Hygiene
VERESS, G., Informatics and Control
VINCZE, L., Inorganic Chemistry
VINCZE, L., Animal Nutrition
ZSOLNAY, F., Pedagogy

PÉCSI TUDOMÁNYEGYETEM
(University of Pécs)

7633 Pécs, Szántó K. J. u. 1/b
Telephone: (72) 510-509
Fax: (72) 501-508
E-mail: rector@pte.hu
Internet: www.pte.hu
Founded 1367, re-f. 1923 as Janus Pannonius Tudományegyetem (Janus Pannonius Univ.); present name 2000 upon integration with Pécsi Orvostudományi Egyetem (Pécs Univ. Medical School) and Illyés Gyula Pedagógiai Főiskola (Gyula Illyés College of Education)
State control
Academic year: September to May (two terms)
Rector: Dr RÓBERT GÁBRIEL
Vice-Rector for Communication: Dr BÉLA HORVÁTH
Sr Vice-Rector for Finances and Strategic Affairs: Dr FERENC FARKAS
Vice-Rector for Research and Education: Dr MÁRTA FONT
Chief Admin.Officer: IMRE GÁTI
Chief Librarian: Dr ÁGNES DÁRDAI
Number of teachers: 2,000
Number of students: 33,248
Publications: *Pécsi Orvostudományi Egyetem Évkönyve* (1 a year), *Specimina Fennica* (irregular), *Specimina Geographica* (irregular), *Specimina Nova Dissertationum ex Institutio Historico* (irregular), *Specimina Sibirica* (irregular), *Studia Iuridica Auctoritatae Universitatis Pécs Publicata* (4 a year), *Studia Oeconomica Auctoritatae Universitatis Pécs Publicata* (4 a year), *Studia Paedagogica Auctoritate Universitatis Pécs Publicata* (irregular), *Studia Philosophica et Sociologica Auctoritatae Universitatis Pécs Publicata* (4 a year), *Szép Literatúrai Ajándék* (4 a year), *Tudományos Dialóg* (6 a year), *Univ Pécs* (every 2 weeks)

DEANS

Faculty of Adult Education and Human Resources Development: Dr DÉNES KOLTAI
Faculty of Business and Economics: Dr GÁBOR RAPPAI
Faculty of Health Sciences: Prof. JÓZSEF BÓDIS
Faculty of Humanities: Dr FERENC FISCHER
Faculty of Law: Dr GYULA BERKE
Faculty of Music and Visual Arts: Prof. COLIN FOSTER
Faculty of Sciences: Prof. ISTVÁN GERESDI
Illyés Gyula Faculty of Education: Dr GYÖRGY FUSZ
Medical School: Prof. PÉTER NÉMETH
Mihály Pollack Faculty of Engineering: Prof. JÓZSEF MECSI

PROFESSORS

Faculty of Business and Economics (7622 Pécs, Rákóczi u. 80; tel. (72) 501-599; fax (72) 501-553; e-mail rappai@ktk.pte.hu; internet www.ktk.pte.hu):

BARAKONYI, K., Strategic Management
BÉLYÁCZ, I., Corporate Finance and Accounting

BUDAY-SÁNTHA, A., Agricultural, Environmental and Regional Economics
DOBAY, P., Business Informatics
FARKAS, F., Management
KOMLÓSI, S., Decision-making
LÁSZLÓ, GY., Corporate Finance and Accounting
OROSZI, S., Economics
REKETTYE, G., Marketing
SIPOS, B., Strategic Management
TAKÁCS, B., Marketing
TÖRŐCSIK, M., Marketing
TÓTH, T., Economic History
VARGA, J., Decision-making
VÖRÖS, J., Decision-making

Faculty of Health Sciences (7621 Pécs, Vörösmarty u. 4; tel. (72) 513-671; e-mail dekan@etk.pte.hu):

BÓDIS, J., Obstetrics and Gynaecology
BUDA, J., Public Health
CHOLNOKY, P., Paediatrics
CSERE, T., Radiology
FARKAS, M., Nuclear Medicine
FIGLER, M., Gastroenterology
GYÓDI, GY., Paediatrics
HARTMANN, G., Physiology
HORVÁTH, B., Obstetrics and Gynaecology
ILLEI, GY., Obstetrics and Gynaecology
JEGES, S., Biostatistics
KELEMEN, J., Chemistry
KISS, T., Biology
KOMÁROMY, L., Biology
KOPA, J., Neurosurgery
KOVÁCS, L. G., Neuroendocrinology
KRÁNITZ, J., Orthopaedics
LAKY, R., Traumatology
ROZSOS, I., Surgery
SULYOK, E., Paediatrics
TAHIN, T., Medical Sociology
TÁRNOK, F., Gastroenterology

Faculty of Humanities (7624 Pécs, Ifjúság u. 6; tel. (72) 503-600; fax (72) 501-558; e-mail dean@btk.pte.hu; internet www.btk.pte.hu):

ANDRÁSFALVY, B., Ethnography
BÓKAY, A., Literature and Culture of the English-Speaking People
BOROS, J., History of Philosophy
ERŐS, F., Psychology
FISHER, F., Modern History
FONT, M., Medieval and Early Modern History
FORRAY, R. K., Linguistics
HETESI, I., Classical Literary History and Comparative Literature
KÁLMÁN, C. GY., Modern Literary History and Theory of Literature
KARSAI, GY., Classical Philology
KASSAI, I., Linguistics
KÉZDI, B., Personality, Development and Clinical Psychology
KISBÁN, E., Ethnography
KOMLÓSI, L., English Linguistics
KUPA, L., Sociology and Social Policy
LÁSZLÓ, J., Psychology
NAGY, E., Sociology and Social Policy
NAGY, I., Classical Literary History and Comparative Literature
ORMOS, M., Modern History
PÓCS, É., Ethnography
ROHONYI, Z., Classical Literary History and Comparative Literature
SZÉPE, GY., Linguistics
TASSONI, L., Italian Studies
THOMKA, B., Modern Literary History and Theory of Literature
VARGYAS, P., Ancient History and Archaeology
VISY, ZS., Ancient History and Archaeology
WEISS, J., History of Philosophy
WILD, K., German Linguistics

Faculty of Law (7622 Pécs, 48-as tér 1; tel. (72) 501-563; fax (72) 215-148; e-mail berke@ajk.pte.hu; internet www.law.pte.hu):

ANDRÁSSY, GY., Political Science and Social Theory
BRUHÁCS, J., International and European Law
KAJTÁR, I., History of Law and Roman Law
KECSKÉS, L., Civil Law
KENGYEL, M., Civil Procedural Law and Sociology of Law
KISS, GY., Labour Law and Social Welfare Law
KISS, L., Administrative Law
KORINEK, L., Criminal Law
TÓTH, M., Criminal Law
TREMMEL, F., Criminal Procedural Law
VISEGRÁDY, A., Philosophy of Law and State

Faculty of Sciences (7624 Pécs, Ifjúság u. 6; tel. (72) 501-512; fax (72) 501-527; e-mail szabgab@gamma.ttk.pte.hu; internet www.ttk.pte.hu):

AGÁRDI, P., Cultural Studies
BERGOU, J., Theoretical Physics
BORHIDI, A., Botany
CSOKNYA, M., Zoology and Neurobiology
ERDŐSI, F., Institute of Geography
FISCHER, E., Zoology and Neurobiology
HÁMORI, J., Zoology and Neurobiology
KLEIN, S., Human Resource Development
KOLLÁR, L., Inorganic Chemistry and Technology
KORPA, CS., Theoretical Physics
KŐSZEGFALVI, GY., Institute of Geography
KOZMA, L., Adult Education
LOVÁSZ, GY., Institute of Geography
MAJER, J., General and Applied Ecology
NAGY, G., General Physics and Chemistry
PESTI, M., General and Environmental Microbiology
SZABÓ, L., Botany
SZEIDL, L., Mathematics
TOMCSÁNYI, T., Genetics and Molecular Biology
TÓTH, J., Institute of Geography
UHRIN, B., Mathematics
VUICS, T., Institute of Geography

Faculty of Music and Visual Arts (7624 Pécs, Damjanich u. 30; tel. (72) 501-540; fax (72) 501-540; e-mail dekan@art.pte.hu; internet www.art.pte.hu):

BENCSIK, I., Sculpture
JOBBÁGY, V., Music
KESERÜ, I., Painting
KIRCS, L., Music
PINCZEHELYI, S., Painting
RÉTFALVI, S., Sculpture
TILLAI, A., Music
VIDOVSZKY, L., Theory of Art

Illyés Gyula Faculty of Education (7100 Szekszárd, Rákóczi u. 1; tel. (74) 528-311; fax (74) 528-301; e-mail titkar@igyfk.pte.hu; internet www.igyfk.pte.hu):

ANDRÁSSY, GY., Philosophy
BAJNER, M., Foreign Languages
BORBÉLY, S., Hungarian Language and Literature
BÚS, I., Education
FUSZ, GY., Visual Education
HORVÁTH, B., Hungarian Language and Literature
KURUCZ, R., Education and Psychology
NAGY, J. T., Philosophy of Law
TOLNAI, GY., Social Policy
TOTHNÉ LITOVKINA, A., Foreign Languages
VÁRADY, Z., History of Science

Medical School (7624 Pécs, Szigeti u. 12; tel. (72) 536-200; fax (72) 536-104; e-mail dekani.hivatal@aok.pte.hu; internet www.aok.pte.hu):

ÁNGYÁN, L., Physiology
BAJNÓCZKY, I., Forensic Medicine
BARTHÓ, L., Pharmacology
BARTHÓNÉ SZEKERES, J., Medical Microbiology and Immunology
BELÁGYI, J., Central Research Laboratory

BELLYEI, Á., Orthopaedics
BOGÁR, L., Anaesthesiology and Intensive Therapy
CZIRJÁK, L., Internal Medicine
CZOPF, J., Neurology
DÓCZI, T., Neurosurgery
EMBER, I., Public Health
EMŐDY, L., Microbiology
ERTL, T., Obstetrics and Gynaecology
FEKETE, M., Paediatrics
FISCHER, E., Pharmacology
GALLYAS, F., Neurosurgery
GÖTZ, F., Urology
GREGUS, Z., Pharmacology
HIDEG, K., Central Research Laboratory
HORVÁTH, L., Radiology
HORVÁTH ÖRS, P., Surgery
KAJTÁR, P., Paediatrics
KARÁTSON, A., Internal Medicine
KELÉNYI, G., Pathology
KELLERMAYER, M., Clinical Biochemistry
KETT, K., Surgery
KILÁR, F., Central Research Laboratory
KOLLÁR, L., Surgery
KOSZTOLÁNYI, GY., Paediatrics
KOVÁCS, B., Ophthalmology
KOVÁCS, S., Pathophysiology
KRÁNICZ, J., Orthopaedics
KROMMER, K., Obstetrics and Gynaecology
LÁZÁR, GY., Anatomy
LÉNÁRD, L., Physiology
LUDÁNY, A., Clinical Chemistry
MÉHES, K., Paediatrics
MEZŐNÉ FARKAS, B., Dermatology
MOLNÁR, D., Paediatrics
MÓZSIK, GY., Internal Medicine
NAGY, L., Family Medicine
NÉMETH, P., Immunology and Biotechnology
NYÁRÁDY, J., Traumatology
PAJOR, L., Pathology
PAPP, L., Cardiology
PÁR, L., Internal Medicine
PINTÉR, A., Paediatrics
PYTEL, J., Otorhinolaryngology
SÁNDOR, A., Biochemistry
SCHNEIDER, I., Dermatology
SÉTÁLÓ, GY., Anatomy
SOLTÉSZ, GY., Paediatrics
SOMOGYI, B., Biophysics
SÜMEGI, B., Biochemistry
SZABÓ, GY., Oral Medicine
SZABÓ, I., Behavioural Science
SZABÓ, I., Obstetrics and Gynaecology
SZEBERÉNYI, J., Biology
SZÉKELY, M., Pathophysiology
SZELÉNYI, Z., Pathophysiology
SZOLCSÁNYI, J., Pharmacology
TEKERES, M., Intensive Therapy and Anaesthesia
TÉNYI, J., Public Health
THAN, G., Obstetrics and Gynaecology
TÓTH, GY., Chemistry
TRIXLER, M., Psychiatry and Medical Psychology
VERECZKEI, L., Behavioural Science
VÉRTES, M., Physiology

Mihály Pollack Faculty of Engineering (7624 Pécs, Boszorkany u. 2; tel. (72) 211-968; fax (72) 214-682; e-mail mecsi@pmmk.pte.hu; internet www.pmmf.pte.hu):

ARADI, L., Public Utilities, Geodesy and Environmental Protection
ÁSVÁNYI, J., Automation
BACHMAN, Z., Design and Architecture
BÁRSONY, J., Statics and Supporting Structures
BUDAY, L., Education
CSÉBFALVI, GY., Statics and Supporting Structures
FÜLÖP, L., Building Structures
HÜBNER, M., Urban Development
JÓZSA, L., Electric Networks
KISS, E., Education
KISTELEGDI, I., Building Structures

KLINCSIK, M., Mathematics
LENKEI, P., Statics and Supporting Structures
ORBAN, F., Mechanical Engineering
ORBÁN, J., Materials, Geotechnics and Transport Engineering
TÓTH, Z., Urban Development
VAJDA, J., Building Construction
VARGA, L., Education
VÍG MIKLÓSNE, L. A., Mathematics

SEMMELWEIS EGYETEM
(Semmelweis University)

1085 Budapest VIII, Üllői u. 26
Telephone: (1) 459-1500
Fax: (1) 317-2220
E-mail: rekhiv@rekhiv.sote.hu
Internet: www.sote.hu

Founded 1769 as Medical Faculty of the Univ. of Nagyszombat, ind. 1951 as Semmelweis Orvostudományi Egyetem (Semmelweis Univ. of Medicine), present name 2000 upon integration with Haynal Imre Egészségtudományi (Imre Haynal Univ. of Health Sciences) and Magyar Testnevelési Egyetem (Hungarian Univ. of Physical Education)
State control
Languages of instruction: Hungarian, English, German
Academic year: September to June
Rector: Prof. Dr T. TULASSAY
Vice-Rector for Education and Int. Relations: Dr MILLOS KELLERMAYER
Vice-Rector for Gen. Affairs: Dr AGOSTON SLEL
Vice-Rector for Science and Innovation: Dr MIKLOS TOTH
Library of 261,624 vols
Number of teachers: 1,171
Number of students: 11,143
Publication: *Pathology Oncology Research* (4 a year)

DEANS

Faculty of Dentistry: Dr I. GERA
Faculty of Health Sciences: Dr J. MÉSZÁROS (Dir-Gen.)
Faculty of Medicine: Dr I. KARÁDI
Faculty of Pharmacy: Dr B. NOSZAL
Faculty of Physical Education and Sport Sciences: Dr J. TIHANYI
School of Doctoral Studies: Dr Á. SZÉL (Pres.)

PROFESSORS

Faculty of Dentistry (tel. (1) 266-0453; fax (1) 266-1967; e-mail gera@szajseb.sote.hu):

BARABAS, J., Oral, Dental and Maxillofacial Surgery
BOROS, I., Oral Biology
DIVINYI, T., Oral, Dental and Maxillofacial Surgery
FÁBIÁN, T., Prosthodontics
FAZEKAS, Á., Preservation Dentistry
FEJÉRDY, P., Prosthetic Dentistry
GERA, I., Periodontics
NAGY, G., Oral Diagnostics
SIMON, GY., Oral Biology
SUBA, Z., Oral and Maxillofacial Surgery
SZABÓ, GY., Oral and Maxillofacial Surgery
VARGA, G., Oral Biology
ZELLES, T., Oral Biology

Faculty of Health Sciences (1088 Budapest, Vas u. 17; tel. (1) 369-1241; fax (1) 369-1241; e-mail meszarosj@seefk.hu):

CZINNER, A., Paediatrics
SZABOLCS, J., Dietetics

Faculty of Medicine (tel. (1) 317-9057; fax (1) 266-0441; e-mail vegan@rekhiv.sote.hu):

ÁCSÁDY, GY., Cardiovascular Surgery
ÁDÁM, É., Medical Microbiology
ÁDÁM, V., Medical Biochemistry

ALFÖLDY, F., Transplantation and Surgery
ARATO, A., Paediatrics
BANHEGY, G., Medical Chemistry
BIRKÁS, J., Military and Disaster Medicine
BITTER, J., Psychiatry and Psychotherapy
BODOR, E., Cardiovascular Surgery
BÖSZÖRMÉNYI NAGY, GY., Pulmonology
CSERMELY, P., Medical Chemistry, Molecular Biology and Pathobiochemistry
CSILLAG, A., Anatomy, Histology and Embryology
DARVAS, K. I., Surgery
DE CHÂTEL, R., Internal Medicine
DEMETER, J., Internal Medicine
DZSINICH, CS., Cardiovascular Surgery
ENYEDI, P., Physiology
FALLER, J., Surgery
FALUDI, G., Psychiatry
FALUS, A., Biology
FARAGÓ, A., Medical Chemistry, Molecular Biology and Pathobiochemistry
FARSANG, G., Internal Medicine
FEHÉR, E., Anatomy, Histology and Embryology
FEKETE, B., Immunology
FEKETE, GY., Paediatrics
FIDY, J., Biophysics and Radiology
FLAUTNER, L., Surgery
FÜRST, ZS., Pharmacology
FÜST, GY., Internal Medicine
GÉHER, P., Pneumatology and Physiotherapy
GERENDAI, I., Human Morphology and Developmental Biology
GERGELY, P., Dermatology and Venereology
GERŐ, L., Internal Medicine
GÖMÖR, B., Rheumatology and Physiotherapy
GYIRES, K., Pharmacology and Pharmacotherapy
HORKAY, F., Cardiology
HORVÁTH, A., Dermatology and Venereology
HUNYADY, L., Physiology
JÁRAY, J., Transplantation and Surgery
KÁDÁR, A., Pathology
KALABAY, L., Family Medicine
KÁLMÁNCHEY, R., Paediatrics
KARÁDI, I., Internal Medicine
KÁRPÁTI, S., Dermatology and Venereology
KELEMEN, Z., Urology
KELLER, E., Forensic Medecine
KELTAI, M., Cardiology
KEMPLER, P., Internal Medicine
KERPEL-FRONIUS, S., Pharmacology and Pharmacotherapy
KOLLAI, M., Physiology and Experimental Laboratory for Clinical Research
KOLLER, Á., Pathophysiology
KOPP, M., Behavioural Sciences
KOPPER, L., Pathology and Experimental Cancer Research
KOVALSZKY, I., Pathology
KÖVES, K., Human Morphology and Developmental Biology
KUPCSULIK, P., Surgery
LAKATOS, P., Internal Medecine
LIGETI, E., Physiology
LIGETI, L., Physiology
LOSONCZY, GY., Pulmonology
MACHAY, T., Paediatrics
MAGYAR, P., Pulmonology
MANDL, J., Medical Chemistry, Molecular Biology and Pathobiochemistry
MATOLCSY, A., Pathology and Experimental Cancer Research
MORAVA, E., Public Health
MORVAI, V., Internal Medicine
MÓZES, T., Traumatology
NAGY, GY., Human Morphology and Developmental Biology
NAGY, P., Pathology
NAGY, Z., Cardiovascular Surgery
NEMES, A., Cardiovascular Surgery
NÉMETH, J., Ophthalmology

NYÁRY, I., Neurosurgery
OLÁH, I., Human Morphology and Developmental Biology
ONDREJKA, P., Surgery
PAJOR, A., Obstetrics and Gynaecology
PÁLÓCZI, K., Immunology
PAPP, J., Internal Medicine
PAPP, Z., Obstetrics and Gynaecology
PAULIN, F., Obstetrics and Gynaeology
PÉNZES, I., Anaesthesiology and Intensive Therapy
PERNER, F., Transplantology and Surgery
POÓR, GY., Rheumatology and Physiology
PRÉDA, I., Cardiology
RÁCZ, K., Internal Medicine
RAJNA, P., Psychiatry and Psychotherapy
REGÖLY-MÉREI, J., Surgery
RÉPÁSSY, G., Otorhinolaryngology, Head and Neck Surgery
RÉTHELYI, M., Anatomy, Histology and Embryology
REUSZ, GY., Paediatrics
ROMICS, I., Urology
ROMICS, L., Internal Medicine
ROSIVALL, L., Pathophysiology
ROZGONYI, F., Microbiology
SALACZ, GY., Ophthalmology
SANDOR, J., Surgery
SÁNDOR, P., Human Physiology
SÁRVÁRY, A., Traumatology
SCHAFF, ZS., Pathology
SIKLÓSI, GY., Obstetrics and Gynaeology
SIMON, T., Public Health
SÓTONYI, P., Forensic Medicine
SPÄT, A., Physiology
SRÉTER, L., Internal Medicine
STAUB, M., Medical Chemistry, Molecular Biology and Pathobiochemistry
SÜVEGES, I., Ophthalmology
SZAGO, A., Paediatrics
SZALAY, F., Internal Medicine
SZÁNTÓ, I., Surgery
SZÉKÁCS, B., Geriatrics
SZÉL, A., Human Morphology and Developmental Biology
SZENDRŐI, M., Orthopaedics
SZIRMAI, I., Neurology
SZOLLÁR, L., Pathophysiology
TAMÁS, GY., Internal Medicine
TIHANYI, T., Surgery
TIMÁR, L., Paediatrics, Infectious Diseases
TOMPA, A., Public Health
TÓTH, M., Medical Chemistry, Molecular Biology and Pathobiochemistry
TRINGER, L., Psychiatry and Psychotherapy
TULASSAY, T., Paediatrics
TULASSAY, ZS., Internal Medicine
UNGVÁRY, GY., Public Health
VEREBÉLY, T., Paediatrics
WENGER, T., Human Morphology and Developmental Biology

Faculty of Pharmacy (tel. (1) 266-0449; fax (1) 317-5340; e-mail nosbel@hogyes.sote.hu):

KLEBOVICH, J., Pharmaceutics
LEDNICZKY, L., Pharmacology
LIPTÁK, J., Medical Regulation
MARTON, S., Pharmaceutics
MÁTYUS, P., Organic Chemistry
NOSZÁL, B., Pharmaceutical Chemistry
PAÁL, T., Medical Regulation
SZŐKE, E., Pharmacognosy
TAKÁCSNÉ NOVÁK, K., Pharmaceutical Chemistry
TEKES, K., Pharmacodynamics
TÖRÖK, T., Pharmacodynamics
VINCZE, Z., University Pharmacy, Pharmacy Administration

Faculty of Physical Education and Sport Sciences (1123 Budapest, Alkotás u. 44; tel. (1) 487-9214; fax (1) 356-6337; e-mail nyerges@mail.hupe.hu):

BERLLES, I., Sports Surgery
DOZSA, I., Rhythmic Dance and Aerobics
FÖLDESY, T., Social Sciences

GOMBOCZ, J., Theory and Teaching of Physical Education
KERTÉSZ, I., Social Sciences
MÉSZÁROS, J., Health Sciences and Sports Medicine
NYAKAS, Cs., Health Sciences and Sports Medicine
PAVLIK, G., Health Sciences and Sports Medicine
RADÁK, Zs., Sport Sciences Research
SIPOS, K., Psychology
TAKÁCS, F., Social Sciences
TIHANYI, J., Biomechanics

SZÉCHENYI ISTVÁN EGYETEM
(Széchenyi István University)

9026 Győr, Egyetem tér 1
Telephone: (96) 503-400
Fax: (96) 329-263
E-mail: sze@sze.hu
Internet: www.sze.hu

Founded 1968 as Széchenyi István Főiskola; present name and status 2002
State control
Academic year: September to June

Rector: Dr TAMÁS SZEKERES
Vice-Rector: JÁNOS RECHNITZER
Vice-Rector for Institutional Devt: Prof. Dr KÁROLY KARDOS
Dir of Int. Project Center: Prof. Dr CSABA KOREN
Dir of Strategy and Devt: TAMÁS L. SZILASI
Sec.-Gen.: Prof. Dr BÉLA ÍRÓ
Library Dir: ANIKÓ FABULA

Library of 240,000 vols, 1,000 periodicals
Number of teachers: 360
Number of students: 10,600 (6,800 undergraduate, 1,200 postgraduate, 2,600 distant learning)
Publications: *Hungarian Electronic Journal of Sciences* (online), *Acta Technica Jaurinensis, Tudományos Füzetek, Law, State, Politics*

DEANS

Deák Ferenc Faculty of Law: Prof. Dr GYULA SZALAY
Faculty of Technical Sciences: Prof. Dr LÁSZLÓ KÓCZY T.
Kautz Gyula Faculty of Economics: Dr LÁSZLÓ JÓZSA

ATTACHED INSTITUTES

Petz Lajos Institute of Health and Social Studies: 9024 Győr, Szent Imre ut. 28; tel. (96) 507-940; fax (96) 507-940; e-mail nagysandor@petz.gyor.hu; Dir Prof. Dr SÁNDOR NAGY.

Varga Tibor Institute of Music: 9025 Győr, Kossuth ut. 5; tel. (96) 329-735; fax (96) 314-862; e-mail ruppert@sze.hu; Dir Prof. Dr ISTVÁN RUPPERT.

SZEGEDI TUDOMÁNYEGYETEM
(University of Szeged)

6720 Szeged, Dugonics tér 13
Telephone: (62) 544-001
Fax: (62) 546-371
E-mail: rekthiv@rekt.u-szeged.hu
Internet: www.u-szeged.hu

Founded 1872, refounded 1921; became József Attila Tudományegyetem (Attila József University) 1962; present name 2000 upon merger with Szent-Györgyi Albert Orvostudományi Egyetem (Albert Szent-Györgyi University of Medicine) and other instns
State control
Academic year: September to June

Rector: Prof. Dr GÁBOR SZABÓ
Vice-Rector for Education: Dr BÉLA PUKÁNSZKY

Vice-Rectors for Gen. Affairs: Prof. Dr IMRE MUCSI, Prof. Dr JÁNOS LONOVICS
Vice-Rector for Scientific Issues: Dr IMRE DÉKÁNY
Vice-Rector for Strategic Issues: Dr BÉLA RÁCZ
Vice-Rector for Student Issues: Dr ATTILA BADÓ
Librarian: PALOTÁSNÉ RÓZA PÁNTI

Library: see Libraries and Archives
Number of teachers: 2,279
Number of students: 31,478
Publications: *Acta Biologica Szegediensis, Acta Climatologica, Acta Cybernetica, Acta Scientarum Mathematicarum*

DEANS

Faculty of Arts: Prof. Dr ÁRPÁD BERTA
Faculty of Economics and Business Administrations: Dr BEÁTA FARKAS
Faculty of Law: Prof. Dr IMRE SZABÓ
Faculty of Medicine: Prof. Dr MAGDOLNA POGÁNY
Faculty of Pharmacy: Prof. Dr GYÖRGY ISTVÁN FALKAY
Faculty of Science: Prof. Dr GÁBOR MEZŐSI
College Faculty of Agriculture: Prof. Dr IMRE MUCSI
College Faculty of Food Engineering: Prof. Dr JÓZSEF FENYVESSY
College Faculty of Health Sciences: Dr GYÖRGY BENEDEK
College Faculty of Music: Prof. Dr FERENC KEREK
College Faculty of 'Juhász Gyula' Teachers' Training College: Prof. Dr GÁBOR GALAMBOS

PROFESSORS

Faculty of Arts (6722 Szeged, Egyetem u. 2; tel. (62) 544-166; fax (62) 425-843; e-mail kelemen@arts.u-szeged.hu; internet www.arts.u-szeged.hu):
  ANDERLE, Á., Hispanic Studies
  BAKRÓ-NAGY, M., Finno-Ugrian Linguistics
  BALÁZS, M., Early Hungarian Literature
  BASSOLA, P., German Linguistics
  BERNÁTH, A., German Literature
  BERTA, Á., Altaic Studies
  CSAPÓ, B., Education
  CSEJTEI, D., Philosophy
  CSÚRI, K., Austrian Culture and Literature
  HAJNAL, M., Early Hungarian Literature
  JUHÁSZ, A., Ethnography
  KARSAI, L., Modern World History and Mediterranean Studies
  KENESEI, I., English and American Studies
  KONTRA, M., English Language Teacher Education and Applied Linguistics
  MAKK, F., Auxiliary Sciences of History
  NAGY, L., Modern World History and Mediterranean Studies
  OLAJOS, T., Auxiliary Sciences of History
  PÁL, J., Italian Language and Literature
  PÁLFY, M., French Language and Literature
  SAJTI, E., Modern World History and Mediterranean Studies
  SZABÓ, J., Hungarian Linguistics
  SZAJBÉLY, M., Classic Hungarian Literature
  SZIGETI, L., Modern Hungarian Literature
  SZÖRÉNYI, L., Comparative Literature
  WOJTILLA, GY., Ancient History

Faculty of Economics and Business Administration (6722 Szeged, Honvéd tér 6; tel. (62) 544-485; fax (62) 544-499; e-mail bfarkas@eco.u-szeged.hu; internet www.eco.u-szeged.hu):
  BENET, I., World Economics and European Economic Integration
  BOTOS, K., Finance
  DINYA, L., Marketing and Management
  GARAI, L., Economic Psychology

LENGYEL, I., Economics and Economic Development
Faculty of Law (6722 Szeged, Tisza L. krt. 54; tel. (62) 544-206; fax (62) 544-204; e-mail ajtk.dekani@juris.u-szeged.hu; internet www.juris.u-szeged.hu):
  BALOGH, E., Legal History
  BESENYEI, L., Civil Law and Civil Procedure
  BLAZOVICH, L., Legal History
  BODNÁR, L., International Law
  CZÚCZ, O., Social and Labour Law
  HERCZEG, J., Statistics and Demography
  JAKAB, É., Roman Law
  KATONA, T., Statistics and Demography
  MARTONYI, J., International Private Law
  NAGY, F., Criminal Law and Criminal Procedure
  PACZOLAY, P., Political Sciences
  POKOL, B., Philosophy and Sociology of Law
  RUSZOLY, J., Legal History
  STIPTA, I., Legal History
  TRÓCSÁNYI, L., Constitutional Law
Faculty of Medicine (6720 Szeged, Dóm tér 12; tel. (62) 545-015; fax (62) 426-529; e-mail aokdh@medea.szote.u-szeged.hu; internet www.szote.u-szeged.hu):
  BÁLINT, G., Psychiatry
  BALOGH, A., Clinical Surgery
  BARI, F., Physiology
  BÁRTFAI, G., Tocology and Gynaecology
  BENEDEK, GY., Physiology
  BODOSI, M., Neurological Surgery
  BORBÉLYI, Z., Internal Medicine and Cardiology
  BOROS, M., Experimental Surgery
  CSANÁDY, M., Internal Medicine
  CZÍGNER, J., Otolaryngology
  DOBOZY, A., Dermatology
  DUDA, E., Medical Microbiology
  DUX, L., Biochemistry
  ENGELHARDT, J., Neurology
  FARKAS, G., Surgery
  FAZEKAS, A., Prosthetic Dentistry
  FORSTER, T., Internal Medicine and Cardiology
  FRÁTER, L., Radiology
  FÜZESI, K., Paediatrics
  GELLEN, J., Toxicology and Immunology
  HANTOS, F., Family Medicine
  HŐGYE, M., Internal Medicine and Cardiology
  HORVÁTH, A. R., Clinical Chemistry
  HUSZ, S., Dermatology and Allergology
  IVÁNYI, B., Pathology
  JANCSÓ, G., Physiology
  JANKA, Z., Neurology and Psychiatry
  JÁRDÁNHÁZY, T., Neurology
  JÓRI, J., Otorhinolaryngology and Head and Neck Surgery
  JULESZ, J., Endocrinology
  KEMÉNY, L., Dermatology and Allergology
  KOLOZSVÁRI, L., Ophthalmology
  KÓSA, F., Forensic Medicine
  KOVÁCS, A., Oral Surgery
  KRASZKÓ, P., Pulmonology
  LÁZÁR, G, Surgery
  LEPRÁN, I., Pharmacology and Pharmacotherapy
  LONOVICS, J., Internal Medicine
  MÁNDI, Y., Medical Microbiology and Immunology
  MÉRAY, J., Anaesthesiology
  MÉSZÁROS, T., Orthopaedics
  MIHÁLY, A., Anatomy, Histology and Embryology
  MIKÓ, T., Pathology
  NAGY, E., Clinical Microbiology
  NAGYMAJTÉNYI, L., Public Health
  PAJOR, L., Urology
  PALKÓ, A., Radiology
  PAPP, G., Paediatrics
  PAPP, J. G., Pharmacology
  PÁL, A., Tocology and Gynaecology

PÁVICS, L., Nuclear Medicine
PENKE, B., Medical Chemistry
PETRI, A., Surgery
POKORNY, G., Rheumatology
PRÁGAI, B., Medical Microbiology and Immunology
PUSZTAI, R., Medical Microbiology and Immunology
RESCH, B., Tocology and Gynaecology
SIMONKA, J. A., Traumatology
SONKODI, I., Oral Medicine
SONKODI, S., Nephrology, Dialysis
SZABAD, J., Medical Biology
SZABÓ, G., Pathophysiology
SZABÓ, J., Medical Genetics
SZÖLLŐSSY, J., Tocology and Gynaecology
TAKÁCS, T., Internal Medicine
TELEGDY, G., Pathophysiology
THURZÓ, L., Oncotherapy
TÓTH, K., Orthopaedics
TÚRI, S., Paediatrics
VARGA, G., Internal Medicine and Cardiology
VARGA, T., Forensic Medicine
VÁRKONYI, Á., Paediatrics
VARRÓ, T., Pharmacology and Pharacotherapy
VÉCSEI, L., Neurology
VÉGH, Á., Pharmacology and Pharmacotherapy
VIMLÁTA, L., Anaesthiology
WITTMANN, T., Internal Medicine

Faculty of Pharmacy (6720 Szeged, Zrinyi u. 9; tel. (62) 545-022; fax (62) 541-906; e-mail gytkdh@medea.szote.u-szeged.hu; internet www.szote.u-szeged.hu):

DOMBI, G., Pharmaceutical Analysis
ERŐS, I., Pharmaceutical Technology
FALKAY, GY., Pharmacodynamics
FÜLÖP, F., Pharmaceutical Chemistry
HÓDI, K., Pharmaceutical Technology
HOHMANN, J., Pharmacognosy
MÁTHÉ, I., Pharmacognosy
PÁAL, T., Drug Regulatory Affairs
RÉVÉSZ, P., Pharmaceutical Technology
STÁJER, G., Pharmaceutical Chemistry

Faculty of Science (6720 Szeged, Aradi vértanúk tere 1; tel. (62) 544-681; fax (62) 426-221; e-mail annuse@sci.u-szeged.hu; internet www.sci.u-szeged.hu):

BECSEI, J., Economic Geography
BOR, ZS., Optics and Quantum Electronics
BOROS, I., Genetic and Molecular Biology
CSIRIK, J., Computer Science
CSÖRGŐ, S., Applied Analysis
CZÉDLI, G., Algebra and Number Theory
DÉKÁNY, I., Colloid Chemistry
ERDEI, L., Plant Physiology
ERDŐHELYI, A., Solid State Chemistry and Radiochemistry
ÉSIK, Z., Principles of Computer Science
FEHÉR, L., Theoretical Physics
FÜLÖP, Z., Foundations of Computer Science
GALLÉ, L., Ecology
GÉCSEG, F., Computer Science
GULYA, K., Zoology and Cell Biology
HANNUS, I., Applied and Environmental Chemistry
HATVANI, L., Analysis
HETÉNYI, M., Mineralogy, Geochemistry and Petrography
IGLÓI, F., Theoretical Physics
KÉRCHY, L., Analysis
KEVEI, F., Climatology and Landscape Ecology
KIRICSI, I., Applied Chemistry
KISS, T., Inorganic Chemistry
KOVÁCS, K., Biotechnology
KRÁMLI, A., Applications of Analysis
KRISZTIN, T., Applied Numerical Mathematics
LEHOCZKI, E., Botany
LEINDLER, L., Analysis
MARÓTI, P., Biophysics

MARÓY, P., Genetic and Molecular Biology
MÉSZÁROS, R., Economic Geography
MEZŐSI, G., Physical Geography
MOLNÁR, A., Organic Chemistry
MÓRICZ, F., Applications of Analysis
NAGY, L., Inorganic and Analytical Chemistry1
NAGYPÁL, I., Physical Chemistry
NEMCSÓK, J., Biochemistry
NOTHEISZ, F., Organic Chemistry
NOVÁK, M., Physical Chemistry
RÁCZ, B., Optics and Quantum Electronics
SIMÁNYI, N., Geometry
SZABÓ, G., Optics and Quantum Electronics
SZATMÁRI, S., Experimental Physics
SZENDREI, Á., Algebra and Number Theory
SZENDREI, M., Algebra and Number Theory
SZENTE, M., Comparative Physiology
TOLDI, J., Comparative Physiology
TOTIK, V., Set Theory and Mathematical Logic
VISY, C., Physical Chemistry

College Faculty of Agriculture (6800 Hódmezővásárhely, Andrássy u. 15; tel. (62) 246-466; e-mail bodnar@mgk.u-szeged.hu; internet www.mgk.u-szeged.hu):

MUCSI, I., Animal Husbandry
PÉTER, J., Nutrition

College Faculty of Food Engineering (6724 Szeged, Mars tér 7; tel. (62) 546-003; fax (62) 546-003; e-mail fotit@szef.u-szeged.hu; internet www.szef.u-szeged.hu):

FENYVESSY, J., Food Technology
KOVÁCS, E. T., Food Science
SZABÓ, G., Unit Operation and Environmental Techniques
TANÁCS, L., Food Science

College Faculty of Health Sciences (6726 Szeged, Temesvári krt. 31; tel. (62) 545-024; fax (62) 545-515; e-mail poma@efk.u-szeged .hu; internet www.efk.u-szeged.hu):

BÁRÁNY, F., Social Work and Social Policy

College Faculty of Music (6722 Szeged, Tisza L. krt. 79–81; tel. (62) 544-600; fax (62) 544-066; e-mail zfk@muzik.u-szeged.hu; internet www.muzik.u-szeged.hu):

HUSZÁR, L., Music Theory
KEREK, F., Piano
SZECSŐDI, F., Strings
TEMESI, M., Voice

College Faculty of 'Juhász Gyula' Teacher Training College (6722 Szeged, Boldogasszony sgt. 6; tel. (62) 546-050; fax (62) 420-953; e-mail galambos@jgytf.u-szeged.hu; internet www.jgytf.u-szeged.hu):

BÉKÉSI, I., Hungarian Language
GALAMBOS, G., Computer Science
GALGÓCZI, L., Hungarian Language
NAGY, J., Hungarian Language
NÁNAI, L., Physics
SERES, L., Chemistry

SZENT ISTVÁN EGYETEM
(Szent István University)

2103 Gödöllő, Páter Károly u. 1
Telephone: (28) 522-000
Fax: (28) 410-804
E-mail: info@szie.hu
Internet: www.szie.hu

Founded 1945 as Gödöllői Agrártudományi Egyetem (Gödöllő University of Agricultural Sciences), merged with Állatorvostudomanyi Egyetem (University of Veterinary Science) (Budapest), Kertészeti és Élelmiszeripari Egyetem (University of Horticulture and Food Technology) (Budapest), Jászberényi Tanitóképző Főiskola (Jászberény Teacher-Training College) and Ybl Miklós Műszaki Főiskola (Miklós Ybl Polytechnic) in 2000, adopting present name

State control
Languages of instruction: Hungarian, English, Russian, French
Academic year: September to May
Rector: Dr SOLTI LÁSZLÓ
Library: attached libraries and archives in Gödöllő, Budapest, Jászberény, Szarvas, Gyula, Békéscsaba
Number of teachers: 809
Number of students: 17,464

DEANS

Faculty of Agricultural Engineering: Dr ATTILA VAS
Faculty of Agricultural and Environmental Sciences (Gödöllő): Dr CSÁNYI SÁNDOR
Faculty of Agricultural, Water and Environmental Management of Tessedik Samuel College (Szarvas): Dr HÁJOS MÁRIA
Faculty of Applied Arts (Jászberény): Dr BARKÓ ENDRE
Faculty of Economics (Békéscsaba): Dr BORZÁN ANITA
Faculty of Economics and Social Sciences (Gödöllő): Dr VILLÁNYI LÁSZLÓ
Faculty of the Food Industry: Prof. Dr ANDRÁS FEKETE
Faculty of Health Care and Medical Sciences of Tessedik Sámuel College (Gyula): Dr KÖTELES LAJOS
Faculty of Horticulture: Dr JENŐ BERNÁTH
Faculty of Landscape Architecture: Dr ILONA BALOGH ORMOS
Faculty of Mechanical Engineering (Gödöllő): Dr SZABÓ ISTVÁN
Faculty of Pedagogy (Szarvas): Dr LIPCSEI IMRE
Faculty of Veterinary Science: Prof. Dr FODOR LÁSZLÓ
College Faculty of Jászberény: (vacant)
Ybl Miklos Technical College Faculty: Prof. Dr GEORGE SAMSONDI KISS
Ybl Miklós School of Architecture (Budapest): Dr MAKOVÉNYI FERENC
Institute of Scientific Training: Dr PÉTER SZENDRŐ

DIRECTORS

College Faculty of Agricultural Economics, Gyöngygös: Dr SÁNDOR MAGDA

PROFESSORS

Faculty of Agricultural Engineering:

BARÓTFY, I., Environmental Engineering
BEER, GY., Agricultural Engineering
FARKAS, I., Physics
GYÜRK, I., Mechanics
JESZENSZKY, Z., Agricultural Engineering
KÓSA, A., Mathematics
SEMBERY, P., Food Engineering
SZENDRŐ, P., Agricultural Mechanization
SZÜLE, ZS., Agricultural Mechanization
VAS, A., Agricultural Engineering

Faculty of Agricultural and Environmental Sciences:

ANDRÁS, D.
ERIKA, M.
ERZSÉBET, K.
FERENC, G.
FERENC, L.
FERENC, S.
FERENC, V.
GÁBOR, B.
GYÖRGY, F.
GYÖRGY, H.
GYÖRGY, V.
JÁNOS, K.
JÁNOS, T.
JÓZSEF, K.
JUDIT, D.
LAJOS, H.
LÁSZLÓ, B.
LÁSZLÓ, HESZKY
LÁSZLÓ, HORNOK

LÁSZLÓ, HORVÁTH
MÁRTA, B.
MÁRTON, J.
MIHÁLY, W.
MIKLÓS, M.
PÉTER GERGELY, P.
SÁNDOR, C.
ZOLTÁN, M.
ZOLTÁN, T.

Faculty of Agricultural, Water and Environmental Management of Tessedik Samuel College:

ISTVÁN, P.
ZOLTÁN, I.

Faculty of Economic and Social Sciences:

ANDRÁS, N.
BÁLINT CSABA, I.
CSABA, M.
CSABA, S.
GYÖRGY IVÁN, C.
IMRE, L.
ISTVÁN, F.
ISTVÁN, S.
JÓZSEF, L.
JÓZSEF, M.
JÓZSEF, V.
LAJOS, S.
LÁSZLÓ, H.
LÁSZLÓ, K.
LÁSZLÓ, V.
MAGDOLNA, C.
PÉTER, H.
TAMÁS, S.
TAMÁS, T.
TOMAY TAMÁS, S.
ZOLTÁN, S.

Faculty of Mechanical Engineering:

ATTILA, V.
CSIZMADIA BÉLA, M.
DEZSŐ, F.
GÁBOR, K.
ISTVÁN, B.
ISTVÁN, F.
ISTVÁN, H.
JÁNOS, B.
LAJOS, L.
LÁSZLÓ, F.
LÁSZLÓ, T.
PÉTER, S.
ZOLTÁN, V.
ZSOLT, S.

Faculty of Veterinary Sciences:

ENDRE, B.
GÁBOR, S.
JÁNOS, F.
JÁNOS, V.
JÁNOS LÁSZLÓ, V.
JÓZSEF ZSIGMOND, S.
LÁSZLÓ, F.
LÁSZLÓ, Z.
KÁROLY, V.
KATALIN, H.
MIKLÓS, R.
OTTÓ, S.
PÁL, R.
PÁL, S.
PÉTER, G.
PÉTER, L.
PÉTER, N.
PÉTER, S.
RÓBERT, F.
SÁNDOR, C.
SÁNDOR GYÖRGY, F.
TIBOR, G.
VILMOS LÁSZLÓ, F.

Ybl Miklós Faculty of Architecture:

KÁROLY, Z.
RUDOLF, K.
GÁBOR, T.

PROFESSORS FROM THE FORMER UNIVERSITY OF HORTICULTURE AND FOOD TECHNOLOGY

BALÁZS, S., Vegetable Production

BALOGH, S., Food Industry Economics
BÉKÁSSY-MOLNÁR, E., Food Technology
BERNÁTH, J., Medicinal Plants
BOROSS, L., Chemistry and Biochemistry
CSEMEZ, A., Landscape Architecture
CSEPREGI, P., Viticulture
DALÁNYI, L., Landscape Architecture
DEÁK, T., Microbiology
DIMÉNY, I., Agricultural Economics
DINYA, L., Economics and Marketing
EPERJESI, I., Oenology
ERDÉLYI, E., Food Technology
FARKAS, J., Food Preservation
FEKETE, A., Food Physics
FODOR, P., Chemistry and Biochemistry
GLITS, M., Plant Pathology
HARNOS, Zs., Mathematics
HORVÁTH, G., Plant Physiology
HOSCHKE, A., Brewing and Distillation
JÁMBOR, I., Landscape Architecture
KISS, I., Food Preservation
KÖRMENDY, I., Food Preservation
KOSÁRY, J., Chemistry and Biochemistry
LÁNG, Z., Technical Department
MÉSZÁROS, Z., Entomology
MŐCSÉNYI, M., Landscape Architecture
PAIS, I., Chemistry
PAPP, J., Fruit Growing
RIMÓCZI, I., Botany
SÁRAI, T., Food Technology
SÁRKÖZY, P., Agricultural Economics
SASS, P., Fruit Growing
SCHMIDT, G., Floriculture and Dendrology
SZABÓ, S. A., Food Chemistry
VARSÁNYI, I., Food Preservation
VELICH, I., Plant Genetics and Selection
VERMES, L., Agrometeorology and Water Management

SZINHÁZ- ÉS FILMMŰVÉSZETI EGYETEM
(University of Drama and Film)

1088 Budapest, Vas u. 2C
Telephone: (1) 318-8111
Fax: (1) 338-4749
E-mail: xan6632@mail.iif.hu
Internet: www.filmacademy.hu
Founded 1865
State control
Rector: GÁBOR SZÉKELY
Vice-Rectors: LÁSZLÓ BABARCZY, ÁDÁM HORVÁTH
Dir of Int. Relations: JÁNOS XANTUS
Sec.-Gen.: L. TISZEKER
Number of teachers: 97
Number of students: 269

ZRÍNYI MIKLÓS NEMZETVÉDELMI EGYETEM
(Zrínyi Miklós University of National Defence)

1101 Budapest, Hungária krt. 9-11
Telephone: (1) 432-9000
Fax: (1) 432-9012
E-mail: rektor@zmne.hu
Internet: portal.zmne.hu
State control
Rector: Dr JÁNOS SZABÓ.

Private Universities

ANDRÁSSY GYULA BUDAPESTI NÉMET NYELVŰ EGYETEM
(Andrássy Gyula University)

1464 Budapest, POB 1422
1088 Budapest, Pollack Mihály tér 3
Telephone: (1) 266-3101
Fax: (1) 266-3099
E-mail: uni@andrassyuni.hu
Internet: www.andrassyuni.hu

Private control
Language of instruction: German
Rector: Prof. Dr MASÁT ANDRÁS
Pro-Rector: Prof. Dr CHRISTIAN SCHUBEL
Library Dir: HEDVIG ZIMMERMANN

DEANS

Faculty of Comparative Law Studies: Prof. Dr OLIVER DIGGELMANN
Faculty of European Studies: Prof. Dr DIETER A. BINDER
Faculty of International Relations: Dr MARTINA ECKARDT

CENTRAL EUROPEAN UNIVERSITY

1051 Budapest, Nádor u. 9
Telephone: (1) 327-3000
Fax: (1) 327-3005
E-mail: contact@ceu.hu
Internet: www.ceu.hu
Founded 1991
Private control
Language of instruction: English
Academic year: September to June
Postgraduate courses only
Pres. and Rector: Prof. YEHUDA ELKANA
Academic Pro-Rector: HOWARD M. ROBINSON
Pro-Rector for Hungarian and EU Affairs: KAROLY BARD
Vice-Pres. for External Relations: ILDIKO MORAN
Vice-Pres. for Student Services: ROSITSA BATESON
Library of 150,000 books, 1,500 periodicals
Number of teachers: 305
Number of students: 1,541

DEBRECENI REFORMÁTUS HITTUDOMÁNYI EGYETEM
(Debrecen University of Reformed Theology)

4044 Debrecen, Kálvin tér 16
Telephone: (52) 414-744
Fax: (52) 516-822
E-mail: info@drhe.drk.hu
Internet: www.drhe.drk.hu
Founded 1538
Private control
Rector: KÁROLY FEKETE
Library of 600,000 vols
Number of teachers: 36
Number of students: 306

EVANGÉLIKUS HITTUDOMÁNYI EGYETEM
(Evangelical-Lutheran Theological University)

1141 Budapest, Rózsavölgyi köz 3
Telephone: (1) 469-1050
Fax: (1) 363-7454
E-mail: teologia@lutheran.hu
Internet: teol.lutheran.hu
Founded 1557
Private control
Rector: Dr ZOLTÁN CSEPREGI
Library of 55,000 vols, 119 periodicals
Number of teachers: 20
Number of students: 200

Departments of Church History, Church Music, New Testament Theology, Old Testament Theology, Practical Theology, Religious and Social Studies and Systematic Theology.

KÁROLI GÁSPÁR REFORMÁTUS EGYETEM
(Gáspár Károli University of the Reformed Church in Hungary)

1092 Budapest, Ráday u. 28
Telephone: (1) 217-2403
Fax: (1) 217-2403
E-mail: dekani.hivvez.htk@kre.hu
Internet: www.kre.hu

Founded 1855
Private control

Rector: Prof. Dr. FERENC SZŰCS

Library of 2,000,000 vols
Number of teachers: 19
Number of students: 190

DEANS

Faculty of Humanities: (vacant)
Faculty of Theology: Prof. Dr DÁVID NÉMETH Dr ERNŐ RAFFAY

ATTACHED INSTITUTE

Institute of Kremlinology: tel. (1) 455-9060; e-mail kemoke@index.hu; Dir Prof. Dr MIKLÓS KUN.

ORSZÁGOS RABBIKÉPZŐ–ZSIDÓ EGYETEM
(Jewish Theological Seminary–University of Jewish Studies)

1084 Budapest, Bérkocsis u. 2
Telephone: (1) 317-2396
Fax: (1) 318-7049
E-mail: vzs@or-zse.hu
Internet: www.or-zse.hu

Founded 1877
Private control

Rector: Rabbi Dr Y. A. SCHÖNER

Library of 110,000 vols
Number of teachers: 87
Number of students: 264

Faculty of Rabbinical Studies; College Faculty/Paedagogium.

PÁZMÁNY PÉTER KATOLIKUS EGYETEM
(Péter Pázmány Catholic University)

1088 Budapest, Szentkirályi u. 28–30
Telephone: (1) 429-7211
Fax: (1) 318-0507
E-mail: rector@ppke.hu
Internet: www.ppke.hu

Founded 1635
Private control
Academic year: September to June

Rector: Rev. Dr GYÖRGY FODOR
Vice-Rector: Rev. Dr SZABOLCS ANZELM SZUROMI

Financial Dir: MIKLÓS RÓKA
Technical Dir: PÉTER BOROSS-TÓBY
Library of 400,000 vols
Number of teachers: 650
Number of students: 8,500

Publications: *Folia Canonica* (review of Eastern and Western Canon Law in five languages, 1 a year), *Folia Theologica* (in five languages, 1 a year), *Kánonjog* (Canon Law, in Hungarian, 2 a year), *Teológia* (in Hungarian, 4 a year), *VERBUM Analecta Neolatina* (in several European languages, 2 a year)

DEANS

Faculty of Humanities: Prof. IDA FRÖHLICH
Faculty of Information Technology: Prof. TAMÁS ROSKA
Faculty of Law and Political Science: Prof. GYULA BÁNDI
Faculty of Theology: Rev. Prof. ZOLTÁN ROKAY

Colleges

Apor Vilmos Katolikus Főiskola (Apor Vilmos Catholic College): 2600 Vác, Konstantin tér 1-5.; tel. (27) 511-140; fax (27) 511-141; e-mail avkf@avkf.hu; internet www.avkf.hu; Private control; Rector Dr PÁL BALÁZS.

Baptista Teológiai Akadémia (Baptist Theological Academy): 1068 Budapest, Benczúr u. 3; tel. (1) 342-0912; fax (1) 342-7534; internet www.bta.hu; Private control; Rector Dr TIBOR ALMÁSI.

Budapesti Gazdasági Főiskola (Budapest Business School): 1149 Budapest, Buzogány u. 11–13; tel. (1) 469-6600; fax (1) 469-6636; internet www.bgf.hu; f. 2000; State control; Rector Dr EVA SANDORNÉ-KRISZT; 17,796 students; Colleges of Commerce, Catering and Tourism; International Management and Business Studies; Finance and Accountancy.

Budapesti Kommunikációs és Üzleti Főiskola (Budapest School of Communication and Business): 1147 Budapest, Nagy Lajos kir.u. 1-9; tel. (1) 273-3090; fax (1) 273-3099; internet www.bkf.hu; Private control; Rector Dr LÁSZLÓ VASS; Librarian KORNÉLIA BÁNHEGYI KOLLÁR; Institutes of Economics and Business Sciences; European Studies; Journalism and Media Studies; Marketing and Business Communication; Social Sciences.

Budapesti Műszaki Főiskola (Budapest Tech (Polytechnical Institution)): 1034 Budapest, Doberdó u. 6; tel. (1) 250-0333; fax (1) 453-4149; e-mail rektor@bmf.hu; internet www.bmf.hu; f. 2000 as a result of the merger of Könnyűipari Műszaki Főiskola

(College of Technology for Light Industry) (Budapest), Bánki Donát Gépipari Műszaki Főiskola (Donát Bánki Polytechnic) (Budapest), Kandó Kálmán Műszaki Főiskola (Kálmán Kandó College of Engineering) (Budapest) and other instns; State control; 417 teachers; 12,500 students; Rector Prof. Dr IMRE RUDAS; Librarian KRASZNAI MIHÁLYNÉ.

Dunaújvárosi Főiskola (Dunaújváros College): 2400 Dunaújváros Táncsics M. u. 1/A; tel. (25) 551-211; fax (25) 551-262; e-mail international@mail.duf.hu; internet www.duf.hu/english; f. 1969; State control; 111 teachers; 3,513 students; Dir-Gen. MÓNIKA RAJCSÁNYI-MOLNÁR.

International Business School – Budapest: 1021 Budapest, Tárogató u. 2-4; tel. (1) 391 2550; e-mail info@ibs-b.hu; internet www.ibs-b.hu; f. 1993; Private control; Chancellor Prof. ISTVÁN TAMÁS.

Károly Róbert Főiskola (Károly Róbert College): 320 Gyöngyös, 1 Mátrai u. 36; tel. (37) 518-305; fax (37) 313-170; internet www.karolyrobert.hu; Private control; Rector Dr SÁNDOR MAGDA; Colleges of Agriculture and Agricultural Management.

Kecskeméti Főiskola (Kecskemét College): 6000 Kecskemét, Izsáki u. 10B; tel. (76) 501-960; fax (76) 501-979; internet www.kefo.hu; State control; f. 2000 by merger of College of Mechanical Engineering and Automation, Teacher Training College and University of Horticulture and Food-Processing, Horticultural Faculty Kecskemét; 105 teachers; 6,000 students; Rector Dr JÓZSEF DANYI.

Magyar Táncművészeti Főiskola (Hungarian Dance Academy): 1145 Budapest, Columbus u. 87–89. POB 1372, Pf. 439; tel. (1) 273-3434; fax (1) 273-3444; e-mail info@mtf.hu; internet www.mtf.hu; f. 1950; State control; academic year September to June; library: 23,000 vols; 103 teachers; 600 students; Rector for Scientific and Admin. Issues Dr GÁBOR BOLVÁRI-TAKÁCS (acting); Rector for Artistic and Educational Issues GYÖRGY SZAKÁLY (acting); Dir Dr MÁRIA ZÓRÁNDI JAKAB; Finance Dir. GABRIELLA JAKUCS; Librarian IRÉN TÓTH BÍRÓ.

Nyíregyházi Főiskola (College of Nyíregyháza): 4401 Nyíregyháza, Sóstói u. 31B; tel. (42) 599-400; fax (42) 404-092; internet www.nyf.hu; State control; Rector Dr ZOLTÁN JÁNOSI.

Veszprémi Érseki Hittudományi Főiskola (Archiepiscopal Theological College of Veszprém): 8200 Veszprém, Jutasi u. 18/2; tel. (88) 426-116; fax (88) 426-865; internet www.vhf.hu; Private control; Rector Dr ISTVÁN VARGA.

ICELAND

The Higher Education System

The Icelandic higher education system dates back to the foundation of the University of Iceland in 1911. The University of Iceland remains the principal institution of higher learning in Iceland, but since the 1970s new institutions of higher education have emerged with a more specialized focus, providing greater diversity at that level. In 2007 there were nine higher education institutions in Iceland and some 17,728 students were enrolled in further and higher education.

Legislation on higher education institutions (the Universities Act, No. 136/1997) enacted in 1997 establishes the general framework for the activities of these institutions. In this Act, the term 'háskóli' is used to refer both to traditional universities and institutions that do not carry out research. Separate legislation for each public higher education institution, and the charters of privately run universities, define their engagement in research, internal organization, etc. Iceland is a signatory of the Bologna Declaration, and all legislative reforms and regulations are handled by a national Bologna follow-up group based in the Ministry of Education, Science and Culture. A two-cycle degree system that conforms to the Bologna regulations is well established for most courses with the exception of medical-related subjects.

Public and private higher education institutions receive individual appropriations from the state budget. The administration of each public university is entrusted to the Senate, the rector, faculty meetings, faculty councils and deans, if the university is divided into faculties. The Senate issues final rulings in the affairs of the university and its institutions, formulates their overall policy and furthers their development. The Senate is the supreme decision-making body in each institution unless otherwise provided for explicitly in the relevant act. The state draws up performance-related contracts with all higher education institutions, defining how the institution intends to achieve its objectives and what the Government's financial contribution shall be.

Entry to undergraduate courses is based on the Stúdentspróf (matriculation examination). Many institutions have restricted admission based on the average mark obtained or marks in subjects that are deemed relevant. Mature students are not always required to hold the Stúdentspróf if they have specific work experience. Courses are assessed in terms of credits.

Short courses resulting in a certificate or diploma are available in a limited number of subjects. The Baccalaureatus (Bachelors degree), usually in arts, science or education, is three to four years in length (a minimum of 90 credits). The University of Iceland awards the Kandidatspróf (Candidatus degree), which is offered in professional subject areas (law, medicine, engineering, etc.) and is four to six years in length. A number of institutions provide one- to two-year programmes following the Baccalaureatus leading to postgraduate certificates in various subjects. The University of Iceland awards the Meistarapróf (Masters degree) after a two-year course for holders of the Baccalaureatus. In some cases, a first-class Baccalaureatus is required. The Magister Paedagogiae degree in education is only offered in Icelandic studies. All courses require completion of a major thesis or research project. The Iceland University of Education offers a two-year Master of Education course. There are two types of Doktorspróf (Doctorate degree) available either at the University of Iceland or the Iceland University of Education. The Doctor Philosophiae is three or four years in length and follows the Meistarapróf. The Doctor Scientiarum and the Doctor Medicinae degree courses are based on the Kandidatspróf or the Meistarapróf degrees. In exceptional circumstances, a holder of a good Baccalaureatus may be allowed to undertake a Doctorate degree; however, studies would have to last for four years. The course is completely research-based.

Specialized vocational schools, known as Sérskóli, offer courses for specialized employment. Since the 1990s many Sérskóli have been upgraded to the higher education level. Students are required to take 25 unit-credits in general academic subjects to complement their technical training. Apprentices completing their studies take the Sveinspróf (Journeyman's examination). Students may progress to become a Meistarabréf (Master Craftsman) after a period of work experience and advanced study. Alternatively, students may progress to university after a specified period of additional studies. The Meistarabréf gives the right to train apprentices, operate a business or manage an enterprise.

Icelandic students have a long tradition of studying abroad for their higher education. About 16% of Icelandic students in higher education study abroad, most of them in postgraduate studies.

Regulatory and Representative Bodies

GOVERNMENT

Ministry of Education, Science and Culture: Sölvhólsgötu 4, 150 Reykjavík; tel. 545-9500; fax 562-3068; e-mail postur@mrn.stjr.is; internet www.menntamalaraduneyti.is; Minister ÞORGERÐUR KATRÍN GUNNARSDÓTTIR.

ACCREDITATION

ENIC/NARIC Iceland: Office for Academic Affairs, Univ. of Iceland, Suðurgata, 101 Reykjavík; tel. 525-4360; fax 525-4317; e-mail thordkri@hi.is; internet www.naric-enic.hi.is; Dir of Academic Affairs ÞÓRÐUR KRISTINSSON.

NATIONAL BODIES

Samstarfsnefnd háskólastigsins (Standing Committee of the Rectors of Icelandic Higher Education Institutions): University of Iceland, Office of the Rector, Suðurgata, 101 Reykjavík; tel. and fax 525-4302; e-mail thordrkri@hi.is; internet www.hi.is; f. 1987; 8 mems; Head KRISTÍN INGÓLFSDÓTTIR; Dir of Academic Affairs ÞÓRÐUR KRISTINSSON.

Learned Societies

AGRICULTURE, FISHERIES AND VETERINARY SCIENCE

Bændasamtök Íslands (Farmers' Association of Iceland): Baendahöllinni við Hagatorg, POB 7080, 127 Reykjavík; tel. 563-0300; fax 562-3058; e-mail vefstjori@bondi.is; internet www.bondi.is; f. 1995; 4,000 farmer mems in 15 district asscns and 13 sector orgs; library of 10,000 vols; Chair. ARI TEITSSON; Dir Dr SIGURGEIR THORGEIRSSON; publs *Bændablaðið* (Farmers' News, 26 a year), *Freyr* (12 a year).

BIBLIOGRAPHY, LIBRARY SCIENCE AND MUSEOLOGY

Information—The Icelandic Library and Information Science Association/Upplýsing—Félag bókasafns- og upplýsingafræða: Lyngási 18, 210 Garðabæ; tel. 864-6220; e-mail upplysing@upplysing.is; internet upplysing.is; f. 1960; 500 mems; strengthenes, encourages, and works for the recognition of the importance of the services of libraries and information centres within the Icelandic soc.; Pres. ÞÓRDÍS T. ÞÓRARINSDÓTTIR; Sec. INGIBJÖRG BALDURSDÓTTIR; publs *Bókasafnið* (1 a year), *Fregnir* (3 a year), *A Leið til Upplýsingar* (History of Icelandic Library Associations, with summary in English).

FINE AND PERFORMING ARTS

Bandalag Íslenzkra Listamanna (Union of Icelandic Artists): POB 637, 121 Reykjavík; tel. 862-4808; e-mail bil@bil.is; internet www.bil.is; f. 1928; Pres. KOLBRÚN HALLDÓRSDÓTTIR; 3,100 mems.

Constituent Organizations:

Arkítektafélag Íslands (Icelandic Architects' Association): Engjateigi 9, 105 Reykjavík; tel. 551-1465; fax 562-0465; e-mail ai@ai.is; internet www.ai.is; 226 mems; Chair. ÞÓRARINN ÞÓRARINSSON.

Félag Íslenzkra Leikara (Icelandic Actors' Association): Lindargötu 6, 101 Reykjavík; tel. 552-6040; fax 562-7706; e-mail fil@fil.is; internet www.fil.is; Chair. RANDVER THORLAKSSON; 310 mems.

Félag Íslenzkra Listdansara (Association of Icelandic Dance Artists): POB 8654, 128 Reykjavík; e-mail olof.i@li.is; 55 mems; Chair. ÓLÖF INGÓLFSDÓTTIR.

Félag Íslenzkra Myndlistarmanna (Association of Icelandic Visual Artists): Klapparstíg 25–27, 101 Reykjavík; e-mail sim@simnet.is; Chair. PJETUR STEFÁNSSON; 263 mems.

Félag Íslenzkra Tónlistarmanna (Icelandic Musicians' Association): Lindargötu 46, 101 Reykjavík; fax 562-6455; e-mail fiston@centrum.is; Chair. MARGRÉT BÓAS-DÓTTIR; 92 mems.

Félag Kvikmyndagerdarmanna (Icelandic Film Makers' Association): POB 5162, 128 Reykjavík; internet www .filmmakers.is; f. 1966; 156 mems; Chair. BJORN BJÖRNSSON.

Félag Leikstjóra á Íslandi (Icelandic Association of Stage Directors): Lindargötu 6, 101 Reykjavík; tel. 562-6656; 68 mems; Chair. PETER EINARSSON.

Rithöfundasamband Íslands (Icelandic Writers' Association): Dyngjuvegi 8, 104 Reykjavík; tel. 568-3190; fax 568-3192; e-mail rsi@rsi.is; internet www.rsi.is; f. 1974; 3,800 mems; Chair. PETUR GUNNARS-SON; Exec. Dir RAGNHEIDUR TRYGGVADÓT-TIR.

Samband Íslenzkra Myndlistarmanna (Icelandic Visual Artists' Association): Hafnarstræti 16, POB 1115, 121 Reykjavík; tel. 551-1346; fax 562-6656; e-mail sim@simnet.is; internet www.sim.is; 355 mems; Chair. SOLVEIG EGGERTSDÓTTIR.

Samtök Kvikmundaleikstjóra (Guild of Icelandic Film Directors): Sudurgata 14, 101 Reykjavík; 50 mems; Chair. FRIDRIK THOR FRIDRIKSSON.

Tónskáldafélag Íslands (Icelandic Composers' Society): Laufásvegi 40, 101 Reykjavík; tel. 552-4972; 50 mems; Chair. JOHN SPEIGHT.

Tónlistarfélagið (Music Society): Bjarmaland 19, 108 Reykjavík; f. 1930; operates a College of Music; affiliated societies in major towns; Chair. BALDVIN TRYGGVASON; Man. RUT MAGNÚSSON; Headmaster of College HALLDÓR HARALDSSON.

HISTORY, GEOGRAPHY AND ARCHAEOLOGY

Íslenzka fornleifafélag (Icelandic Archaeological Society): POB 177, 121 Reykjavík; f. 1879; Pres. THÓR MAGNÚSSON; 600 mems; Sec. GUDMUNDUR ÓLAFSSON; publ. *Arbók* (Year Book).

Sögufélag (Icelandic Historical Society): Fischersundi 3, 101 Reykjavík; tel. 551-4620; e-mail sogufelag@sogufelag.is; internet www.sogufelag.is; f. 1902; 1,600 mems; Pres. Prof. ANNA AGNARSDÓTTIR; Sec. Prof. MÁR JÓNSSON; publs *Ný saga* (1 a year), *Saga* (1 a year).

LANGUAGE AND LITERATURE

Hið Íslenzka bókmenntafélag (Icelandic Literary Society): Skeifan 3B, Reykjavík; tel. 588-9060; fax 581-4088; e-mail hib@islandia .is; internet www.hib.is; f. 1816; research

work and publishing; 2,000 mems; Pres. SIGURDUR LÍNDAL; Sec. REYNIR AXELSSON; publ. *Skírnir* (2 a year).

NATURAL SCIENCES

General

Vísindafélag Íslendinga (Icelandic Academy of Sciences and Letters): Bárugötu 3, 101 Reykjavík; f. 1918; 159 mems; Pres. SIGURDUR STEINTHORSSON; publs *Ráðstefnurit* (irregular), *Rit*.

Biological Sciences

Íslenzka náttúrufrædifélag (Icelandic Natural History Society): Hlemmi 3, POB 5320, 125 Reykjavík; tel. 590-0500; fax 590-0595; e-mail ni@ni.is; internet www.ni.is; f. 1889; 1,600 mems; library of 9,000 vols, 600 periodicals; Pres. JÓN OTTÓSSON; publ. *Náttúrufrædingurinn* (4 a year journal of natural history).

Physical Sciences

Jöklarannsóknafélag Íslands (Iceland Glaciological Society): POB 5128, 125 Reykjavík; fax 552-1347; internet www.jorfi.is; f. 1950; 550 mems; Pres. MAGNÚS T. GUD-MUNDSSON; Sec. STEINUNN JAKOBSDÓTTIR; publ. *Jökull* (1 a year).

TECHNOLOGY

Verkfrædingafélag Íslands (Association of Chartered Engineers in Iceland): Engjateigi 9, Reykjavík 105; tel. 568-8511; fax 568-9703; f. 1912; 1,100 mems; Pres. STEINAR FRID-GEIRSSON; Sec. LOGI KRISTJÁNSSON; publ. *Arbók Verkfrædingafélags Íslands* (1 a year).

Research Institutes

ECONOMICS, LAW AND POLITICS

Hagstofa Íslands (Statistics Iceland): Borgartun 21A, 150 Reykjavík; tel. 528-1000; fax 528-1098; e-mail information@statice.is; internet www.statice.is; f. 1914; Dir-Gen. ÓLAFUR HJÁLMARSSON; publs *Hagskýrslur Íslands* (Statistics of Iceland), *Hagtíðindi* (Statistics Monthly), *Landshagir* (Statistical Yearbook of Iceland).

MEDICINE

Rannsóknastofa Háskólans (University Institute of Pathology): Barónsstígur, POB 1465, 121 Reykjavík; tel. 543-8351; f. 1917; 52 mems; Dir Prof. JOHANNES BJORNSSON.

Tilraunastöð Háskóla Íslands i meinafrædi að Keldum (Institute for Experimental Pathology, University of Iceland): við Vesturlandsveg, 112 Reykjavík; tel. 585-5100; fax 567-3979; e-mail bo@hi.is; internet www.keldur.hi.is; f. 1948; affiliated to University of Iceland; library of 4,000 vols; Dir SIGURDUR INGRARSSON; publ. *Icelandic Agricultural Sciences* (1–2 a year).

NATURAL SCIENCES

General

Rannsóknarrád Íslands (The Icelandic Centre for Research): Laugavegur 13, 101 Reykjavík; tel. 515-5800; fax 552-9814; internet www.rannis.is; f. 1994; attached to Min. of Education, Science and Culture; advises the govt and Parliament on all aspects of science, technology and innovation, and promotes int. cooperation in science and technology; Dir Dr HALLGRIMUR JANASSON.

Attached Research Institutes:

Hafrannsóknastofnunin (Marine Research Institute): Skulagata 4, 121 Rey-

kjavík; tel. 575-2000; fax 575-2001; e-mail hafro@hafro.is; internet www.hafro.is; attached to Min. of Fisheries; researches into marine biological and oceanographic sciences; spec. divs for pelagic fish, demersal fish, flatfish, technology and fishing gear, hydrography, phytoplankton, zooplankton and benthos; Chair. FRIÐRIK BALDURSSON; Dir JÓHANN SIGURJÓNSSON.

Idntæknistofnun Íslands (Technological Institute of Iceland): c/o Rannsóknarrád Islands, Laugavegur 13, 101 Reykjavík; attached to Min. of Industry; research and service institution for industry; research on raw materials, machinery and end products to improve quality and competitiveness of Icelandic industrial production; spec. divs for training and information, industrial devt, technical services and for research; Chair. MAGNÚS FRIÐGEIRSSON; Dir HALLGRÍMUR JÓNASSON.

Rannsóknastofnun byggingaidandarins (Building Research Institute): c/o Rannsóknarrád Islands, Laugavegur 13, 101 Reykjavík; tel. 570-7300; fax 570-7311; f. 1965; attached to Min. of Industry; scientific research and services for the construction and bldg industries; Chair. MAGNUS FRIÐGEIRSSON; Dir HÁKON ÓLAFSSON.

Rannsóknastofnun fiskidnadarins (Icelandic Fisheries Laboratories): Skulagata 4, 101 Reykjavík; tel. 530-8600; fax 530-8601; e-mail info@rf.is; internet www .rfisk.is; attached to Min. of Fisheries; research and services for the fish industry, quality control, etc.; divs for chemistry, bacteriology and technology; Chair. FRIÐRIK FRIÐRIKSSON.

Rannsóknastofnun landbúnadarins (Agricultural Research Institute): Keldnaholti, 112 Reykjavík; internet www.rala.is; attached to Min. of Agriculture; govtfinanced research and experimental devt in agriculture; spec. divs for animal-breeding, ecology and cultivation and farming technology; Chair. PÉTUR HELGASON; Dir THORSTEINN TÓMASSON.

Surtseyjarfélagið (Surtsey Research Society): POB 352, 121 Reykjavík; e-mail surtsey@ni.is; internet www.surtsey.is; f. 1965; promotes and coordinates scientific work in geo- and biological sciences on the island of Surtsey; 104 mems; Chair. HALLGRÍMUR JÓNASSON; Sec. BORGÞÓR MAGNÚSSON; publ. *Surtsey Research*.

Biological Sciences

Náttúrufrædistofnun Íslands (Icelandic Institute of Natural History): Hlemmur 3, POB 5320, 125 Reykjavík; tel. 590-0500; fax 590-0595; e-mail ni@ni.is; internet www.ni .is; f. 1889 by Hið Íslenska Náttúrufrædifélag (The Icelandic Natural History Soc.) and maintained by this Soc. until 1946, taken over by the State 1947; library of 12,000 vols, 500 periodicals; Dir-Gen. JÓN G. OTTÓSSON; publs *Acta Botanica Islandica* (irregular), *Bliki* (irregular), *Fjölrit Náttúrufrædistofnunar* (irregular).

Physical Sciences

Vedurstofa Íslands (Icelandic Meteorological Office): Bústadavegur 9, 150 Reykjavík; tel. 522-6000; fax 522-6001; e-mail office@vedur.is; internet www.vedur.is; f. 1920; weather forecasts, climatology, aerology, sea ice, seismology, avalanches and landslides; library of 10,000 vols; Dir MAGNÚS JÓNSSON; publs *Greinargerd* (Report, irregular), *Vedráttan* (12 a year).

Libraries and Archives
Reykjavík

Borgarbókasafn Reykjavíkur (City Library of Reykjavík): Grófarhús, Tryggvagötu 15, 101 Reykjavík; tel. 563-1750; fax 563-1705; internet www.borgarbokasafn.is; f. 1923; 500,000 vols; Dir ANNA TORFADOTTIR.

Landsbókasafn Íslands-Háskólabókasafn (National and University Library of Iceland): Arngrímsgötu 3, 107 Reykjavík; tel. 525-5600; fax 525-5615; e-mail upplys@bok.hi.is; internet www .landsbokasafn.is; f. 1994 by amalgamation of the Nat. Library of Iceland (f. 1818) and the Univ. Library (f. 1940); 900,000 books, 16,000 MSS; Dir INGIBJÖRG STEINUNN SVERRISDÓTTIR; Deputy Dir THORSTEINN HALLGRIMSSON; Dir for Services ASLAUG AGNARSDÓTTIR; Dir for Nat. Collns. KRISTIN BRAGADÓTTIR.

Thjódskjalasafn Íslands (National Archives of Iceland): Laugavegur 162, 101 Reykjavík; tel. 590-3300; fax 590-3301; e-mail upplysingar@skjalasafn.is; internet www .archives.is; f. 1882; colln of historical documents since 12th century; Dir ÓLAFUR ÁSGEIRSSON.

Museums and Art Galleries
Reykjavík

Listasafn Einars Jónssonar (National Einar Jónsson Museum): Eiriksgata, POB 1051, 121 Reykjavík; tel. 551-3797; fax 562-3909; e-mail skulptur@skulptur.is; internet www.skulptur.is; sculpture and paintings by Einar Jónsson (1874–1954); Dir JULIANA GOTTSKALKSDOTTIR.

Þjóðminjasafn Íslands (National Museum of Iceland): Suðurgötu 41, 101 Reykjavík; tel. 530-2200; fax 530-2201; e-mail thjodminjasafn@thjodminjasafn.is; internet www.natmus.is; f. 1863; 2,000 objects, dating from the Settlement Age to the present; 1,000 photographs since beginning of 20th century; Dir MARGRÉT HALLGRÍMSDÓTTIR.

Universities

HÁSKÓLINN Á AKUREYRI
(University of Akureyri)

Nordurslod, 600 Akureyri

Telephone: 460-8000
Fax: 460-8999
E-mail: international@unak.is
Internet: www.unak.is
Founded 1987
Languages of instruction: Icelandic, English
Academic year: August to June
Rector: THORSTEINN GUNNARSSON
Number of teachers: 90
Number of students: 1,700

DEANS

Education: Dr GUÐMUNDUR HEIÐAR FRÍMANNSSON
Health Sciences: Dr HERMANN ÓSKARSSON
Law and Social Sciences: Dr ELÍN DÍANNA GUNNARSDÓTTIR
Management and Natural Science: Dr EYJÓLFUR GUÐMUNDSSON

ATTACHED RESEARCH INSTITUTES

Research and Development Centre: Rannsóknahúsið Borgir, v/Norðurslóð, 600 Akureyri; tel. 460-8900; fax 460-8919; e-mail

rha@unak.is; internet www.rha.is; Dir JÓN INGI BENEDIKTSSON.

HÁSKÓLINN Á BIFRÖST
(Bifröst University)

311 Borgarnes
Telephone: 433-3000
Fax: 433-3001
E-mail: bifrost@bifrost.is
Internet: www.bifrost.is
Founded 1918
Private, non-profit
Languages of instruction: Icelandic, English
Academic year: September to August

Library of 7,000 vols

Rector: ÁGÚST EINARSSON
Vice-Rector: BRYNDÍS HLÖÐVERSDÓTTUR
Librarian: ANDREA JÓHANNSDÓTTIR
Int. Coordinator: KRISTÍN ÓLAFSDÓTTIR

Library of 10,000 vols
Number of teachers: 60
Number of students: 1,200

DEANS

Faculty of Business: REYNIR KRISTJANSSON
Faculty of Law: BRYNDÍS HLÖÐVERSDÓTTIR
Faculty of Social Sciences and Economics: JÓN ÓLAFSSON

PROFESSORS

BJARNASON, A., Business
EYÞÓRSSON, G., Social Sciences and Economics
LINDAL, S., Law
MÓSESDÓTTIR, L., Business
ÓLAFSSON, J., Social Sciences and Economics

HÁSKÓLI ÍSLANDS
(University of Iceland)

Saemundargata 6, 101 Reykjavík
Telephone: 525-4000
Fax: 552-1331
E-mail: hi@hi.is
Internet: www.hi.is
Founded 1911
State control
Academic year: September to June
Rector: Prof. KRISTÍN INGÓLFSDÓTTIR
Vice-Rector: Prof. EIRÍKUR TÓMASSON
Dir for Academic Affairs: THÓRDUR KRISTINSSON
Dir for Finance: SIGURDUR J. HAFSTEINSSON
Dir for Human Resources: GUDRUN J. GUDMUNDSDOTTIR
Dir for Internal Review: GUNNLAUGUR H. JÓNSSON
Dir for Int. Relations: KARITAS KVARAN
Dir for Marketing and Public Relations: ÁSTA HRONN MAACK
Dir for Operations and Resources: GUÐMUNDUR R. JÓNSSON
Dir for Science and Research: HALLDÓR JÓNSSON

Library: see Libraries and Archives
Number of teachers: 2,340 (480 tenured, 1,860 non-tenured)
Number of students: 9,900
Publications: *Árbók Háskóla Íslands* (1 a year), *Ritaskrá Háskóla Íslands* (1 a year)

DEANS

Faculty of Economics and Business Admin.: Prof. FRIDRIK M. BALDURSSON
Faculty of Engineering: Prof. SIGURDUR BRYNJÓLFSSON
Faculty of Humanities: Assoc. Prof. ODDNÝ G. SVERRISDÓTTIR
Faculty of Law: Prof. PÁLL HREINSSON
Faculty of Medicine: Prof. STEFÁN B. SIGURÐSSON

Faculty of Nursing: Prof. ERLA KOLBRÚN SVAVARSDÓTTIR
Faculty of Odontology: Assoc. Prof. INGA B. ÁRNADÓTTIR
Faculty of Pharmacy: Prof. ELÍN SOFFÍA ÓLAFSDÓTTIR
Faculty of Science: Assoc. Prof. HÖRDUR FILIPPUSSON
Faculty of Social Sciences: Prof. ÓLAFUR HARDARSON
Faculty of Theology: Prof. HJALTI HUGASON

ATTACHED RESEARCH INSTITUTES

Árni Magnússon Institute in Iceland.
Centre for International Studies.
Centre for Research in the Humanities.
Centre for Women's and Gender Studies.
Dental Institute.
Engineering Research Institute.
Ethical Research Institute.
Fisheries Research Institute.
Icelandic Language Institute.
Institute of Anthropology.
Institute of Biology.
Institute of Business Research.
Institute of Economic Studies.
Institute of Experimental Pathology.
Institute of History.
Institute of Lexicography (Ordabók).
Institute of Linguistics.
Institute of Literary Research.
Institute of Nursing Research.
Institute of Philosophy.
Institute of Theology.
Law Institute.
Nordic Volcanological Institute.
Science Institute.
Sigurdur Nordal Institute: medieval and modern Icelandic culture.

HÁSKÓLINN Í REYKJAVÍK
(University of Reykjavík)

Ofanleiti 2, 103 Reykjavík
Telephone: 510-6200
Fax: 510-6201
E-mail: ru@ru.is
Internet: www.ru.is
Founded 1998
Academic year: August to June
Rector: Dr GUÐFINNA S. BJARNADOTTIR
Dir: HANNA KATRÍN FRIÐRIKSSON
Head Librarian: GUÐRÚN TRYGGVADÓTTIR

DEANS

School of Business: AGNAR HANSSON
School of Computer Science: GÍSLI HJÁLMTÝSSON
School of Law: THÓRÐUR S. GUNNARSSON

KENNARHÁSKÓLI ÍSLANDS
(Iceland University of Education)

Stakkahlíð, 105 Reykjavík
Telephone: 563-3800
Fax: 563-3833
E-mail: khi@khi.is
Internet: www.khi.is
Founded 1908, as Teachers' College of Iceland, present name and status 1997
Academic year: August to July

Depts of undergraduate and postgraduate studies.

Rector: Dr ÓLAFUR PROPPÉ
Number of teachers: 170
Number of students: 1,800

LANDBUNAÐARHÁSKÓLI ÍSLANDS
(Agricultural University of Iceland)

Hvanneyri, 311 Borgarnes
Telephone: 433-5000
Fax: 433-5001
E-mail: lbhi@lbhi.is
Internet: www.hvanneyri.is

Founded 1889

Rector: Dr ÁGÚST SIGURÐSSON,

Library of 18,650 vols
Number of teachers: 28
Number of students: 246

Publication: *Fjölrit Bændaskólans* (1 a year).

LISTAHÁSKÓLI ÍSLANDS
(Iceland Academy of Arts)

Skipholt 1, Reykjavík
Telephone: 552-4000
Fax: 562-3629
E-mail: lhi@lhi.is
Internet: www.lhi.is

Founded 1998, following merger of Reykjavik College of Music, Icelandic College of Arts and Crafts, and Icelandic Drama School

State control

Academic year: August to May

Depts of architecture, drama, fine art, graphic design, music, product design

Rector: HJALMAR H. RAGNARSSON
Dir of Academic Affairs: SIGRUN KR. MAGNUS-DOTTIR
Int. Relations Coordinator and Student Counsellor: HANNA BACHMAN
Library Dir: LÍSA VALDIMARSDÓTTIR

Number of teachers: 37 full-time, 200 part-time
Number of students: 400

TÆKNISKÓLI ÍSLANDS
(Icelandic College of Engineering and Technology)

Höfðabakka 9, 110 Reykjavík
Telephone: 577-1400
Fax: 577-1401

E-mail: icet@ti.is
Internet: vefur.ti.is

Founded 1964

Languages of instruction: Icelandic, English

Academic year: August to May

Rector: GUDBRANDUR STEINTHORSSON

Library of 9,000 vols
Number of teachers: 115 (45 full-time, 70 part-time)
Number of students: 700

College

Búnadarskólinn á Hólum i Hjaltadal (Agricultural School): Hólum i Hjaltadal, 551 Sauðárkrókur; tel. 453-6300; fax 453-6301; e-mail holaskoli@holar.is; f. 1882; 4 profs; depts of aquaculture, rural tourism; Int. Center for Icelandic Horses; library: 6,000 vols; 50 students; Dir HAUKUR JØRUNDARSON.

INDIA

The Higher Education System

The modern higher education system was established while India was under British rule. Among the oldest institutions are Presidency College (founded in 1817), Deccan College Postgraduate and Research Institute (founded in 1821) and Sanskrit College (founded in 1824). In 1857 major universities were founded at Mumbai (formerly Bombay), Madras and Kolkata (formerly Calcutta). The main representative body of Indian universities, the Association of Indian Universities, was founded in 1925 and re-established as a statutory body in 1947, when India gained its independence. In 1953 the University Grants Commission was created to act between the Government and States as the coordinating body on higher education. In the same year a National Council for Higher Education in Rural Areas was established. India had a total of 337 universities and institutions with university status in 2005/06, and some 13,413 university and affiliated colleges. University enrolment was about 14.5m.

Universities are autonomous institutions, mostly funded by the States' governments, except for the 'central' universities, which are funded by the central Government. Universities are classified as either 'unitary' or 'affiliating'. Unitary universities conduct all undergraduate and postgraduate teaching, while in affiliating universities the teaching of undergraduates is conducted by affiliated colleges. There are also two other types of universities, 'deemed' and 'institutions of national importance'. Deemed universities are single-discipline institutions that have been granted university status by the University Grants Commission, and the institutions of national importance are funded directly by the Government but are distinct from central universities. The States account for 90% of university funding, with the rest coming from central Government. Student fees account for a small percentage of universities' income. The National Assessment and Accreditation Council (founded 1994) is the national body responsible for accreditation and quality assurance.

Universities have broadly the same administrative structure. The Vice-Chancellor is both the administrative and the academic head of the university. The Senate or Court, Syndicate and Executive Council or Board of Management are the primary administrative bodies, responsible for institutional budgets and management. The Academic Council oversees all academic aspects of the institution, including teaching and research. Faculties are the most important academic divisions, and are headed by Deans. Boards of Study determine programmes of study.

Admission to higher education is on the basis of one of the different Higher Secondary School Certificates. Standard undergraduate Bachelors degrees last three years, although some programmes in professional fields of study last four years (engineering, dentistry and pharmacy) or five years (architecture). The Bachelors of Laws is either a five-year first degree or a two- to three-year second degree. The first postgraduate degree is the Masters. Admission to the Masters may vary depending on the institution; a Bachelors is the most common requirement, but institutions may also set an entrance examination, while applicants for Masters programmes in the fields of architecture, engineering, pharmacy and technology must sit the Graduate Aptitude Test in Engineering. Masters programmes are two to three years in length. Following the Masters, there is a pre-doctoral programme called the Master of Philosophy (MPhil), a one-and-a-half year course. Finally, the Doctorate (PhD) is awarded three years after the Masters and at least two years after the MPhil. The PhD consists of a thesis based on original research.

Technical and vocational education is overseen by several different bodies: the Central Apprenticeship Council, the National Council for Training in Vocational Trades, the National Council of Educational Research and Training, the Joint Council for Vocationalization of Education and the All India Council for Technical Education. The Joint Council for Vocationalization of Education was founded in 1990 and is the body tasked with implementing and maintaining the national standard of vocational education. Universities, polytechnics and colleges offer one- to four-year Diploma courses in most subjects.

In 2010 the Government was planning to establish new universities and colleges, but it was thought these would not be enough to meet demand. India's 11th five-year plan requires an additional 7m. new places in higher education by 2012 and a total of 16m. additional places in higher education by 2020.

Regulatory and Representative Bodies

GOVERNMENT

Bureau of University and Higher Education and Minority Education, Ministry of Human Resource Development: Shastri Bhavan, New Delhi 110 001; tel. (11) 23382298; fax (11) 23070036; e-mail skumar-mail@nic.in; internet education.nic.in; Min. of Human Resource Devt ARJUN SINGH; Jt Sec. (Addl. charge) SUNIL KUMAR; Dirs R. D. SAHAY, ANUPAMA BHATNAGAR, UPAMANYU BASU, UMA SHANKAR.

Ministry of Culture: Room 334, 'C' Wing, Shastri Bhavan, Dr Rajendra Prasad Rd, New Delhi 110 001; tel. (11); fax (11) 23384867; e-mail js.culture@nic.in; internet indiaculture.nic.in; Min. AMBIKA SONI; Sec. JAWHAR SIRCAR; Jt Sec. N. C. GOYAL; publ. Sanskriti.

Ministry of Human Resource Development: Shastri Bhavan, New Delhi 110 001; tel. (11) 23782698; fax (11) 23382365; e-mail hrm@sb.nic.in; internet education.nic.in; Minister ARJUN SINGH.

ACCREDITATION

National Assessment and Accreditation Council: POB 1075, Nagarbhavi, Bangalore 560072, Karnataka; tel. (80) 23210261; fax (80) 23210270; e-mail naac@blr.vsnl.net.in; internet www.naacindia.org; Dir Prof. H. A. RANGANATH (acting).

FUNDING

University Grants Commission (UGC): Bahadur Shah Zafar Marg, New Delhi 110 002; tel. (11) 23232701; fax (11) 23231797; e-mail webmaster@ugc.ac.in; internet www.ugc.ac.in; f. 1953; attached to Dept of Higher Education, Min. of Human Resource Devt; library of 41,850 vols; Chair. Prof. S. K. THORAT; Sec. R. P. AGARWAL; publs *Bulletin of Higher Education, Journal of Higher Education, University Development in India* (annual statistical review).

NATIONAL BODIES

All India Council for Technical Education (AICTE): 7th Fl., Chanderlok Bldg, Janpath, New Delhi 110 001; tel. (11) 23724151; fax (11) 23724183; e-mail admin@aicte.ernet.in; internet www.aicte.ernet.in; f. 1945; Chair. of Ccl Prof. DAMODAR ACHARYA; Vice-Chair. of Ccl Dr R. A. YADAV; publ. *Technical Education in independent India 1999 (Compendium).*

Association of Indian Universities: AIU House, 16 Comrade Indrajit Gupta Marg (Kotla Marg), New Delhi 110 002; tel. (11) 23230059; fax (11) 23232131; e-mail info@aiuweb.org; internet www.aiuweb.org; f. 1925; library of 20,000 vols, 150 periodicals, annual reports, calendars, handbooks and Act of the various univs and Supreme Court of India judgments in the field of education; Pres. Prof. A. M. PATHAN; Sec.-Gen. Prof. DAYANAND DONGAONKAR; publs *Equivalence of Foreign Degrees* (irregular), *Handbook of Computer Education* (1 a year), *Handbook of Distance Education* (1 a year), *Handbook of Engineering Education* (1 a year), *Handbook* *of Library and Information Science* (1 a year), *Handbook of Management Education* (1 a year), *Handbook of Medical Education* (1 a year), *Scholarships for Study Abroad and at Home* (1 a year), *Universities Handbook* (every 2 years).

Indian Adult Education Association: 17B Indraprastha Estate, New Delhi 110 002; tel. (11) 23379306; fax (11) 23378206; e-mail iaea_india@yahoo.com; internet www .iaea-india.org/; f. 1939 under the Indian Socs Registration Act 1860; 2,500 mems; library: Amarnath Jha Library (f. 1957) 23,500 books, 110 periodicals; Pres. Prof. K. C. CHOUDHARY; Gen.-Sec. Dr MADAN SINGH; publs *Indian Journal of Adult Education* (4 a year), *Indian Journal of Population Education* (4 a year), *Jago Aur Jagao* (in Hindi 12 a year), *Proudh Shiksha* (in Hindi, 12 a year).

National Council of Educational Research and Training: Sri Aurobindo Marg, New Delhi 110 016; tel. (11) 26560620; fax (11) 26868419; e-mail director .ncert@nic.in; internet www.ncert.nic.in; f. 1961 with the aim of improving school education; academic adviser to the Min. of Human Resource Devt; coordinates research and devt in all branches of education; organizes pre- and in-service training; publishes school textbooks, instructional material for teachers and educational surveys; 8 major constituent units: Nat. Institute of Education and Central Institute of Educational Technology in New Delhi, Central Institute of Vocational Education in Bhopal and 5 regional Institutes of Education at Ajmer, Bhopal, Bhubaneswar, Mysore and Shillong; Pres. The Union Min. of Human Resource Devt; Dir Prof. KRISHNA KUMAR; publs *Indian Educational Abstracts*, *Indian Educational Review* (2 a year), *Journal of Indian Education*, *Journal of Value Education*, *School Science* (4 a year), *The Primary Teacher*.

Learned Societies

GENERAL

India International Centre: 40 Lodi Estate, Max Mueller Marg, Lodhi Rd H.O., New Delhi 110003; tel. (11) 24619431; internet www.iicdelhi.nic.in; f. 1958; int. cultural organization for promotion of amity and understanding between the different communities in the world; programme of lectures, discussions, film evenings, etc.; mems: 3,746 individuals, 256 corporate (incl. 35 univs); library of 31,000 vols, also houses the India Collection of 3,500 rare documents on British India and the Himalayan Club Library of 900 vols; Pres. Dr KAPILA VATSYAYAN; Dir N. N. VOHRA; Sec. N. H. RAMACHANDRAN; publs *IIC Diary* (6 a year), *IIC Quarterly*.

Indian Council for Cultural Relations (ICCR): Azad Bhawan, Indraprastha Estate, New Delhi 110002; tel. (11) 23379309; fax (11) 23378639; e-mail president@iccrindia .org; internet www.iccrindia.org; f. 1950 to establish and strengthen cultural relations between India and other countries; branch offices in Mumbai, Kolkata, Madras, Bangalore, Chandigarh, Lucknow, Trivandrum and Hyderabad; cultural centres in Georgetown (Guyana), Paramaribo (Suriname), Moscow (Russia), Port Louis (Mauritius), Jakarta (Indonesia), Berlin (Germany), Cairo (Egypt), Tashkent (Uzbekistan), Almaty (Kazakhstan) and London (United Kingdom); activities incl. exchange visits between scholars, artists and people of eminence in the field of art and culture; exchange of exhibitions; int. confs and seminars, lectures

by renowned scholars incl. Azad Memorial Lectures; establishment of chairs and centres of Indian studies abroad and welfare of overseas students in India; admin. of Jawaharlal Nehru Award for Int. Understanding; presentation of books and Indian art objects to univs, libraries and museums in other countries; library: over 55,000 vols on India and other countries; Pres. Dr KARAN SINGH; Dir-Gen. PAVAN K. VARMA; publs interpretations of Indian art and culture and translations of Indian works into foreign languages, *African Quarterly* (in English, 4 a year), *Gagananchal* (Hindi, 4 a year), *Indian Horizons*, *Papeles de la India* (in Spanish, 4 a year), *Rencontre avec l'Inde* (in French, 4 a year), *Thaqafat-ul-Hind* (in Arabic, 4 a year).

Indian Institute of World Culture: No. 6 Shri B. P. Wadia Rd, Basavangudi, Bangalore 560004; tel. (80) 26678581; e-mail iiwc@ vsnl.net; internet www.ultindia.org/ indian_institute_of_world_c.html; f. 1945; a sister instn of ULT dedicated to further the first objective of the Theosophical Movement Universal Brotherhood of Humanity; Mumbai Office; provides opportunities for cultural and intellectual devt; promotes exchange of thought between India and other countries and raises the consideration of nat. and world problems to the plane of moral and spiritual values and to foster a sense of universal brotherhood; 3,100 mems; library of 40,000 vols, 400 periodicals; Pres. Justice M. N. VENKATACHALIAH; Vice-Pres. R. N. NAGARAJ; Hon. Sec. Y. M. BALAKRISHNA; publs *Bulletin* (12 a year), *Transactions*.

Jammu and Kashmir Academy of Art, Culture and Languages: Lal Mandi, Srinagar, Kashmir 190001; tel. (191) 2542640 (Jammu); tel. (8649) 232379 (Srinagar); fax (191) 2542640 (Jammu); fax (8649) 232379 (Srinagar); internet jkc.weebly.com/home .html; f. 1958; promotes arts, culture and languages of the State; library of 20,000 vols, 650 rare MSS, 250 laminated photographs, 90 opera and folk song recordings; collections of gramophone records, cassettes, paintings, jewellery, calligraphy, costumes, contemporary paintings and sculpture; Pres. Gen. K. V. KRISHNA RAO; Sec. ZAFFAR IQBAL KHAN MANHAS; publs *Encyclopaedia Kashmirana*, *Hamara Adab* (1 a year anthology in Urdu, Kashmiri, Gojri, Pahari, Dogri, Punjabi, Hindi, Ladakhi), *Sheeraza* (12 a year in Urdu, 6 a year in Kashmiri, Dogri, Punjabi and Hindi, 4 a year in Ladakhi, Pahari, Gojri and 1 a year in English and Balti).

AGRICULTURE, FISHERIES AND VETERINARY SCIENCE

Agri-Horticultural Society of India: 1 Alipore Rd, Kolkata 700027; tel. (33) 24791713; fax (33) 24793580; e-mail ahsi@ vsnl.net; internet www.agrihorticultureindia .com/; f. 1820; 1,300 mems; library of 400 vols; Pres. B. K. NAHATA; Sr Vice-Pres. GAURAV SWARUP; Vice-Pres. SHARAD KHAITAN; Sec. NIRUPOM SEN; publs *Encyclopedia of Himalayan Medicinal Flora*, *Horticultural Journal* (4 a year).

Agri-Horticultural Society of Madras: New-134 Cathedral Rd, Gopalapuram, Chennai 600086; tel. (44) 28116816; f. 1835; 3,410 mems; Patron HE The GOVERNOR OF TAMIL NADU; Chair. R. SADASIVAM; Hon. Sec. Prof. J. RAMCHANDRAN.

Crop Improvement Society of India: Dept of Plant Breeding and Genetics, Punjab Agricultural University, Ludhiana 141004, Punjab; tel. (161) 2401960; fax (161) 2400945; e-mail info@pau.edu; f. 1974; aims to disseminate knowledge on crop improvement through lectures, symposia, publications, to arrange excursions and

explorations, and to cooperate with national and international organizations; 200 mems; Pres. Dr G. S. SIDHU; Sec. Dr G. S. CHAHAL; publ. *Crop Improvement* (2 a year).

Indian Dairy Association: IDA House, Sector IV, R. K. Puram, New Delhi 110022; tel. (11) 26170781; fax (11) 26174719; e-mail ida@nde.vsnl.net.in; internet www .indairyasso.org; f. 1948; 3,000 mems; library: Mansingh Bhai Patel Library of 700 vols; 100 periodicals; Pres. Dr N. R BHASIN; Vice-Pres N. A. SHAIKH, ARUN NARKE; publs *Indian Dairyman* (12 a year), *Indian Journal of Dairy Science* (6 a year).

Indian Society of Agricultural Economics: Krishi Vikas Sadan, First Floor, (Near Dr. Antonio Da Silva Technical High School) Veer Savarkar Marg, Dadar (W) Mumbai 400028; tel. (22) 24374789; fax (22) 24374790; e-mail isae@bom7.vsnl.net.in; internet www.isaeindia.org; f. 1939; promotes the study of social and economic problems of agriculture and rural areas, and technical competence for teaching and research in agricultural economics and allied subjects; 1,416 mems and subscribers; library of 22,280 vols; Pres. Dr C. RAMASAMY; Vice-Pres. Prof. L. K. MOHANA RAO; Vice-Pres. Dr SUDHA MYSORE; Vice-Pres. Dr R. K. PANDA; Vice-Pres. K. V. KRISHNAN; Vice-Pres. Dr R. S. BAWA; Hon. Sec. and Treas. Dr C. L. DADHICH; Hon. Jt Sec. VIJAYA VENKATESH; publs books, reports, papers, *Comparative Experience of Agricultural Development in Developing Countries of Asia and the South-East Since World War II* (1972), *Evaluation of Land Reforms (with special reference to the Western Region of India)*, *The Indian Journal of Agricultural Economics* (4 a year).

Indian Society of Soil Science: First Fl, National Societies Block, National Agricultural Science Centre Complex, Dev Prakash Shastri Marg, Pusa, New Delhi 110012; tel. (11) 25841991; fax (11) 25841529; e-mail isss .secretary@gmail.com; internet www .isss-india.org/; f. 1934; cultivates and promotes soil science and its allied disciplines and disseminates knowledge of soil science and its applications; cooperation with Int. Soc. of Soil Science and similar orgs; organizes seminars symposia, confs, meetings, etc.; ; 2,350 mems; Pres. Dr A. K. SINGH; Vice-Pres Dr J. P. SHARMA, Dr B. P. SINGH; Sec. Dr R. K. RATTAN; publs *Bulletin* (irregular), *Journal* (4 a year).

ARCHITECTURE AND TOWN PLANNING

Indian Institute of Architects: Prospect Chambers Annexe, Dr D. N. Rd, Fort, Mumbai 400001; tel. (22) 22046972; fax (22) 22832516; e-mail iia@vsnl.com; internet www.iia-india.org; f. 1929; promotes aesthetic, scientific and practical efficiency of the architectural profession; sponsors architectural education; sets qualifying standards for the profession; provides a forum for discussing related subjects,; 10,233 mems, incl. 1,191 Fellows, 28 Hon. Fellows, 8,624 assocs, 95 Licentiates, 1,850 students, 65 retired; library of 3,000 vols; Pres. VINAY M. PARELKAR; Vice-Pres. PANDURANG POTNIS; Hon. Treas. DEBABRATA GHOSH; Jt Hon. Sec. VIJAY GARG; publ. *Journal* (12 a year).

BIBLIOGRAPHY, LIBRARY SCIENCE AND MUSEOLOGY

Indian Association of Special Libraries and Information Centres (IASLIC): P. 291, CIT Scheme No. 6M, Kankurgachi, Kolkata 700054; tel. (33) 3349651; e-mail iaslic@vsnl.net; internet www.iaslic.org; f. 1955; promotes study and research into special librarianship and information science; conducts short-term training courses on the subject, holds confs and coordinates activities among special libraries and spec. interest groups; publishes seminar and conf. papers and books on information and library science; translation and reprographic services; 2,200 mems; library of 2,600 vols, 50 current periodicals; Hon. Pres. Prof. S. B. GHOSH; Hon. Gen. Sec. D. K. NAG; publs *Conference Proceedings, IASLIC Bulletin* (4 a year), *Indian Library Science Abstracts (ILSA)* (1 a year), *Seminar Proceedings.*

Indian Library Association: A/40–41, Flat 201, Ansal Bldgs, Dr Mukherjee Nagar, Delhi 110009; tel. and fax (22) 27651743; internet www.ilaindia.org; f. 1933; 4,000 mems; library of 600 vols; Pres. Prof. C. R. KARISIDDAPPA; Sec. D. V. SINGH; publ. *ILA Bulletin* (4 a year).

Museums Association of India: c/o Dir, State Museum, Banarasi Bagh, Lucknow 226001; tel. (522) 2206157; fax (522) 2206158; f. 1865; professional discussions, seminars, conferences, exhibitions, courses in museology etc.; 700 individual and institutional mems; library of 25,000 books, 5,000 research journals; Dir Dr RAKESH TIWARI (acting); publ. *Bulletin of Museums and Archeology.*

National Book Trust, India: A-5, Green Park, New Delhi 110016; tel. (11) 26568052; fax (11) 26851795; e-mail nbtindia@ndb.vsnl .net.in; internet www.nbtindia.org.in; f. 1957; an autonomous body set up by the Govt; activities incl. publishing moderately priced books for general readers in 12 Indian languages and English, giving assistance to authors, illustrators and publishers for producing books for children, neo-literates and the higher education sector, organizing book fairs, exhibitions, seminars and workshops, and promoting Indian books abroad; Chair. Prof. BIPAN CHANDRA; Dir NUZHAT HASSAN.

ECONOMICS, LAW AND POLITICS

All India Bar Association: DS-423/424, New Rajinder Nagar, New Delhi 110060; tel. (11) 28743284; fax (11) 28743285; e-mail allindiabar@gmail.com; internet www .allindiabar.org; f. 1959; Chair. ADISH C. AGGARWALA.

Indian Council of World Affairs: Sapru House, Barakhamba Rd, New Delhi 110001; tel. (11) 23359159; fax (11) 23311208; internet www.icwa.in; f. 1943; non-governmental instn for the study of Indian and int. relations and world affairs; research library; 1,500 mems; library of 128,000 vols, 376 periodicals, UN and EU depository; Pres. HARCHARAN SINGH JOSH; Hon. Sec.-Gen. S. C. PARASHER; Chief Librarian CHHAYA SHARMA; publs *India Quarterly, Foreign Affairs* (12 a year).

Indian Economic Association: Delhi School of Economics, Delhi 110009; e-mail iejpanch@yahoo.co.in; f. 1918; Pres. Prof. G. K. CHADHA; Vice-Pres. Prof. L. K. MOHANA RAO; Hon. Sec. Dr ANIL KUMAR THAKUR; publ. *Indian Economic Journal.*

The Indian Law Institute: Opposite Supreme Court, Bhagwandas Rd, New Delhi 110001; tel. (11) 23386321; fax (11) 23782140; e-mail ili@ili.ac.in; internet www .ilidelhi.org; f. 1956; Deemed Univ.; promotes advanced studies and research in law and reform of admin. of law and justice; 3,500 mems; library of 75,000 vols; Pres. CHIEF JUSTICE OF INDIA; Dir Prof. D. S. SENGAR; Registrar DALIP KUMAR; publs *Annual Survey of Indian Law, Journal of Indian Law Institute* (4 a year).

Institute of Chartered Accountants of India: ICAI Bhawan, Indraprastha Marg, Post Box No. 7100, New Delhi 110002; tel. (11) 39893989; fax (11) 30110580; e-mail icaiho@icai.org; internet www.icai.org; f. 1949, a statutory body est. under an Act of Parliament; a statutory body for the regulation of the profession of chartered accountants in India; contributes in the fields of education, professional devt, maintenance of high accounting, auditing and ethical standards; 161,859 mems; library: Central Ccl Library 62,000 vols; Pres. AMARJIT CHOPRA; Vice-Pres. G. RAMASWAMY; publs *Gateway to International Trade-E Communiqué of the Committee on Trade Laws & WTO, ICAI Patrika, Management Accounting and Business Finance, The Chartered Accountant* (12 a year).

EDUCATION

All India Association for Educational Research: N1/55 IRC Village, Bhubaneswar 751015; tel. (674) 2550611; e-mail indianeducationalresearch@yahoo.co.in; internet www.aiaer.net; f. 1987; holds annual and periodical confs on various themes and publishes a journal, both print and online; 2,760 mems; Patron Prof. B. K. PASSI; Pres. Prof. SURAJ PRAKASH MALHOTRA; Gen. Sec. and Editor Prof. SUNIL BEHARI MOHANTY; Treas. DHRUBA CHARAN MISHRA; publ. *Journal of All India Association for Educational Research* (2 a year).

Hyderabad Educational Conference: 19 Bachelors' Quarters, Jawaharlal Nehru Rd, Hyderabad, Deccan; f. 1913; promotes academic research, assists needy students and furthers education in Andhra Pradesh; library: over 9,500 vols; Pres. SYED MASOOD ALI; Sec. GHOUSE MOHIUDDIN; publs *Educational Annual* (in Urdu), *Proceedings of Public Sessions* (in Urdu), *Ruh-e-tarraqui* (in Urdu).

J. N. Petit Institute: 312 Dr Dadabhoy Naoroji Rd, Fort, Mumbai 400001; tel. (22) 22048463; e-mail petitheritage_01@yahoo.co .in; f. 1856; organizes lectures and makes accessible literary, scientific and philosophic works; 4,210 mems; library: see Libraries and Archives; Pres. Sir DINSHAW M. PETIT; Hon. Secs RODA ANKALESARIA, N. M. PATEL.

National Bal Bhavan: Kotla Rd, New Delhi 110002; tel. (11) 23232672; e-mail nbb@bol .net.in; internet www.nationalbalbhavan.nic .in/; f. 1956; autonomous institution est. by Min. of Human Resource Devt; provides planned environment and creative activities based on Arts and Science to children between the ages of 5 and 16; provides leadership and guidance to teachers towards fostering a creative approach in teaching of art and science, organizes orientation courses for teachers and parents, runs a repertory theatre for children, the Nat. Children's Museum and a nat. training resource centre; library: children's library of 43,347 vols, reference library of 11,584 vols; Chair. Begum BILKES I. LATIF; Vice-Chair. ZENA BERNADETTE VIJAY KUMAR; Sec. AMITA SHAW; publ. *Akkar Bakkar and Akkar Bakkar Times* (booklet entirely produced by the children).

FINE AND PERFORMING ARTS

All-India Fine Arts and Crafts Society: 1 Rafi Marg, New Delhi 110001; tel. (11) 23711315; fax (11) 23715366; e-mail aifacsarts@yahoo.co.in; internet www.aifacs .org.in; f. 1928; holds art exhibitions incl. the All India Annual Art Exhibition of painting, photography, sculpture, graphics, traditional art and water colours and drawings, exhibitions of Indian art abroad and exhibitions of arts and crafts from foreign countries in India, talks and film shows on art; 550 mems; library of 5,300 vols; Pres. RAM V. SUTAR;

Chair. Prof. PARAMJEET SINGH (acting); publs *Arts News* (12 a year), *Roopa Lekha* (1 a year).

Art Society of India: Sandhurst House, Shop 524 S.V.P. Rd, Bandra East, Mumbai 400051; tel. (22) 23888550; f. 1918; promotes art and artists all over India; colln of rare art books; 650 mems; library of 2,000 vols; Pres. P. DAHANUKAR; Hon. Sec. B. R. KULKARNI.

India International Photographic Council: 21 Bharti Artists Colony, Vikas Marg, New Delhi 110092; tel. (11) 65751099; e-mail iipc@mail.com; f. 1983; promotes art and science of photography; 4,000 mems; publ. *IIPC Photographic Journal* (12 a year).

Indian Society of Oriental Art (Calcutta): 15 Park St, Kolkata 700016; tel. (33) 22174805; f. 1907; 320 mems; promotes and researches all aspects of ancient and contemporary Indian and Oriental art; library of 3,500 vols; Sec. INDIRA NAG CHAUDHURI; publ. *Journal* (1 a year).

Lalit Kala Akademi/National Academy of Art: Rabindra Bhavan, Ferozshah Rd, New Delhi 110001; tel. (11) 23387241; e-mail lka@lalitkala.gov.in; internet lalitkala.gov .in; f. 1954; autonomous, govt-financed; sponsors nat. and int. exhibitions, such as the Nat. Exhibition of Art (annual) and Triennale-India; arranges seminars, lectures, films, etc.; Sec. Dr SUDHANAR SHARMA; publs *Lalit Kala Ancient* (2 a year), *Lalit Kala Contemporary* (4 a year), *Samkaleen Kala* (in Hindi, 4 a year).

National Academy of Music, Dance and Drama/Sangeet Natak Akademi: Rabindra Bhavan, Feroze Shah Rd, New Delhi 110001; tel. (11) 23381833; fax (11) 23385715; e-mail help@sangeetnatak.org; internet www.sangeetnatak.org; f. 1953; preserves and develops the performing arts of India; documents the performing arts through films, tapes and photographs; maintains a museum of musical instruments, costumes, masks and puppets; offers financial assistance to music, dance and theatre institutions; administers the Jawaharlal Nehru Manipur Dance Academy, Imphal, Kathak Kendra, Delhi, and Rabindra Rangashala, Delhi; conducts festivals, seminars; gives awards and fellowships for outstanding work; 66 mems; library of 22,000 vols and audio-visual library of tapes and discs; Chair. Dr RAM NIWAS MIRDHA; Sec. JAYANT KASTUAR; publ. *Sangeet Natak* (4 a year).

South India Society of Painters: No. 13, 111 Trust Cross, Chennai 600028.

The Bombay Art Society: Jehangir Art Gallery, Mahatma Gandhi Rd, Mumbai 400023; tel. (22) 22044058; e-mail contactus@bombayartsociety.org; internet www.bombayartsociety.org; f. 1888; 450 life mems; 150 ord. mems; 200 student mems; holds All India Annual Art Exhibition; Pres. VIJAY RAUT; Chair. VITTHAL LOKHANDKAR; Hon. Secs Prof. NARENDRA VICHARE, SURENDRA JAGTAP; Hon. Treas. CHANDRAJIT YADAV; publs *Art Journal*, illustrated catalogues of exhibitions.

HISTORY, GEOGRAPHY AND ARCHAEOLOGY

Bharata Itihasa Samshodhaka Mandala: 1321 Sadashiva Peth, Pune 411030; tel. (20) 24472581; f. 1910; collects, conserves and publishes historical materials; colln of 3,500 coins; 33,000 Persian, Sanskrit and Marathi MSS; 1,600,000 documents, about 1,200 old Indian paintings; 1,000 copperplates, sculptures and other antiquarian objects, museum of paintings; 675 mems; library of 40,000 vols; Pres. (vacant); Chair. Dr S. GOKHALE; Sec. Dr S. M. BHAVE; publs *Journal* (4 a year), *Puraskrita Granthamala, Sviya Granthamala Series.*

Geographical Society of India: c/o Dept of Geography, Univ. of Calcutta, 35 Ballygunge Circular Rd, Kolkata 700019; tel. (33) 24753681; f. 1933; geographical lectures, seminars, excursions and exhibitions; encouragement of geographical research and training; 750 mems; library of 14,200 vols, 5,709 journals; Pres. S. P. DASGUPTA; Sec. DURGADAS SAHA; publ. *Geographical Review of India* (4 a year).

LANGUAGE AND LITERATURE

Alliance Française: 2 Aurangzeb Rd, New Delhi 110001; tel. (11) 23014682; fax (11) 23014364; e-mail dgaf@afindia.org; internet www.afindia.org; offers courses and examinations in French language and culture and promotes cultural exchange with France; attached teaching centres in Ahmedabad, Bangalore, Bhopal, Chandigarh, Chennai, Coimbatore, Hyderabad, Indore, Jaipur, Karikal, Kochi, Kolkata, Madurai, Mahe, Mumbai, Panjim, Pondichery, Pune, Rajkot, Secunderabad and Trivandrum.

British Council: British High Commission, 17 Kasturba Gandhi Marg, New Delhi 110001; tel. (11) 23711401; fax (11) 23710717; e-mail delhi.enquiry@in .britishcouncil.org; internet www .britishcouncil.org/india; teaching centre; offers courses and exams in English language and British culture and promotes cultural exchange with the UK; attached offices in Hyderabad, Pune, Chandigarh, Bangalore, Chennai, Kolkata and Mumbai; library of 30,000 vols; Dir EDMUND MARSDEN.

Kendriya Hindi Nideshalaya (Central Hindi Directorate): Min. of Human Resource Devt, Dept of Education, West Block 7, R. K. Puram, New Delhi 110066; tel. (11) 26178454; fax (11) 26100758; e-mail pushplata_taneja@rediffmail.com; internet www.hindinideshalaya.nic.in; f. 1960; preparation and publ. of bilingual and trilingual dictionaries of Indian and foreign languages; teaching of Hindi by correspondence courses to Indians and foreigners; extension courses; c. 300 mems; library of 83,100 vols; Dir Dr K. VIJAY KUMAR; publs *Bhasha* (4 a year), *UNESCO DOOT* (12 a year), *Varshiki* (1 a year).

Linguistic Society of India: c/o Dept of Linguistics, Deccan College Postgraduate and Research Institute, Pune 411006; tel. (20) 26698744; e-mail secretaryil@gmail.com; internet www.lsi.org.in; f. 1928; 700 mems; library of 6,000 vols; Pres. K. RANGAN; Vice-Pres. ANVITA ABBI; publ. *Indian Linguistics* (1 a year).

Madras Literary Society: College Rd, Chennai 600006; tel. (44) 28279666; f. 1812, became Auxiliary of the Royal Asiatic Soc. of Great Britain and Ireland 1830; library of 150,000 vols, incl. 30,000 19th-century edns; Pres. M. GOPALAKRISHNAN; Hon. Sec. U. RAMESH RAO; publs *Madras Journal of Literature and Science, Transactions of the Literary Society of Madras.*

Max Müller Bhavan (Goethe-Institut): 3 Kasturba Gandhi Marg, New Delhi 110001; tel. (11) 23329506; fax (11) 23325534; e-mail info@delhi.goethe.org; internet www.goethe .de/newdelhi; the 6 brs of the Goethe-Institut in India are named after the German Indologist Max Müller (1823–1900); offers courses and examinations in German language and culture and promotes cultural exchange with Germany; attached centres in Bangalore, Chennai, Mumbai, Kolkata and Pune; Dir for S Asia Region HEIKO SIEVERS.

Mythic Society: 2 Nrupathunga Rd, Bangalore 560002; tel. (80) 22215034; f. 1909; promotes the study of mythology, archaeology, indology and Karnataka history; 400 mems; library of 24,000 vols, incl. spec. collns of Mysore history; Pres. Dr SURYANATH U. KAMATH; Sec. Dr M. K. L. N. SASTRY; publ. *Journal* (4 a year).

PEN All-India Centre: Theosophy Hall, 40 New Marine Lines, Mumbai 400020; tel. (22) 22032175; e-mail india.pen@gmail.com; f. 1933; Founder SOPHIA WADIA; Pres. Dr DAUJI GUPTA; Sec.-Treas. RANJIT HOSKOTE (acting); publ. *The Indian PEN* (4 a year).

Sahitya Akademi/National Academy of Letters: Rabindra Bhavan, 35 Ferozeshah Rd, New Delhi 110001; tel. (11) 23387064; fax (11) 23382428; e-mail secy@ndb.vsnl.net.in; internet www.sahitya-akademi.org; f. 1954; devt of Indian literature, coordination of literary activities in the Indian languages and research in Indian languages and literature; publ. of literary works; promotion of cultural exchanges with other countries; awards annual prizes for original works and translations; organizes seminars, symposia and workshops on literary subjects; Gen. Ccl consists of 8 eminent persons in the field of letters elected in their personal capacity, nominees of the Central and State Govts, 20 reps of the univs and 1 rep. of each of the 22 languages of India recognized by the Akademi, and 1 rep. each of the Lalit Kala Akademi, the Sangeet Natak Akademi, the Indian Ccl for Cultural Relations, the Raja Rammohun Roy Library Foundation and the Indian Publishers' Asscns; library of 125,000 vols; Pres. Prof. SUNIL GANGOPADHYAY; Vice-Pres. S. S. NOOR; Sec. AGRAHARA KRISHNA MURTHY; publs *Indian Literature* (in English, 6 a year), *Samakaleena Bharatiya Sahitya* (in Hindi, 6 a year), *Sanskrita Pratibha* (in Sanskrit, 2 a year).

Sanskrit Academy: Mandya Dist., Karnataka, Melkote, Karnataka 571431; tel. (8236) 48781; e-mail asrbng@vsnl.com; internet sanskritacademy.org; f. 1927; promotion and propagation of Sanskrit language, publication of studies and expositions of Sanskrit works, org. of oratorical and recitation competitions, regular lectures and seminars in Sanskrit and Tamil on well-known Sanskrit poets and philosophers by eminent scholars, occasional production of Sanskrit drama; library of 25,000 vols of philosophy, literature, culture, vedanta, aesthetics, agriculture, etc.; 200 mems; publ. *Sambhashana Sandeshah* (12 a year).

Tamil Nadu Tamil Development and Research Council: Fort St George, Chennai 600009; f. 1959; development of Tamil in all its aspects, especially as a modern language; library of 27,000 vols, 320 MSS, 85 periodicals; 16 teachers; 50 students; Chair. CHIEF MINISTER; Vice-Chair. MINISTER FOR EDUCATION; Sec. DIRECTOR OF TAMIL DEVELOPMENT; publ. *Tamil Nadu Tamil Bibliography.*

MEDICINE

All-India Ophthalmological Society: c/o Dr Lalit Verma, Dr R. P. Centre for Ophthalmic Sciences, All-India Institute of Medical Sciences, Ansari Nagar, New Delhi 110029; tel. (11) 26593187; fax (11) 26852919; e-mail lalitverma@yahoo.com; internet www.aios.org; f. 1930; cultivation and promotion of the study and practice of ophthalmic sciences with a view to render service to the community and to promote social contacts among ophthalmologists; 7,394 mems; Pres. Dr K. P. S. MALIK; Gen. Sec. Dr LALIT VERMA; publ. *Indian Journal of Ophthalmology* (4 a year).

Association of Medical Physicists of India: c/o Radiological Physics and Advisory Div., Bhabha Atomic Research Centre, CT & CRS Bldg, Anushaktinagar, Mumbai 400094; tel. (22) 24447077; e-mail office@ampi.org.in; internet www.ampi.org.in; f. 1976; organizes annual conf., workshops, lectures, awards, research grants, travel fellowships within India; 680 mems representing medical physicists, radiation oncologists and others interested in this field; Pres. Prof. S. K. KOUL; Vice-Pres. A. M. PENDSE; Sec. Dr R. M. NEHRU; publ. *Journal of Medical Physics* (4 a year).

Association of Surgeons of India: 21 Swamy Sivananda Salai, Chepauk, Chennai 600005; tel. (44) 25383459; fax (44) 25367095; e-mail asi@md5.vsnl.net.in; internet www.asiindia.org; f. 1938; 12,006 mems; library: approx. 12,000 vols; Pres. Dr R. P. SRIVASTAVA; Pres. Elect NARENDRA KUMAR PANDEY; Hon. Sec. Dr A. RATHNASWAMI; publ. *Indian Journal of Surgery* (6 a year).

Bombay Medical Union: Blavatsky Lodge Bldg, Grant Rd, Mumbai 400007; tel. (22) 23612880; f. 1883; 250 mems; Pres. Dr U. N. BASTODKAR; Sec. Dr Smt. M. K. THACKER.

Federation of Obstetric & Gynaecological Societies of India: Model Residency CHS, Ground Floor, 605 Bapurao Jagtap Marg, Jacob Circle, Mahalaxmi East, Mumbai 400011; tel. (22) 23021648; fax (22) 23021383; e-mail fogsi@bom7.vsnl.net.in; internet www.fogsi.org; f. 1950; organizes annual congress for the exchange of views in the various aspects of the subject; organizes workshops on family planning, etc.; medical education programme; holds periodic international seminars; 24,000 mems; Pres. Dr SANJAY GUPTE; Sec.-Gen. Dr P. K. SHAH; publ. *Journal of Obstetrics & Gynaecology of India* (6 a year).

Helminthological Society of India: Dept of Parasitology, UP College of Veterinary Science and Animal Husbandry, Mathura; Pres. Prof. S. N. SINGH; Treas.-Sec. Prof. B. P. PANDE; publ. *Indian Journal of Helminthology* (2 a year).

Indian Association of Parasitologists: 110 Chittaranjan Ave, Kolkata 700012; Pres. Dr H. N. RAY; Sec. Dr A. B. CHAUDHURY.

Indian Cancer Society: Lady Ratan Tata Medical & Research Centre, M. Karve Rd, Cooperage, Mumbai 400021; tel. (22) 22029942; fax (22) 22872745; e-mail info@ indiancancersociety.org; internet www .indiancancersociety.org; f. 1951; charitable trust subsisting on donations; supports cancer research; aids sufferers from cancer, improves facilities for diagnosis, treatment and rehabilitation; educates the public and the profession; and organizes nat. confs; diagnostic, treatment and research centre in South Mumbai (Lady Ratan Tata Medical and Research Centre); Chair. Dr S. H. ADVANI; Vice-Chair. NIHAL KAVIRATHE; Hon. Sec. and Man. Trustee Dr ARUN P. KURKURE; publ. *Indian Journal of Cancer* (4 a year).

Indian Medical Association: I.M.A. House, Indraprastha Marg, New Delhi 110002; tel. (11) 23370009; fax (11) 23379470; e-mail inmedici@vsnl.com; internet www.ima-india.org; f. 1928; 125,000 mems; Pres. Dr ASHOK ADHAO; Hon. Gen. Sec. Dr DHARAM PRAKASH; publs *Apka Swasthya* (12 a year), *Family Medicine India* (4 a year), *I.M.A. News* (12 a year), *Journal* (12 a year), *Your Health* (12 a year).

Indian Pharmaceutical Association: Kalina, Santacruz (East), Mumbai 400098; tel. (22) 26671072; fax (22) 26670744; e-mail ipacentre@ipapharma.org; internet www .ipapharma.org; f. 1939; 10,000 mems; Pres.

Dr B. SURESH; Chair. for Industrial Pharmacy Div. and Vice-Pres. J. A. S. GIRI; Chair. for Community Pharmacy Div. and Vice-Pres. RAJ VAIDYA; Chair. for Regulatory Affairs Div. and Vice-Pres. A. KRISHNA DEV; Chair. for Education Div. and Vice-Pres. T. V. NARAYANA; Chair. for Hospital Pharmacy Div. and Vice-Pres. Dr R. N. GUPTA; Hon. Gen. Sec. S. D. JOAG; publs *Indian Journal of Pharmaceutical Sciences* (6 a year), *Pharma Times* (12 a year).

Indian Public Health Association: 110 Chittaranjan Ave, Kolkata 700073, West Bengal; tel. (33) 32913895; e-mail office@ iphaonline.org; internet www.iphaonline.org; f. 1956; promotion of public health and allied sciences; 22 state and local brs; holds Annual Convention, meetings, confs, etc.; organizes training programme on various areas of interest of public health; 3,890 mems; Pres. Dr ASHOK KUMAR; Gen. Sec. Prof. Dr SANDIP K. RAY; publ. *Indian Journal of Public Health* (4 a year).

Indian Society for Medical Statistics: General Secretary, Tuberculosis Research Centre, Indian Council of Medical Research, Dept of Statistics, Chetpet, Chennai 600031; tel. (44) 28369638; e-mail secretaryisms@ gmail.com; internet www.isms-india.com/; f. 1983; contributes to the devt of medical statistics and strengthens the application of statistics in medicine, health and related disciplines; organizes annual confs, refresher courses, symposia; 480 mems; Pres. Prof. AJIT SAHAI; Pres. (Elect) Prof. ARVIND PANDEY; Gen. Sec. Dr P. VENKATESAN; publs *ISMS Bulletin*, proceedings of annual meetings.

Indian Society of Anaesthetists: c/o Dept of Anaesthesiology, K. E. M. Hospital, Parel, Mumbai 400012; e-mail isanational@gmail .com; internet www.isaweb.in; f. 1947; 4,000 mems; Pres. Dr MANJUSHREE RAY; Vice-Pres. Dr AJIT KUMAR; Hon. Sec. Dr S. S. C. CHAKRA RAO; publ. *Indian Journal of Anaesthesia* (6 a year).

Medical Council of India: Pocket 14, Sector 8, Dwarka Phase 1, New Delhi 110077; tel. (11) 25367033; fax (11) 25367024; e-mail mci@bol.net.in; internet www.mciindia.org; f. 1933; maintenance of uniform standards of medical education; reciprocity in mutual recognition of medical qualifications with other countries; maintenance of Indian Medical Register; Pres. Dr P. C. KESAVANKUTTY NAYAR (acting); Sec. Dr A. R. N. SETALVAD; publs *Indian Medical Register, MCI Bulletin of Information, Report of the Programme on Continuing Medical Education.*

National Academy of Medical Sciences: Ansari Nagar, Mahatma Gandhi Rd, New Delhi 110029; tel. (11) 26588718; fax (11) 26588992; e-mail nams_aca@yahoo.com; internet www.nams-india.org/; f. 1961; 2,039 mems (700 fellows, 1,339 ordinary mems); Pres. Dr PREMA RAMACHANDRAN; Vice-Pres. Dr R. MADAN; Sec. Prof. GITA SUBBA RAO; publs *Measurement of Insulin Resistance in Vivo, Metabolic Syndrome: From Inert Facts to Informed Action, Networking in Disaster Management, Oxidative Stress in the Development and Complications, The Emerging Epidemic of Obesity and Cardiometabolic Risk Factors.*

Pharmacy Council of India: 2nd Fl., Combined Councils' Bldg, Temple Lane, Kotla Rd, Aiwan-E-Ghalib Marg, New Delhi 110002; POB 7020, 110002 New Delhi; tel. (11) 23239184; fax (11) 23239182; e-mail pci@ ndb.vsnl.net.in; internet pci.nic.in; f. 1949; attached to Min. of Health & Family Welfare, New Delhi; statutory body; sets and maintains educational standards for qualification and registration in pharmacy and coordinates the practice; Pres. Prof. B. SURESH; Vice-Pres. P. P. SHARMA; Sec. and Registrar ARCHANA MUDGAL; Asst Sec. ANIL MITTAL.

NATURAL SCIENCES
General

Indian Academy of Sciences: CV Raman Ave, POB 8005, Sadashivanagar, Bangalore 560080, Karnataka; tel. (80) 23612546; fax (80) 23616094; e-mail office@ias.ernet.in; internet www.ias.ac.in; f. 1934; promotes the cause of science in its pure and applied forms; activities incl. publ. of scientific journals and special volumes, organizing meetings of the Fellowship and discussions on important topics, recognizing scientific talent, improvement of science education and supporting issues of concern to the scientific community; 1,073 full individual mems (970 fellows, 49 hon. fellows), 51 assoc. mems; library of 1,000 vols; Pres. Dr A. K. SOOD; Sec. Prof. DIPANKAR CHATTERJI; Sec. Prof. J. SRINIVASAN; Exec. Sec. G. CHANDRAMOHAN; publs *Bulletin of Materials Science* (6 a year), *Current Science* (24 a year), *Journal of Astrophysics and Astronomy* (4 a year), *Journal of Biosciences* (4 a year), *Journal of Chemical Sciences* (6 a year), *Journal of Earth System Science* (6 a year), *Journal of Genetics* (3 a year), *Pramana* (journal of physics, 12 a year), *Pramana-journal of physics* (12 a year), *Proceedings Mathematical Sciences* (4 a year), *Resonance: Journal of Science Education* (12 a year), *Sadhana-engineering sciences* (6 a year), *Year Book.*

Indian National Science Academy (formerly National Institute of Sciences of India): Bahadur Shah Zafar Marg, New Delhi 110002; tel. (11) 23221931; fax (11) 23235648; e-mail esoffice@insa.nic.in; internet www.insa.ac.in; f. 1935; promotes scientific knowledge, coordination between scientific bodies, and safeguards the interests of scientists in India; adhering organization of ICSU; 676 Fellows, 104 Foreign Fellows; library of 21,000 vols; Pres. Dr S. VARADARAJAN; Secs Prof. N. APPAJI RAO, Prof. P. T. MANOHARAN; publs *Indian Journal of History of Science, Indian Journal of Pure and Applied Mathematics, Progress of Science in India.*

Indian Science Congress Association: 14 Dr Biresh Guha St, Kolkata 700017; tel. and fax (33) 22872551; e-mail iscacal@vsnl.net; internet sciencecongress.nic.in; f. 1914; advances and promotes science in India; holds annual congress; 12,001 mems; library of 8,000 vols, 60 periodicals; Pres. Dr T. RAMASAMI; Secs Prof. AVIJIT BANERJI, Dr ASHOK K. SAXENA; publs *Everyman's Science* (4 a year), *Proceedings* (1 a year, in 4 parts).

National Academy of Sciences: 5 Lajpatrai Rd, Allahabad 211002, Uttar Pradesh; tel. (532) 2640224; e-mail allahabad.nasi@ gmail.com; internet www.nasi.nic.in; f. 1930; promotes all brs of science; 2,580 mems excluding 732 fellows, 48 honorary fellows and 23 foreign fellows; Pres. Prof. ASIS DATTA; Gen. Secs Prof. KRISHNA MISRA (HQ) Prof. AKHILESH KUMAR TYAGI (Out station); Exec. Sec. and CPIO Dr M. S. SINHA; publs *Annual Number* (1 a year), *National Academy of Sciences Letters* (12 a year), *Proceedings* in two sections— *Section A: Physical Sciences, Section B: Biological Sciences* (4 a year).

Biological Sciences

Academy of Zoology: Church Rd 2/95, Civil Lines, Agra 282002; f. 1954; 1,500 mems; library of 91,000 vols, exchange service with other zoological institutions; international organization and forum for the advancement of zoology; Pres. and Sec. Dr D. P. S. BHATI; publ. *The Annals of Zoology.*

Association of Microbiologists of India: DDG Fisheries, ICAR, Krishi Bhavan, New Delhi 110001; tel. (11) 25846738; e-mail generalsecretaryami@yahoo.com; internet www.amiindia.info; f. 1938, registered under Socs Registration Act XXI of 1860; 1,500 mems; library of 3,000 vols; Pres. Dr S. AYYAPPAN; Gen. Sec. Prof. R. C. KUHAD; publ. *Indian Journal of Microbiology* (4 a year).

Bombay Natural History Society: Hornbill House, Salim Ali Chowk, Shahid Bhagat Singh Rd, Mumbai 400001; tel. (22) 22821811; fax (22) 22837615; e-mail bnhs@ bom4.vsnl.net.in; internet www.bnhs.org; f. 1883; studies natural history, ecology and conservation in the Indian sub-continent; research programmes in field zoology; 5,000 mems; library of 20,000 vols; Pres. B. G. DESHMUKH; Hon. Sec. J. C. DANIEL; Dir A. R. RAHMANI; Librarian NIRMALA REDDY; publs *Hornbill, Journal.*

Indian Association of Biological Sciences: Life Science Centre, Calcutta University, Kolkata 700019; tel. (33) 224753681; f. 1968; 400 mems; Sec. and Editor Prof. T. M. DAS; publ. *Indian Biologist* (2 a year).

Indian Biophysical Society: c/o Sec., IBS Dept of Chemical Sciences, Tata Institute of Fundamental Research, Homi Bhabha Road, Colaba, Mumbai 400005; tel. (22) 22782278; fax (22) 22804610; internet www.tifr.res.in/ ~ibs; f. 1965; c. 200 mems; Pres. Prof. N. R. JAGANNATHAN; Sec. Prof. K. V. R CHARY; publ. *Proceedings* (1 a year).

Indian Botanical Society: Dept of Botany, University of Madras, Chepauk, Chennai 600005; f. 1920; Pres. K. S. THIND; Sec. Prof. K. S. BHARGAVA; publ. *Journal.*

Indian Phytopathological Society: Division of Plant Pathology, Indian Agricultural Research Institute, New Delhi 110012; tel. (11) 25848418; fax (11) 25843113; e-mail ipsdis@yahoo.com,; internet www.ipsdis.com; f. 1947; 1,600 mems; virology, bacteriology, mycology, nematology and plant pathology; holds seminars, symposia, etc.; Pres. Dr C. MANOHARACHARY; Sec. Dr D. K. AGARWAL; publs *Indian Phytopathology* (4 a year), *IPS* (4 a year).

Indian Society of Genetics and Plant Breeding: F2, 1st Fl., NASC Comple, DPS Marg, New Delhi 110012; fax (11) 25843437; e-mail isgpb@rediffmail.com; f. 1942; plant breeding and genetic research; 1,600 mems; Pres. Dr M. C. KHARKWAL; Sec. S. M. S. TOMAR; publ. *Journal* (4 a year).

Marine Biological Association of India:; tel. (484) 2394420; fax (484) 2394909; e-mail mail@mbai.org.in; internet www.mbai.org.in/ index.html; f. 1958; promotes research on marine sciences in the Asia-Pacific region; organizes lectures, symposia and seminars on specific subjects; offers requisite information to research workers and students undertaking research in marine biological sciences; Pres. Dr G. SYDA RAO; Vice-Pres. Prof. Dr N. R. MENON; Vice-Pres. Dr N. G. K. PILLAI; Sec. Dr K. SUNILKUMAR MOHAMED; publs *Journal of the Marine Biological Association of India* (2 a year), *Memoirs* (irregular), Proceedings of symposia (irregular).

Society of Biological Chemists, India: Indian Institute of Science, Bangalore 560012; tel. (80) 23601412; fax (80) 23601412; e-mail sbcihq@gmail.com; internet www.iisc.ernet.in/sbci/index.htm; f. 1930; symposia and annual meetings; sponsorships of symposia, seminar and workshops for nat. and int. scientists; 1,600 mems; Pres. Dr V. S. CHAUHAN; Vice-Pres.

Dr D. N. RAO (local) Dr ALOK BHATTACHARYA (out station) Dr D. KARUNAGARAN (out station); publs *Biochemical Reviews* (1 a year), *Proceedings and Abstracts* (1 a year).

Zoological Survey of India: Prani Vigyan Bhawan, M-Block New Alipore, Kolkata 700053; tel. (33) 24003925; fax (33) 24003238; f. 1916; attached to Min. of Environment and Forests; exploration and survey of fauna in India; taxonomic studies; status survey of endangered species; publication of results through departmental journals; maintenance and devt of nat. zoological collns; maintenance of museums at HQs and regional stations; environmental impact studies produced on behalf of Min. of Environment and Forests; library of 37,100 vols, 875 periodicals; Dir Dr RAMAKRISHNA; publ. *Journal of Indian Zoology* (1 a year).

Mathematical Sciences

Allahabad Mathematical Society: 10 C. S. P. Singh Marg, Allahabad 211001; tel. (532) 2623553; fax (532) 2623221; e-mail ams10marg@gmail.com; internet www .amsallahabad.org; f. 1958, registered in 1962 under the Socs Registration Act XXI of 1860; furthers the cause of advanced study and research in various brs of mathematics, incl. theoretical physics and mathematical statistics; 270 mems; library of 5,000 vols; Pres. Dr MONA KHARE; publs *Bulletin* (1 a year), *Indian Journal of Mathematics* (3 a year).

Bharata Ganita Parisad: Dept of Mathematics and Astronomy, University, Lucknow 226007; tel. (522) 2740019; f. 1950; mathematics; 475 mems; library of 16,000 vols; Pres. Prof. J. B. SHUKLA; Gen. Sec. Prof. A. NIGAM; publ. *Ganita* (2 a year).

Calcutta Mathematical Society: Asutosh Bhavan, AE-374, Sector I, Saltlake City, Kolkata 700064; tel. (33) 23378882; fax (33) 23376290; e-mail cms@cal2.vsnl.net.in; f. 1908; lectures, seminars, symposia, workshops in mathematical sciences; research projects sponsored by various funding agencies; 1,011 mems; library of 22,612 vols; Pres. Prof. Dr K. RAMACHANDRA; Sec. Prof. Dr MAHIMARANJAN ADHIKARI; publs *Bulletin* (6 a year), *Journal* (2 a year), *News Bulletin* (12 a year), *Review Bulletin* (2 a year).

Indian Mathematical Society: Dept of Mathematics, Univ. of Pune, Pune, Maharashtra 411 007; e-mail sknimbhorkar@yahoo .com; internet www.indianmathsociety.org .in/; f. 1907; 1,400 mems; library of 4,000 vols; Pres. Prof. R. SREEDHARAN; Gen. Sec. Prof. V. M. SHAH; Treas. Prof. S. K. NIMBHORKAR; publs *Journal of the Indian Mathematical Society* (4 a year), *Mathematics Student* (4 a year).

Physical Sciences

Astronomical Society of India: ISRO Satellite Centre, Airport Road, Bangalore, Karnataka 560017; tel. (80) 25265628; fax (80) 25265407; e-mail pati@iiap.ernet.in; internet www.asindia.org/default.aspx; f. 1990; recognizes talented Indian individuals who have made significant contributions in fostering astronautics in India; 750 mems; Pres. G. MADHAVAN NAIR; Vice-Pres. K. V. S. S. PRASADA RAO; Exec. Sec. R. K. RANJANGAM; Treas. V. SUNDARARAMAIAH; publs *Bulletin* (4 a year), *Memoirs* (irregular).

Electrochemical Society of India: Indian Institute of Science Campus, Bangalore 560012; tel. (80) 23340977; fax (80) 23341683; e-mail mahesh@cedt.iisc.ernet.in; f. 1964; promotes the science and technology of electrochemistry, electro-deposition and plating, corrosion incl. high-temperature oxidation, electrometallurgy and metal finish-

ing, semi-conductors and electronics, batteries, solid electrolytes, solid state electrochemistry, and protection of metals and materials against environmental attack; 670 mems; library of 4,000 vols; Pres. M. RAVINDRANATH; Sec. Dr G. ANANDA RAO; publ. *Journal* (4 a year).

Indian Association for the Cultivation of Science: 2A& 2B Raja S. C. Mallick Rd, Kolkata 700032; tel. (33) 24734971; fax (33) 24732805; e-mail helpdesk@iacs.res.in; internet www.iacs.res.in; f. 1876; promotes fundamental research in the developing areas of basic sciences; 703 mems (625 life, 50 ordinary, 10 assoc., 18 hon.); Pres. Dr T. RAMASAMI; publ. *Indian Journal of Physics* (12 a year).

Indian Chemical Society: University Science College Bldgs, 92 Acharya Prafulla Chandra Rd, Kolkata, West Bengal 700009; tel. (33) 23609497; fax (33) 23503478; e-mail indi3478@dataone.in; internet indianchemsoc.org/; f. 1924; 2,000 mems; library of 10,500 vols; Pres. Prof. RAMESH CHANDRA; Hon. Sec. Prof. P. L. MAJUMDER; publ. *Journal* (12 a year).

Optical Society of India: Dept of Applied Optics and Photonics, Applied Physics Bldg, Calcutta Univ., 92 Acharya Prafulla Chandra Rd, Kolkata 700009, West Bengal; tel. (33) 23522411; e-mail info@osiindia.org; internet www.osiindia.org; f. 1965; promotes and diffuses the knowledge of optics in all its branches, pure and applied; organizes seminars, workshops and confs; 678 mems; library of 400 vols; Pres. T. K. ALEX; Gen. Sec. Prof. L. N. HAZRA; publ. *Journal of Optics* (4 a year).

RELIGION, SOCIOLOGY AND ANTHROPOLOGY

Anthropological Society of Mumbai: 209 Dr Dadabhai Naoroji Rd, Fort, Mumbai 400001; f. 1886; Pres. Dr J. F. BULSARA; Hon. Sec. SAPUR F. DESAI.

Asiatic Society: 1 Park St, Kolkata 700016; e-mail aslibcal@cal.vsnl.net.in; internet www .asiaticsocietycal.com; f. 1784; studies humanities and sciences in India; 1,292 mems, 64 research Fellows; library of 149,000 vols; 47,000 MSS in 26 languages, 80,000 journals, 24,000 old coins, 75 oil paintings; research on Indology and Oriental studies; Pres. Prof. BISWANATH BANERJI; Sec. Prof. RAMAKANTA CHAKRABARTY; publ. *Journal* (4 a year).

Asiatic Society of Mumbai: Town Hall, Shahid Bhagatsingh Marg, Fort Mumbai 400023, Maharashtra; tel. (22) 22660956; e-mail asml@mtnl.net.in; internet www .asiaticsociety.org; f. 1804 as Dr P. V. Kane Research Institute for Oriental Studies; investigates and encourages sciences, arts and literature in relation to Asia and India; 2,811 mems; library of 248,953 vols, 2,357 MSS, 10,443 old coins; Chief Patron HE THE GOVERNOR OF MAHARASHTRA; Pres. Dr AROON TIKEKAR; Hon. Sec. Dr VIDYA VENCATESAN; publs *Journal*, reports.

Indian Anthropological Association: Department of Anthropology, Univ. of Delhi, Delhi 110007; tel. (11) 27667329; e-mail iaadelhi@rediffmail.com; internet www .indiananthropology.org; f. 1964; 400 mems; Pres. Prof. Dr S. M. PATNAIK; Vice-Pres. S. N. RATHA; Gen. Sec. S. K. CHAUDHURY; publs *Directory of Anthropologists in India* (every 4–5 years), *Indian Anthropologist* (2 a year), *News Bulletin* (1 a year).

Indian Society for Afro-Asian Studies: 297 Sarswati Kunj, I.P. Ext., New Delhi 110092; tel. (11) 22722801; fax (11) 22725024; f. 1980; analyzes political, eco-

nomic, social and cultural situation of Afro-Asian countries; 621 mems; Pres. LALIT BHASIN; Sec. Dr DHARAMPAL.

Theosophical Society: Int. HQs, Adyar, Chennai 600020; tel. (44) 24912474; e-mail intl.hq@ts-adyar.org; internet www.ts-adyar .org/; f. 1875 in New York, USA, Adyar Library & Research Centre 1886, present location 1986; forms a nucleus of the universal brotherhood of humanity without distinction of race, creed, sex, caste or colour; encourages the study of comparative religion, philosophy and science; investigates unexplained laws of nature and the powers latent in man; 32,000 mems throughout the world; library of 250,000 vols and 20,000 palm-leaf and paper MSS; Pres. RADHA BURNIER; Sec. MARY ANDERSON; publs *Adyar Library Bulletin* (1 a year), *The Theosophist* (12 a year).

TECHNOLOGY

Aeronautical Society of India: 13B, Indraprastha Estate, New Delhi 110002; tel. (11) 23370516; fax (11) 23370768; e-mail aerosoc@ bol.net.in; internet www.aerosocietyindia .com/; f. 1948; promotion and diffusion of knowledge of aeronautical sciences and aircraft engineering, and advancement of the aeronautical profession; 6,500 mems; library of 4,000 vols; Patron-in-Chief Hon'ble PRIME MINISTER OF INDIA; Pres. V. V. THULASIDAS; Pres. (Elect) ASHOK K. BAWEJA; Vice-Pres RAVI MENON B. P. BALIGA, R. SAREEN, BABU PETER, V. P. AGRAWAL, ASHOK NAYAK; Hon. Sec.-Gen. ASHOK BHUSHAN; Officer on Special Duty for Admin. Gp Capt. (Retd) H. C. BHATIA; Sec. Gp Capt. (Retd) R. C. GOYAL; publs *Elastic Stability of Structural Elements*, *Journal* (4 a year).

Geological, Mining and Metallurgical Society of India: c/o Geology Dept, Univ. of Calcutta, 35 Ballygunge Circular Rd, Kolkata 700019; tel. (33) 24753681; e-mail boses_in@yahoo.com; f. 1924; 315 mems; Pres. Prof. A. K. GHOSH; Jt Sec. SANTANU BOSE; Jt Sec. P. SIKDAR; publs *Bulletin*, *Journal* (4 a year).

India Society of Engineers: 12B Netaji Subhas Rd, Kolkata 700001; f. 1934; library of 20,000 vols; 8,000 mems; Pres. A. C. SINHA; Gen. Sec. D. B. CHOWDHURY; publ. *Science and Engineering* (12 a year, in English).

Indian Association of Geohydrologists: c/o Geological Survey of India, 4 Chowringhee Lane, Kolkata 700016; f. 1964; 440 mems; Pres. V. SUBRAMANYAM; Hon. Sec. A. K. ROY; publ. *Indian Geohydrology*.

Indian Ceramic Society: c/o Central Glass and Ceramic Research Institute, Kolkata 700032; tel. (33) 24138878; fax (33) 24730957; e-mail info@incers.org; internet www.incers.org/home.html; f. 1928; 2,000 mems; Pres. Prof. F. D. GNANAM; Vice-Pres. SWAPAN KR. GUHA; Hon. Jt Secs S. CHAKRABARTI, Dr K. G. K. WARRIER; publ. *Transactions* (4 a year).

Indian Institute of Metals: Metal House, Plot 13/4, Block AQ, Sector V, Salt Lake, Kolkata 700091; tel. (33) 2367 9768; fax (33) 23675335; e-mail iiomcal@dataone.in; internet www.iim-india.net; f. 1947; chapters based in Katni, Delhi, Bhopal, Baroda, Burnpur, Coimbatore, Chittorgarh, Chennai, Bangalore, Hyderabad, Hisar, Jaipur, Kharagpur, Korba, Rourkela, Mysore, Roorkee, Raigarh, Varanasi, Trichy, Vijaynagar, Visakhapatnam, Udaipur, Trivandrum, Salem, Surathkal, Sunabeda, Paloncha, Poona, Nagpur, Mumbai, Kolkata, Kolar Fold Field, Keonjhar, Kalpakkam, Khetrinagar, Kanpur, Jamshedpur, Ichapur, Hazira, Ghatsila, Duburi, Durgapur, Chandigarh, Bhadravati, Bhilai, Bhubaneswar, Bokaro, Angul, Ambarnath; 9,000 mems; Pres. L. PUGAZ-

HENTHY; Vice-Pres and Chair. Dr SANAK MISHRA (Ferrous Division), Dr D. BANERJEE (Metal Sciences Division), M. NARAYANA RAO; Sec.-Gen. J. C. MARWAH; publs *IIM Metal News* (6 a year), *Transactions* (6 a year).

Indian National Academy of Engineering (INAE): 6th Fl., Vishwakarma Bhawan, Shaheed Jeet Singh Marg, New Delhi 110016; tel. (11) 2 6582635; fax (11) 26856635; e-mail inaehq@inae.org; internet www.inae.org/; f. 1987; promotes gen. advancement of engineering and technology and related sciences and disciplines; awards professorship, fellowship and scholarship; 299 Fellows; Pres. Dr P. S. GOEL; Vice-Pres. for Acad., Professional and Int. Affairs Dr BALDEV RAJ; Vice-Pres. for Fellowships, Awards and Corporate Communication Prof. PREM KRISHNA; Vice-Pres. for Finance and Establishment Dr M. J. ZARABI.

Indian Society of Mechanical Engineers (ISME): c/o Dept of Mechanical Engineering, Indian Institute of Technology, New Delhi 110016; tel. (11) 26311259; fax (11) 26311261; f. 1975; 480 mems; Pres. Prof. G. S. SEKHON; Sec. Dr S. G. DESHMUKH; publs *Journal of Engineering Design* (4 a year), *Journal of Engineering Production* (4 a year), *Journal of Thermal Engineering* (4 a year).

Institution of Electronics and Telecommunication Engineers (IETE): 2 Institutional Area, Lodi Rd, New Delhi 110003; tel. (11) 24631810; fax (11) 24649429; internet www.iete.org/; f. 1953; promotes the advancement of electronics and telecommunications engineering and related fields; 40,000 mems; Pres. Lt-Gen. ASHOK AGARWAL; Sec.-Gen. Brig. (Retd) V. K. PANDAY; publs *IETE Journal of Education* (4 a year), *IETE Journal of Research* (6 a year), *IETE Technical Review* (6 a year).

Institution of Engineers (India): 8 Gokhale Rd, Kolkata 700020; tel. (33) 22238230; fax (33) 22238345; e-mail sdg@ieindia.org; internet www.ieindia.org; f. 1920; engineering professional soc. in India imparting non-formal engineering education; inc. by Royal Charter 1935; 94 centres; 60 libraries; over 500,000 mems; Pres. Rear Admiral K. O. THAKARE; Sec. and Dir-Gen. Cmdr (retd) ARVIND K. POOTHIA; publs *Divisional Journals (15 engineering journals)* (12 a year), *Inter-Disciplinary* (2 a year), *Technorama* (2 a year).

Mineralogical Society of India: Manasa Gangotri, Mysore 6; f. 1959; advances knowledge of crystallography, mineralogy, petrology, etc., by means of research and the holding of confs, meetings and discussions; 400 mems; library of 1,500 vols; Pres. Dr VISWANATHIAH; Sec. Dr P. N. SATISH; publ. *The Indian Mineralogist*.

Systems Society of India: c/o The Deputy Director, Vikram Sarabhai Space Centre, Control Guidance and Simulation Entity, Thiruvananthapuram 695022; tel. (471) 2565516; fax (471) 2564080; e-mail ds_antuvan@vssc.gov.in; internet www.sysi.org; f. 1981; nat. professional org. for systems science and engineering; numerous chapters incl. Thiruvananthapuram Chapter, Kozhikkode Chapter, Kharagpur Chapter, Vellore Chapter, Manipal Chapter, Aligarh Chapter, Agra Chapter, Hyderabad Chapter; 1,800 mems; Pres. Dr BIJAN B. DAS; Vice-Pres Dr VISHAL SAHNI, Dr ZACHARIAH C. ALEX; Sec. Dr D. S. ANTUVAN; publ. *Journal of Systems Science and Engineering* (journal, 2 a year).

Research Institutes
GENERAL

Council of Scientific and Industrial Research: Anusandhan Bhawan, 2 Rafi Marg, New Delhi 110001; tel. (11) 23711251; fax (11) 23714788; internet www.csir.res.in; f. 1942; attached to Min. of Science and Technology; library of 20,000 vols; Pres. THE PRIME MIN.; Dir-Gen. Prof. SAMIR K. BRAHMACHARI; Jt Sec. for Admin. AJAY KUMAR; publ. *Technical Manpower Bulletin* (12 a year).

Attached Research Institutes:

Central Building Research Institute: Roorkee 247667, Uttar Pradesh; tel. (1332) 272243; fax (1332) 272272; e-mail general@cscbri.ren.nic.in; f. 1947; research and devt in all aspects of building science and technology; work divided into 5 areas: shelter planning, new materials, structural and foundation engineering, disaster mitigation and process devt; library of 44,778 vols; Dir Dr R. NARAYANA IYENGAR; publ. *Bhavanika* (in Hindi, 4 a year).

Central Drug Research Institute: Chattar Manzil Palace, POB 173, Lucknow 226001; tel. (522) 2223286; fax (522) 2223405; e-mail director@cdri.res.in; internet www.cdriindia.org; f. 1951; biochemical, molecular biological, pharmacological, chemical, microbiological, endocrinological, biophysical, parasitological and medical research; library of 21,300 vols; Dir Dr TUSHAR KANTI CHAKRABORTY; publs *Industry Highlights* (4 a year), *Ocean Drugs Alert* (4 a year).

Central Electrochemical Research Institute: Karaikudi 630006, Tamil Nadu; tel. (4565) 222065; fax (4565) 222088; e-mail cecrik@cscecri.ren.nic.in; f. 1953; electrochemical and allied research; library of 31,755 vols; Dir Dr M. RAGHVAN; publ. *Bulletin of Electro-chemistry*.

Central Electronics Engineering Research Institute: Pilani, Rajasthan; tel. (1596) 242111; fax (1596) 242294; e-mail root@ceeri.ernet.in; f. 1953; design and construction of electronic equipment, components and test equipment; Dir Dr S. AHMAD; publ. *CEERI News* (4 a year).

Central Food Technological Research Institute: Cheluvamba Mansion, Food Technology PO, Mysore 570013; tel. (821) 2517760; fax (821) 2516308; e-mail director@nicfos.ernet.in; internet www.mylibnet.org.in/cftri/cftri.htm; f. 1950; library of 36,300 vols; Dir Dr V. PRAKASH; publs *Food Digest* (4 a year), *Food Patents* (4 a year), *Food Technology Abstracts* (12 a year), *Library Bulletin* (4 a year).

Central Glass and Ceramic Research Institute: 196 Raja S. C. Mullick Rd, Jadavpur, Kolkata 700032; tel. (33) 24735829; fax (33) 24730957; e-mail cscgcri@giascl.l.vsnl.net.in; f. 1950; fundamental and applied research on special kinds of glass, ceramics, sol-gel, refractories, ceramic coatings, composites and allied areas; library of 25,000 vols; Dir Dr H. S. MAITY.

Central Institute of Medicinal and Aromatic Plants: PO CIMAP, Lucknow 226015; tel. (522) 2359623; fax (522) 2342666; e-mail roor@cimap.sirnetd.ernet.in; f. 1959; co-ordination of activities in the devt of cultivation and use of medicinal and aromatic plants on organized basis; library of 2,688 vols; Dir Dr SUSHIL KUMAR; publs *Farm Bulletin* (irregular), *Journal of Medicinal and Aromatic Plant Sciences* (4 a year), *Yatharth* (4 a year).

Central Institute of Mining and Fuel Research: PO Fuel Research Institute, Digwadih, Dhanbad 828108, Jharkhand; tel. (326) 2296023; fax (326) 2296025; e-mail dcmrips@yahoo.co.in; f. 1945, fmrly known as Central Fuel Research Institute; research on coal, lignite, allied subjects and other sources of fuel; environmental management and waste utilization; library of 10,129 vols, 35,000 periodicals; Dir Dr AMALENDU SINHA; publ. *Fuel Science and Technology* (4 a year).

Central Leather Research Institute: Adyar, Chennai 600020; tel. (44) 24910846; fax (44) 24912150; e-mail clrim@giasmd01.vsnl.net.in; internet www.clri.org; f. 1948; library of 17,225 vols; Dir Dr T. RAMASAMI; publ. *Leather Science Abstract Services* (12 a year).

Central Mechanical Engineering Research Institute: Mahatma Gandhi Ave, Durgapur 713209, West Bengal; tel. (343) 2546749; fax (343) 2546745; e-mail root@cscmeri.ren.nic.in; internet www.cmeri.com; f. 1958; library of 60,000 vols; Dir Shri HARDYAL SINGH; publ. *Mechanical Engineering Bulletin* (4 a year).

Central Mining Research Institute: Barwa Rd, Dhanbad, 826001 Bihar; tel. (326) 2203043; fax (326) 2205028; e-mail director@csemri.ren.nic.in; f. 1956; research on safety, health and efficiency in mining; library of 26,382 vols; Dir Dr T. N. SINGH.

Central Road Research Institute: PO CRRI, Delhi-Mathura Rd, New Delhi 110020; tel. (11) 26848917; fax (11) 26845943; e-mail director@cscrri.ren.nic.in; f. 1952; research and devt in highway engineering, traffic and transportation, transport environment and safety, bridge engineering, pavement design; library of 90,000 vols; Dir Dr A. K. GUPTA; publs *CRRI Road Abstracts* (4 a year), *CRRI WIN Bulletin* (4 a year), *Highway Documentation* (12 a year), *Roadsearch Bulletin* (2 a year).

Central Salt and Marine Chemicals Research Institute: Waghawadi Rd, Bhavnagar 364002, Gujarat; tel. (278) 2569496; fax (278) 2566970; e-mail general@csmcri.ren.nic.in; f. 1954; preparation of salt, magnesium compounds, bromine and bromides, cultivation and use of marine algae, desalination of water by solar stills, electrodialysis and reverse osmosis, waste water treatment using membrane processes; library of 48,000 vols; Dir Dr P. K. GHOSH.

Central Scientific Instruments Organization: Sector 30-C, Chandigarh 160020; tel. (172) 2657190; fax (172) 2657267; e-mail root@cscsia.ren.nic.in; internet www.nio.org/csir/csio.htm; f. 1959; research, design, devt, repair and maintenance of scientific and industrial instruments; technical training and diploma courses in instrument technology; library of 38,700 vols, 180 periodicals; Dir Dr R. P. BAJPAI (acting); publ. *Communications in Instrumentation* (4 a year).

Centre for Biochemicals Technology: Mall Rd, Delhi Univ. Campus, Delhi 110007; tel. (11) 27257298; fax (11) 27257471; e-mail central@cbt.res.in; internet www.cbt.res.in; f. 1966; uses the results obtained in basic biological research to provide commercially viable technologies for health care; Dir SAMIR K. BRAHAMCHARI.

Centre for Cellular and Molecular Biology: Hyderabad; tel. (40) 27173487; fax (40) 27171195; e-mail lalji@ccmb.ap.nic.in; internet www.ccmbindia.org; f. 1977;

research in frontier areas and multi-disciplinary areas of modern biology with a view to aiding devt of biochemical and biotechnology in India by providing centralized facilities and training; Dir Dr LALJI SINGH; publ. *CCMB Highlights*.

Indian Institute of Chemical Biology: 4 Raja S. C. Mullick Rd, Jadavpur, Kolkata 700032; tel. (33) 24735197; fax (33) 24735197; e-mail iichbio@giascl01.vsnl.net .in; f. 1956; solution of medical problems through fundamental and applied research in the basic biological sciences, with emphasis on projects bearing directly on the country's current biological and medical needs; library of 30,000 vols; Dir Dr D. K. GANGULY (acting).

Indian Institute of Chemical Technology: Hyderabad 500007; tel. (40) 27173874; fax (40) 27173387; e-mail root@ csiict.ren.nic.in; f. 1944; agrochemicals, drugs and pharmaceuticals, inorganic chemicals and materials, organic coatings and polymers, design engineering of chemical plant, oils and fats, biotechnology; library of 40,000 vols, 500 periodicals; Dir Dr K. V. RAGHVAN; publ. *Bulletin* (4 a year).

Indian Institute of Petroleum: Dehradun 248005; tel. (135) 2624508; fax (135) 2671986; e-mail iipddn@de12.vsnl.net.in; f. 1960; research and devt in the field of petroleum, natural gas, and petrochemicals and use of petroleum products; trains technical personnel; assists Bureau of Indian Standards in framing standards for petroleum products; library of 15,000 vols, 14,000 periodicals; the institute is a Patents Inspection Centre of the Indian Patents Office and is open to the public for studying patent specifications; Dir S. SINGHAL (acting); publs *R & D Newsletter* (4 a year), *Vikalp* (4 a year).

Industrial Toxicology Research Centre: Mahatma Gandhi Marg, Lucknow 226001, Uttar Pradesh; tel. (522) 2221856; fax (522) 2228227; e-mail intox@itrc .sirnetd.ernet.in; f. 1965; studies the effects of industrial pollution; library of 25,200 vols; Dir Dr P. K. SETH.

Institute of Himalayan Bioresources Technology, Palampur: Dist. Kangra, 176061 Himachal Pradesh; tel. (1894) 230411; fax (1894) 230433; e-mail director@csihbt.ren.nic.in; f. 1983; biodiversity conservation, tea husbandry and manufacture, agro-technology, processing and post-harvest technologies for floriculture, aromatic and herbal plants; Dir Dr P. S. AHUJA.

Institute of Microbial Technology: Sector 39A, Chandigarh 160036; tel. (172) 2690785; fax (172) 2690585; e-mail root@ imtech.ernet.in; internet www.imtech .ernet.in; f. 1983; research and devt in genetic engineering and microbiology, protein engineering, immunology and fermentation technology; library of 15,809 vols; Dir Dr AMIT GHOSH.

Institute of Minerals and Materials Technology: Council of Scientific and Industrial Research, Bhubaneshwar, Orissa 751013; tel. (674) 2581636; fax (674) 5881637; e-mail bkm@immt.res.in; internet www.immt.res.in; f. 1964 fmrly Regional Research Laboratory; library of 35,000 vols; research in problems relating to minerals and materials resources and technology; Dir Prof. B. K. MISHRA; Librarian Dr D. B. RAMESH.

National Aerospace Laboratories: PB 1779, Kodihalli, Bangalore 560017; tel. (80) 25270584; fax (80) 25260862; e-mail viman@csnal.ren.in; internet www .cmmacs.ernet.in/nal; f. 1959; research and

devt in aircraft design, testing and operation, and support for nat. aerospace programmes; library of 110,000 vols; Dir Dr T. S. PRALAHAD.

National Botanical Research Institute: Rana Pratap Marg, Lucknow 226001; tel. and fax (522) 2282881; e-mail manager@nbri.sirnetd.ernet.in; f. 1953; research into economic botany and collection, introduction, propagation and improvement of ornamental and economic plants; 520 mems; library of 53,414 vols; Dir Dr P. PUSHPANGADAN; publ. *Applied Botany Abstracts* (4 a year).

National Chemical Laboratory: Dr Homi Bhabha Rd, Pune 411008; tel. (20) 25902600; fax (20) 25902601; e-mail director@ncl.res.in; internet www .ncl-india.org; f. 1950; advanced functional materials, biotechnology, catalysis, organic chemical technology, chemical engineering science and polymers; 770 mems; library of 138,452 vols; 700 students; Dir Dr S. SIVARAM; publ. *NCL Bulletin* (4 a year).

National Environmental Engineering Research Institute: Nehru Marg, Nagpur 440020, Maharashtra; tel. (712) 2249885; fax (712) 2249900; e-mail director@neeri.res.in; internet www.neeri .res.in; f. 1958; research and devt in environmental monitoring, environmental biotechnology, solid and hazardous waste management, environmental systems design, modelling and optimization, air and water pollution control, sewage and industrial wastewater treatment, instrumentation and environmental impact studies; library of 46,500 vols, journals, reports, conference proceedings, CDs and audiovisual films; 200 int. and nat. peer-reviewed current periodicals; online access to 3,000 scientific and technical journals; Dir Dr TAPAN CHAKRABARTI (acting); publs *Journal of Environmental Science and Engineering* (4 a year), *Paryavaran Patrika* (2 a year, in Hindi).

National Geophysical Research Institute: Uppal Rd, Hyderabad 500007; tel. (40) 27170141; fax (40) 27171564; e-mail postmast@csngri.ren.nic.in; internet www .ngri.com; f. 1961; basic and applied research into mineral exploration and investigation of the earth's interior through seismic, geomagnetic, electric, geochemical and paleogeophysical studies; library of 19,173 vols, 13,895 bound vols of journals, 120 subscribed journals; Dir Dr HARSH K. GUPTA.

National Institute of Oceanography: Miramar, Panaje, 403004 Goa; tel. (8251) 221322; fax (8251) 223340; e-mail ocean@ csnio.ren.nic.in; internet www.nio.org; f. 1966; investigates physical, chemical, geological and biological oceanography, also functions as the Nat. Oceanographic Data Centre; research on marine geophysics and instrumentation; maintenance of data pertaining to the Indian Ocean at Planning and Data Div.; library of 24,000 vols; Dir Dr E. DESA.

National Institute of Science, Technology and Development Studies: Hillside Rd, New Delhi 110012; tel. (11) 25743227; fax (11) 25754640; e-mail postmast@csnistad.ren.nic.in; f. 1981; research on technological and social change, and resource planning and use for regional devt; library of 15,000 vols, 250 periodicals; Dir Dr S. PRUTHI (acting); publs *CLOSS* (4 a year), *Report* (every 2 years).

National Metallurgical Laboratory: Jamshedpur 831007, Singhbhum District, Bihar; tel. (657) 2431131; fax (657)

2426527; e-mail nml@csnml.ren.nic.in; f. 1950; ore dressing, production, physical and chemical metallurgy; library of 43,875 vols; Dir Prof. P. R. RAO; publs *News Bulletin* (4 a year), *Technical Journal* (4 a year).

National Physical Laboratory: Hillside Rd, New Delhi 110012; tel. (11) 25741440; fax (11) 25752678; f. 1947; fundamental and applied research in physics; maintenance of standards; testing and calibration of equipment; library of 109,000 vols; Dir Prof. A. K. RAYCHAUDHARY; publs *Ionospheric Data* (4 a year), *Sameeksha* (4 a year).

North-East Institute of Science and Technology: Jorhat, 785006 Assam; tel. (376) 2370012; fax (376) 2370011; e-mail director@rrljorhat.res.in; f. 1961; research into coal, petroleum, pulp and paper, natural product chemistry, cement, drugs and pharmaceuticals, synthetic organic chemistry, essential oils and medicinal plants, general and earthquake engineering, biochemistry, biotechnology, material science, building materials, soil engineering, testing and analysis; library of 24,500 books, 22,000 back vols and standards, patents, reports and theses; Dir Dr P. G. RAO; Head B. C. SAIKIA; publs *Bioinformation up to date* (12 a year), *NEIST Highlights* (1 a year), *NEIST Jorhat Technologies* (irregular), *NEIST News* (6 a year).

Regional Research Laboratory: Canal Rd, Jammu-Tawi 180001, Jammu and Kashmir; tel. (191) 2546368; fax (191) 2548607; e-mail rrlj@nde.vsnl.net.in; f. 1957; drug and medicinal plants; introduction of exotic plants, particularly from temperate zones; plant chemistry, extraction and processing of drugs; library of 16,522 vols; Dir Prof. S. S. HANDA.

Regional Research Laboratory: Library Bldg, Hoshangabad Rd, Univ. of Bhopal, Habibganj Naka, Bhopal 462026; tel. (755) 2587105; fax (755) 2587042; e-mail root@rrlbpl.onp.nic.in; f. 1981; research and devt on minerals and materials with particular focus on aluminium; Dir Prof. T. C. RAO.

Regional Research Laboratory: Industrial Estate, Trivandrum; tel. (471) 2490324; fax (471) 2491712; e-mail root@ csrrltd.ren.nic.in; f. 1976 to develop technologies for the optimal use of regional resources, to help industry in the region through research, devt and technology transfer; Dir Dr G. V. NAIR.

Structural Engineering Research Centre: Chennai 600113; tel. (44) 22542139; fax (44) 22540508; e-mail director@sercm.org; internet www.sercm .org; f. 1965; wind engineering and experimentation and earthquake engineering; structural health monitoring and evaluation; forensic analysis; metal structure behaviour, transmission line towers and analysis design and testing; computational structural mechanics; sustainable materials and composites and structural engineering construction and technology; library of 13,500 vols, 146 periodicals; Dir Dr NAGESH R. IYER; publ. *Journal of Structural Engineering* (6 a year).

Structural Engineering Research Centre: Central Govt Enclave, Kamla Nehru Nagar, Ghaziabad 201002, Uttar Pradesh; tel. (575) 2721874; fax (575) 2721882; e-mail root@cssercg.ren.nic.in; f. 1965; research into various aspects of structural engineering, incl. problems connected with bridges and long-span structures and high-rise bldgs, natural disaster mitigations and materials science; library of 8,500 vols; Dir V. K. GHANEKAR; publ. *Journal* (4 a year).

AGRICULTURE, FISHERIES AND VETERINARY SCIENCE

Agro-Economic Research Centre: Visva-Bharati University, Santiniketan 731235, West Bengal; tel. (3463) 252751; fax (3463) 252672; e-mail aere@vbharat.ernet.in; f. 1954; conducts research in agricultural economics; library of 6,000 vols; Dir KAZI M. B. RAHIM.

Central Arid Zone Research Institute: Jodhpur 342003; tel. (291) 2786584; fax (291) 2788706; e-mail kprvittal@cazri.res.in; internet www.cazri.res.in; f. 1959; 7 divs: Resource Survey and Monitoring, Resource Management, Arable Cropping System, Perennial Cropping System, Animal Sciences and Rodent Control, Energy Management, Engineering and Product Processing; Outreach programme; Regional Research Stations in Pali, Bikaner, Jaisalmer, Bhuj; library of 19,000 books, 164 current journals, 1,990 reprints; Dir Dr K. P. R. VITTAL; publs *Annals of Arid Zone* (4 a year), *DEN News* (4 a year).

Central Inland Fisheries Research Institute: Barrackpore 700120, West Bengal; tel. (33) 25920177; fax (33) 25920388; e-mail cifri@vsnl.com; internet www.cifri.ernet.in; f. 1947; researches into ecology of rivers, production functions of inland water bodies in the country, reservoirs, flood plain wetlands, estuaries and lakes; appraisal of inland fisheries resources, fisheries management of selected rivers, reservoirs, ox-bow lakes and estuaries; pen culture of carp and prawns; biology of fish and prawns; water pollution studies, conservation and environmental modelling; fish diseases and their control; also conducts information and training programmes; library of 9,000 vols and 90 journals; Dir Prof. Dr ANIL PRAKASH SHARMA; publ. *Indian Fisheries Abstracts* (2 a year).

Central Rice Research Institute: Cuttack, 753006 Orissa; tel. (671) 2367757; fax (671) 2367663; e-mail crrictc@ori.nic.in; internet crri.nic.in; f. 1946; research on basic and applied aspects of all disciplines of rice culture; 530 mems; library of 12,000 vols, 200 periodicals; Dir Dr T. K. ADITYA; publs *Oryza* (4 a year), *Rice Research News* (4 a year).

Central Tobacco Research Institute: Rajahmundry 533105, Andhra Pradesh; tel. (883) 465995; fax (883) 64341; e-mail ctri@pol .net.in; internet www.indiantobacco.com/rd .php; f. 1947; library of 22,000 vols, 159 periodicals; under the Indian Council of Agric. Research (Ministry of Agriculture and Rural Reconstruction, Govt of India); applied and fundamental research on all types of tobacco grown in India; regional stations at Guntur, Vedasandur, Pusa, Hunsur, Dinhata, Jeelugumilli and Kandukur; 250 mems; Dir Dr KAPIL DEO SINGH.

Indian Agricultural Statistics Research Institute: Library Ave, Pusa Rd, New Delhi 110012; tel. (11) 25847121; fax (11) 25841564; e-mail director@iasri.res.in; internet www.iasri.res.in; f. 1959; part of ICAR; research in experimental designs, sample surveys, biometric techniques, forecasting techniques, econometrics and computer applications; conducts postgraduate courses and in-service training in agricultural statistics and computer application; provides advisory service to agricultural scientists; provides consultancy service in data processing; develops computer software and information systems; library of 26,240 vols, 8,561 journals, 40 online journals, 9,346 reports, 912 theses; Dir Dr V. K. BHATIA;

Nat. Prof. Dr V. K. GUPTA; publ. *Agricultural Research Data Book* (1 a year).

Indian Council of Agricultural Research (ICAR): Krishi Bhavan, Dr Rajendra Prasad Rd, New Delhi 110001; tel. (11) 23382629; e-mail mrai.icar@nic.in; internet www.icar .org.in; f. 1929; attached to Min. of Agriculture; promotes agricultural and animal husbandry research in conjunction with state govts, central and state research institutions; provides consultancy and information on agriculture, horticulture, resource management, animal sciences, agricultural engineering, fisheries, agricultural extension, agricultural education, home science and agricultural communication; coordinates agricultural research and devt programmes and develops links at nat. and int. level with related org. to enhance the quality of life of the farming community; research centres; human resource devt in the field of agricultural sciences; oversees numerous agricultural universities nationally; establishes Krishi Vigyan Kendras (farm training centres) responsible for training, research and demonstration of the latest agricultural technology; Pres. SHARAD PAWAR; Dir-Gen. Dr MANGALA RAI; Sec. A. K. UPADHYAY; publs *Indian Farming* (12 a year), *Indian Horticulture* (4 a year), *Indian Journal of Agricultural Sciences* (12 a year), *Indian Journal of Animal Sciences* (12 a year), *Kheti* (12 a year), *Krishi Chayanika* (4 a year), *PhalPhool* (4 a year).

Indian Council of Forestry Research and Education: P.O. New Forest, Dehradun (Uttarakhand) 248006; tel. (135) 2759382; fax (135) 2755353; e-mail dg@icfre .org; internet www.icfre.org; f. 1906; library of 160,000 vols, 600 periodicals; Dir-Gen. JAGDISH KISHWAN; publs *ENVIS Forestry Bulletin, Indian Forest Records*.

Indian Plywood Industries Research and Training Institute: Post Bag 2273, Tumkur Rd, Yeshwanthpur, Bangalore 560022, Karnataka; tel. (80) 28394341; fax (80) 28396361; e-mail cnpandey@vsnl.net; internet www.ipirti.gov.in/; f. 1962; attached to Min. of Environment and Forests; researches on saw-milling, plywood-manufacturing techniques, preservative treatment of wood and wood-based panels, devt of synthetic and natural adhesives; testing of panel products; training in mechanical wood-processing technology; specialized short-term courses; library of 8,500 vols; Dir Dr C. N. PANDEY.

Indian Veterinary Research Institute: Izatnagar 243122, Uttar Pradesh; tel. (581) 2300096; fax (581) 2303284; e-mail dirivri@ ivri.up.nic.in; internet www.ivri.nic.in; f. 1889, deemed univ. status 1983; campuses at Bangalore, Bhopal, Izatnagar, Kolkata, Mukteswar, Palampur and Srinagar; research divs of animal biochemistry, animal biotechnology, animal genetics and breeding, animal nutrition, animal physiology, avian diseases, biostatistics, livestock production and management, livestock products technology, poultry science, veterinary bacteriology, veterinary epidemiology, veterinary extension education, veterinary gynaecology and obstetrics, veterinary immunology, veterinary medicine, veterinary parasitology, veterinary pathology, veterinary pharmacology, veterinary public health, veterinary surgery, veterinary virology; library of 207,000 vols, 300 periodicals; Dir Dr R. S. CHAUHAN (acting); Dir for Academic and Dean Dr D. DAS; Registrar K. L. MEENA (acting).

National Dairy Research Institute: Karnal 132001, Haryana; tel. (184) 2252800; fax (184) 2250042; e-mail bnm@ndri.hry.nic.in;

internet www.ndri.res.in; f. 1923, deemed univ.; library of 75,000 vols and 22,000 periodicals; regional stations at Bangalore and Kalyani; research divs in animal biochemistry, animal biotechnology, dairy cattle breeding, dairy cattle nutrition, dairy cattle physiology, dairy chemistry, dairy econ., statistics and management, dairy engineering, dairy extension, dairy microbiology, dairy technology; Dir Dr A. K. SRIVASTAVA; Registrar RAMESHWAR SINGH; Dir of Library Services Dr B. R. YADAV; library of 92,555 vols, 350 periodicals; publ. *Dairy Samachar* (4 a year).

National Sugar Institute: PO NSI Kalyanpur, Kanpur 208017, Uttar Pradesh; tel. (512) 2570730; fax (512) 2570247; e-mail nsikanpur@gmail.com; internet nsi.gov.in; f. 1936; attached to Min. of Consumer Affairs, Food and Public Distribution (Dept of Food and Public Distribution); undertakes research, teaching and consultancy activities in all aspects of sugar technology; library of 7,368 vols; Dir Prof. S. K. MITRA; publs *N.S.I. News, Sharkara*.

Rubber Research Institute of India: Kottayam 686009, Kerala; tel. (481) 2353311; fax (481) 2353324; e-mail rrii@ rubberboard.org.in; internet www .rubberboard.org.in; f. 1955; promotes the devt of the industry; scientific, technological and economic research in improved methods of planting, cultivation, processing and consumption of natural rubber; library of 55,000 vols; Chair. SAJEN PETER; Dir of Research Dr JAMES JACOB; Documentation Officer MERCY JOSE; publs *Indian Rubber Statistics* (1 a year), *Natural Rubber Research* (2 a year), *Rubber* (in Malayalam, 12 a year), *Rubber Board Bulletin* (4 a year), *Rubber Growers' Companion* (4 a year), *Rubber Statistical News* (12 a year).

Vasantdada Sugar Institute: Manjari (Bk.), Tal. Haveli, Dist. Pune 412307, Maharashtra; tel. (20) 26902100; fax (20) 26902244; e-mail vsilib@vsnl.com; internet www .vsisugar.com; f. 1975; library of 18,000 vols; Dir-Gen. SHIVAJIRAO C. DESHMUKH; Librarian N. S. PATHAN; publ. *Bulletin* (4 a year).

BIBLIOGRAPHY, LIBRARY SCIENCE AND MUSEOLOGY

Documentation Research and Training Centre (Indian Statistical Institute): 8th Mile, Mysore Rd, R. V. College Post, Bangalore 560059; tel. (80) 28483002; fax (80) 28484265; e-mail drtc@isibang.ac.in; internet drtc.isibang.ac.in/drtc/dspace-india .html; f. 1962; conducts research in the fields of library science, documentation and information science; trains documentalists; provides an advisory service to industry, academic and research institutions; library of 20,000 vols; Head Prof. I. K. RAVICHANDRA RAO; publ. *DRTC Annual Seminar*.

ECONOMICS, LAW AND POLITICS

Indian Institute of Public Administration: Indraprastha Estate, Ring Rd East, New Delhi 110002; tel. (11) 23702400; fax (11) 23702440; e-mail diriipa@bol.net.in; internet www.iipa.ernet.in; f. 1954; promotes the study of public admin.; research, training, consultancy; library of 192,000 vols, 400 periodicals; Dir Dr B. S. BASWAN; Registrar Dr NARESH KUMAR; publs *Documentation in Public Administration* (4 a year), *Nagarlok* (4 a year), *The Indian Journal of Public Administration* (4 a year).

Institute for Defence Studies and Analyses: 1 Development Enclave, Near USI, New Delhi 110010; tel. (11) 26717983; fax (11) 26154191; e-mail idsa@vsnl.com; internet www.idsa.in; f. 1965; researches on nat.

security, undertakes study on methods of warfare, strategy, disarmament and int. relations; library of 45,000 vols, and 1,500 maps; Pres. DINESH SINGH; Dir J. SINGH; publs *News Reviews* (12 a year), *Strategic Analysis* (12 a year), *Strategic Digest* (12 a year).

Institute for Social and Economic Change: Nagarabhavi PO, Bangalore 560072; tel. (80) 23215468; fax (80) 23217008; e-mail registrar@isec.ac.in; internet www.isec.ac.in; f. 1972; social and economic devt in India; library of 121,000 vols of books, reports and bound periodicals, 300 periodicals; Pres. THE GOV. OF KARNATAKA; Dir Dr R. S. DESHPANDE; Registrar Col ASHUTOSH DHAR; Deputy Librarian Dr K. PRAKASH; publ. *Journal of Social and Economic Development* (2 a year).

Madras Institute of Development Studies: 79 Second Main Rd, Gandhinagar, Adyar, Chennai 600020; tel. (44) 24412589; fax (44) 24910872; e-mail office@mids.ac.in; internet www.mids.ac.in; f. 1970; contributes to the economic and social devt of Tamil Nadu State and India; undertakes studies and research in micro-devt problems; aims at upgrading economic research in the south Indian univs through research methodology courses and studies; fosters inter-univ. cooperation of southern states and promotes inter-disciplinary research; recognized by Univ. of Madras for PhD courses; library of 43,500 vols; Chair. Prof. R. RADHAKRISHNA; Dir Dr S. JANAKARAJAN; publ. *Review of Development and Change* (2 a year).

National Council of Applied Economic Research: Parisila Bhavan, 11 Indraprastha Estate, New Delhi 110002; tel. (11) 23379861; fax (11) 23370164; e-mail infor@ncaer.org; internet www.ncaer.org; f. 1956; autonomous research org.; studies economic problems for govt, int. orgs and private business; library of 83,000 vols, 400 periodicals, microfiche collection of census of India 1872–1951, CD databases; Pres. NANDAN M. NILEKANI; Vice-Pres. M. S. VERMA; Sec. N. J. SEBASTIAN; Dir-Gen. SUMAN K.BERY; publs *Artha Suchi* (4 a year), *Macro Track* (12 a year), *Margin* (4 a year).

National Productivity Council: Utpadakta Bhavan, 5–6 Institutional Area, Lodi Rd, New Delhi 110003; tel. (11) 24690331; fax (11) 24615002; e-mail info@npcindia.org; internet www.npcindia.org; f. 1958; helps to increase productivity in every sector of the nat. economy; 12 regional directorates (Kanpur, Chandigarh, Kolkata, Chennai, Bangalore, Guwahati, Mumbai, Ahmedabad, Delhi, Bhopal, Hyderabad, Patna); library of 30,000 vols, 80 journals; Chair. AJAY SHANKAR; Dir-Gen. N. C. VASUDEVAN; publs *Productivity* (4 a year), *Productivity News* (12 a year), *Utpadakta* (Hindi, 12 a year).

Socio-Economic Research Institute: C-19 & C-39 College Street Market, Kolkata 700007; tel. (33) 22410775; economics and economic history, sociology and social history, demography focusing on the historical demography of India; Dir Prof. DURGAPRASAD BHATTACHARYA.

EDUCATION

Indian Institute of Advanced Study: Rashtrapati Nivas, Shimla 171005; tel. (177) 2830006; fax (177) 2831389; e-mail director@iias.org; internet www.iias.org; f. 1965; undertakes postdoctoral research, especially in the humanities and social sciences; also functions as Inter-Univ. Centre for Humanities and Social Sciences on behalf of the Univ. Grants Commission of India; library of 145,000 vols and 340 periodicals; Dir PETER RONALD DE SOUZA; Chair. Prof.

BHAL CHANDRA MUNGEKAR; publs *IIAS Review* (2 a year), *Studies in Humanities and Social Sciences*, *Summerhill* (2 a year).

Indian Psychometric and Educational Research Association: Dept of Education, Patna Training College Campus, Patna 800004; tel. (612) 50985; f. 1969 to promote and develop the study of, and undertake research into, psychology, education, statistics, etc.; 330 mems; library of 3,700 vols; Pres. Dr A. K. P. SINHA; Gen. Sec. Dr R. P. SINGH; publ. *Indian Journal of Psychometry and Education*.

FINE AND PERFORMING ARTS

National Institute of Design: Paldi, Ahmedabad 380007; tel. (79) 26623692; fax (79) 26621167; e-mail info@nid.edu; internet www.nid.edu/; f. 1961; est. by the govt of India as a research, training and service org. in industrial and communication design; Diploma in Design after 2–3 years' training (graduate) or 5 years' training (undergraduate) in Industrial Design or Communication Design; library of 23,000 vols, 130 current periodicals, 75,000 slides, 2,044 tapes and records, 1,545 other audio-visual aids and 600 well-designed objects for reference; Chair. SALMAN HAIDAR; Dir AKHIL SUCCENA (acting); publs *Design and Environment: An Introductory Manual*, *Design Samvad*, *Design the Indian Context*.

National Research Laboratory for Conservation of Cultural Property: Sector E/3, Aliganj, Lucknow 226024; tel. (522) 2372378; fax (522) 2372378; e-mail mv_nair@india.com; internet www.nrlc.gov.in/english/conservation.htm; f. 1976; conducts research into conservation techniques of objects of art and provides technical assistance to museums and related institutions; training in conservation for Asian countries sponsored by UNESCO; regional laboratory at Mysore; library of 12,000 vols, 130 periodical subscriptions; Dir M. V. NAIR.

HISTORY, GEOGRAPHY AND ARCHAEOLOGY

Archaeological Survey of India: Office of the Dir-Gen., Janpath, New Delhi 110011; tel. (11) 23013574; fax (11) 23019487; e-mail directorgeneralasi@gmail.com; internet www.asi.nic.in; f. 1902; excavating, preservation, surveying and maintenance of archaeological sites; advanced archaeological training; library of 80,000 vols containing rare material; Dir-Gen. K. N. SHRIVASTAVA; Additional Dir-Gen. VIJAY S. MADAN; Jt Dir-Gen. (M) Dr B. R. MANI; Jt Dir-Gen. (G) D. R. GEHLOT; publs *Indian Archaeology—A Review*, *Memoirs*.

Bihar Research Society: Museum Bldgs, Patna 800001, Bihar; f. 1915; library of 31,000 vols; Pres. Dr J. C. JHA; Sec. M. S. PANDEY; publ. *Journal*.

Indian Council of Historical Research: 35 Ferozeshah Rd, New Delhi 110001; tel. (11) 23382321; fax (11) 23383421; e-mail support@ichrindia.org; internet www.ichrindia.org; gives grants for doctoral theses, research projects, historical journals, and for bibliographical and documentation works; organizes and supports seminars, workshops and conferences for promotion of historical research; Chair. Dr SABYASACHI BHATTACHARYA; publs *The Indian Historical Review*, *Myth and Reality*.

Jayaswal, K. P., Research Institute: Patna 800001; f. 1904 to promote historical research; library of 31,650 vols; Dir Dr JATA SHANKAR JHA.

Kamarupa Anusandhana Samiti (Assam Research Society): Gauhati, Assam; f. 1912;

historical and archaeological research; 250 mems; Pres. Dr BISWANARAYAN SHASTRI; Jt Sec. ATULANANDA GOSWAMI; publ. *Journal of Assam Research Society* (1 a year).

Karnatak Historical Research Society: Diwan Bahadur Rodda Rd, Dharwad 1, Karnataka; f. 1914; promotes historical research in the Karnataka; popularizes the study of history and culture by lectures, slides, exhibitions, celebrations of historical events, excursions, etc.; sections for research in language, culture and Vedic literature, socio-economic problems; 100 mems; library of 3,000 vols; Pres. RAJA S. G. ACHARYA; Chair. Dr P. R. PANCHAMUKHI; Secs A. R. PANCHAMUKHI, G. G. NADGIR; publs *Karnatak Historical Review* (2 a year in English and Kannada), and research publications.

National Atlas and Thematic Mapping Organisation: C.G.O. Complex, 7th Fl., DF—Blk, Bidhan Nagar, Kolkata 700064; e-mail natmo@vsnl.net; internet www.natmo.gov.in; fax (33) 23346460; f. 1956; cartographical research and preparation of nat. atlas of India; library of 19,000 vols, 78,000 maps, 350 atlases; Dir Dr PRITHVISH NAG; Jt Dirs ASHOK KR. MALIK, Dr RAJENDRA PRASAD; publs *Agricultural Resources Atlas of India* (in English), *Atlas of Forest Resources* (in English), *Atlas of Kolkata*, *Atlas of Water Resources*, *Irrigation Atlas of India* (in English), *National Atlas of India* (English and Hindi edns), *Satellite Atlas of India*, *Tourist Atlas of India* (in English), other maps and monographs.

Survey of India: Post Box No. 37, Hathibarkala Estate, Dehradun 248001, Uttarakhand; tel. (135) 2744064; e-mail sgo@sancharnet.in; internet www.surveyofindia.gov.in; f. 1767; engaged in topographical, geographical and geodetic preparation of large-scale devt project maps; acts as adviser to the Govt of India on all survey matters; Surveyor-Gen. SEC. OF DEPT OF SCIENCE & TECHNOLOGY, MIN. OF SCIENCE AND TECHNOLOGY; Addl. Surveyor Gen. Maj.-Gen. R. S. TANWAR.

LANGUAGE AND LITERATURE

Abul Kalam Azad Oriental Research Institute:; tel. (40) 23230805; e-mail akaoriental@gmail.com; internet www.akaori.org; f. 1959; research in history, philosophy, culture, Islamic studies and languages; library of 14,000 vols, 133 MSS; Pres. MAHMOOD BIN MUHAMMAD; Hon. Sec. and Dir M. K. ALI KHAN.

Academy of Sanskrit Research: Mandya Dist., Melkote 571431, Karnataka; tel. (8236) 299841; fax (8236) 299981; e-mail asrbng@vsnl.com; internet www.sanskritacademy.org; f. 1976; affiliated to Univ. of Mysore, and Kannada Univ., Hampi; affiliated to Rashtriya Sanskrit Sansthan, New Delhi, for undergraduate, postgraduate and doctoral courses; research and study of Vedas, Agamas and comparative philosophy, with primary focus on Visistadvaita; researches Sanskrit speech synthesis, natural language processing, machine translation, Sanskrit teaching through computer media; collects scientific information available in Sanskrit texts; library of 28,000 vols, 10,500 palm-leaf and paper MSS; 300 mems; Pres. C. N. SEETHARAM; Dir Prof. Dr BHASHYAMSWAMY; Sec. L. K. ATHEEQ; Librarian CHANDRASHEKAR; publ. *Tattva Dipah* (1 a year).

All-India Oriental Conference: Bhandarkar Oriental Research Institute, Deccan Gymkhana, Pune 411004; tel. (20) 25656932; f. 1919; 1,500 mems; mem. Int. Union for Oriental and Asian Studies; academic sessions every two years; Sec. Dr

SAROJA BHATE; publ. *Proceedings of Sessions* (every 2 years).

Anjuman-i-Islam Urdu Research Institute: 92 Dr Dadabhoy Nowroji Rd, Mumbai 400001; tel. (22) 22620177; fax (22) 22621610; e-mail anjuman_uri@rediffmail.com; f. 1948; research in Urdu; PhD in Arabic, Persian, Urdu and Islamic Studies; library of 20,200 vols; Chair. SAMI KHATIB; Dir Dr ABDUS SATTAR DALVI; Librarian SAYED MOHAMMED TAHER; publ. *Nawa-e-Adab* (4 a year).

Bhandarkar Oriental Research Institute: 812, Shivajinagar, Law College Rd, Pune 411004; tel. (20) 25656932; fax (20) 25656932; e-mail bori1@vsnl.net; internet www.bori.ac.in; f. 1917; Sanskrit, Indological and Oriental studies; library of 110,000 vols books, 28,000 MSS; Hon. Sec. R. N. DANDEKAR; publ. *Annals of BORI* (1 a year).

Cama, K. R., Oriental Institute: 136 Mumbai Samachar Marg, Fort, Mumbai 400023; tel. (22) 22843893; fax (22) 22876593; e-mail krcamaoi@vsnl.com; f. 1916; library of 27,804 vols, 2,000 MSS, 199 journals; Pres. MUNCHERJI N. M. CAMA; Jt Hon. Sec. H. N. MODI; Jt Hon. Sec. Dr N. B. MODY; publ. *Journal* (1 a year).

Deccan College Postgraduate and Research Institute: Deccan College Rd, Yeravada, Pune 411006; tel. (20) 226683192; fax (20) 26692104; e-mail deccan.college@gems.vsnl.net.in; f. 1939; postgraduate research in linguistics, archaeology, history and Vedic Sanskrit; library of 150,000 books and periodicals, 12,000 rare MSS; Vice-Chancellor Prof. K. PADDAYYA; Registrar S. R. KASHIKAR; publ. *Annual Bulletin*.

Ganganatha Jha Kendriya Sanskrit Vidyapeetha (Central Sanskrit Research Institute): Azad Park, Allahabad 211002, Uttar Pradesh; f. 1943; research into Sanskrit and other Indological subjects; library of 60,000 vols, 50,000 MSS; Principal Dr G. C. TRIPATHI; publs *Quarterly Research Journal*, catalogues, bibliographies, Sanskrit texts and studies.

Gujarat Research Society: Dr Madhuri Shah Campus, Ramkrishna Mission Marg, Khar (W), Mumbai 400052; tel. (22) 26462691; fax (22) 26047398; f. 1936; organizes and coordinates research in social and cultural activities; teacher-training; library of 10,000 vols; Pres. K. P. HAZARAT; publ. *Journal* (4 a year).

International Academy of Indian Culture: J 22 Hauz Khas Enclave, New Delhi 110016; tel. (11) 22665495; f. 1935; studies India's artistic, literary and historic relations with other Asian countries; library of 200,000 vols, 40,000 MSS; Dir Dr LOKESH CHANDRA; publ. *Satapitaka Series*.

Kuppuswami Sastri Research Institute: 84 Thiru V. Kalayanasundaranar Rd, Mylapore, Chennai 600004; tel. (44) 24675281; fax (44) 24675282; e-mail info@ksrisanskrit.in; internet www.ksrisanskrit.in; f. 1944; govt-sponsored and affiliated to University of Madras; promotion of Oriental learning especially Indology; lectures, seminars and workshops; 400 mems; library of 30,000 vols (including palm-leaf manuscripts); Dir Dr S. S. JANAKI; publs *Journal of Oriental Research*, and numerous research publs.

Mumbai Marathi Granth Sangrahalaya: Dadar, Mumbai 400014; tel. (22) 24134211; f. 1898; research in Marathi language and literature; library of 185,020 vols; Pres. S. K. PATIL.

Oriental Institute of Indian Languages: Univ. of Mysore, Kautilya Circle, Mysore 570005, Karnataka; tel. (821) 2423136; promotes inter-regional and inter-continental understanding through the study of languages; Dir Dr H. P. DEVAKI.

Oriental Research Institute: Univ. of Karnataka Mysore, 570005; tel. (81) 2420331; library of 28,300 vols and 50 periodicals; collection of 60,000 ancient MSS; Dir K. RAJAGOPALACHAR.

Sri Venkateswara University Oriental Research Institute: Tirupati 517502, Andhra Pradesh; tel. (877) 2289414; fax (877) 2289544; internet www.svuniversity.in; f. 1939, present bldg 1979, named the 'Tiruppan Alvar Bhavan' in memory of 9th-century Vaisnava St Tiruppan Alvar; given by T. T. DEVASTHANAMS to the Univ. in 1956; researches in language and literature, philosophy and religion, art and archaeology, ancient Indian history and culture; library of 42,000 vols, 16,948 palm-leaf and paper MSS; publs *Sri Venkateswara Oriental Series*, *SVU Oriental Journal*.

Vishveshvaranand Vedic Research Institute: Sadhu Ashram, Hoshiarpur 146021; tel. (1882) 223582; e-mail vvrinstitute@yahoo.co.in; f. 1903; academic and cultural studies on Indian literatures and religion; Pres. Prof. G. P. CHOPRA; Dir Prof. I. D. UNIYAL; publs *Research Bulletin* (1 a year, in English), *Vishva Jyoti* (cultural, Hindi 12 a year), *Vishva Samskritam* (cultural research, Sanskrit, 4 a year).

Attached Institute:

Vishveshvaranand Vishva Bandhu Institute of Sanskrit and Indological Studies: Sadhu Ashram, Hoshiarpur 146021; tel. (1882) 221002; f. 1965; postgraduate teaching, research and study in Indology; Prak-Shastri and Shastri MA classes in Sanskrit; 12 fellows; library of 76,500 vols, 3,000 ancient MSS; Chair. G. D. BHARADWAJ; publs *Acharya Vishva Bandhu Memorial Lecture Series* (1 a year), *Panjab University Indological Series*, *Vishveshvaranand Indological Journal* (research, English and Sanskrit, 2 a year).

MEDICINE

Advanced Centre for Treatment, Research and Education in Cancer (ACTREC): Tata Memorial Centre, Kharghar, Navi Mumbai 410210; tel. (22) 27405000; fax (22) 27405085; e-mail mail@actrec.gov.in; internet www.actrec.gov.in; f. 1952 as Cancer Research Centre; library: 5,481 books, 9,642 bound vols of journals, 51 current periodicals; Dir Dr R. SARIN; publ. *Scientific Report* (1 a year).

B. M. Institute of Mental Health: Ashram Rd, near Nehru Bridge, Maninagar, Ahmedabad 380009, Gujarat; tel. (79) 26578256; fax (79) 26578259; f. 1951; comprehensive mental health services, teaching, and research; psychiatric clinic for the emotionally disturbed; clinic for children with learning difficulties; occupational therapy and rehabilitation services; speech clinic; postgraduate training in psychodiagnostics and counselling; offers diploma in working with the developmentally handicapped; library of 6,484 vols; Dir Dr S. R. APTE; publ. *Mental Health Review* (1 a year).

Central Leprosy Teaching and Research Institute: Min. of Health & Family Welfare, Govt of India, Chengalpattu, Tamil Nadu 603001; tel. (44) 27426274; fax (44) 27429308; internet dirclatri@dataone.in; f. 1955; a WHO regional training centre; library of 13,000 vols, 33 periodicals; Dir Dr P. K. OOMMEN; publ. *News Bulletin* (4 a year).

Central Research Institute: Kasauli, Himachal Pradesh; f. 1905; medical research, graduate and postgraduate training, manufacture of biological products; Institute of the Govt of India; library of 30,000 vols; Dir Dr J. SOKHEY.

Haffkine Institute for Training, Research and Testing: Acharya Donde Marg, Parel, Mumbai 400012; tel. (22) 24160947; fax (22) 24161787; e-mail contact@haffkineinstitute.org; internet www.haffkineinstitute.org/; f. 1897; principal centre of research in communicable diseases, biomedical and allied sciences in India; library of 26,500 back vols of scientific journals, more than 10,500 books, 4,000 micro fiches and a CD-ROM colln; Dir Dr ABHAY CHOWDHARY; publs *Determination Of HIV Seroprevalence In Pulmonary Tuberculosis Patients And Study Of Their Cellular Responses To Recall Antigens*, *Evaluation of three 'ready to formulate' oil adjuvants for foot-and-mouth disease vaccine production*, *Synthesis and antimicrobial activity of 2,4-disubstituted thiazole derivatives containing 1,2,4-triazole ring systems*.

Indian Brain Research Association: Dept of Biochemistry, University of Calcutta, 35 Ballygunge Circular Rd, Kolkata 700019; f. 1964; 300 mems; library of 2,000 vols; Pres. and Ed. Sec. Prof. J. J. GHOSH; publ. *Brain News* (2 a year).

Indian Council of Medical Research: V. Ramalingaswami Bhawan, Ansari Nagar, New Delhi 110029; tel. (11) 26588895; fax (11) 26588662; e-mail icmrhqds@sansad.nic.in; internet www.icmr.nic.in; f. 1911; promotes, coordinates and funds medical research; maintains the National Institute of Nutrition (Hyderabad), National Institute of Virology (Pune), Tuberculosis Research Centre (Chennai), National Institute of Cholera and Enteric Diseases (Kolkata), Institute of Pathology (New Delhi), National Institute of Occupational Health (Ahmedabad), Institute of Immunohaematology (Mumbai), National Institute for Research in Reproductive Health (Mumbai), Entero Virus Research Centre (Mumbai), Vector Control Research Centre (Pondicherry), Central Jalma Institute for Leprosy (Agra), Malaria Research Centre (Delhi), Institute for Research in Medical Statistics (New Delhi), National Institute of Epidemiology (Chennai), Institute of Cytology and Preventive Oncology (New Delhi), Rajendra Memorial Research Institute of Medical Sciences (Patna), National AIDS Research Institute (Pune), National Centre for Laboratory Animal Sciences (Hyderabad), Food and Drug Toxicology Research Centre (both Hyderabad), Centre for Research in Medical Entomology (Madurai), ICMR Genetic Research Centre (Mumbai), and six Regional Medical Research Centres (Bhubaneswar, Dibrugarh, Jabalpur, Jodhpur, Port Blair, Belgaum); library of 20,000 vols; Dir-Gen. Dr VISHWA MOHAN KATOCH; publs *ICMR Bulletin* (12 a year), *ICMR Patrika* (in Hindi, 12 a year), *Indian Journal of Malariology* (4 a year), *Indian Journal of Medical Research* (12 a year, with supplements).

Institute of Child Health: 11 Dr Biresh Guha St, Kolkata 700017; internet www.ichcal.org/index.htm; f. 1956; affiliated to College for Child Health, Univ. of Calcutta; depts of biochemistry, clinical paediatrics, dermatology, ophthalmology and otorhinolaryngology, paediatric surgery, pathology, physiotherapy, preventive paediatrics, psychiatry, radiology; Dir Dr APURBA GHOSH.

King Institute of Preventive Medicine: Guindy, Chennai 600032; f. 1899; postgraduate training in microbiology; library of 20,137 vols; Dir Dr K. V. MURTHY.

National Institute of Communicable Diseases: Directorate Gen. of Health Services, Min. of Health and Family Welfare (GOI), 22 Sham Nath Marg, Delhi 110054; tel. (11) 23971272; fax (11) 23922677; e-mail dirnicd@bol.net.in; internet www.nicd.org; f. 1963, fmrly Malaria Institute of India (f. 1909); research and training centre in field of communicable and vector-borne diseases; brs at Alwar (Rajasthan), Coonoor (Tamil Nadu) and Jagdalpur (Madhya Pradesh) (all for research and training in epidemiology), Calicut (Kerala), Rajahmundry (Andhra Pradesh) and Varanasi (Uttar Pradesh) (all for research and training on helminthology), Patna (medical entomology and vector control), Bangalore (zoonosis); library of 32,000 vols of books and journals, 251 maps, 89 photocopies and 1,400 annual reports from various orgs; f. 1909; Dir Dr SHIV LAL; Jt Dir and HOD Dr S. VENKATESH (Epidemiology Division), Dr A. C. DHARIWAL (Helminthology Division), Dr V. K. SAXENA (Medical Entomology and Vector Division), S. M. KAUL (T & M Division), Dr VEENA MITTAL (Zoonosis Division), Dr S. T. PASHA (Biochemistry and Biotechnology Division); publs CD Alert (12 a year), Health News Clipping (12 a year).

Attached Institute:

National Anti-Malaria Eradication Programme: 22 Sham Nath Marg, Delhi 110054; tel. (11) 22918576; fax (11) 22518329; f. 1958; coordination, technical guidance, planning, monitoring and evaluation of a nationwide malaria control and eradication programme; library of 4,000 vols; Dir Dr SHIV LAL; publ. Malaria Watch (4 a year).

National Institute of Nutrition: Indian Council of Medical Research, Jamai-Osmania, Tarnaka, Hyderabad, 500007, Andhra Pradesh; tel. (40) 27197200; fax (40) 27019074; e-mail nin@ap.nic.in; internet ninindia.org; f. 1918 as Beri-Beri Enquiry Unit, Deficiency Disease Enquiry 1925, Nutrition Research Laboratories 1928; principal research and training centre for South and South-East Asia; incl. centres for Food and Drug Toxicology Research, Nat. Centre for Laboratory Animal Sciences and Nat. Nutrition Monitoring Bureau; library of 60,000 vols, 30,000 periodicals, 12,000 reports, 20,000 books; Dir Dr B. SESIKERAN; Library and Information Officer DEVIDAS MAHINDRAKAR; publs Nutrition (4 a year), Nutrition News (6 a year).

National Jalma Institute for Leprosy and other Mycobacterial Diseases: POB 101, Dr M. Miyazaki Marg, Taj Ganj, Agra 282001, Uttar Pradesh; tel. (562) 2331756; fax (562) 2331755; e-mail jalma@sancharnet .in; internet www.jalma-icmr.org.in/; f. 1966 as India Centre of JALMA; centre officially handed over to the Govt of India and the Indian Ccl of Medical Research, named the Central JALMA Institute for Leprosy in 1976, present status and name in 2005; part of Indian Ccl of Medical Research; treatment, research and training on leprosy, tuberculosis and HIV/AIDS;; library of 2,496 books, 40 journals; Dir Dr V. M. KATOCH; publ. Quarterly Bulletin.

National Tuberculosis Institute: Govt of India, 'Avalon', 8 Bellary Rd, Bangalore 560003; tel. (80) 23361192; fax (80) 23440952; e-mail ntiindia@blr.vsnl.net.in; internet ntiindia.kar.nic.in; f. 1959; research in epidemiology, applied tuberculosis bacteriology, sociological aspects and systems research with regard to tuberculosis control; training and control programme; information centre on tuberculosis; digital library of institute papers published in periodicals and publs; 140 mems; Dir Dr PRAHLAD KUMAR; publ. Bulletin (2 a year).

Pasteur Institute and Medical Research Institute: Shillong, Meghalaya; f. 1915; library of 7,311 vols; Dir N. G. BANERJEE.

Pasteur Institute of India: Coonoor 643103 (Nilgiris), Tamil Nadu; tel. (423) 2231350; fax (423) 2231655; e-mail oty_piicnr@bsnl.in; internet www .pasteurinstituteindia.com/home.htm; f. 1907; work on virus diseases incl. polio and rabies, devt of vaccines; a WHO int. reference centre for quality control and production of rabies vaccines; a WHO Nat. Polio Surveillance Project; library of 20,000 vols; Dir Dr B. SEKAR; Asst Dir Dr K. N. VENKATARAMANA.

Vallabhbhai Patel Chest Institute: POB 2101, Univ. of Delhi, Delhi 110007; tel. (11) 27666180; fax (11) 27667420; e-mail vpci@ delnet.ren.nic.in; internet www.vpci.org.in; f. 1949; attached to Univ. of Delhi; postgraduate teaching and research in respiratory diseases and allied biomedical sciences; library of 25,000 vols; Dir Prof. V. K. VIJAYAN; publ. Indian Journal of Chest Diseases and Allied Sciences (4 a year).

Vector Control Research Centre: Medical Complex, Indira Nagar, Pondicherry 605006; tel. (413) 2272396; fax (413) 2272041; e-mail vcrc@vsnl.com; internet vcrc.res.in/; f. 1975; attached to Indian Ccl of Medical Research; affiliated with Pondicherry Univ.; develops epidemiological surveillance tools and strategies for the prevention and control of vector-borne diseases, incl. malaria, filariasis and dengue fever; research and postgraduate training; library of 10,000 vols; Dir P. K. DAS.

NATURAL SCIENCES
General

Bose Institute: 93/1 Acharya Prafulla Chandra Rd, Kolkata 700009; tel. (33) 23502403; fax (33) 23506790; e-mail dbt@ boseinst.ernet.in; internet www.boseinst .ernet.in; f. 1917; advances the science and diffusion of knowledge; research undertaken by depts of biochemistry, biophysics, botany, chemistry, microbiology, physics,; experimental stations at Falta, Shamnagar, Madhyamgram and Darjeeling; library of 24,883 vols; Dir Prof. SIBAJI RAHA; Registrar TUSHAR K. GHORUI; Information Officer KAJAL CHAUDHURI; publ. Transactions.

Indian Association for the Cultivation of Science (IACS): 2A& 2B Raja S C Mullick Rd, Kolkata 700032; tel. (33) 24734971; fax (33) 24732805; e-mail helpdesk@iacs.res.in; internet www.iacs.res.in; f. 1876; researches in theoretical physics, spectroscopy, material science, solid state physics, physical chemistry, biological chemistry, energy research unit, polymer science unit, organic and inorganic chemistry; library of 63,205 vols; Pres. Prof. S. K. JOSHI; Dir Prof. K. BHATTACHARYYA; publs Bulletin of the IACS, Indian Journal of Physics.

Raman Research Institute: C. V. Raman Ave, Sadashivanagar, Bangalore 560080, Karnataka; tel. (80) 23610122; fax (80) 23610492; e-mail root@rri.res.in; internet www.rri.res.in; f. 1948; astronomy and astrophysics, light and matter physics, soft condensed matter and theoretical physics; library of 26,035 books, 38,666 periodicals, 175 journals (incl. 100 online); Dir Prof. RAVI SUBRAHMANYAN; Librarian MANJUNATH M.

UNESCO Office New Delhi: B-5/29 Safdarjung Enclave, New Delhi 110029; tel. (11) 26713000; fax (11) 26713001; e-mail newdelhi@unesco.org; internet www.unesco .org/newdelhi; f. 1948; UNESCO's first decentralized office in Asia; acts as designated cluster office for four countries in South Asia (Bhutan, India, Maldives and Sri Lanka); science and technology pro-grammes in 11 South and Central Asian countries and including communication, education and culture programmes; library: documentation and information centre, 30,000 UNESCO documents, reports, etc.; spec. collns: science and technology, education, social sciences, culture and communication; films library, posters, CD-ROMs, CDs; Dir ARMOOGUM PARSURAMEN.

Biological Sciences

Birbal Sahni Institute of Palaeobotany: 53 University Rd, Lucknow 226007; tel. (522) 2740008; fax (522) 2740485; e-mail director@ bsip.res.in; internet www.bsip.res.in/; f. 1946; scientific research on the fundamental and applied aspects of fossil plants and their bearing on the origins of life; evolutionary linkages; biostratigraphy; fossil fuel exploration; phytogeography and biodiagenesis; repository of fossil plants; library of 5,000 vols, 10,000 current periodicals, 35,000 reprints and 300 microfilms, etc.; Dir Prof. NARESH CHANDRA MEHROTRA; publ. The Palaeobotanist (3 a year).

Botanical Survey of India: CGO Complex, 3rd MSO Bldg, Blk F (5th & 6th Floor), DF Blk, Sector I, Salt lake City, Kolkata 700064; tel. (33) 23344963; fax (33) 23346040; internet 164.100.52.111; f. 1890; botanical surveys and research; Headquarters: Central Nat. Herbarium and Indian Botanic Garden at Howrah; Industrial Section, Indian Museum at Calcutta; regional circles at Allahabad, Pune, Coimbatore, Jodhpur, Port Blair, Shillong, Dehradun, Itanagar and Gangtok; library of more than 250,000 vols; 491 scientific staff; Dir Dr B. D. SHARMA; publ. Indian Floras.

Indian Association of Systematic Zoologists: c/o Zoological Survey of India, 34 Chittaranjan Ave, Kolkata 700012; f. 1947; Pres. Dr A. P. KAPUR.

Institute of Plant Industry: Indore, Madhya Pradesh; f. 1924; research in cotton genetics, and in crop improvement of cotton and rotation crops; Dir RAI BAHADUR R. L. SETHI.

Tropical Botanic Garden and Research Institute: Pacha-Palode, Thiruvananthapuram, 695562, Kerala; tel. (472) 2869246; fax (472) 2869646; e-mail tbgri@sancharnet .in; internet www.tbgri.in/; f. 1979; botanical garden, an arboretum, a medicinal plant garden and laboratories for botanical, horticultural, plant biotechnical, ethnomedicinal, ethnopharmacological and phytochemical research; conservation of rare and endangered tropical plant species; promotion of research and devt studies of plants of medicinal and economic importance; herbarium of 17,800 mounted specimens and 30,000 duplicates of vascular plants; museum; library of 5,000 vols, 65 journals; Dir Prof. Dr A. SUBRAMONIAM; publs Index Seminum, Information Brochures.

Zoological Survey of India: Prani Vigyan Bhawan, M Block, New Alipore, Kolkata 700053; tel. (33) 24003925; fax (33) 24003238; internet zsi.gov.in/; f. 1916; activities incl. maintenance of Nat. Zoological Collns, conduct of faunistic surveys and research on systematic zoology, wildlife, environmental conservation, etc.; regional stations at Berhampur, Canning, Chennai, Dehradun, Digha, Hyderabad, Itanagar, Jabalpur, Jodhpur, Kozhikode, Patna, Port Blair, Pune, Shillong, Solan; library of 60,000 vols, 800 periodicals; Dir Dr RAMAKRISHNA; publs Bibliography of Indian Zoology, Fauna of India, Handbooks, Memoirs, Occasional Papers, Records (4 a year), State Fauna Series.

Mathematical Sciences

Institute of Mathematical Sciences: CIT Campus, Taramani, Chennai 600113; tel. (44) 22541856; fax (44) 22541586; internet www.imsc.res.in/; f. 1962; research in pure and applied mathematics, theoretical physics and theoretical computer science; library of 44,996 vols, 260 periodicals; Dir Prof. R. BALASUBRAMANIAN; Registrar SARASWATHI RAMARAJ; publ. *I.M.Sc. Reports.*

Physical Sciences

Alipore Observatory and Meteorological Office: Kolkata; f. 1877; publ. *The India Meteorological Department.*

Astronomical Observatory: Presidency College, Kolkata; f. 1898; Dir Dr P. CHOUDHURY.

Astronomical Observatory of St Xavier's College: 30 Mother Teresa Sarani, Kolkata 700016; tel. (33) 22551264; fax (33) 22879966; e-mail shiva@sxccal.edu; internet www.sxccal.edu/pg_physics; f. 1875; Dir Rev. F. GOREUX.

Bhabha Atomic Research Centre: Trombay, Mumbai 400085, Maharashtra; tel. (22) 25505050; fax (22) 25505151; e-mail director@barc.gov.in; internet www.barc.gov.in; f. 1944; nat. centre for research in and devt of atomic energy for non-military purposes; facilities incl. 3 research reactors; Van de Graaff accelerator; laboratories at Srinagar, Gulmarg, and Gauribidanur; isotope production unit; central workshops; pilot plants for production of heavy water, zirconium, titanium; uranium metal plant; food irradiation and processing laboratory; reactor engineering laboratory and test facilities; library of 200,000 vols, 1,200 technical journals, 450,000 technical reports; Dir Dr SRIKUMAR BANERJEE; publ. *Technical Reports.*

Central Seismological Observatory: Shillong; headquarters at New Delhi.

Geodetic and Research Branch, Survey of India: POB 77, Dehradun 248001; f. 1800; geodetic and allied geophysical activities, including development and research of instrumentation; library of 55,000 vols; Dir Dr M. G. ARUR; publs reports, and technical publications.

Geological Survey of India: 27 J. L. Nehru Rd, Kolkata 700016; tel. (33) 22861676; fax (33) 22496956; e-mail gsi_chq@vsnl.com; internet www.gsi.gov.in; f. 1851; devoted to surveying and mapping, mineral exploration, specialized investigations, other exploration, research and development, information dissemination, human resource development and project modernization and replacement; library of 5,003,500 vols; Dir-Gen. K. N. MATHUR; publs *Bulletin, Series A, B, C* (irregular), *Catalogue Series* (irregular), *Indian Minerals* (4 a year), *Manual Series* (irregular), *Memoirs of the Geological Survey of India* (irregular), *Miscellaneous Publications* (irregular), *Palaeontologica Indica* (irregular), *Records of the Geological Survey of India. Part I–VIII* (1 a year), *Special Publications* (irregular).

India Meteorological Department: Mausam Bhawan, Lodi Rd, New Delhi 110003; tel. (11) 24619415; fax (11) 24669216; internet www.imd.ernet.in/main_new.htm; f. 1875; 6 regional offices at New Delhi, Mumbai, Kolkata, Madras, Nagpur and Guwahati; 11 meteorological centres at Thiruvananthapuram, Bangalore, Hyderabad, Bhubaneshwar, Lucknow, Jaipur, Srinagar, Ahmedabad, Patna, Chandigarh and Bhopal; 10 cyclone detection radars; Positional Astronomy Centre at Kolkata; provides weather service; scientific activities cover research in all brs of meteorology, incl. agricultural and hydrometeorology, radio-meteorology, satellite and environmental meteorology, atmospheric electricity, seismology; New Delhi is Regional Telecommunication Hub and Regional Meteorological Centre under WMO World Weather Watch; Regional Specialised Meteorological Centre for Tropical Cyclones; also Regional Area Forecast Centre under ICAO; Dir-Gen. Dr AJIT TYAGI (acting); publs *Indian Astronomical Ephemeris* (1 a year), *Indian Weather Review*, *Mausam* (4 a year), occasional memoirs, *Regional/State Daily Weather Reports*, reviews.

Indian Bureau of Mines: 'Indira Bhavan', Civil Lines, Nagpur 440102; tel. (712) 2560041; fax (712) 2565073; e-mail cgibm@ibm.mah.nic.in; internet ibm.nic.in; f. 1948; govt dept responsible for the conservation and devt of mineral resources and protection of mining environment; aid in mine and mineral devt; technical consultancy in mining and mineral-processing, colln and dissemination of mineral statistics and information, preparation of feasibility reports of mining projects, incl. benefication plants, and preparation of environmental management plans; conducts market surveys on minerals and mineral commodities; regional offices at Ajmer, Bangalore, Bhubaneswar, Chennai, Dehradun, Goa, Hyderabad, Jabalpur, Kolkata, Ranchi, Udaipur; mineral processing laboratory and pilot plant at Nagpur; library of 50,000 vols, 10,000 periodicals; Controller-Gen. A. N. BOSE; publs *Indian Minerals Yearbook*, *Monthly Statistics of Mineral Production*, *Mineral Industry at a Glance* (1 a year).

Indian Institute of Astrophysics: II Block, Koramangala, Bangalore 560034; tel. (80) 25530672; fax (80) 25534043; e-mail hasan@iiap.res.in; internet www.iiap.res.in; f. 1786 as private observatory in Madras; study of solar physics, stellar physics, solar system objects, theoretical astrophysics incl. ionosphere, cosmology, solar-terrestrial relationship and instrumentation; field stations at Gauribidanur, Hanle, Kavalur and Kodaikanal, and a research unit at Hosakote; library: more than 18,000 vols and access to 140 online journals; Dir Prof. S. S. HASAN; publ. *Reprints.*

Indian Institute of Geomagnetism: Kalamboli-Panvel Highway, New Panvel (W), New Mumbai 410218; tel. (22) 27484046; fax (22) 27480762; e-mail divyam@iigs.iigm.res.in; internet www.iigm.res.in; f. 1971; observatories in Alibag, Jaipur, Nagpur, Gulmarg, Shillong, Pondicherry, Rajkot, Silchar, Tirunelveli, Vishakapatnam; World Data Centre WDC-C2 for geomagnetism; operates geomagnetic observatory over Antarctica; basic research in upper atmospheric physics, solid earth geophysics and allied fields, environmental magnetism; research centres at Tirunelveli, Tamil Nadu (Equatorial Geophysical Research Laboratory) and at Allahabad, Uttar Pradesh (K. S. Krishnan Geomagnetic Research Laboratory); library: 20,000 vols (books, bound periodicals, reprints, reports, maps magnetic data and non-book material); Dir Prof. ARCHANA BHATTACHARYYA; publ. *Indian Magnetic Data* (1 a year).

Indian Space Research Organization (ISRO): Antariksh Bhavan, New BEL Rd, Bangalore 560094; tel. (80) 23415474; fax (80) 23412253; e-mail info@isro.gov.in; internet www.isro.gov.in; f. 1972; devt of satellites, launch vehicles and ground stations for satellite-based communications, resources survey and meteorological services; operates Vikram Sarabhai Space Centre, Space Applications Centre at Ahmedabad, ISRO Satellite Centre at Bangalore, SHAR Centre at Sriharikota Island, Liquid Propulsion System Unit at Trivandrum and Bangalore, Devt and Educational Communications Unit at Ahmedabad, ISRO Telemetry Tracking and Command Network at Bangalore, ISRO Inertial Systems Unit, Trivandrum, INSAT Master Control Facility, Hassan; Nat. Remote Sensing Agency at Hyderabad, Physical Research Laboratory at Ahmedabad and Nat. Mesosphere-Stratosphere-Troposphere Radar Facility at Gadanki; Chair. G. MADHAVAN NAIR; Man. Dir., Antrix Corp. Ltd (commercial arm of ISRO) K. R. SRIDHAR MURTHY; publs *Journal of Spacecraft Technology* (2 a year), *Space India* (4 a year).

Indira Gandhi Centre for Atomic Research: Dept of Atomic Energy, Kalpakkam 603102, Tamil Nadu; tel. (44) 27480267; fax (44) 27480060; e-mail dir@igcar.gov.in; internet www.igcar.gov.in; f. 1971; attached to Dept of Atomic Energy, Govt of India; researches in fast reactor technology and related disciplines; library of 65,000 vols, 820 journals, 200,000 research reports; Dir Dr BALDEV RAJ.

Institute for Plasma Research: Bhat, Gandhinagar, Gujarat 382428; tel. (79) 23962001; fax (79) 23962277; e-mail postmaster@ipr.res.in; internet www.ipr.res.in; f. 1986; research in plasma physics; library of 21,260 vols, 11,096 technical reports, 2,568 reprints, 105 periodicals; Dir P. K. KAW; publ. *Plasma Processing Update* (4 a year).

Inter-University Centre for Astronomy and Astrophysics: POB 4, Ganeshkhind, Pune Univ. Campus, Pune 411007; tel. (20) 25604100; fax (20) 25604699; e-mail root@iucaa.ernet.in; internet www.iucaa.ernet.in; f. 1988; fundamental research and training in all aspects of astronomy and astrophysics; MSc and PhD, refresher courses, research workshops, etc.; Dir Prof. NARESH K. DADHICH; Dean Prof. T. PADMANABHAN (Core Academic Programmes), Prof. A. K. KEMBHAVI; publs *Khagol* (4 a year), *Lecture Notes.*

Mining, Geological and Metallurgical Institute of India: GN-38/4, Sector V, Salt Lake, Kolkata 700091; tel. (33) 23573987; fax (33) 23573482; e-mail mgmi@cal2.vsnl.net.in; internet www.mgmiindia.com/home.html; f. 1906; 2,500 mems from 16 brs; library of 3,500 vols; Pres. N. C. JHA; Vice-Pres. R. K. SAHA; Hon. Sec. S. C. ROY; Jt Sec. P. ROY; publ. *Transactions* (2 a year).

National Institute of Rock Mechanics: Champion Reefs P.O., Kolar Gold Fields 563117, Karnataka; tel. (8153) 275004; fax (8153) 275002; e-mail nirm@nirm.in; internet www.nirm.in/home.htm; f. 1989; library of 1,400 vols; Dir Dr P. C. NAWANI; publ. *Bulletin* (3 a year).

Nizamiah and Japal-Rangapur Observatories and Centre of Advanced Study in Astronomy: Dept of Astronomy, Osmania University, Hyderabad 500007; tel. (40) 27017306; e-mail pies@ouastr.ernet.in; f. 1908, transferred to control of Osmania Univ. 1919; library of 15,000 vols, 4,000 periodicals; Dir Prof. P. V. SUBRAHMANYAM; publ. *Astronomical.*

Physical Research Laboratory: Ahmedabad, Gujarat 380009; tel. (79) 26314000; fax (79) 26314900; e-mail info@prl.res.in; internet www.prl.res.in; f. 1947; atomic and molecular physics, nuclear and particle physics, laser physics and quantum optics, gravitational physics, non-linear dynamics and quantum chaos, optical and infrared astronomy, solar physics, astrophysics, atmospheric sciences and planetary aeronomy, oceanography and climate studies, solar system and geochronology, planetary science and exploration; library of 50,000 vols, 2,500 scientific reports and 1,200 maps; Dir

Prof. JITENDRA NATH GOSWAMI; Controller-cum-Registrar Y. M. TRIVEDI.

Saha Institute of Nuclear Physics: 1/AF, Bidhannagar, Kolkata 700064; tel. (33) 23375345; fax (33) 23374637; e-mail library@saha.ac.in; internet www.saha.ac.in; f. 1950; 1,250 Institute mems; 500 external mems; conducts advanced research and teaching in nuclear science (radioactive ion beams, high-energy physics, quark gluon plasma); research in physics (atomic physics, condensed matter physics, high-energy physics, microelectronics, nuclear physics, plasmic physics, surface and general mathematical physics) and biophysical sciences (cell biology genetic toxicology, macromolecular crystallography, membrane biophysics, molecular genetics, nuclear and radiochemistry, photochemistry, radiation chemistry and biology, structural biology and biomolecular spectroscopy, ultrastructural research); library of 33,327 books, 48,369 journals, 21,218 reports, 774 CD-ROMs; Dir Prof. BIKASH SINHA; Registrar V. V. MALLIKARJUNA RAO.

PHILOSOPHY AND PSYCHOLOGY

Pratap Centre of Philosophy: Dept of Philosophy, Univ. of Pune, Amalner, District Jalgaon, Maharashtra 425401; tel. (2587) 222280; e-mail pratap.philosophy@gmail.com; f. 1916 as Indian Inst. of Philosophy, taken over by univ. and renamed 1972; comparative study of Indian and European philosophy; 3 fellowships awarded yearly for research; library of 6,000 vols; Dir Dr ARCHANA DEGAONKAR; publs *The Philosophical Quarterly* (4 a year), *Tatvadnyan Mandir* (in Marathi).

The Yoga Institute: Santa Cruz (East), Shri Yogendra Marg, Prabhat Colony, Mumbai 400055; tel. (22) 26122185; e-mail yogainstitute@gmail.com; internet www.theyogainstitute.org; f. 1918; promotes self-education, physical, mental, moral and psychic, aided by the science of Yoga; conducts academic and scientific research in Yoga culture and technique; runs teacher training Inst. of Yoga and a Psychosomatic Clinic based on Yoga; library of 4,500 vols; Dir HANSA JAYADEVA YOGENDRA; publs *Cyclopaedia Yoga, Yoga and Total Health* (12 a year), *Yoga Studies*.

RELIGION, SOCIOLOGY AND ANTHROPOLOGY

Anjuman-i-Islam Urdu Research Association: 92 Dadabhoy Nowroji Rd, Mumbai 400001; library of 5,000 vols; Pres. Dr M. ISHAQUE JAMKHANAWALA; Dir Prof. N. S. GOREKAR; publ. 12 vols of research work on Islamic studies.

Anthropological Survey of India:; e-mail hohq@ansi.gov.in 27 Jawaharlal Nehru Rd, Kolkata 700016; tel. (33) 22861796; fax (33) 22861685; e-mail director@ansi.gov.in; internet www.ansi.gov.in; f. 1945; research in cultural and physical anthropology, human ecology, linguistics, psychology, folklore, biochemistry and radiology; library of 40,935 vols; Dir Dr V. R. RAO.

Applied Interdisciplinary Development Research Institute, Youth Entrepreneurship Development Organization (YEDO): 20 Thiruvenkadapuram Main Rd, Choolaimedu, Chennai 600094; tel. (44) 65317697; fax (44) 23741564; e-mail peteraidri@hotmail.com; f. 1985; 120 mems; library of 2,000 vols; interdisciplinary devt education, training, research, consultancy, information dissemination in fields of sustainable agricultural devt, youth empowerment, empowerment of street children, women's empowerment, indigenous know-

ledge and local resources devt, environmental education, and entrepreneurship devt; Exec. Dir Dr A. PETER; publ. *Young Entrepreneurs Digest*.

Ethnographic and Folk Culture Society: C-24, K Rd, Mahanagar Extn, Lucknow 226006; tel. and fax (522) 2372362; e-mail efcs@sancharnet.in; internet www.efcsindia.com; f. 1945; research into anthropological sciences; museum of Folk Life and Culture; library; Pres. Prof. T. N. MADAN; Vice-Presidents Prof. R. K. KAR, Prof. P. VENKAT RAO, Prof. J. K. PUNDIR, Prof. R. B. S. VERMA, Prof. P. K. TEWARI; Hon. Gen. Sec. Dr SUKANT K. CHAUDHARY; publs *The Eastern Anthropologist* (4 a year), *Indian Journal of Physical Anthropology and Human Genetics* (2 a year), *Manav* (in Hindi, 2 a year).

Indian Council of Social Science Research (ICSSR): JNU Institutional Area, Aruna Asaf Ali Marg, New Delhi 110067; tel. (11) 26179849; fax (11) 26179836; e-mail info@icssr.org; internet www.icssr.org; f. 1969; sponsors and coordinates research in social science, provides financial assistance for research programmes, awards fellowships and grants; sponsors confs, seminars, training programmes and publs; provides partial support to 28 social science research institutes; collaborates with international bodies in research programmes; Nat. Social Science Documentation Centre (NASSDOC: see Libraries and Archives); Data Archives; regional centres in Mumbai, Kolkata, Chandigarh, Delhi, Hyderabad, and Shillong; library of 35,000 books, 150,000 periodicals; Chair. Prof JAVEED ALAM; Mem.-Sec. Dr RANJIT SINHA; Dir for Research Institute and Regional Centre Dr. S. N. M. KOPPARTY; Dir for Research Project and Research Fellowship Dr G. S. SAUN; Dir for Research Survey, Publications and Sales Dr RANJIT SINHA; Dir for NASSDOC Dr P. R. GOSWAMI; publs *ICSSR Journal of Abstracts and Reviews: Economics* (2 a year), *ICSSR Journal of Abstracts and Reviews: Geography* (2 a year), *ICSSR Journal of Abstracts and Reviews: Political Science* (2 a year), *ICSSR Journal of Abstracts and Reviews: Sociology and Social Anthropology* (2 a year), *Indian Psychological Abstracts and Reviews* (2 a year), *Indian Social Science Review*.

Institute of Applied Manpower Research: Sector A-7, Institutional Area, Narela, Delhi 110040; tel. (11) 27787214; fax (11) 27783467; e-mail iamr@del2.vsnl.net.in; internet www.iamrindia.org; f. 1962; autonomous body under Planning Comm.; studies and disseminates information on the nature, characteristics and utilization of human resources in India; develops methodologies for forecasting demand and supply; compiles information on technical manpower; organizes seminars, confs, study courses and training programmes in techniques of manpower planning at nat. and int. levels and provides consultancy services; conducts degree and diploma courses in Human Resource Planning and Devt for int. participants in collaboration with Commonwealth Secretariat, London, United Kingdom; library of 26,000 vols, 150 journals; Pres. (Gen. Ccl) Hon. SH. MONTEK SINGH AHLUWALIA; Dir R. SRIDHARAN; Librarian NEERJA JAIN; publs *Manpower Documentation* (12 a year), *Manpower Journal* (4 a year), *Manpower Profile India* (1 a year), *Technical Manpower Bulletin* (4 a year), *Technical Manpower Profile* (every 5 years).

Institute of Economic Growth: University of Delhi Enclave, North Campus, Delhi 110007; tel. (11) 27667288; fax (11) 27667410; e-mail system@iegindia.org; internet www.iegindia.org; f. 1958; an

autonomous body recognized by the University of Delhi as a national-level multidisciplinary centre for advanced research and training, including PhD supervision in the fields of economic and social development; specialized library and documentation service; Dir Prof. KANCHAN CHOPRA; publs *Contributions to Indian Sociology: New Series* (2 a year), *Studies in Asian Social Development* (irregular), *Studies in Economic Development and Planning*.

Namgyal Institute of Tibetology/fmrly Sikkim Research Institute of Tibetology: Deorali, 737101 Gangtok, Sikkim; tel. and fax (3592) 281525; e-mail info@tibetology.net; internet www.tibetology.net; f. 1958; research centre for study of Mahayana (Northern Buddhism); museum of icons and art objects; library of 60,000 vols of Tibetan literature (canonical of all sects and secular) in MSS and xylographs; Dir BALMIKI PRASAD SINGH; publ. *Bulletin of Tibetology* (2 a year).

National Institute of Rural Development: Rajendranagar, Hyderabad 500030; tel. (40) 24008526; fax (40) 24016500; e-mail dhiraj@nird.gov.in; internet www.nird.org.in; f. 1958; autonomous servicing and consultancy agency for central and state govts; training for govt and non-govt officials; a Centre on Rural Documentation (CORD) provides computerized library services; devt research into all facets of rural life; offers consultancy service to nat. and int. orgs; repackages govt and other literature on rural devt for wider dissemination; library of 95,000 vols; Dir-Gen. B. K. SINHA; Deputy Dir.-Gen. K. NARAYANA KUMAR; publs *CORD Abstracts* (6 a year), *CORD Alerts* (26 a year), *CORD Index* (12 a year), *Handbook of Rural Development Statistics* (1 a year), *Journal of Rural Development* (4 a year), *Recommendations of Seminars and Workshops* (1 a year), *Research Highlights* (1 a year).

Rural Development Organization: Lamsang Bazar, PO Lamsang, Manipur; tel. (85) 310961; f. 1975; research, socio-economic devt programme for the rural poor, skill training programme; Library and Documentation Centre, AIDS Prevention and Control Programme, Community Health Centre, Micro-credit scheme, rural bank, all set up with govt aid; library of 10,000 vols; Gen. Sec. W. BRAJABIDHU SINGH; publ. *Loyalam* (12 a year).

A. N. Sinha Institute of Social Studies: Patna 800001, Bihar; tel. (612) 2221395; fax (612) 2226226; e-mail root@ssaansi.ren.nic.in; internet www.ansiss.org; f. 1958 to undertake teaching and research in the social sciences, especially economics, sociology, social psychology and political science; library of 58,206 vols; Dir NAVIN VERMA; Sec. JITENDRA PANDEY; publ. *Journal of Social and Economic Studies* (4 a year).

Sri Aurobindo Centre: Adhchini, Junction of Sri Aurobindo Marg and Qutab Hotel Rd, New Mehrauli Rd, New Delhi 110017; e-mail mail@sabda.in; multi-disciplinary research and training in the integral study of Man; research in comparative religions, Indian cultural values; lectures, seminars, study groups, summer programmes; homeopathic dispensary; research facilities; library; Chair. DHARMA VIRA; Hon. Sec. K. M. AGARWALA.

V. V. Giri National Labour Institute: Sector 24, Gautam Budh Nagar, Noida 201301, Uttar Pradesh; tel. (120) 2411472; fax (120) 2411474; e-mail vvgnli@vsnl.com; internet www.vvgnli.org; f. 1964; research, training and consultancy; library of 50,000 vols; Dir S. K. DEV VERMAN; publs *Award Digest* (4 a year), *Labour and Development* (2 a year), *Shram Jagat* (6 a year), *Shram Vidhan* (6 a year).

TECHNOLOGY

Ahmedabad Textile Industries Research Association: PO Ambavadi Vistar, Ahmedabad 380015; tel. (79) 26307921; fax (79) 26304677; e-mail atiraad1@sancharnet.in; internet www.atira-rnd-tex.org; f. 1949; textile consultation, training and research, information and testing services; library of 41,000 vols; Dir Dr A. K. SHARMA; publs *ACT (ATIRA Communications on Textiles)* (4 a year), *TEXINCON* (4 a year).

The Automotive Research Association of India: POB 832, Vetal Hill, Pune 411004; Survey No. 102, Vetal Hill, Off Paud Rd, Kothrud, Pune 411004; tel. (20) 30231111; fax (20) 25434190; e-mail info@araiindia.com; internet www.araiindia.com; f. 1966; research institution of the Automotive Industry with the Ministry of Industry; provides facilities for research and development; product design; evaluation of equipment and standardization; certification for the Indian automotive and component industry; compilation and dissemination of technical information to the automotive and engineering industry; testing laboratories; library of 10,000 vols, 60 periodicals; Dir Shrikant R. MARATHE; publs *Automotive Abstracts* (12 a year), *ARAI Newsletter* (4 a year), *Automotive Abstracts*.

Bengal Textile Institute: Serampore; f. 1904.

Berhampore Textile Institute: Berhampore; f. 1925.

Birla Research Institute for Applied Sciences: Birlagram 456331, Nagda, Madhya Pradesh; tel. (7366) 246760; fax (7366) 244114; e-mail bri@adityabirla.com; f. 1965; registered soc.; helps nat. industrial growth; research in pulp, cellulose fibre and pollution abatement; Pres. SHAILENDRA K. JAIN; Dir-Gen. A. N. SHRIVASTAVA; publ. *Bulletin* (4 a year).

The Bombay Textile Research Association: Lal Bahadur Shastri Marg, Ghatkopar (W), Mumbai 400086, Maharashtra; tel. (22) 25003651; fax (22) 25000459; e-mail btra@vsnl.com; internet www.btraindia.com; f. 1954; researches on process and product devts with emphasis on cleaner processing technologies; textile testing services; technical consultancy services in textile manufacturing; certification and training services; recognized for postgraduate studies by Univ. of Mumbai; library of 20,200 vols; Dir Dr ASHOK N. DESAI; publs *BTRA Bulletin* (12 a year), *BTRA Scan* (4 a year).

Bureau of Indian Standards (BIS): Manak Bhavan, 9 Bahadur Shah Zafar Marg, New Delhi 110002; tel. (11) 23230131; fax (11) 23234062; e-mail info@bis.org.in; internet www.bis.org.in/; f. 1947; library of 740,000 standards and technical publications and 416 periodicals; Dir-Gen. SHARAD GUPTA; Dir for Library Services ROMA ROY; publs *Current Published Information on Standardization, Standards India, Standards Worldover—Monthly Additions to Library*.

Central Institute for Research on Cotton Technology: Adenwala Rd, Matunga, Mumbai 400019; tel. (22) 24127273; fax (22) 24130835; e-mail circot@vsnl.com; internet www.circot.res.in; f. 1924; part of Indian Council of Agricultural Research; library of 11,800 vols; Dir Dr S. SREENIVASAN.

Central Water and Power Research Station: PO Khadakwasla Research Station, Pune 411024; tel. (20) 24103200; fax (20) 24381004; e-mail wapis@cwprs.gov.in; internet www.cwprs.gov.in; f. 1916; basic and applied research in hydraulic engineering and allied subjects; activities in fields of

hydrology and water resources analysis, river engineering, reservoir and appurtenant structures, coastal and offshore engineering, ship hydrodynamics, hydraulic machinery, foundations and structures, mathematical modelling, instrumentation and control, applied earth sciences; library of 70,779 vols, 200 periodicals; Dir Dr ISHWAR D. GUPTA; Jt Dirs A. C. GANGAL, A. R. CHAVAN, S. GOVINDAN, C. N. KANETKAR, F. T. MATHEW, S. G. PATNAIK, P. K. KHARE, B. S. KULKARNI, DHAYALAN S., R. K. KAMBLE, M. D. KUDALE, R. S. RAMTEKE, Dr C. B. SINGH, VIJAYAKUMAR B., R. S WADHWA.

Indian Institute of Natural Resins & Gums: Namkum, Ranchi 834010, Jharkhand; tel. (651) 2260117; fax (651) 2260202; e-mail iinrg@ilri.ernet.in; internet www.icar.org.in/; f. 1924, fmrly Indian Lac Research Institute; library of 40,128 vols; Dir Dr BANGALI BABOO.

Indian Rubber Manufacturers Research Association: Plot No. B–88, Rd No. 24/U–2, Wagle Industrial Estate, Thane 400604, Maharashtra; tel. (22) 25811348; fax (22) 25823910; e-mail rubberin@bom7.vsnl.net.in; internet www.irmra.org; f. 1959; research and devt relating to rubber and allied industries; 45 staff; Dir Dr S. K. CHAKRABORTY (acting); Deputy Dir P. R. CHOUDHURY; Sr Asst Dir P. K. DAS; Asst Dirs K. R. KRISHNAN, K. RAJKUMAR, Dr ARINDAM MUKHERJI.

Institute of Hydraulics and Hydrology: Poondi 602023, (Via) Trivellore, Chingleput District, Tamil Nadu; f. 1945; library of 8,000 vols and 5,870 journals; Dir K. SUBRAMANIAM.

Irrigation and Power Research Station: Amritsar; conducts research in fields of irrigation and hydraulic engineering; Dir J. NATH.

National Council for Cement and Building Materials: 34 Km-Stone, Delhi-Mathura Rd, Ballabgarh 121004, Haryana; tel. (129) 2242051; fax (129) 2242100; e-mail info@ncbindia.com; internet www.ncbindia.com; f. 1966; provides intensive and planned research and devt support to the cement, concrete and allied industries in the fields of new materials, technology devt and transfer, continuing education and industrial services; library of 44,700 vols, 151 periodicals; Dir-Gen. M. VASUDEVA; publs *Cement Standards of the World, NCB Current Contents* (documentation list, 6 a year), *Research Reports*.

National Institute of Hydrology: Jalvigyan Bhawan, Roorkee, Uttarakhand 247667; tel. (1332) 272106; fax (1332) 272123; e-mail nihmail@nih.ernet.in; internet www.nih.ernet.in; f. 1978; under Min. of Water Resources; research in all aspects of water resources; library of 7,000 vols, 3,000 technical reports, 87 periodicals, etc.; Dir R. D SINGH; publs *Jal Vigyan Sameeksha, Research Reports*.

Pulp and Paper Research Institute: Jaykaypur 765017, Dist. Rayagada, Orissa; tel. (6856) 233550; fax (6856) 222238; e-mail contactpapri@gmail.com; f. 1974; researches in pulp and paper technology, forestry, environment and pigment; library of 6,340 vols, periodicals, etc.; 26 mems; Deputy Dir Dr J. C. PANIGRAHI; Librarian R. K. SAHOO; publs *Abstract Index of Periodicals and Information Bulletin* (6 a year), *PAPRI Information Bulletin* (6 a year).

Research Designs and Standards Organization: Min.of Railways, Govt of India, Manak Nagar, Lucknow 226011; tel. (522) 2451221; fax (522) 2457125; e-mail dg@rdso.railnet.gov.in; internet www.rdso.gov.in; f. 1957; conducts studies on the design and standardization of all railway infrastructure and equipment and tests and trials of new

railway stock and other assets, and research into the economic and effective maintenance of operating practices; library of 154,000 vols, 130 periodicals; Dir-Gen. H. S. PANNU; Additional Dir-Gen. RAJEEV BHARGAV; publs *Indian Railway Technical Bulletin* (4 a year), *RDSO Highlights*, Research Reports, Technical Papers, etc.

Synthetic and Art Silk Mills Research Association: Sasmira, Sasmira Marg, Worli, Mumbai 400030; tel. (22) 24935351; fax (22) 24930225; e-mail sasmira@vsnl.com; internet www.sasmira.org; f. 1950; research and devt in man-made textiles; technical textiles; technical education (postgraduate and diploma courses) in the field of man-made fibres, textile technology, textile chemistry, knitting technology and retail, marketing and management; library of 26,000 vols; Pres. MAGANLAL H. DOSHI; Vice-Pres. MIHIR R. MEHTA; Dir U. K. GANGOPADHYAY; publ. *Man Made Textiles in India*.

Libraries and Archives

Ahmedabad

British Council Library: Bhakaka Bhavan, Law Garden Rd, Ellisbridge, Ahmedabad 380006; tel. (79) 26464693; fax (79) 26469493; e-mail bl.ahmedabad@in.britishcouncil.org; internet library.britishcouncil.org.in; f. 1979; 24,000 vols; adult lending, jr colln, English language devt colln, British home DVDs colln, select colln of magazines on contemporary Britain; Man. MOUMITA BHATTACHARYA.

Gujarat Vidyapith Granthalaya: Ahmedabad 380014; tel. (79) 40016260; fax (79) 27542547; e-mail libhod@gujaratvidyapith.org; internet www.gujaratvidyapith.org; f. 1920; Univ., State Central and Public Library combined; 557,321 vols; depository collection; Librarian BHARTI H. DESAI (acting).

Sheth Maheklal Jethabhai Pustakalaya (Free Public Library): Ellisbridge, Ahmedabad, Gujarat; tel. (79) 26578579; fax (79) 26586908; f. 1933; 25,012 mems; 178,317 vols; UNESCO programmes for children's libraries; Librarian SHANTIBHAI BHUDARDAS PATEL.

Allahabad

Allahabad Public Library: Rajkeeya Public Library, Chandra Shekher Azad Park (Alfred Park), Allahabad 211002; tel. (532) 2460197; f. 1864; 102,000 vols; old govt publs, parliamentary papers and blue books of the 19th century, old MSS and journals; reference and research service; Librarian Dr GOPAL MOHAN SHUKLA.

Bangalore

Bangalore State Central Library: Cubbon Park, Bangalore 560001, Karnataka; tel. (80) 22212128; f. 1914; 140,000 vols; State Librarian and Head of Public Libraries N. D. BAGERI.

British Council Library: Prestige Takt, 23 Kasturba Rd Cross, Opposite Visweswaraya Industrial and Technological Museum, Bangalore 560001; tel. (80) 22489220; fax (80) 22240767; e-mail bl.bangalore@in.britishcouncil.org; internet library.britishcouncil.org.in/profiles.asp?id=bl; f. 1960; 28,000 vols; Man. CHARU SAPRA.

Karnataka Government Secretariat Library: Room No. 28, Ground Floor, Vidhana Soudha, Bangalore 560001; tel. (80) 22257686; fax (80) 22200620; e-mail vslib.kar@nic.in; internet vslib.kar.nic.in; f. c.

1919; 117,846 vols, 15 newspapers, 90 periodicals; Chief Librarian DANIEL BARETTO.

Baroda

Central Library: Baroda 390006, Gujarat; f. 1910; 280,000 vols; State Librarian BAKULESH BHUTA; publ. *Granth Deep* (4 a year).

Chandigarh

British Library: SCO 183–187, Sector 9C, Madhya Marg, Chandigarh 160009; tel. (172) 2745195; fax (172) 2745199; e-mail bl .chandigarh@in.britishcouncil.org; f. 2000; 20,000 vols, 300 audio cassettes, 600 CD-ROMs, 2,500 children's books, 3,000 DVDs, 1,500 IT books; Man. BIPIN KUMAR.

Chennai

Adyar Library and Research Centre: International HQ, The Theosophical Soc., Adyar, Chennai 600020; tel. (44) 24913528; e-mail intl.hq@ts-adyar.org; internet www .ts-adyar.org/library.html; f. 1886; research in Indology; specializes in religion, philosophy, civilization; 200,000 vols, 18,000 MSS; Dir Dr S. SANKARANARAYANAN; Librarian Prof. C. A. SHINDE (acting); publ. *Brahmavidya* (1 a year).

Connemara (State Central) Public Library: Pantheon Rd, Egmore, Chennai 600008, Tamil Nadu; tel. (44) 28193751; internet www.connemarapubliclibrary chennai.com; f. 1896; deposit library from 1954 for all Indian publs; information centre for UN and allied agencies and for Asian Devt Bank; 556,003 vols; Librarian N. AVU-DAIAPPAN; publ. *Tamil Nadu State Bibliography* (in Tamil, 12 a year and 1 a year).

Indian Institute of Technology Madras Central Library: Chennai 600036; tel. (44) 22574951; fax (44) 22570509; e-mail hchandra@iitm.ac.in; internet www.cenlib .iitm.ac.in; f. 1959; 2,000,000 vols, 1,000 current periodicals, 400 films, 1,600 microfilms and microfiches; colln of technical and scientific books (German and English); partial archive of scientific films; user education programmes; Chief Librarian Dr HARISH CHANDRA.

Madras Literary Society Library: Chennai 600006; f. 1812; 150,000 vols incl. 30,000 19th-century edns; Man. P. N. BALASUNDARAM; Hon. Sec. S. V. B. ROW.

Tamil Nadu Government Oriental Manuscripts Library: University Bldg, Chepauk, Chennai 600005; tel. (44) 25365130; f. 1869; acquisition, preservation and publication of rare and important collection of MSS in Sanskrit, Islamic and South Indian languages; 25,373 vols, 72,314 MSS; Curator Dr S. SOUNDARAPANDIAN; publ. *Bulletin*.

Delhi

Central Archaeological Library: Second Floor, Annexe bldg of National Archives of India, Janpath, New Delhi 110001; tel. (11) 23387475; fax (11) 23385883; internet asi.nic .in/asi_ca_lib.asp; f. 1902; attached to Archaeological Survey of India; 102,180 vols, 5,776 maps, 85 current periodicals; Dir P. B. S. SENGAR.

Central Secretariat Library: Ministry of Culture, Govt of India, G Wing, Shastri Bhavan, New Delhi 110001; tel. (11) 23389684; fax (11) 23384846; e-mail csl@ delnet.ren.nic.in; f. 1890; lending, reference, reprographic divisions, background material on selected topics and biographies; 810,000 vols, 730 periodicals; spec. colln: area study, Indian official documents, foreign official documents, Hindi and Indian regional languages publs; Dir KALPANA DASGUPTA.

Delhi Public Library: H-Block, nr Main Market, Sarojini Nagar, Delhi 110023; tel. (11) 24101261; fax (11) 24673220; e-mail dpl@dpl.gov.in; internet www.dpl.gov.in; f. 1951 in association with UNESCO; est. as a model for public library devt in SE Asia; central library, 3 br. libraries, Braille section, 4 mobile libraries and 59 sub-br. and community libraries; 1,557,000 vols in English, Hindi, Urdu, Punjabi, Bengali, Sindhi and other Indian languages and in Braille; Dir Dr BANWARI LAL.

Indian Council of World Affairs Library: Sapru House, Barakhamba Rd, New Delhi 110001; tel. (11) 23317246; fax (11) 23310638; e-mail chhayasharma@icwa.in; internet www.icwa.in; f. 1943; research collns on social sciences with spec. reference to int. relations, int. law and int. economics; Press library; maps, microfilms and microfiches; UN and EU documents; 1,500 mems; 128,000 vols, 376 periodicals, 2,458,000 press clippings; Chief Librarian CHHAYA SHARMA; publ. *India Quarterly* (in-house journal).

Indira Gandhi National Centre for the Arts: 1 Central Vista Mess, Janpath, New Delhi 110001; tel. (11) 23384901; fax (11) 23381139; e-mail skojha@ignca.nic.in; internet ignca.nic.in; f. 1987; resource centre with reference material relating to Indian arts and culture; Academic Dir S. K. OJHA.

National Archives of India: Janpath, New Delhi 110001; tel. (11) 23383436; fax (11) 23384127; e-mail archives@nic.in; internet nationalarchives.nic.in; f. 1891 in Calcutta (Kolkata) as the Imperial Record Dept, transferred to New Delhi in 1911 and to present site in 1926; valuable collns of public records, maps, private papers and microfilm covering 35 km of shelf space; 200,000 vols 1,780,000 books and reports, 3,299 proscribed publications, 400 selections from vernacular native newspapers, 4,225 selections from Government of India and State Govt records, 4,590 vols of Indian parliamentary papers, 1,285 vols of Fort William College colln, 3,560 journals and periodicals, 1,778 gazettes, 2,960 publs in foreign languages; Dir-Gen. S. M. R. BAQAR; publs *Bulletin of Research Theses and Dissertations* (every 2 years), *Indian Archives* (2 a year).

National Institute of Science Communication and Information Resources: Dr K. S. Krishnan Marg, Pusa Campus, New Delhi 110012; tel. (11) 25841647; fax (11) 25847062; e-mail gp@niscair.res.in; internet www.niscair.res.in; f. 2002; attached to Ccl of Scientific and Industrial Research; nat. science library; disseminates scientific and technological information to the scientific community and the gen. public; provides networking services and network-based online services; bibliographical information retrieval from national and international online and CD-ROM databases; 178,000 vols; Dir Dr GANGAN PRATHAP; publs *Annals of Library and Information Studies* (4 a year), *Bharatiya Vaigyanic evam Audyogic Anusandhan Patrika* (2 a year, in Hindi), *Indian Journal of Biochemistry and Biophysics* (6 a year), *Indian Journal of Biotechnology* (4 a year), *Indian Journal of Chemical Technology* (6 a year), *Indian Journal of Chemistry, Sec A* (12 a year), *Indian Journal of Chemistry, Sec B* (12 a year), *Indian Journal of Engineering and Materials Sciences* (6 a year), *Indian Journal of Experimental Biology* (12 a year), *Indian Journal of Fibre and Textile Research* (4 a year), *Indian Journal of Marine Sciences* (4 a year), *Indian Journal of Pure and Applied Physics* (12 a year), *Indian Journal of Radio and Space Physics* (6 a year), *Indian Journal of Traditional Knowledge* (4 a year), *Indian Science*

Abstracts (26 a year), *Journal of Intellectual Property Rights* (6 a year), *Journal of Scientific and Industrial Research* (12 a year), *Medicinal and Aromatic Plants Abstracts* (6 a year), *Natural Product Radiance* (6 a year).

National Social Science Documentation Centre: 35 Ferozshah Rd, New Delhi 110001; tel. (11) 23385959; fax (11) 23383091; internet www.icssr.org; f. 1970; div. of Indian Ccl of Social Science Research (ICSSR); provides information and documentation service for social scientists, policymakers and others working in the academic and govt sectors, business and industry; provides library and reference services, document delivery and reprographic services, consultancy service, select bibliography service, training courses; 565 current periodicals, 150,000 serial vols, 5,000 PhD theses, 3,000 research projects and reports, 15,000 books, conf. papers, working papers; Dir Dr P. R. GOSWAMI; Deputy Dir SAVITRI DEVI; publs *Annotated Index of Indian Social Science Journals* (2 a year), *Bibliographic Reprints* (irregular), *Conference Alert* (4 a year).

Nehru Memorial Museum and Library: Teen Murti House, New Delhi 110011; tel. (11) 23015333; fax (11) 23793296; f. 1964; archival collections on modern Indian history with emphasis on Indian nationalism; research centre for interdisciplinary studies in modern Indian history and society; large collection of newspapers, microfilms, private papers, institutional records, photographs and oral history recordings; 226,603 vols; Dir K. JAYAKUMAR.

Dharamsala

Library of Tibetan Works and Archives: Gangchen Kyishong, Dharamsala 176215, Himachal Pradesh; tel. (1892) 222467; fax (1892) 223723; e-mail info@ltwa.net,; internet www.ltwa.net; f. 1971; 80,000 vols 10,000 photographs, 25,000 hours of audio/ video tape, 1,200 icons and artefacts; Dir Ven. Geshe LHAKDOR; publ. *The Tibet Journal* (4 a year).

Hyderabad

British Council Library: 5-9-22 Sarovar Centre, Secretariat Rd, Hyderabad 500063; tel. (40) 23483333; fax (40) 23483100; e-mail bl.hyderabad@in.britishcouncil.org; internet www.britishcouncilonline.org; f. 1979; library services; seminars; workshops; film screening on climate change and low carbon; 25,000 vols, 2,500 DVDs; information on higher education in the UK; Man. AJAY MERCHANT; Asst Man. EASWARAN NAMPOOTHIRI.

State Central Library: Afzalgunj, Hyderabad 500012, Andhra Pradesh; tel. (40) 24615621; fax (40) 24600107; f. 1891; 347,000 vols; Librarian T. V. VEDAMRUTHAM.

Kolkata

Centre for Asian Documentation: K-15, CIT Bldgs, Christopher Rd, POB 11215, Kolkata 700014; provides reference services; Dir S. CHAUDHURI; publs *Index Asia Series in Humanities* (irregular), *Index Indo-Asiasticus* (4 a year), *Index Internationalis Indicus* (every 3 years), *Indian Biography* (1 a year), *Indian Science index* (every 2 years).

National Library: Belvedere, Kolkata 700027, West Bengal; tel. (33) 24791381; fax (33) 24791462; e-mail nldirector@ rediffmail.com; internet www .nationallibrary.gov.in/index2.html; f. 1903 by the amalgamation of the Calcutta Public Library and the Imperial Library; depository and research library; 4,145 microfilms, 94,500 microfiches, 17,650 periodicals; incl. Central Reference Library, at the same address, compiles *Indian National Bibliography*, but does not hold a book colln; 2,186,500 vols, 84,952 maps, 3,127 MSS; Dir Dr R. RAMACHANDRAN; publs *Bibliographical Control in India, Bibliographies, Conservation of Library Materials, General Collection Author and Subject Catalogues, India's National Library—Systematization and Modernization, Indological Studies and South Asia Bibliography, Rabindra Grantha Suchi* (vol 1 part 1), *Reports, The National Library and Public Libraries in India*.

Lucknow

Acharya Narendra Dev Pustakalaya: 10 Ashoka Marg, Lucknow; f. 1959; public library, with special emphasis on social sciences; 79,636 vols; 150 periodicals; Librarian T. N. MISRA.

Ludhiana

Panjab University Extension Library: Civil Lines, Ludhiana, Punjab; tel. (161) 2449558; f. 1960; serves educational institutions within a radius of 60 km; 138,000 vols; Librarian PREM VERMA (acting).

Mumbai

Petit, J. N., Institute Library: 312 Dr Dadabhoy Naoroji Rd, Fort, Mumbai 400001; tel. (22) 22048463; e-mail petitheritage_01@yahoo.co.in; f. 1856 as 'Fort Improvement Library'; 160,000 vols; Admin. J. R. MODY.

Patna

Bihar Secretariat Library: Patna 800015; f. 1885; 106,300 vols; Chief Librarian P. N. SINHA DOSHI.

Khuda Bakhsh Oriental Public Library: Ashok Rajpath, Patna 800004, Bihar; tel. (612) 2300315; e-mail pat_khopl@dataone.in; internet www.kblibrary.nic.in; f. 1891; autonomous instn under Min. of Culture and declared as an instn of nat. importance; awards fellowships for PhD and D.Litt. students; designated as a MSS Resource Centre (MRC) and Manuscript Conservation Centre (MCC) by the Nat. Mission for MSS, Govt of India; contains more than 21,000 MSS in Arabic, Persian, Urdu, Pushto, Pali, Turkish, Hindi and Sanskrit, 247,032 vols, 39,419 bound periodicals, 2,222 audio and video cassettes, Mughal, Iranian, Central Asian and Rajput paintings; Dir Dr IMTIAZ AHMAD; publ. journals.

Shrimati Radhika Sinha Institute and Sachchidananda Sinha Library (State Central Library, Bihar): G.P.O., Sinha Library Rd., Patna 800001; tel. (612) 222254; f. 1924 by Dr Sachidananda Sinha in the memory of his late wife Srimati Radhika Devi in a portion of his house; admin. by State Govt; located on the rd opposite the museum; incl. a reading room, research room, and newspaper reading room; subscriptions to many foreign and Indian journals; books on literature, history, biography, philosophy, sociology, etc.; known as the Sinha Library by the reading public; 157,089 vols, 523 periodicals; Librarian Dr R. S. P. SINGH.

Rajahmundry

Gowthami Regional Library: Rajahmundry 533104, Andhra Pradesh; tel. (883) 2476908; f. 1898, management transferred to Andhra Pradesh Govt in 1979; spec. colln of rare 19th-century periodicals in English and Telugu, rare colln of old Telugu books; research library of 58,643 vols, 428 palm-leaf MSS; Librarian VENNA POLI REDDY.

Trivandrum

Trivandrum Public Library (State Central Library): Palayam, Vikas Bhavan PO, Thiruvananthapuram, Kerala; tel. (471) 2322895; e-mail slscl@statelibrary.kerala.gov.in; internet www.statelibrary.kerala.gov.in/; f. 1829, declared the 'State Central Library' in 1958, given the status of a minor dept under admin. control of the Higher Education Dept with the State Librarian as HOD in 1988; 327,177 vols in English, Malayalam, Hindi, Tamil, Sanskrit in various disciplines; State Librarian P. SUPRABHA.

Museums and Art Galleries

Ahmedabad

Calico Museum of Textiles:; e-mail dsmehta@calicomuseum.com Sarabhai Foundation, Shahibag, Ahmedabad 380004; tel. (79) 22868172; fax (79) 22865759; e-mail info@calicomuseum.com; internet www.calicomuseum.com; f. 1948; colln of 17th- and 18th-century Indian textiles and costumes, shawls, large tents, carpets, religious textiles and artefacts, Indian miniature paintings, Indian bronzes, and reconstructed carved wooden façades from 17th to 19th centuries; Man. Trustee GIRA SARABHAI; Dir D. S. MEHTA; publ. *Historical Textiles of India at Calico Museum.*

Ajmer

Rajputana Museum: Ajmer 305001, Rajasthan; f. 1908; archaeology; rare sculptures, architectural carvings, old coins, epigraphs, Rajput paintings, arms and armour of Rajasthan; Curator R. D. SHARMA.

Banares

Bharat Kala Bhavan: Banaras Hindu University, Varanasi 221005; tel. (542) 316337; fax (542) 316337; e-mail bharatkalabhavan@sify.com; internet www.bhu.ac.in/kala/index_bkb.htm; f. 1920; attached to univ. since 1950; art objects, miniature paintings, sculpture, textiles, archaeology, seals; library: approx. 14,000 vols and periodicals, 26,511 MSS; Dir Prof. R. C. SHARMA; publs *Chhavi*, catalogues.

Bangalore

Government Museum: Kasturba Rd, Bangalore 560001, Karnataka; f. 1866; art, archaeology, industrial art and natural history; library of 2,000 vols; Curator (vacant).

Visvesvaraya Industrial and Technological Museum: Kasturba Rd, PMB 5216, Bangalore 560001, Karnataka; tel. (80) 22866200; fax (80) 22864009; e-mail vitm@vsnl.com; internet www.vismuseum.org; f. 1962; aims to encourage interest in science and technology, and to explain the application of technology in industry and human welfare; library of 10,230 vols, also audiovisual materials; Dir K. V. BHATTA.

Baroda

Baroda Museum and Picture Gallery: Sayaji Bagh, Vadodra 390018, Gujarat; f. 1887, museum completed in 1894 and picture gallery in 1920; Indian archaeology; prehistoric and historic; Indian art: ancient, medieval and modern; numismatic collections; modern Indian paintings; industrial art; Asiatic and Egyptian collections; Greek, Roman, European civilizations and art; European paintings; ethnology, zoology, geology, economic botany; library of 19,000 vols; Dir S. K. BHOWMIK; Curators SATISH SADASIVAN (Art and Archaeology), G. M. PATHAK (Natural History); publ. *Bulletin.*

Bhubaneswar

Orissa State Museum: Bhubaneswar 751006, Orissa; f. 1932; archaeology, epigraphy, numismatics, armoury, arts and crafts, anthropology, palm-leaf MSS, natural history; library of 22,000 vols, 2,000 periodicals; Dir Dr H. C. DAS; publ. *Orissa Historical Research Journal.*

Bikaner

Government Museum: Bikaner 334001, Rajasthan; tel. (151) 2528894; f. 1937; collection of terracottas, sculptures, bronzes, coins, inscriptions, Rajasthani paintings, documents, arms and costumes, specimens of folk-culture; Superintendent P. C. BHARGAVA.

Bodh Gaya

Archaeological Museum: Archaeological Survey of India, Bodh Gaya, District Gaya, Bihar; tel. (631) 2200739; fax (631) 2200739; stone and bronze sculpture, etc.; Asst Superintending Archaeologist S. K. SINHA.

Chennai

Fort Museum: Archaeological Survey of India, Fort St George, Chennai 600009; tel. (44) 25671127; f. 1948; exhibits belong mainly to the days of the East India Co.; Asst Superintending Archaeologist P. S. SRIRAMAN.

Government Museum and National Art Gallery: Pantheon Rd, Egmore, Chennai 600008; tel. (44) 28193238; fax (44) 28193035; e-mail govtmuse@md4.vsnl.net.in; internet www.chennaimuseum.org; f. 1851; archaeology, ancient and modern Indian art, South Indian bronzes, Buddhist sculptures, numismatics, philately, anthropology, botany, zoology, geology, chemical conservation education, contemporary art, design and display; Dir THIRU M. A. SIDDIQUE; publ. *Madras Museum Bulletins.*

Delhi

Archaeological Museum Red Fort, Delhi: Mumtaz Mahal, Red Fort, 110006; tel. (11) 23267961; f. 1909; library of 420 vols; historical collns of the Mughal period; old arms, seals and signets, letters, MSS, coins, miniatures, Mughal dresses and relics of India's War of Independence; Asst Superintending Archaeologist V. D. JADHAV.

Crafts Museum: Pragati Maidan, Bhairon Rd, New Delhi 110001; tel. (11) 23371641; fax (11) 23371515; e-mail nhhm@vsnl.net; internet www.nationalcraftsmuseum.nic.in; f. 1952; attached to Ministry of Textiles; Indian traditional crafts and tribal arts; library of 11,000 vols; Dir Dr JYOTINDRA JAIN.

National Gallery of Modern Art: Jaipur House, India Gate, Sher Shah Rd, New Delhi 110003; tel. (11) 23386111; fax (11) 23384560; e-mail ngma@del3.vsnl.net.in; internet ngmaindia.gov.in/; f. 1954; contemporary art (paintings, sculpture, drawings, graphics, architecture, industrial design, photography, prints and minor arts); Dir Prof. RAJEEV LOCHAN.

National Gandhi Museum and Library: Rajghat, New Delhi 110002; tel. (11) 23310168; fax (11) 23311793; e-mail gandhimk@bol.net.in; internet www.gandhimuseum.org; f. 1953 by the Gandhi Memorial Museum Soc.; collects and displays Gandhi's records and mementos and promotes the study of his life and work; library of 45,000 vols, 25,000 documents, 80 periodicals, films and recordings, 9,000 photographs, large picture galleries; Chair. Prof. BIMAL PRASAD; Dir Dr VARSHA DAS; Head of Library S. K. BHATNAGAR.

National Museum of India: 1 Janpath, New Delhi 110011; tel. (11) 23018159; fax

(11) 23019821; internet www .nationalmuseumindia.gov.in/; f. 1949; depts of art, archaeology, anthropology, modelling, presentation, preservation, publication, library and photography; Indian prehistoric tools, protohistoric remains from Harappa, Mohenjodaro, etc., representative collns of sculptures, terracottas, stuccos and bronzes from 2nd century BC to 18th century AD; illustrated MSS and miniatures; Stein Colln of Central Asian murals and other antiquities; decorative arts; textiles, coins and illuminated epigraphical charts; armour; copperplate etchings; woodwork; library of 43,400 vols; Dir-Gen. R. C. MISHRA; Dirs U. DAS (Colln and Admin.), Dr R. R. S. CHAUHAN (Exhibition and Public Relation), S. P. SINGH; publs *Bulletin* (1 a year), special publs on art and archaeology.

National Museum of Natural History: FICCI Museum Bldg, Barakhamba Rd, New Delhi 110001; tel. (11) 23314849; e-mail sksaraswat@yahoo.co.uk; internet nmnh.nic .in; f. 1978; exhibits on natural history, ecology, environment, conservation; educational programmes for children and other groups, school loan service, mobile museum for rural extension service; controls regional museums of natural history in Mysore, Bhopal and Bhubneshwar; library of 25,000 vols; Dir (vacant).

National Rail Museum: Chanakyapuri, New Delhi 110021; tel. (11) 26881816; fax (11) 26880804; e-mail smehranrm@yahoo.co .in; internet www.nationalrailmuseum.org/ new_nrm; f. 1977; library of 5,000 vols; Dir RAJESH AGRAWAL.

Rabindra Bhavan Art Gallery: 35 Ferozeshah Rd, New Delhi; tel. (11) 23387241; fax (11) 23782485; e-mail lka@bol.net.in; f. 1955; permanent gallery of the Lalit Kala Akademi (National Academy of Art), and venue of the National Exhibition of Art and Triennale-India (international art); Chair. Dr SARAYU V. DOSHI; publs *Lalit Kala Ancient* (2 a year), *Lalit Kala Contemporary* (4 a year), *Samkaleen Kala* (in Hindi, 4 a year).

Shankar's International Dolls Museum: Nehru House, 4 Bahadur Shah Zafar Marg, New Delhi 110002; tel. (11) 23316970; fax (11) 23721090; e-mail cbtnd@cbtnd.com; internet www.childrensbooktrust.com; f. 1965; 6,000 exhibits from all over the world; Advisor SHANTA SRINIVASAN.

Gauhati

Assam State Museum: Guwahati 781001, Assam; f. 1940; indological and archaeological studies; library of 5,850 vols; Dir Dr R. D. CHOUDHURY; publ. *Bulletin* (1 a year).

Guntur

Archaeological Museum: Nagarjunakonda Zone, Vijayapuri South, District Guntur, 522439 Andhra Pradesh; tel. and fax (8642) 278107; e-mail asamnkonda@gmail.com; f. 1966; prehistoric and historical antiquities, mainly sculptures belonging to Buddhism (3rd–4th centuries AD) and Hinduism (15th–16th centuries AD); Asst Superintending Archaeologist CH. BABJI RAO.

Hyderabad

Andhra Pradesh State Museum: Hyderabad 500034; f. 1930; sculpture, epigraphy, arms and weapons, bidriware, bronze objects, miniatures and paintings, MSS, numismatics, European paintings (prints), decorative and modern arts, textiles; excavations at Yeleswaram Pochampal, Peddabankur; Dir Dr V. V. KRISHNA SASTRY; publ. various on numismatics.

Salar Jung Museum: Hyderabad 500002, Andhra Pradesh; tel. (40) 24523211; fax (40) 24572558; e-mail salarjung@hotmail.com; internet www.salarjungmuseum.in; f. 1951; paintings, textiles, porcelain, jade, carpets, MSS, antiques, ivory, glass, silver- and bronze-ware; children's section; library of 60,000 vols incl. Persian, Arabic and Urdu MSS; Dir Dr A. NAGENDER REDDY; publs *Research Journal* (every 2 years), guidebook and MSS catalogue.

Imphal

Manipur State Museum: Polo-ground, Imphal, Manipur; general collection.

Jaipur

Maharaja Sawai Man Singh II Museum: City Palace, Jaipur 302002, Rajasthan; tel. (141) 2615681; fax (141) 2603880; f. 1959; textiles and costumes, armoury, Mughal and Rajasthani miniature paintings, Persian and Mughal carpets, transport accessories, regalia, historical documents, maps and plans, MSS library of 10,000 Sanskrit, Persian, Hindi and Rajasthani MSS; Dir B. M. S. PARMAR.

Kolkata

Asutosh Museum of Indian Art: Centenary Building, University of Calcutta, Kolkata 700073; f. 1937; library: over 2,000 vols and periodicals; Curator NIRANJAN GOSWAMI; publ. catalogues.

Birla Industrial and Technological Museum: National Council of Science Museums, Govt. of India, 19A Gurusaday Rd, Kolkata 700019; tel. (33) 22877241; fax (33) 22906102; e-mail bitm@cal2.vsnl.net.in; internet www.bitmcal.org; f. 1959; administered by the Nat. Ccl of Science Museums; portrays the history and development of science and technology; 8 satellite centres and 8 mobile science exhibition buses in rural areas; educational programmes for students and teachers and the gen. public; film and CD library; archives; special collections on history and development of science and technology, arts, painting, museology, etc.; library of 14,000 vols incl. periodicals; Dir Sk. EMDADUL ISLAM; publ. *Popscience* (2 a year).

Indian Museum: 27 Jawaharlal Nehru Rd, Kolkata 700016; tel. (33) 22861679; fax (33) 22495696; e-mail imbot@cal2.vsnl.net.in; internet www.indianmuseumkolkata.org/; f. 1814; collns of archaeology, art, coins, anthropology, geology, botany, zoology; herbarium; library of 45,000 vols; Dir Dr SAKTI KALI BASU; Librarian Dr PATRA CHITTARANJAN; publ. *Bulletin* (1 a year).

Victoria Memorial Hall: 1 Queens Way, Kolkata 700071; tel. (33) 22231890; fax (33) 22235142; e-mail victomen@cal2.vsnl.net.in; internet www.victoriamemorial-cal.org; f. 1906; museum of medieval Indian history and culture, and British Indian history of the late 18th and early 19th centuries; wide colln of oil-paintings and watercolours by European artists of 18th and 19th centuries; sketches, miniatures, engravings, photographs, sculptures, maps, MSS, furniture, stamps, coins, medals, textiles, arms and armour; library: almost 13,030 vols; Chair. GOVERNOR OF WEST BENGAL; Sec. and Curator Prof. CHITTARANJAN PANDA.

Lucknow

Uttar Pradesh State Museum: Banarasibagh, Lucknow, Uttar Pradesh; tel. and fax (522) 2206158; f. 1863; collns of sculptures, terracottas, copper plates, numismatics, paintings, MSS, textiles and natural history specimens; anthropological colln; library of 15,000 vols; Dir R. C. TIWARI; publ. *Bulletin* (2 a year).

Mathura

Government Museum: Dampier Nagar, Mathura 281001, Uttar Pradesh; f. 1874; 40,000 items, dominated by sculptures, terracottas of Mathura School to Kushana and Gupta period; coins, paintings, etc.; library: reference library of 20,000 vols.

Mumbai

Chhatrapati Shivaji Maharaj Vastu Sangrahalay: 159–161 Mahatma Gandhi Rd, Fort, Mumbai 400023; tel. (22) 22844484; fax (22) 22045430; internet www .bombaymuseum.org; f. 1905; fmrly Prince of Wales Museum of Western India; sections: Art, Painting, Archaeology, Natural History; library of 25,000 vols; publs *Bulletin*, catalogues.

Dr Bhau Daji Lad Mumbai City Museum: Rani Bagh, 19/A Dr B. Ambedkar Rd, Byculla-East, Mumbai 400027; tel. (22) 23731234; fax (22) 23737942; e-mail bdlmuseum@gmail.com; internet www .bdlmuseum.org; f. 1855; reference library on Indian and foreign art, archaeology, ethnology, geology, history, numismatics and museology; exhibits of agriculture and village life, armoury, cottage industries, ethnology, fine arts, crafts, fossils, Indian coins, minerals, misc. colln, Old Mumbai colln; oldest museum in Mumbai; Man. Trustee and Hon. Dir TASNEEM MEHTA; Curator M. GANDHI; Sr Asst Curator POULOMI DAS; publ. catalogues.

Nagpur

Central Museum: Civil Lines, Nagpur 440001 Maharashtra; tel. (712) 2546314; f. 1863; objects relating to archaeology, art, tribal art and culture, natural history, sculpture, weapons and metal objects; Curator Y. KATHANE.

Nalanda

Archaeological Museum: Archaeological Survey of India, Nalanda, District Nalanda, Bihar; tel. (6112) 281824; f. 1958; collns of antiquities, specializing in Buddhist sculptures; Asst Superintending Archaeologist K. C. SRIVASTAVA.

Patna

Patna Museum: Patna-Gaya Rd, Buddha Marg, Patna 800001, Bihar; tel. (612) 2235731; f. 1917; archaeology, bronzes, ethnology, geology, arms and armour, natural history, art, coins, plaster casts, Tibetan paintings; Dr Rajendra Prasad's colln (first Pres. of India); Buddha Relic casket; publishes research on art, archaeology and ethnology; seminars and lectures; Dir J. P. AGRARWAL; Curator K. K. SHARMA.

Rajahmundry

Sri Rallabandi Subbarao Government Museum (formerly the Andhra Historical Research Society): Godavari Bund Rd, Rajahmundry, East Godavari District, Andhra Pradesh 533101; f. 1967; art, archaeology, epigraphy, history and numismatics; collection of coins, sculpture, pottery, terracotta, palm-leaf MSS, inscriptions, etc.; Dir Dr V. V. KRISHNA SASTRY; publ. *Journal of the AHRS*.

Santiniketan

Rabindra-Bhavana (Tagore Museum and Archives): Visva-Bharati, PO: Santiniketan, Dist.: Birbhum, 731235, West Bengal; tel. (3463) 262751; fax (3463) 262672; f. 1942; colln of MSS, letters, books, newspaper clippings, gramophone records, photographs, cine-film, paintings by Tagore and tape recordings of his voice; inside the Uttarayana Campus where the poet spent the last days of his life; library of 40,000 books and over 12,000 bound journals; publ. *Rabindra-Viksa* (2 a year).

Sarnath

Sarnath Archaeological Museum: District Varanasi 221007, Uttar Pradesh; tel. (542) 2595095; archaeological site museum; f. 1904; Buddhist and Hindu collection from 3rd century BC to 12th century AD; Dy. Superintending Archaeologist A. JHA.

Srinagar

Sri Pratap Singh Museum: Lalmandi, Srinagar 190008-72078, Jammu and Kashmir; tel. (8649) 232374; f. 1898; general colln of Jammu and Kashmir; colln of excavated items incl. pottery, terracotta tiles, metal artifacts and stone objects dating back to different time periods, ranging from the 2nd to 12th centuries; also on display life-size statues of the Buddha, Lords Vishnu, Shiva and Brahma, in chronological order; other items incl. Sharda, Persian and Arabic stone inscriptions, 2nd-century terracotta tiles from Hoinar (Pahalgam) and 3rd-century Harwan tiles; library of 1,300 vols about cultural subjects; Curator M. S. ZAHID.

Trichur

Kerala State Museum:; f. 1885; incl. (1) State Museum and Zoo, Trichur, f. 1885; (2) Govt Museums and Zoological and Botanical Gardens, Trivandrum, f. 1857; natural history collns, Indian arts and crafts; (3) Art Gallery and Krishna-Menon Museum, Calicut, f. 1976; (4) Govt Botanical Garden, Olavanna, f. 1991; The Zoo has 315 animals in 46 species, Art Museum consists of antiques and other unique exhibits; Natural History Museum displays array of specimens of different kinds of animals.

Trivandrum

Sri Chitra Art Gallery, Gallery of Asian Paintings: Trivandrum 695001, Kerala; f. 1935; sections: Pure Indian Art, Rajput, Mughal and Persian, Tanjore, Tibetan, Chinese, Japanese, Balinese, Indo-European (watercolours and oils), etchings and woodcuts; Modern Indian Contemporary Art and Murals; library of 736 vols; Dir K. RAJENDRA BABU; publ. *Administration Report*.

Universities

There are three types of university in India: Affiliating and Teaching (most teaching done in colleges affiliated to the university, but some teaching, mostly postgraduate, undertaken by the university); Unitary (all teaching done on one campus); and Central (universities established by Acts of Parliament). It is not possible, for reasons of space, to give details of affiliated colleges.

ACHARYA N. G. RANGA AGRICULTURAL UNIVERSITY

Rajendranagr, Hyderabad 500030, Andhra Pradesh

Telephone: (40) 24015011
Fax: (40) 24015031
E-mail: angrau@ap.nic.in
Internet: www.angrau.net

Founded 1964 as Andhra Pradesh Agricultural Univ.; present name 1996
Languages of instruction: English, Telugu
Academic year: July to June

Composed of 9 Colleges, 58 Research Stations distributed in 9 Agro-climatic zones of the State, 8 Agricultural Polytechnics, 1 Horticultural Polytechnic, 1 Multipurpose Poly-

technic, 22 District Agricultural Advisory and Transfer of Technology Centres (DAATTCs), 12 Krishi Vigyan Kendras (Farmer Science Centres), 1 Agricultural Technology and Information Centre
Chancellor: HE THE GOVERNOR OF ANDHRA PRADESH
Vice-Chancellor: P. RAGHAVA REDDY
Dir of Extension: Dr L. G. GIRI RAO
Dir of Research: Dr G. LAKSHMI KANTHA REDDY
Dean of Student Affairs: Dr S. V. RAMAKRISHNA RAO
Comptroller: N. SRI KALA
Registrar: M. USHA RANI (acting)
Librarian: Dr K. VEERANJANEYULU

Library of 200,000 vols, 500 periodicals
Number of teachers: 1,035
Number of students: 3,853

Publication: *ANGRAU Journal of Research* (4 a year)

DEANS

Faculty of Agriculture: Dr M. SUDARSHAN REDDY
Faculty of Home Science: Dr P. RAJYA LAKSHMI
Postgraduate Studies: Dr SHAIK MOHAMMAD (acting)

ALAGAPPA UNIVERSITY

Alagappa Nagar, Karaikudi 630003, Tamil Nadu

Telephone: (4565) 228080
Fax: (4565) 225202
E-mail: registrar@alagappauniversity.ac.in
Internet: www.alagappauniversity.ac.in
Founded 1985
Academic year: July to April (2 terms)
Chancellor: HE THE GOV. OF TAMIL NADU
Pro-Chancellor: Dr K. PONMUDI
Vice-Chancellor: Dr P. RAMASAMY
Registrar: Dr A. SHENBAGAVALLI
Controller of Examinations: Dr V. MANICKAVASAGAM
Finance Officer: THIRU R. BOOMINATHAN
Dean of College Devt Ccl: Dr T. R. GURUMOORTHY
Dean of Student Welfare: Dr M. SELVAN
Librarian: Dr A. THIRUNAVUKKARASU

Library of 64,000 vols, 121 periodicals
Number of teachers: 150
Number of students: 1,545

DEANS

Faculty of Arts: Dr R. KRISHNARAJ
Faculty of Education: Dr P. PREMA
Faculty of Management: Dr R. M. CHIDAMBARAM
Faculty of Science: Dr P. NATARAJAN

ATTACHED CENTRES

Centre for Rural Development: tel. (4565) 225842; fax (4565) 225202; Dir Dr A. NARAYANAMOORTHY.
Centre for Gandhian Studies: Dir Dr V. S. KANNAN.
Centre for Nehru Studies: Dir Dr B. DHARMALINGAM.

ALIGARH MUSLIM UNIVERSITY

Aligarh 202002, Uttar Pradesh
Telephone: (571) 2700220
Fax: (571) 2700528
E-mail: vcamu@.amu.ac.in
Internet: www.amu.ac.in
Founded 1875 as Anglo-Mohamedan Oriental College; raised to univ. status, 1920
1920, Central Univ.
Language of instruction: English
Indian govt control

Academic year: July to May
Chancellor: (vacant)
Pro-Chancellor: (vacant)
Vice-Chancellor: Prof. P. K. ABDUL AZIS
Registrar: Prof. Dr V. K. ABDUL JALEEL
Finance Officer: YASMIN JALAL BEG
Controller of Examinations: Prof. PERVEZ MUSTAJAB
Proctor: Prof. MOHD. ZUBAIR KHAN
Dean of Student's Welfare: Prof. AINUL HAQUE
Librarian: Prof. SHABAHAT HUSAIN
Library: 1.1m. vols; MSS in Arabic, Persian, Urdu and Hindi
Number of teachers: 1,101
Number of students: 17,954

DEANS

Faculty of Agriculture Sciences: Prof. PERVEZ QAMAR RIZVI
Faculty of Arts: Prof. MARIA BILQUIS
Faculty of Commerce: Prof. ZIAUDDIN KHAIROOWALA
Faculty of Engineering and Technology: Prof. A. K. GUPTA
Faculty of Law: Prof. IQBAL ALI KHAN
Faculty of Life Sciences: Prof. ABSAR MUSTAFA KHAN
Faculty of Management Studies and Research: Prof. JAVAID AKHTAR
Faculty of Medicine: Prof. ABU QAMAR SIDDIQUI
Faculty of Science: Prof. MOHD. ZUBAIR KHAN
Faculty of Social Sciences: Prof. MOHD. MURTAZA KHAN
Faculty of Theology: Prof. MOHAMMAD SAUD ALAM QASMI
Faculty of Unani Medicine: Prof. TAJUDDIN

ALLAHABAD UNIVERSITY

Allahabad 211002, Uttar Pradesh
Telephone: (532) 2461089
Fax: (532) 2545021
E-mail: mkc@allduniv.ac.in
Internet: www.allduniv.ac.in
Founded 1887
Unitary
Languages of instruction: English, Hindi
Academic year: July to April
Chief Rector: THE GOVERNOR OF UTTAR PRADESH
Chancellor: Dr VERGHESE KURIEN
Vice-Chancellor: Prof. RAJENDRA GOVIND HARSHE
Registrar: FIRDOUS A. WANI
Finance Officer: Prof. J. N. MISHRA
Controller of Examinations: Prof. H. S. UPADHYAYA
Librarian: Dr A. P. GAKHAR
Library of 710,000 vols
Number of students: 37,694

DEANS

Faculty of Arts: Prof. N. R. FAROOQI
Faculty of Commerce: Prof. RAMENDU ROY
Faculty of Law: Prof. L. R. SINGH
Faculty of Medicine: Prof. P. C. SAXENA
Faculty of Science: Prof. SATYA GURU PRAKASH

ATTACHED RESEARCH INSTITUTES

Centre for Behavioural and Cognitive Sciences: tel. (532) 2460738; e-mail office@cbcs.ac.in; internet www.cbcs.ac.in; f. 2002; Dir M. P. SHRIVASTAV.
Centre of Biomedical Magnetic Resonance: Sanjay Gandhi Postgraduate Institute of Medical Sciences Campus, Raebareli Road, Lucknow 226014, Uttar Pradesh; tel. (522) 2668700; fax (522) 2668215; e-mail cbmrlko@gmail.com; internet cbmr.res.in/; f. 2002; Dir Prof. C. L. KHETRAPAL.

Centre For Environmental Education and Research (CEEAR): Dir Dr D. R. MISHRA.

Centre of Mobile Communication for Developing Countries: tel. (532) 640012; Dir Prof. G. K. MEHTA.

Motilal Nehru Institute of Research & Business Administration (MONIRBA): Chatham Lines Campus, Allahabad, Uttar Pradesh; tel. (532) 2250840; fax (532) 2644951; e-mail info@monirba.com; internet www.monirba.com; f. 1965.

National Centre of Experimental Mineralogy and Petrology (NCEMP): tel. (532) 2250840; fax (532) 2644951; e-mail ncempald@dataone.in; internet www.ncemp .org; f. 1996; Dir Prof. ALOK KRISHNA GUPTA.

ANDHRA UNIVERSITY

Visakhapatnam 530003, Andhra Pradesh

Telephone: (891) 2844444

Fax: (891) 2755324

E-mail: registrar@andhrauniversity.info

Internet: www.andhrauniversity.info

Founded 1926

Affiliating

Languages of instruction: English, Telugu

Academic year: July to March

Chancellor: HE THE GOVERNOR OF ANDHRA PRADESH

Vice-Chancellor: Dr BEELA SATYANARAYANA

Rector: Dr B. PARVATHISWARA RAO

Registrar: Prof. PRASAD REDDY

Dean of Academic Affairs: Prof. D. HARINARAYANA

Dean of College Devt Council: Prof. S. K. V. S. RAJU

Dean of Postgraduate Examinations: Prof. E. VISWANATHA REDDY

Dean of Student Affairs: Prof. O. S. R. U. BHANU KUMAR

Dean of Undergraduate Examinations: Prof. L. D. SUDHAKARA BABU

Dir of Press and Publs: Prof. U. VIPLAVA PRASAD

Librarian: Prof. C. SASIKALA

Library of 431,800 vols

Number of teachers: 883

Number of students: 100,000.

CONSTITUENT COLLEGES

Autonomous College of Engineering: tel. (891) 2844999; fax (891) 2747969; e-mail principal@aucevizag.ac.in; 16 depts; centres of excellence incl. Int. Centre for Bioinformatics, Advanced Centre for Nano Technology, Centre for Biotechnology, Centre for Phase Equilibrium Thermodynamic, Centre for Energy Systems, Centre for Condition Monitoring and Vibration Diagnostics, Centre for Remote Sensing and Information System, Centre for Research on Off-Shore Structures; Principal Prof. P. S. N. RAJU; Vice-Principal Prof. S. RAMA MOHAN RAO.

College of Arts and Commerce: tel. (891) 2844666; fax (891) 2550158; e-mail principal_arts@andhrauniversity.info; f. 1966; 237 teachers; 1,894 students; 28 depts; Principal Prof. L. K. MOHANA RAO

DEAN/CHAIR.

Prof. M. KRISHNA KUMARI, Faculty of Arts
Prof. B. PARVATHESWARA RAO, Faculty of Commerce
Prof. K. P. SUBBA RAO, Faculty of Education
Prof. V. RAMESH, Faculty of Fine Arts
Prof. APADA RAO, Faculty of Oriental Learning
N. VIJAYA MOHAN, Faculty of Physical Education
Prof. K. MADHU, Faculty of Yoga

College of Pharmaceutical Sciences: tel. (891) 2844922; f. 1975; Prin. Prof. K. P. R. CHOWDARY.

College of Science and Technology: tel. (891) 2844888; fax (891) 2550158; e-mail principal_science@andhrauniversity.info; f. 1931; 232 teachers; 2,000 students; Schools of Chemistry, Earth and Atmospheric Sciences, Life Sciences, Mathematical Sciences, Physics; 7 Research Centres; Prin. Prof. P. RAJENDRA PRASAD; Asst Prins Prof. Y. V. RAO, Prof. K. RAJENDRA PRASAD, Dr T. SIVA RAO.

Dr B. R. Ambedkar College of Law: tel. (891) 2844502; f. 1945; Prin. Prof. A. RAJENDRA PRASAD (acting).

The University also runs Bachelors of Education, undergraduate and postgraduate courses in East and West Godavari, Srikakulam, Visakhapatnam and Vizianagaram Districts

ANNA UNIVERSITY

Sardar Patel Rd, Guindy, Chennai 600025

Telephone: (44) 22351723

Fax: (44) 22350397

E-mail: vc@annauniv.edu

Internet: www.annauniv.edu

Founded 1978 as Perarignar Anna Univ. of Technology, name changed 1982

State control

Language of instruction: English

Academic year: July to May

Affiliating, with 225 self-financing engineering colleges, 6 govt colleges, 3 govt-aided engineering colleges located in various parts of Tamil Nadu

Vice-Chancellor: Prof. Dr P. MANNAR JAWAHAR

Registrar: Dr S. SHANMUGAVEL

Controller of Examinations: Dr V. JAYABALAN

Dir of Admissions: Dr A. RAMALINGAM

Dir of Research: Dr V. MURUGESAN

Dir of Student Affairs: Dr S. GANESAN

Dir of Univ. Library: Dr K. BALU (acting)

Library of 202,503 vols, 615 periodicals

Number of teachers: 614

Number of students: 11,489

CHAIR.

Faculty of Architecture and Planning: Dr RANEE MARIA LEONIE VEDAMUTHU
Faculty of Civil Engineering: Dr K. ILAMPARUTHI
Faculty of Electrical Engineering: Dr M. R. MOHAN
Faculty of Information and Communication Engineering: Dr T. V. GEETHA
Faculty of Management Science: Dr L. SUGANTHI
Faculty of Mechanical Engineering: Dr S. GOWRI
Faculty of Science and Humanities: Dr A. VIJAYAKUMAR
Faculty of Technology: Dr P. GAUTAM
Sports Board: Dr P. GANESAN

ANNAMALAI UNIVERSITY

Annamalai Nagar 608002, Tamil Nadu

Telephone: (4144) 238248

Fax: (4144) 238080

E-mail: info@annamalaiuniversity.ac.in

Internet: www.annamalaiuniversity.ac.in

Founded 1929 with a token deposit of 200 books along with Sri Meenakshi College, moved into its present location from the eastern wing of the admin. bldg in 1959

Unitary, residential

Languages of instruction: Tamil, English

Academic year: July to June

Chancellor: HE Governor of Tamil Nadu THIRU SURJIT SINGH BARNALA

Pro-Chancellor: Dr M. A. M. RAMASWAMY

Vice-Chancellor: Dr M. RAMANATHAN

Registrar: Dr M. RATHINASABAPATHI

Controller of Examinations: Dr R. MEENAKSHISUNDARAM

Librarian: Dr M. SURIYA

Library of 463,000 vols, palm-leaf MSS in Tamil and Sanskrit, gramophone records

Number of teachers: 2,000

Number of students: 18,567

Publications: *Annamalai University—A Short History, Annamalai University Research Journal*

DEANS

Faculty of Agriculture: Dr G. KUPPUSWAMY
Faculty of Arts: Dr S. RAJENDRAN
Faculty of Dentistry: Dr C. R. RAMACHANDRAN
Faculty of Education: Dr K. VAITHIANATHAN
Faculty of Engineering and Technology: Prof. B. PALANIAPPAN
Faculty of Fine Arts: Prof. A. K. PALANIVEL
Faculty of Indian Languages: Dr P. L. MUTHUVEERAPPAN
Faculty of Medicine: Dr N. CHIDAMBARAM
Faculty of Science: Dr VENUGOPAL P. MENON

ASSAM AGRICULTURAL UNIVERSITY

Jorhat 785013, Assam

Telephone: (376) 3340008

Fax: (376) 3340001

E-mail: vc@aau.ren.nic.in

Internet: www.aau.ac.in

Founded 1969

Teaching, research and extension at undergraduate and postgraduate levels in Agriculture (Jorhat campus and Biswanath Chariali), Home Science (Jorhat campus), Veterinary Science (Khanapara campus and Azad, North Lakhimpur) and Fisheries Science (Raha); 6 regional research stations

Language of instruction: English

Autonomous control

Chancellor: HE THE GOVERNOR OF ASSAM

Vice-Chancellor: Dr B. C. BHOWMIK (acting)

Registrar: Dr KRISHNA GOHAIN

Dir of Extension Education: Dr B. C. BHOWMICK

Dir of Postgraduate Studies: Dr D. DAS

Dir of Student Welfare: Dr D. DAS (acting)

Dirs of Research: Dr N. N. SARMAH (Agriculture), Dr M. R. BORKAKOTY (Veterinary Sciences)

Chief Librarian: Dr T. C. BRAHMA

Library of 90,000 vols (main campus)

Number of teachers: 530

Number of students: 2,500

Publications: *Ghare-Pathare* (Assamese, 12 a year), *Journal of Research, Krishibikshan* (Assamese, 4 a year), *Package of Practices for Kharif Crops* (English, 2 a year), *Package of Practices for Rabi Crops* (English, 2 a year)

DEANS

Faculty of Agriculture: Dr L. K. HAZARIKA
Faculty of Home Science: Dr MINAXI PATHAK
Faculty of Veterinary Science: Dr R. N. GOSWAMI

ASSAM UNIVERSITY

Silchar 788011, Assam

Telephone: (3842) 270801

Fax: (3842) 270802

E-mail: auliba@sancharnet.in

Internet: www.assamuniversity.nic.in

Founded 1994

Central university

Academic year: July to June

Chief Rector: Governor of Assam, Lt-Gen. (Retd) A. SINGH

Chancellor: Dr M. S. SWAMINATHAN
Vice-Chancellor: Prof. TAPODHIR BHATTACHAR-
JEE
Pro Vice-Chancellor (Diphu Campus): Prof.
B. MATE
Pro Vice-Chancellor (Silchar Campus): Prof.
G. D. SHARMA
Finance Officer: Dr A. SEN (acting)
Controller of Examinations: Dr P. DEBNATH
Proctor: Dr M. DUTTA CHOUDHRY
Dir, CDC: Dr B. R. CHOUDHURY
Registrar: S. SENGUPTA
Librarian: V. D. SHRIVASTAVA

Library of 52,557 vols, 186 periodicals
Number of teachers: 140
Number of students: 1,446

Publications: *Journal of Assam University,
Science in society: proceedings of regional
symposium, Silchar: Problems of urban
development of a growing city*

DEANS

School of Environmental Sciences: Prof. A.
GUPTA
School of Humanities: Dr N. B. BISWAS
School of Information Sciences: Prof. G. P.
PANDEY
School of Languages: Prof. S. DEVI
School of Life Sciences: Prof. G. D. SHARMA
School of Management Studies: Dr N. B. DEY
School of Physical Sciences: Prof. K. HEMA-
CHANDRAN
School of Social Sciences: Prof. GOPALJI
MISHRA
School of Technology: Prof. A. K. SEN

AWADHESH PRATAP SINGH
UNIVERSITY

Rewa District Rewa 486003, Madhya Pra-
desh
Telephone: (7662) 230050
Fax: (7662) 242175
Internet: www.apsurewa.ernet.in

Founded 1968
Affiliating, Teaching and Research
Languages of instruction: Hindi, English
Academic year: July to June

Chancellor: HE THE GOVERNOR OF MADHYA
PRADESH
Vice-Chancellor: Prof. A. D. N. BAJPAI
Registrar: Dr R. S. PANDEY
Librarian: G. K. SINGH

Library of 31,000 vols
Number of teachers: 841 (42 at univ., 799 at
affiliated colleges)
Number of students: 47,254 (incl. affiliated
colleges)

Publication: *Vindhya Bharati* (4 a year)

DEANS

Faculty of Arts: R. R. MATHUR
Faculty of Ayurveda: Dr R. V. SOHGUNRA
Faculty of Commerce: Prof. I. P. TRIPATHI
Faculty of Education: Dr RASHAMI SHUKLA
Faculty of Home Science: Dr A. K. SHRIVAS-
TAVA
Faculty of Law: R. R. MATHUR
Faculty of Life Science: Dr R. N. SHUKLA
Faculty of Medicine: Dr M. K. RATHORE
Faculty of Prachya Sanskrit: Dr BHASHKAR-
ACHARYA TRIPATHI
Faculty of Science: Dr S. K. NIGAM
Faculty of Social Science: Dr A. K. SHRIVAS-
TAVA

There are 62 affiliated colleges

BABA FARID UNIVERSITY OF
HEALTH SCIENCES

Sadiq Rd, Faridkot 151203, Punjab
Telephone: (1639) 256232
Fax: (1639) 256234

E-mail: generalinfo@bfuhs.ac.in
Internet: www.bfuhs.ac.in
Founded 1998
Affiliating

Faculties of Ayurveda, dental sciences, homeopathy, medical sciences, nursing sciences,
physiotherapy; 133 affiliated and 4 constituent colleges

Chancellor: HE THE GOVERNOR OF PUNJAB
Vice-Chancellor: Dr SHIVINDER SINGH GILL
Registrar: Dr DARSHAN SINGH SIDHU
Librarian: Dr RAJEEV MANHAS

Library of 25,604 vols
Number of students: 21,332

DEANS

Faculty of Ayurveda: Dr RAVINDER KAUR
SHUKLA
Faculty of Dental Sciences: Dr ANIL KOHLI
Faculty of Homeopathy: Dr TEJINDER PAL
SINGH
Faculty of Medical Sciences: Dr J. L. GARGI
Faculty of Nursing Sciences: Dr KANWALJIT
KAUR
Faculty of Physiotherapy: Dr SANJAY
WADHWA

BABASAHEB BHIMRAO AMBEDKAR
UNIVERSITY

Vidya Vihar, Rai Bareilly Rd, Lucknow
226025
Telephone: (522) 2440826
Fax: (522) 2440821
E-mail: info@bbauindia.org
Internet: www.bbauindia.org

Founded 1996
Central university
Academic year: July to June

Chancellor: Prof. U. R. RAO
Vice-Chancellor: Prof. B. HANUMAIAH
Finance Officer: D. K. JAIRAJ
Registrar: Prof. U. S. RAWAT
Librarian: K. L. MAHAWAR (acting)

DEANS

School of Ambedkar Studies: Prof. N. M. P.
VERMA
School for Biosciences and Biotechnology:
Prof. R. B. RAM
School for Environmental Sciences: Prof. D.
P. SINGH
School for Home Sciences: Dr SUNITA MISHRA
School for Information Science and Technol-
ogy: Prof. R. B. RAM
School for Legal Studies: Prof. S. K. BHATNA-
GAR (acting)
Student Welfare: Dr K. L. MAHAWAR

BANARAS HINDU UNIVERSITY

Varanasi 221005, Uttar Pradesh
Telephone: (542) 2316558
Fax: (542) 2317074
E-mail: bhu@banaras.ernet.in
Internet: www.bhu.ac.in

Founded 1915
State control
Central univ. (residential and teaching)
Languages of instruction: Hindi, English
Academic year: July to April (three terms)

Visitor: PRES. OF THE REPUBLIC OF INDIA
Vice-Chancellor: Prof. D. P. SINGH
Rector: Prof. B. D. SINGH
Registrar: K. P. UPADHYAY
Finance Officer: PARAG PRAKASH
Controller of Examinations: K. P. UAPDHYAY
Dean of Students: S. K. SHARMA
Chief Proctor: Prof. H. C. S. RATHOR
Librarian: Prof. H. N. PRASAD

Library of 916,821 vols
Number of teachers: 1,085

Number of students: 16,105
Publications: *BHU Journal, Prajna*

DEANS

Faculty of Agriculture: Prof. R. P. SINGH
Faculty of Arts: Prof. S. N. PANDEY
Faculty of Ayurveda: Prof. M. DWIVEDI
Faculty of Commerce: Prof. S. CHANDRA
Faculty of Dental Science: Prof. N. MITTAL
Faculty of Education: Prof. B. D. SINGH
Faculty of Information Technology: Prof. J.
N. SINHA
Faculty of Law: Dr M. N. P. SRIVASTAVA
Faculty of Management Studies: Prof. DEE-
PAK BARMAN
Faculty of Medicine: Prof. P. SHARMA
Faculty of Performing Arts: Dr RITWIK
SANYAL
Faculty of Sanskrit Vidya Dharma Vijnan
Sankaya: Prof. K. K. SHARMA
Faculty of Science: Prof. S. C. LAKHOTIA
Faculty of Social Sciences: Prof. P. N. PANDEY
Faculty of Visual Arts: Dr MRIDULA SINHA

CONSTITUENT COLLEGE

Mahila Maha Vidyalaya: f. 1929; Principal
Dr SUSHILA SINGH.

ATTACHED INSTITUTES

Institute of Agricultural Sciences: Dir
Prof. S. R. SINGH.

Institute of Medical Sciences: Dir Prof.
GAJENDRA SINGH

DEANS

Faculty of Ayurveda: Dr VINOD KUMAR JOSHI
Faculty of Dental Sciences: Prof. NEELAM
MITTAL
Faculty of Modern Medicine: Prof. P. SHARMA

Institute of Technology: tel. (542)
2368106; fax (542) 2368428; e-mail
director@itbhu.ac.in; internet www.itbhu.ac
.in; Dir Prof. S. N. UPADHYAY.

4 affiliated colleges

BANGALORE UNIVERSITY

Jnana Bharathi Campus, Jnana Bharathi
Post Bangalore 560056, Karnataka
Telephone: (80) 22961006
Fax: (80) 23219295
E-mail: registrar@bub.ernet.in
Internet: www.bub.ernet.in

Founded 1964
Affiliating
Languages of instruction: Kannada, English
Academic year: June to March

Chancellor: HE THE GOVERNOR OF KARNATAKA
Vice-Chancellor: Prof. A. N. PRABHUDEVA
Pro-Chancellor: ARAVIND LIMBAVALI
Finance Officer: SRI VENKATESHAPPA
Registrar: SANJAY VIR SINGH
Librarian: Dr P. V. KONNUR

Library of 315,000 vols
Number of teachers: 456
Number of students: 300,000

Publications: *Bash Bharathi* (2 a year),
Janapriya Vignana (12 a year), *Sadhane*
(Kannada, 4 a year), *Vidya Bharathi,
Vignana Bharathi*

DEANS

Faculty of Arts: Dr G. S. SIVARAMAKRISHNAN
Faculty of Commerce: Dr PUSHPA D. BHATT
Faculty of Education: Dr M. NARAYANA
SWAMY
Faculty of Engineering: Dr K. R. VENUGOPAL
Faculty of Law: Dr T. R. SUBRAMANYA
Faculty of Science: Dr H. T. RATHOD

UNIVERSITY COLLEGES

**University College of Physical Educa-
tion:** Principal Dr M. S. TALWAR.

University Law College: Principal Dr K. M. HANUMANTHARAYAPPA.

University Visvesvaraya College of Engineering: f. 1917.

There are 400 affiliated colleges and 75 postgraduate depts

BARKATULLAH UNIVERSITY

Hoshangabad Rd, Bhopal 462026, Madhya Pradesh

Telephone: (755) 2491800
E-mail: buregistrar@yahoo.co.in
Internet: www.bubhopal.nic.in

Founded 1970 as Bhopal Univ., name changed 1989

Teaching and Affiliating; 170 affiliated colleges

Languages of instruction: English, Hindi

Chancellor: HE THE GOVERNOR OF MADHYA PRADESH
Vice-Chancellor: Prof. RAVINDRA JAIN
Proctor: Prof. P. K. MISHRA
Finance Officer: BUDHOLIYA
Dir for College Devt Council: H. S. YADAV
Dir for Public Relations: Dr V. S. BAIS
Dean for Student Welfare: Dr KALIKA YADAV
Registrar: Dr SANJAY P. TIWARI
Librarian: Dr ARVIND CHOUHAN

Library of 71,259 vols
Number of teachers: 1,100
Number of students: 40,000 (incl. affiliated colleges)

DEANS

Faculty of Arts: Prof. H. KHAN
Faculty of Commerce: Dr D. P. SHARMA
Faculty of Education: M. S. GUPTA
Faculty of Engineering: Dr A. S. MEHTA
Faculty of Law: H. L. JAIN
Faculty of Life Sciences: Dr S. D. BEBARE
Faculty of Management: Dr N. R. BHANDARI
Faculty of Science: Dr K. K. RAO
Faculty of Social Sciences: Dr H. S. YADAV

BENGAL ENGINEERING AND SCIENCE UNIVERSITY

PO Botanic Garden, Howrah 711103, West Bengal

Telephone: (33) 26684561
Fax: (33) 26682916
E-mail: vc@becs.ac.in
Internet: www.becs.ac.in

Founded 1856 as Civil Engineering College, Calcutta, 1992 deemed univ. status as Bengal Engineering College, 2004 univ. status and present name

Depts of applied mechanics, architecture, chemistry, civil, computer science and technology, electrical, electronics and telecommunications, geology, humanities, human resource management, information technology, mathematics, mechanical, metallurgy, mining, physics

Vice-Chancellor: Dr AJOY ROY
Dean of Research: Dr B. N. DATTA
Dean of Students: A. K. GHOSH
Registrar: Dr BIMAN BANDYOPADHYAY
Finance Officer: MANINDRA NATH SARKAR
Controller of Examinations: Dr BHASWATI MITRA
Librarian: Dr H. P. SHARMA

Library of 200,000 vols, 300 periodicals
Number of students: 2,500

DEANS

Faculty Councils for Postgraduate and Undergraduate Studies of Basic and Applied Sciences: Prof. BICHITRA KUMAR GUHA

Faculty Councils for Postgraduate and Undergraduate Studies of Engineering and Technology: Prof. AMIT KUMAR DAS
Faculty Councils for Postgraduate and Undergraduate Studies of Social and Management Sciences: Prof. MANAS KUMAR SANYAL

CONSTITUENT SCHOOLS

Purabi Das School of Information Technology: tel. (33) 26689312; fax (33) 26689313; internet pdsit.becdu.ac.in; Dir Prof. SURYA SARATHI BARAT.
School of Community Science and Technology (SOCSAT): Dir Dr BHASWATI MITRA.
School of Disaster Mitigation Engineering: Dir Prof. S. C. DUTTA.
School of Ecology Infrastructure and Human Settlement Management: Dir Prof. SOUVANIC ROY.
School of Material Science and Engineering (SMSE): f. 2001; Dir Dr NIL RATAN BANDYOPADHYAY.
School of Management Science (SOMS): f. 2004; Dir Prof. S. C. SAHA.
School of Mechatronics & Robotics: Dir Prof. S. R. BHADRA CHOUDHURI.
School of Safety & Occupational Health Engineering: Dir Prof. B. K. BHATTACHARYA.
School of VLSI Technology: Dir Prof. JAYA SIL.

BERHAMPUR UNIVERSITY

Berhampur 760007, Orissa

Telephone: (680) 2242172
Fax: (680) 2243322
Internet: bamu.nic.in

Founded 1967

Teaching and Affiliating
State control
Language of instruction: English
Academic year: June to May

Chancellor: HE THE GOVERNOR OF ORISSA
Vice-Chancellor: Prof. B. K. SAHU
Comptroller: P. K. RAUT
Controller of Examinations: Prof. A. K. MISHRA
Dir of College Devt Council: Prof. J. N. PANDA
Dir of Distance Education: Prof. B. B. KAR
Registrar: SURECH CH. PANDA
Librarian: J. PANIGRAHY (acting)

Library of 96,997 vols
Number of teachers: 168
Number of students: 31,550

Publication: *Research Journal* (1 a year)

PROFESSORS

ACHARYA, S., Oriya
BARAL, J. K., Political Science
DAS, D., Oriya
DAS, G. N., Linguistics
DAS, H. H., Political Science
DAS, N. C., Physics
KHAN, P. A., Botany
MAJHI, J., Electronics
MISHRA, S. K., English
MISRA, B. N., Botany
MISRA, D.
MISRA, P. M., Marine Science
MOHANTY, S. P., Physics
MOHAPATRA, N. C., Physics
PADHISHARMA, R., Economics
PANDA, C. S., Chemistry
PANDA, G. P., Law
PANDA, G. S., Business Administration
PANDA, J., Commerce
PANDA, P., Economics
PANIGRAHY, G. P., Chemistry
PARHI, N., Mathematics
PATI, S. C., Chemistry
PATNAIK, B. K., Zoology

PATRA, G. C., Industrial Relations and Labour Welfare
PRASAD, R., Zoology
RAO, E. R., English
RATH, D., Mathematics
SAHU, P. K., Commerce
SAMAL, J. K., History
VERMA, G. P., Zoology

There are 11 govt, 62 non-govt and 26 professional technical affiliated colleges

BHARATHIAR UNIVERSITY

Coimbatore 641046, Tamil Nadu

Telephone: (422) 2428100
Fax: (422) 2422387
E-mail: regr@b-u.ac.in
Internet: www.b-u.ac.in

Founded 1982

Teaching and Affiliating; incl. Bharathiar School of Management and Entrepreneur Devt and depts of bio-informatics, bio-technology, botany, chemistry, commerce, computer science, econ., educational technology, English, environmental sciences, linguistics, mathematics, physical education, physics, population studies, psychology, sociology, statistics, Tamil, zoology; 85 affiliated colleges and 19 affiliated research institutes

Academic year: July to April

Chancellor: HE THE GOVERNOR OF TAMIL NADU
Pro-Chancellor: HON'BLE MIN. FOR EDUCATION, GOVT OF TAMIL NADU
Vice-Chancellor: Col Prof. Dr G. THIRUVASAGAM
Registrar: Dr K. NATARAJAN
Controller of Examinations: Dr B. KRISHNAMURTHY
Dir of Finance: THIRU S. MOHANDOSS
Dir of Public Relations: N. J. MURALI MOHAN
Dir of Research: P. KANDASAMY
Dean of College Devt Council: Dr KANDHASAMY
Librarian: Dr P. VINAYAGAMOORTHY

Library of 120,000 vols, 150 periodicals
Founded 1981

DEANS

Arts: Dr C. SHUNMUGOM
Commerce: Dr M. MANICKAM
Education: Dr R. ANANTHASAYANAM
Science: Dr S. NATARAJAN
Social Sciences: Dr C. CHANDRAMOHAN

BHARATHIDASAN UNIVERSITY

Palkalaiperur, Tiruchirappalli 620024, Tamil Nadu

Telephone: (431) 2407072
Fax: (431) 2407045
E-mail: office@bdu.ac.in
Internet: www.bdu.ac.in

Founded 1982

Affiliating; incl. 16 schools and 47 depts and centres; 106 affiliated colleges and 25 approved instns.

Languages of instruction: English, Tamil
State control
Academic year: June to April

Chancellor: HE THE GOVERNOR OF TAMIL NADU
Vice-Chancellor: Dr M. PONNAVAIKKO
Registrar: Dr T. RAMASWAMY (acting)
Finance Officer: THIRU S. SUBBURATHINAM
Controller of Examinations: Dr S. SRIDHARAN
Librarian: Dr S. SRINIVASA RAGAVAN (acting)

Library of 90,000 vols, 200 periodicals
Number of teachers: 2,779
Number of students: 99,802

DEANS

Arts: Dr K. PARTHASARATHY

Indian and Other Languages: Dr A. NOEL JOSEPH SEETHARAMAN

Science: Dr M. LAKSHMANAN

BHAVNAGAR UNIVERSITY

Gaurishanker Lake Rd, Bhavnagar 364002, Gujarat

Telephone: (278) 2430002

Fax: (278) 2426706

E-mail: drhc_trivedi@rediffmail.com

Internet: www.bhavuni.edu

Founded 1978

Teaching and Affiliating

State control

Language of instruction: Gujarati

Academic year: June to March (two terms)

Chancellor: HE THE GOVERNOR OF GUJARAT

Vice-Chancellor: Dr H. C. TRIVEDI

Registrar: RAMSINH H. RAJPUT

Controller of Examinations: K. L. BHATT

Dir of External Studies: B. N. DESAI

Librarian: Dr B. M. GOHEL

Library of 102,090 vols

Number of teachers: 400

Number of students: 20,959

DEANS

Faculty of Arts: Prof. VINOD H. JOSHI

Faculty of Commerce: Dr B. K. OZA

Faculty of Education: Dr J. P. MAIYANI

Faculty of Engineering: Prof. M. K. VORA

Faculty of Law: J. A. PANDYA

Faculty of Management: Dr A. KUMAR

Faculty of Medicine: Dr M. P. SINGH

Faculty of Rural Studies: SATISHBHAI PATEL

Faculty of Science: Dr MAYURIBEN PANDYA

There are 28 affiliated colleges

ATTACHED INSTITUTES

B. V. Patel Pharmaceutical Education and Research Institute: Ahmedabad.

Central Salt and Marine Chemicals Research Institute: see under Research Institutes.

Dholakia School of Music: Sihor.

K. K. Jani Institute of Medical Laboratory Technology: Amargadh; Dir Dr R. M. THAKKAR.

K. L. Institute for Deaf and Dumb: Vidyanagar.

Perfect Foundation: Bhavnagar; Dir R. D. MEHTA.

BHUPENDRA NARAYAN MANDAL UNIVERSITY

Laloo Nagar, Madhepura 852113, Bihar

Telephone: (6476) 222059

Fax: (6476) 222068

Founded 1992

State control

Vice-Chancellor: Prof. QAMAR AHSAN

Registrar: B. P. YADAV

27 Constituent colleges, 24 affiliated colleges, 2 postgraduate centres.

BIDHAN CHANDRA KRISHI VISWAVIDYALAYA

PO Krishi Viswavidyalaya, Mohanpur 741252, Nadia, West Bengal

Telephone: (33) 25879772

Fax: (3473) 222275

E-mail: drbckv@vsnl.net

Internet: www.bckv.edu.in

Founded 1974

Residential

Academic year: July to June

Chancellor: HE THE GOVERNOR OF WEST BENGAL

Vice-Chancellor: Dr RANAJIT KUMAR SAMANTA

Registrar: ASOK BANERJEE

Dir of Extension Education: Dr P. BANDYO-PADHYAY

Dir of Farms: Dr T. K. KUMAR

Dir of Research: Prof. SAROJ SANYAL

Dean of Student Welfare: Prof. RANABIR CHATTERJEE

Asst Librarian: DIPIKA NEOGI

Library of 69,430 vols, 208 periodicals

Number of students: 466

DEANS

Faculty of Agriculture: Prof. A. K. DAS

Faculty of Horticulture: Prof. P. CHATTOPAD-HYAY

Postgraduate Studies: Prof. R. K. BISWAS

BIRSA AGRICULTURAL UNIVERSITY

Kanke, Ranchi 834006, Jharkhand

Telephone: (651) 2450500

Fax: (651) 2450850

E-mail: bau@bitsmart.com

Internet: www.baujharkhand.org

Founded 1981

Languages of instruction: English, Hindi

Academic year: July to June

Chancellor: HE THE GOVERNOR OF JHARKHAND

Vice-Chancellor: Dr N. N. SINGH

Dir of Research: Dr B. N. SINGH

Registrar: Dr S. M. PRASAD

Librarian: R. PRASAD

Library of 70,000 vols

Number of teachers: 200

Number of students: 700

Publication: *Journal of Research*

DEANS

Faculty of Agriculture: Dr A. K. SARKAR

Faculty of Forestry: Dr P. KAUSHAL

Faculty of Veterinary Science and Animal Husbandry: Dr A. K. SINHA

BUNDELKHAND UNIVERSITY

Jhansi 284003, Uttar Pradesh

Telephone: (510) 2320496; (510) 2320761

E-mail: admin@bujhansi.org

Internet: www.bujhansi.org

Founded 1975

Affiliating

Vice-Chancellor: Prof. V. K. MITTAL

Registrar: BHAGWAN SINGH

Finance Officer: K. C. VERMA

Dean of Student Welfare: Prof. V. P. KHARE

Proctor: Prof. V. K. SEHGAL

Librarian: Dr S. C. SROTIA

20 Affiliated colleges

Library of 10,000 vols

Number of teachers: 434

Number of students: 38,000

DEANS

Faculty of Agriculture: Dr B. D. PRAJAPATI

Faculty of Arts: Dr M. L. MAURYA

Faculty of Commerce: Prof. PANKAJ ATRI

Faculty of Education: Dr Y. KULSHRESTHA

Faculty of Engineering and Technology: Dr D. SINGH

Faculty of Law: Prof. D. P. GUPTA

Faculty of Medicine: Dr G. KUMAR

Faculty of Science: Prof. S. P. SINGH

UNIVERSITY CENTRE

Veerangna Jhalkaribai Centre for Women Studies and Development: tel. (510) 2321103; e-mail wsc_bu@rediffmail.com; Dir Dr APARNA RAJ; publ. *International Journal for Women and Gender Research* (2 a year).

CENTRAL AGRICULTURAL UNIVERSITY

Iroisemba, Imphal 795004, Manipur

Telephone: (385) 2415933

Fax: (385) 2415196

E-mail: snpuri04@yahoo.co.in

Internet: www.cic.nic.in/cicmanipur/html/cau.asp

Founded 1993

Central university

Academic year: August to July (two semesters)

Chancellor: V. L. CHOPRA

Vice-Chancellor: Dr S. N. PURI

Registrar: Dr M. PREMJIT SINGH

Library of 18,527 vols, 241 periodicals

Number of teachers: 103

Number of students: 437

DEANS

College of Agriculture: Prof. N. I. SINGH

College of Fisheries: Dr M. L. BHOWMIK

College of Home Science: Dr R. S. RAGHUVAN-SHI

College of Horticulture and Forestry: Prof. D. S. RATHORE

College of Veterinary Science and Animal Husbandry: Dr H. C. KALITA

PROFESSORS

BHATTACHARYA, D., Soil Science and Agricultural Chemistry

LAISHRAM, J. M., Plant Breeding and Genetics

MEITEI, W. I., Horticulture

NANDEESHA, M. C., Aquaculture

RAGHUVANSHI, R. S., Food and Nutrition

RATHORE, D. S., Pomology

SINGH, M. D., Animal Husbandry and Dairying

SINGH, M. P., Agricultural Entomology

SINGH, M. R. K., Plant Breeding and Genetics

SINGH, N. I., Plant Pathology

SINGH, N. R., Agricultural Economics

SINGH, R. K. K., Soil Science and Agricultural Chemistry

SINGH, Y. J., Agricultural Engineering

CHANDRA SHEKHAR AZAD UNIVERSITY OF AGRICULTURE AND TECHNOLOGY

Nawabganj, Kanpur 208002, Uttar Pradesh

Telephone: (512) 2534156

Fax: (512) 2533808

E-mail: info@csauk.ac.in

Internet: www.csauk.ac.in

Founded 1975

State control

Languages of instruction: Hindi, English

Academic year: July to June

Chancellor: HE THE GOVERNOR OF UTTAR PRADESH

Vice-Chancellor: Prof. DINESH SINGH

Comptroller: D. PAL

Dir of Agricultural Experiment Station: Dr R. P. KATIYAR

Dir of Extension: Dr V. K. SINGH

Registrar: Dr V. P. KANAUJIA

Librarian: Dr G. S. SINGH

Library of 64,300 vols, 4,481 periodicals

Number of teachers: 318

Number of students: 1,187

DEANS

Faculty of Agricultural Engineering and Technology: Dr K. KUMAR

Faculty of Agriculture: Dr A. N. TIWARI

Faculty of Home Science: Dr P. S. KENDUR-KAR

CHATRAPATI SHAHUJI MAHARAJ UNIVERSITY, KANPUR

Kalyanpur, Kanpur 208024, Uttar Pradesh
Telephone: (512) 2570450
Fax: (512) 2570006
Internet: www.kanpuruniversity.org
Founded 1966 as Kanpur University; present name 1997
Affiliating
State control
Languages of instruction: English, Hindi
Academic year: July to June
Chancellor: HE THE GOVERNOR OF UTTAR PRADESH
Vice-Chancellor: Dr H. K. SEHGAL
Registrar: MAHESH CHANDRA
Librarian: Dr S. P. SINGH
170 Affiliated colleges
Library of 47,000 vols
Number of students: 220,000

DEANS

Faculty of Agriculture: Dr A. K. SRIVASTAVA
Faculty of Arts: G. J. SRIVASTAVA
Faculty of Ayurvedic and Unani Medicine: Dr B. D. AGGARWAL
Faculty of Business Management: Prof. Y. C. MISHRA
Faculty of Commerce: Dr P. C. CHATURVEDI
Faculty of Education: Dr S. SHANTA
Faculty of Law: S. L. VIDYARTHI
Faculty of Life Sciences: Dr L. C. MISRA
Faculty of Medicine: Dr S. K. KATIYAR
Faculty of Science: Dr P. K. MATHUR
Faculty of Social Sciences: (vacant)
Univ. College of Dental Sciences: Prof. Y. C. MISHRA
Univ. Institute of Engineering and Technology: Prof. D. SARAN

CHAUDHARY CHARAN SINGH HARYANA AGRICULTURAL UNIVERSITY

Hissar 125004, Haryana
Telephone: (1662) 289326
Fax: (1662) 23495
E-mail: vc@hau.ernet.in
Internet: hau.ernet.in
Founded 1970
State control
Language of instruction: English
Academic year: July to June
Chancellor: HE THE GOVERNOR OF HARYANA
Vice-Chancellor: Dr DHARAM VIR (acting)
Registrar: Dr R. S. DALAL
Dir of Extension: Dr H. D. YADAV
Dir of Research: Dr S. S. PAHUJA
Controller of Examinations: Dr V. K. KALRA
Librarian: PREM SINGH
Library of 317,343 vols (218,000 books, 97,437 vols of periodicals)
Number of teachers: 730
Number of students: 650
Publications: *Haryana Kheti* (12 a year), *HAU Journal of Research* (2 a year)

DEANS

College of Agricultural Engineering and Technology: Dr M. K. GARG
College of Agriculture: Dr S. S. PAHUJA
College of Animal Sciences: Dr N. SINGH YADAV
College of Basic Sciences and Humanities: Dr V. K. CHOWDHURY
College of Home Science: Dr N. KHETARPAUL
College of Veterinary Science: Dr S. K. NAGPAL
Postgraduate Studies: Dr O. P. TOKY

CHAUDHARY CHARAN SINGH UNIVERSITY

Meerut 250005, Uttar Pradesh
Telephone: (121) 2760551
Fax: (121) 2760577
E-mail: vicechancellor@ccsuniversity.org
Internet: www.ccsum.com
Founded 1966 as Meerut University
Affiliating and Teaching
Languages of instruction: Hindi, English
Chancellor: HE THE GOVERNOR OF UTTAR PRADESH
Vice-Chancellor: Prof. S. P. OJHA
Registrar: Dr V. B. BANSAL
Library of 95,074 vols, 276 periodicals
Number of students: 125,365
Publications: *Indian Journal of Political Science, Journal of Political and Public Administration*

DEANS

Faculty of Agriculture: Prof. P. V. SINGH
Faculty of Arts: Prof. J. K. PUNDIR
Faculty of Commerce: Dr A. B. LAL
Faculty of Education: Prof. S. PAL
Faculty of Law: Dr C. SHEKAR
Faculty of Medicine: Dr U. SHARMA
Faculty of Science: Prof. D. PANDEY
Faculty of Technology: Prof. D. PANDEY
One constituent college and 63 affiliated colleges

CHAUDHARY DEVI LAL UNIVERSITY

Barnala Rd, Sirsa 125055, Haryana
Telephone: (1666) 247104
Internet: cdlu.edu.in
Founded 2003
Teaching and Affiliating
Language of instruction: English
Academic year: July to May (three terms)
Chancellor: HE THE GOVERNOR OF HARYANA
Vice-Chancellor: Dr K. C. BHARDWAJ
Registrar: Dr R. K SEHGAL
Dean of Academic Affairs: Dr R. K. SINGH
Finance Officer: Dr N. C. JAIN
Proctor: Dr R. CHANDER
Controller of Examinations: N. C. JAIN
Librarian: Dr D. P. WARNE
Faculties of Arts and Languages, Commerce and Management, Education, Engineering and Technology, Law, Physical Education, Social Sciences

DEANS

Faculty of Commerce and Management: Prof. SULTAN SINGH
Faculty of Education: Prof. SHAMSHER SINGH JANG BAHADUR
Faculty of Engineering and Technology: Prof. VIKRAM SINGH
Faculty of Humanities: Prof. ANU SHUKLA
Faculty of Law: Prof. HARBANSH
Faculty of Life Sciences: Prof. SURESH KUMAR GAHLAWAT
Faculty of Physical Sciences: Prof. PARVEEN AGHAMKAR
Faculty of Social Sciences: Dr RAJBIR SINGH DALAL

CHAUDHARY SARWAN KUMAR HIMACHAL PRADESH KRISHI VISHVAVIDYALAYA

Palampur 176062, Dist. Kangra, Himachal Pradesh
Telephone: (1894) 230521
Fax: (1894) 230465
E-mail: icuns@hillagric.ernet.in
Internet: www.hillagric.ernet.in
Founded 1978; fmrly Faculty of Agriculture of Himachal Pradesh University

State control
Language of instruction: English
Academic year: July to June
Chancellor: HE THE GOVERNOR OF HIMACHAL PRADESH
Vice-Chancellor: Dr TEJ PARTAP
Registrar: NEERAJ KUMAR
Comptroller: B. R. DHIMAN (acting)
Dir of Education: Dr K. K. KATOCH
Dir of Research: Dr S. C. SHARMA
Registrar: RAJDEV SINGH JASROTIA
Librarian: Dr KAHAN BASSI (acting)
Library of 74,000 vols
Number of teachers: 367
Number of students: 792
Publication: *Himachal Journal of Agricultural Research* (2 a year)

DEANS

College of Agriculture (Palampur): Dr O. P. SHARMA (acting)
College of Basic Sciences: Dr R. G. SUD (acting)
College of Home Science: Dr P. K. SHARMA
College of Veterinary and Animal Sciences: Dr A. C. VARSHNEY (acting)
Postgraduate Studies: Dr P. K. SHARMA (acting)

ATTACHED REGIONAL RESEARCH STATIONS

Regional Research Centre, Bajaura: Bajaura, Dist. Kullu 175125, Himachal Pradesh; tel. (1905) 287235; Assoc. Dir H. L. THAKUR.

Regional Research Centre, Dhaulakuan: Dhaulakuan, Dist. Sirmour 173001, Himachal Pradesh; tel. (1704) 257421; Assoc. Dir V. KALIA.

Regional Research Centre, Kukumseri: Kukumseri, Dist. Lahoul and Spiti, Himachal Pradesh; tel. (1909) 222210; Assoc. Dir VIJAY SINGH THAKUR.

COCHIN UNIVERSITY OF SCIENCE AND TECHNOLOGY

Cochin 682022, Kerala
Telephone: (484) 2575396
Fax: (484) 2577595
E-mail: registrar@cusat.ac.in
Internet: www.cusat.ac.in
Founded 1971
State control
Language of instruction: English
Academic year: July to April
Chancellor: HE THE GOVERNOR OF KERALA
Pro-Chancellor: THE MINISTER FOR EDUCATION, KERALA
Vice-Chancellor: K. M. ABRAHAM
Registrar: Dr A. RAMACHANDRAN
Finance Officer: S. OUSEPH
Controller of Examinations: V. K. RAMACHANDRAN NAIR
Dir of Int. Relations and Academic Admissions: Dr K. SAJAN
Dir of Public Relations and Publs: S. ANILKUMAR
Librarian: Dr S. DEVI ANTHERJANAN
Library of 82,000 vols, 200 periodicals
Number of teachers: 197
Number of students: 2,100
Publications: *Indian Manager, Law Review, Statistical Methods*

DEANS

Faculty of Engineering: Prof. P. O. J. LEBBA
Faculty of Environmental Studies: Dr I. S. BRIGHT SINGH
Faculty of Humanities: Dr A. ARAVINDAKSHAN
Faculty of Law: Dr K. N. CHANDRASEKHARA PILLAI
Faculty of Marine Science: Dr K. MOHAN KUMAR

Faculty of Medical Science and Technology: Dr P. S. JOHN
Faculty of Science: Dr V. UNNIKRISHNAN NAIR
Faculty of Social Sciences: Dr D. RAJASENAN
Faculty of Technology: Dr V. P. NARAYANAN NAMPOORI

PROFESSORS

ALIYAR, S., Hindi
ARAVINDAKSHNAN, A., Hindi
BABU, T. J., Civil Engineering
BABU SUNDAR, S., Computer Application
BALACHAND, A. N., Physical Oceanography
BALAKRISHNAN, K. G., Electronics
CHACKO, J., Chemical Oceanography
CHANDRASEKHARAN, M., Biotechnology
CHANDRASEKHARAN, N. S., Legal Studies
CHANDRASEKHARAN PILLAI, K. N., Legal Studies
DAMODARAN, K. T., Marine Sciences
DAMODARAN, R., Marine Sciences
EASWARI, M., Hindi
FRANCIS, C. A., Management Studies
GEORGE, K. E., Polymer Science and Rubber Technology
GEORGE, K. K., Management Studies
GEORGE VARGHESE, K., Management Studies
GIRIJAVALLABHAN, C. P., Physics
GOPALAKRISHNA KURUP, P., Marine Sciences
HRIDAYANATHAN, C., Industrial Fisheries
JACOB, P. K., Computer Science
JATHAVEDAN, M., Mathematics
JOSEPH, R., Polymer Science and Rubber Technology
KORAKANDY, R., Industrial Fisheries
KRISHNAMURTHY, A., Mathematical Sciences
KRISHNANKUTTY, P., Ship Technology
KURIAKOSE, A. P., Polymer Science and Rubber Technology
KURIAKOSE, V. L., Physics
MADHUROADANA KENUP, B., Industrial Fisheries
MARY JOSEPH, T., Management Studies
MATHAI, E., Physics
MATHEW, K. T., Electronics
MATHEW, S., Industrial Fisheries
MATHEWS ABRAHAM, B., Civil Engineering
MOHAMMED YUSSUF, K., Applied Chemistry
MOHAN KUMAR, K., Atmospheric Science
MOHANAN, N., Hindi
MOHANAN, P., Electronics
MOHANDAS, A., Environmental Studies
MURALEEDHARAN NAIR, K. R., Statistics
MURUGESAN REDDIAR, K., German
NANDAKUMARAN, V. M., Photonics
NARAYANAN NAMPOOTHIRI, V. P., Photonics
PAVITHRAN, K. B., Management Studies
PHILIP, B., Marine Biology, Microbiology and Biochemistry
PHILIP, J., Instrumentation
PILLAI, P. R. S., Electronics
POULOSE JACOB, K., Computer Science
RADHAKRISHNAN, P., Photonics
RAJAN, C. K., Atmospheric Science
RAJAPPAN NAIR, K. P., Physics
RAJASENAN, D., Applied Economics
RAMACHANDRAN, A., Industrial Fisheries
RAMACHANDRAN NAIR, V. K., Statistics
RAM MOHAN, H. S., Marine Sciences
RAVINDRA-NATHA MENON, N. R., Marine Sciences
SABIR, M., Physics
SADASIVAN NAIR, G., Legal Studies
SAJAN, K., Marine Sciences
SALIH, M., Marine Biology, Microbiology and Biochemistry
SASIDHARAN, R., Hindi
SEBASTIAN, K. L., Applied Chemistry
SERALATHAN, P., Marine Geology and Geophysics
SHANMUGHAN, M., Hindi
SIVASANKARA PILLAI, V. N., Environmental Studies
SOMASEKHARAN NAIR, E. M., Ship Technology
SUDARSHANAN PILLAI, P., Management Studies

SUGUNAN, S., Applied Chemistry
SUKUMARAN NAIR, H. K., Applied Economics
SUKUMARAN NAIR, M. K., Applied Chemistry
SUNEETHA BAI, L., Hindi
THRIVIKRAMAN, T., Mathematical Sciences
UNNIKRISHNAN NAIR, N., Statistics
VALLABHAN, G., Photonics
VASUDEVAN, K., Electronics
VIJAYAKUMAR, K. P., Physics
WILSON, P. R., Management Studies
YUSUFF, M., Applied Chemistry

DEEN DAYAL UPADHYAY GORAKHPUR UNIVERSITY

Gorakhpur 273009, Uttar Pradesh
Telephone: (551) 2330767
Fax: (551) 2340459
E-mail: registrar@ddugu.edu.in
Internet: www.ddugu.edu.in

Founded 1958 as Gorakhpur Univ., present name 1997

Teaching and Affiliating; 4 professional and 82 affiliated colleges
Languages of instruction: Hindi, English
Academic year: July to April (two terms)
Chancellor: HE THE GOVERNOR OF UTTAR PRADESH
Vice-Chancellor: Prof. P. K. MAHANTY
Registrar: T. N. UPADHYAY
Librarian: J. L. UPADHYAY

Library of 387,100 vols, 800 periodicals
Number of teachers: 300
Number of students: 115,000, incl. students of the colleges

DEANS

Baba Raghav Das Medical College: Dr R. B. VERMA
Faculty of Agriculture: Prof. A. B. MANI TRIPATHI
Faculty of Arts: Prof. A. K. SAXENA
Faculty of Commerce: Prof. T. P. N. SRIVASTAVA
Faculty of Education: Prof. S. N. TRIPATHI
Faculty of Law: Prof. A. KUMAR MISHRA
Faculty of Science: Prof. J. P. CHATRUWEDI

DEV SANSKRITI VISHWAVIDYALAYA

Gayatrikunj, Shantikunj, Hardwar 249411, Uttaranchal
Telephone: (1334) 261367
Fax: (1334) 260723
E-mail: administrator@dsvv.org
Internet: www.dsvv.org

Founded 2002
Academic year: July to May

Depts of computer science, English, holistic health management, human consciousness and yogic science, Indian culture and tourism studies, journalism and mass communication, psychology, rural management and entrepreneurship, theology

Chancellor: Dr PRANAV PANDYA
Vice-Chancellor: Dr S. P. MISHRA
Registrar: D. S. VISHWAVIDYALAY

Library of 25,000 vols
Number of teachers: 15
Number of students: 136

DEVI AHILYA VISHWAVIDYALAYA

Nalanda Parishar, Indore 452001, Madhya Pradesh
Telephone: (731) 2527532
Fax: (731) 2529540
E-mail: registrar.davv@dauniv.ac.in
Internet: www.dauniv.ac.in

Founded 1964 as University of Indore
Teaching and Affiliating
Languages of instruction: Hindi, English
State control

Academic year: July to May (three terms)
Chancellor: HE THE GOVERNOR OF MADHYA PRADESH
Vice-Chancellor: Dr BHAGIRATH PRASAD
Registrar: Dr R. D. MUSALGOANKAR
Librarian: Dr G. H. S. NAIDU

153 Affiliated colleges
Library of 117,210 vols
Number of teachers: 1,251
Number of students: 6,000 on campus; 120,000 in affiliated colleges

DEANS

Faculty of Arts: Dr C. DEOTALE
Faculty of Ayurved: Dr P. P. AGRAWAL
Faculty of Commerce: Dr D. D. MUNDRA
Faculty of Dentistry: Dr H. C. NEEMA
Faculty of Education: Dr S. VAIDYA
Faculty of Electronics: Dr RAJKAMAL
Faculty of Engineering: (vacant)
Faculty of Engineering Sciences: (vacant)
Faculty of Life and Home Sciences: Dr R. BHARADWAJ
Faculty of Management Studies: Dr R. D. PATHAK
Faculty of Medicine: Dr K. BHAGAWAT
Faculty of Pharmacy: Dr S. C. CHATURVEDI
Faculty of Physical Education: (vacant)
Faculty of Science: Dr K. K. PANDEY
Faculty of Social Sciences and Law: Dr B. Y. LALITHAMA

ATTACHED RESEARCH INSTITUTES

Institute of Engineering and Technology: tel. (731) 2462311; fax (731) 2764385; e-mail dir.iet@dauniv.ac.in; internet www.iet.dauniv.ac.in; Dir Dr M. CHANDWANI.
Institute of Management Studies: internet www.ims.dauniv.ac.in; f. 1969; Dir Dr P. N. MISHRA.

DHARMSINH DESAI UNIVERSITY

POB 35, College Rd, Nadiad 387001, Gujarat
Telephone: (268) 2520502
Fax: (268) 2520501
E-mail: vc@ddu.ac.in
Internet: www.ddu.ac.in

Founded 1968 as Dharmsinh Desai Institute of Technology; Deemed Univ. status 2000; State Univ. status 2005
Pres.: Dr N. D. DESAI
Vice-Chancellor: Dr H. M. DESAI
Registrar: Dr T. R. SHAH

Library of 17,000 vols, 80 periodicals

DEANS

Faculty of Business Admin.: Prof. G. S. SHAH
Faculty of Commerce: Prof. M. K. TRIVEDI
Faculty of Dental Science: Dr B. S. JATHAL
Faculty of Pharmacy: Dr L. D. PATEL
Faculty of Technology: Dr P. A. JOSHI

DIBRUGARH UNIVERSITY

Dibrugarh 786004, Assam
Telephone: (373) 2370231
Fax: (373) 2370323
E-mail: info@dibru.ac.in
Internet: www.dibru.ac.in

Founded 1965

Affiliating and teaching; depts of anthropology, applied geology, Assamese, chemistry, commerce, economics, education, English, history, life science, mathematics, petroleum technology, pharmaceutical sciences, physics, political science, sociology, statistics; 121 affiliated colleges
State control
Languages of instruction: Assamese, English
Academic year: January to December
Chancellor: HE THE GOVERNOR OF ASSAM
Vice-Chancellor: Dr K. K. DEKA

Registrar: Dr P. K. Bhuyan
Controller of Examinations: Dr S. Gogoi
Librarian: (vacant)
Library of 158,481 vols, 5,200 periodicals
Number of teachers: 181 (univ. depts)
Number of students: 58,850 (incl. affiliated colleges)
Publications: *Anthropology Bulletin, Assam Economic Journal, Assam Statistical Review, Dibrugarh University Journal of Education, Dibrugarh University Journal of English Studies, Journal of Historical Research, Life Sciences Bulletin, Mathematical Forum, Padartha Vigyan Patrika* (physics, in Assamese, 1 a year), *Pharmray, The North Eastern Research Bulletin*.

DR B. R. AMBEDKAR OPEN UNIVERSITY

Prof. G. Ram Reddy Marg, Rd 46, Jubilee Hills, Hyderabad 500033, Andhra Pradesh
Telephone: (40) 23544830
Fax: (40) 23544830
E-mail: info@braou.ac.in
Internet: www.braou.ac.in
Founded 1982
Academic year: July to June
Chancellor: HE The Governor of Andhra Pradesh
Vice-Chancellor: Prof. Obulreddy Ramanjula Reddy
Registrar: Dr B. Sunder Rao
Controller of Examinations: Prof. V. C. Rao
Public Relations Officer: A. V. Reddy
Librarian: Dr G. Sujatha
Library of 29,912 vols
Number of teachers: 63
Number of students: 63,575

DEANS

Faculty of Arts: Prof. K. S. Ramana
Faculty of Commerce: Dr A. Sudhakar
Faculty of Science: Prof. S. V. Rajasekhar Reddy
Faculty of Social Sciences: A. Vidyavathi

PROFESSORS

Chandrasekhara Rao, V., Library Science
Damayanthi Devi, I., Zoology
Gnanaprasuna, K., Physics
Hayat, S., Urdu
Jadhao, Y., Hindi
Kiranmayi, Y. S., Business Management
Koteswara Rao, K., Commerce
Kuppuswamy Rao, K., Mathematics
Nethi, G., Zoology
Prasad, V. S., Public Administration
Pushpa Ramakrishna, C., English
Rajashekar Reddy, S. V., Geology
Ramachandraiah, G., Chemistry
Ramachandraiah, M., Botany
Ramaiah, P., Economics
Srinivasacharyulu, G., Evaluation
Sundara Rao, B., Economics
Umapathi Varma, Y. V., Educational Technology
Vasunadan, R., Telugu
Venkaiah, V., Business Management
Vidyavathi, A., Sociology
There are 140 Study Centres located in the state of Andhra Pradesh

DR BABASAHEB AMBEDKAR MARATHWADA UNIVERSITY

Aurangabad 431004, Maharashtra
Telephone: (240) 2400491
Fax: (240) 2403113
E-mail: registrar@bamu.net
Internet: www.bamu.net
Founded 1958
Teaching and Affiliating

Languages of instruction: English, Marathi
Academic year: June to April (2 terms)
Chancellor: HE The Governor of Maharashtra
Vice-Chancellor: Dr N. Kottapalle
Registrar: Dr D. V. Muley
Dir of Board of College and Univ.: Dr A. G. Khan
Finance Officer: B. S. Annasaheb
Controller of Examinations: Dr M. G. Gumaste
Librarian: Dr S. S. Lomate
Library of 304,473 vols
Number of teachers: 3,275 (incl. affiliated colleges)
Number of students: 130,534

DEANS

Arts: N. A. Lavande
Ayurveda: D. V. Kulkarni
Commerce: S. R. Madan
Education: G. V. Shetkar
Engineering and Technology: P. A. Deshmukh
Fine Art: D. D. Bade
Homeopathy: Dr S. M. Desarada
Law: Dr S. P. Pande
Management Science: Dr V. S. Savant
Physical Education: A. B. Humbe
Science: Dr D. R. Mane
Social Science: P. N. Patil
There are 146 affiliated colleges

DR BABASAHEB AMBEDKAR OPEN UNIVERSITY

Sarkhej-Gandhinagar Highway, Ahmedabad 380060, Gujarat
Telephone: (79) 27413747
Fax: (79) 27413751
E-mail: baouvc@yahoo.co.in
Internet: www.baou.org
Founded 1994
State control
Academic year: August to July
Schools of commerce and management, computer science, distance education and education technology, humanities and social sciences; 250 study centres
Chancellor: HE The Governor of Gujarat
Vice-Chancellor: Prof. Avadhesh Kumar Singh
Registrar: S. H. Barot.

DR BABASAHEB AMBEDKAR TECHNOLOGICAL UNIVERSITY

Vidyavihar, District Raigad, Lonere 402103, Maharashtra
Telephone: (2140) 275101
Fax: (2140) 275040
Internet: www.dbatechuni.org
Founded 1989
State control
Depts of chemical engineering, chemistry, computer engineering, electrical engineering, electronics and telecommunications engineering, information technology, mathematics, mechanical engineering, petrochemical engineering, physics
Chancellor: HE The Governor of Maharashtra
Vice-Chancellor: Dr A. A. Ghatol
Registrar: Dr P. D. Sathe
Librarian: S. P. Vaidya
Library of 51,000 vols, 114 periodicals.

DR BALASAHEB SAWANT KONKAN KRISHI VIDYAPEETH

Ratnagiri, Dapoli 415712, Maharashtra
Telephone: (2358) 282411
Fax: (2358) 282074

E-mail: root@kkv.ren.nic.in
Internet: www.dbskkv.org
Founded 1972
State control
Academic year: July to May
Language of instruction: English
Chancellor: HE The Governor of Maharashtra
Vice-Chancellor: Dr V. Mehata
Registrar: R. N. Kulkarni
Librarian: S. M. Rodge
Library of 32,384 vols, 128 periodicals
15 Research Stations

DEANS

Faculty of Agricultural Engineering: Dr A. G. Pawar
Faculty of Agriculture: Dr V. B. Mehta
Faculty of Fisheries: Dr P. C. Raje

CONSTITUENT AND AFFILIATED COLLEGES

College of Agricultural Engineering and Technology: Manki-Palvan, Tal-Chiplun, Ratnagiri 415641; tel. (2355) 233181; fax (2352) 264830; e-mail caetmp@yahoo.co.in; f. 2003; Dir V. N. Gawande.

College of Agriculture: Saralgaon, Tal-Murbad, Thane 421401; tel. (2524) 240770; f. 2001.

College of Fisheries: Ratnagiri 415629, Maharashtra; tel. (2352) 232987; fax (2352) 232241; e-mail rtg_fishcoll@sancharnet.in; f. 1981.

College of Horticulture: Kharawate-Dahiwali, Ratnagiri 415606, Maharashtra; tel. (2355) 264017; fax (2355) 264830; f. 2001.

Govindraoji Nikam College of Agriculture: Mandki-Palvan. Tal-Chiplun, Ratnagiri 415629, Maharashtra; tel. (2355) 233181; fax (2355) 264830; e-mail gncamp@redifmail.com; f. 2001; Dir Dr T. L. Chorage.

DR BHIM RAO AMBEDKAR UNIVERSITY

Senate House, Paliwal Park, Agra 282004, Uttar Pradesh
Telephone: (562) 2820051
Fax: (562) 2520051
E-mail: info@dbrau.ac.in
Internet: www.dbrau.ac.in
Founded 1927 as Agra University; present name 1995
Affiliating and Teaching
Languages of instruction: English, Hindi
Academic year: July to May (one term)
Chancellor: HE The Governor of Uttar Pradesh
Vice-Chancellor: Dr K. N. Tripathi
Registrar: Dr Balji Yadav
Hon. Librarian: Dr Sunder Lal
Library of 169,027 vols
Number of students: 123,000

DEANS

Faculty of Agriculture: Dr J. P. Verma
Faculty of Commerce: Dr K. K. Bansal
Faculty of Education: Dr Chander Hans Pathak
Faculty of Fine Arts: Dr S. Bhargave
Faculty of Homeopathic Medicine: Dr Moti Lal Shukla
Faculty of Home Science: Dr H. Kumar
Faculty of Law: Dr V. K. Kaushik
Faculty of Medicine: Dr U. C. Misra
Faculty of Science: Dr Jai Shanker

CONSTITUENT INSTITUTES

Dau Dayal Institute of Vocational Education: Agra.

Deen Dayal Upadhyay Institute of Rural Development: Agra.

Institute of Basic Sciences: Agra.

Institute of Home Science: Agra; library of 10,218 vols; 10 teachers; Dir Dr H. KUMAR (acting).

Institute of Social Sciences: Agra; library of 18,000 vols; 14 teachers; Dir Dr S. V. PANDEY.

K. M. Institute of Hindi Studies and Linguistics: Agra; library of 39,000 vols; Dir Dr JAI SINGH NEERAD.

Lalit Kala Sansthan (Institute of Fine Arts): Agra.

School of Life Sciences: Agra.

Seth Padam Chandjain Institute of Commerce, Business Management and Economics: Agra; Dir Dr M. R. BANSAL (acting).

There are 144 affiliated colleges

DR HARI SINGH GOUR UNIVERSITY

Gour Nagar, University Campus, Sagar, Madhya Pradesh 470003
Telephone: (7582) 222574
Fax: (7582) 223236
E-mail: sagaruniversity@mp.nic.in
Internet: www.sagaruniversity.nic.in
Founded 1946
Teaching, affiliating and residential; 81 affiliated colleges
Languages of instruction: Hindi, English
Academic year: July to April (two terms)
Chancellor: HE THE GOVERNOR OF MADHYA PRADESH
Vice-Chancellor: Prof. D. P. SINGH
Rector: Prof. Dr K. S. PITRE
Registrar: Dr PARIKCHHIT SINGH
Dean of Student Welfare: Dr A. K. SHANDILYA
Finance Officer: P. N. SINGH
Librarian: MUKESH KUMAR SAHU (acting)
Library of 310,000 vols
Number of teachers: 300
Number of students: 80,000

Publication: *Madhya Bharti—Research Journal* (1 a year, Hindi and English)

DEANS

Faculty of Arts: Prof. A. K. AWASTHI
Faculty of Commerce: Prof. Y. S. THAKUR
Faculty of Education: Dr G. SHANKAR
Faculty of Engineering: Prof. R. K. TRIVEDI
Faculty of Law: Prof. P. K. RAI
Faculty of Life Sciences: Prof. D. C. ATRI
Faculty of Management: Prof. Y. S. THAKUR
Faculty of Science: Prof. D. C. ATRI
Faculty of Social Sciences: Prof. P. K. RAI
Faculty of Technology: Prof. G. P. AGRAWAL

DR N. T. R. UNIVERSITY OF HEALTH SCIENCES, ANDHRA PRADESH

Vijayawada 520008, Andhra Pradesh
Telephone: (866) 2451206
Fax: (866) 2450463
E-mail: ntruhs@hotmail.com
Internet: 203.199.178.93
Founded 1986
Residential and teaching; faculties of dental sciences, indian systems of medicine, medical laboratory technology, modern medicine, nursing, nutrition and physiotherapy; 316 affiliated colleges
Language of instruction: English
State control
Academic year: July to June
Chancellor: HE THE GOVERNOR OF ANDHRA PRADESH
Vice-Chancellor: Prof. A. V. KRISHNAM RAJU
Registrar: Prof. T. VENUGOPAL RAO
Librarian: K. SRINIVASA RAO
Library: Library in process of formation

Number of teachers: 3,000
Number of students: 9,000 undergraduate, 3,000 postgraduate

DR PANJABRAO DESHMUKH AGRICULTURE UNIVERSITY

Krishi Nagar, Akola 444104, Maharashtra
Telephone: (724) 2258200
Fax: (724) 2258219
E-mail: vc@pdkv.mah.nic.in
Internet: pdkv.mah.nic.in
Founded 1969
State control
Languages of instruction: English, Marathi
Academic year: July to June
Chancellor: HE THE GOVERNOR OF MAHARASHTRA
Pro-Chancellor: THE MIN. FOR AGRICULTURE, MAHARASHTRA
Vice-Chancellor: Dr V. M. MYANDE
Registrar: RAM CHIMURKAR
Library of 140,500 vols
Number of teachers: 650
Number of students: 3,650

Publications: *Krishi Patrika* (in Marathi, 12 a year), *PKV Research Journal* (2 a year), *Post Graduate Institute Research Journal* (1 a year)

DEANS

Faculty of Agricultural Engineering: Dr D. S. KHARCHE
Faculty of Agriculture: Dr V. D. PATIL

CONSTITUENT COLLEGES

College of Agricultural Engineering: Akola; f. 1970; Assoc. Dean Dr D. S. KHARCHE.

College of Agriculture: Akola; f. 1950; Assoc. Dean V. D. PATIL.

College of Agriculture: Nagpur; f. 1906; Assoc. Dean Dr C. S. CHOUDHARI.

College of Forestry: Akola; f. 2001; Assoc. Dean Dr J. S. ZOPE.

College of Horticulture: Akola; f. 2001; Assoc. Dean Dr V. K. MAHORKAR.

Postgraduate Institute: Akola; f. 1970; Assoc. Dean Dr R. B. SOMANI.

There are two affiliated colleges and 19 research stations

DR RAM MANOHAR LOHIA AVADH UNIVERSITY

PB 17, Faizabad 224001, Uttar Pradesh
Telephone: (5278) 246223
Fax: (5278) 246330
E-mail: edp@rmlau.ac.in
Internet: www.rmlau.ac.in
Founded 1975 as Avadh University
Teaching and Affiliating
Languages of instruction: English, Hindi
Academic year: July to June
Chancellor: HE THE GOVERNOR OF UTTAR PRADESH
Vice-Chancellor: Prof. ARUN KUMAR MITTAL (acting)
Registrar: K. N. PANDEY
Finance Officer: A. SRIVASTAVA
Librarian: S. K. SINGH
Number of teachers: 19 (univ.), 2,006 (affiliated colleges)
Number of students: 45,220 (univ. and affiliated colleges)

DEANS

Faculty of Agriculture: (vacant)
Faculty of Arts: Prof. S. P. TIWARI
Faculty of Commerce and Management: Dr H. P. PANDEY
Faculty of Dental Science: (vacant)

Faculty of Education: Dr RAKA SINHA
Faculty of Engineering and Technology: (vacant)
Faculty of Home Science: (vacant)
Faculty of Law: Dr U. SINGH
Faculty of Science: Prof. G. C. PANDEY

There are 33 affiliated colleges

DR YASHWANT SINGH PARMAR UNIVERSITY OF HORTICULTURE AND FORESTRY

Nauni (Solan) 173230, Himachal Pradesh
Telephone: (1792) 252219
Fax: (1792) 252009
E-mail: vc@yspuniversity.ac.in
Internet: www.yspuniversity.ac.in
Founded 1985
State control
Academic year: August to July
Chancellor: PRABHA RAO
Vice-Chancellor: Dr K. R. DHIMAN
Registrar: BALDEV RAM THAKUR
Librarian: Dr M. S. PATHANIA
Dir of Extension Education: Dr D. R. GAUTAM
Dir of Research: Dr S. K. SHARMA

Depts of basic sciences, biotechnology, entomology and apiculture, floriculture and landscaping, forest products, fruit breeding, mycology and plant pathology, pomology, post-harvest technology, silviculture and agroforestry, social sciences, soil science and water management, tree improvement and genetic resources, vegetable crops
Library of 57,206 vols
Number of teachers: 222
Number of students: 755

DEANS

College of Forestry: Dr S. D. SHARMA
College of Horticulture: Dr R. C. SHARMA

PROFESSORS

AGNIHOTRI, R. P., Regional Horticultural Research Station, Jachh
BARWAL, V. S., Post-harvest Technology
BAWA, R., Regional Centre, NAEB
BAWEJA, H. S., Directorate of Extension Education
BHALLA, R., Regional Horticultural Research Station, Mashobra
BHARDWAJ, M. L., Krishi Vigyan Kendra, Chamba
BHARDWAJ, S., Regional Horticultural Research Station, Mashobra
BHARDWAJ, S. S., Regional Horticultural Research Station, Bajarua
BHARDWAJ, S. V., Biotechnology
BHATIA, H. S., Regional Horticultural Research Station, Bajarua
BHATIA, R., Regional Horticultural Research Station, Jachh
CHAND, R., Forest Products
CHANDEL, J. S., Fruit Science
CHANDEL, R. P. S., Entomology and Apiculture
CHAUHAN, N. S., Forest Products
CHAUHAN, P. S., Regional Horticultural Research Station, Mashobra
CHAUHAN, U., Entomology and Apiculture
DORHOO, N. P., Directorate of Research
DUBEY, J. K., Directorate of Extension Education
GARG, R. C., Mycology and Plant Pathology
GUPTA, A. K., Mycology and Plant Pathology
GUPTA, B., Silviculture and Forestry
GUPTA, D., Entomology and Apiculture
GUPTA, J. K., Entomology and Apiculture
GUPTA, N. K., Silviculture and Forestry
GUPTA, P. R., Entomology and Apiculture
GUPTA, R., Directorate of Extension Education
GUPTA, S. K., Mycology and Plant Pathology
GUPTA, Y. C., Floriculture and Landscaping

JOSHI, A. K., Horticultural Research Station, Dhaulakuan
JOSHI, V. K., Post-harvest Technology
KANBID, B. R., Directorate of Extension Education
KANWAR, H. S., Seed technology and Production Centre
KANWAR, K., Biotechnology
KASHYAP, S. D., Silviculture and Forestry
KAUR, M., Basic Sciences
KAUR NATH, A., Biotechnology
KAUSHAL, P., Regional Centre (NAEB)
KHAJURIA, D. R., Regional Horticultural Research Station, Bajarua
KHAN, M. L., Entomology and Apiculture
KHANNA, A. S., Entomology and Apiculture
KHURANA, D. K., Tree Improvement and Genetic Resources
KORLA, B. N., Vegetable Science
KUMAR, J., Regional Horticultural Research Station, Bajarua
KUMAR, K., Fruit Breeding and Genetic Resources
KUMAR, P., Basic Sciences
KUMAR, R., Entomology and Apiculture
KUMARI, A., Directorate of Extension Education
MAHAJAN, S., Computer and Instrumentation Centre
MANKOTA, M. S., Regional Horticultural Research Station, Mashobra
MEHTA, K., Fruit Science
NARANG, M. L., Forest Protection Unit
NEGI, Y. S., Business Management
PRASHAR, R. S., Litchi and Mangro Research Station, Nagrota Bagwan
RAI, K., Forest Products
RAINA, J. N., Soil Science and Water Management
RAINA, R., Forest Products
RAM, V., Mycology and Plant Pathology
RANA, B. S., Entomology and Apiculture
RANA, S. S., Regional Horticultural Research Station, Jachh
RANDEV, A. K., Regional Horticultural Research Station, Mashobra
REHALIA, A. S., Pomology
SHAMET, G. S., Silviculture and Forestry
SHARMA, A. K., Regional Horticultural Research Station, Jachh
SHARMA, A. K., Basic Sciences
SHARMA, D. D., Fruit Science
SHARMA, D. D., Social Sciences
SHARMA, D. K., Regional Horticultural Research Station, Jachh
SHARMA, G. C., Horticultural Research Station, Kandaghat, Solan
SHARMA, G. K., Directorate of Extension Education
SHARMA, G. K., Fruit Breeding and Genetic Resources
SHARMA, H. R., Horticultural Research Station, Kandaghat, Solan
SHARMA, I. D., Entomology and Apiculture
SHARMA, I. M., Mycology and Plant Pathology
SHARMA, I. P., Soil Science and Water Management
SHARMA, J. N., Mycology and Plant Pathology
SHARMA, K. C., Temperate Horticultural Research Station, Kotkhai
SHARMA, K. D., Post-harvest Technology
SHARMA, L. R., Social Sciences
SHARMA, N., Fruit Science
SHARMA, O. P., Directorate of Extension Education
SHARMA, P. C., Post-harvest Technology
SHARMA, R., Social Sciences
SHARMA, R. C., Forest Protection Unit
SHARMA, R. L., Mycology and Plant Pathology
SHARMA, S. K., Biotechnology
SHARMA, S. K., Mycology and Plant Pathology
SHARMA, S. S., Basic Sciences
SHARMA, V., Basic Sciences
SHIRKOT, C. K., Basic Sciences
SHUKLA, Y. R., Vegetable Science

SINGH, N. B., Tree Improvement and Genetic Resources
SINGH THAKUR, A., Basic Sciences
SRIVASTAVA, D. K., Biotechnology
SUD, A., Regional Horticultural Research Station, Mashobra
SUMAN, B. C., Mycology and Plant Pathology
THAKUR, B. S., Krishi Vigyan Kendra, Kandaghat, Solan
THAKUR, K. S., Post-harvest Technology
THAKUR, M. C., Vegetable Science
THAKUR, P. D., Mycology and Plant Pathology
THAKUR, P. S., Silviculture and Forestry
THAKUR, S., Regional Horticultural Research Station, Jachh
THAKUR, V., Environmental Science
THAKUR, V. S., Regional Horticultural Research Station, Mashobra
THAPA, C. D., Mycology and Plant Pathology
TOMER, C. S., Fruit Science
TRIPATHI, D., Soil Science and Water Management
VERMA, K. S., Environmental Science

DRAVIDIAN UNIVERSITY

Chitoor District, Kuppam 517425, Andhra Pradesh
Telephone: (8570) 278220
Fax: (8570) 278230
Internet: www.dravidianuniversity.ac.in
Founded 1997

Teaching, residential and affiliating; depts of comparative Dravidian literature and philosophy, computers and allied sciences, Dravidian and computational linguistics, education and human resource devt, English and communication, folklore and tribal studies, history, archaeology and culture, Kannada language and translation studies, Tamil language and translation studies, Telugu language and translation studies

Academic year: July to June
Chancellor: HE THE GOVERNOR OF ANDHRA PRADESH
Vice-Chancellor: Prof. G. LAKSHMINARAYANA
Registrar: Prof. P. RAJASEKHARA REDDY
Dean of Academic Affairs: Prof. D. ANANDA NAIDU
Finance Officer: RAMA DAS
Library of 55,000 vols
Number of students: 165

EFL UNIVERSITY (ENGLISH AND FOREIGN LANGUAGES UNIVERSITY)

Hyderabad 500007, Andhra Pradesh
Telephone: (402) 7098131
Fax: (402) 7098402
E-mail: ciefors@ciefl.ac.in
Internet: www.efluniversity.ac.in
Founded 1958, deemed univ. status 1973; central univ. 2007
Academic year: June to May

Campuses at Lucknow, Shillong; schools of critical humanities, distance education, English language education, foreign languages, language sciences
Vice-Chancellor: Prof. ABHAI MAURYA
Registrar: Dr P. BAPAIAH
Library of 120,000 vols, 470 journals
Number of teachers: 98
Number of students: 2,276
Publications: *ESSAIS* (2 a year), *Journal of English and Foreign Languages* (2 a year), *Occasional Papers in Linguistics, Russian Philology* (1 a year)

DEANS
Academic: NIRUPAMA RASTOGI
Campus Development and Facilities: MEENAKSHI REDDY

Culture: K. G. VIJAYAKRISHNAN
English: T. SRIRAMAN
Examinations: P. MADHAVAN
Foreign Languages: MOHSIN USMANI
International Relations: ABHAI MAURYA
Non-Formal Courses and Resources: MALATHY KRISHNAN
Planning: LAKSHMI CHANDRA
Publications and Library: R. AMRITAVALLI
Research and Studies: M. MADHAVA PRASAD
Student Welfare: SATISH KUMAR PODUVAL
Technical Infrastructure: VINAY S. TOTAWAR

FAKIR MOHAN UNIVERSITY

Vyasa Vihar, Balasore 756019, Orissa
Telephone: (6782) 264244
Fax: (6782) 254881
Internet: www.fmuniversity.org
Founded 1999
Academic year: July to May

Depts of bioscience and biotechnology, business management, environment sciences, information and communication, population studies; 61 affiliated colleges
Chancellor: HE THE GOVERNOR OF ORISSA
Vice-Chancellor: Prof. SUKANTI PRIYA PATTNAIK
Registrar: Dr A. C. KAR
Controller of Finance: S. MARANDI
Library of 2,143 vols
Number of students: 23,542

GAUHATI UNIVERSITY

Main Campus, Gauhati 781014, Assam
Telephone: (3661) 2570415
Fax: (3661) 2570133
Kokrajhar Campus, PO Rangalikhata (Debargaon) Kokrajhar 783370, Assam
Telephone: (3661) 277183
E-mail: vc@gauhati.ac.in
Internet: www.gauhati.ac.in
Founded 1948

Teaching, residential and affiliating
Language of instruction: English
Academic year: July to May (three terms)
Chancellor: HE THE GOVERNOR OF ASSAM
Vice-Chancellor: Prof. O. K. MEDHI
Registrar: Dr UTTAM CHANDRA DAS
Controller of Examinations: Dr PRAFULLA K. DEKA
Treas.: HEM CHANDRA GAUTAM
Librarian: B. C. GOSWAMI
Library of 517,000 vols
Number of teachers: 281
Number of students: 118,213

DEANS

Faculty of Arts: Prof. UMESH DEKA
Faculty of Commerce: Prof. NAYAN BARUAH
Faculty of Engineering: Prof. D. BHATTACHARJEE
Faculty of Law: Prof. B. CHAKRAVERTY
Faculty of Medicine: Dr P. D. BORA
Faculty of Science: Prof. S. K. SARMA

CONSTITUENT COLLEGE

University Law College: Gauhati; Principal Dr B. K. CHAKRABORTY.

ATTACHED RESEARCH INSTITUTES

Population Research Centre: Hon. Dir Dr D. C. NATH.

Women's Studies Research Centre: Dir Dr ARCHANA SHARMA.

There are 194 affiliated colleges

GOA UNIVERSITY

Taleigao Plateau, 403203, Goa
Telephone: (832) 2451345

Fax: (832) 2451182
E-mail: registra@unigoa.ac.in
Internet: www.unigoa.ac.in

Founded 1985

Academic year: June to April

Vice-Chancellor: Prof. DILEEP DEOBAGKAR
Registrar: Dr DOHAN M. SANGODKAR
Finance Officer: DAMODAR J. NAIK
Controller of Examinations: G. J. S. TALAU-LIKAR
Librarian: P. V. KONNUR

46 Affiliated colleges

Library of 120,000 vols, 450 periodicals
Number of students: 7,080

DEANS

Faculty of Commerce: Dr B. RAMESH
Faculty of Design: (vacant)
Faculty of Education: Dr L. VERNAL
Faculty of Engineering: Prof. R. P. ADGAON-KAR
Faculty of Languages and Literature: Dr K. S. BHAT
Faculty of Law: A. S. NADKARNI
Faculty of Life Science and Environment: Dr P. V. DESAI
Faculty of Management Studies: Dr P. R. SARODE
Faculty of Medicine: Prof. PRADEEP NAIK
Faculty of Natural Sciences: Dr J. B. FERNANDES
Faculty of Performing, Fine Art and Music: M. V. VENGURLEKAR
Faculty of Social Sciences: Prof. A. V. AFONSO

ATTACHED RESEARCH INSTITUTES

All India Institute of Local Self Government: tel. (832) 2226358; Principal A. G. KHANOLKAR.

Directorate of Archives and Archaelogy: tel. (832) 2226692; Principal M. L. DICHOLKAR.

Fisheries Survey of India: tel. (832) 2520957; Principal M. E. JOHN.

Malaria Research Centre: tel. (832) 2222444; Principal A. KUMAR.

National Centre for Antarctic and Ocean Research: tel. (832) 2520863; Principal RAVINDRA RASHIK.

National Institute of Oceanography: tel. (832) 2456700; Principal S. SHETYE.

Thomas Stephen's Konkani Kendra: tel. (832) 2415857; Principal P. NAIK.

Xavier Centre of Historical Research: tel. (832) 2414971; Principal D. MENDONCA.

GOVIND BALLABH PANT UNIVERSITY OF AGRICULTURE AND TECHNOLOGY

Udham Singh Nagar, Pantnagar 263145, Uttarakhand

Telephone: (5944) 233330
Fax: (5944) 233473
E-mail: vc@gbpuat.ernet.in
Internet: www.gbpuat.ac.in

Founded 1960

Languages of instruction: English, Hindi

State control

Academic year: July to June (two terms)

Accred. bodies: ICAR and AICTE; 10 constituent colleges and 72 teaching depts out of which 61 offer postgraduate degree programmes, univ. runs 13 on campus research centres/stations and 19 outstation research centres; farm service centres (Krishi Vigyan Kendra), 1 each in 11 dists of Uttarakhand, offer agriculture extension service

Chancellor: HE THE GOVERNOR OF UTTARAKHAND
Vice-Chancellor: Dr B. S. BISHT
Registrar: Dr T. C. THAKUR

Librarian: Dr S. P. JAIN

Library of 386,075 vols, 72,308 periodical titles

Number of teachers: 745

Number of students: 4,010 (2,400 males and 1,610 females)

Publications: *Indian Farmers Digest* (English, 12 a year), *Kisan BHARTI* (Hindi, 12 a year), *Pantnagar Journal of Research* (2 a year)

DEANS

College of Agribusiness Management: Dr V. B. K. SIKKA
College of Agriculture: Dr J. P. TIWARI
College of Basic Sciences and Humanities: Dr B. R. K. GUPTA
College of Fishery Sciences: Dr A. P. SHARMA
College of Home Science: Dr RITA SINGH RAGHUVANSHI
College of Technology: Dr M. P. SINGH
College of Veterinary and Animal Sciences: Dr G. K. SINGH
Hill Campus, Ranichauri: Dr M. C. NAUTIYAL
Postgraduate Studies: Dr J. K. SINGH
VCSG College of Horticulture, Bharsar: Dr P. S. BISHT

GUJARAT AYURVED UNIVERSITY

Chanakya Bhavan, Jamnagar 361008, Gujarat

Telephone: (288) 2676854
Fax: (288) 2555585
E-mail: info@ayurveduniversity.com
Internet: www.ayurveduniversity.com

Founded 1967

Affiliating and teaching

Languages of instruction: Gujarati, Hindi, English, Sanskrit

Academic year: June to April (two terms)

Chancellor: HE THE GOVERNOR OF GUJARAT
Vice-Chancellor: Dr S. S. SAVRIKAR
Registrar: R. M. JHALA (acting)
Dir of Institute of Postgraduate Training and Research: Prof. M. S. BAGHEL
Dir of Pharmacy: (vacant)
Librarian: S. M. JANI

11 Affiliated colleges

Library of 29,000 vols
Number of teachers: 219
Number of students: 2,071

Publications: *Ayu* (research at the University, 12 a year), *Traditional Medicine International* (4 a year).

CONSTITUENT COLLEGE

Shree Gulab Kunverba Ayurved Mahavidyalaya: Principal Dr M. N. GOHIL.

ATTACHED INSTITUTES

Institute of Ayurved Pharmaceutical Sciences: tel. (288) 2555746; fax (288) 2555966; e-mail iaps@ayurveduniversity.com; internet www.iaps.ac.in; f. 1999; Principal Dr SURESH CHANDRA DASH.

Maharishi Patanjali Institute for Yoga Naturopathy Education and Research: tel. (288) 2770103; e-mail info@ayuyoga.com; internet www.ayuyoga.com; f. 2000.

GUJARAT UNIVERSITY

Navrangpura, Ahmedabad 380009, Gujarat

Telephone: (79) 26301341
Fax: (79) 26302654
Internet: www.gujaratuniversity.org.in

Founded 1949

Teaching and affiliating; 250 affiliated colleges, 15 recognized instns

Languages of instruction: Gujarati, Hindi, English

Academic year: June to April (two terms)

Chancellor: HE THE GOVERNOR OF GUJARAT
Vice-Chancellor: Dr P. H. TRIVEDI
Pro-Vice-Chancellor: Dr N. K. PATEL
Registrar: M. S. SHAH
Controller of Examinations: J. LILANI
Librarian: RAMANBHAI L. PATEL

Library of 334,110 vols
Number of teachers: 3,075
Number of students: 187,771 undergraduates; 36,5050 postgraduates

DEANS

Faculty of Arts: Prof. K. B. DESAI
Faculty of Commerce: Principal: K. K. SHAH
Faculty of Engineering and Technology: Prof. H. V. TRIVEDI
Faculty of Law: Principal: R. S. DESAI
Faculty of Medicine: Dr H. P. BHALODIYA
Faculty of Science: Principal: R. G. BHATT

GULBARGA UNIVERSITY

Gulbarga 585106, Karnataka

Telephone: (8472) 263202
Fax: (8472) 263206
E-mail: reggug@rediffmail.com
Internet: www.gulbargauniversity.kar.nic.in

Founded 1980

State (Govt of Karnataka) control

Languages of instruction: English, Kannada

Academic year: June to March

Chancellor: H. R. BHARADWAJ
Pro-Chancellor: ARAVIND S. LIMBAVALI
Vice-Chancellor: Prof. B. G. MULIMANI
Registrar and Finance Officer: Prof. S. L. HIREMATH
Librarian: Dr R. B. GADDAGIMATH

305 Affiliated colleges, 43 univ. depts and postgraduate centres in Bellary, Bidar, Raichur, Sandur

Library of 320,000 vols, 410 journals, 9,500 e-journals

Number of students: 63,000

DEANS

Faculty of Arts: Prof. MOHD ABDUL HAMEED
Faculty of Commerce: Prof. B. M. KANAHALLI
Faculty of Education: Prof. SYEDA AKHTAR
Faculty of Law: Prof. S. S. PATIL
Faculty of Science and Technology: Prof. Y. M. JAYARAJ
Faculty of Social Science: Prof. B. S. MAHESHWARAPPA

GURU GHASIDAS UNIVERSITY

Bilaspur 495009, Chhattisgarh

Telephone: (7752) 260283
Fax: (7752) 260148
E-mail: csit@ggu.ac.in
Internet: www.ggu.ac.in

Founded 1983

Campus at Surguja (Ambikapur)

Vice-Chancellor: Prof. LAKSHMAN CHATURVEDI
Registrar: K. K. CHANDRAKAR
Finance Officer: UMESH AGRAWAL
Dir of College Devt Council: Dr M. S. K. KHOKAR
Dean of Student Welfare: Dr S. V. S. CHOUHAN
Librarian: Dr U. N. SINGH

139 Affiliated colleges

Library of 85,000 vols

DEANS

Faculty of Arts: Dr B. B. SHUKLA
Faculty of Education: A. KUJUR
Faculty of Engineering: Prof. S. M. SAHA
Faculty of Home Science: Dr J. SHARMA
Faculty of Law: Dr A. B. SONI
Faculty of Life Science: Prof. B. M. MUKHERJEE

Faculty of Management and Commerce: Prof. L. M. MALVIYA

Faculty of Medical Science: Dr V. D. TIWARI

Faculty of Natural Resources: Prof. S. S. SINGH

Faculty of Physical Education: Prof. S. S. SINGH

Faculty of Science: Prof. A. K. SAXENA

Faculty of Social Science: Dr J. P. SHARMA

ATTACHED INSTITUTES

Chhattisgarh Institute of Medical Sciences: tel. (7752) 254300; fax (7752) 501684; f. 2001; Dean Prof. ANIL SARANGI

PROFESSORS

BADGAIYA, Y. D.
BEHARA, P. K., Biochemistry
CHHABRA, B., Anaesthesia
DHURIYA, A., Anatomy
HAJARI, S. K., Anatomy
JAINA, R. S., Orthopaedics
KAR, C. R., Surgery
MITRA, J. P., Microbiology
PANDA, B. K., Surgery
PATIL, S. K. B., Biochemistry
PATLE, D. R., Surgery
RATH, S. K., Obstetrics and Gynaecology
SARANGI, A., Dean
SHARMA, D. K., Physiology
SINGH, P. C., Venerology and Dermatology
SINGH, P. D., Pharmacology

Institute of Technology: Dir Prof. S. N. SAHA.

GURU GOBIND SINGH INDRAPRASTHA UNIVERSITY

Kashmere Gate, Delhi 110403

Telephone: (11) 23900166

Fax: (11) 23865941

E-mail: mail@ipu.edu

Internet: ipu.ac.in

Founded 1998

Teaching and affiliating

Academic year: August to July

Chancellor: VIJAI KAPOOR

Vice-Chancellor: Prof. DILIP K. BANDYOPAD-HYAY

Registrar: VINOD K. JAIN

Controller of Examinations: Prof. YOGESH SINGH

Controller of Finance: VANDANA GUPTA

Dir of Corporate Affairs: Prof. O. P. GOYAL

Librarian: SUBHASH DESHMUKH

Library of 15,690 vols

DEANS

School of Basic and Applied Sciences: Prof. N. R. GARG

School of Biotechnology: Prof. P. C. SHARMA

School of Chemical Technology: Prof. S. S. SAMBI

School of Education: Prof. A. BENIWAL

School of Engineering and Technology: Prof. S. WADHWA

School of Environmental Management: Prof. J. K. GARG

School of Humanities and Social Sciences: Prof. A. BENIWAL

School of Information Technology: Prof. B. V. R. REDDY

School of Law and Legal Studies: Prof. S. GUPTA

School of Management Studies: Prof. A. S. LATHER

School of Planning and Architecture: Prof. B. V. R. REDDY

CHAIRMEN

University Centre for Disaster Management Studies: Dr A. KAUR

University Centre for IT Services and Infrastructure Management: Dr C. S. REDDY

University Centre for Media Studies: Prof. S. AGGARWAL

GURU JAMBESHWAR UNIVERSITY OF SCIENCE AND TECHNOLOGY

Delhi Rd, Hisar 125001, Haryana

Telephone: (1662) 263101

Fax: (1662) 276240

E-mail: gju_tech@yahoo.com

Internet: www.gju.ernet.in

Founded 1995

Chancellor: HE THE GOVERNOR OF HARYANA

Vice-Chancellor: Lt-Gen Dr D. D. S. SANDHU

Registrar: Prof. R. S. JAGLAN

Proctor: Prof. RAJESH MALHOTRA

Dean of Academic Affairs: Prof. H. L. VERMA

Dean of Student Welfare: Prof. NAWAL KISHORE

Controller of Examinations: Prof. R. S. JAGLAN

Librarian: Prof. J. K. SHARMA

Library of 73,732 vols, 184 periodicals

DEANS

Faculty of Engineering and Technology: Prof. D. KUMAR

Faculty of Management Studies: Prof. S. C. KUNDU

Faculty of Media Studies: Prof. S. GANDHI

Faculty of Medical Sciences: Prof. S. K. SHARMA

Faculty of Non-conventional Sources of Energy and Environmental Science: Prof. N. RAM

Faculty of Pharmaceutical Sciences: Prof. D. N. MISHRA

Faculty of Religious Studies: Prof. C. P. KAUSHIK

Faculty of Science and Technology Interface: Prof. K. BANSAL

Haryana School of Business: Prof. S. C. KUNDU

GURU NANAK DEV UNIVERSITY

Amritsar 143005, Punjab

Telephone: (183) 2258802

Fax: (183) 2258819

Internet: www.gndu.ac.in

Founded 1969

Autonomous, partly funded by state government

Languages of instruction: English, Hindi, Punjabi

Academic year: July to June

Chancellor: HE THE GOVERNOR OF PUNJAB

Vice-Chancellor: Dr A. S. BRAR

Registrar: Dr INDERJIT SINGH

Library of 430,000 vols

Number of teachers: 316 (in univ. campus)

Number of students: 96,711 (incl. external students)

Publications: *Amritsar Law Journal* (1 a year), *Guru Nanak Journal of Sociology* (2 a year), *Indian Journal of Quantitative Economics* (2 a year), *Journal of Management Studies* (1 a year), *Journal of Regional History* (1 a year), *Journal of Sikh Studies* (English, 2 a year), *Journal of Sports Traumatology and Allied Sports Science* (1 a year), *Khoj Darpan* (Punjabi, 2 a year), *Personality Study and Group Behaviour* (1 a year), *Perspectives on Guru Granth Sahib* (1 a year), *Pradhikrit* (Hindi, 1 a year), *PSE Economic Analyst* (English, 2 a year), *Punjab Journal of English Studies* (1 a year), *Punjab Journal of Politics* (2 a year), *University Samachar* (4 a year)

DEANS

Faculty of Agriculture and Forestry: Dr S. S. CHAHAL

Faculty of Applied Sciences: Prof. J.S. SEKHON

Faculty of Arts and Social Sciences: Prof. NAVDEEP SINGH TUNG

Faculty of Economics and Business: Dr PARMINDER SINGH

Faculty of Education: Dr AMIT KAUTS

Faculty of Engineering and Technology: Dr JASVIR SINGH

Faculty of Humanities and Religious Studies: Dr SHASHI BALA

Faculty of Languages: Dr PREM SAGAR SHARMA

Faculty of Law: VEER SINGH

Faculty of Life Sciences: Prof. A. K. THUKRAL

Faculty of Music and Fine Arts: Dr BHAGWANT KAUR

Faculty of Physical Education: Dr SUKHDEV SINGH

Faculty of Physical Planning and Architecture: Dr S. S. BEHL

Faculty of Sciences: Dr TARSEM GILL

Faculty of Sport Medicine and Physiotherapy: Dr JASPAL SINGH

HEMCHANDRACHARYA NORTH GUJARAT UNIVERSITY

University Rd, POB 21, Patan 384265, Gujarat

Telephone: (2766) 230427

Fax: (2766) 231917

E-mail: vc@ngu.ac.in

Internet: www.ngu.ac.in

Founded 1986

State control

Language of instruction: Gujarati

Academic year: June to April

Chancellor: HE THE GOV. OF GUJARAT

Vice-Chancellor: Dr KIRANKUMAR K. SHAH

Pro-Vice-Chancellor: Dr J. H. PANCHOLI

Registrar: B. J. RATHORE (acting)

Controller of Examinations: Dr B. J. RATHORE

Chief Accounts Officer: A. R. MAKWANA

Deputy Registrar for Academic Affairs: D. M. PATEL

Asst Registrar for Academic Affairs: K. N. PATEL

Asst Registrar for Examinations: DHRUV DAVE

Dir of Physical Eduction: Dr J. D. DAMOR (acting)

Nat. Social Scheme Coordinator: Dr J. D. DAMOR

Dean of Faculty: Prof. M. B. CHAUDHARY

Librarian: M. K. PRAJAPATI

Asst Librarian: Dr M. G. PATEL

248 Affiliated colleges

Library of 55,880 vols, 110 periodicals

Number of teachers: 1,829

Number of students: 43,080 (25,748 males and 17,332 femaless)

Publications: *Anart* (1 a year), *Udichya* (26 a year)

DEANS

Faculty of Arts: Dr J. N. BAROT

Faculty of Commerce: Prin.: S. H. PATEL

Faculty of Education: Dr B. D. DAVE

Faculty of Engineering: K .G. MARADIA

Faculty of Homeopathy: Prin.: Dr B. JAGNNATHAN

Faculty of Law: Prin.: Dr J. U. NANAVATI

Faculty of Management Studies: N. H. BHATT

Faculty of Pharmacy: Prin.: C. N. PATEL

Faculty of Rural Studies: A. B. PATEL

Faculty of Science: Dr B. L. PUNJANI

HEMWATI NANDAN BAHUGUNA GARHWAL UNIVERSITY

Srinagar (Garhwal) 246174, Uttaranchal

Telephone: (1370) 267795

Fax: (1346) 252174
E-mail: root@hnbgugrw.ren.nic.in
Internet: www.garhwaluniversity.org
Founded 1973, fmrly Garhwal University, renamed 1989
Teaching and Affiliating
State control
Languages of instruction: Hindi, English
Academic year: July to May
Campuses at Chauras, Pauri, Tehri
Chancellor: HE The Governor of Uttar Pradesh
Vice-Chancellor: Dr N. Natarajan (acting)
Registrar: C. S. Mehta
Hon. Librarian: Prof. B. S. Semwal
52 Affiliated govt colleges and 28 private professional instns
Library of 280,000 vols
Number of teachers: 251
Number of students: 100,000 (incl. colleges)

DEANS

Faculty of Agriculture: Prof. N. D. Todariya
Faculty of Arts: Prof. B. M. Khanduri
Faculty of Ayurveda: Dr Puja Bardwaj
Faculty of Commerce: Prof. Alok Saklani
Faculty of Education: Prof. K. B. Budhori
Faculty of Engineering: Dr M. L. Dewal
Faculty of Law: Dr S. K. Mittal
Faculty of Medicine: Dr A. N. Mehrotra
Faculty of Non-formal Education: Prof. A. Misra
Faculty of Science: Prof. R. D. Gaur

HIDAYATULLAH NATIONAL LAW UNIVERSITY

HNLU Bhawan, Civil Lines, Raipur 492001, Chhattisgarh
Telephone: (771) 4080114
Fax: (771) 4080118
E-mail: registrar@hnlu.ac.in
Internet: www.hnlu.ac.in
Founded 2003
Residential; schools of Administration of Justice, Continuing and Clinical Legal Education (SAJCCLE), Business and Global Trade Law Devt (SBGTLD), Constitutional and Admin. Governance (SCAG), Int. Legal Studies (SILS), Juridical and Social Sciences (SJSS), Science, Technology and Sustainable Devt (SSTSD); regional centre in Bilaspur
Vice-Chancellor: Prof. M. K. Srivastava
Dir for Bilaspur Centre: T. V. Ramakrishnan.

HIMACHAL PRADESH UNIVERSITY

Summer Hill, Shimla 171005, Himachal Pradesh
Telephone: (177) 2830890
Fax: (177) 2830775
E-mail: gad.hpu@gmail.com
Internet: hpuniv.nic.in
Founded 1970
Affiliating and Teaching
State control
Languages of instruction: English, Hindi
Academic year: July to May
Chancellor: HE The Governor of Himachal Pradesh
Vice-Chancellor: Prof. Sunil Kumar Gupta
Registrar: Prof. Shashi Kant Sharma
Controller of Examinations: A. N. Gupta
Dean of Students Welfare: Prof. Y. P. Sharma
Dean of Studies: Prof. C. L. Chandan
Librarian: (vacant)
272 Affiliated colleges and instns
Library of 188,402 vols
Number of teachers: 260
Number of students: 6,461

DEANS

Faculty of Ayurveda: Dr Y. K. Sharma
Faculty of Commerce and Management Studies: Dr Sadhana Mahajan
Faculty of Dental Sciences: Dr Ashu Gupta
Faculty of Education: Prof. Y. K. Sharma
Faculty of Engineering and Technology: Dr Niraj Sharma
Faculty of Languages: Prof. Vidya Sharda
Faculty of Law: Prof. Suresh Kapoor
Faculty of Life Sciences: Prof. H. S. Banyal
Faculty of Performing and Visual Arts: Dr Jeet Ram Sharma
Faculty of Physical Science: Dr Niraj Sharma
Faculty of Social Sciences: Dr B. S. Marh

ATTACHED RESEARCH INSTITUTE

Institute of Life Sciences: Gachibowli, Hyderabad 500046; tel. (40) 66571500; fax (40) 66571581; e-mail info@ilsresearch.org.

INDIRA GANDHI KRISHI VISHWAVIDYALAYA

Krishak Nagar, Raipur 492006, Madhya Pradesh
Telephone: (771) 2443166
Fax: (771) 2442131
Internet: igau.edu.in
Faculties of agricultural eng., agriculture, dairy technology, veterinary sciences and animal husbandry
Chancellor: HE The Governor of Chhattisgarh
Vice-Chancellor: Dr C. R. Hazra
Registrar: K. C. Painkra
Librarian: Dr R. K. Mishra.

INDIRA GANDHI NATIONAL OPEN UNIVERSITY

Maidan Garhi, New Delhi 110068
Telephone: (11) 29532707
Fax: (11) 26862312
E-mail: vnr.pillai@ignou.ac.in
Internet: www.ignou.ac.in
Founded 1985
Central university
Autonomous control
Languages of instruction: English, Hindi
Academic year: January to December
Vice-Chancellor: Prof. V. N. Rajasekharan Pillai
Pro-Vice-Chancellors: Prof. O. P. Mishra, Prof. P. Sinclair, Dr D. K. Choudhry, Dr L. Pillai, Dr K. R. Srivathsan
Registrar: K. Laxman
Librarian: S. K. Arora
Library of 80,000 vols, 500 periodicals
Number of teachers: 255
Number of students: 594,227
Publication: *Indian Journal of Open Learning* (2 a year)

DIRECTORS

School of Agriculture: Prof. B. S. Hansra
School of Communication: Prof. Madhulika Kaushik
School of Computer and Information Science: Prof. M. Lal
School of Continuing Education: Prof. A. Aneja
School of Education: Prof. M. L. Koul
School of Engineering and Technology: Prof. G. Kansal
School of Health Sciences: Prof. S. B. Arora
School of Humanities: Prof. J. M. Parakh
School of Management Studies: Prof. N. V. Narasimham
School of Sciences: Prof. S. Malhotra
School of Social Sciences: Prof. U. Kanjilal

INDIRA KALA SANGIT VISHWAVIDYALAYA

Khairagarh 491881, Chhattisgarh
Telephone: (7820) 234232
Fax: (7820) 234108
E-mail: reg@iksvv.com
Internet: www.iksvv.com
Founded 1956
Teaching and affiliating; 6 affiliated centres and 33 affiliated colleges
Languages of instruction: Hindi, English
Academic year: July to April (two terms)
Chancellor: HE The Governor of Chhattisgarh
Vice-Chancellor: Prof. Gita Paintal
Registrar: Prof. Dr T. Unnikrishnan
Deputy Librarian: Ramesh Patel
Library of 43,000 vols, 41 periodicals, 90 MSS
Number of teachers: 586
Number of students: 9,680
Publications: *Bharat Bhashyam, Bhatkhande Smriti Granth, Kala Saurabh, Ki Sangit Yatra, Meri Dakshin Bharat, Sangit Suryodaya, Shiv Mangalam*

DEANS

Faculty of Arts: Prof. Mridula Shukla
Faculty of Dance: Prof. Mandavi Singh
Faculty of Folk Music and Arts: Prof. Bharat Patel
Faculty of Music: Prof. Prakash Mahadik
Faculty of Visual Arts: Prof. M. C. Sharma

JADAVPUR UNIVERSITY

Main Campus, 188 Raja S. C. Mullick Rd, Jadavpur, Kolkata 700032
Telephone: (33) 24146414
Fax: (33) 24137121
Salt Lake Campus, Plot 8, Blk LB, Sector 3, Salt Lake City, Kolkata 700098
Telephone: (33) 23355215
E-mail: registrar@admin.jdvu.ac.in
Internet: www.jadavpur.edu
Founded 1955
Residential and teaching; depts of architecture, bengali, chemical engineering, chemistry, civil engineering, comparative literature, computer science and engineering, construction technology, economics, electrical engineering, electronics and telecommunication engineering, English, film studies, food technology and biochemical engineering, geological science, history, information technology, instrumentation and electronics engineering, instrumentation science, international relations, library and information science, life science and biotechnology, mathematics, mechanical engineering, metallurgical engineering, pharmaceutical technology, philosophy, physical education, physics, power engineering, printing engineering, production engineering, Sanskrit, sociology; 20 interdisciplinary schools; 38 centres of research
Language of instruction: English
Academic year: July to June (two terms)
Chancellor: HE The Governor of West Bengal
Vice-Chancellor: Prof. P. N. Ghosh
Pro-Vice-Chancellor: Prof. S. Datta
Dean of Students: Prof. R. Ray
Registrar: R. Bandyopadhyay
Controller of Examinations: Dr S. Bhattacharyya
Finance Officer: G. K. Pattanayak
Chief Librarian: B. B. Das
Library of 551,445 vols, 1,057 journals
Number of teachers: 662
Number of students: 9,441
Publications: *Essays and Studies* (2 a year), *Journal of Comparative Literature* (1 a

year), *Journal of the Department of Bengali* (1 a year), *Journal of History* (1 a year), *Journal of International Relations* (1 a year), *Journal of Philosophy* (2 a year)

DEANS

Faculty of Arts: Prof. B. CHATTERJEE
Faculty of Engineering and Technology: Prof. M. K. MITRA
Faculty of Science: Prof. Dr S. BHATTACHARYA

CENTRES FOR ADVANCED STUDIES

Centre for Ambedkar Studies: Prin. Prof. A. K. BANERJI.

Centre for Cognitive Science: tel. (33) 24147620; e-mail cogsc@center.jdvu.ac.in; internet www.ccsju.org; Prin. Prof. A. CHATTERJEE.

Centre for European Studies: tel. (33) 24839962; e-mail europa_1997@rediffmail.com; f. 1997; Prin. Prof. P. K. BHATTACHARYYA.

Centre for Human Settlement Planning: tel. (33) 4129520; fax (33) 4739852; e-mail monideep@cal.vsnl.net.in; f. 1995; Prin. Prof. M. CHATTERJEE.

Centre of Indology: tel. (33) 24146023; Prin. Prof. M. BANERJEE.

Centre for Knowledge Based Systems: tel. (33) 4736129; fax (33) 4727723; e-mail ckbsjuin@vsnl.com; f. 1987; Prin. Prof. T. K. GHOSHAL.

Centre for Marxian Studies: Prin. Prof. D. CHAKRABORTY.

Centre for Microprocessor Application for Training, Education and Research: tel. (33) 24734866; f. 1983; Prin. Prof. D. K. BASU.

Centre for Mobile Computing and Communication: e-mail pkdas@ieee.org; internet www.cmccju.org; f. 2003; Prin. Prof. P. K. DAS.

Centre for Quality Management System: tel. (33) 4832165; fax (33) 4831890; internet www.cqmsju.org; f. 1994; Prin. Prof. S. K. GHOSH.

Centre for Refugee Studies: tel. (33) 4835019; e-mail opmcrs@cal2.vsnl.net.in; f. 1997; Prin. Prof. O. MISHRA.

Centre for Surface Science: tel. (33) 4838411; e-mail cssju@yahoo.co.uk; f. 1992; Prin. Prof. S. C. BHATTACHARYA.

Computer Aided Design Centre: tel. (33) 24146844; e-mail cadcentr@cadcentreju.org; internet www.cadcentreju.org; Prin. Prof. R. DUTTAGUPTA.

Condensed Matter Physics Research Centre: tel. (33) 4138917; f. 1990; Prin. Prof. D. ROY.

IC Design and Fabrication Centre: tel. (33) 4721833; fax (33) 4732217; e-mail juicc@vsnl.com; f. 1986; Prin. Prof. H. SAHA.

Nuclear and Particle Physics Research Centre: tel. (33) 4138917; f. 2000; Prin. Prof. D. GHOSH.

Plasma Studies Centre: tel. (33) 4731484; fax (33) 4137902; e-mail mk@jufs.ernet.in; f. 1994; Prin. Prof. B. CHAKRABORTY.

Relativity and Cosmology Research Centre: tel. (33) 24138917; e-mail asitb@cal3.vsnl.net.in; f. 1994; Prin. Prof. Dr A. BANERJEE.

Sir C. V. Raman Centre for Physics and Music: Prin. Prof. Dr D. GHOSH.

JAGADGURU RAMANANDACHARYA RAJASTHAN SANSKRIT UNIVERSITY

Rajasthan Textbook Board Bldg, 2–2A Jhalana, Dungri, Jaipur, Rajasthan
Telephone: (141) 2710047

Fax: (141) 2711050
E-mail: jrrsu@yahoo.com
Internet: www.jrrsanskrituniversity.ac.in
Founded 2001
Academic year: July to May
Chancellor: HE THE GOV. OF RAJASTHAN
Vice-Chancellor: Prof. YUGAL KISHORE MISHRA
Registrar: MADAN MOHAN SHARMA
Publications: *Akshara, Wyakhyanmanimala.*

JAGADGURU RAMBHADRACHARYA HANDICAPPED UNIVERSITY

Chitrakoot, Karwi, 210204 Uttar Pradesh
Telephone: (5198) 290454
Fax: (5198) 290111
E-mail: jrhuniversity@yahoo.com
Internet: www.jrhu.com
Founded 2001
Vice-Chancellor: Dr RAMDEO PRASAD SINGH
Registrar: Dr AVANISH C. MISHRA
Finance Officer: R. P. MISHRA

DEANS

Faculty of Humanities, Fine Art and Music: Prof. YOGESH C. DUBEY
Faculty of Social Sciences, Computer Science, Information Technology and Education: Prof. KAPIL D. MISHRA

JAI NARAIN VYAS UNIVERSITY, JODHPUR

Jodhpur 342001, Rajasthan
Telephone: (291) 2649733
Fax: (291) 2649733
E-mail: info@jnvu.edu.in
Internet: www.jnvu.edu.in
Founded 1962
Languages of instruction: English, Hindi
Academic year: July to April
Chancellor: HE THE GOVERNOR OF RAJASTHAN
Vice-Chancellor: Dr J. P. CHANDELIYA
Registrar: G. L. TIWARI
Finance Officer: NIRMLA MEENA
Librarian: Dr R. M. SHARMA
9 Affiliated colleges
Library of 277,229 vols
Number of teachers: 336
Number of students: 24,063

Publications: *The Beacons* (Engineering), *Annals of Economics, International Journal of Finance and Economic Studies* (1 a year), *Journal of Accounting and Control* (1 a year)

DEANS

Faculty of Arts, Social Sciences and Education: Dr A. MATHUR
Faculty of Commerce and Management Studies: Dr K. MATHUR
Faculty of Engineering and Architecture: Prof. S. K. BHARGAVA
Faculty of Law: Dr M. K. BHANDARI
Faculty of Science: Dr A. BOHRA

DIRECTORS

Institute of Evening Studies: Dr P. S. BHATI
K. Nehru College for Women: Dr ANAND MATHUR

PROFESSORS

BANERJI, K. K., Chemistry
BHANDARI, S., Mining Engineering
DHARIWAL, S. R., Physics
GUPTA, V. P., Civil Engineering
LALWANI, S. J., Commerce
MALI, S. L., Electrical Engineering
OHRI, M. L., Civil Engineering
SETRIA, M. R., Structural Engineering
SHARMA, D., Civil Engineering
SHARMA, U. S., Civil Engineering

SHEKHANAT, K. S., Rajasthani
SHRIVASTAVA, R. S., Sociology
SURANA, D. M., Mining Engineering
SURANA, P., Sociology
SURANA, S. L., Electrical Engineering
TIWARI, R. P., Mechanical Engineering

JAI PRAKASH VISHWAVIDYALAYA

Dak Bunglow Rd, Chapra 841301, Bihar
Telephone: (6152) 243898
Fax: (6152) 232607
Internet: jpv.bih.nic.in
Founded 1990
21 Constituent colleges and 9 affiliated colleges
Vice-Chancellor: Prof. Dr RAM PRAVESH SHARMA
Pro Vice-Chancellor: (vacant):
Dean of Student Welfare: Dr RAJESWAR P. SINGH
Proctor: Dr LALAN PRASAD YADAV
Registrar: Prof. Dr M. G. MUSTAFA
Finance Officer: DAYA K. MISHRA
Controller of Examinations: Dr GOPAL P. ARYA

DEANS

Faculty of Commerce: Prof. R. P. SINGH
Faculty of Humanities: Prof. Dr USHA VERMA
Faculty of Science: Prof. Dr RAJENDRA PD. SINGH
Faculty of Social Sciences: Prof. Dr B. P. N. PATHAK

JAMIA MILLIA ISLAMIA

Maulana Mohammad Ali Johar Marg, Jamia Nagar, New Delhi 110025
Telephone: (11) 26981717
Fax: (11) 26980229
E-mail: dir.cit@jmi.ac.in
Internet: jmi.nic.in
Founded 1920
Central university
Autonomous control (government financed)
Languages of instruction: Urdu, Hindi, English
Academic year: July to July
Chancellor: FAKHRUDDIN T. KHORAKIWALA
Vice-Chancellor: Prof. MUSHIRUL HASAN
Registrar: Prof. S. M. AFZAL
Finance Officer: N. U. SIDDIQUI
Dean of Student Welfare: Prof. ZUBAIR MEENAI
Librarian: Dr GAYAS MAKHDUMI
Library of 336,857 vols, 379 periodicals, 3,000 MSS
Number of teachers: 612
Number of students: 12,851

Publications: *Islam and the Modern Age* (4 a year, English), *Islam Aur Asr-i-Jadeed* (4 a year, Urdu), *Jamia Monthly* (in Urdu)

DEANS

Faculty of Architecture: Prof. S. M. AKHTAR
Faculty of Education: Prof. A. SIDDIQUI
Faculty of Engineering and Technology: Prof. S. S. NABI
Faculty of Fine Arts: Prof. S. G. H. ZAIDI
Faculty of Humanities and Languages: Prof. S. I. A. ZAIDI
Faculty of Law: Prof. V. K. GUPTA
Faculty of Natural Sciences: Prof. K. K. DEWAN
Faculty of Social Sciences: Prof. A. S. KOHLI

ATTACHED INSTITUTES

AJK Mass Communication Research Centre: tel. (11) 26987285; fax (11) 26986811; e-mail contact@ajkmcrc.org; internet ajkmcrc.org; f. 1982; Dir B. R. YADAV.

Centre for Culture Media and Governance: tel. (11) 6831717; Dir Prof. BISWAJIT DAS.

Centre for European and Latin American Studies: Dir Prof. SONYA SURABHI GUPTA.

Centre for Ghandian Studies: tel. (11) 26985473; e-mail gandhiancentre.jamia@gmail.com; Dir Dr A. P. SEN.

Centre for Interdisciplinary Research in Basic Sciences: tel. (11) 26981717; e-mail faizan_ahmad@yahoo.com; Dir Prof. FAIZAN AHMAD.

Centre for Jawaharlal Nehru Studies: e-mail dir.cjns@jmi.ac.in; Dir Prof. SHAKTI KAK.

Centre for Management Studies: e-mail furqanq@sify.com; Dir Prof. FURQAN QAMAR.

Centre for Physiotherapy and Rehabilitation Sciences: Dir Dr M. EJAZ HUSSAIN.

Centre for the Study of Comparative Religions and Civilizations: internet www.studyreligion.in; Dir Prof. I. H. AZAD FAROOQUI.

Centre for Theoretical Physics: e-mail ctp@jamia-physics.net; internet www.jmi.nic.in/ctp; Dir Prof. M. SAMI.

Centre for West Asian Studies: f. 2004; Dir Dr RAJENDRA M. ABHIYANKAR.

Dr K. R. Narayanan Centre for Dalit and Minorities Studies: Dir Prof. M. M. KHAN.

Dr Zakir Husain Institute of Islamic Studies: f. 1971; Dir Prof. AKHTARUL WASEY.

Maulana Mohamed Ali 'Jauhar' Academy of Third World Studies: f. 1988; Dir Prof. MUSHIRUL HASAN.

Nelson Mandela Centre for Peace and Conflict Resolution: tel. (11) 26985473; e-mail centreforpeace@rediffmail.com; internet www.jamia4peace.org; f. 2004; Dir Prof. RADHA KUMAR.

Sarojini Naidu Centre for Women Studies: tel. (11) 26981270; e-mail sncwsjmi@yahoo.co.in; f. 2000; Dir Prof. JANAKI RAJAN.

JAWAHARLAL NEHRU AGRICULTURAL UNIVERSITY

PB 80, Krishnagar, Jabalpur 482004, Madhya Pradesh

Telephone: (761) 2681778
Fax: (761) 2681389
E-mail: registrar_jnkvv@yahoo.co.in
Internet: www.jnkvv.nic.in

Founded 1964
Languages of instruction: Hindi, English
Academic year: July to June

Chancellor: HE THE GOVERNOR OF MADHYA PRADESH
Vice-Chancellor: Dr GAUTAM KALLOO
Registrar: Dr S. S. TOMAR
Comptroller: G. S. KURVETI
Dean of Student Welfare: Dr P. K. BISEN (acting)

Library of 202,000 vols, incl. periodicals
Number of students: 2,282

Publication: *JNKVV Research Journal* (4 a year)

DEANS

Faculty of Agricultural Engineering: Dr G. S. RAJPUT (acting)
Faculty of Agriculture: Dr V. S. TOMAR
Faculty of Veterinary Science and Animal Husbandry: Dr K. S. JOHAR

DIRECTORS

Extension and Instruction: Dr J. S. RAGHU
Farms: Dr S. K. RAO
Research: Dr V. S. TOMAR

CONSTITUENT COLLEGES

College of Agricultural Engineering, Jabalpur: Dean Dr S. S. TOMAR.

College of Agriculture, Ganj Basoda: Dean (vacant).

College of Agriculture, Gwalior: Dean Dr H. S. KUSHWAHA.

College of Agriculture, Indore: Dean Dr S. L. NAIK (acting).

College of Agriculture, Jabalpur: Dean Dr G. S. RAJPUT (acting).

College of Agriculture, Khandwa: Dean Dr R. A. SHARMA (acting).

College of Agriculture, Rewa: Dean Dr R. P. SINGH (acting).

College of Agriculture, Sehore: Dean Dr S. K. SHRIVASTAVA (acting).

College of Agriculture, Tikamgarh: Dean Dr R. K. PATHAK (acting).

College of Horticulture, Mandsaur: Dean Dr B. S. BAGHEL (acting).

College of Veterinary Science and Animal Husbandry, Jabalpur: Dean Dr R. P. S. BAGHEL (acting).

College of Veterinary Science and Animal Husbandry, Mhow: Dean Dr N. K. DIXIT (acting).

College of Veterinary Science and Animal Husbandry, Rewa: Dean (vacant).

JAWAHARLAL NEHRU TECHNOLOGICAL UNIVERSITY

Kukatpally, Hyderabad 500072, Andhra Pradesh

Telephone: (40) 23158661
Fax: (40) 23156184
E-mail: info@jntu.ac.in
Internet: www.jntu.ac.in

Founded 1972
State control
Academic year: July to April

Chancellor: HE THE GOVERNOR OF ANDHRA PRADESH
Vice-Chancellor: Dr D. NARASIMHA REDDY
Rector: Dr K. LAL KISHORE
Dir of Academics and Planning: Dr G. TULASIRAM DAS
Registrar: Dr E. SAIBABA REDDY
Librarian: Prof. B. SATYANARAYANA

192 Affiliated Engineering colleges, 12 Pharmacy Colleges, 3 Architectural Colleges
Library of 48,000 books, 128 periodicals
Number of teachers: 457
Number of students: 34,000 (incl. affiliated colleges).

CONSTITUENT COLLEGES

College of Engineering, Anantapur: f. 1946; Principal Dr K. RAJAGOPAL.

College of Engineering, Hyderabad: f. 1965; Principal Dr N. V. RAMANA RAO.

College of Engineering, Kakinada: f. 1946; Principal Dr N. S. V. GHANDI.

College of Fine Arts, Hyderabad: tel. (40) 3314282; f. 1940; Principal Prof. Y. RAO.

ATTACHED INSTITUTES

Bureau of Industrial Consultancy and Research and Development (BICARD), Hyderabad: tel. (40) 23321007; Dir Dr H. S. RAO.

Institute of Science and Technology: tel. (40) 23058729; f. 1989.

Oil Technological Research Institute, Anantapur: f. 1949.

School of Continuing and Distance Education: tel. (40) 3318055; fax (40) 23372662; e-mail scdejntu@hd2.dot.net.in; f. 1976; Principal Dr A. V. BABU.

School of Planning and Architecture, Hyderabad: tel. (40) 23317006; e-mail dir_spa_jntu@yahoo.com; f. 1940; Dir Dr PADMAVATHI.

JAWAHARLAL NEHRU UNIVERSITY

New Mehrauli Rd, New Delhi 110067

Telephone: (11) 26742676
Fax: (11) 26742580
E-mail: webmaster@mail.jnu.ac.in
Internet: www.jnu.ac.in

Founded 1969

Central university
Academic year: July to May

Chancellor: Prof. YASH PAL
Vice-Chancellor: Prof. B. B. BHATTACHARYA
Rectors: Prof. R. PRASAD, Prof. R. KUMAR
Registrar: AVAIS AHMAD (acting)
Dean of Student Welfare: Prof. R. K. KALE (acting)
Librarian: Dr K. GOPAL (acting)

Library of 484,702 vols, 700 periodicals
Number of teachers: 371
Number of students: 3,843

Publications: *Hispanic Horizon* (2 a year), *International Studies* (4 a year), *Journal of School of Languages* (2 a year), *Studies in History* (2 a year)

DEANS

School of Arts and Aesthetics: Prof. H. S. SHIVAPRAKASH
School of Biotechnology: Prof. A. DIXIT
School of Computer and Systems Sciences: Prof. N. PARIMALA
School of Environmental Sciences: Prof. V. K. JAIN
School of Information Technology: Prof. A. BHATTACHARYA
School of International Studies: Prof. P. PANT
School of Language, Literature and Culture Studies: Prof. V. SINGH
School of Life Sciences: Prof. P. K. YADAVA
School of Physical Sciences: Prof. R. GHOSH
School of Social Sciences: Prof. H. SINGH

ATTACHED CENTRES

Centre for the Study of Law and Governance: tel. (11) 26704021; fax (11) 26717506; e-mail dir_cslg@mail.jnu.ac.in; internet www.jnu.ac.in/cslg; Dir Prof. AMITA SINGH.

Special Centre for Molecular Medicine: Dir Dr RAKESH TYAGI.

Special Centre for Sanskrit Studies: tel. (11) 26714128; f. 2001; Dir Prof. VARYAM SINGH.

JAYPEE UNIVERSITY OF INFORMATION TECHNOLOGY

Waknaghat, PO Dumehar Bani, Via-Kandaghat, Dist. Solan, 173215, Himachal Pradesh

Telephone: (1792) 257999
Fax: (1792) 245362
Internet: www.juit.ac.in

Founded 2002
Private control
Language of instruction: English
Academic year: July to June

Chancellor: HE THE GOV. OF HIMACHAL PRADESH
Pro-Chancellor: Dr MANOJ GAUR
Vice-Chancellor: Prof. Y. MEDURY
Registrar: Brig. (Retd) BALBIR SINGH
Dean: Prof. T. S. LAMBA
Registrar: Brig. BALBIR SINGH
Librarian: SHRI RAM

Library of 26,000 vols
Number of teachers: 101
Number of students: 1,829

Depts of bioinformatics and biotechnology, civil engineering, computer science and engineering, electronics and communication engineering, information technology, management studies, mathematics, pharmacy, physics, professional devt and humanities

PROFESSORS

BHOOSAN, S. V., Electronics and Communication Engineering
CHAUDHURI, P., Computer Science and Information Technology
CHAUHAN, R. S., Biotechnology and Bioinformatics
GHRERA, S. P., Computer Science and Information Technology
GUPTA, A. K., Biotechnology and Bioinformatics
KATYAL, S. C., Physics
KULSHRESHTHA, D. C., Electronics and Communication Engineering
SINGH, H., Mathematics
SINGH, K., Mathematics

CONSTITUENT INSTITUTES

Jaypee Institute of Engineering and Technology: A-B Rd, Guna 473226, Madhya Pradesh; tel. (7544) 267051; fax (7544) 267011; e-mail contact@jiet.ac.in; internet www.jiet.ac.in; Dir Prof. N. J. RAO; Dean of Academic Affairs Prof. K. K. JAIN; Registrar Brig. S. K. S. NEGI.

Jaypee Institute of Information Technology: A-10, Sector 62, Noida 201307, Uttar Pradesh; tel. (120) 2400980; e-mail jp .gupta@jiit.ac.in; internet www.jiit.ac.in/jiit; Vice-Chancellor Prof. J. P. GUPTA; Registrar Col V. KUMAR.

JIWAJI UNIVERSITY

Vidya Vihar, Gwalior 474011, Madhya Pradesh
Telephone: (751) 2341896
Fax: (751) 2341450
E-mail: info@idejug.org
Internet: www.jiwaji.edu
Founded 1964
Teaching and Affiliating
Languages of instruction: Hindi, English
Academic year: July to June
Chancellor: HE THE GOVERNOR OF MADHYA PRADESH
Vice-Chancellor: Prof. A. K. KAPOOR
Registrar: Dr D. S. CHANDEL
Librarian: J. N. GAUTAM
Library of 140,000 vols
Number of students: 47,358
Publications: *Humanities*, *Science* (2 a year)

DEANS

Faculty of Arts: Dr H. C. GUPTA
Faculty of Commerce and Management: Dr D. C. SHARMA
Faculty of Life Science: (vacant)
Faculty of Physical Education: (vacant)
Faculty of Science: (vacant)
Faculty of Social Sciences: Dr P. L. SABLOOK

There are over 100 affiliated colleges

KACHCHH UNIVERSITY

Mundra Rd, Kachchh 370001, Gujarat
Telephone: (2832) 290245
Fax: (2832) 235012
E-mail: info@kskvkachchhuniversity.org
Internet: kskvku.digitaluniversity.ac
Founded 2003
Faculties of arts, commerce, education, law, science, technology; 28 affiliated colleges
Number of teachers: 200
Number of students: 15,000
Vice-Chancellor: Dr K. V. GOR

Registrar: A. H. GOR
Controller of Examinations: A. P. MEJTA.

KAKATIYA UNIVERSITY

Vidyaranyapuri, Warangal 506009
Telephone: (8712) 277687
Fax: (8712) 278935
E-mail: registrar@kakatiya.ac.in
Internet: www.kakatiya.ac.in
Founded 1976
Teaching and affiliating
Languages of instruction: English, Telugu, Urdu
Chancellor: HE THE GOVERNOR OF ANDHRA PRADESH
Vice-Chancellor: Prof. N. LINGAMURTHY
Registrar: Prof. SATYANARAIN NALLANI
Controller of Examinations: Prof. T. P. REDDY
Dean of College Devt Council: Prof. T. B. RAO
Deputy Librarian: K. RAMANAIAH
Library of 104,000 vols
Number of teachers: 248
Number of students: 90,000
Publication: *Kakatiya Journal of English Studies and Vimarshini*

DEANS

Faculty of Arts: Prof. K. KATYAYANI
Faculty of Commerce and Business Management: Prof. T. JOGA CHARY
Faculty of Education: Prof. G. RAMESH
Faculty of Engineering: Prof. R. V. CHALAM
Faculty of Law: Justice L. N. REDDY
Faculty of Pharmaceutical Sciences: Prof. A. V. N. APPA RAO
Faculty of Science: Prof. G. R. RAO
Faculty of Social Sciences: Prof. N. VIJAYA

CONSTITUENT COLLEGES

Institute of Advanced Studies in Education: Principal Prof. C. SAMMAIAH.
School of Distance Learning and Continuing Education: tel. (870) 2438S77; fax (870)2438000; e-mail info@sdlceku.ac.in; internet www.sdlceku.ac.in; Dir Prof. K. VENKATANARAYANA.
University Arts and Science College, Warangal: Principal Prof. G. S. REDDY.
University College of Engineering: Principal Prof. SHOWRY.
University College, Warangal: Principal Prof. C. SAMMAIH.
University College of Law, Warangal: Principal Dr K. SUDHAKAR.
University College of Pharmaceutical Sciences, Warangal: Principal Dr M. SARANGAPANI.
University Postgraduate College, Godavarikhani: Principal Dr VENKARAM REDDY.
University Postgraduate College, Karimnagar: Principal Dr BHARATH.
University Postgraduate College, Khammam: Principal Prof. M. RAO.
University Postgraduate College, Nirmal: Principal Prof. N. RAMULU.
University Postgraduate College, Warangal: Principal Prof. M. RAO.

KALYANI UNIVERSITY

Kalyani 741235, Nadia, West Bengal
Telephone: (33) 25828690
Fax: (33) 25828282
E-mail: registrar@klyuniv.ac.in
Internet: www.klyuniv.ac.in
Founded 1960
Teaching and research
Language of instruction: English
Academic year: June to May

Chancellor: HE THE GOVERNOR OF WEST BENGAL
Vice-Chancellor: Prof. ARABINDA KUMAR DAS
Controller of Examinations: Dr PRADIP PRASAD KARURI
Dean of Student Welfare: Dr ASIT KUMAR DAS
Registrar: UTPAL BATTACHARYYA
Librarian: Dr ASITABHA DAS
36 Affiliated colleges
Library of 128,790 vols, 116 periodicals
Number of teachers: 217
Number of students: 4,000

DEANS

Faculty of Arts and Commerce: Dr SUBHAS CHANDRA SARKAR
Faculty of Education: Prof. SUDARSHAN BHOWMICK
Faculty of Engineering, Technology and Management: Dr JYOTSNA KUMAR MANDAL
Faculty of Science: Prof. D. K. BHATTACHARYYA

PROFESSORS

Bengali (tel. (33) 25828220 ext. 233):
BANERJEE, R.
CHOUDHURI, D.
GHATAK, K.
GHATAK, K. S.
SHAW, R.

Biophysics and Biochemistry (tel. (33) 25828750):
BHATTACHARYYA, D. K.
ROY, P. K.

Botany (tel. (33) 25825750 ext. 317):
BHATTACHARYYA, S.
BISWAS, A. K.
CHAUDHURI, S.
GHOSH, P. D.
SEN, T.

Chemistry (tel. (33) 25828220 ext. 305):
DEY, K.
GUHA, A.
LAHIRI, S. C.
MAJUMDER, K. C.
MAJUMDER, M. N.
MUKHERJEE, J.
SARKAR, A. R.

Commerce (tel. (33) 25828750):
BHATTACHARYYA, P. K.
KONAR, D. N.
MAJHI, M. M.

Ecology:
SANTRA, S. C.

Economics (tel. (33) 25828750):
BHATTACHARYYA, R. N.
DUTTA, M.
GHOSH, B.
PAL, D. P.

Education (tel. (33) 25828750):
BASU, M. K.

English (tel. (33) 25828750):
BHATTACHARYYA, D. P.
CHAKRABORTY, B.
DAS, N.
DEB, P. K.

Folklore and History:
CHAKRABORTY, B. K.

Mathematics (tel. (33) 25828750):
BASU, M.
CHAKRABORTY, H.
DAS, A. G.
DEY, U. C.
KONAR, A.
MUKHERJEE, S.
SANYAL, D. C.
SENGUPTA, P. R.

Physical Education (tel. (33) 25820184 ext. 232):
BANERJEE, A. K.
BHOWMICK, S.
GHOSH, S. R.
Physics (tel. (33) 25820184):
BHATTACHARYYA, A. B.
BISWAS, S.
CHAUDHURI, S.
DASGUPTA, P.
DEB, S. K.
ROY, A. C.
ROY, S.
RUDRA, P.
Political Science:
MUKHOPADHYAY, A.
Sociology:
DASGUPTA, H.
DASGUPTA, S. K.
MANNA, S.
Statistics:
DAS, P.
MITRA, T. K.
PANDA, R. N.
Zoology (tel. (33) 25828750):
BHATTACHARYYA, D. K.
CHAKRABORTY, S.
DEY, N. C.
HALDER, D. P.
JANA, B. B.
KHUDA BAX, A. R.
KONAR, S. K.
KUNDU, S.
MANNA, C. K.
MUKHERJEE, D. K.
SAHU, C. R.

KAMESHWAR SINGH DARBHANGA SANSKRIT UNIVERSITY

Darbhanga, Bihar 846004
Telephone: (6272) 222178; (6272) 222217
E-mail: info@ksdsu.edu.in
Internet: www.ksdsu.edu.in
Founded 1961
Teaching and affiliating
Autonomous control
Languages of instruction: Sanskrit, Hindi
Academic year: July to June
Chancellor: HE THE GOVERNOR OF BIHAR
Vice-Chancellor: Dr KULAND JHA
Registrar: KANHALYA JEE CHOUBEY
Librarian: J. MAHTO
Library of 100,000 vols, 15,000 periodicals, 10,000 MSS
Number of students: 515,000
Publication: *Vishwa Maneesha* (4 a year)

DEANS

Faculty of Darshan: R. S. JHA
Faculty of Jyotish: R. C. JHA
Faculty of Puran: (vacant)
Faculty of Samaj Shstra: K. MISHRA
Faculty of Veda: S. MISHRA
Faculty of Vyakaran: V. MISHRA
There are 38 constituent colleges and 37 affiliated colleges

KANNADA UNIVERSITY HAMPI

Vidyaranya, Hospet (Taluk) 583276, Karnataka
Telephone: (8394) 241337
Fax: (8394) 241334
E-mail: mail@kannadauniversity.org
Internet: www.kannadauniversity.org
Founded 1991
Unitary and residential; faculties of fine arts, languages, sciences and social sciences
Vice-Chancellor: Dr A. MURIGEPPA

Registrar: Dr S. S. PUJAR
Publications: *Budakattu Karnataka* (Tribal Karnataka), *Janapada Karnataka* (Folklore of Karnataka), *Journal of Karnataka Studies* (in English), *Kannada Adhyayana*, , (Kannada Studies), *Mahila Adhyayana* (Women Studies), *Namma Kannada* (Kannada Linguistics)

DEANS

Fine Arts: Prof. S. C. PATIL
Languages: Prof. RAHAMATH TARIKERE
Social Sciences: Dr T. R. CHANDRASHEKAR

KANNUR UNIVERSITY

Kannur 670567, Kerala
Telephone: (497) 2782351
Fax: (497) 2782190
E-mail: registrar@kannuruniversity.ac.in
Internet: www.kannuruniversity.ac.in
Founded 1996
105 Affiliated colleges; campuses at Kasaragod, Mananthavady, Mangattuparamba, Nileshwaram, Thalassery, Payyannur
Vice-Chancellor: Dr P. K. MICHAEL THARAKAN
Pro-Vice-Chancellor: Dr A. P. KUTTYKRISHNAN
Registrar: K. M. ABDUR RASHEED
Controller of Examinations: K. M. ABDUR RASHEED
Finance Officer: SHAJEE JOSE
Public Relations Officer: ACHUTHANANDAN KUNIYIL
Library of 26,980 vols, 151 periodicals

DEANS

Faculty of Ayurveda: Dr V. P. SADHANANDAN
Faculty of Commerce and Management: Dr M. BHASI
Faculty of Communication: Dr SUJETHA NAIR
Faculty of Education: Dr M. S. LALITHAMMA
Faculty of Engineering: Dr V. GOPAKUMAR
Faculty of Humanities: Dr K. V. KUNHIKRISHNAN
Faculty of Languages and Literature: Dr T. B. VENUGOPALA PANICKER
Faculty of Law: Dr D. RAJEEV
Faculty of Modern Medicine: Dr K. BHASKARAN
Faculty of Science: Dr P. K. VIJAYAN
Faculty of Social Science: Prof. DAMODARAN NAMBOOTHIRI

KARNATAK UNIVERSITY

Dharwad 580003, Karnataka
Telephone: (836) 2215252
Fax: (836) 2747884
E-mail: webmaster@kud.ernet.in
Internet: www.kud.ernet.in
Founded 1949
Teaching and affiliating; postgraduate centres in Belgaum, Bijapur, Haveri, Karwar; 246 affiliated colleges
Language of instruction: English
Academic year: June to April
Chancellor: HE THE GOVERNOR OF KARNATAKA
Vice-Chancellor: Prof. S. K. SAIDAPUR
Registrar: V. RANGASWAMY
Librarian: Dr S. B. PATIL
Library of 350,000 vols
Number of teachers: 310 postgraduate, 5,556 in colleges
Number of students: 3,779 (postgraduate)
Publications: *Bharati Vidyarthi* (4 a year), *Humanities*, *Journal of the Karnataka University—Science, Social Sciences; Karnataka Bharati* (4 a year)

DEANS

Faculty of Arts: Dr M. S. MULLA
Faculty of Commerce: Dr H. Y. KAMBLE

Faculty of Education: Dr N. N. GANIHAR
Faculty of Law: Dr K. R. AITHAL
Faculty of Management: Dr A. H. CHACHADI
Faculty of Science and Technology: Dr B. P. WAGHMARE
Faculty of Social Sciences: Dr A. S. BALASUBRAMANYA

CONSTITUENT COLLEGES

Karnatak Arts College: Dharwad; f. 1917; Prin. Dr VEENA SHANTESHWAR.
Karnatak Science College: Dharwad; f. 1919; Prin. Dr B. G. NADAKATTI.
University College of Education: f. 1962; Prin. Dr R. T. JANTALI.
University College of Law: f. 1962; Prin. C. S. PATIL.
University College of Music and Fine Arts: f. 1975; Prin. H. A. KHAN.

KARNATAKA STATE OPEN UNIVERSITY

Manasagangotri, Mysore 570006, Karnataka
Telephone: (821) 2512471
Fax: (821) 2500846
E-mail: registrarksou@gmail.com
Internet: www.ksoumysore.com
Founded 1969 as Institute of Correspondence Course and Continuing Education, present name and status 1996
Academic year: August to June
Vice-Chancellor: Dr B. A. VIVEKA RAI
Registrar: K. R. JAYAPRAKASH RAO
Dean of Academic Affairs: Dr JAGADEESH
Dean of Study Centres: Dr M. SUSHEELA URS
Regional Dirs: D. SHIVANNA (Davanagere): Dr K. G. SURESH (Bangalore): Dr KAMBLE ASHOK (Gulbarga): G. V. CHANDRA SHEKAR (Dharwad): Prof. HOOVAJAH GOWDA (Shimoga)
Library of 80,000 vols
Number of teachers: 60
Number of students: 30,000

CHAIRS OF DEPARTMENTS

Commerce and Management: Prof. JAGADEESHA
Economics: S. SHIVANNA
Education: Dr N. LAKSHMI
English: Y. ALIJAZ AHMED
Hindi: B. G. CHANDRALEKHA
History: Dr G. RAMANATHAN
Kannada: D. T. BASAVARAJ
Management: Dr JAGADEESH
Political Science and Public Administration: S. M. SEETHAMMA
Sanskrit: Dr N. RADHAKRISHNA BHAT
Sociology: N. DODDASIDIAH
Tamil: M. TAMILMARAN
Telugu: Dr A. RAMANATHAM NAIDU
Urdu: BALQUEES BANU

KARNATAKA STATE WOMEN'S UNIVERSITY

City Campus, Station Rd, Nr Dr B. R. Ambedkar Circle, Bijapur 586101, Karnataka
Toravi Campus, Toravi, Athani Rd, Bijapur 586109, Karnataka
Telephone: (8352) 240030
Fax: (8352) 242795
E-mail: wu_bij@kar.nic.in
Internet: www.kswubij.ac.in
Languages of instruction: Kannada, English
Academic year: July to June
Founded 2003
Vice-Chancellor: Prof. GEETHA BALI
Registrar: S. A. KAZI
Librarian: P. G. TADASAD
Library of 56,746 vols, 240 periodicals
Number of teachers: 46

Number of students: 16,027
66 Affiliated colleges

DEANS
Faculty of Arts: Dr VIJAYASHREE SABARAD
Faculty of Commerce: Dr S. B. KAMASHETTY
Faculty of Education: Dr T. M. GEETHA
Faculty of Science and Technology: Dr SHARANAPPA HALASE
Faculty of Social Sciences: Dr S. A. KAZI

KARUNYA UNIVERSITY

Karunya Nagar, Coimbatore 641114, Tamil Nadu
Telephone: (42) 22614300
Fax: (42) 22615615
E-mail: info@karunya.edu
Internet: www.karunya.edu
Founded 1986, deemed univ. status 2004, univ. status 2006
Schools of biotechnology, civil eng., computer science and technology, electrical science, management, mechanical sciences, science and humanities; depts of personality devt, value education
Number of teachers: 350
Number of students: 5,400
Vice-Chancellor: Dr P. P. APPASAMY
Registrar: Dr A. M. FERNANDEZ
Dir of Operations: S. JEYAPAUL
Dir of Research: Dr B. C. PILLAI
Dean of Academic Affairs: Dr D. GNANARAJ.

KAVIKULGURU KALIDAS SANSKRIT VISHWAVIDYALAYA

Baghele Bhavan, Mouda Rd, District Nagpur, Ramtek 441106, Maharashtra
Telephone: (7114) 255549
Fax: (7114) 255549
E-mail: admin@sanskrituni.net
Internet: sanskrituni.net
Founded 1997
Academic year: July to May
Chancellor: HE THE GOVERNOR OF MAHARASHTRA
Vice-Chancellor: Dr PANKAJ CHANDE
Registrar: HARSHIDA DAVE (acting)
Dean of Faculty: Dr N. J. PURI
Librarian: Dr HARSHIDA DAVE
Undergraduate and postgraduate courses in Sanskrit
49 Affiliated colleges
Number of teachers: 22
Number of students: 1,148

KERALA AGRICULTURAL UNIVERSITY

Vellanikkara 680656, Thrissur, Kerala
Telephone: (487) 2371619
Fax: (487) 2370019
E-mail: registrar@kau.in
Internet: www.kau.edu
Founded 1972
Language of instruction: English
Academic year: June to March
Chancellor: HE THE GOVERNOR OF KERALA
Vice-Chancellor: K. R. VISWAMBHARAN
Registrar: JOBI V. PAUL
Comptroller: P. V. DEVDAS
Dir of Academic and Postgraduate Studies: Dr D. ALEXANDER
Dir of Extension: Dr M. K. SHEELA
Dir of Research: Dr P. K. ASHOKAN
Dir of Student Welfare: Dr JOSE J. CHUNGATH
Librarian: K. P. SATHIAN (acting)
10 Constituent colleges, 6 regional agricultural research stations, 26 research stations
Library of 115,000 vols
Number of teachers: 823

Number of students: 2,445
Publications: *Journal of Tropical Agriculture* (2 a year), *Journal of Veterinary and Animal Science* (2 a year)

DEANS
Faculty of Agricultural Engineering: Dr V. GANESAN
Faculty of Agriculture: Dr K. HARIKRISHNAN NAIR
Faculty of Fisheries: Dr MOHANA KUMARAN NAIR
Faculty of Veterinary and Animal Sciences: Dr E. NANU

CONSTITUENT COLLEGES
College of Agriculture, Padannakkad: Kasaragod 671328; tel. (467) 2280616; e-mail adpad@kau.
College of Agriculture, Vellayani: Thiruvananthapuram 695522; tel. (471) 2381002; e-mail deanagri@kau.in; (formerly affiliated to University of Kerala).
College of Cooperation, Banking and Management: Thrissur 680656; tel. (487) 2370367; e-mail ccbm@kau.in; f. 1981.
College of Dairy Science and Technology, Idukki: Mannuthy, Thrissur 680651; tel. (487) 2372861; e-mail cdst@kau.in; f. 1994.
College of Fisheries: Panangad, Ernakulam 682651; tel. (484) 2700337; e-mail cofpanangad@kau.in; f. 1979.
College of Forestry: Thrissur 680656; tel. (487) 2370050; e-mail adforestry@kau.in.
College of Horticulture: Thrissur 680656; tel. (487) 2370790; e-mail adhort@kau.in; f. 1972.
College of Veterinary and Animal Science, Thrissur: Mannuthy, Thrissur 680651; tel. (487) 2370451; e-mail vetmannuthy@kau.in; (formerly affiliated to University of Calicut).
College of Veterinary and Animal Science, Wayanad: Pookot, Wayanad 673576; tel. (4936) 256340; e-mail vetpookot@kau.in; f. 1999.
Kelappaji College of Agricultural Engineering and Technology: Tavanur, Malappuram 679573; tel. (494) 2686009; e-mail kcaet@kau.in.

KUMAUN UNIVERSITY

Nainital 263001, Uttar Pradesh
Telephone: (5942) 235068; (5942) 235576
Internet: www.kumaununiversity.org
Founded 1973
Teaching and affiliating; 3 campuses (Almora, Bhimtal, Nainital), 28 affiliated colleges
Languages of instruction: Hindi, English
Academic year: July to June (two terms)
Chancellor: HE THE GOVERNOR OF UTTARAKHAND
Vice-Chancellor: Prof. C. P. BARTHWAL
Registrar: B. C. JOSHI
Finance Officer: B. BANGYAL
Librarian: Prof. C. C. PANT
Library of 90,000 vols
Number of teachers: 573
Number of students: 75,000

DEANS
Faculty of Arts: Prof. N. K. SHAH
Faculty of Commerce and Management: Prof. B. D. AWASTHI
Faculty of Education: Prof. A. BHARTI
Faculty of Law: Prof. S. D. SHARMA
Faculty of Science: Prof. K. PANDEY

PROFESSORS
Faculty of Arts:
BISHT, H. S., Geography
BISHT, L. S., Economics
BISHT, L. S., Hindi
DUBE, M. P., Political Science
GUPTA, R. K., Hindi
PANDE, G. C., Economics
PANDEY, D. C., Economics
PATHAK, S., History
POKHARIA, D. S., Hindi
RAWAT, A. S., History
RUWALI, K. D., Hindi
SAH, N. K., Economics
SAHAI, V., History
SINGH, O. P., Geography
TRIPATHI, D. R., Sanskrit
Faculty of Commerce and Management:
BISHT, N. S., Business Administration
RANA, N. S., Commerce
TIWARI, J. C., Commerce
Faculty of Education:
DURGAPAL, S.
JOSHI, J. K.
JUYAL, P. D.
SHUKLA, S. C.
Faculty of Science:
BHATT, S. D., Zoology
BISHT, C. S., Mathematics
BISHT, G., Chemistry
BISHT, M., Zoology
CHANDRA, M., Chemistry
CHANDRA, S., Botany
DHAMI, H. S., Mathematics
JOSHI, G. C., Botany
JOSHI, L., Chemistry
KAUSHAL, B. R., Zoology
KHAMI, K. S., Chemistry
KHETWAL, K. S., Chemistry
KUMAR, S., Geology
KUMAR, S., Zoology
LOHANI, A. B., Mathematics
MATHELA, C. S., Chemistry
MATHPAL, K. N., Chemistry
MEHROTRA, R. M., Chemistry
MEHTA, S. P. S., Chemistry
MELKANI, K. B., Chemistry
MISHRA, V. N., Chemistry
PANDEY, K., Physics
PANDEY, K. N., Botany
PANDEY, S. B., Mathematics
PANGETI, Y. P. S., Botany
PANT, C. C., Geology
PANT, D. N., Mathematics
PANT, M. C., Physics
PANT, R. P., Mathematics
PANT, T. C., Physics
SHAH, L., Zoology
SINGH, R. P., Forestry
SINGH, S. P., Botany
VARMA, K. R., Botany

KURUKSHETRA UNIVERSITY

Kurukshetra 136119, Haryana
Telephone: (1744) 238039
Fax: (1744) 238277
E-mail: kulib@kuk.ernet.in
Internet: kukinfo.com
Founded 1956
Teaching and affiliating; 3 constituent colleges, 213 affiliated colleges
State control
Languages of instruction: English, Hindi
Academic year: July to June
Chancellor: HE THE GOVERNOR OF HARYANA
Vice-Chancellor: Dr R. P. BAJPAI
Registrar: Dr R. TANWAR
Dean of Academic Affairs: Dr S. P. MALHOTRA
Dean of Colleges: Dr T. R. KUNDU
Dean of Students: Dr R. TANWAR
Dir of Public Relations: Dr K. K. KATHURIA
Librarian: R. D. MEHLA

Library of 299,463 vols, 400 periodicals
Number of teachers: 390
Number of students: 5,584

Publications: *Jeevanti* (in Hindi), *Journal of Haryana Studies* (in English), *Kalanidhi* (magazine, in Hindi), *Kuru Jyoti* (in English, Sanskrit and Hindi), *Kurukshetra Law Journal* (in English), *Praci Jyoti* (in English), *Research Journal for Arts and Humanities* (in English and Hindi), *Sambhawana* (in Hindi)

DEANS

Faculty of Arts and Languages: Dr N. S. KAUSHAL
Faculty of Ayurvedic Medicine: Dr V. V. CHHIKARA (acting)
Faculty of Commerce and Management: Dr M. K. JAIN
Faculty of Education: Dr SUSHMA SHARMA
Faculty of Engineering and Technology: Dr O. P. BAJPAI
Faculty of Indic Studies: Dr ARUN KESARWANI
Faculty of Law: Dr R. K. GUPTA
Faculty of Life Sciences: Dr D. MUKHARJEE
Faculty of Medicine and Dentistry: Dr S. K. KHINDSIA
Faculty of Science: Dr NAND LAL
Faculty of Social Sciences: Dr P. D. SHARMA

PROFESSORS

Faculty of Arts and Languages (tel. (1744) 234374):
GUPTA, L. C., Hindi
KAANG, A. S., Punjabi
SHARMA, S. D., English

Faculty of Commerce and Management:
BANSAL, M. L., Commerce
BHARDWAJ, D. S., Tourism
DWIVEDI, R. S., Management
GUPTA, S. L., Management
HOODA, R. P., Commerce
JAIN, M. K., Management
MITTAL, R. K., Commerce
SHARMA, V. D., Management

Faculty of Education:
MALHOTRA, S. P.
MAVI, N. S.
YADAV, D. S.

Faculty of Indic Studies (tel. (1744) 238347):
KUSHWAHA, S. K., Fine Arts
SAXENA, MADU BALA, Music
SHARMA, INDU BALA, ISIS
SINGH, A., Sanskrit

Faculty of Law:
AGGARWAL, V. K.
KUMARI, D.
VARANDANI, G.

Faculty of Science (tel. (1744) 239235):
ANEJA, K. R., Microbiology
ARYA, S. P., Chemistry
ASTHANA, V. K., Geography
CHATURVEDI, D. K., Physics
CHOPRA, G., Zoology
GEORGE, P. J., Electronics Science
GUPTA, S. C., Chemistry
KAKKAR, L. R., Chemistry
KUMARI, S., Statistics
LUNKAD, S. K., Geology
MATTA, N. K., Botany
MEHTA, J. R., Chemistry
MITTAL, I. C., Zoology
MUKHERJEE, D., Botany
NAND, LAL, Earth Sciences
RANI, S., Botany
ROHTASH, C., Zoology
SHARMA, N. D., Physics
SHARMA, V. K., Geography
SINGH, H., Biochemistry
SURI, P. K., Computer Science
TREHAN, K., Botany
VINOD KUMAR, Mathematics

Faculty of Social Sciences:
KUNDU, T. R., Economics
KHURANA, G., History
SHARMA, P. D., Political Science
SHARMA, R. K., History
SINGH, H., Public Administration
PATHANIA, S., History
TANWAR, R., History
TUTEJA, K. L., History
UPADHYAYA, R. K., Social Work
VASHIST, B. K., Economics

KUVEMPU UNIVERSITY

Jnana Sahyadri, Shankaraghatta 577451, Shimoga District, Karnataka

Telephone: (8282) 256221
Fax: (8282) 256262
E-mail: reg_admn@kuvempu.ac.in
Internet: www.kuvempu.ac.in

Founded 1987
Academic year: August to April

Affiliating; 57 postgraduate depts in arts, commerce, education and law, science; 4 constituent colleges (sahyadri Arts And Commerce College; Sahyadri Science College, Shimoga; B. D. T. College Of Engineering, Davangere; Fine Arts College, Davangere); 3 BEd. colleges, 6 Law colleges and 30 BEd colleges in Shimoga, Chitradurga, Chikmagalur, Davangere; outlying regional postgraduate centres at Davangere and Kadur; 97 affiliated colleges

Chancellor: RAMESHWAR THAKUR
Vice-Chancellor: Prof. B. S. SHERIGARA
Registrar: R. UDAY KUMAR
Dir of College Devt Council: Prof. M. KRISHNAPPA
Dir of Student Welfare: Dr BASAVARAJ NELLISARA
Librarian: Dr K. C. RAMAKRISHNEGOWDA

Library of 70,000 vols, 4,124 vols of periodicals
Number of teachers: 93
Number of students: 950 (postgraduate)

DEANS

Faculty of Arts: Prof. J. S. SADANANDA
Faculty of Commerce: Prof. V. MURUGAIAH
Faculty of Education: Prof. S. M. PRAKASH
Faculty of Engineering: Prof. K. REVANASIDDAPPA
Faculty of Law: Prof. B. S. REDDY
Faculty of Medicine: Dr C. M. RAMESH
Faculty of Science and Technology: Prof. M. KRISHNAPPA

LALIT NARAYAN MITHILA UNIVERSITY

Kameshwarnagar, POB 13, Darbhanga 846004, Bihar

Telephone: (6272) 222463; (6272) 222598
E-mail: vc_lnmu@indiatimes.com
Internet: lnmu.bih.nic.in

Founded 1972

Teaching and affiliating; 43 constituent colleges, 24 affiliated colleges
Languages of instruction: Hindi, English
Academic year: June to May

Chancellor: HE THE GOVERNOR OF BIHAR
Vice-Chancellor: Dr RAJ MANI PRASAD SINGH
Pro-Vice-Chancellor: Dr GOPAL PRASAD SINGH
Registrar: Dr KUMARESH PRASAD SINGH
Librarian: K. K. KAMAL

Library of 173,774 vols, 54 journals
Number of teachers: 1,251
Number of students: 110,355

DEANS

Faculty of Arts: Prof. R. N. THAKUR
Faculty of Commerce: Dr GOPAL LAL
Faculty of Education: (vacant)

Faculty of Law: Prof. D. K. JHA
Faculty of Medicine: Dr S. N. SINGH
Faculty of Science: Prof. S. PANDEY

PROFESSORS

JHA, B. N., Mathematics
JHA, S. M., Maithili
LALL, G., Commerce
PANDEY, S., Zoology
PATHAK, R. K., Hindi
PRASAD, A. B., Botany
RAHMAN, M., Urdu
ROY, B. K., History
THAKUR, B., Economics
THAKUR, R. N., Political Science
THAKUR, Y., Chemistry

MADHYA PRADESH BHOJ (OPEN) UNIVERSITY

Kolar Rd, Raja Bhoj Marg, Damkheda, Chunabhatti Bhopal 462016, Madhya Pradesh

Telephone: (755) 2424670
Fax: (755) 2424670
Internet: www.bhojvirtualuniversity.com

Founded 1992
Academic year: July to June

Vice-Chancellor: Prof. K. SINGH
Registrar: Dr P. N. JOSHI
Librarian: J. P. SONI

Library of 7,000 vols

DIRECTORS OF REGIONAL CENTRES

Bhopal: Dr S. DWIVEDI
Bilaspur: Dr S. L. KOKA
Durg: Dr R. CHOUBEY
Gwalior: Dr A. P. S. CHOUHAN
Indore: Dr D. VARSHNEY
Jabalpur: Dr K. K. TIWARI
Jagdalpur: Dr A. ALI
Raipur: Dr S. K. SINGH
Rewa: Dr S. S. PARIHAR
Sagar: Dr R. S. KASANA
Satna: Dr R. TIWARI

PROFESSORS

DHAKAD, S. K.
DUBEY, S. K.
GARDE, V. D.
GOEL, R. M.
GREWAL, J. S.
MISRA, R. D.
SAXENA, M. C.
SESHADRI, C. S.
TOMAR, S. K.

MADURAI-KAMARAJ UNIVERSITY

Palkalai Nagar, Madurai 625021, Tamil Nadu

Telephone: (452) 2459455
Fax: (452) 2459181
E-mail: registrar@mkuniversity.org
Internet: www.mkuniversity.org

Founded 1966

Teaching and affiliating
Languages of instruction: English, Tamil
Academic year: June to April

Chancellor: HE THE GOVERNOR OF TAMIL NADU
Vice-Chancellor: Dr R. KARPAGA KUMARAVEL
Registrar: Dr I. SINGARAM
Controller of Examinations: Dr S. SHANMUGIAH
Dean of College Devt Council: Dr S. D. AMIRTHA RAJAN
Dean of Curriculum Devt: Dr G. SUBRAMANIAN
Dean of Endowment and Devt: Dr P. M. AJMALKHAN
Dean of Research and Devt: Dr K. VELUTHAMBI
Academic Dean: Dr K. IYAKUTTI

Librarian: A. SRIMURUGAN

18 Schools comprising 73 depts; 109 affiliated colleges (9 autonomous), 7 evening colleges

Library of 300,000 vols, 500 periodicals

Number of teachers: 377 (excluding affiliated colleges)

Number of students: 133,100 (including affiliated colleges)

Publication: *Journal of Biology Education* (4 a year)

PROFESSORS

School of Biological Sciences (tel. (452) 2458471 ext. 369):

GUNASEKARAN, P., Genetics
KANDULA, S., Immunology
MARIMUTHU, G., Animal Behaviour and Physiology
MUNAVAR, H., Molecular Biology
PALIWAL, K., Plant Morphology and Algology
SELVAM, G. S., Biochemistry
SHANMUGASUNDARAM, S., Microbial Technology
SUDHAKARSAMY, P., Plant Sciences

School of Biotechnology (tel. (452) 2458471 ext. 384):

DHARMALINGAM, K., Genetic Engineering
KRISHNASWAMY, S., Bioinformatics
PALANIVELU, P., Molecular Microbiology
VELUTHAMBI, K., Plant Biotechnology

School of Chemistry (tel. (452) 2458471 ext. 347):

ATHAPPAN, P. R., Inorganic Chemistry
GANDHIDASAN, R., Natural Products Chemistry
MURUGESAN, R., Physical Chemistry
MUTHUSUBRAMANIAN, S., Organic Chemistry
PERUMAL, S., Organic Chemistry
PITCHUMANI, K., Natural Products Chemistry
RAJAGOPAL., S., Physical Chemistry
RAMACHANDRAN, M. S., Physical Chemistry
RAMARAJ, R., Physical Chemistry
RAMESH, P., Natural Products Chemistry
RAMU, A., Inorganic Chemistry
SIVAKOLUNTHU, S., Inorganic Chemistry
VAIDYANATHAN, S., Physical Chemistry

School of Business Studies (tel. (452) 2458471 ext. 359):

ALAGAPPAN, V., Commerce
CHANDRAN, C., Management Studies
CHINNIAH, V., Management Studies
PANDIAN, P., Commerce
RAMAMOORTHY, K., Commerce
RAVICHANDRAN, K., Management Studies
SEKAR, P. C., Management Studies
SURYA RAO, U., Management Studies

School of Earth and Atmospheric Sciences (tel. (452) 2458471 ext. 245):

ILANGOVAN, P., Environmental Remote Sensing and Cartography
KRISHNAN, N., Environmental Remote Sensing and Cartography
LAKSHMI, K., Geography
PARTHASARATHY, G. R., Geography
SANTHAKUMARI, A., Geography
SHANMUGANANDAN, S., Geography

School of Economics (tel. (452) 2458471 ext. 353):

DEIVAMANI, K., Human Resources Devt Economics
DHULASI BIRUNDHA, V., Agricultural Economics
HARIDOSS, R., Mathematical Economics
HARIHARAN, S. V., Mathematical Economics
MANONMONEY, N., Industrial Economics
MUTHULAKSHMI, R., Rural Devt Economics
SARASWATHI, N., Rural Devt Economics
VIJAYALAKSHMI, S., Econometrics

School of Education (tel. (452) 2458471 ext. 356):

KRISHNAN, K., Education

School of Energy Environment and Natural Resources (tel. (452) 2458471 ext. 365):

KUMARAGURU, A. K., Environment Studies
MAHADEVAN, A., Futures Studies
PAULRAJ, S., Solar Energy
SUNDARAM, A., Futures Studies

School of English and Foreign Languages (tel. (452) 2458471 ext. 361):

CHELLIAH, S., English and Comparative Literature
PARAMESWARI, D., English and Comparative Literature
SANKARAKUMAR, A., English and Comparative Literature

School of Historical Studies (tel. (452) 2458471 ext. 354):

CHANDRA BABU, B. S., Medieval History
DANIEL, D., Modern History
GOPALKRISHNAN, P. B., Modern History
JAYARAJ, K. V., Modern History
RAMASWAMY, T., Ancient History

School of Indian Languages (tel. (452) 2458471 ext. 362):

GIRIPRAKASH, T. S., Telugu and Comparative Literature
HARIKRISHNA BHAT, B., Kannada

School of Information and Communication Sciences (tel. (452) 2458471 ext. 364):

MANONMANI, T., Communication
SANTHA, A., Journalism and Science Communication

School of Mathematics (tel. (452) 2458471 ext. 339):

ARIVARIGNAN, G., Applied Mathematics & Statistics
BASKARAN, R., Mathematics
KARUNAKARAN, V., Mathematics

School of Performing Arts (tel. (452) 2458471 ext. 248):

AYYANAR, V., Art History, Aesthetics and Fine Arts
MUTHIAH, I., Folklore
SETHURAMAN, G., Art History, Aesthetics and Fine Arts

School of Physics (tel. (452) 2458471 ext. 352):

ARUMUGAM, G, Computer Science
IYAKUTTI, K., Microprocessor and Computer
NATARAJAN, S., Computer Science
NAVANEETHAKRISHNAN, K., Theoretical Physics
RAMACHANDRAN, K., Theoretical Physics
RAMAKRISHNAN, V., Microprocessor and Computer
UMAPATHY, S., Theoretical Physics

School of Religions, Philosophy and Humanist Thought (tel. (452) 2458471 ext. 342):

AJMALKHAN, P. M., Islam and Islamic Tamil Studies
ANDIAPPAN, S., Gandhian Studies and Ramalinga Philosophy
JEYAPRAGASAM, S., Gandhian Studies and Ramalinga Philosophy
MUTHUMOHAN, N., Gurunanak Studies

School of Social Sciences (tel. (452) 2458471 ext. 360):

KANNAN, R., Sociology
MADHANAGOPAL, R., Political Science
NALINI, B., Sociology
PERIAKARUPPAN, P., Political Science
SINGARAM, I., Sociology
THARA BHAI, L., Sociology

School of Tamil Studies (tel. (452) 2458471 ext. 347):

ATHITHAN, A., Linguistics
MANIVEL, M., Manuscriptology, Tamilology

MOHAN, N. R., Comparative Literature
SARADHAMBAL, C., Comparative Literature
SASIREHA, S., Literary Criticism
THIRUMALAI, M., Literary Criticism
VENKATARAMAN, S., Modern Literature

MAGADH UNIVERSITY

Bodh-Gaya 824234, Bihar

Telephone: (631) 2200490
Fax: (631) 2222717
Internet: magadhuniversity.ac.in

Founded 1962

Teaching and Affiliating
Languages of instruction: English, Hindi
Academic year: June to May

Chancellor: HE THE GOVERNOR OF BIHAR
Vice-Chancellor: Prof. B. N. PANDEY
Pro-Vice-Chancellor: (vacant)
Registrar: Dr D. K. YADAV (acting)
Finance Officer: S. SRIVASTAVA
Controller of Examinations: Dr R. SINGH
Librarian: Prof. S. KUMAR

44 Constituent colleges, 60 affiliated colleges

Library of 162,161 vols, 10 journals, 1,381 MSS

Number of teachers: 5,000
Number of students: 170,500

DEANS

Faculty of Commerce: Dr V. K. SINGH
Faculty of Engineering: Dr K. P. SINGH
Faculty of Humanities: Dr I. K. MASIH
Faculty of Law: Dr D. N. MISHRA
Faculty of Management: Dr M. MURARI
Faculty of Medicine: Dr M. S. KUMAR
Faculty of Science: Dr R. L. PRASAD
Faculty of Social Science and Education: Dr B. SINGH

PROFESSORS

AGRAWAL, B. N., Political Science
AGRAWAL, N. C., Commerce
AMBASHTHA, A. V., Commerce
GUPTA, L. N., Commerce
JHA, B. K., Political Science
LAL, B. K., Philosophy
MISHRA, C. N., Sanskrit
NATH, B., Philosophy
PRASAD, B. K., Philosophy
PRASAD, B. N., Mathematics
PRASAD, N., English
ROY, L. M., Economics
ROY, P., Hindi
SAHAI, S., Ancient Indian and Asian Studies
SHRIVASTAVA, J. P., Chemistry
SINGH, A. N., Physics
SINGH, B. K., Psychology
SINGH, B. P., Political Science
SINGH, G. P., Physics
SINGH, H. G., Economics
SINGH, J. P., English
SINGH, R. C. P., Ancient Indian and Asian Studies
SINGH, S., Mathematics
SINGH, S. B., Zoology
SINHA, D. P., Zoology
SINHA, H. P., Philosophy
SINHA, N. C. P., Psychology
SINHA, S. P., Economics
SINHA, V. N., Philosophy
THAKUR, U., Ancient Indian and Asian Studies
TIWARY, P., Mathematics
VERMA, B. B., Commerce
VISHESHWARAM, S., Mathematics

ATTACHED INSTITUTES

Mishra, L. N., Institute of Economic Development and Social Change: Hon. Dir Dr CHAKERDHAR SINGH.

Nava Nalanda Mehavihar: Nalanda; postgraduate teaching in Pali and research in

Pali literature with special reference to Buddhism; Dir Dr U. THAKUR.

Rajendra Memorial Research Institute of Medical Science: postgraduate research in conjunction with the Faculty of Medicine; Dir Dr LALA SURAYNANDAN PRASAD.

Sri D. K. Jain Orient Research Institute: Arrah; postgraduate research in Prakrit, Jain philosophy and religion; Hon. Dir Dr RAJA RAM JAIN.

MAHARAJA SAYAJIRAO UNIVERSITY OF BARODA

Vadodara 390002, Gujarat

Telephone: (265) 2795521
Fax: (265) 2792277
E-mail: registrar@msubaroda.ac.in
Internet: www.msubaroda.ac.in

Founded 1949

Residential and teaching
Language of instruction: English
Academic year: June to April (two terms)

Vice-Chancellor: Dr RAMESH K. GOYAL
Pro-Vice-Chancellor: Prof. SHARADCHANDRA M. JOSHI
Registrar: A. V. GUPTA
Librarian: (vacant)

Library of 404,043 vols
Number of teachers: 1,230
Number of students: 35,000

Publications: *Journal of Animal Morphology and Physiology, Journal of Education and Psychology, Journal of Oriental Institute, Journal of Technology and Engineering* (1 a year), *Pavo, Swadhyaya*

DEANS

Faculty of Arts: Prof. NITIN J. VYAS
Faculty of Commerce: (vacant)
Faculty of Education and Psychology: Prof. S. KUMAR
Faculty of Family and Community Sciences: Prof. P. MOHITE
Faculty of Fine Arts: Prof. D. H. KANNAL
Faculty of Journalism and Communication: (vacant)
Faculty of Law: (vacant)
Faculty of Management Studies: Prof. G. C. MAHESHWARI
Faculty of Medicine: (vacant)
Faculty of Performing Arts: (vacant)
Faculty of Science: (vacant)
Faculty of Social Work: Prof. A. KHASGIWALA
Faculty of Technology and Engineering: Prof. B. S. PAREKH

PROFESSORS

Faculty of Arts:

CHOODAWAT, P. S., Sociology
JUNEJA, O. P., English
KAR, P., English
MEHTA, S. Y., Gujarati
MOHITE, D. H., Political Science
PANDYA, N. M., Economics
PANTHAM, T., Political Science
PAREKH, V. S., Archaeology
PATEL, K. H., Environmental Archaeology
PATEL, P. J., Sociology
REDE, L. A., Economics
SHAH, M. N., Economics
SIDDIQI, M. H., Persian
SONAWANE, V. H., Archaeology

Faculty of Commerce:

BHATT, A. S., Commerce and Business Administration
MOHITE, M. D., Cooperation
PANCHOLI, P. R., Business Economics
PATEL, B. S., Commerce and Business Administration
SANDHE, A. G., Commerce and Business Administration
SHAH, K. R., Economics

SINGH, S. K., Business Economics
SYAN, J. K., Banking and Business Finance
VYAS, I. P., Commerce and Business Administration

Faculty of Education and Psychology:

GOEL, D., Education
JOSHI, S. M., Educational Administration
YADAV, M. S., Education

Faculty of Fine Arts:

PANCHAL, R. R., Sculpture
PATEL, V. S., Graphic Arts

Faculty of Home Science:

BALKRISHNAIH, B., Clothing and Textiles
MANI, U. V., Foods and Nutrition
SARASWATI, T. S., Human Development and Family Studies
SHAH, A., Home Science Extension and Communication

Faculty of Law:

PARIKH, S. N., Law
RATHOD, J. C., Law

Faculty of Management Studies:

DADI, M. M., Management
DHOLAKIA, M. N., Management
JOSHI, K. M., Management
MAHESHWARI, G. C., Management

Faculty of Medicine:

BHOTI, S. J., Ophthalmology
BONDRE, K. V., Anatomy
BUCH, V. P., Radiology
CHANDWANI, S., Physiology
CHAUHAN, L. M., Obstetrics and Gynaecology
DESAI, M. R., Obstetrics and Gynaecology
GHOSH, S., Biochemistry
HATHI, G., Physiology
HEMAVATI, K. G., Pharmacology
JHALA, D. R., Paediatrics
JOSHI, G. D., Preventative and Social Medicine
KARELIA, L. S., Pathology
MAZUMDAR, U., Dentistry
MEHTA, J. P., Surgery
MEHTA, N. C., Medicine
PATHAK, K., Medicine
PATRA, B. S., Surgery
PATRA, S. B., Pathology
RAWAL, H. H., Anaesthesia
SAINATH, M., Ophthalmology
SANGHVI, N. G., Medicine
SAXENA, S. B., Microbiology
SHAH, A. U., Preventative and Social Medicine
SHAH, D. N., Preventative and Social Medicine
SHAK, K. D., Surgery
SHARMA, S. N., Plastic Surgery
SHETH, R. T., Ophthalmology
SHUKLA, G. N., Surgery
TIWARI, R. S., Ear, Nose and Throat
VAISHNAVI, A. J., Orthopaedics
VANKAR, G. K., Psychiatry
VOHRA, P. A., Radiology
VYAS, D. C., Anatomy

Faculty of Performing Arts:

BHONSLE, D. K., Vocal Music
SHAH, P., Dance

Faculty of Science:

AMBADKAR, P. M., Zoology
BHATTACHARYA, P. K., Chemistry
CHATTOO, B., Microbiology
CHHATPAR, H. S., Microbiology
DESAI, N. D., Geology
DESAI, S. J., Geology
DEVI, S. G., Chemistry
GOYAL, O. P., Mathematics
KATYARE, S. S., Biochemistry
MEHTA, T., Biochemistry
PADH, H., Biochemistry
PAREKH, L. J., Biochemistry
PATEL, H. C., Statistics
PATEL, M. P., Geology

PATEL, N. V., Mathematics
PILO, B., Zoology
RAKSHIT, A. K., Chemistry
RAMCHANDRAN, A. V., Zoology
RANGASWAMY, V. C., Geography
RAO, K. K., Microbiology
SHAH, A. C., Chemistry
SHREEHARI, M., Statistics
SOMAYAJULU, D. R. S., Physics
TELANG, S. D., Biochemistry

Faculty of Social Work:

ANJARIA, V. N., Social Work
NAVALE, A. S., Social Work
SAXENA, S. B., Social Work

Faculty of Technology and Engineering:

AGRAWAL, S. K., Metallurgical Engineering
AGRAWAL, S. R., Applied Mathematics
BALARAMAN, R., Pharmacy
BANGLORE, V. A., Textile Engineering
BASA, D. K., Metallurgical Engineering
BHAGIA, R. M., Applied Mechanics
BHATT, G. D., Mechanical Engineering
BHATT, R. D., Civil Engineering
BHAVNANI, H. V., Civil Engineering
BHAVSAR, N., Electrical Engineering
BIYANI, K. R., Applied Mechanics
CHUDASAMA, U. V., Applied Chemistry
DE, D. K., Textile Engineering
DESAI, P. B., Mechanical Engineering
DESHPANDE, S. V., Architecture
DIVEKAR, M. H., Chemical Engineering
ETHIRAJULU, K., Chemical Engineering
GADGEEL, V. I., Metallurgical Engineering
GOROOR, S. P., Water Management
GUHA, S., Textile Chemistry
GUPTE, S. G., Electrical Engineering
JOSHI, S. M., Electrical Engineering
JOSHI, T. R., Applied Physics
KANITKAR, S. A., Electrical Engineering
KAPADIA, V. H., Textile Engineering
LOIWAL, A. S., Mechanical Engineering
MISHRA, A. N. R., Pharmacy
MISHRA, S. H., Pharmacy
MODI, P. M., Water Management
MOINUDDIN, S., Chemical Engineering
MORTHY, R. S. R., Pharmacy
NANAVATI, J. I., Mechanical Engineering
PAI, K. B., Metallurgical Engineering
PAREKH, B. S., Computer Science
PARMAR, N. B., Civil Engineering
PATEL, A. A., Mechanical Engineering
PATEL, B. A., Electrical Engineering
PATEL, H. J., Computer Science
PATEL, N. M., Applied Mechanics
PATHAK, V. D., Applied Mathematics
PATODI, S. C., Applied Mechanics
POTBHARE, V. N., Applied Physics
PRAJAPATI, J. J., Civil Engineering
PURANIK, S. A., Chemical Engineering
PUTHANPURAYIL, P., Mechanical Engineering
RAJPUT, H. G., Training and Placement
SAVANI, A. K., Civil Engineering
SHAH, A. N., Civil Engineering
SHAH, D. L., Applied Mechanics
SHAH, S. G., Electrical Engineering
SHROFF, A. V., Applied Mechanics
SUBRAMANYAM, N., Chemical Engineering
SUKLA, H. J., Mechanical Engineering
SUNDAR MORTI, N. S., Metallurgical Engineering
SUTARIA, P. N., Civil Engineering
THAKUR, S. A., Electrical Engineering
TRIVEDI, A. I., Electrical Engineering
VASDEV, S., Chemical Engineering
VORA, R. A., Applied Chemistry
VYAS, J. K., Applied Mechanics
YADAV, R., Pharmacy

Centre for Continuing and Adult Education and Community Services:

PARALIKAR, K. R.

Oriental Institute:

NANAVATI, R. I.
WADEKAR, M. L.

CONSTITUENT COLLEGES

Baroda Sanskrit Mahavidyalaya: Vadodara; f. 1915; Prin. Y. B. OAZ.

Manibhai Kashibai Amin Arts and Science College and College of Commerce: Padra; f. 1965; Prin. G. S. PATEL.

Oriental Institute: tel. (265) 2425121; e-mail mlwadekar@hotmail.com; Dir Prof. M. L. WADEKAR.

Polytechnic: Vadodara; f. 1957; Prin. K. S. AGRAWAL.

ATTACHED CENTRE

Women's Studies Research Centre: tel. (265) 2792106; Dir Dr P. D. MUKHERJEE.

MAHARANA PRATAP UNIVERSITY OF AGRICULTURE AND TECHNOLOGY

Udaipur 313001, Rajasthan

Telephone: (294) 2471101

Fax: (294) 2470682

E-mail: vc@mpuat.ac.in

Internet: mpuat.digitaluniversity.ac.in

Founded 1999

Chancellor: HE THE GOVERNOR OF RAJASTHAN
Vice-Chancellor: Dr PRATAP NARAIN
Registrar: ASHOK YADAV
Dir of Extension Education: Dr P. M. JAIN
Dir of Research: Dr P. SINGH
Controller of Examinations: Dr S. C. BHANDARI
Librarian: Dr R. SWAMINATHAN
Library of 144,354 vols, 252 journals

DEANS

Rajasthan College of Agriculture: Dr V. N. JOSHI
College of Dairy and Food Science Technology: Dr N. S. RATHORE
College of Fisheries: Dr V. N. JOSHI
College of Home Science: Dr M. CHOUDHARY
College of Horticulture and Forestry (Jhalawar): Dr S. K. SHARMA
College of Technology and Engineering: Dr V. KUMAR

ATTACHED RESEARCH INSTITUTE

Land and Water Management Research Institute: Dir Dr RAJVEER SINGH.

MAHARASHTRA ANIMAL AND FISHERY SCIENCES UNIVERSITY

Seminary Hills, Nagpur 440006, Maharashtra

Telephone: (712) 2511784

Fax: (712) 2511282

E-mail: mafsudet@yahoo.co.in

Internet: www.mafsu.in

Founded 2000

Chancellor: HE THE GOV. OF MAHARASHTRA
Pro-Chancellor: MIN. FOR ANIMAL HUSBANDRY DIARY DEVT AND FISHERY DEVT, MAHARASHTRA STATE
Vice-Chancellor: Dr A. S. NINAWE
Dir of Extension and Training: Dr S. Z. ALI
Dir of Instructions: Dr S. H. NARAYANKHEDKAR
Dir of Research and Registrar: Dr R. L. DHOBLE
Univ. Librarian: S. N. GAWANDE

DEANS

Faculty of Dairy Technology: Dr D. N. BAJAD
Faculty of Fishery Science: Dr D. R. KALORE
Faculty of Veterinary Science: Dr S. G. NARAYANKHEDKAR
Lower Education: Dr D. B. SARODE

CONSTITUENT COLLEGES

Bombay Veterinary College: Parel, Mumbai 400012; tel. (22) 24130162; fax (22) 24172301; e-mail vetsamad@yahoo.com; f. 1886; Dean Dr A. SAMAD.

College of Dairy Technology: Udgir, Dist. Latur 413517; tel. (2385) 257448; fax (2385) 2563506; e-mail cdkhedkar@gmail.com; f. 2008; Dean Dr C. D. KHEDKAR.

College of Dairy Technology: Warud (Pusat), Dist. Yavatmal 445204; tel. (7233) 247269; fax (7233) 247268; e-mail dtc@mafsu.in; f. 1992; Dean Dr D. N. BAJAD.

College of Fishery Science: Nagpur 440006; tel. and fax (712) 2567192; e-mail dewanandkalorey@rediffmail.com; f. 2007; Dean Dr D. R. KALORE.

College of Fishery Science: Udgir , Dist. Latur 413517; tel. (2385) 256672; fax (2385) 256690; e-mail adfish.udgir@gmail.com; f. 2006; Dean Dr B. R. KHARATMOL.

College of Veterinary and Animal Sciences, Parbhani: Parbhani 431402; tel. (2452) 220044; fax (2452) 226188; e-mail bhosle_ns@rediffmail.com; f. 1972; Dean Dr N. S. BHONSLE.

College of Veterinary and Animal Sciences, Udgir: Udgir, Dist. Latur 413517; tel. (2385) 257448; fax (2385) 2563506; e-mail udgirvet@yahoo.com; f. 1987; Dean Dr R. C. TAKARKHEDE.

Krantisinh Nana Patil College of Veterinary Science: Satara Dist., Shirval 412801; tel. (2169) 244227; fax (2169) 244243; e-mail deanknpvet@yahoo.co.in; f. 1988; Dean Dr A. G. KHARPE.

Nagpur Veterinary College: Seminary Hills, Nagpur 440006; tel. (712) 2511259; fax (712) 2510883; e-mail dean_nvc1@rediffmail.com; f. 1958; Dean Dr C. R. JANGDE.

Postgraduate Institute of Veterinary and Animal Sciences, Akola: Murtizapur Rd, Akola 444104; tel. (724) 2258643; fax (724) 2258644; e-mail drvhkalbande@rediffmail.com; f. 1970; Dean Dr V. H. KALBANDE.

MAHARASHTRA UNIVERSITY OF HEALTH SCIENCES

Vani-Dindori Rd, Mhasrul, Nashik 422004, Maharashtra

Telephone: (253) 2539292

Fax: (253) 2539295

E-mail: registrar@muhsnashik.com

Internet: www.muhsnashik.com

Founded 1998

Academic year: June to May

Faculties of allied health sciences, ayurveda, dentistry, homeopathy and medicine; 297 affiliated colleges

Chancellor: HE THE GOV. OF MAHARASHTRA
Vice-Chancellor: Dr NILIMA A. KSHIRSAGAR (acting)
Registrar: Dr SUNIL H. FUGARE

DEANS

Allied Health Sciences Faculty: Dr RESHMA DESAI
Ayurveda Faculty: Dr S. G. DESHMUKH
Dental Faculty: Dr M. G. PAWAR
Homeopathy Faculty: Dr A. N. BHASME
Medical Faculty: Dr S. D. DALVI

MAHARISHI MAHESH YOGI VEDIC VISHWAVIDYALAYA

Karaundi, Sihora, Paan Umariya, Katni 483332, Madhya Pradesh

Telephone: (7625) 220343

E-mail: mmyvv@mahaemail.com

Internet: www.mmyvv.com/mmyvv-e

Founded 1995

Vice-Chancellor: Prof. BHUVNESH SHARMA

Registrar: PYARE L. KADALBAJU.

MAHARSHI DAYANAND SARASWATI UNIVERSITY

Ajmer 305001, Rajasthan

Telephone: (145) 2787055

Fax: (145) 2787049

Internet: www.mdsuajmer.com

Founded 1987 as Ajmer University; present name c. 1992

Vice-Chancellor: Prof. BHAGIRATH SINGH
Registrar: B. L. SUNARIA

There are 89 affiliated colleges

DEANS

Faculty of Commerce: Dr SHER SINGH DOCHANIYA
Faculty of Education: Dr V. G. JADHAV
Faculty of Fine Arts: Dr S. S. CHUG
Faculty of Law: MADAN LAL PEETLIYA
Faculty of Management Studies: Prof. MANOJ KUMAR
Faculty of Science: Dr SARVESH PALRIA
Faculty of Social Science: Dr R. P. JOSHI

PROFESSORS

BHARDWAJ, T. N., Botany
DUBE, S. N., Mathematics
JOSHI, R. P., Political Science
VASHISHTHA, V. K., History

MAHARSHI DAYANAND UNIVERSITY, ROHTAK

Rohtak 124001, Haryana

Telephone: (1262) 274327

Fax: (1262) 294133

E-mail: mduniversity@yahoomail.com

Internet: www.mdurohtak.com

Founded 1976

Affiliating; 448 affiliated colleges
Languages of instruction: English, Hindi
Academic year: July to June

Chancellor: HE THE GOV. OF HARYANA
Vice-Chancellor: Prof. R. P. HOODA
Registrar: Dr S. P. VATS
Dean of College Devt Ccl: Dr D. SINGH
Dean of Student Welfare: Dr R. SINGH
Dir of Distance Education: Prof. N. KUMAR
Librarian: (vacant)

Library of 235,155 vols, 400 periodicals
Number of teachers: 300
Number of students: 186,665

Publication: *Maharishi Dayanand University Rohtak Research Journal (Arts)* (2 a year)

DEANS

Faculty of Commerce: Dr M. S. MALIK
Faculty of Education: Dr I. DHULL
Faculty of Engineering and Technology: Dr V. K. SINGH
Faculty of Humanities: Dr S. P. S. DAHIYA
Faculty of Law: Dr C. P. SHEORAN
Faculty of Life Sciences: Dr S. N. MISHRA
Faculty of Management Sciences: Dr A. K. RAJAN
Faculty of Performing and Visual Arts: Dr B. SHARMA
Faculty of Pharmaceutical Sciences: Dr A. NANDA
Faculty of Physical Sciences: Dr N. SINGH
Faculty of Social Sciences: Dr K. S. SANGWAN

MAINTAINED INSTITUTE

Institute of Law and Management Studies, Gurgaon: tel. (124) 2580098; fax (124) 2383343; e-mail ilmsmdu@gmail.com; f. 2002; Dir Dr R. K. SABHARWAL, Law Programmes: Dr POONAM DATTA, Management Programmes.

MAHATAMA GANDHI ANTARRASHTRIYA HINDI VISHWAVIDYALAYA

Post Manas Mandir, Gandhi Hill, Wardha 442001, Maharashtra
Telephone: (7152) 230907
Fax: (7152) 230903
E-mail: info@hindivishwa.org
Internet: www.hindivishwa.org
Founded 1997
Academic year: July to May

Vice-Chancellor: Prof. VIBHUTI NARAIN RAI
Pro-Vice-Chancellor: Prof. NADEEM HASNAIN
Registrar: Dr K. G. KHAMARE
Finance Officer: M. S. KHAN

Publications: *Bahuvachan* (in Hindi, 4 a year), *Hindi: Language, Discourse, Writing* (in English, 4 a year), *Hindi Vishwa Samachar* (in Hindi, house journal), *Pustak Varta* (in Hindi, 24 a year)

DEANS

School of Culture: Prof. MANOJ KUMAR
School of Language: Prof. UMASHANKAR UPADHYAY
School of Literature: Prof. SURAJ PALIWAL
School of Translation and Interpretation: Prof. A. P. SRIVASTAVA

CENTRES

Adult Continuing Education Extension and Field Outreach Centre: tel. (7151) 242812; e-mail klvp_k@yahoo.com; Dir Prof. K. VASWANI (acting).

Dr Babasaheb Ambedkar Dalit and Tribal Studies Centre: Dir Prof. L. KARUNYAKARA.

Distance Education Centre: Dir Prof. NADEEM HASNAIN.

Indian and Foreign Language Advanced Studies Centre.

Dr Bhadant Anand Kausalyayan, Buddhist Studies Centre: Dir M. L. KASARE.

Technology Studies Centre: e-mail mahendra@hindivishwa.org; Dean Prof. MAHENDRA KUMAR PANDEY.

Mahatma Gandhi Fuiji Guru Ji Peace Studies Centre: Dir Dr MANOJ KUMAR.

MAHATMA GANDHI CHITRAKOOT GRAMODAYA VISHWAVIDYALAYA

District Satna, Chitrakoot 485331, Madhya Pradesh
Telephone: (7670) 265413
Fax: (7670) 265411
E-mail: mgcgv@rediffmail.com
Internet: www.ruraluniversity-chitrakoot.org
Founded 1991
Academic year: July to June

Vice-Chancellor: Prof. G. SINGH
Registrar: Dr R. S. TRIPATHI
Librarian: Dr R. P. BAJPAL

Library of 32,644 vols, 54 journals

DEANS

Faculty of Agriculture and Animal Sciences: Dr A. K. GUPTA
Faculty of Ayurveda: E. A. UPADHYAY
Faculty of Commerce: Dr Y. UPADHYAY
Faculty of Education: Dr S. R. S. SENGAR
Faculty of Fine Arts: Prof. K. D. MISHRA
Faculty of Humanities and Social Sciences: Dr A. VERMA
Faculty of Rural Reconstruction: Dr R. C. SINGH
Faculty of Science: Dr R. C. TRIPATHI

MAHATMA GANDHI KASHI VIDYAPEETH

Varanasi 221002, Uttar Pradesh
Telephone: (542) 2222689
Fax: (542) 2221268
E-mail: support@mgkvp.ac.in
Internet: www.mgkvp.ac.in

Chancellor: HE THE GOVERNOR OF UTTAR PRADESH
Vice-Chancellor: NITIM RAMESH GOKARN
Registrar: BALJI YADAV
Finance Officer: Prof. NAND LAL
Controller of Examinations: PRABHAT RANJAN
Dean of Student Welfare: Dr K. PANDEY

DEANS

Faculty of Commerce and Management: Prof. M. D. SHUKLA
Faculty of Education: Prof. M. K. DAS
Faculty of Humanities: Prof. R. K. RAI
Faculty of Law: Dr S. C. SINGH
Faculty of Medical Sciences: Dr P. N. DWIVEDI
Faculty of Science and Technology: Prof. SATYA SINGH
Faculty of Social Sciences: Prof. O. P. SRIVASTAVA
Faculty of Social Work: Prof. A. S. I. SHASTRI
Mahamana Madan Mohan Malviya Institute of Hindi Journalism: Prof. O. P. SINGH

MAHATMA GANDHI UNIVERSITY

Priyadarshini Hills PO, Kottayam 686560, Kerala
Telephone: (481) 2731050
Fax: (481) 2731009
E-mail: mgu@md2.vsnl.net.in
Internet: www.mguniversity.edu
Founded 1983 as Gandhiji Univ.
State control
Language of instruction: English
Academic year: June to March

21 Univ. depts, 27 engineering colleges, 1 law college, 4 medical colleges, 22 nursing colleges, 8 sme nursing insts, 3 centres of school of technology and applied sciences, 5 pharmacy colleges, 7 dental colleges, 3 ayurveda colleges, 2 homeopathic colleges, 3 allied medical education colleges, 1 music and fine arts college; 127 affiliated arts and science colleges, 43 education training colleges and 12 univ. colleges of teacher education; 76 off-campus centres—62 centres within Kerala, 7 outside Kerala and 7 abroad; 10 interdisciplinary schools of teaching and research, 12 schools of higher learning in applied science and professional studies, with academic autonomy; 245 affiliating colleges of which 163 are in the unaided stream; central library and 21 deptl libraries

Chancellor: HE THE GOV. OF KERALA
Vice-Chancellor: Prof. Dr RAJAN GURUKKAL
Pro-Vice-Chancellor: Prof. Dr RAJAN VARUGHESE
Registrar: Prof. M. R. UNNI
Controller of Examinations: Dr THOMAS JOHN MAMPRA
Finance Officer: ABRAHAM J. PUTHUMANA
Dir of College Devt Council: Dr B. THOMAS
Public Relations Officer: G. SREEKUMAR
Librarian: Dr R. R. NAIR

Library: 2,500 online nat. and int. journals
Number of teachers: 5,000
Number of students: 150,000

DEANS

Medical College: Dr J. JACOB K.
School of Behavioural Sciences: Dr R. PADMAM
School of Chemical Sciences: Dr M. PADMANABHAN,
School of Environmental Sciences: Dr A. P. THOMAS

School of Gandhian Thought and Devt Studies: Dr M. MAHARAJAN
School of Indian Legal Thought: Prof. Dr K. VIKRAMAN NAIR
School of Letters: Dr V. C. HARRIS
School of Management and Business Studies: Dr K. SREERANGANATHAN
School of Medical Education: Prof. K. M. MARIAM
School of Pedagogical Sciences: Prof. Dr P. J. JACOB
School of Pure and Applied Physics: Dr C. VENUGOPAL

MAHATMA JYOTIBA PHULE ROHILKHAND UNIVERSITY

Pilibhit by-pass Rd, Bareilly 243006, Uttar Pradesh
Telephone: (581) 2527263
Fax: (581) 2523334
Internet: mjpru.ac.in
Founded 1975 as Rohilkhand Univ., present name 1997
State control
Languages of instruction: Hindi, English
Academic year: July to June
130 Affiliated colleges

Chancellor: HE THE GOVERNOR OF UTTAR PRADESH
Vice-Chancellor: Prof. SATYA P. GAUTAM
Registrar: B. K. PANDEY
Finance Officer: VIMAL PRAKASH SRIVASTAVA
Librarian: Prof. A. K. SINHA

Library of 27,000 vols, 140 periodicals
Number of teachers: 1,062
Number of students: 65,000

DEANS

Faculty of Advanced Social Sciences: Prof. R. P. YADAV
Faculty of Agriculture: Dr P. VEER
Faculty of Applied Science: Prof. A. K. JAITLY
Faculty of Arts: Dr S. SHARMA
Faculty of Commerce: Dr B. N. CHAURASIA
Faculty of Dental Sciences: (vacant)
Faculty of Education: Dr B. R. GUPTA
Faculty of Engineering and Technology: Prof. A. K. GUPTA
Faculty of Law: Dr S. K. SINGH
Faculty of Management: Prof. A. K. SARKAR
Faculty of Sciences: Prof. Y. K. GUPTA

MAHATMA PHULE KRISHI VIDYAPEETH

Rahuri, Ahmednagar Dist. 413722, Maharashtra
Internet: mpkv.mah.nic.in
Founded 1968
Academic year: July to May

Chancellor: HE THE GOVERNOR OF MAHARASHTRA
Pro-Chancellor: THE MINISTER FOR AGRICULTURE
Vice-Chancellor: Dr R. B. DESHMUKH
Registrar: BABASAHEB R. PARDHE
Librarian: A. G. KARANDE

Library of 62,864 vols
Number of students: 2,200

Publications: *Journal of Maharashtra Agricultural University* (in English, 3 a year), *Shi Suga* (in Marathi, 3 a year)

DEANS

Faculty of Agricultural Engineering: Prof. R. K. PARKALE
Faculty of Agriculture: Dr S. S. KADAM

CONSTITUENT COLLEGES

College of Agricultural Engineering, Rahuri: f. 1969; Assoc. Dean Prof. G. B. BANGAL.

College of Agriculture, Dhule: f. 1960; Assoc. Dean Dr Y. M. SHINDE.

College of Agriculture, Kolhapur: f. 1963; Assoc. Dean Prof. S. T. KANJALE.

College of Agriculture, Pune: f. 1906; library of 37,838 vols, 50 periodicals; Assoc. Dean Dr V. M. PAWAR.

Postgraduate Agricultural Institute, Rahuri: f. 1972; library of 80,000 vols; Assoc. Dean Dr S. S. KADAM.

MAKHANLAL CHATURVEDI RASHTRIYA PATRAKARITA VISHWAVIDYALAYA

POB RSN/560, Trilochan Singh Nagar, Shahpura, Bhopal 462016, Madhya Pradesh

Telephone: (755) 2725307
Fax: (755) 2561970
E-mail: query@mcu.ac.in
Internet: www.mcu.ac.in
Founded 1991
Academic year: August to July

Vice-Chancellor: ACHYUTANAND C. MISHRA
Dir: O. P. DUBEY
Registrar: ANIL CHOUBEY
Librarian: G. N. VYAS

Library of 15,000 vols

Publication: *Vidura* (in Hindi and English)

Depts of Broadcast Journalism, Communication and Public Relations, Computer Applications and Journalism, Library and Information Science.

MANGALORE UNIVERSITY

Mangalagangotri 574199, Karnataka
Telephone: (824) 2287276
Fax: (824) 2287367
E-mail: info@mangaloreuniversity.ac.in
Internet: www.mangaloreuniversity.ac.in
Founded 1980
Languages of instruction: English, Kannada
Academic year: June to April

25 Postgraduate depts; 2 constituent colleges; 4 law, 13 education, 5 autonomous and 119 affiliated colleges/instns

Chancellor: HE THE GOVERNOR OF KARNATAKA
Vice-Chancellor: Prof. K. M. KAVERIAPPA
Registrar: P. PREM KUMAR
Finance Officer: Prof. P. S. YADAPADITHAYA
Dir of College Devt Ccl: Dr W. LINDA CHRISTY
Dir of Student Welfare: Prof. K. CHINNAPPA GOWDA
Librarian: Dr M. K. BHANDI

Library of 150,428 vols
Number of teachers: 2,849
Number of students: 1,303 (university), 41,579 (affiliated colleges)

DEANS

Faculty of Arts: Prof. G. V. JOSHI
Faculty of Commerce: Prof. P. S. YADAPADITHAYA
Faculty of Education: Dr H. NAGALINGAPPA
Faculty of Law: Dr P. D. SEBASTIAN
Faculty of Science: K. K. ACHARY

MANIPUR UNIVERSITY

Canchipur, Imphal 795003, Manipur
Telephone: (385) 2435143
Fax: (385) 2435145
E-mail: vcmu@sancharnet.in
Internet: manipuruniv.ac.in
Founded 1980
Central university 2005
Central control
Language of instruction: English
Academic year: July to June

Chief Rector: HE THE GOVERNOR OF MANIPUR
Chancellor: Prof. P. N. SRIVASTAVA
Vice-Chancellor: Prof. C. AMUBA SINGH
Registrar: Dr N. LOKENDRA SINGH
Finance Officer: M. BIREN SINGH
Controller of Examinatons: H. RAJAMANI SINGH
Dean of Student Welfare: Prof. TH. RATANKUMAR SINGH
Dir of College Devt Council: Prof. R. K. RANJAN SINGH
Librarian: Dr TH. KHOMDON SINGH

72 Affiliated colleges

Library of 156,811 vols, 205 nat. and 38 int. journals
Number of teachers: 163 (postgraduate depts only)
Number of students: 1,792 (postgraduate depts only)

DEANS

School of Humanities: Prof. S. SANATOMBI SINGHA
School of Human and Environmental Science: Prof. W. NABAKUMAR SINGH
School of Life Sciences: Prof. G. JITENDRA SHARMA
School of Mathematical and Physical Sciences: Prof. R. K. GARTIA
School of Medical Sciences: Prof. W. GYANESHWAR SINGH
School of Social Sciences: Prof. AMAR YUMNAM

CONSTITUENT COLLEGE

Manipur Institute of Technology (MIT): Principal Dr TH. KULACHANDRA SINGH.

ATTACHED CENTRES

Centre for Human Rights and Duties Education: Dir Prof. K. IBO SINGH.

Centre for Manipur Studies: f. 2005; Dir Prof. AMAR YUMNAM.

Centre for Myanmar Studies: f. 1989; Dir Prof. W. NABAKUMAR SINGH.

Centre for Social Exclusion & Inclusive Policy: Dir Prof. L. TOMBI SINGH.

Educational Multimedia Research Centre: f. 1989; Dir Dr N. PREMCHAND SINGH.

MANONMANIAM SUNDARANAR UNIVERSITY

Abishekapatti, Tirunelveli 627012, Tamil Nadu
Telephone: (462) 2333741
Fax: (462) 2334363
E-mail: tvl_regismsu@sancharnet.in
Internet: www.msuniversity.org.in
Founded 1990

Teaching and affiliating; depts of information technology and engineering, marine sciences and technology, chemistry, communication, computer science and engineering, criminology and criminal justice, English, environmental sciences, history, library and information science, management studies, mandatory disclosure of information, mathematics, physics, sociology, sports and physical education, statistics, Tamil; 70 affiliated colleges

Chancellor: HE THE GOVERNOR OF TAMIL NADU
Vice-Chancellor: Dr R. T. SABAPATHY MOHAN
Registrar: Dr S. GOPALAKRISHNAN
Finance Officer: S. RAMAKRISHNAN
Controller of Examinations: Dr N. ARUNACHALAM
Librarian: P. ALANGARABABU.

MARATHWADA AGRICULTURAL UNIVERSITY

Parbhani, 431402, Maharashtra
Telephone: (2452) 223801
Fax: (2452) 223582
E-mail: vcmau@rediffmail.com
Internet: mkv2.mah.nic.in
Founded 1972
State control
Language of instruction: English
16 Affiliated research stations
Academic year: June to May

Chancellor: HE THE GOVERNOR OF MAHARASHTRA
Vice-Chancellor: Dr S. S. KADAM
Registrar: Dr K. M. LAWANDE
Librarian: B. T. MUNDHE

Library of 62,405 vols, 229 periodicals
Number of teachers: 282
Number of students: 2,017

Publication: *Sheti Bhati* (Marathi, 12 a year)

PROFESSORS

Faculty of Agricultural Technology:

KULKARNI, D. N., Food Science and Cereal Technology
WANKHEDE, D. B., Biochemistry

Faculty of Agriculture:

CHAVAN, B. N., Agronomy
DHAVAN, A. S., Agricultural Chemistry and Soil Science
GORE, K. P., Agricultural Engineering
JANDHALE, S. G., Agricultural Extension
KULKARNI, U. G., Plant Physiology
NADRE, K. R., Agricultural Extension
NARWADKAR, P. R., Horticulture
PAWAR, N. D., Agricultural Economics and Statistics
SHELKE, D. K., Agronomy
SONTAKKE, M. B., Horticulture

Faculty of Home Science:

MURALI, D., Home Management
PATANAM, V., Child Development and Family Relations
ROHINDEVI, P., Food and Nutrition

CONSTITUENT COLLEGES

College of Agricultural Engineering: Parbhani; Prin. Dr G. R. MORE.

College of Agricultural Technology: Parbhani; Prin. Dr D. B. WANKHEDE.

College of Agriculture, Ambajogai: Ambajogai; Prin. Dr B. K. DHANORKAR.

College of Agriculture, Badnapur: Badnapur; Prin. Dr H. N. PATIL.

College of Agriculture, Latur: Latur; Prin. Dr K. K. ZOTE.

College of Agriculture, Osmanabad: Osmanabad; Prin. Dr V. G. REDDY.

College of Agriculture, Parbhani: Parbhani; Prin. Dr M. V. DHOBALE.

College of Home Science: Parbhani; Prin. Prof. D. MURALI.

College of Horticulture: Parbhani; Prin. Dr B. A. KADAM.

MAULANA AZAD NATIONAL URDU UNIVERSITY

Gochibowli, Hyderabad 500032, Andhra Pradesh
Telephone: (40) 23006612
Fax: (40) 23006603
E-mail: manuu@indiainfo.com
Internet: www.manuu.ac.in
Founded 1998
Central univ.
State control
Chancellor: Dr OBEID SIDDIQUI
Vice-Chancellor: Prof. A. M. PATHAN

Registrar: Prof. K. R. IQBAL AHMED
Finance Officer: Y. JAYANT RAO
Librarian: Dr ABBAS KHAN

Library of 14,500 vols, 54 periodicals
Number of students: 56,000
12 Depts, 104 study centres

DEANS

School of Education and Training: Prof. H. KHATIJA BEGUM
School of Languages, Linguistics and Indology: Prof. K. SAEED
School of Mass Communication and Journalism: Prof. A. NISAM
School of Political Science and Public Admin.: Prof. S. M. RAHMATULLAH

REGIONAL CENTRES

Bangalore Regional Centre—MANUU: Al-Ameen Commercial Complex, POB 27058, 2nd Fl., Hosur Rd, Bangalore 560027, Karnataka; tel. (80) 22228329; Dir KHAZI ZIAULLAH.

Bhopal Regional Centre—MANUU: 12 Ahmedabad Palace, Koh-e-Fiza, Bhopal, Madhya Pradesh; tel. (755) 2736930; Dir Dr MOHD AHSAN.

Darbhanga Regional Centre—MANUU: Super Market, Moula Ganj, Darbhanga 846 004, Bihar; tel. (6272) 258755; Dir Dr S. E. H. IMAM AZAM.

Delhi Regional Centre—MANUU: B-1/275, Ground Fl., Zaidi Apts, TIT Rd Okhla, Jamia Nagar, New Delhi, 110025; tel. (11) 26934762; fax (11) 26838260; Dir Dr SHAHID PERVEZ.

Kolkata Regional Centre—MANUU: Flat 5, 2nd Fl., 9A Lower Range, Kolkata 700017, West Bengal; tel. (33) 22894568; Dir SAHAB SINGH.

New Mumbai Regional Centre—MANUU: A-1, CHS Ltd, F-1/6, 2nd Fl., Dev Hotel, Sector 5, Vahsi, New Mumbai 400703, Maharashtra; tel. 22-27820515; Dir Dr M. ARSHAD EKBAL.

Patna Regional Centre—MANUU: 2nd Fl., Bihar State Co-operative Bank Bldg, Ashok Rajpath, Patna 800004, Bihar; tel. (612) 2300413; Dir Dr HASNUDDIN HAIDER.

Srinagar Regional Centre—MANUU: 18B Jawahar Nagar, Srinagar 190001, Jammu and Kashmir; tel. (914) 2310221; Dir Dr ABDUL GHANI.

MAULANA MAZHARUL HAQUE ARABIC AND PERSIAN UNIVERSITY

Sandal Nagar, Mahendru, Patna 800006
Vice Chancellor: AHMAD MUKHTARUDDIN.

MIZORAM UNIVERSITY

POB 190, Aizwal 796009, Mizoram
Telephone: (389) 2330654
Fax: (389) 2330642
E-mail: registrar@mzu.edu.in
Internet: www.mzu.edu.in
Founded 2000

Central univ.; depts of biotechnology, botany, chemistry, commerce, economics, education, electronic engineering, English, extension education and rural development, forest ecology and forestry, geography, geology, history and ethnography, horticulture, aromatic and medicinal plants, information technology, library and information science, management, mathematics and computer science, physics, political science, psychology, public administration, social work, zoology; 31 affiliated colleges
Academic year: August to July
Language of instruction: English

Vice-Chancellor: Prof. A. N. RAI
Registrar: I. D. A. S. BENJAMINA
Dir of College Devt Ccl: S. K. GHOSH
Librarian: A. S. CHANDEL

Library of 63,538 vols, 369 periodicals
Number of teachers: 129
Number of students: 1,237

DEANS

School of Earth Sciences and Natural Resource Management: Prof. H. LALRAMN-GINGLOVA
School of Economics, Management and Information Sciences: Prof. LIANZELA
School of Education and Humanities: Prof. R. P. VADHERA
School of Engineering and Technology: Prof. R. P. TIWARI
School of Life Sciences: Prof. G. C. JAGETIA
School of Physical Sciences: Prof. R. P. TIWARI
School of Social Science: Prof. J. K. PATNAIK

CONSTITUENT SCHOOL

Pachhunga University College: College Veng, Aizawl; tel. (389) 2322257; fax (389) 2317524; f. 1958 as Aijal College; present name 1979; 2002 became constituent college; 84 teachers; 1,290 students; Prin. Dr TAW-NENGA (acting).

MOHAN LAL SUKHADIA UNIVERSITY

Pratap Nagar, Udaipur 313001, Rajasthan
Telephone: (294) 2471035
Fax: (294) 2471150
E-mail: registrar@mlsu.org
Internet: www.mlsu.org
Founded 1962 as Rajasthan Agricultural University, present name 1982

Teaching and Affiliating
Autonomous control
Languages of instruction: English, Hindi
Academic year: July to June

Chancellor: HE THE GOVERNOR OF RAJASTHAN
Vice-Chancellor: ARPANA ARORA
Registrar: MOHAN LAL SHARMA
Dean of Postgraduate Studies: Prof. I. V. TRIVEDI
Dean of Student Welfare: Prof. S. R. VYAS
Librarian: Prof. M. S. SHARMA

110 Affiliated colleges

Library of 287,000 vols
Number of teachers: 264
Number of students: 47,209

DEANS

Faculty of Commerce: Prof. K. C. SODANI
Faculty of Humanities: Prof. S. R. VYAS
Faculty of Management: Dr P. K. JAIN
Faculty of Science: Prof. MADHU SUDAN SHARMA
Faculty of Social Sciences: Prof. R. N. VYAS

CONSTITUENT COLLEGES

College of Commerce and Management Studies: Udaipur; tel. (294) 2412009; Dean Prof. K. C. SODANI.

College of Law: Udaipur; tel. (294) 2470958; Dean Prof. VIJAY SHRIMALI.

College of Science: Udaipur; tel. (294) 2413955; Dean Prof. MADHU SUDAN SHARMA.

College of Social Sciences and Humanities: Udaipur; tel. (294) 2470143; Dean Prof. R. N. VYAS.

MOTHER TERESA WOMEN'S UNIVERSITY

Kodaikanal 624102, Tamil Nadu
Telephone: (4542) 241122
Fax: (4542) 241122

E-mail: registrar@motherteresawomenuniv.ac.in
Internet: www.motherteresawomenuniv.ac.in

Founded 1984
State control
Languages of instruction: English, Tamil
Academic year: June to May

Depts of biotechnology, computer science, economics, education, English, family life management, historical studies and tourism management, management, music, physics, sociology, Tamil, visual communication; 4 affiliated colleges

Chancellor: HE THE GOV. OF TAMIL NADU
Vice-Chancellor: Dr ARUNA SIVAKAMI ANANTHAKRISHNAN
Registrar: Dr S. MANI
Finance Officer: P. K. SUBRAMANYAN
Controller of Examinations: Dr S. SUNDARI
Asst Librarians: Dr K. P. PADMAVATHI, P. SEMBIANMADEVI

Library of 87,000 vols
Number of teachers: 34
Number of students: 1,000

PROFESSORS

ARAVANAN, T., Tamil
PHIL, M., Education

ATTACHED RESEARCH AND EXTENSION CENTRES

Chennai Centre: Teacher's Training College Campus, Saidapet, Chennai 600015; tel. (44) 24347222.

Madurai Centre: MMSSS Sancta Maria, Chokkalinga Nagar, Bye Pass Rd, Madurai 625010; tel. (452) 2387355.

CONSTITUENT COLLEGES

Government Arts College for Women: Nilakottai.

Mother Teresa Women's University College: Kodaikanal; f. 1985.

M. V. Muthiah Pillai Arts College for Women: Dindigul.

AFFILIATED COLLEGES

Arulmigu Palaniandavar Arts College for Women: Chinnakalayamputhur 624615 Palani Taluk, Dindigul Dist.; tel. and fax (4545) 255128; e-mail admin@apacwomen.ac.in; internet www.apacwomen.ac.in; f. 1970; library of 30,162 vols.; Prin. Dr G. THEMOZHI; Librarian INDIRANI RAJAMANI; depts in Commerce, economics, English, history, mathematics and sciences, Tamil.

Jeyaraj Annapakiyam College for Women: Periyakulam Theni 625601, Tamil Nadu; tel. and fax (4546) 231482; e-mail secretary@annejac.com; internet www.annejac.com; f. 1971; Pres. Mother Xavier MARIA THANGAM; Prin. Dr Sr Y. YESU THANGAM.

Nadar Saraswathi Arts and Science College for Women: POB 55, Vadapudupatty, Annanji Theni 625531; tel. (4546) 269297; fax (4546) 269000; e-mail nsc-principal@yahoo.com; internet www.nadarsaraswathicollege.com; f. 1996; library of 10,000 vols.; Pres. Dr A. S. R. JEYASEELAN; Prin. Dr K. GIRIJA.

St Antony's College of Arts and Science for Women: Dindigul.

Sri Adi Chunchanagiri Women's College: Cumbum.

NAGALAND UNIVERSITY

Lumami, Kohima 797001, Nagaland
Telephone: (370) 2290331
Fax: (370) 2290246
E-mail: nagalanduniversity@yahoo.co.in
Internet: www.nagauniv.org.in

Founded 1994
Central university
State control
Language of instruction: English
Academic year: September to August
Chief Rector: HE THE GOVERNOR OF NAGA-
LAND
Chancellor: Prof. YOGINDER K. ALAGH
Vice-Chancellor: Prof. K. KANNAN
Registrar: T. VIHIENUO
Dean of Student Welfare: Dr B. V. RAO
Finance Officer: (vacant)
Librarian: LUCY BENDANG
Library of 32,916 vols, 75 periodicals
2 Further campuses at Kohima and Medzi-
phema; 42 affiliated colleges
Number of teachers: 112
Number of students: 19,151 (18,349 under-
graduate, 802 postgraduate)

DEANS

School of Agricultural Sciences and Rural
Development: Prof. IMNAYONGDANG
School of Humanities and Education: Prof.
IMTISUNGBA
School of Sciences: Prof. PARDESHI LAL
School of Social Sciences: Prof. A. K. MISHRA

NAGARJUNA UNIVERSITY

Nagarjuna Nagar 522510, Andhra Pradesh
Telephone: (863) 2293238
Internet: www.nagarjunauniversity.ac.in
Founded 1976
Language of instruction: English
Academic year: July to April
292 Affiliated colleges
Chancellor: HE THE GOV. OF ANDHRA PRADESH
Vice-Chancellor: Prof. Y. R. HARAGOPAL
REDDY
Prin.: Prof. NIRMALA MARY TURAKA
Registrar: M. V. N. SARMA
Rector: Prof. K. VIYYANNA RAO
Librarian: J. RAMA RAO
Library of 100,000 vols, 331 periodicals
Number of teachers: 148
Number of students: 1,700

DEANS

Faculty of Commerce: Prof. G. N. BRAHMA-
NANDAM
Faculty of Education: Dr G. BHUVANESWARA
LAKSHMI
Faculty of Engineering: Prof. G. NAGESWARA
RAO
Faculty of Humanities: Prof. G. KRUPACHARY,
Faculty of Law: Prof. A. SUBRAHMANYAM
Faculty of Natural Sciences: Prof. NIRMALA
MARY TURAKA
Faculty of Pharmacy: Prof. N. RAMA RAO
Faculty of Physical Sciences: Prof. LAM
PRAKASA RAO
Faculty of Social Sciences: C. S. N. RAJU

PROFESSORS

Faculty of Commerce:
BRAHMANANDAM, G. N., Commerce
DAKSHINA MURTHY, D., Commerce
GANJU, M. K., Commerce
HANUMANTHA RAO, K., Commerce
NARASIMHAM, V. V. L., Commerce
PRASAD, G., Commerce
UMAMAHESWARA RAO, T., Commerce
VIYYANNA RAO, K., Commerce
Faculty of Engineering:
THRIMURTY, P., Computer Science and
Engineering
Faculty of Humanities:
BALAGANGADHARA RAO, Y., Telugu and Lan-
guages
BHASKARA MURTHY, D., Ancient History
and Archaeology

KRUPACHARY, G., Telugu and Languages
KUMARASWAMY, Y., Ancient History and
Archaeology
NIRMALA, T., Telugu and Oriental Lan-
guages
PUNNA RAO, A., Telugu and Oriental Lan-
guages
RAMA SASTRY, N. A., Telugu and Languages
RAMALAKSHMI, P., Ancient History and
Archaeology
SARASWATHI, R., English
SUBRAHMANYAM, B. R., Ancient History and
Archaeology
Faculty of Law:
HARAGOPAL REDDY, Y. R.
RANGAIAH, N., Law
VIJAYANARAYANA REDDY, D.
Faculty of Natural Sciences:
BALAPARAMESWARA RAO, M., Aquaculture
DURGA PRASAD, M. K., Zoology
GOPALAKRISHNA REDDY, T., Zoology
LAKSHMI, N., Botany
MALLAIAH, K. V., Botany
NARASIMHA RAO, P., Botany
NIRAMALA MARY, T., Botany
RAMAMOHANA RAO, P., Botany
RAMAMURTHY NAIDU, K., Botany
RANGA RAO, V., Geology
SANTHA KUMARI, D., Botany
SHARMA, S. V., Zoology
Faculty of Physical Sciences:
ANJANEYULU, Y., Chemistry
GOPALA KRISHNA MURTHY, P. V., Physics
HARANADH, C., Physics
KOTESWARA RAO, G., Mathematics
NARASIMHAM, V. L., Statistics
NARAYANA MURTHY, P., Physics
PRAKASA RAO, L., Mathematics
PRAKASA RAO, N. S., Chemistry
RAMA BADRA SARMA, I., Mathematics
RAMAKOTAIAH, D., Mathematics
RANGACHARYULU, H., Physics
SATYANANDAM, G., Physics
SATYANARAYANA, P. V. V., Chemistry
SHYAM SUNDAR, B., Chemistry
SIVA RAMA SARMA, B., Chemistry
VENKATACHARYULU, P., Physics
VENKATESWARA REDDY, Y., Mathematics
Faculty of Social Sciences:
ASHEERVADH, N., Political Science
BAPUJI, M., Political Science
BHAVANI, V., Political Science
NARAYANA RAO, C., Political Science
RAGHAVULU, C. V., Political Science and
Public Administration
RAJA BABU, K., Economics
RAJU, C. S. N., Economics
SUDHAKARA RAO, N., Economics

NALANDA OPEN UNIVERSITY

Biscomaun Bhawan, Gandhi Maidan, Patna
800001, Bihar
Telephone: (612) 2201013
Fax: (612) 2201001
E-mail: nalopuni@sancharnet.in
Internet: www.nalandaopenuniversity.com
Founded 1987
Academic year: June to May
Chancellor: HE THE GOVERNOR OF BIHAR
Pro-Vice-Chancellor: Prof. R. B. P. SINGH
Vice-Chancellor: VIJAY SHANKAR DUBEY
Registrar: Dr S. P. SINHA
Study centres in Ara, Bhagalpur, Patna,
Ranchi and Saharsa
Library of 10,000 vols

HEADS OF SCHOOLS

School of Commerce and Social Sciences:
Prof. R. P. SINGH RAHI
School of Computer and Information Sci-
ences: Dr U. M. THACKUR

School of Health and Environmental Sci-
ences: Dr G. K. PRASAD
School of Management Studies and Physical
Sciences: Prof. USHA SINGH
School of Indian Languages and Religions:
Prof. P. C. PANDEY

NARENDRA DEVA UNIVERSITY OF AGRICULTURE & TECHNOLOGY

Narendranagar, Kumarganj, Faizabad
224229, Uttar Pradesh
Telephone: (5270) 262161
Fax: (5270) 262097
E-mail: nduat@up.nic.in
Internet: www.nduat.ernet.in
Founded 1974
State control
Languages of instruction: Hindi, English
Chancellor: HE THE GOVERNOR OF UTTAR
PRADESH
Vice-Chancellor: Prof. BASANT RAM
Registrar: Prof. B. V. S. SISODIA
Library of 42,000 vols
Number of teachers: 67
Number of students: 432
Publication: NDUAT News Bulletin

DEANS

Faculty of Agricultural Engineering and
Technology: Dr R. SINGH
Faculty of Agriculture: Dr M. R. VERMA
Faculty of Home Science: Dr SUMAN BHANOT
Faculty of Veterinary Science and Animal
Husbandry: Dr R. SINGH

CONSTITUENT COLLEGE

**Mahamaya College of Agricultural
Engineering & Technology:** Faizabad
Ambedkar Nagar, Uttar Pradesh; f. 2003 as
Engineering faculty of NDUAT.

NATIONAL ACADEMY OF LEGAL STUDIES AND RESEARCH UNIVERSITY (NALSAR)

3–4–761 Barkatpura, Hyderabad 500027,
Andhra Pradesh
Telephone: (40) 27567955
Fax: (40) 27567310

Justice City, Shameerpet, Rangareddy Dis-
trict, Hyderabad 500078, Andhra Pradesh
Telephone: (40) 23498107
Fax: (8418) 245161
E-mail: admissions@nalsar.ac.in
Internet: www.nalsarlawuniv.ac.in
Founded 1998
Academic year: July to June
Vice-Chancellor: Prof. VEER SINGH
Registrar: Prof. K. V. S. SARMA
Library of 17,000 vols
Publication: NALSAR Law Review (2 a year).

NATIONAL LAW INSTITUTE UNIVERSITY

Bhopal Bhadbhada Rd, Barkheri Kalan, POB
369, Bhopal 462003, Madhya Pradesh
Telephone: (755) 2696965
Fax: (755) 2696965
E-mail: info@nliu.com
Internet: www.nliu.com
Founded 1998
Dir: Dr S. S. SINGH
Finance Officer: N. C. TEKAM
Registrar: C. M. GARG.

NATIONAL LAW UNIVERSITY

NH-65, Nagaur Rd, Mandor, Jodhpur
342304, Rajasthan
Telephone: (291) 2577530

Fax: (291) 2577540
E-mail: nlu-jod-rj@nic.in
Internet: www.nlujodhpur.ac.in
Founded 1999
State control
Language of instruction: English
Chancellor: Chief Justice of Rajasthan JAGDISH BHALLA
Vice-Chancellor: Justice N. N. MATHUR
Registrar: RATAN LAHOTI
Librarian: VINOD D.
Library of 10,500 books, 108 journals, 1,400 electronic journals
Number of teachers: 46
Number of students: 548
Publications: *Journal of Governance* (2 a year), *Scholasticus* (2 a year), *Trade Law and Development* (2 a year)

DEANS

Faculty of Law: Prof. Dr I. P. MASSEY
Faculty of Management: Prof. Dr U. R. DAGA
Faculty of Policy Science: Dr ALOK KUMAR GUPTA (acting)
Faculty of Science: Prof. Dr K. K. BANERJEE

NETAJI SUBHAS OPEN UNIVERSITY

1 Woodburn Park, Kolkata 700020, West Bengal
Telephone: (33) 22835157
Fax: (33) 22835082
E-mail: admin@wbnsou.com
Internet: www.wbnsou.com
Founded 1997
Language of instruction: Bengali
Undergraduate and postgraduate degree programmes in accountancy, Bengali, botany, chemistry, commerce, computer science, economics, education, English, environmental science, geography, history, management, mathematics, physics, political science, public administration, sociology, zoology; 6 campuses in Kolkata; 160 study centres
Chancellor: HE THE GOVERNOR OF WEST BENGAL
Vice-Chancellor: Prof. MANIMALA DAS
Registrar: TARUN KUMAR MANDAL
Dir of Humanities and Social Sciences: Dr UDAYBHANU BHATTACHARYA
Dir of Science: Prof. KAJAL DE
Dir of Study Centre: Prof. ASHIT BARAN AICH
Controller of Examinations: A. DAS
Number of students: 100,000

NIRMA UNIVERSITY OF SCIENCE AND TECHNOLOGY

Sarkhej Gandhinagar Highway, Village Chharodi, Ahmedabad 382481, Gujarat
Telephone: (2717) 241911
Fax: (2717) 241917
E-mail: asst_registrar@nirmauni.ac.in
Internet: www.nirmauni.ac.in
Founded 1994; present name and status 2003
Privately controlled by Nirma Education and Research Foundation
Vice-Chancellor: Dr N. V. VASANI
Exec. Registrar: D. P. CHHAYA

DEANS

Faculty of Law: Dr PURVI POKHARIYA (acting)
Faculty of Management: Prof. UPINDER DHAR
Faculty of Pharmacy: Dr AVANI AMIN (acting)
Faculty of Science: Dr SRIRAM SESHADRI (acting)
Faculty of Technology and Engineering: Prof. K. KOTECHA

CONSTITUENT INSTITUTES

Institute of Diploma Studies

Founded 1997
Prin.: Prof. H. N. PRAJAPATI
Registrar: D. P. CHHAYA
Depts of chemical engineering, computer engineering, electrical engineering, electronics and communication engineering, information technology, mechanical engineering, plastic engineering
Library of 60,000 vols, 400 print periodicals, 8,000 e-journals

Institute of Law

Founded 2007
Dir: Prof. V. S. MALLAR.

Institute of Management

E-mail: grnair@imnu.ac.in
Internet: www.imnu.ac.in
Founded 1996
Dir: Dr UPINDER DHAR
Librarian: Prof. H. ANIL KUMAR
Library of 23,000 vols, 185 periodicals

PROFESSORS

BAHL, S.
BHATTACHARYA, A.
CHUGAN, P. K.
DHANAK, D.
GUPTA, G. S.
GUPTA, P.
MAHAKUD, J.
MALLIKARJUN, M.
MUNCHERJI, N.
NATH, V. V.
PETHE, S.
SAHU, C.
SAHU, S.
SAXENA, S.
TRIVEDI, H.
YADAV, P. K.

Institute of Pharmacy

E-mail: rp.ip@nirmauni.ac.in
Founded 2004
Dir: Dr Y. K. AGRAWAL
Prin.: Dr AVANI F. AMIN
Library of 2,500 vols, 70 periodicals.

Institute of Science

E-mail: hs.is@nirmauni.ac.inn
Founded 2004
Dir: Dr Y. K. AGRAWAL
Postgraduate programmes in biochemistry and biotechnology
Library of 22,000 vols.

Institute of Technology

E-mail: director.it@nirmauni.ac.in
Founded 1995
Dir: Prof. A. B. PATEL
Depts of chemical engineering, civil engineering, electrical engineering, humanities, information technology and computer engineering, mathematics, mechanical engineering
Library of 22,000 vols.

NIZAM'S INSTITUTE OF MEDICAL SCIENCES

Punjagutta, Hyderabad 500082, Andhra Pradesh
Telephone: (40) 23489000

Fax: (40) 23310076
E-mail: nims@ap.nic.in
Internet: nims.ap.nic.in
Founded 1964 as Nizam's Orthopaedic Hospital; present name and status 1989
Residential; depts of anaesthesiology and intensive care, biochemisty, cardio-thoracic surgery, cardiology, chest clinic, clinical pharmacology and therapeutics, dental, dermatology, endocrinology and metabolism, gastroenterology, general medicine, gynaecology, medical oncology, microbiology, nephrology, neurology, neurosurgery, nuclear medicine, orthopaedics, paediatrics, pathology, physiotherapy, plastic surgery, radiation oncology, radiology and imageology, rheumatology, surgical gastroenterology, surgical oncology, transfusion medicine, urology, vascular surgery
Dir: Prof. D. PRASADA RAO
Dean: Prof. M. U. R. NAIDU
Medical Superintendent: Dr N. SATYANARAYANA
Exec. Registrar: Prof. M. SUDERSHANAM
Financial Controller: V. SRIDHAR
Number of teachers: 149

NORTH-EASTERN HILL UNIVERSITY

PO NEHU Campus, Shillong 793002
Telephone: (364) 2550101
Fax: (364) 2550076
Internet: www.nehu.ac.in
Founded 1973
Central univ.; 54 affiliated colleges
Language of instruction: English
Academic year: July to June
Chancellor: Prof. M. G. K. MENON
Vice-Chancellor: Prof. PRAMOD TANDON
Pro Vice-Chancellor: Prof. S. S. KHARE
Registrar: Prof. D. T. KHATHING
Chief Finance Officer: P. C. MAJHI
Controller of Examinations: Prof. D. R. SYIEMLIEH
Dean of Student Welfare: Dr H. J. SYIEMLIEH
Dir of College Devt Council: Dr C. R. DIENGDOH
Librarian: Dr I. MAJAW
Library of 187,000 vols
Number of teachers: 271
Number of students: 23,709
Publication: *NEHU Journal of Social Sciences and Humanities* (4 a year)

DEANS

School of Economics, Management and Information Science: Prof. P. NAYAK
School of Human and Environmental Sciences: Prof. B. K. TIWARI
School of Humanities and Education: Prof. T. AO
School of Life Sciences: Prof. V. TANDON
School of Physical Sciences: Prof. K. ISMAIL
School of Social Sciences: Prof. R. BURGOHAIN
School of Technology: Prof. K. ISMAIL

NORTH MAHARASHTRA UNIVERSITY

PB No. 80, Jalgaon 425002, Maharashtra
Telephone: (257) 2258405
Fax: (257) 2258406
E-mail: info@nmu.ac.in
Internet: www.nmu.ac.in
Founded 1990
State control
Academic year: July to April
Vice-Chancellor: Dr B. P. KHANDERAO
Registrar: Dr M. V. BARIDE
Dir of Public Relations: R. B. CHINCHOLAKAR
Librarian: Dr B. T. RAMCHANDRA
143 Affiliated colleges
Library of 28,728 vols, 85 periodicals

Number of teachers: 3,174
Number of students: 47,974

DIRS OF SCHOOLS

School of Chemical Sciences: Dr D. G. HUNDIWALE
School of Environmental and Earth Sciences: Dr S. T. INGLE
School of Life Sciences: Dr M. V. KULKARNI
School of Mathematical Sciences: Dr R. L. SHINDE
School of Physical Sciences: Dr P. P. PATIL

NORTH ORISSA UNIVERSITY

Sriram Chandra Vihar, Takatpur, Baripada, Mayurbhanj 757003, Orissa
Telephone: (6792) 255127
Fax: (6792) 255127
Internet: nou.nic.in
Founded 1998
State control
Academic year: June to May
Faculties of arts, commerce, computer applications, education, engineering, law, medicine, science, tribal studies; 81 affiliated colleges
Chancellor: HE THE GOV. OF ORISSA
Vice-Chancellor: Dr SHIBA PRASAD RATH
Registrar: Dr HARIPRASAD P. PANDA
Librarian: S. K. TANTI
Library of 2,647 vols
Number of students: 10,320

ORISSA UNIVERSITY OF AGRICULTURE AND TECHNOLOGY

District Khurda, Bhubaneswar 751003, Orissa
Telephone: (674) 2392677
Fax: (674) 2397780
E-mail: ouatmain@hotmail.com
Internet: ouat.ac.in
Founded 1962
Teaching and Research
State control
Language of instruction: English
Academic year: July to July
Chancellor: HE THE GOVERNOR OF ORISSA
Vice-Chancellor: Prof. D. P. RAY
Registrar: DUKHISHYAM SHATAPATHY
Dean of Extension Education: Dr S. S. NANDA
Dean of Research: Dr D. NAIK
Dean of Student Welfare: Dr D. K. DAS
Controller of Examinations: Dr BIRANCHI N. ROUTRAY
Librarian: Dr N. K. DHAL
7 Constituent colleges; Centre for Postgraduate Studies
Library of 900,000 vols, 133 periodicals
Number of teachers: 512
Number of students: 3,046

DEANS

College of Agricultural Engineering and Technology: Dr S. N. MOHANTY
College of Agriculture (Bhubaneswar): Dr P. K. MOHAPATRA
College of Agriculture (Chiplima): Dr S. K. MISHRA
College of Basic Science and Humanities: Dr M. CHAKRABORTY
College of Engineering and Technology: Dr B. S. PATRO
College of Fisheries: Dr S. K. MISHRA
College of Home Science: Prin.: Dr P. DAS
College of Veterinary Science and Animal Husbandry: Dr B. K. SAHOO

OSMANIA UNIVERSITY

Hyderabad 500007, Andhra Pradesh
Telephone: (40) 27098043

E-mail: registrar@osmania.ac.in
Internet: www.osmania.ac.in
Founded 1918
Teaching, residential and affiliating; 120 affiliated colleges and 16 Oriental colleges
Languages of instruction: English, Hindi, Telugu, Urdu, Marathi
Academic year: June to April (two terms)
Chancellor: HE THE GOV. OF ANDHRA PRADESH
Vice-Chancellor: Prof. T. TIRUPATI RAO
Registrar: Prof. Y. C. VENUDHAR
Dean of College Devt Ccl: Prof. P. JETTAIAH
Dean of Devt: Prof. M. NARSIMHA CHARY
Dean of Student Affairs: Dr B. LAXMAIAH
Public Relations Officer: Prof. B. S. RAO
Librarian: V. REVATHI
Library of 422,000 vols
Number of students: 300,000

Publication: *Osmania Journal of English Studies*

DEANS

Faculty of Arts: Prof. M. MANVI
Faculty of Business Management: Prof. A. VIDYADHAR REDDY
Faculty of Commerce: Prof. K. V. ACHALA-PATHI
Faculty of Education: Prof. B. VIJAYA LAKSHMI
Faculty of Engineering: Prof. R. RAMESH REDDY
Faculty of Informatics: Prof. A. VENUGOPAL REDDY
Faculty of Law: Justice L. NARSIMHA REDDY
Faculty of Oriental Languages: Dr M. A. JAMEEL KHAN
Faculty of Science: Prof. U. V. SUBHA RAO
Faculty of Social Sciences: Prof. P. V. LAKSHMI REDDY
Faculty of Technology: Prof. J. S. N. MURTHY

UNIVERSITY COLLEGES

Institute of Advanced Study in Education: f. 1918; Prin. Prof. K. SUBHASHCHANDRA REDDY.

University College of Arts and Social Sciences: tel. (40) 27098298; fax (40) 27091952; e-mail info@ouartscollege.com; internet ouartscollege.com; f. 1918; Prin. Prof. P. L. VISHWESHWER RAO.

University College of Commerce and Business Management: f. 1975; Prin. Prof. M. SHRI NIVAS.

University College of Engineering: tel. (40) 27098254; internet www.uceou.edu; f. 1929; Prin. Prof. D. N. REDDY.

University College of Law: tel. (40) 27098254; internet www.osmanialawcollege .org; f. 1960; Prin. Dr G. B. REDDY.

University College of Physical Education: tel. (40) 27090711; f. 1928; Prin. Prof. S. IBRAHIM.

University College of Science: f. 1918; Prin. Dr K. VEERA REDDY.

University College of Technology: tel. (40) 27682291; fax (40) 27098472; e-mail principal@ouct.org; f. 1969; Prin. Prof. S. VENKATESHWAR.

CONSTITUENT COLLEGES

Nizam College: Basheerbagh, Hyderabad; tel. (40) 23234231; fax (40) 23240806; e-mail principal@nizamcollege.ac.in; internet www .nizamcollege.ac.in; f. 1887; Prin. Prof. B. T. SEETHA.

Postgraduate College of Law, Hyderabad: f. 1954; Prin. G. MANCHAR RAO.

Postgraduate College of Science: Saifabad, Hyderabad; e-mail pgcss@rediffmail .com; internet oupgcollege.ac.in; f. 1951; Prin. Prof. K. SHANKARAIAH.

Postgraduate College, Secunderabad: Sadar Patel Rd, Secunderabad 500003; tel. (40) 27902169; fax (40) 27903688; e-mail principal@oupgcs.ac.in; internet www.oupgcs .ac.in; f. 1947; Prin. Prof. M. DEVA DASS.

University College for Women: Hyderabad; tel. (40) 24657813; fax (40) 24737692; e-mail oucwkoti@rediffmail.com; internet www.oucwkoti.ac.in; f. 1924; Prin. Prof. ZUBAIDA AZEEM.

District Postgraduate Colleges:

Postgraduate College, Biknoor: f. 1976; Prin. Dr U. UMESH KUMAR.

Postgraduate Centre, Mahaboobnagar: f. 1987; Head Dr N. ASHOK.

Postgraduate Centre, Mirzapur: f. 1980; Prin. Dr B. MANOHAR.

Postgraduate Centre, Nalgonda: f. 1987; Prin. Dr S. ANJAIAH.

PANDIT RAVISHANKAR SHUKLA UNIVERSITY, RAIPUR

Amanaka G. E. Rd, Raipur 492010, Chhattisgarh
Telephone: (771) 2262540
Fax: (771) 2262583
Internet: www.prsu.ac.in
Founded 1964
Teaching and Affiliating
Languages of instruction: Hindi, English
Private control
Academic year: July to June (two terms)
Chancellor: HE THE GOVERNOR OF CHHATTIS-GARH
Vice-Chancellor: Prof. SHIV KUMAR PANDEY
Registrar: INDU ANANT
Librarian: M. I. AHMED
180 Affiliated colleges
Library of 160,000 vols
Number of students: 125,000

DEANS

Faculty of Arts: Dr CHITTARANJAN KAR
Faculty of Ayurved: Dr D. K. KATARIA
Faculty of Commerce: AMIR CHAND JAIN
Faculty of Education: Dr B. K. MEHTA
Faculty of Engineering: Dr H. KUMAR
Faculty of Home Science: Dr V. RAJ
Faculty of Law: Dr A. A. KHAN
Faculty of Management: Dr R. P. DAS
Faculty of Science: Dr G. L. MUNDHRA
Faculty of Social Sciences: Dr M. A. KHAN
Faculty of Technology: Dr SHAILENDRA SARAF

CONSTITUENT SCHOOLS

Centre for Regional Studies and Research: f. 1993; Dir Prof. O. P. VERMA.

Centre for Woman Studies: f. 2001.

Institute of Management: f. 1993; Dir Dr R. P. DAS.

Institute of Pharmacy: tel. (771) 2262832; e-mail info@iopraipur.ac.in; internet www .iopraipur.ac.in; f. 2001; Dir Dr S. SARAF.

Institute of Teachers Education.

Institute of Tourism and Hotel Management: f. 2002; Dir Dr L. S. NIGAM.

School of Studies in Adult, Continuing Education and Extension: f. 1985; Dir Dr BINA PATHAK.

School of Studies in Ancient Indian History, Culture and Archaeology: f. 1971; Dir Prof. L. S. NIGAM.

School of Studies in Anthropology: f. 1965; Dir Dr MANJULA GUHA.

School of Studies in Biotechnology: f. 2003; Dir Dr K. L. TIWARI.

School of Studies in Chemistry: f. 1972; Dir Dr RAMA PANDE.

School of Studies in Comparative Religion and Philosophy: f. 1985; Dir Dr BHAGWANT SINGH.

School of Studies in Computer Science: e-mail dropvyas@gmail.com; internet www .prsu.ac.in/soscs.html; f. 1992; Dir Prof. O. P. VYAS.

School of Studies in Economics: f. 1971; Dir Dr USHA DUBEY.

School of Studies in Electronics: f. 1994; Dir Dr KAVITA THAKUR.

School of Studies in Geography: f. 1965; Dir Dr M. P. GUPTA.

School of Studies in Geology and Water Resource Management: f. 1984; Dir Dr M. W. Y. KHAN.

School of Studies in History: f. 1971; Dir Dr M. A. KHAN.

School of Studies in Law: f. 1982; Dir Dr A. ALIM KHAN.

School of Studies in Library and Information Science: f. 1971; Dir Dr A. K. VERMA.

School of Studies in Life Sciences: f. 1977; Dir Dr VIBHUTI RAI.

School of Studies in Literature and Languages: Dir Dr K. L. VERMA.

School of Studies in Mathematics: f. 1991; Dir Dr B. K. SHARMA.

School of Studies in Physical Education: f. 1972; Dir Dr RITA VENU GOPAL.

School of Studies in Physics: f. 1972; Dir Dr S. BHUSHAN.

School of Studies in Psychology: f. 1965; Dir Dr P. SINGH.

School of Studies in Sociology: f. 1965; Dir Dr P. K. SHARMA.

School of Studies in Statistics: f. 1977; Dir Dr GAURI SHANKAR.

PANJAB UNIVERSITY

Sector 14, Chandigarh 160014

Telephone: (172) 2541945

Fax: (172) 2541022

E-mail: regr@pu.ac.in

Internet: www.puchd.ac.in

Founded 1947

Teaching and affiliating; 115 affiliated colleges

Languages of instruction: English, Punjabi, Urdu, Hindi

Academic year: July to April

Chancellor: THE VICE-PRESIDENT OF INDIA

Vice-Chancellor: Dr R. C. SOBTI

Registrar: Prof. PARAMJIT SINGH

Librarian: A. R. SETHI

Library: Libraries of 590,000 vols

Number of teachers: 746

Number of students: 20,554

Publications: *Parakh, Parishodh, P. U. Research Journal* (science), *Social Sciences Research Journal*

DEANS

Faculty of Arts: Dr MADAN MOHAN PURI

Faculty of Business Management and Commerce: Prof. S. P. SINGH

Faculty of Design and Fine Arts: JOGINDER SINGH

Faculty of Education: NIRMAL KAUR

Faculty of Engineering and Technology: Prof. D. K. VOHRA

Faculty of Languages: Dr ANIRUDH JOSHI

Faculty of Law: GOPAL KRISHAN CHATRATH

Faculty of Medical Sciences: Dr K. S. CHUGH

Faculty of Pharmaceutical Sciences: Prof. V. K. KAPOOR

Faculty of Science: (vacant)

PATNA UNIVERSITY

Ashok Raj Path, Patna 800005, Bihar

Telephone: (612) 2670531; (612) 2670877

Internet: puonline.bih.nic.in

Founded 1917

Residential and teaching

Languages of instruction: Hindi, English

Academic year: June to May (three terms)

Chancellor: HE THE GOV. OF BIHAR

Vice-Chancellor: Prof. SHYAM LAL

Pro-Vice-Chancellor: Prof. SYED L. AHSON

Registrar: Dr VIBHASH KUMAR YADAV

Dean of Student Welfare: Dr EJAZ ALI ARSHAD

Controller of Examination: Dr SURENDRA PRASAD YADAV

Finance Office: Dr JATADHAR MISHRA

Librarian: Dr R. N. MISHRA

Library of 300,000 vols

Number of teachers: 895

Number of students: 11,000

Publication: *University of Patna Journal*

DEANS

Faculty of Commerce: Dr JYOTI SHEKHAR

Faculty of Education: G. K. PRAJAPATI

Faculty of Engineering: Dr P. K. SINHA

Faculty of Fine Arts: Dr N. K. P. SINGH

Faculty of Humanities: Dr R. R. SAHAY

Faculty of Law: Dr L. L. B. SHARAN

Faculty of Medicine: Dr B. K. SINGH

Faculty of Science: Dr S. N. GUHA

Faculty of Social Science: Dr SAVITRI SHARMA

PROFESSORS

ADHIKARI, S., Geography
AHMAD, S. U., Sociology
AKHTAR, M. M., Physics
ALAM, M. S., Persian
ALAM, P. A., Urdu
ARSHAD, E. A., Urdu
ARYA, R. S., Philosophy
ASHOK, S. M., English
AZAD, A., Urdu
AZAD, R., Chemistry
BANERJEE, N. N., Botany
BANERJEE, S., Political Science
BEGAM, S., Urdu
BHAKTA, C., Chemistry
BHATT, P., Zoology
BLAKTA, S., Mathematics
CHOUDHARY, A. K., Physics
CHOUDHARY, M. N., Hindi
CHOUDHARY, N. K., Economics
CHOUDHARY, R., Philosophy
CHOUDHARY, R. B., Sanskrit
CHOUDHARY, S., Political Science
DAS, R. N., Mathematics
DUBEY, G. R., Education
DUBEY, S., Psychology
DUBEY, V. S., Geology
DUTTA, P., History
DUTTA, S. A., English
GHOSH, A. K., Chemistry
GHOSH, P., History
GUHA, S. N., Physics
GUPTA, A. D., Sociology
GUPTA, A. K., Botany
GUPTA, F., Sanskrit
HASANARAN, S. J., Mechanical Engineering
JAISWAL, R., Mathematics
JHA, B., Maithili
JHA, H., Sociology
JHA, I., Education
JHA, K., Psychology
JHA, N. N., Physics
JHA, R., Ancient Indian History and Archaeology
JHA, R., English
JHA, S. M., Mathematics
JHA, U., Chemistry
KALIM, Z., English
KARAN, V., Maithili
KATHURIA, S., Botany

KHAN, S. A., Statistics
KUMAR, A., English
KUMAR, A., Sanskrit
KUMAR, B., Chemistry
KUMAR, B., Statistics
KUMAR, B. S., History
KUMAR, N., Mechanical Engineering
KUMAR, R. V., History
KUMAR, S., Civil Engineering
KUMAR, S., Sociology
KUMARI, A., Statistics
KUMARI, R., Sociology
KUMARI, S., Hindi
LAL, S., Chemistry
MAHTO, K., Geography
MAHTO, R. U., Commerce
MALTIYAR, K. K., Geography
MATHUR, K. N. L., Physics
MIRZA, K., Political Science
MISHRA, A., Statistics
MISHRA, B. K., Geology
MISHRA, H., English
MISHRA, J. S., History
MISHRA, N. M., Physics
MISHRA, R. G., Sanskrit
MISHRA, R. N., Statistics
MISHRA, R. S., Statistics
MISHRA, U., Commerce
MITRA, K. A., Physics
MOHAN, M., Zoology
MUKHERJEE, D., Physics
MUKHERJEE, I., Botany
MURARI, R., Economics
NATH, A., Zoology
NILIMA, N., Hindi
OJHA, G. P., Political Science
PADAMDEO, S. R., Botany
PANDEY, B. N., Commerce
PANDEY, M. K., Sanskrit
PANDEY, N. M., English
PANDEY, N. N., Physics
PASWAN, B., Hindi
PASWAN, K. N., Geography
PODAR, P. K., History
PRAJAPATI, G. K., Education
PRAKASH, D., Chemistry
PRASAD, A., Chemistry
PRASAD, A., Statistics
PRASAD, B., Mathematics
PRASAD, D., Mathematics
PRASAD, D., Sociology
PRASAD, K., Geology
PRASAD, K., History
PRASAD, R. D., Hindi
PRASAD, R. K., Chemistry
PRASAD, R. N., Philosophy
PRASAD, R. P., Chemistry
PRASAD, S. A. K., Mathematics
PRASAD, S. L., Geography
QUADRI, E. A., Civil Engineering
RAJGARHIA, C., Mathematics
RANI, P., Zoology
ROHATAGI, A. K., Geology
ROY, D. N., Bengali
ROY, R., English
ROY, R. B. R., Hindi
ROY, S., Chemistry
ROY, V. R., Psychology
RUDRA, S., Economics
SAHAY, R. R., Philosophy
SHARDENDU, Hindi
SHARMA, B., Mathematics
SHARMA, D. K., Mathematics
SHARMA, D. K., Physics
SHARMA, J. P., Education
SHARMA, M. D., Bengali
SHARMA, N. K., Hindi
SHARMA, P. L., History
SHARMA, R. N., Sociology
SHARMA, S., Psychology
SHARMA, S. N., Botany
SHARMA, S. N., Physics
SHARMA, S. N., Political Science
SHAW, G., Home Science
SHEKHAR, J., Commerce
SHREE, V., Philosophy

SHUKLA, H., Political Science
SHUKLA, K. N., Zoology
SHUKLA, P., Psychology
SHUKLA, R., Geology
SIDDIQUI, F. K., Arabic
SIDDIQUI, M. G., Persian
SIDDIQUI, M. O., Botany
SINGH, A., Economics
SINGH, A. K., Ancient Indian History and
  Archaeology
SINGH, A. K., History
SINGH, A. K., Psychology
SINGH, A. K. S., Hindi
SINGH, A. N., History
SINGH, B. P., Economics
SINGH, C., Commerce
SINGH, D. P., Hindi
SINGH, G., Hindi
SINGH, J., Physics
SINGH, J. M. P., Hindi
SINGH, J. P., Sociology
SINGH, K. N., Mechanical Engineering
SINGH, K. P., English
SINGH, K. S. P., Civil Engineering
SINGH, L. K. P., Geography
SINGH, N. K., Geology
SINGH, N. K. P., History
SINGH, N. N. P., History
SINGH, P., Philosophy
SINGH, P. D., Chemistry
SINGH, R. B. P., Geography
SINGH, R. P., Chemistry
SINGH, S., Botany
SINGH, S., Home Science
SINGH, S. C., History
SINGH, S. D. N., Sociology
SINGH, S. K., Mechanical Engineering
SINGH, S. K., Statistics
SINGH, S. K. P., Economics
SINGH, S. K. P., History
SINGH, S. N., Chemistry
SINGH, S. N., Economics
SINGH, S. P. Y., Hindi
SINGH, S. S., Ancient Indian History and
  Archaeology
SINHA, A. K., Civil Engineering
SINHA, A. K., Statistics
SINHA, A. P., Economics
SINHA, B. K., Mathematics
SINHA, G., Psychology
SINHA, H. B. P., Mathematics
SINHA, K., Economics
SINHA, K. S., Mathematics
SINHA, L., Political Science
SINHA, M., Psychology
SINHA, M., Sanskrit
SINHA, M. N., Geology
SINHA, M. P., Zoology
SINHA, M. R., English
SINHA, N., Geology
SINHA, P., Psychology
SINHA, P. K., Mathematics
SINHA, P. K., Mechanical Engineering
SINHA, R. C., Philosophy
SINHA, R. J., Chemistry
SINHA, R. K., Zoology
SINHA, R. M. P., Physics
SINHA, S., English
SINHA, S., Philosophy
SINHA, S. K., Civil Engineering
SINHA, S. S., Education
SINHA, U. K., Botany
SINHA, V., Psychology
SINHA, V. K., Zoology
SINHA, V. N. P., Geography
SIRKAR, J., Economics
SRINIVASAN, P., Physics
SRIVASTAVA, S. K., Zoology
SRIVASTAVA, U. K., Civil Engineering
SUKLA, B., Sociology
TAHAN, K., Persian
THAKUR, B. K., Geology
THAKUR, J., Physics
THAKUR, S. J., English
THAKUR, V. K., History
TIWARI, B., Hindi

TIWARY, N. P., Philosophy
TIWARY, P. N., History
TRIPATHY, A. N., Sanskrit
TULSIYAN, S. S., Economics
VARMA, M., Philosophy
VERMA, C., Zoology
VERMA, J., Psychology
VERMA, M., Economics
VERMA, P. C., Economics
VERMA, R. K., Mathematics
VERMA, S. P., Physics
VERMA, U., Geography
YADAV, A., Physics
YADAV, A. K. P., Physics
YASIN, S., Zoology

CONSTITUENT COLLEGES

Bihar College of Engineering: Mahendru, Patna; f. 1924; 4-year course; 46 teachers; 450 students; Prin. Dr A. K. SINHA.

Bihar National College: Bankipur, Patna 4; tel. (612) 2300619; f. 1917; 84 teachers; 1,263 students; Prin. Dr RAMESH PRASAD.

College of Arts and Crafts: Patna 800001; tel. (612) 2235348; f. 1938; 5 teachers; 150 students; Prin. Dr ANUNAY CHOUBEY.

Directorate of Distance Education: tel. (612) 2672941; e-mail contact@ddepu.org; internet www.ddepu.org; Dir Dr AMARENDRA MISHRA.

Institute of Library and Information Science: tel. (612) 2672941; Prin. Dr R. N. MISHRA.

Institute of Psychological Research and Service: tel. (612) 2690096; Prin. Dr PRABHA SHUKLA.

Institute of Public Administration: tel. (612) 2670284; Dir Dr KHALID MIRZA.

Magadh Mahila College: tel. (612) 2223454; fax (612) 2213738; e-mail info@magadhmahilacollege.org; internet www.magadhmahilacollege.org; f. 1946; 30 teachers; 918 students; Prin. Dr SUKHADA KUMARI.

National Institute of Technology: tel. (612) 2670631; Prin. Dr U. C. RAY.

Patna College: tel. (612) 2671589; f. 1863; the oldest college in the province, and the parent instn of 3 other colleges; 48 teachers; 2,363 students; Prin. Dr RANVIJAY KUMAR.

Patna Dental College: tel. (612) 2665130; Prin. Dr D. K. SINGH.

Patna Law College: tel. (612) 2670510; f. 1906; 20 teachers; 868 students; Prin. Dr RAKESH VERMA.

Patna Medical College: tel. (612) 2300343; f. 1925; under administrative control of the Govt of Bihar; 60 teachers; 900 students; Prin. Dr R. K. P. SINGH.

Patna Science College: tel. (612) 6453576; internet sciencecollege.bih.nic.in; f. 1927; 56 teachers; 1,002 students; Prin. Dr S. N. GUHA.

Patna Training College: tel. (612) 2302037; f. 1908; 10 teachers; 126 students; Prin. Dr JAGDISH PRASAD SHARMA.

Patna Women's College: tel. (612) 2531186; internet www.patnawomenscollege.in; f. 1940; 44 teachers; 2,309 students; Prin. Sister Dr DORIS D'SOUZA.

Vanijya Mahavidyalaya: tel. (612) 2670782; f. 1953; 12 teachers; 704 students; Prin. Dr SHAMBHU NATH SINGH.

Women's Training College: tel. (612) 2222809; f. 1951; 11 teachers; 244 students; Prin. Dr MONAWWAR JAHAN.

PERIYAR UNIVERSITY

Bangalore Main Rd Salem 636011, Tamil Nadu

Telephone: (427) 2345766

Fax: (427) 2345565
E-mail: info@periyaruniversity.ac.in
Internet: periyaruniversity.ac.in

Founded 1997
State control
Academic year: July to June
Languages of instruction: English, Tamil
Chancellor: HE THE GOVERNOR OF TAMIL NADU
Vice-Chancellor: Dr M. THANGARAJU
Registrar: Dr S. GUNASEKARAN
Controller of Examinations: Dr A. JAYAKUMAR
Univ. Librarian: Dr N. SUBRAMANIAN
Library of 48,000 vols, 168 periodicals
Number of teachers: 108
Number of students: 1,100
Faculties of Arts, Commerce, Education, Engineering, Languages and Science
There are 59 affiliated colleges.

PONDICHERRY UNIVERSITY

R. Venkataraman Nagar, Kalapet, Pondicherry 605014

Telephone: (413) 2655179
Fax: (413) 2655734
E-mail: registrar@pondiuni.edu.in
Internet: www.pondiuni.org

Founded 1985
Central university
State control
Languages of instruction: English, French, Tamil, Hindi, Malayalam, Telugu, Sanskrit
Academic year: July to June
Chancellor: HE THE VICE-PRESIDENT OF INDIA
Vice-Chancellor: Prof. J. A. K. TAREEN
Registrar: S. LOGANATHAN
Public Relations Officer: N. ARUNAGIRI
Controller of Examinations: Prof. T. J. SAHAYAM CHELLIAH
Librarian: R. SAMYUKTHA
Number of teachers: 140
Number of students: 1,217 (University), 15,909 (affiliated colleges and institutes)
Publication: *Journal of Social Sciences and Humanities*

DEANS

School of Humanities: Dr V. C. THOMAS
School of Life Sciences: Prof. PRIYA DAVIDAR
School of Management: Dr R. PANNEERSELVAM
School of Performing Arts: Prof. R. RAJU
School of Physical, Chemical and Applied Sciences: Dr S. BALAKRISHNAN
School of Social and Int. Studies: Prof. D. SAMBANDHAN
Ramanujam School of Mathematics and Computer Science: Dr H. P. PATIL
Subramania Bharathi School of Tamil Language and Literature: Dr A. ARIVUNAMBI

ATTACHED INSTITUTES

Bioinformatics Centre: tel. and fax (413) 2655211; e-mail bicpu2001@yahoo.co.in; internet www.bicpu.edu.in; Dir Dr P. P. MATHUR.

Centre for Human Rights: f. 1999; Dir Dr T. S. N. SASTRY.

Centre for Nehru Studies: Dir Dr B. KRISHNAMURTHY.

Centre for Pollution Control and Energy Technology: Dir Dr S. A. ABBASI.

Centre for Women's Studies: f. 1999; Dir Dr V. T. USHA.

Centre for Yoga Studies: f. 2000; Dir Dr D. SAKTHIGNANAVEL.

POTTI SREERAMULU TELUGU UNIVERSITY

Lalitha Kala Kshetram, Public Gardens, Nampally, Hyderabad 500004, Andhra Pradesh

Telephone: (40) 23230435
Fax: (40) 23236045
E-mail: info@teluguuniversity.ac.in
Internet: teluguuniversity.ac.in

Founded 1985

5 Campuses in Hyderabad, Kuchipudi, Rajahmundry, Sri Sailam, Warangal
Chancellor: HE The Gov. of Andhra Pradesh RAMESHWAR THAKUR
Vice-Chancellor: Prof. A. BHOOMAIAH
Registrar: Prof. T. GOWRISHANKER
Librarian: Dr C. M. KRISHANA
Library of 100,000 vols (55,000 Telugu, 43,000 English), 150 periodicals

DEANS

School of Comparative Studies: Prof. S. SUBRAHMANYAM
School of Fine Arts: Prof. BITTU VENKATESH-WARLU
School of Folk and Tribal Lore: Dr B. RAMESH
School of History, Culture and Archaeology: Prof. D. R. RAJU
School of Language Development: Prof. K. ASHIRVADAM
School of Social and Other Sciences: Prof. V.B. SUBRAHMANYAM
School of Telugu Literature: Prof. P. LEELA-VATHI

PUNJAB AGRICULTURAL UNIVERSITY

Ludhiana 141004, Punjab

Telephone: (161) 2401960
Fax: (161) 2400945
E-mail: info@pau.edu
Internet: www.pau.edu

Founded 1962

Teaching, Research and Extension
Autonomous control
Languages of instruction: English, Punjabi
Academic year: August to July (two terms)
Chancellor: HE THE GOVERNOR OF PUNJAB
Vice-Chancellor: Dr MANJIT SINGH KANG
Dir of Extension Education: Dr N. S. MALHI
Dir of Research: Dr PARAMJIT SINGH MINHAS
Dir of Student Welfare: Dr DULCHA SINGH BRAR
Dean of Postgraduate Studies: Dr SATWINDER K. MANN
Registrar: Dr V. K. SHARMA
Librarian: Dr J. K. SANGHA
Library of 257,724 vols, 6,849 journals, 36,043 theses, 101,311 periodicals, 22 e-books
Number of teachers: 1,182
Number of students: 2,067
Publications: *Changi Kheti* (in Punjabi, 12 a year), *Journal of Research* (in English, 4 a year), *Package of Practices for Crops of the Punjab* (2 a year), *Progressive Farming* (in English, 12 a year), *Punjab Agricultural Handbook* (1 a year)

DEANS

College of Agricultural Engineering: Dr P. K. GUPTA
College of Agriculture: Dr M. S. AULAKH
College of Basic Science and Humanities: Dr T. SINGH
College of Home Science: Dr N. GREWAL
College of Veterinary Science: Dr M. S. OBEROI

PUNJAB TECHNICAL UNIVERSITY

Ladowali Rd, Jalandhar 144001, Punjab

Telephone: (1822) 255506
Fax: (1822) 255507
E-mail: ptumail@ptu.ac.in
Internet: www.ptu.ac.in

Founded 1997

Courses in engineering, natural sciences and technology; affiliated colleges: 40 engineering, 56 management, 17 pharmacy, 6 architecture, 2 hotel management, 13 medical lab technology and IT
Chancellor: HE THE GOV. OF PUNJAB
Vice-Chancellor: Dr RAJNEESH ARORA
Registrar: SAROJINI GAUTAM SHARDA.

PUNJABI UNIVERSITY

Patiala 147002, Punjab

Telephone: (175) 3046030
Fax: (175) 2283073
E-mail: regpup@pbi.ac.in
Internet: www.punjabiuniversity.ac.in

Founded 1962

Languages of instruction: Punjabi, English
State control
166 Affiliated colleges
Academic year: July to May (three terms)
Chancellor: HE THE GOVERNOR OF PUNJAB
Vice-Chancellor: Dr JASPAL SINGH
Registrar: Dr S. S. KHEHRA
Dir of Public Relations: Dr GURMEET SINGH MAAN
Librarian: Dr SAROJ BALA
Library of 420,000 books, 50,000 journals
Number of students: 11,386
Publication: *Journal of Religious Studies* (4 a year)

DEANS

Faculty of Arts and Culture: Prof. GURNAM SINGH
Faculty of Business Studies: Dr A. S. CHAWLA
Faculty of Education and Information Science: Dr JAGTAR SINGH
Faculty of Engineering and Technology: Prof. M. S. SAINI
Faculty of Languages: Prof. B. S. KHEHRA
Faculty of Law: Dr C. SINGH
Faculty of Life Sciences: P. SINGHAL
Faculty of Medicine: Dr N. KAUR MULTANI
Faculty of Physical Sciences: Dr R. C. VERMA
Faculty of Social Sciences: Dr MANJU VERMA

ATTACHED RESEARCH INSTITUTE

Advanced Centre for Technical Development of Punjabi Language, Literature and Culture: tel. (175) 3046171; f. 2004; Dir Dr GURPREET SINGH LEHAL.

RABINDRA BHARATI UNIVERSITY

56A Barrackpore Trunk Rd, Kolkata 700050

Telephone: (33) 25568019
Fax: (33) 25568079
Internet: www.rabindrabharatiuniversity.net

Founded 1962

Languages of instruction: Bengali, English
State control
Academic year: June to May (three terms)
Chancellor: HE THE GOVERNOR OF WEST BENGAL
Vice-Chancellor: Prof. KARUNA SINDHU DAS
Registrar: Dr TAPATI MUKHERJEE
Finance Officer: AMIT MUKHERJEE
Public Relations Officer: SURANJANA BHATTA-CHARYA
Librarian: SATYABRATA GHOSAL
Library of 92,500 vols, 258 periodicals
Number of teachers: 165
Number of students: 6,759

Publications: departmental journals (1 a year: Bengali, Sanskrit, English, Education, Economics, Library and Information Science, Vedic Studies, Study and Research on Tagore, Rabindra Sangeet), *Rabindra Bharati Journal* (English, 1 a year), *Rabindra Bharati University Patrika* (Bengali, 1 a year)

DEANS

Faculty of Applied Arts: A. P. MITRA (acting)
Faculty of Arts: Prof. S. K. GHOSH
Faculty of Fine Arts: Prof. A. DUTT
Faculty of Visual Arts: Dr S. DHAR

RAJASTHAN AGRICULTURAL UNIVERSITY, BIKANER

Bikaner 334006, Rajasthan

Telephone: (151) 2250025
Fax: (151) 2250336
E-mail: reg@raubikaner.org
Internet: www.raubikaner.org

Founded 1988

Vice-Chancellor: Prof. PRATAP NARAIN
Registrar: RAM DEV GOYAL
Dean of Postgraduate Studies: Dr ANIL KUMAR
Controller of Examinations: Dr PRAN MEHRO-TRA
Dir of Distance Education: Dr A. K. PUROHIT
Dir of Extension Education: Dr R. N. GOS-WAMI
Dir of Student Welfare: Dr R. N. KACHHAWA
Dirs of Research: Dr S. B. S. YADAV, Dr M. P. SAHU
Librarian: CHETAN RAJPUROHIT
Library: Central Library of 10,000 vols
Number of teachers: 425
Number of students: 2,250

DEANS

College of Agriculture: Dr B. L. POONIA
College of Home Science: Dr M. GOYAL
College of Veterinary and Animal Science: A. K. GAHLOT
Institute of Agri-business Management: Prof. A. K. DAHAMA (Dir)

CONSTITUENT COLLEGES

College of Agriculture: tel. (151) 2250292; e-mail coa@agricolbikaner.org; internet www.agricolbikaner.org; f. 1988.

College of Home Science: tel. (151) 2250692; e-mail chsc_bkn@hotmail.com; internet www.hascraubikaner.org.

College of Veterinary and Animal Science: tel. (151) 2543419; fax (151) 2549348; internet www.bikanervetcol.org; publ. *Journal of Camel Practice and Research*, *Journal of Canine Development and Research*, *Veterinary Practitioner*.

Institute of Agribusiness Management (IABM): tel. (151) 2252981; e-mail director@iabmbikaner.org; internet www.iabmbikaner.org; f. 2000.

S.K.N. College of Agriculture: Jobner; tel. (1425) 254022; Dir B. R. CHIPPA.

RAJASTHAN AYURVEDA UNIVERSITY

Jodhpur 331401, Rajasthan

Telephone: (291) 2111701
Fax: (291) 2111677
E-mail: rau_jodhpur@yahoo.co.in
Internet: www.raujodhpur.com

Founded 2003

Academic year: July to June
Languages of instruction: Sanskrit, Hindi, English
State Control
Vice-Chancellor: Prof. BANWARI LAL GAUR
Registrar: CHAIN SINGH PANWAR

Librarian: Dr RAKESH KUMAR SHARMA
39 Affiliated colleges
Library of 5,791 vols, 23 journals
Number of teachers: 23
Number of students: 6,948

DEANS

Faculty of Ayurved: Prof. MAHESH CHANDRA
  SHARMA
Faculty of Homeopathy: Dr J. D. DARYANI
Faculty of Unani: Prof. G. Q. CHISTI

RAJENDRA AGRICULTURAL UNIVERSITY

Pusa, Samastipur 848125, Bihar
Telephone: (6274) 240239
Fax: (6274) 240266
E-mail: info@pusavarsity.org.in
Internet: www.pusavarsity.org.in
Founded 1970
Languages of instruction: Hindi, English
Academic year: July to June (two terms)
Chancellor: HE THE GOV. OF BIHAR
Vice-Chancellor: Dr M. L. CHOUDHARY
Registrar: Dr A. K. P. SINGH
Librarian: Dr B. N. MISHRA
Library of 54,000 vols and 2,000 MSS
Number of teachers: 400
Number of students: 1,200
Publications: *Adhunik Kisan* (12 a year),
  Research Journal (4 a year)

DEANS

Faculty of Agricultural Engineering: Dr A. P.
  MISHRA
Faculty of Agriculture: Dr K. R. MAURYA
Faculty of Basic Science: Dr V. K. SHAHI
Faculty of Home Science: Dr M. SINGH
Faculty of Veterinary Science: Dr J. N. SINGH
Postgraduate Faculty: Dr V. S. VERMA

PROFESSORS

Faculty of Agricultural Engineering:
  KUMAR, A., Soil Conservation
  RAM, R. B., Farm Machinery
Faculty of Agriculture:
  CHOUDHARY, L. B., Plant Breeding
  MISHRA, S. S., Agronomy
  OJHA, K. L., Plant Pathology
  PRASAD, B., Soil Science
  SAKAL, R., Soil Science
  SHARMA, R. P. ROY, Agronomy
  SINGH, B. K., Agronomy
  SINGH, R. K., Seed Technology
  THAKUR, R., Plant Breeding
  YAZDANI, S. S., Entomology and Agricul-
    tural Zoology
Faculty of Veterinary Science:
  MOHAN, M., Animal Breeding and Genetics
  PRASAD, C. B., Veterinary Microbiology
  SINGH, M. K., Veterinary Pharmacology
  SINHA, R. R. P., Animal Nutrition
  SRIVASTAVA, P. S., Veterinary Parasitology

ATTACHED COLLEGES

Bihar Agriculture College: Sabour, Bhagalpur; f. 1908 as Bengal Provincial College;
library of 24,835 vols, 70 periodicals; Prin. Dr
S. K. CHANDRA.
Bihar Veterinary College: Patna; Prin. Dr
S. R. SINGH.
College of Agricultural Engineering: f.
1983; depts of farm machinery, farm power
and renewable energy, irrigation and drainage engineering, post-harvest technology and
agricultural structures, soil and water conservation engineering; Dean Dr A. P. MIS-
HRA.
**College of Basic Sciences and Human-
ities:** f. 1981; depts of biochemistry and
chemistry, botany and plant physiology, gen-

etics and molecular biology, language, mathematics and computer application,
microbiology, physics, statistics; Dean Dr V.
K. SHAHI.
College of Fisheries: Dholi; f. 1984; Prin.
Dr S. C. RAI.
College of Home Science: Pusa; f. 1982;
depts of child devt, clothing and textiles,
family resource management, foods and
nutrition; Dean Dr MEERA SINGH.
**Sanjay Gandhi Institute of Dairy Tech-
nology:** f. 1982; depts of dairy cattle breeding and production, dairy cattle nutrition and
forage production, dairy chemistry, dairy
economics, statistics and management, dairy
eng., dairy microbiology, dairy technology,
reproduction and physiology; Dir Dr C.
PRASAD.
Tirhut College of Agriculture: Dholi,
Muzaffarpur; f. 1960; Prin. Dr U. K. MISHRA.

RAJIV GANDHI PROUDYOGIKI VISHWAVIDYALAYA (University of Technology of Madhya Pradesh)

Airport By-pass, Gandhi Nagar, Bhopal
  462036, Madhya Pradesh
Telephone: (755) 2678890
Fax: (755) 2742002
E-mail: vc@rgtu.net
Internet: www.rgtu.net
Founded 1998
State Technological Univ.
156 Colleges of engineering, 44 colleges of
MCA, 91 colleges of pharmacy, 3 colleges of
architecture
Vice-Chancellor: Prof. PIYUSH TRIVEDI
Registrar: Dr A. K. S. BHADORIA
Controller of Examinations: Dr A. K. SINGH
Library of 24,720 vols
Number of students: 130,000

RAJIV GANDHI UNIVERSITY

Rono Hills, Itanagar 791112, Arunachal
  Pradesh
Telephone: (360) 2277253
Fax: (360) 2277889
E-mail: vc_au@rediffmail.com
Internet: www.rgu.ac.in
Founded 1984 as Arunachal Univ.; present
  name 2005
State control
Central univ.
Language of instruction: English
Chancellor: MATA PRASAD
Vice-Chancellor: Prof. K. C. BELLIAPPA
Registrar: D. PANDEY
Librarian: (vacant)
Faculties of basic sciences, education, envir-
onmental sciences, languages, life sciences,
management, social sciences, technology; 11
affiliated colleges in Bomdila, Itanagar,
Khonsa, Pasighat, Salaya, Tezu
Library of 35,000 vols, 200 periodicals
Number of teachers: 46
Number of students: 385

DEANS

Faculty of Education: Prof. J. C. SONI
Faculty of Environmental Sciences: Prof. R.
  S. YADAVA
Faculty of Languages: Prof. B. N. SINGH
Faculty of Management: Prof. A. MITRA
Faculty of Social Sciences: Prof. A. C.
  TALUKDAR

RAJIV GANDHI UNIVERSITY OF HEALTH SCIENCES, KARNATAKA

Bangalore 560041, Karnataka
Telephone: (80) 26961926
Fax: (80) 26961927
E-mail: drpsp@rguhs.ac.in
Internet: www.rguhs.ac.in
Founded 1996
Courses in anaesthesia, ayurveda, cardi-
ology, dentistry, homeopathy, hospital man-
agement, medical laboratory technology,
medicine, naturopathy and yogic sciences,
nursing, perfusion technology, pharmacy,
physiotherapy, psycho-social rehabilitation,
radiography, renal dialysis technology,
respiratory technology, surgery, unani medi-
cine
Vice-Chancellor: Dr S. RAMANANDA SHETTY
Registrar: VASANTHA KUMAR S.
Librarian: Dr R. RAMA RAJ URS.

RANCHI UNIVERSITY

Shaheed Chowk Ranchi, 834001 Bihar
Telephone: (651) 2208553; (651) 2301077
E-mail: admin@ranchiuniversity.org.in
Internet: ranchiuniversity.org.in
Founded 1960
Teaching and affiliating; 23 postgraduate
depts; 33 constituent colleges; 24 affiliated
colleges
Chancellor: HE THE GOVERNOR OF BIHAR
Vice-Chancellor: Prof. A. A. KHAN
Registrar: Dr L. N. BHAGAT
Controller of Examinations: Dr A. K. MAHTO
Dean of Student Welfare: Dr C. S. P. LUGUN
Library of 100,000 vols
Number of teachers: *c.* 2,000
Number of students: 67,500
Publications: *Journal of Agricultural Sci-
  ence, Journal of Historical Research, Jour-
  nal of Social Research, Political Scientist,
  Research Journal of Philosophy, The Geo-
  graphical Outlook, The University Journal*

DEANS

Faculty of Commerce: Prof. S. N. L. DAS
Faculty of Education: Dr APARAJITA JHA
Faculty of Engineering: (vacant)
Faculty of Humanities: Prof. S. P. MISHRA
Faculty of Law: Dr B. N. JHA
Faculty of Medicine: Prof. Dr S. N. CHOUDH-
  ARY
Faculty of Science: Prof. G. P. SHARAN
Faculty of Social Sciences: Prof. S. P. MISHRA

RANI DURGAVATI VISHWAVIDYALAYA JABALPUR

Saraswati Vihar, Jabalpur 482001, Madhya
  Pradesh
Telephone: (761) 2600567
Fax: (761) 2603752
E-mail: cc@rdunijbpin.nic.in
Internet: www.rdunijbpin.org
Founded 1957 as Jabalpur University, name
  changed 1983
Teaching and Affiliating
Languages of instruction: Hindi, English
Academic year: July to April (four terms)
Chancellor: HE THE GOVERNOR OF MADHYA
  PRADESH
Vice-Chancellor: Dr S. M. P. KHURANA
Dir of College Devt Council: Dr KAMLESH
  MISHRA
Dean of Student Welfare: Dr R. D. BHARDWAJ
Registrar: M. K. RAI
Librarian: Y. L. CHOPRA
Library of 183,000 vols
Number of teachers: 1,053
Number of students: 95,000

DEANS

Faculty of Arts: (vacant)
Faculty of Ayurveda: Dr K. K. AGNIHOTRI
Faculty of Commerce: (vacant)
Faculty of Education: Dr B. K. SAHU
Faculty of Homeopathic Medicine and Surgery: (vacant)
Faculty of Home Science: (vacant)
Faculty of Law: Prof. A. SHRIVASTAVA
Faculty of Life Sciences: Prof. Y. K. BANSAL
Faculty of Management: (vacant)
Faculty of Mathematical Science: Prof. P. V. JAIN
Faculty of Medicine: Dr D. K. SAKALLE
Faculty of Science: Prof. A. SHRIVASTAVA
Faculty of Social Sciences: Dr C. S. S. THAKUR

There are 116 affiliated colleges

RASHTRASANT TUKADOJI MAHARAJ NAGPUR UNIVERSITY

Chhatrapati Shivaji Maharaj Admin. Premises, Rabindranath Tagore Marg, Nagpur 440001, Maharashtra

Telephone: (712) 2525417
Fax: (712) 2532841
E-mail: info@nagpuruniversity.org
Internet: www.nagpuruniversity.org

Founded 1923, fmrly Nagpur Univ.

Teaching and affiliating; 439 affiliated colleges

Languages of instruction: English, Hindi, Marathi

Academic year: June to March (two terms)

Chancellor: HE THE GOV. OF MAHARASHTRA
Vice-Chancellor: Dr S. N. PATHAN
Registrar: SUBHASH BELSARE
Librarian: Dr P. S. G. KUMAR

Library of 350,171 vols, including 14,313 MSS
Number of teachers: 4,074
Number of students: 95,664

DEANS

Faculty of Arts: A. K. DEY
Faculty of Ayurvedic Medicine: S. SHARMA
Faculty of Commerce: N. H. KHATRI
Faculty of Education: R. S. DAGAR
Faculty of Engineering and Technology: H. THAKARE
Faculty of Home Science: Dr A. G. MOHARIL
Faculty of Law: SUNDARAM
Faculty of Medicine: Dr W. B. TAYADE
Faculty of Science: Dr T. M. KARDE
Faculty of Social Sciences: V. H. GHORPADE

CONSTITUENT COLLEGES

B. R. Ambedkar College of Law: f. 1925; 10 teachers; 2,571 students; Prin. Dr J. L. APARAJIT.

Laxminarayan Institute of Technology: tel. (712) 2561107; fax (712) 2531659; e-mail rajumankar@rediffmail.com; internet www .litnagpur.info; f. 1942; 50 teachers; 510 students; Dir Dr R. B. MANKAR.

University College of Education: Nagpur; f. 1945; 16 teachers; 320 students; Prin. V. MANAPURE.

SAMBALPUR UNIVERSITY

PO Jyoti Vihar, Burla, Sambalpur 768019, Orissa

Telephone: (663) 2430157
Fax: (663) 2430158
E-mail: chairman@sambalpuruniversitypgc .in
Internet: www.sambalpuruniversitypgc.in

Founded 1967

Teaching and Affiliating
Language of instruction: English
Academic year: June to May

Chancellor: THE GOVERNOR OF ORISSA

Vice-Chancellor: Prof. ARUN K. PUJARI
Registrar: R. R. PADHEE
Dir of College Devt Council: Prof. S. MOHANTY
Librarian: Dr B. P. MOHAPATRA

179 Affiliated colleges

Library of 105,000 vols, 15,000 periodicals
Number of teachers: 1,653
Number of students: 36,225

Publications: *Journal* (Science, 1 a year), *Journal of Humanities* (1 a year), *Saptarshi* (12 a year)

DEANS

Faculty of Arts: Prof. S. NANDA
Faculty of Commerce: Prof. D. P. NAYAK
Faculty of Education: (vacant)
Faculty of Engineering: Dr R. K. MISHRA
Faculty of Law: Prof. G. K. RATH
Faculty of Medicine: Prof. A. K. SARANGI
Faculty of Science: Dr M. K. BEHERA

SAMPURNANAND SANSKRIT UNIVERSITY

Varanasi 221002, Uttar Pradesh

Telephone: (542) 2204089; (542) 2206617
Internet: ssvv.up.nic.in

Founded 1958

Teaching and affiliating; faculties of adhunika jnana vijnana, philsophy, sahitya Sanskrit, sramana vidya, veda-vedanga; 2 affiliated on-campus, and 1,998 off-campus colleges

Chancellor: THE GOV. OF UTTAR PRADESH
Vice-Chancellor: Prof. V. KUTUMB SHASTRI
Registrar: YOGANDRA NATH
Dir of Research: Dr RAJA RAM SHUKLA
Librarian: V. N. MISRA

Library of 262,000 vols
Number of students: 35,000

SARDAR PATEL UNIVERSITY

Vallabh Vidyanagar 388120, Gujarat

Telephone: (2692) 226812
Fax: (2692) 236475
Internet: www.spuvvn.edu

Founded 1955

Teaching and affiliating; 26 postgraduate depts, 1 constituent college, 71 affiliated colleges

Languages of instruction: Hindi, English, Gujarati

Academic year: June to April (two terms)

Chancellor: HE THE GOV. OF GUJARAT
Vice-Chancellor: Dr B. G. PATEL
Registrar: Dr B. NATRAJ
Librarian: Dr M. J. TRIVEDI

Library of 212,780 vols
Number of teachers: 172
Number of students: 43,912 , incl. 8,597 postgraduate

Publications: *Arth-Vikas* (Economics Journal), *Journal of Education and Psychology*, *Mimansa* (Journal of English Literature), *Prajna* (Journal of Basic Science), *Prajna* (Journal of Social Science and Business Studies), *Sheel Shrutam* (12 a year)

DEANS

Faculty of Arts: Dr R. P. PANDYA
Faculty of Business Studies: M. K. PATEL
Faculty of Education: Dr V. T. BHAMWARI
Faculty of Engineering and Technology: Prin.: F. S. UMRIGAR
Faculty of Home Science: Dr REMA SUBHASH
Faculty of Homoeopathy: Dr V. D. PATEL
Faculty of Law: APRURVA C. PATHAK
Faculty of Management: Dr NIKHIL M. ZAVERI
Faculty of Medicine: Dr S. H. SHRIVASTAV

Faculty of Pharmaceutical Science: Prof. A. K. SALUJA
Faculty of Science: Dr D. J. DESAI

SARDAR VALLABH BHAI PATEL UNIVERSITY OF AGRICULTURE AND TECHNOLOGY

Modipuram, Meerut 250110, Uttar Pradesh

Telephone: (121) 2411503
Fax: (121) 2411505
E-mail: university@svbpuniversitymerrut .org
Internet: www.svbpmeerut.ac.in

Founded 2000

Colleges of agriculture, agriculture business management, animal husbandry and veterinary science, basic sciences, biotechnology, engineering, home science, horticulture and agroforestry, information technology, postharvest technology and food processing, postgraduate studies

Chancellor: HE THE GOVERNOR OF UTTAR PRADESH
Vice-Chancellor: Dr M. P. YADAV
Registrar: Dr NARENDRA SHARMA
Dean of Student Welfare: Prof. P. L. SAROJ
Dir of Research: Prof. I. B. SINGH

DEANS

College of Agriculture: Prof. B. RAM (acting)
College of Biotechnology: Prof. D. SINGH (acting)
Postgraduate Studies: Prof. Y. P. SINGH

SARDARKRUSHINAGAR DANTIWADA AGRICULTURAL UNIVERSITY

District Banaskantha, Sardar Krushinagar 385506, Gujarat

Telephone: (2748) 278222
Fax: (2748) 278261
E-mail: vc@gauskn.guj.nic.in
Internet: www.sdau.edu.in

Founded 1972

Fmrly Gujarat Agricultural Univ.
Academic year: July to March

Chancellor: SUNDARSINGH BHANDARI
Vice-Chancellor: Dr RAVISH CHANDRA MAHESHWARI
Dir of Research and Dean of Postgraduate Studies: Dr S. B. S. TIKKA
Dir of Student Welfare: Dr VEER SINGH
Registrar: Dr H. N. KHER
Librarian: Dr L. D. PARMER

Library of 24,150 vols, 225 periodicals
Number of teachers: 1,336
Number of students: 2,181

DEANS

Faculty of Agricultural Engineering and Technology: Dr S. C. B. SIRIPURAPU
Faculty of Agriculture: Dr J. G. PATEL
Faculty of Dairy Science: Dr R. S. SHARMA
Faculty of Fisheries Science: Dr A. Y. DESAI (acting)
Faculty of Forestry and Horticulture: Dr B. M. PATEL (acting)
Faculty of Home Science: Dr K. SHREEDHARAN (acting)
Faculty of Veterinary Science and Animal Husbandry: Dr V. P. VADODARIA (acting)

CONSTITUENT COLLEGES

Aspee College of Home Science: Sardar Krushinagar; Prin. Dr M. M. PATEL (acting).

Aspee College of Horticulture and Forestry: Navsari; Prin. Dr B. M. PATEL (acting).

B. A. College of Agriculture: Anand; Prin. Dr D. J. PATEL.

College of Agricultural Engineering and Technology: Junagadh; Prin. Dr S. C. B. SIRIPURAPU.

College of Agriculture, Junagadh: Prin. Dr D. D. MALAVIA.

College of Agriculture, Sardar Krushinagar: Prin. Dr S. R. S. DANGE (acting).

College of Fisheries Science: Veraval; Prin. Dr A. Y. DESAI (acting).

College of Veterinary Science and Animal Husbandry, Anand: Prin. Dr M. B. PANDE (acting).

College of Veterinary Science and Animal Husbandry, Sardar Krushinagar: Prin. Dr M. C. DESAI.

Mansukhlal Chhaganlal College of Dairy Science: Anand; Prin. Dr R. S. SHARMA.

N. M. College of Agriculture: Navsari; Prin. Dr H. N. VYAS.

SAURASHTRA UNIVERSITY

University Campus, University Rd, Rajkot 360005, Gujarat

Telephone: (281) 2576347
Fax: (281) 2581385
E-mail: registrar@sauuni.ernet.in
Internet: www.saurashtrauniversity.edu

Founded 1967
Teaching and affiliating
State control
Languages of instruction: Gujarati, Hindi, English
Academic year: June to March/April (two terms)

Chancellor: HE THE GOV. OF GUJARAT STATE
Vice-Chancellor: Dr KAMLESH P. JOSHIPURA
Pro-Vice-Chancellor: K. T. TRIVEDI
Registrar: G. M. JANI
Controller of Examinations: J. M. MAMTORA
Librarian: N. N. SONI

318 Affiliated colleges

Library of 171,577 vols, 230 periodicals
Number of teachers: 3,614 (incl. affiliated colleges)
Number of students: 140,234 (incl. affiliated colleges)

DEANS

Faculty of Architecture: (vacant)
Faculty of Arts: S. J. JHALA (acting)
Faculty of Business Management: Dr P. L. CHAUHAN
Faculty of Commerce: R. M. TALVANIA
Faculty of Education: B. R. RAMANUJ
Faculty of Engineering: S. PARIKH
Faculty of Home Science: V. CHHICHHIYA
Faculty of Homeopathy: Dr B. M. PANDA (acting)
Faculty of Law: N. C. SHUKLA (acting)
Faculty of Medicine: Dr D. K. SHAH
Faculty of Rural Studies: D. R. MARTHAK
Faculty of Science: Dr G. BHIMANI

SHER-E-KASHMIR UNIVERSITY OF AGRICULTURAL SCIENCES AND TECHNOLOGY JAMMU

Railway Rd, Jammu 180012, Jammu and Kashmir

Telephone: (191) 2473417
Fax: (191) 2473883
E-mail: vc@skuast.org
Internet: www.skuast.org

Founded 1999
State control
Academic year: July to June

Chancellor: HE THE GOVERNOR OF JAMMU AND KASHMIR
Vice-Chancellor: Dr B. MISHRA
Registrar: A. K. KOUL

Librarian: S. C. UPPAL
Library of 11,412 vols, 125 current periodicals

DEANS

Faculty of Agriculture: Dr R. K. SHARMA (Assoc. Dean)
Faculty of Veterinary Sciences and Animal Husbandry: Dr A. K. SRIVASTAVA

SHER-E-KASHMIR UNIVERSITY OF AGRICULTURAL SCIENCES AND TECHNOLOGY OF KASHMIR

Shalimar Campus, Srinagar 191121, Jammu and Kashmir

Telephone: (194) 2462160
Fax: (194) 2462160
E-mail: vcskuastk@jk.nic.in
Internet: www.skuastkashmir.ac.in

Founded 1982
State control
Academic year: August to July

Faculties of agriculture, fisheries, postgraduate studies, veterinary sciences and animal husbandry

Chancellor: HE THE GOVERNOR OF JAMMU AND KASHMIR
Vice-Chancellor: Dr ANWAR ALAM
Registrar: Dr M. A. GORA

Library of 63,738 vols, 110 periodicals.

SHIVAJI UNIVERSITY

Vidyanagar, Kolhapur 416004, Maharashtra

Telephone: (231) 2609000
Fax: (231) 2691533
E-mail: vcoffice@unishivaji.ac.in
Internet: www.unishivaji.ac.in

Founded 1962
Teaching and Affiliating
Languages of instruction: English, Marathi
Academic year: June to April (two terms)

Chancellor: HE THE GOVERNOR OF MAHARASHTRA
Vice-Chancellor: Dr M. M. SALUNKHE
Registrar: Dr D. T. SHIRKE (acting)
Librarian: R. K. KAMAT (acting)

226 Affiliated colleges

Library of 244,729 vols, 6,923 MSS, 361 periodicals
Number of teachers: 3,483
Number of students: 194,314

Publication: *University Journal* (Humanities and Social Sciences sections)

DEANS

Faculty of Arts: Dr J. R. JADHAV
Faculty of Ayurvedic and Homeopathic Medicine: (vacant)
Faculty of Commerce: Dr B. S. SAWANT
Faculty of Education: K. N. SANGLE
Faculty of Engineering and Technology: A. N. JADHAV
Faculty of Law: Prin.: MANGLA S. PATIL
Faculty of Medicine: Dr RAMKRISHNA AYCHIT
Faculty of Science: Dr T. B. JAGTAP
Faculty of Social Sciences: Dr V. P. RASAM

CONSTITUENT CENTRES

Centre for Community Development: tel. (231) 2690571; Dir MANJUSHA DESHPANDE.

Centre of Gandhian Studies: f. 2000; Dir Dr R. B. PATIL.

Centre for Women's Studies: Dir Dr MEDHA NANIVADEKAR.

Shahu Research Centre: f. 1974; Dir Dr M. P. PATIL.

SHREEMATI NATHIBAI DAMODAR THACKERSEY WOMEN'S UNIVERSITY

1 Nathibai Thackersey Rd, Mumbai 400020, Maharashtra

Telephone: (22) 22031879
Fax: (22) 22018226
Internet: sndt.digitaluniversity.ac

Founded 1916
Teaching and affiliating; 210 affiliated colleges
State control
Languages of instruction: English, Gujarati, Marathi, Hindi
Academic year: June to March (two terms)

Chancellor: HE THE GOV. OF MAHARASHTRA
Vice-Chancellor: Dr CHANDRA KRISHNAMURTHY
Pro-Vice-Chancellor: Prof. S. MANTHA
Registrar: Dr MADHU MADAN
Librarian: Dr SUSHAMA POWDWAL

Library of 335,000 vols
Number of teachers: 744 full-time, 238 part-time
Number of students: 50,000

DEANS

Faculty of Arts: Dr SHASHI KASHYAP
Faculty of Commerce: Dr KALYANI VENKATESHWARAN
Faculty of Education: Dr LEENA DESHPANDE
Faculty of Fine Arts: AVIRAJ TAYADE
Faculty of Home Sciences: Dr SHOBHA UDIPI
Faculty of Library Science: PARUL ZAVERI
Faculty of Nursing: NANCY FERNANDES
Faculty of Social Sciences: Dr MANGALA JUNGALE

CONSTITUENT COLLEGES

C. U. Shah College of Pharmacy: Sir Vithaldas Vidyavihar Juhu Rd, Mumbai 400049; tel. (22) 26608551; e-mail cuscp@yahoo.co.in; f. 1980; Prin. Dr S. Y. GABHE.

Janakidevi Bajaj Institute of Management Studies: Sir Vithaldas Vidyavihar Juhu Rd, Mumbai 400049; tel. (22) 26606626; e-mail jdbims@rediffmail.com; internet www.jdbims.net; f. 1997; Dir GULNAR SHARMA.

Leelabai Thackersey College of Nursing: tel. (22) 22087422; e-mail ltcn@rediffmail.com; f. 1952; Prin. ALKA KALAMBI.

Premcoonverbai Vithaldas Damodar Thackersey College of Education for Women: tel. (22) 22063267; e-mail pvdtce@sndt.ac.in; f. 1959; Prin. Dr HARSHA MANCHANT.

Premlila Vithaldas Polytechnic: Sir Vithaldas Vidyavihar Juhu Rd, Mumbai 400049; tel. (22) 26608676; e-mail pvpelex@vsnl.com; internet www.pvpsndt.org; f. 1976; Prin. RAVINDRA KABNURKAR.

Shree Hansraj Pragji Thackersey School of Library Science: e-mail shptsndt@gmail.com; internet www.shpt-econtent.in; f. 1961; Prin. Prof. SUSHAMA POWDWAL.

Shreemati Nathibai Damodar Thackersey College of Arts, and Shreemati Champaben Bhogilal College of Commerce and Economics for Women: tel. (22) 22093789; f. 1931; Prin. Dr B. B. PRADHAN.

Shreemati Nathibai Damodar Thackersey College of Arts and Commerce for Women: Karve Rd, Maharshi Karve Vidyavihar, Pune 411038; f. 1916; Prin. (vacant).

Shreemati Nathibai Damodar Thackersey College of Education for Women: Karve Rd, Maharshi Karve Vidyarihar, Pune 411038; tel. (22) 25433416; e-mail sndt_education_pune@yahoo.co.in; f. 1964; Prin. Dr LEENA DESHPANDE.

Shreemati Nathibai Damodar Thackersey College of Home Science: Karve Rd, Maharshi Karve Vidyarihar, Pune 411038; tel. (22) 25432097; e-mail principal@sndthsc.com; internet www.sndthsc.com; f. 1968; Prin. (vacant).

Sir Vithaldas Thackersey College of Home Science: tel. (22) 26602504; e-mail computerlab@vsnl.net; internet www.svt.ac.in; f. 1959; Prin. Dr INDRAJIT MADAN (acting).

Usha Mittal Institute of Technology: Sir Vithaldas Vidyavihar Juhu Rd, Mumbai 400049; tel. (22) 26606040; e-mail umit@vsnl.net; internet www.umit.ac.in; Dir KUMUD VASNIK.

SHRI JAGANNATH SANSKRIT VISHWAVIDYALAYA

Srivihar, Puri 752003, Orissa

Telephone: (6752) 251663

Fax: (6752) 251073

E-mail: sjsv@ori.nic.in

Internet: sjsv.nic.in

Founded 1981

Depts of dharmashastra, nyaya, sahitya, sarvadarshan, veda, vedanta and vyakarana

Vice-Chancellor: Prof. ALEKHA CHANDRA SARANGI

Registrar: Dr BABAJI CHARAN PATTANAYAK

Librarian: MAHESHWAR MOHAPATRA

Library of 22,731 vols, 1,044 journals

Publication: *Jagannath Jyotih* (irregular).

SHRI MATA VAISHNO DEVI UNIVERSITY

SPO Kakryal, Katra 182320, Distrtict: REASI, Jammu and Kashmir

Telephone: (1991) 285535

Fax: (1991) 285694

E-mail: vc@smvdu.ac.in

Internet: www.smvdu.ac.in

Founded 1999

Residential and teaching

Chancellor: HE THE GOV. OF JAMMU AND KASHMIR

Vice-Chancellor: Prof. N. K. BANSAL

Registrar: Dr R. S. MISRA

Librarian: SUBRATA DEB

Library: approx. 20,000 vols, 1250 online periodicals and 94 print periodicals, e-resources: 500 CDs/DVDs, databases: ABI Inform Global, MathSciNet, EIS Statistical, Memberships: INDEST-AICTE CONSORTIUM, DELNET

DEANS

College of Engineering: Prof. M. L. GARG

College of Management: Prof. J. P. SINGH

College of Philosophy, Culture and Languages: Prof. R. S. MISRA

College of Sciences: Prof. V. VERMA

DIRECTORS

School of Applied Physics and Mathematics: Dr V. K. BHAT

School of Architecture and Landscape Design: Prof. C. L. RAZDAN

School of Business: Dr SUNIL GIRI (acting)

School of Economics: Dr SUPARN SHARMA (acting)

School of Electronics and Communication: Dr S. K. PURI

School of Infrastructure and Resource Management: RAKESH SHARMA (acting)

School of Languages: Dr VANDANA SHARMA (acting)

School of Mechanical Engineering: Dr SUDHIR KUMAR (acting)

SIDO KANHU MURMU UNIVERSITY

Santal Parganas, Dumka 814101, Jharkhand

Internet: skmu.edu.in

Founded 1992 as Siddhu Kanhu Univ., present name 2000

Academic year: June to May

13 Constituent colleges and 15 affiliated colleges

Vice-Chancellor: Dr VICTOR TIGGA

Pro-Vice-Chancellor: Dr ARVIND KUMAR

Dean of Student Welfare: Dr MANOJ KUMAR SINHA

Registrar: Dr A. N. PATHAK (acting)

Librarian: Dr AJIT KUMAR SINGH.

SIKKIM MANIPAL UNIVERSITY OF HEALTH, MEDICAL AND TECHNOLOGICAL SCIENCES

Fifth Mile, Tadong, Gangtok 737102, Sikkim

Telephone: (3592) 232041

Fax: (3592) 232041

E-mail: study@smu.edu.in

Internet: www.smu.edu.in

Founded 1995

Academic year: August to July

Chancellor: HE THE GOV. OF SIKKIM

Pro-Chancellor: Dr RAMDAS PAI

Vice-Chancellor: Dr K. JAYAKUMAR

Registrar: SHERAP SHENGA.

CONSTITUENT INSTITUTIONS

School of Basic and Applied Sciences: Majitar Rangpo 737132, East Sikkim; internet sbas.smu.edu.in.

Sikkim Manipal College of Nursing: Fifth Mile, Tadong, Gangtok 737102, Sikkim; internet cn.smu.edu.in; Principal MRIDULA DAS.

Sikkim Manipal College of Physiotherapy: Fifth Mile, Tadong, Gangtok 737102, Sikkim; internet cp.smu.edu.in; Principal Dr NIKITA JOSHI.

Sikkim Manipal Institute of Medical Science: Fifth Mile, Tadong, Gangtok 737102, Sikkim; Dean Dr P. G. SHIVANANDA.

Sikkim Manipal Institute of Technology: Majitar Rangpo 737132, East Sikkim; tel. (3592) 246353; fax (3592) 246112; e-mail slg smit@sancharnet.in; internet smit.smu.edu.in; f. 1997; Dir Brig. Dr SOMNATH MISHRA; Dean Prof. Dr ACHINTYA CHOUDHURY.

SREE SANKARACHARYA UNIVERSITY OF SANSKRIT

Sree Sankarapuram, Ernakulam, Kalady 683574, Kerala

Telephone: (484) 2463380

Fax: (484) 2463480

E-mail: ssus@vsnl.com

Internet: www.ssus.ac.in

Founded 1994

Academic year: June to April

Faculties of arts, education, sanskrit studies and social sciences; regional Centres in Ettumanoor, Kalady, Koyilandy, Payyannur, Thrissur, Thuravoor and Tirur

Chancellor: HE THE GOV. OF KERALA

Vice-Chancellor: Dr J. PRASAD

Registrar: Dr S. PREMJITH

Prin. and Dean of Studies: Dr N. K. SANKARAN

Library of 53,000 vols, 125 periodicals, 200 MSS.

SRI KRISHNADEVARAYA UNIVERSITY

Sri Venkateswarapuram PO, Anantapur 515003, Andhra Pradesh

Telephone: (8554) 255700

Fax: (8554) 255804

E-mail: registrar@skuniversity.org

Internet: www.skuniversity.org

Founded 1967, univ. status 1981

Postgraduate teaching and research

Language of instruction: English

Academic year: December to October

Chancellor: HE THE GOVERNOR OF ANDHRA PRADESH

Vice-Chancellor: Prof. P. KUSUMA KUMARI

Prin.: Prof. T. PULLAIAH

Dean of College Devt Ccl: Prof. D. SARALA KUMARI

Controller of Examinations: T. K. SRINIVAS

Dir of Centre for Distance Education: Prof. V. REDDAPA REDDY

Registrar: Prof. Y. G. H. PHILIP

Librarian: Dr P. KAMAIAK

112 Affiliated colleges

Library of 114,000 vols, 190 periodicals

Number of teachers: 154

Number of students: 1,500

DEANS

Faculty of Engineering: (vacant)

Faculty of Languages and Literature: Prof. H. S. BRAHMANADA

Faculty of Law: Prof. S. SESHAIAH

Faculty of Life Sciences: Prof. K. RADHAKRISHNAIAH

Faculty of Management: Prof. C. R. REDDY RAO

Faculty of Physical Sciences: Prof. D. R. V. PRASAD RAO

Faculty of Social Sciences: Prof. C. U. MOHAN

PROFESSORS

ANKI REDDY, K. C., Mathematics

BASHA MOHIDEEN, M., Zoology

BRAHMAJI RAO, S., Chemistry

ENOCK, K., Telugu

GHOUSE, M., Law

GOPAL, B. R., History

KAMESWARA RAO, A.

KANTHA RAO, M. L., Economics

KOTESWARA RAO, T., Telugu

KRISHNA, D. V., Mathematics

MANOHARA MURTHY, N., Physics

NAIDU, V. T., Rural Development

NARAYANA, N., Economics

PRAKASHA RAO, C. G., Botany

RAGHUNATHA SARMA, S., Telugu

RAJGOPAL, E.

RAMA MURTHY, V., Physics

RAMAKRISHNA RAO, A., English

RAMAKRISHNA RAO, P., Biochemistry

RAMAKRISHNA RAO, T. V., Physics

RAMAVATHARAM, S. I., Law

SEETHARAMASWAMY, R., Mathematics

SHARMA, D. P., Commerce

SUBBA RAO, C., English

SUBBARAMAIAH, S., Economics

SUBBI REDDY, T., Commerce

SUBRAHMANYAM, S. V., Physics

SUDARSHAN RAO, T. P., Law

SWAMINATHAN, E., Geography

TIRUPATHI NAIDU, V., Rural Development

VENKATA REDDY, C., Economics

VENKATA REDDY, D., Chemistry

VENKATA REDDY, K., English

VENKATA REDDY, K., Rural Development

VENKATASIVA MURTHY, K. N., Mathematics

POSTGRADUATE CENTRE

SKU, Kurnool: f. 1977; library of 25,000 vols, 30 periodicals; courses in area planning and regional devt in economics, microprocessors in physics, MSc. computer science and management studiesnatural products in chemistry, operations research and statistical quality control, telugu; Dir Prof. C. UMASANKAR.

SRI PADMAVATHI MAHILA VISVAVIDYALAYAM

Tirupati 517502, Andhra Pradesh
Telephone: (877) 2248417
Fax: (877) 2248417
E-mail: vcspmvv@yahoo.com
Internet: www.padmavatiwomen-univ.org
Founded 1983
Academic year: July to June

Schools of applied mathematics, business management, communication and information science, computer science, education, home science, legal studies and research, letters, life sciences, music and fine arts, pharmaceutical sciences, physical sciences, social sciences; Univ. College of Eng., Centre for Ambedkar Studies, Centre for Research Studies

Chancellor: HE THE GOV. OF ANDHRA PRADESH
Vice-Chancellor: Prof. G. SAROJAMMA
Rector: Prof. K. UMA DEVI
Registrar: Dr E. MANJUVANI
Deputy Librarian: Dr D. RAJESWARI

Library of 46,000 books, 8,000 vols of periodicals
Number of students: 1,032

SRI VENKATESWARA UNIVERSITY

Tirupati 517502, Andhra Pradesh
Telephone: (877) 2248374
Internet: www.svuniversity.in
Founded 1954 as Residential and Teaching; Affiliating since 1956
Languages of instruction: English, Telugu
Academic year: June to April (two terms)

Chancellor: HE THE GOVERNOR OF ANDHRA PRADESH
Vice-Chancellor: Prof. N. PRABHAKARA RAO
Registrar: Prof. K. RATHNAIAH
Dean of College Devt Council: Prof. M. A. K. SUKUMAR
Dir of Research: Prof. S. BUDDHUDU
Librarian: Dr M. R. CHANDRAN

Library: Libraries of 278,974 vols
Number of teachers: 400
Number of students: 5,000

DEANS

College of Arts: Prof. C. P. KASAIAH
College of Biological and Earth Sciences: Prof. P. SREENIVASULU
College of Commerce, Management and Information Sciences: Prof. S. BALARAMI REDDY
College of Education and Extension Studies: Prof. D. USHA RANI
College of Engineering: Prof. M. M. NAIDU
College of Humanities: Prof. S. G. D. CHANDRASEKHAR
College of Int. Studies: Prof. D. K. KRANTH CHOWDARY
College of Mathematical and Physical Sciences: Prof. C. SUBBARAMI REDDY

POSTGRADUATE CENTRES

Postgraduate Centre, Kadapa: f. 1977; library of 20,000 vols, 40 periodicals; Dir Prof. G. SIVA REDDY.

Postgraduate Centre, Kavali: f. 1929; library of 17,500 vols, 40 periodicals; Dir Prof. B. D. RAMI REDDY.

SWAMI RAMANAND TEERTH MARATHWADA UNIVERSITY

Vishnupuri, Nanded 431606, Maharashtra
Telephone: (2462) 229243
Fax: (2462) 229245
E-mail: nnd_vc@sancharnet.in
Internet: www.srtmun.ac.in
Founded 1994

Teaching and affiliating
Academic year: June to April

Chancellor: HE THE GOV. OF MAHARASHTRA
Vice-Chancellor: Dr S. B. NIMSE
Registrar: Dr RAM B. WAGH
Dir of Student Welfare: D. D. PAWAR
Controller of Examinations: Maj. N. V. CHAVAN
Librarian: Dr S. P. SATARKAR

172 Affiliated colleges

Library of 40,000 vols, 123 nat. and 34 int. periodicals
Publication: *New Vision*

DEANS

Faculty of Arts: Dr B. S. JADHAV
Faculty of Commerce: Dr B. B. JADHAV
Faculty of Education: Dr B. M. GORE
Faculty of Physical Sciences: P. N. DESHMUKH
Faculty of Science: Dr G. D. BAGADE
Faculty of Social Sciences: Dr U. D. SAWANT

TAMIL NADU AGRICULTURAL UNIVERSITY

Coimbatore 641003, Tamil Nadu
Telephone: (422) 6611200
Fax: (422) 6611410
E-mail: registrar@tnau.ac.in
Internet: www.tnau.ac.in
Founded 1971
State control
Language of instruction: English
Academic year: July to June (two semesters)

10 Colleges; 34 research stations

Chancellor: HE THE GOV. OF TAMIL NADU
Pro-Chancellor: THE MIN. OF AGRICULTURE, GOVT OF TAMIL NADU
Vice-Chancellor: Dr C. RAMASAMY
Registrar: Dr S. D. SUNDAR SINGH
Controller of Admissions: Dr B. SANTHANAKRISHNAN
Deputy Librarian: K. PERUMALSAMY

Library of 161,146 vols, 380 periodicals
Number of teachers: 955
Number of students: 2,791

Publications: *Journal of Agriculture Resource Management* (in English, 2 a year), *Journal of External Education* (in English, 4 a year), *Madras Agricultural Journal* (in English, 12 a year), *South Indian Horticulture* (in English, 4 a year)

DEANS

Agricultural College and Research Institute, Coimbatore: Dr R. KRISHNASAMY
Agricultural College and Research Institute, Killikulam: Dr T. M. THIAGARAJAN
Agricultural College and Research Institute, Madurai: Dr N. KEMPUCHETTY
Agricultural Engineering College and Research Institute, Coimbatore: Dr R. MANIAN
Agricultural Engineering College and Research Institute, Kumulur: Dr C. T. DEVADAS
Anbil Dharmalingham Agricultural College and Research Institute, Tiruchirappalli: Dr S. ANTHONI RAJ
Forest College and Research Institute, Mettupalayam: Prof. K. S. NEELAKANDAN
Home Science College and Research Institute, Madurai: Dr K. SHEELA
Horticultural College and Research Institute, Coimbatore: Dr E. VADIVEL
Horticultural College and Research Institute, Periyakulam: Dr S. ANBU
School of Postgraduate Studies, Coimbatore: Dr S. KOMBAIRAJU

DIRECTORS

Centre for Agriculture and Rural Development Studies: Dr N. RAVEENDRAN
Centre for Plant Breeding and Genetics: Dr T. S. RAVEENDRAN
Centre for Plant Molecular Biology: Dr K. RAMASAMY
Centre for Plant Protection Studies: Dr T. MARIMUTHU
Extension Education: Dr G. DORAISWAMY
Open and Distance Learning: Dr V. ALAGESAN
Planning and Mentoring: Dr D. VEERARAGAVATHATHAM
Research: Dr S. RAMANATHAN
Soil and Crop Management Studies: Dr V. MURUGAPPAN
Student Welfare: Dr V. THANDAPANI
Tamil Nadu Rice Research Institute, Aduthurai: Dr B. CHANDRASEKARAN
Water Technology Centre: Dr K. PALANISAMI

CONSTITUENT COLLEGES

Agricultural College and Research Institute, Coimbatore: tel. (422) 6611210; fax (422) 6611410; e-mail deanagri@tnau.ac.in; internet www.tnau.ac.in/agcbe.

Agricultural College and Research Institute, Killikulam: Killikulam, Vallanadu 628252, Tamil Nadu; tel. (4630) 2461226; fax (4630) 2461268; e-mail deankkm@tnau.ac.in; f. 1984; Dir Dr P. VIVEKANANDAN.

Agricultural College and Research Institute, Madurai: Madurai 625104; tel. (452) 2422956; e-mail deanagrimdu@tnau.ac.in; internet www.tnau.ac.in/agrimdu.html; ean Dr N. KEMBUCHETTY.

Agricultural Engineering College and Research Institute, Coimbatore: tel. (422) 5511255; fax (422) 2431672; e-mail deancaecbe@tnau.ac.in; internet www.tnau.ac.in/aecricbe; Dean Dr A. SAMPATHRAJAN.

Agricultural Engineering College and Research Institute, Kumulur: Tiruchirappalli 621712, Tamil Nadu; tel. and fax (431) 2541218; e-mail deancaekum@tnau.ac.in; f. 1972; Dean Dr C. T. DEVADAS.

Anbil Dharmalingam Agricultural College and Research Institute: Tiruchirappalli 620009, Tamil Nadu; f. 1992; Dean Dr A. ANTHONI RAJ.

Forest College and Research Institute: Mettupalayam 641301, Tamil Nadu.

Home Science College and Research Institute, Madurai: Madurai 625104; e-mail manimegalaigobalasamy@yahoo.co.in; f. 1980; Dean Dr G. MANIMEGALAI.

Horticultural College and Research Institute, Coimbatore: tel. (422) 5511371; fax (422) 2430781; e-mail deanhortcbe@tnau.ac.in; internet www.tnau.ac.in/horcbe; Dean Dr D. VEERARAGAVATHATHAM.

Horticultural College and Research Institute, Periyakulam: Periyakulam 625604, Tamil Nadu; tel. (4546) 231726; e-mail deanhcripkm@tnau.ac.in.

School of Postgraduate Studies, Coimbatore: e-mail deanspgs@tnau.ac.in; internet www.tnau.ac.in/pg; f. 1971.

TAMIL NADU DR AMBEDKAR LAW UNIVERSITY

5 Greenways Rd, Chennai 600028, Tamil Nadu
Telephone: (44) 24641212
Fax: (44) 24957414
E-mail: vc@tndalu.org
Internet: www.tndalu.org
Founded 1997
8 Affiliated law colleges

Chancellor: HE THE GOV. OF TAMIL NADU
Vice-Chancellor: Prof. S. SACHIDHANANDAM
Registrar: Dr D. GOPAL
Controller of Examinations: Prof. T. JOHNSON
Public Relations Officer: A. SHAJJATH HUSSAIN
Dean of Postgraduate Studies: Prof. A. RAGHUNATHA REDDY

Library of 13,960 vols
Number of students: 7,300

Publication: *Law Journal* (1 a year).

CONSTITUENT SCHOOLS

School of Excellence in Law: f. 2002; Dir Prof. Dr D. GOPAL.

Tamil Nadu Dr Ambedkar Law University Law College, Chengalpattu: f. 2003.

TAMIL NADU DR M. G. R. MEDICAL UNIVERSITY

69 Anna Salai, Guindy, Chennai 600032, Tamil Nadu

Telephone: (44) 22353574
Fax: (44) 22353698
E-mail: tnmmu@yahoo.com
Internet: www.tnmmu.ac.in

Founded 1987

Teaching and Affiliating

Chancellor: HE THE GOVERNOR OF TAMIL NADU
Vice-Chancellor: Dr K. M. M. HUSSAIN
Librarian: Dr N. C. JAYAMANI

226 Govt and private medical and paramedical instns affiliated

HEADS OF FACULTIES

Faculty of Ayurveda: Dr R. DEVADAS
Faculty of Basic Medical Sciences: Dr R. G. SUKUMAR
Faculty of Biomedical Sciences: Dr R. HARIHARAN
Faculty of Community Health, Social Sciences and History of Medicine: Dr RAJKUMAR
Faculty of Dentistry: Dr S. RAMACHANDRAN
Faculty of Homeopathy: Dr T. K. MOHANDAS
Faculty of Medicine and Medical Specialities: Dr M. THIRUNAVUKKARASU
Faculty of Naturopathy and Yogic Sciences: (vacant)
Faculty of Nursing: Dr M. GOWRI (acting)
Faculty of Obstetrics and Gynaecology and Related Specialities: Dr N. RAJAMAHESHWARI
Faculty of Paediatrics and Paediatric Specialities: Prof. K. M. M. HUSSEIN
Faculty of Pharmacy: Dr T. K. RAVI
Faculty of Siddha: Dr A. M. ABDUL KADHER
Faculty of Surgery and Surgical Specialities: Dr GOVHARDAN
Faculty of Unani: Dr K. R. AHMED

PROFESSORS

Faculty of Ayurveda:
SESHADHRI, V.

Faculty of Basic Medical Sciences:
BANUMATHY, S. P., Anatomy
MANICKAVASAGAM, S.
NALINI, A., Pharmacology
RAJESWARI, C., Microbiology
SHERIFF, Biochemistry
VADIVELU, Forensic Medicine

Faculty of Biomedical Sciences:
SAMUEL, N. M.

Faculty of Community Health, Social Sciences and History of Medicine:
PRITHVI, A.

Faculty of Dentistry:
JAGANNATHAN, J., Conservative Dentistry
SWAMINATHAN, T. N., Prosthodontics

Faculty of Medicine and Medical Specialities:
BHIRMANANDHAM, C. V., Cardiology
JAGANNATHAN, K., Thoracic Medicine
JAYANTHI, Gastroenterology
PALANIAPPAN, V., Psychiatry
PANCHAPAKESA RAJENDRAN, C., Rheumatology
RAJAN, S. K., General Medicine
RAVIKANNAN, Medical Oncology
SENTHAMIL SELVI, G., Dermatology
USMAN, N., Venerology

Faculty of Nursing:
SAHU, G.

Faculty of Obstetrics and Gynaecology and Related Specialities:
ANUSUYA, P., Obstetrics and Gynaecology
MATHAI, M., Obstetrics and Gynaecology
RAMACHANDRAN, M., Obstetrics and Gynaecology
SAMBANDAN, S., Obstetrics and Gynaecology
SOUNDARAM, K., Obstetrics and Gynaecology
TAMILMANI, D., Obstetrics and Gynaecology

Faculty of Paediatrics and Paediatric Specialities:
CHANDRASEKARAN, K., Paediatrics
CHERIAN, T., Paediatrics
SARKUNAM, C. S. R., Paediatrics
TAMILARASU, P. T., Paediatrics
TAMILVANAN, S., Paediatrics

Faculty of Pharmacy:
PRAKASH, M. S.
RAJENDRAN, A.
RAO, G. S.
SRIDHARAN, A.

Faculty of Siddha:
GANAPATHY, G.
IQBAL, P. I.
PATRAYAN, A.
RAJESWARI, A.
SAKUNTHALA, P. R.

Faculty of Surgery and Surgical Specialities:
CHANDRASEKARAN, M., Surgical Endocrinology
DAMODARAN, S., Surgical Gastroenterology
JESUDASON, B., Surgery
PUSHPARAJ, K., Neurosurgery
RATHINAM, T., Ears, Nose and Throat

TAMIL NADU VETERINARY AND ANIMAL SCIENCES UNIVERSITY

Madhavaram Milk Colony, Chennai 600051, Tamil Nadu

Telephone: (44) 25551586
Fax: (44) 25551575
E-mail: tanuvas@vsnl.com
Internet: www.tanuvas.tn.nic.in

Founded 1989

State control

Academic year: July to June

Chancellor: HE THE GOV. OF TAMIL NADU
Vice-Chancellor: Dr P. THANGARAJU
Registrar: Dr N. D. JOY CHANDRAN

Number of teachers: 466
Number of students: 1,457

Publications: *Cheiron* (6 a year), *Tanuvas Newsletter* (12 a year), *Kalnadai Kathir* (6 a year), *Cheidhi Madal* (12 a year).

CONSTITUENT INSTITUTIONS

Centre for Animal Health Studies: Dir Dr B. MURALI MANOHAR.

Centre for Animal Production Studies: Dir Dr R. PRABHAKARAN.

Faculty of Basic Sciences: Dean Dr S. R. SRINIVASAN.

Fisheries College and Research Institute: Thoothukudi 628008, Tamil Nadu; Dean Dr V. K. VENKATARAMANI.

Institute of Animal Nutrition: LRS Campus, Kattankolathur PO, Kattupakkam 603203, Tamil Nadu; Dir Dr M. MURUGAN.

Institute of Food and Dairy Technology: Koduvalli, Chennai 600052, Tamil Nadu; Dir Dr ROBINSON J. J. ABRAHAM.

Madras Veterinary College: Depts of animal genetics and breeding, animal nutrition, animal reproduction, bioinformatics, dairy science, livestock production and management, meat science and technology, obstetrics and gynaecology, poultry science, veterinary anatomy and histology, veterinary and animal husbandry, extension and entrepreneurship, veterinary clinical medicine, ethics and jurisprudence, veterinary microbiology, veterinary parasitology, veterinary pathology, veterinary pharmacology and toxicology, veterinary physiology and biochemistry, veterinary preventive medicine and epidemiology and veterinary surgery, radiology; library of 60,363 vols, 162 periodicals; Dean Dr L. JOHN.

Veterinary College and Research Institute: Namakkal 637001, Tamil Nadu; library of 7,763 vols, 78 periodicals; Dean Dr C. CHANDRAHASAN.

TAMIL UNIVERSITY

Administrative Bldg, Trichy Rd, Thanjavur 613005, Tamil Nadu

Telephone: (4362) 227040
Fax: (4362) 227040
E-mail: contact@tamiluniversity.ac.in
Internet: www.tamiluniversity.ac.in

Founded 1981

Languages of instruction: Tamil, English
Academic year: July to April

Chancellor: HE THE GOV. OF TAMIL NADU
Vice-Chancellor: Dr M. RAJENDRAN
Registrar: Dr A. KARTHIKEYAN
Finance Officer: THIRU P. MOHAN
Public Relations Officer: Dr THIRU G. PANNEER SELVAM
Library Dir: Dr B. SUNDARESAN

Library of 136,324 vols, 393 periodicals
Number of teachers: 74
Number of students: 265

DEANS

Faculty of Arts: Dr M. RAMASAMY
Faculty of Developing Tamil: Dr H. CHITHIRAPUTHIRAPILLAI
Faculty of Languages: Dr A. RAMANATHAN
Faculty of Manuscriptology: V. R. MADHAVAN
Faculty of Science: Dr G. DEIVANAYAGAM

ATTACHED INSTITUTES

Centre for Underwater Archaeology: Dir (vacant).

School of Philosophy: research in philosophy; Dir Dr G. BASKARAN.

Tribal Research Institute: Dir Dr V. CHIDAMBARANATHANPILLAI.

TEZPUR UNIVERSITY

Napaam, Tezpur 784028, Assam

Telephone: (3712) 267007
Fax: (3712) 267006
E-mail: administration@tezu.ernet.in
Internet: www.tezu.ernet.in

Founded 1994

Academic year: July to June

Central university

Vice-Chancellor: Prof. MIHIR K. CHAUDHURI
Registrar: Dr ALAK KUMAR BURAGOHAIN
Finance Officer: RABI RAM BORA

Controller of Examinations: Dr B. SAHARIA
Dean of Student Welfare: Prof. M. SARMA
Library of 25,000 vols
Number of teachers: 100
Number of students: 700

DEANS

School of Energy, Environment and Natural
Resources: Prof. K. K. BARUAH
School of Engineering: Prof. D. K. SAIKIA
School of Humanities and Social Sciences:
Prof. BIJAY KR. DANTA
School of Management Sciences: (vacant)
School of Science and Technology: Prof. B. K.
KONWAR

THIRUVALLUVAR UNIVERSITY

Fort Campus Vellore 632004, Tamil Nadu
Telephone: (416) 2217778
Fax: (416) 2221344
Internet: www.tvuni.in

Founded 2002

Depts of chemistry, economics, zoology; affiliated colleges in dists of Cuddalore, Thiruvannamalai, Vellore, Villupuram

Vice-Chancellor: Dr A. JOTHI MURUGAN
Registrar: Dr B. KRISHNAMURTHY
Controller of Examinations: Dr B. KRISHNAMURTHY.

TILKA MANJHI BHAGALPUR UNIVERSITY

Bhagalpur 812007, Bihar
Telephone: (641) 2620100
Fax: (641) 2620353
E-mail: mustafams@yahoo.com
Internet: www.tmbu.org

Founded 1960 as Bhagalpur University; present name 1991
Teaching and Affiliating
Academic year: June to May

Chancellor: HE THE GOVERNOR OF BIHAR
Vice-Chancellor: Dr PREMA JHA
Registrar: Dr V. K. DAS
Dean of Student Welfare: Dr B. N. SINGH

34 Univ. depts; 29 constituent colleges
Library of 140,000 vols, 125 periodicals
Number of teachers: 1,055
Number of students: 60,000

DEANS

Faculty of Commerce: Dr R. K. SINHA
Faculty of Education: HARENDRA P. SINGH
Faculty of Engineering: Dr C. R. PRATAP
Faculty of Humanities: Dr G. N. JHA
Faculty of Medicine: Dr ANIL KUMAR VERMA
Faculty of Science: Dr R. P. SAHAI
Faculty of Social Science: Dr R. D. SHARMA

TRIPURA UNIVERSITY

PO Suryamaninagar, Tripura West 799130,
Tripura
Telephone: (381) 2374801
Fax: (381) 2374802
E-mail: tripurauniversity@rediffmail.com
Internet: www.tripurauniversity.in

Founded 1987
State control
Teaching and Affiliating
Languages of instruction: English, Bengali
Academic year: June to May

Chancellor: HE THE GOVERNOR OF TRIPURA
Vice-Chancellor: Prof. ARUNODAY SAHA
Registrar: Dr K. B. JAMATIE
Controller of Examinations: B. C. SINHA
Librarian: D. K. RANA

21 Affiliated colleges
Library of 52,560 vols
Number of teachers: 63

Number of students: 19,000 (incl. affiliated
colleges)

DEANS

Arts and Commerce: Prof. M. CHOUDHURI
Science: Prof. BASANT KUMAR AGARWALA

PROFESSORS

AGGARWAL, B. K., Life Science
BHOWMIK, R. N., Mathematics
CHAUDHURIU, M., Bengali
CHAUDHURY, D. K., History
DEBNATH, P., Commerce
DEY, A., Mathematics
DEY, B. K., Physics
DEY, S. N., Sanskrit
DINDA, B., Chemistry
GHOSH, D., Life Science
HALDAR, P. K., Commerce
ROY, A. D., Life Science
SAHA, A., Economics
SRIVASTAVA, R. C., Life Science

UNIVERSITY OF AGRICULTURAL SCIENCES, BANGALORE

Ghandi Krishni Vignan Kendra, Bellary Rd,
Bangalore 560065, Karnataka
Telephone: (80) 23330153
Fax: (80) 23330277
E-mail: registrar@uasbangalore.edu.in
Internet: www.uasbangalore.edu.in

Founded 1964
Residential
Languages of instruction: English, Kannada
State control
Academic year: September to August (two
terms)

Chancellor: HE THE GOVERNOR OF KARNATAKA
Pro-Chancellor: THE MINISTER OF AGRICULTURE, KARNATAKA
Vice-Chancellor: Dr P. G. CHENGAPPA
Dir for Extension: Dr PRABHAKARA SETTY
Dir for Research: Dr H. SHIVANNA
Dir for Student Welfare: Dr K. P. RAMA
PRASANNA
Registrar: Dr B. RAJU
Librarian: Dr K. K. MANJUNATHA

Library of 169,835 vols
Number of teachers: 1,082
Number of students: 2,500 undergraduates
and 1,000 graduates
Publications: *Mysore Journal of Agricultural
Sciences* (4 a year), 10 series (UAS
Research, UAS Extension, UAS Education,
etc.)

PROFESSORS

ABDUL RAHMAN, S., Parasitology
ANANTHANARAYANA, R., Chemistry and Soils
ANILKUMAR, T. B., Plant Pathology
ASHOK, T. H., Horticulture
AVADHANI, K. K., Genetics and Plant Breeding
BHAT, G. S., Dairy Chemistry
CHALLAIAH, Agricultural Extension
CHANDRAKANTH, M. G., Agricultural Economics
CHANDRAMOULI, K. N., Anatomy
CHANDRAPPA, H. M., Plant Breeding
CHANDRASHEKAR GUPTA, T. R., Fishery Oceanography
CHANNAPPA, T. C., Agricultural Engineering
CHENGAPPA, P. G., Agricultural Marketing
CHIKKADEVAIAH, Seed Processing Engineering
CHOWDEGOWDA, M., Agricultural Engineering
DAS, T. K., Animal Nutrition
DEVEGOWDA, G., Poultry
ESHWARAPPA, G., Agricultural Extension
FAROOQ MOHAMMED, Veterinary Physiology
FAROOQI, A. A., Medicinal and Aromatic
Plants

GANGADHAR, K. S., Gynaecology and Obstetrics
GEETHA RAMACHANDRA, Biochemistry
GIRIJA, P. R., Psychology
GOPALA GOWDA, H. S., Agricultural Microbiology
GOPALAKRISHNA HEBBAR, Agricultural Economics
GOPALAKRISHNA RAO, Agricultural Extension
GOVINDAIAH, M. G., Animal Genetics and
Breeding
GOVINDAN, R., Entomology
GOWDA, H., Pharmacology
GUNDURAO, D. S., Mathematics
GURUMURTHY, Statistics
GURURAJ HUNSIGI, Agronomy
HEGDE, S. V., Microbiology
HONNEGOWDA, Pharmacology
HUDDAR, A. G., Horticulture
JAGADISH, A., Entomology
JAGADISH KUMAR, Pharmacology
JAGANNATH, M. S., Parasitology
JANARDHANA, K. V., Crop Physiology
JAVAREGOWDA, S., Agricultural Engineering
JAYADEVAPPA, S. M., Surgery
JAYARAMAIAH, M., Sericulture
JOSEPH BHAGYARAJ, D., Agricultural Microbiology
JOSHI SHAMASUNDAR, Botany
KAILAS, M. M., Dairy Production
KARUNASAGAR, I., Fishery Microbiology
KATTEPPA, Y., Agricultural Extension
KESHAVAMURTHY, K. V., Plant Pathology
KESHAVANATH, P., Aquaculture
KHAN, M. M., Horticulture
KRISHNA, K. S., Agricultural Extension
KRISHNAPPA, A. M., Soil Science
KRISHNAPRASAD, Agricultural Entomology
KRISHNAPRASAD, P. R., Pathology
KRISHNEGOWDA, K. T., Agronomy
KULAKARNI, R. S., Agricultural Botany
KUMARASWAMY, A. S., Water Management
and Plant Breeding
LAKKUNDI, N. H., Agricultural Entomology
LOKANATH, G. R., Poultry for Meat
MALLIK, B., Acarology
MALLIKARJUNAIAH, R. R., Microbiology
MANJUNATH, A., Plant Breeding
MELANTA, R., Horticulture
MOHAN JOSEPH, Fishery Biology
MUNI LAL DUBEY, B., Gynaecology and
Obstetrics
MUNIYAPPA, T. V., Agricultural Extension
MUNIYAPPA, V., Plant Pathology
MUSHTARI BEGUM, J., Home Science
NAGARAJA SETTY, M. V., Plant Breeding
NAGARAJU, Animal Sciences
NANJEGOWDA, D., Nematology
NARASIMHAMURTHY, S., Mathematics
NARAYANA, K., Pharmacology
NARAYANA GOWDA, K., Agricultural Extension
NARAYANAGOWDA, J. V., Horticulture
NARENDRANATH, R., Physiology
PANCHAKSHARAIAH, S., Agronomy
PARAMASHIVAIAH, B. M., Animal Science
PARAMESWAR, N. S., Plant Breeding
PARASHIVAMURTHY, A. S., Soil Science
PARVATHAMMA, S., Mathematics
PARVATHAPPA, H. C., Soil Science and Agricultural Chemistry
PRABHAKAR HEGDE, B., Dairy Production
PRABHAKAR SETTY, T. K., Agronomy
PRABHUSWAMY, H. P., Agricultural Entomology
PRASAD, T. G., Crop Physiology
PRATAP KUMAR, K. S., Poultry Science
PUTTASWAMY, Entomology
RAGHAVAN, R., Veterinary Microbiology
RAJ, J., Microbiology
RAJAGOPAL, D., Apiculture
RAMACHANDRAPRASAD, T. V., Agronomy
RAMANJANEYULU, G., Dairy Technology
RAMAPRASANNA, K. P., Seed Technology
RANGANATHAIAH, K. G., Plant Pathology
RAVI, P. C., Agricultural Marketing
SAMIULLA, R., Horticulture

SATHYAN, B. A., Plant Breeding
SATHYANARAYANA RAO, G. P., Agricultural Extension
SESHADRI, V. S., Agricultural Extension
SHANBHOGUE, S. L., Fishery Biology
SHANKAR, P. A., Dairy Microbiology
SHANKAREGOWDA, B. T., Plant Sciences
SHANTHA JOSEPH, Fishery Economics
SHANTHA R. HIREMATH, Plant Breeding
SHANTHAMALLAIAH, N. R., Crop Production
SHARIEF, R. A., Plant Science
SHESHAPPA, D. S., Fishery Engineering
SHIVAPPA SHETTY, K., Microbiology
SHIVANNA, H., Plant Breeding and Genetics
SHIVARAJ, B., Agronomy
SHIVASHANKAR, K., Agronomy
SIDDARAMAIAH, A. L., Plant Pathology
SIDDARAMAIAH, B. S., Agricultural Extension
SIDDARAMAPPA, R., Soil Science
SIDDARAMEGOWDA, T. K., Biotechnology
SINGLACHAR, M. A., Agronomy
SOMASHEKARAPPA, G., Agricultural Extension
SRIDHARA, S., Zoology
SRIHARI, K., Zoology
SRIKAR, L. N., Biochemistry
SRINIVASA GOWDA, M. V., Economics
SRINIVASA GOWDA, R. N., Poultry Pathology
SURYA PRAKASH, S., Agricultural Economics
SUSHEELA DEVI, L., Soil Science and Agricultural Chemistry
THIMME GOWDA, S., Agronomy
UDAYAKUMAR, M., Crop Physiology
UPADHYA, A. S., Veterinary Microbiology
UTTAIAH, B. C., Horticulture
VAIDEHI, M. P., Home Science
VAJRANABAIAH, S. N., Crop Physiology
VASUDEVAPPA, Inland Fisheries
VEERABHADRAIAH, V., Agricultural Extension
VENKATASUBBAIAH, K., Botany
VENKATESH REDDY, T., Post-Harvest Technology
VENUGOPAL, Agricultural Extension
VENUGOPAL, N., Agricultural Meteorology
VIDYACHANDRA, B., Plant Breeding
VIJAYASARATHI, S. K., Veterinary Microbiology
VIRAKTHAMATH, C. A., Agricultural Entomology
VISHWANATH, D. P., Soil Science
VISWANATH, S., Virology
VISWANATHA, S. R., Plant Breeding
VISWANATHA REDDY, V. N., Gynaecology and Obstetrics
VISWANATHA SASTRY, K. M., Veterinary Medicine
YADAHALLI, Y. H., Agronomy

CONSTITUENT COLLEGES

College of Agriculture—Bangalore: e-mail diagri@bgl.vsnl.net.in; f. 1946; Dir Dr R. GOVINDAN.

College of Agriculture—Hassan: POB 39, Karekere 573201, Hassan; tel. (81) 72290517; e-mail diagri_hassan@rediffmail.co.in; f. 1996; Dir Dr A. S. KUMARA SWARMY.

College of Agriculture—Mandya: Mandya-Melkote Rd, Mandya, Kamataka; f. 1991; Dir Dr C. SHANKARAIAH.

College of Agriculture—Shimoga: f. 1990; Dir Dr K. KENCHAIAH.

College of Forestry: Kunda Rd, Ponnampet, Kodagu; tel. (82) 7449365; f. 1995; Dir Dr N. A. PRAKASH.

College of Horticulture: Mudigere 577132; tel. (82) 63228152; fax (82) 63228022; f. 1991; Dir Dr J. VENKATESHA.

College of Sericulture: Chinthamani; f. 1995; Dir Dr A. N. S. GOWDA.

UNIVERSITY OF BIKANER

Bikaner
Telephone: (151) 2200414
Fax: (151) 2522495
E-mail: info@bikaneruniversity.in
Internet: www.bikaneruniversity.in
Founded 2003
Affiliating; faculties of arts, commerce and management, education, law, science, social science; 69 affiliated colleges in Churu, Sriganganagar, Hanumangarh, Bikaner
Vice-Chancellor: Dr C. B. GENA
Registrar: S. S. RANKAWAT.

UNIVERSITY OF BURDWAN

Rajbati, Bardhaman 713104, West Bengal
Telephone: (342) 2533913
Fax: (342) 2530452
E-mail: pio@buruniv.ac.in
Internet: www.buruniv.ac.in
Founded 1960
Teaching and Affiliating
Languages of instruction: English, Bengali
Academic year: June to May
Chancellor: HE THE GOVERNOR OF WEST BENGAL
Vice-Chancellor: Prof. SUBRATA PAL
Registrar: Dr S. M. DAN
Finance Officer: P. N. GHOSH
Controller of Examinations: S. MUKHOPADHYAY
Librarian: A. M. MIDDA (acting)
Library of 210,481 vols
Number of teachers: 205
Number of students: 3,293
Publications: *Bengali Journal*, *English Journal*, *History Journal*, *Journal of Mass Communication*, *Law Review*, *Philosophy Journal*, *Political Science Journal*, *Sanskrit Journal*, *Science Journal*, *Socio-Political Journal*

PROFESSORS

BAGCHI, S., Chemistry
BAGCHI, S. B., Statistics
BANDOPADHYAY, D. N., English
BANDYOPADHYAY, M. K., Sanskrit
BANDYOPADHYAY, T. C., Zoology
BANERJEE, A. K., Economics
BANERJEE, C., Mathematics
BANERJEE, G., Mathematics
BANERJEE, K., Geography
BANERJEE, M., Chemistry
BASU, D. K., Philosophy
BASU, P. S., Botany
BASU, S., Bengali
BASU, S., Chemistry
BHATTACHARYYA, A., Philosophy
BHATTACHARYYA, A., Sanskrit
BHATTACHARYYA, A. K., Music
BHATTACHARYYA, A. K., Physics
BHATTACHARYYA, G. N., Sanskrit
BHATTACHARAYYA, K., Chemistry
BHATTACHARAYYA, K., Mathematics
BHATTACHARYYA, P. K., Botany
BHATTACHARYYA, R. P., Sanskrit
BISWAS, S. C., Library and Information Science
BISWAS, S. K., Commerce
CHAKRABARTI, T., Sanskrit
CHAKRABORTY, B., Bengali
CHAKRABORTY, C. S., Zoology
CHAKRABORTY, K., Bengali
CHAKRABORTY, N. D., Mathematics
CHAKRABORTY, P., Economics
CHAKRABORTY, P., Zoology
CHAKRABORTY, P. C., English
CHAKRABORTY, P. K., Economics
CHAKRABORTY, S., Bengali
CHAKRABORTY, S., Zoology
CHAKRABORTY, S. K., Mathematics
CHATTERJEE, K. K., English
CHATTERJEE, S. K., Institute of Science Education
CHATTOPADHYAY, A., Statistics
CHATTOPADHYAY, K. C., Mathematics
CHATTOPADHYAY, N. C., Botany
CHATTOPADHYAY, R. R., Bengali
CHAUDHURY, M. K., Bengali
CHAUDHURY, P. K., Zoology
DAS, A. K., Chemistry
DAS, P., Commerce
DAS, T. K., Physics
DASGUPTA, S. S., Physics
DE, A. K., Bengali
DE, G. S., Chemistry
DE, N. K., Geography
DUTTA, D. M., Business Administration
GHOSH, B., Sociology
GUPTA, K., Botany
GUPTA, L. N., Bengali
HOQUE, A., Philosophy
HUI, A. K., English
KHAN, G. C., Philosophy
KUNDU, R. K., English
KUSHARI, D. P., Botany
MAHARATNA, A., Economics
MAJUMDAR, G., Zoology
MALLIK, A. K., Commerce
MALLIK, P., Physics
MALLIK, U. K., Commerce
MITRA, A., Sociology
MITRA, C., Geography
MONDAL, K. K., Mathematics
MONDAL, P. K., Philosophy
MUKHERJEE, A., Botany
MUKHERJEE, B., Sanskrit
MUKHERJEE, R. N., Mathematics
MUKHOPADHYAY, A. K., Botany
MUKHOPADHYAY, A. K., Chemistry
MUKHOPADHYAY, A. K., Political Science
MUKHOPADHYAY, R. N., Botany
MUKHOPADHYAY, S., Computer Science
NANDI, A. P., Zoology
NANDI, B., Botany
PRAMANIK, N. C., Political Science
PRASAD, N., Geography
RAY, A. B., Political Science
RAY, M. K., English
ROY, A., History
ROY, D., Business Administration
ROY, R. K., Physics
ROY, S., Zoology
ROY, S. K., Physics
ROY, S. K., Political Science
ROY CHOUDHURY, S. K., Mathematics
SAMAD, A., Mathematics
SAMANTA, B. C., Physics
SAMANTA, L. K., Physics
SARKAR, A. K., Zoology
SARKAR, B. C., Physics
SARKHEL, J., Commerce
SARMA, P., Botany
SENGUPTA, S. K., Business Administration
SIDDHANTA, U. K., Instrumentation Centre
SINGH, S. S., Law
SINHA, B. C., Hindi
THAKUR, S., Chemistry

There are 101 affiliated colleges

UNIVERSITY OF CALCUTTA

Senate House, 87/1, College St, Kolkata 700073, West Bengal
Telephone: (33) 22410071
Fax: (33) 22413222
E-mail: admin@caluniv.ac.in
Internet: www.caluniv.ac.in
Founded 1857
Teaching and Affiliating
Language of instruction: English
Academic year: July to June
Chancellor: GOVERNOR OF WEST BENGAL
Vice-Chancellor: Prof. ASIS KUMAR BANERJEE
Pro-Vice-Chancellor for Academic Affairs: Prof. SURANJAN DAS
Pro-Vice-Chancellor for Business and Finance: Prof. TAPAN KUMAR MUKHERJEE
Registrar: Dr BASAB CHAUDHURI
Librarian: Dr SOUMITRA SARKAR

Library of 795,000 vols
Number of teachers: 667
Number of students: 91,741
Publications: *Calcutta Review* (4 a year),
UNICAL (4 a year)

DEANS

Faculty of Agriculture and Veterinary Science: Prof. R. K. SARKAR
Faculty of Arts: Prof. A. K. BANDYOPADHYAY
Faculty of Commerce, Social Welfare and Business Management: Prof. R. CHAKRABORTY
Faculty of Education, Journalism and Library Information Science: Prof. T. BASU
Faculty of Engineering and Technology: Prof. S. SEN
Faculty of Fine Arts, Music and Home Science: Prof. S. BANDYOPADHYAY
Faculty of Law: Prof. I. G. AHMED
Faculty of Science: Prof. D. CHATTOPADHYAY

PROFESSORS

University College of Agriculture (5 Ballygunge Circular Rd, Kolkata 700 019):

BASU, R. N.
BHATTACHARYYA, B.
GHOSH, K.
GUPTA, S. K.
MAJUMDAR, B. C.
MAJUMDAR, M. K.
SADHU, M. K.

University College of Arts (1 Reformatory St, Kolkata 700 027; tel. 2241-0071; fax (33) 2241-3222):

ACHARYA, S. N., Sanskrit
ALQUADRI, S. M. S., Ancient Indian History and Culture
BANDYOPADHYAY, A., History
BANDYOPADHYAY, B. N., Sociology
BANDYOPADHYAY, S., Ancient Indian History and Culture
BANERJEE, A. K., Economics
BANERJEE, H., History
BANERJEE, H. K., Economics
BANERJEE, M., Philosophy
BANERJEE, S., Economics
BANERJEE, S., English
BASU, R., Sanskrit
BHATTACHARYA, A., Ancient Indian History and Culture
BHATTACHARYA, A., Philosophy
BHATTACHARYA, B., Pali
BHATTACHARYA, K., Linguistics
BHATTACHARYA, S. K., Sociology
BHAUMIK, A. C., Museology
BURKE, I. K., Ancient Indian History and Culture
CHAKRABARTI, B., Library and Information Science
CHAKRABARTI, D., English
CHAKRABARTI, R., Ancient Indian History and Culture
CHAKRABARTI, R., Philosophy
CHAKRABARTI, S., English
CHATTERJEE, R., Islamic History and Culture
CHATTERJEE, R., Political Science
CHATTOPADHYAY, S.
CHATURVEDI, J., Hindi
CHAUDHURI, A., Economics
CHAUDHURI, B., South and South-East Asian Studies
CHOUDHURI, S., Islamic History and Culture
DAS, S., History
DASGUPTA, A., Economics
DASGUPTA, A., Library and Information Science
DE, B. B., Ancient
DUTTA, P. K., Political Science
DUTTA GUPTA, S., Political Science
GANGULY, M. K., Sanskrit
GANGULY, S. S., Bengali
GHOSH, D., Sanskrit

GHOSH, J., Bengali Language and Literature
GHOSH, P., South and South-East Asian Studies
GOSWAMI, K. R., Philosophy
GUPTA, C., Archaeology
GUPTA, D., Philosophy
KHAN, M., Bengali Language and Literature
MAHAPATRA, R., Tamil
MAITRA, J., Ancient Indian History and Culture
MAJUMDAR, M., Bengali Language and Literature
MALLIK, A., Economics
MUKHERJEE, B., Political Science
MUKHERJEE, B. K., Bengali Language and Literature
MUKHERJEE, S. K., Museology
MUKHOPADHYAY, B. K., Bengali Language and Literature
MUKHOPADHYAY, S. K., Political Science
NATH, M. K., Linguistics
PANDEY, C., Hindi
PARAMANIK, S. K., Sociology
RAY, A., Islamic History and Culture
RAY, J. K., History
ROY, A. K., South and South-East Asian Studies
ROY, D. K., Museology
ROY, S., English
SANYAL, J., English
SANYAL, K., Economics
SEN, K., Philosophy
SEN, P. K., Philosophy
SEN, R., Philosophy
SEN, S. K., Linguistics
SENGUPTA, S., Sanskrit
SHARMA, A., Hindi
SHAW, S., Hindi
SIKDAR, S. N., Economics
TAQI, Y. R., Urdi
VASUDEVAN, H. S., History

University College of Commerce, Social Welfare and Business Management (87/1 College St, Kolkata 700 073; tel. (33) 2241-0071; fax (33) 2241-3222):

BANERJEE, B.
BANERJEE, S.
SINHA, G. C.

University College of Law (51/1 Hazra Rd, Kolkata 700019; tel. (33) 2475-5801):

AHMED, I. G.

University College of Management (1 Reformatory St, Kolkata 700 027; tel. (33) 2479-1645):

CHAKRABARTI, R.
DHAR, S., Business Management
KHASNABIS, R., Business Management

University College of Science (35 Ballygunge Circular Rd, Kolkata 700 019
92 Acharya Prafulla Chandra Rd, Kolkata 700 009):

ACHARYA, S. K., Pure Mathematics
ADHIKARY, M. R., Pure Mathematics
BAGCHI, B., Applied Mathematics
BANDHYOPADHYAY, M. K., Geography
BANERJEE, A., Chemistry
BANERJEE, A. B., Biochemistry
BANERJEE, D., Physics
BANERJEE, J., Chemistry
BANERJEE, M., Botany
BANERJEE, S. B., Zoology
BASU, A., Statistics
BASU, S. R., Geography
BHATTACHARYYA, A., Zoology
BHATTACHARYYA, A., Marine Science
BHATTACHARYYA, A. K., Biochemistry
BHATTACHARYYA, C., Geology
BHATTACHARYYA, D. K., Pure Mathematics
BHATTACHARYYA, M., Anthropology
BHATTACHARYYA, P. K., Physics
CHAKRABARTI, B. C., Pure Mathematics
CHAKRABARTI, C. G., Applied Mathematics

CHATTERJEE, A., Botany
CHATTERJEE, N. B., Zoology
CHATTERJEE, P. K., Psychology
CHATTERJEE, S. P., Physiology
CHATTOPADHYAY, D., Biochemistry
CHOUDHURI, P. K., Applied Mathematics
CHOWDHURY, B., Anthropology
CHOWDHURY, U., Biophysics
DAS, J., Pure Mathematics
DAS, J. N., Applied Mathematics
DAS, K. C., Physics
DAS, K. P., Applied Mathematics
DAS, T. K., Physics
DASCHOWDHURY, A. B., Anthropology
DASGUPTA, C. K., Biophysics
DASGUPTA, U., Biophysics
DATTA GUPTA, A. K., Zoology
DE, S. S., Applied Mathematics
GANGULY, S., Pure Mathematics
GHATAK, K. P., Electronics Science
GHOSH, C. K., Biochemistry
GHOSH, P. N., Physics
GHOSH, S., Botany
LAHIRI, P., Zoology
MAITY, B. R., Zoology
MALLICK, R., Botany
MANNA, B., Zoology
MONDAL, A., Biochemistry
MUKHERJEE, D., Geology
MUKHERJEE, M., Biochemistry
MUKHERJEE, P., Botany
MUKHERJEE, S., Botany
MUKHERJEE, S., Geology
MUKHOPADHYAY, A. S., Zoology
MUKHOPADHYAY, S. C., Geography
NANDA, D. K., Zoology
PAL, S. G., Zoology
PAN, N. R., Physics
PRAMANIK, A. K., Applied Mathematics
PURAKAYASTHA, R., Botany
RAY, S., Botany
ROY, R., Anthropology
ROYCHAUDHURY, P., Applied Mathematics
ROYCHOUDHURY, D., Electronics Science
ROYCHOWDHURY, A., Physics
ROYCHOWDHURY, P., Physics
ROYCHOWDHURY, R., Botany
SAHA, G. B., Psychology
SAHA, P. K., Geography
SAMAJPATI, N., Botany
SAMANTA, B. K., Geology
SANYAL, A. B., Biophysics
SARKAR, S. K., Physics
SEN, R. N., Applied Mathematics
SEN, S., Botany
SENGUPTA, A., Geology
SENGUPTA, D., Biochemistry
SIRCAR, P. K., Botany
THAKUR, A. R., Biophysics

University College of Technology:

BANDHYOPADHYAY, S., Computer Science
BANIK, A. K., Chemical Engineering
BASU, A. K., Chemical Technology
BASU, D. K., Applied Physics
BASU, P. K., Radiophysics and Electronics
BHATTACHARJEE, A. K., Computer Science
BHATTACHARYYA, D. K., Chemical Technology
BHATTACHARYYA, S., Chemical Engineering
BHATTACHARYYA, T. K., Chemical Technology
CHAKRABORTY, A. K., Applied Physics
CHAKRABORTY, A. N., Radiophysics and Electronics
CHATTERJEE, N. K., Chemical Technology
CHATTOPADHYAY, D., Radiophysics and Electronics
DAS, V., Polymer Science and Technology
DASGUPTA, A. K., Radiophysics and Electronics
DAS PODDAR, P. K., Chemical Technology
DATTA, A. K., Applied Physics
DATTA, A. N., Radiophysics and Electronics
DATTA, B. K., Chemical Engineering

GHOSH, P., Polymer Science and Technology

GUPTA, S. N., Polymer Science and Technology

LAHIRI, C. R., Chemical Technology

MAJUMDER, R. N., Chemical Technology

MITRA, N. K., Chemical Technology

MITRA, T. K., Applied Physics

MUKHOPADHYAY, A. K., Applied Physics

NATH, N. G., Radiophysics and Electronics

PARIA, B. B., Chemical Engineering

PARIA, H., Radiophysics and Electronics

PURKAIT, N. N., Radiophysics and Electronics

RAKSHIT, P. C., Radiophysics and Electronics

ROY, P., Chemical Engineering

ROY, S. K., Radiophysics and Electronics

SAHA, P. K., Radiophysics and Electronics

SEN, A. K., Radiophysics and Electronics

SENGUPTA, P. K., Polymer Science and Technology

UNIVERSITY COLLEGES

University College of Agriculture: Kolkata; Sec. M. K. SENGUPTA.

University College of Arts: Kolkata; f. 1954; Sec. Dr D. P. DE.

University College of Commerce, Social Welfare and Business Management: Kolkata; f. 1954; Sec. Dr D. P. DE.

University College of Education, Journalism and Library Science: Sec. Dr A. K. CHAKRABORTI.

University College of Fine Arts, Music and Home Science: Sec. (vacant).

University College of Law: Kolkata; f. 1909; Sec. M. K. NAG.

University College of Medicine: Kolkata; f. 1957; Sec. Dr D. BAGCHI.

University College of Science: Kolkata; f. 1954; Sec. M. K. SENGUPTA.

University College of Technology: Kolkata; f. 1954; Sec. M. K. SENGUPTA.

CONSTITUENT COLLEGES

All India Institute of Hygiene and Public Health: Dir Dr B. N. GHOSH; see under Colleges.

Institute of Postgraduate Medical Education and Research: 244 Acharyya J. C. Bose Rd, Kolkata 700 020; Dir Prof. D. SEN.

Presidency College: 86/1 College St, Kolkata; f. 1817; Principal (vacant).

Sanskrit College: Bankim Chatterjee St, Kolkata; f. 1824; Principal B. P. BHATTACHARYYA.

School of Tropical Medicine: Kolkata; Dir Dr B. D. CHATTERJEE.

There are also 37 professional colleges and 207 affiliated colleges

UNIVERSITY OF CALICUT

PO Calicut University, Malappuram 673635, Kerala

Telephone: (494) 2401144

Fax: (494) 2400269

E-mail: reg@unical.ac.in

Internet: www.universityofcalicut.info

Founded 1968

Teaching and Affiliating

State control

Languages of instruction: English, Malayaam

Academic year: June to March

Chancellor: HE THE GOVERNOR OF KERALA

Vice-Chancellor: Prof. ANWAR JAHAN ZUBERI

Pro-Vice Chancellor: Dr C. GOBINATHAM PILLAI

Controller of Examinations: Dr T. K. NARAYANAN

Finance Officer: T. K. NARAYANAN (acting)

Dir of Public Relations: T. P. RAJEEVAN (acting)

Registrar: Dr T. K. NARAYANAN

Librarian: N. SUSHAMA

There are 285 affiliated colleges, incl. 115 Arts and Science Colleges, 53 Training Colleges, 23 Engineering/Technical Colleges, 5 Medical Colleges, 4 Ayurveda Colleges, 2 Law Colleges, 23 Oriental Title Colleges, 7 IHRD Centres, 1 Fine Arts College, 16 Nursing Colleges, 2 Dental Colleges, 8 Pharmacy Colleges, 1 Homeopathy College, 2 Hotel Management Colleges.

Library of 90,900 vols

Number of teachers: 166 (Univ. Depts), 5,920 (Affiliated Colleges)

Number of students: 305,000 (Univ. Depts and Affiliated Colleges)

Publications: *Calicut University Research Journal* (2 a year), *Interventions, Journal of South Indian History, Malabar, Malyala Vimarsam*

DEANS

Faculty of Ayurveda: Dr P. K. WARRIER

Faculty of Commerce and Management Studies: Dr E. P. SAINUL ABIDEEN

Faculty of Dentistry: Dr M. HARINDRANATH

Faculty of Education: Dr K. P. MANOJ

Faculty of Engineering: Dr M. P. CHANDRA SEKHARAN

Faculty of Fine Arts: Dr VAYALA VASUDEVAN PILLAI

Faculty of Health Science: T. SANKARAN NAIR

Faculty of Homeopathy: Dr M. P. PRAKASAN

Faculty of Humanities: Dr D. P. NAIR

Faculty of Journalism: Dr SYED AMJAD AMAMED

Faculty of Languages and Literature: Dr IQBAL AHAMMAD

Faculty of Law: Prof. K. V. NARAYANIKUTTY

Faculty of Medicine: Dr R. VELAYUDHAN NAIR

Faculty of Science: Dr P. RAMESAN

UNIVERSITY OF DELHI

Delhi 110007

Telephone: (11) 27667011

Fax: (11) 27667049

E-mail: vc@du.ac.in

Internet: www.du.ac.in

Founded 1922

Central univ.

Languages of instruction: English, Hindi

Academic year: July to April (three terms)

Chancellor: VICE-PRESIDENT OF INDIA

Pro-Chancellor: CHIEF JUSTICE OF INDIA

Vice-Chancellor: Prof. DEEPAK PENTAL

Pro-Vice-Chancellor: TANDON KUMAR

Registrar: Dr A. K. DUBEY

Dir of South Campus: Prof. DINESH SINGH

Dean of Colleges: Prof. NAYANJOT LAHIRI

Dean of Examinations: Prof. M. L. SINGHLA

Dean of Int. Relations: Prof. K. SREENIVAS

Dean of Research: Prof. K. N. TRIPATHI

Librarian: M. L. SAINI

Library of 1,450,000 vols, 1,290 journals

Number of teachers: 270

Number of students: 309,203

DEANS

Faculty of Applied Social Sciences and Humanities: Prof. S. K. VIJ

Faculty of Arts: Prof. S. PANJA

Faculty of Ayurvedic and Unani Medicine: K. K. SIJORIA

Faculty of Commerce and Business Studies: Prof. S. JAIN

Faculty of Education: Prof. B. BAJEVA

Faculty of Interdisciplinary and Applied Sciences: Prof. R. C. KUHAD

Faculty of Law: Prof. S. N. SINGH

Faculty of Management Studies: Prof. J. K. MITRA

Faculty of Mathematical Sciences: Prof. M. L. AGGARWAL

Faculty of Medical Sciences: Prof. U. RUSIA

Faculty of Music and Fine Arts: Prof. A. MITTAL

Faculty of Science: Prof. R. PAL

Faculty of Social Sciences: Prof. B. CHAKRABARTY

Faculty of Technology: Prof. P. KUMAR

CONSTITUENT COLLEGES

Atma Ram Sanatan Dharam College: New Delhi; f. 1959.

Bharati Mahila College: New Delhi; f. 1971.

Daulat Ram College: Delhi 7; f. 1960.

Gargi College: New Delhi; f. 1967.

Guru Gobind Singh College of Commerce: Delhi; f. 1984.

Gyan Devi Salwan College: New Delhi; f. 1970.

Hamdard College of Pharmacy: New Delhi; f. 1972.

Hamdard Tibbi College: Delhi; f. 1977.

Hans Raj College: Delhi; f. 1948.

Hindu College: Delhi; f. 1922.

Indraprastha College for Women: Delhi; f. 1925.

Institute of Home Economics: Delhi; f. 1969.

Janki Devi Mahavidyalaya: New Delhi; f. 1959.

Jesus and Mary College: New Delhi; f. 1968.

Kalindi College: New Delhi; f. 1967.

Kamla Nehru College: New Delhi; f. 1964.

Lady Irwin College: New Delhi; f. 1950.

Lady Shri Ram College for Women: New Delhi; f. 1956.

Lakshmibai College: Delhi; f. 1965.

Maitreyi College: New Delhi; f. 1967.

Mata Sundri College: New Delhi; f. 1967.

Moti Lal Nehru College: New Delhi; f. 1964.

P.G.D.A.V. College: New Delhi; f. 1957.

Rajdhani College: New Delhi; f. 1964.

St Stephen's College: Delhi; f. 1922.

Ramjas College: Delhi; f. 1917.

Satyawati Co-educational College: Delhi; f. 1972.

Shaheed Bhagat Singh College: New Delhi; f. 1967.

Shivaji College: New Delhi; f. 1961.

Shri Aurobindo College: New Delhi; f. 1972.

Shri Guru Teg Bahadur Khalsa College: Delhi; f. 1951.

Shri Ram College of Commerce: Delhi; f. 1926.

Shyam Lal College: Delhi; f. 1964.

Shyama Prasad Mukherjee College: New Delhi; f. 1969.

Sri Venkateswara College: New Delhi; f. 1961.

Swami Shardhanand College: Delhi; f. 1967.

Vivekanand Mahila College: Delhi; f. 1970.

Zakir Hussain College: Delhi; f. 1948.

UNIVERSITY MAINTAINED COLLEGES

College of Vocational Studies: New Delhi; f. 1972.

Deshbandhu College: Kalkaji, New Delhi; f. 1952.

Dyal Singh College: New Delhi; f. 1959.

Kirori Mal College: Delhi; f. 1954.

Miranda House for Women: Delhi; f. 1948.

School of Correspondence Courses and Continuing Education: Delhi; f. 1962.

University College of Medical Sciences: Delhi; f. 1971.

Vallabhbhai Patel Chest Institute: see under Research Institutes.

GOVERNMENT MAINTAINED COLLEGES

Ayurvedic and Unani Tabbia College: New Delhi; f. 1974.

College of Art: New Delhi; f. 1972.

College of Nursing: New Delhi; f. 1946.

College of Pharmacy: New Delhi; f. 1971.

Delhi College of Engineering: Kashmeri Gate, Delhi 6; f. 1959.

Delhi Institute of Technology: Delhi; f. 1983.

Lady Hardinge Medical College: New Delhi; f. 1949.

Maulana Azad Medical College: New Delhi; f. 1958.

ATTACHED RESEARCH CENTRES

Agricultural Economics Research Centre: tel. (11) 27667588; Dir P. S. VASHISHTHA.

Centre for Environmental Management of Degraded Ecosystem: tel. (11) 27662402; Dir Prof. INDERJIT.

Centre for Interdisciplinary Studies of Mountain and Hill Environment (CISMHE): f. 1990; Dir Dr V. KUMAR.

Developing Countries Research Centre (DCRC): tel. (11) 27666281; fax (11) 27667049; e-mail dcrc@dcrcdu.org; internet www.dcrcdu.org; f. 1993; Dir Prof. M. MOHANTY.

Dr B. R. Ambedkar Centre For Biomedical Research (ACBR): tel. (11) 27667151; Dir Prof. V. BRAHMACHARI.

Women Study Development Centre: tel. (11) 27667151; f. 1987; Dir Prof. V. CHATURVEDI.

UNIVERSITY OF HYDERABAD

Central University PO, Hyderabad 500046, Andhra Pradesh

Telephone: (40) 23132102
Fax: (40) 23010292
E-mail: yakkala@uohyd.ernet.in
Internet: www.uohyd.ernet.in

Founded 1974

Central university
State control
Language of instruction: English
Academic year: July to April

Chief Rector: HE THE GOVERNOR OF ANDHRA PRADESH
Chancellor: R. CHIDAMBARAM
Vice-Chancellor: Prof. S. E. HASNAIN
Pro-Vice-Chancellors: Prof. V. KANNAN, Prof. B. P. SANJAY
Registrar: Dr PRAKASH SARANGI
Public Relations Officer: A. J. THOMAS
Finance Officer: S. PARABRAHMAIAH
Controller of Examinations: Dr V. RAO
Librarian: Dr M. K. RAO

Library of 257,000 vols
Number of teachers: 200
Number of students: 2,000

DEANS
School of Chemistry: Prof. M. PERIASAMY

School of Engineering Sciences and Technology: Prof. A. T. BHATNAGAR
School of Humanities: M. G. RAMANAN
School of Life Sciences: Prof. A. S. RAGHAVENDRA
School of Management Studies: Prof. V. V. RAMANA
School of Mathematics and Computer and Information Sciences: Prof. T. AMARANATH
School of Medical Sciences: Prof. M. RAMANADHAM
School of Performing Arts, Fine Arts and Communication: Prof. V. PAVARALA
School of Physics: Prof. V. SRIVASTAVA
School of Social Sciences: Prof. E. HARIBABU

UNIVERSITY OF JAMMU

Baba Sahib Ambedkar Rd, Jammu (Tawi) 180006, Jammu and Kashmir

Telephone: (191) 2435248
Fax: (191) 2450014
E-mail: nodalpoint@jammuuniversity.in
Internet: www.jammuuniversity.in

Founded 1969

Affiliating and teaching; 44 constituent colleges and 17 affiliated colleges
Languages of instruction: English, Hindi, Urdu, Sanskrit, Dogri, Punjabi
Academic year: July to March

Chancellor: HE THE GOVERNOR OF JAMMU AND KASHMIR
Vice-Chancellor: Prof. VARUN SAHNI
Registrar: Prof. O. S. SUDAN
Librarian: Prof. VERINDER GUPTA (acting)
Library of 340,810 vols, 250 periodicals
Number of teachers: 259
Number of students: 33,453

Publications: *Distance Education Journal*, *Social Sciences and Arts Journal*

DEANS
Faculty of Arts: Prof. N. SARAF
Faculty of Ayurveda: Dr C. R. GUPTA
Faculty of Behavioural Sciences: Prof. K. SUMBALI
Faculty of Commerce: Prof. S. P. GUPTA
Faculty of Engineering Technology: Dr R. N. SHARMA
Faculty of Law: Prof. S. K. SHARMA
Faculty of Life Sciences: Prof. V. K. ANAND
Faculty of Management Studies: Prof. J. R. DHOTRA
Faculty of Medicine: Dr ANIL GOSWAMY
Faculty of Music and Fine Arts: SAVITA BAKSHI
Faculty of Oriental Learning: Prof. K. H. SIDDIQUI
Faculty of Science: Prof. B. L. KALSOTRA
Faculty of Social Sciences: Prof. K. KOUR

PROFESSORS
AIMA, A., Management Studies
ANAND, V. K., Botany
BADYAL, S. K., Physics and Electronics
BANDHU, D., Distance Education
BHAT, B. L., Economics
CHARAK, P., English
CHOUDHARY, R., Political Science
DHAR, B. L., Geology
DHOTRA, J. R., Management Studies
DUTTA, S. P., Environmental Science
GANAI, N. A., Law
GOHIL, R. N., Botany
GUPTA, N., Hindi
GUPTA, R., Chemistry
GUPTA, R., Economics
GUPTA, S. C., Zoology
GUPTA, S. P., Commerce
GUPTA, V., Dogri
GUPTA, V. K., Physics and Electronics
HAMAL, I. A., Botany
JYOTI, M. K., Zoology
KAHN, S. R., Psychology

KALSOTRA, B. L., Chemistry
KAUR, K., Political Science
KESAR, A., Dogri Studies
KHOSA, S. K., Physics and Electronics
KOMAL, B. S., Mathematics
KOUL, G. L., Computer Science
KUMAR, R., Hindi
LANGER, A., Botany
MAGOTRA, L. K., Physics and Electronics
MAGOTRA, V. P., Law
MALHAN, I. V., Library Science
MANDOKA, R., English
MASOODI, G. S., Law
MOHD, J., History
OM, H., History
PANDA, J. R., Sociology
PARIHAR, L., Law
PRASAD, G. V. R., Geology
RANA, M. R., Management Studies
RAZDAN, K. B., English
SEHGAL, B. P. S., Law
SHARMA, I. B., Chemistry
SHARMA, K., Management Studies
SHARMA, N. R., Education
SHARMA, O. P., Economics
SHARMA, R. D., Commerce
SHARMA, R. L., Chemistry
SHARMA, S. K., Law
SIDDIQUI, K. H., Urdu
SINGH, A. P., Mathematics
SINGH, G., Computer Science
SINGH, G., Geography
SINGH, S., Law
SUDAN, C. S., Geology
SUMBLI, K., Education
SURI, S. P., Education
TIWARI, R. J., Statistics
VERMA, L., Education
WADAN, D. S., Punjabi
WAKHLU, A. K., Botany
WANGOO, C. L., Mathematics

ATTACHED CENTRES
Centre for History and Culture of Jammu and Ladakh Regions: f. 1994; Dir Dr ANITA BILLOWRIA.

Centre for New Literatures: Dir Prof. POSH CHARAK CHOUHAN.

Centre for Strategic and Regional Studies: e-mail csrs@jammuuniversity.in; f. 2002; Dir Dr SANGEETA THAPLIYAL.

Regional Centre for Field Operations and Research on Himalayan Glaciology: e-mail ganjoork@rediffmail.com; Dir Dr KESHAV SHARMA.

UNIVERSITY OF KASHMIR

Hazratbal, Srinagar 190006, Jammu and Kashmir

Telephone: (194) 2420078
Fax: (194) 2421357
E-mail: info@kashmiruniversity.net
Internet: www.kashmiruniversity.net

Founded 1948

Academic year: March to December

Teaching and affiliating

Vice-Chancellor: Prof. RIYAZ PUNJABI
Registrar: Prof. S. FAYAZ AHMAD
Controller of Examinations: Prof. A. M. SHAH
Dean of Academics: Prof. ABDUL AZIZ UL AUZEEM
Dean of College Devt: Prof. NISAR AHMAD SHAH
Dean of Student Welfare: Prof. M. M. MASOODI
Public Relations Officer: SHOWKAT SHAFI
Librarian: REYAZ RUFAI

62 Affiliated colleges

Library of 375,000 vols
Number of teachers: 280
Number of students: 30,000 (incl. affiliated colleges)

Publication: *Journal of Himalayan Ecology and Sustainable Development*

DEANS

Faculty of Arts: Prof. A. H. TAK
Faculty of Commerce and Management Studies: Prof. G. M. DIN DAR
Faculty of Education: Prof. N. A. NADEEM
Faculty of Engineering: Prof. N. A. SHAH
Faculty of Law: Prof. M. A. MIR
Faculty of Medicine: Dr M. AHMAD
Faculty of Music and Fine Arts: Prof. A. AZIZ UL AUZEEM (acting)
Faculty of Oriental Learning: Prof. M. AHMAD KHAN
Faculty of Science: Prof. R. C. BHAGAT
Faculty of Social Science: Prof. N. BABA

PROFESSORS

ABDUL AZIZ, Mathematics
ALVI, W. A., Library and Information Science
AZURDAH, M. Z., Urdu
BABA, N. A., Political Science
BHAT, A. S., Law
BHAT, G. M., Economics
BHAT, M. I., Geology
BHAT, R. C., Zoology
CHANNA, A., Zoology
CHESTI, M. Z., Zoology
DABLA, B. A., Sociology
DHAR, R. L., Zoology
DHAR, T. N., English
DOST, M., Economics
FAROOQ, A., Physics
JAMWAL, K. S., Physics
JAVAID, A. Q., Urdu
KANT, T. A.
KAW, M. A., Central Asian Studies
KHAN, A. H., Distance Education
KHAN, A. M., Central Asian Studies
KHAN, A. R., Zoology
KHAN, B. A., Economics
KHAN, M. I., History
KURSHID, A., Management Studies
LONE, M. S., Kashmiri
MALIK, G. M., Education
MALIK, G. R., English
MALIK, N. A., Urdu
MASOODI, M. M., Persian
MATTOO, A. M., Central Asian Studies
MATTOO, A. R., Management Studies
MIR, A. A., Law
MIR, G. Q., Law
MIR, M., Law
MIR, M. A., Law
MUNSHI, A. H., Botany
MUZAMER, A. M., Urdu
NADEEM, N. A., Education
NIAZMAND, M. S., Persian
NISAR, A., Economics
PEER, M. A., Computer Science
PUNJABI, R., Distance Education
QUADRI, S. M. A., Law
QURESHI, A. W., Economics
QURESHI, M. A., Chemistry
RAFIQUI, A. Q., History
RAIS, A., Geography
RATHER, A. R., Education
SAPRU, B. L., Botany
SHAH, A. M., Environmental Services
SHAH, A. M., Management Studies
SHAH, G. M., Zoology
SHAH, N. A., Electronics
SIKANDAR, F., Botany
SOFI, M. A., Mathematics
SYED, F. A., Commerce
TAK, A. H., English
TANTRAY, G. N., Centre of Adult Continuing Education and Extension
WAFAI, B. A., Botany
WANI, M. A., History

RESEARCH CENTRES

Academic Staff Centre: tel. (194) 2420389; fax (194) 2421357; f. 1987; Dir Prof. MEHRAJ-UD-DIN.

Bioinformatics Centre: tel. (194) 2421353; fax (194) 2428723; e-mail andrabik@ kashmiruniversity.net; internet www .bioinfoku.org; f. 2000; Dir Dr KHURSHID IQBAL ANDRABI.

Centre for Adult Continuing and Extension Education: f. 1978; Dir Prof. ALTAF AHMAD MIR.

Centre of Central Asian Studies: tel. (194) 2422553; fax (194) 2420923; e-mail mkaw@rediffmail.com; f. 1978; publ. *Journal of Central Asian Studies* (1 a year); Dir Prof. MUSHTAQ A. KHAN.

Centre of Distance Education: tel. (194) 2429810; e-mail disedu@kashmiruniversity .net; f. 1976; publ. *Communication* (1 a year), *Tarseel* (1 a year); Dir Dr SHAFIQA PRAVEEN.

Centre of Research for Development: f. 1979; Dir Prof. A. R. YOUSEF.

Educational Multimedia Research Centre: tel. (194) 2420610; e-mail emmrc@ kashmiruniversity.net; f. 1992; Dir SHAHID RASOOL.

Iqbal Institute: tel. (194) 2410201; f. 1977; Dir Prof. B. A. NAHVI.

Population Research Centre: tel. (194) 2427541; fax (194) 2423091; e-mail prcsrinagar@rediffmail.com; f. 1985; Dir Prof. G. M. BHAT.

State Resource Centre: f. 1978; Dir Prof. B. A. WAFAI.

University Science Instrumentation Centre: tel. (194) 2410774; fax (194) 2420405; e-mail gmbhat_ku@yahoo.co.in; f. 1979; Dir Prof. G. M. BHAT.

UNIVERSITY OF KERALA

Thiruvananthapuram 695034, Kerala
Telephone: (471) 2306422
Fax: (471) 2307158
E-mail: kuinform@eth.net
Internet: www.keralauniversity.edu
Founded 1937

Teaching and affiliating; 50 affiliated colleges, 25 professional colleges, 57 recognized research centres
Language of instruction: English
Academic year: June to May
Chancellor: HE THE GOVERNOR OF KERALA
Pro-Chancellor: THE MIN. FOR EDUCATION, GOVERNMENT OF KERALA
Vice-Chancellor: Dr A. JAYAKRISHNAN
Pro-Vice-Chancellor: Dr V. JAYAPRAKAS
Registrar: K. A. HASHIM
Controller of Examinations: Dr M. T. SULE-KHA
Dir of College Devt Ccl: Dr M. JAYAPRAKASH
Dir of Planning and Devt: Dr S. V. SUDHEER
Public Relations Officer: S. D. PRINS
Librarian: J. USHA

Library of 280,804 vols
Number of teachers: 5,799
Number of students: 123,310

DEANS

Faculty of Applied Sciences: Dr M. R. KAIMAL
Faculty of Arts: Dr J. BEEGUM
Faculty of Ayurveda: Dr M. R. VASUDEVAN NAMPOOTHIRI
Faculty of Commerce: Dr K. P. MURALEED-HARAN
Faculty of Dentistry: Dr K. J. KUMAR
Faculty of Education: Dr J. EXEMMAL
Faculty of Engineering and Technology: Dr R. IBRAHIMKUTTY
Faculty of Fine Arts: Dr V. V. PILLAI
Faculty of Homoeopathy: Dr T. M. SREEDEVI
Faculty of Law: Dr K. C. SUNNY
Faculty of Management Studies: Dr J. RAJAN
Faculty of Medicine: Dr D. DALUS

Faculty of Oriental Studies: Dr D. BENJAMIN
Faculty of Physical Education: Dr E. SUNIL
Faculty of Science: Dr P. INDRASENAN
Faculty of Social Sciences: Dr R. N. YESUDAS

UNIVERSITY CENTRES

Centre for Adult Continuing Education and Extension (CACEE): tel. (471) 2302523; e-mail cacee@keralauniversity .edu; Dir Prof. B. VIJAYAKUMAR.

Centre for Bioinformatics: tel. (471) 2412759; e-mail sankar.achuth@gmail.com; internet www.cbi.keralauniversity.edu; f. 2005; Dir Dr A. S. S. NAIR.

Centre for Canadian Studies: tel. (471) 306422; f. 1991; Dir Dr J. BEGUM.

Centre for Convergence Media Studies: tel. (471) 2301045; Dir M. VIJAYAKUMAR.

Centre for Gandhian Studies: f. 1970; Dir Dr J. M. RAHIM.

Centre for Marine Diversity: tel. (471) 2412434; e-mail k.padmakumar@vsnl.com; Dir Dr K. PADMAKUMAR.

Centre for Vedanta Studies: f. 1986; Dir Dr K. MAHESWARAN NAIR.

Centre for Women's Studies: tel. (471) 2441515; f. 1986; Dir Dr G. S. JAYASREE.

International Centre for Kerala Studies: tel. (471) 2412168; f. 1988; Dir Dr N. SAM.

Population Research Centre: tel. (471) 418796; f. 1983; Dir Dr K. KRISHNAKUMARI.

Sree Narayana Study Centre for Social Change: tel. (471) 2418421; f. 1996; Dir Dr K. VIJAYAN.

Survey Research Centre: f. 1979; Dir C. P. SURESH.

University Observatory: tel. (471) 2322732; f. 1837; Dir Dr V. K. VAIDYAN.

V. K. Krishna Menon Study Centre for International Relations: tel. (471) 2418307; Dir Dr G. GOPAKUMAR.

UNIVERSITY OF LUCKNOW

Badshah Bagh, Lucknow 226007, Uttar Pradesh
Fax: (522) 2740086
E-mail: info@lkouniv.ac.in
Internet: www.lkouniv.ac.in
Founded 1921

Residential and teaching
Languages of instruction: English, Hindi
Academic year: July to April
Chancellor: HE THE GOVERNOR OF UTTAR PRADESH
Vice-Chancellor: Prof. AJAIB SINGH BRAR
Pro-Vice-Chancellor: Prof. U. N. DWIVEDI
Registrar: Dr G. P. TRIPATHI
Finance Officer: J. PRASAD
Controller of Examinations: Prof. A. K. S. CHAUHAN
Dean of Student Welfare: Prof. N. PANDEY

Library of 510,000 vols
Number of teachers: 661
Number of students: 48,625

DEANS

Faculty of Architecture: NEHRU LAL
Faculty of Arts: Prof. V. D. PANDEY
Faculty of Commerce: Prof. VAISHAMPAYAN
Faculty of Education: A. CHOUBEY
Faculty of Fine Arts: Dr RAJIV NARAIN
Faculty of Law: A. K. AWASTHI
Faculty of Science: Prof. V. K. TANDON

CONSTITUENT COLLEGES

College of Arts and Crafts: Lucknow; Prin. J. K. AGARWAL.

Government College of Architecture: Lucknow; Prin. Prof. N. LAL.

Institute of Engineering and Technology: Lucknow; Dir Prof. G. N. PANDEY.

King George's Medical College: Lucknow; f. 1911; 4-year postgraduate medical courses have been established; Prin. Dr P. K. MISHRA.

State College of Ayurveda: Lucknow; f. 1954; Prin. Prof. B. N. SINGH.

ATTACHED INSTITUTES

Institute of Development Studies: Dir Prof. A. K. SENGUPTA.

Institute of Management Sciences: tel. (522) 2740032; Chair. Prof. A. S. BRAR.

Institute of Mass Communication in Science and Technology: f. 1995; Dir Prof. D. KUMAR.

Institute of Women's Studies: f. 1997; Dir Prof. R. CHANDRA.

Regional Centre for Urban and Environmental Studies: tel. (522) 2740165; e-mail directorrcueslko@gmail.com; internet www.rcueslko.org; Dir Dr N. K. RAI.

UNIVERSITY OF MADRAS

Chepauk, Triplicane PO, Chennai 600005, Tamil Nadu

Telephone: (44) 25399778
Fax: (44) 25366693
E-mail: vcoffice@unom.ac.in
Internet: www.unom.ac.in

Founded 1857

Teaching and Affiliating
Languages of instruction: English, Tamil
Academic year: July to April

Chancellor: HE THE GOVERNOR OF TAMIL NADU
Vice-Chancellor: Prof. S. RAMACHANDRAN
Pro-Chancellor: Dr K. PONMUDI
Academic Dean: Dr P. DURAISAMY
Dean of Research: Dr D. VELMURUGAN
Dir of Chepauk Campus: Dr P. T. SRINIVASAN
Dir of Guindy Campus: Dr H. DEVARAJ
Dir of Marina Campus: Dr REVATHY
Dir of Taramani Campus: Dr N. SRINIVASAN
Registrar: Dr M. RANGANATHAM
Librarian: Dr R. VENGAN (acting)

Library of 506,295 vols
Number of students: 107,518

Publication: *Annals of Oriental Research*

DEANS

Faculty of Arts: Dr R. THANDAVAN
Faculty of Fine Arts: Dr N. RAMANATHAN
Faculty of Indian and Other Languages: Dr V. JAYADEVAN
Faculty of Law: Dr N. BALU
Faculty of Science: Dr D. LALITHA KUMARI
Faculty of Teaching: Dr D. RAJA GANESAN

There are 276 affiliated colleges

UNIVERSITY OF MUMBAI

University Rd, Fort, Mumbai 400032, Maharashtra

Telephone: (22) 22704390
Fax: (22) 22652832
E-mail: vc@fort.mu.ac.in
Internet: www.mu.ac.in

Founded 1857 as Univ. of Bombay, present name 1996

Teaching and Affiliating
Language of instruction: English
Academic year: June to April (two terms)

Chancellor: HE THE GOV. OF MAHARASHTRA
Vice-Chancellor: Dr VIJAY KHOLE
Pro-Vice-Chancellor: Dr ARUN D. SAWANT
Registrar: K. VENKATRAMANI
Controller of Examinations: V. B. SHINDE
Librarian: Prof. VIJAYA RAJHAMA

315 Constituent colleges and 79 recognized postgraduate instns (mostly listed under Research Institutes)

Library of 837,978 vols
Number of students: 262,350

Publications: *Journal of the University of Bombay, Prakrit and Pali, Sanskrit, University of Bombay Studies, University Economics Series, University Series in Monetary and International Economics, University Sociology Series*

DEANS

Faculty of Arts: Dr P. VENKATESH
Faculty of Commerce: Principal: M. G. SHIRAHATTI
Faculty of Fine Arts: N. L. KENY
Faculty of Law: N. M. RAJADHYAKSHA
Faculty of Science: S. B. PATIL
Faculty of Technology: Prof. S. SAHARE

PROFESSORS

Faculty of Arts:

ABHEDI, R. S. A., Urdu
ANNAKUTY, V. K., German Literature and Russian
BANDIVADEKAR, C. M., Comparative Literature
BHARADWAJ, M. A., Econometrics
BHARUCHA, N., Post-Colonial Literature
BHAT NAYAK, V., Mathematics
BHONGLE, N., 20th-Century Indian Literature in English
BOKIT, S. V., Industrial Policy and Development Banking
BHOWMIK, S. K., Sociology
CHAWATHE, P. D., Graphs Theory
CORREA, R., Economics
DALVI, A. M. I., Urdu
DESHPANDE, J. V., Mathematics
DOSSAL, M., History
GIRI, R. D., Mathematics
GUHA, S. B., Geography
GUMMADI, N., General Economics
JADHAV, A. S., Geography
JANWA, H. L., Algebra
JOGDAND, P. G., Sociology
JOSHI, S. A., Philosophy
JOSHI, S. M., Statistical Inference
KAMATH, P. M., American Studies
KHOKLE, V. S., Socio-linguistics
KUMARESAN, S., Mathematics
LIMAYE, N. B., Mathematics
LUKMANI, V. M., English
MODY, N. B., Civics and Politics
MOHANTY, S. P., Social Demography
MOMIN, A. R., Cultural Anthropology
MUNGEKAR, B. I., Economics
NABAR, S. P., Statistics
NABAR, V., Indo-English Literature
NACHANE, D. N., Quantitative Economics
NADKARNI, M. G., Mathematics
NEMADE, B. V., Comparative Literature
PETHE, A. M., Economics
PHADKE, V. S., Geography
RAJHANSA, V. P., Reference Service
RAO, M. J. M., General Economics
SABNIS, R. S., Monetary and Industrial Economics
SANDESARA, J. C., Industrial Economics
SANE, S. S., Mathematics
SAWANT, S. D., Agricultural Economics
SEETA PRABHU, K., Economics
SEN, M., Experimental Psychology
SIRDESHPANDE, M. R., French
SRIRAMAN, S., Transport Economics
TIKEKAR, A. C., Library Science
TIWARI, R., Hindi
VAIDYA, S. S., Marathi
VANAJA, N., Algebra
VASANT KARNIK, A., Economics
VASANTKUMAR, T., Kannada Literature
VYAS, V. S., Music

Faculty of Commerce:

ANAGOL, M., Banking
GHOSH, P. K., Personnel Management
IYER, V. R., Management
MANERIKAR, V. V., Research Methodology
MURTHY, G. N., Finance and Accounts
SANTANAM, H., Operational Research

Faculty of Law:

KHODIE, N., Mercantile Law
RAO, M., Law
WARKE, P. C., Law

Faculty of Science:

BAGADE, U. S., Life Sciences
FULEKAR, M. H., Life Sciences
GAJBHIYE, N. S., Physics
GOGAVALE, S. V., Experimental Electronic and Plasma Physics
HOSANGADI, B. D., Organic Chemistry
JOSHI, V. N., Computer Science
KULKARNI, A. R., Plant Sciences
NARAYANAN, P., Life Sciences
NARSALE, A. M., Physics
PATEL, S. B., Experimental Nuclear Physics
PRATAP, R., Electronics
RANGWALA, A. A., Theoretical Physics
SHETHNA, Y. I., Life Sciences
SIVAKAMI, S., Life Sciences
VASANTHAKUMAR, T., Kannada

Faculty of Technology:

AKAMANCHI, K. G., Pharmaceutical Chemistry
ATHAWALE, V. D., Chemistry
BHAT, N. V., Physics
CHANDALIA, S. B., Chemical Engineering
DIXIT, S. G., Physics
JOSHI, J. B., Chemical Engineering
KALE, D. D., Polymer Technology
KULKARNI, P. R., Food Science and Technology
KULKARNI, V. M., Medicinal Chemistry
LOKHANDE, H. T., Fibre Science
MALSHE, V. C., Paint Technology
MASHRAQUI, S. H., Chemistry
MHASKAR, R. D., Chemical Engineering
NYAYADHISH, V. B., Mathematics
PAI, J. S., Biochemical Engineering
PANGARKAR, V. G., Chemical Engineering
RAJADHYAKSHA, R. A., Physical Chemistry
RAO, H. M., Engineering
SESHADRI, S., Dyestuffs Technology
SHARMA, M. M., Chemical Engineering
SHENAY, V. A., Textile Chemistry
SUBRAMANIAN, V. V. R., Oil Technology
TELI, M. D., Fibre Science
TIWARI, K. K., Chemical Engineering
TUNGARE, S. A., Architecture
VARADARAJAN, T. S., Applied Physics
VENKATESEN, T. K., Oil Chemistry
YADAV, G. D., Chemical Engineering

UNIVERSITY OF MYSORE

POB 407, Mysore 570005, Karnataka

Telephone: (821) 2438666
Fax: (821) 2421263
E-mail: registrar@uni-mysore.ac.in
Internet: www.uni-mysore.ac.in

Founded 1916

Teaching and affiliating
Languages of instruction: English, Kannada
Academic year: June to March (two terms)

Chancellor: HE THE GOV. OF KARNATAKA
Vice-Chancellor: Dr V. G. TALWAR (acting)
Registrar: B. J. HOSMATH
Registrar for Evaluation: B. RAMU
Finance Officer: M. K. SANNASWAMY
Dir of College Devt Ccl: Prof. K. SRIHARI
Librarian: Dr M. KRISHNAMURTHY

122 Affiliated colleges; 5 constituent colleges; 2 postgraduate centres at Hemagangotri and Mandya

Library of 800,000 vols, 2,400 journals
Number of students: 56,500

DEANS

Faculty of Arts: Prof. C. P. SIDDHASHRAMA
Faculty of Commerce: Prof. B. R. ANANTHAN
Faculty of Education: Prof. A. S. RAGHAVA KUMARI
Faculty of Engineering: Prof. CHENNA VENKATESH
Faculty of Law: Dr H. K. NAGARAJA
Faculty of Medicine: Dr KAMALA
Faculty of Science and Technology: Prof. Y. SRINIVASA REDDY

UNIVERSITY COLLEGES

College of Fine Arts for Women: Prin. Dr C. BHATT.

Maharaja's College: Prin. Dr C. SIDDARAJU.

University College of Physical Education: Prin. Dr M. CHANDRAKUMAR.

University Evening College: Prin. SARVAMANGALA BAI.

Yuvaraja's College: Prin. SUMINTHRA BAI.

ATTACHED INSTITUTES

Ambedkar Research Centre: Dir Dr A. SOMASHEKAR.

Centre for Information Science and Technology: Dir Prof. R. YUSADEV.

Educational Multimedia Research Centre: Dir Prof. A. BALASUBRAMANIAN.

Gandhi Bhavan: Dir Dr S. SHIVARAJAPPA.

Institute for Development Studies: f. 1971; Dir Dr K. S. ARUN KUMAR.

Oriental Research Institute: Dir Dr K. V. RAMESH.

Third Sector Research Resource Centre: e-mail info@tsr.uni-mysore.ac.in; internet tsr .uni-mysore.ac.in; Dir Dr Y. DONGRE.

University School of Design: Dir Prof. DAROGA.

UNIVERSITY OF NORTH BENGAL

PO North Bengal Univ., Raja Rammohunpur 734430, Darjeeling District, West Bengal
Telephone: (353) 2582099
Fax: (353) 2581212
E-mail: regnbu@sancharnet.in
Internet: www.nbu.ac.in

Founded 1962

Teaching and affiliating; 23 postgraduate depts; 18 centres; 86 affilliated colleges
Academic year: July to June
Chancellor: HE THE GOV. OF WEST BENGAL
Vice-Chancellor: Prof. ARUNABHA BASUMAJUMDAR
Registrar: Dr DILIP K. SARKAR
Finance Officer: P. K. GHOSH
Librarian: M. MANDAL

Library of 180,000 vols, 700 periodicals
Number of teachers: 154
Number of students: 51,000

DEANS

Faculty of Arts, Commerce and Law: Prof. R. GHOSH
Faculty of Science: Prof. B. N. CHAKRABARTY

PROFESSORS

Arts, Commerce and Law:

BHADRA, R. K., Sociology
BHATTA, A., Bengali
BHATTACHARJEE, C., Philosophy
CHAKRABORTY, B. B., Philosophy
CHAKRABORTY, U., English
GHOSH, R., Philosophy
MONDAL, SK. R., Centre for Himalayan Studies
MUKHOPADHYAY, C., Economics

MUKHOPADHYAY, R. S., Sociology
ROY MOULIK, S. K., English
SAHU, R., Centre for Himalayan Studies
SENGUPTA, P. K., Political Science
SENGUPTA, P. R., Commerce
UPADHYAY, B. K., Nepali

Science:

BOSE, M. K., Mathematics
DAS, A. P., Botany
DASGUPTA, D., Physics
HAZRA, D. K., Chemistry
KARANJAI, S. B., Mathematics
MANNA, N. R., Computer Science and Applications
MUKHOPADHYAY, A., Zoology
NANDI, K. K., Mathematics
ROY, A., Chemistry
ROY, P. S., Chemistry
SAHA, S. K., Chemistry
SARKAR, P. K., Botany

UNIVERSITY OF PETROLEUM AND ENERGY STUDIES

PO Bidholi, Via-Prem Nagar, Dehradun 284006, Uttaranchal
Telephone: (135) 2102690
Fax: (135) 2694204
E-mail: info@upesindia.org
Internet: www.upesindia.org

Founded 2003

Private, Hydrocarbons Education and Research Soc.

Regional centre in Gurgaon; additional campus at Rajahmundry
Chancellor: Dr S. J. CHOPRA
Pro-Chancellor: Prof. G. C. TEWARI
Vice-Chancellor: Dr PARAG DIWAN
Registrar: SANDEEP MEHTA

Number of teachers: 20

DEANS

College of Engineering Studies: Dr B. P. PANDEY
College of Legal Studies: Dr R. H. GORANE
College of Management and Economic Studies: Prof. G. C. TEWARI

UNIVERSITY OF PUNE

Ganeshkhind Rd, Pune 411007, Maharashtra
Telephone: (20) 25696061
E-mail: regis@unipune.ernet.in
Internet: www.unipune.ernet.in

Founded 1949

Teaching and Affiliating
Languages of instruction: English (optional), Marathi
Academic year: June to March (two terms)
Chancellor: HE THE GOVERNOR OF MAHARASHTRA
Vice-Chancellor: Dr NARENDRA JADHAV
Registrar: Dr MANIK LAXMANRAO JADHAV
Librarian: Prof. S. K. PATIL

41 Postgraduate depts; 269 affiliated colleges; 129 research institutes
Library of 422,000 vols, 435 periodicals
Number of teachers: 288
Number of students: 96,000 (including affiliated colleges)

DEANS

Faculty of Arts: Prof. SUDHAKER PANDEY
Faculty of Ayurvedic Medicine: P. H. KULKARNI
Faculty of Commerce: Dr J. R. GODHA
Faculty of Education: Prof. S. V. KHER
Faculty of Engineering: Prof. H. M. GANESHRAO
Faculty of Law: VIJAYRAO MOHITE
Faculty of Medicine: Dr M. J. JOSHI

Faculty of Mental, Moral and Social Science: Dr D. B. KERUR
Faculty of Science: Dr S. C. GUPTE

ATTACHED INSTITUTES

Centre for Development of Advanced Computing: tel. (20) 25704100; fax (20) 25694004; internet www.cdac.in.

Inter-University Centre for Astronomy and Astrophysics: tel. (20) 25604100; fax (20) 25604699; e-mail nkd@iucaa.ernet.in; internet www.iucaa.ernet.in; Dir N. K. DADHICH.

National Centre for Cell Science: tel. (20) 25708000; fax (20) 25692259; Dir G. C. MISHRA.

National Centre for Radio Astrophysics: tel. (20) 25719000; fax (20) 25692149; e-mail www@ncra.tifr.res.in; Dir P. K. MANOHARAN.

UNIVERSITY OF RAJASTHAN

JLN Marg, Jaipur 302055, Rajasthan
Telephone: (141) 2711070
Fax: (141) 2709582
E-mail: info@uniraj.ernet.in
Internet: www.uniraj.ernet.in

Founded 1947

Teaching and affiliating; 37 postgraduate depts; 206 affiliated colleges
Independent control
Languages of instruction: English, Hindi
Academic year: July to May (two terms)
Chancellor: HE THE GOV. OF RAJASTHAN
Vice-Chancellor: Dr NARENDRA KUMAR JAIN
Registrar: ALOK MATHUR
Controller of Examinations: N. N. GUPTA
Librarian: Prof. PRADEEP BHATNAGAR

Library of 371,500 vols, 65,000 bound periodicals
Number of teachers: 575
Number of students: 175,000

DEANS

Faculty of Arts: Prof. S. RAI
Faculty of Commerce: Dr J. K. TANDON
Faculty of Education: Dr R. ARORA
Faculty of Engineering and Technology: S. G. MODANI
Faculty of Fine Arts: Dr K. GARG
Faculty of Law: Prof. S. S. LAL
Faculty of Management Studies: Dr G. KAPOOR
Faculty of Science: Prof. S. L. KOTHARI
Faculty of Social Sciences: Prof. B. L. GUPTA

UNIVERSITY COLLEGES

Commerce College: f. 1956.

Evening Law College.

Law College.

Maharaja's College: f. 1944.

Maharani's College: f. 1944.

Rajasthan College: f. 1956.

RESEARCH CENTRES

Centre for Converging Technologies: Dir Prof. SARDAR SINGH.

Centre for Development of Physics Education: Dir Prof. SARDAR SINGH.

Centre for Gandhian Studies.

Centre for Jain Studies: Dir Dr P. C. JAIN.

Centre for Non-Conventional Energy Resources: e-mail jain-ip@uniraj.ernet.in; Dir Dr I. P. JAIN.

Indira Gandhi Centre for Human Ecology, Environmental and Population Studies: e-mail jamali-khan@uniraj.ernet .in; Dir Prof. T. I. K. JAMALI.

R. A. Podar Institute of Management: tel. (141) 2711349; Dir Dr RAJESH KOTHARI.

South Asia Studies Centre: e-mail sharma-ml@uniraj.ernet.in; Dir Dr M. L. SHARMA.

UTKAL UNIVERSITY

PO Vani Vihar, Bhubaneswar 751004, Orissa

Telephone: (674) 2581850

Fax: (674) 2581850

Internet: www.utkal-university.org

Founded 1943

Teaching and affiliating
State control
Languages of instruction: English, Oriya
Academic year: July to June

Chancellor: HE THE GOV. OF ORISSA
Vice-Chancellor: Prof. BINAYAK RATH
Registrar: Dr L. N. SAHOO
Dir of College Devt Ccl: Prof. H. K. PATRA
Dir of Student Welfare: Prof. BRAHMANANDA PADHI
Controller of Examinations: Dr BIMAL C. MISHRA
Comptroller of Finance: K. K. MOHANTY
Librarian: Dr P. K. MOHANTY (acting)

267 Affiliated colleges

Library of 237,695 vols, 236 periodicals
Number of teachers: 8,521
Number of students: 200,000

DEANS

Faculty of Arts: Prof. K. M. PATRA
Faculty of Commerce: Dr GUNANIDHI SAHOO
Faculty of Education: M. DAS
Faculty of Engineering: Dr NILAKANTHA PATTANAIK
Faculty of Law: INDRAJIT RAY
Faculty of Medicine: Dr R. N. DASH
Faculty of Science: Dr P. K. JESTHI

CONSTITUENT COLLEGES

Madhusudan Law College: Cuttack; f. 1949; Prin. Dr D. P. KAR.

University Law College: Vani Vihar, Bhubaneswar 751004; f. 1975; Prin. Dr P. K. PADHI.

UTKAL UNIVERSITY OF CULTURE

POB 4, Bhubaneswar 751001, Orissa

Telephone: (674) 2530213

Fax: (674) 2535486

E-mail: mail@utkaluniversityculture.org

Internet: www.utkaluniversityculture.org

Founded 1999

Teaching and affiliating; schools of architecture and archaeology, culture studies, language and literature, occupational studies, Orissan studies, performing arts, visual arts
Academic year: July to June

Chancellor: HE THE GOVERNOR OF ORISSA
Vice-Chancellor: Prof. Dr SADHU CHARAN PANDA
Registrar: Dr HARAPRASAD PARICHA PATNAIK
Finance Officer: R. K. PATRA

Library of 3,000 vols

27 Affiliated colleges (4 govt, 23 private).

UTTAR PRADESH RAJARSHI TANDON OPEN UNIVERSITY

17 Maharshi Dayanand Marg, Thornhill Rd, Allahabad 211001, Uttar Pradesh

Telephone: (532) 2621839

Fax: (532) 2624368

E-mail: contact@uprtou.org.in

Internet: www.uprtou.org.in

Founded 1998

Schools of computer and information technology, health sciences, humanities and languages, journalism and mass communication, management, social sciences, tourism and hotel management

Chancellor: HE THE GOV. OF UTTAR PRADESH
Vice-Chancellor: Prof. NAGESHWAR RAO
Registrar: M. L. KANAUJIA
Finance Officer: Dr S. K. GUPTA

DIRECTORS

School of Education: Prof. S. P. GUPTA
School of Humanities: Dr B. N. SINGH
School of Social Sciences: Dr M. N. SINGH

UTTAR PRADESH TECHNICAL UNIVERSITY

IET Campus, Sitapur Rd, Lucknow 226021, Uttar Pradesh

Telephone: (522) 2732194

Fax: (522) 2732189

Noida Office C-22, Sector 62, Noida 201301, Uttar Pradesh

Telephone: (120) 2400416

Fax: (120) 2400418

E-mail: registrar@uptu.ac.in

Internet: www.uptu.org

Founded 2000

Chancellor: HE THE GOVERNOR OF UTTAR PRADESH
Vice-Chancellor: Prof. PREM VRAT
Registrar: U. S. TOMER
Finance Officer: B. L. RATHORE
Controller of Examinations: Prof. V. K. SINGH
Number of students: 90,000

317 Affiliated colleges.

CONSTITUENT INSTITUTES

Institute of Engineering and Technology: Sitapur Rd, Lucknow; tel. (522) 2361692; e-mail director@ietlucknow.edu; internet ietlucknow.edu; Dir Prof. S. K. SRIVASTAVA.

Lucknow College of Architecture: Tagore Marg, Lucknow 226007; tel. (522) 2740236; e-mail principal@lcoarch.ac.in; internet www.foa.uptu.ac.in.

V. B. S. PURVANCHAL UNIVERSITY

Devkali Jasopur, Saraykhaja, Jaunpur 222001, Uttar Pradesh

Telephone: (5452) 252244

Fax: (5452) 252222

E-mail: registrar@vbspu.ac.in

Internet: vbspu.ac.in

Founded 1987

Residential and affiliating; institutes of biological studies, business management, engineering and technology, pharmacy; depts of applied psychology, business economics, financial studies, human resource devt, mass communication; 331 affiliated colleges

Vice-Chancellor: Prof. R. C. SARASWAT
Registrar: Dr B. L. ARYA
Finance Officer: RANJIT KUMAR SRIVASTAVA
Controller of Examinations: R. S. YADAV
Number of students: 380,000 (incl. affiliated colleges)

DEAN

Faculty of Science: Prof. D. D. DUBEY

VARDHAMAN MAHAVEER OPEN UNIVERSITY

Rawatbatha Rd, Akhelgarh, Kota 324010, Rajasthan

Telephone: (744) 2471254

Fax: (744) 2472525

E-mail: reg@vmoukota.in

Internet: vmou.ac.in

Founded 1987 as Kota Open Univ., present name 2002

Depts of commerce, computer science, economics, education, English, Hindi, history, Indian tradition and culture, journalism, law, library and information science, management and political science; regional centres in Ajmer, Bikaner, Jaipur, Jodhpur, Kota, Udaipur; 85 study centres

Chancellor: HE THE GOV. OF RAJASTHAN
Vice-Chancellor: Prof. NARESH DADHICH
Registrar: B. L. KOTHARI

Library: over 100,000 vols, 200 periodicals.

VEER KUNWAR SINGH UNIVERSITY

Arrah 802301, Bihar

Telephone: (6182) 223559

Fax: (6182) 223559

E-mail: registrar@vksu-ara.org

Internet: www.vksu-ara.org

Founded 1992
Academic year: June to May

20 Postgraduate depts, 17 constituent colleges, 3 Law colleges, 37 affiliated colleges

Chancellor: HE THE GOVERNOR OF BIHAR
Vice-Chancellor: Dr I. C. KUMAR
Registrar: Dr QAMAR AHSAN
Librarian: Dr J. P. SINGH

DEANS

Faculty of Commerce: Dr D. K. TIWARI
Faculty of Humanities: Dr R. P. RAI
Faculty of Science: Dr R. P. PANDEY
Faculty of Social Science: Dr GANDHIJEE RAI

VEER NARMAD SOUTH GUJARAT UNIVERSITY

Udhna-Magdalla Rd, Surat 395007, Gujarat

Telephone: (261) 2227141

Fax: (261) 2227312

E-mail: sgu@sgu.ernet.in

Internet: www.sgu.ernet.in

Founded 1967 as South Gujarat Univ., present name 2004

Teaching and affiliating
State control
Language of instruction: Gujarati
Academic year: June to March (two terms); attached to Nat. Assessment and Accreditation Ccl, Bangalore

Chancellor: HE The Gov. of Gujarat PANDIT NAWAL KISHORE SHARMA
Vice-Chancellor: Prof. Dr B. A. PRAJAPATI
Registrar: J. R. MEHTA (acting)
Librarian: B. J. ANKUYA (acting)

140 Affiliated colleges

Library of 172,134 vols, 242 periodicals
Number of teachers: 105 (univ. postgraduate dept)
Number of students: 3,794 (univ. postgraduate dept)

DEANS

Faculty of Arts: G. P. SANADHYA
Faculty of Commerce: J. M. NAIK
Faculty of Education: Dr K. V. DESAI
Faculty of Law: Dr V. B. DESAI
Faculty of Management: Dr S. K. VAJPEYEE
Faculty of Medicine: Dr S. KUMAR
Faculty of Rural Studies: Dr V. J. SOMANI
Faculty of Science: N. B. MAHIDA

VIDYASAGAR UNIVERSITY

PO Vidyasagar Univ., West Midnapore 721102, West Bengal

Telephone: (32) 22275297

Fax: (32) 22275329

E-mail: registrar@vidyasagar.ac.in

Internet: www.vidyasagar.ac.in

Founded 1981
State control

Teaching and affiliating; 53 affiliated colleges
Languages of instruction: English, Bengali
Academic year: July to June

Chancellor: HE THE GOV. OF WEST BENGAL
Vice-Chancellor: Prof. SWAPAN KUMAR PRA-
MANICK
Registrar: Dr HIMANSU GHOSH
Librarian: AMIYA SARKAR (acting)

Library of 75,000 vols, 135 periodicals
Number of teachers: 105
Number of students: 36,500 (incl. affiliated colleges)

Publications: *Journal of Biological Sciences* (1 a year), *Journal of Commerce* (1 a year), *Journal of Library and Information Science* (1 a year), *Journal of Philosophy and the Life World* (1 a year), *Journal of Physical Sciences* (1 a year), *Politics and Society* (1 a year)

DEANS

Faculty of Arts and Commerce: Prof. SANKAR PRASAD SINGHA
Faculty of Science: Prof. SUSANTA KR. CHAK-RABORTY

PROFESSORS

BANERJEE, T. K., Political Science with Rural Administration
BATTACHARYA, T., Zoology
KHAN, L. A., Bengali
MAHAPATRA, P. K., Physics
MAITI, M., Applied Mathematics
MISRA, P. K., Philosophy and Life-World
MUKHOPADHAYA, S., Computer Science and Electronics
PATI, B. R., Microbiology
RANJAN DE, B., Chemistry and Chemical Technology
SAHA, S. C., Electronics

VIKRAM UNIVERSITY

University Rd, Ujjain 456010, Madhya Pradesh

Telephone: (734) 2514270
Fax: (734) 2514276
E-mail: info@vikramuniversity.ac.in
Internet: www.vikramuniversity.ac.in

Founded 1957

Teaching and Affiliating
Languages of instruction: Hindi, English
Academic year: July to June

Chancellor: HE THE GOVERNOR OF MADHYA PRADESH
Vice-Chancellor: Prof. RAM RAJESH MISHRA
Registrar: Dr M. K. RAI
Librarian: Prof. P. K. GOYAL

Two constituent colleges, 30 depts, 6 special centres

101 Affiliated colleges

Library of 191,793 vols, 48,000 vols of periodicals
Number of students: 31,472

DEANS

Faculty of Arts: Dr N. OBEROI
Faculty of Commerce: Dr R. SONI
Faculty of Education: Dr N. SHINDE
Faculty of Information Technology: Dr S. K. GHOSH
Faculty of Life Science: Dr S. K. BILLORE
Faculty of Management: Dr N. RAO
Faculty of Physical Science: Prof. V. W. BHAGWAT
Faculty of Social Science: Dr S. PANDE

VINOBA BHAVE UNIVERSITY

POB 31, Hazaribag 825301, Jharkhand

Telephone: (6546) 264279
Fax: (6546) 264279
E-mail: info@vbu.co.in

Internet: vbu.co.in

Founded 1992
State control
Academic year: July to May

17 Constituent colleges and 40 affiliated colleges

Chancellor: HE THE GOVERNOR OF JHARKHAND
Vice-Chancellor: Prof. Dr A. KUMAR
Pro-Vice-Chancellor: Dr J. L. ORAON
Registrar: Dr S. P. SINHA
Controller of Examinations: Dr M. K. SINGH
Librarian-in-charge: Dr PARMANAND MAHTO

DEANS

Faculty of Ayurveda: Dr H. P. PANDEY
Faculty of Education: Dr K. SINGH
Faculty of Engineering: Dr S. K. SINGH
Faculty of Homeopathy: Dr K. SINGH
Faculty of Humanities: Dr V. JHA
Faculty of Law: Dr D. K. SHARMA
Faculty of Medicine: Dr S. N. BAIROLIYA
Faculty of Science: Dr R. PRASAD
Faculty of Social Sciences: Dr S. N. SINGH

VISVA-BHARATI

PO Santiniketan, Birbhum 731235, West Bengal

Telephone: (3463) 261531
Fax: (3463) 261156
E-mail: registrar@visva-bharati.ac.in
Internet: www.visva-bharati.ac.in

Founded 1951

Central univ.; institutes of agricultural science, dance, drama and music, education, fine arts, humanities and social sciences, rural reconstruction, science, Tagore studies and research; 15 centres
Central Govt control
Languages of instruction: English, Bengali
Academic year: July to April (three terms)

Rector: HE THE GOV. OF WEST BENGAL
Chancellor: Dr MANMOHAN SINGH
Vice-Chancellor: Prof. RAJAT KANTA RAY
Registrar: Dr MANI MUKUT MITRA
Librarian: Prof. P. JASH (acting)

Library of 750,000 vols
Number of teachers: 516
Number of students: 6,357

Publications: *Visva-Bharati Patrika* (4 a year), *Journal of Philosophy*.

WEST BENGAL NATIONAL UNIVERSITY OF JURIDICAL SCIENCES

Dr Ambedkar Bhavan, 12 LB Block, Sector III, Salt Lake, Kolkata 700098, West Bengal

Telephone: (33) 23350534
Fax: (33) 23357422
E-mail: nujs@vsnl.com
Internet: www.nujs.edu

Founded 1999
State control

Schools of criminal justice and admin., economic and business laws, legal practice and devt, private laws and comparative jurisprudence, public law and governance, social sciences, technology, law and devt; centres for consumer protection and welfare, human rights and citizenship studies, studies in WTO laws, studies for women and law

Vice-Chancellor: Prof. MAHENDRA P. SINGH
Librarian: TUTU MUKHERJEE

Library of 100,000 vols, 124 journals.

VISVESWARAIAH TECHNOLOGICAL UNIVERSITY

Santhibastawad Rd, Machhe, Belgaum 590018, Karnataka

Telephone: (831) 2498100
Fax: (831) 2405467
E-mail: info@vtu.ac.in
Internet: www.Vtu.ac.in

Founded 1994
Academic year: AugustJanuaryFebruaryJuly (2 semesters)

Courses in chemical, civil, computer science, electrical, electronics, industrial production, mechanical, textile engineering; 175 affiliated colleges and regional centres in Bangalore, Belgaum, Gulbarga and Mysore; teaching and affiliating

Chancellor: HE THE GOV OF KARNATAKA
Pro-Chancellor: THE MIN. FOR HIGHER EDUCATION, KARNATAKA
Vice-Chancellor: Dr H. P. KINCHA
Registrar: Prof. K. V. A. BALAJI.

ATTACHED CENTRES

Bosch Rexroth Centre: GSSS Institute of Eng. and Tech., Metagalli Industrial Area, Kasaba Hobli, K. R. S. Rd, Mysore, Karnataka; fax (821) 2581977; e-mail vtubosch@vtu.ac.in.

E-Learning Centre: SJCE STEP SEED Bldg, SJCE Campus, Mysore, 570006; fax (8212) 413223; internet elearning.vtu.ac.in.

WEST BENGAL UNIVERSITY OF ANIMAL AND FISHERY SCIENCES

68 Kshudiram Bose Sarani, Kolkata 700037, West Bengal

Telephone: (33) 25563450
Fax: (33) 25571986
Internet: www.wbuafscl.ac.in

Founded 1995
State control
Academic year: July to June

Faculties of dairy technology, fishery sciences, and veterinary and animal sciences

Chancellor: HE THE GOV. OF WEST BENGAL
Vice-Chancellor: Prof. C. S. CHAKRABARTI
Registrar: Dr D. N. JANA
Librarian-in-charge: Dr RANAJIT KUMAR GHOSH

Library of 22,000 vols

DEANS

Faculty of Dairy Technology: Prof. AJIT K. MISRA
Faculty of Fishery Sciences: Prof. KUSHAN CH. DORA (acting)
Faculty of Veterinary and Animal Sciences: Prof. DIPAK DE

WEST BENGAL UNIVERSITY OF TECHNOLOGY

BF 142, Sector II, Salt Lake City, Kolkata, 700017, West Bengal

Telephone: (33) 23217578
Fax: (33) 23341030
E-mail: registrar@wbut.ac.in
Internet: www.wbut.net

Founded 2001
State control
Academic year: January to December

Chancellor: HE THE GOVERNOR OF WEST BENGAL
Vice-Chancellor: Prof. SABYASACHI
Registrar: Dr S. R. ISLAM
Finance Officer: A. BHOWMIK
Controller of Examinations: Maj. SHANTANU

136 Affiliated colleges.

YASHWANTRAO CHAVAN MAHARASHTRA OPEN UNIVERSITY

Nashik 422222, Maharashtra
Telephone: (253) 2231714
Fax: (253) 2231716
E-mail: registrar@ycmou.com
Internet: www.ycmou.com

Founded 1989
State control
Languages of instruction: English, Hindi, Marathi
Academic year: July to June
8 Regional centres and 2,500 recognized study centres

Chancellor: HE THE GOV. OF MAHARASHTRA
Vice-Chancellor: Dr RAJAN WELUKAR
Registrar: Dr NANASAHEB R. KAPADNIS

Library of 25,000 vols
Number of teachers: 4,300
Number of students: 400,000

Publications: *Dnyangangotri* (4 a year), *Mukta Vidya* (2 a year), *Wamvad* (12 a year)

DIRECTORS

School of Agricultural Science: Prof. SURYA GUNJAL
School of Commerce and Management: Prof. PANDIT PALANDE
School of Computer Science: Prof. RAMCHANDRA TIWARI
School of Continuing Education: Prof. RAJENDRA VADNERE
School of Education: Dr A. N. JOSHI
School of Health Sciences: Dr SHYAM ASHTEKAR
School of Humanities and Social Sciences: Dr RAMESH WARKHEDE
School of Science and Technology: MANOJ KILLEDAR

Institutes of National Importance

Institutes of National Importance are established, or so designated, through Acts of Parliament and are thereby granted degree-awarding powers.

ALL-INDIA INSTITUTE OF MEDICAL SCIENCES

Ansari Nagar, New Delhi 110029
Telephone: (11) 26588500
Fax: (11) 26588663
E-mail: director@aiims.ac.in
Internet: www.aiims.edu

Founded 1956
Depts of anaesthesiology, anatomy, biochemistry, biomedical engineering, biophysics, biostatistics, biotechnology, blood bank, cardiac anaesthesiology, cardiac biochemistry, cardiac pathology, cardiac radiology, cardiology, cardiothoracic and vascular surgery, dental surgery, dermatology and venereology, emergency medicine, endocrinology and metabolism, forensic medicine, gastroenterology and human nutrition, gastrointestinal surgery, haematology, histocompatibility and immunogenetics, hospital administration, laboratory medicine, microbiology, nephrology, neuro-anaesthesiology, neurology, neuropathology, neuro-radiology, neurosurgery, nuclear magnetic resonance, nuclear medicine, obstetrics and gynaecology, orthopaedics, otorhinolaryngology, paediatric surgery, paediatrics, pathology, pharmacology, physical medicine and rehabilitation, physiology, radio diagnosis, reproductive biology, surgical disciplines, urology

Dir: Dr T. D. DOGRA (acting)
Dean of Academics: Dr R. C. DEKA
Dean of Examinations: Dr T. D. DOGRA
Registrar: Dr SANDEEP AGARWALA
Librarian: Dr R. P. KUMAR

Library of 115,000 vols, 570 periodicals
Number of teachers: 475 .
Number of students: 1,000

Publication: *The National Medical Journal of India* (6 a year)

PROFESSORS

Anaesthesiology:
ARORA, M. K.
BATRA, R. K.
CHANDERLEKHA
DUREJA, G. P.
JAYALAKSHMI, T. S.
PAWAR, D. K.
SAXENA, R.

Anatomy:
AJMANI, M. L.
KUCHERIA, K.
KUMAR, R.
MEHRA, R. D.
SABHERWAL, U.
WADHWA, S.

Biochemistry:
RAO, D. N.
SINGH, N.
SINHA, S.

Biomedical Engineering:
ANAND, S.
RAY, A. R.
SINGH, H.
TANDON, S. N.

Biophysics:
MISHRA, R. K.
RAO, G. S.
SINGH, T. P.

Biostatistics:
SUNDARAM, K. R.

Biotechnology:
PRASAD, H. K.
SHARMA, Y. D.
TYAGI, J. S.

Cardiology:
BAHL, V. K.
KOTHARI, S. S.
REDDY, K. S.
SAXENA, A.

Centre of Community Medicine:
KAPOOR, S. K.
PANDAV, C. S.
REDDAIAH, V. P.

Dental Surgery:
PARKASH, H.
SHAH, N.

Dermatology and Venereology:
KHANNA, N.
SHARMA, V. K.
VERMA, K. K.

Endocrinology and Metabolism:
AMMINI, A. C.

Forensic Medicine:
DOGRA, T. D.

Gastroenterology and Human Nutrition:
ACHARYA, S. K.
JOSHI, Y. K.
KAPIL, U.

Gastrointestinal Surgery:
CHATTOPADHYAY, T. K.

Haematology:
CHOUDHRY, V. P.
KUMAR, R.
SAXENA, R.

Hospital Administration:
CHAUBEY, P. C.
SHARMA, R. K.

Laboratory Medicine:
JAILKHANI, B. L.
MUKHOPADHYAY, A. K.

Medicine:
GULERIA, R.
KUMAR, A.
MISRA, A.
SHARMA, S. K.
SOOD, R.

Microbiology:
BANERJEE, U.
BROOR, S.
SAMANTARAY, J. C.
SETH, P.

Nephrology:
DASH, S. C.
TIWARI, S. C.

Nuclear Magnetic Resonance Imaging:
JAGANNATHAN, N. R.

Nuclear Medicine:
BANDOPADHYAYA, G. P.
MALHOTRA, A.
PANT, G. S.

Obstetrics and Gynaecology:
KRIPLANI, A.
KUMAR, S.
MITTAL, S.

Orthopaedics:
BHAN, S.
JAYASWAL, A.
KOTWAL, P. P.
RASTOGI, S.

Otorhinolaryngology:
BAHADUR, S.
DEKA, R. C.
SHARMA, S. C.

Paediatric Surgery:
GUPTA, D. K.
MITRA, D. K.

Paediatrics:
ARORA, N. K.
ARYA, L. S.
BHAN, M. K.
KALRA, V.
PAUL, V. K.

Pathology:
CHOPRA, P.
DAWAR, S.
KAPILA, K.
PANDA, S. K.
SARKAR, C.
SINGH, M. K.
VERMA, K.
VIJAYARAGHAVAN, M.

Pharmacology:
GROVER, J. K.
GUPTA, Y. K.

Physical Medicine and Rehabilitation:
SINGH, U.

Physiology:
BIJLANI, R. L.
KUMAR, V. M.
SENGUPTA, J.

Psychiatry and Deaddiction Centre:
KHANDELWAL, S. K.
MEHTA, M.
RAY, R.
TRIPATHI, B. M.

Radio Diagnosis:
GUPTA, A. K.
MUKHOPADHYAY, S.
VASHIST, S.

Reproductive Biology:
  KUMAR, A.
  SARKAR, N. N.
Surgical Disciplines:
  KUMAR, A.
  MEHTA, S. N.
  MISRA, M. C.
  SRIVASTAVA, A.
Transplant Immunology and Immunogenetics:
  MEHRA, N. K.
Urology:
  GUPTA, N. P.
  HERNAL, A. K.

ATTACHED CENTRES

Cardiothoracic Sciences Centre: f. 1982; Prin. Prof. A. SAMPATH.

Centre for Dental Education and Research: f. 2003; Prin. Dr NASEEM SHAH.

College of Nursing: e-mail mvatsa@aiims.ac.in; Prin. M. VATSA.

Dr R. P. Centre for Ophthalmic Sciences: tel. (11) 26589695; fax (11) 26593101; e-mail pschiefrpc@yahoo.com; f. 1967; Prin. Prof. S. GHOSE.

Jai Prakash Narayan Apex Trauma Centre.

National Drug Dependence Treatment Centre: Sector 19, Kamla Nehru Nagar, Ghaziabad, Uttar Pradesh; tel. (120) 2788974; fax (120) 2788979; e-mail nddtc.aiims@qmail.com; f. 1988; Prin. Dr RAJAT RAY.

Neurosciences Centre: f. 2003; Prin. Prof. H. H. DASH.

DAKSHINA BHARAT HINDI PRACHAR SABHA

Thanikachalam Rd, Chennai 600017, Tamil Nadu
Telephone: (44) 24341824
Fax: (44) 24388420
E-mail: info@dbhps-chennai.com
Internet: www.dbhps-chennai.com
Founded 1918, present name and status 1964
Academic year: July to June
Language of instruction: Hindi
20 Affiliated colleges
Chancellor: R. VENKATARAMAN
Vice-Chancellor: B. D. JATTI
Pro-Vice-Chancellor: V. A. SHARMA
Registrar: R. F. NEERLAKATTI
Registrar: Dr P. H. SETHUMADHAVA RAO
Library of 100,000 vols (within Nat. Hindi Research Library).

INDIAN INSTITUTE OF TECHNOLOGY, BOMBAY

Powai, Mumbai 400076, Maharashtra
Telephone: (22) 25722545
Fax: (22) 25723480
E-mail: director@iitb.ac.in
Internet: www.iitb.ac.in
Founded 1958
Language of instruction: English
Academic year: July to April
Residential; depts of aerospace engineering, chemical engineering, chemistry, civil engineering, computer science and engineering, earth sciences, electrical engineering, humanities and social sciences, mathematics, mechanical engineering, metallurgical engineering and materials science, physics
Dir: Prof. DEVANG V. KHAKHAR
Registrar: B. S. PUNALKAR
Dean of Academic Programme: Prof. S. BISWAS

Dean of Faculty: Prof. A. K. SURESH
Dean of Planning: Prof. K. V. KRISHNA RAO
Dean of Research and Devt: Prof. K. RAMAMRITHAM
Dean of Resource Mobilization: Prof. R. K. SHEVGAONKAR
Dean of Student Affairs: Prof. P. GOPALAN
Librarian: Dr DAULAT JOTHWANI
Library of 414,475 vols, 1,442 periodicals
Number of teachers: 495
Number of students: 5,865.

ATTACHED RESEARCH CENTRES

Advanced Centre for Research in Electronics: tel. (22) 25767690; fax (22) 25723806; e-mail head.acre@iit.ac.in; Head Prof. RAMAN S. SRINIVASA.

Centre for Aerospace Systems Design and Engineering: tel. (22) 25767840; fax (22) 25729511; e-mail head.casde@iit.ac.in; Head Prof. P. M. MUJUMDAR.

Centre for Environmental Science and Engineering: tel. (22) 25767853; fax (22) 25764650; e-mail head.cese@iit.ac.in; Head Prof. S. R. ASOLEKAR.

Centre for Formal Design and Verification of Software: tel. (22) 25768700; fax (22) 25794290; e-mail head.cfdvs@iit.ac.in; Head Prof. G. SIVAKUMAR.

Centre for Studies in Resources Engineering: tel. (22) 25767263; fax (22) 25723190; e-mail head.csre@iit.ac.in; Head Prof. H. S. PANDALAI.

Centre for Technology Alternatives in Rural Areas: tel. (22) 25767500; fax (22) 25767874; e-mail head.ctara@iit.ac.in; Head Prof. A. W. DATE.

Computer Aided Design Centre: tel. (22) 25767796; fax (22) 25723480; e-mail head.cad@iit.ac.in; Head Prof. R. K. MALIK.

Industrial Design Centre: tel. (22) 25767819; fax (22) 25767803; e-mail head.idc@iit.ac.in; Head Prof. R. POOVAIAH.

Sophisticated Analytical Instrumentation Facility: tel. (22) 25767691; fax (22) 25723314; e-mail head.saif@iit.ac.in; Head Prof. A. R. KULKARNI.

ATTACHED SCHOOLS

Kanwal Rekhi School of Information Technology: tel. (22) 25767900; fax (22) 25720022; e-mail head.kresit@iit.ac.in; Head Prof. A. RANADE.

School of Biosciences and Bioengineering: tel. (22) 25767207; fax (22) 25726895; e-mail head.bio@iit.ac.in; Head Prof. K. K. RAO.

Shailesh J. Mehta School of Management: tel. (22) 25767781; fax (22) 25722872; e-mail head.som@iit.ac.in; Head Prof. K. JAIN.

INDIAN INSTITUTE OF TECHNOLOGY, DELHI

Hauz Khas, New Delhi 110016
Telephone: (11) 26582222
Fax: (11) 26582277
E-mail: malhotraas@hotmail.com
Internet: www.iitd.ac.in
Founded 1961, present status 1963
Academic year: July to May
Dir: Prof. SURENDRA PRASAD
Registrar: D. T. SHAHANI (acting)
Dean of Alumni Affairs and Int. Programmes: Prof. A. GUPTA
Dean of Industrial Research and Devt: Prof. V. S. BISARIA
Dean of Postgraduate Studies and Research: Prof. M. BALAKRISHNAN
Dean of Students: Prof. A. SHARMA

Dean of Undergraduate Studies: Prof. S. R. KALE
Librarian: Dr J. ARORA
Library of 307,832 vols
Number of teachers: 484
Number of students: 4,854.

ATTACHED SCHOOLS

Amar Nath and Shashi Khosla School of Information Technology: tel. (11) 26591290; fax (11) 26868765; internet www.it.iitd.ac.in; Head Prof. H. SARAN.

Bharti School of Telecommunication Technology and Management: tel. (11) 6596200; internet www.iitd.ac.in/bsttm; f. 2000; Head Prof. S. PRASAD.

INDIAN INSTITUTE OF TECHNOLOGY, GUWAHATI

North Guwahati, Guwahati 781039, Assam
Telephone: (361) 2690401
Fax: (363) 2692321
E-mail: pro@iitg.ernet.in
Internet: www.iitg.ernet.in
Founded 1994
Depts of biotechnology, chemical engineering, chemistry, civil engineering, computer science and engineering, design, electronics and communication, humanities and social sciences, mathematics, mechanical engineering, physics
Dir: Prof. GAUTAM BARUA
Registrar: Dr BRAJENDRA NATH RAYCHOUDHURY
Dean of Academic Affairs: Prof. SUKUMAR NANDI
Dean of Admin.: (vacant)
Dean of Faculty Affairs: Prof. P. K. BORA
Dean of Research and Devt: Prof. P. S. ROBI
Dean of Student Affairs: Dr ARUP KUMAR SARMA.

ATTACHED CENTRES

Centre for Educational Technology: tel. (361) 2582667; fax (363) 2690762; e-mail cet@iitg.ernet.in; Dir Dr RAJIV TIWARI.

Centre for Energy: tel. (361) 2583150; fax (363) 2690762; e-mail dhirenh@iitg.ernet.in; f. 2004; Dir Dr PINAKESWAR MAHANTA.

Centre for the Environment: tel. (361) 2583050; fax (361) 2690762; e-mail evc_off@iitg.ernet.in; Dir Dr CHANDAN MAHANTA.

Centre for Mass Media Communication: tel. (361) 2582456; Dir Prof. K. RAMACHANDRAN.

Centre for Nanotechnology: tel. (361) 2583075; fax (361) 2690762; e-mail nano_off@iitg.ernet.in; Dir Dr ARUN CHATTOPADHYAY.

INDIAN INSTITUTE OF TECHNOLOGY, KANPUR

IIT PO, Kanpur 208016, Uttar Pradesh
Telephone: (512) 2597258
E-mail: doiitk@iitk.ac.in
Internet: www.iitk.ac.in
Founded 1960
State control
Language of instruction: English
Depts of engineering, humanities, science
Dir: Prof. S. G. DHANDE
Dean of Academic Affairs: Prof. R. K. THAREJA
Dean of Faculty Affairs: Prof. B. DEO
Dean of Research and Devt: Prof. K. MURALIDHAR
Dean of Resource Planning and Generation: Prof. S. V. AGGARWAL
Dean of Student Affairs: Prof. P. SINHA
Registrar: S. S. KASHALKAR

Librarian: R. MISHRA
Library of 390,000 vols and 900 periodicals
Number of teachers: 319
Number of students: 2,061.

ATTACHED RESEARCH CENTRES

Advanced Centre for Materials Science: internet www.iitk.ac.in/acms; f. 1978; Head S. SANGAL.

Centre for Laser Technology: tel. (512) 3927766; e-mail utpal@iitk.ac.in; internet www.iitk.ac.in/celt; Head Prof. U. DAS.

Centre for Mechatronics: tel. (512) 2597995; internet www.iitk.ac.in/robotics; Head S. SEN.

Computer Aided Desgin: tel. (512) 597838; e-mail achat@iitk.ac.in; internet www.iitk.ac.in/cad; Head Prof. S. G. DHANDE.

National Information Centre of Earthquake Engineering: tel. (512) 2597866; fax (512) 2597794; e-mail nicee@iitk.ac.in; internet www.nicee.org; Head Prof. S. K. JAIN.

National Wind Tunnel Facility: tel. (512) 2597843; e-mail kamal@iitk.ac.in; internet www.iitk.ac.in/nwtf; f. 1999; Head Dr K. PODDAR.

Samtel Centre for Display Technologies: tel. (512) 2597582; fax (512) 2597395; e-mail samtel_head@iitk.ac.in; internet www.iitk.ac.in/scdt; f. 2000; Head Prof. S. KUMAR.

SIDBI Innovation and Incubation Centre: tel. (512) 2596646; fax (512) 2597057; e-mail bvphani@iitk.ac.in; internet www.iitk.ac.in/siic; Head Dr B. V. PHANI.

INDIAN INSTITUTE OF TECHNOLOGY, KHARAGPUR

Kharagpur 721302, West Bengal
Telephone: (3222) 255221
Fax: (3222) 255303
E-mail: director@iitkgp.ernet.in
Internet: www.iitkgp.ac.in

Founded 1950
Academic year: July to April

Depts of aerospace engineering, agricultural and food engineering, architecture and regional planning, biotechnology, chemical engineering, chemistry, civil engineering, computer science and engineering, cryogenic engineering, electrical engineering, electronics and electrical communication engineering, geology and geophysics, humanities and social sciences, industrial engineering and management, information technology, materials science, mathematics, mechanical engineering, metallurgical and materials engineering, medical science and technology, mining engineering, ocean engineering and naval architecture, physics and meteorology

Dir: Prof. DAMODAR ACHARYA
Deputy Dir: M. CHAKRABORTY
Registrar: Dr D. GUNASEKARAN
Academic Dean: S. K. SOM
Dean of Continuing Education: A. CHAKRABORTY
Dean of Faculty and Planning: R. N. DATTA
Dean of Postgraduates and Research: P. K. J. MOHAPATRA
Dean of Student Affairs: D. K. TRIPATHY
Chair, Central Library: Prof. P. K. J. MAHAPATRA

Library of 362,852 vols, 1,130 periodicals
Number of teachers: 431
Number of students: 3,604

INDIAN INSTITUTE OF TECHNOLOGY, MADRAS

IIT PO, Chennai 600036, Tamil Nadu
Telephone: (44) 22578100

Fax: (44) 22570509
E-mail: registrar@iitm.ac.in
Internet: www.iitm.ac.in

Founded 1959
State control

Residential; depts of aerospace engineering, applied mechanics, biotechnology, chemical engineering, chemistry, civil engineering, computer science and engineering, electrical engineering, engineering design, humanities and social sciences, management studies, mathematics, mechanical engineering, metallurgical and materials engineering, ocean engineering, physics
Language of instruction: English
Academic year: July to April

Dir: Prof. M. S. ANANTH
Dean of Academic Courses: Prof. SANTHA KUMAR
Dean of Academic Research: Prof. K. KRISHNAIAH
Dean of Admin.: Prof. M. SINGAPERUMAL
Dean of Industrial Consultancy and Sponsored Research: Prof. T. T. NARENDRAN
Dean of Planning: Prof. R. BHASKAR
Dean of Students: Prof. V. G. IDICHANDY
Registrar: Dr K. PANCHALAN
Librarian: Dr H. CHANDRA

Library: see Libraries and Archives
Number of teachers: 460
Number of students: 4,500

Publications: *Journal of Mathematical and Physical Science* (6 a year), *Research Consultancy, Expertise and Facilities* (1 a year).

INDIAN INSTITUTE OF TECHNOLOGY, ROORKEE

Roorkee 247667, Uttaranchal
Telephone: (1332) 285311
Fax: (1332) 273560
E-mail: regis@iitr.ernet.in
Internet: www.iitr.ac.in

Founded 1847; fmrly Univ. of Roorkee

Depts of alternative hydro energy, architecture, biotechnology, chemical engineering, chemistry, civil engineering, earth sciences, earthquake engineering, electrical engineering, electronic and computer engineering, humanities, hydrology, management studies, mathematics, mechanical and industrial engineering, metallurgical engineering, paper technology engineering, physics, water resources

Dir: Prof. S. C. SAXENA
Dean of Admin.: Prof. S. C. JAIN
Dean of Alumni Affairs: Prof. H. SINVHAL
Dean of Faculty Affairs: Prof. D. K. PAUL
Dean of Finance and Planning: Prof. S. KUMAR
Dean of Postgraduate Studies and Research: Prof. H. O. GUPTA
Dean of Saharanpur Campus: Prof. R. P. AGARWAL
Dean of Sponsored Research and Industrial Consultancy: Prof. S. RAY
Dean of Student Welfare: Prof. V. K. GUPTA
Dean of Undergraduate Studies: Prof. G. S. SRIVASTAVA
Registrar: A. K. SRIVASTAVA
Librarian: Y. SINGH

Library of 320,000 vols.

INDIAN STATISTICAL INSTITUTE

203 Barrackpore Trunk Rd, Kolkata 700108, West Bengal
Telephone: (33) 25752001
Fax: (33) 25776680
E-mail: dean@isical.ac.in
Internet: www.isical.ac.in

Founded 1931

State control
Academic year: July to June
ISI regional centres located in Bangalore, Chennai, Coimbatore, Delhi, Giridih, Hyderabad, Mumbai, Pune, Vadodara

Dir: Prof. S. K. PAL
Dean of Studies: Prof. G. M. SAHA
Chief Librarian: Prof. D. DASGUPTA (acting)

Library of 215,000 vols

Publication: *Sankhya: The Indian Journal of Statistics*

HEADS OF DIVISIONS

Applied Statistics: Prof. A. N. BASU
Biological Sciences: Dr B. MUKHOPADHYAY
Computer Science and Communication Science: Prof. B. CHANDA
Physical and Earth Science: Prof. S. BHATTACHARYA
Social Sciences: Prof. T. KABIRAJ
Theoretical Statistics and Mathematics: Prof. G. MISRA

PROFESSORS

BAGCHI, B.
BAGCHI, D. K.
BAGCHI, S.
BAGCHI, S. C.
BANDYOPADHAY, S.
BHAT, B. V. R.
BHATIA, R.
BHATT, A. G.
BHATTACHARYA, B.
BHATTACHARYA, B. B.
BHATTACHARYA, S.
BHIMASANKARAM, P.
BOSE, A.
BOSE, M.
CHAKRAVARTY, S. R.
CHANDA, B.
CHANDA, S.
CHANDRA, T. K.
CHATTOPADHYAY, M.
CHAUDHURI, P.
CHOWDHURI, B. B.
COONDOO, D.
DANDAPAT, B. S.
DAS, A.
DAS, J.
DAS, N.
DAS, S.
DAS, S. P.
DASGUPTA, A. K.
DASGUPTA, D.
DASGUPTA, R.
DELAMPADY, M.
DEWANJI, A.
DEY, A.
DUTTA GUPTA, J.
GHOSE, M.
GOSWAMI, A.
GUPTA, M. R.
GUPTA, R.
JEGANATHAN, P.
KARANDIKAR, R. L.
KUNDU, M. K.
MAITI, P.
MAJUMDER, A.
MAJUMDER, H. P.
MAJUMDER, P. K.
MAJUMDER, P. P.
MAZUMDER, B. S.
MITRA, S.
MONDAL, B. N.
MUKHERJEA, K. K.
MURTHY, C. A.
MUTHURAMALINGAM, P. L.
NARAYANA, N. S. S.
PAL, N. R.
PARUI, S. K.
PAUL, M.
RAHA, A. B.
RAJEEV, B.
RAMACHANDRAN, V. K.
RAMAMURTHY, K.

RAMASUBRAMANIAM, S.
RAMASWAMY, B.
RAO, A. R.
RAO, I. K.
RAO, S. B.
RAO, T. J.
RAO, T. S. S. R. K.
RAY, K. S.
REDDY, B. M.
ROY, B. K.
ROY, P.
ROY, R.
ROY, S.
ROY CHOWDHURY, P.
SAHA, D.
SAHA, G. M.
SAMANTA, T.
SARBADHIKARI, H.
SARKAR, A.
SARKAR, N.
SASTRY, N. S. N.
SEN, A.
SENGUPTA, A.
SENGUPTA, D.
SIKDAR, K.
SINHA, B. P.
SINHA, K. B.
SITARAM, A.
SRIVASTAVA, S. M.
SWAMINATHAN, M.
THANGAVALU, S.
TRIPATHI, T. P.
VIJAYAN, K. S.

ATTACHED CENTRE

International Statistical Education Centre (ISEC): tel. (33) 25752521; fax (33) 25781834; e-mail isec@isical.ac.in; internet www.isical.ac.in/~isec; f. 1950; Principal Prof. M. PAL.

NATIONAL INSTITUTE OF PHARMACEUTICAL EDUCATION AND RESEARCH

Sector 67, SAS Nagar, Mohali 160062, Punjab
Telephone: (172) 2214682
Fax: (172) 2214692
E-mail: director@niper.nic.in
Internet: www.niper.nic.in
Founded 1991
Academic year: July to June

Depts of biotechnology, medicinal chemistry, natural products, pharmaceutical analysis, pharmaceutical management, pharmaceutical technology, pharmaceutics, pharmacology and toxicology, pharmacy practice
Dir: Prof. P. R. RAO
Dean: Prof. SARANJIT SINGH
Registrar: BHUPINDER SINGH (acting)
Library of 3,139 vols, 103 periodicals
Publication: *Current Research & Information on Pharmaceutical Sciences (CRIPS)* (4 a year)

PROFESSORS

BANERJEE, U. C., Pharmaceutical Technology
BANSAL, A. K., Pharmaceutics
BHUTANI, K. K., Natural Products
CHAKRABORTI, A. K., Medicinal Chemistry
DEY, C. S., Biotechnology
RAO, P. R., Pharmacology and Toxicology
SINGH, S., Pharmaceutical Analysis
TIWARI, P., Pharmacy Practice

POSTGRADUATE INSTITUTE OF MEDICAL EDUCATION AND RESEARCH

Sector 12, Chandigarh 160012
Telephone: (172) 2747585
Fax: (172) 2744401
E-mail: pgimer@chd.nic.in

Internet: www.pgimer.nic.in
Founded 1962
Academic year: January to December orJuly to June
Dir: Prof. K. K. TALWAR
Dean: Prof. VINAY SAKHUJA
Deputy Dir for Admin.: ANIL KUMAR GUPTA
Registrar: NARESH VIRDI
Library of 85,000 vols, 577 periodicals

PROFESSORS

BHANSALI, A., Endocrinology
CHAWLA, H. S., Oral Health Sciences
CHAWLA, Y. K., Hepatology
DHALIWAL, L. K., Obstetrics and Gynaecology
GILL, S. S., Orthopaedics
GUPTA, A., Ophthalmology
GUPTA, A. K., Hospital Administration
GUPTA, M., Anatomy
JINDAL, S. K., Pulmonary Medicine
JINDAL, S. K., Telemedicine
JOSHI, K., Histopathology
KANWAR, A. J., Dermatology, Venereology and Leprosy
KHANDELWAL, N., Radio Diagnosis and Imaging
KHANDUJA, K. L., Biophysics
KHOSLA, V. K., Neurosurgery
KOHLI, K. K., Biochemistry
KULHARA, P., Psychiatry
KUMAR, R., School of Public Health
MALLA, N., Parasitology
MANDAL, A. K., Urology
MARWAHA, N., Blood Transfusion
MINZ, M., Renal Transplant Surgery
NARANG, A., Paediatrics
PANDA, N. K., Otolaryngology
PANDHI, P., Pharmacology
PRABHAKAR, S., Experimental Medicine and Biotechnology
PRABHAKAR, S., Neurology
RAJWANSHI, A., Cytology and Gynaecological Pathology
RAO, K. L. N., Paediatric Surgery
RATHO, R. K., Virology
SAKHUJA, V., Nephrology
SHARMA, M., Medical Microbiology
SHARMA, R. K., Plastic Surgery
SHARMA, S. C., Radiotherapy
SINGH, D., Forensic Medicine
SINGH, K., Gastroenterology
TALWAR, K. K., Cardiology
VASISHTA, R. K., Immunopathology
VERMA, S., Internal Medicine
WADHWA, S., Physical and Rehabilitation Medicine
WIG, J., Anaesthesia
WIG, J. D., General Surgery

SANJAY GANDHI POSTGRADUATE INSTITUTE OF MEDICAL SCIENCES

Raebareli Rd, Lucknow 226014
Telephone: (33) 25752004
Fax: (522) 2668017
Internet: www.sgpgi.ac.in
Founded 1983
Autonomous, state funded

Depts of anaesthesiology, biostatistics, cardiology, cardiovascular and thoracic surgery, critical care medicine, endocrine surgery, endocrinology, gastroenterology, haematology, immunology, medical genetics, microbiology, nephrology, neurology, neurosurgery, nuclear medicine, pathology, radiodiagnosis, radiotherapy, surgical gastroenterology, transfusion medicine, urology
Dir: Prof. A. K. MAHAPATRA.

SREE CHITRA TIRUNAL INSTITUTE FOR MEDICAL SCIENCES AND TECHNOLOGY

Thiruvananthapuram 695011, Kerala
Telephone: (471) 2524400
Fax: (471) 2550728
E-mail: director@sctimst.ac.in
Internet: www.sctimst.ac.in
Founded 1973, present status 1980
Academic year: January to December

Depts and divs of anesthesiology, biochemistry, blood transfusion services, cardiology, cardiovascular and thoracic surgery, cellular and molecular cardiology, health science studies, microbiology, neurology, neurosurgery, pathology, radiology
Pres.: Dr R. CHIDAMBARAM
Dir: Dr K. RADHAKRISHNAN
Dean of Academic Affairs: Dr JAGAN MOHAN THARAKAN
Registrar: Dr A. V. GEORGE.

SRI VENKATESWARA INSTITUTE OF MEDICAL SCIENCES

Alipiri Rd, Tirupati 517507, Andhra Pradesh
Telephone: (877) 2287152
Fax: (877) 2286803
E-mail: svimshosp@yahoo.com
Internet: svimstpt.ap.nic.in
Founded 1993

Affiliating; depts of anaesthesiology, biochemistry, cardiology, cardiothoracic surgery, casuality, dietetics, endocrinolgy, gastroenterology, general medicine, genito urinary surgery, nephrology, nuclear medicine, neurology, neurosurgery, oncology, microbiology, pathology, physiotherapy radiology, transfusion medicine
Dir: G. SUBRAMANYAM.

Deemed Universities

Deemed Universities (also known as Deemed-to-be Universities) are institutions that have been conferred the status of a university by virtue of their long tradition of teaching, or specialization and excellence in a particular field of study.

Allahabad Agricultural Institute: Allahabad 211007, Uttar Pradesh; tel. (532) 2684281; fax (532) 2684394; e-mail registrar@aaidu.org; internet www.aaidu.org; f. 1910, deemed univ. status 2000; Faculties of agriculture, arts and culture, business studies, engineering and technology, health and medical sciences, humanities, science, social sciences, theology, veterinary science and animal husbandry; library: 40,000 vols; Chancellor Dr MANI JACOB; Pro-Chancellor Dr J. A. OLIVER; Vice-Chancellor Prof. RAJENDRA B. LAL; Pro-Vice-Chancellor Prof. HENRY SHEPHERD; Registrar Prof. A. K. A. LAWRENCE; Dir of Extension Prof. NAHAR SINGH; Dir of Finance STEPHEN DAS; Dir of Research Prof. S. B. LAL; Librarian S. P. MALLICK.

Amrita Vishwa Vidyapeetham: Ettimadai PO, Coimbatore 641105, Tamil Nadu; tel. (422) 2656422; fax (422) 2656274; e-mail univhq@amrita.edu; internet www.amrita.edu; f. Deemed univ. status 2003; campuses at Amritapuri, Bangalore, Kochi, Mysore; schools of arts and sciences, ayurveda, biotechnology, business, dentistry, education, engineering, journalism, medicine, nursing, pharmacy; Centre for Nanosciences; Vice-Chancellor Dr P. VENKAT RANGAN; Dean of Admin. Dr S. KRISHNAMOORTHY; Dean of Corporate Relations Prof. C. PARAMESHWARAN.

Atal Bihari Vajpayee Indian Institute of Information Technology and Management: Morena Link Rd, Gwalior 474010, Madhya Pradesh; tel. (751) 2449702; fax (751) 2460313; e-mail director@iiitm.ac.in; internet www.iiitm.ac.in; f. 2001; Depts of computer science, electronics, finance, human resources, information technology, marketing and networking; Dir Prof. S. G. DESHMUKH.

Avinashilingam University for Women: Mettupalayam Rd, Coimbatore 641043, Tamil Nadu; tel. (422) 2440241; fax (422) 2438786; e-mail registrar@avinuty.ac.in; internet www.avinashilingam.edu; f. 1957, deemed univ. status 1988; Faculties of engineering, community education and entrepreneurship devt, home science, humanities, management studies, science; library: 130,000 vols; 4,436 students; Vice-Chancellor Dr SAROJA PRABHAKARAN; Registrar Dr GOWRI RAMAKRISHNAN

DEANS

Faculty of Business Administration: Dr SHANTHA B. KURUP
Faculty of Community College and Entrepreneurship Development: Dr VIJAYALAKSHMI PURUSHOTHAMAN
Faculty of Education: Dr R. CHANDRA
Faculty of Engineering: Dr S. MARAGATHAM NATRAJ
Faculty of Home Science: Dr SATHYAVATHIMUTHU
Faculty of Humanities: Dr D. LALITHA
Faculty of Science: Dr R. PARVATHAM.

Attached Centres:

Centre for Women's Studies: Avinashilingam University for Women, Coimbatore; tel. (422) 2435266; fax (422) 2433408; e-mail cws_auw@yahoo.com; internet www.cws-adu.org; f. 2000; Dir K. C. LEELAVATHY.

Gandhian Studies Centre: Avinashilingam University for Women, Coimbatore; f. 2005.

Banasthali Vidyapith (Banasthali University): *Banasthali Campus:* Banasthali 304022, Rajasthan; tel. (1438) 228348; fax (1438) 228365
Jaipur Campus: C-62, Sarojini Marg, C Scheme, Jaipur 302001, Rajasthan; tel. (141) 5118721; e-mail info@banasthali.ac.in; internet www.banasthali.org; f. 1935, deemed univ. status 1983; Faculties of education, fine arts, home science, humanities, management, science, social sciences; library: 180,757 vols, 530 periodicals; 210 teachers; 4,182 students; Vice-Chancellor Prof. ADITYA SHASTRI; Pres. Prof. DIWAKAR SHASTRI; Sec. and Treas. Prof. CHITRA PUROHIT; Librarian Dr S. D. VYAS.

Bharath University: 173 Agharam Rd, Selaiyur, Chennai 600073, Tamil Nadu; tel. (44) 22290742; fax (44) 22293886; e-mail contact@bharathuniv.com; internet www.bharathuniv.com; f. 1984; Deemed University status 2003; constituent instns: Bharath Institute of Science and Technology, Sree Balaji Dental College and Hospital, Sree Balaji Medical College and Hospital, Sree Lakshmi Narayana Institute of Medical Sciences; library: 75,000 vols, 80 periodicals; Chancellor Dr S. JAGATHRAKSHAKAN; Vice-Chancellor Dr K. P. THOOYAMANI; Registrar (vacant).

Bharati Vidyapeeth University: Lal Bahadur Shastri Marg, Pune 411030, Maharashtra; tel. (20) 24331317; fax (20) 24339121; e-mail bharati@vsnl.com; internet www.bharatividyapeeth.edu; f. 1964, Deemed University status 1996; composed of 17 constituent instns: Medical College, Dental College and Hospital, College of

Ayurved, Homoeopathic Medical College, College of Nursing, Yashwantrao Mohite College of Arts, Science and Commerce, New Law College, Yashwantrao Chavan Institute of Social Science Studies and Research, Social Science Centre, Research and Development Centre in Pharmaceutical Sciences and Applied Chemistry, Institute of Environment Education and Research, Pune College of Pharmacy, Institute of Management and Entrepreneurship Development, College of Engineering, College of Physical Education, Rajiv Gandhi Institute of Biotechnology and Information Technology, Interactive Research School for Health Affairs; library: total colln of 99,125 vols; 8,386 students; Vice-Chancellor Prof. SHIVAJIRAO KADAM; Registrar B. R. ARBAD.

Bhatkhande Music Institute University: 1 Kaiserbagh, Lucknow 226001, Uttar Pradesh; tel. (522) 2210318; fax (522) 2222926; e-mail info@bhatkhandemusic.edu.in; internet www.bhatkhandemusic.edu.in; f. Deemed univ. status 2000; Faculties of dance, instrumental music, musicology, training and vocal music; Vice-Chancellor Prof. PURNIMA PANDE; Registrar Dr A. SRIVASTAVA.

Birla Institute of Technology, Ranchi: Mesra 835215, Ranchi, Jharkhand; tel. (651) 2276249; fax (651) 2275401; e-mail birlatech@bitsmart.com; internet www.bitmesra.ac.in; f. 1955, Deemed University status 1986; extension centres in Allahabad, Chennai, Jaipur, Kolkata, Lalpur, Noida and Patna; int. centres in Bahrain, Muscat and Ras Al Khaimah (UAE); depts of applied sciences, architecture, biotechnology, engineering and technology, hotel management and catering technology, management, pharmaceutical sciences; library: 112,470 vols, 100 periodicals; 149 teachers; 1,650 students; Vice-Chancellor Dr P. K. BARHAI; Registrar Dr R. K. VERMA (acting); Treas. S. S. JAJODIA (acting); Librarian Dr V. SREENIVASULU; publs *Journal of Hospitality Application & Research* (1 a year), *Journal of Manufacturing Technology and Research* (4 a year), *PHARMBIT* (2 a year)

DEANS

Academic Coordination: Dr D. SASMAL
Academic Infrastructure: Dr USHA JHA
Admissions: Dr D. JAIRATH
Development Programme: Dr M. MUKHERJEE
Doctoral Research: Dr ASHOK MISRA
Examination: Prof. C. M. PRASAD
Extension Centres: Dr A. K. CHATTERJEE
Faculty Development: Dr GOPAL PATHAK
Finance: Dr P. C. JOSHI
Postgraduate Studies: Dr MOHAN VARMA
Research: Dr P. K. BARHAI
Undergraduate Studies: Prof. C. M. PRASAD

Birla Institute of Technology and Science: Vidhya Vihar Campus, Pilani 333031, Rajasthan; tel. (1596) 242192; fax (1596) 244183; e-mail mmsanand@bits-pilani.ac.in; internet discovery.bits-pilani.ac.in/index .html; f. 1964; Private; Accredited by Nat. Assessment and Accreditation Ccl; campuses in Goa, Hyderabad and Dubai (UAE); academic year July to May (2 terms); library: 223,810 vols, 535 periodicals; 535 teachers; 17,898 students; Chancellor Dr K. K. BIRLA; Vice-Chancellor Prof. L. K. MAHESHWARI; Deputy Dir of Academic Affairs Prof. G. RAGHURAMA; Deputy Dir of Admin. Prof. K. E. RAMAN; Dir of Dubai Campus Prof. M. RAMACHANDRAN; Dir of Goa Campus Prof. K. E. RAMAN; Dir of Hyderabad Campus Prof. V. S. RAO; Registrar Prof. M. M. S. ANAND; Librarian Dr M. I. BHAT; publ. *Journal of Cooperation among University, Research and Industrial Enterprises* (4 a year).

Central Institute of Fisheries Education: Seven Bungalows, University Rd, Anderi, Mumbai 400061, Maharashtra; tel. (22) 26361446; fax (22) 26361573; e-mail contact@cife.edu.in; internet www.cife.edu .in; f. 1961; Deemed University status 1989; centres in Kolkata, Kakinada, Rohtak, Powerkheda; library: 27,326 vols; Dir Dr D. KUMAR; Registrar C. LAL.

Central Institute of Higher Tibetan Studies: Sarnath, Varanasi 221007, Uttar Pradesh; tel. (542) 2585148; fax (542) 2585150; e-mail ngawang_samten@yahoo .com; internet www.smith.edu/cihts; f. 1977, deemed univ. status 1988; faculties of Language and Literature, Philosophy, Social Science, Tibetan Fine Arts, Tibetan Medicine and Astrology; library: 56,000 vols on Buddhist, Tibetan, Indian and Himalayan Studies in Tibetan, Hindi, Sanskrit and other languages; publs *Dhih – A Rare Buddhist Texts Research Journal*, 8 series of research *vols*; Dir NGAWANG SAMTEN; Registrar R. D. AGARWAL.

Datta Meghe Institute of Medical Sciences: Nyss Management Campus, Atrey Layaut, Pratap Nagar, Nagpur 440022; tel. (712) 3956552; fax (712) 2245318; e-mail info@dmims.org; internet www.dmims.org; Vice-Chancellor Dr VEDPRAKASH MISHRA; Dirs SAGAR MEGHE, SAMEER MEGHE; Registrar Dr VIDYA SAGAR

DEANS

Faculty of Ayurveda: (vacant)
Faculty of Dentistry: Dr A. J. PAKHAN
Faculty of Medicine: Dr S. S. PATEL

Dayalbagh Educational Institute: Dayalbagh, Agra 282005, Uttar Pradesh; tel. (562) 2801545; fax (562) 2801226; e-mail admin@dei.ac.in; internet www.dei.ac.in; f. 1981; faculties of arts, commerce, education, engineering, science and social sciences and technical college; library: 101,213 vols; 180 teachers; 2,493 students; Dir Prof. V. G. DAS; Registrar Prof. S. S. SRIVASTAVA; Treas. S. BIJLANI; publ. *Journal of Science and Engineering Research* (1 a year).

Deccan College Postgraduate and Research Institute: Yeravada, Pune 411006, Maharashtra; tel. (20) 26693794; fax (20) 26692104; e-mail deccan.college@ gems.vsnl.net.in; internet www .deccancollegepune.org; f. 1821, deemed univ. status 1990; depts of archaeology, linguistics; library: 128,764 books, 31,647 vols of bound periodicals; 127 students; Dir Dr K. PADDAYYA; Librarian T. MORE.

Dr B. R. Ambedkar National Institute of Technology: Jalandhar 144004, Punjab; tel. (181) 2690301; fax (181) 2690320; e-mail admin@nitj.ac.in; internet www.nitj.ac.in; f. 1987, deemed univ. status 2002; depts of applied chemistry, applied mathematics, applied physics, chemical and biological engineering, civil engineering, computer science, electronics and communication engineering, humanities, industrial engineering, instrumentation and control engineering, leather technology engineering, management, mechanical engineering, textile technology eng.; Dir Prof. MOIN UDDIN; Registrar Dr A. L. SANGAL

DEANS

Academic Programmes: Prof. A AGNIHOTRI
Infrastructure Planning and Devt: Prof. S. P. SINGH
Research and Industrial Liaison: Prof. R. K. GARG
Students and Alumni: Prof. ARVINDER SINGH

Dr M. G. R. Educational and Research Institute: E. V. R. Periyar Salai (NH4

Highway), Maduravoyal, Chennai 600095, Tamil Nadu; tel. (44) 23782176; fax (44) 23783165; e-mail registrar@drmgrdu.ac.in; internet www.drmgrdu.ac.in; f. 1988, deemed univ. status 2003; faculties of engineering and technology, humanities and sciences, medicine and dental sciences; library: 50,000 vols, 302 periodicals; Vice-Chancellor Dr G. GOPALAKRISHNAN; Pro-Chancellor Prof. A.C. S. ARUN KUMAR; Dean of Admin. Prof. R. KALAVATHY; Exec. Dir Prof. G. C. KOTHANDAN; Managing Dir A. C. S. KUMAR; Registrar Prof. S. DINAKARAM.

Forest Research Institute University: Kaulagarh Rd, Dehradun 248195, Uttaranchal; tel. (135) 2751826; fax (135) 2756865; e-mail dir_fri@icfre.org; internet friuniversity.icfre.gov.in; f. 1906, deemed univ. status 1991; MSc degree courses in environment management, forestry, wood science and technology; also offers postgraduate diploma courses and doctorate degree courses; library: 159,286 vols; 82 students; Dean Dr R. K. AIMA; Dir Dr S. S. NEGI; Registrar T. C. NAUTIYAL.

Gandhigram Rural Institute: Dindigul District, Gandhigram 624302, Tamil Nadu; tel. (451) 2452371; fax (451) 2453071; e-mail gricc@vsnl.com; internet www.ruraluniv.ac.in; f. 1956, deemed univ. status 1976; faculties of agriculture and animal husbandry, English and foreign languages, Indian languages, rural development, rural health and sanitation, rural oriented sciences, rural social sciences, Tamil and rural arts; library: 93,422 vols, 320 periodicals; 118 teachers; 2,024 students; Vice-Chancellor Dr M. R. KUBENDRAM; Registrar Dr M. S. VADIVELU; Librarian Dr J. ABRAHAM; library: 103,300 vols, 285 periodicals; publ. *Journal of Extension and Research* (2 a year)

DEANS

Faculty of Agriculture and Animal Husbandry: Dr R. UDHAYAKUMAR
Faculty of English and Foreign Languages: Dr M. R. KUBENDRAN
Faculty of Rural Development: Dr N. NARAYANASAMY
Faculty of Rural Health and Sanitation: Dr V. K. MUTHU
Faculty of Rural Oriented Sciences: Dr N. S. NAGARAJAN
Faculty of Rural Social Sciences: Dr M. WILLIAM BASKARAN
Faculty of Tamil, Indian Languages and Rural Arts: Dr A. PITCHAI

Gokhale Institute of Politics and Economics: BMCC Rd, Deccan Gymkhana, Pune 411004, Maharashtra; tel. (20) 25650287; fax (20) 25652579; e-mail gipelib@gipe.ernet.in; internet www.gipe.ernet.in; f. 1930, deemed univ. status 1993; postgraduate courses in politics and economics; library: 261,537 vols, 440 periodicals; Dir Dr A. SINHA; Registrar Dr N. BENJAMIN; publ. *Artha Vijanana* (in English, 4 a year).

Gujarat Vidyapith: Ashram Rd, Ahmedabad 380014, Gujarat; tel. (79) 40016200; fax (79) 27542547; e-mail registrar@gujaratvidyapith.org; internet www.gujaratvidyapith.org; f. 1920, deemed univ. status 1963; languages of instruction: Gujarati, Hindi; academic year June to April; campuses at Ahmedabad, Anand, Gandhinagar, Kheda, Valsad; Chancellor NARAYANBHAI DESAI; Vice-Chancellor SUDARSHAN AAYANGAR; Registrar Dr RAJENDRA KHIMANI (acting); Librarian BHARTIBEN DESAI (acting); library: 539,945 vols; 105 teachers; 1,774 students; publ. *Vidyapith* (4 a year)

DEANS

College of Education: Dr M. PATEL
College of Hindi Education: Dr K. C. PARMAR

M. D. College of Physical Education: Dr J. K. SAVALIA
M. D. College of Rural Service (Home Science), Randheja: Dr RAMILABEN PATEL
M. D. College of Rural Service, Sadra: KANUBHAI NAIK
M. D. College of Social Sciences: Dr MALTIBEN DUBEY

PROFESSORS

DUBEY, MALTIBEN, Hindi
JOSHI, BHARATBHAI H., Education
PANDYA, JAYAPRAKASH G., Education
PARMAR, KANTIBHAI C., Hindi Education
PATEL, ARTIBEN P., Education
PATEL, MOHANBHAI K., Education
SAVALIYA, JAMNADAS K., Physical Education
SHUKLA, NIMISHA, Rural Economics
UPADHYAY, USHA, Gujarati

Gurukul Kangri Vishwavidyalaya: PO Gurukul Kangri, Hardwar 249404, Uttar Pradesh; tel. (1334) 246811; fax (1334) 246366; e-mail queries@gkvharidwar.org; internet gkvharidwar.org; f. 1902, deemed univ. status 1962; library: 133,667 vols; 103 teachers; 1,558 students; Chancellor SUDERSHAN KUMAR SHARMA; Vice-Chancellor Prof. SWATANTRA KUMAR; Pro-Vice-Chancellor Prof. V. P. SHASTRI; Registrar Prof. A. K. CHOPRA; Librarian Dr J. P. VIDYALANKAR; library: 135,000 vols; publs *Arya Bhatt* (4 a year), *Gurukula Patrika* (12 a year), *Prahlad* (4 a year), *Vedic Path* (4 a year).

Indian Agricultural Research Institute: Pusa Campus, New Delhi 110012; tel. (11) 25847438; fax (11) 25846420; e-mail director@iari.res.in; internet www.iari.res.in; f. 1905, deemed univ. status 1958; postgraduate courses in all major branches of agriculture; schools of basic sciences, crop improvements, crop protection, resource management and social sciences; library: 600,000 vols; 360 teachers; 600 students; Dir Dr S. A. PATIL; Dir of Extension Dr B. SINGH; Dir of Research Dr K. R. KOUNDAL; Registrar P. C. JACOB; Dean Dr H. S. GAUR; Librarian N. S. PAKHALE.

Indian Institute of Foreign Trade: Bhawan, B-21, Qutab Institutional Area, New Delhi 110016; tel. (11) 26965124; fax (11) 26853956; e-mail iift@iift.ac.in; internet www.iift.edu; f. 1963; attached research centres: Centre for International Trade in Technology, Centre for SME Studies, Centre for World Trade Organization Studies; library: 84,000 vols and 800 periodicals; Dir K. T. CHACKO; Registrar L. D. MAGO; Head (Kolkata Centre) Dr K. RANGARAJAN; publs *Focus WTO*, *Foreign Trade Review*.

Indian Institute of Information Technology: Nehru Science Centre, Kamla Nehru Rd, Allahabad 211012, Uttar Pradesh; tel. (532) 2922000; fax (532) 2430006; e-mail contact@iiita.ac.in; internet www.iiita.ac.in; f. 1999; Deemed University status 2000; undergraduate and postgraduate courses in information technology; Dean of Academic Affairs Dr M. D. TIWARI.

Indian Institute of Science: Bangalore 560012, Karnataka; tel. (80) 23600757; fax (80) 23600085; e-mail regr@admin.iisc.ernet.in; internet www.iisc.ernet.in; f. 1909; faculties of engineering and science; library: 411,676 vols; 434 teachers; 1,794 students; Dir Prof. P. BALARAM; Registrar J. LALITHA; Public Relations Officer V. THILAGAM; Librarian Dr S. VENKADESAN.

Indian Law Institute: Bhagwandas Rd, New Delhi 110001; tel. (11) 23387526; fax (11) 23782140; e-mail ili@ilidelhi.org; internet www.ilidelhi.org; f. 1956, deemed univ. status in 2004; courses in admin. law, alternative dispute resolution, corporate laws and management, cyber law, environ-

mental law, human rights law, intellectual property rights law, int. trade law, labour law, securities and banking law, tax law; library: 75,000 vols, 270 periodicals; Dir Prof. S. SIVAKUMAR (acting); Registrar DALIP KUMAR; publ. *Journal of the Indian Law Institute*.

Indian School of Mines University: Dhanbad 826004, Jharkhand; tel. (326) 2296559; fax (326) 2296563; e-mail info@ismdhanbad.ac.in; internet www.ismdhanbad.ac.in; f. 1926; residential; depts of applied chemistry, applied geology, applied geophysics, applied mathematics, applied physics, computer science and engineering, electrical engineering, electronics engineering, fuel and mineral engineering, humanities and social science, management studies, mechanical engineering and mining machinery engineering, petroleum engineering; language of instruction: English; academic year July to June; library: 74,550 books, 550 journals, 3,000 online journals; 105 teachers; 1,035 students; Dir Prof. T. KUMAR; Dean of Academics and Research Prof. KAMPAN MUKHERJEE; Dean of Planning and Devt Prof. A. CHATTOPADHYAY; Dean of Student Welfare Prof. P. S. GUPTA; Registrar P. S. SANDHU; Librarian Dr PARTHA DE.

Indian Veterinary Research Institute: Izatnagar 243122, Uttar Pradesh; tel. (581) 2300096; fax (581) 2303284; e-mail dirivri@ivri.up.nic.in; internet www.ivri.nic.in; f. 1889, deemed univ. status 1983; campuses at Bangalore, Bhopal, Izatnagar, Kolkata, Mukteswar, Palampur and Srinagar; research divs of animal biochemistry, animal biotechnology, animal genetics and breeding, animal nutrition, animal physiology, avian diseases, biostatistics, livestock production and management, livestock products technology, poultry science, veterinary bacteriology, veterinary epidemiology, veterinary extension education, veterinary gynaecology and obstetrics, veterinary immunology, veterinary medicine, veterinary parasitology, veterinary pathology, veterinary pharmacology, veterinary public health, veterinary surgery, veterinary virology; library: 207,000 vols, 300 periodicals; Dir Dr R. S. CHAUHAN (acting); Dir for Academic and Dean Dr D. DAS; Registrar K. L. MEENA (acting).

Indira Gandhi Institute of Development Research: Gen. A. K.Vaidya Marg, Goregaon (E), Mumbai 400065, Maharashtra; tel. (22) 28400919; fax (22) 28402752; e-mail dean@igidr.ac.in; internet www.igidr.ac.in; f. 1987, deemed univ. status 1995; postgraduate courses in economics and devt studies; library: 40,000 vols, 460 periodicals; 30 teachers; Dir Dr D. M. NACHANE; Registrar T. V. SUBRAMANIAN; Librarian G. K. MANJUNATH.

Institute of Advanced Studies in Education/IASE University: Gandhi Vidya Mandir, Sardarshahr 331401, Rajasthan; tel. (1564) 223054; fax (1564) 223682; e-mail info@iaseuniversity.org.in; internet www.iaseuniversity.org.in; f. 1950, deemed univ. status 2002; faculties of education, information technology, management, medicine; campuses at Bhunbeshwar and Bikaner; library: 95,000 vols; 10,000 students; Dir MILAP DUGAR; Registrar R. S. SUROLIA.

Institute of Armament Technology: Girinagar, Pune 411025, Maharashtra; tel. (20) 24389444; fax (20) 24389509; e-mail root@iat.ernet.in; f. 1952; Deemed University status 1999; library: 42,000 vols, 250 periodicals; Dir Prof. G. S. MANI.

International Institute for Population Sciences: Govandi Station Rd, Deonar, Mumbai 400088, Maharashtra; tel. (22)

25563254; fax (22) 25563257; e-mail director@iips.net; internet www.iipsindia .org; f. 1956, deemed univ. status 1985; depts of devt studies, extra mural studies and distance education, fertility studies, mathematical demography and statistics, migration and urban studies, population policies and programmes, public health and mortality studies; 30 teachers; 120 students; library: 76,962 books, 13,108 bound periodicals; Dir Dr FAUJDAR RAM; Registrar Dr M. K. KULKARNI; Librarian D. D. MESTRI.

International Institute of Information Technology: Gachibowli, Hyderabad 500032, Andhra Pradesh; tel. (40) 66531000; fax (40) 66531413; e-mail query@ iiit.net; internet www.iiit.net; f. 1998; undergraduate and postgraduate courses in various disciplines of information technology; research centres in bioinformatics, building science, communications, earthquake engineering, education, data engineering, open software, technology consultancy, visual embedded systems technology, visual information technology; library: 6,000 vols; Dir Prof. RAJEEV SANGAL; Librarian V. PRABHA-KAR SARMA.

Jain Vishva Bharati Institute: Dist. Nagaur, Ladnun 341306, Rajasthan; tel. (1581) 222110; fax (1581) 223472; e-mail registrar@jvbi.ac.in; internet jvbi.ac.in; f. 1970, deemed univ. status 1991; depts of Acharya Kalu Kanya Mahavidhyalaya, computer applications, education, jainology and comparative religion and philosophy, nonviolence and peace, prakrit and jain agama, science of living, preksha meditation and yoga, social work; library: 46,260 books, 116 periodicals, 6,000 MSS; Vice-Chancellor Dr SAMANI M. PRAJNA; Dir of Research Prof. Dr BACHH R. DUGAR; Finance Officer RAKESH K. JAIN; Registrar Prof. Dr G. S. SHRIVASTAVA; Librarian H. C. R. SIDDAPPA.

Jamia Hamdard: Hamdard Nagar, New Delhi 110062; tel. (11) 26059688; fax (11) 26059663; e-mail inquiry@jamiahamdard .edu; internet www.jamiahamdard.edu; f. 1963, deemed univ. status 1989; faculties of allied health sciences, islamic studies and social science, management studies and information technology, medicine, nursing, pharmacy and science; library: 141,021 books, 124 periodicals, 5,000 MSS; 2,100 students; Vice-Chancellor Dr G. N. QAZI; Registrar Prof. NAUSHAD ALAM; Finance Officer C. L. GUPTA; Dean of Student Welfare Prof. R. K. KHAR; Provost Dr E. A. KHAN; Proctor Dr T. A. SIDDIQUI; Librarian K. K. FARUQI.

Janardan Rai Nagar Rajasthan Vidyapeeth: Pratap Nagar, Udaipur 313001, Rajasthan; tel. (294) 2490040; fax (294) 2492440; e-mail info@jrnrvpu.org; internet www.jrnrvu.org; f. 1937, deemed univ. status 1987; faculties of arts and commerce, computer science, management, medical science, science; 12 constituent institutions; library: 244,000 books, 140 periodicals; 5,300 students; Vice-Chancellor Prof. L. BHATT; Registrar Dr V. S. PANWAR; Dir of Distance Education Dr D. JOHAR; Librarian K. L. VAISHNAV.

CONSTITUENT COLLEGES:

Homeopathic Medical College and Hospital: Udaipur; e-mail homoeopathic@jrnrvpu.org.

Institute of Management Studies: Udaipur; tel. and fax (294) 2490632; e-mail imsjrnrvu_director@yahoo.co.in; internet www.fmsrvu.org; Dir Prof. RAJEEV JAIN.

Institute of Rajasthan Studies: Udaipur; e-mail rajasthanstudies@jrnrvpu.org.

Lokmanya Tilak College: Dabok, Udaipur; tel. (294) 2655327; fax (294) 2657753; e-mail info@lokmanyatilakcollege.org; internet www.lokmanyatilakcollege.org; faculty of education; Dean and Prin. Prof. DIVYA NAGAR.

M. V. Shramjeevi College: Town Hall Link Rd, Udaipur; e-mail shramjeevi@ jrnrvpu.org; faculties of commerce, humanities and social sciences; Prin. Prof. N. K. PANDYA.

Udaipur School of Social Work: Dabok, Udaipur; e-mail social@jrnrvpu.org; Prin. (vacant).

Jawaharlal Nehru Centre for Advanced Scientific Research: Jakkur, Bangalore 560064, Karnataka; tel. (80) 22082900; fax (80) 22082766; e-mail admin@jncasr.ac.in; internet www.jncasr.ac.in; f. 1989; Deemed University status 2002; library: 10,000 vols, 71 periodicals; 40 teachers; Pres. M. R. S. RAO; publs *Chemistry and Physics of Materials, Engineering Mechanics, Evolutionary and Organismal Biology, Geodynamics, Molecular Biology and Genetics, Theoretical Science.*

Kalinga Institute of Industrial Technology/KIIT University: Bhubaneshwar 751024, Orissa; tel. (674) 2725113; fax (674) 2725113; e-mail kiit@kiit.ac.in; internet www .kiit.ac.in; f. Deemed University status 2004; schools of biotechnology, computer application, law, management, rural management, technology; constituent instns: Kalinga Institute of Medical Sciences, Kalinga Institute of Social Sciences, KIIT Int. School, KIIT Science College, Kalinga Polytechnic; Vice-Chancellor Prof. S. C. DE SARKAR; Pro-Vice-Chancellor Prof. M. S. MISHRA; Registrar Dr A. K. JHA.

Lakshmibai National Institute of Physical Education: Mela Rd, Shakti Nagar, Gwalior 474002, Madhya Pradesh; tel. (751) 4000918; fax (751) 2340553; e-mail fo@lnipe .gov.in; internet www.lnipe.gov.in; f. 1957; Deemed University status 1995; library: 31,000 vols; depts of coaching, fitness and dance, computer science and applied statistics, health sciences and yoga therapy, research, devt and advanced studies, sports management and journalism, teacher education, youth affairs and sports; Vice-Chancellor Maj.-Gen. SHIBNATH MUKHERJEE; Registrar Dr L. N. SARKAR; Finance Officer VISHAL BANSAL; publs *Journal of Physical Education and Allied Sciences* (1 a year), *Journal of Physical Education and Sports Sciences* (1 a year)

PROFESSORS

DATTA, A. K.

DEBNATH, MONIKA

DEY, R. N., Research, Devt and Advance Studies

MAZUMDAR, INDU

MUKHERJEE, S., Teacher Education

PAL, RAMESH

PANDE, P. K., Health Sciences and Yoga Therapy

SINGH, JASRAJ

VERMA, J. P., Computer Science and Applied Statistics

Malaviya National Institute of Technology: Jaipur 302017, Rajasthan; tel. (141) 2529078; fax (141) 2529029; e-mail director@ mnit.ac.in; internet www.mnit.ac.in; f. 1963, deemed univ. status 2002; depts of architecture, chemical engineering, chemistry, civil engineering, computer engineering, electrical engineering, electronics and communication engineering, humanities, mathematics, mechanical engineering, metallurgical engineering, physics, structural engineering; library: 133,600 vols; 150

teachers; 1,700 students; Dir Prof. R. P. DAHIYA; Dean of Academic Affairs Prof. P. R. SONI; Dean of Admin. Prof. G. AGARWAL; Dean of Faculty Affairs Prof. R. A. GUPTA; Dean of Research and Devt Prof. RAVINDRA NAGAR; Dean of Student Affairs Prof. SUDHIR KUMAR; Registrar P. S. DHAKHA; Librarian DEEP SINGH

PROFESSORS

BHARDWAJ, A. K., Management Studies

CHAURASIA, S. P., Chemical Engineering

GAUR, M. S., Computer Engineering

GUPTA, K. D., Chemistry

JAIN, R., Mathematics

JAIN, V. K., Electrical Engineering

MISRA, A., Structural Engineering

SHARMA, G., Civil Engineering

SHRINGI, R., Architecture

SONI, S. L., Mechanical Engineering

SWAMI, K. C., Physics

TANDON, N., Humanities

YADAV, R. K., Metallurgy and Materials

YADAV, R. P., Electronics and Communication

Manipal Academy of Higher Education: University Bldg, Madhav Nagar, Manipal 576104, Karnataka; tel. (820) 2571000; e-mail admissions@manipal.edu; internet www.manipal.edu; f. 1953, deemed univ. status 1993; privately controlled network of 50 instns run by the Manipal Group, incl. Kasturba Medical College, Manipal Centre for Information Sciences, Manipal College of Allied Health Sciences, Manipal College of Dental Sciences, Manipal College of Nursing, Manipal College of Pharmaceutical Sciences, Manipal Institute of Communication, Manipal Institute of Jewellery Management, Manipal Institute of Management, Manipal Institute of Regenerative Medicine, Manipal Institute of Technology, Manipal Life Sciences Centre, Melaka Manipal Medical College, Welcomgroup Graduate School of Hotel Administration; depts of geopolitics, statistics; Manipal Advanced Research Group; off-campus BSc in animation; library: 50,000 vols, 600 periodicals; Chancellor Dr RAMDAS M. PAI; Pro-Chancellor Dr H. S. BALLAL; Vice-Chancellor Dr RAJ WARRIER; Registrar Dr H. VINOD BHAT.

Maulana Azad National Institute of Technology: Bhopal 462051, Madhya Pradesh; tel. (755) 5206006; fax (755) 2670562; e-mail info@manit.ac.in; internet www.manit .nic.in; f. 1960, deemed univ. status 2002; depts of architecture and planning, computer application, energy centre, eng., humanities, management, physical education, remote sensing and GIS, science; library: 107,923 vols, 100 journals; Dir Prof. K. S. PANDEY; Dean of Admin. Dr S. RANGNEKAR; Dean of Research and Devt Dr K. R. PARDASANI; Dean of Student Affairs Dr A. M. SHANDILYA; Registrar ARVIND MITTAL; Librarian AJAY PANDEY.

Meenakshi University: 12 Vembuli Amman Koil St, Chennai, 600078; tel. (44) 23643955; fax (44) 23643958; e-mail info@ maher.ac.in; internet www.maher.ac.in; f. 2004; constituent colleges: Ammal Dental College and Hospital, College of Nursing, College of Physiotherapy, Dept of Eng. and Technology, Medical College and Research Institute; Vice-Chancellor Dr T. GUNASA-GARAN; Dir Dr C. M. NANDAGOPAL; Registrar A. N. SANTHANAM.

CONSTITUENT COLLEGES:

Arulmigu Meenakshi Amman College of Nursing: Enathur, Kancheepuram.

Meenakshi Ammal Dental College and Hospital: Chennai 600095.

Meenakshi College of Nursing: Chennai 600095.

Meenakshi College of Occupational Therapy: Chennai 600095.

Meenakshi College of Physiotherapy: West K. K. Nagar, Chennai 600078.

Meenakshi Medical College and Research Institute: Enathur, Kancheepuram.

Mody Institute of Technology and Science: Dist. Sikar, Lakshmangarh 332311, Rajasthan; tel. (1573) 225001; fax (1573) 225042; e-mail contact@mitsuniversity.ac.in; internet www.mitsuniversity.ac.in; f. 1998, deemed univ. status 2004; faculties of arts, commerce and law, engineering and technology, management studies, science; library: 23,362 vols; 74 teachers; 1,250 students; Chancellor R. P. MODY; Vice-Chancellor Prof. SHAKTIDEV MUKHERJEE; Registrar Prof. AMAL KUMAR

DEANS

Faculty of Arts, Science and Commerce: Dr SHAKTI BAIJAL

Faculty of Engineering and Technology: Prof. P. K. DAS

Faculty of Juridical Sciences: Prof. SATISH C. SHASTRI

Faculty of Management Studies: Prof. K. V. S. M. KRISHNA

Motilal Nehru National Institute of Technology: Allahabad 211004; tel. (0532) 2445103; fax (0532) 2445101; internet www .mnnit.ac.in; f. 1961, deemed univ. status 2002; depts of applied mechanics, chemistry, civil engineering, computer science and engineering, electrical engineering, electronics and communications engineering, humanities and social science, management studies, mathematics, mechanical engineering, physics; library: 95,409 vols, 268 journals; Dir Prof. A. B. SAMADDAR; Dean of Academic Affairs Dr N. ROY; Dean of Admin. Dr A. K. MISRA; Dean of Student Affairs Dr R. NARAIN; Librarian S. K. TIWARI.

Narsee Monjee Institute of Management Studies (NMIMS)/NMIMS University: V. L. Mehta Rd, Vile Parle (W), Mumbai 400056, Maharashtra; tel. (22) 26134577; fax (22) 26114512; e-mail enquiry@nmims .edu; internet www.nmims.edu; f. 1981, deemed univ. status 2003; schools of architecture, business management, commerce, distance learning, pharmacy, science, technology management and engineering; library: 42,000 books, 308 periodicals; Vice-Chancellor Dr RAJAN SAXENA (acting); Registrar V. K. SRIDHAR; Librarian VRUSHALI RANE; publ. *NMIMS Management Review* (2 a year)

DEANS

Balwant Sheth School of Architecture: TRI-LOCHAN M. CHHAYA

Mukesh Patel School of Technology Management and Engineering: Dr D. J. SHAH

School of Business Management: Dr RAMESH BHAT

School of Pharmacy and Technology Management: Dr R. S. GAUD

Technology Management: Dr PRADEEP KUMAR

National Brain Research Centre: NH 8, Manesar 122050, Haryana; tel. (124) 2338922; fax (124) 2338910; e-mail info@ nbrc.ac.in; internet www.nbrc.ac.in; f. 2003, Deemed University; main research areas: Molecular and Cellular Neuroscience, Systems Neuroscience, Computational Neuroscience; Dir Prof. VIJAYALAKSHMI RAVINDRANATH; Registrar K. V. S. KAMESWARA RAO; Chief Admin. Officer K. V. S. KAMES-WARA RAO.

National Dairy Research Institute: Karnal 132001, Haryana; tel. (184) 2252800; fax (184) 2250042; e-mail bnm@ndri.hry.nic.in; internet www.ndri.res.in; f. 1923, deemed univ.; library: 75,000 vols and 22,000 periodicals; regional stations at Bangalore and Kalyani; research divs in animal biochemistry, animal biotechnology, dairy cattle breeding, dairy cattle nutrition, dairy cattle physiology, dairy chemistry, dairy econ., statistics and management, dairy engineering, dairy extension, dairy microbiology, dairy technology; Dir Dr A. K. SRIVASTAVA; Registrar RAMESHWAR SINGH; Dir of Library Services Dr B. R. YADAV; library: 92,555 vols, 350 periodicals; publ. *Dairy Samachar* (4 a year).

National Institute of Mental Health and Neurosciences: POB 2900, Hosur Rd, Bangalore 560029, Karnataka; tel. (80) 26995005; fax (80) 26564830; e-mail regt@ nimhans.kar.nic.in; internet www.nimhans .kar.nic.in; f. 1974, deemed university status 1994; depts of biophysics, biostatistics, epidemiology, human genetics, mental health education, mental health and social psychology, neuroanaesthesia, neurochemistry, neuroimaging and interventional radiology, neurology, neuromicrobiology, neuropathology, neurophysiology, neurosurgery, neurovirology, nursing, psychiatric and neurological rehabilitation, psychiatric social work, psychiatry, psychopharmacology, speech pathology and audiology; library: 75,000 vols, 315 periodicals; Vice-Chancellor Prof. D. NAGARAJA; Dean Dr N. PRADHAN; Registrar M. V. SAVITHRI; Library and Information Officer Dr H. S. SIDDAMALLAIAH.

National Institute of Technology, Agartala: Barjala, Agartala 799055, Tripura (West); tel. (381) 2346630; fax (381) 2346360; e-mail nitagartala@yahoo.co.in; internet www.tec.nic.in; f. 1965, fmrly Tripura Engineering College; depts of civil engineering, computer science and engineering, electrical engineering, electrical and electronics engineering, mechanical engineering, production engineering, transportation engineering; Prin. Dr S. C. SAHA; Vice-Prin. P. C. DAS; Academic Dean Dr SWAPAN BHAUMIK; Dean of Student Welfare Dr SAROJ K. DAS; Registrar Dr D. BHATTACHARJEE.

National Institute of Technology, Calicut: Calicut 673601, Kerala; tel. (495) 2286101; fax (495) 2287250; e-mail pvr@nitc .ac.in; internet www.nitc.ac.in; f. 1961, deemed univ. status 2002; library: 100,000 vols; depts of architecture and civil engineering, chemical engineering, computer science and engineering, electrical engineering, electronics engineering, humanities, mathematics, mechanical engineering, science; Dir Dr G. R. C. REDDY; Registrar P. ANANTHAKRISHNAN; Librarian Dr S. ASHOK.

National Institute of Technology, Durgapur: Mahatma Gandhi Ave, Durgapur 713209, West Bengal; tel. (343) 2546397; fax (343) 2547375; e-mail director@nitdgp.ac .in; internet www.nitdgp.ac.in; f. 1960, deemed univ. status 2002; depts of applied mechanics and drawing, biotechnology, chemical engineering, chemistry, civil engineering, computer science and engineering, electrical engineering, electronics and communication engineering, geology, humanities, information technology, management studies, mathematics, mechanical engineering, metallurgical and materials engineering, physics; library: 22,000 vols, 150 periodicals; 162 teachers; 1,800 students; Dir Prof. S. BHATTACHARYA; Admin. Dean Prof. A. K. MITRA; Registrar S. K. RAY; Librarian Dr M. MANDAL.

National Institute of Technology, Hamirpur: Hamirpur 177005, Himachal Pradesh; tel. (1972) 254001; fax (1972) 223834; e-mail director@nitham.ac.in; internet www.nitham.ac.in; f. 1986, deemed univ. status 2002; depts of applied science and humanities, architecture, computer science and engineering, civil engineering, electrical engineering, electronics and communications engineering, mechanical engineering; 68 teachers; 900 students; library: 55,870 vols; Dir Dr I. K. BHAT; Academic Dean Dr J. N. SHARMA; Registrar A. L. SHARMA; Librarian D. S. JASWAL.

National Institute of Technology, Jamshedpur: Jamshedpur 831014, Jharkhand; tel. (657) 2373392; fax (657) 2373246; e-mail director@nitjsr.ac.in; internet www.nitjsr.ac .in; f. 1960; depts of applied mechanics, chemistry, civil engineering, computer science and engineering, electrical engineering, electronics engineering, mathematics and humanities, mechanical engineering, metallurgical engineering and materials science, physics, production engineering and science; Dir Dr A. MISHRA; Dean of Academic Affairs Dr R. J. SINGH; Dean of Admin. Dr S. N. SINHA; Dean of Student Affairs N. K. NARAIN; Registrar Dr M. K. BANERJEE; Librarian Dr N. BHARTI.

National Institute of Technology, Karnataka: Surathkal, Dakshina Kannada, Srinivasnagar 575025, Karnataka; tel. (824) 2474000; fax (824) 2476033; e-mail registrar@nitk.ac.in; internet www.nitk.ac .in; f. 1960, deemed univ. status 2002; depts of applied mechanics, chemical engineering, chemistry, civil engineering, computer engineering, electronics and communication, humanities, social sciences and management, information technology, mathematical and computational sciences, metallurgical and materials engineering, mining engineering, physics; library: 100,000 vols; 195 teachers; Dir Dr S. SANCHETI; Dean of Academic Affairs Prof. K. HALEMANE; Dean of Admin. Affairs Prof. P. RAO; Dean of Planning and Devt Prof. S. G. MAYYA; Dean of Student Affairs Prof. V. R. SASTRY; Registrar Dr M. G. RAJ; Librarian M. K. MOHANDAS.

National Institute of Technology, Kurukshetra: Kurukshetra 136119, Haryana; tel. (1744) 238122; fax (1744) 238050; e-mail nit_kkr@rediffmail.com; internet www .nitkkr.ac.in; f. 1963, deemed univ. status 2002; depts of business administration, chemistry, civil engineering, computer engineering, electrical engineering, electronics and communication engineering, humanities and social sciences, mathematics, mechanical engineering, physics; library: 119,314 vols; Dir Dr M. N. BANDYOPADHYAY; Dean of Planning and Devt Dr S. P. JAIN; Academic Dean Dr R. K. BANSAL; Registrar R. P. S. LOHCHAB; Librarian KRISHAN GOPAL.

National Institute of Technology, Patna: Patna 799055, Bihar; tel. (381) 2346630; fax (381) 2346360; internet www.nitp.ac.in; f. 1886 as Pleaders Survey Training School, Bihar College of Engineering 1924, current status 2004; Autonomous; depts of civil engineering, computer science and engineering, electrical engineering, electronics and communications engineering, information technology, mechanical engineering; Dir Dr U. C. RAY; Registrar Dr VIDYA SAGAR.

National Institute of Technology, Raipur: Raipur 492010, Chhattisgarh; tel. (771) 2254200; fax (771) 2254600; internet www .nitrr.ac.in; f. 1963, fmrly Govt Engineering College, Raipur; depts of architecture, biomedical engineering, bio-technology, chemical engineering, civil engineering, computer science and engineering, electrical engineering, electronics and telecommunication engineering, information technology, mechanical engineering, mining engineering, metallurgical engineering; Dir Dr K. K. SUGHANDI

DEANS

Academic Affairs: Dr K. D. PERMAR
Administration: Dr K. K. SUGANDHI
Planing and Development: Prof. M. M. HAMBARDE
Research and Faculty Development: Dr A. M. RAWANI
Student's Welfare: Dr M. K. VERMA

National Institute of Technology, Rourkela: Rourkela 769008, Orissa; tel. (661) 2476773; fax (661) 2462999; e-mail info@ nitrkl.ac.in; internet www.nitrkl.ac.in; f. 1955, deemed univ. status 2002; depts of applied mathematics, biotechnolgy and medical engineering, ceramic engineering, chemical engineering, chemistry, civil engineering, computer science and engineering, electrical engineering, electronics and communication engineering, humanities and social sciences, mechanical engineering, metallurgical and materials engineering, mining engineering, physics; library: 150,000 vols; Dir Prof. SUNIL K. SARANGI; Dean of Academic Affairs Dr S. K. RATH; Dean of Admin. Dr J. K. SATAPATHY; Dean of Planning and Devt Dr U. K. MOHANTY; Dean of Research Dr R. K. SAHOO; Dean of Student Affairs Dr P. C. PANDA; Registrar S. K. UPADHYAY; Librarian Y. S. RAO.

National Institute of Technology, Silchar: Silchar 788010, Assam; tel. (3842) 233179; fax (3842) 233797; e-mail contactus@nits.ac.in; internet www.nits.ac .in; f. 1967; depts of chemistry, civil engineering, electrical engineering, electronics and telecommunication engineering, humanities and social sciences, mathematics, mechanical engineering, physics; library: 45,000 vols, 150 periodicals; 880 students; Dir Prof. P. K. BANIK; Dean of Academic Affairs Prof. A. K. SIL; Dean of Planning and Devt Prof. A. K. ROY; Dean of Research Prof. R. GUPTA; Dean of Student Affairs Prof. A. K. SINHA; Registrar Dr FAZAL A. TALUKDAR.

National Institute of Technology, Srinagar: Hazratbal 190006, Jammu and Kashmir; tel. (194) 2422032; fax (194) 2420475; e-mail director@nitsri.net; internet www .nitsri.net; f. 1960, deemed univ. status 2003; depts of chemical engineering, chemistry, civil engineering, electrical engineering, electronics and communication engineering, humanities, mathematics, mechanical engineering, metallurgical engineering, physics; Dir Prof. R. K. WANCHOO; Registrar A. R. BHATT.

National Institute of Technology, Tiruchirapalli: Tanjore Main Rd, Nat. Highway 67, Tiruchirappalli 620015, Tamil Nadu; tel. (431) 2501801; fax (431) 2500133; e-mail deanac@nitt.edu; internet www.nitt.edu; f. 1964, deemed univ. status 2003; depts of architecture, chemical engineering, chemistry, civil engineering, computer applications, computer science and engineering, electrical and electronics engineering, electronics and communication engineering, english, humanities, instrumentation and control engineering, management studies, mathematics, mechanical engineering, metallurgical engineering, physics, production engineering; Centre for Energy and Environmental Science and Technology; library: 100,000 books, 15,943 bound periodicals, 200 current periodicals, 4,500 online journals; 2,190 undergraduates, 1,025 postgraduates; 192 teachers; Dir Prof. M. CHIDAMBARAM; Dean of Academic Programme Dr P. JAYABALAN; Dean of Admin. Dr M. UDAYAKUMAR; Dean of Industrial Consultancy and Sponsored Research Dr N. AMMASAI GOUNDEN; Dean of Students Dr S. KUMANAN.

National Institute of Technology, Warangal: Warangal 506004, Andhra Pradesh; tel. (870) 2459191; fax (870) 2459547; e-mail director@nitw.ernet.in; internet www.nitw .ac.in; f. 1959; depts of biotechnology, centre for management studies, chemical eng., chemistry, civil eng., computer science and eng., electrical eng., electronics and communication eng., mathematics and humanities, mechanical eng., metallurgical and materials eng., physical education, physics; library: 131,757 vols, 210 periodicals; 200 teachers; 3,000 students; Dir Prof. Y. V. RAO; Dean of Academic Affairs Prof. R. V. CHALAM; Dean of Admin. Prof. G. V. REDDY; Dean of Planning and Devt Prof. C. B. K. RAO; Dean of Student Affairs Prof. R. RAO; Registrar Prof. Y. N. REDDY; Public Relations Officers Dr D. S. K. RAO, Dr M. R. REDDY; Librarian R. S. REDDY.

National Law School of India University: Nagarbhavi, PB 7201, Bangalore 560242, Karnataka; tel. (80) 23213160; fax (80) 23160534; e-mail registrar@nls.ac.in; internet www.nls.ac.in; f. 1987; library: 18,000 books, 15,000 bound periodicals; 30 teachers; 400 students; Vice-Chancellor Prof. A. JAYAGOVIND; Registrar Prof. V. NAGARAJ; publs *Indian Journal of Law and Technology* (1 a year), *National Law School of India Review* (2 a year), *Socio-Legal Review* (1 a year).

Attached Research Institutes:

Centre for Child and the Law: NLSIU, PO 7201, Nagarbhavi, Bangalore 560072; tel. and fax (80) 23160528; e-mail ccl@nls .ac.in.

Centre for Environmental Education, Research and Advocacy: tel. (80) 23160527; e-mail ceera@nls.ac.in.

Centre for Intellectual Property Research and Advocacy: tel. (80) 23160535 ext. 235; e-mail cipra@nls.ac.in; internet www.iprlawindia.org.

Centre for Study of Casteism, Communalism and Law: tel. (80) 23160533.

Centre for Women and the Law: tel. (80) 23160532; e-mail cwl@nls.ac.in.

Institute of Law and Ethics in Medicine: e-mail tilem@nls.ac.in; tel. (80) 23160529.

National Institute for Alternate Disputes Resolution: tel. (80) 23160533.

National Institute of Human Rights: e-mail nihr@nls.ac.in; tel. (80) 23160533.

National Museum Institute of History of Art, Conservation and Museology: Janpath, New Delhi 110011; tel. (11) 23011901; fax (11) 23011899; e-mail dgnationalmuseum@gmail.com; internet nmi .gov.in; f. 1983, deemed univ. status 1989; postgraduate courses in conservation and restoration of works of arts, history of art, museology; library: 2,500 books, 60,000 slides; Vice-Chancellor R. C. MISHRA; Dean Prof. K. K. JAIN; Registrar K. K. KULSHRESHTHA; Librarian Dr B. N. SINGH.

National University of Educational Planning and Administration: 17-B Sri Aurobindo Marg, New Delhi 110016; tel. (11) 26863562; fax (11) 26853041; e-mail nuepa@ nuepa.org; internet www.nuepa.org; f. 1962, current status2006; offers courses for education personnel of developing countries and district education officers; other in-service training courses; research in various aspects of educational planning and management; consultancy service for developing countries, State govts and other orgs; collaboration with UNESCO and other foreign agencies; Vice-Chancellor Prof. VED PRAKASH; Registrar Dr B. K. SINGH; Librarian DEEPAK MAKOL; library: 53,500 vols, 350 current journals; publs *Journal of Educational Planning and Administration* (4 a year), *Pariprakshya* (in Hindi).

Nava Nalanda Mahavihara (Nalanda University): PO Nalanda, Bihar 803111; tel. and fax (6112) 274820; internet navanalandamahavihara.org; f. 1951, deemed univ. status 2006; administered by Dept of Culture, Min. of Human Resources Devt; studies and research in Pali, Buddhism, philosophy, ancient Indian and Asian studies; diploma in languages: Chinese, Japanese, Tibetan, Hindi, Sanskrit and Pali; library: 36,000 vols; Dir Prof. Dr RAVINDRA PANTH; publs *Atthakatha*, *Pali Tipitaki*.

Padmashree Dr D. Y. Patil Vidyapeeth: Sector 15, CBD Belapur, Navi Mumbai 400614, Maharashtra; tel. (22) 39285999; fax (22) 39286197; e-mail info@dypatil.com; internet www.dypatil.in; f. 2002; Vice-Chancellor Prof. JAMES THOMAS; Registrar Dr F. A. FERNANDES; Controller of Examinations RADHA RAMAMURTHY; Finance Officer R. P. NALAWADE.

CONSTITUENT COLLEGES:

Dr D. Y. Patil Dental College and Hospital: Dental Hospital Bldg, Dr D. Y. Patil Vidyanagar, Sector 7, Nerul, Navi Mumbai 400706, Maharashtra; tel. (22) 27731599; fax (22) 27709591; e-mail dentistry@dypatil.edu.

Dr D. Y. Patil Medical College: New Medical College Bldg, Dr D. Y. Patil Vidyanagar, Sector 5 , Nerul, Navi Mumbai 400706, Maharashtra; tel. (22) 39215999; fax (22) 39215911; e-mail medicine@dypatil.edu.

Punjab Engineering College: Sector 12, Chandigarh 160012; tel. (172) 2753064; fax (172) 2745175; e-mail admissions@pec.ac.in; internet www.pec.ac.in; f. 1947; library: 106,000 vols; Dir Dr MANOJ DATTA; Dean of Academic Affairs Dr ASHWANI KUMAR; Dean of Research and Planning Dr GURNAM SINGH; Dean of Student Welfare Prof. M. L. GUPTA; Head Librarian P. S. KANG.

Rashtriya Sanskrit Sansthan: 56-57 Institutional Area, Janakpuri, New Delhi 110058; tel. (11) 28524993; fax (11) 28521948; e-mail rsks@nda.vsnl.net.in; internet www.sanskrit .nic.in; f. 1970; campuses in Allahabad, Bhopal, Jaipur, Jammu, Lucknow, Mumbai, Puri, Sringeri and Trichur; library: total library colln of 213,581 vols, 51,133 MSS; Vice-Chancellor Prof. RADHAVALLABH TRIPATHI; publ. *Sanskrit Vimarsh* (1 a year).

Rashtriya Sanskrit Vidyapeetha: Tirupati 517507, Andhra Pradesh; tel. (8574) 2286799; fax (8574) 2287809; e-mail registrar_rsvp@yahoo.com; internet rsvidyapeetha.ac.in; f. 1961; library: 60,000 vols and 5,000 MSS; Vice-Chancellor Prof. HAREKRISHNA SATAPATHY; Registrar A. GURUMURTHI; Dean of Academic Affairs Prof. K. E. GOVINDAN.

S. R. M. Institute of Science and Technology: *Head Office* 3 Veerasamy St, West Mambalam, Chennai 600033, Tamil Nadu; tel. (44) 24742836; fax (44) 24748925 *Kattankulathur Campus* SRM Nagar, Kattankulathur, Kancheepuram 603203, Tamil Nadu; tel. (44) 27452270; fax (44) 27452343 *Modi Nagar Campus* Delhi-Meerut Rd, Sikrikalan Modi Nagar, Gazhiabad 201204, Uttar Pradesh; tel. (1232) 248618; fax (1232) 245441 *Ramapuram Campus* Bharathi Salai, Ramapuram, Chennai 600089, Tamil Nadu; tel. (44) 43923042; fax (44) 22491777 *Trichy Campus* Irangalur Post, Mannachanallur Taluk, Tiruchirapalli Dist 621105; tel. (431)

2910599; e-mail registrar@srmuniv.ac.in; internet www.srmuniv.ac.in; f. 1985 as S. R. M. Engineering College, deemed univ. status 2002; faculties of engineering, management, medicine, science and humanities; campuses at Kattankulathur, Modi Nagar, Ramapuram; Chancellor T. R. PACHAMUTHU; Vice-Chancellor P. SATHYANARAYANAN.

Sardar Vallabhbhai National Institute of Technology: Ichhchha Nath, Surat 395007, Gujarat; tel. (261) 2223606; fax (261) 2228394; e-mail director@svnit.ac.in; internet www.svnit.ac.in; f. 1961; library: 100,000 vols; depts of applied mechanics, applied science and humanities, chemical engineering, computer engineering, electrical engineering, electronics engineering, mechanical engineering, production engineering; Dir Dr P. D. POREY; Dean of Admin. Dr H. S. PATIL; Registrar H. A. PARMAR; Librarian T. B. GHOSH.

Sathyabama University: Jeppiaar Nagar, Old Mamallapuram Rd, Chennai 600119, Tamil Nadu; tel. (44) 24503150; fax (44) 24502344; e-mail admissions@sathyabamauniv.ac.in; internet www .sathyabamauniv.ac.in; f. 1987, deemed univ. status 2001; depts of architecture, bioinformatics, biomedical engineering, biotechnology, chemical engineering, civil engineering, computer application, computer science and engineering, electrical and electronics engineering, electronics and communication engineering, electronics and control engineering, electronics and instrumentation engineering, electronics and telecommunication engineering, information technology, management sciences, mechanical engineering, production engineering, science and visual communication; library: 50,000 vols, 290 periodicals; Vice-Chancellor Prof. V. S. R. K. MOULY; Registrar Dr S. S. RAU; Controller of Examinations Prof. K. V. NARAYANAN; Dean of Academic Research Dr P. E. SANKARANARAYANAN; Dean of Postgraduate Studies Dr N. MANOHARAN.

School of Planning and Architecture: 4 Block B, Indraprastha Estate, New Delhi 110002; tel. (11) 23702382; fax (11) 23702383; e-mail regspa@indiatimes.com; internet www.spa.ac.in; f. 1955; depts of architectural conservation, architecture, building engineering and management, environmental planning, housing, industrial design, landscape architecture, physical planning, regional planning, transport planning, urban design, urban planning; library: 74,759 vols; 62 teachers; 694 students; Dir Prof. RANJIT MITRA KUMAR; Dean of Studies Prof. A. K. SHARMA; Registrar D. R. BAINS; Librarian NAJMA RIZVI; publ. *SPACE* (4 a year).

Shanmugha Arts, Science, Technology and Research Academy: Shanmugha Campus, Tirumalaisamaduram, Thanjavur 613402, Tamil Nadu; tel. (4362) 264101; fax (4362) 264120; e-mail admissions@sastra .edu; internet www.sastra.edu; f. 1984, deemed univ. status 2001; schools of chemical engineering and biotechnology, civil engineering, computing, electrical and electronics engineering, humanities and sciences, management, mechanical engineering; 600 teachers; 8,000 students; Vice-Chancellor Prof. R. SETHURAMAN; Registrar N. ANANTHARAMAN; Dean of Student Affairs Prof. M. NARAYANAN; Dean of Research Dr T. R. SIVARAMAKRISHNAN.

ATTACHED CENTRES:

Centre for Advanced Research in Indian System of Medicine: internet www.sastra.edu/carism; Dean Dr G. VICTOR RAJAMANICKAM.

Centre for Nanotechnology and Advanced Biomaterials: tel. (4362) 304000; fax (4362) 264120; internet www .sastra.edu/centab; Dir Dr S. SWAMINATHAN.

Shri Lal Bahadur Shastri Rashtriya Sanskrit Vidyapeetha: Qutub Institional Area, New Delhi 110016; tel. (11) 46060606; fax (11) 26533512; e-mail info@slbsrsv.ac.in; internet www.slbsrsv.ac.in; f. 1962; Deemed University status 1987; library: 65,000 vols, 17 periodicals; Vice-Chancellor Prof. VACHASPATI UPADHYAYA; Registrar B. K. MOHAPATRA.

Sri Chandrasekharenda Saraswathi Viswa Mahavidyalaya: Sri Jayendra Saraswathi St, Enathur 631561, Tamil Nadu; tel. (44) 27264301; fax (44) 27264285; e-mail registrar@kanchiuniv.ac.in; internet www .kanchiuniv.ac.in; f. 1993; library: 200,000 vols; depts of ayurvedic medicine, Sanskrit and Indian culture, science and humanities, electrical engineering, mechanical engineering, computer science and engineering, electronics and communications, management studies; Vice-Chancellor Prof. B. VISWANATHAN; Registrar Prof. Dr V. S. VISHNUPOTTY; Dean for Academics G. SUBBA RAO; Dean for Research K. P. V. RAMANA KUMAR.

Sri Ramachandra University: No.1, Ramchandra Nagar, Porur, Chennai 600116, Tamil Nadu; tel. (44) 24768403; fax (44) 24767008; e-mail registrar@srmc.edu; internet www.srmc.edu; f. 1985, deemed univ. status 1994; depts of anaesthesiology, cardiac care, chest and tuberculosis, dermatology, emergency, trauma and critical care, endocrinology, ears, nose and throat, general medicine, general surgery, medical gastroenterology, nephrology, neurology, neurosurgery, obstetrics and gynaecology, ophthalmology, orthopaedics, paediatric medicine, paediatric surgery, paediatric urology, plastic and reconstructive surgery, psychiatry, radiology and imaging sciences, surgical gastroenterology and urology; library: 23,000 vols, 350 periodicals; 3,500 students; Chancellor V. R. VENKATAACHALAM; Vice-Chancellor Dr S. RANGASWAMI; Chief Executive Director RADHA VENKATACHALAM; Dean of Faculties Dr K. V. SOMASUNDARAM.

Sri Sathya Sai University: Prasanthi Nilayam Campus, Anantapur District, Andhra 515134, Andhra Pradesh; tel. (8555) 287239; fax (8555) 287390; e-mail registrar@ sssu.edu.in; internet sssu.edu.in; depts of accounting and finance, biosciences, chemistry, commerce, economics, education, English language and literature, history and Indian culture, home sciences, management, mathematics and computer science, philosophy, physics, political science, Telugu language and literature; campuses at Anantapur, Bangalore; f. 1981; library: 150,000 vols; 115 teachers; 1,100 students; Vice-Chancellor Prof. VISWANATH PANDIT; Registrar Prof. A. V. LAKSHMINARASIMHAM; Controller of Examinations Prof. M. NANJUNDAIAH; Prin. (Prasanthi Nilayam Campus) Prof. U. S. RAO; Prin. (Anantapur Campus) SANJAY SAHNI; Prin. (Brindavan Campus) Dr DWARAKA RANI RAO; publs *Bulletin of Pure and Applied Sciences* (4 a year), *International Journal of Modern Physics* (4 a year), *Journal of Applied Mathematics and Stochastic Analysis* (4 a year), *Third Concept: An International Journal of Ideas* (6 a year).

Swami Vivekananda Yog Anusandhana Samsthana: Bangalore 560019, Karnataka; e-mail info@svyasa.org; internet www.svyasa .org; divs of yoga and humanities, yoga and life sciences, yoga and management studies, yoga and physical sciences, yoga and spirituality; Vice-Chancellor Prof. H. R. NAGENDRA.

Symbiosis International Education Centre: Senapati Bapat Rd, Pune 411004, Maharashtra; tel. (20) 25652444; fax (20) 25659209; e-mail siec@vsnl.net; internet www.symbiosis.ac.in; f. 1979; Deemed University status 2002; constituent institutes: Centre for Information Technology, Centre for Management and Human Resource Development, Centre for Management Studies, College of Nursing, English Language Teaching Institute, Institute of Business Management, Institute of Computer Studies and Research, Institute of Design, Institute of Foreign and Indian Languages, Institute of Geo-informatics, Institute of Health Sciences, Institute of International Business, Institute of Management Studies, Institute of Mass Communication, Institute of Operations Management, Institute of Telecom Management, Law College; 217 teachers (43 full-time, 7 part-time, 167 visiting); 45,000 students; Vice-Chancellor Dr M. S. RASTE; Dir Dr VIDYA YERAVDEKAR; Registrar V. S. POL.

Tata Institute of Fundamental Research: Homi Bhabha Rd, Mumbai 400005, Maharashtra; tel. (22) 22782000; fax (22) 22804610; e-mail webmaster@tifr .res.in; internet www.tifr.res.in; f. 1945, deemed univ. status 2003; attached research centres: National Centre for Biological Sciences (Bangalore), National Centre for Radio Astrophysics (Pune), Homi Bhabha Centre for Science Education (Mumbai); attached field stations: Balloon Facility (Hyderabad), High Energy Gamma Ray Observatory (Panchmarhi), Radio Astronomy Centre (Ooty), TIFR Centre Maths (Bangalore), TIFR Gravitation Laboratory (Gauribidanur); schools of mathematics, natural sciences, technology and computer science; Dir Prof. MUSTANSIR BARMA.

Tata Institute of Social Sciences: POB 8313, Deonar, Mumbai 400088, Maharashtra; tel. (22) 25563289; fax (22) 25562912; e-mail sparasuraman@tiss.edu; internet www.tiss.edu; f. 1936, deemed univ. status 1964; schools of health systems studies, management and labour studies, rural devt, social sciences, social work; independent centres for lifelong learning, media and cultural studies, research methodology, Jamsetji Tata Centre for Disaster Management; library: 105,000 vols; 106 students; Dir Prof. S. PARASURAMAN; Registrar Dr SANDEEP CHATTERJEE; Librarian Dr M. KOGANURAMATH; publ. *The Indian Journal of Social Work.*

TERI University: India Habitat Centre, Lodi Rd, New Delhi 110003; Plot No 10, Institutional Area, Vasant Kunj, New Delhi; tel. (11) 26122222; fax (11) 26122874; e-mail registrar@teri.res.in; internet www .teriuniversity.ac.in; f. 1998, deemed univ. status 1999; faculties of applied sciences, policy and planning; Chancellor Dr R. K. PACHAURI; Vice-Chancellor Dr P. P. BHOJVAID (acting); Registrar RAJIV SETH.

Thapar University: POB 32 Patiala 147004, Punjab; tel. (175) 2393021; fax (175) 2364498; e-mail registrar@tiet.ac.in; internet www.tiet.ac.in; f. 1956, deemed univ. status 1985; schools of chemistry and biotechnology, management and social sciences, mathematics and computer applications, physics and material science; library: 55,000 vols; 102 teachers; 1,340 students; Dir Dr ABHIJIT MUKHERJEE; Registrar Brig. PARAMJIT SINGH; Registrar B. P. CHAUHAN; Dean of Academic Affairs Dr R. K. SHARMA; Dean of Research and Sponsored Projects Dr SUSHEEL MITTAL; Dean of Student Affairs Dr N. K. VERMA.

Tilak Maharashtra Vidyapeeth: Vidyapeeth Bhavan, Gultekdi, Pune 411037; tel.

(20) 24261856; fax (20) 24266068; e-mail timavee@pn2.vsnl.net.in; internet www.tmv .edu.in; f. 1921; faculties of arts and fine arts, ayurveda, education, modern sciences and professional skills, moral and social sciences; campuses at Aurangabad, Delhi, Mumbai; library: 77,674 vols; 35 teachers; 5,508 students; Vice-Chancellor Dr DEEPAK TILAK; Registrar Dr UMESH KESKAR; Finance Officer PRADIP A. KHATAVKAR; Controller of Examinations JAGDISH SALVE; Librarian REVATI DESHMUKH.

Vinayaka Missions Research Foundation: NH-47 Sankari Main Rd, Ariyanoor, Salem 636308, Tamil Nadu; tel. (427) 3987000; fax (427) 2477903; e-mail vmtrust@vinayakamission.com; internet www.vinayakamission.com; f. 2001; faculties of allied health sciences, arts and sciences, dentistry, education, engineering technology and management sciences, homeopathy, int. dentistry, int. medicine, medicine, nursing, pharmacy, physical education, physiotherapy; 13 constituent colleges in Chennai, Karaikal, Pondicherry, Salem; Chancellor Dr A. SHANMUGASUNDARAM; Vice-Chancellor Prof. Dr V. R. RAJENDRAN; Controller of Examinations Dr A. BALASUNDARAM.

Visvesvaraya National Institute of Technology: South Ambazari Rd, Nagpur 440011, Maharashtra; tel. (712) 2226240; fax (712) 2223230; e-mail registrar@vnit.ac .in; internet www.vnitnagpur.ac.in; f. 1960, deemed univ. status 2002; depts of applied chemistry, applied mechanics, applied physics, architecture, civil engineering, electrical engineering, electronics and computer science, humanities, mathematics, mechanical engineering, metallurgical engineering, mining engineering; library: 90,838 vols, 166 periodicals; 1,500 undergraduates, 200 postgraduates; Dir Dr S. S. GOKHALE; Registrar B. M. GANVEER; Librarian Dr H. T. THORAT.

Colleges
BUSINESS

Administrative Staff College of India: Bella Vista, Raj Bhavan Rd, Khairabad, Hyderabad 500082; tel. (40) 66533000; fax (40) 23312954; internet www.asci.org.in; f. 1956; conducts post-experience management devt programmes for officials in govt, execs and mans in industry and non-govt orgs; undertakes research and consultancy assignments for nat. and int. orgs; library: 74,000 vols, 500 periodicals, online databases; Dir-Gen. Dr S. K. RAO; Dean of Research and Consultancy Prof. M. CHANDRASEKHAR; Dean of Training and Confs Dr PARAMITA DAGUPTA; Registrar and Sec. Col (Retd) TEJINDER SINGH; Librarian Dr N. G. SATISH; publ. *ASCI Journal of Management* (2 a year).

Indian Institute of Management, Ahmedabad: Vastrapur, Ahmedabad 380015; tel. (79) 66324599; fax (79) 26306896; e-mail director@iimahd.ernet.in; internet www .iimahd.ernet.in; f. 1962; 2-year postgraduate, 4-year doctoral programme in management; gen. and functional management programmes for practising managers, and special programmes for govt officials, univ. teachers and sectors such as agriculture, public systems; undertakes project research and consulting in the field of management; 80 teachers; 400 postgraduate programme students; 50 PhD-level students; library: 148,600 vols; Chair. Dr VIJAYPAT SINGHANIA; Dir Prof. SAMIR K. BARUA; publ. *Vikalpa* (4 a year).

Indian Institute of Management, Bangalore: Bannerghatta Rd, Bangalore 560076;

tel. (80) 26582450; fax (80) 26584050; e-mail info@iimb.ernet.in; internet www.iimb.ernet .in/iimb; f. 1973; postgraduate programmes; library: 209,000 vols, 34 online databases, 695 print journals, 850 electronic journals; 80 teachers; 425 students; Dir Prof. PANKAJ CHANDRA; publ. *IIMB Management Review* (2 a year).

Indian Institute of Management, Calcutta: Diamond Harbour Rd, Joka, Kolkata 700104, West Bengal; tel. (33) 24678310; fax (33) 24678307; e-mail director@iimcal.ac.in; internet www.iimcal.ac.in; f. 1961 to promote improvement in management through education, research and consultancy; 2-year MBA course in Computer-Aided Management, 3-year part-time MBA in business management; doctoral and extension courses; centres for studies in human values, devt and environment policy, rural devt and environment management; executive devt; faculty devt through research and consulting services; library: Dr B. C. Roy Memorial library of 125,000 vols; 77 teachers; 669 students; Dir Dr SHEKHAR CHAUDHURI; publs *Decision*, *Journal on Human Values* (2 a year).

Indian Institute of Management, Indore: Prabandh Shikhar, Pithampur Rd, Rau, Indore 453331, Madhya Pradesh; tel. (731) 4228400; fax (731) 4228800; e-mail webman@ iimidr.ac.in; internet www.iimidr.ac.in; f. 1997; library: 15,000 vols and 425 periodicals; 27 teachers; Dir Prof. N. RAVICHANDRAN; Chief Admin. Officer K. R. NARENDRA BABU; Librarian KISHOR SATPATHY; publ. *International Journal of Management Practices and Contemporary Thought (IMPACT)*.

Indian Institute of Management, Kozhikode: IIMK Campus P.O., Kozhikode 673570, Kerala; tel. (495) 2803001; fax (495) 2803010; e-mail director@iimk.ac.in; internet www.iimk.ac.in; f. 1996; library: 7,000 books, 1,120 periodicals; Dir Dr KRISHNA KUMAR; Librarian Dr M. G. SREEKUMAR.

Indian Institute of Management, Lucknow: Prabandh Nagar, Off Sitapur Rd, Lucknow 226013, Uttar Pradesh; tel. (522) 2734101; fax (522) 2734025; e-mail admission@iiml.ac.in; internet www.iiml.ac .in; f. 1984; 2-year postgraduate programme in agri-business management, exec. devt programmes; undertakes research and consulting projects in the field of management; main areas: agriculture, health, education, rural development, state public enterprises, corporate management, information technology and systems, entrepreneurship, corporate communication and media relations, leadership and human values; centre for entrepreneur devt and new venture management, agricultural management centre; library: Gyanodaya Library of 60,000 documents; 66 teachers; 480 postgraduate students; Dir Prof. PREM C. PURWAR; Dean of Academic Affairs Prof. YOGESH AGARWAL; Dean of Planning and Development Prof. SUKUMAR NANDI; publ. *Metamorphosis* (2 a year).

EDUCATION

National Institute of Educational Planning and Administration: 17-B Sri Aurobindo Marg, New Delhi 110016; tel. (11) 26863562; fax (11) 26853041; f. 1962; diploma courses for education personnel of developing countries and district education officers; other in-service training courses; research in various aspects of educational planning and management; consultancy service for developing countries, State govts and other orgs; collaboration with UNESCO and other foreign agencies; library: 45,963 vols, 350 current journals; Dir Prof. KULDEEP

MATHUR; publs *Journal of Educational Planning and Administration* (4 a year), *Pariprakshya* (in Hindi).

GENERAL

Christ College Bangalore: Hosur Rd, Bangalore; tel. (80) 40129100; fax (80) 40129000; e-mail principal@christcollege .edu; internet www.christcollege.edu; depts of commerce/management, humanities, sciences, social sciences; College of Education, College of Law; library: 77,500 vols, 173 journals; Prin. Dr THOMAS C. MATHEW; Vice-Prin. Fr ABRAHAM.

Fergusson College: Pune 411004; tel. (20) 25654212; e-mail principal@fergusson.edu; internet www.fergusson.edu; f. 1885; affiliated to Univ. of Pune; library: 300,000 vols; Prin. Dr R. G. PARDESHI; Vice-Prin. Prof. D. V. KULKAMI.

Hans Raj College: Mahatma Hans Raj Marg, Malka Ganj, Delhi 110007; tel. (11) 27667747; fax (11) 27666338; e-mail principal@hrc.du.ac.in; internet www .hansrajcollege.com; f. 1948; Autonomous; BA in economics, English, Hindi, history, mathematics, Sanskrit; BSc in botany, chemistry, computer science, physics, zoology; constituent college of Univ. of Delhi; Prin. Dr S. R. ARORA; Librarian G. R. SHARMA.

Lady Shri Ram College for Women: Lajpat Nagar-IV, New Delhi 110024; tel. (11) 26434459; fax (11) 26216951; e-mail lsrc@vsnl.com; internet www.lsrcollege.org; f. 1956; depts of commerce, economics, education, English, Hhindi, history, journalism, mathematics, philosophy, physical education, political science, psychology, Sanskrit, sociology, statistics; constituent college of Delhi Univ.; 2,000 students; Prin. Dr MEENAKSHI GOPINATH; Librarian A. P. YADAV.

Loyola College: Chennai 600034, Tamil Nadu; tel. (44) 28178200; fax (44) 28175566; e-mail helpdesk@loyolacollege.edu; internet www.loyolacollege.edu; Autonomous; f. 1925; depts of advanced zoology and biotechnology, chemistry, commerce, computer science, economics, English, foreign languages, history and applied history, mathematics, oriental languages, philosophy, physical education, physics, plant biology and biotechnology, social work, sociology, statistics, Tamil, visual communication; Institutes of Dialogue with Cultures and Religions, Entomology Research, Frontier Energy, Industrial and Social Science Research, People Studies, Vocational Education; 116 teachers; 7,021 students; Prin. Fr A. ALBERT MUTHUMALAI; Dean of Students Prof. K. S. ANTONYSAMY; Controller of Examinations Prof. D. P. VENUGOPALAN; Librarian Prof. K. T. DILLI.

Madras Christian College: Tambaram, Chennai 600059, Tamil Nadu; tel. (44) 22397731; internet www.mcc.edu.in; f. 1837; Autonomous; depts of chemistry, commerce, economics, English, history, languages, mathematics, philosophy, physics, public admin., social work, statistics, Tamil; Prin. Dr V. J. PHILIP.

Presidency College, Chennai: Chennai; tel. (44) 28544894; fax (44) 28510732; e-mail info@presidencychennai.com; internet www .presidencychennai.com; f. 1840; Autonomous; faculties of arts and commerce, languages, science; library: 150,000 vols, 95 journals; Prin. Prof. M. DHANUSHKODI; Librarian K. V. RAMALINGAM.

Presidency College, Kolkata: 86/1 College St, Kolkata 700073, West Bengal; tel. (33) 22412738; e-mail contact@ presidencycollegekolkata.ac.in; internet www.presidencycollegekolkata.ac.in; f. 1817 as Hindoo College, present name 1885; depts of Bengali, botany, chemistry, economics, english, geography, geology, Hindi, history, mathematics, philosophy, physics, physiology, political science, sociology, statistics, zoology; Prin. MAMATA RAY; Librarian DEBNARAYAN CHAKRABARTI.

St Joseph's College: PB 27094, 36 Lalbagh Rd, Bangalore 560027; tel. (80) 22211429; fax (80) 22272299; e-mail principal@sjc.ac.in; internet www.sjc.ac.in; Autonomous; f. 1882; Principal Dr. Fr AMBROSE PINTO; Vice-Principal Fr CLARENCE D'SOUZA.

St Stephen's College: University Enclave, Delhi 110007; tel. (11) 27667271; fax (11) 27667965; e-mail info@ststephens.edu; internet www.ststephens.edu; f. 1881; depts of Chemistry, computer science, economics, English, history and political science, mathematics, philosophy, physics, Sanskrit and Hindi, Urdu, Persian; constituent college of Delhi Univ.; library: 12,000 vols; Prin. Rev. VALSON THAMPU; Vice-Prin. Dr M. S. FRANK; Dean NANDITA NARAIN; Dean of Academic Affairs Dr VIJAY TANKHA.

St Xavier's College, Ahmedabad: Navaranpura, Ahmedabad, Gujarat; internet www .stxavierscollege.net; depts of biochemistry, biology, chemistry, computer science, economics, electronics, English, Gujarati and Hindi, mathematics, physics, psychology, Sanskrit, statistics; Pres. Fr WILLIAM K. ABRANCHES; Vice-Pres. Fr AMALRAJ SEBASTIAN; Librarian HARBHAM JADEJA.

INSTITUTIONS:

Katha Xavier's Centre for Translation: f. 2003; conducts seminars on autobiographies of Gujarati mainstream writers; socially and politically marginalized figures in Gujarat's history; storytelling traditions, myths, fables, fantasy tales, partition literature; Muslim narratives in Gujarati; research on literature of marginal communities of Dalits, Tribals, documentation of narratives by Parsis and Kutchis; Dir Dr RITA KOTHARI.

Xavier Research Foundation: f. 1995.

St Xavier's College, Kolkata: 30 Park St, Kolkata 700016; tel. (33) 22875995; fax (33) 22879966; e-mail principal@sxccal.edu; internet www.sxccal.edu; Autonomous; language of instruction: English; f. 1860; faculties of arts, business administration, commerce, education, science; library: 18,800 vols; Rector Rev. Fr GEORGE PONODATH; Prin. Rev. Fr Dr FELIX RAJ; Librarian Fr FELIX RAJ.

St Xavier's College, Mumbai: 5 Mahapalika Marg, Mumbai 400001; tel. (22) 22620661; fax (22) 22620665; e-mail admin@xaviers.edu; internet www.xaviers .edu; f. 1860; affiliated to Univ. of Mumbai; faculties of arts, business management, commerce, mass media, science; Institutes of Communication, Counselling, Management and Research, Social Research and Action; library: 12,000 vols; Prin. Fr FRAZER MASCARENHAS; Librarian MEDHA TASKAR.

Symbiosis College of Arts and Commerce: Senapati Bapat Marg, Pune 411004; tel. (20) 25653903; fax (20) 25651850; e-mail info@symbiosiscollege.org; internet www .symbiosiscollege.org; f. 1983; affiliated to Symbiosis Int. Univ.; Liberal Arts college; Dir Dr S. B. MUJUMDAR.

LANGUAGES

Central Institute of Indian Languages: Department of Higher Education, Language Bureau, Ministry of Human Resource Development, Government of India, Manasagangothri, Hunsur Rd, Mysore 570006; tel. (821) 2345031; fax (821) 2515032; e-mail udaya@ ciil.stpmy.soft.net; internet www.ciil.org; f. 1969; assisting and coordinating the devt of Indian languages; preparation of grammars and dictionaries of tribal and border languages; inter-disciplinary research; preparation of materials for teaching and learning; 290 academic and technical staff; 7 Regional Language Centres in Mysore (languages: Kannada, Telugu, Malayalam, Tamil), Bhubaneswar (languages: Assamese, Bengali, Oriya), Pune (languages: Marathi, Gujarati, Sindhi), Patiala (languages: Urdu, Punjabi, Kashmiri), Solan (Urdu), Lucknow (Urdu) and Guwahati (north-eastern languages); centres for creative writing and lexicography, educational technology and media studies, excellence in classical languages, human resource development, information on language sciences, language planning, language technology, linguistic and cultural documentation, materials production, speech sciences, testing and evaluation, tribal and endangered languages; library: 63,000 vols and 250 periodicals; Dir Prof. UDAYA NARAYANA SINGH; Head, Centre for Applied Language Sciences Dr J. C. SHARMA; Head, Centre for Language Planning and Development Dr K. P. ACHARYA; Head, Centre for Language Technology Dr A. K. BASU; Head, Centre for Material Production, Testing and Evaluation B SYAMALA KUMARI; Head, Centre for Translation, Lexicography and Extension Dr P. N. DATTA BARUAH; publ. *New Language Planning Newsletter* (4 a year).

LAW

Amity Law School: *Delhi Campus* Yasho Bhawan (Adj. Escorts Heart Institute), Okhla Marg, New Delhi 110025; *Noida Campus* Sector 44 Noida (NCR), Uttar Pradesh; tel. (11) 26325901; fax (11) 26325903; internet www.amity.edu/als; affiliated to Guru Gobind Singh Indraprastha Univ.; f. 2000; library: 150,000 vols, 80 periodicals; Dir (Delhi) Prof. M. K. BALACHANDRAN; Dir (Noida) Prof. S. P. SINGH.

Government Law College: A Rd, Churchgate, Mumbai 400020, Maharastra; tel. (22) 22041707; fax (22) 22851315; e-mail principal@glc.edu; internet www.glc.edu; f. 1855; library: 36,000 vols, 38 journals; publs *Journal of Law and Society, Law Review*; Prin. P. R. RAO.

ILS Law College: Law College Rd, Pune 411004, Maharashtra; tel. (20) 25678678; fax (20) 25658665; e-mail ilslaw@vsnl.com; internet www.ilslaw.edu; f. 1923; 3-year and 5-year LLB degree; Masters in Labour Laws, Labour Welfare; diploma in Taxation Laws; 1,600 students; library: 45,000 vols, 100 periodicals; Pres. Y. V. CHANDRACHUD; Vice-Pres. R. SHINDE; Prin. VAIJAYANTI JOSHI.

Indian Academy of International Law and Diplomacy: 9 Bhagwan Dass Rd, New Delhi 110001; tel. (11) 23384458; fax (11) 23383783; e-mail isil@giasdl01.vsnl.net.in; internet www.isil-aca.org/indian-academy-intl-law.htm; f. 1964; part of the Indian Society of International Law; includes a research institute and library; offers courses in int. law and diplomacy, human rights, int. humanitarian and refugee laws, int. trade and business law, law of air transport and aviation liability, int. law and law of int. instns; library: 25,000 vols; Pres. RAM NIWAS MIRDHA; publ. *Indian Journal of International Law* (4 a year).

Symbiosis Law School: Senapati Bapat Rd, Pune 411004; tel. (20) 25655114; fax (20) 25671711; e-mail info@symlaw.ac.in; internet www.symlaw.ac.in; f. 1977; constituent of Symbiosis Int. Univ.; Chancellor Dr S. B. MUJUMDAR; Vice-Chancellor Dr M. S. RASTE; Prin. Dr SHASHIKALA GURPUR; Librarian KALPANA JADHAV.

MEDICINE

All India Institute of Hygiene and Public Health: 110 Chittaranjan Ave, Kolkata 700073; tel. (33) 315286; f. 1932; constituent college of University of Calcutta; administered by Directorate-General of Health Services and Ministry of Health and Family Welfare; facilities for postgraduate work and medical research; depts of behavioural sciences, biochemistry and nutrition, epidemiology and health education, maternal and child health, microbiology, occupational health, public health administration, public health nursing, sanitary engineering, social and preventive medicine, statistics and demography, veterinary public health; Rural Health and Training Centre, Urban Health and Training Centre; offers diploma, certificate, and orientation courses; academic year July to June; 112 teachers (incl. 14 professors); 300 students; library: 85,000 vols, 250 current periodicals; Dir Prof. K. J. NATH.

Armed Forces Medical College: Wanowrie, Pune 411040; internet afmc.nic.in; f. 1948; library: 20,000 bound journals; Dir and Commandant Lt-Gen. S. K. SHARMA; Dean Maj.-Gen. G. RAVINDRANATH; publ. *Medical Journal Armed Forces of India (MJAFI).*

Christian Medical College: Vellore 632004, Tamil Nadu; tel. (416) 2222102; fax (416) 2232035; e-mail directorate@cmcvellore .ac.in; internet www.cmch-vellore.edu; f. 1948; graduate courses in laboratory technology, medical records science, medicine, occupational therapy, physiotherapy; 11 postgraduate medical diploma courses; 23 postgraduate degree courses; 11 higher specialty courses; variety of allied health sciences diploma programmes; Dir Dr SURANJAN BHATTACHARJI; Dean, College of Nursing BHARATHI JACOB.

Jawaharlal Institute of Postgraduate Medical Education: Dhanvantri Nagar, Pondicherry 605006; tel. (413) 2272380; fax (413) 2272067; e-mail director@jipmer.edu .in; internet www.jipmer.edu; f. 1823 as Ecole de Medicine de Pondicherry, present name 1964; Govt control; affiliated to Pondicherry Univ.; depts of anaesthesiology, anatomy, biochemistry, cardiology, cardiothoracic and vascular surgery, dermatology, dentistry, ear, nose and throat, emergency medical services, forensic medicine and toxicology, medicine, medical education, microbiology, neurology, obstetrics and gynaecology, ophthalmology, orthopaedics, paediatrics, pathology, plastic surgery, pharmacology, physiology, preventive and social medicine, psychiatry, radiodiagnosis, radiotherapy, sexually transmitted diseases, surgery, tb and chest diseases, urology; Dir Dr SUBBA RAO; Dean Dr K. S. REDDY.

Kasturba Medical College, Manipal: Manipal Univ., Manipal 576104, Karnataka; tel. (820) 2922367; fax (820) 2571927; e-mail office.kmc@manipal.edu; internet www .manipal.edu; f. 1953; part of Manipal Univ.; depts of anatomy, ayurvedic medicine, biochemistry, biotechnology, community medicine, dermatology, ear, nose and throat, forensic medicine, hospital admin., laser spectroscopy, medical education, nephrology, obstetrics and gynaecology, ophthalmology, orthopaedics, paediatric surgery, pathology, plastic surgery, psychiatry, radiodiagnosis and imaging, surgery, tb and respiratory diseases, urology, yoga; Dean Dr P. SRIPATHI RAO; Librarian Dr SHIVANANDA BHAT.

Lady Hardinge Medical College: New Delhi 110001; e-mail lhmc@vsnl.com; f. 1914; library: 25,000 vols, 18,000 bound and 148 current periodicals; affiliated to Univ. of Delhi; depts of anaesthesiology, anatomy, biochemistry, ear, nose and throat, forensic medicine, microbiology, obstetrics and gynaecology, ophthalmology, orthosurgery, paediatrics, pathology, pharmacology, physiology, psychiatry, radiology, radiotherapy, skin, surgery, venereal diseases; Prin. Dr G. K. SHARMA.

Maulana Azad Medical College: Bahadaur Shah Zafar Marg, New Delhi 110002; tel. (11) 23239271; e-mail info@mamc.ac.in; internet www.mamc.ac.in; f. 1959; depts of anaesthesia, anatomy, biochemistry, community medicine, dentistry, dermatology and sexually transmitted diseases, ear, nose and throat, forensic medicine, microbiology, obstetrics and gynaecology, orthopaedics, paediatrics, pathology, pharmacology, physiology, radiodiagnosis, radiotherapy, surgery; Dean Dr A. K. AGARWAL; Registrar S. M. HAIDER.

National Institute of Health and Family Welfare (NIHFW): Baba Gang Nath Marg, Munirka, New Delhi 110067; tel. (11) 26165959; fax (11) 26101623; e-mail director@nihfw.org; internet www.nihfw.org; f. 1977; in-service training, MD course in community health administration, biomedical research, research and consultancy; regional centre for health management; documentation and reprographic services; library: specialized library of 41,000 vols and 308 periodicals; Dir Prof. DEOKI NANDI; publs *NIHFW Journal* (4 a year), Technical Report series.

TECHNOLOGY

See Institutes of National Importance for details of Indian Institutes of Technology.

Government College of Engineering and Ceramic Technology: 73, Abinash Chandra Banerjee Lane, Kolkata 700010, West Bengal; tel. (33) 23701264; fax (33) 23701264; e-mail gcect@rediffmail.com; internet www.gcect.ac.in; f. 1941 as Bengal Ceramic Institute, Calcutta; renamed the College of Ceramic Technology in 1962; present status in 2001; Prin. Dr ASIS KUMAR BANDYOPADHYAY.

Institute of Radiophysics and Electronics, University of Calcutta: 92 Acharya Prafulla Chandra Rd, Kolkata 700009, West Bengal; tel. (33) 23509115; fax (33) 23515828; e-mail bbandy@vsnl.com; internet www.irpel.org; f. 1949; houses postgraduate teaching and research dept of Univ. of Calcutta, Faculty of Technology; 3-year post-BSc integrated course leading to BTech. degree, and two-year post-BTech./BE course leading to MTech. degrees in radiophysics and electronics and in information technology; conducts training programmes; research facilities in ionosphere, radio wave propagation, radio astronomy, solid state and microwave electronics, millimetre wave technology, solid state devices, plasma and quantum electronics, optoelectronics, control systems and micro-computers, communication theory and systems, microelectronics and VLSI technology; maintains ionosphere field station at Haringhata and radio astronomy field station at Kalyani; recognized as a Centre of Advanced Study by the University Grants Commission; 36 teachers; 240 students; library: 18,000 vols, 5,000 journal issues; Head Dr BIJOY BANDYOPADHYAY.

National Institute of Fashion Technology: Hauz Khas, Near Gulmohar Park, New Delhi 110016; tel. (11) 26965080; fax (11) 26851198; e-mail admission@nift.ac.in; internet www.nift.ac.in; f. 1986; undergraduate and postgraduate diploma courses relevant to the textiles and clothing industries; library of 17,000 books and docs; campuses in New Delhi, Bangalore, Mumbai, Kolkata, Gandhinagar, Hyderabad, Chennai, Rae Bareli; Dir KALPANA SWAMY; Dean of Academics Prof. ASHA BAXI; Registrar MUNISH GIRIDHAR; publ. *Fashion and Beyond* (4 a year).

Schools of Art and Music

Academy of Architecture: 278 Shankar Ghanekar Marg, Prabhadevi, Mumbai 400025, Maharashtra; f. 1955; 5-year Govt Diploma courses in architecture; library: 5,600 vols and 2,000 slides; Prin. P. P. AMBERKAR.

Bharatiya Vidya Bhavan: Munshi Sadan, Bhartiya Vidya Bhavan Chowk, Kulapati Munshi Rd, Mumbai 400007, Maharashtra; tel. (22) 23631261; fax (22) 23630058; e-mail bhavan@bhavans.info; internet www.bhavans.info; f. 1938; revitalizes ancient Indian values to suit modern needs; postgraduate courses in Indology; colleges of arts, science, commerce and engineering; runs schools, Academy of Foreign Languages, College of Sanskrit; dept of Ancient Insights and Modern Discoveries; Ayurveda Research Centre; Institute of Communication and Management; Institute of Management and Research; schools of music, dancing, dramatic art; library: 76,688 vols and 1,404 MSS; 31,450 mems; Pres. SURENDRALAL G. MEHTA; Vice-Pres MURLI S. DEORA B. N. SRIKRISHNA; Dir-Gen. and Exec. Sec. H. N. DASTUR; publs *Astrological Journal* (English and Gujarati, 1 a year), *Bharatiya Vidya* (Sanskrit, 4 a year), *Bhavan's Dimdima* (English, 12 a year children's magazine), *Bhavan's Journal* (26 a year), *Navneet* (Hindi, 12 a year), *Navneet-Samarpan* (Gujarati, 12 a year), *Samvid* (Sanskrit, quarterly), 11 vols of the *History and Culture of the Indian People*, and various series.

ATTACHED COLLEGE:

Bhavan's Sardar Patel College of Engineering: Munshi Nagar, Andheri (West), Mumbai 400058, Maharashtra; tel. (22) 26289777; fax (22) 26237819; e-mail spce01@bom2.vsnl.net.in; internet www.spce.ac.in; f. 1962; depts of civil, electrical, mechanical and structural engineering; Exec. Chair and Dean Dr M. L. SHRIKANT; Principal Dr S. Y. MHAISKAR; Librarian SANJAY JAYARAM SAWANT; library of 44,000 vols.

There are 12 affiliated colleges and 33 other institutions.

Kalakshetra Foundation: Tiruvanmiyur, Chennai 600041, Tamil Nadu; tel. (44) 24524057; fax (44) 24524359; e-mail director@kalakshetra.in; internet www.kalakshetra.in; f. 1936; centre for education in classical music, dancing, theatrical art, painting and handicrafts; maintains a weaving centre for the production of silk and cotton costumes in traditional design and a Kalamkari Unit for dyeing and hand-block printing with vegetable dyes; Dr U. V. Swaminatha Aiyar library noted for classical MSS and literature in Tamil; library: 10,000 books on dance, music, painting, literature and religion; Dir LEELA SAMSON; Sec R. V. RAMANI.

Music Academy: 168 T. T. K. Rd, Royapettah, Chennai 600014, Tamil Nadu; tel. (44) 28112231; fax (44) 42359362; e-mail music@ musicacademymadras.com; internet www.musicacademymadras.in; f. 1927; research and study of Indian music; directs the Teachers' College of Music; library: 5,300 vols; Pres. N. MURALI; Vice-Pres HABIBULLAH BADSHA, C. V. KARTHIK NARAYANAN, L. VISWANATHAN, P. OBUL REDDY, R. SESHSAYEE, R. SRINIVASAN; publ. *Journal*.

National School of Drama: Bahawalpur House, 1 Bhagwandas Rd, New Delhi 110001; tel. (11) 23382821; fax (11) 23384288; e-mail info@nsd.gov.in; internet nsd.gov.in; f. 1959; 3-year diploma course for a maximum of 20 students in each class, short-term theatre training workshops; Theatre-in-Education Company working with and performing for children; library: 28,000 vols, 2,500 slides, records, etc.; 16 teachers; 60 students; Dir Dr ANURADHA KAPUR; Registrar D. R. SARIN; publs *Rang Prasang* (in Hindi, 2 a year), *Theatre India* (in English, 2 a year).

Sri Varalakshmi Academies of Fine Arts: Ramavilas, Kashipathy Agarahar, Chamaraja Double Rd, Mysore 4; f. 1945; educational and cultural research instn; gives advanced courses of study in Karnataka music; library: 5,000 vols; Prin. Vidwan C. V. SRIVATSA; Head Research Dept Prof. R. SATHYANARAYANA.

INDONESIA

The Higher Education System

The oldest institution of higher education is the Institut Teknologi Bandung (Bandung Institute of Technology), which was founded in 1920 when Indonesia was part of the Dutch East Indies. In 1949 Indonesia gained independence from the Netherlands. The Portuguese colony of Timor-Leste (formerly East Timor) was annexed in 1975 and administered as a province of Indonesia until 1999, when it was transferred to a UN transitional administration before achieving sovereign independence in 2002. Higher education facilities consist of different types of institutions, which include public and private universities (universitas), higher colleges (sekolah tinggi), teacher training institutes (institut keguruan dan ilmu pendidikan), Islamic universities (universitas Islam), Christian universities (universitas Kristen), academies (akademi) and polytechnics (politeknik). Universities (including the three technical institutes) offer a full range of undergraduate and postgraduate degrees; teacher training institutes and Islamic universities have degree-awarding powers; academies are specialized institutions of higher education related to a particular profession; and polytechnics are technical and vocational institutions offering diploma-level education. In 2007/08 there were 2,680 tertiary institutions with a total enrolment of 3,805,287 students. The Directorate-General of Higher Education is the government body responsible for overall control of higher education, but the Directorate of Islamic Higher Education is responsible for the Islamic universities.

Admission to public universities is on the basis of the Entrance Examination to State Universities (Ujian Masuk Perguruan Tinggi Negeri), while admission to polytechnics requires the applicant to complete secondary education and sit an entrance examination (Ujian Masuk Politeknik). The Entrance Examination to State Universities is divided into two streams, social sciences and natural sciences. Institutions may also make an offer of admission based on Interest and Ability Tracing (Penelusuran Minat dan Kemampuan), a system for monitoring secondary school students.

Indonesia operates a US-style 'credit semester' system for awarding undergraduate and postgraduate degrees, divided into three stages (sarjana). The first stage is the undergraduate degree (Sarjana Satu), the course for which lasts a minimum of eight semesters (four years) and requires 144–160 credits. Degrees in professional fields, such as medicine, dentistry, veterinary science and engineering, may last for an additional one to three years. The second stage (and first postgraduate degree) is the Magister, a course of study requiring 36–50 credits and lasting at least four semesters (two years). The third and last stage is the Doktor, also lasting at least four semesters (two years) and requiring a further 40–60 credits.

Post-secondary technical and vocational education is offered by polytechnics and academies. Students are awarded one of four diplomas (D1–D4) depending on length of course (one to four years) or area of specialization. The diploma D4 is regarded as equivalent to the Sarjana Satu. There are also two 'specialist' vocational qualifications, Ijazah Spesialis (SP1), awarded after two years and requiring 26–50 credits, and Ijazah Spesialis (SP2), awarded after 40–50 credits have been accrued following SP1.

The National Accreditation Board for Higher Education (Badan Akreditasi Nasional Perguruan Tinggi) was founded in 1994 as part of the Directorate-General of Higher Education and is the body responsible for accrediting both public and private institutions of higher education. Courses are ranked on a scale A–D, with A being 'very good' and D 'unsatisfactory'. C is the minimum requirement for accreditation. The board started piloting institutional accreditation by early 2008.

Regulatory and Representative Bodies

GOVERNMENT

Direktorat Jenderal Pendidikan Tinggi (Directorate-General of Higher Education): Ditjen DIKTI, Jl. Pintu Timur Senayan, Jakarta; e-mail dikti@dikti.go.id; internet www.dikti.go.id; Dir-Gen. Prof. Dr BAMBANG SUDIBYO.

Ministry of Culture and Tourism: Sapta Pesona Bldg, Jl. Medan Merdeka Barat 17, Jakarta 10110; tel. (21) 3838167; fax (21) 3849715; e-mail pusdatin@budpar.go.id; internet www.budpar.go.id; Min. JERO WATJIK.

Ministry of National Education: Jl. Jenderal Sudirman, Senayan, Jakarta 12041; tel. (21) 57950226; e-mail administrator@depdiknas.go.id; internet www.depdiknas.go.id; Min. BAMBANG SOEDIBYO.

ACCREDITATION

Badan Akreditasi Nasional Perguruan Tinggi (National Accreditation Board for Higher Education): Komplek Ditjen Jend. Mandikdasmen, Depdiknas RI, Gd D, Lantai 1, Jl. RS. Fatmawati Cipete, Jakarta 12410; tel. and fax (21) 7668690; e-mail sekretariat.banpt@gmail.com; internet ban-pt.depdiknas.go.id; f. 1994; Chair. Prof. KAMANTO SUNARTO.

Learned Societies

GENERAL

Jajasan Kerja-Sama Kebudajaan (Foundation for Cultural Cooperation): Jl. Gajah Mada 13, Bandung 40115; promotes cooperation and mutual understanding between the countries of Western Europe and Indonesia; Rep. for Indonesia A. KOOLHAAS.

BIBLIOGRAPHY, LIBRARY SCIENCE AND MUSEOLOGY

Asosiasi Museum Indonesia (Indonesian Museum Association): c/o Museum Nasional, Jl. Merdeka Barat 12, Jakarta 10110; tel. (21) 3868172; fax (21) 3811076; e-mail asosiasi_museum_indonesia@yahoo.com; internet www.asosiasimuseumindonesia.or.id; f. 2004; Chair. Drs SOETRISNO.

Ikatan Pustakawan Indonesia (Indonesian Library Association): Jl. Salemba Raya 28A, Jakarta 10430; tel. and fax (21) 7872353; f. 1954; Pres. DADY P. RACHIMANANTA; Sec.-Gen. H. ZULFIKAR ZEN.

EDUCATION

UNESCO Office Jakarta and Regional Science Bureau for Asia and the Pacific: Jl. Galuh (II) No. 5, Kebayoran Baru, POB 1273/JKT, Jakarta 12110; tel. (21) 7399818; fax (21) 72796489; e-mail jakarta@unesco.org; internet www.unesco.or.id; represents Brunei, Indonesia, Malaysia, Philippines and Timor-Leste; Dir Dr HUBERT GIJZEN.

LANGUAGE AND LITERATURE

Alliance Française: Jl. Raya Puputan I, 13A, Denpasar 80235; tel. and fax (361) 234143; e-mail afd@afdenpasar.org; internet www.afdenpasar.org; offers courses and examinations in French language and culture and promotes cultural exchange with France; centres in Balikpapan, Bandung, Denpasar, Lampung, Manado, Medan, Padang and Semarang; Dir AUDREY LAMOU; Librarian FEYBE I. MOKOGINTA.

British Council: S. Widjojo Centre, Jl. Jenderal Sudirman Kav 71, Jakarta 12190; tel. (21) 2524115; fax (21) 2524129; e-mail information@britishcouncil.or.id; internet www.britishcouncil.org/indonesia; teaching centre; offers courses and examinations in English language and British culture and promotes cultural exchange with the UK; attached office in Surabaya; library of 18,000 vols; Dir Dr PATRICK BRAZIER; Man., English Language Services SIMON COLLEDGE.

Goethe-Institut: Jl. Sam Ratulangi 9–15, POB 3640, Jakarta 10350; tel. (21) 23550208; fax (21) 23550021; e-mail info@jakarta.goethe.org; internet www.goethe.de/jakarta; f. 1961; offers courses and examinations in German language and culture and promotes cultural exchange with Germany; attached centre in Bandung; library of 8,500 vols,

1,600 audiovisual items, 40 periodicals; Dir FRANZ XAVER AUGUSTIN.

MEDICINE

Ikatan Dokter Indonesia (Indonesian Medical Association): Jl. Dr Sam Ratulangi 29, Menteng, Jakarta 10350; tel. (21) 3150679; fax (21) 3900473; e-mail pbidi@idola.net.id; internet www.idionline.org; f. 1950; 45,131 mems; Chair. Prof. Dr FACHMI IDRIS; Sec.-Gen. Dr SLAMET BUDIARTO; publs *BIDI* (26 a year), *Majalah Kedokteran Indonesia* (12 a year).

NATURAL SCIENCES

Physical Sciences

Astronomical Association of Indonesia: Jakarta Planetarium, Cikini Raya 73, Jakarta 10330; tel. (21) 2305146; fax (21) 2305147; f. 1920; promotes advancement of astronomical science; Chair. Prof. Dr BAMBANG HIDAYAT; Sec. Drs S. DARSA; Treas. Dr WINARDI SUTANTYO.

TECHNOLOGY

Persatuan Insinyur Indonesia (Indonesian Institute of Engineers): 39 Jl. Halimun, Jakarta 12980; tel. (21) 8352180; fax (21) 83700663; e-mail info@pii.or.id; internet www.pii.or.id; 27,000 mems; Pres. ABURIZAL BAKRIE; Sec.-Gen. I. SUCIPTO UMAR.

Research Institutes

GENERAL

Lembaga Ilmu Pengetahuan Indonesia (Indonesian Institute of Sciences): Jl. Jendral Gatot Subroto 10, Jakarta 12710; tel. (21) 5251542; fax (21) 5207226; e-mail kepala@lipi.go.id; internet www.lipi.go.id; f. 1967; gov agency; promotes the devt of science and technology; serves as the nat. centre for regional and int. scientific cooperation; organizes nat. research centres; library of 150,000 titles; Head Prof. Dr UMAR ANGGARA JENIE; publs *Annales Bogorienses* (2 a year), *Berita Biologi* (4 a year), *Berita Iptek* (4 a year), *IPT Technical Journal* (4 a year), *Jurnal Kimia Terapan Indonesia* (3 a year), *Journal of Tropical Ethnobiology* (2 a year), *Jurnal Ekonomi dan Pembangunan* (2 a year), *Jurnal Elektronika dan Pembangunan* (6 a year), *Jurnal Masyarakat dan Budaya* (2 a year), *Jurnal Penduduk dan Pembangunan* (2 a year), *Jurnal Teknologi Informasi* (3 a year), *Korosi: Majalah Ilmu dan Teknologi* (2 a year), *Limnotek* (2 a year), *Majalah Perencanaan LIPI* (2 a year), *Majalah Widyariset* (12 a year), *Masyarakat Indonesia: Majalah Ilmu-ilmu Sosial Indonesia* (2 a year), *Oseanologi dan Limnologi di Indonesia* (6 a year), *Prosea Newsletter* (4 a year), *Reinwardtia: A Journal on Taxonomic Botany, Plant Sociology and Ecology* (irregular), *Riset Geologi dan Pertambangan, Telaah: Berkala Ilmu Pengetahuan dan Teknologi* (2 a year), *Treubia: Journal on Zoology of the Indo-Australian Archipelago* (irregular), *Warta Biotek* (4 a year), *Warta KIM* (12 a year), *Warta Kimia Analitik* (2 a year), *Warta Oseanografi* (4 a year).

AGRICULTURE, FISHERIES AND VETERINARY SCIENCE

Badan Penelitian dan Pengembangan Kehutanan (Forestry Research and Development Agency): Manggala Wanabakti Bldg Blk 1, 11 Fl., Jl. Jend. Gatot Subroto, Jakarta 10270; tel. (21) 5730392; fax (21) 5720189; e-mail datinfo@forda-mof.org; internet www.forda-mof.org; f. 1983; attached to Kementerian Kehutanan (Min. of Forestry); 390 research scientists; library of 34,005 vols, 2,848 vols in reference colln, 6,321 textbooks; Dir-Gen. TACHRIR FATHONI; Sec. PUTERA PARTHAMA; Sec.-Gen. BOEN M. PURNAMA; publs *Journal of Forestry Research* (2 a year), *Journal of Forestry Policy Analysis* (series, 3 a year), *Journal of Forest and Nature Conservation Research* (5 or 6 a year), *Journal of Forest Products Research* (4 a year), *Forest Product Bulletin* (2 a year), *Forestry Socio Economic Journal* (4 a year), *Info Hutan* (4 or 6 a year), *Info Sosial Ekonomi Kehutanan* (magazine, 4 a year), *Mitra Hutan Tanaman* (3 a year), *Plantation Forest Research Journal* (3 a year), *Tekno Hutan Tanaman* (3 a year).

Balai Besar Industri Agro (Centre for Agro-Based Industry): Jl. Ir H. Juanda 11, Bogor 16122; tel. (251) 8324068; fax (251) 8323339; e-mail cabi@bbia.go.id; internet www.bbia.go.id; f. 1909; attached to Min. of Industry; provides services for agriculture-based industry through training, consultancy, chemical and microbiological testing, research and devt, certification, environmental management, technical inspection, design engineering on food processing and calibration; Dir YANG YANG SETIAWAN; publ. *Warta IHP* (Journal of agro-based industry, 2 a year).

Balai Besar Penelitian Veteriner Bogor (Research Institute for Veterinary Science, Agency of Agricultural Research and Development, Ministry of Agriculture): Jl. R. E. Martadinata 30, POB 151, Bogor 16164; tel. (251) 331048; fax (251) 336425; e-mail balivet@indo.net.id; internet bbalitvet.litbang.deptan.go.id; f. 1908; depts of bacteriology, balitvet culture colln, mycology, parasitology, pathology and epidemiology, toxicology, virology; library of 12,270 vols, 1,136 periodicals; Dir Dr SJAMSUL BAHRI.

Balai Penelitian Bioteknologi Perkebunan Indonesia (Indonesian Biotechnology Research Institute for Estate Crops): Jl. Salak 1A, Bogor 16151; tel. (251) 8333382; fax (251) 8315985; e-mail ipardboo@indo.net.id; internet www.ipard.com; f. 1933; supportive research in plant molecular biology and immunology, microbes and bioprocessing; library of 13,493 vols, 1,597 periodicals, 3,109 reprints, 70 theses; Head of Unit Dr Ir DARMONO TANIWIRYONO; publ. *Menara Perkebunan* (in English and Indonesian, 2 a year).

Pusat Penelitian dan Pengembangan Hortikultura (Indonesian Centre for Horticulture Research and Development (ICHORD)): Jl. Raya Ragunan 29A, Pasarminggu, Jakarta 12520; tel. (21) 7805768; fax (21) 7805135; e-mail puslitbanghorti@litbang.deptan.go.id; internet hortikultura.litbang.deptan.go.id; research and devt of horticultural crops; Dir Drs YUSDAR HILMAN; publs *Jurnal Hortikultura* (4 a year), *Katalog* (1 a year), *IPTEK* (1 a year).

Attached Institutes:

Balai Penelitian Tanaman Buah Tropika (Indonesian Tropical Fruit Research Institute): Jl. Raya Solok-Aripan Km 8, Kotak Pos No. 5, Solok Sumatera Barat 27301; tel. (755) 20137; fax (755) 20592; e-mail balitbu@litbang.deptan.go.id; internet www.balitbu.litbang.deptan.go.id; f. 1985; applied research for fruit crops in breeding and genetics, physiology, tissue culture, biotechnology, soils and plant nutrition, pest and disease management, and agricultural economics; Dir Dr I. NURHADI.

Balai Penelitian Tanaman Hias (Indonesian Ornamental Crops Research Institute (IOCRI)): Jl. Raya Ciherang Segunung, Kotak Pos 8 SdL, Pacet-Cianjur 43253; tel. (263) 512607; fax (263) 514138; e-mail segunung@indoway.net; Dir Dr KUSUMAH EFFENDIE.

Balai Penelitian Tanaman Sayur (Indonesian Vegetable Research Institute (IVEGRI)): Jl. Tangkuban Perahu 517, Lembang; tel. (22) 2786245; fax (22) 2786416; e-mail ivegri@balitsa.or.id; Dir Dr UDIN S. NUGRAHA.

Pusat Penelitian dan Pengembangan Peternakan (Central Research Institute for Animal Sciences): Jl. Raya Pajajaran, Kav E-59, Bogor, West Java 16151; tel. (251) 322185; fax (251) 328283; e-mail criansci@indo.net.id; internet peternakan.litbang.deptan.go.id; f. 1950; researches into farm animals and animal parasites and diseases; library of 14,000 vols, 1,199 periodicals; Dir Dr KUSUMA DIWYANTO; publs *Ilmu Peternakan dan Veteriner* (4 a year), *Proceedings of the National Seminar* (1 a year), *Wartazoa* (2 a year).

Pusat Penelitian dan Pengembangan Tanaman Pangan (Centre for Food Crops Research and Development): Jl. Merdeka 147, Bogor 16111; tel. (251) 334089; fax (251) 312755; internet www.puslittan.bogor.net; f. 1961; food crops research and devt; library of 3,000 vols; Dir Dr ACHMAD M. FAGI; publ. *Contributions of CRIFC* (4–6 a year).

Attached Institutes:

Balai Penelitian Bioteknologi Tanaman Pangan (Research Institute for Biotechnology of Food Crops): Jl. Tentara Pelajar 3A, Bogor 16111; tel. (251) 337975; fax (251) 338820; Dir Dr DJOKO S. DAMARDJATI; publs *Buletin Penelitian* (Research Bulletin, 2–4 a year), *Penelitian Pertanian* (Agricultural Research, 3–4 a year, in Indonesian and English).

Balai Penelitian Tanaman Jagung dan Serealia Lain (Research Institute for Maize and Other Cereals): Jl. Ratulangi, Kotak Pos 173, Maros 90511, Ujung Pandang, Sulawesi Selatan Telp; tel. (411) 371016; fax (411) 318148; Dir Dr MARSUM DAHLAN; publ. *Agrikam: Buletin Penelitian Pertanian* (Agricultural Research Bulletin, 2–4 a year, with English summary).

Balai Penelitian Tanaman Kacang-kacangan dan Umbi-umbian Malang (Research Institute for Legumes and Root Crops): Jl. Raya Kendal Payak, Kotak Pos 66, Malang, Jawa Timur, 65101; tel. (341) 81468; fax (341) 318148; Dir Dr SUYAMTO; publ. *Penelitian Palawija* (Palawija Research, 2 a year, in Indonesian, and abstract in English).

Balai Penelitian Tanaman Padi (Research Institute for Rice): Jl. Raya 9, Sukamandi—Tromol Pos 11, Cikampek Subang, Jawa Barat 41255; tel. (264) 520157; fax (264) 520158; Dir Dr ANDI HASANUDDIN; publ. *Media Sukamandi* (Research at Sukamandi, 2–4 a year, with English summary).

Balai Penelitian Tanaman Pangan Lahan Rawa (Research Institute for Food Crops on Swampy Areas): Jl. Kebun Karet, Lok Tabat, Kotak Pos 31, Kalimantan, Selatan Banjarbaru 70712; tel. (511) 4772534; fax (511) 4773034; Dir ACHMADI; publ. *Pemberitaan Penelitian* (2–4 a year, in Indonesian and English).

Pusat Penelitian Kelapa Sawit (Indonesian Oil Palm Research Institute): Jl. Brigjen Katamso 51, Medan 20158; tel. (61) 7862477; fax (61) 7862488; e-mail admin@iopri.org; internet www.iopri.org; f. 1916; promotes agricultural improvement on the member estates; library of 11,000 vols, 20,000 periodicals; Dir Dr Ir WITJKSANA; publs *Berita* (in Indonesian), *Bulletin* (4 a year, in Indonesian with English summaries), *Oil Palm Statistics* (in Indonesian), *Rainfall Records* (in Indonesian).

Pusat Penelitian Perkebunan Gula Indonesia (Indonesian Sugar Research Institute): Jl. Pahlawan 25, Pasuruan 67126; tel. (343) 421086; fax (343) 421178; e-mail puslitgula@ipard.com; f. 1887; 150 staff; library of 15,000 vols; Dir Dr MIRZAWAN PDN; publs *Berita* (Communications), *Bulletin* (2 a year), *Majalah Penelitian Gula* (Sugar Journal, 4 a year).

Pusat Penelitian Tanah dan Agroklimat (Soil and Agricultural Climate Research Centre): Jl. Ir H. Juanda 98, Bogor 16123; f. 1905; library of 4,000 vols; Dir Dr SYARIFUD-DIN KARAMA.

ARCHITECTURE AND TOWN PLANNING

Research Institute for Human Settlements and United Nations Regional Centre for Research on Human Settlements: Jl. Panyawungan, Cileunyi, Wetan, Kab. Bandung 40393; tel. (22) 798393; fax (22) 798392; e-mail inge@bdg.centrin.net.id; f. 1953; researches on housing, bldgs, etc.; library of 29,000 vols; Dir SUTIKUI UTORO; publs *Buku Petunjuk Pedesaan* (in Bahasa Indonesian), *Jurnal Penelitian Pemutiman* (4 a year, in Bahasa Indonesian), *Masalah Bangunan* (4 a year, in English).

ECONOMICS, LAW AND POLITICS

Badan Pusat Statistik (BPS Statistics Indonesia): Jl. Dr Sutomo 6–8, Jakarta 10710; tel. (21) 3841195; fax (21) 3857046; e-mail bpshq@bps.go.id; internet www.bps.go.id; f. 1960; library of 60,000 vols, 1,100 periodicals; Dir Dr SOEDARTI SURBAKTI.

Centre for Strategic and International Studies: Jakarta Post Bldg, Third Fl., Jl. Palmerah Barat 142–243, Jakarta 10270; tel. (21) 53654601; fax (21) 53654607; e-mail csis@csis.or.id; f. 1971; policy-oriented studies in int. and nat. affairs in collaboration with industry, commerce, and the political, legal and journalistic communities; library of 50,000 vols, 377 journals and 20 newspapers; Exec. Dir Dr HADI SOESASTRO; publs *Analisis CSIS* (4 a year), *The Indonesian Quarterly* (in English).

Indonesian Institute of World Affairs: c/o University of Indonesia, Jakarta; Chair. Prof. SUPOMO; Sec. SUDJATMOKO.

Lembaga Administrasi Negara (National Institute of Public Administration): Jl. Veteran 10, Jakarta 10110; tel. (21) 3868201; fax (21) 3848792; e-mail humas@lan.go.id; internet www.lan.go.id; f. 1957; library of 16,712 vols; Chair. Dr ASMAWI REWANSYAH; publs *Jurnal Administrasi Negara*, *Jurnal Administrasi Publik*, *Jurnal Administrator Borneo*, *Jurnal Diklat Aparatur*, *Jurnal Ilmu Administrasi*, *Manajemen Pembangunan*.

Lembaga Pers dan Pendapat Umum (Press and Public Opinion Institute, Ministry of Information): Pegangsaan Timur 19B, Jakarta; f. 1953; audience research of press, film and radio; library of 4,500 vols; Dir Dr MARBANGUN.

HISTORY, GEOGRAPHY AND ARCHAEOLOGY

Dinas Intelijen Medan & Geografi Jawatan Topografi TNI-AD (Geographical Institute): Jl. Dr Wahidin 1/11, Jakarta; Dir Capt. AMARUL AMRI.

Direktorat Perlindungan dan Pembinaan Peninggalan Sejarah dan Purbakala (Directorate for the Protection and Development of the Historical and Archaeological Heritage): Jl. Cilacap 4, POB 2533, Jakarta; Dir UKA TJANDRASASMITA.

Pusat Penelitian Arkeologi (Research Centre of Archaeology): Jl. Raya Condet Pejaten 4, Pasar Minggu, Jakarta 12510; tel. (21) 7988131; fax (21) 7988187; e-mail arkenas@bit.net.id; brs in Yogyakarta, Denpasar, Palembang, Bandung, Banjarmasin, Makassar, Manado, Ambon and Jayapura; library of 15,000 vols; Dir Dr HARIS SUKEN-DAR; publs *Aspects*, *Amerta*, *Bulletin*, *Kalpataru*.

LANGUAGE AND LITERATURE

Pusat Bahasa. Departemen Pendidikan Nasional (Language Centre of the Ministry of National Education): POB 6259, Jl. Daksinapati Barat IV, Rawamangun, Jakarta 13220; tel. (21) 4706678; fax (21) 4750407; e-mail masterfbs@bahasa-sastra.web.id; f. 1975; language planning policies, research in linguistics and vernaculars, compiling of dictionaries, coordinating and supervising language devt and cultivation, applied research in language education; library of 80,000 vols; Dir DENDY SUGONO; publs *Bahasa dan Sastra* (6 a year), *Informasi Pustaka Kebahasaan* (4 a year), *Lembar Komunikasi* (6 a year).

MEDICINE

Badan Pengawas Obat dan Makanan (National Agency of Drug and Food Control): Jl. Percetakan Negara 23, Jakarta 10560; tel. (21) 42883309; fax (21) 42889117; e-mail informasi@pom.go.id; internet www.pom.go.id; f. 2000; legislation, regulation and standardization of drug and food industries; licensing and certification of pharmaceutical industry; evaluation of products; sampling and laboratory testing of products; inspection of production and distribution facilities; investigation and law enforcement; auditing of product advertisement and promotion; research on drug and food policy implementation; public communication, information and education; Head Drs H. M. SAMPURNO; Sec. Dra MAWARWATI DJAMALUDDIN.

Central Institute for Leprosy Research: Jl. Kimia 17, Jakarta; f. 1935; incl. clinic and laboratory; Dir MOH. ARIF.

Laboratorium Kesehatan Daerah (Pathological Laboratory, Ministry of Health): Jl. Rawasari Slt 2, Jakarta 10510; tel. (21) 4247408; f. 1906; investigation and control of contagious and endemic diseases in Sumatra; library of 3,000 vols; Dir Dr ISKAK KOIMAN.

Laboratorium Kesehatan Pusat Lembaga Eijkman (Eijkman Institute): Library, Clinical Pathology Dept, Medical Faculty of the University of Indonesia, Ciptomangunkusumo Hospital, Jl. Diponegoro 69–71, Jakarta 10010; tel. (21) 332265; fax (21) 3147713; f. 1888; bacteriological-serological dept, chemical dept and virus division; publs reports, papers; Head Dr HENDRO JOEWONO.

Lembaga Malaria (Malaria Institute, Ministry of Health): Jl. Percetakan Negara 29, Jakarta; tel. (21) 417608; fax (21) 4207807; f. 1920; Dir Dr P. R. ARBANI.

Perusahaan Negara Bio-Farma (Pasteur Institute): Jl. Pasteur 9, POB 47, Bandung 40161; Dir M. S. NASUTION.

Pusat Penelitian dan Pengembangan Pelayanan dan Technologi Kesehatan (Health Services and Technology Research and Development Centre): Jl. Indrapura 17, Surabaya 60176; tel. (31) 3528748; fax (31) 3528749; internet www.litbang.depkes.go.id/p4tk Jl. Percetakan Negara 23A, Jakarta 10560; tel. (21) 4243314; fax (21) 4211013; f. 1975; library of 14,500 books, 750 magazine titles; Dir Dr H. SUWANDI MAKMUR; publs

Bulletin of Health System Research (2 a year), *Warta JIP* (4 a year).

Unit Diponegoro (Nutrition Institute): c/o Nutrition Centre, Seameo Tropmed–U.I., Campus University of Indonesia, Salemba 4, Jakarta; f. 1937; Dir Dradjat D. PRAWIR-ANEGARA.

NATURAL SCIENCES
General

Institut de Recherche pour le Développement (IRD): Wisma Anugraha, Jl. Taman Kemang 32B, Jakarta 12730; tel. (21) 71792114; fax (21) 71792179; e-mail ird-indo@rad.net.id; internet www.id.ird.fr; f. 1944; (see main entry under France); agroforestry, agronomy, anthropology, aquaculture, archaeology, ethno-ecology, fishery, geography; Dir Dr PATRICE LEVANG.

Biological Sciences

Pusat Penelitian Biologi (Research Centre for Biology): Jl. Raya Jakarta, Bogor Km 46, Cibinong, Bogor 16911; tel. and fax (21) 8797612; e-mail biologi@mail.lipi.go.id; internet biologi.lipi.go.id; f. 1817; 424 mems; library of 49,180 vols, 4,393 bound periodicals, c. 600 current periodicals, 24,587 reprints, 4,377 unpublished reports, 7,155 newspaper clippings, 2,463 maps; Dir Dr SITI NURAMALIATI PRIJONO; publs *Berita Biologi*, *Reinwardtia*, *Treubia*, *Laporan Tahunan*, *Laporan Teknik* (1 a year), *Laporan Kemajuan* (4 a year), *Warta Kita* (6 a year), *pamphlets*.

Attached Institutes:

Balai Penelitian dan Pengembangan Botani (Research and Development Institute for Botany): Jl. Raya Juanda 22, Bogor; f. 1884; Head Dr JOHANIS PALAR MOGEA.

Balai Penelitian dan Pengembangan Mikrobiologi (Research and Development Institute for Microbiology): c/o Kebun Raya Indonesia; f. 1884; Head Dr SUBADRI ABDULKADIR.

Balai Penelitian dan Pengembangan Zoologi (Research and Development Institute for Zoology): Jl. Raya Juanda 3, Bogor; Head Drs MOHAMAD AMIR.

UPT Balai Pengembangan Kebun Raya (Bogor Botanical Gardens):; f. 1817; Head Dr SUHIRMAN; publs *Alphabetical List of Plant Species*, *Buletin Kebun Raya* (4 a year), *Index Seminum* (1 a year), *Warta Kebun Raya* (irregular).

Physical Sciences

Badan Meteorologi Klimatologi dan Geofisika (Meteorology, Climatology and Geophysics Agency): Jl. Angkasa 1, No. 2, Kemayoran, POB 3540, Jakarta 10720; tel. (21) 2426321; fax (21) 4246703; internet www.bmg.go.id; drafting nat. policies relating to meteorology, climatology and geophysics; data and information services; research and devt; Dir Dr Ir Sri WORO B. HARIJONO.

Dinas Geodesi, Jawatan Topografi TNI-AD (Geodetic Section, Army Topographic Service): Jl. Bangka 1, Bandung; f. 1855; library of 2,000 vols, 2,500 periodicals; Dir MOH TAWIL.

Badan Tenaga Nuklir Nasional (National Atomic Energy Agency): Jl. Kuningan Barat, Mampang Prapatan, POB 4390, Jakarta 12710; tel. (21) 5251109; fax (21) 5251110; e-mail humas@batan.go.id; internet www.batan.go.id; Dir-Gen. DJALI AHIMSA.

Observatorium Bosscha (Bosscha Observatory): Jl. Peneropongan Bintang, Lembang, Java; tel. and fax (22) 2786001; e-mail kunjungan@as.itb.ac.id; internet bosscha.itb.ac.id; f. 1925; since 1951 the observatory has been part of the Dept of Astronomy, Bandung Institute of Technology, Bandung; Dir Dr BAMBANG HIDAYAT; publs *Annals* (irregular), *Contributions* (irregular).

Pusat Penelitian Oseanografi (Research Centre for Oceanography): Jl. Pasir Putih 1, Ancol Timur, POB 4801/JKTF, Jakarta 14430; tel. (21) 64713850; fax (21) 64711948; e-mail p30.lipi@jakarta.wasantara.net.id; internet www.oseanologi.lipi.go.id; f. 1905; library of 2,000 vols, 250 periodical titles; Dir Dr Ir KURNAN SUMADHIHARYA; publs *Marine Research in Indonesia* (irregular), *Oseana* (4 a year), *Oseanologi di Indonesia* (irregular).

Pusat Survei Geologi (Centre for Geological Survey): Jl. Diponegoro 57, Bandung 40122; tel. and fax (22) 7218482; e-mail contact@grdc.esdm.go.id; internet www.grdc.esdm.go.id; f. 1979; geological and geophysical research and systematic mapping; library: see Libraries; Dir Dr A. DJUMARMA WIRAKUSUMAH; publs *Buletin*, *Geofisika dan Tematik*, *Geosurvey Newsletter*, *Journal of Geology and Mineral Resources*, *Peta Geologi*, *Publikasi Khusus* (spec. publs.), *Publikasi Teknik* (Technical Papers: Geophysics, Palaeontology Series).

TECHNOLOGY

Akademi Teknologi Kulit (Academy of Leather Technology): Jl. Ateka Bangunharjo, Sewon, Bantul, POB 1186, Yogyakarta 55187; tel. (274) 383727; e-mail info@atk.ac.id; internet www.atk.ac.id; Dir IR CAHYA WIDIYATI.

Balai Besar Kerajinan dan Batik (Batik and Handicraft Research Institute): Jl. Kusumanegara 7, Yogyakarta; tel. (274) 546111; fax (274) 543582; internet www.batik.go.id; f. 1951; research, testing, and training courses; 108 mems; library of 1,792 vols; Dir SOEPARMAN S. TEKS.

Balai Besar Penelitian dan Pengembangan Industri Barang Kulit, Karet dan Plastik (BBKKP) (Centre for Leather, Rubber and Plastic (CLRP)): Jl. Sokonandi 9, Yogyakarta 55166; tel. (274) 563939; fax (274) 563655; e-mail bbkkp@bbkkp.go.id; internet bbkkp.go.id; f. 1927; library of 4,000 vols; Dir SARDJONO.

Balai Fotogrametri (Institute of Photogrammetry): Jl. Gunung Sahar 90, Jakarta; f. 1937; attached to Min. of Defence; researches on problems relating to photogrammetry, aerotriangulization, topographical maps, etc.; library of 1,500 books and periodicals; Head Maj. R. E. BEAUPAIN.

Dinas Hidro-Oseanografi (Naval Hydro-Oceanographic Office): Jl. Pantai Kuta V1, Jakarta 14430; f. 1947; hydrographical survey of Indonesia; staff of 700; publishes Tide Tables, etc.; Dir Col P. L. KATOPPO.

Direktorat Metrologi (Directorate of Metrology): Jl. Pasteur 27, Bandung 40171; tel. (22) 4203597; fax (22) 4207035; e-mail ditmet@bdg.centrin.net.id; f. 1923; Dir of Metrology AMIR SAHARUDDIN SJABRIAL.

Institut Teknologi Tekstil (Institute of Textile Technology): Jl. Jond. A. Yani 318, Bandung; f. 1922; Dir Maj. JON SEORJOSEOJARSO.

Jajasan Dana Normalisasi Indonesia (Indonesian Standards Institution): Jl. Braga 38, (Atas) Bandung; f. 1920; Chair. Prof. R. SOEMONO; Sec. GANDI.

Lembaga Research dan Pengujian Materiil Angkatan Darat (Military Laboratory for Research and Testing Material, Ministry of Defence): Jl. Ternate 6–8, Bandung; f. 1865; library of 1,500 vols; Dir Brig.-Gen. N. A. KUSOMO.

Pusat Penelitian dan Pengembangan Sumber Daga Air (Research Institute for Water Resources): Jl. Ir. H. Juanda 193, POB 841, Bandung 40135; tel. (22) 2504053; fax (22) 2500163; e-mail pusair@bdg.centrin.net.id; internet www.pusair.domainvalet.com; f. 1966; attached to Agency for Research and Devt, Min. of Settlement and Regional Infrastructure; surveys, investigates and researches in the field of water resources devt; comprises experimental stations for hydrology, water resources, the environment, hydraulic structures and geotechnics, irrigation, swamps and coastal regions, rivers and sabo; library of 6,000 vols, 3,000 reports, 9,000 periodicals; Dir DYAH RAHAYU PANGESTI; publs *Bulletin Pusair* (2 a year), *Jurnal Penelitian dan Pengembangan Pengairan* (2 a year), *Technical and Research Report* (1 a year).

Libraries and Archives

Jakarta

Arsip Nasional Republik Indonesia (National Archives): Jl. Ampera Raya 7, Jakarta 12560; tel. (21) 7805851; fax (21) 7805812; e-mail info@anri.go.id; internet www.anri.go.id; f. 1892; preserves documents as a nat. heritage and nat. account of the planning, execution and performance of the nat. life; provides records for govt and public activities; supervises the management of current operational records and the colln, storage, preservation, safe-keeping and use of historical archives; c. 25 km archives; 8,437 vols of books and other publs, 48,000 films, 10,000 video recordings, 4,000 oral history recordings, 1.6m. photographs; Dir Dr DJOKO UTOMO; publs *Berita Arsip Nasional RI* (2 a year), *Lembaran Berita Sejarah Lisan Arsip Nasional RI* (irregular), *Penerbitan Sumber Sejarah* (irregular), *Penerbitan Sumber Sejarah Lisan* (irregular).

Central Documentation and Library of the Ministry of Information: Medan Merdeka Barat 9, Jakarta; f. 1945; specializes in mass communication, social and political subjects, and supplies regional br. offices; press-cutting service from Indonesian newspapers since 1950; temporarily acting as Exchange Centre for govt publs and official documents; 10,000 vols; Head Drs P. DALIMUNTHE; Librarian SAMPOERNO.

Perpustakaan Bagian Pathologi Klinik R. S. 'Dr Tjipto Mangunkusumo' (Dr Tjipto Mangunkusumo Hospital Library): Jl. Diponegoro 69, Jakarta; 3,000 vols; medicine, public health; Dir Prof. Dr JEANNE LATU.

Perpustakaan Dewan Perwakilan Rakyat Republik Indonesia (Library of Indonesian Parliament): Jl. Jenderal Gatot Subroto, Jakarta 10270; tel. (21) 5715220; fax (21) 584804; f. 1946; 200,000 vols; Librarian ROEMNINGSIH.

Perpustakaan Nasional (National Library of Indonesia): Jl. Salemba Raya 28A, POB 3624, Jakarta 10002; Jl. Merdeka Selatan 11, Pusat, Jakarta 10002; tel. (21) 3922669; fax (21) 3103554; internet www.pnri.go.id; f. 1980, by a merger of four libraries; depository library of Indonesia; 750,000 vols; spec. collns: Indonesian newspapers since 1810, Indonesian periodicals since 1779, Indonesian maps since 17th century, Indonesian dissertations, Indonesian monographs since 17th century; Dir MASTINI HARDJO PRAKOSO; publs *Bibliografi Nasional Indonesia* (4 a year), *Indeks artikel suratkabar* (Press Index, 4 a year), *subject bibliographies*, *catalogues*.

Perpustakaan Sejarah Politik dan Sosial (Library of Political and Social History): Medan Merdeka Selatan 11, Jakarta; f. 1952; 65,000 vols; incl. the Nat.ional Bibliographic Centre (Kantor Bibliografi Nasional) deposit library; Librarian Drs SOEKARMAN; publs *Berita Bulanan* (Bulletin, 12 a year), *Checklist of Serials in the Libraries of Indonesia*, *Publications—Indonesia*, *Regional Bibliography of Social Sciences*, *Publications—Indonesia*, *Checklist of Serials in the Libraries of Indonesia*.

Pusat Dokumentasi dan Informasi Ilmiah—Lembaga Ilmu Pengetahuan Indonesia (PDII-LIPI) (Indonesian Scientific Knowledge Centre): Jl. Jendral Gatot Subroto 10, POB 4298, Jakarta 12042; tel. (21) 5733465; fax (21) 5733467; e-mail admin@pdii.lipi.go.id; internet www.pdii.lipi.go.id; f. 1965; 58,552 books, 4,783 periodicals, 14,022 theses and dissertations, 75,000 microforms, 40,000 research reports, 11,679 patents; Head Dra JUSNI DJATIN; publs *Abstract of Research and Survey Reports* (irregular), *Baca* (Read, 3 a year), *Daftar Terbitan Berkala Indonesia yang Telah Mempunyai ISSN* (Indonesian Serials with ISSN, irregular), *Directory of Special Libraries and Information Sources in Indonesia* (irregular), *FOKUS* (issues covering 17 subjects, 6 a year), *Index of Indonesian Learned Periodicals*, *Index to Papers Submitted to Seminars* (irregular), *Union Catalog of Serials* (irregular).

UPT Perpustakaan dan Dokumentasi, Biro Pusat Statistik (Library and Statistical Documentation, Central Bureau of Statistics): POB 1003, Jl. Dr Sutomo 8, Jakarta; tel. (21) 3810291; fax (21) 3857046; 60,000 vols; Librarian DAME MUNTHE.

South Sulawesi

Perpustakaan Umum Makassar (Makassar Public Library): Jl. Madukelleng 3, POB 16, Ujung Pandang 90112; f. 1969; organizes lending library services in brs throughout South Sulawesi Province; film and music programmes; foreign-language courses; children's library services; exhibitions and talks; 42,000 vols; Dir (vacant).

UPT Perpustakaan Universitas Hasanuddin (Hasanuddin University Library): Kampus UNHAS Tamalanrea, Jl. Perintis Kemerdekaan km 10, Ujung Pandang 90245; tel. (411) 587027; fax (411) 510088; e-mail library@unhas.ac.id; internet www.unhas.ac.id/perpustakaan; f. 1956; open to public; 122,000 vols, 3,821 periodicals, 23,421 dissertations and theses; Head Dra NOER JIHAD SALEH; publs *Iaporan Tahunan*, *Info Pustaka*, *Warta Perpustakan*.

West Java

Perpustakaan (Pusat) Universitas Indonesia: Kampus UI, Depok 16424; tel. (21) 7864134; fax (21) 7863469; e-mail libserv@ui.edu; internet www.lib.ui.ac.id; Head of Library Dra LUKI WIJAYANTI.

Perpustakaan Pusat Institut Teknologi Bandung (Central Library, Bandung Institute of Technology): Jl. Ganesha 10, Bandung 40132; tel. (22) 2500089; fax (22) 2500089; e-mail info@lib.itb.ac.id; internet www.lib.itb.ac.id; f. 1920; colln of rare books, pamphlets and reports on Indonesia; colln on science, technology, fine arts and business; 227,000 vols, 791 current periodicals, 40,000 bound vols; Dir Dr YANNES MARTINUS PASARIBU; publ. *ITB Proceedings*.

Perpustakaan Pusat Penelitian dan Pengembangan Geologi (Library of Geological Research and Development Centre): Jl. Diponegoro 57, Bandung 40122; tel. (22) 772601; fax (22) 702669; e-mail grdc@melsa

.net.id; 11,000 vols, 904 periodicals, 4,609 maps, 11,021 reports, 9,034 reprints, 400 microfiches; Chief Librarian RINI H. MARINO.

Pusat Perpustakaan Angkatan Darat (Central Military Library): Jl. Kalimantan 6, Bandung; 36,000 vols in Central Library, and about 20,000 vols in departmental, territorial and college and office libraries; Dir Brig.-Gen. SOESATYO.

Pusat Perpustakaan Pertanian dan Komunikasi Penelitian (Indonesian Centre for Agricultural Library and Technology Dissemination): Jl. Ir Haji Juanda 20, Bogor 16122; tel. (251) 8321746; fax (251) 8326561; e-mail pustaka@pustaka-deptan.go.id; internet www.pustaka-deptan.go.id; f. 1842; 400,000 vols; Dir Ir NING PRIBADI; publs *Abstrak Hasil Penelitian Pertanian Indonesia* (Indonesian Agricultural Research Abstract, 2 a year), *Indek Biologi dan Pertanian Indonesia* (Indonesian Biology and Agricultural Index, 3 a year), *Indonesian Journal of Agriculture* (2 a year), *Indonesian Journal of Agricultural Science* (2 a year), *Jurnal Bioteknologi Pertanian* (Indonesian Journal of Agricultural Biotechnology, 2 a year), *Jurnal Penelitian dan Pengembangan Pertanian* (Indonesian Journal of Agricultural Research and Development, 2 a year).

UPT Perpustakaan Institut Pertanian Bogor (Bogor Agricultural University Library): Kampus Darmaga, POB 199, Bogor 16680; tel. (251) 8621073; fax (251) 8623166; e-mail perpustakaan@bima.ipb.ac.id; internet perpustakaan.ipb.ac.id; f. 1963; 159,000 vols, 3,500 periodicals; Head Librarian TOHA NURSALAM; publs *Forum Pasca Sarjana*, *Indonesian Journal of Tropical Agriculture*.

Yogyakarta

Perpustakaan Islam (Islamic Library): c/o Min. of Religious Affairs, Jl. Lapangan Banteng Barat 3–4, Jakarta 10710; Jl. P. Mangkubumi 38, Yogyakarta; internet www.perpustakaan-islam.com; f. 1942; attached to Min. of Religious Affairs; 70,000 vols; MSS and periodicals; Dir Drs H. ASYHURI DAHLAN; Librarian MOH. AMIEN MANSOER.

Perpustakaan Jajasan Hatta (Hatta Foundation Library): Malioboro 85, Yogyakarta; 43,000 vols; Librarian R. SOEDJAT-MIKO.

Perpustakaan Wilayah (Regional Library): Malioboro 175, Yogyakarta; f. 1949; 120,000 vols; Librarian ST. KOSTKA SOEGENG.

Museums and Art Galleries

Aceh

Museum Nanggroe Aceh Darussalam: Jl. Sultan Alaidin Mahmudsyah 12, Baiturrahman, Banda Aceh 23241; tel. (651) 23144; fax (651) 21033; f. 1915, as the House of Aceh, present name and status 2002; weaponry, household furnishings, ceremonial costumes, gold jewellery and calligraphy.

Museum Nangguor Pidie: Jl. Teuku Cik Ditiro, Sigli, Pidie Regency.

Museum Perjuangan Iskandar Muda: Jl. Kelurahan Penniti, kecamatan Baiturrahman, Banda Aceh.

Bali

Blanco Renaissance Museum: POB 80571, Ubud, Bali; tel. (361) 975502; fax (361) 975551; e-mail a-blanco@indo.net.id; internet www.blancomuseum.com; f. 1998, fmr studio of artist Antonio Blanco; collns of paintings.

Museum Bali: Jl. Letnan Kolonel Wisnu 1, Denpasar, Bali; f. 1932; exhibits of Bali culture; library of 1,970 vols, 1,605 magazines, 1,023 transcriptions of lontars (palm leaves); Dir Drs PUTU BUDIASTRA; publs *Karya Widia tak berkala, Majalah Saraswati*.

Museum Gedong Kirtya: Jl. Veteran 20, Singaraja; tel. (362) 22645; f. 1928; collns incl. ancient Balinese letters, chronicles and *kakawin* (Balinese poetry) written on palm leaves.

Museum Puri Lukisan: Jl. Raya Ubud, Ubud, Bali; e-mail info@museumpurilukisan.com; internet www.mpl-ubud.com; f. 1956, admin. by Yayasan Ratna Wartha foundation (f. 1953); colln incl. Balinese paintings and woodcarvings.

Museum Seni Agung Rai (Agung Rai Museum of Art): Jl. Pengosekan, Ubud, Gianyar 80571; tel. (361) 975742; fax (361) 975332; e-mail info@armamuseum.com; internet www.armamuseum.com; f. 1996; colln of paintings; special temporary exhibitions; theatre performances; dance, music, and painting classes; bookshop, library and reading room; cultural workshops; seminars and training programmes; centre for visual and performing arts; Chair. AGUNG RAI.

Neka Art Museum: Jl. Raya Campuhan, Kedewatan Village, Ubud, Gianyar 80571; tel. (361) 975074; fax (361) 97563; e-mail info@museumneka.com; internet www.museumneka.com; f. 1982; Dir SUTEJA NEKA.

Rudana Museum: Jl. Cok Rai Pudak 44 Peliatan, Ubud, Bali 80571; tel. (361) 975779; fax (361) 975091; e-mail info@museumrudana.com; internet www.museumrudana.com; f. 1995; Man. Dir PUTU SUPADMA RUDANA.

Central Java

Museum Jawa Tengah Ronggowarsito: Jl. Abdulrahman Saleh 1, Semarang; tel. and fax (6224) 760238; e-mail cs@museumronggowarsito.org; internet www.museumronggowarsito.org; f. 1989; collns in art, ethnography, biology, geology, ceramics and technology; Head Drs PUJI JOHARNOTO.

Museum Masjid Agung Demak: Jl. Sultan Fatah 57, Demak; tel. and fax (291) 685532; f. 1975.

Museum Soesilo Soedarman: Gentasari-Kroya, Cilacap; tel. and fax (282) 494400; f. 2000; collns of rifles, pistols and machine-guns.

Museum Tosan Aji Purworejo: Jl. Mayjend Sutoyo 10, Purworejo; collns of prehistoric artefacts in stone mortar, Hindu religious statues, yonis, statues of Shiva-Parvati.

Jakarta

Fine Art and Ceramic Museum: Jl. Pos Kota 2, West Jakarta; tel. (21) 6907062; f. built 1870, f. as Fine Arts Gallery 1976; colln of 400 items: sculpture, graphics, wood totems and batik paintings; spec. collns incl. masterpieces of Indonesian artists Hendra Gunawan, Raden Saleh; collns of ceramics from various regions.

Jakarta History Museum: Jl. Taman Fatahillah 1, West Jakarta 11110; tel. (21) 6929101; fax (21) 6902387; exhibits from prehistoric Jakarta; est. of Jayakarta in 1527; 16th-century Dutch colonization to independence of Indonesia.

Museum Listrik dan Energi Baru (Electricity and Renewable Energy Museum): Jl. Raya Taman Mini, Jakarta 13560; tel. and fax (21) 8413451; e-mail museumlistrik@yahoo.com; internet www.museumlistrik

.com; history, outdoor exhibits of electric technology; Dir Drs SOETRISNO.

Museum Nasional (National Museum): Jl. Merdeka Barat 12, Pusat Jakarta; tel. 360796; e-mail museumnasional@indo.com; internet www.museumnasional.org; f. 1778, fmrly Museum Pusat; library of 360,000 vols (now part of Nat. Library); depts of ceramics, ethnography, prehistory, classical archaeology, anthropology, MSS and education; publs subject catalogues; Dir Dr ENDANG SRI HARDIATI.

Museum Wayang (Puppet Museum): Jl. Pintu Besar Utara 27, Tamansari, West Jakarta 11110; tel. (21) 6929560; e-mail info@museumwayang.com; displays leather and wood puppets; colln of 4,000 puppets.

Textile Museum: Jl. Aipda K. S. Tubun 4, Central Jakarta; tel. (21) 5606613; f. 1975; displays traditional *kain* (skirt worn by Indonesian men and women).

North Sumatra

Museum Deli Serdang: Lubuk Pakam Kompleks Perkantoran Pemda Deli Serdang, Kelurahan Desa Jati Sari, Kecamatan, Lubuk Pakam, Deli Serdang; f. 2003; attached to Min. of Culture and Tourism.

Museum Karo Lingga: Desa Lingga Kabupaten Karo, Kelurahan Desa Lingga, Kecamatan Simpang Empat, Karo; f. 1977.

Museum Negeri Propinsi Sumatra Utara (State Museum of North Sumatra): Jl. H. M. Joni No. 51, Medan 20217; tel. (61) 7366792; fax (61) 7322220; e-mail info@museum-sumut.org; f. 1982; Museum Head Drs HARTINI.

Museum Simalungun: Jl. Sudirman 20 Pematang Siantar, Kelurahan Proklamasi, Kecamatan Siantar Barat, Siantar; tel. (622) 21954; f. 1940.

Papua

Museum Loka Budaya: Jl. Raya Abeoura-Setani, Kelurahan Hedam, Kecamatan Abepura, Kabupaten Jayapura; f. 1970; colln of 2,000 ethnographic objects of tribes in Papua.

Museum Negeri Provinsi Papua (Papua State Museum): Jl. Raya Sentani Km 17, 8 Waena-Jayapura Kelurahan Waena, Kecamatan Abepura, Kabupaten Jayapura; f. 1981; colln of 3,447 items: geology, biology, ethnography, archaeology, history, numismatics, physiology, ceramics, fine arts, human profiles, maps and dioramas.

Riau

Museum Daerah Riau Sang Nila Utama (Riau Regional Museum of Nila Utama): Jl. Jend. Sudirman 194; tel. (761) 33466; fax (761) 40195; historical relics of the Riau Province.

Museum Sultan Syarif Kasim: Jl. Jend. Sudirman, Bengkalis; collns incl. royal jewellery, hand-woven embroidery, batik fabrics.

South Sumatra

Monumen Perjuangan Rakyat (MONPERA) (People's Struggle Monument): Jl. Merdeka, Palembang 30132; tel. (711) 358514.

Museum Negeri Propinsi Sumatra Selatan (State Museum of South Sumatra): Jl. Srijaya 288, Km 5.5, Kecamatan Sukaramai, Palembang 30139; tel. (711) 411382; fax (711) 412636.

Museum Pahlawan Nasional Dr A. K. Gani (Museum of National Hero Dr A. K. Gani): Jl. MP Mangkunegara 1/RT01, Sukamaju Sako, Palembang 30168; tel. (711) 824046; exhibits related to life of Adenan Kapau Gani, leader of nat. freedom movement.

Museum Sultan Mahmud Badaruddin II: Jl. Sultan Mahmud Badaruddin II 2; tel. (711) 358450; fax (711) 352573; f. museum bldg built 1823, 2004 as museum, fmrly official home of the Dutch resident in Palembang; collns incl. numismatics, ceramics and fine arts.

West Sumatra

Museum Kereta Api Sawahlunto: Jl. Kampung Teleng, Kelurahan Pasar, Kecamatan Lembah Segar, Sawahlunto; tel. and fax (754) 61023; collns of cars, steam locomotives, communication devices; photo documentation.

Museum Mande Rubiah: Kampung Lubuk Sitepung, Nagari Lunang, Kecamatan Lunang Silaut, Kabupaten Pesisir Selatan; collns of MSS, coins, weapons, kitchen utensils, ceremonial tools, traditional wear, porcelain dishes, lamps and canes.

Museum Perjuangan Tridaya Eka Dharma: Jl. Panorama 24 Kelurahan Kayu Kubu, Kecamatan Guguk Panjang, Kecamatan Bukittinggi; collns incl. traditional tools and weapons.

Museum Rumah Kelahiran Bung Hatta: Jl. Soekarno, Hatta 37, Bukit Tinggi; tel. (752) 23503; birth home of Mohammad Hatta.

Yogyakarta

Museum Dewantara Kirti Griya: Jl. Tamansiswa 31, Yogyakarta; tel. (274) 389208; fax (274) 377120; f. 1970.

Museum Geoteknologi Mineral UPN 'Veteran' Yogyakarta: Jl. Babarsari 2, Tambakbayan, Yogyakarta; tel. (274) 486991; fax (274) 487147; e-mail museummgmt@upnyk.ac.id; internet museum.upnyk.ac.id; f. 1988.

Museum KRKB Gembira Loka: Jl. Kebun Raya 2, Yogyakarta; tel. (274) 373861; f. 1953.

Museum Monumen Pergerakan Wanita Indonesia (Museum of the Women's Movement): Jl. Laksda Adisucipto 88, Yogyakarta; tel. (274) 587818; fax (274) 520360; displays household appliances and kitchen equipment.

Museum Pusat AD 'Dharma Wiratama' (Central Army Museum): Jl. Jend. Sudirman 47, Yogyakarta; tel. and fax (274) 561417; f. 1956, present location 1982; collns of weapons, inventory, optical and communications equipment; spec. travelling exhibitions; lectures and workshops.

Museum Rumah Jawa Tembi Bantul: Jl. Parang Tritis, Km 8.4 Tembi, Timbulharjo, Sewon, Bantul, Yogyakarta; tel. (274) 368004; fax (274) 368001; f. 1999.

Museum Wayang Kekayon Yogyakarta (Kekayon Puppet Museum Yogyakarta): Jl. Yogya Wonosari, Km 7 no. 277, Yogyakarta; tel. (274) 513218; puppet masks and clothing.

Ullèn Sentalu (Javanese Culture and Art Museum): Jl. Boyong Kaliurang, Sleman, Yogyakarta; tel. (274) 880158; fax (274) 881743; internet www.ullensentalu.com; f. 1994; art heritage wealth, culture and history from the Javanese civilization.

State Universities

INSTITUT PERTANIAN BOGOR
(Bogor Agricultural University)

Jl. Lingkar Akademik, Kampus IPB Darmaga, Bogor 16680

Telephone: (251) 622642
Fax: (251) 622708

Internet: www.ipb.ac.id

Founded 1963
State control
Languages of instruction: Indonesian, English(for foreign visiting professors)
Academic year: September to June (two semesters)

Rector: Dr Ir HENRY SUHARDIYANTO
Vice-Rector for Academic Affairs and Student Affairs: Prof. Dr Ir H. YONNY KUSMARYONO
Vice Rector for Business and Communication: Dr Ir H. ARIF IMAN SUROSO
Vice-Rector for Resources and Devt: Prof. Dr Ir HERMANTO SIREGAR
Vice-Rector for Research and Collaboration: Dr Ir H. MIFTAH ANAS FAUZI
Registrar: Dr SETYO PERTIWI
Administrator: Ir UDIN M. WAHJUDIN
Librarian: Ir TOHA NURSALAM

Number of teachers: 1,327
Number of students: 19,440

Publications: *Buletin Hama dan Penyakit Tumbuhan, Buletin Ilmu Tanah, Communication Agriculture, Feed and Nutrition Journal, Forum Pasca Sarjana, Gema Penelitian, Indonesian Journal of Tropical Agriculture, Jurnal Ilmu Pertanian Indonesian, Jurnal Primatologi, Media Konservasi, Media Peternakan, Media Veteriner, Teknologi*

DEANS

Faculty of Agriculture: Prof. Dr M. CHOSIN
Faculty of Agricultural Technology: Prof. Dr M. BAMBANG PRAMUDYA NOORACHMAT
Faculty of Animal Science: Prof. Dr H. SOEDARMADI
Faculty of Economics and Management: Prof. Dr BUNASOR SANIM
Faculty of Fisheries and Marine Science: Dr E. HARIS
Faculty of Forestry: Prof. Dr YUSUF SUDOHADI
Faculty of Mathematics and Natural Sciences: Dr SISWADI
Faculty of Veterinary Medicine: Dr F. H. PASARIBU

INSTITUT SENI INDONESIA SURAKARTA
(Indonesia Institute of the Arts Surakarta)

Jl. ki Hajar Dewantara 19, Kentingan, Jebres, Surakarta 57126

Telephone: (271) 647658
Fax: (271) 646175
E-mail: direct@isi-ska.ac.id
Internet: www.isi-ska.ac.id

Founded 1965 as Akademi Seni Karawitan Indonesia (ASKI), merged with Akademi Seni Tari Indonesia (ASTI) to form Sekolah Tinggi Seni Indonesia Surakarta 1983, present status 2006
Public control

Rector: Prof. Dr T. SLAMET SUPARNO

Library of 36,588 vols
Number of teachers: 203
Number of students: 852

INSTITUT SENI INDONESIA YOGYAKARTA
(Indonesia Institute of the Arts Yogyakarta)

Jl. Parangtritis Km 6.5, POB 1210, Yogyakarta 55188

Telephone: (274) 373659
Fax: (274) 371233
E-mail: arts@isi.ac.id
Internet: www.isi.ac.id

Founded 1984, univ. status, fmrly known as Institut Seni Indonesia Yogyakarta
Language of instruction: Indonesian

Academic year: September to June
Rector: Drs SOEPRAPTO SOEDJONO
Vice-Rector for Academic Affairs: Prof. Dr A. M. HERMIN KUSMAYATI
Vice-Rector for Admin. and Financial Affairs: Drs SISWADI
Vice-Rector for Students Affairs: Drs SYAFRUDDIN
Registrar: G. BUDI PRIYATMO
Librarian: Dra HERLIN NOVIAR SUBARYANTI

Library of 44,368 vols
Number of teachers: 329
Number of students: 1,922

Publications: *ARS, Visual Arts Journal, EKSPRESI, Research Journal, FENOMEN, Research Journal, RESITAL, Performing Arts Journal, REKAM, Recorded Media Arts Journal, SENI, Journal for the Arts* (4 a year), *SURYA SENI, Postgraduate Journal*

DEANS
Faculty of Performing Arts: Drs TRIYONO BRAMANTYO PAMUDJO SANTOSO
Faculty of Recorded Media Arts: Drs ALEX ANDRI LUTHFI R.
Faculty of Visual Arts: Dr M. AGUS BURHAN

INSTITUT TEKNOLOGI BANDUNG
(Bandung Institute of Technology)

Jl. Tamansari 64, Bandung 40116
Jl. Ganesha 10, Bandung 40132

Telephone: (22) 2500935
E-mail: webmaster@itb.ac.id
Internet: www.itb.ac.id

Founded 1920, present form 1959 as a merger of the faculties of mathematics, natural sciences and engineering of the Univ. of Indonesia
State control
Language of instruction: Indonesian
Academic year: August to July

Rector: Prof. Dr Ir DJOKO SANTOSO
Vice-Rector for Academic Affairs: Dr Ir ADANG SURAHMAN
Vice-Rector for Gen. Admin.: Prof. Dr Ir DJOKO SANTOSO
Vice-Rector for Devt, Planning, Admin. and Information Systems: Dr Ir RIZAL ZAINUDDIN TAMIN
Librarian: Dr Ir ROBERT MANURUNG

Number of teachers: 1,263
Number of students: 15,031

Publications: *Akta Farmasetika Indonesia* (12 a year), *Buletin Geologi* (3 a year), *Geodesi dan Surveying* (2 a year), *Journal of Mathematics and Science* (2 a year), *Journal Pusat Pengembangan Perencanaan Wilayah Kota* (1 a year), *Jurnal Atap* (1 a year), *Jurnal Teknik dan Manajemen Industri* (3 a year), *Jurnal Teknik Lingkungan* (2 a year), *Jurnal Teknik Sipil* (4 a year), *Jurnal Teknologi Mineral* (3 a year), *Kontribusi Fisika* (4 a year), *Maalah Ilmiah Himpunan Matematika Indonesia* (2 a year), *Majalah Ilmiah Teknik Electro* (3 a year), *Majalah Mesin* (3 a year)

DEANS

Faculty of Civil Engineering and Planning: Prof. Dr Ir TOMMY FIRMAN
Faculty of Fine Arts and Design: Drs SETIAWAN SABANA
Faculty of Industrial Technology: Prof. Dr Ir DJOKO SUJARTO
Faculty of Mathematics and Natural Sciences: Dr Ing. CYNTHIA LINAYA RADIMAN
Faculty of Mineral Technology: Prof. Dr Ir MADE EMMY RELAWAT
Graduate Programme: Prof. Dr Ir SOELARSO (Dir)

School of Business and Management: Prof.
Dr SURNA TJAHJA DJAJADININGRAT

PROFESSORS

ACHMAD, S. A., Chemistry
AGOES, G., Pharmacy
ALGAMAR, K., Environmental Engineering
ANSJAR, M., Mathematics
ARIFIN, A., Mathematics
ARISMUNANDAR, W., Mechanical Engineering
ASIKIN, S., Geology
BAGIASNA, K., Mechanical Engineering
BARMAWI, M., Physics
BINTORO, S. B., City Planning
BRODJONEGRO, S. S., Mechanical Engineering
BROTOSISWOJO, B. S., Physics
CHATIB, B., Environmental Engineering
DHANUTIRTO, H., Pharmacy
DIRAN, O., Mechanical Engineering
DJAJADININGRAT, A. H., Environmental
Engineering
DJAJADININGRAT, S. T., Industrial Engineering
DJAJAPUTRA, A. A., Civil Engineering
DJAJASUGITA, F. A., Electrical Engineering
DJALARI, Y. A., Design
DJAUHARI, M. A., Mathematics
DJOJODIHARDJO, H., Mechanical Engineering
FIRMAN, K., Pharmacy
FIRMAN, T., City Planning
GANI, A. Z., Industrial Engineering
GDE RAKA, I. D., Industrial Engineering
HANDOJO, A., Engineering Physics
HARAHAP, F., Mechanical Engineering
HARJOSUPARTO, S., Chemical Engineering
HARLANDJA, B., Civil Engineering
HAROEN, Y., Electrical Engineering
HARSOKOESOEMO, D., Mechanical Engineering
HENDRADJAYA, L., Physics
HIDAYAT, B., Astronomy
JENJIE, S. D., Mechanical Engineering
KAHAR, J., Geodesy
KAMIL, S., Mechanical Engineering
KANA, J. C., Petroleum Engineering
KARSA, K., Electrical Engineering
KOESOEMADINATA, R. P., Geology
KUSBIANTORO, City Planning
LIANG, O. B., Chemistry
LIONG, T. H., Physics
MANGUNWIJAYA, A., Mining Engineering
MARDIHARTANTO, F. X., Industrial Engineering
MARDISEWOJO, P., Petroleum Engineering
MARTODJOJO, S., Geology
MARTOJO, W., Mining Engineering
MERATI, I. G. W., Civil Engineering
MIRA, S., Geodesy
NABANAN, S. M., Mathematics
ON, T. M., Physics
PADMAWINATA, K., Pharmacy
PIROUS, A. D., Design
PRINGGOPRAWIRO, H., Geology
PRINGGOPRAWIRO, M., Physics
PRODJOSOEMARTO, P., Mining Engineering
PULUNGGONO, A., Geology
RAHAYU, S. I., Chemistry
RAIS, J., Geodesy
RELAWATYI, S. E., Geology
RIDWAN, A. S., Civil Engineering
SAMADIKUN, S., Electrical Engineering
SAMPURNO, Geology
SANTOSO, D., Geophysics
SAPIIE, S., Electrical Engineering
SASMOJO, S., Chemical Engineering
SASTRAMIHARDJA, I., Chemical Engineering
SASTRODIHARDJO, S., Biology
SATIADARMA, K., Pharmacy
SEMBIRING, R. K., Mathematics
SILABAN, P., Physics
SIRAIT, K. T., Electrical Engineering
SIREGAR, C., Pharmacy
SIREGAR, H. P. S., Petroleum Engineering
SISWOSUWARNO, M., Mechanical Engineering
SJAFRUDDIN, A., Civil Engineering
SJUIB, F., Pharmacy

SLAMET, J. S., Environmental Engineering
SOEDIRO, I., Pharmacy
SOEDJITO, B. B., City Planning
SOEGIJANTO, R. M., Engineering Physics
SOEGIJOKO, S., Electrical Engineering
SOELARSO, Mechanical Engineering
SOEMARSO, M., Environmental Engineering
SOEMINTAPOERA, K., Electrical Engineering
SOEMODINOTO, W., Mining Engineering
SOENARKO, B., Engineering Physics
SOEPANGKAT, H. P., Physics
SOERIA-ATMADJA, R., Geology
SOERIAATMADJA, R. E., Biology
SUDARWATI, S., Biology
SUDIRMAN, I., Industrial Engineering
SUDRADJAT, I., Architecture
SUHARTO, D., Mechanical Engineering
SUHUD, R., Civil Engineering
SUJARTO, D., City Planning
SUKARMADIJAYA, H., Environmental Engineering
SULE, D., Mining Engineering
SUMAWIGANDA, S., Civil Engineering
SURAATMADJA, D., Civil Engineering
SURDIA, N. M., Chemistry
SURDIA, T., Metallurgical Engineering
SUTJIATMO, B., Mechanical Engineering
SUWONO, A., Mechanical Engineering
TABRANI, P., Design
TAROEPRATJEKA, H., Industrial Engineering
TJAHJATI, S. B., City Planning
TOHA, I. S., Industrial Engineering
TUAH, H., Civil Engineering
UMAR, F., Mining Engineering
WANGSADINATA, W., Civil Engineering
WARDIMAN, A., Engineering Physics
WAWOROENTOE, W. J., City Planning
WIDAGDO, Design
WIDODO, R. J., Electrical Engineering
WIRASONJAYA, S., Architecture
WIRJOMARTONO, S. H., Mechanical Engineering
WIRJOSUMARTO, H., Mechanical Engineering
WISJNUPRAPTO, Environmental Engineering
ZAINUDDIN, I. M., Design
ZEN, M. T., Geology

INSTITUT TEKNOLOGI SEPULUH NOPEMBER
(Technology Institute of Sepuluh Nopember)

POB 900/SB, Surabaya 60008, East Java
Located at: Kampus ITS, Sukolilo, Surabaya 60111, East Java

Telephone and fax (31) 5923411
E-mail: int_off@its.ac.id
Internet: www.its.ac.id

Founded 1960
State control
Language of instruction: Indonesian
Academic year: September to June

Rector: Dr Ir PRIYO SUPROBO
Vice-Rector for Academic Affairs: Prof. Ir NOOR ENDAH B. MOCTAR
Vice-Rector for Admin.: Ir R. SYARIF WIDJAYA
Vice-Rector for Student Affairs: Dr Ir ACHMAD JAZIDIE
Head of the Academic Admin. and Student Affairs Bureau: Drs HARRY SANTOSO
Head of the Admin. Planning and Information System Bureau: Ir ARIE KISMANTO
Head of the Gen. Admin. and Finance Bureau: NURIJATI HAMID
Librarian: Drs ACHMAD

Library of 45,994 vols
Number of teachers: 1,043
Number of students: 17,384

Publications: Berita ITS, Iptek, various faculty bulletins

DEANS

Faculty of Civil Engineering and Planning: Prof. Dr Ir PRIYO SUPROBO

Faculty of Industrial Technology: Dr Ir TRIYOGI YUWONO
Faculty of Information Technology: Prof. Ir ARIEF DJUNAIDI
Faculty of Mathematics and Sciences: Prof. Dr SUASMORO
Faculty of Ocean Engineering: Ir ASJHAR IMRON

DIRECTORS

Polytechnic of Electronics: Dr Ir TITON DUTONO
Polytechnic of Ship Building: Ir SUWARNO TAHID
Research and Public Service Institute: Prof. Ir I. NYOMAN SUTANTRA

PROFESSORS

ALTWAY, A., Chemical Engineering
ANWAR, N., Civil Engineering
BAKTIR, A., Chemical Engineering
DJANALI, S., Informatics Engineering
DJUNAIDY, A., Information System Engineering
ERSAM, T., Chemical Engineering
HADI, W., Environmental Engineering
KOESTALAM, P., Civil Engineering
LINUWIH, S., Statistics
MOCHTAR, I. B., Civil Engineering
MOCHTAR, N. E., Civil Engineering
NUH, M., Electrical Engineering
NURSUHUD, D., Mechanical Engineering
PENANGSANG, H. O., Electrical Engineering
PRATIKTO, W. A., Ocean Engineering
PURNOMO, M. H., Electrical Engineering
PURWONO, R., Structural Engineering
PUTU RAKA, I. G., Civil Engineering
RACHIMOELLAH, M., Chemistry
RAMELAN, R., Mechanical Engineering
RENANTO, Chemical Engineering
SANTOSA, M., Architecture
SANTOSO, H. R., Architecture
SARNO, R., Informatics Engineering
SILAS, J., Architecture
SOEBAGIO, Electrical Engineering
SOEGIONO, Ocean Engineering
SUASMORO, H., Physics
SUKARDJONO, S., Electrical Engineering
SUPROBO, P., Civil Engineering
SUTANTRA, N., Mechanical Engineering
SUTRISNO, H., Electrical Engineering
SUWARNO, J., Chemical Engineering
SUWARNO, N., Chemical Engineering
TJANDRASA, H., Informatics Engineering
WAHYUDI, H., Civil Engineering

UNIVERSITAS AIRLANGGA
(Airlangga University)

Jl. Mulorejo, Kampus C, Surabaya 60115
Telephone: (31) 5914042
Fax: (31) 5981841
E-mail: sekretaris_ua@unair.ac.id
Internet: www.unair.ac.id

Founded 1954
Language of instruction: Indonesian
Academic year: September to August

Rector: Prof. Dr Dr D. H. FASICH
Vice-Rector for Academic and Learning, Research and Public Service: Prof. Dr MUHAMAD ZAINUDDIN
Vice-Rector for General Admin.: Dr MUSLICH ANSHORI
Vice-Rector for Information and Student Affairs: Dr SUNARKO SETYAWAN
Chief, Bureau for General Academic Admin. and Student Affairs: Dr ZAINAL ARIFIN
Chief, Bureau for General Admin.: Dra Hj. SUNARTI
Chief, Bureau for Planning Admin. and Information Systems: ROSMELYANI
Librarian: RR. RATNANINGSIH

Number of teachers: 1,434
Number of students: 20,719

Publications: *Buletin Toraks Kardiovaskular Indonesia* (4 a year), *Folia Medika Indonesiana* (4 a year), *Majalah Kedokteran Gigi* (4 a year), *Majalah Kedokteran Surabaya* (4 a year), *Majalah Kedokteran Tropis Indonesia* (4 a year), *Majalah Kesehatan Masyarakat* (4 a year), *Majalah Masyarakat Kebudayaan Politik* (4 a year), *Surabaya Journal of Surgery* (4 a year), *Yuridika* (4 a year)

DEANS

Faculty of Dentistry: Prof. Dr Drg. MOHAMAD RUBIANTO
Faculty of Economics: Drs KARJADI MINTAROEM
Faculty of Law: H. MACHSOEN ALI
Faculty of Letters: Prof. HERU SUPRIYADI
Faculty of Mathematics and Natural Sciences: Drs H. ABDUL LATIEF BURHAN
Faculty of Medicine: Prof. Dr Dr H. M. S. WIYADI
Faculty of Pharmacy: Prof. Dr NOOR CHOLIES ZAINI
Faculty of Psychology: Prof. Dr H. M. ZAINUDIN
Faculty of Public Health: Dr Dr TJIPTO SUWANDI
Faculty of Social and Political Sciences: Dr Drs HOTMAN SIAHAAN
Faculty of Veterinary Medicine: Dr Drh. ISMUDIONO
Postgraduate Programmes: Prof. Dr Dr H. MUHAMMAD AMIN

UNIVERSITAS ANDALAS

Kampus Limau Manis, Padang 25163
Telephone: (751) 71181
Fax: (751) 71508
Internet: www.unand.ac.id
Founded 1956
Language of instruction: Indonesian
Academic year: September to June

Rector: MARLIS RAHMAN
Vice-Rector for Academic Affairs: AMIRMUSLIM MALIK
Vice-Rector for Admin. and Finance: DJASWIR ZEIN
Vice-Rector for Student Affairs: FIRMAN HASAN
Head Librarian: MARAMIS

Number of teachers: 1,396
Number of students: 13,009

Publications: *Andalas Medical Journal, Jurnal Antropologi, Jurnal Ekonomi Manajemen, Jurnal Matematika dan Ilmu Pengetahuan Alam, Jurnal Pembangunan dan Perubahan Sosial Budaya, Jurnal Penelitian Andalas, Jurnal Peternakan dan Lingkungan, Jurnal Teknologi Pertanian (Journal of Agricultural Technology), Justisia, Lingua: Jurnal Bahasa dan Sastra, Potetika, Teknika, Warta Pengabdian Andalas*

DEANS

Faculty of Agriculture: BUJANG RUSMAN
Faculty of Animal Husbandry: AZINAR KAMARUDDIN
Faculty of Arts: SYAFRUDDIN SULAIMAN
Faculty of Economics: SJAFRIZAL
Faculty of Engineering: DAHNIL ZAINUDDIN
Faculty of Law and Social Science: AZHAR RAUF
Faculty of Mathematics and Natural Sciences: HAZLI NURDIN
Faculty of Medicine: RUSDAN DJAMIL
Faculty of Political and Social Sciences: DAHRUL DAHLAN
Polytechnic of Agriculture: MASRUL JALAL
Polytechnic of Engineering: ALIZAR HASAN

UNIVERSITAS BENGKULU
(University of Bengkulu)

Jl. Raya Kandang Limun, Bengkulu 38371
Telephone: (736) 21170
Fax: (736) 22105
Internet: www.unib.ac.id
Founded 1982
Rector: Dr Ir SOEKOTJO
Chief Admin. Officer: SYAIFUL AKHMAD
Librarian: Mrs ROSDIANAH ASSAUDI

Library of 20,600 vols
Number of teachers: 444
Number of students: 3,320

DEANS

Faculty of Agriculture: TOEKIDJO MARTOREJO
Faculty of Economics: ILYAS YAKUB
Faculty of Education: AZNAM YATIM
Faculty of Law: HIDJAZIE K.
Faculty of Social Sciences: HASNUL BASRI

UNIVERSITAS BRAWIJAYA

Jl. Veteran, Malang, Jawa Timur 65145
Telephone: (341) 575777
Fax: (341) 565420
E-mail: rektorat@brawijaya.ac.id
Internet: www.brawijaya.ac.id
Founded 1963
State control
Language of instruction: Indonesian
Academic year: September to August

Rector: Prof. Dr Ir YOGI SUGITO
Vice-Rector: Prof. Dr BAMBANG SUHARTO
Vice-Rector: Drs WARKUM SUMITRO
Vice-Rector: Prof. Dr H. R. B. AINURRASYID
Head of Gen. Admin. Bureau: GOERID HARDJITO
Head of Planning and Information System Bureau: Dra Hj. SITI ROMLAH
Head of Student and Academic Admin. Bureau: Dra Haja SITI ROMLAH
Librarian: Dra WELMIN SUNYI ARININGSIH

Number of teachers: 1,271
Number of students: 28,105

Publications: *Administrator* (12 a year), *Agrivita* (12 a year), *Agrotek* (4 a year), *Aqua* (4 a year), *Arena Hukum* (12 a year), *Buletin* (12 a year), *Canopy* (12 a year), *Dian* (12 a year), *Diagnostika* (1 a year), *Febra* (12 a year), *Habitat* (3 a year), *Indicus* (12 a year), *Indikator* (12 a year), *Jurnal* (2 a year), *Jurnal Administrasi Bisnis* (2 a year), *Jurnal Administrasi Negara* (2 a year), *Jurnal Ilmu Peternakan* (2 a year), *Jurnal Penelitian Ilmu—Ilmu Hayati* (2 a year), *Jurnal Penelitian Ilmu—Ilmu Sosial* (2 a year), *Jurnal Penelitian Ilmu—Ilmu Teknik* (2 a year), *Jurnal Teknik* (3 a year), *Jurnal Teknologi Pertanian* (2 a year), *Lintasan Ekonomi* (2 a year), *Mafaterna* (2 a year), *Majalah Kedokteran Universitas Brawijaya* (3 a year), *Manifest* (2 a year), *Media Karya Ilmiah* (2 a year), *Mimbar Universitas Brawijaya* (6 a year), *Mitra Akademika* (2 a year), *Natural Jurnal* (2 a year), *Prasetya* (48 a year), *Solid* (2 a year), *Techno* (2 a year), *Wartamina* (6 a year)

DEANS

Faculty of Administrative Sciences: Dr SUHADAK
Faculty of Agriculture: Prof. Dr Ir SYEKHFANI
Faculty of Agricultural Technology: Prof. Dr Ir SIMON BAMBANG WIDJANARKO
Faculty of Animal Husbandry: Prof. Dr Ir IFAR SUBAGIYO
Faculty of Economics: Prof. Dr BAMBANG SUBROTO
Faculty of Engineering: Ir IMAM ZAKY
Faculty of Fishery: Ir SUKOSO
Faculty of Law: WARKUM SUMITRO

Faculty of Medicine: Dr HARIJANTO
Faculty of Natural Science and Mathematics: Ir ADAM WIRYAWAN
Faculty of Polytechnic: Ir BUDI TJAHJONO
Postgraduate Studies Programme: Prof. Dr Dr DJANGGAN SARGOWO

PROFESSORS

ACHMAD, H., Medicine
ACHMADY, Z. A., Administration
ACHMANU, Animal Husbandry
ALHABSJI, T., Administration
ALI, M. M., Medicine
ARIFFIN, Aeroclimatology
ASHARI, M. S., Agriculture
ASTUTI, M. S., Law
BAISOENI, H., Mathematics
CHUZAEMI, S., Animal Husbandry
FADJAR, A. M., Law
FANANI, Z., Animal Husbandry
FAUZI, A., Administration
GINTING, E., Animal Husbandry
GURITNO, B., Agriculture
HADIASTONO, T., Agriculture
HAIRIAH, K., Agriculture
HAKIM, L., Animal Husbandry
HANDAYANTO, E., Agriculture
HARIJONO, Agricultural Technology
HARSONO, O. S. H., Economics
HIDAYAT, A., Medicine
HIDAYAT, M., Medicine
ICHSAN, M., Administration
IDRUS, M. S., Economics
ISLAMY, M. I., Administration
ISMANI, Administration
KALIM, H., Medicine
KIPTIYAH, S. M., Economics
KOENTJOKO, Animal Husbandry
KUMALANINGSIH, S., Agricultural Technology
LOEKITO, R. M., Medicine
LUTH, T., Law
MARTAWIJAYA, S., Economic Development
MIMBAR, S. M., Agriculture
MISMAIL, B., Electrical Engineering
MOELJADI, H., Economics
MOENANDIR, J., Agriculture
MUNIR, M., Agriculture
MUNIR, M., Law
MUSTADJAB, M. M., Agriculture
NIMRAN, U., Administration
NUGROHO, W. H., Mathematics
PURNOMO, H., Animal Husbandry
RASYID, Y., Agriculture
RUBAI, M., Law
SALEH, M., Economics
SARGOWO, D., Medicine
SASTRAHIDAYAT, I. R., Agriculture
SEMAOEN, M. I., Agriculture
SITOMPUL, S. M., Agriculture
SJAMSUDDIN, S., Administration
SODIKI, A., Law
SOEBAKTININGSIH, Medicine
SOEBARINOTO, Animal Husbandry
SOEHONO, L. A., Mathematics
SOEKARTAWI, Agriculture
SOEMARNO, Agriculture
SOEPARMAN, S., Engineering
SOEPRAPTO, R., Administration
SOETANTO, H., Animal Husbandry
SOEWARTO, S., Medicine
SUBROTO, B., Accounting
SUDARMA, M. S., Accounting
SUGIJANTO, Agriculture
SUGITO, Y., Agriculture
SUHARDJONO, Research Methodology
SUHARTO, B., Agricultural Technology
SUKESI, K., Agriculture
SULISTYOWATI, L., Agriculture
SUMITRO, S. B., Agricultural Technology
SUNUHARYO, B. S., Administration
SUPRIYANTO, E., Fisheries
SUSANTO, M. H., Economics
SUSANTO, T., Agricultural Technology
SYAFRADJI, M. S., Economics
SYAMSIDI, S. R. C., Agriculture
SYAMSULBAHRI, Agriculture

SYEKHFANI, Agriculture
THANTAWI, Economics
TRIADJI, B., Economics
TRISUNUWATI, P., Epidemiology
TROENA, E. A., Economics
UTOMO, W. H., Agriculture
WAHAB, S. A., Administration
WARDANA, N. G., Engineering
WARDIYATI, T., Agriculture
WIDJANARKO, S. B., Agricultural Technology
WIDODO, M. A., Medicine
ZAIN, D., Economics

UNIVERSITAS CENDERAWASIH

Jl. Kamp Wolker, Kampus UNCEN Waena, Jayapura, Papua 99358

Telephone: (967) 572108
Fax: (967) 572102
E-mail: uncen@uncen.ac.id
Internet: www.uncen.ac.id

Founded 1962
Language of instruction: Indonesian
Academic year: September to July

Rector: Ir FRANS A. WOSPAKRIK
Vice-Rector: Drs ISAAK AJOMI
Vice-Rector: Drs DAAN DIMARA
Vice-Rector: Ir ROBERT LALENOH
Gen. Admin. Officer: Ir H. SUMANTO
Academic and Student Admin. Officer: Drs M. HATTU
Librarian: Drs A. C. SUNGKANA HADI

Library of 56,000 vols
Number of teachers: 519
Number of students: 6,789

Publications: *Bulletin of Irian Jaya Development, Tifa Agro*

Faculties of agriculture, civil engineering, economics, education and teacher training, law, mathematics, natural sciences, social and political sciences.

UNIVERSITAS DIPONEGORO
(Diponegoro University)

Jl. Prof. Sudarto, Tembalang, Semarang 50275

Telephone: (24) 7460014
Fax: (24) 7460013
Internet: www.undip.ac.id

Founded 1956
Academic year: September to August

Rector: Prof. Ir EKO BUDIHARDJ
Vice-Rector for Academic Affairs: Prof. Dr S. P. HADI
Vice-Rector for Admin. and Finance: Prof. Dr Ir Y. S. DARMANTO
Vice-Rector for Devt and Collaboration: Dr Dr SUSILO WIBOWO
Vice-Rector for Student Affairs: Dr Ir BAMBANG TRIONO BASUKI
Head of Admin. and Academic Bureau: Drs PRIYO SANTOSO
Head of Gen. Admin. Bureau: Dra KUSRINI
Head of Planning Admin. and Information Systems Bureau: Dra ISMARTINI
Head of Student Admin. Bureau: Dra PRANTIKASIH
University Librarian: Dra ARI WIDJAYANTI

Library of 191,224 vols
Number of teachers: 1,618
Number of students: 38,522

Publications: *Berita Penelitian, Berita UNDIP, Bhakti, Buletin Fekom, Bulletin Dharma Wanita, Bulletin Fakultas Peternakan & Perikanan, Cakrawala, Edent, Forum, Gallery, Gema, Gema Keadilan, Gema Teknologi, Hayam Wuruk, Ilmiah Politeknik, Info, Kinetika, Konsolidasi, Lembaran Imu Sastra, Mahaprika, Majalah, Majalah Kedokteran, Manunggal, Masalah-Masalah Hukum, Masalah Teknik, Media, Media Ekonomi & Bisnis,*

Nuansa, Opini, Prasasti, Publica, Pulsa, Respect, Teknis, Transient, UNDIP Newsletter, Warta Perpustakaan, Zigma

DEANS

Faculty of Animal Husbandry: Dr Ir BAMBANG SRIGANDONO
Faculty of Economics: Dr H. M. CHABACHIB
Faculty of Engineering: Prof. Ir EKO WAHYUNI
Faculty of Fisheries and Marine Science: Prof. Dr Ir YOHANES HUTALIRAT
Faculty of Law: ACHMAD BUSRO
Faculty of Letters: Prof. Dr RAHAYU PRIHATMI
Faculty of Mathematics and Natural Sciences: Dr Drs WALIYU SETIA RUDI
Faculty of Medicine: Prof. Dr KABULRACHMAN
Faculty of Public Health: Dr LUDFI SANTOSO
Faculty of Social and Political Sciences: Drs WARSITO

DIRECTORS

Community Service Institute: Drs SUWARSO
Education Development Institute: Drs YUSMILARSO
Research Institute: Prof. Dr Dr I. RIWANTO

PROFESSORS

ANGGORO, S., Aquatic Biology
ATMOMARSONO, U., Animal Science
BUDIHARDJO, E., Architecture
BUDI PRAYITNO, S., Aquaculture
DARMANTO, Y. S., Fisheries Resources
DARMONO, S., Nutrition
DJOKO MOELJANTO, S., Internal Medicine
DJULIATI SUROYO, A. M., Social and Economic History
FAIK HEYDER, A., Surgery
FATIMA MUIS, S., Nutrition
GHOZALI, I., Methodology
HADIHARDAJA, J., Steel Construction
HADISAPUTRO, S., Public Health
HARRY KISTANO, N., Letters
HARTONO, B., Neurology
HARTONO, S. R., Commercial Law
HUTABARAT, S., Oceanography
HUTABARAT, Y., Aquatic Culture
KABULRACHMAN, Dermatovenerology
KARYANA, S., Traditional Javanese Culture
KELIB, A., Islamic Law
KRISTIANTI, L., Paediatrics
MANGUNWIHARDJO, S., Financial Management
MIYASTO, Economics
MULADI, H., Criminal Law
MUSTAFID, Mathematics
NASUTION, I., Pharmacology and Theraputics
NAWAWI ARIEF, B., Criminal Law
NOTOATMOJO, H., Paediatrics
PARSUDI ABDULROCHIM, I., Internal Medicine
P. HADI, S., Environmental Studies
PRAMONO, N., Obstetrics and Gynaecology
PRAPTOHARDJO, U., Gynaecology and Obstetrics
PRIHATMI, M. S. R., Literature
RACHMATULLAH, P., Physiology
RAHAYU PRIHATMI, S., Literature
REDJEKI, H. S., Law
RIWANTO, Surgery
SARJADI, H., Anatomy, Pathology
SATOTO, Nutrition
SERIKAT PUTRAJAYA, N., Criminal Law
SOEBOWO, Anatomy, Pathology
SOEDARSONO, Animal Production
SOEDJARWO, Indonesian Literature
SOEDJATI, Linguistics
SOEJOENOES, A., Obstetrics and Gynaecology
SOEMANTRI, A., Paediatrics, Haematology
SOENARTO, S., Internal Medicine
SOETOMO, I., Linguistics
SOETOMO, S., Planology
S. TRASTOTENOJO, M., Paediatrics
SUDARYONO, Linguistics
SUDIGBIA, Paediatrics
SUGANGGA, Proscriptive Law
SULTANA, A., Histology

SUNARJO, S., Anaesthiology
SUNARTI, D., Animal Production
SUPRIHARYONO, A., Fishery
SURYANTO, B., Agribusiness Management
SUSANTO, I. S., Criminal Law
SUTRISNO, I., Animal Husbandry
SYA'RANI, L., Fishery
WARASIH, E., Law and Society
WARELLA, Y., Sociology and Politics
WIBOWO, S., Andrology
WILARDJO, S., Ophthalmology

UNIVERSITAS GADJAH MADA

Bulaksumur, Yogyakarta 55281

Telephone: (274) 588688
Fax: (274) 565223
E-mail: rektor@ugm.ac.id
Internet: www.ugm.ac.id

Founded 1949
Language of instruction: Indonesian
Academic year: September to June

Rector: Prof. Ir SUDJARWADI
Senior Vice Rector for Academic, Research, and Community Service: Prof. Dr Ir SUDJARWADI
Sr Vice-Rector for Admin., Finance and Human Resources Devt: Ir AINUN NA'IM
Vice-Rector for Students, Alumni and Business Develt: Prof. Dr Ir ZAENAL BACHARUDDIN
Exec. Sec.: Drs DJOKO MOERDIYANTO

Number of teachers: 2,273
Number of students: 55,000

Publications: *Agritech* (agricultural technology, 4 a year), *Berita Kedokteran Masyarakat* (medicine, 4 a year), *Berkala Ilmiah MIPA* (mathematics and natural sciences, 2 a year), *Berkala Ilmu Kedokteran* (medicine, 4 a year), *Biologi* (biology, 2 a year), *Buletin Kehutanan* (forestry, 4 a year), *Buletin Peternakan* (animal husbandry, 4 a year), *Forum Teknik* (engineering, 3 a year), *Humaniora* (humanities, 4 a year), *Indonesian Food and Nutrition Progress* (2 a year), *Indonesian Journal of Geography* (2 a year), *Jurnal Fisika Indonesia* (mathematics and natural sciences, 4 a year), *Majalah Farmasi Indonesia* (pharmacy, 4 a year), *Majalah Geografi Indonesia* (geography, 2 a year), *Manusia dan Lingkungan* (environmental studies, 3 a year), *Media Teknik* (engineering, 4 a year), *Perlindungan Tanaman Indonesia* (agricultural technology, 2 a year), *Warta Pengabdian* (community service, 3 a year)

DEANS

Faculty of Agricultural Technology: Dr Ir DJAGAL WISESO MARSENO
Faculty of Agriculture: Prof. Ir TRIWIBOWO YUWONO
Faculty of Animal Science: Prof. Dr Ir TRI YUWANTA
Faculty of Biology: Dr RETNO PENI SANCAYANINGSIH
Faculty of Cultural Sciences: Dr IDA ROCHANI ADI
Faculty of Dentistry: Drg. SOEHARDONO
Faculty of Economics: Prof. MARWAN ASRI
Faculty of Engineering: Ir TUMIRAN
Faculty of Forestry: Prof. Dr Ir MOCHAMMAD NA'IEM
Faculty of Geography: Prof. Dr SURATMAN
Faculty of Law: Prof. Dr MARSUDI TRIATMODJO
Faculty of Mathematics and Natural Sciences: Dr CHAIRIL ANWAR
Faculty of Medicine: Prof. Dr ALI GHUFRON MUKTI
Faculty of Pharmacy: Prof. Dr MARCHABAN
Faculty of Philosophy: Dr M. MUKHTASAR SYAMSUDDIN

Faculty of Psychology: Prof. Dr FATUROCH-MAN

Faculty of Social and Political Sciences: Prof. Dr PRATIKNO

Faculty of Veterinary Medicine: Prof. Dr Drh. BAMBANG SUMIARTO MOECHAROM

Graduate Programmes: Prof. Dr HARTONO

UNIVERSITAS HALUOLEO

Kampus Bumi Tridharma Anduonohu, Kendari, Sulawesi Tenggara 93232

Telephone: (401) 25104

Fax: (401) 22006

Founded 1981

Academic year: September to June

Rector: Prof. Dr Ir H. SOLEH SOLAHUDDIN

Vice-Rector: Drs SULEMAN

Vice-Rector: Drs H. AHMAD BAKKARENG

Vice-Rector: Drs LA ODE MUH. ARSYAD TENO

Vice-Rector: Drs H. ALIBAS YUSUF

Librarian: Drs L. HAISU

Library of 43,342 vols

Number of teachers: 452

Number of students: 9,029

Publications: *Agri Plus* (6 a year), *Gema Pendidikan* (6 a year), *Journal Haluoleo* (4 a year), *Majalah Ekonomi* (6 a year), *Sosial Politik* (6 a year)

DEANS

Faculty of Agriculture: Ir H. MAHMUD HAMUNDU

Faculty of Economics: HASAN AEDY

Faculty of Education: Drs H. MUHAMMAD GAZALI

Faculty of Social and Political Sciences: Drs H. M. NUR RAKHMAN

UNIVERSITAS HASANUDDIN

Jl. Perintis Kemerdekaan, Kampus Unhas Tamalanrea, Makassar 90245

Telephone: (411) 584002

Fax: (411) 585188

E-mail: cio@unhas.ac.id

Internet: www.unhas.ac.id

Founded 1959

Academic year: September to February

Rector: Prof. Dr Dr IDRUS A. PATURUSI

Deputy Rector for Academic Affairs: Prof. Dr DJABIR HAMZAH

Deputy Rector for Admin. and Financial Affairs: Prof. Dr Ir H. A. SYAMSUL ARIFIN P.

Deputy Rector for Student and Alumni Affairs: Prof. Dr Ir AMBO ALA

Deputy Rector for Cooperative and Devt Affairs: Prof. Dr Ir A. MAPPADJANTJI AMIEN

Registrar: Dra RATNA ARDJO

Librarian: Dr SYARIFUDDIN ATTJE (acting)

Number of teachers: 1,684

Number of students: 20,816

Publications: *Identitas UNHAS* (12 a year), *Interaski/LPPM* (3 a year), *Jupiter/Perpustakaan* (2 a year)

DEANS

Faculty of Agriculture and Forestry: Prof. Dr Ir SYAWAL

Faculty of Animal Husbandry: Prof. Dr Ir H. BASIT WELLO

Faculty of Dentistry: Dr M. AMIN KANSI

Faculty of Economics: Dr H. FATTAH KADIR

Faculty of Engineering: Dr Ir SALEH PALLU

Faculty of Law: ABDUL RAZAK

Faculty of Letters: Dr H. M. DARWIS

Faculty of Marine Sciences and Fisheries: Ir HAMZAH SUNUSI

Faculty of Mathematics and Natural Sciences: Prof. Dr ALFIAN NOOR

Faculty of Medicine: Prof. Dr Dr IDRUS A. PATURUSI

Faculty of Public Health: Prof. Dr Dr RAZAK THAHA

Faculty of Social and Political Sciences: Prof. Dr HAFIED CANGARA

DIRECTORS

Central Workshop: Dr Ir DUMA HASAN

Language Centre: Dr ETTY BAZERGAN

Postgraduate Studies Programme: Prof. Dr Ir H. M. NATSIR NESSA

UNHAS Information Centre: Dr Ir MUH. IVAN AZIS

UNIVERSITAS INDONESIA

Main Campus Kampus UI Depok Jawa Barat 16424

Jl. Salemba Raya no. 4, Jakarta Pusat 10430

Telephone: (21) 7867222

Fax: (21) 78849060

E-mail: io-ui@ui.ac.id

Internet: www.ui.ac.id

Founded 1950

Languages of instruction: Indonesian, English

Academic year: August to JuneFebruary (two semesters)

Pres.: Prof. Dr GUMILAR RUSLIWA SOMANTRI

Vice-Pres. for Academic Affairs and Student Affairs: Prof. Dr Ir MUHAMMAD ANIS. M. MET

Vice-Pres. for Cooperation and Facilities: AK. TAFSIR NURCHAMID

Vice-Pres. for Devt: SUNARDJI

Univ. Sec.: Prof. Dr KETUT SURAJAYA

Librarian: LUKI WIJAYANTI

Number of teachers: 4,321

Number of students: 42,533

Publications: *Makara* (Health Sciences edition) (3 a year), *Makara* (Science edition) (3 a year), *Makara* (Social Sciences edition) (3 a year), *Makara* (Technology edition) (3 a year), and various faculty bulletins

DEANS

Faculty of Computer Sciences: Dr T. BASARUDIN

Faculty of Dental Medicine: Dr BAMBANG IRAWAN

Faculty of Economics: Dr FIRMANZAH

Faculty of Humanities: Prof. Dr BAMBANG WIBAWARTA

Faculty of Law: Prof. SAFRI NUGRAHA

Faculty of Mathematics and Natural Sciences: Drs ADI BASUKRIADI

Faculty of Medicine: Dr RATNA SITOMPUL

Faculty of Nursing Sciences: Prof. Dra DEWI IRAWATI

Faculty of Psychology: Dr WILMAN DAHLAN MANSOER

Faculty of Public Health: Prof. Dr BAMBANG WISPRIYONO

Faculty of Social and Political Sciences: Dr BAMBANG SHERGI LAKSMONO

Faculty of Technology: Dr Ir RENALDY DALIMI

Programme of Postgraduate Studies: Dr PURNAWAN JUNADI

UNIVERSITAS ISLAM NEGERI SYARIF HIDAYATULLAH JAKARTA (Syarif Hidayatullah State Islamic University (UIN) Jakarta)

Jl. Ir H. Juanda, 95 Ciputat, Banten 15412

Telephone: (21) 7401925

Fax: (21) 7402982

E-mail: info@uinjkt.ac.id

Internet: www.uinjkt.ac.id

Founded 1960, as the State Academy of Islamic Studies, renamed the Syarif Hidayatullah State Institute of Islamic Studies 1998, univ. status 2002

State control

Rector: Prof. Dr KOMARUDDIN HIDAYAT

Vice-Rector for Academic Affairs: Dr JAMHARI

Vice-Rector for Gen. Admin.: Prof. Dr AMSAL BACHTIAR

Vice-Rector for Institutional Development: Dr SUDARNOTO ABDUL HAKIM

Vice-Rector for Students Affairs: Prof. Dr THIB RATA

DEANS

Faculty of Adab and Humanities: Dr H. ABDUL CHOIR

Faculty of Da'wa and Communication: Dr ARIEF SUBHAN

Faculty of Dirasat Islamiya: Prof. Dr ABUDDIN NATA

Faculty of Economics and Social Science: ABDUL HAMID

Faculty of Medicine and Health Sciences: Prof. Dr Dr M. K. TAJUDIN

Faculty of Psychology: Dr YAHYA UMAR

Faculty of Shari'a and Law: Prof. Dr M. AMIN SUMA

Faculty of Science and Technology: Dr Ir SYOPIANSYAH JAYA PUTRA

Faculty of Tarbiya and Teaching Sciences: Prof. Dr DEDE ROSYADA

Faculty of Usul-al Din and Philosophy: Dr AMIN NURDIN

UNIVERSITAS JAMBI

Kampus Universita Jambi, Jl. Raya Jambi, Muara Bulian, Km 15 Mendalo, Jambi 36361

Telephone: (741) 583377

Fax: (741) 583111

E-mail: unja@unja.ac.id

Internet: www.unja.ac.id

Founded 1963

Language of instruction: Indonesian

Academic year: September to August

Rector: H. KEMAS ARSYAD SOMAD

Vice-Rector for Academic Affairs: Drs H. ARDINAL

Vice-Rector for Admin.: Dr Ir. A. RAHMAN

Vice-Rector for External and Internal Affairs: Dr AULIA TASMAN

Vice-Rector for Student Affairs: Dr Drs MAIZAR KARIM

Head of Bureau of Academic Admin., Student Affairs, Planning and Information System: Drs IBRAHIM

Head of Bureau of Gen. Admin. and Finance: Drs H. A. GANI

Librarian: SYAFRI SYAM

Library of 140,000 vols

Number of teachers: 696

Number of students: 13,563

Publication: *Berita UNJA* (12 a year)

DEANS

Faculty of Agriculture: Dr Ir ZILKIFLI

Faculty of Animal Husbandry: Ir AFZALANI

Faculty of Economics: Dr AFRIZAL

Faculty of Education: Drs AFFAN MALIK

Faculty of Law: TAUFIK YAHYA

Postgraduate Programmes: Dr SURATNO

UNIVERSITAS JEMBER

Jl. Kalimantan 37, Jember 68121

Telephone and fax (331) 331042

Internet: www.unej.ac.id

Founded 1964

State control

Languages of instruction: Indonesian, English, French

Academic year: July to June

Rector: Prof. Dr H. KABUL SANTOSO

Vice-Rector for Academic Affairs: Dr Ir IDHA HARIYANTO

Vice-Rector for Admin. and Finance: Prof. Drs KADIMAN

Vice-Rector for Student Affairs: PURNOMO

Registrar: Drs MADE PEDUNGAN SARDHA
Dir of Agricultural Polytechnic: Ir H. SUHARJO WIDODO
Dir of Univ. Research Institute: Drs LIAKIP
Librarian: Drs MAHFUD A.

Library of 117,441 vols
Number of teachers: 783
Number of students: 12,933

Publications: *Argopuro, Dian Wanita, Gema Universitas*

DEANS

Faculty of Agricultural Technology: Ir WAGITO
Faculty of Agriculture: Ir Hj. SITI HARTANTI
Faculty of Dentistry: Drg. BOB SOEBIJANTORO
Faculty of Economics: Drs H. SUKUSNI
Faculty of Law: SAMSI KUSAIRI
Faculty of Letters: Drs SUDJADI
Faculty of Social and Political Sciences: Prof. Drs H. BARIMAN
Faculty of Teacher Training & Educational Sciences: Drs SUKARDJO

UNIVERSITAS JENDERAL SOEDIRMAN

Jl. H. R. Boenyamin 708, Purwokerto, Central Java

Telephone: (281) 635292
Fax: (281) 631802
E-mail: info@unsoed.ac.id
Internet: www.unsoed.ac.id
Founded 1963
Language of instruction: Indonesian
Academic year: September to August (two semesters)

Rector: Prof. RUBIJANTO MISMAN
Vice-Rector for Academic Affairs: Dr SUDJARWO
Vice-Rector for Admin. Affairs: Prof. Dr H. KAMIO
Vice-Rector for Student Affairs: KOMARI
Chief Registrar: Ir BAMBANG PURNOMO
Librarian: Drs CHAMDI

Number of teachers: 750
Number of students: 13,000

Publications: *Journal of Rural Development* (4 a year), *Majalah Ilmiah Unsoed* (biological scientific journal, 4 a year)

DEANS

Faculty of Agriculture: Ir SUMIRAT BRONTO WALUYO
Faculty of Animal Husbandry: Prof. Dr Ir SWANDIARINI
Faculty of Biology: Prof. Dr Haji TRIANI HARDIYATI
Faculty of Economics: Drs GATOT SUPRIHANTO
Faculty of Law: ABDUL AZIS NASIHUDIN
Faculty of Social Sciences and Politics: Drs SUHARI

UNIVERSITAS LAMBUNG MANGKURAT

Kampus UNLAM, Jl. Brigjen H. Hasan Basry, POB 279, South Kalimantan, Banjarmasin 70123

Telephone and fax (511) 54177
E-mail: bjm.unlam@bjm.mega.net.id
Internet: www.unlam.ac.id
Founded 1958 as private univ., state control 1960
Language of instruction: Indonesian
Academic year: September to August

Rector: Prof. MUHAMMAD RASMADI
Vice-Rector for Academic Affairs: Dr Ir ATHAILLAH MURSYID
Vice-Rector for Admin. Affairs: Ir Hj. MAHYAR DIANA
Vice-Rector for Student Affairs: Ir H. MULYADI YUSUF

Head of Academic Admin., Student Affairs, Planning and Information Systems: Drs H. M. SYACHRIAR ACHMAD
Head of General Admin., Financial and Employee Affairs: Dra Hj. SUNDUSIAH
Librarian: H. MARCONY KHALID

Number of teachers: 830
Number of students: 10,734

Publications: *Kalimantan Agriculture* (4 a year), *Kalimantan Scientiae* (2 a year), *Orientasi* (4 a year), *Vidya Karya* (2 a year)

DEANS

Faculty of Agriculture: Ir H. M. RASMADI
Faculty of Economics: Drs H. YUSRIANSYAH AZIS
Faculty of Engineering: Ir H. ZAIN HERNADY ARIFIN
Faculty of Fisheries: Ir SAALUDDIN HUSIN
Faculty of Forestry: Dr Ir H. M. RUSLAN
Faculty of Law: RIDUAN SYACHRANI
Faculty of Medicine: Dr H. HASNI HASAN BASRI
Faculty of Social and Political Sciences: Drs H. BURHAN ACHMAD
Faculty of Teaching Training and Education: Drs RUSTAM EFFENDI

UNIVERSITAS LAMPUNG (University of Lampung)

Jl Prof. Dr Soemantri Brojonegoro No. 1, Bandar Lampung 35145

Telephone: (721) 709611
Fax: (721) 702767
E-mail: info@unila.ac.id
Internet: www.unila.ac.id
Founded 1965
State control
Languages of instruction: Indonesian, English
Academic year: August to June (2 terms)

Rector: Prof. Dr Ir SUGENG P. HARIANTO
Vice-Rector I for Academic Affairs: Prof. Dr Ir HASRIADI MAT AKIN
Vice-Rector II for Admin. and Finance Affairs: Ir SULASTRI RAMLI
Vice-Rector III for Student Affairs: Dr D. M. SUNARTO
Vice-Rector IV for Cooperation, Planning and Information Affairs: Dr SATRIA BANGSAWAN
Admin. Gen. and Finance Bureau Leader: HARSONO SUCIPTO
Admin. Planning, Management Information System and Cooperation Bureau Leader: Drs MARDI SYAHPERI
Research Centre Leader: Prof. JOHN HENDRI
Public Service Leader: Dr BUDI KOESTORO
Mag. Dir: Prof. Dr Ir ABDUL KADIR SALAM
Library Dir: Drs SUGIANTA

Number of teachers: 1,173
Number of students: 25,944

Publications: *Buletin Penelitian, Warta Pengabdian pada Masyarakat*

DEANS

Faculty of Agriculture: Prof. WAN ABBAS ZAKARIA
Faculty of Economics: TOTO GUNARTO
Faculty of Education and Teacher Training: Prof. Dr SUDJARWO
Faculty of Engineering: Dr LUSMELIA
Faculty of Law: ADIUS SEMENGUK
Faculty of Mathematics and Natural Science: Dr SUTYARSO
Faculty of Social and Political Sciences: Drs AGUS HADIAWAN

DIRECTORS

Bureau of Legal Consultation and Aid: M. PULUNG
Centre of Languages: Drs DEDI SUPRIYADI
Centre of Public Services: Drs KANTAN ABDULLAH

Institute of Demography: MUCHSIN BADAR
Institute of Environmental Studies: Prof. Dr K. E. S. MANIK
Institute of Management: SUDANAR
Lampungnese Culture Studies: Dr VIVIT BARTOVEN N
Research Centre: Dr FADDEL DJAUHAR

UNIVERSITAS MALIKUSSALEH

Jl. Tgk Chik Ditiro, 26 Lancang Garam Lhokseumawe, Aceh

Telephone: (645) 41373
Fax: (645) 44450
E-mail: info@unimal.ac.id
Internet: www.unimal.ac.id
Founded 1969
State control

Faculties of agriculture, economics, engineering and law

Rector: Prof. A. HADI ARIFIN
Vice-Rector I: RASYIDIN
Vice-Rector II: AIYUB
Vice-Rector III: BAKHTIAR
Vice-Rector IV: M. AKMAL.

UNIVERSITAS MATARAM

Jl. Majapahit 62, Nusa Tenggara Barat, Mataram 83125

Telephone: (370) 633007
Fax: (370) 636041
E-mail: rektorat@unram.org
Internet: www.unram.ac.id
Founded 1962
Academic year: September to August

Rector: Dr MANSUR MA'SHUM
Vice-Rector for Academic Affairs: Dr ARIFUDDIN SAHIDU
Vice-Rector for Admin. Affairs: Drs HASBULLAH
Vice-Rector for External Cooperation: ROSIADY SAYUTI
Vice-Rector for Student Affairs: MUHAMMAD DARWIN
Registrar: MUHIBAH NASRUDDIN
Admin. Officer: FATHULLAH NATSIR
Librarian: LALU BUDIMAN

Library of 73,156 vols
Number of teachers: 851
Number of students: 11,541

Publications: *Agroteksos* (4 a year), *Komunitas* (2 a year), *Research Journal* (3 a year)

DEANS

Faculty of Agriculture: Dr PARMAN
Faculty of Animal Science: M. S. MUHZIE
Faculty of Economics: SUKARDAN
Faculty of Education and Teaching: Dr SYAHDAN
Faculty of Engineering: Prof. HADI SUTRISNO
Faculty of Law: ZAINAL ASIKIN
Faculty of Medicine: Prof. MULYANTO

UNIVERSITAS MULAWARMAN

Kampus Gunung. Kelua, East Kalimantan, Samarinda 75119

Telephone: (541) 741118
Fax: (541) 732870
E-mail: rektorat@unmul.ac.id
Internet: www.unmul.ac.id
Founded 1962 as Mulawarman School of Higher Learning, present status 1963
Academic year: September to August

Rector: Prof. Dr ARIFFIEN BRATAWINATA
Vice-Rector for Academic Affairs: Prof. Dr MAMAN SUTISNA
Vice-Rector for Admin. and Finance: SUYATNO WIJOYO
Vice-Rector for Devt and Cooperation: Prof. Dra Hj. RUSMILAWATI

Vice-Rector for Student Affairs: Prof. Drs
EDDY SUBANDRIJO
Head of Gen. Admin. and Finance Bureau:
MASRIANI
Library Dir: SUBIANTORO
Number of teachers: 856
Number of students: 26,746
Publication: *Frontir* (2 a year)

DEANS

Faculty of Agriculture: GUSTI HAFIZIANSYAH
Faculty of Economics: Prof. ZAMRUDDIN HASID
Faculty of Education and Teacher Training:
Drs ICHRAR ASBAR
Faculty of Engineering: Ir H. DHARMA
WIDADA
Faculty of Fisheries and Marine Science: Dr
H. HELMINUDDIN
Faculty of Forestry: Prof. Dr AFIF RUCHAEMI
Faculty of Law: LA SINA
Faculty of Mathematics and Natural Sci-
ences: Drs SUDRAJAT
Faculty of Medicine: Dr EMIL BACHTIAR
MOERAD
Faculty of Pharmacy: LAODE RIJAI
Faculty of Public Health: Dra SITI BADRAH
Faculty of Social and Political Sciences: D. B.
PARANOAN

UNIVERSITAS NEGERI GORONTALO

Jl. Jend. Sudirman, 6 Kota, Gorontalo
Telephone: (435) 821125
Fax: (435) 821752
Internet: www.ung.ac.id
Founded 1963
State control
Rector: Prof. Dr Ir H. NELSON POMALINGO
Vice-Rector I: Dr SYAMSU QAMAR BADU
Vice-Rector II: Drs NAWIR SUNE
Vice-Rector III: Drs HAMZAH UNO
Vice-Rector IV: Dr MAHLUDIN BARUADI

DEANS

Faculty of Agriculture: Ir ZULZAIN ILAHUDE
Faculty of Education: Drs SAMATOWA USMAN
Faculty of Engineering: Drs NAWIR SUNE
Faculty of Health Sciences and Sports: Dra
RAMA P. HIOLA
Faculty of Literature and Culture: Dra HJ.
MALABAR SAYAMA
Faculty of Mathematics and Natural Sci-
ences: Dr RAMLI UTINA
Faculty of Social Sciences: Drs MOONTI
USMAN

UNIVERSITAS NEGERI JAKARTA
(State University of Jakarta)

Jl. Rawamangun Muka, Jakarta 13220
Telephone: (21) 4890046
Fax: (21) 4893726
E-mail: administrator@unj.ac.id
Internet: www.unj.ac.id
Founded 1957
State control
Faculties of economy, engineering, languages
and arts, mathematics and natural sciences,
science and education, social sciences, sports
Rector: Dr BEDJO SUJANTO
Vice-Rector I: Dr ZAINAL RAFLI
Vice-Rector II: Dr SYARIFUDIN
Vice-Rector III: Drs FACHRUDDIN ARBAH
Vice-Rector IV: Dr SOEPRIJANTO.

UNIVERSITAS NEGERI MAKASSAR
(State University of Makassar)

Jl. A. P. Pettarani, Makassar 90222
Telephone: (411) 869854
E-mail: admin@unm.ac.id
Internet: www.unm.ac.id
Founded 1961

State control
Faculties of arts and design, economics,
education, engineering, languages and lit-
erature, mathematics and natural sciences,
psychology, sports science
Rector: Prof. Dr H. ARISMUNANDAR
Vice-Rector I: Prof. Dr SOFYAN SALAM
Vice-Rector II: Prof. Dr ANDI ICHSAN
Vice-Rector III: Prof. Dr HAMSU ABDUL GANI
Vice-Rector IV: Dr NURDIN NONI.

UNIVERSITAS NEGERI MALANG
(State University of Malang)

Jl. Semarang 5, Malang 65145
Telephone: (341) 551312
Fax: (341) 551921
E-mail: info@um.ac.id
Internet: www.um.ac.id
Founded 1954
State control
Rector: Prof. Dr H. SUPARNO (acting)
Vice-Rector I: Dr H. KUSMINTARDJO
Vice-Rector II: Prof. Dr H. AH. ROFI'UDDIN
Vice-Rector III: Prof. Dr H. MASJKUR.

UNIVERSITAS NEGERI MANADO
(State University of Manado)

Tondano, Manado
Internet: www.unima.ac.id
Founded 1955
State control
Rector: Prof. Dr PHILOTEUS E. A. TUERAH.

UNIVERSITAS NEGERI MEDAN
(State University of Medan)

Jl. Willem Iskandar Pasar V, Medan 20221
Telephone: (61) 6613365
Fax: (61) 6613319
E-mail: sekretariat@unimed.ac.id
Internet: www.unimed.ac.id
Founded 1956
State control
Rector: SYAWAL GULTOM.

UNIVERSITAS NEGERI PAPUA
(Papua State University)

Manokwari
Internet: www.unipa.ac.id
Founded 2000
State control
Faculties of agriculture and agricultural
technology, animal husbandry, economics,
fisheries and marine science, forestry, math-
ematics and natural sciences
Rector: Prof. Dr Ir FRANS WANGGAI.

UNIVERSITAS NEGERI SEMARANG
(State University of Semarang)

Semarang
Internet: www.unnes.ac.id
Founded 1961
State control
Faculty of economics and law, education,
engineering, languages and arts, mathemat-
ics and natural sciences, social sciences,
sports
Rector: Prof. Dr H. SUDIJONNO SASTROAT-
MODJO
Vice-Rector for Academic Affairs: Prof. Dr
SUPRIADI RUSTAD
Vice-Rector for Gen. Admin.: Drs WAHYONO
Vice-Rector for Devt and Cooperation: Prof.
Dr FATHUR ROKHMAN
Vice-Rector for Student Affairs: Dr MASRU-
KHI.

UNIVERSITAS NEGERI SURABAYA
(State University of Surabaya)

Jl. Ketintang, Surabaya
Telephone: (31) 828009
Fax: (31) 828080
E-mail: rektor@um.ac.id
Internet: www.unesa.ac.id
Founded 1960
State control
Rector: Prof. Dr H. SUPARNO.

UNIVERSITAS NEGERI YOGYAKARTA

Karangmalang, Yogyakarta 55281
Telephone: (274) 586168
Fax: (274) 542185
E-mail: humas@uny.ac.id
Internet: www.uny.ac.id
Founded 1964
State control
Rector: Prof. SUGENG MARDIYONO.

UNIVERSITAS NUSA CENDANA
(Nusa Cendana University)

Jl. Adisucipto, Penfui, Nusa Tenggara
Timur, Kupang 85001
Telephone: (380) 881580
Fax: (380) 881586
E-mail: puskomundana@undana.ac.id
Internet: www.undana.ac.id
Founded 1962
State control
Languages of instruction: Indonesian, Eng-
lish
Academic year: July to June
Rector: Prof. Ir FRANS UMBU DATTA
Vice-Rector for Academic Affairs: Drs I.
GUSTI BAGUS ARJANA
Vice-Rector for Admin. Affairs: Drs DOPPY
ROY NENDISSA
Vice-Rector for Cooperation Affairs: Ir
FABIAN HARRY LAWALU
Vice-Rector for Student Affairs: Drs OCTAVIA-
NUS EOH
Chief Admin. Officer for Academic, Students
and Information System: Drs DAUD U. Z.
KAMURI
Chief Admin. Officer for Finance and Facil-
ities: Drs JOSEPH WULAGENING
Librarian: Drs GORIS SABON
Number of teachers: 900
Number of students: 13,000
Publications: *Liguminesa Journal* (4 a year),
Media Eksakta Journal (4 a year), *Nusa
Cendana Journal* (4 a year), *Sinergia* (12 a
year), *Warta Undana* (12 a year)

DEANS

Faculty of Agriculture: Prof. Dr Ir SAMUEL
PAKAN
Faculty of Animal Husbandry: Ir AGUS
KONDA MALIK
Faculty of Law: Dr SUKARDAN ALOVSIUS
Faculty of Medicine: Dr HERU TJAHYONO
Faculty of Public Health: Ir GUSTAF OEMATAN
Faculty of Science and Engineering: Drs M.
J. PELLA
Faculty of Social and Political Sciences: Prof.
Dr ALOYSIUS LILIWERI
Faculty of Teacher Training and Education:
Drs LUKAS BILI BORA

UNIVERSITAS PADJADJARAN

Jl. Dipati Ukur 35, Bandung 40132
Telephone: (22) 2503271
Fax: (22) 2534498
E-mail: info@unpad.ac.id
Internet: www.unpad.ac.id
Founded 1957
State control

Languages of instruction: Indonesian, English

Academic year: August to July (two semesters)

Rector: Prof. Dr H. A. HIMENDRA WARGAHADI-BRATA

Vice-Rector for Academic Affairs: Prof. Dr H. PONPON S. IDJRADINATA

Vice-Rector for Admin.: M. WAHYUDIN ZARKASYI

Vice-Rector for Cooperation: Prof. Dr H. USMAN HARDI

Vice-Rector for Planning, Information Systems and Supervision: Prof. T. SUGANDA

Vice-Rector for Student Affairs: SYARIF A. BARMAWI

Librarian: Prof. Dr I. NURPILIHAN

Library of 178,441 vols

Number of teachers: 1,868

Number of students: 40,482

Publications: *Agrikulture* (Agriculture, 3 a year), *Bionatura* (Sciences, 3 a year), *Jurnal Ekonomi* (Economics, 2 a year), *Jurnal Kedokteran Bandung* (Medicine, 3 a year), *Jurnal Keperawatan* (Nursing, 2 a year), *Puslitbangkum* (Law, 2 a year), *Sosiohumaniora* (Social Sciences, 3 a year)

DEANS

Faculty of Agriculture: Prof. Dr SADELI NATASASMITA

Faculty of Animal Husbandry: Prof. Dr NASIPAN USRI

Faculty of Communication Science: Drs SOLEH SOEMIRAT

Faculty of Dentistry: Dr SETIAWAN NATASAMITA

Faculty of Economics: Prof. Dr H. SURIPTO SAMID

Faculty of Law: Prof. Dr MAN SUPARMAN SASTRAWIDJAJA

Faculty of Letters: Prof. Dr H. EDI SUHARDI EKADJATI

Faculty of Mathematics and Natural Sciences: Prof. Dr SUPRIATNA

Faculty of Medicine: Dr FIRMAN FUAD WIRAKUSUMAH

Faculty of Psychology: Dr H. SURYANA SUMANTRI

Faculty of Social and Political Science: Drs TACHJAN

UNIVERSITAS PALANGKARAYA

Jl. Yos Sudarso, Kotak Pos 2, Palangka Raya, Kalimantan Tengah 73112

Telephone: (536) 26878

Fax: (536) 21722

E-mail: info@universitaspalangkaraya.ac.id

Internet: www.upr.ac.id

Founded 1963

Language of instruction: Indonesian

Academic year: July to June

Rector: Drs NAPA J. AWAT

Vice-Rector I: Drs HERIYANTO M. GARANG

Vice-Rector II: Drs DADANG LORIDA

Vice-Rector III: H. M. DAMIRI

Vice-Rector IV: Prof. Dr H. AHMADI ISA

Academic and Students' Admin. Officer: Drs LEUNHARD BAN YEN

Librarian: Dra ISTIRAHAYU

Number of teachers: 501

Number of students: 5,265

Publications: *Garantung* (12 a year), *Optimal* (12 a year), *Suara Tunjung Nyaho* (12 a year), *Wahana* (12 a year)

DEANS

Faculty of Agriculture: Ir. SINTO R. NOEHAN

Faculty of Economics: Drs EFENDY D. TIMBANG

Faculty of Education and Teacher Training: Drs HENRY SINGARASA

UNIVERSITAS PATTIMURA AMBON

POB 95, Jl. Ir M. Putuhena Poka, Ambon 97233

Telephone: (911) 322626

Fax: (911) 322691

E-mail: sisdiksat@unpatti.ac.id

Internet: www.unpatti.ac.id

Founded 1956, present status 1962

Language of instruction: Indonesian

Academic year: August to July

Rector: Dr Ir J. L. NANERE

Vice-Rector for Academic Affairs: Prof. P. J. SIWABESSY

Vice-Rector for Admin. and Finance: J. LEIWAKABESSY

Vice-Rector for Student Affairs: Ir J. J. TUHUMURY

Registrar: Drs E. LEUWOL

Librarian: ALI ZAWAWI

Number of teachers: 636

Number of students: 7,516

Publication: *Media Unpatti* (12 a year)

DEANS

Faculty of Agriculture: Ir. J. PUTINELLA

Faculty of Economics: Drs L. A. RASJID

Faculty of Fishery: Ir. J. M. NANLOHY

Faculty of Law: C. M. PATTIRUHU

Faculty of Social and Political Sciences: Drs M. RENUR

Faculty of Teacher Training and Education: Drs T. J. A. UNEPUTTY

Faculty of Technology: Ir. J. ASTHENU

DIRECTORS

Institute of Community Service: Dr MUS. HULISELAN

Institute of Research: Dr Ir. P. SITIAPESSY

UNIVERSITAS PENDIDIKAN GANESHA SINGARAJA

Bali

Telephone: (362) 22570

Fax: (362) 25735

E-mail: humas@undiksha.ac.id

Internet: www.undiksha.ac.id

State control

Faculties of education, languages and arts, mathematics and natural sciences, social education, sports and health, technical and vocational education

Rector: Dr I NYOMAN SUDIANA

Vice-Rector I: Dr I GUSTI PUTU SUHARTA

Vice-Rector II: Dr I NYOMAN JAMPEL

Vice-Rector III: Drs I PUTU SUHARTA

Vice-Rector IV: Dr I KETUT SEKEN

Library of 37,818 vols, 4275 titles.

UNIVERSITAS PENDIDIKAN INDONESIA

Jl. Dr Setiabudhi 229, Bandung 40154

Telephone: (22) 2013161

Fax: (22) 2013651

Internet: www.upi.edu

Founded 1954 as Perguruan Tinggi Pendidikan Guru (Teacher's Education College), reformed as Bandung Institute of Teaching and Educational Sciences 1964, present status 1999

State control

Faculties of educational sciences, language and art, science, social studies, sports and health, technology

Rector: Prof. SUNARYO KARTADINATA

Number of teachers: 1,302

Number of students: 22,700

UNIVERSITAS RIAU

Kampus Bina Widya Km 12.5, Simpang Baru, Pekanbaru, Sumatra 28293

Telephone: (761) 63266

Fax: (761) 63279

E-mail: rektor@unri.ac.id

Internet: www.unri.ac.id

Founded 1962

Academic year: September to July

Rector: Prof. Dr MUCHTAR AHMAD

Vice-Rector for Academic Affairs: Prof. Dr DADANG ISKANDAR

Vice-Rector for Admin.: Drs AMIR HASAN

Vice-Rector for Planning and Cooperation: Ir SUWARDI LOCKMAN

Vice-Rector for Student Affairs: Ir ARIFIEN MANSYOER

Registrar: Prof. Dr DADANG ISKANDAR

Librarian: Ir PUTU SEDANA

Number of teachers: 919

Number of students: 14,223

Publications: *Dawat* (Journal of Malay Language and Culture, 4 a year), *Jurnal Agritek* (Agricultural Technology, 2 a year), *Jurnal Ekonomi* (Economics, 4 a year), *Jurnal Ilmu Sosial dan Politik* (Social and Political Sciences, 4 a year), *Jurnal Natur Indonesia* (2 a year), *Jurnal Penelitian* (General Scientific Research, 4 a year), *Jurnal Perikanan dan Ilmu Kelautan* (Fisheries and Marine Science, 2 a year), *Terubuk* (Fisheries Bulletin, 4 a year)

DEANS

Faculty of Agriculture: Dr ASLIM RASYAD

Faculty of Economics: Drs MUCHTAR MARISO

Faculty of Engineering: Drs RAHMAD

Faculty of Fisheries: Dr Ir FELIATRA

Faculty of Natural Sciences and Mathematics: Dra CHAINULFIFAH

Faculty of Politics and Social Science: Drs ALFIAN

Faculty of Teacher Training and Education: Drs M. ZEIN MAADAP

PROFESSORS

ADAM, D., Government and Law

AHMAD, M., Marine Sciences and Fisheries

DAHRIL, T., Planktonology and Water Quality

DIAH, M., Education

HASAN, K., Education

IMRAN, A., Islamology

ISKANDAR, D., Physics

KASMY, M. F., Physics

KASRY, A., Aquatic Resources Management

MAHMUD, S., Education

MARZUKI, S., History Education

RAB, T., Enzymology

RAHMAN, M., Mathematics

RASYAD, A., Agriculture

SAAD, M., Rural Sociology

SAMAD, R., Education

SUWARDI, History

UMAR, S. M., Education

USMAN, F., Agriculture

UNIVERSITAS SAM RATULANGI

Kampus UNSRAT Bahu, North Sulawesi, Manado 95115

Telephone: (431) 863886

Fax: (431) 822568

E-mail: rektorat@unsrat.ac.id

Internet: www.unsrat.ac.id

Founded 1961

State control

Language of instruction: Indonesian

Academic year: starts September

Rector: Prof. Dr DONALD A. RUMOKOY

Vice-Rector: Prof. Dr J. SH POLIL MANDANG

Vice-Rector: Prof. Dr PAULUS KINDANGEN

Vice-Rector: Prof. Dr B. H. R. KALRUPAN

Vice-Rector: Prof. Dr DAVID A. KALIGIS
Vice-Rector: Prof. Dr Ir JEFREY I KINDANGEN
Vice-Rector: Prof. Drs MAJID ABDULLAH
Head of Bureau for Academic and Student Admin.: H. J. MEWENGKANG
Head of Central Library: D. SILANGEN
Number of teachers: 1,496
Number of students: 12,526
Publication: *Palakat-Inovasi*

DEANS

Faculty of Agriculture: Dr Ir D. T. SEMBEL
Faculty of Animal Husbandry: Prof. Dr D. A. KALIGIS
Faculty of Economics: Prof. NY. I. NAJOEN
Faculty of Engineering: R. J. M. MANDAGI
Faculty of Fisheries and Maritime Sciences: Prof. Dr S. BERHIMPON
Faculty of Law: Prof. ADOLF DAPU
Faculty of Letters: Drs ROBERT TANDI
Faculty of Mathematics and Natural Science: Dr S. RONDONUWU
Faculty of Medicine: Dr J. W. SIAGIAN
Faculty of Social Sciences and Politics: Drs J. J. LONTAAN

PROFESSORS

ALAMSJAH, Soil Physics
BUDIARSO, Technology
DUNDU, B., Microbiology
JAN, H., Statistics
KAKAUHE, R. P. L., Management Accounting
KAPOJOS-MONGULA, I. C. R., Civil Law
KARINDA, D. S., English and Dutch
KASINEM-S., Commercial Law
KORAH, M. W., Marketing Management Science
MANDANG, J. H. A., Ahli Mata
MUNIR, M., Paediatrics
MUSA, A., Modern Indonesian History
MUSA KARIM, Indonesian Literature
PALAR, W. T., Agrarian Studies
PALENEWEN, J. L., Ecology
PANDA, H. O., Surgery
PUNUH-GO, S., Civil Law
ROGI, M., Economic Development
SALEH, M., Indonesian Government System
SINOLUNGAN, J. M., Medical Psychology
SOEPENO, Customary Law
SUPIT, J. T., Sociology
TANGKUDUNG, R. S., Civil Administration
TIMBOELENG, K. W., Physics and Research Methodology
TUSACH, N. A., Civil Law
WANTASEN, D., Soil Physics
WAWOROENTOE, S. A., Physics
WAWOROENTOE, W. J., Urban and Regional Planning
WILAR, A. F., Veterinary Science
WOKAS, F. H. M., Plant Protection
WOWOR, G. E., Gynaecology
WUMU, J., History of Economics

UNIVERSITAS SEBELAS MARET SURAKARTA
(Sebelas Maret University Surakarta)

Jl. Ir Sutami 36A, Surakarta 57126
Telephone and fax (271) 646994
E-mail: io@uns.ac.id
Internet: www.uns.ac.id
Founded 1976
State control
Language of instruction: Indonesian
Academic year: August to July

Rector: Prof. Dr H. MOHAMMED SYAMSULHADI
Vice-Rector for Academic Affairs: Prof. Dr RAVIK KARSIDI
Vice-Rector for Admin. Affairs: Prof. Dr Ir SHOLAHUDDIN
Vice-Rector for Cooperation Affairs: Prof. Dr ADI SULISTYONO
Vice-Rector for Student Affairs: Drs DWI TIYANTO

Librarian: Drs HARMAWAN
Library of 288,024 vols
Number of teachers: 1,571
Number of students: 30,020

Publications: *Issues In Social and Environmental Accounting* (journal), *Mediator* (student magazine, 12 a year)

DEANS

Faculty of Agriculture: Prof. Dr Ir H. SUNTORO
Faculty of Economics: Prof. Dr BAMBANG SUTOPO
Faculty of Engineering: Ir MUKAHAR
Faculty of Law: MOCH. YAMIN
Faculty of Letters and Arts: Drs SUDARNO
Faculty of Mathematics and Natural Sciences: Prof. Dr SUTARNO
Faculty of Medicine: Prof. Dr A. A. SUBIYANTO
Faculty of Social and Political Science: Drs SUPRIYADI
Faculty of Teacher-Training and Education: Prof. Dr M. FURQON HIDAYATULLAH
Postgraduate Programme: Prof. Drs SURANTO

UNIVERSITAS SRIWIJAYA

Jl. Jaksa Agung R. Suprapto, Palembang, South Sumatra
Telephone: (711) 26004
E-mail: yadiutama@ilkom.unsri.ac.id
Internet: www.unsri.ac.id
Founded 1960
State control
Language of instruction: Indonesian
Academic year: July to June

Rector: Prof. Dr BADIA PERIZADE
Vice-Rector I: Dr ZULFIKARI DAHLAN
Vice-Rector II: KENCANA DEWI
Vice-Rector III: H. ANIS SAGAF
Vice-Rector IV: Dr ABDUL HAMID RASYID
Admin. Bureau: Drs HERMAN MURSAL
Librarian: Dra CHUZAIMAH DIEM

Number of teachers: 540 full-time, 617 part-time
Number of students: 8,427

Publications: *Majalah Universitas Sriwijaya* (3 a year), and faculty bulletins

DEANS

Faculty of Agriculture: ZULJATI SYAHRUL
Faculty of Dentistry: Prof. Dr ARSUAD
Faculty of Economics: BADIA PERIZADE
Faculty of Education: Dr ZULKIFLI DAHLAN (acting)
Faculty of Engineering: Dr HASAN BASRI
Faculty of Law: SOFYAN HASAN
Faculty of Teacher Training: Prof. Dr DJAHIR BASIR

PROFESSORS

HALIM, A., Linguistics
HARDJOWIJONO, G., Paediatrics
MUKTI, H. D., Advanced Management
MUSLIMIN, A., Administrative Law
SOELAIMAN, M., Adat Law

UNIVERSITAS SUMATERA UTARA
(University of Sumatera Utara)

Jl. Dr. T. Mansur No. 9, Kampus USU, North Sumatera Medan 20155
Telephone: (61) 8216575
Fax: (61) 8219411
E-mail: usu@karet.usu.ac.id
Internet: www.usu.ac.id
Founded 1952
State control
Languages of instruction: Indonesian, English
Academic year: August to July
Rector: Prof. CHAIRUDDIN P. LUBIS

Vice-Rector for Academic Affairs: Prof. Dr SUMONO
Vice-Rector for Administrative Affairs: Dr SUBHILHAR
Vice-Rector for Asset Management: Ir ISMAN NURIADI
Vice-Rector for Planning, Cooperation and Foreign Affairs: Prof. Dr SUKARIA SINULINGGA
Vice-Rector for Student Affairs: Dr LINDA MAAS
Head of Library and Information System: Drs. A. RIDWAN SIREGAR

Library of 500,000 vols
Number of teachers: 1,750
Number of students: 28,000

DEANS

Faculty of Agriculture: Dr ZULKIFLI NASUTION
Faculty of Dentistry: Prof. ISMET D. NASUTION
Faculty of Economics: Drs JHON T. RITONGA
Faculty of Engineering: Dr NAWAWY LOEBIS
Faculty of Law: Prof. Dr RUNTUNG
Faculty of Letters: Prof. BAHREN UMAR SIREGAR
Faculty of Mathematics and Sciences: Prof. EDDY MARLIANTO
Faculty of Medicine: Dr T. BAHRI ANWAR
Faculty of Political and Social Science: Drs M. ARIF NASUTION
Faculty of Public Health: (vacant)
School of Postgraduate Studies: Dr T. CHAIRUN NISA

UNIVERSITAS SYIAH KUALA

Jl. Darussalam, Kopelma Darussalam Banda Aceh 23111
Telephone: (651) 7410250
E-mail: rektor@unsyiah.ac.id
Internet: www.unsyiah.ac.id
Founded 1961
State control
Language of instruction: Indonesian
Academic year: August to June

Rector: DARNI
Vice-Rector I: Dr SAMSUL RIZAL
Vice-Rector II: Dr EDDY NUR ILYAS
Vice-Rector III: Drs RUSLI YUSUF
Vice-Rector IV: DARUSMAN
Chief Academic Admin. Officer: Drs BACHTIAR EFENDI
Chief Admin. Officer: Drs MUSTAFA USMAN
Librarian: Drs SANUSI

Number of teachers: 1,278
Number of students: 16,715

Publications: *Agripet* (2 a year), *Agrista*, *Ekobis*, *Jurnal Kedokteran Syiah Kuala*, *Jurnal Teknik Sipil* (3 a year), *Kanun Fakultas Hukum*, *Managemen dan Bisnis*, *Medica Veterinaria*, *Mekanikal Komputasi & Numerical*, *Mon Mata* (4 a year), *Natural*, *Rekayasa Elektrika*, *Rekayasa Kimia & Lingkungan*, *Teknorama*, *Telaah dan Riset*, *Wacana Pendidikan* (4 a year), *Warta Unsyiah*

DEANS

Faculty of Agriculture: Ir ISMAYANI
Faculty of Economics: Prof. Dr SAID MUHAMMAD
Faculty of Engineering: Prof. Dr Ir HUSAINI
Faculty of Law: MAWARDI ISMAIL
Faculty of Mathematical and Natural Sciences: Dr MUSTANIR
Faculty of Medicine: Dr SYAHRUL
Faculty of Teacher Training and Education: Dr M. YUSUF AZIZ
Faculty of Veterinary Science: Dr MAHDI ABRAR

UNIVERSITAS TADULAKO

Kampus Bumi, Tadulako Tondo, Sulawesi, Palu 94118

Telephone: (451) 422611
Fax: (451) 422844
E-mail: lemlit@untad.ac.id
Internet: www.untad.ac.id

Founded 1981

Rector: Drs MOHAMMAD RASYID
Vice-Rector: T. A. M. TILAAR
Vice-Rector: ARIFUDDIN BIDIN
Vice-Rector: SAHABUDDIN MUSTAPA
Vice-Rector: Dr MAIN LABASO
Head of General Admin. Bureau: RAFIGA PONULELE
Librarian: Drs MUH. ASRI HENTE

Library of 30,042 vols
Number of teachers: 660
Number of students: 6,500

DEANS

Faculty of Agricultural Sciences: Ir MASRIL BUSTAMI
Faculty of Economics: ARSYAD MAARDANIN
Faculty of Law: ISMAIL KASIM
Faculty of Social and Political Sciences: Drs ZAINUDDIN BOLONG
Faculty of Teacher Training: Drs H. TJATJO THAHA
Diploma Programme for Technical Sciences: Ir GALIB ISHAK

UNIVERSITAS TANJUNGPURA

Jl. Ahmad Yani Pontianak, Kalbar, Pontianak 78124

Telephone and fax (561) 739636
E-mail: untan@untan.ac.id
Internet: www.untan.ac.id

Founded 1959
Language of instruction: Indonesian
Academic year: begins September

Rector: Prof. Hj. ASNIAR ISMAIL
First Vice-Chancellor: Prof. Dr HENDRO S. SUDAGUNG
Registrar: RADJALI HADIMASPUTRA
Head of General Administration Bureau: MAYARANA RANITA
Librarian: SUTARMIN

Number of teachers: 734
Number of students: 9,305

DEANS

Faculty of Agriculture: Prof. Ir ALAMSYAH
Faculty of Economics: ASNIAR SUBAGYO
Faculty of Engineering: Ir Haji PONY SEDYANINGSIH
Faculty of Law: Prof. ANWAR SALEH
Faculty of Social and Political Sciences: Prof. Dr Sy. IBRAHIM ALKADRIE
Faculty of Teaching and Education: Prof. Drs JAWADI HASID

UNIVERSITAS TERBUKA
(Indonesian Open Learning University)

Jl. Cabe Raya, Pondok Cabe, Ciputat Tangerang 15418, POB 6666, Jakarta 15418

Telephone: (21) 7490941
Fax: (21) 7490147
E-mail: info@p2m.ut.ac.id
Internet: www.ut.ac.id

Founded 1984
State control
Language of instruction: Indonesian

Pres.: Prof. Dr ATWI SUPARMAN
Registrar: Drs MUCHSININ
Librarian: Drs EFFENDI WAHYONO

Library of 30,000 vols
Number of teachers: 766
Number of students: 225,203

Publications: *Indonesian Journal of Open and Distance Learning* (2 a year), *Journal of Education* (2 a year), *Journal of Indonesian Studies* (2 a year), *Journal of Mathematics, Science and Technology* (2 a year), *Komunika* (4 a year), *Suara Terbuka* (12 a year)

DEANS

Faculty of Economics: NADIA SRI DAMAYANTI
Faculty of Education: Dr PAULINA PANNEN
Faculty of Mathematics and Natural Science: Dr Ir DJOKOSETYANTO
Faculty of Social and Political Science: Drs ZAINUL ITTIHAD AMIN

UNIVERSITAS TRUNOJOYO MADURA

Bangkalan, East Java

Telephone: (31) 3014091
Fax: (31) 3014463
E-mail: humas@trunojoyo.ac.id
Internet: www.trunojoyo.ac.id

Founded 2001
State control

Rector: Prof. Dr Ir H. ARIFFIN
Vice-Rector I: Drs BAMBANG SABARIMAN
Vice-Rector II: Dr Ir SLAMET SUBARI
Vice-Rector III: H. BOED MUSTIKO

DEANS

Faculty of Agriculture: Ir MOH. FAKHRY
Faculty of Economics: Prof. IWAN TRIYUNWONO
Faculty of Engineering: Ir SOEPRAPTO
Faculty of Law: H. MOH. AMIR HAMZAH

UNIVERSITAS UDAYANA
(Udayana University)

Bukit Jimbaran Campus, Badung 80361

Telephone: (361) 701954
Fax: (361) 701907
E-mail: info@unud.ac.id
Internet: www.unud.ac.id

Founded 1962
State control
Academic year: August to December
Language of instruction: Indonesian

Pres.: Prof. Dr I. MADE BAKTA
Deputy Pres. for Academic Affairs: Prof. Dr I. KOMANG GDE BENDESA
Deputy Pres. for Admin. Affairs: Prof. Dr DEWA PUTU SUTJANA
Deputy Pres. for Cooperation and Information Affairs: Prof. Dr Ir I. G. P. WIRAWAN
Deputy Pres. for Student Affairs: Prof. Dr Ir I. NYOMAN SUTJIPTA
Librarian: Drs I. GUSTI NYOMAN TIRTAYASA

Library of 21,390 vols
Number of teachers: 1,702
Number of students: 16,304

Publications: *Berita Udayana* (12 a year), *Majalah Ilmiah Universitas Udayana* (4 a year), *Majalah Kedokteran Unud* (4 a year)

DEANS

Faculty of Agricultural Technology: I GUSTI NGURAH AGUNG
Faculty of Agriculture: NENGAH ARTHA
Faculty of Animal Husbandry: TJOKORDA GDE OKA SUSULA
Faculty of Economics: Dr MADE KEMBAR SRI BUDHI
Faculty of Engineering: Dr I WAYAN REDANA
Faculty of Law: I. KETUT RAI SETIA BUDHI
Faculty of Letters (Arts): Prof. Dr I. WAYAN ARDIKA
Faculty of Medicine: Prof. Dr D. P. WIDJANA
Faculty of Sciences: Prof. Dr I. WAYAN KASA
Faculty of Veterinary Science: Dr Drh. I MADE DAMRI YASA

PROFESSORS

ADIPUTRA, N., Occupational Health
ARDANA, G. G., History
ARDIKA, W., Archaeology
ARGA, Agricultural Economics
ARHYA, N., Biochemistry
ARKA, B., Veterinary Science
ARYANTA, W. R., Food Microbiology
ASTININGSIH, K., Poultry Production
ASTITI, T. I. P., Custom Law
ATMAJA, D. G., Law
BAGUS, G. N., Indonesian Language
BAGUS, G. N., Social Anthropology
BAKTA, M., Internal Medicine
BAWA, W., Indonesian Language
BHINAWA, N., Animal Production
BUDHA, K., Surgery
BUNGAYA, G., Management
DJAGRA, I. B., Animal Production
KALAM, A. A. R., Arts and Design
LANA, K., Animal Nutrition
LANANG, O., Genetics
MANIK, G., Animal Husbandry
MANUABA, I. B. A., Human Physiology
MARDANI, N. K., Biology (Environmental Studies)
MASTIKA, M., Animal Nutrition
MATRAM, R. B., Veterinary Physiology
NALA, G. N., Human Physiology
NEHEN, K., Economic Devt
NETRA SUBADIYASA, N., Soil Science
NITIS, M., Animal Nutrition
OKA, I. B., Pharmacology
PANGKAHILA, J. A., Sexology
PUTHERA, G. A. G., Human Histology
PUTRA, D. K. H., Animal Physiology
RATA, I. B., Archaeology
RIKA, K., Forage Science
SAIDI, H. S., Islamology
SIRTA, N., Custom Law
SOEWIGIONO, S., Gastroenterology
SUARNA, I. M., Forage Science
SUATA, I. K., Microbiology
SUDHARTA, T. R., Sanskrit Language
SUDJATHA, W., Food and Technology
SUKARDI, E., Human Anatomy
SUKARDIKA, K., Microbiology
SURAATMAJA, S., Paediatrics
SURYADHI, N. T., Public Health
SUTAWAN, N., Social and Agricultural Economics
SUTER, K., Food Technology
SUTHA, G. K., Law
SUTJIPTA, N., Social and Agricultural Economics
SUWETA, G. P., Veterinary Science
SUYATNA, G., Social Economics
TJITARSA, I. B., Public Health
WIDNYANA, M., Law
WINAYA, P. D., Soil Fertility
WIRAWAN, D. N., Public Health
WITA, W., Cardiology

Private Universities

PETRA CHRISTIAN UNIVERSITY

Jl. Siwalankerto 121–131, Surabaya 60236

Telephone: (31) 8439040
Fax: (31) 8436418
E-mail: info@peter.petra.ac.id
Internet: www.petra.ac.id

Founded 1961
Private control
Languages of instruction: Indonesian, English
Academic year: August to August (2 semesters)

Rector: Ir PAUL NUGRAHA
Vice-Rector for Academic Affairs: Ir F. JONES SYARANAMUAL
Vice-Rector for Finance and Admin.: Dra GAN SHU SAN

Vice-Rector for Student Affairs: Drs HERI SAPTONO WARPINDYASMORO
Registrar: Dra WIDIARTI SUPRAPTO
Librarian: LIAW TOONG TJIEK
Library: 110,715 books, 8,277 audiovisual items
Number of teachers: 642
Number of students: 7,242
Publications: *Accounting and Finance Journal* (2 a year), *Architecture Dimension* (2 a year), *Civil Engineering Dimension* (2 a year), *Electrical Journal* (2 a year), *Industrial Engineering Journal* (industrial engineering dept, 2 a year), *Informatic Journal* (2 a year), *Management and Entrepreneur Journal* (2 a year), *Mechanical Engineering Journal* (2 a year), *Nirmana* (visual communication design dept, 2 a year), *K@TA* (language and literature, 2 a year), (published by The Institute of Research and Community Outreach in collaboration with Communication Science Dept)

DEANS

Faculty of Art and Design: Ir RIDUAN SUKARDI
Faculty of Civil Engineering and Planning: Ir HANDOKO SUGIHARTO
Faculty of Communication Studies: Drs IDO PRIJANA HADI (acting)
Faculty of Economics: Drs DEVIE
Faculty of Industrial Technology: Prof. Ir ROLLY INTAN
Faculty of Letters: Drs SAMUEL GUNAWAN

UNIVERSITAS 17 AGUSTUS 1945, JAKARTA
(17 August 1945 University, Jakarta)

Jl. Sunter Permai Raya Sunter Agung, Podomoro, Jakarta Utara 14350
Telephone and fax (21) 6410287
E-mail: untag@untag-jkt.org
Internet: www.untag-jkt.org
Founded 1945
Private control
Faculties of administration, economics, engineering, law, pharmacy, social and political science
Rector: Dr THOMAS NOACH PEEA.

UNIVERSITAS 17 AGUSTUS 1945, SURABAYA
(17 August 1945 University, Surabaya)

Telephone: (31) 5931800
Fax: (31) 5927817
E-mail: info@untag.ac.id
Internet: www.untag-sby.ac.id
Founded 1958
Language of instruction: Indonesian
Academic year: September to August
Faculties of agricultural science, economics, law, letters, psychology, social and political sciences.

UNIVERSITAS AL-AZHAR

Complex of Al-Azhar Mosque, Jakarta 12110
Telephone: (211) 7279275
Fax: (211) 7244767
Internet: www.uai.ac.id
Founded 2000
Private control
Rector: Prof. Dr Ir ZUHAL
Vice-Rector for Corporate Devt: DJOKOSANTOSO MOELJONO
Vice-Rector for Public Admin. and Human Resources: Drs MUHSIN LUBIS
Vice-Rector for Student Affairs and Academic Div.: Dr Ir AHMAD H. LUBIS

DEANS

Faculty of Economics: Prof. Dr SAYUTI HASIBUAN
Faculty of Engineering: Prof. Dr Ir SARDY
Faculty of Islamic Religion: Dr NURHAYATI DJAMAS
Faculty of Law: Prof. Dr ERMAN RAJAGUKGUK
Faculty of Mathematics and Science: Dr Ir WITONO BASUKI
Faculty of Psychology: Prof. HARSONO WIRYOSUMARTO
Faculty of Social and Political Sciences: Prof. Dr YAHYA A. MUHAIMIN

UNIVERSITAS ATMA JAYA YOGYAKARTA

Campus Bldg II, Thomas Aquinas Rd, Babarsari 44, Yogyakarta 55281
Telephone: (274) 487711
Fax: (274) 487748
E-mail: admisi@mail.uajy.ac.id
Internet: www.uajy.ac.id
Founded 1965
Private control
Rector: Ir A. KOESMARGONO
Vice-Rector for Admin., Finance and Human Resources: LUDDY INDRA PURNAMA.

UNIVERSITAS BAITURRAHMAH

Jl. Raya by-pass Km 15, Aie Pacah, Padang
Telephone: (751) 463069
Fax: (751) 463068
Internet: www.unbrah.ac.id
Founded 1979
Private control

DEANS

Faculty of Dentistry: R. RAMA PUTRANTO
Faculty of Economics: Dr H. YANDI SUKRI
Faculty of Medicine: Prof. H. AMIRMUSLIM MALIK
Faculty of Public Health: Dr WINARDI

UNIVERSITAS BAITURRAHMAH

Jl. Raya by-pass Km 15, Aie Pacah, Padang
Telephone: (751) 463069
Fax: (751) 463068
Internet: www.unbrah.ac.id
Founded 1979
Private control

DEANS

Faculty of Dentistry: R. RAMA PUTRANTO
Faculty of Economics: Dr H. YANDI SUKRI
Faculty of Medicine: Prof. H. AMIRMUSLIM MALIK
Faculty of Public Health: Dr WINARDI

UNIVERSITAS BALIKPAPAN

Jl. Pupuk Raya, Gn. Bahagia, Balikpapan
Telephone: (542) 765442
Fax: (542) 764205
E-mail: info@uniba-bpn.ac.id
Internet: www.uniba-bpn.ac.id
Private control
Rector: Prof. Dr ELLYANO S. LASAM

DEANS

Faculty of Economics: Drs HAIRUL ANAM
Faculty of Law: Drs MUHAMAD MUHDAR
Faculty of Sastras: Dra SITI HAFSAH
Faculty of Technology: Ir POEGOEH

UNIVERSITAS BATANGHARI JAMBI

Jl. Slamet Riyadi Broni, Jambi
Telephone: (741) 60673
Fax: (741) 64930
E-mail: rektorat@unbari.ac.id

Internet: www.unbari.ac.id
Private control
Rector: H. FACHRUDDIN RAZI

DEANS

Faculty of Agriculture: Ir M. SUGIHARTONO
Faculty of Economics: OSRITA HAPSARA
Faculty of Law: M. ZEN ABDULLAH
Faculty of Technology: Ir AZWARMAN

UNIVERSITAS BINA DARMA

Jl. Jend. Ahmad Yani, Palembang
Internet: www.binadarma.ac.id
Founded 1993
Private control
Faculties of communication, computer science, economy, engineering, language and literature, psychology
Pres.: Prof. Ir BUCHORI RACHMAN.

UNIVERSITAS BINA NUSANTARA
(Bina Nusantara University)

Kampus Anggrek, Jl. Kebon Jeruk Raya No. 27, Kebon Jeruk, Jakarta Barat 11530
Telephone: (21) 53696969
Fax: (21) 5300244
E-mail: publicrelations@binus.edu
Internet: www.binus.ac.id
Founded 1974
Private control
Rector: Prof. Dr Ir HARJANTO PRABOWO
Vice-Rector for Academic Devt: IMAN HERWIDIANA KARTOWISASTRO
Vice-Rector for Collaboration and Institutional Devt: WAYAH S. WIROTO
Vice-Rector for Operation and Resources: S. KOM. NELLY
Vice-Rector for Student Affairs and Community: Drs ANDREAS CHANG.

UNIVERSITAS BORNEO TARAKAN
(Borneo University)

Jl. Amal Lama 1, POB 170, Tarakan 77123
Telephone: (551) 5507023
E-mail: ubt@borneo.ac.id
Internet: www.borneo.ac.id
Founded 1999
Private control
Rector: ABDUL JABARSYAH
Faculties of agriculture, economics, fisheries, law, technology.

UNIVERSITAS BUNG HATTA

Jl. Sumatra Ulak Karang, Padang, Sumatra Barat 25133
Telephone: (751) 7051678
Fax: (751) 55475
E-mail: rektorat@bung-hatta.ac.id
Founded 1981
Private control
Rector: Prof. Dr HAFRIZAL SJANDRI

DEANS

Faculty of Civil Engineering and Planning: Ir HENRI WARMAN
Faculty of Fisheries and Marine Science: Ir H. YEMPITA EFENDI
Faculty of Industrial Technology: Dr Ir SAIFUL JAMAAN
Faculty of Law: BOY YENDRA TAMIN

UNIVERSITAS DWIJENDRA

Jl. Kamboja 17, Denpasar, Bali
Telephone: (361) 224383
Fax: (361) 233974
E-mail: universitasdwijendra@yahoo.co.id
Internet: www.dwijendra.com

Founded 1984
Private control

DEANS

Faculty of Agriculture: Ir ANAK AGUNG GDE PUSHPHA
Faculty of Engineering: Ir PUTU GDE ERY SUARDANA
Faculty of Law: PUTU DYATMIKAWATI
Faculty of Science and Communication: AYU RATNA WESNAWATI

UNIVERSITAS EKSAKTI

Jl. Veteran Dalam, 26B, Padang, Sumatera Barat 25131
Internet: www.univ-ekasakti-pdg.ac.id
Founded 1973
Private control

Rector: Prof. Dr ANDI MUSTARI
Vice-Rector I: Ir DANG SRI CHAERANI
Vice-Rector II: (vacant)
Vice-Rector III: Ir DANG SRI CHAERANI
Librarian: Dra SAUFNI CHALID
Library of 8,648 titles

DEANS

Faculty of Agriculture: Prof. Dr H. KASLI
Faculty of Economics: Dr AGUS SUTARJO
Faculty of Engineering: Drs ABU RIZAL
Faculty of Law: ADHI WIBOWO
Faculty of Sastras: Dra F. MEUTHIA YUSUF
Faculty of Social Science and Political Science: Drs INTIZHAM JAMIL

UNIVERSITAS HKBP NOMMENSEN
(Huria Kristen Batak Protestan Nommensen University)

Jl. Sutomo 4A, POB 1133, Medan
Telephone: (61) 4522922
Fax: (61) 4571426
E-mail: uhn@nommensen.org
Internet: www.nommensen.org
Founded 1954
Private control: Batak Christian Protestant Church
Language of instruction: Indonesian
Academic year: September to July

Rector: Ir B. RICSON SIMARMATA
Vice-Rector for Academic Affairs: Drs RAFLES D. TAMPUBOLON
Vice-Rector for Financial Affairs: Drs PANTAS SILABAN
Vice-Rector for Student Affairs: Ir HOTMAN MANURUNG
Dir of Community Service: Ir B. T. SIMANJOR-ANG
Dir of Research: Dr Ir JONGKER TAMPUBOLON
Number of teachers: 310
Number of students: 7,549
Publication: VISI (scientific magazine)

DEANS

Faculty of Agriculture: Ir P. PARLIN LUMBAN-RAJA
Faculty of Animal Husbandry: Ir HERLINA SARAGI
Faculty of Arts: Drs BEN M. PASARIBU
Faculty of Economics: Drs ADANAN SILABAN
Faculty of Education: Dr TAGOR PANGARIBUAN
Faculty of Engineering: Ir SINDAK HUTAURUK
Faculty of Law: TULUS SIAMBATON
Faculty of Public and Business Administration: Drs MONANG SITORUS

UNIVERSITAS IBN KHALDUN

Jl. Pemuda, Kav. 97, POB 1224, Rawamangun, Jakarta 13220
Telephone and fax (21) 4702564
Founded 1956

Languages of instruction: Indonesian, English, Arabic

Rector: Prof. Drs H. RAMLY HUTABARAT
Vice-Rector: Drs H. T. ABDUL MADJID
Vice-Rector: TITING HAZARA
Vice-Rector: Drs A. SAEFUDDIN SYAF
Registrar: Drs M. UMAR BAAY
Librarian: Drs H. AIDIL FITRI M. HATTA
Number of teachers: 115
Number of students: 3,000
Publication: Media UIC

DEANS

Faculty of Agriculture: Ir WASIS GUNADI
Faculty of Communication: Drs HAMID SUCHAS
Faculty of Economics: Ir H. LAW SURYANA
Faculty of Islamic Religion: H. AHMAD SOBARI
Faculty of Law: H. MUHYAR NUGRAHA
Faculty of Social and Political Science: (vacant)
Faculty of Theology: ABD. KHALIK NUR ALI
Institute of Islamic Mass Communication: Drs H. MOH. ALI
Institute of Social Research: Ir RUSLI DJOHAN

UNIVERSITAS IBN KHALDUN BOGOR

Jl. K. H. Sholeh Iskandar Km 2, POB 172, Bogor 16162
Telephone and fax (251) 356884
E-mail: rector@mail.uika-bogor.ac.id
Internet: www.uika-bogor.ac.id
Founded 1961
Private control
Language of instruction: Indonesian

Chancellor: Prof. Dr Ir H. AFFENDI ANWAR
Rector: Dr Ir SUNSUN SAEFULHAKIM
Head of Academic Admin.: Dra HERAWATI
Head of General Admin.: Hj. TITING SUHARTI
Librarian: Dra TATI TARSITI
Number of teachers: 300
Number of students: 4,293
Publication: Islamic Journal of Technology, Institutional and Humanity Development (2 a year)

DEANS

Faculty of Economics: H. AHMAD MUBAROK
Faculty of Education: Drs YUSUF SHOBIRI
Faculty of Engineering: Dr Ir PRAWOTO
Faculty of Islamic Studies: Drs H. E. BAH-RUDDIN
Faculty of Law: BARLY
Graduate School of Islamic Studies: Dr K. H. DIDIN HAFIDHUDDIN

UNIVERSITAS ISLAM INDONESIA
(Islamic University of Indonesia)

Gedung Rektorat, Jl. Kaliurang Km 14.5, Yogyakarta 55584
Telephone: (274) 898444
Fax: (274) 898459
E-mail: rektorat@uii.ac.id
Internet: www.uii.ac.id
Founded 1945
Private control
Language of instruction: Indonesian
Academic year: July to June

Rector: Dr LUTHFI HASAN
Vice-Rector for Academic Affairs: Dr S. F. MARBUN
Vice-Rector for Admin. and Financial Affairs: Dr H. MUQODIM
Vice-Rector for Collaborative Affairs: Dr A. AKHYAR ADNAN
Vice-Rector for Student Affairs: Ir H. BACH-NAS
Chief Admin. Officer: Drs H. SYAFARUDDIN ALWI
Librarian: Dra MURYANTI
Library of 73,000 vols

Number of teachers: 365
Number of students: 18,375
Publication: UII News (12 a year)

DEANS

Faculty of Civil Engineering and Planning: Prof. Dr Ir. WIDODO
Faculty of Economics: Drs SUWARSONO
Faculty of Industrial Technology: Ir H. BACHRUN SUTRISNO
Faculty of Islamic Science: Drs H. MUDHOFAR AKHWAN
Faculty of Law: Dr JAWAHIR THONTOWI
Faculty of Mathematics and Science: JAKA NUGRAHA
Faculty of Medical Science: Prof. Dr Dr RUSDI LAMSUDDIN
Faculty of Psychology: Dr SUKARTI

PROFESSORS

AHMAD ANTONO, Concrete Structures
ASYMUNI, H., Islamic Court
ATMADJA, M. K., International Law
BAHARUDDIN LOPA, Criminal Law
BERNADIB, S. I., Methods of Educational Evaluation, Educational Philosophy
CHOTIB, H. A., Ushl al-Fiqh
DAHLAN, H. Z., Principles of Islamic Law
FATKHURRAHMAN, History of Islam and Islamic Law
HADITONO, S. R., Individual Psychology
HARDJOSO, R., Irrigation
HASAN POERBOHADIWIDJAJA, Environmental Planning
KOESNOE, H. M., Private Procedural Law
KUSNADI HARDJOSUMANTRI, Environment Law
MOCHTAR YAHYA, H., General Philosophy
MUH ZEIN, Method and Evaluation of Islamic Education
MULADI, Politics of Law
PARLINDUNGAN, A. P., Agrarian Law
PARTADIREDJA, H. A., Indonesian Economy
PRAGNYONO, R., Fluid Mechanics
PURNOMO, B., Criminal Law
RIYANTO, B., Development Economy
SATJIPTO RAHARDJO, Sociology of Law
SITI RAHAYU, Psychology
SOEDIKNO MERTOKOESOEMO, Civil Law, Jurisprudence
SOEDIRDJO, Educational Counselling, Curriculum Advancement
SOEKANTO, Business Policy
SOELISTYO, International Economy
SOEPARNO, Analytical Geometry
SRI SUMANTRI, Constitutional Law
SUNARDJO, R., Irrigation Technology
SUYUTI, H. Z., Statistics
SYACHRAN BASAH, Administrative Law
SYAFTI MA'ARIF, A., Islamic Cultural History
TUGIMAN, N., Indonesian Language
UMAR, H. M., Modern Islamic Ideology
UMAR ASSASUDDIN, English
WARSITO, Polymer Chemistry
YUSUF, H. H., Hadiths I, II, III

UNIVERSITAS ISLAM INDONESIA CIREBON
(Islamic University of Indonesia in Cirebon)

Jl. Kapten Samadikun 31, Cirebon
Pres.: SA'DILLAH FATHONI
Sec.: M. Z. ABIDIEN

DEANS

Faculty of Economics: Drs ROSYADI
Faculty of Law: S. PRAWIRO
Faculty of Theology: H. MAS'OED

UNIVERSITAS ISLAM JAKARTA

Jl. Balai Takyat, Utan Kayu, Jakarta 13120
Telephone: (21) 8566451
Fax: (21) 8504818
E-mail: informasi@uid.ac.id

Internet: www.uid.ac.id
Founded 1951
Pres.: Prof. Dr SOEMEDI
Rector: SOEDJONO HARDJOSOEDIRO
Registrar: RASJIDI OESMAN
Librarian: ZAINAL ABIDIN
Number of teachers: 34
Number of students: 309

DEANS

Faculty of Economics: TAHER IBRAHIM
Faculty of Education: H. M. NUR ASJIK
Faculty of Law and Social Sciences: Drs H. NAZARUDIN

UNIVERSITAS ISLAM NUSANTARA

Jl. Soekarno-Hatta 530, POB 1579, Bandung 40286
Telephone: (22) 7509655
E-mail: humus@uninus.ac.id
Internet: www.uninus.ac.id
Founded 1959 as Universitas Nahdlatul Ulama, present name 1976
Academic year: September to August
Chancellor: Mayjen H. ACHMAD RUSTANDI
Rector: Dr H. DEDI MULYASANA
Deputy Rector: Drs SUHENDRA YUSUF
Deputy Rector: WAHDI SUARDI
Deputy Rector: H. RUBI ROBANA
Registrar: Drs RUSLI
Librarian: Drs UNDANG SUDAR SANA
Number of teachers: 402
Number of students: 6,574
Publications: *Literat* (4 a year), *Suara UNINUS* (4 a year)

DEANS

Faculty of Agriculture: Ir RUBI ROBANA
Faculty of Communication Sciences: Drs H. S. INSAR MARTADIKUSUMAH
Faculty of Economics: Drs KUSMANA
Faculty of Education and Literature: Dr DIDIN WAHIDIN
Faculty of Engineering: Ir AGUS EDY PRANOTO
Faculty of Islamology: Drs HANAFI
Faculty of Law: Drs ENJANG SURACHMAN

PROFESSORS

Faculty of Agriculture:
  AISYAH, H., Pedology
  SADELI, H.
Faculty of Communication Sciences:
  HUSEIN, S. I., Communications Sciences
Faculty of Economics:
  SURACHMAN, H., Management Economics
Faculty of Education and Literature:
  EFFENDY, E. R., Mathematics
  EMUH, Arabic
  FAISAL, Y. A., Indonesian Literature
  RUSYANA, Y., Indonesian Literature
  SLAMET, H. A., Indonesian Language
  SOEHARTO, B., Non-Formal Education
  SYAMSUDDIN, Curriculum Development and Methodology
Faculty of Engineering:
  HANDALI, D., Mathematics
  SUMARNO, Mathematics
Faculty of Islamology:
  DJATNIKA, H. R., Islamology
  HELMY, H., Islamology
  SALIMUDDIN, Islamology
Faculty of Law:
  BASYAH, S., Public Administration Law
  RASYIDI, L., Family Law
  SANUSI, H. A., Law, Public Administration and Education

UNIVERSITAS ISLAM RIAU
(Islamic University of Riau)

Jl. Kaharuddin Nasution 113, Perhentian, Marpoyan, Pekanbaru, Riau 28284
Telephone and fax (761) 674834
Internet: www.unri.ac.id
Founded 1962
Academic year: July to June
Rector: Prof. Dr MUCHTAR AHMAD
Vice-Rector I: Prof. Dr DADANG ISKANDAR
Vice-Rector II: AMIR HASAN
Vice-Rector III: ARIFFIEN MANSYOER
Vice-Rector IV: Drs SUARDI LOEKMAN
Librarian: FIRDAUS
Library of 5,150 vols
Number of teachers: 660 (160 full-time, 500 part-time)
Number of students: 7,391
Publications: *Alam* (4 a year), *Dinamika Pertanian* (4 a year), *Presfektif* (2 a year), *Saintis* (2 a year), *Siasat* (2 a year)

DEANS

Faculty of Agriculture: Ir T. ISKANDAR JOHAN
Faculty of Economics: Drs SHAHDANUR
Faculty of Education: Drs NAZIRUN
Faculty of Engineering: ALI MUSNAL
Faculty of Islamic Theology: ALI NUR
Faculty of Law: ARIFIN BOER
Faculty of Political and Sociological Sciences: ZAINI ALI

UNIVERSITAS ISLAM SUMATERA UTARA
(Islamic University of North Sumatra)

Campus Munawarah, Teladan, Medan 20217
Telephone and fax (61) 716790
Internet: www.uisu.ac.id
Founded 1952
Private control
Language of instruction: Indonesian
Academic year: July to June
Chancellor: Brig.-Gen. (retd) H. A. MANAF LUBIS
Rector: Drs H. M. YAMIN LUBIS
Registrar: Drs ABDUL HAKIM SIREGAR
Librarian: Drs SUDIAR SUDARGO
Number of teachers: 808
Number of students: 10,000
Publications: *Al Jamiah-UISU* (3 a year), *Buletin Fakultas Hukum* (6 a year), *Buletin Fakultas Pertanian* (4 a year)

DEANS

Faculty of Agriculture: Ir MEIZAL
Faculty of Economics: Drs AHMAD GHAZALI
Faculty of Education and Teaching: Drs H. ADLIN AHMAD
Faculty of Engineering: Ir H. M. ICHWAN NASUTION
Faculty of English: Drs MISRAN SUDIONO
Faculty of Islamic Communication: Drs MUSTAFA KAMIL
Faculty of Islamic Education: H. MAHMUD AZIZ SIREGAR
Faculty of Islamic Law: Drs SAID ALHINDUAN
Faculty of Law: AMRIZAL PULUNGAN
Faculty of Medicine: Prof. Dr H. HABIBAH HANUM NASUTION
Faculty of Political Science: Drs DANAN JAYA

UNIVERSITAS JAYABAYA

Campus A Jl. Pulomas Selatan kav 23, Jakarta Timur 13210
Telephone: (21) 4700877
Fax: (21) 4700893
Campus C Jl. Raya Bogor km 28, Cimanggis, Jakarta Timur 13210
Telephone: (21) 8719958
E-mail: info@jayabaya.ac.id

Internet: www.jayabaya.ac.id
Founded 1958
Chancellor: Dr H. MOESLIM TAHER
Rector: Prof. H. AMIR SANTOSO
Vice-Rector I: Hj. POPON SJARIF ARIFIN
Vice-Rector II: Drs H. SYAHID SUHANDI AZIS
Vice-Rector III: MANSYUR KARDI
Number of teachers: 782
Number of students: 15,000

DEANS

Faculty of Communication Science: DARMA SETIAWAN
Faculty of Economics: Prof. Dr Hj. MIRRIAM
Faculty of Law: Prof. Dr H. YUDHA BHAKTI
Faculty of Law and Management: H. INDARTONO RIVAI
Faculty of Political and Social Sciences: H. AMIR SANTOSO
Faculty of Technology: DARMA SETIAWAN

UNIVERSITAS KADER BANGSA PALEMBANG

Kampus A Jl. Mayjend. H. M. Ryacudu 88, Palembang
Telephone: (711) 510173
Kampus B Jl. Jend. Sudirman 1077–1088, Palembang
Telephone: (711) 318311
Internet: www.ukb.ac.id
Founded 2000
Private control
Programmes in engineering, health studies, legal studies, midwifery, pharmacy
Rector: H. T. WATHAN
Vice-Rector I: FERRY PRESCA
Vice-Rector II: Dr Hj. IRZANITA
Vice-Rector III: AHMAD DINAR.

UNIVERSITAS KATOLIK INDONESIA ATMA JAYA

Semanggi Campus Jl. Jend. Sudirman 51, Jakarta 12930
Telephone: (21) 5703306
Fax: (21) 5708811
Pluit Campus Jl. Pluit Raya 2, Jakarta 14440
Telephone: (21) 6691944
Fax: (21) 6606122
E-mail: rek@atmajaya.ac.id
Internet: www.atmajaya.ac.id
Founded 1960
Languages of instruction: Indonesian, English
Academic year: July to June
Chair. of Board: Drs R. DJOKOPRANOTO
Rector: Prof. Dr BERNADETTE N. SETIADI
Vice-Rector I: Ir ST. NUGROHO KRISTONO
Vice-Rector: Dr MARCELLINUS MARCELLINO
Vice-Rector: Drs. PETRUS PIUS SALAMIN
Vice-Rector: Dr LILIANA SUGIHARTO
Librarian: Dr DIAO AI LIEN
Library of 70,260 vols
Number of teachers: 1,071
Number of students: 13,452
Publications: *Atma nan Jaya* (science, 3 a year), *Gloria Juris* (law and human rights, 2 a year), *Jurnal Administrasi dan Bisnis* (administration and business, 4 a year), *Jurnal Ekonomi dan Bisnis* (economics and business, 2 a year), *Majalah Kedokteran* (medical science, 3 a year), *Metris* (science and technology, 4 a year), *Respons* (social ethics, 2 a year)

DEANS

Faculty of Business Administration: Dr POL A. Y. AGUNG NUGROHO
Faculty of Economics: Drs SOFIAN SUGIOKO
Faculty of Engineering: Dr M. M. LANNY W. PANDJAITAN

Faculty of Law: ANTONIUS P. S. WIBOWO
Faculty of Medicine: Dr SATYA JOEWANA
Faculty of Psychology: Dr ENGELINA TANZIL BONANG
Faculty of Teacher Training and Education: Dr LAURA F. N. SUDARNOTO
Faculty of Technobiology: Prof. Dr ANTONIUS SUWANTO
Graduate School: Dr ALOISIUS AGUS NUGROHO

UNIVERSITAS KATOLIK PARAHYANGAN
(Parahyangan Catholic University)

Ciumbuleit 94, Bandung 40141
Telephone: (22) 2032655
Fax: (22) 2031110
E-mail: humas@home.unpar.ac.id
Internet: www.unpar.ac.id
Founded 1955
Private control
Language of instruction: Indonesian
Academic year: August to June
Chair., Board of Trustees: Prof. Dr B. S. KUSBIANTORO
Rector: Dr CECILIA LAUW JADE SWAN
Vice-Rector for Academic and Student Affairs: Dr PAUL. P. RAHARDJO
Vice-Rector for Financial Affairs: Drs ARTHUR PURBOYO
Vice-Rector for Organization and Personnel: Dr R. ISMADI BEKTI SANTOSO
Librarian: Dra MELINA L. TARDIA
Number of teachers: 1,321 (334 full-time, 687 part-time)
Number of students: 9,781
Publications: Bina Ekonomi (4 a year), Integral (4 a year), Jurnal Administrasi Publik (2 a year), Jurnal PACIS (2 a year), Melintas (4 a year), Profil (4 a year), Pro Justitia (4 a year), Potensia (4 a year), Rekasaya (4 a year), Research Journal (2 a year)

DEANS

Faculty of Economics: Dra CATHARINA TAN LIN SOEI
Faculty of Engineering: Dr Ir R. W. TRIWEKO
Faculty of Industrial Technology: Dr BUDI HUSODO BISOWARNO
Faculty of Law: R. ISMADI S. BEKTI
Faculty of Mathematics and Natural Sciences: Dra ROSA DE LIMA
Faculty of Philosophy: Dr Ir F. X. RUDIYANTO SUBAGIO
Faculty of Social and Political Sciences: Drs DENNY MARCELINUS TRI ARYADI
Graduate School: Prof. Dr Ir PAULUS PRAMANTO RAHARDJO

PROFESSORS

BROTOSISWOJO, B. S., Computer Physics
DIRJOSISWORO, S., Law
DJAJAPUTERA, A., Civil Engineering
NIMPOENO, J. S., Psychology
RAHARDJO, P. P., Geotechnology
SIDHARTA, B. A., Law
SIREGAR, S., Architecture
SJAFRUDDIN, A., Law
SOELARNOSIDJI, D., Geotechnology in Civil Engineering
SUHARTO, IGN., Chemical Engineering
SUNDJAJA, R. S., Management
SURJOATMONO, B., Civil Engineering
WINARDI, Economics

UNIVERSITAS KLABAT

Airmadidi, Manado 95371
Telephone: (431) 891035
Fax: (431) 891036
E-mail: email@unklab.ac.id
Internet: www.unklab.ac.id
Founded 1965

Private control
Rector: A. B. SEPANG.

UNIVERSITAS KRISNADWIPAJANA

Jl. Raya Jati Waringin, Pondok Gede, Jakarta 13077
Telephone: (21) 8462229
Fax: (21) 8462461
E-mail: humas@unkris.ac.id
Founded 1952
Language of instruction: Indonesian
Academic year: February to December
Rector: Dr LODEWIJK GULTOM
Vice-Rector I: PUGUH SANTOSO
Vice-Rector II: Hj. LINDA ISMAIL
Vice-Rector III: Drs EDWARD DOLOKSARIBU
Dir of Postgraduate Programmes: Prof. Dr RUSLI RAMLI
Sec.: WAYAN SUGIYANA
Librarian: Dr DASPAN
Number of teachers: 128
Number of students: 2,000

DEANS

Faculty of Economics: Drs. MUHADI RIYANTO
Faculty of Law: Dr LODEWIJK GULTOM
Faculty of Science Administration: Drs. JACK R. SIDABUTAR
Faculty of Technology: RUSJDI HADJERAT

UNIVERSITAS KRISTEN INDONESIA
(Christian University of Indonesia)

Jl. Mayjen Sutoyo 2, Cawang, Jakarta 13630
Telephone: (21) 8092425
Fax: (21) 80886882
E-mail: humas-uki@uki.ac.id
Internet: www.uki.ac.id
Founded 1953
Rector: Prof. Dr K. TUNGGUL SIRAIT
Vice-Rector for Academic Affairs: Dr A. S. L. RAMPEN
Vice-Rector for Admin. Planning and Devt: E. GUNAWAN
Vice-Rector for Student Affairs: A. SIREGAR
Number of teachers: 739
Number of students: 8,000
Publications: Dialektika, Dinamika Pendidikan, Emas, Honeste Vivere, Jurnal Ekonomi, Logos, UKI Bulletin

DEANS

Faculty of Economics: Drs A. ZABUA
Faculty of Education: TOGAP LINANJUNTAK
Faculty of English Language and Literature: Dr L. S. BANGUN
Faculty of Law: Dr BERNARD HUTABARAK
Faculty of Medicine: Dr S. M. L. TORUAN
Faculty of Social and Political Science: Prof. Dr PAYUNG BANGUN
Faculty of Technology: Dr A. SOEBAGIO

UNIVERSITAS KRISTEN MARANATHA
(Maranatha Christian University)

Jl. Prof. Suria Sumantri 65, Bandung 40164
Telephone: (22) 2012186
Fax: (22) 2015154
E-mail: humas@maranatha.edu
Internet: www.marantha.edu
Founded 1965
Language of instruction: Indonesian
Academic year: September to August
Rector: Prof. Dr Ir H. P. SEPTORATNO SIREGAR
Vice-Rector I: Ir RUDY WAWOLUMAJA
Vice-Rector II: Ir NOEK SULANDARI
Vice-Rector III: Pdt. FERLY DAVID
Vice-Rector IV: Dr FELIX KASIM
Number of teachers: 500
Number of students: 12,000

Publications: Journal Kedoktoran (Medicine Journal, 1 a year), Majalah Ilmiah Maranatha (Maranatha Scientific Magazine, 4 a year), Media Komunikasi Maranatha (Maranatha Communication Media, 3 a year)

DEANS

Faculty of Art and Design, Undergraduate Programme: Dr GAI SUHARJA
Faculty of Economics, Undergraduate Programme: TEDY WAHYUSAPUTRA
Faculty of Engineering, Undergraduate Programme: Prof. Dr Ir BENJAMIN SOENARKO
Faculty of Information Technology, Undergraduate Programme: RADIANT VICTOR IMBAR
Faculty of Letters, Undergraduate Programme: Drs EDWARD ALDRICH LUKMAN
Faculty of Medicine, Undergraduate Programme: Dr SURJA TANURAHARDJA
Faculty of Psychology, Undergraduate Programme: Drs R. SANOESI SUSANTO
Master of Accounting, Postgraduate Programme: RIKI MARTUSA
Master of Management, Postgraduate Programme: Dra IKA GUNAWAN
Master of Psychology, Postgraduate Programme: Dr PARWATI SUPANGAT

UNIVERSITAS KRISTEN SATYA WACANA
(Satya Wacana Christian University)

Jl. Diponegoro 52–60, Salatiga 50711
Telephone: (298) 321212
Fax: (298) 321433
Internet: www.uksw.edu
Founded 1956
Languages of instruction: Indonesian, English(for special programmes only)
Academic year: August to July
Rector: Prof. Dr KRIS HERAWAN TIMOTIUS
Asst Rector I: Dr Ir DANIEL DAUD KAMEO
Asst Rector II: HARIJONO
Asst Rector III: UMBU RAUTA
Asst Rector IV: AGNA SULIS KRAVE
Registrar: SUDI WINARNO
Librarian: Drs DJASMANI
Number of teachers: 306 (full-time)
Number of students: 9,325
Publications: Citra Wacana (4 a year), Dian Ekonomi (2 a year), Kritis (3 a year)

DEANS

Faculty of Agriculture: Ir SUPRIHATI
Faculty of Biology: Drs AGNA SULIS KRAVE
Faculty of Economics: Prof. HENDRAWAN SUPRATIKNO
Faculty of Education and Teacher Training: Drs AUGUS HERMAN NAIOLA
Faculty of Languages and Letters: Drs URIP SUTIYONO
Faculty of Law: J. DANNY ZACHARIAS
Faculty of Pedagogy: Dr LOBBY LUKMONO
Faculty of Performing Arts: Drs AGASTYA RAMA LISTYA
Faculty of Psychology: Dra HARI SUTJININGSIH
Faculty of Science and Mathematics: Dr AGUS KRISTIJANTO
Faculty of Social and Political Sciences: Dr KUTUT SUWONDO
Faculty of Technology: Ir BUDIHARDJA MURTIANTA
Faculty of Theology: Drs. DANIEL NUHAMARA
Professional Programmes: LINA SINATRA
Postgraduate Programmes: Prof. DANIEL DAUD KAMEO

UNIVERSITAS MAHAPUTRA MUHAMMAD YAMIN SOLOK

Jl. Raya Koto Baru 7, Solok 27361
Telephone: (755) 20128
Fax: (755) 20127
Private control

Programmes in accounting, agribusiness, agrotechnology, biology, economic development, legal studies, livestock, management and mathematics.

UNIVERSITAS MAHASARASWATI DENPASAR

Jl. Kamboja 11A, Denpasar, Bali
Telephone: (361) 227019
E-mail: info@unmas.ac.id
Internet: www.unmas.ac.id
Founded 1963
Private control.

UNIVERSITAS MEDAN AREA

Campus 1 Jl. Kolam 1, Medan 20223
Telephone: (61) 7366878
Fax: (61) 736068
Campus 2 Jl. Jend Gatot Subroto 395, Medan 20118
Telephone: (61) 4567330 Campus 3 Jl. Sei Serayu 70A, Medan 20118
Telephone: (61) 8214875
E-mail: uma001@indosat.net.id
Internet: www.universitasmedanarea.com
Founded 1983
Private control
Faculties of agriculture, engineering, law, social and political sciences and psychology.

UNIVERSITAS METHODIST INDONESIA

Campus 1 Jl. Hang Tuah 8, Medan 20152
Telephone: (61) 4536735
Fax: (61) 4567533
Campus 2 Jl. Setia Budi Pasar II, Tg. Sari
Internet: umi-medan.info
Founded 1969
Private control
Rector: Dr THOMSON P. NADAPDAP
Vice-Rector I: Prof. Dr J. NAIBAHO
Vice-Rector II: Dr P. SIMANJUNTAK
Vice-Rector III: Drs OCTAVIAN RAGNAR SITORUS

DEANS

Faculty of Agriculture: Ir BERTON E. LUM-BANTOBING
Faculty of Computer Science: Drs LISTON SIHITE
Faculty of Economics: Drs RAFIDIN HUTAPEA
Faculty of Literature: Drs P. SIMANJUNTAK
Faculty of Medicine: Dr HOPHOPTUA SIAHAAN

UNIVERSITAS MUHAMMADIYAH ACEH

Jl. Muhammadiyah 91, Desa Bathoh Lueng Bata, Banda Aceh 23245
Telephone: (651) 31583
Fax: (651) 34092
Founded 1969
Private control
Library of 1,300 titles.

UNIVERSITAS MUHAMMADIYAH JAKARTA

Campus A Jl. K. H. Ahmad Dahlan, Cirendeu Ciputat, Jakarta Selatan
Telephone: (21) 7401894
Fax: (21) 7430756

Campus B Jl. Cempaka Putih Tengah 27, Jakarta Pusat
Telephone: (21) 4256024
E-mail: info@umj.ac.id
Internet: www.umj.ac.id
Rector: AGUS SUNARTO
Faculties of agriculture, economics, law, medicine, religion, social and political sciences, technology.

UNIVERSITAS MUHAMMADIYAH KUPANG

Jl. K. H. Ahmad Dahlan 17, Kupang, Nusa Tengarra Timur
Telephone: (380) 833693
Fax: (380) 25333
Founded 1987
Private control
Rector: Drs DARSYAD ANTJO
Library of 5,282 vols, 15,882 periodicals.

UNIVERSITAS MUHAMMADIYAH MALANG
(Muhammadiyah University of Malang)

Jl. Raya Tlogomas 246, Malang 65144
Telephone: (341) 464318
Fax: (341) 460782
E-mail: webmaster@unix.umm.ac.id
Internet: www.umm.ac.id
Founded 1966
Languages of instruction: Indonesian, English
Academic year: September to June
Rector: Drs H. MUHADJIR EFFENDY
Vice-Rector for Academic Affairs: Ir H. MUH. HAMZAH
Vice-Rector for Financial Affairs: Drs H. WAKIDI
Vice-Rector for Student Affairs: Ir H. ALI SAIFULLAH
Chief of Academic Admin.: Ir DAMAT
Chief of Public Admin.: Drs H. FAUZAN
Librarian: WAHJOE DWI PRIJONO
Number of teachers: 816
Number of students: 20,274
Publications: Bestari Journal (4 a year), Bestari Tabloid (12 a year)

DEANS

Faculty of Agriculture: Ir MISBAH RUHIYAT
Faculty of Animal Husbandry: Ir ABDUL MALIK
Faculty of Economics: Drs WAHYU HIDAYAT RIYANTO
Faculty of Engineering: Ir SUNARTO
Faculty of Islamic Education: Drs MOH. NURHAKIM
Faculty of Law: MOKH. HAJIH
Faculty of Medicine: Ir H. MUH. HAMZAH (acting)
Faculty of Psychology: Drs LATIPUN
Faculty of Social and Political Science: Dra VINA SALVIANA
Faculty for Teacher Training and Education: Drs AHSANUL IN'AM

UNIVERSITAS MUHAMMADIYAH MATARAM

Jl. K. H. A. Dahlan 1, Pegesangan, Mataram
Telephone: (370) 633723
Founded 1980
Private control
Rector: Ir H. SUHARTO TJITROHADJONO
Library of 8,500 titles
Number of teachers: 80
Number of students: 1,930

UNIVERSITAS MUHAMMADIYAH SUMATERA UTARA

Jl. Kapt. Mukhtar Basri 3, Medan 20238
Telephone: (61) 6619056
Fax: (61) 6625474
Internet: www.umsu.ac.id
Founded 1957
Private control
Rector: H. BAHDIN NUR TANJUNG
Vice-Rector I: Drs H. ARMANSYAH
Vice-Rector II: H. SUHARWADI K. LUBIS
Vice-Rector III: Drs AGUSSANI

DEANS

Faculty of Agriculture: Ir ALRIDIWIRSAH
Faculty of Economics: PASARIBU ZULASPAN TUPTI
Faculty of Engineering: RAHMATULLAH
Faculty of Islamic Religion: AKRIM
Faculty of Law: FARID WAJDI
Faculty of Medicine: TAUFIQ
Faculty of Social and Political Sciences: R. KUSNADI
Faculty of Teacher Training and Education: Hj. NUR'AIN LUBIS

UNIVERSITAS MUHAMMADIYAH TAPANULI SELATAN DI PADANG SIDEMPUAN

Jl. Sutan Moch. Arief 32, Padang Sidempuan, Tapanuli Selatan 22716
Telephone: (634) 21696
Founded 1983
Private control
Rector: H. MARAGINDA HARAHAP.

UNIVERSITAS MUSLIM NUSANTARA AL-WASHLIYAH

Medan
E-mail: admin@umnaw.com
Internet: www.umnaw.com
Private control
Rector: Prof. Hj. Sri SULISTYAWATI

DEANS

Faculty of Agriculture: Ir ERNITA
Faculty of Economics: ARBY BACHTIAR
Faculty of Law: PURBA NELVITIA
Faculty of Mathematics and Natural Sciences: PANDAPOTAN NASUTION
Faculty of Sastras: S. S. SUFATMI
Faculty of Teacher Training and Education: Drs ULIAN BARUS

UNIVERSITAS NAHDLATUL WATHAN MATARAM

Jl. Kaktus 1–3, Mataram 82137
Telephone: (370) 641275
Fax: (370) 641275
Private control.

UNIVERSITAS NASIONAL

Jl. Sawo Manila, Pasar Minggu, Jakarta 12520
Telephone: (21) 7806700
Fax: (21) 7802718
E-mail: info@unas.ac.id
Internet: www.unas.ac.id
Founded 1949
Private control
Accredited by Badan Akreditasi Nasional (Nat. Accreditation Board)
Language of instruction: Indonesian
Academic year: September to August
Rector: Drs EL AMRY BERMAWI PUTERA
Vice-Rector for Academic Affairs: Prof. Ir NGADINO SURIP
Vice-Rector for Community Service: Drs UMAR SAID As

Vice-Rector for Financial and Gen. Admin. Affairs: Drs EKO SUGIYANTO
Vice-Rector for Int. Cooperation and Devt: Drs FALDY RASYIDIE
Univ. Librarian: MUMUH M. B. S. HUM
Library of 18,159 vols, 26,842 books, 205 magazines and journals, 11,048 theses
Number of teachers: 745
Number of students: 10,500
Publications: *Ilmu Dan Budaya* (social science, 12 a year), *Jounal Poelitik* (political science), *Journal Sawo Manila* (literature)

DEANS

Faculty of Agriculture: Ir TRI WALUYO
Faculty of Biology: Drs IMRAN S. L. TOBING
Faculty of Economics: Dr SURYONO EFENDI
Faculty of Engineering and Science: Ir AJAT SUDRAJAT
Faculty of Health Science: Dr ROSMAWATI LUBIS
Faculty of Informatics, Communications and Technology: Dr Ir ISKANDAR FITRI
Faculty of Law: Dr ARRISMAN
Faculty of Literature and Language: Drs WAHYU WIBOWO
Faculty of Social and Political Science: Drs HASTO ATMOJO SUROYO

UNIVERSITAS NGURAH RAI DENPASAR

Jl. Padma Penatih, Denpasar, Timur
Telephone and fax (361) 468349
E-mail: fisip@unr.ac.id
Internet: www.unr.ac.id
Founded 1981
Private control.

UNIVERSITAS PAKUAN

Jl. Pakuan, POB 452, Bogor 16143
Telephone: (251) 8312206
Fax: (251) 356927
Internet: www.unpak.ac.id
Founded 1961
Chancellor: Dr H. MASHUDI
Rector: ACHMAD SUBROTO
Sec.: R. H. NATANEGARA
Number of teachers: 60
Number of students: 350

DEANS

Faculty of Economics: Drs USMAN ZAKARIA
Faculty of Law: BINTATAR SINAGA
Faculty of Mathematics and Natural Science: Ir. SOEDARSONO
Faculty of Technology: DJAUHARI NOOR

UNIVERSITAS PANCASILA

Srengseng Sawah, Jagakarsa, Pasar Minggu, Jakarta Selatan 12640
Telephone: (21) 7270086
Fax: (21) 7271868
E-mail: info@univpancasila.ac.id
Internet: www.univpancasila.ac.id
Founded 1966
Language of instruction: Indonesian
Academic year: September to August
Chair.: Dr Ir SISWONO YUDOHUSODO
Rector: EDIE TOET HENDRATNO
Vice-Rector for Academic Affairs and Finance and Admin.: Prof. Ir ANTONIUS ANTON
Vice-Rector for Student Affairs: H. ALWI ASSEGAF
Vice-Rector: Drs ANANG FADILLAH RIVAI
Registrar: Dr SAPTADI WIDJAYA SETIABUDI
Librarian: WAKIM
Library of 30,906 vols
Number of teachers: 860
Number of students: 12,017

Publications: *Media Humas, Buletin Farmasi, Suara Ekonomi, Retorika, Jurnal Teknik*

DEANS

Faculty of Economy: Dra DEWI TRIRAHAYU
Faculty of Engineering: Prof. Ir ANTONIUS ANTON
Faculty of Law: INDAH HARLINA
Faculty of Pharmacy: Drs I. WAYAN REDJA

UNIVERSITAS PEMBANGUNAN PANCABUDI

Jl. Jend. Gatot Subroto, Km 4, 5 Simpang Sei Sikambing, Medan, Sumatera Utara
Telephone: (61) 8455571
Fax: (61) 4514808
E-mail: unpab@pancabudi.ac.id
Internet: www.pancabudi.ac.id
Founded 1961
Private control
Rector: H. MUHAMMAD ISA INDRAWAN
Vice-Rector for Academic Affairs: RIZAL AHMAD
Vice-Rector for Admin. and Finance: SAIMARA SEBAYANG
Vice-Rector for Student Affairs: RIADIONO.

UNDIKNAS UNIVERSITY

Jl. Bedugul 39 Sidakarya, Denpasar 80225
Telephone: (361) 723868
Fax: (361) 723990
E-mail: info@undiknas.ac.id
Internet: www.undiknas.ac.id
Founded 1969
Private control
Rector: Prof. Dr GEDE SRI DAMA

DEANS

Faculty of Administrative Science and Communication: Dr Drs I NYOMAN SUBANDA
Faculty of Economics and Business: Drs IDA I DEWA MADE RAI MAHAPUTRA
Faculty of Information and Engineering: I WAYAN SUTAMA
Faculty of Law: Prof. Dr I NYM BUDIANA

PETRA CHRISTIAN UNIVERSITY

Jl. Siwalankerto 121–131, Surabaya 60236
Telephone: (31) 8439040
Fax: (31) 8436418
E-mail: info@peter.petra.ac.id
Internet: www.petra.ac.id
Founded 1961
Private control
Languages of instruction: Indonesian, English
Academic year: August to August (2 semesters)
Rector: Ir PAUL NUGRAHA
Vice-Rector for Academic Affairs: Ir F. JONES SYARANAMUAL
Vice-Rector for Finance and Admin.: Dra GAN SHU SAN
Vice-Rector for Student Affairs: Drs HERI SAPTONO WARPINDYASMORO
Registrar: Dra WIDIARTI SUPRAPTO
Librarian: LIAW TOONG TJIEK
Library: 110,715 books, 8,277 audiovisual items
Number of teachers: 642
Number of students: 7,242
Publications: *Accounting and Finance Journal* (2 a year), *Architecture Dimension* (2 a year), *Civil Engineering Dimension* (2 a year), *Electrical Journal* (2 a year), *Industrial Engineering Journal* (industrial engineering dept, 2 a year), *Informatic Journal* (2 a year), *Management and Entrepreneur Journal* (2 a year), *Mechan-

ical Engineering Journal (2 a year), *Nirmana* (visual communication design dept, 2 a year), *K@TA* (language and literature, 2 a year), (published by The Institute of Research and Community Outreach in collaboration with Communication Science Dept)

DEANS

Faculty of Art and Design: Ir RIDUAN SUKARDI
Faculty of Civil Engineering and Planning: Ir HANDOKO SUGIHARTO
Faculty of Communication Studies: Drs IDO PRIJANA HADI (acting)
Faculty of Economics: Drs DEVIE
Faculty of Industrial Technology: Prof. Ir ROLLY INTAN
Faculty of Letters: Drs SAMUEL GUNAWAN

UNIVERSITAS PGRI KUPANG

Jl. Anggur 10 Naikoten I, Kupang 85118
Telephone and fax (380) 821824
E-mail: pgrintt@yahoo.com.

UNIVERSITAS SAMAWA

Jl. Raya Sering, Sumbawa, Besar
Telephone: (371) 625848
E-mail: unsasumbawa@yahoomail.com
Private control.

UNIVERSITAS SERAMBI MEKKAH

Jl. Tengku Imum Lueng Bata Desa Bathoh, Banda Aceh 23249
Telephone: (651) 26160
Founded 1985
Private control
Rector: Prof. Dr M. ISA SULAIMAN.

UNIVERSITAS SISINGAMANGARAJA XII TAPANULI UTARA DI SIBORONG-BORONG

North Tapanuli, Siborongborong
Telephone and fax (633) 41017
Founded 1987
Private control
Rector: Ir ADRIANI SIAHAAN
Vice-Rector: Ir ARVITA SIHALOHO
Vice-Rector: Ir T. B. PAKPAHAN
Vice-Rector: Drs MAULIATE SIMORANGKIR

DEANS

Faculty of Agriculture: ELSERIA SIBURIAN
Faculty of Economics: Dr AGUSNI PASARIBU
Faculty of Engineering: Ir M. SIAHAAN
Faculty of Law: TUNGGUL SIMORANGKIR
Faculty of Teacher Training and Education: Drs DONVER PANGGABEAN

UNIVERSITAS SULTAN AGENG TIRTAYASA

Jl Raya Jakarta KM 4, Pakupatan, Serang, Banten
Telephone: (254) 280330
Fax: (254) 281254
E-mail: info@untirta.ac.id
Internet: www.untirta.ac.id
Founded 2001
Private control
Rector: Ir RAHMAN ABDULLAH
Faculties of economics, engineering.

SWISS GERMAN UNIVERSITY

Kampus BSD City, Bumi Serpong, Damai, Java 15321
Telephone: (21) 5376221
Fax: (21) 5376201
E-mail: rector@sgu.ac.id

Internet: www.sgu.ac.id
Founded 2009
Private control
Rector: Prof. Dr PETER PSCHEID
Pro-Rector I: Prof. Dr MARSUDI W. KISWORO
Pro-Rector II: Dipl.-Ing. KETUT TEJAWIBAWA
Library of 39,000 books, 107 scientific journals, 10 magazines

DEANS

Faculty of Business Administration: (vacant)
Faculty of Engineering: Prof. Dipl.-Ing. JUERGEN GRUENEBERG
Faculty of Information Technology: Dipl.-Ing. KHO I ENG
Faculty of Life Sciences: Dr MARULI PANDJAITAN
Faculty of Social Sciences: (vacant)

UNIVERSITAS TABANAN

Jl. Wagimin 8, Kediri, Tabanan, Bali
Telephone: (361) 811605
Founded 1981
Private control
Rector: Ir IDA BAGUS GDE WIRAKUSUMA
Library of 1,901 vols, 2,356 periodicals.

UNIVERSITAS TRIKARYA

Jl. Gaperta Ujung 58, Perladangan Helvetia, Medan Helvetia, Medan 20124
Telephone: (61) 8450419
E-mail: univ_trikarya@plasa.com
Founded 2002
Private control.

UNIVERSITAS TRISAKTI

Jl. Kyai Tapa 1, Grogol, Jakarta 11440
Telephone: (21) 5663232
Fax: (21) 5644270
E-mail: sekun@trisakti.ac.id
Internet: www.trisakti.ac.id
Founded 1965
Language of instruction: Indonesian
Academic year: September to August
Rector: Prof. Dr THOBY MUTIS
Vice-Rector for Academic Affairs: Prof. Dr H.YUSWAR Z BASRI,
Vice-Rector for Cooperation and Human Resources: Ir ASRI NUGRAHANTI
Vice-Rector for Personnel, Admin. and Finance: Prof. Dr ITJANG D. GUNAWAN
Vice-Rector for Student Affairs: H. I. KOMANG SUKA'ARSANA
Secretariat: H. SOFAN
Head of Library: Dra FARIDA SALIM
Number of teachers: 2,681 (1,691 full-time, 701 part-time)
Number of students: 30,754
Publication: *Masyarakat Kampus* (24 a year)

DEANS

Faculty of Art and Design: Prof. Drs YUSUF AFFENDI DJALARI
Faculty of Civil Engineering and Planning: Dr Ir EKA SEDIADI RASYAD
Faculty of Dentistry: Dr BAMBANG S. TRENGGONO
Faculty of Earth and Energy Technology: Ir H. MOH THAMRIN
Faculty of Economics: Prof. Dr FARIDA JASFAR
Faculty of Industrial Technology: Ir DOCKY SARASWATI
Faculty of Landscape Architecture and Environmental Technology: Ir IDA BAGUS RABINDRA
Faculty of Law: ENDAR PULUNGAN
Faculty of Medicine: Prof. JULIUS E. SURYAWIDJAJA

UNIVERSITAS VETERAN REPUBLIK INDONESIA

Jl. Baruga Raya Kampus II, Ujung Pandang
Telephone: (411) 491203
Faculties of education, history, law.

UNIVERSITAS WARMADEWA

Denpasar, Bali
Internet: www.warmadewa.ac.id
Founded 1983
Private control
Rector: Prof. Dr I MADE SUKARSA
Vice-Rector I: Drs I MADE YUDHIANTARA
Vice-Rector II: IDA BAGUS UDAYANA PUTRA
Vice-Rector III: Ir A. A. NGURAH MAYUN WIRAJAYA

DEANS

Faculty of Economics: Drs I WAYAN ARJANA
Faculty of Engineering: I GUSTI MADE S. DIASA
Faculty of Law: NI LUH MADE MAHENDRAWATI
Faculty of Literature: Drs NYOMAN SUJAYA

Institutes

ABFI Institute Perbanas: Jl. Perbanas, Karet Kuningan, Setiabudi, Jakarta 12940; tel. (21) 5252533; fax (21) 5228460; e-mail info@perbanasinstitute.ac.id; internet www .perbanasinstitute.ac.id; f. 2007, by merger of Sekolah Tinggi Ilmu Ekonomi (College of Economics, f. 1969) and Sekolah Tinggi Manajemen Informatika dan Komputer (College of Information Management and Computers, f. 1993); offers programmes in banking, general management and risk management; Rector Dr Ir FATCHUDIN; Vice-Rector for Academic Affairs Dr STEPH SUBANIDJA; Vice Rector for Graduate Programmes Prof. Dr ADLER HAYMANS MANURUNG; Vice-Rector for Human Resource Devt Dr WILSON R. LUMBANTOBING; Vice-Rector for Student and Alumni Affairs Dr DAVID SITUMORANG.

Balai Pengkajian Teknologi Pertanian Jawa Barat (West Java Research Institute for Agricultural Technology): Jl. Kayuambon 80, Lembang, Bandung 40391; tel. (22) 2786238; fax (22) 2789846; e-mail bptp-jabar@litbang.deptan.go.id; internet jabar.litbang.deptan.go.id; f. 1994.

Institut Filsafat Theologi dan Kepemimpinan Jaffray (IFTK Jaffray Jakarta) (Institute for Theological and Leadership Philosophy Jaffray): Jl. Jatinegara Timur II 35, Jakarta 13350; tel. (21) 8570986; fax (21) 8570988; e-mail iftkj@centrin.net.id; internet www.iftk-jaffray.com; f. 1932, present name and status 1991; Rector Dr Drs JERRY RUMAHLATU; Vice-Rector for Academic Affairs NASOKHILI GIAWA; Vice-Rector for Admin. and Finance Dr MAGDALENA TOMATALA; Vice-Rector for Student Affairs PHILEMON INDAKRAY.

Institut Ilmu Sosial dan Ilmu Politik Jakarta (Institute of Social and Political Sciences): Jl. Raya Lenteng Agung 32, Jakarta Selatan 12610; tel. (21) 7806223; fax (21) 7817630; e-mail admin@iisip.ac.id; internet www.iisip.ac.id; f. 1953; faculties of administration, communication, social and political sciences; Rector MASLINA W. HUTASUHUT.

Institut Keguruan dan Ilmu Pendidikan Budi Utomo: Jl. Simpang Arjuno 14B, Malang; tel. (341) 326019; fax (341) 335070; e-mail info@budiutomo.ac.id; f. 1984; offers programmes in economics, English, history and sociology, mathematics, sports and health.

Institut Keguruan dan Ilmu Pendidikan Mataram (Institute of Teacher Training and Education): Gedung Dwitya Jl. Pemuda 59, Mataram; tel. (370) 632082; internet ikipmataram.ac.id; f. 1967; Rector H. LALU SAID RUHPINA; Head Librarian A. SUNANDAR.

Institut Keguruan dan Ilmu Pendidikan PGRI Bali: Jl. Seroja, Tonya, East Denpasar, Denpasar; tel. (361) 431434; fax (361) 701128; f. 1983; library: 3,100 titles; Rector REDHA GUNAWAN.

Institut Keguruan dan Ilmu Pendidikan PGRI Jember: Jl. Jawa 10, Jember; tel. (331) 335823; fax (331) 335977; internet www .ikip-jember.org; f. 1979; Rector Drs H. M. ARIFIN.

Institut Keguruan dan Ilmu Pendidikan PGRI Madiun: Jl. Setiabudi 85, Madiun; tel. (351) 462986; fax (351) 459400; e-mail rektorat@ikippgri-madiun.ac.id; internet ikippgri-madiun.ac.id; Rector Drs PARJI.

Institut Keguruan dan Ilmu Pendidikan PGRI Semarang: Jl. Cipto Lontar 1, Semarang; tel. (24) 8316377; fax (24) 8448217; internet ikip-pgrismg.net; faculties of language and literature, mathematics and science education; library: 10,771 titles, 35,244 theses; Rector MUHDI.

Institut Keguruan dan Ilmu Pendidikan Saraswati Tabanan: Jl. Pahlawan 2, Delod Peken, Tabanan 82113; tel. (362) 811267.

Institut Pertanian STIPER Yogyakarta: Jl. Nangka II, Maguwoharjo, Depok, Sleman, Yogyakarta 55282; tel. and fax (247) 885479; e-mail info@instiper.ac.id; internet www .instiper.ac.id; f. 1958; faculties of agricultural technology, agriculture, forestry; library: 789 reference titles, 327 journals; Rector Dr Ir PURWADI; Vice-Rector Dr Ir HARSAWARDANA; Vice-Rector I Dr Ir A. SIH AYIEK SAYEKTI.

Institut Sains dan Teknologi AKPRIND Yogyakarta: Jl. Kalisahak 28, Komplek, Balapan 55222; tel. (274) 563029; fax (274) 563847; e-mail ista@indo.net.id; internet www.akprind.ac.id; faculties of applied science, industrial technology and mineral technology.

Institut Sains dan Teknologi TD Pardede: Jl. Dr. TD Pardede 8, Kecamatan, Medan 20153; tel. and fax (61) 4569877; e-mail mail@istp.ac.id; internet www.istp.ac .id; f. 1987; faculties of civil engineering and planning, mineral technology and industrial technology; Rector Ir RUDOLF SITORUS; Vice-Rector I Drs L. SIHOMBING; Vice-Rector II Ir OMNY PARNGARIBUAN; Vice-Rector III Ir SIBARANI.

Institut Teknologi Adhi Tama Surabaya: Jl. Arief Rachman Hakim 100, Surabaya; tel. (31) 5945043; fax (31) 5994620; internet www .itats.ac.id; library: 19,165 book titles; Rector HADI SETIYAWAN; Vice-Rector I ARIEF RACHMAN; Vice-Rector II KUNTO EKO SUSILO; Vice-Rector III BAMBANG SETYONO.

Institut Teknologi Indonesia: Jl. Raya Puspiptek Serpong, Tangerang, Banten 15320; tel. and fax (21) 7561102; internet www.iti.ac.id.

Institut Teknologi Medan: Jl. Gedung Arca 52, Medan 20217; tel. and fax (61) 7363771; e-mail itm@itm.ac.id; internet www .itm.ac.id; f. as Akademi Teknik Dwiwarna, name changed to Institut Teknologi Sumatera 1963, Sekolah Tinggi Teknik Medan 1976, present name and status 1984; Rector Ir MAHRIZAL MASRI; Vice-Rector I Ir ILMI ABDULLAH; Vice-Rector II MUNAJAT; Vice-Rector III MAHYUZAR MASRI.

Institut Teknologi Nasional (National Institute of Technology): Mustafa 23, Bandung 40124; tel. (22) 7272215; internet www .itenas.ac.id; f. 1972 as Akademi Teknologi

Nasional, present name and status 1984; Rector Prof. Dr Ir HARSONO TAROEPRATJEKA; Vice-Rector for Academic and Student Affairs Ir SYAHRIL SAYUTI; Vice-Rector for Finance and Gen. Admin. Ir YANTI HELIANTY; Vice-Rector for Planning and Cooperation Dr IMAM ASCHURI.

Higher Colleges

Sekolah Tinggi Bahasa Asing (STBA) Yapari-ABA Bandung: Jl. Cihampelas 194, Bandung 40131; tel. (22) 2035426; fax (22) 2036765; e-mail info@stbayapariaba.ac.id; internet stbayapariaba.ac.id; Private control.

Sekolah Tinggi Filsafat Driyarkara (School of Philosophy Driyarkara): Jl. Cempaka Putih Indah 100A, Jembatan Serong Rawasari, Jakarta 10520; tel. (21) 4247129; fax (21) 4224866; e-mail stfd@dnet.net.id; internet www.driyarkara.ac.id; f. 1969; offers programmes in philosophy and science theology; 316 students; Chair. Prof. Dr A. EDDY KRISTIYANTO; publ. *Driyarkara* (4 a year).

Sekolah Tinggi Ilmu Ekonomi Malangkuçeçwara (Malangkuçeçwara School of Economics): Jl. Terusan Candi Kalasan, Blimbing, Malang 65142; tel. (341) 491813; e-mail info@stie-mce.ac.id; internet www.stie-mce.ac.id; f. 1971; depts of accounting and finance; Pres. NEVI DANILA; Vice-Pres.

Drs BUNYAMIN; Vice-Pres. Drs TACHJUDDIN; Vice-Pres. Drs KADARUSMAN.

Sekolah Tinggi Ilmu Ekonomi Pasundan (Higher College for Economics Pasundan): Jl. Usman Ambon 4, Kacang Pedang, Pangkalpinang 33125; tel. (717) 438735; fax (717) 438736; e-mail info@stie-ibek.ac.id; internet stiepas.ac.id; f. 2000; offers programmes in accounting and management; Chair. YOLANDA PUSPASARI.

Sekolah Tinggi Ilmu Ekonomi Solusi Bisnis Indonesia (Higher College for Economics and Business Solutions Indonesia): Jl. Ring Rd Utara 17, Condong Catur, Yogyakarta 55283; tel. and fax (274) 887984; internet stie-sbi.ac.id; programmes in accounting and management; Chair. LUCIA IKA FITRIASTUTI.

Sekolah Tinggi Ilmu Sosial dan Ilmu Politik Kebangsaan–Masohi (College of Social and Political Science): Jl. Christina Martha Tiahahu 15, Masohi; tel. (914) 22057; internet www.stisipkebangsaanmasohi.com; f. 1999; administered by Yayasan Perguruan Tinggi Kebangsaan (Nat. Higher Education Foundation) Masohi; Chair. Drs J. KAPRESSY.

Sekolah Tinggi Manajemen Informatika dan Teknik Komputer (STIKOM) Surabaya (Higher College of Information Management and Computer Engineering Surabaya): Jl. Kedung Baruk 98, Surabaya; tel. (31) 8721731; e-mail info@stikom.edu; internet www.stikom.edu; f. 1983.

Sekolah Tinggi Teknik Poliprofesi Medan: Jl. Sei Batanghari 3–4, Medan; tel. (61) 8446729; e-mail layanan@sttp-poliprofesi.ac.id; internet sttp-poliprofesi.ac.id; f. 2002; Dir AKMAN DAULAY.

Sekolah Tinggi Teknologi Jakarta: Jl. Jatiwaringin Raya 278, Pondok Gede, Jakarta; tel. (21) 8462316; fax (21) 8463692; e-mail sttj@cbn.net.id; internet www.sttj.ac.id; f. 1972; Chair. ROSSI SETIADJI.

Sekolah Tinggi Teknologi Nuklir–BATAN (Higher College for Nuclear Technology): Jl. Babarsari POB 6101 YKBB, Yogyakarta 55281; tel. (247) 484085; fax (247) 489715; internet www.sttn-batan.ac.id; f. 1982; research and devt of nuclear technology.

Schools of Art and Music

Akademi Seni Karawitan Indonesia Padang Panjang (Academy for Traditional Music and Dance): Jl. Puti Bungsu 35, Padang Panjang, Sumatra Barat; tel. (752) 82077; fax (752) 82803; f. 1966; offers diploma courses in ballet, dance, music and music performance; library: 6,196 vols; 62 teachers; 428 students; Dir Prof. MARDJANI MARTAMIN; Registrar BAHRUL PADEK; Librarian Drs ANNAS HAMIR.

IRAN

The Higher Education System

The first modern institution of higher education was the Dar al-Fanun, a technical institute founded in 1851. In 1928 two more technical institutes were founded, now known as Iran University of Science and Technology and K. N. Toosi University of Technology. In 1934 Dar al-Fanun was incorporated into the newly established University of Tehran, the first multi-disciplinary institution of higher education. Universities were closed following the Islamic revolution in 1979 but gradually reopened from 1983. Public universities and colleges are administered by the Ministry of Science, Research and Technology, and medical universities (which are classified separately) are controlled by the Ministry of Health and Medical Education. In 1982 an 'open' university, Islamic Azad University, was founded, which now has 80 centres in cities and towns. It is not funded by central government, it administers its own entrance examination and charges tuition fees. Payame Noor University was founded in 1987 and offers correspondence courses and continuing adult education. There are 54 state-operated universities, and by 2008 there were over 3.5m. students enrolled, with 1.7m. of these at the Islamic Azad University. Other higher education institutions include general and professional colleges, technological institutes and vocational establishments.

To enter higher education, students must gain the Pre-University Certificate and sit the National Entrance Examination. (Islamic Azad University administers its own entrance examination—Kunkur.) Iranian higher education is based on a 'credit semester' system; one credit is gained following 17 hours of taught classes, 34 hours of laboratory work or 51 hours of practical ('workshop') experience. The first undergraduate qualification is the Associate degree, awarded after four semesters (two years) and requiring 67–72 credits. Colleges of Further Education offer an equivalent degree known as Kardani. The Bachelors is the second (and main) undergraduate degree, lasting eight semesters (four years) and requiring 130–35 credits. First degrees offering professional titles are available in pharmacy, medicine, dentistry and veterinary science; these last 11 semesters (six years). A student with the Bachelors may progress to postgraduate education, which consists of the Masters (Karshenasi-Arshad or Fogh-Licence) and Doctorate. The Masters is a course lasting four semesters (two years) and requiring 28–32 credits (of which the thesis accounts for four to 10 units). The final university degree is the Doctorate, which consists of two stages: first, the student must complete 12–30 credits of classroom-based learning; second, a period of original research leading to submission of a thesis is required. The course lasts a total of four to five years.

University courses must be accredited by either the Ministry of Science, Research and Technology Directorate of Development or the Ministry of Health and Medical Education.

Regulatory Bodies

GOVERNMENT

Ministry of Culture and Islamic Guidance: Baharestan Sq., Tehran; tel. (21) 32411; fax (21) 33117535; e-mail info@ershad.gov.ir; internet www.ershad.gov.ir; Minister MUHAMMAD HOSSEIN SAFFAR-HARANDI.

Ministry of Education: Si-e-Tir St, Emam Khomeini Sq., Tehran; tel. (21) 32421; fax (21) 675503; e-mail info@medu.ir; internet www.medu.ir; Minister AI REZA ALI AHMADI.

Learned Societies

GENERAL

UNESCO Office Tehran: Bahman Bldg, Sa'ad Abad Palace Complex, Tehran 19894; tel. (21) 22751315; fax (21) 22751318; e-mail tehran@unesco.org; internet www.unesco.org/tehran; designated Cluster Office for Afghanistan, Iran, Pakistan and Turkmenistan; Dir QUNLI HAN.

ECONOMICS, LAW AND POLITICS

Iran Management Association: POB 15855-359, Tehran; Karimkhan Blvd 1/53 corner of Asjodi St, Tehran; tel. (21) 8827878; fax (21) 8835278; e-mail info@iranmanagement.org; internet www.iranmanagement.org; f. 1960 to promote sound management principles and techniques for the improvement of management in Iran, and to create understanding and cooperation among managers in Iran and other countries; 200 individual and 200 institutional mems; library of 8,000 vols; Sec.-Gen. PARVIZ BAYAT; publs *Management Magazine* (in Persian, with summary in English, 12 a year), *Modiriat* (Management, 6 a year).

HISTORY, GEOGRAPHY AND ARCHAEOLOGY

Ancient Iran Cultural Society: Jomhorie Eslamie Ave, Shahrokh St, Tehran; f. 1961; Man. Dir A. QUORESHI.

British Institute of Persian Studies: c/o The British Acad., 10 Carlton House Terrace, London, SW1Y 5AH, United Kingdom; tel. (20) 7969-5203; fax (20) 7969-5401; e-mail bips@britac.ac.uk *in Tehran:* 1553, Khiaban-e Dr Ali Shariati, Qolhak, Tehran 19396–13661; tel. (21) 22601937; fax (21) 22604901; e-mail bips@parsonline.net; internet www.bips.ac.uk; f. 1961; cultural institute, with special emphasis on history, archaeology and all aspects of Iranian studies; 400 mems; library of 10,000 books and MSS; Hon. Sec. (London Office) PETER DAVIES; Librarian (Tehran Office) FARIBA RAYHANPOUR; publ. *Iran* (1 a year).

LANGUAGE AND LITERATURE

British Council: North Entrance British Embassy Compound, Shariati St, Qholhak, Tehran 19396 13661; tel. (21) 2001222; fax (21) 2007604; e-mail info@ir.britishcouncil.org; internet www.britishcouncil.org/iran; offers courses and exams in English language and British culture and promotes cultural exchange with the UK; Dir ANDREW MURRAY.

MEDICINE

Iranian Society of Microbiology: Department of Microbiology and Immunology, Faculty of Medicine, University of Tehran; tel. (21) 88955810; e-mail ijmicrobiology@gmail.com; internet www.ism.ir; f. 1940; 185 mems; Gen. Sec. G. H. NAZARI; publ. *Iranian Journal Microbiology*.

NATURAL SCIENCES

Mathematical Sciences

Iranian Mathematical Society: POB 13145-418, Tehran; tel. (21) 8808855; fax (21) 8807775; e-mail iranmath@ims.ir; internet www.ims.ir; f. 1971; 2,750 mems; Pres. E. S. MAHMOODIAN; publs *Bulletin* (2 a year), *Farhang va Andishaye Riyazi* (2 a year).

Research Institutes

GENERAL

Institute for Humanities and Cultural Studies (IHCS): 64 St, Seyyed Jamal-eddin Ave, Tehran 14374; tel. (21) 88048037; fax (21) 88036317; e-mail info@ihcs.ac.ir; internet www.ihcs.ac.ir; f. 1981; research faculties: Literature, History, History and Philosophy of Science, Religious Studies, Linguistics, Social Sciences, Cultural Studies; languages of instruction: Arabic, English, Persian; library of 120,000 vols; Dir Prof. MEHDI GOLSHANI; publs *Afaq al-Hizarah al-Islamiyyah* (2 a year), *Journal of Humanities* (4 a year), *The Farhang* (4 a year), *Science and Religion Bulletin* (2 a year).

AGRICULTURE, FISHERIES AND VETERINARY SCIENCE

Agricultural Biotechnology Research Institute of Iran (ABRII): POB 4119, Mardabad Ave, Karaj 31585; tel. (261) 2708282; fax (261) 2704539; e-mail khayam@abrii.ac.ir; internet www.abrii.ac.ir; f. 1983 as the Plant Biotechnology Department of Seed and Plant Improvement

Institute; depts of Genomics, Tissue Culture and Gene Transformation, Genetics, Cellular and Molecular Biology, Microorganisms and Biosafety, Physiology and Proteomics, Technical Services and Research Support; Dir-Gen. Dr MOJTABA KHAYYAM NEKOUEI.

Animal Science Research Institute: POB 31585-1483, Karaj, Tehran; tel. (261) 4430010; fax (261) 4413258; e-mail info@asri.ir; internet www.asri.ir; f. 1933; research on cattle, water buffalo, sheep, goats, poultry and honeybees; library of 6,425 books, 176 periodicals; Gen. Dir Dr MOHAMMAD ALI KAMALI; publ. *Animal Husbandry Research Institute.*

Plant Pests and Diseases Research Institute: POB 19395-1454, Evin/Tabnak St, Tehran; tel. (21) 2403012; fax (21) 2403691; e-mail info@ppdri.ac.ir; internet www.ppdri.ac.ir; f. 1943; research on pests and diseases of agricultural crops; botany, entomology, biological control, pesticides and agricultural zoology; library of 55,000 vols (English and Farsi), 480 periodicals (English and Farsi); Dir Dr G. A. ABDOLLAHI; publs *Applied Entomology and Phytopathology* (1 a year, in Farsi and English), *Rostaniha – Botanical Journal of Iran* (1 a year, in Farsi and English), *Iranian Journal of Plant Pathology* (1 a year, in Farsi and English), *Journal of the Entomological Society of Iran* (1 a year, in Farsi and English).

Razi Vaccine and Serum Research Institute: POB 31975–148, Karaj 3197619751; tel. (261) 4570038; fax (261) 4552194; e-mail admin@rvsri.com; internet www.rvsri.com; f. 1930; epizootological and ecological studies of animal diseases and human and animal biology; research and preparation of all veterinary vaccines, some human vaccines and therapeutic sera; postgraduate courses in virology and microbiology; languages of instruction: Persian, English; library of 13,000 books, 800 periodicals; Gen. Dir Prof. ABDOLHOSSEIN DALIMI; publ. *Archives of the Razi Institute* (in English, 1 a year).

ECONOMICS, LAW AND POLITICS

Institute for Political and International Studies (IPIS): Shahid Bahonar Ave, Shahid Aghaee St, POB 19395/1793, Tehran; tel. (21) 22802671; fax (21) 22802649; e-mail cominfo@ipis.ir; internet www.ipis.ir; f. 1983; acts as a research and information centre on int. relations, law, economics and Islamic studies, with emphasis on the Middle East, the Persian Gulf and Central Asia; holds conferences and seminars on contemporary int. issues; library of 200,000 vols; Pres. ALI AHANI; Dir-Gen. Dr SEYED R. MOSAVI; publs *Amyu Darya* (in English and Russian), *Central Asia and Caucasus Review Quarterly* (in Farsi), *Foreign Policy Quarterly* (in Farsi), *Iranian Journal of International Affairs Quarterly* (in English), *Islam and International Relations* (in Farsi), *Journal of Alalaghat Aliranieh* (in Arabic).

Institute for Trade Studies and Research: 240 North Kargar St, POB 14185-671, Tehran 14187; tel. (21) 6425118622378; fax (21) 69383746929634938374; e-mail info@itsr.ir; internet itsr.irtp.comwww.itsr.ir; f. 1980; library of 70,000 vols; DirPres. Dr A. R.MAHMOUOD EFTEKHARIDODANGEH; publs *Commercial Surveys* (6 a year), *Journal of Trade StudiesIranian Journal of Trade Studies (IJTC)* (4 a year).

HISTORY, GEOGRAPHY AND ARCHAEOLOGY

Institut Français de Recherche en Iran: Ave Shahid Nazari, 52 rue Adib, POB 15815-3495, Tehran 94371; tel. (21) 66401192; fax (21) 6405501; e-mail ifri@ifriran.org; internet www.ifriran.org; f. 1897, present name 1983; research into Iranian civilization, contact between French and Iranian scholars; library of 42,000 vols; Dir CHRISTOPHE BALAIJ; publs *Abstracta Iranica* (1 a year), *Cahiers de la DAFI, Bibliothéque Iranienne.*

National Cartographic Centre: POB 13185-1684, Azadi Sq., Meraj Ave, Tehran; tel. (21) 6000031; fax (21) 6001971; internet www.ncc.org.ir; f. 1953; library of 4,000 vols, 2,500 reports; Dir Dr M. MADAD; publ. *Naghshebardari* (Journal of Surveying, 4 a year).

MEDICINE

Institut Pasteur: 69 Pasteur Ave, Tehran; tel. (21) 66953311; fax (21) 66465132; e-mail office@pasteur.ac.ir; internet www.pasteur .ac.ir; f. 1921; vaccines, research in microbiology, biochemistry, biopharmaceuticals, biotechnology and human genetics, molecular biology, parasitology and mycology, physiology and pharmacology; teaching and postgraduate training; Dir-Gen. Dr ABDOLHOSSEIN ROUHOL AMINI NAJAFABADI; publ. *Iranian Biomedical Journal.*

NATURAL SCIENCES

Institute for Research in Fundamental Sciences: POB 19395–5746, Niavaran Bldg, Niavaran Sq., Tehran; tel. (21) 22287013; fax (21) 22290151; e-mail ipminfo@ipm.ir; internet www.ipm.ir; f. 1989; Schools of Astronomy, Cognitive Sciences, Computer Science, Mathematics, Nanoscience, Particles and Accelerators, Philosophy, Physics; Dir M. J. A. LARIJANI; publ. *Akhbar* (4 a year).

RELIGION, SOCIOLOGY AND ANTHROPOLOGY

Anthropological Research Institute: Azadi Ave, Zanjan Int., POB 13445-719, Tehran; tel. (21) 6016367; fax (21) 6018628; f. 1937; attached to Iranian Cultural Heritage Organization; Dir MOHAMMAD MIRSHOKRAEE.

Islamic Research Foundation, Astan Quds Razavi: POB 91735-366, Mashhad; tel. (511) 2232501; fax (511) 2230005; internet www.irf.net; f. 1984; research into Islamic subjects: the Qu'ran, the Hadith, jurisprudence, scholastic theology, Islamic text editing, translating Islamic books, study of Islamic arts, production of Islamic CDs; nat. and int. seminars; 180 mems; library of 62,000 vols; Man. Dir Prof. ALI AKBAR ELAHI KHORASANI; publ. *Mehkat* (4 a year).

TECHNOLOGY

Electric Power Research Centre: POB 15745–448, Shahrak Ghods, Pounak Bakhtari Blvd, Tehran; tel. (21) 8079401; fax (21) 8094774; f. 1983; attached to Min. of Energy; library of 12,000 vols, 151 periodicals; Pres. S. M. TABATABAEE; publ. *Journal of Electrical Science and Technology* (4 a year).

Libraries and Archives

Isfahan

Municipal Library: Shahied Nikbakht St, POB 81638, Isfahan; tel. (31) 621200; fax (31) 621100; f. 1991; 60,000 vols.

University of Isfahan Library: Isfahan; internet book.ui.ac.ir/cgi-bin/lib; 112,150 vols, half in Persian and Arabic, the remainder in European languages; Persian MSS and incunabula; Dir Dr HOSSEIN HARSIJ.

Mashhad

Ferdowsi University of Mashhad Information Centre and Central Library: POB 331-91735, Mashhad; tel. (511) 8789263; fax (511) 8796822; e-mail cent-lib@um.ac.ir; internet c-library.um.ac.ir; f. 1971; 280,000 vols; Dir of Information Centre and Central Library Prof. Dr MEHRDAD MOHRI.

Organizations of Libraries, Museums and Documents Center of Astan-e Quds-e Razavi: POB 91735-177, Mashhad; tel. (511) 2216555; fax (511) 2220845; e-mail info@aqlibrary.org; internet www.aqlibrary .org; f. 15th century; general library and assistance for researchers, 33 br. libraries, document centre, museums; 2m. vols, 65,000 MSS and 6m. other documents; 78,200 vols of foreign books (in 64 languages); Gen. Dir Dr ALI MUHAMMAD BARADRAN RAFIEI.

Tabriz

Tabriz Public Library (Ketabkhaneh Melli Tabriz): Tabriz; 12,816 vols; Dir SEYYED MASOUD NAQIB.

Tarbiat Library: Daneshsara Sq., Tabriz; tel. (41) 5222190; f. 1921; 29,750 vols; Dir HOSSEIN ASADI.

University of Tabriz Central Library and Documentation Centre: Tabriz; tel. (411) 3344705; fax (411) 3355993; e-mail a-assadzadeh@tabrizu.ac.ir; internet www .2tabrizu.ac.ir; f. 1967; 95,871 vols, 6,231 microfiches, 4,300 maps, 6,231 microfilms, 1,643 periodicals, 647 tapes; Librarian A. ASSADZADEH.

Tehran

Central Library and Documentation Centre of Shahid Beheshti University: Evin, Tehran 19834; tel. (21) 293155; f. 1960; 315,529 vols, 3,190 periodicals; Librarian Dr ZAHRA GOOYA; publs *Sourat Ketabhaye Fehrest Shodeh, Tazebaye Ketabkhaneh.*

Central Library and Documentation Centre of Tehran University: Enghelab Ave, Tehran; tel. (21) 61112362; fax (21) 66495388; e-mail libpublic@ut.ac.ir; internet library.ut.ac.ir; f. 1949, re-housed 1970; Central Library of 850,000 vols, faculty libraries of 950,000 vols; Librarian Dr A. A. ENAYATI.

Centre for Socio-Economic Documentation and Publications: Baharestan Sq., Tehran 11365; tel. 3271; fax 301135; f. 1962, reorganized 1982; attached to Planning and Budget Organization; brs in 6 divs: technical services, information services and network affairs, libraries (Central Library, Archive for Development Maps and Projects and 25 regional libraries), editing, graphics and production, distribution; libraries: 49,000 vols, 576 periodicals, 1,627 titles microforms, 16,000 titles devt projects, 18,000 maps and plans, databases of selected articles; Dir MEHDI PAZOUKI; publ. *Periodical Index to Socio-Economic Articles* (4 a year).

Institute for Political and International Studies Library and Documentation Centre: POB 19395-1793, Tajrish, Tehran; tel. (21) 2571010; fax (21) 2802643; internet www.ipis.ir; f. 1983; attached to the Foreign Ministry; spec. library and assistance for researchers; 20,000 vols on Islamic science, history, politics, economics, law, geography, diplomacy, military studies; 400 periodicals; Dir-Gen. Dr S. M. K. SAJJADPOUR; publs *African Studies Journal* (2 a year), *Al-Alaaghaat* (4 a year), *Amu Darya* (4 a year), *Asiyaje Miyaneh va Ghofghaaz* (4 a year), *Iranian Journal of International Affairs* (4 a year), *Siyasat-e-Khare* (Journal of Foreign Policy, 4 a year).

Iran Bastan Museum Library: Khiaban-e Imam Khomeini, Khiaban-e Sium-e Tir,

Tehran 11365; f. 1964; 17,000 vols; Dir M. R. RIYAZI KESHE.

Iran University of Medical Sciences and Health Services Central Library and Documentation Centre: POB 14155-6439, Tehran; tel. (21) 8058644; fax (21) 8054360; e-mail centrlib@iums.ac.ir; internet www .iums.ac.ir; f. 1975; 35,000 books, 1,323 current periodicals, 9,355 theses, 3,000 audiovisual titles; Dir SUSSAN ERTEJAEI.

Iranian Cultural Heritage Organization Documentation Centre: POB 13445-1594, Tehran; tel. (21) 6003126; fax (21) 6003126; e-mail info@ichodoc.ir; internet www.ichodoc .ir; f. 1994; 36,000 vols, 237 periodicals, 15,667 research reports, 2,030 films, 22,180 maps, 70,000 photographs, 155,560 slides, 125,000 negatives, 122 video cassettes, 204 audio cassettes, 771 CDs, 923 posters, 4,000 microfiches; Dir FARIBA FARZAM.

Iranian Information and Documentation Centre (IRANDOC): 1090 Englab St, POB 13185/1371, Tehran; tel. (21) 66494980; fax (21) 66462254; e-mail info@irandoc.ac.ir; internet www.irandoc.ac.ir; f. 1968; attached to Min. of Higher Education; research; training; information and knowledge management services; work in the fields of basic sciences, agriculture, medical sciences, humanities and technology; advises and assists in the establishment of specialized information centres and acts as the nat. reference centre; organizes, processes and disseminates scientific and technologic documents; key role in nat. and ministerial orgs; 24,000 vols, 210 current periodicals, 70,000 student dissertations; Dir of IRANDOC SEYYED OMID FATEMI; publs *Abstracts of Scientific/Technical Papers* (4 a year), *Current Research in Iranian Universities and Research Centres* (4 a year), *Directory of Scientific Meetings held in Iran* (4 a year), *Dissertation Abstracts of Iranian Graduates Abroad* (4 a year), *Ettela s Resani* (Technical Bulletin, 4 a year), *Iranian Dissertation Abstracts* (4 a year), *Iranian Government Reports* (4 a year), *Iranian Scholars and Experts* (1 a year).

Library of the Bank Markazi Jomhouri Islami Iran (Central Bank of the Islamic Republic of Iran): Pegah St, Mirdamad Blvd, POB 11365/8531, Tehran; tel. (21) 29953263; fax (21) 29953290; e-mail libinfoservices@cbi .ir; internet lib.cbi.ir/libcbi; f. 1960; 110,000 books and reports; Dir MAHROKH LOTFI.

Malek Library: Melale Mottahed Ave, Janb e Vezarat Omour Kharege, Tehran; tel. (21) 66743744; fax (21) 66705974; e-mail khoddari@yahoo.com; f. 1937; 70,000 vols covering the sciences, 19,000 titles, 6,400 MSS; attached to the Malek Museum; Museum Dir and Head of Research Dept SAEID KHODDARI NAEINI.

National Library and Archives of Iran: National Library Blvd, Haqani Expressway (West–East), POB 15875-3693, Tehran 1537614111; tel. (21) 88644080; fax (21) 88644082; e-mail pria@nlai.ir; internet www .nlai.ir; f. 1937; 684,465 books (510,479 in Farsi and Arabic, 173,986 in other languages), 1m. periodicals, 172,000 MSS documents and patchworks, 14,729 Arabic and Farsi MSS, 67,280 pamphlets and sheets, 9,848 lithographic prints, 320,093 non-book items; maintains library higher education centre for library science; Dir KAZEM MOOSAVI BOJNOURDI; publ. *Iranian National Bibliography* (online and CD-ROM, 1 a year).

Parliament Library (1): Ketabkhane-ye Majles-e Shora-ye Eslami 1, Baharestan Sq., POB 11365-866, Tehran; tel. (21) 33126092; fax (21) 33130919; internet www .majlislib.com; f. 1912; 272,000 books, 28,000 bound vols of 5,000 Persian, Arabic and Latin periodicals, 24,000 manuscripts vols, 12m. national and historical documents, 10,000 photographs, 460 magnetic tapes, 90 old maps, 17,500 manuscripts on microfilm, 3,000 CDs of manuscripts, 27 vols of theses and dissertations, 12,000 government reports, 300 microfilms and 250 CDs of old Iranian periodicals; UN depository; museum (see Museums and Art Galleries); Dir SEYYED MOHAMMAD ALI AHMADI ABHARI; publs *Name-ye Baharestan* (2 a year), *Payam-e Baharestan* (12 a year).

Attached Library:

Parliament Library (2): Ketabkhaneh Majles-e Shora-ye Eslami 2, Emam Khomeini Ave, Tehran 13174; tel. (21) 6135335; fax (21) 3130919; f. 1959; spec. colln on Iranian, Islamic and Oriental studies: 49,554 printed books, 5,166 bound vols of 395 Persian, Arabic and Latin periodicals; Dir SEYYED MOHAMMAD ALI AHMADI ABHARI.

Museums and Art Galleries

Isfahan

Armenian Museum of All Saviour's Cathedral: POB 81735-115, Julfa, Isfahan; tel. (311) 6243471; fax (311) 6270999; e-mail sourbv@yahoo.com; internet www.newjulfa .org; f. 1930, rehoused 1971 with additions; under the supervision of the Diocesan Council of the Armenians in Isfahan; 750 ancient MSS, 570 paintings, miniatures and antique church vestments, tomb portraits; library of 25,000 vols.

Chehel Sotun Museum: Isfahan; Dir KARIM NIKZAD.

Mashhad

Astan-e Qudse Razavi Museums: Sahn-e-Kausar, Mashhad 91348-43388; tel. (511) 2241105; fax (511) 2224570; e-mail info@ aqlibrary.org; internet www.aqm.ir; f. 1937, inaugurated 1945; Anthropology Museum, Central Museum, Weapons Museum, Koran Museum, Stamp Museum, Astronomical Instruments and Clocks Museum, Natural Objects and Shells Museum, Crystal and Porcelain Museum, Coins and Medals Museum, Carpet Museum, Museum of Holy Qur'an and Precious Objects presented by His Eminence Ayatollah Khamenei, History of Mashhad Museum and Paintings Museum; Dir MOHSEN AMIRY NIA.

Qom

Qom Museum: Eram St, Qom; tel. 7741491; f. 1936; under the supervision of the Archaeological Service; Dir B. YOSEFZADEH.

Shiraz

Pars Museum: Shiraz; tel. (11) 24151; f. 1938; exhibits incl. manuscripts, earthenware, ancient coins; Dir MOHAMMAD HOSSEIN ESTAKHR; Curator HASRAT ZADEH SORUDE.

Tehran

Golestan Palace Museum: Maidan Panzdah Khordad, POB 11365-4595, Tehran 11149; tel. (21) 3113335; fax (21) 3111811; e-mail info@golestanpalace.org; internet www.golestanpalace.ir; f. 1894; Dir PARVIN SADR SEGHT-OL-ESLAMI.

Iran Bastan Museum: Khiaban-e Imam Khomeini, Khiaban-e Sium-e Tir, Tehran 11364; tel. (21) 6672061; f. 1946; archaeological and cultural research; conservation, repair and exhibition of cultural material; 4 depts; library of 15,924 vols; Dir J. GOLSHAN.

Malek Museum: Melale Mottahed Ave, Tehran; tel. (21) 66726613; fax (21) 66717364; e-mail khoddari@yahoo.com; internet www.aqmlm.ir; f. 1937, opened new bldg in 1997; various objects of historical interest: coins, paintings, metalwork and woodwork, royal decrees, carpets, philatelic colln; library: see Libraries and Archives; Museum Dir and Head of Research Dept Dr SAID KHODDARI NAINI.

Mardom Shenassi Museum (Ethnological Museum): Maidan Panzdah Khordad, POB 11365-9595, Tehran 11149; tel. (21) 3110653; fax (21) 3111811; f. 1888; Dir ALIREZA ANISI.

Parliament Museum: Muze-ye Majles-e Shora-ye Eslami, POB 11365–866, Baharestan Sq., Tehran; tel. (21) 3130919; fax (21) 3130919; internet www.majlislib.com; f. 1999; 294 old Iranian paintings, 714 artistic and traditional handicrafts and gifts presented to the speakers of the Islamic Consultative Assembly by foreign dignitaries, 150 rolls of old carpets, 70 chairs and tables, small colln of antiques; Dir SEYYED MOHAMMAD ALI AHMADI ABHARI.

Tehran Museum of Contemporary Art: N Karegar Ave, Laleh Park, Tehran; tel. (21) 98951324; fax (21) 88965664; e-mail info@ tmoca.com; internet www.tmoca.com; f. 1977; library of 24,000 vols in formation; Dir MAHMOOD SHALOOEI.

Universities

AHWAZ JONDISHAPOUR UNIVERSITY OF MEDICAL SCIENCES

Golestan-bol, University City Central Building, Ahwaz 6135715794

Telephone: (611) 3339092

Fax: (611) 3335200

E-mail: info@ajums.ac.ir

Internet: www.ajums.ac.ir

Founded 1988; previously part of Shahid Chamran University

Academic year: September to June

Pres.: Dr HAYAT MOMBEINI

Registrar: Dr M. E. MOTLAQ

Librarian: B. DASHTBOZORGI

Number of teachers: 408

Number of students: 5,276

Publications: *Jondishapour Journal of Pharmaceutical Sciences* (2 a year), *Scientific Medical Journal* (4 a year)

DEANS

College of Dentistry: Dr M. SHOKRI
College of Health: M. LATIFI
College of Nursing: Z. ABBASPOUR
College of Pharmacology: Dr A. HEMATI
College of Physiotherapy: Dr M. J. SHATERZADEH
Medical College: Dr M. FEGHHI
Paramedicine College: Dr M. KARANDISH

PROFESSORS

ASHNAGHAR, A.
BEHROOZ, M.
KALANTARI, H.
MAKVANDI, M.
MARAGHI, S.
MOGHADAM, A. Z.
PEDRAM, M.
ZANDIAN, K.

AL-ZAHRA UNIVERSITY

Vanak, Tehran 1993891176

Telephone: (21) 88035187

Fax: (21) 88044040

E-mail: office@alzahra.ac.ir

Internet: www.alzahra.ac.ir

Founded 1965, name changed 1981
State control
Language of instruction: Persian
Academic year: September to June
Chancellor: Dr MAHBOUBEH MIBASHERI
Vice-Chancellor for Academic Affairs: Dr
  YADOLLAH ORDUKHANI
Vice-Chancellor for Admin. and Finance: Dr
  MAHNAZ MOLLANAZARI
Vice-Chancellor for Research: Dr SIMIN HOS-
  SEINIAN
Vice-Chancellor for Student Affairs: SHAHIN
  GHAHREMAN IZADI
Dir of Int. Relations: Dr AZAM SAZVAR
Librarian: Dr QODSI ZIARANI MOHAMMADI
Library of 121,569 vols
Number of teachers: 600
Number of students: 7,932
Publications: *Journal of Art 'Jelveye Honar'*,
  Journal of Hadith and Qu'ran Studies,
  Journal of Humanities, *Journal of Science*,
  Journal of Women Studies

DEANS

Faculty of Engineering: Dr JAFAR BAGHERI
  NEJAD
Faculty of Fine and Applied Arts: Dr ABUL-
  QASEM DADVAR
Faculty of Literature, Foreign Languages
  and History: Dr ENSIEH KHAZALI
Faculty of Physical Education and Sports
  Science: Dr PARVANEH NAZAR ALI
Faculty of Psychology and Education: Dr
  MOJDEH VAZIRI
Faculty of Sciences: Dr REZA SABET DARIYANI
Faculty of Social Sciences and Economics: Dr
  SUSAN BASTANI
Faculty of Theology: Dr ZAHRA RABBANI

ATTACHED RESEARCH CENTRE

Women's Research Centre: tel. (21)
8049809; fax (21) 8049809; e-mail golkhoo@
alzahra.ac.ir; Dir Dr SHEKOOFEH GOLKHOO.

ALLAMEH TABATABA'I UNIVERSITY

POB 15815/3487, Tehran
Telephone: (21) 8901521
Fax: (21) 8902536
Internet: web.atu.ac.ir
Founded 1984 following merger of the Uni-
  versity Complex for Literature and
  Humanities and the University Centre for
  Public and Business Administration
State control
Languages of instruction: English, Persian
Academic year: September to June
Pres.: Dr SEYED SADRODDIN SHARIATI
Vice-Chancellor for Academic Affairs: Prof.
  Dr AHMAD TAMIMDARI
Vice-Chancellor for Admin. and Finance:
  Prof. Dr JAFAR BABAJANI
Vice-Chancellor for Research and Int. Rela-
  tions: Prof. Dr HOSSEIN RAHMANSERESHT
Vice-Chancellor for Student Affairs: Prof. Dr
  HOSSEIN SALIMI
Registrar: Ms SEPEHRI
Chief Librarian: Dr ZAHRA SEIFKASHANI
Number of teachers: 361 (full-time)
Number of students: 12,177
Publication: Each faculty publishes its own
  journal

DEANS

Faculty of Economics: Prof. Dr HAMID SHOR-
  AKA
Faculty of Law and Politics: Asst Prof. Dr
  GHOLAM-ALI CHEGENIZADE
Faculty of Management and Accounting:
  Asst Prof. Dr ABULFAZL KAZZAI
Faculty of Persian Literature and Foreign
  Languages: Prof. Dr SAEED VAEZ
Faculty of Psychology and Education: MOR-
  TEZA AMINFAR

Faculty of Social Sciences: Asst Prof. Dr
  MAHAMMAD ZAHEDIASL

ATTACHED RESEARCH INSTITUTES

**Center for Studies on Iranian Economy
(CSIE):** Dean Asst Prof. Dr SAEED MOSHIRI.
**International Centre for Insurance Edu-
cation and Research (ICIER):** Dean Asst
Prof. Dr MOHAMMAD-GHOLI YOSEFI.

AMIRKABIR UNIVERSITY OF TECHNOLOGY

424 Hafez Ave, Tehran 15875-4413
Telephone: (21) 64540-1
Fax: (21) 66413969
E-mail: intoff1@aut.ac.ir
Internet: www.aut.ac.ir
Founded 1958 as Tehran Polytechnic
State control
Academic year: September to June
Pres.: Dr ALIREZA REHAI
Vice-Pres. for Academic Affairs: Dr MOHAM-
  MAD HASAN SEBT
Vice-Pres. for Admin. and Finance Affairs:
  Dr ALI MOHAMMAD KIMIAGARI
Vice-Pres. for Research and Technology: Dr
  REZA SAFABAKHSH
Vice-Pres. for Student Affairs: Dr BEHROOZ
  AREZOO
Dir of Int. Affairs: Dr F. SHARIF
Librarian: Dr OROUJALIAN
Number of teachers: 450
Number of students: 9,100
Depts of aerospace engineering, chemical
engineering, civil engineering, computer
and information technology, electrical engin-
eering, industrial engineering, marine engin-
eering, mathematics, medical engineering,
mining and metallurgical engineering, phys-
ics, polymer engineering, textile engineering
Publication: *Amirkabir Journal of Science
  and Technology* (4 a year).

ATTACHED RESEARCH INSTITUTES

**Advanced Textiles Materials and Tech-
nology Research Institute:** internet atmt
.aut.ac.ir.
**Concrete Technology and Durability
Research Centre:** tel. (21) 64543074; fax
(21) 64543074; e-mail concrete@aut.ac.ir;
internet www.aut.ac.ir/ctdr; Dir Prof. ALI
AKBAR RAMEZANIANPOUR.
Energy Research Centre: tel. (21)
64542611; fax (21) 64542611; e-mail erc@
aut.ac.ir; internet www.aut.ac.ir/research/
erc/home.htm; Dir Prof. BAHRAM DABIR.
**Synthetic Fibres and Textile Research
Centre:** Dir Dr MOHAMMAD REZA BABAEI.

UNIVERSITY OF ART

POB 14155-6434, Tehran
42 First St, Parvin Etesami St, Dr Fatemi
  Ave, Tehran 14146
Telephone: (21) 8954606
Fax: (21) 8954609
E-mail: art-university@art.ac.ir
Internet: www.art.ac.ir
Founded 1980 through amalgamation of the
  Conservatory of Music, College of Decora-
  tive Arts, College of Dramatic Arts, College
  of National Music and Farabi University;
  present name 1991
State control
Language of instruction: Farsi
Academic year: October to July
Pres.: Dr MOHAMMAD REZA HAFEZI
Vice-Pres. for Admin. and Finance: SEYED
  ABUTORAB AHMADPANAH
Vice-Pres. for Instruction: Dr MOHAMMAD
  TAGHI ASHOURI
Vice-Pres. for Research: PARVIN PARTOVI

Vice-Pres. for Student Affairs: SEYED JAVAD
  SALIMI
Library of 50,000 vols
Number of teachers: 252 (82 full-time, 170
  part-time)
Number of students: 2,200
Publications: *Dastavard* (4 a year), *Honarna-
  meh* (4 a year)

DEANS

Applied Arts and Graduate Studies: Mr
  HOSSEINI
Architecture and Urban Planning: Dr VAHID
  GHOMASHCHI
Cinema and Theatre: Mr BANI-ARDALAN
Music: Mr LOTFI
Visual and Applied Arts: Mr ESKANDARI

BU-ALI SINA UNIVERSITY

Shariati Ave, University Sq., Hamadan
  65174
Telephone: (811) 8273952
Fax: (811) 8272046
Internet: www.basu.ac.ir
Founded 1973
State control
Academic year: September to June
Pres.: Dr M. GHOLAMI
Vice-Pres. for Admin. and Finance: Dr A.
  KAREGAR BIDEH
Vice-Pres. for Devt: M. R. TAHMASEBI
Vice-Pres. for Education: Dr G. R. KHANLARI
Vice-Pres. for Research: Dr S. J. SABOUNCHI
Vice-Pres. for Student Affairs: Dr M. SHAR-
  IFIAN
Librarian: Dr M. S. GHAEMIZADEH
Number of teachers: 272
Number of students: 7,450
Publication: *Agricultural Research* (2 a year)

DEANS

Faculty of Agriculture: Dr M. J. SOLEIMANI
Faculty of Engineering: Dr M. NILI
Faculty of Letters and Humanities: Dr F.
  MIRZAII
Faculty of Science: Prof. H. ILUKHANI
Faculty of Teacher Training (Malayer): Dr
  M. JALALI
Faculty of the Veterinary College: Dr H.
  SHOKRIAN

FERDOWSI UNIVERSITY OF MASHHAD

Azadi Sq., Ferdowsi University Campus,
  Mashhad 9177948974
Telephone: (511) 8797363
Fax: (511) 8763637
E-mail: intr@um.ac.ir
Internet: www.um.ac.ir
Founded 1949
State control
Language of instruction: Farsi
Academic year: September to June (two
  semesters)
Chancellor: Prof. ALI REZA ASHOURI
Vice-Chancellor for Academic Affairs: Dr
  MAHDI KHAJAVI
Registrar: Dr MAHMOOD REZAI ROKENABAD
Dir of the Int. Office: Dr MOHAMMAD TAGHI
  HAMED MOUSAVIAN
Librarian: Dr BEHROOZ MAHRAM
Library of 13,000 vols
Number of teachers: 650
Number of students: 17,000
Publications: *Agricultural Science and Tech-
  nology* (4 a year), *Iranian Food Science and
  Technology Research Journal* (4 a year),
  Iranian Journal of Field Crop Research (4
  a year), *Journal of the School of Economics
  and Business Administration* (4 a year),
  Journal of the School of Engineering (4 a

year), *Journal of the School of Literature* (4 a year), *Journal of the School of Sciences* (4 a year), *Journal of Theology and Islamic Studies* (4 a year)

DEANS

Faculty of Administration and Economics: Dr M. LOTFALIPOOR
Faculty of Agriculture: Dr REZA VALIZADEH
Faculty of Education and Psychology: Dr BAKHTIYAR SHABANI
Faculty of Engineering: Dr HOSSAIN NOEEI BAGHBAN
Faculty of Letters and Humanities: Dr A. MOHAMMAD ZADEH REZAI
Faculty of Mathematical Sciences: Dr H. R. TAREGHIAN
Faculty of Physical Education: R. HASHEMI JAVAHERI
Faculty of Sciences: Dr REZA EIZADI
Faculty of Theology: Dr H. HAERI
Faculty of Veterinary Science: Dr A. NAGHIBI
Shirvan School of Agriculture: Dr MAHMOOD SHOOR
Nishabour School of Fine Arts: Dr HADI MANSOORI MGHADAM

UNIVERSITY OF GILAN

POB 1841, Mellat Street, Rasht
Telephone: (131) 3221999
Fax: (131) 3227022
E-mail: khazar@cd.gu.ac.ir
Internet: www.gu.ac.ir
Founded 1977
State control
Language of instruction: Farsi
Academic year: September to June (two semesters)

Chancellor: Dr DAWOUD AHMADI DASTJERDI
Vice-Chancellor for Academic Affairs: Dr REZA FOTOUHI GHAZVINI
Vice-Chancellor for Finance and Admin.: ESMAEIL MAGHSODI
Vice-Chancellor for Research Affairs: Dr ABOLFAZL DARVIZEH
Vice-Chancellor for Student Affairs: Dr MALEK-MOHAMMAD RANJBAR
Office of Public Relations: Dr HASSAN TAJIK
Office of Int. and Scientific Relations: Dr MASOUD VAHABI MOGHADDAM
Librarian: Dr REYHANEH SARIRI

Number of teachers: 308
Number of students: 6,705

Publication: *Mahnameh* (12 a year, in Farsi)

DEANS

Faculty of Agriculture: Dr AHAD SAHRAGARD
Faculty of Engineering: Dr HOSSEIN HAFTH-CHENARI
Faculty of Fine Arts and Architecture: HAM-ZEH GHOLAM-ALI-ZADEH
Faculty of Fishery and Aquatic Animals: Dr MSOUD SATTARI
Faculty of Humanities: Dr MOHAMMAD KAZEM YOUSEFPOUR
Faculty of Natural Resources: Dr ZYAEDDIN MIRHOSSEINI
Faculty of Physical Education: Dr ARSALAN DAMIRCHI
Faculty of Sciences: Dr ESMAEIL ANSARI

IRAN UNIVERSITY OF MEDICAL SCIENCES AND HEALTH SERVICES

Crossroads of Shahid Hemmat and Shahid Chamran Expressways, POB 15875-6171, Tehran 144961-4535
Telephone: (21) 98052193
Fax: (21) 88054393
E-mail: ofintrel@iums.ac.ir
Internet: www.iums.ac.ir
Founded 1974 as Iran Medical Centre
State control

Language of instruction: Persian
Academic year: September to June

Chancellor: Dr S. A. HASSANI
Vice-Chancellor for Education: Dr A. PAZOUKI
Vice-Chancellor for Food and Pharmaceutical Affairs: Dr M. BEYGLAR
Vice-Chancellor for Health Affairs: Dr F. EMAMI
Vice-Chancellor for Management Devt and Resources: Dr S. A. RAZAVI
Vice-Chancellor for Research: Dr S. A. MOTE-VALIAN
Vice-Chancellor for Student and Cultural Affairs: Dr A. AMIRFARHANGI
Registrar: Dr M. AFKARI
Head of Central Library: B. JAMEI

Library of 45,244 vols, 3,681 journals, 14,623 theses, 202 research projects
Number of teachers: 684
Number of students: 6,572

Publications: *Annals of Iranian Medicine* (4 a year), *Five Star Doctor* (4 a year), *Iran Journal of Nursing* (4 a year), *Iranian Journal of Pharmacology and Therapeutics* (4 a year, online), *Iranian Journal of Psychiatry and Clinical Psychology* (4 a year), *Journal of Health Management* (4 a year), *Journal of Iran University of Medical Sciences* (4 a year), *Journal of Medical Laboratory Sciences* (4 a year), *Journal of Medical Management* (4 a year), *Journal of Students* (12 a year), *Journal of Thought and Behavior* (4 a year), *Medical Education* (4 a year), *Rehabilitation Message* (4 a year)

DEANS

School of Allied Medical Sciences: Dr A. KAZEMI
School of Management and Medical Information: Dr SH. TOFIGHI
School of Medicine: Dr R. FARASATKISH
School of Nursing and Midwifery: Dr F. HAGHDOOST OSKOUEI
School of Public Health: Dr M. H. TAGHDISI
School of Rehabilitation Sciences: Dr M. S. GHASEMI

PROFESSORS

AGHAKHANI, K., Forensic Medicine
AKBARIAN-NIA, M., Neurology
ARAB MOHAMMAD HOSSEONI, A., Paediatrics
AZAR, M., Neurosurgery
BIDARI, A., Emergency Medicine
BOLOURI, B., Biophysics
DANESHI, A., Otorhinolaryngology
FIROUZRAY, M., Biochemistry
GHAFFARPOUR, G., Dermatology
GHALEHBANDI, M., Psychiatry
HADIZADEH, H., Radiology
HASHEMI, F., Pathology
HASHEMI, M., Ophthalmology
HEYDARI, M., Surgery
HOMAYOUNFAR, H., Physiology
IMANI, F., Anaesthesiology
JAFARI, D., Orthopaedics
JAVAD MOUSSAVI, S. A., Internal Medicine
JOGHATAEI, M. T., Anatomy
KASHANIAN, M., Obstetrics and Gynaecology
KAZAMI, A., Reconstructive Surgery
MAHMOUDIAN, M., Pharmacology
MAJIDPOUR, A., Infectious Diseases
MOLAVI NOJOUMI, M., Social Medicine
MOVAHHED, M., Nuclear Medicine
OURMAZDI, H., Parasitology
RASTEGAR LARI, A., Microbiology
SALEKMOGHADDAM, A., Immunology
SHAHROKH, H., Urology
YEKKEH YAZDANDOUST, R., Clinical Psychology

IRAN UNIVERSITY OF SCIENCE AND TECHNOLOGY

Narmak, Tehran 1684613114
Telephone: (21) 77240303
Fax: (21) 77491031
E-mail: interiust@iust.ac.ir
Internet: www.iust.ac.ir
Founded 1928
State control
Language of instruction: Farsi
Academic year: September to June

Chancellor: Dr M. S. JABALAMELI
Vice-Chancellor for Admin. and Finance: Dr BIJAN GHAFFARI
Vice-Chancellor for Education: Dr MASOOD HADIAN
Vice-Chancellor for Research and Technology: Dr MOHAMMAD HASSAN BAZIAR
Vice-Chancellor for Student and Cultural Affairs: Dr MOHAMMAD FATHIAN
Dir of the Office of Int. and Scientific Cooperation: Dr SAEED MIRZAMOHAMMADI
Head of Graduate Studies: Dr FARZAD BAZ-DID-TEHRANI
Registrar: Dr MASOUD YAGHINI
Librarian: Dr SEYED MAHDI ALAVI AMLASHI

Library of 120,000 vols, more than 1,400 subscriptions to academic magazines, more than 23,000 titles of thesis
Number of teachers: 657 (370 full-time, 287 part-time)
Number of students: 10,971

Publications: *International Journal of Civil Engineering* (4 a year, in English), *International Journal of Engineering* (4 a year, in Persian and English), *Iranian Journal of Electrical and Electronic Engineering* (4 a year, in English), *Iranian Journal of Materials Science and Engineering* (4 a year, in English)

DEANS

Arak College of Technology: Dr ABOLFAZL AHMADI
Behshahr College of Technology: Dr M. MOHAMMADPOUR OMRAN
Dept of Chemistry: Dr MANSOUR ANBIA
Dept of Foreign Languages: Dr SEYED MAH-MOOD MIR TABATABEI
School of Architecture and Urban Design: Dr MOHSEN FAIZI
School of Automotive Engineering: Dr M. H. SHOJAEE FARD
School of Chemical Engineering: Dr TOORAJ MOHAMMADI
School of Civil Engineering: Dr GHOLAMREZA GHODRATI AMIRI
School of Computer Engineering: Dr M. SHARIFI
School of Electrical Engineering: Dr SHAH-RAM MOHAMMAD NEJAD
School of Industrial Engineering: Dr SIAMAK NOURI
School of Mathematics: Dr GHOLAMHOSSEIN YARI
School of Mechanical Engineering: Dr MOHARAM HABIBNEJAD KORAYEM
School of Metallurgy and Materials Engineering: SEYED MOHAMMAD-ALI BOUTORABI
School of Physics: Dr SEYED ROUHOLLAH AGHDAEE
School of Railway Engineering: Dr S. JAVAD MIR MOHAMMAD SADEGHI

PROFESSORS

ABOUTALEBI, M.-R., School of Metallurgy and Materials Engineering
AFSHAR, A., School of Civil Engineering
AHMADIAN, H., School of Mechanical Engineering
ARABI, H., School of Metallurgy and Materials Engineering
ARYANEZHAD, M.-B.-Q., School of Industrial Engineering

AYATOLLAHI, M. R., School of Mechanical Engineering
BAZIAR, M. H., School of Civil Engineering
BEHBAHANI, H., School of Civil Engineering
BEITOLLAHI, A., School of Metallurgy and Materials Engineering
BOUTORABI, S. M.-A., School of Metallurgy and Materials Engineering
DANESHJOU, K., School of Mechanical Engineering
FALLAHI, M., Dept of Foreign Languages
FARMAN, H., School of Physics
GHASEMZADEH, R., School of Metallurgy and Materials Engineering
GHODRATI AMIRI, G., School of Civil Engineering
GOLESTANI-FARD, F., School of Metallurgy and Materials Engineering
HABIBNEJAD KORAYEM, M., School of Mechanical Engineering
HASHEMINEJAD, S. M., School of Mechanical Engineering
HEDJAZI, J., School of Metallurgy and Materials Engineering
HODJAT KASHANI, F., School of Electrical Engineering
JASBI, A., School of Industrial Engineering
JAVADPOUR, J., School of Metallurgy and Materials Engineering
KAVEH, A., School of Civil Engineering
MALEK NEJAD, K., School of Mathematics
MARGHUSSAIN, V., School of Metallurgy and Materials Engineering
MIRDAMADI, S., School of Metallurgy and Materials Engineering
MOHAMMADI, K., School of Electrical Engineering
MOHAMMADI, T., School of Chemical Engineering
NOOROSSANA, R., School of Industrial Engineering
ORAIZI, H., School of Electrical Engineering
RAZAVIZADEH, H., School of Metallurgy and Materials Engineering
SANAEI, E., School of Civil Engineering
SEYED SADJADI, S., Dept of Chemistry
SEYED-HOSSEINI, S. M., School of Industrial Engineering
SHABESTARI, S. G., School of Metallurgy and Materials Engineering
SHAYANFAR, H., School of Electrical Engineering
SHIDFAR, A., School of Mathematics
SHOJAEEFARD, M. H., School of Automotive Engineering
SHOKRIEH, M. M., School of Mechanical Engineering
SHOULAIE, A., School of Electrical Engineering
SOLEIMANI, M., School of Electrical Engineering

ATTACHED RESEARCH INSTITUTES

Analytical Electrochemistry Research Centre: tel. and fax (21) 772491; fax (21) 7724050; Dir Dr SEYED MOHAMMAD-REZA MILANI HOSSEINI.

Asphalt Concrete Mixture and Bitumen Research Centre: tel. (21) 77240281; fax (21) 77240089; Dir Dr HASSAN ZIARI.

Automobile Research Centre: tel. (21) 73913970; fax (21) 77491224; Dir Dr M. H. SHOJAEEFARD.

Cement Research Centre: tel. (21) 77240475; fax (21) 77240397; Dir Dr ALI ALLAHVERDI.

Electronic Research Centre: tel. (21) 77240487; fax (21) 77240486; Dir Dr ALIREZA MOHAMMAD SHAHRI.

Green Research Centre: tel. (21) 77491223; fax (21) 77491242; e-mail jadid@iust.ac.ir; Dir Dr S. JADID.

Information Technology Research Centre: tel. (21) 77491192; fax (21)

77491193; e-mail akbari@iust.ac.ir; Dir Dr A. AKBARI.

Iran Aluminium Research Centre: tel. (21) 77240599; fax (21) 77240500; Dir Dr MOHAMMAD-TAGHI SALEHI.

Iran Composites Institute: tel. (21) 73912887; fax (21) 77491206; e-mail shokrieh@iust.ac.ir; internet www.irancomposits.org; Dir Dr M. M. SHOKRIEH.

Technology Incubator: tel. (21) 77497788; fax (21) 77899955; Dir Dr MOHAMMAD REZA JAHED MOTLAGH.

Transportation Research Centre: tel. (21) 77240399; fax (21) 77240398; Dir Dr AFSHIN SHARIAT.

UNIVERSITY OF ISFAHAN

Isfahan, Darvazeh Shiraz 81746-73441
Telephone: (311) 7932001
Fax: (311) 6687396
E-mail: int-office@ui.ac.ir
Internet: www.ui.ac.ir
Founded 1946, present status 1958
State control
Language of instruction: Persian
Academic year: September to July

Chancellor: Dr MOHAMMAD HOSSEIN RAMESHT
Vice-Chancellor for Academic Affairs and Graduate Studies: Dr SYDE ALI ASGHAR MIR BAGHERI FARD
Vice-Chancellor for Finance and Admin.: Dr MOHAMMED REZA ABDI
Vice-Chancellor for Research and Technology: Dr HOSSEIN HARSIJ
Vice-Chancellor for Student and Cultural Affairs: Dr MOHAMMAD BIDHENDI
Dir for Int. Relations: Dr ARASH SHAHIN
Librarian: Dr HAMID REZA FALLAH

Library of 438,063 vols
Number of teachers: 885
Number of students: 16,000

Publications: *Comparative Theology* (2 a year), *Geography and Environmental Planning* (4 a year), *Geography Researches* (4 a year), *Historical Researches* (4 a year), *International Economics* (2 a year), *Iranian Journal of Petrology* (4 a year), *Iranian Journal of Plant Biology* (2 a year), *Journal of Financial Accounting Research* (2 a year), *Journal of Persian Language and Literature (GOHARE GOYA)* (4 a year), *Journal of Regional and Urban Planning* (4 a year), *Journal of Researches in Linguistics* (4 a year), *Literature Arts* (4 a year), *Metaphysic* (4 a year), *Practical Sociology* (4 a year), *Researches in Sedimentary and Cryptology* (4 a year), *Researches on Persian Language Literature* (4 a year), *Taxonomy and Biosystematics* (2 a year)

DEANS

Faculty of Administrative Sciences and Economics: Dr SEYYED JAVAD EMAM JOMEH ZADEH
Faculty of Educational Sciences and Psychology: Dr REZA HOYEIDA
Faculty of Engineering and Technology: Dr SEYYED FOAD AGHAMIRI
Faculty of Foreign Languages: Dr MAHMOUD REZA GASHMARDI
Faculty of Literature and Humanities: Dr ASGHAR MONTAZEROLGHAEM
Faculty of Mathematics and Computer Studies, Khansar: Dr HESHMATOLLAH YAVARI
Faculty of Physical Education and Sports Sciences: Dr SEYYED MOHAMMAD MARANDI
Faculty of Pure Sciences: SHAHRAM TANGESTANI NEJAD
Faculty of Sciences and New Technology: Dr MOJITABA MOSTAJABODDAVATI

ISFAHAN UNIVERSITY OF MEDICAL SCIENCES

Hezar-Jerib Avenue, Isfahan
Telephone: (311) 7923077
Fax: (311) 6687898
E-mail: international@mui.ac.ir
Internet: www.mui.ac.ir
Founded 1950
State control
Language of instruction: Persian
Academic year: September to June

Chancellor: Dr ABBAS REZAIE
Vice-Chancellor for Academic Affairs: Dr B. SHAMS
Vice-Chancellor for Finance and Admin.: Dr M. B. TAVAKOLI
Vice-Chancellor for Research Affairs: Dr M. NEMATBAKHSH
Vice-Chancellor for Student Affairs: Dr M. JALALI
Registrar: M. MARDANI
Head of Libraries: H. RASTEGARI

Number of teachers: 595
Number of students: 6,105

Publications: *ARYA Atherosclerosis*, *Iranian Journal of Medical Education*, *Journal of Research at the Isfahan Medical School* (4 a year), *Journal of Research in Medical Sciences* (4 a year)

DEANS

Faculty of Dentistry: Dr A. KHADEMI
Faculty of Health: Dr M. ZADEH
Faculty of Management and Information Services: Dr M. YARMOHAMMADIAN
Faculty of Medicine: Dr H. TABAN
Faculty of Nursing and Midwifery: Dr H. ABEDI
Faculty of Pharmacy: Dr J. DEHKORDI
Faculty of Rehabilitation Sciences: Dr F. BAHMANI

ISFAHAN UNIVERSITY OF TECHNOLOGY

Isfahan 8415683111
Telephone: (311) 3912505
Fax: (311) 3912511
E-mail: isco@cc.iut.ac.ir
Internet: www.iut.ac.ir
Founded 1977
State control
Language of instruction: Persian
Academic year: September to July

Pres.: Dr G. R. GHORBANI
Vice-Pres. for Academic Affairs: Dr MOJTABA AZHARI
Vice-Pres. for Finance and Administration: Dr MOHAMMAD HASSAN ABBASI
Vice-Pres. for Research: Dr SEYED HASAN GHAZIASKAR
Vice-Pres. for Student Affairs: Dr ALI AKBAR ALEM RAJABI
Registrar: Dr SOROUSH ALIMORADI
Library Dir: Dr MOSTAFA KARIMAIAN EGHBAL
Library of 88,000 vols, 2,500 periodicals
Number of teachers: 440
Number of students: 9,000

Publications: *Esteghlal* (Journal of Engineering, 2 a year), *Iranian Journal of Physics Research*, *Journal of Sciences and Technology of Agriculture and Natural Resources*

DEANS

Faculty of Chemical Engineering: Dr GH. ETEMAD
Faculty of Chemistry: Dr S. H. GHAZIASKAR
Faculty of Civil Engineering: Dr M. M. SAADATPOUR
Faculty of Electrical and Computer Engineering: Dr M. A. MONTAZERI

Faculty of Industrial Engineering: Dr GH. A. RAISSI ARDALI
Faculty of Materials Engineering: Dr M. A. GOLOZAR
Faculty of Mathematics: Dr H. R. ZOHOURI-ZANGENAH
Faculty of Mechanical Engineering: Dr A. SABONCHI
Faculty of Mining Engineering: Dr J. TAJA-DOD
Faculty of Natural Resources: Dr A. JALALIAN
Faculty of Physics: Dr H. AKBARZADEH
Faculty of Textile Technology: Dr S. H. AMIRSHAHI
College of Agriculture: Dr MORTEZA ZAHEDI

PROFESSORS

AKBARZADEH, H., Physics
AMINI, S. M., Computational Physics
AMINZADEH, A., Chemistry
BASSIR, H., Mining Engineering
HAGHANY, A., Pure Mathematics
HAJRASOOLIHA, SH., Soil Science
KALBASI, M., Soil Science
MALLAKPOUR, S. E., Chemistry
MOLKI, M., Mechanical Engineering
MOUSAVI, S. F., Agriculture
PARSAFAR, GH., Chemistry
PARSIAN, A., Statistics
REZAEI, A., Plant Breeding, Cytogenetics
ROSTAMI, A. A., Mechanical Engineering
SAADATPOUR, M. M., Civil Engineering
TAHANI, V., Electronic Engineering

ISLAMIC AZAD UNIVERSITY

4th Golestan St, Pasdaran Ave, Tehran 1666976113
Telephone: (21) 22565149
Fax: (21) 22547787
E-mail: info@intl.iau.ir
Internet: www.azad.ac.ir
Founded 1982
Academic year: September to September
Pres.: Dr A. JASSBI
Vice-Pres. for Academic Affairs: Dr H. SADE-GHISHOJA
Vice-Pres. for Construction and Devt: A. SHAHRAKI
Vice-Pres. for Coordination Affairs: M. S. KALHOR
Vice-Pres. for Cultural Affairs: M. PIRAYAN-DEH
Vice-Pres. for Financial and Admin. Affairs: M. ZAHABION
Vice-Pres. for Int. Affairs: Dr PAYMAN MAHASTI
Vice-Pres. for Medical Affairs: Dr H. YAHYAVI
Vice-Pres. for Non-profit Schools: M. MIR-SHAMSI
Vice-Pres. for Parliamentary Affairs: Dr F. FARMAND
Vice-Pres. for Research: Dr F. LARIJANI
Vice-Pres. for Student Affairs: Dr J. AZIZIAN
Librarian: P. MAHASTI SHOTORBANI
Library: 4.9m. vols
Number of teachers: 25,310
Number of students: 850,000
Publications: *Armane-e-Pazhouhesh*, *Bassirat* (Vision, 4 a year), *Daneshnameh* (4 a year), *Danesh va Pezhouhesh* (4 a year), *Economics and Management* (4 a year), *Ensan Va Andishe* (Man and Thought, 4 a year), *Geographic Space* (4 a year), *Jelve-gahe-do-payam* (4 a year), *Journal of Agricultural Sciences* (4 a year), *Journal of Medical Sciences* (4 a year), *Journal of Sciences* (4 a year), *Koushk* (4 a year), *Mobin* (4 a year), *Namaye Pazhoohosh* (4 a year), *Nedaye-Daneshgah* (4 a year), *Nedaye Golestan* (4 a year), *Nourolelm* (4 a year), *Omran* (4 a year), *Pazhoheshnameh I* (4 a year), *Pazhuhesh–DINI* (4 a year), *Peyke Dime* (4 a year), *Pooyesh* (4 a

year), *Pouya* (4 a year), *Rah-avar* (v), *Rahavard* (4 a year), *Rouyesh* (4 a year), *Scientific-Cultural Letter of Research* (4 a year), *Scientific Research Journal* (4 a year), *Scientific Research Periodical* (4 a year), *Scientific Research Quarterly*, *Sedaye Didar* (4 a year), *Selselat-Al-Zahab* (4 a year), *Sokhane Ashna* (4 a year), *Tazeha* (4 a year), *Tolu-e-Andishe* (4 a year), *Yeganeh* (4 a year), *Zakaria Razi* (4 a year)

Colleges of agricultural engineering, arts, civil engineering, humanities, medicine and basic sciences; each of the University's 350 branches, which are located throughout Iran, offers a selection of the courses run by the University.

K. N. TOOSI UNIVERSITY OF TECHNOLOGY

POB 15875-4416, 470 Mirdamad Ave W, 19697-64499 Tehran
Telephone: (21) 88881003
Fax: (21) 88882997
E-mail: oisc@kntu.ac.ir
Internet: www.kntu.ac.ir
Founded 1928, present name 1987
State control
Languages of instruction: Farsi, English
Academic year: September to June
Pres.: Dr SEYED MOHAMMAD TAGHI BATHAEE
Vice-Pres. for Admin. and Finance: Dr FARID NAJAFEE
Vice-Pres. for Education: Dr A. SHAHANI
Vice-Pres. for Research: Dr HAMID ABRISHAMI MOGHADAM
Vice-Pres. for Student Affairs: Dr HASSAM KARIMI MAZRAE
Librarian: Dr M. VARSHOSAZ
Library of 44,506 vols
Number of teachers: 233
Number of students: 5,587
Publications: *Abangan Magazine* (4 a year), *Journal of Robotics*, *Olum-o-Mohandesi'ye Nasir* (2 a year)

DEANS

Faculty of Aerospace Engineering: Dr M. MOSAVI NAIENIAN
Faculty of Civil Engineering: Dr MOGHADAS TAFRESHI
Faculty of Electrical and Computer Engineering: Dr AHMADIAN
Faculty of Geodesy and Geomatics Engineering: Dr VOSOOGHI
Faculty of Industrial Engineering: Dr KHOSHALHAN
Faculty of Mechanical Engineering: Dr Z. BASHAR HAGH
Faculty of Science: Dr SALEH KOOTAHI

KERMANSHAH UNIVERSITY OF MEDICAL SCIENCES

Shahid Beheshti Blvd, Kermanshah
Telephone: (831) 8354434
Fax: (831) 8356433
E-mail: info@kums.ac.ir
Internet: www.kums.ac.ir
Founded 1986; previously part of Razi University
State control
Academic year: September to July
Chancellor: Dr SAMAD NORIZAD
Vice-Chancellor for Admin. and Financial Affairs: Dr EBRAHIM SHAKIBA
Vice-Chancellor for Education and Research: Dr HAMIDREZA OMRANI
Vice-Chancellor for the Food and Drug: Dr REZA TAHVILIAN
Vice-Chancellor for Health: Dr HAHAB MOINI MOSTOFI

Vice-Chancellor for Research: Dr FARID NAJAFI
Vice-Chancellor for Treatment: Dr TUORAJ AHMADI JUOYBARI
Librarian: SAYED JALAL KAZEMI OSKUEE
Library of 96,000 vols
Number of teachers: 228
Number of students: 3,072
Publications: *Behbood* (Scientific Quarterly), *Journal of Injury and Violence Research*

DEANS

Faculty Of Dentistry: Dr HAMID REZA MOZAFARI
Faculty of Health: Dr YAHYA SAFARI
Faculty of Medicine: Dr SAYED HAMID MADANI
Faculty of Nursing: Dr ALIREZA KHATONI,
Faculty of Pharmacy: Dr BABAK GHOLAMIN
Faculty of Pormedical: FATEME DARABI

MASHHAD UNIVERSITY OF MEDICAL SCIENCES

Daneshghah Ave, POB 91375-345, Mashhad
Telephone: (511) 8433528
Fax: (511) 8430249
E-mail: info.en@mums.ac.ir
Internet: www.mums.ac.ir
Founded 1945
Academic year: October to July
Pres.: Dr MASOUD MALEKI
Vice-Pres. for Admin. and Financial Affairs: Dr AMANOLLAH KARIMI
Vice-Pres. for Education: Dr AKBAR DARAKH-SHAN
Vice-Pres. for Food and Drug Affairs: Dr NASER VAHDATI
Vice-Pres. for Health: Dr MOHAMMADREZA MAJDI
Vice-Pres. for Research: Dr JALIL TAVAKKOL AFSHARI
Vice-Pres. for Student Affairs: Dr NASER SARGOLZAIE
Vice-Pres. for Treatment Affairs: Dr GHOLAMALI MAEMOORI
Librarians: P. MODIRAMANI, Z. JANGI
Library of 100,000 vols
Number of teachers: 554
Number of students: 5,688
Publications: *Iranian Journal of Basic Medical Sciences* (4 a year), *Iranian Journal of Oto-rhino-laryngology* (4 a year), *Journal* (4 a year)

DEANS

Faculty of Dentistry: Dr MOHAMMAD HASSAN ZARABI
Faculty of Health and Paramedical Sciences: Dr J. MOVAFFAGH
Faculty of Medicine: Dr MOHAMMAD TAGHI RAJABI MASHHADI
Faculty of Nursing and Midwifery: Dr ABBASS HEIDAN
Faculty of Pharmacy: Dr H. HOSSEINZADEH

MAZANDARAN UNIVERSITY

POB 416, Pasdaran St, Babolsar 47415
Telephone: (11252) 32095
Fax: (11252) 33702
E-mail: um@umz.ac.ir
Internet: www.umz.ac.ir
Founded 1975 as Reza Shah Kabir University, name changed 1980
State control
Language of instruction: Farsi
Academic year: September to June
Pres.: Dr GHASEM ALIZADEH AFROUZI
Vice-Pres. for Academic Affairs: Dr SAEED MIRZANEJAD
Vice-Pres. for Admin. and Finance: Dr BAHRAM SADEGHPOUR

Vice-Pres. for Research: Dr AHMAS JAFARI SAMIMI
Vice-Pres. for Student Affairs: Dr MORTEZA ALAVIAN
Registrar: Dr ALI BAGHERI KHALILI
Librarian: Dr REZA NOORZAD
Number of teachers: 320
Number of students: 11,280

DEANS

Faculty of Art and Architecture: Dr GHOLAM-REZA MALEKSHAHI
Faculty of Basic Sciences: Dr YAHYA TALEBI
Faculty of Economics and Admin. Sciences: Dr ALIREZA POURFARAJ
Faculty of Humanities and Social Sciences: Dr GHOLAMREZA PIROUZ
Faculty of Law and Political Science: Dr KIOMARS KALANTARI
Faculty of Physical Sciences: Dr SHADMEHR MIRDAR

PAYAME NOOR UNIVERSITY

POB 19395-4697, Lashkarak Rd, Tehran 19569
Telephone: (21) 22442042
Fax: (21) 22441511
E-mail: int@pnu.ac.ir
Internet: www.pnu.ac.ir
Founded 1987
State control
Languages of instruction: Persian, English
Academic year: September to July (two terms)
Pres.: Prof. HASSAN ZIARI
Vice-Pres. for Admin. and Finance: Dr FEISAL HASSANI
Vice-Pres. for Education and Assessment: Dr ABDOLLAH MOTAMEDI
Vice-Pres. for Information Technology: Dr REZA HAJI HOSSEINI (acting)
Vice-Pres. for Planning and Devt: MAHMOUD KEIMANESH
Vice-Pres. for Research: Dr SEYED AHMAD MIRSHOKRAIE
Vice-Pres. for Student Affairs and Culture: Dr ALIREZA DELAFKAR
Dir of the Int. Office: Dr HOSSEIN SALEHZADEH
Librarian: Dr SEYED ALI ALAMOLHODA
Library: 1.4m. vols (total for all centres)
Number of teachers: 3,500 1.1m.
Publications: *Journal of Basic Sciences* (4 a year), *Journal of Humanities* (4 a year), *Peyke Noor Journal* (6 a year)
Distance education; 30 provincial and 485 local centres in Iran; depts of accountancy, agricultural economics engineering, agricultural machinery and mechanization engineering, agricultural sciences engineering, animal husbandry, Arabic literature, art, biology, business administration, chemistry, computer sciences, economics, education, electronic commerce, English language and linguistics, environmental health, ethics and mysticism, geography, geology, hardware engineering, history, industrial engineering, information technology management, Islamic civilization, history and culture, Islamic studies, jurisprudence and basics of Islamic laws, Koranic sciences and tradition, management of rural devt engineering, mathematics, natural resources and environmental engineering, Persian language and literature, philosophy and speech, physical education, physics, professional health, product management engineering, project management engineering, psychology, public administration, public health, social sciences, software engineering, statistics, water and soil engineering

DEANS

Faculty of Agricultural Sciences: Dr MOHSEN SHOOKAT FADAEE
Faculty of Art and Media: HOOSHANG KHOS-ROBEIGI
Faculty of Basic Sciences: Prof. SEYED AHMAD MIRSHOKRAIE
Faculty of Economics and Social Sciences: Dr MOHAMMAD TAGHI AMINI
Faculty of Engineering: Dr HASSAN FALLAH
Faculty of Humanities: Dr FATEMEH KOUPA
Faculty of Theology: ABEDIN MO'MENI

PETROLEUM UNIVERSITY OF TECHNOLOGY

569 Hafez Ave, Tehran 15996-45313
Telephone: (21) 8804272
Fax: (21) 8807687
E-mail: info@put.ac.ir
Internet: www.put.ac.ir
Founded 1939 as Abadan Institute of Technology
State control, under Ministry of Petroleum
Languages of instruction: English, Farsi
Academic year: September to June
Chancellor: Dr D. H. PANJESHAHI
Vice-Chancellor for Academic Affairs: Dr M. R. SHISHESAZ
Vice-Chancellor for Finance and Admin.: A. ALIMORADY
Vice-Chancellor for Research Affairs: Dr B. ROUZBEHANI
Vice-Chancellor for Research and Postgraduate Studies: Dr A. EMAMZADEH
Vice-Chancellor for Student Affairs: Dr N. NABHANI
Registrar: Dr M. FARZAM
Number of teachers: 100
Number of students: 1,500

DEANS

Faculty of Accounting and Finance (Tehran): Dr A. EMAMZADEH
Faculty of Chemical and Petrochemical Engineering (Abadan): Dr T. JADIDI
Faculty of Petroleum Engineering (Ahwaz): Dr K. SALAHSHOOR

ATTACHED INSTITUTE

Mahmood-Abad Institute for Marine Sciences: POB 161, Mahmood-Abad; Dir H. RAZAEE.

RAZI UNIVERSITY

Kermanshah Azadi Sq., Kermanshah
Telephone: (831) 4277603
E-mail: info@razi.ac.ir
Internet: www.razi.ac.ir
Founded 1974
State control
Academic year: January to September
Chancellor: Prof. MOHAMMAD MEHDI KHODAEI
Vice-Chancellor for Academic Affairs: Dr ALIREZA NIKRAHI
Vice-Chancellor for Research Affairs: Dr ABDOL HAMID PAPZAN
Vice-Chancellor for Student Affairs: Dr ALI BIDMESHKIPOUR
Number of teachers: 175
Number of students: 3,550

DEANS

School of Agriculture: Dr SAEED JALALI HONARMAND
School of Engineering: Dr NAJAF BIGLARI
School of Literature and Humanities: Dr VAHID SABZIANPOUR
School of Physical Education: Dr VAHID TADIBI
School of Science: Dr REZA HASHEMI
School of Social Science: Dr MASOUD AKHA-VANKAZEMI

School of Veterinary Medicine: Dr ABDOL ALI CHALECHALE

SEMNAN UNIVERSITY OF MEDICAL SCIENCES

POB 35195-163, Molavi Blvd, Semnan
Telephone: (231) 3320112
Fax: (231) 3321622
E-mail: info@sem-ums.ac.ir
Internet: www.sem-ums.ac.ir
Founded 1988 as Semnan College of Medical Sciences; present name and status 1990
Academic year: September to June (two semesters)
Works in collaboration with seven hospitals in the Semnan province
Chancellor: Dr ALI RASHIDI-POUR
Vice-Chancellor for Academic and Research Affairs: Dr VAHID SEMNANI
Vice-Chancellor for Drugs and Food: Dr SIAMAK YAGHMAIAN
Vice-Chancellor for Financial and Admin. Affairs: Dr BEHPOUR YOUSEFI
Vice-Chancellor for Health Affairs: Dr JAFAR JANDAGHI
Vice-Chancellor for Student Affairs: Dr MOHAMMAD AMOUZADEH KHALILI
Vice-Chancellor for Treatment: Dr MOHAM-MAD BAGHER SABERI ZAFARGHANDI
Head Librarian: Dr GHOLAMREZA IRAJIAN
Library of 41,863 vols, 125 current periodicals, 417 theses
Number of teachers: 119
Number of students: 1,420
Publications: *Avay-e-Elm* (medical research, in Persian, 2 or 3 a year), *Health communicators, focus on Health* (in Persian, 2 a year), *Health magazine* (in Persian, 2 a year), *Koomesh Medical Journal* (in Persian, 4 a year)

DEANS

Faculty of Health: MOHAMMAD BAGHER DEL-KHOSH
Faculty of Medicine: Dr MOHAMMAD E. AMIN-BEIDOKHTI
Faculty of Nursing and Paramedical Sciences: SAEED HAJIAGHAJANI
Faculty of Rehabilitation: Dr AMIR H. BAKH-TIARI

SHAHED UNIVERSITY

POB 15875-5794, 115 North Kargar Ave, Tehran
Telephone: (21) 6413734
Fax: (21) 6419568
Internet: www.shahed.ac.ir
Founded 1989
State control
Academic year: September to June
Chancellor: Dr MAHMOOD NOORISAFA
Vice-Chancellor for Academic Affairs: Dr SEIYED KAZEM FOROOTAN
Vice-Chancellor for Admin. and Financial Affairs, and Devt: Dr MOSTAFA KIAIE
Vice-Chancellor for Cultural Affairs: Dr ALI AZAM KHOSRARI
Vice-Chancellor for Research: Dr SOGHRAT FAGHIHZADEH
Vice-Chancellor for Student Affairs: Dr KAM-RAR SAGHAFI
Librarian: ABFOLREZA NOROOZI CHACOLI
Library of 215,000 vols, 240 periodicals
Number of teachers: 215
Number of students: 3,000
Publication: *Daneshvar* (4 a year)

DEANS

Faculty of Agriculture: Dr MASOOD ISFAHANI
Faculty of Art: ALI ASGAR SHIRAZI
Faculty of Basic Sciences: Dr IRAJ RASOOLI

Faculty of Dentistry: Dr SEIYED SHOJAEDDIN SHAYEGH

Faculty of Engineering: Dr JALAL NAZARZA-DEH

Faculty of Humanities and Literature: Dr MOHAMMAD REZA IMAM

Faculty of Medical Sciences: Dr SEIYED SAEID SEIYED MORTAZ

SHAHID BAHONAR UNIVERSITY OF KERMAN

POB 76169-133, Kerman
Telephone: (341) 3220041
Fax: (341) 3220065
E-mail: sbuk@mail.uk.ac.ir
Internet: www.uk.ac.ir
Founded 1974, teaching commenced 1975
State control
Languages of instruction: Farsi, English
Academic year: September to June
Pres.: AHMAD AMIRI KHORASANI
Vice-Pres. for Admin. and Finance: AKBAR HOSSEINI POUR
Vice-Pres. for Education: HOSSEIN MOHEBI
Vice-Pres. for Research: MOHAMMAD RANJBAR HAMGHAVANDI
Vice-Pres. for Student Affairs: MANSOUR SAHEBZAMANI
Registrar: Dr M. A. VALI
Librarian: M. SHAFIIE
Library of 150,000 vols
Number of teachers: 400
Number of students: 12,500

Colleges of sgriculture, srt, basic sciences, engineering, literature and human sciences, management and economics, mathematics and computer science, physical education and sport science, veterinary sciences; faculties of agriculture (Jiroft), higher education (Bam), mining (Zarand), technology (Sirjan).

SHAHID BEHESHTI UNIVERSITY

Evin, 19834 Tehran 1983963113
Telephone: (21) 29901
Fax: (21) 22431919
E-mail: info@sbu.ac.ir
Internet: www.sbu.ac.ir
Founded 1960 as National University of Iran; present name 1983
State control
Language of instruction: Farsi
Academic year: September to June
Pres.: Prof. AHMAD SHAABANI
Vice-Pres. for Admin. and Finance: Dr BEH-ROOZ DORI
Vice-Pres. for Education and Graduate Studies: Dr BAHMAN HONARI
Vice-Pres. for Information and Communication Technology: Dr FEREIDOON SHAMS
Vice-Pres. for Research and Technology: Dr PEYMAN SALEHI
Vice-Pres. for Student and Cultural Affairs: Dr MORTEZA SAMNOON MAHDAVI
Dir of Collegiate Relations and Int. Scientific Cooperations: Dr HOSSEIN POUR AHMADI
Dir of Public Relations: HADI SALEHI ZADEH
Registrar: Dr MASOOD SHARIFI
Library: see Libraries and Archives
Number of teachers: 500
Number of students: 13,576
Publications: Ayeneh Isar, Ayeneh Ma'refat (Research Journal of Philosophy and Discourse), Daneshnameh, Journal of Earth Sciences, Journal of Family Research, Journal of Human Sciences, Management Excellence, Management Perspective, Rahyaft (Political and International Approaches, 4 a year), Quarterly Applied Psychology, Revue de Recherche Juridique, Soffeh (architecture)

DEANS

Faculty of Architecture and Urban Planning: Dr AKBAR HAJ EBRAHIM ZARGAR
Faculty of Biological Sciences: Dr MASSOD SHEIDAI
Faculty of Earth Sciences: Dr HASSAN LASH-KARI
Faculty of Economics and Political Sciences: Dr MOHAMMAD NASER SHERAFAT JAHROMI
Faculty of Education and Psychology: HAMID REZA POURETAMAD
Faculty of Electrical and Computer Engineering: Dr SEYED EBRAHIM AFJEII
Faculty of Law: Dr GOODARZ EFTEKHAR JAHROMI
Faculty of Letters and Human Sciences: Dr AKBAR MAJDODINE
Faculty of Management and Accounting: Dr MOHAMMAD ESMAEIL FADAEI
Faculty of Mathematical Sciences: Dr MOHAMMAD ZOKAEI
Faculty of New Technologies and Energy Engineering: Dr ABAS SAIDI
Faculty of Physical Education and Sports Sciences: Dr KHOSRO EBRAHIM
Faculty of Sciences: Dr MEHRDAD FARHOUDI
Faculty of Theology and Religions: Dr HASSAN SAEEDI

PROFESSORS

ABASSI, A., Literature and Human Sciences
ABBAS ZADEGAN, S. M., Education and Psychology
ABBASPOUR, M., Electrical and Computer Engineering
ABDI DANESHPOUR, Z., Architecture and Urban Planning
ABDOLAHI, M., Environmental Sciences Research Institute
ABDOLI, A., Environmental Sciences Research Institute
ABDOLI, B., Physical Education and Sport Sciences
ABEDIN, A., Education and Psychology
ABEDIN, A., Family Research Institute
ABOLGHASEMI, M., Education and Psychology
ABOLGHASEMI, S. M., Literature and Human Sciences
ADABI, M. H., Earth Sciences
ADIB RAD, N., Education and Psychology
ADIBZADEH, B., Architecture and Urban Planning
AFJEI, S. E., Electrical and Computer Engineering
AGHDAEE, M., Physical Education and Sport Sciences
AHARI, Z., Architecture and Urban Planning
AHMAD ZADEH, F., Environmental Sciences Research Institute
AHMADI, F., Architecture and Urban Planning
AHMADI, S. H., Literature and Human Sciences
AHMADZADEH, S., Literature and Human Sciences
AKBARI, M. A., Literature and Human Sciences
AKBARI GHAMSARI, A., Literature and Human Sciences
AKBARIAN, M., Management and Accounting
ALAEI, A., Architecture and Urban Planning
ALAMOL HODA, J., Education and Psychology
ALASKARI, Z., Literature and Human Sciences
ALAVI, S. A., Earth Sciences
ALAVINIA, S., Literature and Human Sciences
ALBORZ, M., Mathematical Sciences
ALEM TABRIZ, A., Management and Accounting
ALIREZAEI, S., Earth Sciences
ALSHAHIR BIFARHANG MAJDODDIN, A., Literature and Human Sciences
AMINI, M., Law
AMINI HOURA, M., Architecture and Urban Planning
AMIR ARJOMAND, A., Law

ANSARINIA, S., Architecture and Urban Planning
ARAB MAZAR, A., Economic and Political Sciences
ARABMAZAR YAZDI, M., Management and Accounting
ARBABI, M., Law
ARBABIAN, A., Management and Accounting
ARDEBILI, M. A., Law
ARDEBILI, M. H., Management and Accounting
AREFI, M., Education and Psychology
ASADI, G., Management and Accounting
ASGHARI, A. H., Mathematical Sciences
ASGHARIAN JEDDI, A., Architecture and Urban Planning
ASHTIANI, M., Education and Psychology
ASLANKHANI, M., Physical Education and Sport Sciences
ASSADI, B., Economic and Political Sciences
AVANI, G., Literature and Human Sciences
AYATOLLAHZADEH SHIRAZI, M. M., Mathematical Sciences
AZADEH, A. A., Mathematical Sciences
AZARI, H., Mathematical Sciences
AZGHANDI, A., Economic and Political Sciences
BA EZAT, F., Education and Psychology
BABAPOOR, M. M., Department of Islamic Teachings
BADIEI, M., Architecture and Urban Planning
BAGHERIAN, F., Education and Psychology
BAHADORI BARCHELOEI, M., Electrical and Computer Engineering
BAHADORIFAR, M., Earth Sciences
BAHAR NEJAD, Z., Department of Islamic Teachings
BAHARI ARDESHIRI, A. A., Literature and Human Sciences
BAHER, G., Management and Accounting
BANA RAZAVI, M., Economic and Political Sciences
BARGH JELVE, S., Environmental Sciences Research Institute
BEHESHTI AVAL, S. B., Architecture and Urban Planning
BEHZAD, M., Mathematical Sciences
BEHZADI SHIRKALA, M., Earth Sciences
BEIGZADEH, E., Law
BERANJEH TORABI, D. M., Literature and Human Sciences
BLACK, J. E., Environmental Sciences Research Institute
BOZORGAN NIA, M. A., Literature and Human Sciences
CHALABI, M., Literature and Human Sciences
CHENARI, A. A., Literature and Human Sciences
CHIME, N., Family Research Institute
DADASHI, M. S., Physical Education and Sport Sciences
DADGAR, U., Law
DADKAN, M. H., Physical Education and Sport Sciences
DANESH, E., Education and Psychology
DANESHPOUR PARVAR, F., Literature and Human Sciences
DARABKOLAIE, E., Department of Islamic Teachings
DARABPOUR, M., Law
DARGAHI, A., Electrical and Computer Engineering
DARGAHI, H., Economic and Political Sciences
DARIUSH HAMEDANI, H., Mathematical Sciences
DARKOOSH, S. A., Economic and Political Sciences
DAVOODI, P., Economic and Political Sciences
DEHGAN, A., Department of Islamic Teachings
DEHGHAN, M., Family Research Institute
DEHZAD, B., Earth Sciences
DELSHAD, S., Literature and Human Sciences
DEYHIMFARD, R., Environmental Sciences Research Institute

DEZFOULIAN, K., Literature and Human Sciences
DIDARI, R., Literature and Human Sciences
DORRI, B., Management and Accounting
EBRAHIM, K., Physical Education and Sport Sciences
EBRAHIMI, M. M., Mathematical Sciences
EBRAHIMI VARKIANI, M., Department of Islamic Teachings
EFTEKHAR JAHROMI, G., Law
EJTEHADI, M., Literature and Human Sciences
EMADZADEH, G., Literature and Human Sciences
ESHGHI, M., Electrical and Computer Engineering
ESLAHCHI, C., Mathematical Sciences
ESLAMI, R., Law
ESMAEILI, J., Electrical and Computer Engineering
ESMAILPOUR MOTLAGH, A., Literature and Human Sciences
ESPANDAR, R., Earth Sciences
ESTARAMI, E., Literature and Human Sciences
ETEZADI, L., Architecture and Urban Planning
FADAEI NEJAD, M. E., Management and Accounting
FAGHIHI, M. R., Mathematical Sciences
FAKHARI, A. H., Law
FAKHARI TEHRANI, F., Architecture and Urban Planning
FALLAHI, A., Architecture and Urban Planning
FALSAFI, H., Law
FANNI, Z., Earth Sciences
FARDANESH, M. A., Economic and Political Sciences
FARSIJANI, H., Management and Accounting
FARZAD, F., Management and Accounting
FATEMI JAHROMI, S. A., Literature and Human Sciences
FATHI VAJAR GAH, K., Education and Psychology
FATTAH, A., Electrical and Computer Engineering
FERDOSI, S., Education and Psychology
FEYZOLLAHZADEH, A., Literature and Human Sciences
FOROOZESH, N., Mathematical Sciences
FOYOZAT, E., Literature and Human Sciences
GADAK, A., Law
GANJALI, M., Mathematical Sciences
GHADIMI, H., Architecture and Urban Planning
GHADIRI, F., Family Research Institute
GHAEM, G., Architecture and Urban Planning
GHAFFARI, A., Architecture and Urban Planning
GHAFOORI, M., Economic and Political Sciences
GHAHREMANI, M., Education and Psychology
GHANAATSHOAR, M., Laser and Plasma Research Institute
GHANBARI, M. J., Law
GHANBARI MAMAN, H., Economic and Political Sciences
GHAREHCHEH, M., Management and Accounting
GHARI SEYED FATEMI, M., Law
GHASEMI HAMED, A., Law
GHASEMPOUR, A., Environmental Sciences Research Institute
GHASEMZADEH, A., Management and Accounting
GHAVAM, A., Economic and Political Sciences
GHAVAMI ZADEH, R., Electrical and Computer Engineering
GHAVIMI, M., Literature and Human Sciences
GHOAMREZAEI, M., Literature and Human Sciences
GHORBANI, M., Earth Sciences
GHOUCHANI, F., Management and Accounting
GOLDOOST JOUYBARI, R., Law

GOLKAR, K., Architecture and Urban Planning
GOOYA, Z., Mathematical Sciences
HADDADI, S. M., Literature and Human Sciences
HADIZADEH, A., Management and Accounting
HAGHIGHAT, R., Earth Sciences
HAGHIGHI, M., Management and Accounting
HAJ EBRAHIM ZARGAR, A., Architecture and Urban Planning
HAJ JABBARI, S., Mathematical Sciences
HAJI GHASEMI, K., Architecture and Urban Planning
HAJI KARIMI, A., Management and Accounting
HAJI MIR ARAB, M., Economic and Political Sciences
HAJIABOLHASAN, H., Mathematical Sciences
HAJI-YOUSEFI, A. M., Economic and Political Sciences
HAMIDIZADEH, M. R., Management and Accounting
HAMIDREZA, G., Laser and Plasma Research Institute
HANAEI KASHANI, M. S., Literature and Human Sciences
HANJANI, S. A., Law
HASAN ZADE KIABI, B., Environmental Sciences Research Institute
HASHEMI, S. A., Economic and Political Sciences
HASHEMI, S. H., Environmental Sciences Research Institute
HASHEMI, S. M., Law
HASHEMIPOUR, O., Electrical and Computer Engineering
HASSANI, A., Literature and Human Sciences
HASSANI, M., Earth Sciences
HEKMAT, N., Literature and Human Sciences
HERAVI, I., Management and Accounting
HERAVI, M., Architecture and Urban Planning
HESHMATZADEH, M. B., Economic and Political Sciences
HEYDARI, M., Education and Psychology
HEYDARI, M., Family Research Institute
HEYDARIAN., M. T., Literature and Human Sciences
HOJJAT, M., Department of Islamic Teachings
HONARI, B., Mathematical Sciences
HOSHI, A., Management and Accounting
HOSSEINABADI, A., Law
HOSSEINALIPOUR, S., Architecture and Urban Planning
HOSSEINI, S. M., Management and Accounting
HOSSEINI BARMAEI, S. F., Law
HOSSEINI BARZI, M., Earth Sciences
HOSSEINPOUR KAZEMI, M., Economic and Political Sciences
HOSSEINZADEH, M., Management and Accounting
HOVANLO, F., Physical Education and Sport Sciences
HOZHABR KIANI, K., Economic and Political Sciences
ILKHANI, M., Literature and Human Sciences
ILKHANI, S. C., Literature and Human Sciences
JABERIPOUR, G., Electrical and Computer Engineering
JAFARI ROHANI, B., Mathematical Sciences
JAHANKHANI, A., Management and Accounting
JALALI, A., Electrical and Computer Engineering
JALALI, M., Architecture and Urban Planning
JAVIDRUZI, M., Architecture and Urban Planning
JOUDAT, M. R., Architecture and Urban Planning
KAFAIE, S. M. A., Economic and Political Sciences
KANANI, M. R., Environmental Sciences Research Institute

KARIMIAN, F., Literature and Human Sciences
KASSAEE, M., Management and Accounting
KHAKZAD, A., Earth Sciences
KHALATBARI, A., Literature and Human Sciences
KHALEDI, S., Earth Sciences
KHALFEH SHOUSHTARI, M. E., Literature and Human Sciences
KHALIGHI, A., Literature and Human Sciences
KHANSARI MOUSAVI, S., Literature and Human Sciences
KHATAMI, A., Literature and Human Sciences
KHATAMI, M. J., Architecture and Urban Planning
KHATTAT, N. K., Literature and Human Sciences
KHEYRANDISH, A., Environmental Sciences Research Institute
KHLLAT, F., Mathematical Sciences
KHODA PANAHI, M. K., Education and Psychology
KHODADADI, A., Mathematical Sciences
KHODAI KALATEBAI, N., Literature and Human Sciences
KHODAIAN, S., Earth Sciences
KHOMAMIZADEH, F., Law
KHORASANI ZADEH, M., Architecture and Urban Planning
KHORSAND, H., Electrical and Computer Engineering
KHORSHIDI, G., Management and Accounting
KHOSH KONESH, A., Education and Psychology
KHOSHBAKHT, K., Environmental Sciences Research Institute
KOOSHA, J., Law
KOUCHAKZADE, M., Environmental Sciences Research Institute
LAJEVARDI, M., Earth Sciences
LAJEVARDI, S. J., Management and Accounting
LARI, A., Physical Education and Sport Sciences
LASHKARI, H., Earth Sciences
LATIFI, H., Laser and Plasma Research Institute
LESSAN PEZESHKI, H., Literature and Human Sciences
LIAGHATI, H., Environmental Sciences Research Institute
LOTF ABADI, H., Education and Psychology
LOTFALIKANI, A., Earth Sciences
MAHDAVI, M. S., Literature and Human Sciences
MAHDAVI DAMGHANI, A. M., Environmental Sciences Research Institute
MAHDAVI HERSINI, S. E., Education and Psychology
MAHMOUDI, H., Environmental Sciences Research Institute
MAHMOUDI, M., Mathematical Sciences
MAJIDI KHAMENEH, B., Earth Sciences
MAKHZAN MOUSAVI, S. A., Literature and Human Sciences
MANAVI TEHRAN, A., Economic and Political Sciences
MANI, M. A., Economic and Political Sciences
MANSOORBAKHT, G., Literature and Human Sciences
MANSOUR, L., Education and Psychology
MARANDI, M. R., Department of Islamic Teachings
MASHAYEKH FARIDANI, S., Architecture and Urban Planning
MASOUDI, R., Laser and Plasma Research Institute
MASOUMZADEH KIAEI, M. A., Economic and Political Sciences
MAZAHERI TEHRANI, M. A., Education and Psychology
MAZAHERI TEHRANI, M. A., Family Research Institute
MAZLOOMNEZHAD, B., Electrical and Computer Engineering

MEHRA, N., Law
MEHRDAD, S. M., Environmental Sciences Research Institute
MEHRPOUR MOHAMMADABADI, H., Law
MEHRSHAHI, E., Electrical and Computer Engineering
MEMARIAN, A., Architecture and Urban Planning
MESGARI, A. A., Literature and Human Sciences
MESHKANI, M. R., Mathematical Sciences
MILANI, V., Mathematical Sciences
MINA KARI, M., Education and Psychology
MINOUEI, S., Environmental Sciences Research Institute
MIR JALILI, M. H., Environmental Sciences Research Institute
MIR RIAHI, S., Architecture and Urban Planning
MIR SHAMS SHAHSHAHANI, S., Literature and Human Sciences
MIRI, S., Architecture and Urban Planning
MIRMOHAMMAD SADEGHI, H., Law
MOEINI, M., Physical Education and Sport Sciences
MOGHIM ESLAM, G., Laser and Plasma Research Institute
MOGHISEH, H., Department of Islamic Teachings
MOHAGHEGH AHMADABADI (DAMAD), S. M., Law
MOHAJERANI, A., Laser and Plasma Research Institute
MOHAMMADI, H. R., Earth Sciences
MOHAMMADZADEH, H., Earth Sciences
MOHSENI ARMAKI, S. M., Laser and Plasma Research Institute
MOMAYEZ, A., Architecture and Urban Planning
MOMENI, I., Earth Sciences
MOMENI, M., Earth Sciences
MOMTAZ, F., Literature and Human Sciences
MONIRI, M., Mathematical Sciences
MONSHIZADEH, R., Earth Sciences
MORTAZAVI, S., Education and Psychology
MOSADEGH RASHTI, A. A., Literature and Human Sciences
MOSHARAFOLMOLK, M., Literature and Human Sciences
MOSHIRI, F., Architecture and Urban Planning
MOSTAFAVI, H., Environmental Sciences Research Institute
MOSTAFAVI KASHANI, S. M., Law
MOSTAFAVI NIA, S. M. K., Department of Islamic Teachings
MOTTAGHI, H., Management and Accounting
MOUSA POUR, N., Education and Psychology
MOUSAVI, M. R., Earth Sciences
MOUTABI, F., Family Research Institute
NADIMI, H., Architecture and Urban Planning
NADIMI, H., Literature and Human Sciences
NAHREYNI, F., Law
NAJAFI ABRANDABADI, H., Law
NAJAFIAN, B., Earth Sciences
NAMAZI, H., Economic and Political Sciences
NAMAZIAN, A., Architecture and Urban Planning
NAMAZIZADEH, M., Physical Education and Sport Sciences
NAMVAR GHAREH SHIRAN, E., Electrical and Computer Engineering
NASSERY, H. R., Earth Sciences
NAVAEI, K., Architecture and Urban Planning
NAVI, K., Electrical and Computer Engineering
NAZARI, A., Architecture and Urban Planning
NAZEMI, E., Electrical and Computer Engineering
NEJAD EBRAHIMI, S., Environmental Sciences Research Institute
NEMATOLLAHI, V., Literature and Human Sciences
NIKBAKHT, H. R., Law

NIKNAM, A., Laser and Plasma Research Institute
NIKPEY, A., Law
NILI, M. Y., Architecture and Urban Planning
NOBAHAR, R., Law
NOFARASTI, M., Economic and Political Sciences
NOJOUMIAN, A. A., Literature and Human Sciences
NOOR BALOOCHI, S., Mathematical Sciences
NOORI NAEINI, S., Economic and Political Sciences
NOURANI POUR, R., Education and Psychology
NOURBAHA, R., Law
NOURI ROUDSARI, O., Environmental Sciences Research Institute
NOURSHAHI, M., Physical Education and Sport Sciences
ORKAMANI AZAR, F., Electrical and Computer Engineering
OSSEINION, S. A., Mathematical Sciences
PADIDAR, M., Architecture and Urban Planning
PAKDAMAN, S., Education and Psychology
PAKZAD, J., Architecture and Urban Planning
PALIZBAN, F., Literature and Human Sciences
PANAGHI, L., Family Research Institute
PARCHAMI, D., Literature and Human Sciences
PARDAKHTCHI, M., Education and Psychology
PARSA, M. A., Architecture and Urban Planning
PARVIN JAHROMI, K., Mathematical Sciences
PAZUKI, A., Architecture and Urban Planning
POOR KAZEMI, M. H., Economic and Political Sciences
POORBARAT, M., Mathematical Sciences
POORSINA, M., Department of Islamic Teachings
POUR AHMADI MIEBODI, H., Economic and Political Sciences
POUR ETEMAD, H. R., Education and Psychology
POUR KERAMATI, V., Architecture and Urban Planning
POUR KERMANI, M., Earth Sciences
POUR MOAFI, S. M., Earth Sciences
POURETEMAD, H., Family Research Institute
POURKIANI, M., Physical Education and Sport Sciences
RAFATI, H., Environmental Sciences Research Institute
RAFIPOOR, F., Literature and Human Sciences
RAHGOSHAI, M., Earth Sciences
RAHMANI, B., Earth Sciences
RAHMANI FAZLI, A., Earth Sciences
RASA, I., Earth Sciences
RASEKH, M., Law
RASHIDIAN, A., Literature and Human Sciences
RASI, M., Literature and Human Sciences
RASOULI NARAGHI, G., Architecture and Urban Planning
RASTKAR, A. R., Laser and Plasma Research Institute
RAZAVI ZADEH, G., Electrical and Computer Engineering
RAZAVIAN, M. T., Earth Sciences
RAZJOUYAN, M., Architecture and Urban Planning
RAZMGAH, F., Architecture and Urban Planning
REZA, M. T., Environmental Sciences Research Institute
REZAEIAN, A., Management and Accounting
REZAZADE VALUJERDI, A., Electrical and Computer Engineering
ROHANI RANKOUHI, M. T., Electrical and Computer Engineering
ROOZBEHAN, M., Economic and Political Sciences
ROSHAN, M., Family Research Institute
ROSOULI, H., Literature and Human Sciences
ROUSTA, A., Management and Accounting

SABAHI, H., Environmental Sciences Research Institute
SABBAGHIAN, Z., Education and Psychology
SADAT KYAIE, M., Department of Islamic Teachings
SADEGHI, A., Earth Sciences
SADEGHI, A., Law
SADEGHI PEY, N., Architecture and Urban Planning
SADJADI, S. A. M., Literature and Human Sciences
SADOOGH VANINI, H., Earth Sciences
SADR, S. K., Economic and Political Sciences
SADRIA, A., Architecture and Urban Planning
SAEIDI, A., Earth Sciences
SAFFAR, M. J., Law
SAFFARI, A., Law
SAHBA YAGHMAEI, M., Laser and Plasma Research Institute
SAIDI, H., Department of Islamic Teachings
SAJADI, J., Earth Sciences
SALAHI MALEK, Y., Economic and Political Sciences
SALEHI, P., Environmental Sciences Research Institute
SALEHI ZADEH, H., Department of Islamic Teachings
SALEHPOUR, Y., Family Research Institute
SALEMI, A., Environmental Sciences Research Institute
SAMNON, M., Department of Islamic Teachings
SAMSAMI, H., Economic and Political Sciences
SANEI DAREHBIDI, M., Literature and Human Sciences
SANIEI, N., Electrical and Computer Engineering
SARAFI, M., Earth Sciences
SARIOLGHALAM, M., Economic and Political Sciences
SARTIPI POUR, M., Architecture and Urban Planning
SAVARAEI, P., Law
SAVOJI, M. H., Electrical and Computer Engineering
SEIFI, S. J., Law
SEIFI, Z., Law
SERVAT, M. M., Literature and Human Sciences
SERVATI, M. R., Earth Sciences
SEYED HASHEMI, S. E., Department of Islamic Teachings
SEYED MIRZAEI, S. M., Literature and Human Sciences
SHABANI, N., Environmental Sciences Research Institute
SHABANI, R., Literature and Human Sciences
SHAEGHI, A. A., Environmental Sciences Research Institute
SHAFIE HOLIHI, K., Mathematical Sciences
SHAH HOSSEINI, H., Electrical and Computer Engineering
SHAHBAZI, E., Environmental Sciences Research Institute
SHAHIDA, M. R., Earth Sciences
SHAHIDI, S., Education and Psychology
SHAHLAEE, A., Mathematical Sciences
SHAHNI KARAMAZADEH, N., Mathematical Sciences
SHAHRIARI, S., Earth Sciences
SHAHSHAHANI, S., Literature and Human Sciences
SHAHVARANI, A., Mathematical Sciences
SHAMLOO, B., Law
SHAMS, A., Law
SHAMSFARD, M., Electrical and Computer Engineering
SHARIF TEHRANI, S. R., Architecture and Urban Planning
SHARIFI, M., Education and Psychology
SHARIFI, M., Family Research Institute
SHARIFI, M. J., Electrical and Computer Engineering
SHEIKH, M. A., Literature and Human Sciences
SHEIKHHASSANI, G. H., Earth Sciences

SHEMIRANI, A., Earth Sciences
SHERAFAT, M. N., Economic and Political Sciences
SHOEIBI, A., Architecture and Urban Planning
SHOKRI, B., Laser and Plasma Research Institute
SIMBAR, F., Economic and Political Sciences
SOHEIL, K., Literature and Human Sciences
SOKHANVAR, J., Literature and Human Sciences
SOLEIMANI, D., Literature and Human Sciences
SONBOLI, A., Environmental Sciences Research Institute
TABARSA, G., Management and Accounting
TABATABEI, S., Electrical and Computer Engineering
TAFAZOLI, F., Economic and Political Sciences
TAGHI, Z., Architecture and Urban Planning
TAHBAZ, M., Architecture and Urban Planning
TAHMASBIAN, K., Family Research Institute
TAJIK, M. R., Economic and Political Sciences
TALEB ZADEH, M., Education and Psychology
TALEBI, D., Management and Accounting
TAVAKKOLI, M., Department of Islamic Teachings
TAVAKOLI, A., Economic and Political Sciences
TAVAKOLINIA, J., Earth Sciences
TAVASOLI, S. H., Laser and Plasma Research Institute
TAVASSOLIZADEH, N., Law
TEHRANCHI, M. M., Laser and Plasma Research Institute
THOMAS ZADEH, R., Literature and Human Sciences
TOUSI ARDEKANI, M., Mathematical Sciences
VAEZ IRAVANI, F., Electrical and Computer Engineering
VAEZI, A., Literature and Human Sciences
VAHDANI MOGHADAM, M., Laser and Plasma Research Institute
VAHID DOSTJERDI, F., Literature and Human Sciences
VAHIDI, T., Architecture and Urban Planning
VAHIDI ASL, M. Q., Mathematical Sciences
VATANKHAH, M., Economic and Political Sciences
VAZIRI FARAHANI, B., Architecture and Urban Planning
VAZIRI FARAHANI, P., Architecture and Urban Planning
VIZEH FAYAZ, O., Literature and Human Sciences
VOSOOGHI ABEDINI, M., Earth Sciences
YAMANI DOUZI SORKHABI, M., Education and Psychology
YAVARI, M. E., Economic and Political Sciences
YAZDI, M., Earth Sciences
YOSOFI, S. A., Mathematical Sciences
ZADE MOHAMMADI, A., Family Research Institute
ZAKER ALHOSSEINI, A., Electrical and Computer Engineering
ZAKERZADEH, A., Literature and Human Sciences
ZAND, E., Environmental Sciences Research Institute
ZAREI, M. H., Law
ZEKAVAT, K., Architecture and Urban Planning
ZIATAVANA, M. H., Earth Sciences
ZOKAEI, M., Mathematical Sciences

SHAHID BEHESHTI UNIVERSITY OF MEDICAL SCIENCES AND HEALTH SERVICES

POB 4139-19395, Shahid Chamran Highway, Evin, Tehran
Telephone: (21) 2401022
Fax: (21) 2400052

E-mail: icrd@sbmu.ac.ir
Internet: www.sbmu.ac.ir
Founded 1961 as Melli University; present name 1986
State control
Language of instruction: Farsi
Academic year: September to June

Chancellor: Dr HABIBOLLA PEYRAVI
Vice-Chancellor for Academic Affairs: Dr D. YADEGARI
Vice-Chancellor for Admin. and Finance: Dr R. ABOUFAZELI
Vice-Chancellor for Curative and Pharmaceutical Affairs: Dr S. S. RAZAVI
Vice-Chancellor for Health: Dr A. RAMEZANKHANI
Vice-Chancellor for Research: Dr M. JORJANI
Vice-Chancellor for Student and Cultural Affairs: Dr M. HOSSEINI KHAMENE
Dir of Int. Relations and Congress Management: Dr F. OKHOVATIAN
Librarian: A. MOHADES RAAD

Library of 5,458 vols, 3,000 current journals, 60 e-books
Number of teachers: 1,039
Number of students: 5,961

Publications: Bina (Journal of Ophthalmology, 4 a year), Digestive Disease Digest (12 a year), International Journal of Endocrinology and Metabolism (4 a year), Iranian Journal of Infectious Disease and Tropical Medicine (4 a year), Iranian Journal of Plastic and Reconstructive Surgery (4 a year), Iranian Journal of Urology (4 a year), Journal of Dentistry (4 a year), Journal of Medical Education (4 a year), Journal of the Pharmaceutical Research Centre (4 a year), Pejouhandeh (4 a year), Research in Medical Subjects (in Farsi, 4 a year), Tanaffos (Respiration, 4 a year)

DEANS

Faculty of Allied Medicine: Dr S. H. MOGHADAM-NIA
Faculty of Dentistry
Faculty of Medicine: Dr M. MARDANI
Faculty of Nutrition and Food Industrial Sciences: Dr N. KALANTARI
School of Nursing and Midwifery: Dr M. YAZDJERDI
Faculty of Pharmacy: Dr M. MOSADEGH
School of Public Health: Dr H. KHATAMI
Faculty of Rehabilitation: Dr M. GHASSEMY BOROMAND

SHAHID CHAMRAN UNIVERSITY

Ahvaz, Khouzestan
Telephone: (611) 3330022
Fax: (611) 3332040
E-mail: webmaster@cua.ac.ir
Internet: www.scu.ac.ir
Founded 1955 as Jundi Shapur University, present name 1983
State control
Language of instruction: Farsi
Academic year: September to June

Chancellor: Dr MORTEZA ZARGAR SHOOSHTARI NOURI
Vice-Chancellor for Academic Affairs: Dr M. A. FIROOZI
Vice-Chancellor for Admin. and Finance: Dr GHOMESHI
Vice-Chancellor for Research and Technology: Dr H. R. GHAFOURI
Vice-Chancellor for Student Affairs: M. MOGHBELAL-HOSSEIN
Dir of Int. Affairs: Mr SADROS-SADAT
Registrar: M. JANNEJAD
Librarian: Dr A. FARAJPAHLOU

Number of teachers: 518
Number of students: 13,308

Publications: Journal of Education and Psychology (in Farsi, 4 a year), Journal of Engineering (in Farsi, 1 a year), Journal of Literature and Islamic Studies (in Farsi, 1 a year), Journal of Veterinary Medicine (in Farsi, 1 a year), Scientific Journal of Agriculture (in Farsi, 4 a year), University Journal of Science (in Farsi, 1 a year)

DEANS

Faculty of Agriculture: Dr NABIPOUR
Faculty of Arts: M. KOLLAHKAJ
Faculty of Economic and Social Science: Dr NABAVI
Faculty of Education and Psychology: Dr M. KOUKABI
Faculty of Engineering: Dr M. JOORABIAN
Faculty of Geology and GIS: G. RANGZAN
Faculty of Literature and Humanities: Dr MOVAHED
Faculty of Mathematics and Computer Science: H. HARIZAVI
Faculty of Physical Education: Dr A. H. HABIBI
Faculty of Science: Dr M. CHITSAZAN
Faculty of Theology and Islamic Studies: Dr A. MATOORI
Faculty of Veterinary Science: Dr M. GHORBANPOUR
Faculty of Water Science Engineering: Dr S. M. KASHEFIPOUR

SHAHID SADOUGHI UNIVERSITY OF MEDICAL SCIENCES

POB 89195-734, 2 Bouali Ave, Yazd
Telephone: (351) 82470171
Fax: (351) 8245446
E-mail: info@ssu.ac.ir
Internet: www.ssu.ac.ir
Founded 1983
State control
Language of instruction: Farsi
Academic year: September to June

Chancellor: Dr AHMAD HAERIAN
Vice-Chancellor for Academic Affairs: Dr MR. MANSORIAN
Vice-Chancellor for Admin. and Financial Affairs: Dr MH. EHRAMPOUSH
Vice-Chancellor for Health: Dr M. KARIMI
Vice-Chancellor for Research Affairs: Dr S. M. YASSINI
Vice-Chancellor for Student Services: Dr HOSSEINI
Dir of Int. Affairs: Dr SM. KALANTAR
Registrar: A. M. ALI HEIDARI

Library of 40,000 vols, 278 journals
Number of teachers: 236
Number of students: 1,800

DEANS

Faculty of Dentistry: Dr TALEBI
Faculty of Medicine: Dr RAFIEAN
Faculty of Nursing and Midwifery: Dr SEYED HASSANI
Faculty of Paramedicine: Dr KHALILI
Faculty of Public Health: Dr EHRAMPOUSH

SHAHREKORD UNIVERSITY OF MEDICAL SCIENCES

POB 88184, Kashany Ave, Shahrekord
Telephone: (381) 34590
Fax: (381) 34588
Internet: www.skums.ac.ir
Founded in 1986
State control
Language of instruction: Persian

Pres.: Dr M. HASHEMZADEH
Vice-Chancellor for Admin. and Financial Affairs: F. SHARAFATI
Vice-Chancellor for Curative, Drug and Food Affairs: Dr E. NOORIAN

Vice-Chancellor for Education and Research:
Dr M. R. SAMIEY NASAB
Vice-Chancellor for Student and Cultural
Affairs: Dr H. DAVOODPOUR
Librarian: Dr A. AMINI
Library of 33,000 vols
Number of teachers: 130
Number of students: 1,357

DEANS

Faculty of Medicine: Dr M. ROGHANY
Faculty of Nursing and Midwifery: M.
RAHIMY
Broujen Faculty of Nursing: S. BANAEYAN

SHARIF UNIVERSITY OF
TECHNOLOGY

POB 11365-8639, Tehran
Telephone: (21) 66005419
Fax: (21) 66012983
E-mail: scientia@sharif.edu
Internet: www.sharif.edu
Founded 1965 as Aryamehr University, present name 1979
State control
Languages of instruction: Farsi, English
Academic year: September to May
Library of 168,000 vols
Pres.: Prof. SAEED SOHRABPOUR
Vice-Pres. for Admin. and Finance: Prof.
SEYED ALI AKBAR EKRAMI
Vice-Pres. for Education and Graduate Studies: Prof. ALI MEGHDARI
Vice-Pres. for Planning and Budget: ALI
ASGHAR ESKANDAR BAYATI
Vice-Pres. for Research: Dr REZA ROOSTA
AZAD
Vice-Pres. for Student Affairs: Dr BIJAN
VOSOOGHI VAHDAT
Chair. of Office of Int. and Scientific
Cooperation (OISC): Prof. ABOLHASSAN
VAFAI
Dean of Assessment: ALI KARIMI TAHERI
Dean of Education: ABOL GHASEM DOLATI
Dean of Extra Curriculum: MOHAMMAD MIR-ZAI
Dean of Financial Affairs: MOHAMMAD FOR-OOTAN
Dean of Graduate Studies: AMIR DANESHGAR
Dean of Human Resources: HAMID REZA
MADAAH HOSSEINI
Dean of Industrial Cooperation: SEYYED
JAMALEDIN HASHEMIAN
Dean of Research Affairs: MASOUD TAJRISHI
Dean of Student Affairs: SEYED REZA NAGHI-NASAB
Librarian: Prof. HAMID MEHDIGHOLI
Library of 242,000 vols (130,000 in English,
12,000 in Farsi), 100,000 periodicals
Number of teachers: 300
Number of students: 8,000, including 2,000
Masters and 400 PhD students
Depts of aerospace engineering, chemical
engineering and petroleum, chemistry, civil
engineering, computer engineering, electrical engineering, industrial engineering,
management and economics, materials science and engineering, mathematical sciences, mechanical engineering, philosophy
of science, physics

Publications: *Scientia Iranica* (6 a year, in
English), *Sharif* (scientific and research, 4
a year, in Farsi).

ATTACHED RESEARCH CENTRES

**Advanced Communications Research
Institute:** tel. (21) 6165910; fax (21)
6036002; e-mail acri@sharif.edu; internet
acri.sharif.ir.

Advanced Information and Communication Technology Centre: internet www
.aictc.com; Dir Dr HAMID REZA RABIEE.

**Advanced Manufacturing Research
Centre (AMRC):** Dir MOJTABA TAHMOURES.
**Centre of Excellence in Earthquake
Engineering:** Dir Prof. M. T. KAZEMI.
Centre of Excellence in Energy Conversion: Azadi St, Tehran; tel. (21) 66165549;
fax (21) 66000021; internet sina.sharif.edu;
languages of instruction: Farsi, English; Dir
Dr S. K. HANNANI.
Electronics Research Centre: tel. (21)
66005517; fax (21) 66030318; e-mail erc@
sina.sharif.edu; internet www.sharif-erc
.com; Dir Prof. MAHMOUD TABIANI.
Institute for Nanoscience and Nanotechnology: tel. (21) 66164123; fax (21)
66164119; e-mail inst@sharif.edu; internet
nano.sharif.ir; Dir Prof. AZAM IRAJI ZAD.
**Institute for Transportation Studies
and Research:** Dir Dr HOSSEIN POURZAHEDI.
**Sharif Applied Physics Research
Centre:** tel. (21) 616-4542; fax (21) 6602-
2711; e-mail appliedphysics@mehr.sharif
.edu; internet physics.sharif.edu/
~appliedphysics; Dir Dr AHMAD AMJADI.
Sharif Energy Research Institute: Dir Dr
YADDOLLAH SABOUHI.
Water Energy Research Centre: tel. (21)
66005118; fax (21) 66164651; e-mail torkian@
sina.sharif.ac.ir; internet sharif.ir/~werc; Dir
Dr AYOOB TORKIAN.

SHIRAZ UNIVERSITY

Jam-e-Jam Ave, Shiraz 71946-84636
Telephone: (71) 6286416
Fax: (71) 6286419
E-mail: sadeghi@shirazu.ac.ir
Internet: www.shirazu.ac.ir
Founded 1946 as Pahlavi University, present
name 1979
State control
Languages of instruction: Farsi, English
Academic year: October to July (two semesters)
Chancellor: Dr MOHAMMAD HADI SADEGHI
Vice-Chancellor for Academic Affairs: Dr
ABDOLHOSAIN JAHANMIRI
Vice-Chancellor for Admin. and Financial
Affairs: Dr EBRAHIM HADIAN
Vice-Chancellor for Research Affairs: Dr
GHOLAMHOSEIN ZAMANI
Vice-Chancellor for Student and Cultural
Affairs: Dr MOHAMMAD MOAZZENI
Dir of Public Relations: MOJTABA TOOBAEI
Librarian: Dr ZAHIR HAYATI
Number of teachers: 573
Number of students: 12,446
Publications: *Iran Agricultural Research*
Journal of Social Sciences and Humanities, *Iranian Journal of Science and Technology*

DEANS

School of Agriculture: Dr YAHYA EMAM
School of Arts and Architecture: Dr MAHYAR
ARDSHIRI
School of Education and Psychology: Dr
MOHSEN KHADEMI
School of Engineering: Dr SEYYED SHAHABE-DIN AYATOLAHI
School of Law: Dr PARVIZ AMERI
School of Literature and Human Sciences: Dr
ABDULMAHDI RIAZI
School of Science: Dr NOZAR SAMANI
School of Veterinary Medicine: Dr SEYYED
SHAHRAM SHEKARFOROUSH
Junior Agricultural College, Darab: SAMAD
ERFANIFAR
Teacher Training College, Kazeroon: SEYYED
MOHTASHAM MOHAMMADI

UNIVERSITY OF SISTAN AND
BALUCHISTAN

POB 98135-987, Zahedan
Telephone: (541) 2445981
Fax: (541) 2446771
Internet: www.usb.ac.ir
Founded 1974
State control
Language of instruction: Farsi
Academic year: September to July (two
semesters)
Chancellor: Dr A. AKBARI
Vice-Chancellor for Academic Affairs: M. H.
SANGTARASH
Vice-Chancellor for Admin. and Finance: Dr
AMIN REZA KAMALYAN
Vice-Chancellor for Research: Dr RAHBAR
RAHIMI
Vice-Chancellor for Student Affairs: Dr A. A.
MORYDI FARIMANI
Registrar: Dr ABDOLLAH WASIGH ABBASI
Dir of Central Library: Dr RAHMATOLLAH
LASHKARIPOUR
Number of teachers: 300
Number of students: 12,000
Publications: *Applied Engineering* (in Farsi,
2 a year), *Divine and Law* (in Farsi, 2 a
year), *Geography & Development* (in Farsi,
2 a year), *History and Archaeology* (in
Farsi, 2 a year), *Iranian Journal of Fuzzy*
System (2 a year), *Journal of Engineering*
and Science (in Farsi, 2 a year), *Journal of*
Humanities (in Farsi, 4 a year), *Persian*
Language and Literature (in Farsi, 2 a
year), *Train Science and Psychology* (in
Farsi, 2 a year)

DEANS

College of Humanities (Iranshar): Eng.
AZARAG
College of Humanities (Zahedan): Dr A. A.
AHANGAR
Engineering College: Dr S. FARAHAT
Fine Arts College: Dr M. MEHRAN
Science College: Dr A. A. MIRZAIE

PROFESSORS

AKBARI, A., Agricultural Economics
ATASHI, H., Chemical Engineering
AZIMI, P., Mathematics
ESHGI, H., Chemistry
KHOSHNOODI, M., Chemical Engineering
LASHKARIPOUR, G. R., Geology
MANSORI-TORSHIZI, H. M., Chemistry
NOORA, A. A., Mathematics
RAHIMI, R., Chemical Engineering
REZVANI, A. R., Chemistry
SARDASHTI, A. R., Chemistry
SHARIATI, H., Mathematics
TORMANZAHI, A., Agriculture
VALIZADEH, J., Agriculture
YAZDANI, B.-O., Humanities

TABRIZ UNIVERSITY OF MEDICAL
SCIENCES

Golgasht Ave, Tabriz
Telephone: (411) 3347345
Fax: (411) 3347345
E-mail: iro@tbzmed.ac.ir
Internet: www.tbzmed.ac.ir
Founded 1985, fmrly part of University of
Tabriz
State control
Languages of instruction: Farsi, English
Academic year: October to July
Chancellor: Dr A. R. JODATI
Vice-Chancellor for Admin. and Finance: Dr
A. JAVAD ZADEH
Vice-Chancellor for Education: Dr J. HANAEE
Vice-Chancellor for Food and Medicines: Dr
A. GARJANI

Vice-Chancellor for Health Services: Dr A. R. NIKNIAZ
Vice-Chancellor for Research: Dr RASHIDI
Vice-Chancellor for Student Affairs: Dr A. A. TAHER AGDAM
Vice-Chancellor for Treatment: Dr M. KHOSH-BATEN
Registrar: Dr M. VARSCHOCHI
Librarian: Mrs MASOOMI
Number of teachers: 500
Number of students: 4,664
Publications: *Journal of Basic Science in Medicine, Journal of Nursing and Obstetrics, Medical Journal, Pharmaceutical Science, Research Journal*

DEANS

Faculty of Dentistry: Dr J. YAZDANI
Faculty of Medical Rehabilitation Science: Dr R. KHANDAGI
Faculty of Medicine: Dr M. BARZEGAR
Faculty of Nursing and Obstetrics: Dr Z. MAYABI
Faculty of Paramedical Sciences: Dr A. RAFI
Faculty of Pharmacy: Dr M. H. ZARRINTAN
Faculty of Public Health and Nutrition: Dr M. R. SIYAHI

ATTACHED RESEARCH CENTRES

Biotechnology Research Center: tel. (411) 3364038; fax (411) 3379420; e-mail brc .info@tbzmed.ac.ir; internet www.tbzmed.ac .ir/biotechnology; Dir Prof. SIAVOUSH DAST-MALCHI.

Haematology Oncology Research Center: tel. (411) 3343811; fax (411) 3343844; e-mail irajkermani@hotmail.com; internet horc.tbzmed.ac.ir; Dir Dr IRAJ ASVADI KER-MANI.

Research Centre for Pharmaceutical Nanotechnology: tel. (411) 3367914; fax (411) 3367929; e-mail yomidi@tbzmed.ac.ir; internet nano.tbzmed.ac.ir; Dir Dr YADOLLAH OMIDI.

Tuberculosis and Lung Disease Center: tel. (411) 3364901; fax (411) 3364901; e-mail ansarink@tbzmed.ac.ir; internet www .tbzmed.ac.ir/tlrc; Dir Dr KHALIL ANSARIN.

UNIVERSITY OF TABRIZ

29th Bahman Blvd, Tabriz 51666-14766
Telephone: (411) 3355994
Fax: (411) 3344272
E-mail: international@tabrizu.ac.ir
Internet: www.tabrizu.ac.ir
Founded 1946, fmrly University of Azaraba-degan
State control
Language of instruction: Farsi
Academic year: September to June (two semesters)
Chancellor: Prof. M. R. POURMOHAMMADIE
Vice-Chancellor for Academic Affairs: Dr M. H. SADEGHI
Vice-Chancellor for Finance and Admin. Affairs: Dr H. KATEBI
Vice-Chancellor for Postgraduate Affairs: Prof. M. MOGHADDAM-VAHED
Vice-Chancellor for Research Affairs: Dr H. NAMAZIE
Vice-Chancellor for Student Affairs: Dr Y. NOZHOOR
Registrar: Dr M. H. REZAEI MOGHADDAM
Dir of Int. Academic Collaboration: Dr FAR-AHMAND FARROKHI
Librarian: Dr M. T. ALAVIE
Library: see Libraries & Archives
Number of teachers: 480
Number of students: 11,500
Publications: *Journal of Agricultural Sciences* (4 a year), *Journal of the Faculty of Engineering* (4 a year), *Journal of the*

Faculty of Humanities and Social Sciences (4 a year), *Pazhoohesh* (Record of University Research Activities, 2 a year)

DEANS

Faculty of Agriculture: Dr A. BABAEI-AHARI
Faculty of Agriculture (Maragheh Campus): M. R. AZAM-PARSA
Faculty of Chemistry: Dr H. ASHASIE
Faculty of Education and Psychology: Dr D. HOSSEINI-NASAB
Faculty of Engineering: Dr A. AGHA GOLZA-DEH
Faculty of Humanities and Social Sciences: Dr M. BEHESHTIE
Faculty of Mathematics: Dr A. A. MEHRVARZ
Faculty of Natural Sciences: Dr Y. SATTARZA-DEH
Faculty of Persian Literature and Foreign Languages: Dr A. ASSADOLLAHI TAJARRAG
Faculty of Physics: Dr D. JASSOR

PROFESSORS

Faculty of Agriculture (tel. (411) 3341316; fax (411) 3345332; e-mail agri-dean@tabrizu .ac.ir):

MASSIHA, S., Horticulture
MOGHADDAM-VAHED, M., Plant Breeding
PEYGHAMIE, E., Plant Pathology
RAHIMZADEH KHOEI, F., Agronomy
VALIZADEH, M., Genetics and Breeding

Faculty of Chemistry (tel. (411) 3355998; fax (411) 3340191; e-mail chemfac@tabrizu.ac .ir):

BLOURCHIAN, S. M., Organosilicon Chemistry
DJOZAN, DJ., Analytical Chemistry
ENTEZAMI, A. A., Polymer Chemistry
GOLABI, S. M., Electroanalytical Chemistry
MANZOORI, J., Analytical Chemistry, Spectroscopy
POURNAGHI AZAR, M. H., Electroanalytical Chemistry
SOROURADDIN ABADI, M. H., Analytical Chemistry
ZAFARANI-MOATTAR, M. T., Physical Chemistry

Faculty of Education and Psychology (tel. (411) 3341133; fax (411) 3356009):

HOSSEINI-NASAB, D., Training Psychology

Faculty of Engineering (tel. (411) 3356022; fax (411) 3346287; e-mail joeng@tabrizu.ac .ir):

BEHRAVESH, A., Structural Engineering
DILMAGHANI, S., Civil Engineering
HASANZADEH, Y., Heat and Fluid Transfer Engineering
HOSSEINI, S. H., Power Electronics
KEYANVASH, A., Metallurgy
KHANMOHAMMADI, S., Automatic Engineering
KHOSHRAVAN-AZAR, M. E., Heat Transfer Engineering
PIROUZ-PANAH, V., Internal Combustion Engines

Faculty of Humanities and Social Sciences (tel. (411) 3344286; fax (411) 3356013):

BANIFATEMEH, H., Social Sciences
ESFAHANIYAN, D., History
HARIRI-AKBARI, M., Political Sociology
RAJAEI ASL, A. H., Physical Geography

Faculty of Mathematics (tel. (411) 3356032; fax (411) 3344015):

MEHRVARZ, A. A., Algebra
N-DEHGAN, Y., Mathematical Analysis
SHAHABI, M. A., Mathematics
TOOMANIAN, A., Differential Geometry

Faculty of Natural Sciences (tel. (411) 3356027; fax (411) 3341244):

HOSSEINPOUR FEIZI, M. A., Radiobiology

Faculty of Persian Literature and Foreign Languages (tel. (411) 3341150; fax (411) 3356017):

BAGHERI, M., Culture and Ancient Languages
EJLALI, A. P., Persian Language and Literature
IRANDOOST, R., French Language and Literature
LOTFIPOUR SAEDI, K., Applied Linguistics
NAVALI, M., Philosophy
SARKARATI, B., Ancient Iranian Languages

Faculty of Physics (tel. (411) 3356030; fax (411) 3341244):

BIDADI, H., Solid-state Physics
JAFARIZADEH, M., Physics of Elementary Particles
KALAFI, M., Solid-state Physics
MOHAMMAD-ZADEH JASSUR, D., Atomic Physics
SOBHANIAN, S., Atomic Physics, Plasma
TAJALLI SAIFI, H., Atomic Physics, Lasers

ATTACHED COLLEGES

College of Engineering (Bonab Campus): Dir M. R. A. PARSA.
College of Engineering (Marand Campus): Dir S. HOSSEINI.
College of Veterinary Medicine: Dir Dr H. KARIMIE.

TARBIAT MODARRES UNIVERSITY

POB 14155-4838, Intersection of Chamran and Ale-Ahmad Highways, Tehran
Telephone: (21) 8011001
Fax: (21) 8006544
E-mail: intl@modares.ac.ir
Internet: www.modares.ac.ir
Founded 1982
Academic year: September to June
Pres.: Dr FARHAD DANESHJOO
Vice-Pres. for Academic Affairs: Dr M. T. AHMADY
Vice-Pres. for Admin. and Financial Affairs: Dr H. BAHRAMI
Vice-Pres. for Research: Dr M. F. MOUSAVI
Vice-Pres. for Student Affairs: Dr A. MALEKI MOGHADDAM
Librarian: Dr AHMAD ZAVARAN HOSEINI
Library of 80,000 vols, 2,552 periodicals
Number of teachers: 433
Number of students: 3,595

DEANS

Faculty of Agriculture: Dr T. TAVAKOLI
Faculty of Arts: Dr M. R. POORJAAFAR
Faculty of Basic Medical Sciences: Dr M. RASAEE
Faculty of Basic Sciences: Dr H. NADERIMA-NESH
Faculty of Engineering: Dr SHOJAOSSADATI
Faculty of Humanities: Dr S. AYEENEVAND
Faculty of Natural Resources and Marine Sciences: Dr SAHARI

TEHRAN UNIVERSITY OF MEDICAL SCIENCES AND HEALTH SERVICES

23 Dameshgh Ave, Vali-e-Asr St, Tehran 14155-14167
Telephone: (21) 8896692
Fax: (21) 8898532
E-mail: iro@sina.tums.ac.ir
Internet: www.tums.ac.ir
Founded 1935 following devolution of medical schools from the University of Tehran and merger with other Tehran-based medical institutions
Chancellor: Dr BAGHER LARIJANI
Vice-Chancellor for Research: Dr AKBAR FOTOUHI
Number of teachers: 1,300

Number of students: 13,000

Publications: *Acta Medica* (4 a year), *Daru* (4 a year), *Journal of Dentistry* (4 a year)

Schools of Advanced Medical Technologies, Allied Medical Services, Dentistry, Medicine, Nursing and Midwifery, Pharmacy, Public Health, Rehabilitation

Research centres: science and technology in medicine, rheumatology, auditory, digestive diseases, skin diseases and leprosy, trauma, haematology and oncology, cardiovascular diseases, endocrinology and metabolism, reproductive health, urology, immunology, asthma and allergies, ethics and medical history, cancer, addiction, bank of transplantation products of Iran; 11 Educational and Health Research Centres in 10 provinces, 15 teaching hospitals; 40 br. libraries and one digital library with access to more than 5,000 full-text medical journals.

UNIVERSITY OF TEHRAN

Enghelab Ave, Tehran 14174

Telephone: (21) 61113358

Fax: (21) 6409348

E-mail: international@ut.ac.ir

Internet: www.ut.ac.ir

Founded 1934

Language of instruction: Farsi

Academic year: September to July (two semesters)

Pres.: Dr FARHAD RAHBAR

Vice-Pres. for Academic Affairs: Dr M. KAMAREIEE

Vice-Pres. for Admin.: Dr S. M. MOGHIMI

Vice-Pres. for Planning: Dr S. R. AMELI

Vice-Pres. for Research and Technology: Dr M. JAFARI

Vice-Pres. for Student Affairs: Dr M. GHAMSARI

Univ. Librarian: Dr F. FAHIMNIA

Library: see Libraries and Archives

Number of teachers: 1,500

Number of students: 32,000

DEANS

Faculty of Agriculture: Dr ALI REZA TALAEI

Faculty of Economics: Dr HOSSEIN ABBASINEJAD

Faculty of Education: Dr KAMAL DORRANI

Faculty of Engineering: Dr MAHMOOD NILI AHMADABADI

Faculty of Environmental Studies: Dr HOSSAIN BAHRINI

Faculty of Fine Arts: Dr M. MEHDI AZIZI

Faculty of Foreign Languages: Dr NADER HAGHANI

Faculty of Geography: Dr GHADIRI

Faculty of Law and Political Science: Dr HASSAN ALI DOROODIAN

Faculty of Literature and Humanities: Dr SHIKHOLSLAMI

Faculty of Management and Business Administration: Dr ALI TASLIMI

Faculty of Natural Resources: Dr MOHAMMAD JAFARI

Faculty of Physical Education: Dr BAGHEZADEH

Faculty of Science: Dr HASSAN EBRAHIMZADEH

Faculty of Social Science: Dr AZAD ARMAKI

Faculty of Theology and Islamic Studies: Dr ALI ALIABADI

Faculty of Veterinary Medicine: Dr S. MEHDI GHAMSARI

DIRECTORS

Aboureihan Educational Complex: Dr MAHMOOD REZA BEHBAHANI

Centre for International Studies: Dr MOSAFA

Ghom Higher Educational Complex: Dr MOHSEN RAHAMI

Institute of Biophysics and Chemistry: Dr OZRA RABANI

Institute of Comparative Law: Dr SAFAEI

Institute of Dehghoda Encyclopaedias: Dr S. JAFAR SHAHEIDI

Institute of Desert Regions and Arid Zones: Dr ZEHTABIAN

Institute of Geography: Dr FARHOODI

Institute of Geophysics: Dr JAVAHERIAN

Institute of Psychology: Dr MOHAMMAD ALI KARDAN

URMIA UNIVERSITY

POB 165, Urmia 57153

Telephone: (441) 3448131

Fax: (441) 3443443

E-mail: chancellor@urmia.ac.ir

Internet: www.urmia.ac.ir

Founded 1965

Academic year: September to July

Chancellor: Dr GOUDARZ SADEGHI-HASHJIN

Vice-Chancellor for Devt: Dr ESFANDYAR MARDANI

Vice-Chancellor for Education: Dr ESMAIL AYAN

Vice-Chancellor for Personnel and Finance: GHOLAMREZA MANSOORFAR

Vice-Chancellor for Research: Dr MOHAMMAD MEHDI BARADARANI

Vice-Chancellor for Student Affairs: Dr MAHMOOD RAZAZADEH

Registrar: Dr ALIREZA MOZAFFARI

Librarians: Dr FARHAD FARROKHI ARDEBILI, MOHAMMADREZA FARHADPOOR

Library of 58,000 vols

Number of teachers: 284

Number of students: 8,431

Publications: *Neda* (12 a year), *Pajooheshgaran* (4 a year)

DEANS

Faculty of Agriculture: Dr ASGHAR KHOSROWSHAHI

Faculty of Engineering: Dr IRAJ MIRZAEE

Faculty of Literature and Humanities: Dr ABDOLLAH TOLOEE-AZAR

Faculty of Science: Prof. M. NOJAVAN ASHGARI

Faculty of Veterinary Medicine: Dr B. DALIR NAGHADEH

YAZD UNIVERSITY

POB 89195-741, Yazd

Telephone: (351) 7250220

Fax: (351) 7250110

E-mail: president-office@yazduni.ac.ir

Internet: www.yazduni.ac.ir

Founded 1988

State control

Languages of instruction: Farsi, English

Academic year: September to June

Pres.: Dr SEYYED ALI MOHAMMAD MIRMOHAMMADI MEYBODI

Vice-Pres. for Education: Dr AHMAD SOHANKAR ESFAHANI

Vice-Pres. for Finance and Admin.: Dr FAZLOLLAH ADIBNIYA

Vice-Pres. for Research: Dr MOHAMMAD HASSAN KHADEMI

Vice-Pres. for Student Affairs: Dr MOHAMMAD ALI AMROLLAHI

Registrar: Dr ALI AKBAR DEHGHAN

Librarian: Dr BAGHIYAN

Library of 45,000 vols

Number of teachers: 314

Number of students: 7,281

Publications: *Bulletin*, *Kavoshnameh* (humanities research, 2 a year)

DEANS

Faculty of Art and Architecture: Dr K. MANDEGARI

Faculty of Engineering: Dr K. BARKHORDARI

Faculty of Humanities: Dr M. MALEKSABET

Faculty of Natural Resources and Desert Studies: Dr M. TAGHI DASTOORANI

Faculty of Science: Dr M. REZA NOORBALA

RESEARCH CENTRES

Desert and Dryland Research Institute: tel. (351) 8211670; fax (351) 82110317; e-mail ddri@yazduni.ac.ir; f. 1998.

Engineering and Applied Science Research Center: tel. (351) 8211670; fax (351) 8210699; e-mail easr@yazduni.ac.ir.

Colleges

There are c. 50 colleges of higher education in Iran, and c. 40 technological institutes, of which the following are a selection only.

College of Surveying: POB 1844, Azadi Sq., Tehran; f. 1965; national training centre for surveyors; 80 students; affiliated to National Cartographic Centre; Dir Dr H. NAHAVANDCHI.

Iran Banking Institute: POB 19395/4814, 207 Pasdaran Ave, Tehran; tel. (21) 2848000; fax (21) 2842618; internet www.ibi.ac.ir; f. 1963; four-year BA degree courses in Banking, Accounting and Computer Science, and MA degree courses in Banking, Accounting and Law; library: 24,000 vols; 2,450 students; Chancellor Dr MEHDI EMRANI.

Military Academy: Sepah Ave, Tehran; depts of general engineering science, international relations and treaties, military armaments, military history, military science and tactics, nuclear warfare, physics and electronics.

IRAQ

The Higher Education System

The University of Baghdad (founded 1957) is the oldest university in Iraq. As a result of increasing petroleum revenues in the 1970s, the higher education sector expanded significantly, and in addition to the universities a large number of technical institutes were established. However, during the 1980s and 1990s higher education was affected by economic privations caused by war with Iran (1980–88) and sanctions imposed by the international community following Iraq's invasion of Kuwait in 1990 and defeat by a US-led coalition in 1991. In March–April 2003 another US-led coalition invaded Iraq, captured Baghdad and toppled the Baathist regime of Saddam Hussain. Since 2003 higher education has been subject to reform, including the establishment of new universities; however, many academics have been killed, moved abroad or taken permanent leave of absence, student numbers have fallen, and in some areas Islamist groups have imposed segregated classes or forced female students to adopt Islamic forms of dress. The Ministry of Higher Education and Scientific Research oversees the administration of the 20 public universities and other colleges and technical institutes. In 2002/03 there were approximately 240,000 undergraduates attending 65 institutions of higher education; however, it was reported in 2006 that a growing number of students were failing to attend school or university as a result of the worsening security situation in many parts of the country.

Students must complete secondary education to be admitted to public universities. Each year the Ministry of Higher Education and Scientific Research determines entry requirements, which vary from programme to programme. The main undergraduate degree is the Bachelors, which lasts four years, although longer periods of study are required for pharmacy, architecture, dentistry, veterinary medicine (all five years) and medicine (six years). The first postgraduate degree is the Masters, lasting two to three years and incorporating both taught and research elements. The final university degree is the Doctor of Philosophy, which also includes both taught and research elements, with students required to pass examinations based on classroom-based work before proceeding to the research element.

Technical and vocational education is dominated by technical colleges and institutes, most of which were founded during the 1970s. The Commission for Technical Education is the government body responsible for administering these institutions and technical degrees and diplomas. The Technician Diploma is a two-year course offered by technical institutes, of which there were 37 in 2004. (Some technical institutes are directly affiliated to government ministries, depending on the area of specialization.) Holders of the Technician Diploma can gain direct entry to the second year of the four-year Bachelor of Technology programme, offered by technical colleges. The majority of these courses are in the fields of engineering and medicine. Following the Bachelor of Technology, technical colleges offer a two-year Higher Diploma of Technology, mainly in engineering disciplines. The Master of Technology is similar to the Higher Diploma of Technology, but contains a greater element of research.

During the US-led military campaign to oust the regime of Saddam Hussain in early 2003, and in the subsequent period of social unrest, damage and looting were reported at a number of Iraq's public institutions.

Regulatory Bodies

GOVERNMENT

Ministry of Culture: POB 624, Qaba bin Nafi Sq., Sadoun St, Baghdad; tel. (1) 5383171; Minister (vacant).

Ministry of Education: Saad State Enterprises Bldg, nr the Convention Centre, Baghdad; tel. (1) 8832571; Minister KHUDAYER AL-KHUZAIE.

Ministry of Higher Education and Scientific Research: Baghdad; tel. (1) 2806315; e-mail ministry@moheiraq.org; internet www.moheiraq.org; Minister (vacant).

Learned Societies

EDUCATION

Arab Literacy and Adult Education Organization (ARLO): POB 3217, 113 Abu Nawas St, Baghdad; tel. 7186246; f. 1966 by ALECSO to promote co-operation in all aspects of literacy and adult education between the Arab states; all Arab states are mems; library of 14,700 vols; Dir HASHIM ABU ZEID EL-SAFI (acting); publ. *The Education of the Masses* (2 a year).

FINE AND PERFORMING ARTS

Iraqi Artists' Society: Damascus St, Baghdad; f. 1956; exhibitions and occasional publs; Pres. NOORI AL-RAWI; Sec. AMER ALU-BIDI.

LANGUAGE AND LITERATURE

British Council: 10 Spring Gardens, London, SW1A 2BN, United Kingdom; tel. (161) 957-7755; fax (161) 957-7762; e-mail iraq@britishcouncil.org; internet www.britishcouncil.org/iraq; f. 1940; offers courses and exams in English language and promotes cultural exchange with the UK; based in London until further notice; Chief Exec. MARTIN DAVIDSON.

Iraqi Academy: Waziriya, Baghdad; tel. (1) 4224202; fax (1) 4222066; e-mail iraqacademy@yahoo.com; internet www.iraqacademy.org; f. 1947 with the aims of maintaining the Arabic language and heritage, supporting research in Arabic and Muslim history, the history of Iraq and Arabic language and heritage, maintaining Kurdish and Assyrian languages; 37 mems; Pres. Prof. Dr AHMED MATLOUB; publ. *Majallat al-Mejmah al-Ilmi* (literary, 4 a year).

MEDICINE

International Iraqi Medical Association: e-mail adilmahd@emirates.net.ae; internet www.iimaonline.net; NGO supporting Iraqi physicians at home and abroad; annual conf.; Pres. Dr ALI HARJAN; Dir of Public Relations Dr ADIL AL-MANSOURI; publ. *Journal*.

Iraqi Medical Association: Maari St, al-Mansoor, Baghdad; tel. (1) 5374209; fax (1) 5372193; e-mail nfo@ima-iq.org; internet www.ima-iq.org; f. 1920; Pres. Prof. Dr NADHIM A. KASIM; publ. *Iraqi Medical Journal* (2 a year, in English and Arabic).

NATURAL SCIENCES

General

Federation of Arab Scientific Research Councils: POB 13027, Baghdad; tel. (1) 8881709; fax (1) 8867511; f. 1976; strengthens collaboration among scientific research ccls, instns, centres and univs in all Arab states; adopts the Arabic language in scientific research and technology and encourages the use of Arabic in scientific research and promotes the Arabization of scientific terminology; plans jt research projects among Arab states, especially those related to Arab devt plans; 15 mem. states; library of 800 vols, 600 periodicals, 1,100,000 patent documents from USA, EPO, WIPO; Sec.-Gen. Prof. Dr TAHA T. AL-NAIMI; publs *Federation News, Journal of Computer Research*.

Research Institutes

GENERAL

Scientific Research Council: POB 2441, Jadiriya, Baghdad; f. 1963; Pres. Dr NAJIH M. KHALIL.

Attached Research Centres:

Agriculture and Water Resources Research Centre: Fudhailiyah; Dir Dr SAMIR A. AL-SHAKER.

Biological Research Centre: Jadiriya; Dir Dr AZWAR N. KHALAF.

Building Research Centre: Jadiriya; Dir Dr M. AL-IZZI.

Educational Studies and Psychological Research Center: Jadiriya; tel. 7785162; e-mail psychocenter@hotmail .com; internet www.psychocenteriraq.com; f. 1986; library of 3,358 vols; Dir Dr GHASSAN H. SALIM; publ. *Psychological Sciences*.

Electronics and Computer Research Centre: Jadiriya; Dir Dr M. N. BEKIR.

Genetic Engineering and Biotechnology Research Centre: Jadiriya; Dir Dr FARUQ YASS AL-ANI.

Petroleum Research Centre: Jadiriya; Dir Dr A. H. A. K. MOHAMMED.

Scientific Affairs Office: Jadiriya; Dir Dr RADHWAM K. A. HALIM.

Scientific Documentation Centre: Jadiriya; library: see under Libraries.

Solar Energy Research Centre: Jadiriya; Dir N. I. AL-HAMDANY.

Space Research Centre: Jadiriya; Dir Dr ALI AL-MASHAT.

AGRICULTURE, FISHERIES AND VETERINARY SCIENCE

Agriculture and Water Resources Research Centre: POB 2416, Karada al-Sharkiya, Baghdad; tel. (1) 7512080; f. 1980 to carry out research to improve and develop water and agricultural resources; 75 researchers; library of 6,000 vols, 450 periodicals; Dir-Gen. Dr SAMIR A. H. AL-SHAKIR; publ. *Journal of Agriculture and Water Resources Research*.

EDUCATION

Centre for Educational and Psychological Research: Univ. of Baghdad, 9 Waziriya, Baghdad; e-mail edu-psychological@uob.edu.iq; f. 1966; educational and psychological research studies to make education an effective power for the acceleration of economic and social devt; library of 6,000 vols; Dir Dr MOHAMMED ALI KHALAF; publ. *Journal of Educational Psychological Research* (2 a year).

HISTORY, GEOGRAPHY AND ARCHAEOLOGY

British Institute for the Study of Iraq: 10 Carlton House Terrace, London, SW1Y 5AH, United Kingdom; tel. (20) 7969-5274; fax (20) 7969-5401; e-mail bisi@britac.ac.uk; internet www.bisi.ac.uk; f. 1932 as the British School of Archaeology; present name 2007; promotes, supports and undertakes research in Iraq and neighbouring countries; covers the subjects of archaeology, history, anthropology, geography, language and other related domains from earliest times to the present; grants are available for research; 800 mems; library: the library is currently housed by the British Embassy in Baghdad, the number of vols is unknown; Chair. Prof. ROGER MATTHEWS; Vice-Chair. Dr HARRIET CRAWFORD; publs *Iraq* (1 a year), *The International Journal of Contemporary Iraqi Studies* (3 a year).

PHILOSOPHY AND PSYCHOLOGY

Psychological Research Center: Univ. of Baghdad Complex, Jaderiyah, Baghdad; tel. (1) 7786678; fax (1) 7785162; e-mail psychocenter@hotmail.com; internet www .psychocenteriraq.com; psychological and parapsychological research and training; library of 3,070 vols (1,992 Arabic, 1,078 English); publs *Journal of Psyche and Life* (6 a year, incl. section in English), *Journal of Psychological Sciences* (4 a year, in Arabic and English), *Psychological Health* (4 a year, in Arabic).

TECHNOLOGY

Department of Scientific and Industrial Research: Directorate-General of Industry, Baghdad; f. 1935; staff 42; Dir-Gen. of Industry SHEETH NA'AMANN; publ. *Technical Bulletin*.

Nuclear Research Centre: Tuwaitha, Baghdad; f. 1967; fmr main establishment of Iraq Atomic Energy Commission, now under control of International Atomic Energy Agency; administrative responsibility assumed by the Iraq Ministry of Science and Technology.

Libraries and Archives

Arbil

University of Salahaddin Central Library: Kirkuk St, Arbil; tel. (66) 2260089; e-mail library@usalah.org; f. 1968; 263,705 vols, 530 current periodicals; Dir Dr MOHAMMAD MUSTAFA.

Baghdad

Al-Awqaf Central Library (Ministry of Endowments and Religious Affairs Central Library): POB 14146, Baghdad; f. 1928; library building looted and burnt down April 2003; library staff were able to preserve approx. 5,250 of the total collection of 7,000 MSS; Contact HASAN FREIH; publ. *Al-Rissala-al-Islamiya*.

Al-Mustansiriya University Library: POB 14022, Waziriya, Baghdad; e-mail library@uomustansiriyah.edu.iq; f. 1963; 311,800 vols, 30,000 vols of periodicals, 330 rolls of film, 280 current periodicals; also 11 college libraries with 33,000 vols, 850 periodicals; part of the colln was looted 2003; Dir FAISAL ANWAN AL-TAEE.

Arab Gulf States Information and Documentation Center: POB 5063, Baghdad; tel. (1) 5433914; f. 1981; affiliated to the Board of Ministers of Information of the Arab Gulf States; aims to gather information from many sources, and to systematize, analyse and exchange it; supports the basic structure of existing information services; seven mem. states; provides a consultancy service; databases, microfilms; specialized library of 8,000 vols; Dir-Gen. HAYFA A. JAJAWI.

Educational Documentation Library: Ministry of Education, Educational Campus, Baghdad; tel. (1) 8860000-2178; f. 1921; 37,000 vols, 73 periodicals; Librarian Dr KADHIM G. AL-KHAZRAJI.

Ibn Hayyan Information House: Iraqi Atomic Energy Commission, POB 765, Tuwaitha, Baghdad; up-to-date references, reports, pamphlets, microcards, magazines and film reels; Dir ISAM ATTA AJAJ.

Iraqi Academy Library: Waziriya, Baghdad; f. 1947; 60,000 vols, 32 original MSS, 1,600 copied MSS, 1,500 microfilms; Librarian SABAH NOAH.

Iraqi Museum Library: Salhiya Quarter, Baghdad West; tel. (1) 8840876; f. 1934; archaeology, history of civilization, art, architecture, cultural heritage; evacuation of colln undertaken before the US-led military intervention 2003, currently in storage; 229,000 vols, 34,000 MSS; Dir ZAINAT AL-SAMAKRI; publ. *Al-Maskukat*.

National Archives of Iraq: POB 594, Baghdad; f. 1964; attached to the Min. of Culture; bldg looted and burnt down April 2003; colln subsequently subject to flooding and is currently frozen to prevent deterioration.

National Library: POB 594, Baghdad; tel. (1) 4164190; f. 1961; building looted and burnt down April 2003; approx. 500,000 vols destroyed in fire; some holdings are subsequently subject to flooding and are currently frozen to prevent deterioration; legal deposit centre and national bibliographic centre; Dir-Gen. SAAD ESKANDER.

Scientific Documentation Centre: Abu Nuas Rd, POB 2441, Baghdad; tel. (1) 7760023; f. 1972; scientific information services to researchers at the institutes/centres of the Scientific Research Council (*q.v.*), and to others working in Iraqi laboratories, incl. UNDP experts; seven libraries are being developed, each attached to a research centre of the Council, incl. the Central Science Library; in-service training for students of Library Science and Documentation and librarians; 20 staff mems; Dir Dr FAIK ABDUL S. RAZZAQ.

University of Baghdad Central Library: POB 47303, Jadiriya, Baghdad; e-mail maktaba.unive@yahoo.com; f. 1959; section in Al-Waziriya looted and some stock stolen April 2003; major reconstruction under way; govt and UN depository library; acts as Exchange and governmental Bibliographical Centre; publ. *Current Contents of Iraqi Universities' Journals* (temporarily ceased publication).

Basrah

University of Basrah Central Library: Basrah; f. 1964; 200,000 vols, 700 MSS, 1,400 current periodicals; Librarian Dr TARIK AL-MANASSIR; publ. catalogue (irregular).

Mosul

University of Mosul Central Library: Mosul; tel. 810162; fax 814765; f. 1967; looted April 2003, although its collns were left intact; 24 br. libraries; 140,000 vols, 3,500 periodicals, depository of UN and Iraqi govt publs; Dir MAHMUD JIRJIS; publs *Adab Al-Rafidarn* (irregular), *Al-Rafidain Engineering* (irregular), *Annals of the College of Medicine-Mosul* (irregular), *Catalogue* (1 a year), *Iraqi Journal of Veterinary Sciences* (irregular), *Journal of Education and Science* (irregular), *Journal of Rafidain Development* (irregular), *Mesopotamia Journal of Agriculture* (irregular), *Research Work of University Faculty Members* (1 a year).

Museums and Art Galleries

Arbil

Arbil Museum: Arbil; tel. (66) 522273; objects from Iraqi history up to Arabic-Islamic period.

Babylon

Babylon Museum: Babylon; f. 1949; contains models, pictures, and paintings of the remains at Babylon; the museum is situated amongst the ruins.

Baghdad

Abbasid Palace Museum: Baghdad; tel. (1) 4164950; a restored palace dating back to the late Caliphs of the Abbasid dynasty (13th century AD); an exhibition of Arab antiquities and scale models of important Islamic monumental buildings in Iraq. Opened as a Museum in 1935.

Baghdad Museum: Sahat al Risafi, Baghdad; tel. (1) 4165317; f. 1970; museum of folklore and costumes, natural history; photographic exhibition on history of Baghdad; Memorial Exhibition, containing the royal relics of King Faisal I; picture gallery; Dir ALAE AL SHIBLI.

Iraq Military Museum: A'dhamiya, Baghdad; f. 1974 by merger of Arms Museum (f. 1940) and Museum of War (f. 1966); contains old Arabian weapons, Othmanic fire-arms and contemporary Iraqi weapons.

Iraq National Museum: Salhiya quarter, Baghdad West; internet www .theiraqmuseum.org; f. 1923; looted April 2003, resulting in theft or destruction of approx. 15,000 items; closed until Feb. 2009 when it was re-opened to select groups; colln incl. antiquities dating from the early Stone Age to the beginning of the 18th century AD, incl. large colln of Islamic objects; Al-Sarraf gallery contains Islamic coins; library: see Libraries; Dir AMIRA EIDAN; publs *Al-Maskukat* (2 a year), *Sumer* (1 a year).

Iraq Natural History Research Centre and Museum: Bab al Muadham, Baghdad; tel. (1) 4165790; f. 1946; attached to the University of Baghdad; incl. sections on zoology, botany and geology; research work in natural history; exhibitions of animals, plants, rocks and minerals pertaining to Iraq; organizes cultural, educational and scientific training programmes; library of 31,000 vols, 850 periodicals; Dir H.-A. ALI; publs *Bulletin of the Iraq Natural History Research Centre*, *Iraq Natural History Research Centre Publications* (series of scientific papers, in English (with Arabic summaries), dealing with the natural history of Iraq and neighbouring countries).

National Museum of Modern Art: Al-Nafoura Square, Bal Al-Sharqi, Baghdad; f. 1962; Supervisor AMER AL UBAIDI.

Basrah

Natural History Museum of the University of Basrah: Corniche St, POB 432, Basrah; tel. (40) 213494; f. 1971; study of flora and fauna of the marshes of South Iraq and the Arabian Gulf; sections on mammals, birds, reptiles and amphibia, and fishes; scientific collns in all sections accessible to specialists and exhibits open to public; Dir Dr KHALAF AL ROBAAE.

Mosul

Mosul Museum: Dawassa, Mosul; tel. (60) 2430; f. 1951; collns of Assyrian antiquities of the 9th and 8th centuries BC found at Nimrud, objects uncovered in the ruins of Hatra dating from the 2nd century BC to the 2nd century AD, agricultural tools and pottery vessels from 5000–4000 BC, photographs of excavated buildings at Tepe Gawra, maps of the Assyrian Empire, Nimrud and Hatra; Prehistoric and Islamic exhibits; assists in discovery and maintenance of several archaeological sites; library: c. 2,000 vols; Dir HAZIM A. AL HAMEED.

Nasiriya

Nasiriya Museum: Nasiriya; tel. (42) 233851; Sumerian and other archaeological objects found in Ur, Al-Abeed and Aridu; Dir ABDUL AMIR HAMDANI.

Samarra

Samarra Museum: Samarra; tel. (21) 722114; f. 1936; it is housed in one of the old city gates, and contains objects excavated in the ruins of ancient Samarra; also historic maps, writings, pictures.

Universities

UNIVERSITY OF AL ANBAR

Ramadi, al Anbar governorate
Telephone: (1) 8864814
Fax: (1) 8178849

E-mail: anb.unv@uruklink.net
Founded 1987
State control
Pres.: ABDUL HADI RAJEB HABEEB (acting)
Vice-Pres. for Admin. and Scientific Affairs: ABDUL MAJEED ABOUL HAMEED ALI AL ANNI (acting)
Number of teachers: 464

AL MUSTANSIRIYA UNIVERSITY

POB 14022, Waziriya, Baghdad
Telephone: (1) 4168501
Fax: (1) 4165521
E-mail: mustuni@uruklink.net
Founded 1963
State control
Languages of instruction: Arabic, English
Academic year: September to June
Pres.: Dr IHSAN K. AL KURSHY (acting)
Vice-Pres. for Admin.: ADEL H. AL BAGHDADI (acting)
Vice-Pres. for Scientific Affairs: Dr KANAN A. ABDUL RAZAK (acting)
Librarian: MAISOON A. AL OBIADY
Library: see Libraries
Number of teachers: 1,555
Number of students: 23,748
Publications: *Al Mustansiriya Journal of Science*, *Al Mustansiriya Literary Review*, *Journal of Administration and Economics*, *Journal of the College of Education*, *Journal of the College of Teachers*, *Journal of Dialah Education*, *Journal of Engineering and Pollution*, *Journal of the Founding Leader for National and Socialist Studies*, *Journal of Medical Research*, *Journal of Middle Eastern Studies*

DEANS
College of Administration and Economics: Dr ALI J. AL OBIADY
College of Arts: Dr MUHAMED O. AL SHEMARY
College of Dental Studies: Dr RAAD M. JADOA
College of Education: Dr SABAH A. ATTY
College of Engineering: Dr ALI M. AL ATHARY
College of Medicine: Dr MUHAMED H. AL WAN
College of Science: Asst Prof. KADUM H. AL MOSSAWI
College of Sports: Asst Prof. Dr SAMEER M. ALAWE

AL NAHRAIN UNIVERSITY

POB 64074, Jadiriyah, Baghdad
Telephone: (1) 7767810
Fax: (1) 7763592
E-mail: saduni@uruklink.net
Internet: www.alnahrain-university.org
Founded 1993 as Saddam Univ.; present name 2003
Pres.: MAHMOOD H. HAMMASH (acting)
Vice-Pres. for Admin.: FAYEK J. AL AZZAWI
Librarian: ZAINAB H. RASHID
Library of 65,963 vols
Number of teachers: 285
Number of students: 1,180

DEANS
College of Engineering: Dr MAZIN A. KADHIM
College of Law: Dr BASIM M. SALEH
College of Medicine: Dr MAHMOOD H. HAMASH
College of Political Sciences: Dr MAZIN I. AL RAMADANI
College of Science: Dr FALAH A. ATTAWI

UNIVERSITY OF AL QADISIYA

POB 88, Diwaniya, al Qadisiya governorate
Telephone: (36) 628066
Fax: (1) 8164160
E-mail: unv.qadisia@uruklink.net

Founded 1988
State control
Pres.: Dr MOHAMMAD H. AL JABIRI (acting)
Vice-Pres. for Admin.: D. HIKMAT (acting)
Library of 2,000 vols
Number of teachers: 407

UNIVERSITY OF AL TA'AMEEM

Baghdad Rd, Kirkuk, al Ta'ameem governorate
Telephone: 418531
E-mail: fqislam@uruklink.net
Founded 2003
State control
Pres.: KAMAK OTHMAN OMEAR (acting)
Vice-Pres. for Admin.: ABRAHIM ATEA SALIH (acting)
Vice-Pres. for Scientific Affairs: NAJAT QADIR OMEAR (acting)
Number of teachers: 60

UNIVERSITY OF BABYLON

POB 4, Hilla, Babylon
Telephone: (30) 246562
Fax: 8851398
E-mail: unihead@babylon-uni.com
Internet: www.babylon-uni.com
Founded 1991
State control
Colleges of agriculture, art, basic education, dentistry, economics and administration, education, engineering, fine arts, law, materials engineering, medicine, nursing, physical education, science, veterinary science; Science College for Girls
Pres.: Prof. Dr NABEEL H. AL A'ARAGI (acting)
Vice-Pres. for Admin.: HAMDIA ABBAS (acting)
Vice-Pres. for Scientific Affairs: ABD-AMEER AL GANEMI (acting)
Number of teachers: 450

UNIVERSITY OF BAGHDAD

POB 17635, Jadiriya, Baghdad
Telephone: (1) 7787819
Fax: (1) 7763592
E-mail: info@univofbaghdad.com
Internet: www.univofbaghdad.org
Founded 1957
State control
Languages of instruction: Arabic, English
Academic year: September to June
Pres.: MOSA JAWAD AZIZ AL MOSAWE
Vice-Pres. for Admin.: Dr NIHAD M. ABDUL RAHMAN
Vice-Pres. for Scientific Affairs: Dr HATAN JABAR ATTIYA
Registrar: TUMADHR ABDULLAH
Librarians: AMIR ABID MAJBOUR, YUSRA R. ZAHAWI
Library: see Libraries. Each institute and college has its own library of Arabic and foreign books
Number of teachers: 3,675
Number of students: 85,000
Publications: *Ibn al Haitham Journal for Pure and Applied Sciences* (2 a year), *Iraqi Journal of Pharmaceutical Sciences* (4 a year), *Iraqi Journal of Science* (4 a yeary), *Iraqi Journal of Veterinary Medicine* (2 a year), *Iraqi Natural History Museum Bulletin* (4 a year), *Journal of Agricultural Sciences* (2 a year), *Journal of the College of Administration and Economics* (4 a year), *Journal of the College of Dentistry* (irregular), *Journal of the College of Education for Women* (2 a year), *Journal of the College of Languages* (1 a year), *Journal of the College of Sharia* (2 a year), *Journal of Engineering* (irregular), *Journal of the*

Faculty of Medicine (4 a year), *Journal of Legal Sciences* (4 a year), *Journal of Political Science* (4 a year), *Journal of Sports Education* (irregular), *Statistical Bulletin* (1 a year), *The Academic* (4 a year), *The Professor* (4 a year)

DEANS

College of Administration and Economics: Dr ADIL H. SALIH
College of Agriculture: Dr BAQIR ABID KHALAF
College of Arts: Dr NOURI HAMMOUDI AL QAYSI
College of Dentistry: Dr ISAM ABDUL AZIZ ALI
College of Education (Ibn al Haitham): Dr FAROUK ABDUL SALAM AWNI
College of Education (Ibn Rushd): Dr MALIK IBRAHIM SALIH
College of Education for Women: Dr FADHIL AL SAQI
College of Engineering: Dr LAITH ISMAIL
College of Fine Arts: Dr ABDUL MURSIL AL ZAYDI
College of Islamic Sciences: Dr ABDUL MUNIM AHMED SALIH
College of Languages: Dr ADNAN AL JUBOURI
College of Law: Dr MUHAMMED AL DOURI
College of Medicine: Dr FAKHRI M. AL HADITHI
College of Nursing: BADIA AL DAGHSTANI
College of Pharmacy: Dr WALEED R. A. SULAIMAN
College of Political Science: Dr SHAFIK AL SAMARRAIE
College of Science: Dr FAROUK AL ANI
College of Sports Education: Dr ALI TURKI
College of Veterinary Medicine: Dr KHALIL IBRAHIM ALTAYIF

AFFILIATED CENTRES

Astronomical Research Unit (attached to the College of Science): Dir Dr HAMEED MIJWIL AL NIAIMI.

Centre for International Studies (attached to the College of Political Science): Dir Dr ABDUL GHAFOUR KARIM ALI.

Centre for Palestinian Studies (attached to the College of Political Science): Dir Dr KHLDOUN NAJI MAROUF.

Centre for the Revival of Arab Scientific Heritage: Dir NABILA ABDUL MUNIM.

Centre for Urban and Regional Planning (Postgraduate studies): Dir Dr WADHAH SAID YAHYA.

Educational and Psychological Research Centre (attached to the College of Education, Ibn Rushd): Dir MAHDI AL SAMARRAE.

UNIVERSITY OF BASRAH

POB 49, Basrah
Telephone: (1) 8868520
Fax: (1) 8862998
E-mail: basrauniversity@satline.net
Founded 1964
State control
Languages of instruction: Arabic, English
Academic year: September to June
Pres.: DAWOOD SULEIMAN
Vice-Pres.: (vacant)
Librarian: Dr AMER ABID MUHSIN AL SAAD
Library of 169,586 vols, 59,000 periodicals
Number of teachers: 1,033
Number of students: 19,781

Publications: *Arab Gulf Journal, Basrah Journal of Agricultural Sciences, Basrah Journal of Sciences, Basrah Journal of Surgery, Economic Studies, Gulf Economics Journal, Iraqi Journal of Polymers, Journal of Arts, Journal of Basrah Research, Journal of Physical Education, Marina Mesopotamica, Medical Journal of Basrah University*

DEANS

Faculty of Administration and Economics: Dr JALIL S. THAMAD
Faculty of Agriculture: Dr NAZAR A. SHUKRI
Faculty of Arts: Dr RAAD ZAHRAW AL MUSAWI
Faculty of Education: Dr GALIB BAKIR M. GALIB
Faculty of Education (at Theequar): Dr MAHDI ORYBY HUSSAIN AL DAKHIL
Faculty of Engineering: Dr ABDULAMIR S. RESAN
Faculty of Fine Arts: MUAYAD ABDULSAMAD
Faculty of Law: Prof. Dr ABDULMAHDI SALEEM AL MUDHAFFAR
Faculty of Medicine: Prof. Dr ALIM ABDULHAMID YACOUB
Faculty of Physical Education: Dr SALAH ATTYA KADHUM
Faculty of Science: Prof. Dr GOURGIS ABIDAL ADAM
Faculty of Teaching-Training: Dr HAMEED HASSAN TAHIR
Faculty of Veterinary Science: Dr ABDULMUTTALIB Y. YOUSIF

DIRECTORS

Centre for Arab Gulf Studies: Dr OWDA SULTAN
Centre for Marine Sciences: Dr ABDULRAZAK MAHMOOD
Computer Centre: Dr WALEED A. J. MOHAMMAD ALI
Medical Centre: Dr ABDULKHALIQ Z. BNAYAN

UNIVERSITY OF DIYALA

POB 2, Baquba Post Office, Baqubah, Diyala Governorate, Al-Muradia, Old Baquba-Baghdad Way
Telephone: (790) 1978420
Fax: (5) 8853610
E-mail: diyala_university@yahoo.com
Internet: www.uodiyala.edu.iq
Languages of instruction: Arabic, English
Founded 1999
State control
Pres.: Prof. Dr MAHMOUD SHAKER RASHEED (acting)
Vice-Pres. for Admin. Affairs: Dr AYAD AL AJEELY
Vice-Pres. for Scientific Affairs: Dr AMER M. IBRAHIM (acting)
Number of teachers: 867
Number of students: 14,782

Publication: *Al Afaak Al Jadida* (in Arabic)

DEANS

College of Administration and Economics: Dr MUHSIN HASSAN ALWAN
College of Agriculture: Dr ADEL NORI GOMA'A
College of Basic Education: Dr ABBAS FADIL GAWAD
College of Education (Al-Razi): Dr ABBAS ABOOD FARHAN
College of Education (Al-Asmaee): Dr MAHMOUD FAIAD HUMMADI
College of Engineering: Dr ADEL KHALEEL MAHMOUD
College of Islamic Sciences: AHMED ABID AL SATTAR GASIM
College of Law: Dr ABID AL-AZIZ SHAABAN KHALID
College of Medicine: Dr KHUDHAIR KH. IBRAHIM
College of Science: Dr DHAHIR ABID AL-HADI
College of Sport Education: Dr MAHIR ABID AL-LATEEF
College of Veterinary Medicine: Dr ABID AL RAZZAQ SHAFEEQ

UNIVERSITY OF DUHOK

Kurdistan Region, Dohuk Governorate
Telephone: (62) 7227060

E-mail: relations@uod.ac
Internet: www.uod.ac
Founded 1992
State control

Pres.: Dr ASMAT MOHAMMED KHALID (acting)
Vice-Pres. for Admin. Affairs: Dr SALEEM H. HAJI (acting)
Vice-Pres. for Scientific Affairs: Dr HASAN AMEEN MOHAMMED (acting)
Vice-Pres. for Int. Relations: Dr DAWOOD S. ATRUSHI
Library of 11,770 vols
Number of teachers: 791
Number of students: 9,876

DEANS

College of Administration and Economics: Dr KHALIL GHAZI HASAN
College of Agriculture: Dr MUSLEH MOHAMMED SAE'D
College of Arts: Dr MOHAMMED SALIH TAYEB
College of Basic Education: Dr LUIS KARO BANDO
College of Commerce: Dr ABDUL HAMID SULAIMAN
College of Education: Dr LAZGEEN ABDI
College of Engineering: Dr ALI FLAIAH HUSAIN
College of Law and Politics: Dr NADHIM YOUNS OTHMAN
College of Medicine: Dr FARHAD KHURSHEED MOHAMMED
College of Nursing: Dr AHMED MOHAMMED SALIH
College of Physical Education: Dr ODEAT ODISHO
College of Science: Dr SARKAWT ALI SAMI
College of Veterinary Medicine: Dr NADHIM SULAIMAN A. AZIZ
Higher Institute of Learning: Dr ASMAT MOHAMMED KHALID (Head)
Scientific Research Centre: JALADET JUBREAL (Head)

ISLAMIC UNIVERSITY

Adhmai, Habiet Khatoun, Baghdad
Telephone: (1) 4254257
E-mail: islamicuniversitybag@yahoo.com
Internet: www.iubaghdad.com
Founded 1989
State control
Language of instruction: Arabic
Pres.: Prof. Dr ZIYAD M. RASHEED AL ANI (acting)
Pres. for Admin. Affairs: Prof. ZIYAD MOHAMED RASHEED AL-ANI (acting)
Vice-Pres. for Admin. Affairs: Dr ANMMAR AHMED MOHAMED
Vice-Pres. for Scientific Affairs: Dr IBRAHEEM ABID SAIL (acting)
Librarian: Dr KAIS ABDULLATIF AHMED
Library of 19,512 vols, 1,270 periodical titles
Number of teachers: 505
Number of students: 6,224

DEANS

College of Art: Dr ABDULLAH HASAN AL-HADITHI
College of Economic and Administration: Dr HIKMET FARIS TA'AAN
College of Education: Dr ADNAN ADNAN ALI AL-FARAJI
College of Education of Girls: Dr OMER MAJEED AID SALEH
College of Fundamental of Religion College: Dr SUBHI FANDI AL-KUBEISI
College of Law: Dr ZIYAD HAMED ABAAS AL-SUMAYDAAI
College of Shariah: Dr ABDULMUNAEM KHALIL AL-HITI

UNIVERSITY OF KARBALA

Al Dhbbat district, Karbala, Karbala governorate

Telephone: (32) 321364
E-mail: info@uokerbala.edu.iq
Internet: www.uokerbala.edu.iq
Founded 2002
State control

Colleges of administration and economics, agriculture, education, engineering, law, medicine, pharmacy, science
Pres.: A. H. ALWAN (acting)
Library of 25,000 vols
Number of teachers: 222

UNIVERSITY OF KUFA

Kufa, al Najaf governorate
Telephone: (33) 346034
E-mail: kufa@uruklink.net
Internet: kuiraq.com
Founded 1987
State control

Pres.: HASSAN ISAA AL HAKEEM (acting)
Vice-Pres. for Admin.: NOORIE AL HAKKNIE (acting)
Vice-Pres. for Scientific Affairs: MAJID KADHUM HUSSAIN (acting)

Number of teachers: 410

Faculties of administration and economics, agriculture, arts, dentistry, education (girls), engineering, law, mathematics and computer science, medicine, nursing, pharmacology, physical education, science, veterinary science

PROFESSORS

ABAS ALSAED SALMAN, J., Agriculture Sciences
ABDUL-AMEER AL-DALEMY, M., Abdominal Medicine
ABDUL-HAMSA AL-SHAMARY, P., Micro Alive
ABDUL-RASSWL AL-GHAKANEI, N., Economy
ABOUD AL-KAFAF, A., Geography
ABU HAMD AL-ALI, R., Economy
ABU RAHEAL AL-FATLAWEI, A., Geography
ADEA EASSA AL-MHANA, J., Medicine and Surgery
AKAB AL-WAIALY, T., Modern History
ALEASA, A., Biochemistry
ALI ALHAKEMI, H., History
ALI SAMEA AL-ALI, M., Geography
ALI AL-FEDAWEE, A., Paediatrics
ALI AL-SAKEAR, M., Arabic Language
ALMOUSA AL-ASADI, K., Geography Natural
AL-HASSENI, H., Mathematics
AL-HASSNWEI, S., Pharmacy
AL-JUMAILI, S., Biology
AL-KHALIDI, A., Turkish
AL-KUTUBI, S., Mathematics
AL-SAEEDI, A., Biology
AL-SHARMANY, M., Agriculture Sciences
ALWAN AL-FATLAWI, A., Arabic Language
ASER MOSSA AL-GORATEI, H., Arabic Literature
HAFAD AL-KAFAGEI, A., Arabic Literature
HAMOD AL-SHAMA, Y., Physiology
HUSSEIN AL-KUFEE, A., Diseases Medicine
HUSSEIN AL-ZAMALY, N., Medicines
HASSAN AL-SNEAD, A., Physics
HASSAN AL-ENASSI, T., History
JALEEL ABDUL-HASSAN AL-GHALEBEI, A., Economy
KADEM THEDAN AL-FATLAWEI, K., Economy
MERZA AL-HUMAIRI, T., Biology
MHASSEN ALBU-AREBI, N., Philosophy
MOHAMED AL-ATHAREI, A., Economy
MOHAMED AL-JANABI, H., Abdominal Medicine
MUHSIN AL-YASIRI, A., Arabic Language
RADEE ABUOD NASAR, M., Islamic Sciences
RAKBAN AL-KAFAGEI, A., Law

RESHED JABBER AL-ABEADI, H., Nutriments Sciences
RWAH ALI AL-MUOSWEAI, S., Administrations
SADAK ALSHIKE RADEA, M., Economy
SADDON AJEAL AL-AJEALI, S., Agriculture Sciences
TALAB AL-MUOSWEA, A., Geography
TARASH ZAOARI AL-JANABI, H., Micro Alive

UNIVERSITY OF MOSUL

al Majmoa al Thaqafia, Mosul
Telephone: (60) 810733
Fax: (60) 815066
E-mail: president@mosuluniversity.org
Internet: www.uomosul.edu.iq
Founded 1967 as a separate univ.; fmrly part of the Univ. of Baghdad
State control
Languages of instruction: Arabic, English
Academic year: September to June (2 terms)
Pres.: OBAY S. AL DEWACHI (acting)
Vice-Pres. for Admin.: Dr BURHAN MAHMOOD AHMAD AL ALI (acting)
Vice-Pres. for Scientific Affairs: Dr NAZAR MAJEED QIBI (acting)
Librarian: Dr NASSER ABDUL RAAZAQ MULLA JASSIM

Number of teachers: 2,548
Number of students: 22,526

Publications: Adab al Rafidian (4 a year), Al Rafidian Engineering Sciences (4 a year), Al Rafidain Dental Journal (4 a year), Al Rafidain Journal of Computer Science (4 a year), Al Rafidain Journal of Earth Science (4 a year), Al Rafidain Journal of Law (4 a year), Al Rafidain Journal of Science (4 a year), Al Rafidain Journal of Statistical Science (4 a year), Al Rafidain Sports Science Journal (4 a year), Annals of The Medical College (4 a year), College of Basic Education Research Journal (4 a year), Iraq Journal of Agricultural Science (4 a year), Iraqi Journal of Pharmacy (4 a year), Iraqi Journal of Veterinary Medicine (4 a year), Journal of Education and Science (4 a year), Regional Studies (4 a year), Studies Mosulia (4 a year), Tanmiat al Rafidain (4 a year)

DEANS

College of Administration: Dr FAWAZ GARALLA AL DOLUMY
College of Agriculture: Dr MOWAFAK TAYEB AL LAYLA
College of Arts: MUHAMMAD-BASIL AL AZZAWI
College of Basic Education: Dr FADHIL KHALHL IBRAHIM
College of Dentistry: Dr ABDUL HAQ ADUL MAGEED SULIMAN
College of Education: Dr ABDL WAHID DH. TAHA
College of Electronics Engineering: Dr BAYEZ K. AL SULAIFANIE
College of Engineering: Dr MOHAMMAD TAYEB AL LAYLA
College of Fine Arts: Dr ADEL SAEED AL SAFAR
College of Islamic Sciences: Dr DURIAD ABDUL QAADER NURI
College of Law: Dr GAFAR MOHAMMAD GAWAD AL FADHLI
College of Mathematics and Computer Science: Dr THAFER RAMATHAN MUTTAR
College of Medicine: Dr MUZHIM AL KHYATT
College of Medicine (Nineveh): Dr NAZAR MAJEED QIBI
College of Nursing: Dr SUBHE HUSEIN AL GUBORE
College of Pharmacy: Dr SABAH G. AL DABBAGH
College of Physical Education: Dr YASSIN TAHA MOHAMMAD ALI
College of Political Science: Dr TALAL YOUNIS AL GALILI

College of Science: Dr IHSAN A. MUSTAFA AL ABDULLAH
College of Veterinary Medicine: Dr FOUAD KASIM MOHAMMAD

ATTACHED INSTITUTES

Centre for Dams and Water Resources: Dir SALIM QASIM AL NAQUIB.
Centre for the Development of Teaching Methods: Dir QUSAY TAWFEQ GHAZAL.
Computer Centre: Dir Dr HYTAM ABD AL WAHAB.
Environmental Research Centre: Dir Dr TARIQ AHMAD MAHMOUD.
Mosul Studies Centre: Dir THANOON Y. AL TAEE.
Regional Studies Centre: Dir GHANIM MOHAMMED AL HAFOU.
Remote Sensing Centre: Dir Dr MOHAMMED Y. AL ALAAF.

UNIVERSITY OF SALAHADDIN

Karkuk St, Runaki 235–323, Erbil, Kurdistan Region
Telephone: (66) 2230409
E-mail: presedent-office@salahaddin-ac.com
Internet: www.salahaddin-ac.com
Founded 1968 in Sulaimaniya as University of Sulaimaniya; present name and location 1981
State control
Languages of instruction: Kurdish, Arabic, English
Academic year: September to June (two terms)
Pres.: Dr MOHAMMAD S. MOHAMMAD
Vice-Pres. for Scientific Affairs: Dr AHMAD ANWAR AMIN DEZAYE
Librarian: Dr MOHAMMAD MUSTAFA
Library: see Libraries
Number of teachers: 800
Number of students: 10,965 (10,597 undergraduate, 368 postgraduate)
Publications: Statistical Abstract (1 a year), University News (12 a year, Arabic), Zanco (scientific journal, Arabic and English)

DEANS

College of Administration and Economics: Asst Prof. Dr DLER ISMAIL HAQI
College of Agriculture: Asst Prof. Dr FARHAD HASSAN AZEEZ
College of Arts: Prof. Dr AZAD MUHAMMAD AMEEN NAQISHBANDI
College of Dentistry: Dr DASHTI BAIZ DZAYI
College of Education: Prof. Dr KAREEM SALIH ABDUL
College of Engineering: Dr FARAYDOON HADI MAROUF
College of Law: NAJDAT SABRI AQRAWI
College of Medicine: Asst Prof. Dr HAMA NAJIM JAFF
College of Nursing: Dr FARHAD JALEEL KHAYAT
College of Pharmacy: Dr TAFUR JALAL KHLEL
College of Physical Education: IIDREES MUHAMMAD TAHIR
College of Political Science: Dr AHMED MUSTAFA SULAIMAN
College of Science: Asst Prof. ROSTEM KAREEM SAED
College of Teacher Training: Asst Prof. Dr AZAD JALAL SHAREEF

UNIVERSITY OF SULAIMANIYA

2/3/205 Kani-Askan, Sulaimaniya
Telephone: (53) 2127453
E-mail: info@univsul.com
Internet: www.univsul.org
Founded 1968
State control

Languages of instruction: Arabic, English, Kurdish

Colleges of administration and economics, agriculture, dentistry and commerce, education, engineering, fine Arts, humanities, languages, nursing, physical education, law, medicine, science, veterinary medicine

Pres.: KAMAL KHOSHNAW (acting)
Vice-Pres. for Admin.: SHAWNM ABDUL QADIR (acting)
Vice-Pres. for Scientific Affairs and Postgraduate Research: NAZAR M. MUHAMMAD AMIN (acting)
Library of 24,689 vols
Number of teachers: 489
Number of students: 8,000

UNIVERSITY OF TECHNOLOGY

al Sinah St, Baghdad
Telephone: (1) 7746532
Fax: (1) 7199446
E-mail: shekhly@uruklink.net
Internet: www.uotiq.org
Founded 1975; fmrly the College of Engineering Technology of the University of Baghdad
State control
Languages of instruction: Arabic, English
Academic year: October to July
Pres.: Dr WAIL NOORALDEN AL RIFAIE (acting)
Vice-Pres. for Admin. and Scientific Affairs: KRIKOR SIROB (acting)
Registrar: Dr ABDU AL HUSAIN SAKHI
Librarian: AYAD J. SHAMIS ELDEN
Library of 25,000 vols
Number of teachers: 961 (668 full-time, 293 part-time)
Number of students: 7,752

PROFESSORS
AL HADEETHI, A., Structural Engineering
AL HAIDARY, J. T., Production Engineering and Metallurgy
AL MUTALIB IBRAHIM, A., Applied Sciences
AL SAMAAUI, A., Structural Engineering
AL SAMRAAI, J. M. A., Electrical Engineering
AL TOORNAJI, M., Production Engineering and Metallurgy
HAMMUDI, W. KH., Applied Sciences
KHAIRI, W., Computer and Control Engineering
KHORSEED, N., Structural Engineering
MAJEED, J., Mechanical Engineering
TAWFICK, H., Mechanical Engineering

UNIVERSITY OF THI-QAR

Nasiriya, Thi-Qar governorate
Internet: www.unidhiqar.com
Founded 2002
State control
Pres.: ISMAIL OBEID ALSNAVI (acting)
Vice-Pres. for Admin.: QASIM MOHAMMAD (acting)
Vice-Pres. for Scientific Affairs: ABBAS HUSSEIN (acting)
Number of teachers: 155
Number of students: 5,639

DEANS
College of Arts: FADEL KAZEM SADIK
College of Education: MOHAMED JASSIM MOHAMMED
College of Engineering: HAIDAR SAAD REFINERY
College of Medicine: NAJI MAJID
College of Sciences: NAJAH RASSOL AL JABBRAI

UNIVERSITY OF TIKRIT

POB 42, Salah al Din, Tikrit
Telephone: (21) 825743

Fax: (21) 825384
E-mail: tikrituniversity@hotmail.com
Founded 1987
State control
Languages of instruction: Arabic, English
Academic year: September to June
Pres.: Prof. Dr MAHER S. AL JUBORI (acting)
Librarian: SABAH S. KHALEFE
Number of teachers: 701
Number of students: 6,824
Publications: *Iraqi Journal of Educational and Psychological Sciences and Sociology* (4 a year), *Surra Min Raa Journal* (4 a year), *Tikrit Journal of Agricultural Sciences* (4 a year), *Tikrit Journal of Economic Sciences* (4 a year), *Tikrit Journal of Engineering Sciences* (4 a year), *Tikrit Journal of Humanities* (4 a year), *Tikrit Journal of Pharmaceutical Sciences* (4 a year), *Tikrit Journal of Pure Sciences* (4 a year), *Tikrit Medical Journal* (4 a year)

DEANS
College of Administration and Economics: Asst Prof. Dr SABAH F. MAHMOOD
College of Agriculture: Prof. Dr ABDULLAH AHMED AL SAMARRAIE
College of Dentistry: Prof. Dr ADNAN H. MOHAMMED
College of Education: Asst Prof. Dr ALI SALIH HUSSEIN
College of Education (Samarra): Asst Prof. Dr MUHAMMAD IBRAHIM HUSSEIN
College of Education for Women: Asst Prof. Dr JAID Z. MUKHLIF
College of Engineering: Asst Prof. Dr HAYDAR SAAD YASEEN AL JUBAIR
College of Law: Asst Prof. Dr DHAMIN HUSSEIN
College of Medicine: Asst Prof. Dr ABID AHMAD SALMAN
College of Pharmacy: Prof. Dr ALI ISMAIL UBEID
College of Science: Asst Prof. Dr SUBHI ATIA MAHMOOD

PROFESSORS
ABDOON, H. F., Islamic Jurisprudence
ABDULLAH, A. A.-M., Veterinary Science
ALAAH, M. M., Microbiology
AL AZIZ, M. A., Veterinary Science
AL BAYDHANI, I. S., Modern History
AL HUSSEIN, S. A., Biology
AL JUBURI, A. H. M., Arabic Language
AL NAJAFEE, H. M., Civil Engineering
AL OMER, A. K., Arabic Language
ALI, A. A.-G. M., Medicine
ALI, K. I., Politics
ALI, N. H., Physical Education
AL-JUBURI, M. S. A., Arabic Language
AL JUMAILI, S. H. A., Arabic Language
AL-KUTUBI, S. H., Mathematics
ALRAHMAN, Y. A. A., Medicine
AL SAMARRAIE, A. A.-K. M., Physical Education
AL SAMARRAIE, A. A.-M. H., Chemistry
AL SHIQARCHI, S. T., Chemistry
AL TAAI, A. A. H., Arabic Language
AUBED, A. I., Pharmacology and Toxicology
AZIZ, A. A., Chemistry
DAWOOD, A. S., Plant Protection
DAWOOD, I. S., Biology
DEKRAAN, S. B., Chemistry
GHANIM, Y. M.-A., Medicine
HAMAD, G. Q., Arabic Language
HANTOSH, F. G., Chemistry
HUSEIN, M. H., Civil Engineering
KAMEL, A. A.-M., Modern History
KAMEL, F. M., Food Technologies
LATEEF, R. A., Crops
MAHMOUD, S. A., Chemistry
MOHAMMED, A. H., Dentistry
MOHAMMED, A. H., Economics
MOHAMMED, M. M., Medicine

MUKHIF, J. Z., Arabic Language
MUSA, M. M., Veterinary Science
RASEED, A. A.-M., Economics
SAIED, J. M., Animal Production
SHIHAB, A. F., Biology
WADY, A. A.-R. A., History

UNIVERSITY OF WASSIT

Kut, Wassit governorate
Telephone: (23) 313861
Internet: www.uowasit.edu.iq
Founded 2003
State control
Pres.: Dr JABBAR YASSER AL MAYAH
Number of teachers: 109

Colleges

Al Imam al A'dham College: Karkh, Baghdad; f. 1967, affiliated to Baghdad Univ. 1978; degree course in Islamic studies; 34 teachers; 516 students; Dean Dr SUBHI MOHAMMAD JAMIL AL KHAYYAT; publ. *Journal* (1 a year).

Foundation for Technical Institutes: Baghdad; f. 1972; attached to the Min. of Higher Education and Scientific Research; groups all the institutes of technology; Pres. H. M. S. ABDUL WAHAB.

Incorporated Institutes:

Institute of Administration: Rissafa, Baghdad; f. 1964; Dean A. S. AL MASHAT.

Institute of Administration, Karkh (Baghdad): f. 1976; Dean T. SHAKER.

Institute of Applied Arts: Baghdad; f. 1969; Dean A. NOOR-EDDIN.

Institute of Technology: Baghdad; f. 1969; Dean N. S. MUSTAFA.

Technical Institute, Basrah: f. 1973; UNDP/UNESCO project; technology and admin.; 1,660 students; Dean H. I. MOHAMMED.

Technical Institute, Hilla: f. 1976; technology and admin.; Dean S. B. DERWISH.

Technical Institute, Kirkuk: f. 1976; technology and admin.; Dean M. ABDUL RAHMAN.

Technical Institute, Mosul: f. 1976; technology and admin.; Dean M. S. SAFFO.

Technical Institute, Missan: f. 1979; technology and admin.

Technical Institute, Najaf: f. 1978; technology and admin.; Dean M. A. JASSIM.

Technical Institute, Ramadi: f. 1977; technology and admin.; Dean J. M. AMIN.

Technical Institute, Sulaimaniya: f. 1973; medical technology and admin.; Dean R. M. ABDULLAH.

Technical Institute of Agriculture: Abu-Ghraib, Baghdad; f. 1964; Dean S. A. HASSAN.

Technical Institute of Agriculture, Arbil: Aski-Kalak, Arbil; f. 1976; Dean M. S. ABBASS.

Technical Institute of Agriculture, Kumait: Kumait, Missan; f. 1976; Dean H. L. SADIK.

Technical Institute of Agriculture, Mussaib-Babylon: Mussaib-Babylon; f. 1979.

Technical Institute of Agriculture, Shatra-Thi Qar: Shatra-Thi Qar; f. 1979.

Technical Institute of Medicine: Baghdad; f. 1964; Dean A. S. AL MASHAT.

IRELAND

The Higher Education System

Higher education in Ireland dates from the foundation of the University of Dublin Trinity College in 1592; the next oldest institutions are the Royal College of Physicians of Ireland (founded 1654) and the National University of Ireland, Maynooth (formerly St Patrick's College, founded 1795). Until 1920 the 32 counties of Ireland were part of the United Kingdom; however, in that year Ireland was partitioned: the six north-eastern counties remained part of the United Kingdom, and the 26 southern counties sought independence. In 1922 the southern counties achieved dominion status, under the British Crown, as the Irish Free State. Ireland achieved full sovereignty within the Commonwealth in 1937, and the Republic of Ireland was declared in 1949. There are seven universities, as well as other institutions of higher education including colleges, institutes of technology, schools of art and music, and professional establishments. Under the Universities Act (1997) and the Qualifications Act (1999), Ireland participates in the Bologna Process. In 2006/07 82,488 full-time students were enrolled at universities and Higher Education Authority Institutions, and 53,358 students were enrolled at technology colleges.

Admission to higher education is administered by the Central Applications Office. In accordance with the Bologna Process, the university awards system consists of Bachelors, Masters and Doctorate degrees. The Bachelors is the main undergraduate degree and lasts for three to four years. However, degrees in some disciplines, such as dentistry, veterinary medicine, architecture (all five years) and medicine (six years), may last longer. Following the Bachelors, a student may take the Masters, the first postgraduate degree. The Masters is a one-to two-year programme of study, and may be either a taught or a research degree. The second postgraduate degree (and final university-level award) is the Doctor of Philosophy, which is a research-based course lasting two to five years. In addition to the universities, higher education is offered by other types of institution, including Institutes of Technology and so-called 'Designated' Institutions. Awards from these establishments are assured by the Higher Education and Training Awards Council (founded 2001). Quality assurance of universities is organized through the independent Irish Universities Quality Board, which was established in 2002, however the devolved statutory responsibility is with the universities. The Higher Education Authority also has a statutory right to review the quality assurance procedures in the universities, having consulted with the universities and the National Qualifications Authority of Ireland.

Technical and vocational education is offered by colleges, the Dublin Institute of Technology and Industrial Training Authority centres. The Higher Education and Training Awards Council oversees all continuing and adult education and administers a wide range of certificated courses. The most prominent vocational award is the National Vocational Certificate (Levels 1–3).

Regulatory and Representative Bodies

GOVERNMENT

Department of Arts, Sport and Tourism: 23 Kildare St, Dublin 2; tel. (1) 6313800; fax (1) 6611201; e-mail seamusbrennan@dast.gov.ie; internet www.dast.gov.ie; Minister SÉAMUS BRENNAN.

Department of Education and Science: Marlborough St, Dublin 1; tel. (1) 8892162; fax (1) 8786712; e-mail info@education.gov.ie; internet www.education.ie; Minister MARY COUGHLAN.

ACCREDITATION

ENIC/NARIC Ireland: Nat. Qualifications Authority of Ireland, 5th Floor, Jervis House, Jervis St, Dublin 1; tel. (1) 8871500; fax (1) 8871595; e-mail info@qualrec.ie; internet www.qualrec.ie; Man. of Operations, Qualifications Recognition NIAMH LENEHAN.

Higher Education and Training Awards Council: 26–27 Denzille Lane, Dublin 2; tel. (1) 6441500; fax (1) 6441577; e-mail info@hetac.ie; internet www.hetac.ie; f. 2001 under the Qualifications (Education and Training) Act 1999; develops higher education outside the univ. system in the Republic of Ireland; approves and recognizes courses; grants and confers nat. awards (degrees, diplomas, certificates); co-ordinates courses within and between institutions; successor to the Nat. Council for Educational Awards (NCEA—f. 1972); may delegate authority to make awards to recognized institutions under the Qualifications (Education and Training) Act 1999; 15 mems; Chief Exec. GEARÓID Ó CONLUAIN.

National Qualifications Authority of Ireland: 5th Floor, Jervis House, Jervis St, Dublin 1; tel. (1) 8871500; fax (1) 8871595; e-mail info@nqai.ie; internet www.nqai.ie; f. 2001; objects: the establishment and maintenance of a framework of qualifications for the devt, recognition and award of qualifications based on standards of knowledge, skill or competence to be acquired by learners; the establishment and promotion of the maintenance and improvement of the standards of awards of the further and higher education and training sector, other than in the existing univs; the promotion and facilitation of access, transfer and progression throughout the span of education and training provision; the Authority is not an awarding body; Chair. PAUL HARAN; Chief Exec. SEÁN Ó FOGHLÚ.

FUNDING

Higher Education Authority: Brooklawn House, Crampton Ave, Shelbourne Rd, Dublin 4; tel. (1) 2317100; fax (1) 2317172; e-mail info@hea.ie; internet www.hea.ie; statutory planning and devt body for higher education and research in Ireland; has wide advisory powers throughout the whole of the tertiary education sector; funding authority for univs and a number of designated higher education instns; Chair. MICHAEL KELLY; Chief Exec. TOM BOLAND.

NATIONAL BODIES

Central Applications Office: Tower House, Eglinton St, Galway; tel. (91) 509800; fax (91) 562344; internet www.cao.ie; f. 1976; processes applications for first-year undergraduate courses offered by the higher-education instns in the Republic of Ireland; CEO IVOR GLEESON.

Further Education and Training Awards Council: East Point Plaza, East Point Business Park, Dublin 3; tel. (1) 8659500; fax (1) 8650067; e-mail information@fetac.ie; internet www.fetac.ie; f. 2001; makes quality-assured awards in accordance with nat. standards within the nat. framework, creating opportunities for all learners in further education and training to have their achievements recognized and providing access to systematic progression pathways; Chief Exec. STAN MCHUGH.

Irish Universities Association (IUA): 48 Merrion Sq., Dublin 2; tel. (1) 6764948; fax (1) 6622815; e-mail info@iua.ie; internet www.iua.ie; the rep. body of the heads of the 7 Irish univs; seeks to advance univ. education and research through the formulation and pursuit of collective policies and actions on behalf of the Irish univs thereby contributing to Ireland's social, cultural and economic wellbeing; Pres. Dr HUGH BRADY; Chief Exec. NED COSTELLO; publ. *IUA Review* (irregular).

Learned Societies

GENERAL

Royal Dublin Society: Ballsbridge, Dublin 4; tel. (1) 6680866; fax (1) 6604014; e-mail info@rds.ie; internet www.rds.ie; f. 1731 for the advancement of agriculture, industry, science and the arts; 6,000 mems; library: see Libraries and Archives; Pres. Dr AUSTIN MESCAIL; Chief Exec. MICHAEL DUFFY; Registrar EILEEN BYRNE; publ. *Minerva* (3 a year).

Royal Irish Academy: Academy House, 19 Dawson St, Dublin 2; tel. (1) 6762570; fax (1) 6762346; e-mail info@ria.ie; internet www

.ria.ie; f. 1785; acad. for the sciences and humanities in the Republic of Ireland; promotes excellence in scholarship, recognizes achievements in learning and undertakes research projects; advises on and contributes to public debate and public policy formation in science, technology and culture; maintains a library; the largest Irish publisher of scholarly and scientific journals, books and monographs; 486 mems (424 ordinary, 65 hon.); library of 35,000 vols, 31,000 pamphlets, 1,800 sets of current periodicals, 2,500 MSS; Pres. Prof. NICHOLAS P. CANNY; Sec. Prof. THOMAS BRAZIL; Exec. Sec. PATRICK BUCKLEY; publs *Biology and Environment Proceedings* (3 a year), *Ériu* (1 a year), *Irish Journal of Earth Sciences* (1 a year), *Irish Studies in International Affairs* (1 a year), *Mathematical Proceedings* (2 a year), *Proceedings Section C* (Archaeology, Celtic Studies, History, Linguistics, Literature, 5 a year).

AGRICULTURE, FISHERIES AND VETERINARY SCIENCE

Royal Horticultural Society of Ireland: Cabinteely House, The Park, Cabinteely, Dublin 18; tel. and fax (1) 2353912; e-mail info@rhsi.ie; internet www.rhsi.ie; f. 1816; 1,000 mems; Pres. MAEVE KEARNS; Sec. CORA KENNEDY; publ. *Newsletter* (12 a year).

Society of Irish Foresters: Enterprise Centre, Ballintogher, Co Sligo; tel. (71) 9164434; fax (71) 9134904; e-mail sif@eircom.net; internet www.societyofirishforesters.ie; f. 1942 to advance and spread the knowledge of forestry in all its aspects, to promote professional standards in forestry and the regulation of the forestry profession in Ireland; annual study tour, field days, annual symposium, lectures; continuous professional development programme; 650 mems; Pres. MICHAEL BULFIN; Sec. CLODAGH DUFFY; publs *Irish Forester* (4 a year), *Irish Forestry* (2 a year).

Veterinary Council: 53 Lansdowne Rd, Ballsbridge, Dublin 4; tel. (1) 6684402; fax (1) 6604373; e-mail info@vci.ie; internet www.vci.ie; f. 1931; 2,370 registered mems; Registrar V. BEATTY.

ARCHITECTURE AND TOWN PLANNING

Architectural Association of Ireland: 8 Merrion Sq., Dublin 2; tel. (1) 6761703; internet www.irish-architecture.com/aai; f. 1896 to promote the practice and study of architecture, and to foster cooperation among architects; 450 mems; Pres. MAXIM LAROUSSI; Hon. Sec. KEVIN DONOVAN; publ. *Building Material* (12 a year).

Royal Institute of the Architects of Ireland: 8 Merrion Sq., Dublin 2; tel. (1) 6761703; fax (1) 6610948; e-mail info@riai.ie; internet www.riai.ie; f. 1839; 3,300 mems; Pres. PAUL KEOGH; Dir. JOHN GRABY; publs *Architecture Ireland* (6 a year), *House* (2 a year).

Society of Chartered Surveyors: 5 Wilton Place, Dublin 2; tel. (1) 6765500; fax (1) 6761412; e-mail info@scs.ie; internet www.scs.ie; constituent body of the Royal Instn of Chartered Surveyors; Dir-Gen. CIARA MURPHY.

BIBLIOGRAPHY, LIBRARY SCIENCE AND MUSEOLOGY

Library Association of Ireland (Cumann Leabharlann na héireann): 53 Upper Mount St, Dublin 2; tel. (1) 6380910; e-mail president@libraryassociation.ie; internet www.libraryassociation.ie; f. 1928, incorporated 1952; 650 mems; courses: continuing professional devt, Assoc. of the Library Assocn

of Ireland (ALAI), Fellow of the Library Asscn of Ireland (FLAI); holds conferences; lobbies govt; Pres. SIOBHÁN FITZPATRICK; Hon. Sec. KIERAN SWORDS; publs *An Leabharlann/ The Irish Library* (4 a year), *Directory of Libraries and Information Services in Ireland* (jtly with Northern Ireland Br. of the Library Asscn, online only).

ECONOMICS, LAW AND POLITICS

Institute of Chartered Accountants in Ireland: Offices and Library: 83 Pembroke Rd, Ballsbridge, Dublin 4; Belfast Office: 11 Donegall Sq. South, Belfast, BT1 5JE, UK; tel. (1) 6680400; fax (1) 6680842; e-mail ca@icai.ie; internet www.icai.ie; inc. by Royal Charter 1888; 10,000 mems; library of 20,000 vols; Pres. JOHN P. GREELY; Chief Exec. PAT COSTELLO; publ. *Accountancy Ireland* (6 a year).

King's Inns, Honorable Society of: Henrietta St, Dublin 1; tel. (1) 8744840; fax (1) 8726048; e-mail info@kingsinns.ie; internet www.kingsinns.ie; f. 1542; provides training course to enable students to be admitted to the degree of barrister-at-law; 4,000 mems; library of 98,900 vols; Under-Treas. CAMILLA MCALEESE; Dir of Education MARCELLA HIGGINS; Dean of School of Law SARAH MACDONALD; Librarian JONATHAN ARMSTRONG; publ. *Irish Student Law Review* (1 a year).

Law Society of Ireland: Blackhall Pl., Dublin 7; tel. (1) 6724800; fax (1) 6724801; e-mail general@lawsociety.ie; internet www.lawsociety.ie; f. 1852; 7,000 mems; library of 14,000 vols; Dir-Gen. KEN MURPHY; Librarian MARGARET BYRNE; publs *Law Directory* (1 a year), *Gazette* (12 a year).

Statistical and Social Inquiry Society of Ireland: c/o Robert Watt, Indecon House, 25 Wellington Quay, Dublin 2; tel. (1) 6600311; e-mail info@ssisi.ie; internet www.ssisi.ie; f. 1847 to promote the study of social and economic developments; c. 500 mems; Pres. Prof. A. PUNCH; Hon. Secs T. N. CAVEN, P. WALSH, S. F. WHELAN; publ. *Journal* (1 a year).

EDUCATION

Church Education Society: c/o Church of Ireland House, Church Ave, Rathmines, Dublin 6; tel. (1) 4978422; fax (1) 4978821; e-mail ces@ireland.anglican.org; f. 1839; Asst Sec. and Treas. JENNIFER BYRNE.

FINE AND PERFORMING ARTS

Aosdána: 70 Merrion Sq., Dublin 2; tel. (1) 6180200; fax (1) 6761302; e-mail aosdana@artscouncil.ie; internet www.artscouncil.ie/aosdana; f. 1981; attached to the Arts Council; an affiliation of artists engaged in literature, music and visual arts; membership limited to 250 mems; Registrar PAUL JOHNSON.

Arts Council: 70 Merrion Sq., Dublin 2; tel. (1) 6180200; fax (1) 6761302; e-mail info@artscouncil.ie; internet www.artscouncil.ie; f. 1951; Irish Govt agency for devt of the arts; promotes and assists the artists; in addition to organizing and promoting exhibitions and other activities itself, the Council gives grant-aid to many organizations including the theatre, opera, arts centres, arts festivals, exhibitions and publishers; also awards bursaries and scholarships to individual artists; offers advice and information on arts to Govt, individuals and orgs; Chair. PAT MOYLAN.

Irish Recorded Music Association: IRMA House, 1 Corrig Ave, Dun Laoghaire, Co Dublin; tel. (1) 2806571; fax (1) 2806579; e-mail irma_info@irma.ie; internet www.irma.ie; f. 1948; organizes schools recital and

workshop scheme, composer workshops, and Irish auditions for the European Union Youth Orchestra; Dir-Gen. DICK DOYLE; publs *Music Events Diary*, *Policy Statement of Music Education*.

Royal Hibernian Academy: 15 Ely Pl., Dublin 2; tel. (1) 6612558; fax (1) 6610762; e-mail info@rhagallery.ie; internet www.royalhibernianacademy.ie; f. 1823; painting, sculpture, installation and mixed media; 4 galleries; 66 mems (13 hon., 44 acads, 9 assoc.); Pres. STEPHEN MCKENNA; Sec. DAVID CRONE.

HISTORY, GEOGRAPHY AND ARCHAEOLOGY

Cork Historical and Archaeological Society: c/o Hon. Treasurer, Lackenroe, Glenmore Cross, Glanmire, Cork; tel. (21) 541076; internet www.ucc.ie/chas; f. 1891; 400 mems; Pres. Dr ELIZABETH TWOHIG; Hon. Sec. MARY LANTRY; publ. *Journal* (1 a year).

Folklore of Ireland Society: c/o UCD Delargy Centre for Irish Folklore and the Nat. Folklore Colln, School of Irish, Celtic Studies, Irish Folklore and Linguistics, Newman Bldg, Belfield, Dublin 4; tel. (1) 7168216; fax (1) 7161144; e-mail eolas@bealoideas.ie; internet www.bealoideas.ie; f. 1926; 650 mems; Pres. ANRAÍ Ó BRAONÁIN; Sec. EMER NÍ CHEALLAIGH; publ. *Béaloideas* (1 a year).

Geographical Society of Ireland: c/o GSI Treasurer, Dept of Geography, St Patrick's College, Drumcondra, Dublin 9; internet www.geographical-society-ireland.org; f. 1934; seeks to provide information and promote discussion about a wide range of topics of geographical interest, within Ireland and abroad; organizes lectures and seminars, field trips; 200 mems; Pres. Dr JOE BRADY; Treas. Dr RONAN FOLEY; publs *Geonews* (2 a year), *Irish Geography* (3 a year).

Military History Society of Ireland: University College Dublin, Newman House, 86 St Stephen's Green, Dublin 2; tel. (1) 2985617; fax (1) 7067211; e-mail patandpatkirby@eircom.net; internet www.mhsi.ie; f. 1949; 1,000 mems; Hon. Secs Dr PATRICK MCCARTHY (Correspondence), Col PATRICK G. KIRBY (Membership); publ. *The Irish Sword* (2 a year).

Old Dublin Society: 44 Warrenhouse Rd, Baldoyle, Dublin 13; f. 1934; promotes study of history and antiquities of Dublin; 325 mems; library of 1,300 vols; Pres. Rev. DUDLEY A. LEVISTONECOONEY; Sec. BARRY FARRELL; publ. *Dublin Historical Record* (2 a year).

Royal Society of Antiquaries of Ireland: 63 Merrion Sq., Dublin 2; tel. (1) 6761749; internet www.rsai.ie; f. 1849; 1,100 mems; library of 13,000 vols; Pres. CHARLES DOHERTY; Hon. Gen.-Sec. Dr NIALL BRADY; Hon. Gen.-Sec. KELLY FITZGERALD; publ. *Journal* (1 a year).

LANGUAGE AND LITERATURE

Alliance Française: 1 Kildare St, Dublin 2; tel. (1) 6761732; fax (1) 6764077; e-mail info@alliance-francaise.ie; internet www.alliance-francaise.ie; offers courses in general French, French conversation, specialized French, French for primary schools; also offers diploma courses and corporate courses; promotes French culture; attached offices in Cork, Kilkenny, Limerick, Waterford and Wexford; Dir JEAN-MICHEL GARCIA.

British Council: Newmount House, 22/24 Lower Mount St, Dublin 2; tel. (1) 6764088; fax (1) 6766945; e-mail info@ie.britishcouncil.org; internet www.britishcouncil.org/ireland; offers courses and exams in English language and British culture and promotes cultural exchange with the UK; promotes creative and knowledge economy of the UK; Dir MATT BURNEY.

Conradh na Gaeilge (Gaelic League): 6 Sráid Fhearchair, Dublin 2; tel. (1) 4757401; fax (1) 4757844; e-mail eolas@cnag.ie; internet www.cnag.ie; f. 1893; 200 brs; Sec.-Gen. JULIAN DE SPÁINN; Deputy Sec.-Gen. PEADAR MAC FHLANNCHADHA; publs *An tUltach* (12 a year), *Feasta* (12 a year).

Goethe-Institut: 37 Merrion Sq., Dublin 2; tel. (1) 6611155; fax (1) 6611358; internet www.goethe.de/dublin; offers courses and examinations in German language and culture and promotes cultural exchange with Germany; library of 12,000 vols; Dir ROLF STEHLE.

Instituto Cervantes: 58 Northumberland Rd, Ballsbridge, Dublin 4; tel. (1) 6682936; fax (1) 6688416; e-mail cendub@cervantes.es; internet dublin.cervantes.es; offers courses and exams in Spanish language and culture and promotes cultural exchange with Spain and Spanish-speaking Latin and Central America; library of 11,000 vols; Dir AURORA SOTELO MORILLO.

Irish PEN: 'Tully', Ballinteer Rd, Dublin 12; e-mail irishpen@ireland.com; internet www.irishpen.com; f. 1921; 62 mems; Chair. MARITA CONLON MCKENNA; Sec. and Treas. NESTA TUOMEY.

Irish Texts Society: c/o Royal Bank of Scotland, 49 Charing Cross Rd, London, SW1A 2DX, UK; e-mail hon.treas@irishtextssociety.org; internet www.irishtextssociety.org; f. 1898 to advance public education by promoting the study of Irish literature, and to publish texts in the Irish language, with translations, notes, etc.; 640 mems; library: archives of the Society have been placed in the Univ. College Cork Library; Pres. Prof. PÁDRAIG Ó RIAIN; Hon. Sec. SEÁN HUTTON; Hon. Treas. MICHAEL J. BURNS; publs *Main Series: 61 vols of Irish-language texts with English translation, Subsidiary Series: 17 vols.*

MEDICINE

Dental Council: 57 Merrion Sq., Dublin 2; tel. (1) 6762226; fax (1) 6762069; e-mail info@dentalcouncil.ie; internet www.dentalcouncil.ie; f. 1928 as the Dental Board, superseded by the Dental Council in 1985; registers dentists and controls standards of education and conduct among dentists in Ireland; Pres. DANIEL I. KEANE; Chief Officer and Registrar THOMAS FARREN.

Irish Medical Organisation: IMO House, 10 Fitzwilliam Place, Dublin 2; tel. (1) 6767273; fax (1) 6612758; e-mail imo@imo.ie; internet www.imo.ie; f. 1936; 6,000 mems; CEO GEORGE MCNEICE; publ. *Irish Medical Journal* (10 a year).

Medical Council: Lynn House, Portobello Court, Lower Rathmines Rd, Dublin 6; tel. (1) 4983100; fax (1) 4983102; e-mail nfo@mcirl.ie; internet www.medicalcouncil.ie; f. 1978; 17,000 mems; Pres. Dr JOHN HILLERY.

Pharmaceutical Society of Ireland: 18 Shrewsbury Rd, Ballsbridge Dublin 4; tel. (1) 2184000; fax (1) 2837678; e-mail info@pharmaceuticalsociety.ie; internet www.pharmaceuticalsociety.ie; f. 1875; Pres. RONAN QUIRKE; Registrar and Sec. Dr AMBROSE MCLOUGHLIN; publ. *Calendar* (1 a year).

Royal Academy of Medicine in Ireland: Frederick House, 2nd Fl., 19 S Frederick St, Dublin 2; tel. (1) 6334820; fax (1) 6334918; e-mail helenmoore@rcpi.ie; internet www.rami.ie; f. 1882; 1,500 fellows; Pres. Prof. THOMAS N. WALSH; Gen. Sec. and Treas. Dr

JOHN O'CONNOR; publ. *Irish Journal of Medical Science* (4 a year).

NATURAL SCIENCES

Biological Sciences

Dublin University Biological Association: Trinity College, Dublin; f. 1874; 400 mems; Pres. Prof. IAN TEMPERLEY; Hon. Sec. EMER LOUGHREY.

Dublin Zoo: Phoenix Park, Dublin 8; tel. (1) 4748900; fax (1) 6771660; e-mail info@dublinzoo.ie; internet www.dublinzoo.ie; f. 1830; 9,000 mems; Pres. MICHAEL MACNULTY; Hon. Sec. DOROTHY KILROY; Dir LEO OOSTER-WEGHEL.

Physical Sciences

Institute of Chemistry of Ireland: POB 9322, Cardiff Lane, Dublin 2; e-mail info@instituteofchemistry.org; internet www.chemistryireland.org; f. 1950; 800 mems; Pres. Dr J. P. JAMES; Hon. Sec. J. P. RYAN; publ. *Irish Chemical News* (2 a year).

Irish Astronomical Society: POB 2547, Dublin 14; tel. (1) 2981268; e-mail ias1937@hotmail.com; internet www.irishastrosoc.org; f. 1937; 150 mems; library: video-cassette and book libraries; Pres. BRIAN KEANE; Sec. ANGELA O'CONNELL; publs *Orbit* (6 a year), *Sky High* (1 a year).

Irish Branch of the Institute of Physics: c/o Department of Experimental Physics, University College Dublin, Belfield, Dublin 4; tel. (1) 7162216; fax (1) 2837275; e-mail alison.hackett@iop.org; internet ireland.iop.org; f. 1964; learned society and professional body for the advancement of physics and physics education on the island of Ireland; 1,700 mems; Chair. Dr MARTIN LAMB; Sec. Dr EMMA SOKELL.

PHILOSOPHY AND PSYCHOLOGY

Psychological Society of Ireland: CX House, 2A Corn Exchange Pl., Poolbeg St, Dublin 2; tel. (1) 4749160; fax (1) 4749161; e-mail pres@psihq.ie; internet www.psihq.ie; f. 1970 to advance psychological knowledge and research in Ireland, to ensure maintenance of high standards of professional training and practice, to seek the devt of psychological services; 2,000 mems; Pres. Dr MITCHEL FLEMING; Hon. Sec. IAN STEWART; publs *The Irish Journal of Psychology, The Irish Psychologist.*

Theosophical Society in Ireland: 31 Pembroke Rd, Dublin 4; tel. (1) 6602517; e-mail theosophy@eircom.net; f. 1919; Pres. Rep. N. CLANCY; Sec. F. O'KELLY DE GALLAGH; publ. *Bulletin* (12 a year).

University Philosophical Society: Graduate Memorial Building, Trinity College, Dublin 2; tel. (85) 1419072; fax (1) 6778996; e-mail president@tcdphil.com; internet www.tcdphil.com; f. 1684, re-founded 1854; 'Major Society' for composition, reading and discussion of papers on literary, political, philosophical and scientific subjects; regular guest speakers; 7,500 mems; Pres. DAIRE HICKEY; Sec. EDWARD GAFFNEY; publs *Laws, Philander* (1 a year).

TECHNOLOGY

Biomedical/Clinical Engineering Association of Ireland: c/o Dept of Biomedical Engineering, Cork University Hospital, Bishopstown Road, Wilton, Cork 24; tel. (21) 49-22-849; internet www.beai.ie; f. 1992; Chair. BERNARD MURPHY; Sec. NOEL MURPHY; publ. *BEAI Spectrum.*

Institution of Civil Engineers (Republic of Ireland Division): 8 Ardglas, Dundrum, Dublin 16; tel. (1) 4114260; f. 1818; c. 550 mems; Chair. DON N. MCENTEE; publs *Muni-*

cipal Engineer (4 a year), *New Civil Engineer* (52 a year).

Institution of Electrical Engineers Ireland Branch: ESB National Grid, Lower Fitzwilliam St, Dublin 2; tel. (1) 7026071; internet local.iee.org/ireland; Chair. KEVIN O'RIORDAN; Hon. Sec. DAVID HEALY.

Institution of Engineers of Ireland: 22 Clyde Rd, Ballsbridge, Dublin 4; tel. (1) 6684341; fax (1) 6685508; e-mail info@engineersireland.ie; internet www.iei.ie; f. 1835; promotes knowledge and advancement of the engineering profession, conducts examinations and confers the designations 'Chartered Engineer', 'Associate Engineer' and 'Engineering Technician'; 21,000 mems; Dir-Gen. KEVIN KERNAN; publs *Academic Reviews, Engineers Journal, Ezine* (electronic), *Papers, Transactions.*

Research Institutes

GENERAL

Science Policy Research Centre: Faculty of Commerce, Univ. College Dublin, Belfield, Dublin 4; tel. (1) 7068263; fax (1) 7061132; f. 1969 to carry out research and to undertake commissioned studies in areas related to technology and innovation policy; small private library; Dir Prof. DENIS J. COGAN.

AGRICULTURE, FISHERIES AND VETERINARY SCIENCE

Teagasc (Agriculture and Food Development Authority): Oak Park, Carlow; tel. (59) 9170200; fax (59) 9182097; e-mail publications@hq.teagasc.ie; internet www.teagasc.ie; f. 1988; national body providing advisory, research, education and training services to the agriculture and food industry; activities are integrated and managed through 6 divisions; Dir JIM FLANAGAN; publ. *Irish Journal of Agricultural and Food Research* (2 a year).

Divisions:

Kildalton College of Agriculture: Piltown, Co Kilkenny; tel. (51) 643105; fax (51) 643797; e-mail mgalvin@kildalton.teagasc.ie; national crops division and headquarters for advisory and training services in Teagasc South; Dir MICHAEL GALVIN.

Kinsealy Research Centre: Malahide Rd, Dublin, 17; tel. (1) 8460644; fax (1) 8460524; e-mail bfarrell@grange.teagasc.ie; national beef division; headquarters for advisory and training services in Teagasc North; Dir DONAL CAREY.

Moorepark Research and Development Division (Teagasc): Fermoy, Co Cork; tel. (25) 42222; fax (25) 42340; national centre for research in dairying and pig production; Head of Dairy Husbandry Dr PATRICK DILLON; Head of Pig Husbandry BRENDAN LYNCH.

National Dairy Products Research Centre: Moorepark, Fermoy, Co Cork; tel. (25) 42222; fax (25) 42340; e-mail ldonnelly@moorepark.teagasc.ie; national centre providing research, development and consultancy services; Dir Dr PATRICK DILLON.

Ashtown Food Research Centre: Ashtown, Dublin 15; tel. (1) 8059500; fax (1) 8059550; e-mail declan.troy@teagasc.ie; internet www.teagasc.ie/ashtown; centre providing research, development and consultancy services for all aspects of food production (except dairy products), food safety and nutrition, and market studies; Head Dr DECLAN TROY.

Rural Development Division (Teagasc): Athenry, Co Galway; tel. (91) 845845; fax (91) 845847; e-mail pseery@ athenry.teagasc.ie; national centre for rural development; Dir PETER SEERY.

BIBLIOGRAPHY, LIBRARY SCIENCE AND MUSEOLOGY

Irish Manuscripts Commission: 45 Merrion Sq., Dublin 2; tel. (1) 6761610; fax (1) 6623832; e-mail support@irishmanuscripts .ie; internet www.irishmanuscripts.ie; f. 1928; publishes primary manuscript sources for Irish history located in public and private archives in Ireland and abroad; 21 mems; Chair. Prof. JAMES MCGUIRE; Administrator Dr CATHY HAYES; publ. *Analecta Hibernica* (irregular).

ECONOMICS, LAW AND POLITICS

Economic and Social Research Institute: Whitaker Sq., Sir John Rogerson's Quay, Dublin 2; tel. (1) 6671525; fax (1) 6686231; e-mail admin@esri.ie; internet www.esri.ie; f. 1960; 130 individual mems, 400 corporate mems; library of 40,000 vols; Dir Prof. FRANCES RUANE; publs *Economic and Social Review* (4 a year), *Medium Term Review* (every 2 years), *Quarterly Economic Commentary*.

HISTORY, GEOGRAPHY AND ARCHAEOLOGY

Office of the Chief Herald of Ireland: 2 Kildare St, Dublin 2; tel. (1) 6030311; fax (1) 6621062; e-mail herald@nli.ie; internet www .nli.ie; f. 1552; granting, confirming and registering of armorial bearings; 1,000 MSS since the 16th century, 100,000 archive items since 1800; Keeper FERGUS GILLESPIE.

LANGUAGE AND LITERATURE

Institiúid Teangeolaíochta Éireann/Linguistics Institute of Ireland: 31 Fitzwilliam Pl., Dublin 2; tel. (1) 6765489; fax (1) 6610004; internet www.ite.ie; f. 1972; research in applied linguistics with special reference to the Irish language and teaching and learning of languages generally; 30 mems; library of 10,000 books, 151 periodicals; Chair. CLÍONA DE BHALDRAITHE MARSH; Dir EOGHAN MAC AOGÁIN; publs *Language, Culture and Curriculum* (3 a year), *Teangeolas* (2 a year).

MEDICINE

Health Research Board: 73 Lower Baggot St, Dublin 2; tel. (1) 2345000; fax (1) 6611856; e-mail hrb@hrb.ie; internet www .hrb.ie; f. 1987; Chief Exec. ENDA CONNOLLY.

NATURAL SCIENCES

Physical Sciences

Dunsink Observatory: School of Cosmic Physics, Castleknock, Dublin 15; tel. (1) 8387911; fax (1) 8387090; e-mail astro@ dunsink.dias.ie; internet www.dunsink.dias .ie; f. 1785; part of Dublin Institute for Advanced Studies; library of 5,000 vols, 75 periodicals; Dir Prof. EVERT MEURS; Sec. CAROL WOODS.

Libraries and Archives

Cork

Cork City Libraries: 57–61 Grand Parade, Cork; tel. (21) 4924900; fax (21) 4275684; e-mail libraries@corkcity.ie; internet www .corkcitylibraries.ie; f. 1892; 465,000 vols, incl. extensive local studies and reference collns in books, newspapers and journals;

large music colln in Rory Gallagher Music Library; City Librarian LIAM RONAYNE.

Cork County Library: Cork County Library and Arts Service, County Library Bldg, Carrigrohane Rd, Cork; tel. (21) 4546499; e-mail corkcountylibrary@corkcoco .ie; internet www.corkcoco.ie/library; 1,080,000 vols, 90 periodicals; 28 brs, 5 mobile libraries; Librarian (vacant).

Cork Institute of Technology Bishopstown Library: Bishopstown Campus, Cork; tel. (21) 4326501; internet library.cit.ie; brs at Crawford College of Art and Design, Cork School of Music and National Maritime College of Ireland; Librarian DERRY DELANEY.

University College Cork Library: The Boole Library, University College Cork, College Rd, Cork; tel. (21) 4902794; fax (21) 4273428; e-mail library@ucc.ie; internet booleweb.ucc.ie; f. 1849; 500,000 vols, including Irish Manuscript collection (microfilm), Senft (philosophy), Torna (Irish), Cooke (travel), John E. Cummings Memorial Collection (humour), Langlands Collection (Africa); Postgraduate Research Library currently under construction; EU documentation centre; Irish copyright privilege; Librarian JOHN FITZGERALD.

Dublin

Central Catholic Library: 74 Merrion Sq., Dublin 2; tel. (1) 6761264; e-mail catholiclibrary@imagine.ie; internet www .catholiclibrary.ie; f. 1922; controlled by the Central Catholic Library Asscn; open to the public; lending and reference depts containing material on every aspect of Catholicism, on other Christian denominations and other religions, Irish history and culture, philosophy; 90,000 vols, incl. large journal colln, spec. colln of 2,000 vols on Christian art, Ireland Colln; Librarian Dr TERESA WHITINGTON; Hon. Librarian PETER COSTELLO.

Chester Beatty Library: Dublin Castle, Dublin 2; tel. (1) 4070750; fax (1) 4070760; e-mail info@cbl.ie; internet www.cbl.ie; f. 1953; donated to the Irish nation by Sir Alfred Chester Beatty in 1968; contains one of the world's leading collns of Islamic and East Asian art, important Western and Biblical MSS and miniatures; incunabula and other printed books; Dir Dr MICHAEL RYAN.

Dublin City Public Libraries: 138–144 Pearse St, Dublin 2; tel. (1) 6744800; fax (1) 6744879; e-mail dublinpubliclibraries@ dublincity.ie; internet www .dublincitypubliclibraries.ie; f. 1884; 2,400,000 vols; spec. collns incl. early Dublin printing and fine binding, incunabula, political pamphlets and cartoons, Dublin periodicals and 18th-century plays, Abbey Theatre material, Swift and Yeats material; extensive local history colln in books, newspapers and pictures; representative holdings of modern Dublin presses; spec. music library; language learning centre; City Librarian DEIRDRE ELLIS-KING.

Irish Theatre Archive: c/o Dublin City Library and Archive, 138–144 Pearse St, Dublin 2; tel. (1) 6744800; fax (1) 6744881; e-mail cityarchives@dublincity.ie; internet www.dublincity.ie; f. 1981 to collect and preserve Ireland's theatre heritage; large colln of material: programmes, posters, play-scripts, prompt-books, etc.; organizes lecture series, exhibitions; Archivist Dr MARY CLARK.

Law Library of Ireland: Four Courts, Dublin 7; tel. (1) 8720622; fax (1) 8720455; internet www.lawlibrary.ie; controlled by the Council of the Bar of Ireland; open to mems of the Irish Bar only; 100,000 vols; Chair., Professional Services Cttee RODERICK MAGUIRE; publ. *The Bar Review*.

Library Council: 53–54 Upper Mount St, Dublin 2; tel. (1) 6761167; fax (1) 6766721; e-mail info@librarycouncil.ie; internet www .librarycouncil.ie; f. 1947 by Public Libraries Act; advises local authorities and the Min. for the Environment, Heritage and Local Govt on the devt of public library services; provides an information service on libraries and librarianship; operates the inter-library lending system for Ireland, and provides the Secretariat for the Cttee on Library Co-operation in Ireland; operates Public Lending Remuneration Office est. by the Copyright and Related Rights (Amendment) Act 2007; Dir NORMA MCDERMOTT; publ. *Irish Library News*.

Marsh's Library: St Patrick's Close, Dublin 8; tel. and fax (1) 4543511; e-mail keeper@ marshlibrary.ie; internet www.marshlibrary .ie; f. 1701; 25,000 vols and 300 MSS; Keeper MURIEL MCCARTHY.

National Archives of Ireland: Bishop St, Dublin 8; tel. (1) 4072300; fax (1) 4072333; e-mail mail@nationalarchives.ie; internet www.nationalarchives.ie; f. 1988 (merger of Public Record Office, f. 1867, and State Paper Office, f. 1702), under the Nat. Archives Act, to preserve and make accessible the records of Depts of State, courts, other public service orgs and private donors; 50,000 linear metres of archives; Dir Dr DAVID CRAIG.

National Library of Ireland: Kildare St, Dublin 2; tel. (1) 6030200; fax (1) 6766690; e-mail info@nli.ie; internet www.nli.ie; f. 1877; more than 8,000,000 vols including Irish printing colln, pamphlets, periodicals, newspapers, 70,000 MSS, including 1,200 Gaelic MSS, 630,000 photographic negatives, 90,000 prints and drawings, ephemera and music; Dir FIONA ROSS; Keeper of Manuscripts and Chief Herald COLETTE O'FLAHERTY; publ. *National Library of Ireland News* (4 a year).

Oireachtas Library and Research Service: Leinster House, Dublin 2; tel. (1) 6184701; fax (1) 6184109; internet www .oireachtas.ie; f. 1922; information and research services to support the work of both Houses of the Oireachtas (Parliament) cttees and individual mems of Parliament; Head of Library and Research Service MADELAINE DENNISON.

Representative Church Body Library: Braemor Park, Churchtown, Dublin 14; tel. (1) 4923979; fax (1) 4924770; e-mail library@ ireland.anglican.org; internet www.ireland .anglican.org; f. 1932; theological library controlled by the Representative Body of the Church of Ireland; 40,000 vols, mainly theology, history, ethics and education; Church of Ireland archives; MSS colln, mainly ecclesiastical; Librarian and Archivist Dr RAYMOND REFAUSSÉ.

Royal College of Surgeons in Ireland Library (The Mercer Library): Mercer St Lower, Dublin 2; tel. (1) 4022407; fax (1) 4022457; e-mail library@rcsi.ie; internet www.rcsi.ie/library; f. 1784; 75,000 vols; spec. collns: archives of RCSI and Dublin hospitals, 10,000 rare books, medical pamphlets from 17th century; Librarian KATE KELLY.

Royal Dublin Society Library (RDS Library): Ballsbridge, Dublin 4; tel. (1) 2407254; fax (1) 6604014; e-mail librarydesk@rds.ie; internet www.rds.ie/ library; f. 1731; 100,000 vols, including more than 4,000 relating to Ireland, many of them old and rare; 6,000 works and pamphlets on all branches of agricultural science up to 1920, including 1,500 works of equestrian interest; reference collection of more than 2,000 vols, including the 'Thoms Street' directory on Dublin, since the 1840s; the scientific and private correspondence of Professor George Francis Fitzgerald (1851–1901, physicist at Trinity College, Dublin, who first suggested a method of producing radio waves) of which there are more than 1,000 letters; Irish local history colln and genealogical information; Dublin horse show archives, incl. the Maymes Ansell archive of equestrian photographs, archival colln incl. the written and visual heritage of the Society manuscript material from 1731, rare first edns of science publs, the papers of Dr Horace H. Poole, Richard M. Barrington and John Edmund Carew; the records of the Radium Institute and the Maymes Ansell Archive of Equestrian Photographs; 100,000 vols, incl. more than 4,000 relating to Ireland; Dir of Library JOANNA QUINN; Librarian GERARD WHELAN.

Trinity College Library: College St, Dublin 2; tel. (1) 8961665; fax (1) 8963774; internet www.tcd.ie/library; f. 1592; Univ. and British/Irish legal deposit library; 4,500,000 printed vols, 6,000 MSS, incl. the Book of Kells and other medieval MSS; collns of 17th- and 18th-century French printed materials and caricatures; extensive colln of music scores and maps; visitor centre; Librarian and College Archivist ROBIN ADAMS; publ. *Long Room* (1 a year).

University College Dublin Library: Belfield, Dublin 4; tel. (1) 7167067; fax (1) 2837667; e-mail library@ucd.ie; internet www.ucd.ie/library; f. 1908; 1,200,000 vols, 8,000 periodicals; spec. collns incl. pre-1850 imprints, Baron Palles (Law) Library of 2,500 vols, Zimmer (Celtic) Library of 2,000 vols, C. P. Curran (Irish literature), John McCormack (music), Colm Ó Lochlainn (Irish printing), F. J. O'Kelley (Irish printing) and John L. Sweeney (Literature) collns; MSS colln; literary archives and papers incl. those of Sean O'Riordain, Patrick Kavanagh, Mary Lavin, Maeve Binchy and Frank McGuinness; Univ. Librarian Dr JOHN BROOKS HOWARD.

Galway

Galway City Library: St Augustine St, Galway; tel. (91) 561666; fax (91) 565039; e-mail info@galwaylibrary.ie; internet www.galwaylibrary.ie; Librarian PAT MCMAHON.

Galway County Libraries: Island House, Cathedral Square, Galway; tel. (91) 562471; fax (91) 565039; e-mail info@galwaylibrary.ie; internet www.galwaylibrary.ie; f. 1927; 350,000 vols; County Librarian PATRICK MCMAHON.

National University of Ireland, Galway, James Hardiman Library: National University of Ireland, Galway; tel. (91) 524411; fax (91) 522394; e-mail info@nuigalway.ie; internet www.library.nuigalway.ie; f. 1849; 257,000 vols; extensive collection of books in Irish published since 1890; EEC Documentation Centre; enjoys Irish copyright privilege; Librarian MARIE REDDAN.

Limerick

Limerick City Library: City Hall, Merchants Quay, Limerick; tel. (61) 407510; fax (61) 415266; e-mail citylib@limerickcity.ie; internet www.limerickcity.ie/services/library; 3 br. libraries; Librarian DOLORES DOYLE.

Limerick County Library: 58 O'Connell St, Limerick; tel. (61) 496526; fax (61) 318570; e-mail libinfo@limerickcoco.ie; internet www.lcc.ie/library; 5 brs and 19 part-time brs; Librarian DAMIEN BRADY.

Maynooth

John Paul II Library, National University of Ireland, Maynooth: Maynooth, Co Kildare; tel. (1) 7083884; fax (1) 6286008;

e-mail library.information@nuim.ie; internet www.library.nuim.ie; f. 1795; 442,500 vols, 26,000 full-text electronic journals 50,000 eBooks; Librarian CATHAL MCCAULEY.

Waterford

Waterford City Council Central Library: Lady Lane, Waterford; tel. (51) 849975; e-mail library@waterfordcity.ie; internet www.waterfordcity.ie/library; 3 brs; audio-listening and language-learning facilities; Librarian JANE CANTWELL.

Waterford County Library Headquarters: Lismore, Co Waterford; tel. (58) 21370; e-mail libraryhq@waterfordcoco.ie; internet www.waterfordcountylibrary.ie; 8 brs; County Librarian DONALD BRADY.

Museums and Art Galleries

Cork

Cork Public Museum: Fitzgerald Park, Cork; tel. (21) 4270679; fax (21) 4270931; e-mail museum@corkcity.ie; f. 1910; sections devoted to Irish history and archaeology, also municipal, social and economic history, Cork glass, silver and lace; items of special interest include the Cork helmet horns, the Garryduff gold bird, the Roche silver collar, civic maces, municipal oar, freedom boxes and Grace Cup of Cork Corporation; Curator STELLA CHERRY.

Dublin

Civic Museum: 58 South William St, Dublin; tel. (1) 6794260; f. 1953; attached to Dublin Public Libraries; original exhibits of antiquarian and historical interest pertaining to Dublin; subjects in the permanent colln incl. streets and buildings of Dublin, traders, industry, transport, political history, maps; Curator THOMAS P. O'CONNOR.

Dublin City Gallery The Hugh Lane: Charlemont House, Parnell Sq. North, Dublin 1; tel. (1) 2225550; fax (1) 8722182; e-mail info.hughlane@dublincity.ie; internet www.hughlane.ie; f. 1908; works of Irish, English and European schools of painting, and pictures from the Sir Hugh Lane colln; sculptures; Dir BARBARA DAWSON.

Dublin Writers Museum: 18 Parnell Sq., Dublin 1; tel. (1) 8722077; fax (1) 8722231; e-mail writers@dublintourism.ie; internet www.writersmuseum.com; f. 1991; history of Irish literature; library; Operations Man. MARIA O'CALLAGHAN; Curator ROBERT NICHOLSON.

Irish Museum of Modern Art: Royal Hospital, Military Rd, Kilmainham, Dublin 8; tel. (1) 6129900; fax (1) 6129999; e-mail info@modernart.ie; internet www.modernart.ie; f. 1991; works by Irish and non-Irish artists since the beginning of the 20th century; Dir PHILOMENA BYRNE (acting).

James Joyce Museum: Martello Tower, Sandycove, Co Dublin; tel. and fax (1) 2809265; e-mail joycetower@dublintourism.ie; f. 1962; papers and personal effects of the writer (1882–1941) and critical works about him; library of 550 vols; Curator ROBERT NICHOLSON.

National Botanic Gardens Glasnevin: Glasnevin, Dublin 9; tel. (1) 8377596; fax (1) 8360080; e-mail botanicgardens@opw.ie; internet www.botanicgardens.ie; f. 1795; includes Irish National Herbarium; visitor centre combines a lecture hall, restaurant and display area with exhibits relating to the history and purpose of the gardens; library of 40,000 vols, including colln of illustrated botanical works; Dir DONAL SYNNOTT; publ.

Glasra–Contributions from the National Botanic Gardens, Glasnevin (1 a year).

National Gallery of Ireland: Merrion Sq. W, Dublin 2; tel. (1) 6615133; fax (1) 6615372; e-mail info@ngi.ie; internet www.nationalgallery.ie; f. 1854; nat., historical and portrait galleries; continental European, British and Irish masters since 1250; 2,500 oil paintings, 300 sculptures, 5,200 drawings and watercolours, 3,000 prints; library of 70,000 vols; research services incorporate the Fine Art Library, NGI Archive, Centre for the Study of Irish Art and the Yeats Archive; Dir RAYMOND KEAVENEY.

National Museum of Ireland: Kildare St, Dublin 7; tel. (1) 6777444; fax (1) 6777450; e-mail marketing@museum.ie; internet www.museum.ie; f. 1877 by the Science and Arts Museums Act; incl. (1) Irish Antiquities Div. (Keeper EAMONN P. KELLY); (2) Art and Industrial Div. (Keeper MICHAEL KENNY); (3) Irish Folklife Div. (Keeper TONY CANDON); (4) Natural History Div., which incl. zoological and geological sections (Keeper NIGEL MONAGHAN); Dir Dr PATRICK F. WALLACE.

Royal College of Surgeons in Ireland Museum: St Stephen's Green, Dublin 2; f. 1820; Asst Curator Prof. DOROTHY BENSON.

Strokestown

Strokestown Park House Garden and Famine Museum: Strokestown Park, Strokestown, Co Roscommon; tel. (78) 9633013; fax (78) 9633712; e-mail info@strokestownpark.ie; internet www.strokestownpark.ie/museum.html; f. 1994; collns related to the history of the Great Irish Famine of the 1840s; Man. JOHN O'DRISCOLL.

Universities

DUBLIN CITY UNIVERSITY

Dublin 9
Telephone: (1) 7005000
Fax: (1) 8360830
E-mail: registry@dcu.ie
Internet: www.dcu.ie

Founded 1980 as National Institute for Higher Education, Dublin; University status 1989
State control
Academic year: September to May
Pres.: Prof. FERDINAND VON PRONDZYNSKI
Vice-Pres. for Learning Innovation: MARIA SLOWEY
Vice-Pres. for Research: DERMOT DIAMOND
Registrar: KEVIN GRIFFIN
Sec.: MARTIN CONRY
Librarian: PAUL SHEEHAN
Number of teachers: 264
Number of students: 10,000
Publication: *NewsLink* (3 a year)

DEANS

Faculty of Engineering and Computing: Prof. CHARLES MCCORKELL
Faculty of Humanities and Social Sciences: Prof. EITHNE GUILFOYLE
Faculty of Science and Health: Prof. MALCOLM SMYTH
Joint Faculty of Education: PÁID MAGEE
Joint Faculty of Humanities: Prof. MICHAEL CRONIN

Dublin City University Business School:
Prof. BERNARD PIERCE
Oscail–National Distance Education Centre:
Dr RONNIE SAUNDERS

HEADS OF SCHOOLS

Faculty of Engineering and Computing:
Computing: Prof. MICHAEL RYAN
Electronic Engineering: Prof. MICHAEL
MCCORKELL
Mechanical and Manufacturing Engineer-
ing: Prof. SALEEM HASHMI
Faculty of Humanities and Social Sciences:
Applied Language and Intercultural Stud-
ies: Prof. JENNY WILLIAMS
Communications: BRIAN TRENCH
Education Studies: Dr GERARD MCNAMARA
Fiontar (Business Studies, taught in
Gaelic): Dr CAOILFHIONN NIC PHÁIDÍN
Law and Government: Prof. ROBERT ELGIE
Faculty of Science and Health:
Biotechnology: Prof. IAN W. MARISON
Chemical Sciences: Prof. HAN VOS
Health and Human Performance: Dr NIALL
MOYNA
Mathematical Sciences: Prof. JOHN CAR-
ROLL
Nursing: Prof. ANNE SCOTT
Physical Sciences: Prof. JOHN COSTELLO

ATTACHED INSTITUTE

National Distance Education Centre:
Dublin 9; a faculty of the universityf. 1982;
the executive arm of the Nat. Distance
Education Ccl; Dir Dr DENIS BANCROFT.

ATTACHED COLLEGES

Mater Dei Institute of Education: Clon-
liffe Ave, Dublin 3; tel. (1) 8376027; fax (1)
8370776; e-mail info@materdei.dcu.ie;
internet www.materdei.ie; f. 1966; College
of the University since 1999; courses in Irish
Studies and Theology; 50 teachers; 545 students; library of 160,000 vols; Pres. Rev. Dr
MICHAEL DRUMM; Registrar Rev. Dr EOIN G.
CASSIDY; publ. *Religion, Education and the
Arts* (1 a year).

St Patrick's College: Drumcondra, Dublin
9; tel. (1) 8842000; fax (1) 8376197; e-mail
presidents.office@spd.dcu.ie; internet www
.spd.dcu.ie; f. 1875; College of the University
since 1993; academic depts participate in the
Joint Faculties of Education and Humanities; 58 teachers; 2,000 students; library of
100,000 vols; Pres. Dr PÁURIC TRAVERS;
Registrar Dr LIAM MAC MATHÚNA; publ.
Studia Hibernica (1 a year), *The Irish Journal of Education* (2 a year).

NATIONAL UNIVERSITY OF IRELAND

49 Merrion Sq., Dublin 2
Telephone: (1) 4392424
Fax: (1) 4392466
E-mail: registrar@nui.ie
Internet: www.nui.ie
Founded 1908
Chancellor: Dr GARRET FITZGERALD
Vice-Chancellor: Prof. JOHN G. HUGHES
Registrar: Dr ATTRACTA HALPIN
Publications: *Calendar* (1 a year), *Éigse: A
Journal of Irish Studies* (irregular).

CONSTITUENT COLLEGES

University College Cork

Western Rd, Cork
Telephone: (21) 4903000
Fax: (21) 4273428
E-mail: registrar@ucc.ie
Internet: www.ucc.ie

Founded 1845 as Queen's College, Cork;
changed to above in 1908
Academic year: October to September
Pres.: Prof. G. T. WRIXON
Vice-Pres.: Prof. AINE HYLAND (Research,
Policy and Support)
Vice-Pres. for Academic Affairs and Regis-
trar: Prof. PAUL GILLER
Vice-Pres. for Finance and Admin., and Sec.
and Bursar: MICHAEL F. KELLEHER
Vice-Pres. for Planning, Communications
and Devt: MICHAEL O'SULLIVAN
Vice-Pres. Research, Policy and Support:
Prof. J. KEVIN COLLINS
Librarian: JOHN A. FITZGERALD
Number of teachers: 2,280 (539 full-time,
1,741 part-time)
Number of students: 15,556 full-time (12,622
undergraduate, 2,923 postgraduate)
Publication: *Chimera* (1 a year)

DEANS

Faculty of Arts and Celtic Studies: Prof.
DAVID H. COX
Faculty of Commerce: Prof. DENIS I. F. LUCEY
Faculty of Engineering: Dr RICHARD KAVA-
NAGH (acting)
Faculty of Food Science and Technology:
Prof. YRJO H. ROOS
Faculty of Law: Prof. CAROLINE FENNELL
Faculty of Medicine and Health: Prof.
MICHAEL MURPHY
Faculty of Science: Prof. PATRICK FITZPATRICK

PROFESSORS
(Some professors also have responsibilities in
other faculties)

Faculties of Arts and Celtic Studies (tel. (21)
4902773; fax (21) 4903364; e-mail
artsfaculty@arts.ucc.ie):
CLARKE, D., Philosophy
COX, D. H., Music
HOWARD, M. P., German
HYLAND, A., Education
KEARNEY, C. J., Modern English
KEOGH, D. F., Modern History (European
Integration Studies)
LEE, J. J., Modern History
MACKENZIE, D., Hispanic Studies
Ó CARRAGÁIN, E., Old and Middle English
Ó COILEÁIN, S., Modern Irish Language
O'CORRAIN, D., History
Ó DONOVAN, P. T., French
Ó RIAIN, P. S., Early Irish Language and
Literature
POWELL, F. W., Applied Social Studies
SACCONE, E., Italian
SCAKOLCZAI, A. I., Sociology
SMYTH, W. J., Geography
TAYLOR, M., Applied Psychology
WOODMAN, P. C., Archaeology

Faculty of Commerce (tel. (21) 4902136; fax
(21) 4903251; e-mail commerce@ucc.ie):
CAHILL, E. P., Accounting and Finance
COLLINS, N., Government
FANNING, C. M., Economics
GREEN, S., Management and Marketing
MURPHY, C. M., Business Information Sys-
tems

Faculty of Engineering (tel. (21) 4903081; fax
(21) 4276648; e-mail engfac@ucc.ie):
CAMPBELL, J.
CREAN, G.
KENNEDY, P.
KIELY, G.
MURPHY, P.
O'KANE, J. P. J., Civil Engineering
OLIVEIRA, F. A., Process Engineering

Faculty of Food Science and Technology (tel.
(21) 4902007; fax (21) 4276389; e-mail
fcoyne@foodscience.ucc.ie):
CASHMAN, K. D., Food Science and Technology

CONDON, J. J., Microbiology
DALY, C., Food Technology
LUCEY, D. I. F., Food Economics
MORRIS, E. R., Food Chemistry
MORRISSEY, P. A., Nutrition
ROSS, Y. H., Food Science and Technology

Faculty of Law (Aras Na Laois, Cork; tel. (21)
4903249; fax (21) 4903413; e-mail lawfac@ucc
.ie):
CARROLL, B. A., Law
MORGAN, D. G., Law

Faculty of Medicine and Health (3 Elder-
wood, College Rd, Cork; tel. (21) 4902455; fax
(21) 4270339; e-mail medfac@ucc.ie):
BRADLEY, C. P., General
DALY, R. J., Psychiatry
FRAHER, J. P., Anatomy
HALL, W. J., Physiology
HIGGINS, J. R., Obstetrics and Gynaecology
KEARNEY, P. J., Paediatrics
MCCARTHY, G., Nursing Studies
MCCONNELL, R. J., Restorative Dentistry
MURPHY, M. B., Clinical Pharmacology
O'MULLANE, D. M., Preventive and Paedia-
tric Dentistry
PARFREY, N., Pathology
PERRY, I. J., Epidemiology and Public
Health
QUIGLEY, E. M., Medicine
REDMOND, H. P., Surgery
SHANAHAN, F. L. J., Medicine
SHORTEN, N., Surgery
SLEEMAN, D., Dental Surgery

Faculty of Science (tel. (21) 4902299; fax (21)
4270380; e-mail sciencefaculty@ucc.ie):
BOWEN, J. A., Software Engineering
BRÜCK, P. M., Geology
CASSELLS, A. C., Plant Science
CONDON, J. J., Microbiology
COTTER, T. G., Biochemistry
DAVENPORT, J., Zoology and Animal Ecol-
ogy
GUILBAULT, G. G., Analytical Chemistry
JENNINGS, W. B., Organic Chemistry
MCINERNEY, J. G., Physics
MORAN, M. A., Applied Statistics
MORTELL, M. P., Applied Mathematics
O'REILLY, E., Physics
O'SULLIVAN, F., Statistics
PAWLTAN, Y., Statistics
SODEAU, J., Physical Chemistry
SPALDING, T. R., Inorganic Chemistry
SREENAN, C. J., Computer Science

University College Dublin

Belfield, Dublin 4
Telephone: (1) 7160000
Fax: (1) 7161160
E-mail: communications@ucd.ie
Internet: www.ucd.ie
Languages of instruction: English, Irish
Founded 1908
Academic year: September to May
Pres.: Dr HUGH BRADY
Registrar, Deputy Pres. and Vice-Pres.: Dr
PHILIP NOLAN
Vice-Pres. for Research: Prof. DESMOND FITZ-
GERALD
Vice-Pres. for Staff and Administrative Sys-
tems: Mr EAMON DREA
Vice-Pres. for Students: Dr MARTIN BUTLER
Vice-Pres. for Univ. Relations: Dr PADRAIC
CONWAY
Librarian: SEAN PHILLIPS
Library: see Libraries and Archives
Number of teachers: 2,531 (837 full-time,
1,694 part-time)
Number of students: 22,000
Publication: *Irish University Review* (2 a
year)

DEANS

Arts and Celtic Studies, Principal of College: Prof. MARY E. DALY
Business and Law, Principal of College: Mr PAUL HARAN
Engineering, Mathematical and Physical Sciences, Principal of College: Prof. NICK QUIRKE
Human Sciences, Principal of College: Prof. BRIGID LAFFAN
Life Sciences, Principal of College: Prof. BRIAN M. MCKENNA

PROFESSORS

(Many professors are members of more than one faculty; entry here is shown under one faculty only)

College of Arts and Celtic Studies (Newman Bldg, Belfield, Dublin 4; tel. (1) 7168101; e-mail artsceltic@ucd.ie):

BARNES, J. C., Italian
BARTLETT, T., Modern Irish History
BREATNACH, P. A., Classical Irish
CALDICOTT, C. E. J., French
CLAYTON, M., Old and Middle English
CRUICKSHANK, D. W., Spanish
FANNING, J. R., Modern History
KIBERD, D., Anglo-Irish Literature and Drama
MCCARTHY, M. J., History of Art
MAYS, J. C. C., Modern English and American Literature
MEIKLE, J. L., American Studies
NÍ CATHÁIN, M. P., Early (incl. Medieval) Irish Language and Literature
Ó CATHÁIN, S., Irish Folklore
RAFTERY, B., Celtic Archaeology
RIDLEY, H. M., German
SMITH, A., Classics
WATSON, S., Modern Irish Language and Literature
WHITE, H., Music

College of Business and Law (Carysfort Ave, Blackrock, Dublin 4; tel. (1) 7168852; fax (1) 7168954):

BOURKE, P., Banking and Finance
BRADLEY, M. F., International Marketing
BRENNAN, N., Management
CASEY, J. P., Law
DEEGAN, A., Management Information Systems
HOURIHAN, A. P., Management of Financial Institutions
KELLY, W. A., Business Administration
LAMBKIN, M. V., Marketing
O'BRIEN, F. J., Accountancy
OSBOROUGH, W. N., Jurisprudence and Legal History
ROCHE, W. K., Industrial Relations and Human Resources
WALSH, E., Accounting

College of Engineering, Mathematical and Physical Sciences (UCD Engineering and Materials Science Centre, Belfield, Dublin 4; tel. (1) 7161864; fax (1) 7161155; e-mail engscience@ucd.ie):

BOLAND, P.
BRAZIL, T.
BYRNE, G., Mechanical Engineering
DINEEN, S.
GARDINER, S. J.
GRUNEWALD, M.
IVANKOVIC, A.
KEALY, L., Architecture
LYNCH, P.
MACELROY, J. M. D.
O'BRIEN, E. J., Civil Engineering
OTTEWILL, A.
SHANNON, P. M.
SMYTH, B.

College of Human Sciences (Newman Bldg (Room G210), Belfield, Dublin 4; tel. (1) 7168619; fax (1) 7168355; e-mail mary.buckley@ucd.ie):

BENSON, C., Psychology
BOLAND, P. J., Statistics
BURKE, M., Library and Information Studies
BUTTIMER, A., Geography
DINEEN, S., Mathematics
DRUDY, S., Education
GARVIN, T. C., Politics
LAFFAN, B., European Politics
LAFFEY, T. J., Mathematics
MENNELL, S., Sociology
MORAN, D., Philosophy
NEARY, J. P., Political Economy
OUHALLA, J., Linguistics
WALSH, B. M., National Economics of Ireland and Applied Economics

College of Life Sciences (Belfield, Dublin 4; tel. (1) 7162684; fax (1) 7162685; e-mail life-sciences@ucd.ie):

BAIRD, A., Veterinary Physiology and Biochemistry
BANNIGAN, J. G., Anatomy
BELLENGER, C. R., Veterinary Surgery
BOLAND, M. P., Animal Husbandry
BRADY, H. R., Medicine and Therapeutics
BRESNIHAN, B., Rheumatology
BURY, G., General Practice
CARRINGTON, S., Veterinary Anatomy
CASEY, P. R., Clinical Psychiatry
COLLINS, J. D., Farm Animal Clinical Studies
CURRY, J., Agricultural Zoology
CUSACK, D. A., Legal Medicine
DAWSON, K. A., Physical Chemistry
DERVAN, P. A., Pathology
DRUMM, B., Paediatrics
DUKE, E., Zoology
ENGEL, P. C., Biochemistry
ENNIS, J. T., Radiology
FITZGERALD, M. X., Medicine
FITZPATRICK, C., Child and Adolescent Psychiatry
FITZPATRICK, J. M., Surgery
GARDINER, J. J., Forestry
GREEN, A., Medical Genetics
HALL, W. W., Medical Microbiology
HEGARTY, A. F., Organic Chemistry
HENNERTY, M. J., Horticulture
JONES, B. R., Small Animal Clinical Studies
KEANE, M., Computer Science
KENNEDY, M. J., Geology
MACERLEAN, D. P., Radiology
MCKENNA, B., Food Science
MCKENNA, T. J., Investigative Endocrinology
MCNICHOLAS, F., Child and Adolescent Psychiatry
MORIARTY, D. C., Anaesthesiology
O'BRIEN, C., Ophthalmology
O'CALLAGHAN, E., Mental Health Research
O'HERLIHY, C., Obstetrics and Gynaecology
O'HIGGINS, N. J., Surgery
POWELL, D., Investigative Endocrinology
QUINN, P. J., Veterinary Microbiology and Parasitology
ROCHE, J. F., Animal Husbandry and Production
RYAN, M. P., Pharmacology
SHEAHAN, B., Veterinary Pathology
STEER, M., Botany
TREACY, M. M., Nursing
WALSH, E., Crop Science

ATTACHED SCHOOL

Michael Smurfit Graduate School of Business: Dean Dr DAMIEN MCLOUGHLIN.

National University of Ireland, Galway
Galway
Telephone: (91) 524411
Fax: (91) 525700
Internet: www.nuigalway.ie

Founded 1845 as Queen's College, Galway; became University College, Galway in 1908; present name 1997
Languages of instruction: English, Irish
Academic year: September to June
Pres.: Dr I. Ó MUIRCHEARTAIGH
Deputy Pres.: Prof. J. BROWNE
Vice-Pres.: Prof. G. HURLEY
Vice-Pres.: MARY O'RIORDAN
Vice-Pres.: Prof. J. J. WARD
Sec. for Academic Affairs: Dr S. MAC MATHÚNA
Bursar: Dr MARY DOOLEY
Library: see Libraries and Archives
Number of teachers: 550
Number of students: 15,000

DEANS

Faculty of Arts: Prof. J. MARSHALL
Faculty of Celtic Studies: Dr M. NÍ DHONNCHADHA
Faculty of Commerce: Prof. R. GREEN
Faculty of Engineering: Prof. P. O'DONOGHUE
Faculty of Law: G. QUINN
Faculty of Medicine: Dr P. A. CARNEY
Faculty of Science: Dr P. MORGAN

PROFESSORS

Faculties of Arts and Celtic Studies:

BARRY, K., English
BRADLEY, D., Spanish
CANNY, N. P., History
CURTIN, C. A., Political Science and Sociology
ERSKINE, A. W., Classics
JAMES, J., Psychology
MAC CRAITH, M., Modern Irish
NÍ DHONNCHADHA, M., Old and Middle Irish and Celtic Philology
O'BRIEN, C., Italian
Ó GORMAILE, P., French
RICHARDSON, W., German
SCHMIDT-HANISSA, H., German
STROHMAYER, U., Geography
WADDELL, J., Archaeology
WORNER, M. H., Philosophy

Faculty of Commerce:

COLLINS, J. F., Accountancy and Finance
CUDDY, M. P., Economics
GREEN, R. H., Management
WARD, J. J., Marketing

Faculty of Engineering:

CUNNANE, C., Hydrology
LYONS, G. J., Information Technology
MCNAMARA, J. F., Mechanical Engineering
O'DONOGHUE, P. E., Civil Engineering
WILCOX, D., Electronic Engineering

Faculty of Law:

O'MALLEY, W. A., Business Law
QUINN, G., Law
SCHABAS, W., Human Rights Law

Faculty of Medicine:

CALLAGY, G., Pathology
CORMICAN, M., Bacteriology
DOCKERY, P., Anatomy
KERIN, M., Surgery
LOFTUS, B. G., Paediatrics
MCCARTHY, P. A., Radiology
MCDONAGH, C., Psychiatry
MORRISON, J., Obstetrics and Gynaecology
MURPHY, A., General Practice
O'BRIEN, T., Medicine

Faculty of Science:

BUTLER, R., Chemistry
COLLERAN, E., Microbiology
GUIRY, M. D. R., Botany
HINDE, J. P., Statistics
HURLEY, T. C., Mathematics
KANE, M. T., Physiology
LOWNES, N., Biochemistry
RICHARDSON, W., Spanish
RYAN, P. A., Geology

SMITH, T. J., Biomedical Engineering and Science
WALTON, P. W., Applied Physics

National University of Ireland Maynooth

Maynooth, Co Kildare
Telephone: (1) 7086000
E-mail: admissions@nuim.ie
Internet: www.nuim.ie

Founded 1795 as St Patrick's College, Maynooth, which divided in 1997 into National University of Ireland, Maynooth, and a continuing St Patrick's College, Maynooth
State control
Languages of instruction: Irish, English
Academic year: September to June
Pres.: Prof. JOHN G. HUGHES
Vice-Pres. for Innovation: Dr JAMES A. WALSH
Registrar: DAVID REDMOND
Librarian: CATHAL MCCAULEY

Library: see Libraries and Archives
Number of teachers: 256
Number of students: 7,300

Publications: *Presidents Report, ReSearch Magazine, The Bridge Alumni Magazine*

DEANS

Faculty of Arts, Celtic Studies and Philosophy: Dr PETER DENMAN
Faculty of Science and Engineering: Prof. BERNARD P. MAHON
Faculty of Social Sciences: Dr ROBERT GALAVAN.

RECOGNIZED COLLEGES OF THE UNIVERSITY

Institute of Public Administration: 57–61 Lansdowne Rd, Ballsbridge, Dublin 4; tel. (1) 2403600; fax (1) 6689135; e-mail information@ipa.ie; internet www.ipa.ie; 1,500 individual mems; library of 40,000 vols, 300 periodicals; 1,400 students; Dir-Gen. JOHN CULLEN; publ. *Administration* (4 a year), *Administration Yearbook & Diary* (1 a year), *Personnel & Industrial Relations Directory* (every two years).

Milltown Institute of Theology and Philosophy: Milltown Park, Ranelagh, Dublin 6; tel. (1) 2698388; fax (1) 2692528; e-mail info@milltown-institute.ie; internet www.milltown-institute.ie; Pres. Dr BRIAN GROGAN.

National College of Art and Design: 100 Thomas St, Dublin 8; tel. (1) 6364200; fax (1) 6364207; e-mail fios@ncad.ie; internet www.ncad.ie; f. 1746; faculties of design, education, fine art, and history of art and design and complementary studies; 75 teachers; 750 students; Dir COLM O BRIAIN.

HEADS OF FACULTIES

Design: Prof. ANGELA WOODS
Education: Prof. GARY GRANVILLE
Fine Art: Prof. BRIAN MAGUIRE
History of Art and Design and Complementary Studies: Prof. JOHN TURPIN

Royal College of Surgeons in Ireland: 123 St Stephens Green, Dublin 2; tel. (1) 4022100; e-mail info@rcsi.ie; internet www.rcsi.ie; f. 1784; faculties of dentistry, nursing, radiologists, sports science and exercise medicine; college of anaesthetists; 125 teachers; 900 students; Chief Exec. and Registrar MICHAEL HORGAN; publ. *Journal* (4 a year)

DEANS OF POSTGRADUATE FACULTIES

Faculty of Dentistry: SEAN SHERIDAN
Faculty of Nursing: Prof. SEAMUS COWMAN (Head)

Faculty of Radiologists: Dr ÉAMANN BREATNACH
Faculty of Sports Science and Exercise Medicine: Dr MICHAEL G. MOLLOY
College of Anaesthetists: Prof. HOWARD FEE (Pres.)

PROFESSORS

BOUCHIER-HAYES, D., Surgery
CAHILL, K. M., Tropical Medicine
COLLINS, P. B., Biochemistry
COLLUM, L., Ophthalmology
CUNNINGHAM, A., Anaesthesia
DINAN, T., Psychiatry
DOHERTY, J., Physiology
GILL, D. G., Paediatrics
GRAHAM, I., Epidemiology and Preventive Medicine
HARBISON, J., Forensic Medicine and Toxicology
HARRISON, R., Obstetrics and Gynaecology
HUMPHRIES, H., Microbiology
LEADER, M., Pathology
LYONS, J. B., History of Medicine
MCELVANEY, N., Medicine
MCGEE, H., Psychology
MONKHOUSE, S., Anatomy
NOLAN, K., Chemistry
O'BOYLE, C., Psychology
SHANNON, W., General Practice
WADDINGTON, J., Clinical Neuroscience
WALSH, M., Otolaryngology

St Angela's College of Education: Lough Gill, Sligo; tel. (71) 9143580; fax (71) 9144585; e-mail mcapilitan@stacs.edu.ie; internet college.stangelas.ie; undergraduate courses in education, home economics and nursing; Pres. Dr ANNE TAHENY.

Shannon College of Hotel Management: Shannon International Airport, Shannon, Co Limerick; tel. (61) 712210; fax (61) 475160; internet www.shannoncollege.com; Dir PHILLIP SMYTH.

TRINITY COLLEGE DUBLIN, THE UNIVERSITY OF DUBLIN

College Green, Dublin 2
Telephone: (1) 8961000
Internet: www.tcd.ie

Founded 1592
Academic year: July to August
Chancellor: MARY TERESE WINIFRED ROBINSON,
Pro-Chancellor: Sir ANTHONY O'REILLY
Pro-Chancellor: T. D. SPEARMAN
Pro-Chancellor: VINCENT JOHN SCATTERGOOD
Provost: J. HEGARTY
Vice-Provost: PATRICK JOHN PRENDERGAST
Registrar: JÜRGEN BARKHOFF
Sec.: (vacant): A. FITZGERALD
Librarian: D. R. H. ADAMS

Library: see Libraries and Archives
Number of teachers: 809
Number of students: 15,428 (incl. postgraduate)

Publication: *Hermathena*

DEANS

Faculty of Arts, Humanities and Social Sciences): MICHAEL ANTHONY MARSH
Faculty of Engineering, Mathematics and Science: DAVID CLIVE WILLIAMS
Faculty of Health Sciences: COLM ANTOINE O'MORÁIN
Graduate Studies: CAROL ANN O'SULLIVAN
Research: DAVID GEORGE LLOYD

PROFESSORS

AHMAD, K., Computer Science
ANWYL, R., Neurophysiology
BACIK, I., Criminal Law, Criminology and Penology

BARNES, L., Dermatology
BARRY, F., International Business and Development
BARRY, J., Population Health Medicine
BEGLEY, C., Nursing and Midwifery
BERGIN, C., Infectious Diseases
BINCHY, W., Laws
BLAU, W., Physics of Advanced Materials
BOLAND, J., Chemistry Research
BRADLEY, D., Population Genetics
CAFFREY, M., Membrane Structural and Functional Biology
CAMPBELL, N., Phonetics and Speech Sciences
CASSIDY, L., Ophthalmology
CHAHOUD, A., Latin
CLAFFEY, N., Periodontology
COAKLEY, D., Medical Gerontology
COEY, J., Natural and Experimental Philosophy
COFFEY, U. C., Electrical Engineering
COLEMAN, D., Oral and Applied Microbiology
CONLON, K., Surgery
CUNNINGHAM, E., Animal Genetics
DASILVA, L, Telecommunications
DORMAN, C., Microbiology
DRURY, L., Astronomy
DYER, M., Construction Innovation
FALLON, P., Translational Immunology
FEARSON, P., Psychiatry
FITZGERALD, M., Child and Adolescent Psychiatry
FITZPATRICK, D., Modern History
FITZPATRICK, J., Mechanical Engineering
FLINT, S., Oral Medicine
FOSTER, T., Molecular Microbiology
FRODL, T., Integrated Neuroimaging
GALLAGHER, M., Comparative Politics
GILL, M., Psychiatry
GILLIGAN, R., Social Work and Social Policy
GRAHAM, I., Cardiovascular Medicine
GRATTON, J., French
GREENE, S., Childhood Research
GRENE, N., English Literature
GRENFELL, M., Education
GRIMSON, J., Health Informatics
GUNNLAUGSSON, T., Chemistry
HARDIMAN, O., Neurology
HARRISON, W., Computer Science
HASLETT, J., Statistics
HEGNER, M., Physics
HENNESSY, M., Computer Science
HINTON, J., Microbial Pathogenises
HOGAN, L., Ecumenics
HOLLYWOOD, D., Clinical Oncology
HORNE, J., Modern European History
HUMPHRIES, P., Medical Molecular Genetics
JONES, M., Botany
KEARNEY, C., International Business
KELLEHER, D., Medicine
KELLY, J., Chemistry
KENNEDY, H., Forensic Psychiatry
KENNY, R., Geriatric Medicine
KRAMER, A., European History
LANE, S., Respiratory Medicine
LANE, S., Physiology
LAWLOR, B., Old Age Psychiatry
LUCEY, J., Psychiatry
LYNCH, M., Cellular Neuroscience
MARSH, M., Comparative Political Behaviour
MARTIN, S., Medical Genetics
MCCANN, S., Haematology
MCCONNELL, D., Genetics
MCGILP, J., Surface and Interface Optics
MCGING, B., Greek
MCLOUGHAN, D., Psychiatry
MCMANUS, P., Early Irish
MEAMY, J., Radiology
MILLS, K., Experimental Immunology
MURPHY, D., Obstetrics
MURRAY, J., Business Studies
NORMAND, C., Health Policy and Management
NUNN, J., Special Care Dentistry
O'BYRNE, K., Oncology
O'CONNELL, B., Restorative Dentistry
O'CONNOR, H., Gastroenterology

O'DOWD, T., General Practice
O'FARRELLY, C., Comparative Immunology
O'KEANNE, V., Psychiatry
O'HAGAN, J., Economics
O'HALPIN, E., Contemporary Irish History
O'KELLY, F., General Practice
O'LEARY, J., Pathology
O'MAHONY, M., Civil Engineering
O'MORÁIN, C., Medicine
O'NEILL, L., Biochemistry
O'ROURKE, K., Economics
PETHICA, J., Physics
PRENDERGAST, P., Bio-Engineering
RAMASWAMI, M., Neurogenetics
REYNOLDS, J., Surgery
ROBERTSON, I., Psychology
ROBINSON, I., History
ROGERS, T., Clinical Microbiology
ROSS, I., Eighteenth-Century Studies
ROWAN, M., Neuropharmacology
REILLY, R., Neural Engineering
SCOTT, D., French and Visual Studies
SENGE, M., Organic Chemistry
SHATASHVILI, S., Natural Philosophy
SHVETS, I., Applied Physics
SIMONS, P., Moral Philosophy
SMITH, O., Haematology
STALLEY, R., History of Art
STASSEN, L., Oral and Maxillofacial Surgery
SWANWICK, G., Psychiatry
TAYLOR, D., Geography
TAYLOR, D., Materials Engineering
TIMON, C., Otolaryngology
VIJ, J., Electronic Materials
WALSH, J., Medical Gerontology
WOLFE, K., Genome Evolution

RECOGNIZED COLLEGES

Church of Ireland College of Education: 96 Upper Rathmines Rd, Dublin 6; tel. (1) 4970033; 3-year course leading to BEd pass degree; Principal SYDNEY BLAIN.

Coláiste Mhuire, Marino: Griffith Ave, Dublin 9; tel. (1) 8057700; 3-year course leading to BEd pass degree; Principal (vacant).

Froebel College of Education: Sion Hill, Blackrock, Co Dublin; tel. (1) 2888520; 3-year course leading to BEd pass degree; Principal SISTER DARINA HOSEY.

Irish School of Ecumenics (Trinity College Dublin): Bea House, Milltown Park, Dublin 6; tel. (1) 2601144; Dir J. D. A. MAY.

St Catherine's College of Education for Home Economics: Sion Hill, Blackrock, Co Dublin; tel. (1) 2884989; f. 1929; 4-year course leading to BEd (home economics) honours degree; Pres. MADELEINE MULRENNAN.

UNIVERSITY OF LIMERICK

Limerick
Telephone: (61) 202700
Fax: (61) 330316
Internet: www.ul.ie
Founded 1972 as National Institute for Higher Education, Limerick; University status 1989
State control
Language of instruction: English
Academic year: September to May
Pres. and Vice-Chancellor: Prof. ROGER G. H. DOWNER
Vice-Pres. for Academic and Registrar: Prof. DON BARRY
Vice-Pres. for Admin. and Sec.: JOHN O'CONNOR
Vice-Pres. for External Affairs: Prof. NOEL WHELAN
Vice-Pres. for Research: Prof. VINCENT CUNNANE
Dir, Human Resources: ANNA DOUGHAN
Library of 330,000 vols

Number of teachers: 554
Number of students: 10,500
Publications: *Degree Programmes* (undergraduate brochure, 1 a year), *President's Report* (1 a year), *Prospectus: postgraduate* (every 2 years), *Prospectus: undergraduate* (1 a year).

University-Level Institutions

DUBLIN INSTITUTE FOR ADVANCED STUDIES

10 Burlington Rd, Dublin 4
Telephone: (1) 6140100
Fax: (1) 6680561
E-mail: registrarsoffice@admin.dias.ie
Internet: www.dias.ie
Founded 1940
Chair. of Council: Prof. D. M. X. DONNELLY
Registrar: CECIL KEAVENEY.

CONSTITUENT SCHOOLS

School of Celtic Studies: Chair. Prof. B. Ó MADAGÁIN

SENIOR PROFESSORS
BREATNACH, L.
KELLY, F.
Ó MURCHÚ, M.

School of Cosmic Physics: Chair. Prof. G. WRIXON

SENIOR PROFESSORS
DRURY, L. O'C.
JONES, A. G.
MEURS, E. J. A.

School of Theoretical Physics: Chair. Sir M. ATIYAH

SENIOR PROFESSORS
DORLAS, T. C.
NAHM, W.
O'CONNOR, D.

ROYAL COLLEGE OF PHYSICIANS OF IRELAND

2nd Fl., International House, 20–22 Lower Hatch St, Dublin 2
Telephone: (1) 6616677
Fax: (1) 6762920
E-mail: info@rcpi.ie
Internet: www.rcpi.ie
Founded 1654
President: Prof. T. J. McKENNA
Registrar: Prof. N. G. McELVANEY
Secretary: J. W. BAILEY

Faculties of obstetrics and gynaecology, occupational medicine, paediatrics, pathology, public health medicine; awards a Fellowship, a Membership, and a Diploma in Obstetrics and Women's Health.

Institutes of Technology

Athlone Institute of Technology: Dublin Rd, Athlone, Co Westmeath; tel. (902) 24400; fax (902) 24417; internet www.ait.ie; f. 1970; two-year Nat. Certificate courses, three- and one-year Nat. Diploma courses, four-year degree/professional courses, one-year post-Diploma degree courses, graduate Diploma courses, Masters degree courses, postgraduate research; library: 50,000 vols; 300 teach-

ers; 4,000 students; Dir Prof. CIARÁN Ó CATHÁIN; Registrar Dr JOSEPH RYAN

HEADS OF SCHOOLS
Business Studies: J. CUSACK
Engineering: A. HANLEY
Humanities and Hospitality Studies: Dr M. FITZGIBBON
Science: Dr P. TOMKINS

Cork Institute of Technology: Rossa Ave, Cork; tel. (21) 326100; fax (21) 545343; f. 1912; library: 65,000 vols, 550 periodicals; 1,050 teachers; 12,200 students; Dir P. KELLEHER; Registrar B. GOGGIN

HEADS OF DEPARTMENTS
Applied Physics and Instrumentation: Dr E. M. CASHELL
Biological Sciences: Dr J. O'MULLANE
Building and Civil Engineering: L. F. HODNETT
Business Studies: T. J. RIGNEY
Chemical and Process Engineering: J. T. O'SHEA
Chemistry: Dr J. O. WOOD
Electrical and Electronics Engineering: L. J. M. POLAND
Mathematics and Computing: Dr B. J. BRENDAN MURPHY
Mechanical and Manufacturing Engineering: D. A. FITZPATRICK
Nautical Studies: D. C. BURKE
Printing, Graphics and Editorial Studies: D. POWER
Social and General Studies: D. A. COURTNEY
Tourism and Catering Studies: J. KILLILEA
Transport and Automobile Engineering: D. DEMPSEY
Continuing Adult Education: P. MAHONY.

Attached Centres:
Centre for Advanced Manufacturing and Management Systems: Dir M. COTTERELL.
Centre for Clean Technology: Dir D. CUNNINGHAM.
Centre for Educational Opportunities: Dir M. BERMINGHAM.
Centre for Innovation in Education: Dir R. P. COUGHLAN.
Centre for Nautical Enterprise: Dir G. TRANT.
Centre for Surface and Interface Analysis: Dirs E. M. CASHELL, L. McDONNELL.

Constituent Schools:
Cork School of Music: Union Quay, Cork; tel. (21) 270076; fax (21) 276595; f. 1878; Principal G. SPRATT.
Crawford College of Art and Design: Sharman Crawford St, Cork; tel. (21) 966343; fax (21) 962767; f. 1884; Principal GEOFFREY STEINER-SCOTT.

Dublin Institute of Technology: Fitzwilliam House, 30 Upper Pembroke St, Dublin 2; tel. (1) 4023000; fax (1) 4023399; internet www.dit.ie; f. 1978 by bringing together 6 established colleges; formally established 1993; academic year September to June; 1,500 teachers, (incl. part-time); 25,000 students, (incl. part-time); Pres. Prof. B. NORTON; Dir of Academic Affairs Dr F. McMAHON; Dir of Finance R. WILLS; Director of Human Resources D. CAGNEY; Dir of Research and Enterprise Dr D. GLYNN; Registrar Dr T. DUFF

DIRECTORS OF FACULTIES
Faculty of Applied Arts: Dr E. HAZELKORN
Faculty of the Built Environment: Prof. J. RATCLIFFE
Faculty of Business: P. O'SULLIVAN
Faculty of Engineering: Dr M. MURPHY

Faculty of Science: Dr M. Hussey
Faculty of Tourism and Food: Dr M. Mulvey

HEADS OF SCHOOLS

Faculty of Applied Arts (Rathmines Rd, Dublin 6):
School of Art, Design and Printing: J. O'Conner
School of Conservatory of Music and Drama: B. Grant
School of Languages: H. Conway
School of Media: Dr B. O'Neill
School of Social Sciences and Legal Studies: Dr N. Hayes

Faculty of the Built Environment (Bolton St, Dublin 2):
School of Architecture: J. Horan
School of Construction: P. Murray
School of Environmental Planning and Management: H. Van der Kamp
School of Real Estate and Construction Economics: T. Dunne

Faculty of Business (Aungier St, Dublin 2):
School of Accounting and Finance: Dr T. Barrett
School of Management: R. Burns
School of Marketing: K. Ui Ghallachoir
School of Retail and Services Management: J. Jameson
Graduate Business School: Dr J. Urquhart

Faculty of Engineering (Bolton St, Dublin 1):
School of Civil and Building Services Engineering: J. Turner
School of Control Systems and Electrical Engineering: Dr E. Coyle
School of Electronic and Communication Engineering: Dr G. Farrell
School of Manufacturing Engineering: J. Lawlor
School of Mechanical and Transport Engineering: Dr J. McGovern

Faculty of Science (Kevin St, Dublin 8):
School of Biological Sciences: B. A. Ryan
School of Chemistry: Dr N. Russell
School of Computing: Dr B. O'Shea
School of Mathematical Sciences: Dr J. M. Golden
School of Physics: Dr V. Toal

Faculty of Tourism and Food (Cathal Brugha St, Dublin 1):
School of Culinary Arts and Food Technology: Dr J. Hegarty
School of Food Science and Environmental Health: Dr S. Cassidy (acting)
School of Tourism and Hospitality Management: Dr J. Ruddy (acting)

Dun Laoghaire Institute of Art, Design and Technology: Carraiglea Park, Kill Ave, Dun Laoghaire, Co Dublin; tel. 2144600; fax 2144700; certificate, diploma and degree programmes; Dir Roisin Hogan; Registrar Jim Devine.

Dundalk Institute of Technology: Dundalk; tel. (42) 34785; fax (42) 33505; f. 1970; certificate, diploma and degree courses; library: 30,000 vols; Dir Sean McDonagh; Registrar S. McManus

HEADS OF SCHOOLS

Business Studies: Peter Fuller
Engineering: John Connolly
Science: Dr Simon O'Brien

Galway-Mayo Institute of Technology: Dublin Rd, Galway; tel. (91) 753161; fax (91) 751107; internet www.gmit.ie; f. 1972; degree, diploma and certificate courses; library: 95,000 vols; 300 teachers; 9,000 students (5,000 full-time, 4,000 part-time); Dir Marion Coy; Registrar Bernard O'Hara; Librarian Ann Joyce Walsh

HEADS OF SCHOOLS

Art, Design and Humanities: John Tunney
Business Studies: Larry Elwood
Engineering: Gerard MacMichael
Hotel and Catering: Stuart Jauncey
Science: Des Foley

HEADS OF CENTRES

Castlebar Campus: Katie Sweeney
Letterfrack Campus: Michael Hannon

Institute of Technology Blanchardstown: Blanchardstown Road North, Dublin 15; tel. (1) 8851000; fax (1) 8851001; e-mail college.support@itb.ie; internet www.itb.ie; f. 1999; Bachelors and Masters degrees; national certificates, national and graduate diplomas; 67 teachers; 1,060 students (626 full-time, 356 part-time, 78 apprentices); Dir Dr Mary Meaney; publ. *Journal* (2 a year)

HEADS OF SCHOOLS

School of Business and Humanities: Des Moore
School of Informatics and Engineering: Larry McNutt

Institute of Technology Carlow: Kilkenny Rd, Carlow; tel. (59) 9170400; fax (59) 9170500; e-mail info@itcarlow.ie; internet www.itcarlow.ie; f. 1970; higher certificate, ordinary degree, honours degree and postgraduate courses; library: 25,000 vols; 200 teachers; 4,000 students; Dir Dr Ruaidhrí Neavyn; Registrar Brian L. Bennett

HEADS OF DEPARTMENTS

Applied Biology and Chemistry: Dr David Ryan
Business and Management Studies: Colm Kelly
Computing, Physics and Mathematics: Mike Baker
Electronic Engineering: Brendan Laffan
Humanities and Applied Languages: Martin Meagher
Mechanical, Civil and Construction Engineering: John Doyle

Institute of Technology Sligo: Ballinode, Sligo; tel. (71) 9155222; fax (71) 9144096; internet www.itsligo.ie; f. 1970; national certificate and diploma courses; degree courses; professional courses; library: 23,000 vols; 180 teachers; 3,385 full-time students; 732 part-time students; 250 apprentices; Dir Dr Richard Thorn

HEADS OF SCHOOLS

Business and Humanities: T. Young
Engineering: B. McCormack
Science: J. P. Timpson
Development: D. McConville

Institute of Technology Tallaght: Tallaght, Dublin 24; tel. (1) 4042000; fax (1) 4042700; e-mail info@it-tallaght.ie; internet www.it-tallaght.ie; f. 1992; higher Certificates, ordinary Bachelors degrees and honours Bachelors degrees; Dir Dr Tim Creedon; Registrar John Vickery

HEADS OF DEPARTMENTS

School of Business and Humanities: Dr Damien Roche
School of Engineering: Pat McLaughlin
School of Science: Dr Mike Ahern

Institute of Technology Tralee: Clash, Tralee, Co Kerry; tel. (66) 7145600; fax (66) 7125711; e-mail info@ittralee.ie; internet www.ittralee.ie; f. 1977; full-time Nat. Certificate courses, Nat. Diploma courses, Bachelors and Masters degrees and doctorates, part-time degree courses; library: 30,000 vols; 200 teachers; 4,000 students; Dir Michael Carmody; Administration Officer Dick Carmody

HEADS OF SCHOOL

Business Studies: Brian O'Connor
Engineering: Kevin Lynch
Science: Seamus O'Shea

Letterkenny Institute of Technology: Port Rd, Letterkenny, Co Donegal; tel. (74) 64100; fax (74) 64111; courses at certificate, diploma and degree levels in engineering, science, design and business studies; library: 30,000 vols; 170 teachers; 1,300 students; Dir Paul Hannigan; Registrar Daniel Brennan

HEADS OF SCHOOLS

Business Studies: S. Ó Cnáimhsí
Engineering: C. Ó Somacháin
Science: W. J. W. Hines

Limerick Institute of Technology: Moylish Park, Limerick; tel. (61) 208209; fax (61) 208209; e-mail information@lit.ie; internet www.lit.ie; f. 1852; 500 teachers; 6,000 students; Dir V. N. McCarthy; Registrar T. Twomey (acting)

HEADS OF SCHOOLS AND DEPARTMENTS

School of Art and Design: R. Ruth
School of the Built Environment: J. Healy (acting)
School of Business: H. Chadda (acting)
Department of Electrical and Electronic Engineering: B. Callan
Department of Humanities: T. Mangan
Department of Information Technology: I. Kavanagh (acting)
Department of Mechanical and Automobile Engineering: P. Ryan
Department of Science: F. Barry (acting)

Tipperary Institute: Nenagh Rd, Thurles, Co Tipperary; tel. (504) 28000; fax (504) 28001; e-mail info@tippinst.ie; internet www.tippinst.ie; f. 1998; Bachelors degrees and higher certificates; library: 17,479 vols, 330 periodicals; 600 students; Chief Exec. Pádraig Culbert

HEADS OF DEPARTMENT

Department of Business: Moya Breen
Department of Information and Communications Technology: James Greenslade
Department of Sustainable Rural Development: Ciaran Lynch

Waterford Institute of Technology: Cork Rd, Waterford; tel. (51) 302000; fax (51) 378292; e-mail enquiries@wit.ie; internet www.wit.ie; f. 1969; degree courses, doctorates, Diplomas, Certificates; library: 90,000 vols, 400 periodicals; 200 full-time teachers; 10,000 students (6,000 full-time 4,000 part-time); Dir Prof. Kieran R. Byrne; Registrar P. Downey

HEADS OF SCHOOLS

Accountancy and Business: Dr Tom O'Toole
Engineering: D. Moran
Humanities: Dr J. P. Ennis
Science and Information Technology: Dr E. Martin

Other Institutions of Higher Education

National College of Ireland: Sandford Rd, Ranelagh, Dublin 6; tel. (1) 4060504; fax (1) 44972200; e-mail info@ncirl.ie; internet www.ncirl.ie; f. 1951; 30 teachers; 4,000 students; PhD, Masters degree, diploma and certificate courses, full-time and part-time; also short courses; specialist areas: human resource management, personnel management, industrial relations, trade union studies, accountancy, business management, languages and European studies, computing, information technology law, management of change, leadership, community-based learning; Pres. Prof. JOYCE O'CONNOR.

St Patrick's College: Maynooth, Co Kildare; tel. (1) 6285222; fax (1) 6289063; f. 1795; comprises National Seminary and Pontifical University; Bachelors, Masters and Doctoral degrees, and Diplomas and Licentiates; library: 65,000 vols; 24 teachers; 392 students; Pres. Mgr DERMOT FARRELL.

Schools of Art and Music

National College of Art and Design: see under National University of Ireland–Recognized Colleges of the University.

ROYAL IRISH ACADEMY OF MUSIC

36–38 Westland Row, Dublin 2

Telephone: (1) 6764412

Fax: (1) 6622798

E-mail: info@riam.ie

Internet: www.riam.ie

Founded 1848, incorporated 1889

Dir: JOHN O'CONOR

Sec.: DOROTHY SHIEL

Registrar: TONY MADIGAN

Number of teachers: 75 teachers

Number of students: 1,000 students

ISRAEL

The Higher Education System

The earliest institutions of higher education were founded when Palestine was a province of the Ottoman Turkish Empire, and tended to be religious, technical or arts schools. The oldest specialist institution is the Etz Hayim, General Talmud, Torah and Grand Teshivah (founded 1847), and the oldest university-level institution is Technion—Israel Institute of Technology (founded 1912; inaugurated 1924). Following the First World War (1914–18), Palestine became a League of Nations mandate under British administration and increased Jewish immigration led to the expansion of the higher education sector: the Hebrew University of Jerusalem was founded in 1918 and inaugurated in 1925. The Arab and Jewish communities began to develop parallel forms of communal government, including separate education systems. In May 1948 the United Kingdom terminated its Palestinian mandate, and an independent Jewish State of Israel was declared. Several university-level institutions were established shortly after, including the Weizmann Institute of Science (founded 1949), Bar-Ilan University (founded 1953; inaugurated 1955) and Tel-Aviv University (founded 1953; inaugurated 1956). In addition to the eight universities, other institutions of higher education include colleges and higher institutes. The Council for Higher Education Law (1958) established the Council for Higher Education to oversee Israeli higher education, including accreditation of institutions and quality assurance. There is a three-stage process of accreditation. First, the institution is allowed to advertise programmes of study, invite applications from students and start teaching courses; however, the institution is not allowed to award degrees or other qualifications. Secondly, an institution is permitted to be opened and maintained as a provisional institution of higher education but without accreditation and without awarding the relevant qualifications. Thirdly, and finally, the institution is accredited as an institution of higher education and authorized to award degrees.

In 2005/06 there were 209,500 students in institutions of higher education compared with 76,000 in 1990. In addition, there were 41,150 students in the Open University compared with 13,000 in 1990. In 2006 there were 41,800 studying for a Masters degree. Studies for the Doctoral degree are offered only in the research universities. The number of doctoral students increased steadily from 3,910 in 1990 to 9,835 in 2006.

The school leavers' certificate or bagrut (matriculation) is the main criterion for admission to higher education. Applicants may also be required to undergo psychometric testing and attend a personal interview, depending on the institution. The Bachelors degree is the standard university-level undergraduate qualification, and the course usually lasts three years. However, some disciplines require longer periods of study, such as nursing (four years) and medicine (six years). Bachelors degrees from non-university institutions, usually Colleges and Higher Institutes, tend to be awarded in conjunction with a professional title or indicate the area of specialization. The first postgraduate-level degree is the Masters, a one- to two-year programme of study that may or may not include a thesis component. A Masters with a thesis component (Type A) allows admission to doctoral studies; a Masters without a thesis (Type B) does not. The second (and highest) postgraduate qualification is the Doctorate (most commonly a PhD) and lasts two years.

Technical and vocational education at the post-secondary level is offered by technical colleges and non-university institutions of higher education. The first qualification at this level is the Technai (Qualified Technician), which lasts one year. The other main qualification is the Handassai (Practical Engineer), which is divided into two tracks, Type A and Type B. Handassai (Type A) is a one-year programme of study, and Handassai (Type B) lasts two years. Admission to Technai and Handassai courses requires a bagrut or completion of 12 years of education.

The proportion of ultra-Orthodox adults outside the labour force increased steadily over much of the late 20th and early 21st centuries. In 2010 the Council for Higher Education formulated a plan to encourage these ultra-Orthodox adults into higher education in order to improve their employability. This formed part of a five-year plan for the whole higher education system.

Regulatory and Representative Bodies

GOVERNMENT

Ministry of Education: POB 292, 34 Shivtei Israel St, 91911 Jerusalem; tel. (2) 5602222; fax (2) 5602223; e-mail info@education.gov.il; internet www.education.gov.il; Minister GIDEON SA'AR.

Ministry of Science, Culture and Sport: POB 49100, Kiryat Hamemshala, Hamizrachit, Bldg 3, 91490 Jerusalem; tel. (2) 5411115; fax (2) 5323497; e-mail minister@most.gov.il; internet www.most.gov.il; Minister GALEB MAJADELE.

ACCREDITATION

Council for Higher Education: POB 4037, 91040 Jerusalem; tel. (2) 5679911; fax (2) 5679955; internet www.che.org.il; f. 1958; recommends to the Govt the granting of licences to higher education institutes, and accreditation, and authorizes awarding of degrees; 24 mems; Chair. THE MINISTER OF EDUCATION; Dir-Gen. STEVEN G. STAV.

ENIC/NARIC Israel: Dept for Evaluation of Foreign Academic Degrees, Ministry of Education, 2 Devora Haneviah St, 91911 Jerusalem; tel. (2) 5603702; fax (2) 5603876; e-mail diplomot@education.gov.il; Dir TZIPY WEINBERG.

Quality Assessment Unit: 38 Keren Hayesod St, cnr of 2 Jabotinsky St, David Brothers Bldg, 4th Fl., Jerusalem; tel. (2) 5669938; fax (2) 5611914; e-mail michal@che.org.il; internet www.che.org.il; f. 2004 to improve the quality of higher education, increase awareness of the quality assessment process, and develop systems in higher education instns for the continual evaluation of academic quality; periodical assessment of study programmes; Head MICHAL NEUMAN.

Learned Societies

GENERAL

Israel Academy of Sciences and Humanities: POB 4040, 91040 Jerusalem; tel. (2) 5676222; fax (2) 5666059; e-mail academy@academy.ac.il; internet www.academy.ac.il; f. 1959; sections of Humanities and Natural Sciences; academic centre in Cairo, Egypt; 87 mems; Pres. Prof. MENAHEM YAARI; Vice-Pres. Prof. RUTH ARNON; Exec. Dir Dr MEIR ZADOK; Chair. of Humanities Prof. YOHANAN FRIEDMANN; Chair. of Natural Sciences Prof. RAPHAEL MECHOULAM.

BIBLIOGRAPHY, LIBRARY SCIENCE AND MUSEOLOGY

Israel Librarians' Association: POB 303, 61002 Tel-Aviv; f. 1952; gen. organization of librarians, archivists and information specialists; promotes the interests and advances the professional standards of librarians; professional and examining body; 850 mems; Chair. BENJAMIN SCHACHTER; Sec. NAAMA RAVID; publs Meida La Sefran, Yad-La-Kore (Libraries and Archives Magazine).

Israel Society of Libraries and Information Professionals (ASMI): 8 Blum St, 44253 Kefar Saba; tel. (77) 2151800; fax (77) 2151800; e-mail asmi@asmi.org.il; internet www.asmi.org.il; f. 1966; promotes the utilization of recorded knowledge by disseminating information in the fields of science, technology and the humanities, and facilitates written and oral communication; 400 mems; Chair. Dr SHAHAF HAGAFNI; publs

Igeret (irregular), *Information and Librarianship* (1 a year).

Israeli Center for Libraries: POB 3251, 51103 Benei Berak; tel. (3) 6180151; fax (3) 5798048; e-mail icl@icl.org.il; internet www.icl.org.il; f. 1965; provides centralized processing and other services for libraries; organizes non-academic librarianship courses; Chair. JACOB AGMON; Dir ORLY ONN; publs *Basifriyot* (12 a year), *Yad Lakore* (1 a year).

Museums Association of Israel: POB 7, 75100 Rishon Le-Zion; tel. (3) 9565977; fax (3) 9565788; e-mail secretariat@icom.org.il; internet www.icom.org.il; f. 1964 to foster public interest in museums and cooperation among asscn members; affiliated to International Council of Museums (ICOM); 55 mems; Chair. ITZHAK BRENNER.

ECONOMICS, LAW AND POLITICS

International Association of Jewish Lawyers and Jurists: 10 Daniel Frish St, 64731 Tel-Aviv; tel. (3) 6910673; fax (3) 6953855; e-mail iajj@goldmail.net.il; internet www.intjewishlawyers.org; f. 1969 to contribute towards establishing int. order based on law and the promotion of human rights; examines legal problems related to Jewish communities; holds int. congresses and seminars; 10 centres (in Israel and abroad); affiliated with the World Jewish Congress (WJC); Pres. ALEX HERTMAN; Exec. Dir RONIT GIDRON-ZEMACH; publ. *Justice* (4 a year).

Israel Bar: 10 Daniel Frish St, 64731 Tel-Aviv; tel. (3) 6362200; fax (3) 6918696; e-mail vaadmerkazi@israelbar.org.il; internet www.israelbar.org.il; f. 1961; autonomous statutory body to incorporate and represent lawyers in Israel; 16,000 mems; Pres. YORI GEIRON; Gen. Dir LINDA SHAFIR; Chair., Nat. Council AMOS VAN EMDEN; publs *Hapraklit* (12 a year), *Orech Hadin* (2 a year).

Attached Organizations:

David Rotlevi National Mediation Institute of the Israel Bar:tel. (3) 6362221; fax (3) 6091641; Jt Chairs SHAY SEGAL, MOSHE TCHETCHIK.

Institute for Continuing Legal Studies: 82 Menachem Begin Rd, 67138 Tel Aviv; tel. (3) 5616550; fax (3) 5616551; e-mail machon@israelbar.org.il; Jt Chairs Dr YORAM DANZIGER, Prof. AHARON NAMDAR.

International Association of Jewish Lawyers and Jurists Secretariat:tel. (3) 6910673; fax (3) 6953855; e-mail iajlj@goldmail.net.il; internet www.intjewishlawyers.org; Man. ARIEL AINBINDER.

Israel Political Science Association: c/o Dept of Political Studies, Bar-Ilan University, 52900 Ramat Gan; tel. (3) 5318578; fax (3) 9234511; e-mail ispsa.mail@gmail.com; internet www.ispsa.org; 100 mems; Chair. Prof. SAM LEHMAN WILZIG.

FINE AND PERFORMING ARTS

ACUM (Society of Authors, Composers and Music Publishers in Israel): ACUM House, 9 Tuval St, POB 1704, 52117 Ramat Gan; tel. (3) 6113400; fax (3) 6122629; e-mail acum@acum.org.il; internet www.acum.org.il; f. 1936; copyright; promotion of music and literature; 4,000 mems; Chief Exec. Officer YORIK BEN-DAVID.

Israel Music Institute: 55 Menachem Begin Rd, POB 51197, 67138 Tel-Aviv; tel. (3) 6247095; fax (3) 5612826; e-mail musicinst@bezeqint.net; internet www.imi.org.il; f. 1961; publishes and promotes Israeli music and musicological works throughout the world; produces CDs on Israeli music celebration festival; Israel Music Information Centre; Central Library of Israeli Music; mem. of the Int. Asscn of Music Information Centres and Int. Fed. of Serious Music Publishers; library: 2,500 scores, 2,000 audio recordings; Chair. DANIELA RABINOWITZ; Dir PAUL LANDAU; publ. *IMI News* (3 a year).

Israel Painters and Sculptors Association: 9 Alharizi St, 64244 Tel-Aviv; tel. (3) 5246685; fax (3) 5226433; e-mail artassoc@netvision.net.il; f. 1934 to advance plastic arts in Israel and protect artists' interests; affiliated to the International Association of Art; organizes group exhibitions and symposia; provides assistance to immigrant artists; maintains a gallery for members' exhibitions; graphic arts workshop and materials supply store; 3 brs; 2,000 mems; Chair. RACHEL SHAVIT.

HISTORY, GEOGRAPHY AND ARCHAEOLOGY

Historical Society of Israel: 2 Betar St, POB 4179, 91041 Jerusalem; tel. (2) 5650444; fax (2) 6712388; e-mail info@shazar.org.il; internet www.shazar.org.il; f. 1926 to promote the study of general and Jewish history; 1,000 mems; library: Library of Jewish History, Judaica, 25,000 vols; Chair. Prof. MICHAEL HEYD; Sec.-Gen. ZVI YEKUTIEL; publs *Historia* (general history, in Hebrew, with summary in English, 2 a year), *Zion* (Jewish history, in Hebrew with summary in English, 4 a year).

Israel Antiquities Authority: POB 586, 91004 Jerusalem; tel. (2) 6204622; fax (2) 6289066; internet www.antiquities.org.il; f. 1948; govt authority; engages in archaeological excavations and surveys, inspection and preservation of antiquities and ancient sites, scientific publs; custodianship of all antiquities; Dir of Antiquities SHUKA DORFMAN; Sec. H. MENAHEM; publs *Archaeological Survey of Israel* (irregular), *Atiqot* (irregular), *Excavations and Surveys in Israel* (2 a year).

Israel Geographical Association: c/o Dept of Geography, Bar-Ilan University, 52900 Ramat-Gan; internet www.geography.org.il; f. 1961; 650 mems; Pres. YEHUDA CRADUS; Sec. Dr GABI LIPSHITZ; publ. *Ofakim*.

Israel Prehistoric Society: POB 1502, Jerusalem; f. 1958; 100 mems; incl. the 'M. Stekelis' Museum of Prehistory; Chair A. GOPHER; Sec. N. GOREN; publ. *Mitekufat Haeven* (1 a year).

Jerusalemer Institut der Görres-Gesellschaft (Jerusalem Institute of the Görres Society): Notre Dame of Jerusalem Center, POB 4595, 91044 Jerusalem; tel. (2) 6271170; f. 1908; fmrly Orientalisches Institut der Görres-Gesellschaft; art, history, archaeology, biblical studies, Christian iconography; library, photo archive, computerized index of Christian monuments in the Holy Land; Pres. Prof. WOLFGANG BERGSDORF.

LANGUAGE AND LITERATURE

Academy of the Hebrew Language: Givat Ram Campus, 91904 Jerusalem; tel. (2) 6493555; fax (2) 5617065; e-mail acad2u@huji.ac.il; internet hebrew-academy.huji.ac.il; f. 1953; studies the vocabulary, structure and history of the Hebrew language and is the official authority for its devt; is compiling a historical dictionary of the Hebrew language; library: library specializing in Hebrew and Semitic languages; 38 mems (23 full, 15 advisory); Pres. Prof. M. BAR-ASHER; Chief Scientific Sec. R. GADISH; publs *Leshonenu* (4 a year), *Leshonenu La'am* (4 a year), *Zikhronot*.

Association of Religious Writers: POB 7440, Jerusalem; tel. (2) 5660478; fax (2) 5660478; f. 1963; Chair. Dr ZAHAVA BEN-DOV; publ. *Mabua*.

British Council: Crystal House, 12 Hahilazon St, Ramat Gan, 52136 Tel-Aviv; tel. (3) 6113600; fax (3) 6113640; e-mail info@britishcouncil.org.il; internet www.britishcouncil.org/israel; promotes cultural relations between the UK and other countries by offering opportunities for inter-cultural dialogue and knowledge sharing in science, education, English language, sports and arts; offers preparation and testing for IELTS and administers various British professional and academic exams; attached offices in Nazareth and W Jerusalem; Dir JIM BUTTERY; Head of ELT HELEN SYKES.

Goethe-Institut: 15 Sokolov St, 92144 Jerusalem; tel. (2) 5610627; fax (2) 5618431; e-mail info@jerusalem.goethe.org; internet www.goethe.de/jerusalem; offers courses and exams in German language and culture and promotes cultural exchange with Germany; attached centre in Tel-Aviv; Dir Dr FRIEDRICH DAHLHAUS.

Hebrew Writers Association in Israel: POB 7111, Tel-Aviv; tel. (3) 6953256; fax (3) 6919681; f. 1921; 400 mems; publ. *Moznayim* (12 a year).

Instituto Cervantes: Shulamit 7, 64371 Tel Aviv; tel. (3) 5279992; fax (3) 5299558; e-mail centel@cervantes.es; internet telaviv.cervantes.es; offers courses and exams in Spanish language and culture and promotes cultural exchange with Spain and Spanish-speaking Latin and Central America; library of 14,000 vols; Dir ROSA MARÍA MORO DE ANDRÉS.

Palestinian PEN Centre: Wadi al-Juz, Al-Khaldi St 4, Jerusalem; tel. (2) 6262970; fax (2) 6280103; f. 1992; 50 mems; Pres. HANAN AWWAD.

MEDICINE

Israel Gerontological Society: POB 2371, 55000 Kiryat Ono; tel. (3) 5357161; fax (3) 6359399; e-mail igs@netvision.net.il; internet www.gerontology.org.il; f. 1956; 600 mems; Chair. Prof. JACOB LOMRANZ; Vice-Chair. Dr YITSHAL BERNER; publ. *Gerontology* (4 a year).

Israel Medical Association: POB 3604, 52136 Ramat Gan; 35 Jabotinsky St, 2 Twin Towers, Level 11, 52136 Ramat Gan; tel. (3) 6100444; fax (3) 5753303; e-mail tguvot@ima.org.il; internet www.ima.org.il; f. 1912; Pres. Dr YORAM BLACHAR; publs *Harefuah* (26 a year, in Hebrew, abstracts in English), *Israel Medical Association Journal* (12 a year).

Israel Society for Neuroscience: POB 666, 75106 Rishon Le Zion; tel. (3) 9694126; fax (3) 9660841; e-mail michal.gilady@isfn.org.il; internet www.isfn.org.il; Pres. ILIANA GOZES.

Israel Society of Internal Medicine: Division of Medicine, Sapir Medical Centre, Meir Hospital, 44281 Kfar Sava; tel. (9) 7472591; fax (9) 7472671; e-mail mlahav@post.tau.ac.il; internet www.isim.org.il; f. 1958; four regional centres; a division of the Israel Medical Association (IMA), and affiliated to the International Society of Internal Medicine (ISIM); organizes scientific meetings and congresses; participates in the planning of postgraduate education in internal medicine and improving conditions of internal medicine practitioners; 750 mems; Chair. Prof. MORDECHAI RAVID; Sec. Dr MEIR LAHAV.

Society for Medicine and Law in Israel: 30 Arlozerov St, Petach-Tikva; tel. (3) 9231047; e-mail acarmi@research.haifa.ac.il;

f. 1972; 3 brs; affiliated to the World Association for Medical Law (WAML); examines and recommends amendments to medical laws; organizes int. conferences; 1,600 mems; Pres. A. CARMI; publ. *Refuah U Mishpat* (Medicine & Law, in Hebrew, 4 a year).

NATURAL SCIENCES
General
Association for the Advancement of Science in Israel: c/o Prof. M. Jammer, Dept of Physics, Bar-Ilan University, 52100 Ramat-Gan; tel. (3) 5318433; fax (3) 5353298; f. 1953; 5,200 mems; Pres. Prof. M. JAMMER; publ. *Proceedings of Congress of Scientific Societies.*

Biological Sciences
Entomological Society of Israel: POB 6, 50250 Bet-Dagan; tel. (3) 9683729; fax (3) 9604428; e-mail vtada@volcani.agri.gov.il; internet entomology.org.il; f. 1962; promotes, improves and disseminates the science of entomology (incl. acarology) in Israel; holds 1 full-day meeting per year; 224 mems; Pres. Prof. ADA RAFAELI; Sec. Dr VICTORIA SOROKER; publ. *Israel Journal of Entomology.*

Israel Society of Plant Sciences: c/o Hebrew University of Jerusalem, 76100 Rehovot; tel. (4) 9489443; fax (4) 9489899; e-mail ispb@post.tau.ac.il; internet www.tau.ac.il/lifesci/ispb; f. 1936; aims to promote the advancement of the fundamental and applied branches of botanical science; conducts research, organizes lectures and field work; over 300 mems; Pres. Dr SHAHAL ABBP; publ. *Israel Journal of Plant Sciences.*

Israel Society of Biochemistry and Molecular Biology: POB 9095, 52 190 Ramat Efal; tel. (3) 6355038; fax (3) 5351103; e-mail isbmb1@gmail.com; internet www.tau.ac.il/lifesci/isbmb; 350 mems; Pres. Prof. MICHAEL EISENBACH; Sec. Prof. ORNA ELROY-STEIN.

Society for the Protection of Nature in Israel: 4 Hashfela St, Tel-Aviv 66183; tel. (3) 5375063; fax (3) 5377695; internet www.teva.org.il; f. 1953 to promote nature conservation and quality of the environment; operates 24 local brs, 26 field-study centres, 7 biological information centres; research centres on birds, mammals, reptiles, insects, plants and caves; maintains close cooperation with the Nature Reserves Authority, the Environmental Protection Service and the Council for Beautiful Israel; organizes int. seminars on nature conservation education; 100,000 mems; Chair. YOAV SAGI; Exec. Dir EITAN GEDALIZON; publs *Eretz Magazine* (in English, 6 a year), *Pashosh* (children's, in Hebrew, 12 a year), *Teva Va'aretz* (Nature & Land, in Hebrew, 6 a year).

Zoological Society of Israel: c/o Dept of Zoology, Tel-Aviv University Ramat Aviv; internet telem.openu.ac.il/zoosoc; f. 1940; 300 mems; Chair. B. S. GALIL.

Mathematical Sciences
Israel Mathematical Union: c/o Israel Mathematical Union, Faculty of Mathematics and Computer Sciences, Weizmann Institute, 76100 Rehovot; fax (8) 9344278; e-mail imu@imu.org.il; internet imu.org.il; f. 1953; 210 mems; Pres. HARRY DYM; Sec. VERED ROM-KEDAR.

Physical Sciences
Israel Chemical Society: POB 26, 76100 Rehovot; tel. (8) 9343829; fax (8) 9344142; e-mail ics.sec@gmail.com; internet www.weizmann.ac.il/ics; a scientific and professional asscn; holds two conventions each year and organizes lectures and symposia in vari-

ous parts of Israel; the society represents Israel in the International Union of Pure and Applied Chemistry; Pres. Prof. HERBERT BERNSTEIN; Sec. Prof. MOSHE KOL.

Israel Geological Society: POB 1239, 91000 Jerusalem; e-mail gsi@igs.org.il; internet www.igs.org.il; f. 1951; 400 mems; Pres. ARIEL HEIMANN; Vice-Pres. DOV AVIGAD; publ. *Israeli Journal of Earth Sciences.*

Israel Physical Society: c/o Dept of Physics, Technion, 32000 Haifa; tel. (3) 5318431; fax (3) 5353298; e-mail dekel@phys.huji.ac.; internet physics.technion.ac.il/~ips; f. 1954; 250 mems; Pres. Prof. AVISHAI DEKEL; Sec. Prof. AVRAHAM SCHILLER; publ. *Annals of the IPS.*

PHILOSOPHY AND PSYCHOLOGY
Israel Psychological Association: 74 Frishman St, POB 11497, 61114 Tel-Aviv; tel. (3) 5239393; fax (3) 5230763; e-mail psycho@zahav.net.il; internet www.psychology.org.il; f. 1958; 2,623 mems; Chair. DAN ZAKAY.

RELIGION, SOCIOLOGY AND ANTHROPOLOGY
Israel Oriental Society: The Hebrew University, Jerusalem; tel. (2) 5883633; f. 1949; aims to promote interest in and knowledge of history, politics, economics, culture and life in the Middle East; arranges lectures and symposia to study all aspects of contemporary Middle Eastern, Asian and African affairs; Chair. NEHEMIA LEVTZION; Sec. NIMROD GOREN; publ. *Hamizrah Hehadash* (The New East, 1 a year).

TECHNOLOGY
Association of Engineers and Architects in Israel: 200 Dizengoff Rd, POB 6429, 61063 Tel-Aviv; tel. (3) 5240274; fax (3) 5235993; e-mail eng-1@aeai.org.il; internet www.engineers.org.il; f. 1922; brs in Tel-Aviv, Jerusalem, Haifa, Beersheba; 20,000 mems; Pres. Prof. Y. NEEMAN; Chair. Eng. E. COHEN-KAGAN; publs *Chemical Engineering* (6 a year), *Electrical Engineers* (6 a year), *Journal of Engineering and Archaeology* (12 a year, in Hebrew with English summaries).

Israel Society of Aeronautics and Astronautics: POB 2956, 61028 Tel-Aviv; e-mail biaf@aerospace.org.il; internet www.aerospace.org.il; f. 1951 as Israel Soc. of Aeronautical Sciences, merged 1968 with Israel Astronautical Soc.; lectures and confs to foster the growth of aerospace science; 300 mems; Chair. Prof. OVADIA HARARI; Sec. YEHUDA BOROVIK; publ. *BIAF-Israel Aerospace e-Magazine* (4 a year).

Society of Electrical and Electronics Engineers of Israel: 200 Dizengoff St, Tel-Aviv; e-mail seeei@bezeqint.com; internet www.seeei.org.il; f. 1937; 120 mems; Pres. Ing. J. KOEN; Sec. Ing. J. KORNBLUM; publ. *Electricity and People* (in Hebrew, 6 a year).

Research Institutes
GENERAL
Samuel Neaman Institute for Advanced Studies in Science and Technology: Technion City, 32000 Haifa; tel. (4) 8292329; fax (4) 8231889; e-mail info@neaman.org.il; internet www.neaman.org.il; f. 1978; independent public policy institute researching nat. problems in science and technology, education, and economic, health and social devt; Dir Prof. MOSHE MOSHE.

Technion Research and Development Foundation Ltd: Senate House, Technion City, 32000 Haifa; tel. (4) 8292497; fax (4) 8320186; e-mail oshmu@cs.technion.ac.il; internet www.trdf.co.il; f. 1952; operates Industrial Testing Laboratories (building materials, geodetic research, soils and roads, hydraulics, chemistry, metals, electro-optics, vehicles); administers sponsored research at Technion—Israel Institute of Technology (see under Universities) in aeronautical, agricultural, biomedical, chemical, civil, computer, electrical, food and biotechnology, industrial, management and mechanical engineering; biology, chemistry, mathematics and physics (sciences); and architecture and town planning, education in technology and science, general studies, medicine; 22 subsidiaries in fields of electronics, energy, agriculture, food and medicine; Man. Dir Prof. ODED SHMUELI.

AGRICULTURE, FISHERIES AND VETERINARY SCIENCE
Agricultural Research Organization: Volcani Center, POB 6, 50250 Bet-Dagan; tel. (3) 9683226; fax (3) 9665327; e-mail research@volcani.agri.gov.il; internet www.agri.gov.il; f. 1921; fundamental and applied research in agriculture; numerous scientific projects at 7 institutes and 3 experiment stations; part of the Min. of Agriculture and Rural Devt; library of 30,000 vols and periodicals; Dir Prof. YITZHAK SPIEGEL; publ. *Israel Agresearch* (Hebrew with English summaries and captions).

Attached Institutes:

Institute of Agricultural Engineering: tel. (3) 9683303; fax (3) 9604704; Dir Dr ZE'EV SCHMILOVITCH.

Institute of Animal Science: Volcani Center, POB 6, 50250 Bet-Dagan; tel. (8) 9484400; fax (8) 9475075; e-mail harpaz@volcani.agri.gov.il; internet www.agri.gov.il/en/units/institutes/3.aspx; basic and practical research to support Israeli animal breeders and farmers; depts (i) Poultry and Aquaculture, (ii) Ruminant Science and Genetics; Head of Institute Prof. SHEENAN HARPAZ.

Institute of Plant Protection: tel. (3) 9683437; fax (3) 9604180; e-mail frtir@volcani.agri.gov.il; Dir Prof. ABED GERA.

Institute of Plant Sciences: tel. (3) 9683482; fax (3) 9669583; e-mail vcfield@volcani.agri.gov.il; Dir Prof. ITAMAR GLAZER.

Institute of Soils, Water and Environmental Sciences: tel. (3) 9683640; fax (3) 9604017; e-mail etty@volcani.agri.gov.il; Dir Dr MENACHEM BEN-HUR.

Institute for Technology and the Storage of Agricultural Products: tel. (3) 9683588; fax (3) 9604428; e-mail gadit@volcani.agri.gov.il; Dir Prof. ELAZAR FALLIK.

Beth Gordon, A. D. Gordon Agriculture, Nature and Kinnereth Valley Study Institute: Deganya A, 15120 Emeq Ha-Yarden; tel. (6) 750040; f. 1935; inaugurated 1941; regional and research centre and museum of natural history and agriculture and history of the Kinneret (Lake of Galilee) Region; library of 60,000 vols; Dir S. BEN NOAM; Curator of Archaeology Z. VINOGRADOV; Curator of Natural History S. LULAV.

ECONOMICS, LAW AND POLITICS
Institute for Counter-Terrorism (ICT): Interdisciplinary Center Herzliya, POB 167, 46150 Herzliya; tel. (9) 9527277; fax (9) 9513073; e-mail webmaster@ict.org.il; internet www.ict.org.il; f. 1996; research into terrorism worldwide; Chair. SHABTAI SHAVIT; Exec. Dir BOAZ GANOR.

Jerusalem Institute for Israel Studies: 20 Radak St, 92186 Jerusalem; tel. (2) 5630175; fax (2) 5639814; internet www.jiis .org.il; f. 1981; independent non-profit organization to study policy issues and social, economic and political processes in Jerusalem in order to facilitate and improve public policy-making; and to study and disseminate research and environmental policy issues in Israel; Dir ORA AHIMEIR; Exec. Dir Prof. JAACOV BAR SIMON TOV.

Research Institute of the Yitzhak Rabin Centre for Israel Studies: 77 Rokach Blvd, POB 17538, 61175 Tel-Aviv; tel. (3) 7453333; fax (3) 7453355; e-mail info@rabincenter.org .il; internet www.rabincenter.org.il; f. 1997; history, society and culture of the State of Israel; associated Rabin archive, library and museum; Chair. Prof. YAAKOV NEEMAN; Exec. Dir of Research Institute YOSSI LAHMANY.

Weitz Center for Development Studies: POB 12, 76100 Rehovot; tel. (8) 9474111; fax (8) 9475884; e-mail training@netvision.net.il; internet www.weitz-center.org; f. 1963; research, training and planning activities related to the promotion of rural regional devt, tourism and entrepreneurship in Israel and the developing world; library of 50,000 vols, World Bank depository library; Gen. Dir JULIA MARGULIES.

EDUCATION

Henrietta Szold Institute—National Institute for Research in the Behavioural Sciences: 9 Columbia St, Kiryat Menachem, Jerusalem; tel. (2) 6494444; fax (2) 6437698; e-mail szold@szold.org.il; internet www.szold.org.il; f. 1941; non-profit organization undertaking research on psychology, psychometry, sociology and education; information retrieval centre for the social sciences in Israel; database of 40,000 records; Dir Prof. ISAAC FRIEDMAN; publ. *Megamot—Behavioral Sciences Quarterly*.

HISTORY, GEOGRAPHY AND ARCHAEOLOGY

Albright, William Foxwell, Institute of Archaeological Research in Jerusalem: 26 Salah ed-Din St, POB 19096, Jerusalem; tel. (2) 6288956; fax (2) 6264424; e-mail director@albright.org.il; internet www.aiar .org; f. 1900 as the American School of Oriental Research; 2,000 mems; library of 30,000 vols; research projects in Semitic languages, literatures, and history; archaeological surveys and excavations; Pres. J. EDWARD WRIGHT; Dir S. GITIN.

Israel Exploration Society: Avida St 5, POB 7041, 91070 Jerusalem; tel. (2) 6257991; fax (2) 6247772; e-mail ies@vms.huji.ac.il; internet israelexplorationsociety.huji.ac.il; f. 1914 as the Soc. for the Reclamation of Antiquities; excavations and allied research into the history, archaeology and geography of Israel; publishes research results; educates the public in these matters by means of congresses, general meetings, etc.; 4,000 mems; Chair. of Exec. Cttee Prof. E. STERN; Dir HILLEL GEVA; publs *Eretz-Israel* (in Hebrew and English, every 3 years), *Israel Exploration Journal* (in English, 2 a year), *Qadmoniot* (in Hebrew, 2 a year).

Joe Alon Centre for Regional and Folklore Studies: Kibbutz Lahav, 85335 Negev; tel. (8) 9913322; fax (8) 9919889; e-mail joealon@lhv.org.il; internet www.joealon.org .il; f. 1972; centre for research, study and survey of the Southern Shefelah (the hilly region between Jerusalem and Beersheba); incl. an Archaeological Museum, a Museum of Bedouin Culture, a Museum for the New Jewish Settlement in the Negev, the Fehalin Exhibit, housed in a restored dwelling cave

complex, at the foot of a major site; awards grants for research in the region; library of 900 vols, 3,500 slides; Exec. Dir UZZI HALAMISH.

Kenyon Institute: POB 19283, 91192 Jerusalem; tel. (2) 5828101; fax (2) 5323844; e-mail kenyon@cbrl.org.uk; internet www .britac.ac.uk/institutes/cbrl/; f. 1920 as British School of Archaeology in Jerusalem; part of the Council for British Research in the Levant (see parent institution in Research Institutes in Jordan); undertakes and promotes study of all aspects of the archaeology, history and culture of the Levant from prehistoric times to the present; library and hostel; library of 10,000 vols, 100 periodicals; Dir Dr JAIMIE LOVELL; Research Scholar CHLOE MASSEY.

Leo Baeck Institute Jerusalem: 33 Bustenai St, Jerusalem; tel. (2) 5633790; fax (2) 5669505; e-mail leobaeck@leobaeck.org; internet www.leobaeck.org; f. 1955; research and publs on history and culture of Central European Jewry; academic and cultural events, maintenance of library and archives; library: library and archive of items in German, English and Hebrew; special colln: microfilm archive of Jewish newspapers; publs *Juedischer Almanach*, *Innovations in the Study of German Jewry*, *Yearbook*.

MEDICINE

Sheba Medical Center: 52621 Tel Hashomer; tel. (3) 5302473; fax (3) 5356851; internet eng.sheba.co.il; f. 1948; Dir Prof. ZEEV ROTSTEIN; research centres in regenerative medicine, neuroscience, cancer, heart disease and genetics; incl. Israel National Center for Health Policy and Epidemiology Research, Israel National Center for Medical Simulation, Middle East Pediatric Congenital Heart Center, Israel Center for Newborn Screening, Israel National Center for Rehabilitation.

NATURAL SCIENCES

General

Israel Science Foundation: Albert Einstein Sq., 43 Jabotinsky St, 91040 Jerusalem; tel. (2) 5885412; fax (2) 5635782; e-mail tamar@isf.org.il; internet www.isf.org.il; f. 1995; Dir Dr TAMAR JAFFE-MITTWOCH.

Biological Sciences

Israel Institute for Biological Research: POB 19, 74100 Ness-Ziona; tel. (8) 9381656; fax (8) 9401404; internet www.iibr.gov.il; f. 1952; conducts biomedical research in drug design, synthesis of fine chemicals and devt of newly advanced products and processes in biotechnology; three research divs: Chemistry, Biology and Environmental Sciences; 320 scientists and supporting staff; library of 50,000 vols and 800 periodicals; Head of Biological Sciences Dr ARIE ORDENTLICH; Head of Medicinal Chemistry Dr ZVI TEITELBAUM; Head of Environmental Sciences Dr MOSHE KLEIMAN; publ. *OHOLO Annual International Scientific Conference*.

National Institute for Psychobiology in Israel: Hebrew University, Givat Ram Campus, 91904 Jerusalem; tel. (2) 6584086; fax (2) 5635267; e-mail psychobi@cc.huji.ac.il; internet www.psychobiology.org.il; f. 1971 with funds from the Charles E. Smith Family Foundation, to create a network of scientists engaged in research in psychobiology, to further co-operative programmes between existing institutions, and to train personnel in the field of psychobiology; administers Charles E. Smith Family Laboratory for Collaborative Research in Psychobiology; operates through the Research and Development Authority of the Hebrew University;

Pres. DAVID BRUCE SMITH; Dir Prof. SHAUL HOCHSTEIN; Sec. Prof. ELLIOT GERSHON.

Physical Sciences

Earth Sciences Research Administration: 30 Malkhei Israel, 95501 Jerusalem; tel. (2) 5314246; fax (2) 5380688; e-mail mbeyth@gsi.gov.il; Ministry of National Infrastructures; f. 1949; defines scientific issues involved in energy, environment and infrastructure; Dir-Gen. HEZI KUGLER.

Subordinate Institutions:

Geological Survey of Israel: 30 Malkhei Israel St, 95501 Jerusalem; tel. (2) 5314211; fax (2) 5380688; e-mail ask_gsi@ gsi.gov.il; internet www.gsi.gov.il; f. 1949; geological mapping, research and exploration of mineral, water and energy resources; environmental geology; mitigation of earthquake hazards; Dir Dr ORA SHAPIRA.

Geophysical Institute of Israel: 1 Hamashbir St, POB 2286, 58122 Holon; tel. (8) 9785801; fax (8) 9208811; internet www.gii.co.il; f. 1957; activities devoted chiefly to the exploration of petroleum, water and mineral resources and to engineering studies in Israel and abroad, using geophysical methods; documentation unit; data-processing centre; monitoring and mitigation of earthquake hazards; Dir Dr Y. ROTSTEIN.

Israel Oceanographic and Limnological Research: POB 1793, 31000 Haifa; tel. (4) 8526639; fax (4) 8511911; e-mail barak@ocean.org.il; internet www.ocean .org.il; f. 1967; physical, chemical and biological oceanography and limnology; aquaculture; Dir Prof. BARAK HERUT.

Israel Meteorological Service: POB 25, 50250 Bet Dagan; tel. (3) 9682121; fax (3) 9604065; e-mail ims@ims.gov.il; internet www.ims.gov.il; f. 1936; provides general service to public and detailed service to various orgs; library; various publs; Dir Z. ALPERSON.

RELIGION, SOCIOLOGY AND ANTHROPOLOGY

Harry Fischel Institute for Research in Talmud and Jewish Law: Bucharim Quarter, 14 David St (Corner Fischel St), POB 5289, 91052 Jerusalem; tel. (2) 5322517; fax (2) 5326448; e-mail harry_@netvision.net.il; f. 1932; seminary for Rabbis and Rabbinical Judges; legislation and research publications; codification of Jewish law; Jewish adult education centre; 80 mems; Chancellor Chief Rabbi SHEAR-YASHUV COHEN.

World Jewish Bible Center: POB 7024, Jerusalem; tel. (2) 6255965; f. 1957; aims to disseminate a knowledge of the Bible and of Bible research by publications, lectures and exhibitions; Chair. S. J. KREUTNER; publ. *Beit Mikra* (in Hebrew, 4 a year).

Yad Izhak Ben-Zvi: POB 7660, 91076 Jerusalem; tel. (2) 5398888; fax (2) 5638310; e-mail ybz@ybz.org.il; internet www.ybz.org .il; f. 1964; encourages research into the history of Israel and Jerusalem; promotes the study of Jewish communities in the Middle East, Izhak Ben-Zvi and the Zionist and labour movements of Israel; library; library of 65,000 vols; Dir Dr ZVI ZAMERET; publs *Cathedra* (4 a year), *Et-mol* (6 a year), *Pe'amim* (4 a year), *Sefunot* (irregular), *Shalem* (irregular).

Subordinate Institutions:

Ben-Zvi Institute for the Study of Jewish Communities in the East: POB 7660, 91076 Jerusalem; tel. (2) 5398844; fax (2) 5612329; e-mail mbz@ybz.org.il; internet www.ybz.org.il; f. 1947; operated jtly with the Hebrew Univ. of Jerusalem; sponsors research into the history and culture of Jewish communities in Muslim countries since the 7th century; maintains a large colln of MSS, and other historical documents; library; Chair. Prof. YOM TOV ASSIS; publs *Ginzei Qedem- Genizah Reseach Annual* (1 a year, Hebrew and English), *Jewish Communities in the East in the 19th and 20th centuries*, *Pe'amim* (in Hebrew, 4 a year), *Sefunot* (in Hebrew, irregular).

Institute for Research of Eretz Israel: POB 7660, 91076 Jerusalem; tel. (2) 5398888; fax (2) 5638310; e-mail ybz@ybz .org.il; internet www.ybz.org.il; promotes research on the history of Eretz Israel from Biblical times to the mid-20th century, and publishes studies on the history and culture of the Jewish people in Israel from the destruction of the Second Temple to the first years of the State of Israel's existence; research and studies based on the work of scientists at the main univs; Dir Prof. URI BIALER.

TECHNOLOGY

Israel Atomic Energy Commission: POB 7061, 61070 Tel-Aviv; 26 Rehov Chaim Levanon, Ramat Aviv, Tel-Aviv; tel. (3) 6462922; fax (3) 6462570; internet www.iaec .gov.il; f. 1952; advises the Government on long-term policies and priorities in the advancement of nuclear research and devt; supervises the implementation of policies approved by the Govt, incl. the licensing of nuclear power plants; promotion of technological industrial applications; represents Israel in relations with scientific instns and organizations abroad (Israel is a mem. of IAEA); Chair. The PRIME MINISTER; Dir-Gen. G. FRANK.

Attached Research Centres:

Negev Nuclear Research Centre: Dimona; natural uranium-fuelled and heavy water- moderated reactor IRR-2 of 26 MW thermal; Dir MICHA DAPHT.

Soreq Nuclear Research Centre: 81800 Yavne; tel. (8) 9434290; internet www .soreq.gov.il; f. 1958; swimming-pool research reactor IRR-1 of 5 MW thermal; Dir URI HALAVEE.

Office of the Chief Scientist—Industrial Research Administration, Ministry of Industry and Trade: 5 Bank Israel St, POB 3166, 91036 Jerusalem; tel. (2) 6662486; fax (2) 6662928; f. 1970; promotes industrial research and devt in industry, research institutes and higher education institutes by financing projects; encourages establishment of science-based industrial parks near universities and research institutes; proposes policies to promote innovative industry through legislation, developing physical and technical infrastructure and intergovernmental industrial R&D agreements; Chief Scientist ELI OPER.

Associated Institutions:

Institutes for Applied Research, Ben-Gurion University of the Negev: POB 1025, 84110 Be'ersheva; tel. (8) 5778382; f. 1956; engages in applied research in water desalination, membrane and ion-exchange technologies, chemical technologies, irrigation with brackish and seawater, development of salt- and drought-resistant crops and ornamentals, natural products from higher plants and algae, devt of mechanical and electromechanical products, utilization of non-conventional energy sources; 120 staff; library of 13,200 vols; Dir Prof. A. SHANI; publ. *Scientific Activities* (2 a year).

Israel Ceramic and Silicate Institute: Technion City, 32000 Haifa; tel. (4) 8222107; fax (4) 8325339; e-mail isracer@ actcom.co.il; internet www.isracer.org; f. 1962; provides the local ceramic industry with technical assistance and with research and devt into advanced and new fields in ceramics technology; 12 staff; Dir Dr ADRIAN GOLDSTEIN.

Israel Fiber Institute: POB 8001, 91080 Jerusalem; tel. (2) 5707377; fax (2) 5245110; attached to Technion—Israel Institute of Technology; f. 1953; advances textile, polymer, paper, leather and related industries; applied R&D, testing services, quality control, training courses for engineers and technicians, MSc and PhD courses in conjunction with the Hebrew Univ.; 45 staff; library of 4,000 vols and 30 periodicals; Dir Dr HILDA GUTTMAN.

Israel Institute of Metals: Technion City, 32000 Haifa; tel. (4) 8294473; f. 1962; serves industry in metallurgy and powder technology, foundry, corrosion and coating technology, vehicle and mechanical engineering; Dir Prof. A. ROSEN.

Israel Institute of Plastics: POB 7293, 31072 Haifa; tel. (4) 8225174; fax (4) 8225173; f. 1981; R&D and information centre for promoting the plastic industry; Dir Dr S. ABRAHAMI.

Israel Wine Institute: POB 2329, 4 Ha-Raz St, 76310 Rehovot; tel. (8) 9475693; f. 1957; improves the country's wines by means of quality control and applied research and promotes their export; Dir SHLOMO COHEN.

National Physical Laboratory: Hebrew Univ., Danziger A Bldg, Givat Ram Campus, 91904 Jerusalem; tel. (2) 6303501; fax (2) 6303516; attached to Min. of Industry and Trade; f. 1950; applied research with industrial orientation, basic physical and chemical standards, energy saving, ecology, solar energy; Dir Dr ILYA KUSELMAN.

Rubber Research Association Ltd: Technion City, 32000 Haifa; tel. (4) 8222124; fax (4) 8227582; f. 1951; the advancement of the rubber industry in Israel; Dir D. CZIMERMAN.

Standards Institution of Israel: POB 39020, 61390 Tel-Aviv; tel. (3) 5454154; fax (3) 5419683; internet www.iso.co.il; f. 1923; tests the compliance of commodities with the requirements of standards and specifications; grants standards mark; conducts technological research; publishes the Nat. Standards Specifications and Codes; 550 staff; library of 300,000 standards; Dir-Gen. ELI HADAR; publ. *Mati* (4 a year).

Libraries and Archives

Be'ersheva

Ben Gurion University of the Negev Aranne Library: POB 653, 84105 Be'ersheva; tel. (8) 6461413; fax (8) 6472940; e-mail yaatz@bgu.ac.il; internet www.bgu.ac .il/aranne; f. 1966; 1,000,000 vols, 25,000 current periodicals incl. e-journals, 3,200 microfilms, 300 audiovisual cassettes, 76 DVDs, 1,200 CD-ROMs and books, 1,500 online theses; spec. collns; David Tuviyahu Archives of the Negev; Isaiah Berlin Room; Dir HAYA ASNER.

Haifa

Borochov Library: c/o Haifa Labour Council, POB 5226, Haifa; f. 1921; 40,000 vols, in central library, 60,000 vols in 24 brs; Chief Librarian EZECHIEL OREN.

Haifa AMLI Library of Music: 23 Arlosoroff St, POB 4811/25, Haifa; tel. (4) 8644485; fax (4) 8644485; f. 1958; lending library incl. books, scores, records and cassettes; Librarian LEAH MARCUS.

Pevsner Public Library: 54 Pevsner St, POB 5345, Haifa; tel. (4) 8667766; f. 1934; 200,000 vols covering all fields of literature and science, in Hebrew, English and German; 15 brs; Chief Librarian Dr S. BACK.

Technion—Israel Institute of Technology, Library System: Technion City, 32000 Haifa; tel. (4) 8292507; fax (4) 8295662; e-mail ddalia@tx.technion.ac.il; internet library.technion.ac.il; f. 1925; science, technology, architecture and medicine; Elyachar (Central) Library, 17 departmental libraries; 1,000,000 vols, 12,700 current periodicals, 281 databases, 695 electronic books; Dir DALIA DOLEV.

University of Haifa Library: Mount Carmel, 31905 Haifa; tel. (4) 8240289; fax (4) 8257753; e-mail libmaster@univ.haifa.ac.il; internet lib.haifa.ac.il; f. 1963; 1,050,000 vols, 17,000 periodical titles; 8,000 current periodicals; 480,000 micro-fiches and -films, 27,000 maps; 168,000 slides; 5,600 films (incl. video cassettes); special collns incl. integrated law colln, rare books, media centre, laboratory for children's librarianship; Dir OREN WEINBERG; Admin. Dir. HUMI REKEM.

Jerusalem

Archive and Library of Ashkenaz House Synagogue Memorial: 58 King George St, POB 7440, 91073 Jerusalem; tel. (2) 6233225; fax (2) 6233226; e-mail synagog@netvision .net.il; internet www.ashkenazhouse.org; f. 1988; research into German communities and synagogues destroyed during 'Kristallnacht' in Germany, November 1938; collects material about Ashkenaz Jewry and docs relating to 'Kristallnacht'; ongoing compilation of a series of memorial books in German (of which 5 have already appeared in print), documenting the synagogues and Jewish communities destroyed in the early 20th century in greater Germany; preparation of English-language memorial books on the above subjects, for the American public; research into history of the ship *Exodus* and the subsequent deportation of holocaust survivors back to Europe; Founder and Dir-Gen. Prof. em. Dr MEIER SCHWARZ.

Awkaf Supreme Council Library: c/o Supreme Muslim Council, POB 19859, Jerusalem; Haram al-Sharif, Jerusalem; f. 1931; contains Arabic and Islamic MSS.

Bibliothèque de l'Ecole Biblique et Archéologique Française de Jérusalem: POB 19053, 6 Nablus Rd, 91190 Jerusalem; tel. (2) 6264468; fax (2) 6282567; e-mail biblio@ebaf.edu; internet www.ebaf.edu; f. 1890; 145,000 vols; archaeology and epigraphy of the ancient Near East, biblical studies; Dir Dr HERVÉ PONSOT; Librarian Rev. PAWEL TRZOPEK; publs *Cahiers de la Revue Biblique*, *Etudes Bibliques*, *Revue Biblique* (4 a year).

Central Archives for the History of the Jewish People (formerly Jewish Historical General Archives): POB 39077, 91390 Jerusalem; tel. (2) 6586249; fax (2) 6535426; e-mail archives@vms.huji.ac.il; internet sites .huji.ac.il/archives; f. 1969; Dir HADASSAH ASSOULINE; 13,000 vols on Jewish history, 1,600 community archives, 12,000 photographs, 8,000 statutes; intended to serve as the central archives of Jewish history.

Central Zionist Archives: POB 92, Jerusalem; tel. (2) 6204800; fax (2) 6204837; e-mail cza@wzo.org.il; internet www .zionistarchives.org.il; f. 1919; official repository of the World Zionist Org., the Jewish Agency, the Jewish Nat. Fund Keren Hayesod and the World Jewish Congress; 70,000 books, 10,000m. original documents, 900,000 photographs and negatives, 70,000 maps, 26,000 posters and announcements, 6,000 newspaper titles; 500 audio recordings, 2m. genealogical records; Admin. Dir GILI SIMHA; Deputy Dir for Archival Matters ROCHELLE RUBINSTEIN.

Gulbenkian Library: Armenian Patriarchate, POB 14106, 91140 Jerusalem; tel. (2) 6282331 ext. 222; e-mail ibrary@ armenian-patriarchate.org; f. 1929; donated by the late Calouste Gulbenkian; one of the three great Armenian libraries in the diaspora, the others being the Mekhitarist Fathers' Library in Venice, Italy and another in Vienna, Austria; public library of 100,000 vols, of which one-third are in Armenian and the rest in foreign languages, primarily English and French; receives more than 360 newspapers, magazines, periodicals (of which more than one-half are Armenian) from foreign countries; collns of newspapers and magazines since the 1850s; a copy of the first printed Armenian Bible (1666); 3,890 Armenian MSS; Dir Rev. Fr NORAYR KAZAZIAN; Sec. RINA DJERNAZIAN; Librarian MALINA ZAKIAN LA-PORTA; publ. *Sion* (official organ of the Armenian Patriarchate, 12 a year).

Israel Antiquities Authority Archives Branch: POB 586, 91004 Jerusalem; tel. (2) 6204680; fax (2) 6271173; e-mail arieh@ israntique.org.il; internet www.antiquities .org.il; f. 1926; written, computerized, photographic and digitized records, maps and plans; Head BARUCH BRANDL; Asst to Head of Archives ARIEH ROCHMAN-HALPERIN.

Israel State Archives: Prime Minister's Office, Kiryat Ben-Gurion, 91950 Jerusalem; tel. (2) 5680680; fax (2) 6793375; e-mail research@archives.gov.il; internet www .archives.gov.il; f. 1949; comprises 7 sections: Department of Files and Manuscripts, Library Department, Records Management, Supervision Department of Public and Private Archives, Services to the Public, Technical Services Department and Publication of State Papers; holdings incl. files occupying 30 kilometres of shelving, 150,000 printed items and 25,000 books; administrative records, incl. foreign relations, are available after 30 years and records on defence after 50 years; State Archivist E. FRIESEL; Dir M. MOSSEK; publs *Documents on the Foreign Policy of Israel*, *Israel Government Publications* (bibliography, 1 a year).

Jerusalem City (Public) Library: POB 1409, Jerusalem; tel. (2) 6256785; fax (2) 6255785; f. 1961; 750,000 vols; 20 brs and 2 Bookmobiles; Dir ABRAHAM VILNER.

Library of the Central Bureau of Statistics: 66 Kanfei Nesharm St, POB 34525, 95464 Jerusalem; tel. (2) 6592666; fax (2) 6521340; internet www.cbs.gov.il; f. 1948; 40,000 vols; spec. colln: all publs of (British) Palestine Dept of Statistics (due to be transferred to the Israel State Archives); most publs available for exchange; Librarian MARIAN ROMAN.

Library of the Knesset: Knesset, 91950 Jerusalem; tel. (2) 6753333; fax (2) 6662733; internet www.knesset.gov.il; f. 1949; principally for members' use; 150,000 vols, incl. books, bound periodicals and colln of all Israeli Govt publs, UN publs and foreign parliamentary papers; Librarian NAOMI KIMHI.

Library of the Studium Biblicum Franciscanum: POB 19424, Monastery of the Flagellation, Via Dolorosa, 91193 Jerusalem; tel. (2) 6270485; fax (2) 6264519; e-mail secretary@studiumbiblicum.org; f. 1924; 50,000 vols chiefly on archaeology, judaeo-christianism, biblical and patristic studies,

420 periodicals; 20 mems; Librarian D. ROBAERT.

Muriel and Philip Berman Medical Library, Library Authority, Hebrew University of Jerusalem: POB 12272, 91120 Jerusalem; tel. (2) 6758795; fax (2) 6758376; e-mail mdlibinfo@savion.huji.ac.il; internet library.md.huji.ac.il; f. 1919; serves faculty and students of the Hebrew Univ. of Jerusalem Faculty of Medicine, Faculty of Dental Medicine, School of Pharmacy, Nursing School and School of Public Health and the Hadassah-Hebrew Univ. Hospital; 65,000 book titles (electronic and print), 5,000 electronic journal titles, 80 annual print periodical subscriptions; history of medicine colln and museum; Dir SHARON LENGA.

Schocken Library: 6 Balfour St, 92102 Jerusalem; tel. (2) 5631288; fax (2) 5636857; e-mail jtspress@schocken-jts.org.il; internet www.schocken-jts.org.il; f. 1900; 55,000 vols, 200 MSS, 20,000 photostats (Hebrew Liturgy and Poetry); Dir Dr SHMUEL GLICK; Bibliographer and Research Librarian DAVID KERSCHEN.

Supreme Court Library: Supreme Court of Israel, Rehov Sha'arei Mishpat, Kiryat Ben Gurion, 91 950 Jerusalem; tel. (2) 6759665; e-mail liba@supreme.court.gov.il; internet www.court.gov.il; f. 1949; 85,000 vols; Dir LIBA BORCK.

The National Library of Israel: POB 39105, 91390 Jerusalem; tel. (2) 6584651; fax (2) 6511771; e-mail orenw@savion.huji.ac .il; internet www.jnul.huji.ac.il; f. 1892; 10,000 MSS; 49,000 microfilmed Hebrew MSS; microfilms of Jewish and Israeli newspapers; 200 incunabula (120 Hebrew and 80 in other languages); 15,000 current periodicals; special collns incl. the Abraham Schwadron Colln of Jewish Autographs and Portraits, the Harry Friedenwald Colln on the History of Medicine, the National Sound Archives and the Jacob Michael Colln of Jewish Music, the Sidney M. Edelstein Colln on the History of Chemistry, the Eran Laor Cartographic Colln, the Archives of Albert Einstein; 5,000,000 vols, incl. those in departmental libraries; Dir OREN WEINBERG; Chief Librarian RIVKA SHVEIKY; publs *Index of Articles on Jewish Studies* (1 a year), *Kiryat Sefer* (bibliography, 4 a year).

Kfar Giladi

Kfar Giladi Library: 12210 Kfar Giladi, Upper Galilee; f. 1934; 35,000 vols, 110 periodicals; Librarian SHULAMIT ROSENTHAL.

Kiryat Shmona

Library of Tel-Hai Academic College: Upper Galilee, 12210, nr Kiryat Shmona; tel. (4) 8181785; fax (4) 8181787; e-mail sagim@telhai.ac.il; internet www.telhai.ac.il; incl. the Calvary Colln, the Ofer Colln, the Kapeliuk Middle East colln, Dvir Colln in Environmental Studies, the Lubin art colln and the Gail Chasin art colln, Littauer Judaic Colln, Silvia Sheim Colln; 80,000 vols, 600 periodicals, 1,200 videotapes, 4,200 e-Journals; Library Dir IRIS CHAI.

Nahariya

Municipal Library in Memory of William and Chia Boorstein: 61 Herzl St, Nahariya; tel. (4) 9879870; f. 1946; under the supervision of the Ministry of Education , Jerusalem; 70,000 vols; Chief Librarian SHOSHANA GIBLEY.

Ramat-Gan

Bar-Ilan University Library System: Central Library, 52900 Ramat-Gan; tel. (3) 5318165; fax (3) 5353116; e-mail tchiya .dagan@mail.biu.ac.il; internet www.biu.ac .il/lib; f. 1955; serves faculties of humanities,

Judaica, law, social sciences, exact sciences, and life sciences; 1,000,000 vols, 4,500 current journals; spec. collns incl. the Mordecai Margulies colln of rare 16th and 17th century Hebrew books and 800 Hebrew Oriental MSS, Berman colln of early E European Hebrew imprints, rare Latin and German books on Jewish studies, Old Testament criticism, material on the Dead Sea Scrolls and the Samaritans; a colln of material on the devt of Religious Zionism; colln of Responsa and Jewish studies; Moussaieff colln of 220 Kabbalistic MSS; Head Periodicals Dept T. DAGAN; publs *Hebrew Subject Headings* (online), *Index to Literary Supplements of the Daily Hebrew Press* (online).

'Dvir Bialik' Municipal Central Public Library: Hibat-Zion St 14, Ramat-Gan; f. 1945; 400,000 vols, incl. special Rabbinic literature and Social Sciences colln; maintains 11 brs; Chief Librarian HADASSAH PELACH.

Rehovot

Hebrew University of Jerusalem, Central Library of Agricultural Science: POB 12, 76100 Rehovot; tel. (8) 9481270; f. 1960; Nat. Agricultural Library, operated jtly by the Volcani Centre of the Min. of Agriculture's Agricultural Research Org. and the Hebrew Univ. Faculty of Agriculture; maintains exchange relations all over the world; 300,000 vols, 3,200 current periodicals and serials, 180,000 docs; regional libraries at Gilath, Dor and N've Ya'ar; Dir SUSANA GURMAN.

Weizmann Archives: POB 26, 76100 Rehovot; tel. (8) 9343390; fax (8) 9344176; internet www.weizmann.ac.il/wis-library/archive .htm; f. 1973; contains assembled letters, papers, photographs, and other docs relating to political and scientific activities of Dr Chaim Weizmann, first President of Israel; approx. 180,000 items; Archivist ORNA ZELTZER.

Weizmann Institute of Science Libraries: POB 26, 76100 Rehovot; tel. (8) 9343873; fax (8) 9344176; e-mail ilana.pollack@ weizmann.ac.il; internet www.weizmann.ac .il/library; f. 1934 as Ziff Institute Libraries; renamed 1949; Wix Central Library, 3 faculty libraries, 1 departmental library and approx. 50 departmental collections; 260,000 vols, incl. bound periodicals and 1,032 current print periodicals in science and technology, and access to several databases and several thousand electronic journals; Chief Librarian ILANA POLLACK.

Tel-Aviv

Felicja Blumental Music Center and Library: 26 Bialik St, 61048 Tel-Aviv; tel. (3) 6201185; fax (3) 6201323; e-mail info@ fbmc.co.il; internet www.fbmc.co.il; f. 1950; 75,920 vols, 64 periodicals, 18,000 records, 3,446 compact discs, 170 video cassettes; Bronislav Huberman archive, Joachim Stutschewsky archive, Shulamith Conservatory (1910), Beit Levi'im (1919), etc.; Dir IRIT SCHÖNHORN.

General Archives of the City of Tel-Aviv-Yafo: City Hall, Kikar Malkhei Israel, 64162 Tel-Aviv; tel. (3) 6438554; f. 1967; Archivist JUDITH Z. FASTOVSKY.

Library of the Kibbutzim College of Education: 149 Namir Rd, 62507 Tel-Aviv; tel. (3) 6902323; fax (3) 6992791; internet www.smkb.ac.il; f. 1940; 75,000 vols; Librarian EDNA NAAMAN.

Sourasky Central Library, Tel-Aviv University: POB 39038, Ramat-Aviv, 61930 Tel-Aviv; tel. (3) 6408745; fax (3) 6407833; e-mail miril@tauex.tau.ac.il; internet www.cenlib .tau.ac.il; f. 1954; 880,000 vols, 4,800 current periodicals and 96,000 microforms; 7 specialized br. libraries; 788,000 vols; incl. the Pevsner Colln of Hebrew Press, the Faitlovitch colln, the Colln of Yiddish Literature and Culture in memory of Benzion and Pearl Margulies, the Wiener Library colln, which concerns the Second World War, spec. the Holocaust, and the history of anti-Semitism, the Herbert Cohen colln of rare books, the Dr Horodisch colln on the history of books and the Jaffe colln of Hebrew poetry; Dir MIRA LIPSTEIN.

Tel-Aviv Central Public Library 'Shaar Zion': 25 King Saul Blvd, POB 33235, Tel-Aviv; tel. (3) 6910141; fax (3) 6919024; internet www.tel-aviv.gov.il/english/culture/ariela.htm; f. 1922; 900,000 vols (in 25 brs); General Library in 8 languages; spec. collns: Rambam Library, Ahad ha-Am Library (history and geography of Eretz Israel), Dance Library, Graphoteque (lending library of artist prints), Legal Library; Dir ORA NEBENZAHL.

Museums and Art Galleries

Acre

Okashi Art Museum, Acre: Old City of Akko, El-Jazz'ar St, Acre; permanent exhibition of works by Avsalom Okashi (1916–1980); temporary exhibitions by Israeli artists.

Be'ersheva

Negev Museum: 60 Ha'atsmaut Rd, POB 5188, 84100 Be'ersheva; tel. (7) 6206570; fax (7) 6206536; e-mail br7museum@br7.org.il; f. 1954; exhibits from regional excavations, mainly from the Chalcolithic, Israelite, Roman and Byzantine periods; exhibitions of Israeli contemporary art; Dir GALIA GAVISH.

Haifa

Haifa Museum of Art: 26 Shabbetai Levy St, 33043 Haifa; tel. (4) 8523255; fax (4) 8552714; e-mail curator@hma.org.il; internet www.hma.org.il; f. 1951; collns of Israeli and world contemporary art, prints, art posters, paintings and sculptures; library of 10,000 vols; Curator Dir TAMI KATZ-FREIMAN.

National Maritime Museum: 198 Allenby Rd, POB 44855, 31447 Haifa; tel. (4) 8536622; fax (4) 8539286; e-mail curator@nmm.org.il; internet www.nmm.org.il; f. 1954; large colln of artefacts and ship models illustrating 5,000 years of navigation and shipbuilding, old maps and engravings, undersea archaeology, a Hellenistic bronze ram, and stamps and ancient coins connected with seafaring and maritime symbols; archaeology and civilizations of ancient peoples; scientific instruments; library: research library of 6,000 vols; Dir-Gen. NISSIM TAL; publ. *Sefunim*.

Tikotin Museum of Japanese Art: 89 Hanassi Ave, 34529 Haifa; tel. (4) 8383554; fax (4) 8379824; e-mail curator@tmja.org.il; internet www.tmja.org.il; f. 1960; paintings, prints, drawings, textiles, netsuke, lacquer work, ceramics, metalwork, collection of Mingei (folk art); courses for children and adults; library of 3,000 vols; Chief Curator Dr ILANA SINGER.

Jerusalem

Archaeological (Rockefeller) Museum: POB 71117, 91710 Jerusalem; tel. (2) 6282251; fax (2) 6708906; e-mail fawziib@imj.org.il; internet www.imj.org.il; f. 1938; fmrly Palestine Archaeological Museum; archaeology of Israel from earliest times up until end of Islamic period; largely material found in excavations before 1948; Dir JAMES S. SNYDER.

Beit Ha'Omanim (Jerusalem Artists' House): 12 Shmuel Hanagid St, Jerusalem; tel. (2) 6253653; fax (2) 6258594; e-mail artists@zahav.net.il; f. 1965; Israeli and foreign contemporary art exhibitions and permanent gallery of works by Israeli artists; Dir RUTH ZADKA.

Bible Lands Museum Jerusalem: POB 4670, 91046 Jerusalem; 25 Granot St, 93706 Jerusalem; tel. (2) 5611066; fax (2) 5638228; e-mail contact@blmj.org; internet www.blmj.org; f. 1992; ancient Near Eastern history and Biblical archaeology; Dir BATYA BOROWSKI; Curator YEHUDA KAPLAN.

Israel Museum: POB 71117, 91710 Jerusalem; tel. (2) 6708811; fax (2) 5631833; e-mail info@imj.org.il; internet www.imj.org.il; f. 1965; fine art, Judaica and archaeology from Biblical times to the present; Shrine of the Book housing Dead Sea Scrolls; Billy Rose Sculpture Garden; a renovation project to extend the museum bldgs is to be completed by the end of 2009; library of 65,000 vols; Dir JAMES S. SNYDER; publ. *Journal* (1 a year).

Mayer, L. A., Museum for Islamic Art: POB 4088, 2 Hapalmach St, 91040 Jerusalem; tel. (2) 5661291; fax (2) 5619802; e-mail islamart@netvision.net.il; internet www.islamicart.co.il; f. 1974; colln of Islamic art: metalwork, glass, miniatures, ceramics, ivories, jewellery; Sir David Salomons colln of antique clocks and watches; educational activities in Jewish and Arab sectors; library of 14,000 vols, 50 periodicals; photographs and slides; Dir RACHEL HASSON.

Museum of Prehistory, Institute of Archaeology, Hebrew University: Mt Scopus Campus, Jerusalem; tel. (2) 5882099; fax (2) 5825548; internet archaeology.huji.ac.il; f. 1955; large colln of objects from prehistoric sites in Israel; library.

Museum of Taxes: 42 Agripas St, POB 3100, 91036 Jerusalem; tel. (2) 6257597; fax (2) 6252381; e-mail misim@mof.gov.il; internet ozar.mof.gov.il/museum; f. 1964; 5 sections: artefacts from the Land of Canaan and environs, taxes levied specifically on Jews in the Diaspora, gen. section for tax-related items from all over the world, taxation in Israel, prevention of smuggling and importation of illegal goods and other customs-related issues; Dir MIRA DROR; publ. *Israeli Tax Review* (4 a year).

Museum of the Studium Biblicum Franciscanum: POB 19424, Monastery of the Flagellation, Via Dolorosa, Jerusalem; tel. (2) 6282936; fax (2) 6264519; e-mail sbfnet@netvision.net.il; internet 198.62.75.1/www1/ofm/sbf/sbfmuse.html; f. 1923; Palestinian archaeology: city coins of Palestine, Roman-Byzantine-Crusader pottery and objects; Curator M. PICCIRILLO; publ. *S. B. F Museum*.

Yad Vashem, Holocaust Martyrs' and Heroes' Remembrance Authority: POB 3477, Mount of Remembrance, 90435 Jerusalem; tel. (2) 6443400; fax (2) 6443409; e-mail general.information@yadvashem.org.il; internet www.yadvashem.org; f. 1953; the Jewish people's nat. memorial to the Holocaust; Holocaust History museum: permanent exhibition of photographs, documents, artefacts and testimonies; Hall of Names; Hall of Remembrance; Children's Memorial; Valley of the Communities; Memorial to the Deportees; Ave and Garden of the Righteous Among the Nations; Holocaust art museum; Int. Institute for Holocaust Research is responsible for expanding academic and research activities; Int. School for Holocaust Studies organizes seminars and develops teaching materials; library of 123,000 vols; world's largest repository of archival and documentary information on the Holocaust: approx. 68m. pages of documents, microfilms, testimonies, diaries, artefacts; Chair. AVNER SHALEV; publ. *Yad Vashem Studies*.

Kibbutz Hazorea

Wilfrid Israel Museum of Oriental Art and Studies: Kibbutz Hazorea, 30060 Post Hazorea; f. 1947; opened 1951 in memory of the late Wilfrid Israel; a cultural centre for study and art exhibitions incl. modern art and all areas of the plastic arts; houses the Wilfrid Israel colln of Near and Far Eastern art and cultural materials; local archaeological exhibits from neolithic to Byzantine times; art library; Dir EHUD DOR.

Kibbutz Lahav

Museum of Bedouin Culture: Joe Alon Centre, Kibbutz Lahav, 85335 Negev D. N.; tel. (8) 9913322; fax (8) 9919889; e-mail joealon@lhv.org.il; internet www.joealon.org.il; f. 1985; part of the Colonel Joe Alon Centre for Regional and Folklore Studies; exhibition of contemporary arts and crafts, educational lectures and guided tours, photographs, demonstrations of Bedouin life (weaving, cooking, etc.); museum of Jewish settlement in the Negev; art gallery; museum of the Bar-Kokba Rebellion; awards grants for research in Bedouin and regional studies; library of 150 vols, 3,000 slides; Gen. Dir RACHEL ALON-MARGALIT.

Kiryat Shmona

Tel Hai Museum: 12210 Tel Hai, Upper Galilee; tel. (4) 6951333; reconstruction of a Jewish settlement from the beginning of the 20th century; documents of Joseph Trumpeldor and his defence of the region in 1920.

Ma'ayan Baruch

Ma'ayan Baruch Prehistory Museum of the Huleh Valley: 12220 Ma'ayan Baruch, Upper Galilee; tel. (4) 523791649; fax (4) 6950724; f. 1952; prehistory of the Huleh Valley from the Palaeolithic (incl. large colln of Ashulian handaxes) to the Chalcolithic period; locally excavated Bronze Age and Roman-Byzantine objects; colln of stone grain mills and oil presses; the Earliest Dog in the World, buried with a woman from the Natufian period (10,000 BC); plaster skull from Neolithic era (7000 BC); world ethnographic exhibition of tools fashioned by people who still live as in prehistoric times; Dir A. ASSAF.

Nazareth

Terra Sancta Museum: Terra Sancta Monastery, POB 23, 96100 Nazareth; tel. (4) 6572501; fax (4) 6460203; f. 1920; Byzantine (and later) remains, coins, Roman and Byzantine glass; colln of antiquities from excavations made in the monastery compound; Vicar of Monastery Rev. P. JOSÉ MONTALVERNE DE LANCASTRE.

Safad

Israel Bible Museum: c/o POB 1396, Safed; tel. (4) 6999972; internet www.israelbiblemuseum.com; f. 1984; exhibition of the biblical art of Phillip Ratner; permanent and changing exhibitions incl. Kabbalah and art for children; Dir AMI SHOSHAN.

Sha'ar Ha-Golan

Museum of Prehistory: Sha'ar Ha-Golan, Jordan Valley; f. 1950; large number of exhibits from the neolithic Yarmukian culture excavated in the region; Dir Y. ROTH.

Tel-Aviv

Ben-Gurion House: 17 Ben-Gurion Blvds, 63454 Tel-Aviv; tel. (3) 5221010; fax (3) 5247293; f. 1974; residence of David Ben-Gurion, first Prime Minister of the State of Israel; museum and research and study centre; library of 20,000 vols and periodicals on history of Zionist movement, land and state of Israel, ancient peoples, cultures, religions and philosophies, gen. and military history; Dir HANNI HERMOLIN.

Beth Hatefutsoth (The Nahum Gold-mann Museum of the Jewish Diaspora): POB 39359, 61392 Tel-Aviv; tel. (3) 7457890; fax (3) 7457831; e-mail armoni@bh.org.il; internet www.bh.org.il; f. 1978; permanent exhibition tells the story of Jewish survival and life in the Diaspora; temporary exhibitions portray Jewish communities all over the world; seminars and youth educational activities; photographic and film archives; Jewish Genealogy and music centre; CEO AVINOAM ARMONI.

Eretz-Israel Museum: 2 Chaim Levanon St, POB 17068, Ramat Aviv, 61170 Tel-Aviv; tel. (3) 6415244; fax (3) 6412408; internet www.eretzmuseum.org.il; Tel-Aviv region archaeology and history, Jewish ethnography and folklore, ceramics, ancient glass, numismatics, history of Jewish theatre, tools and technology, planetarium; library of 40,000 vols.

Tel-Aviv Museum of Art: POB 33288, 27 Shaul Hamelech Blvd, 64329 Tel-Aviv; tel. (3) 6077000; fax (3) 6958099; e-mail cliffs@tamuseum.com; internet www.tamuseum.com; f. 1932; art colln consisting of works since 16th century; Israeli art; library: art library of 60,000 vols, periodicals, microfiches, databases; Dir and Chief Curator Prof. MORDECHAI OMER.

Tiberias

Municipal Museum of Antiquities: Lake Front, Tiberias; f. 1953; colln of antiquities from Tiberias and region, mainly of the Roman, Byzantine and Arab periods; Dir ELISHEVA BALLHORN.

Universities

BAR-ILAN UNIVERSITY

52900 Ramat-Gan
Telephone: (3) 5318111
Fax: (3) 5344622
E-mail: director-general.office@mail.biu.ac.il
Internet: www.biu.ac.il

Founded 1953; inaugurated 1955
State control
Language of instruction: Hebrew
Academic year: October to June
Pres.: Prof. MOSHE KAVEH
Vice-Pres. for Research: Prof. HAROLD BASCH
Assoc. Vice-Pres.: JUDITH HAIMOFF
Rector: Prof. JOSEPH MENIS
Dir-General: HAIM GLICK
Academic Registrar: M. MISHAN
Librarian: (vacant)
Library: see Libraries and Archives
Number of teachers: 1,350
Number of students: 31,678

Four regional colleges; Ashkelon College, Jordan Valley College, Safed College, Western Galilee College; 76 research centres

Publication: *Philosophia* (4 a year)

DEANS

Faculty of Exact Sciences: Prof. A. AMIR
Faculty of Humanities: Prof. B. ABRAHAMOV
Faculty of Jewish Studies: Prof. M. ORFALI
Faculty of Law: Prof. A. REICH

Faculty of Life Sciences: Prof. H. BREITBART
Faculty of Social Sciences: Prof. S. SANDLER

PROFESSORS

Faculty of Exact Sciences (tel. (3) 5318585; fax (3) 5344766; e-mail exacts@mail.biu.ac.il; internet www.esc.biu.ac.il):

AGRONOVSKY, M., Mathematics
AMIR, A., Computer Science
BASCH, H., Chemistry
BERKOWITZ, R., Physics
DEUTSCH, M., Physics
EHRENBERG, B., Physics
EISENBERG, L., Mathematics
FREULIKHER, V., Physics
FREUND, Y., Physics
FRIEDMAN, L., Mathematics
FRIMER, A., Chemistry
GEDANKEN, A., Chemistry
GOLDSCHMIDT, Z., Chemistry
GORDON, A., Chemistry
HALPERN, H., Physics
HAVLIN, S., Physics
HOCHBERG, K., Mathematics
HOZ, S., Chemistry
KANTOR, I., Physics
KAVEH, M., Physics
KAY, K., Chemistry
KESSLER, D., Physics
KRAUSS, S., Computer Science
KRUSHKAL, S., Mathematics
MARGEL, S., Chemistry
MARGOLIS, S., Mathematics
MARZBACH, E., Mathematics
NUDELMAN, A., Chemistry
ORBACH, D., Chemistry
PERSKY, A., Chemistry
RABIN, I., Physics
RAPPAPORT, D., Physics
ROSENBLUH, M., Physics
ROWEN, L., Mathematics
SHAPIRA, B., Physics
SHLIMAK, I., Physics
SHNIDER, S., Mathematics
SUKENIK, H., Chemistry
TEICHER, M., Mathematics
ULMAN, A., Chemistry
YESHURUN, Y., Physics
ZALCMAN, L., Mathematics

Faculty of Humanities (tel. (3) 5318370; fax (3) 5347601; e-mail segalil@mail.biu.ac.il; internet www.biu.ac.il/hu):

ABRAHAMOV, B., Arabic
FINE, J., English
HALAMISH, M., Philosophy
HANDELMAN, S., English
HARVEY, S., Philosophy
HASSINE, J., Comparative Literature
KATZOFF, R., Classical Studies
KOREN, R., French Culture
LANGERMAN, Z., Arabic
PERL, J., English
REICHELBERG, R., Comparative Literature
ROTHSTEIN, S., English
SAGUY, A., Philosophy
SCHWARTZ, D., Philosophy
SPOLSKY, E., English
WIDOKER, D., Philosophy

Faculty of Jewish Studies (tel. (3) 5318233; fax (3) 5351233; e-mail jsfcty@mail.biu.ac.il; internet www.biu.ac.il/js):

BAR TIKVAH, B., Literature of the Jewish People
BAUMGARTEN, A., Jewish History
COHEN, M., General History
COHEN, T., Literature of the Jewish People
DISHON, Y., Literature of the Jewish People
FEINER, S., Jewish History
GENIZI, H., General History
HAVLIN, S. Z., Talmud and Information Sciences
HAZAN, E., Literature of the Jewish People
KASHER, R., Bible
KLONER, A., Land of Israel Studies

KOGEL, J., Bible
LIPSKER, A., Literature of the Jewish People
MICHMAN, D., Jewish History
MILIKOWSKI, H., Talmud
ORFALI, M., Jewish History
ROSMAN, M., Jewish History
SAFRAI, Z., Land of Israel Studies
SCHWARTZ, J., Land of Israel Studies
SCHWARTZWALD, O., Hebrew Language
SHARVIT, S., Hebrew Language
SOKOLOFF, M., Hebrew and Semitic Languages
SPERBER, D., Talmud
SPIEGEL, Y., Talmud
TABORI, Y., Talmud
TAUBER, E., History of the Middle East
TOAFF, A., Jewish History
VARGON, S., Bible
WEISS, H., Literature of the Jewish People

Faculty of Law (tel. (3) 5318417; fax (3) 5351856; e-mail olmertr@mail.biu.ac.il; internet www.law.biu.ac.il):

COHEN, Z.
LERNER, S.

Faculty of Life Sciences (tel. (3) 5318721; fax (3) 7369928; e-mail landmar@mail.biu.ac.il; internet life-sciences.biu.ac.il):

ACHITUV, Y.
BREITBART, H.
BRODIE, C.
COHEN, Y.
HAAS, E.
KISLEV, M.
MALIK, Z.
MAYEVSKY, A.
SAMPSON, S.
SHAINBERG, A.
SHOHAM, Y.
SREDNI, B.
STEINBERGER, J.
SUSSWEIN, A.

Faculty of Social Sciences (tel. (3) 5318452; fax (3) 5351825; e-mail socials@mail.biu.ac.il; internet www.biu.ac.il/soc):

ADAD, M., Criminology
ALPEROVITCH, G., Economics
BABKOFF, H., Psychology
COHEN, S., Political Science
DON-YEHIEH, E., Political Science
FRIEDMAN, M., Sociology
GAZIEL, H., School of Education
GOLDREICH, Y., Geography
GREILSAMMER, I., Political Studies
HALEVY-SPIRO, M., Social Work
HILLMANN, A., Economics
INBAR, E., Political Science
IRAM, Y., Education
JAFFE, E., Business Administration
KATZ, J., Geography
KLEIN, P., Education
KOSLOWSKY, M., Psychology
KRAWITZ, S., Psychology
LAUTERBACH, B., School of Business Administration
LAVEE, H., Geography
LEVI-SHIFF, R., Psychology
MENIS, J., Education
MEVARECH, Z., Education
MIKULINCER, M., Psychology
NACHSHON, I., Criminology
NITZAN, S., Economics
ORBACH, I., Psychology
RABINOWITZ, J., Social Work
SANDLER, S., Political Science
SCHWARZWALD, J., Psychology
SHULMAN, S., Psychology
SILBER, J., Economics
TAPIERO, C., Economics
TZURIEL, D., School of Education
VAKIL, E., Psychology
WELLER, A., Psychology
WOLF, Y., Criminology
YEHUDA, S., Psychology

YITZCHAKI, H., Social Work
ZIDERMAN, A., Economics
ZISSER, B., Political Science

BEN GURION UNIVERSITY OF THE NEGEV

POB 653, 84105 Be'ersheva
Telephone: (8) 6461223
Fax: (8) 6479434
E-mail: rector@bgu.ac.il
Internet: www.bgu.ac.il
Founded 1965
Languages of instruction: Hebrew, English
Academic year: October to June
Pres.: Prof. RIVKA CARMI
Rector: Prof. JIMMY WEINBLATT
Vice-Pres. and Dir-Gen.: DAVID BAREKET
Vice-Pres. and Dean for Research and Devt: Prof. MORDECHAY HERSKOWITZ
Vice-Pres. for External Affairs: Prof. AMOS DRORY
Dir of Public Affairs: NINA PERLIS
Librarian: AVNER SCHMUELEVITZ

Library: see Libraries and Archives
Number of teachers: 1,000
Number of students: 17,000

Publications: *Geography Research Forum, HAGAR—International Social Science Review, Israel Social Science Research Journal, Israel Studies, JAMA'A—Interdisciplinary Journal for the Study of the Middle East, MIKAN—Research Journal of Hebrew Literature, Shvut—Studies in Russian and East European Jewish History and Culture*

DEANS

Faculty of Engineering Sciences: Prof. GABI BEN-DOR
Faculty of Health Sciences: Prof. SHAUL SOFER
Faculty of Humanities and Social Sciences: Prof. MOSHE JUSTMAN
Faculty of Natural Sciences: Prof. AMIR SAGI
Guilford Glazer School of Business and Management: Prof. ARIE REICHEL
Kreitman School of Advanced Graduate Studies: Prof. RAMY BRUSTEIN

PROFESSORS

Faculty of Engineering Sciences (tel. (8) 6479270; fax (8) 6479401; e-mail offcdean@bgumail.bgu.ac.il; internet cmsprod.bgu.ac.il/eng/engn):

AHARONI, H., Electrical and Computer Engineering
ALFASSI, Z., Nuclear Engineering
APELBLAT, A., Chemical Engineering
ARAZI, B., Electrical and Computer Engineering
BEN-DOR, G., Mechanical Engineering
BEN-YAAKOV, S., Electrical and Computer Engineering
CENSOR, D., Electrical and Computer Engineering
DARIEL, M., Materials Engineering
DINSTEIN, I., Electrical and Computer Engineering
DUBI, A., Nuclear Engineering
EILON, A., Electrical and Computer Engineering
ELIEZER, D., Materials Engineering
ELPERIN, T., Mechanical Engineering
FINGER, N., Industrial Engineering and Management
FUKS, D., Materials Engineering
GALPERIN, A., Nuclear Engineering
GOTTLIEB, M., Chemical Engineering
HAVA, S., Electrical and Computer Engineering
HERSKOWITZ, M., Chemical Engineering
IGRA, O., Mechanical Engineering
JACOB, I., Nuclear Engineering

KAPLAN, B., Electrical and Computer Engineering
KOPEIKA, N., Electrical and Computer Engineering
KOST, J., Chemical Engineering
LADANY, S., Industrial Engineering and Management
LETAN, R., Mechanical Engineering
MENIPAZ, E., Industrial Engineering and Management
MERCHUK, J., Chemical Engineering
MOND, M., Mechanical Engineering
PERL, M., Mechanical Engineering
PLISKIN, J., Industrial Engineering and Management
PLISKIN, N., Industrial Engineering and Management
PORTMAN, V., Mechanical Engineering
RONEN, Y., Nuclear Engineering
ROTMAN, S., Electrical and Computer Engineering
SCHULGASSER, K., Mechanical Engineering
SEGEV, R., Mechanical Engineering
SHACHAM, M., Chemical Engineering
SHANI, G., Nuclear Engineering
SHER, E., Mechanical Engineering
SHINAR, D., Industrial Engineering and Management
SHUVAL, P., Information Systems Engineering
SINUANI-STERN, Z., Industrial Engineering and Management
SLONIM, M., Electrical and Computer Engineering
TALYANKER, M., Materials Engineering
TAMIR, A., Chemical Engineering
VILNAY, O., Construction Engineering
VOLLICH, D., Electrical and Computer Engineering
WISNIAK, J., Chemical Engineering
ZARETSKY, E., Mechanical Engineering

Faculty of Health Sciences (tel. (8) 6477409; fax (8) 6477632; e-mail rtemes@bgumail.bgu.ac.il; internet www.fohs.bgu.ac.il):

ABOUD, M., Microbiology and Immunology
ALKAN, M., Internal Medicine
APPELBAUM, A., Cardiology
APTE, R., Microbiology and Immunology
BASHAN, N., Clinical Biochemistry
BENJAMIN, J., Psychiatry
BUSKILA, D., Internal Medicine
CARMEL, S., Health Sociology
CARMI, R., Clinical Genetics
CLARFIELD, M., Geriatrics
FRASER, D., Epidemiology
GROSSMAN, Y., Physiology
GURMAN, G., Anaesthesiology
HALEVI, S., Dermatology
HALLAK, M., Gynaecology
HELDMAN, E., Physiology
HERZANO, Y., Radiology
ILIA, R., Cardiology
ISAKOV, N., Microbiology and Immunology
KATZ, M., Gynaecology
LEVY, R., Biochemistry
LEVY, Y., Biochemistry
LUNENFELD, E., Gynaecology
MARGULIS, C., Medical Education
MAZOR, M., Gynaecology
MEYERSTEIN, N., Physiology
MORAN, A., Physiology
NAGGAN, L., Epidemiology
NEUMANN, L., Epidemiology
PIURA, B., Gynaecology
PORATH, A., Internal Medicine
POTASHNIK, G., Gynaecology
RAGER, B., Microbiology and Immunology
SCHLESINGER, M., Paediatrics
SCHVARTZMAN, P., Family Medicine
SEGAL, S., Microbiology and Immunology
SHARONI, Y., Clinical Biochemistry
SCHLAEFFER, F., Internal Medicine
SHANY, SH., Clinical Biochemistry
SIKULER, E., Internal Medicine
SOFER, S., Paediatrics

SUKENIK, S., Internal Medicine
TAL, A., Paediatrics
WEINSTEIN, J., Microbiology
WHITE, E., Morphology

Faculty of Humanities and Social Sciences (tel. (8) 6461105; fax (8) 6472945; e-mail henik@bgumail.bgu.ac.il; internet www.bgu.ac.il/html/academics.html):

ALEXANDER, T., Hebrew Literature
BAR-ON, D., Behavioural Sciences
BENZION, U., Economics
BLIDSTEIN, G., Jewish Thought
BORG, A., Hebrew Language
BOWMAN, D., Geography and Environmental Development
BRAVERMAN, A., Economics
BREGMAN, D., Hebrew Literature
CASPI, D., Communication Studies
DANZINGER, L., Economics
DREMAN, S., Behavioural Sciences
EINY, E., Economics
GELMAN, Y., Philosophy
GILAD, I., Bible and Ancient Near-Eastern Studies
GORDON, D., Education
GORDON, H., Education
GORODETSKY, M., Education
GRADUS, Y., Geography and Environmental Development
GRIES, Z., Jewish Thought
GRUBER, I., Bible and Ancient Near-East Studies
HENIK, A., Behavioural Sciences
HOCHMAN, O., Economics
HUROWITZ, V., Bible and Ancient Near-Eastern Studies
ISRALOWITZ, R., Social Work
JUSTMAN, M., Economics
KRAKOVER, S., Geography and Environmental Development
KREISEL, H., Jewish Thought
LARONNE, J., Geography and Environmental Development
LASKER, D., Jewish Thought
LAZIN, F., Behavioural Sciences
LIBERLES, R., History
LURIE, Y., Philosophy
MEIR, A., Geography and Environmental Development
MORRIS, B., Middle East Studies
OREN, E., Bible and Ancient Near-Eastern Studies
PARUSH, A., Philosophy
POZNANSKI, R., Politics and Government
PRIEL, B., Behavioural Sciences
QIMRON, E., Hebrew Language
REGEV, U., Economics
ROSEN, S., Bible and Ancient Near-Eastern Studies
SALMON, Y., History
SHAROT, S., Behavioural Sciences
SHINAR, D., General Studies
SIVAN, D., Hebrew Language
STERN, E., Geography and Environmental Development
TALSHIR, Z., Bible and Ancient Near-East Studies
TOBIN, I., Foreign Languages and Literature
TROEN, I., History
TSAHOR, Z., History
TSOAR, H., Geography and Environmental Development
TZELGOV, Y., Behavioural Sciences
VINNER, S., Science and Technology Education
WEINBLATT, J., Economics

Faculty of Natural Sciences (tel. (8) 6461633; fax (8) 6472954; e-mail mia@math.bgu.ac.il; internet www.bgu.ac.il/html/academics.html):

ABRAHAM, U., Mathematics
ABRAMSKY, Z., Life Sciences
ALPAI, D., Mathematics
ALTSHULER, A., Mathematics

AVISHAI, Y., Physics
BAHAT, D., Geological and Environmental Sciences
BAND, Y., Chemistry
BARAK, Z., Life Sciences
BECKER, J., Chemistry
BELITSKI, H., Mathematics
BEREND, D., Mathematics
BERNSTEIN, J., Chemistry
BITTNER, S., Chemistry
BRUSTEIN, R., Physics
CHIPMAN, D., Life Sciences
COHEN, M., Mathematics
DAVIDSON, A., Physics
EFRIMA, S., Chemistry
EICHLER, D., Physics
EISENBERG, T., Mathematics
FEINTUCH, A., Mathematics
FONF, V., Mathematics
FUHRMANN, P. A., Mathematics
GEDALIN, M., Physics
GERSTEN, A., Physics
GLASER, R., Chemistry
GOLDSHTEIN, V., Mathematics
GOREN, S., Physics
GORODETSKY, G., Physics
GRANOT, Y., Life Sciences
HODORKOVSKY, V., Chemistry
HOROVITZ, B., Physics
HOROWITZ, Y., Physics
KISCH, H., Geological and Environmental Sciences
KOJMAN, M., Mathematics
KOST, D., Chemistry
LIN, M., Mathematics
MEIR, Y., Physics
MIZRAHI, Y., Life Sciences
MOALEM, A., Physics
MORDECHAI, S., Physics
MOREH, R., Physics
OWEN, D., Physics
PAROLA, A., Chemistry
POLAK, M., Chemistry
PRIEL, Z., Chemistry
PROSS, A., Chemistry
RABINOVITSCH, A., Physics
ROSENWAKS, S., Physics
RUBIN, M., Mathematics
SCHARF, B., Chemistry
SEGEV, Y., Mathematics
SHOSHAN-BARMATZ, V., Life Sciences
SHUKER, R., Physics
TKACHENKO, V., Mathematics
ZARITSKY, A., Life Sciences

Guilford Glazer School of Business and Management (tel. (8) 6472190; fax (8) 6472868; e-mail sompr@nihul.bgu.ac.il; internet www.bgu.ac.il/som):

BAR-ELI, M., Business Administration
DRORY, A., Business Administration
GIDRON, B., Business Administration
MALACH-PINES, A., Business Administration
PREISS, K., Business Administration
REICHEL, A., Hotel and Tourism Management

ATTACHED RESEARCH INSTITUTES

Ben-Gurion Research Institute for the Study of Israel: tel. (8) 6596936; fax (8) 6596939; e-mail moreshet@bgu.ac.il; internet cmsprod.bgu.ac.il/eng/centers/bgi; f. 1976; publ. *Israel Studies* (3 a year), *Iyunim Bitkumat Israel* (1 a year); Dir MICHAL MOUYAL.

Homeland Security Research Institute: tel. (8) 6596936; fax (8) 6596939; e-mail doronhav@bgu.ac.il; internet cmsprod.bgu.ac.il/eng/centers/hsri; Dir Prof. DORON HAVAZALET.

Jacob Blaustein Institute for Desert Research: Sde Boker Campus, 84990 Be'ersheva; tel. (8) 6596777; fax (8) 6596703; e-mail bidr@bgu.ac.il; internet www.bgu.ac.il/bidr; f. 1974; Dir Prof. AVIGAD VONSHAK.

National Institute for Biotechnology in the Negev: tel. (8) 6461963; fax (8) 6472983; e-mail vardasb@bgu.ac.il; internet cmsprod.bgu.ac.il/eng/centers/nibn; Dir Prof. VARDA SHOSHAN BARMATZ.

Research Institute for Jewish and Israeli Literature and Culture: tel. (8) 6596936; e-mail heksher@bgu.ac.il; internet cmsprod.bgu.ac.il/eng/centers/heksherim; f. 2001; Dir Prof. YIGAL SCHWARTZ.

UNIVERSITY OF HAIFA

Mount Carmel, 31905 Haifa
Telephone: (4) 8240111
Fax: (4) 8342104
E-mail: rector@research.haifa.ac.il
Internet: www.haifa.ac.il

Founded 1963
Independent
Language of instruction: Hebrew
Academic year: October to June

Pres.: Prof. AARON BEN-ZE'EV
Rector: Prof. YOSSI BEN-ARTZI
Vice-Rector: Prof. DAVID FARAGGI
Vice-Pres. for Admin.: Prof. BARUCH MARZAN
Vice-Pres. for External Relations and Resource Devt: AMOS GAVER
Vice-Pres. and Dean of Research: Prof. MAJID AL-HAJ
Registrar: RUTH RABINOWITZ
Academic Sec.: SHOSHANA LANDMAN
Dean of Graduate Studies: Prof. SOPHIA MENACHE
Librarian: Prof. HAYA BAR-ITZHAK

Number of teachers: 1,125
Number of students: 16,000

Publications: *Dappim—Research in Literature* (1 a year, Hebrew, with English abstracts), *Jewish History* (every 2 years), *JTD Haifa University Studies in Theatre and Drama* (1 a year), *Mishpat Umimshal Law and Government in Israel* (every 2 years, Hebrew), *Studies in Children's Literature* (1 a year, Hebrew), *Studies in Education* (every 2 years, Hebrew)

DEANS AND HEADS OF SCHOOLS

Faculty of Education: Prof. OFRA MAYSELLES
Faculty of Humanities: Prof. MENACHEM MOR
Faculty of Law: Prof. ELI SALZBERGER
Faculty of Sciences and Science Education: Prof. ABRAHAM HAIM
Faculty of Social Sciences: Prof. SAMMY SAMOOHA
Faculty of Social Welfare and Health Sciences: Prof. PERLA WERNER
School of Political Sciences: Prof. GABRIEL BEN DOR
School of Social Work: Dr AMNON LAZAR
Graduate School of Management: Prof. SHEIZAF RAFAELI

PROFESSORS

Faculty of Education (tel. (4) 8240726; fax (4) 8240911; internet www.edu.haifa.ac.il):

ALEXANDER, H., Education
BARAK, A., Education
BEN-PERETZ, M., Education
BREZNITZ, Z., Education
COHEN, A., Education
HERTZ-LAZAROWITZ, R., Education
KATRIEL, T., Education
KLINGMAN, A., Education
LINN, R., Education
NESHER, P., Education
SALOMON, G., Education
SCHECHTMAN, Z., Education
SEGINA, R., Education
SHIMRON, J., Education
YERUSHALMY, M., Education
ZEIDNER, M., Education

Faculty of Humanities (tel. (4) 8240125; fax (4) 8240128; e-mail mmor@univ.haifa.ac.il; internet hcc.haifa.ac.il):

AVISHUR, Y., Hebrew Language
AZAR, M., Hebrew Language
BARAM, A., Middle Eastern History
BARNAI, J., Land of Israel Studies
BEN-ARTZI, Y., Land of Israel Studies
CHETRIT, J., French
CHISICK, H., History
DAVID, E., General History
DIMANT, D., Jewish History
DOLGOPOLSKY, A., Hebrew Language
ELBAZ, R., French
ELDAR, I., Hebrew Language
EVRON., M., Archaeology
FREEDMAN, W., English
GELBER, Y., Land of Israel Studies
GILBAR, G., Middle East History
GILEAD, A., Philosophy
GINAT, J., Land of Israel Studies
GOLDSTEIN, Y., Land of Israel Studies
GOODITCH, M., General History
GRABOIS, A., History
HAHLILI, R., Archaeology
HELTZER, M., Bible
HOFFMAN, J., Hebrew Language
KAGAN, Z., Hebrew and Comparative Literature
KANAZI, G., Arabic Language and Literature
KELLNER, M., Jewish History
KOCHAVI, A., History
KUSHNIR, D., Middle East History
LAUFER, M., English
LUZ, E., Jewish Thought
MALUL, M., Biblical Studies
MANSOUR, Y., Hebrew Language
MART, Y., Maritime Civilizations
MENACHE, S., General History
MICHEL, J., French
ODED, B., Jewish History
ORKIN, M., Theatre, English Literature
PECHTER, M., Jewish History
RAPPAPORT, U., Jewish History
REICH, R., Archaeology
ROBIN, R., General History
RONEN, A., Archaeology
ROZEN, M., Jewish History
SANDLER, W., English
SCHATZKER, C., Jewish History
SEGAL, A., Archaeology
SHENHAR, A., Hebrew and Comparative Literature
SHICHOR, Y., Multidisciplinary Studies
SHOHAM, R., Hebrew and Comparative Literature
SMILANSKY, S., Philosophy
SOBEL, M., History
SPANIER, E., Maritime Civilizations
STATMAN, D., Philosophy
STOW, K., Jewish History
TOBI, J., Hebrew and Comparative Literature
WARBURG, G., Middle Eastern History
YARDENI, M., History
YEHOSHUA, A. B., Hebrew and Comparative Literature
ZINGUER, I., French

Faculty of Law (tel. (4) 8240633; fax (4) 8249247; internet law.haifa.ac.il):

EDREY, Y., Law
GROSS, E., Law

Faculty of Sciences and Science Education (tel. (4) 8288076; fax (4) 8288108; e-mail sciences@research.haifa.ac.il; internet science.haifa.ac.il):

BUTNARIO, D., Mathematics
CARO, Y., Mathematics
CENSOR, Y., Mathematics
DAFNI, A., Biology
GOLAN, J., Mathematics
GORDON, A., Physics
HAIM, A., Biology

KOZENIKOV, A., Mathematics
MORAN, G., Mathematics
NEVO, E., Biology
REISNER, S., Mathematics
RUBINSTEIN, Z., Mathematics
SKOLNICK, A., Biology
SOKER, N., Physics
VAISMAN, I., Mathematics
WASSER, S., Biology
WEIT, I., Mathematics
YITZHAKI, I., Biology
ZACKS, J., Mathematics
ZOLLER, U., Chemistry

Faculty of Social Sciences (tel. (4) 8240331;
fax (4) 8246814; e-mail ssmooha@univ.haifa
.ac.il; internet hevra.haifa.ac.il):

AL-HAJ, M., Sociology
ARAZY, J., Mathematics and Computer
  Science
ARIAN, A., Political Science
BARAK, A., Psychology
BAR-GAL, Y., Geography
BAR-LEV, S., Statistics
BEIT-HALLAHMI, B., Psychology
BEN-DOR, G., Political Science
BERG, M., Statistics and Business Admin-
  istration
BERMAN, E., Psychology
BIGER, N., Business Administration
BRAUN, A., Mathematics and Computer
  Science
BREZNITZ, S., Psychology
CENSOR, Y., Mathematics and Computer
  Science
DAFNI, A., Biology
EDEN, B., Economics
FARAGGI, D., Statistics
FELZENTAL, D., Political Science
FISHMAN, G., Sociology
GOLAN, J., Mathematics and Computer
  Science
GOLOMBIC, M., Computer Science
GUIORA, A. Z., Psychology
HARPAZ, Y., Sociology and Business Admin-
  istration
HAYUTH, Y., Geography
INBAR, M., Geography
ISHAI, Y., Political Science
KATRIEL, T., Communication
KELLERMAN, A., Geography
KEREN, G., Psychology
KIPNIS, B., Geography
KLIOT, N., Geography
KORIAT, A., Psychology
KRAUS, V., Sociology
KUTIEL, H., Geography
LANDAU, G., Computer Science
LANDSBERGER, M., Economics
LANGBERG, N., Statistics
LIEBERMAN, O., Economics
MAKOV, E., Land of Israel Studies
MATTRAS, Y., Sociology
MELNIK, A., Economics
MESHIULAM, I., Business Admin.
MINTZ, A., Political Science
MORAN, G., Mathematics and Computer
  Science
NAVON, D., Psychology
NEVO, B., Psychology
PERRY, D., Statistics
RAFAELI, S., Business Admin.
RAKOVER, S., Psychology
REISER, B., Statistics
RICHTER-LEVIN, G., Psychology
ROITMAN, M., Mathematics
ROSENFELD, H., Sociology
ROSNER, M., Sociology
ROZENBLATT, M., Business Admin.
RUBIN, S., Psychology
RUBINSTEIN, Z., Mathematics and Com-
  puter Science
SAFIR, M., Psychology
SAGI-SCHWARTZ, A., Psychology
SAMUEL, Y., Sociology
SHECHTER, M., Economics

SHITOVITZ, B., Economics
SHLIFER, E., Business Admin.
SMOOHA, S., Sociology
SOBEL, Z., Sociology
SOFFER, A., Geography
VAINSHTEIN, A., Mathematics and Com-
  puter Science
VAISMAN, I., Mathematics and Computer
  Science
WATERMAN, S., Geography
WEIMAN, G., Sociology and Communication
WEISS, G., Statistics
WEIT, I., Mathematics and Computer Sci-
  ence
ZAKS, J., Mathematics and Computer Sci-
  ence

Faculty of Social Welfare and Health Sciences (tel. (4) 8249950; fax (4) 8249946;
e-mail werner@research.haifa.ac.il; internet
hw.haifa.ac.il):

EISIKOVITS, Z., Social Work
GILBAR, O., Social Work
GUTTMAN, D., Social Work
LEV-WIESEL, R., Social Work
LINN, S., Public Health
LOEWENSTEIN, A., Gerontology
RIMMERMAN, A., Social Work
SHARLIN, S., Social Work
WEISS, T., Occupational Therapy
WERNER, P., Gerontology

HEBREW UNIVERSITY OF JERUSALEM

Mount Scopus, 91905 Jerusalem
Telephone: (2) 5882111
Fax: (2) 5322545
E-mail: admission@savion.huji.ac.il
Internet: www.huji.ac.il
Founded 1918; inaugurated 1925
Private control, partially supported by the
Govt
Academic year: October to June
Language of instruction: Hebrew
Chair., Bd of Govs: CHARLES H. GOODMAN
Pres.: Prof. MENACHEM MAGIDOR
Vice-Pres. and Dir-Gen.: ELHANAN HACOHEN
Vice-Pres. for External Relations: CARMI
  GILLON
Vice-Pres. for Research and Devt: Prof.
  HILLEL BERCOVIER
Rector: Prof. SARA STROUMSA
Vice-Rector: Prof. MIRI GUR-ARYE
Dean of Students: Prof. ESTHER SHOHAMI
Number of teachers: 998
Number of students: 23,000

Publications: *ACTA-Analysis of Current
  Trends in Antisemitism* (research papers,
  in English, 2–3 a year), *Aleph:Historical
  Studies in Science and Judaism* (in Eng-
  lish, 1 a year), *Antisemitism International*
  (in English, 1 a year), *Edah Velashon*
  (Publn of the Hebrew Univ. Jewish Oral
  Traditions Research Centre, Hebrew, 1 a
  year), *Hispania Judaica Bulletin* (History,
  Culture, Thought, Literature, Art and
  Language of Jews in the Iberian Peninsula, in English), *Israel Journal of Math-
  ematics* (in English, 6 a year), *Israel Law
  Review* (in English, 3 a year), *Italia* (His-
  tory, Culture and Literature of the Jews of
  Italy, annual, multilingual), *Iyyun* (Jour-
  nal of Philosophy, quarterly, 2 a year in
  Hebrew and 2 in English), *Jerusalem
  Studies in Arabic and Islam (JSAI)* (1 a
  year, mostly with English contributions
  but also French, German and Arabic),
  Jerusalem Studies in Hebrew Language
  (in Hebrew, 1 a year), *Jerusalem Studies in
  Hebrew Literature* (in Hebrew, 1 a year),
  Jerusalem Studies in Jewish Folklore (in
  Hebrew, 1 a year), *Jerusalem Studies in
  Jewish Thought* (in Hebrew, 1 a year),
  Jews in Russia Eastern Europe (in Eng-

lish, published in co-operation with the
Leonid Nevzlin Research Centre), *Journal
d'Analyse Mathématique* (3 a year), *Journal of Experimental Criminology* (in English, 4 a year), *Massorot* (Studies in
Language Traditions of Hebrew and Ara-
maic, in Hebrew, 1 a year), *Mishpatim*
(Law, in English and Hebrew, 3 a year),
Partial Answers (Journal of Literature and
the History of Ideas, in English), *Perspec-
tives* (Humanistic Studies, in particular
Literature, History and Arts, in French, 1
a year), *Politika* (Journal of Israeli political
science and int. relations, in Hebrew),
*QAEDEM: Monographs of the Institute of
Archaeology* (in English, 1-2 a year),
QEDEM Reports (Archaeology, in English,
1-2 a year), *Shnaton Hamishpat Haivri*
(Jewish Law, in Hebrew), *Shnaton:
Annual for Biblical and Ancient Near
Eastern Studies* (Hebrew, 1 a year), *Stud-
ies in Contemporary Jewry* (Studies in
Contemporary Jewry, 1 a year, in English
published in conjunction with Oxford Univ.
Press), *Studies in Jewish Education*
(Multi-disciplinary, annual, bi-lingual
(English, Hebrew)), *Tarbiz* (Jewish stud-
ies, in Hebrew, 4 a year)

DEANS AND DIRECTORS

Faculty of Agricultural, Food and Environ-
  mental Science: Prof. ELI FEINERMAN
Faculty of Dental Medicine: Prof. ADAM
  STABHOLZ
Faculty of Humanities: Prof. ISRAEL BARTAL
Faculty of Law: Prof. YOAV DOTAN
Faculty of Mathematics and Natural Science:
  Prof. GAD MAROM
Faculty of Medicine: Prof. EHUD RAZIN
Faculty of Social Sciences: Prof. BOAZ SHAMIR
Jerusalem School of Business Admin.: Prof.
  TSVI PIRAN
School of Education: Prof. PHILIP WEXLER
School of Pharmacy: Prof. ISRAEL RINGEL
Paul Baerwald School of Social Work and
  Social Welfare: Prof. GAIL AUSLANDER
Centre for Pre-Academic Studies: Prof. URI
  BIALER
Hebrew Univ.—Hadassah School of Occupa-
  tional Medicine: Dr SHULA PARUSH
Hebrew Univ.—Hadassah School of Public
  Health and Community Medicine: Prof.
  SHMUEL SHAPIRA
Koret School of Veterinary Medicine: Prof.
  SHIMON HARRUS
Rothberg School for Overseas Students: Prof.
  YONATA LEVI

PROFESSORS

Faculty of Agricultural, Food and Environmental Science

(including the School of Nutritional Sciences
and the Koret School of Veterinary Medicine)

ADAM, Z., Plant Sciences and Genetics in
  Agriculture
ADIN, A., Soil and Water Sciences
CAHANER, A., Plant Sciences and Genetics
  in Agriculture
CHEN, Y., Soil and Water Sciences
CZOSNEK, H., Sciences and Genetics in
  Agriculture
FEINERMAN, E., Agricultural Economics
FRIEDMAN, A., Animal Sciences
GUTNICK, J. M., School of Veterinary Medi-
  cine
HADAR, Y., Plant Pathology and Microbiol-
  ogy
KIGEL, J., Plant Sciences and Genetics in
  Agriculture
LERMAN, Z., Agricultural Economics
MADAR, Z., Biochemistry, Food Science and
  Nutrition
MAHRER, Y., Soil and Water Sciences
MEIDAN, R., Animal Sciences

MUALEM, Y., Soil and Water Sciences
NAIM, H., Food Science and Nutrition
NUSSINOVITCH, A., Biochemistry, Food Science and Nutrition
OKON, Y., Plant Pathology and Microbiology
RUBIN, B., Plant Sciences and Genetics in Agriculture
SAGUY, I., Biochemistry, Food Science and Nutrition
TEL-OR, E., Plant Sciences and Genetics in Agriculture
TSUR, Y., Agricultural Economics
VAINSTEIN, A., Plant Sciences and Genetics in Agriculture
WALLACH, R., Soil and Water Sciences
WEISS, D., Plant Sciences and Genetics in Agriculture
WOLF, S., Plant Sciences and Genetics in Agriculture
WOLFENSON, D., Animal Sciences
YARDEN, O., Plant Pathology and Microbiology
YUVAL, B., Entomology
ZAMIR, D., Plant Sciences and Genetics in Agriculture

Faculty of Dental Medicine (En Karem Campus, POB 12272, 91120 Jerusalem; tel. (2) 6158595; fax (2) 6439219; e-mail dentistry_sa@savion.huji.ac.il; internet dental.huji.ac.il):

(Hebrew Univ.—Hadassah School of Dental Medicine)

BAB, I., Oral Pathology
CHEVION, M., Biochemistry
DEUTSCH, D., Oral Biology
GAZIT, D., Oral Pathology
HOROWITZ, M., Physiology
MANN, J., Community Dentistry
NITZAN, D., Oral and Maxillofacial Surgery
SCHWARTZ, Z., Periodontics
SELA, J., Oral Pathology
SELA, M., Maxillofacial Rehabilitation
SELA, M., Oral Biology
SHAPIRA, L., Periodontics
SOSKOLNE, A., Periodontics
STABHOLZ, A., Endodontics
TAL, M., Anatomy and Cell Biology

Faculty of Humanities
(the Joseph and Ceil Mazer Centre for the Humanities, incl. the Asian and African Studies; Archaeology; Contemporary Jewry; Languages, Literatures and Art; Philosophy and History; Institutes of: Jewish Studies)

AMITAI, R., Islamic and Middle Eastern Studies
ASCHHEIM, S., History
ASSIS, Y.-T., Jewish History
BAR-ELLI, G., Philosophy
BARTAL, I., Jewish History
BAR YAFFE, Y., Spanish and Latin American Studies
BELFER-COHEN, A., Archaeology
BEN-MENAHEM, Y., Philosophy, History and Philosophy of Science
BEN-SASSON, M., Jewish History
BESSERMAN, L., English Literature
BRODY, R., Talmudic Studies
BUDICK, E., American Studies
BUDICK, S., English Literature
BUNIS, D., Hebrew Language
COHEN, E., History
COHEN, R., Jewish History
COTTON, H., History and Classics
DELLA PERGOLA, S., Contemporary Jewry
DINER, D., History
ELIOR, R., Jewish Thought
ELIZUR, S., Hebrew Literature
GAFNI, I., Jewish History
GOLOMB, J., Philosophy
GOREN-INBAR, N., Archaeology

HALBERTAL, M., Jewish Thought and Philosophy
HARVEY, Z., Jewish Thought
HASAN-ROKEM, G., Hebrew Literature and Folklore
HEVER, H., Hebrew Literature
HEYD, D., Philosophy
HEYD, M., History
HOPKINS, S. A., Arabic Language and Literature
IDEL, M., Jewish Thought
KADISH, A., History
KAHANA, M., Talmudic Studies
KAPLAN, S., Comparative Religion and African Studies
KAPLAN, Y., Jewish History
KISTER, M., Jewish Studies
KÜHNEL, B., Art History
LECKER, M., Arabic Language and Literature
MAMAN, A., Hebrew Language
MAZAR, A., Archaeology
MENDELS, D., History
PATRICK, J., Archaeology
PITOWSKY, I., History and Philosophy of Science
POZY, C., Philosophy
RAPPAPORT-HOVAV, M., English Literature
RAVITZKY, A., Jewish Thought
RICCI, D., American Studies and Political Science
ROJTMAN, B., French Language and Literature, General and Comparative Literature
ROSENTHAL, D., Talmudic Studies
SCHULMAN, D., Indian Studies and Comparative Religion
SCHWARTZ, D., Jewish History
SCOLNICOV, S., Education, Philosophy
SEROUSSI, E., Musicology
SHESHA-HALEVY, A., General and Egyptian Philology
SHINAN, A., Hebrew Literature
STEINER, M., Philosophy
STEWART, F., Islamic Studies
STROUMSA, G., Comparative Religion
STROUMSA, S., Jewish Thought, Arabic Language and Literature
SZEINTUCH, Y., Yiddish
TAUBE, M., Linguistics and Slavic Studies
TIMENCHIK, R., Russian and Slavic Studies
TOCH, M., History
TOKER, L., English Literature
TOV, E., Bible
WISTRICH, R., History, Jewish History
WOLOSKY, S., English Literature
YAHALOM, Y., Hebrew Literature
YUVAL, I., History of Jewish Studies
ZAKOVITCH, Y., Bible
ZIMMERMANN, M., History

School of Education:

BABAD, E., Education
GATI, I., Education, Psychology
KAREEV, Y., Education
NURIT, Y., Education, Psychology
RAPOPORT, T., Education, Social Work
RITOV, I., Education
SCOLNICOV, S., Education, Philosophy
ULLMAN-MARGALIT, E., Education
WEXLER, P., Education

Faculty of Law (tel. (2) 5882528; fax (2) 5823042; e-mail law_sa@savion.huji.ac.il; internet law.mscc.huji.ac.il):

(incl. the Harry Sacher Institute for Legislative Research and Comparative Law, the Israel Matz Institute for Research in Jewish Law)

BEN-MENAHEN, H., Jewish Law, Philosophy of Law
DOTAN, Y., Public Law
FASSBERG, C., Private International Law, Comparative Law, Legal History

GAVISON, R., Philosophy of Law and Public Law
GILEAD, I., Tort Law
GUR-ARYE, M., Criminal Law
HAREL, A., Jurisprudence, Theory of Rights, Economic Analysis of Law
KREMITZER, M., Criminal and Constitutional Law
LIBSON, G., Islamic Law
LIFSCHITZ, B., Jewish Law
SHETREET, S., Public Law and the Judiciary
WEISBURD, D., White Collar Crime, Policing
ZAMIR, E., Contract Law

Faculty of Medicine
(the Hebrew Univ.—Hadassah Medical School, incl. the Hadassah-Henrietta Szold School of Nursing, the School of Occupational Therapy, the School of Pharmacy, School of Social Medicine and Public Health,)

ABRAMSKY, O., Neurology
ARGOV, A., Neurology
ARIEL, I., Pathology
BACH, G., Genetics
BARENHOLZ, Y., Biochemistry
BEERI, E., Public Health, Nutrition
BELLER, U., Obstetrics
BEN-CHETRIT, E., Medicine
BEN-EZRA, D., Ophthalmology
BEN-NERIAH, Y., Immunology
BEN-SASSON, Z., Immunology
BEN-YEHUDA, D., Haematology
BENITA, S., Pharmacy
BERCOVIER, H., Clinical Microbiology
BERGMAN, H., Physiology
BERGMAN, Y., Experimental Medicine, Cancer Research
BIALER, M., Pharmacology
BRANSKY, D., Paediatrics
BRENNER, T., Neurology
BREUER, R., Medical Imaging
BREZIS, M., Medicine
CEDAR, H., Cellular Biochemistry, Human Genetics
CHAJEK-SHAUL, T., Internal Medicine
DOMB, A., Medicinal Chemistry
EILAT, D., Immunology, Internal Medicine
ELIDAN, J., Laryngology
ELPELEG, O., Paediatrics
FAINSOD, A., Cellular Biochemistry and Human Genetics
FIBACH, E., Experimental Haematology
FREUND, H., Surgery
FRIEDLANDER, Y., Epidemiology, Public Health
FRIEDMAN, G., Medicine, Geriatrics
FRIEDMANN, M., Pharmacy
GABIZON BARCHILOM, A., Oncology
GALUN, E., Gene Therapy
GLASER, B., Endocrinology
GOLDBERG, I., Microbiology, Molecular Genetics
GOLOMB, G., Pharmaceutics
GOMORI, M. (acting), Radiology
GRANOT, E., Paediatrics
GRETZ, D., Anatomy
HANANI, M., Surgery
HANSKY, E., Microbiology
HEMERMAN, C., Paediatrics
HEYMAN, S., Internal Medicine
HONIGMAN, A., Virology
ILAN, Y., Medicine
JAFFE, C., Parasitology
KAEMPFER, R., Molecular Virology
KAISER, N., Endocrinology
KALCHEIM, C., Anatomy
KANNER, B. I., Biochemistry
KAPLAN, M., Paediatrics
KARK, J., Social Medicine
KEDAR, E., Immunology
KEREM, E., Paediatrics
KEREN, A., Cardiology
KESHET, E., Molecular Biology

KOHEN, R., Pharmacy
LAUFER, N., Obstetrics and Gynaecology
LEWIN, A., Obstetrics and Gynaecology
LIBSON, Y., Medical Imaging
LEITERSDORF, E., Internal Medicine
LERER, B., Psychiatry
LEV-TOV, A., Anatomy and Cell Biology
LEVY-SHAFFER, F., Pharmacology
LICHTENSTEIN, D., Physiology
LIEBERGALL, M., Orthopaedic Surgery
MANNY, J., Surgery
MARGALIT, H., Genetics
MAYER, M., Clinical Biochemistry
MEYUCHAS, O., Biochemistry
MILGROM, CH., Orthopaedics
MINKE, B., Physiology
MITRANI-ROSENBAUM, S., Molecular Biology, Gene Therapy
NAPARSTEK, J., Internal Medicine
ORNOY, A., Anatomy
PANET, A., Virology
PEER, J., Ophthalmology
PERETZ, T., Oncology
RAZ, I., Internal Medicine
RAZIN, E., Biochemistry
RECHES, A., Neurology
ROTSHENKER, S., Anatomy
RUBINSTEIN, A., Psychiatry
SAMUELOFF, A., Obstetrics
SHALEV, A., Psychiatry
SHOUVAL, D., Internal Medicine
SHPIRA, S., Medical Management
SHLOMAI, J., Molecular Biology
SHOHAMI, E., Pharmacology
SIEGAL, T., Neurology and Neuro-Oncology
SILVER, J., Nephrology
SPRUNG, CH. L., Medicine
STEINER, I., Neurology
TOVITO, E., Pharmacology
TZIVONI, D., Medicine, Cardiology
UMANSKY, F., Neurosurgery
VAADIA, E., Physiology
VARON, D., Haematology
VLODAVSKY, I., Oncology
WEINSTEIN, D., Obstetrics and Gynaecology
WEISSMAN, CH., Anaesthesiology
YAARI, E., Physiology
YAGEL, S., Obstetrics and Gynaecology
YANAI, J., Anatomy and Embryology
YEDGAR, S., Biochemistry
YEFENOF, E., Immunology

Faculty of Science
(incl. the Amos de Shalit Science Teaching Centre; Alexander Silberman Institute of Life Sciences; Heinz Schteinitz Interuniversity; Institute of Computer Science; Institute of Earth Sciences; Institute for Marine Biological Research; Institute of Mathematics Institute of Chemistry; Racah Institute of Physics

AGMON, N., Chemistry
AGRANAT, A., Applied Physics
AIZENSHTAT, Z., Applied Chemistry
ARKIN, I., Biological Chemistry
ASSCHER, M., Physical Chemistry
ATLAS, D., Biological Chemistry
AVNIR, D., Organic Chemistry
BAER, R., Physical Chemistry
BALBERG, Y., Experimental Physics
BANIN, U., Physical Chemistry
BARAK, A., Computer Science
BECKENSTEIN, Y., Theoretical Physics
BEERI, C., Computer Science
BELKIN, S., Life Sciences
BEN-ARTZI, M., Mathematics
BEN-OR, M., Computer Science
BEN-SHAUL, A., Theoretical Chemistry
BENVENISTY, N., Life Sciences
BIALI, S., Organic Chemistry
BINO, A., Theoretical and Analytical Chemistry
BUCH, V., Chemistry
CABANTCHIK, Y., Biophysics

CAMHI, J. M., Cell and Animal Biology
COHEN, A., Atmospheric Sciences
COHN, D., Applied Chemistry
DAVIDOV, D., Experimental Physics
DEKEL, A., Theoretical Physics
DE-SHALIT, E., Mathematics
DEVOR, M., Zoology
DOLEV, D., Computer Science
DROR-FARJOUN, E., Mathematics
ELITZUR, S., Theoretical Physics
ENZEL, Y., Earth Sciences
EREL, Y., Geology
EREZ, J., Oceanography
FARKAS, H., Mathematics
FEINBERG, J., Physics
FELDMAN, Y., Applied Physics
FELNER, I., Experimental Physics
FRIEDLAND, L., Theoretical Physics
FRIEDMAN, N., Computer Science
GAL, A., Theoretical Physics
GARTI, N., Applied Chemistry
GENIN, A., Ecology and Oceanography
GERBER, R. B., Theoretical Chemistry
GIVEON, A., Physics
GLABERSON, W., Experimental Physics
GRUENBAUM, Y., Genetics
HART, S., Mathematics
HIRSCHBERG, J., Genetics
HOCHSTEIN, S., Neurobiology
HRUSHOVSKI, E., Mathematics
JOSKOWICZ, L., Computer Science
KALAI, G., Mathematics
KAPLAN, A., Plant Sciences
KEREM, B., Life Sciences
KHAIN, A., Atmospheric Sciences
KHAZDAN, D., Mathematics
KIFER, Y., Mathematics
KOSLOFF, R., Physical Chemistry
KUPFERMAN, O., Computer Science
LEV, O., Ecology
LEVIN, G., Mathematics
LEVITAN, A., Physics
LEVITSKI, A., Biological Chemistry
LEWIS, A., Applied Physics
LINIAL, M., Biological Chemistry
LINIAL, N., Computer Science
LIVNE, R., Mathematics
LUBOTZKY, A., Mathematics
LURIA, M., Applied and Environmental Science
LUZ, B., Plant Sciences
MAGDASSI, S., Applied Chemistry
MAGIDOR, M., Mathematics
MANDELZWEIG, V., Theoretical Physics
MANDLER, D., Chemistry
MAROM, G., Applied Chemistry
MATTHEWS, A., Geology
MEERSON, B., Experimental Physics
MILO, O., Physics
MOSHEIOV, G., Statistics
MOZES, S., Mathematics
NAVON, O., Geology
NECHUSHTAI, R., Plant Sciences
NELKEN, I., Neurobiology
NEYMAN, A., Mathematics and Economics
NISAN, N., Computer Science
OREN, A., Ecology
ORLY, J., Biological Chemistry
OVADYAHU, Z., Experimental Physics
PALDOR, N., Plant Sciences
PAUL, M., Experimental Physics
PELEG, S., Computer Science
PIRAN, Z., Theoretical Physics
POST, A., Molecular Ecology
RABINOVICI, E., Theoretical Physics
RIPS, E., Mathematics
ROSENFELD, D., Plant Sciences
ROSENSCEIN, J., Computer Science
RUBINSKY, B., Bioengineering
RUHMAN, S., Chemistry
SAGIV, S., Computer Science
SARI, R., Physics
SASSON, Y., Applied Chemistry
SCHULDINER, S., Microbial Ecology
SEGEV, I., Neurobiology
SELA, Z., Mathematics

SHAIK, S. S., Organic Chemistry
SHALEV, A., Mathematics
SHASHUA, A., Computer Science
SHELAH, S., Mathematics
SHMIDA, A., Botany
SOLOMON, S., Theoretical Physics
SOMPOLINSKY, H., Physics
SOREQ, H., Biological Chemistry
SPIRA, M., Neurobiology
TIKOCHINSKY, Y., Physics
TISHBY, N., Computer Science
WEINSHALL, D., Computer Science
WEISS, B., Mathematics
WERMAN, M., Computer Science
WILLNER, I., Organic Chemistry
YAROM, Y., Neurobiology
ZIGLER, A., Physics

Faculty of Social Sciences:
BAR-SIMAN-TOV, Y., Int. Relations
BEN-ARI, E., Sociology, Anthropology
BEN-SHAKHAR, G., Psychology
BEN-YEHUDA, N., Sociology
BENTIN, S., Psychology and Education
BIALER, U., Int. Relations
BIENSTOCK, M., Economics
BILO, Y., Psychology and Sociology
BORNSTEIN, G., Psychology
COHEN, A., Psychology
COHEN, R., Int. Relations
DAYAN, U., Geography
DE-SHALIT, A., Political Sciences
EBSTEIN, R., Psychology
EZRAHI, Y., Political Science
FROST, R., Psychology
GALNOOR, I., Political Science
GATI, I., Psychology and Education
GILULA, Z., Statistics and Social Work
HART, S., Economics
HASSON, S., Geography and Urban Studies
HAVIV, M., Statistics
ILOUZ, E., Sociology
KARK, R., Geography
KELLA, O., Statistics
LAVIH, V., Economics
LIEBES, T., Communication
LIEBLICH, A., Psychology
METZER, J., Economics
MOSHEIOV, G., Statistics
NINIO, A., Psychology
OMAN, S., Statistics
PERRY, M., Economics, Rationality Centre
PFEFFERMAN, D., Statistics
POLLAK, M., Statistics
RICCI, D., Political Science
RINOTT, Y., Statistics
RITOV, Y., Statistics
RUBIN, R., Geography
SALOMON, I., Geography and Urban Studies
SCHUL, Y., Psychology
SHAMIR, B., Sociology, Anthropology
SHANON, B., Psychology
SHAVIT, Y., Psychology
SHEFFER, G., Political Science
TEUBAL, M., Economics
VERTZBERGER, Y., Int. Relations
WINTER, E., Economics
WOLFSFELD, G., Political Science
YERMIYA, R., Psychology
YIRMIYA, N., Psychology
YITZHAKI, S., Economics
ZUCKER, D., Statistics

Jerusalem School of Business Administration (tel. (2) 5883235; fax (2) 5881576; internet bschool.huji.ac.il):
BAR-YOSEF, S., Accounting
GALAI, D., Banking
KORNBLUTH, J., Business Admin.
LANDSKRONER, Y., Business Admin.
MAZURZKY, O., Marketing
MOSHEIOV, G., Business Admin., Statistics
VENEZIA, I., Business Admin.

Paul Baerwald School of Social Work and Social Welfare (tel. (2) 5881477; fax (2) 5823587; e-mail social-work@savion.huji.ac.il; internet www.sw.huji.ac.il):

AUSLANDER, G.
BENBEMISHTY, R.
LITWIN, H.
RAPOPORT, T.
SCHMID, H.

RESEARCH CENTRES AND INSTITUTES

Alexander Silberman Institute of Life Sciences: Givat Ram, 91904 Jerusalem; tel. (2) 6585420; fax (2) 6586103; e-mail arkin@cc.huji.ac.il; internet www.bio.huji.ac.il; Chair. Prof. ISAIAH ARKIN.

Asper Centre for Entrepreneurship: Jerusalem School of Business Admin., Jerusalem; tel. (2) 5882994; fax (2) 5883685; e-mail refo@mscc.huji.ac.il; internet bschool.huji.ac.il; Dir Prof. JACOB GOLDENBERG.

Benjamin Triwaks Bee Research Centre: Hebrew Univ. of Jerusalem, POB 12, 76100 Rehovot; tel. (8) 9489401; fax (8) 9489842; e-mail shafir@agri.huji.ac.il; internet departments.agri.huji.ac.il/entomology/staff_pages/shafir.html; Dir Dr SHARONI SHAFIR.

Ben-Zvi Institute for the Study of Jewish Communities in the East: POB 7660, Jerusalem; tel. (2) 5398844; fax (2) 5612329; e-mail bzi@ybz.org.il; internet www.ybz.org.il; Chair. YOM TOV ASSIS.

Brian Y. Davidson Centre for Agribusiness: Jerusalem School of Business Admin., Jerusalem; tel. (2) 5883224; fax (2) 5883685; e-mail dinam@savion.huji.ac.il; internet bschool.huji.ac.il; Dir Prof. CHEZI OFIR.

Centre for Agricultural Economic Research: Hebrew Univ. of Jerusalem, POB 12, 76100 Rehovot; tel. (8) 9489230; fax (8) 9466267; e-mail finkelsh@agri.huji.ac.il; Dir Prof. ISRAEL FINKELSHTAIN.

Centre for Agricultural Research in Desert and Semi-Arid Zones: Hebrew Univ. of Jerusalem, POB 12, 76100 Rehovot; tel. (8) 9489234; fax (8) 9468565; e-mail yonachen@agri.huji.ac.il; internet departments.agri.huji.ac.il/economics/econocene.html; Dir Prof. YONA CHEN.

Centre for Diabetes Research: tel. (2) 6758798; fax (2) 6758741; e-mail sassolo@cc.huji.ac.il; Chair. Prof. SHLOMO SASSON.

Centre for Integrated Pest Management: Hebrew Univ. of Jerusalem, POB 12, 76100 Rehovot; tel. (8) 9489223; fax (8) 9466768; e-mail coll@agri.huji.ac.il; Dir Dr MOSHE COLL.

Centre for Jewish Art: tel. (2) 5882281; fax (2) 5400105; e-mail cja@vms.huji.ac.il; internet cja.huji.ac.il; Dir Dr RINA TALGAM.

Centre for Literary Studies: tel. (2) 5883925; fax (2) 5880203; e-mail cis@savion.huji.ac.il; Dir Dr JON DAVID WHITMAN.

Centre for Nanoscience and Nanotechnology: Givat Ram, Jerusalem; tel. (2) 6584515; fax (2) 6584148; e-mail banin@chem.ch.huji.ac.il; internet www.nanoscience.huji.ac.il; Dir Prof. URI BANIN.

Centre for Rationality and Interactive Decision Theory: Givat Ram, Jerusalem; tel. (2) 6584135; fax (2) 6513681; e-mail ratio@math.huji.ac.il; internet www.ratio.huji.ac.il; Dir Prof. EDNA ULLMANN-MARGALIT.

Centre for Research on Dutch Jewry: Rabin Bldg, Mt Scopus, Jerusalem; tel. (2) 5880242; fax (2) 5880241; e-mail dutchjew@cc.huji.ac.il; internet dutchjewry.huji.ac.il; Dir Prof. YOSEF KAPLAN.

Centre for Research on Romanian Jewry: Rabin Bldg, Mt Scopus, Jerusalem;

tel. (2) 5881672; fax (2) 5881673; e-mail rumjewry@vms.huji.ac.il; Dir Dr ODED IR-SHAI.

Centre for Research on the History and Culture of Polish Jews: tel. (2) 5881769; Dir Dr DANIEL BLATMAN.

Centre for Slavic Languages and Literatures: tel. (2) 5883901; fax (2) 5881245; e-mail romantimenchik@excite.com; Dir Prof. WOLF MOSCOWICH.

Centre for the Study of Christianity: tel. (2) 5883819; fax (2) 5883819; e-mail centerc@savion.cc.huji.ac.il; Dir Dr DAVID SATRAN.

Centre for the Study of Jewish Languages and Literature: Rabin Bldg, Mt Scopus, Jerusalem; tel. (2) 5880244; fax (2) 5881206; e-mail otirosh@mscc.huji.ac.il; Dir Prof. MOSHE BAR-ASHER.

Centre for the Study of Pain: internet paincenter.huji.ac.il; Dir Prof. YAIR SHARAV.

Centre for Trauma Research: fax (2) 6417997; e-mail rivkind@hadassah.org.il; Dir Prof. AVI RIVKIND.

Chais Centre for Jewish Studies in Russian: tel. (2) 5881770; fax (2) 5881795; e-mail chais_center@savion.cc.huji.ac.il; Dir Dr SEMION GOLDIN.

Chanock Centre of Virology: tel. (2) 6758554; fax (2) 6784010; Dir Prof. AMOS PANET.

Cherrick Centre for the Study of Zionism, the Yishuv and the State of Israel: tel. (2) 5882867; fax (2) 5882986; e-mail cherrick@mscc.huji.ac.il; internet cherrick.huji.ac.il; Dir Dr UZI REBHUN.

D. Walter Cohen DDS Middle East Centre for Dental Education: tel. (2) 6758596; fax (2) 6439219; e-mail hujident@cc.huji.ac.il; Dir Prof. GIDEON HOLAN.

Dinur Centre for Research in Jewish History: Rabin Bldg, Mt Scopus, Jerusalem; tel. (2) 5884894; fax (2) 5883894; e-mail dinurcenter@mscc.huji.ac.il; internet www.dinur.org; Dir Dr ODED IR-SHAI.

Edmund Landau Minerva Centre for Research in Mathematical Analysis and Related Areas: Institute of Mathematics, Givat Ram, Jerusalem; tel. (2) 6584091; fax (2) 5630702; e-mail mbartzi@math.huji.ac.il; internet www.ma.huji.ac.il; Dir Prof. MATANIA BEN-ARTZI.

Eliezer Ben-Yehudah Research Centre for History of Hebrew, The: Rabin Bldg, Mt Scopus, Jerusalem; tel. (2) 5881816; fax (2) 5881206; internet www.hum.huji.ac.il/benyehuda; Dir Prof. STEVE FASSBERG.

European Forum at the Hebrew University: tel. (2) 5883286; fax (2) 5881535; e-mail mseuro@mscc.huji.ac.il; internet www.ef.huji.ac.il; Dir Prof. BIANCA KUHNEL.

Folklore Research Centre: Rabin Bldg, Mt Scopus, Jerusalem; tel. (2) 5881797; e-mail hasan@mscc.huji.ac.uk; Dir Prof. GALIT HASAN-ROKEM.

Franz Rosenzweig Centre for the Study of German Culture and Literature: tel. (2) 5881909; fax (2) 5811369; e-mail rosenzweig@vms.huji.ac.il; Dir Prof. PAUL MENDES FLOHR.

Fritz Haber Research Centre for Molecular Dynamics: Institute of Chemistry, Givat Ram, Jerusalem; tel. (2) 6585271; fax (2) 5618033; e-mail abs@fh.huji.ac.il; internet www.chemistry.huji.ac.il; Dir Prof. AVINOAM BEN-SHAUL.

G. W. Leibnitz Minerva Centre for Research in Computer Sciences: School of Computer Science and Engineering, Jerusalem; tel. (2) 6586299; fax (2) 6585439; e-mail josko@cs.huji.ac.il; internet www.cs.huji.ac.il; Dir Prof. LEO JOSKOWICZ.

Gal-Edd Centre for Industrial Development: Jerusalem School of Business Admin., Jerusalem; tel. (2) 5883224; fax (2) 5883685; e-mail dainam@savion.huji.ac.il; internet bschool.huji.ac.il; Dir Dr NIRON HASHAI.

Germania-Judaica: tel. (2) 5882658; Dir Prof. ISRAEL YUVAL.

Gilo Citizenship, Democracy and Civil Education Centre: tel. (2) 5882267; fax (2) 5881532; e-mail gilocenter@mscc.huji.ac.il; internet www.gilocenter.huji.ac.il; Dir Dr JEFF MACY.

Goldie Rotman Centre for Cognitive Science in Education: tel. (2) 5882102; Dir Prof. YAAKOV KAREEV.

Harry and Michael Sacher Institute for Legislative Research and Comparative Law: tel. (2) 5882535; fax (2) 5882565; e-mail sacher.institute@gmail.com; internet law.mscc.huji.ac.il/law1/sache; Dir Prof. SHIMON SHETREET.

Harry S. Truman Research Institute for the Advancement of Peace: tel. (2) 5882300; fax (2) 5828076; e-mail truman@savion.huji.ac.il; internet truman.huji.ac.il; Dir (vacant).

Harry Stern National Centre for the Study and Treatment of Alzheimer's Disease and Related Topics: Life Sciences Bldg, Givat Ram, 91904 Jerusalem; tel. (2) 6584086; fax (2) 5635267; internet psychobiology.org.il; Dir Prof. SHAUL HOCHSTEIN.

Hebrew University Bible Project: Rabin Bldg, Mt Scopus, Jerusalem; tel. (2) 5880246; fax (2) 5880248; e-mail rzer@mscc.huji.ac.il; Dir Prof. SHMARYAHU TALMON.

Hebrew University Centre for Converging Sciences and Technologies: Hadassah Ein Kerem, POB 12272, Jerusalem; tel. (2) 6757627; fax (2) 6757628; e-mail dgaz@cc.huji.ac.il; Dir Prof. DAN GAZIT.

Herb and Frances Brody Centre for Food Sciences: Hebrew Univ. of Jerusalem, POB 12, 76100 Rehovot; tel. (8) 9489292; fax (8) 9462384; e-mail feiner@agri.huji.ac.il; Dir Prof. ELI FEINERMAN.

Hubert H. Humphrey Centre for Experimental Medicine and Cancer Research: tel. (2) 6758350; fax (2) 6414583; e-mail katzav@md.huji.ac.il; Dir Prof. SHULAMIT KATZAV-SHAPIRA.

Institute for Advanced Studies: Givat Ram, 91904 Jerusalem; tel. (2) 6584735; fax (2) 6523429; e-mail advance@vms.huji.ac.il; internet www.as.huji.ac.il; Dir Prof. ELIEZER RABINOVICI.

Institute for Dental Science: tel. (2) 6758596; fax (2) 6439219; e-mail hujident@cc.huji.ac.il; Dir Dr GIDEON HOLAN.

Institute for Medical Research: POB 12272, 91120 Jerusalem; tel. (2) 6757527; fax (2) 6757529; e-mail eitony@ekmd.huji.ac.il; Dir Prof. EITAN YEFENOF.

Interdisciplinary Centre for Neural Computation: Givat Ram, Jerusalem; tel. (2) 6584563; fax (2) 6586152; e-mail haim@fiz.huji.ac.il; internet www.icoc.huji.ac.il; Dir Prof. HAIM SOMPOLIMSKY.

International Centre for University Teaching of Jewish Civilization: tel. (2) 5881773; fax (2) 5819096; e-mail msjewciv@mscc.huji.ac.il; internet jewishcivilization.huji.ac.il; Dir Prof. CYRIL ASLANOV.

Israel Matz Institute for Research in Jewish Law: tel. (2) 5882501; fax (2) 5882567; e-mail jewishlaw@savion.cc.huji.ac.il; internet law.mscc.huji.ac.il/law1/newsite/hebrew.html; Dir Prof. GIDEON LIBSON.

Jewish Music Research Centre: POB 39105, 91390 Jerusalem; tel. (2) 6585059;

fax (2) 5611156; e-mail jmrc_inf@savion.huji
.ac.il; internet www.jewish-musc@huji.ac.il;
Dir Prof. EDWIN SEROUSSI.

Jewish Oral Traditions Research Centre: Rabin Bldg, Mt Scopus, Jerusalem; tel. (2) 5881828; e-mail dornirit@zahav.net.il; Dir Prof. AHARON MAMAM.

K Mart International Retail and Marketing Centre: Jerusalem School of Business Admin., Jerusalem; tel. (2) 5883224; fax (2) 5883685; e-mail dinam@savion.huji.ac.il; internet bschool.huji.ac.il; Dir Prof. DAVID MAZURSKY.

Kennedy Leigh Centre for Horticultural Research: Hebrew Univ. of Jerusalem, POB 12, 76100 Rehovot; tel. (8) 9489251; fax (8) 9489899; e-mail shimony@agri.huji.ac.il; internet departments.agri.huji.ac.il/horticulture/kennedy.html; Dir Prof. BARUCH RUBIN.

Knune Minerva Farkas Centre for the Study of Light Induced Processes: Institute of Chemistry, Givat Ram, Jerusalem; tel. (2) 6585067; fax (2) 5618033; e-mail yehuda@chem.cc.huji.ac.il; internet www.chemistry.huji.ac.il; Dir Prof. YEHUDA HAAS.

Krueger Centre for Finance: Jerusalem School of Business Admin., Jerusalem; tel. (2) 5883224; fax (2) 5883685; e-mail dinam@savion.huji.ac.il; internet bschool.huji.ac.il; Dir Prof. HAIM LEVY.

Kühne-Minerva Centre for Studies of Visual Transduction: Faculty of Medicine, POB 12272, 91120 Jerusalem; tel. (2) 6758407; fax (2) 6431736; e-mail minb@md.huji.ac.il; Dir Prof. BARUCH MINKE.

Lafer Centre for Women and Gender Studies: tel. (2) 5883455; fax (2) 5883364; e-mail mslaferc@mscc.huji.ac.il; internet www.lafer.huji.ac.il; Dir Dr MIMI AIZENSTADT.

Lautenberg Centre for General and Tumour Immunology: Faculty of Medicine, POB 12272, 91120 Jerusalem; tel. (2) 6758726; fax (2) 6430834; e-mail daniellak@savion.huji.ac.il; internet immunology.huji.ac.il; Dir Prof. YINON BEN-NERIAH.

Leo Picard Groundwater Research Centre: tel. (8) 9489174; fax (8) 9475181; e-mail mualem@agri.huji.ac.il; Dir Prof. YECHEZKEL MUALEM.

Leonard Davis Institute for International Relations: tel. (2) 5882312; fax (2) 5825534; e-mail msdavis@mscc.huji.ac.il; internet davis.huji.ac.il; Dir Prof. ALFRED TOVIAS.

Leonid Nevzlin Research Centre for Russian and East European Jewry: tel. (2) 5881959; fax (2) 5881950; e-mail merkaznev@savion.huji.ac.il; internet www.nevzlin.huji.ac.il; Dir Dr JONATHAN DEKEL-CHEN.

Levi Eshkol Institute for Economic, Social and Political Research: tel. (2) 5883032; fax (2) 5324339; e-mail eshkol@mscc.huji.ac.il; internet eshkol.huji.ac.il; Dir Prof. GAD WOLSFELED.

Levin Centre for the Study of Normal Child and Adolescent Development: tel. (2) 5883370; fax (2) 5881159; e-mail levinc@mscc.huji.ac.il; internet psychology.mscc.huji.ac.il; Dir Prof. NURIT YIRMIYA.

Lisa Meitner-Minerva Centre for Computational Quantum Chemistry: Institute of Chemistry, Givat Ram, Jerusalem; tel. (2) 6585909; fax (2) 6585345; e-mail sason@yfaat.ch.huji.ac.il; internet www.chemistry.huji.ac.il; Dir Prof. SASSON SHAIK.

Louis Frieberg Centre for East Asian Studies, The: tel. (2) 5881371; fax (2) 5881371; e-mail eacenter@mscc.huji.ac.il;

internet www.eacenter.huji.ac.il; Dir Dr GIDEON SHELACH.

Minerva Avron Even-Ari Centre of Photosynthesis Research: Institute of Life Sciences, Givat Ram, Jerusalem; tel. (2) 6585338; fax (2) 6586103; e-mail hirschu@vms.huji.ac.il; internet www.bio.huji.ac.il; Dir Prof. JOSEPH HIRSCHBERG.

Minerva Centre for Human Rights: tel. (2) 5881156; fax (2) 5819371; e-mail mchr@savion.huji.ac.il; internet law.mscc.huji.ac.il/law1/minerva/english; Dir Prof. YUVAL SHANY.

Minerva Centre for the Study of Bone Metabolism: Nephrology Services, Hadassah Hebrew Univ. Hospital, POB 12000, 91120 Jerusalem; tel. (2) 6436778; fax (2) 6421234; e-mail silver@cc.huji.ac.il; internet www.hadassah.org.il/atarim/medicine/e1.htm; Dir Prof. JUSTIN SILVER.

Misgav Yerushalaim Centre for the Study of Sephardi and Oriental Jewry: Rabin Bldg, Mt Scopus, Jerusalem; tel. (2) 5815460; fax (2) 5815460; e-mail misgav@savion.huji.ac.il; internet www.hum.huji.ac.il/misgav/index2.htm; Dir Prof. JOSEPH HACKER.

Mordechai Zagagi Centre for Finance and Accounting: Jerusalem School of Business Admin., Jerusalem; tel. (2) 5883224; fax (2) 5883685; e-mail dinam@savion.huji.ac.il; internet bschool.huji.ac.il; Dir Prof. YORAM LANDSKRONER.

Moshe Shilo Centre for Marine Biogeochemistry: Institute of Life Sciences, Givat Ram, Jerusalem; tel. (8) 6374329; fax (8) 6360122; e-mail anton@pob.huji.ac.il; internet www.ivi-eilat.ac.il; Dir Prof. ANTON POST.

Multi-Disciplinary Centre for Environmental Research: tel. (8) 9489916; fax (8) 9467763; e-mail kigel@agri.huji.ac.il; internet www.sites.huji.ac.il/cfer; Dir Prof. JAIME KIGEL.

National Council of Jewish Women Research Institute for Innovation in Education: tel. (2) 5882015; fax (2) 5882174; e-mail ayalab@savion.huji.ac.il; internet ncjw.res.mscc.huji.ac.il; Dir Dr MEIR BUZAGLO.

National Institute for Psychobiology in Israel: Life Sciences Bldg, Givat Ram, 91904 Jerusalem; tel. (2) 6584086; fax (2) 5635267; e-mail psychobi@cc.huji.ac.il; internet psychobiology.org.il; Dir Prof. SHAUL HOCHSTEIN.

Nehemia Levzion Centre for Islamic Studies: tel. (2) 5881541; fax (2) 5880258; e-mail islamic@mscc.huji.ac.il; internet islam-center.huji.ac.il; Dir Prof. REUVEN AMITAI.

Niznick Dental Implant and Research Centre: tel. (2) 6776170; fax (2) 6776175; e-mail kohavi@cc.huji.ac.il; internet www.hadassah.org.il; Dir Prof. D. KOHAVI.

Orion Centre for the Study of the Dead Sea Scrolls and Associated Literature, The: Rabin Bldg, Mt Scopus, Jerusalem; tel. (2) 5881966; fax (2) 5883584; e-mail msdss@mscc.huji.ac.il; internet orion.mscc.huji.ac.il; Dir Prof. STEVEN FASSBERG.

Otto Loewi Centre for Cellular and Molecular Neurobiology: Institute of Life Sciences, Givat Ram, Jerusalem; tel. (2) 6583172; fax (2) 6586103; e-mail yarom@vms.huji.ac.il; internet www.bio.huji.ac.il; Dir Prof. YOSEF YARAM.

Otto Warburg Minerva Centre for Agricultural Biotechnology: Hebrew Univ. of Jerusalem, POB 12, 76100 Rehovot; tel. (8) 9489973; fax (8) 9363882; e-mail ingel@agri

.huji.ac.il; internet departments.agri.huji.ac.il/biotech; Dir Prof. SHMUEL WOLF.

Philip and Muriel Berman Centre for Biblical Archaeology: Institute of Archaeology, Hebrew Univ., 91905 Jerusalem; tel. (2) 5882403; fax (2) 5825548; Dir Prof. YOSEF GARFINKEL.

Recanati Centre for Research in Business Administration: Jerusalem School of Business Admin., Jerusalem; tel. (2) 5883224; fax (2) 5883685; e-mail dainam@savion.huji.ac.il; internet bschool.huji.ac.il; Dir Prof. ZVI WIENER.

Richard Koebner Centre for German History: Hebrew Univ., Jerusalem; tel. (2) 5883766; fax (2) 5816501; e-mail mskoeb@pluto.mscc.huji.ac.il; Dir Prof. MOSCHE ZIMMERMAN.

Robert H. and Clarice Smith Centre for Art History: Hebrew Univ., Mt Scopus, 91905 Jerusalem; tel. (2) 5883872; fax (2) 5883944; e-mail anat@savion.huji.ac.il; internet www.smithcenter.huji.ac.il; Dir Prof. ZIVA AMISHAI-MAISELS.

Roland Centre for the Research of Neurodegenerative Disease: Faculty of Medicine, Hebrew Univ., POB 12272, 91120 Jerusalem; tel. (2) 6757388; fax (2) 6439736; e-mail hagaib@md.huji.ac.il; Dir Prof. HAGAI BERGMAN.

Ronald E. Goldstein DDS Research Centre for Dental Materials and Aesthetics in Dentistry: Faculty of Dental Medicine, Hebrew Univ., POB 12272, 91120 Jerusalem; tel. (2) 6776193; fax (2) 6429683; e-mail nitzan@bichacho.net; Dir Prof. NITZAN BICHACHO.

Sanford F. Kuvin Centre for the Study of Infectious and Tropical Diseases: Institute for Medical Research, POB 12272, 91120 Jerusalem; tel. (2) 6758089; fax (2) 6727425; e-mail josephs@ekmd.huji.ac.il; internet kuvin.huji.ac.il; Dir Prof. JOSEPH SHLOMAI.

Scheinfeld Centre for Human Genetics in the Social Sciences: tel. (2) 536855; fax (2) 536853; e-mail ebstein@mscc.huji.ac.il; Dir Prof. RICHARD EBSTEIN.

Scholion Interdisciplinary Research Centre in Jewish Studies: tel. (2) 5882430; fax (2) 5881196; e-mail scholion@savion.huji.ac.il; internet scholion.huji.ac.il; Dir Prof. ISRAEL J. YUVAL.

Seagram Centre for Soil and Water Sciences: Hebrew Univ. of Jerusalem, POB 12, 76100 Rehovot; tel. (8) 9489340; fax (8) 9475181; e-mail soil@agri.huji.ac.il; internet departments.agri.huji.ac.il/soils; Dir Prof. YECHEZKEL MUALEM.

S. H. Bergman Centre for Philosophical Studies: tel. (2) 5883762; fax (2) 5880148; Dir Prof. DAVID HEYD.

Shaine Centre for Research in the Social Sciences: tel. (2) 5883032; fax (2) 5324339; e-mail msschein@mscc.huji.ac.il; Dir Prof. ZALI GUREVITCH.

Sidney M. Edelstein Centre for the History and Philosophy of Science, Technology and Medicine: Givat Ram, 91905 Jerusalem; tel. (2) 6585652; fax (2) 6586709; e-mail travis@cc.huji.ac.il; Dir Prof. ITAMAR PITOWSKY.

Sigmund Freud Centre for Study and Research in Psychoanalysis: tel. (2) 5883380; fax (2) 5322132; e-mail msfreud@pluto.mscc.huji.ac.il; internet atar.mscc.huji.ac.il/%7efreud; Dir Prof. GABY SHEFLER.

Smart Family Foundation Communication Institute: tel. (2) 5883210; fax (2) 5817008; e-mail msmartc@mscc.huji.ac.il; internet smart.huji.ac.il; Dir Prof. MENACHEM BLONDHEIM.

Sturman Centre for Human Development: tel. (2) 5883409; fax (2) 5881159; e-mail msmerava@mscc.huji.ac.il; Dir Prof. RAM FROST.

Sudarsky Centre for Computational Biology: Givat Ram, Jerusalem; tel. (2) 6585425; fax (2) 6586103; e-mail michall@cc .huji.ac.il; internet www.cbc.huji.ac.il; Dir Prof. MICHAL LINEAL.

Vidal Sassoon International Centre for the Study of Antisemitism: tel. (2) 5882494; fax (2) 5881002; e-mail sicsa@mscc .huji.ac.il; internet sicsa.huji.ac.il; Dir Prof. ROBERT WISTRICH.

Zigi and Lisa Daniel Swiss Centre: tel. (2) 5883056; fax (2) 5880004; e-mail crmr@ savion.huji.ac.il; internet www.crmr.huji.ac .il; Dir Prof. YAACOV BAR SIMAN TOV.

OPEN UNIVERSITY OF ISRAEL

108 Ravutski St, POB 808, 43107 Raanana

Telephone: (9) 7780778

Fax: (9) 7780642

E-mail: president@openu.ac.il

Internet: www.openu.ac.il

Founded 1974; fmrly Everyman's Univ.; present name 1989; a distance-learning institution serving students on a nationwide basis. Academic and general adult education using written material and integrating technology (incl. online and satellite transmission) in a self-study system supplemented by tutorial instruction; offers 500 courses in the arts, democracy, computer science and natural sciences, communication, education, economics, management, history, Judaic studies, literature, language, mathematics, philosophy, political science, psychology, sociology

Language of instruction: Hebrew

Academic year: September to June (two semesters) and summer semester

Chancellor: Lord WOOLF

Deputy Chancellor: Lord ROTHSCHILD

Vice-Chancellor: Prof. ABRAHAM GINZBURG

Pres.: Prof. HAGIT MESSER-YARON

Vice-Pres. for Academic Affairs: Prof. JUDITH GAL-EZER

Dir -Gen.: DAVID KLIBANSKI

Dean of Academic Studies: Prof. TAMAR S. HERMANN

Dean of Students: Dr HAIM SAADOUN

Dir of the Library: HAVA MUSTIGMAN

Library of 75,000 vols, 500 e-books, 92 databases, 20,000 electronic periodicals

Number of teachers: 1,693 (55 senior faculty members, 428 junior faculty members and 1,210 tutors throughout Israel teaching in 100 study centres)

Number of students: 36,315, 2,598 graduate students, 7,000 students in countries of the former USSR

TEL-AVIV UNIVERSITY

Ramat-Aviv, 69978 Tel-Aviv

Telephone: (3) 6407777

Fax: (3) 6408601

Internet: www.tau.ac.il

Founded 1953; inaugurated 1956

Private control, partially supported by the Govt

Language of instruction: Hebrew

Academic year: October to June (2 terms)

Pres.: Prof. ZVI GALIL

Vice-Pres. for Public Affairs: Dr GARY SUSSMAN

Vice-Pres. for Research and Devt: Prof. EHUD GAZIT

Rector: Prof. DANY LEVIATAN

Vice-Rector: Prof. ARON SHAI

Dir-Gen.: Prof. MORDEHAI KOHN

Academic Sec.: SARA KINEL

Dean of Students: Prof. YOAV ARIEL

Library: see Libraries and Archives

Number of teachers: 2,200

Number of students: 26,000

Publications: *Hasifrut* (4 a year), *Iunei Mishpat* (4 a year), *Poetics Today* (4 a year), *Zemanim* (4 a year), *Mideast File* (4 a year), *Middle East Contemporary Survey* (1 a year), *Jahrbuch des Instituts für Deutsche Geschichte* (1 a year), *Dinei Israel* (1 a year), *Israel Yearbook in Human Rights* (1 a year), *Studies in Zionism* (2 a year), *Mediterranean Historical Review* (2 a year), *Michael* (8 every 18 months), *Shvut* (9 a year), *Studies in Educational Evaluation* (4 a year), *International Perspective on Education and Society* (1 a year), *Theoretical Inquiries in Law* (2 a year), *Israeli Society* (in Hebrew), *Kesher*

DEANS

Yolanda and David Katz Faculty of Arts: Prof. HANNAH NAVEH

Iby and Aladar Fleischman Faculty of Engineering: Prof. EHUD HEYMAN

Raymond and Beverly Sackler Faculty of Exact Sciences: Prof. HAIM WOLFSON

Lester and Sally Entin Faculty of Humanities: Prof. SHLOMO BIDERMAN

Buchmann Faculty of Law: Prof. HANOCH DAGAN

George S. Wise Faculty of Life Sciences: Prof. YOEL KLOOG

Faculty of Management (Leon Recanati Graduate School of Business Administration): Prof. ASHER TISHLER

Sackler Faculty of Medicine: Prof. JOSEPH MEKORI

Gershon H. Gordon Faculty of Social Sciences: Prof. NOAH LEWIN-EPSTEIN

PROFESSORS

AARONSON, J., Mathematics
ABBOUD, S., Biomedical Engineering
ABRAMOWICZ, H., Physics
AHARONOWITZ, Y., Microbiology
AHARONY, A., Physics
AHITUV, N., Management
AKSELROD, S., Physics
ALGOM, D., Psychology
ALON, N., Mathematics
ALONI, R., Botany
ALPERT, P., Geophysics and Planetary Sciences
AMIRAV, A., Chemistry
AMIT, Y., Bible
AMOSSY, R., French Literature
ANDELMAN, D., Physics
ANILY, S., Management
APTER, A., Psychiatry
ARBEL, A., Industrial Engineering
ARBEL, B., History
ARBER, N., Medicine
ARON, S., History
ASHKENAZI, S., Paediatrics
AVERBUCH, A., Computer Sciences
AVRON, A., Computer Sciences
AYALON, A., History of the Middle East and Africa
AZAR, Y., Computer Sciences
AZRIEL, P., Anaesthiology and Intensive Care
BANKS-SILLS, L., Mechanical Engineering
BAR-KOCHVA, B., History of the Jewish People
BAR-MEIR, S., Medicine
BAR-NAVI, E., History
BAR-NUN, A., Planetary Sciences
BAR-TAL, D., Education
BARBASH, G., Preventive Medicine, Social Medicine
BARKAI, R., History
BARNEA, D., Mechanical Engineering
BARZILAY, Z., Paediatrics
BATTLER, A., Cardiology
BE'ERY, Y., Electrical Engineering

BEER, S., Plant Sciences
BELHASSEN, B., Cardiology
BELKIN, A., Theatre Arts
BELKIN, M., Ophthalmology
BEN, E. S., Psychology
BEN-AVRAHAM, Z., Geophysics
BEN-BASSAT, I., Haematology
BEN-DAVID, Y., Anatomy and Anthropology
BEN-JACOB, E., Physics
BEN-RAFAEL, E., Sociology and Anthropology
BEN-RAFAEL, Z., Gynaecology and Obstetrics
BEN-ZVI, A., Political Science
BEN-ZVI, L., Theatre Arts
BENAYAHU, Y., Zoology
BENJAMINI, Y., Statistics
BENNINGA, S., Management
BENVENISTE, Y., Mechanical Engineering
BENVENISTI, E., Law
BERECHMAN, J., Urban Planning
BERGMAN, D., Physics
BERNHEIM, J., Medicine
BERNSTEIN, J., Mathematics
BIDERMAN, S., Philosophy
BIXON, M., Chemistry
BOXMAN, R., Electrical and Electronic Engineering
BRACHA, B., Law
BRAUNER, N., Mechanical Engineering
BREIMAN, A., Plant Sciences
BUCHNER, A., Oral Pathology
CARMELI, S., Physics
CASHER, A., Physics
CHEN, R., Physics
CHESHNOVSKY, O., Chemistry
CHESKIS, S., Chemistry
CHOR, B., Computer Sciences
COHEN, A., Communication
COHEN, G., Molecular Microbiology and Biotechnology
COHEN, J., History of the Jewish People
COHEN, N., Law
CUKIERMAN, A., Economics
DAGAN, H., Law
DASCAL, M., Philosophy
DASCAL, N., Physiology
DAVIDSON, M., Psychiatry
DAYAN, D., Oral Pathology
DAYAN, T., Zoology
DEKEL, E., Economics
DERSHOWITZ, N., Computer Sciences
DEUTCH, M., Law
DINARI, G., Paediatrics
DOR, J., Obstetrics and Gynaecology
DRAZEN, A., Economics
DREYFUS, T., Teaching of Science
DYN, N., Applied Mathematics
ECKSTEIN, Z., Economics
EDEN, D., Management
EINAV, S., Biomedical Engineering
ELAD, D., Biomedical Engineering
ELDAR, M., Cardiology
ENTIN, O., Physics
EPEL, B. L., Botany
ESHEL, I., Statistics
EVEN, U., Chemistry
EVEN-ZOHAR, I., Theory of Literature
FABIAN, I., Cell Biology and Histology
FAINARU, M., Medicine
FARBER, M., Mathematics
FARFEL, Z., Medicine
FEDER, M., Electrical Engineering
FERSHTMAN, CH., Economics
FIAT, A., Computer Sciences
FINKELBERG, M., Classics
FINKELSTEIN, I., Archaeology
FISHELSON, Z., Cell and Development Biology
FISHER, M., Classical Archaeology
FLEUROV, V., Physics
FRANKFURT, L. L., Physics
FREEMAN, A., Biotechnology
FRENK, H., Psychology
FRENKEL, J., Economics
FRENKEL, N., Cell Research and Immunology
FRIEDLAND, N., Psychology
FRIEDMAN, M. A., Talmud
FUCHS, C., Statistics

FUCHS, M., Mechanical Engineering
GADOTH, N., Neurology
GAFTER, U., Medicine
GANS, CH., Law
GANZACH, Y., Management
GAT, A., Political Sciences
GAZIT, A., Human Microbiology
GERCHAK, Y., Industrial Engineering
GERSHONI, I., History of the Middle East
GERSHONI, Y., Cell Research and Immunology
GILBOA, I., Management, Economics
GINSBURG, D., Mathematics
GITIK, M., Mathematics
GLASNER, S., Mathematics
GLAZER, J., Management
GLEZERMAN, M., Obstetrics and Gynaecology
GLUSKIN, E., Mathematics
GOFER, A., Archaeology
GOLANI, I., Zoology
GOLDBERG, I., Chemistry
GOLDBOURT, U., Preventive Medicine, Social Medicine
GOLDHIRSCH, I., Mechanical Engineering
GOLDMAN, B., Genetics
GORODETSKY, G., History
GOVER, A., Electrical and Electronic Engineering
GOZES, I., Clinical Biochemistry
GRAUR, D., Zoology
GREEN, M., Preventive Medicine, Social Medicine
GREENSTEIN, E., Bible
GRODEZINSKY, Y., Psychology
GROSSMAN, E., Medicine
GUREVITZ, M., Plant Sciences
GUTNIK, D., Microbiology
HALKIN, H., Medicine
HALPERN, Z., Medicine
HAMMEL, I., Pathology
HARAN, D., Mathematics
HARATS, D., Medicine
HARDY, A., Electrical and Electronic Engineering
HASSIN, R., Statistics
HATIVA, N., Education
HAZAN, H., Sociology and Anthropology
HEFETZ, A., Zoology
HENIG, M., Management
HENIS, Y., Biochemistry
HERSHKOVITZ, I., Anatomy and Anthropology
HEYMAN, E., Electrical Engineering
HILDESHEIMER, M., Communication Disorders
HIZI, A., Cell Biology
HOCHBERG, Y., Statistics
HOFFMAN, Y., Bible
HOLZMAN, A., Hebrew Literature
HOMBURG, R., Obstetrics and Gynaecology
HORNIK, J., Management
HOROWITZ, A., Geology
HOROWITZ, M., Cell Research and Immunology
HUPPERT, D., Chemistry
ICHILOV, O., Education
ISAAC, B., Classics
ITZCHAK, Y., Diagnostic Radiology
IZRE'EL, S., Semitic Linguistics
JARDEN, M., Mathematics
KAFFE, I., Oral Radiology
KAHANE, Y., Management
KALAY, A., Management
KALDOR, U., Chemistry
KANDEL, SH., Management
KANTOR, Y., Physics
KARLINER, M., Physics
KARNIOL, R., Psychology
KASHMAN, Y., Chemistry
KATZ, D., History
KATZIR, A., Physics
KAUFMAN, G., Biochemistry
KEISARI, Y., Human Microbiology
KENAAN-KEDAR, N., History of Arts
KEREN, G., Cardiology
KIT, E., Mechanical Engineering
KLAFTER, J., Chemistry
KLEIN, A., Mathematics
KLEIN, S., Jewish Philosophy

KLIEMAN, A., Political Science
KLOOG, Y., Biochemistry
KORCZYN, A., Neurology
KORENSTEIN, R., Physiology
KOSLOFF, D., Geophysics
KREITLER, S., Psychology
KRONFELD, I., Geophysics and Planetary Sciences
KUPIEC, M., Microbiology
LAMED, R., Biotechnology
LANDMAN, F., Linguistics
LANGHOLZ, G., Electrical Engineering
LAOR, D., Hebrew Literature
LAOR, N., Psychiatry
LASS, Y., Physiology
LAVI, S., Cell Biology
LEDERMAN, E., Law
LEHRER, E., Statistics
LEIBOWITZ, E., Physics and Astronomy
LEIDERMAN, L., Economics
LESSING, J., Gynaecology and Obstetrics
LEVANON, N., Electrical and Electronic Engineering
LEVIATAN, D., Mathematics
LEVIN, D., Applied Mechanics
LEVIN, E., Physics
LEVIN, Z., Atmospheric Sciences
LEVO, Y., Medicine
LEVY, A., Physics
LEVY, S., Theatre Arts
LEWIN, N., Sociology and Anthropology
LIBERMAN, U. A., Statistics
LICHTENBERG, D., Pharmacology
LICHTENSTADT, J., Physics
LITSYN, S., Electrical Engineering
LIVSHITS, Z., Anatomy and Anthropology
LOBEL, T., Psychology
LOTAN, I., Physiology
LOYA, Y., Zoology
MAIMON, O., Industrial Engineering
MALKIN, I., Ancient History
MANSOUR, Y., Computer Sciences
MAOZ, D., Physics and Astronomy
MAOZ, Z., Political Science
MARGALIT, M., Education
MARGALIT, R., Biochemistry
MATZKIN, H., Surgery
MAUTNER, M., Law
MAZEH, T., Physics
MEDIN, Z., History
MEILIJSON, I., Statistics
MEKORI, Y., Medicine
MELAMED, E., Neurology
MENASHIRI, D., History of the Middle East
MESSER, H., Electrical Engineering
MEVARECH, M., Microbiology
MICHAELSON, D., Biochemistry
MILMAN, V., Mathematics
MILOH, T., Engineering
MIMOUNI, F., Paediatrics
MINTS, R., Physics
MOHR, R., Surgery
MOTRO, M., Cardiology
MULLER, E., Management
NAAMAN, N., History of the Jewish People
NADLER, A., Psychology
NAOR, Z., Biochemistry
NAVON, R., Human Genetics
NELSON, N., Biochemistry
NETZER, H., Physics
NEVO, D., Education
NITZAN, A., Chemistry
NUSSINOV, R., Biochemistry
NUSSINOV, S., Physics
OFEK, I., Human Microbiology
OFER, A., Management
OLEVSKII, A., Mathematics
OPPENHEIMER, A., History of the Jewish People
OR, U. G., Surgery
ORON, U., Zoology
ORON, Y., Pharmacology
OVADIA, M., Zoology
PASSWELL, J., Paediatrics
PAZ, G., Physiology
PELED, E., Chemistry

PHILLIP, M., Paediatrics
PIASETZKY, E., Physics
PICK, E., Immunology
PITARU, S., Oral Biology
PODOLACK, M., Planetary Science
POLAK, F., Bible
POLTEROVICH, L., Mathematics
PORAT, A., Law
PORTUGALI, J., Geography
RABEY, M., Neurology
RABINOVICH, I., History of the Middle East
RABINOWITZ, B., Cardiology
RAK, Y., Anatomy and Anthropology
RAVID, M., Medicine
RAVIV, A., Psychology
RAZ, A., Biochemistry
RAZ, J., East Asian Studies
RAZ, T., Management
RAZI, Z., History
RAZIN, A., Economics
RECHAVI, G., Haematology
REHAVI, M., Pharmacology
REIN, R., History
REPHAELI, Y., Physics
RISHPON, J., Biotechnology
ROKEM, F., Theatre Arts
ROLL, I., Classical Archaeology
RON, E., Microbiology
RON-EL, R., Gynaecology and Obstetrics
RONEN, B., Management
ROSENAU, P., Applied Mathematics
ROSENBAUM, M., Psychology
ROSENBERG, M., Human Microbiology
ROSENMAN, G., Electrical Engineering
ROSSET, SH., Mathematics
ROZEN, S., Chemistry
RUBIN, U., Arabic Language and Literature
RUBIN, Z., History
RUBINSTEIN, A., Economics
RUBINSTEIN, E., Medicine
RUDNICK, Z., Mathematics
RUPIN, E., Computer Science
RUPIN, E., Physiology
RUSCHIN, SH., Electrical Engineering
SABAR, B., Education
SADAN, J., Islamic Culture, Arabic Literature
SADKA, E., Economics
SAFRA, Z., Management
SAMET, D., Management
SAND, SH., History
SARNE, Y., Physiology
SAVION, N., Clinical Biochemistry
SCHMEIDLER, D., Statistics and Economics
SCHWARTZ, M., Physics
SEMYONOV, M., Sociology
SHACHAM-DIAM, Y., Electrical Engineering
SHAI, A., History
SHAKED, U., Electrical and Electronic Engineering
SHALGI, R., Embryology
SHAMIR, M., Political Science
SHAMIR, R., Computer Sciences
SHAMIR, Z., Hebrew Literature
SHANI, M., Health Systems Management
SHAPIRA, A., History of the Jewish People
SHAPIRA, Y., Electrical and Electronic Engineering
SHAPIRO, Y., Physiology
SHARIR, M., Computer Sciences
SHAVIT, Y., History of the Jewish People
SHAVIT, Y., Sociology and Anthropology
SHAVIT, Z., Semiotics and Cultural Research
SHEMER, J., Medicine
SHEMER, L., Mechanical Engineering
SHENKMAN, L., Medicine
SHILOH, Y., Human Genetics
SHOENFELD, Y., Medicine
SHOHAMY, E., Education
SHOHAT, M., Paediatrics
SHUSTIN, E., Mathematics
SIDI, Y., Medicine
SINGER, I., Cultures of the Ancient East
SINGER, S., Electrical Engineering
SIVASHINSKY, G., Applied Mathematics
SKORNICK, Y., Surgery
SKUTELSKY, E., Pathology

SNEH, B., Botany
SNYDERS, I., Electrical Engineering
SODIN, M., Mathematics
SOLOMON, B., Biotechnology
SOLOMON, Z., Social Work
SOUDRY, D., Mathematics
SPIEGLER, I., Management
STAVY, R., Teaching of Science
STEINBERG, B., Electrical Engineering
STERN, N., Medicine
STERNBERG, A., Physics
STERNBERG, M., Theory of Literature
STONE, L., Zoology
STRAUSS, S., Educational Psychology
TAL, H., Periodontology
TAMARKIN, M., History of Africa
TAMIR, A., Statistics
TAMSE, A., Endodontology
TARSI, M., Computer Sciences
TAUMAN, Y., Management
TEBOULLE, M., Operation Research and Statistics
TE'ENI, D., Management
TEICHMAN, M., Psychology
TEICHMAN, Y., Psychology
TERKEL, J., Zoology
TIROSH, D., Teaching of Science
TISHLER, A., Management
TODER, V., Embryology
TOLEDANO, E., History of the Middle East
TOURY, G., Theory of Literature, Comparative Literature
TSAL, Y., Psychology
TSIRELSON, B., Statistics
TUR, M., Electrical and Electronic Engineering
TUR-KASPA, R., Medicine
TURKEL, E., Mathematics
TYANO, S., Psychiatry
URBAKH, M., Chemistry
VERED, Z., Cardiology
VIDNE, B., Surgery
VOLKOV, S., History
WEINER, I., Psychology
WEINSTEIN, E., Electrical and Electronic Engineering
WEISMAN, Y., Paediatrics
WEISS, A., Electrical Engineering
WEISS, Y., Economics
WEIZMAN, A., Psychiatry
WEIZMAN, R., Psychiatry
WIENTROUB, S. H., Orthopaedic Surgery
WOLFSON, H., Computer Sciences
YAKAR, J., Archaeology
YANKIELOWICZ, S., Physics
YAROSLAVSKY, L., Electrical Engineering
YASSIF, E., Hebrew Literature
YEHUDAI, A., Computer Sciences
YINON, U., Physiology
YOGEV, A., Sociology of Education
YOM-TOV, Y., Zoology
ZADOK, R., History of the Jewish People and Cultures of the Ancient East
ZAGAGI, N., Classical Studies
ZAHAVI, J., Management
ZAKAY, D., Psychology
ZALTZMAN, N., Law
ZANG, I., Management
ZILCHA, I., Economics
ZISAPEL, N., Biochemistry
ZONNENSCHEIN, J., Physics
ZWICK, U., Computer Sciences

TECHNION—ISRAEL INSTITUTE OF TECHNOLOGY

32000 Haifa

Telephone: (4) 8292111
Fax: (4) 8292000
E-mail: president@technion.ac.il
Internet: www.technion.ac.il

Founded 1912; inaugurated 1924
State control
Language of instruction: Hebrew
Academic year: October to July

Pres.: Prof. YITZHAK APELOIG
Sr Exec. Vice-Pres.: Prof. PAUL D. FEIGIN
Exec. Vice-Pres. and Dir-Gen.: Prof. ZVI KOHAVI
Exec. Vice-Pres. for Academic Affairs: Prof. MOSHE SIDI
Exec. Vice-Pres. for Research: Prof. ODED SHMUELI
Vice-Pres. for Resource Devt and External Relations: Prof. RAPHAEL ROM
Dean of Undergraduate Studies: Prof. YAACOV MAMANE
Dean of Graduate School: Prof. MOSHE SHPITALNI
Dean of Students: Prof. MICHAL GREEN
Library: see Libraries and Archives
Number of teachers: 993
Number of students: 13,291 (9,273 undergraduate, 4,018 postgraduate)
Publications: *HaTechnion* (3 a year), *Shlomo Kaplansky Memorial Series* (inc. in *Israel Journal of Technology*), *The Joseph Wunsch Lectures* (1 a year)

DEANS

Faculty of Aerospace Engineering: Prof. O. RAND
Faculty of Architecture and Town Planning: Prof. A. CHURCHMAN
Faculty of Biology: Prof. G. SCHUSTER
Faculty of Biotechnology and Food Engineering: Prof. S. MIZRAHI
Faculty of Chemical Engineering: Prof. Y. TALMON
Faculty of Chemistry: Prof. M. EISEN
Faculty of Civil and Environmental Engineering: Prof. A. BENTUR
Faculty of Computer Science: Prof. E. BIHAM
Faculty of Electrical Engineering: Prof. I. CIDON
Faculty of Industrial Engineering and Management: Prof. B. GOLANY
Faculty of Materials Engineering: Prof. E. ZOLOTOYABKO
Faculty of Mechanical Engineering: Prof. Z. PALMOR
Faculty of Medicine: Prof. I. PERLMAN
Faculty of Physics: Prof. J. AVRON
Dept of Biomedical Engineering: Prof. J. MIZRAHI (Head)
Dept of Education in Technology and Science: Assoc. Prof. M. MOORE (Head)
Dept of Humanities and Art: Prof. C. SCHAPIRA
Dept of Mathematics: Prof. J. RUBINSTEIN

PROFESSORS

Faculty of Aerospace Engineering (tel. (4) 8292308; fax (4) 8292030; e-mail aerdean@ aerodyne.technion.ac.il; internet ae-www .technion.ac.il):

BAR-ITZHACK, I., Navigation, Guidance and Control
DURBAN, D., Aerospace Structure
GANY, A., Rocket Propulsion
GIVOLI, D., Aerospace Structures, Computational Mechanics
GREENBERG, B., Combustion Theory
GUELMAN, M., Space Engineering
KARPEL, M., Aeroelasticity, Optimization
RAND, O., Rotary Wings, Aerospace Structures
ROSEN, A., Rotary Wings, Aerospace Structure
TAMBOUR, Y., Combustion of Fuel Sprays
WEIHS, D., Fluid Mechanics, Bio-Mechanics and Stability Theory
WELLER, T., Aerospace Structures, Smart Structures Technology

Faculty of Architecture and Town Planning (tel. (4) 8294001; fax (4) 8294617; e-mail deanarc@tx.technion.ac.il; internet architecture.technion.ac.il):

ALTERMAN, R., Land Development

AMIR, S., Regional Planning
BURT, M., Ocean Architecture
CARMON, N., Social Policy
CHURCHMAN, A., Environmental Psychology
SHAVIV, E., Energy and Architecture
SHEFER, D., Urban and Regional Economics

Faculty of Biology (tel. (4) 8294211; fax (4) 8225153; e-mail ddafna@tx.technion.ac.il; internet biology.technion.ac.il):

CASSEL, D., G-Proteins and Membrane Traffic
SCHUSTER, G., Molecular Biology

Department of Biomedical Engineering (tel. (4) 8294129; fax (4) 8294599; e-mail office@ bm.technion.ac.il; internet www.bm.technion .ac.il):

DINNAR, U., Cardiovascular Fluid Dynamics, Minimal Invasive Diagnosis
LANIR, Y., Tissues Mechanics and Structure, Cardiac Mechanics, Coronary Circulation
MIZRAHI, J., Orthopaedic and Rehabilitation Biomechanics

Faculty of Biotechnology and Food Engineering (tel. (4) 8293068; fax (4) 8293399; e-mail biotech@tx.technion.ac.il; internet biotech .technion.ac.il):

COGAN, U., Food Chemistry
LEVI, B. Z., Mammalian Cell Biotechnology, Transcriptional Regulation, Innate Immunity
MILTZ, J., Packaging Engineering
SHOHAM, Y., Biochemical Engineering, Industrial Microbiology, Applied Enzymology

Faculty of Chemical Engineering (tel. (4) 8292820; fax (4) 8295672; e-mail chemeng@ technion.ac.il; internet chemeng.technion.ac .il):

COHEN, Y., Polymer Science and Engineering
GRADER, G., Ceramic Materials, Sol-Gel Systems
LEWIN, D. R., Process Design and Control
MARMUR, A., Interfaces and Colloids
NIR, A., Fluid Mechanics, Transport Phenomena
SEMIAT, R., Process Development, Separation Processes, Desalination, Electro-Optical Techniques for Fluid-Flow
SHEINTUCH, M., Chemical Reaction Engineering, Catalysis, Non-linear Dynamics
TALMON, Y., Complex Liquids, Electron Microscopy

Faculty of Chemistry (tel. (4) 8293727; fax (4) 8295860; e-mail chsabine@tx.technion.ac.il; internet schulich.technion.ac.il):

APELOIG, Y., Organosilicon and Computational Chemistry
BAASOV, T., Bio-organic Chemistry, Enzymology
EISEN, M., Polymer Chemistry, Organometallic Chemistry
GROSS, Z., Catalysis, Inorganic Chemistry, Bioinorganic Chemistry
KAFTORY, M., Chemical Crystallography
KEINAN, E., Biocatalysis, Organic Synthesis, Molecular Computing
KOLODNEY, E., Molecular Beams, Surface Chemistry
MAREK, I., Organic Synthesis
MOISEYEV, N., Quantum Chemistry
SCHLECTER, I., Analytical Chemistry
SPEISER, S., Laser Photophysics

Faculty of Civil and Environmental Engineering (tel. (4) 8293066; fax (4) 8220133; e-mail deansecr@technion.ac.il; internet cee .technion.ac.il):

BENTUR, A., Cementitious and Composite Building Materials

CEDER, A., Transportation Planning and Operation

DOYTSHER, Y., Mapping and Geo-Information Engineering

EISENBERGER, M., Computational Mechanics-Static, Dynamics, Stability Analysis

FROSTIG, Y., Sandwich Structures, Pre-stressed Concrete, Retrofitting of Concrete Structures, Tile-Wall Systems

FRYDMAN, S., Geotechnical Engineering

KIRSCH, U., Structural Engineering

LAUFER, A., Project Management

MAMANE, Y., Air Pollution Meteorology, Atmospheric Aerosols

MURAVSKI, G., Soil Structure Interaction

NEUMANN, P. M., Plant Physiology

POLUS, A., Traffic Flow and Congestion Modelling, Safety of Transportation Systems

RUBIN, H., Contaminant Hydrology

SHEINMAN, I., Post-Buckling, Dynamics, Static, Damage, Vibration Induced by People

STIASSNIE, M., Water Waves

UZAN, J., Pavement Engineering

YANKELEVSKY, D., Impact Engineering, Mechanics of Reinforced Concrete, Earthquake Engineering

ZIMMELS, Y., Environmental and Process Engineering

Faculty of Computer Science (tel. (4) 8294313; fax (4) 8294353; e-mail itai@cs.technion.ac.il; internet www.cs.technion.ac.il):

BARAM, Y., Pattern Recognition, Artificial Neural Network

BIHAM, E., Cryptology

BRUCKSTEIN, A., Image Processing

BSHOUTY, N., Computational Learning Theory

FRANCEZ, N., Semantics and Verification, Computational Linguistics

GRUMBERG, O., Formal Verification

ISRAELI, M., Scientific Computing, Numerical Methods, Computational Linguistics

ITAI, A., Analysis of Algorithms and Data Structures, Computational Linguistics

KUSHILEVITZ, E., Complexity and Cryptography

MAKOWSKY, J., Mathematical Logic Computability and Complexity, Combinatorial Algorithms, Database Theory

MORAN, S., Search Methods on the Web

ROTH, R., Coding Theory

SIDI, A., Theoretical Numerical Analysis and Scientific Computing

SHMUELI, O., Databases: Systems and Theory

UNGARISH, M., Modelling and Numerical Simulation of Fluid Flows

ZAKS, S., Distributed Computing and Communication Networks

Faculty of Electrical Engineering (tel. (4) 8294680; fax (4) 8295757; e-mail eedean@ee.technion.ac.il; internet www.ee.technion.ac.il):

CIDON, I., Communication Networks

EISENSTEIN, G., Optoelectronics

FEUER, A., Automatic Control

FINKMAN, E., Quantum Hetrostructure

FISCHER, B., Optoelectronics

LEVIATAN, Y., Electromagnetic Waves

MALAH, D., Digital Signal Processing of Speech and Images

MERHAV, N., Information Theory

ROM, R., Communication Networks

SALZMAN, J., Optoelectronics

SCHIEBER, D., Energy Conversion

SEGALL, A., Computer Networks

SHAMAI, S., Information Theory

SHWARTZ, A., Large Deviations Theory

SIDI, M., Computer Networks

TANNENBAUM, A., Robust Control Theory

ZEEVI, Y., Vision and Image Sciences

ZEITOUNI, Z., Large Deviations Theory

ZIV, J., Statistical Communication, Information Theory

Faculty of Industrial Engineering and Management (tel. (4) 8294444; fax (4) 8295676; e-mail iedean@ie.technion.ac.il; internet iew3.technion.ac.il):

ADLER, R., Stochastic Processes

BEN-TAL, A., Non-linear Optimization

EREV, I., Behavioural Sciences and Experimental Economics

EREZ, M., Organizational Psychology

DE-HAAN, U., Entrepreneurship

FEIGIN, P., Applied Statistics

GOLANY, B., Industrial Engineering

GOPHER, D., Human Factors

KASPI, H., Probability and Stochastic Processes

MANDELBAUM, A., Operations Research, Stochastic Processes and their Applications

MONDERER, D., Game Theory

NEMIROVSKY, A., Optimization Complexity Theory

NOTEA, A., Non-Destructive Testing

ROTHBLUM, U. G., Operations Research

RUBINSTEIN, R., Stochastic Systems

SHTUB, A., Project Management

TENNENHOLTZ, M., Artificial Intelligence

WEISSMAN, I., Probability and Statistics

Faculty of Materials Engineering (tel. (4) 8294591; fax (4) 8295677; e-mail oilana@tx.technion.ac.il; internet materials.technion.ac.il):

EIZENBERG, M., Electronic Materials

GUTMANAS, E., Processing of High-Performance Material

KOMEM, Y., Electronic Materials

LIFSHITZ, Y., Nanostructured Inorganic Materials

SHECHTMAN, D., Properties and Microstructure of Intermetallic Compounds

SIEGMANN, A., Polymers and Plastic Structuring

ZOLOTOYABKO, E., X-Ray Diffraction

Faculty of Mathematics (tel. (4) 8223071; fax (4) 8324654; e-mail mathsee@tx.technion.ac.il; internet www.math.technion.ac.il):

AHARONI, R., Combinatorics

AHARONOV, D., Complex Analysis

BENYAMINI, Y., Banach Spaces

BERMAN, A., Matrix Theory

BSHOUTY, D., Complex Analysis, Probability Theory, Mathematical Statistics

CHILLAG, D., Algebra Group Theory

CWIKEL, M., Functional Analysis and Interpolation Space

GOLDBERG, M., Numerical Analysis

GORDON, Y., Functional Analysis

HERSHKOWITZ, D., Matrix Theory

IOFFE, A., General Theory of Sub-differentials

KATCHALSKI, M., Combinatorial Geometry

LERER, L., Linear Algebra, Operator Theory

LIRON, N., Applied Mathematics

LOEWY, R., Linear Algebra

MARCUS, M., Partial Differential Equations, Non-linear Analysis

NEPOMNYASHCHY, A., Fluid Mechanics

PINKUS, A., Approximation Theory

PINSKY, R., Probability and Stochastic Processes, Partial Differential Equations

REICH, S., Non-linear Analysis

RUBINSTEIN, J., Applied Mathematics

SOLEL, B., Operator Theory, Functional Analysis

SONN, J., Algebraic Number Theory

WAJNRYB, B., Algebraic Geometry

ZEITOUNI, O., Probability and Stochastic Processes

ZIEGLER, Z., Theory of Approximation

Faculty of Mechanical Engineering (tel. (4) 8292079; fax (4) 8295710; e-mail iritg@technion.ac.il; internet meeng.technion.ac.il):

ALTUS, E., Micro-Mechanics of Solids

BAR-YOSEPH, P., Finite Element Analysis

BEN-HAIM, Y., Decisions under Uncertainty, Reliability

DEGANI, D., Computational Fluid Dynamics

ELIAS, E., Thermohydraulics, Nuclear Engineering

ETSION, I., Tribology, Lubrication

GROSSMAN, G., Thermodynamics, Heat Pumps, Cooling and Air-Conditioning

GUTMAN, S., Relative Stability of Linear Dynamic Systems

HABER, S., Particulate Systems

PALMOR, Z., Digital Control of Industrial and Mechanical Systems

RUBIN, M., Continuum Mechanics

SHAPIRO, M., Porous Media, Aerosols

SHITZER, A., Bio-Heat Transfer

SHOHAM, M., Robotics and Medical Robotics

SHPITALNI, M., CAD/CAM, Manufacturing

TIROSH, J., Fracture Mechanics

YARIN, A., Rheology, Fluid Mechanics

YARIN, L. P., Two-Phase Flow, Combustion

ZVIRIN, Y., Solar Energy, Internal Combustion Engines

Faculty of Medicine (POB 9649, Bat Galim, 31096 Haifa; tel. (4) 8292111; fax (4) 8517008; e-mail md@tx.technion.ac.il; internet md.technion.ac.il):

AVIRAM, M., Lipid Research Laboratory

BENJAMIN, B., Haematology

BEYAR, R., Invasive Cardiology

CIECHANOVER, A., Intercellular Breakdown of Proteins

ETZIONI, A., Paediatrics and Immunology

FINBERG, J., Neuropharmacology

FINSOD, M., Neurosurgery

FRY, M., Enzymology of DNA Replication

GAVISH, M., Molecular Pharmacology

HASIN, Y., Cardiology

HERSHKO, A., Intracellular Protein Degradation

ITSKOVITZ, J., Human Embryonic Stem Cells

KRAUSZ, M., General Surgery

LAVIE, P., Psychobiology, Sleep Research

LEWIS, B., Cardiology

NEUFELD, G., Angiogenesis

PALTI, Y., Physiology and Biophysics

PERLMAN, I., Vision Neurophysiology

PRATT, H., Behavioural Sciences

ROWE, Y., Haematology

SHALEV, E., Obstetrics and Gynaecology

SKORECKI, K., Nephrology, Molecular Medicine

VOLDAVSKY, I., Vascular and Tumour Biology, Biochemistry

YOUDIM, M., Neuropharmacology

Faculty of Physics (tel. (4) 8293909; fax (4) 8295755; e-mail office@physics.technion.ac.il; internet physics.technion.ac.il):

AKKERMANS, E., Theory of Condensed Matter Physics, Mesoscopic Quantum

AUERBACH, A., Condensed Matter Theory

AVRON, J., Mathematical Physics

BRAUN, E., Biophysics, Non-linear Dynamics of Systems out of Equilibrium

COHEN, E., Spectroscopic Properties of Laser Materials

DADO, S., High-Energy Physics Experimentation

DAR, A., Astroparticle Physics

EHRENFREUND, E., Semiconducting Quantum Structures and Polymers

EILAM, G., Elementary Particle Physics

FELSTEINER, J., Condensed Matter Physics, Plasma Physics

FISHMAN, S., Quantum Chaos

GERSHONI, D., Semiconducting Quantum Heterostructures

GRONAU, M., Theoretical High Energy Physics

KALISH, R., Ion-Implantation—Hyperfine Interactions

KOREN, G., Superconductivity and Lasers

LIPSON, S., Low Temperature Physics

MANN, A., Theoretical Physics

MOSHE, M., Theoretical High Energy Physics

ORI, A., General Relativity, Black Holes, Gravitational Radiation

POLTURAK, E., High Temperature Superconductors

REGEV, O., Astrophysics

RIESS, I., Solid State Electrochemistry

SEGEV, M., Nonlinear Optics

SHAPIRO, B., Theory of Condensed Matter

SHAVIV, G., Astrophysics

SIVAN, U., Mesoscopic Physics, Bio-Electronics

SOKER, N., Astrophysics Theory

WEIZMANN INSTITUTE OF SCIENCE

POB 26, 76100 Rehovot

Telephone: (8) 9342111

Fax: (8) 9344107

E-mail: news@weizmann.ac.il

Internet: www.weizmann.ac.il

Founded 1949; incl. the Daniel Sieff Research Institute (f. 1934).

The Institute is a private non-profit corporation for fundamental and applied research in the natural and exact sciences. The Feinberg Graduate School offers MSc and PhD courses

Pres.: Prof. DANIEL ZAJFMAN

Vice-Pres.: Prof. HAIM GARTY

Vice-Pres. for Admin. and Finance: GAD KOBER

Vice-Pres. for Resource Devt and Public Affairs: Prof. ISRAEL BAR-JOSEPH

Vice-Pres. for Technology Transfer: Prof. MORDECHAI SHEVES

Chief Librarian: Mrs I. POLLACK

Library: see Libraries and Archives

Number of teachers: 300

Number of students: 785 postgraduates

DEANS

Faculty of Biochemistry: Prof. B.-Z. SHILO

Faculty of Biology: Prof. B. GEIGER

Faculty of Chemistry: Prof. YEHIAM PRIOR

Faculty of Mathematics and Computer Science: Prof. ZVI ARTSTEIN

Faculty of Physics: Prof. YOSEF NIR

Feinberg Graduate School: Prof. LIA ADDADI

DIRECTORS OF CENTRES

Faculty of Biochemistry:

Avron-Wilstätter Minerva Center for Research in Photosynthesis: Prof. A. SCHERZ

Charles W. and Tillie K. Lubin Center for Plant Biotechnology: Prof. GAD GALILI

Crown Human Genome Center: Prof. DORON LANCET

David and Fela Shapell Family Center for Genetic Disorders Research: Prof. YORAM GRONER

Dr Joseph Cohn Minerva Center for Biomembrane Research: Prof. ZVI LIVNEH

Harry and Jeanette Weinberg Center for Plant Molecular Genetics Research: Prof. GAD GALILI

Kekst Family Center for Medical Genetics: Prof. YORAM GRONER

Leo and Julia Forchheimer Center for Molecular Genetics: Prof. A. KIMCHI

M. D. Moross Institute for Cancer Research: Prof. YORAM GRONER

Mel Dobrin Center for Nutrition: Prof. GAD GALILI

Y. Leon Benoziyo Institute for Molecular Medicine: Prof. BEN-ZION SHILO

Faculty of Biology:

Belle S. and Irving E. Meller Center for Biology of Ageing: Prof. ZELIG ESHHAR

Carl and Micaela Einhorn-Dominic Institute for Brain Research: Prof. YADIN DUDAI

Gabrielle Rich Center for Transplantation Biology Research: Prof. YAIR REISNER

Murray H. and Meyer Grodetsky Center for Research of Higher Brain Functions: Prof. A. GRINVALD

Nella and Leon Benoziyo Center for Neurological Diseases: Prof. MENAHEM SEGAL

Nella and Leon Benoziyo Center for Neurosciences: Prof. YADIN DUDAI

Norman and Helen Asher Center for for Brain Imaging: Prof. YADIN DUDAI

Wilner Family Center for Vascular Biology: Prof. NAVA DEKEL

Women's Health Research Center: Prof. VARDA ROTTER

Yad Abraham Research Center for Cancer Diagnostics and Therapy: Prof. VARDA ROTTER

Faculty of Chemistry:

Center for Energy Research: Prof. JACOB KARNI

Fritz Haber Center for Physical Chemistry: Prof. SHIMON VEGA

Gerhard M. J. Schmidt Minerva Center for Supermolecular Architecture: Prof. R. TENNE

Helen and Martin Kimmel Center for Archaeological Sciences: Prof. STEPHEN WEINER

Helen and Martin Kimmel Center for Molecular Design: Prof. DAVID MILSTEIN

Helen and Martin Kimmel Center for Nanoscale Science: Prof. RESHEF TENNE

Helen and Milton A. Kimmelman Center for Biomolecular Structure and Assembly: Prof. A. E. YONATH

Ilse Katz Institute for Material Sciences and Magnetic Resonance Research: Prof. MORDECHAI SHEVES

Joseph and Ceil Mazer Center for Structural Biology: Prof. AMNON HOROVITZ

Sussman Family Center for the Study of Environmental Sciences: Prof. DAN YAKIR

Faculty of Mathematics and Computer Science:

Arthur and Rochelle Belfer Institute of Mathematics and Computer Science: Prof. ZVI ARTSTEIN

Ida Cohen Centre for Mathematics: Prof. ZVI ARTSTEIN

Minerva Center for Formal Verification of Reactive Systems: Prof. A. PNUELI

Faculty of Physics:

Albert Einstein Minerva Center for Theoretical Physics: Prof. ELI WAXMAN

Center for Experimental Physics: Prof. YARON SILBERBERG

Joseph H. and Belle R. Braun Center for Submicron Research: Prof. M. HEIBLUM

Maurice and Gabriela Goldschleger Center for Nanophysics: Prof. ISRAEL BAR-JOSEPH

Minerva Center for Non-linear Physics of Complex Systems: Prof. ITAMAR PROCACCIA

Nella and Leo Benoziyo Center for High Energy Physics: Prof. G. MIKENBERG

Feinberg Graduate School:

Aharon Katzir-Katchalsky Center: Prof. Y. YARDEN

Colleges and Higher Institutes

Academic Centre Ruppin: PO Academic Center Ruppin, 40250 Emek Hefer; tel. (9) 8983005; fax (9) 8983021; e-mail rani@ruppin.ac.il; internet www.ruppin.ac.il; f. 1949; three-year degree courses in accounting, business admin. and behavioural sciences, economics; two-year courses in architecture, basic trades, computers, electrical engineering, industrial management, landscape architecture, megatronics, soil and water engineering; short courses in accounting and mechanics, basic economics; school of engineering: electrical, industrial and computer science; library: 30,000 vols; 350 teachers; 5,000 students; Pres. Prof. SHOSH ARAD; Dir ZVIKA LEVIN.

Academic Centre of Law and Business: 26 Ben Gurion St, 52275 Ramat-Gan; tel. (3) 6000800; fax (3) 6000801; e-mail info@rg-law.ac.il; internet www.clb.ac.il; depts of communication and technology, criminal law and criminology and law, human rights; 1,000 students; Dean Prof. PINHAS SHIFMAN.

Academic College of Tel-Aviv-Yaffo: 4 Antokolsky St, POB 16131, 61161 Tel-Aviv; tel. (3) 5211840; fax (3) 5211870; e-mail mirsham@mta.ac.il; internet www.mta.ac.il; Bachelors of Arts degrees in computer science, behavioural science, management, society and politics.

Bezalel Academy of Arts and Design: Mount Scopus, POB 24046, 91240 Jerusalem; tel. (2) 5893333; fax (2) 5823094; e-mail mail@bezalel.ac.il; internet www.bezalel.ac.il; f. 1906; degree courses in architecture, design, animation, ceramics and glass design, fine arts, Gold- and Silver-smithingindustrial design, jewellery and fashion accessories design,photography, visual communication, video and computer imaging; library: 35,000 vols; 300 teachers; 1,600 students; Pres. Prof. ARNON ZUCKERMAN.

Ecole Biblique et Ecole Archéologique Française: 6 Nablus Rd, POB 19053, 91190 Jerusalem; tel. (2) 6264468; fax (2) 6282567; e-mail directeur@ebaf.edu; internet ebaf.op.org; f. 1890; research, Biblical and Oriental studies, exploration and excavation in Palestine; 14 professors; library, see Libraries; Dir PAULINE BOILARD; publs *Cahiers de la Revue Biblique, Etudes Annexes, Etudes Bibliques, Littératures anciennes du Proche Orient, Revue Biblique* (4 a year).

Hadassah College: 37 Hanevi'im St, POB 1114, 91010 Jerusalem; tel. (2) 6291911; fax (2) 6250619; e-mail info@hadassah.ac.il; internet www.hadassah.ac.il; f. 1970; comprises Hadassah Academic College (depts of communication disorders, computer sciences, medical laboratory sciences, optometry, , Hadassah College of Technology (depts of dental technology, cinema and television production, hotel management, photography and digital media, industrial design, printing and computer graphics, technical software engineering), Tachlit Centre for Lifelong Learning; Pres. Prof. NAVA BEN ZVI.

Hebrew Union College—Jewish Institute of Religion: 13 King David St, 94101 Jerusalem; tel. (2) 6203333; fax (2) 6251478; e-mail mzakai@huc.edu; internet www.huc.edu; f. 1963; br. of the same instn in the United States of America; the first year of graduate rabbinic studies, Jewish education, cantorial training and programme in biblical archaeology, incl. summer excavations; Rabbinic programme for Israel Reform (Progressive); English 'Lehrhaus' study programmes in classical Jewish Literature for gen. public (Bet Midrash); Skirball Museum of Biblical

Archaeology; library: Abramov library of 40,000 vols; microfilm colln from American Jewish Archives; 35 teachers; 150 students; Pres. Dr DAVID ELLENSON; Dean Rabbi MICHAEL MARMUR.

International Institute of Histadrut: Beit Berl, 44905 Kfar Saba; tel. (9) 7612303; fax (9) 7456962; e-mail info@peoples.org.il; internet www.peoples.org.il; f. 1958 to train labour and cooperative movements, professional assocs and women's and youth orgs; candidates nominated by trade unions, cooperatives, univs, int. labour orgs, etc.; courses and seminars in fields of labour, social and economic devt and cooperative studies in Arabic, English, French, Russian and Spanish; 41,400 graduates from 140 countries; library: 15,000 vols, and monographs and periodicals; 8 teachers; 1,400 students; Dir-Gen. MICHAEL FROHLICH; Academic Dir SERDIO GRYN.

Jerusalem Academy of Music and Dance: Givat Ram Campus, 91904 Jerusalem; tel. (2) 6759911; fax (2) 6512824; e-mail schul@jamd.ac.il; internet www.jamd.ac.il; f. 1947; performing arts, composition, conducting and theory, music education, dance; awards BMus., BEdMus., Dance and Artists' Diplomas; courses leading to BAMus., MAMus. and MMus. in cooperation with the Hebrew University; Conservatory and High School (Music and Dance); 190 teachers; 550 students; library: 60,000 vols; colln of musical instruments; electroacoustic laboratory; Pres. Prof. ILAN SCHUL; Dir-Gen. MICHA TAL.

Jerusalem College of Technology: 21 Havaad Haleumi St, POB 16031, 91160 Jerusalem; tel. (2) 6751111; fax (2) 6751068; e-mail pr@jct.ac.il; internet www.jct.ac.il; f. 1969; 4-year first degree courses; library: 20,000 vols; 106 teachers (66 full-time, 40 part-time); 2,660 students; Pres. Prof. JOSEPH S. BODENHEIMER; Rector Prof. MENACHEM STEINER; Librarian ZVI SOBEL.

Jerusalem University College: POB 1276, Mount Zion, 91012 Jerusalem; tel. (2) 6718628; fax (2) 6732717; e-mail paulwright@juc.edu; internet www.juc.edu; f. 1957; also known as American Institute of Holy Land Studies; Christian study centre at univ. level; graduate and undergraduate courses in the geography, history, languages, religions and cultures of Israel in the Middle East context; field trips and archaeological excavation programme; 20 teachers; 200 students; Pres. Dr PAUL WRIGHT.

Mosad Harav Kook: POB 642, Jerusalem; tel. (2) 6526231; fax (2) 6526968; internet www.mosadharavkook.com; f. 1937 to educate and train young men for research in the field of Torah Literature and to infuse the original Hebrew culture in all classes of the people; library: Rav Maimon Library of Judaica; religious Zionist Archives; publs Torah-Science books, incl. the printing of MSS of previously unpublished *Rishonim* works that are still retained in Genizah form, popular commentary to the entire Bible; incorporates Institute for Chasiduth; Dir Rabbi JOSEPH MOVSHOVITZ.

ORT Braude College: POB 78, 21982 Karmiel; tel. (4) 9901911; fax (4) 9901715; e-mail rishum@braude.ac.il; internet www .braude.ac.il; f. 1988; B.Tech degree programmes in Biotechnology Engineering, Electrical and Electronics Engineering, Mechanical Engineering, Industrial and Management Engineering, and Software Engineering; also Practical Engineering 2-year degree programmes; library: 50,000 vols; 320 teachers; 1,200 undergraduate students; Pres. Prof. YOHANAN ARZI.

Pontifical Biblical Institute: POB 497, 3 Paul-Emile Botta St, 91004 Jerusalem; tel. (2) 6252843; fax (2) 6241203; e-mail admipib@gmail.com; internet www.biblico.it/jerusalem.html; f. 1913 as a br. of the Pontifical Biblical Institute of Rome, Italy; fosters the study of Biblical geography and archaeology; provides courses for students and graduates of Roman Institute; Prehistorical Museum containing discoveries of Teleilat Ghassul, a chalcolithic site in the Jordan valley, excavated by the Institute; library: 26,000 vols for biblical studies; Dir Rev. JOSEPH DOAN CÔNG NGUYÊN.

Shenkar College of Engineering and Design: 12 Anne Frank St, 52526 Ramat-Gan; tel. (3) 6110045; fax (3) 7521141; e-mail info@shenkar.ac.il; internet www.shenkar.ac .il; f. 1970; Bachelors degrees and research in industrial management and marketing, computer science, plastics engineering, industrial chemistry, industrial engineering, fashion design, textile and interior design, jewellery design, industrial design; library: 20,000 vols, 250 periodicals; 50 teachers; 2,180 students (680 full-time, 1,500 part-time); Pres. Prof. AMOTZ WEINBERG; Man. Dir GUY PERETZ.

Studium Biblicum Franciscanum: POB 19424, Monastery of the Flagellation, 91193 Jerusalem; tel. (2) 6270485; fax (2) 6264519; e-mail secretary@studiumbiblicum.org; internet www.custodia.org/sbf; f. 1927; centre of archaeological research sponsored by the Franciscan Custody of the Holy Land, biblical and archaeological faculty of the *Pontificium Athenaeum Antonianum*, Rome, for degrees of Bachelors in theology, Licentiate and Doctorate in biblical sciences and archaeology, and diploma in oriental biblical studies and archaeology and in biblical formation; 15 teachers; 80 students; Dean G. C. BOTTINI; publs *Analecta, Collectio Maior, Collectio Minor, Liber Annuus, Museum*.

Tel Hai Academic College: 12210 Upper Galilee; tel. (4) 8181785; fax (4) 6900919; e-mail telhai@telhai.ac.il; internet www .telhai.ac.il; f. 1957; Bachelors degree courses in biotechnology and environmental sciences, nutrition sciences, education, economics and management, social work, computer science, multidisciplinary studies; Diploma courses in architecture, construction, electronics and electricity, computers, mechanics and machinery, industrial management, telemedia and communication, drama therapy; art institute courses in sculpture, drawing, ceramics, photography and ethnic crafts; 500 teachers; 4,000 students; Pres. Prof. ZEKI BERK; Vice-Pres. for Academic Affairs Prof. SHMUEL SHAMAI.

Ulpan Akiva Netanya, International Hebrew Study Centre: POB 6086, 42160 Netanya; tel. (9) 8352312; fax (9) 8652919; e-mail ulpanakv@netvision.net.il; internet www.ulpan-akiva.org; f. 1951; basic and supplementary courses in Hebrew and Arabic; cultural studies; 45 teachers; Dir ESTHER PERRON.

Yeshivat Dvar Yerushalayim (Jerusalem Academy of Jewish Studies): 53 Katzenellenbogen, Har Nof, POB 34580, 344 Jerusalem; tel. (2) 6522817; fax (2) 6522827; e-mail dvar@dvar.org.il; internet www.dvar.org.il; f. 1970; runs courses in English, French, Spanish, Russian and Hebrew on the Bible, Hebrew, Talmud, philosophy, ethics and Halacha; 500 mems; library: 5,000 vols; 7 teachers; 70 students; Dean Rabbi B. HOROVITZ; Exec. Dir Rabbi E. ALTHEIM; publ. *Jewish Studies Magazine* (1 a year).

Zinman College of Physical Education and Sport Sciences at the Wingate Institute: 42902 Netanya; tel. (9) 8639222; fax (9) 8650960; e-mail zinman@wincol.macam.ac.il; internet www.wincol.ac.il; f. 1944; four-year BEd programme, M.P.E. programme at the college, MA programme in conjunction with Haifa Univ.; in-service training; library: 52,000 vols, 180 periodicals; 450 teachers; 950 regular students, 3,000 students on other courses; Rector Prof. Dr MICHAEL SAGIV.

ITALY

The Higher Education System

Italy's first universities were established during the 10th to the 13th century and are among the oldest in Europe; in fact, Università degli Studi di Parma (AD 962) is Europe's oldest university, and other long-established universities include Università di Bologna (founded 1088), Università degli Studi di Modena e Reggio Emilia (founded 1175) and Università degli Studi di Perugia (founded 1200). Several universities date from the 14th to the 16th century. In 2006/07 there were 1.8m. undergraduate students in higher education in Italy; the largest universities were La Sapienza in Rome, with around 170,000 students, and Bologna, with more than 100,000 students. In 2005/06 there were 74 institutes of higher education. Italian universities operate on the European Credit Transfer System (ECTS), and Italy also participates in the Bologna Process to establish a European Higher Education Area. The Ministry of Universities and Research is the government agency responsible for higher education. In addition to universities, there are four other types of State-recognized institutions of higher education: academies of arts education, higher institutes of applied arts, the national school for cinema studies and national institutes or schools for cultural restoration and preservation.

Admission to higher education is primarily based on the higher secondary school certificate (Diploma di Esame di Stato), though institutions may also administer entrance examinations. Since the implementation of the Bologna Process in 1999 the universities have adopted a two-tier Bachelors and Masters degree system. The Bachelors degree (Laurea) is a three-year programme that requires 180 credits. Undergraduates in specialized or professional fields that require longer periods of study, such as medicine (six years), pharmacy, architecture and law (all five years), may carry credits over into the Laurea Specialistica. Alternatively, the Laurea Specialistica may be awarded as a conventional Masters-type degree after one to three years study following the Laurea. Dottorato di Ricerca is the standard doctoral degree programme, and admission is on the basis of the Laurea Specialistica and institutional requirements.

A decree was made in 2008 allowing universities to become private sector foundations, though by 2010 none had yet taken up the option.

Regulatory and Representative Bodies

GOVERNMENT

Ministry of Cultural Assets and Activities: Via del Collegio Romano 27, 00186 Rome; tel. 06-67231; fax 06-6798441; e-mail urp@beniculturali.it; internet www .beniculturali.it; Minister FRANCESCO RUTELLI.

Ministry of Education: Viale Trastevere 76A, 00153 Rome; tel. 06-58491; fax 06-5803381; e-mail uffstampa@istruzione.it; internet www.istruzione.it; Minister BEPPE FIORONI.

Ministry of Universities and Research: Piazzale Kennedy 20, 00144 Rome; tel. 06-58491; e-mail ufficio.stampa@miur.it; internet www.miur.it; Minister FABIO MUSSI.

ACCREDITATION

Comitato Nazionale per la Valutazione del Sistema Universitario (National Committee for the Evaluation of the University System): Piazzale Kennedy 20, 00144 Rome; tel. 06-97726401; fax 06-97726480; e-mail valuniv@miur.it; internet www.cnvsu.it; Pres. Prof. LUIGI BIGGERI.

ENIC/NARIC Italy/Centro di Informazione sulla Mobilità e le Equivalenze Accademiche (Information Centre on Academic Mobility and Equivalence): Viale Ventuno Aprile 36, 00162 Rome; tel. 06-86321281; fax 06-86322845; e-mail cimea@ fondazionerui.it; internet www.cimea.it; f. 1984; Dir Dott. CARLO FINOCCHIETTI.

Istituto Nazionale per la Valutazione del Sistema Educativo di Istruzione e di Formazione (National Institute for the Assessment of the Educational System): Villa Falconieri, Via Borromini 5, 00044 Frascati; tel. 06-941851; fax 06-94185215; e-mail biblioteca@invalsi.it; internet www.invalsi.it; f. 1974; library of 9,500 vols, 235 current periodicals; Dir ANTONIO PILEGGI; Head Librarian RITA MARZOLI.

NATIONAL BODIES

Conferenza dei Rettori delle Università Italiane (Italian University Rectors' Conference): Palazzo Rondanini, Piazza Rondanini 48, 00185 Rome; tel. 06-684411; fax 06-68441399; e-mail segreteria@crui.it; internet www.crui.it; f. 1963; Pres. Prof. GUIDO TROMBETTI; Exec. Dir Dott.ssa EMANUELA STEFANI.

Consiglio Universitario Nazionale (National University Council): Piazzale Kennedy 20, 00144 Rome; tel. 06-97727502; fax 06-97726031; e-mail cun@miur.it; internet www.cun.it; f. 1997; 57 mem. univs; Pres. Prof. ANDREA LENZI; Sec. Dott. ANTONIO VALEO.

Istituto per la Cooperazione Universitaria Onlus (Institute for University Co-operation): Viale G. Rossini 26, 00198 Rome; tel. 06-85300722; fax 06-8554646; e-mail info@icu.it; internet www.icu.it; f. 1967 to promote cultural relations between different countries, chiefly through univ. cooperation, int. meetings and study groups; int. technical cooperation by sending volunteers and experts to developing countries; Pres. Prof. UMBERTO FARRI; Gen. Sec. CARLO DE MARCHI; publs *Educazione e Sviluppo* (irregular), *SIPE—Servizio Stampa Educazione e Sviluppo* (6 a year).

Fondazione Rui: Viale XXI Aprile 36, 00162 Rome; tel. 06-86321281; fax 06-86322845; e-mail info@fondazionerui.it; internet www.fondazionerui.it; f. 1959; library of 3,000 vols; Pres. Prof. CRISTIANO CIAPPEI; Dir Dr FABIO MONTI; publs *Documenti di Lavoro* (4 a year), *Fondazione Rui* (4 a year), *Universitas*.

Learned Societies

GENERAL

Accademia delle Scienze dell'Istituto di Bologna (Academy of Sciences of the Bologna Institute): Via Zamboni 31, 40126 Bologna; tel. 051-222596; fax 051-265249; e-mail accademiascienze@libero.it; internet www.unibo.it/portale/divulgazione+scienti-fica/accademia/default.htm; f. 1711; organizes national and international conventions and conferences; promotes studies of art restoration and art history; 60 mems; 200 corresp. mems; Pres. Prof. ILLIO GALLIGANI; Sec. Prof. RUGGERO BORTOLAMI.

Accademia delle Scienze di Ferrara (Academy of Sciences of Ferrara): Via Romei 3, 44100 Ferrara; tel. 0532-205209; fax 0532-205209; internet web.unife.it/associazioni/accademia_delle_scienze; f. 1823; sections of Medical Sciences, Mathematics, Physics and Natural Sciences, Law, Economics, History and Moral Sciences; 270 mems; library of 12,500 vols; Pres. Prof. Avv. GIOVANNA CAVALLARO; Sec. Avv. VINCENZO CAPUTO; publ. *Atti*.

Accademia delle Scienze di Torino (Academy of Sciences of Turin): Via Maria Vittoria 3, 10123 Turin; tel. 011-5620047; fax 011-532619; e-mail info@accademia.csi.it; internet www.accademiadellescienze.it; f. 1783; sections of Physics, Mathematics and Natural Sciences, Moral Sciences, History and Philology; 310 mems; library: see Libraries and Archives; Pres. Prof. PIETRO ROSSI; publs *Atti* (edns for physical, mathematical and natural sciences, and for the philosophy, law, history and philology, 1 a year each), *Memorie* (edns for physical, mathematical and natural sciences, and for philosophy, law, history and philology, 1 a year each), *Quaderni* (irregular).

Accademia Etrusca (Etruscan Academy): Palazzo Casali, Piazza Signorelli 9, 52044 Cortona; tel. 0575-637248; fax 0575-637248; e-mail accademia_etrusca@libero.it; internet www.accademia-etrusca.org; f. 1727; promotes knowledge of the culture and history of the Cortona area and of Etruscan archaeological discoveries; 80 mems; 50 hon. mems; 80 corresp. mems; Pres. Dott. GUGLIELMO MAETZKE; Vice-Pres. and Sec. Prof. EDOARDO MIRRI; publs *Annuario* (every

2 years), *Cortona Francescana, Fonti e Testi, Note e Documenti*.

Accademia Gioenia di Catania: Via Fragalà 10, 95100 Catania; e-mail malber@unict .it; internet www.unict.it/gioenia; f. 1824; sections of Natural Sciences, Physics, Chemistry and Mathematics, and Applied Sciences; 56 mems, 57 corresp. mems; library of 20,000 vols, 400 periodicals; Pres. Prof. SALVATORE FOTI; Gen. Sec. Prof. GIORGIO MONTAUDO; publs *Atti della Accademia Gioenia di Scienze Naturali in Catania, Bollettino delle Sedute della Accademia Gioenia di Scienze Naturali in Catania*.

Accademia Ligure di Scienze e Lettere (Ligurian Academy of Sciences and Letters): Piazza G. Matteotti 5, 16123 Genoa; tel. 010-565570; fax 010-566080; f. 1798; 180 mems (30 ordinary and 50 corresp. in each class; 20 hon.); library of 60,000 vols; Pres. Prof.ssa PAOLA MASSA; Sec.-Gen. Dr G. P. PELOSO; publs *Atti* (1 a year), *Studi e Ricerche*.

Accademia Nazionale dei Lincei: Palazzo Corsini, Via della Lungara 10, 00165 Rome; tel. 06-680271; fax 06-6893616; e-mail segreteria@lincei.it; internet www.lincei.it; f. 1603; sections of Physical, Mathematical and Natural Sciences (Academic Secs Prof. GIANCARLO SETTI, Prof. ANNIBALE MOTTANA), Moral, Historical and Philological Sciences (Academic Secs Prof. ANTONIO GIULIANO, Prof. FULVIO TESSITORE); 540 mems (180 nat., 180 corresp., 180 foreign); library: see Libraries and Archives; Pres. Prof. LAMBERTO MAFFEI; Vice-Pres. Prof. ALBERTO QUADRIO CURZIO; Academic Administrator Prof. LUCIANO MARTINI; Academic Administrator Prof. PIETRO RESCIGNO; publs *Memorie: Classe di Scienze Morali, Storiche e Filologiche* (irregular), *Memorie Lincee, Classe di Scienze Morali, Storiche e Filologiche* (4 a year), *Memorie Lincee, Matematica e Applicazioni* (irregular), *Memorie Lincee, Scienze Fisiche e Naturali* (irregular), *Notizie degli Scavi di Antichità, Rendiconti: Classe di Scienze Morali, Storiche e Filologiche* (4 a year), *Rendiconti Lincei: Matematica e Applicazioni* (4 a year), *Rendiconti Lincei: Scienze Fisiche e Naturali* (4 a year).

Accademia Nazionale di San Luca (National Academy of San Luca): Piazza dell'Accademia di San Luca 77, 00187 Rome; tel. 06-6798850; fax 06-6789243; e-mail segreteria@accademiasanluca.it; internet www.accademiasanluca.it; f. 14th century; sections of Painting, of Sculpture, of Architecture; 54 mems; 90 corresp. mems; 30 foreign mems; 47 cultural and hon. mems; library: see Libraries and Archives; Pres. CARLO AYMONINO; Sec.-Gen. GIORGIO CIUCCI.

Accademia Nazionale di Santa Cecilia (National Academy of Santa Cecilia): Auditorium Parco della Musica, l.go Luciano Berio 3, 00196 Rome; tel. 06-80242501; fax 06-80242301; e-mail info@santacecilia.it; internet www.santacecilia.it; f. 1566; promotes symphonic concert music, has own symphony orchestra and chorus, carries out professional music training; 100 mems (70 nat., 30 foreign); Pres. BRUNO CAGLI; publs *E. M. Rivista degli Archivi di Etnomusicologia* (1 a year), *Studi Musicali* (2 a year).

Accademia Nazionale Virgiliana di Scienze, Lettere e Arti (Virgilian National Academy of Sciences, Literature and Arts): Via dell'Accademia 47, 46100 Mantua; tel. 0376-320314; fax 0376-222774; internet www .accademiavirgiliana.it; f. early 17th century, present name 1981; 170 mems (90 full, 20 hon., 60 corresp.); library: see Libraries and Archives; Pres. Prof. GIORGIO BERNARDI PERINI; Sec. LIVIO VOLPI GHIRARDINI; publ. *Atti e Memorie N. S.* (1 a year).

Accademia Petrarca di Lettere, Arti e Scienze (Petrarch Academy of Literature, Arts and Science): Via dell'Orto 28, 52100 Arezzo; tel. 0575-24700; internet www .accademiapetrarca.it; f. 1810; 413 mems; library of 15,000 vols; Pres. Prof. GIULIO FIRPO; Sec. Prof. ANTONIO BATINTI; publs *Atti e Memorie* (1 a year), *Studi Petrarcheschi* (1 a year).

Accademia Pugliese delle Scienze (Puglia Academy of Sciences): Palazzo dell'Ateneo, Piazza Umberto I, 70121 Bari; tel. and fax 080-5714578; e-mail accademia .pugliese@ateneo.uniba.it; internet www .ateneo.uniba.it/accademiapugliese; f. 1925; divided into two classes: physical, medical and natural sciences, and moral sciences; library of 6,600 vols, 270 periodical titles; 120 ordinary mems, 200 corresp. mems and 20 hon. mems; Pres. Prof. VITTORIO MARZI; Sec. GIOVANNA PANEBIANCO; publ. *Atti e Relazioni* (1 a year).

Accademia Roveretana degli Agiati: Piazza Rosmini 5, 38068 Rovereto; tel. 0464-436663; fax 0464-487672; e-mail info@ agiati.org; internet www.agiati.org; f. 1750; fosters the development of sciences, literature and art; 330 mems; library of 50,000 vols; Pres. Prof. LIVIO CAFFIERI; publs *Atti* (Series A (human sciences, literature, art), online), *Atti* (Series B (mathematics, physics, natural science), online).

Accademia Tiberina: Via del Vantaggio 22, 00186 Rome; tel. 06-3619305; internet www .pontificiaaccademiatiberina.it; f. 1813; 200 mems and 2,000 assoc., corresp., resident and hon. mems; applied sciences, psychology, arts, hygiene and health, anthropology, Yoga-Vedanta centre; library of 10,000 vols; Pres. Prof. Dott. FERNANDO MARIOTTI; Sec. (vacant).

Accademia Toscana di Scienze e Lettere 'La Colombaria' (La Colombaria Tuscan Academy of Science and Literature): Via S. Egidio 23, 50122 Florence; tel. and fax 055-2396628; internet www.colombaria.it; f. 1735; library of 30,000 vols; Pres. Prof. FRANCESCO ADORNO; Gen. Sec. STEFANO SPILLI; publs *Atti e Memorie* (1 a year), *Corpus dei papiri filosofici greci e latini* (irregular), *Studi* (4 or 5 a year).

Fondazione Internazionale Premio E. Balzan—'Premio': Piazzetta U. Giordano 4, 20122 Milan; tel. (2) 76002212; fax (2) 76009457; e-mail balzan@balzan.it; internet www.balzan.org; f. 1957; annual prizes for the worldwide promotion of the arts and sciences; Pres. Amb. B. BOTTAI; Sec.-Gen. Dr S. WERDER; publ. *Premi Balzan* (1 a year).

Istituto Lombardo Accademia di Scienze e Lettere: Via Brera 28, 20121 Milan; tel. 02-864087; fax 02-86461388; e-mail istituto.lombardo@unimi.it; internet www.istitutolombardo.it; f. 1802; 120 mems; 193 corresp. assocs; 80 foreign mems; library of 495,000 vols, 330 Italian periodicals, 600 foreign periodicals; Pres. Prof. ANTONIO PADOA SCHIOPPA; Vice-Pres. Prof. GIANANTONIO SACCHI LANDRIANI; divided into 2 classes: Mathematics and Natural Sciences (Sec. Prof. FIORENZA DE BERNARDI); Moral Sciences (Sec. Prof. ISABELLA GUALANDRI);; publs *Cicli di Conferenze, Memorie della Classe di Scienze Matematiche e Naturali, Memorie della Classe di Scienze Morali, Rendiconti–Classe di Lettere e Scienze Morali, Rendiconti–Parte Generale e Atti Ufficiali, Rendiconti: Scienze Matematiche e Naturali*.

Istituto Veneto di Scienze, Lettere ed Arti (Venetian Institute of Sciences, Literature and Arts): Campo S. Stefano 2945, 30124 Venice; tel. 041-2407711; fax 041-5210598; e-mail ivsla@istitutoveneto.it; internet www.istitutoveneto.it; f. 1838; func-

tions as academy; also organizes postdoctoral courses; sections of Physical, Mathematical and Natural Sciences (Academic Sec. Prof. GIAN ANTONIO DANIELI), Moral Sciences, Literature and Arts (Academic Sec. Prof. MANLIO PASTORE STOCCHI); 78 mems; 110 corresp. mems; 29 foreign mems; library of 200,600 vols; Pres. Prof. LEOPOLDO MAZZAROLLI; publs *Atti* (Proceedings (moral sciences series), 4 a year), *Atti* (Proceedings (physical sciences series), 4 a year), *Memorie*.

Società di Letture e Conversazioni Scientifiche (Scientific Society): Palazzo Ducale ammezzato ala est, Piazza Matteotti 5, Genoa; tel. and fax 010-565141; e-mail letturescientifiche@libero.it; internet www .letturescientifiche.it; f. 1866; holds conferences and debates on scientific, historical, literary and political topics; library of 15,310 vols; Pres. UMBERTO COSTA.

Società Nazionale di Scienze, Lettere ed Arti (National Society for Sciences, Literature and Art): Via Mezzocannone 8, 80134 Naples; tel. and fax 081-5527549; e-mail socnazsla@virgilio.it; internet www .socnazsla.unina.it; library of 35,000 vols; Pres. Prof. FULVIO TESSITORE; Sec.-Gen. Prof. CARLO SBORDONE.

UNESCO Office in Venice–UNESCO Regional Bureau for Science and Culture in Europe (BRESCE): 4930 Castello–Palazzo Zorzi, 30122 Venice; tel. 041-2601511; fax 041-5289995; e-mail veniceoffice@unesco.org; internet www .unesco.org/venice; f. 1988; science policy, education and research throughout SE Europe; environmental policy in local govt (incl. management of water resources and prevention of natural disasters); devt of cultural activities and identifying priorities in SE Europe, such as protection and promotion of cultural heritage; training programmes for cultural conservation; promotes cultural dialogue and artistic creation, and handicraft as a symbol of cultural diversity; library of 2,000 UNESCO publs; Dir Dr ENGELBERT RUOSS.

AGRICULTURE, FISHERIES AND VETERINARY SCIENCE

Accademia di Agricoltura di Torino (Academy of Agriculture of Turin): Via Andrea Doria 10, 10123 Turin; tel. 011-8127470; fax 011-8127470; e-mail to0323@ biblioteche.reteunitaria.piemonte.it; internet web.tiscali.it/accagri; f. 1785; 155 mems; library of 26,000 vols, 50 current periodicals; Pres. Dott. Prof. SILVANO SCANNERINI; publs *Annali Dell'Accademia di Agricoltura di Torino* (1 a year), *Nuovo Calendario Georgico* (1 a year).

Accademia dei Georgofili (Academy of Georgofili): Logge degli Uffizi, 50122 Florence; tel. 055-212114; fax 055-2302754; e-mail accademia@georgofili.it; internet www.georgofili.it; f. 1753; promotes the application of sciences to agriculture and environmental protection, and the development to rural areas; 522 mems; library of 60,000 vols; Pres. Prof. FRANCO SCARAMUZZI; publs *Atti, Quaderni, Rivista di Storia della Agricoltura*.

Accademia Italiana di Scienze Forestali (Italian Academy of Forestry Science): Piazza Edison 11, 50133 Florence; tel. 055-570348; fax 055-575724; e-mail info@aisf.it; internet www.aisf.it; f. 1951; 327 mems; library of 6,000 vols; Pres. Prof. O. CIANCIO; publs *Annali* (1 a year), *L'Italia Forestale e montana* (6 a year).

Accademia Nazionale di Agricoltura (National Academy of Agriculture): Via Castiglione 11, 40124 Bologna; tel. 051-268809; fax 051-263736; e-mail segreteria@ accademia-agricoltura.it; internet www

.accademia-agricoltura.unibo.it; f. 1807; 80 mems and 140 corresponding mems; library of 20,000 vols; Pres. Prof. GIORGIO AMADEI; Sec. Dott. ANDREA SEGRÈ; publ. *Annali* (4 a year).

Istituto Agronomico per l'Oltremare (Agronomic Institute for Overseas): Via Antonio Cocchi 4, 50131 Florence; tel. 055-50611; fax 055-5061333; e-mail iao@iao .florence.it; internet www.iao.florence.it; f. 1904; 50 mems; library of 127,000 vols, 800 current periodicals; Dir-Gen. Dott. ALICE PERLINI; publ. *Journal of Agriculture and Environment for International Development* (4 a year).

Società Italiana delle Scienze Veterinarie (Italian Society of Veterinary Sciences): Via Istria 3B, 25125 Brescia; tel. 030-223244; fax 030-2420569; e-mail sisvet@ fondiz.it; internet www.sisvet.it; f. 1947; 1,700 mems; Pres. Prof. ANTONIO PUGLIESE; Gen. Sec. Prof. MASSIMO DE MAJO; publ. *Atti.*

Società Italiana di Economia Agraria (Italian Agrarian Economics Society): Istituto di Zooeconomia, Coviolo, 42100 Reggio Emilia; tel. 0522-21745; e-mail mario .prestamburgo@econ.univ.trieste.it; internet brezza.iuav.it/~ramirez; f. 1962; 300 mems; Pres. Prof. MARIO PRESTAMBURGO; publ. *Atti* (1 a year).

ARCHITECTURE AND TOWN PLANNING

Centro Internazionale di Studi di Architettura 'Andrea Palladio' (Andrea Palladio International Centre for the Study of Architecture): Palazzo Barbaran da Porto, contra' Porti 11, CP 835, 36100 Vicenza; tel. 0444-323014; fax 0444-322869; e-mail segreteria@ cisapalladio.org; internet www.cisapalladio .org; f. 1959 to make known the work of Andrea Palladio, born Padua 1508, and to encourage the study of Palladianism and of Venetian architecture of all ages; Pres. AMALIA SARTORI; Dir GUIDO BELTRAMINI; publ. *Annali* (online, 1 a year).

Istituto Nazionale di Architettura (IN-ARCH) (National Architectural Institute): Via Crescenzio 16, 00193 Rome; tel. 06-68802254; fax 06-6868530; e-mail inarch@ inarch.it; internet www.inarch.it; f. 1959; organizes meetings, debates and exhibitions; 2,000 mems; Pres. Ing. ADOLFO GUZZINI.

Istituto Nazionale di Urbanistica (INU) (National Institute of Town Planning): Piazza Farnese 44, 00186 Rome; tel. 06-68801190; fax 06-68214773; e-mail amministrazione@inu.it; internet www.inu .it; f. 1930; 2,654 mems (960 ordinary, 1,694 assoc.); Pres. Prof. Arch. PAOLO AVARELLO; Sec. MASSIMO GIULIANI; publs *Urbanistica* (3 a year), *Urbanistica Dossier* (12 a year), *Urbanistica Informazioni* (6 a year).

Italia Nostra—Associazione Nazionale per la Tutela del Patrimonio Storico, Artistico e Naturale della Nazione (Italia Nostra—National Association for the Preservation of the Historical, Artistic and Natural Heritage of the Nation): Viale Liege, 33, 00198 Rome; tel. 06-8537271; fax 06-85350596; e-mail italianostra@italianostra .org; internet www.italianostra.org; f. 1955; 20,000 mems, subscribers, delegates; library of 4,500 vols; brs in 206 towns; Pres. JOHN LOSAVIO; Sec.-Gen. GAIA PALLOTTINO; publ. *Italia Nostra* (9 a year).

BIBLIOGRAPHY, LIBRARY SCIENCE AND MUSEOLOGY

Associazione Italiana Biblioteche (Italian Library Association): CP 2461, 00185 Rome AD; c/o Biblioteca nazionale centrale, viale Castro Pretorio 105, 00185 Rome; tel. 06-4463532; fax 06-4441139; e-mail aib@aib

.it; internet www.aib.it; f. 1930 to support the org. and devt of libraries and a library service in Italy, and to act as a professional representative in all cultural, scientific, technical, legal and legislative spheres; 4,500 mems; library of 8,000 vols, 500 journals; Pres. Prof. MAURO GUERRINI; Sec. MARCELLO SARDELLI; publs *AIB Notizie* (12 a year), *Bollettino AIB* (4 a year).

Associazione Nazionale dei Musei Italiani (National Association of Italian Museums): Piazza San Marco 1, 00186 Rome; tel. and fax 06-6791343; Pres. Prof. D. BERNINI; Sec. Dott. L. BARBACINI; publ. *Musei e Gallerie d'Italia.*

Istituto Centrale per il Restauro e la Conservazione del Patrimonio Archivistico e Librario (Central Institute for the Restoration and Conservation of Archives and Libraries): Via Milano 76, 00184 Rome; tel. 06-482911; fax 06-4814968; e-mail icapl@ beniculturali.it; internet www.icpal .beniculturali.it; f. 2007 by merger of Istituto Centrale per la Patologia del Libro (ICPL) with Centro di Fotoriproduzione Legatoria e Restauro Degli Archivi di Stato (CFLR) attached to Italian Min. of Cultural Heritage and Activities; book and document restoration and preservation; research on the safeguarding and conservation of library and archival heritage; 77 mems; library of 15,000 vols; Dir Dott.ssa ARMIDA BATORI.

ECONOMICS, LAW AND POLITICS

Accademia Italiana di Economia Aziendale (Academy of Business Economics): Via Farini 14, 40124 Bologna; tel. 051-558798; fax 051-6492446; e-mail redazione@ accademiaaidea.it; internet www .accademiaaidea.it; f. 1813; divided into 3 classes; 375 national mems; 50 foreign mems; 10 hon. mems; reps from all Italian universities; Pres. Prof. ROBERTO CAFFERATA; Vice-Pres. Prof. GIORGIO INVERNIZZI; Vice-Pres. Prof. LUCIANO MARCHI.

CIRGIS (International Centre for Juridical Research and Scientific Initiatives): Via Manzoni 45, 20121 Milan; tel. 02-6552167; fax 02-6570144; e-mail segreteria@cirgis.it; internet www.cirgis.it; f. 1979 to promote cultural relations between scholars of Italian and foreign law; aims for the realization of exchanges of thought and experience between Italian and foreign jurists, the knowledge of laws and institutions of different countries through meetings, publs, etc.; c. 400 mems; Pres. Avv. Prof. FRANCESCO OGLIARI; International Sec. Avv. GIUSEPPE AGLIALORO.

Istituto di Diritto Romano e dei Diritti dell'Oriente Mediterraneo (Institute of Roman Law and Laws of the Near East): Facoltà di Giurisprudenza, Piazzale Aldo Moro 5, 00185 Rome; tel. 06-49910608; fax 06-49910241; e-mail marilena.zanatatritto@ uniroma1.it; internet 151.100.28.159; f. 1937; library of 70,000 vols, 80 current periodicals; Dir Prof. ANDREA DI PORTO; Academic Sec. Dott.ssa MARILENA ZANATA TRITTO.

Società Italiana degli Economisti (Italian Economists' Society): Piazzale Martelli, 8, 60121 Ancona; tel. 071-2207111; fax 071-200494; internet www.sie.unian.it; f. 1950; 594 mems; Pres. Prof. GIORGIO LUNGHINI; Gen. Sec. Prof. GIULIANO CONTI; publs *Bollettino dei Soci, Lettera* (1 a year), *Rivista Italiana degli Economisti.*

Società Italiana di Economia, Demografia e Statistica (Italian Society of Economics, Demography and Statistics): Piazza Tommaso de Cristoforis 6, 00159 Rome; tel. 06-43589008; fax 06-43589008; e-mail sieds@tin.it; internet www .sieds.it; f. 1938; c. 600 mems; Pres. Prof. ORNELLO VITALI; Sec.-Gen. Prof. FRANCO VACCINA; publs *Collana di Studi e Monografie*

(irregular), *Demografia e Statistica* (4 a year), *Rivista Italiana di Economia.*

Società Italiana di Filosofia Giuridica e Politica: c/o Ist. di Filosofia del Diritto, Facoltà di Giurisprudenza, Università La Sapienza, 00185 Rome; tel. 06-490489; fax 06-49910951; f. 1936; 200 mems; Pres. GAETANO CARCATERRA; Sec. MAURIZIO BASCIU; publ. *Rivista internazionale di filosofia del diritto* (4 a year).

Società Italiana di Statistica (Italian Statistics Society): Salita de' Crescenzi 26, 00186 Rome; tel. 06-6869845; fax 06-6540742; internet www.ips.it/musis/ scheda77.html; f. 1939; 1,000 mems; statistics and demography; Pres. Prof. LUIGI BIGGERI; Gen. Sec. Prof. MAURIZIO VICHI; publs Proceedings of the Scientific Meetings, *Journal of the Italian Statistical Society* (4 a year), *SIS-Bollettino* (4 a year), *SIS-Informazioni* (12 a year).

Società Italiana per l'Organizzazione Internazionale (SIOI) (UN Association for Italy): Piazza di S. Marco 51, Palazzetto di Venezia, 00186 Rome; tel. 06-6920781; fax 06-6789102; e-mail sioi@sioi.org; internet www.sioi.org; f. 1944; sections in Florence, Milan, Naples, Turin; library: see Libraries; Pres. UMBERTO LA ROCCA; Sec.-Gen. FABIO MIGLIORINI; publ. *La Comunità Internazionale* (4 a year).

EDUCATION

Associazione Pedagogica Italiana (Italian Educational Association): Via Zamboni 34, 40126 Bologna; tel. 051-2098442; fax 051-228847; e-mail info@aspei.it; internet www .aspei.it; f. 1950; aims to promote the development of schools in general and all other institutions of education, also studies and research in education; 50 brs; 5,000 mems; Pres. SIRA SERENELLA MACCHIETTI; Sec.-Gen. ALDO D'ALFONSO; publ. *Bollettino* (4 a year).

FINE AND PERFORMING ARTS

Accademia di Francia (French Academy in Rome): Villa Medici, Viale Trinità dei Monti 1, 00187 Rome; tel. 06-6761291; fax 06-6761278; e-mail standard@villamedici.it; internet www.villamedici.it; f. 1666; organizes exhibitions, concerts, symposia and seminars on artistic and literary topics, and on their history; library of 27,000 vols; Dir RICHARD PEDUZZI; Gen. Sec. ELIZABETH FLEURY.

Accademia Raffaello: Via Cesare Battisti 54, 61029 Urbino; tel. (0722) 329695; e-mail segreteria@accademiaraffaello.it; internet www.accademiaraffaello.it; f. 1869; promotes fine art; 108 mems; library of 6,000 vols; Pres. Dr GAETANO SAVOLDELLI PEDROCCHI.

Fondazione Istituto Italiano per la Storia della Musica (Italian Institute for the History of Music): c/o Accademia Nazionale di Santa Cecilia, Via Vittoria 6, 00187 Rome; tel. and fax 06-36000146; e-mail istmusica@virgilio.it; internet www.iism.it; f. 1938; Pres. Prof. AGOSTINO ZIINO; publ. *Bollettino.*

Istituto Nazionale di Studi Verdiani (National Institute of Verdi Studies): Via Melloni 1B, 43100 Parma; tel. 0521-285273; e-mail direzione@studiverdiani.it; internet www.studiverdiani.it; f. 1960 under the patronage of the International Music Council and the Italian Ministry of Culture to study the life and works of Giuseppe Verdi; library of 15,000 vols, archives of 25,000 documents; Pres. MARIA MERCEDES CARRARA VERDI; Dir PIERLUIGI PETROBELLI; publs *Carteggi Verdiani, Premio Internazionale Rotary Club di Parma 'Giuseppe Verdi', Proceedings of Congresses, Quaderni, Studi Verdiani* (1 a year).

Istituto Universitario Olandese di Storia dell'Arte (Dutch University Institute for the History of Art): Viale Torricelli 5, 50125 Florence; tel. 055-221612; fax 055-221106; internet www.iuoart.org; f. 1958; library of 50,000 vols; Dir BERT W. MEIJER.

Kunsthistorisches Institut in Florenz–Max-Planck-Institut/Istituto di Storia dell'Arte di Firenze (Institute for the History of Art in Florence): Via Giuseppe Giusti 44, 50121 Florence; tel. 055-249111; fax 055-2491155; internet www.khi.fi.it; f. 1897; 32 mems; library of 270,000 vols, 2,450 periodicals and 560,000 reproductions; spec. collns incl. art in N Italy, Italian art since 19th century; Dirs Prof. Dr GERHARD WOLF, Prof. Dr ALESSANDRO NOVA; publs *Kleine Schriftenreihe des KHI* (1 a year), *Mitteilungen* (1 a year), *Monographienreihe: Italienische Forschungen* (every 2 years).

Real Academia de España en Roma (Royal Spanish Academy in Rome): Piazza San Pietro in Montorio 3, 00153 Rome; tel. 06-5812806; fax 06-5818049; e-mail info@raer.it; internet raer.it; f. 1873; Dir ENRIQUE PANÉS; Gen. Sec. FERNANDO VALERO.

Società d'Incoraggiamento d'Arti e Mestieri (Society for the Encouragement of Arts and Crafts): Via Santa Marta 18, 20123 Milan; tel. 02-86450125; fax 02-86452542; e-mail segreteria@siam1838.it; internet www.siam1838.it; f. 1838; education in mechanics, electronics, electrotechnics, chemistry, computer studies; library of 6,000 vols; Pres. BRUNO SORESINA; Gen. Sec. ALBERTO PIANTA.

Società Italiana di Musicologia (Italian Musicological Society): CP 7256, Ag. Roma Nomentano, 00162 Rome; Via dei Greci 18, 00187 Rome; tel. 338-1957796; e-mail segreteria@sidm.it; internet www.sidm.it; f. 1964; 800 mems; Pres. GUIDO SALVETTI; Sec. SARA CICCARELLI; publs *Bollettino* (2 a year), *Fonti Musicali Italiane* (1 a year), *Rivista Italiana di Musicologia* (2 a year).

Società Italiana Musica Contemporanea: Via Domenichino 12, 20149 Milan; tel. 02-468157; fax 02-468157; e-mail simc@fastwebnet.it; internet www.simc-italia.it; Pres. M. PERAGALLO; Sec. M. R. MANN.

HISTORY, GEOGRAPHY AND ARCHAEOLOGY

Associazione Archeologica Romana (Roman Archaeological Society): Piazza B. Cairoli 117, 00186 Rome; tel. 06-6865647; internet www.associazionearcheologicaromana.it; f. 1902; 400 mems; library of 3,000 vols; Pres. Prof. CLAUDIO STRINATI; Sec. PAOLA MANETTO; publ. *Romana Gens* (4 a year).

Istituto Geografico Militare (Military Geographical Institute): Via C. Battisti 10, 50122 Florence; tel. 055-27321; fax 055-282172; e-mail info@geomil.esercito.difesa.it; internet www.igmi.org; f. 1872; geodetic and topographical surveying; official cartography; library of 120,000 vols, 700 atlases, 19,000 cartographic items; Dir-Gen. Lt-Gen. MICHELE CORRADO; publs *Bollettino di Geodesia e Scienze Affini* (4 a year), *L'Universo* (6 a year).

Istituto Italiano di Numismatica (Italian Numismatics Institute): Palazzo Barberini, Via Quattro Fontane 13, 00184 Rome; tel. 06-4743603; fax 06-4743603; e-mail istituto@istitutoitalianonumismatica.it; internet www.istitutoitalianonumismatica.it; f. 1936; library of 22,000 vols; Pres. Prof. ATTILIO STAZIO; Dir Prof. SARA SORDA; publ. *Annali* (1 a year).

Istituto Italiano di Paleontologia Umana (Italian Institute of Human Palaeontology): Piazza Mincio 2, 00198 Rome; tel. 06-8557598; internet w3.uniroma1.it/isipu; f.

1913; quaternary environment, geology, palaeontology, palaeoanthropology, archaeology; 250 mems; library of 5,800 vols, 31 periodicals; extensive offprints series; Pres. Prof. AMILCARE BIETTI; Gen. Sec. GIORGIO MANZI; publs *Memorie* (irregular), *Quaternaria* (1 a year).

Istituto Italiano per la Storia Antica (Italian Institute for Ancient History): Via Milano 76, 00184 Rome; tel. and fax 06-4880597; e-mail storia.antica@virgilio.it; f. 1935; library of 17,000 vols; Pres. Prof. ANDREA GIARDINA; publs *Dizionario Epigrafico di Antichità Romane*, *Miscellanea Greca e Romana*, *Quaderni della Scuola di Storia Antica* (3 a year), *Studi pubblicati dall'Istituto Italiano per la Storica Antica*.

Istituto Nazionale di Archeologia e Storia dell'Arte (National Institute of Archaeology and History of Art): Piazza San Marco 49, 00186 Rome; tel. 06-6780817; fax 06-6798804; e-mail inasa@inasa-roma.it; internet www.inasa-roma.it; f. 1918; library of 500,000 vols; Pres. Prof. ADRIANO LA REGINA; publ. *RIASA - Rivista dell'Istituto Nazionale di Archeologia e Storia dell'Arte* (1 a year).

Istituto Nazionale di Studi Etruschi ed Italici (National Institute for Etruscan and Italic Studies): Via della Pergola 65, 50121 Florence; tel. 055-2396846; fax 055-2396846; e-mail studietruschi@interfree.it; f. 1932; 206 mems; library of 14,915 vols; Pres. Prof. GIOVANNANGELO CAMPOREALE; Sec. Prof. LUIGI DONATI; publ. *Studi Etruschi* (1 a year).

Istituto per la Storia del Risorgimento Italiano (Institute for the History of the Italian Revival): Vittoriano, Piazza Venezia, 00186 Rome; tel. 06-6793598; fax 06-6782572; e-mail ist.risorgimento@tiscalinet.it; internet www.risorgimento.it/risorgimento/home_istituto.htm; f. 1935; 3,400 mems; Pres. Prof. GIUSEPPE TALAMO; Gen. Sec. Prof. SERGIO LA SALVIA; publs *Biblioteca Scientifica* (3 series), *Rassegna Storica del Risorgimento dal 1914* (4 a year).

Istituto Storico Italiano per il Medio Evo (Italian Institute of Medieval History): Piazza dell'Orologio 4, 00186 Rome; tel. 06-68802075; fax 06-68195963; e-mail istituto@isime.it; internet www.isime.it; f. 1883; library of 120,000 vols; Pres. MASSIMO MIGLIO; publs *Bullettino*, *Fonti per la storia dell'Italia medievale*, *Nuovi Studi Storici*, *Repertorium Fontium Historiae Medii Aevi*.

Istituto Storico Italiano per l'Età Moderna e Contemporanea (Italian Historical Institute for the Contemporary and Modern Era): Via Michelangelo Caetani 32, 00186 Rome; tel. 06-68806922; fax 06-6875127; e-mail iststor@libero.it; f. 1934; historical research and publications; Pres. Prof. LUIGI LOTTI; publ. *Annuario*.

Società di Minerva: Piazza Hortis 4, 34123 Trieste; tel. 040-660245; fax 040-661030; e-mail societadiminerva@gmail.com; internet www.retecivica.trieste.it/minerva/home.htm; f. 1810; studies history, art and culture of Trieste, Istria and Gorizia; 150 mems; Pres. Prof. arch. GINO PAVAN; Sec. Dott. GIULIANA MARINI; publs *Archeografo Triestino* (1 a year), *Extra serie dell'Archeografo Triestino* (irregular), *Quaderni di Minerva* (irregular).

Società di Studi Geografici (Society for Geographical Studies): Via San Gallo 10, 50129 Florence; tel. 055-2757956; fax 055-2757956; e-mail info@societastudigeografici.it; internet www.societastudigeografici.it; f. 1895; 600 mems; library of 20,000 vols; Pres. MARIA TINACCI MOSSELLO; Sec. CRISTINA CAPINERI; publ. *Rivista Geografica Italiana* (4 a year).

Società Geografica Italiana: Palazzetto Mattei in Villa Celimontana, Via della Naviocella 12, 00184 Rome; tel. 06-7008279; fax 06-77079518; e-mail segretaria@societageografica.it; internet www.societageografica.it; f. 1867; library: see Libraries and Archives; Pres. Prof. FRANCO SALVATORI; publs *Bollettino* (4 a year), *Memorie, Ricerche e Studi*.

Società Napoletana di Storia Patria (Neapolitan Society of Italian History): Via Vittorio Emanuele III (Maschio Angioino), 80133 Naples; tel. 081-5510353; fax 081-5510353; e-mail snsp@unina.it; internet www.storia.unina.it/snsp; f. 1875; library of 350,000 vols, 900 current periodicals; 650 mems; Pres. Prof. GIUSEPPE GALASSO; Vice-Pres. Prof. RAFFAELE AJELLO; publ. *Archivo Storico per le Province Napoletane*.

Società Romana di Storia Patria (Roman Society of Italian History): Piazza della Chiesa Nuova 18, 00186 Rome; tel. 06-68307513; e-mail srsp@libero.it; f. 1876; c. 100 mems; Pres. LETIZIA ERMINI PANI; Sec. PASQUALE SMIRAGLIA; publs *Archivio della Società* (1 a year), *Codice diplomatico di Roma e della Regione Romana* (irregular), *Miscellanea della Società* (irregular).

Società Storica Lombarda (Lombardy Historical Society): Via Morone 1, 20121 Milan; tel. 02-860118; fax 02-72002108; e-mail storica@tiscalinet.it; internet www.societastoricalombarda.it; f. 1873; 450 mems; library of 27,000 vols; Pres. Co. Ing. GAETANO BARBIANO DI BELGIOJOSO; Sec. Dott. LUIGI OROMBELLI; publ. *Archivio Storico Lombardo* (1 a year).

LANGUAGE AND LITERATURE

Accademia della Crusca: Villa Medicea di Castello, Via di Castello 46, 50141 Florence; tel. (55) 454277; fax (55) 454279; internet www.accademiadellacrusca.it; f. 1583; library of 121,000 vols; Pres. Prof. NICOLETTA MARASCHIO; Dir of Philological Studies ROSANNA BETTARINI; Dir of Lexicographical Studies Prof. LUCA SERIANNI; Dir of Grammatical Studies Prof. TERESA POGGI SALANI; Sec. PIERO FIORELLI; publs *La Crusca Per Voi* (2 a year), *Studi di Filologia Italiana* (1 a year), *Studi di Grammatica Italiana* (1 a year), *Studi di Lessicografia Italiana* (1 a year).

Alliance Française: Via Giulia 251, 00186 Rome; tel. 06-4474061; fax 06-4456370; e-mail federation@alliancefr.it; internet www.alliancefr.it; offers courses and exams in French language and culture and promotes cultural exchange with France; attached offices in Aosta, Avellino, Bari, Biella, Bologna, Borgomanero, Catania, Catanzaro, Fermo, Foggia, Forli, Ivrea, L'Aquila, La Spezia, Lecce, Livorno, Lucques, Messina, Pavia, Piacenza, Sassari, Sulmona, Trieste, Venice, Verona, Ventimiglia and Viareggio; Dir CHARLES DE TINGUY DE LA GIROULIÈRE.

British Council: Via Quattro Fontana 20, 00184 Rome; tel. 06-478141; fax 06-4814296; e-mail studyandcultureuk@britishcouncil.it; internet www.britishcouncil.org/italy; teaching centre; offers courses and exams in English language and British culture and promotes cultural exchange with the UK; attached teaching centres in Bologna, Milan and Naples (Vomero and Chiaia); Dir, Italy PAUL DOCHERTY.

Goethe-Institut: Via Savoia 15, 00198 Rome; tel. 06-8440051; fax 06-8411628; e-mail vl@rom.goethe.org; internet www.goethe.de/it/rom/deindex.htm; offers courses and exams in German language and culture and promotes cultural exchange with Germany; attached centres in Genoa, Milan,

Naples and Turin; library of 29,000 vols; Dir MICHAEL KAHN-ACKERMANN.

Instituto Cervantes: Via di Villa Albani 14–16, 00198 Rome; tel. 06-8537361; fax 06-8546232; e-mail cenrom@cervantes.es; internet roma.cervantes.es; offers courses and exams in Spanish language and culture and promotes cultural exchange with Spain and Spanish-speaking Latin and Central America; attached centres in Milan and Naples; library of 24,000 vols; Dir LUIS JAVIER RUÍZ SIERRA.

PEN Club Italiano: Via Daverio 7, 20122 Milan; e-mail infopen@penclubitalia.org; internet www.penclubitalia.org; promotes freedom of expression; 250 mems; Pres. FERDINANDO CAMON; Sec.-Gen. VITTORIO SOZZI; publ. *Scritture* (4 a year).

Società Dante Alighieri: Palazzo di Firenze, Piazza Firenze 27, 00186 Rome; tel. 06-6873694; fax 06-6873685; e-mail segreteria@ladante.it; internet www.ladante.it; f. 1889; promotes Italian language and culture throughout the world; Sec.-Gen. Comm. Dott. ALESSANDRO MASI; publ. *Pagine della Dante* (3 a year).

Società Dantesca Italiana (Italian Dante Society): Palagio dell'Arte della Lana, Via Arte della Lana 1, 50123 Florence; tel. 055-287134; fax 055-211316; e-mail sdi@dantesca.it; internet www.dantesca.it; f. 1888; library of 25,000 vols, 1,500 microfilms; Pres. Prof. ENRICO GHIDETTI; publs *Collana, Dantesca, Edizione Nazionale delle Opere di Dante Alighieri, Manoscritti Danteschi e d'Interesse Dantesco, Quaderni degli Studi Danteschi, Quaderni del Centro di Studi e Documentazione Dantesca e Medievale, Rivista Annuale, Studi Danteschi.*

Società Filologica Romana: Dipartimento di Studi Romanzi, Sapienza Università di Roma, Facoltà di Scienze Umanistiche, P. le Aldo Moro 5, 00185 Rome; tel. 06-72595105; e-mail beggiato@lettere.uniroma2.it; internet cisadu2.let.uniroma1.it/fil_rom/sfr/frame_vi sualizzazione.htm; f. 1901; library of 8,000 vols; Pres. FABRIZIO BEGGIATO; Sec. SERGIO MARRONI; publ. *Studi Romanzi.*

Società Italiana degli Autori ed Editori (SIAE) (Italian Authors' and Publishers' Society): Viale della Letteratura 30, 00144 Rome; tel. 06-59901; fax 06-59647050; e-mail urp@siae.it; internet www.siae.it; f. 1882; protects authors' and publishers' rights; 50,000 mems; administers the Museo e Biblioteca Teatrale del Burcardo (35,000 vols); Pres. SILVANO GUARISO (acting); Gen. Dir Prof. GIANNI PROFITA; publs *Bollettino SIAE, Il Diritto d'Autore, Lo Spettacolo* (4 a year), *Lo Spettacolo in Italia* (1 a year), *Teatro in Italia* (1 a year).

Società Letteraria di Verona (Verona Literary Society): Piazzetta Scalette Rubiani 1, 37121 Verona; tel. 045-595949; fax 045-595949; e-mail societaletteraria@societaletteraria.it; internet www.societaletteraria.it; f. 1808; promotes appreciation of sciences, literature and art; library of 200,000 vols; Pres. Dott. GIAMBATTISTA RUFFO; publ. *Bollettino* (1 a year).

MEDICINE

Accademia delle Scienze Mediche di Palermo: c/o Policlinico universitario Paolo Giaccone, Dip. di Biopatologia e Metodologie Biomediche, corso Tukory 211, 90134 Palermo; tel. 091-6552456; fax 091-6555901; e-mail accademiascienze@unipa.it; internet www.unipa.it/accademiascienze; f. 1621; library; Pres. Prof. A. SALERNO; Sec. Prof. A. GULLOTTI; publ. *Atti* (1 a year).

Accademia di Medicina di Torino (Turin Academy of Medicine): Via Po 18, 10123 Turin; tel. and fax 011-8179298; internet www.accademiadimedicina.unito.it; f. 1846; 120 ordinary mems, 30 hon. mems, 29 corresp. mems; library of 11,240 vols; Pres. Prof. GIUSEPPE POLI; Sec.-Gen. Prof. GIOVANNI CARLO ISAIA; publ. *Giornale* (2 a year).

Accademia Medica di Roma: Policlinico Umberto I, Viale del Policlinico, 00161 Rome; tel. 06-4957818; f. 1875; 400 mems; Pres. Prof. ANDREA SCIACCA; Sec. Prof. MARIO STEFENINI; publ. *Bolletino ed Atti* (1 a year).

Associazione Italiana di Dietetica e Nutrizione Clinica (Italian Association for Dietetics and Clinical Nutrition): Via Sallustio Bandini 10, 00191 Rome; tel. and fax 06-36306018; e-mail info@adiitalia.com; internet www.adiitalia.com; f. 1950; education and training; application of research in nutrition; 200 mems; Pres. Prof. MARIA ANTONIA FUSCO; Gen. Sec. Dr GIUSEPPE FATATI; publ. *ADI Magazine* (4 a year).

Associazione Italiana di Medicina Aeronautica e Spaziale (Italian Association for Aeronautical and Space Medicine): Servizio Medicina Gruppo Alitalia, Largo Forlanini, Aeroporto Leonardo da Vinci, 00050 Fiumicino; tel. 06-65632660; e-mail info@aimas.it; internet www.aimas.it; f. 1963; Pres. GIACOMO C. MODUGNO; Gen. Sec. FLAVIO BARETTI; publ. *Bollettino* (irregular).

Fondazione Luigi Villa: Via Pace 9, 20122 Milan; tel. 02-5510709; fax 02-54100125; f. 1969; research in molecular biology, genetics and haematology; library of 9,500 vols; Pres. Prof. PIER MANNUCCIO MANNUCCI; Sec.-Gen. Dott. OLGA MOSCA.

Società Italiana di Anestesia, Rianimazione e Terapia Intensiva: Corso Bramante 83, 10126 Turin; tel. 011-678282; fax 011-674502; internet www.siaarti.it; f. 1934; 2,000 mems; Pres. LUCIANO GATTINONI; Sec./Treas. FERDINANDO RAIMONDI; publ. *Minerva Anestesiologica* (12 a year).

Società Italiana di Cancerologia (Italian Society of Cancerology): Via G. Venezian, 1, 20133 Milan; tel. 02-2666895; fax 02-2664342; e-mail sic@istitutotumori.mi.it; internet www.cancerologia.it; f. 1952; Pres. MARCO A. PIEROTTI; publ. *Tumori.*

Società Italiana di Chirurgia (Italian Society for Surgery): Viale Tiziano, 19, 00196 Rome; tel. 06-3221867; fax 06-3220676; e-mail sic@sichirurgia.org; internet www.sichirurgia.org; f. 1882; Pres. Prof. CLAUDIO CORDIANO; Gen. Sec. Prof. ALDO ROMALDI; publ. *Chirurgia Italiana* (6 a year).

Società Italiana di Farmacologia (Italian Pharmacological Society): Viale Abruzzi 32, 20131 Milan; tel. 02-29520311; fax 02-29520179; e-mail sif.farmacologia@segr.it; internet sif.unito.it; f. 1939 to develop pharmacological studies and their applications; 1,152 mems (1,115 ordinary, 13 hon., 24 assoc.); Pres. Prof. ACHILLE CAPUTI; Exec. Sec. Prof. PIER LUIGI CANONICO; publs *Pharmacological Research* (12 a year), *Quaderni della SIF* (4 a year).

Società Italiana di Ginecologia ed Ostetricia (Italian Society for Gynaecology and Obstetrics): Via dei Soldati 25, 00186 Rome; tel. 06-6875119; fax 06-6868142; e-mail federazione@sigo.it; internet www.sigo.it; f. 1892; 5,300 mems; Pres. ANTONIO AMBROSINI; Sec. NICOLA COLACURCI; publs *Atti* (1 a year), *Italian Journal of Gynaecology and Obstetrics* (4 a year), *SIGO Notizie* (3 a year).

Società Italiana di Medicina Interna (Italian Society for Internal Medicine): Viale dell'Università 25, 00185 Rome; tel. 06-44340373; fax 06-44340474; e-mail info@simi.it; internet www.simi.it; f. 1887; annual nat. congress; 2,597 mems; Pres. Prof. FRAN-CESCO VIOLI; Sec. Prof. NICOLA MONTANO; publ. *Internal and Emergency Medicine* (official journal, in English).

Società Italiana di Medicina Legale e delle Assicurazioni (Italian Society for Legal Medicine and Assurance): Istituto di Medicina Legale, Via Mangiagalli 37, 20133 Milan; e-mail staff@simlaweb.com; internet www.simlaweb.com; f. 1897; Pres. Prof. ANTONIO FARNETI; publ. *Rivista Italiana di Medicina Legale.*

Società Italiana di Odontostomatologia e Chirurgia Maxillo-Facciale (Italian Society for Odontostomatology and Maxillofacial Surgery): Via Eugubina 42, 06122 Perugia; tel. 075-5729867; fax 075-5737378; e-mail siocmf@tin.it; internet main .netemedia.net/siocmf; f. 1957; 2,000 mems; Pres. Prof. PIERLUIGI SAPELLI; Sec.-Gen. and Treas. Prof. MAURIZIO PROCACCINI; publ. *Minerva Stomatologica* (12 a year).

Società Italiana di Ortopedia e Traumatologia (Italian Society for Orthopaedics and Traumatology): Via Nicola Martelli 3, 00197 Rome; tel. 06-80691593; fax 06-80687266; e-mail segreteria@siot.it; internet www.siot .it; f. 1906; 3,100 mems; Pres. Prof. VITTORIO MONTELEONE; Sec. Dott. VINCENZO CASTELLI; publ. *Giornale Italiano di Ortopedia e Traumatologia* (4 a year).

Società Italiana di Radiologia Medica: Via della Signora 2, 20122 Milan; tel. 02-76006094; fax 02-76006108; e-mail segretario .amministrativo@sirm.org; internet www .sirm.org; f. 1913; Pres. ALFREDO SIANI; publ. *La Radiologia Medica* (in Italian and English).

Società Italiana di Reumatologia (Italian Society for Rheumatology): Corso Plebisciti 9, 20129 Milan; tel. 02-7382330; fax 02-7385763; e-mail reumatologia@unipd.it; internet www.reumatologia.it; f. 1950; 915 mems; Pres. STEFANO BOMBARDIERI; Gen. Sec. VITTORIO MODENA; publs *Bollettino, Reumatismo* (4 a year).

Società Italiana di Traumatologia della Strada (Italian Society for Road Accident Traumatology): Via Monte delle Gioie 1/D, 00199 Rome; tel. 06-49982399; fax 06-49982553; e-mail socitras@socitras.org; internet www.socitras.org; f. 1984; studies on road trauma, safety campaigns, dissemination of knowledge, training courses; 200 mems; Pres. Prof. ANDREA COSTANZO; Sec.-Gen. Dr ROBERTO SAPIA.

Società Medica Chirurgica di Bologna (Society of Medicine and Surgery): Palazzo dell'Archiginnasio, Piazza Galvani 1, 40124 Bologna; tel. and fax 051-231488; e-mail info@medchir.bo.it; internet www.medchir .bo.it; f. 1802; holds scientific meetings; 250 mems; library of 15,000 vols; Pres. Prof. LUIGI BOLOMDI; Sec. RITA GOLFIERI; Dir of Library Prof. STEFANO ARIETI; publ. *Bullettino delle Scienze Mediche.*

NATURAL SCIENCES

General

Accademia Nazionale delle Scienze, detta dei XL (National Academy of Sciences, known as the Forty): Via L. Spallanzani 7, 00161 Rome; tel. 06-44250465; fax 06-44250871; e-mail segreteria@accademiaxl.it; internet www.accademiaxl.it; f. 1782 as the Italian Society of Sciences; 65 mems (40 Italian, 25 foreign); Pres. Prof. G. T. SCARASCIA MUGNOZZA; Sec. Prof. M. CUMO; publs *Annuario* (every 2 years), *Memorie di Matematica* (1 a year), *Rendiconti: Memorie Scienze Fisiche e Naturali* (1 a year), *Scritti e Documenti* (irregular).

Federazione delle Associazioni Scientifiche e Tecniche (Federation of Scientific and Technological Associations): Piazzale R. Morandi 2, 20121 Milan; tel. 02-77790300; fax 02-782485; e-mail fast@fast.mi.it; internet www.fast.mi.it; f. 1897; aims at fostering cultural debate and promotion of the fields of science policy, technological and industrial research and development, with particular reference to: energy and resources, chemistry and materials, electronics and information, biotechnology, technological research and innovation, ecology and environment, training, professionalism and job organization; mems: 40 scientific orgs, 55,000 individuals; Pres. Prof. ADOLFO COLOMBO; Gen. Sec. Dr ALBERTO PIERI.

Società Adriatica di Scienze (Adriatic Society of Sciences): CP 1029, 34100 Trieste; e-mail adriscie@univ.trieste.it; internet www .units.it/~adriscie; f. 1874; 200 mems; library of 27,000 vols; Pres. Prof. FRANCO CUCCHI; Sec. BERNARDINO CRESSERI; publ. *Bollettino* (1 a year).

Società Italiana di Scienze Naturali (Italian Society of Natural Sciences): Museo Civico di Storia Naturale, Corso Venezia 55, 20121 Milan; tel. 02-795965; fax 02-795965; e-mail info@scienzenaturali.org; internet www.scienzenaturali.org; f. 1857; promotes and carries out scientific research; organizes meetings to present and discuss members' research results; 1,000 mems; library: library of 1,600 periodicals; Pres. CARLO VIOLANI; Sec. MAMI AZUMA; publs *Atti* (2 a year), *Memorie, Natura* (2 a year), *Paleontologia Lombarda, Rivista di Ornitologia* (2 a year).

Società Italiana per il Progresso delle Scienze (Italian Society for Scientific Progress): Viale dell'Università 11, 00185 Rome; tel. 06-4451628; fax 06-4440515; e-mail sips@ sipsinfo.it; internet www.sipsinfo.it; f. 1839; library of 30,000 vols; Pres. Prof. MAURIZIO CUMO; Sec. Prof. ROCCO CAPASSO; publs *Atti Riunioni SIPS* (1 a year), *Scienza e Tecnica* (12 a year).

Società Toscana di Scienze Naturali (Tuscan Society of Natural Sciences): Via S. Maria 53, 56126 Pisa; e-mail info@stsn.it; internet www.stsn.it; f. 1847; 412 mems; library of 75,000 vols, 300 current periodicals; Pres. Prof. STEFANO MERLINO; Gen. Sec. FRANCO RAPETTI; publs *Atti—Memorie serie A (abiologica)* (electronic, 1 a year), *Atti—Memorie serie B (biologica)* (electronic, 1 a year), *Palaeontographia Italica* (1 a year).

Biological Sciences

Società Botanica Italiana Onlus (Italian Botanical Society Onlus): Via Giorgio La Pira 4, 50121 Florence; tel. 055-2757379; fax 055-2757467; e-mail sbi@unifi.it; internet www .societabotanicaitaliana.it; f. 1888; 1,300 mems; library of 9,000 vols; Pres. Prof. FRANCESCO MARIA RAIMONDO; Sec. Prof. CONSOLATA SINISCALCO; publs *Informatore Botanico Italiano* (2 a year with supplements), *Plant Biosystems* (3 a year).

Società Entomologica Italiana (Italian Entomological Society): c/o Museo Civico di Storia Naturale, Via Brigata Liguria 9, 16121 Genoa; tel. (10) 586009; e-mail socentomit.info@alice.it; internet www .socentomit.it; f. 1869; pure and applied entomology; library (Corso Torino 19/4 sc. A. Genoa); 750 mems; Pres. Prof. A. VIGNA TAGLIANTI; publs *Bollettino* (3 a year), *Memorie* (1 a year).

Società Italiana di Biochimica Clinica e Biologia Molecolare Clinica (Italian Society of Clinical Biochemistry and Clinical Molecular Biology): Via Libero Temolo 4, 20126 Milan; tel. 02-87390041; fax 02-87390077; e-mail segreteria@sibioc.it; internet www.sibioc.it; f. 1969; 2,500 mems; mem. of Int. Federation of Clinical Chemis-

try; Pres. Prof. LUCA DEIANA; publ. *Biochimica Clinica* (12 a year).

Società Italiana di Biochimica e Biologia Molecolare (Italian Society for Biochemistry and Molecular Biology): Dipartimento di Scienze Biochimiche 'A. Rossi Fanelli', Università di Roma 'La Sapienza', Piazzale Aldo Moro 5, 00185 Rome; tel. 06-4450291; fax 06-4440062; e-mail info@biochimica.it; internet www .biochimica.it; f. 1951; 1,100 mems; Pres. Prof. ANTONIO DE FLORA; Sec. Prof. LUCIANA AVIGLIANO; publ. *Biochimica in Italia*.

Società Italiana di Ecologia (SItE) (Italian Ecological Society): c/o Dipartimento di Scienze Ambientali, Università di Parma, Area Parco delle Scienze 33A, 43100 Parma; fax 0521-905402; e-mail site@dsa.unipr.it; internet www.dsa.unipr.it/site; f. 1976; aims to promote theoretical and applied ecological research, to disseminate knowledge of ecology, encourage the devt of cultural exchange among researchers, and to facilitate nat. and int. cooperation; operates working groups, congresses, etc.; 705 mems; Pres. Prof. PIERLUIGI VIAROLI; Sec.-Gen. ALBERTO BASSET; publ. *SITE Atti* (proceedings of congresses and symposia, 1 a year).

Società Italiana di Microbiologia (Italian Microbiological Society): c/o Istituto di Microbiologia, Via Androne 81, 95124 Catania; tel. 095-312633; e-mail sim@societasim.org; internet www.societasim.org; f. 1962; promotes the study of microbiology, holds congresses and conventions; Pres. GIUSEPPE NICOLETTI; Sec. and Treas. S. RIPA; publ. *Bollettino* (online, 1 a year).

Physical Sciences

Associazione Geofisica Italiana (Italian Geophysical Association): c/o CNR, V.le dell'Università 11, 00185 Rome; tel. and fax 06-44702989; e-mail info@associazionegeofisica .it; internet www.associazionegeofisica.it; f. 1951; promotes, coordinates and disseminates knowledge, studies and research on pure and applied geophysics; 200 mems; library of 1,500 vols; Pres. Prof. Dr H. COLACINO; Sec. Dr M. AVERSA; publ. *Bollettino Geofisico* (4 a year).

Associazione Geotecnica Italiana (Italian Geotechnical Association): Viale dell'Università 11, 00185 Rome; tel. 06-44704349; fax 06-44361035; e-mail agiroma@iol.it; internet www.associazionegeotecnica.it/~agi; f. 1947; independent; aims to encourage, carry out and support geotechnical studies and research in Italy through publications, conferences, scholarships, etc.; 1,100 mems; Pres. Prof. GIOVANNI BARLA; publ. *Rivista Italiana di Geotecnica* (4 a year).

Associazione Italiana Nucleare: Corso Vittorio Emanuele II 244, 00186 Rome; tel. 06-94005401; fax 06-94005314; e-mail info@ assonucleare.it; internet www.assonucleare .it; f. 1998 by merger of ANDIN (Associazione Italiana di Ingegneria Nucleare e Sicurezza Impiantistica), FIEN (Forum Italiano dell'Energia Nucleare) and SNI (Società Nucleare Italiana); promotes debate and research into the role of nuclear power, in order to promote the peaceful and safe use of nuclear technology, in the national interest; Chair. Prof. RENATO ANGELO RICCI.

Società Astronomica Italiana (Italian Astronomical Society): Largo E. Fermi 5, 50125 Florence; tel. and fax 055-2752270; e-mail sait@arcetri.astro.it; internet www .sait.it; f. 1920; 700 mems; Pres. Prof. ROBERTO BUONANNO; Sec. Dr FABRIZIO MAZZUCCONI; publs *Giornale di Astronomia* (print and electronic versions, 4 a year), *Memorie* (4 a year).

Società Chimica Italiana (Italian Chemical Society): Viale Liegi 48/C, 00198 Rome; tel. 06-8549691; fax 06-8548734; e-mail soc .chim.it@agora.it; internet www.soc.chim.it; f. 1909; 5,000 mems; library of 2,300 vols; Pres. Prof. LUIGI CAMPANELLA; publs *Annali di Chimica* (6 a year), *Il Farmaco* (medicinal and pharmaceutical chemistry, in English, 12 a year), *La Chimica e l'Industria* (12 a year), *La Chimica nella Scuola* (6 a year).

Società Geologica Italiana (Italian Geological Society): c/o Dipartimento di Scienze della Terra, Università La Sapienza, Piazzale Aldo Moro 5, 00185 Rome; tel. (6) 4959390; fax (6) 49914154; e-mail sgi@ socgeol.it; internet www.socgeol.it; f. 1881; 1,700 mems; Sec. Dott. ACHILLE ZUCCARI; publs *Bollettino* (3 a year), *Memorie* (irregular), *Rendiconti*.

Società Italiana di Fisica (Italian Physics Society): Via Saragozza 12, 40123 Bologna; tel. 051-331554; fax 051-581340; e-mail sif@ sif.it; internet www.sif.it; f. 1897; 1,500 mems; library of 6,500 vols; Pres. Prof. FRANCO BASSANI; publs *Bollettino* (6 a year), *European Physical Journal* (owned in conjunction with 2 other learned socs, 12 a year), *Europhysics Letters* (24 a year), *Giornale di Fisica* (4 a year), *Il Nuovo Cimento B* (12 a year), *Il Nuovo Cimento C* (6 a year), *Rivista del Nuovo Cimento* (12 a year).

PHILOSOPHY AND PSYCHOLOGY

Società Filosofica Italiana (Italian Philosophical Society): c/o Dip. di Studi Filosofici ed Epistemologici, Università di Roma 'La Sapienza', Villa Mirafiori, Via Nomentana 118, 00161 Rome; tel. and fax 06-8604360; e-mail sfi@sfi.it; internet www.sfi.it; f. 1902; ind. org.; promotes philosophical research on a scientific level; safeguards the professional status of philosophy lecturers; encourages contact and collaboration in Italy and internationally between philosophic disciplines; helps set up local centres of study; 1,350 mems; Pres. STEFANO POGGI; Sec. and Treas. Prof. CARLA GUETTI; publ. *Bollettino* (3 a year).

Società Italiana di Psicologia: Via Tagliamento 76, 00198 Rome; tel. 06-8845136; fax 06-8845136; e-mail sipsit@tin.it; internet www.sips.it; f. 1910; carries out activities in conjunction with university institutions for study and research; organizes national congresses every 3 years; Pres. LEONARDO ANCONA; publ. *Psicologia Italiana*.

RELIGION, SOCIOLOGY AND ANTHROPOLOGY

Fondazione Marco Besso (Marco Besso Foundation): Largo di Torre Argentina 11, 00186 Rome; tel. 06-6865611; fax 06-68216313; e-mail segreteriadue@ fondazionemarcobesso.it; internet www .fondazionemarcobesso.it; f. 1918; promotes development of Roman cultural world; library: see Libraries and Archives; Pres. GLORIA SONAGLIA LUMBROSO; Dir ANTONIO MARTINI.

Gruppo Interdisciplinare per la Ricerca Sociale (Interdisciplinary Group for Social Research): Facoltà di Scienze Statistiche, Demografiche e Attuariale, Piazzale Aldo Moro 5, 00185 Rome; tel. 06-4453828; f. 1937; Italian section of Int. Institute of Sociology; library of 8,000 vols, 100 current periodicals; Pres. Prof. AMMASSARI.

Società Italiana di Antropologia e Etnologia: Via del Proconsolo 12, 50122 Florence; tel. 055-2396449; fax 055-219438; e-mail musant@unifi.it; f. 1871; 200 mems; library of 5,760 vols, 70 periodicals; Pres. Prof. CLETO CORRAIN; Librarian CATERINA SCAR-

SINI; publ. *Archivio per l'Antropologia e la Etnologia* (1 a year).

TECHNOLOGY

Associazione Elettrotecnica ed Elettronica Italiana (AEI) (Italian Electrical and Electronics Association): Central Office, Via Mauro Macchi 32, 20124 Milan; tel. 02-87389960; fax 02-66989023; e-mail federaeit.it; internet www.aei.it; f. 1896; Pres. FRANCESCO GAGLIARDI; Gen. Sec. ANDREA BONATI; publs *AEIT—Federazione di Elettrotecnica, Elettronica, Automazione, Informatica e Telecomunicazioni* (12 a year), *European Transactions on Telecommunications* (6 a year, in English), *L'Energia Elettrica* (6 a year), *Mondo Digitale* (12 a year).

Associazione Idrotecnica Italiana (Italian Water Resources Association): Via di Santa Costanza 7, 00198 Rome; tel. 06-8845064; fax 06-8852974; e-mail info@idrotecnicaitaliana.it; internet www.idrotecnicaitaliana.it; f. 1923; study of problems concerning the utilization and management of water resources, and the safeguarding of the environment; 1,500 mems; library of 200 vols; Pres. UGO MAJONE; Gen. Sec. OLIMPIA ARCELLA; publ. *L'Acqua* (6 a year).

Associazione Italiana di Aeronautica e Astronautica (Italian Association of Aeronautical and Space Sciences): Casella Postale 227, 00187 Rome; tel. and fax (6) 88346460; e-mail info@aidaa.it; internet www.aidaa.it; f. 1920; promotes and coordinates research in aeronautical and space sciences; cooperates with nat. and int. bodies in this field; 400 mems in 8 sections; Pres. Prof. FRANCO PERSIANI; Gen. Sec. Prof. ANTONIO CASTELLANI; publ. *Aerotecnica Missili e Spazio* (4 a year).

Associazione Italiana di Metallurgia (Italian Metallurgical Association): Piazzale R. Morandi 2, 20121 Milan; tel. 02-76021132; fax 02-76020551; e-mail aim@aimnet.it; internet www.aimnet.it; f. 1946; promotes and develops all aspects of science, technology and use of metals and materials closely related to metals; 2,000 mems; Pres. OTTAVIO LECIS; Gen. Sec. (vacant); publ. *La Metallurgia Italiana* (12 a year).

Associazione Italiana Nucleare (Italian Nuclear Association): Corso Vittorio Emanuele II 244, 00186 Rome; tel. 06-94005401; fax 06-94005314; Chair. Prof. RENATO ANGELO RICCI; Sec.-Gen. Ing. UGO SPEZIA.

Comitato Elettrotecnico Italiano (CEI) (Italian Electrotechnical Committee): Via Saccardo 9, 20134 Milan; tel. 02-210061; fax 02-21006210; internet www.ceiweb.it; Pres. Ing. ALDO BOLZA.

Comitato Termotecnico Italiano (CTI) (Italian Thermotechnical Committee): Via G. Pacini 11, 20131 Milan; tel. 02-2662651; fax 02-26626550; e-mail cti@cti2000.it; internet www.cti2000.it; f. 1933; Pres. CESARE BOFFA; Gen. Sec. Prof. GIOVANNI RIVA; publ. *La Termotecnica* (10 a year).

Ente Nazionale Italiano di Unificazione (UNI) (Italian National Standards Association): Via Battistotti Sassi 11B, 20133 Milan; tel. 02-700241; fax 02-70106149; e-mail uni@uni.com; internet www.uni.com; f. 1921; Pres. PAOLO SCOLARI; Exec. Vice-Pres. Dr Ing. ENRICO MARTINOTTI; publ. *Unificazione* (4 a year).

Ente di Studi Nucleari per l'Agricoltura (ISNA) (Institute of Nuclear Studies applied to Agriculture): Via IV Novembre 152, 00187 Rome; tel. 06-6784991; f. 1959; Pres. Avv. Prof. GIUSEPPE GESUALDI; Sec.-Gen. Prof. M. L. SCARSELLI; publs *Agricoltura*

d'Italia (12 a year), *Il Corriere di Roma*, *Quaderni ISNA*.

Istituto Italiano del Marchio di Qualità (IMQ) (Italian Institute of the Quality Mark): Via Quintiliano 43, 20138 Milan; tel. 02-50731; fax 02-5073271; e-mail mkt@imq.it; internet www.imq.it; f. 1951; tests electrical and gas products to grant the IMQ safety mark; undertakes EU Directives conformity assessment and certifies company quality and management systems as part of the CSQ scheme; Pres. GIORGIO SCANAVACCA; Man. Dir GIANCARLO ZAPPA; publs *Guida agli Acquisti IMQ* (list of products and companies approved by IMQ, 2 a year), *IMQ Notizie* (News, 4 a year).

Istituto Italiano della Saldatura (Italian Welding Institute): Lungobisagno Istria 15A, 16141 Genoa; tel. 010-83411; fax 010-8367780; e-mail iis@iis.it; internet www.iis.it; f. 1948; consultancy training, research, standardization, certification, laboratory tests and diploma courses in welding; 800 mems; library of 15,000 vols; Sec.-Gen. Dott.-Ing. MAURO SCASSO; publ. *Rivista Italiana della Saldatura* (6 a year).

Research Institutes

GENERAL

Consiglio Nazionale delle Ricerche (CNR) (National Research Council of Italy): Piazzale Aldo Moro 7, 00185 Rome; tel. 06-49931; fax 06-4461954; e-mail urp@urp.cnr.it; internet www.cnr.it; f. 1923; research is carried out by 110 institutes in 5 groups: Basic Sciences; Earth and Environmental Sciences; Human and Social Sciences; Life Sciences; and Technological, Engineering and Information Sciences; 20 Aree di Ricerca provide the institutes with logistical, technical and administrative support: Bari (Pres. Prof. ANGELO VISCONTI), Bologna (Pres. Dott. GIANCARLO SECONI), Cosenza (Pres. Dott. MARINO SORRISO VALVO), Florence (Pres. Prof. PIER LUIGI EMILIANI), Genoa (Pres. Ing. FILIPPO GRASSIA), Milan 1 (Pres. Dott. ALCIDE BERTANI), Milan 2 (Pres. Dott. VALTER ESPOSTI), Milan 3 (Pres. Dott. EMILIO OLZI), Milan 4 (Pres. Prof. ALBERTO ALBERTINI), Naples 1 (Pres. Prof. CATELLO POLITO), Naples 2 (Pres. Prof. MOSÈ ROSSI), Naples 3 (Pres. Dott. GUIDO CIMINO), Padua (Pres. Dott. SERGIO DAOLIO), Palermo (Pres. Dott. PIERLUIGI SAN BIAGIO), Pisa (Pres. Prof. LUIGI DONATO), Potenza (Pres. Prof. VINCENZO CUOMO), Rome 1—Montelibretti (Pres. Dott. SESTO VITICOLI), Rome 2—Tor Vergata (Pres. Dott. PAOLO PERFETTI), Rome 3 (Pres. Prof. PIETRO CALISSANO), Turin (Pres. Prof. MAURIZIO CONTI); Pres. Prof. FABIO PISTELLA; Dir-Gen. Dott. ANGELO GUERRINI; publs *Almanacco della Scienza* (electronic, 26 a year), *CNR Report* (1 a year), *Ricerca e Futuro* (print and electronic versions, 4 a year), *Notiziario Neutroni e Luce di Sincrotrone* (print and electronic versions, in Italian and English, 2 a year).

Basic Sciences:

Istituto per le Applicazioni del Calcolo 'Mauro Picone' (Institute for Applied Mathematics): Viale del Policlinico 137, 00161 Rome; tel. 06-884701; fax 06-4404306; e-mail direttore@iac.cnr.it; internet www.iac.cnr.it; f. 2000; Dir Prof. MICHIEL BERTSCH.

Istituto di Astrofisica Spaziale e Fisica Cosmica (Cosmic Physics and Space Astrophysics Institute): Via del Fosso del Cavaliere 100, 00133 Rome; tel. 06-49934472; fax 06-20660188; e-mail gev@

rm.iasf.cnr.it; internet www.rm.iasf.cnr.it; f. 2000; Dir Dott. GABRIELE VILLA.

Istituto di Chimica dei Composti Organo Metallici (Institute of Organometallic Compounds Chemistry): Via Madonna del Piano snc, 50019 Sesto Fiorentino; tel. 055-52251; fax 055-5225203; e-mail claudio.bianchini@iccom.cnr.it; internet www.iccom.cnr.it; f. 2001; Dir Dott. CLAUDIO BIANCHINI.

Istituto di Chimica Inorganica e delle Superfici (Institute of Inorganic and Surface Chemistry): Corso Stati Uniti 4, 35127 Padua; tel. 049-8295940; fax 049-8702911; e-mail zanella@icis.cnr.it; internet www.icis.cnr.it; f. 2000; Dir Dott. PIERINO ZANELLA.

Istituto di Chimica e Tecnologia dei Polimeri (Institute of Polymer Chemistry and Technology): Via Campi Flegrei 34, 80078 Pozzuoli; tel. 081-8675077; fax 081-8675230; e-mail direttore@ictp.cnr.it; internet www.ictp.cnr.it; f. 2001; Dir Prof. COSIMO CARFAGNA.

Istituto di Cibernetica 'Edoardo Caianiello' (Cybernetics Institute): Via Campi Flegrei 34, 80078 Pozzuoli; tel. 081-8675111; fax 081-8675128; e-mail s.termini@cib.na.cnr.it; internet www.cib.na.cnr.it; f. 2001; Dir Prof. SETTIMO TERMINI.

Istituto di Cristallografia (Institute of Crystallography): Via Giovanni Amendola 122/O, 70126 Bari; tel. 080-5929140; fax 080-5929170; e-mail carmelo.giacovazzo@ic.cnr.it; internet www.ic.cnr.it; f. 2001; Dir Prof. CARMELO GIACOVAZZO.

Istituto per l'Energetica e le Interfasi (Institute for Energetics and Interphases): Corso Stati Uniti 4, 35127 Padua; tel. 049-8295850; fax 049-8295853; e-mail s.daolio@ieni.cnr.it; internet www.ieni.cnr.it; f. 2000; Dir Dott. SERGIO DAOLIO.

Istituto di Fisica Applicata 'Nello Carrara' (Institute of Applied Physics): Via Madonna del Piano, 10 50019 Sesto Fiorentino, Florence; tel. 055-52251; fax 055-5225000; e-mail r.salimbeni@ifac.cnr.it; internet www.ifac.cnr.it; f. 2001; Dir Dott. RENZO SALIMBENI.

Istituto di Fisica del Plasma 'Piero Caldirola' (Institute for Plasma Physics): Via Roberto Cozzi 53, 20125 Milan; tel. 02-66173238; fax 02-66173239; e-mail direttore@ifp.cnr.it; internet www.ifp.cnr.it; f. 1974; library of 3,000 vols, 100 periodical titles; Dir Dott. ENZO LAZZARO.

Istituto di Fisica dello Spazio Interplanetario (Institute for Interplanetary Space Physics): Via del Fosso del Cavaliere 100, 00133 Rome; tel. 06-4993460; fax 06-49934383; e-mail angioletta.coradini@ifsi.rm.cnr.it; internet www.ifsi.rm.cnr.it; f. 2001; Dir Dott.ssa ANGIOLETTA CORADINI.

Istituto di Fotonica e Nanotecnologie (Institute for Photonics and Nanotechnologies): Via Cineto Romano 42, 00156 Rome; tel. 06-415221; fax 06-41522220; e-mail evangelisti@ifn.cnr.it; internet www.ifn.cnr.it; f. 2000; study and development of photonics from points of view of radiation-matter interaction and of developing materials, devices and systems; study and development of nanotechnologies for the fabrication of nanoscale-size devices; development of microelectronic and micromechanical devices; Dir Prof. FLORESTANO EVANGELISTI.

Istituto di Matematica Applicata e Tecnologie Informatiche (Institute of Applied Mathematics and Information Technology): Via Ferrata 1, 27100 Pavia; tel. 0382-548211; fax 0382-548300; e-mail direttore@imati.cnr.it; internet www.imati .cnr.it; f. 2000; Dir Prof. FRANCO BREZZI; Librarian M. GRAZIA FUSARI.

Istituto per i Materiali Compositi e Biomedici (Institute for Composite and Biomedical Materials): Piazzale Vincenzo Tecchio 80, 80125 Naples; tel. 081-7682401; fax 081-7682666; e-mail nicolais@unina.it; f. 2001; Dir Prof. LUIGI NICOLAIS.

Istituto dei Materiali per l'Elettronica ed il Magnetismo (Institute of Materials for Electronics and Magnetism): Parco Area delle Scienze 37A, 43124 Fontanini, Parma; tel. 0521-2691; fax 0521-269206; e-mail direttore-imem@imem.cnr.it; internet www.imem.cnr.it; f. 2001; library of 1,300 vols; Dir Dott. SALVATORE IANNOTTA.

Istituto di Metodologie Chimiche (Institute for Methodological Chemistry): Via Salaria Km 29.3, CP 10, 00016 Monterotondo Stazione; tel. 06-9062511; fax 06-90672519; e-mail imc@imc.cnr.it; internet www.mlib.rm.cnr.it; f. 2001; Dir Dott. GIANCARLO ANGELINI.

Istituto di Metodologie Inorganiche e dei Plasmi (Institute of Inorganic Methodologies and Plasmas): Via Salaria Km 29.3, CP 10, 00016 Monterotondo Stazione; tel. 06-90672213; fax 06-90672238; e-mail direttore.imip@imip.cnr.it; internet www .imip.cnr.it; f. 2000; Dir Dott. MARIO CACCIATORE.

Istituto per la Microelettronica e Microsistemi (Institute for Microelectronics and Microsystems): Stradale Primosole 50, 95121 Catania; tel. 095-5968211; fax 095-5968312; e-mail emanuele.rimini@imm.cnr.it; internet www.imm.cnr.it; f. 2000; Dir Prof. EMANUELE RIMINI.

Istituto per i Processi Chimico-Fisici (Institute for Chemical and Physical Processes): Via Giuseppe Moruzzi 1, 56124 Pisa; tel. 050-3152234; fax 050-3152234; e-mail direttore@ipcf.cnr.it; internet www .ipcf.cnr.it; f. 2000; Dir Dott. MASSIMO MARTINELLI.

Istituto di Radioastronomia (Institute of Radioastronomy): Via Piero Gobetti 101, 40129 Bologna; tel. 051-6399385; fax 051-6399431; e-mail gtofani@ira.cnr.it; internet www.ira.cnr.it; f. 2000; Dir Prof. GIANNI TOFANI.

Istituto di Scienze e Tecnologie Molecolari (Institute of Molecular Science and Technologies): Via Camillo Golgi 19, 20133 Milan; tel. 02-70635452; fax 02-50314300; e-mail g.casalone@istm.cnr.it; internet www.istm.cnr.it; f. 2000; Dir Dott. GIANLUIGI CASALONE.

Istituto per la Sintesi Organica e la Fotoreattività (Institute for Organic Syntheses and Photoreactivity): Via Piero Gobetti 101, 40129 Bologna; tel. 051-6399770; fax 051-6399844; e-mail direzione@isof.cnr.it; internet www.isof .cnr.it; f. 2000; Dir Dott. GIANCARLO SECONI.

Istituto dei Sistemi Complessi (Sperimentale) (Institute for Experimental Complex Systems): Via dei Taurini 19, 00185 Rome; tel. 06-49934598; fax 06-49934003; e-mail luciano.pietronero@isc .cnr.it; internet www.isc.cnr.it; f. 2004; Dir Prof. LUCIANO PIETRONERO.

Istituto Sperimentale di Acustica 'Orso Mario Corbino' (Institute of Acoustics): Via del Fosso del Cavaliere 100, 00133 Rome; tel. 06-49934482; fax 06-20660061; e-mail damico@idac.rm.cnr.it;

internet www.idac.rm.cnr.it; f. 2001; Dir Prof. ARNALDO D'AMICO.

Istituto di Struttura della Materia (Institute for the Structure of Matter): Via del Fosso del Cavaliere 100, 00133 Rome; tel. 06-49934476; fax 06-49934153; e-mail perfetti@ism.cnr.it; internet www .ism.cnr.it; f. 2000; Dir Dott. PAOLO PERFETTI.

Istituto per lo Studio delle Macromolecole (Institute for Macromolecular Studies): Via Edoardo Bassini 15, 20133 Milan; tel. 02-23699366; fax 02-2362946; e-mail locatelli@ismac.cnr.it; internet www.ismac .cnr.it; f. 2000; Dir Dott. PAOLO LOCATELLI.

Istituto per lo Studio dei Materiali Nanostrutturati (Institute of Nanostructured Materials): Via dei Taurini 19, 00185 Rome; tel. 06-90672484; fax 06-90672372; e-mail mariaester.moresi@ismn.cnr.it; internet www.ismn.cnr.it; f. 2000; Dir Dr.ssa. GIUSEPPINA PADELETTI.

Istituto per la Tecnologia delle Membrane (Institute for Membrane Technology): Via P. Bucci, 87030 Rende; tel. 0984-402706; fax 0984-402103; e-mail e.drioli@ itm.cnr.it; internet www.itm.cnr.it; f. 2001; Dir Prof. ENRICO DRIOLI.

Earth and Environmental Sciences:

Istituto per l'Ambiente Marino Costiero (Institute for the Coastal Marine Environment): Calata Porta di Massa, 80133 Naples; tel. 081-5423811; fax 081-5423888; e-mail dargenio@gms01.geomare .na.cnr.it; f. 2001; Dir Prof. BRUNO D'ARGENIO.

Istituto per la Dinamica dei Processi Ambientali (Institute for the Dynamics of Environmental Processes): Calle Larga Santa Marta 2137, 30123 Venice; tel. 041-2348547; fax 041-2578549; e-mail paolo .cescon@idpa.cnr.it; internet www.idpa.cnr .it; f. 2001; Dir Prof. PAOLO CESCON.

Istituto di Geologia Ambientale e Geoingegneria (Institute of Environmental Geology and Geoengineering): Via Bolognola 7, (Via Salaria Km 11.6), 00138 Rome; tel. 06-88070001; fax 06-8804463; e-mail giovannimaria.zuppi@igag.cnr.it; internet www.igag.cnr.it; f. 2001; Dir Dott. GIUSEPPE CAVARRETTA.

Istituto di Geoscienze e Georisorse (Institute of Geosciences and Earth Resources): Via Giuseppe Moruzzi 1, 56124 Pisa; tel. 050-3152384; fax 050-3152323; e-mail direttore@igg.cnr.it; internet www.igg.cnr.it; f. 2001; Dir Prof. PIERO MANETTI.

Istituto sull'Inquinamento Atmosferico (Institute for Atmospheric Pollution): Via Salaria Km 29.3, CP 10, 00016 Monterotondo Stazione; tel. 06-90625349; fax 06-90672660; e-mail allegrini@iia.cnr.it; internet www.iia.cnr.it; f. 2001; Dir Dott. IVO ALLEGRINI.

Istituto di Metodologie per l'Analisi Ambientale (Institute of Methodologies for Environmental Analysis): Contrada S. Loja, CP 27, 85050 Tito Scalo; tel. 0971-427262; fax 0971-427222; e-mail cuomo@ imaa.cnr.it; internet www.imaa.cnr.it; f. 2001; Dir Prof. VINCENZO CUOMO.

Istituto di Ricerca sulle Acque (Water Research Institute): Via Reno 1, 00198 Rome; tel. 06-8841451; fax 06-8417861; e-mail direzione@irsa.rm.cnr.it; internet www.irsa.rm.cnr.it; f. 2001; Dir Prof. ROBERTO PASSINO.

Istituto di Ricerca per la Protezione Idrogeologica (Research Institute for Geo-hydrological Protection): Via Madonna Alta 126, 06128 Perugia; tel. 075-5014402;

fax 075-5014420; e-mail direzione@irpi.cnr .it; internet www.irpi.cnr.it; f. 2001; Dir Prof. LUCIO UBERTINI.

Istituto di Scienze dell'Atmosfera e del Clima (Institute of Atmospheric Sciences and Climate): Via Piero Gobetti 101, 40129 Bologna; tel. 051-6399619; fax 051-6399658; e-mail direzione@isac.cnr.it; internet www.isac.cnr.it; f. 2000; Dir Prof. FRANCO PRODI.

Istituto di Scienze Marine (Institute of Marine Sciences): San Polo 1364, Palazzo Papadopoli, 30125 Venice; tel. 041-5216811; fax 041-2602340; e-mail direttore@ismar.cnr.it; internet www .ismar.cnr.it; f. 2001; Dir Prof. ENRICO BONATTI.

Istituto per lo Studio degli Ecosistemi (Institute of Ecosystem Study): Largo Vittorio Tonolli 50–52, 28922 Pallanza; tel. 0323-518300; fax 0323-518349; e-mail r.debernardi@ise.cnr.it; internet www.ise .cnr.it; f. 2001; Dir Dott. RICCARDO DE BERNARDI.

Human and Social Sciences:

Ceris—Istituto di Ricerca sull'Impresa e lo Sviluppo (Institute of Research on Business Firms and Development): Via Real Collegio 30, 10024 Moncalieri; tel. 011-6824911; fax 011-6824966; e-mail s.rolfo@ceris.cnr.it; internet www .ceris.cnr.it; f. 1956; research for National Research Council; Dir Dott. SECONDO ROLFO.

Istituto per i Beni Archeologici e Monumentali (Institute of Archaeological Heritage—Monuments and Sites): Prov.le Lecce-Monteroni, 73100 Lecce; tel. 0832-422200; fax 0832-422225; e-mail francesco .dandria@unile.it; internet www.ibam.cnr .it; f. 2001; Dir Prof. FRANCESCO D'ANDRIA.

Istituto per la Conservazione e Valorizzazione dei Beni Culturali (Institute for the Conservation and Promotion of Cultural Heritage): Vai Madonna del Piano, 10 Edificio C, 50019 Sesto Fiorentino; tel. 055-5225484; fax 055-5225403; e-mail direttore@icvbc.cnr.it; internet www.icvbc.cnr.it; f. 2001; Dir Prof. PIERO FREDIANI.

Istituto per il Lessico Intellettuale Europeo e la Storia delle Idee (Institute for the European Intellectual Lexicon and the History of Ideas): Villa Mirafiori, via Carlo Fea 2, 00161 Rome; tel. 06-86320527; fax 06-49917215; e-mail iliesi@iliesi.cnr.it; internet www.iliesi.cnr.it; f. 1964; 25 mems; library of 4,600 microfilms; Dir Prof. RICCARDO POZZO; publs *Bruniana and Campanelliana*, *Elenchos*.

Istituto di Linguistica Computazionale (Institute of Computational Linguistics): Via Giuseppe Moruzzi 1, 56124 Pisa; tel. 050-3152870; fax 050-3152839; e-mail direttore@ilc.cnr.it; internet www.ilc.cnr .it; f. 2001; Dir Dott.ssa NICOLETTA ZAMORANI CALZOLARI.

Istituto Opera del Vocabolario Italiano (The Italian Dictionary): Via di Castello 46, 50141 Florence; tel. 055-452841; fax 055-4250678; e-mail beltrami@ovi.cnr.it; internet www.ovi.cnr .it; f. 2001; Dir Prof. PIETRO BELTRAMI.

Istituto di Ricerche sulle Attività Terziarie (Institute for Service Industry Research): Via Michelangelo Schipa 115, 80122 Naples; tel. 081-2470911; fax 081-2470933; e-mail a.morvillo@irat.cnr.it; internet www.irat.cnr.it; f. 2001; Dir Dott. ALFONSO MORVILLO.

Istituto di Ricerche sulla Popolazione e le Politiche Sociali (Institute for Research on Population and Social Policies): Via Nizza 128, 00198 Rome; tel. 06-49932805; fax 06-85834506; e-mail e .pugliese@irpps.cnr.it; internet www.irpps .cnr.it; f. 2001; Dir Prof. ENRICO PUGLIESE.

Istituto di Ricerca sui Sistemi Giudiziari (Institute for Research on Judicial Systems): Via Zamboni 26, 40126 Bologna; tel. 051-237044; fax 051-260250; e-mail direttore@irsig.cnr.it; internet www.irsig .cnr.it; f. 2002; Dir Prof. GIUSEPPE DI FEDERICO.

Istituto di Storia dell'Europa Mediterranea (Institute of Mediterranean European History): Via G. B. Tuveri 128, 09129 Cagliari; tel. 070-40367; fax 070-498118; e-mail casula@isem.cnr.it; internet www .isem.cnr.it; f. 2001; Dir Prof. FRANCESCO CESARE CASULA.

Istituto per la Storia del Pensiero Filosofico e Scientifico Moderno (Institute for the History of Philosophical and Scientific Thought in the Modern Age): Via Porta di Massa 1, 80133 Naples; tel. 081-2535580; fax 081-2535515; e-mail sanna@ unina.it; internet www.ispf.cnr.it; f. 2001; Dir Dott.ssa MANUELA SANNA.

Istituto di Studi sulle Civiltà dell'Egeo e del Vicino Oriente (Institute for Aegean and Near Eastern Studies): Via Giano della Bella 18, 00162 Rome; tel. 06-4416131; fax 06-44237724; e-mail direzione@icevo.cnr.it; internet www.icevo .cnr.it; f. 1968, present status in 2001; library of 15,000 vols; Aegean and Early Greek Civilization; Aegean Archaeology; Mycenaean Philology; Cretan Archaeology; Cypriot Archaeology; Mediterranean Protohistory; Anatolian and Near Eastern Civilization; Near Eastern Archaeology; Anatolian Archaeology; Iranian Archaeology; Hittitology; Hurritology; Urartian Civilization; Assyriology; 13 mems; Dir Dr MARIE-CLAUDE TRÉMOUILLE (acting); publ. *Studi Micenei ed Egeo Anatolici.*

Istituto di Studi sulle Civiltà Italiche e del Mediterraneo Antico (Institute for the Study of the Italic and Ancient Mediterranean Civilizations): Viale di Villa Massimo 29, 00161 Rome; tel. 06-85301934; fax 06-44239379; e-mail etruschi@iaei.rm.cnr.it; internet soi.cnr.it/ iscima; f. 2001; Dir Prof. FRANCESCO RONCALLI DI MONTORIO.

Istituto di Studi Giuridici Internazionali (Institute for International Legal Studies): Via dei Taurini 19, 00185 Rome; tel. 06-49937660; fax 06-44340025; e-mail sergio.marchisio@isgi.cnr.it; internet www .isgi.cnr.it; f. 1986, present name 2001; research in international law; the international protection of human rights; international environmental law; library of 2,000 vols; Dir Prof. SERGIO MARCHISIO.

Istituto di Studi sui Sistemi Regionali Federali e sulle Autonomie 'Massimo Severo Giannini' (Institute for Regional and Federal Studies): Via dei Taurini 19, 00185 Rome; tel. 06-49937740; fax 06-490704; e-mail info.issirfa@issirfa.cnr.it; internet www.issirfa.cnr.it; f. 2001; Dir Prof. ANTONIO D'ATENA.

Istituto di Studi sulle Società del Mediterraneo (Institute of Studies on Mediterranean Societies): Via Pietro Castellino 111, 80131 Naples; tel. 081-6134086; fax 081-5799467; e-mail malanima@issm.cnr.it; internet www.issm .cnr.it; f. 2001; growth, convergence and divergence in Mediterranean economies in the past and present; 30 mems; library of 15,000 vols; Dir Prof. PAOLO MALANIMA; publ. *Global environment.*

Istituto per le Tecnologie Applicate ai Beni Culturali (Institute for Technologies Applied to Cultural Heritage): Via Salaria Km. 29.3, CP 10, 00016 Monterotondo Stazione; tel. 06-90625274; fax 06-90672373; e-mail direttore@itabc.cnr.it; internet www.itabc.cnr.it; f. 2001; Dir Dott. SALVATORE GARRAFFO.

Istituto di Teoria e Tecniche dell'Informazione Giuridica (Institute of Legal Information Theory and Technology): Via Panciatichi 56/16, 50127 Florence; tel. 055-43995; fax 055-4221637; e-mail nicola .palazzolo@ittig.cnr.it; internet www.ittig .cnr.it; f. 2001; Dir Prof. NICOLA PALAZZOLO.

Life Sciences:

Istituto di Biochimica delle Proteine (Institute of Protein Biochemistry): Via Guglielmo Marconi 10, 80125 Naples; tel. 081-6132273; fax 081-6132277; e-mail m .rossi@ibp.cnr.it; internet www.ibp.cnr.it; f. 2001; Dir Prof. MOSÈ ROSSI.

Istituto di Biofisica (Institute of Biophysics): Via De Marini 6, Torre di Francia, 16149 Genoa; tel. 010-6475592; fax 010-6475500; e-mail direttore@pi.ibf.cnr.it; internet www.ibf.cnr.it; f. 2001; Dir Dott. FRANCO CONTI.

Istituto di Bioimmagini e Fisiologia Molecolare (Institute of Molecular Bioimaging and Physiology): Via Fratelli Cervi 93, 20090 Segrate; tel. 02-21717514; fax 02-21717558; e-mail ferruccio.fazio@hsr.it; internet www.ibfm.cnr.it; f. 2001; Dir Prof. FERRUCCIO FAZIO.

Istituto di Biologia Agro-ambientale e Forestale (Institute of Agro-environmental and Forest Biology): Via Guglielmo Marconi 2, 05010 Porano; tel. 0763-374911; fax 0763-374980; e-mail giuseppe .scarascia@ibaf.cnr.it; internet www.ibaf .cnr.it; f. 2001; Dir Prof. GIUSEPPE SCARASCIA MUGNOZZA.

Istituto di Biologia e Biotecnologia Agraria (Institute of Agricultural Biology and Biotechnology): Via Edoardo Bassini 15, 20133 Milan; tel. 02-23699403; fax 02-23699411; e-mail direttore@ibba.cnr.it; internet www.ibba.cnr.it; f. 2001; Dir Dott. ALCIDE BERTANI.

Istituto di Biologia Cellulare (Institute of Cell Biology): Via E. Ramarini 32, 00016 Monterotondo Scalo; tel. 06-90091207; fax 06-90091260; e-mail gtocchini@ibc.cnr.it; f. 1969; research areas in functional genomics, systems of signal transduction, molecular aspects of the construction logic and the functioning of complex organisms, RNA, molecular aspects of the relationship between parasite and host in tropical diseases, construction of mutant strains and phenocopies of mice, cryo-conservation, rederivation, distribution of mutant strains, production and telematic distribution of databases of mutant strains; Dir Prof. GLAUCO TOCCHINI-VALENTINI.

Istituto di Biologia e Patologia Molecolari (Institute of Molecular Biology and Pathology): Piazzale Aldo Moro 5, 00185 Rome; tel. (6) 4940543; fax (6) 4440062; e-mail emilia.chiancone@uniroma1.it; internet www.ibpm.cnr.it; f. 2001; Dir Prof.ssa EMILIA CHIANCONE.

Istituto di Biomedicina e di Immunologia Molecolare 'Alberto Monroy' (Institute of Biomedicine and Molecular Immunology): Via Ugo La Malfa 153, 90146 Palermo; tel. 091-6809134; fax 091-6809122; e-mail bonsignore@ibim.cnr.it; internet www.ibim.cnr.it; f. 2001; Dir Prof. GIOVANNI BONSIGNORE.

Istituto di Biomembrane e Bioenergetica (Institute of Biomembrane and Bioe-

nergetics): Via Giovanni Amendola 165/A, 70126 Bari; tel. 080-5443389; fax 080-5443317; e-mail papabchm@cimedoc.uniba .it; f. 2001; Dir Prof. SERGIO PAPA.

Istituto di Biometeorologia (Institute for Biometeorology): Via Giovanni Caproni 8, 50145 Florence; tel. 055-301421; fax 055-308910; e-mail maracchi@ibimet.cnr.it; internet www.ibimet.cnr.it; f. 2000; Dir Prof. GIAMPIERO MARACCHI.

Istituto di Biostrutture e Bioimmagini (Institute of Biostructure and Bioimaging): Via Mezzocannone 16, 80134 Naples; tel. 081-2536651; fax 0825-34560; e-mail pedone@chemistry.unina.it; internet www .ibb.cnr.it; f. 2001; Dir Prof. CARLO PEDONE.

Istituto di Chimica Biomolecolare (Institute of Biomolecular Chemistry): Via Campi Flegrei 34, 80078 Pozzuoli; tel. 081-8675024; fax 081-8041770; e-mail gcimino@icmib.na.cnr.it; internet www .icmib.na.cnr.it; f. 2001; Dir Dott. GUIDO CIMINO.

Istituto di Chimica del Riconoscimento Molecolare (Institute of Chemistry of Molecular Recognition): Via Mario Bianco 9, 20131 Milan; tel. 02-28500024; fax 02-28901239; e-mail direttore@icrm .cnr.it; internet www.icrm.cnr.it; f. 2001; Dir Dott. GIACOMO CARREA.

Istituto per l'Endocrinologia e l'Oncologia 'Gaetano Salvatore' (Institute for Experimental Endocrinology and Oncology): Via Sergio Pansini 5, 80131 Naples; tel. 081-7463036; fax 081-7701016; e-mail consigli@ieos.cnr.it; internet ieos.cnr.it; f. 2001; Dir Prof. EDUARDO CONSIGLIO.

Istituto di Fisiologia Clinica (Institute of Clinical Physiology): Via Giuseppe Moruzzi 1, 56124 Pisa; tel. 050-3152216; fax 050-3152166; e-mail ldonato@ifc.cnr.it; internet www.ifc.cnr.it; f. 2001; Dir Prof. LUIGI DONATO.

Istituto di Genetica e Biofisica 'Adriano Buzzati Traverso' (Institute of Genetics and Biophysics): Via Pietro Castellino 111, 80131 Naples; tel. 081-6132401; fax 081-6132706; e-mail polito@ igb.cnr.it; internet www.igb.cnr.it; f. 2000; Dir Prof. CATELLO POLITO.

Istituto di Genetica Molecolare (Institute of Molecular Genetics): Via Abbiategrasso 207, 27100 Pavia; tel. 0382-5461; fax 0382-422286; e-mail riva@igbe.pv.cnr .it; internet www.igm.cnr.it; f. 2000; Dir Dott. SILVANO RIVA.

Istituto di Genetica delle Popolazioni (Institute of Population Genetics): Casella Postale, 07040 Santa Maria la Palma; tel. 079-946706; fax 079-946714; e-mail pirastu@igm.ss.cnr.it; f. 2001; Dir Dott. MARIO PIRASTU.

Istituto di Genetica Vegetale (Institute of Plant Genetics): Via Giovanni Amendola 165/A, 70126 Bari; tel. 080-5583400; fax 080-5587566; e-mail direttore.igv@igv.cnr .it; internet www.igv.cnr.it; f. 2001; Dir Prof. LUIGI MONTI.

Istituto di Neurobiologia e Medicina Molecolare (Institute of Neurobiology and Molecular Medicine): Viale Marx 15, 00137 Rome; tel. 06-86090246; fax 06-86090370; e-mail calissano@in.rm.cnr.it; f. 2000; Dir Prof. PIETRO CALISSANO.

Istituto di Neurogenetica e Neurofarmacologia (Institute of Neurogenetics and Neuropharmacology): Cittadella Universitaria di Cagliari, 09042 Monserrato CA Sardinia; tel. 070-6754543; fax 070-6754652; e-mail c.flore@inn.cnr.it; f. 2001; Dir Dr MARIA SERAFINA RISTALDI (acting).

Istituto di Neuroscienze (Neuroscience Institute): Via Giuseppe Moruzzi 1, 56124 Pisa; tel. 050-3153211; fax 050-3153220; e-mail maffei@in.cnr.it; internet www.in .cnr.it; f. 2001; Dir Prof. LAMBERTO MAFFEI.

Istituto per la Protezione delle Piante Consiglio Nazionale delle Ricerche (Plant Protection Institute): Via Madonna del Piano (edificio E), 50019 Sesto Fiorentino; tel. 055-5225589; fax 055-5225666; e-mail f.loreto@ipp.cnr.it; internet www .ipp.cnr.it; f. 2001; Dir Dott. FRANCESCO LORETO.

Istituto di Scienza dell'Alimentazione (Institute of Food Science): Via Roma 52 a/c, 83100 Avellino; tel. 0825-299111; fax 0825-781585; e-mail leone@isa.cnr.it; internet www.isa.cnr.it; f. 2001; Dir Prof. ANTONIO MALORNI.

Istituto di Scienze Neurologiche (Institute of Neurological Sciences): Località Burga, Piano Lago, 87050 Mangone; tel. 0984-98011; fax 0984-969306; e-mail a .quattrone@isn.cnr.it; internet www.isn .cnr.it; f. 2001; Dir Prof. ALDO QUATTRONE.

Istituto di Scienze delle Produzioni Alimentari (Institute of Food Production Sciences): Via Amendola 122/O, 70126 Bari; tel. 080-5929333; fax 080-5929373; e-mail angelo.visconti@ispa.cnr.it; internet www.ispa.cnr.it; f. 2001; Dir Dott. ANGELO VISCONTI.

Istituto di Scienze e Tecnologie della Cognizione (Institute of Cognitive Sciences and Technologies): Viale Carlo Marx 15, 00137 Rome; tel. 06-86090235; fax 06-824737; e-mail c.castelfranchi@istc.cnr.it; internet www.istc.cnr.it; f. 2001; Dir Prof. CRISTIANO CASTELFRANCHI.

Istituto per i Sistemi Agricoli e Forestali del Mediterraneo (Institute for Mediterranean Agriculture and Forest Systems): Via Patacca 85, 80056 Ercolano; tel. 081-7717325; fax 081-7718045; e-mail r .dandria@isafom.cnr.it; internet www .isafom.cnr.it; f. 2001; Dir Dr RICCARDO D'ANDRIA.

Istituto per il Sistema Produzione Animale in Ambiente Mediterraneo (Institute for Animal Production in the Mediterranean Environment): Via Argine 1085, 80147 Ponticelli; tel. 081-5966006; fax 081-5965291; e-mail lino@iabbam.na .cnr.it; internet www.iabbam.na.cnr.it; f. 2001; Dir Dott. LINO FERRARA.

Istituto di Tecnologie Biomediche (Institute of Biomedical Technologies): Via Fratelli Cervi 93, 20090 Segrate; tel. 02-26422702; fax 02-26422770; e-mail director@itb.cnr.it; internet www.itb.cnr .it; f. 2001; Dir Prof. ALBERTO ALBERTINI.

Istituto per i Trapianti d'Organo e Immunocitologia (Organ Tranplantation and Immunology Institute): Piazzale Collemaggio, 67100 L'Aquila; tel. 0862-27129; fax 0862-410758; e-mail d.adorno@itoi.cnr .it; internet www.itoi.cnr.it; f. 2001; Dir Prof. DOMENICO ADORNO.

Istituto di Virologia Vegetale (Institute of Plant Virology): Strada delle Cacce 73, 10135 Turin; tel. 011-39771; fax 011-343809; e-mail m.conti@ivv.cnr.it; internet www.ivv.cnr.it; f. 2001; Dir Prof. MAURIZIO CONTI.

Technological, Engineering and Information Sciences:

Consorzio RFX: Corso Stati Uniti 4, 35127 Padua; tel. 049-8295000; fax 049-8700718; e-mail segrgen@igi.cnr.it; internet www.igi.cnr.it; f. 1996; Dir Prof. FRANCESCO GNESOTTO.

Istituto di Analisi dei Sistemi ed Informatica 'Antonio Ruberti' (Institute for Systems Analysis and Computer Science): Viale Manzoni 30, 00185 Rome; tel. 06-77161; fax 06-7716461; e-mail bertolazzi@iasi.cnr.it; internet www.iasi .cnr.it; f. 2001; Dir Dott.ssa PAOLA BERTO-LAZZI.

Istituto di Calcolo e Reti ad Alte Prestazioni (Institute for High-performance Computing and Networking): Via Pietro Bucci, Cubo 41C, 87030 Rende; tel. 0984-831720; fax 0984-839054; e-mail sacca@icar.cnr.it; internet www.icar.cnr.it; f. 2001; Dir Prof. DOMENICO SACCÀ.

Istituto di Elettronica e di Ingegneria dell'Informazione e delle Telecomunicazioni (Institute of Electronics, Computer and Telecommunications Engineering): Corso Duca degli Abruzzi 24, 10129 Turin; tel. 011-5645400; fax 011-5645429; e-mail ajmone@polito.it; internet www.ieiit.cnr.it; f. 2001; Dir Prof. MARCO AJMONE MARSAN.

Istituto di Informatica e Telematica (Institute for Informatics and Telematics): Via Giuseppe Moruzzi 1, 56124 Pisa; tel. 050-3152112; fax 050-3152593; e-mail franco.denoth@iit.cnr.it; internet www.iit .cnr.it; f. 2001; Dir Prof. FRANCO DENOTH.

Istituto di Ingegneria Biomedica (Institute of Biomedical Engineering): Corso Stati Uniti 4, 35127 Padua; tel. 049-829570; fax 049-8295763; e-mail isib .cnr@polimi.it; internet www.isib.cnr.it; f. 2001; Dir Dott. FERDINANDO GRANDORI.

Istituto di Ricerche sulla Combustione (Institute for Research on Combustion): Piazzale Vincenzo Tecchio 80, 80125 Naples; tel. 081-7682245; fax 081-5936936; e-mail grusso@irc.na.cnr.it; internet www .irc.na.cnr.it; f. 2001; Dir Prof. GENNARO RUSSO.

Istituto di Scienza e Tecnologia dei Materiali Ceramici (Institute of Ceramics Science and Technology): Via Granarolo 64, 48018 Faenza; tel. 0546-699711; fax 0546-699719; e-mail babini@istec.cnr.it; internet www.istec.cnr.it; f. 2001; Dir Dott. GIAN NICOLA BABINI.

Istituto di Scienza e Tecnologie dell'Informazione 'Alessandro Faedo' (Institute of Information Science and Technology 'Alessandro Faedo'): Via Giuseppe Moruzzi 1, 56124 Pisa; tel. 050-3152878; fax 050-3152811; e-mail direttore@isti.cnr .it; internet www.isti.cnr.it; f. 2000; Dir Dr CLAUDIO MONTANI.

Istituto di Studi sui Sistemi Intelligenti per l'Automazione (Institute of Intelligent Systems for Automation): Via Giovanni Amendola 122/D-I, 70126 Bari; tel. 080-5929420; fax 080-5929460; e-mail distante@ba.issia.cnr.it; internet www .issia.cnr.it; f. 2001; Dir Dott. ARCANGELO DISTANTE.

Istituto di Tecnologie Avanzate per l'Energia 'Nicola Giordano' (Institute for Advanced Energy Technologies): Via Salita S. Lucia sopra Contesse 5, 98126 Messina; tel. 090-6241; fax 090-624247; e-mail cacciola@itae.cnr.it; internet www .itae.cnr.it; f. 2000; Dir Dott. Ing. GAETANO CACCIOLA.

Istituto di Tecnologie Industriali e Automazione (Institute of Industrial Technologies and Automation): Viale Lombardia 20A, 20131 Milan; tel. 02-23699995; fax 02-23699941; e-mail f.jovane@itia.cnr .it; internet www.itia.cnr.it; f. 2000; Dir Prof. FRANCESCO JOVANE.

Istituto Motori (Motors Institute): Via Marconi 8, 80125 Naples; tel. 081-7177111; fax 081-2396097; e-mail a.dilorenzo@im .cnr.it; internet www.im.cnr.it; f. 2001; Dir Dott. ALDO DI LORENZO.

Istituto Nazionale di Ricerca Metrologica (National Institute of Research in Metrology): Strada delle Cacce 91, 10135 Turin; tel. 011-39191; fax 011-346384; e-mail a.sacconi@imgc.cnr.it; internet www.inrim.it; f. 2006; science of measurements; researches materials; develops innovative technologies and devices; provides nat. measurements traceability to the SI; represents Italy in int. metrological organisms; library of 20,000 vols; Pres. Prof. ELIO BAVA.

Istituto Nazionale di Ottica Applicata (INOA) (National Institute of Applied Optics): Largo Enrico Fermi 6, 50125 Florence; tel. 055-23081; fax 055-2337755; e-mail direttore@ino.it; internet www.ino .it; f. 1927; quantum, instrumental and physiological optics; library of 7,000 vols; Pres. Prof. FABIO PISTELLA; Gen. Dir Dr CARLO CASTELLINI.

Istituto per le Macchine Agricole e Movimento Terra (Institute for Agricultural and Earth-moving Machines): Via Canal Bianco 28, 44124 Ferrara; tel. 0532-735611; fax 0532-735666; e-mail r .paoluzzi@imamoter.cnr.it; internet www .imamoter.cnr.it; f. 2001; Dir Ing. ROBERTO PAOLUZZI.

Istituto per il Rilevamento Elettromagnetico dell'Ambiente (Institute for Electromagnetic Sensing of the Environment): Via Diocleziano 328, 80124 Naples; tel. 081-5707999; fax 081-5705734; e-mail bucci.om@irea.cnr.it; internet www.irea .cnr.it; f. 2001; active microwave remote sensing; passive remote sensing in optics; modelling of electromagnetic interaction processes; multi source data fusion and integration for environmental monitoring; sensors and techniques for electromagnetic diagnostics; biological effects and clinical diagnostic and therapy applications related to electromagnetic fields; 36 mems; Dir Prof. OVIDIO MARIO BUCCI.

Istituto per la Valorizzazione del Legno e delle Specie Arboree (Tree and Timber Institute): Via Madonna del Piano snc, 50019 Sesto Fiorentino; tel. 055-52251; fax 055-5225507; e-mail ario .ceccotti@ivalsa.cnr.it; internet www .ivalsa.cnr.it; f. 2002; Dir Prof. ARIO CECCOTTI.

Istituto per le Tecnologie della Costruzione (Construction Technologies Institute): Via Lombardia 49, 20098 San Giuliano Milanese; tel. 02-98061; fax 02-98280088; e-mail valter.esposti@itc.cnr.it; internet www.itc.cnr.it; f. 2001; Dir Ing. VALTER ESPOSTI.

Istituto per le Tecnologie Didattiche-ITD (Institute for Educational Technology-ITD): Via De Marini 6, Torre di Francia, 16149 Genoa; tel. 010-6475303; fax 010-6475300; e-mail itd@itd.cnr.it; internet www.itd.cnr.it; f. 2001 by merging of Istituto per le Tecnologie Didattiche, based in Genoa and founded in 1970, and the Istituto Tecnologie Didattiche e Formative, established in 1993 in Palermo; research in educational technology; computer science, engineering, mathematics, physics, pedagogy, psychology, languages; library of 5,000 vols; Dir Dr ROSA BOTTINO; publ. *TD-Tecnologie Didattiche* (Italian, abstract in English, 3 a year).

AGRICULTURE, FISHERIES AND VETERINARY SCIENCE

Istituto Sperimentale per la Cerealicoltura (Experimental Institute for Cereal Crops): Via Cassia 176, 00191 Rome; tel. 06-3295705; fax 06-36306022; e-mail cerealicoltura@cerealicoltura.it; internet www.cerealicoltura.it; f. 1919; cereal crops improvement; cereal genetics; library of 10,000 vols, 318 current periodicals; Dir Dott. NATALE DI FONZO; publs *Journal of Genetics and Breeding* (4 a year), *Maydica* (maize and allied species, 4 a year).

Istituto Sperimentale per la Zoologia Agraria (Experimental Institute of Agricultural Zoology): Via Lanciola 12A, Cascine del Riccio, 50125 Florence; tel. 055-24921; fax 055-209177; e-mail isza@isza.it; internet www.isza.it; f. 1875; library of 55,000 vols; Dir Dott. MARCO VITTORIO COVASSI; publ. *Redia* (1 a year).

Ufficio Centrale di Ecologia Agraria (Meteorological and Ecological Centre): Via del Caravita 7A, 00186 Rome; tel. 06-695311; fax 06-69531215; e-mail ucea@ucea.it; internet www.ucea.it; f. 1876; controls 100 observatories; 18 mems; Dir Dott. DOMENICO VENTO; publs *Bollettino Agrometeorologico Nazionale* (12 a year), *Bollettino Avversità Meteo*, *Osservazioni Meteo Collegio Romano* (electronic, 1 a year), *Indici Agroclimatici: Velocità e direzione del vento*.

ECONOMICS, LAW AND POLITICS

Centro di Ricerche Economiche e Sociali (CERES) (Centre for Economic and Social Research): Via Po 102, 00198 Rome; tel. 06-8541016; fax 06-85355360; internet www.ce-res.org; f. 1970 as an autonomous body promoted by a trade union (CISL); improves economic and social conditions of workers; fosters contact and collaboration between nat. and int. centres and institutes interested in problems of economic and social devt; Pres. Prof. RENATA LIURAGHI; Sec.-Gen. Prof. GABRIELLA PAPPADA; publs *Benessere degli Anziani* (12 a year), *Quaderni di Economia del Lavoro* (3 a year).

Fondazione Giangiacomo Feltrinelli: Via Romagnosi 3, 20121 Milan; tel. 02-874175; fax 02-86461855; e-mail segretaria@fondazionefeltrinelli.it; internet www.feltrinelli.it/fondazione; f. 1949; history of international socialism, communism and the labour movement; economic and social history; library of 400,000 vols, 20,000 periodicals; Pres. CARLO FELTRINELLI.

Istituto Affari Internazionali (International Affairs Institute): Via Angelo Brunetti 9, 00186 Rome; tel. (6) 3224360; fax (6) 3224363; e-mail iai@iai.it; internet www.iai.it; f. 1965; promotes understanding of the problems of int. politics through studies, research, meetings and publications; library of 25,000 vols; Pres. STEFANO SILVESTRI; Exec. Vice-Pres. GIANNI BONVICINI; Dir and Legal Rep. ETTORE GRECO; publs *Affar Internazionali* (online, in Italian), *FP Global* (6 a year), *IAI Quaderni* (in English and Italian, 6 a year), *La politica estera dell'Italia* (yearbook, in Italian), *The International Spectator* (in English, 4 a year).

Istituto di Studi Europei 'Alcide De Gasperi': Via Poli 29, 00187 Rome; tel. 06-6784262; fax 06-6794101; e-mail kipsc@tin.it; internet www.ise-ies.org; f. 1953; promotes research and organizes meetings on legal, economic, political and social issues in the field of European co-operation and integration, and within a broader pan-European context; the Postgraduate School of European Studies organizes courses of varying duration and specialized seminars; courses are also held on the specialized English and French terminology of European int. orgs; library of 5,000 vols; Pres. Prof. Dott. GIUSEPPE SCHIAVONE; Admin. Officer CLAUDIA BATTISTI.

Istituto Italiano di Studi Legislativi (Italian Institute for Legislative Studies): Via del Corso 267, 00186 Rome; tel. 06-6789488; fax 06-69941306; e-mail gianpierorsello@inwind.it; f. 1925 to promote the scientific and technical studies of legislation; Pres. Prof. GIAN PIERO ORSELLO; Gen. Sec. Dssa FRANCA CIPRIGNO; publs *L'Italia e l'Europa*, *Yearbook of Comparative Law and Legislative Studies*.

Istituto Nazionale di Statistica (National Institute of Statistics): Via Cesare Balbo 16, 00184 Rome; tel. 06-46731; fax 06-46733107; internet www.istat.it; f. 1926; library of 500,000 vols, 2,700 current periodicals; Pres. LUIGI BIGGERI; Dir-Gen. P. GARONNA; publs *Annuario statistico italiano*, *Bollettino mensile di statistica* (12 a year).

Istituto per gli Studi di Politica Internazionale (Institute for the Study of International Politics): Palazzo Clerici, Via Clerici 5, 20121 Milan; tel. 02-8633131; fax 02-8692055; e-mail ispi.segreteria@ispionline .it; internet www.ispionline.it; f. 1933; public and private funding; aims to provide information and analysis of the great global issues of today, to identify opportunities for more effective Italian participation in int. affairs, to identify the domestic factors that constrain or enhance Italy's int. role; research in int. politics and economics, strategic problems and the history of foreign relations, European integration, int. economic cooperation, consolidation of peace and security among nations, strengthening of political freedoms and democratic instns; library of 100,000 vols, historical archive, press archive; postgraduate training courses; organizes conferences, lectures, etc.; Pres. BORIS BIANCHERI; Dir PAOLO MAGRI; publs *ISPI Relazioni Internazionali* (electronic, 3 a year), *L'Italia e la Politica Internazionale* (1 a year).

Istituto per le Relazioni tra l'Italia e i Paesi dell'Africa, America Latina e Medio Oriente (IPALMO) (Institute for Relations between Italy and the Countries of Africa, Latin America and the Middle East): email ipalmo@ipalmo.com; internet www .ipalmo.com; f. 1971 to promote and develop political, economic and cultural relations between countries in these regions; research and promotion of information at all levels of Italian society; to organize conferences, seminars, etc.; library of 20,000 vols, 500 periodicals; Pres. GIANNI DE MICHELIS; Scientific Dir UMBERTO TRIULZI; publ. *Politica Internazionale* (6 a year).

UNICEF Innocenti Research Centre: Piazza SS. Annunziata 12, 50122 Florence; tel. 055-20330; fax 055-2033220; e-mail florence@unicef.org; internet www.unicef-irc .org; f. 1988; conducts research vital to the work of the United Nations Children's Fund (UNICEF), especially in the field of children's rights; addresses emerging issues in areas of social and economic policies and implementation of int. standards for children in all countries; Deputy Dir DAVID PARKER.

EDUCATION

Istituto per Ricerche ed Attività Educative (Institute for Educational Research and Activity): Riviera di Chiaia 264, 80121 Naples; tel. 081-2457074; e-mail ipe@ ipeistituto.it; internet www.ipeistituto.it; f. 1979; aims to give young people access to education, culture and jobs; offers grants, promotes study and research in education; 32 mems; library of 6,500 vols; Pres. Prof. RAFFAELE CALABRÓ; Sec.-Gen. Dott. LORENZO BURDO; publ. *IPEnews* (12 a year).

FINE AND PERFORMING ARTS

Istituto Centrale per il Restauro (Central Institute for the Restoration of Works of Art): Piazza S. Francesco di Paola 9, 00184 Rome; tel. 06-488961; fax 06-4815704; e-mail icr@ arti.beniculturali.it; internet www.icr.arti .beniculturali.it; f. 1939; research on the influence of environment on cultural property and on prevention of deterioration; studies formulation of rules on theory of conservation and restoration and on techniques to be used; advises institutes of the Min. of Cultural Assets and Activities, and regional organizations; in-service teaching and refresher courses; carries out restoration of complex works or those of interest in research and teaching; library of 43,000 vols, 800 periodicals; archive of 51,600 negatives, 4,664 X-rays, 31,900 slides on restoration; Dir CATERINA BON VALSASSINA; publs *Bollettino ICR* (2 a year), *DIMOS* (series), preprints of International Conferences on non-destructive testing, micro-analytical methods and environment evaluation for study and conservation of works of art (every 5 years), *News.Icr* (electronic, Italian and English versions, 6 a year).

Istituto Internazionale per la Ricerca Teatrale (International Institute for Theatre Research): Casa di Goldoni, S. Tomà 2794, 30124 Venice; tel. 041-714883; f. 1953 by the Int. Fed. for Theatre Research; library of 30,000 vols; spec. collns: critical works, Italian and foreign dramatic works, Venetian musical theatre scores, periodicals, edns of the playwright Carlo Goldoni, Maddelena (miscellany), Ortolani miscellany, Vendramin Archive; Pres. Prof. CARMELO ALBERTI; Gen. Sec. Doc. MARIA IDA BIGGI.

Villa I Tatti/Harvard University Center for Italian Renaissance Studies: Via di Vincigliata 26, 50135 Florence; tel. 055-603251; fax 055-603383; e-mail info@itatti .it; internet www.itatti.it; f. 1961; fmr residence of Bernard Berenson, who left his library and art colln to Harvard; offers postdoctoral study of the Italian Renaissance: history of art, political, economic and social history, history of philosophy and religion, history of literature, music and science; library of 150,000 vols, 500 current periodicals, 300,000 photographs; Dir JOSEPH CONNORS; publ. *I Tatti Studies* (every 2 years).

HISTORY, GEOGRAPHY AND ARCHAEOLOGY

Academia Belgica (Belgian Academy in Rome): Via Omero 8, 00197 Rome; tel. 06-20398631; fax 06-3208361; e-mail direttore@ academiabelgica.it; internet www .academiabelgica.it; f. 1939; research centre and residence; congress centre; promotion of science and culture from Belgium and its Regions; library of 80,000 vols; Dir Prof. WALTER GEERTS; publ. *Belgian Historical Institute in Rome* (series and annual bulletin since 1919).

Accademia di Danimarca (Danish Institute of Science and Art in Rome): Via Omero 18, 00197 Rome; tel. 06-3265931; fax 06-3222717; e-mail accademia@acdan.it; internet www.acdan.it; f. 1956; archaeology, philology, art and architecture, history of art, history of music, literature; library of 25,000 vols; Dir Dr ERIK BACH (acting); Sec. and Librarian Dr MARIA ADELAIDE ZOCCHI; publ. *Analecta Romana Instituti Danici*.

Accademia Tedesca (German Academy in Rome): Villa Massimo, Largo di Villa Massimo 1–2, 00161 Rome; tel. 06-4425931; fax

06-44259355; e-mail villamassimo.roma@katamail.com; Dir Dr JOACHIM BLÜHER.

American Academy in Rome: Via Angelo Masina 5, 00153 Rome; tel. 06-58461; fax 06-5810788; f. 1894; fellowships for independent study and advanced research in fine arts, classical studies, art history, Italian studies and archaeology; library of 135,000 vols; Pres. ADELE CHATFIELD-TAYLOR; Dir CARMELA VIRCILLO FRANKLIN; Librarian CHRISTINA HUEMER; publ. *Memoirs* (1 a year).

British Institute of Florence: Piazza Strozzi 2, 50123 Florence; tel. 055-26778200; fax 055-26778222; e-mail info@britishinstitute.it; internet www.britishinstitute.it; f. 1917; develops cultural understanding between the UK and Italy through the teaching of their respective languages and cultures; offers a range of Italian language and history of art courses, and an extensive programme of English language courses for the host population; a number of special programmes are run in conjunction with British and American univs; archive containing material relating to the British community in Tuscany in 19th and early 20th centuries incl. the Waterfield family, Susan Horner, Maquay family, Edward Gordon Craig and Edward Hutton; Vernon Lee colln contains a number of books from her library with her annotations; library of 50,000 vols; 1,700 students; Dir VANESSA HALL-SMITH.

British School at Rome: Via Gramsci 61, 00197 Rome; tel. 06-3264939; fax 06-3221201; e-mail info@bsrome.it; internet www.bsr.ac.uk; f. 1901, inc. by Royal Charter 1912; postgraduate residential centre for higher research in the humanities and for the practice of the fine arts and architecture; 40 residents; library of 60,000 vols, 600 current periodicals; Dir Prof. C. J. SMITH; Librarian VALERIE SCOTT; publ. *Papers of the British School at Rome* (1 a year).

Centro Camuno di Studi Preistorici (Centre for Prehistoric Studies): Via Marconi 7, 25044 Capo di Ponte Valcamonica; tel. 0364-42091; fax 0364-42572; e-mail ccspreist@tin.it; internet www.ccsp.it; f. 1964; research centre specializing in prehistoric rock art; archaeological research, early religions, anthropology and ethnology; seminars, int. symposia, individual tutoring in prehistoric and tribal art; coordinator of World Archives of Rock Art; provides advisers and consultants on conservation, exhibition and evaluation of prehistoric and tribal art; park and museum planning; field research in Europe, Asia and Australia; Valcamonica summer school; library of 38,000 vols, 300,000 photographs; Dir Prof. EMMANUEL ANATI; publs *Archivi*, *BCSP: The World Journal of Prehistoric and Tribal Art*.

Centro Italiano di Studi sul Basso Medioevo – Accademia Tudertina: Via Ciuffelli 31, 06059 Todi; tel. 075-8942521; all aspects of late medieval civilization; Pres. Prof. TULLIO GREGORY; Dir Prof. ENRICO MENESTÒ.

Deutsches Archäologisches Institut Rom (German Archaeological Institute Rome): Via Sardegna 79, 00187 Rome; tel. 06-4888141; fax 06-4884973; e-mail sekretariat@rom.dainst.org; internet www.dainst.org; f. 1829; library of 220,000 vols, 1,200 current periodicals; Dirs Prof. Dr HENNER VON HESBERG, Prof. Dr KLAUS S. FREYBERGER; Library Dir Dr THOMAS FRÖHLICH; publs *Römische Mitteilungen*, *Series*, *Sonderschriften des Deutschen Archäologischen Instituts Rom*.

Ecole Française de Rome/Scuola Francese di Roma (French School in Rome): Piazza Farnese 67, 00186 Rome; tel. 06-686011; fax 06-6874834; f. 1873; French school of archaeology and history, specializing in Rome and medieval and modern Italy; library of 180,000 vols, 1,650 periodicals and 32,000 off-prints; Dir MICHEL GRAS; Dirs of Studies JEAN-FRANÇOIS CHAUVARD, MARILYN NICOUD, YANN RIVIÈRE; Librarian YANNICK NEXON; publ. *Mélanges de l'Ecole Française de Rome* (series *Antiquité, Moyen Age, Italie et Méditerranée*).

Escuela Española de Historia y Arqueología, CSIC Roma (Spanish School of History and Archaeology in Rome): Via di Torre Argentina 18-3°, 00186 Rome; tel. 06-6810001; fax 06-68309047; e-mail escuela@csic.it; internet www.csic.it; f. 1910; history of Italian-Spanish interaction; organizes confs, seminars; research programmes and support for Spanish historians and archaeologists in Italy; 15 mems; library of 20,000 vols; special collns: Monumenta Albornotiana, documents on Spanish music in Italy; Dir Prof. RICARDO OLMOS ROMERA.

Fondazione Centro Italiano di Studi sull'Alto Medioevo (Central Italian Foundation for Studies on Early Medieval Civilization): Palazzo Ancaiani, Piazza della Libertà 12, 06049 Spoleto; tel. 0743-225630; fax 0743-49902; e-mail cisam@cisam.org; internet www.cisam.org; f. 1951; promotes research, conferences and scientific publications on all aspects of early medieval civilization; library of 3,000 vols; Pres. Prof. ENRICO MENESTÒ; publ. *Studi Medievali III Serie* (4 a year).

Institutum Romanum Finlandiae: Passeggiata del Gianicolo 10, 00165 Rome; tel. 06-68801674; fax 06-68802349; e-mail orma@irfrome.org; internet www.irfrome.org; f. 1954; Classical and Italian studies; library of 19,000 vols; Dir Prof. KAJ SANDBERG; publ. *Acta Instituti Romani Finlandiae*.

Istituto di Norvegia in Roma (Norwegian Institute in Rome): Viale Trenta Aprile 33, 00153 Rome; tel. 06-58391007; fax 06-5880604; internet www.hf.uio.no/roma; f. 1959; library of 24,000 vols; Dir T. K. SEIM; publ. *Acta ad Archaeologiam et Artium Historiam Pertinentia* (1 a year).

Istituto Ellenico di Studi Bizantini e Postbizantini di Venezia (Hellenic Institute of Byzantine and Post-Byzantine Studies of Venice): Castello 3412, 30122 Venice; tel. 041-5226581; fax 041-5238248; internet www.institutoellenico.org; f. 1951; library of 25,000 vols, and archives containing 200,000 documents from 16th–19th centuries relating to the Greek Orthodox community of Venice; Dir CHRYSSA MALTEZOU; Sec. DEMETRA FARASI; publ. *Thesaurismata* (1 a year).

Istituto Italiano di Studi Germanici (Italian Institute for Germanic Studies): Via Calandrelli 25, 00153 Rome; tel. 06-588811; fax 06-5888139; e-mail chiarini@studigermanici.it; internet www.studigermanici.it; f. 1932; library of 80,000 vols; Dir Prof. PAOLO CHIARINI; publs *Atti, Poeti e prosatori tedeschi, Strumenti, Studi e ricerche, Studi Germanici* (3 a year), *Wissenschaftliche Reihen: Testi e Materiali*.

Istituto Italiano per gli Studi Storici (Italian Institute for Historical Studies): Via Benedetto Croce 12, 80134 Naples; tel. 081-5512390; fax 081-5514813; e-mail istituto@iiss.it; internet www.iiss.it; f. 1947; studies and teaching in history, philosophy and the humanities; awards 20 student grants annually and offers scholarships to Italian and non-Italian postgraduates; library of 130,000 vols, 1,500 periodicals, 400 current periodicals; Pres. Prof. NATALINO IRTI; Dir Prof. GENNARO SASSO; Gen. Sec. Dott.ssa MARTA HERLING; Librarian Dott.ssa ELLI CATELLO; publs *Annali* (1 a year), *Carteggi di Bene-*

detto Croce (2 a year), *Collana delle monografie* (2 a year), *Inventari* (1 a year), *Ristampe Anastatiche* (4 a year), *Saggi e Studi, Testi storici filosofici e letterari* (1 a year).

Istituto Nazionale di Studi Romani (National Institute of Roman Studies): Piazza dei Cavalieri di Malta 2, 00153 Rome; tel. 06-5743442; fax 06-5743447; e-mail studiromani@studiromani.it; internet www.studiromani.it; f. 1925; promotes the study of Rome from ancient to modern times in all aspects; 120 mems; library of 26,000 vols, 1,500 periodicals; Pres. Prof. MARIO MAZZA; Dir Dott. FERNANDA ROSCETTI; publs *Rassegna d'Informazioni* (12 a year), *Studi Romani* (4 a year).

Istituto Nazionale di Studi sul Rinascimento (National Institute of Renaissance Studies): Palazzo Strozzi, 50123 Florence; tel. 055-287728; fax 055-280563; e-mail insr@iris.firenze.it; internet www.insr.it; f. 1938; publishes critical texts and results of research; 10-mem. ccl; library of 45,000 vols, 500 periodicals, special colln 'Machiavelli-Serristori', art photo library of 78,000 items, 700 microfilms; Pres. Prof. MICHELE CILIBERTO; publ. *Rinascimento* (1 a year).

Istituto Papirologico 'Girolamo Vitelli' (Papyrological Institute): Borgo degli Albizi 12–14, 50122 Florence; tel. 055-2478969; fax 055-2480722; f. 1908; study of Greek and Latin papyri; library of 20,000 vols; colln of papyri; Scientific Dir Prof. GUIDO BASTIANINI; publs *Comunicazioni, Notiziario di Studi e Ricerche in Corso, Papiri Greci e Latini della Società Italiana, Studi e Testi di Papirologia*.

Istituto Siciliano di Studi Bizantini e Neoellenici 'B. Lavagnini' (Sicilian Institute for Byzantine and Neo-hellenic Studies): Via Noto 34, 90141 Palermo; tel. 6259541; fax 308996; e-mail istbizantino@issbi.org; f. 1952; 120 mems (60 ordinary, 60 corresp.); library of 10,000 vols; Pres. Prof. VINCENZO ROTOLO; Sec.-Gen. Prof. RENATA LAVAGNINI.

Istituto Storico Austriaco a Roma (Austrian Historical Institute in Rome): Viale Bruno Buozzi 113, 00197 Rome; tel. 06-36082601; fax 06-3224296; e-mail info@oehirom.it; internet www.oehirom.it; f. 1881; Dir Dr RICHARD BOESEL; publs *Publikationen des Historischen Instituts beim ÖKI in Rom* (irregular), *Römische Historische Mitteilungen* (1 a year).

Istituto Storico Germanico di Roma/Deutsches Historisches Institut in Rom (German Historical Institute in Rome): Via Aurelia Antica 391, 00165 Rome; tel. 06-6604921; fax 06-6623838; e-mail verwaltung@dhi-roma.it; internet www.dhi-roma.it; f. 1888; medieval, modern and contemporary history; history of music; library of 222,300 vols, 861 current periodicals; Dir Prof. Dr MICHAEL MATHEUS; Head Librarian Dr THOMAS MENZEL; publs *Analecta musicologica, Bibliographische Informationen zur neuesten Geschichte Italiens, Bibliothek des Deutschen Historischen Instituts, Quellen und Forschungen aus italienischen Archiven und Bibliotheken, Ricerche dell'Istituto Storico Germanico di Roma*.

Real Colegio de San Clemente de los Españoles (Royal College of Spain): Via del Collegio di Spagna 4, 40123 Bologna; tel. 051-330408; f. 1364 under Will of Cardinal Don Gil de Albornoz; study centre for 20 Spanish postgraduates; library of 25,000 vols; Rector Prof. Dr JOSÉ GUILLERMO GARCÍA VALDECASAS; publ. *Studia Albornotiana* (irregular).

Reale Istituto Neerlandese a Roma (Royal Netherlands Institute): Via Omero 10–12, 00197 Rome; tel. 06-3269621; fax 06-3204971; e-mail info@knir.it; internet www.knir.it; f. 1904; classical archaeology, history of art, history of Rome and Italy; residence for scholars from Dutch univs; library of 50,000 vols; Dir Prof. Dr BERNARD STOLTE; publ. *Fragmenta* (1 a year).

Svenska Institutet i Rom (Swedish Institute in Rome): Via Omero 14, 00197 Rome; tel. 06-3201966; fax 06-3230265; internet www.isvroma.org; f. 1926; library of 60,000 vols; Swedish courses for students of classical archaeology and history of art; fellowships in classical philology, archaeology, architecture, history of art and conservation; excavations at various sites in Italy; Dir Prof. BARBRO SANTILLO FRIZELL; publs *Acta Instituti Romani Regni Sueciae, Opuscula Romana, Suecoromana*.

MEDICINE

Istituto di Ricerche Farmacologiche 'Mario Negri' (Institute of Pharmacological Research): Via Eritrea 62, 20157 Milan; tel. 02-390141; fax 02-3546277; e-mail mnegri@ marionegri.it; internet www.marionegri.it; f. 1961; non-profit org. for research and education in pharmacology and biomedicine; library of 8,848 scientific publications; Pres. Dott. PAOLO MARTELLI; Dir Prof. SILVIO GARATTINI; publs *Negri News* (12 a year), *Research and Practice* (6 a year).

Istituto Nazionale di Ricerca per gli Alimenti e la Nutrizione (National Institute for Research on Food and Nutrition): Via Ardeatina 546, 00178 Rome; tel. 06-514941; fax 06-51494550; e-mail dgferrari@inran.it; internet inn.ingrm.it; f. 1936 as part of CNR, independent 1958 on budget of Min. of Agricultural Resources, supported by contracts and grants from Min. of Health, CNR and int. bodies; biological research in human nutrition, analyses and surveys on composition and nutritive value of foods; Pres. Prof. FERDINANDO ROMANO; Gen. Dir Dr PATRIZIA FERRARI.

Istituto Nazionale per la Ricerca sul Cancro (National Institute for Cancer Research): Largo Rosanna Benzi 10, 16132 Genoa; tel. 010-56001; fax 010-358032; internet www.istge.it; f. 1978; research in all fields of cancer prevention, diagnosis, cure and rehabilitation; holds conferences, seminars, training courses; library of 1,808 books, 148 periodicals; Chief Exec. Dr MAURIZIO MAURI; Scientific Dir RICCARDO ROSSO; publ. *IST Insieme* (6 a year).

Istituto Superiore di Sanità (Higher Institute of Health): Viale Regina Elena 299, 00161 Rome; tel. 06-49901; fax 06-49387118; e-mail web@iss.it; internet www .iss.it; f. 1934; aims to promote public health through scientific research, surveys, controls and analytical tests in the various fields of health sciences; library of 200,000 vols, 3,500 current periodicals; Pres. Prof. ENRICO GARACI; Dir-Gen. Dr SERGIO LICHERI; publs *Annali dell' Istituto Superiore di Sanità* (4 a year), *Istisan Congressi* (5 a year), *Notiziario dell' Istituto Superiore di Sanità* (12 a year), *Rapporti ISTISAN* (40 a year), *Strumenti di Riferimento* (irregular).

NATURAL SCIENCES
General
Istituto per l'Interscambio Scientifico (Institute for Scientific Interchange): Viale Settimo Severo 65, 10133 Turin; tel. 011-6603090; fax 011-6600049; internet www.isi .it; f. 1982; promotes basic research in molecular biology, chemistry, computer sciences, economics, mathematics, theoretical physics; Pres. Prof. TULLIO REGGE; Exec. Dir TIZIANA BERTOLETTI.

Biological Sciences
Herbarium Universitatis Florentinae—Sezione Botanica, Museo di Storia Naturale Università di Firenze: Via La Pira 4, 50121 Florence; tel. 055-2757462; f. 1842; systematic botany, plant geography; Dir Dr PIERO CUCCUINI; publ. *Pubblicazioni del Museo Botanico*.

Stazione Zoologica 'Anton Dohrn' (Zoological Station 'Anton Dohrn'): Villa Comunale, 80121 Naples; tel. (81) 5833111; fax (81) 7641355; e-mail stazione.zoologica@szn.it; internet www.szn.it; f. 1872; conducts biological research on marine organisms and marine ecosystems; library of 90,000 vols, 159 periodicals, 1,000 electronic resources; Pres. Prof. ROBERTO DI LAURO; Dir-Gen. Ing. MARCO CINQUEGRANI; publs *History and Philosophy of Life Sciences, Marine Ecology*.

Mathematical Sciences
Istituto Nazionale di Alta Matematica Francesco Severi (National Institute of Higher Mathematics): Piazzale Aldo Moro 5, 00185 Rome; tel. 06-490320; fax 06-4462293; e-mail indam@altamatematica.it; internet www.altamatematica.it; f. 1939; promotes training of researchers in mathematics, conducts research in pure and applied mathematics; Pres. Prof. CORRADO DE CONCINI; publs *Rendiconti di Matematica, Symposia Mathematica*.

Physical Sciences
Comitato Glaciologico Italiano (Italian Glaciological Committee): Corso Massimo D'Azeglio 42, 10125 Turin; tel. 011-3977251; fax 011-6707155; e-mail comitato@glaciologia .it; internet www.glaciologia.it; f. 1895; glaciology and alpine climatology; library of 700 books, 15,000 photographs; Pres. Prof. CARLO BARONI; Gen. Sec. Dr GIOVANNI MORTARA; publ. *Geografia Fisica e Dinamica quaternaria* (2 a year).

Dipartimento di Ingegneria Nucleare, Centro Studi Nucleari Enrico Fermi (CESNEF) (E. Fermi Centre for Nuclear Studies): Politecnico di Milano, Via Ponzio 34/3, 20133 Milan; tel. 02-23996300; fax 02-23996309; internet www.cesnef.polimi.it; f. 1957; one of the Departments of the Politecnico di Milano; trains technical personnel in the fields of nuclear energy, physics of materials, and electronics; library of 7,000 vols, 31 current periodicals; Dir Prof. GIUSEPPE CAGLIOTI.

INAF—Osservatorio Astronomico di Trieste (National Institute for Astrophysics—Trieste Astronomical Observatory): Via Tiepolo 11, 34143 Trieste; tel. 040-3199111; fax 040-309418; e-mail segreteria@oats.inaf .it; internet www.ts.astro.it; f. 1753; attached to Istituto Nazionale di Astrofisica; research in astrophysics, astrophysical techniques; 65 staff with further 21 researchers working on temporary basis (fixed-term contractors, postdoctoral fellows and other fellowship holders); library of 23,900 vols, 300 periodicals; Dir Prof. STEFANO CRISTIANI.

Istituto Gemmologico Italiano (Italian Gemmological Institute): Piazza San Sepolcro, 1, 20123 Milan, Lombardy; tel. 02-80504992; fax 02-80505765; e-mail info@igi .it; internet www.igi.it; f. 1973; courses in gemmology, laboratory analysis, research; 1,500 mems; Pres. GIAN-MARIA BUCCELLATI.

Istituto Idrografico della Marina (Naval Institute of Hydrography): Passo dell'Osservatorio 4, 16100 Genoa; tel. 010-24431; fax 010-261400; e-mail iim.sre@marina.difesa.it; internet www.marina.difesa.it/idro; f. 1872; library of 35,000 vols; Library Dir P. PRESCIUTTINI BELLEZZA.

Istituto Italiano di Speleologia: Dip. Scienze della Terra e Geologico-Ambientali, Via Zamboni 67, 40127 Bologna; tel. 051-2094547; fax 051-2094522; e-mail paolo .forti@unibo.it; f. 1929; exploration and scientific research in natural caves; 5 mems; library of 65,000 vols; Dir Prof. PAOLO FORTI; publ. *Memorie* (irregular).

Istituto Nazionale di Astrofisica: Viale del Parco Mellini 84, 00136 Rome; tel. 06-355331; fax 06-35533219; e-mail inaf@inaf.it; internet www.inaf.it; promotes, carries out and co-ordinates research in the fields of astronomy, radioastronomy, spatial astrophysics and cosmic physics; has observatories in: Bologna, Cagliari, Catania, Florence, Milan, Naples, Padua, Palermo, Rome, Teramo, Trieste and Turin; finances the Telescopio Nazionale Galileo (q.v.) located on La Palma, Canary Islands; has a part ownership in the Large Binocular Telescope at the Mount Graham Int. Observatory (q.v.), AZ, USA; Pres. Prof. SERGIO DE JULIO.

Istituto Nazionale di Fisica Nucleare (INFN) (National Institute of Nuclear Physics): Via Enrico Fermi 40, 00044 Rome; tel. 06-6840031; fax 06-68307924; e-mail prot_ac@inf.infn.it; internet www.infn.it; f. 1951; promotes and undertakes research in fundamental nuclear physics; consists of: Central Administration (Frascati), 19 sections, 4 National Laboratories (Frascati, Legnaro, Gran Sasso (L'Aquila), Catania), the National Centre for Informatics and Networking (CNAF Bologna) and 8 groups; the sections are at the Institutes of Physics at the Universities of Turin, Milan, Padua, Genoa, Trieste, Bologna, Pisa, Pavia, Florence, Rome, Rome II, Rome III, Naples, Bari, Catania, Cagliari, Ferrara, Perugia, Lecce; the groups are at the Institutes of Physics at the Universities of Parma, Trento, Udine, Salerno, Messina, L'Aquila, Cosenza, Sanità; Pres. ROBERTO PETRONZIO.

Istituto Nazionale di Geofisica e Vulcanologia (National Institute of Geophysics and Volcanology): Via di Vigna Murata 605, 00143 Rome; tel. 06-518601; fax 06-5041181; e-mail info@ingv.it; internet www.ingv.it; f. 1936; seismology, geomagnetism, aeronomy, environmental geophysics; library of 6,000 vols, 150 current periodicals; Pres. Prof. ENZO BOSCHI; publs *Annali di Geofisica* (6 a year), *Annuario geomagnetico, Bollettino dei valori istantanei alle ore 0, Bollettino indici K* (12 a year), *Bollettino ionosferico* (12 a year), *Bollettino macrosismico* (1 a year), *Bollettino sismico* (4 a year), *Tavole di previsione ionosferica* (26 a year), *2* (3 a year).

Istituto Nazionale di Oceanografia e di Geofisico Sperimentale (National Institute for Oceanography and Experimental Geophysics): Borgo Grotta Gigante 42/C, 34010 Sgonico; tel. 040-21401; fax 040-327307; e-mail mailbox@ogs.trieste.it; internet www.ogs.trieste.it; f. 1958; library of 3,000 vols; Pres. Prof. IGINIO MARSON; publ. *Bollettino di Geofisica Teorica e Applicata* (4 a year).

Laboratori Nazionali di Frascati dell' INFN (National Laboratories of INFN, Frascati): Via E. Fermi 40, 00044 Frascati; tel. 06-94031; fax 06-94032582; e-mail dirlnf@lnf .infn.it; internet www.lnf.infn.it; f. 1953; 450 MeV Linear accelerator for electrons and positrons, 1.5 GeV electron positron storage ring; theoretical research group, high-energy and nuclear physics research, electronics and radio-frequency laboratory, laboratory of technology and vacuum; library of 20,000 vols; Dir MARIO CALVETTI.

Osservatorio Astronomico di Capodimonte (Astronomical Observatory at Capodimonte): Salita Moiariello 16, 80131 Naples; tel. 081-5575111; fax 081-456710; e-mail capaccioli@na.astro.it; internet www.na .astro.it; f. 1819; uses a 1.6 m mirror telescope for studies and research; library of 24,000 vols; Dir Prof. MASSIMO CAPACCIOLI; publ. *Annuario* (online, 1 a year).

Osservatorio Astronomico di Padova (Padua Astronomical Observatory): Vicolo dell' Osservatorio 5, 35122 Padua; tel. 049-8293411; fax 049-8759840; e-mail oa-padova@pd.astro.it; internet www.pd .astro.it; f. 1767; attached to Istituto Nazionale di Astrofisica; library of 10,000 vols; Dir Prof. MASSIMO CALVANI.

Osservatorio Astronomico di Roma (Rome Astronomical Observatory): Viale del Parco Mellini 84, 00136 Rome; tel. 06-35347056; fax 06-35347802 and at Via Frascati 33, 00040 Monteporzio Catone; tel. 06-9428641; fax 06-9447243; e-mail buonanno@mporzio.astro.it; internet www.mporzio.astro .it; f. 1923; library of 25,000 vols, 51 astronomical and astrophysical periodicals; astronomical museum; attached astronomical station at Campo Imperatore; Dir Prof. ROBERTO BUONANNO; publ. *Solar Phenomena*.

Osservatorio Vesuviano (Vesuvius Observatory): Via Diocleziano 328, 80124 Naples; tel. 081-6108483; fax 081-6100811; e-mail info@ov.ingv.it; internet www.ov.ingv.it; f. 1841; chiefly concerned with monitoring the active volcanic areas of Mount Vesuvius, Campi Flegrei Caldera and the island of Ischia; Dir Prof. GIOVANNI MACEDONIO; publs *Monitoring Report* (online, irregular), *Open File Report* (online, 1 a year).

PHILOSOPHY AND PSYCHOLOGY

Centro Superiore di Logica e Scienze Comparate (Centre for Logic and Comparative Science): Via Belmeloro 3, 40126 Bologna; f. 1969; promotes the study of logic and contributes to research in this field; 1,250 mems; library and archives; Pres. Prof. FRANCO SPISANI.

Istituto di Studi Filosofici 'Enrico Castelli' (Institute of Philosophy): Via Nomentana 118, c/o Facoltà di Filosofia, Università, 00161 Rome; tel. 06-44238062; f. 1939; Chair. JEAN-LUC MARION; Dir Prof. PIERLUIGI VALENZA; publs *Archivio di Filosofia* (4 a year), *Bibliografia filosofica Italiana*, *Edizione Naz. A. Rosmini*, *Edizione Naz. dei Classici del pensiero italiano*, *Edizione Naz. V. Gioberti*, *Settimana di studi filosofici internazionali* (1 a year).

RELIGION, SOCIOLOGY AND ANTHROPOLOGY

Fondazione di Ricerca 'Istituto Carlo Cattaneo' ('Istituto Carlo Cattaneo' Research Foundation): Via Santo Stefano 11, 40125 Bologna; tel. 051-239766; fax 051-262959; e-mail istitutocattaneo@cattaneo .org; internet www.cattaneo.org; f. 1965; studies and researches in the field of social science with particular regard to education, electoral behaviour, politics, crime, terrorism, family, immigration and public policy; Pres. Prof. RAIMONDO CATANZARO; Dir Prof. GIANCARLO GASPERONI; Deputy Dir Prof. GIANFRANCO BALDINI; publs *Cattaneo* (irregular), *Cultura in Italia* (1 a year), *Elezioni,- Governi, Democrazia* (irregular), *Italian Politics—A Review* (1 a year), *Misure/Materiali di ricerca dell'Istituto Carlo Cattaneo* (irregular), *Polis-Ricerche e studi su società e politica in Italia* (3 a year), *Stranieri in Italia* (irregular).

Istituto Italiano di Antropologia (Italian Institute of Anthropology): Università di Roma 'La Sapienza', Dipart. di Biologia Animale e dell'Uomo, P.le Aldo Moro 5,

00185 Rome; tel. 06-49912273; fax 06-49912771; e-mail isita@uniroma1.it; internet www.isita-org.com; f. 1893 as Società Romana di Antropologia; adopted current name in 1937; promotes interdisciplinary approach to anthropology, which encompasses a synthesis of the biological, social and cultural aspects of human evolution; organizes scientific meetings; runs courses and seminars; 120 mems; library of 6,500 vols; Pres. BERNARDINO FANTINI; Sec. Assoc. Prof. GIOVANNI DESTRO-BISOL; publ. *Journal of Anthropological Sciences* (1 a year).

Istituto Italiano per l'Africa e l'Oriente (IsIAO) (Italian Institute for Africa and the East): Via Ulisse Aldrovandi 16, 00197 Rome; tel. 06-328551; e-mail info@isiao.it; internet www.isiao.it; f. 1995; Pres. Prof. GHERARDO GNOLI; Gen. Dir GIANCARLO GARGARUTI; a library and museum of oriental art are attached to the Institute; publs *Africa* (4 a year), *Archaeological reports*, *Cina* (1 a year), *East and West* (in English, 4 a year), *Il Giappone* (1 a year), *Ming Qing Yanjiu* (1 a year), *Reports and Memoirs*, *Restorations*, *Rome Oriental Series*, *Yemen* (irregular).

Istituto Luigi Sturzo: Via delle Coppelle 35, 00186 Rome; tel. 06-6840421; fax 06-68404244; e-mail segretaria@sturzo.it; internet www.sturzo.it; f. 1951; sociological and historical research; library of 120,000 vols; Pres. Dott. ROBERTO MAZZOTTA; Sec.-Gen. Dott. FLAVIA NARDELLI; publs *Civitas* (3 a year), *Sociologia* (3 a year).

Istituto per l'Oriente C. A. Nallino: Via Alberto Caroncini 19, 00197 Rome; tel. (6) 8084106; fax (6) 8079395; e-mail ipocan@ ipocan.it; internet www.ipocan.it; f. 1921; researches on modern and ancient Near East; library of 35,000 vols, 300 periodicals; Pres. Prof. CLAUDIO LO JACONO; publs *Eurasian Studies* (2 a year), *Oriente Moderno* (2 a year), *Quaderni di Studi Arabi* (1 a year), *Rassegna di Studi Etiopici* (1 a year).

TECHNOLOGY

Centro Radioelettrico Sperimentale 'Guglielmo Marconi' (Marconi Experimental Radio-electric Centre): Padriciano 99, 34012 Trieste; tel. 040-3755517; fax 040-3755519; internet marconi.area.trieste.it; f. 1933; attached to the Istituto Superiore delle Poste e Telecomunicazioni; experimental research on radio waves; Pres. Prof. GIANCARLO CORAZZA.

Centro Sviluppo Materiali SpA: Via di Castel Romano 100, 00128 Rome; tel. 06-5055829; fax 06-5055202; e-mail info@c-s-m .it; internet www.c-s-m.it; f. 1963; reference centre for innovation in materials and in related production, design and application technologies; library of 40,000 vols; Man. Dir Dr R. BRUNO; Gen. Man. Dr A. MASCANZONI.

Ente per le Nuove Tecnologie, l'Energia e l'Ambiente (ENEA) (Agency for New Technology, Energy and the Environment): Lungotevere Thaon di Revel 76, 00196 Rome; tel. 06-36271; fax 06-36272591; internet www .enea.it; f. 1960; scientific research and technological devt, implementing advanced research programmes and conducting complex projects for Italy's social and economic devt; library of 250,000 vols; Pres. Prof. CARLO RUBBIA; Gen. Dir Ing. GIOVANNI LELLI; publs *Energia Ambiente e Innovazione* (6 a year), *Rapporto Energia e Ambiente* (online, 1 a year).

Fondazione Guglielmo Marconi (Guglielmo Marconi Foundation): Via Celestini 1, 40044 Pontecchio Marconi; tel. 051-846121; fax 051-846951; e-mail fgm@fgm.it; internet www.fgm.it; f. 1938; research in telecommunications; library of 3,500 vols; Chair. Prof. GABRIELE FALCIASECCA.

Istituto Elettrotecnico Nazionale 'Galileo Ferraris' (Galileo Ferraris National Electrotechnical Institute): Strada delle Cacce 91, 10135 Turin; tel. 011-39191; fax 011-346384; e-mail info@ien.it; internet www .ien.it; f. 1934; carries out research in metrology and on new materials and devices; tests materials, components and apparatus; contributes to education and training of students; 155 mems; library of 11,000 vols, 1,000 periodicals, CEI standards; Pres. ELIO BAVA; Gen. Dir PAOLO A. MASTROENI; publ. *Scientific Report* (1 a year).

Istituto Nazionale per Studi ed Esperienze di Architettura Navale (National Institute of Naval Architecture Studies and Experiments): Via di Vallerano 139, 00128 Rome; tel. 06-50299222; fax 06-5070619; e-mail secretary@insean.it; internet www .insean.it; f. 1927; library of 3,500 vols; Pres. GIANO PISI; Dir Dr GIACOMO GRANDE; publ. *Quaderni* (1 a year).

SORIN Biomedica SpA: Via Benigno Crespi 17, 20159 Milan; tel. (02) 69969711-509; internet www.sorin.com; f. 1956; applied research in biomedicine; production and development of radiopharmaceuticals and immunodiagnostic kits (using radioactive and enzymatic tracers), pacemakers, artificial cardiac valves (mechanical and biological), oxygenators, dialysers, haemodialysis and haemoperfusion accessories; 2,112 staff; Chair. ROSARIO BIFULCO; CEO ANDRÉ MICHEL BALLESTER.

Libraries and Archives
Alessandria

Biblioteca Civica: Piazza Vittorio Veneto 1, (ang. Via Machiavelli), 15100 Alessandria; tel. 0131-515911; internet www.comune .alessandria.it/flex/cm/pages/serveblob.php/l/ it/idpagina/1315; f. 1806; 180,000 vols, 217 current periodicals; Dir (vacant).

Ancona

Archivio di Stato di Ancona: Via Maggini 80, 60127 Ancona; tel. 071-2802053; fax 071-2800356; e-mail asan@archivi.beniculturali .it; internet archivi.beniculturali.it/asan; f. 1941; provincial archives dating from before Italian unification; 8,000 vols, 280 periodicals; Dir Dott.ssa GIOVANNA GIUBBINI; publ. *Archivio di Stato-Ancona* (series, irregular).

Biblioteca Comunale Luciano Benincasa: Via Bernabei 32, Piazza Plebiscito 33, 60121 Ancona; tel. 071-222-5020; fax 071-222-5020; e-mail aiaale@comune.ancona.it; f. 1669; 160,000 vols, 62 incunabula, 124 periodicals, 347 MSS, 3,000 *cinquecentine*; Dir ALESSANDRO L. AIARDI.

Arezzo

Biblioteca della Città di Arezzo: Palazzo Pretorio, Via dei Pileati 8, 52100 Arezzo; tel. 0575-22849; fax 0575-370419; e-mail direzione@bibliotecaarezzo.it; internet www .bibliotecaarezzo.it; f. 1603; 250,000 vols, pamphlets and miscellanea, 587 MSS and 197 incunabula; Dir Dott. SILVIO SANTINI.

Ascoli Piceno

Biblioteca Comunale 'Giulio Gabrielli': Piazza Arringo 6, 63100 Ascoli Piceno; tel. 0736-298212; fax 0736-298232; internet www .cultura.marche.it/musamarche/arim/11 .html; f. 1849; 180,000 vols, 265 incunabula, 900 MSS, 2,000 *cinquecentine*, 340 periodicals; Dir Dott.ssa EMANUELA IMPICCINI.

Avellino

Biblioteca Provinciale Scipione e Giulio Capone: Corso Europa 41, 83100 Avellino;

tel. and fax 0825-782382; e-mail info@
mediateca.avellino.it; internet avellino
.ebiblio.it; f. 1913; 120,000 vols; Dir Dott.
MARIO SARRO.

Bari
Archivio di Stato di Bari: Via Demetrio
Marin 3, 70125 Bari; tel. 080-5024860; fax
080-5024870; e-mail archivio.stato@teseo.it;
internet www.teseo.it/archiviodistato; f.
1835; 6,192 vols, 224 periodicals, 139 MSS;
Dir Dr GIUSEPPE DIBENEDETTO.

Bergamo
Biblioteca Civica 'Angelo Mai': Piazza
Vecchia 15, 24129 Bergamo; tel. 035-
399430; fax 035-240655; e-mail info@
bibliotecamai.org; internet www
.bibliotecamai.org; f. 1760; 650,000 vols,
9,380 MSS, 37,478 documents, 2,140 incunabula; Dir GIULIO ORAZIO BRAVI.

Bologna
Archivio di Stato di Bologna: Piazza dei
Celestini 4, 40123 Bologna; tel. 051-223891;
fax 051-220474; e-mail asbo@archivi
.beniculturali.it; internet www
.archiviodistatobologna.it; f. 1874; 230,000
items, 23,000 vols, 331 periodicals; Dir
Dott.ssa MARIA ROSARIA CELLI GIORGINI.

Biblioteca Carducci: Piazza Carducci 5,
40125 Bologna; tel. 051-347592; fax 051-
4292820; e-mail casacarducci@comune
.bologna.it; internet www.casacarducci.it/
htm/info_cont/bibl1.htm; given to the commune of Bologna in 1907 by Marguerite of
Savoy, inaugurated in 1921; the library
preserves the surroundings of the poet
Giosuè Carducci and contains his collected
works, as well as many rare editions of other
works; 35,000 vols; Dir PIERANGELO BELLET-
TINI.

**Biblioteca Comunale dell'Archiginna-
sio:** Piazza Galvani 1, 40124 Bologna; tel.
051-276811; fax 051-261160; e-mail
archiginnasio@comune.bologna.it; internet
www.archiginnasio.it; f. 1801; 951,535 vols
(incl. 2,500 incunabula, 20,000 16th-century
edns), 12,000 MSS, 500,000 letters and documents; Dir Dott. PIERANGELO BELLETTINI;
publ. *L'Archiginnasio—Bollettino della Biblioteca Comunale di Bologna* (1 a year).

**Biblioteca del Dipartimento di Scienze
Giuridiche 'A. Cicu':** Via Zamboni 27–29,
40126 Bologna; tel. 051-2099626; fax 051-
2099624; e-mail bibgiur@giuri.unibo.it;
internet www.jus.unibo.it; f. 1926; 292,000
vols; Chief Librarian LEONARDA MARTINO.

Biblioteca San Domenico: Piazza San
Domenico 13, 40124 Bologna; tel. 051-
6400493; fax 051-6400492; e-mail biblsand@
iperbole.bologna.it; internet www.comune
.bologna.it/iperbole/biblsand; f. 1218; more
than 75,000 vols, incunabula and MSS;
spec. collns incl. philosophy and theology;
Dir ANGELO PIAGNO.

Biblioteca Universitaria di Bologna: Via
Zamboni 33–35, 40126 Bologna; tel. 051-
243420; fax 051-252110; e-mail direzione@
bub.unibo.it; internet www.bub.unibo.it; f.
1712; 1,348,688 vols, 309,475 pamphlets,
12,820 MSS, 1,021 incunabula, 76,708 microforms, 11,224 periodicals; Dir Dr BIANCAS-
TELLA ANTONINO; publ. *BUBLife* (3 a year).

Brescia
Biblioteca Queriniana: Via Mazzini 1,
25121 Brescia; tel. 030-2978200; fax 030-
2400359; e-mail queriniana@comune.brescia
.it; internet queriniana.comune.brescia.it; f.
1747; 500,511 vols; Dir ALDO PIROLA.

Cagliari
Archivio di Stato di Cagliari: Via Gallura
2, 09125 Cagliari; tel. 070-669450; fax 070-
653401; e-mail as-ca@beniculturali.it;
internet www.archiviostatocagliari.it; f.
19th century; 29,525 vols, 2,690 periodicals,
21 MSS, 407,000 microfiches; Dir Dott.ssa
ANNA PIA BIDOLLI.

Biblioteca Universitaria: Via Università
32A, 09124 Cagliari; tel. 070-660017; fax 070-
652672; f. 1792; 460,470 vols, 1,033 MSS,
5,469 letters and documents, 241 incunabula,
2,784 magazines; Gabinetto delle Stampe
'Anna Marongiu Pernis' contains 4,541 etchings; Dir Dott. GRAZIELLA SEDDA DELITALA.

Campobasso
Archivio di Stato di Campobasso: Via
Orefici 43, 86100 Campobasso; tel. 0874-
411488; fax 0874-411525; e-mail ascb@
archivi.beniculturali.it; f. 1818; 19,000 vols,
802 periodicals, 29 MSS; Dir Dott.ssa ELENA
GLIELMO.

Catania
Archivio di Stato di Catania: Via Vittorio
Emanuele 156, 95131 Catania; tel. 095-
7159860; fax 095-7150465; e-mail asct@
archivi.beniculturali.it; internet archivi
.beniculturali.it/asct; f. 1854; 161,790 items;
11,700 vols; Dir Dott. ALDO SPARTI.

Biblioteca Regionale Universitaria:
Piazza Università 2, 95124 Catania; tel.
095-7366111; fax 095-326862; f. 1755;
400,000 vols, 117 incunabula, 590 MSS; Dir
UGO GIOVALE.

**Biblioteche Riunite Civica e A. Ursino
Recupero:** Via Biblioteca 13, 95124 Catania;
tel. 090-316883; f. 1931 as municipal library,
fmrly a Benedictine monastery library, nationalized in 1867; 210,000 vols, specializing in
Sicily and Catania; Dir Prof.ssa MARIA
SALMERI.

Cesena
Istituzione Biblioteca Malatestiana:
Piazza Bufalini 1, 47023 Cesena; tel. 0547-
610892; fax 0547-21237; e-mail
malatestiana@sbn.provincia.ra.it; internet
www.malatestiana.it/manoscritti/index.htm;
f. 1452; 400,000 vols, 286 incunabula, 2,180
MSS; Dir Dott.ssa DANIELA SAVOIA.

Como
Biblioteca Comunale: Via Indipendenza
87, 22100 Como; tel. 031-270187; fax 031-
240183; e-mail biblioteca@comune.como.it; f.
17th century; 370,000 vols; Dir RICCARDO
TERZOLI.

Cremona
Biblioteca del Seminario Vescovile: Via
Milano 5, 26100 Cremona; tel. 03-7220267;
fax 03-7229135; e-mail seminario.cr@libero
.it; f. 1592; 138,450 vols, 400 MSS, 18
incunabula; Dir Prof. FOGLIA DON ANDREA.

Biblioteca Statale: Via Ugolani Dati 4,
26100 Cremona; tel. 0372-495611; fax 0372-
495615; e-mail bs-cr@beniculturali.it; f. c.
1600; 700,000 vols, 2,380 MSS, 18,600 letters
and documents, 374 incunabula, 6,000 16th-
century editions; Dir Dr STEFANO CAMPAG-
NOLO; publs *Annali*, *Fonti e Sussidi*, *Mostre*.

Fermo
Biblioteca Comunale: Piazza del Popolo 7,
63023 Fermo; tel. 0734-284310; fax 0734-
215112; e-mail biblioteca@comune.fermo.net;
internet www.fermo.net/ita/egov/biblioteca
.html; f. 1688; 332,000 vols, 681 incunabula,
15,000 *cinquecentine*, 3,000 MSS, 110 current periodicals; Dir NATALIA TIZI.

Ferrara
Biblioteca Comunale Ariostea: Via
Scienze 17, 44100 Ferrara; tel. 0532-418200;
fax 0532-204296; e-mail info.ariostea@
comune.fe.it; internet www.artecultura.fe.it/
index.phtml; f. 1753; 420,000 vols; Dir Dott.
E. SPINELLI.

Florence
Archivio di Stato di Firenze: Viale G.
Italia 6, 50122 Florence; tel. 055-263201; fax
055-2341159; internet www.archiviodistato
.firenze.it; f. 1852; 604,580 items; 43,000 vols,
350 periodicals; Dir Dott.ssa ROSALIA MANNO
TOLU.

Biblioteca degli Uffizi: Loggiato degli
Uffizi, 50122 Florence; tel. 055-2388647; fax
055-2388648; internet www.polomuseale
.firenze.it/biblioteche/bib_uffizi.asp; f. 1770;
64,000 vols; Dir Dr CLAUDIO DI BENEDETTO.

**Biblioteca del Gabinetto Scientifico Let-
terario G. P. Vieusseux:** Palazzo Strozzi,
Piazza Strozzi, 50123 Florence; tel. 055-
288342; fax 055-2396743; e-mail biblioteca@
vieusseux.fi.it; internet www.vieusseux.fi.it/
biblio.html; f. 1819; 600,000 vols; Dir Prof.
ENZO SICILIANO; publ. *Antologia Vieusseux* (4
a year).

Attached Archive:

> **Archivio Contemporaneo 'Alessandro
> Bonsanti':** Palazzo Corsini-Suarez, Via
> Maggio 42, 50125 Florence; tel. 055-
> 290131; fax 055-213188; e-mail archivio@
> vieusseux.fi.it; internet www.vieusseux.fi
> .it/archivio_contemporaneo.html; f. 1975;
> 500,000 vols, 85,000 records; Man. GLORIA
> MANGHETTI.

Biblioteca Marucelliana: Via Cavour 43–
47, 50129 Florence; tel. 055-27221; fax 055-
294393; e-mail marucelliana@maru.firenze
.sbn.it; internet www.maru.firenze.sbn.it; f.
1752; 553,992 vols; 2,574 MSS; 489 incunabula, 3,200 drawings, 53,000 prints, 8,000
16th-century editions, 30,405 letters and
documents, 9,322 periodicals; Dir MARIA
PRUNAI FALCIANI.

Biblioteca Medicea-Laurenziana: Piazza
S. Lorenzo 9, 50123 Florence; tel. 55-210760;
fax 55-2302992; e-mail b-mela@beniculturali
.it; internet www.bmlonline.it; f. 1571; contains the private Medici Library, collns of
MSS from the Medici family, the Grand
Dukes of Lorena, S. Croce, S. Marco, Badia
Fiesolana, cathedral of Florence, and private
family collns; 15th- and 16th-centuries first
edns; 14,000 MSS of the 5th–19th century;
2,500 papyri, 80 ostraca, 150,000 vols; Dir Dr
MARIA PRUNAI FALCIANI.

Biblioteca Moreniana: Via dei Ginori 10,
50123 Florence; tel. and fax 055-2760331;
e-mail moreniana@provincia.fi.it; internet
www.provincia.fi.it/moreniana.htm; f. 1869;
34,000 vols, c. 2,000 MSS, specializing in
ancient Tuscan history; Dir Dott.ssa SIMO-
NETTA MERENDONI.

Biblioteca Nazionale Centrale: Piazza
Cavalleggeri 1, 50122 Florence; tel. 055-
249191; fax 055-2342482; e-mail info@bncf
.firenze.sbn.it; internet www.bncf.firenze.sbn
.it; f. 1747; 5,300,000 vols, pamphlets,
115,000 periodicals, 25,000 MSS, 4,000 incunabula, 29,000 16th-century edns; Dir Dr
ANTONIA IDA FONTANA; publ. *Bibliografia
nazionale italiana* (12 a year, 1 a year
accumulations, 4 a year CD-ROM).

Biblioteca Pedagogica Nazionale: c/o
Biblioteca di Documentazione Pedagogica,
Palazzo Gerini, Via M. Buonarroti 10,
50122 Florence; tel. 055-2380364; fax 055-
2380330; e-mail biblioteca@indire.it; f. 1941;
80,000 vols, 1,600 periodicals, rare books,
drawings, etc.; data banks on education;
Pres. Dott.ssa MARIA CRISTINA DOTTORINI;

publs *Schedario* (review of children's literature, 3 a year), *Segnalibro* (review of literature for young people, 1 a year).

Biblioteca Riccardiana: Via dei Ginori 10, 50123 Florence; tel. 055-212586; fax 055-211379; e-mail riccardiana@riccardiana .firenze.sbn.it; internet www.riccardiana .firenze.sbn.it; f. 1815; 61,675 vols, 4,415 MSS, 725 incunabula, 3,856 16th-century editions, 192 periodicals; Dir Dott.ssa GIOVANNA LAZZI.

Biblioteca Umanistica dell' Università: Piazza Brunelleschi 3, 50121 Florence; tel. 055-2757811; fax 055-243471; e-mail floriana .tagliabue@unifi.it; internet www.sba.unifi .it/biblio/umanistica; f. 1959; 1,600,000 vols; Dir Dr FLORIANA TAGLIABUE.

Forlì

Biblioteca Comunale 'Aurelio Saffi': Corso della Repubblica 72, 47100 Forlì; tel. 0543-712600; fax 0543-712616; e-mail biblioteca-saffi@comune.forli.fo.it; internet www.provincia.forli-cesena.it/cultura/biblioteche/ita/saffi.htm; 490,000 vols, 250 incunabula, 8,000 16th-century editions, 2,000 MSS, 2,200 periodicals; Dir Dr FRANCO FABBRI.

Genoa

Archivio di Stato di Genova: Piazza S. Maria in Via Lata, 7, 16128 Genoa; tel. 010-5957581; fax 010-5538220; e-mail asge@ archivi.beniculturali.it; internet archivi .beniculturali.it/asge/asge.htm; f. 1817; 13,000 vols, 145 periodicals; Dir PAOLA CAROLI.

Biblioteca Durazzo Giustiniani: Via XXV Aprile 12, 16123 Genoa; tel. 010-2476232; fax 010-2474122; f. 1760–1804; 20,000 17th- and 18th-century vols, 1,000 *cinquecentine*, 448 incunabula, 300 MSS; Curator Dott.ssa SANDRA MACCHIAVELLO.

Biblioteca di Storia dell'Arte: Via ai Quattro Canti di San Francesco, 16121 Genoa; tel. 010-5574957; fax 010-5574970; e-mail biblarte@comune.genova.it; internet www.comune.genova.it/turismo/biblioteche/bibliociv/welcome.htm; f. 1908; 56,000 vols; specialized library relating to Italian and Genoese fine arts (since 11th century); Curator Dr ELISABETTA PAPONE; publ. *Bollettino dei Musei Civici Genovesi*.

Biblioteca Universitaria: Via Balbi 3 e 38B, 16126 Genoa; tel. 010-254641; fax 010-2546420; e-mail bu-ge@beniculturali.it; internet www.bibliotecauniversitaria.ge.it; f. 18th century; 617,109 vols, 1,039 incunabula, 1,949 MSS, 19,287 letters and documents; Dir Reg. SIMONETTA BUTTÒ.

Gorizia

Biblioteca Statale Isontina di Gorizia: Via Mameli 12, 34170 Gorizia; tel. 0481-580210; fax 0481-580260; e-mail bs-ison@ beniculturali.it; internet www.isontina .librari.beniculturali.it; f. 1629; lending and reference library; bibliographical information service; 367,000 vols, 41 incunabula, 690 *cinquecentine*, 873 current periodicals, 547 MSS, 1,181 microfiches, 270 pictures; Dir Dott. MARCO MENATO; publ. *Studi Goriziani* (2 a year).

Imola

Biblioteca Comunale: Via Emilia 80, 40026 Imola; tel. 0542-602636; fax 0542-602602; e-mail bim@comune.imola.bo.it; f. 1761; 419,000 vols, 520 current periodicals, 1,692 MSS, 140 incunabula; Dir Dott.ssa GRAZIA-VITTORIA GURRIERI.

L'Aquila

Biblioteca Provinciale 'Salvatore Tommasi': Piazza Palazzo 30, 67100 L'Aquila; tel. 0862-299431; fax 0862-299450; e-mail biblioteca@provincia.laquila.it; internet www .provincia.laquila.it/biblioteca; f. 1848; 250,000 vols, 300 current periodicals, 131 incunabula, 1,011 MSS, 3,200 *cinquecentine* (rare 16th-century editions), 900 video cassettes; Dir Dr PAOLO COLLACCIANI.

Livorno

Biblioteca Comunale 'Labronica' Francesco Domenico Guerrazzi: Via del Forte S. Pietro 15, 57123 Livorno; tel. 0586-219265; fax 0586-219151; e-mail bottinidellolio@ comune.livorno.it; internet www.comune .livorno.it/_livo/pages.php?id=127; f. 1816; 380,000 vols incl. 2,000 15th- and 16th-century edns, 850 current periodicals, various MSS, and 60,000 letters and documents; Dir Dott. DUCCIO FILIPPI; publ. *Quaderni della Labronica* (4 a year).

Lucca

Biblioteca Statale di Lucca: Via S. Maria Corteorlandini 12, 55100 Lucca; tel. 0583-491271; fax 0583-496770; e-mail bs-lu@ beniculturali.it; internet www.bslu.librari .beniculturali.it; f. 1794; 480,000 vols, 594 current periodicals, 10,000 *cinquecentine*, 835 incunabula, 4,321 MSS, 19,850 letters and documents, 2,595 graphic items; musical colln of 68 MSS, 500 scores; Dir Dott.ssa MARCO PAOLI.

Macerata

Biblioteca Comunale Mozzi-Borgetti: Piazza Vittorio Veneto 2, 62100 Macerata; tel. 0733-256360; fax 0733-256338; e-mail biblioteca@comune.macerata.it; internet www.comune.macerata.it/entra/engine/ raservepg.php3/p/2508110417; f. 1773; 350,000 vols, 10,000 MSS, 300 incunabula, 20,000 photographs; Dir Dott.ssa ALESSANDRA SFRAPPINI.

Mantua

Biblioteca Comunale Teresiana: Via Roberto Ardigò 13, 46100 Mantua; tel. 0376-321515; fax 0376-310801; e-mail biblioteca.comunale@domino.comune.mantova.it; internet www.bibliotecateresiana.it; f. 1780; 330,000 vols, 1,375 MSS, 1,425 incunabula, 8,500 *cinquecentine*; Dir Dr CESARE GUERRA.

Biblioteca dell' Accademia Nazionale Virgiliana: Via dell'Accademia 47, 46100 Mantua; tel. 0376-320314; fax 0376-222774; e-mail cgallic@tin.it; f. early 17th century; 30,000 vols; Librarian Prof. MARIO VAINI; publs *Atti e Memorie* (1 a year), *Nuova Serie* (1 a year).

Messina

Biblioteca Regionale Universitaria di Messina: Via I Settembre 117, 98122 Messina; tel. 090-663332; fax 090-771909; e-mail brs.me@regione.sicilia.it; internet www .regione.sicilia.it/beniculturali/brum/index .htm; f. 1731; 449,926 vols, 461 current periodicals, 1,307 MSS, 423 incunabula, 3,637 *cinquecentine*; Dir Dott. GIOVANNI GRILLO.

Milan

Archivio di Stato di Milano: Via Senato 10, 20121 Milan; tel. 02-7742161; fax 02-774216230; e-mail as-mi@beniculturali.it; internet www.archiviodistatomilano.it; f. 1886; 27,096 vols and pamphlets, 18,814 periodicals; Dir Dott. MARIA BARBARA BERTINI.

Archivio Storico Civico e Biblioteca Trivulziana: Castello Sforzesco, 20121 Milan; tel. 02-88463690; fax 02-88463698; e-mail c.ascbibliotrivulziana@comune.milano .it; internet www.comune.milano.it; f. 1872 as Archivio Storico Civico, renamed Biblioteca Trivulziana 1935; 170,000 vols, 1,500 MSS dating from the 8th century, 2,000 incunabula, and rare edns of works on history and literature, local historical artefacts; Dir Dott.ssa ISABELLA FIORENTINI; publ. *Libri E Documenti* (1 a year).

Biblioteca Archeologica e Numismatica: Castello Sforzesco, 20121 Milan; tel. 02-88463772; fax 02-88463800; e-mail c .bibliocasva@comune.milano.it; internet www.comune.milano.it/casva; 35,000 vols; f. 1808; prehistoric, Roman, Etruscan, Greek and Egyptian archaeology; coins and medals; library and historical archives; Dir Dr RINA LA GUARDIA; publ. *Rassegna di Studi* (2 a year).

Biblioteca d'Arte: Castello Sforzesco, 20121 Milan; tel. 02-88463737; fax 02-88463819; e-mail c.biblioarte@comune.milano.it; internet www.comune.milano.it/casva; f. 1930; art history, applied arts, museology, graphics, design, visual arts; art library and Leonardo da Vinci Colln; 115,000 vols, 21,000 periodicals, 286 current periodicals; Dir RINA LA GUARDIA.

Biblioteca d'Ateneo dell'Università Cattolica del Sacro Cuore: Largo Gemelli 1, 20123 Milan; tel. 02-72342230; fax 02-72342701; e-mail biblioteca.direzione-mi@ unicatt.it; internet www.unicatt.it/library; f. 1921; 1,906,500 vols and pamphlets, 32,500 periodicals, 11,450 electronic journals, 270 online and CD-ROM-based databases; Head of Library Dott.ssa ELLIS SADA.

Biblioteca Centrale di Ingegneria–Leonardo: Piazza Leonardo da Vinci 32, 20133 Milan; tel. 02-23992550; fax 02-23992560; internet bci.biblio.polimi.it; 153,400 vols, 350 MSS, 3,780 periodicals, 270 current periodicals; Head of Library SIMONETTA MORELLI.

Biblioteca del Centro Nazionale di Studi Manzoniani: Via Morone 1, 20121 Milan; tel. 02-86460403; fax 02-875618; e-mail cnsm@tiroli.it; f. 1937; 25,000 vols; Dir Prof. GIANMARCO GASPARI; Vice-Pres. Prof. ANGELO STELLA; publs *Annali*, *Bollettino Bibliografico*, *Edizione Nazionale ed Europea delle Opere di Alessandro Manzoni*.

Biblioteca Comunale: Palazzo Sormani, Corso di Porta Vittoria 6, 20122 Milan; tel. 02-88463397; fax 02-88463353; e-mail c .bibliocentrale@comune.milano.it; internet www.comune.milano.it/biblioteche; f. 1886; 644,432 vols, 2,414 current periodicals, 48,909 audio and video items, 483 electronic resources; Dir Dr ANNA MARIA ROSSATO.

Biblioteca del Conservatorio di Musica 'Giuseppe Verdi': Via Conservatorio 12, 20122 Milan; tel. 02-762110219; fax 02-76003097; e-mail biblioteca@consmilano.it; internet www.consmilano.it; f. 1808; 500,000 items; 50,000 MSS, 30,000 books on music, 400 periodicals; Librarian LICIA SIRCH; publ. *Annuario del Conservatorio*.

Biblioteca della Facoltà di Agraria: Università degli Studi di Milano, Via G. Celoria 2, 20133 Milan; tel. 02-50316428; fax 02-50316427; e-mail bib.agraria@unimi.it; internet users.unimi.it/biblioteche/agraria; f. 1871; 51,000 vols; Scientific Dir Prof. A. SCHIRALDI; Librarian Dott. ANGELO BOZZOLA.

Biblioteca delle Facoltà di Giurisprudenza e di Lettere e Filosofia dell' Università: Via Festa del Perdono 7, 20122 Milan; tel. 02-50312273; fax 02-50312598; e-mail alessandra.dallera@unimi.it; internet users.unimi.it/~biblio; f. 1923; 930,000 vols; Dir MARIA ALESSANDRA DALL'ERA.

Biblioteca dell' Istituto Lombardo Accademia di Scienze e Lettere: Via Borgonuovo 25, 20121 Milan; tel. 02-864087; fax 02-86461388; e-mail istituto.lombardo@unimi.it; internet www.istitutolombardo.it/biblioteca.html; f. 1802; 495,000 vols, 2,600 periodicals; Dir Dr ADELE BIANCHI ROBBIATI.

Biblioteca Nazionale Braidense: Via Brera 28, 20121 Milan; tel. 02-86460907; fax 02-72023910; e-mail b-brai.@beniculturali.it; internet www.braidense.it; f. 1770; 1,500,000 vols, 17,149 periodicals, 26,455 autographs, 2,107 MSS; Dir AURELIO AGHEMO.

Biblioteca dell' Università Commerciale Luigi Bocconi: Via Gobbi 5, 20136 Milan; tel. 02-58365101; fax 02-58365100; e-mail library.staff@unibocconi.it; internet www.unibocconi.it/biblioteca; f. 1903; borrowing and reference services, user instruction services; European Documentation Centre; Asian Devt Bank Repository; 697,249 vols, 10,614 paper periodicals, 13,324 e-journals, 48,763 theses, 52 databases, 1,662 ancient books (from 16th to 18th centuries); Head Librarian Dr MARISA SANTARSIERO.

Raccolte Storiche del Comune di Milano, Biblioteca e Archivio: Palazzo De Marchi, Via Borgonuovo 23, 20121 Milan; tel. 02-8693549; fax 02-72001483; e-mail risorgi@energy.it; f. 1884; 250,000 vols, newspapers and pamphlets, 3,825 files of documents since 1750; Dir Dott. ROBERTO GUERRI.

Veneranda Biblioteca Ambrosiana: Piazza Pio XI 2, 20123 Milan; e-mail info@ambrosiana.it; internet www.ambrosiana.eu; tel. 02-806921; fax 02-80692212; f. 1607, opened to the public in 1609; 900,000 vols and rare prints, 35,000 MSS mostly Latin, Greek, and Oriental, 2,100 incunabula, 12,000 parchments, 20,000 prints, 10,000 drawings; Dir Dott. GIANANTONIO BORGONOVO; publs *Accademia Ambrosiana. Fonti e Studi, Accademia Ambrosiana. Studia Ambrosiana* (1 a year), *Accademia Ambrosiana. Studia Asiatica, Accademia Ambrosiana. Studia Borromaica* (1 a year).

Modena

Biblioteca Estense Universitaria: Palazzo dei Musei, Largo Porta S. Agostino 337, 41121 Modena; tel. 059-222248; fax 059-230195; e-mail b-este@beniculturali.it; internet www.cedoc.mo.it/estense; 556,889 vols, 11,025 MS vols, 158,464 loose MSS, 1,662 incunabula, 15,966 *cinquecentine*, 128,610 pamphlets, 8,582 periodicals; Dir Dott. LUCA BELLINGERI; Librarian ANNALISA BATTINI.

Naples

Archivio di Stato di Napoli: Piazzetta Grande Archivio 5, 80138 Naples; tel. 081-5638111; e-mail asna@archivi.beniculturali.it; internet archivi.beniculturali.it/asna; f. 1808; 544,000 items; 25,000 vols; Dir Dott.ssa FELICITA DE NEGRI.

Biblioteca del Conservatorio S. Pietro a Majella: Via S. Pietro a Majella 35, 80138 Naples; tel. (81) 5644427; fax (81) 5644415; e-mail biblioteca@sanpietroamajella.it; f. 1791; 300,000 vols, 18,000 MSS, 10,000 costume designs, 8,000 opera libretti, 10,000 letters, 200 *cinquecentine*; Dir Dr FRANCESCO MELISI.

Biblioteca della Facoltà di Scienze Agrarie dell' Università degli Studi di Napoli Federico II: Via Università 100, 80055 Portici; tel. 081-2539321; e-mail petricci@unina.it; internet www.agraria.unina.it/biblio; f. 1872; 65,000 vols, 3,130 periodicals, 441 current periodicals; Dir OLIMPIA PETRICCIONE.

Biblioteca della Pontificia Facoltà Teologica dell' Italia Meridionale, sezione 'San Tommaso d'Aquino': Viale Colli Aminei 2, 80131 Naples; tel. 081-7410000; fax 081-7437580; e-mail presidenzapftim@libero.it; internet www.teologia.it/pftim; f. 1687; 120,000 vols; 11 incunabula, 600 MSS, 1,000 periodicals, 450 current periodicals; Dir Prof. ANTONIO PORPORA.

Biblioteca della Società Napoletana di Storia Patria: Piazza Municipio, Maschio Angioino, 80133 Naples; tel. 081-5510353; fax 081-5529238; e-mail bibl.snsp@libero.it; internet www.storia.unina.it/snsp; f. 1875; 300,000 vols, 2,400 MSS, 2,955 periodicals, 900 current periodicals, 1,300 *cinquecentine*, 59 incunabula; Librarian MARIA CONCETTA VILLANI; publ. *Archivio Storico per le Province Napoletane*.

Biblioteca di Castelcapuano: Piazza Amore Nicola 1, 80100 Naples; tel. 081-269416; fax 081-282367; f. 1848; 40,000 vols; Dir Dott. ROSSI BUSSOLA RAFFAELLO.

Biblioteca Nazionale 'Vittorio Emanuele III': Palazzo Reale, 80132 Naples; tel. 081-7819111; fax 081-403820; e-mail emanuele@librari.beniculturali.it; internet www.bnnonline.it; f. 1804; 1,800,000 vols, 19,000 MSS, 8,300 periodicals, 4,563 incunabula, 1,792 papyri from Herculaneum; Dir Dott. MAURO GIANCASPRO; publ. *I Quaderni*.

Biblioteca Statale Oratoriana del Monumento Nazionale dei Girolamini: Via Duomo 142, 80138 Naples; tel. and fax 81-294444; e-mail biblioteca@girolamini.it; internet www.girolamini.it/biblioteca.htm; f. 1586; 169,000 vols, 120 incunabula, 5,000 *cinquecentine*, 485 periodicals, 57 current periodicals; Dir P. GIOVANNI FERRARA.

Biblioteca Universitaria di Napoli: Via G. Paladino 39, 80138 Naples; tel. (81) 5517025; fax (81) 5528275; e-mail bu-na@beniculturali.it; internet www.bibliotecauniversitarianapoli.beniculturali.it; f. 1816; 776,211 vols, 5,820 periodicals, 3,654 *cinquecentine*, 462 incunabula, 144 MSS; open to the public; Dir ORNELLA FALANGOLA.

Novara

Biblioteca Comunale Negroni: Corso Felice Cavallotti 4, 28100 Novara; tel. 0321-3702800; fax 0321-628068; e-mail no0054@biblioteche.regioni.piemonte.it; f. 1906; 250,000 vols, 3,052 periodicals, 5,540 records, 131 incunabula, 771 microfilms, 420 MSS, maps, etc.; Dir Dr M. CARLA UGLIETTI.

Padua

Biblioteca Antoniana: Piazza del Santo 11, 35123 Padua; tel. and fax 049-8751492; e-mail info@bibliotecaantoniana.191.it; internet www.basilicadelsanto.org/ita/chiostri/biblio.asp; f. 13th century; 85,000 vols, 800 MSS; Dir Prof. SERGIO CATTAZZO.

Biblioteca Civica: Via Altinate 71, 35121 Padua; tel. 049-8204811; fax 049-8204804; e-mail biblioteca.civica@comune.padova.it; internet www.padovanet.it/biblioteche; f. 1858; art, Italian literature, history, local history (Padua and Veneto); 500,000 vols, 5,500 MSS, 385 incunabula, 2,000 periodicals; Head Librarian Dr GILDA P. MANTOVANI; publ. *Bollettino del Museo Civico di Padova*.

Biblioteca del Seminario Vescovile: Via Seminario 29, 35122 Padua; tel. 049-9983635; fax 049-8761934; e-mail biblio.seminariopadova@unipd.it; internet www.seminariopadova.it; f. 1671; 300,000 vols, 1,135 MSS, 417 incunabula, 800 periodicals; Dir Prof. RICCARDO BATTOCCHIO; Librarian Dr ACHILLE CANTAMESSA; Librarian Dr MARIA CRISTINA FAZZINI.

Biblioteca Universitaria: Via S. Biagio 7, 35121 Padua; tel. 049-8240211; fax 049-8762711; e-mail info.bupd@unipd.it; internet www.bibliotecauniversitariapadova.it; f. 1629; 676,982 vols; 2,798 MSS, 1,283 incunabula, 1,530 music scores, 1,055 maps, 6,681 periodicals, 592 current periodicals, 9,622 *cinquecentine*, 3,000 prints and engravings; Dir Dott. FRANCESCO ALIANO.

Palermo

Archivio di Stato di Palermo: Corso Vittorio Emanuele 31, 90133 Palermo; tel. 091-589693; fax 091-6110594; e-mail aspa@archivi.beniculturali.it; internet archivi.beniculturali.it/aspa; f. 1814; 386,918 items; 22,000 vols; Dir CLAUDIO TORRISI.

Biblioteca Centrale della Regione Siciliana: Corso Vittorio Emanuele 429–431, 90134 Palermo; tel. 091-7077642; fax 091-7077644; e-mail bcrs@regione.sicilia.it; internet www.regione.sicilia.it/beniculturali/bibliotecacentrale; f. 1782; 580,000 vols; 1,930 MSS, 1,044 incunabula, 5,907 periodicals, 15,000 letters and documents, 5,066 rare books, 4,125 maps, prints and engravings, 47,664 microforms, 3,541 photographs and slides; Dir GAETANO GULLO.

Biblioteca Comunale: Casa Professa, 90134 Palermo; tel. 091-7407570; fax 091-7407584; internet librarsi.comune.palermo.it; f. 1760; 365,000 vols; 1,038 incunabula, 15,000 *cinquecentine*; Dir Dott. FILIPPO GUTTUSO.

Parma

Biblioteca Palatina: Strada alla Pilotta 3, 43121 Parma; tel. 0521-220411; fax 0521-235662; e-mail b-pala@beniculturali.it; internet www.bibliotecapalatina.beniculturali.it; f. 1761; 715,000 vols, 6,671 MSS, 556 periodicals, 3,044 incunabula, 52,601 engravings and drawings; Dir ANDREA DE PASQUALE.

Biblioteca Palatina–Sezione Musicale presso il Conservatorio di Musica 'A. Boito': Strada Conservatorio 27, 43100 Parma; tel. 0521-289429; fax 0521-235662; internet www.bibliotecapalatina.beniculturali.it; f. 1889; 72,449 vols, 16,288 MSS, 30 periodicals; Dir Dr ANDREA DE PASQUALE.

Pavia

Biblioteca Civica 'Carlo Bonetta': Piazza Petrarca 2, 27100 Pavia; tel. 0382-21635; fax 0382-33580; e-mail fmilani@comune.pv.it; internet www.comune.pv.it/on-line/index.jsp?instance=1&node=198; f. 1887; Dir Dott. FELICE MILANI.

Biblioteca Universitaria: Strada Nuova 65, 27100 Pavia; tel. 0382-24764; fax 0382-25007; e-mail bupv.infbib@librari.beniculturali.it; internet siba.unipv.it/buniversitaria; f. 1763; 500,000 vols, 1,402 MSS, 689 incunabula, 5,391 periodicals, 718 current periodicals, 7,000 *cinquecentine*, 1,394 microfilms; Librarian Dott.ssa ANNA MARIA CAMPANINI STELLA.

Perugia

Biblioteca Augusta del Comune di Perugia: Palazzo Conestabile della Staffa, Via delle Prome 15, 06122 Perugia; tel. 075-5772500; fax 075-5722231; e-mail augusta@comune.perugia.it; internet www.comune.perugia.it/canale.asp?id=2822; f. 1615; 380,000 vols, 3,380 MSS, 1,330 incunabula, 3,800 periodicals, 16,500 *cinquecentine*; Dir Dott. MAURIZIO TARANTINO.

Pesaro

Biblioteca e Musei Oliveriani: Via Mazza Domenico 97, 61100 Pesaro; tel. 0721-33344; f. 1793; 250,000 vols on general culture and local history; Librarian Prof. Dott. ANTONIO BRANCATI; publ. *Studia Oliveriana* (1 a year).

Piacenza

Biblioteca Comunale Passerini Landi: Via Carducci 14, 29100 Piacenza; tel. (523) 492401; fax (523) 492400; e-mail biblio .amministrazione@comune.piacenza.it; internet www.biblioteche.piacenza.it/passerini; f. 1774; 50,000 vols, 1,000 incunabula, 5,000 *cinquecentine*; Dir Dott. CARLO EMANUELE MANFREDI.

Pisa

Biblioteca Universitaria: Via Curtatone e Montanara 15, 56126 Pisa; tel. 050-913411; fax 050-42064; e-mail bupi@librari .beniculturali.it; internet www.pisa.sbn.it; f. 1742; 668,000 vols, 1,389 MSS, 24,087 documents, 161 incunabula, 1,034 current periodicals; Dir Dott.ssa ALESSANDRA PESANTE.

Pistoia

Biblioteca Comunale Forteguerriana: Piazza della Sapienza 5, 51100 Pistoia; tel. 0573-24348; fax 0573-371466; e-mail biblioteca@comune.pistoia.it; internet www .comune.pistoia.it/museibiblioteche/forte-guerriana/index.htm; f. 1696; 300,000 vols, 223 current periodicals, 1,000 MSS, 126 incunabula, 3,000 *cinquecentine*, 1,000 CDs; Dir Dr MAURIZIO VIVARELLI.

Portici

Biblioteca del Dipartimento di Entomologia e Zoologia Agraria, Università degli Studi di Napoli Federico II: Via Università 100, 80055 Portici; tel. 081-2539188; fax 081-7755145; e-mail gaeiorio@ unina.it; f. 1872; applied entomology and biological control; 100,000 vols; Dir GAETANO IORIO; publ. *Bollettino del Laboratorio di Entomologia Agraria 'Filippo Silvestri'*.

Potenza

Archivio di Stato: Via Nazario Sauro 1, 85100 Potenza; tel. 0971-56144; fax 0971-56223; e-mail aspz@aspz.it; internet aspz.it; f. 1818; 10,000 linear miles of records (since the 11th century); administrative and judicial archives since 1687; notarial archives since 1524; archives of religious houses dissolved in the 19th century; private and feudal archives since 1500; collns of parchments (since the 10th century) and municipal statutes; also archives of ecclesiastical bodies incl. those of the Venosa cathedral chapter (since the 11th century); 17,000 vols, 2,500 periodicals; Dir Dott.ssa VALERIA VERRASTRO.

Biblioteca Nazionale: Via del Gallitello, 85100 Potenza; tel. 0971-54829; fax 0971-55071; internet www.bnpz.librari .beniculturali.it; f. 1985; functions as univ. library (Univ. della Basilicata) and regional library; 300,000 vols, 1,681 periodicals; Dir Dott. MAURIZIO RESTIVO.

Ravenna

Istituzione Biblioteca Classense: Via Baccarini 3, 48100 Ravenna; tel. 0544-482112; fax 0544-482104; e-mail informazioni@classense.ra.it; internet www .classense.ra.it; f. 1707–1711; 790,000 vols; Dir Dott. DONATINO DOMINI; publ. *Letture Classensi*.

Reggio Emilia

Biblioteca Panizzi: Via Farini 3, 42100 Reggio Emilia; tel. 0522-456084; fax 0522-456081; e-mail panizzi@comune.re.it; internet panizzi.comune.re.it; f. 1796; 500,000 vols, 10,000 MSS; Dir Dr MAURIZIO FESTANTI.

Rimini

Biblioteca Civica Gambalunga: Via Gambalunga 27, 47900 Rimini; tel. 0541-51105; fax 0541-26167; e-mail gambalunghiana@ comune.rimini.it; internet www.comune .rimini.it/servizi/citta/cultura/biblioteca; f. 1619; 220,000 vols (including 7,000 *cinquecentine*), 384 incunabula, 1,350 MSS, 350 current periodicals, 1,960 bound periodicals, 8,000 drawings and engravings, 40,000 photographs; Dir Prof. MARCELLO DI BELLA.

Rome

Archivio Centrale dello Stato: Piazzale degli Archivi 27, 00144 Rome; tel. 06-545481; fax 06-5413620; e-mail acs@archivi .beniculturali.it; internet archivi .beniculturali.it/acs; f. 1875; 130,000 vols, also periodicals, etc.; political, administrative, cultural and judicial archives of the Kingdom of Italy and Italian Republic; Dir ALDO G. RICCI.

Archivio di Stato di Roma: Corso del Rinascimento 40, 00186 Rome; tel. 06-6819081; fax 06-6864123; e-mail asroma@ asrm.archivi.beniculturali.it; internet archivi.beniculturali.it/asrm/index.html; f. 1871; conservation of archives produced by the central offices of the Papal State from the Middle Ages to 1870, together with documents produced by other agencies in the Rome area; papal provincial treasuries (incl. Avignon and Benevento); archives of religious orders since the 14th century and of brotherhoods, academies, corporate bodies, the University of Rome and notary registers since the 13th century; conservation of govt office records of the Italian State with seat in Rome; School of Archival Science, Latin Palaeography and Diplomatics; 52,000 vols, with 3 important collns: Statutes, MSS, Decrees; Dir Dott. LUIGI LONDEI.

Biblioteca Angelica: Piazza Sant'Agostino 8, 00186 Rome; tel. 06-6840801; fax 06-68408053; e-mail b-ange@beniculturali.it; internet www.biblioangelica.it; f. 1605; 15th–18th-century literature; Augustinian, Jansenist, Reformation and counter-Reformation collns; 220,000 vols, 2,704 MSS, 1,156 incunabula; Dir Dott.ssa FIAMMETTA TERLIZZI.

Biblioteca Archeologia e Storia dell'Arte: Piazza Venezia 3, 00187 Rome; tel. 06-6780982; fax 06-6781167; e-mail archeologica@librari.beniculturali.it; internet www.archeologica.librari.beniculturali .it; f. 1922; 599,000 vols, 3,500 periodicals, 1,489 MSS, 16 incunabula, 20,000 prints, 59,411 microfiches, 740 *cinquecentine*; Dir STEFANIA MURIANNI.

Biblioteca Casanatense: Via S. Ignazio 52, 00186 Rome; tel. (6) 6976031; fax (6) 69902254; e-mail casanatense@biblioroma .sbn.it; internet www.casanatense.it; f. 1701; preserves and enhances the collns of Cardinal Girolamo Casanate; 400,000 vols; spec. collns: MSS colln, 6,000 vols of great value incl. exultet, liturgical codes, medical-scientific texts, Oriental and Hebraic codes, famous autographs incl. that of Niccolò Paganini; Incunabula colln, 2,200 vols incl. unique first edns and plaques; Engravings colln, 30,000 engravings incl. Abbot Antonio Ricci's donation and endowment of the Chamber of Calligraphy; Musical works colln, 1,700 MSS and 2,000 published works; Theatre colln, 7,000 copies of dramatic works and musical librettos, Edicts and Bans colln, 70,000 from 1550 to 1870, esp. from the Pontiff State; Periodicals: colln, 2,000 titles (220 current subscriptions) incl. Roman and Pontifical State journals; Heraldry colln, 1,200 works; Sanctification actions colln, Decisions of the Sacred Rota and other ecclesiastical tribunals; the library's holdings

are currently being increased by the acquisition of antiquarian materials and new publs; Dir IOLANDA OLIVIERI.

Biblioteca Centrale del Consiglio Nazionale delle Ricerche (Central Library of National Research Council): Piazzale Aldo Moro 7, 00185 Rome; tel. 06-49933221; fax 06-49933834; e-mail biblioce@bice.rm.cnr.it; internet www.bice.rm.cnr.it; f. 1927; 1,000,000 vols, 10,000 periodicals, EU depository library; scientific and technical subjects; Dir Prof. BRUNELLA SEBASTIANI.

Biblioteca Centrale Giuridica del Ministero della Giustizia: Palazzo di Giustizia, Piazza Cavour, 00193 Rome; tel. 06-68834900; e-mail bcg@giustizia.it; internet www.giustizia.it/giustizia/it/mg_7.wp; f. 1866; 200,000 vols, 2,300 periodicals, 1,000 current periodicals; Dir Dr ORAZIO FRAZZINI.

Biblioteca Centrale del Ministero dell'Interno: Palazzo del Viminale, Via Agostino Depretis, 00184 Rome; tel. 06-46525703; fax 06-46536689; internet www.interno.it/ sezioni/viminale; f. 1872; 110,000 vols; Dir ARTURO LETIZIA.

Biblioteca del Ministero degli Affari Esteri: Piazza della Farnesina 1, 00194 Rome; tel. 06-36913279; e-mail giuseppina .dipietro@esteri.it; internet www.esteri.it/ita/ 5_47_188.asp; f. 1850; 200,000 vols, 1,500 periodicals, 168 current periodicals; international relations, contemporary history; Dir Dott.ssa MARIA ADELAIDE FRABOTTA.

Biblioteca del Ministero delle Risorse Agricole, Alimentari e Forestali: Via XX Settembre 20, 00187 Rome; tel. 06-4743482; fax 06-4743079; internet biblioteca.dsmc .uniroma1.it/ricerca/cittanascosta.html; f. 1860; 500,000 vols, 300 current periodicals; Dir Dott.ssa MILVIA SVIBENS.

Biblioteca del Senato 'Giovanni Spadolini': Piazza della Minerva, 38, 00186 Rome; tel. 06-67063717; fax 06-67064338; e-mail bibliotecaminerva@senato.it; internet www .senato.it/biblioteca; f. 1848; 700,000 vols, 3,000 periodicals, 1,100 current periodicals, 209 MSS, 30 incunabula; chiefly works on law, history and politics; medieval statutes; Head of Library Dott. SANDRO BULGARELLI.

Biblioteca dell'Accademia Nazionale dei Lincei e Corsiniana: Via della Lungara 10, 00165 Rome; tel. 06-6861983; fax 06-68027343; e-mail segreteria@lincei.it; internet www.lincei.it/biblioteca/index.php; f. 1754; 552,000 vols on history of arts, sciences and culture, 7,000 periodicals, 4,600 MSS, 2,307 incunabula; oriental section on Arabic and Islamic civilization, with 35,000 books, 350 periodicals, 500 MSS; online catalogue for modern collection; Dir Dott. MARCO GUARDO; Librarian (Ancient Printed Books) Dr EBE ANTETOMASO; Librarian (Bibliographical Exchanges) Dott.ssa LAURA FORGIONE; Librarian (Oriental Section) Dott.ssa VALENTINA SAGARIA ROSSI; Librarian (Manuscripts) Dott.ssa ENRICA SCHETTINI; Librarian (Periodicals) MARINA TOMEI.

Biblioteca della Camera dei Deputati: Via del Seminario 76, 00186 Rome; tel. 06-67603476; fax 06-6786886; e-mail bib_segreteria@camera.it; f. 1848 in Turin; 1,000,000 vols, 10,000 bound periodicals, 2,500 current periodicals; Dir Dr ANTONIO CASU; publ. *Bollettino Nuove Accessioni* (12 a year).

Biblioteca della Fondazione Marco Besso: Largo di Torre Argentina 11, 00186 Rome; tel. 06-6865611; fax 06-68216313; e-mail biblioteca@fondazionemarcobesso.it; internet www.fondazionemarcobesso.it/ nuovobesso; 60,000 vols and 5,000 pamphlets; special collections: Rome, Dante, Proverbs, Tuscia; Curator ANNA MARIA AMADIO.

Biblioteca della Società Geografica Italiana: Villa Celimontana, Via della Navicella 12, 00184 Rome; tel. 06-7008279; fax 06-77079518; e-mail biblioteca@ societageografica.it; internet www .societageografica.it/archivio/biblioteca/index .htm; f. 1867; 400,000 vols; Library Counsellor LINA MARIA VITALE; publs *Bollettino della Società geografica italiana, Memorie della Società geografica italiana, Ricerche e studi.*

Biblioteca della Società Italiana per l'Organizzazione Internazionale (SIOI): Piazza di S. Marco 51, Palazzetto di Venezia, 00186 Rome; tel. 06-6920781; fax 06-6789102; e-mail sioi@sioi.org; f. 1944; 70,000 vols, 800 periodicals, 500,000 UN documents; Librarian Dr SARA CAVELLI.

Biblioteca della Soprintendenza Speciale alla Galleria Nazionale d'Arte Moderna e Contemporanea: Viale delle Belle Arti 131, 00196 Rome; tel. 06-32298246; fax 06-3221579; e-mail biblioteca .gnam@arti.beniculturali.it; internet www .gnam.arti.beniculturali.it/biblioteca.htm; f. 1945; 65,000 vols, 1,500 periodicals, 40,000 miscellaneous items, on art since the 19th century; Dir Prof. LEANDRO VENTURA; Assoc. Dir Dr MARINA GARGIULO; Librarian Dott. DINA MACERA; publ. *Bollettino mensile delle nuove accessioni* (12 a year, online).

Biblioteca di Storia Moderna e Contemporanea: Via M. Caetani 32, 00186 Rome; tel. 06-6828171; fax 06-68807662; e-mail b-stmo@beniculturali.it; internet www.bsmc .it; f. 1917; 450,000 vols, 11,000 MSS, 7,200 bound periodicals, 600 current periodicals, 3,000 microfilms and microfiches; Dir STEFANIA MURIANNI.

Biblioteca Istituto Italo-Latino Americano: Piazza Benedetto Cairoli 3, 00186 Rome; tel. 06-68492241; fax 06-6872834; e-mail biblioteca@iila.org; internet www.iila .org; f. 1966; specializes in contemporary Latin-American life; services offered: offsets of any item in library, in-service library loans, information service; 80,000 vols, 1,000 periodicals, 100 CD-ROMs; Librarian Prof. RICCARDO CAMPA.

Biblioteca Lancisiana: Borgo S. Spirito 3, 00193 Rome; tel. 06-68352449; fax 06-68352442; internet www.lancisiana.it; f. 1711; history of medicine, history of science; 18,013 vols, 374 MSS, 60 incunabula, 2,000 *cinquecentine*; Dir Dr SAVERIO MARCO FIORILLA.

Biblioteca Medica Statale: Viale del Policlinico 155, 00161 Rome; tel. 06-490778; fax 06-4457265; e-mail bs-medi@beniculturali.it; internet bms.beniculturali.it; f. 1925; 145,000 vols, 1,193 periodicals; Dir Dr GIOVANNI ARGANESE; publ. *Bollettino bimestrale nuove accessioni.*

Biblioteca Musicale del Conservatorio 'S. Cecilia': Via dei Greci 18, 00187 Rome; tel. 06-36096736; fax 06-36001800; internet www.conservatoriosantacecilia.it; f. 1875; 300,000 vols, 10,000 MSS, 100 current periodicals; Dir Prof. DOMENICO CARBONI.

Biblioteca Nazionale Centrale di Roma: Viale Castro Pretorio 105, 00185 Rome; tel. 06-49891; fax 06-4457635; internet www .bncrm.librari.beniculturali.it; f. 1876; 6,000,000 vols, 84,000 MSS, 1,938 incunabula, 25,000 *cinquecentine*, 20,000 maps, 44,000 periodicals, 10,000 prints and drawings; Dir Dott. OSVALDO AVALLONE.

Biblioteca Storica dei Ministeri delle Finanze e del Tesoro: Via XX Settembre 97, 00187 Rome; tel. 06-47613120; fax 06-4814086; internet www.tesoro.it/web/ area_biblioteche/biblioteca_storica.htm; f.

1857; 100,000 vols; Dir Prof. WALTER D'AVANZO.

Biblioteca Universitaria Alessandrina: Piazzale Aldo Moro 5, 00185 Rome; tel. 06-4474021; fax 06-44740222; internet alessandrina.librari.beniculturali.it; f. 1661; 1,000,000 vols, 16,000 bound periodicals, 6,000 current periodicals, 450 MSS, 680 incunabula; Dir MARIA CRISTINA DI MARTINO.

Biblioteca Vallicelliana: Piazza della Chiesa Nuova 18, 00186 Rome; tel. 06-68802671; fax 06-6893868; e-mail b-vall@ beniculturali.it; internet www.vallicelliana .it; f. 1581; 150,000 vols, 2,659 MSS, 404 incunabula; also contains library of 'Società Romana di Storia Patria' (50,000 vols); Dir Dr MARIA CONCETTA PETROLLO PAGLIARANI.

Bibliotheca Hertziana—Max-Planck-Institut für Kunstgeschichte: Via Gregoriana 28, 00187 Rome; tel. 06-69993-1; fax 06-69993333; e-mail info@biblhertz.it; internet www.biblhertz.it; f. 1913; 280,000 vols on the history of Italian art, 1,130 current periodicals, 2,520 bound periodicals, 787,000 photographs of Italian art; Librarian Dr ANDREAS THIELEMANN; publs *Römisches Jahrbuch der Bibliotheca Hertziana, Römische Forschungen der Bibliotheca Hertziana, Römische Studien der Bibliotheca Hertziana, Studi della Bibliotheca Hertziana.*

Cineteca Nazionale: Via Tuscolana 1524, 00173 Rome; tel. 06-72294278; fax 06-7211619; e-mail biblioteca@snc.it; internet www.csc-cinematografia.it/csc/pages/info .php; f. 1935; includes the National Film Archive and the Luigi Chiarini Library; 42,763 vols, 10,976 scenarios, 871 bound periodicals, 170 current periodicals; Dir GABRIELE TESTI; Library Dir Dott.ssa FIAMMETTA LIONTI; publ. *Bianco e Nero* (3 a year).

David Lubin Memorial Library, Food and Agriculture Organization (FAO) of the United Nations: Viale delle Terme di Caracalla, 00153 Rome; tel. 06-57053784; fax 06-57052002; e-mail fao-library-reference@ fao.org; internet www.fao.org/library; f. 1946; reference and information services, briefings and seminars, and electronic reproduction of FAO documents; 1,000,000 vols and more than 8,000 current journals, of which 2,500 electronic; Colln and Devt Group PATRICIA MERRIKIN.

Discoteca di Stato e Museo dell'Audiovisivo (National Sound Archive): Via M. Caetani 32, 00186 Rome; tel. 06-68406901; fax 06-6865837; e-mail discoteca@dds.it; internet www.dds.it; f. 1928; collection of recordings of eminent Italians; 220,000 records of classical and light music, jazz; 25,000 records and tapes on anthropology and folklore; collection of sound reproduction equipment; 9,000 vols; Dir Dott. MASSIMO PISTACCHI.

Istituto Centrale per il Catalogo Unico delle Biblioteche Italiane e per le Informazioni Bibliografiche (Central Institute of the Union Catalogue of Italian Libraries and Bibliographical Information): Viale del Castro Pretorio 105, 00185 Rome; tel. 06-4989484; fax 06-4959302; internet www.iccu .sbn.it; f. 1951; Dir Dr MARCO PAOLI.

Rovigo

Pinacoteca dell'Accademia dei Concordi: Piazza V. Emanuele II 14, 45100 Rovigo; tel. 0425-27991; fax 0425-27993; e-mail concordi@concordi.it; internet www .concordi.it; f. 1580; Egyptian and Roman colln; numismatic colln of 2,000 items; colln of paintings from 15th–19th centuries; 250,000 vols.

Sassari

Biblioteca Universitaria: Piazza Università 21, 07100 Sassari; tel. 079-235179; fax 079-235787; internet www.comune.sassari.it/ guida/biblioteche/biblioteca_universitaria .htm; f. between 1558 and 1562; 350,000 vols, 1,200 bound periodicals, 1,000 current periodicals, 2,864 MSS, 1,431 microfilms, 71 incunabula, 3,500 *cinquecentine*; Dir Dott.ssa PINA ULERI.

Siena

Biblioteca Comunale degli Intronati: Via della Sapienza 5, 53100 Siena; tel. 0577-280704; fax 0577-44293; e-mail biblio@ comune.siena.it; internet www.biblioteca .comune.siena.it; f. 1758; 386,419 vols, 3,679 bound periodicals, 1,091 current periodicals, 5,699 MSS, 1,038 incunabula, 20,000 prints, 5,810 microfiches, 32,500 slides; Dir Dott. DANIELE DANESI.

Teramo

Biblioteca Provinciale 'Melchiorre Delfico': Via Dèlfico 16, 64100 Teramo; tel. 0861-252744; fax 0861-254197; e-mail biblioteca@ provincia.teramo.it; internet www.provincia .teramo.it/?area=1066381515305; f. 1816; 260,000 vols, 5,000 bound periodicals, 600 current periodicals, 1,200 *cinquecentine*, 55 incunabula, 15,000 MSS, 100,000 photographs; Dir LUIGI PONZIANI.

Trento

Biblioteca dell' Archivio di Stato di Trento: Via Maccani 161, 38100 Trento; tel. 0461-829008; fax 0461-828981; e-mail astn@archivi.beniculturali.it; internet www .biblio.unive.it/sba/biblioteche/altrebiblio-teche.asp; f. 1919; administered by the Ministero per i Beni Culturali e Ambientali; cultural function and to promote historical research; 7,141 vols, 100 periodicals, holds archives of state offices from pre-unification Italy and single documents and archives belonging to or deposited with the State; Dir Dr SALVATORE ORTOLANI.

Biblioteca Comunale: Via Roma 55, 38100 Trento; tel. 0461-275521; fax 0461-275552; e-mail tn.viaroma@biblio.infotn.it; internet www.bibcom.trento.it; f. 1856; 735,587 vols, 536 incunabula and 4,244 16th-century edns, music section of 18,365 vols; 25,250 MSS, 8,450 periodicals, 10,247 maps; colln of 166,636 vols on history and culture of Trentino-Alto Adige; Austrian Library (7,821 vols); Dir Dr FABRIZIO LEONARDELLI; publs *A TUTTO BIB—Novita per Ragazzi* (4 a year), *BIB—Notiziario della Biblioteca Comunale di Trento* (4 a year), *Trentine* (1 a year).

Treviso

Biblioteca Comunale: Borgo Cavour 20, 31100 Treviso; tel. 0422-545342; fax 0422-583066; internet www.bibliotecatreviso.it; f. 1770; 450,000 vols, 4,000 MSS, 810 incunabula; Dir Dr EMILIO LIPPI; publ. *Studi Trevisani.*

Trieste

Archivio di Stato di Trieste: Via A. La Marmora 17, 34139 Trieste; tel. 040-390020; fax 040-9380033; e-mail as-ts@beniculturali .it; internet www.archivi.beniculturali.it/ asts; f. 1926; 44,688 vols, 1,116 periodicals; Dir Dott. GRAZIA TATÒ.

Biblioteca Civica 'A. Hortis': Piazza Attilio Hortis 4, 34123 Trieste; tel. 040-6758200; fax 040-6758199; e-mail bibcivica@comune .trieste.it; internet www.retecivica.trieste.it/ triestecultura/biblioteche/bibciv/civicaframe .htm; f. 1793; 400,000 vols, 401 MSS, drawings and maps; Petrarch, Piccolomini, Svevo and Joyce sections and historical archives; Dir Dott. BIANCA CUDERI.

Biblioteca Statale di Trieste: Largo Papa Giovanni XXIII 6, 34123 Trieste; tel. 040-300725; fax 040-301053; e-mail bsts@librari .beniculturali.it; internet www.bsts.librari .beniculturali.it; f. 1956; 196,000 vols; Dir MARCO MENATO.

Narodna in študijska knjižnica v Trstu (Slovene National Study Library): Via S. Francesco 20, 34133 Trieste; tel. 040-635629; fax 040-3484684; e-mail bibslo@spin .it; internet www.nsk-trst.sik.si; f. 1947; 100,000 vols, 500 periodicals.

Turin

Archivio di Stato di Torino: Piazza Castello 209, 10124 Turin; tel. (11) 540382; fax (11) 546176; e-mail as-to@beniculturali.it; internet www.archiviodistatotorino.it; f. 12th century, bldg 1731; houses documents of the House of Savoy (county, duchy, kingdom) up to 1861, and those of the provincial state admins of the 19th century; archives: 81 shelf-km; 50,000 vols, MSS collns; Dir Dr MARCO CARASSI.

Biblioteca dell' Accademia delle Scienze di Torino: Via Maria Vittoria 3, 10123 Turin; tel. 011-5620047; fax 011-532619; e-mail biblioteca@accademia.csi.it; internet www.accademiadellescienze.it; f. 1783; a conservation library covering most fields of the sciences and humanities; rare books dating from the 15th–19th centuries; colln of books, letters and MSS from the late 18th–19th centuries; 200,000 vols, 500 current periodicals and 3,500 others, 35,000 letters, MSS; online catalogue; Head Librarian Dott.ssa ELENA BORGI; publs *Atti della Accademia* (1 a year), *Memorie della Accademia* (1 a year), *Quaderni della Accademia* (1 a year).

Biblioteche Civiche e Raccolte Storiche: Via Cittadella 5, 10122 Turin; tel. 011-4429812; fax 011-4429830; e-mail biblioteche.civiche@comune.torino.it; internet www.comune.torino.it/cultura/ biblioteche; f. 1869; 1,417,683 vols, 67 incunabula, 1,359 MSS, 1,445 16th- century books, 18,762 rare vols, 7,721 microfilms, 1,427 current periodicals; 14 br. libraries; Dir Dott. PAOLO MESSINA.

Biblioteca del Politecnico di Torino: Castello del Valentino, Viale Mattioli 39, 10125 Turin; tel. 011-5646710; fax 011-5646799; e-mail direttore@sb.polito.it; internet www.biblio.polito.it; 15,000 vols; Dir Dott.ssa MARIA VITTORIA SAVIO.

Biblioteca Reale: Piazza Castello 191, 10122 Turin; tel. 011-543855; fax 011-5178259; e-mail to0263@biblioteche .reteunitaria.piemonte.it; f. 1831; 187,614 vols, 4,391 MSS, 1,491 parchments, 3,096 drawings, 1,107 periodicals, 188 incunabula; library of the Savoy family; historical documents on heraldry, military matters, the Sardinian States, the *Risorgimento* and the Piedmont; Dir GIOVANNA GIACOBELLO BERNARD.

Biblioteca Speciale di Matematica 'Giuseppe Peano': Dipartimento di Matematica, Università degli Studi di Torino, Via Carlo Alberto 10, 10123 Turin; fax 011-6702824; f. 1883; 70,000 vols; Dir Prof. FERDINANDO ARZARELLO.

Udine

Biblioteca Civica 'Vincenzo Joppi': Piazza Marconi 8, 33100 Udine; tel. 0432-271583; fax 0432-271580; e-mail bcu@ comune.udine.it; internet www.comune .udine.it/biblioteca.htm; f. 1864; 527,647 vols, 11,000 MSS, 124 incunabula; Dir Dott. ROMANO VECCHIET.

Urbino

Biblioteca Universitaria: Via Aurelio Saffi 2, 61029 Urbino; tel. 0722-305212; fax 0722-305286; e-mail bibhum@uniurb.it; internet www.uniurb.it/bib/home.htm; f. 1720; 436,755 vols; Dir Dott. GOFFREDO MARANGONI.

Venice

Biblioteca dell' Accademia Armena di S. Lazzaro dei Padri Mechitaristi: Isola S. Lazzaro, 30126 Venice; tel. 041-5260104; fax 041-5268690; f. 1701; 100,000 vols, 4,000 MSS; Dir Dr SAHAK DJEMDJEMIAN.

Biblioteca del Civico Museo Correr: Piazza S. Marco 52, Procuratie Nuove, 30124 Venice; tel. 041-2405211; fax 041-5200935; e-mail biblioteca.correr@ fmcvenezia.it; internet www .museicivicivenezian.it; f. 1830; specializes in history of art and Venetian history; 116,933 vols, 1,022 periodicals, 13,018 MSS, 700 MSS on microfiche; Dir GIANDOMENICO ROMANELLI.

Biblioteca Nazionale Marciana: Piazzetta San Marco 7, 30124 Venice; tel. 041-2407211; fax 041-5238803; internet marciana.venezia .sbn.it; f. 1468; 900,000 vols, 3,731 periodicals, 2,883 incunabula, 24,055 *cinquecentine*, 13,000 MSS; Dir Dott. MARINO ZORZI.

Fondazione Scientifica Querini-Stampalia: Castello 5252, 30122 Venice; tel. (41) 2711411; fax (41) 2711445; e-mail biblioteca@ querinistampalia.org; internet www .querinistampalia.it/biblioteca; f. 1869; 300,000 vols, 400 current periodicals; Dir ENRICO ZOLA.

Verona

Biblioteca Civica: Via Cappello 43, 37121 Verona; tel. 045-8079710; fax 045-8009727; e-mail civica@comune.verona.it; internet www.comune.verona.it; f. 1792; 540,000 vols; 1,188 incunabula; 3,477 MSS; Dir Dott. AGOSTINO CONTO.

Vicenza

Biblioteca Civica Bertoliana: Contrà Riale 5, 36100 Vicenza; tel. 0444-578211; fax 0444-578234; e-mail bertoliana@ bibliotecabertoliana.it; internet www .bibliotecabertoliana.it; f. 1696; 800,000 vols, 850 incunabula, 3,564 MSS, 615 current periodicals; Librarian GIORGIO LOTTO.

Museums and Art Galleries

Ancona

Museo Archeologico Nazionale delle Marche: Palazzo Ferretti, Via Ferretti 1, 60121 Ancona; tel. 071-202602; fax 071-202134; internet www.archeomarche.it/ museoanc.htm; f. 1906; prehistoric and Roman archaeology; large colln from Iron Age Picene and Celtic cultures; Dir Prof. Dr GIULIANO DE MARINIS.

Aquileia

Museo Archeologico Nazionale: Via Roma 1, 33051 Aquileia; tel. 0431-91016; fax 0431-919537; e-mail archeologico@ museoarcheo-aquileia.it; internet www .museoarcheo-aquileia.it; f. 1882; collection of Roman architecture, sculpture, inscriptions, mosaics, etc. from excavations in the town; library of 10,000 vols; Dir Dott.ssa FRANCA MASELLI SCOTTI; publ. *Aquileia Nostra* (1 a year).

Attached Museum:

Museo Paleocristiano: Via Monastero, 33051 Aquileia; tel. 0431-91131; fax 0431-919537; e-mail paleocristiano@ museoarcheo-aquileia.it; internet www .museoarcheo-aquileia.it; f. 1961; mosaics and inscriptions from the palaeo-Christian era; Dir Dott.ssa FRANCA MASELLI SCOTTI.

Arezzo

Museo Archeologico: Via Margaritone 10, 52100 Arezzo; tel. and fax 0575-20882; internet www.mega.it/archeo.toscana/ samuar.htm; f. 1832; Etruscan, Greek and Roman antiquities, coralline vases of Augustan period, sarcophagi, mosaics, coins and bronzes; Dir Dott.ssa P. ZAMARCHI.

Museo Statale d'Arte Medievale e Moderna: Palazzo Bruni Ciocchi, Via San Lorentino 8, 52100 Arezzo; tel. 0575-409050; fax 0575-299850; internet brunelleschi.imss.fi.it/ ist/luogo/museostataleartemedievalemo derna.html; f. 1957; Italian paintings from 13th–19th centuries, Majolica ware, glass, ivories, seals and coins; Curator Dott. STEFANO CASCIU.

Assisi

Museo del Tesoro della Basilica di S. Francesco in Assisi: Piazza S. Francesco, 2, 06081 Assisi; tel. 075-819001; fax 075-8190035; e-mail museosc@gmail.com; internet www.sanfrancescoassisi.org; f. 1927; historical and artistic collns relating to the Basilica church of St Francis, F. M. Perkins colln of 13th–15th-century European art; Dir Fr LUIGI MARIOLI.

Bari

Museo Archeologico: Palazzo dell'Ateneo, Piazza Umberto I, 70121 Bari; tel. 080-5211559; internet www.archeologia .beniculturali.it/pages/atlante/s89.html; f. 1882; library of 2,500 vols; Dir Dott. GIUSEPPE ANDREASSI.

Pinacoteca Provinciale: Via Spalato 19, 70121 Bari; tel. 080-5412421; fax 080-5583401; e-mail pinacotecaprov.bari@tin.it; f. 1928; Apulian, Venetian and Neapolitan paintings and sculpture from 11th to 19th centuries; paintings from the 'Macchiaioli'; library of 3,000 vols; Dir Dott.ssa CLARA GELAO.

Bergamo

Accademia Carrara di Belle Arti–Museo: Accademia Carrara di Belle Arti, Piazza Giacomo Carrara 82/A, 24121 Bergamo; tel. 035-399640; fax 035-224510; e-mail segr@ accademiacarrara.bergamo.it; internet www .accademiacarrara.bergamo.it; f. 1796; colln incl. paintings by Bellini, Raffaello, Pisanello, Mantegna, Botticelli, Beato Angelico, Previtali, Tiepolo, Lotto, Moroni, Baschenis, Galgario; drawings, prints and sculptures since 15th century; Pres. Dott. WILLI ZAVARITT; Curator GIOVANNI VALAGUSSA.

Bologna

Museo Civico Archeologico: Via dell'Archiginnasio 2, 40124 Bologna; tel. 051-2757211; fax 051-266516; e-mail mca@comune.bologna .it; internet www.comune.bologna.it/bologna/ museoarcheologico; f. 1881; prehistoric, Egyptian, Greek, Roman, Villanovan, Etruscan and Celtic antiquities; numismatic colln; library of 28,000 vols; Dir Dott.ssa CRISTIANA MORIGI GOVI.

Pinacoteca Nazionale: Via Belle Arti 56, 40126 Bologna; tel. 051-4209411; e-mail spsadbo@arti.beniculturali.it; internet www .pinacotecabologna.it; f. 1808; Bolognese paintings and other Italian schools from 14th–18th centuries; German and Italian engravings; Dir Prof. ANDREA EMILIANI.

Bolzano

Museo Archeologico dell'Alto Adige/ Südtiroler Archäologiemuseum (South Tyrol Museum of Archaeology): Via Museo 43, 39100 Bolzano; tel. 0471-320100; fax 0471-320122; e-mail museum@iceman.it; internet www.iceman.it; history and archaeology of the South Tyrol region from the Palaeolithic to the Carolingian period (AD 800); also 'Ötzi', 5,000-year old mummified man discovered in the Schnalstal Glacier in 1991; Dir Dr ANGELIKA FLECKINGER.

Museo Civico di Bolzano: Via Cassa di Risparmio 14, 39100 Bolzano; tel. 0471-974625; fax 0471-980144; e-mail museo .civico@comune.bolzano.it; internet www .comune.bolzano.it; f. 1902; history of art since medieval period; archaeology, numismatics, furniture, liturgical items; library of 27,000 vols, 77 periodicals; Dir Dr STEFAN DEMETZ.

Brescia

Fondazione Brescia Musei: Via Musei 81, 25121 Brescia; tel. 030-2400640; fax 030-2990267; internet www.bresciamusei.com; Dir Dott.ssa RENATA STRADIOTTI.

Constituent Museums and Galleries:

Museo delle Armi 'Luigi Marzoli': Via Castello 9, 25121, Brescia; tel. 030-293292; f. 1988; 14th- to 18th-century arms.

Museo del Risorgimento: Via Castello 9, 25121 Brescia; tel. 030-293292; f. 1959; 19th-century historical exhibits.

Pinacoteca Tosio Martinengo: Piazza Moretto 4, 25121 Brescia; tel. 030-3774999; f. 1906; art from the 13th to 18th centuries.

Santa Giulia–Museo della Città: Via dei Musei 81/bis, 25121 Brescia; tel. 030-2977834; f. 1882; art and archaeology and 3 churches; incl. colln of the former Museo Romano (prehistoric, pre-Roman and Roman artefacts).

Museo Civico di Scienze Naturali: Via Ozanam 4, 25128 Brescia; tel. 030-2978672; fax 030-3701048; e-mail museoscienze@ comune.brescia.it; internet www.comune .brescia.it/museoscienzenaturali; f. 1949; botanical, geological, zoological and palaeoethnographical collns; library of 60,000 vols; Dir MARCO TONON; publs *Annuario Civica Specola Cidnea*, *Natura Bresciana*.

Museo Diocesano d'Arte Sacra: Via Gasparo da Salò 13, 25122 Brescia; tel. 030-3751064; fax 030-40233; internet www .mus-dioc.bs.it; f. 1978; Dir IVO PANTEGHINI.

Cagliari

Museo Archeologico Nazionale: Cittadella dei Musei, Piazza Arsenale 1, 09124 Cagliari; tel. 070-662496; f. 1806; Sardinian antiquities (prehistorical, Punic, Roman periods); library of 8,000 vols; Dir Dr VINCENZO SANTONI.

Capua

Museo Provinciale Campano: Via Roma, 81043 Capua; tel. 0823-620076; fax 0823-620035; e-mail museocampano@provincia .caserta.it; internet www.provincia.caserta .it/museocampano; f. 1870; library of 70,000 vols, 2,956 MSS; Pres. ON. DOMENICO ZINZI; Dir (vacant).

Chieti

Museo Archeologico Nazionale d'Abruzzo: Via Villa Comunale 3, 66100 Chieti; tel. 0871-331668; fax 0871-330946; e-mail musarc@muvi.org; internet www .muvi.org/musarc; f. 1959; pottery, weapons and ornaments from 9th to 4th century BC,

burial sites, sculpture from 6th and 5th centuries BC; Dir Dott.ssa MARIA RUGGERI.

Cividale

Museo Archeologico Nazionale: Piazza del Duomo 13, 33043 Cividale; tel. 0432-700700; fax 0432-700751; e-mail museoarcheocividale@beniculturali.it; f. 1817; prehistoric, Roman and medieval archaeology, jewellery and miniatures, MSS; library of 15,000 vols and archives; Dir Dott.ssa SERENA VITRI; publ. *Forum Iulii* (1 a year).

Cosenza

Museo Civico di Rovereto: Bgo S. Caterina 41, 38068 Rovereto; tel. 0464-439055; fax 0464-439487; e-mail museo@museocivico .rovereto.tn.it; internet www.museocivico .rovereto.tn.it; f. 1898; history and archaeology; Dir Dr VINCENZO ZUMBINI; publ. *Guide*.

Faenza

Museo Internazionale delle Ceramiche: Via Campidori 2, 48018 Faenza; tel. 0546-697311; fax 0546-27141; e-mail info@ micfaenza.org; internet www.micfaenza.org; f. 1908; history, art and techniques of ceramics; library of 53,000 vols; Dir (vacant); publ. *Faenza* (6 a year).

Ferrara

Gallerie d'Arte Moderna e Contemporanea: Corso Porta Mare 9, 44100 Ferrara; tel. 0532-243415; e-mail artemoderna@ comune.fe.it; Dir Dott. ANDREA BUZZONI.

Constituent Galleries:

Museo Michelangelo Antonioni: Corso Ercole i d'Este 17, 44100 Ferrara; tel. 0532-209988; e-mail diamanti@comune.fe.it.

Palazzo dei Diamanti: Corso Ercole I d'Este 21, 44100 Ferrara; tel. 0532-209988; fax 0532-203064; e-mail diamanti@comune .fe.it; incorporates Galleria d'Arte Moderna e Contemporanea.

Palazzo Massari: Corso Porta Mare 5–9, 44100 Ferrara; tel. 0532-243415; fax 0532-205035; e-mail artemoderna@comune.fe.it; incorporates Museo d'Arte Moderna e Contemporanea Filippe de Pisis, Museo dell'Ottocento, Museo G. Boldini, Padiglione d'Arte Contemporanea.

Museo Archeologico Nazionale di Ferrara: Via XX Settembre 124 (Palazzo di Ludovico il Moro), 44100 Ferrara; tel. 0532-66299; fax 0532-741270; e-mail sba-ero .museoarchferrara@beniculturali.it; internet www.archeobo.arti.beniculturali.it/ferrara; f. 1935; Greco-Etruscan vases, statuettes, bronzes and gold ornaments from the graves of Spina; Dir Dott.ssa CATERINA CORNELIO.

Florence

Comune di Firenze–Direzione Cultura– Servizio Musei: Via delle Conce 28, 50122 Florence; tel. 055-2625961; fax 055-2625984; internet www.comune.fi.it; Dir Dott.ssa CHIARA SILLA.

Attached Museums and Galleries:

Cappella Brancacci: Piazza del Carmine, 50124 Florence; tel. 055-2382195; frescoes in the Church of Santa Maria del Carmine painted by Masolino (1383–1447) and Masaccio (1401–28), and completed by Filippino Lippi (1457–1504).

Fondazione Romano nel Cenacolo di Santo Spirito: Piazza Santo Spirito 29, 50125 Florence; tel. 055-287043; colln of sculptures given by Salvatore Romano; incl. 2 pieces by Tino di Camaino, and 2 fragments attributed to Donatello.

Galleria Rinaldo Carnielo: Piazza Savonarola 3, 50132 Florence; works by the sculptor Rinaldo Carnielo (1853–1910).

Museo Bardini: Piazza dei Mozzi 1, 50125 Florence; tel. 055-2342427; f. 1925; paintings by Pollaiuolo, Beccafumi, Lucas Cranach, Mirabello Cavalori, Giovanni da S. Giovanni, Cecco Bravo, Guercino, Carlo Dolci, Luca Giordano, Il Volterano; sculptures by Nicola and Giovanni Pisano, Tino di Camaino, Andrea della Robbia, Donatello, Michelozzo; oriental rugs, bronzes, arms, furniture, medals, etc.

Museo Marino Marini: Piazza San Pancrazio, 50123 Florence; tel. 055-219432; fax 055-289510; e-mail info@ museomarinomarini.it; internet www .museomarinomarini.it; f. 1988; 183 sculptures, paintings, drawings by the sculptor Marino Marini (1901–80) in a permanent exhibition; Pres. CARLO SISI.

Museo di Palazzo Vecchio: Quartieri Monumentali, Piazza della Signoria, 50122 Florence; tel. 055-2768325; paintings, furnishings; frescoes by Ghirlandaio, Salviati, Bronzino, Vasari; Michelangelo's 'Victory' statue.

Museo di Santa Maria Novella: Piazza S. Maria Novella, 50123 Florence; tel. 055-282187; museum built in part of a Dominican church; 15th-century frescoes of the Genesis story by Paolo Uccello, Dello Delli; 14th-century frescoes by Andrea di Bonaiuto depicting the Dominican order and the Church Triumphant.

Museo Stibbert: Via F. Stibbert 26, 50134 Florence; tel. 055-486049; fax 055-475721; e-mail info@museostibbert.it; internet www.museostibbert.it/web.it; f. 1908; Etruscan, Roman and medieval arms and armour; European and Oriental arms from 15th to 19th centuries; holy objects and vestments; European and Oriental costumes, etc., from 18th to 19th centuries; Flemish tapestries from 15th to 17th centuries; Italian and foreign paintings and furniture from 14th to 19th centuries; library of 3,500 vols; Dir KIRSTEN ASCHENGREEN.

Museo Storico Topografico 'Firenze com' era': Via dell'Oriolo 24, 50122 Florence; tel. 055-2616545; depicts the history of the city.

Raccolta d'Arte Contemporanea 'Alberto della Ragione': Via S. Egidio, 21, 50122 Florence; tel. 055-283078; c. 250 works donated by Alberto della Ragione in 1970; Italian art 1914–60.

Gabinetto Disegni e Stampe degli Uffizi: Via Ninna 5, 50123 Florence; tel. 055-2388671; fax 055-2388624; internet www .polomuseale.firenze.it; Dir MARZIA FAIETTI.

Galleria d'Arte Moderna di Palazzo Pitti: Piazza Pitti 1, 50125 Florence; tel. 055-2388601; fax 055-2654520; e-mail gam@ polomuseale.firenze.it; internet www .polomuseale.firenze.it/musei/artemoderna; f. 1914; paintings and sculptures since the 19th century; library of 2,000 vols on the history of art; Dir Dott. CARLO SISI.

Galleria dell' Accademia: Via Ricasoli 58–60, 50122 Florence; tel. 055-2388609; fax 055-2388764; e-mail galleriaaccademia@ polomuseale.firenze.it; internet www .polomuseale.firenze.it; f. 1784; contains the most complete colln of Michelangelo's statues in Florence and works of art of 13th–19th-century masters, mostly Tuscan; colln of musical instruments from the Medici and Lorena families; Dir Dott.ssa FRANCA FALLETTI.

Galleria Palatina: Palazzo Pitti, Piazza Pitti 1, 50125 Florence; tel. 055-2388614;

fax 055-2388613; e-mail galleriapalatina
.galleri@tin.it; internet www.polomuseale
.firenze.it/musei/palatina; f. 17th century;
contains a colln of paintings from the 16th
and 17th centuries; library of 2,000 vols on
the history of art; Dir SERENA PADOVANI.

Galleria Palatina e Appartamenti Reali:
Palazzo Pitti, Piazza Pitti 1, 50125 Florence;
tel. 055-2388611; fax 055-2388613; e-mail
galleriapalatina.galleri@tin.it; internet www
.sbas.firenze.it; f. 18th and 19th centuries;
Italian and European masterpieces from the
16th and 17th centuries, incl. works by
Raphael, A. del Sarto, Carvaggio, Titian,
Rubens and Van Dyck; Dir Dott.ssa SERENA
PADOVANI.

Galleria degli Uffizi: Piazzale degli Uffizi,
50122 Florence; tel. 055-2388651; fax 055-
2388694; e-mail direzione.uffizi@
polomuseale.firenze.it; internet www
.polomuseale.firenze.it/uffizi; f. 16th century;
Florentine Renaissance paintings and sculpture, and paintings by German, Dutch and
Flemish masters; library of 64,000 vols, 470
MSS relating to the Florentine collections, 5
incunabula, 996 bound periodicals, 140 current periodicals; Dir ANTONIO PAOLUCCI.

Museo Archeologico Nazionale: Via della
Colonna 38, 50121 Florence; tel. 055-23575;
fax 055-242213; e-mail sat@comune.firenze
.it; internet www.comune.firenze.it/soggetti/
sat; f. 1870; Egyptian, Etruscan and Greco-
Roman archaeology; Dir Dott. ANGELO BOT-
TINI.

Museo degli Argenti: Palazzo Pitti, Piazza
Pitti 1, 50125 Florence; tel. 055-2388709; fax
055-2388710; internet www.polomuseale
.firenze.it/musei/argenti; summer state
apartments of the Medici Grand Dukes;
collns of gold, silver, enamel, *objets d'art*,
hardstones, ivory, amber, cameos and jewels,
principally from the 15th–18th centuries; Dir
ORNELLA CASAZZA.

Attached Gallery:

> **Galleria del Costume:** Palazzo Pitti,
> 50125 Florence; tel. and fax 055-2388763;
> e-mail costume.pitti@virgilio.it; internet
> www.polomuseale.firenze.it/musei/cos-
> tume; period costumes, principally since
> the 18th century, shown in the neo-clas-
> sical Meridiana wing of the palace; Dir Dr
> CARLO SISI.

Museo della Casa Buonarroti: Via Ghi-
bellina 70, 50122 Florence; tel. 055-241752;
fax 055-241698; e-mail fond@casabuonarroti
.it; internet www.casabuonarroti.it; f. 1858;
works by Michelangelo and others; large
collection of drawings by Michelangelo,
sculptures, majolica and archaeological items
from the Buonarroti family collections; Dir P.
RAGIONIERI.

Museo Horne: Fondazione Horne, Via dei
Benci, 50122 Florence; tel. 055-244661; furniture and works of art from the 14th–16th
centuries; Pres. Dr UMBERTO BALDINI.

Museo Mediceo: Palazzo Medici-Riccardi,
Via Cavour 1, 50129 Florence; tel. 055-
2760340; fax 055-2760451; e-mail a
.belisario@provincia.fi.it; internet www
.palazzo-medici.it; chapel built by Michelozzo
and frescoed by Benozzo Gozzoli (1459);
gallery with frescoes by Luca Giordano
(1680); Dir ALESSANDRO BELISARIO.

Museo Nazionale del Bargello: Via del
Proconsolo 4, 50122 Florence; tel. 055-
2388606; fax 055-2388756; e-mail
museobargello@libero.it; internet www.sbas
.firenze.it/bargello; f. 1859; medieval and
modern sculpture and *objets d'art*; Dir BEA-
TRICE PAOLOZZI STROZZI; publs *Inventari Med-
icei*, *Lo Specchio del Bargello*, *Mostre del
Museo Nazionale del Bargello*.

Museo dell' Opera del Duomo: Piazza del
Duomo 9, 50122 Florence; tel. 055-2302885;
fax 055-2302898; e-mail opera@operaduomo
.firenze.it; internet www.operaduomo.firenze
.it; f. 1891; Dir PATRIZIO OSTICRESI.

**Museo di Palazzo Davanzati (Casa Fior-
entina Antica):** Via Porta Rossa 13, 50123
Florence; tel. 055-2388610; fax 055-2388699;
internet www.sbas.firenze.it; f. 1956; applied
arts, specializing in lace and ceramics; Dir
Dott.ssa ROSANNA CATERINA PROTO PISANI.

Museo delle Porcellane: Piazza Pitti,
50125 Florence; tel. 055-2388709; fax 055-
2388710; internet www.polomuseale.firenze
.it/musei/porcellane; collection of European
porcelain from c. 1720–1850; Dir Dr MARIA
MADDALENA MOSCO.

Museo di S. Marco o dell' Angelico:
Piazza San Marco 3, 50121 Florence; tel.
055-2388608; fax 055-2388704; e-mail
museosanmarco@polomuseale.firenze.it;
internet www.polomuseale.firenze.it/musei/
sanmarco; f. 1869; contains the largest existing colln of paintings by Fra Angelico; Dir
Dott.ssa MAGNOLIA SCUDIERI.

**Museo Galileo—Istituto e Museo di
Storia della Scienza:** Piazza dei Giudici 1,
50122 Florence; tel. 055-265311; fax 055-
2653130; e-mail info@museogalileo.it;
internet www.museogalileo.it; f. 1927;
museum of scientific instruments and institute dedicated to the research, documentation and dissemination of the history of
science; library of 110,000 vols; Dir Prof.
PAOLO GALLUZZI; publs *Galilaeana* (1 a year),
Nuncius Annali di Storia della Scienza (2 a
year).

Forlì

Istituti Culturali ed Artistici: Corso della
Repubblica 72, 47100 Forlì; tel. 0543-712600;
fax 0543-712616; comprises a picture gallery,
collection of prints and engravings, archaeological and ethnographical museums, ceramics, sculpture and local history; Piancastelli
collection of paintings, medals and coins; Dir
Dr FRANCO FABBRI.

Pinacoteca e Musei del Comune: Corso
Repubblica 72, 47100 Forlì; tel. 0543-712606;
fax 0543-712616; e-mail servizio.pinacoteca
.musei@cofo.it; Dir Dr FRANCO FABBRI.

Genoa

**Comune di Genova Direzione Cultura,
Sport e Turismo—Settore Musei:** Largo
Pertini 4, 16121 Genoa; tel. 010-5574700; fax
010-5574701; e-mail museicivici@comune
.genova.it; internet www.comune.genova.it/
turismo/musei/welcome.htm; f. 1908; library
of 40,000 vols; Dir GUIDO GANDINO; publ.
Bollettino dei Musei Civici Genovesi (4 a
year).

Attached Museums and Galleries:

> **Archivio Storico del Comune di Gen-
> ova:** Palazzo Ducale, Piazza Matteotti 10,
> 16123 Genoa; tel. 010-5574808; fax 010-
> 5574823; e-mail archiviostorico@comune
> .genova.it; internet www
> .archiviostoricogenova.it; f. 1906; docu-
> ments since 15th century; coins, weights
> and measures; Curator RAFFAELLA PONTE.

> **Castello D'Albertis Museo delle Cul-
> ture del Mondo:** Corso Dogali 18, 16136
> Genoa; tel. 010-2723820; fax 010-2721456;
> e-mail castellodalbertis@comune.genova.it;
> internet www.castellodalbertis
> .museidigenova.it; f. 2004; housed in a
> Neo-Gothic castle with archaeological and
> ethnological collns from pre-Columbian
> civilizations of Central and South America,
> Indians of North American plains, Hopi of
> Arizona, cultures of Oceania and Africa;
> also houses Museo delle Musiche dei Popoli
> (Folk Music Museum) that preserves

musical instruments from all over the
world; Curator MARIA CAMILLA DE PALMA.

**Centro di Documentazione per la
Storia, l'Arte, l'Immagine di Genova:**
Via ai 4 Canti di San Francesco 59–61 r,
16124 Genoa; tel. 010-5574956; fax 010-
5574970; e-mail archiviofotografico@
comune.genova.it; internet www
.museidigenova.it; f. 1910; art library;
topographic colln; 200,000 photographs
(1860–1946) on Genoese customs and history, 19th-century landscapes, war damage, Italian and Genoese art and
architecture 11th–19th centuries; photographs of museum collns; topographical
and cartographical documents on Genoa
and Liguria; library of 50,000 vols, 50,000
photos, 7,000 documents; Curator ELISA-
BETTA PAPONE.

**Civico Museo di Storia e Cultura
Contadina Genovese e Ligure:** Salita
al Garbo 47, 16159 Genoa Rivarolo; tel.
010-7401243; fax 010-5574701; f. 1983;
colln of tools and utensils relating to local
rural life since 19th century; Curator
PATRIZIA GARIBALDI.

Galata Museo del Mare: Calata de Mari
1, Darsena, Porto Antico, 16128 Genoa; fax
010-2345655; e-mail info@
galatamuseodelmare.it; internet www
.galatamuseodelmare.it; maritime history
of the city; exhibits incl. 17th-century
galleon, arsenal, docks, ancient atlases
and naval instruments.

Galleria di Palazzo Bianco: Via Garibaldi 11, 16124 Genoa; tel. 010-5572193;
fax 010-5572269; e-mail
museidistradanuova@comune.genova.it;
internet www.museidigenova.it; f. 1889;
paintings by Genoese and Flemish masters
and other schools (16th–18th centuries);
Dir PIERO BOCCARDO; Curator RAFFAELLA
BESTA.

Galleria di Palazzo Rosso: Via Garibaldi
18, 16124 Genoa; tel. 010-2476351; fax
010-2475357; e-mail museopalazzorosso@
comune.genova.it; internet www
.museopalazzorosso.it; f. 1874; the fine art
colln of a noble Genoese family: paintings
and sculpture, frescoes and stuccos, nativity models, ceramics; also a colln of textiles;
Curator PIERO BOCCARDO.

Museo di Archeologia Ligure: Villa
Durazzo-Pallavicini, Via Pallavicini 11,
16155 Genoa–Pegli; tel. 010-6981048; fax
010-6974040; e-mail archligure@mail.it; f.
1892; Ligurian archaeology of the periods
up to the Roman era; colln of Greek and
Roman antiquities; Curators PATRIZIA GAR-
IBALDI, GUIDO ROSSI.

**Museo d'Arte Contemporanea Villa
Croce:** Via Jacopo Ruffini 3, 16128 Genoa;
tel. 010-585772; fax 010-532482; e-mail
museocroce@comune.genova.it; internet
www.museovillacroce.it; f. 1985; works by
key Italian artists; documentation on artistic research in Genoa and Liguria from
the Second World War onwards; sculpture
by Genoese and Ligurian artists; specialized library and archive open to the public;
library of 20,000 books and exposition
catalogues; Curator SANDRA SOLIMANO.

**Museo d'Arte Orientale 'Edoardo
Chiossone':** Villetta di Negro, Piazzale
Mazzini 4N, 16122 Genoa; tel. 010-542285;
fax 010-580526; e-mail museochiossone@
comune.genova.it; internet www.chiossone
.museidigenova.it; f. 1905; Japanese works
of art from 11th–19th centuries (about
20,000 pieces), collected in Japan during
the Meiji period by Edoardo Chiossone; Dir
DONATELLA FAILLA.

Museo Civico di Storia Naturale 'Giacomo Doria': Via Brigata Liguria 9, 16121 Genoa; tel. 010-564567; fax 010-566319; e-mail museodoria@comune.genova.it; internet www.museodoria.it; f. 1867; zoology, botany and geology; library of 89,000 vols; Dir Dr ROBERTO POGGI; publs *Annali* (every 2 years), *Doriana* (irregular).

Museo 'Giannettino Luxoro': Via Mafalda di Savoia 3, 16167 Genoa–Nervi; tel. 010-322673; fax 010-322396; f. 1945; Flemish and Genoese paintings of the 17th and 18th centuries, furniture, ceramics and pottery in the rooms of an early 20th-century villa; Curator LOREDANA PESSA.

Museo Navale: Villa Doria, Piazza Bonavino 7, 16156 Genoa–Pegli; tel. 010-6969885; fax 010-5574701; f. 1930; models of ships, nautical instruments, navigation maps, prints; Curator PIERANGELO CAMPODONICO.

Museo del Risorgimento e Istituto Mazziniano: Casa di Mazzini, Via Lomellini 11, 16124 Genoa; tel. 010-2465843; fax 010-2541545; e-mail museorisorgimento@comune.genova.it; internet www.istitutomazziniano.it; f. 1934; exhibits illustrating life and work of Mazzini, 19th-century documents and arms, specialized library containing works since 18th century; Curator LEO MORABITO.

Museo di Sant'Agostino: Piazza Sarzano 35r., 16128 Genoa; tel. 010-2511263; fax 010-2464516; e-mail museosagostino@comune.genova.it; internet www.museosantagostino.it; f. 1939, closed due to damage sustained during the Second World War, reopened 1984; sculpture from 10th–18th centuries, architecture and paintings; Curator ADELMO TADDEI.

Museo del Tesoro della Cattedrale di San Lorenzo: Piazza San Lorenzo, 16123 Genoa; tel. 010-2471831; fax 010-5574701; e-mail info@arti-e-mestieri.it; internet www.museosanlorenzo.it; f. 1892; gold and silver objects; Curator CLARIO DI FABIO.

Padiglione del Mare e della Navigazione: Porto Antico—Magazzini del Cotone, 16126 Genoa; tel. 010-2463678; fax 010-2467746; f. 1996; maritime colln; works of art, models and reproductions; Curator PIERANGELO CAMPODONICO.

Raccolte Frugone in Villa Grimaldi: Villa Grimaldi Fassio, Via Capolungo 9, Nervi, 16167 Genoa; tel. 010-322396; fax 010-3724405; e-mail raccoltefrugone@comune.genova.it; internet www.raccoltefrugone.it; f. 1993; colln of sculpture and paintings by Italian artists since 19th century; Curator MARIA FLORA GIUBILEI.

Galleria Nazionale di Palazzo Spinola: Piazza Pellicceria 1, 16123 Genoa; tel. 010-2705300; fax 010-2705322; e-mail palazzospinola@beniculturali.it; internet www.palazzospinola.it; f. 1958; Dir Dott.ssa FARIDA SIMONETTI; publ. *Quaderni* (1 a year).

Soprintendenza per i Beni Archeologici della Liguria: Palazzo Reale, Via Balbi 10, 16126 Genoa; tel. 010-27181; fax 010-2465925; e-mail sba-lig@beniculturali.it; internet www.archeoge.arti.beniculturali.it; f. 1939; preservation of monuments and excavations of Liguria (prehistoric, Roman and medieval); conservation of the ancient city of Luni, prehistoric caves of Balzi Rossi and archeological area of Varignano Vecchio; library of 14,000 vols; Superintendent Dott. FILIPPO MARIA GAMBARI.

Grosseto

Museo Archeologico e d'Arte della Maremma: Piazza Baccarini 3, 58100 Grosseto; tel. 0564-488750; fax 0564-488753; e-mail maam@gol.grosseto.it; internet www.gol.grosseto.it/maam; f. 1865; archaeological and medieval findings from the Maremma; library of 3,000 vols; Dir Dott.ssa MARIAGRAZIA CELUZZA.

L'Aquila

Museo Nazionale d'Abruzzo: Forte Spagnolo, 67100 L'Aquila; tel. 0862-6331; fax 0862-413096; e-mail mna@muvi.org; internet muvi.org/museonazionaledabruzzo; f. 1949; art from the early Middle Ages to contemporary times; Dir Dott. CALCEDONIO TROPEA.

Lecce

Museo 'Sigismondo Castromediano': Viale Gallipoli 28, 73100 Lecce; tel. 0832-307415; fax 0832-304435; f. 1868; archaeology and art gallery; library of 1,900 vols, 2,500 pamphlets and offprints; Dir ANTONIO CASSIANO.

Lucca

Museo Nazionale di Villa Guinigi: Villa Guinigi, Via della Quarquonia, 55100 Lucca; tel. and fax 0583-496033; e-mail luccamuseinazionali@libero.it; internet www.liberologico.com/sbaaaspi/flash/musei/villa guinigi; colln of Roman and late Roman sculptures and mosaics; Romanesque, Gothic, Renaissance and Neoclassical sculpture; paintings from the 12th–18th centuries incl. Fra Bartolomeo and Vasari; wood inlays, textiles, medieval goldsmiths' art; Dir Dott.ssa MARIA TERESA FILIERI.

Museo e Pinacoteca Nazionale di Palazzo Mansi: Via Galli Tassi 43, 55100 Lucca; tel. 0583-55570; fax 0583-312221; f. 1868; paintings by Titian, Tintoretto, etc., and Tuscan, Venetian, French and Flemish Schools; Dir Dr MARIA TERESA FILIERI.

Mantua

Palazzo Ducale: Piazza Sordello 40, 46100 Mantua; tel. 0376-352100; fax 0376-366274; e-mail info@mantovaducale.it; internet www.mantovaducale.it; incorporates Museo e Galleria di Pittura (13th–18th-century paintings) and Museo Statuario d'Arte Greca e Romana; Dir Dott. FABRIZIO MAGANI.

Matera

Museo Nazionale D. Ridola: Via D. Ridola 24, 75100 Matera; tel. 0835-310058; internet www.archeologia.beniculturali.it/pages/atlante/s201.html; f. 1910; local prehistory; funerary items from 6th–4th centuries BC, bronzes; Dir Dott.ssa MARIA LUISA NAVA.

Messina

Museo Regionale: Viale della Libertà 465, 98191 Messina; tel. 090-361292; fax 090-361294; internet www.regione.sicilia.it/beniculturali/dirbenicult/musei/musei2/engarmessina.htm; f. 1922; local art and culture from 12th–18th centuries; Dir Dott.ssa CARMELA ANGELA DI STEFANO.

Milan

Galleria d'Arte Moderna: Villa Belgiojoso Bonoparte, Museo Dell'Ottocento, Via Palestro 16, 20121 Milan; tel. and fax 02-77809761; f. 1861; painting and sculpture from Neo-Classical period until late 19th century; incl. the Grassi and Vismara collns and Museo Marino Marini; Dir Dott.ssa MARIA TERESA FIORIO.

Museo d'Arte Antica: Castello Sforzesco, 20121 Milan; tel. 02-88463695; fax 02-88463650; f. 1893; sculpture from the middle ages to the 16th century, incl. the *Pietà* of Michelangelo; paintings, incl. works by Mantegna, Foppa, Lippi, Bellini, Lotto, Tintoretto, Tiepolo, Guardi; furniture, silver, bronzes, ivories, ceramics, musical instruments, tapestries by Bramantino, Bertarelli stamp colln; library of 41,000 vols; Dir Dr CLAUDIO SALSI (engravings, drawings); Dir Dr FRANCESCA TASSO (art collns).

Museo Civico di Storia Naturale di Milano: Corso Venezia 55, 20121 Milan; tel. 02-88463280; fax 02-88463281; internet www.comune.milano.it/museostorianaturale; f. 1838; all brs of natural history; depts of vertebrate palaeontology, invertebrate palaeontology, mineralogy, vertebrate zoology, invertebrate zoology, entomology, botany; library of 140,000 vols; Dir Dr ENRICO BANFI; publs *Atti della Società Italiana di Scienze Naturali e del Museo Civico di Storia Naturale di Milano* (2 a year), *Memorie della Società Italiana di Scienze Naturali e del Museo Civico di Storia Naturale di Milano* (irregular), *Natura* (2 a year).

Museo Nazionale della Scienza e della Tecnica 'Leonardo da Vinci': Via San Vittore 21, 20123 Milan; tel. 02-485551; fax 02-48010016; e-mail museo@museoscienza.org; internet www.museoscienza.org; f. 1953; scientific and technical activities, displaying relics, models and designs, with particular emphasis on Leonardo's work; library of 32,000 vols, mostly history of science and technology, 150 16th-century vols, large section on Leonardo, including facsimile of every MS; Dir FIORENZO GALLI; publ. *Museoscienza* (2 a year).

Museo Poldi Pezzoli: Via A. Manzoni 12, 20121 Milan; tel. 02-796334; fax 02-45473811; e-mail info@museopoldipezzoli.it; internet www.museopoldipezzoli.it; f. 1881; paintings from 14th–19th centuries; armour, tapestries, rugs, jewellery, porcelain, glass, textiles, furniture, clocks and watches, etc.; library of 5,500 vols; Dir Dott. ANNALISA ZANNI.

Pinacoteca Ambrosiana: Piazza Pio XI 2, 20123 Milan; tel. 02-806921; fax 02-80692210; e-mail info@ambrosiana.it; internet www.ambrosiana.it; f. 1618; paintings by Raphael, Botticelli, Titian, Luini, Jan Brueghel, Leonardo da Vinci, Jacobo Bassano, Bramantino, etc.; miniatures, enamels, ceramics and medallions; Dir Dott. GIANFRANCO RAVASI.

Pinacoteca di Brera: Via Brera 28, 20121 Milan; tel. 02-722631; fax 02-72001140; e-mail brera.artimi@arti.beniculturali.it; internet www.brera.beniculturali.it; f. 1809; pictures of all schools, especially Lombard and Venetian; paintings by Mantegna, Bellini, Crivelli, Lotto, Titian, Veronese, Tintoretto, Tiepolo, Foppa, Bergognone, Luini, Piero della Francesca, Bramante, Raphael, Caravaggio, Rembrandt, Van Dyck, Rubens; also 20th-century works, mostly Italian; Dir Dott.ssa MARIA TERESA FIORIO.

Raccolte Storiche del Comune di Milano, Museo del Risorgimento: Palazzo De Marchi, Via Borgonuovo 23, 20121 Milan; tel. 02-88464170; fax 02-88464181; e-mail risorgi@energy.it; internet www.museidelcentro.mi.it; f. 1884; documents, relics, etc., of the period 1796–1870; library of 130,000 vols; Dir Dott. ROBERTO GUERRI.

Modena

Galleria Estense: Palazzo dei Musei, Piazza Sant' Agostino 337, 41100 Modena; tel. 059-4395711; fax 059-230196; e-mail sbsae-mo@beniculturali.it; internet www.galleriaestense.beniculturali.it; f. 15th century in Ferrara, transferred to Palazzo Ducale, Modena, 1598, to Palazzo dei Musei

1894; collns include about 2,000 paintings and drawings of 14th–18th centuries, sculpture, engravings, medals; library of 15,000 vols; Superintendent MARIA GRAZIA BERNARDINI.

Museo Civico Archeologico Etnologico: Palazzo dei Musei, Viale Vittorio Veneto 5, 41100 Modena; tel. 059-200100; fax 059-200110; e-mail museo.archeologico@comune.modena.it; internet www.comune.modena.it/museoarcheologico; f. 1871; prehistory and ethnology; library of 5,000 vols, 2,700 pamphlets; Curator Dott. ILARIA PULINI; publ. *Quaderni*.

Museo Civico d'Arte: Largo Porta Sant'Agostino 337, 41100 Modena; tel. 059-200100; fax 059-200110; e-mail museo.arte@comune.modena.it; internet www.comune.modena.it/museoarte; f. 1871; paintings, sculpture, decorative arts; library of 7,500 vols, 3,500 pamphlets; Curator Dott.ssa FRANCESCA PICCININI.

Museo Lapidario Estense: Piazza Sant'Agostino 337, 41100 Modena; tel. 059-4395711; fax 059-230196; e-mail galleria.estense@beniculturali.it; internet www.galleriaestense.it; f. 1828; Roman and medieval archaeological collections; Dir Dott. MARIA GRAZIA BERNARDINI.

Naples

Museo Archeologico Nazionale: Piazza Museo 19, 80135 Naples; tel. 081-4422111; fax 081-440013; e-mail ssba-na@beniculturali.it; internet marcheo.napolibeniculturali.it; f. 18th century; Greek, Roman, Italian and Egyptian antiquities; Superintendent Prof. Dr PIETRO GIOVANNI GUZZO; publ. *Rivista di studi pompeiani* (1 a year).

Museo Civico 'Gaetano Filangieri': Via Duomo 288, 80138 Naples; tel. 081-203211; fax 081-203175; internet www.cib.na.cnr.it/remuna/filang/indice.html; f. 1888; paintings, furniture, archives, photographs, majolica, arms and armour; library of 30,000 vols, and coin collection of Neapolitan history; Dir ANTONIO BUCCINO GRIMALDI.

Museo 'Duca di Martina' alla Floridiana: Via Cimarosa 77, 80127 Naples; tel. and fax 081-5788418; e-mail martina.artina@beniculturali.it; f. 1931; decorative art; exhibits donated by the Duke; spec. colln of oriental art; Dir Dr LUISA AMBROSIO.

Museo e Gallerie Nazionali di Capodimonte: Via Miano 1, 80131 Naples; tel. 081-7499111; fax 081-7445032; e-mail capodimonte.artina@arti.beniculturali.it; f. 1738; paintings from 13th–19th centuries; sculpture from 19th century; contemporary art; colln of arms and armour; medals and bronzes of the Renaissance; porcelain; library of 2,000 vols; Dir Prof. MARCIELLA UTILI.

Museo Nazionale di S. Martino: Largo S. Martino 5, 80129 Naples; tel. 081-5585942; e-mail artina@arti.beniculturali.it; f. 1872; ancient church of S. Martino with 16th–18th century pictures, 13th–19th century sculpture, majolica and porcelain, Neapolitan historical records and topographical collection, naval colln, arms and military costumes, opaline glass, section of modern painting, prints and engravings; Dir Dott.ssa ROSSANA MUZII.

Soprintendenza Archeologica di Pompei: Via Villa dei Misteri 2, 80045 Pompei; tel. 081-8575111; fax 081-8613183; e-mail info@pompeiisites.org; internet www.pompeiisites.org; f. 1982; Supt Prof. PIETRO GIOVANNI GUZZO.

Supervised Sites:

  Antiquarium Nazionale di Boscoreale: Via Settetermini 15, Loc. Villa Regina,

80041 Boscoreale; tel. 081-5368796; fax 081-8613183; e-mail info@pompeiisites.org; internet www.pompeiisites.org; Dir Dott.ssa GRETE STEFANI.

  Scavi di Ercolano: Corso Resina, 80056 Ercolano; tel. 081-7324311; fax 081-8613183; e-mail info@pompeiisites.org; internet www.pompeiisites.org; Dir Dott.ssa MARIA PAOLA GUIDOBALDI.

  Scavi di Oplontis: Via Sepolcri, 80058 Torre Annunziata; tel. 081-8621755; fax 081-8613183; e-mail info@pompeiisites.org; internet www.pompeiisites.org; Dir Dott. LORENZO FERGOLA.

  Scavi di Pompei: Via Villa dei Misteri 2, 80045 Pompei; tel. 081-8575400; fax 081-8613183; e-mail info@pompeiisites.org; internet www.pompeiisites.org; Dir Dott. ANTONIO D'AMBROSIO.

  Scavi di Stabia: Via Passeggiata Archeologica, 80053 Castellammare di Stabia; tel. 081-8714541; fax 081-8613183; e-mail info@pompeiisites.org; internet www.pompeiisites.org; Dir Dott.ssa GIOVANNA BONIFACIO.

Padua

Musei Civici di Padova: Piazza Eremitani 8, 35121 Padua; tel. 049-82045450; fax 049-8204585; e-mail musei@comune.padova.it; internet padovacultura.padovanet.it/musei/archivio/000046.html; f. 1825; Dir DAVIDE BANZATO; publ. *Bollettino del Museo Civico di Padova*.

Constituent Institutions:

  Cappella degli Scrovegni: Piazza Eremitani 8, 35121 Padua; tel. 049-82045450; fax 049-8204585; e-mail musei@comune.padova.it; internet padovacultura.padovanet.it/musei/archivio/000071.html; f. 1300; Giotto frescoes; Dir DAVIDE BANZATO.

  Museo Archeologico: Piazza Eremitani, 35121 Padua; tel. 049-82045450; fax 049-8204585; e-mail zampierig@comune.padova.it; internet padovacultura.padovanet.it/musei/archivio/000065.html; f. 1825; pre- and early historic and Roman finds; Curator Dott. GIROLAMO ZAMPIERI.

  Museo d'Arte Medioevale e Moderna: c/o Musei Civici, Piazza Eremitani 8, 35121 Padua; tel. 049-82045450; fax 049-8204585; e-mail musei@comune.padova.it; internet padovacultura.padovanet.it/musei/archivio/000066.html; f. 1825; paintings, sculptures, bronzes, ceramics; Curator Dott.ssa FRANCA PELLEGRINI.

  Museo Bottacin: Palazzo Zuckermann, Corso Garibaldi 33, 35122 Padua; tel. 049-8766959; fax 049-8774671; internet padovacultura.padovanet.it/musei/archivio/000148.html; f. 1865; Graeco-Roman, Paduan, Venetian, Italian, Napoleonic coins, seals and medals, 19th-century sculptures and paintings; Curator Dott.ssa ROBERTA PARISE.

  Palazzo della Ragione 'Il Salone': Piazza delle Erbe, 35122 Padua; tel. 049-8205006; fax 049-8204566; e-mail musei@comune.padova.it; internet padovacultura.padovanet.it/musei/archivio/000082.html; f. 1218; works by Fra Giovanni degli Eremitani, frescoes by Nicolò Miretto and Stefano Da Ferrara; Dir DAVIDE BANZATO.

Palermo

Museo Archeologico Regionale A. Salinas: Via Bara all'Olivella 24, 90133 Palermo; tel. 091-6116805; fax 091-6110740; e-mail a.salinas@tin.it; f. 1866; prehistoric, Egyptian, Greek, Punic, Roman and Etruscan antiquities; library of 25,000 vols and pamphlets;

Superintendent Prof. Dott.ssa CARMELA ANGELA DI STEFANO.

Parma

Galleria Nazionale: Piazzale della Pilotta 15, 43100 Parma; tel. 0521-233309; fax 0521-206336; e-mail sbaspr@libero.it; internet www.artipr.arti.beniculturali.it/htm/galleria.htm; f. 1752, later reconstructed and added to; paintings from 13th–19th centuries, incl. works by Correggio, Parmigianino, Cima, El Greco, Piazzetta, Tiepolo, Holbein, Van Dyck, Mor, Nattier, and several painters of the school of Parma; 19th-century paintings by Parmesan painters; library of 15,000 vols; Superintendent LUCIA FORNARI SCHIANCHI.

Museo Archeologico Nazionale: Via della Pilotta 5, 43100 Parma; tel. 0521-233718; fax 0521-386112; e-mail manpr@libero.it; f. 1760; archaeological collection of sculptures and other monuments from Veleia; Prehistoric and Bronze Age collections; Roman monuments from province of Parma; Egyptian, Greek, Etruscan and Roman art documents; Dir Dr MARIA BERNABÒ BREA.

Museo Bodoniano: c/o Biblioteca Palatina, Palazzo della Pilotta 3A, 43121 Parma; tel. 0521-220411; fax 0521-235662; e-mail museobodoni@beniculturali.it; internet www.museobodoni.beniculturali.it; f. 1963; dedicated to art of printing: punches, original matrices and moulds (approx. 80,000) from Bodoni's printing works; rare edns, technical manuals, press and tools of 'the prince of printers'; Dir ANDREA DE PASQUALE; Curator CATERINA SILVA; publ. *Crisopoli. Bollettino del museo Bodoniano di Parma* (1 a year).

Pavia

Civici Musei—Castello Visconteo: Viale XI Febbraio 35, 27100 Pavia; tel. 0382-33853; fax 0382-303028; e-mail museicivici@comune.pv.it; internet www.museicivici.pavia.it; f. 1838; library of 24,000 vols; Dir Dott. SUSANNA ZATTI.

Perugia

Galleria Nazionale dell'Umbria: Palazzo dei Priori, Corso Vannucci 19, 06123 Perugia; tel. 075-586681; fax 075-58668400; internet www.gallerianazionaleumbria.it; f. 1918; paintings of Umbrian school, 13th–19th centuries; also sculptures and jewellery; library of 5,300 vols; Dir Dott.ssa VITTORIA GARIBALDI.

Museo Archeologico Nazionale dell'Umbria: Piazza Giordano Bruno 10, 06121 Perugia; tel. 075-5720345; fax 075-5728200; e-mail archeopg@arti.beniculturali.it; internet www.archeopg.arti.beniculturali.it; f. 1948; prehistoric, Roman, Hellenistic and Etruscan remains; primitive pottery, bone tools, funerary urns, amulets, archaic bronzes, coins; Dir A. E. FERUGLIO.

Pesaro

Musei Civici di Pesaro (Pinacoteca e Museo delle Ceramiche): Piazza Toschi Mosca 29, 61100 Pesaro; tel. (721) 387541; fax (721) 387524; e-mail musei@comune.pesaro.ps.it; internet www.museicivicipesaro.it; f. 1936; art gallery and ceramics and decorative arts museum; Dir Prof. GIAN CARLO BOJANI.

Pisa

Museo Nazionale di S. Matteo: Piazza San Matteo in Soarta, Lungarno Mediceo, 56127 Pisa; tel. 050-541865; fax 050-500099; internet www.humnet.unipi.it/linguistica/corsiit/pisa/museo_nazionale_di_san_matteo.htm; f. 1949; sculptures by the Pisanos and their school; colln of the Pisan school from the 12th–14th centuries, and paintings and sculpture of the 15th–17th centuries (works by Simone Martini, Masaccio, Beato Angel-ico, Benozzo Gozzoli, Ghirlandaio, Donatello, Della Robbia), 10th–17th-century ceramics, colln of coins and medals; Dir Dott.ssa MARIAGIULIA BURRESI.

Portoferraio

Museo Napoleonico di Villa S. Martino: San Martino, 57037 Portoferraio; tel. 0565-914688.

Ravenna

Museo Nazionale di Ravenna: Via Bene-detto Fiandrini, 48100 Ravenna; tel. 0544-34424; fax 0544-37391; e-mail sbapravenna@beniculturali.it; f. 1885; State property since 1885; art, numismatics and archaeology; Dir Dott. CETTY MUSCOLINO.

Reggio Calabria

Museo Nazionale: Piazza De Nava 26, 89122 Reggio Calabria; tel. 0965-812255; fax 0965-25164; e-mail archeorc@arti .benicultura.it; internet www .museonazionalerc.it; f. 1958; archaeological objects from Calabria from prehistoric era to Roman times; also Antiquarium di Locri (Locri), Museo Archaeologico (Vibo Valentia), Museo Archaeologico (Crotone), Museo della Sibaritide (Sibari); art gallery; library of 10,000 vols; Dir Dott.ssa ELENA LATTANZI; publ. *Klearchos* (1 a year).

Rome

Galleria Borghese: Piazzale del Museo Borghese, 5, 00197 Rome; tel. 06-8413979; e-mail info.servizimusei@libero.it; internet www.galleriaborghese.it; f. c. 1616; picture gallery, collections of classical and Baroque sculpture; Dir Dott.ssa ALBA COSTAMAGNA.

Galleria Nazionale d'Arte Antica di Palazzo Barberini: Via Quattro Fontane 13, 00184 Rome; tel. 06-4824184; fax 06-4880560; internet www.galleriaborghese.it; Italian and European paintings from 12th–18th centuries, Baroque architecture; Corsini colln at Galleria Corsini, Via della Lungara 10; Dir Dott. SIVIGLIANO ALLOISI.

Istituto Nazionale per la Grafica: Calco-grafia, Via della Stamperia 6, 00187 Rome; tel. 06-699801; fax 06-69921454; internet www.grafica.arti.beniculturali.it; f. 1895; Ita-lian and foreign prints and drawings from 14th century onwards; collection of matrices since 16th century; Dir Dott.ssa SERENITA PAPALDO.

Keats-Shelley House: Piazza di Spagna 26, 00187 Rome; tel. (6) 6784235; fax (6) 6784167; e-mail info@keats-shelley-house .org; internet www.keats-shelley-house.org; f. 1903; access by appointment and depend-ent upon a letter of recommendation from an academic instn or publisher; Dir's permission required prior to consulting books published before 1900; library: reference library of 9,000 vols; Dir CATHERINE PAYLING; publ. *The Keats-Shelley Review.*

Musei Capitolini: Piazza del Campidoglio 1, 00186 Rome; tel. 06-67102475; fax 06-6785488; e-mail info.museicapitolini@comune.roma.it; internet www .museicapitolini.org; f. 1471; archaeology, art history; Dir Dott.ssa ANNA MURA SOMMELLA.

Museo Barracco: Corso Vittorio Emanuele 168, 00186 Rome; tel. and fax 06-68806848; e-mail info.museobarracco@comune.roma.it; internet en.museobarracco.it; f. 1905; evolu-tion of sculpture from Egyptian to Roman styles; Dir Dott.ssa MARESITA NOTA.

Museo della Civiltà Romana: Piazza G. Agnelli 10, 00144 Rome; tel. 06-5926041; fax 06-5926135; internet www2.comune.roma.it/museociviltaromana; f. 1952; history of Rome

from its origins; Curator Dott.ssa ANNA MURA SOMMELLA.

Museo di Palazzo Venezia: Via del Plebis-cito 118, 00186 Rome; tel. 06-69994284; fax 06-69994394; internet museopalazzovenezia .beniculturali.it; f. 1921; 13th–16th century paintings; bronze, marble and terracotta sculptures; medieval and Renaissance dec-orative art; 16th–17th century ceramics; furniture, prints, textiles; Dir ROSSELLA VODRET.

Museo di Roma: Via di San Pantaleo (Piazza Navona), 00186 Rome; tel. 06-67108346; fax 06-67108303; e-mail museodiroma@comune.roma.it; internet www.museodiroma.it; f. 1930; topographic, cultural, social, historical and artistic devel-opment of Rome since medieval times; Dir Dott.ssa MARIA ELISA TITTONI.

Museo Nazionale d'Arte Orientale: Palazzo Brancaccio, Via Merulana 248, 00185 Rome; tel. 06-4874415; fax 06-4870624; e-mail orientale@arti.beniculturali .it; internet www.viavenetoroma.it/it/musei/dettamusei.asp?id=69; f. 1957; library of 8,000 vols; Dir Dott.ssa DONATELLA MAZZEO.

Museo Nazionale delle Arti e Tradizioni Popolari: Piazza Marconi 8/10, 00144 Rome; tel. 06-5926148; fax 06-5911848; e-mail popolari@arti.beniculturali.it; internet www .popolari.arti.beniculturali.it; f. 1923; library of 30,000 vols; archives of musical, spoken and photo-cinematographic material; Dir Dott.ssa STEFANIA MASSARI.

Museo Nazionale di Castel Sant'Angelo: Lungotevere Castello 50, 00193 Rome; tel. 06-6819111; fax 06-6819196; internet www .galleriaborghese.it/castello/it; f. 1925; ancient armoury; architectural and monu-mental remains, frescoes, sculptures, pic-tures and period furniture; library of 13,000 vols, 60 periodicals; Dir MARIA GRAZIA BER-NARDINI.

Museo Nazionale di Villa Giulia: Piazzale di Villa Giulia 9, 00196 Rome; tel. 06-3226571; fax 06-3202010; internet www .roma2000.it/zvilagiu.htm; f. 1889; Etruscan and Italian antiquities; Dir Dott.ssa FRAN-CESCA BOITANI.

Museo Nazionale Preistorico Etnogra-fico 'Luigi Pigorini': Piazzale G. Marconi 14, 00144 Rome; tel. 06-549521; fax 06-54952310; e-mail pigorini@arti.beniculturali .it; internet www.pigorini.arti.beniculturali .it; f. 1875; prehistory and ethnology; library of 63,000 vols, 500 bound periodicals, 500 current periodicals; Superintendent Dr MARIA ANTONIETTA FUGAZZOLA; publ. *Bullet-tino di Paletnologia Italiana* (1 a year).

Scavi di Ostia: Viale dei Romagnoli 717, 00119 Ostia Antica, Rome; tel. 06-56358099; fax 06-5651500; e-mail ostia@arti .beniculturali.it; internet www.itnw.roma.it/ostia/scavi; Roman antiquities, monuments, paintings, sculptures, mosaics; Curator Dott.ssa ANNA GALLINA ZEVI.

Soprintendenza alla Galleria Nazionale d'Arte Moderna e Contemporanea: Viale delle Belle Arti 131, 00196 Rome; tel. 06-322981; fax 06-3221579; e-mail comunicazione.gnam@arti.beniculturali.it; internet www.gnam.arti.beniculturali.it; Superintendent Dott.ssa SANDRA PINTO.

Attached Sites:

Galleria Nazionale d'Arte Moderna: Viale delle Belle Arti 131, 00196 Rome; tel. 06-322981; fax 06-3221579; e-mail comunicazione.gnam@arti.beniculturali.it; internet www.gnam.arti.beniculturali.it/gnamco.htm; f. 1883; art since 19th cen-tury; library of 60,000 vols, 1,500 period-icals; Dir Dott.ssa SANDRA PINTO.

Museo Boncompagni Ludovisi: Via Boncompagni 18, 00187 Rome; tel. 06-42824074; e-mail gnam@arti.beniculturali .it; internet www.gnam.arti.beniculturali .it/boncco.htm; modern decorative arts and fashion; Dir GIANNA PIANTONI.

Museo Hendrik Christian Andersen: Via Pasquale Stanislao Mancini, 20 (Piaz-zale Flaminio), 00196 Rome; tel. 06-3219089; fax 06-3221579; e-mail edimajo .gnam@arti.beniculturali.it; internet www .gnam.arti.beniculturali.it/andeco.htm; f. 1998; paintings and sculpture by Hendrik Christian Andersen (1872–1940); Dir ELENA DI MAJO.

Museo Mario Praz: Palazzo Primoli, Via Zanardelli 1, 00186 Rome; tel. and fax 06-6861089; e-mail museopraz@museopraz .191.it; internet www.museopraz .beniculturali.it; f. 1995; furniture, paint-ings, sculpture, carpets, miniatures and objects made of bronze, crystal, porcelain, silver and marble collected by Mario Praz (1896–1982); Dirs Dott. PATRIZIA ROSAZZA FERRARIS, Dott. CHIARA STEFANI.

Raccolta Manzù: Via Laurentina Km 32.8, 00040 Ardea; tel. 06-9135022; e-mail gnam@arti.beniculturali.it; internet www .gnam.arti.beniculturali.it/manzco.htm; f. 1981; work by the sculptor Manzù; Dir LIVIA VELANI.

Soprintendenza Speciale per i Beni Archeologici di Roma: Piazza dei Cinque-cento 67, 00185 Rome; tel. 06-480201; fax 06-4880445; e-mail info@archeorm.arti .beniculturali.it; internet www.archeorm.arti .beniculturali.it/sar2000; Superintendent Prof. ADRIANO LA REGINA.

Attached Sites:

Il Colosseo (The Colosseum): Anfiteatro Flavio (Colosseo), Piazza del Colosseo, 00184 Rome; tel. 06-39967700; internet www.archeorm.arti.beniculturali.it/sar2000/colosseo/colosseo.asp; f. AD 80.

Terme di Caracalla: Viale Terme di Caracalla 52, 00153 Rome; tel. 06-39967700; internet www.archeorm.arti .beniculturali.it/sar2000/caracalla/cara-calla.asp; f. AD 216; remains of large com-plex of Roman baths.

Terme di Diocleziano (Baths of Diocle-tian): Via Enrico de Nicola 78, 00185 Rome; tel. 06-39967700; internet www.archeorm .arti.beniculturali.it/sar2000/diocleziano/default.asp; f. 3rd century AD; museum f. 1889; sculpture, sarcophagi, inscriptions, mosaics and frescoes.

Villa dei Quintili: Via Appia Nuova 1092, 00178 Rome; tel. 06-39967700; internet www.archeorm.arti.beniculturali.it/sar2000/villa_quintili/villa_dei_quintili .asp; f. 2nd century AD; extensive villa with rooms for masters and servants, bath quarters.

Museo Nazionale Romano: Piazza dei Cinquecento 79, 00185 Rome; tel. 06-483617; fax 06-4814125; f. 1889; Greek, Hellenistic and Roman sculpture and bronzes, paintings and mosaics, numis-matics; archaeological colln; Dir Prof. ADRIANO LA REGINA.

Constituent Centres:

Crypta Balbi: Via delle Botteghe Oscure 31, 00186 Rome; tel. 06-39967700; internet www.archeorm.arti.beniculturali.it/sar2000/cripta/cripta.asp; f. 13BC; remains of an arcaded courtyard and theatre; material and tools from a 7th-century workshop.

Domus Aurea (Golden House): Via della Domus Aurea, 00184 Rome; tel. 06-39967700; internet www.archeorm.arti

.beniculturali.it/sar2000/domus/domus_
aurea.asp; remains of Nero's villa built
after the great fire of AD 64.

Mausoleo di Cecilia Metella: Viale
Appia Antica 161, 00179 Rome; tel. 06-
39967700; internet www.archeorm.arti
.beniculturali.it/sar2000/cecilia_metella/
cecilia_metella.asp; f. AD 20–30; funeral
monument.

Palatino (Palatine Hill): Piazza S. Maria
Nova 53, 00186 Rome; tel. 06-39967700;
internet www.archeorm.arti.beniculturali
.it/sar2000/palatino/palatino.asp; history of
Rome from 8th century BC.

Palazzo Altemps: Piazza di Sant'Apolli-
nare 48, 00186 Rome; tel. 06-39967700;
internet www.archeorm.arti.beniculturali
.it/sar2000/altemps/pal_altemps.asp; f.
1997; Greek and Roman sculpture.

Palazzo Massimo: Largo di Villa Peretti,
1, 00185 Rome; tel. 06-480201; fax 06-
48903504; internet www.archeorm.arti
.beniculturali.it/sar2000/museo_romano/
pal_massimo.asp; f. 1998; statues, mosaic
pavement, numismatics, frescoes, bronzes
and jewellery from 1st century BC to 4th
century AD

Villa Farnesina: Via della Lungara 230,
00165 Rome; tel. 06-68027268; fax 06-
68027513; e-mail farnesina@lincei.it;
internet www.lincei.it/informazioni/
villafarnesina; now the property of the
Accademia Nazionale dei Lincei; built 1509
by Peruzzi; decorated by Raphael, Peruzzi
and others; Curator Geom. RODOLFO DON-
ZELLI.

Rovigo

Museo dell'Accademia dei Concordi:
Palazzo Roverella, via Laurenti 8/10, 45100
Rovigo; tel. 0425-460093; fax 0425-27993;
internet www.concordi.it; contains 650 Venetian paintings from the 15th–18th centuries;
colln of Flemish paintings; Dir WIGI COSTATO.

**Pinacoteca dell'Accademia dei Con-
cordi:** Piazza Vittorio Emanuele 14, 45100
Rovigo; tel. 0425-21654; fax 0425-27993;
internet www2.regione.veneto.it/cultura/
musei/inglese/pag4176e.htm; f. 1833; contains 650 Venetian paintings (15th–18th
centuries), incl. work by Seminario Vescovile
di Rovigo; Dir ADRIANO MAZZETTI.

Sarsina

Museo Archeologico Nazionale: Via Cesio
Sabino 39, 47027 Sarsina; tel. 0547-94641;
internet www.comune.sarsina.fo.it/
museoarch/museo.htm; f. 1890; exhibition of
archaeological remains from the Roman age;
Dir Dott.ssa CHIARA GUARNIERI.

Sassari

**Museo Nazionale Archeologico Etnogra-
fio G. A. Sanna:** Via Roma 64, 07100
Sassari; tel. 079-272203; fax 079-271524;
e-mail museosanna@beniculturali.it;
internet www.museosannasassari.it; f. 1932;
archaeology, medieval and modern art, ethnography; Dir Dott. LUISANNA USAI.

Siena

Museo Archeologico: Piazza Duomo 2,
53100 Siena; tel. 0577-224811; fax 0577-
224829; e-mail infoscala@comune.siena.it;
internet www.santamaria.comune.siena.it;
antiquities from the local area; Etruscan
section; numismatic collection; Dir ENRICO
TOTI.

Museo Aurelio Castelli: Via dell'Osser-
vanza 7, 53100 Siena; tel. 0577-332444;
internet www.museionline.it/ita/cerca/museo
.asp?id=4060; 14th–15th-century sculpture,
paintings and drawings from the 15th–18th
centuries; library of 28,000 vols.

Pinacoteca Nazionale: Palazzo Buon-
signori, Via San Pietro 29, 53100 Siena; tel.
0577-286143; fax 0577-286143; internet www
.spsae-si.beniculturali.it/index.php?it/77/
musei; f. 1930; 650 paintings exhibited; Dir
Dott.ssa ANNA MARIA GUIDUCCI.

Syracuse

**Museo Archeologico Regionale 'Paolo
Orsi':** Viale Teocrito 66, 96100 Syracuse;
tel. 0931-464022; fax 0931-462347; e-mail
museo.orsi@tin.it; internet www.regione
.sicilia.it/beniculturali/dirbenicult/musei/
musei2/orsi.htm; f. 1886; prehistory, statuary and antiques from the excavations of the
Greco-Roman city and from prehistoric and
classical sites of Eastern Sicily; Dir Dott.
GIUSEPPE VOZA.

Taranto

Museo Archeologico Nazionale: Corso
Umberto 141, 74100 Taranto; tel. 099-
4532112; fax 099-4594946; e-mail
archeologica.taranto@libero.it; internet www
.tarantocitta.it/museo.htm; f. 1887; local prehistory and Greco-Roman remains; Dir Dott.
GIUSEPPE ANDREASSI.

Tarquinia

Museo Nazionale Tarquiniense: Palazzo
Vitelleschi, 01016 Tarquinia; tel. 0766-
856036; internet www.tarquinia.net/citta/
turismo/museo_nazionale.asp; f. 1924; Etruscan sarcophagi from the 4th and 3rd centuries BC, Etruscan and Greek vases, bronzes,
ornaments; Etruscan paintings; Dir Dott.ssa
MARIA CATALDI.

Trento

**Castello del Buonconsiglio–Monumenti
e Collezioni Provinciali:** Via B. Clesio 5,
38100 Trento; tel. 0461-233770; fax 0461-
239497; e-mail castellodelbuonconsiglio@
provincia.tn.it; internet www.buonconsiglio
.it; f. 1924; ancient, medieval and modern
art; Dir Dott. FRANCO MARZATICO.

Trieste

Civici Musei di Storia ed Arte: Via
Cattedrale 15, 34121 Trieste; tel. 040-
310500; fax 040-300687; e-mail
museostoriaarte@comune.trieste.it; internet
www.triestecultura.it; Dir Dott. ADRIANO
DUGULIN.

Constituent Museums and Galleries:

**Castello di San Giusto e Civico Museo
del Castello, Lapidario Tergestino:**
Piazza Cattedrale 3, 34121 Trieste; tel.
040-309362; fax 040-300687; e-mail
museostoriaarte@comune.trieste.it; internet www.triestecultura.it; f. 1936, Lapidario 2001; Dir Dott. ADRIANO DUGULIN.

Civico Museo d'Arte Orientale: Via S.
Sebastiano 1, 34121 Trieste; tel. 040-
3220736; fax 040-300687; e-mail
museoarteorientale@comune.trieste.it;
internet www.triestecultura.it; f. 2001; Dir
Dott. ADRIANO DUGULIN.

**Civico Museo di Guerra per la Pace
'Diego de Henriquez':** Via Revoltella 37,
34139 Trieste; tel. 040-948430; fax 040-
944390; e-mail museodehenriquez@
comune.trieste.it; internet www
.triestecultura.it; f. 1998; Dir Dott.
ADRIANO DUGULIN.

**Civico Museo della Risiera di S.
Sabba—Monumento Nazionale:** Ratto
della Pileria 43, 34148 Trieste; tel. 040-
826202; fax 040-300687; e-mail
museostoriaarte@comune.trieste.it; internet www.triestecultura.it; f. 1975; Dir
Dott. ADRIANO DUGULIN.

**Civico Museo del Risorgimento e
Sacrario Oberdan:** Via XXIV Maggio 4,

34133 Trieste; tel. 040-361675; fax 040-
300687; e-mail museostoriaarte@comune
.trieste.it; internet www.triestecultura.it;
f. 1934; Dir Dott. ADRIANO DUGULIN.

Civico Museo Sartorio: Largo Papa
Giovanni XXIII 1, 34123 Trieste; tel. 040-
301479; fax 040-300687; e-mail
museostoriaarte@comune.trieste.it; internet www.triestecultura.it; f. 1947; Dir
Dott. ADRIANO DUGULIN.

**Civico Museo di Storia ed Arte e Orto
Lapidario:** Via Cattedrale 15, 34121
Trieste; tel. 040-308686; fax 040-300687;
e-mail museostoriaarte@comune.trieste.it;
internet www.triestecultura.it; f. Orto
Lapidario 1843, Civico Museo di Storia
1873; Dir Dott. ADRIANO DUGULIN.

**Civico Museo di Storia Patria—Civico
Museo Morpurgo de Nilma:** Via
Imbriani 5, 34122 Trieste; tel. 040-
636969; fax 040-636969; e-mail
museostoriaarte@comune.trieste.it; internet www.triestecultura.it; f. Museo Morpurgo 1947, Civico Museo di Storia Patria
1950; Dir Dott. ADRIANO DUGULIN.

**Civico Museo Teatrale 'Carlo
Schmidl':** Via Rossini, 4, 34122 Trieste;
tel. 040-366030; fax 040-636969; e-mail
museoschmidl@comune.trieste.it; internet
www.triestecultura.it; f. 1950; Dir Dott.
ADRIANO DUGULIN.

**Museo Postale e Telegrafico della
Mitteleuropa:** Piazza Vittorio Veneto 1,
34132 Trieste; tel. 040-6764264; fax 040-
6764570; e-mail museopostaletrieste@
posteitaliane.it; internet www
.triestecultura.it; f. 1997, in association
with Poste Italiane S.p.A.; Dir Dott.
ADRIANO DUGULIN.

Turin

Armeria Reale: Piazza Castello 191, 10122
Turin; tel. 011-543889; fax 011-5188063;
e-mail armeriareale@artito.arti
.beniculturali.it; internet www.artito.arti
.beniculturali.it; f. 1837; collection of arms;
includes the equestrian armour of Otto
Heinrich and works by Pompeo della Chiesa,
Etienne Delaune and the engravers of the
Munich school, Emanuel Sadeler, Daniel
Sadeler and Caspar Spät; Dir FULVIO CER-
VINI.

Città di Torino—Settore Musei: Via San
Francesco da Paola 3, 10123 Turin; tel. 011-
4434470; fax 011-4434494; e-mail daniele
.jalla@comune.torino.it; internet www
.comune.torino.it/musei; Dir DANIELE LUPO
JALLÀ.

Attached Museums:

Borgo e Rocca Medioevale: Parco del
Valentino, Viale Virgilio, 10126 Turin; tel.
011-4431701; fax 011-4431719; e-mail
borgo.medioevale@comune.torino.it; internet www.comune.torino.it/musei/civici/bm;
Superintendent Dott.ssa ENRICA PAGELLA.

**Galleria Civica d'Arte Moderna e Con-
temporanea:** Via Magenta 31, 10128
Turin; tel. 011-5629911; fax 011-4429550;
e-mail gam@comune.torino.it; internet
www.gamtorino.it; f. 1953; Pres. GIOVANNA
INCISA CATTANEO; Dir PIERGIOVANNI CAS-
TAGNOLI.

**Palazzo Madama—Museo Civico
d'Arte Antica:** Piazza Castello, 10122
Turin; tel. 011-4433501; fax 011-4429929;
e-mail palazzomadama@
fondazionetorinomusei.it; internet www
.palazzomadamatorino.it; f. 1863; Dir
ENRICA PAGELLA.

**Museo Civico Pietro Micca e dell'asse-
dio di Torino del 1706** (Pietro Micca and
1706 Siege of Turin Civic Museum): Via
Guicciardini 7/A, 10121 Turin; tel. 011-

546317; fax 011-533772; internet www .museopietromicca.it; f. 1861; Hon. Curator and Dir-Gen. SEBASTIANO PONSO.

Galleria Sabauda: Via Accademia delle Scienze 6, 10123 Turin; tel. (11) 547440; fax (11) 549547; e-mail galleriasabauda@artito .arti.beniculturali.it; f. 1832; one of principal Flemish and Dutch collns, and early Italian, also Bronzino, Veronese, Tiepolo and Lombard and Piedmontese schools, furniture, sculpture and jewellery; Dir Dott.ssa PAOLA ASTRUA.

Museo di Antichità: Via XX Settembre 88C, 10124 Turin; tel. 011-5211106; fax 011-5213145; e-mail info@museoarcheologico.it; internet www.museoantichita.it; f. 1940; Piedmontese prehistory; Etruscan, Sardinian and Gallo-Roman remains; Greek and Cypriot ceramics; Roman statues; silverware; Dir Dott.ssa LILIANA MERCANDO.

Museo Egizio: Via Accademia delle Scienze 6, 10123 Turin; tel. 011-5617776; fax 011-5623157; e-mail ufficio.segreteria@ museoegizio.org; internet www.museoegizio .org; f. 1824; Pharonic, Ptolemaic and Coptic antiquities; entire furnishings of the tomb of architect Kha and his wife from Deir el-Medina, Temple of Ellesija (reconstructed Nubian temple of 18th dynasty) presented by the Egyptian Govt; objects from Droveth colln and Schiaparelli excavations in Egypt; Dir ELENI VASSILIKA.

Udine

Civici Musei e Gallerie di Storia e Arte: Castello, Piazza Libertà, 33100 Udine; tel. 0432-271591; fax 0432-271932; f. 1866; history, art; Dir Dott. MAURIZIO BUORA.

Urbino

Galleria Nazionale delle Marche—Palazzo Ducale: Piazza Duca Federico 107, 61029 Urbino; tel. 0722-27601; fax 0722-377483; e-mail info.servizimusei@ libero.it; internet www.galleriaborghese.it/ nuove/einfourbino.html; f. 1912; medieval and Renaissance works of art originating in the town of Urbino and the provinces of Marche; Dir Prof. PAOLO DAL POGGETTO.

Venice

Biennale di Venezia: Ca' Giustinian, San Marco 1364, 30124 Venice; tel. 041-5218711; fax 041-2728329; e-mail infogruppi@ labiennale.org; internet www.labiennale.org; f. 1895; an autonomous body; organizes artistic and cultural events throughout the year: visual arts, architecture, cinema, theatre, music, dance; the Biennale owns historical archives of contemporary art; library of 100,000 vols and catalogues, photographs, etc.; Pres. DAVIDE CROFF; Gen. Dir GAETANO GUERCI.

Galleria Giorgio Franchetti alla Ca' d'Oro: Cannaregio 3932, 30121 Venice; tel. (41) 5238790; fax (41) 5222349; e-mail polve .franchetti@arti.beniculturali.it; internet www.artive.arti.beniculturali.it; f. 1928; sculpture, bronzes, medals, coins, tapestries, ceramics, and Venetian, central Italian and Flemish art; Dir Dott.ssa ADRIANA AUGUSTI; Curator Dott.ssa CLAUDIA CREMONINI; Ceramics Curator Dott.ssa FRANCESCA SACCARDO; Paintings Restorer Dott.ssa GLORIA TRANQUILLI.

Gallerie dell'Accademia: Campo della Carità, Dorsoduro 1050, 30130 Venice; tel. 041-5222247; fax 041-5212709; e-mail polve .accademia@arti.beniculturali.it; internet www.artive.arti.beniculturali.it; f. 1807; Venetian painting 1310–1700; Superintendent Dott.ssa GIOVANNA SCIRÈ NEPI.

Musei Civici Veneziani: Piazza San Marco 52, 30124 Venice; tel. 041-5225625; fax 041-

5200935; e-mail info@fmcvenezia.it; internet www.museiciviciveneziani.it; Dir Prof. GIANDOMENICO ROMANELLI.

Constituent Institutions:

Ca' Rezzonico: Dorsoduro 3136, 30123 Venice; tel. and fax 041-2410100; e-mail info@fmcvenezia.it; internet www .museiciviciveneziani.it; f. 1935; 18th-century Venetian art, sculpture, etc.

Casa di Carlo Goldoni: San Polo 2794, 30125 Venice; tel. 041-2759325; fax 041-2440081; e-mail mkt.musei@comune .venezia.it; internet www .museiciviciveneziani.it; house of the comic playwright (1707–93).

Galleria Internazionale d'Arte Moderna di Ca' Pesaro: Santa Croce 2076, 30135 Venice; tel. 041-5240695; fax 041-5241075; e-mail mkt.musei@comune .venezia.it; internet www .museiciviciveneziani.it; f. 1897; works of art since the 19th century.

Museo Correr: Piazza San Marco 52, 30124 Venice; tel. 041-2405211; fax 041-5200935; e-mail info@fmcvenezia.it; internet www.museiciviciveneziani.it; f. 1830 by Teodoro Correr who bequeathed his collns to the City; Venetian art (13th–16th centuries) and history of the Serenissima, Renaissance coins, ceramics; publ. *Bollettino* (4 a year).

Museo Fortuny: San Marco 3780, 30124 Venice; tel. 041-5200995; fax 041-5223088; e-mail mkt.musei@comune.venezia.it; internet www.museiciviciveneziani.it; closed for restoration.

Museo del Merletto: Piazza Galuppi 187, 30012 Burano; tel. 041-730034; fax 041-735471; e-mail mkt.musei@comune .venezia.it; internet www .museiciviciveneziani.it; f. 1981; examples of lace since 19th century in the former Lace School.

Museo di Storia Naturale: Santa Croce 1730, 30125 Venice; tel. 041-2750206; fax 041-7210000; e-mail mkt.musei@comune .venezia.it; internet www .museiciviciveneziani.it; f. 1923; natural history; entomology, malacology, ornithology, icthyology, African ethnology.

Museo del Vetro: Fondamenta Giustinian 8, 30121 Murano; tel. and fax 041-739586; e-mail mkt.musei@comune .venezia.it; internet www .museiciviciveneziani.it; f. 1861; Venetian glass from middle ages to the present; also collns of Roman glass from 1st century AD, Spanish, Bohemian and English collns; archives and photographic colln; spec. exhibitions and educational projects.

Palazzo Ducale (Doge's Palace): Piazza San Marco 1, 30124 Venice; tel. 041-2715911; fax 041-5285028; e-mail mkt .musei@comune.venezia.it; internet www .museiciviciveneziani.it; f. 1340; doge's apartments, institutional chambers, armoury and prisons.

Palazzo Mocenigo: Santa Croce 1992, 30126 Venice; tel. 041-721798; fax 041-5241614; e-mail mkt.musei@comune .venezia.it; internet www .museiciviciveneziani.it; palace of the noble Venetian family that provided several of the doges; colln of fabrics and costumes; library on history of fashion.

Planetario di Venezia: Ass.Astrofili Veneziani, Casella Postale 36, Venice Lido; tel. 041-731518; e-mail planetario@ astrovenezia.net; internet www .astrovenezia.net.

Torre Civica di Mestre: Piazza Erminio Ferretto, 30174 Mestre; tel. 041-2749062;

fax 041-2749049; internet www.comune .venezia.it/torre_mestre; f. 13th century.

Torre dell'Orologio (Clock Tower): Piazza San Marco, 30124 Venice; tel. 041-2715911; fax 041-5285028; e-mail mkt .musei@comune.venezia.it; internet www .museiciviciveneziani.it; f. 15th century; closed for restoration.

Museo Archeologico: Piazza S. Marco 17, 30122 Venice; tel. 041-5225978; fax 041-5210547; e-mail artive@arti.beniculturali.it; f. 1523, reorganized 1923–26 and again after 1945; Greek and Roman sculpture, gems and coins, mosaics and sculptures from the 5th century BC–11th century AD; library of 3,000 vols; Dir Dott.ssa GIOVANNA NEPI SCIRÈ.

Museo Civico di Storia Naturale: Fontego dei Turchi, Santa Croce 1730, 30135 Venice; tel. 041-721852; fax 041-5242592; e-mail nat .mus.ve@comune.venezia.it; internet www2 .regione.veneto.it/cultura/musei/scheda .asp?id=36; f. 1921; marine fauna of the Adriatic, ornithology, entomology, minerals and fossils, plants and algae of the world; library of 30,000 vols, 2,350 periodicals; Dir Dr E. RATTI; publs *Bollettino* (1 a year), *Quaderni* (irregular).

Museo d'Arte Orientale: Santa Croce 2076, 30135 Venice; tel. and fax 041-5241173; e-mail polve.orientale@arti.beniculturali.it; internet www.artive.arti.beniculturali.it/ index_x.htm; 17th–19th-century decorative arts from the Far East; Dir Dott.ssa FIORELLA SPADAVECCHIA.

Museo della Fondazione Querini Stampalia: Palazzo Querini Stampalia, Castello 5252, 30122 Venice; tel. 041-2711411; fax 041-2711445; e-mail museo@ querinistampalia.org; internet www .querinistampalia.org; f. 1869; 14th- to 19th-century Italian paintings, 18th- and 19th-century furniture, china; Dir Dr ENRICO ZOLA.

Museo Storico Navale: Riva S. Biasio Castello 2148, 30122 Venice; tel. 041-2441399; fax 041-5200276; internet www .marina.difesa.it/venezia; f. 1919; library of 3,000 vols; Dir RUDY GUASTADISEGNI.

Peggy Guggenheim Collection (Solomon R. Guggenheim Foundation, New York): Palazzo Venier dei Leoni, 701 Dorsoduro, 30123 Venice; tel. 041-2405411; fax 041-5206885; e-mail info@guggenheim-venice.it; internet www.guggenheim-venice.it; f. 1980; permanent collection includes masterpieces of cubism, futurism, metaphysical painting, European abstraction, surrealism, and American abstract expressionism; Italian futurist works on loan from the Gianni Mattioli collection; sculpture garden; Dir PHILIP RYLANDS.

Pinacoteca Manfrediniana: Dorsoduro 1, 30123 Venice; tel. 041-2411018; fax 041-2743998; e-mail seminario@patriarcato .venezia.it; internet www.marcianum.it; f. 1827; paintings and sculpture of the Roman, Gothic, Renaissance, Baroque, Neo-classical periods; library of 80,000 vols; Dir LUCIO CILIA.

Verona

Musei Civici d'Arte di Verona: Corso Castelvecchio 2, 37121 Verona; tel. 045-8062611; fax 045-8010729; e-mail castelvecchio@comune.verona.it; internet www.comune.verona.it; f. 1857; Dir Dott.ssa PAOLA MARINI.

Constituent Museums and Galleries:

Art Library and Graphic Collections: Corso Castelvecchio 2, 37121 Verona; tel. 045-8005817; fax 045-8010729; e-mail castelvecchio@comune.verona.it; internet www.comune.verona.it; f. 1957; library of

33,000 vols, 14,000 prints and drawings; Dir Dott. GIORGIO MARINI.

Galleria Comunale d'Arte Moderna e Contemporanea: Via Forti 1, 37121 Verona; tel. 045-8001903; fax 045-8003524; Dir Dott. G. ROSSI CORTENOVA.

Museo degli Affreschi e Tomba di Giulietta: Via del Pontiere, 37122 Verona; tel. 045-8000361; e-mail castelvecchio@comune.verona.it; f. 1973; Dir Dr PAOLA MARINI.

Museo Archeologico al Teatro Romano: Regaste Redentore 2, 37129 Verona; tel. 045-8000360; fax 045-8010587; e-mail castelvecchio@comune.verona.it; Dir Dott.ssa PAOLA MARINI.

Museo di Castelvecchio: Corso Castelvecchio 3, 37121 Verona; tel. 045-8005817; fax 045-8010729; e-mail castelvecchio@comune.verona.it; Dir Dott.ssa PAOLA MARINI.

Museo Lapidario Maffeiano: Piazza Brà, 37121 Verona; tel. 045-590087; f. 1745; Curator Dra MARGHERITA BOLLA.

Vicenza

Musei Civici: Piazza Matteotti, 36100 Vicenza; tel. 0444-4222811; fax 0444-4546619; e-mail assturismo@comune.vicenza.it; internet www.comune.vicenza.it/ente/musei/index.php; Dir Dott.ssa MARIA ELISA AVAGNINA.

Attached Museums:

Museo Naturalistico Archeologico: Contrà S. Corona 4, 36100 Vicenza; tel. 0444-320440; e-mail museonatarcheo@comune.vicenza.it; internet www.museicivicivicenza.it; f. 1991; fossils, flora and fauna; Palaeolithic and local Roman remains; Dir Dott. ANTONIO DAL LAGO; publ. *Natura Vicentina* (1 a year).

Museo del Risorgimento e della Resistenza: Villa Guiccioli, Viale X Giugno 115, 36100 Vicenza; tel. 0444-322998; fax 0444-326023; e-mail museorisorgimento@comune.vicenza.it; internet www.comune.vicenza.it/vicenza/musei/risorgimento.php; Dir Dott. MAURO PASSARIN.

Pinacoteca Civica: Palazzo Chiericati, Piazza Matteotti 37–39, 36100 Vicenza; tel. 0444-321348; fax 0444-546619; e-mail museocivico@comune.vicenza.it; internet www.comune.vicenza.it/vicenza/musei/pinacoteca.php; f. 1855; 13th–19th century paintings and sculpture by artists incl. Montagna, Veronese, Tintoretto and Tiepolo; MSS, drawings, prints and coins; Dir Dott.ssa MARIA ELISA AVAGNINA.

Viterbo

Museo Civico: Piazza Crispi 2, 01100 Viterbo; tel. 0761-348275; fax 0761-348276; e-mail museocivico@comune.viterbo.it; internet www.viterbonline.com/muscivicus.html; f. 1912; archaeology, art history; Dir Dott.ssa ADRIANA EMILIOZZI.

Volterra

Museo Diocesano d'Arte Sacra: Palazzo Vescovile, Via Roma 13, 56048 Volterra; tel. 058-886290; fax 058-886290; e-mail museoartesacravolterra@nemail.it; internet www.diocesivolterra.it; f. 1932; sculpture, paintings, costumes, ornaments; Dir Dott. UMBERTO BAVONI.

Museo Etrusco Guarnacci: Via Don Minzoni 15, 56048 Volterra; tel. 0588-86347; fax 0588-90987; e-mail musei@comune.volterra.pi.it; internet www.comune.volterra.pi.it/english/museiit/metru.html; f. 1761; Roman and Etruscan coins, urns, bronzes, etc.; Dir (vacant).

State Universities

UNIVERSITÀ DEGLI STUDI DI ANCONA

Piazza Roma 22, 60121 Ancona
Telephone: 071-2201
Fax: 071-2202324
Internet: www.unian.it
Founded 1969
Academic year: November to October

Rector: Prof. MARCO PACETTI
Vice-Rector: Prof. MARIO GOVERNA
Director: Dott. SANDRO FERRI
Librarian: Dott.ssa SILVIA SOTTILI

Library of 26,000 vols
Number of teachers: 430
Number of students: 13,000

DEANS

Faculty of Agronomy: Prof. EDOARDO BIONDI
Faculty of Economics: Prof. ENZO PESCIARELLI
Faculty of Engineering: Prof. GIOVANNI LATINI
Faculty of Medicine and Surgery: Prof. TULLIO MANZONI
Faculty of Sciences: Prof. ETTORE OLMO

UNIVERSITÀ DEGLI STUDI DI BARI

Piazza Umberto I, 70121 Bari
Telephone: 080-311111
Internet: www.uniba.it
Founded 1924

Rector: Prof. CORRADO PETROCELLI
Admin. Dir: Dott. GIORGIO DE SANTIS

Number of teachers: 700
Number of students: 42,439

DEANS

Faculty of Agriculture: Prof. E. BELLITTI
Faculty of Economics and Commerce: Prof. G. CHIASSINO
Faculty of Education: Prof. M. DELL'AQUILA
Faculty of Engineering: Prof. B. MAIONE
Faculty of Foreign Languages: Prof. V. MASIELLO
Faculty of Jurisprudence: Prof. G. PIEPOLI
Faculty of Letters and Philosophy: Prof. F. TATEO
Faculty of Medicine: Prof. V. MITOLO
Faculty of Pharmacology: Prof. V. TORTORELLA
Faculty of Science: Prof. A. COSSU
Faculty of Veterinary Medicine: Prof. G. O. MARCOTRIGIANO

UNIVERSITÀ DEGLI STUDI DELLA BASILICATA

Via Nazario Sauro 85, 85100 Potenza
Telephone: 0971-201111
Fax: 0971-474102
Internet: www.unibas.it
Founded 1982

Rector: Prof. GIANFRANCO BOARI
Vice-Rector: Prof. PASQUALE PIAZZOLLA
Admin. Dir: Dr MARIO ROSARIO CAVALIERE
Librarians: Prof. CARLO MARIA SIMONETTI, Prof. GABOR KORCHMAROS

Library of 85,000 vols
Number of teachers: 307
Number of students: 4,845
Publications: *Basilicata Università, Collana 'Atti e Memorie', Collana 'Strutture e Materiali', Quaderni*

DEANS

Faculty of Agriculture: Prof. F. BASSO
Faculty of Engineering: Prof. V. COPERTINO
Faculty of Letters and Philosophy: Prof. A. DE FRANCESCO
Faculty of Sciences: Prof. A. M. TAMBURRO

UNIVERSITÀ DEGLI STUDI DI BERGAMO

Via Salvecchio 19, 24129 Bergamo
Telephone: 035-227111
Fax: 035-243054
E-mail: postmaster@unibg.it
Internet: www.unibg.it
Founded 1968

Rector: Prof. ALBERTO CASTOLDI
Admin. Dir: Dott. GIUSEPPE GIOVANELLI
Librarian: Dott. ENNIO FERRANTE

Library of 142,000 vols
Number of teachers: 211
Number of students: 6,317

DEANS

Faculty of Economics: Prof. MARIA IDA BERTOCCHI
Faculty of Engineering: Prof. ANTONIO PERDICHIZZI
Faculty of Foreign Languages and Literature: Prof. ALBERTO CASTOLDI

PROFESSORS

Faculty of Economics:
AMADUZZI, A., Business Administration
ARCUCCI, F., International Trade and Finance
BERTOCCHI, M. I., Financial Mathematics
BIFFIGNANDI, S., Statistics Applied to Economics
FENGHI, F., Commercial Law
FERRI, P. E., Economic Analysis
GAMBARELLI, G., General Mathematics
GRAZIOLA, G., Economics of Enterprise
LEONI, R., Labour Economics
MASINI, M., Banking
RENOLDI, A., Value Management
SACCHETTO, C., Tax Law
SPEDICATO, E., Operations Research
TAGI, G., Industrial Operations Management
TAGLIARINI, F., Commercial Penal Law
Faculty of Engineering:
BUGINI, A., Industrial Management of Quality
COLOMBI, R., Statistics and Probability
PERDICHIZZI, A., Energetic Powerplants
RIVA, R., Theoretical and Applied Mechanics
SALANTI, A., Economics
Faculty of Foreign Languages and Literature:
BELLER, M., German Language and Literature
CASTOLDI, A., French Language and Literature II
CERUTI, M., Epistemology
CORONA, M., Anglo-American Languages and Literature
GOTTI, M., History of the English Language
LOCATELLI, A., English Language and Literature
MARZOLA, A., English Language and Literature
MIRANDOLA, G., French Language and Literature I
MOLINARI, M. V., Germanic Philology
MORELLI, G., Spanish Language and Literature
PAPA, E., Modern and Contemporary History
VILLA, C., Medieval and Humanist Philology

UNIVERSITÀ DI BOLOGNA

Via Zamboni 33, 40126 Bologna
Telephone: 051-2099111
Fax: 051-2099372
Internet: www.unibo.it
Founded 1088

Academic year: October to July

Rector: Prof. PIER UGO CALZOLARI
Admin. Dir: Dott.ssa INES FABBRO

Library of 1,250,000 vols and 400 video cassettes; additional departmental libraries
Number of teachers: 3,001
Number of students: 101,488

DEANS

Faculty of Agriculture: Prof. DOMENICO REGAZZI
Faculty of Architecture: Prof. GIANNI BRAGHIERI
Faculty of Arts and Philosophy: Prof. GIUSEPPE SASSATELLI
Faculty of Economics: Prof. SANDRO SANDRI
Faculty of Economics, Forli: Prof. GIUSEPPE FARNETI
Faculty of Economics, Rimini: Prof. GUIDO CANDELA
Faculty of Education: Prof. FRANCO FRABBONI
Faculty of Engineering: Prof. FRANCO PERSIANI
Faculty of Engineering II: Prof. GUIDO MASETTI,
Faculty of Foreign Languages and Literature: Prof. ALBERTO DESTRO
Faculty of Industrial Chemistry: Prof. FERRUCCIO TRIFIRÒ
Faculty of Jurisprudence: Prof. STEFANO CANESTRARI
Faculty of Mathematics, Physics and Natural Sciences: Prof. LORENZO DONATIELLO
Faculty of Medicine: Prof. MARIA PAOLA LANDINI
Faculty of Pharmacy: Prof. GIORGIO CANTELLI FORTI
Faculty of Political Science: Prof. ANNA STAGNI
Faculty of Political Science, Forli: Prof. GILIBERTO CAPENA
Faculty of Psychology: Prof. GUIDO SARCHIELLI
Faculty of Sport Science: Prof. SALVATORE SQUATRITO
Faculty of Statistics and Demography: Prof. PAOLA MONARI
Faculty of Veterinary Medicine: Prof. STEFANO CINOTTI
School of Modern Languages for Interpreters and Translators: Prof. CHRISTOPHER GUY ASTON

UNIVERSITÀ DEGLI STUDI DI BRESCIA

Piazza del Mercato 15, 25121 Brescia
Telephone: 030-29881
Fax: 030-2988329
Internet: www.unibs.it
Founded 1982

Rector: Prof. AUGUSTO PRETI
Vice-Rector: Prof. GIANCARLO PROVASI
Admin. Dir: Dr ANGELO BRESCIANI
Librarians: RICCARDO FAINI (Economics and Law), FRANCESCO GENNA (Engineering), PIER FRANCO SPANO (Medicine and Surgery)
Number of teachers: 355
Number of students: 12,020

DEANS

Faculty of Economics: GIANCARLO PROVASI
Faculty of Engineering: ANDREA TARONI
Faculty of Law: VINCENZO ALLEGRI
Faculty of Medicine and Surgery: LUIGI CAIMI

UNIVERSITÀ DI CAGLIARI

Via Università 40, 09124 Cagliari, Sardinia
Telephone: 070-662493
Internet: www.unica.it
Founded 1606 by Pope Paul V

Rector: Prof. PASQUALE MISTRETTA
Admin. Dir: Dott. FABRIZIO CHERCHI
Librarian: Dott.ssa GRAZIELLA SEDDA DELITALA

Number of teachers: 1,000
Number of students: 18,000

Publication: *Studi economico-giuridici* and publs from each faculty

DEANS

Faculty of Economics and Commerce: Prof. G. USAI
Faculty of Education: Prof. S. TAGLIAGAMBE
Faculty of Engineering: Prof. CARLO VIVANET
Faculty of Law: Prof. F. SITZIA
Faculty of Letters and Philosophy: Prof. G. RESTAINO
Faculty of Medicine: Prof. A. BALESTRIERI
Faculty of Pharmacy: Prof. A. MACCIONI
Faculty of Political Science: Prof. G. SOTGIU
Faculty of Science: Prof. F. RAGA

UNIVERSITÀ DI CALABRIA

Via P. Bucci, 87036 Arcavacata di Rende
Telephone: (984) 4911
Fax: (984) 493616
E-mail: diramm@unical.it
Internet: www.unical.it
Founded 1972
Academic year: November to October

Rector: Prof. GIOVANNI LaTORRE
Admin. Officer: Dott. BRUNA ADAMO

Number of teachers: 865 (incl. professors and researchers)
Number of students: 34,266

Library of 400,000 vols

DEANS

Faculty of Economics: Prof. FRANCO RUBINO
Faculty of Engineering: Prof. PAOLO VELTRI
Faculty of Letters and Philosophy: Prof. RAFFAELE PERRELLI
Faculty of Mathematical, Physical and Natural Sciences: Prof. GINO MIROCLE CRISCI
Faculty of Pharmacy: Prof. SEBASTIANO ANDÒ
Faculty of Political Sciences: Prof. GUERINO D'IGNAZIO

UNIVERSITÀ DI CAMERINO

Via Gentile III Da Varano, 62032 Camerino
Telephone: 0737-4011
Fax: 0737-402085
Internet: www.unicam.it
Founded 1336; University status 1727
Academic year: November to October

Rector: Prof. FULVIO ESPOSITO
Admin. Dir: Dr LUIGI TAPANELLI

Number of teachers: 301
Number of students: 10,055

Publications: *Documents Phytosociologiques*, *Index—International Survey of Roman Law*, *Laboratorio di Studi linguistici*, *Medicina legale—Quaderni camerti*, *Quaderni Camerti*, *Studi geologici camerti*

DEANS

Faculty of Architecture: Prof. GIOVANNI GUAZZO
Faculty of Jurisprudence: Prof. GUIDO BISCONTINI
Faculty of Pharmacy: Prof. MAURIZIO MASSI
Faculty of Science: Prof. RICARDO PIERGALLINI
Faculty of Veterinary Medicine: Prof. BENIAMINO TESEI

ATTACHED INSTITUTES

School of Clinical-Chemical Research: Dir Prof. ROSALIA TACCONI.

School of Postgraduate Studies in Civil Law: Dir Prof. ANTONIO FLAMINI.

School of Specialization in Hospital Pharmacy: Dir Prof. IPPOLITO ANTONINI.

UNIVERSITÀ DEGLI STUDI DI CASSINO

Via G. Marconi 10, 03043 Cassino (Frosinone)
Telephone: 0776-2993209
Fax: 0776-310562
E-mail: info@unicas.it
Internet: www.unicas.it
Founded 1979
State control

Rector: PAOLO VIGO
Admin. Dir: ANDREA MARZOCCHI

Number of teachers: 160
Number of students: 9,500

DEANS

Faculty of Economics and Commerce: Prof. MARIA CLAUDIA LUCCHETTI
Faculty of Education: Prof. GIANFRANCO RUBINO
Faculty of Engineering: Prof. GUIDO CARPINELLI
Faculty of Letters and Philosophy: GIANFRANCO RUBINO

UNIVERSITÀ DEGLI STUDI DI CATANIA

Piazza dell' Università 2, 95124 Catania
Telephone: 095-321112
Fax: 095-325194
E-mail: rettore@unict.it
Internet: www.unict.it
Founded 1434

Rector: Prof. ANTONINO RECCA
Pro-Rector: Prof.ssa MARIA LUISA CARNAZZA
Admin. Dir: Dr FEDERICO PORTOGHESE

Number of teachers: 1,517
Number of students: 53,674

DEANS

Faculty of Agriculture: Prof. GIUSEPPE PERROTTA
Faculty of Architecture: Prof. UGO CANTONE
Faculty of Economics and Commerce: Prof. EMILIO GIARDINA
Faculty of Education: Prof. ROSARIO SORACI
Faculty of Engineering: Prof. GIUSEPPE COZZO
Faculty of Jurisprudence: Prof. VINCENZO ZAPPALA
Faculty of Literature and Philosophy: Prof. GIUSEPPE GIARRIZZO
Faculty of Mathematics, Physics, Chemistry and Natural Sciences: Prof. RENATO PUCCI
Faculty of Medicine: Prof. GIOVANNI RUSSO
Faculty of Pharmacy: Prof. GIUSEPPE RONSISVALLE
Faculty of Political Science: Prof. VINCENZO SCIACCA

UNIVERSITÀ DEGLI STUDI DI FERRARA

Via Savonarola 9, 44100 Ferrara
Telephone: 0532-293111
Fax: 0532-248927
E-mail: mgn@dns.unife.it
Internet: www.unife.it
Founded 1391
Academic year: November to October

Rector: Prof. PATRIZIO BIANCHI
Pro-Rector: (vacant)
Admin. Dir: Dott. ALESSANDRO FABBRI

Number of teachers: 714
Number of students: 17,000

Publications: *Annali dell' Università*, *Ateneo* (6 a year)

DEANS

Faculty of Architecture: Prof. GRAZIANO TRIPPA
Faculty of Economics: (vacant)
Faculty of Engineering: Prof. ROBERTO POMPOLI
Faculty of Law: Prof. GIOVANNI CAZZETTA
Faculty of Letters and Philosophy: Prof. CARLO ALBERTO CAMPI
Faculty of Mathematical, Physical and Natural Sciences: Prof. REMIGIO ROSSI
Faculty of Medicine and Surgery: Prof. ADOLFO SEBASTIANI
Faculty of Pharmacy: Prof. ALESSANDRO BRUNI

PROFESSORS

Faculty of Architecture (Via Quartieri 8, 44100 Ferrara; tel. 0532-293613; fax 0532-293611; e-mail faf@unife.it; internet architettura.fe.infn.it):

ACOCELLA, A., Architectural Technology
ALESSANDRI, C., Construction Theory
CECCARELLI, P., Urban Planning
DI FEDERICO, I., Industrial Technical Physics
LAUDIERO, F., Construction Methods
MINARDI, B., Urban and Architectonic Composition
TRIPPA, G., Architectural Technology

Faculty of Economics (Vicolo del Gregorio 13–15, 44100 Ferrara; tel. 0532-293000; fax 0532-293012; internet www.economia.unife .it):

BIANCHI, P., Applied Economics
CALAMANTI, A., Economics of Financial Mediators
COCOZZA, F., Economic Law
PINI, P., Political Economy
POLA, G., Finance
SEGALA, F., Mathematical Analysis

Faculty of Engineering (Via Saragat 1, 44100 Ferrara; tel. 0532-974871; fax 0532-760162; internet www.unife.it/facolta/facolta-300076 .htm):

BEGHELLI, S., Automatic Controls
BETTOCCHI, R., Energy and Environmental Systems
DAL CIN, R., Stratigraphic and Sedimentological Geology
DALPIAZ, G., Applied Machine Mechanics
DEL PIERO, G., Construction Theory
FERRETTI, P., Experimental Physics
FRANCHINI, M., Hydraulic and Marine Hydraulic Engineering
FRONTERA, F., Experimental Physics
LAMMA, E., Information Processing Systems
OLIVO, P., Electronics
PADULA, M., Mathematical Physics
PIVA, S., Industrial Technical Physics
POMPOLI, R., Environmental Technical Physics
RUSSO, P., Topography and Cartography
TRALLI, A., Construction Theory
ZUCCHI, F., Chemical Foundations of Technology

Faculty of Law (Corso Ercole I d'Este 37, 44100 Ferrara; tel. 0532-205521; fax 0532-200188; e-mail infogiur@unife.it; internet www.giuri.unife.it):

ADAMI, F. E., Canon and Ecclesiastical Law
BALANDI, G. G., Labour Law
BERNARDI, A., Penal Law
BIN, R., Constitutional Law
BORGHI, P., Agrarian Law
BRUNELLI, G., Institutions of Public Law
BRUZZO, A., Political Economy
CARIELLO, V., Commercial Law
CASAROTTO, G., Agrarian Law
CAZZETTA, G., History of Medieval and Modern Law
CIACCIA, B., Civil Procedure Law
COSTATO, L., Agrarian Law

DE GIORGI, M. V., Private Law
GRIPPO, G., Commercial Law
MANFREDINI, A., Roman Law and Laws of Antiquity
NAPPI, P., Agrarian Law
PASTORE, B., Philosophy of Law
PELLIZZER, F., Administrative Law
PUGIOTTO, A., Constitutional Law
SALERNO, F., International Law
SCARANO USSANI, V., Roman Law and Laws of Antiquity
SOMMA, A., Comparative Private Law
ZAMORANI, P., Roman Law and Laws of Antiquity

Faculty of Letters and Philosophy (Via Savonarola 38, 44100 Ferrara; tel. 0532-293416; fax 0532-202689; internet www .unife.it/facolta/facolta-300035.htm):

BELLATALLA, L., History of School and Educational Institutions
BOLLINI, M., Roman History
CAMPI, C. A., Geography
CHERCHI, P., Italian Literature
FABBRI, P., Musicology and Musical History
FAVA, E., Glottology and Linguistics
FOLLI, A., Contemporary Italian Literature
GALLI, M., German Literature
GENOVESI, G., General and Social Pedagogy
MATARRESE, S., Italian Language
MAZZI, M. S., Medieval History
MAZZOCCHI, G., Spanish Literature
MERCI, P., Romance Philology and Linguistics
NESPOR, M. A., Glottology and Linguistics
PANCERA, C., History of Schools and Educational Institutions
RICCI, G., Modern History
SECHI, S., Contemporary History
TEMPERA, M., English Literature
TROVATO, P., Italian Language
VARESE, R., History of Modern Art
ZANOTTI, A., General Sociology

Faculty of Mathematical, Physical and Natural Sciences (Via Luigi Borsari 46, 44100 Ferrara; tel. 0532-291347; fax 0532-291348; internet www.unife.it/facolta/facolta-275017 .htm):

ABELLI, L., Comparative Anatomy and Cytology
ALBERTI, A., Mineralogy
BARBUJANI, G., Genetics
BECCALUVA, L., Petrology and Petrography
BERNARDI, F., Biochemistry
BIASINI, L., Numerical Analysis
BIGNOZZI, C. A., General and Inorganic Chemistry
BOSELLINI, A., Stratigraphic and Sedimentological Geology
BROGLIO, A., Anthropologyy
CANESCHI, L., Theoretical Physics and Mathematical Models and Methods
CIMIRAGLIA, R., Physical Chemistry
COLTORTI, M., Petrology and Petrography
CORALLINI, A., General Microbiology
DALPIAZ, P., General Physics
DEL CENTINA, A., Geometry
DI CAPUA, E., Experimental Physics
DONDI, F., Analytical Chemistry
DONDONI, A., Organic Chemistry
ELLIA, P., Geometry
FAGIOLI, F., Environmental and Conservation Chemistry
FASULO, M. P., General Botany
FIORENTINI, G., Nuclear and Subnuclear Physics
FOA', A. G., Zoology
GERDOL, R., Environmental and Applied Botany
GILLI, G., Physical Chemistry
LASCU, A., Geometry
MARTINELLI, G., Experimental Physics
MASSARI, U., Mathematical Analysis
MENINI, C., Algebra
NANNI, T., Applied Geology

NIZZOLI, F., Solid-State Physics
PEPE, L., Complementary Mathematics
PERETTO, C., Anthropology
PICCOLINO, M., Physiology
PRODI, F., Earth Physics
ROSSI, R., Ecology
RUGGIERO, V., Numerical Analysis
SACCHI, O., Physiology
SACERDOTI, M., Mineralogy
SALVATORELLI, G., Comparative Anatomy and Cytology
SCANDOLA, F., General and Inorganic Chemistry
SCHIFFRER, G., Theoretical Physics and Mathematical Models and Methods
SIENA, F., Petrology and Petrography
SOLONNIKOV, V., Mathematical Physics
TRAVERSO, O., General and Inorganic Chemistry
TRIPICCIONE, R., Theoretical Physics and Mathematical Models and Methods
ZANGHIRATI, L., Mathematical Analysis

Faculty of Medicine and Surgery (Via Fossato di Mortara 64/b, 44100 Ferrara; tel. 0532-291545; fax 0532-291546; e-mail preside.medicina@unife.it; internet web .unife.it/facolta/medicina):

AVATO, F. M., Forensic Medicine
AZZENA, G. F., General Surgery
BERGAMINI, C., Clinical Biochemistry and Clinical Molecular Biology
BERTI, G., General Pathology
BOREA, P. A., Pharmacology
BORGNA, C., General and Specialized Paediatrics
CALURA, G., Odontostomatological Diseases
CALZOLARI, E., Medical Genetics
CAPITANI, S., Human Anatomy
CARUSO, A., Histology
CASSAI, E., Microbiology and Clinical Microbiology
CASTOLDI, G. L., Haematology
CAVAZZINI, L., Anatomical Pathology
CIACCIA, A., Diseases of the Respiratory Tract
CONCONI, F., Biochemistry
CROCE, C. M., Medical Oncology
DALLOCCHIO, F. P. F., Biochemistry
DE ROSA, E., Industrial Medicine
DEGLI UBERTI, E., Endocrinology
DEL SENNO, L., Molecular Biology
DI VIRGILIO, F., General Pathology
DONINI, I. G., General Surgery
DURANTE, E., General Surgery
FAVILLA, M., Physiology
FELLIN, R., Internal Medicine
FERRARI, R., Cardiovascular Diseases
GRANIERI, E., Neurology
GRAZI, E., Biochemistry
GREGORIO, P., General and Applied Hygiene
GUALDI, E., Anthropology
LIBONI, A., General Surgery
LONGHINI, C., Internal Medicine
MANNELLA, P., Imaging and Radiotherapy Diagnostics
MARTINI, A., Audiology
MOLINARI, S., Clinical Psychology
MOLLICA, G., Obstetrics and Gynaecology
NENCI, I., Anatomy and Pathological Histology
PASTORE, A., Otolaryngology
PINAMONTI, S., Applied Biology
RAMELLI, E., Psychiatry
REGOLI, D., Pharmacology
SEBASTIANI, A., Eyesight Diseases
SICILIANI, G., Odontostomatological Diseases
SPIDALIERI, G., Physiology
TOGNON, M., Applied Biology
TRAINA, G. C., Ambulatory Diseases
TROTTA, F., Rheumatology
TURINI, D., Urology
VIGI, V., General and Specialized Paediatrics

VIRGILI, A., Skin and Venereal Diseases

Faculty of Pharmacy (Via Fossato di Mortara 17/19, 44100 Ferrara; tel. 0532-291265; fax 0532-291296; e-mail farmline@unife.it; internet web.unife.it/facolta/farmacia):

BARALDI, P. G., Pharmaceutical Chemistry
BIANCHI, C., Pharmacology
BIONDI, C., Physiology
BRANDOLINI, V., Food Chemistry
BRUNI, A., Pharmocological Biology
GAMBACCINI, M., Applied Physics (Conservation, Environmental, Biological and Medical)
GAMBARI, R., Biochemistry
MANFREDINI, S., Pharmaceutical Chemistry
MANSERVIGI, R., Microbiology and Clinical Microbiology
MENEGATTI, E., Applied Pharmaceutical Technology
POLLINI, G. P., Organic Chemistry
RIZZUTO, R., General Pathology
SALVADORI, S., Pharmaceutical Chemistry
SCATTURIN, A., Applied Pharmaceutical Chemistry
SIMONI, D., Pharmaceutical Chemistry
TANGANELLI, S., Pharmacology
TOMATIS, R., Pharmaceutical Chemistry
TRANIELLO, M. S., Biochemistry

UNIVERSITÀ DEGLI STUDI DI FIRENZE

Piazza San Marco 4, 50121 Florence
Telephone: 055-27571
Fax: 055-264194
Internet: www.unifi.it
Founded 1321
Academic year: September to August
Rector: AUGUSTO MARINELLI
Vice-Rector: ALFREDO CORPACI
Admin. Dir: Dott. MICHELE OREFICE
Dir of Library System: Dott.ssa GIULIA MARAVIGLIA
Number of teachers: 2,236
Number of students: 59,847

DEANS

Faculty of Agriculture and Forestry: Prof. AUGUSTO MARINELLI
Faculty of Architecture: Prof. FRANCESCO GURRIERI
Faculty of Economics: Prof. CARLO VALLINI
Faculty of Education: Prof. PAOLO OREFICE
Faculty of Engineering: Prof. ENNIO CARNEVALE
Faculty of Jurisprudence: Prof. PAOLO CARETTI
Faculty of Letters and Philosophy: Prof. PAOLO MARRASSINI
Faculty of Mathematical, Physical and Natural Sciences: Prof. P. MALESANI
Faculty of Medicine and Surgery: Prof. GIOVANNI ORLANDINI
Faculty of Pharmacy: Prof. SERGIO PINZAUTI
Faculty of Political Sciences: Prof. CLAUDIO FRANCHINI

UNIVERSITÀ DEGLI STUDI 'GABRIELE D'ANNUNZIO'

Via dei Vestini 31, 66013 Chieti Scalo
Telephone: 0871-3551
Fax: 0871-3556007
E-mail: segreteriarettore@unich.it
Internet: www.unich.it
Founded 1965 as a private univ.; became a state univ. 1982
State control
Rector: Prof. FRANCO CUCCURULLO
Gen. Dir: Dr MARCO NAPOLEONE
Number of students: 19,000

DEANS

Faculty of Architecture: Prof. TOMMASO SCALESSE
Faculty of Commerce: Prof. MARIO GIACCIO
Faculty of Foreign Languages and Literature: Prof. FRANCESCO MARRONI
Faculty of Literature and Philosophy: Prof. GAETANO BONETTA
Faculty of Mathematical, Physical and Natural Sciences: Prof. BRUNO DI SABATINO
Faculty of Medicine and Surgery: Prof. CARMINE DI ILIO
Faculty of Pharmacy: Prof. MICHELE VACCA

UNIVERSITÀ DEGLI STUDI DI GENOVA

Via Balbi 5, 16126 Genoa
Telephone: 010-20991
Fax: 010-2099227
E-mail: webmaster@unige.it
Internet: www.unige.it
Founded 1670
Academic year: November to October
Rector: Prof. S. PONTREMOLI
Vice-Rector: (vacant)
Admin. Dir: Dott. D. PELLITTERI
Number of teachers: 1,719
Number of students: 40,125
Publications: *Annuario dell'Università di Genova* (sections on research and teaching units, each annual), *Genuense Atenaeum* (6 a year)

DEANS

Faculty of Jurisprudence: Prof. V. PIERGIOVANNI
Faculty of Political Sciences: Prof. A. M. DEL GROSSO
Faculty of Economics and Commerce: Prof. L. CASELLI
Faculty of Letters and Philosophy: Prof. M. G. ANGELI
Faculty of Education: Prof. A. DAL LAGO
Faculty of Medicine and Surgery: Prof. U. MARINARI
Faculty of Mathematics, Physics and Natural Science: Prof. M. GIANNINI
Faculty of Pharmacy: Prof. G. BIGNARDI
Faculty of Engineering: Prof. A. SQUARZONI
Faculty of Architecture: Prof. A. E. CALCAGNO
Faculty of Foreign Languages: Prof. P. CROVETTO

UNIVERSITÀ DELGI STUDI DELL'INSUBRIA

Via Ravasi 2, 21100 Varese
Telephone: 0332-219780
Fax: 0332-219009
E-mail: rettore@uninsubria.it
Internet: www.uninsubria.eu
Founded 1998
Rector: Prof. RENZO DIONIGI
Vice-Rector: Prof. GIORGIO CONETTI
Administrative Director: Dr MARINO BALZANI
Library Dir: ALESSANDRA BEZZI
Library of 81,570 vols, 648 journals, 13,000 electronic journals
Number of teachers: 393
Number of students: 9,546

DEANS

Faculty of Economics: Prof. MATTEO ROCCA
Faculty of Law: Prof. MARIA PAOLA VIVIANI SCHLEIN
Faculty of Medicine in Varese: Prof. PAOLO CHERUBINO
Faculty of Sciences in Como: Prof. STEFANO SERRA CAPIZZANO
Faculty of Sciences in Varese: Prof. ALBERTO COEN PORISINI

SPECIAL RESEARCH CENTRES

International Research Centre for Local History and Cultural Diversities: Via Ravasi 2, 21100 Varese; tel. 332-219801; fax 332-219809; e-mail info@cslinsubria.it; internet www.cslinsubria.it.

Insubria Centre on International Security (ICIS): Via Valleggio 11, 21100 Como; e-mail maurizio.martellini@uninsubria.it.

Research Centre for Political Symbolism and Cultural Forms: Via Valleggio 11, 21100 Como; e-mail giuliomaria.chiodi@uninsubria.it.

UNIVERSITÀ DEGLI STUDI DELL'AQUILA

Piazza Rivera 1, 67100 L'Aquila
Telephone: 0862-4311
Fax: 0862-412948
Internet: www.univaq.it
Founded 1952
Rector: Prof. FERDINANDO DI ORIO
Admin. Dir: Dott. FILIPPO DEL VECCHIO
Library of 171,356 vols
Number of teachers: 509
Number of students: 8,260

DEANS

Faculty of Business Economics: STELIO VALENTINI
Faculty of Education: Prof. ENRICO MONTANARI
Faculty of Engineering: Prof. LUIGI BIGNARDI
Faculty of Medicine: Prof. FERDINANDO DI ORIO
Faculty of Sciences: Prof. ARMANDO REALE

UNIVERSITÀ DEGLI STUDI DI LECCE

Viale Gallipoli 49, 73100 Lecce
Telephone: 0832-291111
Fax: 0832-292204
E-mail: rettore@unile.it
Internet: www.unile.it
Founded 1956
Academic year: November to October
Rector: Prof. ORONZO LIMONE
Admin. Dir: Dott. ANTONIO SOLOMBRINO
Librarian: Dott.ssa GIOVANNA BASCIA
Library of 500,000 vols
Number of teachers: 673
Number of students: 28,403
Publication: *Unile* (4 a year)

DEANS

Faculty of Arts: Prof. MARCELLO GUAITOLI
Faculty of Economics: Prof. NICOLA DI CAGNO
Faculty of Education: Prof. MARCELLO STRAZZERI
Faculty of Engineering: Prof. DOMENICO LAFORGIA
Faculty of Foreign Languages: Prof. ANTONIO FINO
Faculty of Law: Prof. NICOLA DE LISO
Faculty of Letters and Philosophy: Prof. BRUNO PELLEGRINO
Faculty of Science: Prof. CARLO STORELLI

UNIVERSITÀ DEGLI STUDI DI MACERATA

Piaggia dell'Università 11, 62100 Macerata
Telephone: 0733-2581
Fax: 0733-2582689
E-mail: rel.esterne@unimc.it
Internet: www.unimc.it
Founded 1290
Rector: Prof. ROBERTO SANI
Vice-Rector: Prof. LUIGI LACCHÉ
Head of Administration: Dr ROLANDO GARBUGLIA

Deputy Rector for Budget and Financial Planning: Prof. ANTONELLA PAOLINI
Deputy Rector for Buildings and Property: Prof. ADRIANO BALLARINI
Deputy Rector for Computing and Multi-media Centre (CAIM): Prof. MAURO MARCONI
Deputy Rector for e-Learning and Integrated Teacher Training Centre (CELFI): Prof. PIER GIUSEPPE ROSSI
Deputy Rector for Equal Opportunities Committee: Prof. MARINA CAMBONI
Deputy Rector for International Relations: Prof. ANDREA SIMOCINI
Deputy Rector for Library System: Prof. ENZO CANIZZARO
Deputy Rector for Organization and Staff: Prof. CARLO MENGHI
Deputy Rector for Orientation Centre: Prof. BARBARA POJAGHI
Deputy Rector for Professional and Corporate Relations: Prof. CRISTIANA MAMMANA
Deputy Rector for Public Relations: Prof. DIEGO POLI
Deputy Rector for Theatre and Artistic Events: Prof. MARCELLO VERDENELLI
Deputy Rector for University of Macerata Publications Centre: Prof. LUIGI LACCHÉ
Deputy Rector for University Language Centre (CLA): Prof. DANIELLE LÉVY

Number of teachers: 300
Number of students: 15,000

DEANS

Faculty of Arts and Humanities: Prof. DANIELE MAGGI
Faculty of Communication Sciences: Prof. MAURIZIO CIASCHINI
Faculty of Economics: Prof. MAURO MARCONI
Faculty of Educational Sciences: Prof. MICHELE CORSI
Faculty of Law: Prof. RINO FROLDI
Faculty of Political Sciences: Prof. VITANTONIO GIOIA

ATTACHED RECORDS AND RESEARCH CENTRES

Antoine Barnave Laboratory of Constitutional History: Dir Prof. ROBERTO MARTUCCI.
Attilio Moroni Centre of Studies: Dir Prof. GINESIO MANTUANO.
Centre for Autobiographical Studies: Dir (vacant).
Centre for European Records (CDE): Dir Prof. ENZO CANNIZZARO.
Centre for Legal Computing (CIG): Dir Prof. ENRICO DEL PRATO.
Centre for Records on Contemporary Parties and Political Movements in Le Marche: Dir Prof. ANGELO VENTRONE.
Centre for Records and Research on the History of the School Textbook and Children's Literature: Dir Prof. ROBERTO SANI.
Centre for Records and Research on North African Archaeology: Dir Prof. ANTONINO DI VITA.
Centre for Research into the Psychology of Communication: Dir Prof. ANDRZEJ ZUZCKOWSKI.
Centre for Research into the Psychology of Development and Education: Dir Prof.ssa ANNA ARFELLI.
Centre for Studies on Juvenile Justice: Dir Prof. GLAUCO GIOSTRA.
Centre for Studies and Records of the University of Macerata: Dir Prof. SANDRO SERANGELI.
Fausto Vicarelli Laboratory for the Study of the Relations between Banks and Industry: Dir Prof. ANDREA NIUTTA.

Ghino Valenti Laboratory on Agricultural, Environmental and Alimentary Policies: Dir Prof. FRANCESCO ADORNATO.
Interdepartmental Centre on the Reform of the State of Welfare Policies: Dir Prof.ssa PAOLA OLIVELLI.
Inter-University Centre for Research, Teaching and Teacher Training (CIRDIFOR): Dir Prof. MICHELE CORSI.
Laboratory of Computer Records: Dir Prof. STEFANO PIGLIAPOCO.
Laboratory of European Mediterranean and Oriental History: Dir Prof. ANGELO VENTRONE.
Laboratory of Experimental Phonetics (LAFOS): Dir Prof. DIEGO POLI.

UNIVERSITÀ DEGLI STUDI DI MESSINA

Piazza Salvatore Pugliatti 1, 98122 Messina
Telephone: 090-6761
Fax: 1717762
E-mail: prorettore.vicario@unime.it
Internet: www.unime.it

Founded 1548
Academic year: November to June

Rector: Prof. FRANCESCO TOMASELLO
Pro-Rector: Prof. GIOVANNI DUGO
Admin. Dir: Dr VINCENZO FERLUGA

Number of teachers: 1,300
Number of students: 40,000

DEANS

Faculty of Economics: Prof. L. FERLAZZO NATOLI
Faculty of Education: Prof. A. PENNISI
Faculty of Engineering: Prof. S. GALVAGNO
Faculty of Jurisprudence: Prof. S. BERLINGÒ
Faculty of Literature and Philosophy: Prof. V. FERA
Faculty of Mathematics, Physics and Natural Sciences: Prof. M. GATTUSO
Faculty of Medicine: Prof. E. SCRIBANO
Faculty of Pharmacy: Prof. M. G. VIGORITA
Faculty of Politics: Prof. A. ROMANA
Faculty of Statistical Sciences: Prof. L. LA TONA
Faculty of Veterinary Medicine: Prof. G. GERMANÀ

UNIVERSITÀ DEGLI STUDI DI MILANO

Via Festa del Perdono 7, 20122 Milan
Telephone: 02-503111
Fax: 02-50312627
Internet: www.unimi.it

Founded 1923
Academic year: October to September

Rector: Prof. E. DECLEVA
Vice-Rector: Prof. D. CASATI
Admin. Dir: Dott. FILIPPO SORI
Librarian: Dott. GIULIANA GIUSTINO

Number of teachers: 716
Number of students: 63,000

Publication: *Sistema Università* (online at www.sisuni.unimi.it)

DEANS

Faculty of Agriculture: Prof. C. SORLINI
Faculty of Law: Prof. V. FERRARI
Faculty of Letters and Philosophy: Prof. E. FRANZINI
Faculty of Medicine: Prof. G. COGGI
Faculty of Motor Sciences: Prof. G. PIZZINI
Faculty of Pharmacy: Prof. R. PAOLETTI
Faculty of Political Sciences: Prof. M. REGINI
Faculty of Sciences: Prof. M. PIGNANELLI
Faculty of Veterinary Medicine: Prof. G. POLI

PROFESSORS

Faculty of Agriculture (Via Celoria 2, 20133 Milan; tel. 02-50316500; fax 02-50316508; e-mail preside.agraria@unimi.it; internet www.unimi.it/ateneo/facol/agraria.htm):
ANDREONI, V., Agricultural Microbiology
BASSI, D., Fruit Farming
BELLI, G., Plant Pathology
BIANCO, P. A., Plant Pathology
BODRIA, L., Agricultural Mechanics
BONOMI, F., Biochemistry
CASATI, D., Agrofood Economy
CASTELLI, G., Agricultural Mechanics
CASTROVILLI, C. M., Zooculture
COCUCCI, M., Physiology of Farmed Plants
CORTESI, P., Plant Pathology
CROVETTO, G. M., Animal Nutrition and Foodstuffs
DE WRACHIEN, D., Irrigation and Drainage
DESIMONI, E., Analytical Chemistry
DURANTI, M. M., Biochemistry
ECCHER, T., General Arboriculture
ELIAS, G., Environmental Technical Physics
FRISIO, D. G., Rural Economics and Surveying
GALLI, A., Foods Microbiology
GANDOLFI, C., Agricultural and Forest Hydraulics
GARLASCHI, F. M., Vegetable Physiology
GASPARETTO, E., Agricultural Mechanization
GAVAZZI, G., Plant Genetic Improvement
GENEVINI, P., Soil Chemistry
GIURA, R., Agricultural Hydraulics
GREPPI, M., Hydraulic Systems, Forestry
LOCATELLI, D. P., General and Applied Entomology
LOZZIA, G. C., General and Applied Entomology
LUCISANO, M., Food Science and Technology
MAGGIORE, T., Herbaceous Farming
MANACHINI, P., General Microbiology
MANNINO, S., Chemico-Physical and Sensory Analysis of Food
MERLINI, L., Organic Chemistry
MONDELLI, R., Organic Chemistry
PAGANI, S., Enzymology
PELLEGRINO, L. M., Food Science and Technology
PIERGIOVANNI, L., Food Science and Technology
POLELLI, M., Rural Evaluation
POMPEI, C., Food Technology Processes
PORRINI, M., Physiology
PRETOLANI, R., Rural Economics and Surveying
QUARONI, S., Vegetable Pathology
RAGG, E. M., Organic Chemistry
RESMINI, P., Agricultural Industry
ROSSI, M., Food Science and Technology
SACCHI, G. A., Organic Chemistry
SALAMINI, F., Genetics and Biotechnology
SANGIORGI, F., Rural and Forest Construction
SCHIRALDI, A., Physical Chemistry
SCIENZA, A., General Arboriculture and Tree Cultivation
SORLINI, C., Agricultural and Forest Microbiology
SUCCI, G., Special Animal Husbandry
SÜSS, L., Agricultural Entomology
TANO, F., Herbaceous Farming
TATEO, F., Food Science and Technology
TESTOLIN, G., Human Food and Nutrition
TOCCOLINI, A., Rural and Forest Construction
VOLONTERIO, G., Agricultural Industry
ZOCCHI, G., Food Science and Technology

Faculty of Law (Via Festa del Perdono 7, 20122 Milan; tel. 02-50312400; fax 02-50312653; e-mail presidenza.giurisprudenza@unimi.it; internet www.unimi.it/ateneo/facol/giurisp.htm):

ALBISETTI, A., Ecclesiastical Law
AMODIO, E., Procedural Penal Law
ANGIOLINI, V., Constitutional Law
BARIATTI, S., International Law
BENATTI, F., Institutions of Private Law
BOSCHIERO, N., International Law
CANDIAN, A., Comparative Private Law
CANTARELLA, E., Institutions of Roman Law
CARINCI, M. T., Labour Law
CARNEVALI, U., Institutions of Private Law
CASTAGNOLA, A., Civil Procedural Law
CASUSCELLI, G., Ecclesiastical Law
CAVALLONE, B., Civil Procedural Law
CONDINANZI, M., International Law
D'AMICO, M. E., Constitutional Law
DE NOVA, G., Civil Law
DENOZZA, F., Commercial Law
DI RENZO, M. G., History of Italian Law
DOLCINI, E., Penal Law
DOMINIONI, O., Procedural Penal Comparative Law
FERRARI, E., Administrative Law
FERRARI, S., Canon Law
FERRARI, V., Sociology of Law
FLORIDA, G., Comparative Public Law
FRASSI, P. A., Commercial Law
GAFFURI, G., Tributary Law
GALANTINI, M. N., Procedural Penal Law
GAMBARO, A., Comparative Private Law
GITTI, G., Institutions of Private Law
GNOLI, F., Roman Law
GOISIS, G., Political Economy
GRECO, G., Administrative Law
GREZZI, M. L., Philosophy of Law
GUERCI, C. M., Political Economy
JAEGER, P., Commercial Law
JORI, M., Philosophy of Law
LANCELLOTTI, E., Financial Science
LUZZATI, C. R., Philosophy of Law
LUZZATTO, R., International Law
MARINUCCI, G., Penal Law
MASSETTO, G., History of Italian Law
MERLIN, E., Civil Procedural Law
MORELLO, U. M., Private Law
NASCIMBENE, B., European Community Law
PADOA SCHIOPPA, A., History of Italian Law
PALIERO, C., Penal Law
PARISI, F., Institutions of Private Law
PELOSI, A. C., Institutions of Private Law
PERICU, G., Administrative Law
PISANI, M., Procedural Penal Law
POCAR, F., International Law
POLARA, G., Institutions of Roman Law
RICCI, E., Bankruptcy Law
RIMINI, E., Commercial Law
ROSSIGNOLI, B., Economics of Credit Institutions
SACCHI, R., Commercial Law
SALETTI, A., Civil Procedural Law
SANTA MARIA, A., International Law
SPAGNUOLO VIGORITA, L., Labour Law
TENELLA SILLANI, C., Institutions of Private Law
TREVES, T., International Private and Procedural Law
TRIMARCHI, F., Administrative Law
TRIMARCHI, P., Civil Law
VIGANÒ, F., Penal Law
VILLA, G., Institutions of Private Law
VILLATA, R., Administrative Law
VIOLINI, L., Constitutional Law
VITALI, E. G., Ecclesiastical Law
ZANON, N., Constitutional Law

Faculty of Letters and Philosophy (Via Festa del Perdono 7, 20122 Milan; tel. 02-50312701; fax 02-50312543; e-mail elio .franzini@unimi.it; internet www.unimi.it/ ateneo/facol/letfil.htm):

ALBINI, G., Medieval History
ANTONIELLI, L., History of Political Institutions
ANZI, A., History of the English Theatre
BARONI, M. F., Palaeography
BEJOR, G., Classical Archaeology

BERRA, C., Italian Literature
BIANCHI, E., Geography
BIGALLI, D., History of Philosophy
BIGNAMI, M., English Language and Literature
BOCCALI, G., Sanskrit Language and Literature
BOELLA, L., Moral Philosophy
BOLOGNA, M., Archives, Bibliography and Library Science
BOLOGNA, M. P., Glottology and Linguistics
BONOMI, A., Philosophy of Language
BONOMI, I., Italian Linguistics
BOSISIO, P., Dramatic Arts
BRAMBILLA, E., Modern History
BRIOSCHI, F., History of Literary Criticism
BROGI, G., History of the Russian Language
BRUTI LIBERATI, L., Modern History
CADIOLI, A. V., Contemporary Italian Literature
CAIZZI, F., History of Ancient Philosophy
CANAVERO, A., Modern History
CANZIANI, G., History of Philosophy
CAPRA, C., Modern History
CASALEGNO, P., Philosophy and Theory of Languages
CATTANEO, M. T., Spanish Language and Literature
CAVAJONI, G., Latin Language and Literature
CERCIGNANI, F., German Language and Literature
CHIAPPA, M. L., Medieval History
CHITTOLINI, G., Medieval History
CIANCI, G., English Language and Literature
CICALESE, M. L., Theory and History of Historiography
COLOMBO, M., French
COMBA, R., Medieval History
COMETTA, M., German Philology
CONCA, F., History of the Greek Language
CORDANO, F., Greek History
D'AGOSTINO, A., Romance Philology
DAVERIO, G., Greek History
DE ANGELIS, V., Humanistic Philology
DECLEVA, E., Contemporary History
DE FRANCESCO, A., Modern History
DEGRADA, F., History of Modern and Contemporary Music
DE MARINIS, R. C., Early and Recorded History
DEVECCHI, P., History of Modern Art
DI SALVO, M. G., Slavonic Philology
DOGLIO, M., French Literature
DONATI, C., History of the Ancient Italian States
DONINI, P., History of Ancient Philosophy
FIACCADORI, G., Christian and Medieval Archaeology
FORABOSCHI, D., Roman History
FRANZINI, E., Aesthetics
FUMAGALLI, M. J., History of Medieval Philosophy
GALLAZZI, C., Papyrology
GIACOMELLI, R., Glottology and Linguistics
GIORELLO, G., Philosophy of Science
GORI, G., History of Modern Philosophy
GUALANDRI, I., Latin Literature
IAMARTINO, G., English
LANARO, G. V., History of Philosophy
LEHNUS, L. A., Classical Philology
MARI, M., Italian Literature
MASINI, A., Italian Linguistics
MAZZOCCA, F., Museology, Art Criticism and Restoration Criticism
MENEGHETTI, M. L., Romance Philology
MERLO, G., History of the Medieval Church and Heresy
MERZARIO, R., Economic History
MICHELI, G., History of Science and Technology
MILANINI, C., Italian Literature
MODENESI, M., French Literature
MONTALEONE, C., Moral Philosophy

MONTECCHI, G., Bibliography and Archive and Library Science
MORGANA, S., Italian Language History
NEGRI, A., History of Modern Art
NISSIM, L., French Language and Literature
ORLANDI, G., Medieval Latin Literature
PAGETTI, C., English Language and Literature
PERASSI, E., Hispano-American Languages and Literatures
PETTOELLO, R., History of Philosophy
PEYRONEL, S., Medieval and Early Modern History
PIACENTINI, P., Egyptology and Coptic Civilization
PIRETTO, G. P., Slavic Studies
PIVA, P., History of Medieval Art
PUNZO, M., Modern History
RAMBALDI, E., Moral Philosophy
ROSA, G., Contemporary Italian Literature
RUMI, G., Contemporary History
SAMPIETRO, L., Anglo-American Languages and Literatures
SAPELLI, G., Economic History
SCARAMELLINI, G., Geography
SCARAMUZZA, G., Aesthetics
SCARAMUZZA, M. E., Spanish Literature
SINI, C., Theoretical Philosophy
SPAGGIARI, W., Italian Literature
SPERA, F., Italian Literature
TREVES, A. L., Geography
VALOTA, B., History of Eastern Europe
VISMARA, P., History of Christianity and the Churches
ZANETTO, G., Greek Language and Literature
ZECCHI, S., Aesthetics
ZERBI, M. C., Geography

Faculty of Medicine (Via Festa del Perdono 7, 20122 Milan; tel. 02-50312360; fax 02-50312365; e-mail preside.medicina@unimi .it; internet www.unimi.it/ateneo/facol/ medchir.htm):

AGUS, G. B., Vascular Surgery
ALESSI, E., Dermatology
ALLEGRA, L., Diseases of the Respiratory System
ALLEVI, P., Biochemistry
ALTAMURA, A. C., Psychiatry
ALTOMARE, G., Dermatology
ANASTASIA, M., Chemistry and Biochemical Propaedeutics
AUSTONI, E., Urology
AUXILIA, F., Hygiene
BA, G., Psychiatry
BALDISSERA, F. G., Human Physiology
BALSARI, A., General Pathology
BEK PECCOZ, P., Endocrinology
BELLINI, T., Applied Physics (Arts, Environment, Biology and Medicine)
BERTAZZI, P. A., Industrial Medicine
BIANCHI PORRO, G., Gastroenterology
BIGLIOLI, P., Cardiac Surgery
BLASI, F. B., Diseases of the Respiratory System
BOCK, G., History of Medicine
BOLIS, G., Obstetrics and Gynaecology
BORTOLANI, E., General Surgery
BRAGA, P., Pharmacology
BRESOLIN, N., Neurology
BRESSANI DOLDI, S., General Surgery
BRUSATI, R., Maxillofacial Surgery
BUSACCA, M., Obstetrics and Gynaecology
CABITZA, P., Orthopaedics and Traumatology
CAIRO, G., General Pathology
CAJONE, F., General Pathology
CANTALAMESSA, L., Internal Medicine
CAPETTA, P., Obstetrics and Gynaecology
CAPPELLINI, M. D., Internal Medicine
CAPUTO, R., Dermatology
CARACCIOLO, E., Clinical Psychology
CARRASSI, A., Special Odontostomatological Pathology

CARRUBA, M., Pharmacology
CATTANEO, M. N., Internal Medicine
CAVAGNA, G., Human Physiology
CAVAGNINI, F., Endocrinology
CAVALLARI, P., Physiology
CESARANI, A., Audiology
CESTARO, B. A., Biological Chemistry
CHIESARA, E., Toxicology
CHIGORNO, V. L., Clinical Biochemistry and Molecular Biology
CIANCAGLINI, R., Clinical Gnathology
CICARDI, M., Internal Medicine
CLEMENTI, F., Cellular and Molecular Pharmacology
CLERICI, M. S., General Pathology
COGGI, G., Pathological Anatomy and Histology
COLOMBI, A., Industrial Medicine
COLOMBO, M., Internal Medicine
COMI, P., General Pathology
CONTE, D., Gastroenterology
CORNALBA, G., Imaging and Radiotherapy Diagnostics
CORTELLARO, M., Internal Medicine
CORTI, M., Medical Physics
CROSIGNANI, P., Obstetrics and Gynaecology
CROSTI, C., Dermatology
CUSI, D. M., Nephrology
D'ANGELO, E., Human Physiology
DE FRANCHIS, R., Gastroenterology
DECARLI, A., Medical Statistics
DELLE FAVE, A., General Psychology
DESIDERIO, M. A., General Pathology
DI FIORE, P. P., General Pathology
DI GIULIO, A. M., Pharmacology
DONATELLI, F., Cardiac Surgery
DUBINI, F., Microbiology
FANTINI, F., Rheumatology
FARGION, S. R., Internal Medicine
FARNETI, A., Forensic Medicine
FARRONATO, G., Odontostomatological Diseases
FASSATI, L. R., General Surgery
FEDELE, L., Obstetrics and Gynaecology
FERRARIO, V. F., Human Anatomy
FERRERO, M. E., General Pathology
FIORENTINI, C., Cardiology
FOÀ, V., Industrial Hygiene
FOSCHI, D., General Surgery
GABRIELLI, L., Vascular Surgery
GAINI, S. M., Neurosurgery
GALLI, M., Infectious Diseases
GALLI, M. G., Hygiene
GALLUS, G. V., Medical Statistics and Biometrics
GATTINONI, L., Anaesthesiology and Resuscitation
GELMETTI, C., Dermatology
GHIDONI, R., Biological Chemistry
GIANNI, A., Medical Oncology
GINELLI, E., General Biology
GIOIA, M. A., Human Anatomy
GIOVANNINI, M., Paediatrics
GRANDI, M. A., Forensic Medicine
GROPPETTI, A., Pharmacology
GUAZZI, M., Cardiology
GUIDOBONO CAVALCHIN, F., Pharmacology
IAPICHINO, G., Anaesthesiology
INVERNIZZI, G., Psychiatry
LAMBERTENGHI DELILIERS, G., Internal Medicine
LARIZZA, L., Medical Genetics
LEDDA, M., Histology
LENTI, C., Child Neuropsychiatry
LEONETTI, G., Medical Semiology and Methodology
LODI, F., Forensic Toxicology
LUCIGNANI, G., Imaging and Radiotherapy Diagnostics
MAGRINI, F., Internal Medicine
MALCOVATI, M., Molecular Biology
MALLIANI, A., Internal Medicine
MANNUCCI, P. M., Internal Medicine
MANTOVANI, A., General Pathology
MARIANI, C., Neurology

MARIOTTI, M., Physiology
MARONI, M., Industrial Medicine
MASSIMINI, F., General Psychology
MATTINA, R., Microbiology
MATTURRI, L., Pathological Anatomy and Histology
MELZI D'ERIL, G., Clinical Biochemistry and Molecular Biology
MEOLA, G., Neurology
MERONI, P., Internal Medicine
MEZZETTI, M., Thoracic Surgery
MILANESI, G., Cellular Biology
MILANI, F., Radiotherapy
MOJA, E., General Psychology
MONTORSI, M., General Surgery
MORABITO, A., Medical Statistics
MORACE, G., Microbiology and Clinical Microbiology
MORGANTI, A., Internal Medicine
MORONI, M. E., Infectious Diseases
MÜLLER, E., Pharmacology
NICOLIN, A. N., Pharmacology
ORECCHIA, R., Radiotherapy
ORZALESI, N., Ophthalmology
OTTAVIANI, F., Otorhinolaryngology
PAGANI, M., Internal Medicine
PAGANO, A., Hygiene
PARDI, G., Obstetrics and Gynaecology
PELICCI, P. G., General Pathology
PERETTI, G., Orthopaedics and Traumatology
PERRELLA, M., Physical Biochemistry
PODDA, M., Internal Medicine
POLI, M., General Psychology
PONTIROLI, A., Internal Medicine
PRINCIPI, N., Paediatrics
RATIGLIA, R., Ophthalmology
RIVA, E., General and Specialist Paediatrics
ROCCO, F., Urology
RONCALLI, M., Pathological Anatomy
RONCHETTI, F., Chemistry and Biochemical Propaedeutics
RONCHI, E., Forensic Medicine
ROVIARO, G. C., General Surgery
SALVATO, A., Orthognathodontics
SAMBATARO, G., Otorhinolaryngology
SANTAMBROGIO, L., Thoracic Surgery
SANTANIELLO, E., Chemistry and Biochemical Propaedeutics
SANTORO, F., Odontostomatology
SCALABRINO, G., General Pathology
SCARONE, S., Psychiatry
SCORZA, R., Clinical Immunology and Allergology
SCORZA, R., General Surgery
SETTEMBRINI, P., Vascular Surgery
SICCARDI, A., General Biology
SMIRNE, S., Neurology
SONNINO, S., Biological Chemistry
SPINNLER, H., Neurology
STEFANI, M., Anatomy and Pathological Histology
STROHMENGER, L., Pedodontics
SURACE, A., Orthopaedics and Traumatology
TAROLO, G. L., Nuclear Medicine
TASCHIERI, A., General Surgery
TEALDI, D. G., Vascular Surgery
TENCHINI, M. L. G., General Biology
TETTAMANTI, G., Human Systematic Biochemistry
TRABUCCHI, E., General Surgery
VAGO, G., Pathological Anatomy
VERGANI, C., Gerontology and Geriatrics
VIALE, G., Pathological Anatomy and Histology
VICENTINI, L., Pharmacology
VILLA, M. L., Immunology
WEINSTEIN, R., Parodontology
ZANETTI, A., Hygiene
ZOCCHI, L., Physiology

Faculty of Motor Sciences (Via Kramer 4A, 20129 Milan; tel. 02-50315151; fax 02-50315152; e-mail scienze.motorie@unimi.it;

internet www.unimi.it/ateneo/facol/scmot .htm):

CARANDENTE, F., Internal Medicine
FIORILLI, A., Applied Dietetics
LUZI, L., Physiology
PETRUCCIOLI, M. G., Human Anatomy
PIZZINI, G., Human Anatomy
SFORZA, C., Human Anatomy
VEICSTEINAS, A., Physiology
VENERANDO, B., Biochemistry

Faculty of Pharmacy (Viale Balzaretti 9, 20133 Milan; tel. 02-50318402; fax 02-50318266; e-mail presidenza.farmacia@unimi.it; internet www.unimi.it/ateneo/facol/farmacia.htm):

ABBRACHIO, M. P., Pharmacology
ALBINATI, A., General and Inorganic Chemistry
BARLOCCO, D., Pharmaceutical Chemistry
BECCALLI, E., Organic Chemistry
BERINGHELLI, T., General and Inorganic Chemistry
BERRA, B., Biological Chemistry
BOMBIERI, G., Drug Analysis
CARINI, M., Pharmaceutical Chemistry
CASTANO, P., Human Anatomy
CATAPANO, A. L., Pharmacology
CATTABENI, F., Applied Pharmacology
CATTANEO, E., Pharmacology
CELOTTI, F., General Pathology
CESAROTTI, E., General and Inorganic Chemistry
COLONNA, S., Organic Chemistry
CORSINI, A., Pharmacology
D'ALFONSO, G., General and Inorganic Chemistry
DALLA CROCE, P., Heterocyclic Chemistry
DE AMICI, M., Pharmaceutical Chemistry
DE GIULI MORGHEN, C., General Microbiology
DE MICHELI, C., Pharmaceutical and Toxicological Chemistry
DEL PRA, A., General and Inorganic Chemistry
FERRI, V., Pharmaceutical and Toxicological Chemistry
FOLCO, G., Pharmacology and Pharmacognosy
FRANCESCHINI, G., Pharmacology
GALLI, C., Pharmacological Tests and Measuring
GALLI, C. L., Pharmacology
GAVEZZOTTI, A., Physical Chemistry
GAZZANIGA, A., Applied Pharmaceutical Technology
GELMI, M. L., Organic Chemistry
MAFFEI FACINO, R., Drug Analysis
MAGGI, A. C., Pharmacology
MONTANARI, L., Pharmaceutical Technology, Socioeconomy and Legislation
MOTTA, M., General Physiology
PALLAVICINI, M., Pharmaceutical Chemistry
PIVA, F., Physiology
POCAR, D., Organic Chemistry
RACAGNI, G., Pharmacology and Pharmacognosy
SIRTORI, C., Clinical Pharmacology
SPARATORE, A., Pharmacological Chemistry
STRADI, R., Physical Methods in Organic Chemistry
TARAMELLI, D., General Pathology
TOMÈ, F., Pharmaceutical Biology
TREMOLI, E., Pharmacology
VALOTI, E., Pharmaceutical Chemistry

Faculty of Political Sciences (Via Conservatorio 7, 20122 Milan; tel. 02-50321000; fax 02-50321005; e-mail presidenza.scienze.politiche@unimi.it; internet www.unimi.it/ateneo/facol/scpol.htm):

ALBERICI, A., Economics of Credit Institutions
ANTONIOLI, M., Contemporary History
BARBA NAVARETTI, G., Political Economy

BECCALLI, B. Z., Sociology of Economic and Labour Processes
BERNAREGGI, G. M., Public Economy
BESUSSI, A., Political Philosophy
BILANCIA, P., Institutions of Public Law
BOGNETTI, G., Financial Sciences
BORDOGNA, L., Sociology of Economic and Labour Processes
CAFARI PANICO, R., European Community Law
CALVI, M. V., Spanish Language and Translation
CELLA, G. P., Economic Sociology
CHECCHI, D., Political Economy
CHIARINI, R., History of Political Parties and Political Movements
CHIESI, A. M., General Sociology
CLERICI, R., International Private Law
DE CARLI, P. G., Economics and Law
DE MARCO, E., Institutions of Public Law
DONZELLI, F., Political Economy
ESCOBAR, R., Political Philosophy
FACCHI, A., Philosophy of Law
FERRARA, M., Political Science
FERRARI, A., Contemporary History
FERRARI, P. A., Statistics
FLORIO, M., Financial Science
FRIGO, M., International Law
GALEOTTI, M. D., Political Economy
GANINO, M., Comparative Public Law
GARAVELLO, O., Economic Politics
GARZONE, G. E., English
ICHINO, P., Labour Law
ISENBURG, T., Political and Economic Geography
ITALIA, V., Institutions of Public Law
JULLION, M. C., French Language and Translation
LACAITA, G. C., Contemporary History
LAMBERTI ZANARDI, P., International Law
LAVAGNINO, A., Chinese and South East Asian Languages and Literatures
LEONINI, L., Sociology of Cultural and Communicative Processes
LIVORSI, F., History of Political Doctrine
LUPONE, A. M. G., International Law
MARAFFI, M., General Sociology
MARTELLI, P., Political Science
MARTINELLI, A., Political Science
MAURI, A., Economics of Credit Institutions
MAZZOLENI, F., Sociology of Cultural and Communicative Processes
MISSALE, A., Political Economy
MOIOLI, A., Economic History
MOLTENI, C., Japanese and Korean Languages and Literatures
MOSS, D. M., Demo-etno-anthropology
NICOLINI, G., Statistics
OLLA, M. P., History of International Relations
PEDRAZZI, M., International Law
PILOTTI, L., Economics and Management Studies
REGALIA, I., Sociology of Economic and Labour Processes
REGINI, M., Industrial Relations
REGONINI, G., Political Science
RIMINI, C. P., Institutions of Private Law
RIOSA, A., Contemporary History
RIVOLTA, G. C., Commercial Law
RONFANI, P., Juridical Sociology of Deviance and Social Change
RUFFINI, M. L., Comparative Private Law
SALVATI, M. A., Political Economy
SANTONI, M., Public Economy
SEGATTI, P., Political Phenomena and Sociology
TURSI, A., Labour Law
VENTURINI, G., International Law
VIARENGO, I., International Law
VIVAN, I., English Literature
ZICCARDI, F. E., Comparative Private Law

Faculty of Sciences (Via Saldini 50, 20133 Milan; tel. 02-50316001; fax 02-50316004;

e-mail presidenza.scienze@unimi.it; internet www.unimi.it/ateneo/facol/smfn.htm):

ACERBI, E., Physics Experiments
ANNUNZIATA, R., Organic Chemistry
APOLLONI, B., Informatics
ARDIZZONE, S., Physical Chemistry
ARTIOLI, G., Mineralogy
BAMBUSI, D. P., Mathematical Physics
BELLINI, G., Physics Experiments
BELLOBONO, I. R., General and Inorganic Chemistry
BELLONE, E., History of Science and Technology
BERETTA, G. P., Applied Geology
BERTIN, G., Astronomy and Astrophysics
BERTINO, E., Database and Information Systems
BERTOLINI, M., Geometry
BERTONI, A., Theoretical Computer Science
BIRATTARI, C., Physics
BLASI, A., Mineralogy
BOLOGNESI, M., Biochemistry
BONETTI, R., Nuclear and Sub-Nuclear Physics
BONIFACIO, R., Institutions of Theoretical Physics
BORIANI, A., Petrography
BORTIGNON, P. F., Nuclear and Sub-Nuclear Physics
BOTTAZZINI, U., Complementary Mathematics
BRACCO, A., Physics Experiments
BROGLIA, R. A., Theory of Nuclear Structures
BRUSCHI, D., Informatics
CAMPADELLI, P., Informatics
CANDIA, M. D., Zoology
CANUTO, G., Geometry
CAPASSO, V., Mathematical Statistics
CARACCIOLO, S., Theoretical Physics and Mathematical Models and Methods
CASTANO, S., Computer Science
CAVALLINI, G., General Pedagogy
CENINI, S., General and Inorganic Chemistry
CESA BIANCHI, N. A., Informatics
CIANI, G. F., Inorganic Chemistry
CINQUINI, M., Organic Chemistry
COLOMBO, R., Cytology and Histology
COTTA RAMUSINO, P., Theoretical Physics and Mathematical Models and Methods
COZZI, F., Organic Chemistry
DAMIANI, E., Informatics
DANIELI, B., Physical Methods in Organic Chemistry
D'ANTONA, O., Informatics
DE BERNARDI, F., Zoology
DEDÒ, M., Geometry
DE FALCO, D., Calculus of Probability and Mathematical Statistics
DEGLI ANTONI, G., Applied Computer Science (Programming)
DEHÒ, G., Genetics
DEJANA, E., General Pathology
DE MICHELIS, M., Plant Physiology
D'ESTE, G., Algebra
DESTRO, R., Physical and Chemical Laboratory
DI FRANCESCO, D., General Physiology
ERBA, E., Palaeontology and Palaeoecology
FAELLI, A., General Physiology
FERRAGUTI, M., Zoology
FERRARI, R., Statistical Mechanics
FERRARIO, A., Mineral Deposits
FERRUTI, P., Macromolecular Chemistry
FOIANI, M., Molecular Biology
FORNI, L., Physical Chemistry
FORNILI, S. L., Physics
FORTE, S., Theoretical Physics and Mathematical Models and Methods
GADIOLI, E., Nuclear Physics
GAETANI, M., Geology
GALASSI, S., Ecology
GALGANI, L., Pure Mechanics
GALLI, E. A., General Microbiology

GARLASCHELLI, L., General and Inorganic Chemistry
GENNARI, C., Organic Chemical Laboratory
GHILARDI, S., Logic and Philosophy of Science
GIANINETTI, E., Theoretical Chemistry
GIAVINI, E., Comparative Anatomy
GIGLIO, M., Physics Experiments
GORLA, M., Genetics
GOSSO, G., Structural Geology
GRAMACCIOLI, C., Physical Chemistry
GREGNANIN, A., Petrography
HAUS, G., Computer Science
JADOUL, F., Regional Geology
JENNINGS, R., Photobiology
LANDINI, D., Industrial Chemistry
LANTERI, A., Geometry
LANZ, L., Institutions of Theoretical Physics
LICANDRO, E., Physical Chemistry
LONGHI, P., Electrochemistry
LONGO, C., Botany
LORENZI, A., Mathematical Analysis
MAIORANA, S., Organic Chemistry
MANDELLI, L., General Physics
MANITTO, P. M., Chemistry of Natural Organic Substances
MANTOVANI, R., Genetics
MARANESI, P., Electronics
MARTELLA, G., Information Systems
MERONI, E., Experimental Physics
MILANI, P., Material Structure
MILAZZO, M., Physical Methodology in the Arts
MOSCA, A., Clinical Biochemistry and Molecular Biology
MUSSINI, T., Electrochemistry
MUSSIO, P., Informatics
NALDI, G., Numerical Analysis
NICOLA, P. C., Mathematical Economics
NICORA, A., Palaeontology and Palaeoecology
ORSINI, F., Organic Chemistry
PAGANONI, L., Mathematical Analysis
PALLESCHI, M., Institutions of Advanced Geometry
PANERAI, A., Pharmacology
PAULMICHL, M., Physiology
PAVARINO, L. F., Numerical Analysis
PAVERI, F. S., Institutions of Mathematics
PEROTTI, M. E., Cytology and Histology
PESOLE, G., Molecular Biology
PIGHIZZINI, G., Computer Science
PIGNANELLI, M., Institutions of Nuclear and Subnuclear Physics
PIURI, V., Information Processing Systems
PIZZOTTI, M., General and Inorganic Chemistry
PLEVANI, P., Molecular Biology
POLI, S., Petrology and Petrography
POZZOLI, R., Material Structure
PREMOLI SILVA, I., Micropalaeontology
PROVINI, A., Ecology
RAGAINI, V., Chemical Industrial Processes and Systems
RAGUSA, F., Experimental Physics
RAIMONDI, M., Physical Chemistry
REATTO, L., Material Structure
RIGOLI, M., Geometry
ROSSI, G. P., Informatics
ROSSI, M., General and Inorganic Chemistry
RUF, B., Mathematical Analysis
RUSSO, G., Organic Chemistry
SABADINI, R., Terrestrial Physics
SAINO, N., Ecology
SALA, F., Botany
SAMARATI, P., Computer Science
SANNICOLÒ, F., Organic Chemistry
SCARABOTTOLO, N., Computer Science
SCOLASTICO, C., Organic Chemistry
SEGALE, A., Rural Economics and Surveying
SERRA, E., Mathematical Analysis
SIRONI, A., General and Inorganic Chemistry

SIRONI, G., Genetics
SMIRAGLIA, C., Physical Geography and Geomorphology
SOAVE, C., Plant Physiology
SPERANZA, G., Organic Chemistry
STURANI, E. P., Cellular Biochemistry
TANTARDINI, G. F., Physical Chemistry
TINTORI, A., Palaeontology and Palaeoecology
TONELLI, C., Genetics
TRASATTI, S., Electrochemistry
TUCCI, P., History of Physics
UGO, R., General Inorganic Chemistry
VALLE, C., Computer Science
VAN GEEMAN, L., Geometry
VANONI, M. A., Biochemistry
VERDI, C., Institutions of Mathematics
VITELLARO, L., Comparative Anatomy and Cytology
ZAMBELLI, V., Algebra
ZANETTI, G., Biological Chemistry
ZANON, D., Theory of Physics, Mathematical Models and Methods

Faculty of Veterinary Medicine (Via Celoria 10, 20133 Milan; tel. 02-50318002; fax 02-50318004; e-mail presveter@unimi.it; internet www.unimi.it/ateneo/facol/medvet .htm):

ADDIS, F., Clinical Veterinary Surgery
BALDI, A., Animal Nutrition and Foodstuffs
BELLOLI, A. G., Medical Veterinary Semiology
BERETTA, C., Pharmacology, Pharmacodynamics and Veterinary Pharmacy
BONIZZI, L., Veterinary Microbiology and Immunology
BONTEMPO, V., Animal Nutrition and Diet
CAIROLI, F., Clinical Obstetrics and Veterinary Gynaecology
CANTONI, C. A., Animal Food Products Inspection and Control
CARENZI, C., Morpho-Functional Evaluation of Animal Production
CARLI, S., Veterinary Pharmacology and Toxicology
CATTANEO, P., Animal Food Products Inspection and Control
CLEMENT, M. G., Veterinary Physiology
CODAZZA, D. M., Infectious Diseases of Domestic Animals
CORINO, C., Animal Foodstuffs and Nutrition
CREMONESI, F., Veterinary Obstetrics and Gynaecology
CRIMELLA, C., Special Zootechnics
DE GRESTI DI SANLEONARDO, A., Surgical Veterinary Semiology
DELL' ORTO, V., Animal Foodstuffs and Nutrition
DOMENEGHINI, C., Systematic and Comparative Veterinary Anatomy
FERRANDI, B., Systematic and Comparative Veterinary Anatomy
FERRO, E., Clinical Veterinary Medicine
FINAZZI, M., Veterinary Pathological Anatomy
FONDA, D., Surgical Veterinary Semiology
GALLAZI, D., Infectious Diseases of Domestic Animals
GANDOLFI, F., Anatomy of Domestic Animals
GENCHI, C., Parasitic Diseases
GUIDOBONO CAVALCHINI, A., Mechanization of Farming Processes.
GUIDOBONO CAVALCHINI, L., Aviculture
LANFRANCHI, P., Veterinary Parasitology
LAURIA, A., Veterinary, Systematic and Comparative Anatomy
MORTELLARO, C., Veterinary Surgical Pathology
NAVAROTTO, P., Rural and Forest Construction
PAGNACCO, G., Animal Genetic Improvement and General Husbandry
PEZZA, F., Clinical Veterinary Medicine

PIRANI, A., Rural Economics and Surveying
POLI, G., Veterinary Microbiology and Immunology
POMPA, G., Veterinary Toxicology
PONTI, W., Infectious Diseases of Domestic Animals
PORCELLI, F., General and Special Histology and Embryology
POZZA, O., Pathology of Domestic Animals
RONCHI, S., Biochemistry
RUFFO, G., Infectious Diseases, Prophylaxis and Veterinary Inspection
SALA, V., Infectious Diseases of Domestic Animals
SARTORELLI, P., Veterinary General Pathology and Pathological Anatomy
SAVOINI, G., Foodstuffs Technology
SCANZIANI, E., General and Veterinary Anatomical Pathology
SECCHI, C. L., Biochemistry
VALFRÈ, F., Supply, Markets and Rural Industries
VERGA, M., Specialized Zootechnics
ZECCONI, A., Infectious Diseases of Domestic Animals

UNIVERSITÀ DEGLI STUDI DI MILANO-BICOCCA

Piazza dell'Ateneo Nuovo 1, 20126 Milan
Internet: www.unimib.it

Director: Rag. PIERO CASSANI.

UNIVERSITÀ DEGLI STUDI DI MODENA E REGGIO EMILIA

Via Università 4, 41100 Modena
Telephone: 059-2056511
Fax: 059-245156
E-mail: rettore@unimo.it
Internet: www.casa.unimo.it
Founded 1175
Academic year: November to October
Rector: Prof. ALDO TOMASI
Admin. Dir: Dott. STEFANO RONCHETTI
Library of 294,000 vols
Number of teachers: 700
Number of students: 14,564
Publications: *Annuario, Notiziario*

DEANS

Faculty of Economics: Prof. A. FERRARI
Faculty of Engineering: Prof. G. S. BAROZZI
Faculty of Jurisprudence: Prof. R. LAMBERTINI
Faculty of Mathematics, Physics and Natural Sciences: Prof. C. JACOBONI
Faculty of Medicine and Surgery: Prof. M. PONZ DE LEON
Faculty of Pharmacy: Prof. F. FORNI

PROFESSORS

Faculty of Agricultural Science and Technology (Via Kennedy 17, 42100 Reggio Emilia; tel. 0522-383232; fax 0522-304217; internet www.rcs.re.it/corsi/agraria.htm):

BIANCHI, U., Genetics
GIUDICI, P., Agroalimentary and Environmental Microbiology
PELLEGRINI, M., Applied Geology
TONGIORGI, P., Zoology

Faculty of Arts and Philosophy (Via Berengario 51, 41100 Modena; tel. 059-2056911; fax 059-2056917):

BONDI, M., English Linguistics
DRUMBL, J., German Linguistics
TOCCI, G., Modern History

Faculty of Economics (Via Berengario 51, 41100 Modena; tel. 059-2056911; fax 059-2056917; e-mail preside.economia@unimo.it; internet www.economia.unimo.it):

BISONI, C., Professional and Banking Procedures

BOSI, P., Finance and Financial Law
BRUSCO, S., Economics and Industrial Policy
BURSI, T., Industrial and Commercial Techniques
FERRARI, A., Stock Exchange Techniques
GINZBURG, A., Economic and Financial Policy
GOLZIO, L. E., Work Study
GRANDORI, A., Personnel Management
LANE, D. A., Statistics
RICCI, G., Financial Mathematics

Faculty of Engineering (Via Campi 213/A, 41100 Modena; tel. 059-2055107; fax 059-366293; e-mail preside.ingegneria@unimo.it; internet www.ing.unimo.itViale Allegri 15, 42100 Reggio Emilia; tel. 0522-406356; fax 0522-496466; e-mail preside.ingre@unimo.it; internet www.ingre.unimo.it):

ALBERIGI, A., Electronics
ANDRISANO, A. O., Industrial Design
BAROZZI, G. S., Technical Physics
BERGAMASCHI, S., Information Elaboration Systems
BISI, O., General Physics
CAMPI, S., Mathematical Analysis
CANALI, C., Applied Electronics
CANNAROZZI, M., Construction Theory
CANTORE, G.
CECCHI, R., Environmental Sanitary Engineering
FANTINI, F., Industrial Electronics
FRANCESCHINI, V., Rational Mechanics
GRASSELLI, L., Geometry
IMMOVILLI, G., Electronic Communications
NANNARONE, S., Physics
PELLACANI, G. C., General and Inorganic Chemistry
PILATI, F., Macromolecular Chemistry
RIMINI, B., Industrial Plant Mechanics
SANDROLINI, S., Hydraulic Machinery
STROZZI, A.
TIBERIO, P., Information Elaboration Systems
ZOBOLI, M.

Faculty of Jurisprudence (tel. 059-2056589; fax 059-417522; e-mail preside .giurisprudenza@unimo.it; internet www .giurisprudenza.unimo.it):

ALESSANDRINI, S., Economic Policy
ANTONINI, A., Navigation Law
BIONE, M., Commercial Law
BONFATTI, S., Banking Law
BORGHESI, D., Law of Civil Procedure
CALANDRA BUONAURA, V., Commercial Law
DONINI, M., Penal Law
GALANTINO, L., Labour Law
GASPARINI CASARI, V., Administrative Law
GIANOLIO, R. C., Administrative Law
GUERZONI, L., Ecclesiastical Law
LAMBERTINI, R., Institutions of Roman Law
LUBERTO, S., Anthropology and Criminology
MARANI, F., General Private Law
PANFORTI, M. D., Comparative Private Law
SILINGARDI, G., Transport Law
VIGNUDELLI, A., Constitutional Law

Faculty of Mathematics, Physics and Natural Sciences (Via Campi 213/A, 41100 Modena; tel. 059-371834; fax 059-270809; e-mail preside.scienze@unimo.it; internet www .scienze.unimo.it):

ACCORSI, C. A., Phytogeography
BERTOLANI, R., Zoology
BERTONI, C. M., Theoretical Physics
BONI, M., Mathematical Analysis
BORTOLANI, V., Solid State Physics
CALANDRA BUONAURA, C., Structure of Materials
CAPEDRI, S., Petrography
CAVICCHIOLI, A., Institutes of Advanced Geometry
CHITI, G., Mathematical Analysis
CREMA, R., Ecology

DEL PRETE, C., Botany
DIECI, G., Micropalaeontology
FANTIN, A. M., Histology and Embryology
FAZZINI, P., Geology
FUNARO, D., Numerical Analysis
GAGLIARDI, C., Geometry II
JACOBONI, C., Atomic Physics
LARATTA, A., Numerical Analysis and Programming
LAZZERETTI, P., Physical Chemistry
LEVONI, S., Foundations of Mathematical Physics
MAGHERINI, P. C., General Physiology
MARINI, M., Comparative Anatomy
MENABUE, L., General and Inorganic Chemistry
MESCHIARI, M., Geometry
MIRONE, P., Physical Chemistry
MOMICCHIOLI, F., Physical Chemistry
OTTAVIANI, E., Comparative Anatomy and Cytology
OTTAVIANI, G., Physics (Preparation of Experiments)
PAGLIAI, A. M., Zoology
PAGNONI, U. M., Organic Chemistry
PALYI, G., Chemical Composition
PANIZZA, M., Physical Geography
PASSAGLIA, E., Mineralogy
PRUDENZIATI, M., Applied Electronics
QUATTROCCHI, P., Advanced Elementary Mathematics
RIVALENTI, G., Metamorphic Petrography
RUSSO, A., Palaeoecology
SANTANGELO, R., Terrestrial Physics
SEGRE, U., Electrochemistry
SERPAGLI, E., Palaeontology
SIGHINOLFI, G., Geochemistry
TADDEI, F., Advanced Organic Chemistry
TORRE, G., Organic Chemistry

Faculty of Medicine and Surgery (Via del Pozzo 71, 41100 Modena; tel. 059-422398; fax 059-374037; e-mail preside.medicina@unimo.it; internet wwww.medicina.unimo.it):

AGGAZZOTTI, G., Hygiene and Dentistry
AGNATI, L. F., Human Physiology
ALBERTAZZI, A., Nephrology
ARTIBANI, W., Urology
BAGGIO, G. G., Pharmacology
BALLI, R., Otorhinolaryngology
BARBOLINI, G., Anatomy, Histology and Pathology
BEDUSCHI, G., Forensic Medicine
BERGOMI, M., Hygiene and Odontology
BERNASCONI, S., Paediatrics
BERTOLINI, A., Pharmacology
BLASI, E., Microbiology
BOBYLEVA, V., General Pathology
BON, L., Human Physiology
BORELLA, P., General and Applied Hygiene
CALANDRA BUONAURA, S., General Pathology
CANÉ, V.
CARULLI, N., Medical Pathology and Clinical Methodology
CAVAZZUTI, G. B., Clinical Paediatrics
CELLI, L., Orthopaedics and Traumatology
CONSOLO, U., Odontostomatological Special Surgery
CORAZZA, R., Human Physiology
CORTESI, N., General Clinical Surgery and Surgical Therapy
CORTI, A., Biological Chemistry
CURCI, P., Psychiatry
DE BERNARDINIS, G., General Surgery
DE FAZIO, F. A., Forensic and Insurance Medicine
DE GAETANI, C., Foundations of Medicine and Histological Pathology
DELLA CASA, L., Infectious Diseases
ESPOSITO, R., Infectious Diseases
FABBRI, L., Respiratory Diseases
FABIO, U., Microbiology
FAGLIONI, P., Clinical Neurology
FERRARI, F., Pharmacology
FERRARI, S., Applied Biology

FERRARI, S., Biological Chemistry
FORABOSCO, A., Histology and Embryology
GALETTI, G., Clinical Otorhinolaryngology
GIANNETTI, A., Clinical Dermatology
GUARALDI, G. P., Clinical Psychiatry
GUERRA, R., Clinical Ophthalmology
JASONNI, V. M., Obstetrics and Gynaecology
LODI, R. G., Thoracic Surgery
MANENTI, F., Gastroenterology
MAROTTI, G., Human Anatomy
MATTIOLI, G., Cardiology
MODENA, M. G., Cardiology
MONTI, M. G., Biological Chemistry
MORUZZI, M. S., Chemical Biology
MUSCATELLO, U., General Pathology
PASETTO, A., Anaesthesiology
PONZ DE LEON, M., Internal Medicine
PORTOLANI, M., Virology
ROMAGNOLI, R., Radiology
SALVIOLI, G., Surgical Pathology
SAVIANO, M., Surgical Pathology
SEIDENARI, S., Allergological Dermatology
SILINGARDI, V., Special Medical Pathology and Clinical Methodology
STELLA, A., Vascular Surgery
STERNIERI, E., Clinical Pharmacology
TOMASI, A., General Physiopathology
TORELLI, G., Haematology
TORELLI, U., General Clinical Medicine and Therapy
TRENTINI, G. P., Anatomy and Pathological History
VENTURA, E., General Clinical Medicine and Therapy
VIVOLI, G., Hygiene
VOLPE, A., Physiopathology of Human Reproduction
ZENEROLI, M. L., Semiotics
ZINI, I., Human Physiology

Faculty of Pharmacy (Via Campi 183, 41100 Modena; tel. 059-2055169; fax 059-373602; e-mail preside.farmacia@unimo.it; internet www.farmacia.unimo.it):

ALBASINI, A., Applied Pharmaceutical Chemistry and Toxicology
BARALDI, M., Pharmacology
BERNABEI, M. T., Pharmaceutical Procedures and Legislation
BRASILI, L., Pharmaceutical and Toxicological Chemistry
CAMERONI, R., Applied Pharmaceutical Chemistry
FORNI, F., Pharmaceutical Procedures and Legislation
GALLI, E., Mineralogy
GAMBERINI, G., Pharmaceutical Chemical Analysis
MELEGARI, M., Pharmaceutical Chemical Analysis II
MONZANI, V. A., Pharmaceutical Chemical Analysis
PECORARI, P., Pharmaceutical Chemical Analysis
PIETRA, P., General Physiology
QUAGLIO, G., Hygiene

UNIVERSITÀ DEGLI STUDI DEL MOLISE

Via de Sanctis, 86100 Campobasso
Telephone: 0874-4041
Fax: 0874-63968
Internet: www.unimol.it
Founded 1982
Rector: Prof. LUCIO D'ALESSANDRO
Admin. Dir: Dr GIUSEPPE PATRIZI

DEANS

Faculty of Agriculture: Prof. RAIMONDO CUBADDA
Faculty of Economics and Social Sciences: Profa LUCIANA FRANGIONI

Faculty of Law: Prof. ANTONIO PROCIDA MIRABELLI DI LAURO

UNIVERSITÀ DI NAPOLI 'FEDERICO II'

Corso Umberto I, 80138 Naples
Telephone: 081-5477111
Fax: 081-2537330
E-mail: uffpubrel@ceda.unina.it
Internet: www.unina.it
Founded 1224
Rector: Prof. G. TROMBETTI
Admin. Dir: Dott. T. PELOSI
Number of teachers: 1,668
Number of students: 83,975

DEANS

Agriculture: A. SANTINI
Architecture: A. CESARANO
Economics: M. MARRELLI
Engineering: V. NASO
Law: L. LABRUNA
Literature and Philosophy: A. V. NAZZARO
Mathematics and Natural Sciences: A. DI DONATO
Medicine: A. RUBINO
Pharmacy: E. NOVINELLO
Political Science: T. D'APONTE
Sociology: E. PUGLIESE
Veterinary Medicine: F. ROPERTO

UNIVERSITÀ DEGLI STUDI DI NAPOLI – L'ORIENTALE

Via Partenope 10/A, 80121 Naples
Telephone: 081-7643230
Fax: 081-6909112
Internet: www.iuo.it
Founded 1732
Chancellor: LIDA VIGANONI
Admin. Dir: Dr CLAUDIO BORRELLI

DEANS

Faculty of Foreign Languages and Literatures: Prof. G. DE CESARE
School of Islamic Studies: Prof. L. SERRA
Faculty of Letters and Philosophy: Prof. G. D'ERME
Faculty of Political Science: Prof. P. FRASCANI

UNIVERSITÀ DEGLI STUDI DI NAPOLI 'PARTHENOPE'

Via Ammiraglio Acton 38, 80133 Naples
Telephone: 081-5475111
Fax: 081-5521485
E-mail: rettore@uniparthenope.it
Internet: www.uninav.it
Founded 1920 as Istituto Universitario Navale; present name c. 2000
Rector: Prof. GENNARO FERRARA
Administrative Director: Dr ENRICO DE SIMONE
Library of 50,000 vols
Number of teachers: 102
Number of students: 5,689
Publication: Annali
Faculties: economics, engineering, law, maritime sciences, motor sciences.

UNIVERSITÀ DEGLI STUDI DI PADOVA

Via 8 Febbraio 2, 35122 Padua
Telephone: 049-8275111
Fax: 049-8273009
Internet: www.unipd.it
Founded 1222
Rector: Prof. VINCENZO MILANESI
First Pro-Rector: Prof. GIUSEPPE ZACCARIA
Admin. Dir: Arch. GIUSEPPE BARBIERI

Librarian: Prof. P. DEL NEGRO
Number of teachers: 1,382
Number of students: 65,579
Publications: *Annuario, Bollettino-Notiziario* (1 a year), *Guida dello Studente*

DEANS

Faculty of Agriculture: Prof. U. ZILIOTTO
Faculty of Economics: (vacant)
Faculty of Education: Prof. M. CHIARANDA
Faculty of Engineering: Prof. G. B. GUARISE
Faculty of Jurisprudence: Prof. A. BURDESE
Faculty of Letters and Philosophy: Prof. S. COLLODO
Faculty of Mathematics, Physics, and Natural Sciences: Prof. C. PECILE
Faculty of Medicine and Surgery: Prof. A. GATTA
Faculty of Pharmacy: Prof. F. DALL' ACQUA
Faculty of Political Science: Prof. G. ZACCARIA
Faculty of Psychology: Prof. V. RUBINI
Faculty of Statistical Sciences: Prof. L. BERNARDI
Faculty of Veterinary Medicine: Prof. B. BIOLATTI

UNIVERSITÀ DEGLI STUDI DI PALERMO

Piazza Marina 61, 90133 Palermo
Telephone: 091-270111
Internet: www.unipa.it
Founded 1777
Rector: Prof. GIUSEPPE SILVESTRI
Admin. Dir: CARMELO MAZZÈ
Number of teachers: 1,300
Number of students: 20,000
Publications: *Annali della Facoltà di Economia e Commercio, Annali del Seminario Giuridico, Circolo Giuridico L. Sampolo*

DEANS

Agriculture: G. FIERROTTI
Architecture: M. DE SIMONE
Economics: V. FAZIO
Education: G. A. PUGLISI
Engineering: E. OLIVIERI
Law: S. MAZZAMUTO
Letters and Philosophy: A. BUTTITA
Mathematics: F. MAGGIO
Medicine: A. GULLOTTI
Pharmacy: S. GIAMMANCO

UNIVERSITÀ DEGLI STUDI DI PARMA

Via Università 12, 43100 Parma
Telephone: 0521-032111
E-mail: uniparma@unipr.it
Internet: www.unipr.it
Founded 962
Academic year: November to October
Rector: Prof. GINO FERRETTI
Admin. Dir: Dott. RODOLFO POLDI
Number of teachers: 1,074
Number of students: 29,853

DEANS

Faculty of Agricultural Science: Prof. R. MARCHELLI
Faculty of Arts: Prof. G. BIONDI
Faculty of Architecture: Prof. G. BASSANELLI
Faculty of Economics and Commerce: Prof. A. GUENZI
Faculty of Engineering: Prof. A. VILLA
Faculty of Jurisprudence: Prof. G. BONILINI
Faculty of Medicine: Prof. A. NOVARINI
Faculty of Pharmacy: Prof. G. PELIZZI
Faculty of Physical, Mathematical and Natural Sciences: Prof. A. MANGIA
Faculty of Veterinary Medicine: Prof. C. F. FLAMMINI

UNIVERSITÀ DEGLI STUDI DI PAVIA

Corso Strada Nuova 65, 27100 Pavia
Telephone: 0382-504217
Fax: 0382-504529
Internet: www.unipv.it
Founded 1361 by Emperor Charles IV
Academic year: November to October
Rector: Prof. ROBERTO SCHMID
Vice-Rector: Prof. PAOLA VITA-FINZI
Admin. Dir: Dr GAETANO SERAFINO
Number of teachers: 1,033
Number of students: 22,789
Publications: *Annuario, Guida dello Studente* (for each faculty), *Guida dello Studente Straniero* and many faculty publs

DEANS

Faculty of Arts and Philosophy: Prof. G. FRANCIONI
Faculty of Economics: Prof. L. RAMPA
Faculty of Engineering: Prof. N. CANTONI
Faculty of Law: Prof. S. SEMINARA
Faculty of Mathematics, Physics and Natural Science: Prof. G. FLOR
Faculty of Medicine and Surgery: Prof. C. MELONI
Faculty of Pharmacology: Prof. C. CARAMELLA
Faculty of Musicology: Prof. G. BORIO
Faculty of Political Sciences: Prof. S. VECA

UNIVERSITÀ DEGLI STUDI DI PERUGIA

Piazza dell' Università 1, 06100 Perugia
Telephone: 075-5851
Fax: 075-5852067
E-mail: gestione@unipg.it
Internet: www.unipg.it
Founded 1200
State control
Academic year: November to October
Rector: Prof. FRANCESCO BISTONI
Admin. Dir: Dott.ssa ANGELA MARIA LACAITA
Pro-Rector: Prof. ANTONIO PIERETTI
Librarian: Dott. M. PIERONI
Number of teachers: 312
Number of students: 31,746
Publications: *La Salute Umana, L'Università, Rivista di Biologia, Rivista di Dermatologia, Rivista di Idrobiologia*

DEANS

Faculty of Agrarian Science: Prof. B. ROMANO
Faculty of Economics: Prof. T. SEOIARI
Faculty of Education: Prof. E. MIRRI
Faculty of Engineering: Prof. R. SORRENTINO
Faculty of Jurisprudence: Prof. S. CAPRIOLI
Faculty of Letters and Philosophy: Prof. A. PIERETTI
Faculty of Mathematical, Physical and Natural Sciences: Prof. C. MANTOVANI
Faculty of Medicine and Surgery: Prof. R. ROSSI
Faculty of Pharmacy: Prof. C. M. FIORETTI CECCHERELLI
Faculty of Political Science: Prof. M. RAVERAIRA
Faculty of Veterinary Medicine: Prof. A. GAITI

PROFESSORS

Faculty of Agrarian Science:

ABBOZZO, P., Farm Evaluation
BENCIVENGA, M., Systematic Agricultural Botany
BERNARDINI BATTAGLINI, M., Animal Husbandry
BIANCHI, A. A., Herbaceous Cultivation
BIN, F., Biological Techniques
BONCIARELLI, F., Cultivation of Special Herbaceous Plants
BUSINELLI, M., Soil Chemistry

CIRICIOFOLO, E., Biology, Production and Technology of Seeds
COSTANTINI, F., Animal Nutrition and Feeding
COVARELLI, G., Weed Control
DURANTI, E., Physiology of Animals in Stockbreeding
FALCINELLI, M., Genetic Improvement in Cultivated Plants
FANTOZZI, P., Alimentation
FATICHENTI, F., Agrarian and Arboreal Microbiology
GIOVAGNOTTI, C.
LORENZETTI, F., Agrarian Genetics
MANNOCCHI, F., Agrarian Hydraulics
MARTE, M., Plant Pathology
MARTINI, A., Agrarian Microbiology
MARUCCHINI, C., Introductory Agrarian Chemistry
MENNELLA, V. G., Agricultural and Forestry Planning
MONOTTI, M., General Agriculture
MONTEDORO, G., Agricultural Industries
PENNACCHI, F., Agrarian Economics
RAGGI, V., Plant Pathology
ROMANO, B., Morphology and Plant Physiology
ROSSI, A. C., Economics and Agrarian Policy
ROSSI, J., Dairy Food Microbiology
SARTI, D. M., Stockbreeding
SCARPONI, L., Agrarian Biochemistry
SOLINAS, M., Agricultural Entomology
STANDARDI, A., Specialist Fruit Growing
TOMBESI, A., General Fruit Growing
VERONESI, F., Genetic Biotechnology
ZAZZERINI, A., Phytotherapy

Faculty of Economics:

BORGIA, R., Institutions of Private Law
BRACALENTE, B., Economics Statistics
CALZONI, G., Political Economy
CAVAZZONI, G., Accountancy
CHIARELLE, R., Institutions of Public Law
CICCHITELLI, G., Statistics
CORALLINI, S., Banking
FORCINA, A., Statistics
GRASSELLI, P. M., Political Economy
MEZZACAPO, V., Banking Legislation
MORICONI, F., Mathematics
PAGLIACCI, G., General Mathematics
PERONI, G., Marketing
RIDOLFI, M., Political Economy
SEDIARI, T., Agrarian Economics and Politics
SEVERINO, P., Commercial Penal Law

Faculty of Education:

BALDINI, M., History of Philosophy
BUCCI, S., General Education
DOTTI, U., Italian Language and Literature
FINZI, C., History of Political Doctrine
FISSI MIGLIORINI, R., Dantesque Philology
FURIOZZI, G. B., History of Umbria
MANCINI, F. F., History of Umbrian Art
MIRRI, E., Philosophy
PERUGI, M., Romance Philology
PETRONI, F., History of Modern and Contemporary Italian Literature
RICCIOLI, G., French Language and Literature
ROSATI, L., Teaching
SANTINI, C., Latin Language and Literature
SETAIOLI, A., Latin Grammar
UGOLINI, R., Contemporary History
ZURLI, L., Latin Philology

Faculty of Engineering:

BALLI, R., Applied Mechanics
BASILI, P., Electromagnetic Fields
BATTISTON, R., Physics
BERNA, L., Urban Technology
BIDINI, G., Machines
BORRI, A., Construction Theory
BRANDI, P., Mathematical Analysis
BURRASCANO, P., Electrotechnology

CANDELORO, D., Mathematical Analysis I
CONTI, P., Industrial Technical Drawing
CORRADINI, C., Technical Hydrology
FELLI, M., Technical Physics
LA CAVA, M., Automatic Controls
LIUTI, G., Chemistry
MAZZOLAI, F. M., Physics
PALMIERI, L., Physics
PARDUCCI, A., Construction Technology
PUCCI, E., Advanced Mechanical Engineering
SOCINO, G., Physics
SOLETTI, A. C., Design
SORRENTINI, R., Electromagnetic Fields
TACCONI, P., Applied Geology
VECCHIOCATTIVI, F., Chemistry

Faculty of Jurisprudence:

AZZARITI, G., Constitutional Law
BADIALI, G., International Law
BARBERINI, G., Ecclesiastical Law
CAPRIOLI, S., History of Modern Italian Law
CARDI, E., Procedural Law
CAVALAGLIO, A., Bankruptcy Law
CAVALLO, B., Administrative Law
CINELLI, M., Labour Law
DALLERA, G. F., Finance and Financial Law
GAITO, A., Penal Law
MIGLIORINI, L., Administrative Law
MORSELLI, E., Penal Law
PALAZZO, A., Institutions of Private Law
PALAZZOLO, N., History of Roman Law
PEPPE, L., Roman Law
SALVI, C., Civil Law
SASSANI, M., Civil Procedural Law
TALAMANCA, A., Canon Law
TINELLI, G., Tax Law
VOLPI, M., Constitutional Comparative Law

Faculty of Letters and Philosophy:

AGOSTINIANI, L., Linguistics
BONAMENTE, G., Roman History
CARANCINI, G. L., European Protohistory
COARELLI, F., Greek and Roman Antiquity
DI PILLA, F., French Language and Literature
FALASCHI, G., Italian Literature
FROVA, C., Medieval History
GIORDANI, R., Christian Archaeology
ISOLA, A., Ancient Christian Literature
MADDOLI, G., Greek History
MELELLI, A., Geography
MENESTÒ, E., Medieval Latin Literature
MORETTI, G., Italian Dialectology
PICCINATO, S., Anglo-American Literature
PIERETTI, A., Theoretical Philosophy
PIZZANI, U., Latin Literature
PRIVITERA, G. A., Greek Literature
RONCALLI DI MONTORIO, F., Etruscan Studies and Italic Antiquity
RUFINI, S., English Language and Literature
SANTACHIARA, U., Church History
SCARPELLINI PANCRAZI, P., History of Medieval Art
SEPPILLI, T., Cultural Anthropology
SPAGGIARI PERUGI, B., Romance Philology
TORELLI, M., Archaeology and History of Greek and Roman Art
TORTI, A., English Language and Literature

Faculty of Mathematical, Physical and Natural Sciences:

ALBERTI, G., Inorganic Chemistry
AMBROSETTI, P. L., Palaeontology
ANTONIELLI, M., Plant Physiology
AQUILANTI, V., General and Inorganic Chemistry
AVERNA, A.
BARSI, F., Theory and Application of Mechanical Calculation
BARTOCCI, U., Geometry
CATALIOTTI, R. S., Physical Chemistry

CIOFI DEGLI ATTI, C., Institutions of Nuclear Physics
CIONINI, P. G., Botany
CIROTTO, C., Cytology and Histology
CLEMENTI, S., Organic Chemistry
COLETTI, G., Institutions of Mathematics
DE TOLLIS, B. A., Institutions of Theoretical Physics
DI GIOVANNI, M. V., Zoology
FAINA, G., Geometry
FAVARO MAZZUCATO, G., Physical Chemistry
FRINGUELLI, F., Organic Chemistry
GAINO, E., Zoology
GIANFRANCHESCHI, G. L., General Physiology
GRANETTI, B., Botany
GUAZZONE, S., Algebra
IORIO, A. M., Virology
LAGANÀ, A., General and Inorganic Chemistry
LARICCIA, P., Physics Laboratory
MAFFEI, P., Astrophysics
MANTOVANI, G., General Physics
MARINO, G., Organic Chemistry
MAZZUCATO, U., Physical Chemistry
MONTANINI MEZZASOMA, I., Biochemistry
MOROZZI, G., Hygiene
MORPURGO, G. P., Genetics
NAPPI, A., General Physics
ONORI, G., Physics
ORLACCHIO, A., Biochemistry
PASCOLINI, R., Comparative Anatomy
PASSERI, L., Sedimentology
PECCERILLO, A., Petrography
PERUZZI, M. I., General Physics
PIALLI, G., Geology
PIOVESANA, O., General and Inorganic Chemistry
PUCCI, P., Mathematical Analysis
RINALDI, R., Mineralogy
SACCHETTI, F., Solid State Physics
SANTUCCI, S., Physics Laboratory
SAVELLI, G., Organic Chemistry
SGAMELLOTTI, A., Inorganic Chemistry
SRIVASTAVA YOGENDRA, N., Quantum Theory
TATICCHI, A., Organic Chemistry
TATICCHI, M. I., Ecology
TULIPANI, S., Computer Science
VERDINI, L., Structure of Matter
VOLPI, G., General and Inorganic Chemistry
ZANAZZI, P. F., Crystallography

Faculty of Medicine and Surgery:

ABBRITTI, G., Industrial Medicine
AMBROSIO, G., Cardiology
ARIENTI, G., Biological Chemistry
BARTOLI, A., General Surgery
BECCHETTI, E., Histology
BINAGLIA, L., Chemistry and Biomedicine
BISTONI, F., Microbiology
BOLIS, G. B., Anatomy and Pathological Histology
BOLLI, G., Metabolic Diseases
BORRI, P. F., Psychiatry
BRUNETTI, P., Internal Medicine
BUCCIARELLI, E., Anatomy and Pathological Histology
CALANDRA, P., Dermatology
CAPRINO, G., Radiology
CASALI, L., Diseases of the Respiratory System
DADDI, G., Surgical Pathology and Clinical Propaedeutics
DELOGU, A., Ophthalmology
D'ERRICO, P., Dental Prosthesis
DONATO, R. F., Neuroanatomy
FABRONI, F., Forensic Medicine
FALORNI, A., Paediatrics
FIORE, C., Physiopathological Optics
FRONGILLO, R. F., Infectious Diseases
FURBETTA, M., Preventive and Social Paediatrics
GALLAI, V., Neurology

GIOVANNINI, E., General Biology
GORACCI, G. F., Biological Chemistry
GRIGNANI, F., Internal Medicine
LATINI, P., Radiotherapy
LAURO, V., Gynaecology and Obstetrics
LIOTTI, F. S., General Biology
LISI, P., Dermatology
MAGNI, F., Human Physiology
MAIRA, G., Neurosurgery
MANNARINO, E., Internal Medicine
MARCONI, P., Immunology
MARTELLI, M. F., Haematology
MASTRANDREA, V., Hygiene
MODOLO, M. A., Hygiene
MOGGI, L., General Surgery
MORELLI, A., Gastroenterology
NEGRI, P. L., Paradontology
NENCI, G. G., Internal Medicine
NORELLI, G. A., Forensic Medicine
PALUMBO, R., Nuclear Medicine
PAULUZZI, S., Infectious Diseases
PECORELLI, F., Orthopaedics and Traumatology
PEDUTO, V. A., Anaesthesia and Resuscitation
PETTOROSSI, V. E., Human Physiology
PORENA, M., Urology
PUXEDDU, A., Internal Medicine
RIBACCHI, R., Anatomy and Pathological Histology
RICCARDI, C., Pharmacology
RINONAPOLI, E., Orthopaedics and Traumatology
ROSI BARBERINI, G., Cellular Biology
ROSSI, R., General Pathology
SALVADORI, P., Physics
SANTEUSANIO, F., Endocrinology
SENIN, U., Geriatrics and Gerontology
STAFFOLANI, N., Oral Surgery
STAGNI, G., Infectious Diseases
TRISTAINO, B., General Surgery
VACCARO, R., Paediatrics
VALORI, C., Internal Medicine
VILLANI, C., Oncological Gynaecology
VIOLA MAGNI, M. P., General Pathology

Faculty of Pharmacy:

CORSANO LEOPIZZI, S., Pharmaceutical and Toxicological Chemistry
COSTANTINO, U., General and Inorganic Chemistry
DAMIANI, P., Food Science Chemistry
FIORETTI CECCHERELLI, M. C., Pharmacology and Pharmacognosy
FLORIDI, A., Biochemistry
FRAVOLINI, A., Pharmaceutical and Toxicological Chemistry
GRANDOLINI, G., Socioeconomic Technology and Pharmaceutical Legislation
MENGHINI, A., Pharmaceutical Botany
PELLICCIARI, R., Pharmaceutical and Toxicological Chemistry
PUCCI, P., Pharmacology
ROSSI, C., Applied Pharmaceutical Chemistry
SCASSELLATI, S. G., Hygiene
TESTAFERRI, L., Organic Chemistry
TIECCO, M., Organic Chemistry
VECCHIARELLI, A., Microbiology

Faculty of Political Science:

BONO, S., History and Institutions of Afro-Asian Countries
CARINI, C., History of Political Doctrine
COMPARATO, V. I., Modern History
CRESPI, F., Sociology
D'AMOJA, F., History of International Relations
DI GASPARE, G., Economic Law
GALLI DELLA LOGGIA, E., History of Political Parties and Movements
GROHMANN, A., Economic History
MARCHISIO, S., International Law
MELOGRANI, P., Contemporary History
MERLONI, F., Administrative Justice
RAVERAIRA, M., Institutions of Public Law
TEODORI, M., American History

Tosi, L., History of Treaties and International Politics
Tramontana, A., Finance

Faculty of Veterinary Medicine:

Asdrubali, G., Pathology of Birds
Avellini, G., Clinical Veterinary Medicine
Battistacci, M., Clinical Veterinary Surgery
Beghelli, V., Veterinary Physiology and Ethology
Bellucci, M., Veterinary Radiology and Nuclear Medicine
Boiti, C., Veterinary Physiology and Ethology
Castrucci, G., Infectious Diseases and Prophylaxis
Ceccarelli, P., Topographical Veterinary Anatomy
Chiacchiarini, P., Obstetrics and Gynaecology
Debenedetti, A., Endocrinology of Domestic Animals
Di Antonio, E., Inspection and Control of Foodstuffs of Animal Origin
Fruganti, G., Veterinary Medical Pathology
Gaiti, A., Biochemistry
Gargiulo Bersiani, A. M., Histology and General Embryology
Lorvik, S., Anatomy of Domestic Animals
Malvisi, J., Pharmacology and Pharmacodynamics
Mangili Pecci, V., Laboratory Diagnosis
Manocchio, I., Pathological Anatomy
Moriconi, F., Veterinary Surgical Pathology
Olivieri, O., Animal Nutrition
Polidori Girolamo, A. B., Veterinary Parasitology
Ranucci, S., Veterinary Medical Semiology and Clinical Methodology
Silvestrelli, M., Special Stockbreeding
Valente, C., Infectious Diseases
Vitellozzi, G., Veterinary Pathological Anatomy

UNIVERSITÀ DEGLI STUDI DI PISA

Lungarno Pacinotti 43, 56126 Pisa
Telephone: 050-920115
Fax: 050-42446
E-mail: rettore@unipi.it
Internet: www.unipi.it
Founded 1343
State control
Academic year: November to October
Rector: Prof. Luciano Modica
Chief Admin. Officer: Dott. Giorgio Coluccini
Librarian: Dott. Renato Tamburrini
Number of teachers: 300
Number of students: 47,000

DEANS

Faculty of Agrarian Science: A. Alpi
Faculty of Economics: Prof. R. Ferraris
Faculty of Engineering: Prof. P. Corsini
Faculty of Foreign Languages and Literature: Prof. G. di Stefano
Faculty of Law: Prof. U. Santarelli
Faculty of Letters and Philosophy: Prof. G. Fioravanti
Faculty of Mathematical, Physical and Natural Sciences: Prof. M. Pasquali
Faculty of Medicine and Surgery: Prof. M. Campa
Faculty of Pharmacy: Prof. A. Lucacchini
Faculty of Political Science: Prof. A. Massera
Faculty of Veterinary Medicine: A. Buonacorsi

UNIVERSITÀ DEGLI STUDI MEDITERRANEA DI REGGIO CALABRIA

Via Zecca 4, 89125 Reggio Calabria
Telephone: 0965-331701
Fax: 0965-332201
E-mail: rettore@unirc.it
Internet: www.unirc.it
Founded 1982
Rector: Prof. Alessandro Bianchi
Pro-Rector: Prof. Rosario Giuffre'

DEANS

Faculty of Agriculture: Prof. R. C. Fichera
Faculty of Architecture: Prof. M. Giovannini
Faculty of Engineering: C. Morabito
Faculty of Law: S. Ciccarello

UNIVERSITÀ DEGLI STUDI DI ROMA 'LA SAPIENZA'

Piazzale Aldo Moro 5, 00185 Rome
Telephone: 06-49911
Fax: 06-49910348
E-mail: rettore@uniroma1.it
Internet: www.uniroma1.it
Founded 1303 by Pope Boniface VIII, with the Papal Bull 'In Supremae praeminentia dignitatis'
Rector: Prof. Giuseppe D'Ascenzo
Director: Carlo Musto D'Amore
Librarian: Prof. Giovanni Ciclotti
Number of teachers: 4,312
Number of students: 189,000

DEANS

School of Aerospace Engineering: Prof. U. Ponzi
Faculty of Architecture I: Prof. Lucio Valerio Barbera
Faculty of Architecture II: Prof. Roberto Palumbo
Faculty of Communication Studies: Prof. Domenico De Masi
Faculty of Economics and Commerce: Prof. Attilio Celant
Faculty of Engineering: Prof. Tullio Bucciarelli
Faculty of Humanities: Prof. Paolo Matthiae
Faculty of Jurisprudence: Prof. Carlo Angelici
Faculty of Letters and Humanities: Prof. Guido Pescosolido
School of Librarianship and Archivists: Prof. Attilio De Luca
Faculty of Mathematics, Physics and Natural Science: Prof. Francesco Bossa
Faculty of Medicine I: Prof. L. Frati
Faculty of Medicine II: Prof. Aldo Vecchione
Faculty of Oriental Studies: Prof. Federico Nasini
Faculty of Pharmacy: Prof. Domenico Misiti
Faculty of Philosophy: Prof. Marco Maria Olivetti
Faculty of Political Science: Fulco Lanchester
Faculty of Psychology I: Stefano Puglisi Allegra
Faculty of Psychology II: Prof. Francesco Avallone
Faculty of Sociology: Luciano Benadusi
Faculty of Statistics, Demography and Actuarial Science: Prof. Renato Guarini

ATTACHED CENTRES

Interdepartmental Research Centre of European and International Studies: internet www.eco.uniroma1.it/europe; Dir Prof. Giuseppe Burgio.

Interuniversity Research Centre on Developing Countries (CIRPS): internet www.cirps.it; Dir Prof. Vincenzo Naso.

UNIVERSITÀ DEGLI STUDI DI ROMA 'TOR VERGATA'

Via Orazio Raimondo 18, 00173 Rome
Telephone: 06-72591
Fax: 06-7234368
Internet: web.uniroma2.it
Founded 1985
Rector: Prof. Renato Lauro
Admin. Dir: Dr Ernesto Nicolai
Publications: *I Quaderni di Tor Vergata*, *L'Osservatorio*

DEANS

Faculty of Economics: Prof. Luigi Paganetto
Faculty of Engineering: Prof. Franco Maceri
Faculty of Law: Prof. Filippo Chiomenti
Faculty of Literature and Philosophy: Prof. Franco Salvatori
Faculty of Mathematics, Physics and Natural Sciences: Prof. Paolo Luly
Faculty of Medicine and Surgery: Prof. Renato Lauro

UNIVERSITÀ DEGLI STUDI DI SALERNO

Via Ponte don Melillo, 84084 Fisciano (Salerno)
Telephone: 089-961111
Internet: www.unisa.it
Founded 1970
Rector: Prof. Raimondo Pasquino
Admin. Dir: Dr Giuseppe Paduano

DEANS

Faculty of Economics and Commerce: Prof. N. Postiglione
Faculty of Education: Prof. A. Mango
Faculty of Engineering: Prof. R. Pasquino
Faculty of Law: Prof. M. Panebianco
Faculty of Letters and Philosophy: Prof. A. Trimarco
Faculty of Political Science: Prof. A. Musi
Faculty of Science: Prof. G. Sodano

UNIVERSITÀ DEGLI STUDI DI SASSARI

Piazza Università 21, 07100 Sassari, Sardinia
Telephone: 079-228811
Fax: 079-228820
Internet: www.uniss.it
Founded 1562
State control
Academic year: November to October
Rector: Prof. Alessandro Maida
Admin. Dir and Sec.: Dott. Giovannino Sircana
Librarian: Dott. Elisabetta Pilia
Number of teachers: 604
Number of students: 16,319
Publication: *Annuario*

DEANS

Faculty of Agronomy: Prof. Gavino Del Rio
Faculty of Economics and Commerce: Prof. Carlo Ibba
Faculty of Languages: Prof. Simonetta Sanna
Faculty of Law: Prof. Giovanni Lobrano
Faculty of Letters and Philosophy: Prof. Giovanni Meloni
Faculty of Mathematics, Physics and Natural Sciences: Prof. Bruno Masala
Faculty of Medicine and Surgery: Prof. Giulio Rosati
Faculty of Pharmacy: Prof. Riccardo Cerri
Faculty of Political Science: Prof. Virgilio Mura
Faculty of Veterinary Medicine: Prof. Antonello Leoni

UNIVERSITÀ DEGLI STUDI DI SIENA

Via Banchi di Sotto 55, 53100 Siena
Telephone: 0577-232111
Fax: 0577-298202
E-mail: rettore@unisi.it
Internet: www.unisi.it

Founded 1240

Rector: Prof. SILVANO FOCARDI
Admin. Dir: Dr EMILIO MICCOLIS
Number of teachers: 514
Number of students: 19,093

Publication: *Annuario Accademico*

DEANS

Faculty of Arts and Humanities: T. DETTI
Faculty of Economics: G. ROLLA
Faculty of Education: F. ABBRI
Faculty of Engineering: R. TIBERIO
Faculty of Law: R. MARTINI
Faculty of Letters and Philosophy: M. BETTINI
Faculty of Mathematics, Physics and Natural Sciences: R. DALLAI
Faculty of Medicine and Surgery: L. ANDREASSI
Faculty of Pharmacy: C. PELLERANO

UNIVERSITÀ DEGLI STUDI DI TERAMO

Viale Crucioli 122, 64100 Teramo
Telephone: 0861-2661
Fax: 0861-245350
E-mail: webmaster@unite.it
Internet: www.unite.it

Founded 1993 upon independence of Teramo campus of Università degli Studi 'Gabriele D'Annunzio'

Rector: Prof. RITA TRANQUILLI LEALI
Pro-Rector: Prof. FULVIO MARSILIO
Admin. Dir: Dott. LUIGI RENZULLO
Librarian: Dott. VALERIA DE BARTOLOMEIS
Number of teachers: 257
Number of students: 10,262

Publication: *Trimestre* (2 a year)

DEANS

Faculty of Agriculture: Prof. DINO MASTROCOLA
Faculty of Communication Studies: Prof. FRANCESCO BENIGNO
Faculty of Law: Prof. FLORIANA CURSI
Faculty of Political Science: Prof. ADOLFO PEPE
Faculty of Veterinary Medicine: Prof. FULVIO MARSILIO

UNIVERSITÀ DEGLI STUDI DI TORINO

Via Verdi 8, 10124 Turin
Telephone: 011-6702200
Fax: 011-6702218
E-mail: rettore@unito.it
Internet: www.unito.it

Founded 1404
Academic year: October to September

Rector: Prof. EZIO PELIZZETTI
Pro-Rector: Prof. SERGIO RODA
Admin. Dir: Dott. PASQUALE MASTRODOMENICO
Number of teachers: 2,050
Number of students: 65,000

DEANS

Agriculture: Prof. BRUNO GIAU
Arts and Philosophy: Prof. LORENZO MASSOBRIO
Economics: Prof. SERGIO CONTI
Education: Profa ANNAMARIA POGGI
Foreign Languages: Prof. LIBORIO TERMINE
Law: Prof. MARIO DOGLIANI

Mathematics, Physics and Natural Sciences: Prof. ENRICO PREDAZZI
Medicine: Prof. GIORGIO PALESTRO
Pharmacy: Prof. CARLO BICCHI
Political Sciences: Prof. FRANCO GARELLI
Psychology: Prof. GIAN PIERO QUAGLINO
Veterinary Medicine: Prof. CARLO GIRARDI

UNIVERSITÀ DEGLI STUDI DI TRENTO

Via Belenzani 12, 38100 Trento
Telephone: 0461-881111
Fax: 0461-881258
E-mail: direzionegenerale@amm.unitn.it
Internet: www.unitn.it

Founded 1962
State control (since 1982)
Academic year: October to September

President: Dott. INNOCENZO CIPOLLETTA
Rector: Prof. DAVIDE BASSI
Admin. Dir: Dott. MARCO TOMASI
Librarian: Dott. PAOLO BELLINI
Library of 350,000 vols and 12,400 periodicals
Number of teachers: 474
Number of students: 14,183

Publications: *Unitn* (12 a year), *Unitrentomagazine* (3 a year)

DEANS

Faculty of Arts and Philosophy: Prof. FABRIZIO CAMBI
Faculty of Cognitive Science: Prof. REMO JOB
Faculty of Economics: Prof. CARLO BORZAGA
Faculty of Engineering: Prof. RICCARDO ZANDONINI
Faculty of Law: Prof. ROBERTO TONIATTI
Faculty of Mathematics, Physics and Natural Sciences: Prof. MARCO ANDREATTA
Faculty of Sociology: Prof. ANTONIO SCAGLIA

UNIVERSITÀ DEGLI STUDI DI TRIESTE

Piazzale Europa 1, 34127 Trieste
Telephone: 040-5587111
Fax: 040-6763093
E-mail: rettore@units.it
Internet: www.univ.trieste.it

Founded 1924

Rector: Prof. FRANCESCO PERONI
Vice-Rector: Prof. FABIO RUZZIER
Admin. Dir: Dott. ANTONINO DI GUARDO
Librarian: M. LUISA NESBEDA

Number of teachers: 1,200
Number of students: 24,500

Publication: *Piazzale Europa* (3 a year)

DEANS

Faculty of Economics: L. COSSAR
Faculty of Education: L. LAGO
Faculty of Engineering: L. DELCARO
Faculty of Humanities: S. MONTI
Faculty of Law: F. TOMMASEO
Faculty of Medicine: A. LEGGERI
Faculty of Natural Sciences: L. FONDA
Faculty of Pharmacy: G. STEFANCICH
Faculty of Political Science: D. COCCOPALMERIO
Faculty of Psychology: W. GERBINO
Data Processing Centre: Dr M. GREGORI (Dir)
Modern Languages for Interpreters and Translators: J. M. DODDS

ATTACHED INSTITUTES

Institute of Anaesthesiology and Intensive Care: Dir A. GULLO.

Institute of Dentistry: Dir M. SILLA.

Institute of Forensic Medicine: Dir B. M. ALTAMURA.

Institute of General Clinical Medicine: Dir G. GUARNIERI.

Institute of General Pathology: Dir L. PATRIARCA.

Institute of General Surgery: Dir A. LEGGERI.

Institute of History of Medieval and Modern Art: Dir R. GIORDANI.

Institute of Hygiene: Dir C. CAMPELLO.

Institute of Industrial Medicine: Dir F. GOBBATO.

Institute of Law: Dir P. CENDON.

Institute of Nervous and Mental Diseases: Dir G. CAZZATO.

Institute of Obstetrics and Gynaecology: Dir S. GUASCHINO.

Institute of Ophthalmology: Dir G. RAVALICO.

Institute of Orthopaedics: Dir F. MAROTTI.

Institute of Otorhinolaryngology: Dir M. RUSSOLO.

Institute of Paediatrics: Dir F. PANIZON.

Institute of Pathological Anatomy: Dir L. DI BONITO.

Institute of Physiology: Dir A. BAVA.

Institute of Psychiatry: Dir E. AGUGLIA.

Institute of Radiology: Dir L. DALLA PALMA.

Institute of Surgical Pathology: Dir A. NEMETH.

Institute of Urology: Dir E. BELGRANO.

Institute of Venereal Diseases and Dermatology: Dir C. SCARPA.

UNIVERSITÀ DEGLI STUDI DELLA TUSCIA

Via. S. Maria in Gradi 4, 01100 Viterbo
Telephone: 0761-357900
Fax: 0761-321771
E-mail: rettore@unitus.it
Internet: www.unitus.it

Founded 1979
State control
Academic year: November to October

Rector: Prof. MARCO MANCINI
Vice-Rector: Prof. STEFANO GREGO
Admin. Dir: Dr GIOVANNI CUCULLO

Number of teachers: 320
Number of students: 10,000

DEANS

Faculty of Agriculture: Prof. E. RUGINI
Faculty of Conservation of Cultural Heritage: Prof. M. ANDALORO
Faculty of Economics: Prof. E. PERRONE
Faculty of Mathematics, Physics and Natural Sciences: Prof. V. BUONOCORE
Faculty of Modern Languages and Literature: Prof. G. PLATANIA
Faculty of Political Sciences: Prof. M. FERRARI ZUMBINI

UNIVERSITÀ DEGLI STUDI DI UDINE

Palazzo Florio, Via Palladio 8, 33100 Udine
Telephone: 0432-556111
Fax: 0432-507715
Internet: www.amm.uniud.it

Founded 1978
State control

Rector: Prof. FURIO HONSELL
Pro-Rector: Prof. MARIA AMALIA D'ARONCO
Admin. Dir: Dr DANIELE LIVON
Librarian: Dr PIER GIORGIO SCLIPPA

Library of 630,000 vols
Number of teachers: 780
Number of students: 16,800

Publication: *RES* (5 a year)

DEANS

Faculty of Agriculture: Prof. ANGELO VIA-
NELLO
Faculty of Economics: Prof. FLAVIO PRESS-
ACCO
Faculty of Education: Prof. FRANCO FABBRO
Faculty of Engineering: Prof. ANDREA STELLA
Faculty of Law: Prof. MARIA RITA D'ADDEZIO
Faculty of Literature: Prof. CATERINA FURLAN
Faculty of Medicine and Surgery: Prof.
FRANCO QUADRIFOGLIO
Faculty of Medicine and Veterinary Medi-
cine: Prof. MARCO GALEOTTI
Faculty of Modern Languages: Prof. VIN-
CENZO ORIOLES
Faculty of Sciences: Prof. CARLO TASSO

UNIVERSITÀ DEGLI STUDI DI URBINO

Via Saffi 2, 61029 Urbino
Telephone: 0722-374203
Fax: 0722-374242
E-mail: rettore@uniurb.it
Internet: www.uniurb.it

Founded 1506
Academic year: November to October

Rector: Prof. Dott. GIOVANNI BOGLIOLO
Vice-Rector: Prof. Dott. MAURO MAGNANI
Admin. Dir: Dott. ROBERTO PETRUCCI

Library: see Libraries
Number of teachers: 483
Number of students: 22,088

Publications: *Documents de Travail* (semiotics, in 6 series), *Fonti e Documenti* (history), *Hermeneutica* (philosophy), *Le Carte*
(history), *Notizie da Palazzo Albani* (art
review), *Quaderni dell'Istituto di Filosofia*
(philosophy), *Quaderni di Hermeneutica*
(philosophy), *Quaderni Urbinati di Cultura Classica* (philology), *Storie Locali*
(history), *Studi Urbinati—A* (law and economics), *Studi Urbinati—B* (history, philosophy and literature)

DEANS

Faculty of Economics: GIANCARLO FERRERO
Faculty of Education: NANDO FILOGRASSO
Faculty of Environmental Sciences: FILIPPO
MANGANI
Faculty of Foreign Languages: STEFANO
PIVATO
Faculty of Law: LUIGI MARI
Faculty of Letters and Philosophy: GIORGIO
CERBONI BAIARDI
Faculty of Mathematics, Physics and Natural
Sciences: PAOLO COLANTONI
Faculty of Pharmacy: GIORGIO TARZIA
Faculty of Physical Education and Health:
VILBERTO STOCCHI
Faculty of Political Sciences: VITTORIO PAR-
LATO
Faculty of Sociology: GRAZIELLA MAZZOLI

PROFESSORS

(Some staff serve in more than one faculty)

Faculty of Economics (Via Saffi 42, 61029
Urbino; tel. 0722-305500; fax 0722-305566;
e-mail presecon@uniurb.it; internet www
.econ.uniurb.it):

ANTONELLI, G., Marketing of Agroindus-
trial Products
CIAMBOTTI, M., Economic Planning and
Auditing
FERRERO, G., Marketing
GARDINI, L., Mathematics for Economic
Applications
GIAMPAOLI, A., Banking
MARCHINI, I., Business Economics
PAOLONI, M., General and Applied
Accountancy
PENCARELLI, T., Economics and Manage-
ment
POLIDORI, G., Transport Economics

RINALDI, R., Financial Law
STEFANINI, L., General Mathematics

Faculty of Education (Via Bramante 17,
61029 Urbino; tel. 0722-327628; fax 0722-
327628; e-mail lisa@uniurb.it; internet www
.uniurb.it/sciform/home.htm):

BALDACCI, M., General Pedagogy
CUBELLI, R., General Psychology
FILOGRASSO, N., General Pedagogy
LOSURDO, D., History of Philosophy
PERSI, P., Geography
PIRANI, P., Educational Psychology
RIPANTI, G., Theoretical Philosophy
ROSSI, S., Theory and Techniques of Psy-
chological Discourse
SALA, G., Dynamic Psychology

Faculty of Environmental Sciences (Località
Crocicchia, 61029 Urbino; tel. 0722-304271;
fax 0722-305265; e-mail sc.ambientali@
uniurb.it; internet www.uniurb.it/sa/index
.html):

CECCHETTI, G., Principles of Environmen-
tal Protection
CONFORTO, G., Laboratory of General Phys-
ics
MAGNANI, F., Environmental Chemistry
WEZEL FORESE, C., Stratigraphy
ZUMINO, M. E., Biogeography

Faculty of Foreign Languages (Piazza Rinascimento 7, 61029 Urbino; tel. 0722-328506;
fax 0722-328506; e-mail pres.facolta.lingue@
uniurb.it):

BOGLIOLO, G., French Literature
MORISCO, G., Anglo-American Languages
and Literatures
MULLINI, R., English Literature
OSSANI, A. T., Italian Literature
PIVATO, S., Contemporary History
SAURIN DE LA IGLESIA, M. R., Spanish
Literature
VENTURELLI, A., History of German Culture
ZAGANELLI, G., Romance Philology

Faculty of Law (Via Matteotti 1, 61029
Urbino; tel. 0722-3031; fax 0722-2955;
e-mail presidigiur@giur.uniurb.it; internet
www.uniurb.it):

DONDI, A., Civil Procedural Law
FANTAPPIÈ, C., History of Canon Law
FERRONI, L., Institutes of Private Law
GILIBERTI, G., Roman Law
MARI, L., International Law
MOROZZO DELLA ROCCA, P., Civil Law
ROZO ACUNA, E., Comparative Public Law

Faculty of Letters and Philosophy (Piano S.
Lucia 6, 61029 Urbino; tel. 0722-320125; fax
0722-320125; e-mail preslet@lettere.uniurb
.it):

ARBIZZONI ARTUSI, G., Philosophy of Italian
Literature
BERNARDINI, P., Greek Language and Lit-
erature
BOLDRINI, S., Latin Language and Litera-
ture
CECCHINI, E., Humanist Medieval Latin
Literature
CECCHINI, F. M., Contemporary History,
History of the Risorgimento
CERBONI BAIARDI, G., Italian Literature
CUBEDDU, I., Theoretical Philosophy
FRANCHI, A., Glottology and Linguistics
GORI, F., History of Christianity and the
Church
GUERCIO, M., Archives, Bibliography and
Librarianship
ILLUMINATI, A., History of Philosophy
LANCIOTTI, S., Latin Language and Litera-
ture
PERINI, G., Museum Organization and Art
and Restoration Criticism
PERUSINO, F., Greek Language and Litera-
ture
QUESTA, C., Classical Philology

RAFFAELLI, R., Latin Language and Litera-
ture
RINALDI TUFI, S., Classical Archaeology
SCODITTI, G., Anthropological Demoethnic
Studies
TAROZZI, G., Logic and Philosophy of Sci-
ence

Faculty of Mathematics, Physics and Natural
Sciences (Località Crocicchia, 61029 Urbino;
tel. 0722-304283; fax 0722-304240; e-mail
scienze.mmffnn@uniurb.it):

ATTANASI, O. A., Organic Chemistry
BALSAMO, M., Zoology
BERETTA, E., Mathematical Analysis
COCCIONI, R., Micropalaeontology
COLANTONI, P., Sedimentology
DEL GRANDE, P., Comparative Anatomy
GAZZANELLI, G., Cytochemistry and Histo-
chemistry
GORI, U., Applied Geology
MAGNANI, M., Biological Chemistry
MICHELONI, M., General and Inorganic
Chemistry
NINFALI, P., Comparative Biochemistry
PAPA, S., Human Anatomy
PERRONE, V., Stratigraphic Geology

Faculty of Pharmacy (Via Saffi 2, 61029
Urbino; tel. 0722-329881; fax 0722-2737;
e-mail farmacia@uniurb.it):

ACCORSI, A., Biological Chemistry
CANTONI, O., Pharmacotherapy
DACHÀ, M., Applied Biochemistry
PIATTI, E., Food Science
TARZIA, G., Pharmaceutical Chemistry and
Toxicology
VETRANO, F., Physics

Faculty of Physical Education and Health
(Via Oddi 14, 61029 Urbino; tel. 0722-
3517278; fax 0722-328829; e-mail presid
.smotorie@uniurb.it):

FALCIERI, E., Human Anatomy
STOCCHI, V., Applied Biochemistry

Faculty of Political Sciences (Via Bramante
17, 61029 Urbino; tel. 0722-328557; fax 0722-
328656; e-mail sc.politiche@uniurb.it):

DELLA CANANEA, G., Administrative Law
GREGOIRE, R., History of Christianity
GUDERZO, M., History of International
Relations
MAZZONI, R., Political Economy
PARLATO, V., Canon Law
TENELLA-SILLANI, C., Institutes of Private
Law

Faculty of Sociology (Via Saffi 15, 61029
Urbino; tel. 0722-327343; fax 0722-322343;
e-mail presidenza@soc.uniurb.it; internet
www.soc.uniurb.it):

ALFIERI, L., Political Philosophy
DEI, M., Sociology of Education
DEL TUTTO, L., General Linguistics
DIAMANTI, I., Political Science
FRANCI, A., Social Statistics
GRASSI, P., Philosophy of Religions
MAGGIONI, G., Sociology of Law
MAZZOLI, G., Communication Sociology
NEGROTTI, M., Methodology in Human Sci-
ences
PIAZZI, G., Sociological Theory
VALLI, B., Mass-Media Sociology

UNIVERSITÀ DEGLI STUDI DI VENEZIA

Dorsoduro 3246, Ca' Foscari, 30123 Venice
Telephone: 041-2348111
Fax: 041-52101112
E-mail: help@unive.it
Internet: www.unive.it

Founded 1868, formerly Istituto Universitario di Economia e Commercio e di Lingue
e Letterature Straniere
Academic year: November to October

Rector: Prof. PIER FRANCESCO GHETTI
Pro-Rector: Prof.ssa ELIDE PITTARELLO
Admin. Dir: Dott.ssa FRANCESCA BITETTI
Librarian: Sig. ALESSANDRO BERTONI
Number of teachers: 494
Number of students: 17,427
Publications: *Annuario, Cafoscariappunta-menti* (6 a year), *Cafoscarinotizie* (4 a year)

DEANS

Faculty of Economics and Commerce: Prof. F. MASON
Faculty of Foreign Languages and Literature: Prof. M. CICERI
Faculty of Letters and Philosophy: Prof. G. LEVI
Faculty of Mathematical, Physical and Natural Sciences: Prof. G. A. MAZZOCCHIN

UNIVERSITY CENTRES AND SCHOOLS

Administrative Computer Centre: Dorsoduro 2169, Santa Marta, 30123 Venice; Pres. Dott. G. BUSETTO.

Computer Centre: Dorsoduro 3861, 30123 Venice; tel. 5229823; Pres. Prof. G. PACINI.

Interdepartmental Experimental Centre: Dorsoduro 2137, 30123 Venice; tel. 5298111; Pres. Prof. G. A. MAZZOCCHIN.

Interfaculty Linguistics Centre: Santa Croce 2161, 30125 Venice; tel. 5241642; Dir Prof. G. CINQUE.

Interuniversity Centre for Venetian Studies: San Marco 2945, Ca' Loredan, 30124 Venice; tel. 5200996; Dir Prof. G. PADOAN.

Statistical Documentation Centre: Dorsoduro 3246, 30123 Venice; tel. 5298111; Dir Prof. R. VEDALDI.

UNIVERSITÀ DEGLI STUDI DI VERONA

Via dell'Artigliere 8, 37129 Verona
Telephone: 045-8028111
Fax: 045-8098255
Internet: www.univr.it
Founded 1982
Rector: Prof. ALESSANDRO MAZZUCCO
Pro-Rector: Prof.ssa BETTINA CAMPEDELLI
Admin. Dir: Dott. ANTONIO SALVINI
Number of teachers: 258
Number of students: 13,087

DEANS

Faculty of Arts and Philosophy: Prof. L. SECCO
Faculty of Economics and Commerce: Prof. G. BORELLI
Faculty of Languages and Foreign Literature: Prof. E. MOSELE
Faculty of Mathematics, Physics and Natural Sciences: Prof. E. BURATTINI
Faculty of Medicine and Surgery: Prof. R. CORROCHER

POLITECNICO DI MILANO

Piazza Leonardo da Vinci 32, 20133 Milan
Telephone: 02-23991
Fax: 02-23992206
Internet: www.polimi.it
Founded 1863
Academic year: November to October
Rector: Prof. ADRIANO DE MAIO
Vice-Rector: Prof. MARIA CRISTINA TREU
Pro-Rector: Prof. GIAMPIO BRACCHI
Admin. Dir: Dott. PIERO ZANELLO
Librarians: Prof. MAURIZIO BORIANI, Prof. ENNIO LAZZARINI, Prof. MARIA GIOVANNA SAMI
Number of teachers: 1,013
Number of students: 42,402

Publication: *Politecnico* (4 a year)

DEANS

Faculty of Architecture (Milano Bovisa): Prof. ANTONIO MONESTIROLI
Faculty of Architecture (Milano Bovisa—Industrial Design): Prof. ALBERTO SEASSARO
Faculty of Architecture (Milano Leonardo): Prof. CESARE STEVAN
Faculty of Engineering: Prof. OSVALDO DE DONATO
Faculty of Engineering (Como): Prof. PIERLUIGI DELLA VIGNA
Faculty of Engineering (Lecco): Prof. MICHELE GASPARETTO
Faculty of Engineering (Milano Bovisa): Prof. LUIGI PUCCINELLI
Faculty of Engineering (Milano Leonardo): Prof. NICOLA SCHIAVONI

POLITECNICO DI TORINO

Corso Duca degli Abruzzi 24, 10129 Turin
Telephone: 011-5646666
Fax: 011-5646329
Internet: www.polito.it
Founded 1859
Higher Institute of Engineering and Architecture
Academic year: November to October
Rector: FRANCESCO PROFUMO
Admin. Dir: MARCO TOMASI
Librarian: Prof. G. GHIONE
Library of 175,000 vols
Number of teachers: 774
Number of students: 23,000

DEANS

Faculty of Architecture (Turin): Prof. V. COMOLI
Faculty of Engineering (Turin): Prof. R. CONTI
Faculty of Engineering (Vercelli): Prof. A. GUGLIOTTA
Faculty of Information Engineering (Turin): Prof. C. NALDI

Other Universities, Colleges and Institutes

AMERICAN UNIVERSITY OF ROME

Via Pietro Roselli 4, 00153 Rome
Telephone: 06-58330919
Fax: 06-58330992
E-mail: aurinfo@aur.edu
Internet: www.aur.edu
Office in USA: 1025 Connecticut Ave, NW, Suite 601, Washington, DC 20036, USA
Telephone: (202) 331-8327
Fax: (202) 296-9577
Founded 1969
Academic year: August to July
President: MARGARET MELADY
Provost: ROBERT MARINO
Student Services: JAMES LYNCH
Admissions: MARIA NISDEO
Library of 8,000 vols, ProQuest databases containing 4,336 periodicals
Number of teachers: 60
Number of students: 450
Depts of anthropology, art and art history, biology, business administration, cinema, classics, communications, computer science, drama, economics, English, English as a Foreign Language (EFL), history, Italian, mathematics, music, philosophy, political science, psychology, sociology, Spanish, studio art.

BOLOGNA CENTER OF THE JOHNS HOPKINS UNIVERSITY PAUL H. NITZE SCHOOL OF ADVANCED INTERNATIONAL STUDIES (SAIS)

Via Belmeloro 11, 40126 Bologna
Telephone: 051-2917811
Fax: 051-228505
E-mail: admission@jhubc.it
Internet: www.jhubc.it
Founded 1955
Language of instruction: English
Academic year: September to May
Interdisciplinary graduate programme in int. relations with an emphasis on int. economics, European studies, int. devt, and the many subfields of int. relations (conflict management, global theory and history, int. law and orgs, int. policy, strategic studies). 1- and 2-year programmes are available, with the possibility of combining a year in Bologna and Washington, DC (USA). A strong language programme is available to enable students to achieve a foreign language proficiency, necessary for any career in int. relations.
Dir: Prof. KENNETH KELLER
Dir of Finance and Admin.: BART DRAKULICH
Registrar: HANNELORE ARAGNO
Librarian: GAIL MARTIN
Library of 76,000 vols
Number of teachers: 50
Number of students: 185
Publication: *Bologna Center Journal of International Affairs*.

ENI CORPORATE UNIVERSITY— SCUOLA ENRICO MATTEI

Via S. Salvo 1, 20097 San Donato Milanese
Telephone: 02-52057969
Fax: 02-52057908
E-mail: info.scuolamattei@eni.it
Internet: www.enicorporateuniversity.it/scuolamattei/
Founded 1957
Academic year: September to June
Dean: Prof. PIERANGELO CIGNOLI
Library of 15,000 vols
Number of teachers: 50
Number of students: 55 new students per year
Publication: *Quaderni* (3 a year)
Economic and management studies; higher degree in energy and environmental economics.

EUROPEAN UNIVERSITY INSTITUTE

Via dei Roccettini 9, 50016 San Domenico di Fiesole (FI),
Telephone: 055-46851
Fax: 055-4685298
E-mail: webmaster@iue.it
Internet: www.iue.it
Founded 1972 by the member states of the European Communities (present-day EU)
Academic year: September to June
Language of instruction: EU languages
Pres.: Prof. YVES MÉNY
Sec.-Gen.: Dott. MARCO DEL PANTA RIDOLFI
Librarian: VEERLE DECKMYN
Library of 500,000 vols
Number of teachers: 50 (full-time)
Number of students: 600 (postgraduate)
Publications: *EUI Review, EUI Working Papers, European Foreign Policy Bulletin, European Journal of International Law, European Law Journal, President's Annual Report, Robert Schuman Centre Newsletter*.

ATTACHED INSTITUTIONS

Academy of European Law: Dirs B. DE WITTE, G. DE BÚRCA F. FRANCIONI.

European Forum: Dir H. WALLACE.

Robert Schuman Centre for Advanced Studies: Dir H. WALLACE.

FREIE UNIVERSITÄT BOZEN/LIBERA UNIVERSITÀ DI BOLZANO
(Free University of Bozen/Bolzano)

Via Sernesi 1, 39100 Bolzano
Telephone: 0471-012200
Fax: 0471-012209
E-mail: info@unibz.it
Internet: www.unibz.it
Founded 1997
Provincial state control
Languages of instruction: German, Italian, English
Rector: Prof. Dr JOHANN DRUMBL
President: Dr FRIEDRICH SCHMIDL
Library of 77,300 books, 1,036 periodicals, 4,250 online journals, 68 databases
Number of teachers: 25
Number of students: 1,965

DEANS

Faculty of Computer Science: Prof. MICHAEL BÖHLEN
School of Economics: Prof. MAURIZIO MURGIA
Faculty of Education: Prof. GERALD WALL-NÖFER
Faculty of Design and Art: Prof. KUNO PREY

ISTITUTO REGIONALE DI STUDI E RICERCA SOCIALE

Piazza S. Maria Maggiore 7, 38100 Trento
Telephone: 0461-273611
Fax: 0461-233821
E-mail: emma.stefano@irsrs.tn.it
Internet: irsrs.isite.it
Founded 1947; until c. 1993, Scuola Superiore Regionale di Servizio Sociale
Pres.: Dott. ITALO MONFREDINI
Dir: Dott.ssa LAURA RAVANELLI
Library of 15,000 vols
Number of teachers: 350
Number of students: 6,000
Publication: *Annali* (1 a year).

CONSTITUENT INSTITUTES

Scuola per Educatore Professionale (School for Professional Educators).

Scuola per Operatore Socio-Assistenziale (School for Social Service Workers).

Università della Terza Età e del Tempo Disponibile (Open University): training for social workers, and adult education.

ISTITUTO UNIVERSITARIO DI ARCHITETTURA

Tolentini 191, 30135 Venice
Telephone: 041-2571111
Fax: 041-2571760
E-mail: comesta@iuav.it
Internet: web.iuav.it
Founded 1926
State control
Academic year: November to October
Rector: Prof. M. FOLIN
Admin. Dir: Dott. PIERPAOLO MINELLI
Librarian: Dott.ssa LAURA CASAGRANDE
Library of 123,000 vols, 2,500 periodicals
Number of teachers: 372
Number of students: 12,000

ISTITUTO UNIVERSITARIO DI STUDI EUROPEI
(University Institute of European Studies)

Via Maria Vittoria 26, 10123 Turin
Telephone: 011-8394660
Fax: 011-8394664
E-mail: info@iuse.it
Internet: www.iuse.it
Founded 1952
Offers postgraduate courses and researches in law and int. econ.
Pres.: Prof. RAFFAELE CATERINA
Library of 35,000 vols, 23,000 documents from int. orgs.

JOHN CABOT UNIVERSITY

Via della Lungara 233, 00165 Rome
Telephone: 06-6819121
Fax: 06-5897429
E-mail: admissions@johncabot.edu
Internet: www.johncabot.edu
Office in USA: POB 11427, Southport, NC 28461, USA
E-mail: usoffice@johncabot.edu
Founded 1972
Independent, four-year institution of liberal arts
President: JAMES CREAGAN
Dean of Academic Affairs: FRANCO PAVON-CELLO
Dean of Students and Director of Administration and Enrolment: L. CHRIS CURRY
Registrar: CARMEN SCARPATI
Director of Admissions: FRANCESCA R. GLEASON
Library Supervisor: SUSAN FULLER
Library: Frohring Library: reference material, curriculum-related items, newspapers, 1,000 online journals
Number of teachers: 50

PROFESSORS

CREAGAN, J. F., International Relations
GRAY, L. E., Political Science

LIBERA UNIVERSITÀ DI LINGUE E COMUNICAZIONE IULM

Via Carb Bo 1, 20143 Milan
Telephone: 02-891411
Fax: 02-89141410
E-mail: iulm.orienta@iulm.it
Internet: www.iulm.it
Founded 1968
Academic year: October to May
Rector: Prof. GIOVANNI A. PUGLISI
Admin. Dir: Dott. CIRO FRACCACRETA
Librarian: Dott. GIOVANNI MOSCATI
Library of 122,000 vols
Number of teachers: 350
Number of students: 8,500

DEANS

Faculty of Communications Science: Prof. CARLO A. RICCIARDI
Faculty of Foreign Languages and Literature: Profa PATRIZIA NEROZZI

LIBERA UNIVERSITÀ INTERNAZIONALE DEGLI STUDI SOCIALI GUIDO CARLI IN ROMA
(Independent International University of Social Studies in Rome)

Viale Pola 12, 00198 Rome
Telephone: 06-852251
Fax: 06-85225300
E-mail: direzionegenerale@luiss.it
Internet: www.luiss.it

Founded 1945, recognized by the Government 1966
Pres.: LUCA CORDERO DI MONTEZEMOLO
Rector: MASSIMO EGIDI
Gen. Man.: PIER LUIGI CELLI
Library of 118,000 vols and 2,133 periodicals
Number of teachers: 515
Number of students: 4,800

DEANS

Faculty of Economics: Prof. F. FONITANE
Faculty of Law: Prof. M. FOSCHINI
Faculty of Political Science: Prof. G. C. DE MARTIN

LIBERA UNIVERSITÀ MARIA SS. ASSUNTA

Via della Traspontina 21, 00193 Rome
Telephone: 06-684221
Fax: 06-6878357
E-mail: lumsa@lumsa.it
Internet: www.lumsa.it
Founded 1939
Academic year: October to July
Pres.: GIUSEPPE DALLA TORRE DEL TEMPIO DI SANGUINETTO
Registrar: Dott. GIANNINA DI MARCO
Librarian: Dott. GIUSEPPINA D'ALESSANDRO
Library of 100,000 vols
Number of teachers: 350
Number of students: 5,200
Faculties of education, law, letters and philosophy
Publications: *I Quaderni della Lumsa* (1 a year), *Nuovi Studi Politici* (4 a year).

SCUOLA INTERNAZIONALE SUPERIORE DI STUDI AVANZATI IN TRIESTE

Via Beirut 2–4, 34014 Trieste
Telephone: 040-37871
Fax: 040-3787528
Internet: www.sissa.it
Founded 1978; sponsored by the Italian Government
Languages of instruction: English, Italian
Academic year: November to October
Director: Prof. STEFANO FANTONI
Administrator: GIULIANA ZOTTA VITTUR
Library of 10,000 vols
Number of teachers: 62
Number of students: 220

Higher degrees in physics, mathematics and neuroscience; research; fellowships for students from developing countries.

SCUOLA NORMALE SUPERIORE DI PISA

Piazza dei Cavalieri 7, 56126 Pisa
Telephone: 050-509111
E-mail: direzione@sns.it
Internet: www.sns.it
Founded 1813
State control
Dir: Prof. SALVATORE SETTIS
Chief Admin. Officer: Dott. CLAUDIO CAPECCHI
Librarian: Dott.ssa SANDRA DI MAJO
Library of 500,000 vols
Number of teachers: 36
Number of students: 279
Publications: *Annali* (Arts series, Science series), *Italia dialettale*, *Quaderni di Matematica*, *Studi Linguistici e Filologici*, *Studi e Testi*, *Testi umanistici inediti o rari*.

UNIVERSITÀ CATTOLICA DEL SACRO CUORE
(Catholic University of the Sacred Heart)

Largo A. Gemelli 1, 20123 Milan
Telephone: 02-72345407
Fax: 02-72343796
Internet: www.unicatt.it

Founded 1920; recognized by the Government 1924

Rector: Prof. L. ORNAGHI
Admin. Officer: Dott. A. CICCHETTI
Librarian: Dott. ELLIS SADA
Number of teachers: 3,292
Number of students: 41,519

Publication: various, published by individual faculties

DEANS

Faculty of Agrarian Sciences: Prof. G. PIVA
Faculty of Banking, Finance and Insurance Sciences: Prof. B. V. FROSINI
Faculty of Economics (Milan): Prof. A. COVA
Faculty of Economics (Piacenza): Prof. E. CICIOTTI
Faculty of Educational Sciences: Prof. M. LENOCI
Faculty of Jurisprudence: Prof. G. PASTORI
Faculty of Jurisprudence (Piacenza): Prof. G. NEGRI
Faculty of Letters and Philosophy: Prof. G. PICASSO
Faculty of Linguistic Sciences and Foreign Literatures: Prof. S. CIGADA
Faculty of Mathematical, Physical and Natural Sciences: Prof. M. DEGIOVANNI
Faculty of Medicine and Surgery: Prof. P. MARANO
Faculty of Political Sciences: Prof. A. QUADRIO CURZIO
Faculty of Psychology: Prof.ssa E. SCABINI
Faculty of Sociology: Prof. M. COLASANTO

UNIVERSITÀ COMMERCIALE LUIGI BOCCONI

Via R. Sarfatti 25, 20136 Milan
Telephone: 02-58361
Fax: 02-58362000
Internet: www.uni-bocconi.it

Founded 1902; private control
Academic year: November to October

Pres.: Prof. MARIO MONTI
Rector: Prof. CARLO SECCHI
Vice-Pres.: Prof. LUIGI GUATRI
Chief Exec. and General Manager: Dott. GIOVANNI PAVESE
Librarian: MARISA SANTASIERO
Number of teachers: 971
Number of students: 12,600

Publications: *Azienda Pubblica, Commercio, Economia delle Fonti di Energia, Economia e Management, Economia e Politica Industriale, Finanza Marketing e Produzione, Giornale degli Economisti e Annali di Economia, Sviluppo e Organizzazione*

DEANS

CESDIA Centre for Teaching and Learning: Prof. V. CODA (Dir)
Department of Business Administration: Prof. PAOLO MOTTURA
Department of Economics: Prof. ALDO MONTESANO
SDA Bocconi School of Management: Prof. MAURIZIO DALLOCCHIO (Dir)

PROFESSORS

AIROLDI, G., Business Administration
ALESSANDRI, A., Commercial Law
AMATORI, F., Economic History
AMIGONI, F., Business Administration
ARTONI, R., Public Finance

BATTIGALLI, P., Economics
BELTRATTI, A., Economics
BERTONI, A., Corporate Finance
BIANCHI, L. A., Company and Business Law
BINI, M., Corporate Finance
BORGONOVI, E., Public Administration
BRUGGER, G., Corporate Finance
BRUNETTI, G., Business Administration
BRUNI, F., International Monetary Theory and Policy
BUSACCA, B., Business Administration and Management
CASTAGNOLA, A., Civil Law
CASTAGNOLI, E., Mathematics
CATTINI, M., Economic History
CIFARELLI, D. M., Statistics
CODA, V., Business Administration
DE PAOLI, L., Business Administration and Management
DEMATTÈ, C., Financial Intermediaries
FABRIZI, P. L., Securities Market
FAVERO, C. A., Monetary Economics
FERRARI, G., Monetary Economics
FILIPPINI, C., Economic Development
FORESTIERI, G., Financial Intermediaries
FRACCHIA, F., Administrative Law
FROVA, A., Corporate Finance
GIAVAZZI, F., Economics
GOLFETTO, F., Business Administration and Management
GRANDORI, A., Corporate Organization
GUARNERI, A., Comparative Civil Law
INVERNIZZI, G., Business Administration
IUDICA, G., Civil Law
LIEBMAN, S., Labour Law
MALERBA, F., Business Administration
MARCHETTI, P., Industrial Law
MASSARI, M., Capital Budgeting
MONTESANO, A., Economics
MONTI, M., Economics
MOTTURA, P., Financial Intermediaries
MULIERE, P., Statistics
ONIDA, F., International Economics
PACI, S., Management of Insurance Companies and Savings Institutions
PECCATI, L., Mathematics for Economics and Finance
PERRONE, V., Organization Theory
PEZZANI, F., Business Administration
PIVATO, S., Industrial Management
PODESTÀ, S., Commercial Management
PORTA, A., Monetary Theory and Policy
PROVASOLI, A., Cost Accounting and Management Control Systems
ROMANI, A., Economic History
RUOZI, R., Banking
SACERDOTI, G., International Law
SALVEMINI, S., Human Resources Management
SECCHI, C., Economics of the European Communities
SENN, L., Regional Economics
SITZIA, B., Econometrics
TABELLINI, G., Economics
URBANI, G., Political Science
VALDANI, E., Marketing
VALOTTI, G., Business Administration
VERONESE, P., Statistics
VICARI, S., Management of Industrial Companies
VIGANO, A., Cost Accounting and Management Control Systems

UNIVERSITÀ ITALIANA PER STRANIERI

Palazzo Fortebraccio 4, 06123 Perugia
Telephone: 075-57461
Fax: 075-62014
Internet: www.unistrapg.it

Founded 1921
Academic year: January to December

Founded for the diffusion abroad of Italian language and culture; courses in Italian language and civilization for foreigners of all nationalities. There are courses in advanced culture on Italian institutions, literature, pedagogy, history of art, the geography of Italy, Italian history, and Italian thought throughout the centuries; also courses in Italian language and culture, divided into three sections: Preparatory, Intermediate, Advanced; there are also in the summer term special courses in Etruscology, history of art and modern Italian and a course for teachers of Italian abroad. Lectures and classes are given by professors of Italian universities, leading members of academies, etc.

Rector: Prof. GIORGIO SPITELLA
Pro-Rector: ALBERTO MAZZETTI
Admin.: Dott. CARMELO SAETTA
Library of 70,000 vols
Number of teachers: 100
Number of students: 7,000

Publication: *Annali dell'Università*.

VENICE INTERNATIONAL UNIVERSITY

Isola di S. Servola, 30100 Venice
Telephone: 041-2719511
Fax: 041-2719510
E-mail: viu@univiu.it
Internet: www.univiu.org

Founded 1997
Academic year: September to May

Pres.: UMBERTO VATTANI
Dean: IGNAZIO MUSU
Sec.-Gen.: ANTONELLA ATTARDO

Staff and students provided by the constituent univs.

RESEARCH AND TRAINING CENTRES

Centre for Studies on Technologies in Distributed Intelligence Systems (TeDIS).

International Centre of Economics and Finance (ICEF).

Thematic Environmental Networks (TEN).

Schools of Music and Art
MUSIC

Accademia Filarmonica Romana (Rome Philharmonic Academy): Via Flaminia 118, 00196 Rome; tel. 06-3201752; fax 06-3210410; e-mail info@filarmonicaromana .org; internet www.filarmonicaromana.org; f. 1821; library: 1,500 vols; Pres. ROMAN VLAD.

Accademia Musicale Chigiana: Via di Città 89, 53100 Siena; tel. 0577-22091; fax 0577-288124; e-mail accademia.chigiana@ chigiana.it; internet www.chigiana.it; f. 1932; master classes, seminars, lectures, concerts, operas, international research conventions; 26 teachers; 351 students; Artistic Director Maestro ALDO BENNICI.

Conservatorio 'Claudio Monteverdi': Piazza Domenicani 19, 39100 Bolzano; tel. 0471-978764; e-mail info@ conservatoriobolzano.it; internet www .conservatoriobolzano.it; f. 1940; library: 10,000 vols; international Busoni Piano Competition held annually; Dir Prof. FELIX RESSCH; Admin. Dir Dott. MARIO BELLI.

Conservatorio di Musica 'A. Boito': Via Conservatorio 27A, 43100 Parma; tel. 0521-381911; fax 0521-200398; e-mail direzione .cons-pr@iol.it; internet www.conservatorio .pr.it; f. 1825; library: 70,000 vols; 140 teachers; 800 students; Dir EMILIO GHEZZI.

Conservatorio di Musica 'Benedetto Marcello': Palazzo Pisani, San Marco 2810, 30124 Venice; tel. 041-5225604; fax 041-5239268; e-mail direttoreamministrativo@ conseve.it; internet www.conseve.it; f. 1877; 90 teachers; 480 students; library: 50,000 vols, 70 periodicals; Dir GIOVANNI UMBERTO BATTEL.

Conservatorio di Musica 'G. B. Martini': Piazza Rossini 2, 40126 Bologna; tel. 051-221483; fax 051-223168; e-mail segreteria@ conservatorio-bologna.com; internet www .conservatorio-bologna.com; f. 1804; Dir (vacant).

Conservatorio di Musica 'Giuseppe Tartini': Via Carlo Ghega 12, 34132 Trieste; tel. 040-6724911; fax 040-370205; e-mail erasmus@conservatorio.trieste.it; internet www.conservatorio.trieste.it; f. 1903; 93 teachers; 630 students; Dir MASSIMO PAROVEL.

Conservatorio di Musica 'Giuseppe Verdi': Via Conservatorio 12, 20122 Milan; tel. 02-7621101; fax 02-76020259; e-mail info@consmilano.it; internet www .consmilano.it; f. 1808; library: see Libraries; Dir MARCELLO ABBADO.

Conservatorio di Musica 'L. Cherubini': Piazzetta delle Belle Arti 2, 50121 Florence; tel. 055-292180; fax 055-2396785; e-mail conservatoriofirenze@tin.it; internet www .bdp.it/conservatorio-firenze; f. 1861; 107 teachers; 702 students; Dir Maestro GIOVANNI CICCONI; Sec. Dott.ssa M. POLLICINA.

Conservatorio di Musica 'Niccolò Piccinni': Via Cifarelli 26, 70124 Bari; tel. 080-5740022; fax 080-5794461; internet www .conservatoriopiccinni.it; f. 1959; library: 11,000 vols; Dir MARCO RENZI; Admin. Sec. Dott.ssa ANNA MARIA SFORZA.

Conservatorio di Musica 'S. Pietro a Majella': Via S. Pietro a Majella 35, 80138 Naples; tel. 081-5644411; fax 081-5644415; e-mail info@sanpietroamajella.it; internet www.sanpietroamajella.it; Dir Dr A. COLLUCCI.

Conservatorio di Musica 'Santa Cecilia': Via dei Greci 18, 00187 Rome; tel. 06-3609671; internet www .conservatoriosantacecilia.it; Dir Maestro GIORGIO CAMBISSA.

Conservatorio di Musica 'V. Bellini': Via Squarcialupo 45, 90133 Palermo; tel. 091-580921; fax 091-586742; f. 1721; library: 40,000 vols, collection of 18th- and 19th-century MSS; Pres. (vacant); Dir CARMELO CAPUSO; publ. *Quaderni del Conservatorio* (irregular).

Conservatorio Statale di Musica 'G. Pierluigi da Palestrina': Piazza Porrino 1, 09128 Cagliari; tel. 070-493118; fax 070-487388; internet www.conservatoriocagliari .it; f. 1939; Dir NINO BONAVOLONTÀ.

Conservatorio Statale di Musica 'Gioacchino Rossini': Piazza Olivieri 5, 61100 Pesaro; tel. 0721-33671; fax 0721-35295; e-mail segreteria@conservatoriorossini.it; internet www.conservatoriorossini.it; f. 1882; library: 25,000 vols; Dir MARCO GIANNOTTI.

Conservatorio Statale di Musica 'Giuseppe Verdi': Via Mazzini 11, 10123 Turin; tel. 011-8178458; fax 011-885165; internet www.conservatoriotorino.eu; f. 1867; Dir GIORGIO FERRARI.

ART

Accademia Albertina di Belle Arti: Via Accademia Albertina 6, 10123 Turin; tel. 011-889020; fax 011-8125688; e-mail albertina@ itbox.net; internet www.accademialbertina .torino.it; f. 1652; 70 teachers; 550 students; Pres. Dott. Proc. A. M. MAROCCO; Dir Prof. CARLO GIULIAMO.

Accademia di Belle Arti di Bologna (Academy of Fine Arts of Bologna): Via Belle Arti 54, 40126 Bologna; tel. 051-4226411; fax 051-253032; e-mail info@ accademiabelleartibologna.it; internet www .accademiabelleartibologna.it; f. 1710; library: 15,000 vols; Dir Prof. A. BACCILIERI; Librarian Prof. M. V. RICCARDI SCASSELLATI; publ. *Prontuario* (1 a year).

Accademia di Belle Arti di Carrara (Academy of Fine Arts): Via Roma 1, 54033 Carrara; tel. 0585-71658; e-mail info@ accademiacarrara.it; internet www .accademia.carrara.ms.it; courses in painting, sculpture and scene-painting; Dir Prof. MARCO BAUDINELLI; Admin. Dir Dr LINO BUSELLI.

Accademia di Belle Arti di Firenze (Academy of Fine Arts of Florence): Via Ricasoli 66, 50122 Florence; tel. 055-215449; fax 055-2396921; e-mail segreteria@ accademia.firenze.it; internet www .accademia.firenze.it; f. 1801; library: 22,000 vols; Pres. Sen. L. BAUSI; Dir Prof. D. VIGGIANO.

Accademia di Belle Arti di Lecce (Academy of Fine Arts of Lecce): Via Libertini 3, 73100 Lecce; tel. 0832-258611; fax 0832-301490; e-mail accademialecce@libero.it; internet www.accademiabelleartilecce.com; Dir Prof. Arch. GIACINTO LEONE.

Accademia di Belle Arti di Milano (Academy of Fine Arts of Milan): Palazzo di Brera, Via Brera 28, 20121 Milan; tel. 02-869551; fax 02-86403643; e-mail accademia@ accademiadibrera.milano.it; internet www .accademiadibrera.milano.it; f. 1776; library: 25,000 vols; 400 teachers; 3,500 students; Pres. Prof. STEFANO ZECCHI; Dir Prof. FERNANDO DE FILIPPI.

Accademia di Belle Arti di Napoli (Academy of Fine Arts of Naples): Via S. M. Constantinopoli 107, 80138 Naples; tel. 081-444245; fax 081-444245; e-mail napoli_accademia@libero.it; internet www .accademianapoli.it; f. 1838; library: 7,000 vols; Dir Prof. ALFREDO SCOTTI.

Accademia di Belle Arti di Palermo (Academy of Fine Arts of Palermo): Via Papireto 20, 90134 Palermo; tel. 091-580876; fax 091-583746; e-mail amministrazione@accademiadipalermo.it; internet www.accademiadipalermo.it; Dir UMBERTO DE PAOLA.

Accademia di Belle Arti 'Pietro Vannucci' di Perugia (Academy of Fine Arts of Perugia): Piazza S. Francesco al Prato 5, 06123 Perugia; tel. 075-5730631; fax 075-5730632; internet www.abaperugia.org; f. 1573; 96 Academicians, 143 Hon. Academicians; collections of paintings, engravings, drawings, etc.; library: 13,330 vols; Pres. On.le Dott. ALFREDO DE POI; Dir Prof. FABRIZIO FABBRONI.

Accademia di Belle Arti di Ravenna (Academy of Fine Arts of Ravenna): Via delle Industrie 76, 48100 Ravenna; tel. 0544-453125; fax 0544-451104; e-mail accademia@comune.ravenna.it; internet www.accademiabellearti.ra.it; f. 1827; library: 10,000 vols; Dir Prof. MAURO MAZZALI; Admin. Dir Dott.ssa ORIELLA GARAVINI.

Accademia di Belle Arti di Roma (Academy of Fine Arts of Rome): Via Ripetta 222, 00186 Rome; tel. 06-3227025; fax 06-3218007; internet www .accademiabelleartiroma.it; f. 1873; Dir Prof. ANTONIO PASSA.

Accademia di Belle Arti di Venezia (Academy of Fine Arts of Venice): Campo della Carità 1050, 30123 Venice; tel. 041-5225396; fax 041-5230129; e-mail info@ accademiavenezia.edu; internet www .accademiavenezia.edu; f. 1750; 76 teachers; 870 students; Dir Prof. RICCARDO RABAGLIATI.

Istituto Statale d'Arte: Piazza Duca Federico 1, 61029 Urbino; tel. 0722-329892; fax 0722-4830; e-mail ia.scuolalibro@provincia .ps.it; f. 1865; engraving techniques, cartoon drawing, ceramics, photography, editorial graphics, publicity art; library: 20,000 vols; 110 teachers; 714 students; Pres. Prof. MAURIZIA RAGONESI.

Istituto Statale d'Arte 'Enrico e Umberto Nordio': Via di Calvola 2, 34143 Trieste; tel. 040-300660; fax 040-311646; e-mail info@isanordio.it; internet www .isanordio.it; f. 1955; courses in architecture, design and printing of textiles, interior decorating; library: 5,450 vols; Dir Prof. TEODORO GIUDICE.

Istituto Statale d'Arte 'Filippo Figari': Piazza d'Armi 16, CP 105, 07100 Sassari; tel. 079-234466; fax 079-2012665; e-mail sssd020006@istruzione.it; woodwork, metalwork, weaving, painting, ceramics, graphic art and architecture; Pres. Prof. NICOLÒ MASIA.

Istituto Statale d'Arte per la Ceramica: Corso Baccarini 17, 48018 Faenza; tel. 0546-21091; fax 0546-680093; e-mail iaballardini@ provincia.ra.it; internet www .istitutoarteceramicafaenza.com; f. 1916; basic courses in ceramic art and technology; higher courses in stoneware, ceramic building coatings, porcelain, restoration, technology of special ceramics, traditional ceramics.

DANCE AND DRAMA

Accademia Nazionale di Arte Drammatica 'Silvio d'Amico': Via Vincenzo Bellini 16, 00198 Rome; tel. 06-8543680; fax 06-8542505; f. 1935; 45 teachers; 100 students; Dir Prof. LUIGI MARIA MUSATI.

Accademia Nazionale di Danza: Largo Arrigo VII 5, 00153 Rome; tel. 06-5717621; fax 06-5780994; e-mail sd@ accademianazionaledanza.it; internet www .accademianazionaledanza.com; f. 1948; Pres. CARLO SCARASCIA MUGNOZZA; Dir LIA CALIZZA.

JAMAICA

The Higher Education System

The University of Technology, Jamaica (formerly Jamaica Institute of Technology) was founded in 1958, while Jamaica was under British colonial administration. In 1962 Jamaica achieved full independence within the Commonwealth, and in the same year the University of the West Indies (founded 1948), which has a campus on the island at Mona, was elevated to university status. In 2003/04 there were 15 institutions providing tertiary education with 11,600 students enrolled. By 2005 the University of the West Indies alone had over 13,000 students. The Tertiary Unit of the Ministry of Education is the Government agency responsible for higher education.

Admission to higher education is on the basis of two or more GCE A-Levels. The Bachelors is the standard undergraduate degree and lasts three years, followed by the Masters, the first postgraduate degree. The University of the West Indies offers either a two-year, coursework-based Masters programme or a research-based Master of Philology (MPhil). The highest university degree is the Doctorate, which lasts for two years after award of the Masters.

Technical and vocational education at the post-secondary level is supervised by the Human Employment and Resource Training Agency and National Council on Technical and Vocational Education and Training. The Human Employment and Resource Training Agency runs several academies and vocational training centres and the National Council on Technical and Vocational Education and Training is the official body responsible for awarding the National Vocational Qualification of Jamaica (Levels 1–4). A three-year Associate of Science degree is offered by the College of Agriculture, Science and Education.

The University Council of Jamaica is responsible for quality assurance and accreditation of higher education institutions.

Regulatory and Representative Bodies

GOVERNMENT

Ministry of Education: 2 National Heroes Circle, Kingston 4; tel. 922-1400; fax 948-7755; e-mail maria.jones@moey.gov.jm; internet www.moey.gov.jm; Minister ANDREW HOLNESS.

Ministry of Information, Culture, Youth and Sports: Jamaica House, Kingston 6; tel. 927-9941; e-mail maria.jones@moey.gov.jm; Minister OLIVIA GRANGE.

ACCREDITATION

University Council of Jamaica: 6B Oxford Rd, Kingston 5; tel. 929-7299; fax 929-7312; e-mail ucj@cwjamaica.com; internet www.universitycouncilja.com; f. 1987 to increase the availability of univ.-level training in Jamaica, through accreditation of instns, courses and programmes for recognition and acceptability; has the power to confer degrees, diplomas, certificates and other academic awards and distinctions on those who have pursued courses approved by the Council at associated tertiary instns; Chair. Dr LLOYD BARNETT; Exec. Dir Dr ETHLEY D. LONDON.

Learned Societies

GENERAL

Institute of Jamaica: 12–16 East St, Kingston; tel. 922-0620; fax 922-1147; internet www.instituteofjamaica.org.jm; f. 1879; comprises the National Library of Jamaica (see Libraries); two Junior Cultural Centres; Natural History Division; Arawak (Indian) Museum; Jamaica Folk Museum; Military Museum; Maritime Museum; the National Gallery of Jamaica; the African-Caribbean Institute/Jamaica Memory Bank; Institute of Jamaica Publications; Exec. Dir. VIVIAN CRAWFORD (acting); publ. *Jamaica Journal*.

UNESCO Office Kingston: 3rd Fl., The Towers, 25 Dominica Drive, Kingston 5; tel. 929-7087; fax 929-8468; e-mail kingston@unesco.org; internet www.unescocaribbean.org; designated Cluster Office for Antigua and Barbuda, Bahamas, Barbados, Belize, Dominica, Grenada, Guyana, Jamaica, St Christopher and Nevis, St Lucia, St Vincent and the Grenadines, Suriname, Trinidad and Tobago; Dir HELENE-MARIE GOSSELIN.

AGRICULTURE, FISHERIES AND VETERINARY SCIENCE

Jamaican Association of Sugar Technologists: c/o Sugar Industry Research Institute, Kendal Rd, Mandeville; tel. 962-2241; fax 962-1288; f. 1937 by the local sugar industry to conduct research and investigate technical problems of the Jamaican sugar industry; 266 mems; uses library of Sugar Industry Research Institute; Pres. MICHAEL G. HYLTON; Sec. H. M. THOMPSON; publ. *JAST Journal* (1 a year).

ARCHITECTURE AND TOWN PLANNING

Jamaican Institute of Architects: POB 251, Kingston 10; 2A Caledonia Crescent, Kingston 5; tel. 926-8060; fax 920-3589; e-mail jia@cwjamaica.com; internet www.jia.org.jm; f. 1957; 71 mems (56 full, 15 assoc.); Pres. CHRISTOPHER WHYMS-STONE; Vice-Pres. KARIN HAY; Hon. Sec. LAURIE FERRON; publ. *Jamaica Architect* (1 a year).

BIBLIOGRAPHY, LIBRARY SCIENCE AND MUSEOLOGY

Library and Information Association of Jamaica: POB 125, Kingston 5; tel. and fax 927-1614; e-mail liajapresident@yahoo.com; internet www.liaja.org.jm; f. 1949 as Jamaica Library Asscn; 227 mems; Pres. MARVA BRADFORD; Sec. CHRISTA STEWART-FULLERTON; publs *LIAJA Bulletin* (1 a year), *LIAJA News* (2 a year).

HISTORY, GEOGRAPHY AND ARCHAEOLOGY

Jamaica National Heritage Trust: POB 8934, 79 Duke St, Kingston CSO; tel. 922-1287; fax 967-1703; e-mail jnht@cwjamaica.com; internet www.jnht.com; f. 1958; protection, preservation, restoration and promotion of Jamaica's material and cultural heritage, particularly through declaration of national monuments and designation of protected national heritage; Chair. Rev. DEVON DICK; Exec. Dir SUSANNE LYON.

LANGUAGE AND LITERATURE

Alliance Française: 12B, Lilford Ave (off Lady Musgrave Rd), Kingston 10; tel. 978-4622; fax 978-1836; e-mail alliance.francaisekingston@laposte.net; offers courses and examinations in French language and culture and promotes cultural exchange with France.

British Council: The British High Commission, 28 Trafalgar Rd, Kingston 10; tel. 929-7090; fax 960-3030; e-mail bcjamaica@britishcouncil.org.jm; internet www.britishcouncil.org/caribbean; offers courses and examinations in English language and British culture and promotes cultural exchange with the UK; Man. NICOLA JOHNSON.

MEDICINE

Medical Association of Jamaica: 19A Windsor Ave, Kingston 5; tel. 946-1105; fax 946-1102; internet www.medicalassnjamaica.com; f. 1877 as br of British Medical Asscn; ind. body 1966; for the promotion of medical and allied sciences and of the medical profession; 707 mems; Pres. Dr ALVERSTON BAILEY; Hon. Sec. Dr ANN JACKSON-GIBSON; publ. *Journal* (1 a year).

TECHNOLOGY

Jamaica Institution of Engineers: 2 Winchester Rd, Kingston 10; tel. 929-6741; fax 929-4655; e-mail jie@anngel.com.jm; internet www.jieng.org; f. 1960, present name 1977; to promote the advancement of the engineering profession and the practice and science of engineering, and to facilitate the exchange of information and ideas on those subjects among the mems and others; Pres. HOWARD CHIN; Hon. Sec. HERMON EDMONSON; publ. *JIE Advisor* (12 a year).

Research Institutes

AGRICULTURE, FISHERIES AND VETERINARY SCIENCE

Sugar Industry Research Institute: Kendal Rd, Mandeville; tel. 962-2241; fax 962-1288; e-mail sirijam@jamaicasugar.org; internet www.jamaicasugar.org; f. 1973; research into sugar cane cultivation and environmental management; library of 660 vols, 2,500 bound vols of periodicals; Dir of Research EARLE ROBERTS.

ECONOMICS, LAW AND POLITICS

Planning Institute of Jamaica: 16 Oxford Rd, POB 634, Kingston 5; tel. 960-9339; fax 906-5011; e-mail info@pioj.gov.jm; internet www.pioj.gov.jm; f. 1955, fmrly the Central Planning Unit, present name in 1984; policy advice on economic, social and sustainable devt issues to the govt; Dir-Gen. Dr PAULINE KNIGHT; publs *Economic and Social Survey,- Jamaica* (1 a year), *Economic Update and Outlook* (4 a year), *JA People Magazine* (1 a year), *Jamaica Survey of Living Conditions* (1 a year), *The Labour Market Information Newsletter* (2 a year).

MEDICINE

Caribbean Food and Nutrition Institute (CFNI): Jamaica Centre, POB 140, Mona, Kingston 7; tel. 927-1540; fax 927-2657; e-mail e-mail@cfni.paho.org; internet www.cfni.paho.org; f. 1967; conducts research and training courses and provides technical advisory services to 18 govts of the English-speaking Caribbean on matters relating to food and nutrition; library of 4,500 vols; there is a centre in Trinidad; Dir Dr FITZROY HENRY; publs *Cajanus* (4 a year), *Nyam News* (24 a year).

Medical Research Council Laboratories: University of the West Indies, Mona, Kingston 7; tel. 927-2471; fax 927-2984; e-mail grserjnt@uwimona.edu.jm; f. 1974; attached to Medical Research Council, London; research into sickle-cell disease; 20 staff; Dir G. R. SERJEANT.

NATURAL SCIENCES

General

Scientific Research Council: POB 350, Kingston 6; tel. 927-1771; fax 927-1990; e-mail adminsrc@toj.com; internet www.src-jamaica.org; f. 1960; undertakes, fosters and coordinates scientific research in the island; library of 10,000 vols; Exec. Dir Dr AUDIA BARNETT; publs *Conference Proceedings* (1 a year), *Jamaican Journal of Science and Technology* (1 a year).

Libraries and Archives

Kingston

Jamaica Library Service: POB 58, 2 Tom Redcam Dr., Kingston 5; tel. 926-3310; fax 926-2188; internet www.jamlib.org.jm; f. 1948; provides an island-wide network of 656 service points, including 13 parish libraries, and 121 branch libraries; oversees 925 school and higher education libraries; total bookstock 2,711,000 vols, 70 periodicals; 1,121,000 vols in primary schools and 428,000 vols in secondary schools; Dir PATRICIA ROBERTS; publ. *Statistical Report of the Jamaica Library Service* (1 a year).

National Library of Jamaica: 12 East St, POB 823, Kingston; tel. 967-2494; fax 922-5567; e-mail nljresearch@cwjamaica.com; internet www.nlj.org.jm; f. 1979; 47,000 printed items, 29,600 maps and plans, 4,400 serials, 27,100 photographs, 3,150 MSS, 2,550 items of audiovisual material on Jamaica and the West Indies; Exec. Dir WINSOME HUDSON; publs *Jamaica National Bibliography* (4 a year), *National Library News* (4 a year).

University of the West Indies Library: Mona, Kingston 7; tel. 512-3569; fax 927-1926; e-mail main.library@uwimona.edu.jm; internet www.mona.uwi.edu/library/; f. 1948; 518,981 vols incl. 6,349 current and 6,495 non-current periodicals in the Main Library and 2 br. libraries for the Medical (32,896 vols) and Scientific (97,634 vols) Collns; Campus Librarian NORMA Y. AMENU-KPODO.

Spanish Town

Jamaica Archives: cnr King and Manchester Sts, Spanish Town PO; tel. 984-2581; fax 984-8254; e-mail jarchives@jard.gov.jm; internet www.jard.gov.jm; f. 1659; nat. archives of Jamaica; spec. colln of ecclesiastical and private records of historical value; Govt Archivist CLAUDETTE THOMAS.

Museum

Kingston

Institute of Jamaica Museum: see Institute of Jamaica.

Universities

UNIVERSITY OF TECHNOLOGY, JAMAICA

237 Old Hope Rd, Kingston 6

Telephone: 927-1680

Fax: 927-4388

E-mail: regist@utech.edu.jm

Internet: www.utechjamaica.edu.jm

Public control

Accredited by University Council of Jamaica

Founded 1958 as Jamaica Institute of Technology; became College of Arts, Science and Technology 1959; present name and status 1995

Academic year: August to May

Chancellor: Sir WILLIAM MORRIS

Pro-Chancellor: EDWARD SEAGA

Pres.: Prof. ERROL MORRISON,

Vice-Pres. for Academic Affairs and Quality Assurance: GEORGE ROPER

Vice-Pres. for Admin. and Univ. Registrar: DIANNE MITCHELL

Vice-Pres. for Devt: Dr NEVILLE SADDLER

Vice-Pres. for Finance, IT and Business Services: KOFI NKRUMAH-YOUNG

Vice-Pres. for Graduate Studies, Research and Entrepreneurship: Prof. GOSSETT OLIVER

Hon. Treasurer: VIVIAN CRAWFORD

Univ. Librarian: HERMINE SALMON

Univ. Orator: PAMELA KELLY

Number of teachers: 600

Number of students: 10,000

Serves Antigua and Barbuda, Anguilla, Barbados, Bahamas, Belize, British Virgin Islands, Dominica, Grenada, Guyana, Jamaica, St Lucia, St Vincent, Trinidad and Tobago, and Turks and Caicos Islands

Publication: *Journal*

DEANS

Faculty of the Built Environment: Dr CAROL ARCHER (acting)

Faculty of Business and Management: GARTH KIDDOE

Faculty of Education and Liberal Studies: Dr HALDANE JOHNSON

Faculty of Engineering and Computing: CHARMAINE DELISSER

Faculty of Health and Applied Science: Dr EUGENIE BROWN-MYRIE

UNIVERSITY OF THE WEST INDIES, MONA CAMPUS

Mona, Kingston 7

Telephone: 927-1661

Fax: 927-2765

E-mail: oadmin@uwimona.edu.jm

Internet: www.mona.uwi.edu

Founded 1948, University 1962

Serves 16 territories: Jamaica, Anguilla, Bahamas, Belize, British Virgin Islands, Cayman Islands, Barbados, Antigua and Barbuda, Dominica, Grenada, Montserrat, St Christopher and Nevis, St Lucia, Turks and Caicos, St Vincent and the Grenadines, Trinidad and Tobago. The faculties of humanities and education, medical sciences and social sciences are located on all three campuses. The faculty of law is in Barbados, agriculture and engineering in Trinidad, and the faculties of pure and applied sciences are in Barbados and Jamaica

Academic year: August to July

Chancellor: Sir GEORGE ALLEYNE

Vice-Chancellor: Prof. NIGEL HARRIS

Prin.: Prof. KENNETH HALL

University Registrar: GLORIA BARRETT-SOBERS

Librarian: STEPHNEY FERGUSON

Number of teachers: 400

Number of students: 11,000

Publications: *Arts Review* (2 a year), *Caribbean Journal of Criminology and Social Psychology* (2 a year), *Caribbean Journal of Education*, *Caribbean Law Bulletin* (2 a year), *Caribbean Law Review* (2 a year), *Caribbean Quarterly*, *Journal of Tropical Agriculture* (4 a year), *Social Economics Studies* (4 a year), *West Indian Journal of Engineering* (2 a year), *West Indian Law Journal* (1 a year), *West Indian Medical Journal* (4 a year)

DEANS AT MONA

Faculty of Humanities and Education: Prof. AGGREY BROWN

Faculty of Medical Sciences: Prof. ARCHIBALD MCDONALD

Faculty of Pure and Applied Sciences: Prof. RONALD YOUNG

Faculty of Social Sciences: MARK FIGUEROA

PROFESSORS

AHMAD, M., Biotechnology
BAILEY, W., Geography and Geology
BAIN, B., Community Health and Psychiatry
BENNETT, F., Pathology
BORNHOP, D., Applied Chemistry
BRANDAY, J., Surgery, Radiology, Anaesthesia and Intensive Care
BROWN, A., Mass Communication
BURTON, E., Medicine
CAMPBELL, C., History
CHEN, A., Physics
CHEVANNES, B., Social Anthropology
CHRISTIE, C., Obstetrics, Gynaecology and Child Health
DASGUPTA, T., Inorganic Chemistry
DENBOW, C., Medicine
DEVONISH, H., Language, Linguistics and Philosophy
DONOVAN, S., Palaeozoology
DURRANT, F., Library and Information Studies
FLETCHER, P., Clinical Surgery
FORRESTER, T., Tropical Medicine
FREEMAN, B., Ecology
HANCHARD, B., Anatomical Pathology
HICKLING, F., Psychiatry

JACKSON, T., Igneous Petrology
JACOBS, H., Chemistry
JONES, E., Public Administration
LENNARD, J., English and American Literature
LEO-RHYNIE, E., Women and Development Studies
LEWIS, R., Political Thought
MILLER, E., Teacher Education
MORGAN, O., Medicine
MOORE, B., History
MORRIS, M., Creative Writing and West Indian Literature
MORRISON, E., Biochemistry
MUNROE, T., Government and Politics
NETTLEFORD, R. N., Continuing Studies
REICHGELT, J., Computer Science
REID, H., Clinical Haemorheology
ROBINSON, E., Geology
SHIRLEY, G., Management Studies
SPENCER, H., Cardiothoracic Surgery
THOMAS-HOPE, E., Environmental Development
UCHE, C., Sociology and Social Work
WALKER, S., Epidemiology
WARNER-LEWIS, M., African Caribbean Language and Orature
WILKS, R., Epidemiology
WINT, A., International Business
YOUNG, R., Physiology

ATTACHED INSTITUTES

Biotechnology Centre: Dir Prof. M. AHMAD.

Caribbean Institute of Media and Communication: Dir Drs M. DE BRUIN.

Centre for Environment and Development: Dir Prof. A. BINGER.

Centre for Gender and Development Studies: Dir Dr B. BAILEY.

Centre for Management Development: Dir Dr J. COMMA.

Centre for Marine Sciences: Dir Dr G. WARNER.

Chronic Disease Research Centre: Dir Prof. H. FRASER.

Institute of Caribbean Studies: Dir J. PEREIRA.

Institute of Education: Dir J. TUCKER.

International Centre for Environment and Nuclear Sciences: Dir Prof. G. C. LALOR.

Philip Sherlock Centre for Creative Arts: Mona, Kingston 7; f. 1967; term-to-term activity in painting, sculpture, dance, theatre, writing, exhibitions, readings, etc.; acting as the home for ICC Week activities; the mounting of a small Caribbean Arts Festival; Sec. CAROLYN ALLEN.

School of Business: Dir Prof. G. SHIRLEY.

School of Continuing Studies: Mona, Kingston 7; Dir Prof. L. CARRINGTON.

Sir Arthur Lewis Institute for Social and Economic Studies: Mona, Kingston 7; tel. (92) 72409; applied research relating to the Caribbean; Dir Prof. N. DUNCAN (Mona; Dir Prof. A. DOWNES (Cave Hill; Dir Prof. S. RYAN (St. Augustine).

Trade Union Education Institute: Mona, Kingston 7; Dir of Studies Prof. L. CARRINGTON.

Tropical Medicine Research Institute: Mona, Kingston 7; Dir Prof. TERRENCE FORRESTER.

AFFILIATED INSTITUTIONS

Caribbean Institute for Meteorology and Hydrology: Dir Dr COLIN DEPRADINE.

Mico Teachers' College: Dir Dr CLAUDE PACKER.

St John Vianney and the Uganda Martyrs: Dir Rev. MICHAEL DE VERTEUIL.

St Michael's Seminary: Mona, Kingston 7; awards degrees of the Univ. of the West Indies; Director Sr THERESA LOWE CHING.

United Theological College of the West Indies: Mona, Kingston 7; awards degrees and licentiates of the Univ. of the West Indies; Pres. Dr LEWIN WILLIAMS (acting).

College

College of Agriculture, Science and Education: POB 170, Passley Gardens, Port Antonio, Portland; tel. 993-3246; fax 993-2208; internet www.case.edu.jm; f. 1995 by merger of College of Agriculture and Passley Gardens Teachers' College; two-year degree course in all aspects of agriculture; 47 faculty mems; 533 full-time students; 86 part-time; 24 evening; faculties of agriculture, education and science; community college and continuing education programmes; library: 35,000 vols, spec. colln: UN publs, West Indian works, Jamaica Govt publs; Pres. Dr PAUL IVEY (acting); Registrar PATRICIA WRIGHT-CLARKE.

JAPAN

The Higher Education System

Higher education in Japan consists of four categories of institution: universities (daigaku), junior colleges (tanki-daigaku), vocational colleges and technology colleges (koto-senmongakko) and professional graduate schools (the latter since 2003). Institutions are either publicly or privately administered. In 2005 there were 726 universities and graduate schools, with 2.9m. students, and 551 junior and technical colleges, with 278,515 students. Universities offer the full range of undergraduate and postgraduate degrees, and since incorporation in 2004 have become autonomous from the Ministry of Education, Culture, Sports, Science and Technology with regard to decisions about finance, staffing and self-assessment. Junior colleges specialize in two- or three-year Associate Degrees (Jun-Gakushi), credits from which may be accepted towards completion of the university Bachelors degrees. Technology colleges offer five-year training programmes in specialist fields of engineering and technology and professional graduate schools, first established in 2003, offer two-year programmes of study aimed at bridging the gap between formal education and professional experience. The Ministry of Education, Culture, Sports, Science and Technology is responsible for education at all levels, sets the centrally compiled curriculum guidelines and authorizes textbooks. The Japan University Accreditation Association (JUAA) carries out the Certified Evaluation System, whereby all universities are evaluated periodically by a Ministry-approved third party. (The JUAA was originally established in 1947 and had voluntary membership.)

Admission to university is a three-stage process, based on completion of secondary education, results in the Unified First Stage Examination, administered by the National Centre for University Entrance, and each institution's entrance examination. Applicants can only take an institution's entrance examination depending upon their results in the Unified First Stage Examination. The Bachelors (Gakushi) is the under-graduate degree, and is awarded on a 'credit' system following four (or up to six, for some subjects) years of study. Students must accrue at least 124 credits in 'major' and 'minor' subjects. The two-year Associate Degree offered by junior colleges requires a minimum of 62 credits and the three-year Associate Degree 93 credits. The first postgraduate degree is the Masters (Shushui), and is only available at university postgraduate schools (daigaku-in). The Masters is mainly a research-based degree, lasting two years and requiring 30 credits. The Doctorate (Hakushi) is the second postgraduate degree and highest university-level qualification. It is an entirely research-based programme of study, culminating in the submission of a thesis.

Technical and vocational education qualifications include the Special Training School Advanced Course Certificate (Senshu gakko Senmon-ka shuryo shosho), Special Training School Upper Secondary Certificate (Senshu gakko koto-ka sotsugyuo menjo), Technical Associate Degree or Diploma from a Special Training College (Senmonshi) and Vocational Training Certificate or Diploma (awarded by Vocational Training College of the Ministry of Labour).

In 2005 a report entitled The Future of Higher Education in Japan was published. The report identified that as from 2007 university capacity would be at saturation point. It specified a number of goals including increased funding and quality assurance, a review of undergraduate liberal arts education and the introduction of a system for approving new institutions and departments.

The economic downturn since 2009, and Japan's long-term economic problems, may accelerate higher education reforms but not reshape them in any significant way. Reforms include a plan to reduce government funding for national and city-controlled universities, subsidization of private institutions, and a series of targeted programmes—including a university excellence initiative, an evolving quality assurance programme, and an effort to recruit foreign students.

Regulatory and Representative Bodies

GOVERNMENT

Ministry of Education, Culture, Sports, Science and Technology: 3-2-2, Kasumigaseki, Chiyoda-ku, Tokyo 100-8959; tel. (3) 5253-4111; fax (3) 3595-2017; internet www.mext.go.jp; Minister KISABURO TOKAI.

ACCREDITATION

Daigaku Kijun Kyokai (Japan University Accreditation Association): 2-7-13, Ichigaya Sadohara-cho, Sinjuku-ku, Tokyo 162-0842; tel. (3) 5228-2020; fax (3) 5228-2323; internet www.juaa.or.jp; f. 1947; promotes the qualitative improvement of univs in Japan through the voluntary efforts and mutual assistance of mem. univs; Pres. TOYOOMI NAGATA.

Daigaku-hyoka Gakui-juyo Kiko (National Institution for Academic Degrees and University Evaluation (NIAD-UE)): 1-29-1 Gakuen-nishimachi, Kodaira-shi, Tokyo 187-8587; tel. (42) 307-1500; fax (42) 307-1552; e-mail dir-intl@niad.ac.jp; internet www.niad.ac.jp; f. 1991; ind. agency conducting evaluations of teaching and research activities at univs, junior colleges, colleges of technology and inter-univ. research insti-tutes to raise the quality of education and research; awards academic degrees to learners recognized as having fulfilled required academic standards; Pres. SHIN-ICHI HIRANO.

NATIONAL BODIES

Chuo Kyoiku Shingikai (Central Council for Education): Min. of Education, Culture, Sports, Science and Technology, 3-2-2, Kasumigaseki, Chiyoda-ku, Tokyo 100-8959; tel. (3) 5253-4111; internet www.mext.go.jp; f. 1952; advises the Minister; carries out research and considers issues relating to the promotion of education, lifelong learning and sports; has 5 working groups concerned with: education systems, lifelong learning, elementary and lower secondary education, univs, and sports and youth; Chair. MASAKAZU YAMAZAKI.

Kokuritsu Daigaku Kyokai (Japan Association of National Universities): 4F, Nat. Center of Sciences Bldg, 1-2, Hitotsubashi 2-chome, Chiyoda-ku, Tokyo 101-0003; tel. (3) 4212-3506; fax (3) 4212-3509; e-mail info@janu.jp; internet www.janu.jp; Pres. HIROSHI KOMIYAMA.

Kokuritu Kyoiku Seisaku kenkyu Sho (National Institute for Educational Policy Research): 3-2-2 Kasumigaseki, Chiyoda-ku, Tokyo 100-8951; tel. (3) 6733-6833; e-mail info@nier.go.jp; internet www.nier.go.jp; f. 1949; conducts research on specific issues for use in the planning and formulation of educational policy; carries out research into social education; conducts jt int. initiatives (incl. research studies) in the education field; Dir-Gen. SHIGENORI YANO.

Koritsu Daigaku Kyokai (Japan Association of Municipal and Prefectural Colleges and Universities): Toranomon-Yoshiara Bldg, 9th Floor, 1-6-13 Nishi-Shimbashi, Minato-ku, Tokyo 105-0003; tel. (3) 3501-3336; fax (3) 3501-3337; e-mail jimu@kodaikyo.jp; internet www.kodaikyo.jp; f. 1949; 74 mems; Pres. TAKAO KODAMA.

Nihon Shiritsu Daigaku Kyokai (Association of Private Universities of Japan): Shigakukaikan Bekkan 9F, 4-2-25 Kudankita, Chiyoda-ku, Tokyo 102-0073; tel. (3) 3261-7048; fax (3) 3261-0769; e-mail koei@shidaikyo.or.jp; internet www.shidaikyo.or.jp; f. 1946; 384 private univs and colleges; Chair. Dr SUNAO ONUMA; Sec.-Gen. HIDEBUMI KOIDE; publ. Kyoikugakujutsu.

Learned Societies

GENERAL

Nihon Gakujutsu Kaigi (Science Council of Japan): 22–34 Roppongi 7-chome, Minato-ku,

Tokyo 106; tel. (3) 3403-6291; fax (3) 3403-6224; internet www.scj.go.jp; f. 1949; governmental org. coordinating Japan's scientific research; divisions of Agriculture, Commerce and Business Administration, Dentistry and Pharmacology, Economics, Engineering, Law and Political Science, Literature, Medicine, Pedagogy, Philosophy, Psychology, Pure Science, Sociology and History; 210 mems; library: see Libraries and Archives; Pres. Dr ICHIRO KANAZAWA; Sec.-Gen. YASUHIKO NAGA-SHIMA.

Nihon Gakujutsu Shinko-kai (Japan Society for the Promotion of Science): 6 Ichibadncho, Chiyoda-ku, Tokyo 102-8471; tel. (3) 3263-1722; fax (3) 3221-2470; internet www.jsps.go.jp; f. 1932; independent admin. institution and funding agency; administers grants-in-aid for scientific research, research fellowships for young scientists, univ./industry cooperation, scientific outreach, etc.; has cooperative agreements with 82 overseas orgs; operates JSPS overseas offices in 10 cities; 99 mems; Pres. MOTOYUKI ONO; publs *Japanese Scientific Monthly, JSPS Quarterly.*

Nippon Gakushiin (Japan Academy): 7–32 Ueno Park, Taito-ku, Tokyo 110-0007; tel. (3) 3822-2101; fax (3) 3822-2105; e-mail international@japan-acad.go.jp; internet www.japan-acad.go.jp; f. 1879; 150 mems; Pres. Prof. MASAAKI KUBO; Vice-Pres. Prof. TAKASHI SUGIMURA; Section Chair. (Humanities and Social Sciences) Prof. CHIE NAKANE; Section Chair. (Pure and Applied Sciences) Prof. YOSHIHIDE KOZAI; publs *Proceedings* (2 series, 10 a year), *Nippon Gakushiin Kiyo* (3 a year).

AGRICULTURE, FISHERIES AND VETERINARY SCIENCE

Engei Gakkai (Japanese Society for Horticultural Science): Business Center for Academic Societies Japan, 16–9 Honkomagome 5-chome, Bunkyo-ku, Tokyo 113; tel. (3) 5814-5801; fax (3) 5814-5820; f. 1923; 2,795 mems; Pres. ICHIRO KAJIURA; Sec. TADASHI BABA; publ. *Journal* (6 a year).

Nihon Ikushu Gakkai (Japanese Society of Breeding): c/o Faculty of Agriculture, University of Tokyo, Bunkyo-ku, Tokyo 113-8657; tel. (3) 5841-5065; fax (3) 5841-5063; e-mail kishima@abs.agr.hokudai.ac.jp; internet www.nacos.com/jsb/e; f. 1951; 2,300 mems; Pres. ATSUCHI HIRAI; publs *Breeding Science* (4 a year), *Ikushugaku Kenkyu* (4 a year).

Nihon Ju-í Gakkai (Japanese Society of Veterinary Science): Tokyo RS Bldg 8th Fl., 6-26-12 Hongo, Bunkyo-ku, Tokyo 113-0033; tel. (3) 5803-7761; fax (3) 5803-7762; e-mail office@jsvs.or.jp; internet www.soc.nii.ac.jp/jsvs; f. 1885; 4,100 mems; Pres. KUNIO DOI; publ. *The Journal of Veterinary Medical Science* (12 a year).

Nihon Oyo Toshitsu Kagaku Kai (Japanese Society of Applied Glycoscience): c/o National Food Research Institute, 2-1-2 Kannondai, Tsukuba, Ibaraki 305; tel. (298) 38-7991; fax (298) 38-8005; internet www.soc.nii.ac.jp/jsag; f. 1952; 1,147 mems; Pres. YASUHITO TAKEDA; Vice-Pres. HIROKAZU MATSUI, KENJI YAMAMOTO, TAKASHI KURIKI; publ. *Journal of Applied Glycoscience* (4 a year).

Nihon Sanshi Gakkai (Japanese Society of Sericultural Science): c/o Nat. Institute of Agrobiological Sciences, 1-2 Ohwashi, Tsukuba, Ibaraki 305-8634; tel. and fax (29) 838-6056; e-mail jsss@silk.or.jp; internet www.soc.nii.ac.jp/jsss2; f. 1930; 557 mems; Pres. Prof. MICHIHIRO KOBAYASHI; Man. HIDETOSHI TERAMOTO; publs *Journal of Insect Biotechnology and Sericology* (3 a year), *Journal of*

Sericultural Science of Japan (Sanshi Konchu Biotec, 3 a year).

Nippon Seibutsu-Kogaku Kai (Society for Biotechnology, Japan): c/o Faculty of Engineering, Osaka Univ., 2–1 Yamadaoka, Suita, Osaka 565-0871; tel. (6) 6876-2731; fax (6) 6879-2034; e-mail sbbj@bio.eng.osaka-u.ac.jp; internet www.sbj.or.jp; f. 1923; provides training and development opportunities for students and young researchers; 3,500 mems; Pres. Prof. SHINJI IIJIMA; publs *Journal of Bioscience and Bioengineering* (in English, 12 a year), *Seibutsu-kogaku Kaishi* (in Japanese, 12 a year).

Nihon Shinringakkai (Japanese Forestry Society): c/o Japan Forest Technical Association, Rokubancho 7, Chiyoda-ku, Tokyo; tel. and fax (3) 3261-2766; f. 1914; forestry research; 2,900 mems; Pres. KAZUMI KOBAYASHI; publs *Journal* (6 a year), *Shinrin Kagaku* (bulletin, 3 a year).

Nippon Chikusan Gakkai (Japanese Society of Animal Science): 201 Nagatani Corporas, Ikenohata 2-9-4, Taito-ku, Tokyo 110-0008; tel. (3) 3828-8409; fax (3) 3828-7649; e-mail tikusan@blue.ocn.ne.jp; internet www.soc.nii.ac.jp/jszs; f. 1924; animal science; 2,706 mems; Pres. HIDEO YANO; publs *Animal Science Journal* (6 a year), *Nihon Chikusan Gakkaihou* (4 a year).

Nippon Dojo-Hiryo Gakkai (Japanese Society of Soil Science and Plant Nutrition): 26-10-202 Hongo, 6 chome, Bunkyo-ku, Tokyo; tel. (3) 3815-2085; fax (3) 3815-6018; e-mail jssspm@wwwsoc.nii.ac.jp; f. 1914; 2,300 mems; Pres. TADAKATU YONEYAMA; publs *Journal* (6 a year), *Soil Science and Plant Nutrition* (6 a year).

Nippon Nougei Kagaku Kai (Japan Society for Bioscience, Biotechnology and Agrochemistry): 4–16 Yayoi 2-chome, Bunkyo-ku, Tokyo 113-0032; fax (3) 3815-1920; e-mail shomu-b@jsbba.or.jp; internet www.jsbba.or.jp; f. 1924; 12,546 mems; library of 742,010 vols; Pres. Prof. SAKAYU SHIMIZU; publs *Bioscience, Biotechnology and Biochemistry* (in English, 12 a year), *Nippon Nôgeikagaku Kaishi* (in Japanese, 12 a year), *Kagaku To Seibutsu* (in Japanese, 12 a year).

Nippon Sakumotsu Gakkai (Crop Science Society of Japan): 2F Shin-Kyoritsu Bldg, Shinkawa 2-22-4, Chuo-ku,, Tokyo 104-0033; fax (3) 3553-2047; e-mail cssj-jim@bridge.ocn.ne.jp; internet www.soc.nii.ac.jp/cssj; f. 1927; 1,500 mems; Pres. Dr SHIGEMI AKITA; Sec. YUSEKE GOTO; publs *Japanese Journal of Crop Science* (4 a year), *Plant Production Science* (4 a year).

Nippon Shokubutsu-Byori Gakkai (Phytopathological Society of Japan): Shokubo Bldg, Komagome 1-43-11, Toshima-ku, Tokyo 170; tel. (3) 3943-6021; fax (3) 3943-6021; internet www.ppsj.org; f. 1916 to promote research on plant diseases; 1,880 regular mems; Pres. SHINJI TSUYUMU; Vice-Pres. TOMONORI SHIRAISHI; publ. *Journal* (4 a year).

Nippon Suisan Gakkai (Japanese Society of Fisheries Science): c/o Tokyo University of Fisheries, 4-5-7 Konan, Minato-ku, Tokyo 108-8477; tel. (3) 3471-2165; fax (3) 3471-2054; f. 1932; research in fishing science and technology, mariculture, aquaculture, marine environmental science and related fields; 4,879 mems; library of 69 vols; Pres. Prof. T. WATANABE; publs *Fisheries Science* (in English, 6 a year), *Nippon Suisan Gakkaishi* (6 a year).

Nogyokikai Gakkai (Japanese Society of Agricultural Machinery): c/o BRAIN, 1-40-2 Nisshin-cho, Saitama 331-8537; tel. (48) 652-4119; fax (48) 652-4119; e-mail jsam@iam.brain.go.jp; internet www.soc.nii.ac.jp/jsam; f. 1937; 1,500 mems; Pres. TOMOHIKO ICHI-

KAWA; publ. *Journal of the Japanese Society of Agricultural Machinery* (6 a year).

ARCHITECTURE AND TOWN PLANNING

Nihon Zoen Gakkai (Japanese Institute of Landscape Architecture): Zoen Kaikan 6th Fl., 1-20-11 Jinnan, Shibuya-ku, Tokyo 150-0041; tel. (3) 5459-0515; fax (3) 5459-0516; e-mail info@landscapearchitecture.or.jp; internet www.landscapearchitecture.or.jp; f. 1924; 1,800 mems; Pres. AKIRA HOMMA; publ. *Journal.*

Nihon Zosen Gakkai (Japanese Society of Naval Architects and Ocean Engineers):internet www.jasnoe.or.jp; f. 2005 by merger of Society of Naval Architects of Japan, Kansai Society of Naval Architects, Japan, and the West-Japan Society of Naval Architects; publ. *Kanrin.*

Nippon Toshi Keikaku Gakkai (City Planning Institute of Japan): Ichibancho-West Building 6F, Ichibancho 10, Chiyoda-ku, Tokyo 102-0082; tel. (3) 3261-5407; fax (3) 3261-1874; internet wwwsoc.nii.ac.jp/cpij; f. 1951; 5,349 mems; Pres. TAKASHI ONISHI; publ. *City Planning Review* (6 a year).

BIBLIOGRAPHY, LIBRARY SCIENCE AND MUSEOLOGY

Gakujutsu Bunken Fukyu-Kai (Association for Science Documents Information): c/o Tokyo Institute of Technology, 2-12-1 O-okayama, Meguro-ku, Tokyo 152-8550; fax (3) 3726-3118; e-mail gakujyutubunken@mvd.biglobe.ne.jp; f. 1933; Pres. SHU KANBARA; publ. *Reports on Progress in Polymer Physics in Japan* (English, 1 a year).

Information Processing Society of Japan: Kagaku-kaikan (Chemistry Hall) 4F, 1–5 Kanda-Surugadai, Chiyoda-ku, Tokyo 101-0062; tel. (3) 3518-8374; fax (3) 3518-8375; e-mail somu@ipsj.or.jp; internet www.ipsj.or.jp; f. 1960; 30,000 mems; Pres. Dr HAJIME SASAKI; publ. *Journal of Information Processing.*

Joho-Jigyo, Kagaku-Gijutsu Shinko Kiko (S&T Information Services, Japan Science and Technology Agency (JST)y): 5-3 Yonban-cho, Chiyoda-ku, Tokyo 102-0081; tel. (3) 5214-8402; fax (3) 5214-8400; e-mail sti@jst.go.jp; internet sti.jst.go.jp; f. 1957; an integrated org. of S&T; prepares abstracts, online and manual search services, translation and photo-duplication service, library service, computer processing; 470 mems; Pres. K. KITAZAWA; publs *Current Bibliography on Science and Technology* (Abstracts from about 16,200 journals, 12 series), *Journal of Information Processing and Management* (12 a year), *Current Science and Technology Research in Japan* (in English and Japanese), *JST Thesaurus*, *JST Holding List of Serials and Proceedings* (online).

Joho Kagaku Gijutsu Kyokai (Information Science and Technology Association): Sasaki Bldg, 5–7 Koisikawa 2, Bunkyo-ku, Tokyo 112; tel. (3) 3813-3791; fax (3) 3813-3793; e-mail infosta@infosta.or.jp; internet www.infosta.or.jp; f. 1950; 2,020 mems; Pres. T. GONDOH; publ. *Journal* (1 a year).

Nihon Hakubutsukan Kyokai (Japanese Association of Museums): Shoyu-Kaikan 3-3-1, Kasumigaseki, Chiyoda-ku, Tokyo 100-8925; tel. (3) 3591-7190; fax (3) 3591-7170; e-mail webmaster@j-muse.or.jp; internet www.j-muse.or.jp; f. 1928; Gen. Man. YOKO NIIZUMA; 1,330 mems; publ. *Museum Studies* (12 a year).

Nihon Toshokan Kyokai (Japan Library Association): 1-11-14, Shinkawa, Chuo-ku, Tokyo 104-0033; tel. (3) 3523-0811; fax (3) 3523-0841; e-mail info@jla.or.jp; internet www.jla.or.jp; f. 1892; all aspects of library development; 8,900 mems; library of 10,000 vols; Sec.-Gen. KATSURA YOKOYAMA; publs *Gendai no Toshokan* (4 a year), *Nihon no Sankotosho Shikiban* (4 a year), *Nihon no Toshokan* (1 a year), *Toshokan Nenkan* (1 a year), *Toshokan Zasshi* (12 a year).

Nippon Toshokan Joho Gakkai (Japan Society of Library and Information Science): c/o Graduate School of Library and Information Science, Univ. of Tsukuba, 1–2 Kasuga, Tsukuba-shi, Ibaraki-ken 305-8550; fax (29) 859-1380; e-mail jslis-info@slis.tsukuba.ac .jp; internet www.soc.nii.ac.jp/jslis; f. 1953; 750 mems; Pres. SHUICHI UEDA; Sec. YUKO YOSHIDA; publ. *Journal* (4 a year).

ECONOMICS, LAW AND POLITICS

Aziya Seikei Gakkai (Japan Association for Asian Studies): c/o Ochanomizu University, 2-1-1 Otsuka, Bunkyo-ku, 112-8610; tel. 5976-1478; e-mail jaas-info@ npo-ochanomizu.org; internet www.jaas.or .jp; f. 1953; 900 mems; Pres. SATOSHI AMAKO; publ. *Aziya Kenkyu* (Asian Studies, 4 a year).

Hikaku-ho Gakkai (Japan Society of Comparative Law): c/o Faculty of Law, Tokyo University, Hongo, Bunkyo-ku, Tokyo 113; internet www.soc.nii.ac.jp/jscl; f. 1950; studies in comparative law; holds conferences; issues publications; 780 mems; Pres. H. TANAKA; publ. *Hikakuhô Kenkyû* (Comparative Law Journal, 1 a year).

Hogaku Kyokai (Jurisprudence Association): Faculty of Law, University of Tokyo, Hongo, Bunkyo-ku, Tokyo; tel. (3) 3812-2111; f. 1884; 600 mems; Pres. TAKESHI SASAKI; publs *Hogaku Kyokai Zasshi, Journal*.

Hosei-shi Gakkai (Japan Legal History Association): Kyoto University, Yoshida-hommachi, Sakyo-ku, Kyoto 606-8501; tel. (75) 753-3235; fax (75) 753-3290; e-mail jalha@wwwsoc.nii.ac.jp; internet www.soc .nii.ac.jp/jalha; f. 1949; 495 mems; Pres. S. KOYAMA; publ. *Legal History Review* (1 a year).

Hosokai (Lawyers' Association): 1, 1-chome, Kasumigaseki, Chiyoda-ku, Tokyo; tel. (3) 3581-2146; internet www.hosokai.or.jp; f. 1891; 20,000 mems; library of 30,000 vols; Pres. RYOHACHI KUSABA; Dir ISAO IMAI; publ. *Hoso Jiho.*

Japan Institute of International Affairs: 11th Fl., Kasumigaseki Bldg, 3-2-5 Kasumigaseki, Chiyodaku, Tokyo 100-6011; tel. (3) 3503-7261; fax (3) 3503-7292; e-mail jiiajoho@jiia.or.jp; internet www.jiia.or.jp; f. 1956; 512 mems; Pres. YOSHIJI NOGAMI; Exec. Dir TOSHIYUKI FUJIWARA; publ. *Kokusai Mondai* (International Relations, in Japanese, 4 a year).

Japan Institute of Public Finance: c/o Institute of Statistical Research, Japan Life Insurance Bldg 7th fl., 1-18-16 Shinbashi Minatoku, Tokyo 105-0004; tel. (3) 3591-8496; fax (3) 3595-2220; e-mail zaisei@isr.or .jp; internet wwwsoc.nii.ac.jp/jipf; f. 1940 as Japanese Association of Fiscal Science; 1,000 mems; publ. *Zaisei Kenkyu* (1 a year).

Keizai Riron Gakkai (Japan Society of Political Economy): Faculty of Economics, Rikkyo University, 3 Ikebukuro, Toshima-ku, Tokyo; internet www.jspe.gr.jp; f. 1959; 865 mems; Pres. H. OOUCHI; publ. *Political Economy Quarterly.*

Keizaigaku-shi Gakkai (Japan Society for the History of Economic Thought): Dept of Economics, Tohoku University, Kawauchi, Sendai; tel. (22) 217-6275; fax (22) 217-6231; e-mail mawatari@econ.tohoku.ac.jp; internet society.cpm.ehime-u.ac.jp/shet/shet .html; f. 1949; 810 mems; Pres. SHOHKEN MAWATARI; publ. *History of Economic Thought, Society Newsletter.*

Kokusaiho Gakkai (Association of International Law): Faculty of Law, Univ. of Tokyo, Hongo, Bunkyo-ku, Tokyo; tel. (3) 3812-2111; f. 1897; 804 mems; Pres. M. OTSUKA; publs *Kokusaiho Gaiko Zasshi, Journal of International Law and Diplomacy.*

Labour Lawyers Association of Japan: 4F Sohyo-Kaikan, 3-2-11 Kanda-Surugadai Chiyoda-ku, Tokyo; tel. (3) 3251-5363; fax (3) 3258-6790; f. 1957; 1,400 mems; publ. *Rodosha no Kenri* (Workers' Rights, 4 a year).

Nichibei Hougakukai (Japanese American Society for Legal Studies): c/o Faculty of Law, Univ. of Tokyo, Hongo, Bunkyo-ku, Tokyo 113-0033; f. 1964; seeks and develops mutual understanding of Japanese and American law and legal scholarship, especially through cooperation of members of the legal profession; 800 mems; Dir M. OTSUKA; publ. *Amerika Hō* (Law in the USA, 2 a year).

Nihon Keizai Gakkai (Japanese Economics Association): c/o The Institute of Statistical Research, 1-18-16 Shimbashi, Minato-ku, Tokyo 105-0004; tel. (3) 3591-8496; fax (3) 3595-2220; internet www.jeaweb.org; f. 1934; 3,063 mems; Pres. TAKENORI INOKI; publ. *Japanese Economic Review* (4 a year).

Nihon Kinyu Gakkai (Japan Society of Monetary Economics): 1-2-1 Nihonbashi Hongokucho, Chuo-ku, Tokyo; tel. (3) 3231-1372; fax (3) 3241-3649; e-mail jsme@d8.dion .ne.jp; internet www.soc.nii.ac.jp/jsme; f. 1943; 1,318 mems; Pres. Prof. YOSHIRO TSUTSUI; publ. *Review of Monetary and Financial Studies* (2 a year).

Nihon Koho Gakkai (Japan Public Law Association): Univ. of Tokyo, 7-3-1 Hongo, Bunkyo-ku, Tokyo; f. 1948; 1,200 mems; Pres. K. TAKAHASHI; publ. *Koho-Kenkyu* (Public Law Review, 1 a year).

Nihon Minji Soshoho Gakkai (Japan Association of Civil Procedure Law): c/o Faculty of Law, Osaka City University, 3-3-138 Sugimoto, Sumiyoshi-ku, Osaka; tel. (6) 6605-2327; fax (6) 6605-2920; f. 1949; 815 mems; Pres. H. MATSUMOTO; publ. *Journal of Civil Procedure* (1 a year).

Nihon Tokei Gakkai (Japan Statistical Society): c/o SINFONICA, Nohgakushorin Bldg 5F, 3-6 Kanda Jimboucho Chiyoda-ku, Tokyo 101-0051; tel. (3) 3234-7738; fax (3) 3234-7738; internet www.jss.gr.jp; f. 1931; 1,312 mems; Pres. Prof. YASUTO YOSHIZOE; Pres. Prof. MANABU IWASAKI; publ. *Journal* (2 a year).

Nippon Hoshakai Gakkai (Japan Association of Sociology of Law): University of Tokyo, Hongo, Bunkyo-ku, Tokyo; internet wwwsoc.nii.ac.jp/hosha; f. 1947; 805 mems; Pres. N. TOSHITANI; publ. *Sociology of Law* (1 a year).

Nippon Hotetsu-Gakkai (Japan Association of Legal Philosophy): Chiba University, Faculty of Law and Economics, 1-33, Yayoi-cho, Inage-ku, Chiba-shi, Chiba 263-8522; tel. (43) 290-2362; fax (43) 290-2362; e-mail jalp@wwwsoc.nii.ac.jp; internet wwwsoc.nii .ac.jp/jalp; f. 1948; 486 mems; Pres. Prof. ITARU SHIMAZU; publ. *The Annals of Legal Philosophy.*

Nippon Keiei Gakkai (Japan Society of Business Administration): Hitotsubashi Univ., 2-1 Naka, Kunitachi, Tokyo 186-8601; tel. (42) 580-8571; internet www.soc .nii.ac.jp/jsba; f. 1926; 2,193 mems; Pres. A. SAKASHITA; publs *Annual Review of Business Administration, Journal of Business Management.*

Nippon Keiho Gakkai (Criminal Law Society of Japan): University of Tokyo, Hongo,

Bunkyo-ku, Tokyo; f. 1949; 1,000 mems; Pres. K. SHIBAHARA; publ. *Journal* (4 a year).

Nippon Keizai Seisaku Gakkai (Japan Economic Policy Association): School of Political Science and Economics, Waseda University, 1-6-1 Nishiwaseda, Shinjuku-ku, Tokyo 169-8050; tel. (3) 5286-2193; fax (3) 5286-2193; e-mail jepa-mail@list.waseda.jp; internet wwwsoc.nii.ac.jp/jepa; f. 1940; 1,150 mems; Pres. Prof. YASUMI MATSUMOTO; publ. *International Economic Policy Studies.*

Nippon Seizi Gakkai (Japanese Political Science Association): Faculty of Law, Rikkyo University, 3-34-1, Nishi-Ikebukuro, Toshima-ku, Tokyo 171; fax (3) 3705-4530; e-mail ykobayas@hs.catv.ne.jp; internet www.soc.nii.ac.jp/jpsa2; 820 mems; Sec.-Gen. Dr YOSHIAKI KOBAYASHI; publ. *Annals* (1 a year).

Nippon Shogyo Gakkai (Japan Society of Commercial Sciences): Meiji University, Surugadai Kanda, Chiyoda-ku, Tokyo; f. 1951; 980 mems; Pres. K. FUKUDA.

Private International Law Association: Chuo University Faculty of Law, 742-1 HIgashinakano Hachioji-shi, Tokyo 192-0393; tel. (42) 674-3154; fax (42) 674-3133; f. 1949; 244 mems; Pres. KORESUKE YAMAUCHI.

Tokyo Daigaku Keizai Gakkai (Society of Economics): Faculty of Econ., Univ. of Tokyo, 7-3-1 Hongo, Bunkyo-ku, Tokyo 113-0033; f. 1922; 200 mems; Pres. HIROSHI YOSHIRAWA; publ. *Journal of Economics* (4 a year).

EDUCATION

Asia–Pacific Cultural Centre for UNESCO (ACCU): 6 Fukuromachi, Shinjuku-ku, Tokyo 162-8484; tel. (3) 3269-4435; fax (3) 3269-4510; e-mail general@accu.or.jp; internet www.accu.or.jp; f. 1971; adult learning materials, children's books, literacy materials development, music, personnel exchange programmes, photo contest, protection of cultural heritage, training programmes and other regional cultural activities; library of 29,000 vols; Pres. KAZUO SUZUKI; Dir-Gen. KOJI NAKANISHI; publs *Activity Report* (1 a year), *ACCU News* (Japanese, 6 a year), *Asian / Pacific Book Development* (English, 4 a year).

Nihon Gakko-hoken Gakkai (Japanese Association of School Health): Dept of Health Education, Faculty of Education, University of Tokyo, Hongo 7-3-1, Bunkyo-ku, Tokyo 113; tel. (3) 3812-2111; fax (3) 5991-3741; e-mail jash@shobix.co.jp; internet www.soc .nii.ac.jp/jash; f. 1954; 1,500 mems; Pres. ATSUHISA EGUCHI; publ. *Gakko-hoken Kenkyu* (Japanese Journal of School Health, 12 a year).

Nihon Hikaku Kyoiku Gakkai (Japan Comparative Education Society): c/o Dept of Education, Graduate School of Human Environment Studies, Kyushu University, 6-19-1, Hakozaki, Higashi-ku, Fukuoka City, Fukuoka Prefecture 812-8581; tel. and fax (92) 632-8426; f. 1965; 905 mems; Pres. K. MOCHIDA; Sec.-Gen. H. TAKEKUMA; publs *Comparative Education* (2 a year), *Newsletter* (2 a year).

Nihon Kyoiku Gakkai (Japanese Educational Research Association): 2-29-3-3F Hongo, Bunkyo-ku, Tokyo 113-0033; tel. (3) 3818-2505; fax (3) 3816-6898; e-mail jsse@ oak.ocn.ne.jp; f. 1941; 3,300 mems; Pres. MANABU SATO; publ. *The Japanese Journal of Educational Research* (4 a year).

Nihon Kyoiku-shakai Gakkai (Japan Society of Educational Sociology): Faculty of Education, University of Tokyo, Hongo 7-3-1, Bunkyo-ku, Tokyo 113; tel. (3) 5800-6813; fax (3) 5800-6814; e-mail jses2@wwwsoc.nii.ac

.jp; internet www.soc.nii.ac.jp/jses2; f. 1949; 1,200 mems; Pres. HIDENORI FUJITA; publ. *Journal of Educational Sociology* (2 a year).

Nihon Kyoiku-shinri Gakkai (Japanese Association of Educational Psychology): Yaguchi Bldg, 5th Fl., Hongo 2-11-7, Bunkyo-ku, Tokyo 113-0033; tel. (3) 3818-1534; fax (3) 3818-1575; internet www.soc.nii.ac.jp/jaep; f. 1952; 7,300 mems; Pres. YUJI MORO; publ. *Japanese Journal of Educational Psychology* (4 a year).

Nippon Kagaku Kyoiku Gakkai (Japan Society for Science Education): c/o Nakanishi Printing Co. Ltd., Shimotachiuri Ogawa-Higashi, Kamikyo-ku, Kyoto 602 8048; tel. (75) 41-53-661; fax (75) 41-53-662; e-mail jsse@nacos.com; internet www.jsse.jp; f. 1977; science and mathematics education and educational technology; 1,200 mems; Pres. J. YOSHIDA; publs *Journal* (4 a year), *Letter* (6 a year), *Proceedings of Annual Meeting*.

Nippon Sugaku Kyoiku Gakkai (Japan Society of Mathematical Education): POB 18, Koishikawa, Tokyo 112-8691; tel. (3) 3946-2267; fax (3) 3946-3736; internet www.sme.or.jp; f. 1919; 3,334 mems; Pres. Prof. T. SAWADA; publs *Journal* (12 a year), *Supplementary issue* (report on mathematical education, 2 a year), *Yearbook* (1 a year).

Nippon Taiiku Gakkai (Japanese Society of Physical Education, Health and Sport Sciences): Kishi Memorial Hall (Rm 508), Jinnan 1-1-1, Shibuya-ku, Tokyo 150; tel. (3) 3481-2427; fax (3) 3481-2428; internet www.soc.nii.ac.jp/jspe3; f. 1950; 6,752 mems; Pres. Dr JUJIRO NARITA; publ. *Int. Journal of Sport and Health Science* (4 a year).

FINE AND PERFORMING ARTS

Bijutsu-shi Gakkai (Japanese Art History Society): c/o Tokyo National Research Institute of Cultural Properties, 13–27 Ueno Park, Taito-ku, Tokyo 110; internet www.soc.nii.ac.jp/jahs2; f. 1949; 2,300 mems; publ. *Journal* (4 a year).

Nihon Engeki Gakkai (Japanese Society for Theatre Research): Waseda University, 1-6-1 Nishi-Waseda, Shinjuku-ku, Tokyo 169-8050; tel. (3) 3203-4141; f. 1949; Pres. T. MORI.

Nippon Ongaku Gakkai (Musicological Society of Japan): 3-3-3-201 Iidabashi, Chiyoda-ku, 102-0072 Tokyo; tel. (3) 3288-5616; f. 1952; 1,350 mems; Pres. T. ISOYAMA; publ. *Ongaku Gaku* (Journal, 3 a year).

HISTORY, GEOGRAPHY AND ARCHAEOLOGY

Keizai Chiri Gakkai (Japan Association of Economic Geographers): Institute of Economic Geography, Faculty of Economics, East Bldg, Hitotsubashi University, Naka 2-1, Kunitachi-shi, Tokyo 186; tel. (425) 72-1101, ext 5374; fax (425) 71-1893; internet wwwsoc.nii.ac.jp/jaeg; f. 1954; 700 mems; Pres. K. TAKEUCHI; publ. *Annals* (4 a year).

Nihon Kokogakkai (Archaeological Society of Japan): c/o Tokyo National Museum, Ueno Park, Taito-ku, Tokyo; f. 1895; 2,200 mems; Pres. Dr FUJITA KUNIO; publ. *Kokogaku Zasshi* (4 a year).

Nippon Kokogaku Kyokai (Japanese Archaeological Association): 5-15-5, Hirai, Edogawa-ku, Tokyo 132-0035; tel. (3) 3618-6608; fax (3) 3618-6625; internet www.soc.nii.ac.jp/jaa2; f. 1948; 4,072 mems; library of 37,790 vols; Pres. TADASHI NISHTANI; publ. *Nihon Kōkogaku* (journal).

Nippon Oriento Gakkai (Society for Near Eastern Studies in Japan): Tokyo-Tenrikyokan 9, 1-chome 9, Kanda Nishiki-cho, Chiyoda-ku, Tokyo 101-0054; tel. (3) 3291-

7519; fax (3) 3291-7519; f. 1954; 800 mems; Pres. KOJI KAMIOKA; publs *Oriento* (in Japanese, 2 a year), *Orient* (in European languages, 1 a year).

Nippon Seibutsuchiri Gakkai (Biogeographical Society of Japan): c/o Prof. Dr S. Sakai, 2-26-12 Sendagi, Bunkyo-ku, Tokyo 113; tel. (3) 3828-0445; fax (3) 3828-0445; e-mail qyv04336@nifty.ne.jp; internet wwwsoc.nii.ac.jp/tbsj; f. 1928; 300 mems; Pres. Prof. Dr SEIROKU SAKAI; publs *Bulletin, Biogeographica, Fauna Japonica*.

Nippon Seiyoshigakukai (Japanese Society of Western History): Dept of Western History, Graduate School of Letters, Osaka Univ., 1–5 Machikaneyama-cho, Toyonaka, Osaka 560-8532; tel. (6) 6850-5105; fax (6) 6850-5105; e-mail seiyousihgaku@mti.biglobe.ne.jp; f. 1948; 880 mems; Pres. Prof. A. EGAWA; publ. *Studies in Western History* (4 a year).

Shigaku-kai (Historical Society of Japan): University of Tokyo, Hongo, Bunkyo-ku, Tokyo 113; f. 1889; c. 2,470 mems; Pres. OSAMU NARUSE; publ. *Shigaku-Zasshi* (Historical Journal of Japan).

Tokyo Chigaku Kyokai (Tokyo Geographical Society): 12–2 Nibancho, Chiyoda-ku, Tokyo 102-0084; tel. (3) 3261-0809; fax (3) 3263-0257; e-mail chigaku@abox9.so-net.ne.jp; internet www.soc.nii.ac.jp/tokyogeo; f. 1879; 810 mems; Pres. ISAMU KOBAYASHI; publ. *Journal of Geography* (6 a year, and 1 special issue a year).

Toyoshi-Kenkyu-Kai (Society of Oriental Researches): Kyoto University, Sakyo-ku, Kyoto City; tel. (75) 753-2790; internet wwwsoc.nii.ac.jp/toyoshi/index.html; f. 1935; 1,400 mems; Pres. I. MIYAZAKI; publ. *Toyoshi-Kenkyu* (Journal of Oriental Researches, 4 a year).

LANGUAGE AND LITERATURE

Alliance Française: Imamura Bldg, 9th Fl., 2-2-11 Tenjinbashi, Kita-Ku, Osaka 530-0041; tel. (6) 358-7391; fax (6) 358-7393; e-mail info@calosa.com; internet www.calosa.com; offers courses and examinations in French language and culture and promotes cultural exchange with France; attached teaching centres in Nagoya, Sapporo, Sendai and Tokushima; Dir ERIC GALMARD.

British Council: 1–2 Kagurazaka, Shinjuku-ku, Tokyo 162-0825; tel. (3) 3235-8031; fax (3) 3235-8040; e-mail enquiries@britishcouncil.or.jp; internet www.britishcouncil.org/japan; teaching centre; offers courses and examinations in English language and British culture and promotes cultural exchange with the UK; attached teaching centres in Kyoto, Nagoya and Osaka; Dir, Japan JOANNA BURKE.

Goethe-Institut: Doitsu Bunka Kaikan, 7-5-56 Akasaka, Minato-ku, Tokyo 107-0052; tel. (3) 3584-3201; fax (3) 3586-3069; e-mail info@tokyo.goethe.org; internet www.goethe.de/os/tok/deindex.htm; offers courses and examinations in German language and culture and promotes cultural exchange with Germany; attached centres in Kyoto and Osaka; library of 10,000 vols, 40 periodicals; Dir RAIMUND WOERDEMANN.

Japan Comparative Literature Association: Aoyamagakuin University, Shibuya-ku, Tokyo; tel. (3) 5421-3238; fax (3) 5421-3238; internet wwwsoc.nii.ac.jp/jcla; f. 1948; 400 mems; Pres. KEN INOUE; Sec.-Gen. Prof. TAKASHI ARIMITSU; publ. *Journal* (1 a year).

Japanese Centre of International PEN: 20-3 Kabuto-cho, Nihonbashi, Chuo-ku, Tokyo 103-0026; e-mail secretariat01@

japanpen.or.jp; internet www.japanpen.or.jp; f. 1935; Pres. KAZUNARI YOSHIZAWA.

Kokugogakkai (Society for the Study of Japanese Language): Faculty of Letters, University of Tokyo, Hongo, Bunkyo-ku, Tokyo 113; fax 5802-0615; e-mail office@jpling.gr.jp; internet wwwsoc.nii.ac.jp/jpling; f. 1944; 1,500 mems; Pres. ETSUTARO IWABUCHI; publ. *Studies in the Japanese Language* (4 a year).

Manyo Gakkai (Society for Manyo Studies): 3-3-138 Sugimotocho Sumiyoshiku, Osaka 558-0022; tel. (6) 6605-2414; f. 1951; 810 mems; publ. *The Manyo* (4 a year).

Nihon Dokubungakkai (Japanese Society of German Literature): c/o Ikubundo, Hongo 5-30-21, Bunkyo-ku, Tokyo 113-0033; tel. (3) 3813-5861; fax (3) 3813-5861; e-mail jgg@tokyo.email.ne.jp; internet wwwsoc.nii.ac.jp/jgg; f. 1947; 2,600 mems; Pres. Prof. TERUAKI TAKAHASHI; publs *Doitsu Bungaku / German Literature* (2 a year), *Doitsugo Kyoiku / Deutschunterricht in Japan* (1 a year).

Nihon Eibungakkai (English Literary Society of Japan): 501 Kenkyusha Bldg, 9 Surugadai 2-chome, Kanda, Chiyoda-ku, Tokyo 101-0062; tel. (3) 3293-7528; fax (3) 3293-7539; e-mail ejimu@elsj.org; internet www.elsj.org; f. 1928; 4,000 mems; Pres. YOSHIYUKI FUJIKAWA; publ. *Studies in English Literature* (3 a year).

Nihon Esperanto Gakkai (Japan Esperanto Institute): Waseda-mati 12-3, Sinzyuku-ku, Tokyo 162-0042; tel. (3) 3203-4581; fax (3) 3203-4582; e-mail chb71944@biglobe.ne.jp; f. 1919; 1,435 mems; linguistics; Pres. YAMASAKI SEIKŌ; Sec. ISINO YOSIO; publ. *La Revuo Orienta* (12 a year).

Nihon Gengogakkai (Linguistic Society of Japan): Shimotachiuri Ogawa Higashi, Kami Kyoku, Kyoto 602-8048; tel. (75) 415-3661; fax (75) 415-3662; e-mail lsj@nacos.com; internet www.tooyoo.l.u-tokyo.ac.jp/~lsj/jap; f. 1938; 2,050 mems; publ. *Gengo Kenkyu* (Journal, 2 a year).

Nippon Onsei Gakkai (Phonetic Society of Japan): National Institute for Japanese Language 10-2 Midori-cho, Tachikawa, Tokyo 190-8561; tel. (42) 540-4515; fax (42) 540-4524; e-mail psj@nacos.com; internet www.psj.gr.jp; f. 1926; study of sound phenomena of human speech; 780 mems; library of 30,000 vols; Pres. SHOSUKE HARAGUCHI; publ. *Journal* (3 a year).

Nippon Seiyo Koten Gakkai (Classical Society of Japan): Dept of Classics, Faculty of Letters, Kyoto Univ., Kyoto 606-8501; tel. (75) 753-2767; e-mail hiroyuki.takahashi@bun.kyoto-u.ac.jp; internet www.bun.kyoto-u.ac.jp/classics/csj/csj.html; f. 1950; 500 mems; Pres. KATSUTOSHI UCHIYAMA; Sec. HIROYUKI TAKAHASHI; publ. *Journal of Classical Studies* (1 a year).

MEDICINE

Japanese Society for the Study of Pain: Department of Anaesthesiology, Nihon University School of Medicine, 30-1, Oyaguchi-kamicho, Itabashi-ku, Tokyo 173-8610; tel. (3) 3972-8111; fax (3) 5917-4766; e-mail s-ogawa@med.nihon-u.ac.jp; f. 1973; research into pain mechanism and pain management; 698 mems; Pres. Prof. K. IWATA; publ. *Pain Research* (4 a year).

Nihon Eisei Gakkai (Japanese Society for Hygiene): Osaka University, Graduate School of Medicine, Dept of Social and Environmental Medicine, 2-2 Yamada-oka, Suita, Osaka 565-0871; tel. (6) 6879-3928; fax (6) 6879-3928; internet www.nacos.com/jsh; f. 1929; 2,750 mems; Pres. Prof. KANEHISA MORIMOTO; publs *Environmental Health and Preventive Medicine* (in English, 4 a year),

Japanese Journal of Hygiene (in Japanese, 4 a year).

Nihon Hinyokika Gakki: (Japanese Urological Association); Saito Bldg, 5F, 2-17-15 Yushima, Bunkyo-ku, Tokyo 113-0034; f. 1912; 7,200 mems; Pres. Prof. AKIHIKO OKUYAMA; publs *International Journal of Urology* (12 a year), *Japanese Journal of Urology* (6 a year).

Nihon Hotetsu Shika Gakkai (Japan Prosthodontic Society): 1-43-9 Komagome, Toshima-ku, Tokyo; tel. (3) 5940-5451; fax (3) 5940-5630; e-mail hotetsu-gakkai01@max .odn.ne.jp; internet www.hotetsu.com; f. 1931; meetings, confs, seminars; researches on new prosthodontics; liaisons with other prosthodontic societies worldwide; 6,611 mems; Pres. Prof. KEIICHI SASAKI; Vice-Pres. and Pres. Elect KIYOSHI KOYANO; Vice-Pres. YOSHINOBU TANAKA; Gen. Affairs HIDEO MAT-SUMURA; publs *Journal of Prosthodontic Research* (4 a year), *Nihon Hotetsu Shika Gakkai zasshi* (Journal of Japan Prosthodontic Society, 4 a year).

Nihon Ishi-Kai (Japan Medical Association): Bunkyo-ku, Tokyo 113; f. 1916; 121,514 mems; Pres. Y. KARASAWA; publs *Japan Medical Association Journal* (in English, 6 a year), *Journal* (in Japanese, 12 a year).

Nihon Junkanki Gakkai (Japanese Circulation Society): Kinki Invention Center, 14 Yoshida Kawahara-cho, Sakyo-ku, Kyoto 606-8305; tel. (75) 751-8643; fax (75) 771-3060; e-mail admin@j-circ.or.jp; internet www.j-circ.or.jp; f. 1935; cardiology; 21,096 mems; Chief Dir AKIRA TAKESHITA; publs *Circulation Journal* (in English, 12 a year; supplement in Japanese, 3 a year), *Journal of Board of Certified Members of the Japanese Circulation Society* (in Japanese, 2 a year).

Nihon Kakuigakukai (Japanese Society of Nuclear Medicine): c/o Japan Radioisotope Association, 2-28-45 Honkomagome, Bunkyo-ku, Tokyo 113-0021; tel. (3) 3947-0976; fax (3) 3947-2535; e-mail anm@xvg.biglobe.ne.jp; internet www.jsnm.org; f. 1963; 3,500 mems; Pres. Dr NAGARA TAMAKI; publs *Annals of Nuclear Medicine* (10 a year), *Japanese Journal of Nuclear Medicine* (4 a year).

Nihon Koku Eisei Gakkai (Japanese Society for Dental Health): c/o Koku Hoken Kyokai 43-9, Komagome 1-chome Toshima-ku, Tokyo 170-0003; tel. (3) 3947-8891; fax (3) 3947-8341; internet www.kokuhoken.or.jp/jsdh; f. 1952; 2,500 mems; Pres. M. YONE-MITSU; publ. *Journal* (4 a year).

Nihon Koku Geka Gakkai (Japanese Society of Oral and Maxillofacial Surgeons): Seven-Ster Mansion Takanawa (2nd floor), 20-26-202 Takanawa 2-chome, Minato-Ku, Tokyo; tel. (3) 5791-1791; fax (3) 5791-1792; internet www.jsoms.org; f. 1952; 8,500 mems; Gen. Sec. Dr KAN-ICHI SETO; publ. *Japanese Journal of Oral and Maxillofacial Surgery* (12 a year).

Nihon Kokuka Gakkai (Japanese Stomatological Society): Department of Oral Surgery, School of Medicine, University of Tokyo, 7-3-1 Hongo, Bunkyo-ku, Tokyo 113-8549; tel. (3) 5803-5400; fax (3) 5803-0101; f. 1947; 3,600 mems; Dir ICHIRO YAMASHITA; publ. *Journal* (4 a year).

Nihon Kyosei Shikagakkai (Japan Orthodontic Society): c/o Koku Hoken Kyokai, 1-44-2 Komagome, Toshima-ku, Tokyo 170-0003; tel. (3) 3947-8891; fax (3) 3947-8841; e-mail info@jos.gr.jp; internet www.jos.gr.jp; f. 1932; 4,200 mems; Pres. Dr KUNIMICHI SOMA; publ. *Orthodontic Waves* (in English and Japanese, 6 a year).

Nihon Masuika Gakkai (Japan Society of Anaesthesiologists): TY Bldg 6F, 18-11 Hongo 3-chome, Bunkyo-ku, Tokyo 113-0033; tel. (3) 3815-0590; fax (3) 3814-0464; internet www.anesth.or.jp; f. 1954; 8,677 mems; Pres. K. HANAOKA; Sec. Y. SHIMIDA; publs *Masui* (12 a year), *Journal of Anaesthesia* (4 a year).

Nihon Naika Gakkai (Japanese Society of Internal Medicine): 28–8, 3-chome, Bunkyo-ku, Tokyo 113-8433; fax (3) 3818-1556; e-mail iminfo@naika.or.jp; internet www.naika.or .jp; f. 1903; 73,000 mems; Chief Dir ICHIRO KANAZAWA; publs *Internal Medicine* (in Japanese, 12 a year), *Internal Medicine* (in English, 12 a year).

Nihon No-Shinkei Geka Gakkai (Japan Neurosurgical Society): Ishikawa Bldg 4F, 5-25-16 Hongo, Bunkyo-ku, Tokyo; tel. (3) 3812-6226; fax (3) 3812-2090; e-mail jns@ss .iij4u.or.jp; internet jns.umin.ac.jp; f. 1948; 8,088 mems; Chair. TAKASHI YOSHIMOTO; publ. *Neurologia Medico-Chirurgica* (in English, 12 a year).

Nihon Ronen Igakukai (Japan Geriatrics Society): Kyorin Bldg No 702, 4-2-1 Yushima, Bunkyo-ku, Tokyo 113; internet www .jpn-geriat-soc.or.jp; f. 1959; 4,500 mems; Chair. Prof. H. ORIMO; publ. *Japan Journal of Geriatrics* (6 a year).

Nihon Seishin Shinkei Gakkai (Japanese Society of Psychiatry and Neurology): Wing Bldg 52, 5-25-18 Hongo, Bunkyo-ku, Tokyo 113-0033; tel. (3) 3814-2991; fax (3) 3814-2992; e-mail info@jspn.or.jp; internet www .jspn.or.jp; 8,200 mems; Pres. Dr TAKUYA KOJIMA; publ. *Seishin Shinkeigaku Zasshi* (in Japanese,12 a year).

Nihon Shika Hoshasen Gakkai (Japanese Society for Oral and Maxillofacial Radiology): c/o Hitotsubashi Printing Co. Ltd, Gakkai Business Center, 2-4-11 Fukagawa, Koutou-ku, Tokyo 135-0033; tel. (3) 5620-1953; fax (3) 5620-1960; e-mail tsuchimochi@ngt.ndu.ac .jp; f. 1951; 1,200 mems; Sec.-Gen. S. KANDA; publs *Dental Radiology* (in Japanese, 4 a year), *Oral Radiology* (in English, 2 a year).

Nihon Shika Igakkai (Japanese Association for Dental Science): 4-1-20 Kudankita, Chiyoda-ku, Tokyo; tel. (3) 3262-9214; fax (3) 3262-9885; internet www.jads.jp; f. 1949; 94,000 mems; 14 mem. socs; Pres. Prof. K. ETO; publs *Dentistry in Japan* (1 a year), *Japanese Dental Science Review* (2 a year).

Nihon Shokaki-byo Gakkai (Japanese Society of Gastroenterology): Ginza Orient Bldg, 8F, Ginza 8-9-13, Chuo-ku, Tokyo; tel. (3) 3573-4297; fax (3) 3289-2359; e-mail info@ jsge.or.jp; internet www.jsge.or.jp; f. 1898; 25,000 mems; Pres. KENJI FUJIWARA; publs *Journal of Gastroenterology* (in English, 12 a year), *Nihon Shokaki-byo Gakkai Zasshi* (in Japanese, 12 a year).

Nihon Shonika Gakkai (Japan Paediatric Society): 4F Daiichi Magami Bldg, 1-1-5 Koraku, Bunkyo-ku, Tokyo 112-0004; tel. (3) 3818-0091; fax (3) 3816-6036; internet www.jpeds.or.jp; f. 1896; 16,311 mems; Pres. Dr SHUMPEI YOKOTA; Sec. Gen. Dr MAKIKO OKUYAMA; publs *Paediatrics International* (in English, 6 a year), *Journal of the Japan Paediatric Society* (in Japanese, 12 a year).

Nihon Syoyakugakkai (Japanese Society of Pharmacognosy): Business Centre for Academic Societies, 4–16, Yayoi 2-chome, Bunkyo-ku, Tokyo 113; tel. (3) 5206-6007; fax (3) 5206-6008; e-mail shoyaku@asas.or.jp; internet www.jsphcg.gr.jp; f. 1946; 1,027 mems; Pres. M. KONOSHIMA; publ. *Japanese Journal of Pharmacognosy* (4 a year).

Nihon Teii Kinou Shinkei Geka Gakkai (Japan Society for Stereotactic and Functional Neurosurgery): c/o Dept of Neuro-

logical Surgery, School of Medicine, Nihon University, 30-1 Ohyaguchi Kamimachi, Itabashi-ku, Tokyo 173-8610; tel. (3) 3972-8111, ext. 2481; fax (3) 3554-0425; e-mail teii@med .nihon-u.ac.jp; internet jssfn.umin.ac.jp; f. 1963; 518 mems; Sec.-Gen. Dr C. FUKAYA; publ. *Functional Neurosurgery* (2 a year).

Nihon Yakuri Gakkai (Japanese Pharmacological Society): Yayoi 2-4-16, Bunkyo-ku, Tokyo 113-0032; tel. (3) 3814-4828; fax (3) 3814-4809; e-mail society@pharmacol.or.jp; internet www.pharmacol.or.jp; f. 1927; 6,100 mems; Chair. KEITARO HASHIMOTO; publs *Folia Pharmacologica Japonica* (in Japanese, 12 a year), *Journal of Pharmacological Sciences* (in English, 12 a year).

Nippon Bitamin Gakkai (Vitamin Society of Japan): 2nd Floor, Kyodai Kaikan, 15–9 Kawaramachi Yoshida, Sakyo-ku, Kyoto 606-8305; tel. (75) 751-0314; fax (75) 751-2870; e-mail vsojkn@mbox.kyoto-inet.or.jp; internet web.kyoto-inet.or.jp/people/vsojkn; f. 1947; 2,000 mems; Pres. KENJI FUKUZAWA; Chief Sec. TAKESHI MATUMOTO; publs *Journal of Nutritional Science and Vitaminology* (in English, 6 a year), *Vitamins* (in Japanese, 12 a year).

Nippon Byorigakkai (Japanese Society of Pathology): New Akamon Bldg 4F, 2-40-9 Hongo, Bunkyo-ku, Tokyo 113-0033; tel. (3) 5684-6886; fax (3) 5684-6936; internet jsp .umin.ac.jp; f. 1911; 4,200 mems; Chair. SHIGEO MORI; publs *Annual of Pathological Autopsy Cases in Japan* (in Japanese), *Pathology International* (in English, 12 a year), *Proceedings* (in Japanese).

Nippon Gan Gakkai (Japanese Cancer Association): c/o Cancer Institute, Kami-Ikebukuro 1-37-1, Toshima-ku, Tokyo 170-0012; tel. (3) 3918-0111, ext. 4231; fax (3) 3918-5776; f. 1907; 16,976 mems; Pres. Dr TOMOYUKI KITAGAWA; publs *Japanese Journal of Cancer Research* (12 a year), *Gann Monograph on Cancer Research* (irregular).

Nippon Ganka Gakkai (Japanese Ophthalmological Society): 2-4-11-402, Sarugaku-cho, Chiyoda-ku, Tokyo 101-8346; fax (3) 3293-9384; internet www.nichigan.or.jp; f. 1897; 13,690 mems; Pres. MAKOTO ARAIE; publs *Japanese Journal of Ophthalmology* (6 a year), *Journal of Japanese Ophthalmological Society* (12 A YEAR).

Nippon Geka Gakkai (Japan Surgical Society): World Trade Center Bldg, 2-4-1 Hamamatsu-cho, Minato-ku, Tokyo 105-6108; tel. (3) 5733-4094; fax (3) 5473-8864; e-mail info@jssoc.or.jp; internet www.jssoc.or .jp; f. 1899; 37,405 mems; Pres. TAKASHI KANEMATSU; publ. *Surgery Today* (12 a year).

Nippon Hifu-ka Gakkai (Japanese Dermatological Association): Taisei Bldg, 3-14-10 Hongo, Bunkyo-ku, Tokyo 113-0033; tel. (3) 3811-5099; fax (3) 3812-6790; e-mail gakkai@ dermatol.or.jp; internet www.dermatol.or.jp; f. 1901; 8,567 mems; Pres. S. HARADA; publs *Japanese Journal of Dermatology* (in Japanese, 14 a year), *Journal of Dermatology* (in English, 12 a year).

Nippon Hoi Gakkai (Medico-Legal Society of Japan): Dept of Forensic Medicine, Faculty of Medicine, Univ. of Tokyo, 7-3-1 Hongo, Bunkyo-ku, Tokyo 113; tel. (3) 5800-5416; fax (3) 5800-5416; e-mail legalmed@m.u-tokyo.ac .jp; internet web.sapmed.ac.jp/jslm; f. 1914; 1,400 mems; Pres. Dr KENJI KAMIYA; publs *Japanese Journal of Legal Medicine* (2 a year), *Legal Medicine* (2 a year).

Nippon Hoshasen Eikyo Gakkai (Japan Radiation Research Society): National Institute of Radiological Sciences, 9-1 Anagawa-4, Inage-ku, Chiba 263-8555; tel. (43) 251-2111; fax (43) 251-4531; f. 1959; 1,052 mems; Pres.

KENJI KAMIYA; publ. *Journal of Radiation Research* (4 a year).

Nippon Igaku Hōshasen Gakkai (Japan Radiological Society): NP-II Bldg, 5-1-16 Hongo, Bunkyo-ku, Tokyo 113-0033; tel. (3) 3814-3077; fax (3) 5684-4075; e-mail qa@radiology.or.jp; internet www.radiology.jp; f. 1950; 7,500 mems; Pres. Dr OSAMU MATSUI; publ. *Radiation Medicine.*

Nippon Jibi-Inkoka Gakkai (Otorhinolaryngological Society of Japan, Inc.): 3-23-14-807 Takanawa, Minato-ku, Tokyo; tel. (3) 3443-3085; fax (3) 3443-3037; e-mail office@jibika.or.jp; internet www.jibika.or.jp; f. 1893; 10,500 mems; Pres. TAKUYA UEMURA; publ. *Nippon Jibi-Inkoka Gakkai Kaiho (Tokyo)* (12 a year).

Nippon Kaibo Gakkai (Japanese Association of Anatomists): c/o Business Center for Academic Societies Japan, 5-16-9 Honkomagome, Bunkyo-ku, Tokyo 113; e-mail gakkai5@kokuhoken.or.jp; internet www.anatomy.or.jp; f. 1893; 2,700 mems; Pres. Dr SHIGEO UCHINO; publ. *Anatomical Science International* (4 a year).

Nippon Kansenshoh Gakkai (Japanese Association for Infectious Diseases): Nichinai Bldg, 2F, 3-28-8, Hongo, Bunkyo-ku, Tokyo 113-0033; tel. (3) 5842-5845; fax (3) 5842-5846; e-mail info@kansensho.or.jp; internet www.kansensho.or.jp; f. 1926; 10,500 mems; Pres. AIKICHI IWAMOTO; publs *Journal of the Japanese Association for Infectious Diseases* (online, 6 a year), *Journal of Infection and Chemotherapy* (online).

Nippon Kekkaku-byo Gakkai (Japanese Society for Tuberculosis): 1-24, Matsuyama 3-chome, Kiyose-shi, Tokyo 204-8533; tel. 0424-92-2091; fax 0424-91-8315; f. 1923; 3,000 mems; Chair. Dr K. AOKI; publ. *Kekkaku* (12 a year).

Nippon Ketsueki Gakkai (Japanese Society of Haematology): c/o Kinki Chiho Invention Center, 14 Kawahara-cho, Yoshida, Sakyo-ku, Kyoto 606-8305; tel. (75) 752-2844; fax (75) 752-2842; e-mail info@jshem.or.jp; internet www.jshem.or.jp; f. 1937; academic year September to August; organizes research, symposia, seminars; 7,500 mems; Pres. Prof. YUZURU KANAKURA; publs *International Journal of Hematology* (10 a year with 1 supplement), *The Japanese Journal of Clinical Hematology* (12 a year).

Nippon Kisei-chu Gakkai (Japanese Society of Parasitology): Dept of Tropical Medicine and Parasitology, Keio University School of Medicine, 35 Shinanomachi Shinjuku-ku, Tokyo 160-8582; tel. (3) 3353-1211; fax (3) 3353-5958; internet jsp.tm.nagasaki-u.ac.jp; f. 1929; 998 mems; Pres. Prof. T. HORII; Chair Prof. T. TAKEUCHI; publ. *Parasitology International* (4 a year).

Nippon Koshu-Eisei Kyokai (Japan Public Health Association): Koei Bldg, 1-29–8, Shinjuku, Shinjuku-ku, Tokyo 160-0022; tel. (3) 3352-4281; fax (3) 3352-4605; e-mail info@jpha.or.jp; internet www.jpha.or.jp; f. 1883; 5,000 mems; Pres. MINORU SEIJO; publs *Japanese Journal of Public Health, Public Health Information* (12 a year).

Nippon Rai Gakkai (Japanese Leprosy Association): 4-2-1, Aoba-cho, Higashimurayama-shi, Tokyo 189-0002; tel. (42) 391-8085; fax (42) 394-9092; e-mail jla-hp-admin@hansen-gakkai.jp; internet www.hansen-gakkai.jp; f. 1927; 355 mems; Pres. NORIHASA ISHII; publ. *Japanese Journal of Leprosy* (3 a year).

Nippon Saikingakkai (Japanese Society for Bacteriology): c/o Oral Health Association of Japan, 1-44-2 Komagome, Toshima-ku, Tokyo 170; tel. (3) 3947-8891; fax (3) 3947-8341; e-mail gakkai@kokuhiken.or.jp;

internet wwwsoc.nii.ac.jp/jsb; f. 1927; 3,400 mems; Pres. Dr HIDEO HAYASHI; publs *Japanese Journal of Bacteriology* (4 a year), *Microbiology and Immunology* (12 a year).

Nippon Sanka-Fujinka Gakkai (Japan Society of Obstetrics and Gynaecology): Twin View Ochanomizu Bldg, 2-3-9 Hongo, Bunkyo-ku, Tokyo 113-0033; tel. (3) 5842-5452; fax (3) 5842-5470; e-mail nissanfu@jsog.or.jp; internet www.jsog.or.jp; f. 1949; 15,434 mems; Chair. Prof. YASUNORI YOSHIMURA; publ. *Acta Obstetrica et Gynaecologica Japonica* (12 a year).

Nippon Seikei Geka Gakkai (Japanese Orthopaedic Association): 2-40-18, Hongo, Bunkyo-ku, Tokyo 113-8418; tel. (3) 3816-3671; fax (3) 3818-2337; internet www.joa.or.jp; f. 1926; 20,742 mems; Pres. Prof. HIROSHI YAMAMOTO; publs *Journal* (in Japanese, 12 a year), *Journal of Orthopaedic Science* (in English, 6 a year).

Nippon Seiri Gakkai (Physiological Society of Japan): 3-30-10 Hongo, Bunkyo-ku, Tokyo 113-0033; tel. (3) 3815-1624; fax (3) 3815-1603; e-mail psj@qa2.so-net.ne.jp; internet int.physiology.jp; f. 1922; 3,700 mems; Pres. YASUNOBU OKADA; publs *Journal of the Physiological Society of Japan* (in Japanese, 12 a year), *Journal of the Physiological Society of Japan* (in English, 6 a year).

Nippon Shika Hozon Gakkai (Japanese Society of Conservative Dentistry): c/o Oral Health Association of Japan (Koku Hoken Kyokai), Komagome TS Bldg, 1-43-9 Komagome, Toshima-ku, Tokyo 170-0003; tel. (3) 3947-8891; fax (3) 3947-8341; e-mail gakkai8@kokuhoken.or.jp; internet wwwsoc.nii.ac.jp/jscd; f. 1955; 4,540 mems; Pres. HIDEAKI SUDA; publ. *Journal of Conservative Dentistry* (6 a year).

Nippon Shinkei Gakkai (Japanese Society of Neurology): Ichimaru Bldg 31-21 Yushima 2-chome, Bunkyo-ku, Tokyo 113-0034; tel. (3) 3815-1080; fax (3) 3815-1931; internet www.neurology-jp.org; f. 1960; 6,895 mems; Chair. ICHIRO KANAZAWA; publ. *Clinical Neurology* (12 a year).

Nippon Shinkeikagaku Gakkai (Japan Neuroscience Society): Inagaya Bldg 504, 37-6 Hongo 2-chome, Bunkyo-ku, Tokyo 113-0033; tel. (3) 3813-0272; fax (3) 3813-0272; internet www.jnss.org; f. 1974; 4,000 mems; Pres. K. OBATA; publs *Neuroscience Research* (12 a year), *News.*

Nippon Tonyo-byo Gakkai (Japan Diabetes Society): 5-25-18, Hongo, Bunkyo-ku, Tokyo 113-0033; tel. (3) 3815-4364; fax (3) 3815-7985; f. 1958; 15,533 mems; Pres. KOICHI YOKONO; publ. *Journal* (12 a year).

Nippon Uirusu Gakkai (Society of Japanese Virologists): Business Centre for Academic Societies, 5-16-9 Honkomagome, Bunkyo-ku, Tokyo 113; f. 1953; 3,000 mems; Pres. Dr HIROSHI YOSHIKURA; publs *Microbiology and Immunology* (12 a year), *Virus* (Japanese text with English summary, 2 a year).

Nippon Yakugaku-Kai (Pharmaceutical Society of Japan): 12-15, Shibuya 2-chome, Shibuya-ku, Tokyo 150-0002; tel. (3) 3406-3321; fax (3) 3498-1835; e-mail doi@pharm.or.jp; internet www.pharm.or.jp; f. 1880; 21,541 mems; Pres. O. YONEMITSU; Exec. Dir M. OHZEKI; publs *Biological and Pharmaceutical Bulletin* (12 a year), *Chemical and Pharmaceutical Bulletin* (12 a year), *Farumashia* (12 a year), *Japanese Journal of Toxicology and Environmental Health* (6 a year).

Nippon Yuketsu Gakkai (Japan Society of Blood Transfusion): Metropolitan Tokyo Red Cross Blood Centre, 1-31-4 Hiroo, Shibuya-ku, Tokyo; tel. (3) 5485-6020; fax (3) 5466-

3111; internet www.yuketsu.gr.jp; f. 1954; 3,000 mems; Pres. TAKEO JUJI; publ. *Japanese Journal of Transfusion Medicine* (6 a year).

Oto-Rhino-Laryngological Society of Japan: 3-25-22 Takanawa, Minato-Ku, Tokyo 108-0074; tel. (3) 3443-3085; fax (3) 3443-3037; f. 1893 as the Tokyo Oto-Rhino-Laryngological Society; 1947 present name; 10,604 mems; Chair GINICHIRO ICHIKAWA; publs *Auris Nasus Larynx, Nippon Jibiinkoka Gakkai Kaiho* (12 a year).

NATURAL SCIENCES

General

Nihon Kagakushi Gakkai (History of Science Society of Japan): Shimazu Bldg 202, 2-13-1 Hirakawa-cho, Chiyoda-ku, Tokyo 102-0093; tel. and fax (3) 3239-0545; internet www.soc.nii.ac.jp/jshs; f. 1941; 1,000 mems; Pres. TATSUMASA DOUKE; publs *Kagakushi Kenkyu* (4 a year), *Historia Scientiarum* (3 a year).

Biological Sciences

Nihon Hassei Seibutsu Gakkai (Japanese Society of Developmental Biologists): Center for Developmental Biology, RIKEN Kobe 2-2-3 Minatojima-minami Chuo-ku Kobe, Hyogo 650-0047; tel. and fax (78) 306-3072; e-mail jsdbadmin@jsdb.jp; internet www.jsdb.jp; f. 1968; 1,400 mems; Pres. SHINICHI AIZAWA; publ. *Development, Growth and Differentiation* (in English, 9 a year).

Nihon Jinrui Iden Gakkai (Japan Society of Human Genetics): Dept of Medical Genomics, Tokyo Medical and Dental University, 1-5-45 Yushima, Bunkyo-ku, Tokyo 113-8510; tel. (3) 5803-5820; fax (3) 5803-0244; internet jshg.jp; f. 1956; 1,046 mems; Pres. YU-SUKE NAKAMURA; publ. *Journal* (4 a year).

Nihon Kairui Gakkai (Malacological Society of Japan): National Science Museum, 3-23-1, Hyakunin-cho, Shinjuku-ku, Tokyo 169-0073; tel. (3) 3364-7124; e-mail msj_manager@hotmail.com; f. 1928; scientific research on molluscs; 900 mems; Pres. T. OKUTANI; publs *Chiribotan* (in Japanese with English abstract, 4 a year), *Venus* (4 a year).

Nihon Kontyû Gakkai (Entomological Society of Japan): c/o Dept of Zoology, National Science Museum (Natural History), 3-23-1 Hyakunin-chô, Shinjuku, Tokyo 169; e-mail ueno@kintaro.grt.kyushu-u.ac.jp; f. 1917; 1,300 mems; Pres. HIROSHI SHIMA; publs *Entomological Science, Insects of Japan* (irregular).

Nihon Mendel Kyokai (Japan Mendel Society): Editorial and Business Office, Cytologia, c/o Toshin Bldg, Hongo 2-27-2, Bunkyo-ku, Tokyo 113-0033; fax (3) 3814-5352; f. 1929; 1,100 mems; Pres. HIDEO HIROKAWA; publ. *Cytologia* (4 a year).

Nihon Seitai Gakkai (Ecological Society of Japan): 1–8 Nishihanaikecho, Koyama, Kitaku Kyoto 603-8148; tel. and fax (75) 384-0250; e-mail office@mail.esj.ne.jp; internet www.esj.ne.jp/es; f. 1953; research in all aspects of ecology; 4,000 mems; Pres. T. NAKASHIZUKA; Sec.-Gen. E. KASUYA; publs *Japanese Journal of Ecology* (in Japanese, 3 a year), *Ecological Research* (in English, 6 a year), *Japanese Journal of Conservation Ecology* (in Japanese, 2 a year).

Nihon Shokubutsu Bunrui Gakkai (Japanese Society for Plant Systematics): Faculty of Symbiotic Systems Science, Fukushima University, Fukushima 960-1296; internet wwwsoc.nii.ac.jp/jsps; f. 2001; 900 mems; plant taxonomy and phytogeography; Pres. JIN MURATA; Sec. TAKAHIDAE

KUROSAWA; publ. *Acta Phytotaxonomica et Geobotanica* (3 a year).

Nippon Chô Gakkai (Ornithological Society of Japan): c/o National Science Museum, 3-23-1 Hyakunin-cho, Shinjuku-ku, Tokyo 169-0073; tel. (3) 3364-7131; fax (3) 3364-7104; e-mail nihon-chogakkai@lagopus.com; internet www.soc.nii.ac.jp/osj; f. 1912; 1,200 mems; library of 600 vols; Pres. HIROSHI NAKAMURA; Sec.–Gen. ISAO NISHIUMI; publs *Japanese Journal of Ornithology* (in Japanese, 2 a year), *Ornithological Science* (in English, 2 a year).

Nihon Dobutsu Gakkai (Zoological Society of Japan): Toshin Bldg, Hongo 2-27-2, Bunkyo-ku, Tokyo 113-0033; tel. (3) 3814-5461; fax (3) 3814-6216; e-mail zsj-society@umin .net; internet www.zoology.or.jp; f. 1878; 2,610 mems; Pres. NORI SATOH; Sec. Gen. YUKO NAGAI; publ. *Zoological Science* (12 a year).

Nippon Eisei-Dobutu Gakkai (Japanese Society of Medical Entomology and Zoology): c/o Dept of Parasitology, School of Medicine, Aichi Medical University, Nagakute, Aichi 480-1195; tel. (561) 62-3311; fax (561) 63-3645; internet www.jsmez.gr.jp; f. 1943; 750 mems; Pres. Prof. YASUO CHINZEI; publ. *Medical Entomology and Zoology* (4 a year).

Nippon Iden Gakkai (Genetics Society of Japan): National Institute of Genetics, 1, 111 Yata, Mishima, Shizuoka 411-8540; tel. 55-981-6736; fax 55-981-6736; e-mail japgenet@ lab.nig.ac.jp; internet wwwsoc.nii.ac.jp/gsj3; f. 1920; 1,500 mems; Pres. SADAO ISHIWA; publ. *Genes and Genetic Systems* (6 a year).

Nippon Kin Gakkai (Mycological Society of Japan): c/o Forest Health Group, Kansai Research Center, Forestry and Forest Products Research Institute, Nagai-Kyutaro 68, Momoyama-cho, Fushimi-ku, Kyoto 612-0855; tel. (75) 366-9912; fax (75) 611-1207; e-mail msj_office@remach.kais.kyoto-u.ac.jp; internet wwwsoc.nii.ac.jp/msj7; f. 1956; 1,600 mems; Pres. MAKOTO KAKISHIMA; publ. *Mycoscience* (4 a year).

Nippon Kumo Gakkai (Arachnological Society of Japan): c/o Faculty of Education, Kumamoto Univ., Kurokami 2-chome 40-1, Kumamoto 860-8555; tel. (96) 342-2532; e-mail tanabe@gpo.kumamoto-u.ac.jp; f. 1936; 300 mems; Pres. Dr NOBUO TSURUSAKI; Sec. TSUTOMU TANABE; publ. *Acta Arachnologica* (2 a year).

Nippon Oyo-Dobutsu-Konchu Gakkai (Japanese Society of Applied Entomology and Zoology): c/o Japan Plant Protection Association, 43-11, 1-chome, Komagome, Toshima-ku, Tokyo 170; internet odokon .org; f. 1957; 2,000 mems; Pres. Prof. KENJI FUJISAKI; Exec. Dir HIROSHI HONDA; publs *Applied Entomology and Zoology* (in English, 4 a year), *Japanese Journal of Applied Entomology and Zoology* (in Japanese with English synopsis, 4 a year).

Nippon Rikusui Gakkai (Japanese Society of Limnology): c/o School of Environmental Science, University of Shiga Prefecture, 2500 Hassaka-cho, Hikone, Shiga 522-8533; tel. (749) 28-8307; fax (749) 28-8463; e-mail ban@ ses.usp.ac.jp; internet wwwsoc.nii.ac.jp/jslim; f. 1931; 1,288 mems; Pres. Dr NORIO OGURA; Gen. Sec. Dr OSAMU MITAMURA; publs *Japanese Journal of Limnology* (3 a year), *Limnology* (3 a year).

Nippon Shokubutsu Gakkai (Botanical Society of Japan): c/o Toshin Bldg, 2-chome 27-2 Hongo, Bunkyo-ku, Tokyo; tel. (3) 3814-5675; fax (3) 3814-5352; e-mail bsj@bsj.or.jp; internet bsj.or.jp; f. 1882; 2,300 mems; Pres. M. WADA; publ. *Journal of Plant Research* (6 a year).

Nippon Shokubutsu Seiri Gakkai (Japanese Society of Plant Physiologists): Shimotachiuri Ogawa Higashi, Kamikyoku, Kyoto 602-8048; tel. (75) 415-3661; fax (75) 415-3662; e-mail jspp@nacos.com; internet www .nacos.com/jspp; f. 1959; 3,201 mems; Pres. KIYOTAKA OKADA; Sec.-Gen. AKIRA NAGATANI; publ. *Plant and Cell Physiology* (12 a year).

Mathematical Sciences

Nihon Sugaku Kai (Mathematical Society of Japan): 34–8, Taito-1-chome, Taito-ku, Tokyo 110-0016; tel. (3) 3835-3483; fax (3) 3835-3485; f. 1877; 5,000 mems; Pres. SADAYOSHI KOJIMA; publs *Journal* (4 a year), *Sugaku* (4 a year), *Sugaku-Tsushin* (bulletin, 4 a year), *Japanese Journal of Mathematics* (2 a year), *MSJ Memoirs* (irregular), *Advanced Studies in Pure Mathematics* (irregular).

Physical Sciences

Butsuri Tansa Gakkai (Society of Exploration Geophysicists of Japan): 2F MK5 Bldg, 1-5-6 Higashikanda, Chiyoda-ku, Tokyo 101-0031; tel. (3) 6804-7500; fax (3) 6804-7500; e-mail office@segj.org; internet www.segj .org; f. 1948; 1,420 mems; Pres. S. ROKUGAWA; publ. *Butsuri Tansa* (Geophysical Exploration, every 2 months).

Chigaku Dantai Kenkyu-kai (Association for Geological Collaboration in Japan): Kawai Bldg, 2–24–1, Minami-Ikebukuro, Toshima-ku, Tokyo 171-0022; tel. (3) 3983-3378; fax (3) 3983-7525; e-mail chidanken@ tokyo.email.ne.jp; internet wwwsoc.nii.ac.jp/ agcj/index.html; f. 1947; study of geology, mineralogy, palaeontology and related earth sciences; 2,500 mems; Pres. YUKIO OHTOMO; Sec. SATORU TAKEGOSHI; publs *Sokuhō* (News, 12 a year), *Chikyu-Kagaku* (Earth Science, 6 a year), *Senpō* (Monograph, irregular), *Chigaku Kyoiku To Kagaku-undo* (Education of Earth Science, 3 a year).

Chikyu-Denjiki   Chikyu-Wakuseiken Gakkai (Society of Geomagnetism and Earth, Planetary and Space Science): c/o Business Centre for Academic Societies, 5-16-9 Honkomagome, Bumkyo-ku, Tokyo 113-8622; tel. (3) 5814-5801; fax (3) 5814-5820; internet www.kurasc.kyoto-u.ac.jp/sgepss; f. 1947; frmly Nippon Chikyu Denki Ziki Gakkai; 695 mems; Pres. Prof. RYOICHI FUJII; publ. *Earth, Planets and Space* (12 a year).

Japan Weather Association: Sunshine 60 Bldg 3-1-1, Higashi-Ikebukuro, Toshima-ku, Tokyo 170-6055; tel. (3) 5958-8161; fax (3) 5958-8162; e-mail webmaster@jwa.go.jp; internet www.jwa.or.jp; f. 1950; Pres. MICHI-HIKO MATSUO; publs *Geophysical Magazine*, *Journal of Meteorological Research* (12 a year), *Kisho*, *Oceanographical Magazine* (4 a year).

Japanese Society of Microscopy: Akihabara Konoike Bldg 3F, 1-25 Kanda-sakuma Cho, Chiyoda-ku, Tokyo 101-0025; fax (3) 702-8816; e-mail kenbikyo@realize-se.co.jp; internet wwwsoc.nii.ac.jp/jsm; f. 1949; 2,690 mems; Pres. KAZUO OGAWA; publ. *Journal of Electron Microscopy* (4 a year).

Kobunshi Gakkai (Society of Polymer Science, Japan): Shintomicho Tokyu Bldg, 3-10-9 Irifune, Chuo-ku, Tokyo 104-0042; tel. (3) 5540-3771; fax (3) 5540-3737; e-mail intnl@ spsj.or.jp; internet www.spsj.or.jp; f. 1951; 12,598 mems; Pres. MITSUO SAWAMOTO; publs *Kobunshi* (High Polymers, 12 a year), *Kobunshi Ronbunshu* (Journal of Polymer Science and Technology, abstracts in English, 12 a year), *Polymer Journal* (in English, 12 a year), *Polymer Preprints* (CD-ROM, in English, 2 a year).

Nihon Bunseki Kagaku-Kai (Japan Society for Analytical Chemistry): Gotanda San-haitsu, 26-2, Nishigotanda 1-chome, Shinagawa-ku, Tokyo 141-0031; tel. (3) 3490-3351; fax (3) 3490-3572; e-mail analytsci@jsac.or.jp; internet www.soc.nii.ac .jp/jsac; f. 1952; 9,108 mems; Pres. M. TANAKA; Sec.-Gen. Dr TADASHI FUJINUKI; publs *Bunseki Kagaku* (12 a year), *Analytical Sciences* (6 a year).

Nihon Kobutsu Kagaku Kai (Japan Association of Mineralogical Sciences): c/o Graduate School of Science, Tohoku Univ., Sendai 980-8578; tel. (22) 224-3852; fax (22) 224-3852; e-mail kyl04223@nifty.ne.jp; internet wwwsoc.nii.ac.jp/jams3/jmps.htm; f. 2007 by merger of Japanese Association of Mineralogists, Petrologists and Economic Geologists (f, 1929) and The Mineralogical Society of Japan; 1,000 mems; library of 17,000 vols; Pres. Dr EIJI OHTANI; Sec. MASUMI MIYACHI; publ. *Journal of Mineralogical and Petrological Sciences* (6 a year).

Nihon Nensho Gakkai (Combustion Society of Japan): c/o Department of Mechanical Engineering, Osaka Prefecture University, 1-1 Gakuen-cho, Sakai, Osaka 599-8531; tel. (72) 255-7037; fax (72) 255-7037; e-mail office@combustionsociety.jp; internet combustionsociety.jp; f. 1953; 700 mems; Pres. TOSHIKAZU KADOTA; publ. *Journal* (4 a year).

Nihon Nogyo-Kisho Gakkai (Society of Agricultural Meteorology of Japan): c/o Yokendo Co. Ltd., 5-30-15 Hongo, Bunkyo-ku, Tokyo 113-0033; tel. (3) 3814-0915; fax (3) 3814-2615; e-mail nogyo-kisho@yokendo.co .jp; internet www.soc.nii.ac.jp/agrmet; f. 1942; studies protected cultivation, agricultural meteorology and resources of food production; 831 mems; Pres. Prof. MASUMI OKADA; publ. *Nogyo-Kisho* (Journal of Agricultural Meteorology, 4 a year).

Nihon Seppyo Gakkai (Japanese Society of Snow and Ice): 3rd Fl., Kagaku-Kaikan, Kanda Surugadai 1-5, Chiyoda-ku, Tokyo 101-0062; tel. (3) 5259-5245; fax (3) 5259-5246; e-mail jimu@seppyo.org; internet www .seppyo.org; f. 1939; 950 mems; Pres. Dr YOSHIYUKI FUJII; publs *Seppyo* (Journal of the Japanese Society of Snow and Ice, in Japanese and English, 6 a year), *Bulletin of Glaciological Research* (in English, 1 a year), occasional papers and bibliography.

Nippon Bunko Gakkai (Spectroscopical Society of Japan): c/o Industrial Hall, 1-13, Kanda-Awaji-cho, Chiyoda-ku, Tokyo 101; tel. (3) 3253-2747; fax (3) 3253-2740; f. 1951; 1,300 mems; Pres. M. TASUMI; Sec. Y. F. MIZUGAI; publ. *Bunko Kenkyu* (6 a year).

Nippon Butsuri Gakkai (Physical Society of Japan): 5th Fl., Eishin-kaihatsu Bldg, 5-34-3 Shimbashi, Minato-ku, Tokyo 105-0004; tel. (3) 3434-2671; fax (3) 3432-0997; e-mail jps-office@jps.or.jp; internet wwwsoc.nii.ac .jp/jps; f. 1946; 18,223 mems; Pres. SUKE-KATSU USHIODA; publs *Butsuri* (in Japanese, 12 a year), *Journal of the Physical Society of Japan* (12 a year), *Physics Education in Universities* (in Japanese, 3 a year), *Progress of Theoretical Physics* (12 a year).

Nippon Chishitsu Gakkai (Geological Society of Japan): Igeta Bldg, 8-15 Iwamoto-cho 2-chome, Chiyoda-ku, Tokyo 101-0032; tel. (3) 5823-1150; fax (3) 5823-1156; e-mail main@geosociety.jp; internet www.geosociety .jp; f. 1893; stratigraphy, petrology, tectonics, volcanology, etc; 5,000 mems; library of 10,000 vols; Pres. ASAHIKO TAIRA; publ. *Journal* (12 a year).

Nippon Dai-Yonki Gakkai (Japan Association for Quaternary Research): 3rd Fl., Rakuyo Bldg, Waseda-Tsurumaki-cho 519, Shinjuku, Tokyo 162-0041; tel. (3) 5291-6231; fax (3) 5291-2176; e-mail daiyonki@ shunkosha.com; internet wwwsoc.nii.ac.jp/

qr/index.html; f. 1956; 1,800 mems; Sec. of Exec. Cttee SUMIKO KUBO; publ. *Quaternary Research* (5 a year).

Nippon Kagakukai (Chemical Society of Japan): 1-5 Kanda-Surugadai, Chiyoda-ku, Tokyo 101-8307; tel. (3) 3292-6161; fax (3) 3292-6318; e-mail info@chemistry.or.jp; internet www.csj.jp; f. 1878; 31,000 mems; Pres. Prof. YASUHIRO IWASAWA; Man. HIROKO IHIDA; publs *Bulletin of the Chemical Society of Japan* (12 a year), *Chemistry: An Asian-Journal* (12 a year), *Chemistry Letters* (12 a year), *Chemical Record* (6 a year).

Nippon Kaisui Gakkai (Society of Sea Water Science, Japan): c/o Sea Water Science Research Laboratory, Salt Industry Centre of Japan, 4-13-20, Sakawa, Odawara-shi, Kanagawa; f. 1950; 414 mems; Pres. SHINICHI NAKAO; publ. *Journal*.

Nippon Kaiyo Gakkai (Oceanographic Society of Japan): MACAS, 9th Fl., Paleseside Bldg, 1-1-1 Hitotsubashi, Chiyoda-ku, Tokyo 100-0003; tel. (3) 3211-1412; fax (3) 3211-1413; e-mail jos@mycom.co.jp; internet wwwsoc.nii.ac.jp/kaiyo; f. 1941; 2,379 mems; Pres. ISAO KOIKE; publs *Journal of Oceanography* (6 a year), *Umi no Kenkyu* (Oceanography in Japan, 6 a year).

Nippon Kazan Gakkai (Volcanological Society of Japan): c/o Earthquake Research Institute, University of Tokyo, 1-1-1 Yayoi, Bunkyo-ku, Tokyo 113-0032; tel. (3) 3813-7421; fax (3) 5684-7421; e-mail kazan@khaki .plala.or.jp; internet wwwsoc.nii.ac.jp/kazan; f. 1932; 1,200 mems; Pres. TADAHIDE UI; publ. *Bulletin* (6 a year).

Nippon Kessho Gakkai (Crystallographic Society of Japan): Nissei Otuka 3-chome Bldg, 3-11-6 Otuka, Bunkyo-ku, Tokyo 112-0012; tel. (3) 5940-7640; fax (3) 5940-7980; internet wwwsoc.nii.ac.jp/crsj/index.html; f. 1950; 1,000 mems; Pres. KAZUMAZA OHSUMI; Sec-Gen. MASAKI TAKATA; publ. *Journal* (6 a year).

Nippon Kisho Gakkai (Meteorological Society of Japan): c/o Japan Meteorological Agency, 1-3-4 Ote-machi, Chiyoda-ku, Tokyo 100-0004; tel. (3) 3212-8341; fax (3) 3216-4401; e-mail metsoc-j@aurora.ocn.ne.jp; internet wwwsoc.nii.ac.jp/msj; f. 1882; 4,300 mems; Pres. T. ASAI; publs *Journal* (6 a year), *Tenki* (in Japanese, 12 a year).

Nippon Kokai Gakkai (Japan Institute of Navigation): c/o Tokyo University of Mercantile Marine, 2-1-6 Etchujima, Koto-ku, Tokyo; tel. (3) 3630-3093; fax (3) 3630-3093; internet homepage2.nifty.com/navigation; f. 1948; 1,011 mems; Pres. Prof. S. KUWASIMA; publs *Journal* (2 a year), *Navigation* (4 a year).

Nippon Koseibutsu Gakkai (Palaeontological Society of Japan): 3rd Fl., Toshin Bldg, 2-27-2 Hongo, Bunkyo-ku, Tokyo 113-0033; tel. (3) 3814 5490; fax (3) 3814 6216; e-mail psj-office@world.ocn.ne.jp; internet www.soc .nii.ac.jp/psj5; f. 1935; 1,050 mems; Pres. NORIYUKI IKEYA; publs *Paleontological Research* (4 a year), *Fossils* (2 a year).

Nippon Onkyo Gakkai (Acoustical Society of Japan): Nakaura 5th Bldg, 2-18-20 Sotokanda, Chiyoda-ku, Tokyo 101-0021; fax (3) 5256-1022; e-mail asj-www@asj.gr.jp; internet www.asj.gr.jp; f. 1936; 4,530 mems; Pres. T. SONE; publs *Acoustical Science and Technolgy* (12 a year, online), *Reports of Spring and Autumn Meetings* (2 a year).

Nippon Sokuchi Gakkai (Geodetic Society of Japan): c/o Japanese Association of Surveyors, 1-3-4 Koishikawa, Bunkyo-ku, Tokyo, 112-0002; tel. (3) 5684-3358; fax (3) 5684-3366; e-mail nihonsokuchi@jsurvey.jp; internet wwwsoc.nii.ac.jp/geod-soc; f. 1954; studies astronomy, crustal activity, earth

tide, geodesy, geomagnetism, gravity, etc; 600 mems; library of 5,000 vols; Pres. Dr SHUHEI OKUBO; publ. *Journal* (4 a year).

Nippon Temmon Gakkai (Astronomical Society of Japan): National Astronomical Observatory, 2-21-1 Osawa, Mitaka-shi, Tokyo 181-8588; tel. (422) 31-1359; fax (422) 31-5487; e-mail jimu@asj.or.jp; internet www .asj.or.jp; f. 1908; 2,640 mems; Pres. Y. UCHIDA; publs *Publications* (6 a year), *The Astronomical Herald* (in Japanese, 12 a year).

Nippon Yukagaku Kai (Japan Oil Chemists' Society): 7th Floor, Yushi Kogyo Kaikan, 13-11, Nihonbashi 3-chome, Chuo-ku, Tokyo 103-0027; tel. (3) 3271-7463; fax (3) 3271-7464; e-mail yukagaku@jocs-office.or.jp; internet www.soc.nii.ac.jp/jocs; f. 1951; 2,426 mems; Pres. ISAO IKEDA; publ. *Journal of Oleo Science* (12 a year).

Sen-i Gakkai (Society of Fibre Science and Technology, Japan): 3-3-9-208 Kamiosaki, Shinagawa-ku, Tokyo 141; tel. (3) 3441-5627; fax (3) 3441-3260; e-mail office@fiber .or.jp; internet www.fiber.or.jp; f. 1943; c. 3,000 mems; Pres. HIROSHI INAGAKI; publ. *Journal* (12 a year).

Shokubai Gakkai (Catalysis Society of Japan): Shin-Ikeda-yama Mansions, Room 302, 5-21-13, Higashi-Gotanda, Shinagawa-ku, Tokyo 141; tel. (3) 3444-2126; fax (3) 3444-8794; internet www.shokubai.org; f. 1958; 2,370 mems; Pres. Y. MOROOKA; publ. *Shokubai* (Catalyst, 8 a year).

Zisin Gakkai (Seismological Society of Japan): 6-26-12 Tokyo RS Building, Hongo, Bunkyo-ku, Tokyo 113-0033; tel. (3) 5803-9570; fax (3) 5803-9577; e-mail zisin@tokyo .email.ne.jp; internet wwwsoc.nii.ac.jp/ssj; f. 1929; 2,400 mems; Chair. MASAKAZU OHTAKE; publs *Zisin* (Journal, 4 a year), *Earth Planets and Space* (12 a year), *Newsletter* (6 a year).

PHILOSOPHY AND PSYCHOLOGY

Bigaku-Kai (Japanese Society for Aesthetics): Univ. of Tokyo, Graduate School of Humanities and Sociology, Dept. of Aesthetics, 7-3-1, Hongo, Bunkyo-ku, Tokyo 113-0033; e-mail bigakukai@nifty.ne.jp; internet wwwsoc.nii.ac.jp/bigaku; f. 1950; 1,500 mems; Pres. KIYOKAZU NISHIMURA; publs *Bigaku* (in Japanese, 2 a year), *Aesthetics* (every 2 years).

Moralogy Kenkyusho (Institute of Moralogy): 1-1, 2-chome, Hikarigaoka, Kashiwashi, Chiba-ken 277-8654; tel. (4) 7173-3252; fax (4) 7173-3263; internet rc.moralogy.jp; f. 1926; 231 mems; library of 71,624 vols; Pres. M. HIROIKE; publ. *Studies in Moralogy* (2 a year).

Nihon Rinrigakukai (Japanese Society for Ethics): Dept of Ethics, Faculty of Letters, University of Tokyo, Bunkyo-ku, Tokyo 113; tel. (3) 727-147; e-mail jse@logos.tsukuba.ac .jp; internet jse.trustyweb.jp; f. 1950; 800 mems; Pres. YÔKICHI YAZIMA; Man. MASAHIRO NAKAGAWA; publ. *Rinrigakunenpo* (1 a year).

Nippon Dobutsu Shinri Gakkai (Japanese Society for Animal Psychology): c/o K. & U. Co. Ltd, MSK Bldg 3F, 3-32-7 Hongo Bunkyo-ku, Tokyo 113-0033; tel. (3) 3815-4800; fax (3) 3815-4807; e-mail dousin-gakkai@umin.ac.jp; internet www.soc .nii.ac.jp/jsap2; f. 1933; 400 mems; Pres. MASATAKA WATANABE; publ. *The Japanese Journal of Animal Psychology* (2 a year).

Nippon Shakai Shinri Gakkai (Japanese Society of Social Psychology): c/o International Academic Printing Co. Ltd, 4-4-19 Takadanobaba, Shinjuku-ku, Tokyo 169-0075; tel. (3) 5389-6217; fax (3) 3368-2822; e-mail jssp-post@bunken.co.jp; internet wwwsoc.nii.ac.jp/jssp; f. 1950; 1,896 mems;

Pres. IKUO DAIBO; publs *Japanese Journal of Social Psychology*, *Bulletin* (3 a year).

Nippon Shinri Gakkai (Japanese Psychological Association): 5-23-13-7F, Hongo, Bunkyo-ku, Tokyo 113; tel. (3) 3814-3953; fax (3) 3814-3954; internet www.psych.or.jp; f. 1927; 7,000 mems; Pres. KEIICHIRO TSUJI; publs *Japanese Journal of Psychology* (6 a year), *Japanese Psychological Research* (4 a year).

RELIGION, SOCIOLOGY AND ANTHROPOLOGY

Japanese Society of Cultural Anthropology: 2-1-1-813 Mita, Minato-ku, Tokyo 108-0073; tel. (3) 5232-0920; fax (3) 5232-0922; e-mail hoya@jasca.org; internet wwwsoc.nii .ac.jp/jasca; f. 1934; 2,000 mems; publ. *Bunkajinruigaku* (Japanese Journal of Cultural Anthropology, 4 a year).

Nihon Indogaku Bukkyôgakukai (Japanese Association of Indian and Buddhist Studies): Hongo Bldg 2F, 3-33-5 Bunkyo-ku, Hongo Tokyo 113-0033; e-mail jaibs@l .u~tokyo.ac.jp; f. 1951; 2,350 mems; Pres. KIYOTAKA KIMURA; publ. *Indogaku Bukkyôgaku Kenkyû* (Journal of Indian and Buddhist Studies).

Nihon Shūkyō Gakkai (Japanese Association for Religious Studies): 1-29-7-205 Hongo, Bunkyo-ku, Tokyo 113-0033; tel. (3) 5684-5473; fax (3) 5684-5474; internet wwwsoc.nii.ac.jp/jars; f. 1930; 2,100 mems; Pres. FUJIO IKADO; publ. *Journal of Religious Studies* (4 a year).

Nippon Dokyo Gakkai (Japan Society of Taoistic Research): Kansai University, Faculty of Letters, 3-35 Yamate-cho 3-chome, Suita-shi, Osaka 564-8680; tel. (6) 368-0326; f. 1950; 650 mems; Pres. Y. SAKADE; publ. *Journal of Eastern Religions* (2 a year).

Nippon Jinruigaku Kai (Anthropological Society of Nippon): Business Center for Academic Societies, 5-16-9 Honkomagome, Bunkyo-ku, Tokyo 113-8622; tel. (3) 5814-5801; fax (3) 5814-5820; internet www.soc.nii.ac.jp/ jinrui; f. 1884; 700 mems; Pres. TASUKU KIMURA; publs *Anthropological Science* (4 a year), *Anthropological Science (Japanese Series)* (2 a year).

Nippon Shakai Gakkai (Japanese Sociological Society): Department of Sociology, Faculty of Letters, University of Tokyo, 7-3-1 Hongo, Bunkyo-ku, Tokyo 113-0033; tel. (3) 5841-8933; fax (3) 5841-8932; e-mail jss@ wwwsoc.nii.ac.jp; internet www.gakkai.ne.jp/ jss; f. 1923; 3,600 mems; Pres. TAKASHI HOSOYA; publs *International Journal of Japanese Sociology* (in English, 1 a year), *Shakaigaku Hyóron* (4 a year).

Tōhō Gakkai (Institute of Eastern Culture): 4-1, Nishi Kanda 2-chome, Chiyoda-ku, Tokyo 101-0065; tel. (3) 3262-7221; fax (3) 3262-7227; e-mail iec@tohogakkai.com; internet www.tohogakkai.com; f. 1947; Asian studies; 1,600 mems; Chair. YOSHIO TOGAWA; Sec.-Gen. HIDEO KAWAGUCHI; publs *Acta Asiatica* (bulletin, 2 a year), *Tōhōgaku* (Eastern Studies, 2 a year), *Transactions of the International Conference of Eastern Studies* (1 a year).

TECHNOLOGY

Denki Gakkai (Institute of Electrical Engineers of Japan (IEEJ)): Homat Horizon Bldg, 6-2 Goban-cho, Chiyoda-ku, Tokyo 102-0076; tel. (3) 3221-7256; fax (3) 3221-3704; e-mail jimkyoku@iee.or.jp; internet www.iee .or.jp; f. 1888; 26,000 mems; Pres. HISAO OKA; publs *IEEJ Transactions on Electronics, Information and Systems* (in Japanese and English, 12 a year), *IEEJ Transactions on Fundamentals and Materials* (in Japanese and English, 12 a year), *IEEJ Transactions* *on Industry Applications* (in Japanese and English, 12 a year), *IEEJ Transactions on Power and Energy* (in Japanese and English, 12 a year), *IEEJ Transactions on Sensors and Micromachines* (in Japanese and English, 12 a year), *Journal of the IEEJ* (in Japanese, 12 a year).

Denshi Joho Tsushin Gakkai (Institute of Electronics, Information and Communication Engineers): Kikai-Shinko-Kaikan Bldg, 5-8, Shibakoen 3-chome, Minato-ku, Tokyo 105-0011; tel. (3) 3433-6691; fax (3) 3433-6659; f. 1917; 40,000 mems; Pres. HISASHI KANEKO; publs *Journal, Transactions* (9 series, incl. *Original Contributions in English and Abstracts in English from the Transactions*, 12 a year).

Doboku-Gakkai (Japan Society of Civil Engineers): Yotsuya 1-chome, Shinjuku-ku, Tokyo; tel. (3) 3355-3452; fax (3) 5379-2769; e-mail iad@jsce.or.jp; internet www.jsce-int.org; f. 1914; 40,742 mems; library of 45,000 vols; Pres. Dr TORU KONDO; Exec. Dir. MORIYASU FURUKI; publs *Journal* (12 a year), *Coastal Engineering in Japan* (in English, 2 a year), *Transactions* (12 a year), *Civil Engineering, JSCE* (1 a year).

Keikinzoku Gakkai (Japan Institute of Light Metals): Tukamoto-Sazan Bldg, 2-15, Ginza 4 chome, Chuo-ku, Tokyo 104-0061; tel. (3) 3538-0232; fax (3) 3538-0226; e-mail jilm1951@jilm.or.jp; internet www.jilm.or.jp; f. 1951; 2,222 mems; Pres. AKIHIKO KAMIO; publ. *Journal* (in Japanese and synopsis in English, 12 a year).

Keisoku Jidouseigyo Gakkai SICE (Society of Instrument and Control Engineers): 1-35-28-303, Hongo, Bunkyo-ku, Tokyo 113-0033; tel. (3) 3814-4121; fax (3) 3814-4699; internet www.sice.or.jp; f. 1962; 9,183 mems; Pres. SUSUMU TACHI; Vice-Pres RYOICHI TAKAHASHI, KAZUO KYUMA; publ. *Journal* (12 a year).

Kuki-Chowa Eisei Kogakkai (Society of Heating, Air-conditioning and Sanitary Engineers of Japan): 8-1, 1-chome, Kitashinjuku, Shinjuku-ku, Tokyo; f. 1917; 17,000 mems; Pres. M. KAMATA; publs *Journal* (12 a year), *Transactions* (12 a year).

Nihon Genshiryoku Gakkai (Atomic Energy Society of Japan): Shimbashi 2-3-7, Minato-ku, Tokyo 105-0004; tel. (3) 3508-1261; fax (3) 3581-6128; e-mail atom@aesj.or.jp; internet wwwsoc.nii.ac.jp/aesj; f. 1959; peaceful uses of atomic energy; 7,700 mems; Pres. Dr M. TAKUMA; Sec.-Gen. Y. TARUISHI; publs *Journal of Nuclear Science and Technology* (12 a year), *Nihon-Genshiryoku-Gakkai Shi* (12 a year), *Transactions of the Atomic Energy Society of Japan* (4 a year).

Nihon Kasai Gakkai (Japanese Association for Fire Science and Engineering): 3F Gakkai Center Bldg, 2-4-16 Yayoi, Bunkyo-ku, Tokyo 113-0032; tel. (3) 3813-8308; fax (3) 5689-3577; e-mail kasai50@sepia.ocn.ne.jp; f. 1951; 2,000 mems; Pres. TAKAO WAKAMATU; publ. *Kasai* (Fire, 6 a year).

Nihon Kikai Gakkai (Japan Society of Mechanical Engineers): Shinanomachi-Rengakan 5F, 35 Shinanomachi, Shinjuku, Tokyo 160-0016; tel. (3) 5360-3500; fax (3) 5360-3508; e-mail wwwadmin@jsme.or.jp; internet www.jsme.or.jp; f. 1897; 40,000 mems; Pres. MASAKI SHIRATORI; publs *Journal* (12 a year), *JSME International Journal* (in English, 12 a year, online), *Transactions* (12 a year).

Nippon Kinzoku Gakkai (Japan Institute of Metals): 1-14-32 Ichibancho, Aoba-ku, Sendai 980-8544; tel. (22) 223-3685; fax (22) 223-6312; e-mail secgnl@jim.or.jp; f. 1937; 10,000 mems; Pres. KIYOHITO ISHIDA; publs *Bulletin* (12 a year), *Journal* (12 a year),

Materials Transactions (in English, 12 a year).

Nippon Kogakukai (Japan Federation of Engineering Societies): Nogizaka Bldg, 6-41, Akasaka 9-chome, Minato-ku, Tokyo 107; internet www.jfes.or.jp; f. 1879.

Nippon Koku Ūchu Gakkai (Japan Society for Aeronautical and Space Sciences): c/o Meiko Bldg, Bekkan, 1-18-2 Shinbash, Minato-ku, Tokyo 105-0004; tel. (3) 3501-0463; fax (3) 3501-0464; e-mail office@jsass.or.jp; internet www.jsass.or.jp; f. 1934; 4,400 mems; Pres. Prof. KANICHIROU KATO; publs *Journal* (12 a year), *Transactions* (4 a year).

Nippon Seramikusu Kyoukai (Ceramic Society of Japan): 22-17, 2-chome, Hyakunin-cho, Shinjuku-ku, Tokyo 169-0073; fax (3) 3362-5714; e-mail information@cersj.org; internet www.ceramic.or.jp; f. 1891; 5,546 mems; Pres. YOSHINORI KOKUBU; publs *Journal, Ceramics Japan* (Bulletin).

Nippon Shashin Gakkai (Society of Photographic Science and Technology of Japan): Tokyo Polytechnic Institute, 2-9-5 Hon-cho, Nakano-ku, Tokyo 164-8678; tel. (3) 3373 0724; fax (3) 3299 5887; internet www.spstj.org; f. 1925; 1,550 mems; Pres. T. WAKABAYASHI; publ. *Journal* (6 a year).

Nippon Tekko Kyoukai (Iron and Steel Institute of Japan): Niikura Building, 2-Kanda-Tsukasacho 2-chome, Chiyoda-ku, Tokyo 101-0048; tel. (3) 5209-7011; fax (3) 3257-1110; internet www.isij.or.jp; f. 1915; 9,274 mems; Exec. Dir Dr AKIRA KOJIMA; publs *Ferrum* (bulletin, in Japanese, 12 a year), *ISIJ International* (in English, 12 a year), *Tetsu-to-Hagané* (Iron and Steel, in Japanese, 12 a year).

Nippon Tribologi Gakkai (Japanese Society of Tribologists): c/o Kikai Shinko Kaikan No. 407-2, 3-5-8, Shibakoen, Minato-ku, Tokyo 105-0001; tel. (3) 3434-1926; fax (3) 3434-3556; e-mail jast@tribology.jp; internet www.tribology.jp; f. 1956; 3,044 mems; Pres. TAKASHI YAMAMOTO; publs *Journal of Japanese Society of Tribologists* (12 a year), *Tribology* (online).

Nogyo-Doboku Gakkai (Japanese Society of Irrigation, Drainage and Reclamation Engineering): Nogyo Doboku-Kaikan, 34-4 Shinbashi 5-chome, Tokyo 105-0004; tel. (3) 3436-3418; fax (3) 3435-8494; e-mail suido@jsidre.or.jp; internet www.jsidre.or.jp; f. 1929; 13,000 mems; Pres. Prof. TSUYOSHI MIYAZAKI; publs *Journal* (12 a year), *Journal of Rural and Environmental Engineering* (in English, 2 a year), *Transactions* (6 a year).

Seisan Gijutsu Kenkyusho (Institute of Industrial Science): c/o University of Tokyo, 4-6-1 Komaba, Meguro-ku, Tokyo 153-8505; tel. (3) 5454-6024; fax (3) 5452-6094; e-mail kokusai@iis.u-tokyo.ac.jp; internet www.iis.u-tokyo.ac.jp; f. 1949; Dir-Gen. Prof. S. NISHIO; publ. *Seisan-Kenkyu* (12 a year).

Shigen Sozai Gakkai (Mining and Materials Processing Institute of Japan): Nogizaka Bldg, 9-6-41 Akasaka, Minato-ku, Tokyo 107; tel. (3) 3402-0541; fax (3) 3403-1776; e-mail info@mmij.or.jp; internet www.mmij.or.jp; f. 1885; 2,627 mems; Sec.-Gen. YAMAGUCHI TAKASHI; publs *Journal* (12 a year), *Metallurgical Review* (2 a year), *MMIJ Proceedings* (2 a year).

Sisutemu Seigyo Jyouhou Gakkai (Institute of Systems, Control and Information Engineers): 14 Yoshidakawaharacho, Sakyo ward, Kyoto City, Kyoto 606-8305; tel. (75) 751-6413; fax (75) 751-6037; e-mail shomu@iscie.or.jp; internet www.iscie.or.jp; f. 1957; 2,744 mems; Pres. MINORU ABE; publ. *Systems, Control and Information* (12 a year).

Yosetsu Gakkai (Japan Welding Society): 1-11 Sakuma-cho, Kanda, Chiyoda-ku, Tokyo;

tel. (3) 3253-0488; fax (3) 3253-3059; internet wwwsoc.nii.ac.jp/jws; f. 1925; 5,000 mems; Pres. Dr SHUZO SUSEI; publ. *Journal* (12 a year).

Research Institutes
GENERAL

Kokusai Nihon Bunka Kenkyu Center (International Research Center for Japanese Studies): 3–2 Oeyama-cho, Goryo, Nishikyo-ku, Kyoto 610-1192; tel. (75) 335-2222; fax (75) 335-2091; e-mail www-admin@nichibun.ac.jp; internet www.nichibun.ac.jp; f. 1987; attached to Nat. Institutes for the Humanities (an Inter-Univ. Research Institute Corporation); interdisciplinary and comprehensive research on Japanese studies, and research cooperation; library of 420,000 vols, 6,700 periodicals; Dir-Gen. Dr TAKENORI INOKI; publs *Japan Review* (in English), *Nihon Kenkyu* (in Japanese).

Sogo Kenkyu Kaihatsu Kiko (National Institute for Research Advancement): POB 5004, 34F Yebisu Garden Place Tower, 4-20-3 Ebisu, Shibuya-ku, Tokyo 150-6034; tel. (3) 5448-1700; fax (3) 5448-1743; e-mail info@nira.or.jp; internet www.nira.or.jp; f. 1974 under parliamentary legislation to promote and conduct interdisciplinary research that focuses on the problems facing modern society and their alleviation; conducts its own research, also commissions and subsidizes research by other bodies; promotes international exchange of research affecting policy-making around the world; research results are made public through lectures, symposia or publication of reports; Chair. YOTARO KOBAYASHI; Pres. MOTOSHIGE ITO; Executive Vice-Presidents YOSHIO EZAKI, YASUO SAWAI; publs *Almanac of Think Tanks in Japan, NIRA Kenkyu Hokokusho, NIRA News, NIRA Research Output* (in English), *NIRA Review* (in English), *NIRA Seisaku Kenkyu, NIRA's World Directory of Think Tanks* (in English).

AGRICULTURE, FISHERIES AND VETERINARY SCIENCE

Forest and Forest Products Research Institute: 1 Matsunosato, Tsukuba Ibaraki 305-8687; tel. (29) 873-3211; fax (29) 874-3720; internet www.ffpri.affrc.go.jp; f. 1878; library of 386,000 vols (incl. br. stations); Pres. KAZUO SUZUKI; publ. *Bulletin* (4 a year).

National Agriculture Research Center: 3-1-1 Kannondai, Tsukuba, Ibaraki 305-8666; tel. (29) 838-8481; fax (29) 838-8484; e-mail www@narc.affrc.go.jp; internet narc.naro.affrc.go.jp; f. 1981; library of 62,000 vols, 5,800 periodicals; Dir-Gen. AKHIRO SASAKI; publs *Bulletin* (2 a year), *Miscellaneous* (1 a year), *Farming System Research* (1 a year).

National Food Research Institute: 2-1-12 Kannondai, Tsukuba, Ibaraki 305-8642; tel. (29) 838-7971; fax (29) 838-7996; internet www.nfri.affrc.go.jp; f. 1934; food processing, chemistry, technology, storage, engineering, distribution, nutrition; applied microbiology, analysis, radiation, etc.; 121 mems; library of 40,000 vols; Dir Dr S. TANIGUCHI; publs *Report of the National Food Research Institute, Food Science and Technology.*

National Institute for Rural Engineering: 2-1-6 Kannondai, Tsukuba-shi, Ibaraki-ken 305-8609; tel. (298) 38-7513; fax (298) 38-7609; internet www.nkk.affrc.go.jp; f. 1988; research on engineering technologies for agriculture and rural community areas; 115 mems; library of 38,000 vols; Dir-Gen. HIR-

OSHI SATO; publs *Bulletin* (12 a year), *Technical Report* (irregular).

National Institute of Agrobiological Sciences (NIAS): 2-1-2 Kannondai, Tsukuba, Ibaraki 305-8602; tel. (298) 38-7406; fax (298) 38-7408; e-mail niasl@nias.affrc.go.jp; internet www.nias.affrc.go.jp; f. 2001 by merger of National Institute of Agrobiological Resources (NIAR) and National Institute of Sericultural and Entomological Sciences (NISES); life science research on plants, animals and insects to facilitate the devt of Japan's domestic agricultural industry; 400 mems; library of 75,000 vols; Pres. TERUO ISHIGE; publ. *Gamma Field Symposia* (1 a year).

National Institute of Animal Health: 3-1-5, Kannondai, Tsukuba-shi, Ibaraki 305-0856; tel. (29) 838-7708; fax (29) 838-7907; e-mail ref-niah@ml.affrc.go.jp; internet niah.naro.affrc.go.jp; f. 1921; animal husbandry, biology, veterinary medicine; 3 br. laboratories; library of 21,422 vols, 2,465 serial titles; Dir-Gen. Dr YOSUKE MURAKAMI; publs *Animal Health* (research report, 1 a year), *Bulletin* (1 a year).

National Institute of Crop Science: 2-1-18 Kannondai, Tsukuba, Ibaraki 305-8518; tel. (298) 38-8260; fax (298) 38-7488; e-mail www-nics@naro.affrc.go.jp; internet nics.naro.affrc.go.jp; f. 1893; library of 130,000 vols; publ. *Bulletin* (irregular).

National Institute of Fruit Tree Science: 2-1 Fujimoto, Tsukuba, Ibaraki 305-8605; tel. (29) 838-6451; fax (29) 838-6437; e-mail www-fruit@naro.affrc.go.jp; internet fruit.naro.affrc.go.jp; f. 1902; library of 60,000 vols; Dir Dr YOSHINORI HASEGAWA.

National Institute of Livestock and Grassland Science: 2 Ikenodai, Kukizaki, Inashiki Ibaraki 305-0901; tel. (298) 38-8618; fax (298) 38-8573; e-mail www@nilgs-t.affrc.go.jp; internet www.nilgs.naro.affrc.go.jp; f. 1916; library of 51,000 vols; publ. *Bulletin* (irregular).

National Institute of Vegetable and Tea Science: 360 Kusawa, Ano, Age Mie 514–2392; tel. (59) 268-4621; fax (59) 268-1339; internet vegetea.naro.affrc.go.jp; f. 1902; publ. *Bulletin* (1 a year).

Policy Research Institute, Ministry of Agriculture, Forestry and Fisheries: 2-2-1 Nishigahara, Kita-ku, Tokyo; tel. (3) 3910-3946; fax (3) 3940-0232; e-mail www@primaff.affrc.go.jp; internet www.primaff.affrc.go.jp; f. 1946; library of 331,495 vols; Dir T. SHINOHARA; publ. *Journal of Agricultural Policy Research* (in Japanese).

ECONOMICS, LAW AND POLITICS

Chuto Chosakai (Middle East Institute of Japan): Sanko Park Bldg, 5th Fl., 7-3-1 Nishi-Shinjuku-ku, Tokyo 160-0023; tel. (3) 3371-5798; fax (3) 3371-5799; internet www.meij.or.jp; f. 1960; government-aided; exchanges information with other countries; research activities in 4 areas: political and diplomatic affairs, industry, economy, natural resources; library in process of formation; Chair. KOSAKU INABA; publs *Chuto Kenkyu* (Journal of Middle East Studies, 12 a year), *Chuto Kitaafurika Nenkan* (Yearbook of the Middle East and North Africa).

Japan Center for International Exchange: 4-9-17 Minami-Azabu, Minato-ku, Tokyo 106-0047; tel. (3) 3446-7781; fax (3) 3443-7580; e-mail admin@jcie.or.jp; internet www.jcie.or.jp; f. 1971 to promote dialogue between Japan and the rest of the world; int. conferences and seminars, overseas programme planning, promotion of policy studies and exchange programmes among philanthropic organizations; Japanese Secretariat of the Trilateral Commission; Pres. TADASHI YAMAMOTO.

Japan Economic Research Institute: 6th Floor, Kowa 32 Bldg, 2-32, Minami-Azabu 5-chome, Minato-ku, Tokyo 106-0047; tel. (3) 3442-9400; fax (3) 3442-9403; e-mail web@nikkeicho.or.jp; internet www.nikkeicho.or.jp; f. 1962; research and study of domestic and foreign economic and business management; library of 8,000 vols; Exec. Dir KATSUZO YAMADA; Chair. KENJIRO NAGASAKA; publ. research reports.

Japan Maritime Development Association: Kaiun Bldg, 6-4, 2-chome, Hirakawa-cho, Chiyoda-ku, Tokyo; tel. (3) 3265-5231; fax (3) 3265-5035.

Kabushikikaisha Mitsubishi Sogo Kenkyusho (Mitsubishi Research Institute, Inc.): 3-6, Otemachi 2-chome, Chiyoda-ku, Tokyo 100-8141; tel. (3) 3270-9211; fax (3) 3279-1308; internet www.mri.co.jp; f. 1970; aims to meet new social, economic and industrial requirements in an age of advanced information systems and internationalization; research on nat. and int. scale to serve the needs of government agencies and industry in the fields of economic, political, industrial and management affairs, techno-economics, social engineering, technology and data processing; 900 mems; library of 63,000 vols, 1,000 periodicals; Chair. TAKESHI YANO; Pres. MASAYUKI TANAKA; publs *Outlook for the Japanese Economy* (2 a year), *Journal* (2 a year), *MRI Analysis of Japanese Corporations* (2 a year).

National Institute of Population and Social Security Research: 6th Fl., Hibiya Kokusai Bldg, 2-2-3 Uchisaiwaicyo, Chiyoda-ku, Tokyo 100-0011; tel. (3) 3595-2984; fax (3) 3591-4816; e-mail soumuka@ipss.go.jp; internet www.ipss.go.jp; f. 1939; part of Ministry of Health and Welfare; library of 16,000 vols; Dir TAKANOBU KYOGOKU; publ. *Journal of Population Problems* (4 a year).

Nihon Boeki Shinkokiko Ajia Keizai Kenkyusho (Institute of Developing Economies, Japan External Trade Organization (IDE-JETRO)): 3-2-2 Wkaba, Mihama-ku, Chiba-shi, Chiba 261-8454; tel. (43) 299-9500; fax (43) 299-9724; e-mail info@ide.go.jp; internet www.ide.go.jp; f. 1960; library of 600,000 vols; 400 mems; researches on economic, political and social issues in developing economies to support Japan's expansion of harmonious trade and investment; provision of int. economic cooperation focused on developing economies; Chair.and CEO YASUO HAYASHI; Pres. TAKASHI SHIRAISHI; publs *Ajia Keizai* (in Japanese, 12 a year), *The Developing Economies* (in English, 4 a year), *Ajiken World Trend* (in Japanese, 12 a year).

Nihon Keizai Kenkyu Center (Japan Center for Economic Research): Nikkei Kayabacho Bldg, 2-6-1 Nihombashi-kayabacho, Chuo-ku, Tokyo 103; tel. (3) 3639-2801; fax (3) 3639-2839; e-mail jcernet@jcer.or.jp; internet www.jcer.or.jp; f. 1963; 372 institutional, 280 individual mems; library of 45,813 vols, 920 periodicals; Pres. S. TOSHIDA; publ. *Asian Economic Policy Review*.

Nippon Keidanren (Japan Business Federation): 1-9-4, Otemachi, Chiyoda-ku, Tokyo 100-8188; tel. (3) 5204-1500; fax (3) 5255-6255; internet www.keidanren.or.jp; f. 2002 by merger of Keidanren (Japan Federation of Economic Organizations) and Nikkeiren (Japan Federation of Employers' Associations); 1,662 mems; library of 100,000 vols; Chair. FUJIO MITARAI.

Nippon Research Center Ltd: 2-7-1 Nihonbashi-honchou, Chuo-ku, Tokyo 103-0023; tel. (3) 6667-3400; fax (3) 6667-3470; internet www.nrc.co.jp; f. 1960 by interdisciplinary researchers and business men to meet the needs of industrial and economic circles; marketing and public opinion research, marketing consultancy, public relations, economic forecasting and urban and regional development; 96 staff; library of 3,000 vols; Pres. INAHIRO SUZUKI; publ. *Bulletin of Marketing Research* (in Japanese, 1 a year).

Rôdô Kagaku Kenkyusho (Institute for Science of Labour): 2-8-14, Sugao, Miyamae-ku, Kawasaki-shi, Kanagawa-ken 216-8501; tel. (44) 977-2121; fax (44) 977-7504; internet www.isl.or.jp; f. 1921; systems safety, chemical health risk management, employment and working life conditions, human–technology interaction, human work environment management, local industries, occupational epidemiology, systems safety, welfare support, work stress,; Pres. YUJIROU HAYASHI; Dir Dr NAOKI MAEHARA; publs *Rôdô Kagaku* (Journal of Science of Labour, 12 a year), *Rôdô no Kagaku* (Digest of Science of Labour, 12 a year).

EDUCATION

Kokuritsu Kyoiku Seisaku Kenkyujo (National Institute for Educational Policy Research): 6-5-22 Shimomeguro, Meguro-ku, Tokyo 153-8681; tel. (3) 5721-5150; fax (3) 3714-7073; e-mail info@nier.go.jp; internet www.nier.go.jp; f. 1949; conducts basic research on specific issues for use in the planning and formulation of education policy and also pursues a wide range of activities such as providing academic sectors with information about educational studies, conducting research studies in conjunction with schools, pursuing practical research into social education, and conducting joint int. initiatives (incl. research studies) in the education field; library: see Libraries; Dir-Gen. SHIGERU YOSHIDA; publs *Bulletin* (in Japanese, annual; in English, irregular), *Kenkyushuroku* (in Japanese, 2 a year), *Koho* (in Japanese, 6 a year), *Unesco-NIER Newsletter* (in English, 3 a year).

FINE AND PERFORMING ARTS

Tokyo Bunkazai Kenkyu-jo (Tokyo National Research Institute of Cultural Properties): 13–43 Ueno Park, Taito-ku, Tokyo 110-8713; tel. (3) 3823-2241; fax (3) 3828-2434; internet www.tobunken.go.jp; f. 1930; depts incl. Intangible Cultural Heritage, Research Programming; also Center for Conservation Science and Restoration Techniques, Japan Center for Int. Co-operation in Conservation and Div. of General Affairs; library of 110,000 vols; Dir-Gen. SUZUKI NORIO; publs *Bijutsu Kenkyu* (Journal of Art Studies, 4 a year), *Hozon Kagaku* (Science for Conservation, 1 a year), *Nihon Bijutsu Nenkan* (Year Book of Japanese Art), *Proceedings of the International Symposium on the Conservation and Restoration of Cultural Property* (1 a year).

Tōyō Ongaku Gakkai (Society for Research in Asiatic Music): 201 Daini Hachikou House, 5-9-25 Yanaka, Taito-ku, Tokyo 110-0001; tel. (3) 3823-5173; fax (3) 3823-5174; internet wwwsoc.nii.ac.jp/tog; f. 1936; aims to promote research in Japanese and other Asian music and ethnomusicology; 750 mems; Pres. KAZUYUKI TANIMOTO; publ. *Tōyō Ongaku Kenkyū* (1 a year).

HISTORY, GEOGRAPHY AND ARCHAEOLOGY

Geographical Survey Institute: Kitasato-1, Tsukuba-shi, Ibaraki-ken 305-0811; tel. (29) 864-1111; fax (29) 864-8087; f. 1869; part of Ministry of Construction; library of 32,000 vols; Dir YOSHIHISA HOSHINO; publ. *Bulletin* (irregular).

LANGUAGE AND LITERATURE

Kokubungaku Kenkyu Siryokan (National Institute of Japanese Literature): Midorityou 10-3 Tachikawa, Tokyo 190-0014; tel. (50) 5533-2900; fax (42) 526-8604; e-mail so-mu@nijl.ac.jp; internet www.nijl.ac.jp; f. 1972 by the Min. of Education, Science and Culture at the recommendation of the Japan Science Council and in response to requests for a centre for the preservation of Japanese classical literature; surveys, collects (largely in microfilm), studies, processes, preserves and provides access to MSS and old printed books relating to Japanese literature before 1868; also undertakes research in this field; provides scholarly community with facilities for consultation and reproduction of materials; historical documents division collects and preserves documents of *kinsei* (1600–1867); library: see Libraries; Dir-Gen. Dr YUICHIRO IMANISHI; publs *Bulletin* (1 a year), *Bibliographic Reports* (1 a year), *Bibliography of Research in Japanese Literature* (1 a year), *Proceedings of the International Conference on Japanese Literature in Japan* (1 a year).

Kokuritu Kokugo Kenkyuzyo (National Institute for Japanese Language): 3-9-14, Nisigaoka, Kita-ku, Tokyo 115; tel. (3) 3900-3111; fax (3) 3906-3530; internet www.kokken.go.jp; f. 1948; library of 105,000 vols; Pres. SEIJU SUGITO; Dir MICHITERU TOKUSHIGE; publs *Kokugo Nenkan* (Japanese Language Studies, 1 a year), *Nihongo Kagaku* (Japanese Linguistics), *Nihongo Kyouiku Ronshu* (Japanese Language Education, 1 a year).

MEDICINE

Cancer Institute, Japanese Foundation for Cancer Research: 3-10-6 Ariake, Koto ward, Tokyo, 135-8550; tel. (3) 3520-0111; fax (3) 3520-0141; internet www.jfcr.or.jp; f. 1908; departments of biochemistry, cancer chemotherapy, cell biology, experimental pathology, gene research, human genome analysis, pathology, physics, molecular biotherapy and viral oncology; library of 5,000 vols, 10,000 periodicals; Cancer Chemotherapy Center, Cancer Institute Hospital and Genome Center attached; Dir Dr TETSUO NODA; publ. *Japan Journal for Cancer Research* (12 a year).

Institute of Brain and Blood Vessels: 6-23 Ootemachi, Isezaki-city, Gumma; tel. (270) 24-3355; fax (270) 24-3359; f. 1963; clinical and basic research on cerebrovascular disease; 356 mems; Dir Dr TATSURU MIHARA; publ. *Nosotchu No Kenkyu* (Studies on Apoplexy).

Institute of Chemotherapy: 6-1-14 Kohnodai, Ichikawa-city, Chiba; tel. (473) 75-1111; fax (473) 73-4921; f. 1939; Dir Prof. TSUGUO HASEGAWA; publ. *Bulletin of the Institute of Chemotherapy*.

Institute of Public Health: 4-6-1 Shirokanedai, Minato-ku, Tokyo 108-8638; tel. (3) 3441-7111; fax (3) 3446-4314; internet www.iph.go.jp; f. 1938; part of Ministry of Health and Welfare; postgraduate education and research in public health; library of 68,000 vols, 1,500 periodicals; Dir K. FURUICHI; publ. *Bulletin* (4 a year).

Kekkaku Yobo Kai Kekkaku Kenkyujo (Research Institute of Tuberculosis, Japan Anti-Tuberculosis Association): 3-1-24 Matsuyama Kiyose-shi, Tokyo 204-8533; tel. (424) 93-5711; fax (424) 92-4600; internet www.jata.or.jp; f. 1939; research on health education campaign against tuberculosis: information, surveillance and training center: tuberculosis and respiratory diseases;; 56 mems; library of 15,000 vols; Dir Dr NOBUKATSU ISHIKAWA; publs *Information and Review of Tuberculosis and Respiratory Disease Research* (in Japanese, 4 a year), *Red Double-Barred Cross* (in Japanese, 6 a year), *Review of Tuberculosis for Public Health Nurses* (in Japanese, 2 a year).

Kitasato Institute Research Center for Biologicals: 6-111 Arai, Kitamoto-shi, Saitama 108; tel. (3) 3444-6161; internet www.kitasato.ac.jp; f. 1914; research on the cause, prevention and therapy of various diseases; 1,100 mems; library of 86,000 vols; Dir S. OMURA.

Kohno Clinical Medicine Research Institute: 1-28-15 Kita-Shinagawa, Shinagawa-ku, Tokyo; tel. (3) 472-4630; fax (3) 474-1355; internet kcmi.or.jp; f. 1951; 62 staff; library of 3,000 vols; Dir M. KOHNO; publs *Archives, Bulletin*.

Miyake Medical Institute: 1-3 Tenjin-mae, Takamatsu-city, Kagawa; internet www.miyake.or.jp; f. 1949; Dir T. MIYAKE.

National Cancer Center: 5-1-1 Tsukiji, Chuo-ku, Tokyo 104-0045; tel. (3) 3542-2511; fax (3) 3542-3567; e-mail www-admin@ncc.go.jp; internet www.ncc.go.jp; f. 1962; diagnosis, treatment and research of cancer and allied diseases; Dept of Ministry of Health and Welfare; 800 staff; library of 56,000 vols, 17,000 monographs, 500 periodicals; Pres. SETSUO HIROHASHI; Dirs RYOSUKE TSUCHIYA (Hospital), KEIJI WAKABAYASHI (Research Institute); publs *Collected Papers of Hospital* (in Japanese and English, 1 a year, distributed free to libraries), *Collected Papers of Research Inst.* (in English, 1 a year, distributed free to libraries), *Tumour Registration of Bone, Lung, Stomach, Blood, Brain, etc.* (in Japanese, distributed free to libraries).

National Institute of Genetics: 1111, Yata, Mishima-city, Shizuoka 411-8540; tel. (55) 981-6707; fax (55) 981-6715; e-mail shomuka@lab.nig.ac.jp; internet www.nig.ac.jp/home.html; f. 1949; part of Ministry of Education, Science, Sports and Culture; library of 20,000 vols; Dir Dr YOSHIKI HOTTA.

National Institute of Health and Nutrition: 1-23-1 Toyama, Shinjuku-ku, Tokyo 162-8636; tel. (3) 3203-5721; fax (3) 3202-3278; e-mail eiken-office@nih.go.jp; internet www.nih.go.jp; f. 1920; part of Ministry of Health and Welfare; library of 30,000 vols; Dir NOBUAKI SHIBAIKE; publ. *Japanese Journal of Nutrition* (in Japanese, every 2 months).

National Institute of Health Sciences: 1-18-1 Kamiyoga, Setagaya, Tokyo 15-8501; tel. (3) 3700-1141; fax (3) 3707-6950; internet www.nihs.go.jp; f. 1874; research in connection with the cosmetics, drugs, environmental chemicals, medical devices and regulation of foods; Dir MASAHIRO NISHIJIMA; publ. *Bulletin* (1 a year).

National Institute of Occupational Safety and Health: 6-21-1, Nagao Tamaku, Kawasaki-city, Kanagawa 214-8585; tel. (44) 865-6111; fax (44) 865-6124; e-mail info@niih.go.jp; internet www.jniosh.go.jp/en; f. 1956; part of Ministry of Health, Labour and Welfare; library of 26,000 vols; Dir YUTAKA MAEDA; publ. *Industrial Health* (6 a year).

National Institute of Infectious Diseases: Toyama 1-23-1, Shinjuku-ku, Tokyo 162-8640; tel. (3) 5285-1111; fax (3) 5285-1150; e-mail info@nih.go.jp; internet www.nih.go.jp/niid; f. 1947; part of Ministry of Health, Labour and Welfare; research on communicable diseases, including an AIDS Research Centre; assay of biological products and antibiotics; library of 30,000 vols; Dir TATSUO MIYAMURA; publ. *The Japanese Journal of Infectious Diseases* (6 a year).

National Institute of Mental Health, National Center of Neurology and Psychiatry: 4-1-1 Higashimaci, Kodairashi, Tokyo 187-8553; tel. (42) 341-2711; fax (42) 346-1944; internet www.ncnp.go.jp/nimh; f. 1952; part of Ministry of Health and Welfare; Dir A. FUJINAWA; publ. *Journal of Mental Health* (1 a year).

Neuropsychiatric Research Institute: 91 Benten-cho, Shinjuku-ku, Tokyo; tel. (3) 3260-9171; fax (3) 3260-9191; internet www.seiwa-hp.com; f. 1951; research on sleep disorders, mood disorders; art therapy; Chief Dir T. HIROSE.

Nukada Institute for Medical and Biological Research: 5-18 Inage-cho, Chiba-city, Chiba; f. 1939; Dir Dr H. NUKADA; publ. *Report* (irregular).

Ogata Institute for Medical and Chemical Research: 2-10-14 Higashi-Kanda, Chiyoda-ku, Tokyo 101-0031; tel. (3) 3865-7500; fax (3) 3865-7510; f. 1962; library of 12,000 vols; Pres. MASAHIDE ABE; publ. *Igaku to Seibutsugaku* (Medicine and Biology, 12 a year).

Tokyo Metropolitan Institute of Medical Science: Honkomagome 3-18-22, Bunkyoku, Tokyo 113-8613; tel. (3) 3823-2105; fax (3) 3823-2965; e-mail ui@rinshoken.or.jp; internet www.rinshoken.or.jp; f. 1975; research in aetiology and pathogenesis of intractable diseases and application of molecular and cellular biology to the aetiology of these diseases; library of 30,000 vols; Dir KEIJI TANAKA; publ. *Rinshoken News* (in Japanese, 12 a year).

NATURAL SCIENCES

General

Kokuritsu Kyokuchi Kenkyujyo (National Institute of Polar Research): 9–10 Kaga 1-chome, Itabashi-ku, Tokyo 173-8515; tel. (3) 3962-4712; fax (3) 3962-2529; e-mail shomu@nipr.ac.jp; internet www.nipr.ac.jp; f. 1973; attached to Joho Shisutemu Kenkyu Kiko (Research Organization of Information Systems); replaces the former Polar Research Centre of the National Science Museum; government-sponsored; implements programmes of the Japanese Antarctic Research Expeditions (JARE), organizes postgraduate courses in polar subjects, offers research facilities to national and foreign universities and individual researchers; library of 44,200 vols and bound periodicals57 full-time staff; Dir Prof. OKISUGU WATANABE; publs include *Nankyoku Shiryo* (Antarctic Record, 3 a year), *Memoirs of the National Institute of Polar Research* (Special Issue), *JARE Data Reports* (10 a year), *Journal* (1 a year), *Arctic Data Reports*, *Antarctic Geological Map Series*.

Biological Sciences

Kihara Institute for Biological Research: Yokohama City University, Maioka-cho 641, Totsuka-ku, Yokohama 244; tel. (45) 820-1900; fax (45) 820-1901; f. 1942; library of 20,000 vols; Dir KAORU MIYAZAKI; publs *Seiken Ziho* (1 a year), *Wheat Information Service* (2 a year).

Mitsubishi Kasei Institute of Life Sciences: 11 Minamiooya, Machida-shi, Tokyo 194-8511; tel. (427) 24-6248; fax (427) 24-6312; e-mail lspr@mitils.jp; internet www.mitils.co.jp; f. 1971; research in human and general life science; library of 5,000 vols; Pres. Dr TAKAO SEKIYA; Chair Dr AKIHIRO TOBE.

Osaka Bioscience Institute: 6-2-4 Furue-dai, Suita-shi, Osaka 565-0874; tel. (6) 6872-4812; fax (6) 6872-4818; e-mail office@obi.or.jp; internet www.obi.or.jp; f. 1987; library of 12,000 vols; Dir Dr HIDESABURO HANAFUSA; Librarian ATSUKO TAKIKAWA.

Tokyo Biochemical Research Institute: Kyobashi NS Bldg, 2-5-21 Kyobashi, Chuo-ku, Tokyo 104-0031; tel. (3) 3562-5705; fax (3) 3562-5730; e-mail asia@tokyobrf.or.jp; internet www.tokyobrf.or.jp; f. 1950; Dir M. OKADA.

Mathematical Sciences

Institute of Statistical Mathematics: 4-6-7 Minami Azabu, Minato-ku, Tokyo 106-8569; tel. (3) 5421-8719; fax (3) 5421-8719; internet www.ism.ac.jp; f. 1944; Nat. Inter-Univ. Research Institute; research in statistics; library of 52,000 vols, 2,250 periodicals; Dir Prof. GENSHIRO KITAGAWA; publs *Annals* (4 a year), *Proceedings* (2 a year).

Physical Sciences

Fukada Geological Institute: 2-13-12 Hon-Komagome, Bunkyo-ku, Tokyo 113-0021; tel. (3) 3944-8010; fax (3) 3944-5404; e-mail fgi@fgi.or.jp; internet www.fgi.or.jp; f. 1954; Chair TADASHI SATO; publs *Fukadaken Library* (10 a year), *Nenpo* (in Japanese or English, both with English abstract, 1 a year).

Institute of Physical and Chemical Research (RIKEN): 2–1 Hirosawa, Wako-shi, Saitama 351-0198; tel. (48) 462-1111; fax (48) 462-1554; e-mail koho@riken.jp; internet www.riken.go.jp; f. 1917; studies related to science and technology; 621 mems; library of 100,000 vols; Pres. RYOJI NOYORI; publs *RIKEN Accelerated Progress Report* (1 a year), *RIKEN Review* (6 a year).

Japan Atomic Energy Agency (JAEA): 4–49 Muramatsu, Tokai-mura, Naka-gun, Ibaraki 319-1184; tel. (29) 282-1122; internet www.jaea.go.jp; f. 2005 by merger of Japan Atomic Energy Research Institute (JAERI) and Japan Nuclear Cycle Development Institute (JNC); library of 36,000 vols; Pres. TOSHIO OKAZAKI; Exec. Dir ICHIRO NAKAJIMA.

Kobayasi Institute of Physical Research: 3-20-41 Higashi-Motomachi, Kokubunji, Tokyo 185-0022; tel. (42) 321-2841; fax (42) 322-4698; e-mail info@kobayasi-riken.or.jp; internet www.kobayasi-riken.or.jp; f. 1940; acoustics (noise and vibration, acoustic material, piezoelectric material); Pres. M. YAMASHITA; Dir K. YAMAMOTO.

Meteorological Research Institute: 1–1 Nagamine, Tsukuba, Ibaraki 3050052; tel. (29) 853-8546; fax (29) 853-8545; www.mri-jma.go.jp; f. 1942; 174 mems; meteorology, geophysics, seismology, oceanography, geochemistry; Dir S. KADOWAKI; publ. *Papers in Meteorology and Geophysics* (4 a year).

National Astronomical Observatory, Mizusawa VERA Observatory: 2-12 Hoshigaoka-cho, Oshu-shi Mizusawa, Iwate-ken 023-0861; tel. (197) 22-7111; fax (197) 22-7120; internet www.miz.nao.ac.jp; f. 1899; astronomy, geophysics, geodesy; part of Institute of Natural Sciences; library of 68,400 vols; Prof. H. KOBAYASHI; publ. *National Astronomical Observatory Technical Reports of the Mizusawa Kansoku Centre*.

National Institute for Materials Science: 1-2-1 Sengen, Tsukuba, Ibaraki 305-0047; tel. (29) 859-2000; e-mail info@nims.go.jp; internet www.nims.go.jp; f. 2001; Pres. Prof. TERUO KISHI.

Space Activities Commission: 2-2-1 Kasumigaseki, Chiyoda-ku, Tokyo 100-8966; tel. (3) 3581-5271; fax (3) 3503-2570; f. 1968; contributes to a comprehensive and stream-lined execution of government programmes on space development, incl. organization of administrative agencies, planning of general policies and outlining training programmes for researchers and technicians; Chair. SADA-KAZU TANIGAKI.

RELIGION, SOCIOLOGY AND ANTHROPOLOGY

Okura Institute for the Study of Spiritual Culture: 706 Futoo-cho, Kohoku-ku, Yokohama; tel. (45) 542-0050; fax (45) 542-0051; f. 1929; Dir N. SASAI; publ. *Okuravama Ronshu.*

TECHNOLOGY

Building Research Institute: 1 Tachihara, Tsukuba-shi, Ibaraki Pref.; tel. (29) 864-2151; fax (29) 864-2989; e-mail bri@kenken.go.jp; internet www.kenken.go.jp; f. 1946; 101 mems; building design and use, building economics, building materials, construction techniques, earthquake engineering, environmental engineering, fire safety, structural engineering, town planning; library of 50,000 vols; Dir-Gen. H. YAMANOUCHI; publ. *BRI Research Papers.*

Civil Engineering Research Institute of Hokkaido/Hokkaido Development Agency: Hiragishi 1-3, Toyohira-ku Sapporo 062-8602; internet www.ceri.go.jp; f. 1937; library of 36,000 vols; Pres. TOMONORI SAITO; publ. *Report* (4 a year).

Communications Research Laboratory: 4-2-1 Nukui-Kitamachi, Koganei, Tokyo 184-8795; tel. (42) 327-5392; fax (42) 327-7587; e-mail publicity@crl.go.jp; internet www.crl.go.jp; f. 1952; next-generation information-communication networks, radio, space and optical communication, space weather forecasting, and related fields; library of 160,000 vols; Dir T. IIDA; publs *CRL Annual Bulletin* (in Japanese), *CRL News* (in Japanese, 12 a year), *Ionospheric Data in Japan* (12 a year), *Journal* (4 a year), *Review* (in Japanese, 4 a year).

Engineering Research Institute: Faculty of Engineering, University of Tokyo, 11-16, Yayoi, 2 chome, Bunkyo-ku, Tokyo; f. 1939; 67 staff; library of 6,747 vols; Dir YOICHI GOSHI.

Institute for Fermentation, Osaka: 17-85, Juso-honmachi 2-chome, Yodogawaku, Osaka 532; tel. (6) 6300-6555; fax (6) 6300-6814; e-mail desk@ifo.or.jp; internet www.ifo.or.jp; f. 1944; preservation and distribution of micro-organisms and animal cells; 23 staff; library of 800 vols; Dir Dr TORU HASEGAWA; publs *List of Cultures*, *IFO Research Communications* (every 2 years).

Institute for Future Technology: Tomiokabashi Bldg, 2-6-11 Fukagawa, Koto-ku, Tokyo; tel. (3) 5245-1011; fax (3) 5245-1061; internet www.iftech.or.jp; f. 1971; research in the fields of technology forecasting, technology assessment and other socio-economic research in future technologies (electronics, telecommunications, space and energy); library of 15,000 vols; Pres. HIROEI FUJIOKA; Chief Sec. TAKAMITSU KOSHIKAWA; publ. *Kenkyu Seika Gaiyo* (research results, in Japanese, 1 a year).

Institute of Research and Innovation, Japan: 1-6-8 Yushima, Bunkyo-ku, Tokyo 113; tel. (3) 5689-6356; fax (3) 5689-6350; f. 1959; fmrly Industrial Research Institute, Japan; independent; research and development in technology and socio-technology, including alternative energy sources, nuclear technologies and related innovative problems; 70 research staff; library of 2,000 vols; Pres. SHO NASU; Dir JIRO MIYAMOTO; publ. *Bulletin* (in Japanese, 4 a year).

International Association of Traffic and Safety Sciences: 6-20, 2-chome, Yaesu, Chuo-ku, Tokyo 104-0028; f. 1974; aims to contribute to the realization of a better traffic soc. through the practical application of research conducted in a variety of fields; research surveys on traffic and its safety; colln and retrieval of information on traffic-related sciences; sponsorship of domestic and int. symposia and study meetings; provision of awards; IATSS Forum, human resource devt programme for south-east Asian countries; Exec. Dir HIROSHI ISHIZUKI; publs *IATSS Research* (in English, 2 a year), *IATSS Review* (in Japanese with English abstracts, 4 a year), *Statistics: Road Accidents in Japan* (in English, 1 a year), *White Paper on Traffic Safety* (in English, 1 a year).

Japan Aerospace Exploration Agency (JAXA): 1-6-4 Marunouchi, Chiyoda-ku, Tokyo 100-0005; tel. (3) 6266-6400; fax (3) 6266-6910; internet www.jaxa.jp; f. 2003 by merger of Institute of Space and Astronautical Science (ISAS), National Aerospace Laboratory of Japan (NAL) and National Space Development Agency of Japan (NASDA); Pres. KEIJI TACHIKAWA.

Japan Construction Method and Machinery Research Institute: 3154 Obuchi, Fuji-shi, Shizuoka-ken; tel. (545) 35-0212; fax (545) 35-3719; e-mail nakashima@cmi.or.jp; f. 1964; construction machine testing and associated research; Dir HIDESUKE NAKASHIMA.

Kokudo Gijyutsu Seisaku Sougou Kenkyujo (National Institute for Land and Infrastructure Management, Ministry of Land, Infrastructure and Transport): 1 Asahi, Tsukuba-shi, Ibaraki-ken 305-0804; tel. (29) 864-4593; fax (29) 864-4322; e-mail kokusai@nilim.go.jp; internet www.nilim.go.jp; f. 2001; 43 research divisions; 386 staff; research on advanced information technology, airports, building, coastal and marine environments, disaster risk management, environment, harbours, housing, land and construction management, ports, rivers, roads, water quality control, and urban planning; library of 193,000 vols; Dir TSU-NEYOSHI MOCHIZUKI; publ. *NILIM News Letter* (in English).

National Institute of Advanced Industrial Science and Technology: Tokyo Headquarters, 1-3-1, Kasumigaseki, Chiyoda-ku, Tokyo 100-8921; tel. (3) 5501-0900; e-mail presec@m.aist.go.jp; internet www.aist.go.jp; f. 2001; government-sponsored research institute; Dir Dr HIROYUKI YOSHIKAWA.

National Marine Research Institute: 6-38-1, Shinkawa, Mitaka, Tokyo 181-0004; tel. (422) 41-3015; fax (422) 41-3247; e-mail info2@nmri.go.jp; internet www.nmri.go.jp; f. 1916; 2001 present name; attached to Ministry of Transport; shipbuilding and marine engineering; library of 68,000 vols; Pres. SHIRO INOUE; publ. *Papers* (6 a year).

Independent Administration Institution National Research Institute for Earth Science and Disaster Prevention (NIED): 3-1 Tennodai, Tsukuba-shi, Ibaraki-ken 305-0006; tel. (29) 851-1611; fax (29) 851-1622; e-mail toiawase@bosai.go.jp; internet www.bosai.go.jp; f. 1963; library of 71,232 vols; Dir YOSHIMITSU OKADA; publs *Report of the NIED* (2 a year), *Technical Note of the NIED*, *Disaster Research Report of the NIED*, *Strong-motion Earthquake Records in Japan* (1 a year), *Prompt Report of Strong-motion Earthquake Records* (irregular).

Branches:

Nagaoka Institute of Snow and Ice Studies: 187-16, Maeyama, Suyoshi Omachi, Nagaoka-shi, Niigata-ken 940; study of techniques for the prevention of snow damage.

Shinjyo NIED Branch of Snow and Ice Studies: 1400, Takadan, Toka-machi, Shinjo-shi, Yamagata-ken 996; study of the prevention of disasters caused by snow and ice.

National Research Institute of Brewing: 2-6-30 Takinogawa, Kita-ku, Tokyo 114-0023; tel. (3) 3910-6237; fax (3) 3910-6236; e-mail info@nrib.go.jp; internet www.nrib.go .jp; f. 1904; Pres. JYUNICHI HIRAMATSU; Exec. Dir YASUZOU KIZAKI.

Noguchi Institute: 1-8-1 Kaga, Itabashi-ku, Tokyo 173-0003; tel. (3) 3961-3255; fax (3) 3964-4071; internet www.noguchi.or.jp; f. 1941; research into carbohydrate chemistry, solid-state catalysts for ecoprocess; Pres. KAGEYASU AKASHI.

Port and Airport Research Institute: 3-1-1 Nagase, Yokosuka, Kanagawa 239-0826; fax (468) 44-5010; fax (468) 44-1274; internet www.pari.go.jp; f. 1962 as Port and Harbour Research Institute; later reorganized into 2 institutes: National Institute for Land and Infrastructure Management and Port and Airport Research Institute; attached to Ministry of Transport; research on all aspects of port, harbour and airport construction technology; library of 20,000 vols; Exec. Researcher Dr SHIGEO TAKAHASHI; publs *Report* (4 a year), *Technical Notes* (4 a year).

Railway Technical Research Institute: 2-8-38 Hikari-cho, Kokubunji-shi, Tokyo 185-8540; tel. (425) 73-7258; fax (425) 73-7356; internet www.rtri.or.jp; f. 1907; research in railway engineering and magnetic levitated vehicles; 530 mems; library of 350,000 vols; Chair. YOSHIJI MATSUMOTO; Pres. HIROUMI SOEJIMA; publs *Quarterly Report of RTRI*, *Railway Research Review* (in Japanese, 12 a year), *Souken Hokoku* (RTRI Report, in Japanese, 12 a year).

Research Institute for Production Development: 15 Shimo Kamomori Honmachi, Sakyo-ku, Kyoto 606-0805; tel. (75) 781-1107; fax (75) 791-7659; f. 1947; Pres. TAKAO YAMAMURO.

Research Institute of Printing Bureau: 6-4-20 Sakawa, Odawara, Kanagawa; tel. (465) 49-4246; f. 1891; Dir H. NONAKA; publ. *Research Bulletin* (2 a year).

Shobo-kenkyujo (National Research Institute of Fire and Disaster): 35-3, Jindaiji-Higashicho 4-Chome, Chofu, Tokyo 182-8508; tel. (422) 44-8331; fax (422) 42-7719; e-mail toiawase2008@fri.go.jp; internet www .fri.go.jp; f. 1948; library of 17,500 vols; Dir AKIRA TERAMURA; publs *Shobo-kenkyujo Hokoku*, *Shoken Syuho* (1 a year).

Tensor Society: c/o Kawaguchi Institute of Mathematical Sciences, Matsu-ga-oka 2-7-15, Chigasaki 253; fax (467) 86-4713; e-mail tensorsociety@ybb.ne.jp; f. 1937; undertakes original research in the field of tensor analysis and its applications; library of 23,000 vols; Pres. Prof. Dr T. KAWAGUCHI; Sec. Prof. Dr H. KAWAGUCHI; publ. *Tensor* (3 a year).

The Institute of Energy Economics, Japan: Inui Bldg, 13–1 Kachidoki 1-chome, Chuo-ku, Tokyo 104-0054; tel. (3) 5547-0211; fax (3) 5547-0223; e-mail otoiawase@tky.ieej .or.jp; internet eneken.ieej.or.jp; f. 1966; coordinates information related to energy, its use, supply, conservation and economic aspects; provides material as basis for planning and policy formation by govt and private business; int. cooperation on energy projects; 188 mems incl. energy-related industries and research instns; library of 53,800 vols; Chair. and CEO MASAHISA NAITOH; Man. Dirs MASAKI CHIBA, KOKICHI ITO, KENSUKE KANEKIYO KENJI KOBAYASHI HIDEKI OKAMOTO,

TSUTOMU TOICHI, Dr KEN KOYAMA, Dr KOICHIRO TANAKA AKIHIRO KUROKI; publs *IEEJ Energy Journal* (in English, 4 a year), *EDMC Handbook of Energy & Economic Statistics in Japan* (in English, 1 a year), *EDMC Energy Trend* (in Japanese, 12 a year).

Libraries and Archives

Akita

Akita Prefectural Library: 14-31 Sannousinmati, Akita-shi, Akita 010-0952; tel. (18) 866-8400; fax (18) 866-6200; e-mail apl@apl .pref.akita.jp; internet www.apl.pref.akita.jp; f. 1899; 403,162 vols; Librarian N. FUJITA.

Chiba

Chiba Prefectural Central Library: 11-1 Ichibacho Chuo-ku, Chiba City 260-8660; tel. (43) 222-0116; internet www.library.pref .chiba.lg.jp; 268,488 vols; Librarian S. TATEISHI.

Hakodate

Hakodate City Library: 17-2 Aoyagi-cho, Hakodate City; tel. (138) 22-7447; fax (138) 22-0837; 122,500 vols (including branch library); Librarian I. FUKUDA.

Hiroshima

Hiroshima Prefectural Library: 3-7-47 Senda-machi, Naka-ku, Hiroshima City; tel. (82) 241-4995; fax (82) 241-9799; f. 1951; public library; 399,957 vols; Librarian K. HATAKEYAMA.

Ise

Jingu Bunko: 1711 Kodakushimoto-cho, Ise, Mie Prefecture 516-0016; tel. (596) 222737; fax (596) 225066; internet www .isejingu.or.jp/bunka/bunbody4.htm; 260,000 vols on Shinto; Librarian KUNIO KOBORI.

Kagoshima

Kagoshima Prefectural Library: 1-1 Shiroyama-machi, Kagoshima City; 222,357 vols; Librarian H. KUBOTA.

Kanazawa

Kanazawa City Libraries: 2-20 Tamagawa-cho, Kanazawa City 920; internet www.lib.kanazawa.ishikawa.jp; 510,000 vols; Librarian N. YOSHIMOTO.

Kanazawa Municipal Izumino Library: 22-22, 4-chome Izumino-machi, Kanazawa City 921-8034; tel. (76) 280-2345; fax (76) 280-2342; e-mail m-m@lib.kanazawa .ishikawa.jp; internet www.lib.kanazawa .ishikawa.jp; f. 1995; 360,000 vols; Dir S. KIDO.

Kobe

Kobe City Library: 7-2 Kununoki-cho, Ikuta, Kobe; f. 1911; 240,000 vols; Librarian S. AKAI.

Kobe University Library: Rokkodai-cho, Nada-ku, Kobe; tel. (78) 803-7315; fax (78) 803-7320; e-mail kikaku@lib.kobe-u.ac.jp; internet www.lib.kobe-u.ac.jp; f. 1908; 2,958,000 vols; Dir TAKESHI SASAKI.

Kochi

Kochi Prefectural Library: 3 Marunouchi, Kochi City; 141,927 vols; Librarian N. SHIMESHINO.

Kyoto

Institute for Research in Humanities Library: Yoshida-Honmachi, Sakyo-ku, Kyoto 606-8501; attached to Kyoto University; 564,000 vols; institute divided into 2 sections: humanities and oriental studies; Dir Prof. NAOKI MIZUNO.

Kyoto Prefectural Library and Archives: 1-4 Hangi-cho, Shimogamo, Sakyo-ku, Kyoto-shi, Kyoto 606-0823; tel. (75) 723-4831; fax (75) 791-9466; internet www.pref.kyoto .jp/shiryokan; f. 1898; 350,000 vols; Dir MINORU SHIBATA.

Kyoto University Library: Yoshida Honmachi, Sakyo-ku, Kyoto 606-8501; tel. (75) 753-2613; fax (75) 753-2629; e-mail w3adm3@kulib.kyoto-u.ac.jp; internet www .kulib.kyoto-u.ac.jp; f. 1899; 6,357,421 vols; central library and 54 libraries of 15 graduate schools and 13 research institutes; Dir Dr JOJI FUJII; publ. *Seishu* (Library Bulletin, 4 a year).

Ryukoku University Library: 67 Tsukamoto-cho, Fukakusa, Fushimi-ku, Kyoto 612; tel. (75) 645-7885; fax (75) 641-7955; e-mail f-lib@ad.ryukoku.ac.jp; internet opac.lib .ryukoku.ac.jp; f. 1639; 1,800,000 vols; 3 brs: Fukakusa, Omiya and Seta libraries; Librarian JITSUZO SHIGETA.

Matsuyama

Matsuyama University Library: 4-2 Bunkyo-cho, Matsuyama 790; tel. (89) 925-7111; fax (86) 926-9116; e-mail mu-libs@ matsuyama-u.jp; internet www.matsuyama .ac.jp; f. 1923; 540,000 vols; collection of rare books, including first editions of 18th- and 19th-century works on political economy; Librarian Prof. K. SHISHIDO.

Nagoya

Nagoya City Tsuruma Central Library: 43 Tsurumai-cho, Tsurumai 1-1-155, Showa-ku, Nagoya City; tel. (52) 741-3131; fax (52) 732-9872; internet www.tsuruma-lib.showa .nagoya.jp; f. 1923; 1,040,400 vols; Librarian Y. WADA.

Nagoya University Library: Furo-cho, Chikusa-ku, Nagoya 464-8601; tel. (52) 789-3678; fax (52) 789-3694; internet www.nul .nagoya-u.ac.jp; f. 1939; central library and 9 school and 3 institute libraries; 2,635,000 vols; Dir Dr M. KAINOH.

Naha

Ryukyu Islands Central Library: Central Library Building, Naha, Okinawa; f. 1950; 45,926 vols; central deposit library.

Nara

Nara Prefectural Library: 48 Nobori Ooji-cho, Nara City 630-8135; tel. (742) 34-2111; fax (742) 34-5514; e-mail info@library.pref .nara.jp; internet www.library.pref.nara.jp; f. 1909; 296,000 vols; Librarian KATSUKO TOYODA; publ. *Untei*.

Niigata

Niigata Prefectural Library: 3-1-2 Meike Minami, Niigata City; tel. (25) 284-6001; fax (25) 284-6832; f. 1915; 610,000 vols; Librarian K. SHIBUYA.

Niigata University Library: 8050 Ikarashi 2-nocho, Nishi-ku, Niigata City 950-2181; f. 1949; 1,672,410 vols; Dir T. YATA.

Nishinomiya

Kwansei Gakuin University Library: 1-1-155 Uegahara, Nishinomiya, Hyogo 662-8501; tel. (798) 54-6121; fax (798) 54-6448; internet library.kwansei.ac.jp; f. 1889; 1,200,000 vols, nearly 40% in foreign languages; br. libraries for 8 schools, 11 graduate schools, 2 satellite campuses; Dean of University Library Services TAKUTOSHI INOUE; publ. *Tokeidai* (Bulletin).

Okayama

Okayama University Library: 1-1 Naka 3-chome, Tsushima, Okayama City 700-8530; tel. (86) 252-1111; fax (86) 251-7314; internet www.lib.okayama-u.ac.jp; f. 1949; 2 br.

libraries; 1,870,000 vols; Dir H. INOUE; publ. *Kai* (Library News, 2 a year).

Osaka

Kansai University Library: 3-3-35 Yamate-cho, Suita-shi, Osaka; tel. (6) 368-1121; fax (6) 330-1464; internet www .kansai-u.ac.jp/english/library; f. 1914; 2,028,000 vols; Librarian K. URANISHI.

Osaka Prefectural Nakanoshima Library: 1-2-10 Nakanoshima, Kita-ku, Osaka 530-0005; tel. (6) 6203-0474; fax (6) 6203-4914; internet www.library.pref.osaka .jp; f. 1903; 545,000 vols; Head Librarian HIROKAZU OMOKI; publ. *Osaka Furitsu Tosyokan Kiyou* (1 a year).

Sapporo

Hokkaido University Library: Kita 8 Nishi 5, Kita-ku, Sapporo 060-0808; tel. (11) 716-2111; fax (11) 747-2855; internet www .lib.hokudai.ac.jp/index_e.html; f. 1876; 20 br. libraries; 3,688,129 vols (incl. 1,798,649 foreign language texts); spec. collns on Slavic studies and N Eurasian culture studies; Librarian Dr MASAAKI HEMMI; publ. *Yuin* (4 a year).

Sendai

Tohoku University Library: Kawauchi, Aoba-ku, Sendai 980-77; internet www .library.tohoku.ac.jp; f. 1911; 2,247,000 vols, incl. Kano Colln (108,000 vols) in Japanese and Chinese, the Tibetan Buddhist Canons (6,652 vols), Wundt Colln (15,800 vols) and several other special collns; Dir Prof. KEICHI NOE.

Shizuoka

Shizuoka Prefectural Central Library: 53–1 Yada, Shizuoka City; tel. (54) 262-1242; fax (54) 264-4268; e-mail mailmaster@ tosyokan.pref.shizuoka.jp; internet www .tosyokan.pref.shizuoka.jp; f. 1925; 430,000 vols, 7,500 periodicals, 4,000 films and videotapes; Librarian YOSHIHIKO SUZUKI; publs *Aoi* (1 a year), *Toshokan-Dayori* (6 a year).

Tenri

Tenri Central Library: 1050 Somanouchi, Tenri, Nara 632-8577; tel. (743) 63-9200; fax (743) 63-7728; e-mail info@tcl.gr.jp; internet www.tcl.gr.jp; f. 1930; 2m. vols (incl. 480,000 in foreign languages); spec. libraries: Yorozuyo Library on Christian Missions (incl. Jesuit mission printings in Japan), Kogido Library of Africana Colln (6,000 vols), Ito Jinsai on Confucian Studies, Wataya Library on Renga and Haikai Works (20,000 items); Chief Librarian KEIICHIRO MOROI; publ. *Biblia* (in Japanese, 2 a year).

Tokyo

Chuo University Library: 742-1 Higashinakano, Hachioji-shi, Tokyo 192-0393; tel. (4) 2674-2511; fax (4) 2674-2514; f. 1885; 2m. vols (577,826 in foreign languages), 14,561 periodicals; Librarian Prof. NOBUO YASUI.

Hitotsubashi University Library: Naka 2-1, Kunitachi-city, Tokyo 186-8601; tel. (42) 580-8237; fax (42) 580-8251; internet www .lib.hit-u.ac.jp; f. 1887; 1,793,877 vols, 16,149 periodicals; Librarian MASAO WATANABE; houses br. library for Institute of Economic Research; f. 1940; 242,500 vols; Dir Y. KIKOKAWA.

Imperial Household Agency Library: 1–1 Chiyoda, Chiyoda-ku, Tokyo; tel. (3) 3213-1111; fax (3) 3214-2792; e-mail information@ kunaicho.go.jp; f. 1948; 87,946 vols; Librarian Mr MOMOTA.

International Christian University Library: 10-2 Osawa 3-chome, Mitaka-shi, Tokyo 181-8585; tel. (422) 33-3301; fax (422) 33-3305; e-mail library@icu.ac.jp; internet

www-lib.icu.ac.jp; f. 1953; 685,655 vols (incl. 326,327 foreign), 2,105 periodicals; Dir TAMAMI HATAKEYAMA (acting); Man. FUJIKI YUKO.

Japan Meteorological Agency Library: 1-3-4 Ote-machi, Chiyoda-ku, Tokyo 100-8122; e-mail jma-library@met.kishou.go.jp; f. 1875; 110,000 vols; Chief Librarian EIJU TAKAHASI.

Keio University Media Center: 2-15-45 Mita, Minato-ku, Tokyo 108; Chair. S. SUGIYAMA.

Kokugakuin University Library: 4-10-28 Higashi, Shibuya-ku, Tokyo; f. 1882; 1,087,663 vols; Librarian Prof. TOSHIO SAWANOBORI; publ. *Kokugakuin Daigaku Toshokan Kiyo* (Library Journal).

Kokuritsu Kobunshokan (National Archives): 3-2 Kitanomaru Park, Chiyoda-ku, Tokyo 102-0091; tel. (3) 3214-0621; fax (3) 3212-8806; internet www.archives.go.jp; f. 1971; attached to Cabinet office; archives, Cabinet Library of 480,000 vols, and government records of 406,000 vols; Pres. MITSUOKI KIKUCHI; publs *Kitanomaru* (1 a year), *Archives* (3 a year).

Kokuritsu Kyoiku Seisaku Kenkyujo, Kyoiku Kenkyu Joho Senta, Kyoiku Toshokan (Library of Education, Educational Resources Research Centre, National Institute for Educational Research of Japan): 3-2-2 Kasumigaseki, Chiyoda-ku, Tokyo 100-8951; tel. (3) 6733-6536; fax (3) 6733-6957; e-mail library@nier.go.jp; internet www.nier .go.jp/library; f. 1949; 490,000 vols; publ. *Kyoiku Kenkyu Ronbun Sakuin* (Education Index, online, quarterly).

Ministry of Foreign Affairs Library: 2-2 Kasumigaseki, Chiyoda-ku, Tokyo 100; 90,638 vols and 175 periodicals; Librarian YOSHIMASA KIMURA.

Ministry of Justice Library: 1-1, 1-chome, Kasumigaseki, Chiyoda-ku, Tokyo 100-8977; f. 1928; 300,000 vols; Chief Librarian T. OYAMA.

National Diet Library: 1-10-1 Nagatacho, Chiyoda-ku, Tokyo 100-8924; tel. (3) 3506-5147; fax (3) 3508-2934; e-mail kokusai@ndl .go.jp; internet www.ndl.go.jp; f. 1948; deposit library for Japanese publs and publs of the UN, UNESCO, ILO, WHO, ICAO, WTO, etc.; IFLA PAC centre for Asia, ISSN centre for Japan; is divided into 1 bureau and 6 depts: Acquisitions, Admin., Books, Research and Legislative Reference, Serials, Special Materials and Library Co-operation; consists of the Main Library, Detached Library in the Diet, Int. Library of Children's Literature, Toyo Bunko (Oriental) Library and 27 br. libraries in the Exec. and Judicial agencies of the Govt; 33,639,985 items, 8,833,407 books; 502,838 maps; 598,900 audio materials and CDs; 12,957,816 items of microform materials; 63,921 optical discs; 472,447 Japanese doctoral dissertations; 276,509 manuscripts; other catalogued items; subscriptions: 11,848,762 serials (periodicals and newspapers); Librarian MAKOTO NAGAO; publs *National Diet Library Newsletter* (online, in English, 6 a year)), *CDNLAO Newsletter* (online, in English, 3 a year), *Books on Japan* (online, in English, 4 a year), *National Bibliography Weekly List* (online, in Japanese), *Current Awareness* (online and print; most issues are in Japanese; a few are in English), *Japanese National Library monthly bulletin* (online, in Japanese).

National Institute of Japanese Literature Library: Midorityou 10-3, Tachikawa Tokyo 190-0014; tel. (50) 553-32926; fax (42) 526-8607; e-mail service@nijl.ac.jp; internet www.nijl.ac.jp; f. 1972; 188,397 vols; microforms of woodcuts, old printed books and

MSS; 46,434 reels of microfilm, 57,358 sheets of microfiche, 74,362 vols of paper copy, 6,773 titles of serials; archives for Japanese historical documents: 500,000 items; Dir N. YAMASHITA.

Norin Suisansho Toshokan: (Ministry of Agriculture, Forestry and Fisheries Library): 2-2-1, Nishigahara, Kita-Ku, Tokyo 114-0024; tel. (3) 3910-3978; fax (3) 3940-0232; e-mail ref-primaff@ml.affrc.go.jp; f. 1948; 275,000 vols; Librarian TATEKI ARAI; publs *Norin Suisan Tosho Shiryo Geppo* (12 a year review of publs on agriculture, forestry and fisheries), *Norin Suisan Bunken Kaidai* (1 a year annotated bibliography).

Ochanomizu University Library: 1-1 Otsuka 2-chome, Bunkyo-ku, Tokyo 112-8610; tel. (3) 5978-5839; fax (3) 5978-5933; e-mail lib-ref@cc.ocha.ac.jp; internet www.lib .ocha.ac.jp; f. 1874, reorganized 1949; 563,000 (including 179,000 foreign) vols; Dir YUJIRO OGUCHI.

Science Council of Japan Library: 22-34, Roppongi 7-chome, Minato-ku, Tokyo 106; tel. (3) 3403-6291; internet www.scj.go.jp; f. 1949; 54,000 vols; Librarian MASATO OKAMOTO.

Seikado Bunko Library and Art Museum: 2-23-1 Okamoto, Setagaya-ku, Tokyo; tel. (3) 3700-0007; internet www .seikado.or.jp; 200,000 vols of Chinese and Japanese classics.

Sophia (Jôchi) University Library: 7-1 Kioi-cho, Chiyoda-ku, Tokyo 102-8554; tel. (3) 3238-3511; fax (3) 3238-3268; f. 1913; 920,000 vols, 10,500 periodicals; Librarian MIKITO HAYASHI.

Statistical Library, Statistics Bureau, Management and Coordination Agency: 19-1, Wakamatsu-cho, Shimjuku-ku, Tokyo 162; tel. (3) 3202-1111; internet www.stat.go .jp; f. 1946; 400,000 vols; Librarian KENJI OKADA; publs numerous reports, statistical handbooks.

Supreme Court Library: 4-2 Hayabusacho, Chiyoda-ku, Tokyo 102-8651; f. 1949; 260,000 vols; Librarian S. OGAWA.

Tokyo Geijutsu Daigaku Toshokan (Tokyo University of the Arts Library): Ueno Park 12–8, Taito-ku, Tokyo 101-8714; tel. (50) 5525-2420; fax (50) 5525-2531; internet www.lib.geidai.ac.jp; f. 1887; over 365,377 vols, 2,212 microfilms, 4,359 microfiches; also music and audiovisual collns (97,722 scores, 19,831 records, 6,290 CDs, 3,396 video recordings); Dir E. TAGUCHI.

Tokyo Metropolitan Central Library: 5-7-13 Minami-Azabu, Minato-ku, Tokyo 106-8575; tel. (3) 3442-8451; fax (3) 3447-8924; internet www.library.metro.tokyo.jp; f. 1972; research and reference center, center of library co-operation in Tokyo; 1,471,000 vols and 10,000 periodicals; Morohashi Colln (Chinese classics), Sanetoh Colln (Chinese literature), Yedo Colln, Kaga Colln (rare books of the Yedo Era) and others; Dir TETSUYA SAITO; publs *Hibiya*, *Library Science Bulletin* (1 a year).

Tokyo University of Foreign Studies Library: 3-11-1 Asahicho, Fuchu-shi, Tokyo 183-8534; f. 1899; 733,003 vols (including 464,320 foreign); Dir H. TATEISHI.

Tokyo University of Marine Science and Technology Library: Konan 4-5-7, Minato-ku, Tokyo 108-8477; tel. (3) 5463-0444; fax (3) 5463-0445; e-mail to-joho@s.kaiyodai.ac.jp; internet lib.s.kaiyodai.ac.jp; f. 1888; 296,000 vols (including 74,000 foreign); Chief Librarian HIROSHI OKADA; publ. *Journal* (1 a year).

Toyo Bunko (Oriental Library): Honkomagome 2-28-21, Bunkyo-ku, Tokyo 113-0021; tel. (3) 3942-0121; fax (3) 3942-0258; e-mail webmaster@toyo-bunko.or.jp; internet www

.toyo-bunko.or.jp; f. 1924; 898,542 vols; research library specializing in Asian studies; special collections: Iwasaki collection of old and rare Japanese and Chinese books and manuscripts, Kawaguchi collection of Tibetan and Buddhist classics, Morrison collection of Western books on Asia; Dir YOSHINOBU SHIBA; publs *Toyo Gakuho* (4 a year), *Memoirs of the Research Department of the Toyo Bunko* (1 a year, jt publ. with National Diet Library).

University of Tokyo Library System: Hongo 7-3-1, Bunkyo-ku, Tokyo 113-0033; tel. (3) 5841-2612; fax (3) 5841-2636; e-mail kikaku@lib.u-tokyo.ac.jp; internet www.lib .u-tokyo.ac.jp; f. 1877; 8,120,000 vols, including Nanki collection (96,000 vols) and several other spec. colln; general library, Komaba library, Kashiwa library and 52 faculty and institute libraries; Dir K. SAIGO; publ. *Bulletin*.

Waseda University Library: 1-6-1 Nishiwaseda, Shinjuku-ku, Tokyo 169-8050; fax (3) 5272-2061; e-mail info@wul.waseda.ac.jp; internet www.wul.waseda.ac.jp; f. 1882; 5,323,682 vols; Dir TETSUO KATO; publ. *Bulletin* (1 a year).

Toyonaka

Osaka University Library: 1–4, Machikaneyama-cho, Toyonaka, Osaka 560-0043; tel. (6) 6850-5045; fax (6) 6850-5052; internet www.library.osaka-u.ac.jp; f. 1931; 3,050,000 vols; Main library and 2 branch libraries; Dir MINORU KAWAKITA.

Utsunomiya

Tochigi Prefectural Library: 1-2-23 Hanawada, Utsunomiya, Tochigi 320-0027; tel. (28) 622-5111; fax (28) 624-7855; e-mail tochilib@lib.pref.tochigi.jp; internet www.lib .pref.tochigi.jp; 196,579 vols; Librarian T. IZUMI.

Yamaguchi

Yamaguchi Prefectural Library: 150–1 Matsue, Ushirogawa, Yamaguchi City 753-0083; tel. (3) 924-2111; fax (3) 932-2817; internet library.pref.yamaguchi.lg.jp; f. 1903; 389,104 vols; Librarian TANAKA HIROSHI; publ. *Toshokan Yamaguchi*.

Yamaguchi University Library: 1667-1 Yoshida, Yamaguchi-shi, Yamaguchi 753-8511; tel. (3) 933-5182; e-mail toshokan@ yamaguchi-u.ac.jp; f. 1949; 2 br. libraries; 1,552,323 vols, 29,501 periodicals.

Yokohama

Kanagawa Prefectural Library: 9-2 Momijigaoka, Nishi-ku, Yokohama City; f. 1954; 76 mems; 540,875 vols; Librarian M. ANDO; publ. *Kanagawa Bunka* (6 a year).

Yokohama National University Library: 79-6 Tokiwadai, Hodogayaku, Yokohama 240-8501; tel. (45) 339-3217; fax (45) 339-3229; e-mail libref@ynu.ac.jp; internet www .lib.ynu.ac.jp; f. 1949; 1,386,472 vols; Dir Prof. K. YANAI.

Museums and Art Galleries

Abashiri

Abashiri Kyodo Hakubutsukan (Abashiri Municipal Museum): Katsuramachi 1-1-3, Abashiri-shi, Hokkaido 093-0041; tel. (152) 43-3090; fax (152) 61-3020; f. 1936; 600 local products, 25,000 articles of historical, geographical and archaeological interest, and 1,800 ethnological objects; Dir HIDEAKI WADA.

Atami

MOA Museum of Art: 26-2, Momoyama, Atami 413-85 11; tel. (557) 84-2511; fax (557) 84-2570; internet www.moaart.or.jp; f. 1957, reorganized 1982 by Mokichi Okada Asscn; Japanese and Oriental fine arts: paintings, ceramics, lacquers, calligraphy and sculptures; library of 25,000 vols; Dir YOJI YOSHIOKA; publs *Digest Catalogue*, *MOA Museum Members Club* (4 a year), *Selected Catalogue* (5 vols).

Gora

Hakone Museum of Art: 1300 Gora, Kanagawa Pref.; tel. (460) 2-2623; fax (460) 2-0124; internet www.moaart.or.jp/english/ hakone; f. 1952; private collection of Japanese ceramic works of art belonging to Okada Mokichi; Dir YOJI YOSHIOKA (Director of MOA Foundation).

Hakodate

Hakodate City Museum: 21-7 Suehiro-cho, Hakodate City; tel. (138) 22-4128; f. 1879; oldest local museum in Japan; Dir M. ISHIKAWA.

Hiraizumi

Chuson-ji Sanko-zo (Chuson-ji Temple Sanko Repository): Hiraizumi-machi, Nishi-Iwai-gun; internet www.chusonji.or.jp; f. 1955 to preserve treasures and possessions of the Fujiwara family who were important in the late period of Heian (801–1185).

Hiroshima

Hiroshima Children's Museum: 5-83, Moto-machi, Naka-ku, Hiroshima City 730; tel. (82) 222-5346; fax (82) 502-2118; e-mail riyou-annai@pyonta.city.hiroshima.jp; internet www.pyonta.city.hiroshima.jp; f. 1980; scientific and cultural programmes; planetarium; exhibits on science, transport, astronomy; Dir HIROSHI OKIMOTO; publs *Kagakukan Dayori* (12 a year), *Planetarium* (4 a year).

Ikaruga

Hōryuji (Hōryūji Temple): Aza Hōryūji, Ikaruga-cho, Ikoma-gun, Nara Prefecture; a large number of Buddhist images and paintings; the buildings date from the Asuka, Nara, Heian, Kamakura, Ashikaga, and Tokugawa periods.

Ise

Jingu Chokokan (Jingu Historical Museum): 1754-1 Koda-kushimoto, Ise-city, Mie 516-0016; tel. (596) 22-1700; fax (596) 22-5515; internet www.isejingu.or.jp/museum; 1,734 exhibits, incl. treasures of the Grand Shrine of Ise (Naiku Shrine and Geku Shrine) and many objects of historical interest; library of 1,082 vols, MSS and pictures; Dir and Chief of Cultural Section of the Grand Shrine of Ise YASUJI AKIOKA.

Jingu Nogyokan (Agricultural Museum): 1754-1 Koda-kushimoto-cho, Ise, Mie 516-0016; tel. (596) 22-1700; fax (596) 22-5515; internet www.isejingu.or.jp/museum; f. 1905; 9,583 exhibits connected with agriculture, forestry, and fishing (incl. colln of over 40 species of shark); Dir YASUJI AKIOKA.

Itsukushima

Itsukushima Jinja Homotsukan (Treasure Hall of the Itsukushima Shinto Shrine): Miyajima-cho, Saeki-gun; f. 1934; 4,000 exhibits of paintings, calligraphy, sutras, swords, and other ancient weapons; Curator and Chief Priest MOTOYOSHI NOZAKA.

Kamakura

Kamakura Kokuhokan (Kamakura Museum): 2-1-1 Yukinoshita, Kamakura City, Kanawaga; tel. (467) 22-0753; fax (467) 23-5953; internet www.city.kamakura .kanagawa.jp/kokuhoukan/index.htm; f. 1928; Japanese art and history in the Middle Ages; 3,521 valuable specimens of Japanese fine arts; 12 mems; library of 6,587 vols; Dir TATSUTO NUKI; publ. *Kokuhokan-zuroku*.

Museum of Modern Art, Kamakura: 2-1-53 Yukinoshita, Kamakura, Kanagawa 248-0005; tel. (467) 22-5000; fax (467) 23-2464; e-mail kinbi.4313@pref.kanagawa.jp; internet www.planet.pref.kanagawa.jp/city/ kinbi.htm; f. 1951; modern and contemporary art in Japan and Europe; Dir TADAYASU SAKAI.

Kobe

Hakutsuru Bijutsukan (Hakutsuru Fine Art Museum): 6-1-1 Sumiyoshiyamate, Higashinada-ku, Kobe 658-0063; tel. (78) 851-6001; fax (78) 851-6001; f. 1934; 1,300 specimens of fine art, incl. noted Chinese ceramics, old bronze vases and silverware, and oriental carpets; library of 10,000 vols; Dir HIDEO KANO.

Kobe City Museum: 24 Kyo-machi, Chuo-ku, Kobe 650-0034; tel. (78) 391-0035; fax (78) 392-7054; internet www.city.kobe.jp/ cityoffice/57/museum; f. 1982; theme of museum is the historical view of international cultural intercourse, especially contact between Eastern and Western cultures; 38,000 items including 21 national treasure items, important collections of Namban and Kohmoh arts, 17th–19th-century maps, also historical and archaeological items; library of 55,000 vols; Sec.-Gen. KAZUO KOBAYASHI; publs *Yearbook*, *Museum Tayori* (newsletter, 3 a year), *Bulletin* (1 a year).

Kochi

Kochi Kaitokukan (Kochi Castle): 1-2-1 Marunouchi, 780-0850 Kochi City, Kochi Prefecture; tel. (888) 24-5701; fax (888) 24-9931; internet www.pref.kochi.jp/~kochijo; f. 1913; 800 exhibits, including autographs and material of interest in Japanese historical research; Dir YUTAKA KONDO.

Kotohira

Kotohira-gü Hakubutsukan (Museum in the Kotohira Shrine): Kotohira-gü Shrine, Kotohira-machi, Nakatado-gun; 3,011 exhibits; Chair. MITSUSHIGE KOTOOKA; Sec. HAZIME HIRAO KOTOHIRA.

Kumamoto

Kumamoto Arts and Crafts Museum: 3–35 Chibajo-machi, Kumamoto City 860-0001; tel. (96) 324-4930; f. 1982; traditional arts and crafts; 3,000 ancient and contemporary items.

Kurashiki

Ohara Bijutsukan (Ohara Museum of Art): 1-1-15 Chuo, Kurashiki City; tel. (86) 422-0005; fax (86) 427-3677; e-mail info@ohara.or .jp; internet www.ohara.or.jp; f. 1930; Western paintings since the 19th century and contemporary arts; modern Japanese ceramics and fabrics; modern Japanese oil paintings; Asiatic art; artwork from Ancient Egypt and Medieval Islam; Dir SHUJI TAKASHINA.

Kushiro

Kushiro-shiritsu Hakubutsukan (Kushiro City Museum): Harutori Park 1-7, Shunkodai, Kushiro; tel. (154) 41-5809; fax (154) 42-6000; e-mail ku7011@city.kushiro .hokkaido.jp; internet www.city.kushiro .hokkaido.jp; f. 1936; 12,130 earthenware articles, natural history museum; Dir FUMIO NISHIYAMA; publs *Memoirs of the Kushiro City Museum* (1 a year), *Science Report of the Kushiro City Museum* (4 a year).

Kyoto

Chishakuin (Treasure Hall of the Chishakuin Temple): 964 Higashi-Kawaramachi, Higashiyama-ku, Kyoto; tel. (75) 541-5361; fax (75) 541-5364; Buddhist equipment and utensils, old documents, paintings, calligraphy, sutras, and books in Japanese and in Chinese.

Daigoji Reihokan (Treasure Hall of the Daigoji Temple): Daigo, Fushimi-ku, Kyoto; tel. (75) 571-0002; fax (75) 571-0101; f. 1936; contains 1,500 old art objects and 120,000 historical documents relating chiefly to Buddhism.

Jishoji (Ginkakuji) (Silver Temple): Ginkakuji-cho, Sakyo-ku, Kyoto; f. 1482 by Yoshimasa, eighth Shogun of Ashikaga, as 12 separate bldgs in the grounds of his villa; only the Ginkaku or Silver Hall, and the Togudo are now left; Curator R. ARIMA.

Kitano Temmangu Homotsuden (Treasure Hall of Kitano-Temmangu shrine): Kitano Bakuro-cho, Kamigyo-ku, Kyoto; tel. (75) 461-0005; fax (75) 461-6556; internet www.kitanotenmangu.or.jp; shrine dedicated to Michizane Sugawara, statesman and great scholar of Heian period; exhibits of treasure hall include the 'Kitano-Tenjin' history picture scrolls and an ancient copy of the 'Nihon Shoki'.

Korūji Reihōden (Treasure Museum of the Koryuji Temple): Koryuji Temple, Uzumasa, Ukyo-ku, Kyoto; f. 1922; many Buddhist images and pictures, including the two images of 'Miroku Bosatsu'; Curator EIKO KIYOTAKI.

Kyoto Kokuritsu Hakubutsukan (Kyoto National Museum): 527 Chaya-machi, Higashiyama-ku, Kyoto; tel. (75) 541-1151; fax (75) 531-0263; e-mail welcome@kyohaku.go.jp; internet www.kyohaku.go.jp; f. 1897 as Imperial Kyoto Museum; 52,692 books and 188,528 research photographs; 11,513 exhibits, incl. fine art and applied art exhibits and historical materials of Asia, chiefly of Japan; Dir Dr JOHEI SASAKI; Chief Curator KENICHI YUYAMA; publs *Bulletin* (Research journal in Japanese, 1 a year), *Ueno Memorial Foundation for the Study of Buddhist Art* (in Japanese, 1 a year).

Kyoto-shi Bijutsukan (Kyoto Municipal Museum of Art): Okazaki Park, Sakyo-ku, Kyoto 606-8344; tel. (75) 771-4107; fax (75) 761-0444; internet www.city.kyoto.jp/bunshi/kmma; f. 1933; contemporary fine art objects (mostly Japanese); Dir MITSUGI UEHIRA.

Myōhōin (Treasure House of the Myōhōin Temple): Myohoin-maegawa-cho, Higashiyama-ku, Kyoto; possessions of Toyotomi-Hideyoshi and many other national treasures.

National Museum of Modern Art, Kyoto: Enshoji-cho, Okazaki, Sakyo-ku, Kyoto; tel. (75) 761-4111; fax (75) 752-0509; e-mail info@momak.go.jp; internet www.momak.go.jp; f. 1963; Japanese-style painting, oil painting, print, modern art, crafts, design, photography, sculpture; Dir TAKEO UCHIYAMA; Chief Curator YASUHIRO SHIMADA; publs *Museum News* (6 a year), *Membership* (4 a year).

Ninnaji Reihóden (Treasure Hall of the Ninnaji Temple): Ninnaji Temple, Omuro Daimon-cho, Ukyo-ku, Kyoto.

Rengeoin (Sanjusangendo) (Treasure House of the Rengeoin Temple): Mawaricho, Higashiyama-ku, Kyoto; 'One Thousand Images' and many other Buddhist images.

Rokuonji (Treasures of the Rokuonji Temple): Kinkakuji-cho, Kita-ku, Kyoto; famed for its garden and gold pavilion.

Shoren-in (Treasure House of the Shōren-in Temple): Sanjōbō-machi, Awadaguchi, Higashiyama-ku, Kyoto; internet www.shorenin.com; f. 1153; Dir JIKO HIGASHIFUSHIMI; library of 5,000 vols; rare books, writings, paintings, etc.

Taiten Kinen Kyoto Shokubutsuen (Kyoto Prefectural Museum Botanical Garden): Hangi-cho, Shimogamo, Sakyô-ku, Kyoto 606-0823; tel. (75) 701-0141; fax (75) 701-0142; 120,000 plants and 5,500 botanical specimens.

Toyokuni Jinja Hómotsuden (Treasure Hall of the Toyokuni Shrine): Shomen Chaya-machi Yamato-Ooji, Higashiyama-ku, Kyoto; treasures and possessions of Toyotomi-Hideyoshi, incl. paintings, painted screens, swords, etc.

Yogen-In (Treasure Hall of the Yōgen-In Temple): Sanju-sangendō-mae, Yamato-ōji Shichijō Higashi Iru, Higashiyama-ku, Kyoto.

Yūrinkan (Yurinkan Collection): 44 Okazaki-Enshōjichyô, Sakyô-ku, Kyoto 606-8344; tel. (75) 761-0638; f. 1926; privately owned by the Fujii Foundation; rare antique Chinese fine arts and curios, incl. bronze and jade ware, porcelain, seals, Buddhist images, pictures, and calligraphy; Dir Z. FUJII.

Matsue

Koizumi-Yakumo Kinenkan (Lafcadio Hearn Memorial Museum): 322 Okudanimachi, Matsue City 690-0872; tel. (852) 21-2147; fax (852) 21-2156; f. 1933; collection of items belonging to Lafcadio Hearn; library of 492 vols (works by and on Hearn); Dir TOSHIO UCHIDA.

Shimane Prefectural Museum: 1 Tonomachi, Matsue City; tel. (852) 22-6727; fax (852) 22-6728; e-mail kodai@izm.ed.jp; internet www2.pref.shimane.jp/kodai; f. 1959; bronze bells, bronze swords and other ancient heritage; Dir SYO KATSUBE; publs *Ancient Culture in Shimane* (1 a year), *News of the Institution for Ancient Study* (4 a year), *Studies of Ancient Culture* (1 a year).

Matsumoto

Matsumoto City Museum: 4-1 Marunouchi, Matsumoto City, Nagano 390-0873; tel. (263) 32-0133; fax (263) 32-8974; e-mail mcmuse@city.matsumoto.nagano.jp; internet www.city.matsumoto.nagano.jp; f. 1906; folklore, history, archaeology, star festival dolls, popular belief tools, fine art, agricultural tools; Dir KENICHI KUMAGAI.

Minobu

Minobusan Homotsukan (Treasury of the Kuonji Temple): Kuonji Temple, Minobumachi, Minami-Koma-gun; 300 articles, examples of the fine arts, and materials connected with the history of the Nichiren Sect of Buddhism, the biography of Saint Nichiren.

Mount Koya

Kōyasan Reihōkan (Museum of Buddhist Art on Mount Kōya): Kōyasan, Kōya-cho, Itogun; f. 1921; 50,000 exhibits, incl. Buddhist paintings and images, sutras and old documents, some of them registered National Treasures and Important Cultural Properties; a centre of Buddhism in Japan; Dir CHIKYŌ YAMAMOTO.

Nagoya

Nagoya Castle Donjon: 1-1 Hon-maru, Naka-ku, Nagoya; tel. (52) 231-1700; built in 1612 by Ieyasu Tokugawa; destroyed by fire 1945; restored to its original form 1959; exhibition rooms, galleries and observatory; 1,049 paintings of the Kano school on sliding doors and ceilings; armoury and swords.

Nara

Kasugataisha Homotsuden (Treasure Hall of the Kasugataisha Shrine): Kasugataisha Shrine, 160 Kasugano-cho, Nara City; f. 1934; the ancient, curvilinear style of architecture is called 'Kasuga Zukuri' after this shrine; Shrine Master CHIKATADA KASANNOIN.

Museum Yamato Bunkakan: 1-11-6 Gakuen-minami, Nara; tel. (742) 45-0544; fax (742) 49-2929; internet www.kintetsu.jp/kouhou/yamato; f. 1960; art objects of East Asia, chiefly Japan, China and Korea; library of 20,000 vols; Dir Prof. SHUGO ASANO; publs *Yamato Bunka* (2 a year), *Catalogues of the Museum Collection* (in English), *Bi-no-Tayori* (4 a year).

Nara National Museum: 50 Nobori-oji-cho, Nara-shi 630-8213; tel. (742) 22-7771; fax (742) 26-7218; internet www.narahaku.go.jp; f. 1895; Buddhist sculptures, paintings, applied arts, calligraphy, archaeological objects, etc.; also special exhibitions; library of 59,750 vols; Dir KENICHI YUYAMA.

Neiraku Museum: Isuien Park, 74 Suimoncho, Nara City; tel. (742) 22-2173; fax (742) 25-0781; f. 1939; ancient Chinese bronze mirrors, seals, etc., and Korean potteries; Dir JUNSUKE NAKAMURA.

Todaiji: 406-1 Zōshi-cho, Nara; tel. (742) 22-5511; fax (742) 22-0808; f. 752; HQ of Kegonshū Buddhist sect; Daibutsuden: Main Hall of the Todaiji Temple, the largest wooden edifice in the world, the world-famous Great Image of Buddha and 2 Bodhisattvas; attached bldgs are the Hokkedō, Kaidanin, Nigatsudō, which contain many famous images of Buddha and Bodhisattva; library of 70,000 vols, 10,000 manuscripts; Dir D. UENO; publ. *Nanto Bukkyō: Journal of the Nanto Society for Buddhist Studies* (1 a year).

Yakushiji (Yakushiji Temple): 457 Nishi-no-Kyō-machi, Nara City 630-8563; tel. (742) 33-6001; fax (742) 33-6004; e-mail yksj8@mahoroba.or.jp; internet www.nara-yakushiji.com; f. 697; famous bronze images of the Yakushi Trinity; a pagoda 1,300 years old; Dir Lord Abbot S. MATSUKUBO.

Narita

Naritasan Reikokan Museum (Treasure Hall of the Naritasan-Shinshoji Temple): Narita Park, Narita-City, Chiba Pref. 286-0023; tel. (476) 22-2111; fax (476) 24-2210; internet www.naritasan.or.jp; f. 1947; contains treasures dedicated to the shrine and archaeological pieces from the region, 12,113 MSS and books, sculptures, botanical specimens; Curator SHOSEKI TSURUMI.

Omishima

Oyamazumi Jinja Kokuhokan (Treasure Hall of the Oyamazumi Shrine): Oyamazumi Shrine, Omishima Town, Ochigun; f. AD 1; 2,000 exhibits, incl. a large colln of ancient armour, swords, and the oldest mirrors in Japan; library of 20,000 vols; Curator YASUHISA MISHIMA.

Osaka

National Museum of Ethnology: 10-1 Senri Expo Park, Suita, Osaka 565-8511; tel. (6) 6876-2151; fax (6) 6875-0401; internet www.minpaku.ac.jp; f. 1974; 256,436 artefacts from Japan and abroad; conducts anthropological research and promotes general understanding and awareness of peoples, societies and cultures around the world; established as Inter-Univ. Research Institute; library of 587,115 vols, 15,586 journals, 69,325 audiovisual items; Dir-Gen. KEN'ICHI SUDO; publs *Bulletin* (in Japanese,

English, French, Spanish, Russian, Chinese and German, 4 a year), *Minpaku Anthropology Newsletter* (2 a year, in English), *Minpaku Tsushin* (newsletter, in Japanese), *Senri Ethnological Reports* (irregular), *Senri Ethnological Studies* (in English and selected other European languages, irregular).

Osaka Municipal Museum of Art: 1–82 Chausuyama-cho, Tennoji-ku, Osaka 543-0063; tel. (6) 6771-4874; fax (6) 6771-4856; internet www.city.osaka.jp/museum-art; f. 1936; Chinese, Korean and Japanese fine art; library of 11,000 vols; Dir YUTAKA MINO; publ. *Miotsukushi* (Bulletin, 2 a year).

Osaka Museum of Natural History: Nagai Park, Higashisumiyoshi-ku, Osaka 546-0034; tel. (6) 6697-6221; fax (6) 6697-6225; internet www.mus-nh.city.osaka.jp; f. 1952; botany, entomology, geology, palaeontology and zoology; Dir TAKAYOSHI NASU; Head Curator MOTOHARU OKAMOTO; publs *Bulletin, Nature Study, Occasional Paper* (1 a year), *Special Publications* (1 a year).

Tenri

Tenri University Sankokan Museum: 250 Morimedo-cho, Tenri City, Nara Prefecture 632-8540; tel. (743) 63-8414; fax (743) 63-7721; f. 1930; attached to Tenri University; ethnographic and archaeological items from all parts of the world.

Tokyo

Ancient Orient Museum: 1–4 Higashi Ikebukuro 3-chome, Toshima-ku, Tokyo 170-8630; tel. (3) 3989-3491; fax (3) 3590-3266; e-mail museum@orientmuseum.com; internet www.sa.il24.net; f. 1978; archaeology and art history of Middle and Near East, Egypt, India and Central Asia; library of 9,000 vols; Dir Prof. TAKUYA IWASAKI; publ. *Bulletin* (1 a year).

Bridgestone Museum of Art, Ishibashi Foundation: 10-1, Kyobashi 1-chome, Chuo-ku, Tokyo 104-0031; tel. (3) 3563-0241; fax (3) 3561-2130; f. 1952 by Shojiro Ishibashi; private museum of 19th- and 20th-century European paintings and modern Japanese Western-style paintings; Dir NORIO SHIMADA.

Gotoh Museum: 9–25 3-chome Kaminoge, Setagaya-ku, Tokyo; tel. (3) 3703-0662; fax (3) 3703-0440; internet www.gotoh-museum .or.jp; f. 1960; Japanese, Chinese and Korean art; c. 4,000 exhibits, incl. the 'Tales of Genji' scroll and the 'Diary of Lady Murasaki' scroll.

Inokashira Onshi Koen Shizen Bunkaen (Natural Science Park in Inokashira Park): 1-17-6 Gotenyama, Musashinoshi, Tokyo; zoo, botanical garden, research room, marine biology room.

Kokuritsu Kagaku Hakubutsukan (National Museum of Nature and Science): Ueno Park 7–20, Taito-ku, Tokyo 110-8718; tel. (3) 3822-0111; fax (3) 5814-9898; e-mail webmaster@kahaku.go.jp; internet www .kahaku.go.jp; f. 1877, merged with Research Institute for Natural Resources in 1971; exhibits of natural history, physical science and engineering; colln of over 3.6m. specimens; library of 99,782 vols; Dir SHINJI KONDO; publs *Bulletin* (in 5 series), *Memoirs* (irregular), *Monographs* (irregular).

Kotsu Hakubutsukan (Transportation Museum): 25 1-chome, Kanda-Sudacho, Chiyoda-ku, Tokyo; tel. (3) 3251-8481; fax (3) 3251-8489; e-mail gakugei@kouhaku.or .jp; internet www.kouhaku.or.jp; f. 1921; aircraft, electric equipment, locomotives, motor-cars, ships, etc.; Dir TATSUHIKO SUGA.

Meguro Parasitological Museum: 4-1-1 Shimomeguro, Meguro-ku, Tokyo 153-0064; tel. (3) 3716-1264; fax (3) 3716-2322; internet

kiseichu.org; f. 1953; science of parasites; Dir MASAAKI MACHIDA.

Meiji Jingu Homotsuden (Meiji Shrine Treasure Museum): Yoyogi, Shibuya-ku, Tokyo; f. 1921; 102 treasures and possessions of Emperor Meiji and 74 objects belonging to Empress Shoken; there is also a Memorial Picture Gallery.

Mori Art Museum: 53rd Fl., Roppongi Hills, Mori Tower, 6-10-1 Roppongi, Minato-ku, Tokyo; tel. (3) 5777-8600; fax (3) 6406-9351; internet www.mori.art.museum; f. 2003; Dir FUMIO NANJO.

Museum of Contemporary Art, Tokyo: Metropolitan Kiba Park, 4-1-1 Miyoshi Koto-ku, Tokyo 135-0022; tel. (3) 5245-4111; fax (3) 5777-8600; internet www.mot-art-museum .jp; Japanese and foreign art since 1945.

Nezu Institute of Fine Arts: 6-5-1 Minami-Aoyama, Minato-ku, Tokyo 107-0062; tel. (3) 3400-2536; fax (3) 3400-2436; e-mail nezu@ nezu-muse.or.jp; internet www.nezu-muse.or .jp; f. 1940; private colln by Kaichiro Nezu of 7,195 paintings, calligraphy, sculpture, swords, ceramics, lacquer-ware, archaeological exhibits; 187 items designated as nat. treasures; Dir KOICHI NEZU.

Nippon Mingeikan (Japan Folk Crafts Museum): 4-3-33 Komaba, Meguro-ku, Tokyo 153-0041; tel. (3) 3467-4527; fax (3) 3467-4537; internet www.mingeikan.or.jp; f. 1936; Japanese traditional folk craft and craft from around the world; spec. collns from founding mems of Mingei Movement: Soetsu Yanagi, Kanjiro Kawai, Shoji Hamada, Keisuke Serizawa, Bernard Leach, Shiko Munakata, Kenkichi Tomimoto and others; Dir YOTARO KOBAYASHI; publ. *Mingei* (12 a year).

Okura Cultural Foundation Okura Shukokan Museum: 2-10-3, Toranomon, Minato-ku, Tokyo; f. 1917; 1,700 articles of fine arts; library of 36,000 vols Chinese classics; Pres. NOBORU NISHITANI.

Shitamachi Museum: 2–1 Ueno-koen, Taito-ku, Tokyo; tel. (3) 3823-7451; internet www.taitocity.net/taito/shitamachi; f. 1980; re-creation of the old commercial district of Tokyo; incl. typical street, wooden houses, life-size figures, furniture, pictures, books and letters, religious material, domestic utensils, Second World War items, games and musical instruments, cosmetics and accessories, etc.; Dir HIDENOBU HIROSE.

Shodo Hakubutsukan (Calligraphy Museum): 2-10-4 Negishi, Taito-ku, Tokyo 110-0003; tel. (3) 3872-2645; f. 1936; colln of the calligrapher, the late F. Nakamura; 1,000 rubbed copies of the stone tablets and 'hōjō', ancient texts of calligraphy (10,000 articles).

The National Museum of Modern Art, Tokyo: 3–1 Kitanomaru Koen, Chiyoda-ku, Tokyo 102-8322; tel. (3) 5777-8600; internet www.momat.go.jp; f. 1952; art museum and crafts gallery; colln of modern artworks, and related references dating from the beginning of the 20th century to present; art museum incls paintings, sculptures, prints, watercolours, drawings, photographs and other works; crafts gallery incls textiles, glass, lacquer, wood, bamboo and metalwork, dolls, industrial and graphic design; also nat. film centre holdings films and non-film materials; Dir KAMOGAWA SACHIO; publs *Gendai no Me* (in Japanese, 6 a year), *National Film Center Newsletter* (in Japanese, 6 a year).

The National Museum of Western Art: 7-7 Ueno-koen, Taito-ku, Tokyo 110-0007; tel. (3) 3828-5131; fax (3) 3828-5135; e-mail wwwadmin@nmwa.go.jp; internet www .nmwa.go.jp; f. 1959 (building designed by Le Corbusier); 19th-century European paintings and sculptures collected by the late Kojiro

Matsukata and new acquisitions of old masters; Dir Dr MASANORI AOYAGI.

Tokyo Daigaku Rigaku Kenkyu-ka Fuzoku Shokubutsuen (Botanical Gardens, Graduate School of Science, University of Tokyo): 7-1, Hakusan 3, Bunkyo-ku, Tokyo 112; tel. (3) 3814-2625; fax (3) 3814-0139; f. 1684, transferred to Univ. 1877; Nikko br.; research in systematic botany and conservation of plants; 6,000 kinds of plants; 2,500 in Nikko; associated with the herbarium TI with approx. 700,000 specimens; library of 20,000 vols; Dir Prof. Dr JIN MURATA.

Tokyo Kokuritsu Hakubutsukan (Tokyo National Museum): 13-9 Ueno Park, Taito-ku, Tokyo 110-8712; tel. (3) 5405-8686; fax (3) 3822-2081; internet www.tnm.jp; f. 1872; largest museum in Japan; Japanese and E fine arts, incl. paintings, calligraphy, sculpture, metalwork, ceramic art, textiles, lacquer-ware, archaeological exhibits; Dir-Gen. MASAMI ZENIYA; publs *Museum* (12 a year), *Tokyo National Museum News* (12 a year).

Tokyo-to Bijutsukan (Tokyo Metropolitan Art Museum): Ueno Park 8–36, Taito-ku, Tokyo; tel. (3) 3823-6921; fax (3) 3823-6920; e-mail tobi@tobikan.jp; internet www .tobikan.jp; f. 1926; ancient and modern art exhibition, educational service, art library and gallery for group exhibitions; closed from April 2010 to March 2012 for renovation; Dir YOSHITAKE MAMURO; Curator ATSUKO TAKEUCHI; publ. *Bulletin* (1 a year).

University Art Museum, Tokyo University of the Arts: Ueno Park, Taito-ku, Tokyo 110-8714; tel. (3) 5525-2200; fax (3) 5525-2532; internet www.geidai.ac.jp/museum; paintings, sculptures and applied art of Japan, China and Korea.

Waseda Daigaku Tsubouchi Hakase Kinen Engeki Hakubutsukan (Tsubouchi Memorial Theatre Museum, Waseda University): 1-6-1 Nishi-Waseda, Shinjuku-ku, Tokyo 169-8050; tel. (3) 5286-1829; fax (3) 5276-4398; e-mail enpaku@list.waseda.jp; internet www.waseda.jp/enpaku; f. 1928; 92,000 (Japanese), 30,000 (foreign) books on drama, 46,000 woodblock colour prints, 23,000 pictures and 518 costumes, properties, and other items used on the stage; Dir BUNZO TORIGOE; publ. *Studies in Dramatic Art.*

Yasukuni Jinja: Kudan Kita, 3-1-1, Chiyoda-ku, Tokyo 102-8246; Chiyoda-ku, Tokyo; tel. (3) 3261-8326; fax (3) 3261-0081; internet www.yasukuni.or.jp; f. 1869; nat. shrine dedicated to the war dead; museum displays items from wars fought by Japan since the establishment of the shrine.

Ueno

Iga-ryu Ninja Museum: 117-13-1 Ueno-marunouchi, Iga City, Mie Prefecture; tel. (595) 23-0311; fax (595) 23-0314; e-mail ninpaku@ict.ne.jp; internet www.iganinja.jp; history and exhibits on Ninjas, spies who played an important role during periods of civil war in medieval Japan.

Yokohama

Kanagawa Prefectural Kanazawa Bunko Museum: 142 Kanazawa-cho, Kanazawa-ku, Yokohama; tel. (45) 701-9069; fax (45) 788-1060; internet www.planet.pref .kanagawa.jp/city/kanazawa.htm; f. 1972; nat. treasures (figure of Hojo-Sanetoki, etc.); library: f. 1275; 20,000 old books and 4,149 documents; Curator MAKOTO NAGAMURA.

National Universities

AICHI PREFECTURAL UNIVERSITY

1522-3 Ibaragabasama, Kumabari, Naga-kute-cho, Aichi-gun, Aichi 480-1198
Telephone: (561) 64-1111
E-mail: jim@bur.aichi-pu.ac.jp
Internet: www.aichi-pu.ac.jp
Founded 1947
Pres.: MASAO MORI
Library of 450,000 vols

PROFESSORS

Faculty of Foreign Studies:

HAYAMIZU, Y., Department of French Studies
HIOKI, M., Department of German Studies
KICHISE, S., Department of British and American Studies
KURAHASHI, M., Department of Chinese Studies
SHIGA, I., Department of Spanish and Latin American Studies

Faculty of Information Science and Technology:

HANDA, N., Department of Applied Information Science and Technology
SAKURAI, K., Department of Information Systems

Faculty of Letters:

KAWAGUCHI, A., Department of Childhood Education
KOTANI, S., Department of Japanese Language and Letters
SHIMIZU, K., Department of Social Welfare
TOUYAMA, I., Department of English
YAMADA, M., Department of Japanese History and Culture

ASAHIKAWA MEDICAL COLLEGE

2-1-1-1 Midorigaoka, Asahikawa 078-8510
Telephone: (166) 65-2111
Fax: (166) 66-0025
E-mail: ipc@asahikawa-med.ac.jp
Internet: www.asahikawa-med.ac.jp
Founded 1973
Independent (National University Corporation)
Academic year: April to March
Pres.: SUNAO YACHIKU
Exec. Dirs: HIYOSHI SHIONO, MUTSUO ISHIKAWA
Exec. Sec.-Gen.: SUSUMU OHTA
Library Dir: KATSUHIRO OGAWA
Library of 139,000 vols
Number of teachers: 263
Number of students: 953 (845 undergraduate, 108 postgraduate)
Publication: Asahikawa Medical College (1 a year).

BUNKYO UNIVERSITY

3-2-17 Hatanodai, Shinagawa-ku, Tokyo 142-0064
Telephone: (3) 3783-5511
Fax: (3) 3783-8300
E-mail: iec@stf.bunkyo.ac.jp
Internet: www.bunkyo.ac.jp
Founded 1927
Pres.: TSUNEYOSHI ISHIDA
Number of teachers: 226
Number of students: 8,649
Library of 546,000 vols
Faculties of Culture, Education, Human Science, Information and Communications, International Studies, Language and Literature.

CHIBA UNIVERSITY

1-33 Yayoi-cho, Inage-ku, Chiba-shi, Chiba 263-8522
Telephone: (43) 251-1111
Fax: (43) 290-2041
E-mail: kokusai@office.chiba-u.jp
Internet: www.chiba-u.jp
Founded 1949
Independent
Academic year: April to March
Pres.: TOYOKI KOZAI
Dir-Gen.: TETSUO YAMANE
Library Dir: SYUN TUTIYA
Number of teachers: 1,267 full-time
Number of students: 14,460
Publications: Bulletin of the Faculty of Education (1 a year), Chemical Analysis Center Research Achievements, Chiba University Social Sciences and Humanities (1 a year), Economics Journal, Journal of Humanities (1 a year), Journal of Law and Politics, Journal of the School of Nursing (1 a year), Laboratory Waste Treatment Plant Bulletin (1 a year), Newsletter of the Research Center for Pathogenic Fungi and Microbial Toxicoses (2 a year), Outline of the Research Center for Pathogenic Fungi and Microbial Toxicoses (every 2 years), Record of Research Activities of the Faculty of Pharmaceutical Science, Research Activities and Interests of the Faculty of Engineering (2 a year), Research Report of the Center for Co-operative Research, Technical Bulletin of the Faculty of Horticulture (1 a year), Technical Reports of Mathematical Sciences

DEANS

Faculty of Education: H. FUJISAWA
Faculty of Engineering: K. MIYAZAKI
Faculty of Horticulture: H. AMANO
Faculty of Law and Economics: R. MIYAZAKI
Faculty of Letters: Y. NISHIMURA
Faculty of Science: K. OGAWA
Graduate School of Humanities and Social Sciences: S. MIURA
Graduate School of Medical and Pharmaceutical Sciences: T. ISHIKAWA
Graduate School of Pharmaceutical Sciences: K. YAMAMOTO
Graduate School of Science and Technology: T. OBINATA
School of Medicine: Y. FUKUDA
School of Nursing: K. ISHIGAKI

DIRECTORS

Center of Cooperative Research: O. SAITO
Center for Environment, Health and Field Sciences: T. KOZAI
Center for Environmental Remote Sensing: T. TAKAMURA
Center for Foreign Languages: M. KUBOTA
Center for Frontier Electronics and Photonics: T. UEMATSU
Center for Frontier Science: N. UENO
Chemical Analysis Center: T. IMAMOTO
Gene Research Center: T. TOKUHISA
Health Sciences Center: K. NAGAO
Institute of Media and Information Technology: S. SHIMAKURA
International Student Center: M. HIROHASHI
Marine Biosystems Research Center: T. YAMAGUCHI
Radioisotope Research Center: Y. ARANO
Research Center for Frontier Medical Engineering: Y. MIYAKE
Research Center for Pathogenic Fungi and Microbial Toxicoses: K. NISHIMURA
Toxic Waste Treatment Plant: K. MIYAZAKI
University Hospital: T. FUJISAWA

PROFESSORS

Center for Environment, Health and Field Sciences (6-2-1 Kashiwanoha, Kawashi-shi, Chiba 277-0882; tel. (4) 7134-8401; fax (4) 7134-8437):

ANDO, T., Ornamental Plant Science
KOZAI, T., Environmental Control Engineering
KURIYAMA, T., Respirology
NOMA, Y., Experimental Farms
OHGAMA, T., Wood Science and Technology
TOKUYAMA, I., Sports Pedagogy

Center for Environmental Remote Sensing (tel. (43) 290-3832; fax (43) 290-3857; internet www.cr.chiba-u.jp):

MIWA, T., Dept of Geoinformation Analysis
NISHIO, H., Dept of Database Research
SUGIMORI, Y., Dept of Geoinformation Analysis
TAKAMURA, T., Dept of Sensor and Atmospheric Radiation
TAKEUCHI, N., Dept of Sensor and Atmospheric Radiation

Center for Foreign Languages:

BOSWELL, P. D., Psychology of Teaching
KUBOTA, M., Linguistics
MIKOSHIBA, M., Russian Intellectual History
SHIINA, K., Methodology for English Teaching
TABATA, T., Linguistics, Phonology
YAMAOKA, K., French Literature

Center for Frontier Science (1–33 Yayoi-cho, Inage-ku, Chiba-shi, Chiba 263-8522; tel. (43) 290-3522; fax (43) 290-3523; e-mail info@cfs.chiba-u.jp; internet www.cfs.chiba-u.ac.jp):

HANAWA, T., Astrophysics
OHTAKA, K., Applied Physics

Graduate School of Science and Technology:

ANDO, A., Proteins Engineering
ASANO, Y., Environmental Plant Science
FUJIKAWA, T., XAFS Theory
FURUYA, T., Applied Geomorphology
HATTORI, M., Architectural Design Study
HIRATA, H., Systems Engineering
ICHIKAWA, A., Knowledge Engineering
INABA, T., Differential Topology
IWADATE, Y., Physics and Chemistry of Liquids and Amorphous Materials
KOHMOTO, S., Organic Photochemistry
MAJIMA, T., Mechanics and Strength of Materials
MATSUDA, T., Electronic Commerce and Agribusiness
NATSUME, Y., Condensed Matter Theory
NISHIKAWA, K., Physical Chemistry
OHNO, T., Imaging Materials
SATO, T., Plant Molecular Biology
SHIGA, H., Complex Manifolds
SHIMAKURA, S., Fundamentals of Electrical and Electronic Engineering
SUGIYAMA, K., Design Systems Planning
TAGAWA, A., Agricultural Process Engineering
TAMURA, T., Molecular Biology
UESUGI, H., Fireproofing of Buildings
YAHAGI, T., Digital Signal Processing
YOSHIDA, H., Complex Analysis

Faculty of Education (fax (43) 290-2519; e-mail hd2504@office.chiba-u.jp; internet www.e.chiba-u.jp):

ABE, A., Physical Education and School Health Education
AKASHI, Y., Sociology of Education
AMAGAI, Y., Developmental Clinical Psychology
AMAGASA, S., School Management
FUJII, T., Constitutional Law
FUJIKAWA, D., Development of Teaching
FUJISAWA, H., Art Education
FUSHIMA, Y., Psychology of School Learning

HIRAIDE, S., English and American Literature

HOSAKA, T., Clinical Studies in School Education

INABA, H., Physical Chemistry

INAGAKI, K., Early Childhood Education

INOUE, T., Sociology

ISAKA, J., Japanese Linguistics

ISHII, K., Food and Cookery Science

ISOBE, K., Orthopaedics

ISOZAKI, I., Political Science

IWAGAKI, O., Teaching Methods

IWATA, M., Developmental Psychology

IWATSUKI, K., Educational Psychology

KAMIYA, N., Musical Expression in Early Childhood Education

KAMO, H., Philosophy

KANAMORI, R., Painting

KATAOKA, Y., Sports Physiology

KATAYAMA, T., Sports Management

KATO, S., Chinese Literature

KENMOCHI, N., Analysis and Applied Mathematics

KIKUCHI, T., Teaching Methods of Physical Education and Sports

KOBAYASHI, K., Theory of School Nursing and School Health

KOMIYAMA, T., Motor Control

KOSHIKAWA, H., Differential Topology

KUMABE, T., Mechanics

KURANO, M., Analysis and Applied Mathematics

KUSAKARI, H., Nuclear Physics

MISAWA, M., Climatology

MIWA, S., School Management

MIYAMOTO, M., Sociology of the Family

MIYANO, M., Teaching of Music

MIYASHITA, K., Adolescent Psychology

MIZUUCHI, H., Curriculum Development

MOROTOMI, Y., Educational Counselling

MURAMATSU, S., Sports and Nutrition

NAGANE, M., School Psychology

NAGASAWA, S., Social Education

NAGATA, K., Comparative Theory of Art

NAKAZAWA, J., Developmental Psychology

NUKUI, M., Teaching of Science

OASHI, O., Psychology of Learning

OHGAMA, T., Wood Science and Technology

OHKOCHI, N., Agriculture Education

OHTA, T., Special Education

OI, K., English Pedagogy

OKAMOTO, K., Solid State Physics

OKI, T., Industrial Design

OTSUKA, T., English Linguistics

SADAHIRO, S., Educational Administration

SATO, F., Home Economics Education

SATO, K., Ethics

SATO, M., Children's Literature

SATO, M., Movement Theory of Sport

SHIBATA, M., Aesthetics of Costume

SHIMADA, K., Teaching of Mathematics

SHIMIZU, T., English and American Literature in School Education

SHUTO, H., Japanese Language Education

SUGITA, K., Paediatric Neurology

SUZUKI, A., Physiology and Ecology of Fungi

TAKEUCHI, H., Teaching of Social Studies

TAKIZAWA, F., Philosophy of Physical Education and Sport

TAMURA, T., Greek History

TANAKA, T., Teaching of Social Studies

TERAI, M., Japanese Language Education

TERAKADO, Y., Housing and the Living Environment

TOKUYAMA, I., Sports Pedagogy

TOZAKI, K., Physics

TSURUOKA, Y., Science Education

UENO, H., Sculpture

UESUGI, K., Moral Education

UKAWA, M., Music Education (Piano)

UMETANI, T., Psychology of Handicapped Children

URANO, T., Teaching of Calligraphy

WATANABE, S., Vocal Music

YAMAMURA, J., Human Geography

YAMANO, Y., Electrical Engineering

YAMAUCHI, K., Group Representation Theory

YAMAZAKI, Y., Geology

YODA, A., Technology Education

Faculty of Engineering:

AKUTSU, F., Synthetic Polymer Chemistry

ANDO, M., Construction and Production of Buildings

AOKI, H., Materials Planning for Design

AOYAGI, S., Bio-organic Chemistry

FUJITA, T., Synthetic Organic Chemistry

FUKASAWA, A., Communication and Information Networks

FUKUKAWA, Y., Urban Planning and Design, Historic Conservation

HASEGAWA, A., Photophysics

HATTORI, T., Ceramic Sciences

HIBINO, H., Design Psychology and Colour Science

HIROHASHI, M., Materials Science

HISIDA, M., Heat Engine Engineering

HONDA, T., Optical Engineering, Image Processing

HOTTA, A., Industrial Design

IKEDA, H., Computer Science

ITO, K., Antenna Engineering

KAGEGAWA, K., Inorganic Material

KAMAIKE, M., Product Design

KATO, H., Optimization of Manufacturing

KATSUURA, T., Ergonomics

KITAHARA, T., City Planning

KITAMURA, A., Fundamentals of Materials Science

KITAMURA, T., Electronic Image Processing

KOBAYASHI, H., Organic Memory and Display Materials

KOTERA, H., Printing Image Processing

KUDO, K., Physical Electronics

KURYU, A., Architectural Design

LIU, H., Biomechanical Engineering

MAENO, K., Thermofluid Dynamics

MATSUBA, I., Engineering of Information Processing

MIYAKE, Y., Measurement and Analysis of Image Information

MIYATA, T., Interior Design

MIYAZAKI, K., Philosophy and History of Design

MIYAZAKI, M., Visual Communication Design

MORITA, H., Laser Chemistry on Nanomaterials

MORITA, K., Structural Planning

NAKAHIRA, T., Polymer Chemistry

NAKAI, S., Disaster Prevention

NAKAMOTO, T., Micro Machining

NAKAMURA, M., Plastic Working

NISHIKAWA, N., Fluids Engineering

NOGUCHI, K., Visual Perception

NONAMI, K., Control and Robotics

OCHIAI, Y., Advanced Device Materials

OGUMA, K., Analytical Chemistry

OGURA, K., Synthetic Organic Chemistry

OKAMOTO, H., Optical Properties of Semiconductors

OTANI, S., Earthquake Engineering

OTSUBO, Y., Rheology

SAITO, O., Semiconductor Rhotonics

SHIMIZU, T., Environmental Design

SUGITA, K., Information Recording Materials

TAMAI, T., History of Architecture

TANAKA, K., Physical Electronics

TATEDA, M., Opto-electronics

TATSUMOTO, H., Systems Design in Water and Wastewater Treatment

UEMATSU, T., Industrial Physical Chemistry

UENO, N., Molecular Quantum Assemblies

UNO, M., Architecture and Urban Design

WATANABE, T., Micro-machine Elements

YAGUCHI, H., Visual Science

YAMAGUCHI, M., Electrical Circuits

YAMAMOTO, M., Synthetic Organic Chemistry

YAMAOKA, T., Imaging Materials

YASHIRO, K., Microwave Theory and Technology

YOSHIKAWA, A., Quantum Electronics

Faculty of Horticulture (648 Matsudo, Matsudo-shi, Chiba 271-8510; tel. (47) 308-8706; fax (47) 308-8720; e-mail n8703@office.chiba-u.jp; internet www.h.chiba-u.ac.jp):

AMANO, H., Applied Entomology and Zoology

AMEMIYA, Y., Green Space Environmental Technology

AMEMIYA, Y., Plant Pathology

ANDO, T., Ornamental Plant Science

FUJII, T., Microbial Engineering

HARADA, K., Genetics and Plant Breeding

HONJO, T., Planting Design

IIMOTO, M., Plant Production Engineering

INUBUSHI, K., Soil Science

KEINO, S., Agricultural Marketing

KIKUCHI, M., Agricultural Economics

KON, H., Green Space Meteorology

KOZAI, T., Environmental Control Engineering

MASADA, M., Biochemistry

MATSUI, H., Fruit Science

MII, M., Plant Cell Technology

MINAMIDA, S., Horticultural Management and Information

MOTOYAMA, N., Pesticide Toxicology

NAGATA, Y., Molecular Biology

NAKAGAWA, H., Biotechnology of Agroresources

NAKAMURA, O., Town and Country Planning

OHE, Y., Horticultural Information Science

OKITSU, S., Forest Ecology

ONO, S., Garden Design

SAITO, O., Farm Business Management

SANADA, H., Food and Nutrition

SHINOHARA, Y., Vegetable Science

TASHIRO, Y., Urban Landscape Design

WATANABE, Y., Plant Nutrition

YAMAUCHI, S., Humanistic Study on Environment

Faculty of Law and Economics:

ABE, K., International Economics

ABIKO, S., Contemporary Economic Theory

AKIMOTO, E., American Economic History

AMANO, M., Monetary Economics, Business Cycles

AMEMIYA, A., German Socio-economic History

AOTAKE, S., Corporate Law

ENDOH, Y., Commercial Law, Anti-monopoly Law

FURUUCHI, H., Modern European Economic History

HANDA, Y., Civil Law

HAYASHI, W., International Cooperation Law, Anglo-Japanese Alliance Relations

HAYASHI, Y., Criminal Law

HIROI, Y., Social and Health Policy

INABA, H., Econometrics

IWAMA, A., Constitutional Law, Parliamentary System

IWATA, M., Comparative Economic Systems, Yugoslav Politics and Political Economy

KAKIHARA, K., Macroeconomics

KAMANO, K., Civil Law, Environmental Law

KINPARA, K., Religion and Law, Civil Procedure

KUDO, H., History of Social Thought

KURITA, M., Economic Law, Competition Law

MARUYAMA, E., Condominium Law, Housing Law, Urban Law, Property Law, Civil Law

MARUYAWA, T., German Studies

MATSUDA, C., Public Finance

MIYAZAKI, R., Japanese Government and Politics
MURAYAMA, M., Sociology of Law
MUSASHI, T., Industrial Organization
NAKAHARA, H., International Research and Development, Company Management
NAKAKUBO, H., Labour and Employment Law
NOMURA, Y., Mathematical Economics
NOZAWA, T., History of Political Economy
OGANO, S., Civil Law, Environmental Law, Property Law
OKUMOTO, Y., Economic Statistics, Seasonal Adjustment
OMORI, W., Public Administration, Local Government
SAKAKIBARA, K., Macroeconomics, Money, Constitutional Economics
SAKAMOTO, T., Japanese Legal History
SHIMAZU, I., Philosophy of Law
SHINDO, M., Public Administration
SUZUKI, T., Administrative Law, Local Government Law
TAGAYA, K., Information Law, Administrative Law
TEZUKA, K., Foreigners and Law, Employment Security in Japan, Germany and USA
UEKI, S., Comparative Studies of Civil Law, Contracts and Torts
WATANABE, Y., Constitutional Law
YAMASHINA, T., Middle High German
YUMOTO, K., Political Consciousness in the Chinese Republican Era
YOSHIZUMI, Y., Financial Accounting

Faculty of Letters:

AKIYAMA, K., Comparative Literature, French Modern Literature, Japanese Modern Literature
CHOI, K., History of Korea
GORYO, K., Psychology
IIDA, N., Ethics, Bioethics
INUZUKA, S., Industrial Sociology, Theory of Organization
JITSUMORI, M., Comparative Cognition, Animal Learning
KUROSAWA, K., Social Psychology, Law and Psychology, Personality Psychology
MAEDA, S., German and Austrian Literature, Narratology
MATSUMOTO, H., Japanese Linguistics (Grammar, Dialectology)
MINAMIZUKA, S., History of Europe, History of Hungary, Rural Society
MITSUI, Y., 18th-century French Literature, Philosophy of the Enlightenment
MIURA, S., Japanese Ancient Literature, Japanese Oral Literature
MIYAKE, A., Modern Japanese History, Labour History
MIYANO, H., Psychology
MIZUKAMI, T., German Literature
NAGAI, H., Contemporary Western Philosophy
NAKAGAWA, H., Linguistics, Oral Literature, Ainu Language and Literature
NISHIMURA, Y., Comparative Studies of Modern Art and Literature
OGATA, T., Labour Sociology, Foreign Worker Problems, Sociology of Traffic Problems
OGIHARA, S., Cultural Anthropology of Northern Asia, Ethnology of the Ainu, Oral Traditions of the Ainu and the Northern Peoples
OGURA, M., Medieval English Philology
OKAMOTO, T., Japanese Archaeology
ONO, K., American Literature
OZAWA, H., Modern and Contemporary History of Europe
SAKURAI, A., Life—History Approach, Sociology of Social Problems, Research of Japanese Minorities (Buraku People, etc.)
SATO, H., History

SUGAHARA, K., History of Tokugawa Shogunate
TAKAGI, G., Japanese Early Modern Literature
TAKAHASHI, K., Ancient Philosophy
TAKEI, H., Medical Anthropology, Cultural Anthropology, Amazonian Aboriginal Culture
TAKITO, M., Modern Japanese Literature
TOKIZANE, S., American Literature, Novel, Theory of Literature
TUTIYA, S., Philosophy, Ethics, Cognitive Science, Spoken Dialogue Studies, Document Processing
YANAGISAWA, S., Prehistory of Japan
YASUDA, H., Modern Japanese Literature

Faculty of Science:

FUNABASHI, M., Carbohydrate Chemistry
HINO, Y., Mathematical Analysis
HIROI, Y., Metamorphic Petrology
IMAMOTO, T., Organic Chemistry
INOUE, A., Clay Mineralogy
ISEZAKI, N., Geophysics
ISIMURA, R.
ITO, M., Sedimentology
ITO, T., Structural Geology
KANEKO, K., Surface Solid State Chemistry, Molecular Science, Adsorption Science
KIMURA, T., High Energy Physics
KITAZUME, M., Finite Group Theory, Algebraic Combinatorics
KOBAYASHI, K., Cell Biology
KOHORI, Y., Low-temperature Physics
KOSHITANI, S., Algebra
KOYAMA, N., Biochemistry
KURASAWA, H., Nuclear Physics
MATSUMOTO, R., Astrophysics
NAGISA, M., Operator Algebra
NAKAGAMI, J., Statistics, Mathematical Programming
NAKAMURA, K., Coding Theory, Cryptography and Information Security
NAKANO, M., Biochemistry
NAKAYAMA, T., Nanoscience
NISHIDA, T., Mineralogy
NOZAWA, S., Algebra
OBINATA, T., Developmental Biology
OGAWA, K., Nuclear Physics
OHARA, S., Environmental Geology
OHASHI, K., Cell Physiology
SAKURA, Y., Hydrogeology
TAGURI, M., Statistics
TAKAGI, R., Geometry
TAKEDA, Y., Coordination Chemistry, Solution Chemistry
TSUJI, T., Computer Software, Theory of Programmes
TUTIYA, T., Echophysiology
YAMADA, I., Solid State Physics
YAMAMOTO, K., Molecular Physiology
YANAGISAWA, A., Organic Chemistry
YASUDA, M., Statistics
WATANO, Y., Plant Biosystems, Molecular Ecology

Graduate School of Medical and Pharmaceutical Sciences:

CHIBA, T., Neurobiology

Graduate School of Medicine (1-8-1 Inohana, Chuo-Ku, Chiba-shi, Chiba 260-8670; tel. (43) 222-7171; fax (43) 226-2005; e-mail g5004@office.chiba-u.jp; internet www.m.chiba-u.ac.jp):

BUJO, H., Genome Research and Clinical Application
FUJISAWA, T., Thoracic Surgery
FUKUDA, Y., Autonomic Physiology
HARIGAYA, K., Molecular and Tumour Pathology
HATA, A., Public Health
HATTORI, T., Neurology
HIRASAWA, H., Emergency and Critical Care Medicine
ICHINOSE, M., Plastic Surgery

ISHIKURA, H., Molecular Pathology
ITO, H., Radiology
ITO, H., Urology
IWASE, H., Legal Medicine
IYO, M., Psychiatry
KIMURA, S., Biochemistry and Molecular Pharmacology
KOHNO, Y., Paediatrics
KOMURO, I., Cardiovascular Science and Medicine
KOSEKI, H., Molecular Embryology
KURIYAMA, T., Respirology
KUWAKI, T., Molecular and Integrative Physiology
MIYAZAKI, M., General Surgery
MORI, C., Bioenvironmental Medicine
MORIYA, H., Orthopaedic Surgery
NAKAYA, H., Pharmacology
NAKAYAMA, T., Medical Immunology
NISHINO, T., Anaesthesiology
NODA, M., Molecular Infectology
NOGAWA, K., Occupational and Environmental Medicine
NOMURA, F., Molecular Diagnosis
OCHIAI, T., Academic Surgery
OHNUMA, N., Paediatric Surgery
OKAMOTO, Y., Otorhinolaryngology
SAISHO, H., Medicine and Clinical Oncology
SAITO, T., Molecular Genetics
SAITO, Y., Clinical Cell Biology
SEKIYA, S., Reproductive Medicine
SHINKAI, H., Clinical Biology of Extracellular Matrix
SHIRASAWA, H., Molecular Virology
SUZUKI, N., Environmental Biochemistry
TAKIGUCHI, M., Biochemistry and Genetics
TANIGUCHI, M., Molecular Immunology
TANZAWA, H., Clinical Molecular Biology
TOKUHISA, T., Developmental Genetics
TOSHIMORI, K., Anatomy and Developmental Biology
YAMAMOTO, S., Ophthalmology and Visual Science
YAMAURA, A., Neurological Surgery
YANO, A., Infection and Host Disease

Graduate School of Pharmaceutical Sciences (1-33 Yayoi-cho, Inage-ku, Chiba-shi, Chiba 263-8522; tel. (43) 251-1111; fax (43) 290-2974):

AIMI, N., Molecular Structure and Biological Function
ARANO, Y., Radiopharmaceutical Chemistry
CHIBA, K., Pharmacology and Toxicology
HAMADA, Y., Pharmaceutical Chemistry
HORIE, T., Biopharmaceutics
IGARASHI, K., Clinical Biochemistry
ISHIBASHI, M., Natural Products Chemistry
ISHIKAWA, T., Medicinal Organic Chemistry
KOBAYASHI, H., Biochemistry
MURAYAMA, T., Chemical Pharmacology
NEYA, S., Physical Chemistry
NISHIDA, A., Synthetic Organic Chemistry
SAITOH, K., Molecular Biology and Biotechnology
SUZUKI, K. T., Toxicology and Environmental Health
TOIDA, T., Bio-analytical Chemistry
UEDA, S., Drug Information and Communication
UENO, K., Geriatric Pharmacology and Therapeutics
YAMAGUCHI, N., Molecular Cell Biology
YAMAMOTO, K., Pharmaceutical Technology
YAMAMOTO, T., Microbiology and Molecular Genetics
YANO, S., Molecular Pharmacology and Pharmacotherapeutics

Health Sciences Center (1-33 Yayoi-cho, Inage-ku, Chiba-shi, Chiba 263-8522; tel. (47) 290-2210; fax (47) 290-2220; e-mail inf@hsc.chiba-u.ac.jp; internet hschome-gw.hsc.chiba-u.ac.jp):

NAGAO, K., Internal Medicine

Institute of Media and Information Technology (1–33 Yayoi-cho, Inage-ku, Chiba-shi, Chiba 263-8522; tel. (43) 290-3535; fax (43) 290-3581; internet www.imit.chiba-u.jp):

KOMORI, Y., Mathematical Logic
SOHMIYA, Y., German Linguistics, Semantics, Corpus Linguistics
ZEN, H., Intelligent Information Media

International Student Center (tel. (43) 290-2197; fax (43) 290-2198; e-mail bm2198@office.chiba-u.jp):

HATA, H., Teaching Japanese as a Second Language
NIIKURA, R., Cross-cultural Psychology

Marine Biosystems Research Center (1 Uchiura, Amatsu-kominato-cho, Awagun, Chiba 299-5502; tel. (47) 095-2201; fax (47) 095-2271; internet www-es.s.chiba-u.ac.jp/kominato/index_eng.html):

MIYAZAKI, T., Aquatic Ecology
YAMAGUCHI, T., Palaeobiology

School of Nursing (1-8-1 Inohana, Chuo-Ku, Chiba-shi, Chiba 260-8672; tel. (43) 222-7171):

FUNASHIMA, N., Nursing Education
HONDA, A., Continuing Nursing
ISHIGAKI, K., Home Care Nursing
IWASAKI, Y., Psychiatric Nursing
KITAIKE, T., Health Science
MASAKI, H., Gerontological Nursing
MIYAZAKI, M., Community Health Nursing
MORI, M., Maternity Nursing
NAKAMURA, N., Child Nursing
OHTA, S., Gerontological Nursing
OMURO, R., Nursing Administration
SATO, R., Adult Nursing
TESHIMA, M., Hospital Nursing Care
YAMADA, S., Physiology and Biochemistry
YOSHIMOTO, T., Geriatric Community Nursing, Care Systems Management

Research Center for Frontier Medical Engineering:

HACHIYA, H., Medical Image Processing
IGARASHI, T., Surgical Device Design
ITO, K., Antenna Engineering
SHIMOYAMA, I., Human Neurophysiology
TATSUOKA, H., Neuroscience

Research Center for Pathogenic Fungi and Microbial Toxicology (1-8-1 Inohana, Chuo-ku, Chiba 260-8670; tel. (43) 222-7171; fax (43) 226-2486; internet www.pf.chibau.ac.jp; f. 1946; Dir: YUZURU MIKAMI):

FUKUSHIMA, K., Division of Fungal Resources and Development
KAMEI, K., Division of Fungal Infection
MIKAMI, Y., Division of Molecular Biology and Therapeutics
NISHIMURA, K., Division of Phylogenetics
TAKEO, K., Division of Ultrastructure and Function

University Hospital (1-8-1 Inohana, Chuo-ku, Chiba-shi, Chiba 260-8670; tel. (43) 222-7171; fax (43) 224-3830; e-mail wad6005@office.chiba-u.jp; internet www.ho.chiba-u.jp):

IKUSAKA, M., Dept of General Medicine
KITADA, M., Pharmacy
KOUZU, T., Dept of Endoscopic Diagnostics and Therapeutics
SATOMURA, Y., Medical Informatics
TONABE, M., Postgraduate Education Center

CHUKYO UNIVERSITY

101-2 Yagoto Honmachi, Showa-ku, Nagoyashi, Aichi-ken 466-8666
Telephone: (52) 835-7111
E-mail: ic@mng.chukyo-u.ac.jp
Internet: www.chukyo-u.ac.jp
Founded 1954
Pres.: KAORU KITAGAWA

Chancellor and Chair. of the Board of Dirs: KIYOHIRO UMEMURA
Dir of the Library: HITOSHI YASUMURA
Dir, Admin. Bureau: KAZUHIRO HANAMURA

DEANS

Faculty of English: HIROSHI YOSHIKAWA
Faculty of Economics: KIYOHIDE UMEMURA
Faculty of Law: YUKIO HIYAMA
Faculty of Letters: SUMIAKI MORISHITA
Faculty of Psychology: MAREHIRO MUKAI
Faculty of Sociology: NOBORU MATSUDA
School of Health and Sport Sciences: KAGEMOTO YUASA
School of Information Science and Technology: HIROYASU KOSHIMIZU
School of International Liberal Studies: SUSUMU ITO
School of Management: MASAAKI NAKAMURA
School of Policy Design: NOBUHIRO OKUNO

CHUO GAKUIN UNIVERSITY

451 Kujike, Abiko, Chiba 270-1196
Telephone: (4) 7183-6501
Fax: (4) 7183-6502
Internet: www.cgu.ac.jp
Founded 1900
President: TERUO OKUBO
Faculties of Commerce and Law.

EHIME UNIVERSITY

10-13 Dogo-Himata, Matsuyama City 790-8577
Telephone: (89) 927-9000
Fax: (89) 927-9025
Internet: www.ehime-u.ac.jp
Founded 1949
Independent
Academic year: April to March (2 terms)
Pres.: MASAYUKI KOMATSU
Admin. Officer: I. KUBONIWA
Dean of Students' Affairs Office: T. SAITO
Library Dir: KOJI SANUKI
Library of 1,144,000 vols
Number of teachers: 976 full-time
Number of students: 9,858

DEANS

Faculty of Agriculture: MASAYA SHIRAISHI
Faculty of Education: YASUNOBU KINTO
Faculty of Engineering: KOICHI SUZUKI
Faculty of Law and Arts: MOTOJI IMAIZUMI
Faculty of Medicine: KOJI HASHIMOTO
Faculty of Science: YASUNOBU YANAGISAWA
United Graduate School of Agricultural Sciences: TADAAKI WAKIMOTO

FUKUI UNIVERSITY

9-1 Bunkyo 3-chome, Fukui City 910-8507
Telephone: (776) 23-0500
Fax: (776) 27-8030
E-mail: kaiho@sec.icpc.fukui-u.ac.jp
Internet: www.fukui-u.ac.jp
Founded 1949
Independent
Academic year: April to March
Pres.: SHINPEI KOJIMA
Dir of Admin.: YUZO SATO
Librarian: TOSHIYUKI KODAIRA
Library of 453,403 vols
Number of teachers: 367
Number of students: 4,159

DEANS

Faculty of Education and Regional Studies: YOSHIHIKO HAYATA
Faculty of Engineering: SHINGO TAMAKI

FUKUSHIMA UNIVERSITY

1 Kanayagawa, Fukushima 960-1296
Telephone: (24) 548-8084
Fax: (24) 548-3180
E-mail: hpc@fukushima-u.ac.jp
Internet: www.fukushima-u.ac.jp
Pres.: TOSHIO KONNO
Number of students: 4,309

Faculties and Graduate Schools of Administration and Social Sciences, Economics. and Business Administration, Human Development and Culture, Symbiotic Systems Science.

FUKUYAMA UNIVERSITY

985-1 Aza-Sanzou, Higashimuracho, Fukuyama-shi, Hiroshima 729-0292
Telephone: (84) 936-2111
Fax: (84) 936-2213
E-mail: soumu@fucc.fukuyama-u.ac.jp
Internet: www.fukuyama-u.ac.jp
Founded 1975
Chancellor: TAKASHI MIYACHI
Pres.: TAIZO MUTA
Vice-Pres: HIRAKU SHIMADA, RYUUSUKE YOSHIHARA
Librarian: TOSHIRO KATAOKA
Library of 222,700 vols
Number of teachers: 240
Number of students: 5,500

DEANS

Faculty of Economics: ISAO OOKUBO
Faculty of Engineering: KAZUO KOBAYASHI
Faculty of Human Cultures: FUMIKO MATSUDA
Faculty of Life Science and Biotechnology: KIYOSHI SATOUCHI
Faculty of Pharmacy: SATOSHI HIBINO

GIFU UNIVERSITY

1-1 Yanagido, Gifu-shi, Gifu-ken 501-1193
Telephone: (58) 230-1111
Fax: (58) 230-2021
E-mail: gjea04007@jim.gifu-u.ac.jp
Internet: www.gifu-u.ac.jp
Founded 1949
Independent
Pres.: T. KINJOH
Sec.-Gen.: Y. KIJIMA
Librarian: T. UNO
Library of 822,409 vols, 13,000 periodicals
Number of teachers: 738 full-time
Number of students: 5,995

DEANS

Faculty of Agriculture: T. NAKAMURA
Faculty of Education: YOSHIMI SASAKI
Faculty of Engineering: H. SHIMIZU
Faculty of Regional Studies: Y. MATSUDA
School of Medicine: Y. NOZAWA

GUNMA UNIVERSITY

4–2 Aramaki-machi, Maebashi City, Gunma 371-8510
Telephone: (27) 220-7111
E-mail: s-research@jimu.gunma-u.ac.jp
Internet: www.gunma-u.ac.jp
Founded 1949
Academic year: April to March
President: MAMORU SUZUKI
Vice-Pres. for General, Financial Affairs and Facilities: HIROYUKI SHIRAI
Vice-Pres. for Research: SEIJI OZAWA
Vice-Pres. for Student Affairs: KIMIO NAKAMURA
Dir of University Hospital: YASUO MORISHITA
Dir of Management: MOTOHARU IUE
Admin.: TADEDNORI IKENOUE

Librarian: YOUICHI NAKAZATO
Library of 651,576 vols
Number of teachers: 849 full-time
Number of students: 7,021
Publication: *Journal of Social and Information Studies* (1 a year)

DEANS

Faculty of Education: TADASHI MATSUDA
Faculty of Engineering: TAKAYUKI TAKARADA
Faculty of Medicine: FUMIO GOTO
Faculty of Social and Information Studies: NOBUTAKA OCHIAI
Institute of Molecular and Cellular Regulation: ITARU KOJIMA

HIROSAKI UNIVERSITY

1 Bunkyo-cho, Hirosaki 036-8560
Telephone: (172) 36-2111
Fax: (172) 37-6594
E-mail: webmaster@cc.hirosaki-u.ac.jp
Internet: www.hirosaki-u.ac.jp
Founded 1949
Independent
Academic year: April to March
Pres.: MASAHIKO ENDO
Vice-Pres.: Y. MIZUNE
Registrar: R. SHIBATA
Librarian: E. OKAZAKI
Dir of the Hospital: S. HARATA
Number of teachers: 692
Number of students: 5,512
Publication: *School Outline* (1 a year)

DEANS

Faculty of Agriculture and Life Science: K. TOYOKAWA
Faculty of Education: H. OZAWA
Faculty of Humanities: T. TANNO
Faculty of Science and Technology: H. OHNUKI
School of Medicine: M. ENDO

PROFESSORS

Faculty of Agriculture and Life Science (3 Bunkyo-cho, Hirosaki 036-8561; internet nature.cc.hirosaki-u.ac.jp):

ANDO, Y., Entomology
AOYAMA, M., Soil Science
ARAKAWA, O., Pomology
ASADA, Y., Applied Microbiology, Microbial Technology
BOKURA, T., Agricultural Meteorology
FUKUDA, H., Horticulture
HARADA, Y., Plant Pathology
ISHIGURO, S., Biochemistry of the Eye, Developmental Biology
KANDA, K., Cooperative Study
KUDO, A., Irrigation, Drainage and Hydraulic Engineering
MAKITA, H., Vegetation Geography, Environmental Science
MIYAIRI, K., Biochemistry
MOTOMURA, Y., Science of Horticultural Bioproducts
MUTO, A., Molecular Engineering
NAKAMURA, S., Biochemical Engineering
NIIZEKI, M., Plant Breeding and Genetics
OBARA, Y., Cytogenetics
OHMACHI, T., Molecular Biology, Applied Microbiology
OKUNO, T., Organic Chemistry and Biochemistry
SASAKI, C., Agricultural Land Engineering
SAWADA, S., Plant Ecophysiology
SAWARA, Y., Animal Behaviour
SHIOZAKI, Y., Pomology
SUGIYAMA, K., Virology, Molecular Biology
SUGIYAMA, S., Crop Science, Plant Evolutionary Biology
TAKAHASHI, H., Regional Economy
TAKAMURA, K., Morphogenesis
TAKEDA, K., Microbial Ecology

TANIGUCHI, K., Rural Planning
TOYOKAWA, K., Feeds and Feeding
UNO, T., Agricultural Economics
YURUGI, M., Structural Mechanics, Construction Materials, Concrete

Faculty of Education (internet siva.cc .hirosaki-u.ac.jp):

ANDO, F., Education for Children with Disabilities
ANNO, M., Japanese History
ASANO, K., Piano
FUMOTO, N., Psychology of Sport and Physical Activity
GION, Z., Social Studies Education
HAGA, T., Clothing Science
HANDA, S., Mathematics Education
HAYAKAWA, M., Health Education
HIKAGE, Y., Home Economics Education, Laundering and Finishing
HIRAKI, K.
HIRAOKA, K., Adolescent Development, Learning Theory
HONMA, M., Movement Theory
HORIUCHI, H., Earth Materials Science
HOSHI, K., Art Education
HOSHINO, H., Condensed Matter Physics
IMAI, T., Musicology
ITOH, S., Analysis
IWAI, Y., Oil Painting, Tempera and Etching
KAMADA, K., Sedimentology
KAMIYA, K., Rural Sociology
KATO, Y., Food Chemistry
KITADA, T., Harmonic Analysis
KON, M., Differential Geometry
MARUYAMA, M., Japanese Literature
MENZAWA, K., School Health Education and Safety Education, School Health Promotion
MORI, A., School Health Education
MORI, R., Home Economics Education
MURAKAMI, O., Animal Physiology
MURAYAMA, M., Educational Methodology
NANBA, K., Algebra, Foundations of Mathematics, Discrete Mathematics
OHSHIMA, Y., Biomechanics
OHTAKA, A., Animal Taxonomy
OKADA, K., Sculpture, Clay Working (Pottery)
OKUNO, T., English Linguistics
OTA, S., Mathematics Education
OTSUBO, S., Sociology of Education
OYAMA, S., Health and Physical Education
OZAWA, H., Educational System and Administration
SAITO, S., Science Education, Phycology, Limnology
SAITO, T., History of Medieval Japan
SATO, K., Exercise Physiology
SATO, S., Adult Education
SATO, Y., Paediatrics
SATOH, Y., Magnetics
SEKI, H., Photochemistry
TAKANASHI, T., English Teaching Methodology
TANDOH, S., Educational Psychology
TOYOSHIMA, A., Social Clinical Psychology
UEDA, K., Timber Engineering
WATANABE, K., Voice
YAJIMA, T., Philosophy
YAMAGUCHI, T., Sinology
YOSHINO, H., Developmental Psychology, Psychology of Personality

Faculty of Humanities (internet human.cc .hirosaki-u.ac.jp):

AKAGI, K., Public Economics, Law and Economics
ARAI, K., Behavioural Accounting
CARPENTER, V., International Politics
FUJINUMA, K., Japanese Archaeology
FUJITA, M., Business Behaviour, Public Utilities
FUNAKI, Y., Statistics, and Operations Research

HASEGAWA, S., Early Modern Japanese History
HORIUCHI, T., Constitutional Law
HOSHINO, Y., Accounting and Control
IGARASHI, Y., Ethics
ISHIDOU, T., English, American Literature, American Studies, Robert Frost, Mark Twain, McCarthyism
KATORI, K., Science of Information and Systems
KITAJIMA, S., Regional Economy and Regional Policy
MOROOKA, M., Science of Religion
MURAMATSU, K., Political Theory
MURATA, S., English Literature
NAKAZAWA, K., Western Economic History
NITTA, S., Modern German Literature
OKAZAKI, E., Philosophy
OKUNO, K., Linguistics
PHILIPS, J. E., History of Africa, America and Islam
SAKUMICHI, S., Social Psychology, Anthropology
SATO, N., English Literature
SATOH, K., Japanese Linguistics
SHIMUZU, A., Philosophy of Information
SHINOMIYA, T., Business History
SUDO, H., History of Art
SUGIYAMA, Y., Cultural Anthropology
SUZUKI, K., Economic Theory
TANAKA, I., German Literary Arts
TERADA, M., French Literature
UEKI, H., Chinese Classical Literature
USUDA, S., Japanese Literature
WARASHINA, K., Japanese Language
YASUDA, M., Marketing

Faculty of Science and Technology (3 Bunkyo-cho, Hirosaki 036-8561; internet www.st .hirosaki-u.ac.jp):

AMENOMORI, M., Cognitive Science, Superhigh Energy Physics
ARAKI, T., Applied Electronics
FUKASE, M., VLSI Computer
FURUYA, Y., Intelligent Materials Design and Systems, Materials Processing, Solid State Sensors and Actuators, Non-destructive Evaluation
GOTO, T., Applied Chemistry
IIKURA, Y., Instrumentation Physics, Remote Sensing
INAMURA, T., Spray Engineering and Combustion, Propulsion Engineering
ITO, A., Combustion, Fire Science, Multiple Phase Flow
ITO, S., Organic Syntheses
KATO, H., Solid State Physics, Synchrotron-Radiation Science
KAWAGUCHI, S., Cosmic-ray Physics
KURAMATA, S., Space Physics
KURATSUBO, S., Harmonic Analysis
MAKINO, E., Micro Electromechanical Systems
MASHITA, M., Thin Film and Surface Physics
MIYATA, H., Solid Mechanics, Fracture Mechanics, Strength Evaluation Systems
MORI, T.
MOTOSE, K., Algebra
NAKAZATO, H., Functional Analysis
NANJO, H., High Energy Astrophysics
NENCHEV, D. N., Robotics
OHZEKI, K., Analytical Chemistry
RIKIISHI, K., Physical Oceanography, Meteorology, Glaciology
SAITO, M., Computational Science Approach to Biomolecular Recognition
SAKISAKA, Y., Solid State Physics, Synchrotron-radiation Science
SASAKI, K., Surface Physics
SATO, H., Phase Transformation, Plastic Deformation
SATO, T., Raman Spectra
SATO, T., Seismology
SHIBA, M., Disaster Prevention Geology

SHIMIZU, T., Bioinformatics, Biophysics
SUDO, S., Physical Chemistry
SUTO, S., Physical Chemistry of Polymers
TAJIRI, A., Organic Physical Chemistry
TAKAGUCHI, M., Matrix Analysis
TAKEGAHARA, K., Theoretical Solid State Physics
TANAKA, K., Physical Vulcanology, Seismology
TSURUMI, M., Environmental Chemistry, Geochemistry
UJIIE, Y., Petroleum Geology, Organic Geology
YOSHIOKA, Y., Computer Networks, Computer Architecture
YOSHIZAWA, A., Organic Materials Science

School of Medicine (53 Hon-cho, Hirosaki 036-8563; internet hippo.med.hirosaki-u.ac.jp):

ABE, Y., Radiation Oncology
ENDO, M., Glycobiology of Glycoconjugates
HADA, R., Medical Informatics
HANADA, K., Sun Protection, Laser Therapy, Atopic Dermatitis, Photodynamic Therapy
ICHIMARU, T., Medical Apparatus and Engineering
ICHINOHE, T., Paediatric Nursing, Guidance in Nursing Practice
ITO, E., Paediatric Haematology and Oncology
IWASAKI, A., Medical (Radiation) Physics
KACHI, T., Anatomy
KAGIAYA, A., Obstetrics and Gynaecology
KAMIYA, H., Immunopathology of Parasitic Infection
KANEKO, S., Epiteptology, Clinical and Basic Neuropsychopharmacology
KAWAHARA, R., Gerontological Nursing
KIKUCHI, H., Endocrinology
KIMURA, H., Oral and Maxillo-facial Surgery
KIMURA, K., Nursing of Adults
KUDO, H., Tumour Pathology
KURATA, K., Neurophysiology
KURODA, N., Forensic Pathology
MATSUKI, A., Anaesthesiology, Intensive Care, Pain Clinic
MATSUMOTO, M., Neurophysiology
MATSUNAGA, M., Clinical Neurology, Neuroepidemiology
MINAGAWA, T., Cancer Nursing
MITA, R., Public Health
MIURA, H., Existence Philosophy, Medical Philosophy and Ethics
MIURA, T., Orthopaedic Surgery, Rehabilitation Medicine
MIZUSHIMA, Y., Respirology, Gerontology
MOTOMURA, S., Cardiovascular Pharmacology
MUNAKATA, A., Gastroenterology
MUNAKATA, H., Paediatric Surgery
NAKAMURA, T., Chronic Pancreatitis, Pancreatic Steatorrhoea, Pancreatic Diabetes, Gastric Emptying, Clinical Laboratory Medicine
NAKANE, A., Bacteriology, Immunology
NAKAZAWA, M., Basic and Clinical Research for Retinal Diseases
NIKARA, T., Physiology
OHGUSHI, Y., Nursing Science
OKUMURA, K., Internal Medicine, Cardiology
SASAKI, J., Tumour Immunology, Pathogenic Bacteriology, Food Science
SASAKI, M., Surgery for Digestive Diseases, Hepato-pancreaticobiliary Surgery, Liver Transplantation
SATO, T., Pathology
SATO, Y., Neuroscience
SATOH, K., Basic Studies on the Pathogenesis of Cerebrovascular Diseases
SATOH, K., Biochemistry, Enzymology, Chemical Larcinogenesis

SAWADA, Y., Study of Wound Healing, Burns, Hypertrophic Scan and Keloids, Microcirculation of the Flap
SEIMIYA, Y., Analysis of Daily Activity
SHINKAWA, H., Inner and Middle Ear Morphology, Middle Ear Surgery
SHOMURA, K., Neural Anatomy
SUDA, T., Endocrinology and Metabolism
SUGAMARA, K., Pharmacological and Pharmaceutical Drugs Interaction
SUGAWARA, K., Physical Fitness, Nutrition, Immunology
SUZUKI, S., Neurosurgery, Cerebro-vascular Diseases
SUZUKI, T., Oncology of the Urogenital Region
TAKAHASHI, G., Microscopic Anatomy, Cell Biology
TATEISHI, T., Clinical Pharmacology, Pharmacokinetics and Pharmacodynamics
TSUCHIDA, S., Cancer Biochemistry, Biochemical Pharmacology
TSUSHIMA, H., Physical Therapy
WADA, K., Clinical Research in Adult Epilepsy
WAKABAYASHI, K., Neuropathology
WAKUI, M., Cellular Physiology
WAKUI, M., Physiology I
YAGIHASHI, S., Pathology
YAMABE, H., Nephrology
YAMADA, C., Community Health, Public Health, International Health, International Cooperation
YASUJIMA, M., Laboratory Medicine, Hypertension
YODONO, H., Research of Interventional Radiology
YONESAKA, S., Paediatric Cardiology

ATTACHED RESEARCH INSTITUTES

Center for Computing and Communications: 3 Bunkyo-Cho, Hirosaki 036-8561; Dir Y. YOSHIOKA.

Center for Education and Research of Lifelong Learning: 1 Bunkyo-cho, Hirosaki 036-8560; Dir S. SATO.

Center for Educational Research and Practice: 1 Bunkyo-cho, Hirosaki 036-8560; Dir K. FUKIGAI.

Center for Joint Research: 3 Bunkyo-cho, Hirosaki 036-8561; Dir A. TAJIRI.

Earthquake and Volcano Observatory: 3 Bunkyo-cho, Hirosaki 036-8561; Dir K. TANAKA.

Gene Research Center: 3 Bunkyo-cho, Hirosaki 036-8561; Dir M. NIIZEKI.

Institute of Brain Science: 5 Zaifu-cho, Hirosaki 036-8562; Dir M. MATSUNAGA.

Institute for Experimental Animals: 5 Zaifu-cho, Hirosaki 036-8562; Dir H. KAMIYA.

University Farms: 7-1 Shitafukuro, Fujisaki-machi, Aomori-ken 038-3802; Dir T. NOMURA.

HIROSHIMA UNIVERSITY

3-2 Kagamiyama 1-chome, Higashi-Hiroshima 739-8511

Telephone: (82) 422-7111
Fax: (82) 424-6179
E-mail: www-admin@hiroshima-u.ac.jp
Internet: www.hiroshima-u.ac.jp/index-j.html

Founded 1949
Independent
Academic year: April to March (2 semesters)

Pres.: TAIZO MUTA
Exec. Vice-Pres. for Education and Student Affairs: S. TAKAHASHI
Exec. Vice-Pres. for Finance: K. MAEKAWA
Exec. Vice-Pres. for Information: Y. TSUBAKI
Exec. Vice-Pres. for Medical Affairs: O. YUGE

Exec. Vice-Pres. for Personnel and General Affairs: T. KUDO
Exec. Vice-Pres. for University Relations: N. OKI
Vice-Pres. for Attached Schools: S. ISHII
Library of 3,197,044 vols, including 1,286,724 in foreign languages
Number of teachers: 1,836
Number of students: 15,294 (incl. 4,346 postgraduate)

Publications: *Hiroshima Mathematical Journal, Journal of Science of the Hiroshima University, Series C (Earth and Planetary Sciences), The Hiroshima University Studies—Graduate School of Letters, Bulletin of the Graduate School of Education, Hiroshima Journal of Mathematics Education, Hiroshima Journal of School Education, Studies in Educational Science, Studies in English Language Education, Hiroshima Journal of Medical Sciences, The Journal of Hiroshima University Dental Society, Bulletin of the Graduate School of Engineering, Proceedings of the Research Institute for Radiation Biology and Medicine, The Hiroshima Economic Studies, The Hiroshima Economic Review, Economic Studies, The Hiroshima Law Journal, Journal of the Graduate School of Biosphere Science, Studies in Area Culture, Studies in Social Sciences, Studies in Culture and the Humanities, Science Reports, Studies in Language and Culture, Journal of International Development and Co-operation, Bulletin of the Institute for Cultural Studies of the Seto Inland Sea, Reports of the Miyajima Natural Botanical Garden, Journal of International Co-operation in Education, Bulletin of the Department of Teaching Japanese as a Second Language, The Annual of Research on Early Childhood, Journal of Learning Science, Bulletin of Music Culture Education, Bulletin of Training and Research Center for Clinical Psychology, Hiroshima Psychological Research, Research in Higher Education in Japan, Higher Education Forum, Hiroshima Law Review*

DEANS AND DIRECTORS

Faculty of Economics: S. TOMIOKA
Faculty of Integrated Arts and Sciences: M. SATO
Graduate School of Advanced Sciences of Matter: T. JO
Graduate School of Biomedical Sciences: T. USUI
Graduate School of Biosphere Sciences: K. SUZUKI
Graduate School of Education: T. NAKAHARA
Graduate School of Engineering: M. OKADA
Graduate School for International Development and Cooperation: K. SAITO
Graduate School of Letters: H. KISHIDA
Graduate School of Medicine: T. MURAKAMI
Graduate School of Science: M. TANIGUCHI
Graduate School of Social Sciences: N. KAWASAKI
Hiroshima University Hospital: T. ASAHARA (Dir)
Law School: M. TANABE
Research Institute for Radiation Biology and Medicine: F. SUZUKI (Dir)

PROFESSORS

Faculty of Integrated Arts and Sciences (7-1 Kagamiyama 1-chome, Higashi- Hiroshima 739-8521; tel. (82) 422-7111; fax (82) 424-0751; e-mail souka-bucho-sien@office.hiroshima-u.ac.jp; internet home .hiroshima-u.ac.jp/souka/e/ias.html):

Division of Area Studies:

FUJITA-SANO, M., Cultural Anthropology, American Studies
IIDA, M., English Literature and Culture

ITOH, S., American Literature and Culture
KASHIHARA, O., Modern Japanese Literature
KOHATA, F., Biblical Studies
KUSUNOSE, M., Modern Chinese History
MIKI, N., Contemporary Chinese Culture
OKAMOTO, M., American Social History
SATAKE, A., Japanese History and Culture
SATO, M., History of German Literature, Everyday Life and Customs in the Early Modern Age
TAKATANI, M., Cultural Anthropology, Southeast Asian Studies

Division of Behavioural and Biological Sciences:

ANDO, M., Integrative Physiology
FURUKAWA, Y., Neurobiology
HORI, T., Psychophysiology
IWATA, K., Comparative Politics and Diplomacy
KAWAHARA, A., Developmental Biology
KUSUDO, K., History of Sport
SEIWA, H., Psychology of Personality
TSUTSUI, K., Brain Science
URA, M., Social Psychology
WADA, M., Biochemistry of Exercise
YAMASAKI, M., Exercise Physiology

Division of Creative Arts and Sciences:

GOLDSBURY, P. A., Philosophy of Language, Comparative Culture
HARA, M., Comparative Philosophy and Music Aesthetics
KOTOH, T., Comparative Philosophy
MURASE, N., French Theatre, French Studies
NAKAMURA, H., Shakespeare, Cinema Studies, Cultural Semiotics
SAITO, T., Modern Science and Mysticism
TAKAHASHI, N., Ancient Greek Philosophy

Division of Language and Culture:

ANIYA, S., Linguistics
HIGUCHI, M., English Philology
IMAZATO, C., History of the English Language, Lexicography
INOUE, K., Linguistics
KOBAYASHI, H., Applied Linguistics, TESOL
NISHIDA, T., Applied Linguistics
OGAWA, Y., Comparative Study of Japanese and Chinese
SKAER, P. M., Linguistics
TANAKA, S., German Literature
YAMADA, J., Psycholinguistics
YOON, K. B., Korean Literature
YOSHIDA, M., Linguistics

Division of Materials Science:

FUKAMIYA, N., Bioactive Natural Products Chemistry
HATAKENAKA, N., Theoretical Condensed Matter Physics
HIKOSAKA, M., Soft Materials Physics
HOSHINO, K., Condensed Matter Physics
ITOH, T., Molecular Spectroscopy and Quantum Chemistry
KOJIMA, K., Condensed Matter Physics
KOMINAMI, S., Biophysical Chemistry
NAGAI, K., Theoretical Solid State Physics
TAKEDA, T., Condensed Matter Physics
UDAGAWA, M., Condensed Matter Physics

Division of Mathematical and Information Sciences:

AGAOKA, Y., Differential Geometry
HARADA, K., Geometry Graphics
KUWADA, M., Experimental Design
MIZUTA, Y., Function Theory
YOSHIDA, K., Applied Analysis

Division of Natural Environmental Sciences:

FUKUOKA, M., Research of Earth Resources
HAYASE, K., Environmental Sciences
HONDA, K., Chemical Ecology
HORIKOSHI, T., Microbiology
KAIHOTSU, I., Hydrology
NAKAGOSHI, N., Landscape Ecology

NARISADA, K., Science Studies
OHO, Y., Environmental Geology
SAKURAI, N., Environmental Plant Physiology
TOGASHI, K., Applied Ecology

Division of Socio-Environmental Studies:

AKIBA, S., Rural Sociology
FUKIHARA, S., Regions and Economy
ICHIKAWA, H., History of Technology
YASUNO, M., Contemporary History

Graduate School of Biosphere Sciences:

NAKANE, K., Environmental Ecosystem Ecology
SAKUGAWA, H., Environmental Chemistry

Graduate School of Education (1-1 Kagamiyama 1-chome, Higashi- Hiroshima 739-8524; tel. (82) 422-7111; fax (82) 422-7171; e-mail kyoiku-kyo-sien@office.hiroshima-u.ac.jp; internet www.ed.hiroshima-u.ac.jp/index.html):

Doctoral Programme in Learning and Curriculum Development; and Master's Programme in Learning Science—Learning Development Major:

DOBASHI, T., Lifespan Developmental Education
HIGUCHI, S., Philosophy and Aesthetics of Learning
ISHII, S., Environmental Psychology
MORI, T., Psychology of Learning
NISHINE, K., Sociology of Education
TAKAHASHI, S., Social Psychology

Doctoral Programme in Learning and Curriculum Development; and Master's Programme in Learning Science—Curriculum and Instruction Development Major:

KIHARA, S., Physical Education
KIMURA, H., Social Studies Education
KUROSE, M., Keyboard Music
MAEDA, S., Human Geography
MATSUDA, Y., Psychology of Physical Education
MOCHIZUKI, T., Food Science
MORITA, N., Japanese Language Education
SHIBA, K., Science Education
TAINOSHO, J., Home Economics Education
WAKAMOTO, S., Art Education

Doctoral Programme in Learning and Curriculum Development; and Master's Programme in Special Education:

FUNATSU, M., Psychology of Children with Disabilities
HAYASAKA, K., Speech and Language Pathology
OCHIAI, T., Special Educational Systems, Inclusive Education
SHIMIZU, Y., Audiology and Education of Children with Hearing Impairment
YAMANASHI, M., Methods of Teaching Children with Visual Impairment

Doctoral Programme in Arts and Science Education; and Master's Programme in Science, Technology and Science Education—Science Education Major:

FURUKAWA, Y., Solid State Chemistry, Magnetic Resonance
HAYASHI, T., Regional Geology, Geoinformatics, Earth Science Education
KADOYA, S., Science Education
MAEHARA, T., Particles and Fields, Physics Education
SUZUKI, M., Petrology
TANAKA, T., Inorganic Chemistry
TOKUNAGA, T., Solid State Physics
TORIGOE, K., Zoology, Biology Education
TSUTAOKA, T., Solid State Physics
YAMASHITA, Y., Nuclear Physics, Physics Education

Doctoral Programme in Arts and Science Education; and Master's Programme in Science, Technology and Science Education—Mathematics Education Major:

IMAOKA, M., Geometry
IWASAKI, H., Mathematics Education
KAGEYAMA, S., Statistics and Combinatorics
MARUO, O., Algebra
NAKAHARA, T., Mathematics Education

Doctoral Programme in Arts and Science Education; and Master's Programme in Science, Technology and Science Education—Technology and Information Education Major:

BANSHOYA, K., Woodworking
MONDEN, Y., Computer Science
TASHIMA, S., Mechanical Processing
UEDA, K., Technology Educations
YAMAMOTO, T., Computer Control Technology

Doctoral Programme in Arts and Science Education; and Master's Programme in Science, Technology and Science Education—Social Studies Education Major:

IKENO, N., Social Studies Education
KATAKAMI, S., Social Studies Education
KOBARA, T., Social Studies Education
MIYAKE, T., Modern Japanese History
NAKAYAMA, T., Medieval Japanese History
OBI, T., Eastern History
SATO, S., Western History
SHIMOMUKAI, T., Ancient and Medieval Japanese History
TANAHASHI, K., Social Studies Education

Doctoral Programme in Arts and Science Education; and Master's Programme in Language and Culture Education—Japanese Language and Culture Education Major:

EBATA, Y., Japanese Language
IWASAKI, F., Japanese Literature
TAKAHASHI, K., Linguistic Geography
TAKEMURA, S., Japanese Literature
YOSHIDA, H., Japanese Language Education

Doctoral Programme in Arts and Science Education; and Master's Programme in Language and Culture Education—English Language and Culture Education Major:

FUKAKAWA, S., Pragmatics, Classroom Research
HAMAGUCHI, O., American Literature
MIURA, S., English Language Education
NAKAO, Y., English Philology and Linguistics
TANAKA, M., Language Testing in English Language Teaching

Doctoral Programme in Arts and Science Education; and Master's Programme in Language and Culture Education—Japanese Pedagogy, Linguistics and Culture Studies Major:

KURACHI, A., Intercultural Education
MACHI, H., Study of Japanese Composition and Style
MIZUMACHI, I., Educational Language Technology
MIZUSHIMA, H., Comparative Cultures and Comparative Literature
NAKAMURA, S., Japanese Intellectual History
NUIBE, Y., Japanese Language Pedagogics
NUMOTO, K., Historical Study of Japanese Language
SAKODA, K., Second Language Acquisition
TAWATA, S., Japanese Linguistics and Japanese Language Education

Doctoral Programme in Arts and Science Education; and Master's Programme in Lifelong Activities Education—Health and Sports Sciences Education Major:

ESASHI, Y., Physical Education

KUROKAWA, T., Sports Training
KUSUDO, K., History of Sport
MATSUOKA, S., Physical Education
WATANABE, K., Physiology, Sports Biomechanics
YANAGIHARA, E., Kinematical Analysis in Sport (Ball Games)

Doctoral Programme in Arts and Science Education; and Master's Programme in Lifelong Activities Education—Human Life Sciences Education Major:

HIRATA, M., Management of Life
IKAWA, Y., Science of Food Preparation
IWASHIGE, H., House Environment Science
MIYAMOTO, S., Clothing Science
SHIBA, S., Home Economics Education

Doctoral Programme in Arts and Science Education; and Master's Programme in Lifelong Activities Education—Music Culture Education Major:

CHIBA, J., Musicology
KUROSE, M., Keyboard Music
OKANO, S., Piano
OKUDA, M., Vocal Music
YOSHITOMI, K., Music Education

Doctoral Programme in Arts and Science Education; and Master's Programme in Lifelong Activities Education—Art Education Major:

ESAKI, A., Product Design
SUGAMURA, T., Science of Arts (History of Japanese Arts)
UCHIDA, M., Drawing and Painting

Doctoral Programme in Education and Human Science; and Master's Programme in Educational Studies:

KOGA, K., Educational Administration and Policy
KOHNO, K., Studies of Educational Leadership
KOIKE, G., Adult and Continuing Education
NAKANO, K., Curriculum Research
NINOMIYA, A., Comparative Education
OKATO, T., Educational Management
OTSUKA, Y., Comparative Education
SAKAKOSHI, M., Educational Thought and Philosophy in Germany
SATOH, H., History of Japanese and Eastern Education
TORIMITSU, M., Early Childhood Education
YAMASAKI, H., Sociology of Higher Education
YASUHARA, Y., History of Western Education

Doctoral Programme in Education and Human Science; and Master's Programme in Psychology:

FUKADA, H., Social Psychology
KODAMA, K., Clinical Psychology
MAEDA, K., Developmental Psychology
MIYATANI, M., Cognitive Psychology
OKAMOTO, Y., Developmental Clinical Psychology
TOSHIMA, T., Neuropsychology
YAMAZAKI, A., Child Psychology

Doctoral Programme in Education and Human Science; and Master's Programme in Higher Education Research and Development:

ARIMOTO, A., Sociology of Higher Education
DAIZEN, T., Sociology of Higher Education
HATA, T., History of Higher Education in Japan
KITAGAKI, I., Education Technology, Fuzzy Science
YAMAMOI, A., Sociology of Higher Education

Graduate School of Advanced Sciences of Matter (3-1 Kagamiyama 1-chome, Higashi-Hiroshima 739-8530; tel. (82) 422-7111; fax (82) 424-7000; internet www.hiroshima-u.ac.jp/en/adsm/):

Department of Molecular Biotechnology:

HIRATA, D., Molecular Biology
KATO, J., Molecular Environmental Biotechnology
KINASHI, H., Microbiology and Natural Product Chemistry
KURODA, A., Biochemistry
MIYAKAWA, T., Molecular Biotechnology in Yeast
NISHIO, N., Environmental Bioengineering
ONO, K., Molecular Biochemistry
TSUCHIYA, E., Molecular Cell Biology
YAMADA, T., Plant/Microbe Interactions

Department of Quantum Matter:

ENDO, I., Photon Physics
JO, T., Theory of Condensed Matters
KADOYA, Y., Solid State Quantum Optics
OGUCHI, T., Computational Physics
OKAMOTO, H., Beam Physics
SERA, M., Experimental Researches of Strongly Correlated Electron Systems
SUZUKI, T., Low Temperature Physics
TAKABATAKE, T., Magnetism and Magnetic Materials
TAKAHAGI, T., Nanotechnology

Department of Semiconductor Electronics and Integration Science:

IWATA, A., Integrated Circuits
MIURA-MATTAUSCH, M., Semiconductor Device Technology
MIYAZAKI, S., Semiconductor Electronics

Graduate School of Biomedical Sciences (2-3 Kasumi 1-chome, Minami-ku, Hiroshima 734-8513; tel. (82) 257-5555; fax (82) 257-5278; e-mail bimes-kyou@office.hiroshima-u.ac.jp; internet www.hiroshima-u.ac.jp/bimes/):

Programmes for Applied Biomedicine:

AKAGAWA, Y., Advanced Prosthodontics, Implantology
EBOSHIDA, A., Public Health and Health Policy, Health Science, Epidemiology, Environmental Health
HAMADA, T., Geriatric Dentistry, Prosthodontics, Stomatognathic Dysfunction
HIRAKAWA, K., Otorhinolaryngology, Head and Neck Surgery and Oncology, Rhinology
INAI, K., Pathology, Tumour Pathology
ITO, K., Radiology, Diagnostic Imaging, Interventional Radiology
KAMATA, N., Oral and Maxillofacial Surgery
KANBE, M., Clinical Laboratory Medicine, Clinical Physiology, ME, Medical Informatics, Gene Engineering
KAWAHARA, M., Dental Anaesthesiology, Pain Clinic
KIMURA, K.
KOBAYASHI, M., Paediatrics, Child Health
KOHNO, N., Molecular and Internal Medicine, Respiratory Diseases, Cancer Therapeutics
KOZAI, K., Paediatric Dentistry
KUDO, Y., Obstetrics and Gynaecology
MAEDA, N., Oral Growth and Developmental Biology, Development of Masticatory System
MORIKAWA, N., Clinical Pharmacotherapy, Pharmacokinetics, Therapeutic Drug Monitoring
OCHI, M., Orthopaedic Surgery, Sports Medicine, Knee Surgery
OZAWA, K., Pharmacotherapy, Clinical Pharmacology
SUEDA, T., Surgery, Thoracic and Cardiovascular Surgery, Bioengineering
TAKAHASHI, I., Preventive Dentistry, Mucosal Immunology
TANIGAWA, K., Emergency and Critical Care Medicine, Cardiopulmonary Resuscitation, Airway Management, Free Radicals and Reperfusion Injury
TANIMOTO, K., Oral and Maxillofacial Radiology, Dysphagia
TANNE, K., Orthodontics and Craniofacial Developmental Biology, Biomechanics
YAJIN, K., Otorhinolaryngology, Head and Neck Surgery, Head and Neck Oncology, Rhinology
YOSHIZAWA, K., Infectious Disease Control and Prevention, Seroepidemiology of Viral Hepatitis
YUGE, O., Anaesthiology and Critical Care

Programmes for Biomedical Research:

AOYAMA, H., Anatomy and Developmental Biology
ASAHARA, T., Surgery, Gastroenterological Surgery, Organ Transplantation
CHAYAMA, K., Medicine and Molecular Science, Gastroenterology, Hepatology
DOHI, T., Dental Pharmacology
HAZEKI, O., Physiological Chemistry, Cellular Signal Transduction
HIDE, M., Dermatology, Allergology and Immunopharmacology in Skin
IDE, T., Cellular and Molecular Biology
KANNO, M., Immunology, Parasitology, Molecular Immunology
KATAOKA, K., Histology and Cell Biology, Histochemistry and Cell Biology of the Digestive Organs
KATO, Y., Dental and Medical Biochemistry, Biochemistry and Oral Biology
KIKUCHI, A., Biochemistry, Intracellular Signal Transduction
KURIHARA, H., Periodontal Medicine, Periodontal Tissue Regeneration, Endodontology
KURISU, K., Neurosurgery, Neuro-oncology, Neuroradiology, Surgery of Brain Tumours and Cerebro-vascular Disease, Skull Base Surgery
MASUJIMA, T., Analytical Molecular Medicine and Devices, Videonanoscopes, Cell Dynamics, Pharmaco-dynamics, Bioanalysis
MATSUMOTO, M., Clinical Neuroscience and Therapeutics, Neurology, Strokology, Gerontology
MISHIMA, H., Ophthalmology and Visual Science, Glaucoma, Ocular Cell Biology, Ocular Pharmacology, Retinal Disease
OGATA, N., Neurophysiology
OHTA, S., Xenobiotic Metabolism and Molecular Toxicology, Neurochemistry, Drug Metabolism
OKAMOTO, T., Molecular Oral Medicine and Maxillofacial Surgery
OKAZAKI, M., Biomaterials Science, Dental Materials
SAKAI, N., Molecular and Pharmacological Neuroscience, Molecular Neurobiology, Neuropharmacology
SHIBA, Y., Oral Physiology
SUGAI, M., Bacteriology, Oral Microbiology
SUGIYAMA, M., Molecular Microbiology and Biotechnology, Antibiotics, Enzymology, Molecular Genetics, Applied Microbiology
TAKATA, T., Oral Maxillofacial Pathobiology, Oral Oncology, Periodontal Tissue Engineering, Diagnostic Pathology
UCHIDA, T., Oral Biology, Oral Anatomy
USUI, T., Urology, Andrology, Oncology, Endo-urology
YAMAWAKI, S., Psychiatry and Neurosciences, Biological Psychiatry, Psychopharmacology, Affective Disorders, Neuroleptic Malignant Syndrome, Psychosomatic Medicine, Liaison Psychiatry, Psycho-oncology
YASUI, W., Molecular Pathology, Molecular Pathology of Gastrointestinal Cancer
YOSHIDA, T., Virology, Paramyxovirus, Bacteriology

YOSHIZUMI, M., Cardiovascular Physiology and Medicine, Cardiology and Vascular Biology

Programmes for Pharmaceutical Sciences:

KOIKE, T., Functional Molecular Sciences, Medicinal Chemistry, Bioinorganic Chemistry

NAKATA, Y., Pharmacology, Neuropharmacology, Molecular Pharmacology

OOTSUKA, H., Pharmacognosy and Natural Product Chemistry, Molecular Pharmaceutics

TAKANO, M., Pharmaceutics and Therapeutics, Drug Transporters and Metabolizing Enzymes, Drug Delivery Systems

TAKEDA, K., Synthetic Organic Chemistry, Mechanistic Organic Chemistry, Synthetic Methodology

Graduate School of Biosphere Sciences (4-4 Kagamiyama 1-chome, Higashi- Hiroshima 739-8528; tel. (82) 424-7905; fax (82) 424-2459; e-mail sei-bucho-sien@office .hiroshima-u.ac.jp; internet home .hiroshima-u.ac.jp/gsbstop/english/top/ index-e.html):

Department of Bioresource Science and Technology:

ESAKA, M., Function and Biosynthesis of Ascorbic Acid in Plants

FUJITA, M., Environmental Physiology of Farm Animals

FURASAWA, S., Basic and Applied Immunobiology

GOTO, N., Enology and Viticulture

GUSHIMA, K., Foraging Ecology of Coral Reef Fishes

HORI, K., Structures, Functions and Applications of Lectins from Marine Organisms

IEFUJI, H., Environmental and Food Biotechnology

IMABAYASHI, H., Larval Settlement of Benthic Organisms

KATO, N., Nutrition and Cancer

KONO, K., Cellular Immunology

MATSUDA, H., Chicken Monoclonal Antibodies

MITANI, K., Holistic Management of Farm Animals

MIZUTA, K., Molecular and Cellular Biology of Yeast

NAGAMATSU, Y., Applied Biochemistry of Microbial Proteins

NAKANO, H., Behaviour and Control of Foodborne Bacterial Pathogens

NISHIMURA, T., Structure and Function of Proteases in Muscle Foods

OHTA, T., Physiological Phenomena and Molecules, Identification and Mechanism Analysis

SATO, K., Physical Chemistry of Lipids

SUZUKI, K., Emulsifying Characteristics and Properties of Food Emulsions

SUZUKI, N., Bio-organic Chemistry, Active Oxygen, Antioxidative Activity, Bio- and Chemiluminescence

TANIGUCHI, K., Ruminant Nutrition and Feeding

TERADA, T., Nuclear Transfer in the Bovine and Porcine Embryo

TSUDUKI, M., Animal Breeding and Genetics

YOSHIMURA, Y., Endocrine Control of Avian Reproductive Functions

Department of Environmental Dynamics and Management:

FUJITA, K., Source–Sink Relationship

HOSHIKA, Y., Mechanism of Material Circulation and its Control in Coastal Seas

ISEKI, K., Marine Ecology and Biogeochemical Cycle

KONO, K., Biology and Fertility of Soils

MARAYAMA, T., Biology of Symbiotic Relationships between Marine Invertebrates

and Micro-organisms, Biology of Hyperthermophiles

MASAOKA, Y., Enhancement of Metal Stress Tolerance in Plants

NAKANE, K., Environmental Chemistry

SAKUGAWA, H., Environmental Ecosystem Ecology

TAKASUGI, Y., Monitoring and Diagnosis of the Physical Environment in Semi-enclosed Sea

UYE, S., Production Ecology of Marine Zooplankton

YAMAMOTO, K., Microbial Ecology and Marine Ecology

YAMAMOTO, T., Aquatic Environmental Management

YAMAUCHI, M., Development of Ecophysiological Soil and Water Management Technology for Environmental Protection

Department of Sciences for Biospheric Coexistence:

NAKAI, T., Fish-pathogenic Bacteria and Viruses

TANAKA, H., Consumer Food Cooperatives

UEMATSU, K., Neural Basis for Fish Swimming

YAMAO, M., Locally Based Coastal Resource Management in Asia, Sustainable Coastal Fisheries Management and 'Code of Conduct for Responsible Production', People's Participation in Community Development and their Responsibility, Development and Export-oriented Food Production and its Impact on the Resource Environment

Graduate School of Engineering (4-1 Kagamiyama 1-chome, Higashi- Hiroshima 739-8527; tel. (82) 422-7111; fax (82) 422-7039; internet www.eden.hiroshima-u.ac.jp):

Mechanical Systems Engineering:

ISHIZUKA, S., Combustion Science and Technology

KIKUCHI, Y., Heat Transfer, Biomass Energy, Carbon Nanotube

KUROKI, H., Powder Metallurgy and Ceramics

MAEKAWA, H., Fluid Engineering

NAGAMURA, K., Machine Elements, Gear Design and Vibration, Tribology

NAKAGAWA, N., Dynamics of Machines

NAKASA, K., Strength and Fracture of Materials, Vibration and Sound, Acoustic Energy

OBA, F., Manufacturing Systems

SAEKI, M., Automatic Control

SAWA, T., Strength of Material, Elasticity, Solid Mechanics

SHINOZAKI, K., Welding and Joining

SHIZUMA, K., Quantum Energy Applications

TAKI, S., Reactive Gas Dynamics

TAKIYAMA, K., Plasma Spectroscopy

YAMANE, Y., Machining, Machine Tools and Mechatronics

YANAGISAWA, O., Control of Material Properties

YOSHIDA, F., Engineering Elasto-Plasticity

Artificial Complex Systems Engineering:

HINAMOTO, T., Electronic Control, Digital Signal Processing

IWASE, K., Mathematical Statistics and Data Analysis

KADO, T., Nano-electronics

KANEKO, M., Robotics, Active Sensing

NAKANO, K., Computer Engineering

NISHIZAKI, I., Decision Analysis and Game Theory

SAKAWA, M., Systems Optimization

SHIBATA, T., Differential Equations and their Application

TAKAHASHI, K., Production Systems Engineering

TSUJI, T., Biological Systems Engineering

YOKOGAWA, K., Computational Materials Science

YORINO, N., Electric Power System Engineering

Information Engineering:

DOHI, T., Systems Reliability Engineering

HARADA, K., Graphics Geometry

HIRASHIMA, T., Computer-based Learning Environment

KUBO, F., Algebraic Deformation Theory

KUWADA, M., Experimental Designs

MORITA, K., Theoretical Computer Science

SHIBA, M., Complex Analysis and its Applications

WATANABE, T., Computer Science and Information Technology

Chemistry and Chemical Engineering:

ASAEDA, M., Separation and Purification Technology

HARIMA, Y., Materials Physical Chemistry

HIROKAWA, T., Applied Instrumental Analysis

KUNAI, A., Organic Materials Chemistry

OKADA, M., Environmental Chemical Engineering

OKUYAMA, K., Thermal Fluids Engineering

OTSUBO, T., Applied Organic Chemistry

SAKOHARA, S., Polymer Technology

SHIONO, T., Advanced Polymer Chemistry

TAKISHIMA, S., Chemical Engineering Thermodynamics

YAMANAKA, S., Applied Inorganic Materials Chemistry

YOSHIDA, H., Fine Particle Technology

Social and Environmental Engineering:

DOI, Y., Marine Hydrodynamics

FUJIKUBO, M., Strength of Structures

FUJIMOTO, Y., Reliability of Structures and Systems

KANEKO, A., Ocean–Atmosphere Environment

KAWAHARA, Y., Hydraulic Engineering

KITAMURA, M., Computational Mechanics for Structural Design

KOSE, K., Management of Human-Technology–Environment Systems

MATSUO, A., Building Structures

MIURA, K., Building Disasters Prevention

MURAKAWA, S., Community Environmental Science

NAKAMURA, H., Structural Engineering

OHKUBO, T., Building Materials and Components

SASAKI, Y., Soil Mechanics and Earthquake Geotechnical Engineering

SATO, R., Concrete and Concrete Structural Engineering

SUGANO, S., Earthquake Engineering

SUGIE, Y., Transportation Planning

SUGIMOTO, T., Architectural History and Design Theory

TAKAKI, M., Ocean Space Engineering

TSUCHIDA, T., Geotechnical and Geo-environmental Engineering

YASUKAWA, H., Naval Architecture

YOKOBORI, H., Architecture, Urban Planning and International Cooperation

Graduate School for International Development and Co-operation (5-1 Kagamiyama 1-chome, Higashi- Hiroshima 739-8529; tel. (82) 424-6905; fax (82) 424-6904; e-mail idec@hiroshima-u.ac.jp; internet home .hiroshima-u.ac.jp/idec):

Division of Development Science:

FUJIWARA, A., Transportation Planning, Environmental Engineering

HIGO, Y., Ocean Engineering

KINBARA, T., Management and Organization

KOMATSU, M., Development Economics

MATSUOKA, S., Environmental Economics

NAKAZONO, K., International Relations

NOHARA, H., Comparative Study of Industrial Organizations

SAITO, K., Marine Development Technology

TOMINAGA, K., Disaster Prevention on Geotechnical Engineering

Division of Educational Development and Cultural and Regional Studies:

IKEDA, H., Content-based Science Education (Biology Education), International Cooperation in Science Education

KASAI, T., Motor Neurophysiology and Motor Rehabilitation Medicine

TABATA, Y., Educational Administration (Educational System, Teacher Education)

UEHARA, A., Intercultural Communication

Graduate School of Letters (2-3 Kagamiyama 1-chome, Higashi- Hiroshima 739-8522; tel. (82) 422-7111; fax (82) 424-0315; e-mail bun-kyo-sien@office.hiroshima-u.ac.jp; internet home.hiroshima-u.ac.jp/bungaku/index .html):

ARIMOTO, N., Modern and Contemporary Japanese Literature

FURUSE, K., Archaeology

HARANO, N., French Language and Literature

ICHIKI, T., Chinese Philosophy

IMADA, Y., Linguistics

ITOH, K., Medieval Japanese Literature

ITOH, S., American Literature and Culture

IWAI, T., Ancient History of Europe

JIMURA, A., English Language Studies

KANO, M., Chinese Linguistics

KATSUBE, M., Japanese Modern History

KAWAHARA, T., German Plays and Opera

KISHIDA, H., Ancient and Medieval Japanese History

KONDO, Y., History of Ethical Thought

KUBOTA, K., Modern and Contemporary Japanese Literature

MATSUI, F., History of Ethical Thought, Bioethics

MATSUMOTO, M., Japanese Language Studies

MATSUMOTO, Y., French Language and Literature

MIURA, M., History of Japanese Architecture

MIZUTA, H., History of Western Philosophy

NAKAMURA, H., Shakespeare, Cinema Studies, Cultural Semiotics

NISHIBEPPU, M., Ancient History of Japan

NOMA, F., History of Ancient and Medieval Chinese Thought

OCHI, M., Ethics

OKAHASHI, H., Human Geography, Regional Geography

OKAMOTO, A., Modern and Contemporary Western History

OKUMURA, K., Physical Geography, Quaternary Geology

SATO, T., Chinese Literature

SODA, S., Modern Chinese History

TANAKA, H., Modern Contemporary American Literature

TOMINAGA, K., Chinese Literature

UEDA, Y., Linguistics

UEKI, K., English Literature

UEMURA, Y., Asian History

YAMASHIRO, H., Medieval Western History

YAMAUCHI, H., Western Philosophy

YOSHINAKA, T., English Literature

Graduate School of Medicine (2-3 Kasumi 1-chome, Minami-ku, Hiroshima 734-8553; tel. (82) 257-5555; fax (82) 257-5278; e-mail bimes-kyou@office.hiroshima-u.ac.jp; internet www.hiroshima-u.ac.jp/hsc/):

Health Sciences:

INAMIZU, T., Sports Medicine and Sciences

INOUE, M., Gastroenterology, Gastrointestinal Physiology and Treatment of Acid-related Diseases

KAKEHASHI, M., Health Science, Health Statistics, Mathematical Modelling, Public Health

KATAOKA, T., Health Care for Adults

KAWAMATA, S., Anatomy of Musculoskeletal System, Anatomy of Calcified Tissue

KINJYO, T., Geriatric Nursing

KOBAYASHI, T., Health Development

MATSUKAWA, K., Physiology, Neural Control of the Cardiovascular System, Motor Control

MIYAGUCHI, H., Occupational Behavioural Science Laboratory

MIYAKOSHI, Y., Fundamentals of Nursing Theory and Practice, Nursing Management and Education

MORIYAMA, M., Medical–Surgical Nursing, Adult Health Nursing

MURAKAMI, T., Rheumatoid Surgery, Elbow Surgery, Sports Medicine

OKAMURA, H., Psycho-oncology, Psychosocial Rehabilitation

ONO, M., Community Health and Home Care Nursing

SHIMIZU, H., Science of Occupational Therapy

SHINKODA, K., Physical Therapy, Kinesiology

TANAKA, Y., Paediatrics, Health Science, Nursing Education

TOBIMATSU, Y., Rehabilitation Medicine and Science for the Elderly and People with Disabilities

TSUSHIMA, H., Community and School Health Nursing

URABE, Y., Athletic Rehabilitation

YAMAKATSU, H., Occupational Therapy for Physical Dysfunction and ADL Disorder

YOKOO, K., Neonatal Nursing, Maternal and Child Health Nursing, Midwifery

YUGE, R., Nerve and Muscle Regeneration

Graduate School of Science (3-1 Kagamiyama 1-chome, Higashi- Hiroshima 739-8526; tel. (82) 422-7111; fax (82) 424-0709; e-mail ri-bucho-sien@office.hiroshima-u.ac.jp; internet www.sci.hiroshima-u.ac.jp/english):

Mathematics:

ENOMOTO, H., Graph Theory, Discrete Mathematics

KAMADA, S., Knots, Topology

MATSUMOTO, M., Galois Group, Arithmetic Fundamental Group, Random Number Generation

MATUMOTO, T., Topology

MIZUTA, Y., Potential Theory

MORITA, T., Dynamic Systems, Ergodic Theory

NAGAI, T., Differential Equations

TSUZUKI, N., Arithmetic Geometry, Number Theory

YOSHINO, M., Differential Equations

Physical Science:

HASHIMOTO, E., Physics of Perfect Crystals, Synchrotron Radiation Physics

HIRAYA, A., Molecular Photophysics and Photochemistry

HORI, T., Particle Accelerator Physics, Synchrotron Radiation Physics

KOJIMA, Y., Theory of Relativity and Astrophysics

MARUYAMA, H., Solid State Physics, X-Ray Spectroscopy

NAMATAME, H., Solid State Physics, Synchrotron Radiation Physics

OHSUGI, T., High Energy Particle Physics, Gamma-ray Astrophysics

OKAWA, M., Elementary Particle Theory, Lattice QCD

SUGITATE, T., High Energy Nuclear Physics

TANAKA, K., Photochemistry and Photophysics

TANIGUCHI, M., Solid State Physics, Synchrotron Radiation Science

Chemistry:

AIDA, M., Quantum Chemisty

EBATA, T., Laser Chemistry and Molecular Spectroscopy

FUJIWARA, T., Analytical Chemistry

FUKAZAWA, Y., Organic Stereochemistry

INOUE, K., Molecular Magnetism

MIYOSHI, K., Coordination and Organometallic Chemistry

OHKATA, K., Synthesis and Isolation of Natural Products

OHNO, K., Physical Chemistry and Vibrational Spectroscopy

YAMAMOTO, Y., Organic Main Group Element Chemistry

YAMASAKI, K., Chemical Kinetics and Dynamics

Biological Science:

DEGUCHI, H., Plant Taxonomy and Ecology, Bryology

HOSOYA, H., Cell Biology, Signal Transduction

MICHIBATA, H., Molecular Physiology

SUZUKI, K., Molecular Genetics, Yeast and Agrobacterial Genetics

TAKAHASHI, Y., Plant Molecular Biology

YOSHIZATO, K., Developmental Biology, Regeneration Biology

Earth and Planetary Systems Science:

HIDAKA, H., Isotope Geochemistry

SHIMIZU, H., Trace Element Geochemistry

TAJIMA, F., Solid Earth Geophysics

WATANABE, M., Ore Petrology and Ore Genesis

Mathematical and Life Sciences:

GEKKO, K., Physical Chemistry of Biopolymers

HIRATA, T., Biological Chemistry and Biotechnology

IDE, H., DNA Damage and Repair

KOBAYASHI, R., Self-organization in Material and Life Science

MORIKAWA, H., Molecular Plant Biology

NISHIMORI, H., Complex Systems and Nonlinear Dynamics

SAKAMOTO, K., Dynamical Systems

TANIMOTO, Y., Magneto-science

YAMAMOTO, T., Molecular Developmental Biology

YOSHIDA, K., Partial Differential Equations

Marine Biological Laboratory:

YASUI, K., Development and Bio-history of Marine Deuterostomes

Miyajima Natural Botanical Garden:

DEGUCHI, H., Plant Taxonomy and Ecology, Bryology

Institute for Amphibian Biology:

KASHIWAGI, A., Endocrine Disruptors, Space Biology, Apoptosis, Transgenesis

SUMIDA, M., Evolutionary Genetics, Molecular Phylogeny

YAOITA, Y., Developmental Biology, Metamorphosis, Programmed Cell Death

Laboratory of Plant Chromosome and Gene Stock:

KONDO, K., Plant Demography, Chromosome Science and Gene Resources

Graduate School of Social Sciences (Higashi-Hiroshima Campus: 2-1 Kagamiyama 1–chome, Higashi-Hiroshima 739-8525 Higashi-Senda Campus: 1-89 Higashisenda-machi 1–chome, Hiroshima 730-0053; tel. (82) 422-7111 (Higashi-Hiroshima), (82) 542-7014 (Higashi-Senda); fax (82) 424-7212 (Higashi-Hiroshima), (82) 542-6964 (Higashi-Senda); e-mail syakai-bucho-sien@office .hiroshima-u.ac.jp):

AGAOKA, Y., Medieval Western History

AIZAWA, Y., Private International Law

EGASHIRA, D., Sociology

FUKIHARU, T., Microeconomics

FUTAMURA, H., Public Finance
GINAMA, I., Macroeconometrics
HINO, S., Product Development Theory
HOSHINO, I., Financial Accounting
INOUE, Z., Management (Strategy Theory)
ISHIDA, M., International Finance
ITOH, T., Economic Policy
KAN, T., Fiscal Policy
KANNO, R., Finance
KATOH, F., Occidental Economic History
KAWASAKI, N., Public Administration
MAEKAWA, K., Financial Econometrics
MAKINO, M., Political History
MATSUDA, M., Political Economy
MATSUMIZU, Y., World Economic Conditions
MATSUIKE, H., Criminal Law
MATSUURA, K., Finance and Econometrics
MORIBE, S., Japanese Politics
MORIOKA, T., Labour Economics
MORITA, K., Comparative Economic Systems
MURAMATSU, J., Marketing Theory
NISHIMURA, H., Constitutional Law
NISHITANI, H., International Law
NOMOTO, R., Industrial Organization
ODAKI, M., Statistics
OKAMURA, M., International Economics, Applied Microeconomics
OTANI, T., Sociology of Law
SAKAGUCHI, K., Management Accounting
SAKANE, Y., Economic History of Japan
TAKAHASHI, H., Civil Law
TAKI, A., Industrial Relations
TERAMOTO, Y., Diplomacy and Diplomatic History
TODA, T., Regional Development Policy
TOMIOKA, S., Economic History
TSUBAKI, Y., Information Resource Management
TSUJI, H., Labour Law
UEDA, Y., Public Choice and Institutional Economics
WAKIMOTO, S., Economic Policy
WATANABE, M., Social Policy
YAMADA, S., History of Political Thought
YANO, J., Macroeconomics
YOSHIDA, O., Asian Politics
YOSHIHARA, T., Legal History

Law School (1-89 Higashisenda 1-chome, Hiroshima 730-0053; tel. (82) 542-7014; fax (82) 542-6964; e-mail senda-bk-sien@office .hiroshima-u.ac.jp; internet www.law .hiroshima-u.ac.jp/lawschool/ls-top.htm):

GOTOH, K., Commercial Law
HIRANO, T., Legal Philosophy
KAMITANI, Y., Civil Law
KATAGI, H., Commercial Law
KINOSHITA, M., Commercial Law
KOHAMA, S., Civil Law
KOHARI, Y., International Law
MITSUI, M., Labour Law
MONDEN, T., Constitutional Law
NAKA, T., Administrative Law
ODA, N., Criminal Law
OHKUBO, T., Criminal Procedure
OKAMOTO, T., Civil Law
SAEKI, Y., Administrative Law
TANABE, M., Civil Procedure
TORIYABE, S., Civil Law

Research Institute for Radiation Biology and Medicine (2-3 Kasumi 1-chome, Minami-ku, Hiroshima 734-8553; tel. (82) 257-5555; fax (82) 255-8339; e-mail bimes-gen@office .hiroshima-u.ac.jp; internet www.rbm .hiroshima-u.ac.jp/index.html):

HONDA, H., Developmental Biology
HOSHI, M., Radiation Biophysics
INABA, T., Molecular Oncology, Haematology
KAMIYA, K., Radiation Biology, Oncology
KIMURA, A., Haematology and Oncology
MATSUURA, S., Human Genetics
MIYAGAWA, K., Molecular Oncology

NISHIYAMA, M., Molecular Oncology, Preclinical Development
OHTAKI, M., Biometrics, Environmetrics
SUZUKI, F., Radiation Biology
TAKIHARA, Y., Stem Cell Biology, Haematology, Regenerative Medicine
TASHIRO, S., Molecular Cell Biology

ATTACHED INSTITUTES

Beijing Research Center: College of International Education, Capital Nomal University, 105 Xisanhuan Beilu, Beijing 00037, China; Dir T. SATO.

Center for the Study of International Co-operation in Education: 5-1 Kagamiyama 1-chome, Higashi-Hiroshima 739-8529; Dir A. NINOMIYA.

Collaborative Research Center: 10-31 Kagamiyama 3-chome, Higashi-Hiroshima 739-0046; Dir Y. YAMANE.

Community Co-operation Center: 3-2 Kagamiyama 1-chome, Higashi-Hiroshima 739-8511; Dir T. ANDO.

Environmental Research and Management Centre: 5-3 Kagamiyama 1-chome, Higashi-Hiroshima 739-8513; Dir S. OTA.

Health Service Center: 7-1 Kagamiyama 1-chome, Higashi-Hiroshima 739-8511; Dir M. YOSHIHARA.

Hiroshima Synchrotron Radiation Center: 313 Kagamiyama 2-chome, Higashi-Hiroshima 739-8526; Dir M. TANIGUCHI.

Information Media Center: 4-2 Kagamiyama 1-chome, Higashi-Hiroshima 739-8526; Dir T. WATANABE.

Institute for Peace Science: 1-89, Higashisenda-machi 1-chome, Naka-ku, Hiroshima 730-0053; Dir M. MATSUO.

International Student Center: 1-2 Kagamiyama 1-chome, Higashi-Hiroshima 739-8523; Dir S. TAWADA.

Natural Science Center for Basic Research and Development: 3-1 Kagamiyama 1-chome, Higashi-Hiroshima 739-8526; Dir I. YAMASHITA.

Research Center for Nanodevices and Systems: 4-2 Kagamiyama 1-chome, Higashi-Hiroshima 739-8527; Dir A. IWATA.

Research Center for Regional Geography: 2-3 Kagamiyama 1-chome, Higashi-Hiroshima 739-8522; Dir H. OKAHASHI.

Research Institute for Higher Education: 2-2 Kagamiyama 1-chome, Higashi-Hiroshima 739-8521; Dir A. ARIMOTO.

Saijo Seminar House: Misonou, Saijo-cho, Higashi-Hiroshima 739-0024; Dir S. TAKAHASHI.

HITOTSUBASHI UNIVERSITY

2-1 Naka, Kunitachi-city Tokyo 186-8601
Telephone: (42) 580-8000
Fax: (42) 580-8006
Internet: www.hit-u.ac.jp
Independent
Founded 1875
Academic year: April to March
Pres.: HIROMITSU ISHI
Vice-Pres: JYURO TERANISHI
Dir-Gen.: SAKASHI KAMATA
Dean of Students: TAKEHIKO SUGIYAMA
Librarian: MAKOTO IKEMA
Library of 1,739,884 vols
Number of teachers: 465 full-time
Number of students: 6,429
Publications: *The Hitotsubashi Review* (12 a year), *Hitotsubashi Journal of Commerce and Management* (1 a year), *Hitotsubashi Journal of Economics* (2 a year), *Hitotsubashi Journal of Law and Politics* (1 a year), *Hitotsubashi Journal of Social Stud-*

ies (2 a year), *Hitotsubashi Arts and Sciences* (1 a year), *Gengo Bunka—Cultura Philologica* (1 a year)

DEANS

Graduate School and Faculty of Commerce and Management: K. ITO
Graduate School and Faculty of Economics: E. TAJIKA
Graduate School and Faculty of Law: T. YAMAUCHI
Graduate School and Faculty of Social Sciences: N. TASAKI
Graduate School of International Corporate Strategy: H. TAKEUCHI
Graduate School of Language and Society: Y. SANO

ATTACHED INSTITUTES

Institute of Economic Research: Tokyo; f. 1940; 41 teachers; Dir M. KUBONIWA; publ. *Economic Review* (4 a year).

Institute of Innovation Research: Tokyo; f. 1997; 11 teachers; Dir S. NAGAOKA; publ. *Hitotsubashi Business Review* (4 a year).

HOKKAIDO UNIVERSITY

Kita 8 Nishi 5, Kita-ku, Sapporo 060-0808
Telephone: (11) 706-2334
Fax: (11) 706-2095
E-mail: kouryu@general.hokudai.ac.jp
Internet: www.hokudai.ac.jp
Founded 1876
Independent
Academic year: April to March
Pres.: Prof. HIROSHI SAEKI
Vice-Pres: Prof. MASAAKI HEMMI, Prof. TADAYUKI HAYASHI, Prof. HISATAKE OKADA, Prof. MINORU WAKITA, Prof. TAKEO HONDOH
Chief Admin. Officer: KAZUO SHIMANUKI
Dir of Univ. Library: Prof. MASAAKI HEMMI
Dir of Univ. Hospital: Prof. MASAHIRO ASAKA
Library of 3,711,309 vols
Number of teachers: 2,050
Number of students: 18,264
Publication: *Hokudai Jiho* (12 as year)

DEANS

Faculty of Advanced Life Science: ISAO TANAKA
Faculty of Pharmaceutical Sciences: AKIRA MATSUDA
Graduate School and Faculty of Education: OSAMU AOKI
Graduate School and Faculty of Public Policy: TAKAO SASAKI
Graduate School and Faculty of Science: KEIZO YAMAGUCHI
Graduate School and Research Faculty of Agriculture: AKIHITO HATTORI
Graduate School of Dental Medicine: MASAMITSU KAWANAMI
Graduate School of Economics and Business Administration: HISASHI INOUE
Graduate School of Engineering: TAKASHI MIKAMI
Graduate School of Environmental Science and Faculty of Environmental Earth Science: TOSHIO IWAKUMA
Graduate School of Health Sciences and Faculty of Health Sciences: SEIICHI KOBAYASHI
Graduate School of Information Science and Technology: MASANORI KOSHIBA
Graduate School of International Media, Communication, and Tourism Studies and Research Faculty of Media and Communication: SHYUUICHI SUGIURA
Graduate School of Law: NOBUHISA SEGAWA
Graduate School of Letters: TSUNEKO MOCHIZUKI
Graduate School of Life Science: AKIRA MATSUDA

Graduate School of Medicine: KENICHI HOMMA
Graduate School of Veterinary Medicine: TAKASHI UMEMURA

PROFESSORS

Faculty and School of Fisheries Science (3-1-1 Minato-cho, Hakodate; tel. (13) 840-5505; fax (13) 843-5015; e-mail shomu@fish.hokudai.ac.jp; internet www.fish.hokudai.ac.jp):

ABE, S., Aquagenomics and Resources Management
ADACHI, S., Molecular Cell Biology and Histology
ARAI, K., Genetics, Genomics and Developmental Biology
GOSHIMA, S., Marine Ecology; Behaviour; Benthos
GOTO, A., Evolutionary Biology of Fishes
HARA, A., Comparative Biochemistry of Fish Serum Protein
HIROYOSHI, K., Fisheries Business Economics
IIDA, K., Underwater Acoustics; Fisheries and Plankton Acoustics; Bio-Acoustics
IKEDA, T., Zooplankton Ecology
ISSHIKI, K., Food Safety; Food Protection
ITABASHI, Y., Lipid Chemistry and Chromatography
KAERIYAMA, M., Conservation Ecology; Salmonology; Fish Ecology
KAWAI, Y., Food Preservation; Food Chemistry; Food Hygiene
KIMURA, N., Fishing Informatics; Seakeeping Qualities of Fishing Vessels
KISHI, J., Numerical Modelling of Marine Ecosystems
KONNO, K., Marine Food Science
KUMA, K., Chemical Oceanography and Marine Biogeochemistry
MEGURO, T., Marine Biology
MIURA, T., Scientific Gears for Fish Sampling
MIYASHITA, K., Liquid Oxidation and Antioxidant
MONTANI, S., Biogeochemical Oceanography
NAKAYA, K., Phylogeny; Taxonomy; Sharks
OJIMA, T., Molecular Biology and Biotechnology of Marine Organisms
OKAMOTO, J., Fisheries Policy
SAEKI, H., Health Benefit of Marine Food Proteins and Marine Food Allergy
SAGA, N., Marine Biology; Developmental Biology
SAITOH, S., Satellite Oceanography
SAKURAI, Y., Marine Ecology; Reproductive Ecology of Marine Fish and Cephalopods
SIGA, N., Zooplankton Taxonomy and Ecology
TAKAGI, Y., Mechanism of Biomineralization
TAKAHASHI, K., Conversion of Fisheries By-products into Value Added Products
TAKAHASHI, T., Life History of Righteye Flounders
YABE, M., Systematic Ichthyology
YANADA, M., Marine Organic Chemistry
YOSHIMIZU, M., Viral and Bacterial Fish Diseases
YOSHIMURA, Y., Control and Design of Fishing Boats and Fisheries Machinery

Faculty of Advanced Life Science (Kita 10, Nishi 8, Kita-ku, Sapporo; tel. (11) 716-3026; fax (11) 756-1244; e-mail shomu@sci.hokudai.ac.jp; internet www.lfsci.hokudai.ac.jp):

AYABE, T., Innate Intestinal Immunity
DEMURA, M., Membrane Protein NMR and Bioinformatics
IGARASHI, Y., Sphingolipid Biology and Biochemistry
KAMO, N., Biophysical Chemistry
KODA, T., Molecular Biology

KOIKE, T., Molecular and Cellular Neurobiology
NAITO, S., Molecular Genetics
NISHIMURA, S., Advanced Chemical Biology
OBUSE, C., Molecular and Cellular Biology
SEYA, T., Microbiology and Immunology
SUGAHARA, K., Glycoscience and Glycobiology
TAKAHASHI, T., Reproductive Biology
TANAKA, I., Protein Crystallography
YAMASHITA, M., Reproductive Biology
YAMAGUCHI, J., Plant Biology and Biochemistry
YAZAWA, M., Biochemistry

Faculty of Education (Kita 11, Nishi 7, Kita-ku, Sapporo; tel. (11) 707-6586; fax (11) 706-4951; e-mail shomu@edu.hokudai.ac.jp; internet www.hokudai.ac.jp/educat):

ANEZAKI, Y., Higher and Continuing Education
AOKI, O., Education and Poverty
CHEN, S., Developmental Psychology of Infancy
KAWAGUCHI, A., Prevention and Health
Education for Lifestyle Related Diseases: (vacant)
MIYAZAKI, T., Adult Education
MIZUNO, M., Muscle Physiology
MUROHASHI, H., Clinical Cognitive Neuroscience
NISHIO, T., History of Physical Education and Sport
OHTSUKA, Y., Health Resort Medicine
ONAI, T., Sociology of Education
SATO, K., Psychology of Learning
SHINDO, S., Teaching Methods for Physical Education
Practical Training in Physical Education: (vacant)
SUDA, K., Teaching Methods for Mathematics
SUZUKI, T., Community Adult Education
TANAKA, Y., Developmental Psychopathology
TOKORO, S., Comparative History of Education
TSUBOI, Y., Educational Administration
YANO, T., Physiology of Exercise

Faculty of Environmental Earth Science (Kita 10, Nishi 5, Kita-ku, Sapporo; tel. (13) 728-4715; fax (13) 706-4867; e-mail somu@ees.hokudai.ac.jp; internet www.ees.hokudai.ac.jp):

FUGETSU, B., Ion/Membrane Interactions
HASEBE, F., Weather/Oceanic Physics/Hydrology; Environmental Dynamic Analysis
HIGASHI, S., Animal Ecology
HIRAKAWA, K., Landform Development under Periglacial and Glacial Environment; Active Tectonics and Paleo-Mega-Tsu
IKEDA, M., Effects of Ocean and Sea Ice on Climate Variability
IWAKUMA, T., Ecology/Environment; Environmental Dynamic Analysis; Resource Maintenance Studies
KIMURA, M., Ecology/Environment; Animal Physiology/Behaviour Heredity/Genome Dynamics
KOHYAMA, T., Maintenance Mechanisms of Species Diversity; Scale Issue of Forest Ecosystem Response to Global Change
KUBOKAWA, A., Weather/Oceanic Physics/Hydrology
MATSUDA, F., Synthetic Organic Chemistry and Natural Product Chemistry
MINAGAWA, M., Isotope Biogeochemistry
MORIKAWA, M., Applied Microbiology; Living Organism Molecular Science
NAKAMURA, H., Organic Chemistry/Physical Chemistry/Analytical Chemistry
NORIKI, S., Analytical Chemistry; Earth Astrochemistry; Environmental Dynamic Analysis

OHARA, M., Evolution of Life History of Plants and Conservation
OKUHARA, T., Environmental Catalyst
ONO, Y., Environmental Geography
SAKAIRI, N., Synthetic Carbohydrate Chemistry
SHIMAZU, K., Environmental Chemistry; Functional Material Chemistry
SUGIMOTO, A., Environmental Dynamic Analysis; Earth Astrochemistry; Weather/Oceanic Physics/Hydrology
TANAKA, S., Analytical Chemistry; Environmental Technology/Environmental Material
TAKADA, T., Ecology/Environment
YAMAZAKI, K., Weather/Oceanic Physics/Hydrology
YOSHIKAWA, H., Environmental Dynamic Analysis; Weather/Oceanic Physics/Hydrology

Faculty of Pharmaceutical Sciences (Kita 12, Nishi 6, Kita-ku, Sapporo; tel. (11) 706-3486; fax (11) 706-4989; e-mail shomu@pharm.hokudai.ac.jp; internet www.pharm.hokudai.ac.jp):

ARIGA, H., Molecular Biology
HARASHIMA, H., Molecular Design of Pharmaceutics
HASHIMOTO, S., Synthetic and Industrial Chemistry
INAGAKI, F., Structural Biology
ISEKI, K., Clinical Pharmaceutics and Therapeutics
KOBAYASHI, J., Natural Products Chemistry
MATSUDA, A., Medicinal Chemistry
MATSUDA, T., Hygienic Chemistry
MINAMI, M., Pharmacology
MIURA, T., Analytical Chemistry
SATO, Y., Fine Synthetic Chemistry
SHUTO, S., Organic Chemistry for Drug Development
SUZUKI, T., Neuroscience
YOKOSAWA, H., Biochemistry

Faculty of Public Policy (Kita 9, Nishi 7, Kita-ku, Sapporo; tel. (11) 706-3074; fax (11) 706-4948; e-mail shomu@juris.hokudai.ac.jp; internet www.hops.hokudai.ac.jp):

ISHII, Y., Regional Policy
KEN ENDO, I., Int. Politics
KURATA, K., Technology Policy
MATSUURA, M., Japanese Political History
MIYAWAKI, A., Public Administration
NAKAMURA, K., International Politics
NAKATSUJI, T., Transportation and Traffic Engineering
SASAKI, T., International Political Economy
SHIBATA, F., Social Security Administration
SHUNJI KANIE, S., Structural Mechanics
WATARI, T., Administrative Law
YAMADA, H., Macroeconomic Policy
YAMAGUCHI, J., Public Administration
YAMAZAKI, M., Local Government and Politics
YOSHIDA, F., Environmental Economics

Faculty of Science (Kita 10, Nishi 8, Kita-ku, Sapporo; tel. (11) 716-3026; fax (11) 756-1244; e-mail shomu@sci.hokudai.ac.jp; internet www.sci.hokudai.ac.jp):

AIKAWA, H., Potential Theory
AMITSUKA, H., Condensed Matter Physics
ARAI, A., Mathematical Physics
FUJIMOTO, M., Theoretical Physics
FUJINO, K., Mineralogy
GONG, J., Polymer Science
HAYASHI, M., Function Theory
HEKI, K., Space Geodesy
HINATSU, Y., Solid State Chemistry
HORIGUCHI, T., Phycology and Protistology
IDO, M., Solid State Physics
IKEDA, R., Geophysical Hydrology
INABE, T., Solid State Chemistry
ISHIKAWA, G., Geometry
ISHIKAWA, K., Theoretical Physics

ISHIMORI, K., Structural Chemistry
IZUMIYA, S., Geometry
JIMBO, S., Applied Analysis, Partial Differential Equations
KASAHARA, M., Seismology and Geodesy
KATAKURA, H., Speciation of Terrestrial Invertebrates
KATO, A., Plant Molecular Genetics
KATO, K., Nuclear Physics
KATO, M., Coordination Chemistry
KAWABATA, K., Biophysics
KAWAMOTO, N., Theoretical Physics
KAWANO, K., Structural Biology
KISHIMOTO, A., Operator Algebra
KITAMURA, N., Analytical Chemistry
KOIKE, K., Solid State Physics
KOYAMA, J., Solid Earth Science
KOZASA, T., Astrophysics and Planetary Science
KUMAGAI, K., Solid State Physics
KURAMOTO, K., Planetary Science
MATSUOU, M., Philosophy of Science
MAWATARI, S., Taxonomy of Invertebrates
MINOBE, S., Physical Oceanography, Climate and Meteorology
MOGI, T., Subsurface Geophysics
MURAKOSHI, K., Material Chemistry
NAGASAKA, Y., Theory of Function
NAKAGAWA, M., Volcanology and Petrology
NAKAMURA, G., Inverse Problems, Partial Differential Equations
NAKAMURA, I., Algebraic Geometry
NAKAZI, T., Functional Analysis
NOMURA, K., Solid State Physics
OHKAWA, F., Theoretical Physics
OIKAWA, H., Bio-organic Chemistry
ONO, K., Differential Geometry and Topology
ONODERA, A., Solid State Physics
OZAWA, T., Partial Differential Equations
SAKAGUCHI, K., Biological Chemistry
SASAKI, N., Tissue Science and Mechanobiology
SAWAMURA, M., Organometallic Chemistry
SUGIYAMA, S., History of Science
SUZUKI, N., Molecular Cell Biology
SUZUKI, N., Organic Geochemistry
SUZUKI, F., Physical Organic Chemistry
TAKAHATA, M., Behavioural Physiology
TAKEDA, S., Physical Chemistry
TAKESHITA, T., Structural Geology and Tectonics
TAKETSUGU, T., Quantum Chemistry
TANINO, K., Synthetic Organic Chemistry
TERAO, H., Combinatorics, Singularities
UOSAKI, K., Physical Chemistry
URANO, A., Neuroendocrinology
WATANABE, S., Planetary Atmosphere
YAMAGUCHI, K., Differential Geometry
YAMAMOTO, K., Plant Physiology
YAMAMOTO, S., Condensed-Matter Theory
YAMASHITA, H., Representation Theory
YOMOGIDA, K., Seismology
YOSHIDA, T., Group Theory and Combinatorics
YURI, M., Complex Systems and Ergodic Theory
YURIMOTO, H., Geochemistry

Graduate School of Dental Medicine (Nishi 7, Kita 13, Kita-ku, Sapporo 060-8586; tel. (11) 706-4313; fax (11) 706-4919; e-mail d-syomu@jimu.hokudai.ac.jp; internet www.den.hokudai.ac.jp):

FUKUSHIMA, K., Oral Pathobiological Science
IIDA, J., Oral Functional Science
INOUE, N., Oral Health Science
KAWANAMI, M., Oral Health Science
KITAGAWA, K., Oral Pathobiological Science
MORITA, M., Oral Health Science
NAKAMURA, M., Oral Pathobiological Science
OHATA, N., Oral Functional Science
SANO, H., Oral Health Science
SHIBATA, K., Oral Pathobiological Science

SHINDOH, M., Oral Pathobiological Science
SUZUKI, K., Oral Pathobiological Science
TAMURA, M., Oral Health Science
TOTSUKA, Y., Oral Pathobiological Science
WATARI, F., Oral Health Science
YAWAKA, Y., Oral Functional Science
YOKOYAMA, A., Oral Functional Science

Graduate School of Economics and Business Administration (Kita 9, Nishi 7, Kita-ku, Sapporo; tel. (11) 706-4058; fax (11) 706-4947; e-mail keizai@pop.econ.hokudai.ac.jp; internet www.econ.hokudai.ac.jp/en05):

HAMADA, Y., Money and Banking
HASEGAWA, H., Econometrics
INOUE, H., International Investment and Finance
ITAYA, J., Public Economics
IWATA, S., Corporate Behaviour
KANDA, K., Disclosure System and Financial Accounting
KANIE, A., Auditing
KIMURA, T., Operations Research
KOJIMA, H., Management of Non-Profit Organizations
KOYAMA, K., Public Finance
MACHINO, K., Applied Game Theory
MIYAMOTO, K., Economic History of Asia
MOHRI, S., Management by Networking
NISHIBE, M., Evolutionary Economics
OKABE, H., Social Economy
SASAKI, K., History of Economics
SEKIGUCHI, Y., Managerial Informatics
SONO, S., Foundations of Statistics
TANAKA, S., Socioeconomic History
UCHIDA, K., Macroeconomics
YONEYAMA, Y., Financial Accounting
YOSHIMI, H., Auditing and Public Sector Accounting
YOSHINO, E., Comparative Socioeconomic Systems

Graduate School of Engineering (Kita 13, Nishi 8, Kita-ku, Sapporo; tel. (11) 716-8832; fax (11) 706-7895; e-mail shomu@eng.hokudai.ac.jp; internet www.eng.hokudai.ac.jp):

AKERA, H., Quantum Matter Physics
ARAI, M., Chemical Engineering
ASAKURA, K., Atmospheric and Terrestrial Engineering
BABA, N., Optical Science and Technology
CHIKAHISA, T., Applied Energy Systems
ENAI, M., Planning and Performances for Built Environment
FUJII, Y., Geoenvironmental Engineering
FUJIKAWA, S., Materials and Fluid Mechanics
FUJITA, O., Space Systems Engineering
FUNAMIZU, N., Water Metabolic System
FURUICHI, T., Policy for Engineering and Environment
FURUSAKA, M., Applied Quantum Beam Engineering
GOHARA, K., Complex Material Physics
GOTO, Y., Building Science and Space Planning
HABAZAKI, H., Functional Materials Chemistry
HARA, S., Industrial Organic Chemistry
HAYASHIKAWA, T., Sustainable Infrastructure System
HINO, T., Plasma Science and Engineering
ICHIKAWA, T., Functional Materials Chemistry
IGUCHI, M., Ecological Materials
IKEGAWA, M., Micromechanical Systems
ISHIMASA, T., Complex Material Physics
ITAGAKI, M., Plasma Science and Engineering
IZUMI, N., Hydraulic and Aquatic Environment Engineering
KADO, Y., Human Settlement Design
KAGAYA, S., Construction Engineering for Cold Regional Environment
KAGIWADA, T., Biomechanics and Robotics

KAKUCHI, T., Chemistry of Functional Molecules
KAMIDATE, T., Chemistry of Functional Molecules
KANEKO, K., Atmospheric and terrestrial Engineering
KIKKAWA, S., Inorganic Materials Chemistry
KIYANAGI, Y., Applied Quantum Beam Engineering
KOBAYASHI, H., Human Settlement Design
KOBAYASHI, Y., Biomechanics and Robotics
KONNO, H., Functional Materials Chemistry
KOSHIZAWA, A., Planning and Performances for Built Environment
KUDO, K., Micromechanical Systems
MASUDA, T., Chemical Engineering
MATSUI, Y., Water Metabolic System
MATSUTO, T., Solid Waste Resources Engineering
MATSUURA, K., Materials Design
MIDORIKAWA, M., Structural and Urban Safety Design
MIKAMI, T., Construction Engineering for Cold Regional Environment
MITACHI, T., Geoenvironmental Engineering
MIURA, S., Geoenvironmental Engineering
MIYAURA, N., Industrial Organic Chemistry
MOHRI, T., Materials Design
MORITA, R., Optical Science and Technology
MUKAI, S., Chemical Engineering
MUNEKATA, M., Biotechnology
MUTO, S., Solid State Physics and Engineering
NAGANO, K., Planning and Performances for Built Environment
NAGATA, H., Space Systems Engineering
NAKAMURA, T., Materials and Fluid Mechanics
NAKANO, T., Chemistry of Functional Molecules
NAKAYAMA, T., Quantum Matter Physics
NARABAYASHI, T., Nuclear and Environmental Systems
NARITA, Y., Micromechanical Systems
NAWA, T., Solid Waste Resources Engineering
OGAWA, H., Applied Energy Systems
OHKUMA, T., Industrial Organic Chemistry
OHNUKI, S., Energy Materials
OHNUMA, H., Construction Engineering for Cold Regional Environment
OHTA, S., Atmospheric and Terrestrial Engineering
OHTSUKA, T., Ecological Materials
ORIHARA, H., Complex Material Physics
OSHIMA, N., Space Systems Engineering
SASAKI, K., Materials and Fluid Mechanics
SASATANI, T., Structural and Urban Safety Design
SATO, S., Nuclear and Environmental Systems
SATOH, K., Policy for Engineering and Environment
SENBU, O., Building Science and Space Planning
SHIMADA, S., Inorganic Materials Chemistry
SHIMAZU, Y., Nuclear and Environmental Systems
SHIMIZU, Y., Policy for Engineering and Environment
SUGIYAMA, K., Nuclear and Environmental Systems
SUGIYAMA, T., Sustainable Infrastructure System
SUMIYOSHI, T., Applied Quantum Beam Engineering
SUZUKI, R., Ecological Materials
TADANO, S., Biomechanics and Robotics
TAGUCHI, S., Biotechnology
TAKAGI, M., Biotechnology

TAKAHASHI, H., Materials Design
TAKAHASHI, J., Inorganic Materials Chemistry
TAKAHASHI, M., Hydraulic and Aquatic Environment Engineering
TAKEDA, Y., Applied Energy Systems
TAMURA, S., Solid State Physics and Engineering
TANAKA, K., Solid State Physics and Engineering
TANDA, S., Quantum Matter Physics
TSUNEKAWA, M., Solid Waste Resources Engineering
UEDA, M., Structural and Urban Safety Design
UEDA, T., Sustainable Infrastructure System
UKAI, S., Energy Materials
WATANABE, Y., Water Metabolic System
WRIGHT, O., Quantum Matter Physics
YAMASHITA, M., Optical Science and Technology
YAMASHITA, T., Hydraulic and Aquatic Environment Engineering
YOKOYAMA, S., Planning and Performances for Built Environment
YONEDA, T., Geoenvironmental Engineering

Graduate School of Information Science and Technology (Kita 14, Nishi 9, Kita-ku, Sapporo; tel. (11) 706-6514; fax (11) 706-7890; e-mail jimusitu@ist.hokudai.ac.jp; internet www.ist.hokudai.ac.jp):

AMEMIYA, Y., Integrated Systems Engineering
ARAKI, K., Information Media Science and Technology
ARIMURA, H., Knowledge Software Science
ENDO, T., Bioinformatics
FUKUI, T., Integrated Systems Engineering
FURUKAWA, M., Complex Systems Engineering
HARAGUCHI, M., Knowledge Software Science
HASEYAMA, M., Information Media Science and Technology
HOMMA, T., Informatics for System Synthesis
IGARASHI, H., Informatics for System Synthesis
KANAI, S., Informatics for System Creation
KANEKO, S., Informatics for System Creation
KAWAHARA, K., Biomedical Systems Engineering
KITA, H., Informatics for System Synthesis
KOSHIBA, M., Information Communication Systems
KUDO, M., Mathematical Information Science
KURIHARA, M., Complex Systems Engineering
MISHIMA, T., Advanced Electronics
MIYAKOSHI, M., Mathematical Information Science
MIYANAGA, Y., Information Communication Systems
MOTOHISA, J., Integrated Systems Engineering
NOJIMA, T., Information Communication Systems
OGASAWARA, S., Informatics for System Synthesis
OGAWA, Y., Information Communication Systems
OHUCHI, A., Complex Systems Engineering
ONOSATO, M., Informatics for System Creation
SAKAI, Y., Integrated Systems Engineering
SATO, Y., Mathematical Information Science
SHIMIZU, K., Biomedical Systems Engineering
SUEOKA, K., Advanced Electronics
TAKAHASHI, Y., Advanced Electronics

TANAKA, Y., Knowledge Software Science
WADA, M., Complex Systems Engineering
WATANABE, H., Bioinformatics
YAMAMOTO, K., Biomedical Systems Engineering
YAMAMOTO, M., Advanced Electronics
YAMAMOTO, T., Information Media Science and Technology
YAMASHITA, Y., Informatics for System Creation
ZEUGMANN, T., Knowledge Software Science

Graduate School of Law (Kita 9, Nishi 7, Kita-ku, Sapporo; tel. (11) 706-3074; fax (11) 706-4948; e-mail shomu@juris.hokudai.ac.jp; internet www.juris.hokudai.ac.jp):

DOKO, T., Labour Law
FUJIWARA, M., Civil Law
GONZA, T., History of Political Theory
HASEGAWA, K., Philosophy of Law
HAYASHI, T., Commercial Law
HAYASHIDA, S., Economic Analysis of Law
HIENUKI, T., Economic Law
HITOMI, T., Administrative Law
ICHIRO OZAKI, S.
IKEDA, S., Civil Law
IMAI, H., Philosophy of Law
KOMORI, T., International Law
MACHIMURA, Y., Law of Civil Procedure
MATSUHISA, M., Civil Law
MIYAMOTO, T., Comparative Political Economy
MURAKAMI, H., Administrative Law
NAGAI, C., Criminal Law
NAKAYAMA, H., Law of Criminal Procedure
OHTSUKA, R., Commercial Law
OKADA, N., Constitutional Law
ONAGI, A., Criminal Law
SASADA, E., Constitutional Law
SEGAWA, N., Civil Law
SHIRATORI, Y., Law of Criminal Procedure
SORAI, M., Modern Political Analysis
SUZUKI, K., Asian Law
TAGUCHI, M., Western Legal History
TAKAMI, S., Law of Civil Procedure
TAMURA, Y., Intellectual Property Law
TANAKA, H., Legal Ethic
TSUJI, Y., Political Theory
TSUNEMOTO, T., Constitutional Law
YAMAMOTO, T., Commercial Law
YAMASHITA, R., Administrative Law
YOSHIDA, K., Civil Law

Graduate School of Letters (Kita 10, Nishi 7, Kita-ku, Sapporo; tel. (11) 726-7728; fax (11) 706-4803; e-mail wwwadmin@let.hokudai.ac.jp; internet www.hokudai.ac.jp/letters):

ABE, J., Psychology
AKASHI, M., Occidental History
ANDO, A., Western Literature
ANZAI, M., Western Literature
CHIBA, K., Philosophy
FUJII, K., Religious Studies and Indian Philosophy
GOTO, Y., Japanology
HANAI, K., Philosophy
HISHITANI, S., Psychology
HOSODA, N., Religious Studies and Indian Philosophy
IKEDA, S., Linguistics Sciences
IKEDA, T., Regional Sciences
INOUE, K., Japanese History
IRIMOTO, T., Northern Culture Studies
KADOWAKI, S., Linguistic Sciences
KAMEDA, T., Behavioural Sciences
KANEKO, I., Sociology
KITAMURA, K., Theory and History of Art
KURYUZAWA, T., Occidental History
KUWAYAMA, T., History and Anthropology
MATSUOKA, M., Sociology
MIKI, S., Asian History
MISAKI, H., Japanology
MIYATAKE, K., History and Anthropology
MOCHIZUKI, T., Linguistics and Western Languages
NAKA, M., Psychology

NAKATOGAWA, K., Philosophy
NAMBU, N., Japanese History
NITTA, T., Ethics and Applied Philosophy
ONO, Y., Linguistics Sciences
OTA, K., History and Anthropology
SAKURAI, Y., Sociology
SATO, R., Sinology
SOTO, J., Filmology and Cultural Studies of Representation
SEKI, T., Regional Sciences
SHIMIZU, M., Linguistics and Western Languages
SHIRAKIZAWA, A., Japanese History
SUTO, Y., Sinology
TAKAHASHI, H., Linguistics and Western Languages
TAKAHEI, H., Philosophy
TAKEDA, M., Sinology
TAKIGAWA, T., Psychology
TAYAMA, T., Psychology
TOMITA, Y., Japanology
TSUMAGARI, T., Northern Culture Studies
TUDA, Y., Asian History
URAI, Y., Linguistics and Western Languages
UTSUNOMIYA, T., Religious Studies and Indian Philosophy
WADA, H., Psychology
YAMADA, T., Philosophy
YAMADA, T., Western Literature
YAMAGISHI, T., Behavioural Sciences
YUHAZU, K., Sinology

Graduate School of Medicine (Kita 15, Nishi 7, Kita-ku, Sapporo; tel. (11) 716-5003; fax (11) 717-5286; e-mail shomu@med.hokudai.ac.jp; internet www.med.hokudai.ac.jp):

AKITA, H., Medical Oncology
ARIGA, T., Paediatrics
ARIKAWA, J., Infectious Disease
CHIBA, H., Biomedical Informatics
DAIGUJI, M., Clinical Occupational Therapy
DATE, H., Medical Engineering and Science
FUJITA, H., Environmental Biology
FUKUDA, S., Otolaryngology, Head and Neck Surgery
FUKUSHIMA, J., Basic Physical Therapy
FUKUSHIMA, K., Sensorimotor and Cognitive Research
GANDO, S., Acute and Critical Care Medicine
HATAKEYAMA, S., Medical Chemistry
HATTA, T., Clinical Occupational Therapy
HONMA, K., Chronobiology
IMAMURA, M., Haematology and Oncology
INOUE, K., Basic Occupational Therapy
ISHIZU, A., Clinical Pathophysiology
IWANAGA, T., Histology and Cytology
IWASAKI, Y., Neurosurgery
IWATA, G., Maternal Nursing and Child Nursing
KAMIYA, H., Neurobiology
KASAHARA, M., Pathology
KAWAGUCHI, H., Laboratory Medicine
KISHI, R., Public Health
KOBAYASHI, S., Biomedical Informatics
KOIKE, T., Clinical Immunology
KONDO, S., Surgical Oncology
KOYAMA, T., Psychiatry
MAEZAWA, M., Healthcare Research and Quality
MATSUNO, K., Clinical Pathophysiology
MATSUSHITA, M., Adult and Gerontological Nursing
MIKAMI, T., Clinical Pathophysiology
MINAKAMI, H., Obstetrics
MINAMI, A., Orthopaedic Surgery
MIWA, S., Cellular and Molecular Pharmacology
MIYAMOTO, K., Clinical Physical Therapy
MORIMOTO, Y., Anaesthesia and Perioperative Medicine
MORISHITA, S., Fundamental Nursing
MORIYAMA, T., Biomedical Informatics
MURATA, W., Basic Occupational Therapy

NISHIMURA, M., Respiratory Medicine
NISHIOKA, T., Radiological Technology
NONOMURA, K., Renal and Genito-urinary Surgery
OGASAWARA, K., Medical Engineering and Science
OHMIYA, Y., Photobiology
OHNO, S., Ophthalmology
SAEKI, K., Community Health Nursing
SAGAWA, T., Maternal Nursing and Child Nursing
SAITO, T., Community Health Nursing
SAKAI, M., Radiological Technology
SAKURAGI, N., Reproductive Endocrinology and Oncology
SAKURAI, T., Medical Informatics
SASAKI, F., Paediatric Surgery
SASAKI, H., Neurology
SATO, Y., Maternal Nursing and Child Nursing
SHIMIZU, H., Dermatology
SHIMIZU, T., Radiological Technology
SHIRATO, H., Radiology
TAKANAMI, S., Community Health Nursing
TAKEDA, N., Basic Physical Therapy
TAMAKI, N., Nuclear Medicine
TAMASHIRO, H., Global Health and Epidemiology
TERAZAWA, K., Forensic Medicine
TODO, S., General Surgery
TSUTSUI, H., Cardiovascular Medicine
WATANABE, M., Anatomy and Embryology
YAMAGUCHI, H., Biomedical Informatics
YAMAMOTO, T., Medical Engineering and Science
YAMAMOTO, Y., Plastic Surgery
YAMANAKA, M., Clinical Physical Therapy
YASUDA, K., Sports Medicine and Joint Reconstruction Surgery
YOKOSAWA, K., Medical Engineering and Science
YOSHIMURA, S., Fundamental Nursing
YOSHIOKA, M., Neuropharmacology

Graduate School of Veterinary Medicine (Kita 18, Nishi 9, Kita-ku, Sapporo; tel. (11) 706-5173; fax (11) 706-5190; e-mail syomu@ vetmed.hokudai.ac.jp; internet www.vetmed .hokudai.ac.jp):

AGUI, T., Disease Control
FUJINAGA, T., Veterinary Clinical Sciences
FUJITA, S., Environmental Veterinary Sciences
HABARA, Y., Biomedical Sciences
HORIUCHI, M., Prion Diseases
INABA, M., Veterinary Clinical Sciences
INANAMI, O., Environmental Veterinary Sciences
ITO, S., Biomedical Sciences
KATAKURA, K., Disease Control
KIDA, H., Disease Control
KIMURA, K., Biomedical Sciences
KON, Y., Biomedical Sciences
TAKAHASHI, Y., Veterinary Clinical Sciences
TAKASHIMA, I., Environmental Veterinary Sciences
TSUBOTA, T., Environmental Veterinary Sciences
UMEMURA, T., Veterinary Clinical Sciences

Research Faculty of Agriculture (Kita 9, Nishi 9, Kita-ku, Sapporo; tel. (11) 706-4123; fax (11) 706-4893; e-mail shomu@agr .hokudai.ac.jp):

ARIGA, S., Environmental Molecular Bioscience
ASANO, K., Applied Microbiology
BANDO, H., Applied Molecular Entomology
DEMURA, K., Agricultural and Environmental Policy
FUJIKAWA, S., Woody Plant Biology
HARA, H., Nutritional Biochemistry
HASEGAWA, S., Soil Conservation
HASHIDOKO, Y., Ecological Chemistry
HATANO, R., Soil Science
HATTORI, A., Meat Science

HIRAI, T., Timber Engineering
HIRANO, T., Environmental Informatics
IIZAWA, R., Agricultural Marketing
IWAMA, K., Crop Science
KAKIZAWA, H., Forest Policy
KAWABATA, J., Food Biochemistry
KIMURA, A., Molecular Enzymology
KIMURA, T., Agricultural and Food Process Engineering
KITAMURA, K., Plant Genetics and Evolution
KOBAYASHI, Y., Animal Nutrition
KODA, Y., Crop Physiology
KOIKE, T., Silviculture and Forest Ecology
KONDO, S., Animal Production System
KONDO, T., Environmental Horticulture and Landscape Architecture
KUROKAWA, I., Farm Management
MARUTANI, T., Earth Surface Processes and Land Management
MASUDA, K., Plant Functional Biology
MASUTA, C., Cell Biology and Manipulation
MATSUDA, J., Agricultural Circulative Engineering
MATSUI, H., Biochemistry
MIKAMI, T., Genetic Engineering
NABETA, K., Natural Product Chemistry
NAGASAWA, T., Land Improvement and Management
NAITO, S., Molecular Biology
NAKAMURA, F., Animal By-product Science
NAKAMURA, F., Forest Ecosystem Management
NOGUCHI, N., Vehicle Robotics
OSAKI, M., Plant Nutrition
OSANAMI, F., Agricultural Development
SAITO, Y., Animal Ecology
SAKASHITA, A., Agricultural Cooperative
SANO, Y., Plant Breeding
SHIMAZAKI, K., Dairy Food Science
SUZUKI, M., Horticultural Science
UBUKATA, M., Wood Chemistry
URANO, S., Agricultural and Environmental Physics
UYEDA, I., Pathogen–Plant Interactions
WATANABE, T., Animal Breeding and Reproduction
YAJIMA, T., Forest Resource Biology
YOKOTA, A., Microbial Physiology

Research Faculty of Media and Communication (Kita 17, Nishi 8, Kita-ku, Sapporo; tel. (11) 716-2111; fax (11) 706-7801; e-mail soumu@ilcs.hokudai.ac.jp; internet www .hokudai.ac.jp/imcts/rfmc.html):

Most of the Professors in this Faculty also belong to the Foreign Language Education Center

EGUCHI, Y., German
HASHIMOTO, H., English
ISHIBASHI, M., German
ISHIKAWA, K., German
KOBAYAKAWA, M., International Public Relations
KOGA, H., Italian
MIYASHITA, M., English
NAGAI, Y., Chinese
NISHI, M., French
NOZAWA, Y., Chinese
OGAWA, Y., English
OHIRA, T., French
OHNO, K., English
SATOH, S., German
SONODA, K., English
STAPLETON, P., English
SUGIURA, S., Russian
TAKAHASHI, Y., German
TAKAI, K., Chinese
TAKEMOTO, K., English
TAKENAKA, M., French
TERADA, T., German
TSUKUWA, M., German
UEDA, M., English
USAMI, S., Russian

YAMADA, K., Russian
YAMADA, Y., English
YOSHIDA, T., German

ATTACHED RESEARCH INSTITUTES

Admission Center: f. 2005; Dir MINORU WAKITA.

Catalysis Research Center: f. 1989; Dir WATARU UEDA.

Center for Advanced Research of Energy Conversion Materials: f. 2004; Dir KAZUYA KUROKAWA.

Center for Advanced Tourism Studies: f. 2006; Dir SHUZO ISHIMORI.

Center for Ainu and Indigenous Studies: f. 2007; Dir TERUKI TSUNEMOTO.

Center for Experimental Research in Social Sciences: f. 2007; Dir TOSHIO YAMAGISHI.

Center for Instrumental Analysis: f. 1979; Dir TOSHIAKI MIURA.

Center for Research and Development in Higher Education: f. 1995; Dir MINORU WAKITA.

Central Institute of Radioisotope Science: f. 1978; Dir NAGARA TAMAKI.

Creative Research Initiative 'Sousei': f. 2005; Dir HISATAKE OKADA.

Environmental Preservation Center: f. 1995; Dir MASAYA SAWAMURA.

Field Science Center for the Northern Biosphere: f. 2001; Dir KAICHIRO SASA.

Foreign Language Education Center: f. 2007; Dir YUTAKA EGUCHI.

Health Administration Center: f. 1972; Dir MANABU MUSASHI.

Hokkaido University Archives: f. 2005; Dir MASAAKI HEMMI.

Hokkaido University Museum: f. 1999; Dir SHUNSUKE MAWATARI.

Information Initiative Center: f. 2003; Dir TSUYOSHI YAMAMOTO.

Institute for Genetic Medicine: f. 2000; Dir TOSHIMITSU UEDE; publ. *Collected Papers* (1 a year).

Institute of Low Temperature Science: f. 1941; Dir AKIRA KOUCHI.

International Student Center: f. 1991; Dir TAKEO HONDOH.

Meme Media Laboratory: f. 1996; Dir YUZURU TANAKA.

Research and Education Center for Brain Science: f. 2003; Dir SHINYA KURIKI.

Research Center for Integrated Quantum Electronics: f. 2001; Dir TAKASHI FUKUI.

Research Center for Zoonosis Control: f. 2005; Dir HIROSHI KIDA.

Research Institute for Electronic Science: f. 1943; Dir KEIJI SASAKI.

Slavic Research Center: f. 1990; Dir KIMITAKA MATSUZATO; publ. *Acta Slavica Iaponica* (1 a year).

IBARAKI UNIVERSITY

1-1, Bunkyo 2-chome, Mito-Shi, Ibaraki-ken 310-8512

Telephone: (29) 228-8007
Fax: (29) 228-8019
Internet: www.ibaraki.ac.jp

Founded 1949
Independent
Academic year: April to March

Pres.: TAKEO MIYATA
Admin.: T. MIYATA
Dean of Student Affairs: F. IKEYA
Librarian: Y. ASANO

Library of 939,000 vols
Number of teachers: 584 full-time
Number of students: 8,864
Publications: Bulletins (in Japanese), Journals of the faculties (in Japanese)

DEANS

Faculty of Education: R. KIKUCHI
Faculty of Engineering: K. YAMAGATA
Faculty of Humanities: T. MURANAKA
Faculty of Science: T. WATANABE
School of Agriculture: T. MATUDA

PROFESSORS

Faculty of Education:

ADACHI, K., School Education
AKISAKA, M., Clinical Medicine
AKUTA, N., Clinical Psychology
ARAKAWA, C., Housing and Domestic Science
EBATA, H., School Education
FUJIHIRA, S., German Literature
HASEGAWA, S., Vocal Music
HASHIURA, H., Japanese Literature
HATTORI, K., Physical Activity Science
HAYAKAWA, K., Composition
HAYAKAWA, T., Geomorphology
HONNDA, T., Information Education
IKEYA, F., European History
INABA, K.
INAMI, Y., Computer Science
KAIZU, S., Applied Mathematics
KAJIWARA, S., Instrumental Music
KANEKO, K., Art Education
KIKUCHI, R., Adult Education
KIMURA, K., Philosophy
KOIZUMI, S., Art History
KOJIMA, H., Information Education
KOMURO, K., Technical Education
KUSAKA, Y., Physical Education
MAEKAWA, Y., Sinology
MAKINO, Y., Geology
MATSUDA, M., Art Education
MATSUI, M., Information Sciences
MATSUMURA, T., Education for Handicapped Children
MATSUZAKA, A., Health and Physical Education
MIURA, T., Health and Physical Education
NAGASAWA, K., English Language Teaching
NAKAMURA, T., Health Education
NAMIKI, T., English Morphology
OGATA, T., Health and Physical Education
OKAMOTO, K., Physical Education
ONO, Y., Mycology
ONODERA, A., Historical Geography
OSHIMA, K., Earth Science
OTA, S., Physical Education
OTAKE, H., Women's Studies
OTANI, H., School Nursing
OTSUKI, I., Economic History of Modern Japan
OUCHI, Z., Language Ethics Education
OZAKI, H., Physiology for Handicapped Children
SASAKI, Y., Japanese Language Teaching
SATO, A., Musicology
SATO, E., Mathematical Education
SATO, H., Technical Education
SOGA, H., Mathematical Science
SOGO, M., Painting
SUGANUMA, K., Clinical Psychology
SUZUKI, E., Social Studies Teaching
TAKIZAWA, T., Hygienics
TANAKA, K., Music Education
TANIGUCHI, T., School Education
TASHIRO, T., School Education
TATSUMI, N., Physical Education
TERAMOTO, T., Industrial Arts
TOGASHI, T., Physical Education
TOSHIYASU, Y., Science Education
YAMAMOTO, H., Organic Chemistry
YAMAMOTO, K., Household Management Education
YAMANE, S., Insect Ecology

YAMASHITA, T., School Education
YANAGIDA, N., Mathematics
YASUDA, K., Home Economics Education
YOSHIDA, H., Home Economics Education

Faculty of Engineering:

ABE, O., Ceramics Engineering
ARAKI, T., Computer Science
EDA, H., Production Engineering and Machine Tools
ENOMOTO, M., Materials Physics
FUJII, K., Laser and Plasma
FUKUZAWA, K., Concrete Engineering
HAMAMATSU, Y., Modelling and Simulation
HARIU, T., Electronic Material Systems
HOSHI, T., Systems Information and Remote Sensing
ICHIMURA, M., Materials Physics
IGARASHI, S., Analytical Chemistry
IKEHATA, T., Plasma Science
IMAI, Y., Communication Engineering
INUI, M., Systems Engineering
ISHIGURO, M., Computer Applications
ITO, G., Plastic Working Science
KAGOSHIMA, K., Antennae
KAMINAGA, H., Energy Conversion
KANO, M., Discrete Mathematics and its Application
KAZITANI, S., Energy Conservation
KIKUMA, I., Electronic Materials
KISHI, Y., Intelligent Systems
KOBAYASHI, M., Systems Information
KOBIYAMA, M., Electromagnetic Systems
KOUNOSU, S., Design Engineering
KOYAMADA, Y., Photonic Systems
KOYANAGI, T., Landscape Planning and Design
KUROSAWA, K., Plasma Science
MAEKAWA, K., Materials Science and Engineering
MASUI, M., Electronic Materials
MASUZAWA, T., Dynamics of Machines
MIMURA, N., Global Environment Engineering
MOMOSE, Y., Surface Chemistry
MOTOHASHI, Y., Materials Science and Engineering
MURANOI, T., Electronic Materials for Functionality
NAITO, K., Analytical Chemistry
NAKAMOTO, R., Functional Analysis
NARA, K., Electrical Power Systems
NIIMURA, N., Physics
NIREI, H., Environmental Asset Science
NUMAO, T., Architecture
OGUCHI, K., Dynamics of Machines
OKADA, Y., Dynamics of Machines
ONO, K., Polymer Science
ONUKI, J., Materials Technology
OZAWA, S., Computational Physics
SASAKI, Y., Foundation and Design of Precision Engineering
SENBA, I., Computer Science
SHIRAISHI, M., Systems and Controls
SIOHATA, K., Design Engineering
SUGITA, R., Electrical and Electronics Engineering
SUZUKI, H., Mechanical Design
SUZUKI, T., Energy Conversion
TAKAHASHI, M., Organic Chemistry
TAKEUCHI, M., Electrical Materials
TAZUKE, Y., Applied Physics
TOMODA, Y., Mechanical Metallurgy
TOZUNE, A., Electric Machines
TURUTA, K., High Voltage and Plasma Science
WU, Z., Structural Engineering
YAMANAKA, K., Systems and Controls
YASUHARA, K., Geotechnical Engineering
YOKOYAMA, K., Structural Engineering
ZYOU, M., CAD/CAM/CAE

Faculty of Humanities:

AIZAWA, Y., English and American Culture
AMEMIYA, S., Politics
AOKI, K., French
ARIIZUMI, S., Economic Structure

ARITOMI, M., Psychology
ASANO, Y., Human Geography
CHEANG, K., Linguistics
FUJII, F., Linguistics
FUKAYA, N., Law
FUKAZAWA, Y., European History
FUSHIMI, K., German
IIZUKA, K., Law
IIJIMA, H., Management Science
KAMATA, A., Social Structure
KAMIYA, T., Social Structure
KANAMOTO, S., Japanese Education
KANOU, Y., Asian Culture
KATAYAMA, Y., Philosophy
KIMURA, M., Southeast Asia Area Study
KISHIMOTO, N., Linguistics
KOIDO, M., French and European Culture
KOIZUMI, Y., English and American Culture
KOMIYAJI, M., Business Administration
LIENG, J., Sinology
MATUMURA, N., Social Structure
MAYANAGI, M., Oriental History
MOGI, M., Comparative Culture
MORIYA, S., Logic
MORIYA, T., Sociology
MURANAKA, M., Sociology
NAKURA, B., Economic Structure
NOSAKA, M., Law
OHATA, K., English and American Culture
OKUBO, N., French Culture
SAITO, M., Regional Societies
SAITO, Y., Local Administration
SANO, H., Media Studies
SASAKI, H., History
SASAKURA, S., English
SATO, K., Economic Structure
SATO, K., German Culture
SIBUYA, A., Sociology
SIMAOKA, S., English
SUGII, K., Oriental History
SUGISHITA, T., International Cooperation Theory
SUMIKAWA, H., European and American Economy Theory
SUZUKI, T., Communication
SUZUKI, Y., Psychology
SUZUKI, Y., German
TAKAHASHI, T., English
TAMURA, T., Law
TANAKA, S., Regional Societies
TATEWAKI, I., Regional Societies
TATEYAMA, Y., International Economics
TOKUE, K., Economic Policy
UENO, H., Social Anthropology
UMEDA, T., Law
WATANABE, K., European Culture
YAMAMOTO, H., Asian Economics

Faculty of Science:

AMANO, T., Science of Cosmic Matter
FUJII, Y., Coordination Chemistry
FUJIWARA, T., Physics
HORI, Y., Botany
HORIUCHI, T., Analysis
ICHIMASA, M., Cell Biology
ICHIMASA, Y., Physiology
IKEDA, Y., Geochemistry
IMURA, H., Analytical Chemistry
ISIZUKA, T., Astrophysics
IZUOKA, A., Physical Chemistry
KANEKO, M., Chemistry
KANNO, S., Atomic Physics
KAWADA, Y., Chemistry
KIMURA, M., Geochemistry
KOJIMA, J., Entomology
MATSUDA, R., Algebra
MISHIMA, S., Biology
MIWA, I., Biology
MORINO, H., Systematics
NAKANO, Y., Structural Chemistry
NISHIHARA, Y., Magnetism and Superconductivity
NODA, F., Theoretical High Energy
OHASHI, K., Analytical Chemistry
ONISHI, K., Applied Mathematics

ONOSE, H., Statistics
ORIYAMA, T., Organic Chemistry
OSHIMA, H., Topology
SAKATA, F., Mathematical Science
SAKUMA, T., Solid-State Physics
TAGIRI, M., Earth and Planetary Physics
TAKANO, K., Mathematics
URABE, T., Geometry
WATANABE, T., Earth Science
YAMADA, M., Physics
YAMAGAMI, S., Quantum Physics
YANAGIDA, R., Cosmic Ray Physics
YOKOSAWA, M., Astrophysics

School of Agriculture:

AKUTSU, K., Plant Pathology
GOTO, T., Applied Physics
KARUBE, J., Farmland Engineering
KASHIWAGI, M., Regional Planning Science
KINOSE, K., Hydraulic Engineering
KODAMA, O., Bio-regulation Chemistry
KOSUGIYAMA, M., Animal Breeding
KOUNO, Y., Chemical Ecology
KUBOTA, M., Soil Science and Plant Nutrition
KURUSU, Y., Industrial Microbiology
MACHIDA, T., Agricultural Systems
MARUBASHI, W., Plant Breeding
MASAKI, T., Enzymatic Chemistry
MATSUDA, T., Horticulture
MATSUZAWA, Y., Animal Husbandry and Behaviour
MORIIZUMI, S., Agricultural Machinery
NAKAGAWA, M., Agricultural Economics
NAKAJIMA, M., Farm Science
NAKAMURA, Y., Feed Science
NAKANE, K., Algebra
NAKASONE, H., Agricultural and Environmental Engineering
OTA, H., Microbial Ecology
SAGO, R., Cultivation Science
SHIO, K., Information Science
SHIRAI, M., Molecular Microbiology
TAKAHARA, H., Bioresource Engineering
TSUKIHASHI, T., Horticulture
YONEKURA, M., Crop Production

IWATE UNIVERSITY

3-18-8 Ueda, Morioka, Iwate 020-8550
Telephone: (19) 621-6006
Fax: (19) 621-6014
E-mail: ssomu@iwate-u.ac.jp
Internet: www.iwate-u.ac.jp
Founded 1949
Independent
Academic year: April to March
Pres.: KENICHI HIRAYAMA
Chief Admin. Officer: TOSHIAKI KIKUCHI
Librarian: YOSHIYA NAKASHIMA
Library of 760,434 vols
Number of teachers: 835
Number of students: 6,218
Publications: *Journal of the Faculty of Agriculture*, *Report on Technology of Iwate University*, *Artes Liberales*

DEANS

Faculty of Agriculture: YOSHINOBU OTA
Faculty of Education: TAKAO FUJIWARA
Faculty of Technology: KUNIO MORI
College of Humanities and Social Sciences: TATSUYUKI TAKATSUKA

JAPAN ADVANCED INSTITUTE OF SCIENCE AND TECHNOLOGY

1-1 Asahidai, Nomi, Ishikawa 923-1292
Telephone: (761) 51-1111
Fax: (761) 51-1088
E-mail: kouhou@jaist.ac.jp
Internet: www.jaist.ac.jp
Founded 1990
State control

Pres.: TAKUYA KATAYAMA
Vice-Pres.: YASUSHI HIBINO
Vice-Pres.: YUSUKE KAWAKAMI
Vice-Pres.: KOZO SUGIYAMA
Dir of the Library: ATSUKO MIYAJI
Number of teachers: 166
Number of students: 925

DEANS

School of Information Science: MASATO AKAGI
School of Knowledge Science: SUSUMU KUNIFUJI
School of Materials Science: HIDEKI MATSUMURA

KAGAWA UNIVERSITY

1-1 Saiwai-cho, Takamatsu-shi 760-8521
Telephone: (87) 832-1025
Fax: (87) 832-1053
E-mail: kokusait@jimu.ao.kagawa-u.ac.jp
Internet: www.kagawa-u.ac.jp
Founded 1949
Independent
Academic year: April to March
Pres.: Dr YOSHITSUGU KIMURA
Vice-Pres: Dr HIROAKI TAKEUCHI, Dr TAKUMI YOSHIZAWA
Sec.-Gen.: KUNIO SEKI
Librarian: MASAYUKI SATO
Library of 650,000 vols
Number of teachers: 473 (incl. teachers at attached schools)
Number of students: 5,261

DEANS

Faculty of Agriculture: MASAHIKO ICHII
Faculty of Economics: MICHIYO IHARA
Faculty of Education: YOSHIMASA KANO
Faculty of Engineering: HIROSHI ISHIKAWA
Faculty of Law: SADAMI UEMURA
Faculty of Medicine: AKINOBU OKABE

KAGOSHIMA UNIVERSITY

1-21–24, Korimoto, Kagoshima 890-8580
Telephone: (992) 85-7111
Internet: www.kagoshima-u.ac.jp
Founded 1949
State control
Pres.: HIROKI YOSHIDA
Dir.-Gen.: CHIKARA MORIMOTO
Library of 1,338,169 vols
Number of teachers: 1,200 full-time
Number of students: 11,000

DEANS

Faculty of Agriculture: I. IWAMOTO
Faculty of Dentistry: K. SUGIHARA
Faculty of Education: A. TAKEKUMA
Faculty of Fisheries: T. NORO
Faculty of Law, Economics and the Humanities: H. ISHIKAWA
Faculty of Medicine: Y. EIZURU
Faculty of Science: S. KIYOHARA
Graduate School of Health Science: A. YOSHIDA
Graduate School of Medical and Dental Sciences: T. MATSUYAMA
Graduate School of Science and Engineering: Y. FUKUI
Law School: H. UNIEME
Professional Graduate School of Clinical Psychology: T. ABE
United Graduate School of Agricultural Sciences: T. SUGANUMA

KANAGAWA UNIVERSITY

3-27-1 Rokkakubashi, Kanagawaku, Yokohama 221-8686
Telephone: (45) 491-1701
Fax: (45) 481-6011

E-mail: kohou-info@kanagawa-u.ac.jp
Internet: www.kanagawa-u.ac.jp
Founded 1949
Library of 1,110,000 vols
Number of students: 19,129
Faculties of Business Administration, Economics, Engineering, Foreign Languages, Law, Science.

KANAZAWA UNIVERSITY

Kakuma-machi, Kanazawa-shi 920-1192
Telephone: (76) 264-5111
Fax: (76) 234-4010
E-mail: now@kanazawa-u.ac.jp
Internet: www.kanazawa-u.ac.jp
Founded 1949
Independent
Academic year: April to March
Pres.: YUJIRO HAYASHI
Vice-Pres. for Finance: S. NAKAMURA
Vice-Pres. for General Affairs and Human Resources: N. ASAKURA
Vice-Pres. for Hospital: Y. WATANABE
Vice-Pres. for Information: T. HASHIMOTO
Vice-Pres. for Research and International Affairs: A. OMURA
Dir for Office of Community Relations: T. HASHIMOTO
Dir for Office of Intellectual Property: N. YOSHIKUNI
Dir for University Library: T. HASHIMOTO
Library of 1,749,982 vols
Number of teachers: 1,031
Number of students: 10,794

DEANS

Faculty of Economics: T. YOKOYAMA
Faculty of Education: K. KATAGIRI
Faculty of Engineering: J. ODA
Faculty of Law: T. MAEDA
Faculty of Letters: I. KUBOTA
Faculty of Medicine: M. FURUKAWA
Faculty of Pharmaceutical Sciences: H. ISHIBASHI
Faculty of Science: S. NAKAO
Graduate School of Medical Science: H. YAMAMOTO
Graduate School of Natural Science and Technology: (vacant)
Graduate School of Socio-environmental Studies: K. GOGA
Law School: Y. HATA

DIRECTORS

Advanced Science Research Center: K. YAMAGUCHI
Cancer Research Institute: H. SATO
Center for Cooperative Research: S. MURAKAMI
Environmental Preservation Center: S. MORI
Extension Institute: M. SOMEI
Foreign Language Institute: T. YABUCHI
Health Service Center: H. NAKABAYASHI
Information Media Center: M. IWAHARA
Institute for Nature and Environmental Technology: K. KASHIWAYA
International Student Center: M. KITAURA
Research Center for Higher Education: T. AONO
University Hospital: S. KOIZUMI

PROFESSORS

Advanced Science Research Center (13-1 Takara-machi, Kanazawa, Ishikawa; tel. (76) 265-2771; fax (76) 234-4537; e-mail yamaguti@kenroku.kanazawa-u.ac.jp; internet web.kanazawa-u.ac.jp/~asrc):

ASANO, M., Experimental Animal Science
MORI, H., Nuclear Medicine
YAMAGUCHI, K., Molecular Genetics

Cancer Research Institute (13-1 Takara-machi, Kanazawa, Ishikawa; tel. (76) 265-2799; fax (76) 234-4527):

HARADA, F., Molecular and Cellular Biology
HIRAO, A., Molecular and Cellular Biology
MINAMOTO, T., Basic and Clinical Oncology
MUKAIDA, N., Molecular Oncology
MURAKAMI, S., Molecular Genetics
SATO, H., Molecular Oncology
SAWABU, N., Basic and Clinical Oncology
SUDA, T., Molecular and Cellular Immunology
TAKAKURA, N., Molecular and Cellular Biology
YAMAMOTO, K., Molecular and Cellular Biology
YOSHIOKA, K., Molecular and Cellular Biology

Center for Co-operative Research (tel. (76) 264-6111; fax (76) 234-4019):

SERYO, K., Mechanical Engineering
YOSHIKUNI, N., Intellectual Property Management

Faculty of Economics (tel. (76) 264-5440; fax (76) 264-5444):

BENNOU, S., Economic History of Modern China
GOKA, K., Labour Economics
HORIBAYASHI, T., Theory of Economic Planning
IKARIYAMA, H., Public Finance
KAMIJO, I., History of Economic Thought
MAEDA, T., Modern Economics
MARUYAMA, K., Comparative Social Philosophy
MIYATA, M., Banking and Financial Systems
MURAKAMI, K., Principles of Economics
NAKASHIMA, K., World-System Theory and the Financial History of Medieval and Modern Europe
NAMU, S., Education
NISHIDA, Y., Japanese Contemporary Agricultural History
NISHIJIMA, Y., Contrastive Sociolinguistics
NOMURA, M., History of Social Thought
SAWADA, M., Industrial Relations and Human Resource Management in Japan and the USA, General Theory of Business Management
SHIRAISHI, H., Business Administration
TSURUZONO, Y., Korean History
UNNO, Y., Economic Policy
YOKOYAMA, T., Social Security
YOSHINO, Y., Sports Science

Faculty of Education (tel. (76) 264-5555; fax (76) 234-4100):

DEMURA, S., Lifelong Sports
EMORI, I., Pedagogy
GOMI, T., Historical Geography
HATANAKA, H., Magnetic Resonance
IHARA, Y., Inorganic Chemistry
IKEGAMI, K., Developmental Psychology
ISHIMURA, U., Physical Education
ITOH, S., Geography and Planning
IZUMI, H., Dielectrics
KATAGIRI, K., Developmental Neuropsychology of Mental Retardation
KATOH, K., Japanese Linguistics
KAWABATA, K., Freshwater Biology
KAYAHARA, M., Clinical Psychology
KIMURA, M., Education for the Handicapped
KONDOH, A., Japanese Linguistics
KUJIRA, Y., Crop Science
KUROBORI, T., Applied Optics
MAEDA, H., Modern Japanese Literature
MATSUBARA, M., Teaching of Science
MATSUDAIRA, M., Textile Science
MATSUNAKA, H., Instrumental Music
MATSUSHITA, R., Philosophy of Education
MATSUURA, N., Graphic Design
MIYASHITA, T., History of European Art

MIYOSHI, Y., Information Science
MORI, E., Japanese Literature
MOROOKA, K., Teaching Methods
MURAI, A., Research on Method of Teaching 'Social Studies'
OHTSUKA, I., English Linguistics
OI, M., Communication Disorders
OKAZAKI, F., Philosophy
OKUBO, H., History of Physical Education and Sports
OKUDA, H., Japanese History
SAKAYORI, A., Igneous Petrology
SASAK, T., Materials Science and Engineering
SHINOHARA, H., Music Education
SUGIMOTO, M., Geology
SUNADA, R., Practice and Research for Clinical Psychology and Education
TANABE, S., Educational Administration and Management
UEDA, J., Chemistry
YAKURA, K., Plant Molecular Biology
YAMAGISHI, M., Housing Science
YAMAMOTO, H., Biomechanics in Sports
YAMAMOTO, H., Classic Japanese Literature
YAMAMOTO, T., Teaching Methods
YASUKAWA, T., History of Foreign Education

Faculty of Law (tel. (76) 264-5403; fax (76) 264-5405):

CHEN, I., Conflict of Laws
INOUE, H., Social Security Law
KASHIMA, M., International Relations
KUSUNE, S., International Communication
MAEDA, T., Labour Law
NAKAMASA, M., Social Philosophy
NAKAMURA, M., Chinese Legal History
NAKAYAMA, H., Criminal Procedure
NISHIMURA, S., Political Sociology
SAKURAI, T., European Legal History
TAKAHASHI, R., Sociology
TOKUMOTO, S., Civil Law
UMEDA, Y., Japanese Legal History
YAMAGATA, K., Developmental Psychology

Faculty of Letters (tel. (76) 264-5360; fax (76) 264-5362):

FUJII, S., Prehistory of the Near East
FURUHATA, T., Oriental History
HASHIMOTO, K., Sociology
HONMA, T., American Literature
IKUTA, S., English Literature
IWATA, R., Chinese Linguistics
KAGAMI, H., Cultural Anthropology
KAJIKAWA, A., Russian History
KAJIKAWA, Y., Geography
KAMIYA, H., Geography
KASAI, J., Japanese History
KASUYA, Y., French Literature
KIGOSHI, O., Japanese Literature
KUBOTA, I., German Literature
KUBUKI, S., Comparative Culture
MATSUHARA, J., Cognitive Psychology
MIZOBE, A., Sociology
MOCHII, Y., Oriental History
MURAKAMI, K., American Literature
NAKABAYASHI, N., Cultural Anthropology
NAKAMURA, Y., English Language
NISHIMURA, S., Japanese Literature
NITTA, T., Linguistics
OHTAKI, S., Chinese Language
SASAKI, T., Archaeology
SHIBATA, M., Philosophy
SHIMA, I., Comparative Culture
SUNAHARA, Y., Philosophy
TAKADA, S., English Literature
TAKAHAMA, S., Archaeology
TAKEUCHI, Y., German Linguistics
TOHDA, M., British History
TSUGE, Y., Linguistics
UCHIDA, H., French Literature
UEDA, M., Japanese Literature
YASUMURA, N., Classical Greek and Latin Literature

Faculty of Medicine (5-11-80 Kodatsuno, Kanazawa, Ishikawa; tel. (76) 265-2500; fax (76) 234-4351):

AMANO, R., Radiochemistry and Radiobiology
ASAI, H., Physical Therapy
HASEGAWA, M., Mental Health and Psychiatric Nursing
HOSO, M., Pathology and Anatomy
HOSOMI, H., Ethics and Bioethics
HOSONO, R., Neurobiology
IKUTA, M., Human Activity Analysis
INAGAKI, M., Fundamental Nursing and Division of Health Science
IZUMI, K., Gerontological and Rehabilitation Nursing
KARASAWA, T., Bacterial Pathogenesis
KAWAHARA, E., Pathology
KAWAI, K., Radiopharmaceutical Chemistry
KIDO, T., Occupational and Environmental Health
KIKUCHI, Y., Radiation Oncology
KIMURA, R., Child Development and Paediatric Nursing
KOJIMA, K., Medical Electronics and Information Sciences
KOSHIDA, K., Medical Radiation Protection
KOYAMA, Y., Psychiatry and Neuropsychology
MIZUKAMI, Y., Radiation Pathology
NAKASHIMA, H., Bioinformatics
NAKATANI, T., Anatomy and Biology of Cutaneous Wound
NEMOTO, T., Medical Engineering, Bioengineering, Biomedical Measurement
NOTOYA, M., Neuropsychology and Speech Pathology
OGIWARA, S., Physical Therapy
OHTAKE, S., Haematology and Oncology
SAEKI, K., Community Health Nursing
SAKAI, A., Maternal and Child Nursing and Midwifery
SANADA, S., Radiological Technology and Medical Physics
SEKI, H., Child and Adolescent Health
SHIMADA, K., Women's Health and Midwifery
SHOSAKU, T., Neurophysiology
SOMEYA, F., Rehabilitation Medicine
SUZUKI, M., Neuroradiology
TACHINO, K., Rehabilitation Medicine
TAKATA, S., Clinical Physiology
TAKAYAMA, T., Nuclear Medicine Technology
TANAKA, J., Virology
YACHIE, A., Immunology and Host Defence

Graduate School of Medical Science (13-1 Takara-machi, Kanazawa, Ishikawa; tel. (76) 265-2100; fax (76) 234-4202):

FUJIWARA, K., Human Movement and Health
FUKUDA, R., Molecular Genetics (Dept. of Biochemistry)
FURUKAWA, M., Otorhinolaryngology, Head and Neck Surgery
HASHIMOTO, T., Laboratory Medicine
HIGASHIDA, H., Biophysical Genetics
ICHIMURA, H., Viral Infection and International Health
INABA, H., Emergency Medical Science (Department of Emergency and Critical Care Medicine)
INOUE, M., Molecular Reproductive Biology
ISEKI, S., Histology and Embryology
KANEKO, S., Cancer Gene Regulation, Gastroenterology and Nephrology
KANO, M., Cellular Neurophysiology
KATO, S., Molecular Neurobiology
KOIZUMI, S., Angiogenesis and Vascular Development (Department of Paediatrics)
KOSHINO, Y., Psychiatry and Neurobiology
MATSUI, O., Radiology

NAKANISHI, Y., Molecular and Cellular Biochemistry

NAKANUMA, Y., Morpho-Functional Pathology (Department of Human Pathology)

NAKAO, S., Cellular Transplantation Biology (Haemato-oncology and Respiratory Medicine)

NAMIKI, M., Integrative Cancer Therapy and Urology

OGAWA, S., Biotargeting

OGINO, K., Environmental and Preventive Medicine

OHSHIMA, T., Forensic and Social Environmental Medicine

OOI, A., Molecular and Cellular Pathology

SAIJOH, K., Environmental and Molecular Bio-informatics

SHIMIZU, T., Bacteriology

SUGIYAMA, K., Ophthalmology

TAKEHARA, K., Angiogenesis and Connective Tissue Metabolism (Department of Dermatology)

TAKUWA, Y., Molecular Vascular Physiology

TANAKA, S., Anatomy and Neuroembryology

TOMITA, K., Restorative Medicine of Neuromusculoskeletal System (Department of Orthopaedic Surgery)

TONAMI, N., Biotracer Medicine (Department of Nuclear Medicine)

WATANABE, G., Thoracic, Cardiovascular and General Surgery (Department of Surgery I)

YAMADA, M., Neurology and Neurobiology of Ageing

YAMAMOTO, E., Oral and Maxillofacial Surgery

YAMAMOTO, H., Biochemistry and Molecular Vascular Biology

YAMAMOTO, K., Organ Function Restoratology (Department of Anaesthesiology and Intensive Care Medicine)

YOKOI, T., Drug Metabolism and Molecular Toxicology

YOKOTA, T., Stem Cell Biology

YOSHIMOTO, T., Molecular and Medical Pharmacology

Graduate School of Natural Science and Technology (tel. (76) 264-6821; fax (76) 234-6844):

ADACHI, M., Optical Metrology

ANDO, T., Biophysics

AOKI, K., Theoretical Physics

ARAI, S., Petrology

CHIKATA, Y., Bridge Maintenance Management

ENDO, K., Theoretical Chemistry

FUJIMAGARI, T., Mathematical Analysis

FUJISHITA, H., Quantum Physics of Condensed Matter

FUJIWARA, N., Systems and Control

FUKUMORI, Y., Physiological Chemistry

FUNADA, T., Vehicle Automation

FURUMOTO, M., Geophysics

HASHIMOTO, H., Visual Communication, Video Coding, Multimedia Processing

HATANE, I., Numerical Analysis, Computational Physics and Mathematics

HAYAKAWA, K., Hygienic Chemistry

HAYASHI, Y., Separation Engineering

HIRAO, M., Production Engineering

HIROSE, Y., Computational Mechanics

HIWATARI, Y., Theory of Material Physics

HOJO, A., Strength of Materials

HONJO, T., Analytical Chemistry

ICHINOSE, T., Functional Analysis

IKEDA, O., Electrochemistry

INOMATA, K., Organic Chemistry

ISHIBASHI, H., Synthetic Organic Chemistry

ISHIDA, H., Coastal Engineering

ISHIWATARI, A., Geology and Petrology

ISOBE, K., Inorganic Chemistry

ITO, H., Differential Equations

ITO, S., Discrete Dynamical System and its Application

ITO, T., Algebraic Combinatorics

IWAHARA, M., Power Electronics, Applied Magnetics

IWATA, Y., Dynamics of Machinery

KAJIKAWA, Y., Structural Engineering

KAMIYA, Y., Robotics

KANJIN, Y., Harmonic Analysis

KANOH, S., Synthetic Polymer Chemistry

KASUE, A., Geometry

KATO, M., Stratigraphy and Palaeontology

KAWAKAMI, M., Urban and Regional Planning

KIHARA, K., Mineralogy and Crystallography

KIMATA, N., Infrastructure Planning, System Simulation

KIMURA, H., Artificial Intelligence

KIMURA, K., Drug Management and Policies

KIMURA, S., Fluid Mechanics and Thermal Sciences

KINOSHITA, H., Organic Chemistry

KITAGAWA, K., Mechanical Properties of Engineering Materials

KITAGAWA, M., Deformation and Strength of Man-made and Naturally Produced Materials

KITAURA, M., Earthquake Engineering

KODAMA, A., Geometry

KOMURA, A., Electrochemistry

KUBO, J., Theoretical Physics

KUMEDA, M., Electronic Materials

KUNIMOTO, K., Bio-organic Chemistry, Environmental Technology

MAEGAWA, K., Structural Engineering

MAGAI, T., Defects in Solids

MASUYA, H., Structural Engineering

MATSUDA, Y., Integrated Circuits

MATSUMOTO, T., Pile Foundations, Pile Dynamics, Numerical Analysis

MATSUNAGA, T., Molecular Human Genetics

MATSUURA, K., Instrumentation by Image Processing

MIKAGE, M., Herbal Medicine and Natural Resources

MIYAGISHI, S., Applied Physical Chemistry

MIYAJIMA, M., Earthquake Engineering

MIYAKAWA, T., Partial Differential Equations

MONZEN, R., Metallic Materials

MORI, S., Heat and Mass Transfer

MORIMOTO, A., Electronic Materials

MOTOI, M., Organic Chemistry of Polymers

MUKAI, C., Pharmaceutical and Organic Chemistry

MURAKAMI, T., Astrophysics

MURAMOTO, K., Image Information Systems

NAGANO, I., Radio Wave Engineering

NAKAGAKI, R., Physical Chemistry

NAKAMOTO, Y., Polymer Chemistry

NAKANISHI, T., Radiochemistry

NAKAO, S., Applied Mathematics

NAKAYAMA, K., Adaptive Systems

NAOE, S., Optical Properties of Materials

NISHIKAWA, K., Digital Signal Processing

NISHIKAWA, K., Theoretical Chemistry

NITTA, K., Polymer Physics

ODA, J., Bionic Design

OHASHI, N., Molecular Physics

OHGISHI, M., Cognitive Engineering

OHKUMA, S., Biochemistry and Molecular Cell Biology

OHTA, T., Pharmacognosy and Chemistry of Natural Products

OKUNO, M., Mineralogy and Non-crystalline Material Science

OMATA, S., Partial Differential Equations and Numerical Analysis

OTANI, Y., Aerosol Technology

SAITOU, M., Computational Materials Science

SAKURAI, S., Developmental Biology

SAKURAI, T., Biochemistry

SATO, H., Non-linear Vibration

SATO, Y., Organic Physical Chemistry

SEKI, H., Environmental Engineering

SEKIZAKI, M., Physical Chemistry of Crystals

SENDA, H., Coordination Chemistry

SHIMADA, K., Clinical Analytical Sciences

SHINTAKU, S., Textile Machinery

SOMEI, M., Chemistry

SUGANO, T., Algebra

SUZUKI, H., Solid–State Physics

SUZUKI, M., Coordination Chemistry

SUZUKI, N., Holistic Pharmacotherapy

TAGO, Y., Computational Science

TAKAHASHI, K., Photo-function Material Chemistry

TAKAMIYA, S., Microwave/Optoelectronic Semiconductor Devices

TAKANOBU, S., Stochastic Analysis

TAKAYAMA, J., Traffic Engineering and Transport Planning

TAKIMOTO, A., Heat and Mass Transfer, Energy Conversion and Environmental Conservation

TAMAI, N., River Engineering, River Planning

TAMURA, K., Chemical Engineering Fundamentals and Thermodynamics

TANAKA, I., History of Science and Technology

TAZAKI, K., Environmental Earth Science

TORII, K., Civil Engineering Materials

TSUCHIYA, M., Mathematics (Theory of Stochastic Processes)

TSUJI, A., Innovative Pharmaceutics

UCHIYAMA, Y., Tribology (Friction and Wear Mechanisms of Rubbers and Plastics)

UEDA, K., Phylogenetics

UEDA, K., Separation and Analytical Chemistry

UEDA, T., Precision Machining, Laser Processing

UENO, H., Fluid Machinery, Fluid Power

UESUGI, Y., Plasma Science, Fusion Plasma Engineering

USUDA, M., Materials Working

YAJIMA, T., Ecology

YAMADA, K., Neuropsychopharmacology

YAMADA, M., Combinatorics

YAMADA, M., Opto-electronics

YAMADA, T., Polymer Processing, Reaction Engineering and Phase Equilibria

YAMADA, Y., Mechanical Properties of Materials

YAMAKOSHI, K., Biomedical Engineering

YAMANE, S., Computer Science

YAMAZAKI, K., Structural Optimization

YATOMI, C., Non-linear Continuum Mechanics

YOKOI, T., Drug Metabolism and Molecular Toxicology

YONEDA, Y., Molecular Pharmacology

YONEYAMA, T., Metal Forming, Machine Design

Law School (tel. (76) 264-5968; fax (76) 234-4167):

ATARASHI, M., Constitutional Law

FURITSU, T., Criminal Law

HASEGAWA, T., Civil Law

HATA, Y., Comparative Constitutional Law

HIGASHI, I., Criminal Procedure

HOSOKAWA, T., Administrative Law

KASHIMI, Y., Civil Law

NAKAJIMA, F., Commercial Law

NAKO, M., Labour Law

NISHIMURA, S., Criminal Law

NOSAKA, Y., Civil Law

OJIMA, S., Family Law

SATO, M., Criminal Procedure

TAJIMA, J., Civil Law

Environmental Preservation Center (tel. (76) 234-6893; fax (76) 234-6895):

OHTA, T., Chemical Engineering Thermodynamics

Extension Institute (tel. (76) 264-5271; fax (76) 234-4045):

HATTORI, E., Adult Education (Life-long Education), Extramural Education

Foreign Language Institute (tel. (76) 264-5760; fax (76) 264-5993):

AISAWA, K., German
KANEKO, Y., German
KIKUCHI, E., German
KUWANO, H., English
MIKAMI (KIMURA), J., French
OYABU, K., English
SANBAI, R., English
SAWADA, S., English
WATANABE, A., English
YABUCHI, T., Chinese

Health Service Center (tel. (76) 264-5251; fax (76) 234-4044; e-mail nakabaya@kenroku .kanazawa-u.ac.jp):

NAKABAYASHI, H., Endocrinology and Metabolism

Information Media Center (tel. (76) 264-6911; fax (76) 234-6918):

SHAKO, M., Network Security
SUZUKI, T., Computational Physics, Particle Physics

Institute for Nature and Environmental Technology (tel. (76) 264-6141; fax (76) 234-4016):

IWASAKA, Y.
KASHIWAYA, K., Hydro-geomorphology
KIMURA, S., Heat Transfer and Fluid Mechanics
KOMURA, K., Environmental Radioactivity
NAKAMURA, K., Ecology
SASAYAMA, Y., Biodiversity
SHIMIZU, N., Bioengineering
YAMADA, S., Magnetic Technology
YAMAMOTO, M., Nuclear Geochemistry

International Student Center (tel. (76) 264-5188; fax (76) 234-4043):

MATSUSHITA, M., Psychology
MIURA, K., Japanese Language Education
OKAZAWA, T., Insect Ecology

Research Center for Higher Education (tel. (76) 264-5837; fax (76) 234-4172):

AONO, T., Medical Law
HAYATA, Y., Evaluation

University Hospital (13-1 Takara-machi, Kanazawa, Ishikawa; tel. (76) 265-2000; fax (76) 234-4320):

KOIZUMI, J., Department of General Medicine
MIYAMOTO, K., Department of Hospital Pharmacy

KITAMI INSTITUTE OF TECHNOLOGY

165 Koen-cho, Kitami, Hokkaido 090-8507
Telephone: (157) 26-9106
Fax: (157) 26-9117
Internet: www.kitami-it.ac.jp
Founded 1960
Independent
Academic year: April to March (2 semesters)
Pres.: HIDEYUKI TSUNEMOTO
Vice-Pres: KOICHI AYUTA, NOBUO TAKAHASHI
Dir of Admin.: AKIHIRO SHIBAZAKI
Library Dir: TOSHIYUKI OSHIMA

Number of teachers: 150 full-time
Number of students: 2,103

Publication: *Memoirs of Kitami Institute of Technology*.

KOBE UNIVERSITY

1-1 Rokkodai-cho, Nada-ku, Kobe 657-8501, Hyogo
Telephone: (78) 881-1212
E-mail: www-admin@kobe-u.ac.jp
Internet: www.kobe-u.ac.jp
Founded 1902
Independent
Academic year: April to March
Pres.: TOMOYUKI NOGAMI
Dirs: KUNIO SAKAMOTO, MASAHIRO TAKASAKI, MASAYUKI SUZUKI, OSAMI NISHIDA, SADAO KAMIDONO, SHIGEYUKI MAYAMA, SHINZO KITAMURA, SHOJI NISHIJIMA
Dir of Admin.: KUNIO SAKAMOTO
Library Dir: KENICHI SUDO
Library of 3,365,000 vols
Number of teachers: 1,674 full-time
Number of students: 17,598

Publications: *Law Review* (1 a year), *Economic Review* (1 a year), *Business Research* (irregular), *Journal of Mathematics* (2 a year), *Kobe Journal of Medical Sciences* (6 a year), *Bulletin of Allied Medical Sciences* (1 a year), *Memoirs of the Graduate School of Science and Technology* (1 a year), *Journal of International Cooperation Studies* (3 a year), *Economic and Business Review* (1 a year), *Journal of Economics and Business Administration* (12 a year), *Kobe Economic and Business Review* (1 a year)

DEANS

Faculty of Agriculture: CHIHARU NAKAMURA
Faculty and Graduate School of Letters: TAKAJI MATSUSHIMA
Faculty of Cross-cultural Studies: SATOSHI MUNAKATA
Faculty of Human Development: SUSUMU WADA
Faculty and Graduate School of Law: EIJI TAKIZAWA
Faculty and Graduate School of Economics: TAKASHI NAKATANI
Faculty and Graduate School of Business Administration: HISAKATSU SAKURAI
School and Graduate School of Medicine: SAKAN MAEDA
Faculty of Engineering: HIROMOTO USUI
Faculty of Maritime Sciences: KINZO INOUE
Faculty of Science: HIROSHI TAKEDA
Graduate School of Cultural Studies and Human Science: SUSUMU WADA
Graduate School of Humanities and Social Sciences: TAKAJI MATSUSHIMA
Graduate School of International Cooperation Studies: YUTAKA KATAYAMA
Graduate School of Science and Technology: HIDEKI FUKUDA
Research Institute for Economics and Business Administration: HIDETOSHI YAMAJI

PROFESSORS

Biosignal Research Center (tel. (78) 803-5332; fax (78) 803-5972; e-mail drkikaku@ ofc.kobe.u.ac.jp; internet inherit:biosig .kobe.u.ac.jp/biosignal/english/index.html):

KIKKAWA, U., Biochemistry
ONO, Y., Biology of Living Functions
SAITO, N., Pharmacology
YONEZAWA, K., Biochemistry

Faculty of Agriculture (1-1 Rokkodai-cho, Nada-ku, Kobe 657-8501; tel. (78) 803-5921; fax (78) 803-5931; e-mail ashomu@ofc.kobe-u .ac.jp; internet www.ans.kobe-u.ac.jp/indexe .html):

AE, N., Soil Science and Plant Nutrition
AOKI, K., Applied Biofunctional Chemistry
ASHIDA, H., Applied Biofunctional Chemistry
HASEGAWA, S., Animal Nutrition, Morphology and Microbiology

HATA, T., Regional and Environmental Engineering
HORIO, H., Biosystems Engineering
HOSAKA, K., Food Resources Education and Research Centre
HOSHI, N., Animal Nutrition, Morphology and Microbiology
INAGAKI, N., Horticultural Science
KAKO, T., Food and Environmental Economics
KAMIJIMA, O., Plant Breeding and Production Science
KANAZAWA, K., Biofunctional Molecules
KAWAMURA, T., Biosystems Engineering
MAYAMA, S., Plant Protection
MIYAKE, H., Biofunctional Chemistry
MIYANO, T., Animal Breeding and Reproduction
MIZUNO, M., Plant Resource Science
MUKAI, F., Animal Breeding and Reproduction
NAITO, T., Plant Protection
NAKAMURA, C., Plant Genetics and Physiology
NAKANISHI, T., Horticultural Science
OHNO, T., Biofunctional Molecules
OHSAWA, R., Animal Science
OKAYAMA, T., Applied Biofunctional Chemistry
SHIMIZU, A., Animal Nutrition, Morphology and Microbiology
SUGIMOTO, T., Genetics and Physiology
SUGIMOTO, Y., Applied Biofunctional Chemistry
TAKADA, O., Food and Environmental Economics
TANAKA, T., Regional and Environmental Science
TERAI, H., Horticultural Science
TOYODA, K., Biosystems Engineering
UCHIDA, K., Regional and Environmental Science
UCHIDA, N., Plant Breeding and Production Science
YAMAGATA, H., Biofunctional Molecules
YASUDA, T., Plant Genetics and Physiology

Faculty of Cross-cultural Studies (1-2-1 Tsurukabuto, Nada-ku, Kobe 657-8501; tel. (78) 803-7515; fax (78) 803-7509; e-mail shomudai@ofc.kobe-u.ac.jp; internet ccs.cla .kobe-u.ac.jp/kohou/eigo/):

AMANO, K., Comtemporary Culture and Society Division
CHO, S., Comtemporary Culture and Society Division
FUJINO, K., Contemporary Culture and Society Division
GODA, T., Intercultural Communication Division
HAYASHI, H., Human Communication and Information Science Division
ICHIDA, Y., Comtemporary Culture and Society Division
ISHIHARA, K., Area Studies Division
ISHIKAWA, T., Area Studies Division
ISHIZUKA, H., Area Studies Division
KABURAGI, M., Human Communication and Information Science Division
KAGEYAMA, S., Area Studies Division
KIBA, H., Intercultural Communication Division
KINOSHITA, M., Area Studies Division
KOMURASAKI, S., Intercultural Communication Division
LU, X., Area Studies Division
MIKAMI, T., Contemporary Culture and Society Division
MIKIHARA, H., Comtemporary Culture and Society Division
MIURA, N., Intercultural Communication Division
MIZUGUCHI, S., Human Communication and Information Science Division
MIZUTA, K., Comtemporary Culture and Society Division

MORIMOTO, M., Intercultural Communication Division
MORISHITA, J., Human Communication and Information Science Division
MUNAKATA, S., Comtemporary Culture and Society Division
NOTANI, K., Intercultural Communication Division
OHTSUKI, K., Human Communication and Information Science Division
SADANOBU, T., Human Communication and Information Science Division
SAKAMOTO, C., Area Studies Division
SAKANO, T., Intercultural Communication Division
SASAE, O., Area Studies Division
SHIBATA, Y., Intercultural Communication Division
SONE, H., Area Studies Division
SUDO, K., Area Studies Division
SUZAKI, S., Area Studies Division
TANIMOTO, S., Area Studies Division
TERAUCHI, N., Area Studies Division
TODA, M., Intercultural Communication Division
UCHIDA, M., Intercultural Communication Division
UOZUMI, K., Contemporary Culture and Society Division
UTSUKI, N., Human Communication and Information Science Division
WANG, K., Area Studies Division
YAMAZAKI, Y., Contemporary Culture and Society Division
YOKOYAMA, K., Area Studies Divison
YOSHIDA, N., Contemporary Culture and Society Division
YOSHIOKA, M., Intercultural Communication Division

Faculty of Engineering (tel. (78) 803-6333; fax (78) 803-6396; e-mail kousyomu@ofc.kobe-u.ac.jp; internet www.eng.kobe-u.ac.jp/index.html):

ADACHI, H., Theory and History of Architecture
DEKI, S., Applied Inorganic Chemistry
FUJII, S., Energy Conversion Engineering
FUJITA, I., Hydraulic Engineering
HAYASHI, S., Mathematical Theory of Programming
HIRASAWA, S., Heat Transfer and Thermal Engineering
KAKUDA, Y., Mathematical Logic and Mathematical Design Theory
KANKI, H., Machine Dynamics and Control
KAWATANI, M., Structural Dynamics
KAYA, N., Space Solar Power Systems
KIKYO, H., Mathematical Logic and Computer Science
KONDO, A., Biochemical Engineering
KURODA, K., Transportation Engineering and Infrastructure Planning
MASUDA, S., Algorithms and Data Structures
MATSUYAMA, H., Membrane Technology
MICHIOKU, K., River Hydraulics
MITANI, I., Ultimate Design of Steel and Composite Structures
MIYOSHI, T., Quantum Electronics
MORII, M., Information Theory, Computer Networks, Internet Security and Cryptography
MORIMOTO, M., Environmental Acoustics
MORIWAKI, T., Intelligent Manufacturing Systems and Ultraprecision Machining
MORIYAMA, M., Architectural and Urban Environmental Engineering
NAGAO, T., Design and Performance of Building Structures
NAKAGIRI, S., Control and Identification of Distributed Systems
NAKAI, Y., Fatigue and Fracture of Engineering Materials
NAMBU, T., Control of PDE
NISHINO, T., Polymer Chemistry

NUMA, M., VLSI Design and CAD
OGAWA, M., Semiconductor Electronics
OHI, K., Quake-proof Structural Engineering
OHMAE, N., Micro- and Nano-Tribology and Surface Engineering
OHMURA, N., Transport Science
OHTA, Y., Control Engineering
OKUBO, M., Polymer Colloid Chemistry
OSUKA, K., Advanced Control Engineering
SHIBUYA, S., Geotechnical Engineering
SHIGEMURA, T., Urban and Architectural Design
SHIOZAKI, Y., Urban and Housing Study
SHIRASE, K., Autonomous Machine Tools and Intelligent Manufacturing Systems
TADA, Y., Optimum Design of Systems
TAKADA, S., Earthquake Engineering
TAKENAKA, N., Multiphase Flow Engineering
TAKI, K., Computer Science and Engineering
TOMITA, Y., Solid Mechanics
TOMIYAMA, A., Energy and Environmental Engineering
TSUKAMOTO, M., Computer Systems and Networking
TSURUYA, S., Catalytic Chemistry
UEDA, Y., Applied Physical Chemistry
USUI, H., Non-Newtonian Fluid Mechanics
WADA, O., Optoelectronic Materials and Devices
YASAKA, Y., Plasma Science and Power Engineering
YASUDA, C., Architectural Planning and Urban Design
YASUDA, H., Nanomaterials Science
YOSHIMOTO, M., VLSI System Engineering
YOSHIMURA, T., Applied Optics and Image Processing

Faculty of Letters (tel. (78) 803-5591; fax (78) 803-5589; e-mail lsoumu@lit.kobe-u.ac.jp; internet www.lit.kobe-u.ac.jp):

DONOHASHI, A., Art History
EDAGAWA, M., French Literature
FUJI, M., Sociology
FUJITA, H., Geography
FUKUNAGA, S., Japanese Literature and Language
HASEGAWA, K., Geography
HISHIKAWA, E., British and American Literature
IWASAKI, N., Sociology
KAMATANI, T., Chinese Language and Literature
KAZASHI, N., Philosophy
KUBOZONO, H., Linguistics
MATSUDA, H., French Literature
MATSUDA, T., Philosophy
MATSUMOTO, Y., Linguistics
MATSUSHIMA, T., Psychology
MOHRI, A., European and American History
MORI, N., Asian History
NAGANO, J., Art Theory
NISHIMITSU, Y., Linguistics
OGURA, T., Psychology
OHTSURU, A., European and American History
RINBARA, S., Japanese Literature and Language
SAITO, S., British and American Literature
SASAKI, M., Sociology
SUZUKI, Y., Japanese Literature and Language
TAKAHASHI, M., Japanese History
YAMAGUCHI, K., German Literature
YAMAMOTO, M., Philosophy
YUI, K., Sociology

Faculty of Human Development (3-11 Tsurukabuto, Nada-ku, Kobe 657-8501; tel. (78) 803-7905; fax (78) 803-7939; e-mail info@h.kobe-u.ac.jp; internet www.h.kobe-u.ac.jp):

AMAKAWA, T., Sciences for the Natural Environment

AOKI, T., Human Life Environment
ASANO, S., Studies of Social Environment
EBINA, K., Sciences for the Natural Environment
ENOMOTO, T., Sciences for the Natural Environment
FUNAKI, T., Educational Science
FUNAKOSHI, S., Childhood Development and Education
GOMI, K., Childhood Development and Education
HAMAGUCHI, H., Human Life Environment
HIRAKAWA, K., Sports Science
HIRAYAMA, Y., Human Life Environment
HIROKI, K., Childhood Development and Education
HOUNOKI, K., Adult Learning
ICHIHASHI, H., Human Life Environment
IMATANI, N., Studies of Social Environment
INAGAKI, N., Educational Science
ISHIKAWA, T., Health Education
ITO, K., Development Psychology
IWAI, M., Music
JOH, H., Human Life Environment
KAWABATA, T., Health Education
KAWABE, S., Sports Science
KISHIMOTO, H., Childhood Development and Education
MARUYA, N., Human Life Environment
MIKAMI, K., Educational Science
NAKABAYASHI, T., Developmental Psychology
NAKAGAWA, K., Sciences for the Natural Environment
NAKAMURA, K., Developmental Psychology
NAKAYAMA, S., Art and Design
NINOMIYA, A., Studies of Social Environment
ODA, T., Behavioural Development Studies
ODAKA, N., Art and Design
OGAWA, M., Educational Science
OKADA, S., Behavioural Development Studies
SAIDA, Y., Music
SAITO, K., Sciences for the Natural Environment
SATO, M., Developmental Psychology
SHIBA, M., Sports Performance
SHIRAKURA, T., Mathematics and Computer Studies
SUEMOTO, M., Adult Learning
SUGINO, K., Developmental Psychology
TAINOSHO, Y., Sciences for the Natural Environment
TAKAHASHI, J., Mathematics and Computer Studies
TAKAHASHI, M., Mathematics and Computer Studies
TAKAHASHI, T., Mathematics and Computer Studies
TANAKA, Y., Health Education
TERAKADO, Y., Sciences for the Natural Environment
TSUCHIYA, M., Educational Science
TSUKAWAKI, J., Art and Design
UEZI, S., Sciences for the Natural Environment
WADA, S., Studies of Social Environment
WAKAO, Y., Music
YAMAGUCHI, Y., Sport Sciences
YAMASAKI, T., Studies of Social Environment
YANAGIDA, Y., Sport Sciences
YANO, S., Human Life Environment

Faculty of Maritime Sciences (5-1-1 Fukaeminamimachi, Higashinada-ku, Kobe 658-0022; tel. (78) 431-6206; fax (78) 431-6355; e-mail mssoumu@ofc.kobe-u.ac.jp; internet www.maritime.kobe-u.ac.jp):

AZUKIZAWA, T., Marine Mechatronics
FUKUDA, K., Maritime Energy Engineering
FUKUOKA, T., Machine Design Engineering
FUKUSHI, K., Analytical Chemistry
FURUSHO, M., Seamanship and Traffic Psychology at Sea

HASHIMOTO, M., Internal Combustion Engines
HAYASHI, Y., Ship Navigation
IMAI, A., Logistics Planning
INOUE, K., Marine Traffic Engineering and Maritime Safety Management
INOUE, T., Network and Communication Systems Engineering
ISHIDA, H., Marine Meteorology
ISHIDA, K., Disaster Science
ISHIDA, T., Marine Power and System Engineering
ISOGAI, T., Statistical Science and Quality Management
KATO, E., Functional Polymer Materials Science
KIMURA, R., Acoustical Engineering and Maintenance Engineering
KITAMURA, A., Particle Beam Engineering
KOBAYASHI, E., Maritime Science and Naval Architecture
KOGUCHI, N., Navigation
KOZAI, K., Satellite Oceanography
MARUO, K., Partial Differential Equations
NISHIDA, O., Energy and Environmental Engineering
NISHIO, S., Naval Architecture
NISHIOKA, T., Fracture Mechanics, Computational Mechanics, Experimental Mechanics
ODA, K., Radiation Dosimetry and Applications
OTSUJI, T.
SADAKANE, H., Naval Architecture
SAKAMOTO, K., Power Electronics
SATO, M., Material Chemistry for Transportation
SHIOTANI, S., Numerical Ship Hydrodynamics
SIMADA, H., Cognitive Science
SUGITA, H., Management for Marine Power Plants
SUZUKI, S., Marine Traffic Laws
TAKAHASHI, R., Statistics
TANAKA, S., Fluid Mechanics of Engineering
YAMAMURA, S., Information Engineering
YOSHIDA, S., Shipping Economics

Faculty of Science (tel. (78) 803-5761; fax (78) 803-5770; e-mail rishomu@ofc.kobe.ac.jp; internet www.sci.kobe-u.ac.jp):

FUKE, K., Physical Chemistry
FUKUDA, Y., Optical Physics
FUKUYAMA, K., Analysis
GUNJI, Y., Planetary Science
HARIMA, H., Condensed Matter Theory
HAYASHI, F., Biology of Living Functions
HAYASHI, M., Organic Chemistry
HIGUCHI, Y., Applied Mathematics
HIMENO, S., Inorganic Chemistry
IKEDA, H., Applied Mathematics
KADONO, Y., Biology of Living Structures
LIM, C. S., High Energy Theory
MATSUDA, T., Planetary Science
MIMURA, T., Biology of Living Structures
MIYATA, T., Earth Science
NAKAGAWA, Y., Planetary Science
NAKAMURA, N., Planetary Science
NAKANISHI, Y., Algebra and Geometry
NORO, M., Applied Mathematics
ONISHI, H., Physical Chemistry
OTOFUJI, Y., Earth Science
SAITO, M., Algebra and Geometry
SAKAMOTO, H., Biology of Living Functions
SASAKI, T., Algebra and Geometry
SATO, H., Earth Science
SETSUNE, J., Inorganic Chemistry
TAKANO, K., Analysis
TAKAYAMA, N., Analysis
TAKEDA, H., Particle Physics
TOMEOKA, K., Planetary Science
TSUCHIYA, T., Biology of Living Functions
WADA, S., Condensed Matter Physics
WATANABE, K., Biology of Living Structures
YAMADA, Y., Analysis

YAMAMURA, K., Organic Chemistry
YAMAZAKI, T., Algebra and Geometry

Graduate School of Business Administration (2-1 Rokkodai-cho, Nada-ku, Kobe, 657-8501; tel. (78) 803-7256; fax (78) 803-6969; e-mail bwebmstr@kobe-u.ac.jp; internet www.b.kobe-u.ac.jp):

DEI, F., International Economics, International Investments
FUJIWARA, K., Money and Financial Systems
GOTOH, M., Financial Reporting and Accounting Systems
HARADA, T., Industrial Organization
ISHII, J., Marketing Management and Business Strategy
KAGONO, T., Business Strategy and Corporate Behaviour
KANAI, T., Organizational Behaviour
KATO, H., Finance
KATO, Y., Management Accounting
KOGA, T., International Accounting
KOKUBU, K., Social and Environmental Accounting
KOMBAYASHI, N., Human Resource Management
KOU, L., Marketing
KUTSUNA, K., Entrepreneurial Finance
KUWAHARA, T., Business History
MARUYAMA, M., Applied Microeconomics, Distribution Systems
MATSUO, H., Supply Chain Management, Production Planning and Scheduling
MIZUTANI, F., Public Utility Economics and Regulatory Economics
NAITO, F., Financial Accounting and Auditing
NAKANO, T., Accounting Systems and History
OGAWA, S., Marketing
SAKAKIBARA, S., Corporate Finance and Portfolio Management
SAKASHITA, A., Organizational Behaviour and Corporate Culture
SAKURAI, H., Financial Accounting, Financial Statement Analysis
SHOJI, K., Transport Economics and Policy
TAKAO, A., Insurance Industry Analysis
TAKASHIMA, K., Marketing and Distribution Systems
TANI, T., Management Accounting and Control

Graduate School of Economics (2-1 Rokkodai-cho, Nada-ku, Kobe 657-8501; tel. (78) 803-7246; fax (78) 803-7293; e-mail esoumu@ofc.kobe-u.ac.jp; internet www.econ.kobe-u.ac.jp):

ADACHI, M., Social Policy
AMANO, M., Modern Japanese Economic History
FUJITA, S., International Monetary System
FUKUDA, W., Economic System Theory
HAGIWARA, T., Contemporary Technology Theory
HAMORI, S., Statistical Analysis of Economic Time Series Data
HARA, M., International Investment Theory
HARUYAMA, T., Economic Growth Theory
IRITANI, J., Public Finance Policy
ISHIGURO, K., International Politics and Economics
ISHIKAWA, M., Environmental Economics
JINUSHI, T., American Economy
KATO, H., Chinese Economy
KUBO, H., European Economy
MARUYA, R., Theory of Economic Policy
MATSUBAYASHI, Y., Empirical Analysis of International Macroeconomy
MITANI, N., Labour Economics
NAKAMURA, T., Macroeconomics, Investment Theory
NAKANISHI, N., International Economics
NAKATANI, T., Macrodynamic Theory
OHKUBO, H., Monetary Policy

OHTANI, K., Theory of Statistical Inference
OKUNISHI, T., European Economic History
OSHIO, T., Social Security
SHIGETOMI, K., Economic History of Modern Britain
TAKAHASHI, S., World Economic Geography
TAKIGAWA, Y., Monetary Economics
TANAKA, Y., Theory of Economic Structure
TANIZAKI, H., On Estimation and Test in Simulation-base Econometrics
UEMIYA, S., History of Economic Theory
URANAGASE, T., Japanese Economic History
YAMAGUCHI, M., Agricultural Policy
YANAGAWA, T., Industrial Organization
YOSHII, M., Comparative Economics

Graduate School of Cultural Studies and Human Science (3-1-1 Tsurukabuto, Nada-ku, Kobe 657-8501; tel. (78) 803-7905; fax (78) 803-7939; e-mail inkouhou@ccs.cla.kobe-u.ac.jp; internet www.cla.kobe-u.ac.jp/sojinka):

HARIMA, T., Clinical Psychology
HOUNOKI, K., Human and Community Empowerment
KAWABATA, T., Human and Community Empowerment
SUEMOTO, M., Human and Community Empowerment

Graduate School of Humanities and Social Sciences (1-1 Rokkodai-cho, Nada-ku, Kobe 657-8501; tel. (78) 803-5591; fax (78) 803-5589; e-mail lsoumo@lit.kobe-u.ac.jp; internet www.lit.kobe-u.ac.jp/index_bunka.html):

IWASAKI, N., Theory of Social Risks

Graduate School of International Cooperation Studies (2-1 Rokkodai-cho, Nada-ku, Kobe 657-8501; tel. (78) 803-7265; fax (78) 803-7295; e-mail kokusomu@ofc.kobe-u.ac.jp; internet www.kobe-u.ac.jp/~gsics/indexj.html):

ALEXANDER, R. B., Endogenous Security
CHEN, K., Economic Development and Regional Inequality
FUKUI, S., Development Microeconomics
IGARASHI, M., International Law
KATAYAMA, Y., Political Development in Southeast Asia
KIMURA, K., Nation-building and State Formation in Korea
MATSUNAGA, N., International Trade and Economic Growth
MATSUNAMI, J., Comparative Study on Deregulation, Privatization and Local Government
MIZUNO, T., Review and Future Assessment on International Issues
NISHINA, K., Development Finance
OHTA, H., Applied Microeconomics
SHIBATA, A., International Law
SURUGA, T., Economic Development and Employment
TAKADA, H., Local Public Administration and Finance
TAKAHASHI, M., African Economics
TATEBAYASHI, M., Policy Activities of Political Elites in Japan
TOSA, H., Critical Theory and its Application in International Relations
UCHIDA, Y., Social Sector Management in Developing Countries
UENO, H., Transition Economy Policies

Graduate School of Law (2-1 Rokkodai-cho, Nada-ku, Kobe 657-850; tel. (78) 803-7232; fax (78) 803-7292; e-mail j1shomu@ofc.kobe-u.ac.jp; internet www.law.kobe-u.ac.jp):

AKASAKA, M., Constitutional Law
AMIYA, R., Western Political History
BABA, K., Sociology of Law
FUJIWARA, A., Japanese Legal History
HAMADA, F., Labour Law
HASUNUMA, K., Philosophy of Law

HATA, M., Civil Procedure
IIDA, F., Political Theory
INOUE, N., Constitutional Law
INOUE, Y., Intellectual Property Law
IOKIBE, M., Japanese Political History, Comparative Politics
ISHIKAWA, T., Professional Legal Education
ISOMURA, T., Civil Law
ITO, M., Comparative Politics
JI, W. D., Chinese Law, Comparative Studies in Legal Culture
KASHIMURA, S., Sociology of Law
KIKKAWA, G., International Relations
KOMURO, N., International Economic Law
KONDO, M., Commercial Law, Securities Regulation
KUBOTA, A., Civil Law
MARUYAMA, E., Anglo-American Law, Medical Law
MASUJIMA, K., International Relations
MORISHITA, T., Russian Law, Principles of Social Sciences
NAKAGAWA, T., Administrative Law
NAKANISHI, M., Civil Procedure
NAKANO, S., Private International Law, International Civil Procedure
NEGISHI, A., Economic Law
OSHIMA, S., Professional Legal Education
OTSUKA, H., Criminal Law
OUCHI, S., Labour Law
SAITO, A., International Trade Law, Private International Law
SAKAMOTO, S., International Law
SATO, H., Tax Law
SENSUI, F., Economic Law
SHINADA, Y., Political Data Analysis, Election System
SHITANI, M., Commercial Law
SUDO, M., Professional Legal Education
TAKIZAWA, E., Western Legal History, Roman Law
TEJIMA, Y., Civil and Medical Law
TSUKIMURA, T., International Relations
USHIMA, K., Criminal Law
YAMADA, S., Civil Law
YAMADA, T., Professional Legal Education
YAMAMOTO, H., Civil Procedure
YAMAMOTO, K., Civil Law
YASUNAGA, M., Civil Law
YONEMARU, T., Administrative Law
YUKIZAWA, K., Commercial Law, Commercial Transactions

Graduate School of Science and Technology (tel. (78) 803-5332; fax (78) 803-5349; e-mail drkikaku@ofc.kobe-u.ac.jp; internet www.scitec.kobe-u.ac.jp/english/index.html):

ABE, S., Function Control
ARAI, T., Information Mathematics
ASAKURA, Y., Space Formation Engineering
BOKU, S., Environmental Science of Bioresource Production
FUKUDA, H., Applied Molecular Assembly
KANAZAWA, Y., Bioresource and Energy Creation
KATO, S., Material Production Process Engineering
KITAGAWA, H., Relational Biosystems
KOJIMA, F., Structural Design
MAEKAWA, S., Bioinformation
MATSUSHITA, T., Fire Safety Engineering, Thermal Environmental Engineering in Building
MIYAKE, M., Biosystem Applications
MUKAI, T., Space and Planetary Materials
NAKAYAMA, A., Regional Environment
NANBA, T., Material Functions
NOUMI, M., Mathematical Structures
NOZAKI, M., Material Structures
ODANI, M., Urban Transportation Planning, Urban and Regional Planning
OHKAWA, T., Intelligent Bioinformatics
ONO, M., Food Marketing
SASAKI, M., Organic Chemistry
TABUCHI, M., Creation of Spatial Systems
TAKEDA, M., Molecular Cellular Science

TAKEUCHI, T., Molecular Structure and Function
TANAKA, S., Theoretical Life Science and Computational Molecular Biology
TAURA, T., Intelligent Artificial Systems
TSUBAKI, M., Functional Molecular Assembly
TSUTAHARA, M., Biological Resource Utilization
UEHARA, K., Media Technology and its Production
YAMANAKA, M., Earth Sciences

International Student Center (tel. (78) 803-5265; fax (78) 803-5289; e-mail ryugaku@ofc.kobe-u.ac.jp; internet www.kobe-u.ac.jp/~kisc):

NAKANISHI, Y., Education in Japanese Language
SEGUCHI, I., Intercultural and Transcultural Education

Medical Center for Student Health (tel. (78) 803-5245; fax (78) 803-5254; e-mail healthy@kobe-u.ac.jp; internet www.kobe-u.ac.jp/medicalc):

BABA, H., Internal Medicine, Biosignal Pathophysiology

Molecular Photoscience Research Center (tel. (78) 803-5761; fax (78) 803-5770; e-mail rishomu@ofc.kobe-u.ac.jp; internet www.kobe-u.ac.jp/mprc):

OHTA, H., Condensed Matter Physics
TOMINAGA, K., Condensed Phase Dynamics

Research Center for Environmental Genomics (tel. (78) 803-5332; fax (78) 803-5349; e-mail drkikaku@ofc.kobe-u.ac.jp; internet www.rceg.biosig.kobe-u.ac.jp/hpj.html):

FUKAMI, Y., Biology of Living Structures
NANMORI, T., Plant Molecular Biology
OONO, K., Plant Cell Biology

Research Center for Inland Seas (tel. (78) 803-5761; fax (78) 803-5770; e-mail rishomu@ofc.kobe-u.ac.jp; internet www.kobe-u.ac.jp/kurcis):

HYODO, M., Earth Science
KAWAI, H., Marine Biology
NAGATA, S., Environmental Biochemistry

Research Center for Urban Safety and Security (tel. (78) 803-6437; fax (78) 803-6394; e-mail rcuss@kobe-u.ac.jp; internet www.kobe-u.ac.jp/~tosi):

ARIKI, Y., Media Engineering
IIZUKA, A., Geo-environmental Engineering and Geoinformatics
ISHIBASHI, K., Seismotectonics
KAMAE, I., Health Informatics and Decision Sciences
OKIMURA, T., Slope Stability and Geotechnical Engineering
TANAKA, Y., Soft Ground Engineering and Earthquake Geotechnical Engineering

Research Institute for Economics and Business Administration (2-1 Rokkodai-cho, Nada-ku, Kobe 657-8501; tel. (78) 803-7270; fax (78) 803-7059; e-mail office@rieb.kobe-u.ac.jp; internet www.rieb.kobe-u.ac.jp):

GOTO, J., International Economy and Business
IGAWA, K., International Economy and Business
ISOBE, T., International Economy and Business
IZAWA, H., International Economy and Business
KAMIHIGASHI, T., Information Economy and Business
KATAYAMA, S., International Economy and Business
KOJIMA, K., Information Economy and Business
KONISHI, Y., Information Economy and Business

LEE, H., Information Economy and Business
MIYAO, R., RIEB Liaison Centre
NISHIJIMA, S., International Economy and Business
NOBEOKA, K., RIEB Liaison Centre
SHIMOMURA, K., Information Economy and Business
TOMITA, M., International Economy and Business
YAMAJI, H., Information Economy and Business

Research Institute for Higher Education (1-2-1- Tsurukabuto, Nada-ku, Kobe 657-8501; tel. (78) 803-7522; fax (78) 803-7539; e-mail dakaikei@ofc.kobe-u.ac.jp; internet www.kurihe.kobe-u.ac.jp):

KAWASHIMA, T., Sociology of Education
MAIYA, K., Experimental Psychology
YAMANOUCHI, K., Sociology of Education

School and Graduate School of Medicine (7-5-1 Kusunoki-cho, Chuo-ku, Kobe 650-0017; tel. (78) 382-5111; fax (78) 382-5050; e-mail webmst@med.kobe-u.ac.jp; internet www.med.kobe-u.ac.jp/welcomej.html):

AIBA, A., Cell Biology
AKITA, H., General Medical Science
ANDO, H., Basic Allied Medicine
AZUMA, T., Polygenic Disease Research
CHIHARA, K., Endocrinology; Metabolism, Neurology and Haematology; Oncology
FUJIMARA, M., Urulogy
FURUKAWA, H., Applied Occupational Therapy
GU, E., Advanced Medical Research and Treatment
HASHIMOTO, T., Basic Occupational Therapy
HAYASHI, Y., Molecular Medicine and Medical Genetics
HOTTA, H., Microbiology and Genomics
ISHII, N., Disaster and Emergency Medicine
ISHIKAWA, Y., Health Sciences and Basic Nursing
KASUGA, M., Diabetes, Digestive and Kidney Diseases
KATAOKA, T., Molecular Biology
KAWABATA, M., International Health
KAWAGUCHI, Y., Psychiatric Nursing and Mental Health
KAWAMATA, T., Applied Occupational Therapy
KITA, A., Maternal Nursing and Midwifery
KOHMURA, E., Neurosurgery
KOMORI, T., Oral and Maxillofacial Functional Science
KUMAGAI, S., Clinical Pathology and Immunology
KUNO, T., Molecular Pharmacology and Pharmacogenomics
KURODA, Y., Gastroenterological Surgery
KUROSAKA, M., Orthopaedic Surgery
MAEDA, K., Psychiatry and Neurology
MAEDA, S., Molecular Pathology
MARUO, T., Women's Medicine
MATSUDA, N., Community Health Nursing
MATSUMURA, S., Biochemistry
MATSUO, H., Maternity Nursing
MATSUO, M., Paediatrics
MIKI, A., Basic Physical Therapy
MINAMI, Y., Biomedical Regulation and Parasitology
MURATA, K., Clinical Nursing
NAKAMURA, S., Biochemistry
NAKAZONO, N., Applied Medical Technology
NEGI, A., Ophthalmology
NIBU, K., Otorhinolaryngology—Head and Neck Surgery
NISHIGORI, C., Dermatology
NISHIO, H., Public Health
NISHIYAMA, K., Basic Medical Technology
OBARA, H., Perioperative Medicine and Pain Management
OKAMURA, H., Molecular Brain Science

OKITA, Y., Cardiovascular, Thoracic and Paediatric Surgery

OKUMURA, K., Clinical Pharmacokinetics

RYO, R., Applied Medical Technology, Haematology and Blood Transfusion Medicine

SAKAMOTO, N., Medical Informatics

SEINO, S., Cell Biology and Neurophysiology

SEKI, K., Applied Occupational Therapy

SHIMADA, T., Applied Physical Therapy

SHIOZAWA, S., Rheumatology

SUGIMURA, K., Radiology

TABUCHI, Y., Clinical Oncology and Surgical Nursing

TAHARA, S., Plastic Surgery

TAKADA, S., Maternal and Child Health Science

TAMURA, Y., Basic Nursing

TERASHIMA, T., Developmental Neurobiology

TSUTOU, A., Basic Allied Medicine

UENO, Y., Legal Medicine

UGA, S., Parasitology

USAMI, M., Basic Medical Technology, Surgical Metabolism and Nutrition

WATANABE, M., Applied Medical Technology

YADA, M., Clinical Nursing

YAMAGUCHI, M., Applied Occupational Therapy

YAMAMURA, H., Proteomics

YAMAZAKI, I., Applied Occupational Therapy

YOKONO, K., Internal and Geriatric Medicine

YOKOYAMA, M., Cardiovascular and Respiratory Internal Medicine

YOKOZAKI, H., Surgical Pathology

School of Languages and Communication (1-2-1 Tsurukabuto, Nada-ku, Kobe 657-8501; tel. (78) 803-7522; fax (78) 803-7539; e-mail dakaikei@ofc.kobe-u.ac.jp; internet solac.cla .kobe-u.ac.jp):

GREER, T., Conversation Analysis, Applied Linguistics, Bilingualism

IGUCHI, J., Applied Linguistics

ISHIKAWA, S., Applied Linguistics

KASHIWAGI, H., English Language Education

KATO, M., English Education

MASUDA, Y., German Linguistics

MIKI, Y., European Maritime Culture

MURATA, R., The Later Enlightenment in Germany

NAKAGAWA, M., Contrastive Linguistics

OKIHARA, K., Applied Linguistics and English Language Education

SHIMAZU, A., American Literature

TSUJIMOTO, Y., British Journalism of the 18th and 19th centuries

URITA, S., English Literature

YOKOKAWA, H., Psycholinguistics

ZHU, C., Phonetics and Foreign Language Education

KUMAMOTO UNIVERSITY

39-1 Kurokami 2-chome, Kumamoto-shi 860-8555

Telephone: (96) 344-2111

Fax: (96) 342-3110

E-mail: message@svml.jimu.kumamoto-u.ac .jp

Internet: www.kumamoto-u.ac.jp

Founded 1949

Independent

Academic year: April to March (2 terms)

Pres.: Dr TATSURO SAKIMOTO

Dir of Admin. Bureau: MASAHARU CHOKI

Vice-Pres: Prof. CHIUCHI HIRAYAMA, Prof. TOMOMICHI ONO

Librarian: Prof. NAKAMASA IWAOKA

Number of teachers: 1,022

Number of students: 9,836

Publications: *Kumamoto Journal of Culture and Humanities* (1 a year), *Kumamoto Law Review* (4 a year), *Kumamoto Journal of Mathematics* (1 a year), *Kumamoto Journal of Science (Earth Sciences)* (1 a year), *Memoirs of the Faculty of Engineering* (2 a year), *Physics Report of Kumamoto University* (every 2 years), *Cryogenics Report of the Shockwave and Condensed Matter Research Center* (1 a year), *Kumamoto University Studies in Social and Cultural Sciences* (1 a year)

DEANS

Faculty of Education: Prof. SHOICHI ISHIHARA

Faculty of Engineering: Prof. ISAO TANIGUCHI

Faculty of Law: Prof. YATARO YOSHINAGA

Faculty of Letters: Prof. MASATO MORI

Faculty of Medical and Pharmaceutical Sciences: Prof. NOBUO SAKAGUCHI

Faculty of Science: Prof. MITSUHIKO KOHNO

Graduate School of Science and Technology: Prof. KATSUHIKO SUGAWARA

Graduate School of Social and Cultural Sciences: Prof. YASUTOSHI YUKAWA

School of Law: Prof. ITARU YAMANAKA

PROFESSORS

Faculty of Education (40-1 Kurokami 2-chome, Kumamoto 860-8555; tel. (96) 342-2514; fax (96) 342-2510; e-mail kyo-somu@ jimu.kumamoto-u.ac.jp; internet www.educ .kumamoto-u.ac.jp):

ASAKAWA, M., Food

BABA, K., Biology

CHIKUMA, Y., Educational Philosophy

FUKUSHIMA, K., Physics

HARADA, I., Electricity

HIGASHI, T., Electricity

HIRAMINE, Y., Algebra

HIRAWA, T., Vocal Music

HORIHATA, M., Japanese Linguistics

ICHIMURA, K., School Health

ISHIHARA, S., Sculpture

ITOH, J., Algebra

KAWAMINAMI, H., Teaching of Social Studies

KIMURA, M., School Health

KIYOZUMI, M., School Health

KOGA, N., Sociology

KUWAHATA, M., Teaching of Domestic Sciences

MAEDA, K., Teaching of Science

MASAMOTO, K., Biology

MIYAMOTO, M., Teaching of Social Studies

NAGATA, N., Teaching of School Health

NAKATA, Y., Educational Administration

NAKAYAMA, T., Theory and History of Music

NISHIKAWA, M., English Linguistics

OGATA, A., Psychology of Handicapped Children

OGAWA, K., Japanese Literature

OGO, K., Exercise and Hygiene

SHIBAYAMA, K., Clinical Psychology

SHIN, K., Education of Handicapped Children

SHINOHARA, H., Educational Psychology

SUGI, S., Teaching of Japanese

SUGOU, H., History of Handicraft Education

SUZUKI, R., English and American Literature

SUZURIKAWA, S., Social Welfare

TAKAGI, N., Teaching of English

TAKAMORI, H., Clothing

TANIGUCHI, K., Physiology of Exercise

TODA, T., English Linguistics

TORIKAI, K., Home Management

TSURUSHIMA, H., History

TSUZINO, T., Mechanics

UMEDA, M., Design and Crafts

WATANABE, K., Earth Science

YAMAMOTO, S., Teaching of Mathematics

YAMANAKA, M., Economics

YANAGI, H., Educational Sociology

YOKOYAMA, S., Geography

YONEMURA, K., Clinical Medicine and Nursing

YOSHIDA, M., Group Dynamics

YOSHIKAWA, N., Theory and History of Art

YOSHINAGA, S., Teaching of Music

Faculty of Engineering (39-1 Kurokami 2-chome, Kumamoto 860-8555; tel. (96) 342-3513; fax (96) 342-3510; internet www.eng .kumamoto-u.ac.jp/english/index.htm):

AKIYAMA, H., Electrical Energy Systems

EBIHARA, K., Electrical Energy Systems

FURUKAWA, K., Water Environmental Engineering

GOTO, M., Bio-related Molecular Science

HARADA, H., Intelligent Systems Engineering

HIROE, T., High Pressure Science and Materials Processing

HIROSE, T., Biochemical Engineering

IHARA, H., Bio-related Molecular Science

IKEGAMI, T., Advanced Technology of Electrical and Computer Systems

IKUNO, H., Electronic and Communication Systems

IMURA, H., Thermal and Fluid Energy Systems

INOUE, T., Electronic and Communication Systems

ISHIHARA, O., Regional Planning and Management

IWAI, Z., Intelligent Systems for Measurement and Control

JYO, A., Chemistry of Molecular Engineering

KASHIWAGI, H., Intelligent Systems for Measurement and Control

KAWAJI, S., Computer Science and Engineering

KAWAMURA, Y., Advanced Materials Technology

KITANO, T., Regional Planning and Management

KITAZANO, Y., Water Environmental Engineering

KOBAYASHI, I., Water Environmental Engineering

KURODA, N., Advanced Materials Technology

MACHIDA, M., Chemistry for Molecular Engineering

MAKINO, Y., Architectural Planning and Design

MAZDA, T., Structural Engineering

MITA, N., Advanced Technology of Electrical and Computer Systems

MITSUI, Y., Architectural Planning and Design

MIYAHARA, K., Electronic and Communication Systems

MIZOKAMI, S., Disaster Prevention Engineering

MOROZUMI, M., Regional Planning and Management

MURAYAMA, N., Advanced Technology of Electrical and Computer Systems

NAITOU, K., Mathematical Science

NAKAMURA, R., Intelligent Systems Engineering

NAKAMURA, Y., Advanced Technology of Electrical and Computer Systems

NISHIDA, M., Advanced Materials Technology

NONAKA, T., Chemistry for Material Science

OBARA, Y., Geotechnical Engineering

ODA, I., Intelligent Machine Design and Manufacturing

OGAWA, K., Architectural Planning and Design

OHMOTO, T., Water Environmental Engineering

OHNO, Y., Materials Development Systems

OHTANI, J., Water Environmental Engineering
OSHIMA, Y., Mathematical Science
SADATOMI, M., Thermal and Fluid Energy Systems
SAISHO, M., Disaster Prevention Engineering
SAKURADA, K., Disaster Prevention Engineering
SATONAKA, S., Intelligent Machine Design and Manufacturing
SHOSENJI, H., Chemistry for Molecular Engineering
SUEYOSHI, T., Computer Science and Engineering
SUZUKI, A., Geotechnical Engineering
TAKADA, Y., Mathematical Science
TANIGUCHI, I., Bio-related Molecular Science
TONDA, H., Materials Development Systems
TORII, S., Intelligent Machine Design and Manufacturing
UCHIYAMA, O., Architectural Planning and Design
UMENO, H., Computer Science and Engineering
USAGAWA, T., Intelligent Systems Engineering
WATANABE, J., Thermal and Fluid Energy Systems
YAMAO, T., Structural Engineering
YANO, T., Structural Engineering
YASUI, H., Intelligent Machine Design and Manufacturing
YOKOI, Y., Mathematical Science

Faculty of Law (40-1 Kurokami 2-chome, Kumamoto 860-8555; tel. (96) 342-2315; fax (96) 342-2310; e-mail jsj-somu@jimu .kumamoto-u.ac.jp; internet www.law .kumamoto-u.ac.jp):

FUKAMATI, K., International Law
HAYASHI, I., International Law
INADA, T., Criminal Procedure
ITO, H., Politics
IWAOKA, N., Politics
KAWAMOTO, T., English Literature
KITAGAWA, K., Philosophy
KIZAKI, Y., Civil Law
MORI, M., German Literature
NAKAMURA, N., Philosophy of Law
OHSAWA, H., Politics
SATO, M., Economic Policy
SUZUKI, K., Politics
WAKASONE, K., European Legal History
YAMASHITA, T., Economics
YAMAZAKI, K., Tax Law
YOSHIDA, I., Sociology of Law
YOSHINAGA, Y., Social Law

Faculty of Letters (40-1 Kurokami 2-chome, Kumamoto 860-8555; tel. (96) 342-2313; fax (96) 342-2310; e-mail bun-somu@jimu .kumamoto-u.ac.jp; internet www.let .kumamoto-u.ac.jp/let/index.html):

FUKAHORI, K., German Literature
FUKUZAWA, K., Linguistics
HOHGETSU, T., Geography
IHARA, S., Japanese Language
IKEDA, M., Cultural Anthropology and Medical Humanities
KAMIMURA, N., German Language
KINOSHITA, N., Archaeology
KOMATSU, H., Cultural History
KOMOTO, M., Archaeology
KUMAMOTO, S., English Language
MARUYAMA, N., Regional Sociology
MORI, M., Japanese Literature
OGINO, K., German Language
OKABE, T., Aesthetics
OOKUMA, K., French Literature
SAKATA, M., German Literature
SHINOZAKI, S., Ethics
SUGITANI, K., German Literature
TAGUCHI, H., Sociology
TAKAHASHI, T., Ethics

TANAKA, Y., German Literature
TANIKAWA, N., English Literature
TERADA, M., French Literature
TOKUNO, S., Regional Sociology
TONE, T., Psychology
WATANABE, I., Psychology
YASUDA, M., Folklore
YOSHIKAWA, E., Chinese Language
YOSIMURA, T., Japanese History

Faculty of Medical and Pharmaceutical Sciences (1-1 Honjo 1-chome, Kumamoto 860-8556; tel. (96) 373-5904; fax (96) 373-5906; e-mail iys-somu@jimu.kumamoto-u.ac.jp; internet www.medphas.kumamoto-u.ac.jp):

ARAKI, E., Metabolic Medicine
EKINO, S., Histology
ENDO, F., Paediatrics
FUTATUKA, M., Public Health
GOTO, M., Structure-Function Physical Chemistry
HARADA, S., Medical Virology
HARANO, K., Computational Molecular Design
HORIUCHI, S., Medical Biochemistry
IMAI, T., Drug Metabolism and Disposition
INOMATA, Y., Paediatric Surgery
IRIE, T., Clinical Chemistry and Informatics
ITO, T., Pathology and Experimental Medicine
KAI, H., Molecular Medicine
KAMASUJI, M., Cardiovascular Surgery
KIKAWA, K., General Medicine
KINOSHITA, Y., Aggressology and Critical Care Medicine
KITAMURA, T., Clinical Behavioural Sciences
KODAMA, K., Anatomy
KURATSU, J., Neurosurgery
MIIKE, T., Child Development
MITSUYA, H., Haematology
MITSUYAMA, S., Pharmacology and Molecular Therapeutics
MIURA, R., Molecular Enzymology
MIYATA, T., Chemico-Pharmacological Sciences
MIZUSHIMA, T., Pharmaceutical Microbiology
MORI, M., Molecular Genetics
NAKAGAWA, K., Pharmacology and Therapeutics
NAKAJIMA, M., Organic Chemistry
NAKANISHI, H., Molecular Pharmacology
NAKAYAMA, H., Molecular Cell Function
NISHIMURA, Y., Immunogenetics
NOHARA, T., Natural Medicines
OGAWA, H., Cardiovascular Medicine
OGAWA, H., Sensory and Cognitive Physiology
OHTSUKA, M., Bio-organic Medicinal Chemistry
OKABE, H., Diagnostic Medicine
OKAMURA, H., Reproductive Medicine and Surgery
OTAGIRI, M., Biopharmaceutics
SAITO, H., Pharmacy
SAKAGUCHI, N., Immunology
SASAKI, Y., Gastroenterology and Hepatology
SAYA, H., Tumour Genetics and Biology
SHIGA, K., Molecular Physiology
SHINOHARA, M., Oral and Maxillofacial Surgery
SHOJI, S., Pharmaceutical Biochemistry
TAKAHAMA, K., Environmental and Molecular Health Sciences
TAKEYA, M., Cell Pathology
TANAKA, H., Developmental Neurobiology
TANIHARA, H., Ophthalmology and Visual Science
TERASAKI, H., Anaesthesiology
TOMITA, K., Nephrology
TSUNENARI, S., Forensic Medicine
UCHINO, M., Neurology
UEDA, M., Pharmaceutical Microbiology

UEDA, S., Urology
UEKAMA, K., Physical Pharmaceutics
UNO, T., Analytical and Biophysical Chemistry
YAMAGATA, Y., Structural Biology
YAMAMOTO, T., Molecular Pathology
YAMASHITA, Y., Diagnostic Imaging
YOSHIHARA, H., Medical Informatics
YUMOTO, E., Otolaryngology—Head and Neck Surgery

Faculty of Science (39-1 Kurokami 2-chome, Kumamoto 860-8555; tel. (96) 342-3314; fax (96) 342-3320; e-mail rig-some@jimu .kumamoto-u.ac.jp; internet www.sci .kumamoto-u.ac.jp/index.html):

ABE, S. I., Developmental Biology
ANIYA, M., Fundamental Physics
ARAI, K., Fundamental Physics
FUJII, A., Solid State Spectroscopy
FURUSHIMA, M., Algebra and Geometry
HAMANA, Y., Probability Theory
HARAOKA, Y., Analysis and Applied Analysis
HASE, Y., Palaeobotany and Environmental Science
HASEGAWA, S., Palaeontology and Environmental Science
HASENAKA, T., Volcanology and Igneous Petrology
ICHIKAWA, F., Superconductivity
ICHIMURA, K., Physical Chemistry
IMAFUKU, K., Organic Chemistry
ISHIDA, A., Dynamics of Environments
ITOH, K., Magnetic Thin Films
KIMURA, H., Analysis and Applied Analysis
KOBAYASHI, O., Algebra and Geometry
KOHNO, M., Analysis and Applied Analysis
MATSUMOTO, N., Inorganic Chemistry
MATSUSAKA, T., Dynamics of Environments
MATSUZAKI, S., Physical Chemistry
MITSUNAGA, M., Quantum Optics
MOMOSHIMA, N., Environmental Analysis
MOTOYOSHI, A., Fundamental Physics
NISHINO, H., Organic Chemistry
NISHIYAMA, T., Petrology, Mineralogy and Geodynamics
NOHDA, S., Environmental Analysis
OHWAKI, S., Integrated Mathematics
SAKAMOTO, N., Polymer Chemistry
SANEMASA, I., Environmental Analysis
SHIBUYA, H., Palaeomagnetism and Geodynamics
SHIMADA, J., Groundwater Circulation
SHIODA, M., Molecular Cell Biology
TANI, T., Molecular Biology
UCHINO, A., Dynamics of Environments
WATANABE, A., Algebra and Geometry
YAMAKI, H., Algebra and Geometry
YOSHIASA, A., Geodynamics and Condensed Matter Physics

Graduate School of Social and Cultural Sciences (40-1 Kurokami 2-chome, Kumamoto 860-8555; tel. (96) 342-2313; fax (96) 342-2130; e-mail bun-somu@jimu.kumamoto-u.ac .jp; internet www.let.kumamoto-u.ac.jp/ gsscs/index_e.html):

YAMANAKA, S., Geography
YUKAWA, Y., Linguistics

Graduate School of Science and Technology (39-1 Kurokami 2-chome, Kumamoto 860-8555; tel. (96) 342-3013; fax (96) 342-3010; e-mail dcjimu@gpo.kumamoto-u.ac.jp; internet 133.95.161.1/index-en.html):

HASEGAWA, S., Natural Environmental Sciences
HIYAMA, T., Energy Systems
ICHIMURA, K., Basic Chemistry and Physics for Materials Sciences
IKI, K., Human-Environmental Engineering
ISHITOBI, M., Intelligent Manufacturing Systems
KAWAHARA, M., Materials Science and Technology

KIDA, K., Applied Chemistry for Materials and Life Sciences
MATSUMOTO, Y., Applied Chemistry of Materials
OHBA, H., Mechanical Systems Design
OHTSU, M., Disaster-preventive Structural Engineering
OKUNO, Y., Electrical and Computer Engineering
SUGAWARA, K., Environmental Conservation Engineering
UCHIMURA, K., Intelligent Systems and Computer Science
YAMAKI, H., Mathematics
YOSHITAMA, K., Bioinformational Science

School of Law (40-1 Kurokami 2-chome, Kumamoto 860-8555; tel. (96) 342-2315; fax (96) 342-2310; e-mail jsj-somu@jimu.kumamoto-u.ac.jp; internet www.kumamoto-ua.ac.jp/lawschool):

FUKUYAMA, M., Law
HARADA, T., Law
HASHIMOTO, M., Civil Law
HAYASHI, M., Local Government Law
HIRATA, H., Criminal Procedure
ISHIBASHI, H., Social Law
KUBOTA, M., Commercial Law
MATSUBARA, H., Civil Procedure Law
NAKAGAWA, Y., Administrative Law
NAKAMURA, S., Criminal Law
ONO, Y., Civil Law
ONODERA, M., Prosecutor
SAWATARI, K., Law
TADA, N., International Private Law
YAMAMOTO, E., Constitutional Law
YAMANAKA, I., Legal Theory and History

Center for AIDS Research (2-1 Honjo 2-chome, Kumamoto 860-0811; tel. (96) 373-6531; fax (96) 373-6532; internet www.caids.kumamoto-u.ac.jp):

MATSUSHITA, S., Clinical Retrovirology and Infectious Diseases
OKADA, S., Haematopoiesis
TAKIGUCHI, M., Viral Immunology

Center for Marine Environment Studies (39-1 Kurokami, 2-chome, Kumamoto 860-8555; tel. (96) 342-3448; fax (96) 342-3448; internet www.engan.dc.kumamoto-u.ac.jp/index.html):

HENMI, Y., Analysis of Cyclization Systems for Natural Resources
TAKIKAWA, K., Hydro- and Geosphere Environments
TAKIO, S., Conservation and Development of Natural Resources

Center for Multimedia and Information Technologies (39-1 Kurokami 2-chome, Kumamoto 860-8555; tel. (96) 342-3824; fax (96) 342-3829; internet www.cc.kumamoto-u.ac.jp):

IRIGUCHI, N.
NAKANO, Y.
SUGITANI, K.

Co-operative Research Center (2081-7 Tabaru, Mashiki-machi, Kumamoto 861-2202; tel. (96) 286-1212; fax (96) 286-1067; internet www.kcr.kumamoto-u.ac.jp/index-j.html):

HIROSUE, H., Liaison between University and Industry
MATSUSHITA, H., Technology Transfer between University and Industry

Institute of Molecular Embryology and Genetics (24-1 Kuhonji 4-chome, Kumamoto 862-0976; tel. (96) 344-2111; fax (96) 373-6638; e-mail imeg@kaiju.medic.kumamoto-u.ac.jp; internet www.imeg.kumamoto-u.ac.jp):

KUME, S., Stem Cell Biology
NAGAFUCHI, A., Cellular Interactions
NAKAO, M., Organ Development
NISHINAKAMURA, R., Integrative Cell Biology
OGAWA, M., Cell Differentiation

OGURA, T., Molecular Cell Biology
OKUBO, H., Molecular Neurobiology
SHIMAMURA, K., Morphogenesis
TAGA, T., Cell Fate Modulation
YAMAIZUMI, M., Cell Genetics
YAMAMURA, K., Developmental Genetics
YOKOUCHI, Y., Pattern Formation

Institute of Resource Development and Analysis (2-2-1 Honjo, Kumamoto 860-0811; tel. (96) 373-6637; fax (96) 373-6638; e-mail iys-senter@jimu.kumamoto-u.ac.jp):

NAKAGATA, N., Reproductive Engineering
URANO, T., Microbiology and Genetics
YAMADA, G., Transgenic Technology

International Student Center (40-1 Kurokami 2-chome, Kumamoto 860-8555; tel. (96) 342-2133; fax (96) 342-2130; e-mail gji-ryugaku@jimu.kumamoto-u.ac.jp; internet center.ryu.kumamoto-u.ac.jp/index_e.html):

KOWAKI, M., Linguistics (Semitic Languages)

Research Center for Higher Education (40-1 Kurokami 2-chome, Kumamoto 860-8555; tel. (96) 342-2716; fax (96) 342-2710; e-mail gak-kyomu@jimu.kumamoto-u.ac.jp; internet www.ge.kumamoto-u.ac.jp):

OHMORI, F., Education Policy
SUGAWARA, T., Educational Evaluation
YAMADA, M., Advanced and Applied Education of European History

Research Center for Lifelong Learning (40-1 Kurokami 2-chome, Kumamoto 860-8555; tel. (96) 342-3281; fax (96) 342-3281; e-mail sos-tiiki@kumamoto-u.ac.jp; internet www.lifelong.kumamoto-u.ac.jp):

SAGA, S., Philosophy, Bio-ethics
UENO, S., Political Science
YANAGI, H., Educational Sociology

Shock Wave and Condensed Matter Research Center (39-1 Kurokami 2-chome, Kumamoto 860-8555; tel. (96) 342-3299; fax (96) 342-3293; internet www.shocomarec.kumamoto-u.ac.jp):

FUJII, A., Low Temperature Science
ITO, S., Shock Processing and its Applications
KUBOTA, H., Solid State Physics under Multi-Extreme Conditions

KYOTO INSTITUTE OF TECHNOLOGY

Hashigami-cho, Matsugasaki, Sakyo-ku, Kyoto 606-8585
Telephone: (75) 724-7111
Fax: (75) 724-7010
E-mail: webmaster@adm.kit.ac.jp
Internet: www.kit.ac.jp/index.html
Founded 1949
Independent
Academic year: April to March
Pres.: YOSIMITI EJIMA
Vice-Pres: KATSUHIKO YAMAGUCHI, SATOSHI HIRAYAMA
Dir-Gen.: KIMIO MURAMATSU
Librarian: SHIGEYUKI YAMAGUCHI

Library of 363,140 vols
Number of teachers: 317
Number of students: 4,327
Publications: *Memoirs of the Faculty of Engineering and Design—JINBUN* (Series of Science and Technology, 1 a year), *Bulletin of the Faculty of Textile Science* (1 a year)

DEANS

Faculty of Engineering and Design: RIKUO OTA
Faculty of Textile Science: SHIGERU KUNUGI

KYOTO UNIVERSITY

Yoshida-Honmachi, Sakyo-ku, Kyoto 606-8501
Telephone: (75) 753-7531
E-mail: koryu52@mail.adm.kyoto-u.ac.jp
Internet: www.kyoto-u.ac.jp
Founded 1897
Independent
Academic year: April to March
Pres.: KAZUO OIKE
Vice-Pres: AKIHIRO KINDA, BUNZO TSUJI, HIROHISA HIGASHIYAMA, KOJIRO IRIKURA, MASAO HOMMA, SHIGEAKI TANAKA
Library: see Libraries and Archives
Number of teachers: 2,911
Number of students: 22,192

DEANS

Graduate School of Agriculture and Faculty of Agriculture: S. YAZAWA
Graduate School of Asian and African Area Studies: M. ICHIKAWA
Graduate School of Biostudies: S. YONEHARA
Graduate School of Economics and Faculty of Economics: S. NISHIMURA
Graduate School of Education and Faculty of Education: Y. KAWASAKI
Graduate School of Energy Science: M. KASAHARA
Graduate School of Engineering and Faculty of Engineering: M. ARAKI
Graduate School of Global Environmental Studies: M. NAITO
Graduate School of Human and Environmental Studies and Faculty of Integrated Human Studies: H. TOMITA
Graduate School of Informatics: Y. NAKAMURA
Graduate School of Law and Faculty of Law: S. MORIMOTO
Graduate School of Letters and Faculty of Letters: J. FUJII
Graduate School of Medicine and Faculty of Medicine: T. HONJO
Graduate School of Pharmaceutical Sciences and Faculty of Pharmaceutical Sciences: M. HASHIDA
Graduate School of Science and Faculty of Science: K. YOSHIKAWA
Law School: Y. NAKAMORI

PROFESSORS

Graduate School of Agriculture and Faculty of Agriculture (Kitashirakawa, Oiwake-cho, Sakyo, Kyoto, 606-8502; tel. (75) 753-6490; fax (75) 753-6020; internet www.kais.kyoto-u.ac.jp):

ADACHI, S., Bioengineering
AOYAMA, S., Agricultural Facility Engineering
AZUMA, J., Forest Biochemistry
ENDO, T., Plant Genetics
FUJISAKI, K., Insect Ecology
FUJITA, M., Structure of Plant Cells
FUJIWARA, T., Fisheries, Oceanography
FUSHIKI, T., Nutrition Chemistry
FUTAI, K., Environmental Mycoscience
HIRATA, T., Marine Bioproducts Technology
HIROOKA, H., Animal Science
HORIE, T., Crop Science
IMAI, H., Animal Reproduction
INOUYE, K., Enzyme Chemistry
IWAI, Y., Forest Resources and Society
KAGATSUME, M., Regional Environmental Economics
KANO, K., Bioelectroanalytical Chemistry
KAWACHI, T., Water Resources Engineering
KAWADA, T., Food Biochemistry
KITA, K., Bioenergy Conversion
KITABATAKE, N., Food and Environmental Science
KOSAKI, T., Soil Science
KUME, S., Environmental Physiology

MATSUMOTO, T., Fibrous Biomaterials

MATSUMURA, Y., Quality Analysis and Assessment

MITSUNO, T., Irrigation, Drainage and Hydrological Environment Engineering

MIYAGAWA, H., Bioregulation Chemistry

MIZUYAMA, T., Erosion Control

MORIMOTO, Y., Landscape Architecture

MURATA, K., Molecular Biotechnology

NAKAHARA, H., Marine Microbial Ecology

NAKATSUBO, F., Chemistry of Biomaterials

NIIYAMA, Y., Farm Management

NISHIDA, R., Chemical Ecology

NISHIO, Y., Chemistry of Composite Materials

NISHIOKA, T., Biofunction Chemistry

NOBUCHI, T., Forest Utilization

NODA, K., Comparative Agricultural History

ODA, S., Farm Management Information and Accounting

OHIGASHI, H., Organic Chemistry in Life Science

OHNISHI, O., Crop Evolution

OHTA, S., Tropical Forest Resources and Environments

OIDA, A., Agricultural Systems Engineering

OKUMURA, S., Wood Processing

OKUNO, T., Plant Pathology

SAKO, Y., Marine Microbiology

SAKUMA, M., Behavioural Physiology and Chemical Ecology of Insects

SAKURATANI, T., Tropical Agriculture

SASAKI, Y., Animal Breeding and Genetics

SEKIYA, J., Plant Nutrition

SHIMIZU, S., Fermentation Physiology and Applied Microbiology

SUEHARA, T., Principles of Agricultural Science

TAKAFUJI, A., Ecological Information

TAKEBE, T., Agricultural and Environmental Policy

TAKEDA, H., Forest Ecology

TANAKA, M., Fish Biology

TANI, M., Forest Hydrology

TANISAKA, T., Plant Breeding

TOMINAGA, T., Weed Ecology

UEDA, K., Cellular Biochemistry

UEDA, M., Biomacromolecular Chemistry

UMEDA, M., Field Robotics

UTSUMI, S., Food Quality Design and Development

YAMADA, T., Plant Production Management

YAMASUE, Y., Physiological Aspects of Agricultural Systems

YANO, H., Animal Nutrition

YAZAWA, S., Vegetable and Ornamental Horticulture

YONEMORI, K., Pomology

YOSHIDA, M., Forest Policy and Economics

YOSHIKAWA, M., Physiological Function of Food

Graduate School of Asian and African Area Studies (46 Shimoadachi-cho, Yoshida, Sakyo-ku, Kyoto 606-8501; tel. (75) 753-7302; fax (75) 753-7350; e-mail soumu@cseas.kyoto-u.ac.jp; internet www.asafas.kyoto-u.ac.jp):

ADACHI, A., The Hindu World

ARAKI, S., Agricultural Ecology

HIRAMATSU, K., Natural Hisory

ICHIKAWA, M., Socio-ecological History

KAJI, S., Culture and Ethnicity

KAKEYA, M., Livelihood and Economy

KOBAYASHI, S., Environmental Ecology

KOSUGI, Y., The Islamic World

OHTA, I., Nature–Human Interaction

SHIMADA, S., Socio-cultural Integration

SUGISHIMA, T., Comparative Social Transformation

Graduate School of Biostudies:

INABA, K., Laboratory of Science Communication and Bioethics

INOUE, T., Laboratory of Gene Biodynamics

ISHIKAWA, F., Laboratory of Cell Cycle Regulation

KAKIZUKA, A., Laboratory of Functional Biology

KOCHI, T., Laboratory of Plant Molecular Biology

KOZUTUMI, Y., Laboratory of Membrane Biochemistry and Biophysics

MINATO, N., Laboratory of Immunology and Cell Biology

NAGAO, M., Laboratory of Biosignals and Response

NEGISHI, M., Laboratory of Molecular Neurobiology

NISHIDA, E., Laboratory of Signal Transduction

SATO, F., Laboratory of Molecular and Cellular Biology of Totipotency

TAKEYASU, K., Laboratory of Plasma Membrane and Nuclear Signalling

UEMURA, T., Laboratory of Cell Recognition and Pattern Formation

YAMAMOTO, K., Laboratory of Molecular Biology of Bioresponse

YONEHARA, S., Laboratory of Molecular and Cellular Biology

Graduate School of Economics and Faculty of Economics (tel. (75) 753-3400; fax (75) 753-3492; e-mail kyoumu@econ.kyoto-u.ac.jp; internet www.econ.kyoto-u.ac.jp):

FUJII, H., International Accounting

FURUKAWA, A., Money and Finance

HIOKI, K., Organization Theory

HISAMOTO, N., Labour Economics

HORI, K., Economic History

IMAKUBO, S., Economic Policy

IWAMOTO, T., International Economics

KAZUSA, Y., Managerial Accounting

KIJIMA, M., Financial Engineering

KOJIMA, H., Principles of Economics

MORIMUNE, K., Econometrics

MOTOYAMA, Y., World Economy

NARIU, T., Applied Economics

NEI, M., Modern Economics

NISHIMURA, S., Applied Economics

NISHIMUTA, Y., Business History

OHNISHI, H., Economic Statistics

OKADA, T., Regional Economy

SHIMOTANI, M., Japanese Economy

SHIOJI, H., Japanese Economy

TACHIBANAKI, T., Economic Policy

TANAKA, H., History of Social Thought

TAO, M., Business Policy

TOKUGA, Y., Accounting for Venture Business

UETA, K., Public Finance

UNI, H., Economic Theory

WAKABAYASHI, Y., Marketing

YAGI, K., Economic Theory

YAMAMOTO, H., Chinese Economy

YOSHIDA, K., Contemporary Economics

Graduate School of Education and Faculty of Education (tel. (75) 753-3010; fax (75) 753-3025; e-mail kyoumu@kyoumu.educ.kyoto-u.ac.jp; internet www.educ.kyoto-u.ac.jp):

FUJIWARA, K., Clinical Psychology

INAGAKI, K., Sociology of Education

ITOH, Y., Clinical Psychology

IWAI, H., Sociology of the Course of Life

KAWAI, T., Clinical Psychology

KAWASAKI, Y., Library and Information Science

KOYASU, M., Cognitive Psychology in Education

MAEHIRA, Y., Lifelong Education

OKADA, Y., Clinical Personality Psychology

SUGIMOTO, H., Comparative Education

SUZUKI, S., Pedagogy

TAKAMI, S., Educational Finance

TANAKA, K., Curriculum Development and Assessment

TSUJIMOTO, M., Japanese History of Education

YAMADA, Y., Developmental Psychology

YANO, S., Clinical Pedagogy

YOSHIKAWA, S., Cognitive Psychology in Education

Graduate School of Energy Science (tel. (75) 753-4871; fax (75) 753-4745; internet www.energy.kyoto-u.ac.jp/index-eng.html):

HOSHIDE, T., Fracture Mechanics for System Integrity

ISHIHARA, K., Social Engineering of Energy

ISHII, R., Space Energy and Resources

ISHIYAMA, T., Combustion Engine Technology

IWASE, M., Physical Chemistry of Iron- and Steelmaking and Related High-Temperature Processes

KASAHARA, M., Atmospheric Environmental Engineering

KONDO, K., Plasma Diagnostics

MABUCHI, M., Materials Science and Engineering

MAEKAWA, T., Plasma Physics

MATSUMOTO, E., Non-linear Continuum Mechanics

NOZAWA, H., Physics and Technology of VLSI

SAKA, S., Ecosystems of Biomass for Energy Use

SHIOJI, M., Combustion Science and Engineering

SHIOTSU, M., Thermal Hydraulics in Energy Systems

TAKUDA, H., Advanced Processing of Resources and Energy

TEZUKA, T., Energy Economics

YAO, T., Solid-state Energy Chemistry

YOSHIKAWA, H., Man–Machine Systems

Graduate School of Engineering and Faculty of Engineering:

AOKI, K., Rarefied Gas Dynamics

AOKI, K., Resources Development Engineering

AOYAMA, Y., Biorecognition

AOYAMA, Y., Urban and Regional Planning

ARAKI, M., Control Engineering

ASAKURA, T., Tunnel Engineering

ASHIDA, Y., Exploration Geophysics

AWAKURA, Y., Materials Electrochemistry

CHUJO, Y., Polymerization Chemistry

EGUCHI, K., Catalyst Science and Catalyst Design Engineering

FUJII, S., Division of Environmental Quality Control

FUKUYAMA, A., Basic Quantum Engineering

HAGIWARA, T., Automatic Control Engineering

HAMACHI, I., Bio-organic Chemistry

HASEBE, S., Process Systems Engineering

HAYASHI, Y., Disaster Risk Management of Built Environment

HIGASHITANI, K., Surface Control Engineering

HIGUCHI, T., Landscape and Environmental Planning

HIKIHARA, T., Power Conversion and Control Laboratory

HIRAO, K., Inorganic Structural Chemistry

HIYAMA, T., Organic Chemistry of Natural Products

HOJO, M., Continuum Mechanics

HOKOI, S., Thermal Analysis and Design

HOSODA, T., River Engineering

ICHIKAWA, A., Systems and Control

IEMURA, H., Earthquake Engineering

IMAHORI, H., Applied Molecular Science

IMANAKA, T., Biotechnology

INAMURO, T., Fluid Dynamics

INOUE, K., Space Development and Structural Systems

INOUE, M., Energy Conversion Chemistry

INUI, H., Intermetallic Alloys for Structural and Functional Uses

ISHIKAWA, J., Charged Particle Devices

ITO, S., Polymer Structure and Function

ITOH, A., Applied Beam Materials Engineering

ITOH, S., Urban Sanitary Engineering

KAKIUCHI, T., Functional Solution Chemistry

KATO, N., Architectural Information Systems

KAWAI, J., Process Chemical Physics

KIDA, S., Fluid Dynamics

KIMURA, K., Mesoscopic Materials Engineering

KIMURA, S., Design of Functional Materials

KITAGAWA, S., Functional Chemistry

KITAMURA, R., Transport Planning and Engineering

KITAMURA, T., Mechanical Behaviour of Materials

KITANO, M., Quantum Optical Engineering

KOBAYASHI, K., Civil Engineering Systems Analysis

KOBAYASHI, T., Biomedical Engineering

KOMORI, S., Fluids Engineering

KOTERA, H., Mechanical Systems

KUBO, A., Machine Design

MAE, K., Environmental Process Engineering

MAEDA, T., Theory of Architecture and Environmental Design

MAKI, T., Mechanical Properties of Steel

MAKINO, T., Thermophysical Properties of Materials

MASUDA, H., Powder Technology

MASUDA, T., Polymer Physics and Rheology

MATSUBARA, A., Precision Measurement and Machining

MATSUBARA, E., Structural Characterization by X-ray Diffraction

MATSUHISA, H., Vibration Engineering

MATSUMOTO, M., Wind Engineering

MATSUOKA, T., Engineering Geology

MATSUSHIGE, K., Molecular Nano-electronics

MITSUDO, T., Catalysis

MIURA, K., Environmental Process Engineering

MIYAGAWA, T., Durability of Reinforced Concrete

MIYAHARA, M., Fluids Confined in Nanospace Order Formation by Nano-colloids

MIYAZAKI, N., Computational Solid Mechanics

MONNAI, T., Architecture and Human Environmental Planning

MORI, Y., Molecular Biology

MORISAWA, S., Environmental Risk Analysis

MORISHIMA, N., Neutron Science

MORIYAMA, H., Nuclear Materials

MUNEMOTO, J., Architectural Planning

MURAKAMI, M., Organometallic Chemistry

MURAKAMI, M., Thin Film Metallurgy

NAGATA, M., Gas Dynamics

NAKATSUJI, H., Quantum Chemistry

NEZU, I., Fluid Mechanics and Hydraulics

NISHIMOTO, S., Excited-state Hydrocarbon Chemistry

NODA, S., Quantum Optoelectronics Engineering

OGUMI, Z., Electrochemistry

OHE, K., Organometallic Chemistry

OHNISHI, Y., Rock Mechanics

OHSAWA, Y., Electric Power System Engineering

OHSHIMA, M., Materials Process Engineering

OKA, F., Soil Mechanics

ONO, K., Propulsion Engineering

OSAMURA, K., Science of Materials

OSHIMA, K., Organic Reaction Chemistry

OTSUKA, K., Analytical Chemistry of Materials

SAITO, T., Mining and Rock Mechanics

SAKAI, T., Coastal Engineering

SAKAKI, S., Quantum Molecular Science and Technology

SAWAMOTO, M., Living Cationic Polymerization

SAWARAGI, T., Design Systems Engineering

SCAWTHORN, C., Natural Hazard Risk Management

SERIZAWA, A., Nuclear Reactor Engineering

SHIMA, S., Engineering Plasticity

SHIMASAKI, M., Computational Electromagnetic Field Analysis

SHIRAKAWA, M., Biophysical Chemistry

SUGIMURA, H., Nanoscopic Surface Architecture

SUGINOME, M., Organic Synthesis and System Design

SUZUKI, M., Integrated Function Engineering

TABATA, O., Micro Electro-Mechanical Systems

TACHIBANA, A., Quantum Theory of Condensed Matter

TACHIBANA, K., Plasma Physics and Technology

TAKADA, M., Housing and Environmental Design

TAKAHASHI, H., Architectural Design and Theory

TAKAHASHI, Y., History of Architecture

TAKAMATSU, S., Architectural Design

TAKAOKA, G., Ion Engineering, Cluster Science

TAKEDA, N., Solid Waste Management

TAKEWAKI, I., Earthquake Resistant Engineering

TAKIGAWA, T., Physics of Polymer Materials

TAMON, H., Separation Engineering

TAMURA, K., Structural Properties of Materials

TAMURA, M., Environmental Remote Sensing

TAMURA, T., Applied Mechanics

TANAKA, F., Polymer Core Physical Chemistry

TANAKA, H., Environmental Evaluation

TANAKA, I., Ceramic Materials Science

TANAKA, K., Inorganic Solid-State Chemistry

TANAKA, K., Molecular Energy Conservation

TANAKA, T., Molecular Science and Technology of Catalysis

TANIGUCHI, E., Urban Infrastructure Systems

TSUCHIYA, K., Dynamics and Control of Space Vehicles

TSUNO, H., Water Quality Conservation

UCHIYAMA, I., Environmental Health

UETANI, K., Mechanics of Building Structures

WADA, O., Circuit Theory and Applications

WATANABE, F., Reinforced and Pressed Concrete Structures

YAMAMOTO, K., Quantum Physics

YAMASHINA, H., Computer-integrated Manufacturing

YOSHIDA, H., Urban Environment and Safety Engineering

YOSHIDA, J., Organic Chemistry

YOSHIKAWA, T., Robotics

YOSHIMURA, M., Knowledge and Information Systems

YOSHIZAKI, T., Polymer Statistical Mechanics

YOSIDA, H., Thermal Systems Engineering

Graduate School of Global Environmental Studies (tel. (75) 753-9167; fax (75) 753-9187; internet www.adm.kyoto-u.ac.jp/ges):

KAMON, M., Environmental Infrastructure Engineering

KAWASAKI, M., Environmental Atmospheric Chemistry

KOBAYASHI, M., Global Environment Architecture

KOBAYASHI, S., Regional Planning

KOSAKI, T., Terrestrial Ecosystems Management

MATSUI, S., Environmentally Friendly Industries for Sustainable Development

MATSUOKA, Y., Global Integrated Assessment Modelling

MATSUSHITA, K., Global Environmental Policy

MIMURO, M., Environmental Biotechnology

MORIMOTO, Y., Landscape Ecology and Planning

NAKAHARA, H., Conservation of Coastal Ecosystems

OGAWA, T., Philosophical Theory of Human and Environmental Symbiosis

SHIIBA, M., Circulation of Environmental Resources

TAKEBE, T., Global Resource Economics

TAMURA, R., Environmental Materials Science

UETA, K., Global Ecological Economics

YOKOYAMA, T., Towards a Theory of Global Civilization

Graduate School of Human and Environmental Studies and Faculty of Integrated Human Studies (Yoshida Nihonmatsu-cho, Sakyo, Kyoto; tel. (75) 753-2950; fax (75) 753-2957; internet www.adm.kyoto-u.ac.jp/jinkan):

ADACHI, Y., Socio-cultural Environments

ATSUJI, T., Chinese Linguistics

BECKER, C., Comparative Religion, Ethics, Death and Dying

EDA, K., History of Modern China

FUKUI, K., Cultural Anthropology of Ethiopia

FUKUOKA, K., American Literature

FUNAHASHI, S., Neurophysiology

HATTORI, F., Linguistics and Slavonic Languages

HORI, T., Natural Environments

INAGAKI, N., Modern French Literature

ISHIDA, A., Modern German Philology and Literature

ISHIHARA, A., Neurochemistry and Physiology

IYORI, T., Common Environmental System

KAMATA, H., Volcanology

KANASAKA, K., Human Societies

KATO, M., Coexisting Systems of Nature and Human Beings

KAWASHIMA, A., Modern British History

KIMURA, T., Russian Literature

KIWAMOTO, Y., Plasma Physics

KOYAMA, S., History of Japanese Education

KUJIRAOKA, T., Human Environment

MAEGAWA, S., Low Temperature Magnetism

MAMIYA, Y., Common Environmental System

MARUHASHI, Y., English Drama

MATSUDA, K., History of Western Learning in Japan

MATSUI, M., Systematic Zoology

MATSUMARU, M., Neurophysiology

MATSUURA, S., History of North-Eastern Asia

MICHIHATA, T., German Literature

MIHARA, O., German Literature

MITANI, K., Slavic Linguistics

MIYAMOTO, Y., Polymer Physics

MORIMOTO, Y., Theory of Partial Differential Equations

MORITANI, T., Environmental Conservation and Development

MOTOKI, Y., Medieval History of Japan

MURANAKA, S., Solid State Chemistry

NAGAYA, M., History and Theory of Social Statistics

NAKANISHI, T., International Relations

NISHII, M., Environmental Conservation and Development

NISHIMURA, M., History of Western Law

NISHIWAKI, T., History of Chinese Philosophy

NISHIYAMA, R., Ancient History of Japan

NIWA, T., American Literature

OKADA, A., Art History and Criticism

OKADA, K., Pedagogy

OKI, M., Linguistics and French Language

ONO, S., Middle High German Literature
OTAGI, H., History of Medieval China
SAEKI, K., Social-environmental System
SAITO, H., Comparative Linguistics and German Language
SAKAGAMI, M., Gravity and Relativity
SHIKAYA, T., Philosophy of Aesthetics
SHIMADA, M., Contemporary History of the United States
SHINGU, K., Fundamental Human Ontology
SHINOHARA, M., Aesthetics and Philosophy
SUGAWARA, K., Social Anthropology and Communication
SUGIMAN, T., Group Dynamics
SUZUKI, M., 18th-century English Culture and Literature
TAKAHASHI, Y., Environmental Conservation and Development
TAKASAKI, K., Algebraic Analysis and Mathematical Physics
TAMADA, O., Environmental Conservation and Development
TANABE, R., German Literature
TOGO, Y., French Linguistics
TOMIDA, Y., Philosophy and History of Philosophy
TOMITA, H., Statistical Physics
TORISSEN, E., Comparative Culture
TSUDA, K., Internal Medicine
UCHIDA, M., Grammar of the Japanese Language
USHIKI, S., Coexisting Systems of Nature and Human Beings
YAMADA, M., Urban Geography
YAMADA, T., Anthropology and Cognition, Shamanism and Ethnicity
YAMAGUCHI, R., Coexisting Systems of Nature and Human Beings
YAMAMOTO, Y., Organic Chemistry
YAMANASHI, M., Cognitive Linguistics
YASUI, K., Human Development
YODA, Y., Shakespeare

Graduate School of Informatics (tel. (75) 753-3599; fax (75) 753-5379; e-mail jimu-soumu@i.kyoto-u.ac.jp; internet www.i.kyoto-u.ac.jp):

EIHO, S., Image Processing Systems
FUJISAKA, H., Non-equilibrium Dynamics
FUKUSHIMA, M., Systems Optimization
FUNAKOSHI, M., Nonlinear Dynamics
GOTOH, O., Bioinformatics
INUI, T., Cognitive Science
ISHIDA, T., Global Information Network
ISO, Y., Analysis of Inverse Problems
IWAI, T., Dynamical Systems Theory
IWAMA, K., Logic Circuits, Algorithms and Complexity Theory
KATAI, O., Symbiotic Systems
KATAYAMA, T., Control Systems Theory
KIGAMI, J., Nonlinear Analysis
KOBAYASHI, S., Biological Information
KUMAMOTO, H., Human Systems
MATSUDA, T., Biomedical Engineering
MATSUYAMA, T., Visual Information Processing
MORIHIRO, Y., Integrated-media Communications
MORIYA, K., Bioresource Informatics
MUNAKATA, T., Physical Statistics
NAKAMURA, Y., Applied Mathematical Analysis
NAKAMURA, Y., Processor Architecture and Systems Synthesis
NISHIDA, T., Artificial Intelligence
NOGI, T., Fundamentals of Complex Systems
OKUNO, H. G., Speech Media Processing
ONODERA, H., Integrated Circuits Design Engineering
SAKAI, H., Mathematical Systems Theory
SAKAI, T., Environmental Informatics
SATO, M., Foundations of Software Science
SATO, T., Advanced Signal Processing
SUGIE, T., Mechanical Systems Control

TAKAHASHI, T., Intelligent Communication Networks
TAKAHASHI, Y., Information Systems
TANAKA, K., Digital Library
TOMITA, S., Computer Architecture
YAMAMOTO, A., Foundations of Artificial Intelligence
YAMAMOTO, Y., Intelligent and Control Systems
YOSHIDA, S., Digital Communications
YUASA, T., Computer Software

Graduate School of Law and Faculty of Law (fax (75) 753-3290; internet www.kyodai.jp/i-english.htm):

AKIZUKI, K., Public Administration
ASADA, M., International Law
DOI, M., Constitutional Law
HATTORI, T., German Law
HAYASHI, N., Roman Law
IDA, R., Law of International Organizations
ITO, T., Japanese Legal History
ITO, Y., Political and Diplomatic History of Japan
KAMEMOTO, H., Legal Philosophy
KARATO, T., Political and Diplomatic History
KASAI, M., Law of Civil Procedure
KAWAHAMA, N., Economic Law
KAWAKAMI, R., European Legal History
KIMURA, M., Comparative Politics
KINAMI, A., Anglo-American Law
KITAMURA, M., Commercial Law
MABUCHI, M., Public Policy
MAEDA, M., Commercial Law
MATOBA, T., Political Science
MATSUOKA, H., Civil Law
MORI, T., Constitutional Law
MORIMOTO, S., Commercial Law
MURANAKA, T., Labour Law
NAKAMORI, Y., Criminal Law
NAKANISHI, H., International Politics
NISHIGORI, S., Civil Law
NISHIMURA, K., Social Security Law
OISHI, M., Constitutional Law
OKAMURA, S., Administrative Law
OKAMURA, T., Tax Law
ONO, N., History of Political Thought
OTAKE, H., Political Process
SAKAI, H., International Law
SAKAMAKI, T., Criminal Law
SAKUMA, T., Civil Law
SAKURADA, Y., Private International Law
SHIBAIKE, Y., Administrative Law
SHINKAWA, T., Political Process
SHIOMI, J., Criminal Law
SHIOMI, Y., Civil Law
SHIYAKE, M., Constitutional Law
SUZAKI, H., Commercial Law
SUZUKI, M., International Politics and Economy
TAKAYAMA, K., Criminal Law
TANAKA, S., Legal Philosophy
TANASE, T., Sociology of Law
TERADA, H., Oriental Legal History
TOKUDA, K., Law of Civil Procedure
YAMAMOTO, K., Civil Law
YAMAMOTO, K., Law of Civil Procedure
YAMAMOTO, Y., Civil Law
YOKOYAMA, M., Civil Law
YOSHIOKA, K., Criminology

Graduate School of Letters and Faculty of Letters:

AKAMATSU, A., History of Indian Philosophy
FUJII, J., Japanese History
FUJITA, K., Psychology
FUJITA, M., Japanese Philosophy
FUMA, S., Oriental History
HAMADA, M., Asian History
HATTORI, Y., European History
HAYASHI, S., Humanistic Informatics
HIRATA, S., Chinese Language and Literature
IKEDA, S., History of Chinese Philosophy

ISHIKAWA, Y., Geography
ITO, K., Philosophy
ITO, K., Sociology
IWAKI, K., Aesthetics and Art History
IZUMI, T., Archaeology
KAMADA, M., Japanese History
KATAYANAGI, E., Christian Studies
KATSUYAMA, S., Japanese History
KAWAI, K., Chinese Language and Literature
KAWAZOE, S., History of Western Medieval Philosophy
KETA, M., Philosophy of Religion
KIDA, A., Japanese Language and Literature
KIHIRA, E., Contemporary History
KINDA, A., Geography
KOBAYASHI, M., History of Western Philosophy
MATSUDA, M., Sociology
MIMAKI, K., Buddhist Studies
MINAMIKAWA, T., European History
MIYAUCHI, H., English Language and Literature
NAGAI, K., Contemporary History
NAKAMURA, K., American Literature
NAKAMURA, T., Art History
NAKATSUKASA, T., Greek and Latin Classics
NEDACHI, K., Aesthetics and Art History
NISHIMURA, M., German Language and Literature
OCHIAI, E., Sociology
OSAKA, N., Psychology
OTANI, M., Japanese Language and Literature
SAITO, Y., Italian Language and Literature
SAKURAI, Y., Psychology
SATO, A., Slavic Languages and Literature
SHOGAITO, M., Linguistics
SUGIMOTO, Y., 20th-century Studies
SUGIURA, K., Geography
SUGIYAMA, M., Oriental History
TAGUCHI, N., French Language and Literature
TAKAHASHI, H., Greek and Latin Classics
TAKUBO, Y., Linguistics
TOKUNAGA, M., Sanskrit Language and Literature
UCHII, S., Philosophy and History of Science
UEHARA, M., Archaeology
WAKASHIMA, T., English Language and Literature
YOSHIDA, J., French Language and Literature
YOSHIDA, K., Linguistics
YOSHIMOTO, M., Oriental History

Graduate School of Medicine and Faculty of Medicine (Yoshida konoe-cho, Sakyo-ku, Kyoto 606-8501; tel. (75) 753-4300; fax (75) 753-4348; e-mail shomu06@mail.adm.kyoto-u.ac.jp; internet www.med.kyoto-u.ac.jp):

CHIBA, T., Gastroenterology and Hepatology
FUJII, S., Gynaecology and Obstetrics
FUJITA, J., Clinical Molecular Biology
FUKUDA, K., Anaesthesia
FUKUHARA, S., Epidemiology and Health Care Research
FUKUI, T., Clinical Epidemiology
FUKUSHIMA, M., Pharmacoepidemiology
FUKUYAMA, H., Functional Brain Imaging
HASHIMOTO, N., Neurosurgery
HAYASHI, T., Psychiatry
HIRAIDE, A., Center for Medical Education
HIRAOKA, M., Radiation Oncology and Image-applied Therapy
HONJO, T., Immunology and Genomic Medicine
ICHIYAMA, S., Clinical Laboratory Medicine
IDE, C., Anatomy and Neurobiology
IMANAKA, Y., Healthcare Economics and Quality Management

INAGAKI, M., Metabolism and Clinical Nutrition
INUI, K., Pharmacy
ITO, J., Otolaryngology, Head and Neck Surgery
KANEKO, T., Morphological Brain Science
KAWANO, K., Integrative Brain Science
KIHARA, M., Global Health and Socio-Epidemiology
KITA, T., Cardiovascular Medicine
KOIZUMI, A., Health and Environmental Sciences
KOMEDA, M., Cardiovascular Surgery
KOSUGI, S., Biomedical Ethics
MAEKAWA, T., Transfusion Medicine and Cell Therapy
MANABE, T., Diagnostic Pathology
MATSUDA, F., Genome Epidemiology
MIMORI, T., Rheumatology and Clinical Immunology
MINATO, N., Immunology and Cell Biology
MISHIMA, M., Respiratory Medicine
MITSUYAMA, M., Microbiology
MIYACHI, Y., Dermatology
NABESHIMA, Y., Pathology and Tumour Biology
NAKAHARA, T., Public Health and International Health
NAKAHATA, T., Paediatrics
NAKAMURA, T., Orthopaedic and Musculoskeletal Surgery
NAKANISHI, S., Biological Sciences
NAKAO, K., Medicine and Clinical Science
NARUMIYA, S., Cell Pharmacology
NODA, M., Molecular Oncology
NOMA, A., Physiology and Biophysics
OGAWA, O., Urology
OHMORI, H., Physiology and Neurobiology
SAKAMOTO, J., Epidemiological and Clinical Research Information Management
SATO, T., Biostatistics
SERIKAWA, T., Laboratory Animals
SHIMIZU, A., Human Genome Analysis
SHINOHARA, T., Molecular Genetics
SHIOTA, K., Anatomy and Developmental Biology
SHIRAKAWA, T., Health Promotion and Human Behaviour
SUZUKI, S., Plastic and Reconstructive Surgery
TAKAHASHI, R., Neurology
TAKEDA, S., Radiation Genetics
TAKETO, M., Pharmacology
TAMAKI, K., Legal Medicine
TANAKA, K., Transplantation and Immunology
TOGASHI, L., Diagnostic Imaging and Nuclear Medicine
TSUKITA, S., Cell Biology
UCHIYAMA, T., Haematology and Oncology
WADA, H., Thoracic Surgery
YOKODE, M., Clinical Innovative Medicine
YOSHIHARA, H., Medical Informatics
YOSHIMURA, N., Ophthalmology and Visual Sciences

Graduate School of Pharmaceutical Sciences and Faculty of Pharmaceutical Sciences (46-29 Yoshida Shimoadachi-cho, Sakyo-ku, Kyoto 606-8501; tel. (75) 753-4510; fax (75) 753-4502; internet www.pharm.kyoto-u.ac.jp):

AKAIKE, A., Pharmacology
FUJII, N., Bio-organic Medicinal Chemistry
HANDA, T., Biosurface Chemistry
HASHIDA, M., Drug Delivery Research
HONDA, G., Pharmacognosy
ITOH, N., Genetic Biochemistry
KANEKO, S., Molecular Pharmacology
KATO, H., Structural Biology
KAWAI, A., Molecular Microbiology
SAJI, H., Patho-Functional Bioanalysis
TAKAKURA, Y., Biopharmaceutics and Drug Metabolism
TAKEMOTO, Y., Organic Chemistry

TOMIOKA, K., Synthetic Medicinal Chemistry
TSUJIMOTO, G., Genomic Drugs Discovery

Graduate School of Science and Faculty of Science:

AGATA, K., Developmental Biology
AOYAMA, H., Theory of Elementary Particles
ARUGA, T., Surface Chemistry
AWAJI, T., Physical Oceanography
FUJIYOSHI, Y., Molecular Biophysics
FUKAYA, K., Geometry
HANADA, T., Inorganic Materials Chemistry
HARA-NISHIMURA, I., Plant Cell Biology
HATA, H., Theoretical Particle Physics
HAYASHI, K., Organic Chemistry
HIRAJIMA, T., Petrology
HIRANO, T., Neurobiology
HORI, M., Animal Ecology
HORIUCHI, H., Theoretical Nuclear Physics
IKAWA, M., Partial Differential Equations
IMAFUKU, M., Ethology
IMAI, K., Experimental Nuclear Physics
IMANISHI, H., Foliation and Symplectic Geometry
INAGAKI, S., Astrophysics
IYEMORI, T., Solar Terrestrial Physics
KAJIMOTO, O., Physical Chemistry
KATAYAMA, K., Biological Anthropology
KATO, K., Number Theory
KATO, S., Representation Theory
KATO, S., Theoretical Chemistry
KAWAI, H., Theoretical Particle Physics
KIDA, H., Climate Physics
KITAMURA, M., Mineralogy
KONO, A., Topology
KOYAMA, K., Cosmic Ray Physics
KUROKAWA, H., Solar Physics
MACHIDA, S., Geomagnetism and Space Physics
MAIHARA, T., Astrophysics
MARUOKA, K., Synthetic Organic Chemistry
MARUYAMA, M., Algebraic Geometry
MASUDA, F., Stratigraphy and Sedimentology
MATSUDA, Y., Solid State Physics
MATSUKI, T., Lie Groups
MIKI, K., Structural Biochemistry and Protein Crystallography
MIWA, T., Algebraic Analysis
MIZUSAKI, T., Low-Temperature Physics
MORI, K., Molecular Biology
MORIWAKI, A., Algebraic Geometry
NAGATA, T., Astrophysics
NAGATANI, A., Plant Physiology
NAKAJIMA, H., Representation Theory and Geometry
NAKAMURA, T., Nuclear Astrophysics
NISHIDA, G., Algebraic Topology
NISHIKAWA, K., Experimental High Energy Physics
NISHIWADA, K., Differential Equations, Financial Mathematics
OBATA, M., Petrology
OIKE, K., Seismology and Physics of the Earth's Interior
OKADA, A., Active Tectonics and Geomorphology
OKADA, K., Plant Molecular Genetics
ONUKI, A., Statistical Physics
OSUKA, A., Organic Chemistry
SAITO, G., Organic Solid State Chemistry
SAITO, H., Number Theory
SASAO, N., Experimental High Energy Physics
SATOH, N., Developmental Genomics
SETOGUCHI, T., Vertebrate Palaeontology
SHIBATA, K., Solar and Cosmic Plasma Physics
SHICHIDA, Y., Molecular Physiology
SHIGEKAWA, I., Probability Theory
SHIMAMOTO, T., Structural Geology and Rock Rheology

SHIRAYAMA, Y., Marine Biology
SHISHIKURA, M., Dynamical System
SUGIYAMA, H., Chemical Biology, Bio-organic Chemistry
TAKEMOTO, S., Geodesy
TAKEMURA, K., Quaternary Geology and Geothermal Sciences
TAKADA, S., Developmental Biology
TANAKA, K., Solid State Spectroscopy, Laser Spectroscopy
TANAKA, Y., Volcano Magnetism
TANIMORI, T., Cosmic Ray Physics
TANIMURA, Y., Theoretical Chemical Physics
TERAO, T., Chemical Physics
TERAZIMA, M., Physical Chemistry, Biophysical Chemistry
TOBE, H., Plant Systematics and Evolution
TSUTSUMI, Y., Nonlinear Partial Differential Equations
UE, M., Low-dimensional Topology
UEDA, T., Complex Analysis in Several Variables
UEMATSU, T., Theory of Elementary Particles
UENO, K., Theory of Complex Manifolds
YAMADA, K., Theory of Condensed Matter
YAMAGIWA, J., Primatology and Anthropology
YAMAUCHI, J., Physical Chemistry and Electron Spin Resonance
YAMAUCHI, M., Number Theory
YAO, M., Physics of Disordered Systems
YODEN, S., Meteorology
YONEI, S., Radiation Biology
YOSHIDA, H., Number Theory
YOSHIKAWA, K., Chemical Physics, Biological Physics
YOSHIMURA, K., Inorganic Chemistry, Solid State Chemistry and Physics, Nuclear Magnetic Resonance
YUSA, Y., Hydrology and Geothermal Sciences

School of Health Sciences, Faculty of Medicine (53 Syogoin Kawahara-cho, Sakyo-ku, Kyoto 606-8507):

AMANO, S., Experimental Epileptology and Neuropathology
EGAWA, T., Diabetes, Teaching Renal Failure, Foot Care
FUJITA, M., Cardiology
FUKUDA, K., Nuclear Magnetic Resonance
FUKUDA, Y., Hepatology, Clinical Immunology
FUNATO, T., Laboratory Medicine and Molecular Diagnostics
HAYASHI, Y., Adult Health Nursing
HINOKUMA, F., Maternal Nursing, Midwifery
INAMOTO, T., Surgery and Clinical Oncology
KABEYAMA, K., Midwifery, Mother and Child Nursing, Women's Health
KATSURA, T., Preventive Nursing, Community Health Nursing
KAWASAKI, N., Biochemistry and Glycobiology
KONISHI, N., Occupational Therapy, Developmental Delay
MITANI, A., Rehabilitation and Brain Science
MIYAJIMA, A., Environmental Health Nursing
NARUKI, H., Community Health Nursing
NOMURA, S., Neuroanatomy and Functional Human Anatomy
SAITO, Y., Basic Nursing, Hospital Infection Control
SAKURABA, S., Psychiatric and Mental Health Nursing
SASADA, M., Haematology and Infectious Diseases
SUGA, S., Clinical Psychology
TOICHI, M., Psychiatry, Cognitive Neuroscience

TSUBOYAMA, T., Orthopaedics, Musculoske-
letal Oncology, Bone Metabolism
TSUKITA, S., Cell Biology
UMEMURA, S., Biomedical Ultrasonics
YAMANE, H., Occupational Therapy for
Mental Disorders

Law School (fax (75) 753-3290; internet www
.kyodai.jp/i-ls.htm):

ASADA, M., International Law
DOI, M., Constitutional Law
ENDO, K., Law Practice Unit
HAMAMOTO, S., Law Practice Unit
HATTORI, T., German Law
HAYASHI, N., Roman Law
HONDA, M., Law Practice Unit
IDA, R., International Law
IIMURA, Y., Law Practice Unit
ITO, T., Japanese Legal History
ITO, Y., Political and Diplomatic History of
Japan
KAMEMOTO, H., Legal Philosophy
KAMIKO, A., Law Practice Unit
KASAI, M., Law of Civil Procedure
KAWAHAMA, N., Economic Law
KAWAKAMI, R., European Legal History
KINAMI, A., Anglo-American Law
KITAGAWA, K., Law Practice Unit
KITAMURA, M., Commercial Law
MAEDA, M., Commercial Law
MATSUDA, K., Law Practice Unit
MATSUOKA, H., Civil Law
MORI, T., Constitutional Law
MORIKAWA, S., Law Practice Unit
MORIMOTO, S., Commercial Law
MURAKAMI, K., Law Practice Unit
MURANAKA, T., Labour Law
NAKAGAWA, H., Law Practice Unit
NAKAMORI, Y., Criminal Law
NISHIGORI, S., Civil Law
NISHIMURA, K., Social Security Law
OISHI, M., Constitutional Law
OKAMURA, S., Administrative Law
OKAMURA, T., Tax Law
SAKAI, H., International Law
SAKAMAKI, T., Criminal Law
SAKUMA, T., Civil Law
SAKURADA, Y., Private International Law
SHIBAIKE, Y., Administrative Law
SHIMIZU, M., Law Practice Unit
SHIOMI, J., Criminal Law
SHIOMI, Y., Civil Law
SHIYAKE, M., Constitutional Law
SUZAKI, H., Commercial Law
TAKAYAMA, K., Criminal Law
TANASE, T., Sociology of Law
TERADA, H., Oriental Legal History
TOKUDA, K., Law of Civil Procedure
YAMAGAMI, K., Law Practice Unit
YAMAMOTO, K., Law of Civil Procedure
YAMAMOTO, K., Civil Law
YAMAMOTO, Y., Civil Law
YASUKI, K., Law Practice Unit
YOKOYAMA, M., Civil Law
YOSHIOKA, K., Criminology

ATTACHED RESEARCH INSTITUTES

**Academic Center for Computing and
Media Studies:** Yoshida-Honmachi, Sakyo-
ku, Kyoto; f. 2002; Dir Prof. T. MATSUYAMA.

Center for African Area Studies: Shimoadachi-cho 46, Yoshida, Sakyo-ku, Kyoto; f.
1986; Dir Prof. Dr S. ARAKI.

Center for Archaeological Operations:
Yoshida Honmachi, Sakyo-ku, Kyoto; f. 1977;
Dir Prof. Dr M. UEHARA.

Center for Ecological Research: 509-3 2-
chome, Hirano, Otsu, Shiga 520-2113; f.
1991; Dir Prof. Y. TSUBAKI.

Center for Southeast Asian Studies:
Shimoadachi-cho 46, Yoshida, Sakyo-ku,
Kyoto; f. 1965; Dir Prof. Dr K. TANAKA;
publ. *Southeast Asian Studies* (4 a year),
Kyoto Review of Southeast Asia (in English).

**Center for the Promotion of Excellence
in Higher Education:** Yoshida-nihon-
matsu-cho, Sakyo-ku, Kyoto; f. 2003; Dir
Prof. Dr T. TANAKA.

Disaster Prevention Research Institute:
Gokasho, Uji City, Kyoto; f. 1951; Dir Prof. K.
ISHIHARA.

Environment Preservation Center:
Yoshida Honmachi, Sakyo-ku, Kyoto; f.
1977; Dir Prof. K. OSHIMA.

**Field Science Education and Research
Center:** Oiwake-cho, Kitashirakawa, Sakyo-
ku, Kyoto; f. 2003; Dir Prof. M. TANAKA.

**Fukui Institute for Fundamental Chem-
istry:** Takanonishihiraki-cho, Sakyo-ku,
Kyoto; f. 2002; Dir Prof. H. NAKATSUJI.

Institute of Advanced Energy: Gokasho,
Uji City, Kyoto; f. 1941; Dir Prof. A.
KOHYAMA.

Institute for Chemical Research: Gokasho, Uji City, Kyoto; f. 1926; Dir Prof. N.
ESAKI.

Institute of Economic Research: Yoshida
Honmachi, Sakyo-ku, Kyoto; f. 1962; library
of 75,722 vols; Dir Prof. Dr T. SAWA.

Institute for Frontier Medical Sciences:
53 Kawahara-cho, Shogoin, Sakyo-ku, Kyoto
606-8507; f. 1998; Dir Prof. N. NAKATSUJI.

Institute for Research in Humanities:
Ushinomiya-cho, Yoshida, Sakyo-ku, Kyoto;
f. 1939; Dir Prof. B. KIN; publ. *Journal of
Oriental Studies* (1 a year), *Journal of
Humanities Studies* (in Japanese, annual),
Annual Bibliography of Oriental Studies,
Annals ZINBUN (in European languages,
irreg.).

Institute for Virus Research: Kawara-
cho, Shogoin, Sakyo-ku, Kyoto; f. 1956; Dir
Prof. R. KAGEYAMA.

Kyoto University Archives: Yoshida Honmachi, Sakyo-ku, Kyoto; f. 2000; Dir Prof. Dr
J. SASAKI.

**Kyoto University International Innov-
ation Center:** Kyoto-Daigaku-katsura,
Nishikyo-ku, Kyoto; f. 2001; Dir Prof. K.
MAKINO.

Kyoto University Museum: Yoshida Honmachi, Sakyo-ku, Kyoto; f. 1997; Dir Prof. Dr
I. YAMANAKA.

Primate Research Institute: Kanrin 41-2,
Inuyama City, Aichi Prefecture; f. 1967; Dir
Prof. N. SHIGEHARA.

Radiation Biology Center: Yoshida
Konoecho, Sakyo-ku, Kyoto; f. 1976; research
and postgraduate training in radiation biology; Dir Prof. T. MATSUMOTO.

Radioisotope Research Center: Yoshida
Konoecho, Sakyo-ku, Kyoto; f. 1971; Dir Prof.
Dr Y. ISOZUMI.

**Research Center for Low Temperature
and Materials Science:** Oiwake-cho, Kitashirakawa, Sakyo-ku, Kyoto; f. 2002; Dir
Prof. T. MIZUSAKI.

**Research Institute for Mathematical
Sciences:** Kitashirakawa, Sakyo-ku, Kyoto;
f. 1963; research and postgraduate training
in mathematical sciences; library of 78,931
vols; Dir Prof. Y. TAKAHASHI.

**Research Institute for Sustainable
Humanosphere:** Gokasho, Uji City, Kyoto;
f. 2004; Dir Prof. S. KAWAI.

Research Reactor Institute: Kumatori-
cho, Sennan-gun, Osaka; f. 1963; library of
45,300 vols; Dir Prof. S. SHIROYA.

**Yukawa Institute for Theoretical Phys-
ics:** Kitashirakawa, Sakyo-ku, Kyoto; f. 1953;
Dir Prof. T. KUGO; publ. *Progress of Theoretical Physics* (12 a year).

KYUSHU INSTITUTE OF DESIGN

Shiobaru 4-9-1, Minami-ku, Fukuoka-shi
815-8540

Telephone: (92) 553-4407
Fax: (92) 553-4593
E-mail: syomuka@kyushu-id.ac.jp
Internet: www.kyushu-id.ac.jp

Founded 1968
Independent
Academic year: April to March (2 semesters)

Pres.: SHO YOSHIDA
Dir-Gen.: MAKOTO OHYA
Dean of Students: MASAMICHI OHKUBO
Library Dir: RYUZO TAKIYAMA

Number of teachers: 96
Number of students: 1,208 (929 undergraduate, 279 postgraduate)

PROFESSORS

Department of Environmental Design:

DOI, Y., History of Architecture and Indus-
trial Design
HIROKAWA, S., Theory of Environmental
Design
ISHII, A., Environmental Systems, Building
and Environment Engineering
KATANO, H., Environmental Systems and
Building Construction
KATO, H. M., Environmental Planning and
Design
MIYAMOTO, M., Environmental Planning
and Design
OHKUBO, M., Environmental Systems and
Structural Engineering
SHIGEMATSU, T., Theory of Environmental
Design

Department of Industrial Design:

FUKATA, S., Intelligent Mechanics and
Control
ISHIMURA, S., Industrial History
ITOI, H., Industrial Design
MORITA, Y., Public Space and Element
Design
SAKATA, T., Mathematical Statistics
SAKI, K., Tribology
SATO, H., Ergonomics
TOCHIHARA, Y., Environmental Ergonomics
YASUKOUCHI, A., Physiological Anthropol-
ogy

Department of Visual Communication
Design:

FUKUSHIMA, S., Artificial Intelligence
GENDA, E., Image Design
NAGASHIMA, K., Image Engineering
SATO, M., Research and Design on Sign
Communication
URAHAMA, K., Image Information Process-
ing
WAKIYAMA, S., Visual Image Design
YAMASHITA, S., Vision Science and Neuro-
biology
YAMASHITA, Y., Vision Science and Psycho-
physics

Department of Acoustic Design:

FUJIEDA, M., Science of Sound Culture
FUJIWARA, K., Science of Acoustical Envir-
onment
IWAMIYA, S., Science of Acoustical Environ-
ment
KAWABE, T., Science of Acoustical Environ-
ment
NAKAJIMA, Y., Science of Acoustic Informa-
tion
NAKAMURA, S., Science of Sound Culture
YOSHIKAWA, S., Science of Acoustic Infor-
mation

Department of Art and Information Design:

FUJIMURA, N., Media Design
KUROSAWA, S., Media Art and Culture
OHNISHI, S., Media Art and Culture
OTA, S., Information Environment Sci-
ences

SASABUCHI, S., Information Environment Sciences

KYUSHU INSTITUTE OF TECHNOLOGY

1-1 Sensui-sho, Tobata-ku, Kitakyushu-shi, Fukuoka 804-8550

Telephone: (93) 884-3008
Fax: (93) 884-3015
E-mail: sou-kikaku@jimu.kyutech.ac.jp
Internet: www.kyutech.ac.jp

Founded 1909
Independent
Language of instruction: Japanese
Academic year: April to March

Pres.: TERUO SHIMOMURA
Registrar: MAKOTO YOSHIDA
Librarian: MORIO MATSUNAGA

Library of 489,867 vols
Number of teachers: 636 full-time
Number of students: 6,307

Deans

Faculty of Computer Science and Systems Engineering: T KODAMA
Faculty of Engineering: T. KOBAYASHI
Graduate School of Computer Science and Systems Engineering: H. TSUKAMOTO

Publications: *Bulletin*, *Memoirs*.

KYUSHU UNIVERSITY

6-10-1 Hakozaki, Higashi-ku, Fukuoka 812-8581

Telephone: (92) 642-2111
Fax: (92) 642-2113
Internet: www.kyushu-u.ac.jp

Founded 1911
Independent
Academic year: April to March

Pres.: T. KAJIYAMA
Vice-Pres: S. ARIKAWA, Y. IMANISHI, W. KOTERAYAMA, H. NAKANO, Y. SHIBATA, M. YANAGIHARA
Admin.: K. HAYATA
Librarian: Y. IMANISHI

Library of 3,741,114 vols
Number of teachers: 2,338
Number of students: 18,202

DEANS

Faculty of Agriculture: K. IMAIZUMI
Faculty of Dental Science: A. AKAMINE
Faculty of Design: H. SATO
Faculty of Economics: Y. OGINO
Faculty of Engineering: K. OGI
Faculty of Engineering Sciences: T. TSUTSUI
Faculty of Human–Environment Studies: T. WATANABE
Faculty of Humanities: Y. KAWAMOTO
Faculty of Information Science and Electrical Engineering: M. TATEIBA
Faculty of Languages and Cultures: K. YAMASHITA
Faculty of Law: N. UEDA
Faculty of Mathematics: M. T. NAKAO
Faculty of Medical Sciences: H. KANAIDE
Faculty of Pharmaceutical Sciences: YUKIHIRO SHOYAMA
Faculty of Sciences: T. ODAGAKI
Faculty of Social and Cultural Studies: K. TAKADA
Graduate School of Systems Life Sciences: T. MURAKAMI
Law School (Professional Graduate School): Y. ODE
School of Education: T. INABA

DIRECTORS

Admission Center: Y. SHIBATA
Art, Science and Technology Center for Cooperative Research: W. KOTERAYAMA
Bio-Architecture Center: S. KUHARA

Biotron Institute: J. CHIKUSHI
Center for Future Chemistry: S. SHINKAI
Center of Advanced Instrumental Analysis: K. MATSUMOTO
Computing and Communications Center: K. MURAKAMI
Hydrogen Technology Research Center: T. KONOMI
Institute for Materials Chemistry and Engineering: N. IMAISHI
Institute for Ionized Gas and Laser Research: M. TSUJI
Institute for Irradiation and Analysis of Quantum Radiation: K. ISHIBASHI
Institute of Health Science: K. UEZONO
Institute of Tropical Agriculture: H. YAHATA
International Student Center: M. YANAGIHARA
Kansei Center for Arts and Science: K. OGI
Kyushu University Asia Research Organization: T. OKAZAKI
Kyushu University Museum: T. MURAE
Laboratory for Waste Water Treatment: H. KOYAMA
Medical Institute of Bioregulation: Y. YOSHIKAI
Natural Disaster Information Center of Western Japan: K. ZEN
Radioisotope Center: M. HIRATA
Research and Development Center for Higher Education: H. SHIMA
Research Center for Education in Health Care Systems: M. TSUNEYOSHI
Research Center for Korean Studies: S. ISHIKAWA
Research Institute for Applied Mechanics: S. IMAWAKI, Research Institute of Superconductor Science and System: K. FUNAKI
Research Laboratory for High Voltage Electron Microscopy: Y. TOMOKIYO
Space Environment Research Center: K. YUMOTO
Steel Research Center: S. TAKAKI
System LSI Research Center: H. YASUURA
Venture Business Laboratory: A. SUEOKA

PROFESSORS

Admission Center (6-10-1 Hakozaki, Higashi-ku, Fukuoka 812-8581; tel. (92) 642-4488; fax (92) 642-4485; e-mail info@ac.kyushu-u.ac.jp; internet www.ac.kyushu-u.ac.jp):

TAKEYA, S., Information Science

Art, Science and Technology Center for Cooperative Research (6-1 Kasuga-koen, Kasuga, Fukuoka 816-8580; tel. (92) 583-7883; fax (92) 573-8729; internet www.astec.kyushu-u.ac.jp):

KUWANO, N., Advanced Functional Materials
MASE, A., Ionized Gas and Laser
MIURA, N., Environment and New Energy
NAKASHIMA, H., Advanced Functional Devices
TANIGAWA, T., Liaison Division
YUMOTO, N., Design Division

Bio-Architecture Center (6-10-1 Hakozaki, Higashi-ku, Fukuoka 812-8581; tel. (92) 642-7282):

FURUYA, S., Metabolic Regulation Research
KONDO, T., Biomaterial Design
SHIRAISHI, F., Bioprocess Design

Biotron Institute (6-10-1 Hakozaki, Higashi-ku, Fukuoka 812-8581; tel. (92) 642-3066; fax (92) 642-3069; e-mail seikan@agr.kyushu-u.ac.jp; internet 133.5.207.201/index.html):

CHIKUSHI, J., Soil Environment

Center for Future Chemistry (6-10-1 Hakozaki, Higashi-ku, Fukuoka 812-8581; tel. and fax (92) 642-3609; e-mail ogawatcm@mbox.nc.kyushu-u.ac.jp):

OGAWA, M., Functional Materials Technology, Life Sciences

Computing and Communications Center (6-10-1 Hakozaki, Higashi-ku, Fukuoka 812-8581; tel. (92) 642-2303; fax (92) 642-2294; e-mail syomu@cc.kyushu-u.ac.jp; internet www.cc.kyushu-u.ac.jp):

AOYAGI, M., Computational Science
FUJINO, S., Computing
HIROKAWA, S., Information Science
TABATA, Y., German

Faculty of Agriculture (6-10-1 Hakozaki, Higashi-ku, Fukuoka 812-8581; tel. (92) 642-2802; fax (92) 642-2804; internet www.agr.kyushu-u.ac.jp):

EGASHIRA, K., Soil Mineralogy and Chemistry
FUJII, H., Silkworm Genetic Resources
FURUKAWA, K., Applied Microbiology
FURUSE, M., Advanced Animal and Marine Bioresources
HATTORI, M.-A., Reproductive Physiology and Biotechnology
HIRAMATSU, K., Water Environmental Engineering
HONJO, T., Marine Environmental Science
IIDA, S., Forest Resources Management
IKEDA, M., Plant Nutrition and Soil Fertility
IKEUCHI, Y., Chemistry and Technology of Animal Products
IMAIZUMI, K., Nutrition Chemistry
ISHINO, Y., Protein Chemistry and Engineering
ITO, M., Marine Bioresource Chemistry and Technology
IWAMOTO, H., Functional Anatomy of Domestic Animals
IWAYA-INOUE, M., Crop Science
KAI, S., Agricultural Marketing
KANAZAWA, S., Microbiological Biochemistry of Soils
KAWAGUCHI, Y., Silkworm Science
KIMURA, M., Biochemistry
KOBAYASHI, Y., Plant Metabolic Physiology
KONDO, R., Systematic Forest and Forest Products Sciences
KUBOTA, F., Plant Production Physiology
KUHARA, S., Molecular Gene Technology
KURODA, K., Wood Chemistry
KUWANO, E., Pesticide Chemistry
MAKI, T., Applied Meteorology
MASUDA, Y., Grassland Science
MATSUI, S., Fish Production Technology
MATSUMOTO, K., Food Analysis
MATSUYAMA, M., Marine Biology
MIYAMOTO, T., Food Hygiene Chemistry
MOHRI, T., Zoology and Reproductive Biology
MORI, K., Bioproduction and Environment Information Sciences
MORITA, M., Biomacromolecular Materials Science
MURASE, Y., Wood Material Technology
NADA, Y, Agricultural Ecology
NAKANO, Y., Irrigation and Water Utilization
NAKAO, M., Marine Biochemistry
NAKAZONO, A., Fish Ecology and Fisheries Biology
ODA, K., Wood Science
OHBA, M., Bioresources and Management
OHTSUBO, M., Environmental Soil Engineering
OKAMOTO, M., Applied Biological Regulation Technology
OKUBO, H., Horticultural Science
OMURA, H., Erosion Control
OTSUKI, K., Forest Ecosphere Sciences and Management
RYUKOH, H., Forest Policy and Resource Management
SATOH, H., Plant Genetic Resources
SHIMIZU, S., Insect Pathology and Microbial Control
SHIMODA, M., Food Process Engineering

SHIRAHATA, S., Cellular Regulation Technology
SHIRAISHI, S., Silviculture
SONOMOTO, K., Microbial Technology
SUZUKI, N., Quantitative Analysis of Agricultural Economics
TADAUCHI, O., Entomology
TAKAGI, M., Insect Natural Enemies
TAKANAMI, Y., Plant Pathology
TANAKA, S., Postharvest Sciences
TSUJI, M., Farm Management
WARIISHI, H., Bioresources Chemistry
YAMADA, K., Food Chemistry
YAMASHITA, A., Agricultural Biophysics
YOKOGAWA, H., Agricultural Economics
YOSHIDA, S., Forest Management
YOSHIMURA, A., Plant Breeding

Faculty of Dental Science (3-1-3 Maidashi, Higashi-ku, Fukuoka 812-8582; tel. (92) 641-1151; internet www.dent.kyushu-u.ac.jp):

AKAMINE, A., Endodontology and Operative Dentistry
HIRATA, M., Molecular and Cellular Biochemistry
IIJIMA, T., Oral Anatomy and Cell Biology
IKEMOTO, Y., Dental Anaesthesiology
ISHIKAWA, K., Biomaterials
KOYANO, K., Removable Prosthodontics
MAEDA, K., Periodontology
NAKAMURA, S., Oral and Maxillofacial Oncology
NAKANISHI, H., Oral Ageing Science
NAKASIMA, A., Orthodontics
NINOMIYA, Y., Oral Neuroscience
NONAKA, K., Paediatric Dentistry
SAKAI, H., Oral Pathology and Medicine
SHIRASUNA, K., Oral and Maxillofacial Surgery
TANAKA, T., Mineralized Tissue Biology
TERADA, Y., Fixed Prosthodontics
YAMAMOTO, K., Biochemical and Molecular Pharmacology
YAMASHITA, Y., Preventive Dentistry
YOSHIURA, K., Oral and Maxillofacial Radiology

Faculty of Design (4-9-1 Shiobaru, Minami-ku, Fukuoka 815-8540; tel. (92) 553-4400; fax (92) 553-4593; internet www.design.kyushu-u.ac.jp):

DOI, Y., History of Architecture and Urban Design
FUJIEDA, M., Composition
FUJIMURA, N., Contents Engineering
FUJIWARA, K., Architectural Acoustics
FUKATA, S., Mechatronics
FUKUSHIMA, S., Image Information Engineering
GENDA, E., Image Design
ISHIDA, T., Architecture Design Theory
ISHII, A., Industrial Design
ISHII, A., Urban and Building Environmental Engineering
ISHIMURA, S., Industrial History
ITABASHI, Y., Contact Comparative Linguistics
IWAMIYA, S., Psychological Acoustics and Acoustic Engineering
KADOTA, H., Media-processing Architecture and Algorithm
KANEKIYO, H., Landscape Architecture
KATANO, H., Building Construction
KAWABE, T., Elementary Particle Physics, High Energy Physics
KIYOSUMI, M., Design Strategy and Design for Branding
KUROSAWA, S., Copyright
MIYAMOTO, M., History of Japanese Cities and Architecture
MORITA, Y., Public Space and Element Design, Industrial Design
NAKAJIMA, Y., Perceptual Psychology
NAKAMURA, S., Composition and Media Art
NISHIYAMA, N., Urban Planning and Design, Landscape Architecture

OHNISHI, S., Art History of Korea and Japan
OTA, S., Functional Analysis
SAKAMOTO, H., Image Engineering
SAKATA, T., Mathematical Statistics
SAKI, K., Tribology
SASABUCHI, S., Mathematical Statistics
SATO, H., Ergonomics
SATO, M., Design and Research on the Sign Communication
SHIGEMATSU, T., Landscape Conservation and Restoration
TAKEDA, T., Virtual Reality
TOCHIHARA, Y., Environmental Ergonomics
URAHAMA, K., Image Information Processing
WAKIYAMA, S., Multiple Image
WATANUKI, S., Kansei Science
YAMASHITA, S., Neurobiology
YAMSHITA, Y., Psychophysics of Vision
YASUKOUCHI, A., Physiological Anthropology
YOSHIKAWA, S., Musical Instrument Acoustics

Faculty of Economics (6-19-1 Hakozaki, Higashi-ku, Fukuoka 812-8581; tel. (92) 642-2357; fax (92) 642-2349; e-mail kzssyomu@jimu.kyushu-u.ac.jp; internet www.en.kyushu-u.ac.jp):

FUJII, Y., International Economic Analysis
FUKAGAWA, H., International Economic Analysis
FURUKAWA, T., Mathematics and Computer Sciences
HAMASUNA, K., International Economic Analysis
HISANO, K., Industrial Systems
HORIE, Y., Economic Analysis and Policy
HOSOE, M., Economic Systems Analysis
INATOMI, M., International Business Analysis
IWAMOTO, S., Mathematics and Computer Sciences
IWASAKI, I., Business and Technology Management
IWATA, K., International Economic Analysis
KAKU, S., Management Systems
KAWANAMI, Y., International Economic Analysis
KONISHI, Y., Business and Technology Management
MAESONO, Y., Mathematics and Computer Sciences
MIURA, I., Economic Systems Analysis
MURAFUJI, I., Business and Technology Management
MUROYAMA, Y., Economic Analysis and Policy
NAGAIKE, K., Business and Technology Management
NAKAI, T., Mathematics and Computer Sciences
NAKAMURA, H., Business and Technology Management
OGINO, Y., Industrial Systems
OSHITA, J., Accounting Systems
OSUMI, K., Economic Systems Analysis
SAEKI, C., Economic Systems Analysis
SEKI, G., Economic Analysis and Policy
SHINOZAKI, A., International Business Analysis
SHIOTSUGU, K., Management Systems
SHUTTO, N., Business and Technology Management
TAKITA, H., International Economic Analysis
TOKINAGA, S., Mathematics and Computer Sciences
USHIYAMA, M., Management Systems
YOSHIDA, M., Business and Technology Management

Faculty of Engineering (6-10-1 Hakozaki, Higashi-ku, Fukuoka 812-8581; tel. (92) 642-3244; fax (92) 642-3243; e-mail

kossyomu@jimu.kyushu-u.ac.jp; internet www.eng.kyushu-u.ac.jp/research):

AKIMOTO, F., Urban and Regional Planning
ANDO, J., Marine Hydrodynamics
ARAI, Y., Molecular Systems Chemistry
ASO, S., Space Systems Dynamics
EHARA, S., Geothermics
ESAKI, T., Environmental Geotechnology
FUKAI, J., Heat Transfer
FUKUCHI, N., Functional Design of Marine Systems
FUKUDA, K., Energy Environment, Economic Systems and Hydrodynamics in Nuclear Reactors
FUKUSHIMA, H., Electrochemistry of Materials
FURUKAWA, A., Hydraulic Machinery
FURUKAWA, M., Aerodynamics of Machinery
FURUTA, H., Applied Organic Chemistry
GOTO, M., Biochemical Engineering, Separation Technology
GOTO, N., Guidance and Control
HARA, K., Gel Properties and Applications in Environmental Engineering
HASHIMOTO, N., Coastal Engineering
HINO, S., Structural Mechanics
HIRAJIMA, T., Mineral Processing and Recycling
HIROKAWA, S., Graphic Science, Biomechanics
HISAEDA, Y., Artificial Enzyme Chemistry, Electroorganic Chemistry
HOJO, J., Applied Inorganic Chemistry
HORITA, Z., Microstructure Control and Characterization
IDEMITSU, K., Nuclear Fuel and Waste Management
IDOGAKI, T., Applied Quantum Physics
IKEDA, N., Applied Nuclear Physics
IMASAKA, T., Applied Analytical Chemistry
IMATO, T., Electroanalytical Chemistry
IRIE, M., Advanced Materials Chemistry
ISHIBASHI, K., Radiation Measurement and Safety
ISHIHARA, T., Inorganic Advanced Materials Chemistry
ITOI, R., Geothermal Reservoir Engineering
JINNO, K., Water Resources Engineering
KAI, S., Applied Physics
KAJIWARA, H., Systems Engineering
KAJIWARA, T., Polymer Engineering, Biochemical Engineering
KAMIHIRA, M., Biotechnology, Cell and Tissue Engineering
KANAYAMA, H., Computational Mechanics
KANEMITSU, Y., Sound and Vibration Control of Mechanical System
KATAYAMA, Y., Bioengineering, DDS and Biochip
KAWAKAMI, K., Bioreaction Engineering
KIDO, H., Reactive Gas Dynamics
KIJIMA, K., Hydrodynamics and Ship Dynamics
KIMIZUKA, N., Molecular Organization Chemistry
KISHIDA, M., Reaction Engineering and Advanced Materials Processing
KOMATSU, T., Environmental Hydraulics
KONDO, E., Systems Mathematics and Engineering
KONDO, Y., Materials Strength, Fatigue
KONDOU, T., Dynamics of Machinery, Mechanical Vibration
KONOMI, T., Fuel Cell Systems
KUDO, K., Nuclear Reactor Engineering
KUNOO, K., Aerospace Structural Systems
KUSUDA, T., Environmental Engineering
MASUDA, M., Materials Science
MATSUI, K., Rock Engineering and Mining Machinery
MATSUMIYA, H., Fluid Dynamics
MATSUMURA, S., Irreversible Processes in Materials

MATSUSHITA, H., Construction Materials and Concrete Structure
MINEMOTO, M., Fluid Mechanics and Transport Phenomena
MIURA, H., Advanced Powder Metallurgy
MORI, H., Thermal Energy Conversion
MOTOOKA, T., Materials Science
MUKAIDA, M., Materials Science
MURAKAMI, T., Bionic Design, Biomechanics and Biotribology
MURAKAMI, Y., Fatigue and Fracture
MURASE, E., Engine Systems
NAGAMURA, T., Polymer Science and Ultra-fast Molecular Photonics
NAGAYAMA, K., Advanced Microphysics
NAKAO, Y., Fusion Plasma Science
NAKASHIMA, K., Physicochemical Property for Materials
NAKASHIMA, N., Nanocarbon and Supramolecular Chemistry
NOGUCHI, H., Solid Mechanics
OCHIAI, H., Geotechnical and Geoenvironmental Engineering
OGI, K., Processing of Composite Materials
OHTA, H., Space Utilization Science and Technology
OHTA, K., Vibration and Acoustics
ONIKURA, H., Machining Systems
OTSUKA, H., Earthquake Engineering
SAKAGUCHI, K., Innovation System Analysis
SAKURAI, A., Flight Dynamics
SAWADA, R., Nano and Micro Systems, Bioengineering
SHIMAOKA, T., Environmental Engineering and Solid Waste Management
SHIMATANI, Y., River Engineering
SHIMIZU, M., Reaction Engineering for Materials
SHINKAI, A., Ship Design and Maritime Intelligence Technology
SHINKAI, S., Molecular Recognition Chemistry
SUEOKA, A., Dynamics of Machinery
SUGIMURA, J., Machine Design and Tribology
SUMI, T., Transport Planning
TAKAKI, S., Phase Transformation and Structure Control
TAKAMATSU, H., Bio–heat and Mass Transfer, Thermal Engineering
TAKATA, Y., Thermal Engineering
TOYOSADA, M., Fracture and Welding Mechanics
TSUGE, Y., Process Systems Engineering
USHIJIMA, K., Engineering Geophysics
WATANABE, K., Economic Geology
YAMADA, S., Applied Photochemistry, Nanoparticle Technology
YAMAMOTO, Y., Tribology
YAMASAKI, N., Aerospace Propulsion
YOSHIKAWA, T., Structural Design of Marine Systems
ZEN, K., Geotechnical and Disaster Prevention Engineering

Faculty of Engineering Sciences (6-1 Kasuga-koen, Kasuga, Fukuoka 816-8560; tel. (92) 583-7555; fax (92) 583-7060; internet www.tj.kyushu-u.ac.jp):

AOKI, T., High Speed Gas Dynamics
AOKI, Y., Theoretical Chemistry
HARATA, A., Analytical Chemistry
HAYASHI, T., Thermal Environment Systems
HONJO, H., Nonlinear Physics
KUWABARA, M., Electroceramics
KYOZUKA, Y., Coastal Environmental Research
MASUDA, M., Laser-aided Fluid Diagnostics
MATSUNAGA, N., Environmental Fluid Dynamics
MIYOSHI, E., Quantum Materials Physics
NAKASHIMA, H., Advanced Energy Conversion Engineering

NISHIKAWA, M., Energy Chemical Engineering
OHTA, S., Complex Dynamic Systems
SASADA, I., Applied Electromagnetics
SHIMANOE, K., Functional Materials
SHIMIZU, A., Thermal Hydraulics in Extreme Conditions
TAKASAKI, K., Engines and Combustion
TANABE, T., Energy Materials Science and Engineering
TANIMOTO, J., Urban Architectural Environmental Engineering
TERAOKA, Y., Functional Inorganic Materials Chemistry
TOCHIHARA, H., Surface Science
TOMOKIYO, Y., Crystal Physics and Engineering
TSUTSUI, T., Organic Materials Chemistry
UCHINO, K., Plasma and Quantum Electronics
YOKOYAMA, S., Electric Energy Systems

Faculty of Human–Environment Studies (6-19-1 Hakozaki, Higashi-ku, Fukuoka 812-8581; tel. (92) 642-2353; fax (92) 642-3104; internet www.human.kyushu-u.ac.jp):

FUJIMOTO, K., Environmental Planning in Architecture
FURUKAWA, H., Social and Organizational Psychology
HAKODA, Y., Cognitive Psychology
HARIZUKA, S., Clinical Psychology for Disabled Children
HORI, Y., History of Ancient Roman Architecture and Urbanization
INABA, T., Comparative and International Education III
KAWANO, A., Steel Structures and Structural Analysis
KAWASE, H., Earthquake Disaster Mitigation
KIKUCHI, S., Housing Design and Planning
KITAYAMA, O., Psychoanalysis
MAEDA, J., Wind Disaster Mitigation
MARUNO, S., Cognitive Developmental Psychology
MATSUDA, T., Sociology of Educational Organization
MATSUZAKI, Y., Clinical Psychology
MINAMI, H., Environmental Psychology
MIURA, K., Psychology of Art and Cognition
MOCHIDA, K., Comparative and International Education I
NAKAMIZO, S., Psychology and Visual Perception
NANRI, Y., Planning of Adult and Community Education
NOJIMA, K., Counselling Psychology
OBA, N., Clinical Psychology
OGAWA, T., Sociology
OHGAMI, H., Developmental Psychology
SAKINO, K., Reinforced Concrete Structures and Structural Mechanics
SEKI, K., Comparative Religion
SINYA, Y., History of Japanese Education
SUZUKI, Y., Sociology
TAJIMA, S., Clinical Psychology
TAKESHITA, T., Architectural Planning
TOMOEDA, T., Sociology
TSUCHIDO, T., Philosophy of Education II
WATANABE, T., Building, Environmental Design and Control
YAOSAKA, O., Educational Administration
YOSHITANI, T., Intercultural Education

Faculty of Humanities (6-19-1 Hakozaki, Higashi-ku, Fukuoka 812-8581; tel. (92) 642-2351; fax (92) 642-2349; internet www.lit.kyushu-u.ac.jp):

ANDO, T., Japanese History
ASAI, K., German Literature
HAMADA, K., Korean History
HOSOKAWA, R., Ethics
IDE, S., Aesthetics and History of Fine Arts
IMANISHI, Y., Japanese Literature
INADA, T., Linguistics
KAWAMOTO, Y., East Asian History

KIKUCHI, E., Occidental Philosophy
MIYAMOTO, K., Archaeology
OKANO, K., Indian Philosophy
SAEKI, K., Japanese History
SAKAMOTO, T., Linguistics
SAKAUE, Y., Japanese History
SAKONO, F., Japanese Language
SHIBATA, A., Chinese Philosophy
SHIMIZU, K., History of Islamic Civilization
SHINPO, H., Occidental History
TAKAGI, A., Geography
TAKEMURA, N., Chinese Literature
TANI, R., Occidental Philosophy
TUBURAYA, Y., Occidental Philosophy
UENO, Y., Japanese Literature
USHIROSHOJI, M., Aesthetics and History of Fine Arts
YAMANOUCHI, A., Occidental History
YOSHII, A., French Literature

Faculty of Information Science and Electrical Engineering (6-10-1 Hakozaki, Higashi-ku, Fukuoka 812-8581; tel. (92) 642-3244; fax (92) 642-3243; e-mail kossyomu@jimu.kyushu-u.ac.jp; internet www.isee.kyushu-u.ac.jp/indexe.html):

AKAIWA, Y., Digital Radio Communications
AMAMIYA, M., Architecture of Intelligent Systems
ARAKI, K., Software Engineering and Internetworking
ARIKAWA, S., Discovery Science
ENPUKU, K., Superconducting Electronics
FUKUDA, A., Systems Software
FUNAKI, K., Applied Superconductivity
HARA, M., Electric Power Engineering
HASEGAWA, R., Machine Intelligence and Systems Architecture
HASEGAWA, T., Robotics
IRAMINA, K., Biomedical Engineering
KAWABE, T., Robust Control
KAWAHARA, Y., Theoretical Computer Science
KOHDA, T., Communication Systems
KUROKI, Y., Microelectronics
MAKINOUCHI, A., Data and Knowledge Science
MATSUYAMA, K., Solid-State Functional Devices
MIYAO, M., Silicon Heterostructural Materials and Devices
MURAKAMI, K., Computer Systems Architecture
NIIJIMA, K., Signal and Image Analysis
NINOMIYA, T., Electronic Circuits and Systems
OKADA, T., Laser Engineering
SAKOE, H., Media Signal Recognition
SAKURAI, K., Cryptography and Information Security
TAKEDA, M., Text Algorithms and Data Mining
TAKEO, M., Superconducting Magnet and Device Technology
TANIGUCHI, R., Computer Vision
TATEIBA, M., Electromagnetic Wave Sensing and Satellite Communications
TOKO, K., Advanced Biomimetic Materials and Sensors
WADA, K., Control Engineering
YAMASHITA, M., Theoretical Computer Science
YASUMOTO, K., Microwave Engineering and Photonics
YASUURA, H., VLSI Systems Design
YOKOO, M., Multi-agent Systems, Artificial Intelligence
YOSHIDA, K., Electrical Machinery and Control
YOSHIDA, K., RF Microelectronics

Faculty of Languages and Cultures (4-2-1 Ropponmatsu, Chuo-ku, Fukuoka 810-8560; tel. (92) 726-4508; fax (92) 726-4511; internet www.rc.kyushu-u.ac.jp/~ilc/index-e.html):

ABE, Y., German
AO, Y., French

FUJISAKI, M., English
HAGA, K., French
INOUE, N., English
KOTANI, K., English
MATSUMURA, Y., English
MICHEL, W., German
MORI, S., French
OHTA, K., English
OKANO, S., German
TAJIMA, M., English
TANAKA, T., German
TANAKA, Y., French
TANIGUCHI, H., English
TOKUMI, M., English
TSUMURA, M., German
TSUNEKAWA, M., German
TSUNEYOSHI, N., German
YAMAMURA, H., Spanish
YAMASHITA, K., English

Faculty of Law (6-19-1 Hakozaki, Higashi-ku, Fukuoka 812-8581; tel. (92) 642-2354; fax (92) 642-2349; e-mail kashomu3@jimu.kyushu-u.ac.jp; internet www.law.kyushu-u.ac.jp):

ABE, M., International Business Law
AGO, S., International Economic Law
DOI, M., Criminology and Criminal Policy
EGUCHI, A., Legal Culture
GONG, R., Legal Culture
ISHIDA, M., International Political History
ISHIKAWA, S., Political History
ISOGAWA, N., Civil Law
KAWASHIMA, S., Civil Procedure
KISA, S., Administrative Law
KOCHI, H., Civil Law
KONO, T., International Private Law
KUMAGAI, K., Intellectual Property Law
KUMANO, N., Political History
MATSUO, M., Criminal Law
NAKAKUBO, H., Labour and Social Law
NAOE, S., Western Legal History
NISHIMURA, S., Roman Law
NISHIYAMA, Y., Commercial Law, Company Law
NODA, S., Labour Law
ODE, Y., Law of Criminal Procedure
OHASHI, Y., Administrative Law
OHKAWARA, N., Comparative Politics
OHKUMA, Y., Constitutional Law
PEJOVIC, C., Maritime Law
SAKAMOTO, M., Constitutional Law
SAKO, I., Philosophy of Law
SEKIGUCHI, M., History of Political Thought
SHICHINOHE, K., Civil and Water Law
SHIMIZU, I., Commercial Law I, Consumer Law
TANAKA, N., Civil Law
UCHIDA, H., Criminal Law
UEDA, K., Criminal Defence
UEDA, N., Japanese Legal History
WATANABE, T., Tax Law
WATANABE, Y., Constitutional Law
YABUNO, Y., Contemporary Japanese Politics
YANAGIHARA, M., International Law

Faculty of Mathematics (6-10-1 Hakozaki, Higashi-ku, Fukuoka 812-8581; tel. (92) 642-2773; fax (92) 642-2522; internet www.math.kyushu-u.ac.jp):

BANNAI, E., Algebra and Combinatorics
EI, S.-I., Nonlinear Analysis
FUKUMOTO, Y., Fluid Mechanics
HAMACHI, T., Dynamic Systems
HARA, T., Mathematical Physics
IWASAKI, K., Geometry and Differential Equations
KANEKO, M., Number Theory
KATO, M., Topology
KAWASHIMA, S., Partial Differential Equations
KAZAMA, H., Complex Analysis
KOIKE, M., Number Theory
KONISHI, S., Mathematical Statistics
KOSAKI, H., Operator Algebra and Operator Theory

MATSUI, T., Mathematical Physics
MIYAOKA, R., Differential Geometry
MORISHITA, M., Topology and Number Theory
NAKAO, M., Partial Differential Equations
NAKAO, M. T., Computational Mathematics
NISHII, R., Statistical Learning Theory
NOMURA, T., Representation Theory and Harmonic Analysis
OSADA, H., Probability Theory
SAEKI, O., Topology
SATO, E., Algebraic Geometry
SUZUKI, M., Complex Analysis
TABATA, N., Numerical Analysis
TANIGUCHI, S., Stochastic Differential Equations and the Malliavin Calculus
TEZUKA, S., Statistical Computation, Randomness and Computational Finance
WAKAYAMA, M., Representation Theory and Zeta Functions
WATATANI, Y., Operator Algebra
YAMADA, K., Differential Geometry
YOSHIDA, M., Complex Analysis
YOSHIKAWA, A., Mathematical Analysis

Faculty of Medical Sciences (3-1-1 Maidashi, Higashi-ku, Fukuoka 812-8582; tel. (92) 641-1151; internet www.med.kyushu-u.ac.jp):

ARAKI, T., Health Care Administration and Management
FURUE, M., Dermatology
HAMASAKI, N., Clinical Chemistry and Laboratory Medicine
HARA, T., Paediatrics
HARADA, M., Medicine and Biosystemic Science
HASHIZUME, M., Disaster and Emergency Medicine
HAYASHI, J., Environmental Medicine and Infectious Diseases
HIMENO, K., Parasitology
HONDA, H., Clinical Radiology
IIDA, M., Medicine and Clinical Science
IKEDA, N., Forensic Pathology and Science
ISHIBASHI, T., Ophthalmology
ITO, Y., Pharmacology and Cell Signalling
IWAKI, T., Neuropathology
IWAMOTO, Y., Orthopaedic Surgery
KANAIDE, H., Molecular Cardiology
KANBA, S., Neuropsychiatry
KATANO, M., Cancer Therapy and Research
KIRA, J., Neurology
KOMUNE, S., Otorhinolaryngology
KONO, S., Preventive Medicine
KOSAKA, T., Anatomy and Neurobiology
KUBO, C., Psychosomatic Medicine
MAEHARA, Y., General Surgery
MATSUDA, T., Biomedical Engineering
MIHARA, K., Molecular Biology
MOHRI, S., Biomedicine
NAITO, S., Urology
NAKANISHI, Y., Respiratory Medicine
NISHIOKA, K., Health Care Administration and Management
NOBUTOMO, K., Health Services Management and Policy
NOSE, Y., Medical Information Science
OGATA, H., Health Care Administration and Management
SASAGURI, T., Clinical Pharmacology
SASAKI, T., Neurosurgery
SHIBATA, Y., Developmental Molecular Anatomy
SUEISHI, K., Pathophysiological and Experimental Pathology
SUNAGAWA, K., Cardiovascular Medicine
TAKAHASHI, S., Anaesthesiology and Critical Care Medicine
TAKAYANAGI, R., Geriatric Medicine
TAKESHIGE, K., Molecular and Cellular Biology
TANAKA, M., Surgery and Oncology
TOBIMATSU, S., Clinical Neurophysiology
TSUNEYOSHI, M., Anatomic Pathology
TSUZUKI, T., Medical Biophysics and Radiation Biology

YANAGI, Y., Virology
YOSHIDA, M., Medical Education
YOSHIDA, S., Bacteriology
YOSHIMURA, M., Integrative Physiology

Faculty of Pharmaceutical Sciences (3-1-1 Maidashi, Higashi-ku, Fukuoka 812-8582; tel. (92) 641-1151; internet www.phar.kyushu-u.ac.jp):

HIGUCHI, R., Natural Products Chemistry
HIGUCHI, S., Clinical Pharmacokinetics
INOUE, K., Pharmacology
KATAYAMA, T., Molecular Biology
KOGA, N., Functional Molecular Science
KUROSE, H., Pharmacology and Toxicology
MAEDA, M., Biomolecular Recognition Chemistry
MINE, K., Clinical Pharmacology
OHDO, S., Medico-pharmaceutical Sciences
SASAKI, S., Bio–organic and Synthetic Chemistry
SHOYAMA, Y., Medicinal Resources Regulation
SUEMUNE, H., Pharmaceutical Synthetic Chemistry
TANAKA, Y., Pharmaceutical Cell Biology
UEDA, T., Immunology
UTSUMI, H., Bio–functional Science
YAMADA, H., Molecular Life Sciences
ZAITSU, K., Bio–analytical Chemistry

Faculty of Sciences (6-10-1 Hakozaki, Higashi-ku, Fukuoka 812-8581; tel. (92) 642-2521; fax (92) 642-2522; internet www.science.scc.kyushu-u.ac.jp):

ANNAKA, M., Physical Chemistry
ARATONO, M., Physical Chemistry
FUJIKI, Y., Molecular Cell Biology
HASHIMOTO, M., Theoretical Astrophysics
HIROOKA, T., Middle Atmosphere Dynamics
IBA, K., Plant Physiology and Plant Molecular Biology
INOUE, S., Solid–State Physics
ISHIGURO, S., Solution Chemistry
ISHIHARA, T., Molecular Genetics
ITOH, H., Large-scale Atmospheric Dynamics
IWASA, Y., Theoretical Biology
KATO, T., Mineral Physics
KATSUKI, T., Synthetic Organic Chemistry
KAWABATA, S., Protein Chemistry
KAWAGUTI, T., Low-dimensional Systems
KAWATO, T., Constructive Organic Chemistry
KIMURA, M., Quantum Chemistry
KIMURA, Y., Soft Condensed Matter Physics
KITAGAWA, H., Inorganic Chemistry
KOYAMA, H., Constructive Organic Chemistry
KUGE, O., Biological Chemistry
MAEDA, Y., Radiochemistry
MATSUKUMA, A., Palaeobiology
MIYAHARA, S., Geophysical Fluid Dynamics
MURAE, T., Organic Cosmochemistry and Geochemistry
NAKADA, M., Mantle Dynamics
NAKANISHI, H., Statistical Physics
NAKANO, H., Quantum Chemistry
NORO, T., Experimental Nuclear Physics
ODAGAKI, T., Condensed Matter Theory
OOMI, G., Solid State Physics
SAGARA, K., Experimental Nuclear Physics
SAGATA, N., Molecular and Developmental Cell Biology
SAKAI, K., Coordination Chemistry
SANO, H., Stratigraphy and Sedimentology
SEKIYA, H., Structural Chemistry
SEKIYA, M., Planetary System Formation
SHIMAZAKI, K., Plant Physiology
SHIMIZU, H., Seismology, Volcanic Seismology
SHIMOHIGASHI, Y., Biological Chemistry
SHINOZAKI, B., Low-dimensional Systems
SUGIYAMA, H., Molecular and Cellular Neurobiology

TACHIDA, H., Molecular Evolution, Population Genetics
TAKAHASHI, K., Marine Geology
TAKEDA, S., Liquids and Disordered Systems
TANAKA, T., Solar–Terrestrial Physics
TOH, Y., Animal Physiology
TOKESHI, M., Aquatic Ecology, Community Ecology
TOKITA, M., Polymer Physics
TORAMARU, A., Volcanology
TSURIMOTO, T., DNA Replication and Chromosomal Functions
WADA, H., Magnetism
WATANABE, Y., Solid State Physics
YAHARA, T., Ecology and Evolution
YAHIRO, M., Theoretical Nuclear Physics
YOKOYAMA, T., Inorganic Reaction Chemistry
YOSHIMURA, K., Analytical Chemistry
YUMOTO, K., Space and Earth Electromagnetism

Faculty of Social and Cultural Studies (4-2-1 Ropponmatsu, Chuo-ku, Fukuoka 810-8560; tel. (92) 726-4508; fax (92) 726-4511; internet www.scs.kyushu-u.ac.jp/index.html):

ARIMA, M., Japanese History
FURUYA, Y., Cultural Anthropology
GOYAMA, K., Chinese Classical Literature
HATTORI, H., Japanese History
KITA, I., Geochemistry
KOIKE, H., Prehistoric Ecology
KUSAKA, M., Chinese Literature
MATSUMOTO, T., Modern Japanese Literature
MIYAKAWA, Y., Regional Studies
MORI, T., Greek Philosophy
MORIKAWA, T., Asian History
NAKAHASHI, T., Physical Anthropology
NEI, Y., Philosophy
OSANAI, Y., Geology and Petrology
OTA, Y., Cultural Anthropology
SAKAI, H., Sedimentological Sciences
SHIMA, H., Environmental Biology and Entomology
SHIMIZU, H., Cultural Anthropology
SHIMIZU, Y., Japanese Political Thought
TAKADA, K., International Relations
TAKAHASHI, K., History of Science
TAKANO, N., Japanese History
TANAKA, Y., Archaeology
YATA, O., Environmental Biology and Entomology
YOSHIDA, M., Modernization of Japan
YOSHIOKA, H., Political Economy of Sciences

Institute for Materials Chemistry and Engineering (6-1 Kasuga-koen, Kasuga, Fukuoka 816-8580; tel. (92) 583-7555; fax (92) 583-7060; internet www.cm.kyushu-u.ac.jp):

FUJII, M., Physical Properties
HAYAMI, H., Nanoscale Evaluation
IMAISHI, N., Photonic Materials
INANAGA, J., Synthetic Methodology and Catalysis
KANEMASA, S., Advanced Organic Synthesis
KIKUCHI, H., Design of Nanosystems
KOYAMA, S., Microprocess Control
MARUYAMA, A., Integrated Biomaterials
MATAKA, S., Systems of Functional Molecules
MISHIMA, M., Physical Organic Chemistry
MORI, A., Chemistry of Functional Molecules
NAGASHIMA, H., Cluster Chemistry
NARUTA, Y., Advanced Molecular Conversion
SATO, O., Nanostructured Integrated Materials
SHINMYOZU, T., Chemistry of Molecular Assemblies
TAKAHARA, A., Hybrid Molecular Assemblies

TSUJI, M., Heterogeneous Integrated Materials
YAMAKI, J., Energy Storage Materials
YOSHIZAWA, K., Theoretical Chemistry

Institute of Health Science (6-1 Kasuga-koen, Kasuga, Fukuoka 816-8580; tel. (92) 583-7555; fax (92) 583-7060):

HASHIMOTO, K., Sports Psychology
ICHIMIYA, A., Psychiatry, Mental Health
KUMAGAI, S., Health and Exercise Epidemiology
NISHIMURA, H., Sports Psychology
OGAKI, T., Exercise Physiology
UEZONO, K., Applied Chronobiology
YAMAMOTO, K., Applied Physiology

Institute of Tropical Agriculture (6-10-1 Hakozaki, Higashi-ku, Fukuoka 812-8581; tel. (92) 642-3076; e-mail njm3076@agr.kyushu-u.ac.jp; fax (92) 642-3077; internet www.agr.kyushu-u.ac.jp/english/tropic):

OGATA, K., Tropical Crops and Environment
YAHATA, H., Global Environment Conservation (Forest Ecophysiology)

International Student Centre (6-10-1 Hakozaki, Higashi-ku, Fukuoka 812-8581; tel. (92) 642-2141; fax (92) 642-2144; e-mail intlrkoryu@jimu.kyushu-u.ac.jp; internet www.isc.kyushu-u.ac.jp):

KASHIMA, E., Japanese Language Education
OKAZAKI, T., Japanese Language Education
POLLACK, J., Exchange Student Programmes (Anthropology)
SCULLY, E., Multicultural Education
SHIMIZU, Y., Japanese Language Education

Kyushu University Museum (6-10-1 Hakozaki, Higashi-ku, Fukuoka 812-8581; tel. and fax (92) 642-4252; e-mail office@museum.kyushu-u.ac.jp; internet www.museum.kyushu-u.ac.jp):

IWANAGA, S., Japanese Prehistory
MATSUKUMA, A., Paleobiology

Medical Institute of Bioregulation (3-1-1 Maidashi, Higashi-ku, Fukuoka 812-8582; tel. (92) 641-1151; internet www.bioreg.kyushu-u.ac.jp):

FUKUI, Y., Immunogenetics
FUKUMAKI, Y., Disease Genes
HAYASHI, K., Genome Analysis
KOHDA, D., Structural Biology
MAKINO, N., Molecular and Clinical Gerontology
MORI, M., Molecular and Surgical Oncology
NAKABEPPU, Y., Neurofunctional Genomics
NAKAYAMA, K., Cell Biology
NISHIMURA, J., Clinical Immunology
SUMIMOTO, H., Biochemistry and Molecular Biology
TAKEDA, K., Embryonic and Genetic Engineering
TANI, K., Molecular and Clinical Genetics
TOH, H., Genome Informatics
WAKE, N., Molecular and Cell Therapeutics
YOSHIKAI, Y., Host Defence
YOSHIMURA, A., Molecular and Cellular Immunology

Radioisotope Center (6-10-1 Hakozaki, Higashi-ku, Fukuoka 812-8581; tel. (92) 642-2703; fax (92) 642-2706; e-mail jimurad@mbox.nc.kyushu-u.ac.jp; internet www.scc.kyushu-u.ac.jp/ri):

OSAKI, S., Radiation Protection

Research and Development Center for Higher Education (4-2-1 Ropponmatsu, Chuo-ku, Fukuoka 810-8560; tel. (92) 726-4508; fax (92) 726-4511; internet www.rche.kyushu-u.ac.jp/index-e.html):

FUCHITA, Y., Organometallic Chemistry
KIRA, Y., Clinical Psychology
SOEJIMA, Y., Crystal Physics

TAKEYA, S., Student Selection, Information Science, Databases

Research Center for Korean Studies (6-10-1 Hakozaki, Higashi-ku, Fukuoka 812-8581; tel. (92) 642-4358; fax (92) 642-4359; e-mail rcks.uok@mbox.nc.kyushu-u.ac.jp; internet rcks.isc.kyushu-u.ac.jp):

MATSUBARA, T., Cultural History of Japanese–Korean Relations

Research Institute for Applied Mechanics (6-1 Kasuga-koen, Kasuga, Fukuoka 816-8580; tel. (92) 583-7502; fax (92) 583-7701; internet www.riam.kyushu-u.ac.jp):

ARAKAWA, K., Fracture Mechanics and Materials
HANADA, K., Advanced Fusion Research Center
IMAWAKI, S., Ocean Eddy Dynamics
ITOH, S.-I., High-energy Plasma Physics
KAKIMOTO, K., Nano-mechanics
KASHIWAGI, M., Free Surface/Interface Dynamics
KOTERAYAMA, W., Ocean Engineering
KURAMOTO, E., High-energy Solid State Physics
MASUDA, A., Dynamics Simulation Research Center
MATSUNO, T., Ocean Circulation Dynamics
NAKAMURA, K., Plasma Surface Interaction
OHYA, Y., Wind Engineering
OIKAWA, M., Nonlinear Dynamics
SATO, K., Advanced Fusion Research Center
TAKAO, Y., Heterogeneous Solid Mechanics
UNO, I., Atmospheric Dynamics
WAKATA, Y., Geophysical Fluid Dynamics
YANAGI, T., Dynamics Simulation Research Center
YOON, J.-H., Dynamics Simulation Research Center
YOSHIDA, N., Extreme-circumstances Structural Materials
ZUSHI, H., Advanced Fusion Research Center

MIE UNIVERSITY

1515 Kamihama-cho, Tsu-shi, Mie 514

Telephone: (592) 32-1211
Fax: (592) 31-9000
Internet: www.mie-u.ac.jp

Founded 1949
Independent
Academic year: April to March

Pres.: RYUICHI YATANI
Chief Admin. Officer: KATSUYUKI KUROSAKI
Librarian: HIROYUKI NODA

Library of 783,000 vols
Number of teachers: 1,740
Number of students: 7,505

Publications: *Outline of Mie University* (every 2 years), *The Journal of Law and Economics* (Hōkei Ronsō), various faculty bulletins

DEANS

Faculty of Bioresources: HITOSHI OBATA
Faculty of Education: TAKESHI KINOSHITA
Faculty of Engineering: GORO SAWA
Faculty of Humanities and Social Sciences: HIDEKAZU HIROSE
School of Medicine: RYUICHI YATANI
College of Medical Sciences: KATSUMI DEGUCHI

UNIVERSITY OF MIYAZAKI

1-1 Gakuen Kibanadai Nishi, Miyazaki-shi, Miyazaki 889-2192

Telephone: (985) 58-7104
Fax: (985) 58-2896
E-mail: kokusai@miyazaki-u.ac.jp
Internet: www.miyazaki-u.ac.jp

Founded 1949; present name and status 2003 following integration of Miyazaki Medical College
Independent
Academic year: April to March (2 semesters)
Pres.: A. SUMIYOSHI
Registrar: K. OHTANI
Librarian: C. TAMURA

Number of teachers: 624
Number of students: 5,450

Publications: Bulletins and memoirs of the faculties

DEANS

Faculty of Agriculture: S. KOBAYE
Faculty of Education and Culture: T. IWA-MOTO
Faculty of Engineering: K. HIRANO
Miyazaki Medical College: H. KANNAN

MURORAN INSTITUTE OF TECHNOLOGY

Mizumoto-cho 27-1, Muroran 050-8585, Hok-kaido
Telephone: (143) 46-5022
Fax: (143) 46-5033
Internet: www.muroran-it.ac.jp
Founded 1949
Independent
Academic year: April to March
Pres.: HIROAKI TAGASHIRA
Admin. Officer: YASHUTO UEMARA
Chief Librarian: KEN-ICHI MATSUOKA

Library of 284,300 vols
Number of teachers: 360
Number of students: 3,500

Publication: *Memoirs* (1 a year).

NAGAOKA UNIVERSITY OF TECHNOLOGY

1603-1 Kamitomioka, Nagaoka, Niigata 940-2188
Telephone: (258) 46-6000
Fax: (258) 47-9000
E-mail: syomugroup@jcom.nagaokaut.ac.jp
Internet: www.nagaokaut.ac.jp
Founded
State control
Language of instruction: Japanese, English
Academic year: April to March
President: Prof. YO KOJIMA
Vice-Pres. for Academic Affairs: Prof. YASU-NORI MIYATA
Vice-Pres. for Evaluation: Prof. IKUZO NISHI-GUCHI
Vice-Pres. for Graduate School: Prof. YASU-NOBU INOUE
Vice-Pres. for Industry–Academia Cooperation and Information: ATSUSHI KAWASAKI
Vice-Pres. for International Affairs: Prof. KOZO ISHIZAKI
Vice-Pres. for Research, Admission and Student Affairs: Prof. KYUICHI MARUYAMA
Dir of Admin.: SATO MASARU

Library of 140,000 vols
Number of teachers: 212
Number of students: 2,469

Departments of Bioengineering, Civil and Environmental Engineering, Electrical Engineering, Management and Information System Science, Materials Science and Technology, Mechanical Engineering, System Safety

DEANS

Graduate School of Engineering: Prof. YASU-NOBU INOUE
Graduate School of Management of Technology: Prof. YASUNORI MIYATA
School of Engineering: Prof. YASUNOBU INOUE

NAGASAKI UNIVERSITY

1-14 Bunkyo-machi, Nagasaki 852-8521
Telephone: (95) 819-2042
Fax: (95) 819-2044
E-mail: www_admin@ml.nagasaki-u.ac.jp
Internet: www.nagasaki-u.ac.jp
Founded 1949
Academic year: April to March
Independent
Pres.: HIROSHI SAITO
Vice-Pres: TSUYOSHI SAKIYAMA, HARUHIKO MASAKI, SHIGERU KATAMINE
Dir-Gen.: SYUSUKE MORITA
Library Dir: TAKATOSHI OKABAYASHI

Library of 1,078,347 vols
Number of teachers: 1,067 full-time
Number of students: 8,935

Publications: *Bulletin of the Faculty of Education*, *Journal of Business and Economics* (4 a year), *Annual Review of South East Asian Studies*, *Annual Review of Economics*, *Nagasaki Medical Journal* (4 a year), *Acta Medica Nagasakiensia* (2 a year), *Report of the Faculty of Engineering* (2 a year), *Journal of Environmental Studies* (2 a year), *Bulletin of the Faculty of Fisheries*, *Bulletin of the School of Allied Medical Sciences*, *Seasonal Report of the Education and Research Centre for Life-long Learning*

DEANS

Faculty of Economics: Prof. TOSHIO SUGIHARA
Faculty of Education: Prof. TATEO HASHIMOTO
Faculty of Engineering: Prof. JUN OYAMA
Faculty of Environmental Studies: Prof. YOSHIHIKO INOUE
Faculty of Fisheries: Prof. MUTSUYOSHI TSU-CHIMOTO
Graduate School of Biomedical Sciences: Prof. KOHTARO TANIYAMA
Graduate School of Science and Technology: Prof. TADASHI ISHIHARA
Institute of Tropical Medicine: Prof. YOSHIKI AOKI
School of Allied Medical Sciences: Prof. AKEMI TERASAKI
School of Dentistry: Prof. MITSURU ATSUTA
School of Medicine: Prof. TAKASHI KANEMATSU
School of Pharmaceutical Sciences: Prof. KENICHIRO NAKASHIMA

DIRECTORS

Animal Research Center: Prof. MICHIO NAKA-MURA
Atomic Bomb Disease Institute: Prof. MASAO TOMONAGA
Center for Educational Research and Training: Prof. AKIFUMI FUKUI
Center for Frontier Life Sciences: Prof. HIROSHI SATO
Center for Instrumental Analysis: Prof. SUSUMI HATAKEYAMA
Division of Comparative Medicine: HIROSHI SATO
Division of Functional Genomics: NORIO NIIKAWA
Division of Radiation Biology and Protection: Prof. YUTAKA OKUMURA
Education and Research Center for Life-long Learning: Prof. KAGEHIRO ITOYAMA
Environmental Protection Center: Prof. TAKEHIRO TAKEMASA
Garden for Medicinal Plants: Prof. ISAO KONO
Health Center: Prof. NOBUKO ISHII
International Student Center: Prof. YOSHI-HIRO MATSUMURA
Joint Research Center: Prof. MAKOTO EGA-SHIRA
Marine Research Institute: Prof. HIDEAKI NAKATA
Research and Development Center for Higher Education: Prof. SHIGERU KATAMINE
Research Center for Tropical Infectious Diseases: Prof. MASAAKI SHIMADA

Science Information Center: Prof. HIDEO KURODA
University Hospital attached to School of Dentistry: Prof. HIROYUKI FUJII
University Hospital attached to School of Medicine: Prof. KOJI SUMIKAWA

PROFESSORS

Faculty of Economics (4-2-1 Katafuchi, Nagasaki 850-8506; tel. (95) 820-6300; fax (95) 820-6370; internet www.econ.nagasaki-u.ac.jp):

AOYAMA, S., Development Economics
BASU, D., International Economics
FUJINO, T., Japanese Corporations and Management
FUJITA, W., Economics of Natural Resources and Energy
FUKAURA, A., Monetary Economics
FUKUZAWA, K., Labour Economics
FURUYAMA, M., Law and Finance
GUNN, G., International Relations
IDE, K., Modern Asian Economies
IMADA, T., Accounting
KANKE, M., Business Management
KASAHARA, T., Business Enterprise and Human Evolution
KAWAMURA, Y., Corporate Planning of Financial Institutions, Investment Banking
KIHARA, T., Cooperation among Nations and International Economics
KOREEDA, M., Microeconomics
MARUYAMA, Y., Decision Making
MATSUMOTO, M., Economic History of the British Empire
MATSUNAGA, A., Small Business Administration
MIHARA, Y., Human Resource Management
MURATA, S., Microeconomics
MURATA, Y., Mathematics
OKADA, H., Financial Accounting
SHIBATA, K., Japanese Economic History
SUGIHARA, T., Management Engineering
SUSAI, M., International Finance
TAGUCHI, N., International Investment
TAKAHASHI, Y., Intellectual Property and Licensing
TAKAURA, Y., Political Economy
TATEYAMA, S., Business Enterprises and Asian Economics
UCHIDA, S., Monetary Economics
UENO, K., Financial Accounting
UNOTORO, Y., Japanese Economy
YAJIMA, K., Derivative Securities

Faculty of Education (fax (95) 819-2265; internet www.edu.nagasaki-u.ac.jp):

ADACHI, K., Analysis and Applied Mathematics
AIKAWA, K., School for Intellectually Iimpaired Children
AKASAKI, M., Teaching of Home Economics
ARITA, Y., Teaching of Social Studies
AZUMA, M., Biology
FUKUI, A., Music Education
FUKUYAMA, Y., Physics
FUNAKOE, K., Law
FURUYA, Y., Materials Science and Engineering
GOTO, Y., Early Childhood Education and Care
HAMASAKI, K., German Literature
HARADA, J., Educational Psychology
HASHIMOTO, T., Science Education
HIGUCHI, S., Analytical Chemistry
HORIUCHI, I., Pianoforte Playing
IIZUKA, T., Philosophy
IKAWA, S., Painting
INOUE, I., American Literature
ITOYAMA, K., Teaching of Technology
IYAMA, K., Social Education
JINNO, N., Biology
KABASHIMA, S., Physics
KAMIZONO, K., Moral and Philosophy Education

KATSUMATA, T., Japanese Literature
KITAMURA, Y., Analysis
KOGA, M., Solid State Physics
MATUNAGA, J., Teaching of Health and Physical Education
MIYAZAKI, M., Developmental Psychology
MURATA, Y., Developmental Psychology
NAKAMURA, M., American Literature
NAKAMURA, Y., English and American Literature
NAKANISHI, H., Biology
NISHIZAWA, S., Physical Fitness
OBARA, T., Exercise Physiology
ODA, M., Design
OSAKI, Y., Astronomy
OTSUBO, Y., Teaching of English
SATO, K., Sculpture
SINNO, T., Psychological Study of Preschool Children's Play
SINOHARA, S., Philosophy
SUGAWARA, M., Exercise Physiology
SUGAWARA, T., Geometry
SUGIYAMA, S., Woodworking
TAHARA, Y., School Health and Sports Physiology
TAKAHASHI, S., International Law, Constitutional Law
TAKAHASHI, S., Sociology
TAMARI, M., Food and Nutritional Chemistry
TANIGAWA, M., Politics
TOMONAGA, S., Psychology
WASHIO, T., Algebra
YAMAGUCHI, T., History
YAMAMOTO, T., Teaching of Japanese
YAMANO, S., Theory of Music
YAMAUCHI, M., Physical Education
YANAGIDA, Y., Educational Sociology
YASUKOUCHI, Y., Teaching of Japanese
YOKOYAMA, M., Politics
YOSHIOKA, H., Educational Psychology

Faculty of Engineering (fax (95) 849-4999; internet www.eng.nagasaki-u.ac.jp):

AOYAGI, H., Biochemistry
EGASHIRA, M., Materials Chemistry
FUJIYAMA, H., Plasma Science
FUKUNAGA, H., Magnetics
FURUMOTO, K., Hydraulics
HARADA, T., Reinforced and Prestressed Concrete Structures
HASAKA, M., Materials Physics and Engineering
IMAI, Y., Fracture Mechanics
ISHIMATSU, T., Measurement and Control Engineering
IWANAGA, H., Analysis of Crystal Structure
IWAO, M., Synthetic Organic Chemistry
KAGAWA, A., Metal Science
KANEMARU, K., Heat Transfer
KAWAZOE, T., Tribology
KISU, H., Computational Mechanics
KOBAYASHI, K., Network Systems
KODAMA, Y., Fluid Dynamics
KUDO, A., Algebra
KUDO, T., Solid–State Electrochemistry
MATSUDA, H., Structural and Engineering Mechanics
MATSUO, H., High-voltage Engineering
MIYAHARA, S., Pattern Recognition and Information Retrieval Systems
NOGUCHI, M., Hydraulics
OGURI, K., Computer and Information Science
OKABAYASHI, T., Dynamics and Control of Structures
ONISHI, M., Coordination Chemistry
OYAMA, J., Electrical Machinery
SAKIYAMA, T., Structural Analysis
SETOGUCHI, K., Fatigue
SHIGECHI, T., Thermal Engineering
SHUGYO, M., Inelastic Behaviour of Steel Structures
TAKAHASHI, K., Structural Vibration
TAKENAKA, T., Electromagnetic Wave Theory

TAMARU, Y., Organic Chemistry
TANABASHI, Y., Soil Mechanics
TANAKA, K., Engineering Optics
TSUJI, M., Electrical Control Systems
UCHIYAMA, Y., Ceramics Science and Technology

Faculty of Environmental Studies (fax (95) 819-2716; internet www.env.nagasaki-u.ac.jp/mainj.shtml):

ARAO, K., Meteorology and Climatology
FUKUSHIMA, K., Anthropology of Religion
GOTO, N., Solid State Physics
HAMA, T., Labour Environment
HAYASE, T., Environmental Politics
HIMENO, J., History of Economics
IDE, Y., Environmental Business Management
IKENAGA, T., Plant Functional Science
IKUNO, M., Civil Law
INOUE, Y., Philosophy
ISHIZAKI, K., Environmental Engineering
KOHRA, S., Environmental Chemistry
MASAKI, H., Oriental Philosophy and Bioethics
MIYA, Y., Crustacean Taxonomy
NAKAMURA, T., Biostatistics and Risk Analysis
NAKAMURA, T., Coastal Oceanography
ONO, T., Environment Economics
SAKUMA, T., Japanese Intellectual History
SONODA, N., German Literature
TAIMURA, A., Exercise Physiology
TAKAZANE, Y., French Culture and Culture Exchange
TAKEMASA, T., Soil Physics
TANIMURA, K., Living Environment
TSUCHIYA, K., Environmental Physiology
UEDA, K., Peptide Chemistry
WAKAKI, T., Japanese Literature
YAMAZAKI, S., Environmental Biochemistry
YOSHIDA, M., Greek Philosophy
YOSHIKAWA, I., Radiation Genetics

Faculty of Fisheries (fax (95) 819-2799; internet www.fish.nagasaki-u.ac.jp/index.htm):

ARAKAWA, O., Marine Food Hygiene
GODA, M., Navigation, Nautical Instruments
HARA, K., Biochemistry
HASHIMOTO, J., Deep-sea Biology
ISHIHARA, T., Aquatic Biochemistry
ISHIMATSU, A., Fish Physiology
ISHIZAKA, J., Biological Oceanography, Ocean Colour Remote Sensing
KATAOKA, C., Marine Social Science
KITAMURA, H., Marine Chemical Ecology, Effects of Pollution on Marine Life
MATSUBAYASHI, N., Colloid and Interface Science
MATSUOKA, K., Micropalaeontology and Coastal Environment Science
MATSUYAMA, M., Limnology and Oceanography
MORII, H., Ecology and Physiology of Marine and Food Bacteria
NAKATA, H., Fisheries Oceanography and Coastal Oceanography
NATSUKARI, Y., Fisheries Biology, Invertebrates, Cephalopoda
NISHINOKUBI, H., Fishing Boat Seamanship, Fishing Gear Engineering
NOZAKI, Y., Chemistry and Technology of Marine Food Materials
ODA, T., Marine Biochemistry
TACHIBANA, K., Nutritional Chemistry of Marine Food
TAKEMURA, A., Acoustical Behaviour of Marine Animals, Life History of Marine Mammals and Sharks
TAMAKI, A., Ecology of Marine Benthos
TSUCHIMOTO, M., Nutritional Physiology of Marine Food
YAMAGUCHI, Y., Fishing Technology Science, Fishing Ground Ecology
YOSHIKOSHI, K., Fish Pathology

Graduate School of Science and Technology (fax (95) 819-2491; internet www.seisan.nagasaki-u.ac.jp):

FUJITA, Y., Marine Phycology
FURUKAWA, M., Polymer Science
GOTOH, K., Remote Sensing
HAGIWARA, A., Marine Invertebrate Zoology, Live Food Science, Applied Planktology
ISHIDA, M., Diesel Combustion Engineering
KURODA, H., Computer and Information Science
MATSUO, H., Electronic and Digital Control
NAKASHIMA, N., Chemistry and Materials Science of Nanocarbons
YOSHITAKE, Y., Vibration of Structures

Institute of Tropical Medicine (1-12-4 Sakamoto, Nagasaki 852-8523; tel. (95) 849-7800; fax (95) 849-7805; internet www.tm.nagasaki-u.ac.jp):

AOKI, Y., Parasitology
HIRAYAMA, K., Molecular Immunogenetics
HIRAYAMA, T., Bacteriology
IWASAKI, T., Pathology
KANBARA, H., Protozoology
MIZOTA, T., Social Environment
MOJI, K., Human Ecology
MORITA, K., Virology
NAGATAKE, T., Internal Medicine
NAKAMURA, M., Biochemistry
SHIMADA, M., Eco-epidemiology
TAKAGI, M., Medical Entomology
YAMAMOTO, N., Preventive Medicine and AIDS Research

School of Dentistry (1-7-1 Sakamoto, Nagasaki 852-8588; tel. (95) 849-7600; fax (95) 849-7608; internet www.de.nagasaki-u.ac.jp):

ATSUTA, M., Fixed Prosthodontics
FUJII, H., Removable Prosthodontics
FUJIWARA, T., Paediatric Dentistry
HARA, Y., Periodontology
HAYASHI, Y., Endodontics and Operative Dentistry
HISATSUNE, K., Dental Materials Science
INOKUCHI, T., Oral and Maxillofacial Surgery II
KATO, Y., Dental Pharmacology
MIZUNO, A., Oral and Maxillofacial Surgery I
NAKAMURA, T., Radiology and Cancer Biology
NAKAYAMA, K., Oral Bacteriology
NEMOTO, T., Oral Biochemistry
OI, K., Dental Anaesthesiology
ROKUTANDA, A., Oral Anatomy
SHINSHO, F., Preventive Dentistry
TAKANO, K., Oral Histology
TODA, K., Oral Physiology
YAMAGUCHI, A., Oral Pathology
YOSHIDA, N., Orthodontics

School of Medicine (1-12-4 Sakamoto, Nagasaki 852-8523; tel. (95) 849-7000; fax (95) 849-7166; internet www.med.nagasaki-u.ac.jp):

AIKAWA, T., Physiology of Visceral Function and Body Fluid
AOYAGI, K., Preventive Health Sciences and Community Health
EGUCHI, K., Immunology, Endocrinology and Metabolism
EISHI, K., Cardiovascular Surgery
FUNASE, K., Human Motor Control, Exercise Physiology
HAMANO, K., Foundations of Nursing
HAYASHI, K., Radiological Science
ISHIHARA, K., Adult Nursing, Cancer Nursing
ISHIMARU, T., Obstetrics and Gynaecology
ITO, T., Biochemistry
KAMIHIRA, S., Laboratory Medicine
KANEMATSU, T., Surgery
KANETAKE, H., Nephro-urology

KATAMINE, S., Cellular and Molecular Biology
KATAYAMA, I., Dermatology
KATO, K., Anatomy of Locomotor Systems, Physical Anthropology
KOHNO, S., Molecular and Clinical Microbiology
KOJI, T., Histology and Cell Biology
KONDO, T., Clinical Biochemistry and Molecular Biology in Ageing-related Vascular Diseases and Cancer
MATSUMOTO, T., Paediatrics
MATSUSAKA, N., Rehabilitation Medicine, Orthopaedic Surgery
MATSUYAMA, T., Cytokine Signalling
MIYASHITA, H., Child Nursing, Rehabilitation
MORISHITA, M., Community Health Nursing
MORIUCHI, H., Medical Virology
NAGAO, T., Occupational Therapy, Assistive Technology
NAGASHIMA, S., Macroscopic Morphology
NAGATA, I., Clinical Neuroscience, Neurology and Neurosurgery
NAKAGOMI, O., Molecular Epidemiology
NAKAJIMA, H., Gynaecological Oncology, Obstetrics
NAKAZONO, I., Forensic Pathology and Science
NIIKAWA, N., Human Genetics
NIWA, M., Neurosensory Pharmacology
OHISHI, K., Midwifery
OHTA, Y., Psychiatry, Mental and Physical Health
OKUMURA, Y., Radiation Biophysics
SATO, H., Comparative Medicine
SEKINE, I., Molecular Pathology
SENJYU, H., Physical Therapy, Pulmonary Rehabilitation
SHIBATA, Y., Radiation Epidemiology
SHIMOKAWA, I., Pathology and Gerontology
SHINDO, H., Orthopaedic Pathomechanism
SHINOHARA, K., Physiology
SUMIKAWA, K., Anaesthesiology
TAGAWA, Y., Thoracic Surgery and Cytometry
TAGUCHI, T., Pathology
TAHARA, H., Physical Therapy, Quality of Life
TAKAHASHI, H., Otorhinolaryngology
TANIYAMA, K., Pharmacology and Therapeutics
TASHIRO, T., Respirology, Infectious Diseases
TERASAKI, A., Adult Health Nursing
TOKUNAGA, M., Public Health Nursing
TOMONAGA, M., Molecular Medicine and Haematology
URATA, H., Adult Nursing, Surgical Nursing
YAMASHITA, S., Molecular Medicine
YANO, K., Cardiovascular Medicine
YOSHIMURA, T., Neurology (Morphology in Neuromuscular Diseases)
YUI, K., Immunology

School of Pharmaceutical Sciences (fax (95) 819-2412; internet www.ph.nagasaki-u.ac.jp/indexj.html):

FUJITA, K., Pharmaceutical Chemistry
HATAKEYAMA, S., Pharmaceutical Organic Chemistry
KAI, M., Chemistry of Biofunctional Molecules
KOBAYASHI, N., Molecular Biology of Diseases
KOHNO, M., Cell Regulation
KOUNO, I., Pharmacognosy
KURODA, N., Analytical Chemistry for Pharmaceutics
MURATA, I., Pharmacotherapeutics
NAKAMURA, J., Pharmaceutics
NAKASHIMA, K., Analytical Research for Pharmacoinformatics
NAKAYAMA, M., Hygienic Chemistry

NATSUMARA, Y., Synthetic Chemistry for Pharmaceutics
UEDA, H., Molecular Pharmacology and Neuroscience
WATANABE, M., Radiation and Life Science
YOSHIMOTO, T., Biotechnology

NAGOYA INSTITUTE OF TECHNOLOGY

Gokiso-cho, Showa-ku, Nagoya 466-855
Telephone: (52) 735-5000
Fax: (52) 735-5009
Internet: www.nitech.ac.jp
Founded 1949
Independent
Language of instruction: Japanese
Academic year: April to March
Pres.: HIROAKI YANAGIDA
Vice-Pres: IWATA AKIRA, NOBUYUKI MATSUI, TETSUMI HORIKOSHI
Dir-Gen.: HIDESHI SUDA
Dir for Univ. Library: KOICHIRO KAWASHIMA
Library of 463,169 vols
Number of teachers: 372
Number of students: 6,516
Publication: *Bulletin* (1 a year).

ATTACHED INSTITUTES

Center for Information and Media Studies: Gokiso-cho, Showa-ku, Nagoya 466-8555; e-mail staff@center.nitech.ac.jp; Dir YUKIE KOYAMA.

Ceramics Research Laboratory: 6–29 Asahigaoka 10-chome, Tajimi, Gifu; Dir SUGURU SUZUKI.

Co-operative Research Center: Gokiso-cho, Showa-ku, Nagoya; Dir KOICHI NAKAMURA.

Instrument and Analysis Center: Gokiso-cho, Showa-ku, Nagoya 466-8555; Dir YOSHIHARU TSUJITA.

Research Center for Micro-structure Devices: Gokiso-cho, Showa-ku, Nagoya; Dir MASAYOSHI UMENO.

NAGOYA UNIVERSITY

Furo-cho, Chikusa-ku, Nagoya 464-8601
Telephone: (52) 789-2044
Fax: (52) 789-2045
E-mail: intl@post.jimu.nagoya-u.ac.jp
Internet: www.nagoya-u.ac.jp
Founded 1939
Independent
Language of instruction: Japanese
Academic year: April to March (two semesters)
Pres.: SHIN-ICHI HIRANO
Vice-Pres: HIDEKI MORI, KOJUN YAMASHITA, SHIN-ICHI YAMAMOTO, YASUO SUGIURA, YUJI WAKAO
Dir-Gen. for Admin.: SABURO TOYODA
Dir of the Library: YOSHITO ITOH
Library: see Libraries and Archives
Number of teachers: 1,831 full-time
Number of students: 16,537
Publication: *Nagoya University Bulletin*

DEANS

Graduate School of Bioagricultural Sciences: T. MATSUDA
Graduate School of Economics: Y. TOMOSUGI
Graduate School of Education and Human Development: T. MURAKAMI
Graduate School of Engineering: N. SAWAKI
Graduate School of Environmental Studies: T. KURODA
Graduate School of Information Science: K. AGUSA
Graduate School of International Development: H. NAKANISHI

Graduate School of Languages and Culture: K. KONDO
Graduate School of Law: H. SABURI
Graduate School of Letters: H. SUGIYAMA
Graduate School of Mathematics: Y. NAMIKAWA
Graduate School of Medicine: M. HAMAGUCHI
Graduate School of Science: I. OHMINE
School of Agricultural Sciences: T. MATSUDA
School of Economics: Y. TOMOSUGI
School of Education: T. MURAKAMI
School of Engineering: N. SAWAKI
School of Informatics and Sciences: M. SANO
School of Law: H. SABURI
School of Letters: H. SUGIYAMA
School of Medicine: M. HAMAGUCHI
School of Science: I. OHMINE

DIRECTORS

Bioscience and Biotechnology Center: M. KOBAYASHI
Center for Asian Legal Exchange: K. SUGIURA
Center for Chronological Research: K. SUZUKI
Center for Cooperative Research in Advanced Science and Technology: G. OBINATA
Center for Developmental Clinical Psychology and Psychiatry: S. HONJO
Center for Gene Research: M. ISHIURA
Center for Information Media Studies: I. YAMAMOTO
Center for Studies of Higher Education: K. TODAYAMA
EcoTopia Science Institute: T. MATSUI
Education Center for International Students: M. EZAKI
Hydrospheric Atmospheric Research Center: H. UYEDA
Information Technology Center: T. WATANABE
International Cooperation Center for Agricultural Education: H. TAKEYA
Nagoya University Museum: M. ADACHI
Radioisotope Research Center: K. NISHIZAWA
Research Center for Materials Science: K. TATSUMI
Research Center of Health, Physical Fitness and Sports: K. SHIMAOKA
Research Institute of Environmental Medicine: I. KODAMA
Solar–Terrestrial Environment Laboratory: R. FUJII
University Hospital: A. IGUCHI

PROFESSORS

Center for Gene Research (Furo-cho, Chikusa-ku, Nagoya 464-8602; tel. (52) 789-3080; fax (52) 789-3081; internet www.gene.nagoya-u.ac.jp/index-e.html):

ISHIURA, M., Genome Biology, Molecular Biology
SUGITA, M., Plant Molecular Biology

Center for Studies of Higher Education (tel. (52) 789-5696; fax (52) 789-5695; e-mail webmaster@cshe.nagoya-u.ac.jp; internet www.cshe.nagoya-u.ac.jp):

NATSUME, T., Comparative Study on Higher Education

Radioisotope Research Center (Furo-cho, Chikusa-ku, Nagoya 464-8602; tel. (52) 789-2563; fax (52) 789-2567; internet www.ric.nagoya-u.ac.jp):

NISHIZAWA, K., Radiation Protection

Nagoya University Museum (Furo-cho, Chikusa-ku, Nagoya 464-8601; tel. (52) 789-5767; fax (52) 789-5896; internet www.num.nagoya-u.ac.jp):

ADACHI, M., Sedimentation and Tectonics
NISHIKAWA, T., Taxonomy and Phylogeny of Marine Invertebrates

Center for Co-operative Research in Advanced Science and Technology (tel. (52) 789-3921; fax (52) 789-3922; internet www .ccrast.nagoya-u.ac.jp):

IWATA, S., Magnetic Materials and Magnetic Devices
KASAHARA, K., Quantum Electronics, Optical Communication
MORI, S., Environment Process Technology
OBINATA, G., Modelling and Control in Robotics, Human–Robot Interfaces, Biocybernetics
OGAWA, M., Semiconductor Devices
TAKAHASHI, H., Copyright

Center for Information Media Studies (tel. (52) 789-3903; fax (52) 789-3900; internet www.media.nagoya-u.ac.jp):

NAGAO, K., Digital Content Technology, Media Informatics, Image and Language Processing, Agent Technology, Artificial Intelligence

Center for Chronological Research (Furo-cho, Chikusa-ku, Nagoya 464-8602; tel. (52) 789-2579; fax (52) 789-3092; internet www .nendai.nagoya-u.ac.jp/en/index.html):

NAKAMURA, T., Geochemistry and Radiochronometry
SUZUKI, K., Petrology and Geochronology

Bioscience and Biotechnology Center (tel. (52) 789-5194; fax (52) 789-5195; internet www.agr.nagoya-u.ac.jp/~nubs/index.html):

HATTORI, T., Plant Cell Function
KITAJIMA, K., Animal Cell Function
KITANO, H., Plant Bioresources
MATSUOKA, M., Plant Molecular Breeding
UOZUMI, T., Molecular Biosystems
WAKAMATSU, Y., Freshwater Fish Stocks

Hydrospheric–Atmospheric Research Center (tel. (52) 789-3466; fax (52) 789-3436; e-mail koho@hyarc.nagoya-u.ac.jp; internet www .hyarc.nagoya-u.ac.jp/hyarc):

NAKAMURA, K., Satellite Meteorology
SAINO, T., Ocean Climate Biology
UYEDA, H., Meteorology
YASUNARI, T., Meteorology, Climate System Study

Center for Asian Legal Exchange (tel. (52) 789-2325; fax (52) 789-4902; e-mail cale@ nomolog.nagoya-u.ac.jp; internet www .nomolog.nagoya-u.ac.jp):

AIKYO, M., Asian Law

Information Technology Center (tel. (52) 789-4352; fax (52) 789-4385; internet www.itc .nagoya-u.ac.jp):

ISHII, K., Computational Fluid Dynamics
MASE, K., Computer Mediated Communication
MIYAO, M., Ergonomics
YOSHIKAWA, M., Database Systems

Center for Developmental Clinical Psychology and Psychiatry (tel. (52) 789-2656; fax (52) 789-5059):

HONJO, S., Child Psychiatry
TSURUTA, K., School Counselling
UJIIE, T., Clinical Support of the Mother–Child Relationship

Education Center for International Students (tel. (52) 789-2198; fax (52) 789-5100; internet www.ecis.nagoya-u.ac.jp):

KASHIMA, T., Phonetics, Teaching Pronunciation of Japanese as a Foreign Language
MATSUURA, M., International Student Advisory and Resource Services
MURAKAMI, K., Teaching Japanese as a Foreign Language
NOMIZU, T., Instrumental Analytical Chemistry, Student Exchange Programme Education
OZAKI, A., Teaching Japanese as a Foreign Language

EcoTopia Science Institute (tel. (52) 789-5262; fax (52) 789-5265; e-mail jimu@esi .nagoya-u.ac.jp; internet www.esi.nagoya-u .ac.jp):

ENOKIDA, Y., Nuclear Fuel Engineering
FUJISAWA, T., High Temperature Physical Chemistry
HASEGAWA, T., Environmental Thermo-Fluid Technologies
HASEGAWA, Y., Energy Science
ICHIHASHI, M., Electron Optics
ITHO, H., Solid Waste Treatment
KATAYAMA, A., Bioremediation and Bioreclamation
KATAYAMA, M., Communication and Information Systems
KITAGAWA, K., Advanced Energy Conversion Systems and Technologies
NAGASAKI, T., Materials Science
OKUBO, H., Electric Power Engineering
SUZUKI, K., Environmental Research
TAKAI, O., Materials Science and Engineering
TANAKA, N., High Resolution Electron Microscopy and Electron Diffraction of Clusters, Wires and Think-Film Related to Nanotechnology
TATEISHI, K., Structural Engineering
TONOIKE, T., Linguistics, Lexicology and Optimality Theory
WATANABE, T., Fluid Informatics and Computational Fluid Dynamics
YOGO, T., Materials Chemistry

Graduate School of Environmental Studies (tel. (52) 789-3454; fax (52) 789-3452; internet www.env.nagoya-u.ac.jp):

AGETA, Y., Glaciology
ANDO, M., Seismology and Geodesy
ENAMI, M., Metamorphic Petrology and Rock-forming Mineralogy
FUJII, N., Volcanology and Planetary Physics
FUKUWA, N., Earthquake Engineering
HATTA, T., Neuropsychology
HAYASHI, N., Economic and Urban Geography
HAYASHI, Y., Sustainable Transport and Spatial Development
HIBINO, T., Electrochemistry
HIRAHARA, K., Seismology
HIROSE, Y., Environmental Social Psychology
HOSHINO, M., Surface Material Systems
IKADATSU, Y., Jurisprudence
IMURA, H., Environmental Systems Analysis and Planning
ISHII, K., Associative Learning
ITAKURA, T., Sociology
ITO, Y., Counselling and Clinical Psychology (Person-centered Approach and Focusing-oriented Psychotherapy)
KAI, K., Meteorology, Climatology and Remote Sensing
KAINUMA, J., Sociology
KANZAWA, H., Meteorology
KATAGI, A., Architectural Design and Theory
KAWABE, I., REE Geochemistry, Geochemical Earthquake Prediction
KAWADA, M., History of Political Thought in Japan
KAWAGUCHI, J., Cognitive Psychology, Human Memory
KAWAI, T., Environmental Science
KAWASAKI, S., Economics
KUNO, S., Environmental Engineering, Environmental Psychology
KURODA, T., Urban Economics, Regional Science, Economic Theory
MASUZAWA, T., Inorganic Biogeochemistry
MATSUBARA, T., Environmental Science, Microbiology, Biochemistry
MATSUMOTO, E., Geochemistry
MIZOGUCHI, T., Historical Geography, Regional Study of South Asia

MORIKAWA, T., Transport Planning
MORIMOTO, H., Mathematical Biology
MURATA, S., Organic Chemistry, Physical Organic Chemistry, Environmental Materials Science
NISHIHARA, K., Sociology, Phenomenological Sociology, Social Theory
OHKAWA, M., Constitutional Law, Environmental Law
OHMORI, H., Structural Mechanics and Computational Analysis
OKAMOTO, K., Geography, Behavioural Geography, Urban Geography
OKUMIYA, M., Optimization of Energy Supplies in Building and Urban Scale
OZAWA, T., Geobiology, Evolutionary Biology
SANO, M., Fuel Cell, Secondary Battery, Energy Systems
SHIMIZU, H., Architectural Planning and Design, Theatre Planning and Administration
SUGIMOTO, T., Heterocyclic Chemistry
SUZUKI, Y., Active Tectonics
TANAKA, S., Urban Sociology
TANAKA, T., Isotope Geochemistry
TANOUE, E., Marine Biogeochemistry
TESHIGAWARA, M., Reinforced Concrete Structures
UMITSU, M., Geomorphology, Quaternary Geology, Geo-environmental Studies
YAMADA, I., Seismology and Planetary Physics
YAMADA, K., Structural Engineering, Bridge Engineering
YAMAGUCHI, Y., Remote Sensing for Environmental Monitoring

Graduate School of International Development (tel. (52) 789-4952; fax (52) 789-4951; e-mail webmaster@gsid.nagoya-u.ac.jp; internet www.gsid.nagoya-u.ac.jp):

EZAKI, M., Development Information Systems
FUTAMURA, H., Drug Trafficking in Latin America
HIROSATO, Y., Educational Development
KIMURA, H., Dynamics of Regional Politics, International Cooperation Policy I, II, Dynamics of Regional Politics
KINOSHITA, T., Second Language Acquisition, Learning, Language Assessment, TESOL and Applied Linguistics
NAKANISHI, H., International and Regional Politics, Organization for International Cooperation
NISHIMURA, Y., Development Management
OHASHI, A., South-east Asian Studies
OMURO, T., Dynamic Theory of Language
OSADA, H., Integrated Development Planning
OTSUBO, S., International Development Economics
SAKURAI, T., Theory of Intercultural Communication
SUGIURA, M., Second Language Acquisition
TAKAHASHI, K., Multiculturalism I, Social Change during Modernization
YASUDA, N., Comparative Asian Legal Systems, Introduction to Law and Development Studies

Graduate School of Languages and Cultures (tel. (52) 789-4881; fax (52) 789-4873; e-mail lcoffice@lang.nagoya-u.ac.jp; internet www .lang.nagoya-u.ac.jp):

ANDO, S., 16th- and 17th-century English Poetry
ARIKAWA, K., German Literature in the Age of the Enlightenment
FUKUDA, M., Comparative Literature and Culture, Medical History
HIGH, P., Intellectual History of Japanese Film
IIDA, H., Contrastive Study of Japanese, Korean and English
INOUE, I., English Linguistics

KAMIYA, O., Modern Chinese Language

KATO, S., American Literature, Japanese and American Environmental Literature

KONDO, K., Language Typology

KOSAKA, K., Contrastive Linguistics

MAENO, M., Cultural History of Early Modern Europe

MATSUMOTO, I., Women's Studies

MATSUOKA, M., Victorian Literature

MURANUSHI, K., William Shakespeare

NAGAHATA, A., American Literature

NAKAI, M., Trend of Thought in Modern Chinese Literature

NAKAJIMA, T., German Lyric Poems of the 19th Century

OCHI, K., Obliteration of Feminine in the Western Culture

SHIBATA, S., Modern Literature in Japan and Germany

SUZUKI, S., Emblems and Religious Poetry in the 16th and 17th Centuries

TADOKORO, M., Comparative Literature and Culture

TANO, I., Modern American Literature and Culture

YANAGISAWA, T., Language Typology, North-western Caucasian Languages

YOSHIMURA, M., English Romanticism

Graduate School of Mathematics (Furo-cho, Chikusa-ku, Nagoya 464-8602; tel. (52) 789-2429; fax (52) 789-2829; internet www.math.nagoya-u.ac.jp/en):

FUJIWARA, K., Algebraic Geometry

GYOJA, A., Representation Theory

KANAI, M., Geometry and Dynamic Systems

KANNO, H., Mathematical Physics

KIMURA, Y., Fluid Dynamics

KOBAYASHI, R., Differential Geometry

KONDO, S., Algebraic Geometry

MATSUMOTO, K., Number Theory

MIYAKE, M., Partial Differential Equations

NAMIKAWA, Y., Algebraic Geometry

NAYATANI, S., Conformal Geometry

OHSAWA, T., Complex Analysis

SATO, H., Geometry

SHIOTA, M., Real Algebraic Geometry

SHOJI, T., Representational Theory

TSUCHIYA, A., Geometry and Mathematical Physics

UMEMURA, H., Algebraic Geometry

UZAWA, T., Representational Theory

International Cooperation Center for Agricultural Education (tel. (52) 789-4225; fax (52) 789-4222; e-mail iccae@agr.nagoya-u.ac.jp; internet www.agr.nagoya-u.ac.jp/~iccae/index-j.html):

ASANUMA, S., Network Development

MATSUMOTO, T., Project Development

Research Center for Materials Science (Furo-cho, Chikusa-ku, Nagoya 464-8602; tel. (52) 789-5902; fax (52) 789-5902; internet www.rcms.nagoya-u.ac.jp/intro/):

IMAE, T., Physical Chemistry

KITAMURA, M., Synthetic Organic Chemistry

SEKI, K., Physical Chemistry

TATSUMI, K., Inorganic Chemistry

Research Center of Health, Physical Fitness and Sports (tel. (52) 789-3946; fax (52) 789-3957; internet www.htc.nagoya-u.ac.jp):

HIRUTA, S., Workload in Care Services

IKEGAMI, Y., Biomechanical Analysis of Human Movement

ISHIDA, K., Cardio-respiratory Responses during Exercise

IZUHARA, Y., Class Work Study of Physical Education

KONDO, T., Exercise and Gastrointestinal Function, Pancreatic Diseases, Breath and Skin Gas in Health and Diseases

NISHIDA, T., Achievement Motivation in Physical Education and Sports

OGAWA, T., Phenomenological Psychopathology, Psychoanalytic Psychotherapy of Adolescents

OSHIDA, Y., Exercise for Insulin Resistance

SHIMAOKA, K., Teaching of Exercise in Health Promotion Programmes

SHIMAOKA, M., Health and Physical Fitness in Workers

YAMAMOTO, Y., Motor Control and Learning from a Dynamical System Approach

Research Institute of Environmental Medicine (tel. (52) 789-3886; fax (52) 789-3887; internet www.riem.nagoya-u.ac.jp/e/index.html):

KAMIYA, K., Molecular and Genomic Regulation of the Heart

KODAMA, I., Molecular and Cellular Cardiology

KOMATSU, Y., Synaptic Plasticity in the Visual Cortex

MIZUMURA, K., Neurophysiology of Pain

MURATA, Y., Molecular Genetics

SAWADA, M., Molecular and Cellular Neuroscience

SEO, H., Molecular Mechanism of Hormone Action

SUZUMURA, A., Neuroimmunology

YASUI, K., Bioinformation Analysis

School of Agricultural Sciences and Graduate School of Bioagricultural Sciences (tel. (52) 789-5266; fax (52) 789-4005; e-mail info@agr.nagoya-u.ac.jp; internet www.agr.nagoya-u.ac.jp):

AOI, K., Polymer Chemistry

DOKE, N., Plant Pathology

EBIHARA, S., Animal Behavioural Physiology

FUKUSHIMA, K., Forest Chemistry

FUKUTA, K., Animal Morphology and Function

HATTORI, K., Plant Genetics and Breeding

HATTORI, S., Forest Resources Utilization

HIRASHIMA, Y., Biomaterials Engineering

ISOBE, M., Organic Chemistry

KIMURA, M., Soil Biology and Chemistry

KITAGAWA, Y., Stem Cell Engineering

KOBAYASHI, M., Biodynamics of Insect–Virus Interactions

KOBAYASHI, T., Gene Regulation

MAEDA, K., Reproductive Science

MAESHIMA, M., Cell Dynamics

MAKI, M., Molecular and Cellular Regulation

MATSUDA, T., Molecular Bioregulation

MIYAKE, H., Plant Resources and Environment

MIZUNO, T., Molecular Biology and Molecular Genetics

MORI, H., Developmental Signalling Biology

NAKAMURA, K., Biological Chemistry

NAKANO, H., Molecular Biotechnology

NAMIKAWA, T., Animal Genetics

NOGUCHI, T., Molecular Physiological Chemistry

OHTA, T., Forest Meteorology and Hydrology

OJIKA, M., Molecular Function Modelling

OMATA, T., Molecular Plant Physiology

OSAWA, T., Food and Biodynamics

SAKAGAMI, Y., Bioactive Natural Products Chemistry

SHIBATA, E., Forest Protection

SHIMADA, K., Animal Physiology

SOMIYA, H., Animal Information Biology

TAKABE, T., Biosphere Symbiosis

TAKENAKA, C., Forest Environment and Resources

TAKEYA, H., Socioeconomic Science of Food Production

TANAKA, T., Applied Entomology

TOMARU, N., Forest Ecology and Physiology

TSUCHIKAWA, S., Mechanical Engineering for Biological Materials

TSUGE, T., Microbes and Plant Production

YAGINUMA, T., Sericulture Entomological resources

YAMAUCHI, A., Biosphere Resources Cycling

YAMAKI, S., Horticultural Science

YOKOTA, H., Animal Feeds and Production

YOSHIMURA, T., Biomacromolecules

School and Graduate School of Economics (tel. (52) 789-4920; fax (52) 789-4921; internet www.soec.nagoya-u.ac.jp):

ANDO, T., History of European Economic Thought

ARAYAMA, Y., Agricultural Policy and Economic Growth

HIRAKAWA, H., Asian Economics

KANAI, Y., British Monetary History during the Inter-war Period

KIMURA, S., Management Accounting

KISIDA, T., Organization

MINAGAWA, T., Microeconomic Foundations of Macroeconomics

NABESHIMA, N., History of Economic Thought, Political Economy

NAGAO, S., History of Economic and Social Thought, Political Economy

NAKANISHI, S., Japanese Economic History

NEMOTO, J., Applied Econometrics and Productivity Analysis

NOGUCHI, A., Financial Accounting

OHTA, S., Labour Economics

OKUMURA, R., Intertemporal Open-economy Macroeconomics

SATO, M., Conceptual Framework of Business Accounting

TAKAKUWA, S., Business Administration

TAKEUCHI, J., Comparative Study on Economic Development

TAKEUCHI, N., Stabilization Policy

TAMARU, M., Globalization and Japanese Economy

TAWADA, M., International Trade Theory

TOMOSUGI, Y., Management Audit

TSUKADA, H., Mathematical Finance

WAGO, H., Econometrics Analysis

YAMAMOTO, T., Financial Statement Analysis

YAMORI, N., Monetary Economics and Banking Theory

School and Graduate School of Education and Human Development (tel. (52) 789-2602; fax (52) 789-2666; internet www.educa.nagoya-u.ac.jp):

HAYAKAWA, M., Philosophy of Human Becoming

HAYAMIZU, T., Psychology of Personality

IMAZU, K., Sociology of Education

KAGEYAMA, H., School Psychology

KANAI, A., Clinical Psychology

KATOH, S., History of Education

MATOBA, M., Methods of Education

MATUSHITA, H., Philosophy of Human Becoming

MORITA, M., Family Psychology

MURAKAMI, T., Psychometrics

NAKAJIMA, T., Educational Administration

NISHINO, S., Comparative Education

NOGUCHI, H., Psychometrics

OKADA, T., Cognitive Psychology

OTANI, T., Technologies in Education

TAKAGI, Y., School Environment

TERADA, M., Vocational and Technical Education

UEDA, T., Educational Management

YOSHIDA, T., Social Psychology

School and Graduate School of Engineering (Furo-cho, Chikusa-ku, Nagoya 464-8603; tel. (52) 789-3405; fax (52) 789-3100; internet www.engg.nagoya-u.ac.jp):

ANDO, H., Mathematical Information Systems

ASAI, S., Electromagnetic Processing of Materials

ASAOKA, A., Soil Mechanics

BABA, Y., Applied Analytical Chemistry

FUJIMAKI, A., Integrated Quantum Devices Engineering
FUKUDA, T., Micro-nano System Control Engineering
FURUHASHI, T., Complex Systems
HAYAKAWA, Y., Intelligent Mechatronics
HIRASAWA, M., Nano-integration Engineering
HONDA, H., Bio-process Engineering
HOSOE, S., Mechatronics Control
ICHIMIYA, A., Fundamental Quantum Engineering
IGUCHI, T., Quantum Beam Measurement and Instrumentation
IIDA, T., Energy Environmental Safety Engineering
IIJIMA, S., Molecular Biology and Genetic Engineering
IKUTA, K., Biomedical Micro–and Nano–Mechatronics
INOUE, J., Solid-State Engineering
IRITANI, E., Mechanical Separation Process Engineering
ISHIDA, Y., Intelligent Manufacturing Machinery
ISHIHARA, K., Chemistry of Biologically Active Materials
ISHIKAWA, T., Deformation Processing of Materials
ITOH, Y., Infrastructure System Design
KAMIGAITO, M., Organic Chemistry of Macromolecules
KANEDA, Y., Computational Fluid Mechanics
KANETAKE, N., Structure and Morphology Control Engineering
KAWAIZUMI, F., Diffusional Process Engineering
KITANO, T., Radiation Chemistry
KODA, S., Chemical Physics of Condensed Matters
KONO, A., Optical Electronics
KOUMOTO, K., Solid–State Materials
KUKITA, Y., Energy Transport Engineering
KURODA, K., Nano-material Characterization
KURODA, S., Quantum Material Physics and Engineering
KUWABARA, M., Materials Reaction Process Engineering
MATSUDA, H., Thermal Energy Engineering
MATSUDA, I., Design of Catalytic Reactions
MATSUI, M., Magnetism of Materials and Magnetics
MATSUI, T., Energy Functional Materials Engineering
MATSUMOTO, T., Knowledge-based Design
MATSUMURA, T., High Current and Power Engineering
MATSUSHITA, Y., Physical Chemistry of Materials
MITAKU, S., Biophysical Engineering
MITSUYA, Y., Micro- and Nano-instrumentation Engineering
MIYATA, T., Fatigue and Fracture of Materials
MIZUTANI, N., Coastal and Maritime Engineering
MIZUTANI, T., Quantum Nano-devices Engineering
MORINAGA, M., Materials Design
MURAMATSU, N., Human System Engineering
MUTO, S., Energy Materials Science under Extreme Conditions
NAKAMURA, A., Optical Physics
NAKAMURA, H., Concrete Materials and Structures
NAKAMURA, M., Resources and Environment
NAKAMURA, Y., Fluid Dynamics
NAKAZATO, K., Intelligent Devices
NIIMI, T., Micro Thermofluid Engineering
NISHIYAMA, H., Selective Organic Synthesis

NOMURA, H., Casting and Solidification Process Engineering
OHNO, N., Computational Solid Mechanics
OKIDO, M., Surface-interface Engineering
OKUMA, S., Information and Control Systems
ONOGI, K., Process Systems Engineering
SAITO, Y., Nano-structure Analysis
SAKAI, Y., Statistical Fluid Engineering
SAKATA, M., Structural Physics Engineering
SATO, K., Micro- and Nano-process Engineering
SATO, K., Communication Networks
SATSUMA, A., Catalyst Design
SAWADA, Y., Disaster Prevention, Geotechnical Engineering
SAWAKI, N., Semiconductor Electronics
SEKI, T., Molecular Assembly, Systems Engineering
SHAMOTO, E., Ultra Precision Engineering
SHIMADA, T., Super Microcomputing
SHINODA, T., Fabrication of Materials Engineering
SODA, K., Quantum Beam Materials Engineering
SOGA, T., Physical Gas Dynamics
SUGAI, H., Plasma Electronics
SUZUOKI, Y., Energy System and Engineering
TAGAWA, T., Chemical Reaction Engineering
TAKAGI, K., Functional Crystalline Chemistry
TAKAI, Y., Energy Device Engineering
TAKAMURA, S., Plasma Science and Technology
TAKEDA, K., Physical Chemistry of Materials
TAKEDA, Y., Nano-materials and Devices
TANAKA, E., Biomechanics
TANAKA, K., Materials and Mechanics
TANIGUCHI, G., Architectural Planning
TANIMOTO, M., Visual Information
TORIMOTO, T., Material Design Chemistry
TSUBAKI, J., Processes for the Functional Development of Materials
TSUJIMOTO, T., River, Coastal and Estuarine Hydro-morphodynamics
TSUNASHIMA, S., Spin Electronics
UEDA, T., Structural Mechanics
UMEHARA, N., Manufacturing Process Technology
UMEMURA, A., Propulsion Energy Systems Engineering
URITANI, A., Applied Nuclear Physics
USAMI, T., Structural Analysis
YAMADA, K., Control Systems Engineering
YAMAMOTO, I., Energy Materials Recycling Engineering
YAMANE, T., Protein Crystallography and Structural Biology
YAMANE, Y., Reactor Physics and Engineering
YAMASHITA, H., Heat Transfer and Combustion
YAMAZAKI, K., Energy Materials Science Engineering
YASHIMA, E., Polymer Materials Design
YOSHIKAWA, N., Aerospace Microsystems
ZAIMA, S., Nano-structured Electronic Device Engineering

School and Graduate School of Law (tel. (52) 789-4910; fax (52) 789-4900; e-mail info@nomolog.nagoya-u.ac.jp; internet www.nomolog.nagoya-u.ac.jp):

AIKYO, K., Constitutional Law
AKANE, T., Criminal Procedure
CHIBA, E., Civil Law
FUJITA, S., Role of the Attorney in Legal Practice
FUKE, T., Public Finance Law and Tax Law
HACHISUKA, T., Role of the Attorney in Legal Practice
HAMADA, M., Corporate Law

HASEGAWA, Y., Civil Procedure
HASHIDA, H., Criminal Law
HONMA, Y., Civil Procedure
ICHIHASHI, K., Administrative Law
ISHII, M., Western Legal History
ISOBE, T., History of Western Political Thought
JIMBO, F., Japanese Legal History
KAGAYAMA, S., Civil Law
KAMINO, K., Administrative Law
KATO, H., Environmental Law
KATO, M., Civil Law
KAWANO, M., Civil Procedure
KITAZUMI, K., Western Political History
KOBAYASHI, R., Commercial Law
MAKINO, J., Business Law Practice
MASUDA, T., Japanese Political History
MATSUURA, Y., Legal Informatics, History of Legal Thought
MORI, H., Constitutional Law
MORIGIWA, Y., Jurisprudence
MOTO, H., Constitutional Law
NAKAHIGASHI, ~M., Corporate Law
NAKAYA, H., Civil Law
OBATA, K., International Law
OHSAWA, Y., Criminal Procedure
ONO, K., Political Science
SABURI, H., International Law
SADAKATA, M., International Politics
SINDO, H., Urban Politics
SUGAWARA, I., Sociology of Law
SUGIURA, K., Russian Law
SUZUKI, M., Intellectual Property Law
URABE, N., Constitutional Law
USHIRO, F., Public Administration
WADA, H., Labour Law
YAMAMOTO, T., Criminal Law

School and Graduate School of Letters (tel. (52) 789-2202; fax (52) 789-2272; internet www.lit.nagoya-u.ac.jp):

ABE, Y., Anthropology, Study of Religions and the History of Japanese Thought
AMANO, M., English Linguistics
EMURA, H., Asian History
HAGA, S., Japanese History
IKEUCHI, S., Japanese History
INABA, N., Japanese History
INOUE, S., Asian History
KAMIO, M., English and American Literature
KAMITSUKA, Y., Chinese Philosophy
KANAYAMA, Y., Philosophy
KASUGA, Y., Japanese Culture
KIMATA, M., Aesthetics and Art History
KUGINUKI, T., Japanese Linguistics
MACHIDA, K., Linguistics
MATSUZAWA, K., French Literature
MIYAJI, A., Aesthetics and Art History
ODA, Y., Japanese Culture
OGAWA, M., Classics
SATO, S., Western History
SHIMADA, Y., Anthropology, Study of Religions and the History of Japanese Thought
SHIMIZU, S., German Literature
SHIOMURA, K., Japanese Literature
SUGIYAMA, H., Chinese Literature
SUTO, Y., Western History
TAKAHASHI, T., Japanese Literature
TAKEUCHI, H., Chinese Philosophy
TAKIKAWA, M., English and American Literature
TAMURA, H., Philosophy
TSUBOI, H., Japanese Culture
WADA, T., Indian Studies
WAZAKI, H., Anthropology, Study of Religions and the History of Japanese Thought
YAMADA, H., Philosophy
YAMAMOTO, N., Archaeology
YOSHIDA, J., Chinese Philosophy

School and Graduate School of Medicine (65 Tsurumai-cho, Showa-ku, Nagoya 466-8550; tel. (52) 744-2500; fax (52) 744-2428; internet www.med.nagoya-u.ac.jp):

ANDO, H., Paediatric Surgery
ANDO, S., Clinical Nursing
AOYAMA, A., International Health
AOYAMA, T., Basic Radiological Technology
ASANO, M., Human Development Nursing and Midwifery
BAN, N., Family and Community Medicine
FUJIMOTO, T., Molecular Cell Biology
FURUKAWA, K., Molecular and Cellular Biology
GOTO, H., Therapeutic Medicine
GOTO, S., Fundamentals of Nursing
HAMAGUCHI, M., Molecular Pathogenesis
HAMAJIMA, N., Preventive Medicine
HIRAI, M., Public Health and Home Care Nursing
HIROSE, K., Cell Physiology
HOSHIYAMA, M., Basic Occupational Therapy
IDA, K., Basic Physical Therapy
IGUCHI, A., Geriatrics
IKEMATSU, Y., Clinical Nursing
ISHIGAKI, T., Radiology
ISHIGURE, N., Medical Radiological Technology
ISHIGURO, N., Orthopaedics
ISOBE, K., Immunology
ITO, H., Basic Medical Technology
ITO, K., Medical Administration and Politics
ITO, S., Basic Radiological Technology
KAIBUCHI, K., Cell Pharmacology
KAJITA, E., Public Health and Home Care Nursing
KATSUMATA, Y., Legal Medicine and Bioethics
KAWAMURA, M., Basic Physical Therapy
KAWATSU, Y., Fundamentals of Nursing
KIKKAWA, F., Obstetrics and Gynaecology
KIKUCHI, A., Molecular Mycology and Medicine
KIUCHI, T., Transplant Surgery
KOBAYASHI, K., Basic Physical Therapy
KODERA, Y., Medical Radiological Technology
KOIKE, Y., Medical Laboratory Technology
KOJIMA, S., Paediatrics
KOJIMA, T., Medical Laboratory Technology
KOMORI, K., Vascular Surgery
MAEDA, H., Medical Radiological Technology
MAEKAWA, A., Public Health and Homecare Nursing
MATSUMURA, Y., Clinical Nursing
MATSUO, S., Clinical Immunology
MIYATA, T., Cell Biology
MIZUTANI, M., Clinical Nursing
MORI, N., Biological Response
MORITA, S., Human Development Nursing and Midwifery
MURATE, T., Medical Laboratory Technology
MUROHARA, T., Cardiology
NABESHIMA, T., Clinical Pharmacy
NAGASE, F., Medical Laboratory Technology
NAKAMURA, S., Clinical Pathophysiology
NAKAO, A., Gastroenterological Surgery
NAKASHIMA, T., Otorhinolaryngology
NAOE, T., Haematology
NARAMA, M., Human Development Nursing and Midwifery
NASU, T., Occupational and Environmental Health
NIMURA, Y., Surgical Oncology
NISHIYAMA, Y., Molecular Virology
OBATA, Y., Medical Radiological Technology
OHNO, K., Neurogenetics and Bioinformatics
OHTA, M., Molecular Bacteriology
OISO, Y., Diabetology and Endocrinology
OTA, K., Fundamentals of Nursing
OZAKI, N., Psychiatry
SAKAKIBARA, H., Public Health and Home Care Nursing

SHIMADA, Y., Anaesthesiology
SHIMAMOTO, K., Medical Radiological Technology
SHIMOKATA, K., Clinical Preventive Medicine
SOBUE, G., Neurology
SOKABE, M., Cell Biophysics
SUGIMURA, K., Basic Occupational Therapy
SUZUKI, K., Basic Occupational Therapy
SUZUKI, K., Human Development Nursing and Midwifery
SUZUKI, S., Applied Physical Therapy
TABUSHI, K., Basic Radiological Technology
TACHIKAWA, K., Hospital and Healthcare Business Management
TAGAWA, Y., Applied Occupational Therapy
TAKAGI, K., Basic Medical Technology
TAKAHASHI, M., Tumour Pathology
TAKAHASHI, T., Molecular Carcinogenesis
TAKAMATSU, J., Transfusion Medicine
TAKEZAWA, J., Emergency and Critical Care Medicine
TERASAKI, H., Protective Care for Sensory Disorders
TOMITA, Y., Dermatology
TORII, S., Plastic and Reconstructive Surgery
TOYOSHIMA, H., Public Health
UEDA, M., Maxillofacial Surgery
UEDA, Y., Cardio-thoracic Surgery
WAKUSAWA, S., Basic Medical Technology
WATANABE, N., Clinical Nursing
YAMADA, S., Applied Physical Therapy
YAMAUCHI, K., Medical Information and Management Science
YAMAUCHI, T., Fundamentals of Nursing
YOKOI, T., Medical Laboratory Technology
YOSHIDA, J., Neurosurgery

School and Graduate School of Science (Furo-cho, Chikusa-ku, Nagoya 464-8602; tel. (52) 789-2394; fax (52) 789-2800; internet www .sci.nagoya-u.ac.jp/index.html):

AIBA, H., Molecular Biology
AWAGA, K., Materials Chemistry
ENDO, T., Biochemistry
FUKUI, Y., Astrophysics
HIRASHIMA, D., Condensed Matter Physics
HOMMA, M., Bioenergetics
HORI, H., Evolutionary Genetics
IIO, T., Biophysics
ISHII, K., Theoretical Biology
ITOH, M., Solid–State Physics
ITOH, S., Biophysics, Bioenergetics
KATOU, K., Physiology of Plant Growth
KONDO, S., Pattern Formation
KONDO, T., Plant Physiology
KOUYAMA, T., Biophysics
KUNIEDA, H., Astrophysics
KUROIWA, A., Developmental Biology
MACHIDA, Y., Molecular Biology
MATSUMOTO, K., Molecular Biology
MORI, I., Molecular Neurobiology
NAKANISHI, T., Nuclear and Particle Physics
NISHIDA, Y., Animal Development
NIWA, K., Nuclear and Particle Physics
NOZAKI, K., Nonlinear Physics
ODA, Y., Developmental Biology
OHMINE, I., Physical Chemistry
OHSAWA, Y., Plasma Physics
OHSHIMA, T., Nuclear and Particle Physics
OKAMOTO, Y., Theoretical Biophysics
OWARIBE, K., Cell Adhesion and Cytoskeleton
SANDA, I., Particle Physics and Fields
SATO, M., Solid–State Physics
SATO, S., Astrophysics
SAWADA, H., Marine Biochemistry
SHIBAI, H., Astrophysics
SHINOHARA, H., Physical Chemistry
SUGAI, S., Solid–State Physics
SUZUMURA, Y., Solid–State Physics
TOMIMATSU, A., Theory of Gravitation
UEMURA, D., Organic Chemistry
WADA, N., Low Temperature Physics

WATANABE, Y., Bioinorganic Chemistry
YAMAGUCHI, S., Organic Chemistry
YAMAWAKI, K., Elementary Particle Physics and Fields

School of Informatics and Sciences and Graduate School of Information Science (tel. (52) 789-4716; fax (52) 789-4800; e-mail syomuk@info.human.nagoya-u.ac.jp; internet www.is.nagoya-u.ac.jp):

AGUSA, K., Information Engineering
ARITA, T., Complex Systems Science
AZEGAMI, H., Complex Systems Science
HAYAKAWA, Y., Complex Systems Science
HIRATA, T., Computer Science and Mathematical Informatics
HIROKI, S., Complex Systems Science
ISHII, K., Systems and Social Informatics
JINBO, M., Computer Science and Mathematical Informatics
KOGA, N., Complex Systems Science
MATSUBARA, Y., Computer Science and Mathematical Informatics
MATSUMOTO, H., Computer Science and Mathematical Informatics
MATSUO, S., Complex Systems Science
MITSUI, T., Computer Science and Mathematical Informatics
MIWA, K., Media Science
MORI, M., Complex Systems Science
MORI, T., Complex Systems Science
MURASE, H., Media Science
NAGAOKA, M., Complex Systems Science
OHNISHI, N., Media Science
SAITO, H., Media Science
SAKABE, T., Information Engineering
SAKAI, M., Computer Science and Mathematical Informatics
SASAI, M., Complex Systems Science
SUENAGA, Y., Media Science
SUGIYAMA, Y., Complex Systems Science
TAKADA, H., Information Engineering
TAKAGI, N., Information Engineering
TAKAHAMA, M., Information Engineering
TAKEDA, K., Media Science
TODAYAMA, K., Systems and Social Informatics
WATANABE, T., Systems and Social Informatics
YASUDA, T., Systems and Social Informatics
YASUMOTO, M., Computer Science and Mathematical Informatics
YOKOI, S., Systems and Social Informatics
YOKOSAWA, H., Complex Systems Science
YONEYAMA, M., Systems and Social Informatics

Solar–Terrestrial Environment Laboratory (Honohara 3-13, Toyokawa, Aichi Pref., 442-8507; tel. (533) 86-3154; fax (533) 86-0811; internet www.stelab.nagoya-u.ac.jp):

FUJII, R., Space Science (Magnetosphere and Ionosphere Physics
ITOW, Y., Cosmic Ray, Dark Matter and Neutrino Physics
KAMIDE, Y., Solar–Terrestrial Physics
KIKUCHI, T., Solar–Terrestrial Physics
KOJIMA, M., Interplanetary Space Physics
MATSUMI, Y., Atmospheric Photochemistry and Chemical Kinetics
MIZUNO, A., Atmospheric Chemistry and Radio Astronomy
MURAKI, Y., Solar Cosmic Ray Physics
OGAWA, T., Upper Atmosphere Physics
OGINO, T., Space Plasma Physics

NARA WOMEN'S UNIVERSITY

Kita-Uoya-Higashi-Machi, Nara City 630-8506

Telephone: (742) 20-3204
Fax: (742) 20-3205
E-mail: admin@jimu.nara-wu.ac.jp
Internet: www.nara-wu.ac.jp
Founded 1908

Independent
Academic year: April to March

Pres.: MASAKO NIWA
Sec-Gen.: MASAMI KOTANI
Librarian: NANAKO SHIGESADA

Library of 514,000 vols
Number of teachers: 222
Number of students: 2,746

Publications: *Studies in Home Economics*, *Graduate School of Human Culture*

DEANS

Faculty of Human Life and Environment: Prof. M. MIYOSHI
Faculty of Letters: Prof. T. HIRAI
Faculty of Science: Prof. Y. TAKAGI
Graduate School of Human Culture (Doctorate Course): Prof. N. FUJIWARA

NIIGATA UNIVERSITY

8050 Ikarashi Ni-no-cho, Nishi-ku, Niigata 950-2181

Telephone: (25) 262-6246
Fax: (25) 262-7519
E-mail: kokusai@adm.niigata-u.ac.jp
Internet: www.niigata-u.ac.jp

Founded 1949
Independent
Academic year: April to March

Pres.: AKIRA HASEGAWA
Vice-Pres: MASAHIRO SHIMADA, SHOJI KOHNO, SUKEO FUKASAWA, TADAO ITO, TAKEHIKO BANDO
Dir of Univ. Library: TAKASHI OOKUMA

Library: see Libraries and Archives
Number of teachers: 1,226
Number of students: 12,901

DEANS

Faculty of Agriculture: T. OHYAMA
Faculty of Dentistry: T. MAEDA
Faculty of Economics: Y. SUGAHARA
Faculty of Education and Human Sciences: T. MORITA
Faculty of Engineering: H. OHKAWA
Faculty of Humanities: H. HONDA
Faculty of Law: T. KATO
Faculty of Medicine: M. UCHIYAMA
Faculty of Science: K. SHUTO
Graduate School of Education: T. MORITA
Graduate School of Health Sciences: M. TAKAHASHI
Graduate School of Management of Technology: M. MASUDA
Graduate School of Medical and Dental Sciences: M. UCHIYAMA
Graduate School of Science and Technology: T. HASEGAWA
Graduate School of the Study of Modern Society and Culture: Y. SUZUKI
School of Law: K. HONMA

OBIHIRO UNIVERSITY OF AGRICULTURE AND VETERINARY MEDICINE

Inada-cho, Obihiro, Hokkaido 080-8555

Telephone: (155) 49-5111
Fax: (155) 49-5229
E-mail: soumu@obihiro.ac.jp
Internet: www.obihiro.ac.jp

Founded 1941
Independent
Academic year: April to March

Pres.: NAOYOSHI SUZUKI
Dir of Admin. Bureau: M. KIKUCHI
Dir of Univ. Library: T. KAWABATA

Library of 190,426 vols
Number of teachers: 149
Number of students: 1,431

Department of Agro-Environmental Science: JUNKO MARUYAMA

Department of Applied Veterinary Science: TOSHIKAZU SHIRAHATA
Department of Basic Veterinary Science: JUNZO YAMADA
Department of Clinical Veterinary Science: TAKAO SARASHINA
Department of Pathobiological Science: MASAKAZU NISHIMURA
Research Unit of Animal Physiology and Function: IKICHI ARAI
Research Unit of Animal Production Science: MIKAMI MASAYUKI
Research Unit of Engineering in Agricultural and Biological Systems: KENICHI ISHIBASHI
Research Unit of Environmental and Rural Engineering: FUJIO TSUCHIYA
Research Unit of Farm Management: ICHIO SASAKI
Research Unit of Food and Resource Economics: SHIGERU ITO
Research Unit of Molecular Cell-Regulation Science: HIROSHI MASUDA
Research Unit of Plant Bioscience: SOUHEI SAWADA
Research Unit of Socio-Environmental Science: MASARU UMETSU

Publication: *Research Bulletin* (on Natural Sciences and on Humanities and Social Sciences, each 2 a year).

OCHANOMIZU UNIVERSITY

2-1-1, Otsuka, Bunkyo-ku, Tokyo 112-8610

Telephone: (3) 5978-5106
Fax: (3) 5978-5890
E-mail: syomu2@cc.ocha.ac.jp
Internet: www.ocha.ac.jp

Founded 1874; reorganized 1949 as Nat. Univ.
Independent
Academic year: April to March

Pres.: MASUKO HONDA
Admin.: HIDETOSHI YAKABE

Number of teachers: 322
Number of students: 2,738

Publications: *Natural Science Report* (2 a year), *Studies in Art and Culture* (1 a year)

DEANS

Faculty of Human Life and Environmental Science: ITAKURA TOSHIRO
Faculty of Letters and Education: YAMAMOTO HIDEYUKI
Faculty of Science: KASAHARA YUJI
Graduate School of Humanities and Sciences: TOKUMARU YOSHIHIKO

OITA UNIVERSITY

700 Dannoharu, Oita City

Telephone: (97) 569-3311
Fax: (97) 554-7413
E-mail: webmaster@ad.oita-u.ac.jp
Internet: www.oita-u.ac.jp

Founded 1949
Independent
Language of instruction: Japanese
Academic year: April to March (2 semesters)

Pres.: IWAO NAKAYAMA
Dir-Gen. of Admin. Bureau: TAKANOBU IRIE
Dir of Univ. Library: KOICHI OBA

Library of 541,000 vols
Number of teachers: 569
Number of students: 5,802

DEANS

Faculty of Economics: MINORU UNO
Faculty of Education and Welfare Science: MAKOTO OSHIMA
Faculty of Engineering: TADAO EZAKI
Graduate School of Social Service Administration: TAKATOMI NINOMIYA

ATTACHED INSTITUTE

Tsurumi Seaside Research Institute: Aza-Hirama, Oaza-Ariakeura, Tsurumimachi, Minamiamabe-gun, Oita 876-1204; tel. (972) 33-1133.

OKAYAMA UNIVERSITY

1-1-1, Tsushima-Naka, Okayama 700-8530

Telephone: (86) 252-1111
Fax: (86) 254-6104
E-mail: ace7038@adm.okayama-u.ac.jp
Internet: www.okayama-u.ac.jp

Founded 1949
Independent
Academic year: April to March (2 semesters)

Pres.: IICHIRO KONO
Vice-Pres: KYOZO CHIBA, KIICHI MATSUHATA, HIROKAZU OSAKI, HAJIME INOUE
Dir-Gen.: T. ABE

Library: see Libraries and Archives
Number of teachers: 1,341 full-time
Number of students: 14,091

Publication: *Okayama University Bulletin*

DEANS

Dental School: T. WATANABE
Faculty of Agriculture: T. SHIRAISHI
Faculty of Economics: T. MATSUMOTO
Faculty of Education: N. MORIKAWA
Faculty of Engineering: H. TOTSUJI
Faculty of Environmental Science and Technology: T. ADACHI
Faculty of Law: S. TANI
Faculty of Letters: F. TAKAHASHI
Faculty of Pharmaceutical Sciences: T. KIMURA
Faculty of Science: K. KASE
Graduate School of Environmental Science (Doctorate Course): F. NAKASUJI
Graduate School of Humanities and Social Sciences (Doctorate Course): T. TAKAHASHI
Graduate School of Medicine, Dentistry and Pharmaceutical Science (Doctorate Course): H. KUMON
Medical School: K. OGUMA
School of Law: M. OKADA, Graduate School of Natural Science and Technology (Doctorate Course): J. TAKADA

PROFESSORS

Faculty of Agriculture (tel. (86) 251-8273; fax (86) 251-8388):

BABA, N., Chemistry of Biological Functions
ICHINOSE, Y., Genetic Engineering
INABA, A., Postharvest Agriculture
INAGAKI, K., Applied Biochemistry and Biotechnology
IZUMIMOTO, M., Animal Food Technology
KAMIMURA, K., Microbial Function
KANZAKI, H., Chemistry and Biochemistry of Bioactive Compounds
KIMURA, Y., Bioapplied Enzymology
KOMATSU, Y., Farm Management and Data Processing Methods
KONDO, Y., Animal Physiology and Pharmacology
KUBOTA, N., Horticultural Crop Production
KUNIEDA, T., Animal Genetics
KURODA, T., Crop Production Science
MASUDA, M., Olericulture
MIYAMOTO, T., Animal Food Function
NAKAJIMA, S., Chemistry and Biochemistry of Bioactive Compounds
NAKASUJI, F., Integrated Pest Management
NIWA, K., Animal Reproduction
OIKAWA, T., Animal Genetics and Breeding
OKAMOTO, G., Pomology
OKUDA, K., Animal Reproduction
SAKAGUCHI, E., Animal Nutrition
SAKAMOTO, K., Applied Plant Ecology
SASAKAWA, H., Rhizosphere Biological Chemistry

SATO, K., Animal Genetics and Breeding
SATOH, T., Resources Management
SHIMOISHI, Y., Biological Information of Chemistry
SHIRAISHI, T., Plant Pathology
SUGIO, T., Microbial Function
TADA, M., Biological Chemistry of Foods
TAHARA, M., Cell Engineering
TSUDA, M., Crop Whole-plant Physiology
YOKOMIZO, I., Farm Management and Date Processing Methods
YOSHIKAWA, K., Physiological Plant Ecology

Faculty of Economics (tel. (86) 251-7345; fax (86) 251-7350):

CHINO, T., Health Economics
ENOMOTO, S., Strategic Management
GENKA, T., Comparative Economic Systems
HARUNA, S., Industrial Organization
HIRANO, M., Local Public Finance
KONISHI, N., Accounting
KOYAMA, Y., Financial Management
KUROKAWA, K., Economic History of the United States
MATSUDA, Y., Organizational Behaviour and Organizational Change
MATSUMOTO, T., Economic History of Modern Asia
NAGAHATA, H., Statistics, Information Science
NAKAMURA, R., Urban and Regional Economics
NIIMURA, S., History of Economic Thought
OTA, Y., History of Economic Thought
SHIMONO, K., Economic History of Modern Japan
TAKEMURA, S., Theory of the Firm, Industrial Organisation
WADA, Y., Social Economics
YOSHIDA, T., Social Statistics, Econometrics
ZHANG, X., Economic Statistics

Faculty of Education (tel. (86) 251-7584; fax (86) 251-7755):

ARIYOSHI, H., Teacher Training
DOI, Y., Algebra
FUCHIGAMI, K., School Organizational Psychology
FUJITA, R., Housing and Living Design
FUKUNAGA, S., British Literature
FURUICHI, Y., Educational Psychology
IDO, K., Music Education
IKEDA, A., Geometry
INADA, T., Japanese Literature
INOUE, S., Educational Psychology
KAGA, M., Biomechanics
KANETA, Y., Composition
KANI, K., Material Engineering
KASAI, Y., Science of Food Preparation
KAWATA, T., Food Science
KISHIMOTO, H., Political Science
KITA, H., Chemistry
KITAGAMI, M., School Management
KONDO, I., Information Technology
KOSAKO, M., English Philology
KUSACHI, I., Mineralogy
MATSUOKA, Y., Clinical Psychology
MIZUNO, M., Developmental Psychology
MONDEN, S., Education for School Health Care
MORI, K., Chinese Philosophy
MORIKAWA, N., Pedagogy
MUSHIAKI, M., Vocal Music
NAKAO, Y., Chemistry
NII, I., Arts and Crafts Education
NISHIYAMA, M., Paintings
NOBE, M., Sociology
OGAWA, T., Paintings
OGURA, H., Biology
OHASHI, K., Manufacturing Education
OHASHI, Y., Physical Education
OKU, S., Music Education
ONO, H., Curriculum Development
ONOYAMA, K., Ceramics
SAKATA, N., Physical Education

SANADA, S., Education for Handicapped Children
SANEKATA, N., Mathematical Analysis
SUGAHARA, M., Japanese Education
SUGIHARA, R., Clothing Science
TAKAHASHI, K., Medicine for School Health Care
TAKAHASHI, T., Mathematics Education
TAKATSUKA, S., English Language Teaching
TAKAYAMA, Y., Social Studies Education
TANAKA, K., Science Education
TANAKA, K., Social Psychology
TANAKA, M., European History
TOKUNAGA, T., Sport Education
UEHARA, K., History
YAMAGUCHI, H., Computer Education
YAMAGUCHI, S., Psychology of Pre-school Children
YAMAMOTO, H., Musicology
YAMAMOTO, H., Systems Engineering
YAMAMOTO, T., Clinical Psychology
YAMANAKA, Y., History of Japanese Education
YAMASHITA, N., Solid State Spectroscopy
YANAGIHARA, M., Psychology of Handicapped Children
YOSHIDA, N., Japanese Language

Faculty of Engineering (tel. (86) 251-8004; fax (86) 251-8021):

FUNABIKI, N., Distributed Systems
GOFUKU, A., Systems Applications
GOTO, K., Functional Materials Chemistry
HASHIGUCHI, K., Foundations of Information Science
HATA, M., Distributed Systems
INABA, H., Energy Engineering
INOUE, A., Systems Theory
KAMIURA, Y., Electronics
KANATANI, K., Foundations of Information Science
KISHIMOTO, A., Functional Materials Chemistry
KOGA, R., Network Architecture
KONISHI, M., Electrical Engineering
MASAKI, A., Information-based Engineering Systems
MIYAZAKI, S., Systems Intelligence
MORIKAWA, Y., Foundations of Information and Communication
NAKANISHI, K., Biotechnology
NARA, S., Electronics
NOGI, S., Electronics
NORITSUGU, T., Systems Control
OHMORI, H., Applied Bioscience
OSAKA, A., Bioactive Materials
SAITO, S., Bioactive Materials
SAKAI, H., Biotechnology
SAKAI, T., Molecular Transformation Chemistry
SAKATA, Y., Functional Materials Chemistry
SENUMA, T., Control of Material Properties
SHAKUNAGA, T., Artificial Intelligence
SHIMAMURA, K., Functional Materials Chemistry
SISHIDO, M., Biomolecular Engineering
SUGIYAMA, Y., Foundations of Information and Communication
SUZUKI, K., Systems Theory
SUZUMORI, K., Systems Control
TADA, N., Material Engineering
TAKADA, J., Functional Materials Chemistry
TAKAHASHI, N., Electrical Engineering
TAKAI, K., Molecular Transformation Chemistry
TANAKA, H., Molecular Transformation Chemistry
TANAKA, Y., Systems Applications
TANIGUCHI, H., Information Based Engineering Systems
TOMITA, E., Energy Engineering
TORAYA, T., Applied Bioscience
TORII, T., Materials Engineering

TOTSUJI, H., Electronics
TUKADA, K., Electronics
TUKAMOTO, S., Manufacturing Engineering
UNEYAMA, K., Molecular Transformation Chemistry
UNO, Y., Design and Manufacturing Technology
WASHIO, S., Engineering Measurement
YAMADA, H., Biomolecular Engineering
YAMASAKI, S., Artificial Intelligence
YANASE, S., Engineering Measurement
YOKOHIRA, T., Network Architecture
YOSHIDA, A., Design and Manufacturing Technology

Faculty of Law (tel. (86) 251-7345; fax (86) 251-7350):

ARAKI, M., Western Political History
ATAKA, K., Local Tax and Finance Law
HARANO, A., Administrative Law
HATANO, S., European Legal History
KAWAHARA, Y., International Politics
KOYAMA, H., Administrative Law
KUROKAMI, N., Law of International Organizations
NAKAMURA, M., Information Law and Policy
NAKATOMI, K., Constitutional Law
NISHIHARA, J., Civil Law
OBATA, T., Japanese Political History
SANO, H., Private International Law
TANI, S., Political Process
TONAI, K., Labour Law
YAMAGUCHI, K., Constitutional Law
YONEYAMA, K., Commercial
ZHANG, H., Chinese Law

Faculty of Letters (tel. (86) 251-7345; fax (86) 251-7350):

EGUCHI, Y., Japanese Linguistics
HASEGAWA, Y., Psychology
HISANO, N., History of Japanese Culture
INADA, T., Archaeology
INAMURA, S., Ethics
JIANG, K., Modern History of Japanese Culture
KANASEKI, T., Comparative Study of Cultures
KITAMURA, K., Cultural Anthropology
KITAOKA, T., Religious Philosophy
KOBAYASHI, T., Sociology
KURACHI, K., History of Japanese Culture
MATSUMOTO, M., English Historical Linguistics
MIYAKE, S., Operatic Studies
NAGASE, H., French Literature
NAGATA, R., European History
NIIMURA, Y., History of Chinese Culture
NIIRO, I., Archaeology
NISHIMAE, T., American Literature
SHIMOSADA, M., Chinese Literature
TAKAHASHI, F., Ethics
TAKAHASHI, T., Old German Language and Literature
TAKUMA, F., Modern German History
TANAKA, T., Psychology
TAYA, R., Psychology
TERAOKA, T., History of German Literature
TSUJI, S., Linguistics
UCHIDA, K., Geography
WADA, M., Linguistics
WATANABE, M., Japanese Literature
YAMAGUCHI, K., Aesthetics
YAMAGUCHI, N., History of French Thought
YOSHIOKA, F., English Literature

Faculty of Pharmaceutical Sciences (tel. (86) 251-7913; fax (86) 251-7926):

HARAYAMA, T., Synthetic and Medicinal Chemistry
HIROTA, T., Pharmaceutical Chemistry
KAMEI, C., Pharmacology
KAWASAKI, H., Clinical Pharmaceutical Science
KIMURA, T., Pharmaceutics
KUROSAKI, Y., Pharmaceutics
MORIYAMA, Y., Neurochemistry

NARIMATSU, S., Health Chemistry
OKAMOTO, K., Bio-organic Chemistry
SAITO, Y., Pharmaceutical Analytical Chemistry
SASAKI, K., Pharmaceutical Fundamental Science
SHINODA, S., Environmental Hygiene
TAMAGAKE, K., Pharmaceutical Physical Chemistry
TSUCHIYA, T., Microbiology
WATAYA, Y., Medicinal Information
YAMAMOTO, I., Immunochemistry
YAMAMOTO, S., Molecular Microbiology
YOSHIDA, T., Pharmacognosy

Faculty of Science (tel. (86) 251-7764; fax (86) 251-7777):

ASAMI, M., Petrology
CHIBA, H., Isotope Geochemistry
HARADA, I., Theoretical Physics
HIROKAWA, M., Mathematical Physics
ISHIDA, H., Structural Chemistry
IWAMI, M., Thin Films and Surface Physics
KAGAWA, H., Molecular Biology
KAMADA, T., Molecular Cell Biology
KASE, K., Resources Geology
KAWAGUCHI, K., Molecular Spectroscopy
KIMURA, M., Organic Function Chemistry
KIYOHARA, K., Differential Geometry
KOBAYASHI, T., Physics of Strongly Correlated Systems
KOJIMA, M., Coordination Chemistry
KURODA, Y., Inorganic Chemistry
KUTSUKAKE, K., Molecular Genetics
MACHIDA, K., Mathematical Physics
MOTOMIZU, S., Analytical Chemistry
NAGAO, M., Surface Chemistry
NAKAMURA, H., Number Theory
NAKANO, I., High Energy Physics
NARAOKA, H., Organic Cosmogeochemistry
NOGAMI, Y., Low Dimensional Material Physics
ODA, H., Seismology
OSHIMA, K., Physics of Quantum Materials
ONO, F., Physics of Materials under Extreme Conditions
SAKAI, T., Differential Geometry
SAKAMOTO, T., Marine Biology
SAKUDA, M., Neutrino Physics
SATAKE, K., Organic Chemistry
SATO, R., Analysis
SAWADA, A., Quantum Electromagnetic Physics
SHEN, J.-R., Plant Physiology and Structural Biology
SHIBATA, T., Geology
SHIMAKAWA, K., Petrology and Marine Geology
SUZUKI, I., Geophysics
TAKAGI, K., Synthetic Organic Chemistry
TAKAHASHI, S., Endocrinology
TAKAHASHI, T., Plant Molecular Genetics
TAKAHASHI, Y., Plant Physiology and Plant Molecular Biology
TAMURA, H., Analysis
TANAKA, H., Theoretical Chemistry
TOMIOKA, K., Chronobiology
TSUKAMOTO, O., Atmospheric Science
UEDA, H., Molecular and Developmental Biology
YAMADA, H., Representation Theory
YAMAMOTO, H., Organic Chemistry
YAMAMOTO, S., Physical Chemistry
YAMAMOTO, Y., Plant Physiology and Biochemistry
YOKOYA, T., Photo-emission Condensed Matter Physics
YOSHIKAWA, Y., Inorganic Chemistry
YOSHIMURA, H., Particle Physics-based Cosmology
YOSHINO, Y., Algebra
ZHENG, G.-Q., Low Temperature Condensed Matter Physics

Graduate School of Medicine, Dentistry and Pharmaceutical Sciences:

ABE, K., Neuroscience

AWAYA, T., Legal Medicine and Bioethics
DATE, I., Neuroscience
FUKUI, K., Oral Pathobiology
GOHDA, E., Immunochemistry
HARAYAMA, T., Synthetic and Medicinal Chemistry
HATANO, T., Natural Product Chemistry
HIRAMATSU, Y., Obstetrics and Gynaecology
HIROTA, T., Pharmaceutical Chemistry
HUH, N., Basic Oncology
ISHIZU, H., Legal Medicine and Bioethics
IWATSUKI, K., Sensory and Locomotory Function Medicine
KAMEI, C., Pharmacology
KANAZAWA, S., Radiology and Laboratory Medicine
KATO, N., Basic Oncology
KATSU, T., Pharmaceutical Physical Chemistry
KAWAKAMI, N., Social Medicine and Environmental Health Sciences
KAWASAKI, H., Clinical Pharmaceutical Science
KIMATA, Y., Sensory and Locomotory Function Medicine
KIMURA, T., Pharmaceutics
KISHI, K., Oral and Maxillofacial Surgery and Diagnostic Medicine
KITAYAMA, S., Oral Pathobiology
KOIDE, N., Radiology and Laboratory Medicine
KUBOKI, T., Oral Functional Reconstruction
KUMON, H., Basic and Clinical Pathophysiology
KURODA, S., Basic and Clinical Neuroscience
KUROSAKI, Y., Pharmaceutics
MAKINO, H., Basic and Clinical Pathophysiology
MATSUI, H., Basic and Clinical Neuroscience
MATSUO, R., Oral Biology
MINAGI, S., Oral Functional Reconstruction
MIYOSHI, S., Environmental Hygiene
MORISHIMA, T., Obstetrics and Gynaecology
MORITA, K., Anaesthesiology and Emergency Medicine
MORIYAMA, Y., Neurochemistry
NAGAI, N., Oral Pathobiology
NAKAYAMA, E., Infection and Immunology
NARIMATSU, S., Health Chemistry
NINOMIYA, Y., Human Biology
NISHIZAKI, K., Sensory and Locomotory Function Medicine
OGAWA, N., Basic and Clinical Neuroscience
OGUMA, K., Infection and Immunology
OHE, T., Cardiovascular Medicine
OHTSUKA, A., Human Biology
OHTSUKA, Y., Basic and Clinical Neuroscience
OKAMOTO, K., Bio-organic Chemistry
SAITO, Y., Pharmaceutical Analytical Chemistry
SANO, S., Cardiovascular Pathophysiology
SASAKI, A., Oral and Maxillofacial Surgery and Diagnostic Medicine
SASAKI, J., Anatomy
SASAKI, K., Pharmaceutical Fundamental Science
SHIMADA, M., Oral and Maxillofacial Surgery and Diagnostic Medicine
SHIMIZU, K., Basic Oncology
SHIMIZU, N., Basic and Clinical Pathophysiology
SHIMONO, T., Oral Health, Growth and Devlopment
SHIRATORI, Y., Basic and Clinical Pathophysiology
SUGAHARA, T., Oral and Maxillofacial and Diagnostic Medicine
SUGIMOTO, T., Oral Biology
SUZUKI, K., Oral Functional Reconstruction

TAKASHIBA, S., Oral Health, Growth and Development
TAKEI, K., Human Biology
TAKIGAWA, M., Oral Biology
TANAKA, N., Basic and Clinical Pathophysiology
TANIMOTO, M., Basic and Clinical Pathophysiology
TSUCHIYA, T., Microbiology
TSUTSUI, K., Human Biology
WATANABE, T., Oral Health, Growth and Development
WATAYA, Y., Medicinal Information
YAMADA, M., Infection and Immunology
YAMAMOTO, S., Molecular Microbiology
YAMAMOTO, T., Oral Biology
YAMAMOTO, T., Oral Health, Growth and Development
YASUDA, T., Basic and Clinical Pathophysiology
YOSHINO, T., Basic and Clinical Pathophysiology
YOSHIYAMA, M., Oral Functional Reconstruction

Medical School:

AKIMOTO, N., Adult Nursing
ARAO, Y., Clinical Biology
ASARI, S., Adult Nursing
FUJINO, F., Adult Nursing
FUKAI, K., Human Nursing
IKEDA, S., Clinical Pathology
JOJA, I., Medical Radiotechnology
KAGEYAMA, J., Adult Nursing
KANDA, A., Community Health Nursing
KATAOKA, M., Clinical Biology
KATO, H., Medicinal Radioscience
KATO, K., Human Nursing
KAWASAKI, S., Medical Radioscience
KURAZONO, H., Clinical Biology
KUSACHI, S., Clinical Pathology
NAKAGIRI, Y., Medical Radiotechnology
NAKATA, Y., Clinical Pathology
NISHIDA, M., Adult Nursing
ODA, M., Maternal and Child Health Nursing
OHTA, N., Maternal and Child Health Nursing
OKA, H., Clinical Biology
OKAMOTO, M., Clinical Biology
OKANO, H., Community Health Nursing
OKUDA, H., Maternal and Child Health Nursing
ONO, K., Maternal and Child Health Nursing
SENDA, Y., Adult Nursing
SUMIMOTO, T., Medical Radioscience
TAKAHASHI, K., Clinical Pathology
TAGUCHI, T., Medical Radiotechnology
TAKEDA, Y., Medical Radiotechnology
YAMAMOTO, Y., Medical Radioscience
YAMAOKA, K., Medical Radioscience
YOKOYAMA, Y., Community Health Nursing

School of Law (tel. (86) 251-7345; fax (86) 251-7350):

AKAMATSU, H., Civil Law
FUJITA, H., Civil Law
FUJIWARA, K., Criminal Procedure
HAGA, R., Commercial Law
HAGIWARA, S., Criminal Law
IGUCHI, F., Constitutional Law
KITAGAWA, K., Criminal Law
MATSUMURA, K., Civil Procedure
MIURA, O., Commercial Law
OKADA, M., Administrative Law
SATO, S., Investigative Law
UEDA, S., Criminal Procedure

ATTACHED INSTITUTES

Institute for Study of the Earth's Interior: 827, Yamada, Misasa-cho, Tohaku-gun, Tottori 682-0193; tel. (858) 43-1215; fax (858) 43-2184; f. 1985; Dir Prof. E. NAKAMURA.

Research Institute for Bioresources: 2-20-1, Chuo, Kurashiki, Okayama 710-0046;

tel. (86) 424-1661; fax (86) 434-1249; f. 1914; affiliated 1951; Dir Prof. K. Takeda.

OPEN UNIVERSITY OF JAPAN

2-11 Wakaba, Mihama-ku, Chiba City 261-8586

Telephone: (43) 276-5111
Fax: (43) 298-4378
Internet: www.u-air.ac.jp
Founded 1983
Chair.: Yasushi Mitarai
Pres.: Hiromitsu Ishi
Vice-Pres: Yoichi Okabe, Hiroshi Ogino, Hirofumi Honma
Dir-Gen.: Mitsuhiro Ikehara
Librarian: Hitoshi Abe

Library of 630,643 vols
Number of teachers: 94
Number of students: 87,169

OSAKA UNIVERSITY

1-1 Yamadaoka, Suita, Osaka 565-0871

Telephone: (6) 6877-5111
Fax: (6) 6879-7106
E-mail: kokusai@hpc.cmc.osaka-u.ac.jp
Internet: www.osaka-u.ac.jp
Founded 1931
Independent
Academic year: April to March

Pres.: Dr Hideo Miyahara
Vice-Pres (Trustees): Akemichi Baba, Kazuhiko Nishina, Kiyokazu Washida, Naoshi Suzuki, Yukichi Umakoshi
Chief Dir-Gen. of Admin. Bureau: Koichi Kitami
Dir of Univ. Library: Hironobu Nakamura
Library: see Libraries and Archives
Number of teachers: 2,387
Number of students: 21,104

Publications: *Osaka Journal of Mathematics, Medical Journal, Law Review, Osaka Economic Papers, Journal of Osaka University Dental Society, Memoirs of the Graduate School of Letters, Memoirs of the Institute of Scientific and Industrial Research, Studies in Language and Culture, Journal of the Faculty of Health and Spirit Science, International Public Policy Studies, Osaka University Papers in English Linguistics, Machikaneyama Ronso*

DEANS

Graduate School and Faculty of Medicine: Masaya Tohyama
Graduate School and School of Dentistry: Kenji Takada
Graduate School and School of Economics: Hiroaki Nagatani
Graduate School and School of Engineering: Masao Toyoda
Graduate School and School of Engineering Science: Shogo Nishida
Graduate School and School of Human Sciences: Junji Koizumi
Graduate School and School of Letters: Takao Kashiwagi
Graduate School and School of Pharmaceutical Sciences: Hiroshi Yamamoto
Graduate School and School of Science: Shinichi Kotani
Graduate School of Frontier Biosciences: Toshio Hirano
Graduate School of Information Science and Technology: Shojiro Nishio
Graduate School of Language and Culture: Kenji Kimura
Graduate School of Law: Ken-ichi Yoshimoto
Graduate School of Law and Politics and School of Law: Kenji Mitsunari
Osaka School of International Public Policy: Akira Kohsaka

PROFESSORS

Graduate School and Faculty of Medicine (2-2 Yamadaoka, Suita, Osaka 565-0871; fax (6) 6879-3070; internet www.med.osaka-u.ac.jp):

Aozasa, K., Molecular Pathology
Arakida, M., Health Promotion Science
Aso, Y., Health Promotion Science
Beppu, S., Functional Diagnostic Physics
Fujikado, T., AppliedVisual Science
Fujiwara, C., Child and Reproductive Health
Fujiwara, H., Medical Physics and Engineering
Fukuzawa, M., Paediatric Surgery
Haruna, M., Medical Physics and Engineering
Hatazawa, J., Nuclear Medicine
Hayakawa, K., Health Promotion Science
Hayashi, N., Molecular Therapeutics
Hirano, T., Immunology and Molecular Biology
Hori, M., Cardiovascular Medicine
Hosokawa, K., Plastic Surgery
Inagaki, S., Bioinformatics
Inoue, O., Medical Physics and Engineering
Inoue, T., Radiation Oncology
Iwatani, Y., Bioinformatics
Johkoh, T., Functional Diagnostic Science
Kanakura, Y., Haematology and Oncology
Kaneda, Y., Gene Therapy Science
Kanoh, M., Cellular Neuroscience
Katayama, I., Dermatology
Kawano, S., Functional Diagnostic Science
Kawase, I., Respirology
Kido, Y., Evidence-based Clinical Nursing
Kinoshita, H., Biomechanic and Motor Control
Kubo, T., Otorhinolaryngology
Kurachi, Y., Pharmacology
Kurokawa, N., Pharmacy
Makimoto, K., Evidence-based Clinical Nursing
Mashimo, T., Anaesthesiology and Critical Care Medicine
Matoba, R., Legal Medicine
Matsuura, N., Functional Diagnostic Science
Mikami, H., Health Promotion Science
Miyasawa, M., Immunodynamics
Miyazaki, J., Stem Cell Regulation Research
Monden, M., Surgery
Morimoto, K., Hygiene and Preventive Medicine
Murase, K., Medical Physics and Engineering
Murata, Y., Obstetrics and Gynaecology
Nagai, H., Child and Reproductive Health
Nagata, S., Genetics
Nakamura, H., Radiology
Nakamura, T., Molecular Regenerative Medicine
Nakano, T., Stem-cell Biology
Noguchi, S., Surgical Oncology
Ogasawara, C., Health Promotion Science
Ogihara, T., Geriatric Medicine
Ogino, S., Evidence-based Clinical Nursing
Ohashi, K., Child and Reproductive Health
Ohira, Y., Applied Psychology
Ohno, Y., Health Promotion Science
Okamoto, M., Molecular Physiological Chemistry
Okumiya, A., Evidence-based Clinical Nursing
Okuyama, A., Urology
Ozono, K., Paediatrics
Sakoda, S., Neurology
Sato, H., Cognitive Neuroscience
Shimada, M., Child and Reproductive Health
Shimomura, I., Internal Medicine
Shirakura, R., Organ Transplantation
Sobue, K., Neuroscience

Sugimoto, H., Traumatology and Acute Critical Medicine
Sugimoto, N., Applied Bacteriology
Sugiyama, H., Functional Diagnostic Science
Suzuki, S., Evidence-based Clinical Nursing
Toda, T., Clinical Genetics
Takai, Y., Molecular Biology and Biochemistry
Takeda, H., Medical Information Science
Takeda, J., Environmental Genetics
Takeda, M., Psychiatry
Tamura, S., Interdisciplinary Image Analysis
Taniguchi, N., Biochemistry
Tano, Y., Ophthalmology
Teshima, T., Medical Physics and Engineering
Tohyama, M., Anatomy and Neuroscience
Tsujimoto, Y., Molecular Genetics
Uchiyama, Y., Cell Biology and Neuroscience
Yamamoto, Y., Bioinformatics
Yamamura, T., Bioinformatics
Yamatodani, A., Medical Physics and Engineering
Yanagida, T., Physiology and Biosignalling
Yoneda, Y., Anatomy and Cell Biology
Yorifuji, S., Functional Diagnostic Science
Yoshida, T., Applied Psychology
Yoshikawa, H., Orthopaedic Surgery
Yoshimine, T., Neurosurgery

Graduate School and School of Dentistry (1-8 Yamadaoka, Suita, Osaka 565-0871; fax (6) 6879-2832; internet www.dent.osaka-u.ac.jp/index-e.html):

Amano, A., Oral Science Methodology
Ebisu, S., Endodontology
Furukawa, S., Oral and Maxillofacial Radiology
Kamisaki, Y., Pharmacology
Kan, Y., Oral Physiology
Kogo, M., Management of Oral and Maxillofacial Diseases
Maeda, Y., Interdisciplinary Dentistry
Morisaki, I., Nursing Dentistry
Murakami, S., Periodontology
Niwa, H., Dental Anaesthesiology
Nokubi, T., Oromaxillofacial Prosthodontics
Ohshima, T., Paediatric Dentistry
Shizukuishi, S., Preventive Dentistry
Takada, K., Orthodontics and Dentofacial Orthopaedics
Toyosawa, S., Oral Pathology
Wakisaka, S., Oral Anatomy and Developmental Biology
Yatani, H., Occlusion, TMD and Advanced Prosthodontics
Yoneda, T., Molecular and Cellular Craniofacial Biology
Yoshida, A., Oral Anatomy and Neurobiology
Yura, Y., Oral and Maxillofacial Oncology

Graduate School and School of Economics (1-7 Machikaneyama-cho, Toyonaka, Osaka 560-0043; tel. (6) 6850-6111; fax (6) 6850-5205):

Abe, K., Economics
Abe, T., Historical Analysis
Asada, T., Business Information
Ban, K., Economics
Dome, T., Political Analysis
Fukushige, M., Management of Technology
Futagami, K., Economics
Honda, Y., Policy Analysis
Honma, M., Economics
Imai, Y., Theoretical Analysis
Kanai, K., Business Information
Kobayashi, T., Business Information
Mino, K., Theoretical Analysis
Miyamoto, M., Historical Analysis
Nagatani, H., Theoretical Analysis

NAKAJIMA, N., Business
OHNISHI, M., Business
OHYA, K., Business Analysis
SAITO, S., Policy Analysis
SAMURA, T., Historical Analysis
SAWAI, M., Historical Analysis
SUGIHARA, K., Economics
TABATA, Y., Business Analysis
TAKAO, H., Business
TAKEDA, E., Business Analysis
YAMADA, M., Theoretical Analysis

Graduate School and School of Engineering (2-1 Yamadaoka, Suita, Osaka 565-0871; fax (6) 6879-7210; internet www.eng.osaka-u.ac.jp):

Department of Advanced Science and Biotechnology:

AONO, M., Applied Surface Science
FUKUI, K., Dynamic Cell Biology
FUKUZUMI, S., Physical Chemistry for Life Science
HARASHIMA, S., Molecular Genetics
ITO, K., Applied Optics and Optical Information Processing
KANAYA, S., Biological Extremity Engineering
KOBAYASHI, A., Cell Technology
MIYATA, M., Molecular Recognition Chemistry
OHTAKE, H., Biochemical Engineering
SHIOYA, S., Bioprocess Systems Engineering
TAKAI, Y., Theoretical Computation Physics
URABE, I., Enzyme Engineering
YOKOYAMA, M., Molecular System Engineering

Department of Applied Chemistry:

AKASHI, M., Industrial Organic Chemistry
BABA, A., Resources Chemistry
CHATANI, N., Molecular Interaction Chemistry
HIRAO, T., Material Synthetic Chemistry
IMANAKA, N., Material Synthetic Chemistry
INOUE, Y., Molecular Interaction Chemistry
KAI, Y., Structural Physical Chemistry
KAMBE, N., Synthesis and Catalysis
KOMATSU, M., Synthetic Organic Chemistry
KUROSAWA, H., Organometallic Chemistry
KUWABATA, S., Applied Chemistry
OHSHIMA, T., Theoretical Organic Chemistry
UYAMA, H., Theoretical Organic Chemistry

Department of Materials Chemistry:

HIRAO, T., Materials Synthetic Chemistry
IMANAKA, N., Materials Synthetic Chemistry
KAI, Y., Structural Physical Chemistry
KOMATSU, M., Synthetic Organic Chemistry
KUWABATA, S., Applied Electrochemistry
OSHIMA, T., Theoretical Organic Chemistry
UYAMA, H., Structural Organic Chemistry

Department of Biotechnology:

FUKUI, K., Dynamic Cell Biology
HARASHIMA, S., Molecular Genetics
KOBAYASHI, A., Cell Technology
OTAKE, H., Biochemical Engineering
SHIOYA, S., Bioprocess Systems Engineering
URABE, I., Enzyme Engineering

Department of Precision Science, Technology and Applied Physics:

HIROSE, K., Computational Physics
KASAI, H., Materials Physics Theory
KATAOKA, T., Quantum Measurement and Instrumentation
KAWAKAMI, N., Condensed Matter Physics and Statistical Physics

MASUHARA, H., Laser Photochemistry and Microspectroscopy
MORITA, M., Scientific Hardware Systems
SUGAWARA, Y., Engineering Physics
YAGI, A., Non-linear Analysis and its Applications
YAMAUCHI, K., Ultra-precision Machining
YASUTAKE, K., Atomically-controlled Processes
YOSHII, K., Functional Materials

Department of Applied Physics:

KASAI, H., Materials Physics Theory
KAWAKAMI, N., Condensed Matter Physics and Statistical Physics
MASUHARA, H., Laser Photochemistry and Microspectroscopy
SUGAWARA, Y., Engineering Physics
YAGI, A., Nonlinear Analysis and its Applications

Department of Adaptive Machine Systems:

ASADA, M., Emergent Robotics
ISHIGURRO, H., Evolution Dynamics
MINAMINO, Y., Intelligent Materials
NAKATANI, A., Microdynamics
OHJI, T., Advanced Materials Processing
YASUDA, H., Materials Processing and Devices

Department of Mechanophysics Engineering:

FUJITA, K., Design and Manufacturing Engineering
HURUSHO, J., Real-world Active Intelligence
IKEDA, M., Control Engineering
INABA, T., Morphology in Machine Phenomena
KAJISHIMA, T., Fluid Engineering and Thermohydrodynamics
KATAOKA, I., Quantum Measurement
KUBO, S., Materials and Structures Evaluation
MINOSHIMA, K., Intelligent Materials
MIYOSHI, T., Production and Measurement Systems Engineering
MORI, N., Complex Fluid Mechanics
OTA, Y., Control Engineering
SHIBUTANI, Y., Solid Mechanics
TAKEISHI, K., Thermal Science and Engineering
TAKEUCHI, Y., Design and Manufacturing Engineering
TANAK, T., Mechanical Systems Analysis and Solid Mechanics
TSUJI, Y., Complex Fluid Mechanics
UMEDA, Y., Design and Manufacturing Engineering

Department of Mechanical Engineering and Systems:

KUBO, S., Materials and Structures Evaluation
MINOSHIMA, K., Materials and Structures Evaluation
MIYOSHI, T., Production and Measurement Systems Engineering
SHIBUTANI, Y., Solid Mechanics
TANAKA, T., Mechanical Systems Analysis and Solid Mechanics

Department of Computer-controlled Mechanical Systems:

FUJITA, K., Design and Manufacturing Engineering
FURUSHO, J., Real-world Active Intelligence
IKEDA, M., Control Engineering
OTA, Y., Control Engineering
SHIRAI, Y., Real-world Active Intelligence
TAKEUCHI, Y., Design and Manufacturing Engineering

Department of Materials Science and Processing:

ARAI, E., Advanced Manufacturing Systems
FUJIMOTO, K., Micro-nano Systems

FUJIMOTO, S., Environmental Materials and Surface Processing
FUJIWARA, Y., Crystal Growth
HIRATA, Y., Intelligent Materials Processing Systems
HIROSE, K., Computational Physics
HUJIMOTO, S., Environmental Materials and Surface Processing
KAKESHITA, T., Quantum Physics of Solids
KOBAYASHI, K., Smart Materials Processing
MATSUO, S., Intelligent Materials Processing
MINAMI, F., Materials Evaluation for Structuring
NISHIMOTO, K., Materials Joining
TANAKA, T., Interface Science and Technology
TOYODA, M., Strength/Fracture Evaluation for Manufacturing
USUI, T., Materials Processing and Metallurgy
YAMAMOTO, M., Physics of Surface and Interface
YAMASHITA, H., Thermophysics of Materials

Department of Materials Science and Engineering:

FUJIWARA, Y., Crystal Growth
KAKESHITA, T., Quantum Physics of Solids
YAMAMOTO, M., Physics of Surface and Interface

Department of Manufacturing Science:

ARAI, E., Advanced Manufacturing Systems
FUJIMOTO, K., Micro-nano Systems
HIRATA, Y., Intelligent Materials Processing Systems
KOBAYASHI, K., Smart Materials Processing
MINAMI, F., Materials Evaluation for Structuring
MIYAMOTO, I., Intelligent Materials Processing Systems
NISHIMOTO, K., Materials Joining
TOYODA, M., Strength/Fracture Evaluation for Manufacturing

Department of Communications Engineering:

BABAGUCHI, N., Telecommunications and Systems Engineering
IIDA, T., Fusion Engineering
ISE, T., Systems and Electric Power Engineering
ITO, T., Electro-materials Engineering
KAWASAKI, Z., Fundamentals for Communications Engineering
KODAMA, R., Laser Engineering
KOMAKI, S., Microwave and Optical Communication Systems
KUMAGAI, S., Control Engineering
MORITA, S., Microscopic Quantum Engineering
NISHIKAWA, M., Supra-high-temperature Engineering
SANPEI, S., Telecommunication and Systems Engineering
SASAKI, T., Applied Electrophysics
SUGINO, T., Science and Technology of Electrical Materials
SUHARA, T., Integrated Electronic Engineering
TAKINE, T., Advanced Communications and Photonic Networks
TANAKA, K., Laser Engineering
TANIGUCHI, T., Quantum Devices
TANINO, T., Systems Analysis and Optimization
TSUJI, K., Systems Engineering
YAGI, T., Control System Engineering

Department of Sustainable Energy and Environmental Engineering:

HORIIKE, H., Neutronics and Nuclear Instrumentation
KAGA, A., Engineering for the Atmospheric Environment

MIZUNO, M., Environment and Energy Systems
MORIOKA, T., Environmental Management
NISHIJIMA, S., Nuclear Chemical Engineering
SAWAKI, M., Environmental Management
TAKEDA, T., Nuclear Reactor Physics
YAMANAKA, S., Nuclear Fuels

Department of Global Architecture:

DEGUCHI, I., Social Systems Engineering
HASEGAWA, K., Naval Architecture
IMAI, K., Regional Environment and Global Transport
KATO, N., Naval Architecture
KOHZU, I., Structural Engineering
MATSUI, S., Structural and Geotechnical Engineering
NAITO, S., Marine Systems Engineering
NAKATSUJI, K., Social Systems Engineering
NITTA, Y., Social Systems Engineering
OHNO, Y., Structural Engineering
SAGARA, K., Architectural Design
TACHIBANA, E., Structural Engineering
TANIMOTO, C., Sustainable Development and Strategy
TOKIDA, K., Structural and Geotechnical Engineering
YAMAGUCHI, K., Sustainable Development and Strategy
YAO, T., Naval Architecture

Department of Environmental Engineering:

FUJITA, M., Water Science and Environmental Biotechnology
KAGA, A., Engineering for the Atmospheric Environment
MIZUNO, M., Environment and Energy Systems
MORIOKA, T., Environmental Management

Department of Management for Industry and Technology:

NARUMI, S., Management of Technology Knowledge
SATO, T., Technology Design
YAMAMOTO, T., Management of Technology Knowledge
ZAKO, M., Technology Design

Science Center for Atoms, Molecules and Ions Control:

FUKUDA, T., Plasma Particle Control Division
HAMAGUCHI, S., Plasma Particle Control Division
NAKATANI, R., Micro-composite Research Division
OKADA, S., Plasma Particle Control Division
SHIRAI, Y., Micro-structures Division

Research Center for Ultra-Precision Science and Technology:

ENDO, K., Precision Science and Technology

Graduate School and School of Engineering Science (1-3 Machikaneyama-cho, Toyonaka, Osaka 560-8531; tel. (6) 6850-6111; fax (6) 6850-6151; internet www.es.osaka-u.ac.jp/index-e.html):

Department of Materials Engineering Science:

HIRAI, T., Solar Energy Chemistry
HIRATA, Y., Environment and Energy System
HIYAMIZU, S., Quantum Physics of Nanoscale Materials
IMOTO, N., Quantum Physics of Nanoscale Materials
INOUE, Y., Environment and Energy System
ITOH, T., Dynamics of Nanoscale Materials
IWAI, S., Molecular Organization Chemistry
KANEDA, K., Chemical Reaction Engineering

KITAOKA, Y., Frontier Materials
KITAYAMA, T., Synthetic Chemistry
KUBOI, R., Bioprocess Engineering
MASHIMA, K., Synthetic Chemistry
MATSUMURA, M., Solar Energy Chemistry
MIYAKE, K., Electron Correlation Physics
MIYASAKA, H., Dynamics of Nanoscale Materials
NAKANO, M., Chemical Reaction Engineering
NAKATO, Y., Molecular Organization Chemistry
NAOTA, T., Synthetic Chemistry
OHGAKI, K., Environment and Energy System
SHIMIZU, K., Quantum Science in Extreme Conditions
SUGA, S., Electron Correlation Physics
SUZUKI, N., Frontier Materials
SUZUKI, Y., Electron Correlation Physics
TADA, H., Quantum Physics of Nanoscale Materials
TAYA, M., Bioprocess Engineering
TOBE, Y., Frontier Materials
UEYAMA, K., Chemical Reaction Engineering
YOSHIDA, H., Quantum Science in Extreme Conditions

Department of Mechanical Science and Bioengineering:

ARAKI, T., Biomedical and Biophysical Measurements
HIRAO, M., Mechanics of Solid Materials
KOBAYASHI, H., Mechanics of Solid Materials
MIYAZAKI, F., Mechano-informatics
NOMURA, T., Biophysical Engineering
OHSHIRO, O., Biomedical and Biophysical Measurements
OSAKADA, K., Mechano-informatics
SUGIMOTO, N., Mechanics of Fluids and Thermo-fluids
TANAKA, M., Biomedical Engineering
TSUJIMOTO, Y., Propulsion Engineering
WAKABAYASHI, K., Biophysical Engineering

Department of Systems Innovation:

AIDA, S., Mathematical and Statistical Finance
AKASAKA, Y., Solid–State Electronics
ARAI, T., Intelligent Systems
FUJII, T., System Theory
IIGUNI, Y., System Theory
INAGAKI, N., Mathematical and Statistical Finance
INUIGUCHI, M., Theoretical Systems Science
ITOSAKI, H., Advanced Quantum Devices and Electronics
KANO, Y., Statistical Science
KITAGAWA, M., Advanced Quantum Devices and Electronics
KOBAYASHI, T., Optical Electronics
NAGAI, H., Mathematical and Statistical Finance
NAWA, H., Mathematical Modelling
NISHIDA, S., Intelligent Systems
OKAMOTO, H., Solid-State Electronics
OKAMURA, Y., Optical Electronics
OKUYAMA, M., Solid-State Electronics
SATO, K., Intelligent Systems
SHIRAHATA, S., Statistical Science
SUZUKI, T., Mathematical Modelling
URABE, S., Optical Electronics
USHIO, T., Theoretical Systems Science
YACHIDA, M., Intelligent Systems

Graduate School and School of Human Sciences (1-2 Yamadaoka, Suita, Osaka 565-0871; tel. (6) 6877-5111; fax (6) 6879-8010; internet www.hus.osaka-u.ac.jp/english):

ABE, A., Educational Policy and Administration
ADACHI, K., Behavioural Data Science
DAIBO, I., Social Psychology
FUJIOKA, J., Educational Psychology

FUJITA, A., Clinical Thanatology and Geriatric Behavioural Science
HINOBAYASHI, T., Comparative and Developmental Psychology
HIRASAWA, Y., Lifelong Education
IMURA, O., Clinical Psychology
KASUGA, N., People and Culture
KAWABATA, A., Advanced Empirical Sociology
KIMAE, T., Sociology of Modern Society
KOIZUMI, J., Cultural and Social Anthropology
KONDO, H., Sociology of Education
KOTO, Y., Sociological Theory
KUGIHARA, N., Social Psychology
KUMAKURA, H., Biological Anthropology
KURIMOTO, E., Cultural and Social Anthropology
KUWANO, S., Environmental Psychology
MAESAKO, T., Communication and Media
MINAMI, T., Comparative and Developmental Psychology
MIURA, T., Applied Cognitive Psychology
MIYATA, K., Clinical Psychology
MORIKAWA, K., Fundamental Psychology
MUTA, K., Sociology of Communication
NAKAGAWA, S., Cultural and Social Anthropology
NAKAMURA, T., Quantitative Psychology of Expression and Cognition
NAKAMURA, Y., International Collaboration
NAKAYAMA, Y., Logical Studies, Foundation of Science
NAOI, A., Information Technology and Human Sciences
OIMATSU, K., Clinical Psychology
ONODA, M., Educational Policy and Administration
SHIMIZU, K., Cultural Studies of Education
SUGAI, K., Educational Technology
SUGENO, T., Philosophical Anthropology
TSUTSUMI, S., Social Policy and Community Empowerment Studies
USUI, S., Human Risk Studies
UTSUMI, S., International Collaboration
YAMAMOTO, T., Behavioural Physiology

Graduate School and School of Letters (1-5 Machikaneyama-cho, Toyonaka, Osaka 560-8532; tel. (6) 6850-6111; fax (6) 6850-5091; e-mail web-admin@www.let.osaka-u.ac.jp; internet www.let.osaka-u.ac.jp):

AKITA, S., Western History
AMANO, F., Theatre Studies
AOKI, N., Japanese Linguistics
ARAKAWA, M., Central Asian History
EGAWA, A., Western History
ENOMOTO, F., Indian Philosophy and Buddhist Studies
FUJIKAWA, T., Western History
FUJITA, H., Environmental Aesthetics
FUKUNAGA, S., Archaeology
GOTO, A., Japanese Language and Literature
HACHIYA, M., Japanese Language and Literature
HAYASHI, M., German Literature
IIKURA, Y., Japanese Language and Literature
IKAI, T., Japanese History
IRIE, Y., Philosophy and History of Philosophy
IZUHARA, T., Japanese Language and Literature
KAMIKURA, T., Aesthetics
KASHIWAGI, T., French Literature
KATAYAMA, T., Asian History
KAWAMURA, K., Historical Studies of Cultural Exchanges
KINSUI, S., Japanese Language and Literature
KOBAYASHI, S., Human Geography
KODERA, T., Art History
KUDO, M., Japanese Linguistics
MOMOKI, S., Asian History
MORIOKA, Y., American Literature

MORIYASU, T., Central Asian History
MURATA, M., Japanese History
NAGATA, Y., Theatre Studies
NAITO, T., Comparative Literature
NAKAOKA, N., Clinical Philosophy and Ethics
NEGISHI, K., Musicology
OBA, Y., English Linguistics
OHASHI, R., Philosophy and Aesthetics
OKUDAIRA, S., Art History
SANADA, S., Japanese Linguistics
SUGIHARA, T., Historical Studies of Cultural Exchanges
SURO, N., Philosophy, Modern Thought and Cultural Studies
TAIRA, M., Japanese History
TAKAHASHI, B., Chinese Literature
TAKENAKA, T., Western History
TAMAI, A., English Literature
TOKI, S., Japanese Linguistics
UENO, O., Philosophy and History of Philosophy
UMEMURA, T., Japanese History
WADA, A., French Literature
WAKAYAMA, E., Art History
WASHIDA, K., Clinical Philosophy and Ethics
YUASA, K., Chinese Philosophy

Graduate School and School of Pharmaceutical Sciences (1-6 Yamadaoka, Suita, Osaka 565-0871; fax (6) 6879-8154; internet www.phs.osaka-u.ac.jp):

AZUMA, J., Clinical Evaluation of Medicines and Therapeutics
BABA, A., Molecular Neuropharmacology
DOI, T., Protein Molecular Engineering
HIRATA, K., Environmental Bioengineering
IMANISHI, T., Bioorganic Chemistry
KITA, Y., Synthetic Organic Chemistry
KOBAYASHI, M., Natural Product Chemistry
MAEDA, M., Biochemistry and Molecular Biology
MATSUDA, T., Medicinal Pharmacology
MURAKAMI, N., Medicinal Plant Resource Exploration
NAKAGAWA, S., Biopharmaceutics
NASU, M., Environmental Science and Microbiology
NISHIKAWA, J., Environmental Biochemistry
OHKUBO, T., Biophysical Chemistry
TAKAGI, T., Pharmaceutical Information Science
TANAKA, K., Toxicology
TANAKA, T., Medicinal and Organic Chemistry
UNO, T., Analytical Chemistry
YAGI, K., Bio-functional Molecular Chemistry
YAMAMOTO, H., Immunology

Graduate School and School of Science (1-1 Machikaneyama-cho, Toyonaka, Osaka 560-0043; tel. (6) 6850-6111; fax (6) 6850-5288; internet www.sci.osaka-u.ac.jp):

AKAI, H., Quantum Physics
AKUTSU, Y., Quantum Physics
AOSHIMA, S., Polymer Synthesis
ASAKAWA, M., Hadronic Physics
DOI, S., Analysis
FUJIKI, A., Global Geometry and Analysis
FUKASE, K., Natural Product Chemistry
FUKUYAMA, K., Structural Biology
HARADA, A., Supermolecular Science
HASE, S., Organic Biochemistry
HAYASHI, N., Applied Mathematics
HIGASHIJIMA, K., Particle Physics
HOSOTANI, Y., Fundamental Physics
IBUKIYAMA, T., Algebra
INABA, A., Structural Thermodynamics
KAIZAKI, S., Inorganic Chemistry
KANAZAWA, H., Molecular Biology
KASAI, T., Reaction Dynamics, Molecular Thermodynamics
KATAKUSE, I., Interdisciplinary Physics

KAWAMURA, H., Solid-State and Statistical Physics
KAWARAZAKI, S., Solid-State Physics
KISHIMOTO, T., Particle and Nuclear Physics
KOISO, N., Geometry
KONNO, K., Algebra
KONNO, T., Coordination Chemistry
KOTANI, S., Analysis
KUNO, Y., Elementary Particle Physics
KURAMITSU, S., Biophysical Chemistry
MABUCHI, T., Global Mathematics
MASUKATA, H., Molecular Genetics
MATSUDA, J., Planetary Science
MUNAKATA, T., Chemistry
MURATA, M., Biomolecular Chemistry
NAKASHIMA, S., Physical Geochemistry
NAKAZAWA, Y., Condensed Matter Physical Chemistry
NAMIKAWA, Y., Algebra
NISHIDA, H., Development Biology
NISHITANI, T., Analysis
NOMACHI, M., Quark Nuclear Physics
NORISUYE, T., Polymer Solutions
NOZUE, Y., Condensed Matter Physics
OGAWA, T., Quantum Physics
OGIHARA, S., Cell Biology
OHSHIKA, K., Geometry
ONUKI, Y., Condensed Matter Physics
SATO, T., Polymer Chemical Physics
SHIMODA, T., Nuclear Physics
SHINOHARA, A., Nuclear Chemistry
SUGITA, H., Analysis
SUZUKI, S., Bioinorganic Chemistry
TAJIMA, S., Condensed Matter Physics
TAKAHARA, F., Theoretical Astrophysics
TAKEDA, S., Condensed Matter Physics
TAKISAWA, H., Molecular Cell Biology
TERASHIMA, I., Plant Ecophysiology
TOKUNAGA, F., Extreme-environment Biology
TSUCHIYAMA, A., Experimental Planetology
TSUNEKI, K., Comparative Zoology
TSUNEMI, H., Astrophysics
UMEHARA, M., Global Mathematics
USUI, S., Algebra
WATANABE, T., Algebra
WATARAI, H., Analytical Chemistry
YAMAGUCHI, K., Quantum Chemistry, Physical Chemistry of Condensed Matter
YAMANAKA, T., High Energy Physics
YAMANAKA, T., Physics of Matter
YONESAKI, T., Microbial Genetics

Graduate School of Information Science and Technology (1-5 Yamadaoka, Suita, Osaka 565-0871; tel. (6) 6877-5111; fax (6) 6879-4570; internet www.ist.osaka-u.ac.jp):

Department of Pure and Applied Mathematics:

DATE, E., Mathematical Science
HIBI, T., Combinatorics
KAWANAKA, N., Discrete Structures
MATSUMURA, A., Applied Analysis
ODANAKA, S., Computer-assisted Mathematics
SAKANE, Y., Applied Geometry

Department of Information and Physical Sciences:

ISHII, H., Operations Research
MORITA, H., Computing with Complexity and Nonlinearity
NUMAO, M., Architecture for Intelligence
TANIDA, J., Physical Sciences
UOSAKI, K., Nonlinear Systems, Modelling and Optimization

Department of Computer Science:

HAGIHARA, K., Supercomputing Engineering
INOUE, K., Software Engineering
KUSOMOTO, S., Software Science
MASUZAWA, T., Algorithm Engineering
YAGI, Y., Intelligent Media Systems

Department of Information Systems Engineering:

CHIBA, T., Advanced System Architecture
IMAI, M., Integrated System Design
KAWATA, T., Advanced Systems Architecture
KIKUNO, T., Dependability Engineering
ONOYE, T., Information Systems Synthesis
TAKEMURA, H., Integrated Media Environment

Department of Information Networking:

HIGASHINO, T., Mobile Computing
IMASE, M., Information Sharing Platform
MURAKAMI, K., Intelligent Networking Systems
NAKANO, H., Advanced Network Architecture
OBASHI, Y., Cyber Communication
SATO, T., Cyber Communication

Department of Multimedia Engineering:

FUJIWARA, T., Information Security Engineering
KATAGIRI, Y., Multimedia Agent Systems
KISHINO, F., Human Interface Engineering
KOGURE, K., Multimedia Agent Systems
KOMODA, N., Business Information Systems
NISHIO, S., Multimedia Data Engineering
SHIMOJO, S., Applied Media Engineering

Department of Bioinformatic Engineering:

AKAZAWA, K., Human Information Engineering
KASHIWABARA, T., Bio-network Engineering
MATSUDA, H., Genome Information Engineering
SHIMIZU, H., Metabolic Engineering

Graduate School of Language and Culture (1-8 Machikaneyama-cho, Toyonaka, Osaka 560-0043; tel. (6) 6850-6111; fax (6) 6850-5865):

DYUBOVSKI, A., Language and Technology
HARUKI, Y., Language and Communication
HAYASHI, Y., Language and Information Science
HUKAZAWA, Y., Language and Communication
IWANE, H., Language and Technology
KANASAKI, H., Area Studies in Language and Culture
KANEKO, M., Area Studies in Language and Culture
KIMURA, K., Area Studies in Language and Culture
KIMURA, S., Interdisciplinary Cultural Studies
KITAMURA, T., Interdisciplinary Cultural Studies
NAKA, N., Language and Culture in International Relations
NAKANO, Y., Language and Culture in International Relations
NARITA, H., Education in Language and Culture
OKADA, N., Education in Language and Culture
OKITA, T., Education in Language and Culture
SENBA, Y., Language and Technology
TAKAOKA, K., Language and Culture in International Relations
TSUDA, A., Language and Communication
TSUKUI, S., Area Studies in Language and Culture
WATANABE, S., Language and Information Science
YOKOTA, G., Interdisciplinary Cultural Studies

Graduate School of Law (1-6 Machikaneyama-cho, Toyonaka, Osaka 560-0043; tel. (6) 6850-6111; fax (6) 6850-5091):

AOE, H., Legal Practice
AOTAKE, S., Legal Practice
CHAEN, S., Legal Practice

HIRATA, K., Legal Practice
IKEDA, T., Legal Practice
KOJIMA, N., Legal Practice
KOSUGI, S., Legal Practice
MATSUI, S., Legal Practice
MATSUKAWA, T., Legal Practice
MATSUMOTO, K., Legal Practice
MISAKA, Y., Legal Practice
MIZUTANI, N., Legal Practice
MURAKAMI, T., Legal Practice
SAKUMA, O., Legal Practice
SHIMOMURA, M., Legal Practice
SUENAGA, T., Legal Practice
SUZUKI, H., Legal Practice
TANIGUTCHI, S., Legal Practice
YOSHIDA, M., Legal Practice
YOSHIMOTO, K., Legal Practice

Graduate School of Frontier Biosciences (1-3 Yamadaoka, Suita, Osaka 565-0871; fax (6) 6879-4420; internet www.fbs.osaka-u.ac.jp):

FUJITA, I., Neuroscience
HAMADA, H., Organismal Biosystems
HANAOKA, F., Integrated Biology
HIRANO, T., Organismal Biosystems
KAWAMURA, S., Nanobiology
KINOSHITA, S., Biophysical Dynamics
KONDOH, H., Biomolecular Networks
KURAHASHI, T., Biophysical Dynamics
MURAKAMI, F., Neuroscience
NAGATA, S., Integrated Biology
NAKANO, T., Integrated Biology
NAMBA, K., Nanobiology
NORIOKA, S., Biophysical Dynamics
OGURA, A., Neuroscience
OHZAWA, I., Neuroscience
OKAMOTO, M., Biomolecular Networks
SHIMOMURA, I., Organismal Biosystems
SUGINO, A., Biomolecular Networks
TANAKA, K., Organismal Biosystems
YAGI, T., Integrated Biology
YAMAMOTO, N., Neuroscience
YANAGIDA, T., Nanobiology
YONEDA, Y., Biomolecular Networks

Graduate School of Law and Politics and School of Law (1-6 Machikaneyama-cho, Toyonaka, Osaka 560-0043; tel. (6) 6850-6111; fax (6) 6850-5091):

HAYASHI, T., Comparative Law and Politics
KAWATA, J., Center for Legal and Political Practice
KUNII, K., Comparative Law and Politics
MITSUNARI, K., Independent Study Center
NAKAO, T., Comparative Law and Politics
NAKAYAMA, R., Governance and Law
OKUBO, N., Governance and Law
SAKAMOTO, K., Governance and Law
TAGO, K., Governance and Law
TAKADA, A., Governance and Law
TAKAHASHI, A., Independent Study Course
TAKENAKA, Y., Independent Study Course
TAKIGUCHI, T., Comparative Law and Politics
YAMASHITA, M., Comparative Law and Politics
YOON, K. C., International and Comparative Law Course

Osaka School of International Public Policy (1-31 Machikaneyama-cho, Toyonaka, Osaka 560-0043; tel. (6) 6850-6111; fax (6) 6850-5208):

HASHIMOTO, Y., Comparative Public Policy
HOSHINO, T., Systems Integration
KOHSAKA, A., Systems Integration
KOJIMA, N., Comparative Corporate Behaviour
KUROSAWA, M., International Public System
MATSUSHIGE, H., Systems Integration
MURAKAMI, M., International Public System
NAKANO, T., Comparative Corporate Behaviour
NOMURA, Y., Systems Integration

SAITO, S., Comparative Economic Development
SAWAI, M., Comparative Economic Development
SUGIHARA, S., Contemporary Japanese Law and Economy
TAKENAKA, H., International Trade Relations
TANIGUCHI, S., International Trade Relations
TOKOTANI, F., Comparative Public Policy
YAMAUCHI, N., Contemporary Japanese Law and Economy
YONEHARA, K., Contemporary Japanese Law and Economy

ATTACHED INSTITUTES

Institute for Protein Research: Suita Campus, Yamadaoka, Suita, Osaka; Dir HIDEO AKUTSU.

Institute of Scientific and Industrial Research: Suita Campus, Mihogaoka, Ibaraki, Osaka; Dir TOMOJI KAWAI.

Institute of Social and Economic Research: Suita Campus, Mihogaoka, Ibaraki, Osaka; Dir SHINSUKE IKEDA.

Joining and Welding Research Institute: Suita Campus, Mihogaoka, Ibaraki, Osaka; Dir KIYOSHI NOGI.

Research Institute for Microbial Diseases: Suita Campus, Yamadaoka, Suita, Osaka; Dir TAROH KINOSHITA.

OSAKA UNIVERSITY OF FOREIGN STUDIES

8-1-1 Aomatani-higashi, Minoo City, Osaka 562-8558

Telephone: (727) 30-5005
Fax: (727) 30-5009
E-mail: sosoumu@post01.osaka-gaidai.ac.jp
Internet: www.osaka-gaidai.ac.jp

Founded 1949
Independent
Academic year: April to March (two semesters)

Pres.: SHUN KORENAGA
Librarian: Prof. MASARU HASHIMOTO

Library of 612,340 vols
Number of teachers: 206
Number of students: 4,528 (Faculty of Foreign Studies), 354 (Graduate School), 127 (Center for Japanese Language)

Publications: *Journal, Japanese Language and Culture: Bulletin of the Center for Japanese Language, Journal of the Association for Integrated Studies in Language and Society.*

OTARU UNIVERSITY OF COMMERCE

3-5-21, Midori, Otaru, 047-0851, Hokkaido
Telephone: (134) 27-5200
Fax: (134) 27-5213
E-mail: inl@office.otaru.ac.jp
Internet: www.otaru-uc.ac.jp

Founded 1949
Independent

Pres.: IEMASA YAMADA
Chief Admin. Officer: HIROSHI AIBA
Librarian: YOICHIRO YUKI

Library of 420,000 vols
Number of teachers: 134
Number of students: 2,260

Depts of economics, commerce, law, information and management sciences, teacher-training programme in commerce and graduate school

PROFESSORS

Department of Commerce: HAJIME ITOH
Department of Economics: HAJIME IMANISHI

Department of Information Technology: HARUHIKO OGASAWARA
Department of Law: MASAHIRO MICHINO

UNIVERSITY OF THE RYUKYUS

1 Senbaru, Nishihara-cho, Okinawa 903-0213

Telephone: (98) 895-2221
Fax: (98) 895-8037
E-mail: webmaster@www.u-ryukyu.ac.jp
Internet: www.u-ryukyu.ac.jp

Founded 1950
Academic year: April to March
Independent
Language of instruction: Japanese

Pres.: TERUO IWAMASA
Vice-Pres. for Financial, Facilities and Hospital Management: HAYAO MIYAGI
Vice-Pres. for Gen. Affairs: TAKASHI MARUYAMA
Vice-Pres. for Planning and Management Strategy: HAJIME OSHIRO
Vice-Pres. for Research Education and Student Affairs: RISHUN SHINZATO
Vice-Pres. for Research Outreach and Int. Affairs: KEISUKE TAIRA
Dean of Students: KATSUMA YAGASAKI
Library Dir: K. OYAKAWA

Library of 930,000 vols
Number of teachers: 879
Number of students: 8,195

DEANS

Faculty of Agriculture: S. GIBO
Faculty of Education: T. NAKAMURA
Faculty of Engineering: T. YAMAKAWA
Faculty of Law: K. UEZATO
Faculty of Medicine: Y. SATO
Faculty of Science: M. TSUCHIYA
Faculty of Tourism Sciences and Industrial Management: T. HESHIKI
Graduate School of Health Sciences: T. HOKAMA
Graduate School of Law: T. TAKARA

PROFESSORS

Faculty of Agriculture:

AKINAGA, T., Postharvest Handling
CHINEN, I., Applied Biochemistry
GIBO, S., Land Conservation
HAYASHI, H., Woody Materials and Processing
HIGA, T., Tropical Horticulture
HIGOSHI, H., Animal Hygiene
HIRATA, E., Forestry Measurement
HONGO, F., Chemistry of Animal Products and Applied Bioresource Utilization
ISHIMINE, Y., Economic Plants
IWAHASHI, O., Insect Ecology
KAWASHIMA, Y., Comparative Anatomy
KOBAMOTO, N., Applied Biophysics
KOKI, Z., Preventive Forestry Engineering
KURODA, T., Environmental Information Sciences
MIYAGI, N., Soil Engineering
MURAYAMA, S., Crop Science
NAKADA, T., Animal Reproduction
NAKASONE, Y., Food Chemistry
OSHIRO, S., Animal Science, Environmental Physiology
SATO, S., Genetics and Breeding of Rice Plants
SHINJO, A., Animal Breeding
SHINJO, T., Geomechanics
SHINOHARA, T., Forest Policy and Economics
TAWATA, S., Pesticide Chemistry
TOKASHIKI, Y., Soil Science
UENO, M., Agricultural Engineering
UESATO, K., Floricultural Plant Science
YAGA, S., Wood Chemistry and Wood Preservation
YAMASHIRO, S., Agricultural Engineering

YASUDA, M., Food Microbiology
YONAHA, T., Plant Pathology
YOSHIDA, S., Agricultural Marketing Theory

Faculty of Education:

AIZAWA, T., Chinese Literature
ARATA, Y., Biophysics Engineering
FUJIE, T., Homemaking Education, Aesthetics in Costume
FUJIWARA, Y., Didactics
HAMAMOTO, M., Sports Methodology
HANASHIRO, R., Consumer Education
HIGA, Z., Technical Education
HIGASIMORI, K., Food Science
HIRATA, E., Education for the Handicapped
IKEDA, K., Judo
INOUE, K., Lifelong Education
ISHIGURO, E., Optics
ISHIKAWA, K., Social Development in Children
ITOKAZU, T., Educational Music of Wind Instruments
IZUMI, K., Vocal Music
KAKAZU, T., Psychology
KAMIYAMA, T., Woodcut
KAMIZONO, S., Developmental Psychology of Mentally Retarded and Handicapped Children
KATO, M., Complex Analysis
KAWANA, T., Physical Geography
KINJO, M., Mathematics Education
KINJO, S., Culinary Science
KINJO, Y., Inorganic Chemistry
KOBASHIGAWA, H., Sports Psychology
KOBAYASHI, M., Theory and History of Art
KOJIMA, Y., Japanese Literature
KOYANAGI, M., Physical Chemistry
MAEHARA, H., Discrete Geometry
MAEHARA, T., Psychology
MAESHIRO, R., Regional Economics
MATSUMOTO, S., Mathematical Physics
MIZUNO, M., Criminal Law
NAGAYAMA, T., Piano Playing
NAKAMURA, I., Meteorology
NAKAMURA, T., Education for the Handicapped
NAKAMURA, T., Theory of Music
NAKASONE, Y., Ecology
NAKAZATO, H., Algebra
NISHIMURA, S., Sculpture
NISHIZATO, K., History of East Asia
NOHARA, T., Palaeontology
OKUDA, M., Ceramic Art
OZAWA, Y., Japanese Literature
SEKINE, H., Electricity and Electrical Engineering
SHIMABUKURO, Z., English Linguistics
SHIMOJANA, M., Animal Ecology and Taxonomy (especially spiders)
SHINZATO, R., Clinical Psychology
SHINZATO, S., Kinematics and Dynamics of Mechanisms
SIMABUKURO, T., Psychology of Personality
TAIRA, K., Health Promotion
TAIRA, T., Physical Education
TAKASHIMA, N., Social Studies
TAKEDA, H., International Peace Studies
TAMAKI, A., Physical Education
TOMINAGA, D., Psychophysiology
UEZU, E., Nutrition and Physiology
YAMAUTI, S., TESL/TEFL
YONEMORI, T., Educational Information Technology

Faculty of Engineering:

AMANO, T., Wind Engineering for Building Structures
ASHARIF, M. R., Adaptive Digital Signal Processing, Speech in Images
FUKUSHIMA, S., Architectural Planning
IKEDA, T., Urban and Regional Planning
KANESHIRO, H., Fatigue Fracture
KINA, S., Sanitary Engineering
KODAMA, M., Microwave
MEKARU, S., Plastic Working
MIYAGI, H., Intelligent Systems

MIYAGI, K., High Velocity Impact
MORITA, D., Conservation Science and Environmental Planning for Architecture
NAGAI, M., Mechanics and Fluid Engineering
NAGATA, T., Thermal Engineering
NAKAMURA, I., Electronic Circuits
NAKAO, Z., Mathematical Informatics
OSHIRO, T., Structural Analysis and Materials
OYAKAWA, K., Heat Transfer Augmentation
SHINZATO, T., Thermal Engineering
TAKAHASHI, H., Power Systems Engineering and Surge Analysis
TAKARA, T., Spoken Language Processing
TAMAKI, S., Digital Control
TOGUCHI, M., Electronic Materials
TSUKAYAMA, S., Coastal Engineering
TSUTSUI, S., Coastal Engineering
UEZATO, K., Electric Machinery
YABUKI, T., Bridge and Structural Engineering
YAFUSO, T., Strength of Materials
YAMAKAWA, T., Reinforced Concrete Structures
YAMAMOTO, T., Neuro-control
YAMASHIRO, Y., Electrical Materials
YARA, H., Welding Engineering
YOSHIYA, K., Intelligent Information Processing
ZUKERAN, C., Multiple-valued Logic Circuit

Faculty of Law and Letters:

AKAMINE, K., American Literature
AKAMINE, M., Japanese Folklore
AKAMINE, M., Modern Chinese History, Modern Okinawa History
ANDO, Y., Sociology
ARAKAKI, S., Civil Law
ASHITOMI, T., Civil Law
CHINEN, S., Monetary Economics
CHINEN, Y., Public Finance
EGAMI, T., Science of Public Administration, Comparative Politics
ENDO, M., Cognitive Psychology
GABE, M., International Relations
HAMASAKI, M., Greek Philosophy
HESHIKI, T., International Marketing
HIYANE, T., History of Political Thought, Political Science
HOSAKA, H., Journalism
IHA, M., Marketing
IKEDA, Y., Japanese Archaeology, Museography
IKEMIYA, M., Ryukyuan Literature
IMURA, O., Clinical Psychology
INABA, Y., Criminal Procedure
IREI, T., Human Resources Management, Business Administration
ISHIKAWA, T., Regional Geography, Human Geography
ISHIMINE, K., Constitutional Law
KABIRA, N., Economic History
KARIMATA, S., Japanese Linguistics, Study of Ryukyuan Dialects
KAWASOE, M., Social Services for the Aged
KOMATSU, M., Economic History
KUDEKEN, K., Community Development in Social Welfare
MACHIDA, M., Settlement Geography, Geographical Information Systems
MAEKADO, A., Geomorphology
MIYARA, S., Linguistics
NAKACHI, H., Administrative Law
NAKACHI, K., American Literature
NAKAHARA, T., Business and Corporation Laws
NAKAHODO, M., Modern Japanese Literature
NAKAMURA, T., Social Psychology
NAMIHIRA, T., Political Philosophy and Theory, Political Science
NISHIKAWA, H., Contemporary Philosophy
OSABE, Y., Asian History
OSHIRO, H., International Economics

OSHIRO, I., Theoretical Economics
OSHIRO, M., Managerial Finance
OSHIRO, T., Regional Development Policy
OYAKAWA, T., Linguistics
SAKIMA, N., European History
SHIMABUKURO, S., Human Geography
SHIMABUKURO, T., Commercial Law, Law of Securities Regulation
SHIMIZU, K., Criminal Law
SHIMOJI, Y., English Linguistics
SHIMURA, K., Quality Management
SUZUKI, N., International Sociology
TAIRA, M., American Literature
TAIRA, T., Applied Linguistics
TAKARA, K., Ryukyuan History
TAKARA, T., Constitutional Law, Administrative Law
TAMAKI, I., Civil Procedure Law
TAMAKI, M., Ryukyuan Literature
TANAKA, H., Economic Statistics
TOMA, S., Theoretical Economics
TOMINAGA, H., Econometrics
TOYOOKA, T., Accounting Information Theory, Accounting Systems
TSUHA, T., Social Anthropology
TSUNODA, M., Civil Law, European Private Law
UEZATO, K., Chinese Literature
UEZU, Y., Accounting
YAMAZATO, J., Japanese History
YAMAZATO, K., American Literature
YOGI, K., Linguistics
YONAHARA, T., Strategic Management
YOSHII, K., German
YOSHIMURA, K., English Literature
YOSHIZAWA, T., Sociology of Education

Faculty of Medicine:

ANIYA, Y., Biochemical Pharmacology
ARAKI, K., Haematology
ARIIZUMI, M., Preventive Medicine
FUKUNAGA, T., Virology
HOKAMA, T., Health Care
IMAMURA, T., Bacteriology
ISHIZU, H., Mental Health Science
ISIDA, H., Anatomy
ITO, E., Pathology
IWAMASA, T., Pathology
IWANAGA, M., Bacteriology
KANAYA, F., Hand Surgery, Microsurgery
KANAZAWA, K., Gynaecological Oncology, Reproductive Immunology
KARIYA, K., Biochemistry
KOJA, K., Surgery
KONO, S., Obstetrics and Gynaecology, Endocrinology
KOSUGI, T., Physiology, Haematology
MAEHIRA, F., Clinical Biochemistry, Biochemistry
MIYAGI, I., Medical Entomology
MIYAZAKI, T., Forensic Medicine
MURAYAMA, S.
MUTO, Y., Digestive Surgery
NAKA, K., Health Administration
NODA, A., Otorhinolaryngology, Head and Neck Surgery
NONAKA, S., Dermatology, Photobiology
OGAWA, Y., Urology
OGURA, C., Neuropsychiatry
OHTA, T., Paediatrics
SAITO, A., Internal Medicine
SAKANASHI, M., Pharmacology
SAKIHARA, S., Health Sociology, Community Health
SATO, Y., Parasitology
SAWAGUCHI, S., Ophthalmology
SHIMADA, K., Human Pathology
SHIMAJIRI, S., Maternal Nursing
SUGAHARA, K., Anaesthesiology
SUNAGAWA, Y., Adult Nursing, Geriatric Nursing
SUNAKAWA, H., Oral and Maxillofacial Surgery
TAKASU, N., Internal Medicine
TANAKA, T., Biochemistry
TERASHIMA, S., Physiology

UZA, M., Health Care
YAMANE, N., Laboratory Medicine
YASUZUMI, F., Anatomy
YOSHII, Y., Neurosurgery

Faculty of Science:

FUKUHARA, C., Inorganic Chemistry
GINOZA, M., Condensed Matter Physics
GOYA, E., Functional Analysis
HAGIHARA, A., Forest Ecophysiology
HAYASHI, D., Structural Geology
HENNA, J., Mathematical Statistics
HIDAKA, M., Coral Biology
HIGA, M., Organic Chemistry
HIGA, T., Marine Natural Products Chemistry
HOSOYA, M., Computer Physics
IKEHARA, N., Physiology and Biochemistry
ISA, E., Calcification
ISHIJIMA, S., Atmospheric Science
KAKAZU, K., Mathematical Physics
KATO, Y., Petrology
KIMURA, M., Marine Geology
KODAKA, K., Functional Analysis
KUNIYOSHI, M., Marine Natural Products Chemistry
MAEDA, T., Algebraic Geometry
MAEHARA, R., Topology
MATAYOSHI, S., Quantum Physics
MIYAGI, Y., Molecular Spectroscopy
NAKAMURA, S., Cytology
NIKI, H., Solid State Physics
NISHIHIRAHO, T., Approximation Theory
OHMURA, Y., Condensed Matter Physics
OOMORI, T., Marine Geochemistry
SHIGA, H., Topology
SHOKITA, S., Fisheries Biology
SUZUKI, T., Number Theory
TAIRA, H., Analytical Chemistry
TAKUSHI, E., Solid State Optics
TEZUKA, M., Topology
TOKUYAMA, A., Environmental Chemistry
TOMOYOSE, T., Solid State Physics
TSUCHIYA, M., Ecology
UEHARA, T., Embryology
UEHARA, Y., Physical Chemistry
YAGASAKI, K., Solid State Physics
YAMAGUCHI, M., Coral-reef Biology
YAMAMOTO, S., Sedimentology
YAMAZATO, M., Probability Theory
YOGI, S., Organic Chemistry
YONASHIRO, K., Condensed Matter Physics

Education and Research Center for Lifelong Learning (Senbaru, Nishihara-cho, Okinawa):

DAIZEN, T., Sociology of Schooling, Sociology of Higher Education

Okinawa–Asia Research Center of Medical Science (Uehara, Nishihara-cho, Okinawa):

JINNO, Y., Molecular Genetics
TANAKU, Y.

Tropical Biosphere Research Center:

ARAMOTO, M., Terrestrial Resources
FUJIMORI, K., Cell Biology
KUMAZAWA, N., Environmental Microbiology Epidemiology
MURAI, M., Animal Ecology
NAKAMURA, M., Reproductive Biology
TAKASO, T., Plant Morphology

University Hospital (Uehara, Nishihara-cho, Okinawa):

HIROSE, Y., Hospital Information System, Knowledge-base System
HOBARA, N., Pharmacokinetic Drug Interaction, Quality Control of Medicine

ATTACHED INSTITUTES

Academic Museum (Fujukan): Senbaru, Nishihara-cho, Okinawa; Dir Y. KAWASHIMA.

Center for Cooperative Research: Senbaru, Nishihara-cho, Okinawa; Dir H. YARA.

Center for Educational Research and Practice: Senbaru, Nishihara-cho, Okinawa; Dir T. YONEMORI.

Center for Educational Research and Training of Handicapped Children: Senbaru, Nishihara-cho, Okinawa; Dir S. KAMIZONO.

Computing and Networking Center: Senbaru, Nishihara-cho, Okinawa; Dir H. MIYAGI.

Education and Research Center for Lifelong Learning: Senbaru, Nishihara-cho, Okinawa; Dir T. YOSHIZAWA.

Environmental Science Center: Senbaru, Nishihara-cho, Okinawa; Dir Y. MIYAGI.

Gene Research Center: Senbaru, Nishihara-cho, Okinawa; Dir N. KOBAMOTO.

Health Administration Center: Senbaru, Nishihara-cho, Okinawa; Dir H. TAKARA.

Institute for Animal Experiments: Uehara, Nishihara-cho, Okinawa; Dir E. ITO.

Instrumental Research Center: Senbaru, Nishihara-cho, Okinawa; Dir Y. UEHARA.

Language Center: Senbaru, Nishihara-cho, Okinawa; Dir Y. SHIMOJI.

Low Temperature Center: Senbaru, Nishihara-cho, Okinawa; Dir H. NIKI.

Okinawa–Asia Research Center of Medical Science: Uehara, Nishihara-cho, Okinawa; Dir K. NARITOMI.

Radioisotope Laboratory: Senbaru, Nishihara-cho, Okinawa; Dir E. ISA.

Research Laboratory Center: Uehara, Nishihara-cho, Okinawa; Dir M. SAKANASHI.

Tropical Biosphere Research Center: Senbaru, Nishihara-cho, Okinawa; Dir K. FUJIMORI.

Attached Stations:

Iriomote Station: Uehara Taketomi-cho, Yaeyama Okinawa; Chief T. TAKASO.

Sesoko Station: Sesoko Motobu-cho, Okinawa; Chief M. MURAI.

University Education Center: Senbaru, Nishihara-cho, Okinawa; Dir H. NAKACHI.

University Experimental Farm: Senbaru, Nishihara-cho, Okinawa; Dir Y. ISHIMINE.

University Experimental Forest: Yona, Kunigami-son, Okinawa; Dir E. HIRATA.

University Hospital: Uehara, Nishihara-cho, Okinawa; Dir K. KANAZAWA.

SAGA UNIVERSITY

Honjo-cho 1, Saga City 840
Telephone: (952) 28-8168
Fax: (952) 28-8819
Internet: www.saga-u.ac.jp
Founded 1949
Academic year: April to March
Pres.: HARUO UEHARA
Vice-Pres: GUNJI ARAMAKI, YASUHISA SHINTOMI
Dir of Gen. Admin. Bureau: TOSHIJI UEDA
Dir of Univ. Library: KEIICHI MIYAJIMA
Library of 600,341 vols
Number of teachers: 471
Number of students: 595 graduate, 5,808 undergraduate
Publication: various faculty reports and bulletins

DEANS

Faculty of Agriculture: TAKAYUKI KOJIMA
Faculty of Culture and Education: KENJI TSUJI
Faculty of Economics: KAZAFUMI KOGA
Faculty of Science and Engineering: AKIRA HASEGAWA

DIRECTORS

Analytical Research and Development Center: KEIICHI WATANABE

Coastal Bioenvironment Center: OSAMU KATO
Computer and Network Center: YOSHIAKI WATANABE
Institute of Lowland Technology: SHIGENORI HAYASHI
Institute of Ocean Energy: MASANORI MONDE
International Student Center: TATSUYA KOMOTO
Joint Research and Development Center: KOHEI ARAI
Synchrotron Light Application Center: HIROSHI OGAWA
Venture Business Laboratory: MASAYOSHI AIKAWA

SAITAMA UNIVERSITY

255 Shimo-Okubo, Sakura-ku, Saitama City, Saitama 338-8570
Telephone: (48) 858-9624
Fax: (48) 858-9675
E-mail: kokusai@mail.saitama-u.ac.jp
Internet: www.saitama-u.ac.jp
Founded 1949
Independent
Academic year: April to March
Pres.: YOSHIHIKO KAMII
Exec. Dirs: MAKOTO HORI, MASAAKI KAWAHASHI, TAKASHI MARUYAMA, YASUTAKE KATO
Library of 788,368 vols, 19,720 periodicals
Number of teachers: 561
Number of students: 8,779
Publications: *Saitama Mathematical Journal* (1 a year), *Research Report of Department Civil and Environmental Engineering* (1 a year), *Asian Economy and Social Environment* (1 a year)

DEANS

Faculty of Economics: OSAMU ITO
Faculty of Education: KAZUTAKA YAMAGUCHI
Faculty of Liberal Arts: EIJI TAKAGI
Graduate School of Cultural Science: EIJI TAKAGI
Graduate School of Economic Science: OSAMU ITO
Graduate School of Education: KAZUTAKA YAMAGUCHI
Graduate School of Science and Engineering: TADAYOSHI MIZUTANI
School of Engineering: HIROKI YAMAGUCHI
School of Science: KINJI INOUE

SHIGA UNIVERSITY

1-1-1 Banba, Hikone, Shiga 522-8522
Telephone: (749) 27-1172
Fax: (749) 27-1174
E-mail: koho@biwako.shiga-u.ac.jp
Internet: www.shiga-u.ac.jp
Founded 1949
Independent
Academic year: April to March
Pres.: KENICHI MIYAMOTO
Vice-Pres: SEIJI OGURI, HIDEKI SUMIOKA
Admin. Dir: OSAHIRO TODOROKI
Librarian: TAKEO TERAYOKO
Library of 550,208 vols
Number of teachers: 315
Number of students: 3,981
Publications: *Fuzoku-shiryo-kan Kenkyu-Kiyo* (Bulletin of the Archival Museum, 1 a year), *Kenkyu-Nenpo* (Annals of Human and Social Sciences, 1 a year), *The Hikone Ronso* (economics, irregular), *Kyoiku-Gakubu Kiyo* (Memoirs of the Faculty of Education, 1 a year), *Shiga-Eibun-Gakkai-Ronbunshu* (English Studies Review, every 2 years)

DEANS

Faculty of Economics: HIROAKI KITAMURA

Faculty of Education: SHOBU SATO
Graduate School of Economics: HIROAKI KITA-
MURA
Graduate School of Education: SHOBU SATO

ATTACHED RESEARCH INSTITUTES

Archives Museum: Dir HIDEKI USAMI.

**Center for Educational Research and
Practice:** 2-5-1 Hiratsu, Otsu, Shiga 520-
0862; Dir TSUTOMU KUBOSHIMA.

**Center for Environmental Education
and Lake Science:** 2-5-1 Hiratsu, Otsu,
Shiga 520-0862; Dir SHUICHI ENDO.

**Institute for Economic and Business
Research:** Dir NAOKI UMEZAWA.

Information Processing Center: Dir
SABURO HORIMOTO.

Joint Research Center: Dir ISAO OGAWA.

Research Center for Lifelong Learning:
2-5-1 Hiratsu, Otsu, Shiga 520-0862; Dir
OSAMU UMEDA.

SHIMANE UNIVERSITY

1060 Nishikawatsu-cho, Matsue-shi, Shi-
mane-ken 690-8504

Telephone: (852) 32-6100
Fax: (852) 32-6019
E-mail: webinfo@jn.shimane-u.ac.jp
Internet: www.shimane-u.ac.jp

Founded 1949
Independent
Academic year: April to March

Pres.: YUICHI HONDA
Registrar: T. KAMADA
Librarian: S. WATANABE

Library of 692,000 vols
Number of teachers: 500
Number of students: 5,550

DEANS

Faculty of Education: M. YAMASHITA
Faculty of Law and Literature: Y. MATSUI
Faculty of Life and Environmental Sciences:
H. YAMAMOTO
Faculty of Science and Engineering: A.
TAKUNA

SHINSHU UNIVERSITY

Asahi 3-1-1, Matsumoto, 390-8621 Nagano-
ken

Telephone: (263) 35-4600
Fax: (263) 36-6769
E-mail: shinhp@jm.shinshu-u.ac.jp
Internet: www.shinshu-u.ac.jp

Founded 1949
Independent

Pres.: ATSUSHI KOMIYAMA

Number of teachers: 1,107 full-time
Number of students: 11,478 (9,344 undergraduates, 2,134 in Graduate School)

DEANS

Faculty of Agriculture: Y. KARASAWA
Faculty of Arts: S. OSHIMA
Faculty of Economics: T. MATASAKA
Faculty of Education: S. AKAHANE
Faculty of Engineering: A. NOMURA
Faculty of Science: T. ITO
Faculty of Textile Science and Technology: A.
HACHIMORI
School of Medicine: T. OHHASHI

SHIZUOKA UNIVERSITY

Ohya 836, Shizuoka-shi 422-8529

Telephone: (54) 238-4407
Fax: (54) 237-0089
E-mail: koho@gene1.adb.shizuoka.ac.jp
Internet: www.shizuoka.ac.jp

Founded 1949

Independent
Pres.: YOSHIMITSU AMAGISHI
Vice-Pres: NOBUYUKI ARAKI, HIROKAZU NAKAI
Dir-Gen.: SHIGENOBU MORI
Dir of Univ. Library: KIMIO BAMBA
Number of teachers: 744 full-time
Number of students: 11,112

DEANS

Faculty of Agriculture: KIYOSHI OKAWA
Faculty of Education: SHOJI KANAI
Faculty of Engineering: HITOSHI ISHII
Faculty of Humanities and Social Sciences:
YOSHIHIKO YAMAMOTO
Faculty of Information Sciences: HIROYUKI
TOKUYAMA
Faculty of Science: KATSUTOSHI ISHIKAWA

DIRECTORS

Center for Education and Research Lifelong
Learning: KINJI TAKI
Center for Joint Research: NAOMICHI OKA-
MOTO
Information Processing Center: NAOKAZU
YAMAKI
Institute for Genetic Research and Biotech-
nology: KOICHI YOSHINAGA
International Student Center: TAKASHIGE
HONDA
Research Institute of Electronics: KENZO
WATANABE
Satellite Venture Business Laboratory: NOR-
IHIRO INAGAKI

TOHOKU UNIVERSITY

2-1-1 Katahira, Aoba-ku, Sendai 980-8577

Telephone: (22) 217-4844
Fax: (22) 217-4846
E-mail: kokusai@bureau.tohoku.ac.jp
Internet: www.tohoku.ac.jp

Founded 1907
Independent
Academic year: April to March

Pres.: TAKASHI YOSHIMOTO
Vice-Pres: HIROYUKI YOSHIKAWA, HITOSHI
OHNISHI, KUNIAKI SUGAI, TETSUO SHYOJI,
MICHITERU TOKUSHIGE, TOSHIFUMI TAKADA,
YOSHIO WASEDA
Dir of Main Library: KEIICHI NOE

Library: see Libraries and Archives
Number of teachers: 2,581
Number of students: 18,035 (10,912 under-
graduate, 7,123 postgraduate)

Publications: *Tohoku University Bulletin* (1 a
year), *Tohoku Journal of Experimental
Medicine* (12 a year), *Annual Research
Bulletin of the Graduate School of Pharma-
ceutical Sciences* (1 a year), *Graduate
School of Engineering and Faculty of
Engineering* (1 a year), *Tohoku Journal of
Agricultural Research* (2 a year), *Reports of
the Institute of Fluid Science* (1 a year),
*Research Report of the Laboratory of
Nuclear Science* (1 a year), *Northeast
Asian Study* (1 a year), *Interdisciplinary
Information Science* (2 a year), *Tohoku
Geophysical Journal* (3 a year)

DEANS

Graduate School of Educational Informatics,
Research Division: TOSHIRO HAGIHARA
Graduate School of Environmental Studies:
AKITSUGU OKUWAKI
Graduate School of Information Sciences:
AKIRA MARUOKA
Graduate School of International Cultural
Studies: CHIKAYOSHI YONEYAMA
Graduate School of Life Sciences: HIROYUKI
IDE
School of Agriculture and Graduate School of
Agricultural Science: YUKIO AKIBA
School and Graduate School of Arts and
Letters: KEIICHI NOE

School and Graduate School of Dentistry:
MAKOTO WATANABE
School and Graduate School of Economics
and Management: SHUITSU HINO
School and Graduate School of Education:
KATSUHIRO ARAI
School and Graduate School of Engineering:
MITSUNOBU MIYAGI
School and Graduate School of Law: TOSHIYA
UEKI
School and Graduate School of Medicine:
MAKOTO TAMAI
School and Graduate School of Pharmaceut-
ical Sciences: HIDEO TAKEUCHI
School and Graduate School of Science:
OSAMU HASHIMOTO

PROFESSORS

Botanical Gardens (12-2 Kawauchi, Aoba-ku,
, Sendai 980-0862; tel. (22) 795-6760; fax (22)
795-6766; e-mail garden-tu@biology.tohoku
.ac.jp; internet www.biology.tohoku.ac.jp/
garden):

SUZUKI, M., Plant Anatomy

Center for Interdisciplinary Research (Aoba,
Aramaki, Aoba-ku, Sendai 980-8578; tel. (22)
795-5757; fax (22) 795-5756; e-mail office@cir
.tohoku.ac.jp; internet www.cir.tohoku.ac.jp):

KASUYA, A., Materials Science
SUEMITSU, M., Materials Science
YAMANE, H., Solid-state Chemistry
YAO, T., Department of Applied Physics

Center for Low-temperature Science (2-1-1
Katahira, Aoba-ku, Sendai 980-8577; tel. (22)
215-2181; fax (22) 215-2184; e-mail ltcenter@
imr.tohoku.ac.jp; internet www.clts.tohoku
.ac.jp):

AOKI, H., Low-temperature Physics

Center for North-east Asian Studies (41
Kawauchi, Aoba-ku, Sendai 980-8576; tel.
(22) 795-6009; fax (22) 795-6010; e-mail
asiajimu@cneas.tohoku.ac.jp; internet www
.cneas.tohoku.ac.jp/index-j.html):

HIRAKAWA, A., Political Economy
ISOBE, A., Cultural Studies
KIKUCHI, E., Regional Ecosystem Studies
KUDOH, J., North Asian Societies
KURIBAYASHI, H., Linguistic Studies
MIYAMOTO, K., Socio-economic Studies on
the Environment
SATO, M., Environmental and Resources
Survey
SEGAWA, M., Social Ecology
TANIGUCHI, H., Geochemistry
YAMADA, K., Social Structure

Center for the Advancement of Higher Education (41 Kawauchi, Aoba-ku, Sendai 980-
8576; tel. (22) 795-7551; fax (22) 795-7647;
e-mail center@high-edu.tohoku.ac.jp;
internet www.he.tohoku.ac.jp/index.html):

HIDA, W., Respiratory Medicine
HORIE, K., Linguistic Typology and Japa-
nese–Korean Contrastive Linguistics
NAWATA, T., Applied Research Section
SAITOH, K., Applied Research Section
SEKIUCHI, T., Basic Research Section
SHIZUYA, H., Theoretical Computer Science
SUZUKI, T., Applied Clinical Psychology
YOSHIMOTO, K., Formal Linguistics, Cogni-
tive Science

Cyclotron Radioisotope Center (6-3 Aoba,
Aramaki, Aoba-ku, Sendai 980-8578; tel.
(22) 795-7800; fax (22) 795-7997; e-mail
admin@cyric.tohoku.ac.jp; internet www
.cyric.tohoku.ac.jp):

BABA, M., Radiation Physics
ITOH, M., Nuclear Medicine
IWATA, R., Radioisotope Production and
Radiopharmaceutical Chemistry
OKAMURA, H., Nuclear Physics

Graduate School of Educational Informatics, Research Division (Kawauchi, Aoba-ku, Sendai 980-8576; tel. (22) 795-6103; fax (22) 795-6110; internet www.ei.tohoku.ac.jp):

HAGIHARA, T., Theory of an Open University

IWASAKI, S., Information Technology Educational Architecture

MURAKI, E., Information Technology Education System Theory

WATABE, S., Information Technology Cognitive Science

Graduate School of Environmental Studies (Aobayama, Sendai 980-8579; tel. (22) 795-4504; fax (22) 795-4309; e-mail s-ara@bureau.tohoku.ac.jp; internet www.kankyo.tohoku.ac.jp):

ARAI, K., Environmental Chemical Engineering

ASANO, Y., East Asian Philosophy

CHIDA, T., Geoenvironmental Remediation

ENOMOTO, H., Environmental Processing for Energy Resources

HATTORI, T., Environmentally Benign Sythesis

HOSHINO, H., Analytical Environmental Chemistry

ISHIDA, H., Environmentally Harmonized Materials

KAYA, K., Environmental Ecology Design

KIMUTA, Y., Middle Eastern and Central Asian Studies

MARUYAMA, K., Structural Materials for Eco-friendly Systems

MATSUE, T., Environmental Bioengineering

MATSUKI, K., Environmental Geomechanics

NAGASAKA, T., Environmental Impact Assessment

NARISAWA, M., Korean Ethnoculture

NIITSUMA, H., Earth System Monitoring and Instrumentation

SAITO, T., Urban Environment

SAKAIDA, K., Physical Environmental Geography

SATAKE, M., International Economic and Environmental Studies

TAKAHASHI, H., Earth Exploitation Environmental Studies

TANIGUCHI, S., Materials Process for Circulatory Society

TOHJI, K., Design of Eco-nanomaterials

TSUCHIYA, N., Environmental Geochemistry

YAMASAKI, N., Environmental Hydrothermal Processes

YOSHIOKA, T., Recycling Chemistry

Graduate School of Information Sciences (Aoba, Aramaki, Aobu-ku, Sendai 980-8579; tel. (22) 795-5813; fax (22) 795-5815; e-mail is-syom@bureau.tohoku.ac.jp; internet www.is.tohoku.ac.jp):

ADACHI, Y., Media and Semiotics

AKAMATSU, T., Road Transportation and Traffic

ANDO, A., Econometric System Analysis

AOKI, T., Computer Structures

DEGUCHI, K., Image Analysis

EBISAWA, H., Physical Fluctuomatics

FUKUCHI, H., Verbal Text Analysis

HASHIMOTO, K., Intelligent Control Systems

HIAI, F., Mathematical Systems Analysis III

HIDA, W., Health Informatics

HORIGUCHI, S., Firmware Science

INAMURA, H., International and Intermodal Transportation

ITOI, K., Information Biology

IWASAKI, S., Cognitive Psychology

KAMEYAMA, M., Intelligent Integrated Systems

KANEKO, M., Mathematical Structures II

KATO, N., Information Technology

KINOSHITA, T., Communication Software Science

KOBAYASHI, H., Ultra-high-speed Information Processing Algorithm

KOBAYASHI, K., Theory of Social Structure and Change

KOBAYASHI, N., Foundations of Software Science

KUDOH, J., Environmental Informatics

MARUOKA, A., Computation Theory

MORISUGI, H., Regional and Urban Planning

MUNEMASA, A., Mathematical Structures I

NAKAJIMA, K., Brain Function Integration

NAKAMURA, T., Computer Architecture

NAKAO, M., Biomodelling

NEMOTO, Y., Communication Science

NISHIZEKI, T., Algorithm Theory

NUMASAWA, J., Information Storage Systems

OBATA, N., Mathematical Systems Analysis II

OBAYASHI, S., Fusion Flow Informatics

OHORI, A., Logic for Information Science

OZAWA, M., Mathematical Structures III

SASAKI, K., Socio-economic Analysis of Urban Systems

SASOH, S., Flow System Informatics

SEKIMOTO, E., Media and Culture

SHINOHARA, A., System Information Sciences

SHIOIRI, S., Visual Recognition and Systems

SHIRATORI, N., Communication Theory

SHIZUYA, H., Information Security

SONE, H., Information Network Systems

SUNOUCHI, C., Mathematical Structures IV

SUZUKI, Y., Acoustic Information

TADOKORO, S., Human–Robot Informatics

TAKEUCHI, O., Philosophy of Human Information

TOKUYAMA, T., Design and Analysis of Information Systems

TOYAMA, Y., Logic for Information Science

TSUBOKAWA, H., Life Fluctuomatics

URAKAWA, H., Mathematical Systems Analysis I

YAMAMOTO, H., Political Analysis of the Information Society

YAMAMOTO, S., Mathematical Modelling

Graduate School of International Cultural Studies (Kawauchi, Aoba-ku, Sendai 980-8576; tel. (22) 795-7541; fax (22) 795-7583; internet www.intcul.tohoku.ac.jp):

ASAKAWA, T., Language System

ASANO, Y., Asian Cultural Studies

FUJITA, M., Comparative Cultural Studies

FUJIWARA, I., Comparative Cultural Studies

HOLDEN, T., Multicultural Societies

ICHIKAWA, M., Cultural Uses of Language

IGAWA, M., American Studies

ISHIHATA, N., Cultural Uses of Language

ISHIKAWA, H., Asian Cultural Studies

KAWAHIRA, Y., Language Generation

KITAGAWA, S., Islamic Areas and Cultural Studies

KOBAYASHI, F., European Cultural Studies

KUSUDA, I., Language Systems

NUNOTA, T., European Cultural Studies

SASAKI, K., Linguistic Communication

SATO, K., Language Systems

SATO, S., Language Generation

SHIGAKI, M., Language Education

SUZUKI, M., Cultural Uses of Language

TAKAHASHI, R., Science, Technology and Environment

TAKENAKA, K., American Studies

TANAKA, K., Multicultural Societies

TATSUYOSHI, T., Monetary Economics

YAMAGUCHI, N., Linguistic Function

YAMASHITA, H., Multicultural Societies

YOKOKAWA, K., International Economic Relations

YONEYAMA, C., Linguistic Function

Graduate School of Life Sciences (tel. (22) 795-5702; fax (22) 795-5704; internet www.lifesci.tohoku.ac.jp/index.html):

ARIMOTO, H., Biostructrual Chemistry

HIGASHITANI, A., Genomic Reproductive Biology

IDE, H., Organogenesis

IIJIMA, T., Systems Neuroscience

KATOW, H., Developmental Biology

KAWATA, M., Evolutionary Biology

KUMAGAI, T., Genetic Ecology in Critical Environments

KUSANO, T., Plant Molecular and Cellular Biology

MAEDA, Y., Control of Growth and Differentiation

MINAMISAWA, K., Environmental Microbiology

MIZUNO, K., Molecular Cell Biology

MURAMOTO, K., Functional Biomolecules

NAKAMURA, K., Molecular Neurobiology

NISHITANI, K., Plant Physiology

OHSHIMA, Y., Bio-organic Chemistry

SASAKI, M., Biostructural Chemistry

SOGAWA, K., Gene Regulation

TAKAGI, T., Molecular Diversity

TAKAHASHI, H., Space and Adaptation Biology

TSUDA, M., Microbial Genetics

URABE, J., Community and Ecosystem Ecology

WATANABE, M., Plant Reproductive Biology

WATANABE, T., Organella Research

YAMAMOTO, D., Neurogenetics

YAMAMOTO, K., Molecular Genetics

YAWO, H., Molecular and Cellular Neurosciences

Information Synergy Center (6-3 Aoba, Aramaki, Aoba-ku, Sendai 980-8578; tel. (22) 795-3407; fax (22) 795-6098; internet www.isc.tohoku.ac.jp):

KINOSHITA, T., Knowledge Engineering

KOBAYASHI, H., High-performance Computer Systems

SONE, H., Communication Networks

YOSHIZAWA, M., Communication Networks

Institute for Materials Research (2-1-1 Katahira, Aoba-ku, Sendai 980-8577; tel. (22) 215-2181; fax (22) 215-2184; e-mail imr-som@imr.tohoku.ac.jp; internet www.imr.tohoku.ac.jp):

CHEN, M., International Frontier Center for Advanced Materials

FUKUYAMA, H., International Frontier Center for Advanced Materials

GOTO, T., Multifunctional Materials Science

HASEGAWA, M., Irradiation Effects in Nuclear and Related Materials

INOUE, A., Non-equilibrium Materials

IWASA, Y., Low-temperature Condensed State Physics

KAWASAKI, M., Superstructured Thin Film Chemistry

KAWAZOE, Y., Materials Design by Computer Simulation

KOBAYASHI, N., Low-temperature Physics

MAEKAWA, S., Theory of Solid State Physics

MATSUI, H., Nuclear Materials Engineering

MATSUOKA, T., Advanced Electronic Materials

NAKAJIMA, K., Crystal Physics

NOJIRI, H., Magnetism

SAKURAI, T., Surface and Interface Research

SATO, Y., Non-equilibrium Materials

SHIKAMA, T., Nuclear Materials Science

SHIOKAWA, Y., Radiochemistry of Metals

TAKANASHI, K., Magnetic Materials

UDA, S., Crystal Chemistry

WAGATSUMA, K., Analytical Science

WATANABE, K., High Field Laboratory for Superconducting Materials
YAMADA, K., Neuron and Gamma-ray Spectroscopy on Condensed Matters

Institute of Development, Ageing and Cancer (4-1 Seiryo-machi, Aoba-ku, Sendai 980-8575; tel. (22) 717-8443; fax (22) 717-8452):
FUKUDA, H., Radiation Medicine
FUKUMOTO, M., Pathology
ISHIOKA, C., General Internal Medicine, Gastroentorology, Molecular Biology
KONDO, T., Thoracic Surgery, Lung Cancer, Lung Transplantation
MATSUI, Y., Developmental Biology
NUKIWA, T., Chest Physician, Molecular Biology
OBINATA, M., Cell Biology
OGURA, T., Developmental Neurobiology, Developmental Biology, Molecular Biology
SATAKE, M., Molecular Biology
SATO, Y., Vascular Biology
TAKAI, T., Experimental Immunology
TAMURA, S., Biochemistry and Molecular Biology
TSUCHIYA, S., Paediatrics
YAMAMOTO, T., Molceular Biology, General Medical Chemistry, Pathological Medical Chemistry
YAMBE, T., Artificial Organs, Cardiovascular Medicine
YASUI, A., DNA Repair and Ageing

Institute of Fluid Science (2-1-1 Katahira, Aoba-ku, Sendai 980-8577; tel. (22) 795-5302; fax (22) 795-5311; e-mail shomu@ifs.tohoku.ac.jp; internet www.ifs.tohoku.ac.jp):
FUJISHIRO, I., Complex Dynamics
HAYASE, T., Super-real-time Medical Engineering
HAYASHI, K., Molten Geomaterials
IKOHAGI, T., Complex Flow Systems
INOUE, O., Advanced Computational Fluid Dynamics
ISHIMOTO, J., Reality-coupled Computation
KOBAYASHI, H., Complex Dynamics
KOHAMA, Y., Ultimate Flow Environment
MARUYAMA, S., Heat Transfer Control
NANBU, K., Gaseous Electronics
NISHIYAMA, H., Electromagnetic Intelligent Fluids
OBAYASHI, S., Integrated Fluid Informatics
OHARA, T., Molecular Heat Transfer
OHIRA, K., Cryogenic Flow
OTA, M., Biofluids Control
QIU, J., Intelligent Systems
SAMUKAWA, S., Intelligent Nano-process
SASOH, A., Ultra-high Enthalpy Flow
SUN, M., Interdisciplinary Shockwave Research
TAKAGI, T., Advanced Systems and Materials Evaluation
TAKEUCHI, S., Advanced Systems
TOKUYAMA, M., Theoretical Fluid Dynamics
TSUCHIYAMA, T., Advanced Technology for Environment and Energy

Institute of Multidisciplinary Research for Advanced Materials (2-1-1 Katahira, Aoba-ku, Sendai 980-8577; tel. (22) 795-5202; fax (22) 795-5211; internet www.tagen.tohoku.ac.jp):
AJIRI, T., Organic Resources Chemistry
ARIMA, T., Strongly Correlated Electron Systems
HARADA, N., Chemistry of Molecular Chirality
ISSHIKI, M., High Purity Materials
ITAGAKI, K., Nonferrous Chemical Metallurgy
ITO, O., Photochemistry
KAINO, T., Materials Chemistry
KAKIHANA, M., Chemical Engineering
KASAI, E., Iron and Steel Engineering
KAWAMURA, J., Solid State Ion Physics

KITAKAMI, O., Magnetic Materials and Devices
KITAMURA, S., Ferrous Process Metallurgy
KOMEDA, T., Molecular Chemistry
KONO, S., Surface Physics
KOYAMA, T., Biochemistry
KURIHARA, K., Surface Forces
KYOTANI, T., Applied Chemistry
MIYASHITA, T., Materials Chemistry
MIZUSAKI, J., Solid State Ion Devices
MURAMATSU, A., Solid State Chemistry
NAKAMURA, T., Physical Process Engineering
NAKANISHI, H., Materials Chemistry
NODA, Y., Electronic Properties of Solids
OKA, Y., Solid State Spectroscopy
OTSUKA, Y., Catalytic and Chemical Processes
SAITO, F., Chemical Engineering, Powder Technology
SAITO, M., Chemistry
SATO, S., Metal Industrial Engineering
SATO, T., Inorganic Materials Chemistry
SHIMIZU, T., Bio-inorganic Chemistry
SINDO, D., Atomic Scale Morphology Analysis
SODEOKA, M., Chemistry
SUITO, H., Physico-chemical Metallurgy
SUZUKI, S., Physical Metallurgy
TERAUCHI, M., Electronic Diffraction and Spectroscopy
TERO, S., Physical Chemistry
TOCHIYAMA, O., Atomic Energy Engineering
TSAI, A., Materials Control
UDAGAWA, Y., X-ray Physics
UEDA, K., Molecular Physics
UMETSU, Y., Aqueous Processing, Physical Chemistry of Metals
YAMAMOTO, M., Soft X-ray Microscopy
YAMAUCHI, S., Physical Chemistry
YANAGIHARA, M., Soft X-ray Microscopy
YOKOYAMA, T., Chemical Engineering

International Exchange Center (Kawauchi, Aoba-ku, Sendai 980-8576; tel. (22) 795-7776; fax (22) 795-7826; e-mail ryugaku@bureau.tohoku.ac.jp; internet www.insc.tohoku.ac.jp):
HORIE, K., Linguistic Typology and Japanese–Korean Comparative Linguistics
KASUKABE, Y., Development of the Short-term Student Exchange Programme
SATO, S., Japanese Language Teaching
SHIGENO, Y., Technologies of Resource and Material Processing
UEHARA, S., Linguistics and Phonetics
YOSHIMOTO, K., Formal Syntax and Japanese Intonation

New Industry Creation Hatchery Center (Aoba 6-6-10, Aramaki, Aoba-ku, Sendai 980-8579; tel. (22) 795-7105; fax (22) 795-7985; e-mail liaison-office@niche.tohoku.ac.jp; internet www.niche.tohoku.ac.jp):
ICHIE, M., Music and Acoustical Medicine
ISHIDA, K., Advanced Materials based on Computer-aided Design and Microstructural Control
KAWASHIMA, R., Functional Brain Imaging
KOHNO, M., Research and Development on Genomics-protemics Technology and Free Radical Control
MIYAMOTO, A., Quantum Design of Nano-functional Materials
OHMI, T., DIIN (New Intelligence for IC Differentiation) Project
TAKAHASHI, M., Development of Self-assembled Monodisperse Nano-particles, Thin-film Media for Terabit Recording
TERASAKI, T., Drug Discovery and Development
UEMATSU, Y., Development of Technology for Preserving the Environment and Reducing Wind-induced Disaster
YAMANAKA, K., Advanced Ultrasonic Nondestructive Evaluation and Sensing

YOKOYAMA, H., Ultrabroadband Coherent Light Sources

Research Institute of Electrical Communication (2-1-1 Katahira, Aobaku, Sendai 980-8577; tel. (22) 795-5420; fax (22) 795-5426; e-mail shomu@jm.riec.tohoku.ac.jp; internet www.riec.tohoku.ac.jp/index-j.html):
AOI, H., Information Storage Systems
CHO, Y., Dialectric Nano-devices
EDAMATSU, K., Quantum Optics and Optical Spectroscopy
HANYU, T., Next-generation VLSI Computing
ITO, H., Quantum and Optoelectronics
MASUOKA, F., Electron Devices
MATSUOKA, H., Advanced Practical Information Technology Development
MIZUNO, K., Electron Devices
MURAOKA, H., Information Recording Devices
MUROTA, J., Atomically Controlled Processing
NAKAJIMA, K., Intelligent Integrated Systems
NAKAMURA, Y., Information Storage Engineering
NAKAZAWA, M., Ultra High Speed Optical Communication
NIWANO, M., Molecular Electronics, Silico-bioelectronics
NUMAZAWA, J., Video Storage Systems
OHNO, H., Compound Semiconductors, Quantum Structures and Spintronics
OHORI, A., Computer Science
OTSUJI, H., Ultrafast and Ultrabroadband Electronics
SHIRAI, M., Advanced Functional Materials
SHIRATORI, N., Information Communication Systems
SIOIRI, S., Visual Cognition and Systems
SUGIURA, A., Electromagnetic Compatibility
SUZUKI, Y., Acoustic Signal Processing
TAKAGI, T., Wireless Mobile Systems
TANEICHI, M., Advanced Practical Information Technology Development
TOYAMA, Y., Computer Science
TSUBOUCHI, K., Wireless Internet System, Circuits and Devices
YANO, M., Informatics in Biological Systems

School and Graduate School of Arts and Letters (Kawanchi, Aoba-ku, Sendai 980-8576; tel. (22) 795-6003; fax (22) 795-6086; e-mail art-syom@bureau.tohoku.ac.jp; internet www.sal.tohoku.ac.jp/index-j.html):
ABE, H., Western Literature and Languages
AKOSHIMA, K., Japanese History and Archaeology
CHIGUSA, S., Linguistics
GOTO, H., Linguistics
GOTO, T., Indology and History of Indian Buddhism
GYOBA, J., Psychology
HANATO, M., Sinology
HARA, E., Western Literature and Languages
HARA, J., Behavioural Science
HARA, K., Western Literature and Languages
HASEGAWA, K., Sociology
IMAIZUMI, T., Japanese History and Archaeology
KANEKO, Y., Western Literature and Languages
KAWAI, Y., Oriental History
KOBAYASHI, T., Japanese Linguistics
KUMAMOTO, T., Oriental History
MASAMURA, T., Sociology
MATSUMOTO, N., European History
MIURA, S., Sinology
MORIMOTO, K., Western Literature and Languages
NAKAOKA, R., History of Fine Arts

NAKAJIMA, R., Sinology
NAKAMURA, M., Western Literature and Languages
NIHEI, M., Japanese Literature and History of Japanese Philosophy
NIHEI, Y., Psychology
NOE, K., Philosophy and Ethics
NUMAZAKI, I., Cultural Anthropology and Science of Religions
OHBUCHI, K., Psychology
OHTO, O., Japanese History and Archaeology
ONO, Y., European History
OZAKI, A., History of Fine Arts
SAITA, I., Applied Japanese Linguistics
SAITO, M., Japanese Linguistics
SAITO, Y., Western Literature and Languages
SAKURAI, M., Indology and History of Indian Buddhism
SATO, H., Japanese Literature and History of Japanese Philosophy
SATO, M., European History
SATO, N., Japanese Literature and History of Japanese Philosophy
SATO, Y., Behavioural Science
SHIMA, M., Cultural Anthropology and Science of Religions
SHIMIZU, T., Philosophy and Ethics
SHINO, K., Philosophy and Ethics
SUTO, T., Japanese History and Archaeology
SUZUKI, A., Applied Japanese Linguistics
SUZUKI, I., Cultural Anthropology and Science of Religions
TAKAGI, K., Sociology
UMINO, M., Behavioural Science
YOSHIHARA, N., Sociology
ZAKOTA, Y., Philosophy and Ethics

School and Graduate School of Dentistry (4-1 Seiryo-machi, Aoba-ku, Sendai 980-8575; tel. (22) 717-8244; fax (22) 717-8279; e-mail den-syom@bureau.tohoku.ac.jp; internet www.ddh.tohoku.ac.jp/index.html):

ECHIGO, S., Oral Surgery
HAYASHI, H., Oral Physiology
IGARASHI, K., Oral Dysfunction Science
KAWAMURA, H., Maxillofacial Surgery
KIKUCHI, M., Oral and Craniofacial Anatomy
KIMURA, K., Fixed Prosthodontics
KOMATSU, M., Operative Dentistry
KOSEKI, T., Preventive Dentistry
MAYANAGI, H., Paediatric Dentistry
OKUNO, O., Dental Biomaterials
ŌOYA, K., Oral Pathology
OSAKA, K., International Oral Health
SASAKI, K., Advanced Prosthetic Dentistry
SASANO, T., Oral Diagnosis and Radiology
SASANO, Y., Craniofacial Development and Regeneration
SHIMAUCHI, H., Periodontology and Endodontology
SHINODA, H., Dental Pharmacology
SUGAWARA, S., Oral Molecular Bioregulation
SUZUKI, O., Craniofacial Function Engineering
TAKADA, H., Oral Microbiology
TAKAHASHI, M., Dento-oral Anaesthesiology
TAKAHASHI, N., Oral Ecology and Biochemistry
WATANABE, M., Ageing and Geriatric Dentistry

School and Graduate School of Economics and Management (27-1 Kawauchi, Aoba-ku, Sendai 980-8576; tel. (22) 795-6263; fax (22) 795-6270; e-mail webmaster@econ.tohoku.ac .jp; internet www.econ.tohoku.ac.jp/indexj .html):

AKITA, J., International Finance
AOKI, K., Comparative Economic Systems
AOKI, M., Cost Accounting
DOLAN, D., Business Communication

FUJII, T., International Accounting
FUKAI, T., Auditing
HASEBE, H., History of Japanese Economy
HAYASHIYAMA, Y., Environmental Economics
HINO, S., Modern Political Economy
HIRAMOTO, A., Japanese Economy
HOSOYA, Y., Econometrics
IPPOSHI, N., Accounting
ITO, T., Information Systems Management
KAMOIKE, O., Money and Banking
KANAZAKI, Y., Financial Management
KOHNO, D., Business Administration
KOHNO, S., Personnel Administration
KWEON, K. C., Research and Development Management
MASUDA, S., Regional Planning
MIYAKE, M., Macroeconomics
MORI, K., Political Economy
NAKAGAWA, T., International Management
NISHIZAWA, A., Policies for New Venture Creation
NOMURA, M., Social Policy
ODONAKA, N., Socio-intellectual History
OMURA, I., Political Economy
OTAKI, S., Business Policy
OTOMASA, S., Corporate Governance
SARUWATARI, K., Comparative Business Studies
SATO, H., International Economics
SEKITA, Y., Welfare Information System
SHIMOMURA, H., Tax Law
SUZUKI, T., Business History
TANIGUCHI, A., Types of Business Enterprise
TERUI, N., Marketing
TSUGE, N., Agricultural Economics
TSUKUDA, Y., Business Statistics
YASUDA, K., Management Information System

School and Graduate School of Education (Kawauchi, Aoba-ku, Sendai 980-8576; tel. (22) 795-6103; fax (22) 795-6110; internet www.sed.tohoku.ac.jp/index-j.html):

AKINAGA, Y., Sociology of Education
ARAI, K., Educational Policy and Planning
HASEGAWA, K., Clinical Psychology
HONGO, K., Psychology and Disability
HOSOKAWA, T., Developmental Disorders
IKUTA, K., Philosophy of Education
KAJIYAMA, M., History of Japanese Education
KATO, M., History of Foreign Education
KAWASUMI, R., Compensation and Welfare of Disabilities
KIKUCHI, T., Developmental Psychology
KOIZUMI, S., Educational Process Studies
MIYAKOSHI, E., Comparative Educational Systems
MIZUHARA, K., Curriculum Studies
NAKAZIMA, N., Socio-cultural Study of Sport
OMOMO, T., Educational Administration
ONODERA, T., Educational Psychology
TAKAHASHI, M., Adult Education
UENO, T., Clinical Community Psychology
UNO, S., Educational Psychology

School and Graduate School of Engineering (6-6-04, Aramaki Aza Aoba, Aoba-ku, Sendai 980-8579; tel. (22) 795-5817; fax (22) 795-5824; e-mail dean@eng.tohoku.ac.jp; internet www.eng.tohoku.ac.jp):

ABE, H., Urban Design
ABE, K., Fusion Reactor Engineering
ADACHI, F., Communication Systems
ANZAI, K., Casting and Advanced Solidification Processing
ASAI, H., Experimental Aerodynamics
ASAI, K., Solid State Physical Chemistry
ASO, H., Network Theory
CHONAN, S., Biomechatronics
EMURA, T., Intelligent Mechatronics
ESASHI, M., Micromachines
FUKINISHI, Y., Fluid Mechanics
FUKUNAGA, H., Space Structures

GALSTER, W., Energy Physics Engineering
HAMAJIMA, T., Applied Power Systems Engineering
HANE, K., Mechanoptics Design
HARA, N., Materials Electrochemistry
HARAYAMA, Y., Technology Policy
HASHIDA, T., Complex Fracture Systems Design
HASHIZUME, H., Fusion and Electromagnetic Engineering
HATAKEYAMA, R., Basic Plasma Engineering
HINO, M., Ferrous Process Metallurgy
HOKKIRIGAWA, K., Intelligent Systems Engineering
HOSHIMIYA, N., Biomedical Electronics
ICHINOKURA, O., Power Electronics
IGUCHI, Y., Socio-engineering
IIBUCHI, K., History of Architecture
IKEDA, K., Mathematical Systems Design
IMAMURA, F., Tsunami Engineering
INOMATA, H., Supercritical Fluid Technology
INOMATA, K., Spin-electronics Materials
INOUE, K., Machine Design
INOUE, N., Structural Engineering
INOUE, Y., Applied Organic Synthesis
INUTAKE, M., Magneto–Plasma–Dynamics Engineering
ISHIDA, K., Computational Microstructure Design
ISHII, K., Radiation Science and Engineering
ITAYA, K., Electrochemical Science and Technology
ITO, T., Solid State Electronics
IWAKUMA, T., Structural Mechanics
IWASAKI, S., Engineers Education and Educational Informatics
KAJITANI, T., Applied X-ray and Neutron Spectroscopy
KANAI, H., Electronic Control Engineering
KANNO, M., Architectural Planning
KATO, K., Tribology
KAWAMATA, M., Intelligent Electronic Circuits
KAWASAKI, A., Micro-power Processing and Systems
KAZAMA, M., Geotechnical Engineering
KISHINO, Y., Mechanics of Materials
KIYONO, S., Nanosystem Engineering
KOIKE, J., Device Reliability Science and Engineering
KOIKE, Y., Low Temperature Physics and Superconductivity Physics
KOKAWA, H., Interface Science and Engineering of Joining
KONNO, M., Material Processing
KOSUGE, K., System Robotics
KOYANAGI, M., Advanced Bio-nano Devices
KUMAGAI, I., Protein Technology
KURIYAGAWA, T., Nanoprecision Mechanical Fabrication
KUSHIBIKI, J., Instrumentation and Ultrasonic Micro-spectroscopy Technology
KUWANO, H., Informative Nanotechnology
MAKINO, S., Intelligent Communication Engineering
MANO, A., Disaster Potential Research
MASUYA, G., Aerospace Systems
MATSUBARA, F., Applied Mathematical Physics
MATSUKI, H., Bio-electromagnetics
MATSUMOTO, S., Process Control
MIHASHI, H., Building and Materials Science
MIMURA, H., Nuclear Energy Flow, Environmental Engineering
MIURA, H., Fracture Control of Microstructures
MIURA, T., Energy Process Engineering
MIYAZAKI, T., Magnetism and Magnetic Materials
MIZOGUCHI, T., Environmental Chemistry
MOTOSAKA, M., Earthquake Engineering
NAGAHIRA, A., Management of Technology

NAKAHASHI, K., Aerodynamic Design
NAKAMURA, K., Acoustic Physics Engineering
NISHIMURA, O., Ecological Engineering
NISHIZAWA, M., Biomicromachine Engineering
NISINO, T., Applied Life Chemistry
NOIKE, T., Environmental Protection Engineering
NITTA, J., Materials Quantum Science
OHMI, T., Urban Planning and Analysis
OHTSU, H., Applied Nuclear Medical Engineering
OKADA, M., Energy Materials
OMURA, T., Water Quality Engineering
OOJI, A., Energy Conversion Technology
OTA, T., Control of Heat Transfer
OUCHI, C., Biomedical Materials
OYAMA, Y., Opto-electronic Materials
SAHASHI, M., Magnetic Microelectronics
SAITOH, H., Engineering for Information Society
SAKA, M., Mechanics of Materials Systems
SAKUMA, A., Solid-state Physics
SASAO, M., Fusion Plasma Diagnostics
SATO, M., Cell Biomechanics
SAWADA, K., Computational Aerodynamics
SAWAMOTO, M., Hydro-environment Systems
SAWAYA, K., Electromagnetic Wave Engineering
SEKINE, H., Smart System for Materials and Structures
SHINDO, Y., Mechanics and Design of Material Systems
SHODA, S., Functional Macromolecular Chemistry
SHOJI, K., Precision Machining
SMITH, R. L., Supercritical Fluid Technology
SOYAMA, H., Intelligent Sensing of Materials
SUGAWA, S., Advanced Functional Systems Engineering
SUGIMURA, Y., Structural Mechanics
SUZUKI, M., Structural Design Engineering
SUZUKI, M., Physicochemistry of Biomolecular Systems
TAKIZAWA, H., Synthetic Chemistry of Advanced Materials
TANAKA, H., Environmental Hydrodynamics
TOCHIYAMA, O., Nuclear Fuel Engineering
UCHIDA, S., Science and Engineering of Particle Beams
UCHIDA, T., Image Electronics
UCHIYAMA, M., Science and Engineering of Particle Beams
UEMATSU, Y., Wind Engineering
WADA, H., Biomechanical Engineering
WAKABAYASHI, T., Foundation of Risk Assessment and Management
WAKABAYASHI, T., Nuclear Energy Systems Safety Engineering
WATANABE, T., Material Design and Interface Engineering
YAMADA, M., Hydrocarbon Chemistry
YAMADA, M., Architectural Disaster Prevention Engineering
YAMADA, Y., Particle-beam Substance Reaction Engineering
YAMAGUCHI, M., Electromagnetic Theory
YAMAGUCHI, T., Computational Biomechanics
YAMAMURA, T., Physics and Chemistry of Fluids
YAMANAKA, K., Materials Evaluation and Sensing
YOKOBORI, T., Materials Design and Interface Engineering
YONEMOTO, T., Reaction Process Engineering
YOSHIDA, K., Space Exploration
YOSHINO, H., Building Environmental Engineering
YOSHINOBU, T., Biomedical Electronics

YUGAMI, H., New Energy Engineering

School and Graduate School of Law (27-1 Kawauchi, Aoba-ku, Sendai 980-8576; tel. (22) 795-6173; fax (22) 795-6249; e-mail law-jm@bureau.tohoku.ac.jp; internet www.law.tohoku.ac.jp):

AOI, H., Jurisprudence
ARIKAWA, T., Constitutional Law
HIRATA, T., European Political History
IKUTA, O., Land Law
INABA, K., Administrative Law
KAISE, Y., International Civil Procedure
KAWAKAMI, S., Civil Law
KAWATO, S., Political Science, Modern Political Analysis
KOGAYU, T., Civil Law
MIZUNO, N., Civil Law, Family Law
MORITA, K., Administrative Law
OHNISHI, H., International Politics
OKAMOTO, M., Criminal Law
OUCHI, T., Western Legal History
OZAKI, K., International Law
SAITO, T., Criminology
SAKATA, H., Civil Procedure
SERIZAWA, H., Anglo-American Law, Transnational Law of Information
SHIBUYA, M., Tax Law
TSUJIMURA, M., Constitutional Law, Comparative Constitutional Law
UEKI, T., International Law
UEMURA, T., Current Japanese Administration
YAGYU, K., History of Political Theory
YAMAMOTO, H., Constitutional Law, Comparative Constitutional Law
YOSHIDA, M., Japanese Legal History
YOSHIHARA, K., Commercial Law, Commercial Law

School and Graduate School of Medicine (2-1 Seiryo-machi, Aoba-ku, Sendai 980-8575; tel. (22) 717-8005; fax (22) 717-8021; e-mail med-som@bureau.tohoku.ac.jp; internet www.med.tohoku.ac.jp/index-j.html):

ABE, T., Clinical Cell Biology
AIBA, S., Dermatology
ARAI, Y., Urology
DODO, Y., Anatomy and Anthropology
DOHURA, K., Prion Biology
FUKUDO, S., Behavioural Medicine
FUNAYAMA, M., Forensic Medicine
HANDA, Y., Restorative Neuromuscular Rehabilitation
HATTORI, T., Allergy and Infectious Diseases
HAYASHI, Y., Paediatric Surgery
HONGO, M., Comprehensive Medicine (University Hospital)
HORII, A., Molecular Pathology
IGARASHI, K., Biochemistry
ITOH, S., Nephrology, Endocrinology and Vascular Medicine
ITOH, T., Immunology and Embryology
ITOYAMA, Y., Neurology
IZUMI, S., Physical Medicine and Rehabilitation
KAKU, M., Molecular Diagnostics
KASAI, N., Institute for Animal Experimentation
KATAGIRI, H., Advanced Therapeutics for Metabolic Diseases
KATOH, M., Anaesthesiology
KITAMOTO, T., Creutzfeldt–Jakob Disease Science and Technology
KOBAYASHI, T., Otolaryngology, Head and Neck Surgery
KOHZUKI, M., Internal Medicine and Rehabilitation Science
KOINUMA, N., Health Administration and Policy
KOKUBUN, S., Orthopaedic Surgery
KONDO, H., Histology
KONDO, Y., Medical Informatics
MARUYAMA, Y., Physiology I
MATSUBARA, Y., Medical Genetics
MATSUOKA, H., Psychiatry

MORI, E., Behavioural Neurology and Cognitive Neuroscience
NAGATOMI, R., Medicine and Science in Sport and Exercise
NAKAYAMA, K., Developmental Genetics
NODA, T., Molecular Genetics
OHUCHI, N., Surgical Oncology
OKA, Y., Molecular Metabolism and Diabetes
OKAMURA, K., Obstetrics
ONO, T., Genome and Radiation Biology
OSUMI, N., Developmental Neuroscience
SAIJO, Y., Molecular Medicine
SASAKI, I., General Surgery, Biological Regulation and Oncology
SASAKI, T., Rheumatology and Haematology
SASANO, H., Anatomical Pathology
SATOH, H., Environmental Health Sciences
SATOMI, S., Advanced Surgical Science and Technology
SHIBAHARA, S., Molecular Biology and Applied Physiology
SHIMOSEGAWA, T., Gastroenterology
SHINOZAWA, Y., Emergency and Critical Care Medicine
SHIRATO, K., Cardiovascular Medicine
SORA, I., Psychobiology
SUGAMURA, K., Immunology
TABAYASHI, K., Cardiovascular Surgery
TAKAHASHI, A., Neuroendovascular Therapy
TAKAHASHI, S., Diagnostic Radiology
TAKESHIMA, H., Biochemistry and Molecular Biology
TOMINAGA, T., Neurosurgery
TSUJI, I., Epidemiology
UEHARA, N., International Health
YAEGASHI, N., Gynaecological Oncology
YAMADA, A., Plastic and Reconstructive Surgery
YAMADA, S., Therapeutic Radiology
YAMAMURO, M., Pain Control
YANAGISAWA, T., Molecular Pharmacology
YANAI, K., Pharmacology
YOSHIMOTO, T., Neurosurgery

School and Graduate School of Pharmaceutical Sciences (Aoba, Aramaki, Aoba-ku, Sendai 980-8578; tel. (22) 795-6801; fax (22) 795-6805; e-mail ph-som@bureau.tohoku.ac.jp; internet www.pharm.tohoku.ac.jp):

ANZAI, J., Pharmaceutical Physicochemistry
ENOMOTO, T., Molecular Cell Biology
FUKUNAGA, K., Pharmacology
IHARA, M., Medicinal Chemistry
IMAI, Y., Clinical Pharmacology and Therapeutics
IWABACHI, Y., Synthetic Chemistry
KONDO, Y., Molecular Transformation
KOSUGI, H., Organoreaction Chemistry
NAGANUMA, A., Molecular and Biochemical Toxicology
NAKAHATA, N., Cellular Signaling
OHIZUMI, Y., Pharmaceutical Molecular Biology
OHUCHI, K., Pathophysiological Biochemistry
OSHIMA, Y., Natural Products Chemistry
SAKAMOTO, T., Heterocyclic Chemistry
TAKEUCHI, H., Bio-structural Chemistry
TERASAKI, T., Membrane Transport and Drug Targeting
YAMAGUCHI, M., Organometallic Chemistry
YAMOZOE, Y., Drug Metabolism and Molecular Toxicology

School and Graduate School of Science (6-3 Aoba, Aramaki, Aoba-ku, Sendai 980-8578; tel. (22) 795-6346; fax (22) 795-6363; e-mail sci-syom@bureau.tohoku.ac.jp; internet www.sci.tohoku.ac.jp):

AOKI, S., Atmospheric Physics
ASANO, S., Atmospheric Radiation, Physical Climatology
BANDO, S., Differential Geometry

CHIBA, M., Astrophysics
EZAWA, Z. F., Theoretical High Energy Physics, Condensed Matter Physics
FUJIMAKI, H., Geochemistry and Petrology
FUJIMOTO, H., Geodynamics of Subduction Zones
FUJIMURA, Y., Theoretical Chemistry
FUKUMURA, H., Physical Chemistry
FUKUNISHI, H., Upper Atmosphere Physics
FUTAMASE, T., Cosmology, General Relativity
HAMA, H., Beam Physics
HANAMURA, M., Algebraic Geometry
HANAWA, K., Physical Oceanography
HASEGAWA, A., Seismology
HASHIMOTO, O., Experimental Nuclear Physics
HATTORI, T., Mathematical Physics
HIKASA, K., Theoretical High Energy Physics
HINO, M., Human Geography
HIRAMA, M., Organic Chemistry
IGARASHI, G., Volcanology and Planetary Science
IMAIZUMI, T., Active Tectonics
INOUE, K., Experimental Particle Physics
ISHIDA, M., Algebraic Geometry
ISHIHARA, T., Solid State Photophysics
IWASAKI, T., Atmospheric Science
KABUTO, K., Organic Chemistry
KAIHO, K., Palaeontology
KASAGI, J., Nuclear Physics
KAWAKATSU, T., Physics of Soft Materials
KAWAMURA, H., Satellite Oceanography
KENMOTSU, K., Differential Geometry
KIRA, M., Organometallic Chemistry
KOBAYASHI, N., Functional Molecular Chemistry
KOBAYASHI, T., Experimental Nuclear Physics
KOZONO, H., Functional Analysis
KUDOH, Y., Mineralogy and Crystallography
KURAMOTO, Y., Theoretical Condensed Matter Physics
MIKAMI, N., Physical Chemistry
MINOURA, K., Palaeontology
MIYASE, H., Experimental Nuclear Physics
MORIOKA, A., Planetary Space Science
MORITA, N., Organic Chemistry
MORITA, Y., Number Theory
MURAKAMI, Y., Solid State Physics
NAKAMURA, T., Number Theory
NAKAZAWA, T., Atmospheric Physics
NIIZEKI, K., Theoretical Condensed Matter Physics
NISHIKAWA, S., Differential Geometry
ODA, M., Micropalaeontology
OGAWA, T., Partial Differential Equations and Applied Analysis
OHKI, K., Biophysics
OHNO, K., Physical Chemistry
OHTANI, E., Geochemistry and Planetology
OKAMOTO, H., Atmospheric Radiation
OKANO, S., Planetary Spectroscopy
ONO, T., Planetary Plasma Physics
ONODERA, H., Microscopic Research on Magnetism
OTSUKI, K., Tectonics and Structural Geology
SAIKAN, S., Non-linear Laser Spectroscopy
SAIO, H., Astrophysics
SAITO, R., Solid State Theory Nanotube
SATO, H., Seismology
SATOH, T., Experimental Ultra Low Temperature Physics
SEKI, M., Astrophysics
SHIMIZU, H., Nuclear Physics
SUTO, S., Surface Physics
SUZUKI, A., Experimental Particle Physics
SUZUKI, M., Plant Anatomy
TAKAGI, I., Partial Differential Equations
TAKAHASHI, T., Photoemission Solid State Physics
TAKAHASHI, T., Number Theory
TAKEDA, M., Probability Theory

TAKIGAWA, N., Theoretical Nuclear Physics
TAMURA, S., Astronomy
TANAKA, K., Mathematical Logic and Foundations of Mathematics
TANIGAKI, K., Solid State Physics
TERAMAE, N., Analytical Chemistry
TOBITA, H., Inorganic Chemistry
TOSA, M., Astronomy
TOYOTA, N., Molecular Metals
TSUBOTA, H., Experimental Nuclear Physics
UEDA, M., Natural Product Chemistry
UMINO, N., Seismotectonics
YAMAGUCHI, A., Experimental High Energy Physics
YAMAMOTO, H., Experimental High Energy Physics
YAMAMOTO, Y., Organic Chemistry
YAMASHITA, M., Coordination Chemistry
YANAGIDA, E., Partial Differential Equations
YASUDA, N., Meteorology
YOSHIDA, T., Volcanology and Petrology
YOSHIFUJI, M., Organic Chemistry
YUKIE, A., Number Theory

School of Agriculture and Graduate School of Agricultural Science (1-1 Tsutsumidori-Amamiyamachi, Aoba-ku, Sendai 981-8555; tel. (22) 717-8603; fax (22) 717-8607; e-mail agr-syom@bureau.tohoku.ac.jp; internet www.agri.tohoku.ac.jp):

AKIBA, Y., Animal Nutrition
GOMI, K., Microbial Biotechnology
HASEBE, T., Environmental Economics
IKEDA, I., Food and Biomolecular Science
IKEGAMI, M., Plant Pathology
KAMIO, Y., Applied Microbiology
KANAHAMA, K., Horticultural Science
KATSUMATA, R., Animal Microbiology
KIJIMA, A., Ecological Genetics (Field Science Center)
KOKUBUN, M., Crop Science
KOMAI, M., Nutrition
KUDO, A., Farm Business Management
KUWAHARA, S., Applied Bio-organic Chemistry
MAE, T., Plant Nutrition and Function
MATSUDA, K., Insect Science and Bioregulation
MINAMI, T., Fisheries Biology and Ecology
MIYAZAWA, T., Biodynamic Chemistry
MOROZUMI, K., Regional Planning
MUROGA, K., Aquacultural Biology
NAKAI, Y., Animal Health and Management
NANZYO, M., Soil Science
NISHIDA, A., Animal Breeding and Genetics
NISHIMORI, K., Molecular Biology
NISHIO, T., Plant Breeding and Genetics
OBARA, Y., Animal Physiology
OHKAMA, K., Agricultural and Resource Economics
OMORI, M., Fisheries Biology and Ecology
SAIGUSA, M., Environmental Crop Science (Field Science Center)
SAITO, G., Remote Sensing (Field Science Center)
SAITO, T., Animal Products Chemistry
SATO, E., Animal Reproduction
SATO, M., Marine Biochemistry
SATO, S., Land Ecology
SEIWA, K., Forest Ecology
SUZUKI, T., Marine Biotechnology
TANIGUCHI, A., Biological Oceanography
TANIGUCHI, K., Applied Aquatic Botany
TANIGUCHI, N., Applied Population Genetics
TORIYAMA, K., Environmental Biotechnology
YAMAGUCHI, T., Functional Morphology
YAMASHITA, M., Biophysical Chemistry
YAMAYA, T., Plant Cell Biochemistry
YONEKURA, H., Resource Management and Development Policy

School of Health Science, Faculty of Medicine (2-1 Seiryo-machi, Aoba-ku, Sendai 980-8575; tel. (22) 717-7903; fax (22) 717-7910; e-mail cms-syom@bureau.tohoku.ac.jp; internet www.cms.tohoku.ac.jp):

HAYASHI, S., Molecular Oncology
ISHIDA, M., Management of Nursing
ITAGAKI, K., Fundamental Nursing
KOBAYASHI, K., Clinical Investigation
KUROKAWA, T., Microbiology
MARUOKA, S., Nuclear Medicine
MASUDA, T., Pathology
MORI, I., Medical Imaging
NEMOTO, R., Adult Nursing
OISHI, M., Image Engineering
OOTAKA, T., Haematology
SAITO, H., Community Health Nursing
SAITO, H., Psychiatry
SAITO, K., Midwifery
SHINDOH, C., Respiratory Physiology
SHIWAKU, H., Child Health Nursing
TAKABAYASHI, T., Maternity Investigation
TAMURA, H., Neuroradiology
ZUGUCHI, M., Diagnostic Radiology

Tohoku University Museum (Aoba 6-3, Aramaki, Aoba-ku, Sendai 980-8578; tel. (22) 795-6767; fax (22) 795-6767; e-mail staff@museum.tohoku.ac.jp; internet www.museum.tohoku.ac.jp):

EHIRO, M., Geology and Palaeontology
YANAGIDA, T., Archaeology

UNIVERSITY OF TOKUSHIMA

2-24 Shinkura-cho, Tokushima 770-8501
Telephone: (88) 656-7000
Fax: (88) 656-7012
E-mail: hibunsyok@jim.tokushima-u.ac.jp
Internet: www.tokushima-u.ac.jp
Founded 1949
National University Corporation
Academic year: April to March
Pres.: TOSHIHIRO AONO
Vice-Pres: HIROSHI NAKAMURA, HIROSHI KAWAKAMI, HISASHI KITAJIMA, MASAYUKI. SHIBUYA, YASUHIRO KURODA
Sec.-Gen.: HIROSHI NAKAMURA
Dir of Univ. Library: KAZUO HOSOI

Number of teachers: 895 full-time
Number of students: 7,744

Publications: *Bulletin of the Faculty of Engineering* (1 a year), *Journal of Human Sciences* (1 a year), *Journal of Human Sciences and Arts* (1 a year), *Journal of Language and Literature* (1 a year), *Journal of Mathematics* (1 a year), *Journal of Medical Investigation* (2 a year), *Natural Science Research* (1 a year), *Social Sciences Research* (1 a year)

DEANS

Faculty of Dentistry: EIICHI BANDO
Faculty of Engineering: YONEO YANO
Faculty of Integrated Arts and Sciences: MAKOTO WADA
Faculty of Medicine: SABURO SONE
Faculty of Pharmaceutical Sciences: TAKSAHI YAMAUCHI
Institute of Health Biosciences, Graduate School: SABURO SONE

PROFESSORS

Faculty of Dentistry, Graduate School of Oral Sciences and Institute of Health Biosciences (3-18-15 Kuramoto-cho, Tokushima 770-8504; tel. (88) 633-9100; fax (88) 631-4215; e-mail isysoumu2k@jim.tokushima-u.ac.jp):

ASAOKA, K., Biomaterials and Bio-engineering
BANDO, E., Fixed Prosthodontics
HANEJI, T., Anatomy and Histology
HAYASHI, Y., Oral Molecular Pathology

HONDA, E., Oral and Maxillofacial Radiology

HOSOI, K., Molecular Oral Physiology

ICHIKAWA, T., Removable Prosthodontics and Oral Implantology

KAWANO, F., Oral Care and Clinical Education

KITAMURA, S., Anatomy

MATSUO, T., Conservative Dentistry

MIYAKE, Y., Microbiology

MORIYAMA, K., Orthodontics and Dentofacial Orthopaedics

NAGATA, T., Periodontology and Endodontology

NAGAYAMA, M., Oral and Maxillofacial Surgery

NAKAJO, N., Dental Anaesthesiology

NISHINO, M., Paediatric Dentistry

NOMA, T., Molecular Biology

SATO, M., Oral and Maxillofacial Surgery and Oncology

YOSHIMOTO, K., Molecular Pharmacology

Faculty of Engineering (2-1 Minamijosanjima-cho, Tokushima 770-8506; tel. (88) 656-7304; fax (88) 656-7328; e-mail kgsoumuk@jim.tokushima-u.ac.jp; internet www.e.tokushima-u.ac.jp/english/main.html):

AKAMATSU, N., Neural Networks and Speech Recognition

AOE, J., Intelligent Systems Engineering

FUKUI, M., Optoelectronics

FUKUTOMI, J., Fluid Engineering and Turbomachinery

HANABUSA, T., Production Systems Engineering

HASHIMOTO, C., Construction Materials

HASHINO, M., Stochastic Hydrology, Water Resources Engineering

HIRAO, K., Structural Engineering and Seismic Design

HORI, H., Biological Science

IMAEDA, M., Process Dynamics and Control

IMAI, H., Mathematics and Applied Mathematics

INOUE, K., Applied Superconductivity and High-Field Generation

INOUE, T., Crystal Growth and Crystal Engineering

IRITANI, T., Spread Spectrum Communications

ISAKA, K., Electric Energy Engineering

IWATA, T., Applied Spectroscopy and Optical Measurement

KAIEDA, Y., Plastic Forming and Powder Metallurgy

KANESHINA, S., Biological Science

KAWAMURA, Y., Organic Chemistry

KAWASHIRO, K., Enzyme Engineering

KINOUCHI, Y., Biomedical Electronics

KITAYAMA, S., Digital Signal Processing

KONAKA, S., Integrated Circuits

KONDO, A., Geotechnical Engineering

KONISHI, K., Robot and Computer Vision

KORAI, H., Microbiology and Microbiological Control

MASUDA, S., Synthetic and Polymer Chemistry

MIWA, K., Combustion Engineering and Energy Conversion

MIZUGUCHI, H., Urban Planning and Landscape Design

MOCHIZUKI, A., Foundations Engineering and Soil Mechanics

MORIOKA, I., Heat Transfer

MOTONAKA, J., Analytical Chemistry

MURAKAMI, H., Risk and Environmental Assessment

MURAKAMI, R., Metal Fatigue, Surface Modification

NAGAMACHI, S., Mathematics and Applied Mathematics

NIKI, N., Medial Imaging, Pattern Recognition

NISHIDA, N., Optical Information Science

NOJI, S., Molecular Biology and Devlopmental Biology

OHNO, T., Nuclear Magnetic Resonance

OHNO, Y., Electron Devices

OKABE, T., River Engineering, Environmental Hydraulics

ONISHI, T., Power Engineering

ONO, N., Multi-agent Systems and Reinforcement Learning

OOSHIKA, T., Enzymology and Genome Engineering

OUSAKA, A., Thermal Engineering, Multiphase Flow

OYA, K., Particle-surface Collisions and Nuclear Fusion

REN, F., Computer Science Technology, Natural Language Processing

SAKAI, S., Semiconductor Photonic Devices

SAWADA, T., Structural Engineering, Earthquake Engineering

SHIMOMURA, T., Soft Engineering, Algorithnic Debugging

SUEDA, O., Well-being Engineering and Assistive Engineering

TAJIMA, K., All-optical Devices

TAKEUCHI, T., Numerical Analysis

TAMESADA, T., Design and Test of Electronic Circuits

TAMURA, K., Biophysical Chemistry

TANAKA, H., Polymer Synthesis and Functional Organic Materials

TOMIDA, T., Chemical Processes Engineering

TSUJI, A., Biochemistry and Protein Engineering

TSUKAYAMA, M., Synthetic and Polymer Chemistry

YAMADA, K., Elasticity and Micromechanics

YAMAGAMI, T., Geotechnical and Landslide Engineering

YAMANAKA, H., Urban Transport Planning and Design

YANO, Y., Intelligent Systems Engineering

YOSHIDA, K., Material Evaluation and Acoustic Emission

YOSHIMURA, T., Vehicle Suspensions and Fuzzy Control

Faculty of Integrated Arts and Sciences (1-1 Minamijosanjima-cho, Tokushima 770-8502; tel. (88) 656-7103; fax (88) 656-7298; e-mail sksoumks@jim.tokushima-u.ac.jp; internet www.ias.tokushima-u.ac.jp):

ABE, E., Kimono Cloth Shrinkage and Repair

ANDO, M., Chinese Literature

ARAKI, H., Motor and Behavioural Physiology

ARIMA, T., Philosophy of the Qin and Han Dynasties

AZUMA, K., Calligraphy

AZUMA, U., Asian Archaeology

BABA, T., German Language and Literature

GOTO, T., Comparative Biochemistry and Physiology

HAMADA, J., Visual Perception

HARAMIZU, T., Japanese Literature

HAYASHI, H., Environmental Biology

HAYASHI, K., Constitutional Law

HIOKI, Z., Theoretical High Energy Physics

HIRAI, S., Historical Geography

HIRAKI, M., Study of Painting Expression

IMAI, S., Applied Spectrocopy, Atomic Spectrometry and Trace Analysis

INOUE, N., English Corpus Linguistics, English Lexicography

ISHIDA, K., Microfossil Geology

ISHIDA, M., Philosophy of the Mind–Body Problem

ISHIHARA, T., Differential Geometry

ISHII, K., Image Conservation Techniques

ISHIKAWA, E., German Language and Literature

ITO, M., Partial Differential Equations

ITO, T., Computational Mathematics and Sciences

ITO, Y., Functional Analysis

KATAOKA, K., Musicology

KATAYAMA, S., Algebraic Number Theory

KATSURA, S., German Language and Literature

KAWAKAMI, S., German Language and Literature

KISHIE, S., Japanese Dialects

KOORI, N., Nuclear Physics

KOYAMA, K., Solid-State Physics

KUWABARA, M., Japanese History

KUWABARA, R., Global Analysis

MAEDA, S., Applied Mathematics

MASUDA, T., Bio-organic Chemistry

MATOBA, H., Exercise Physiology

MATSUMOTO, M., Physical Chemistry

MATSUO, Y., Genetics

MATSUSHITA, M., English Literature

MAYUMI, K., Environmental Economics

MIKI, M., Financial Accounting

MITSUI, A., Industrial Technology

MIURA, T., Physical Education

MIYAZAKI, T., English Literature

MIYAZAWA, K., Composition, Music using Computers

MIZUSHIMA, T., Middle Eastern Economics

MORI, Y., Psychotherapy

MORIOKA, Y., English Linguistics

MOTOKI, Y., English Linguistics

MURATA, A., Geology

NAKAGAWA, H., Marine Physiology and Biochemistry

NAKAJIMA, M., Economic History

NAKAMURA, H., Physical Education

NAKAYAMA, S., Nuclear Physics

NISHIDE, K., American History

OBARA, S., Exercise Physiology

OHASHI, M., Mathematical Programming

OHASHI, M., Immunobiology

OHBUCHI, A., Algebraic Geometry

OYAMA, Y., Analytical Cytology

SAKUMA, R., Social and Imperial History of Modern Britain

SANO, K., Physiological Psychology

SEKIZAWA, J., Risk Assessment for Environmental Protection and Safety

SENBA, M., Japanese Linguistics

SEO, I., English Literature

SHIOTA, T., Geology

TACHIBANA, Y., Economic Theory

TAJIMA, T., French Literature

TAKEDA, Y., Natural Products Chemistry

TERAO, H., Inorganic Chemistry

UENO, K., Sociology of Social Problems

WADA, M., Organic Chemistry

YAMADA, K., Labour Law

YAMAMOTO, M., Developmental Disorders

YOKOIGAWA, K., Applied Microbiology

YOSHIDA, H., Theoretical Sociology

YOSHIDA, S., Ancient Greek Philosophy

YOSHIMORI, K., Chinese Medieval History

Faculty of Medicine, Graduate School of Medical Sciences and Institute of Health Biosciences (3-18-15 Kuramoto-cho, Tokushima 770-8503; tel. (88) 633-9116; fax (88) 633-9028; e-mail isysoumu1k@jim.tokushima-u.ac.jp; internet www.hosp.med.tokushima-u.ac.jp/university/servlet/index):

ADACHI, A., Virology

ARASE, S., Dermatological Science

DOI, T., Clinical Biology and Medicine

FUKUI, Y., Anatomy and Developmental Neurobiology

IRAHARA, M., Gynaecology and Obstetrics

ISHIMURA, K., Anatomy and Cell Biology

ITO, S., Digestive and Cardiovascular Medicine

IZUMI, K., Molecular and Environmental Pathology

KAJI, R., Clinical Neuroscience

KITAGAWA, T., Cardiovascular Surgery

KISHI, K., Nutritional Physiology

KUBO, S., Legal Medicine

MATSUMOTO, T., Medicine and Bioregulatory Sciences
MIYAMOTO, K., Nutritional Biochemistry
MORITA, Y., Integrative Physiology
NAGAHIRO, S., Neurosurgery
NAKAHORI, Y., Human Genetics and Public Health
NAKANISHI, H., Plastic and Reconstructive Surgery
NAKAYA, Y., Nutrition and Metabolism
NISHITANI, H., Radiology
OHMORI, T., Psychiatry
OSHITA, S., Anaesthesiology
OTA, F., Food Microbiology
SANO, T., Human Pathology
SASAKI, T., Biochemistry
SHIOTA, H., Ophthalmology and Visual Science
SONE, S., Internal Medicine and Molecular Therapeutics
TAKEDA, E., Clinical Nutrition
TAKEDA, N., Otorhinolaryngology and Communicative Neuroscience
TAMAKI, T., Pharmacology
TASHIRO, S., Digestive and Paediatric Surgery
TERAO, J., Food Science
YAMAMOTO, S., Applied Nutrition
YASUI, N., Orthopaedic Surgery
YASUMOTO, K., Immunology and Parasitology
YOSHIZAKI, K., Physiology

Faculty of Pharmaceutical Sciences and Graduate School of Pharmaceutical Sciences (1-78-1 Shomachi, Tokushima 770-8505; tel. (88) 633-7245; fax (88) 633-9517; e-mail isysoumu3k@jim.tokushima-u.ac.jp; internet www.ph.tokushima-u.ac.jp):

ARAKI, T., Drug Metabolism and Therapeutics
BABA, Y., Molecular and Pharmaceutical Biotechnology
CHUMAN, H., Molecular and Analytical Chemistry
FUKUI, H., Molecular Pharmacology
FUKUZAWA, K., Health Chemistry
HIGUCHI, T., Molecular Cell Biology and Medicine
ITO, K., Medicinal Biotechnology
KIHARA, M., Pharmaceutical Information Science
KIWADA, H., Pharmacokinetics and Biopharmaceutics
KUSUMI, T., Marine Medicinal Resources
NAGAO, Y., Molecular Medicinal Chemistry
OCHIAI, M., Pharmaceutical Organic Chemistry
SHIMABAYASHI, S., Physical Pharmacy
SHISHIDO, K., Organic Synthesis
TAKAISHI, Y., Pharmacognosy
TAKIGUCHI, Y., Clinical Pharmacology
YAMAUCHI, T., Biochemistry

School of Health Sciences (3-18-15 Kuramoto-cho, Tokushima 770-8503; tel. (88) 633-9003; fax (88) 633-9015; e-mail isysoumu4k@jim.tokushima-u.ac.jp; internet www2.medsci.tokushima-u.ac.jp):

FUJII, M., Neuroradiology
HARADA, M., Neuroradiology
KAGAWA, N., Human Pathology
KAWANISHI, C., Fundamental Nursing
KONDO, H., Fundamental Nursing
KONDO, T., Nutritional Biochemistry
MAEZAWA, H., Radiation Medicine
MORIMOTO, T., Breast Surgery
NAGAMINE, I., Clinical Neurpsychiatry
NAGASHINO, H., Biomedical Engineering
NINOMIYA, T., Psychosomatic Medicine
ONISHI, C., Adult and Gerontological Nursing
ONO, T., Bacterial Genetics
SAITOH, K., Cardiology
SEKIDO, K., Dermatological Science
TADA, T., Gerontological Nursing
TAKEGAWA, Y., Radiotherapy

TAMURA, A., Adult Nursing
TERAO, T., Maternal Health
UENO, J., Diagnostic Radiology
YAMANO, S., Artificial Reproductive Technology
YOSHINAGA, T., Medical Image Reconstruction

Center for Advanced Information Technology (2-1 Minamijosanjima-cho, Tokushima 770-8506; tel. (88) 656-7555; fax (88) 656-9122; e-mail kokusai1@jim.tokushima-u.ac.jp; internet www.ait.tokushima-u.ac.jp):

KITA, K., Computer Science, Information Retrieval, Natural Language Processing
OE, S., Image Processing and Visual Pattern Processing

Center for University Extension (1-1 Minamijosanjima-cho, Tokushima 770-8502; tel. (88) 656-7276; fax (88) 656-7277; e-mail kygakusk@jim.tokushima-u.ac.jp; internet www.cue.tokushima-u.ac.jp):

HIROWATARI, S., Adult and Continuing Education
MORITA, H., Analytical Chemistry
SODA, K., Function of Narrative
WAKAIZUMI, S., High Energy Physics
YOSHIDA, A., Educational Technology

Institute for Animal Experimentation, Institute of Health Biosciences (3-18-15 Kuramoto-cho, Tokushima 770-8503; tel. (88) 633-9116; fax (88) 633-9028; e-mail isysoum1k@jim.tokushima-u.ac.jp; internet www.anex.med.tokushima-u.ac.jp):

SASAKI, T., Biochemistry

Institute for Enzyme Research (3-18-15 Kuramoto-cho, Tokushima 770-8503; tel. (88) 633-9420; fax (88) 633-9422; e-mail kenkyu@jim.tokushima-u.ac.jp; internet mms1.ier.tokushima-u.ac.jp/index2.html):

EBINA, Y., Molecular Genetics
FUKUI, K., Gene Regulatorics
KIDO, H., Molecular Enzyme Chemistry
MATSUMOTO, M., Informative Cytology
SUGINO, H., Molecular Cytology
TANIGUCHI, H., Molecular Enzyme Physiology

Institute for Genome Research (3-18-15 Kuramoto-cho, Tokushima 770-8503; tel. (88) 633-9420; fax (88) 633-9422; e-mail kenkyu@jim.tokushima-u.ac.jp; internet www.genome.tokushima-u.ac.jp):

HARA, E., Division of Protein Information
ITAKURA, M., Division of Genetic Information
SHINOHARA, Y., Division of Gene Expression
SIOMI, H., Division of Gene Function Analysis
TAKAHAMA, Y., Division of Experimental Immunology

Institute for Medicinal Resources, Institute of Health Biosciences (1-78-1 Shomachi, Tokushima 770-8505; tel. (88) 633-7245; fax (88) 633-9517; e-mail isysoum3k@jim.tokushima-u.ac.jp; internet www.ph.tokushima-u.ac.jp):

ITO, K., Medicinal Biotechnology

International Student Center (1-1 Minamijosanjima-cho, Tokushima 770-8502; tel. (88) 656-7082; fax (88) 656-9873; e-mail ryugakuk@jim.tokushima-u.ac.jp; internet www.isc.tokushima-u.ac.jp):

JIN, C. H., Computing Science
MISUMI, T., Teaching Japanese as a Foreign Language
OISHI, Y., Teaching Japanese as a Foreign Language

Radioisotope Center (3-18-15 Kuramoto-cho, Tokushima 770-8503; tel. (88) 633-9416; fax (88) 633-9417; e-mail kenkyu@jim.tokushima-u.ac.jp; internet ricb.ri.tokushima-u.ac.jp/rirc.html):

ADACHI, A., HIV/AIDS treatment

TOKYO INSTITUTE OF TECHNOLOGY

2-12-1, Ookayama, Meguro-ku, Tokyo 152-8550

Telephone: (3) 5734-3827
Fax: (3) 5734-3685
E-mail: iad@jim.titech.ac.jp
Internet: www.titech.ac.jp

Founded 1881
Independent
Academic year: April to March

Pres.: MASUO AIZAWA
Vice-Pres: CHITOSHI MIKI (Academic), MITSUHARU SEKIGUCHI (Finance), YOSHIMORI HONKURA (Planning), AKIRA SHIMOKOHBE (Research)
Dir-Gen. of Admin. Bureau: DAISUKE IKEDA
Dir of Institute Library: EIJI FUJIWARA

Library of 886,484 vols
Number of teachers: 743 full-time
Number of students: 5,007

DEANS

School of Bioscience and Biotechnology: SHIGEHISA HIROSE
School of Engineering: NOBUO FUJII
School of Science: KIYOSHI NAZAKAWA
Graduate School of Bioscience and Biotechnology: SHIGEHISA HIROSE
Graduate School of Decision Science and Technology: HIROMITSU MUTA
Graduate School of Engineering: NOBUO FUJII
Graduate School of Information Science and Engineering: YUKIO TAKAHASHI
Graduate School of Innovation Management: TAKAO ENKAWA
Graduate School of Science and Engineering: KIYOSHI NAKAZAWA
Interdisciplinary Graduate School of Science and Engineering: YOSHINAO MISHIMA

DIRECTORS

Chemical Resources Laboratory: MASASUKE YOSHIDA
Materials and Structures Laboratory: KENICHI KONDOU
Precision and Intelligence Laboratory: SHINICHI YOKOTA
Research Laboratory for Nuclear Reactors: MASAO OGAWA

PROFESSORS

Graduate School of Bioscience and Biotechnology:

AKAIKE, T., Biomaterial Design
AONO, R., Microbial Physiology, Genetic Engineering
FUJIHIRA, M., Biomolecular Processes
HAMAGUCHI, Y., Cell Biology
HANDA, H., Biotechnology
HASHIMOTO, H., Bio-organic Chemistry
HIROSE, S., Biochemistry
ICHINOSE, H., Neurochemistry and Neuropharmacology
IKAI, A., Biodynamics
INOUE, Y., Enzyme Functions
ISHIKAWA, T., Biofunctional Engineering
KISHIMOTO, T., Cell and Developmental Biology
KITAMURA, N., Molecular Biology
KITAZUME, T., Bio-organic Chemistry
KUDO, A., Molecular Immunology
MOTOKAWA, T., Animal Physiology
NAKAMURA, S., Genetic Engineering
OKADA, N., Molecular Evolution
OKAHATA, Y., Fundamentals of Biomolecules
OKURA, I., Biophysical Chemistry, Enzyme Chemistry
SATO, F., Molecular Design of Biological Importance

SEKINE, M., Bio-organic Chemistry
SHISHIDO, K., Molecular Biology
TAKAMIYA, K., Plant Physiology
TANAKA, N., Protein Crystallography
UENO, A., Bio-organic Chemistry, Molecular Recognition
UNNO, H., Biochemistry

Graduate School of Decision Science and Technology:

ENKAWA, T., Production Management
HASHIZUME, D., Sociology
HAYASAKA, M., History of Politics (Slavic Studies)
HIDANO, N., Regional Planning and Infrastructure Project Appraisal
HIGUCHI, Y., Socioeconomic Networks
IGUCHI, T., Japanese Literature
IIJIMA, J., Systems Theory
IMADA, T., International Relations
ISHII, M., Sports Psychology
ITO, K., Ergonomics, Production Control
KIJIMA, K., Management Systems
KIMOTO, T., History of Technology
KUWAKO, T., Philosophy
KYOMOTO, N., Intellectual Property Strategy, Licensing, Software Protection
MAYEKAWA, S., Psychometrics, Educational Statistics, Multivariate Data Analysis
MIYAJIMA, M., Industrial Management
MIYAKAWA, M., Applied Statistics, Quality Control
MIZUNO, S., Operations Research
MURAKI, M., Process Management
MUTA, H., Educational Planning, Economics of Education
MUTO, S., Game Theory
NAKAGAWA, M., Educational Psychology
NAKAHARA, Y., Exercise Physiology
NAKAI, N., Urban Planning
SAIKI, T., Patenting of Pharmaceutical Inventions
SAITO, T., Sociometrics
SAITO, U., Regional Landscape Planning and Design
TANAKA, Z., Political Science
WARAGAI, T., Philosophy, Logic
WATANABE, C., Technology Policy, Technology Management
YAMAMURO, K., Document Analysis
YAMATO, T., Economic Theory
YAMAZAKI, M., History of Science
YANO, M., Social Planning

Graduate School of Information Science and Engineering:

FUJII, S., Environmental Engineering
FUJIWARA, E., Coding Theory, Computer Systems
FURUI, S., Speech Recognition, Human Interfaces
HIGUCHI, Y., Socioeconomic Networks
HIROSE, S., Applied Solid Mechanics, Ultrasonic Nondestructive Evaluation, Numerical Analysis using Boundary Element Method
KIMEI, H., Geophysical Prospecting
KIMURA, K., Vibration, Stochastic Dynamics, Nonlinear Dynamics
KOJIMA, M., Mathematical Programming
KOJIMA, S., Geometry and Topology
MASE, S., Spatial Statistics
MORI, K., Computer Systems, Distributed Computing
NADAOKA, K., Environmental Systems Analysis, Coastal and Ocean Engineering, Mesoscale Meteorology, Applied Remote Sensing, Coastal-space Design, Applied Fluid Dynamics
NAKAJIMA, M., Computer Graphics, Image Processing
NAKAMURA, H., Strength of Materials
OGAWA, H., Pattern Recognition, Image Processing
SAEKI, M., Software Engineering
SASAJIMA, K., Precision Engineering, Measuring Systems

SASSA, M., Computer Software, Programming Environments
SATO, T., Artificial Intelligence and Logic Programming
SHIBAYAMA, E., Software Science, Parallel and Distributed Computing
SHIMIZU, M., Biomechanics, Fluid Dynamics
TAKAHASHI, W., Functional Analysis and its Applications
TAKAHASHI, Y., Applied Probability, Operations Research
TAKIGUCHI, K., Mechanics of Building Structures, Disaster Prevention Systems, Concrete Engineering
TANAKA, H., Natural Language Processing
TOKUDA, T., Software Engineering
UJIHASHI, S., Biomechanics, Sports Engineering, Safety Engineering
WATANABE, O., Theory of Computation
YONEZAKI, N., Applied Logic, Software Science

Graduate School of Science and Engineering:

ABE, M., Electronic Properties of Matter
AKAGI, H., Power Engineering, Power Electronics, Electrical Machines
ANDO, I., Polymer Structure, NMR Spectroscopy, Electronic Structure of Polymers
ANDO, M., Antennas, Electromagnetic Wave Theory
ANDO, T., Physics, Condensed Matter Theory, Quantum Hall Effect, Semiconductor Quantum Structures
AOKI, Y., Urban Planning
ARAKI, K., Coding Theory, Digital Communication Systems
ASAHI, K., Experimental Nuclear Physics
DAIMON, M., Cement Chemistry, Porous Materials, Hydrochemical Synthesis
ENDO, M., Solid Vibrations
ENOKI, T., Physical Chemistry
FUJII, N., Electronic Circuits and Networks
FUJIMOTO, Y., Bio-organic Chemistry
FUJIOKA, H., History of Architecture, Architectural Design
FUJITA, T., Algebraic Geometry
FURUYA, K., Optical and Quantum Electronics
FUTAKI, A., Differential Geometry
HAGIWARA, I., Collaboration Engineering
HANNA, J., Imaging Materials
HASHIMOTO, T., Polymer Processing, Thermal Properties of Polymers
HIGUCHI, Y., Exercise Physiology
HINODE, H., Inorganic Synthesis of Solids, Inorganic Industrial Chemistry
HIRAO, A., Polymer Syntheses
HIROSE, S., Robotics, Biomechanics
HONKURA, Y., Geophysics
HOSOYA, A., Theoretical Cosmology
ICHIMURA, T., Molecular Spectroscopy
IGUCHI, I., Condensed Matter Physics and Superconducting Electronics
IIO, K., Experimental Condensed Matter Physics
IKARIYA, T., Homogeneous Catalysis, Synthetic Organic Chemistry
IKEDA, S., Hydraulics and Environmental Fluid Mechanics
INOU, N., Biomechanics, Autonomous Decentralized Systems, Robotics
INOUE, A., Singularity, Algebraic Geometry
INOUE, T., Physical Chemistry of Polymer Materials
ISHII, S., Singularity and Bifurcation
ISHII, S., Electric Power Engineering, Plasma
ISHIZU, K., Polymer Syntheses, Polymer Reactions
IWAMOTO, M., Electronic Materials
IWASAWA, N., Synthetic Organic Chemistry
IWATSUKI, N., Robotics
KAIZU, Y., Coordination Chemistry

KAJIUCHI, T., Biochemical Engineering, Environmental Chemical Engineering
KAKIMOTO, F., Experimental Cosmic Ray Physics
KAKIMOTO, M., Polymer Syntheses, Thin Polymer Films
KAKINUMA, K., Bio-organic Chemistry
KAWAI, N., Astrophysics
KAWAMURA, K., Physics, Inorganic Chemistry, Mineral Physics
KAWASAKI, J., Mass Transfer Operations
KAWASHIMA, K., Earthquake Engineering
KIKUTANI, T., Fibre and Polymer Processing, Physical Properties of Polymers
KISHIMOTO, K., Strength of Materials, Computational Mechanics
KITAGAWA, A., Fluid Power Control
KOBAYASHI, A., Industrial Measurement
KOBAYASHI, H., Fracture Mechanics and Fatigue
KONAGAI, M., Semiconductors
KOSHIHARA, S., Materials Science
KOUCHI, N., Physical Chemistry of Atomic and Molecular Processes
KUMAZAWA, I., Human Interface
KUNIEDA, H., Integrated Circuits, Signal Processing
KURODA, C., Process Information Systems
KUROKAWA, N., Number Theory
KUSAKABE, O., Geotechnical Engineering
KYOGOKU, K., Tribology, Machine Elements
MARUYAMA, S., Geology, Tectonics
MARUYAMA, T., Physical Chemistry in Advanced Materials
MATSUI, Y., Advanced Thermo-fluid Dynamics
MASUKO, M., Tribology, Applied Surface Chemistry
MATSUO, T., Physical Metallurgy of Iron and Steels, High Temperature Deformation in Alloys
MATSUO, Y., Mechanical Properties of Ceramics
MATSUZAWA, A.
MIKI, C., Structural Mechanics and Engineering
MIMACHI, K., Special Functions, Material Physics, Representation Theory, Holonomic Systems
MINAMI, F., Solid–State Physics and Laser Spectroscopy
MITA, T., Control Theory, Applications of Control Theory, Robotics
MIYAUCHI, T., Fluid Dynamics, Reactive Gas Dynamics
MIYAZAKI, K., Technology Strategy and Diffusion
MIZUTANI, N., Advanced Ceramics, Ceramic Processing, Electro-ceramics, Thin Films
MOCHIMARU, Y., Computational Fluid Dynamics
MORIIZUMI, T., Bioelectronics
MUNEKATA, H., Applied Physics of Property and Crystallography
MURAI, T., Wanderology
MURAKAMI, H., Workshop Processes and Production Engineering
MURATA, M., Differential Equations
NAGAHASHI, H., Image Processing
NAGAI, T., Solar–Terrestrial Physics
NAGATA, K., High Temperature Physical Chemistry and Electronic Materials
NAKAHARA, T., Lubrication Technology, Two-Phase Flow, Oil Hydraulics
NAKAMURA, K., Chemical Engineering
NAKAMURA, Y., Diffraction Crystallography, Magnetic Thin Film
NAKASHIMA, S., Experimental Physical Geochemistry, Geochemical Spectroscopy and Kinetics, Physicochemical Properties of Water in the Earth, Organic–Inorganic Interactions and the Origin of Life, Geochemistry of Resources and the Environment

NAKAZAWA, K., Planetary Physics

NISHI, T., Polymer Alloys, Soft Materials, Polymer Nanotechnology

NISHIDA, N., Experimental Condensed Matter Physics, Low Temperature Physics

NISHIMORI, H., Statistical Physics

NIWA, J., Structural Concrete

OBIKAWA, T., Machining, Materials Science, Mechanical Processing Systems

OGAWA, K., Mechanical Operations

OGAWA, T., Steel and Shell Structures

OGUNI, M., Physical Inorganic Chemistry

OHASHI, H., Power Semiconductor Devices

OHASHI, Y., Crystal Chemistry

OHTA, H., Geotechnical Engineering

OHTAGUCHI, K., Biochemical Reaction Engineering

OKA, M., Theoretical Nuclear Physics

OKADA, K., Ceramic Raw Materials, Mineralogical Science

OKADA, T., Analytical Chemistry

OKAZAKI, K., Thermal and Environmental Engineering

OKUDA, Y., Low Temperature Physics

OKUI, N., Organic Thin Films, Physical Properties of Polymers

OKUMA, M., Dynamics, Optimum Design

OKUTOMI, M., Computer Vision

ONO, K., Dynamics of Machinery

ONZAWA, T., Welding and Materials Science

OTSUKA, K., Heterogeneous Catalysis, Electrocatalysis

OTSUKI, N., Construction Materials, Environmental Materials Design

SAITO, A., Thermal Engineering

SAITO, S., Theoretical Condensed Matter Physics

SAITO, Y., Manufacturing Engineering, CAD, CAM, Computer Intelligent Manufacturing

SAJI, T., Electrochemistry, Surface Chemistry

SAKAI, N., Theoretical Elementary Particle Physics

SAKAI, Y., Communication Systems

SAKAMOTO, K., Architectural Design

SAKANIWA, K., Communication Theory

SAMPEI, M., Control Theory (Linear and Non-linear) and its Application, Non-holonomic Systems

SATO, T., Materials Development, Magnetic Materials, Amorphous Metals

SATOH, I., Thermal Engineering, Heat Transfer Measurement

SENDA, M., Environmental Design

SHIBATA, S., Inorganic Materials Engineering

SHIBATA, T., Experimental Nuclear Physics

SHIBUYA, K., Physical Chemistry

SHIGA, H., Complex Analysis

SHIGA, T., Stochastic Processes

SUMITA, M., Solid Structure and Physical Properties of Organic Materials, Polymer Composites

SUSA, M., Physical Chemistry of Materials

SUZUKI, H., Organometallic Chemistry

SUZUKI, H., Radio Communications Engineering

SUZUKI, K., Organic Chemistry

SUZUKI, M., Plasma Engineering, Nuclear Chemical Engineering

SUZUMURA, A., Joining, High Temperature Materials

TAKAGI, S., Analogue Integrated Circuits, Analogue Signal Processing

TAKAHASHI, E., Petrology, Geochemistry, Solid Geophysics

TAKAHASHI, T., Synthetic Organic Chemistry, Synthetic Processes for Natural Products

TAKATA, T., Supramolecular and Polymer Chemistry

TAKAYANAGI, K., Diffraction, Crystal Physics, Surface Physics

TAKEZOE, H., Optical and Electrical Properties of Organic Materials

TANIOKA, A., Physical Chemistry of Organic Materials, Membrane Science

TOKIMATSU, K., Geotechnical Engineering

TOKURA, H., Processing Technologies

TSUDA, K., Chemical Plant Materials

TSUNAKAWA, H., Geophysics

TSURU, T., Chemistry of Metal Surfaces, Electrochemistry, Corrosion and Passivity of Metals

TSURUMI, T., Electrical Properties and Structure of Inorganic Materials

UCHIYAMA, K., Stochastic Processes and Applied Probability

UEDA, M., Condensed Matter Theory, Quantum Optics

UEDA, M., Polymer Syntheses

UEDA, M., Wave Information Processing

UENO, S., Theory of Parallel and VLSI Computation

UYEMATSU, T., Information Theory, Data Compression

WAKIHARA, M., Inorganic Solid-State Chemistry

WATANABE, J., Structure and Properties of Polymer Liquid Crystals

WATANABE, Y., Experimental Particle Physics

YABE, T., Laser Nuclear Fusion, Computational Fluid Dynamics

YAGI, K., Experimental Condensed Matter Physics, Crystal and Surface Physics

YAI, T., Transport Planning and Engineering

YAMAJI, A., Materials Science

YOSHIDA, T., Topology

YOSHINO, J., Experimental Condensed Matter Physics

Interdisciplinary Graduate School of Science and Engineering (4259 Nagatsuta-cho, Midori-ku, Yokohama 226-8502; tel. (45) 922-1111):

AOYAGI, Y., Information Devices

ASADA, M., Quantum Electronics

DEGUCHI, H., Polymer Synthesis

DOI, Y., Polymer Synthesis

FUCHIGAMI, T., Catalytic Chemistry

HARA, M., Nanotechnology

HARASHINA, S., Environmental Planning, Conflict Resolution

HATORI, Y., Visual Communication System, Network Interface

HIROTA, K., Information Systems

HORIOKA, K., High Power Beam Technology, Laser Engineering

HOTTA, E., Plasma Engineering, Pulsed Power Technology

HOYANO, A., Urban and Building Environment

ISHIKAWA, T., Hydraulics and Hydrology

ISHIWARA, M., Nanomaterials

ITO, K., Computational Brain Science, Design and Control of Robotics and Prostheses

KABASHIMA, Y., Information and Communication Engineering

KANNO, R., Lithium Battery, Solid-State Ionics, Inorganic Materials Chemistry, Solid State Electrochemistry, High Pressure and Thin-film Synthesis

KATO, M., Fracture and Deformation

KINUGASA, Y., Earthquake Geology, Environmental Geology

KOBAYASHI, S., Knowledge Information Processing

KOBAYASHI, T., Digital Signal Processing

KOHNO, T., Nuclear Physics, Heavy Ion-Beam Science

KOSUGI, Y., Neural Networks

KUMAI, S., Nano-electronics

MAEJIMA, H., Microprocessors, Special Purpose Processors, On-chip Systems

MIDORIKAWA, S., Earthquake Engineering

MISHIMA, Y., Physical Metallurgy and Alloy Design

NAKAMURA, K., Computational Neuroscience

NAKANO, Y., Environmental Engineering, Separation Process Engineering

NITTA, K., Artificial Intelligence, Regal Reasoning

ODAWARA, O., Electrochemistry of Metals

OHMACHI, T., Earthquake Engineering

OHNO, R., Architectural Design and Planning, Environmental Psychology

OHSAKA, T., Molten Salt Chemistry, Electrochemistry, Electroanalytical Chemistry, Bioelectrochemistry

OHTSU, M., Opto-quantum Electronics

OKAMURA, T., Cryogenic and Energy Conversion Engineering

ONAKA, S., Mechanical Properties of Materials

SAKAI, T., Semiconductor Devices

SASANO, S., History of Urban and Architectural Design

SATO, A., Strengthening Mechanism and Lattice Imperfections

SEO, K., Engineering Seismology

TAMURA, T., Environmental Atmospheric Turbulence, Urban Wind Climate, Aerodynamic Control

TEHRANO, T., Intelligent Informatics

UCHIKAWA, K., Visual Information Processing

WATANABE, M., Physical Geography

YAI, T., Transport Planning and Engineering

YAMAMURA, M., DNA Computing

YAMASAKI, H., Energy Conversion Engineering

YAMAZAKI, Y., Solid-State Physics and Chemistry

YOKOYAMA, M., Automated Machine Design

YOSHIKAWA, K., High Temperature Energy Conversion, Environmental Fluid Dynamics

Chemical Resources Laboratory:

AKITA, M., Organometallic Chemistry

DOMEN, K., Surface Chemical Reaction

FUJII, M.

IKEDA, T., Polymer Chemistry and Photochemistry

ISHIDA, M., Chemical Engineering and Chemical Environmental Process Design

IWAMOTO, M., Heterogeneous Catalysis

IYODA, T., Functional Molecular Materials, Nano-structured Materials, Materials Electrochemistry

NAKA, Y., Process Systems Engineering

OSAKADA, K., Coordination and Organometallic Chemistry

SHODA, M., Biochemical Engineering, Applied Microbiology

TANAKA, M., Industrial Organic Chemistry

YAMAMOTO, T., Inorganic and Organometallic Chemistry

YAMASE, T., Photochemistry and Photoelectrochemistry

YOSHIDA, M., Biochemistry

Materials and Structures Laboratory:

ATAKE, T., Materials Science, Physical Chemistry

HAYASHI, S., Structural Engineering

ITOH, M., Physical Properties of Inorganic Materials

KASAI, K., Structural Engineering, Earthquake Engineering

KONDO, K., Inorganic Materials and Properties, Applied Physics of Property and Crystallography

SASAKI, S., Synchotron Radiation Science, X-Ray Crystallography, Solid-State Physics

TANAKA, K., Inorganic Materials and Properties, Building Materials

WAKAI, F., Inorganic Materials and Properties

YAMAUCHI, H., Materials Science, Applied Physics of Property and Crystallography, Strongly Correlated Electron Materials, Superconducting Oxides

YASUDA, E., Ceramic Base Composites, Carbon Alloys and Materials

YOSHIMURA, M., Inorganic Materials and Properties, Soft Processing, Advanced Ceramics

Precision and Intelligence Laboratory:

HATSUZAWA, T., Precise Measurement

HIGO, Y., Physical Metallurgy, Nondestructive Evaluation

HORIE, M., Kinematics of Machinery

HOUJOH, H., Acoustic Measurement, Machine Dynamics

KAGAWA, T., Process Control

KOBAYASHI, K., Opto-electronics, Optical Communications, Photonic Integrated Semiconductor Devices

KOYAMA, F., Optical Semiconductor Devices

MASU, K., Advanced Microdevices

OHTSUKI, S., Bio-medical Ultrasonics, Acoustic Engineering

SATO, M., Pattern Recognition Image Processing

SHINNO, H., Ultraprecision Machining, Machine Tool Engineering

SIMOKOBE, A., Dynamics and Control of Precision Mechanisms

UEHA, S., Ultrasonic Engineering, Applied Optics

WAKASHIMA, K., Materials Science, Micromechanics of Composites

WATANABE, S., Mathematics and Information Science

YOKOTA, S., Fluid Power Control

Research Laboratory for Nuclear Reactors:

ARITOMI, M., Nuclear Thermal Engineering

FUJII, Y., Fusion Fuel Chemistry, Tritium Chemistry

HATTORI, T., Accelerator Physics, Heavy Ion Inertial Fusion

KATO, Y., Advanced Nuclear Reactor Systems Design, Complex Flow Computer Simulation

NINOKATA, H., Reactor Safety, Reactor Physics

OGAWA, M., Beam Plasma Sciences, Nuclear Fusion, Nuclear Physics

SEKIMOTO, H., Neutronics, Nuclear Reactor Design

SHIMADA, R., Fusion Reactor Control, Plasma Engineering

TORII, H., Energy Policy

YANO, T., Composite Materials and their Properties

YOSHIZAWA, Y., Thermal Engineering, Energy System, Combustion

TOKYO MEDICAL AND DENTAL UNIVERSITY

5-45, Yushima 1-chome, Bunkyo-ku, Tokyo 113

Telephone: (3) 3813-6111

E-mail: webmaster.isc@tmd.ac.jp

Internet: www.tmd.ac.jp

Founded 1946

Independent

Academic year: April to March (2 semesters)

Pres.: AKIO SUZUKI

Dir-Gen.: O. KIKUKAWA

Dir for Univ. Library: KEIICHI OHYA

Library of 334,132 vols

Number of teachers: 696

Number of students: 2,921

Publications: *Bulletin, Bulletin of the Department of General Education, Reports of the Medical Research Institute, Reports of the*

Institute for Medical and Dental Engineering

DEANS

College of Liberal Arts and Sciences: SAKUMI ITABASHI

Faculty of Dentistry: KAZUHIRO ETO

Faculty of Medicine: KATSUIKU HIROKAWA

Graduate School of Allied Health Sciences: RYUICHI KAMIYAMA

ATTACHED INSTITUTES

Institute for Medical and Dental Engineering: 3-10, Kandasurugadai 2-chome, Chiyoda-ku, Tokyo 101; Dir T. TOGAWA.

Medical Research Institute: 3-10, Kandasurugadai 2-chome, Chiyoda-ku, Tokyo 101; Dir A. SAKUMA.

TOKYO NATIONAL UNIVERSITY OF FINE ARTS AND MUSIC

12-8 Ueno Park, Taito-ku, Tokyo 110-8714

Telephone: (3) 5685-7500

Fax: (3) 5685-7760

Internet: www.geidai.ac.jp

Founded 1949

Pres.: IKUO HIRAYAMA

Dir of Univ. Library: HIROMICHI UENO

Sec.-Gen.: YOSHIYUKI OTAWA

Library: see Libraries and Archives

Number of teachers: 218 full-time

Number of students: 2,785

DEANS

Faculty of Fine Arts: KIJO ROKKAKU

Faculty of Music: AKIO SONODA

DIRECTORS

Media Art Center: TAKAMICHI ITO

Performing Arts Center: TERUO SANBAYASHI

Training centre for Foreign Languages and Declamation: SHUN'ICHIRO HATA

University Art Museum: JUNICHI TAKEUCHI

UNIVERSITY OF TOKYO

7-3-1 Hongo, Bunkyo-ku, Tokyo 113-8654

Telephone: (3) 3812-2111

Fax: (3) 5689-7344

E-mail: kokusai@ml.adm.u-tokyo.ac.jp

Internet: www.u-tokyo.ac.jp

Founded 1877

Independent

Academic year: April to March

Pres.: HIROSHI KOMIYAMA

Univ. Librarian: KAZUHIKO SAIGO

Library: see Libraries and Archives

Number of teachers: 4,165

Number of students: 28,386

DEANS

Graduate School of Agricultural and Life Sciences and Faculty of Agriculture: KATSUMI AIDA

Graduate School of Arts and Sciences and College of Arts and Sciences: Y. KIBATA

Graduate School of Economics and Faculty of Economics: N. JINNO

Graduate School of Education and Faculty of Education: M. SATOH

Graduate School of Engineering and Faculty of Engineering: K. HIRAO

Graduate School of Frontier Sciences: MICHIKATA KONO

Graduate School of Humanities and Sociology and Faculty of Letters: TAKESHI INAGAMI

Graduate School of Information Science and Technology: M. TAKEICHI

Graduate School for Law and Politics: H. TAKAHASHI

Graduate School of Mathematical Sciences: J. SATSUMA

Graduate School of Medicine and Faculty of Medicine: NOBUTAKA HIROKAWA

Graduate School of Pharmaceutical Sciences and Faculty of Pharmaceutical Sciences: Y. EBIZUKA

Graduate School of Public Policy: A. MORITA

Graduate School of Science and Faculty of Science: Y. IWASAWA

Interfaculty Initiative in Information Studies and Graduate School of Interdisciplinary Information Studies: T. HANADA

PROFESSORS

Graduate School of Agricultural and Life Sciences and Faculty of Agriculture (1-1-1 Yayoi, Bunkyo-ku, Tokyo 113-8657; tel. (3) 5841-5486; fax (3) 5841-8122; e-mail oice@ofc.a.u-tokyo.ac.jp; internet www.a.u-tokyo.ac.jp/english/index.html):

ABE, H., Biochemistry of Aquatic Animals

ABE, K., Biological Function Development

AIDA, K., Fish Physiology

AKASHI, H., Veterinary Microbiology

ANDO, N., Wood-based Materials and Timber Engineering

AOKI, I., Fisheries Biology

CHIDA, K., Cell Regulation

DOI, K., Veterinary Pathology

FUKUDA, K., Biological Function Development

FUKUI, Y., Biological Chemistry

FUKUYO, Y., Aquatic Biology

FURUYA, K., Fisheries Oceanography

HAYASHI, Y., Veterinary Anatomy

HIGUCHI, H., Wildlife Biology

HINO, A., Aquaculture Biology

HOGETSU, T., Plant Physiology and Plant Ecology, Silviculture

HONMA, M., Economics

HORI, S., Landscape and Sustainable Tourism

HORINOUCHI, S., Microbiology and Fermentation

IDE, Y., Forestry Gene Science

IGARASHI, Y., Applied Microbiology

INOUE, M., Forest Policy

ISOGAI, A., Pulp and Paper Sciences

ITOH, K., Veterinary Public Health

IWAMOTO, N., Agricultural History and History of Agricultural Sciences

IZUMIDA, Y., International Food System

KISHINO, H., Biometrics and Statistical Genetics

KITAHARA, T., Organic Chemistry

KOBAYASHI, H., Forest Utilization

KOBAYASHI, K., Agricultural Ecosystems

KUGA, S., Structural Biopolymers

KUMAGAI, S., Veterinary Public Health

KUMAGAI, Y., Evaluation of the Natural Environment

KURATA, K., Bio-environmental Engineering

KUROHMARU, M., Veterinary Anatomy

KUROKURA, H., Aquatic Biology

MASAKI, H., Molecular and Cellular Breeding

MATSUNAGA, S., Aquatic Natural Products Chemistry

MESHITSUKA, G., Wood Chemistry and Pulping Chemistry

MIYAZAKI, T., Soil Physics and Soil Hydrology

MORI, Y., Veterinary Ethology

NAGASAWA, H., Bio-organic Chemistry

NAGATA, S., Forest Ecology and Society

NAGATO, Y., Plant Breeding and Genetics

NAKANISHI, T. M., Radio–Plant Psychology

NANBA, S., Bioresource Technology

NISHIHATA, M., Veterinary Physiology

NISHIYAMA, M., Cell Biotechnology

NISHIZAWA, N. K., Plant Nutrition and Biotechnology

OGAWA, H., Veterinary Emergency Medicine

OGAWA, K., Fish Pathology

OHSHITA, S., Bioprocess Engineering
OHSUGI, R., Crop Physiology
OHTA, A., Cellular Genetics
OHTA, M., Wood-based Materials and Timber Engineering, Wood Physics
OMASA, K., Biological and Environmental Information Engineering
ONO, H., Polymeric Materials
ONO, K., Veterinary Clinical Pathobiology
ONODERA, T., Molecular Immunology
OYAIZU, H., Soil Science
OZAKI, H., Veterinary Pharmacology
SAGARA, Y., Food Informatics and Engineering
SAKAI, H., Forest Utilization
SAKAI, S., Animal Breeding
SAMEJIMA, M., Forest Chemistry
SASAKI, N., Veterinary Surgery
SATO, R., Food Chemistry
SENOO, K., Soil Microbiology
SHIMADA, T., Insect Genetics and Bioscience
SHIMIZU, K., Bioinformation Engineering
SHIMIZU, M., Food Chemistry
SHIMOMURA, A., Forest Landscape Planning and Design
SHIOTA, K., Cellular Biochemistry
SHIOZAWA, S., Physical Planning and Environmental Engineering
SHIRAISHI, N., Forest Management
SHIRAKO, Y., RNA Virology
SHOGENJI, S., Food and Resource Economics
SHOUN, H., Enzymology and Applied Microbiology
SUGIYAMA, N., Horticultural Science
SUZUKI, M., Forest Hydrology and Erosion Control
TAKAHASHI, N., Nutritional Biochemistry
TAKEUCHI, K., Landscape Ecology and Planning
TANAKA, T., Water Environmental Engineering
TANGE, T., Forest Ecophysiology
TANIGUCHI, N., Agricultural Structure and Policy
TANOKURA, M., Food Engineering
TATSUKI, S., Applied Entomology
TOJO, H., Applied Genetics
TSUBONE, H., Comparative Pathophysiology
TSUJIMOTO, H., Veterinary Internal Medicine
TSUTSUMI, N., Plant Molecular Genetics
WASHITANI, I., Conservation Ecology
WATABE, S., Aquatic Molecular Biology and Technology
WATANABE, H., Organic Chemistry
YAGI, H., Farm Business Management
YAMAGUCHI, I., Pesticide and Natural Products Chemistry
YAMAGUCHI-SHINOZAKI, L., Plant Molecular Biology
YAMAMOTO, H., Forest Planning
YAMANE, H., Environmental Biochemistry
YATAGAI, M., Plant Material Sciences
YODA, K., Microbiology Biotechnology
YOKOYAMA, S., Biomass Energy Conversion Technology
YONEYAMA, T., Plant Nutrition and Fertilizers
YOSHIKAWA, Y., Laboratory Animal Science
YOSHIMURA, E., Plant Molecular Physiology

Graduate School of Arts and Sciences and College of Arts and Sciences (3-8-1 Komaba, Meguro-ku, Tokyo 153-8902; tel. (3) 5454-6827; fax (3) 5454-4319; e-mail info-komaba@ adm.c.u-tokyo.ac.jp; internet www.c.u.-tokyo .ac.jp):

ADACHI, H., History of Japanese Technology
ADACHI, N., Area Studies
AIZAWA, T., German, German History
AOKI, M., German
ARAI, Y., Human Geography

ARAMAKI, K., International Finance
ASASHIMA, M., Developmental Biology
ATOMI, Y., Sports Sciences
BOCCELLARI, J., English, Comparative Literature
ELLIS, T., Japanese as a Foreign Language
ENDO, Y., American Studies
ENDO, Y., Physical Chemistry
ERIGUCHI, Y., Astrophysics
FUKAGAWA, Y., Development Studies, Korean Studies
FUNABIKI, T., Cultural Anthropology
GOTO, N., Environmental Economics
HASEGAWA, T., Behavioural Ecology
HAYAKAMA, S., Law
HAYASHI, F., American Literature
HIKAMI, S., Statistical Physics
HIROMATSU, T., Statistics
HYODO, T., Physics
IKEDA, N., German
IKEGAMI, S., European Medieval History
IKEUCHI, M., Biology
IMAI, T., Philosophy
ISHIDA, A., International Relations
ISHIDA, Y., German History, Comparative Genocide Studies
ISHII, A., International Relations
ISHII, N., Sports Sciences
ISHII, Y., French
ISHIMITSU, Y., German Literature
ISHIURA, S., Neuroscience
ISOZAKI, Y., Earth Science
ITO, A., Cultural Anthropology
ITOH, T., English
IWASA, T., French, Contemporary Art
IWASAWA, Y., International Law
KADOWAKI, S., Philosophy
KAGOSHIMA, S., Solid-State Physics
KAJI, T., German
KANEKO, K., Nonlinear Physics, Statistical Physics
KARIMA, F., Chinese
KATO, M., Architectural Composition Theory
KAWAI, S., Graphics
KAWANAGO, Y., German, History of Christian Thought
KAWATO, S., Biophysics
KAZAMA, Y., Theory of Elementary Particles
KIBATA, Y., English, British History
KIMURA, H., Anthropology
KITAGAWA, S., Philosophy
KOBAYASHI, K., Sports Sciences
KOBAYASHI, Y., French, Modern Thought
KODA, H., German
KOJIMA, N., Chemistry
KOJO, Y., Political Science
KOMAKI, K., Radiation Physics
KOMIYAMA, S., Theory of Solid-State Physics
KOMORI, Y., Japanese Literature
KONDOH, A., Japanese
KONOSHI, T., Japanese Literature
KOTERA, A., International Law
KUBOTA, S., Sports Science
KUGA, T., Quantum Electronics, Quantum Optics
KURODA, R., Biochemistry of DNA
KUROZUMI, M., Ethics, Japanese Intellectual History
LAMARRE, C., Linguistic Analysis
MABUCHI, I., Biochemistry and Biophysics
MARUYAMA, M., Economics
MASUDA, K., French, French Philosophy
MASUDA, S., Chemistry
MATSUBARA, R., Economic Thought, Social Economics
MATSUI, T., Theoretical Nuclear Physics
MATSUO, M., Environmental and Analytical Chemistry
MATSUOKA, S., Japanese Literature
MATSUURA, H., Multimedia Analysis
MISUMI, Y., Japanese Literature
MITANI, H., Japanese History
MIYAMOTO, H., Philosophy

MIYASHITA, S., French
MORI, M., Political and Social Philosophy
MOTOMURA, R., European History
MURATA, J., Philosophy
MURATA, M., Cell Biology and Biophysics
MURATA, Y., China Studies
NAGATA, T., Physical Chemistry
NAKAI, K., International Relations
NAKANISHI, T., Economics
NAKAZAWA, H., Crosscultural Communication
NAMIKI, Y., Chinese History
NISHINAKAMURA, H., Russian
NIWA, K., Research Management
NOMURA, T., Japanese
NOTOJI, M., American Literature
OE, H., International Relations, Human Security
OGOSHI, N., Korean
OHTA, K., Theoretical Nuclear Physics
OKA, H., English
OKABE, Y., German, Comparative Literature
OKOSHI, Y., Criminal Law
ONAKA, M., Catalysis Chemistry
ONUKI, T., Hellenistic and Early Christian Literature
OTSUKI, T., Sports Sciences
ROSSITTER, P., English
SAKAHARA, S., French
SAKAI, T., Political Science
SASAKI, C., History and Philosophy of Science
SATO, N., Plant Biology
SATO, Y., English, American Literature
SATO, Y., Law, Dispute Processing, Peace Building
SATOMI, D., Biology
SHIBA, N., Serbo-Croat, History
SHIBATA, T., History of Political Thought
SHIGEMASU, K., Bayesian Statistics
SHIMADA, M., Population and Evolutionary Ecology
SHIMOI, M., Inorganic Chemistry, Coordination Chemistry
SHIROTA, T., Chinese Literature
SUGAWARA, K., English
SUGAWARA, T., Physical Organic Chemistry
SUGIHASHI, Y., German, Literature and Aesthetics
SUGITA, H., Arabic
SUTOH, K., Molecular Cell Biology
SUYAMA, A., Biophysics
SUZUKI, H., English and Music
SUZUKI, K., French
SUZUKI, K., Graphics
TAJIRI, M., German
TAKADA, Y., English Literature
TAKAHASHI, H., History
TAKAHASHI, N., Political Science
TAKAHASHI, S., German Literature
TAKAHASHI, T., Philosophy
TAKATSUKA, K., Theoretical Molecular Science
TAKEUCHI, N., French, Comparative Literature
TAKITA, Y., English
TAMAI, T., Software Engineering
TANIUCHI, T., Human Geography
TANJI, A., English Literature
TOMODA, S., Organic Chemistry
TSUNEKAWA, K., Political Science
UCHIDA, R., Contemporary Society
UEDA, H., Spanish
URA, M., Russian Literature
USUI, R., German
WAKABAYASHI, M., Chinese, Modern History of East Asia
WILSON, B., English
YAMADA, H., French Literature, Psychoanalytic Criticism
YAMAKAGE, S., International Relations
YAMAMOTO, S., English
YAMAMOTO, T., Philosophy
YAMAMOTO, Y., Culture and Social Change
YAMASHITA, S., Cultural Anthropology

YAMAUCHI, M., Asian History
YAMAWAKI, N., History of Social Thought
YAMAZAKI, Y., Atomic Physics
YONEYA, T., Theoretical Physics
YOSHIE, A., Japanese History
YOSHIOKA, D., Theory of Solid-State Physics
YUASA, H., French
YUI, D., American and International History

Graduate School of Economics and Faculty of Economics (7-3-1 Hongo, Bunkyo-ku, Tokyo 113-0033; tel. (3) 5841-5543; fax (3) 5841-5521; e-mail advisefs@e.u-tokyo.ac.jp; internet www.e.u-tokyo.ac.jp):

ABE, M., Marketing
ARAI, T., Corporate Finance, Securities Investment
BABA, S., Economic History of the Western World, History of Industrialization and Urbanization in Germany
DAIGO, S., Financial Accounting
FUJIMOTO, T., Technology and Operations Management
FUJIWARA, M., Applied Microeconomics
FUKUDA, S., Money and Banking, Macroeconomics
HANNAH, L., Comparative Business History
HAYASHI, F., Applied Econometrics, Macroeconomics
HIROTA, I., Economic History of Modern France
ICHIMURA, H.
IHORI, T., Public Finance and Economics
ITO, T., International Finance, Finance and Macroeconomics
ITOH, MASANAO, Japanese Economy, Financial History in Japan
ITOH, MOTOSHIGE, International Economics
IWAI, K., Economic Theory
IWAMI, T., International Economics
IWAMOTO, Y., Public Economics, Macroeconomics
JINNO, N., Public Finance
KAMIYA, K., Microeconomics, Mathematical Programming
KANDORI, M., Microeconomic Theory, Game Theory
KANEMOTO, Y., Urban Economics
KOBAYASHI, T., Theory of Investments and Capital Markets
KUBOKAWA, T., Mathematical Statistics
KUNITOMO, N., Statistics, Econometrics and Financial Econometrics
MATSUI, A., Game Theory, Information Economics, Monetary Theory
MATSUSHIMA, H., Microeconomics, Game Theory, Theory of Finance, Informational Economics
MIWA, Y., Economics of Regulations, Corporate Governance, Law and Economics
MOCHIDA, N., Public Finance, Intergovernmental Fiscal Relations
MORI, T., Industrial Relations
OBATA, M., Economic Theory
OKAZAKI, T., Japanese Economic History
OKUDA, H., Russian Economic History
ONOZUKA, T., Economic History of the Western World
SAGUCHI, K., Industrial Relations
SHIBATA, T., Modern Capitalism, Institutional Economics
TABUCHI, T., Urban Economics
TAKAHASHI, N., Organization Theory
TAKEDA, H., Japanese Economic History
TAKENOUCHI, M., International Economics
UEDA, K., Macroeconomics, Financial Theory, Theory of International Finance
WADA, K., Comparative Business History
YAJIMA, Y., Statistics and Econometrics
YOSHIKAWA, H., Macroeconomics

Graduate School of Humanities and Sociology and Faculty of Letters (7-3-1 Hongo, Bunkyo-ku, Tokyo 113-0033; tel. (3) 5841-3705; fax (3) 5841-3817; e-mail shomu@l.u-tokyo.ac.jp; internet www.l.u-tokyo.ac.jp):

AKIYAMA, H., Social Psychology of Ageing
AMANO, M., Philosophy
FUJII, S., Modern Chinese Literature
FUJITA, K., Aesthetics
FUJITA, S., Early Modern Japanese History
FUJIWARA, K., Japanese Literature of Heian Era
FUKASAWA, K., History of Early Modern Europe
GOMI, F., Medieval Japanese History
GOTO, T., Japanese Archaeology
HASEMI, K., Russian and Polish Literature
HATTORI, T., Korean Studies (Sociology)
HAYASI, T., Turkic Languages
HIRAISHI, T., American Literature
HIRANO, Y., German Language and Literature
ICHIKAWA, H., History of Religion, the Bible and Judaism
IKEDA, K., Political Behaviour and Communication, Social Reality and Mediated Communication
IMAMURA, K., Japanese and Asian Archaeology
IMANISHI, N., English Linguistics and Syntax Theory
ISHII, N., History of Modern Europe
ITUMI, K., Classical Languages and Literature
KANAZAWA, M., Russian Literature
KANNO, K., Japanese Ethical Thoughts
KATAYAMA, H., Classical Languages and Literature
KAWAHARA, H., History of the Science of Chance
KIMURA, H., Chinese Language
KINOSHITA, N., Cultural Resource Studies
KISHIMOTO, M., Chinese History
KOJIMA, T., Medieval Japanese Literature
KOMATSU, H., Central Asian History
KONDO, K., History of Modern Europe
KONO, M., History of Japanese Art
KUMAMOTO, H., Indo-European Linguistics
MARUI, H., Indian Philosophy
MATSUMOTO, M., Sociology of Science and Technology, Environmental Sociology
MATSUMURA, K., Uralic Linguistics
MATSUNAGA, S., Philosophy
MATSUURA, J., German Language
MIZUSHIMA, T., South Asian History
MURAI, S., Medieval Japanese History
NAGAMI, S., Italian Language and Literature
NAGASHIMA, H., Early Modern Japanese Literature
NAKAJI, Y., French Language and Literature
NISHIMURA, K., Aesthetics
NITAGAI, K., Urban Sociology
NUMANO, M., Russian and Polish Literature
OHASI, Y., English Literature
ONUKI, S., East Asian Archaeology
OSANO, S., History of Western Art
SAITO, A., Indian Philosophy
SAKURAI, M., Ancient Greek History
SAKURAI, Y., Southeast Asian History
SATO, M., Ancient Japanese History
SATO, S., Intellectual History of Modern China
SATO, T., Visual Perception
SATO, Y., Ethics and Social Thought
SATO, Y., History of Japanese Art
SEIYAMA, K., Mathematical Sociology
SEKINE, S., Occidental Ethical Thought
SHIBATA, M., American Literature
SHIGETO, M., German Linguistics
SHIMAZONO, S., Japanese Religious Thought
SHIOKAWA, T., French Language and Literature
SHITOMI, Y., West Asian History
SUEKI, F., Japanese Buddhism

SUZUKI, T., Japanese Language
TACHIBANA, M., Visual Neuroscience
TADA, K., Ancient Japanese Literature
TAKAHASHI, K., English Literature
TAKAHASHI, T., Dravidian Language and Literature
TAKANO, Y., Cognitive Psychology
TAKAYAMA, H., Medieval European History
TAKAYAMA, M., Philosophy
TAKEGAWA, S., Sociology of Social Policy
TAKESHITA, M., Islamic Studies
TAKEUCHI, S., Japanese Ethical Thought
TAMURA, T., French Language and Literature
TOKURA, H., Chinese Literature
TSUCHIDA, R., Sanskrit Language and Literature
TSUKIMURA, T., French Language and Literature
TSUNODA, T., Australian Aboriginal Linguistics
TSURUOKA, Y., Christian Mysticism
UENO, C., Family and Gender Studies
UTAGAWA, H., East Asian Archaeology
UWANO, Z., Accentology and Dialectology
WATANABE, H., Aesthetics
YAMAGUCHI, S., Experimental Social Psychology
YOSHIDA, M., Korean History
YOSHIDA, N., Early Modern Japanese History

Graduate School of Education and Faculty of Education (7-3-1 Hongo, Bunkyo-ku, Tokyo 113-0033; tel. (3) 5841-3904; fax (3) 5841-3914; e-mail edushomu@p.u-tokyo.ac.jp; internet www.p.u-tokyo.ac.jp/index-j.html):

AKITA, K., Action Research on Training
ETO, T., Health Education
HAEBARA, T., Educational Measurement
HIJIKATA, S., History of Japanese Education
HIROTA, T., Sociology of Education
ICHIKAWA, S., Cognitive Psychology
KAMEGUCHI, K., Clinical Psychology
KANAMORI, O., Methods of Education
KANEKO, M., Higher Education
KARIYA, T., Sociology of Education
KAWAMOTO, T., History of Western Education
MUTOH, Y., Physical Education
NAKADA, M., Methods of Education
NEMOTO, A., Library and Information Science
OGAWA, M., Educational Administration
SASAKI, M., Methods of Education
SATOH, K., Lifelong Learning
SATOH, M., Action Research on Teaching
SHIMOYAMA, H., Clinical Psychology
SHIOMI, T., Science of Education
SHIRAISHI, S., Anthropology of Education
TANAKA, C., Clinical Psychology
WATANABE, H., Educational Measurement
YAMAMOTO, Y., Physiology of Education
YANO, M., Higher Education

Graduate School of Engineering and Faculty of Engineering (7-3-1 Hongo, Bunkyo-ku, Tokyo 113-8656; tel. (3) 5841-7662; fax (3) 5841-7446; e-mail octo@t-adm.t.u-tokyo.ac.jp; internet www.t.u-tokyo.ac.jp):

AIDA, T., Macromolecular Chemistry, Supramolecular Chemistry, Bioinorganic Chemistry
AOKI, T., Aerospace Structures, Mechanics of Composite Materials, Smart Structures
ARAI, T., Automatic Assembly, Robotics, Artificial Intelligence and Service Engineering
ARAKAWA, Y., Electric Propulsion
DOI, M., Soft Matter Physics, Polymer Physics, Rheology
DOMEN, K., Heterogeneous Catalysis
FUJIMOTO, K., Deformation and Fracture of Solids, Tribology

FUJINO, Y., Structural Engineering, Dynamics, Control and Monitoring of Structures and Bridges, Wind and Earthquake

FUJITA, M., Organic Coordination Chemistry

FUJITA, T., Mineral and Material Processing, Recycling Technology, Intelligent Fluid

FUJIWARA, T., Solid-State Physics, Electronic Structure in Condensed Matter

FURUMAI, H., Urban Drainage and Water Quality Management

FURUTA, K., Cognitive Systems Engineering, Technology for Safe and Secure Society

GONOKAMI, M., Non-linear Optics, Quantum Optics, Quantum Electronics, Optical Processes in Solids

HANAKI, K., Urban and Global Environmental Management, Urban Environment Systems

HARATA, N., Urban Transport Planning

HASHIMOTO, K., Intelligent Materials

HASHIMOTO, T., Science and Technology Studies

HIDAKA, K., High Voltage Engineering, Electrical Insulation, Electrical Discharge and Plasma Physics

HIGUCHI, T., Mechatronics, Micro Electromechanical Systems

HIRAO, K., Theoretical Chemistry and Electronic Structure Theory

HORI, K., Artificial Intelligence

HORII, H., Sociotechnology, Rock Mechanics, Applied Mechanics

HOTATE, K., Photonic Sensing, Photonic Signal Processing, Optical Devices

ICHIKAWA, M., Semiconductor Nano-science and Technology

IEDA, H., Transport and City Planning

IIZUKA, Y., Systems Analysis and Design, Structured Knowledge Engineering, Health Care Social System Engineering

IKUHARA, Y., Interface and Grain Boundary Engineering

ISHIHARA, K., Biomaterials

ISHIHARA, S., Nanomechanics, Nanofabrication

ITO, T., Urban and Architectural History

KAGEYAMA, K., Composite Materials Engineering, Smart Material and Structure Systems

KAMATA, M., Equipment and Environmental Engineering

KAMATA, M., Noise and Vibration Control, Vehicle Engineering, Assistive Technology

KANEKO, S., Flow-induced Vibration, Vibration Control, Micro Gas Turbine Engineering

KANNO, M., Metallic Materials

KANODA, K., Experimental Physics of Low-dimensional Correlated Electronic Systems

KASAGI, N., Thermal and Fluids Engineering, Energy Systems Engineering, Turbulence Engineering

KATAOKA, K., Biomaterials and Drug Delivery Systems

KATO, T., Materials Chemistry, Polymer Chemistry, Supramolecular Chemistry

KATO, T., Surface Engineering, Tribology, Nanotribology

KATSUMURA, Y., Radiation Chemistry, Applied Radiation Chemistry

KAWACHI, K., Flight Dynamics, Biokinetics, Helicopter Engineering

KIMURA, F., Design Engineering, CAD/CAM, Manufacturing Systems, Computer-aided Technology in Manufacturing Engineering

KISHIO, K., Solid-State Chemistry, Ionic and Electronic Transport in Solids, Superconductivity

KITAMORI, T., Integration of Micro Chemical Systems, Micro Space Chemistry

KOBAYASHI, I., Environmental Information Network, Light Communications

KOIDE, O., Evaluation of Regional Risks and Multimedia Database System for Historical Disasters

KOIKE, T., Hydrology and Water Resources, Remote Sensing

KOMIYAMA, H., Global Environmental Engineering, Materials Science and Engineering

KOSAKO, T., Radiation Safety, Radiation shielding, radiation Dosimetry

KOSEKI, T., Metals and Alloys

KOSHI, M., Chemical Reaction Kinetics, Laser-induced Chemistry

KOSHIZUKA, S., Computational Fluid Dynamics

KUBO, T., Structural and Earthquake Engineering, Reinforced Concrete Structures

KUWAMURA, H., Structural Engineering, Steel Structures, Welding Mechanics, Reliability Analysis and New Materials

MABUCHI, K., Advanced Biomedical Engineering and Life Sciences

MADARAME, H., Nuclear Safety

MAEDA, K., Defects in Solids, Nanoscopic Analysis

MAEKAWA, K., Concrete Engineering, Modelling of Concrete Performance

MARUYAMA, S., Science and Technology of Carbon Nanotubes, Nanoscale Thermal Engineering

MATSUMOTO, Y., Fluid Engineering, Molecular Dynamics

MATSUSHIMA, K., Business and Innovation Modelling

MITSUISHI, M., Intelligent Manufacturing Systems, Network-based Manufacturing Systems, Active Thermal Compensation for High-speed Machine Tools

MIYATA, H., Computational Fluid Dynamics, Systems Design, Technology Management

MIZUNO, N., Catalytic Chemistry, Inorganic Chemistry

MOHRI, N., Manufacturing Systems Control, Precision Machining

MORISHITA, E., High-speed Gas Dynamics

NAGAMUNE, T., Biotechnology, Biochemical Engineering, Protein Engineering

NAGAOSA, N., Condensed Matter Theory, Superconductivity

NAGASAKI, S., Safety Research on the Nuclear Fuel Cycle

NAGASAWA, Y., Architectural Planning and Design

NAGASHIMA, T., Aerospace Propulsion

NAGASUKA, S., Space Engineering

NAITO, H., Architectural Design, Landscape Design

NAKAO, M., Nano-micro Manufacturing, Information Instrument Design, Mechanical Engineering for Science

NAKAO, S., Membrane Science and Technology

NAKAZAWA, M., Radiation Measurement, Quantum Beam Engineering

NAMBA, K., Sustainable Design in Architecture and Urban Space

NAWATA, K., Econometrics, Statistics

NISHIMURA, Y., Urban Conservation Planning, Urban Design

NITTA, T., Applied Superconductivity, Electrical Machinery, Power Systems

NOZAKI, K., Organometallic Chemistry, Homogeneous Catalysis

ODA, T., Electrostatics, Plasma Application for Environmental Protection and Magnetic Separation

OHASHI, H., Thermal Hydrodynamics, Advanced Models for Complex Phenomena

OHBA, Z., Education Systems Project

OHGAKI, S., Environmental Engineering

OHTSU, M., Nanophotonics

OKA, Y., Nuclear Reactor Design and Analysis

OKABE, A., Urban and Regional Analysis, Geographical Information Science

OKABE, Y., Information Devices, Superconductive Electronics, Brain Computer

OKAMOTO, K., Visualization, Micro-,Nano- and Biofluids

OKATA, J., Urban Planning

OKUBO, S., Mining Machinery, Rock Mechanics

OKUDA, H., Computational Mechanics, Digital Value Engineering

OSHIMA, M., Semiconductor Surface Chemistry, Synchrotron Radiation Science

OZAWA, K., Construction, Project and Infrastructure Management

RINOIE, K., Aircraft Design, Separated Flow Aerodynamics

ROKUGAWA, S., Exploration Geophysics, Earth Observing Systems

SAKAI, S., Strength of Materials, Life Cycle Assessment, Fracture Mechanics

SAKAMOTO, I., Building Construction, Timber Structures

SAKAMOTO, Y., Environmental Control Engineering, Air Conditioning

SATO, K., Petroleum Engineering

SATO, S., Coastal and Environmental Engineering

SEKIMURA, N., Maintenance Engineering, Nuclear Materials, Effects of Radiation on Materials

SHIBATA, T., Semiconductor Devices and Integrated Circuits, Integrated Human Intelligence Systems

SHIMIZU, E., Geoinformatics, Regional Planning

SHINOHARA, O., Landscape Planning and Civic Design

SHIOYA, T., Aerospace Materials, Mechanical Behaviour of Materials

SUGA, T., Microsystem Integration and Packaging, Eco-design

SUZUKI, H., Computer-aided Design and Manufacture, Geometric Modelling

SUZUKI, H., History of Architecture, History of Modern Architecture

SUZUKI, H., Structural Engineering, Ocean Engineering

SUZUKI, S., Flight Mechanics, Control Engineering

SUZUKI, T., Systems Engineering in Materials Science

TAIRA, K., RNA as Origin of Life and RNA Technology

TAKADA, T., Structural Reliability, Earthquake Engineering, Computational Mechanics, Risk Analysis, Decision Theory

TAKAHASHI, H., Digital Signal Processing

TAKAMASU, K., Precision Metrology, Nanometer Measurement, Coordinate Metrology

TAMAKI, K., Marine Geology

TANAKA, M., Materials and Device Physics, Spintronics

TANAKA, S., Fusion Engineering, Nuclear Waste Management

TARUCHA, S., Electronic Properties of Semiconductor Nanostructures

TERAI, T., Materials Science for Nuclear Systems, Fusion Reactor Engineering, Synthesis and Property Control of Advanced Materials by High-energy Particle Processing

TOKURA, Y., Materials Physics

TORIUMI, A., Advanced Devices Engineering

TOWHATA, I., Geotechnical Engineering

UEDA, T., Cost-Benefit Analysis, Infrastructure Economics

UESAKA, M., Quantum Beam Engineering and Applied Electro-Magnetics

WADA, K., Microphotonics

WASHIZU, M., Bio-nanotechnology

WATANABE, S., Computational Engineering of Nanomaterials

YAGI, O., Applied Microbiology

YAMADA, I., Lifestyle and Environmental Information Technology, Network Sensing, Telecommunication Energy Systems

YAMAGUCHI, H., Polar Environment Engineering, Cavitation

YAMAGUCHI, S., Solid-State Ionics

YAMAGUCHI, Y., Nanomaterials Technology, Chemical System Engineering

YAMAJI, K., Energy Systems Engineering

YAMASHITA, K., Theoretical Chemistry and Chemical Reaction Dynamics, Computational Molecular Engineering

YAMATOMI, J., Rock Engineering and Mining Engineering

YOKOYAMA, A., Power Systems Engineering, Control Engineering

YOSHIDA, M., Education Systems Project

YOSHIDA, T., Plasma Materials Engineering

YUHARA, T., Energy Engineering and Policy, Engineering for Naval Architecture and Ocean Engineering, Management of Engineering Projects

Graduate School of Frontier Sciences (5-1-5 Kashiwanoha, Kashiwa-shi, Chiba 277-8562; tel. (4) 7136-5506; fax (4) 7136-4021; e-mail souiki@k.u-tokyo.ac.jp; internet www.k .u-tokyo.ac.jp):

AIDA, H., High-quality Networking, Parallel and Distributed Processing

AIZAWA, K., Image Processing, Multimedia Technologies

AMEMIYA, Y., X-ray Physics and Instrumentation

ASAI, K., Stochastic Models in Bioinformatics

CHIKAYAMA, T., Information Engineering

FUJIMORI, A., Condensed Matter Physics

FUJIWARA, H., Insect Molecular Biology

HAMANO, Y., Content Production

HARATA, N., Urban Transport Planning, Environmental Information Systems in Spatial Planning and Policy

HASEZAWA, S., Plant Cell Biology

HIHARA, E., Refrigeration Engineering, Heat Transfer, Multi-phase Flows

HIROSE, K., Speech Information Processing

HISADA, T., Finite Element Method, Biomechanics

HOSAKA, H., Information Mechatronics and Microdynamics

IBA, H., Evolutionary Computation, Evolutionary Robotics, Genome Informatics

ISOBE, M., Coastal Environment

ITO, K., Polymer Physics

ITO, T., Functional Genomics

IWATA, S., Design Science, Environmental Studies

KAGEMOTO, H., Environmental Hydrodynamics

KAJI, M., Forest Ecology

KANDA, J., Structural Engineering

KATAOKA, H., Biochemistry

KAWAI, M., Surface Science, Nano-Science

KAWANO, S., Molecular Cell Biology

KIMURA, K., Nano-space Function Design, Applied Solid-State Physics

KITOH, S., Environmental Ethics

KOBAYASHI, I., Laboratory of Social Genome Sciences

KOJI, O., Environmental Visualization

KONO, M., Energy Conversion, Aerospace Propulsion

KUMAGAI, Y., Landscape Architecture, Forest Landscape Planning and Design

KUNISHIMA, M., International Infrastructure Development and Management

MATSUHASHI, R., Environment Systems and Economics

MATSUI, T., Comparative Planetology

MINO, T., Water Environment Control, Environmental Biotechnology

MITANI, H., Molecular Genetics, Radiation Biology

MIYAMOTO, Y., Molecular Physiology

MORISHITA, S., Computational Biology, Bioinformatics, Data Mining, Database Systems, Computational Logic

NAGATA, M., Insect Pathology

NAKAYAMA, M., Weather Resources Management and Regional Planning

NAMBA, S., Molecular Plant-microbe Interactions

NISHITA, T., Computer Graphics

OHMORI, H., Natural Environmental Structures

OHNO, H., Living Environmental Design

OHSAWA, M., Plant Ecology

OHYA, Y., Signal Transduction

OKADA, M., Brain Science Information Theory and Physics

ONABE, K., Semiconductor Materials Engineering

SAIGO, K., Synthetic Organic Chemistry, Synthetic Macromolecular Chemistry

SAIKI, K., Surface Science

SAKUMA, I., Biomedical Engineering, Computer-aided Surgery, Precision Engineering

SASAKI, K., Mechatronics, Signal Processing

SHIBATA, T., Semiconductor Electronics

SUGANO, S., Functional Genomics

SUGIURA, S., Cardiology, Physiology of Cardiac Muscle

TAKAGI, H., Solid-State Physics and Chemistry

TAKAGI, S., Semiconductor Device Engineerinf

TAKAGI, T., Computational Biology

TAKAGI, Y., Development Economics

TAKASE, Y., Plasma Physics

TAKEDA, N., Smart Structures and Composite Materials

TAKEDA, T., Brain Science

TORIUMI, M., Petrology, Structural Geology

TORO, S., Ocean Environmental Engineering

TSUJI, S., Environmental Archaeology and Ethnology

TSUJI, T., Biomedical Engineering, Cardiovascular Surgery, Biomaterials

TSUKIHASHI, F., Physical Chemistry of Materials

UEDA, T., Molecular Biology

WADA, H., Magneto-Science and Technology

WATANABE, S., Natural Environment Formation

WATANABE, T., Molecular Oncology, Human Retrovirology

YAMAJI, E., Agro-environmental Engineering

YAMAJI, K., Energy Systems Analysis

YAMAMOTO, H., Information Theory and Cryptology

YAMAMOTO, K., Glycobiology

YAMATO, H., Industrial Information Systems and Environment

YANAGISAWA, Y., Chemical Analysis of Air and Indoor Air Pollution, Systems Analysis of Global Environment

YANAGITA, T., International Monetary Economics

YOSHIDA, T., Transnational Infrastructure Management

YOSHIDA, Z., Plasma Physics and Nonlinear Sciences

YOSHIMURA, S., Simulation and Virtual Environment

Graduate School of Information Science and Technology (7-3-1 Hongo, Bunkyo-ku, Tokyo 113-8656; tel. (3) 5841-7662; fax (3) 5841-7446; e-mail octo@t-adm.t.u-tokyo.ac.jp; internet www.i.u-tokyo.ac.jp):

ANDO, S., Sensors, Measurement, Image Processing

AOYAMA, T., Communication Networks and Systems

DOHI, T., Computer-aided Surgery

ESAKI, H., Computer Networks, Internet Architecture

FUJII, M., Economics and Finance

HAGIYA, M., Formal Verification, Programming Languages, Biocomputing

HARA, S., Control Theory, Learning and Optimization

HARASHIMA, H., Human Communications Engineering

HIRAKI, K., Parallel Processing, Computer Architecture, High Speed Networks

HIROSE, K., Speech Information Processing

HIROSE, M., Virtual Reality, Human Interface

IMAI, H., Alogorithms, Optimization, Complexity, Quantum Computing

ISHIKAWA, M., Robotics, Vision, VLSI, Optics in Computing

ISHIZUKA, M., Artificial Intelligence, Multimodal Lifelike Agents, WWW Intelligence

KANZAKI, R., Neural Mechanisms of Behaviour

MABUCHI, K., Advanced Biomedical Engineering and Life Science

MUROTA, K., Discrete Mathematics

NAKAMURA, Y., Robotics, Mechatronics, Automatic Control

NANYA, T., Dependable Computing and VLSI Design

OKABE, Y., Time Series Analysis and Financial Technology

OTSU, N., Real-world Intelligence, Pattern Recognition

OYANAGI, Y., Numerical Analysis, Parallel Processing

SAGAYAMA, S., Speech Recognition, Signal Processing, Spoken Dialogue System, Music Information Processing

SAKAI, S., Computer Systems and Applications

SATO, T., Intelligent Mechanics Human Machine Systems, Human Cooperative Robotics

SHIMOYAMA, I., Micro Electromechanical Systems, Robotics

SUGIHARA, K., Computational Geometry, Robust Scientific Computation

SUGIHARA, M., Numerical Analysis

TACHI, S., Advanced Robotics, Virtual Reality, Telexistence and Retro-reflective Projection Technology

TAKEICHI, M., Programming Language Theory and its Implementation

TAKEUCHI, I., Real-time Distributed Cooperative Systems

TAKEMURA, A., Statistical Science

YONEZAWA, A., Foundation for Computer Software, Programming Language, Software Security

Graduate School for Law and Politics (7-3-1 Hongo, Bunkyo-ku, Tokyo 113-0033; tel. (3) 5841-3104; fax (3) 5841-3291; e-mail jshomu@j.u-tokyo.ac.jp; internet www.j .u-tokyo.ac.jp):

AIHARA, R., Litigation, Finance and Corporate Law

ARAKI, T., Labour and Employment Law

ASAKA, K., Anglo-American Law

BABA, Y., European Political History

CH'EN, P. H.-C., Principles of Comparative Law, Chinese Legal System

DOGAUCHI, H., Civil Law, Trust Law

EBIHARA, A., German Law

EGASHIRA, K., Commercial Law

FOOTE, D. H., Sociology of Law

FUJITA, T., Commercial Law

FUJIWARA, K., International Politics, Southeast Asian Studies

FURUE, Y., Criminal Procedure

HASEBE, Y., Constitutional Law
HIBINO, T., Constitutional Theory
HIGUCHI, N., Anglo-American Law
HIROSE, H., Consumer Law
IGARASHI, T., Comparative Politics
INOUE, T., Philosophy of Law
INOUYE, M., Criminal Procedure
ISHIGURO, K., Private International Law, Conflict of Laws
ISHIKAWA, K., Constitutional Law
ITO, M., Civil Procedure
ITO, Y., European Law
IWAHARA, S., Corporation Law, Regulation of Financial Institutions
IWAMURA, M., Social Security Law
KABASHIMA, I., Japanese Politics
KANDA, H., Commercial Law
KANSAKU, H., Commercial Law
KATO, J., Comparative Politics
KAWAIDE, Y., History of Western Political Thought
KITAMURA, I., French Law
KOBA, A., Roman Law
KOBAYAKAWA, M., Administrative Law
KOKETSU, H., Administrative Law
KUBO, F., American Government and History
MASUI, Y., Tax Law
MATSUSHITA, J., Insolvency Law
MIYASAKO, Y., International Business Law
MORITA, A., Public Administration
MORITA, H., Civil Law
MORITA, O., Civil Law
NAKATANI, K., International Law
NAKAYAMA, N., Intellectual Property Law
NAKAZATO, M., Tax Law
NISHIDA, N., Criminal Law
NISHIKAWA, Y., Occidental Legal History
NITTA, I., Japanese Legal History
NOMI, Y., Civil Law, Trust Law
NOZAKI, K., General Legal Practice
OBUCHI, T., Intellectual Property Law
OCHIAI, S., Commercial Law
OHGUSHI, K., Latin American Politics
OKUWAKI, N., International Law
OMURA, A., Civil Law
ONUMA, Y., International Law
OTA, S., Law and Social Science, Law and Economics, Civil Dispute Resolution, Legal Negotiation
SAEKI, H., Criminal Law
SAITO, M., Administrative Law, Law of Local Government
SHIOKAWA, N., Russian and Post-Soviet Politics
SHIRAISHI, T., Competition Law
TAKAHARA, A., Politics of East Asia
TAKAHASHI, H., Civil Procedure
TAKAHASHI, K., Constitutional Law
TAKAHASHI, S., History of International Politics
TAKATA, H., Civil Procedure
TANABE, K., Policy Studies
TERAO, Y., Anglo-American Law
UCHIDA, T., Civil Law
UGA, K., Administrative Law
USUI, M., Public Finance Law
WATANABE, H., History of Japanese Political Thought
YAMAGUCHI, A., Criminal Law
YAMAMOTO, R., Administrative Law
YAMAMURO, M., Criminal Procedure
YAMASHITA, T., Commercial Law

Graduate School of Science and Faculty of Science (7-3-1 Hongo, Bunkyo-ku, Tokyo 113-0033; tel. (3) 5841-4570; fax (3) 5841-8776; e-mail shomu@adm.s.u-tokyo.ac.jp; internet www.s.u-tokyo.ac.jp):

AIHARA, H., High Energy Physics
AKASAKA, K., Evolutional and Developmental Biology
AOKI, H., Theoretical Condensed-matter Physics
AOKI, K., Population Biology
EGUCHI, T., Theoretical Particle Physics

FUKADA, Y., Biochemistry and Molecular Biology
FUKUDA, H., Plant Cell Biology
GELLER, R., Seismology
HAMAGUCHI, H., Physical Chemistry
HAMANO, Y., Earth Dynamics
HASEGAWA, T., Solid-State Chemistry
HATSUDA, T., Theoretical Hadron Physics
HAYANO, R., High Energy Nuclear Physics Experiment
HIBIYA, T., Ocean Dynamics
HIRANO, H., Evolutionary Genetics
HOSHINO, M., Space Physics
IWASAWA, Y., Surface Chemistry and Catalysis
KAMIYA, R., Cell Biology
KAWASHIMA, T., Organic Chemistry
KIMURA, G., Tectonics, Structural Geology
KOBAYASHI, A., Materials Chemistry, Structural Chemistry
KOBAYASHI, T., Quantum Electronics
KOMAMIYA, S., Experimental Elementary Particle Physics
KOMEDA, Y., Plant Molecular Genetics
KUBO, T., Physiological Chemistry, Molecular Biology
KUBONO, S., Nuclear Physics, Nuclear Astrophysics
KUWAJIMA, K., Biophysics
MAKISHIMA, K., Experimental High Energy Astrophysics
MATSUMOTO, R., Sedimentology and Geochemistry
MATSU'URA, M., Earthquake Physics, Tectonics
MINOWA, M., Experimental Particle Physics without Accelerators
MIYAMOTO, M., Evolution of Planetary Material
MIYASHITA, S., Statistical Mechanics, Magnetism, Condensed Matter
MURAKAMI, T., Environmental Mineralogy
MURATA, J., Plant Systematics
NAGAHARA, H., Petrology, Planetary Science
NAGAO, K., Geochemistry
NAGATA, T., Plant Physiology and Plant Molecular Biology
NAKADA, Y., Stellar Astrophysics
NAKAMURA, E., Organic Chemistry
NAKANO, A., Developmental Cell Biology
NARASAKA, K., Synthetic Organic Chemistry
NISHIHARA, H., Inorganic Chemistry
NOMOTO, K., Theoretical Astrophysics
NONAKA, M., Molecular Immunology
NOTSU, K., Geochemistry
OHTA, T., Solid-State Physical Chemistry
OKA, Y., Neurobiology
OKAMURA, S., Extragalactic Astronomy
ONAKA, T., Astrophysics
OTSUKA, T., Nuclear Theory
OZAWA, K., Petrology
SAIGO, K., Molecular Biology
SAKAI, H., Nuclear Physics
SAKANO, H., Molecular Biology
SANO, M., Nonlinear Dynamics, Fluid Dynamics
SATO, K., Astrophysics and Cosmology
SHIBAHASHI, H., Theoretical Astrophysics
SHIMOURA, S., Nuclear Physics
SHIONOYA, M., Bioinorganic Chemistry
SOFUE, Y., Radio Astronomy
SUGIURA, N., Planetary Science
TACHIBANA, K., Chemistry of Natural Products
TADA, R., Sedimentology and Palaeoceanography
TAJIMA, F., Molecular Population Genetics
TAKEDA, H., Developmental Genetics
TANABE, K., Palaeontology
TERASAWA, T., Space and Magnetospheric Physics
TOHE, A., Yeast Genetics
TSUBONO, K., Experimental Relativity

UCHIDA, S., Solid-State Physics, High-Tc Superconductivity
UEDA, S., Human Molecular Evolution
UMEZAWA, Y., Analytical Chemistry
URABE, T., Chemical Geology, Economic Geology
WADATI, M., Statistical Physics and Condensed-matter Physics
YAMAGATA, T., Ocean–Atmosphere Dynamics
YAMAGISHI, A., Clay Mineralogy
YAMAMOTO, M., Molecular Genetics
YAMAMOTO, S., Astrophysics, Astrochemistry, Molecular Spectroscopy
YAMANOUCHI, K., Physical Chemistry
YANAGIDA, T., Elementary Particle Physics
YOKOYAMA, J., Cosmology and Astrophysics
YOKOYAMA, S., Biophysics, Biochemistry and Molecular Biology
YOSHII, Y., Galactic Astronomy

Graduate School of Mathematical Sciences (3-8-1 Komaba, Meguro-ku, Tokyo 153-8914; tel. (3) 5465-7014; fax (3) 5465-7012; e-mail suriso@ms.u-tokyo.ac.jp; internet www.ms.u-tokyo.ac.jp):

ARAI, H., Real Analysis, Harmonic Analysis, Theory of Function Spaces
FUNAKI, T., Probability Theory
FURUTA, M., Global Analysis, Low-dimensional Topology
GIGA, Y., Nonlinear Analysis
HORIKAWA, E., Algebraic Geometry
JIMBO, M., Integrable Systems, Representation Theory
KATAOKA, K., Partial Differential Equations
KATSURA, T., Algebraic Geometry
KAWAHIGASHI, Y., Operator Algebras
KAWAMATA, Y., Algebraic Geometry and Complex Manifolds
KIKUCHI, F., Numerical Analysis
KOHNO, T., Three-manifolds, Quantum Groups
KUSUOKA, S., Probability Theory and its Application
MATANO, H., Nonlinear Partial Equations, Dynamical Systems
MATSUMOTO, Y., Topology
MIYAOKA, Y., Algebraic Geometry
MORITA, S., Topology of Manifolds
NAKAMURA, S., Differential Equations and Mathematical Physics
NOGUCHI, J., Complex Analysis in Several Variables, Complex Geometry
ODA, T., Number Theory
OKAMOTO, K., Differential Equations Complex Analysis
OSHIMA, T., Algebraic Analysis, Theory of Unitary Representations
SAITO, S., Arithmetic Geometry, Algebraic Geometry
SAITO, T., Arithmetic Geometry
TOKIHIRO, T., Mathematical Physics, Solid-State Physics
TSUBOI, T., Foliations, Diffeomorphism Groups
YOSHIDA, N., Mathematical Statistics, Stochastic Analysis

Graduate School of Medicine and Faculty of Medicine (7-3-1 Hongo, Bunkyo-ku, Tokyo 113-0033; tel. (3) 5841-3303; fax (3) 5841-3670; e-mail liaison@m.u-tokyo.ac.jp; internet www.m.u-tokyo.ac.jp):

AKABAYASHI, A., Biomedical Ethics
ANDO, J., Systems Physiology
ARAIE, M., Ophthalmology
ETO, F., Rehabilitation Medicine
FUJITA, T., Nephrology and Endocrinology
FUKAYAMA, M., Human Pathology and Diagnostic Pathology
HANAOKA, K., Anaesthesiology and Pain Medicine
HASHIZUME, K., Paediatric Surgery
HIROKAWA, N., Cell Biology and Anatomy
IGARASHI, T., Paediatrics

IHARA, Y., Neuropathology
IINO, M., Cellular and Molecular Pharmacology
KADOWAKI, T., Nutrition and Metabolism
KAGA, K., Otorhinolaryngology, Head and Neck Surgery
KAI, I., Social Gerontology
KAMINISHI, M., Gastrointestinal Surgery, Surgical Sensory Motor Neuroscience, Metabolic Care and Endocrine Surgery
KANDA, K., Nursing Administration
KATO, N., Neuropsychiatry
KAZUMA, K., Adult Nursing; Terminal and Long-term Care Nursing
KIRINO, T., Neurosurgery
KITA, K., Biomedical Chemistry
KITAMURA, T., Urology
KIUCHI, T., Medical Information Network Research
KOBAYASHI, Y., Public Health
KOIKE, K., Infection Control and Prevention
KOSHIMA, I., Plastic and Reconstructive
KURIHARA, H., Physiological Chemistry and Metabolism
MAKUUCHI, M., Hepatobiliary Pancreatic Surgery, Artificial Organ and Transplantation
MATSUSHIMA, K., Molecular Preventive Medicine
MISHINA, M., Molecular Neurobiology
MIYASHITA, Y., Physiology
MIYAZONO, K., Molecular Pathology
MORI, K., Cellular and Molecular Physiology
MURASHIMA, S., Community Health Nursing
NAGAI, R., Cardiology
NAGASE, T., Respiratory Medicine
NAGAWA, H., Surgical Oncology
NAKAMURA, K., Orthopaedic Surgery
NOMOTO, A., Microbiology
OHASHI, Y., Biostatistics; Epidemiology and Preventive Health Sciences
OHE, K., Medical Informatics and Economics
OHTOMO, K., Diagnostic Radiology
OKAYAMA, H., Molecular Biology
OMATA, M., Gastroenterology
OUCHI, Y., Ageing Science, Geriatric Medicine
OYAMA, H., Clinical Bioinformatics
SANADA, H., Gerontological Nursing
SHIMIZU, T., Cellular Signalling
SUZUKI, H., Pharmaceutical Services
TAKAHASHI, K., Transfusion Medicine
TAKAHASHI, T., Neurophysiology
TAKAMOTO, S., Cardiothoracic Surgery
TAKATO, T., Oral and Maxillofacial Surgery
TAKETANI, Y., Obstetrics and Gynaecology
TAMAKI, K., Dermatology
TANIGUCHI, T., Immunology
TOHYAMA, C., Disease Biology and Interpretative Medicine
TOKUNAGA, K., Human Genetics
TSUJI, S., Neurology
TSUTSUMI, O., Obstetrics and Gynaecology
UENO, S., Bioimaging and Biomagnetics
USHIDA, T., Biomedical Materials and Systems
USHIJIMA, H., Developmental Medical Sciences
WAKAI, S., International Community Health
WATANABE, C., Human Ecology
YAHAGI, N., Emergency and Critical Care Medicine
YAMAMOTO, K., Allergology and Rheumatology
YAMAZAKI, T., Clinical Bioinformatics
YATOMI, Y., Clinical Laboratory Medicine
YOSHIDA, K., Forensic Medicine

Graduate School of Pharmaceutical Sciences and Faculty of Pharmaceutical Sciences (7-3-1 Hongo, Bunkyo-ku, Tokyo 113-0033; tel. (3) 5841-4878; fax (3) 5841-4711; e-mail adviser@mol.f.u-tokyo.ac.jp; internet www.f.u-tokyo.ac.jp/index-e.html):

ARAI, H., Health Chemistry
EBIZUKA, Y., Natural Products Chemistry
FUKUYAMA, T., Synthetic Natural Products Chemistry
FUNATSU, T., Biophysics
ICHIJO, H., Cell Signalling
IRIMURA, T., Cancer Biology and Molecular Immunology
IWATSUBO, T., Neuropathology and Neuroscience
KATADA, T., Physiological Chemistry
KIRINO, Y., Neurobiophysics
KOBAYASHI, S., Organic and Organometallic Chemistry
MATSUKI, N., Neuropharmacology and Neuroscience
MIURA, M., Molecular Neurobiology
NAGANO, T., Chemical Biology and Medicinal Chemistry
OHWADA, T., Organic and Medicinal Chemistry
SATOW, Y., Protein Structural Biology
SEKIMIZU, K., Biochemistry, Molecular Biology
SHIBASAKI, M., Synthetic Organic Chemistry
SHIMADA, I., Structural Biology, NMR Spectroscopy, Physical Chemistry
SUGIYAMA, Y., Molecular Pharmacokinetics

Graduate School of Public Policy (7-3-1 Hongo, Bunkyo-ku, Tokyo 113-0033; tel. (3) 5841-3104; fax (3) 5841-3291; e-mail ppin@j.u-tokyo.ac.jp; internet www.pp.u-tokyo.ac.jp):

HAYASHI, R., Economic Policy
ICHIMURA, H., Econometrics
IHORI, T., Public Finance, Public Economics
ITO, T., International Finance, Macroeconomics
KANEMOTO, Y., Urban Economics
KAWAI, M., Basic Macroeconomics
MORITA, A., Public Management
OKUWAKI, N., International Law and Organization, Law of the Sea, Air and Outer Space
TANABE, K., Politics, Policy Analysis, Policy Process

Interfaculty Initiative in Information Studies and Graduate School of Interdisciplinary Information Studies (7-3-1 Hongo, Bunkyo-ku, Tokyo 113-0033; tel. (3) 5841-5900; fax (3) 3811-5970; e-mail info@iii.u-tokyo.ac.jp; internet www.iii.u-tokyo.ac.jp):

ARAKAWA, C., Computational Fluid Dynamics, Simulation
BABA, A., Historical Informatics, Japanese Early Modern Economic History, Digital Archive Science
EINCO, S., Indian Philology, Ritual and Religion in India
HAMADA, J., Information Law and Policy
HANADA, T., Media Studies
HARA, Y., Economic Development Theory, Southeast Asian Economics
HARASHIMA, H., Communication Engineering and Face Studies
HASHIMOTO, Y., Social Psychology
HIROI, O., Social Psychology, Sociology of Disasters
IKEUCHI, K., Computer Vision
ISHIDA, H., Information Semiotics
KAN, S., Investigation of Possibilities for Regional Union in North-east Asia
KAWAGUCHI, Y., Computer Art
KUNIYOSHI, Y., Intelligent Systems and Informatics
NISHIGAKI, T., Information and Media Studies
SAKAMURA, K., Computer Architecture
SASAKI, M., Ecological Psychology

SUDOH, O., Economics of the Knowledge-based Society
TSUJII, J., Computational Linguistics, Natural Language Processing
YAMAGUCHI, Y., Graphics
YOSHIMI, S., Popular Culture and Media Events

ATTACHED RESEARCH INSTITUTES

Asian Natural Environmental Science Center: 1-1-1 Yayoi, Bunkyo-ku, Tokyo 113-8657; f. 1995; Dir K. TAKEUCHI.

Biotechnology Research Center: 1-1-1 Yayoi, Bunkyo-ku, Tokyo 113-8657; f. 1993; Dir S. HORINOUCHI.

Center for Climate System Research: 5-1-5 Kashiwanoha, Kashiwa-shi, Chiba 277-8568; f. 1991; Dir T. NAKAJIMA.

Center for Collaborative Research: 4-6-1 Komaba, Meguro-ku, Tokyo 153-8505; f. 1996; Dir H. YOKOI.

Center for Research and Development of Higher Education: 7-3-1 Hongo, Bunkyo-ku, Tokyo 113-0033; f. 1996; Dir K. OKAMOTO.

Center for Spatial Information Science: 5-1-5 Kashiwanoha, Kashiwa-shi, Chiba 277-8568; f. 1998; Dir R. SHIBASAKI.

Cryogenic Center: 2-11-16 Yayoi, Bunkyo-ku, Tokyo 113-0032; f. 1967; Dir M. MINOWA.

Earthquake Research Institute: 1-1-1 Yayoi, Bunkyo-ku, Tokyo 113-0032; f. 1925; Dir S. OKOBU; publ. *Bulletin of the Earthquake Research Institute* (4 a year).

Environmental Science Center: 7-3-1 Hongo, Bunkyo-ku, Tokyo 113-0033; f. 1975; Dir K. YAMAMOTO.

Health Service Center: 7-3-1 Hongo, Bunkyo-ku, Tokyo 113-0033; f. 1967; Dir (vacant); publ. *Kenko Kanri Gaiyo* (1 a year).

High Temperature Plasma Center: 5-1-5 Kashiwanoha, Kashiwa-shi, Chiba 277-8568; f. 1999; Dir Y. OGAWA.

Historiographical Institute: 7-3-1 Hongo, Bunkyo-ku, Tokyo 113-0033; f. 1869; Dir M. HOTATE; publ. *Shiryo Hensan—Sho Ho* (1 a year), *Shiryo Hensan—Jo Kenkyu Kiyo* (1 a year).

Information Technology Center: 2-11-16 Yayoi, Bunkyo-ku, Tokyo 113-8658; f. 1999; Dir Y. OKABE.

Institute for Cosmic Ray Research: 5-1-5 Kashiwanoha, Kashiwa-shi, Chiba 277-8582; f. 1953; Dir Y. SUZUKI; publ. *ICRR Report* (irregular), *ICRR News* (4 a year), *ICRR Hokoku.*

Institute of Industrial Science: 4-6-1 Komaba, Meguro-ku, Tokyo 153-8505; f. 1949; Dir M. MAEDA; publ. *Seisan-Kenkyu* (12 a year).

Institute of Medical Science: 4-6-1 Shirokanedai, Minato-ku, Tokyo 108-8639; f. 1892; Dir T. YAMAMOTO.

Institute of Molecular and Cellular Biosciences: 1-1-1 Yayoi, Bunkyo-ku, Tokyo 113-0032; f. 1953; Dir A. MIYAJIMA.

Institute of Oriental Culture: 7-3-1 Hongo, Bunkyo-ku, Tokyo 113-0033; f. 1941; Dir A. TANAKA; publ. *Memoirs* (2 a year), *Oriental Culture* (1 a year).

Institute of Social Science: 7-3-1 Hongo, Bunkyo-ku, Tokyo 113-0033; f. 1946; Dir A. KOMORIDA; publ. *Shakai Kagaku Kenkyu* (Journal of Social Science, 6 a year), *Social Science Japan Journal* (2 a year), *Social Science Japan* (newsletter, 3 a year).

Institute for Solid-State Physics: 5-1-5 Kashiwanoha, Kashiwa-shi, Chiba 277-8581; f. 1957; Dir K. UEDA; publ. *Technical Report* (irregular).

Intelligent Modelling Laboratory: 2-11-16 Yayoi, Bunkyo-ku, Tokyo 113-8656; f. 1996; Dir K. HIRAO.

International Center: 7-3-1 Hongo, Bunkyo-ku, Tokyo 113-8654; f. 1990; Dir G. MESHITSUKA; publ. *Bulletin* (1 a year), *News* (4 a year).

International Center for Elementary Particle Physics: 7-3-1 Hongo, Bunkyo-ku, Tokyo 113-0033; f. 2004; Dir S. KOMAMIYA.

International Research Center for Medical Education: 7-3-1 Hongo, Bunkyo-ku, Tokyo 113-0033; f. 2000; Dir K. KAGA; publ. *Newsletter* (2 a year).

Komaba Open Laboratory: 4-6-1 Komaba, Meguro-ku, Tokyo 153-8904; f. 1998; Dir T. NANYA.

Molecular Genetics Research Laboratory: 7-3-1 Hongo, Bunkyo-ku, Tokyo 113-0033; f. 1983; Dir M. YAMAMOTO.

Ocean Research Institute: 1-15-1 Minamidai, Nakano-ku, Tokyo 164-8639; f. 1962; Dir M. TERAZAKI; publ. *Bulletin*, *Preliminary Cruise Report* (irregular).

Radioisotope Center: 2-11-16 Yayoi, Bunkyo-ku, Tokyo 113-0032; f. 1970; Dir Y. MAKIDE.

Research Center for Advanced Science and Technology: 4-6-1 Komaba, Meguro-ku, Tokyo 153-8904; f. 1987; Dir K. HASHIMOTO.

Research into Artifacts Center for Engineering: 5-1-5 Kashiwanoha, Kashiwa-shi, Chiba 277-8568; f. 1992; Dir K. UEDA.

VLSI Design and Education Center: 2-11-16 Yayoi, Bunkyo-ku, Tokyo 113-8656; f. 1996; Dir K. ASADA.

University Museum: 7-3-1 Hongo, Bunkyo-ku, Tokyo 113-0033; f. 1965; Dir S. TAKAHASHI; publ. *Ouroboros* (newsletter, 3 a year), *Bulletin* (irregular), *Material Reports* (irregular), *UMUT Monograph* (irregular).

TOKYO UNIVERSITY OF AGRICULTURE AND TECHNOLOGY

2-8-1 Harumi-cho, Fuchu-shi, Tokyo 183

Telephone: (423) 64-3311
Fax: (423) 60-7376
Internet: www.tuat.ac.jp

Founded 1949
Independent
Language of instruction: Japanese
Academic year: April to March

Pres.: HIDEFUMI KOBATAKE
Vice-Pres: TADASHI MATSUNAGA, TAKAHIKO ONO, AKIRA SASAO, HIROFUMI TAKEMOTO
Library Dir: HIROYUKI OHNO

Library of 524,018 vols
Number of teachers: 442
Number of students: 5,966 (4032 undergraduate, 1934 graduate)

Publication: faculty bulletins (1 a year)

DEANS

Faculty of Agriculture: YASUHISA KUNIMI
Faculty of Technology: AKINORI KOKITSU
Graduate School of Bio-applications and Systems Engineering: MASANORI OKAZAKI
Graduate School of Technology Management: HIDEO KAMEYAMA
United Graduate School of Agricultural Science: YUTARO SENGA

TOKYO UNIVERSITY OF FISHERIES

5–7 Konan 4, Minato-ku, Tokyo 108-8477

Telephone: (3) 5463-0400
Fax: (3) 5463-0359
E-mail: www-master@tokyo-u-fish.ac.jp
Internet: www.tokyo-u-fish.ac.jp

Founded 1888
Academic year: April to March

Pres.: Dr FUMIO TAKASHIMA
Vice-Pres: Dr K. SATO, Dr R. TAKAI
Admin. Dir: M. SATO
Librarian: Dr E. WATANABE

Library of 268,000 vols
Number of teachers: 171
Number of students: 1,745

Publication: *Journal of the TUF* (2 a year)

HEADS OF LABORATORIES

Aquatic Biosciences:

Aquatic Biology: Dr K. FUJITA, Prof. M. OMORI, Dr S. SEGAWA, Prof. J. TANAKA, Dr S. WATANABE
Aquaculture: Dr T. TAKEUCHI, Dr M. NOTOYA, Dr N. OKAMOTO, Dr T. WATANABE, Dr H. FUKUDA
Genetics and Biochemistry: Dr T. AOKI

Fisheries Resource Management:

Fisheries Resource Management System: Dr T. KITAHARA, Dr S. YAMADA, Dr K. TAYA, Y. SATO, Dr K. UENO, Prof. Y. SATO
Ecology and Economics of Fisheries Resources: Dr Y. NAKAI, Dr A. OHNO, Dr R. ISEDA, Dr N. KOIWA, Prof. Y. NAKAI
International Economics of Fisheries and Food Industries: Dr K. SAKURAI

Food Science and Technology:

Food Chemistry: Dr T. SUZUKI, Dr T. FUJII, Dr S. WADA, Dr M. TANAKA
Food Engineering: Dr H. WATANABE, Prof. T. MIHORI, Dr R. TAKAI
Marine Biochemistry: Dr S. KIMURA, Dr K. SHIOMI, Dr H. YAMANAKA, Dr T. HAYASHI, Dr T. WATANABE
Applied Microbiology: Dr E. WATANABE

International and Interdisciplinary Studies:

English: Dr S. MIURA
Ethics: T. AMEMIYA
French: T. SHIMANO
History: O. KANAMORI
Psychology: Dr K. NAKAMURA

Marine Science and Technology:

Fishing Science and Technology: Dr T. ARIMOTO, Dr C. ITOSU, Dr H. KANEHIRO, Dr T. TOKAI
Ocean Systems Engineering: Dr T. AKITA, Prof. Y. NAKAMURA, Dr K. SATOHH, Dr M. FURUSAWA, Dr S. YADA, Dr S. MURAMATSU

Ocean Sciences:

Marine Ecosystem Studies: Dr T. ISHIMARU, Dr M. MAEDA, Dr M. NAMIKOSHI, Dr Y. YAMAGUCHI
Physics and Environmental Modelling: Prof. Y. ANDO, Dr K. KIHARA, Dr M. MATSUYAMA, Dr T. MORINAGA, Dr H. NAGASHIMA, Dr H. OHASHI, Dr N. SHIOTANI

TOKYO UNIVERSITY OF FOREIGN STUDIES

3-11-1 Asahicho, Fuchu-shi, Tokyo 183-8534

Telephone: (42) 330-5126
Fax: (42) 330-5140
E-mail: ml-zhenhp@tufs.ac.jp
Internet: www.tufs.ac.jp/index-j.html

Founded 1899; reorganized 1949
Semi-private institution

Pres.: SETSUHO IKEHATA
Dir-Gen.: M. KOTANI
Library Dir: N. TOMIMORI

Library: see Libraries and Archives
Number of teachers: 241 full-time
Number of students: 4,282

Publication: *Area and Culture Studies* (2 a year)

DEANS

Faculty of Foreign Studies: AKIRA BABA

ATTACHED INSTITUTE

Research Institute for Languages and Cultures of Asia and Africa: 3-11-1 Asahicho, Fuchu-shi, Tokyo 183-8534; tel. (42) 330-5600; fax (42) 330-5610; f. 1964; Dir Dr K. MIYAZAKI; publ. *Journal of Asian and African Studies* (2 a year), *Newsletter* (3 a year).

TOKYO UNIVERSITY OF MERCANTILE MARINE

2-1-6 Etchujima, Koto-ku, Tokyo 135-8533

Telephone: (3) 5245-7312
Internet: www.tosho-u.ac.jp

Founded 1875
Independent

Pres.: AKIO M. SUGISAKI
Dir of Admin. Bureau: TAKAO OKA
Library Dir: SUUSHIN SATO

Number of teachers: 110 full-time
Number of students: 1,093

Publication: *Journals* (natural sciences, humanities and social sciences)

PROFESSORS

Electric Power: YOSHIHIRO HATANAKA
Floating Facilities: KUNIAKI SHOJI
Information Systems Engineering and Navigation Systems: HAYAMA IMAZU
Internal Combustion Engines: HIROSHI OKADA
International Cultural Studies: TAKAKO NIWA
Logistics Engineering: IWAO TAMINAGA
Machinery and Equipment: TOSHIHIKO FUJITA
Marine Engineering and Guidance Control: KOHEI OHTSU
Marine Science and Technology: HIROSHI YAMAGISHI
Mathematical Science: OSAMU MATSUSHITA
Navigational Electronics: SHOGO HAYASHI
Nuclear Power: TOMOJI TAKAMASA
Power Systems Engineering and Steam Power: MASAHIRO OSAKABE

UNIVERSITY OF ELECTRO-COMMUNICATIONS

1-5-1 Chofugaoka, Chōfu City, Tokyo 182-8585

Telephone: (424) 43-5014
Fax: (424) 43-5108
E-mail: kenkyo-k@office.uec.ac.jp
Internet: www.uec.ac.jp

Founded 1949
Independent
Academic year: April to March

Pres.: M. KAJITANI
Dir of Secretariat: I. ISHIOKA
Library Dir: T. MIKI

Number of teachers: 360 full-time
Number of students: 5,452 (4,347 undergraduate, 1,105 postgraduate)

Publication: *Bulletin* (2 a year)

PROFESSORS

Computer and Media Science: KAZUHIKO OZEKI
Information and Communications Systems: TAKASHI S. FUKUDA
Information Photonics and Wave Signal Processing: YOSHIO KAMI
Information Transfer: Theory and Practice: KIYOSHI ANDO
Department of Applied Physics and Chemistry: K. HAKUTA
Department of Computer Science: RIKIO ONAI
Department of Electronic Engineering: KIMURA TADAMASA

Department of Human Communications: HARUYUKI INOUE
Department of Mechanical Engineering and Intelligent Systems: S. KURODA
Department of Systems Engineering: MASAYUKI MATSUI

TOTTORI UNIVERSITY

4-101 Minami, Koyama-cho, Tottori City 680-0945

Telephone: (857) 31-5010
Fax: (857) 31-5018
E-mail: net_adm@jim.tottori-u.ac.jp
Internet: www.tottori-u.ac.jp
Founded 1949
Academic year: April to March
Pres.: MASANORI MICHIUE
Dir-Gen. of Admin.: Y. SUZUKI
Librarian: K. KOSAKA
Number of teachers: 762 full-time
Number of students: 6,090

DEANS

Faculty of Agriculture: M. IWASAKI
Faculty of Education and Regional Sciences: M. NAGAYAMA
Faculty of Engineering: H. KIYAMA
Faculty of Medicine: T. NOSE

TOYAMA UNIVERSITY

3190 Gofuku, Toyama City 930-8555

Telephone: (764) 45-6011
E-mail: info@toyama-u.ac.jp
Internet: www.toyama-u.ac.jp
Founded 1949; Toyama Medical and Pharmaceutical University, Takaoka National College and Toyama University merged May 2003
Academic year: April to March (2 terms)
Pres.: HIROSHI TAKIZAWA
Chief Admin. Officer: O. IMADA
Librarian: H. FUJITA
Library of 965,300 vols
Number of teachers: 445 full-time
Number of students: 7,400

DEANS

Faculty of Economics: S. YOSHIHARA
Faculty of Education: M. KASE
Faculty of Engineering: M. TOKIZAWA
Faculty of Humanities: N. KOTANI
Faculty of Science: K. MATSUMOTO

TOYOHASHI UNIVERSITY OF TECHNOLOGY

Tempaku, Toyohashi, Aichi 441-8580

Telephone: (532) 47-0111
Fax: (532) 44-6509
Internet: www.tut.ac.jp
Founded 1976
Independent
Academic year: April to March
Pres.: Dr TATAU NISHINAGA
Vice-Pres: TOSHIRO KOBAYASHI, HIROYUKI MATSUI
Dir-Gen. of Admin. Bureau: TAKASHI NORIZUKI
Librarian: HIROO YONEZU
Library of 170,000 vols
Number of teachers: 213
Number of students: 2,144

DEANS

Department of Architecture and Civil Engineering: AKIRA OHGAI
Department of Ecological Engineering: TOSHIHIRO KITADA
Department of Electrical and Electronic Engineering: AKIO OOTA

Department of Humanities and Management Science and Engineering: JUN YAMAMOTO
Department of Information and Computer Sciences: SEIICHI NAKAGAWA
Department of Knowledge-based Information Engineering: YOSHIMASA TAKAHASHI
Department of Materials Science: KATSUYUKI AOKI
Department of Mechanical Engineering: MASAO UEMURA
Department of Production Systems Engineering: MASAHIRO KAWAKAMI

UNIVERSITY OF TSUKUBA

1-1-1 Tennodai, Tsukuba, Ibaraki-ken 305-8577

Telephone: (29) 853-2056
Fax: (29) 853-2059
E-mail: koryuka@sakura.cc.tsukuba.ac.jp
Internet: www.tsukuba.ac.jp
Founded 1973
Independent
Language of instruction: Japanese
Academic year: April to March
Pres.: YOICHI IWASAKI
Vice-Pres: AKIHIDE TANIKAWA, HIROMICHI YOSHITAKE, HIROSHI MIZUBAYASHI, NORIO KUDO, SHIN-ICHIRO IZUMI, SUMIO HATANO, TAKESHI KOSHIZUKA
Exec. Advisers to the Pres.: AKIRA UKAWA, ISAO INOUE, YUTAKA TSUJINAKA
Dir of Univ. Hospital: NOBUHIRO YAMADA
Dir of Education Bureau of Attached Laboratory Schools: AKIHIDE TANIKAWA
Dir of Univ. Library: SADAO UEMATSU
Library of 2,457,258 vols, 23,001 periodicals
Number of teachers: 1,659
Number of students: 16,241

PROVOSTS AND DEANS
Undergraduate Programmes

School of Art and Design:
KIYOSHI NISHIKAWA (Provost)
College of Humanities: MAKOTO ITOH (Dean)
College of Comparative Culture: KIICHIROU TAKEMURA (Dean)
College of Japanese Language and Culture: HIDEICHI ETO (Dean)
School of Health and Physical Education:
YOSHIKAZU NOMURA (Provost)
School of Humanities and Culture:
NORIO YAMADA (Provost)
College of Social Sciences: MIYOKO MOTOZAWA (Dean)
College of International Studies: YUKIO FUKUI (Dean)
School of Human Sciences:
SHINYA MIYAMOTO (Provost)
School of Informatics:
YOSHIHIKO EBIHARA (Provost)
College of Education: KAZUO HORI (Dean)
College of Psychology: TOSHIKI OGAWA (Dean)
College of Disability Sciences: SHIGEKI SONOYAMA (Dean)
School of Life and Environmental Sciences:
JUN-ICHI HAYASHI (Provost)
College of Biological Sciences: SHINOBU SATOH (Dean)
College of Agro-Biological Resource Sciences: YUKIO KANAI (Dean)
College of Geoscience: KATSUO SASHIDA (Dean)
School of Medicine and Medical Sciences:
FUJIO OTSUKA (Provost)
School of Medicine: AKIRA HARA (Dean)
School of Nursing: YUKA SAEKI (Dean)

School of Medical Sciences: OSAMU URAYAMA (Dean)
School of Science and Engineering:
KEN-ICHI OKAMOTO (Provost)
College of Mathematics: MITSUHIRO ITO (Dean)
College of Physics: KAZUHIRO YABANA (Dean)
College of Chemistry: TATSUO ARAI (Dean)
College of Engineering Sciences: KEN-ICHI OHSHIMA (Dean)
College of Engineering Systems: SEIJI YASUNOBU (Dean)
College of Policy and Planning Sciences: REIJJI OBASE (Dean)
School of Social and International Studies:
NOBUHIKO KITAWAKI (Provost)
College of Information Science: YOSHINORI YAMAGUCHI (Dean)
College of Media Arts, Science and Technology: JUN'ICHI ISOYA (Dean)
College of Knowledge and Library Sciences: HIROTOYO ISHII (Dean)

Masters Degree Programmes:
NORIO KUDO (Provost)

Doctoral Degree Programmes
Graduate School of Business Sciences:
TAKAHIRO EGUCHI (Provost)
Graduate School of Comprehensive Human Sciences:
KAZUHIKO SHIMIZU (Provost)
Graduate School of Humanities and Social Sciences:
YOSHIKI TSUBOI (Provost)
Graduate School of Library, Information and Media Studies:
SHIN-ICHI NAKAYAMA (Provost)
Graduate School of Life and Environmental Sciences:
OSAMU NUMATA (Provost)
Graduate School of Pure and Applied Sciences:
MASAFUMI AKAHIRA (Provost)
Graduate School of Systems and Information Engineering:
JIRO TANAKA (Provost)

DIRECTORS OF CENTERS
Academic Computing and Communications Center: KOUZOU ITANO
Admission Center: TOMONORI SHIRAKAWA
Agricultural and Forestry Research Center: NAOKI SAKAI
Alliance for Research on North Africa: KAZUKO SHIOJIRI
Center for Computational Physics: MITSUHISA SATO
Center for Research on International Cooperation in Educational Development: HIDEO NAKATA
Center for Tsukuba Advanced Research Alliance: AKIYOSHI FUKAMIZU
Foreign Language Center: IZUMI YASUI
Gene Research Center: HIROSHI KAMADA
International Student Center: STEFAN KAISER
Laboratory Animal Resource Center: KEN-ICHI YAGAMI
Plasma Research Center: TERUJI CHO
Proton Medical Research Center: AKIRA MATSUMURA
Radioisotope Center: HIROKI OSHIO
Research Center for Knowledge Communities: SHIGEO SUGIMOTO
Research Center for University Studies: HISATOSHI SUZUKI
Research Facility for Science and Technology: KAZUO MATSUUCHI
Shimoda Marine Research Center: KAZUO INABA

Special Support Education Research Center: HISAO MAEKAWA

Sport and Physical Education Center: KEN MIYASHITA

Sugadaira Montane Research Center: SEIJI TOKUMASU

Terrestrial Environment Research Center: TADASHI TANAKA

Tsukuba Critical Path Research and Education Integrated Leading Center: NAOYUKI OCHIAI

Tsukuba Industrial Liaison and Cooperative Research Center: SHIN'ICHI YUTA

Tsukuba Research Center for Interdisciplinary Materials Science: YOUICHI OOTSUKA

University Health Center: MORIO OHTSUKA

UTSUNOMIYA UNIVERSITY

350 Mine-machi, Utsunomiya-shi, Tochigi 321-8505

Telephone: (286) (36) 1515
Internet: www.utsunomiya-u.ac.jp
Founded 1949
Independent
Language of instruction: Japanese
Academic year: April to March

Pres.: HIROTO TABARA
Vice-Pres: HIDEKI KASUYA, SHIGERU KITAJIMA
Dir of Univ. Library: HIROTAKA KOIKE

Library of 551,376 vols
Number of teachers: 476
Number of students: 5,411

DEANS

Faculty of Agriculture: TADATAKE MIZUMOTO
Faculty of Education: KIYOSHI NAKAMURA
Faculty of Engineering: YASUSHI NISHIDA
Faculty of International Studies: KAZUKO FUJITA

WAKAYAMA UNIVERSITY

Sakaedani 930, Wakayama-shi 640-8510

Telephone: (73) 454-0361
Fax: (73) 457-7000
Internet: www.wakayama-u.ac.jp
Founded 1949
Academic year: April to March

Pres.: S. MORIYA
Chief Admin. Officer: M. TANIGUCHI
Librarian: H. TACHIBANA

Library of 741,765 vols
Number of teachers: 371
Number of students: 4,460

Publications: *Bulletin of the Faculty of Education*, *The Wakayama Economic Review*

DEANS

Faculty of Economics: T. KINOUCHI
Faculty of Education: K. MORISUGI
Faculty of Systems Engineering: O. OTSUKI

YAMAGATA UNIVERSITY

1-4-12, Koshirakawa-machi, Yamagata 990-8560

Telephone: (23) 628-4006
Fax: (23) 628-4013
Internet: www.yamagata-u.ac.jp
Founded 1949
Independent
Academic year: April to March (2 semesters)

Pres.: FUJIRO SENDO
Sec.-Gen.: DAISUKE IKEDA
Librarian: MASANOBU HAYAKAWA

Library of 991,330 vols
Number of teachers: 1,800
Number of students: 9,436

Publications: *Bulletin of Humanities* (1 a year), *Bulletin of Social Sciences* (2 a year), *Bulletin of Educational Science* (1 a year), *Bulletin of Natural Sciences* (1 a year), *Medical Journal* (2 a year), *Bulletin of Engineering* (1 a year), *Bulletin of Agricultural Science* (1 a year)

DEANS

Faculty of Agriculture: TAKESHI SASSA
Faculty of Education: TSUNEO ISHIJIMA
Faculty of Engineering: TAKESHI ENDO
Faculty of Literature and Social Sciences: KOICHI TAKAGI
Faculty of Science: SEIGO KATO
School of Medicine: MASAO ENDOH

YAMAGUCHI UNIVERSITY

1677-1 Yoshida, Yamaguchi 753-8511

Telephone: (83) 933-5026
Fax: (83) 933-5029
E-mail: sh033@office.cc.yamaguchi-u.ac.jp
Internet: www.yamaguchi-u.ac.jp
Founded 1949
National University Corporation
Academic year: April to March

Pres.: HIROSHI KATO
Vice-Pres: KYOSUKE SAKATE, OSAMU FUKUMASA, SHINYA KAWAI TAKUYA MARUMOTO YOSHIKAZU SUGIHARA
Sec.-Gen.: YUTAKA MATSUYAMA
Dir of Univ. Library: OSAMU FUKUMASA

Library: see Libraries and Archives
Number of teachers: 889
Number of students: 10,785 (9,099 undergraduates, 1,686 postgraduates)

DEANS

Faculty of Agriculture: DAIZO KOGA
Faculty of Economics: OSAMU TAKIGUCHI
Faculty of Education: ISSEI YOSHIDA
Faculty of Engineering: TOSHIKATSU MIKI
Faculty of Humanities: SUSUMU TANAKA
School of Medicine: TOKUHIRO HIROSHI ISHIHARA
Faculty of Science: HIROYUKI MASHIYAMA
Graduate School of East Asian Studies: NORIKO OTANI
Graduate School of Innovation and Technology Management: KEN KAMINISH
United Graduate School of Veterinary Science: TOSHIHARU HAYASHI

UNIVERSITY OF YAMANASHI, NATIONAL UNIVERSITY CORPORATION

4-4-37 Takeda Kofu, Yamanashi 400-8510

Telephone: (55) 220-8004
Fax: (55) 220-8024
Internet: www.yamanashi.ac.jp
Founded 1949
Independent
Academic year: April to March

Pres.: YOJI YOSHIDA
Registrar: KENJI TAMARU
Dean of Students: KUNIO OOHARA
Librarian: TOSHIAKI OTOMO

Library of 556,439 vols
Number of teachers: 600
Number of students: 5,150

Publications: *Bulletin of the Faculty of Education and Human Sciences* (2 a year), *Report of the Faculty of Engineering* (1 a year), *Journal of Applied Educational Research* (1 a year), *Report of the Faculty of Medicine*

DEANS

Faculty of Education: TETSUO HORI
Faculty of Engineering: KOKI YOKOTSUKA
Faculty of Medicine: HIDEAKI NUKUI

ATTACHED INSTITUTES

Center for Crystal Science and Technology: attached to the Faculty of Engineering.

Center for Instrumental Analysis: 4-3-11 Takeda, Kofu 400-8511.

Center for Life Science Research: 1110 Shimokato, Tamaho-cho, Nakakoma-gun 409-3898.

Clean Energy Research Center: 7 Miyamae-cho, Kofu 400-0021.

Cooperative Research and Development Center: 4-3-11 Takeda, Kofu 400-8511.

Institute of Enology and Viticulture: attached to the Faculty of Engineering.

Integrated Information Processing Center: 4-3-11 Takeda, Kofu 400-8511; Dir KOJI IWANUMA.

International Student Center: 4-4-37 Takeda, Kofu 400-8510.

YOKOHAMA NATIONAL UNIVERSITY

79-1 Tokiwadai, Hodogayaku, Yokohama 240-8501

Telephone: (45) 339-3036
Fax: (45) 339-3039
E-mail: international@nuc.ynu.ac.jp
Internet: www.ynu.ac.jp
Founded 1949
National University Corporation
Language of instruction: Japanese
Academic year: April to March (2 semesters)

Pres.: YOSHIHIRO IIDA
Exec. Dirs: S. KISUGI, A. NAGASHIMA, K. SUZUKI, S. WATANABE
Sec.-Gen.: K. SAITOM

Library: see Libraries and Archives
Number of teachers: 613 full-time
Number of students: 10,527

DEANS

Faculty of Business Administration: H. MOGAKI
Faculty of Economics: T. AKIYAMA
Faculty of Education and Human Sciences: S. FUKUDA
Faculty of Engineering: Y. KOKOBUN
Faculty of Environment and Information Sciences: M. ARIMA
Graduate School of Education: S. FUKUDA
Graduate School of Engineering: Y. KOKOBUN
Graduate School of Environment and Information Sciences: M. ARIMA

PROFESSORS

Faculty of Business Administration (79-4 Tokiwadai, Hodogayaku, Yokohama 240-8501; tel. (45) 339-3654; fax (45) 339-3656; e-mail int.somu@nuc.ynu.ac.jp; internet www.business.ynu.ac.jp):

CHO, D., Business Admin.
MOGAKI, H., Int. Personnel Management
MORITA, H., Fiscal Studies, Finance Theory
NAKAMURA, H., Strategic Accounting, Capital Budgeting
OHTSUKA, E., Game Theory
SHIRAI, H., Management Information Systems, Business Modelling
TORII, A., Economic Policy
YAGI, H., Ecological Accounting
YAMAKURA, K., Management
YAMASHITA, S., Nat. Economic Accounting
YOSHIKAWA, T., Cost Accounting, Management Accounting

Faculty of Economics (79-3 Tokiwadai, Hodogayaku, Yokohama 240-8501; tel. (45) 339-3510; fax (45) 339-3504; e-mail int.somu@nuc.ynu.ac.jp; internet www.econ.ynu.ac.jp):

AKIYAMA, T., Theoretical Economics
FUKAGAI, Y., History of Economic Thought, Economic Ethics
HAGIWARA, S., US Economic Policy
HASEBE, Y., Input–Output Analysis
KAMIKAWA, T., Int. Finance, Money and Banking

KANAZAWA, F., Public Finance, Local Finance

KIZAKI, M., Modern Chinese Economy, Corporate Governance in China, Chinese Labour Affairs

KOBAYASHI, M., Statistical Science

OKADO, M., Japanese Economic History

OMORI, Y., Labour Economics

TOMIURA, E., Int. Economics

UI, T., Theoretical Economics

YAMAZAKI, K., Economic Policy

Faculty of Education and Human Sciences (79-2 Tokiwadai, Hodogayaku, Yokohama 240-8501; tel. (45) 339-3253; fax (45) 339-3264; e-mail edu.somu@nuc.ynu.ac.jp; internet www.edhs.ynu.ac.jp):

ARAI, H., Pedagogy

ARAI, M., Production Engineering, Processing Studies

BABA, Y., Gen. Mathematics

CHOMABAYASHI, T., Exercise Physiology

EBIHARA, O., Sociology of Physical Education and Sport

ETO, T., Geology

FUJIMORI, T., Sculpture

FUKAWA, G., Subject Pedagogy

FUKUDA, S., Experimental Psychology

HARADA, H., Soil Zoology

HASHIMOTO, Y., Science Education

HAYASHIBE, H., Developmental Psycholinguistics

HORI, M., Environmental Chemistry

ICHIYANAGI, H., Japanese Modern Literature, Japanese Modern Culture

IMOTO, S., German Literature, European Culture History

INOUE, K., Clinical Psychology

ISHIDA, J., Primary Mathematics Education

KANAI, Y., Ethics

KANAZAWA, H., Japanese Linguistics

KANEKO, K., Eating Habits Studies

KASAHARA, M., Cultural Anthropology

KATO, C., Japanese Modern History

KIKUCHI, T., Ecology, Environment

KIMURA, M., Sports Science

KITAGAWA, Y., Constitutional Law

KOBAYASHI, K., History of Thought

KOBAYASHI, N., Form, Structure

KOBAYASHI, Y., Movement Education Therapy

KOIZUMI, H., Teaching Methods

MAEDA, M., Geometry

MAJIMA, R., Palaeontology

MATSUISHI, T., Neuropsychiatric Studies

MIYAKE, A., Japanese Literature

MIYAZAKI, T., Philosphy, Ethics

MOCHIDA, Y., Ecology, Environment

MORIMOTO, S., Physiology and Applied Physiology, Exercise Physiology

MORIMOTO, S., Science Education

MOTEKI, K., Applied Musicology

MURATA, T., Modern Chinese History

MUROI, H., Aesthetics, Semiotics, Cultural Studies, Philosophy

NAKAGAWA, T., Education for the Hearing-imparied

NAKAMURA, E., Analytical Chemistry

NEGAMI, S., Topological Graph Theory

NISHIMURA, T., Consumer Policy

NISHIMURA, T., Geometry

NISHIWAKI, Y., Geographic Education

NUKATA, J., Cognitive Engineering

NUSHI, A., Educational Psychology

OCHIAI, M., Subject Pedagogy

OGAWA, M., Music Education

OKADA, M., Classical Chinese Literature

ONO, Y., Aesthetics, History of Art

OOISHI, A., Commutative Algebra

OSATO, T., Musicology

OSHIMA, A., Educational Technology

OTAKI, F., Piano Performance

SAKAI, Y., Computer Science

SANO, F., Outdoor Recreation

SASAKI, H., Pedagogy

SATO, Y., Form, Structure

SHIMOJO, H., Ethics

SHIROUZU, N., Modern Chinese Literature

SUGIMURA, H., Organic Chemistry

SUGIYAMA, T., Piano Performance

SUKAWA, H., Korean Economic History

SUZUKI, K., Weather, Oceanic Physics, Hydrology

SUZUKI, T., Home Economics Education, Family Studies

TAJIMA, F., Optical Measurement

TAKAGI, H., Adolescent Psychology

TAKAGI, M., Curriculum Studies

TAKAGI, N., Teaching Methodology

TAKAHASHI, K., Dance Education

TAKAHASHI, K., English Linguistics

TAKAHASHI, M., Educational Anthropology

TAKAYAMA, Y., Psychology of the Disabled

TAKUSARI, D., Aesthetics, History of Art

TANAKA, H., Environmental Physiology

TANEDA, Y., Colony Specificity

TANJI, Y., American Literature, Realism, Naturalism, Women's Studies

TANISHO, S., Biochemical Engineering

UMEMOTO, Y., History of French Theatre, Cinema Theory

WATABE, M., Sociology

YAMAMOTO, I., Experimental Condensed Matter Physics, Physics Education

YANAI, K., Philosophy

YOKOYAMA, N., Physical Education, Sports Science, Budo, Kendo

Faculty of Engineering (79-5 Tokiwadai, Hodogayaku, Yokohama 240-8501; tel. (45) 339-3804; fax (45) 339-3827; e-mail eng.somu@nuc.ynu.ac.jp; internet www.eng.ynu.ac.jp):

ADACHI, T., Electronic Devices, Electronic Equipment

AMEMIYA, N., Electric Power Engineering, Electronic Equipment Engineering

ANDO, K., Structural Ceramics

ARAI, H., Electromagnetics

ARAI, M., Ship Marine Engineering

ASAMI, M., Synthetic Chemistry

AZUSHIMA, A., Material Processing, Treatment

BABA, T., Applied Optics, Quantum Optical Engineering

FUKUTOMI, H., Structural/Functional Materials

HABUKA, H., Applied Physical Properties, Crystal Engineering

HANEJI, N., Electronic Device, Electronic Equipment

HIRAYAMA, T., Aeronautics

HIROSE, Y., Electronic Device, Electronic Equipment

IIDA, Y., Architectural History, Design

ISHIHARA, O., Plasma Science

ISHII, R., Digital Signal Processing

ITOH, K., Physical Chemistry

KAMEMOTO, K., Fluidics

KAMINOYAMA, M., Chemical Engineering

KAWAI, K., Metal Forming and Numerical Simulation

KAWAMURA, A., Power Electronics

KIMISHIMA, Y., Applied Solid-State Physics

KITADA, Y., Differential Topology

KITAYAMA, K., Architectural History, Design

KOBAYASHI, K., Earth Astrochemistry

KOBAYASHI, S., City Planning

KOHNO, R., Information Communication Technology

KOIZUMI, J., Bio-function, Bioprocessors

KOKUBUN, K., Opto-electronics

KONNO, N., Mathematics

KUROKAWA, J., Fluid Engineering

MAEKAWA, T., Computer-aided Design

MATSUMOTO, K., Chemical Engineering Materials Properties, Transfer Operation, Unit Operation, Separation Engineering

MIURA, K., Metallic Physical Properties

MIZUGUCHI, J., Electronic Properties of Organic Semiconductors and Oxide Semiconductors

NAITO, A., Biophysics

NAKAMURA, F., Urban Transportation Planning

NISHINO, K., Thermal Engineering

OGINO, T., Surface Science and Nanotechnology of Semiconductors

OHARA, K., Theory of Architecture

OHNO, K., Mathematical Physics, Fundamental Theory of Physical Properties

OKUYAMA, K., Heat Transfer

ONO, T., Mathematical Physics, Fundamental Theory of Physical Properties

OTA, K., Energy

OYAMA, T., Power Systems Engineering

SAKAKIBARA, K., Physical Organic Chemistry

SANADA, K., Control Engineering

SASAKI, K., Elementary Particle Physics

SHIBATA, M., Elementary Particle Physics, Atomic Nucleus, Cosmic Ray, Space Physics

SHIBAYAMA, T., Civil Engineering

SHIRATORI, M., Machine Material, Material Mechanics

SUMI, Y., Naval Architecture and Ocean Engineering

SUZUKI, K., Naval Architecture and Ocean Engineering

SUZUKI, K., Physical Properties II

TAGAWA, Y., Building Construction/Material

TAKADA, H., Intelligent Mechanics, Mechanical Systems

TAKAGI, J., Production Engineering, Processing Studies

TAKAHASHI, A., Organic Polymer Chemistry, High Performance Polymers for Microelectronics

TAKANO, S., Mathematics

TAKEDA, J., Physical Properties II

TAKEMURA, Y., Magnetics

TAMANO, K., Geometry

TAMURA, A., Architectural Environment/Equipment

TANAKA, H., Machine Element

TANAKA, M., Thin Film and Surface Interface Physical Properties

TANI, K., Rock Engineering

TASAI, A., Building Structure

TSUBAKI, T., Concrete Engineering

TSUBOI, T., Thermal Engineering

UEDA, K., Polymer/Textile Materials

UMEZAWA, O., Structural/Functional Materials

UTAKA, Y., Thermal Engineering

WATANABE, M., Carcinogenesis

WATANABE, M., Polymer Structure

YABUTA, T., Sensitivity Informatics, Soft Computing

YAGI, M., Physical Chemistry

YAKOU, T., Strength of Materials

YAMAMOTO, M., Architecture

YAMAZAKI, Y., Earthquake Engineering

YOKOYAMA, Y., Organic Industrial Materials

YOSHIDA, K., Architectural History, Design

YOSHIKAWA, N., Electronic Device, Electronic Equipment

Faculty of Environmental and Information Sciences (79-7 Tokiwadai, Hodogayaku, Yokohama 240-8501; tel. (45) 339-4422; fax (45) 339-4430; e-mail env-inf.somu@nuc.ynu.ac.jp; internet www.eis.ynu.ac.jp):

ARIMA, M., Petrology

ARISAWA, H., Media Informatics, Database

FUJIWARA, K., Ecology, Environment

GOTOH, T., Perception Information Processing, Intelligent Robotics

HARA, T., Catalysis by Metal Complexes

HIRANO, N., Functional Analysis

HIRATSUKA, K., Applied Molecular Cell Biology

INOUE, S., Synthetic Chemistry
INOUE, Y., Naval Architecture and Ocean Engineering
KAGEI, S., Fuzzy Control
KANEKO, N., Ecology
KONDO, M., Industrial Technology Policy
MASUNAGA, S., Environmental Dynamic Analysis
MATSUDA, H., Environmental Ecology
MATSUMOTO, T., Information Security
MEGURO, T., Inorganic Materials
MITSUI, I., Regional Industrial Policy
MIYAKE, A., Safety Engineering
MORI, T., Natural Language Processing
MORISHITA, S., Machine Mechanics, Control
NAGAO, T., Biological/Living Body Informatics
NAKAI, S., Environmental Health
OGAWA, T., Safety Engineering
OHNO, K., Landscape Ecology
OHTANI, H., Safety Engineering
OKUTANI, T., Inorganic Material, Physical Properties
SADOHARA, S., Social System Engineering, Safety Systems
SASAMOTO, H., Plant Physiology
SEKINE, K., Material Processing, Treatment
SHIDA, K., Mathematical Sociology
SHUSA, Y., Globalization of Firms
SUZUKI, A., Materials Science
TAKEDA, Y., Management Information Systems
TAMURA, N., Natural Language Processing
TERADA, T., Mathematics
UENO, S., Control Engineering
UESUGI, S., Molecular Biology
YAMADA, H., Structural Engineering
YAMADA, T., Computational Mechanics

Graduate School of Education (79-2 Tokiwadai, Hodogayaku, Yokohama 240-8501; tel. (45) 339-3253; fax (45) 339-3264; e-mail edu.somu@nuc.ynu.ac.jp; internet www.edhs.ynu.ac.jp):

INUZUKA, F., Guidance

International Graduate School of Social Sciences (79-4 Tokiwadai, Hodogayaku, Yokohama 240-8501; tel. (45) 339-3602; fax (45) 339-3661; e-mail int.somu@nuc.ynu.ac.jp; internet www.igss.ynu.ac.jp):

ABE, S., Marketing, Consumer Behaviour
ARAKI, I., Int. Law
ARIE, D., Economic Doctrine, Economic Thought
ASANO, Y., Finance
DOI, H., Economic Theory
FUJIMORI, T., Resolution Process in Interpersonal Conflicts
HAMAMOTO, M., Accounting
HARADA, K., Constitutional Law
HIGASHIDA, A., Economic Statistics
IGARASHI, A., Int. Accounting, Int. Auditing
IKEDA, T., Devt Economics
IMAMURA, Y., Civil Law
INOWE, T., Finance, Macroeconomics
ISHIYAMA, Y., Economic History
IWASAKI, M., Tax Law
IZUMI, H., Accounting and Book-keeping Systems
KATO, M., Environmental Law
KAWABATA, Y., Public Law
KAWASHIMA, K., Gen. Civil and Commercial Practice
KIMIZUKA, M., Public Law
KOBAYASHI, M., Linguistics
KODA, K., Macroeconomics
KOIKE, O., Politics
KURASAWA, M., Theoretical Economics
KURUSHIMA, T., Commercial Law
MATSUI, Y., Business Admin.
MITO, H., Business Admin.
MIZOGUCHI, S., Management Accounting
MORIKAWA, T., Int. Law
NAGAI, K., Mathematical Statistics

NAKAMURA, K., Regional and Local Political Economy
NAKAMURA, Y., English Studies
NAKAMURA, Y., Gen. Theory of Economics
NEMOTO, Y., Int. Law
NOMURA, H., Civil Law
OKABE, J., Economic Statistics
OKADA, E., Business Admin.
OKUMURA, T., Monetary Economics
OKUYAMA, K., Sociology of Law
OSAWA, Y., Commercial Law
SAINO, H., Criminal Law
SAITO, S., Accounting
SANBE, N., Admin. Law
SATO, M., Criminal Law
SHIBATA, H., Int. and Comparative Human Resource Management
SUGIHARA, M., Financial, Commercial and Civil Law
TAKAHASHI, J., Civil Law, Land Law, Sociology Law
TAKAHASHI, M., Fiscal Studies, Finance Theory
TANAKA, M., Business Admin.
TANAKA, T., Criminal Law
TASHIRO, Y., Agricultural Policy
TOKUE, Y., Criminal and Procedure Law
UEMURA, H., Theoretical Economics
YAMAGUCHI, O., Pension Mathematics
YOO, H., Int. Law

ATTACHED RESEARCH INSTITUTES

Center for Future Medical Social Infrastructure Based on Information Communications Technology: 79-7 Tokiwadai, Hodogayaku, Yokahama; tel. and fax (45) 339-4490; e-mail mict@ynu.ac.jp; internet www.mict-ynu.ac.jp; Dir RYUJI KOHNO.

Center for Risk Management and Safety Sciences: 79-5 Tokiwadai, Hodogayaku, Yokohama 240-8501; tel. (45) 339-3776; fax (45) 339-4294; e-mail anshin@ynu.ac.jp; internet www.anshin.ynu.ac.jp; Dir KAZUYOSHI SEKINE.

Cooperative Research and Development Center: 79-5 Tokiwadai, Hodogayaku, Yokohama 240-8501; tel. (45) 339-4381; fax (45) 339-4387; e-mail cordec@nuc.ynu.ac.jp; internet www.crd.ynu.ac.jp; Dir SHIN MORISHITA.

Education Center: 79-1 Tokiwadai, Hodogayaku, Yokohama 240-8501; tel. (45) 339-3135; fax (45) 339-3141; e-mail kyomu.gakumu@nuc.ynu.ac.jp; internet www.yec.ynu.ac.jp; Dir KUNIO SUZUKI.

Global–Local Education Research Center: 79-3 Tokiwadai, Hodogayaku, Yokohama 240-8501; tel. and fax (45) 339-3579; e-mail chiki-ct@ynu.ac.jp; internet www.crd.ynu.ac.jp/chiki-ct; Dir SHIGETAKA KOBAYASHI.

Health Service Center: 79-1 Tokiwadai, Hodogayaku, Yokohama 240-8501; tel. (45) 339-3153; fax (45) 339-3156; e-mail healths@nuc.ynu.ac.jp; internet www.hoken.ynu.ac.jp; Dir ETSUKO TANAKA.

Information Technology Service Center: 79-5 Tokiwadai, Hodogayaku, Yokohama 240-8501; tel. (45) 339-4390; fax (45) 339-4393; e-mail joho.kikaku@nuc.ynu.ac.jp; internet www.ipc.ynu.ac.jp; Dir EISAKU OTSUKA.

Instrumental Analysis Center: 79-5 Tokiwadai, Hodogayaku, Yokohama 240-8501; tel. (45) 339-4406; fax (45) 339-4406; e-mail iac@nuc.ynu.ac.jp; internet www.iac.ynu.ac.jp; Dir YASUSHI YOKOYAMA.

International Student Center: 79-1 Tokiwadai, Hodogayaku, Yokohama 240-8501; tel. (45) 339-3186; fax (45) 339-3189; e-mail ryugakusei.center@nuc.ynu.ac.jp; internet www.isc.ynu.ac.jp; Dir TOMOYA SHIBAYAMA.

Office of Industry and Community Liaison: 179-5 Tokiwadai, Hodogayaku,

Yokahama 240-8501; tel. (45) 339-4449; fax (45) 339-4456; e-mail sangaku.sangaku@nuc.ynu.ac.jp; internet www.crd.ynu.ac.jp; Dir SHINSUKE WATANABE.

Radioisotope (RI) Center: 79-5 Tokiwadai, Hodogayaku, Yokohama 240-8501; tel. (45) 339-4410; fax (45) 339-4410; internet www.ric.ynu.ac.jp; Dir SHIGEMARU TANISHO.

Venture Business Laboratory: 79-5 Tokiwadai, Hodogayaku, Yokohama 240-8501; tel. (45) 339-4280; fax (45) 339-4280; e-mail ec-kanri@ynu.ac.jp; internet www.vbl.ynu.ac.jp; Dir AKIHIRO TAMURA.

Municipal Institutions

AOMORI UNIVERSITY OF HEALTH AND WELFARE

Mase 58-1 Hamadate, Aomori 030-8505

Telephone: (17) 765-2000
Fax: (17) 765-2188
E-mail: webmaster@auhw.ac.jp
Internet: www.auhw.ac.jp

Founded 1999

Pres.: SACHIE SHINDO

Faculty of Health Sciences, incl. divs of Human Sciences, Nursing, Social Welfare, Therapy.

DAIDO INSTITUTE OF TECHNOLOGY

10-3 Takiharu-cho, Minami-ku, Nagoya
Internet: www.daido-it.ac.jp

Founded 1961

Pres.: AKIRA SAWAOKA

Library of 170,000 vols
Number of teachers: 97
Number of students: 3,530

Schools of Informatics, Engineering, Liberal Arts and Sciences; Graduate School of Technology.

EDOGAWA UNIVERSITY

Komaki 474, Nagareyama-shi, Chiba-ken 270-0198

Telephone: (4) 7152-0661
Fax: (4) 7154-2490
E-mail: webmaster@edogawa-u.ac.jp
Internet: www.edogawa-u.ac.jp

Founded 1990

College of Sociology.

FUJI WOMEN'S UNIVERSITY

Kita 16-jo Nishi 2, Kita-ku, Sapporo-shi, Hokkaido 001-0016

Telephone: (11) 736-0311
Fax: (11) 709-8541
E-mail: somu@fujijoshi.ac.jp
Internet: www.fujijoshi.ac.jp

Founded 1961

Pres.: YOSHIKO NAGATA

Library of 300,000 vols
Number of teachers: 89
Number of students: 2,250

Faculties of Humanities, Life Sciences.

FUJITA HEALTH UNIVERSITY

1–98 Dengakugakubo, Kutsukake-cho, Toyoake, Aichi-ken 470-1192

Telephone: (562) 93-2504
Fax: (562) 93-4595

Founded 1964

Pres.: HIROSHI NAKANO

Library of 172,000 vols, 1,068 periodicals

Faculties of Medical Technology, Nursing, Radiological Technology, Rehabilitation.

FUKUI UNIVERSITY OF TECHNOLOGY

3-6-1 Gakuen, Fukui City, Fukui 910-8505
Telephone: (776) 29-2620
Fax: (776) 29-7891
E-mail: kouhou@fukui-ut.ac.jp
Internet: www.fukui-ut.ac.jp
Pres.: Prof. MASAHIRO JOHNO
Chancellor: Prof. KEN KANAI

Number of teachers: 160

Departments of Applied Nuclear Technology, Architecture and Civil Engineering, Electrical and Electronic Engineering, Environmental and Biotechnological Frontier Engineering, Management Information Science, Mechanical Engineering, Space Communication Engineering.

FUKUOKA INSTITUTE OF TECHNOLOGY

3-30-1 Wajiro-Higashi, Higashi-ku, Fukuoka 811-0295
Telephone: (92) 606-0607
Fax: (92) 606-7357
E-mail: www-staff@fit.ac.jp
Internet: www.fit.ac.jp
Pres.: KAORU YAMAFUJI

Faculties of Engineering, Information Engineering, Social and Environmental Studies.

FUKUSHIMA MEDICAL UNIVERSITY

1 Hikariga-oka, Fukushima City 960-1295
Telephone: (24) 547-1111
Fax: (24) 547-1995
E-mail: sshigeta@fmu.ac.jp
Internet: www.fmu.ac.jp
Founded 1950
Academic year: April to March
Pres.: SHIRO SHIGETA
Dir of Library: T. SUZUKI
Sec.: Y. YOSHIDA
Hospital Dir: S. NIWA

Library of 138,738 vols
Number of teachers: 330
Number of students: 820

Publications: *Fukushima Igaku Zasshi* (Fukushima Medical Journal, 4 a year), *Fukushima Journal of Medical Science* (2 a year)

Faculty of Medicine, Faculty of Nursing, Postgraduate Research Institute, Hospital

DEANS

Faculty of Medicine: HIDEO KOCHI
Faculty of Nursing: YOKO NAKAYAMA

GIFU PHARMACEUTICAL UNIVERSITY

5-6-1, Mitahora-higashi, 5-chome, Gifu 502-8585
Telephone: (58) 237-3931
Fax: (58) 237-5979
E-mail: iinuma@gifu-pu.ac.jp
Internet: www.gifu-pu.ac.jp
Founded 1932
Municipal Control
Academic year: April to March
Pres.: Prof. MASAYUKI KUZUYA
Chief Admin. Officer: TAKASHI SHINODA
Library Dir: Prof. HIROICHI NAGAI

Library of 59,000 vols
Number of teachers: 70
Number of students: 649

Publications: *Bulletin of Liberal Arts, Proceedings* (1 a year)

DEANS

Faculty of Manufacturing Pharmacy: Prof. TADASHI KATAOKA
Faculty of Pharmaceutical Science: Prof. KAZUYUKI HIRANO

PROFESSORS

FURUKAWA, S., Molecular Biology
GOTO, M., Pharmaceutical Analytical Chemistry
HARA, A., Biochemistry
HIRANO, K., Pharmaceutics
HIROTA, K., Medicinal Chemistry
INOUE, K., Pharmacognosy
KATAOKA, T., Pharmaceutical Chemistry
KAWASHIMA, Y., Pharmaceutical Engineering
KUZUYA, M., Pharmaceutical Physical Chemistry
MASAKI, Y., Pharmaceutical Synthetic Chemistry
MORI, H., Microbiology
NAGAI, H., Pharmacology
NAGASE, H., Hygienics

HACHINOHE INSTITUTE OF TECHNOLOGY

88-1 Ohbiraki Myo, Hachinohe, Aomori 031-8501
Telephone: (178) 25-3111
E-mail: www-admin@hi-tech.ac.jp
Internet: www.hi-tech.ac.jp
Founded 1972
Pres.: Dr SHOYA MASAMI

Library of 100,000 vols, 300 periodicals
Number of students: 5,000

Faculties of Architectural Engineering, Chemical Engineering on Biological Environments, Electronic Intelligence and Systems, Environmental and Civil Engineering, Mechanical Systems on Information Technology, System and Information Engineering, Liberal Arts and Technology.

HAKUOH UNIVERSITY

1117 Daigyoji, Oyama City, Tochigi Prefecture 323-8585
Telephone: (285) 22-1111
Fax: (285) 22-8989
E-mail: nyuushi@hakuoh.ac.jp
Internet: www.hakuoh.ac.jp
Pres.: MAYUMI MORIYAMA
Founded 1915
Number of students: 4,000
Library of 175,000 vols

Faculties of Business Management, Education and Law.

HAMAMATSU UNIVERSITY SCHOOL OF MEDICINE

1-20-1 Handayama Hamamatsu-shi Sizuoka, Hamamatsu City 431-3192
Telephone: (53) 435-2111
Fax: (53) 433-7290
Internet: www.hama-med.ac.jp
Founded 1974
Number of teachers: 273
Medical school.

HANNAN UNIVERSITY

5-4-3 Amami, Higashi, Matsubara, Osaka 580-8502
Telephone: (72) 332-1224
E-mail: webmaster@hannan-u.ac.jp
Internet: www.hannan-u.ac.jp
Founded 1965
Pres.: SHINICHI OTSUKI

Faculties of business, economics, international communication, management information.

HEALTH SCIENCES UNIVERSITY OF HOKKAIDO

1757 Kanazawa, Tobetsu-cho, Ishikari-gun, Hokkaido 061-0293
Telephone: (1332) 3-1211
Fax: (1332) 3-1669
E-mail: nice@hoku-iryo-u.ac.jp
Internet: www.hoku-iryo-u.ac.jp
Founded 1974
Library of 145,000 vols
Number of students: 2,400

Faculty of Pharmaceutical Sciences, Schools of Dentistry, Nursing and Social Services, Psychological Science.

HIMEJI INSTITUTE OF TECHNOLOGY

2167 Shosha, Himeji City, Hyogo 671-2201
Telephone: (792) 66-1661
Fax: (792) 66-8868
E-mail: www-adm@cnth.himeji-tech.ac.jp
Internet: www.himeji-tech.ac.jp
Founded 1944 as Hyogo Prefectural Special College of Technology, 1949 under present name
Academic year: April to March
President: TADAO HAKUSHI
Dean of Students: HIROSHI NAKAYAMA
Dir of Administration: TOSHIAKI SUZUKI
Library Dir: HIDEHIKO NAKANO
Library of 173,000 vols
Number of teachers: 354
Number of students: 3,222
Publication: *Reports of Himeji Institute of Technology* (1 a year)

DEANS

Department of General Education: YASUKAGE ODA
Faculty of Engineering: MOTOYOSHI HASEGAWA
Faculty of Science: SHIGERU TERABE
School of Humanities for Environmental Policy and Technology: JUNJI KIHARA

HOSHI UNIVERSITY

2-4-41 Ebara, Shinagawa, Tokyo 142-8501
Telephone: (3) 5498-5821
Fax: (3) 3787-0036
E-mail: www@hoshi.ac.jp
Internet: www.hoshi.ac.jp
Library of 85,000 vols, 716 periodicals
Number of students: 1,200

Faculty of Pharmaceutical Sciences.

IWATE PREFECTURAL UNIVERSITY

152-52 Takizawa-aza-sugo, Takizawa, Iwate 020-0193
Telephone: (19) 694-2012
Fax: (19) 694-2011
Internet: www.iwate-pu.ac.jp
Founded 1988
President: TANIGUCHI MAKOTO
Vice-President: (vacant)

DEANS

Faculty of Nursing: TSUBOYAMA MICHIKO
Faculty of Policy Studies: KOMARU MASAAKI
Faculty of Social Welfare: SATO TADASHI
Faculty of Software and Information Science: SUGAWARA MITSUMASA

KITAKYUSHU UNIVERSITY

4-2-1 Kitagata, Kokuraminami-ku, Kita-kyushu-shi, Fukuoka 802-8577

Telephone: (93) 962-1837
E-mail: shomu@kitakyu-u.ac.jp
Internet: www.kitakyu-u.ac.jp

Founded 1946, university status 1950
Library of 379,000 vols
Number of students: 5,456

KOBE CITY UNIVERSITY OF FOREIGN STUDIES

9-1 Gakuen-higashi-machi, Nishi-ku, Kobe 6512187

Telephone: (78) 794-8121
E-mail: info@office.kobe-cufs.ac.jp
Internet: www.kobe-cufs.ac.jp

Founded 1946
Academic year: April to March

Pres.: EIICHI KIMURA
Registrar: MASAAKI OMORI
Librarian: SHIRO WADA

Library of 390,000 vols
Number of teachers: 90
Number of students: 2,300

KOBE UNIVERSITY OF COMMERCE

Gakuen-nishimachi, Nishi-ku, Kobe 651-2197

Telephone: (78) 794-6161
Fax: (78) 794-6166
E-mail: shomuka@kobuec.ac.jp
Internet: www.kobeuc.ac.jp/index_e.htm

Founded 1929
State control
Language of instruction: Japanese
Academic year: April to March

President: YASUO SAKAMOTO
Registrar: NOBUHIDE FUJIWARA
Librarian: KENTARO NOMURA

Library of 406,000 vols
Number of teachers: 103
Number of students: 2,050

KUMAMOTO PREFECTURAL UNIVERSITY

3-1-100 Tsukide, Kumamoto City 862-8502

Telephone: (96) 383-2929
Fax: (96) 384-6765
E-mail: www-admin@pu-kumamoto.ac.jp
Internet: www.pu-kumamoto.ac.jp

Founded 1947

Library of 300,000 vols

Faculties of Administration, Cultural Studies, Environmental and Symbiotic Sciences, Letters.

KYOTO PREFECTURAL UNIVERSITY OF MEDICINE

465 Kajii-cho, Kawaramachi, Hirokoji, Kami-kyo-ku, Kyoto 602-8566

Telephone: (75) 251-5111
E-mail: kikaku01@koto.kpu-m.ac.jp
Internet: www.kpu-m.ac.jp

Founded 1873

President: IBATA YASUHIKO
Dean of Students: MARUNAKA YOSHINORI
Director of University Hospital: YAMAGISHI HISAKAZU
Director of Library: NISHIMURA TSUNEHIKO

Library of 218,000 vols
Number of teachers: 304
Number of students: 649 undergraduate, 193 postgraduate

Publication: *Kyoto Furitsu Ikadaigaku Zasshi* (Journal)

College of Medical Technology: T. REIKO
Faculty of Culture and Education: M. SANO
Graduate School: F. SHINJI

KYOTO SANGYO UNIVERSITY

Motoyama, Kamigamo, Kita-ku, Kyoto City 603-8555

Telephone: (75) 705-1408
Fax: (75) 705-1409
E-mail: info-adm@star.kyoto-su.ac.jp
Internet: www.kyoto-su.ac.jp

Founded 1965

Pres.: TOYOH SAKAI

Number of teachers: 297
Number of students: 12,949 undergraduates, 301 graduates

Faculties of Business Administration, Cultural Studies, Economics, Engineering, Foreign Languages, Law, Science.

KYUSHU SANGYO UNIVERSITY

3-1 Matsukadai 2-chome, Higashi-ku, Fukuoka 813-8503

Telephone: (92) 673-5050
Fax: (92) 673-5599
Internet: www.ip.kyusan-u.ac.jp

Founded 1960

Chair.: YAMASHITA HIROHIKO
Pres.: SAGO TAKASHI

Library of 712,310 vols
Number of teachers: 330
Number of students: 15,200

Faculties of Commerce, Economics, Engineering, Fine Arts, Information Science, International Culture, Management.

NAGANO UNIVERSITY

Shimonogo 658-1, Ueda-shi, Nagano-ken 386-1298

Telephone: (268) 39-0001
Fax: (268) 39-0002
E-mail: kouhou@nagano.ac.jp
Internet: www.nagano.ac.jp

Founded 1966

Pres.: RIKIO SHIMADA

Library of 127,000 vols
Number of teachers: 120
Number of students: 1,656

Faculties of Social Science and Social Welfare.

NAGASAKI PREFECTURAL UNIVERSITY

123 Kawashimo-cho, Sasebo-shi, Nagasaki-ken 858-8580

Telephone: (956) 47-2191
Fax: (956) 47-6941
Internet: www.nagasakipu.ac.jp

Founded 1967

Depts of Distributive Science and Business Administration, Economics, Regional Policy; Graduate School of Economics.

NAGOYA CITY UNIVERSITY

1 Kawasumi, Mizuho-cho, Mizuho-ku, Nagoya

Telephone: (52) 841-6201
Fax: (52) 841-6201
E-mail: admin@cc.nagoya-cu.ac.jp
Internet: www.nagoya-cu.ac.jp

Founded 1950

Pres.: YOSHIRO WADA
Sec.-Gen.: S. ISOBE
Library Dir: S. SAITO

Library of 502,973 vols
Number of teachers: 536
Number of students: 3,500

Publications: *Nagoya Medical Journal* (in English, 4 a year), *NCU* (in Japanese), *Oikonomika* (in Japanese, 4 a year)

Faculty of Economics: Y. NAITO
Faculty of Pharmaceutical Sciences: H. IKEZAWA
Medical School: M. SASAKI
School of Design and Architecture: T. YANAGISAWA
School of Humanities and Social Sciences: T. KIDO

OSAKA CITY UNIVERSITY

3-3-138, Sugimoto, Sumiyoshi-ku, Osaka-Ski 558-8585

Telephone: (6) 6605-3411
Fax: (6) 6692-1295
E-mail: koho@ado.osaka-cu.ac.jp
Internet: www.osaka-cu.ac.jp

Founded 1949
Academic year: April to March

Pres.: Y. NISHIZAWA
Vice-President: T. KIRIYAMA
Vice-Pres.: M. MIYANO
Vice-Chair.: T. KASHIWAGI
Dean of Bureau for Admissions and Education: K. TAMAI
Dean of Bureau for Students' Affairs: K. MIURA
Dir of Media Centre: H. HASHIMOTO

Library of 2,400,000 books, 9,500 periodicals
Number of teachers: 929
Number of students: 9,096

Publications: *Geosciences News Letter* (1 a year), *Journal of Geosciences, Osaka City University* (1 a year), *OCU Business News Letter* (1 a year), *OCU Prospectus* (every 2 years), *Osaka Journal of Mathematics* (4 a year)

Graduate School and Faculty of Business: K. AOYAMA
Graduate School and Faculty of Economics: K. WAKIMURA
Graduate School and Faculty of Engineering: H. OOSHIMA
Graduate School and Faculty of Law: T. YASUTAKE
Graduate School and Faculty of Literature and Human Science: M. MURATA
Graduate School and Faculty of Human Life Science: S. TAJIMI
Graduate School and Faculty of Science: H. SAKURAGI
Graduate School for Creative Cities: S. NAKAMOTO
Graduate School of Medicine and Medical School: O. ISHIKO
Graduate School of Nursing: M. IMANAKA

OSAKA GAKUIN UNIVERSITY

2-36-1 Kishibe-Minami, Suita-shi, Osaka 564-8511

Telephone: (6) 6381-8434
Fax: (6) 6382-4363
E-mail: www-admin@uta.osaka-gu.ac.jp
Internet: www.osaka-gu.ac.jp

Pres.: YOSHIYASU SHIRAI

Library of 990,000 vols

Faculties of Business Administrative Sciences, Corporate Intelligence, Distribution and Communication Sciences, Economics, Foreign Languages, Informatics, International Studies, Law.

OSAKA PREFECTURE UNIVERSITY

1-1 Gakuen-cho, Sakai, Osaka 599-8531

Telephone: (72) 252-1161

Fax: (72) 254-9900

Internet: www.osakafu-u.ac.jp

Founded 1949 as Naniwa University; present name 1955

Prefectural control

Academic year: April to March

Pres.: TSUTOMU MINAMI

Admin.: TOSHIHIKO HONDA

Dir. of Library and Science Information Centre: YOJI HIMENO

Library of 1,072,033 vols

Number of teachers: 871

Number of students: 6,332

Publications: *British and American Language and Culture, DMSIS Research Report, Journal of Economics, Business and Law*

DEANS

College of Agriculture: MITSUNORI KIRIHATA

College of Economics: KATSUHIRO MIYAMOTO

College of Engineering: YOJI TAKEDA

College of Integrated Arts and Sciences: SIGEMITSU NAKANISI

College of Social Welfare: YOICHI DOI

SAPPORO MEDICAL UNIVERSITY

Nishi 17-chome, Minami 1-jo, Chuo-ku, Sapporo, Hokkaido 060

Telephone: (11) 611-2111

Fax: (11) 612-5861

E-mail: info@sapmed.ac.jp

Internet: www.sapmed.ac.jp

Founded 1945 as Hokkaido Prefectural School of Medicine; became Sapporo Medical College 1950; present name 1993

Academic year: April to March

Pres.: A. YACHI

Chief Admin. Officer: M. WATANABE

Librarian: S. URASAWA

Library of 214,000 vols

Number of teachers: 373

Number of students: 1,026

Publication: *Sapporo Igaku Zassi* (Sapporo Medical Journal, with English summaries, 6 a year)

DEANS

School of Health Sciences: T. SATO

School of Medicine: M. MORI

SHIMONOSEKI UNIVERSITY

2-1-1 Daigakucho, Shimonoseki City, Yamaguchi Prefecture 751-8510

Telephone: (832) 52-0288

Fax: (832) 52-8099

E-mail: www-admin@shimonoseki-cu.ac.jp

Internet: www.shimonoseki-cu.ac.jp

Founded 1962

Library of 171,200 vols

Number of students: 2,270

Schools of Economics and International Commerce.

TOKYO METROPOLITAN UNIVERSITY

Minami-Ohsawa 1-1, Hachioji-shi, Tokyo 192-0397

Telephone: (426) 77-1111

Fax: (426) 77-1221

Internet: www.metro-u.ac.jp

Founded 1949

Municipal control

Language of instruction: Japanese

Academic year: April to March (2 terms)

President: K. OGIUE

Director of Administrative Bureau: T. MORUOKA

Librarian: M. MAEDA

Library: see Libraries and Archives

Number of teachers: 646

Number of students: 6,540

Publications: *Bulletin* (1 a year), *Daigaku-hiroba* (6 a year), *Gakuhou* (2 a year)

DEANS

Center for Urban Studies: TOSHIHIKO MOGI

Faculty of Economics: TOSHINAO NAKATSUKA

Faculty of Engineering: KOHEI SUZUKI

Faculty of Law: MASAHIDE MAEDA

Faculty of Science: HIDEYUKI SATO

Faculty of Social Sciences and Humanities: SATORU NAGUMO

PROFESSORS

Center for Urban Studies:

AKIYAMA, T., City Transportation Planning

HAGAI, M., Comparative Urban Public Administration

HAGIHARA, K., Urban and Regional Economics

HOSHI, T., Health Science

MATSUMOTO, Y., Social Network Theory

NAKABAYASHI, I., Urban Geography and City Planning

TAMAGAWA, H., Urban Space Analysis

Faculty of Economics:

ASANO, H., Marketing Science

ASANO, S., Econometrics

CHIBA, J., Financial Accounting

FUKAGAI, Y., History of Economic Thought

FUKUSHIMA, T., Public Economics, International Economics

HIGANO, M., Money and Banking

KANAYA, S., Fiscal and Monetary Policy

KUWATA, K., Management Strategy

MIYAKAWA, A., Marxian Economic Theory, History of Economic Thought

MURAKAMI, N., Chinese Enterprise Location

NAKAMURA, J., Labour Economics

NAKATSUKA, T., Business Administration, Operations Research

OMORI, Y., Econometrics

TODA, H., Econometrics

WAKITA, S., Japanese Labour Market

YAGO, K., French Economic History

YAMATO, T., Distribution Mechanism

YAMAZAKI, S., Distribution Policy

Faculty of Engineering:

ANDO, Y., River Engineering, Applied Hydrology

ASAKO, Y., Heat and Mass Transfer

CHIKAZAWA, M., Physical Chemistry of Solid Surfaces

FUKAO, S., Building Construction

FURUKAWA, Y., Precision Machining and Computer-Aided Manufacturing Systems

FURUKAWA, Y., Precision Machining and Computer-Aided Manufacturing Systems

HOBO, T., Analytical Chemistry and Instrumental Analysis

IGOSHI, M., Computer-Aided Design and Manufacturing

IKUTA, S., Parallel Algorithms

INOUE, H., Physical Organic Photochemistry

ISHIKAWA, H., E-business Model and Database

ISHINO, H., Building Service Engineering

ITO, D., Superconductors and their Applications

IWASAKI, K., Computer Architecture

IWATATE, T., Geomechanics

IYODA, T., Molecular Functional Materials

KATAKURA, M., Traffic Engineering and Infrastructure Planning

KAWAI, T., Organic Chemistry

KAWATA, S., Control Engineering

KIMURA, G., Electrical Machinery and Power Electronics

KITSUTAKA, Y., Building Material Engineering

KIYA, T., Digital Signal Management

KOBAYASHI, K., Architectural Theory and Design

KOIZUMI, A., Sanitary Engineering

KOKUBU, K., Concrete Technology

MAEDA, K., Bridge and Structural Engineering

MASUDA, H., Electrical Chemistry

MISAWA, H., Strength of Materials

MORIYA, T., Applications of Ultrasonics

NAGAHAMA, K., Chemical Engineering, Phase Equilibrium and Related Properties

NAGAOKA, S., Functional Materials

NAGASAWA, S., Applications of Lasers and Remote Sensing

NAKAMURA, I., Robotics and Mechatronics

NISHIKAWA, T., Structural Engineering

NISHIMURA, K., Geomechanics

NISHIMURA, H., Plasticity and New Materials Processing

OKUMURA, T., Semiconductor Physics, Optoelectric Devices

OTA, Y., Power Engineering

SAKAKI, T., Strength of Metals and Alloys

SEKIMOTO, H., Piezo-electrical Vibrations and their applications

SUZUKI, K., Structural Dynamics

TAKAMIZAWA, K., City Planning

TAKI, M., Bioelectromagnetics, Noise Control Engineering

UENO, J., Architectural Planning

UMEGAKI, T., Ceramics, Inorganic Phosphate Chemistry

UMEYAMA, M., Water Environmental Engineering

WATANABE, K., Hydrodynamics, Hydraulic Machinery

WATANABE, T., Environment and Energy Saving

YAMADA, M., Chemical Sensing and Instrumentation

YAMAGISHI, T., Synthetic Organic Chemistry

YAMAZAKI, S., Structural Engineering

YOKOYAMA, R., Control and Optimization of Large-Scale Systems

YOSHIBA, M., High Temperature Material

Faculty of Law:

ASAKURA, M., Labour Law, Social Security Law

FUCHI, M., European Legal History

HITOMI, T., Decentralization and Local Autonomy

IKEDA, T., Civil Law, Law of Land Property

ISHIDA, A., Domestic Politics and International Politics

ISHII, M., Civil Law, Medical Law

ISHIKAWA, K., Constitutional Law

ISOBE, T., Administrative Law

KIMURA, M., Criminal Law

MAEDA, M., Criminal Law

MIYAMURA, H., History of Japanese Political Thought

MIZUBAYASHI, T., Japanese Legal History

MORIYAMA, S., East Asian Politics

MORITA, A., Outside Application of National Control

NAKAJIMA, H., Civil Procedure

NAWATA, Y., Philosophy of Law

NOGAMI, K., Political History of Western Countries

NOMURA, Y., Civil Law, Environmental Law

SHIBUYA, T., Commercial Law, Intellectual Property Law, Competition Law

Faculty of Science:

ABE, T., Physical Training

ACHIBA, Y., Laser Chemistry

AIHARA, Y., Ageing and Temperature Regulation

EBIHARA, M., Space Chemistry

FUKUSAWA, H., Classical Oceanography

GUEST, M., Geometry
HIROSE, T., Experimental High-Energy Physics
HISANAGA, S., Cell Biology
HORI, N., Environmental Geography
HUYAMA, Y., Genetics
IKEMOTO, I., Solid-State Chemistry
IMANAKA, K., Human Motor Behaviour, Perception and Motor Control
ISOBE, T., Biological Chemistry
ISOZAKI, H., Partial Differential Equations
IWATA, S., Glacial Geomorphology
IYODA, M., Organic Chemistry
IZAWA, T., Biochemistry and Physiology of Exercise
KACHI, N., Botanical Ecology
KAINOSHO, M., Biochemistry
KAMIGATA, N., Organic Chemistry
KAMISHIMA, Y., Topology
KATADA, M., Physical Inorganic Chemistry and Radiochemistry
KATO, T., Physical Chemistry
KIKUCHI, T., Topography
KOBAYASHI, N., Atomic and Molecular Physics (Experimental)
KOMANO, T., Molecular Genetics
KORANAGA, T., Micro-nano System
KOUGI, M., Neutron Scattering and Solid-State Physics
KUWASAWA, K., Neurobiology
MIKAMI, T., Climatology, Climate Change, Urban Climate
MINAKATA, H., High-energy Physics
MIYAHARA, T., Solid-State Spectroscopy
MIYAKE, K., Number Theory
MIZOGUCHI, K., Solid-State Physics and Magnetic Resonance
MOCHIZUKI, K., Partial Differential Equations
NAKAMURA, K., Algebraic Number Theory and Algorithms
OHASHI, T., X-ray Astronomy
OHNITA, Y., Differential Geometry and Lie Groups
OKA, M., Singularity Theory and Algebraic Geometry
OKABE, Y., Theoretical Condensed-Matter Physics
OKADA, M., Harmonious Analysis
OKUNO, K., Atomic Physics
PRICE, W. S., Biochemistry
SAITO, S., Elementary Particle Basic Theory
SAKAI, M., Analytic Functions
SATO, H., Electron Theory of Metals
SHIMADA, K., Bacteriology
SUGIURA, Y., Human Geography
SUZUKI, T., Atomic Nuclear Physics
TAKII, S., Microbial Ecology
TERAO, H., Singularities and Combinatorics
WADA, M., Photobiology
WAKABAYASHI, M., Systematic Botany
WATANABE, Y., Aquatic Ecology
YAMASAKI, H., Seismo-tectonics, Quaternary Geology
YAMASAKI, T., Systematic Zoology
YASUGI, S., Developmental Biology
YOMASHITA, M., Inorganic Chemistry

Faculty of Social Sciences and Humanities:
EBARA, Y., Theoretical Sociology
FUKUI, A., French Philosophy
FUKUMA, K., Modern English Poetry
FUKUMOTO, Y., German Linguistics
FUKUSHIMA, F., African Literature
HARA, K., European Culture
HIRAI, H., Modern Chinese Literature
ICHIHARA, S., Psychology of Perception
IDE, H., English Novels
INADA, A., Classical Literature
INUI, A., Secondary Education and Educational Practice
ISHIHARA, K., Family Studies, Social Research

ISHIKAWA, T., French Philosophy of the 17th Century
ISHINO, K., French Semantics
ITO, C., English Novels
JIN, K., Comparative Linguistics
JITSUKAWA, T., French Philosophy
KAI, H., Ethics
KANZAKI, S., Ancient Greek Philosophy
KATO, M., Modern English Poetry
KIMURA, M., Ancient Korean History
KISHI, Y., German Literature
KOBAYASHI, K., History of Japanese Language
KOBAYASHI, R., Social Studies and Administration
KOTANI, H., Indian History
KUROSAKI, I., Educational Administration
MANZAWA, M., Modern German Literature
MOGI, T., Educational Psychology
MORIOKA, K., Urban Sociology, Comparative Sociology
MURAYAMA, K., American Novels
NAGAI, T., Clinical Psychology
NAGUMO, S., Modern Chinese Literature
NAKAJIMA, H., Theoretical Linguistics
NAKANO, T., Modern French History
NARASAKI, H., Contemporary American Novel
NISHIKAWA, N., French Poetry of the 19th Century
OCHIAI, M., Chinese Dialectology
OGINO, T., Sociolinguistics
OHGUSHI, R., Adult Education
OKABE, H., Modern German Literature
OKABE, T., Social Welfare System
OKADA, E., History of Social Welfare
OKADA, M., Middle French Literature
OKADA, N., German Philosophy
OKAZAWA, S., Contemporary German Literature
OKUBO, Y., French Literature of the 16th Century
OKUMURA, S., Capitalism in Pre-Communist China
ONO, A., Archaeology
ORISHIMA, M., American Novels
OTSUKA, K., Social Anthropology
PEARSON, H. E., Applied Linguistics, TESOL
SATAKE, Y., Federal Chinese History
SATO, S., Chinese Philology
SEO, I., German Literature of the 20th Century
SOEDA, A., Social Methodology
SUDA, O., Developmental Study of Communication
SUZUKI, T., Contemporary Austrian Literature
TAKAHASHI, K., Political Sociology
TAKAYAMA, H., English Poetry of the 18th Century
TANJI, N., Philosophy of Science
UENO, Y., Shakespearian Studies
WATANABE, K., Social Anthropology
YASUDA, T., Reading Process Research
YOSHIKAWA, K., French Literature of the 20th Century

WAKAYAMA MEDICAL UNIVERSITY

811-1 Kimiidera Wakayama City 641-8509
Telephone: (73) 447-2300
E-mail: admin@wakayama-med.ac.jp
Internet: www.wakayama-med.ac.jp
Founded 1945
President: HIROYUKI YAMAMOTO

Library of 63,250 vols
Number of teachers: 260
Number of students: 399
Publications: *Wakayama Igaku* (in Japanese, 4 a year), *Wakayama Medical Reports* (in English, 4 a year).

YOKOHAMA CITY UNIVERSITY

22-2 Seto, Kanazawa-ku, Yokohama 236-0027
Telephone: (45) 787-2311
Fax: (45) 787-2316
E-mail: netadmin@yokohama-cu.ac.jp
Internet: www.yokohama-cu.ac.jp
Founded 1928
Municipal control
Academic year: April to March
Chancellor and Pres.: KEICHI OGAWA
Chief Admin. Officer: ROKUROU TAKAI
Library Dir: MASATAKA OZAKI

Library of 677,610 vols
Number of teachers: 640
Number of students: 5,480

Publications: *Yokohama Shiritu Daigaku Ronso* (Bulletin, 8 a year), *Yokohama Shiritu Daigaku Kiyo* (Journal, 1 a year), *Keizai-to-Boeki* (Industry and Trade, 2 a year), *Yokohama Medical Bulletin* (in English, 1 a year), *Yokohama Igaku* (Medical Journal, 6 a year), *Yokohama Mathematical Journal* (in English, 2 a year)

DEANS

Faculty of Economics and Business Administration: KAWAUCHI YOSHITADA
Faculty of Humanities and International Studies: FUNIO KANEKO
Faculty of Science: MAKI KUNISUKE
School of Medicine: OKUDA KENJI

Private Universities and Colleges

AICHI UNIVERSITY

1-1 Machihata-cho, Toyohashi-shi, Aichi-ken 441-8522
Telephone: (532) 47-4131
Fax: (532) 47-4144
E-mail: inted@aichi-u.ac.jp
Internet: www.aichi-u.ac.jp
Founded 1946
Academic year: April to March
President: NOBUTERU TAKEDA
Registrar: MASASHI WATANABE
Librarian: MITSUSHI TAMAKI

Library of 1,458,362 vols
Number of teachers: 714 (254 full-time, 460 part-time)
Number of students: 10,084

DEANS

Faculty of Business Administration: TATSUHISA MINAMI
Faculty of Economics: MOTOHIKO SATO
Faculty of International Communication: KENICHI TAMOTO
Faculty of Law: KOUJI SHINDO
Faculty of Letters: MASAYOSHI KATANO
Faculty of Modern Chinese Studies: SATOSHI IMAI
Graduate School of Business Administration: MITSUO FUJIMOTO
Graduate School of Chinese Studies: TSUYOSHI BABA
Graduate School of Economics: KOICHI MIYAIRI
Graduate School of Humanities: KAZUYOSHI SHIMIZU
Graduate School of International Communication: SHIN KOUNO
Graduate School of Law: KATSUYOSHI KATO
Junior College: TAKAO KUROYANAGI

AICHI GAKUIN UNIVERSITY

12 Araike, Iwasaki-cho, Nisshin-shi, Aichi-ken 470-0195

Telephone: (5617) 3-1111
Fax: (5617) 3-6769
E-mail: nyushi@dpc.agu.ac.jp
Internet: www.agu.ac.jp

Founded 1876
Private control
Language of instruction: Japanese
Academic year: April to March

Pres.: HIDETO OONO
Registrar: TAICHI HAYAKAWA
Librarian: KUNIHIRO TAKARADA

Library of 1,151,388 vols
Number of teachers: 506
Number of students: 13,273

Publications: *Transactions of the Institute for Cultural Studies* (1 a year), *Business Review of Aichi Gakuin University* (1 a year), *Aichi Gakuin Law Review* (4 a year), *Journal of the Research Institute of Zen* (1 a year), *The Journal of Aichi Gakuin University* (4 a year), *Foreign Languages and Literature* (1 a year), *Journal of Aichi Gakuin University Dental Society* (4 a year), *Regional Analysis* (2 a year)

DEANS

Faculty of Business and Commerce: MAKOTO OZAKI
Faculty of Dentistry: TOSHIHIDE NOGUCHI
Faculty of General Education: MASAMI INAGAKI
Faculty of Law: KEIICHI TAKAGI
Faculty of Letters: MITSURU ANDO
Faculty of Management: ICHIRO MUKAI
Faculty of Pharmacy: TAKUMA SASAKI
Faculty of Policy Studies: TSUDZUKI TAKAHIKO
Faculty of Psychological and Physical Science: YUZOU SATOU
Japanese Language Course for Foreign Students: KATSUSHI KONDO
Junior College: MASASHI MUKAI

UNIVERSITY OF AIZU

Aizu-Wakamatsu, Fukushima-ken 965-8580

Telephone: (242) 37-2500
Fax: (242) 37-2528
E-mail: daigakuin@u-aizu.ac.jp
Internet: www.u-aizu.ac.jp

Founded 1993

Pres.: SHIGEAKI TSUNOYAMA

Number of teachers: 89
Number of students: 1,039

AOYAMA GAKUIN UNIVERSITY

4-4-25 Shibuya, Shibuya-ku, Tokyo 150-8366

Telephone: (3) 3409-8111
Fax: (3) 3409-0927
E-mail: iec-office@iec.aoyama.ac.jp
Internet: www.aoyama.ac.jp

Founded 1874
Academic year: April to March

Chancellor: M. FUKAMACHI
President: Dr M. HANDA
Vice-Press: Dr M. NISHIZAWA, Dr M. TSUJI
Admin. Officer: T. MUNEKATA
Library Dir: Dr H. TAKAMORI

Library of 1,442,666 vols, 16,262 periodicals
Number of teachers: 1,422 (including 976 part-time)
Number of students: 19,372

Publications: *Aoyama Journal of Business* (4 a year), *Aoyama Journal of Economics* (4 a year), *Aoyama Law Review* (4 a year), *Aoyama Journal of General Education*, *Thought Currents in English Literature*, *Educational Inquiry*, *KIYO* (Journal of Literature), *Aoyama Gobun* (Journal of Japanese Literature), *Aoyama Shigaku* (Journal of History), *Aoyama Business Review*, *Aoyama Journal of International Politics, Economics and Business*, *Etudes Françaises*, *Aoyama International Communication Studies*, *Aoyama Management Review*

DEANS

College of Economics: Dr Y. YOSHIZOE
College of Law: Dr T. YAMAZAKI
College of Literature: H. ISHIZAKI
College of Science and Engineering: Dr K. UOZUMI
Graduate School of International Management: Dr F. ITOH
School of Business Administration: S. HASEGAWA
School of International Politics, Economics and Business Administration: S. HAKAMADA

CHAIRS OF DEPARTMENTS

College of Economics (internet www.econ.aoyama.ac.jp):

　Department of Economics: N. HIRASAWA
　Department of Economics (Evening Division): S. SUGIURA

College of Law (internet www.als.aoyama.ac.jp):

　Department of Law: T. DOBASHI

College of Literature (internet www.cl.aoyama.ac.jp):

　Department of Education: Y. SAKAI
　Department of Education (Evening Division): Dr M. KITAMOTO
　Department of English: M. AKIMOTO
　Department of English (Evening Division): Y. SAKUMA
　Department of French: Dr T. TSUYUZAKI
　Department of Japanese: Y. HIJIKATA
　Department of History: Dr S. WATANABE
　Department of Psychology: K. ENDO

College of Science and Engineering (internet www.agnes.aoyama.ac.jp):

　Department of Physics: Dr I. NISHIO
　Department of Chemistry: Dr H. ITOH
　Department of Mechanical Engineering: Dr S. OHISHI
　Department of Electrical Engineering and Electronics: Dr A. SAWABE
　Department of Industrial and Systems Engineering: Dr M. KURODA
　Deparment of Integrated Information Technology: Dr S. NINOMIYA

School of Business Administration (internet www.agub.aoyama.ac.jp):

　Department of Business Administration: Dr O. SATO
　Department of Business Administration (Evening Division): Dr N. IWATA

School of International Politics, Economics and Business (internet www.sipeb.aoyama.ac.jp):

　Department of International Politics: Dr J. TSUCHIYAMA
　Department of International Economics: K. SENBA

ASIA UNIVERSITY

5-24-10 Sakai, Musashino-shi, Tokyo 180-8629

Telephone: (422) 36-3255
Fax: (422) 36-4869
E-mail: koryu@asia-u.ac.jp
Internet: www.asia-u.ac.jp/english

Founded 1941
Academic year: April to March

President: SHINICHI KOIBUCHI
Librarian: SEIJI NAKAMURA

Library of 548,000 vols

Number of teachers: 466 (174 full-time, 292 part-time)
Number of students: 8,029

DEANS

Asia University Junior College: S. USUI
Faculty of Business Administration: H. OSHIMA
Faculty of Economics: T. KATO
Faculty of International Relations: H. OGAWA
Faculty of Law: H. NAKANO
Faculty of Liberal Arts: T. WATANABE
Graduate School of Business Administration: K. KASAI
Graduate School of Economics: Y. TOZAWA
Graduate School of Law: T. MORIMOTO

AZABU UNIVERSITY

1-17-71 Fuchinobe, Sagamihara City, Kanagawa 229-8501

Telephone: (42) 754-7111
Fax: (42) 754-7661
Internet: www.azabu-u.ac.jp

Founded 1890

President: TSUNENORI NAKAMURA
Librarian: HIDEO FUJITANI

Library of 135,000 vols
Number of teachers: 182
Number of students: 2,300

Publication: *Bulletin*

DEANS

College of Environmental Health: TSUYOSHI HIRATA
School of Veterinary Medicine: TOSHIO MASAOKA

BUKKYO UNIVERSITY

96 Kitahananobo-cho, Murasakino, Kita-ku, Kyoto 603-8301

Telephone: (75) 491-2141
Fax: (75) 495-5723
E-mail: mmc-info@bukkyo-u.ac.jp
Internet: www.bukkyo-u.ac.jp

Founded 1868
Private control
Academic year: April to March

Pres.: RYUZEN FUKUHARA
Vice-Pres.: E. NAKAMURA
Registrar: H. OHKITA
Librarian: Y. YAMADA

Library of 684,000 vols
Number of teachers: 164
Number of students: 6,457

Publications: *Journal of the Faculty of Letters* (1 a year), *Journal of the Faculty of Education* (1 a year), *Journal of the Faculty of Sociology* (1 a year), *Bukkyo University Graduate School Review* (1 a year)

DEANS

Faculty of Letters: M. SHIMIZU
Faculty of Education: J. KAKUMOTO
Faculty of Sociology: M. HAMAOKA
Postgraduate Programmes in Literature: M. SHIMIZU
Postgraduate Programmes in Education: J. KAKUMOTO
Postgraduate Programmes in Sociology: M. HAMAOKA
Independent Postgraduate Programmes in Buddhism: S. ONODA
Training Programme for the Jodo Priesthood: T. TODO

CHIKUSHI JOGAKUEN UNIVERSITY

2-12-1 Ishizaka, Dazaifu City, Fukuoka Prefecture 818-0192

Telephone: (92) 925-3511
Fax: (92) 924-4369

Internet: www.chikushi.ac.jp

Founded 1988

Depts of Asian Studies, Clinical Psychology, English, English and Multimedia Studies, Human Welfare, Japanese Language and Literature,.

CHUBU UNIVERSITY

1200 Matsumoto-cho, Kasugai-shi, Aichi-ken 487-8501

Telephone: (568) 51-1111
Fax: (568) 51-1141
E-mail: cucip@office.chubu.ac.jp
Internet: www.chubu.ac.jp

Founded 1964
Language of instruction: Japanese
Academic year: April to March

Chancellor: KAZUO YAMADA
President: ATSUO IIYOSHI

Library of 427,000 vols
Number of teachers: 491 (including 244 part-time)
Number of students: 8,000 (including 200 postgraduate)

Publications: *Memoirs of the College of Engineering* (1 a year), *Sogo Kogaku* (Journal of the Research Institute for Science and Technology, 1 a year), *Journal of the College of Business Administration and Information Science* (2 a year), *Journal of the College of International Studies* (2 a year), *Journal of the Research Institute for International Studies* (1 a year), *Journal of the Research Institute for Industry and Economics* (1 a year), *Journal of Information Science* (1 a year), *Journal of the College of Humanities* (1 a year)

DEANS

College of Business Administration and Information Science: Dr NOBUO KAMATA
College of Engineering: Dr MAKOTO WATANABE
College of Humanities: YUKIO AKATSUKA
College of International Studies: Dr NOBUHIRO NAGASHIMA
Graduate School of Business Administration and Information Science: Dr NOBUO KAMATA
Graduate School of Engineering: Dr MAKOTO WATANABE
Graduate School of International Studies: Dr NOBUHIRO NAGASHIMA

CHUO UNIVERSITY

742-1 Higashinakano, Hachioji-shi, Tokyo 192-0393

Telephone: (426) 74-2111
Fax: (426) 74-2214
E-mail: intlcent@tamajs.chuo-u.ac.jp
Internet: www.chuo-u.ac.jp

Founded 1885
Academic year: April to March (2 semesters)

Pres. and Chancellor: KOJI SUZUKI
Sec.-Gen.: SHUNSUKE HODOSHIMA
Dean of Students: HISAO FUKUCHI
Library Dir: KEN NAGASAKI

Library: see Libraries and Archives
Number of teachers: 2,009
Number of students: 29,573 (3,171 evening course), 1,833 graduates

Publications: various faculty bulletins, journals

DEANS

Correspondence Division, Faculty of Law: M. SUGAWARA
Faculty of Commerce: K. KITAMURA
Faculty of Economics: A. ICHII
Faculty of Law: K. NAGAI
Faculty of Literature: S. HAYASHI

Faculty of Policy Studies: M. KONO
Faculty of Science and Engineering: N. OKUBO
Graduate School of Commerce: M. TATEBE
Graduate School of Economics: H. TANAKA
Graduate School of Law: T. SHIIBASHI
Graduate School of Literature: S. MUTO
Graduate School of Policy Studies: T. MASUJIMA
Graduate School of Science and Engineering: K. SUGIYAMA

DIRECTORS

Computer Center: T. SEKIGUCHI
Health Center: T. TSUKADA
Institute of Accounting Research: Y. WATABE
Institute of Business Research: T. ISHIZAKI
Institute of Comparative Law in Japan: T. KINOSHITA
Institute of Cultural Science: M. IRINODA
Institute of Economic Research: Y. KOGUCHI
Institute of Health and Physical Science: A. NISHITANI
Institute of Science and Engineering: M. IRI
Institute of Social Science: Y. KAWASAKI
International Center: H. HAYASHIDA

DAITO BUNKA UNIVERSITY

1-9-1 Takashimadaira, Itabashi-ku, Tokyo 175-8571

Telephone: (3) 5399-7323
Fax: (3) 5399-7823
E-mail: info@ic.daito.ac.jp
Internet: www.daito.ac.jp

Founded 1923
Private Control
Academic year: April to March

Chair. of Board: T. TAKEUCHI
Pres.: M. WADA
Managing Dirs: K. SOEDA, S. TSUJINO
Dir of Admin. Office: S. TSUJINO
Dir of Academic Affairs: S. WATABE
Librarian: I. MIYOSHI

Library of 1,204,490 vols
Number of teachers: 1,070
Number of students: 13,315

Publications: *Daito Bunka Daigaku* (Bulletin), *Daito Bunka News* (10 a year)

DEANS

Faculty of Business Administration: M. IMASHIRO
Faculty of Economics: K. UENO
Faculty of Foreign Languages: S. YAMAZAKI
Faculty of International Relations: N. OSHIKAWA
Faculty of Law: Y. FURUKAWA
Faculty of Literature: M. OTA
Faculty of Social–Human Environmentology: Y. TAKAYAMA
Faculty of Sports and Health Science: Y. AOBA

HEADS OF GRADUATE SCHOOLS

Asian Area Studies: M. TAKAKUWA
Business Administration: K. SUZUKI
Economics: H. SUESHIGE
Foreign Languages: E. NISHIKAWA
Law: H. TOKI
Law School: K. ONO
Literature: J. KOYANO

JAPANESE LANGUAGE PROGRAMME FOR FOREIGN STUDENTS

Japanese Language Course: T. MIKAMI

DOHTO UNIVERSITY

149 Nakanoswawa, Kitahiroshima-shi, Hokkaido 061-1196

Telephone: (11) 372-3111
Fax: (11) 376-9706
E-mail: kokusai@dohto.ac.jp

Internet: www.dohto.ac.jp

Founded 1964

Chancellor: Dr JUN SAKURAI

Faculties of Fine Arts, Management, Social Welfare.

DOKKYO UNIVERSITY

1-1 Gakuen-cho, Soka-shi, Saitama-ken 340-0042

Telephone: (489) 42-1111
Fax: (489) 41-6621
E-mail: info@dokkyo.ac.jp
Internet: www.dokkyo.ac.jp

Founded 1964
Private control

Pres.: YASUO KUWAHARA
Head Admin.: IKUO TOI
Librarian: KO KAJIYAMA

Library of 675,000 vols
Number of teachers: 410
Number of students: 8,925

Publication: *Dokkyo International Review* (1 a year)

DEANS

Faculty of Economics: MASAMICHI CHIYOURA
Faculty of Foreign Languages: YUJI NAKAJIMA
Faculty of Law: SHOICHI KOSEKI
Graduate School of Economics: MASAMICHI CHIYOURA
Graduate School of Foreign Languages: YUJI NAKAJIMA
Graduate School of Law: SHOICHI KOSEKI

DOSHISHA UNIVERSITY

Karasuma Imadegawa, Kamigyo-ku, Kyoto 602-580

Telephone: (75) 251-3110
Fax: (75) 251-3075
E-mail: ji-shomu@mail.doshisha.ac.jp
Internet: www.doshisha.ac.jp

Founded 1875
Academic year: April to March

Chancellor: M. OYA
President: E. HATTA
Dean of Academic Affairs: N. TABATA
Dean of Student Affairs: A. MORITA
Administrative Officer: I. HARA

Library: Libraries with 715,027 vols
Number of teachers: 489 full-time
Number of students: 24,166

Publications: *Studies in Christianity, Studies in Humanities, Doshisha Studies in English, Social Science Review, Doshisha Law Review, Economic Review, Doshisha Business Review, Science and Engineering Review of Doshisha University, Doshisha American Studies, The Social Sciences, The Humanities, The Study of Christianity and Social Problems, Shuryu, Doshisha Literature, L.L.L., Studies in Cultural History, Annual of Philosophy, Philosophical Review, Journal of Education and Culture, Doshisha Psychological Review, Bigaku Geijutsugaku, Doshisha Kokungaku, Doshisha Review of Sociology, Doshisha Kogaku Kaiho, Doshisha Studies in Language and Culture, Doshisha Policy and Management Review, Doshisha Hokentaiiku, Doshisha Danso, Neesima Studies*

DEANS

Faculty of Commerce: T. UKAI
Faculty of Economics: T. NISHIMURA
Faculty of Engineering: M. SENDA
Faculty of Law: A. SEGAWA
Faculty of Letters: Y. KUROKI
Faculty of Theology: K. MORI

Graduate School of American Studies: T. KAMATA
Graduate School of Policy and Management: S. OTA

DIRECTORS

Center for American Studies: N. YAMAUCHI
Institute for Language and Culture: I. KOIKE
Institute for the Study of Humanities and Social Sciences: T. TAKITA
Science and Engineering Research Institute: O. YAMAGUCHI

DOSHISHA WOMEN'S COLLEGE OF LIBERAL ARTS

Kodo, Kyotanabe-shi, Kyoto-fu 610-0395
Telephone: (774) 65-8411
Fax: (774) 65-8461
E-mail: somu-t@dwc.doshisha.ac.jp
Internet: www.dwc.doshisha.ac.jp
Founded 1876
Academic year: April to March

Chancellor: M. OYA
Pres.: J. MORITA
Registrar: Y. HONMA
Librarian: Y. YODEN

Library of 445,983 vols
Number of teachers: 750
Number of students: 5,948

DEANS

Academic Affairs: Y. HONMA
Academic Research Promotion Center: K. MOROI
Accounting and Finance: S. TAKAMOTO
Admissions Center: N. YOSHIKAI
Career Support Center: N. MORISHITA
Contemporary Social Studies: T. KONO
General Affairs: K. KOSAKA
Human Life and Science: N. NISHIMURA
International Exchange Center: T. TAGUCHI
Liberal Arts: M. TERAKAWA
Library and information Services Center: Y. YODEN
Pharmaceutical Sciences: K. MORITA
Religious Affairs: J. KONDO
Student Affairs: Y. KOMOTO

FUKUOKA UNIVERSITY

8-19-1, Nanakuma, Jonan-ku, Fukuoka 814-0180
Telephone: (92) 871-6631
Fax: (92) 862-4431
E-mail: fupr@adm.fukuoka-u.ac.jp
Internet: www.fukuoka-u.ac.jp
Founded 1934
Private control
Academic year: April to March

Pres.: HIROYUKI YAMASHITA
Vice-Press: KENROU KAWAIDA, KUNIHIDE MIHASHI, MASAHIRO KIKUCHI
Sec.-Gen.: K. SUETSUGU
Librarian: H. NAGATA

Library of 1,400,000 vols
Number of teachers: 928 full-time
Number of students: 22,319
Publication: *Bulletin*

DEANS

Faculty of Commerce: T. ETO
Faculty of Economics: T. TANAKA
Faculty of Engineering: H. YAMASHITA
Faculty of Humanities: S. MAMOTO
Faculty of Law: N. ASANO
Faculty of Pharmaceutical Sciences: H. SHIMENO
Faculty of Science: M. SAIGO
Faculty of Sports and Health Science: K. KANAMORI
School of Medicine: Y. IKEHARA

DIRECTORS

Animal Care Unit: S. KASHIMURA
Central Research Institute: Y. TOMINAGA
Computer Centre: K. SHUDO
Fukuoka University Chikushi Hospital: T. YAO
Fukuoka University Hospital: A. ARIYOSHI
Language Training Centre: K. TACHIBANA
Radioisotope Centre: S. TASAKI
Takamiya Evening School: M. MORI

GAKUSHUIN UNIVERSITY

1-5-1 Mejiro, Toshima-ku, Tokyo 171-8588
Telephone: (3) 3986-0221
Fax: (3) 5992-1005
E-mail: webmaster@gakushuin.ac.jp
Internet: www.gakushuin.ac.jp/univ
Founded 1949
Private control
Language of instruction: Japanese
Academic year: April to March

Chancellor: Y. TAJIMA
Pres.: Y. NAGATA
Chief Admin. Officer: M. MUNAKATA
Dean of Students: H. ENDO
Librarian: I. ARAKAWA

Library of 1,300,000 vols
Number of teachers: 202 full-time, 645 part-time
Number of students: 8,616 (8,082 undergraduate, 534 postgraduate)
Publications: *Gakushuin Daigaku Bungaku-Bu Kenkyu Nenpo* (Annual Collection of Essays and Studies, Faculty of Letters), *Gakushuin Daigaku Hogakkai Zasshi* (Gakushuin Review of Law and Politics, 2 a year), *Gakushuin Daigaku Keizai Ron-shu* (Gakushuin Economic Papers, 4 a year), *Gakushuin Daigaku Kenkyusosho* (Gakushuin University Studies, 1 a year)

DEANS

Faculty of Economics: Y. SUGITA
Faculty of Law: T. INOUE
Faculty of Letters: N. FUKUI
Faculty of Sciences: D. FUJIWARA

CHAIRMEN

Graduate School of Economics: T. KAWASHIMA
Graduate School of Humanities: N. FUKUI
Graduate School of Law: T. OKA
Graduate School of Management: Y. AOKI
Graduate School of Politics: T. KATSURAGI
Graduate School of Sciences: D. FUJIWARA

PROFESSORS

Faculty of Economics:

AOKI, Y., Consumer Behaviour
ARAI, K., Stochastic Processes and Statistics
ASABA, S., Business Economics and Strategic Management
ENDO, H., Health Economics and Business Policy
FUKUCHI, J., Statistics, Statistical Finance
HOSONO, K., Macroeconomics
IMANO, K., Human Resource Management
ISHII, S., Economic History of Japan
ITSUMI, Y., Public Finance
IWATA, K., Japanese Economic Studies, Land and Housing Economics
KAMBE, S., Microeconomic Theory and Game Theory
KANEDA, N., Accounting
KATSUO, Y., Financial Accounting
KAWASHIMA, T., Special Economics and Econometrics
KOYAMA, A., Business Finance and International Management
MITSUI, K., Public Economics
MIYAGAWA, T., Macroeconomics, Japanese Economy

MORITA, M., Management Science and Strategic Management
MUKUNOKI, H., International Economics
NAMBU, T., Industrial Economics
OKUMURA, H., Japanese Economic Studies, International Finance
SHIROTA, Y., Computer Science
SUGITA, Y., Marketing Science
SUZUKI, T., Business History
TANAKA, N., Systems and Simulation
TATSUMI, K., Financial Markets and Investment
UCHINO, T., Management and Organization Theory
UEDA, T., Marketing
WADA, T., Business Economics and Strategic Management
WAKISAKA, A., Economics of Work and Pay
WAKOH, J., Game Theory, Mathematical Economics
YUZAWA, T., Business History

Faculty of Law:

ENDO, K., Sociology
FUKUMOTO, K., Politics
HASEBE, Y., Law of Civil Procedure
HASHIMOTO, Y., Labour and Employment Law
HIRANO, H., Social Psychology
IIDA, Y., Political History of Europe
INOUE, T., History of Politics and Diplomacy in Japan
ISOZAKI, N., Political Change in East Asia
KAMIYA, M., Anglo-American Law
KANZAKI, T., Conflict of Laws
KATSUNAGI, T., Public Policy and Jurisprudence
MAEDA, A., Commercial Law
MIZUNO, K., Civil Law
MORINAGA, T., History of Western Political Thought
MURAMATSU, M., Public Administration
MURANUSHI, M., International Politics
NAKAI, Y., Comparative Politics
NOMURA, T., Civil Law
NONAKA, N., Principles of Political Science
NOSAKA, Y., Constitutional Law
OKA, T., Civil Law
OKINO, M., Civil Law
SAKAMOTO, K., Political Process of Japan
SAKURAI, K., Administrative Law
SASAKI, T., Political Theory
SHIBAHARA, K., Criminal Law
SHIZUMI, M., Criminal Law
SUDO, N., Sociology
SUNADA, I., American Government and Politics
TAKAGI, H., Administrative Law
TOMATSU, H., Constitutional Law
TSUMURA, M., Law of Criminal Procedure
TSUNEOKA, T., Administrative Law

Faculty of Letters:

ABE, S., History of Japanese Language and Dialectology
ARIKAWA, H., History of European Art
CHUJOH, S., 19th-century French Novel
FITZSIMMONS, A., Irish Literature, Modern British Poetry
FUKUI, N., Contemporary European History
HARADA, Y., French 17th-century Philosophy and Literature
HASHIMOTO, M., Modern English Literature, Irish Literature
HOSAKA, Y., Semantics, Syntax (German)
HYODO, H., Japanese Medieval Literature, Culture of Japanese Performing Arts
IENAGA, J., Medieval Japanese History
INOUE, I., Modern Japanese History
ITOH, K., Clinical Psychology, Supportive Psychotherapy
IWASAKI, H., 20th-century French Novel
KAMENAGA, Y., Medieval European History
KAMIOKA, N., Contemporary American Novels
KANDA, T., Medieval Japanese Literature

KANEGAE, H., Ancient Japanese History
KAWAGUCHI, Y., Educational Methodology
KAWASAKI, Y., Psychotherapy, Transference
KOBAYASHI, T., History of Japanese Art
KOMATSU, E., Linguistics
MAEDA, N., Modern Japanese Linguistics
MANO, Y., British Novels
MARÉ, T., French Literature
MATSUSHIMA, S., English Romantic Poetry
MIYASHITA, S., German Poetry
MURANO, R., Cross-cultural Communication, Teaching Japanese as a Foreign Language
NAGANUMA, Y., Volunteer Learning
NAGASHIMA, Y., Linguistics (Semantics)
NAGATA, Y., Social Psychology
NAKAJIMA, H., English Linguistics
NAKAMURA, I., History of Japanese Thought
NAKANO, H., Elizabethan Drama
NINOMIYA, R., 17th- and 18th-century French Literature
NOMURA, R., 17th- and 18th-century French Literature
OHNUKI, A., Cultural Studies
OKAMOTO, J., German Linguistics, Cognitive Semantics, Linguistic Theory
PEKAR, T., German Literature, Cultural Studies
SAEKI, T., French Drama
SAITOH, T., Educational History
SAKAI, K., Comparative Philosophy, Modern (18th- and 19th-century) Philosophy, Phenomenology
SAKONJI, S., Greek Philosophy, Neoplatonism, Renaissance Philosophy
SANO, M., History of Japanese Art
SASAKI, T., Ancient Japanese Linguistics
SHIMADA, M., Ancient Roman History
SHIMOKAWA, K., British Philosophy (Locke and Hume), Ethics and Political Philosophy
SHINKAWA, T., Medieval Thought and Buddhism in Japan
SHINODA, A., Comparative Psychology
SHINOHARA, S., Learning Theories
SHIOTANI, K., 18th- and 19th-century English Literature
SUGIYAMA, N., French Philosophy
SUWA, T., Cultural Geography
TAKADA, H., German Linguistics, History of the German Language, Historical Pragmatics
TAKAHASHI, H., History of European Art
TAKAMI, K., Linguistics (Syntax and Semantics)
TAKANO, T., Early Modern Japanese History
TAKETSUNA, S., Educational Psychology
TAKEUCHI, F., Modern Asian History
TANABE, C., American Literature
TOGAWA, S., Modern Japanese Literature
TOYAMA, M., Social Cognition, Causal Attribution
TSURUMA, K., Ancient Chinese History
UCHIDA, T., American Literature
WATANABE, M., History of German Linguistics, Sociolinguistics, Comparative Linguistics
YAHAGI, S., 19th-century American Literature
YAMAMOTO, M., Child Development, Developmental Disorder
YAMAMOTO, Y., Modern Japanese Literature
YOSHIDA, K., French Poetry and Poets
YOSHIKAWA, M., Clinical Psychology, Clinical Assessment

Faculty of Science (tel. (3) 3986-0221 ext.6450; fax (3) 5992-1029; e-mail sci-off@gakushuin.ac.jp):

AKAO, K., Complex Manifolds
AKAOGI, M., Science of the Earth's Materials under High Pressure

AKIYAMA, T., Synthetic Organic Chemistry
ARAKAWA, I., Surface and Vacuum Science
FUJIWARA, D., Functional Analysis, Theory of Partial Differential Equations
HIRANO, T., Quantum Optics
IDA, D., Gravity and Relativistic Cosmology
IITAKA, S., Algebraic Geometry, Birational Geometry
ISHII, K., Vibrational Spectroscopy of Molecular Systems
KATASE, K., Differential Topology, Complex Dynamic Systems
KAWABATA, A., Theory of Solid-State Physics, Mesoscopic Physics
KAWASAKI, T., Topology and Geometry of Surfaces
KOTANI, M., Photochemistry and Photophysics of Organic Solids
MIZOGUCHI, T., Materials Science, Spin-polarized Electron Spectroscopy, Magnetism, Amorphous Materials
MIZUTANI, A., Numerical Analysis
MOCHIDA, K., Organometallic Chemistry of Group 14 Elements
MURAMATSU, Y., Geo- and Environmental Chemistry of Trace Elements and Isotopes
NAKAJIMA, S., Number Theory
NAKAMURA, H., Organic Synthesis
NAKANO, S., Number Theory
NISHIZAKA, T., Biophysics of Macromolecular Motion
TAKAHASHI, T., Electronic Properties of Small-dimensional Conductors, Organic Conductors and Superconductors
TASAKI, H., Theoretical Physics and Mathematical Physics
WATANABE, M., Physics of Crystal Growth
YAJIMA, K., Mathematical Physics, Partial Differential Equations

Center for Sports and Health Science (tel. (3) 3971-8989; fax (3) 5992-9306):

HANEDA, Y., Sports Biomechanics
HIRO, N., Sports Methodology
ONO, T., Exercise Physiology
SATO, Y., Applied Physiology, General Principle of Ball Game Strategy and Tactics
TAKAMARU, Y., Coaching Sciences
YAGI, Y., Sports Psychology

ATTACHED INSTITUTES

Gakushuin Daigaku Gaikokugo Kyoiku Kenkyu Sentah (Gakushuin University Foreign Language Teaching and Research Center): f. 1997; Dir K. MOCHIDA.

Gakushuin Daigaku Jinbun Kagaku Kenkyujo (Research Institute for Humanities): f. 1976; Dir Y. NAGASHIMA.

Gakushuin Daigaku Keisanki Sentah (Gakushuin University Computer Center): f. 1974; Dir K. ARAI.

Gakushuin Daigaku Keizai Keiei Kenkyujo (Gakushuin University Research Institute for Economics and Management): f. 1984; Dir K. IMANO.

Gakushuin Daigaku Kokusai Kouryu Sentah (Gakushuin University Center for International Exchange): f. 1990; Dir K. SHIOTANI.

Gakushuin Daigaku Seimei Bunshi Kagaku Kenkyujo (Gakushuin University Institute for Biomolecular Science): f. 1991; Dir T. HAGA.

Gakushuin Daigaku Shiryokan (Gakushuin University Museum of History): f. 1975; Dir T. SHINKAWA.

Gakushuin Daigaku Sports Kenkoh Kagaku Sentah (Gakushuin University Center for Sports and Health Sciences): f. 1994; Dir Y. YAGI.

Gakushuin Daigaku Toyo Bunka Kenkyu-Jo (Gakushuin University Research Institute for Oriental Cultures): f. 1952; Dir T. OKA.

HAKODATE UNIVERSITY

5-1 Takaoka-cho, Hakodate 042-0955
Telephone: (138) 57-1181
Fax: (138) 57-0298
E-mail: post@hakodate-u.ac.jp
Internet: www.hakodate-u.ac.jp
Founded 1938
Pres.: HAKUSHI KAWAMURA
Number of students: 1,200
Faculty of Commerce.

HIROSHIMA JOGAKUIN UNIVERSITY

4-13-1, Ushita-higashi, Higashi-ku, Hiroshima 732-0063
Telephone: (82) 228-0386
Fax: (82) 227-4502
E-mail: kokusai@gaines.hju.ac.jp
Internet: www.hju.ac.jp
Founded 1886, as college 1949
Academic year: April to March
Pres.: HIROSHI IMADA
Vice-Pres.: SHIGEKI SATOH
Registrar: YUJI MAEWAKA
Chief Admin. Officer: SHIGENOBU HATAKEYAMA
Library of 200,000 vols
Number of teachers: 75
Number of students: 2,062
Publication: *Bulletin* (1 a year)

Departments of English Studies, Environmental Culture, Environmental Science, , Graduate School of Language and Culture, Human and Cultural Studies, Human Life Science, Japanese Language and Literature.

HIROSHIMA UNIVERSITY OF ECONOMICS

5-37-1 Gion, Asaminami-ku, Hiroshima City 731-0192
Telephone: (82) 871-1002
Fax: (82) 871-1666
E-mail: int-sc@hue.ac.jp
Internet: www.hue.ac.jp
Founded 1967
Academic year: April to March
Chancellor: MASAO ISHIDA
President: TSUNEO ISHIDA
Chief Administrative Officer: SHIGEMITSU ARICHI
Librarian: HIROSHI SEIKE
Library of 281,050 vols
Number of teachers: 256 (150 full-time, 106 part-time)
Number of students: 5,000

DEANS

Faculty of Economics: TOSHIYUKI MIZOGUCHI
Graduate School of Economics: TOSHIYUKI MIZOGUCHI

HIROSHIMA SHUDO UNIVERSITY

1-1-1 Ozuka-higashi, Asaminami-ku, Hiroshima 731-3195
Telephone: (82) 830-1103
Fax: (82) 830-1303
Internet: www.shudo-u.ac.jp
President: MASANORI KODAMA
Library of 640,594 vols in Japanese and other languages; 4,999 periodicals, 655,112 other items
Number of teachers: 179
Number of students: 6,204

Publications: *Monographs of the Institute for Advanced Studies, Papers of the Research Society of Commerce and Economics, Studies in the Humanities and Sciences, Shudo Hogaku: Shudo Law Review, Journal of Human Environmental Studies, Journal of Economic Sciences*

Faculties of Commercial Sciences, Economic Sciences, Human Environmental Sciences, Humanities and Human Sciences and Law.

HOKKAI-GAKUEN UNIVERSITY

4-1-40, Asahi-machi, Toyohira-ku, Sapporo 062-8605

Telephone: (11) 841-1161
Fax: (11) 824-3141
Internet: www.hokkai-s-u.ac.jp
Founded 1952
Academic year: April to March

Chair.: MASAO MORIMOTO
Pres.: T. ASAKURA
Librarian: N. TSUNEMI
Library of 856,542 vols
Number of teachers: 243 full-time
Number of students: 9,084

Publications: *Keizai Ronshu* (Journal of Economics, 4 a year), *Hogaku Kenkyu* (Journal of the Faculty of Law, 4 a year), *Gakuen Ronshu* (Journal of Hokkai-Gakuen University, 4 a year), *Kogakubu Kenkyu Hokoku* (Bulletin of the Faculty of Engineering, 1 a year), *Jinbun Ronshu* (Studies in Culture, 3 a year), *Keiei Ronshu* (Journal of Business Administration, 4 a year)

DEANS

Faculty of Business Administration: A. FUKU-NAGA
Faculty of Economics: M. KOBAYASHI
Faculty of Engineering: T. YAMANOI
Faculty of Humanities: C. OISHIO
Faculty of Law: N. MUKAIDA

CHAIRMEN

Graduate School of Business Administration: Y. HAYAKAWA
Graduate School of Economics: K. KODA
Graduate School of Engineering: T. KUWA-HARA
Graduate School of Law: N. KATO
Graduate School of Literature: T. HAMA
Law School: O. MARUYAMA

ATTACHED INSTITUTES

Center for Academic Affairs: Dir H. MORISHITA.

Center for Development Policy Studies: f. 1957; Dir K. TAKAHARA; publ. *Kaihatsu Ronshu* (Journal of Policy Studies, 2 a year).

HOKURIKU UNIVERSITY

1-1 Taiyogaoka, Kanazawa City, Ishikawa Prefecture 920-1180

Telephone: (76) 229-1161
Fax: (76) 229-1393
E-mail: koho@hokuriku-u.ac.jp
Internet: www.hokuriku-u.ac.jp
Founded 1975
Academic year: April to March

Pres.: S. KAWASHIMA
Librarian: Y. KITANO
Library of 209,000 vols
Number of teachers: 144
Number of students: 3,000

Publications: *Hokuriku Daigaku Kiyo* (bulletin, 1 a year), *Hokuriku Hogaku* (journal of law and political science, 4 a year)

DEANS

Faculty of Future Learning: S. SONOYAMA

Faculty of Pharmaceutical Sciences: T. SAWA-NISHI
Graduate School of Pharmaceutical Research: T. SAWANISHI (Chair.)

HOSEI UNIVERSITY

2-17-1, Fujimi, Chiyoda-ku, Tokyo 102-8160
Telephone: (3) 3264-9662
Fax: (3) 3238-9873
Internet: www.hosei.ac.jp
Founded 1880
Private control
Language of instruction: Japanese
Academic year: April to March

Pres.: TOSHIO MASUDA
Vice-Press: AKIRA HAMAMURA, HOSHINO TSU-TOMU, YUTAKA KATO, AKIRA TOKUYASU
Registrar: (vacant)
Library Dir: MITSUO NESAKI
Library of 1,590,000 vols
Number of teachers: 2,740 (746 full-time, 1,994 part-time)
Number of students: 37,200, incl. graduate 2,007, correspondence education 6,661

Publications: *Daigakuin Kiyo* (Graduate School Bulletin, 2 a year), *Gendaifukushi Kenkyu* (Bulletin of the Faculty of Social Policy and Administration, 1 a year), *Hogaku-Shirin* (Law and Political Sciences Review, 4 a year), *Hosei Daigaku Bungakubu Kiyo* (Bulletin of Faculty of Letters, 1 a year), *Hosei Daigaku Kogakubu Kenkyu Shuho* (College of Engineering Bulletin, 1 a year), *Hosei Daigaku Kyariadezaingakubu Kiyo* (Bulletin of the Faculty of Lifelong Learning and Career Studies, 1 a year), *Ibunka* (Journal of Intercultural Communication, 1 a year), *Keiei Shirin* (Business Journal, 4 a year), *Keizai-Shirin* (Economic Review, 4 a year), *Ningen Kankyo Ronshu* (Journal of Humanity and the Environment, 2 a year), *Shakai Shirin* (Sociology and Social Sciences, 4 a year)

DEANS

Faculty of Bioscience and Applied Chemistry: TOSHIYUKI NAGATA
Faculty of Business Administration: MASAO YOKOUCHI
Faculty of Computer and Information Sciences: HIROSHI HANAIZUMI
Faculty of Economics: YOSHIKAZU SATO
Faculty of Engineering: YASUHIRO YAMAMOTO
Faculty of Engineering and Design: YOSHI-TAKA TSUBOI
Faculty of Global and Interdisciplinary Studies: YUTAI WATANABE
Faculty of Humanity and the Environment: TOKIO NAGAMINE
Faculty of Intercultural Communication: SHISAI SO
Faculty of Law: ATSUSHI SUGITA
Faculty of Letters: KOICHI NAKAGAMA
Faculty of Lifelong Learning and Career Studies: KOICHIRO KOMIKAWA
KIYOTAKA SAKIKO, Faculty of Science and Engineering
Faculty of Social Policy and Administration: IKUJI ISHIKAWA
Faculty of Social Sciences: MIZUHITO KANE-HARA
Faculty of Sports and Health Studies: HARUO KARIYA
Graduate School Committee: HARUTOSHI FUNAHASHI (Chair.)
Graduate School of Art and Technology: NORIO TAKEUCHI
Graduate School of Business Administration: YASUHIRO INAGAKI
Graduate School of Computer and Information Sciences: NOBUHIKO KOIKE

Graduate School of Engineering: HIROTAKE KATAYAMA
Graduate School of Environmental Management: RYO FUJIKURA
Graduate School of Humanities: MICHI SHIINA
Graduate School of Economics: TETSUJI KAWA-MURA
Graduate School of Intercultural Communication: YOSHIAKI OSHIMA
Graduate School of Law: SUMIMASA SUDO
Graduate School of Regional Policy Design: YOSHIYUKI OKAMOTO
Graduate School of Policy Sciences: MASAHIDE MAJIMA
Graduate School of Politics: NOBUO SHIMOTO-MAI
Graduate School of Social Well-Being Studies: KENICHI BABA
Graduate School of Sociology: MAFUMI FUJITA
Business School of Innovation Management: KOSUKE OGAWA
Business School of Accountancy: KIKUYA MASATO
International Japan-Studies Institute: YUKO TANAKA
Professional Schools: AKIMICHI IWAMA

ATTACHED INSTITUTES

Boissonade Institute of Modern Laws and Politics: 2-17-1 Fujimi, Chiyoda-ku, Tokyo 102-8160; f. 1977; Dir T. OHNO.

Computational Science Research Center: 3-7-2 Kajino-cho, Koganei-shi, Tokyo 184-8584; f. 1969; Dir M. KUSAKABE.

Information Research Institute, California: 800 Airport Blvd, Suite 504, Burlingame, CA 94010, USA; f. 2000; Dir K. YANA.

Information Research Technology Center: 2-17-1 Fujimi, Chiyoda-ku, Tokyo 102-8160; f. 2000; Dir G. SHIRAI.

Institute of Comparative Economic Studies: 4342 Aihara-machi, Machida-shi, Tokyo 194-0298; f. 1984; Dir K. ODAKA; publ. *Journal* (1 a year).

Institute of Nogaku Studies: 2-17-1 Fujimi, Chiyoda-ku, Tokyo 102-8160; f. 1952; Dir H. NISHINO; publ. *Catalogue Noh Drama Collections.*

Institute of Okinawan Studies: 2-17-1 Fujimi, Chiyoda-ku, Tokyo 102-8160; f. 1972; Dir T. YASUE; publ. *Bulletin.*

Japan Statistics Research Institute: 4342 Aihara-machi, Machida-shi, Tokyo 194-0298; f. 1946; Dir H. MORI; publ. *Bulletin* (1 a year).

Ohara Institute for Social Research: 4342 Aihara-machi, Machida-shi, Tokyo 194-0298; f. 1919; Dir S. HAYAKAWA; publ. *Labour Yearbook of Japan* (1 a year), *Report* (12 a year).

Research and Service Center for Tama Community: 2-17-1 Fujimi, Chiyoda-ku, Tokyo 102-8160; Dir C. HIRABAYASHI; publ. *Newsletter* (4 a year).

Research Center of Ion Beam Technology: 3-7-2 Kajino-cho, Koganei-shi, Tokyo 184-8584; f. 1979; Dir T. NAKAMURA.

Sports and Physical Education Research Center: 2-17-1 Fujimi, Chiyoda-ku, Tokyo 102-8160; f. 1976; Dir K. GOMYO.

INTERNATIONAL CHRISTIAN UNIVERSITY

10-2, Osawa 3-chome, Mitaka-shi, Tokyo 181-8585

Telephone: (422) 33-3038
Fax: (422) 33-9887
E-mail: webmaster@icu.ac.jp
Internet: www.icu.ac.jp
Founded 1949

An ecumenical university, accepting students of high academic ability from all countries

Languages of instruction: Japanese, English

Academic year: April to March or September to June

Pres.: NORIHIKO SUZUKI
Vice-Pres. (Academic Affairs): KAZUAKI SAITO
Vice-Pres.(Financial Affairs): ICHIRO NISHIDA
Library Dir: YUKI NAGANO
Library: see Libraries and Archives
Number of teachers: 147 (full-time)
Number of students: 2,887

Publications: *Asian Cultural Studies, Educational Studies, Humanities–Christianity and Culture, Language Research Bulletin, Social Science*

DEANS

College of Liberal Arts: M. OKANO
Graduate School: S. KAWASHIMA
Student Affairs: A. AOI

ATTACHED INSTITUTES

Hachiro Yuasa Memorial Museum: f. 1982; collections of Japanese archaeology and folk art; Dir K. SAITO.

Institute of Asian Cultural Studies: f. 1971, replacing Committee f. 1958; Dir W. STEELE; publ. *Asian Cultural Studies* (1 a year).

Institute of Educational Research and Service: f. 1953; Dir J. MAHER; publ. *Educational Studies* (1 a year).

Institute for the Study of Christianity and Culture: f. 1963; Dir A. TANAKA; publ. *Humanities-Christianity and Culture* (1 a year).

Peace Research Institute: f. 1991; Dir J. WASILEWSKI.

Research Center for Japanese Language Education: f. 1991; Dir M. HIROSE.

Social Science Research Institute: f. 1953; Dir S. ISHIWATA; publ. *The Journal of Social Science* (2 a year).

ISHINOMAKI SENSHU UNIVERSITY

1 Shinmito, Minamisakai, Ishinomaki-shi, Miyagi 986-8580
Telephone: (225) 22-7711
Fax: (225) 22-7710
Internet: www.isenshu-u.ac.jp
Chair.: Dr MASAYOSHI DEUSHI
Pres.: RYOUJI KOBAYASHI
Library of 100,000 vols

Faculty of Business Administration and Faculty of Science.

IWATE MEDICAL UNIVERSITY

19-1 Uchimaru, Morioka, Iwate 020-8505
Telephone: (19) 651-5111
Fax: (19) 624-1231
E-mail: webmaster@iwate-med.ac.jp
Internet: www.iwate-med.ac.jp
Founded 1928, University 1952
Private control
President: SHIGERU ONO
Librarian: TOKIO NAWA
Library of 249,221 vols
Number of teachers: 500
Number of students: 1,037

Publications: *Journal of the Iwate Medical Association* (6 a year), *Dental Journal* (4 a year)

DEANS

School of Dentistry: KIMIO SAKAMAKI
School of Liberal Arts and Sciences: KOKI KANNO

School of Medicine: CHUICHI ITO

JAPAN WOMEN'S UNIVERSITY

2-8-1 Mejirodai, Bunkyou-ku, Tokyo 112-8681
Telephone: (3) 3943-3131
E-mail: n-abroad@atlas.jwu.ac.jp
Internet: www.jwu.ac.jp
Founded 1901
Pres.: SHOKO GOTO
Number of teachers: 200
Number of students: 5,900

Faculties of Home Economics, Humanities, Integrated Arts and Social Sciences, Science.

JIKEI UNIVERSITY

3-25-8 Nishi-Shinbashi, Minato-ku, Tokyo 105-8461
Telephone: (3) 3433-1111
Fax: (3) 3435-1922
Internet: www.jikei.ac.jp
Founded 1881
Private control
Academic year: April to March
President: SATOSHI KURIHARA
Library of 227,036 vols
Number of teachers: 2,151
Number of students: 1,545

Publications: *Tokyo Jikeikai Medical Journal* (in Japanese, 6 a year), *Jikeikai Medical Journal* (in English, 4 a year), *Kyoiku Kenkyu Nenpo* (in Japanese, 1 a year), *Research Activities* (in English, 1 a year)

DEANS

School of Medicine and School of Nursing: S. KURIHARA

KANSAI UNIVERSITY

3-3-35 Yamate-cho, Suita-shi, Osaka 564-8680
Telephone: (6) 6368-1121
Fax: (6) 6330-3027
E-mail: www-adm@www.kansai-u.ac.jp
Internet: www.kansai-u.ac.jp
Founded 1886
Academic year: April to March
Pres.: TEIICHI KAWATA
Chair. of Board of Trustees: SEIICHIRO MORIMOTO
Dir of Educational Affairs Bureau: YASUHIRO KONISHI
Librarian: NOBORU TANAKA
Library: see Libraries and Archives
Number of teachers: 1,827
Number of students: 26,674

Publications: *Bungaku Ronshu* (Literary Essays, 3 a year), *Hogaku Ronshu* (Law Review, 4 a year), *Shakaigaku Kiyo* (Journal of Sociological Research, 2 a year), *Keizai Ronshu* (Economic Review, 6 a year), *Shogaku Ronshu* (Business Review, 5 a year), *Kogaku Kenkyu Hokoku* (Technology Reports, 1 a year), *Keizai-Seiji Kenkyusho Kenkyu Shoho* (Economic and Political Studies), *Tozaigakujutsu Kenkyusho Kiyo* (Bulletin of Institute of Oriental and Occidental Studies), *Kogaku to Gijutsu* (Engineering and Technology), *Hogaku Kenkyusho Kenkyu Shoho, Gien* (Industrial Technology), *Review of Law and Politics, Review of Economics, Review of Business and Commerce, Joho Kenkyu* (Informatics Research), *Senri eno Muchii* (Journal of Graduate School of Foreign Language Education and Research, 1 a year), *Hakubatsukan Kiyo* (1 a year), *Kokogakutsu Shiryoshitsu Kiyo* (1 a year), *Jinken Mondai Kenkyu Kiyo* (1 a year)

DEANS

Faculty of Commerce: Prof. HIROMI TSURUTA
Faculty of Economics: Prof. KANJI MORIOKA
Faculty of Engineering: Prof. TETSUAKO TSUCHIDO
Faculty of Informatics: Prof. TAKASHI KATO
Faculty of Law: Prof. KUMIHIRO OHNUMA
Faculty of Letters: Prof. KEIJI SHIBAI
Faculty of Sociology: Prof. ICHIRO MATSUHARA
Institute of Foreign Language Education and Research: Prof. TAICHI USAMI
School of Law: Prof. KEIICHI YAMANAKA

PROFESSORS

Faculty of Law

Department of Jurisprudence:

FUKUTAKI, H., Commercial Law
GOTO, M., Civil Law
ICHIHARA, Y., History of Legal Thought
ICHIKAWA, K., Japanese Legal History
IKEDA, T., Administrative Law
IWASAKI, K., Insurance Law and Shipping Law
KAMEDA, K., Administrative Law II
KOCHU, N., Constitutional Law
KOIZUMI, Y., Constitutional Law
KOKUBU, T., Family Law and Succession Law
KURITA, K., Maritime Law
KURITA, T., Debtors' and Creditors' Rights
KUZUHARA, R., Criminal Law
NAGATA, S., Civil Law
OHNUMA, K., Labour Law
OHNUMA, K., Labour Law II
OKA, T., European Legal History
SASAMOTO, Y., Insurance Law
SATO, Y., Private International Law
SENTO, Y., Family Law and Succession Law
TSUKIOKA, T., Law of Real Property
YOSHIDA, E., Comparative Constitutional Law
YOSHIDA, N., Emancipation of Buraku

Department of Politics:

MANABE, S., Diplomatic History
MORIMOTO, T., Political and Governmental Organization
OTSURU, C., International Politics
TERAJIMA, T., Political Philosophy
TOKURA, K., European Politics
WAKATA, K., Political Psychology
YAMAMOTO, K., Information Processing
YAMANO, H., Political History of Modern Japan

Faculty of Letters

Course of English Language and Literature:

AKIMOTO, H., American Literature
AOYAMA, T., Linguistics
HASEGAWA, A., English Linguistics
HOSHII, Y., Introductory Seminar
IRIKO, F., Study of American Literature
ISHIZAKA, K., Middle English
KAMIMURA, T., Modern British Novels
KIRWAN, J.
MAKIN, P. J., Modern British and American Poetry
SAKAMOTO, T., History of English Literature
SHIMAZAKI, M., British and American Prose
TANIGUCHI, Y., Modern American Literature
TSUTSUI, O., British and American Drama

Course of Japanese Language and Literature:

ENDO, K., Japanese Linguistics
FUJITA, S., Japanese Literature (Edo Period)
KAMITANI, E., Japanese Linguistics
OHHAMA, M., Early Ancient Japanese Literature
SEKIYA, T., Textual Criticism of Noh Plays
TANAKA, N., Literature in the Heian Period
URANISHI, K., Modern and Contemporary Japanese Literature

YAMAMOTO, T., Early Modern Japanese Fiction

YAMAMOTO, T., Literature in the Heian Period

YOSHIDA, N., History of Modern Japanese Literature

Course of Philosophy:

INOUE, K., Comparative Study of Eastern and Western Thought

KIOKA, N., Philosophy

NAKATANI, N., History of Art in the Far East

ODA, Y., History of Religions

SHINAGAWA, T., Ethics

YAMAMOTO, I., Philosophy

Course of French Language and Literature:

HIRATA, S., Modern French Literature

HONDA, T., French Linguistics

ITOH, M., French Philology

KASHIWAGI, O., French Literature

KAWAKAMI, M., Modern French Literature

NONAMI, T., French Literature

OKU, J., History of French Literature

Course of German Language and Literature:

HAMAMOTO, T., German Cultural Studies

KUDO, Y.

SHIBATA, T., German Literature

TAKEICHI, O., German Linguistics

USAMI, Y., Modern German Literature

WATANABE, Y., German Linguistics

YAKAME, T., German Literature

Course of History and Geography:

ASAJI, K., European Medieval History

FUJITA, T., History of Early China

HASHIMOTO, S., Human Geography

ITOH, O., Human Geography

KOBA, M., Physical Geography

MATSUURA, A., History of Early Modern China

MORI, T.

NAKAMURA, H., History of Modern Russia

NISHIMOTO, M., History of Ancient Japan

NOMA, H., Human History

OHYA, W., History of Modern Japan

SHIBAI, K., History of Modern and Contemporary Europe

SHINTANI, H., History of West Asia

SUITA, H., History of Ancient Orient

TAKAHASHI, S., Human Geography

TAKAHASHI, T., History of Medieval Japan

YABUTA, Y., History of Early Modern Japan

YONEDA, F., Archaeology

Course of Chinese Language and Literature:

AZUMA, J., History of Chinese Philosophy

HAGINO, S., Modern and Contemporary Chinese Literature

INOUE, T., Early Modern Chinese Literature

KAWATA, T., History of Chinese Philosophy

KITAOKA, M., Modern Chinese Literature

KUSAKA, T., Chinese Linguistics

MORISE, T., Classical Chinese Poetry

NIKAIDO, Y., Chinese Popular Religion

TAKEUCHI, Y., Sociology of Education

TAO, D., History of Chinese Philosophy

UCHIDA, K., Chinese Linguistics

Course of Education:

AKAO, K., Adult Education Theory

FUJII, M., Psychology

HATASE, N., Clinical Psychology

MATSUMURA, N., Developmental Psychology

NAKATA, Y., Psychology

NOMURA, Y., Experimental Psychology

OKAMURA, T., Public Administration of Education

TAMADA, K., Pedagogy

TANAKA, T., Psychology

TANAKA, Y., Sociology of Education

YAMAMOTO, F., Pedagogy

YAMAZUMI, K., Educational Research

Inter-Departmental Course:

HAZAMA, K., Social Welfare

KURAHASHI, E., Library and Information Science

SAWAI, S.

SHIBATA, H., Information Processing

UEDA, Y., Liberation of Buraku

Course of Physical Arts:

AOKI, S., Health and Physical Education

BAN, Y., Health and Physical Education

KAWAMOTO, T., Health and Physical Education

KIMURA, S., Health and Physical Education

MIURA, T., Health and Physical Education

MIZOHATA, K., Health and Physical Education

OITA, K., Health and Physical Education

SHIRAFUJI, I., Health and Physical Education

TAKECHI, H., Health and Physical Education

TAMURA, N., Health and Physical Education

ZAKO, T., Health and Physical Education

Faculty of Economics:

AKIOKA, H., Microeconomics

HAMANO, K., Economic History of Japan

HASHIMOTO, K., Public Finance

HASHIMOTO, N., Econometrics

HASHIMOTO, S., History of Economic Theories

HAYASHI, H., Public Finance

HIROE, M., Monetary Policy

ICHIEN, M., Social Security

ICHIKAWA, K., Commercial Economics

ISHIDA, H., Economics of Modern China

IWAI, H., Economic Statistics

KASEDA, H., Economic History

KASHIHARA, M., Agricultural Economics

KASUGA, J., Principles of Economics

KITAGAWA, K., European Economic History

KOIKE, H., Introduction to Political Economy

KUSUNOKI, S., International Economics

LEE, Y., Social Economics

MATSUO, A., Mathematical Statistics

MATSUSHITA, K., Demography

MORIOKA, K., Introduction to Political Economy

MOTOKI, H., Macrodynamics

NAGAHISA, R., Principles of Economics

OTSUKA, T., Social Policy

SATO, M., Macroeconomics

TAKESHITA, K., Theory of Economic Systems

TANIDA, N., Information Processing

UEMURA, K., History of Social Thought

WAKAMORI, F., Political Economy

YASUKI, H., Industrial Organization

YOSHINAGA, K., Economic Statistics

Faculty of Commerce:

ABE, S., Public Sector Economics

ARAKI, T., Information Processing Practice

HABARA, K., Non-Life Insurance

HATORI, Y., International Relations

HIROSE, M., General Management

HIROTA, T., Corporate Strategy

IKEJIMA, M., Securities Markets

INOUE, S., Business History

ITO, K., Human Resources Management

IWASA, Y., Financial Intermediation and Institutions

KATO, Y., Distribution Theory

MATSUMOTO, Y., Monitoring Theory for Fair Disclosure

MATSUO, N., Financial Accounting

MIKAMI, H., Economics of Transport and Communication

MIZUNO, I., Management Accounting

MYOJIN, N., Book-keeping

NAGANUMA, H., History of Commerce

NAKAJIMA, M., Cost Accounting and Accounting History

NAKAMURA, M., Business Communication

OKU, K., Theory of International Trade

OKURA, Y., Tax Accounting

SASAKURA, A., International Accounting

SHIBA, K., Accounting Information Theory

SUYAMA, K., Marketing Management

TAKAHASHI, N., International Transport

TAKAYA, S.

TSURUTA, H., Public Finance

UE, K., Monetary Theory

YOKOTA, S., European and American Economy

YOSHIDA, T., Management of International Trade

Faculty of Sociology

Major in Sociology:

ISHIMOTO, K., Theory of Buraku Liberation

IWAMI, K., Understanding Modern Societies

KAKEBA, H., Sociology of Knowledge

KATAGIRI, S., Theoretical Sociology

KUMANO, T., Cultural Anthropology

MATSUHARA, I., Social Policy and Planning

NAGAI, Y., Urban Studies

SUGINO, A., Social Welfare Policy and Planning

YAMAMOTO, Y., Sociology of Knowledge

YAMATO, R., Sociology of Family

Major in Industrial Psychology:

AMEMIYA, T., Ergonomics

ENDO, Y., Social Cognition

HIGASHIMURA, T., Information Processing

IIDA, N., Psychiatry

KAWASAKI, T., Vocational Guidance

KURATO, Y., Clinical Psychology

SEKIGUCHI, R., Experimental Psychology

SHIMIZU, K., Psychometrics

TAKAGI, O., Interpersonal Psychology

TERASHIMA, S., Clinical Psychology

TSUCHIDA, S., Social Psychology

Major in Mass Communication:

FUJIOKA, S., Journalism

KIMURA, Y., Social Communication

KURODA, I., Sociology of Broadcasting Culture

MIZUNO, Y.

OGAWA, H., Media and Culture

SENO, G., Human Communication

TSUNEKI, T., Communication Behaviour

YOSHIOKA, I., Communication Theory

Major in Industrial Sociology:

ASADA, M., Policy for Economic Stabilization

FUNABA, T., Human Resource Studies

HASHIMOTO, K., Philosophy of Science

MORITA, M., Personnel Management

OH, Y., Industrial Information Theory

ONISHI, M., Labour–Management Relations

SAITOU, Y., Industrial Technology

TAKASE, T., Industrial Sociology

WAKABAYASHI, M., Business Administration

YANO, H., Economic Theory

YOSANO, A., Mathematical Sociology

Faculty of Informatics:

AOYAMA, C., Global Environmentology

ATSUJI, S., Organizational Decision Making

COOK, N. D., General Systems Theory

EZAWA, Y., Computer Science

FUKADA, Y., Image Processing and Pattern Recognition

FUKE, H., International Networks

FURUTA, H., Fuzzy Logic, Theory and Application

HAYASHI, I., Information Systems Management

HAYASHI, T., Computer Graphics

HIJIKATA, H., Mathematics

HIROKAME, M., Mathematics

HORI, M., File Structure

ITO, T., Computer Simulation

KAMEI, K., Management

KATO, M., Philosophy
KATO, T., Cognitive Science
KATO, T., Computer Crime
KITAJIMA, O., Business Behaviour
KITANI, S., Public Administration
KOMATSU, Y., Business Administration
KUBOTA, K., Audiovisual Media Production
KUBOTA, M., Communication
KUROKAMI, H., Multimedia Education
KUROKUZU, H., Accounting Information Systems
KUWABARA, T., Psychology
MIYASHITA, F., Computer Science
NAKAGAWA, Y., Data Structure and Algorithm
NOGUCHI, H., Business Information
OKAMOTO, T., Public Policy
SANO, M., Community Networks
SHIOMURA, T., Microeconomic Models
SHYI, S. C., Management Information Systems
SUGA, T., Computer-based Communication
TANAKA, S., Knowledge Information Processing
TSUJI, M., Software Architecture
UESHIMA, S., Principles of Database Management
UKAI, Y., Economic Policy
YAMAGUCHI, S., Cultural Studies of Information Society
YAMANA, T., Macroeconomic Models
YOSHIDA, N., Principles of Computer Electronics

Faculty of Engineering

Department of Mechanical Engineering:
ARAI, Y., Measurement Systems
ISHIHARA, I., Thermal Engineering
KITAJIMA, K., Manufacturing Processes
SHINGUABARA, S., Nanophysics and Nanofabrication Technology
SHINKE, N., Strength of Materials
TAGAWA, N., Micromechatronics
TAKUMA, M., Experiments on Mechanical Engineering

Department of Mechanical Systems Engineering:
BANDO, K., Computational Fluid Dynamics
FUJITA, T., Analytical Dynamics
HIGUCHI, M., Production Engineering
IWATSUBO, T., Measurement Systems
MORI, A., Machine Design and Engineering Tribology
OHBA, K., Fluids Engineering and Biomechanics
OZAWA, M., Engineering Thermodynamics
UCHIYAMA, H., Control Engineering

Department of Electrical Engineering and Computer Science:
HARA, T., Theory of Electricity and Magnetism
HORIBA, Y., System LSI
KUMAMOTO, A., Flexible and Intelligent Image Processing
MAEDA, Y., Control Theory and Neural Computation
OHNISHI, M., Study of Ion Beam Colliding Fusion Neutron Source
TAMURA, H., Applied Systems Science
YAMAMOTO, M., Computer Networking

Department of Electronics:
IIDA, Y., Microwave and Millimetre-Wave Engineering
KOJIMA, T., Optical and Electromagnetic Engineering
MUNEYASU, M., Image Processing
MURAMAKA, N., Computer Systems Engineering
NOMURA, Y., Information and Intelligent Systems
OKADA, H., Information Networks
OMURA, Y., Device Physics and Modelling
YOKOTA, K., Semiconductor Engineering

Department of Chemical Engineering:
MIYAKE, T., Catalyst Engineering
MIYAKE, Y., Separation Engineering
MUROYAMA, K., Chemical Reaction Engineering
ODA, H., Physical Chemistry
OKADA, Y., Nanoparticle Engineering
SHIBATA, J., Physical Chemistry
SUZUKI, T., Catalyst Engineering
YAMAMOTO, H., Experimental Chemical Engineering

Department of Applied Chemistry:
ARAKAWA, R., Analytical Chemistry
ISHII, Y., Organometallic Chemistry
ISHIKAWA, T., Electrochemistry and Electrochemical Devices
MATSUMOTO, A., Polymer Chemistry
OCHI, M., Polymer Engineering
OUCHI, T., Functional Polymers
TANEKA, K., Organic Supramolecular Chemistry

Department of Materials Science and Engineering:
AKAMATSU, K., Functional Materials
IKEDA, M., Environmental Conscious Materials Laboratory
KOBAYASHI, T., Processing of Molten Metals
KOMATSU, S., Strength of Materials
KOZUKA, H., Ceramic Engineering
MIYAKE, H., Foundry Engineering
OISHI, T., Physical Chemistry of Materials Processing
SUGIMOTO, T., Nonferrous Metallic Materials

Department of Systems Management Engineering:
AOYAGI, S., Automatic Control Theory
FUYUKI, M., Production Systems Engineering
HORII, K., Human Factors Engineering
MORI, K., Production Management
NAKAI, T., Operations Research
UEMURA, T., Visual Information Engineering

Department of Civil and Environmental Engineering:
DOGAKI, M., Structural Mechanics
ISHIGAKI, T., Hydraulic Engineering for Environment and Disaster Prevention
KAWAKAMI, S., Traffic Engineering
KUSUMI, H., Rock Mechanics and Geological Engineering
MIKAMI, I., Design of Civil Engineering Structures
SAKANO, M., Structural Engineering
TOYOFUKU, T., Construction Materials
WADA, Y., Sanitary Engineering

Department of Architecture:
ASANO, K., Structural Engineering
EGAWA, N., Architectural Environmental Design Laboratory
KAWAI, Y., Environmental Engineering
KAWAMICHI, R., Architectural Theory and Design
MARUMO, H., Urban Design
NAGAI, N., History of Architecture
NOGUCHI, T., Environmental Engineering
YAO, S., Structural Engineering

Department of Biotechnology:
HASEGAWA, Y., Genetic Engineering
OBATA, H., Microbial Technology
TSUCHIDO, T., Biocontrol Technology
UESATO, S., Pharmaceutical Technology
YAGI, H., Biochemical Engineering
YOSHIDA, M., Food Biotechnology

General Education in Natural Sciences:
AKI, S.
FUKUSHIMA, M., Probability Theory
ICHIHARA, K., Probability Theory
IKEUCHI, I., Intracellular Signals Transduction Mechanism of Neuronal Cells
KURISU, T., Game Theory

KURIYAMA, A., Mathematical Physics
KUSUDA, M., Functional Analysis
SAITO, T.
SEKI, M., Fluid Dynamics
SHIRAIWA, T., Chiral Molecular Chemistry
TAJITSU, Y.
TAMURA, H., Naturally Occurring Polymer Chemistry
TATSUMI, M., Applied Analytical Chemistry
URAGAMI, T., Functional Polymer Science
YAMAMURA, M., Quantum Many-body Physics
YAMAUCHI, O., Bio-inorganic Chemistry
YANAGAWA, T., Knot Group Theory

Institute of Foreign Language Education and Research:
FUKUI, N., Study of Japanese Culture and Ruth Benedict
GEN, YUKIKOI, Diachronic Study of Colloquial Chinese
GIBBS, A. S., Approach to Foreign Language Communication through Pragmatics, Stylistics and Discourse Analysis, Reading and Writing for Academic Purposes
HIRATA, W., Spanish and Latin American Literature
ISHIHARA, T., American Literature
JOHNSON, G. S., Presentation, Oral Interpretation
KAWAI, T., English Education, English Linguistics
KIKUCHI, A., Linguistics
KIKUCHI, U., Experimental Phonetics
KITAMURA, Y., Cognitive Science, Education Technology
KITE, Y., Sociolinguistics, Second Language Acquisition
KONDO, M., Russian Literature
KUMATANI, A., Korean Linguistics, Sociolinguistics
MOCHIZUKI, M., Applied Linguistics, Japanese Linguistics
NISHIKAWA, K., Chinese Linguistics
SAITO, E., English Education
SCHAUWECKER, D. F., Japanese–German Relationships
SHEN, G., Chinese Language Education
SUGITANI, M., German Language, Education and Intercultural Communication
TAKAHASHI, H., Sociolinguistics
TAKAHASHI, T., English Language Education
TAKEUCHI, O., Applied Linguistics, Educational Technology
USAMI, T., English Literature, English Education
WADA, Y., Medieval Manuscript Studies
YAMAMOTO, E., English Linguistics
YAMANE, S., English Phonetics
YASHIMA, T., Applied Linguistics, Intercultural Communication
YOSHIZAWA, K., Applied Linguistics

School of Law:
FUJITA, H., International Law
HAYAKAWA, T., Commercial Law
IMANISHI, Y., Civil Law
ISHII, K., Criminal Procedure
KAMEDA, K., Administrative Law
KAWAGUCHI, M., Labour Law
KIMURA, T., Civil Law
KINOSHITA, S., Constitutional Law
KITAGAWA, T., Law of International Transactions
KUBO, H., Civil Law
MURATA, H., Constitutional Law
MUROTA, G.
NOVO, M., Administrative Law
ODO, Y., Civil Law
SHIMADA, R., Civil Procedure
TAKESHITA, K., Philosophy of Law
TAKIGAWA, T., Economic Law, International Economic Law
TATSUMI, N., Intellectual Property Law
WAKAMATSU, Y., Civil Law

YAMANAKA, K., Criminal Law
YAMATO, M., Commercial Law

KEIO UNIVERSITY

2-15-45 Mita, Minato-ku, Tokyo 108-8345
Telephone: (3) 5427-1517
Fax: (3) 3769-1564
E-mail: www@info.keio.ac.jp
Internet: www.keio.ac.jp/index-en.html

Founded 1858
Private control
Academic year: April to March

Pres.: ATSUSHI SEIKE
Vice-Press: AKIRA HASEYAMA, MAKOTO IDA, MASAHIKO SHIMIZU, NAOKI WATANABE, NAOYUKI AGAWA, TADASHI KASAHARA, TOSHIAKI MAKABE, YOSHIAKI TOYAMA
Sec.-Gen.: MASAHIRO KOYA
Registrar: BUNJI KURIYA
Dirs of Libraries: YUKIO ITO (Hiyoshi Media Centre), YOSHIKAZU SUGIMOTO (Information and Media Center for Pharmaceutical Sciences), KAZUO SHIIKI (Information and Media Center for Science and Technology), SHINYA SUGIYAMA (Mita Media Centre), ATSUKO KOISHI (SFC Media Center), KEIICHI FUKUDA (Shinanomachi Media Center)

Library of 4,783,740 vols
Number of teachers: 2,383 full-time
Number of students: 33,170 (regular course), 9,383 (correspondence course)

Publications: *Keio Business Review* (1 a year), *Keio Communication Review* (1 a year), *Keio Economic Studies* (2 a year), *Keio Journal of Medicine* (4 a year), *Okajima's Folia Anatomica Japonica* (4 a year), *Keio Economic Observatory* (irregular)

DEANS

Faculty of Business and Commerce: YOSHIO HIGUCHI
Faculty of Economics: SHUHEI SHIOZAWA
Faculty of Environment and Information Studies: HIDEYUKI TOKUDA
Faculty of Law: RYOSEI KOKUBUN
Faculty of Letters: SUMIO NAKAGAWA
School of Medicine: MAKOTO SUEMATSU
Faculty of Nursing and Medical Care: KAEKO YAMASHITA
Faculty of Pharmacy: TADASHI KASAHARA
Faculty of Policy Management: NAOYUKI AGAWA
Faculty of Science and Technology: TOSHIAKI MAKABE

CHAIRPERSONS

Graduate School of Business Administration: KYOICHI IKEO
Graduate School of Business and Commerce: YOSHIO HIGUCHI
Graduate School of Economics: MASAMICHI KOMURO
Graduate School of Health Management: SHOHEI ONISHI
Graduate School of Human Relations: NORIYUKI SUGIURA
Graduate School of Law: RYOSEI KOKUBUN
Graduate School of Letters: SUMIO NAKAGAWA
Graduate School of Media and Governance: IKUYO KANEKO
Graduate School of Media Design: MASA INAKAGE
Graduate School of Medicine: HIDEYUKI OKANO
Graduate School of Pharmaceutical Sciences: TADASHI KASAHARA
Graduate School of Science and Technology: TOSHIAKI MAKABE
Graduate School of System Design and Management: YOSHIAKI OHKAMI
Law School: KANTARO TOYOIZUMI

DIRECTORS

Fukuzawa Memorial Center for Modern Japanese Studies: MASAMICHI KOMURO
Institute of Cultural and Linguistic Studies: SUMIO NAKAGAWA
Institute for Economic and Industry Studies (Sangyo Kenkyujo): HITOSHI HAYAMI
Institute for Media and Communications Research: YUTAKA OISHI
Institute of Physical Education: FUMIO UEDA
Keio Institute of East Asian Studies: YOSHIHIDE SOEYA
Keio Research Center for Foreign Language: KAZUMI SAKAI
Sports Medicine Research Center: SHOHEI ONISHI

KINKI UNIVERSITY

Kowakae 3-4-1, Higashiosaka-shi, Osaka 577-8502
Telephone: (6) 6721-2332
Fax: (6) 6721-2353
E-mail: koho@msa.kindai.ac.jp
Internet: www.kindai.ac.jp

Founded 1925
Private control
Language of instruction: Japanese
Academic year: April to March

Pres.: HIROYUKI HATA
Head Administrator: HIROAKI SEKOH

Library of 1,200,000 vols
Number of teachers: 1,563
Number of students: 29,794

Publications: *Acta Medica Kinki University* (2 a year), *Annals of the Molecular Engineering Institute* (1 a year), *Bulletin of the Fisheries Laboratory of Kinki University* (irregular), *Bulletin of the Pharmaceutical Research and Technology Institute* (1 a year), *Bulletin of the School of Literature, Arts and Cultural Studies* (1 a year), *Ikoma Journal of Economics* (2 a year), *Journal of Business Administration and Marketing Strategy* (3 a year), *Journal of the Faculty of Science and Engineering at Kinki University* (1 a year), *Law Review of Kinki University* (4 a year), *Medical Journal of Kinki University* (2 a year), *Memoirs of the Faculty of Agriculture of Kinki University* (1 a year), *Memoirs of the Institute of Advanced Technology* (2 a year), *Memoirs of the School of Biology-Oriented Science and Technology* (1 a year), *Multimedia Education* (1 a year), *Research Journal of the Department of Teacher Education* (2 a year), *Research Reports of the Faculty of Engineering of Kinki University* (1 a year), *Science and Technology* (1 a year)

DEANS

School of Agriculture: KOICHIRO KOMAI
School of Biology-Oriented Science and Technology: KAZUO YAMAMOTO
School of Business Administration: HIROYASU OKITSU
School of Economics: KYOUZOU TAKECHI
School of Engineering: HIROSHI TSUBAKIHARA
School of Humanity-Oriented Science and Engineering: MASAYUKI ONO
School of Law: HIDEJIRO ISHIDA
School of Literature, Arts and Cultural Studies: YUTAKA ARAMAKI
School of Medicine: HARUMASA OYANAGI
School of Pharmaceutical Sciences: KAZUAKI KAKEHI
School of Science and Engineering: MEGUMU MUNAKATA

KOBE GAKUIN UNIVERSITY

518 Arise, Ikawadani-cho, Nishiku, Kobe 651-2180
Telephone: (78) 974-1551
Fax: (78) 974-5689
E-mail: kgu@j.kobegakuin.ac.jp
Internet: www.kobegakuin.ac.jp

Founded 1966
Academic year: April to March
Campuses at Nagata and Port Island

Pres.: YOSHIO OKADA
Dir-Gen. for Admin.: TTETSUAKI TAKENAKA
Librarian: HIROMI YOSHIDA

Library of 955,062 vols
Number of teachers: 284
Number of students: 10,172

Publications: *Kobe Gakuin Hogaku* (Law and Politics Review), *Kobe Gakuin Economic Papers*, *Memoirs of the Faculty of Pharmaceutical Sciences*, *Journal of Business Management*

DEANS

Faculty of Business Admin.: NOBUO TSUNO
Faculty of Economics: YOSHIO TANAKA
Faculty of Humanities and Sciences: HIRONORI MIZUMOTO
Faculty of Law: TOYOKI OKADA
Faculty of Nutrition: KIYOSHI GODA
Faculty of Pharmaceutical Sciences: HIROSHI OKAMOTO
Faculty of Rehabilitation: ISAO NARA
Graduate School of Economics: YOSHIO TANAKA
Graduate School of Food and Medicinal Sciences: KIYOSHI GODA
Graduate School of Humanities and Sciences: HIRONORI MIZUMOTO
Graduate School of Law: TOYOKI OKADA
Graduate School of Law Practices: KENJI SANEKATA
Graduate School of Nutrition: KIYOSHI GODA
Graduate School of Pharmaceutical Sciences: HIROSHI OKAMOTO

KOGAKUIN UNIVERSITY

1-24-2, Nishi-shinjuku, Shinjuku-ku, Tokyo 163-8677
Telephone: (3) 3342-1211
Fax: (3) 3342-5304
E-mail: kokusai@sc.kogakuin.ac.jp
Internet: www.kogakuin.ac.jp

Founded 1887, university status 1949
Academic year: April to March

Pres.: AKISATO MIZUNO
Vice-Pres.: YAUSHI NAGASAWA
Library Dir: KIYOSHI KATO

Library of 256,000 vols, 2,462 periodicals
Number of teachers: 222
Number of students: 6,617 (6,061 undergraduates, 531 graduates, 25 doctoral students)

Publications: *Kogakuin Daigaku Kenkyu Hokoku* (research reports, 2 a year), *Kogakuin Daigaku Kyotukatei Kenkyu Ronso* (research reports, 2 a year)

DEANS

Faculty of Engineering: Prof. YASUSHI NAGASAWA
Faculty of Global Engineering: Prof. OKITSUGU FURUYA
Faculty of Informatics: Prof. YOSHIO OYANAGI
Graduate School of Engineering: Prof. HIROMICHI FUJIE (Chair.)

KOKUGAKUIN UNIVERSITY

4-10-28, Higashi, Shibuya-ku, Tokyo 150-8440
Telephone: (3) 5466-0111

Fax: (3) 5778-7061
E-mail: kokusai@kokugakuin.ac.jp
Internet: www.kokugakuin.ac.jp

Founded 1882
Academic year: April to March

President: Prof. MASAHIKO ASOYA
Secretary-General: SHOZO SANAGI
Librarian: T. SAWANOBORI

Library: see Libraries and Archives
Number of teachers: 790
Number of students: 10,319

Publications: *Kokugakuin Zasshi* (Journal of
Kokugakuin University), *Kokugakuin Kei-
zaigaku* (Kokugakuin University Economic
Review), *Kokugakuin Hogaku* (Journal of
the Faculty of Law and Politics), *Kokuga-
kuin Daigaku Kiyo* (Transactions of Koku-
gakuin University), *Kokugakuin Daigaku
Daigakuin Bungaku Kenkyuka ronshu*
(Journal of the Graduate School, Kokuga-
kuin University), *Kokugakuin Daigaku
Kenzaigaku Kenkyuka Kiyo* (Kokugakuin
University Economic Studies), *Kokugakuin
Hokenronso* (Journal of Law and Politics,
Graduate School of Law), *Nihonbunka-
Kenkyusho-Kiyo* (Transactions of the Insti-
tute for Japanese Culture and Classics)

DEANS

Faculty of Economics: HIRONORI KON'I
Faculty of Law: SEIICHI NAGAMORI
Faculty of Letters: SHUHEI AOKI
Faculty of Shinto Studies: SOJI OKADA
Graduate School: TSUYOSHI FUJIMOTO
Law School: KATSUMASA HIRABAYASHI

ATTACHED RESEARCH INSTITUTE

**Institute for Japanese Culture and Clas-
sics:** 4-10-28, Higashi, Shibuya-ku, Tokyo
150-8440.

KOKUSHIKAN UNIVERSITY

4-28-1 Setagaya, Setagaya-ku, Tokyo 154-
8515

Telephone: (3) 5481-3112
Fax: (3) 3413-7420
E-mail: wwwadmin@kiss.kokushikan.ac.jp
Internet: www.kokushikan.ac.jp

Founded 1917
Private control
Academic year: April to March

Chairman: HARUO NISHIHARA
Pres.: HIDEO OSAWA
General Dir: ATSUSHI MATSUMOTO
Librarian: SHOICHI YAMAMOTO

Library of 630,638 vols
Number of teachers: 310
Number of students: 12,677

Publications: *Politics and Economics Review,
Kokushikan Law Review*, various faculty
journals and reviews

DEANS

Faculty of Engineering: KATSUHIKO WAKA-
BAYASHI
Faculty of Law: NORIYOSHI WATANABE
Faculty of Letters: AKIRA ABE
Faculty of Political Science and Economics:
HIROYUKI YAMAZAKI
Faculty of Political Science and Economics
(Evening Session): RYOZO SHIROGANE
Faculty of Physical Education: KAZUYUKI
NISHYAMA
Junior College: HIROSHI TASHIRO
School of Asia 21: KAGEAKI KAJIWARA

KOMAZAWA UNIVERSITY

1-23-1 Komazawa, Setagaya-ku, Tokyo 154-
8525

Telephone: (3) 3418-9011
Fax: (3) 3418-9017

E-mail: info-soumu@komazawa-u.ac.jp
Internet: www.komazawa-u.ac.jp
Academic year: April to March

Pres.: KIYOZUMI ISHII
Vice-Pres.: TADASHI SAITO
Registrar: TAKASHI SHIMIZU
Librarian: MITSUYOSHI OKUNO

Library of 1,149,255 vols
Number of teachers: 354
Number of students: 16,649

Publications: *Journal of the Faculty of Bud-
dhism, Journal of Buddhist Studies,
Komazawa Educational Review, Regional
Views, Journal of the Faculty of Letters,
Komazawa Japanese Literature, Studies in
British and American Literature, Koma-
zawa Geography, Journal of the Historical
Association of Komazawa, Komazawa
Journal of Sociology, Journal of the Fac-
ulty of Economics, The Economic Review of
Komazawa Univ., Journal of the Faculty of
Law of Komazawa University, Komazawa
Law and Political Science Review, Koma-
zawa Business Studies, Komazawa Busi-
ness Review, Journal of the Faculty of
Foreign Languages, The Review of Foreign
Languages, Bunka* (Komazawa University
Journal of Culture), *Journal of Health
Sciences of Komazawa University, Journal
of Radiological Sciences of Komazawa
University, Komazawa Annual of Soci-
ology, Komazawa University Journal of
Health and Physical Education*

DEANS

Faculty of Buddhism: MASASHI NAGAI
Faculty of Business Administration: MIT-
SUAKI TAKADA
Faculty of Economics: YOSHIHARU HYAKUTA
Faculty of Health Sciences: YUSUKE YAMA-
MOTO
Faculty of Law: NORIO KOBORI
Faculty of Letters: MASAKI KUBOTA

CHAIRMEN

Graduate Division of Arts and Sciences I:
KANAZAWA ATSUSHI
Graduate Division of Arts and Sciences II:
MASATOSHI KAWASAKI
Graduate Division of Business Administra-
tion: SHIGERU HATORI
Graduate Division of Commerce: NOBUTAKA
SOGA
Graduate Division of Economics: TADAMITSU
YASHIKI
Graduate Division of Health Sciences: KOUKI
YOSHIKAWA
Graduate Division of Law: SHOHEI KANEKO
Graduate Division of Legal Research and
Training: YUTAKA USUKI

KONAN UNIVERSITY

8-9-1 Okamoto, Higashinada-ku, Kobe 658-
8501

Telephone: (78) 431-4341
Fax: (78) 435-2306
E-mail: d-jimu@adm.konan-u.ac.jp
Internet: www.konan-u.ac.jp

Founded 1918

President: Y. SUGIMURA

Library of 775,000 vols
Number of teachers: 240 full-time
Number of students: 9,578

Publications: *Journal of Konan University
Faculty of Letters* (irregular), *Memoirs of
Konan University* (science and engineering
series, 2 a year), *Konan Economic Papers*
(irregular), *Konan Hogaku* (Konan Law
Review, irreg.), *Konan Business Review*
(irregular), *Journal of the Institute for
Language and Culture* (irregular)

DEANS

Faculty of Business Administration: Y.
NAKATA
Faculty of Economics: H. KOBAYASHI
Faculty of Law: T. MAEDA
Faculty of Letters: T. HISATAKE
Faculty of Science and Engineering: T.
SHIGEMATSU

KOSHIEN UNIVERSITY

Momijigaoka, Takarazuka, Hyogo 665-0006

Telephone: (797) 87-5111
Fax: (797) 87-5666
E-mail: nyuushi@koshien.ac.jp
Internet: www.koshien.ac.jp

Founded 1967

President: TOMIO KINOSHITA

Library of 106,942 vols
Number of teachers: 170
Number of students: 1,428

Colleges of Business Administration,
Humanities, Information Sciences, Nutrition.

KURUME UNIVERSITY

67 Asahi-Machi, Kurume 830-0011

Telephone: (942) 35-3311
Fax: (942) 32-5191
E-mail: soumu@med.kurume-u.ac.jp
Internet: www.kurume-u.ac.jp

Founded 1928

Pres.: KYOZO KOKETSU
Dir of Admin. Office: KATSUMI YOSHIHISA

Library of 415,000 vols
Number of teachers: 534
Number of students: 5,808

Publications: *The Kurume Medical Journal*
(4 a year), *The Journal of the Kurume
Medical Association* (12 a year), *The Journal for Studies on Industrial Economics* (4
a year)

Faculties of Commerce, Economics, Law,
Literature and Medicine.

KWANSEI GAKUIN UNIVERSITY

1-1-155 Uegahara, Nishinomiya, Hyogo 662-
8501

Telephone: (798) 51-0952
Fax: (798) 51-0954
E-mail: ciec@kwansei.ac.jp
Internet: www.kwansei.ac.jp

Founded 1889
Academic year: April to March

Chancellor: MICHIYA HATA
President: KAZUO HIRAMATSU
Vice-Presidents: KOHEI ASANO, TOKUTOSHI
INOUE, HIDEKI MINE
Library Director: TAKUTOSHI INOUE

Library: see Libraries and Archives
Number of teachers: 435 full-time
Number of students: 18,702

Publications: *Theological Studies, Human-
ities Review, Journal of the School of
Sociology, Journal of Law and Politics,
Journal of Economics, Journal of Business
Administration, Law Review, Economic
Review, Journal of Policy Studies, Review
of Economics and Business Management,
Studies in Computer Science, Language
and Culture, Studies in Teacher Develop-
ment, Social Sciences Review, Natural
Sciences Review*

DEANS

School of Business Administration: AKIRA
MIYAMA
School of Economics: SHIN NEGISHI
School of Humanities: ATSUHIDE SAKAKURA
School of Law and Politics: YOZO SAWADA

School of Policy Studies: TOYOO FUKUDA
School of Science: YAICHI SHINOHARA
School of Sociology: MICHIHITO TSUSHIMA
School of Theology: ETSURO KINOWAKI
Graduate School of Language, Communication and Culture: TAKAAKI KANZAKI
Institute of Business and Accounting: MARTIN COLLICK
Law School: TOORU KATO

KYOTO PHARMACEUTICAL UNIVERSITY

5, Misasagi-Nakauchi-cho, Yamashina-ku, Kyoto 607-8414

Telephone: (75) 595-4600
Fax: (75) 595-4750
E-mail: kpu-koho@mb.kyoto-phu.ac.jp
Internet: www.kyoto-phu.ac.jp

Founded 1884

Pres.: MASAZUMI IKEDA
Registrar: Dr NORIAKI FUNASAKI
Librarian: Dr TAKESI NISINO

Library of 91,260 vols
Number of teachers: 104
Number of students: 1,821

PROFESSORS

FUJIMOTO, S., Environmental Biochemistry
FUNASAKI, N., Physical Chemistry
HAMAZAKI, H., Health and Sports Sciences
HATAYAMA, T., Biochemistry
HIRAYAMA, T., Public Health
KAMBE, T., Mathematics
KIM, J., Cell Biology
KISO, Y., Medicinal Chemistry
KITAMURA, K., Analytical Chemistry
KOHNO, S., Pharmacology
KOIKE, C., Physics Laboratory
KONOSHIMA, T., Pharmaceutical Sciences and Natural Resources
MURANISHI, S., Pharmaceutics
NAKATA, T., Clinical Pharmacology
NISHINO, T., Microbiology
NODE, M., Pharmaceutical Manufacturing Chemistry
OHTA, S., Chemistry of Functional Molecules
OKABE, S., Applied Pharmacology
SAKURAI, H., Analytical and Bioinorganic Chemistry
SATO, T., Pathological Biochemistry
TAKADA, K., Pharmacokinetics
TAKEUCHI, K., Pharmacology and Experimental Therapeutics
TANIGUCHI, T., Neurobiology
UENISHI, J., Pharmaceutical Chemistry
YAMAMOTO, A., Biopharmaceutics
YOKOYAMA, T., Hospital Pharmacy
YOSHIKAWA, M., Pharmacognosy

MATSUYAMA UNIVERSITY

4–2 Bunkyo-cho, Matsuyama Ehime 790-8578

Telephone: (89) 925-7111
Fax: (89) 922-6064
E-mail: mu-koho@matsuyama-u.ac.jp
Internet: www.matsuyama-u.ac.jp

Founded 1923
Academic year: April to March

President: Prof. SATORU KANIMORI
Registrar: SANIMOTU OCHI

Library: see Libraries and Archives
Number of teachers: 308
Number of students: 5,730

Publications: Matsuyama Daigaku Ronshu (6 a year), Studies in Language and Literature (2 a year)

DEANS

Faculty of Business Administration: Prof. N. IDIIDA
Faculty of Economics: Prof. J. IRIE, Prof. Y. SEINO

Faculty of Humanities: Prof. T. KANAMURA
Faculty of Law: Prof. T. TAKEMIYA
Junior College: Prof. K. YAGI

MEIJI UNIVERSITY

1-1 Kanda-Surugadai, Chiyoda-ku, Tokyo 101-8301

Telephone: (3) 3296-4545
Fax: (3) 3296-4339
E-mail: koho@isc.meiji.ac.jp
Internet: www.meiji.ac.jp

Founded 1881
Private control
Academic year: April to March (2 semesters)

Pres.: Prof. HIROMI NAYA
Dir of Library: SHUICHI NOGAMI

Library of 2,150,000 vols
Number of teachers: 2,517 (859 full-time, 1,658 part-time)
Number of students: 32,056 (29,064 undergraduate, 2,001 postgraduate, 991 women's junior college)

DEANS

Graduate School: AKIRA NAKAMURA
School of Agriculture: KATSUMI YONEYAMA
School of Arts and Letters: TAKEHIKO YOSHIMURA
School of Business Administration: KATSUHIKO HIRAI
School of Commerce: KENICHI FUKUMIYA
School of Information and Communication: YOSHIYUKI NAKAMURA
School of Law: KEIICHIRO TSUCHIYA
School of Political Science and Economics: KAZUTO IIDA
School of Science and Technology: MASAO MUKAIDONO

GRADUATE SCHOOL CHAIRMEN

Dept of Agriculture: YUKIO KATO
Dept of Arts and Letters: AKIRA NAGAOKA
Dept of Business Administration: ETSUO ABE
Dept of Commerce: RYOKICHI TSUDA
Dept of Global Business: TAKEAKI KARIYA
Dept of Governance Studies: HIROO ICHIKAWA
Dept of Law: YUTAKA MASUDA
Dept of Political Science and Economics: MASAMI ITO
Dept of Professional Accountancy: HISASHI YMAMAURA
Dept of Science and Technology: MASAO MUKAIDONO

MEIJI GAKUIN UNIVERSITY

1-2-37 Shirokanedai, Minato-ku, Tokyo 108-8636

Telephone: (3) 5421-5165
Fax: (3) 5421-5185
E-mail: koho@mguad.meijigakuin.ac.jp
Internet: www.meijigakuin.ac.jp

Founded 1877
Private control
Language of instruction: Japanese
Academic year: April to July, September to March

Chancellor: Prof. SATORU KUZE
Pres.: Prof. YOSHIKAZU WAKITA
Vice-Pres.: Prof. MIKIKO YAMAZAKI, Prof. TOMOYOSHI KOIZUMI, Prof. TOSHIO HASHIMOTO
Admin. Officer: SHUJI SHIBASAKI
Librarian: Prof. KUNIO IWAYA

Library of 825,000 vols
Number of teachers: 256
Number of students: 13,639

Publications: Meiji Gakuin Review, English Language and Literature, Papers and Proceedings of Economics, Proceedings of Integrated Arts and Sciences, Law Review (3 a year), International and Regional Studies (2 a year), French Literature, Art Studies,

Psychology, Sociology and Social Welfare Review (1 a year)

DEANS

Faculty of Economics: Prof. TAKESHI OSHIO
Faculty of General Education: Prof. YASUO IKEGAMI
Faculty of International Studies: Prof. NOZOMO AKIZUKI
Faculty of Law: Prof. MITSURU ABE
Faculty of Literature: Prof. RYUUICHI HIGUCHI
Faculty of Sociology and Social Work: Prof. KATSUYOSHI KAWAI
Graduate School of Economics: Prof. MASAAKI TAKAMATSU
Graduate School of International Studies: Prof. SHIGEMOCHI HIROSHIMA
Graduate School of Law: Prof. AKIRA OKI
Graduate School of Literature: Prof. MASAAKI TSUTSUI
Graduate School of Sociology and Social Work: Prof. KIYOSHI MATSUI

MEIJO UNIVERSITY

1-501 Shiogamaguchi, Tempaku-ku, Nagoya, Aichi 468-8502

Telephone: (52) 832-1151
Fax: (52) 833-9494
E-mail: kikaku@meijo-u.ac.jp
Internet: www.meijo-u.ac.jp

Founded 1949
Private control
Academic year: April to March

President: MASAKI AMINAKA
Administrative Officer: RYOICHI ARAI
Library Director: YUICHIROU OZAKI

Library of 735,994 vols, 7,047 periodicals
Number of teachers: 431 (full-time)
Number of students: 15,495

Publications: Meijo Hogaku, Meijo Ronsou, faculty bulletins and reports

DEANS

Faculty of Agriculture: NAOSUKE NII
Faculty of Business: HITOSHI IMAI
Faculty of Economics: UMEGAKI
Faculty of Education: KOUJI ITOU
Faculty of Law: YUZOU KIMURA
Faculty of Pharmacy: YOSHIO SUZUKI
Faculty of Science and Technology: TETSO HUJIMOTO
Faculty of Urban Science: TODASHI USHIJIMA
Junior College: SHINJI MORITA

MEISEI UNIVERSITY

2-1-1 Hodokubo, Hino-shi, Tokyo 191-8506
Campuses at Hino and Ome

Telephone: Hino: (42) 591-5111; Ome: (428) 25-5111
Fax: Hino: (42) 591-8181; Ome: (428) 25-5182
E-mail: office@flc.meisei-u.ac.jp
Internet: www.meisei-u.ac.jp

Founded 1964
Private control
Academic year: April to March

Pres.: JUN'ICHI UJIHARA
Vice-Press: TAKEHIKO MARUYAMA, TETSUO OGAWA
Dirs of Student Affairs: TOSHIAKI UEDA, KAZUYOSHI YAMANAKA
Sec.-Gen.: KATSUNORI KANATANI
Library Dir: YOSHIAKI FIUNATSU

Library of 880,305 vols, 4,300 periodicals
Number of teachers: 243
Number of students: 8,651 (correspondence courses 8,152)

Publications: Research Bulletin of Meisei University. Humanities and Social Sciences (1 a year), Research Bulletin of Meisei University. Physical Sciences and

Engineering (1 a year), *Bulletin of Meisei University. Department of Arts, Faculty of Japanese Culture* (1 a year), *Research Bulletin of Meisei University. Faculty of Informatics* (1 a year), *Annual Bulletin of the Graduate School of Humanities and Social Sciences, Meisei University*

DEANS

Faculty of Economics (Hino): Prof. YOSHIHIKO NISHINO
Faculty of Humanities (Hino): Prof. KOICHI TSUKADA
Faculty of Informatics (Ome): Prof. KANJI OTSUKA
Faculty of Japanese Culture (Ome): Prof. KENJI IKAWA
Faculty of Physical Sciences and Engineering (Hino): Prof. MUNEKAZU TAKANO

MEJIRO UNIVERSITY

4-31-1 Nakaochiai, Shinjuku-ku, Tokyo 161-8539

Telephone: (3) 5996-3121
Fax: (3) 5996-3238
E-mail: webmaster@mejiro.ac.jp
Internet: www.mejiro.ac.jp

Founded 1923

Pres.: KOKI SATO

DEANS

Faculty of Business Administration: (vacant)
Faculty of Human and Social Sciences: OSAMI HUKUSHIMA
Faculty of Humanities: KISAKU KUDO

MOMOYAMA GAKUIN UNIVERSITY (ST ANDREW'S UNIVERSITY)

1-1 Manabino, Izumi, Osaka 594-1198

Telephone: (725) 54-3131
Fax: (725) 54-3215
E-mail: kokusai@andrew.ac.jp
Internet: www.andrew.ac.jp

Founded 1959
Languages of instruction: Japanese, English
Academic year: April to March

President: MICHIO MATSUURA
Vice-Presidents: AKIRA HASEGAWA, YOJI IWATSU, JIRO KIMURA
Library Director: NORIO KITAGAWA

Library of 646,000 vols
Number of teachers: 156
Number of students: 7,387

Publications: *Economic & Business Review, English Review, Human Sciences Review, Intercultural Studies, Journal of Christian Studies, Pan-Pacific Business Review, Research Institute Bulletin, St. Andrew's University Law Review, Sociological Review*

DEANS

Faculty of Business Administration: KICHIZO AKASHI
Faculty of Economics: NORIO TAKEHARA
Faculty of Law: NORIYUKI HONMA
Faculty of Letters: NATSUKI KUNIMATSU
Faculty of Sociology: YOSHIFUMI SHIMIZU

CHAIRS OF GRADUATE SCHOOLS

Graduate School of Business Administration: SHINSHI KATAOKA
Graduate School of Economics: MITSUHIKO IYODA
Graduate School of Letters: NOBUAKI TERAKI
Graduate School of Sociology: OSAMU UEDA

MIYAGI GAKUIN WOMEN'S COLLEGE

9-1-1 Aoba-ku, Sendai Miyagi 981-8557

Telephone: (22) 279-1311
Fax: (22) 279-7566

E-mail: www-admin@mgu.ac.jp
Internet: www.mgu.ac.jp

Founded 1886; first degree courses
Private control
Language of instruction: Japanese
Academic year: April to March

Chancellor: K. MATSUZAKI
President: M. ANBE
Librarian: T. ONODERA

Library of 320,000 vols
Number of teachers: 100
Number of students: 3,094

Publications: *Bulletin of English Department* (1 a year), *Christianity and Culture* (1 a year), *Japanese Literature Note* (1 a year), *Journal of Miyagi College for Women* (1 a year), *Annals of the Institute for Research in Humanities and Social Sciences* (1 a year)

DEANS

Department of Cultural Studies: W. TAKAHASHI
Department of Developmental and Clinical Studies: T. ADAOHI
Department of Domestic and Cultural Sciences: N. OKABO
Department of English Literature: K. ISOZAKI
Department of Food and Nutritional Science: H. HIRAMOTO
Department of Intercultural Studies: M. KUROTAKI
Department of Japanese Literature: M. HAKAZAWA
Department of Music: T. SUMIKAWA

NAGOYA UNIVERSITY OF COMMERCE AND BUSINESS

4-4 Sagamine, Komenoki-cho, Nisshin-shi, Aichi 470-0193

Telephone: (561) 73-2111
Fax: (561) 75-2430
Internet: www.nucba.ac.jp

Founded 1953
Private control
Language of instruction: Japanese
Academic year: April to February (2 terms)

Pres.: HIROSHI KURIMOTO
Dir: MASAHIDE KURIMOTO
Dir of Library: (vacant)

Library of 70,000 vols
Number of teachers: 160 (102 full-time, 58 part-time)
Number of students: 3,389

Publications: *Journal of Economics and Management* (2 a year), *Journal of Language, Culture and Communication* (2 a year), *Bulletin of the Yuichi Kurimoto Memorial Graduate School of Business Administration* (1 a year)

DEANS

Faculty of Accounting and Finance: Prof. AKIRA KOBASHI
Faculty of Business Administration: Prof. HIROKO KAKITANI
Faculty of Foreign Languages and Asian Studies: Prof. GEORGE WATT
Faculty of Management Information Science: Prof. NAMIO HONDA

NANZAN UNIVERSITY

18 Yamazato-cho, Showa-ku, Nagoya 466-8673

Telephone: (52) 832-3111
Fax: (52) 833-6985
E-mail: webmaster@nanzan-u.ac.jp
Internet: www.nanzan-u.ac.jp

Founded 1949
Academic year: April to March

Pres.: MICHAEL CALMANO

Vice-Pres.: K. AOKI, N. KINOSHITA, M. NORO
Chief of Gen. Affairs Section: H. MAKITA
Librarian: H. HOSOYA

Library of 745,014 vols, 16,655 periodicals, 7,425 audiovisual titles
Number of teachers: 807 (317 full-time, 490 part-time)
Number of students: 10,489

Publications: *Academia (Humanities and Social Sciences)* (in Japanese and English, 2 a year), *Academia (Information Sciences and Engineering)* (in Japanese and English, 1 a year), *Academia (Literature and Language)* (in Japanese and English, 2 a year), *Academia (Natural Science and Health and Physical Education)* (in Japanese and English, 1 a year), *Nanzan Journal of Theological Studies* (in Japanese and English, 1 a year), *Nanzan Law Review* (in Japanese, 4 a year), *Nanzan Management Review* (in Japanese and English, 3 a year), *Nanzan Studies on Japanese Language and Culture* (in Japanese, 1 a year), *The Nanzan Journal of Economic Studies* (in Japanese and English, 3 a year)

DEANS

Faculty of Business Administration: Y. KAORU
Faculty of Economics: Y. ARAI
Faculty of Foreign Studies: H. FUJIMOTO
Faculty of Humanities: S. SAKAI
Faculty of Information Sciences and Engineering: A. SUZUKI
Faculty of Law: T. SOEDA
Faculty of Policy Studies: T. MATSUDO
General Education: Y. NAKA

ATTACHED INSTITUTES

Center for American Studies: study of American politics, economics, diplomacy, culture and society and US relationship with Japan; publ. *Nanzan Review of American Studies* (in English, 1 a year).

Center for Asia–Pacific Studies: interdisciplinary study of the politics, int. relations, economics, society, history, culture, and literature of the Asia–Pacific region; publ. *Bulletin* (1 a year).

Center for European Studies: interdisciplinary study of European politics, economics and society; publ. *Bulletin* (in Japanese, 1 a year).

Center for Japanese Studies: a one-semester or one-year programme for int. students from all countries who wish to study all aspects of Japanese language, culture and area studies.

Center for Latin American Studies: study of Latin America, particularly the humanities and social sciences (history, anthropology, education, economics, literature, philosophy, politics, archaeology and linguistics); publ. *Perspectivas Latinoamericanas* (in Spanish, Portuguese and English, 1 a year).

Center for Linguistics: internet www.nanzan-u.ac.jp/linguistics; research in comparative syntax and language acquisition: int. jt research projects with Cambridge, Siena, Connecticut, Hyderabad, and Tsing Hua; publ. *Nanzan Linguistics* (in English, 1 or 2 a year).

Center for Legal Practice-Education and Research: research and practice of legal practical education; implement business studies and lectures about legal practice.

Center for Management Studies: specializing in the study of management issues.

Center for Research in Mathematical Sciences and Information Engineering:

research into information engineering and quantitative sciences; coordination of collaboration between industry and academia.

Center for the Study of Human Relations: publ. *The Nanzan Journal of Human Relations* (in Japanese, 1 a year).

Institute for Social Ethics: research on the principles of social ethics and the ethical problems of contemporary society; publ. *Society and Ethics* (in Japanese, 1 a year).

Nanzan Anthropological Institute: research in cultural anthropology, mainly in SE, E and S Asia; publ. *Nanzan Studies in Cultural Anthropology* (in Japanese, irregular).

Nanzan Institute for Religion and Culture: research in the area of world religions with spec. reference to the religions of Asia and to the dialogue between religions; publ. *Nanzan Symposia* (in Japanese, irregular), *Religious Studies Today* (in Japanese, irregular), *Bulletin* (in Japanese and English, 1 a year), *Japanese Journal of Religious Studies* (in English, 2 a year), *Asian Ethnology* (fmrly Asian Folklore Studies, in English, 2 a year), *Nanzan Library of Asian Religion and Culture* (in English, irregular), *Nanzan Studies in Asian Religions* (in English, irregular), *Nanzan Studies in Religion and Culture* (in English, irregular).

NIHON UNIVERSITY

8–24, Kudan-Minami 4-chome, Chiyoda-ku, Tokyo 102-8275

Telephone: (3) 5275-8116
Fax: (3) 5275-8315
E-mail: intldiv@adm.nihon-u.ac.jp
Internet: www.nihon-u.ac.jp

Founded as Nihon Law School 1889, University status 1903
Private control
Academic year: April to March

Chair. of Board: H. TANAKA
Pres.: T. SAKAI
Vice-Pres.: H. ONAGI
Vice-Pres.: M. MAKIMURA
Vice-Pres.: K. IDEMURA

Library of 5,894,567 vols
Number of teachers: 3,041 full-time
Number of students: 82,677

Publications: *Johokagaku Kenkyu* (information science studies), *Journal of Oral Science*, *Kaikeigaku Kenkyu* (accounting), *Kenkyu Kiyo* (humanities and social sciences), *Kenkyu Kiyo* (proceedings of the Institute of Natural Sciences), *Kenkyu Kiyo Nihon Daigaku Shigakubu (Ippan Kyouiku)* (transactions of the School of Dentistry (General Studies)), *Kokusai Kankei Gakubu Nenpo* (international relations), *Kokusai Kankei Kenkyu* (international relations), *Kokusai Chiiki Kenkyujo Shoho* (RRIAP proceedings of symposium), *Nichidai Igaku Zasshi* (journal of Nihon University Medical Association), *Nihon Daigaku Geijutsu Gakubu Kiyo Ronbunhen* (research in fine art at the College of Art), *Nihon Daigaku Geijutsu Gakubu Kiyo Sousakuhen* (artistic works of the College of Art), *Nihon Daigaku Kokusai Kankei Gakubu Seikatsu Kagaku Kenkyujo Hokoku*, *Nihon Daigaku Kou Gakubu Kiyo* (journal of the College of Engineering), *Nihon Daigaku Kyouiku Seido Kenkyujo Kiyo* (bulletin of the Educational Systems Research Institute), *Nihon Daigaku Igakubu Kiyo* (bulletin of the liberal arts and sciences), *Nihon Daigaku Seibutsushigenkagakubu Sogokenkyujo Kenkyugyosekishu* (proceedings of the General Research Institute, College of Bioresource Sciences), *Nihon Daigaku Sei-*

butsushigenkagakubu ei Kenkyu (proceedings of the Life Science Research Center, College of Bioresource Sciences), *Nihon Daigaku Seisanko Gakubu Kenkyu Houkoku* (journal of the College of Industrial Technology, in editions A and B), *Nihon Daigaku Seisankogaku Kenkyujo Shohou* (journal of the College of Industrial Technology), *Nihon Daigaku Seishin Bunka Kenkyujo Kiyo* (bulletin of the Culture Research Institute), *Nihon Daigaku Tsushinkyoikubu Kenkyu Kiyo* (bulletin of the Correspondence Division of Nihon University), *Nihon Daigaku Yakugakubu Kenkyu Kiyo* (bulletin of the College of Pharmacy), *Nihon Hogaku* (law), *Nihon University Comparative Law*, *Rikogaku Kenkyu Shoho* (journal of the Institute of Science and Technology), *PRIAP Circular*, *Sou-Ka-Ken Nyusu* (URC news), *Seikei Kenkyu* (political science and economics), *Shogaku Kenkyu* (business and industry), *Nihon University Journal of Medicine*

DEANS
College of Art: Y. NODA
College of Bioresource Sciences: T. TOKUYAMA
College of Commerce: S. KATSUYAMA
College of Economics: H. ONAGI
College of Engineering: K. IDEMURA
College of Humanities and Sciences: N. KATO
College of Industrial Technology: S. ISHII
College of International Relations: S. SATO
College of Law: M. SUGIMOTO (acting)
College of Pharmacy: T. KUSAMA
College of Science and Technology: T. TAKIDO
Correspondence Division: H. TAKATSUNA
Junior College: T. SAKAI
School of Dentistry: K. OOTSUKA
School of Dentistry at Matsudo: M. MAKIMURA
School of Medicine: Y. KATAYAMA

NIPPON DENTAL UNIVERSITY

1-9-20 Fujimi, Chiyoda-ku, Tokyo 102-8159

Telephone: (3) 3261 8311
Fax: (3) 3264-8399
E-mail: web-master@tokyo.ndu.ac.jp
Internet: www.ndu.ac.jp

Founded 1907
Academic year: April to March
Pres.: SEN NAKAHARA
Deans: SEN NAKAHARA (Niigata Faculty), SHIGEO YOKODUKA (Tokyo Faculty)
Registrars: KENEI OHBA (Niigata), SHINICHI TAKIZAWA (Tokyo)
Librarians: KAN KOBAYASHI (Niigata Faculty), TAKEJI AYUKAWA (Tokyo Faculty)
Library of 96,822 vols (Tokyo Faculty), 89,217 vols (Niigata Faculty)
Number of teachers: 1,000
Number of students: 2,000

Publication: *Odontology* (6 a year)

PROFESSORS
Tokyo:
AIYAMA, S., Anatomy
AOBA, T., Pathology
FURUTA, Y., Anatomy
FURUYA, H., Anaesthesiology
ISHIKAWA, H., Orthodontics
KAMOI, K., Periodontology
KATSUUMI, I., Conservative Dentistry
KOBAYASHI, Y., Prosthodontics
MATSUMOTO, S., Physiology
NAKAHARA, S., Dentistry in Society
NIWA, M., Hygiene
OGIWARA, K., Paedodontics
SANADA, K., Biochemistry
SATO, T., Anatomy
SIRAKAWA, M., Oral Surgery
SUZUKI, T., Surgery
TANAKA, H., Conservative Dentistry

TSUTSUI, T., Pharmacology
UCHIDA, M., Oral and Maxillofacial Surgery
YOKOZUKA, S., Prosthodontics
YOSHIDA, T., Dental Materials Science
YOSIKAWA, M., Microbiology
YOSUE, T., Radiology

Niigata
1-8 Hamauracho, Niigata-shi, Niigata 951; tel. (25) 267-1500; fax (25) 267-1134

HASEGAWA, A., Periodontology
HATA, Y., Prosthodontics
HATATE, S., Prosthodontics
IGARASHI, F., Otorhinolaryngology
KAMEDA, A., Orthodontics
KANRI, T., Anaesthesiology
KATAGIRI, M., Oral Pathology
KATOH, Y., Conservative Dentistry
KAWASAKI, K., Conservative Dentistry
KIMURA, T., Dental Pharmacology
KOBAYASHI, K., Oral Anatomy
MATAGA, I., Oral Surgery
MATSUKI, H., Surgery
MORITA, O., Prosthodontics
MURAKAMI, T., Oral Physiology
NAKAHARA, S., Dentistry in Society
OGURA, H., Dental Materials Science
NISHIMURA, K., Oral Surgery
SAITO, K., Oral Microbiology
SHIBAZAKI, K., Internal Medicine
SHIMAMURA, H., Oral Biochemistry
SHIMOOKA, S., Paedodontics
SUETAKA, T., Oral Hygiene
TSUCHIKAWA, K., Oral Surgery
TSUCHIMOTO, M., Radiology

NIPPON SPORT SCIENCE UNIVERSITY

Tokyo Campus: 1-1 Fukasawa 7-chome, Setagaya-ku, Tokyo 158-8508

Telephone: (3) 5706-0900
Fax: (3) 5706-0912

Yokohama Campus: 1221-1 Kamoshida-cho, Aoba-ku, Yokohama 227-0033, Kanagawa Pref.

Telephone: (45) 963-7900
Fax: (45) 963-7903
E-mail: international@nittai.ac.jp
Internet: www.nittai.ac.jp

Founded 1891, present status 1949
Private
Academic year: April to March (2 semesters)
Rector and Pres.: Prof. TAKEO TOHNO (acting)
Vice-Pres. for Academic and Student Affairs: Prof. NAOKI ITO
Vice-Pres. for Management and Planning: Prof. Dr TAKEO TAKAHASHI
Exec. Dir., Admin. Office: MASAHIRO FUJINO

Library of 411,397, 6,367 periodicals

DEANS
Graduate School of Health and Sport Science: Dr TAKEO TAKAHASHI
NSSU Faculty of Sport Science: NAOKI ITO
NSSU Teaching Credential Course in PE: KEIJI HONMA
Women's Junior College of NSSU: HAJIME SAKAI

PROFESSORS
ABE, S., Physical Education (Graduate School)
AKIYAMA, A., Cultural Education (Graduate School)
ARAKI, T., Physical Education
ENDA, Y., Physical Education
FUJIMOTO, H., Physical Education
FUJITA, S., Cultural Education
FUJIWARA, S., Physical Education
FUNATO, K., Physical Education (Graduate School)

GUSHIKEN, K., Physical Education
HAKAMADA, D., Martial Arts
HIRANUMA, K., Health Science (Graduate School)
HONMA, K., Cultural Education
HOSOKAWA, S., Early Child Education
IGAWA, S., Health Science (Graduate School)
IRIE, K., Health Science (Graduate School)
ITO, N., Physical Education (Graduate School)
ITO, T., Health Science (Graduate School)
IWASA, K., Physical Education
KENMOTSU, E., Lifelong Sports and Recreation (Graduate School)
KIBAMOTO, H., Physical Education
KIMURA, N., Health Science (Graduate School)
KIYOTA, H., Health Science (Graduate School)
KOBAYAKAWA, Y., Health Science
KOIZUMI, N., Lifelong Sports and Recreation
KUBO, T., Physical Education
KURODA, M., Cultural Education
KUSUMOTO, Y., Cultural Education (Graduate School)
MATSUI, K., Physical Education (Graduate School)
MATSUMOTO, S., Physical Education (Graduate School)
MIYAKE, K., Martial Arts (Graduate School)
MORISHIMA, A., Cultural Education
MORITA, J., Physical Education
MURAKAMI, O., Physical Education (Graduate School)
MURAMOTO, K., Physical Education
NARITA, K., Cultural Education
NISHIDA, T., Physical Education
NISHIO, S., Lifelong Sports and Recreation (Graduate School)
OCHIAI, T., Cultural Education
ODE, K., Lifelong Sports and Recreation (Graduate School)
OGAWA, K., Physical Education
OKADA, A., Cultural Education
OKUIZUMI, K., Early Childhood Education
ONO, M., Health Science
OSAFUNE, T., Cultural Education
OSAKABE, H.I, Cultural Education
OUCI, T., Physical Education
SAIJO, O., Physical Education (Graduate School)
SAKAI, H., Early Childhood Education
SAKURAI, T., Health Science (Graduate School)
SEKIGUCHI, O., Physical Education
SEKINE, Y., Physical Education
SHIMZU, Y, Physical Education
SUGAWARA, I., Physical Education
TAKADA, R., Physical Education
TAKAHASHI, K., Health Science (Graduate School)
TAKAHASHI, T., Physical Education (Graduate School)
TAKIZAWA, K., Physical Education (Graduate School)
TANIGMA, R., Martial Arts
TOKIMOTO, K., Early Childhood Education
UEDA, Y., Lifelong Sports and Recreation
UENO, J., Health Science (Graduate School)
WATANABE, I., Physical Education
YAMADA, T., Health Science (Graduate School)
YAMAMOTO, I., Health Science
YASUHIRO, Y., Physical Education

NOTRE DAME WOMEN'S COLLEGE

1–2 Minami Nonogami-cho, Shimogamo, Sakyo-ku, Kyoto 606-0847

Telephone: (75) 781-1173
Fax: (75) 702-4060
E-mail: international@notredame.ac.jp
Internet: www.notredame.ac.jp

Founded 1961
Private control
Language of instruction: Japanese

Academic year: April to March

Pres.: M. HONDA
Sec.-Gen.: K. TOI
Librarian: Y. OKAZAKI

Library of 133,000 vols
Number of teachers: 105 (36 full-time, 69 part-time)
Number of students: 1,443

Publications: Kiyo, Insight (1 a year)

Departments of English Language and Literature.

OBIRIN UNIVERSITY

3758 Tokiwa-machi, Machida-shi, Tokyo 194-0294

Telephone: (42) 797-5419
Fax: (42) 797-0790
E-mail: cis@obirin.ac.jp
Internet: www.obirin.ac.jp

Founded 1966

President: TOYOSHI SATOW
Number of students: 7,000

Colleges of Business and Public Administration, Economics, Humanities, International Studies.

OSAKA MEDICAL COLLEGE

2–7 Daigakumachi, Takatsuki City, Osaka 569-8686

Telephone: (72) 683-1221
Fax: (72) 683-3723
E-mail: hp-info@poh.osaka-med.ac.jp
Internet: www.osaka-med.ac.jp

Founded 1927
Private control
Language of instruction: Japanese
Academic year: April to March

Chair.: TADAHIRO TANAKA
Pres.: MASAHISA SHIMADA
Sec.-Gen: (vacant)
Librarian: AKIRA SHIMIZU

Library of 221,160 vols
Number of teachers: 362
Number of students: 601

Publications: Journal (in Japanese, 1 a year), Bulletin (in English, 1 a year).

OSAKA SANGYO UNIVERSITY

3-1-1 Nakagaito, Daito-shi, Osaka 574-8530

Telephone: (72) 875-3001
Fax: (72) 875-6551
Internet: www.osaka-sandai.ac.jp

Founded 1965

Chair. of the Board of Trustees: SHIMEJI FURUTANI
Pres.: JUN-ICHIRO SEJIMA

Number of teachers: 250
Number of students: 15,634

Faculties of Business Management, Economics, Engineering, Human Environment; College of General Education; Graduate School.

OTEMON GAKUIN UNIVERSITY

1-15 Nishiai 2-chome, Ibaraki, Osaka 567-8502

Telephone: (72) 641-9631
Fax: (72) 643-5651
E-mail: kokusai@jimu.otemon.ac.jp
Internet: www.otemon.ac.jp

Founded 1966

Pres.: TAKASHI SUZUKI

Library of 450,000 vols

Faculties of economics, international liberal arts, management, psychology, sociology.

RIKKYO UNIVERSITY
(St Paul's University)

3-34-1 Nishi-Ikebukuro, Toshima-ku, Tokyo 171-8501

Telephone: 3985-2204
Fax: 3986-8784
E-mail: cis@grp.rikkyo.ne.jp
Internet: www.rikkyo.ne.jp

Founded 1874
Private control
Academic year: April to March

Chancellor: Rev. TOSHIHIKO HAYAMI
President: TERUO OSHIMI
Registrar: Prof. Y. HIKITA
Librarian: Prof. H. SENGOKU

Library of 1,540,558 vols
Number of teachers: 1,110
Number of students: 15,000

Publications: Rikkyo (4 a year), Rikkyo Daigaku Toshokan Dayori (library news), Rikkyo Daigaku Shokuin Kiyo (administrative staff research proceedings, 1 a year), Kiristokyo Kyoiku Kenkyu (Studies in Christian Education), Rikkyo University Bulletin (every 2 years), Rikkyo Koho (Rikkyo news bulletin, 6 a year), and numerous faculty journals

DEANS
Faculty of Arts: H. MAEDA
Faculty of Community and Human Services: M. SEKI
Faculty of Economics: N. OIKAWA
Faculty of General Curriculum Development: Y. SHOJI
Faculty of Law and Politics: T. AWAJI
Faculty of Science: T. MOTOBAYASHI
Faculty of Social Relations: N. SHIRAISHI
Faculty of Tourism: N. OKAMOTO

RISSHO UNIVERSITY

4-2-16 Osaki, Shinagawa-ku, Tokyo 141

Telephone: (3) 3492-5262
Fax: (3) 5487-3343
E-mail: kint@ris.ac.jp
Internet: www.ris.ac.jp

Founded 1872
Private control
Language of instruction: Japanese
Academic year: April to March

Chancellor: N. TANAKA
President: H. SAKAZUME
Vice-President: Z. KITAGAWA
Registrar: (vacant)
Chief Librarians: H. FUJITA (Osaki), Y. IKOMA (Kumagaya)

Number of teachers: 700 (217 full-time, 483 part-time)
Number of students: 11,900

Publications: Bulletin (1 a year), Journal of Buddhist Studies, Journal of Nichiren Buddhism (1 a year), Quarterly Report of Economics, etc

DEANS
Faculty of Buddhist Studies: K. MITOMO
Faculty of Business and Management: Y. KATO
Faculty of Economics: K. FUKUOKA
Faculty of Geo-Environmental Science: Y. YOSHIDA
Faculty of Law: S. IWAI
Faculty of Letters: S. TEGAWA
Faculty of Social Welfare: T. HOSHINO
Graduate School (Business Administration): T. OKUMURA
Graduate School (Economics): K. FUKUOKA
Graduate School (Law): T. SUZUKI
Graduate School (Literature): Y. TAKAGI

RITSUMEIKAN UNIVERSITY

56-1 Tojiin Kitamachi, Kita-ku, Kyoto 525-8577

Telephone: (75) 465-1111
E-mail: kokusai@st.ritsumei.ac.jp
Internet: www.ritsumei.ac.jp

Founded 1900
Private control
Academic year: April to March

President: TOYO OMI NAGATA
Vice-Presidents: SADAO KAWAMURA, KIMIO YAKUSHIJI
Dean (Academic Affairs): MITSURU SATO
Dean (Graduate Affairs): YOSHINOBU KUSAKABE
Dean (Research Affairs): MAKOTO SATO
Dean (Student Affairs): KATSUO NAKAGAWA
Dean (Library): YOSHIHIRO TANIGUCHI

Library of 2,532,945 vols
Number of teachers: 1,312 full-time
Number of students: 35,604 full-time

Publications: *Ritsumeikan Business Review, Ritsumeikan Economic Review, Ristumeikan Journal of International Studies, Ritsumeikan Journal of International Relations and Area Studies, Ritsumeikan International Affairs, Ritsumeikan Shigaku, Memoirs of Research Institute of Humanities and Social Science, Journal of Ritsumeikan Geographical Society, Proceedings of the Philosophical Society of Ritsumeikan University, Ritsumeikan Law Review, Memoirs of the SR Center, Ritsumeikan University, Ritsumeikan Annual Review of International Studies (in English), Ritsumeikan Eibei Bungaku, Ritsumeikan Torena Haiho, Ritsumeikan Toyoshigaku, Core Ethics, Ritsumeikan Sangyo Shyakaironsyu, Memoirs of the Institute of Humanities, Human and Social Science, Ritsumeikan Seisaku Kagaku, Studies in Language and Culture, Ritsumeikan Bungaku, Journal of Human Science, Art Research, Ritsumeikan Ronkyu Nihon Bungaku, Ritsumeikan Gakurin, Social Systems Studies*

DEANS

College and Graduate School of Business Administration: TERUYOSHI TANAKA
College and Graduate School of International Relations: HIROFUMI OGI
College and Graduate School of Policy Science: KIYOFUMI KAWAGUCHI
College and Graduate School of Science and Engineering: HIDEYUKI TAKAKURA
College and Graduate School of Social Sciences: KUNIHIRO TOSHIFUMI
College of Economics: JUNICHI HIRATA
College of Law: RYOICHI YOSHIMURA
College of Letters: KAZUAKI KIMURA
College of Information Science and Engineering: TAKEO IIDA
Graduate School for Core Ethics and Frontier Sciences: KOZO WATANABE
Graduate School of Economics: SHUJI MATSUKAWA
Graduate School of Language Education and Information Science: JUNSAKU NAKAMURA
Graduate School of Science for Human Services: CHUICHIRO TAKAGAKI
Graduate School of Law: SHIRO AKAZAWA
Graduate School of Letters: HIROHIDE TAKEYAMA
Law School: MASATO ICHIKAWA

PROFESSORS

College and Graduate School of Business Administration:

ANDO, T., Technology Transfer
BAILEY, A., English
CHIYODA, K., Accounting
DOI, Y., Transportation
ENNO, B., Corporate Culture and Governance
FUJITA, T., Business Accounting
HARA, Y., International Corporations
HASHIMOTO, T., Business Administration History
HATTORI, Y., Modern Financial Markets
HIRAI, T., Environmental Accounting Theory
HYOUDO, T., Contemporary Science and Technology
IDA, T., English
IKEDA, S., Cultural Studies, Total Quality Management
IMADA, O., Production Management
ITO, T., Politics and Literature in the Weimar Republic
IWATA, N., Japanese Language Education and Linguistics
KINOSHITA, A., Distribution Procedures
KOEZUKA, H., Product Planning, Marketing Channels
KOKUBO, M., Industrial and Social Psychology
KOSAKA, K., Communicative and Cognitive Mechanisms
MATSUI, T., Medium Enterprises
MATSUMURA, K., Business Financial Management
MIURA, I., Japanese Retail Business
MIURA, M., Health Science
MIYOSAWA, T., Managerial Accounting
MUKAI, J., International Finance
MURAYAMA, T., International Investment
NAGASHIMA, O., Japanese Economy
NAKAMURA, M., Multinationals
NAKANISHI, I., Industrial Economics, Comparative Economic Studies
NAKATA, M., General Business Administration
NAMIE, I., Labour Problems
OKAMOTO, N., Physical Fitness
OKUMURA, Y., Business Strategies
SAITO, M., Business Administration
SASABE, A., History of Science and Engineering
SATO, N., Design Management
SCHLUNZE, R. D., International Management, Economic Geography
SHIOMI, K., Cross-cultural Communication
SUZUKI, Y., French
TAKEDA, M., Management Organization and Information Systems
TAKI, H., Corporations and Accounting
TAMAMURA, H., Privatization
TANAKA, A., Asian Enterprises
TANAKA, T., History of Business Thought
TANAKA, T., Statistics
TANEDA, Y., Managerial Accounting
WATANABE, T., Business Management
YAMAZAKI, S., Spanish
YAMAZAKI, T., Business Administration
YANAGASE, K., Public Finance, Public Economics, Development Policy
YOSHIDA, K., Mathematical Programming

College and Graduate School of Economics:

AGATSUMA, N., Economic Policy
ASADA, K., Public Finance, Money and Banking
FUJIOKA, A., Economic Analysis of Nuclear-based Military Expansion
FURUKAWA, A., Economic Policy
HAMADA, S., Corporate Law
HATANAKA, T., Early Modern Japanese History
HIRATA, J., Economic Statistics
INABA, K., Economic Statistics
IWATA, K., International Economics
IZAWA, H., Economic Theory
KAJIYAMA, N., Currency Exchange System and Economic Development
KAKIHARA, H., Economic Policy, Medicine
KAKUTA, S., Economic Theory
KANEMARU, Y., East Asian Economic History and Modern Chinese History
KASAI, T., International Economic Cooperation
MATSUBARA, T., Agricultural Economics
MATSUI, S., Political Economy, Economic Philosophy
MATSUKAWA, S., General Theory of Economics
MATSUMOTO, A., Political, Financial and Monetary Economics
MATSUNO, S., East Asian Economic Relations
NISHIGUCHI, K., Economic Theory of Developing Nations
NOZAWA, T., Phonology, Psycholinguistics
OHKAWA, M., Economic Theory, International Economics
OHKAWA, T., Industrial Organization
OKAO, K., History of Modern Sports
SAITO, T., Modern Chinese Literature
SAKAMOTO, K., Economic Policy
SATO, T., Social Policy
SATOU, Y., Sport Psychology
SHIMADA, Y., Area Environmental Systems
SHIMIZU, Y., Educational Technology, Intercultural Communication
TAKAGI, A., Contemporary Capitalism
TANAKA, H., Russian and Eastern European Economic Studies
TANAKA, Y., International Economics
TANIGAKI, K., International Trade Theory
TOMATSURI, T., Tourism
TSUJII, E., English
UCHIYAMA, A., Public Finance
WAKABAYASHI, H., Comparative Research of Policy Theories, Regional Policy
YAMADA, H., Econometrics
YAMAI, T., German Economics
YAMAMOTO, S., Actuarial Economics, Insurance, US–Japanese Comparative Economics and Portfolio Theory
YOKOYAMA, M., International Economics
YOSHIDA, C., International Economics
ZHENG, X., Urban and Regional Economics

College and Graduate School of Law:

AKAZAWA, S., Politics, History
ARAKAWA, S., Civil Law, Sociology of Law
DEGUCHI, M., Civil Procedure Law
HANATATE, F., Civil Law
HIRANO, H., Basic Science of Law
HISAOKA, Y., Criminal Law, Criminal Procedure Law
HONDA, M., German Criminal Law
HORI, M., Politics
IKUTA, K., Criminal Law, Criminal Procedure Law
ISHIHARA, H., English Literature
KATSUI, H., Civil Law
KOBORI, M., Modern British Politics
KOYAMA, Y., Civil Law
KURATA, M., Human Rights Theory, Constitutional Law
KUZUNO, H., Criminal Justice and Juvenile Justice
MIKI, Y., Taxation Law
MIYAI, M., International Economic Law
MIZUGUCHI, N., Public Administration, Regional Autonomy
MOTOYAMA, A., Family Law
MURAKAMI, H., Political Science
NAKAJIMA, S., Public Law
NAKAMURA, Y., French Modern Legal History, French Criminal Procedure
NAKATANI, Y., Politics
NISHIMURA, M., International Politics
NOGUCHI, M., English
OHGAKI, H., Financial Law
OHIRA, Y., Japanese Legal History
OKAWA, S., Civil Law
SATO, K., Social Law
SO, S., East Asian Law and Human Rights
SUTO, Y., Proportional Doctrines
TAKEHAMA, O., Insurance
TAKEHARU, S., German, German Literature
TANIMOTO, K., German Language and Literature

TOKUGAWA, S., Civil Law
UNOKI, Y., Chinese Language and Literature
YAKUSHIJI, K., International Law
YAMAMOTO, T., Social Security Law
YASUMOTO, N., Public Administrative Law
YOSHIDA, M., Labour Law
YOSHIMURA, R., Law of Damage
YOSHIOKA, K., Literary Theory

College and Graduate School of Letters:

AKAMA, R., Modern Drama, Literature and Ukiyoe
ASAO, K., Applied Linguistics
EGUCHI, N., Caribbean Studies
FOX, C. E., Modern Japanese Verse
FUJI, K., Experimental Analysis of Behaviour
FUJIMAKI, M., Human Geography, Urban Social Geography
HATTORI, K., Philosophy of Nature and Social Philosophy
HAYASHI, N., Study of True Human Education
HIEDA, Y., Comparative Literature
HIGASHIYAMA, A., Psychology of Sensation and Perception, Geometry of Visual Space
HIKOSAKA, Y., History of Japanese Dialects
HONDA, O., History of Agricultural Development
HONGO, M., National Law of Ancient Japan, Royal Authority and Religion
HOSHINO, Y., Human Memory and Learning, Cognitive Processes
HOSOI, K., Personality
IKEDA, Y., Modern Philosophy
IKUTA, M., Comparative Study of Large Asian Cities
ISE, T., Philosophy
ISHII, F., German Literature in the Pre-March Revolution Period
KASUGAI, T., Clinical Education
KATAHIRA, H., Land Use in the Semi-arid Regions of Australia, Landscape Reproduction
KATSURAJIMA, N., Japanese Early Modern History, Tokugawa Intellectual History
KAWAGUCHI, Y., The English Novel: Forster, Austen, Golding
KAWASHIMA, N., Study of Artisan Guilds and the Rural Traditional Handicraft Industry
KAWASHIMA, M., Life and Culture in Late Medieval Japan
KIDACHI, M., Archaeology
KIMURA, K., Modern Japanese Literature
KITAMURA, M., Political and Cultural Development in the Republic of China
KITANO, K., Film Studies
KITAO, H., Ethics and Philosophy
KO, J. Y., Korean Archaeology
KOBAYASHI, K., Poetry and Painting of William Blake
KUSAKABE, Y., Greek Philosophy, History of Ontology
MACLEAN, R., English and American Literature since the 18th-century
MARUYAMA, M., 20th-century American Literature
MASHIMO, A., Ancient Japanese Literature, Manyoshu and Oral Literature
MATSUDA, K., English Romantic Poets of the 18th and 19th Centuries
MATSUDA, T., Perception and Cognition
MATSUMOTO, H., Late 19th- to Early 20th-century Politics
MATSUMOTO, Y., Medieval Chinese History, Political System of the Tang Dynasty
MOCHIZUKI, A., Applied Behaviour Analysis, Behavioural Human Serviceology
MUKAI, T., Hegelian Philosophy, Culture and Ideology
MURASHIMA, Y., Educational Philosophy, Moral Education

NAGATA, T., Modern and Contemporary American History
NAKAGAWA, S., Modern Japanese Literature
NAKAGAWA, Y., American Literature, Women's Studies
NAKAGAWA, Y., Holistic Education, Women's Studies
NAKANISHI, K., Heian Literature
ODA, M., Cognitive Science, Concept and Imagery
ODAUCHI, T., Religious Movements and Heresy in Medieval Europe
OHTO, C., Greek and Hellenistic History
OKADA, H., Contemporary Chinese Literature
OUJI, T., Area Studies
OZEKI, M., Political Thought and History in Modern Japan, Cultural Theory
PEATY, D., English Language Education
SAITO, T., Research on Altered States of Consciousness
SANO, M., Generative-grammatical Analyses of Japanese and English
SATO, T., Educational and Social Psychology, Experimental Psychology
SHIMA, H., Studies in Tang Dynasty Thought
SHIMIZU, Y., Medieval Chinese Literature and Criticism
SHIMOKAWA, S., Life and Works of Stendhal
SUGIHASHI, T., History of the Warrior Government Formation
TADAI, T., Evidence-based Clinical Psychology and Psychiatry
TAKAGI, K., Developmental Psychology
TAKAHASHI, H., Contemporary German History
TAKAHASHI, M., Natural Environmental Changes and Relationship to Human Lifestyles
TAKASHIMA, K., 19th-century American Literature
TAKEYAMA, H., Italian Literature, Ethnography and Comparative Culture
TAKIMOTO, K., Modern Japanese Literature, Mori Ogai
TANI, T., Phenomenology and Contemporary Philosophy
TOBINO, K., Philosophical Study in Education and Human Relations
TSUCHIDA, Y., Developmental Psychology
TSUKAMA, Y., Linguistics, Phonetics, Foreign Language Education
UEDA, H., Meiji Japanese Literature
UEDA, T., History of Contemporary Western Art, Art Criticism
UENO, R., Classical Chinese Literature
WADA, S., Archaeological Research of the Yayoi and Kofun Peirods
WELLS, K., American Poetry, Folklore and Folksong, Comparative Culture
YAGI, Y., Psychology of Self; Personality and Social Psychology
YAMAMOTO, M., Psychotherapy and Psychoanalysis
YANO, K., Archaeology
YANO, K., Human Geography
YONEYAMA, H., American History, Japanese American History
YOSHIDA, H., Learning Psychology
YOSHIKOSHI, A., Human Impact on the Hydrological Environment
YOSHIMURA, H., Chinese Tang Dynasty Literature
YUKAWA, E., Applied Linguistics and Bilingualism

College and Graduate School of International Relations:

ANDO, T., Western Political History
ANZAI, I., International Peace Theory
ASAHI, M., Contemporary Global Economics
HARA, T., South American Anthropology

HOSHINO, K., European Economics, Monetary Integration
INOUE, J., Cultural Sociology
ITAKI, M., Social Science Methodology
KA, G., Japanese and Chinese Comparative Studies
KANEKO, H., Contemporary German Poetry
KATO, T., Black African-American Literature
KATSURA, R., Asian and International Social Welfare, Family Welfare and Policy
KIMIJIMA, A., Peace Studies, Constitutional Law
KIYOMOTO, O., Contemporary South East Asian History
KOBAYASHI, M., Political Science
KOYAMA, M., International Relations
MATSUSHITA, K., Politics of Developing Countries
MINAMINO, Y., Comparative Politics, Political History, Irish Political History
MIYAKE, M., Linguistic Analysis
MUN, G. S., North East Asian History
NAGASU, M., Japanese Development Assistance, International Cooperation
NAKAGAWA, R., Asian Economics
NAKAMURA, Y., French Thought and Literature, Contemporary Japanese Literature
NAKATSUJI, K., Modern Political History
ODAIRA, K., International Cooperation Law, Francophone and EU Studies
OGI, H., Asian Studies, Chinese Education and Literature
OIKAWA, M., Contemporary American Theatre
OKUDA, H., International Finance
OZORA, H., Mass Media
SATO, M., Comparative Sociology, African Politics
SHAWBACK, M., Foreign Languages, General Studies
TAKAHASHI, N., Japanese Economy
TAKEUCHI, T., Comparative Analysis of Family Structure
TATSUZAWA, K., International Law Relations, Islamic Law, Space Law
WAKANA, M., American Literature
WASSERMAN, M., Theatrical Arts of the West and Japan
YAMADA, H., Japanese Language
YAMAMOTO, S., American Drama

College and Graduate School of Policy Science:

HIRAO, H., Use of Computers in English Education
HONDA, Y., Econometrics
HOSOI, K., Modern Management Theory
JIDOU, Y., History of Industrial Technology
KAWAGUCHI, K., Citizen Participation, Cooperatives and NPOs
KISHIMOTO, T., International Politics and Economics
MIKAMI, T., Artificial Intelligence, Memory and Decision-Making
MIKAMI, T., Administrative Law, Planning Law
MURAYAMA, H., Political Attitude and Political Behaviour
OBATA, N., Environmental Policy
SATOH, M., Policy Formation
SHIGEMORI, T., Political Theory
SHIRAKAWA, I., Economic Policy, International Economics
TAKADA, S., Urban and Regional Planning
TAKAO, K., Environmental Policies, Development Economics
TONEGAWA, K., System Simulation and Management Problems
YAMAMOTO, R., Obligation, Medical Malpractice and Consumer Law
YAMANE, H., Post-war German Literature
YASUE, N., EU and Other International Organizations

ZHOU, W., Environmental Policy, Energy Systems Engineering

College and Graduate School of Science and Engineering:

ABE, A., Technology Management

AKISHITA, S., Active Noise Control in Machinery, Robotics

AMANO, K., Environmental Systems Analysis

AMASAKI, S., Concrete Engineering

AMEYAMA, K., Physical Metallurgy, Microstructure Control, Electron Microscopy

AOYAMA, A., Life-Cycle Engineering

ARAI, M., Spectral Theory of Differential Operators

ARAKI, Y., Educational Technology

ARASE, M., Linguistics, English, Japanese, Substance-Dependence Research

ARIMOTO, S., Robotics, Mechatronics, Machine Intelligence

CHEN, E., Image-Processing, Radioactive Rays Image Measurement, Soft Computing

EGASHIRA, S., Solid Particle and Water Tow Phase Flows, Watercourse and Riverbed Variations

ENDO, A., Community Structure of Terrestrial Invertebrate Animals

FUJIEDA, I., Graphic Information Machinery

FUJIMURA, S., Riemannian Geometry

FUJINO, T., Electrical Engineering

FUKAGAWA, R., Geomechanics, Geomechatronics

FUKUI, M., System LSIs

FUKUMOTO, T., Soil Mechanics and Geotechnical Engineering

FUKUYAMA, T., Elementary Particles, High Energy Astrophysics

HARUNA, M., Urban and Regional Planning Systems

HAYAKAWA, K., Traffic-induced Ground Vibration Propagation and Reduction Measures

HIRAI, S., Robotic Manipulation

IIDA, T., Ergonomics

IKEDA, K., Nonlinear Physical Phenomena

IMAI, S., Atomic Layer CVD and Fabrication of Single Electron Devices

IMAMURA, N., Chemistry of Bio-active Compounds produced by Micro-organisms

ISAKA, T., Sports Biomechanics, Analysis of Human Movement

ISHII, A., Robot Vision, Sensors and Image Analysis

ISHII, H., Number Theory of Automorphic Forms

ISONO, Y., Computational Material Science

ITO, M., Strength and Design of Steel Structures

IWASHIMIZU, Y., Solid Mechanics, Ultrasonic Materials Evaluation

IZUNO, K., Earthquake Resistant Design of Structures

KAITO, C., Quantum Dots Formation

KASAHARA, K., Optical Communication Devices

KATO, M., Physical Chemistry

KAWABATA, T., Power Electronics

KAWAGUCHI, A., Preparation of Functional Polymer Materials Using Epitaxies, and Study of their Properties

KAWAMURA, S., Robotics

KIDO, Y., Investigation of Surface and Interface Structures

KIMATA, M., Engineering

KITAZAWA, T., Numerical Analysis of Electromagnetic Wave Problems

KOBAYASHI, H., Wind-tunnel Experiments and Analyses of Long Bridges Subject to Wind Load

KOJIMA, K., Material and Inorganic Chemistry, Optical Materials

KOJIMA, T., FEM Analysis of Hybrid Concrete Structures Using Discrete Elements

KOMATSU, Y., Online Parameter Estimations of the Induction Machine Utilizing Extension Slip Method

KONDO, K., Synthesis of Functional Polymers

KONISHI, S., Micronanomechatronics and Micromachines, Systems Engineering, Electronic Devices

KOYANAGI, S., Parallel Computation, Database Computer Engineering, Data Mining

KUBO, M., Applied Microbiology

KURATSUJI, H., Quantum Phenomenology

KUSAKA, T., Fracture Mechanics

MAEDA, H., Robot Intelligence for Action and Tasks

MAKIKAWA, M., Biomedical Engineering, Application of Human Motion for Engineering

MATSUDA, T., Separation Analysis, Electro-analysis, Environmental Analysis Chemistry

MATSUOKA, M., Nickel-hydride Batteries, Solar Cells Electrocatalysis, Titanium Dioxide Photocatalysis

MIKI, H., Semiconductor Materials, Solid-state Devices

MIYANO, T., Complex Systems Science, Artificial Intelligence

MIZOSHIRI, I., Medical Electronics and Biological Engineering

MORIMOTO, A., Ultrafast Photonics, Ultrafast Laser Technology, and Terahertz Optoelectronics

MORISAKI, H., Analysis of the Surface Characteristics of Microbial Cells, and the Interaction between Micro-organisms and Interfaces

MURAHASHI, M., Regional and Urban Structure Analyses and Development Techniques

NAKADA, T., Surface Properties

NAKAJIMA, H., Theoretical Analysis of the Interaction Structures of Multi-component Systems

NAKAJIMA, J., Waste Water Treatment Systems, Nitrogen and Phosphorus Removal

NAKAJIMA, K., Homogeneous Kähler Manifolds

NAKAMURA, N., Structure and Physical Properties of Normal Long Chain Compounds, Ionomers and Liquid Crystals

NAKANISHI, T., Measurement and Estimation of Automobile Traffic Flow

NAKAYA, Y., Human Interface, Artificial Intelligence, Recognition Engineering

NAMBA, H., Surfaces as New Materials, Surface Chemical Dynamics

NANISHI, Y., Semiconductor Optoelectronic Devices, Physical Properties of Quantum Structures, Plasma-excited Semiconductor Processes

NARUKI, I., Analysis and Geometry of Complex Manifolds

NISHIO, S., Surface Science

NISHIWAKI, K., Gas Flow, Turbulence, Heat Transfer and Combustion in Combustion Chambers

NUMAI, T., Optical Electronics

OGAMI, Y., Fluid Dynamics

OGASAWARA, H., Geophysics

OGAWA, H., Intelligence Information Science

OGAWA, S., Analysis of Moduli Spaces

OGURA, T., Si System Architecture

OIKAWA, K., Architectural and Urban Space Planning, Environmental Design

OKADA, M., Magnetic and Dielectric Materials, Semiconductor Lasers

ONO, B., Cellular and Molecular Study of the Biological Functions of the Budding Yeast

ONO, Y., Optical Periodic Microstructure

OSAKA, H., Operator Algebras

OZUTSUMI, K., Structural and Thermodynamic Studies of Metal Complexes in Solution

SAITO, S., Optical Communications

SAKAI, J., Optical Fibre Communications and Optical Information Processing

SAKAI, T., Statistical Research on Reliability Engineering

SAKANE, M., Strength Evaluation of Heat-resistant Materials at High Temperatures

SATOMI, J., Basic Physiological and Biochemical Study of Sports Training

SAWAMURA, S., High-pressure Physical Chemistry of Solutions

SHIMAKAWA, H., Social Systems, Computer Software, Information Systems

SHINODA, H., Environmental Studies

SHINYA, H., Functional Analysis

SHIRAISHI, H., Electro-analytical Chemistry

SUGIMOTO, S., Systems and Control Engineering

SUGINO, N., Teaching English as a Foreign Language

SUGIYAMA, S., Microsystem Technology

SUZUKI, K., MEMS for Information and Telecommunication

SUZUKI, K., Pharmaceutical Development, Molecular Biology

TACHIKI, T., Physiology, Biochemistry and the Breeding of Useful Micro-organisms

TAKAKURA, H., High-efficiency Solar Cell Research

TAKANO, N., Computational Mathematics

TAKAYAMA, S., Advanced Sensing Systems and Measurement Science

TAKAYAMA, Y., Computative Algebra

TAKENAKA, A., Properties of Elementary Particles and their Interactions

TAMAKI, J., Design of Functional Interface between Inorganic Materials for Gas-sensing Devices

TAMIAKI, H., Bio-organic Chemistry

TAMURA, H., Information Engineering, Virtual Reality

TANAKA, H., Computer Vision, Visual Communication, Intelligent Information Systems

TANAKA, K., Micro-electric Machine Systems

TANAKA, S., Computer Graphics Systems

TANAKA, T., Precision Processing

TANIGUCHI, Y., High-pressure Physical Chemistry of Liquids, Solutions and Biological Materials

TANIKAGA, R., Organic Synthesis Using Biocatalysts and Organic Sulphurous Reagents

TATEYAMA, K., Construction Engineering

TERAI, H., Research into Computer and LSI Design Automation Systems

THAWONMAS, R., Artificial Intelligence, Entertainment Computing

TOKI, K., Earthquake Engineering, Natural Disaster Science

TORIYAMA, T., Optical Applied Measurements

TSUDAGAWA, M., Analysis and Application of Space Filters

TSUKAGUCHI, H., Transport System Planning and Management

UKITA, H., Optomechatronics

WAKAYAMA, M., Food and Nutrition

WAKAYAMA, M., Food and Nutrition, Micro-organisms

WATANABE, T., Control Engineering

XU, G., Pattern Recognition, Computer Science, Robotics

YAMADA, H., Development of Free-electron Laser

YAMADA, K., Water Demand Analyses and Predictions

YAMADA, O., Mathematical Analysis

YAMADA, T., Probability and Statistics

YAMADA, T., Telecommunication
YAMAMOTO, N., Biomechanics and Function of Living Systems
YAMASAKI, M., Urban Landscape Planning
YAMAUCHI, H., System VLSI Architecture and Implementation
YAMAZAKI, K., Parallel Computing, Computer Graphics, Case-based Reasoning
YOSHIDA, M., Ecology, Ethology
YOSHIHARA, Y., Formation Mechanisms of Harmful Combustion Products and Methods for their Reduction
YOSHIMURA, Y., Structural Phase Transition in Alkali Metal Cyanide

College and Graduate School of Social Sciences:

AKAI, S., Sociology
ARAKI, H., Human Development
ARUGA, I., Turn-Verein
FUKASAWA, A., French Labour and Social History
HIGASHI, J., Critical Applied Linguistics, Sociology of Education
HOGETSU, M., Sociology of Deviance and Sociological Theories
IIDA, T., Sociology
IKEUCHI, Y., American Playwrights
IKUTA, M., Welfare and Information Technology
INUI, K., Social Planning
ISHIKURA, Y., Welfare Sociology, Child and Clinical Psychiatry
JINBO, T., Alternative Media, Media Ethics and Journalism
KANAI, J., Sports Sociology
KIDA, A., Japanese Sociology
KOIZUMI, H., Advertising
KUNIHIRO, T., Political Sociology
KUSAFUKA, N., Physical Education
KUTSUNAI, K., French Literature
LIM, B., Urban Planning
MAEDA, N., Welfare Sociology and Comparative Research in Welfare
MATSUBA, M., German Capitalism
MATSUDA, H., History of Modern Social Thought
MINESHIMA, A., Welfare of the Disabled
MIYASHITA, S., History of Science and Technology
MONDEN, K., History of Science and Technology
MORINISHI, M., History of the Performing Arts
NAGASAWA, K., General Theory of Economics, Economical Statistics
NAKAFUMI, S., Chinese Language and Study of the Tale of the Heike
NAKAGAWA, K., Sociology
NAKAMA, Y., Art History
NAKAMURA, T., Cultural Anthropology
NODA, M., Judicial Welfare
OGAWA, E., Elderly Home Care
OKADA, M., Health Education and Social Work
OKUGAWA, O., Cross-cultural Communication
OZAWA, W., Cross-cultural Communication
SAKAMOTO, T., Sociology
SAKATA, K., Local Media Theory, Broadcast Media Theory
SAKURADANI, M., Sociology
SASAKI, K., Cultural Anthropology
SATO, Y., Sociology, Philosophy
SATOU, H., Sociology, Social Security
SHIBATA, H., Social Security
SHINODA, T., Theory of Political Economy
SUDO, Y., Modern Capitalism
SUZUKI, M., Social Consciousness
TAKAGAKI, C., Mass Communication
TAKAGI, H., Clinical Psychology
TAKAHASHI, M., Sociology
TAKEHAMA, A., Consumer Behaviour
TSUDA, M., Public Access
TSUDOME, M., Social Welfare
TSUJI, K., Disaster Behaviour

WADA, T., Labour Sociology
WEN, C., the Tale of the Heike, Chinese Language
YAMAMOTO, T., Welfare Budget and Administration
YAMASHITA, T., Leisure and Sports Sociology
YANAGISAWA, S., Sociology
YOSHIDA, M., Psycholinguistics

College of Information Science and Engineering:

ASANO, S., Bioscience and Bio-informatics
CHEN, Y. W., Media Technology
ENDO, H., Computer Science
FUJITA, N., Bioscience and Bio-informatics
FUKUMOTO, J., Natural Language Processing
FUSAOKA, A., Human and Computer Intelligence
HACHIMURA, K., Media Technology
HAGIWARA, H., Human and Computer Intelligence
HATTORI, F., Information and Communication Science
HAYANO, T., Proteomics, Molecular Biology, Biochemistry
HAYASHI, T., Media Technology
HIGUCHI, N., Media Technology
IIDA, T., Human and Computer Intelligence
IKEDA, H., Computer Science
INOUE, Y., Information Systems Engineering
KAMEI, K., Human and Computer Intelligence
KAWAI, M., Wireless and Network Systems
KAWAGOE, K., Information and Communication Science
KIKUCHI, M., Bioscience and Bio-informatics
KIKUCHI, T., Bioscience and Bio-informatics
KISHIMOTO, R., Information and Communication Science
KITAMOTO, S., Computer-Generated Animation
KOTSUKI, S., Genetic Informatics
KUNIEDA, Y., Computer Science
KUWABARA, K., Knowledge Processing, Communication Science
MAEDA, T., Electromagnetic Waves and Data Transmission
NAGANO, S., Systems Biology
NAKATANI, Y., Information and Communication Science
NISHIKAWA, I., Human and Computer Intelligence
NISHIO, N., Computer Science
NOZAWA, K., Educational Technology, Inter-cultural Communication
OGAWA, E., Knowledge Engineering
OHNISHI, A., Operating Systems
OKUBO, E., Computer Science
OSHIMA, T., Artificial Reality
OYANAGI, S., Computer Science
RINALDO, F. J., Artificial Intelligence, Expert Systems and Knowledge Information Processing
SHIMAKAWA, H., Computer Science
SHINODA, H., Human and Computer Intelligence
SHIRAI, Y., Robot Intelligence
SUGINO, N., Teaching English as a Foreign Language
SUZUKI, K., Bioscience and Bio-informatics
TAMURA, H., Media Technology
TANAKA, H., Human and Computer Intelligence
TANAKA, S., Media Technology
THAWONMAS, R., Intelligent Entertainment Computing
XU, G., Media Technology
YAMASHITA, Y., Media Technology
YOSHIKAWA, T., Mechatronics, Control Engineering and Robotics

Graduate School for Core Ethics and Frontier Sciences:

AKAMA, R., Japanese Literature
DUMOUCHEL, P., Economic Philosophy
ENDO, A., Symbiosis Theory
GOTO, R., Economic Philosophy
KAMBAYASHI, T., Aesthetics, Art
KOIZUMI, Y., Philosophy
MATSUBARA, Y., History of Science, Scientific Theory
NISHI, M., Comparative Literature
NISHIKAWA, N., French Language, Japanese History, European History
TATEIWA, S., Ethics
UEMURA, M., Television Gaming
WATANABE, K., Cultural Anthropology, African Studies, History of Anthropology

Graduate School of Sciences for Human Services:

AKIRA, H., Genetic Psychology
DAN, S., Family Medical Treatment Methods
FUJI, N., Clinical Psychology
HAYASHI, N., Education, Theory of Character Building
MOCHIZUKI, A., Experimental Action Analysis
MURAMOTO, K., Clinical Psychology, Trauma
NAKAGAWA, Y., Clinical Pedagogics
NAKAMURA, J., Intelligence Development, Life-Span development, Counselling
NAKAMURA, T., Sociology, Social Welfare
NODA, M., Administration of Welfare Justice, Child Welfare
TADAI, T., Clinical Psychology, Psychiatry
TAKAGAKI, C., Clinical Psychology
TAKINO, I., Clinical Psychology
TOKUDA, K., Clinical Psychology

Graduate School of Language Education and Information Science:

AZUMA, S., Code-switching, Socio-linguistic Significance
LEE, N., Linguistics
KAWAMURA, K., English as a Foreign or Second Language
MATSUDA, K., English Literature
NAKAMURA, J., English Corpus Linguistics
NOZAWA, K., Teaching English as a Foreign Language
OHNO, Y., Japanese Pedagogics, Formal Language Studies
OKURA, M., Japanese Language Teaching Methodology
RATZLAFF, G., Second Language Pedagogy and Acquisition
SHIMIZU, Y., Teaching English as a Foreign Language
SUGIMORI, M., Applied Linguistics
TSUKUMA, Y., Linguistics, Phonetics
UMESAKI, A., English Education
YAMADA, H., Linguistics, Phonetics
YOSHIDA, S., Psychology Linguistics

Law School:

DANBAYASHI, K., Women and Law, Trial Procedure
FUJITA, M., Criminal Practice Law
HANATATE, F., Civil Law
HIRAI, T., Civil, Merchant and Medical Law
IBUSUKI, M., Legal Informatics, Criminal Procedure
ICHIKAWA, M., Constitutional Case Law
KATSUI, H., Civil Law
KITAMURA, K., Public Law
KOMATSU, Y., Bankruptcy Law, Consumer Law and Intellectual Property Law
KURONO, Y., Civil Law
MATSUI, Y., International Law
MATSUMIYA, T., Criminal Law
MATSUMOTO, K., Civil Liability, Limitation Act
MORISHITA, H., Criminal Law and Criminal Defence
NINOMIYA, S., Civil Law

OKAHARA, F., Civil Law
OKAMOTO, M., Real Estate Law
OKAWA, S., Civil Case Law, Criminal Case Law
OKUBO, S., Public Law
SAGAMI, Y., Civil Law
SAKAI, H., International Civil Procedure
SHINATANI, T., Corporate Law, Securities Regulation
TANAKA, T., Enterprise Law
UEDA, K., Criminology
WADA, S., Civil Law
WATANABE, S., International Private Law and Civil Procedure
YAMAGUCHI, K., Consumer Protection and International Trade
YAMAMOTO, T., International Conflict Management
YAMANA, T., Tax and Inheritance Tax Law
YASUMOTO, N., Administrative Law, Tax Law

RITSUMEIKAN ASIA PACIFIC UNIVERSITY

1-1 Jumonjibaru, Beppu-shi, Oita 874-8577
Telephone: (977) 78-1111
Fax: (977) 78-1123
Internet: www.apu.ac.jp
Founded 2000
Private control
Languages of instruction: English, Japanese
Academic year: September to July andApril to February

President: Prof. MONTE CASSIM
Vice-Presidents: Prof. NAKAGAMI KEN'ICHI, Dr HAYASHI KENTARO, NISHIDA MUNEAKI, Prof. YAKUSHIJI KIMIO
Dean of Academic Affairs: Prof. NAKANO MASAHIRO
Dean of International Affairs: Dr A. MANI
Dean of Student Affairs: Prof. YAMAGAMI SUSUMU

Library of 65,000 vols
Number of teachers: 120
Number of students: 4,240 (4,000 undergraduate, 240 postgraduate)
Publications: *Journal of Asia Pacific Studies* (3 a year), *Polyglossia* (2 a year)

DEANS

College of Asia Pacific Management: KUNIO IGUSA
College of Asia Pacific Studies: Dr HAYAO FUKUI
Graduate School of Asia Pacific Management: Dr RONALD PATTEN
Graduate School of Asia Pacific Studies: Dr HAYAO FUKUI

RYUKOKU UNIVERSITY

67 Tsukamoto-cho, Fukakusa, Fushimi-ku, Kyoto 612-8577
Telephone: (75) 642-1111
Fax: (75) 642-8867
E-mail: ric@rnoc.fks.ryukoku.ac.jp
Internet: www.ryukoku.ac.jp
Founded 1639
Private control
Academic year: April to March

Chancellor: KOSHO FUJIKAWA
Pres.: DOSHO WAKAHARA
Vice-Pres: TAKESHI HORIKAWA, YOSHIO KAWAMURA
Sec.-Gen.: CHIKO IWAGAMI
Librarian: JITSUZO SHIGETA

Library: see libraries and Archives
Number of teachers: 501
Number of students: 19,830
Publications: *Ryukoku Law Review* (4 a year), *Journal of Economic Studies* (4 a year), *Journal of Ryukoku University* (2 a year), *Ryukoku Journal of Humanities and Sciences* (2 a year), *Journal of Intercultural Communication* (1 a year)

DEANS

Faculty of Business Administration: RINPACHI MISHIMA
Faculty of Economics: HIROKUNI TERADA
Faculty of Intercultural Communication: MASANORI HIGA
Faculty of Law: KEIJI NAGARA
Faculty of Letters: EGUN MIKOGAMI
Faculty of Science of Technology: YOUICHI KOBUCHI
Faculty of Sociology: KAZUNORI KOGA
Japanese Culture and Language Programme: ITSUYO HIGASHINAKA
Junior College: DOSHO WAKAHARA

PROFESSORS

Faculty of Business Administration:

ABE, D., Theoretical Economics
FUJITA, N., Japanese Business History
HARA, M., International Accounting Theory
HAYASHI, A., Corporate Accounting
HAYASHI, K., Cost Accounting
HITOMI, K., Manufacturing Systems Engineering
HONDA, H., Corporate Finance Theory
INOUE, H., Business Management
INOUE, K., Finance Theory
KAMEI, M., International Business Management
KANEKO, A., Insurance Theory
KATAGIRI, M., Marketing Theory
KAWASHIMA, M., Marketing Theory
KITAZAWA, Y., Small Business Management
KOIKE, T., Information Processing Management
KONNO, T., Information Processing Management
MASAOKA, M., Managerial Accounting
MISHIMA, R., Business Administration Psychology
MORIYA, H., Merchandise Studies
NAKAYAMA, J., German Literature
NATSUME, K., International Business Strategy
NISHIHARA, J., Japanese Language Education
NISHIKAWA, K., Labour Management
NOMA, K., Marketing Research
OHGAI, T., International Business
OHNISHI, K., Information Industry
OHSUGI, M., International Finance Theory
ONO, K., Accounting
SATO, K., Marketing
SHIGEMOTO, N., Business Organization Theory
SHIMADA, H., Business Management
SHIMADA, M., English Linguistics
SUGIMURA, M., French Literature
TAKADA, S., Religion
TERASHIMA, K., Information Management
TOGAMI, M., Sociology
TOYOSHIMA, M., Engineering Management
YAMASHITA, A., Macroeconomics
YOKOYAMA, K., Regional Sociology
YOSHIHIRO, S., Primate Ecology
YUI, H., Industrial Engineering

Faculty of Economics:

AZUMA, T., Applied Physiology
HATA, N., Health Industry Economics
HIGUCHI, M., Middle Spanish Literature
IGUCHI, T., Industrial Organization
ISHIKAWA, R., Labour Economics
ITOH, T., Mathematics
KANEKO, H., Economic Theory
KAWAMURA, T., German Literature
KAWAMURA, Y., Development Sociology
LAKSHMAN, W. D., Economic Theory
MATSUOKA, K., Economic Policy
MATSUOKA, T., Theory of Modern Capitalism

MISAKI, S., Economic Theory
MIZUHARA, S., Economic Thought
NAKAMURA, H., Regional Economics
NISHIBORI, F., Theoretical Economics
OBAYASHI, M., African American Development
OISHI, M., English Language
OKACHI, K., International Economic Theory
OMAE, S., Social Policy
OTSUKI, M., German Economic History
SHIMUZU, K., American Literature
TAJIRI, E., Teaching Japanese
TAKADA, M., Public Finance
TAKENAKA, E., Labour Economics
TANAKA, Y., Economic Systems Theory
TERADA, H., Financial Theory
TSUBOUCHI, R., Sociology
YAMAMOTO, S., International Economics
YOSHIMURA, H., Indian Mahayanist Buddhist Thought
YUNO, T., International Finance

Faculty of Intercultural Communication:

AKAGI, H., Japanese Industrial Arts
FUKUDA, K., The United Nations and Japan
FURMANOVSKY, M., American History, TESOL
HABITO, R., Indian and Buddhist Philosophy
HAMANO, S., Human Rights Law, Western Political Thought
HIGA, M., Applied Linguistics
KIGLICS, I., Economics
KIMURA, B., Psychiatry
KOIZUMI, T., Comparative Study of Civilizations
KWON, O., Education
MACADAM, J., Comparative Culture
MATSUBARA, H., Western History
MATSUI, K., Energy Economics
MIYAKAWA, C., French Literature and Language
MURATA, S., Comparative Study of Educational Systems
NAGASAKI, N., Modern South Asian History
PANG, C., Japanese Language, Chinese Language
SAKAMOTO, S., Food Culture, Ethnobotany
SIMPSON, J., World Agriculture
SUDO, M., Comparative Study of Folklore
SUEHARA, T., Cultural Anthropology, Economic Anthropology
SUGIMURA, T., History of Middle Eastern Art
TOH, N., International Communications and Relations
TSURUTA, K., Comparative Literature
UEYAMA, D., Buddhist Studies

Faculty of Law:

FUJIWARA, H., Civil Law
FUKUSHIMA, I., Criminal Law
HAYASHI, T., Buddhism
HIGASHI, F., Physical Education
HIRANO, T., Political Processes
HIRANO, T., The Constitution; Religious Law
HONMA, Y., Civil Proceedings Act
ISHIDA, T., Political Theory
ISHII, K., Philosophy of Law
ISHIZUKA, S., Criminology
IWATA, N., Chinese Language
KATSURA, F., English Language and Literature
KAWABATA, M., African Politics
KAWASUMI, Y., Civil Law
KIM, D., International Human Rights Laws
KISAKA, J., Japanese Political History
KONDO, H., 18th-century English Novel
KUBOTA, M., Sports Sociology
MIKAMI, T., Administrative Law
MIZUNO, T., Tax Law
NAGARA, K., Administrative Law
NISHIO, Y., Commercial Law
SAKAI, S., Current Middle East Politics

SAKAMOTO, M., Administration
SHIRAISHI, K., Public Administration
TAKAHASHI, S., Italian Fascism
TAKEHISA, S., Commercial Law
TAKITA, R., Commercial Politics
TANAKA, N., International Law
TODORIKI, K., Sports Sociology
TOMINO, K., Regional Autonomy
TSUJITA, J., Astrophysics
UEDA, K., Constitutional Law
WAKITA, S., Labour Law
YOROI, T., Labour Law

Faculty of Letters:

AKAMATSU, T., History of Japanese Buddhism
AKIMOTO, M., Japanese Language and Literature
ASADA, M., Japanese Tendai Sect
ASAI, N., Shin Buddhism
CHIN, K., Chinese Language and Literature
DOI, J., Modern Japanese Literature
ECHIZENYA, H., Modern Japanese Culture
FUJIMOTO, M., American Culture
FUKUSHIMA, H., Modern Japanese History
FUROMOTO, T., Anglo-Irish Literature
HAYASHIDA, Y., Eastern History
HIGASHINAKA, I., English Romantic Literature
HIRATA, A., Modern Japanese Thought
ICHIMURA, T., Psychology
INOUE, Y., English Language
ITOI, M., Japanese Language
IZUMOJI, O., Japanese Literature
KAGOTANI, M., Japanese History
KATSUBE, M., Japanese Archaeology
KIDA, T., Modern Chinese History
KITANO, A., Modern Japanese Literature
KODAMA, D., History of Indian Buddhism
KODAMA, S., History of Japanese Religion
KODANI, S., English Literature
KOJIMA, M., Intercultural Pedagogy
KUDARA, K., Buddhism
LAZARIN, M., Philosophy
MARUYAMA, T., Philosophy
MASUDA, R., English Literature
MIKOGAMI, E., Indian Philosophy
MIKOGAMI, E., Modern Western Philosophy
MITSUKAWA, T., Indian Buddhism
MIYAMA, Y., Japanese Literature of the Edo Period
MIYAMOTO, S., Modern English Novels
MIZOGUCHI, K., Philosophy
NAGAKAWA, H., American Literature
NAKAYAMA, S., Chinese Buddhism
NISHIYAMA, R., Mathematics
ODA, Y., Eastern History
OHMINE, A., Philosophy
OHTA, T., Shin Buddhism
OHTORI, K., Tanka Poetry in the Middle Ages
OKA, R., Thought of Shiran
OKAZAKI, K., Japanese Archaeology
SHIYOUBO, T., English Linguistics
TAKEDA, H., History of Indian Buddhism
TAKEDA, R., Buddhism
TANAKA, M., Educational Psychology
TANAKA, S., Psychology
TATSUGUCHI, M., Buddhist Theology
TOKUNAGA, D., Shin Buddhism
TOMITA, M., Educational Technology
TSUNEYOSHI, K., Methods and Curriculum of Education
TSUZUKI, A., East Asian History
UESUGI, T., Philosophy of Education
UMITANI, N., Philosophy of Education
UWAYOKOTE, M., Japanese History
WATANABE, K., History of Sports Philosophy
WATANABE, T., Chinese Buddhist Theory
YAMADA, Y., English Literature
YATA, R., History of Shin Buddhism

Faculty of Science and Technology:

ABE, H., Plasma Physics
ARIKI, Y., Pattern Recognition

DOHSHITA, S., Speech and Audio Media Processing
ENAMI, K., Materials Science and Engineering
FUJIMOTO, Y., Information Engineering
GOTOH, Y., Materials Science
HARADA, T., Catalytic Chemistry
HAYASHI, H., Polymer Science
HORIKAWA, T., Mechanical Engineering and Materials Science
IIDA, S., Solid State Physics
IKEDA, T., Applied Analysis and Computational Science
IWAMOTO, T., Robot Engineering
JIKU, F., Environmental Engineering
KAIYOH, H., Communications Engineering
KAMIJOH, E., Inorganic Functional Materials
KATOH, K., Multivariable Functions
KAWASHIMA, H., Mechanical Engineering
KOBAYASHI, K., Metallic Materials Chemistry
KOBUCHI, Y., Information Science
KOKUBU, H., Mathematics and Dynamic Systems
KONDOH, H., Germanic Literature and Languages
KUNIHIRO, T., Nuclear and Elementary Particle Physics
KUTSUNA, H., Mechanical Engineering
MATSUMOTO, W., Mathematics (Analysis)
MATSUSHITA, T., Coordination Chemistry
MIYASHITA, T., Mechanical Physics
MORITA, Y., Nonlinear Differential Equations
NAKAMURA, T., Computer Science
NAKANISHI, S., Mechanical Engineering
NISHIHARA, H., Superconductivity; Physics
OHJI, K., Mechanical Engineering
OHTSUKA, N., Materials Strength and Fracture Mechanics
OKADA, Y., Information Processing
OKAMOTO, Y., Anglo-Irish Literature
OZAWA, T., Information Technology
SAITOH, M., Optics
SOHMA, K., Buddhism
TAGUCHI, T., Health and Physical Education
TAKAHASHI, T., Science Education and Educational Technology
TAKAYANAGI, K., Astronomy
TSUBOI, Y., Mechatronics and Electronic Control
TSUTSUMI, K., Intelligent Robotic Systems
UDO, A., Systems Engineering
URABE, K., Ceramics
WADA, T., Inorganic Materials Chemistry
YOTSUTANI, S., Mathematics (Analysis)
YUKIMOTO, Y., Semiconductor Electronics

Faculty of Sociology:

FUKUZAKI, S., Health Science
FUNAHASHI, K., Community and Regional Studies
FUSHIMI, Y., Social Welfare Finance
HAYASE, K., Senior Citizens' Welfare
KAMEYAMA, Y., Sociology
KANBAYASHI, S., Social Technology for the Disabled
KASAHARA, S., Industrial Sociology
KISHIDA, H., Clinical Psychology
KODAMA, N., Sociology
KOGA, K., Religion
KOSHII, I., Social Psychology
KUCHIBA, M., Comparative Sociology
MATSUSHITA, K., Population Economics
MATSUTANI, N., Social Security Theory
MORI, Y., Social Welfare Institutions
MUKAI, T., Rural Sociology
MURAI, R., Welfare for the Disabled
NORIKUMO, S., Information Engineering
ODA, K., Social Welfare
OGASAWARA, M., Theoretical Sociology
OSHIDA, E., Mass Media Civilization
SASAKI, M., Social Work
SEKIGUCHI, S., Psychology

SHIMIZU, H., Everyday Life and Religion
SHIMIZU, K., Social Welfare
TAKEHARA, H., Principles of Education
TANAKA, S., Industrial Sociology
TANO, T., Health and Physical Education
TERAKAWA, Y., Religious Psychology
WATARI, H., English Philology

Junior College:

ASAEDA, Z., History of Japanese Buddhism
HAMAGAMI, Y., Child Welfare
IHARA, K., Nursing Technology
IIDA, K., International Social Welfare
IKUTA, M., Social Welfare for the Elderly
KATOH, H., History of Social Welfare Policy
KAWAZOE, T., Shin Buddhism
NAGAI, T., Developmental Psychology
OHNISHI, M., Community Health
TANIMOTO, M., Philosophy
TATSUDANI, A., History of Shin Buddhism
WAKAHARA, D., Pedagogy
YAMADA, M., Indian Buddhism
YAMADA, Y., Shin Buddhism
YOSHIDA, K., Discrimination Problems

ATTACHED RESEARCH INSTITUTES

Institute of Buddhist Cultural Studies:
Shichijo Ohmiya, Shimogyo-ku, Kyoto 600; Dir KYOSHIN ASANO.

Joint Research Centre for Science and Technology: 1-5 Yokoya, Seta Ohe-cho, Otsu, Shiga 520-21; Dir KEISUKE KOBAYASHI.

Research Institute for the Social Sciences: 67 Tsukamoto-cho, Fukakusa, Fushimi-ku, Kyoto; Dir TAKESHI HIRANO.

Socio-cultural Research Institute: 1-5 Yokoya, Seta Ohe-cho, Otsu, Shiga 520-21; Dir KENICHI MATSUI.

UNIVERSITY OF THE SACRED HEART, TOKYO

Hiroo 4 chome 3-1, Shibuya-ku, Tokyo 150-8938

Telephone: (3) 3407-5811
Fax: (3) 5485-3884
E-mail: wwwadmin@u-sacred-heart.ac.jp
Internet: www.u-sacred-heart.ac.jp

Founded 1948
Private control
Academic year: April to March

Pres.: Prof. HEIJI TERANAKA
Vice-Pres. for Graduate Studies: YOSHIKO OKAZAKI
Vice-Pres. for Students: MITSUKO KANEKO
Vice-Pres. for Studies: KENSUKE SUGAWARA
Business Chief: KIMIO MURAMATSU
Registrar: YORIKO YOSHIDA
Librarian: Prof. HITOSHI OBARA

Library of 390,000 vols
Number of teachers: 68 full-time, 318 part-time
Number of students: 2,241

Publications: *Seishin Ronso* (Seishin Studies, 2 a year), *Religion and Civilization* (Bulletin of the Research Institute for the Study of Christian Culture, 1 a year).

SANNO INSTITUTE OF MANAGEMENT

6-39-15 Todoroki, Setagaya, Tokyo 158-8630
Telephone: (3) 3704-1111
Fax: (3) 3704-1608
Internet: www.sanno.ac.jp

Founded 1925

Consists of SANNO Graduate School (MBA Programme), SANNO University Isehara (4-year degree course in Management and Informatics, and distance education course), SANNO College Jiyugaoka (2-year degree course, and distance education course)
Academic year: April to March

Chair.: SHUNICHI UENO
Pres., Sanno University: MASAAKI HARADA
Exec. Dir: TOSHIKAZU TAMURA

Library of 345,000 vols
Number of teachers: 126
Number of students: 7,410 (excluding distance education course students)

Publications: *SANNO College Bulletin* (2 a year), *SANNO College Jiyugaoka Bulletin* (1 a year), *Journal of the Management Research Centre* (irregular)

DEANS

Business Administration: MICHIKO MORIWAKI
Graduate School: TOSHIKAZU TAMURA
School of Management and Information Science: MINAMI MIYAUCHI

SAPPORO GAKUIN UNIVERSITY

11-Banchi, Bunkyodai, Ebetsu, Hokkaido 069-8555

Telephone: (11) 386-8111
Fax: (11) 386-8113
E-mail: kouhou@ims.sgu.ac.jp
Internet: www.sgu.ac.jp

Founded 1946

Pres.: AKIKO FUSE

Faculties of Commerce, Economics, Humanities, Law, Social Information.

SAPPORO UNIVERSITY

3-7-3-1 Nishioka, Toyohira-ku, Sapporo 062-8520

Telephone: (11) 852-1181
E-mail: koho@sapporo-u.ac.jp
Internet: www.sapporo-u.ac.jp

Founded 1967
Private Control
Academic year: April to March

Pres.: MASAYUKI KIMURA
Head Administrator: K. KUROSAWA
Librarian: N. TAKAMATSU

Library of 426,000 vols
Number of teachers: 162
Number of students: 6,700

Publications: *Sapporo Law Review* (2 a year), *Journal of Comparative Cultures* (2 a year), *Sapporo University Journal* (2 a year), *Industrial and Business Journal* (2 a year)

DEANS

Faculty of Business Administration: J. ARAKAWA
Faculty of Cultural Studies: M. YAMAGUCHI
Faculty of Economics: K. MOTODA
Faculty of Foreign Languages: M. KATO
Faculty of Law: H. TANAKA
Graduate School of Law: K. SAKAI
Women's Junior College: A. TODA

SEIJO UNIVERSITY

6-1-20 Seijo, Setagaya-ku, Tokyo 157-8511

Telephone: (3) 3482-2101
Fax: (3) 3482-9698
E-mail: info@seijo.ac.jp
Internet: www.seijo.ac.jp

Founded 1950
Private control
Academic year: April to March

Pres.: YUJI YUI
Admin. Sec.: M. SHIMANO
Librarian: H. FUKUMITSU

Library of 688,395 vols
Number of teachers: 584 (148 full-time, 436 part-time)
Number of students: 5,999

DEANS

Faculty of Arts and Literature: EIJI UENO
Faculty of Economics: YOSHIO ASAI
Faculty of Law: HIROYUKI KONNO
Faculty of Social Innovation: MITSUNOBU SHINOHARA
Junior College: MASUMI ISHINABE

SEIKEI UNIVERSITY

3-3-1 Kichijoji-Kitamachi, Musashino City, Tokyo 180-8633

Telephone: (422) 37-3531
Fax: (422) 37-3883
Internet: www.seikei.ac.jp

Founded 1949
Academic year: April to March

President: KEISUKE KURITA
Librarian: HARUO TANAKA

Library of 742,000 vols
Number of teachers: 183 full-time
Number of students: 8,840 (8,584 undergraduate, 256 postgraduate)

Publications: *Seikei Daigaku Ippankenkyu Hokoku* (Bulletin), *Seikei Daigaku Kogaku Hokoku* (Technology Report), *Journal of Asian and Pacific Studies*

DEANS

Faculty of Economics: C. KOMURA
Faculty of Engineering: Y. KAWADA
Faculty of Humanities: K. AONO
Faculty of Law: E. UEMURA

DIRECTORS

Center for Asian and Pacific Studies: T. TOMITA
Information Processing Center: A. NAKAZATO

SENSHU UNIVERSITY

8 Kandajimbo-cho 3-chome, Chiyoda-ku, Tokyo 101-8425

Telephone: (44) 911-1250
Fax: (44) 911-1243
E-mail: iaffairs@acc.senshu-u.ac.jp
Internet: www.senshu-u.ac.jp

Founded 1880
Academic year: April to March

Pres.: YOSHIHIRO HIDAKA
Librarian: T. OBA

Library of 1,110,000 vols
Number of teachers: 400 full-time
Number of students: 20,472

DEANS

School of Business Administration: K. UOTA
School of Commerce: K. ONISHI
School of Economics: S. SAKAI
School of Law: B. KOHATA
School of Literature: T. ARAKI
School of Network and Information: M. SAKAMOTO
Graduate School of Business Administration: N. TAKEMURA
Graduate School of Commerce: N. OGUCHI
Graduate School of Economics: M. YABUKI
Graduate School of Humanities: T. SUZUKI
Graduate School of Law: T. TAKAGAI
Professional School of Legal Affairs: Y. HIRAI

SETSUNAN UNIVERSITY

17-8 Ikedanakamachi, Neyagawa-shi, Osaka 572-8508

Telephone: (72) 839-9102
Fax: (72) 826-5100
Internet: www.setsunan.ac.jp

Founded 1975

Chair.: MASAO SAKAGUCHI
Pres.: MITSUNORI IMAI

DEANS

Faculty of Business Administration and Information: TATSUMI SHIMADA
Faculty of Engineering: YOSHIO NAMITA
Faculty of International Languages and Cultures: MITSUNORI IMAI
Faculty of Law: MASUYUKI MORIMOTO
Faculty of Pharmaceutical Sciences: NOBORU YATA

SHIKOKU UNIVERSITY

Ojin-cho, Tokushima-shi, Tokushima, 771-1192

Telephone: (88) 665-9911
Fax: (88) 665-8037
E-mail: oip@shikoku-u.ac.jp
Internet: www.shikoku-u.ac.jp

Founded 1966

Pres.: NOBORU FUKUOKA

Library of 317,470 vols
Number of teachers: 163
Number of students: 3,114

Faculty of Literature; Graduate School of Management and Information Science.

SOKA UNIVERSITY

1-236, Tangi-cho, Hachioji, Tokyo 192-8577

Telephone: (426) 91-8200
Fax: (426) 91-2039
E-mail: adm@j.soka.ac.jp
Internet: www.soka.ac.jp

Founded 1971
Private control
Academic year: April to March

Pres.: Prof. Dr MASAMI WAKAE
Vice-Press: Prof. KATSUHIKO FUKUSHIMA, Prof. MASASUKE NIHEI
Librarian: Prof. EIICHI IMAGAWA

Library of 1,005,000 vols
Number of teachers: 295
Number of students: 7,842

Publication: *SUN* (Soka University News, 4 a year)

DEANS

Division of Correspondence Education: Prof. TADASHIGE TAKAMURA
Faculty of Business Administration: Prof. KAORU YAMANAKA
Faculty of Economics: Prof. Dr HIDETAKA HASEBE
Faculty of Education: Prof. RIKIO KIMATA
Faculty of Engineering: Prof. YOSHIMI TESHIGAWARA
Faculty of Law: Prof. AKIRA KIRIGAYA
Faculty of Letters: Prof. YUTAKA ISHIGAMI
Graduate School of Economics: Prof. KINJI UEDA
Graduate School of Engineering: Prof. KOJIRO KOBAYASHI
Graduate School of Law: Prof. KAZUO KAWASAKI
Graduate School of Letters: Prof. KAZUNORI KUMAGAI
Institute of Japanese Language: Prof. KEIKO ISHIKAWA

DIRECTORS

Institute for the Comparative Study of Cultures: M. KITA
Institute of Asian Studies: E. IMAGAWA
Institute of Life Science: M. WAKAE
Institute of Systems Science: M. WAKAE
International Research Institute for the Advanced Study of Buddhism: H. KANNO
Peace Research Institute: T. TAKAMURA

SOPHIA UNIVERSITY
(Jôchi University)

Chiyoda-ku, Kioicho 7-1, Tokyo 102-8554

Telephone: (3) 3238-3111
Fax: (3) 3238-3885
Internet: www.sophia.ac.jp

Founded 1913
Private control (Society of Jesus)
Languages of instruction: Japanese, English
Academic year: April to March

Chancellor: TOSHIAKI KOSO
President: YOSHIAKI ISHIZAWA
Vice-Presidents: L. GROVE, S. IKEO, S. YAMAOKA
Registrar: H. YAMAMOTO
Library: see Libraries and Archives
Number of teachers: 526
Number of students: 11,714

Publications: *Monumenta Nipponica* (in English, 4 a year), *Sophia* (in Japanese, 4 a year)

DEANS

Faculty of Comparative Culture: R. GARDNER
Faculty of Economics: T. SUGIMOTO
Faculty of Foreign Studies: K. YOSHIDA
Faculty of Human Sciences: H. OKAMOTO
Faculty of Humanities: A. OSHIMA
Faculty of Law: M. KOJO
Faculty of Science and Technology: K. SOGABE
Faculty of Theology: T. SAKUMA

DIRECTORS

Counselling Institute: Y. YAMANAKA
Iberoamerican Institute: K. IMAI
Institute for Studies of the Global Environment: K. SEGAWA
Institute for the Study of Social Justice: H. MACHINO
Institute of American and Canadian Studies: T. OTSUKA
Institute of Asian Cultures: Y. MURAI
Institute of Christian Culture and Oriental Religions: K. MATSUOKA
Institute of Comparative Culture: J. OKADA
Institute for the Culture of German-speaking Areas: S. KOIZUMI
Institute of Medieval Thought: H. OGINO
Life Science Institute: K. KUMAKURA
Linguistic Institute for International Communication: K. YOSHIDA

TAKUSHOKU UNIVERSITY

3-4-14 Kohinata, Bunkyo-ku, Tokyo 112

Telephone: (3) 3947-2261
E-mail: web_int@ofc.takushoku-u.ac.jp
Internet: www.takushoku-u.ac.jp

Founded 1900

Campuses at Hachioji and Bunkyo

Chancellor: S. ODAMURA
Pres.: TOSHIO WATANABE
Chair. of Board of Directors: T. FUJITO
Librarian: S. KORI

Library of 440,000 vols
Number of teachers: 528
Number of students: 10,377

Publications: *Hokoku* (1 a year), *Kaigai Jijo* (Journal of World Affairs, 12 a year), *Takushoku Daigaku Ronshu* (6 a year)

DEANS

Faculty of Commerce: T. TAKAHASHI
Faculty of Engineering: M. SAKATA
Faculty of Foreign Languages: T. WADA
Faculty of Political Science and Economics: K. KOBAYASHI
Graduate School: T. OSAKAI
Hokkaido Takushoku Junior College: T. ISHIKAWA
Special Japanese Language Course for Foreign Students: M. ARAKI

Takushoku Junior College: T. GOTO

TAMAGAWA UNIVERSITY

6-1-1 Tamagawa Gakuen 6-chome, Machida, Tokyo 194-8610

Telephone: (427) 39-8111
Fax: (427) 39-1181
E-mail: webmaster@tamagawa.ac.jp
Internet: www.tamagawa.ac.jp

Founded 1929
Private control
Language of instruction: Japanese
Academic year: April to March

Pres.: YOSHIAKI OBARA
Registrar: TAKASHI URATA
Librarian: HARUA TODA

Library of 860,000 vols, 8,000 periodicals
Number of teachers: 787 (351 full-time, 436 part-time)
Number of students: 7,774

Publications: *Mitsubachi Kagaku* (4 a year), *Shoho* (1 a year), *Zenjin Education* (12 a year)

DEANS

Associate Degree Junior College for Women: TOMIO OZAWA
Department of Education by Correspondence: HIROSHI YONEYAMA
Faculty of Agriculture: TADAYUKI ISHIYAMA
Faculty of Arts and Education: HIROSHI YONEYAMA
Faculty of Engineering: HIDETAKE TANIBAYASHI
Graduate School for Agriculture: MITSUO MATSUKA
Graduate School for Education and Letters: YASUTADA TAKAHASHI
Graduate School for Engineering: TAKURO KOIKE
Junior College for Women: MICHIAKI NAGAI

TEZUKAYAMA UNIVERSITY

7-1-1 Tezukayama, Nara City 631-8501

Telephone: (742) 48-9122
Fax: (742) 48-9135
E-mail: webmaster@tezukayama-u.ac.jp
Internet: www.tezukayama-u.ac.jp

Founded 1941

Library of 280,000 vols
Number of teachers: 109
Number of students: 4,166

Faculties of Business Administration, Economics, Humanities, Law and Policy.

TOHOKU GAKUIN UNIVERSITY

1-3-1 Tsuchitoi, Aoba-ku, Sendai 980-8511

Telephone: (2) 264-6425
Fax: (2) 264-6515
E-mail: ico@tscc.tohoku-gakuin.ac.jp
Internet: www.tohoku-gakuin.ac.jp

Founded 1886
Private control
Language of instruction: Japanese
Academic year: April to March

Library of 1,200,000 vols
President: NOZOMU HOSHIMIYA
Vice-Presidents: YOSHITAKA SHIBATA, MAKOTO SAITO
Number of teachers: 511
Number of students: 12,518

Publications: *Church and Theology* (2 a year), *Economics* (3 a year), *History and Geography* (2 a year), *Human, Jurisprudence* (2 a year), *Linguistic and Information Sciences* (3 a year), *Science and Engineering Report* (2 a year), *Tohoku Gakuin University Review English Language and Literature* (2 a year)

DEANS

Faculty of Economics: YOSHINORI HARADA
Faculty of Engineering: GINRO ENDO
Faculty of Fitness and Administration: NOBUMASA YAMAMOTO
Faculty of Law: RYUICHIRO TAKAGI
Faculty of Letters: KENICHI ENDO
Faculty of Liberal Arts: MASAHIRO SAKUMA

TOKAI UNIVERSITY EDUCATIONAL SYSTEM

2-28-4 Tomigaya, Shibuya-ku, Tokyo 151-8677

Telephone: (3) 3467-2211
Fax: (3) 3467-0197
E-mail: pr@yyg.u-tokai.ac.jp
Internet: www.pr.tokai.ac.jp

Founded 1942

Chairman and President: TATSURO MATSUMAE

DIRECTORS

Okinawa Regional Research Center: SOUNOSUKE KATORI
Research Institute for Educational Development: SOUNOSUKE KATORI
Research Institute of Modern Civilization: TATSURO MATSUMAE
Research Institute of Science and Technology: SOUNOSUKE KATORI
Strategic Peace and International Affairs Research Institute: NORIO MATSUMAE
Tokai University European Center (Denmark): MORITO TAKAHASHI
Tokai University Pacific Center (Hawaii): KIYOSHI YAMADA
Tokai University Research and Information Center: YOSHIAKI MATSUMAE
Tokai University Space Information Center: HARUHISA SHIMODA

CONSTITUENT UNIVERSITIES

Hokkaido Tokai University

Telephone: (11) 571-5111
Fax: (11) 571-7879
E-mail: kikaku@ss.htokai.ac.jp
Internet: www.htokai.ac.jp

Sapporo Campus: 5-1-1-1 Minamisawa, Minami-ku, Sapporo, Hokkaido 005-8601; tel. (11) 571-5111; fax (11) 571-7879.

Asahikawa Campus: 224 Chuwa, Kamui-cho, Asahikawa, Hokkaido 070-8601; tel. (166) 61-5111; fax (166) 62-8180.

Founded 1977
Academic year: April to March

President: SHUNMEI MITSUZAWA
Librarian: EIICHI SATO

Library of 179,000 vols
Number of teachers: 112 full-time
Number of students: 2,515

DEANS

School of Art and Technology: JUN MIKAMI
School of International Cultural Relations: KOUJI KOBAYASHI
School of Engineering: MINORU KOUTAKI

CHAIRMEN

Graduate School of Arts: JUN MIKAMI
Graduate School of Science and Engineering: TETSUO SHIMONO

DIRECTORS

Research Institute for Higher Education Programmes: YASUNARI KURIHARA
Cultural Institute of Northern Region: TSUTOMU KOKAWA
Environmental Research Institute: HIROYUKI NISHIMURA

Kyushu Tokai University

Telephone: (96) 382-1141
Fax: (96) 381-7956
E-mail: kikaku@jsmail.js.ktokai-u.ac.jp
Internet: www.ktokai-u.ac.jp
Kumamoto Campus: 9-1-1 Toroku, Kumamoto-shi, Kumamoto 862-8652; tel. (96) 382-1141; fax (96) 381-7956.
Aso Campus: Kawayou, Choyo-son, Aso-gun, Kumamoto 869-1404; tel. (9676) 7-0611; fax (9676) 7-2053.
Founded 1973
Academic year: April to March
President: YOSHIAKI MATSUMAE
Librarian: TAKAAKI TSUKIJI
Library of 240,965 vols
Number of teachers: 138 full-time
Number of students: 3,437

DEANS

School of Agriculture: KIHACHIROU NOBUKUNI
School of Engineering: CHIKAE WATANABE
School of Information Science: SHOJI KAIDA

CHAIRMEN

Graduate School of Agriculture: KIHACHIROU NOBUKUNI
Graduate School of Engineering: CHIKAE WATANABE

DIRECTORS

Institute of Industrial Science and Technology: ICHIRO TAKAGI
Agricultural Research Institute: TAKAO TORIKATA

Tokai University

Telephone: (463) 58-1211
Fax: (463) 50-2052
E-mail: kikaku@tsc.u-tokai.ac.jp
Internet: www.u-tokai.ac.jp
Shonan Campus: 1117 Kitakaname, Hiratsuka-shi, Kanagawa 259-1292; tel. (463) 58-1211; fax (463) 35-2458.
Yoyogi Campus: 2-28-4 Tomigaya, Shibuya-ku, Tokyo 151-8677; tel. (3) 3467-2211.
Shimizu Campus: 3-20-1 Orido, Shimizu-shi, Shizuoka 424-8610; tel. (543) 34-0411.
Isehara Campus: Bouseidai, Isehara-shi, Kanagawa 259-1193; tel. (463) 93-1121.
Numazu Campus: 317 Nishino, Numazu-shi, Shizuoka 410-0395; tel. (559) 68-1111.
Founded 1946
Academic year: April to March
President: JIRO TAKANO
Librarian: TASUKU HAYAMI
Library of 1,801,220 vols
Number of teachers: 1,461 full-time
Number of students: 31,481
Publications: *Tokai Journal of Experimental and Clinical Medicine*, bulletins of the various schools, etc.

DEANS

Foreign Language Centre: KIYOICHI ONO (Head)
International Student Education Center: FUSATO TANIGUCHI (Head)
Japanese Language Course for Foreign Students: FUSATO TANIGUCHI (Head)
Licensed Professional Training Center: YUUKO MIYASAKA (Head)
School of Engineering: HIROHISA UCHIDA
School of Engineering II (Evening Session): HIROHISA UCHIDA
School of Health Sciences: RIYUUKO FUJIMURA
School of High Technology for Human Welfare: CHIKAO UEMURA

School of Humanities and Culture: HIROSHI NINOMIYA
School of Information Technology and Electronics: NOBUAKI TAKAHASHI
School of Law: SHIGERU OTSUKA
School of Letters: YASUO TANAKA
School of Marine Science and Technology: YOSHIMASA TOYOTA
School of Medicine: TOMOMITSU HOTTA
School of Physical Education: NOBUYUKI SATO
School of Political Science and Economics: YASUSHI INOUE
School of Science: KENZOU NANRI

CHAIRMEN

Graduate School of Arts: HARUMI KOSHIBA
Graduate School of Economics: OSAMU TAKENAKA
Graduate School of Engineering: HIROMASA TAKEUCHI
Graduate School of Health Sciences: KEIKO SHICHITA
Graduate School of High Technology for Human Welfare: MASAAKI SHINJI
Graduate School of Law: SHIGERU OTSUKA
Graduate School of Letters: NOBUYUKI WATASE
Graduate School of Marine Science and Technology: YOSHIMASA TOYOTA
Graduate School of Medicine: KIYOSHI KUROKAWA
Graduate School of Physical Education: NAOHISA MATSUNAGA
Graduate School of Political Science: YOSHITERU MAKITA
Graduate School of Science: JIRO TAKANO

TOKIWA UNIVERSITY

1-430-1 Miwa, Mito-shi, Ibaraki Prefecture 310-8585
Telephone: (29) 232-2511
Fax: (29) 231-6078
E-mail: kouhou@tokiwa.ac.jp
Internet: www.tokiwa.ac.jp
Founded 1983
Chair.: HIDEMICHI MOROSAWA
Pres.: ISATO TAKAGI
Colleges of Applied International Studies, Community Development, Human Science; Graduate School of Human Science.

TOKYO UNIVERSITY OF PHARMACY AND LIFE SCIENCES

1432-1 Horinouchi, Hachioji, Tokyo 192-03
Telephone: (426) 76-5111
Internet: www.toyaku.ac.jp
Founded 1880
Pres.: Dr T. YAMAKAWA
Librarian: Prof. A. OHTA
Library of 100,000 vols, 500 periodicals
Number of teachers: 200
Number of students: 2,200

Schools of Life Sciences and Pharmacy.

TOKYO DENKI DAIGAKU
(Tokyo Denki University)

2-2 Kanda-Nishiki-cho, Chiyoda-ku, Tokyo 101-8457
Telephone: (3) 5280-3555
Fax: (3) 5280-3623
E-mail: gakuchoshitsu@jim.ac.jp
Internet: www.dendai.ac.jp
Founded 1907
Academic year: April to March
President: Dr YOSHIHIRO TOMA
General Director of Multimedia Resource Centre and Library: Dr T. SAITO
Library of 321,481 vols, 2,975 periodicals
Number of teachers: 748 (355 full-time, 393 part-time)

Number of students: 11,563

DEANS

Graduate School of Engineering: J. IWAMOTO
Graduate School of Science and Engineering: M. TAKIZAWA
School of Engineering: T. IBAMOTO
School of Engineering (Evening Programme): S. MURAKAMI
School of the Information Environment: S. NAKAMURA
School of Science and Engineering: Y. KASHIMURA

DIRECTORS

Applied Superconductivity Research Laboratory: I. NEMOTO
Centre for Research Collaboration: H. TOMITA
Frontier Research and Development Centre: Y. UCHIKAWA
Research Institute for Construction Technology: M. TACHIBANA
Research Institute for Technology: H. INABA

TOKYO DENTAL COLLEGE

1-2-2 Masago, Mihama-ku, Chiba 261-8502
Telephone: (43) 270-3764
Fax: (43) 270-3765
E-mail: int@tdc.ac.jp
Internet: www.tdc.ac.jp
Founded 1890
Academic year: April to March
Dean: Prof. YUZURU KANEKO
Vice-Deans: Prof. MASASHI YAKUSHIJI
Library of 198,000 vols
Number of teachers: 306
Number of students: 983 (802 undergraduate, 181 postgraduate)
Publications: *Bulletin* (in English, 4 a year), *Shikwa Gakuho* (research journal, in Japanese, every 2 months).

TOKYO KEIZAI UNIVERSITY

1-7-34 Minami-cho, Kokubunji-shi, Tokyo 185-8502
Telephone: (42) 328-7711
Internet: www.tku.ac.jp
Founded 1900 as Okura Commerce School
Private control
Academic year: April to March
President: KATSUHIKO MURAKAMI
Chief Administrative Officer: TOURU SASAKI
Librarian: SHIGEKAZU KUKITA
Library of 640,000 vols
Number of teachers: 445
Number of students: 7,673
Publications: *Journal of Tokyo Keizai University* (6 a year), *Journal of Humanities and Natural Sciences* (2 a year), *Journal of Communication Studies* (2 a year), *Tokyo Kezai Law Review* (2 a year)

DEANS

Faculty of Business Administration: YOSHIAKI JINNAI
Faculty of Communication Studies: KAORU YAMAZAKI
Faculty of Contemporary Law: KAZUO SHIMADA
Faculty of Economics: MASAHIRO FUKUSHI
Graduate School of Business Administration: KENJI OMORI (Chair.)
Graduate School of Communication Studies: TERUO ARIYAMA (Chair.)
Graduate School of Contemporary Law: YOSHIO MIYAZAKI (Chair.)
Graduate School of Economics: HISASHI WATANABE (Chair.)

TOKYO UNIVERSITY OF AGRICULTURE

1-1-1 Sakuragaoka, Setagaya-ku, Tokyo 156-8502

Telephone: (3) 5477-2560
Fax: (3) 5477-2635
E-mail: tuacip@nodai.ac.jp
Internet: www.nodai.ac.jp
Founded 1891
Academic year: April to March
President: Dr ISOYA SHINJI
Chief Administrative Officer: Dr AKIO SHIBA-KAZI
Librarian: Dr SHIGEYUKI MIYABAYASHI
Library of 665,000 vols
Number of teachers: 357
Number of students: 13,000
Publication: *Journal of Agricultural Science* (1 a year)

DEANS

Faculty of Agriculture: Dr TAKASHI AMANO
Faculty of Applied Bioscience: Dr KANJU OSAWA
Faculty of Bio-Industry: Dr MASAO ITO
Faculty of International Agriculture and Food Studies: Dr KATSUTOSHI NIINUMA
Faculty of Regional Environmental Science: Dr MASAHARU KOMAMURA
Graduate School of Agriculture: Dr TAI UCHIMURA
Graduate School of Bio-Industry: Dr YOSHIE MOMONOKI
Junior College: Dr TADASHI YASUHARA

TOKYO UNIVERSITY OF SCIENCE

1-3 Kagurazaka, Shinjuku-ku, Tokyo 162-8601

Telephone: (3) 3260-4271
Internet: www.tus.ac.jp
Founded 1881
Private control
President: HIROYUKI OKAMURA
Deputy Presidents: YOSHIMOTO ABE, TSUNE-HIRO MANABE
Librarian: MASAAKI UEKI
Library of 948,592 vols
Number of teachers: 782
Number of students: 19,825
Publication: *Science Forum* (12 a year)

DEANS

Faculty of Engineering Division I: SHINJI HONAMI
Faculty of Engineering Division II: TAKAYUKI TERAMOTO
Faculty of Industrial Science and Technology: TSUNEO WATANABE
Faculty of Pharmaceutical Sciences: KEN TAKEDA
Faculty of Science Division I: TETSUO KANAMOTO
Faculty of Science Division II: HIROSHI NIITSUMA
Faculty of Science and Technology: HIROYUKI SETO
School of Management: MASAYOSHI HIROTA

ATTACHED INSTITUTES

Research Education Organization for Information Science and Technology: 1–3 Kagurazaka, Shinjuku-ku, Tokyo 162-8601; tel. (3) 3260-4271; Principal MASANORI OHYA.
Research Institute for Biological Sciences: 2641 Yamazaki, Noda-shi, Chiba 278-8510; tel. (4) 7124-1501; Principal TAKA-CHIKA AZUMA.
Research Institute for Science and Technology: 2641 Yamazaki, Noda-shi,

Chiba 278-8510; tel. (4) 7124-1501; Principal YOSHIMASA NIHEI.

TOKYO WOMEN'S CHRISTIAN UNIVERSITY

2-6-1, Zempukuji, Suginami-ku, Tokyo 167-8585

Telephone: (3) 5382-6340
Fax: (3) 3395-1037
E-mail: iec@office.twcu.ac.jp
Internet: www.twcu.ac.jp
Founded 1918
Private control
Language of instruction: Japanese
Academic year: April to March
Pres.: AKIKO MINATO
Librarian: SHINSUKE MUROFUCHI
Library of 600,000 vols
Number of teachers: 142
Number of students: 4,208, including 78 graduates
Publications: *Annals of Institute for Comparative Studies of Culture* (1 a year), *Essays and Studies in British and American Literature* (2 a year), *Historica* (1 a year), *Japanese Literature* (2 a year), *Science Reports* (1 a year), *Sociology and Economics* (1 a year)

DEANS

College of Arts and Sciences: SANAE INOUE
College of Culture and Communication: YUKO KOBAYASHI
Graduate School: HIROSHI IMAI

CHAIRMEN

Graduate School of Culture and Communication: RYOICHI SATO
Graduate School of Humanities: HIROSHI IMAI
Graduate School of Science: MASAHIKO SHINOHARA

TOKYO WOMEN'S MEDICAL UNIVERSITY

8-1 Kawada-cho, Shinjuku-ku, Tokyo 162-8666

Telephone: (3) 3353-8111
Fax: (3) 3353-6793
Internet: www.twmu.ac.jp
Founded 1900
Private control
Language of instruction: Japanese
Academic year: April to March
President: K. TAKAKURA
Registrar: H. YOSHIOKA
Librarian: M. KOBAYASHI
Library of 227,850 vols
Number of teachers: 2,178
Number of students: 961
Publication: *Journal of Tokyo Women's Medical University* (in English or Japanese, 12 a year).

TOYO UNIVERSITY

28-20 Hakusan 5-chome, Bunkyo-ku, Tokyo 112-8606

Telephone: (3) 3945-7557
Fax: (3) 3942-2489
E-mail: ipo@hakusrv.toyo.ac.jp
Internet: www.toyo.ac.jp
Founded 1887
Private control
Academic year: April to March
Pres.: TOMONORI MATSUO
Dirof Academic Affairs: MIKIO AKIYAMA
Librarian: TAKITARO MORIKAWA
Library of 1,101,256 vols
Number of teachers: 1,269 (523 full-time, 746 part-time)

Number of students: 29,819
Publications: faculty bulletins, journals, etc.

DEANS

Undergraduate School of Business Administration: YOUICHI KAKIZAKI
Undergraduate School of Economics: SHUN-ICHI KIGAWA
Undergraduate School of Engineering: MASA-HIDE YONEYAMA
Undergraduate School of Law: HIDETOSHI KOBAYASHI
Undergraduate School of Life Sciences: AKIRA SAKURAI
Undergraduate School of Literature: TASHIAKI YAMADA
Undergraduate School of Regional Development Studies: HAJIME NAGAHAMA
Undergraduate School of Sociology: MAMORA FUNATSU
Graduate School of Business Administration: YASUHIRO OGURA
Graduate School of Economics: KIYOSHI ASUNO
Graduate School of Engineering: TOHRU IUCHI
Graduate School of Law: MASUO IMAGAMI
Graduate School of Life Sciences: AKIRA INOUE
Graduate School of Literature: KAZUO ARITA
Graduate School of Regional Development Studies: TOMONORI MARSUO
Graduate School of Sociology: KOJUN FURU-KAWA

TSUDA COLLEGE

2-1-1 Tsuda-machi, Kodaira-shi, Tokyo 187-8577

Telephone: (42) 342-5111
Fax: (42) 341-2444
E-mail: info-admin@tsuda.ac.jp
Internet: www.tsuda.ac.jp
Founded 1900
Academic year: April to March
Chair.: REIJIROU HATTORI
Library of 350,000 vols, 3,400 periodicals
Number of teachers: 83 full-time
Number of students: 2,830 (incl. 85 postgraduate)
Publications: *Journal of Tsuda College* (1 a year), *The Study of International Relations* (1 a year), *The Tsuda Review* (1 a year)
Faculty of liberal arts, departments of English language and literature, international and cultural studies, mathematics and computer science; postgraduate schools of international and cultural studies, literary studies, mathematics.

TSURU UNIVERSITY

3-8-1 Tahara, Tsuru, Yamanashi 402-8555
Telephone: (554) 43-4341
Fax: (554) 43-4347
E-mail: gakusei@tsuru.ac.jp
Internet: www.tsuru.ac.jp
Founded 1955
Number of teachers: 74 (full-time)
Number of students: 3,000
Teacher training college.

WASEDA UNIVERSITY

1-104 Totsuka-machi, Shinjuku-ku, Tokyo 169-8050
Telephone: (3) 3203-4141
Fax: (3) 3203-7051
E-mail: intl-ac@list.waseda.jp
Internet: www.waseda.jp
Founded 1882
Private control
Academic year: April to February

Pres.: KATSUHIKO SHIRAI

Vice-Pres: KENICHI ENATSU, SEIGO HIRAYAMA, SEIJI HONDA, KENJI HORIGUCHI, YOSHIJI HORIKOSHI, EI'ICHIRO KOBAYASHI, EIKO KONO, ISAO MURAOKA, AKIRA NISHITANI, EI'ICHIRO NOJIMA, AKIRA SESHIMO, SATOSHI SHIMIZU, NAOJI TAKAGI, HIDEAKI TAUCHI, TERUAKI TAYAMA, KENJIRO TSUCHIDA, NOBU-HIRO TSUMOTO, KATSUICHI UCHIDA, YASU-MASA UMESATO, SHOTARO WATANABE

Dir of Library: NOBUYUKI KAMIYA

Library of 5,100,000 vols

Number of teachers: 5,885

Number of students: 54,228 (45,757 undergraduate, 8,471 postgraduate)

The Schools of Letters, Arts and Sciences I and II will be terminated when all existing students graduate; they are replaced from 2007 by the School of Culture, Media and Society and the School of Humanities and Social Sciences. The Schools of Science and Engineering will also be terminated when all existing students graduate; they are replaced from 2007 by the School of Fundamental Science and Engineering, the School of Creative Science and Engineering and the School of Advanced Science and Engineering.

DEANS

Graduate School of Accountancy: YOSHITAKA KOBAYASHI

Graduate School of Advanced Science and Engineering: ATSUSHI ISHIYAMA

Graduate School of Asia Pacific Studies: SATOSHI AMAKO

Graduate School of Commerce: MASATAKA OTA

Graduate School of Creative Science and Engineering: HIROSH YAMAKAWA

Graduate School of Economics: RYO NAGATA

Graduate School of Education: TOSHIMICHI MIYAGUCHI

Graduate School of Environment and Energy Engineering: KATSUYA NAGATA

Graduate School of Finance, Accounting and Law: JUN UNO

Graduate School of Global Information and Telecommunication Studies: YOSHIYORI URANO

Graduate School of Information Production, and Systems: KOTARO HIRASWA

Graduate School of Japanese Applied Linguistics: YOSHIKAZU KAWAGUCHI

Graduate School of Law: TAKEHIKO SONE

Graduate School of Letters, Arts and Sciences: TERUHISA TAJIMA

Graduate School of Science and Engineering: SHUJI HASHIMOTO

Graduate School of Fundamental Science and Engineering: SUNAO KAWAI

Graduate School of Political Science: SEISHI SATO

Graduate School of Social Sciences: YASUHIRO ONISHI

Graduate School of Sport Sciences: TETSUO FUKUNAGA

School of Advanced Science and Engineering: ATSUSHI ISHIYAMA

School of Commerce: NOBUTAKE YOKOTA

School of Creative Science and Engineering: HIROSHI YAMAKAWA

School of Culture, Media and Society: TER-UHISA TAJIMA

School of Education: TOMOKI WARAGAI

School of Fundamental Science and Engineering: SUNAO KAWAI

School of Human Sciences: MIHO SAITO

School of Humanities and Social Sciences: TERUHISA TAJIMA

School of International Liberal Studies: PAUL SNOWDEN

School of Law: TATSUO UEMURA

School of Letters, Arts and Sciences I: TERUHISA TAJIMA

School of Letters, Arts and Sciences II: TERUHISA TAJIMA

School of Political Science and Economics: SHOZO IIJIMA

School of Science and Engineering: SHUJI HASHIMOTO

School of Social Science: YASUHIRO ONISHI

School of Sport Science: TSUNEO SOGAWA

The Okuma School of Public Management: MITSUYOSHI ISHIDA

Waseda Law School: KAORU KAMATA

Schools of Art and Music

Elizabeth University of Music: 4–15 Noboricho, Naka-ku, Hiroshima; tel. (82) 221-0918; fax (82) 221-0947; internet www.eum.ac.jp; f. 1952; library: 88,750 vols, 18,000 sound recordings; 47 full-time, 70 part-time teachers; 656 undergraduates, 53 postgraduates; Pres. HIDEAKI NAKAMURA; Dean of Academic Affairs K. NAGAI; publ. *Kenkyuu Kiyoo* (1 a year).

Kanazawa College of Art: 5-11-1, Kodat-suno, Kanazawa, Ishikawa 920-8656; tel. (76) 262-3531; fax (76) 262-6594; e-mail admin@kanazawa-bidai.ac.jp; internet www.kanazawa-bidai.ac.jp; f. 1946; depts of Fine Art, Design, Crafts; Graduate School; Research Institute of Art and Craft, f. 1972; 67 full-time staff, 200 part-time staff; 665 students; library: 72,000 vols; Pres. YOSHIAKI INUI.

Kunitachi College of Music: 5-5-1 Kashiwa-cho, Tachikawa-shi, Tokyo 190-8520; tel. (42) 536-0321; fax (42) 535-2313; internet www.kunitachi.ac.jp; f. 1950; library: 155,000 books, 120,000 vols of sheet music, 170,000 audio-visual items; 417 teach-

ers; 2,439 students; Pres. NORIKO TAKANO; publs *Kenkyu Kiyo* (Memoirs, 1 a year), *Daigakuin Nempo* (1 a year publication of the postgraduate school), *Ongaku Kenkyujo Nempo* (1 a year publication of the research institute).

Kyoto City University of Arts: 13-6 Kut-sukake-cho, Ohe, Nishikyo-ku, Kyoto 610-1197; tel. (75) 332-0701; fax (75) 332-0709; internet w3.kcua.ac.jp; Pres. Dr YASUNORI NISHIJIMA; 740 undergraduate students, 134 graduates; Faculties of Fine Arts and Music.

Musashino Academia Musicae: 1-13-1 Hazawa, Nerima-ku, Tokyo 176-8521; tel. (3) 3992-1121; fax (3) 3991-7599; internet www.musashino-music.ac.jp; f. 1929; 382 teachers; 2,269 students; library: 200,000 vols; Pres. NAOKATA FUKUI; Librarian HACHIRO CHIKURA; publ. *Review of Studies* (in Japanese, 1 a year).

Osaka College of Music: 1-1-8, Shonai-saiwaimaohi, Toyonaka City, Osaka 561-8555; tel. (6) 6334-2131; fax (6) 6333-0286; e-mail info@daion.ac.jp; internet www.daion.ac.jp; f. 1915; courses in composition, vocal music and instrumental music; library: 123,500 vols; 376 teachers; 1,171 students; Pres. NOBUO NISHIOKA.

Tama Art University: 3-15-34 Kaminoge, Setagaya-ku, Tokyo 158; tel. (3) 3702-1141; fax 03-702-2235; e-mail pro@tamabi.ac.jp; internet www.tamabi.ac.jp; f. 1935; undergraduate division established 1953; departments within the Faculty of Art and Design: ceramic, glass and metal works; environmental design; graphic design; information design; art science; painting; product and textile design; sculpture; 415 teachers; 4,718 students, incl. 3,491 undergraduates and 235 graduates; Pres. SHIRO TAKAHASHI.

Toho Gakuen School of Music: 41-1 1-chome, Wakaba-cho, Chofu-shi, Tokyo 182-8510; tel. (3) 3307-4101; fax (3) 3307-4354; internet www.tohomusic.ac.jp; f. 1961; 83 teachers; 1,400 students; library: 133,000 vols; Pres. T. TSUTSUMI.

Tokyo College of Music: 3-4-5, Minami-Ikebukuro, Toshima-ku, Tokyo 171-8540; tel. (3) 3982-3186; fax (3) 3982-2883; internet www.tokyo-ondai.ac.jp; f. 1907; 1,702 students; library: 130,000 vols, 11,300 CDs; Pres. YOSHIO UNNO.

Ueno Gakuen University: Department of Music, Faculty of Music and Cultural Studies, 24-12 Higashi-Ueno 4-chome, Taito-ku, Tokyo 110-8642; tel. (3) 3842-1021; fax (3) 3843-7548; e-mail info@uenogakuen.ac.jp; internet www.uenogakuen.ac.jp; f. 1904; library: 175,000 vols; 184 teachers; 580 students; Pres. Prof. HIRO ISHIBASHI.

JORDAN

The Higher Education System

In 1920 Jordan (formerly Transjordan) became a League of Nations mandate under British administration. The mandate was terminated in 1946 and Jordan became an independent sovereign state. Wars with Israel in 1948 and 1967 led to an influx of Palestinian refugees; moreover, after the Six Day War (1967) Jerusalem and the West Bank fell wholly under Israeli control. Until 1967 the oldest institution of higher education in Jordan was Birzeit University in the West Bank, which was founded as a school in 1924, added post-secondary courses in 1953 and became a two-year junior college in 1961. However, after 1967 Birzeit University came under Israeli jurisdiction and since 1994 has been part of the Palestinian (National) Authority (PA). The oldest university is now the University of Jordan (founded 1962). The Ministry of Higher Education and Scientific Research and the Council of Higher Education are the bodies responsible for higher education, which consists of public and private universities. In addition, there are approximately 40 community colleges offering diploma-level post-secondary programmes of study. In 2009 there were 23 public and private universities with approximately 220,000 students enrolled. Enrollment in higher education was growing rapidly; the projected number of students entering university was 92,000 per year by 2013, up from 50,469 in 2005.

Universities admissions operate on the basis of the General Secondary Examination. Jordanian universities operate a US-style 'credit semester' system, under which students are required to accumulate a given number of credits each semester in order to graduate. The standard undergraduate Bachelors degree is a four-year programme of study and requires at least 132 credits. Degrees in professional fields of study, such as medicine, engineering and dentistry, may last from five to six years. In 2005 the Council of Higher Education introduced the University Achievement Examination, to be taken by all undergraduates in the final year of the Bachelors degree. The purpose of this examination is to develop a standard measure for evaluating students and courses at both public and private institutions on a subject by subject basis. Success in this examination leads to the award of the University Achievement Examination Qualification Certificate. There are three post-graduate degrees: the Higher Diploma, Masters and Doctor of Philosophy. The Higher Diploma is a one- to three-year course in a professional field of study. The Masters is often a two-year course requiring at least 33 credits. Finally, the Doctor of Philosophy lasts for three to five years, and is a combination of both coursework and original research. The full scope of postgraduate degrees is only available at public universities.

Post-secondary vocational and technical education is serviced in the main by community colleges. There are also accredited workplace-based training schemes. Courses at community colleges last two to three years, require at least 66 credits for completion and lead to the award of a Diploma. All public community colleges are affiliated to Al-Balqa' Applied University. In 1999 a law was passed establishing a five-tier framework for post-secondary non-university education, graded Semi-Skilled, Skilled, Craftsman, Technician and Professional.

As a part of the Ministry of Higher Education and Scientific Research, the Accreditation Council was responsible for quality assurance until June 2007 when it was dissolved and the Higher Education Accreditation Commission was set up in its place. The Commission Council consists of a president, a vice-president, two full-time members, and three part-time members. In 2006 Jordan signed the Catania Declaration to put into place a "Euro-mediterranean Higher Education Area" which seeks to carry out the directives of the Barcelona Declaration of 1995, which later became the Bologna Process. In 2007 a number of priorities were highlighted to bring Jordan's higher education system into line with the European model.

The Higher Education Reform for Knowledge Economy, a project to improve the higher education system in Jordan through policy reforms, was approved in 2009. It was expected to be fully completed by December 2015.

Regulatory and Representative Bodies

GOVERNMENT

Council of Higher Education: Ministry of Higher Education and Scientific Research, POB 35262, Amman; tel. (6) 5347671; fax (6) 5337616; e-mail mohe@mohe.gov.jo; internet www.mohe.gov.jo; f. 1982; controls the devt of private higher education and ensures that minimum standards are maintained; Chair. THE MINISTER OF HIGHER EDUCATION AND SCIENTIFIC RESEARCH.

Ministry of Culture: POB 6140, Amman; tel. (6) 5696218; fax (6) 5696598; e-mail info@culture.gov.jo; internet www.culture.gov.jo; Minister NANCY BAKIR.

Ministry of Education: POB 1646, Amman 11118; tel. (6) 5607181; fax (6) 5666019; e-mail moe@moe.gov.jo; internet www.moe.gov.jo; Minister TAYSEER NUEIMI.

Ministry of Higher Education and Scientific Research: POB 35262, Amman; tel. (6) 5347671; fax (6) 5337616; e-mail mohe@mohe.gov.jo; internet www.mohe.gov.jo; Minister Dr OMAR SHDEIFAT.

ACCREDITATION

Higher Education Accreditation Commission: POB 138, Amman 11941; tel. (6) 5347671; fax (6) 5354562; e-mail a_hunaiti@mohe.gov.jo; f. 2007; Pres. ABDELRAHIM A. HUNAITI.

Learned Societies

GENERAL

Aal Albayt Foundation for Islamic Thought: POB 950361, Amman 11195; tel. (6) 4633642; fax (6) 4633887; e-mail aalal-bayt@rhc.jo; internet www.aalalbayt.org; f. 1980; research is divided into 2 main categories: long-term projects such as the issuing of the *Encyclopedia of Arab Islamic Civilization*, the *Comprehensive Catalogue of Arab Islamic MSS*, the *Annotated Bibliographies of Islamic Economy and Islamic Education* and the Great Tafsirs project; and medium-term projects dealing with contemporary Muslim life and thought; 130 mems from 42 countries; library of 26,146 vols, 562 periodicals; special collns: Hashemite and Jordanian Collns; Dir FARUK JARRAR; Librarian NOUZAT ABU LABAN.

UNESCO Office Amman: POB 2270, Amman 11181; Wadi Saqra St, Amman 11181; tel. (6) 5516559; fax (6) 5532183; e-mail amman@unesco.org; f. 1973; Dir MOHAMED DJELID.

BIBLIOGRAPHY, LIBRARY SCIENCE AND MUSEOLOGY

Jordan Library and Information Association: POB 6289, Amman; tel. (6) 4629412; fax (6) 4629412; internet www.jorla.org; f. 1963; 600 mems; Pres. FADIL KLAYB; Sec. YOUSRA ABU AJAMIEH; publs *Directory of the Libraries in Jordan, Directory of Periodicals in Jordan, Jordanian National Bibliography 1979–, Palestinian Bibliography, Palestinian-Jordanian Bibliography, Rissalat al-Maktaba* (The Message of the Library, 4 a year).

LANGUAGE AND LITERATURE

British Council: First Circle, Jebel Amman, POB 634, Amman 11118; tel. (6) 4603420; fax (6) 4656413; e-mail info@britishcouncil.org.jo; internet www.britishcouncil.org/jordan.htm; teaching centre; offers courses and examinations in English language and British culture and promotes cultural exchange with the UK; Dir TIM GORE.

Goethe Institut Jordanien: POB 1676, Amman 11118; 5 Abdel Mun'im Al Rifa'i St, Amman 11118; tel. (6) 4641993; fax (6)

4612383; e-mail info@amman.goethe.org; internet www.goethe.de/na/amm/enindex .htm; offers courses and exams in German language and culture and promotes cultural exchange with Germany; library of 3,000 vols; Dir Dr CHRISTIANE KRÄMER-HUS-HUS.

Instituto Cervantes: Mohammad Hafiz Ma'ath St 10, POB 815467, Amman 11180; tel. (6) 4610858; fax (6) 4624049; e-mail cenamm@cervantes.es; internet amman .cervantes.es; offers courses and examinations in Spanish language and culture and promotes cultural exchange with Spain and Spanish-speaking Latin and Central America; library of 14,000 vols; Dir MARÍA CARMEN ORDÓÑEZ CARVAJAL.

NATURAL SCIENCES
Biological Sciences

Royal Marine Conservation Society of Jordan: POB 831051, Amman 11183; tel. (6) 5676173; fax (6) 5676183; e-mail information@jreds.org; internet www.jreds .org; f. 1993; conservation and sustainable use of the marine environment through conservation programmes, advocacy, education, outreach and empowerment; 250 mems; Exec. Dir FADI SHARAIHA.

Research Institutes

AGRICULTURE, FISHERIES AND VETERINARY SCIENCE

National Center for Agricultural Research and Extension: POB 226, Amman; internet www.ncartt.gov.jo; f. 1958 as Dept of Agricultural and Scientific Research and Extension; 1985 became the National Center for Agricultural Research and Technology Transfer; present name 2007; covers all branches of agricultural research, information and extension; library of 18,500 vols; Dir SAID GHEZAWI.

HISTORY, GEOGRAPHY AND ARCHAEOLOGY

Council for British Research in the Levant: POB 519, Jubaiha, Amman 11941; tel. (6) 5341317; fax (6) 5337197; e-mail info@ cbrl.org.uk; internet www.cbrl.org.uk; f. 1996 as the merger of the British Institute in Amman for Archaeology and History with the British School of Archaeology in Jerusalem; supports British post-doctoral research in social sciences and the contemporary Levant; provides some limited grant funding and a hostel, library and laboratory facilities to members; 296 individual mems, 27 institutional mems; library of 24,000 vols, divided between Amman and Jerusalem; Dir Dr ALEX BELLAM; publs *Levant* (1 a year), *Bulletin* (1 a year), *Levant Supplementary Series* (monograph series).

TECHNOLOGY

Royal Scientific Society: POB 1438, Al-Jubaiha 11941; tel. (6) 5344701; fax (6) 5344806; e-mail rssinfo@rss.gov.jo; internet www.rss.gov.jo; f. 1970; independent, non-profit industrial research and development centre; electronic services and training centre, computer systems, mechanical engineering, chemical industry, building research centre, economics, wind and solar energy research centre; 10 technical centres housing 38 specialized laboratories; library: see Libraries and Archives; Exec. Vice-Pres. Dr SEYFEDDIN MUAZ.

Libraries and Archives
Amman

Abdul Hameed Shoman Public Library: POB 940255, Amman 11194; tel. (6) 4633627; fax (6) 4633565; e-mail library@shoman.org; internet www.shoman.org; f. 1986; 120,000 vols, 1,200 periodicals; Librarian EMAD ABU-EID.

Greater Amman Public Library: POB 182181, Amman; tel. (6) 4627718; fax (6) 4649420; f. 1960; 257,179 vols in Arabic and English; 500,000 vols, 256 current periodicals; 31 brs for adults and children, Deposit Library for UNESCO (5,000 vols); Jordanian publications; Chief Officer MOHAMED AL-KFA-WIN.

National Library: POB 6070, Amman 11118; 9 Haroun al-Rasheed St, Amman 11118; tel. (6) 5662845; fax (6) 5662865; e-mail nl@nl.gov.jo; internet www.nl.gov.jo; f. 1994; prepares and issues the nat. bibliography and union catalogue; responsible for copyrights and legal deposits; responsible for enforcing Jordanian copyright law; depository for nat., UNESCO and WIPO publs; 123,076 vols, 49,784 titles; Dir-Gen. MAMOUN THARWAT TALHOUNI.

El Hassan Library and Media Centre, Princess Sumaya University for Technology: POB 1438, Amman; tel. (6) 5359949; fax (6) 5347295; e-mail info@psut.edu.jo; internet www.psut.edu.jo; f. 2004; core collection includes energy, civil engineering, construction, industrial chemistry, mechanical engineering, computer science, economics, electronics; 72,000 vols, 106 periodical titles, 200 theses, 2,000 non-print media, 450 maps, 15,000 specifications; online service from Dialog, BRS, Infoline; Dir Dr NERMEEN SHUQOM.

University of Jordan Library: University of Jordan, Amman; tel. (6) 5355000; fax (6) 5355570; e-mail library@ju.edu.jo; internet library.ju.edu.jo; f. 1962; 789,000 vols, 350 current Arabic periodicals, 19,977 online periodicals, mainly in English; 15 reading rooms; legal deposit for UN, WHO, FAO, World Bank, UNESCO, IMF, SIPRI, UNU, ILO, Institute for Peace Research documents; legal deposit for dissertations from all Arab universities; Dir Dr MOHAMMAD RAQAB; publs *Bibliographical list and indexes* (irregular), Directory for Theses Deposited at University Library (2 a year), *Library Guide* (1 a year).

Irbid

Irbid Public Library: POB 348, Irbid; f. 1957; 30,000 vols; Librarian ANWAR ISHAQ AL-NSHIWAT.

Museums and Art Galleries
Amman

Folklore Museum: POB 88, Amman; housed by the Department of Antiquities; f. 1972; colln of nat. traditional costumes; Curator Mrs SA'DIYA AL-TEL.

Jordan Archaeological Museum: POB 88, Amman; tel. (6) 46319768; fax (6) 46319768; e-mail doa@nic.net.jo; f. 1951; 13,000 objects, 36,000 coins; 20 staff; library of 3,560 vols; Curator AIDA NAGHAURY.

Museum of Popular Traditions: POB 88, Amman; f. 1971; local domestic history; brs in Petra, Madaba, Salt and Kerak; Curator IMAN QUDA.

Universities

AL-AHLIYYA AMMAN UNIVERSITY

Al-Ahliyya Amman Univ. PO, Amman 19328

Telephone: (5) 3500211
Fax: (6) 5336104
E-mail: info@ammanu.edu.jo
Internet: www.ammanu.edu.jo

Founded 1990
Private control
Language of instruction: Arabic,
Language of instruction: English

Pres.: Prof. Dr MAHER SALIM

DEANS

Faculty of Administrative and Financial Science: Dr HUSSEIN EL-YASEEN
Faculty of Arts: Dr WAFA EL-KHADRA
Faculty of Engineering: Prof. Dr SADIQ HAMED
Faculty of Information Technology: Dr MUSTAFA YASEEN
Faculty of Law: Dr OMAR EL-BOURINI
Faculty of Nursing: Prof. Dr WASEELA PETRO
Faculties of Pharmacy and Medical Sciences: Dr MAHER SHORBAJI

AL-BALQA' APPLIED UNIVERSITY

POB 19117, Al-Salt, Al-Balqa' Governorate

Telephone: (5) 349111
Fax: (5) 353231
E-mail: davana@bau.edu.jo
Internet: www.bau.edu.jo

Founded 1997
State control

There are 14 affiliated univ. colleges and around 36 affiliated private, military and UN-operated colleges

Pres.: Prof. Dr OMAR ABDALKARIM RIMAWI
Vice-Pres.: Prof. ABDALLAH S. AL-ZOUBI
Vice-Pres.: Prof. NAIM M. ALJOUNI
Dean of Student Affairs: Dr HAMDAN AWAM-LEH
Librarian: NIDAL AL-AHMAD

Library of 38,500 vols
Number of teachers: 1,460
Number of students: 45,000

DEANS

Faculty of Agricultural Technology: Dr YASIN ALZU'BI
Faculty of Engineering: Dr MAHER KHAKISH
Faculty of Graduate Studies and Scientific Research: Dr GHANDI ANFOKA
Faculty of Planning and Management: JIHAD ABU AL SONDOS
Faculty of Science and Information Technology: Dr IBRAHIM HAMARNEH

AL AL-BAYT UNIVERSITY

POB 130040, Mafraq 25113

Telephone: (2) 6297000
Fax: (2) 6297021
E-mail: programmer@aabu.edu.jo
Internet: www.aabu.edu.jo

Founded 1993
State control

Pres.: Prof. NABIL T. SHAWAGFEH
Vice-Pres. for Admin. and Finance: Prof. JIHAD SHAHER AL-MAJALI
Registrar: QFTAN AL-MONANI

Library of 164,890 vols, 121 periodicals
Number of teachers: 200
Number of students: 11,733

Publications: *Al-Manara* (Journal of Academic Research, English and Arabic, 4 a year), *Al-Zahra* (English and Arabic, 12 a year)

DEANS

College for Information Technology: Prof. ADNAN M. AL-SMADI

Faculty of Arts and Humanities: Prof. FAWWAZ M. AL-ABED AL-HAQ

Faculty of Educational Sciences: Prof. YAHYA SHDIFAT

Faculty of Finance and Business Administration: Dr SALEM AL-OUN

Faculty of Islamic Jurisprudence and Law: Dr ZIAD AL-DAGAM

Faculty of Nursing: Dr INSAF SHABAN

Faculty of Science: Dr HASAN TASHTOUSH

AL-HUSSEIN BIN TALAL UNIVERSITY

POB 20, Ma'an

Telephone: (3) 2179000

Fax: (3) 2179050

E-mail: ahu@go.com.jo

Internet: www.ahu.edu.jo

Founded 1999

State control

Pres.: ALI KHALAF AL-HROOT

Dean of Academic Research: Prof. KAMAL AYOUB MOMANI

Number of teachers: 58

Number of students: 1,948

Publication: Al-Haq Ya'lu (2 a year)

DEANS

College of Archaeology, Tourism and Hotel Management: Prof. HANI HAYAJNEH

College of Arts: Dr TAISIR KHALIL EL-ZAWAREH

College of Business Administration and Economics: (vacant)

College of Computer Engineering and Information Technology: Dr FARES FRAIJ

College of Education: Dr MONA ALI ABU DARWESH

College of Mining and Environmental Engineering: Dr MARWAN BATIHA

College of Science: Dr ALI MAHMUD ATEIWI

AL-ISRA PRIVATE UNIVERSITY

POB 22/33, Amman 11622

Telephone: (6) 4711710

Fax: (6) 4711505

E-mail: info@isra.edu.jo

Internet: www.isra.edu.jo

Founded 1991

Private control

Language of instruction: Arabic,

Language of instruction: English

Pres.: ABDUL BARI DURA

Vice-Pres.: NAYEF KHARMA

Dean of Research: GHANEM EL-HASAWI

Dean of Student Affairs: HOSNI AL-SHEYYIB

DEANS

Faculty of Administrative and Financial Sciences: MUSA ALMADHOON

Faculty of Engineering: AHMAD AL-FAHED NUSEIRAT

Faculty of Law: AHMED ABU SHANAB

Faculties of Pharmacy and Medical Sciences: MAZEN QATTO

Faculty of Science and Information Technology: AYMAN AL-NSOUR

AL-ZAYTOONAH UNIVERSITY

POB 130, Amman 11733

Telephone: (6) 591600

Fax: (6) 591571

E-mail: information@alzaytoonah.edu.jo

Internet: www.alzaytoonah.edu.jo

Founded 1993

Private control

Language of instruction: Arabic,

Language of instruction: English

Pres.: Prof. NASR SALEH

Number of teachers: 300

Number of students: 8,000

DEANS

Faculty of Arts: ISAM MAHMOOD ABU SALEEM

Faculty of Economics and Administrative Science: GHALIB AWAD RIFA'I

Faculty of Law: HUSSEIN ATTA HAMDAN

Faculties of Nursing: AHLAM YOUSSEF HAMDAN

Faculty of Pharmacy: SAYYED ISMAIL MOHAMMAD

Faculty of Science: ABDEL FATAH ARIF TAMIMI

APPLIED SCIENCE UNIVERSITY

POB 926296, Amman 11931

Telephone: (6) 5609999

Fax: (6) 5232899

E-mail: info@aspu.edu.jo

Internet: www.aspu.edu.jo

Private control

Language of instruction: Arabic,

Language of instruction: English

Chair.: ABDALLAH ABU KHADEJEH

Pres.: ZEYAD RAMADAN

DEANS

College of Arts: KAYED QUR'OUSH

College of Basic Science: TALAL AL-ALLAF

College of Economics and Business Administration: SAAD AL-SAAD

College of Engineering: BASSAM AL-ASEER

College of Law: YUSSEF ATARTI

College of Medical Science: RULA AL-KHUZAIE

College of Pharmacy: LU'AY RASHAN

THE HASHEMITE UNIVERSITY

POB 150459, Zarqa 13115

Telephone: (5) 3903333

Fax: (5) 3826613

E-mail: huniv@hu.edu.jo

Internet: www.hu.edu.jo

Founded 1992

State control

Pres.: Prof. SULAIMAN ARABIAT

Vice-Pres: Prof. SULTAN ABU TAYEH, Prof. MOHAMAD HIYASSAT, Prof. SALEH AL-OQEILLI

Dean of Student Affairs: Prof. ADNAN HAYAJNEH

Librarian: MOHAMMAD T. S. D. DARWISH

Library of 120,000 vols, 5,000 periodicals

Number of teachers: 329

Number of students: 9,254

DEANS

Faculty of Allied Health Sciences: Prof. ABDELFATTAH SHIHADA

Faculty for Childhood: Prof. MAHMOUD WEHER

Faculty of Economics and Administrative Science: Prof. KHALED ABDELAL

Faculty of Educational Sciences: Prof. SIHAM ABU EITA

Faculty of Engineering: Prof. HASAN TANTAWI

Faculty of Information Technology: Prof. SALEH AL-OQEILLI

Faculty of Literature: Prof. NEDAL AL-MOUSA

Faculty of Medicine: Prof. MADI JAGHABIR

Faculty of Natural Resources and Environment: Prof. EID AL-TARAZ

Faculty of Nursing: Prof. MAJD T. MRAYYAN

Faculty of Physical Education and Sports Sciences: Prof. HAZIM AL-NAHAR

Faculty of Research and Graduate Studies: Prof. MOUSA MOHSEN

Faculty of Sciences: Prof. KHALED ABU ELTEEN

UNIVERSITY OF JORDAN

Amman 11942

Telephone: (6) 5355000

Fax: (6) 5355522

E-mail: admin@ju.edu.jo

Internet: www.ju.edu.jo

Founded 1962

State and autonomous control

Languages of instruction: Arabic, English

Academic year: September to August (two semesters and a summer session)

Pres.: KHALED AL-KARAKI

Dir of Registration and Admission: GHALEB AL-HOURANI

Dir of the Library: Dr HANI AL-AMAD

Number of teachers: 931

Number of students: 23,623

Publication: Dirasat (scientific research)

DEANS

Faculty of Agriculture: Prof. MOHAMMED ISAM YAMAMI

Faculty of Arts: Dr SALAMEH NAIMT

Faculty of Arts and Design: Dr ABDUL-HAMEED HAMAM

Faculty of Business: Prof. HANI AL-DMOUR

Faculty of Dentistry: Prof. LAMIS RAJAB

Faculty of Educational Sciences: Prof. MOHAMMAD NAZIH HAMDI

Faculty of Engineering and Technology: Prof. RAED M. SAMRA

Faculty of Foreign Languages: Prof. AHMAD MAJDOUBEH

Faculty of Graduate Studies: Prof. MUNA S. AL-HADIDI

Faculty of International Studies: Prof. ABDULLAH NAGRASH

Faculty of Law: Prof. GEORGE HAZBOUN

Faculty of Medicine: Dr SLAM SALEH DARADKEH

Faculty of Nursing: Dr INAAM KHALAF

Faculty of Pharmacy: Dr KHALED M. AIEDEH

Faculty of Physical Education: Prof. SUHA ADEEB DAOUD

Faculty of Rehabilitation Sciences: Prof. BASSAM AMMARI

Faculty of Science: Dr HALA KHYAMI-HORANI

Faculty of Shari'a (Islamic Studies): Prof. MOHAMMAD KHAZER AL-MAJALI

King Abdullah II Faculty for Information Technology: Dr FAWAZ AHMAD M. MASOUD AL-ZAGHOUL

JORDAN UNIVERSITY OF SCIENCE AND TECHNOLOGY (JUST)

POB 3030, Irbid 22110

Telephone: (2) 7201000

Fax: (2) 7095123

E-mail: just@just.edu.jo

Internet: www.just.edu.jo

Founded 1986

State control

Languages of instruction: Arabic, English

Academic year: September to September

Pres.: Prof. WAJIH M. OWAIS

Dean of Research: Prof. FAWZI BANAT

Dir of Public Relations: MUHANNAD MALKAWI

Registrar: FAISAL AL RIFAIE

Librarian: ISSA LELLO

Library of 90,000 vols

Number of teachers: 750

Number of students: 18,850 undergraduate and 1,559 graduate students

DEANS

College of Architecture and Design: Dr NATHEER ABU OBEID

Faculty of Agriculture: Prof. MUNIR J. RUSAN

Faculty of Applied Medical Sciences: Prof. LAILA NIMRI

Faculty of Computer Information Technology: Dr MOHAMMAD AL-ROUSAN

Faculty of Dentistry: Prof. ANWAH BATAINEH
Faculty of Engineering: Prof. KHALED A. MAYYAS
Faculty of Medicine: Prof. KAMAL E. BANI-HANI
Faculty of Nursing: Dr MUNTAHA GHARAIBEH
Faculty of Pharmacy: Dr KHOULOUD ALKHAMIS
Faculty of Science and Arts: Prof. AHMED M. ELBETIEHA
Faculty of Veterinary Medicine: Prof. SAEB AL-SUKHON

MU'TAH UNIVERSITY

POB 7, Mu'tah, Al Karak 61710
Telephone: (3) 2372380
Fax: (3) 2375540Amman Liaison Office: POB 5076, Amman
Telephone: (6) 4617860
Fax: (6) 4654061
E-mail: hunaiti@hu.edu.jo
Internet: www.mutah.edu.jo
Founded 1981
State control
Languages of instruction: Arabic, English
Academic year: September to June
Pres.: Prof. Dr ABDELRAHIM A. HUMAITI
Vice-Pres. for Academic Affairs: Prof. MOHAMMAD ABBADI
Vice-Pres. for Admin. Affairs: Prof. QUBLAN AL-MAJALI
Vice-Pres. for Humanities and Science: Prof. MOHANNAD AMIN ABBADI
Vice-Pres. for Military Affairs: ESMAEL E. AL-SHOBAKI
Dean for Academic Research: Prof. MOHAMMAD AL-TARAWNEH
Dean for Graduate Studies: Prof. NIDAL HAWAMDEH
Dean for Student Affairs: Prof. AHMAD BATTAH
Dir of Cultural and Public Affairs: JAZA' MOHAMMAD AL-MASARWEH
Registrar: YASER KASASBEH
Librarian: Dr ABDEL WAHAB MOBIDEEN
Library of 534,753 vols
Number of teachers: 530
Number of students: 16,000
Publication: Mu'tah Journal for Research and Studies

DEANS

Faculty of Agriculture: Dr AMER MAMKAGH
Faculty of Arts: Prof. HUSSAM ALDEEN MUBAIDEEN
Faculty of Business Administration: Dr FAHAD S. KHATEEB
Faculty of Education: Prof. MOHAMMAD RABABAA
Faculty of Engineering: Prof. AYMAN AL-MAAYTEH
Faculty of Law: Dr NIZAM AL-MAJALI
Faculty of Medicine: Prof. ADEL ABU AL-HAIJA
Faculty of Nursing: Prof. SAMEER AL-TAWEEL
Faculty of Physical Education: Prof. MOUTASEM SHATNAWI
Faculty of Sciences: Prof. MAHDI LATAIFEH
Faculty of Shari'ah: Prof. NAEL ABU ZAID
Faculty of Social Sciences: Prof. IBRAHIM AL-OROUD

PHILADELPHIA UNIVERSITY

POB 1, Amman 11932
Telephone: (2) 6374444
Fax: (2) 6374440
Internet: www.philadelphia.edu.jo
Founded 1989
Languages of instruction: Arabic, English
Vice-Pres.: ABDEL RAHIM HUNAITI
Dean of Scientific Research: RAED ABU ZITAR
Dean of Student Affairs: GHASSAN ABDEL KHALEQ

Dir of Admissions: Dr KHALDOUN M. BATIHA

DEANS

Faculty of Administrative and Financial Sciences: MARWA AHMAD
Faculty of Arts: SALEH ABU ISBAA
Faculty of Engineering: IBRAHIM BADRAN
Faculty of Information Technology: MOHAMMAD BETTAZ
Faculty of Law: GHAZI SABARINI
Faculty of Pharmacy: ADI ARIDA
Faculty of Science: ELIAS SALIBA

PRINCESS SUMAYA UNIVERSITY FOR TECHNOLOGY

POB 1438, Al-Jubaiha 11941
Telephone: (6) 5359967
Fax: (6) 5347295
E-mail: info@psut.edu.jo
Internet: www.psut.edu.jo
Founded 1991
Private control
Pres.: Prof. HISHAM GHASSIB
Librarian: NERMEEN SHUQOM
Library of 68,000 vols
Number of teachers: 10 teachers
Number of students: 120 students

DEANS

King Abdullah II School For Electrical Engineering: Prof. BASSAM KAHHALEH
King Hussein School for Information Technology: Prof. YAHIA AL-HALABI
King Abdullah II School For Electrical Engineering: Prof. BASSAM KAHHALEH

UNIVERSITY OF PETRA

POB 961343, Amman 11196
Telephone: (6) 5799555
Fax: (6) 5715570
E-mail: registrar@uop.edu.jo
Internet: www.uop.edu.jo
Founded 1991 as Jordan Univ. for Women
Languages of instruction: Arabic, English
Private control
Pres.: Prof. ADNAN BADRAN
Vice-Pres. for Academic Affairs and Dean of Research and Graduate Studies: Prof. NIZAR EL-RAYYES
Dean of Admissions and Registration: Dr NASER AL-JARNAL
Dean of Student Affairs: Dr MOUHAMAD EL-KASASBEH
Library of 91,411 vols, 65,387 titles, 52,000 e-books
Number of teachers: 266
Number of students: 6,000
Publications: Al-Basair (scientific journal, 2 a year), Awraq Jamie'ya (2 a year)

DEANS

Faculty of Administrative and Financial Services: Dr RAFIQ OMAR
Faculty of Architecture and Arts: Dr AHMAD ABDEL-JAWAD
Faculty of Arts and Sciences: Prof. MOHAMMAD ISHAQ AL-ANANI
Faculty of Information Technology: Dr GASSAN ISSA
Faculty of Pharmacy and Medical Sciences: Prof. TAWFEEQ ARAFAT

YARMOUK UNIVERSITY

POB 566, Irbid 21163
Telephone: (2) 7211111
Fax: (2) 7211199
E-mail: yarmouk@yu.edu.jo
Internet: www.yu.edu.jo
Founded 1975
National and autonomous control

Languages of instruction: Arabic, English
Academic year: October to June
Pres.: Prof. Dr FAYEZ I. KHASAWNEH
Vice-Pres. for Academic Affairs: Prof. Dr HISHAM S. GHARAIBEH
Vice-Pres. for Admin. Affairs: Prof. Dr MOHAMMED S. SUBBARINI
Registrar: ZACHARIAH ABU-ALDAHAB
Librarian: Dr MOHAMMAD SARAYRAH
Library: Central Library of 300,000 vols, 800 current periodicals
Number of teachers: 687
Number of students: 21,205
Publications: Abhath al-Yarmouk (Yarmouk Research Journal), Yarmouk Numismatics (journal)

DEANS

Faculty of Archaeology and Anthropology: Prof. ZAIDON AL-MUHASIN
Faculty of Arts: Prof. FAHMI GHAZWI
Faculty of Economics and Administrative Sciences: Prof. WALEED HMEDAT
Faculty of Education: Prof. YOUSEF SAWALMEH
Hijjawi Faculty of Engineering Technology: Prof. FAROQ AL-OMARY
Faculty of Fine Arts: Prof. KHALID AL-HAMZEH
Faculty of Information Technology: Prof. SULEIMAN MUSTAFA
Faculty of Law: Dr AYMEN MASADEH
Faculty of Physical Education: Prof. Dr ALI AL-DEIRY
Faculty of Science: Prof. IBRAHIM ABU AL-JARAIESH
Faculty of Shari'a (Islamic Law): Dr MUHAMMAD AL-OMARI

PROFESSORS

ABDUL-ALMAJED, M., Usul al-Din
ABDUL-HAFEZ, S., Biology
ABDULHAY, W., Political Science
ABDUL-RAHMAN, A., Arabic
ABO-ZEID, M., Electronic Engineering
ABU AL-JARAYESH, I., Physics
ABU HELOU, Y., Education
ABU-HILAL, A., Geology
ABU-RAHMAH, K., Arabic
ABU-SALEH, M., Statistics
ABUL-UDOUSS, Y., Arabic
ADWAN, Y., Public Administration
AL-ADWAN, S., Chemistry
AL-AHMADI, A., Usul al-Din
ALARAIBI, M., Fine Arts
ALAWNEH, S., Education Psychology
AL-FAYOUMI, I., Arabic
AL-HAQ, F., Linguistics
AL-HASSAN, K., Chemistry
AL-HASSAN, S., English
AL-HIARY, H., Education
AL-JUBOORY, K., Epigraphy
AL-KATIB, R., Education
AL-KAYSI, M., Islamic Studies
AL-MUHEISEN, Z., Archaeology
AL-NOURI, Q., Anthropology
AL-QUDAH, M., Chemistry
AL-QURAISH, T., Semitic and Oriental Languages
AL-SAADI, W., Public Law
AL-SALEM, H., Physical Education
AL-SALIM, M., Business Administration
AL-SHEIKH, K., Arabic
AL-SHMAI, F., Private Law
AL-TELL, SH., Education
ARAJI, A., Public Administration
AREDAH, F., Sports Science
ASFAR, O., Engineering Science and Mechanics
ATHAMNEH, N., English
ATIYYAT, A., Chemistry
ATOUM, A., Education
AWAD, A., History
AYYOUB, N., Physics
BADER, Y., Linguistics
BAKKAR, Y., Arabic

BANI HANI, A., Economics
BARQAWI, K., Chemistry
BATAYNEH, M., History
DAIRY, A., Physical Education
DARABSEH, M., Arabic
DWAIRI, I., Geology
ESMADI, F., Chemistry
FAOURI, R., Public Administration
FARGHAL, M., English
FATAFTAH, Z., Chemistry
FORA, A., Mathematics
GHARAIBEH, H., Banking and Finance
GHARAIBEH, S., Geology
GHAWANMEH, Y., History
GHAZWI, F., Sociology
GHAZZAWI, M., Education
HADDAD, H., Arabic
HADDAD, M., Anthropology
HADDAD, N., Arabic
HAJ-HUSSEIN, A. T., Chemistry
HAMAD, A., Arabic
HAMAM, A., Music
HAMDAN, A., Linguistics
HAMMAD, KH., Economics
HIJAZI, M., Usul al-Din
HIJJEH, M., Mathematics
HMEDAT, W., Economics
HUNAITI, A., Biology
IDRES, A., Fiqh
JIBRIL, I., Chemistry
KAFAFI, Z., Archaeology
KHARBUTLI, M., English
KHASAWNEH, F., Biology
KHASAWNEH, I., Chemistry
KHATEEB, A., Education
KHAWALDEH, M., Education
KHRAIWISH, H., Arabic
KOFAHI, M., Physics
KURDI, Z., Physical Education
LAHAM, N., Physics
LAHHAM, J., Biology
MADAN, K., Statistics
MAHADIN, R., Linguistics
MAHMOUD, S., Physics
MAKKI, A., Electrical Power Engineering
MARI, T. A., Education
MASHAGBAH, F., English
MOMANI, Q., Arabic
MOMANI, R., Economics
MOMANI, R., Islamic Economy
MRYYAN, N., Economics
NAFI, A., Arabic
NAJJAR, M., Anthropology
NUSAIR, N., Public Administration
ODEH, A., Education

OGLAH, A., Biology
OLAIMAT, M., Education
OLWAN, M., Law
OMARI, M, Usul al-Din
OWEIS, W., Biology
QASSEM, W., Biomechanics
QUDAH, S., Arabic
QUTTOUS, B., Arabic
RABABAH, M., Arabic
RABBA'I, A., Arabic
RASHID, M., Chemistry
RAWI, Z., Statistics
RAYYAN, M., History
REFAI, M., Mathematics
REFAIE, S., Electronic Engineering
RHAYYEL, A., Mathematics
SABBAGH, Z., Business Administration
SADEDDIN, W., Geology
SADIQ, M., Fine Arts
SAFA, F., Arabic
SALEM, A., Physics
SALHIEH, M., History
SARI, S., Archaeology
SERYANI, M., Geography
SHARE'E, M., Economics
SHARI, A., Arabic
SHAYEB, F., Arabic
SHORFAT, M., Linguistics
SMADI, A., Education Psychology
STATIYYEH, S., Arabic
SUBBARINI, M., Education
SULEIMAN, I., Journalism
TALAFHA, H., Economics
TALIB, M., Chemistry
TASHTOUSH, H., Chemistry
THALJI, A., English
UGAILI, S., Computer Science
UGLAH, M., Fiqh and Islamic Studies
WARDAT, R., Linguistics
WAZARMAS, I., Physical Education
YOUNIS, M., Mathematics
YUSUF, N., Physics
ZAGHAL, A., Sociology
ZAGHAL, M., Chemistry
ZIADAT, A., Journalism
ZUBI, A., Arabic
ZUGHOUL, M., English

ZARQA PRIVATE UNIVERSITY

POB 2000, al Zarqa 13110
Telephone: (5) 3821100
Fax: (5) 3821100
E-mail: info@zpu.edu.jo

Internet: www.zpu.edu.jo
Founded 1994
Languages of instruction: Arabic, English
Private control
Pres.: Prof. ADNAN HASAN NAYFEH
Vice-Pres. and Dean of Scientific Research: Prof. SAADI M. S. ABDUL JAWAD
Dean of Student Affairs: Dr BASSAM A. AL-BTOOSH

DEANS

Faculty of Art: ABDALLAH AWAD AL KHABASS
Faculty of Economics and Administrative Sciences: MAHMOOD HUSSEIN WADI
Faculty of Educational Sciences: MOHAMMAD ABDEL KAREEM ABU SUL
Faculty of Islamic Studies (Shari'ah): ABDALLAH AWAD AL KHABASS
Faculty of Law: MUNIR HAMID BAYATI
Faculty of Medical Sciences: MUSA TAWFIQ AQTAM
Faculty of Science: IMAD EL DIN MOHAMMAD SADIQ ABU AL RAB

Colleges

Al-Husn Polytechnic: POB 50, Al-Husn; tel. (2) 7210397; f. 1981; library: 10,000 vols; 60 teachers; 800 students; 2-year diploma courses; Dean Dr HUSEIN SARHAN.

Amman University College for Applied Engineering: POB 15008, Marka, Amman; tel. (6) 4892345; f. 1975; two-year diploma course; four-year Bachelors of Applied Engineering; library: 17,000 vols; 91 teachers; 2,000 students; Dean MOHAMMAD A. K. ALIA.

Jordan Statistical Training Centre: POB 2015, Amman; tel. (6) 4842171; fax (6) 4833518; f. 1964 for the training of government employees and other applicants in statistical methods; library: c. 700 vols; Dir ABDULHADI ALAWIN.

National Institute of Training: POB 960383, Amman; tel. (6) 4664155; fax (6) 4680731; f. 1968 as the Jordanian Institute for Public Administration; present name and status 2001; administrative training, research and consultation; library: 5,386 vols; Dir-Gen. ABDULLAH ELAYYAN.

KAZAKHSTAN

The Higher Education System

The Kazakh (formerly Kyrgyz) Autonomous Soviet Socialist Republic was founded in 1920 and became a full Union Republic of the USSR in 1936. In 1991 Kazakhstan declared independence from the USSR, and was renamed the Republic of Kazakhstan. The oldest institutions of higher education date from the Soviet period, and include Almaty Abai State University (founded 1928), Western Kazakhstan State University (founded 1932; current name and status 2000) and Al-Farabi Kazakh National University (founded 1934; current name and status 1994). The Ministry of Education and Science oversees higher education, which is governed according to the Law on Higher Education (1993). The languages of instruction are Kazakh and Russian, although Kazakhs constitute the majority of students in higher education and ethnic Russians mostly choose to attend institutions outside Kazakhstan. Among institutions offering higher education are universities, academies, institutes, conservatories, higher schools and higher vocational schools. In 2005/06 there was a total of 181 State-run higher schools (including universities), with a total enrolment of 775,800 students. Additionally, in 2003/04 there were 134 non-governmental higher education institutes with 297,900 students. In 2008/09 there were 108,000 students enrolled in professional-technical schools and 633,800 in higher education at 143 state higher schools, including universities.

Since 2004 admission to higher education has been on the basis of both the old Diploma of Completed Secondary Education and the new Unified National Testing Examination. The university awards system is moving away from the Soviet-era Specialist Diploma (undergraduate), Candidate of Sciences and Doctor of Sciences (both postgraduate) and towards the European-style Bachelors, Masters and Doctor of Philosophy (PhD) degrees. Although it is not a signatory to that agreement, Kazakhstan in effect, is implementing the Bologna Process to establish a European Higher Education Area, the first phase of which is to adopt a credit-based system of comparable degrees with two main cycles (undergraduate and graduate). The undergraduate-level Specialist Diploma is still offered in most disciplines, notably professional fields of study, and lasts up to six years. Graduates with this degree may advance straight to doctoral-level studies. The Bachelors is a four-year degree; students pursue a general programme of studies in the first two years before majoring in one subject in the final two years. Graduates with the Bachelors may then study for a Masters degree, a two-year course of study (or one year following the Specialist Diploma). The Candidate of Sciences (Aspirantura) is a research-based degree lasting two to three years, following which the student must defend a thesis. Finally, the highest university-level degree is the Doctor of Sciences, a period of study with no fixed duration, which allows the student to pursue a career in academia or research.

Technical and vocational education at post-secondary level is offered by vocational schools, technical schools and colleges. The standard entry requirement is 11–12 years of completed education or the Diploma of Completed Secondary Education. Courses leading to the award of the Diploma of Completed Vocational Secondary Education last between six months to one year. There are also vocational colleges, which administer courses of two to three years leading to the award of the Specialized Secondary Education in a professional field of study.

The National Accreditation Centre at the Ministry of Education and Science is responsible for quality assurance and accreditation, which consists of a three-stage process: licensing, attestation and accreditation. First, an institution's legal status is affirmed by the award of an operational licence. Second, a process of attestation assesses the institution's compliance with minimum educational standards defined by the Ministry of Education and Science. Third, and finally, institutions that have met the appropriate standards of quality assurance receive accreditation, which is then dependent on future five-yearly attestation processes.

Regulatory Bodies

GOVERNMENT

Ministry of Culture and Information: 010000 Astana, pr. Respubliki 24; tel. (7172) 33-32-82; e-mail prmin@mininfo.katelco.kz; internet www.sana.gov.kz; Minister YERMUKHAMET K. YERTYSBAYEV.

Ministry of Education and Science: 010000 Astana, Beibitshilik 11; tel. (7172) 75-20-27; fax (7172) 75-28-71; e-mail pressa@edu.gov.kz; internet www.edu.gov.kz; Minister ZHANSEIT K. TUIMEBAYEV.

ACCREDITATION

National Accreditation Centre: Astana, Office 504, 19 Imanova St; tel. (7172) 78-71-63; e-mail nshakhanova@mail.ru; internet nac.edu.kz; Dir NURILYA SHAKHANOVA.

Learned Societies

GENERAL

National Academy of Sciences of Kazakhstan: 050021 Almaty, Shevchenko 28; tel. (7272) 69-55-93; fax (7272) 69-57-09; f. 1947; sections of Biological and Medical Sciences, Chemical Engineering, Earth Sciences, Humanities and Social Sciences, Physical and Mathematical Sciences; attached research institutes: see Research Institutes; Pres. SERIKBEK DAUKEYEV; Sec.-Gen. MURAT MUKHAMEDZHANOV.

UNESCO Office Almaty: 480091 Almaty, Ul. Tole Bi 67, 4th Fl., UN Bldg; tel. (7272) 58-26-46; fax (7272) 69-58-63; e-mail almaty@unesco.org; internet www.unesco.kz; designated Cluster Office for Kazakhstan, Kyrgyzstan and Tajikistan; Dir (vacant).

LANGUAGE AND LITERATURE

British Council: 050013 Almaty, Republic Sq. 13; tel. (7272) 72-01-11; fax (7272) 72-01-13; e-mail general@kz.britishcouncil.org; internet www.britishcouncil.kz; offers courses and examinations in English language and British culture and promotes cultural exchange with the UK; attached office in Astana; also responsible for British Council work in Kyrgyzstan; library of 10,000 vols; Dir JAMES KENNEDY.

Goethe-Institut: 050040 Almaty, Dschandosowa 2; tel. (7272) 47-27-04; fax (7272) 47-29-72; internet www.goethe.de/oe/alm/deindex.htm; offers courses and examinations in German language and culture and promotes cultural exchange with Germany; library of 5,000 vols; Dir RICHARD KÜNZEL.

Research Institutes

AGRICULTURE, FISHERIES AND VETERINARY SCIENCE

Akmola Agricultural Research Institute: 021231 Akmola obl., Zerendinsky raion, Selo Charlinka; tel. (71172) 2-41-86; fax (71172) 2-17-33; f. 1984; Dir BAKYTZHAN ZHANAIDAROVICH KHAMZIN.

Aral Scientific and Research Institute of Agroecology and Agriculture: 467918 Kyzylorda obl., Aralsk, Lenina 2A; fax (72422) 7-45-63; f. 1995; Dir TOREKHAN KARLKIKHANOVICH KARLIKHANOV.

Atyrau Scientific and Research Institute of Agriculture: 060002 Atyrau, Azattyk 1; tel. (71022) 2-90-46; fax (71022) 2-91-41; f. 1995; Dir GULSYM SISENGALIYEVA.

Barayev, A. I., Research Centre for Grain Farming: 021600 Akmola obl., Shortandy, Nauchnyi; tel. and fax (71631) 2-10-59; e-mail kanal@kepter.kz; f. 1956; library of 56,000 vols; Dir ZH. A. KASKARBAYEV.

Central Kazakhstan Scientific and Research Institute of Agriculture: 100435 Karaganda obl., Buchar Zhyrau raion, Selo Tsentralnoye; tel. (72138) 3-12-51; fax (72138) 3-18-48; f. 1937; Dir ELAMAN SHAKHANOVICH SHAKHANOV.

East Kazakhstan Scientific and Research Institute of Agriculture: 070512 Eastern Kazakhstanv obl., Glubokovsky raion, Pos. Opytnoye Pole, Ul. Nagornaya 3A; tel. (7272) 29-56-54; fax (7272) 29-56-65; Dir SAINELHAN ZHEKSEKENOVICH ZHEKSEKENOV.

Kazakh Research Technological Institute for Operation and Maintenance of Agricultural Machinery: 020100 Akmola obl., Akkol, Lenina 176; tel. (71638) 2-12-75; fax (71638) 2-06-43; e-mail kazniti@mail.kz; f. 1962; Dir A. P. SOLOMKIN.

Kazakh Scientific and Research Institute of Astrakhan Sheep Breeding: 160019 Shymkent, Pr. Lenina 3; tel. (7252) 12-04-09; f. 1962; Dir ABDRAHMAN MOLDANASAROVICH OMBAEV.

Kazakh Scientific and Research Institute of Feedstuffs Production and Pasture: 050035 Almaty, Ul. Dzhandosova 51; tel. (7272) 21-45-86; f. 1969; Dir KASYM ABUOVICH ASANOV.

Kazakh Scientific and Research Institute of Fruit Growing and Viticulture: 050035 Almaty, Pr. Gagarina 238A; tel. (7272) 48-47-92; fax (7272) 48-10-50; f. 1978; Dir EDUARD DAULETOVICH MADENOV.

Kazakh Scientific and Research Institute of Grain and Processed Grain Products: 478000 Astana, Ul. Ugolnaya 26; tel. (7172) 31-01-93; fax (7172) 31-01-96; f. 1953; Dir A. A. OSPANOV.

Kazakh Scientific and Research Institute of Mechanization and Electrification in Agriculture: 050005 Almaty, Pr. Raimbeka 312; tel. (7272) 40-48-00; fax (7272) 77-52-61; f. 1978; Dir ASAN BEKENOVICH OSPANOV.

Kazakh Scientific and Research Institute of Poultry: 040933 Almaty obl., Karasaisky raion, Pos. 50 Let Kazakhskoi SSR, Ul. Maslieva 8; tel. (72771) 9-56-31; fax (72771) 9-56-45; f. 1966; Dir AIDAR KALDYBEKOVICH SABDENOV.

Kazakh Scientific and Research Institute of the Economics and Organization of the Agroindustrial Complex: 050057 Almaty, Ul. Tsatpaeva 30B; tel. (7272) 43-64-11; f. 1934; Dir GANI ALIMOVICH KALIEV.

Kazakh Scientific and Research Institute of the Fishing Industry: 050016 Almaty, Ul. Suyunbay 89A; fax (7272) 30-47-93; Dir SHOKAN ASHENOVICH ALPEYISOV.

Kazakh Scientific and Research Institute of the Food Industry: 050060 Almaty, Pr. Gagarina 238A; tel. (7272) 48-28-90; fax (7272) 48-10-50; f. 1993; Dir DUISENBAY SAILAUBAYEVICH IZBASAROV.

Kazakh Scientific and Research Institute of Water Management: 0800003 Taraz, Ul. Kogueldy 12; tel. (7262) 42-60-71; fax (7262) 42-55-40; e-mail iwre@nursat.kz; internet www.kaziwr.isd.kz; f. 1950; Dir Prof. SAGHIT RAHMATULLAEVICH IBATULLIN.

Kazakh Scientific, Research and Design Institute of the Meat and Milk Industry: 490035 Semipalatinsk, Ul. Baitursunova 29; tel. (7222) 44-26-15; fax (7222) 44-09-90; e-mail nikimmp@ok.kz; f. 1958; Dir MEIRAM ARYNOVICH MYRZABAYEV.

Kazakh Veterinary Scientific and Research Institute: 480029 Almaty, Pr. Raimbeka 223; tel. (7272) 32-17-55; fax (7272) 32-16-11; f. 1925; Dir ABYLAI RYSBAIULY SANSYZBAI.

Kostanai Scientific and Research Institute of Agriculture: 485000 Kostanai, 50 Let Oktobra 94; tel. (7142) 27-80-34; fax (7142) 54-24-72; f. 1984; Dir BERIKZHAN BALAPANULY KAIYPAI.

National Academic Centre of Agrarian Research: 480091 Almaty, 79 Abylai Khan; tel. (7272) 62-52-17; fax (7272) 62-38-31; depts of economics and information in agriculture, crop science and plant breeding, farming, agrochemistry, water and forest production and agroecology, livestock production and veterinary science, mechanization of agricultural production, processing and storing agricultural produce.

Northern Kazakhstan Research Institute of Animal Breeding and Veterinary Science: 150700 Northen Kazakhstan obl., Bishkul raion, Bishkul, Ul. Institutskaya 1; tel. (71538) 2-13-44; fax (71538) 2-12-53; f. 1962; library of 41,000 vols; Dir KANAT. R. MYNZHASOV.

Pavlodar Scientific and Research Institute of Agriculture: 140909 Pavlodar obl., Pavlodar raion, Pos. Krasnoarmeika; fax (7182) 32-50-61; f. 1993; Dir KENZHE KOZHAHMETOVICH ABDULLAYEV.

Research and Technological Institute of Livestock Raising: 040918 Almaty obl., Kaskelensky raion, Tausamaly; tel. (7272) 34-16-45; f. 1974; library of 18,000 vols, 3,300 journals; Dir A. M. MELDEBEKOV.

Research Institute for Plant Protection: 040924 Almaty obl., Karasai raion, Selo Rakhat; fax (7272) 29-56-22; e-mail kazniizr@nursat.kz; f. 1958; library of 29,134 vols; Dir ABAI ORAZULY SAGITOV.

Research Institute of Forestry and Agroforestry Reclamation: 020000 Akmola obl., Shchuchinsk, Ul. Kirova 58; tel. (71622) 2-14-62; f. 1957; library of 140,000 vols; Dir V. M. KOSTROMIN.

Research Institute of Potato and Vegetable Growing: 040917 Almaty obl., Karasai raion, Pos. Kainar; tel. and fax (7272) 98-37-06; f. 1945; Dir TIMUR AITPAYEV.

Research Institute of Sheep Breeding: 040622 Almaty obl., Zhambulsky raion, Mynbayeva; tel. (72770) 6-41-20; f. 1933; sheep, goat, horse and camel breeding; library of 100,000 vols; Dir B. S. SEYIDALIYEV.

South Kazakhstan Scientific and Research Institute of Agriculture: 160813 Shymkent, Soviyetskaya 111; tel. (7252) 22-20-98; fax (7252) 55-16-30; f. 1988; Dir MUHTAR ZHANBYRBAYEVICH ZHANBYRBAYEV.

Taldykorgan Agricultural Research Institute: 040000 Almaty obl., Taldykorgan raion, Pos. Zarya; tel. (72822) 9-94-45; fax (72822) 7-12-34; f. 1992; Dir M. K. KOZHAHMETOV.

Tselinny Scientific and Research Institute of Mechanization and Electrification in Agriculture: 110011 Kostanai, Pr. Abaya 34; fax (7142) 55-81-47; e-mail celin@mail.kz; Dir VLADIMIR LEONIDOVICH ASTAFEV.

Uspanov Institute of Soil Science: 050060 Almaty, Akademgorodok; fax (7272) 48-14-69; e-mail soil@nursat.kz; f. 1945; attached to Nat. Acad. of Sciences of Kazakhstan; Dir A. S. SAPAROV.

ECONOMICS, LAW AND POLITICS

Institute of Economics: 050010 Almaty, Kurmangazy 29; tel. (7272) 93-01-75; fax (7272) 62-78-19; e-mail ieconom@academset.kz; f. 1952; attached to Nat. Acad. of Sciences of Kazakhstan; Dir M. B. KENGHEGUZIN.

Institute of State and Law: 050000 Almaty, Kurmangazy 29; tel. (7272) 69-59-11; f. 1961; attached to Nat. Acad. of Sciences of Kazakhstan; Dir E. K. NURPEISOV.

HISTORY, GEOGRAPHY AND ARCHAEOLOGY

Institute of Geography: 050010 Almaty, Ul. Kalinina 69A; tel. (7272) 61-81-29; f. 1983; attached to Nat. Acad. of Sciences of Kazakhstan; Dir N. K. MUKITANOV.

Margulan Institute of Archaeology: 050010 Almaty, Pr. Dostvyk 44; tel. and fax (7272) 61-86-63; e-mail margulan@freenet.kz; f. 1991; attached to Nat. Acad. of Sciences of Kazakhstan; Dir A. K. MARGULANA.

Valikhanov, Ch. Ch., Institute of History and Ethnology: 050021 Almaty, Ul. Shevchenko 28; tel. (7272) 62-92-37; f. 1945; attached to Nat. Acad. of Sciences of Kazakhstan; Dir M. K. KOZYBAYEV.

LANGUAGE AND LITERATURE

Auezov, M. O., Institute of Literature and Arts: 050010 Almaty, Ul. Kurmangazy 29; tel. (7272) 72-74-11; fax (7272) 72-79-43; e-mail lit_art@academset.kz; internet litart.mindlab.kz; f. 1934; attached to Min. of Education and Science and Nat. Acad. of Sciences of Kazakhstan; Dir SEIT ASKAROVICH KASKABASOV; publ. Keruen (4 a year).

Baitursynov Institute of Linguistics: 050021 Almaty, Ul. Kurmangazy 29; tel. (7272) 61-56-35; fax (7272) 72-80-59; e-mail tilbilimi@bk.ru; f. 1961; attached to Dept of Science of Min. of Education and Science; researches in Kazakh linguistics; library of 500,000 vols; Dir Dr SHERUBAI KURMANBAIULY; publ. Linguistic.

MEDICINE

Central Asian Plague Prevention Research Institute: 050034 Almaty, Kopalskaya ul. 14; tel. (7272) 35-75-48; Dir V. M. STEPANOV.

Dermatovenereological Research Institute of the Committee for Health: Ministry of Education and Science, 050002 Almaty, Ul. Raimbeka 60; tel. (7272) 30-40-85; fax (7272) 50-23-77; f. 1931; library of 250,000 vols; Dir ZURA B. KESHILEVA.

Institute of Microbiology, Epidemiology and Infectious Diseases: 050002 Almaty, Ul. Pastera 34; tel. (7272) 33-04-26; Dir I. K. SHURATOV.

Institute of Nutrition: 050008 Almaty, Ul. Klochkova 66; tel. (7272) 42-92-03; fax (7272) 42-97-20; f. 1974; attached to Nat. Acad. of Sciences of Kazakhstan; Dir T. SH. SHARMANOV; publs Voprosy pitaniya, Zdravookhranenie Kazakhstana (8–10 a year).

Kazakhstan Paediatrics Research Institute: 050000 Almaty, Al-Farabi 146; tel. (7272) 48-81-21; fax (7272) 63-12-07; f. 1932; library of 36,000 vols; Dir A. K. MASKAKEYEV.

National Centre of Labour Hygiene and Occupational Diseases: 100012 Karaganda, 15 Mustafina; tel. and fax (7212) 56-52-63; e-mail ncgtpz@gmail.com; f. 1958 as Institute of Physiology and Occupational Diseases; present name 2002; attached to Healthcare Min.; Dir Dr ZHAMILYA BATTAKOVA; publ. Occupational Hygiene and Medical Ecology (4 a year).

National Centre for Tuberculosis Problems: 050000 Almaty, Bekhozhin ul. 5; tel. (7272) 91-86-57; fax (7272) 91-86-58; e-mail ncpt@itte.kz; f. 1932; library of 11,000 vols; Dir Prof. SH. ISMAILOV.

Research Institute of Clinical and Experimental Surgery: 050003 Almaty, Ul. Mira 62; Dir M. A. ALIEV.

NATURAL SCIENCES

Biological Sciences

Aitkhozhin, M. A., Institute of Molecular Biology and Biochemistry: 050012 Almaty, ul. Dosmuhamedova 86; tel. (7272) 67-63-06; fax (7272) 67-19-47; f. 1983; attached to Nat. Acad. of Sciences of Kazakhstan; Dir Prof. N. A. AITKHOZHIN (acting).

Institute of Botany: 050029 Almaty, Timiryazeva 36D; tel. (7272) 47-66-92; fax (7272) 47-90-42; f. 1995; attached to Nat. Acad. of Sciences of Kazakhstan; Dir S. A. ABIYEV.

Institute of Experimental Biology: 050022 Almaty, Pr. Abaya 38; tel. (7272) 67-23-03; attached to Min. of Education and Science; Dir A. M. MURZAMADIEV.

Institute of General Genetics and Cytology: 050040 Almaty; f. 1995; attached to Nat. Acad. of Sciences of Kazakhstan.

Institute of Human and Animal Physiology: 480032 Almaty, Akademgorodok; tel. (7272) 48-04-88; f. 1945; attached to Nat. Acad. of Sciences of Kazakhstan; Dir KH. D. DUISEMBIN.

Institute of Microbiology and Virology: 050010 Almaty, Ul. Kirova 103; tel. (7272) 61-84-97; e-mail adm@imv.academ.alma-ata .su; f. 1956; attached to Nat. Acad. of Sciences of Kazakhstan; Dir A. N. ILYALETDINOV.

Institute of Zoology: 050034 Almaty, Akademgorodok; tel. (7272) 48-19-32; e-mail common@zoo/2.academ.alma-ata.su; f. 1943; attached to Nat. Acad. of Sciences of Kazakhstan; Dir T. N. DOSZHANOV.

Mathematical Sciences

Institute of Mathematics: 050010 Almaty, Pushkina 125; tel. (727) 272-70-95; fax (727) 272-33-99; e-mail dzhenali@math.kz; internet www.math.kz; f. 1965; attached to Nat. Acad. of Sciences of Kazakhstan; Dir Prof. M. T. DZHENALIEV; Scientific Sec. SHOLPAN BALGIMBAEVA.

Institute of Theoretical and Applied Mathematics: 050021 Almaty, Ul. Pushkina 125; tel. (7272) 61-37-40; f. 1965; attached to Nat. Acad. of Sciences of Kazakhstan; Dir N. K. BLIEV.

Physical Sciences

Akhmedsafin, U. M., Institute of Hydrogeology and Hydrophysics: 050010 Almaty, Ul. Krasina 94; tel. (7272) 61-50-51; f. 1965; attached to Nat. Acad. of Sciences of Kazakhstan; Dir V. V. VESELOV.

Bekturov Institute of Chemical Sciences: 050010 Almaty, Ualikhanov 106; tel. (7272) 91-23-89; fax (7272) 91-24-80; e-mail labsp@ics.scinet.kz; internet www.chemistry .kz; f. 1945; attached to Min. of Education and Science; library of 83,000 vols; Dir Prof. Dr E. E. ERGOZHIN; publ. *Chemical Journal of Kazakhstan* (4 a year).

Chemical-Metallurgical Institute: 100009 Karaganda, Ermekov 63; tel. and fax (7212) 43-31-61; e-mail hmi@mail.krg.kz; f. 1958; attached to Nat. Acad. of Sciences of Kazakhstan; Dir Dr BOLAT KHASSEN.

Fesenkov Astrophysical Institute: 480068 Almaty, Kamenskoe plato; tel. (7272) 65-00-40; e-mail adm@afi.academ .alma-ata.su; f. 1950; attached to Nat. Acad. of Sciences of Kazakhstan; Dir B. T. TASHENOV.

Geological Surveying Oil Research Institute: 060002 Atyrau, Ul. Ordzhonikidze 43; tel. (71222) 3-33-86; Dir S. U. UTGALIYEV.

Institute of Nuclear Physics: 050032 Almaty, Ibragimova 1; tel. (7272) 54-64-67; fax (7272) 54-65-17; internet inp1.sci.kz; f.

1957; attached to Nat. Acad. of Sciences of Kazakhstan; Dir K. K. KADYRZHANOV.

Institute of Organic Catalysis and Electro-chemistry: 050010 Almaty, D. Kunayev 142; tel. (7272) 61-58-08; fax (7272) 91-57-22; e-mail orgcat@nursat.kz; internet www .catalysis.nsk.su; f. 1969; attached to Nat. Acad. of Sciences of Kazakhstan; Dir M. Z. ZHURINOV.

Institute of Organic Synthesis and Carbon Chemistry: 100000 Karaganda, Ul. 40-let Kazakhstana; tel. (7272) 52-60-85; f. 1983; attached to Nat. Acad. of Sciences of Kazakhstan; Dir S. M. MOLDAKHMETOV.

Institute of Petroleum Chemistry and Natural Salts: 060002 Atyrau, Ul. Lenina 2; tel. (7122) 22-26-74; f. 1960; attached to Nat. Acad. of Sciences of Kazakhstan; Dir N. R. BUKEIKHANOV.

Institute of Physics and Technology: 050032 Alatau, Ibragimova 11; tel. (7272) 26-24-95; fax (7272) 26-25-11; e-mail mukashev@sci.kz; internet www.sci.kz; f. 1991; attached to Nat. Acad. of Sciences of Kazakhstan; depts of Condensed matter physics, Material science and nanotechnology, Spectroscopic methods of research, High-energy physics and cosmic rays, Information technology; Dir Dr B. N. MUKASHEV.

Institute of Phytochemistry: 100009 Karaganda, Ministry of Education and Science, ul. Gazalieva, 4; e-mail kms@phyto .karaganda.su; f. 1995; attached to Nat. Acad. of Sciences of Kazakhstan.

Institute of Seismology: 050060 Almaty, Pr. Al-Farabi 75; tel. (7272) 48-21-34; fax (7272) 49-44-17; e-mail adm@seism.academ .alma-ata.su; f. 1976; attached to Nat. Acad. of Sciences of Kazakhstan; Dir A. K. KURSKEYEV.

Institute of Space Research: 050034 Almaty, Akademgorodok; tel. (7272) 62-38-96; e-mail silakaziki@akma-ata.su; f. 1991; attached to Nat. Acad. of Sciences of Kazakhstan; Dir U. M. SULTANGAZIN.

Institute of the Ionosphere: 050020 Almaty, Kamenskoe plato; tel. (7272) 54-80-74; fax (7272) 65-09-93; f. 1983; attached to Nat. Acad. of Sciences of Kazakhstan; Dir V. I. DROBZHEV.

National Nuclear Centre: 071100 Kurchatov, Lenina 6; tel. (72251) 2-33-33; fax (72251) 2-38-58; internet www.nnc.kz; f. 1992; Dir S. T. TUKHVATULIN.

Physical Technical Institute: 050032 Almaty, Alatau; tel. (7272) 69-05-66; fax (7272) 54-52-24; e-mail mukashev@sci.kz; internet www.sci.kz; f. 1991; attached to Nat. Acad. of Sciences of Kazakhstan; Dir Prof. B. N. MUKASHEV.

Satpaev, K. I., Institute of Geological Sciences: 050010 Almaty, Ul. Kalinina 69A; tel. (7272) 61-56-08; e-mail adm@geol .academ.alma-ata.su; f. 1940; attached to Nat. Acad. of Sciences of Kazakhstan; Dir A. A. ABDULLIN.

PHILOSOPHY AND PSYCHOLOGY

Institute of Philosophy: 050021 Almaty, Ul. Kurmangazy 29; tel. and fax (7272) 69-59-11; f. 1991; attached to Nat. Acad. of Sciences of Kazakhstan; Dir Prof. A. N. NYSANBAYEV.

RELIGION, SOCIOLOGY AND ANTHROPOLOGY

Institute of Orient Studies: 050010 Almaty, Ul. Pushkina 111/113; tel. (7272) 61-53-71; f. 1996; attached to Nat. Acad. of Sciences of Kazakhstan; Dir K. T. TALIPOV.

TECHNOLOGY

Eastern Mining and Metallurgical Research Institute of Non-ferrous Metals: 070002 Ust-Kamenogorsk, Promyshlennaya 1; tel. (7232) 47-37-73; fax (7232) 47-37-71; e-mail vcmnauka@mail .east.telecom.kz; internet vcm.ukg.kz; f. 1950; attached to Min. of Industry and New Technologies; carries out research and semi-commercial scale tests; provides scientific and technical assistance in the introduction of technologies and equipment in the fields of polymetal ores mining and dressing, heavy non-ferrous metals metallurgy, applied and analytical chemistry, environment protection; library of 169,000 vols; Dir Dr NIKOLAY USHAKOV.

Institute of Informatics and Control Problems: 050010 Almaty, Pushkina str. 125; tel. and fax (7272) 72-37-11; e-mail office@ipic.kz; internet www.ipic.kz; f. 1991; attached to Science Cttee of MES RK; Dir M. N. KALIMOLDAYEV.

Institute of Metallurgy and Ore Enrichment: 050010 Almaty, Ul. Shevchenko 29/33; tel. (7272) 91-57-81; fax (7272) 91-46-60; e-mail imo-almaty@nursat.kz; internet www .imo.nursat.kz; f. 1945; attached to Nat. Acad. of Sciences of Kazakhstan; Dir Prof. Dr BAGDAULET KENZHALIEV; publ. *Kompleksnoe Ispolzovanie Mineralnogo Siria* (6 a year).

Kunayev Institute of Mining: 050046 Almaty, Ave. Abai 191; tel. (727) 376-53-00; fax (727) 376-52-97; e-mail igdkpms@mail.ru; internet www.igd.kz; f. 1944; attached to Nat. Centre for Integrated Minerals Recycling of the Republic of Kazakhstan; scientific and research activity in mining; devt of rational methods of design and management of production processes at mining companies; creation of effective and environmentally safe technologies and minerals mining equipment; postgraduate training of scientific personnel, training of mining specialists, scientific and technical popularization of latest achievements of science and equipment; editorial activity; int. cooperation; economic activity; library of 70,153 vols incl. 21,724 periodicals; 255 teachers; Dir Prof. Dr GALIEV SEITGALI JOLDASOVICH; publ. *Scientific and Technical Provision of Mining Production* (2 a year).

National Centre for Complex Processing of Mineral Raw Materials: 050036 Almaty, Dzhandosov 67; tel. (7272) 59-00-70; fax (7272) 59-00-75; internet www .innovation.kz; attached to Nat. Academy of Sciences of Kazakhstan; Dir A. ZHARMENOV.

Scientific and Technological Centre of Machinery Construction: 480064 Almaty, Pr. Abaya 191; tel. (7272) 46-97-50; e-mail mntc@mail.ru; f. 1998; Dir S. U. JOLDASBEKOV.

Libraries and Archives

Almaty

Al-Farabi Kazakh National University Central Library: 050010 Almaty, Timiryazeva ul. 42; tel. (7272) 47-27-61; fax (7272) 49-26-09; e-mail guljan_m@kazsu.kz; internet lib.kazsu.kz; f. 1934; 1.5m. vols; Dir E. D. ABULKAYIROVA.

Central Scientific Library of the Ministry of Education & Science of the Republic of Kazakhstan: 050010 Almaty, Ul. Shevchenko 28; tel. (7272) 72-83-41; fax (7272) 61-00-37; e-mail cnb@library.kz; internet www.library.kz; f. 1932; 5.5m. vols, 2,041 MSS; Dir KULZHIKHAN ABUGALIYEVA;

publ. *Kitapkhana Alemi* (Library World, 4 a year).

National Library of the Republic of Kazakhstan: 480013 Almaty, Abaya ave 14; tel. (7272) 62-28-83; fax (7272) 69-28-83; e-mail intrel@nlrk.kz; internet www.nlrk.kz; f. 1931; legal deposit library; 6m. vols; Dir-Gen. ORYNBASSAR ISSAKHOV.

Scientific and Technical Library of Kazakhstan: 050026 Almaty, S. Mukanov 223B; tel. and fax (7272) 68-26-79; internet www.rntb.kz; f. 1960; 22.6m. vols (incl. patents); Dir-Gen. K. G. URMURZINA.

Karaganda

Karaganda State University Library: 100026 Karaganda, Ul. Universitetskaya 28; tel. (7212) 74-53-00; fax (7212) 74-47-67; internet library.ksu.kz; 400,000 vols; Dir S. M. ZHERZHISOVA.

Museums and Art Galleries

Almaty

Central State Museum of Kazakhstan: 050059 Almaty, Samal-1 44; tel. (7272) 64-22-00; e-mail csmrk@hn.freenet.kz; internet www.unesco.kz/heritagenet/kz/hn-english/csmrk/engl/index_en.htm; history and natural history of Kazakhstan; Dir NURSAN ALIMBAY.

Kasteyev Kazakh State Art Museum: 050040 Almaty, Ul. Satpayeva 30A; tel. (7272) 47-82-49; fax (7272) 47-86-69; e-mail kazart@nursat.kz; internet www.art.nursat.kz; f. 1976; Kazakh art, Folk art, Soviet and European art; library of 23,000 vols; Dir BAYTURSUN E. UMORBEKOV.

Universities

AKTAU SH. YESENOV UNIVERSITY

466200 Aktau, Mikro raion 14
Telephone: (7292) 43-85-68
Fax: (7292) 33-42-21
State control
Rector: ASHIMZHAN S. AKHMETOV.

AKTOBE K. ZHUBANOV STATE UNIVERSITY

030014 Aktobe, Molgagulova 34
Telephone: (7132) 55-37-56
Fax: (7132) 57-78-43
E-mail: zhubanov@samgau.kz
State control.

AL-FARABI KAZAKH NATIONAL UNIVERSITY

050038 Almaty, Al-Farabi 71
Telephone: (7272) 47-14-88
Fax: (7272) 47-26-09
E-mail: anurmag@kazsu.kz
Internet: www.kazsu.kz
Founded 1934 (fmrly Kazakh S. M. Kirov State University), present name and status 1994
State control
Languages of instruction: Kazakh, Russian
Academic year: September to July (two semesters)
Rector: Prof. T. A. KOZHAMKULOV
Pro-Rectors: Dr G. K. AKHMETOVA, Prof. ZH. D. DADEBAYEV, Prof. A. I. KUPCHISHIN, Prof. Z. A. MANSUROV, Prof. N. O. OMASHEV, Dr S. T. SHALGYMBAYEV

Librarian: E. DZ. ABULKAIROVA
Library: see Libraries and Archives
Number of teachers: 1,618
Number of students: 14,500
Publication: *Vestnik KazGNU* (1 a year)

DEANS

Dept of Biology: Prof. R. I. BERSIMBAYEV
Dept of Chemistry: Prof. Z. A. ABILOB
Dept of Economics and Business: Prof. R. Y. YELEMESSOV
Dept of Geography: Dr K. M. BAIMYRZAYEV
Dept of History: Prof. ZH. K. TAIMAGAMBETOV
Dept of Int. Relations: Prof. Y. B. ZHATKAN-BAYEV
Dept of Journalism: Prof. B. O. ZHAKYP
Dept of Law: Prof. D. L. BAIDELDINOV
Dept of Literary and Language Studies: Prof. K. A. ABDEZULY
Dept of Mechanics and Mathematics: Prof. M. K. ORUNKHANOV
Dept of Oriental Studies: Prof. S. M. SYZDY-KOV
Dept of Philosophy and Political Science: Prof. G. Y. YESSIM
Dept of Physics: Prof. A. S. ASKAROVA
Preparatory Dept for Foreign Citizens: Dr G. Y. UTEBALIYEVA

ALMATY ABAI STATE UNIVERSITY

050010 Almaty, Dostyk 12
Telephone: (7272) 91-63-39
Fax: (7272) 91-30-50
E-mail: rector@bai.uni.sci.kz
Internet: www.abai.uni.sic.kz
Founded 1928
State control
Languages of instruction: Kazakh, Russian
Academic year: September to June
Rector: TOKMUKHAMED S. SADYKOV
Library: 1m. vols
Number of teachers: 730
Number of students: 8,877

DEANS

Arts and Graphics: BAIMURAT OSPANOV
Finance and Economics: MIRSEDA ALIM-BAYEVA
Geography and Ecology: AZIMKHAN SEITZHA-NOV
History: SAIYN BORBASOV
Int. Relations: EUGENI KUZNETSOV
Kazakh Philology: SAUL DAUTOVA
Law: KAMAL BURKHANOV
Physics and Mathematics: MAKTAGALI BEKTE-MISOV
Psychology and Pedagogy: ROMSEIT KOJAN-BAYEV
Russian Philology: MANAT MUSATAYEVA

ALMATY TECHNOLOGICAL UNIVERSITY

050012 Almaty, Tole-bi 100
Telephone: (7272) 68-83-35
Fax: (7272) 68-63-30
E-mail: atukz@mail.kz
Internet: www.atu.kz
Founded 1952
State control
Rector: K. S. KULAZHANOV
Faculties of Cybernetics, Economics, Extra-mural studies, Food science and technology.

ATYRAU H. DOSMUHAMEDOV STATE UNIVERSITY

465017 Atyrau, Ul. Pushkina 12
Telephone: (7122) 23-30-44
Fax: (7122) 23-30-17
State control
Rector: ASHAT IMANGALIYEV.

DZHAMBUL UNIVERSITY

080003 Taraz, Dzhambul 16A
Telephone: (7262) 23-19-78
State control.

EAST KAZAKHSTAN STATE UNIVERSITY

070002 Ust-Kamenogorsk, 30 Gvardeiskoy Divisii 34B
Telephone: (7232) 540-411
Fax: (7232) 540-407
E-mail: rector@vkgu.kz
Internet: www.vkgu.kz
Founded 1952
State control
Languages of instruction: Kazakh, Russian
Academic year: September to June
Rector: BEIBIT MAMRAYEV
First Vice-Rector: GAINELGAZY ADILGAZINOV
Library of 992,710 vols
Number of teachers: 700
Number of students: 11,079

DIRECTORS

Adult Education: FARXAD KURMANOV
Continuing Education: MAJAK ZHAKSILIKOV
Economics and Finance: TOXTAR BOLGAUOV
Law: KUAT RAKHIMBERDINOV
History and International Relations: RIZABEK SARMULDINOV
Natural Sciences, Ecology: ANAR MYRZAGA-LIYEVA
Philology: SLYAMBEK ORAZALIN
Physics, Mathematics and Technology: BEI-SEN AKHMETZHANOV

GUMILEV, L. N., EURASIAN UNIVERSITY

010008 Astana, Tsiolkovsky 6
Telephone: (7172) 24-32-93
Fax: (7172) 24-30-90
E-mail: root@lceu.ricc.kz
Founded 1962 as teacher-training institute; became Akmola University 1992; present name 1996
State control
Languages of instruction: Kazakh, Russian
Academic year: September to June
Rector: Prof. Dr AMANGHELDY HUSSAYNOVICH HUSSAINOV
Pro-Rector for Coordination and Academic Programmes: MUKHTAR USSINOVICH ISMA-GAMBETOV
Pro-Rector for Financial Admin.: MUKHTAR MUKHAMEDIEVICH URAZALIN
Pro-Rector for Research and Int. Relations: Prof. Dr RAHMETULLA SHARAPIDENOVICH YERKASSOV
Pro-Rector for Social Activities: MINA EMA-NUILOVNA ROMANENKO
Senior Adminstrative Officer: Prof. AMAN-GHELDY ZHAKSYLIKOVICH ISMAILOV
Library: 1m. vols

DEANS

Faculty of Culture and Art: IRINA UMAN-GIREEVNA AUSHEVA
Faculty of Economics: Prof. SAYRAN KAB-DRAKHMANOVNA SURAGANOVA
Faculty of Engineering: Prof. Dr SERIK NURAKOV
Faculty of Engineering and Economics (extramural): Prof. VYACHESLAV VIKTORO-VICH TARASSOV
Faculty of Foreign Languages: SAULE BAZY-LOVNA ZAGATOVA
Faculty of History and Int. Relations: KADYR ABILZHANOVICH AKHMETOV
Faculty of Humanities (extramural): MARAT TOKENOVICH ZHOLBARISSOV

Faculty of Law: ZHUMAHAN ZHARKINBEKOVICH UTENOV

Faculty of Natural Sciences and Physical Education: Prof. AMANZHOL KUSSEPOVICH KUSSEPOV

Faculty of Oriental Studies: Prof. Dr SEYIT ASKAROVICH KASKABASOV

Faculty of Philology: GALINA ALEKSANDROVNA CHERNETSKAYA

Faculty of Physics and Mathematics: YERLAN SERIKOVICH BAIGOZHIN

KARAGANDA E. A. BUKETOV STATE UNIVERSITY

100028 Karaganda, Universitetskaya ul. 28

Telephone: (7212) 77-03-89

Fax: (7212) 77-03-84

E-mail: office@ksu.kz

Internet: www.ksu.kz

Founded 1972

State control

Academic year: September to June

Rector: YERKIN KINAYATOVICH KUBEYEV

Number of teachers: 1,200

Number of students: 13,000

Publication: *Vestnik* (4 a year)

Faculties of biology, chemistry, economics, education, foreign languages, history, law, mathematics, philology, philosophy and psychology, physical culture and sport, physics, social sciences, vocational and continuing improvement.

KAZAKH HUMANITARIAN LAW UNIVERSITY

050008 Almaty, Pr. Abaya 50A

Telephone: (7272) 42-52-25

Fax: (7272) 77-97-53

Founded 1994

State control

Languages of instruction: Kazakh, Russian

Academic year: September to June

Rector: MAKSUT NARIKBAYEV

Vice-Rector: BOLAT BEYEKENOV

Library of 100,237 vols

Number of teachers: 545

Number of students: 1,883

Publication: *State and Law* (3 a year)

DEANS

Commercial Law: SERGEY MARKIN

Criminal Law and Trial Investigation Law: RAMASAN NURTAYEV

Int. Law: IRINA KHAN

Judicial and State Prosecution Law: OMIRBAY KYSTAUBAY

KAZAKH K. I. SATBAYEV NATIONAL TECHNICAL UNIVERSITY

050013 Almaty, Satbayev 22

Telephone: (7272) 92-60-25

Fax: (7272) 92-60-26

E-mail: allnt@kazntu.sci.kz

Internet: www.ntu.kz

Founded 1934 as Kazakh Polytechnic Institute; present name and status c. 1996

State control

Academic year: September to July

Rector: Prof. DOSYM K. SULEYEV

Library: 1.2m. vols

Number of teachers: 1,354

Number of students: 10,142

Attached Institutes of Ecology, Geological Prospecting, Information Technology, Machinery Construction, Metallurgy and Polygraphy, Mining, Natural Humanities, Oil and Gas.

KAZAKH STATE WOMEN'S PEDAGOGICAL INSTITUTE

480083 Almaty, Aiteke-bi 99

Telephone: (7272) 39-42-83

Founded 1944

State control

Languages of instruction: Kazakh, Russian

Academic year: September to July

Rector: SELIKBEK ISAYEV

Library of 860,000 vols

Number of teachers: 650

Number of students: 2,600

Faculties of economics, Education, history, library science, modern languages, music education, natural sciences, philology, philosophy, primary education, sports, teacher training.

KAZAKH-TURKISH HODJA AHMET YESEVI INTERNATIONAL UNIVERSITY

487010 Turkistan, Maydan Yesim-Khan 2

Telephone: (7253) 34-11-44

Fax: (7253) 34-14-47

E-mail: webmaster@mktu.turkistan.kz

Internet: www.turkistan.kz

Founded 1991 jtly by govts of Kazakhstan and Turkey

State control

Languages of instruction: Kazakh, Turkish, Russian, English

Academic year: September to July

Rector: MURAT ZHURINOV

Library of 480,000 vols

Number of teachers: 700

Number of students: 10,200

Publication: *Scientific Methodological Articles* (fortnightly)

Faculties of Art, Art studies, Ecology, Economics, History, History and philology, Languages and literature, Law, Mathematics and econ., Medicine, Natural sciences, Oriental studies.

KOKSHETAU SH. VALIHANOV UNIVERSITY

100001 Kokshetau, Ul. Karla Marksa 76

Telephone: (7162) 25-55-84

Fax: (7162) 25-55-83

E-mail: universi@kokc.kz

Founded 1962

State control

Languages of instruction: Kazakh, Russian

Academic year: September to July

Rector: ABAI A. AITMUHAMBETOV

Library of 600,000 vols

Number of teachers: 450

Number of students: 4,900

DEANS

Faculty of Agriculture and Technology: ALEKSANDR PODDUBNY

Faculty of Chemistry and Biology: TOLEGEN SEILHANOV

Faculty of Economics: KOSYBAI AITKOZHIN

Faculty of Foreign Languages: NATALYA ZHUMANGULOVA

Faculty of History and Art: ZHARAS ERMEKBAYEV

Faculty of Philology: OLGA ANITSHENKO

Faculty of Physics and Mathematics: KADYRHAN MUSABAYEV

KOSTANAI A. BAITURSYNOV STATE UNIVERSITY

110000 Kostanai, Ul. Baitursynova 47

Telephone: (7142) 54-25-94

Fax: (7142) 54-25-94

E-mail: ksu47@mail.kz

Internet: www.ksu.kst.kz

Founded 1939, present status 1992

State control

Rector: KHUSAIN KH. VALIYEV

Publications: *Bilim zharysy* (12 a year), *Zharsken-Kostanai* (6 a year), *Mezhvuzovskii nauchnyi zhurnal* (Intercollegiate Scientific Journal), *Vestnik Nauki* (Herald of Science, 4 a year)

Faculty of journalism; institutes of agriculture, economy and management, engineering and physics, humanities, law, mathematics and information technology, veterinary studies; college of Kazakh State University.

KYZYLORDA KORKYT ATA HUMANITARIAN UNIVERSITY

120000 Kyzylorda, Zheltoksan 40

State control.

KYZYLORDA KORKYT ATA STATE UNIVERSITY

467021 Kyzylorda, Aiteke-bi 29A

Telephone: (72422) 6-17-95

Fax: (72422) 6-17-25

E-mail: ksu@kyzstun.asdc.kz

Founded 1937

State control

Languages of instruction: Kazakh, Russian

Academic year: September to June

Rector: KYLYSHBAI A. BISSENOV

Library: 1.8m. items

Number of teachers: 460

Number of students: 8,000

Publications: *Vestnik* (sciences, quarterly), *Syr Tulegu* (news)

Faculties of Correspondence and Evening Courses, Economics and Ecology, Economics and Engineering, History and Law, Natural Sciences, Philology and Arts, Physics and Mathematics.

M. KOZEYBAYEV NORTH KAZAKHSTAN STATE UNIVERSITY

150000 Petropavlovsk, Pushkin St 86

Telephone: (152) 49-33-52

Fax: (152) 49-33-42

E-mail: mail@nkzu.kz

Internet: www.nkzu.kz

Founded 1937

State control

Languages of instruction: Kazakh, Russian

Academic year: September to August

Rector: ASHIMOV UNDASSYN BAIKENOVICH

Vice-Rector for Academic Work: GUSAKOV VIKTOR PETROVICH

Vice-Rector for Scientific Work and External Relations: TUKACHYOV ALEXANDER ANDREEVICH

Vice-Rector for Educational Work: TAIZHANOVA MUKARAM MURZATOVNA

Vice-Rector for House-Keeping Unit: KUSHUMBAEV AKBAY BAGYTKEREEVICH

Library: 1m. vols

Number of teachers: 440

Number of students: 10,000

DEANS

Faculty of Economics: A. S. ISMAGULOVA

Faculty of Energetic and Mechanical Engineering: KAIRAT T. KOSHEKOV

Faculty of History and Law: SABYR I. IBRAEV

Faculty of Information Technology: B. E. BATYROV

Faculty of Music: N. I. PYSTOVALOVA

Faculty of Natural Sciences: NIKOLAI N. SEMENOV

Faculty of Physical Education: VICTOR K. KULAYEV

Faculty of Transport-Building Engineering: R. S. IMAMBAEVA

Institute of Language and Literature: ZH. S. TALASPAEVA

Qualification Development Institute: A. SH. YASHKINA

SEMEY STATE SHAKARIM UNIVERSITY

490035 Semipalatinsk, Ul. Gleynky 20A

Telephone: (7222) 42-29-37
Fax: (7222) 35-95-49
E-mail: info@semgu.kz
Internet: www.semgu.kz

Founded 1995
State control
Languages of instruction: Kazakh, Russian
Academic year: September to June

Rector: YERLAN SYDYKOV
Vice-Rector: MIKHAIL PANIN

Library: 1m. vols
Number of teachers: 648
Number of students: 8,682

DEANS

Faculty of Economcs: SERIKTAY BAIMUKHANOV
Faculty of Engineering and Technology: SERIK TUMENOV
Faculty of Finance: BEGMAN KOZHEGELDIYEV
Faculty of Humanities: ALMAGUL MUKHAMED-KHANOVA
Faculty of Natural Sciences: BENUR MUSABA-LINA
Faculty of Philology: FARIDA ZHAKSYBAYEVA
Faculty of Veterinary Medicine and Agriculture: ZEINOLLA TOKAYEV

SOUTHERN KAZAKHSTAN AUZEV HUMANITIES UNIVERSITY

160018 Shymkent, Beibitshilik 3
Telephone: (72522) 44-99-88
E-mail: ukrgi-smh@nursat.kz
State control.

SOUTHERN KAZAKHSTAN MEDICAL ACADEMY

160000 Shymkent, Lenina 1
Founded 1944
State control.

STATE FINANCIAL INSTITUTE

071403 Semipalatinsk, Ul. Shugajeva 159
Telephone: (7222) 63-59-20
Fax: (7222) 66-28-83

Founded 1995
State control

Rector: GENNADI N. GARMANIC.

TARAZ M. KH. DULATI STATE UNIVERSITY

080000 Jambul obl., Taraz, Tole
Telephone: (7262) 45-36-64
Fax: (7262) 43-24-02
E-mail: info@targu.kz
Internet: www.tarsu.kz

Founded 1998
State control

Rector: ASHIMZHAN S. AKHMETOV
Number of teachers: 500
Number of students: 6,326

ZHETYSU I. ZHANSUGUROV UNIVERSITY

040009 Taldykorgan, Ul. I. Zhansugurova 187A

Telephone: (72722) 2-00-20
Fax: (72722) 1-22-61

E-mail: tk_jgu@mail.ru
Founded 1972
State control
Languages of instruction: Kazakh, Russian
Academic year: September to June

Rector: ESENGELDY MEDEUYOV
Pro-Rector: ASKHAT SARSENBAYEV

Number of teachers: 307
Number of students: 6,985

Faculties of Business and commerce, Computer education, Finance, Foreign languages, Humanities, Law, Mathematics, Pedagogy.

ZHEZKAZGAN O. A. BAIKONUROV UNIVERSITY

100600 Zhezkazgan, Pr. Alashahana 1
Telephone: (7102) 73-63-24
Fax: (7102) 73-01-15
E-mail: univer@iftc.zhez.kz
Founded 1956
State control
Languages of instruction: Kazakh, Russian, English

Rector: ZHUMAGALI NAURYZBAI
Vice-Rector: KALI KISHAUOV

Library: 1.1m. vols
Number of teachers: 1,035
Number of students: 3,061

DIRECTORS

Institute of Economics and Law: GULNAR TEMIRBAYEVA
Institute of Mining Engineernig: MUHAMEDZ-HAN AUEZOV
Institute Natural Sciences: OMITRAI ZHALE-LOV
Institute of Philology and Arts: MURAT ABEUOV

Other Higher Educational Institutes

Aktobe State Medical Institute: 463022 Aktobe, Ul. Lenina 52; tel. (7132) 54-39-04; library: 62,000 vols.

Almaty Institute of Power Engineering and Telecommunication: 050013 Almaty, Ul. Baytursynova 126; tel. (7272) 92-57-40; fax (7272) 92-50-57; e-mail aipet@aipet.kz; internet www.aipet.kz; f. 1975; faculties of Power engineering, Radio engineering, Thermal engineering; part-time courses and retraining; pre-institutional training; ENTEL College; br. in Ust Kamenogorsk; library: 465,000 vols; 284 teachers; 4,856 students; Rector GUMARBEK ZH. DAUKEYEV; publs *Collections of Scientific Works* (2 a year), *Collections of Postgraduate Works* (1 a year).

Almaty Kurmangazy State Conservatoire: 480091 Almaty, Ablaikhan pr. 90; tel. (7272) 62-76-40; courses in Academic and folk singing, Choral and symphonic conducting, Composition, Cultural management, Musicology, Orchestral and folk instruments, Piano; library: 266,060 vols.

Almaty State Theatrical and Cinema Institute: 480091 Almaty, Ul. Bogenbai Batyr 136; tel. (7272) 63-66-52; fax (7272) 50-62-84; f. 1992; acting and directing apprenticeship; 10 teachers; library: 400 vols.

Astana State Medical Academy: 473013 Astana, Pr. Mira 51A; tel. (7172) 26-07-829; fax (7172) 26-39-18; e-mail akma@asdc.kz; f. 1964, present name and status 1997; faculties of Medicine and biological sciences, Medicine, Paediatrics; library: 381,500 vols; 370 teachers; 2,100 students; Rector R. K. TULEBAYEV.

D. Serikbaev East Kazakhstan State Technical University: 69 H. K. O., 070004 Ust-Kamenogorsk; tel. (7232) 26-28-89; fax (7232) 26-74-09; e-mail ekstu@ektu.kz; internet www.ektu.kz; f. 1958; academic divisions: Institute of Economics and Management, Institute of Mining and Metallurgical Engineering, Institute of Building Technologies and Architecture, Institute of Mechanics and Technology, Postgraduate and New Technologies Institute, Institute of Information Technologies, Faculty with the Kazakh Language of Instruction, Virtual Institute, Centre of Humanities Education; Bachelors degrees, specialist diplomas, Masters degrees and Doctoral programmes; library: 859,800 vols; 660 teachers; 10,400 students; Rector GALYMKAIR MUTANOV; First Vice-Rector ZHENIS KULSEITOV; Vice-Rector for Science and Int. Cooperation Matters TULEGEN IPALAKOV; publs *Collections of Scientific Works* (1 a year), *Vestnik* (scientific journal, 4 a year), *Za znanie!* (To Knowledge!, 12 a year).

Karaganda Kazpotrebsoyuz University of Economics: 100009 Karaganda, Ul. Akademicheskaya 9; tel. (7212) 44-16-22; fax (7212) 44-16-32; e-mail keu@city.krg.kz; internet www.keu.pmicro.kz; f. 1966; Accountancy and audit, Commodity management and analysis, Computer systems, Customs business, Econ. and management, Law, Finance and credit, Marketing and commerce, Merchandizing, State and local govt, Standardization and certification; brs in Aktobe, Astana, Kostanai, Pavlodar, Shymkent; library: 580,000 vols; 170 teachers; 5,000 students; Rector Prof. Dr ERKARA AIMAGAM-BETOV.

Karaganda Metallurgical Institute: 101400 Temirtau, Pr. Lenina 34; tel. (7213) 91-56-26; fax (7213) 91-62-80; e-mail karmeti@temirtau.kz; f. 1963; library: 288,000 vols; faculties of Chemical eng., Mechanical eng., Metallurgy; 175 teachers; 2,500 students; Rector Prof. ABDRAKHMAN NAIZABEKOV.

Karaganda State Medical Academy: 100008 Karaganda, Ul. Gogolya 40; tel. (7212) 51-34-79; fax (7212) 51-89-31; e-mail kgma@nursat.kz; internet www.ksma.kz; f. 1950, present name and status 1997; faculties of biology, dentistry, eastern medicine, medicine, paediatrics, pharmacy, postgraduate studies, public health; 520 teachers; 2,954 students; library: 400,000 vols, 186 periodicals; Rector I. KOOLMAGEMBETOV; publ. *Medicine and Ecology* (6 a year).

Karaganda State Technical University: 100027 Karaganda, Bulvar Mira 56; tel. (7212) 56-88-95; fax (7212) 56-88-95; e-mail ivc@kstu.kz; internet www.kstu.kz; f. 1953 as Karaganda Mining Institute; present name and status 1996; faculties of business management, economics and management, civil engineering, information technology, electromechanical engineering, geoecology, machine building, mining, transport and road engineering; library: 1.5m. books; 762 teachers; 8,166 students; Rector GENNADY G. PIVEN.

Kazakh Ablai Khan University of International Relations and World Languages: 050022 Almaty, Muratbaev 200; tel. (7272) 92-19-97; fax (7272) 92-19-91; e-mail kazumo@ablaikhan.kz; internet www.ablaikhan.kz; f. 1941; faculties of English, French, German; 668 teachers; 5,000 students; library: 630,000 vols; Rector SALIMA S. KUNANBAEVA; Vice-Rector for Study Dept NAGIMA A. SARSEMBAEVA; Vice-Rector for Scientific and Research Work KUSAYIN T. RYSSALDY; Vice-Rector for Study and Methodical Work SATIMA S. ZHUMAGULOVA; Vice-Rector

for Social Work ZHUMAGUL A. ISMAGAMBE-
TOVA; publ. scientific papers.

**Kazakh Leading Academy of Architec-
ture and Civil Engineering:**e-mail inter
.rel@mail.ru 050043 Almaty, Ul. Ryskulbe-
kov 28; tel. (7272) 29-46-11; fax (7272) 20-59-
79; e-mail kazgasa@itte.kz; internet www
.kazgasa.kz; f. 1980; State control; academic
year September to July; undergraduate and
postgraduate courses and scientific research,
PhD programmes; faculties of architecture,
civil engineering, environmental engineering, economics. and management in construction, social sciences; 309 teachers;
4,262 students; Pres. AMIRLAN KUSSAINOV;
Rector GULZADA MUKTAPOVA; publ. *Messenger
of KazGASA* (4 a year).

**Kazakh S. D. Asfendijarov National
Medical University:** 050012 Almaty, Ul.
Tole-bi 88; tel. (7272) 92-78-85; fax (7272) 92-
69-97; e-mail kaznmu@arna.kz; internet
www.kaznmu.kz; f. 1931; present name and
status 2001; faculties of dentistry, gen. medicine, health sciences, paediatrics, pharmacy,
public health; library: 221,000 vols; 883
teachers; 5,349 students; Rector T. MUMINOV.

Kazakh S. Seifullin Agrarian University:
473032 Astana, Pr. Pobedy 116; tel. (7172)
31-75-47; fax (7172) 32-22-94; e-mail agun@
kepter.kz; internet www.agun.kz; f. 1957;
library: 400,000 vols; 402 teachers; 2,043
students; Rector B. ALIMZHANOV.

Kazakh State University of Agriculture:
050010 Almaty, Pr. Abaya 8; tel. (7272) 65-
19-48; fax (7272) 62-44-09; e-mail info@kgau
.almaty.kz; internet www.agriun.almaty.kz;
f. 1996 by merger of Kazakh State Institute
of Agriculture (f. 1929) and Alma-Ata Veter-

inary Institute (f. 1910); depts of agricultural
biology, engineering, forestry and horticulture, microbiology, veterinary medicine;
library: 800,000 vols; 670 teachers; 7,600
students; Rector K. A. SAGADIYEV.

**Kazakh T. Ryskulov Economic Univer-
sity:** 050035 Almaty, Ul. Dzhandosova 55;
tel. (7272) 20-28-45; fax (7272) 21-96-31;
e-mail kazeu@pisem.net; internet www
.kazeu.com; f. 1963; faculties of accounting
and information technology, finance and
credit, management and marketing, world
economy and int. relations; banking and
finance management research institute, Faculty development institute; market economy
research institute; Kazakh economic, finance
and int. trade univ.; 520 teachers; 5,177
students; Rector N. K. MAMYROV.

**Kazakhstan Institute of Management,
Economics and Strategic Research:**
050100 Almaty, Ul. Abaya 4; tel. (7272) 70-
42-00; fax (7272) 70-43-38; internet www
.kimep.kz; f. 1992; colleges of Business, Continuing education, Social sciences; 184 teachers; 3,529 students; Pres. Dr CHAN YOUNG
BANG.

Kustanai Agricultural Institute: 110000
Kustanai, Pr. Sverdlova 28; tel. (7142) 25-12-
23; fax (7142) 25-34-76; f. 1966; library:
341,000 vols; Dirs L. M. OVCHINIKOVA, V. S.
PROKURATOVA.

Rudnyi Industrial Institute: 111500 Rudnyi, Ul. 50 let Oktyabrya 38; tel. and fax
(71431) 5-07-03; e-mail rii@krcc.kz; f. 1958;
faculties of automation of production processes, construction, economics, mining;
attached institute in Lisakovsk; 200 teach-

ers; 4,250 students; Rector Prof. U. T.
ABDRAKHIMOV.

Semipalatinsk State Medical Academy:
490019 Semipalatinsk, Abaya ul. 103; tel.
(7222) 62-39-65; fax (7222) 66-34-01; f. 1953;
library: 315,000 vols; 900 teachers; 2,500
students; Rector T. K. RAISSOV.

**South Kazakhstan Technical Univer-
sity:** 160018 Shymkent, Tauke-han 5; tel.
(7252) 53-50-48; f. 1943; faculties of Chemical
technology, economics, mechanical technology; library: 524,000 vols; Rector T. SH.
KALMENOV; publ. *Science and Education in
South Kazakhstan.*

Taraz State Pedagogical University:
080000 Taraz, Zhambyl obl., Ul. Tole-bi 62;
tel. (7262) 45-13-94; fax (7262) 34-35-30;
e-mail gylym_targpi@mail.ru; f. 1967;
teacher training and research; Rector Prof.
Dr MACHMETGALY N. SARYBEKOV.

Western Kazakhstan State University:
090000 Uralsk, Ul. Krasnoarmejskaja 19; tel.
and fax (7112) 51-26-32; e-mail zapkazgu@
wkau.kz; internet www.wkau.kz; f. 1932;
current name and status following merger
of Western Kazakhstan Agrarian University,
Western Kazakhstan Humanities University
and Western Kazakhstan Dauletkerey Institute of Arts 2000; faculties of agri-business
and ecology, culture and library science,
economics, finance and accountancy, fine
arts, geography and natural sciences, history
and human rights, musical arts, oil and gas,
pedagogy, philology, physics and mathematics, polytechnic, sports and physical training,
veterinary medicine and sanitation; library:
1.2m. vols; 899 teachers; 17,052 students;
Rector B. K. DAMITOV.

KENYA

The Higher Education System

Until independence was achieved in 1963 Kenya was part of British East Africa. The oldest institutions of higher education were established during British colonial rule, such as Egerton University (founded 1939; current name and status 1987), the University of Nairobi (founded 1956; current name and status 1970) and Strathmore University (founded 1961; current name and status 1993). There are public and private universities, which are both accredited by the Commission for Higher Education. In 2007 an estimated 118,000 students were enrolled in universities. In both public and private universities the senior officer is the Chancellor, who in public universities is appointed by the President and in private universities is an appropriate or distinguished personage. University governance is handled by the Governing Council or Board of Trustees, and the chief executive is the Vice-Chancellor, who is also head of the University Senate, which is responsible for academic affairs, and financial and administrative management. Faculty boards and Departments are the main units of academic administration. The Ministry of Education, Science and Technology is the government ministry in charge of higher education, acting through the aegis of the Commission for Higher Education. Universities are funded by the state budget and by students' tuition fees.

Admission to university undergraduate degree programmes is on the basis of at least an average C+ score in the Kenya Certificate of Secondary Education. Admission to Diploma or Certificate programmes requires at least C− or D+, respectively. Students who have been awarded the Diploma or Certificate may be admitted to degree-level programmes.

Diplomas and Certificates are awarded after up to a year of intensive study at universities and polytechnics or through 'open' and distance learning schemes. The standard undergraduate Bachelors degree lasts for four years, except in disciplines such as veterinary medicine (five years), architecture and medicine (both six years). Upon completion of the Bachelors degree, students may take either a one-year Postgraduate Diploma course or a one- to three-year Masters degree. The most advanced university-level degree programme is the Doctorate, which requires two years of study following award of the Masters.

Post-secondary vocational and technical education is available through a number of different institutions: craft training institutes, youth polytechnics, institutes of technology and polytechnics. Although there is not yet a uniform national framework for vocational qualifications, they are roughly separated into four levels: artisan, craftsman, technician and technologist. The Kenya Institute of Education and Kenya National Examinations Council are responsible for developing curriculum and testing at these four levels. Qualifications offered include Higher Diploma, Higher Technician Diploma, Ordinary Diploma and Ordinary Technician Diploma.

In the late 2000s Kenya's higher education, science and technology sector was preparing for major legislative and institutional reforms aimed at promoting a knowledge-based economy to improve national prosperity and global competitiveness. Three new bills were being developed in 2009 to ensure quality, equity and reliability in the delivery of post-secondary education.

Regulatory and Representative Bodies

GOVERNMENT

Ministry of Education, Science and Technology: Jogoo House 'B', Harambee Ave, POB 30040, Nairobi; tel. (20) 334411; e-mail info@education.go.ke; internet www .education.go.ke; Minister of Education Prof. SAM ONGERI; Minister of Science and Technology NOAH M. WEKESA.

Ministry of Gender, Sports, Culture and Social Services: Jogoo House 'A', Taifa Rd, POB 30520, Nairobi; tel. (20) 228411; internet www.kenya.go.ke/gender; Minister (vacant).

ACCREDITATION

Commission for Higher Education: POB 54999, 00200 Nairobi; Red Hill Rd, off Limuru Rd, Gigiri; tel. (20) 720500; fax (20) 2021172; e-mail che@kenyaweb.com; internet www.che.or.ke; f. 1985; plans for the establishment and devt of higher education and training; organizes resources for higher education and training; accredits and regularly inspects univs; co-ordinates and regulates admission to univs; 28 mems; library of 4,284 vols; Sec. and CEO Prof. EVERRETT M. STANDA.

Learned Societies

GENERAL

African Network of Scientific and Technological Institutions (ANSTI): UNESCO Nairobi Office, POB 30592, Nairobi; tel. (20) 622620; fax (20) 622750; e-mail info@ansti .org; internet www.ansti.org; f. 1980 under the auspices of UNESCO and UNDP, aided by the Fed. Repub. of Germany and based at the UNESCO Regional Bureau for Science and Technology (q.v.); aims to bring about collaboration between African engineering, scientific and technological institutions involved in postgraduate training, and to undertake research and development in areas of developmental significance in the region; mems: 85 institutions in 32 countries; Coordinator Prof. J. G. MASSAQUOI; publs *African Journal of Science and Technology*, *Directory of ANSTI Institutions*.

Kenya National Academy of Sciences: POB 39450, Nairobi; tel. (20) 311714; fax (20) 311715; e-mail secretariat@knascience.org; internet www.knascience.org; f. 1977; advancement of learning and research; 200 mems; Hon. Chair. Prof. JOSEPH O. MALO; Hon. Sec. Prof. FELIX M. LUTI; publs *Kenya Journal of Science and Technology* (2 a year), *Newsletter*, *Post Magazine*, *Proceedings of Symposia*.

National Council for Science and Technology: POB 30623, Nairobi; tel. (20) 336173; f. 1977; attached to Ministry of Education, Science and Technology; semi-autonomous government agency; provides advisory services to the Government; 35 council mems; library of 3,000 vols, collection of research reports; Sec. Prof. P. GACII; publ. *NCST Newsletter*.

UNESCO Nairobi Regional Bureau for Science and Technology for Sub-Saharan Africa and Cluster Office: POB 30592, Nairobi 00100 GPO; United Nations Offices, Gigiri, Block C, United Nations Ave, Gigiri, Nairobi; tel. (20) 622353; fax (20) 622750; e-mail nairobi@unesco.org; internet www.unesco-nairobi.org; f. 1965; regional office for 47 African countries; designated Cluster Office for Burundi, Kenya, Rwanda and Uganda; library of 10,000 vols, 400 periodicals; Dir PAUL VITTA; publ. *African Journal of Science and Technology* (2 a year).

AGRICULTURE, FISHERIES AND VETERINARY SCIENCE

Agricultural Society of Kenya: POB 30176, Nairobi; tel. (20) 566655; fax (20) 573838; e-mail chiefexecutive@ask.kenya .com; f. 1901; encourages and assists agriculture in Kenya; holds 12 shows a year and farming competitions; sponsors Young Farmers' Clubs of Kenya; 12,000 mems; Chair. TIMOTHY O. OMATO; Chief Exec. BATRAM M. MUTHOKA; publ. *The Kenya Farmer* (12 a year).

BIBLIOGRAPHY, LIBRARY SCIENCE AND MUSEOLOGY

Kenya Library Association: POB 46031, 00100 Nairobi; tel. 736625237; fax (20) 811455; e-mail ekobachi@yahoo.com; internet www.kla.or.ke; f. 1956; organizes, unites and represents the professions concerned with information work in Kenya;

promotes professional integrity and governs the members of the asscn in all matters of professional practice; 200 mems; Chair. Prof. NYAMBOGA; Nat. Sec. HELLEN AMUNGA; Nat. Sec. ESTHER K. OBACHI; publs *Kelias News* (6 a year), *Maktaba—Official Journal* (2 a year).

ECONOMICS, LAW AND POLITICS

Law Society of Kenya: POB 72219-00200, Nairobi; Professional Centre, First Floor, Parliament Rd, Nairobi; tel. (20) 311337; fax (20) 223997; e-mail lsk@lsk.or.ke; internet www.lsk.or.ke; f. 1949; 4,000 mems; Sec. GEORGE KEGORO; publ. *The Advocate* (4 a year).

HISTORY, GEOGRAPHY AND ARCHAEOLOGY

Historical Association of Kenya: c/o Prof. B. A. Ogot, Moi University, POB 3900, Eldoret; f. 1966; Chair. Prof. BETHWELL A. OGOT; Sec. Dr KARIM K. JANMOHAMED; publs *Hadith Series* (1 a year), *Kenya Historical Review* (2 a year).

LANGUAGE AND LITERATURE

Alliance Française: Maison Française Monrovia, Loila St, POB 45475, 0100 Nairobi; tel. (20) 340054; fax (20) 315207; offers courses and examinations in French language and culture and promotes cultural exchange with France; attached teaching centre in Mombasa.

British Council: Upperhill Rd, POB 40751, 00100 Nairobi; tel. (20) 2836000; fax (20) 2836500; e-mail information@britishcouncil.or.ke; internet www.britishcouncil.org/kenya; teaching centre; offers courses and examinations in English language and British culture and promotes cultural exchange with the UK; Dir for Kenya and Regional Dir for East Africa PHILIP GOODWIN.

Goethe-Institut: Maendeleo House, POB 49468, 00100 Nairobi; tel. (20) 2224640; fax (20) 340770; e-mail info@nairobi.goethe.org; internet www.goethe.de/nairobi; offers courses and examinations in German language and culture and promotes cultural exchange with Germany; provides information on Germany's cultural, social and political life; library of 6,000 vols; Dir JOHANNES HOSSFELD.

MEDICINE

Kenya Medical Association: Chyulu Road, Upper Hill, POB 48502, Nairobi; tel. (20) 724617; f. 1962; 1,500 mems; Chair. Dr JAMES W. NYIKAL; Sec. Dr KAVOO KILONZO; publs *East African Medical Journal* (12 a year), *Medicus* (12 a year).

NATURAL SCIENCES

Biological Sciences

East African Wildlife Society: POB 20110, 00200 City Sq., Riara Rd, off Ngong Rd, Nairobi; tel. (20) 574145; fax (20) 570335; e-mail info@eawildlife.org; internet www.eawildlife.org; f. 1961; non-profit org.; safeguards and promotes the conservation and sustainable management of wildlife resources and their natural habitats in East Africa; 6,000 mems; Exec. Dir ALI AKBER KAKA; publs *African Journal of Ecology* (4 a year), *Swara* (4 a year), *Wildlife Info* (4 a year).

Nature Kenya, the East Africa Natural History Society: POB 44486, GPO, 00100 Nairobi; tel. (20) 3749957; fax (20) 3741049; e-mail office@naturekenya.org; internet www.naturekenya.org; f. 1909; 1,000 mems; library of 10,000 vols; Chair. Dr IAN GORDON; publs *Journal of East African Natural History* (2 a year), *Kenya Birds* (2 a year), *Nature East Africa (the EANHS Bulletin)* (2 a year).

Physical Sciences

Kenya Astronomical Society: POB 59224, Nairobi.

RELIGION, SOCIOLOGY AND ANTHROPOLOGY

Theosophical Society: 55A Third Parklands Ave, POB 45928, Nairobi; e-mail cprdunn@nbnet.co.ke; Gen. Sec. C. P. ROBERTSON-DUNN; publ. *The Theosophical Light* (2 a year).

TECHNOLOGY

Institution of Engineers of Kenya: 1st Fl., KRBC Annex, POB 41346, 00100 Nairobi; tel. (20) 729326; fax (20) 716922; e-mail iek@iekenya.org; internet www.iekenya.org; f. 1945, present name 1973; 2,100 mems; Hon. Sec. Eng. J M. WANYOIKE; publ. *Kenya Engineer* (6 a year).

Research Institutes

AGRICULTURE, FISHERIES AND VETERINARY SCIENCE

Coffee Research Foundation: CRF Coffee Research Station, POB 4, Ruiru; tel. (151) 54027; fax (151) 54133; f. 1949; research on coffee cultivation, agronomy and management, marketing and economics of production; Dir W. R. OPILE; publ. *Kenya Coffee Bulletin*.

Interafrican Bureau for Animal Resources: Maendeleo House, Monrovia St, POB 30786, Nairobi; tel. (20) 338544; fax (20) 220546; internet www.au-ibar.org; f. 1951; veterinary and livestock health and production covering all mem. states of the OAU; library of 5,000 vols; Dir Dr J. T. MUSIIME; publ. *Bulletin of Animal Health and Production in Africa* (4 a year).

Kenya Agricultural Research Institute: City Square, POB 57811, Nairobi; tel. (20) 4183720; fax (20) 4183344; e-mail resource.center@kari.org; internet www.kari.org; f. 1979; agricultural and veterinary sciences research; Dir Dr R. M. KIOME.

Attached Centre:

National Veterinary Research Centre (MUGUGA): POB 32, Kikuyu; preparation and issue of biological products and research into animal health and animal diseases; Dir D. P. KARIUKI; publ. *Record of Research*.

Ministry of Agriculture and Livestock Development, Department of Veterinary Services: Private Bag Kangemi (00625), Nairobi; tel. (20) 632231; fax (20) 631273; f. 1903; control and diagnosis of animal diseases, advisory service to farmers, animal health policy formulation, veterinary research and investigation services, veterinary regulation services; library of 27,500 vols; Dir Dr WILLIAM TOROITICH K. GHONG'.

National Agricultural Research Laboratories: POB 14733, Nairobi; tel. and fax (20) 444144; f. 1908; soil science research, crop protection research; library of 4,000 vols; Dir Dr F. N. MUCHENA; publ. *Soil Survey Report*.

National Horticultural Research Centre: POB 220, Thika; tel. (67) 21283; fax (67) 21285; e-mail karithika@africaonline.co.ke; internet www.kari.org; f. 1955; research into crop protection, seed production, citriculture, viticulture, floriculture, temperate and tropical fruits, post-harvest physiology, vegetables; breeds for multiple disease resistance to common bean diseases; Dir Dr C. N. WATURU.

Plant Breeding Station: Ministry of Agriculture, PO Njoro; tel. (51) 48150; fax (51) 47986; f. 1927; improvement of wheat, barley and oats; 20 professional staff; Officer-in-Charge Dr R. C. MCGINNIS.

Pyrethrum Board of Kenya: POB 420, Nakuru; tel. (51) 2211567; fax (51) 2210466; e-mail marketing@kenya-pyrethrum.com; internet www.kenya-pyrethrum.com; f. 1948; research and information on pyrethrum as a natural insecticide; Dir SAMUEL KIHIU; publ. *Pyrethrum Post* (2 a year).

Tea Research Foundation of Kenya: POB 820, 20200 Kericho; tel. (52) 20598; fax (52) 20575; e-mail lib-trfk@kenyaweb.com; internet www.tearesearch.or.ke; f. 1951; research and technology devt on the production and manufacture of tea, with spec. emphasis on agronomic, botanical, environmental and physical parameters; pests and diseases management; tea biochemistry and processing of tea, technology, knowledge and information transfer, training and advisory services; value addition, product diversification and market research; library of 12,000 vols; Dir Dr FRANCIS N. WACHIRA; publs *Tea Growers Handbook*, *Tea Journal* (2 a year), *TRFK Quarterly Bulletin*.

HISTORY, GEOGRAPHY AND ARCHAEOLOGY

British Institute in Eastern Africa: POB 30710, GPO 0100 Nairobi; tel. (20) 4343190; fax (20) 4343365; e-mail office@biea.ac.uk; internet www.biea.ac.uk; f. 1960; library of 5,000 vols, 100 periodicals; research into the history and archaeology of Eastern Africa, for which occasional grants and studentships are offered; 350 mems; Dir Dr JUSTIN WILLIS; publ. *Azania* (1 a year).

MEDICINE

Alupe Leprosy and Other Skin Diseases Research Centre (The John Lowe Memorial): POB 3, Busia; tel. and fax (55) 22410; f. 1952; part of KEMRI; Dir Dr P. A. OREGE.

Institute for Medical Research and Training: National Public Health Laboratory Services, POB 20750, Nairobi; f. 1964 for research and medical training; see also College of Health Professions, Medical School, under Colleges.

Kenya Medical Research Institute (KEMRI): POB 54840-00200, Nairobi; tel. (20) 722541; fax (20) 720030; internet www.kemri.org; f. 1979; under the Min. of Health; research in biomedical sciences, cooperates with other instns in training programmes and research, cooperates with the relevant ministries, the Nat. Ccl for Science and Technology and the Medical Science Advisory Research Cttee; 11 centres: Centre for Biotechnology Development Research, Centre for Clinical Research, Centre for Virus Research, Centre for Infections and Parasitic Diseases Research, Centre for Traditional Medicines and Drugs Research, Centre for Microbiology Research, Centre for Respiratory Diseases Research, Centre for Vector Biology and Control Research, Centre for Geographic Medicine Research, Centre for Public Health Research, Eastern and Southern Africa Centre of International Parasite Control (ESACIPAC); coordinates the annual African Health Sciences Congress and is secretariat for African Forum for Health Sciences (AFHES); library of 3,000 vols, collection of scientific reprints, theses and dissertations; Dir Dr DAVY KOECH; publs *African Journal of Health Sciences* (4 a year), *AIDS Update* (6 a year), *KEMRI Abstracts*.

National Public Health Laboratory Services (Medical Department): POB 20750, Nairobi; tel. (20) 725601; fax (20) 729504; all branches of medicine; library; Dir Dr JACK NYAMONGO.

Respiratory Diseases Research Centre: POB 47855, Nairobi; tel. (20) 724262; fax (20) 720030; f. 1960; part of KEMRI; research on all aspects of respiratory diseases, with special reference to diagnostic and treatment procedures relevant to developing country situations and to the epidemiology of respiratory diseases; Dir Dr J. A. ODHIAMBO.

NATURAL SCIENCES

Biological Sciences

Institute of Primate Research: National Museums of Kenya, POB 24481, Nairobi; tel. (20) 882571; fax (20) 882546; e-mail directoripr@museums.or.ke; internet www.primateresearch.org; research in primate medicine, virology, reproductive biology, infectious diseases, and ecology and conservation; Dir Dr THOMAS M. KARIUKI; publ. *IPR Report* (1 a year).

TECHNOLOGY

Kenya Industrial Research and Development Institute: Lusaka Rd, Dunga, POB 30650, Nairobi; tel. (20) 535966; fax (20) 555738; e-mail kirdi@arcc.or.ke; internet www.kirdi.go.ke; f. 1948; provides advice for established local industrial concerns and gives assistance in the establishment of new industries on the utilization of local materials; Dir Dr P. M. MUTURI.

Mines and Geological Department: Madini House, Machakos Rd, POB 30009, 00100 Nairobi; tel. (20) 541040; e-mail cmg@bidii.com; f. 1932; geological survey and research; mineral resources development; administers mineral and explosives laws; library of 32,000 vols, 10,000 periodicals; Commr L. K. BIWOTT; publs *Mineral Statistics Data*, bulletins, maps, reports, statistics.

National Fibre Research Centre, Kibos: POB 1490, Kisumu; Dir J. H. BRETTELL.

Libraries and Archives
Mombasa
British Council Library: Jubilee Insurance Bldg, Moi Ave, POB 90590, Mombasa; tel. (41) 2223076; fax (41) 2315349; 3,000 vols, 32 periodicals; Information Centre Man. MARY STEVENS.

Nairobi
Desai Memorial Library: POB 1253, Nairobi; f. 1942; public library and reading room; 31,800 vols; books in Swahili, English, Gujarati, Gurumukhi, Hindi and Urdu; reference, newspaper and periodic sections; 1,151 mems; Pres. A. M. SADARUDDIN; Sec. HARSHAD JOSHI.

High Court of Kenya Library: Law Courts, POB 30041, Nairobi; tel. (20) 221221; f. 1935; comprises High Court Library and Court of Appeal Library in Nairobi and 10 major br. libraries at Mombasa, Kisumu, Eldoret, Kakamega, Nakuru, Nyeri, Kisumu, Bungoma, Machakos and Kisii; 100,000 vols, 65 periodicals on practitioner's law, with special emphasis on Kenyan and English law; Head Librarian E. N. JUMA.

Ismail Rahimtulla Trust Library: POB 40333, Nairobi; tel. (20) 212660; f. 1953; 7,200 vols; Librarian P. GITAU.

Kenya Agricultural Research Institute Library: POB 57811, Nairobi; tel. (20) 4183301; fax (20) 4183344; e-mail resource .centre@kari.org; internet www.kari.org; f. 1928; extends current scientific awareness service to all agricultural research and academic centres and official depts within Kenya; 150,000 vols; Asst Dir Information and Documentation Services REGE RACHEL; Librarian PATRICK MAINA; publ. *East African Agricultural and Forestry Journal* (4 a year).

Kenya National Archives and Documentation Service: POB 49849, Moi Ave, 00100 Nairobi; tel. (20) 250576; fax (20) 316187; e-mail info@kenyarchives.go.ke; internet www.kenyarchives.go.ke; f. 1965; preservation and custody of public records; assists government offices in the maintenance of public records; over 1 million items, incl. reports, maps, films, microfilms, photographs, slides; archival materials accessible to national and international researchers; five records centres in Mombasa, Nairobi, Nakuru, Kisumu and Kakamega; 50,000 vols and periodicals, incl. 9,000 government monographs; 600 annual reports from government ministries and depts; Kenya Gazette, Laws of Kenya and parliamentary debates; 20,000 general and Africana vols; 700 theses and dissertations; 5,000 legal deposit collections; 1,600 periodicals and journals, incl. 30 current titles; the library prepares accession lists for all collections, and alphabetical lists for annual reports and periodicals, and publs indexes and guides to public records; databases accessible via website; Dir L. I. MWANGI.

Kenya National Library Services: POB 30573, Ngong Rd, Nairobi; tel. (20) 725550; fax (20) 721749; e-mail knls@nbnet.co.ke; internet www.knls.or.ke; f. 1967; 621,000 vols, 120 periodicals; public library services through Nat. Lending Library in Nairobi, 19 brs and 8 mobile units; Nat. Reference and Bibliographic Dept f. 1980; special collections: East Africana and Kenyana; Chair. Archbishop STEPHEN ONDIEKI; Dir S. K. NG'ANG'A; publs *Kenya National Bibliography* (1 a year), *Kenya Periodical Directory* (every 2 years).

McMillan Memorial Library: POB 40791, Banda St, Nairobi; tel. (20) 221844; f. 1931; two branch libraries at Kaloleni and Eastlands; comprises Nairobi City Library Services; collns of old photographs, microfilms of East Africa, serial publs; Africana colln of 20,000 vols; 400,000 vols; Chief Librarian A. O. ESILABA.

University of Nairobi Libraries: POB 30197, 00100 Nairobi; tel. (20) 318262; internet www.library.uonbi.ac.ke; f. 1959; 850,000 vols, 600 periodicals, 7,000 electronic journals; 11 brs; acts as legal nat. depository and UN deposit library; Librarian SALOME MUNAVU (acting).

Museums and Art Galleries
Nairobi
National Museums of Kenya: Museum Hill, POB 40658, 00100 Nairobi; tel. (20) 742131; fax (20) 741424; e-mail dgnmk@museums.or.ke; internet www.museums.or .ke; f. 1910 by the E African Natural History Soc.; all brs of natural sciences, prehistory, geology, education, ethnography; library: joint library with E African Natural History Soc., 30,000 vols; Dir Dr IDLE OMAR FARAH; Librarian A. H. K. OWANO; publs *Horizons*, *Journal of East Africa Natural History*, *Kenya Past and Present*.

Attached Museums:

Fort Jesus Museum: POB 82412, Mombasa; tel. (41) 312839; fax (41) 227797; e-mail nmkfortj@swiftmombasa.com; f. 1960; inside 16th-century Portuguese fortress overlooking Mombasa harbour; finds from various coastal Islamic sites, from Fort Jesus, and from a 17th-century Portuguese wreck show the history of the Kenyan coast; library of 1,000 vols and numerous offprints; Curator ALI BAAKABE.

Kisumu Museum: POB 1779, Kisumu; tel. (57) 40804; e-mail kisumuse@africaonline.co.ke; Curator PETER NYAMENYA.

Kitale Museum: POB 1219, Kitale; tel. (54)30996; f. 1926; natural and cultural museum; history and science, emphasis on education; library of 5,000 vols; Curator DANIEL KIPLOROR.

Lamu Museum: POB 48, Lamu; tel. (42) 633073; e-mail lamuse@hotmail.com; internet www.museums.or.ke; Curator ATHMAN HUSSEIN.

Universities
AFRICA NAZARENE UNIVERSITY
POB 53067-00200, Nairobi

Telephone: (45) 24350
Fax: (45) 24352
E-mail: admit@anu.ac.ke
Internet: www.anu.ac.ke

Founded 1994
Private control; administered by Church of the Nazarene International
Academic year: September to August (3 trimesters)

Vice-Chancellor: Prof. LEAH MARENGU
Deputy Vice-Chancellor for Academic Affairs: Prof. MARY JONES

Number of teachers: 50
Number of students: 850

Departments of Commerce, Computer Science and Theology.

AFRICAN VIRTUAL UNIVERSITY
POB 25405, Nairobi
71 Maalim Juma Rd, Kilimani, POB 25405-00603, Nairobi

Telephone: (20) 2712056
Fax: (20) 2712071
E-mail: contact@avu.org
Internet: www.avu.org

Founded 1997
Independent distance-learning institution sponsored by the World Bank, providing education in 18 African countries through a network of 33 Learning Centres
Languages of instruction: English, French

Rector: KUZVINETSA PETER DZVIMBO
Chief Financial Officer: DEREK PIERSON
Dir of Academic Programmes Management and Development: Dr FRED BARASA

Bachelors degree and diploma courses in business studies and computer science; short courses in journalism, information technology and business communication.

CATHOLIC UNIVERSITY OF EASTERN AFRICA
POB 62157-00200, Nairobi

Telephone: (20) 891601
Fax: (20) 891261
E-mail: linkages@cuea.edu
Internet: www.cuea.edu

Founded 1984 as Catholic Higher Institute of Eastern Africa; present name and status 1992

Private control

Rector: Rev. Prof. JOHN C. MAVIIRI

Vice-Rector and Deputy Vice-Chancellor for Academic Affairs: Prof. PAUL OGULA

Vice-Rector and Deputy Vice-Chancellor for Admin.: FRANCIS MUCHOKI

Dir of Academic Linkages: Rev. Dr PETER I. GICHURE

Library of 61,705 vols, 11,553 periodicals

Number of teachers: 261 (141 full-time, 120 visiting)

Number of students: 4,328

Publications: *African Christian Studies* (4 a year), *Eastern Africa Journal of Humanities and Science* (1 a year)

DEANS

Faculty of Arts and Social Sciences: CALLISTO LOCHENG

Faculty of Commerce: ATHERU KALENYWA

Faculty of Education: Rev. Dr MARCELLUS KAWASONG

Faculty of Science: THUO GATHOGO

Faculty of Theology: Rev. Dr CLEMENT MAJAWA

DAYSTAR UNIVERSITY

Athi River Campus, POB 17, 90145 Nairobi

Telephone: (45) 6622601

Fax: (45) 6622420

E-mail: vc@daystar.ac.ke*Nairobi Campus*, POB 44400-00100, Nairobi

Telephone: (20) 2723002

Fax: (20) 2728338

E-mail: vc@daystar.ac.ke*Mombasa Campus*, POB 99483-80107, Kilindini, Mombasa

Telephone: (20) 2416916

E-mail: vc@daystar.ac.ke

Internet: www.daystar.ac.ke

Founded 1974

Private control; non-profit, non-denominational Christian

Vice-Chancellor: Rev. Prof. GODFREY MBITI NGURU

Deputy Vice-Chancellor for Finance, Admin. and Planning: Dr PHILIP KITUI

Library of 73,600 vols, 365 audio/visual resources, 13,600 electronic journals, 40 print journals

Number of teachers: 230

Number of students: 3,937

DEANS

Arts: PURITY KIAMBI

Science and Technology: Dr JON MASSO

Social Sciences: Dr ALICE MUNENE

UNIVERSITY OF EASTERN AFRICA, BARATON

POB 2500, Eldoret

Telephone: (53) 52625

Fax: (53) 52263

E-mail: dvc@ueab.ac.ke

Internet: www.ueab.ac.ke

Private control; Seventh-Day Adventist

Founded 1980

Chancellor: GEOFFREY MBWANA

Vice-Chancellor: Prof. R. TIMOTHY MCDONALD

Deputy Vice-Chancellor: Dr NATHANIEL WALEMBA

Dean of Students: BENSON NYAGWENCHA

Library of 50,000 vols

Number of teachers: 89

Number of students: 1,502 (1,286 full-time, 216 part-time)

DEANS

School of Business: SAMUEL OYIEKE

School of Education: Prof. DENFORD MUS-VOSVI

School of Humanities and Social Sciences: Prof. WA-GITHUMO MWANGI

School of Science and Technology: Prof. ASAPH MARADUFU

EGERTON UNIVERSITY

POB 536, 20115 Egerton

Telephone: (51) 2217891

Fax: (51) 2217827

E-mail: info@egerton.ac.ke

Internet: www.egerton.ac.ke

Founded 1939; university status 1987

State control

Language of instruction: English

Academic year: August to May

Vice-Chancellor: Prof. J. K. TUITOEK

Deputy Vice-Chancellor for Academic Affairs: Prof. ROSE MWONYA

Deputy Vice-Chancellor for Administration and Finance: Prof. L. M. MUMERA

Deputy Vice-Chancellor for Research and Extension: Prof. JUDE M. MATHOOKO

Academic Registrar: Prof. S. M. NGARE

Registrar for Administration and Finance: Dr T. K. SEREM

Prin. of Chuka Constituent College: E. M. NJOKA

Prin. of Kisii Constituent College: Prof. JOHN AKAMA

Prin. of Laikipia Campus: Prof. F. K. LELO

Dean of Students: J. K. KIBET (acting)

Librarian: S. C. OTENYA

Library of 77,439 vols

Number of teachers: 570

Number of students: 10,149

Publications: *Agricultural Bulletin* (2 a year), *Egerton Journal of Humanities, Social Sciences and Education* (2 a year), *Egerton Journal of Science and Technology* (2 a year), '*Kumekucha*' (2 a year)

DEANS

Agriculture: I. K. KOSKEY

Arts and Social Sciences: Dr F. WAKO

Commerce (Kisii Campus): P. A. C. KAPSOOT

Education (Laikipia Campus): Dr M. MATEE

Education and Human Resources: Dr B. N. GITHUA

Engineering: P. K. KIMANI

Environmental Science and Natural Resources: Prof. F. K. LELO

Health Sciences: Dr D. K. NGOTHO

Humanities and Development Studies (Laikipia Campus): Dr F. A. YIEKE

Science: Dr M. K. ROTICH

Graduate School: Prof. B. K. KITUR (Dir)

School of Continuing Education: Prof. F. N. WEGULO (Dir)

School of Education: Dr F. S. BARASA (Dir)

College of Open and Distance Learning: Prof. J. CHANGEIYWO

JOMO KENYATTA UNIVERSITY OF AGRICULTURE AND TECHNOLOGY

POB 62000, City Sq., 0200 Nairobi

Telephone: (67) 52711

Fax: (67) 52030

E-mail: jkuat.main@gmail.com

Internet: www.jkuat.ac.kec

Founded 1981; university status 1994

State control

Language of instruction: English

Academic year: May to April

Chancellor: Prof. FRANCIS JOHN GICHAGA

Vice-Chancellor: Prof. NICK G. WANJOHI

Deputy Vice-Chancellor for Academic Affairs: Prof. MABEL IMBUGA

Deputy Vice-Chancellor for Administration, Planning and Development: Prof. FRANCIS M. NJERUH

Deputy Vice-Chancellor for Research, Production and Extension: Prof. ESTHER M. KAHANGI

Registrar for Academic Affairs: Dr SULEMAN AKECH

Registrar for Administration, Planning and Development: Prof. ISAAC INOTI

Registrar for Research, Production and Extension: P. D. MUCHAI MBUGUA

Dean for Students Welfare: Dr MARANGI MBOGHO

Librarian: LAWRENCE M. WANYAMA

Library of 85,302 vols

Number of teachers: 546

Number of students: 15,000

Publications: *Horizon DAT* (architecture, 1 a year), *Journal of Agriculture Science and Technology* (2 a year), *Journal of Civil Engineering* (1 a year)

DEANS

Civil, Environmental and Construction Engineering: Dr ALFRED MAYABI

Faculty of Agriculture: Dr KAMAU NGAMAU

Faculty of Engineering: Dr MARY NDUNG'U

Faculty of Science: Prof. R. O. ODHIAMBO

School of Architecture and Building Sciences: Dr CRISPINO C. OCHIENG

School for Human Resource Development: Dr ELEGWA MUKULU

School of Electrical, Electronics & Information Engineering: Dr JOHN NDERU

School of Mechanical, Manufacturing and Materials Engineering: Dr BERNARD IKUA

KENYA METHODIST UNIVERSITY

POB 267, Meru

Telephone: (164) 30301

Fax: (164) 30162

E-mail: info@kemu.ac.ke

Internet: www.kemu.ac.ke

Founded 1997

Private control

Chancellor: Dr Rev. STEPHEN KANYARU M'IMPWI

Vice-Chancellor: Prof. MUTUMA MUGAMBI

Registrar: Dr Rev. STEPHEN KANYARU M'IMPWI

Librarian: JOE C. NYAMULUI

CHAIRS OF FACULTIES

Agriculture and Natural Resources: Prof. KABURU M'RIBU

Applied Biology: Prof. ALICE N. MURITHI

Business Administration: Prof. BENJAMIN MAKUYU

Education and Counselling: JOHN GIKUNDA MARIENE

Maths and Computer Science: Prof. LUHAHI LAHI

Theology: Rev. PETER MUKUCCIA

KENYATTA UNIVERSITY

POB 43844, GPO 00100, Nairobi

Telephone: (20) 810901

Fax: (20) 811575

Internet: www.ku.ac.ke

Founded 1972 as constituent college of University of Nairobi, present status 1985

State control

Language of instruction: English

Academic year: September to July

Chancellor: Prof. HARRIS MULE

Vice-Chancellor: Prof. OLIVE M. MUGENDA

Deputy Vice-Chancellor for Academic Affairs: Prof. G. M. MULUVI (acting)

Deputy Vice-Chancellor for Administration: Prof. G. M. MULUVI

Deputy Vice-Chancellor for Finance, Planning and Development: Prof. D. M. MUGENDA

Registrar for Academic Affairs: Dr J. F. KOGA

Registrar for Administration: Dr G. S. MSE
Registrar for Finance, Planning and Development: Dr N. M. KARAGU
Librarian: J. K. GAKOBO (acting)
Library of 335,321 vols, 6,550 vols of periodicals
Number of teachers: 747
Number of students: 24,484
Publications: *African Journal of Educational Studies, Chemchemi, International Journal of the School of Humanities and Social Sciences, East African Journal of Life Sciences, East African Journal of Physical Sciences*

DEANS

School of Agriculture and Enterprise Development: Prof. GITONGA N. MBURUGU
School of Applied Human Sciences: Prof. KEREN MBURUGU
School of Business: Dr J. M. CHEGE
School of Economics: Dr TOM KIMANI
School of Education: Prof. J. OGENO
School of Engineering and Technology: Dr W. MUTHUMBI
School of Environmental Studies: Prof. S. G. NJUGUNA
School of Graduate Studies: Prof. J. WAUDO
School of Health Sciences: Dr B. M. OKELLO-AGINA
School of Hospitality and Tourism Management: Dr ALICE ONDIGI
School of Humanities and Social Sciences: Prof. OLUOCH OBURA
School of Law: Dr LINDA A. MUSUMBA
School of Pure and Applied Sciences: Dr G. MUTHAKIA
School of Visual and Performing Arts: Dr BEATRICE DIGOLO

MASENO UNIVERSITY

Private Bag, Maseno
Telephone: (57) 351620
Fax: (57) 351221
E-mail: vc@maseno.ac.ke
Internet: www.maseno.ac.ke
Founded 2000 upon independence of Moi University's Maseno Univ. College
State control
3 Univ. campuses; constituent college: Bondo Univ. College
Chancellor: FLORIDA A. KARANI
Chair.: Prof. NIMROD BWIBO
Vice-Chancellor: Prof. FREDRICK N. ONYANGO
Deputy Vice-Chancellor for Academic Affairs: Prof. DOMINIC MAKAWITI
Deputy Vice-Chancellor for Admin. and Finance: Prof. MARY K. WALINGO
Deputy Vice-Chancellor for Planning and Extension Services: Prof. GEORGE MARK ONYANGO
Prin.: Prof. STEPHEN AGONG
Librarian: SYLVIA OGOLA
Library of 150,000 vols
Number of teachers: 320
Number of students: 5,250
Publications: *Equator News* (4 a year), *General Information Booklet* (1 a year), *Graduation Bulletin* (1 a year), *Maseno Journal of Education, Arts and Science* (1 a year), *Maseno University Calendar* (every 5 years)

DEANS

Faculty of Arts and Social Sciences: Prof. CALEB OKUMU
Faculty of Education: Dr EDWARDS KOCHUNG'
Faculty of Science: Prof. AGURE JOHN OGONJI
School of Medicine: Prof. JOASH ALUOCH

DIRECTORS

Bondo University College: STEPHEN AGONG (Prin.)
City Campus: Dr KATHERINE MUHOMA
School of Development and Strategic Studies: Dr FREDRICK WANYAMA
School of Environment and Earth Sciences: Prof. JOSEPHINE NGAIRA
School of Public Health and Community Development: Prof. WILSON ODERO
School of Graduate Studies: Prof. PHILIP OKINDA

MOI UNIVERSITY

POB 3900, Eldoret 30100
Telephone: (53) 43620
Fax: (53) 43047
E-mail: vcmu@mu.ac.ke
Internet: www.mu.ac.ke
Founded 1984
State control
Language of instruction: English
Academic year: September to June
Chancellor: Prof. BETHWEL ALLAN OGOT
Vice-Chancellor: Prof. DAVID K. SOME
Deputy Vice-Chancellor for Planning and Development: Prof. S. GUDU
Deputy Vice-Chancellor for Research and Extension: Dr M. J. KAMAR
Chief Academic Officer: Prof. K. OLE KAREI
Chief Administrative Officer: Dr J. K. SANG
Principal of Chepkoilel Campus: Dr J. K. LONYANGAPUO
Finance Officer: BENSON MUIRURI
Librarian: TIRONG ARAP TANUI
Library of 200,000 vols, 50,000 periodicals
Number of teachers: 709
Number of students: 5,266

DEANS

School of Agriculture and Biotechnology: Dr REUBEN M. MUASYA
School of Arts and Social Sciences: Dr PETER O. NDEGE
School of Economics and Business Management: Prof. HENRY K. MARITIM
School of Education: Prof. RUTH N. OTUNGA
School of Engineering: Prof. ABEL N. MAYAKA
School of Environmental Sciences: Prof. WILSON K. YABANN
School of Human Resources Development: Dr MARY C. LUTTA-MUKKHEBI
School of Information Sciences: Prof. JOSEPH B. OJIAMBO
School of Law: Prof. JOHN K. CHEBII
School of Medicine: Dr FABIAN ESAMAI
School of Natural Resources Management: Prof. ERICK KOECH
School of Public Health: Prof. JOSEPH ROTICH
School of Science: Dr PETER K. TORONGEY

UNIVERSITY OF NAIROBI

POB 30197, Nairobi
Telephone: (20) 318262
Fax: (20) 2246655
E-mail: postmaster@unics.gn.apc.org
Internet: www.uonbi.ac.ke
Founded 1956 as Royal Technical College of E Africa; present name 1970
State control
Language of instruction: English
Academic year: October to July
Chancellor: JOE B. WANJUI
Vice-Chancellor: Prof. GEORGE A. O. MAGOHA
Deputy Vice-Chancellor for Academic Affairs: Prof. JACOB T. KAIMENYI
Deputy Vice-Chancellor for Administration and Finance: Prof. PHILIP M. F. MBITHI
Registrar for Academic Affairs: BERNARD M. WAWERU
Registrar for Administration: CHRISTOPHER O. OMBATI

Registrar for Planning: WYCLIFFE J. ASILLA
Librarian: SALOME N. MUNAVU
Number of teachers: 1,662
Number of students: 45,548
Publications: *Academic Calendar, University of Nairobi Varsity Focus* (research activity newsletter)

PRINCIPALS

College of Agriculture and Veterinary Medicine: Prof. AGNES W. MWANG'OMBE
College of Architecture and Engineering: Prof. BERNARD N. K. NJOROGE
College of Biological and Physical Sciences: Prof. LUCY W. IRUNGU
College of Education and External Studies: Prof. HENRY W. MUTORO
College of Health Sciences: Prof. ISAAC O. KIBWAGE
College of Humanities and Social Sciences: Prof. ISAAC M. MBECHE

DEANS

Faculty of Agriculture: Prof. JOHN H. NDERITU
Faculty of Arts: Prof. ENOS H. N. NJERU
Faculty of Veterinary Medicine: Prof. JOHN MUNENE NJENGA
School of Biological Sciences: Dr ELIJAH AKUNDA
School of Business: Prof. STEPHEN NZUVE
School of Continuing and Distance Education: Dr GUANTAI MBOROKI
School of Dental Sciences: Dr EVELYN G. WAGAIYU
School of Economics: FRANCIS M. MWEGA
School of Education: Prof. L. KIBERA
School of Engineering: Dr PATTIS M. A. ODIRA (acting)
School of Law: Prof. BEN SIHANYA
School of Mathematics: JAMES H. WERE
School of Medicine: Prof. ZIPPORAH W. NGUMI
School of Pharmacy: Prof. GRACE N. THOITHI
School of Physical Sciences: Prof. PAUL M. SHIUNDU
School of the Arts and Design: WALTER H. ONYANGO
School of the Built Environment: HEZEKIAH GICHUNGE

PROFESSORS

Faculty of Agriculture (POB 29053, Nairobi; tel. (20) 631340; fax (20) 632121):

IMUNGI, J. K., Food Technology and Nutrition
KANYARI, P. W. N., Veterinary Pathology and Microbiology
KARUE, C. N., Range Management
LARMAT, NANCY K. KARANJA
MARIBEI, JAMES M., Clinical Studies
MBUGUA, SAMUEL K., Food Technology and Nutrition
MICHIEKA, R. W., Crop Protection
MITARU, B., Animal Production
MUKUNYA, D. M., Crop Protection
MWANGOMBE, A., Crop Protection
OGUTU, A., Agricultural Economics
WAITHAKA, K., Crop Science

Faculty of Architecture (tel. (20) 2724521):

ROSTOM, R. S., Geospatial and Space Technology
SYAGGA, P. M., Land Development

Faculty of Arts (tel. (20) 318362; e-mail arts@uonbi.ac.ke):

ABDULAZIZ, M. H., Linguistics and African Languages
CHESAINA, C., Literature
INDANGASI, H., Literature
KIMUYU, PETER K.
MUGAMBI, J. N. K., Religious Studies
MUREITHI, L. P., Economics
MURIUKI, G., History
MWABU, G. M., Economics
NYASANI, J., Philosophy

ODINGO, R. S., Geography
OJANY, F. F., Geography
OMONDI, L. N., Linguistics and African Languages
OYUGI, W. O., Political Science and Public Administration
WANYANDE, PETER, Political Science and Public Administration

Faculty of Veterinary Sciences (POB 29053, Nairobi; tel. (20) 631007; fax (20) 631007; e-mail deanfvm@uonbi.ac.ke):

AGUMBAH, G. J. O., Clinical Studies
GATHUMA, J. M., Public Health, Pharmacology and Toxicology
KIPTOON, J. C., Clinical Studies
MAINA, J. N., Veterinary Anatomy
MAITHO, T. E., Public Health, Pharmacology and Toxicology
MALOIY, G. M. O., Physiology
MITEMA, S. E. O., Public Health, Pharmacology and Toxicology
MUNYUA, W. K., Veterinary Pathology
MUTIGA, E. R., Clinical Studies
NYAGA, P. N., Veterinary Pathology
ODUOR-OKELLO, D., Veterinary Anatomy

School of Business (tel. (20) 2059163):
KIBERA, F. N., Business Administration

School of Dental Sciences (tel. (20) 2720322; fax (20) 723252):

GUTHUA, S. W., Oral Surgery
KAIMENYI, J. T., Periodontology and Community Dentistry
MAKAWITI, DOMINIC W., Biochemistry
MWANG'OMBE, JOSEPH K., Community Health
OPINYA, G. N., Paediatric Dentistry, Orthodontics

School of Education (POB 97, Kikuyu; tel. (66) 6750940; e-mail deanedu@uonbi.ac.ke):

KARANI, F. A., Educational Communication and Technology
MACHARIA, D., Education
OKOMBO, O., Linguistics and Literature
WANJALA, Linguistics and Literature

School of Engineering (tel. (20) 339061):

ADUOL, F. W. O., Surveying
GICHAGA, F. J., Civil Engineering
LUTI, F. M., Mechanical Engineering
OBUDHO, R. A., Urban and Regional Planning
OTIENO, A. V., Electrical and Electronics Engineering
SHARMA, T. C., Agricultural Engineering

School of Law (tel. (20) 3740366):
MUTUNGI, O. K., Commercial Law
OJWANG, J. B., Private Law

School of Medicine (tel. (20) 2726300; fax (20) 714048):

ATINGIA, J. E. U., Orthopaedic Surgery
BHATT, S. M., Medicine
BWIBO, N. O., Paediatrics
KIGONDU, C., Clinical Chemistry
KUNGU, A., Human Pathology
KYAMBI, J. M., Surgery
MALEK, A. K., Human Anatomy
MATTA, W. M., Human Anatomy
MEME, J. S., Paediatrics
NDELE, J., Pharmacology
NDETEI, D. M., Psychiatry
ODHIAMBO, P. A., Surgery
OJWANG, S. B. O., Obstetrics and Gynaecology
OLIECH, J. S., Surgery
OTIENO, L. S., Medicine
PAMBA, H. O., Medical Microbiology
SINEI, S. K., Obstetrics and Gynaecology
THAIRU, K., Physiology
WAMOLA, I. A., Medical Microbiology
WASUNA, A. E. U., Surgery

School of Pharmacy (tel. (20) 2726771):
GUANTAI, A.

KOKWARO, G. O., Pharmaceutics and Pharmacy Practice
MAITAI, C. K., Pharmacology and Pharmacognosy
MWANGI, J. W., Pharmacology and Pharmacognosy

School of Physical Sciences (tel. (20) 4443181; e-mail deanscience@uonbi.ac.ke):

GENGA, R., Physics
GITU, P. M., Chemistry
JUMBA, ISAAC, Chemistry
KAMAU, G. N., Chemistry
KHAMALA, C. P. M., Zoology
KOKWARO, J. O., Botany
MAVUTI, KENNETH M., Zoology
MIBEY, R. K., Botany
MIDIWO, J. O., Chemistry
MUKIAMA, T. K., Botany
MUNAVU, R. M., Chemistry
MWANGI, R. W., Zoology
NYAMBOK, I. O., Geology
ODADA, E., Geology
ODHIAMBO, J. W., Mathematics
OGALLO, L. T., Meteorology
OGANA, B. W., Mathematics
ONYANGO, F. N., Physics
OTIENO-MALO, J. B., Physics
PATEL, P. J., Physics
POKHRIYAL, G. P., Mathematics
WANDIGA, S. O., Chemistry

Institutes:

ALILA, P., Institute for Development Studies
OCHOLLA-AYAYO, A. B. C., Population Studies and Research Institute
OKIDI, C. O., Institute for Development Studies
RODRIGUES, A. J., School of Informatics and Computing
SUDA, C., Institute of African Studies
WANDIBBA, S. B. A., Institute of African Studies

ATTACHED INSTITUTES

Institute of African Anthropology and Gender Studies: tel. (20) 3742078; e-mail director-aags@uonbi.ac.ke; Dir Prof. I. K. NYAMONGO.

Institute for Development Studies: tel. (20) 334244; e-mail idsdirector@swiftkenya.com; Dir Prof. M. JAMA.

Institute of Diplomacy and International Studies: tel. (20) 339014; fax (20) 339014; e-mail director-idis@uonbi.ac.ke; Dir Dr M. MWAGIRU.

Institute of Nuclear Science: e-mail director-ins@uonbi.ac.ke; Dir D. M. MAINA.

Population Studies and Research Institute: tel. (20) 318262; e-mail psri@uonbi.ac.ke; Dir Dr L. E. IKAMARI.

School of Computing and Informatics: e-mail director-sci@uonbi.ac.ke; Dir Prof. W. OKELO-ODONGO.

School of Journalism and Mass Communication: tel. (20) 229168; e-mail soj@uonbi.ac.ke; Dir W. KIAI.

STRATHMORE UNIVERSITY

POB 59857, City Sq., 00200 Nairobi

Telephone: (20) 606155
Fax: (20) 607498
E-mail: admissions@strathmore.edu
Internet: www.strathmore.edu

Founded 1961 as Strathmore College; present name c. 1993
Private control (non-profit)
Academic year: July to June

Vice-Chancellor: Prof. JOHN ODHIAMBO
University Sec.: Dr CHARLES SOTZ
Deputy Vice-Chancellor for Academic Affairs: Dr FLORENCE OLOO

Librarian: GEORGE GITAU
Library of 60,000 vols
Number of teachers: 167
Number of students: 2,476 full-time, 1,825 part-time

DEANS
Faculty of Commerce: DAVID WANG'OMBE
Faculty of Information Technology: Dr REUBEN MARWANGA
Faculty of Tourism and Hospitality: Dr JOSEPH WADAWI
Institute of Continuous Education: Dr RUTH KIRAKA
Institute of Humanities, Education and Development Studies: MARGARET ROCHE
School of Accountancy: GODFREY MADIGU
Strathmore Business School: Dr EDWARD MUNGAI

Colleges

Bukura Agricultural College: POB 23, Sigalagala-Butere Rd, Bukura; tel. (56) 20023; f. 1958; language of instruction: English; academic year October to October; departments: agricultural engineering, agronomy, basic sciences, horticulture, home economics, agricultural economics, agricultural education and extension; 240 students; Principal F. O. ANDITI.

Eldoret Polytechnic: POB 4461, Eldoret; tel. (53) 32661; fax (53) 33188; e-mail eldopoly@africaonline.co.ke; offers certificate and diploma courses in library and information studies; Principal CLEOPHAS LAGAT.

Kenya Conservatoire of Music: POB 41343, Nairobi; tel. (20) 222933; f. 1944; library of instrumental and vocal scores; Dir CAROL NGANGA.

Kenya Institute of Administration: POB 23030, Lower Kabete, Nairobi; tel. (20) 582311; fax (20) 582306; e-mail kia@africaonline.co.ke; f. 1961; residential training for the Kenya Public Service in public administration, project development and management, senior management seminars, research and consultancy, computer courses, effective management communication, management information systems, policy analysis, management of public enterprises, French courses, finance management, environmental management, performance improvement programmes, human resource management, customer care and ethics, disaster management, training for trainers; library: 47,067 vols, 30 current periodicals and a fully equipped audiovisual aids centre; 30 teachers; 280 students; Dir TITUS J. K. GATEERE; publs K. I. A. Occasional Papers (12 a year), Newsline (3 a year).

Kenya Medical Training College: POB 30195, Nairobi; tel. (20) 725711; fax (20) 722907; e-mail kmtc@nbnet.ke; f. 1924; library: 18,000 vols, 150 periodicals; 195 teachers; 2,000 students; Principal W. K. A. BOIT.

Kenya Polytechnic: POB 52428, Nairobi; f. 1961 with UNDP aid; depts of mechanical, electrical and electronic engineering, science, building, business studies, printing, institutional management, library and archive studies, general studies, mathematics, statistics, computing, media services; library: 40,000 vols, 150 periodicals; 300 teachers; 6,504 students; Principal P. O. OKAKA; Librarian S. K. NG'ANG'A.

Kenya School of Law: POB 30369, Nairobi; tel. (20) 890044; fax (20) 891722; e-mail lawschool@kenyaschooloflaw.com; f. 1963; library: 4,730 vols; 13 teachers; 400 students; Principal Prof. W. KULUNDU-BITONYE; Senior

Principal Lecturer ANTHONY MUNENE; Librarian BENTA NARKISO.

Kiambu Institute of Science and Technology: POB 414, Kiambu; tel. (66) 22236; fax (66) 22319; f. 1973; library: 10,000 vols; depts of building, business education, electrical engineering, electronics, computer studies, bakery technology; 61 teachers; 600 students; Principal SIMON IRUNGU.

Kisumu Polytechnic: POB 143, Kisumu; tel. (35) 40161; fax (35) 44417; f. 1997; courses offered in electrical engineering, electronics, mechanical engineering, automo-tive engineering, analytical chemistry, food and beverage management, building, computer studies, personnel management, accounting and business administration; 112 teachers; 2,000 students; Principal FRANCIS IMBO.

Mombasa Polytechnic: POB 90420, Mombasa; tel. (41) 492222; fax (41) 495632; e-mail msapoly@kenyaweb.com; internet www.mombasapoly.ac.ke; f. 1948; full-time, sandwich, block-release and day-release courses; library: 20,000 vols; 200 teachers; 4,037 students; Principal C. T. AKUMU OWUOR;

Registrar A. M. GEKONGE; Librarian R. KASINA.

Rift Valley Institute of Science and Technology: POB 7182, Nakuru; tel. (37) 211974; fax (37) 45656; f. 1972; library: 9,000 vols; 125 teachers; 1,200 students; Principal FRANCIS Z. K. MENJO.

Western University College of Science and Technology: POB 190, Kakamega; tel. (56) 20724; e-mail weco@africaonline.co.ke; f. 1977; library: 4,000 vols; 56 teachers; 500 students; Principal ALFRED F. O. MACHUKI; Librarian ROBERT KIMAKWA.

KIRIBATI

The Higher Education System

In 1979 the Gilbert Islands became an independent republic within the Commonwealth, under the name of Kiribati. Higher education consists mostly of a branch of the University of the South Pacific. In addition, there are the Kiribati Teachers College and the Tarawa Technical Institute, both operated by the Government. All these institutions are located on the Tarawa Atoll. Students from Kiribati also attend establishments of higher education in Australia, New Zealand and Canada. The Ministry of Youth, Education and Sport Development is responsible for tertiary education. The Ministry of Health and Medical Services runs a School of Nursing, also based on Tarawa. There were 198 students enrolled in teacher training and 1,303 in other vocational training in 2001.

Regulatory Body
GOVERNMENT

Ministry of Education, Youth and Sport Development: POB 263, Bikenibeu, Tarawa; tel. 28091; fax 28222; Minister JAMES TAOM.

Library
Bairiki

National Library and Archives: POB 6, Bairiki, Tarawa; tel. 21337; fax 28222; f. 1979 (fmrly Gilbert Islands Nat. Archives); lending section of 30,000 vols; reference library of 2,000 vols; 18,000 vols in small library units throughout Kiribati; Nat. Colln (housed in Archives) of 3,500 published items; archives records of 70,000 items; spec. collns incl. 600 rolls of microfilm and 4,000 microfiches; small philatelic, photograph, and sound recording collns; Librarian and Archivist KUNEI ETEKIERA.

Museum
Bairiki

National Museum: POB 75, Bairiki, Tarawa; in process of formation; items stored in Nat. Archives; Cultural Affairs Officer BWERE ERITAIA.

College

University of the South Pacific, Kiribati Extension Centre: POB 59, Bairiki, Tarawa; tel. 21085; fax 21419; e-mail mackenzie_u@usp.ac.fj; internet www.usp.ac.fj; f. 1973; an external campus of the University of the South Pacific; part-time undergraduate and diploma courses; 5 staff; library: 5,000 vols; 300 students; Dir URIAM TIMITI (acting).

Attached Institute:

Atoll Research Activities: POB 206, Bikenibeu, Tarawa; marine science and biology; Programme Man. TEMAKEI TEBANO; publ. *Atoll Bulletin*.

DEMOCRATIC PEOPLE'S REPUBLIC OF KOREA

The Higher Education System

The Democratic People's Republic of Korea (North Korea) occupies the northern part of the Korean peninsula. In 1945 Korea was divided into military occupation zones, with Soviet forces in the North and US forces in the South. A provisional People's Committee, led by Kim Il Sung of the Korean Communist Party, was established in the North in 1946 and accorded government status. In 1948 the Democratic People's Republic of Korea was proclaimed. The oldest university is Kim Il Sung University, founded in 1946. A report submitted to UNESCO by the North Korean Government in 2000 stated that there were more than 300 universities and colleges with 1.89m. students and academics. In March 2001 the Ministry of Education announced plans for the establishment of a university of information science and technology in Pyongyang, in cooperation with a South Korean education foundation. The new university, named the Pyongyang University of Science and Technology (PUST), officially opened in September 2009 and 250 faculty members, mostly from South Korea, are expected to teach around 200 North Korean postgraduate students.

Regulatory Bodies

GOVERNMENT

Ministry of Culture: Pyongyang; Minister KANG, NUNG SU.

Ministry of Education: Pyongyang; Minister KIM, YONG JIN.

Learned Societies

GENERAL

Academy of Sciences: Ryonmot-dong, Jangsan St, Sosong District, Pyongyang; tel. 51956; f. 1952; brs of Biology (Pres. SON KYONG NAM), Construction and Building Materials (Pres. KIM MAN HYONG), Electronics and Automation Design (Pres. LI SON BONG), Light Industry (Pres. PYON SOK CHON), and brs in Pyongsong (Chair. HAN BYONG HUI) and Hamhung (Pres. RI HYO SON); attached research institutes: see Research Institutes; libraries: see Libraries and Archives; Pres. JANG CHOL; publs *Bulletin* (6 a year), journals for Physics, Mathematics, Biology, Mechanical Engineering, Metals, Analysis (4 a year each) and for Chemistry and Chemical Engineering, Mining, Electronic and Automatic Engineering, Geology and Geography (6 a year each).

Academy of Social Sciences: Central District, Pyongyang; f. 1952; attached research institutes: see Research Institutes; library: see Libraries and Archives; Pres. KIM SOK HYONG.

AGRICULTURE, FISHERIES AND VETERINARY SCIENCE

Academy of Agricultural Science: Ryongsong District, Pyongyang; f. 1948; attached to Acad. of Sciences; attached research institutes: see Research Institutes; Pres. KYE YONG SAM.

Academy of Fisheries: Namgang-dong, Sung Ho District, Pyongyang; attached to Acad. of Sciences; f. 1969; 6 attached research institutes; Chair. SO GYONG HO.

Academy of Forestry: Samsin-dong, Taesong District, Pyongyang; f. 1948; attached to Acad. of Sciences; 5 attached research institutes; Pres. IM ROK JAE.

LANGUAGE AND LITERATURE

Goethe-Informationszentrum: Chollima Cultural House, 8-33 Jonggwang St, Central Area, Pyongyang; internet www.goethe.de/seoul; library of 4,000 vols; promotes cultural exchange with Germany; Dir Dr UWE SCHMELTER (based in Seoul).

MEDICINE

Academy of Medical Sciences: Saemaul-dong, Pyongchon District, POB 305, Pyongyang; tel. 46924; attached to Acad. of Sciences; attached research institutes: see Research Institutes; Pres. RI CHOL.

TECHNOLOGY

Academy of Light Industry Science: Kangan 1-dong, Songyo District, Pyongyang; f. 1954; 7 attached research institutes; Chair. LI JU UNG.

Academy of Railway Sciences: Namgyo-dong, Hyongjaesan District, Pyongyang; attached to Acad. of Sciences; 5 attached research institutes; Chair. MAENG YUN CHOL.

Research Institutes

AGRICULTURE, FISHERIES AND VETERINARY SCIENCE

Agricultural Chemical Research Institute: Ryongsong District, Pyongyang; attached to DPRK Acad. of Agricultural Science; Dir PAK JAE KUN.

Agricultural Irrigation Research Institute: Onchon County, South Pyongan Province; attached to DPRK Acad. of Agricultural Science; Dir HWANG CHANG HONG.

Agricultural Mechanization Research Institute: Sadong District, Pyongyang; attached to DPRK Acad. of Agricultural Science; Dir KANG SONG RYONG.

Crop Cultivation Research Institute: Ryongsong District, Pyongyang; attached to DPRK Acad. of Agricultural Science; Dir RYEM DOK SU.

Crop Science Research Institute: Sunchon City, South Pyongan Province; attached to DPRK Acad. of Agricultural Science; Dir PAK BYONG MUK.

Fruit Cultivation Research Institute: Sukchon County, South Pyongan Province; attached to DPRK Acad. of Agricultural Science; Dir JANG HY KUNG.

Poultry Science Research Institute: Hyongjaesan District, Pyongyang; attached to DPRK Acad. of Agricultural Science; Dir CHOI MAN SANG.

Reed Research Institute: Haeju City, South Hwanghae Province; attached to DPRK Acad. of Agricultural Science; Dir KIM IN SU.

Rice Research Institute: Ryongsong District, Pyongyang; attached to DPRK Acad. of Agricultural Science; Dir KIM SANG RYEN.

Sericulture Research Institute: Dongrim County, North Pyongan Province; attached to DPRK Acad. of Agricultural Science; Dir KIM SUN JONG.

Soil Science Research Institute: Ryongsong District, Pyongyang; attached to DPRK Acad. of Agricultural Science; Dir LI KUN HAENG.

Vegetable Science Research Institute: Sadong District, Pyongyang; attached to DPRK Acad. of Agricultural Science; Dir KIM HAK SON.

Veterinary Science Research Institute: Ryongsong District, Pyongyang; attached to DPRK Acad. of Agricultural Science; Dir PAK WON KUN.

Zoology Research Institute: Sariwon City, North Hwanghae Province; attached to DPRK Acad. of Agricultural Science; Dir KIM KYANG JUNG.

ARCHITECTURE AND TOWN PLANNING

Institute of Architecture and Building Engineering: c/o Academy of Sciences, Namgang-dong, Sung Ho District, Pyongyang; attached to DPRK Acad. of Sciences; Dir SIN DONG CHOL.

ECONOMICS, LAW AND POLITICS

Institute of International Affairs: c/o Academy of Social Sciences, Central District, Pyongyang; attached to DPRK Acad. of Social Sciences; Dir KIM HYONG U.

Institute of Law: c/o Academy of Social Sciences, Central District, Pyongyang; attached to DPRK Acad. of Social Sciences; Dir SIM HYONG IL.

Institute of Trade and Economics: c/o Academy of Social Sciences, Central District, Pyongyang; attached to DPRK Acad. of Social Sciences; Dir (vacant).

HISTORY, GEOGRAPHY AND ARCHAEOLOGY

Institute of Archaeology: c/o Academy of Social Sciences, Central District, Pyongyang; attached to DPRK Acad. of Social Sciences; Dir KIM MYONG NAM.

Institute of Geography: Ryonmot-dong, Jangsan St, Sosong District, Pyongyang; attached to DPRK Acad. of Sciences; Dir KIM JONG RAK.

Institute of History: c/o Academy of Social Sciences, Central District, Pyongyang; attached to DPRK Acad. of Social Sciences; Dir CHON YONG RYUL.

LANGUAGE AND LITERATURE

Institute of Ethnic Classics: c/o Academy of Social Sciences, Central District, Pyongyang; attached to DPRK Acad. of Social Sciences; Dir KIM SUNG PHIL.

Institute of Juche Literature: c/o Academy of Social Sciences, Central District, Pyongyang; attached to DPRK Acad. of Social Sciences; Dir KIM HA MYONG.

Institute of Linguistics: c/o Academy of Social Sciences, Central District, Pyongyang; attached to DPRK Acad. of Social Sciences; Dir JONG SUN GI.

MEDICINE

Industrial Medicine Institute: Sapo-dong, Sapo District, Hamhung City; tel. 2810; attached to DPRK Acad. of Medical Sciences; Dir JO UN HO.

Research Institute for the Cultivation of Medicinal Herbs: Wonju-dong, Sariwon City, North Hwanghae Province; attached to DPRK Acad. of Medical Sciences; Dir KIM KWANG SOP.

Research Institute of Antibiotics: Ryonpo-dong, Sunchon City, South Pyongan Province; attached to DPRK Acad. of Medical Sciences; Dir CHOE SUN JONG.

Research Institute of Biomedicine: Dongsan-dong, Rangnang District, Pyongyang; tel. 23545; attached to DPRK Acad. of Medical Sciences; Dir PAK YUI SUN.

Research Institute of Child Nutrition: Dangsan-dong, Mangyongdae District, Pyongyang; tel. 73430; attached to DPRK Acad. of Medical Sciences; Dir KIM YONG KWANG.

Research Institute of Endocrinology: Mirim-dong, Sadong District, Pyongyang; tel. 623828; attached to DPRK Acad. of Medical Sciences; Dir JANG HON CHOL.

Research Institute of Experimental Therapy: c/o Academy of Medical Sciences, Chonsong-dong, Haesang District, Hamhung City, South Hamgyong Province; attached to DPRK Acad. of Medical Sciences; Dir NAM ON GIL.

Research Institute of Hygiene: Dangsandong, Mangyongdse District, Pyongyang; tel. 44925; attached to DPRK Acad. of Medical Sciences; Dir JE HYONG DO.

Research Institute of Microbiology: Pyongsong City, South Pyongan Province; attached to DPRK Acad. of Medical Sciences; Dir KIM CHANG JIN.

Research Institute of Natural Drugs: Somun-dong, Donghumsan District, Hamhung City, South Hamgyong Province; tel. 53905; attached to DPRK Acad. of Medical Sciences; Dir LI HWAI SU.

Research Institute of Oncology: Saemaul-dong, Pyongchon District, Pyongyang; tel. 42208; attached to DPRK Acad. of Medical Sciences; Dir KIM CHUN WON.

Research Institute of Pharmacology: Daehung-dong, Songyo District, Pyongyang;

tel. 623868; attached to DPRK Acad. of Medical Sciences; Dir RYU GYONG HUI.

Research Institute of Psychoneurology: Uiju County, North Pyongan Province; attached to DPRK Acad. of Medical Sciences; Dir LI GYUN.

Research Institute of Radiological Medicine: Saemaul-dong, Pyongchon District, Pyongyang; tel. 45347; attached to DPRK Acad. of Medical Sciences; Dir O SOK ROK.

Research Institute of Respiratory Ducts and Tuberculosis: c/o Academy of Medical Sciences, Chongsong-dong, Haesang District, Hamhung City, South Hamgyong Province; attached to DPRK Acad. of Medical Sciences; Dir LI CHU WAN.

Research Institute of Surgery: c/o Academy of Medical Sciences, Chongsong-dong, Haesang District, Hamhung City, South Hamgyong Province; attached to DPRK Acad. of Medical Sciences; Dir HAN BYONG GAP.

Research Institute of Synthetic Pharmacy: Sapo-dong, Sapo District, Hamhung City, South Hamgyong Province; attached to DPRK Acad. of Medical Sciences; Dir LI GI SOP.

NATURAL SCIENCES

General

Central Institute of Experimental Analysis: c/o Academy of Sciences, Kwahak-Idong, Unjong District, Pyongsong City, South Pyongan Province; tel. (02) 422-5044; f. 1983; attached to DPRK Acad. of Sciences; Dir RIM CHUN RYOB; publs *Punsok* (analysis, 4 a year), *Bulletin*.

Institute of Environmental Protection: Ryusong-dong, Central District, Pyongyang; attached to DPRK Acad. of Sciences; Dir KIM YONG CHAN.

Biological Sciences

Institute of Botany: Kosan-dong, Daesong District, Pyongyang; attached to DPRK Acad. of Sciences; Dir GUAK JONG SONG.

Institute of Genetics: c/o Academy of Sciences, Ryonmot-dong, Jangsan St, Sosong District, Pyongyang; attached to DPRK Acad. of Sciences; Dir BAEK MUN CHAN.

Institute of Molecular Biology: c/o Academy of Sciences, Ryonmot-dong, Jangsan St, Sosong District, Pyongyang; attached to DPRK Acad. of Sciences; Dir KO GWANG UNG.

Institute of Plant Physiology: c/o Academy of Sciences, Ryonmot-dong, Jangsan St, Sosong District, Pyongyang; attached to DPRK Acad. of Sciences; Dir KIM SONG OK.

Institute of Zoology: Daesong-dong, Daesong District, Pyongyang; attached to DPRK Acad. of Sciences; Dir BAEK JONG HWAN.

Mathematical Sciences

Institute of Mathematics: c/o Academy of Sciences, Doksan-dong, Pyongsong City, South Pyongan Province; attached to DPRK Acad. of Sciences; Dir HO GON.

Physical Sciences

Institute of Analytical Chemistry: c/o Academy of Sciences, Chongsong-dong, Hoesang District, Hamhung City, South Hamgyong Province; attached to DPRK Acad. of Sciences; Dir RIM CHUN RYOP.

Institute of Ferrous Metals: Sae Goridong, Chollima District, Nampo City; attached to DPRK Acad. of Sciences; Dir LI BANG GUN.

Institute of Geology: c/o Academy of Sciences, Doksan-dong, Pyongsong City, South

Pyongan Province; attached to DPRK Acad. of Sciences; Dir KIM ZONG HUI.

Institute of Inorganic Chemistry: c/o Academy of Sciences, Chongsong-dong, Hoesang District, Hamhung City, South Hamgyong Province; attached to DPRK Acad. of Sciences; Dir CHU SUNG.

Institute of Macromolecular Chemistry: c/o Academy of Sciences, Chongsong-dong, Hoesang District, Hamhung City, South Hamgyong Province; attached to DPRK Acad. of Sciences; Dir LI JANG HYOK.

Institute of Non-Ferrous Metals: Jungdaedu-dong, Hangku District, Nampo City; attached to DPRK Acad. of Sciences; Dir KIM MYONG RIN.

Institute of Physical Chemistry: c/o Academy of Sciences, Chongsong-dong, Hoesang District, Hamhung City, South Hamgyong Province; attached to DPRK Acad. of Sciences; Dir KIM JUNG BAE.

Institute of Physics: c/o Academy of Sciences, Doksan-dong, Pyongsong City, South Pyongan Province; attached to DPRK Acad. of Sciences; Dir RYO IN KWANG.

Institute of Pure Metals: Kumbit-dong, Ryongsong District, Hamhung City, South Hamgyong Province; attached to DPRK Acad. of Sciences; Dir LI SANG BOM.

Pyongyang Astronomical Observatory: Daesong-dong, Daesong District, Pyongyang; attached to DPRK Acad. of Sciences; Dir KIM YONG HYOK.

Research Centre for Atomic Energy: Mangyongdae District, Pyongyang; fax (2) 3814416; attached to General Dept of Atomic Energy; Pres. RIM PONG SIK.

PHILOSOPHY AND PSYCHOLOGY

Institute of Philosophy: c/o Academy of Social Sciences, Central District, Pyongyang; attached to DPRK Acad. of Social Sciences; Dir KIM CHANG WON.

TECHNOLOGY

Institute of Chemical Engineering: c/o Academy of Sciences, Chongsong-dong, Hoesang District, Hamhung City, South Hamgyong Province; attached to DPRK Acad. of Sciences; Dir LI JAE OP.

Institute of Constructional Mechanization: c/o Academy of Sciences, Namgangdong, Sung Ho District, Pyongyang; attached to DPRK Acad. of Sciences; Dir PAK RYANG SOP.

Institute of Electricity: c/o Academy of Sciences, Doksan-dong, Pyongsong City, South Pyongan Province; attached to DPRK Acad. of Sciences; Dir CHOE WON GYONG.

Institute of Fuel: Dongsan-dong, Songrim City, North Hwanghe Province; attached to DPRK Acad. of Sciences; Dir KO YONG JIN.

Institute of Hydraulic Engineering: c/o Academy of Sciences, Namgang-dong, Sung Ho District, Pyongyang; attached to DPRK Acad. of Sciences; Dir KIM RYONG GYUN.

Institute of Industrial Biology: c/o Academy of Sciences, Doksan-dong, Pyongsong City, South Pyongan Province; attached to DPRK Acad. of Sciences; Dir LI CHUN HO.

Institute of Mechanical Engineering: c/o Academy of Sciences, Doksan-dong, Pyongsong City, South Pyongan Province; attached to DPRK Acad. of Sciences; Dir KIM UNG SAM.

Institute of Ore Dressing Engineering: c/o Academy of Sciences, Doksan-dong, Pyongsong City, South Pyongan Province; attached to DPRK Acad. of Sciences; Dir LI WON SOK.

Institute of Organic Building Materials: c/o Academy of Sciences, Namgang-dong,

Sung Ho District, Pyongsong; attached to DPRK Acad. of Sciences; Dir PAK CHANG SUN.

Institute of Paper Engineering: Songdori, Anju City, South Pyongan Province; attached to DPRK Acad. of Sciences; Dir RYU SAM JIP.

Institute of Silicate Engineering: Sijong-gu, Taedong County, South Pyongan Province; attached to DPRK Acad. of Sciences; Dir KIM UNG SANG.

Institute of Thermal Engineering: c/o Academy of Sciences, Doksan-dong, Pyongsong City, South Pyongan Province; attached to DPRK Acad. of Sciences; Dir HAN DONG SIK.

Institute of Tideland Construction: c/o Academy of Sciences, Namgang-dong, Sung Ho District, Pyongyang; attached to DPRK Acad. of Sciences; Dir CHO SOK.

Institute of Welding: Ponghwa-dong, Chollima District, Nampo City; attached to DPRK Acad. of Sciences; Dir CHAE HON MUK.

Research Centre of Electronics and Automation: c/o Academy of Sciences, Doksan-dong, Pyongsong City, South Pyongan Province; attached to DPRK Acad. of Sciences; incorporates institutes of Electronics, of Computer Science, of Automation, of Technical Cybernetics, of Electronic Materials; Gen. Dir LI SON BONG.

Research Institute of Medical Instruments: Daesin-dong, Dongdaewon District, Pyongyang; tel. 623839; attached to DPRK Acad. of Medical Sciences; Dir JO MYONG SAM.

Libraries and Archives

Chongjin

Chongjin City Library: Chongjin; Librarian KANG CHAE GUM.

Chongjin Historical Library: Chongjin; Curator EU JAI GYONG.

North Hamgyong Provincial Library: Chongjin; Librarian CHOI MYONG OK.

Haeju

South Hwanghae Provincial Library: Haeju; Librarian CHOI CHI DO.

Hamhung

South Hamgyong Provincial Library: Hamhung; Librarian KIM SOOK JONG.

Hesan

Ryanggang Provincial Library: Hesan; Librarian KIM CHOL WOO.

Kaesong

Kaesong City Library: Kaesong; Librarian HAN IL.

Kaesong Historical Library: Kaesong; Curator CHOI SAE YONG.

Kangge

Chagang Provincial Library: Kangge; Librarian SONG AAI GUN.

Pyongsong

South Pyongan Provincial Library: Pyongsong; Librarian KIM DUK KWAN.

Pyongyang

Academy of Sciences Library: POB 330, Kwahakdong 1, Unjong District, Pyongyang; tel. 32353968; fax 814580; f. 1952; 3.2m. vols; Dir Prof. KIM HYON OK; Chief Librarian Assoc. Prof. HONG SANG SU; publ. *Bulletin*.

Academy of Social Sciences Library: Central District, Pyongyang; Chief Librarian KIM SAE SONG.

Grand People's Study House/State Central Library: POB 200, Pyongyang Central District; tel. (2) 321-5614; fax (2) 381-4427; f. 1982; in charge of nat. bibliography; also functions as correspondence univ.; 20m. vols; Dir CHOE HUI JONG.

Pyongyang Scientific Library: Central District, POB 109, Pyongyang; tel. (2) 321-2314; f. 1978.

Sariwon

North Hwanghae Provincial Library: Sariwon; Librarian KIM HYO DAL.

Shinuiju

North Pyongan Provincial Library: Shinuiju; Librarian LI YONG SIK.

Wonsan

Kangwon Provincial Library: Wonsan; Librarian JI GYU HYOK.

Museums and Art Galleries

Haeju

Haeju Historical Museum: Haeju, South Hwanghae Province.

Hamhung

Hamhung Historical Museum: Hamhung, South Hamgyong Province; Curator KIM IK MYON.

Hyangsan County

Mt Myohyang-san Museum: Hyangsan County, North Pyongan Province; Curator CHOI HYONG MIN.

Pyongyang

Korean Art Gallery: Pyongyang; Curator KIM SANG CHOL.

Korean Central Historical Museum: Central District, Pyongyang; prehistory to early 20th century; Curator JANG JONG SIN.

Korean Ethnographic Museum: Central District, Pyongyang; Curator JON MOON JIN.

Korean Revolutionary Museum: Central District, Pyongyang; history from second half of 19th century to the present; Dir HWANG SUN HUI.

Memorial Museum of the War of Liberation: Moranbong District, Pyongyang; history from second half of the 19th century to the present; Dir THAE PYONG RYOL.

Shinchon County

Shinchon Museum: Shinchon County, South Hwanghae Province; Curator PAK IN CHAIK.

Shinuiju

Shinuiju Historical Museum: Shinuiju, North Pyongan Province; Curator PAK YONG GWAN.

Wonsan

Wonsan Historical Museum: Wonsan, Kangwon Province; Curator JO GANG BAIK.

Universities and Colleges

KIM IL SUNG UNIVERSITY

Daesong District, Pyongyang

Telephone: 54946

Founded 1946

State control

Academic year: September to August

President: SONG JA RIP

Vice-Presidents: CHOE JAND RYONG, JO CHOL, KIM IL GWANG, O KIL BANG, PAEK CHOL, PAEK JAE UK, RI JAE MYON, RI SONG CHOL, RO SONG CHAN

Number of teachers: 2,000

Number of students: 12,000

Publications: natural science magazine, social science magazine

Faculties of atomic energy, biology, chemistry, computer science, economics, foreign literature, geography, geology, history, law, philosophy, physics and mathematics, religion.

ATTACHED RESEARCH INSTITUTES

Computer Science College: Dir KIM YONG JUN.

Doctoral Institute: Dir HAN YONG GU.

Literature College: Dir UN JONG SOP.

Kim Chaek University of Technology: Waesong District, Pyongyang; faculties of geology, mining, metallurgy, mechanical and electrical engineering, shipbuilding, electronics, nuclear technology; Pres. HONG SO HON.

Kim Hyong-Jik University of Education: Pyongyang; f. 1946; Faculties of revolutionary history, pedagogy, history and geography, language and literature, foreign languages, mathematics, physics, biology, music, fine arts, physical education; 2,500 students; 5-year degree course, short-term courses for teachers, correspondence and postgraduate courses; Pres. HONG IL CHON.

Pyongyang University of Agriculture: Pyongyang; f. 1981; depts of fruit and vegetable cultivation, stockbreeding, poultry; Pres. CHON SI GON.

Pyongyang University of Medicine: Woesong District, Pyongyang; Pres. RI WON GIL; There are colleges of higher and professional education (engineering, agriculture, fisheries, teacher training) situated in all the main towns; there are also Factory (Engineering) Colleges.

REPUBLIC OF KOREA

The Higher Education System

The country's oldest institutions of higher education were founded during the final years of the Joseon dynasty (1392–1910), among them Yonsei and Paichai Universities (both founded 1885), Ewha Women's University (founded 1886), Korea University (founded 1905; formerly Posung College) and Dongguk University (founded 1906). Several were established during the early years of the Japanese occupation of the Korean peninsula (1910–45), including Jinju National University (founded 1910), Seoul Theological University (founded 1911), Chung-Ang University (founded 1918) and Miryang National University (founded 1923). Consequently, the Korean education system at all levels displayed strong Japanese influences. Following the Allied defeat of Japan in 1945, Korea was divided at latitude 38°N into military occupation zones, with Soviet forces in the north and US forces in the south. In 1948 the US-administered south became the independent Republic of Korea, while the Democratic People's Republic of Korea was proclaimed in the Soviet-administered north. A three-year war between north and south ended in 1953, and the two countries remain divided at the cease-fire line, separated by a UN-supervised demilitarized zone. Post-1945 education became influenced by the US system and from 1945 has been structured with six years of primary education, six years of secondary education and four years of higher education. A consequence of military control from the 1960s, and particularly during the 1980s, was that specialized and technical education became more respected than the general cultural knowledge traditionally held in high esteem. In recent years a high value has been placed upon scientific education, which resulted in South Korea becoming one of the world's most technologically advanced countries by the 1980s.

Higher education consists of seven types of institution: Junior Colleges, Colleges and Universities, Broadcast and Correspondence Universities, Industrial Universities, Universities of Education, Technical Colleges and miscellaneous colleges. Junior Colleges are distinguished from the other types of institution by the fact that they do not offer four-year undergraduate Bachelors degree programmes. Instead, they offer two- to three-year mainly technical and professionally oriented programmes. Junior Colleges are regulated by the Korean Council for College Education. The remaining six types of institution are grouped under the term Colleges and Universities, and are coordinated by the Korean Council for University Education (KCUE). The acronym 'SKY' is used to denote the three most prestigious universities: Seoul National University, Korea University and Yonsei University. In 2007 there were 175 colleges and universities, with a student enrolment of 1,919,504. A further 296,576 students were enrolled in 1,042 graduate schools.

Since 1993 the US-style College Scholastic Aptitude Test has been the main basis for admission to higher education. Applicants are also assessed on their scholastic record and institutions may set their own entrance examination. The College Scholastic Aptitude Test is administered by the Institute of Curriculum and Evaluation. The main undergraduate degree is the four-year Bachelors (Haksa), although programmes in professional disciplines such as dentistry and medicine last up to six years. Degrees are awarded on the basis of the US-style 'credit semester' system, and students usually need to accrue 140 credits for award of the Bachelors, of which 35 must be in a designated 'major' subject. The postgraduate (or graduate), Masters (Suksa) and Doctorate (Paksa) degrees are offered primarily by university graduate schools. The Masters lasts two years and requires 24–36 credits, the Doctorate two years and 36 credits. Junior colleges, specialist vocational schools and technical schools are the leading institutions of vocational and technical education. Students usually work towards a vocational qualification and then sit the examination for the National Technical Certificate.

Regulatory and Representative Bodies

GOVERNMENT

Ministry of Culture, Sports and Tourism: 42, Sejong-no, Jongno-gu, Seoul 110-703; tel. (2) 3704-9114; fax (2) 3704-9154; e-mail webadmin@mcst.go.kr; internet www.mcst.go.kr; Minister YU, IN-CHON.

Ministry of Education, Science and Technology: 77-6, Sejong-no, Jongno-gu, Seoul 110-760; tel. (2) 2100-6060; fax (2) 2100-6133; internet www.mest.go.kr; Minister AHN, BYONG MAN.

ACCREDITATION

Korean Council for University Education (KCUE): KGIT Sangam Centre, 11 fl, Mapo-gu Sangam-dong 1601 , Seoul 121-270; tel. (2) 6393-5225; fax (2) 6393-5230; e-mail intl@kcue.or.kr; internet english.kcue.or.kr; f. 1982; 201 , incl. most four-year univs in Republic of Korea; Chair. LEE, BAE YONG; Sec.-Gen. Prof. PARK, CHONG YUL; publ. *Daehak Gyoyuk* (Higher Education, in Korean).

NATIONAL BODY

Korean Federation of Teachers' Associations: 142 Woomyeon-dong, Seocho-Ku, Seoul 137-715; tel. (2) 570-5500; fax (2) 576-1081; e-mail kfta2@kfta.or.kr; internet www.kfta.or.kr; f. 1947; Pres. LEE, WON-HEE; Dir JEONG, DONG-SEOB.

Learned Societies

GENERAL

Korea Foundation: 10-11F Diplomatic Centre Bldg, 2558 Nambusunhwanno, Seocho-gu, Seoul 137-863; 1F Joongang Ilbo Bldg, Sunhwa-dong 7, Jung-gu, Seoul 100-759; tel. (2) 2046-8500; fax (2) 3463-6076; e-mail kfcenter@kf.or.kr; internet www.kf.or.kr; f. 1991 (fmrly Int. Cultural Soc. of Korea); promotes mutual understanding and friendship between Korea and the rest of the world; 60 mems; library of 8,000 vols; Pres. YIM SUNG-JOON; publs *Koreana* (in English and Chinese, 4 a year), *Korea Focus* (in English, 6 a year).

National Academy of Sciences: San-94-4, Banpo 4-dong, Seocho-gu, Seoul 137-044; tel. (2) 534-0737; fax (2) 537-3183; internet www.nas.go.kr; f. 1954; 150 mems; library of 15,000 vols; Pres. KIM SANG-JOO; Vice-Pres. PARK YOUNG-SIK; publs *Development of Science Study in Korea* (in Korean, 1 a year), *Journal of NAS* (in Korean, 1 a year), *NAS Annual Bulletin* (in Korean), *NAS Bulletin* (in English, every 2 years), *Proceedings of the International Symposium* (in Korean, 1 a year).

Royal Asiatic Society, Korea Branch: CPO Box 255, Seoul; tel. (2) 763-9483; fax (2) 766-3796; f. 1900 to encourage interest in, and promote study and dissemination of knowledge about, the arts, history, literature and customs of Korea and the neighbouring countries; 1,600 mems; library: reference library of 1,000 vols; Gen. Man. SUE J. BAE; publ. *Transactions* (1 a year).

AGRICULTURE, FISHERIES AND VETERINARY SCIENCE

Korean Forestry Society: c/o Dept of Forest Resources, Seoul National University, Suwon, Kyonggido Seoul 441-744; tel. (331) 290-2330; f. 1960 to foster the study of all aspects of forestry, to promote cooperation among members; 800 mems; Pres. Prof. JONG HWA YOUN; Sec. Assoc. Prof. JOO SANG CHUNG; publ. *Journal* (4 a year).

BIBLIOGRAPHY, LIBRARY SCIENCE AND MUSEOLOGY

Korean Library Association: San 60-1, Banpo-dong, Seocho-gu, Seoul 137-702; tel. (2) 535-4868; fax (2) 535-5616; e-mail klanet@hitel.net; internet www.korla.or.kr; f. 1945; a social and academic instn comprising all the libraries and librarians in Korea;

1,115 institutional, 1,865 individual mems; Pres. KI-NAM SHIN; Exec. Dir KYUNG-KU LEE; publs *KLA Bulletin* (6 a year), *Statistics on Libraries in Korea* (1 a year).

Korean Museum Association: c/o National Museum of Korea, 168-6 Yongsan-dong, Yongsan-gu, Seoul 140-026; tel. (2) 795-0937; fax (2) 795-0939; e-mail webmaster@ museum.or.kr; internet www.museum.or.kr; f. 1976; devt of museums through collaborative networking and of institutional museum policies for the benefits of the preservation of culture and education; Pres. KIDONG BAE.

Korean Research and Development Library Association: Room 0411, KIST Library, POB 131, Cheongryang, Seoul; tel. 967-3692; fax (82) 2963-4013; f. 1979; Pres. KE HONG PARK; Sec. KEON TAK OH.

ECONOMICS, LAW AND POLITICS

Korean Association of Sinology: c/o Asiatic Research Centre, Korea University, Anam-dong, Seoul; f. 1955; 100 mems; Chair. JUN-YOP KIM; publ. *Journal of Chinese Studies.*

Korean Economic Association: 45, 4-ga, Namdae-mun-ro, Chung-gu, Seoul; tel. (2) 3210-2522; fax (2) 3210-2555; e-mail kea1952@kea.ne.kr; internet www.kea.ne.kr; f. 1952; theory, policy and history of economics and business administration; 2,800 mems; library of 3,000 vols; Pres. PYUNG-JOO KIM; Sec.-Gen. JOON-WOO NAHM; publ. *Korean Economic Review* (2 a year).

FINE AND PERFORMING ARTS

Music Association of Korea: Bldg 1-117, Dongsung-dong, Chongro-gu, Seoul 110-765; tel. (2) 744-8060; fax (2) 741-2378; e-mail music@mak.or.kr; internet www.mak.or.kr; f. 1961 to develop Korean nat. music and to promote and protect Korean musicians; organizes concerts, encourages musical composition and nationwide singing; is active in the int. musical exchange and in music education; awards the Prize of Musical Culture; 700 mems; small library; Pres. Dr KIM YONG-JIN.

HISTORY, GEOGRAPHY AND ARCHAEOLOGY

Korean Geographical Society: Dept of Geography, College of Social Sciences, Seoul National University, Seoul 151-746; tel. (2) 875-1463; fax (2) 876-2853; e-mail geography77@daum.net; internet www .kgeography.or.kr; f. 1945 to promote mutual cooperation in academic work and int. understanding; 772 individual mems, 69 institutional mems; Pres. LEE JEONG ROCK; Sec.-Gen. YONG-CHUL SHIN; publ. *Journal* (5 a year).

LANGUAGE AND LITERATURE

Alliance Française: 63-2, Hoehyun-dong 1-ga, Jung-gu, Seoul 100-873; tel. (2) 755-5702; fax (2) 774-4252; e-mail alliance@nuri.net; internet www.afcoree.co.kr; offers courses and examinations in French language and culture and promotes cultural exchange with France; attached teaching centres in Busan, Chonju, Daegu, Daejon, Gwangju, Jeonju; Dir MARC SARRAZIN.

British Council: 4th Fl., Hungkuk Life Insurance Bldg, 226 Shinmunro 1-ga, Jongro-gu, Seoul 110-786; tel. (2) 3702-0600; fax (2) 3702-0660; e-mail info@britishcouncil.or .kr; internet www.bckorea.or.kr; teaching centre; offers courses and examinations in English language and British culture and promotes cultural exchange with the UK; Dir ROLAND DAVIES.

Goethe-Institut: 339-1, Huam-dong, Yongsan-ku, Seoul 140-901; tel. (2) 754-9831; fax (2) 754-9834; e-mail info@seoul.goethe.org; internet www.goethe.de/os/seo/deindex.htm; offers courses and examinations in German language and culture and promotes cultural exchange with Germany; library of 12,000 vols; Dir JURGEN KEIL.

MEDICINE

Korean Medical Association:; tel. (02) 794-2474; fax (02) 793-9190; e-mail intl@ kma.org; internet www.kma.org; f. 1908 to develop the medical sciences and medical education by encouraging research and investigation; 59,292 mems; library of 10,000 vols; Pres. KYUNG MAN HO; publs *Journal* (12 a year), *The KMA News* (2 a week).

PHILOSOPHY AND PSYCHOLOGY

Korean Psychological Association: Dept of Psychology, Seoul National University, Shinrim 2-dong, Kwanak-gu, Seoul; tel. 877-0101, ext. 2528; e-mail kpa0102@chol .com; internet www.koreanpsychology.or.kr; f. 1946; 420 mems; Pres. KIM MYUNG UN; Sec.-Gen. JUNGOH KIM; publs *Korean Journal of Psychology* (2 a year), *Korean Journal of Clinical Psychology* (2 a year), *Korean Journal of Social Psychology* (1 a year), *Korean Journal of Industrial Psychology* (1 a year), *Korean Journal of Developmental Psychology* (1 a year).

Research Institutes

GENERAL

Academy of Korean Studies: 110 Haogogae-gil, Bundang-gu, Seongnam-si, Gyeonggi-do, Seoul 463-791; tel. (31) 709-8111; fax (342) 709-1531; internet www.aks .ac.kr; f. 1978 to research and re-evaluate traditional Korean culture; library of 361,000 vols incl. 35,000 in Western languages; Pres. KIM JEONG-BAE; publ. *Chongsin Munhwa/ Academy News* (3–4 a year).

AGRICULTURE, FISHERIES AND VETERINARY SCIENCE

Rural Development Administration: Suin-ro, 150 (250 Seodun-dong), Gwonseon-gu, Suwon Gyeonggi-do, Seoul 441-707; tel. (31) 299-2200; fax (31) 299-2469; e-mail rda@ rda.go.kr; internet www.rda.go.kr; f. 1906 to carry out agricultural research and rural community devt; 11 subordinate research orgs, 9 provincial offices, 34 regional specialized crop stations; library of 190,000 vols; Administrator KIM JAE-SOO; publs *Agricultural Technology* (in Korean, 12 a year), *Annual Research Report* (Korean and English editions), *Research and Extension* (in Korean, 12 a year).

ECONOMICS, LAW AND POLITICS

Korea Development Institute: POB 113, Cheongnyang, Seoul 130-868; tel. (2) 958-4114; e-mail kdiweb@kdi.re.kr; internet www .kdi.re.kr; f. 1971 to help determine the basic direction of the nation's development by formulating long-term goals and strategies based on accurate economic analysis; to conduct policy-oriented research relating to individual sectors of the economy that will help the country to maintain high economic growth with price stability; to provide consultation on policy issues relating to short-term economic management and planning; library of 100,000 vols, 39,000 research reports, govt documents, also data bank; Pres. OH SEOK HYUN; publs *KDI Journal of*

Economic Policy (in Korean, 4 a year), *KDI Economic Outlook* (in Korean, 4 a year).

Korea Institute for Industrial Economics and Trade (KIET): 66 Hoegiro, Dongdaemun-gu, Seoul 130-742; tel. (2) 3299-3114; internet www.kiet.re.kr; f. 1976 as Korea Foundation for Middle East Studies; separated from Centre for Industrial and Technical Information and took present name 1991; advises govt on industrial, trade and commercial policies; analyses Korean industry, int. economies, new technology and promotion of trade; library of 45,000 vols, 1,500 periodicals; Pres. OH SANG-BONG; publs *KIET Real Economy* (fortnightly), *Journal of Industrial Competitiveness* (1 a year), *KIET Economic Outlook* (2 a year).

Korea Research Center: 228 Pyong-dong, Chongno-gu, Seoul; f. 1956; research in social sciences; library; Pres. MUNAM CHON; publs *Journal of Social Sciences and Humanities, Korean Studies Series.*

EDUCATION

Korean Educational Development Institute: 92–6 Umyeon-dong, Seocho-gu, Seoul 137-791; tel. (2) 3460-0216; fax (2) 3460-0156; e-mail international@kedi.re.kr; internet eng .kedi.re.kr; f. 1972; ind., govt-funded research and devt institute; undertakes research and devt activities on education; assists govt in formulation of educational policies and in long-term devt of education; library of 121,197 vols, 88 periodicals, 499,018 microfiches; Pres. TAE-WAN KIM; publs *KEDI Journal of Education Policy* (in English, 2 a year), *Research Abstracts* (in English, 1 a year), *Statistical Yearbook of Education* (in Korean and English, 1 a year).

National Institute for Training of Educational Administrators: c/o Ministry of Education, Science and Technology, 77-6, Sejong-ro, Jongno-gu, Seoul 110-760; tel. (2) 733-2741; fax (2) 733-0149; f. 1970; government institute; attached to Min. of Education, Science and Technology; library of 21,000 vols; Dir CHONG-TAEK CHANG.

NATURAL SCIENCES

Physical Sciences

Korea Meteorological Administration: 45 Gisangcheong-gil, Dongjak-gu, Seoul 156-720; tel. (2) 836-2385; fax (2) 836-2386; e-mail pb_int@kma.go.kr; internet web.kma .go.kr; under the control of the Min. of Education, Science and Technology; Administrator CHUN BYUNG-SEONG.

PHILOSOPHY AND PSYCHOLOGY

Korean Institute for Research in the Behavioural Sciences: 1606-3 Socho-Dong, Kangnam-gu, Seoul 137-071; tel. 581-8611; f. 1968; basic and applied research in 5 areas: social, child, learning, organization, and psychological testing; 70 researchers; library of 5,000 vols; Dir SUNG JIN LEE; publs *Research Bulletin, Research Notes, Research Monograph.*

TECHNOLOGY

Electronics and Telecommunications Research Institute (ETRI): 138 Gajeongno, Yuseong-gu, Daejeon City, Seoul 305-700; tel. (42) 860-6114; e-mail sloh@etri .re.kr; internet www.etri.re.kr; f. 1976; undertakes research and devt in field of advanced information technology; library of 40,000 vols, 30,000 technical reports, and ETLARS databases; Pres. CHOI MUN-KEE; publs *Electronics and Telecommunications Trends* (4 a year), *ETRI Journal* (4 a year), *Patent Announcement* (26 a year), *Patent*

Information (12 a year), *Weekly Technology Trends* (52 a year).

Korea Atomic Energy Research Institute (KAERI): POB 105, Yu-Seong, Taejon, Seoul 305-600; tel. (42) 868-2000; fax (42) 862-8465; internet www.kaeri.re.kr; f. 1959; reactor-related research and devt, security and R&D of nuclear fuel, nuclear policy research, radiation application technology devt and research and treatment of nuclear radiation, nuclear personnel training and other aspects of nuclear energy; library of 61,000 vols, 700,000 technical reports and 950 periodicals; Pres. MYUNG SEUNG YANG; publs *Journal*, *KAERI Research Papers* (1 a year), *Won Woo* (6 a year).

Korea Institute of Energy Research: 102 Gajeong-ro, Yuseong-gu, Daejeon, Seoul 305-343; tel. (42) 860-3114; fax (42) 861-6224; e-mail webadmin@kier.re.kr; internet www.kier.re.kr; f. 1977 to conduct research on energy and technology; supported by Min. of Education, Science and Technology; 500 mems; library of 30,000 vols; Pres. HAN MOON-HEE; publs *Energy R&D*, *Technical Trends on NRSE*.

Korea Institute of Science and Technology (KIST): 39-1 Hawolkok-dong, Songbuk-ku, Seoul 136-791; tel. (2) 958-6114; fax (2) 958-5478; e-mail cglee@kist.re.kr; internet www.kist.re.kr; f. 1966; research in applied science, chemical engineering, polymer engineering, materials science and engineering, mechanical and control systems, electronics and information technology, environment and CFC alternatives technology, systems engineering, genetic engineering, science and technology policy; library of 50,000 vols, 15,000 technical reports; Pres. Dr HAHN HONG THOMAS; publ. *Collection of Abstracts* (in Korean and English, 1 a year).

Libraries and Archives

Busan

Banyeo Library: San 129-9, Banyeo 3-dong, Haeundae-gu, Busan; tel. (51) 749-5731; fax (51) 749-5739; internet www.banyeolib.or.kr.

Dong-Eui University Central Library: Kaya-Dong, Pusanjin-ku, Busan, Seoul 614-714; tel. (51) 890-1155; fax (51) 890-1165; e-mail hjahn@deu.ac.kr; internet lib.deu.ac.kr; f. 1979; 810,000 vols; Library Dean Dr NAM SOO-HYUN.

Gang Seo Public Library: 2011-2 Daeju 2-dong, Ganseo-gu, Busan 618-807; tel. (51) 973-5274; fax (51) 973-5275; internet library.bsgangseo.go.kr.

Pusan National University Library: 30 Jangjeon-dong, Keumjeong-gu, Pusan 609-735; tel. (51) 510-1800; fax (51) 513-9787; f. 1946; 650,000 vols, 5,000 periodicals; Dir DONG-HYUN JUNG.

Daegu

Bukbu Library: 447-10 Chimsan 3-dong, Buk-gu, Daegu, Seoul 702-857; tel. (53) 350-0800; fax (53) 358-2535; internet www.bukbu-lib.daegu.kr; f. 1982.

Daebong Library: Daebong-dong, Jung-gu, Daegu; tel. (53) 422-0958; internet www.db.dblib.daegu.kr.

Dongbu Library: 664-19 Sinam 4-dong, Dong-gu, Daegu, Seoul 701-014; tel. (53) 603-6100; fax (53) 941-8076; internet www.dongbu-lib.daegu.kr.

Duryu Public Library: 154 Duryu 3-dong, Dalseo-gu, Daegu; tel. (53) 650-0200; internet www.duryu-lib.daegu.kr.

Jungang Library: 42 Dongin-dong 2-ga, Munhwa-gil, Jung-gu, Daegu, Seoul 700-

422; tel. (53) 420-2700; fax (53) 420-2750; internet www.tglnet.or.kr; f. 1918 as Daegu Bu Library, renamed in 1995; Dir HONG-MAN KIM.

Kyungpook National University Library: 1370 Sankyuk-dong, Puk-ku, Taegu 702-701; tel. (53) 950-6510; fax (53) 950-6533; e-mail mspark@kyungpook.ac.kr; internet kudos.knu.ac.kr; f. 1952; 2.1m. vols; Dir SEO, JONG-MOON.

Nambu Metropolitan Library: San 192-4 Daemyeong 9-dong, Nam-gu, Daegu; tel. (53) 620-5511; fax (53) 623-2308; e-mail nbl@edunavi.kr; internet www.nbl.or.kr; f. 1995; Curator JOHOSIK.

Seobu Public Library: 1230-1 Pyeongni 3-dong, Seo-gu, Daegu; tel. (53) 560-8800; fax (53) 560-8819; internet www.seobu-lib.daegu.kr.

Suseong Library: 54 Art Gallery park-route (gil), Manchon 1 (il)-dong, Suseong-gu, Daegu, Seoul 706-707; tel. (53) 740-5532; internet www.hyomok-lib.daegu.kr; f. 1988. as Hyomok Library; present name in 2008.

Daejeon

Daejeon Student Education and Culture Centre: 701 Jung-gu, Daejeon, Seoul 301-807; tel. (42) 229-1490; internet www.djsecc.or.kr.

Daejeon University Library: Daejeon, Seoul 300-718; tel. (42) 280-2681; fax (42) 283-7174; internet libweb.dju.ac.kr.

Hanbat Library: Daejeon, Seoul 301-711; tel. (42) 580-4114; fax (42) 580-4204; e-mail hanbat@its.daejeon.kr; internet hanbat.metro.daejeon.kr; 568,028 vols.

National Archives of Korea: Govt Complex, Seonsaro, 139 (920 Dusan 2-Dong), Seo-Gu, Daejeon 302-701; tel. (42) 481-6300; fax (42) 472-3906; f. 1969, relocated from Seoul in 1998; 336,275 vols, 1.2m. diagrams, 1.5m. cards, 181,311 rolls of microfilm, 740,463 audiovisual items; colln of records of the Yi dynasty.

Branches:

National Archives, Busan: 2-dong, Geoje-dong San 126, Girokgwan 1st Fl, Busan; tel. (51) 550-8025; fax (51) 504-6963.

National Archives, Seoul: Gwanghwa-mun Jeokseondong Platinum 201, 156-dong, Jongro-gu, Seoul; tel. 720-2721; fax 739-8944.

Gwangju

Chonnam University Library: Buk-gu, Yongbong to 77 Daechulbannap-sil, Gwangju, Seoul 500-757; tel. (62) 530-3571; fax (62) 530-3529; internet library.chonnam.ac.kr; f. 1953; 2m. vols, 680,000 books, 20,000 journals and periodicals.

Honam University Library: Gwangsan Seobongdong 59-1, Gwangju, Seoul 506-714; tel. (62) 940-5185; fax (62) 940-5183; e-mail bss@honam.ac.kr; internet library.honam.ac.kr; f. 1979.

Gyeonggi-do

Gamgol Library: 83-8 Sa-dong, Sangrok-gu, Ansan-si, Gyeonggi-do, Seoul 425-170.

Gwacheon Provincial Library of Gyeonggi: 12 Dosegwangil, Gwacheon, Gyeonggi-do; tel. (2) 3677-0371; e-mail webmaster@kwalib.or.kr; internet eng.kwalib.kr; f. 1984; 298,587 vols, 778 periodicals and magazines; Dir LEE WOON SUN.

Seoul

Chung-Ang University Library: 221 Huk-suk-dong, Dongjak-ku, Seoul; f. 1949; 442,667 vols; Dir TOO YOUNG LEE.

Dongguk University Library: 263-ga, Pil-dong, Seoul; internet lib.dongguk.edu; f. 1906; Buddhist and Oriental studies; 350,000 vols, 1,100 periodicals; Dir Dr JAE HO SHIN.

Ewha Woman's University Library: 11–1, Daehyun-dong, Sudaemun-gu, Seoul 120-750; tel. 3277-3124; fax 3277-2857; e-mail jnam@mm.ewha.ac.kr; internet lib.ewha.ac.kr; f. 1923; 1.7m. vols; Dir BONG HEE KIM.

Korea Foundation and Cultural Centre Library: Joogang Ilbo Bldg, 1st Fl., Sunhwa-dong 7, Jung-gu, Seoul 100-759; tel. (2) 2151-6500; fax (2) 2151-6590; e-mail kfcenter@kf.or.kr; internet library.kfcenter.or.kr; f. 2005.

Korea University Library: 1 Anam-dong, Sungbuk-gu, Seoul 136-701; tel. (2) 3290-1470; f. 1937; 400,132 vols; Dir SUNG GI JON.

Korean Braille Library: 510-23, Amsa-dong, Kang dong-ku, Seoul 134-052; tel. (2) 3426-7411; fax (2) 3426-7415; e-mail kbl@kbll.or.kr; internet www.infor.kbll.or.kr; f. 1969; Dir KEUN HAE YOUK.

National Assembly Library: 1 Yoido-dong, Seoul; tel. (2) 784-3565; fax (2) 788-4193; e-mail webw3@nanet.go.kr; internet www.nanet.go.kr; f. 1952; library service for members of the National Assembly, the Executive, the Judiciary, and for scholars and legislative research activities and int. book exchange with 360 institutions worldwide; 900,000 vols, 12,101 current periodicals, 700 newspapers; Librarian JONG PIL YOO; publs *Acquisitions List* (1 a year), *Index to Korean-Language Periodicals* (6 a year and 1 a year), *Index to Korean Laws and Statutes* (2 a year), *Index to National Assembly Debates* (irregular), *Issue Briefs* (irregular), *Legislative Information Analysis* (4 a year), *List of Theses for the Doctor's and Master's Degree in Korea* (1 a year), *National Assembly Library Review* (12 a year).

National Library of Korea: Banpo-Ro 664, Seocho-Gu, Seoul 137-702; tel. (2) 535-4142; fax (2) 590-0530; e-mail nlkpc@www.nl.go.kr; internet www.nl.go.kr; f. 1945; 3.9m. vols; legal deposit library for Korean publications, ISBN, ISSN nat. centre, KOLIS-NET (Korean Library Information System Network) centre, international exchange, research in library and information science, publishes nat. bibliographies, operates National Digital Library (www.dlibrary.go.kr) and training centre for librarians; Dir GI-YOUNG JEONG; publ. *Doseogwan* (4 a year).

Seoul National University Library: San 56-1, Shillim-dong, Kwanak-gu, Seoul 151-742; tel. (2) 880-5284; fax (2) 871-2972; internet library.snu.ac.kr; f. 1946; 2.1m. vols, 13,000 periodicals, incl. Agricultural Library (121,000 vols), Medical Library (123,000 vols), Law Library (65,000 vols), Business Library (11,000 vols), Social Sciences Library (20,000 vols), Dental Library (9,000 vols) and Kyujang-gak Archives (special collection on Choseon Dynasty, 152,000 vols); collns on the arts, sciences, law, education, music, medicine, engineering, economics and commerce; Dir CHONG SUH KIM; publs *Kyujang-gak* (1 a year), *Ko-munseo* (1 a year).

Transport Library: 168, 2-ka, Bongnae-dong, Seoul; f. 1920; 32,000 vols; Dir CHO WOO HYUN; Chief Librarian KIM DOO HO; publ. *Korean National Railroad Bulletin* (12 a year).

United Nations Depository Library: Korea University, 1 An-Am-dong, Sungbuk-gu, Seoul; tel. (2) 3290-1492; fax (2) 922-4633; f. 1957; 38,000 vols; Dir HWA-YOUNG KIM; Librarian MI-GYOUNG CHO.

Yonsei University Library: Yonsei University, 134 Sinchon-dong, Sudaemoon-gu,

Seoul; tel. 361-3308; e-mail leehg@yonsei.ac
.kr; internet library.yonsei.ac.kr; f. 1915;
1.5m. vols, incl. Korean archives, 10,700
periodicals; Dir JONG CHUL HAN; publs *Dong
Bang Hak Chi* (Journal of Korean Studies),
Inmun Kwahak (Journal of Humanities),
International Journal of Korean Studies,
Journal of East and West Studies, *Kyo Yuk
Non Jib* (Journal of Education), *Yonsei Non-
Chong* (Journal of Graduate School), *Yonsei
Social Science Review*, *Abstracts of Faculty
Research Report*, *Yonsei Magazine*.

Museums and Art Galleries

Busan

Busan Museum: 48-1 Daeyeon 4-dong,
Namgu, Busan, Seoul 608-092; tel. (51) 610-
7111; fax (51) 610-7130; e-mail museum@
metro.busan.kr; internet museum.busan.kr;
f. 1978, renovated in 2002; collns from prehistoric period to the present.

Attached Museums:

Bokcheon Museum: 50 Bokcheon-dong
Dongnae-gu, Busan, Seoul 607-020; tel.
(51) 554-4263; fax (51) 554-4265; f. 1996;
displays artifacts excavated from the
tumulus group in Bokcheon-dong that
show the history of Busan from the prehistoric age to the Three Kingdoms Era.

Busan Modern History Museum.

Dongsam-dong Shell Midden Museum:
750-1 Dongsam-dong, Yeongdo-gu Busan.

Busan Museum of Modern Art: 1413 Woo
2 dong, Haeundae-gu, Busan; tel. (51) 744-
2602; fax (51) 740-4280; internet www
.busanmoma.org; f. 1998; exhibitions, scholastic research, archive and presentation, int.
exchange, education, cultural events; Dir
CHO IL SANG.

Pusan National University Museum: San
30, Jangjeon-dong, Geumjeong-gu, Busan,
609-735; internet www.pnu-museum.org;
tel. (51) 510-1838; tel. (51) 581-2455; f.
1956; Korean archaeology with special collection of historical remains of Kyongsang-
Namdo province, arts, ethnology, etc.; Dir
Prof. GYEONGCHEOL SHIN; publ. *Research
Reports* (irregular).

Daegu

Daegu Bangjja Yugi Museum: 399 Dohak-
dong, Dong-gu, Daegu; tel. (53) 606-6171; fax
(53) 606-6179; internet artcenter.daegu.go
.kr/bangjja; f. 2000, opened in 2007; built to
preserve Bangjja Yugi (Korean Bronzewear)
considered a traditional cultural property;
major items of the Bangjja Yugi incl. musical
instruments, utensils and other items for
religious services, tableware and living
goods.

Daegu National Museum: San 41, Hwang-
geum-dong, Suseong-gu, Daegu; tel. (53) 768-
6051; fax (53) 768-6053; e-mail webadmin@
daegu.museum.go.kr; internet daegu
.museum.go.kr; f. 1994; 30,000 items, art and
archaeology; main collns on the material
culture of Daegu, and western and northern
parts of the Gyeongsangbuk-do province.

Daegu University Central Museum:
Daegu University Museum, 15 Naeri, Jillyang, Daegu, Gyeongbuk 712-714; tel. (53)
850-5621; fax (53) 850-5629; internet
museum.daegu.ac.kr; f. 1981; 19 cultural
property excavations, 33 cultural property
surfaces and 37 academic reports.

Daejeon

Daejeon Metropolitan Museum of Arts:
near 396 Mannyeon-dong, Seo-gu, Expo Park

Daejeon; tel. (42) 602-3225; fax (42) 602-
3299; e-mail mintae@daejeon.go.kr; internet
dmma.metro.daejeon.kr; f. 1998; features
modern art from both domestic and foreign
artists; outdoor sculpture park.

Daejeon Prehistoric Museum: Oeun-
dong, Yuseong-gu, Daejeon, Seoul 305-330;
tel. (42) 826-2814; fax (42) 826-2811; internet
museum.daejeon.go.kr; f. 2007; prehistory of
the Daejeon region, collns and artifacts.

Geological Museum: Daejeon, Seoul 305-
350; tel. (42) 868-3797; fax (42) 868-3424;
internet museum.kigam.re.kr; history of the
earth, fossils, evolution; rocks and geological
structures, minerals and human, environment and geology.

Ungno Lee Museum: 396 Mannyon-dong,
Seo-gu, Daejeon; tel. (42) 602-3270; fax (42)
602-3280; internet www.ungnolee-museum
.daejeon.kr; f. 2007, in memory of late
Korean painter Goam Ungno Lee.

**Yeojin Buddhist Art Gallery and
Museum:** 442-1 Tablib-dong, Yuseong-gu,
Daejeon, Seoul 450-702; tel. (42) 934-8466;
fax (42) 933-8477; internet www
.yeojingallery.co.kr.

Gwangju

Gwangju Museum of Art: 48 Bagmulgwan,
Ro Buk-gu, Gwangju, Seoul 500-170; tel. (62)
510-0113; fax (62) 510-0119; internet www
.artmuse.gjcity.net; f. 1992.

Gwangju National Museum: 114 Bak-
mulgwan-lo St, Maegok-dong, Buk-gu,
Gwangju, Seoul 500-150; tel. (62) 570-7014;
fax (62) 570-7015; e-mail webadmin@
gwangju.museum.go.kr; internet gwangju
.museum.go.kr; f. 1978; cultural heritage of
Gwangju.

Gyeonggi-do

Ansan Fishing Village Folk Museum: 717
Seongam-dong, Danwon-gu, Ansan-si,
Gyeonggi-do; tel. (32) 886-0126; preserves
and exhibits traditional folk customs and
fishing culture of Ansan fishing village.

Bucheon Museum of Bow: 8 Sports Complex, Chunui-dong, Wonmi-gu, Bucheon-si,
Gyeonggi-do; tel. (32) 614-2678; internet
www.bcmuseum.or.kr; f. 2004; preserving
traditional bow kukgung culture.

Chunghyeon Museum: 1085-16 Soha 2-
dong, Gwangmyeong-si, Gyeonggi-do 423-
828; tel. (2) 898-0505; fax (2) 898-2507;
e-mail manager@chunghyon.com; internet
www.chunghyeon.org; f. 2003; Dir HAM
GEUMJA.

Deung-Jan Museum: 258-9 Nyeoungwon,
Myonhun-myeon, Yongin-si, Gyeonggi-do
449-850; tel. (31) 334-0797; e-mail
deungjan@deungjan.or.kr; internet www
.deungjan.or.kr; f. 1997; colln of ethnic
antique lamps.

Gyeonggi Museum of Modern Art: Dong-
sangil 36, 667-1 Choji-Dong, Danweon-gu,
Ansan-si, Gyeonggi-do 425-866; tel. (31) 481-
7007; fax (31) 481-7045; e-mail minerva8@
hanmir.com; internet www.gma.or.kr; f.
2006; Dir KIN HONG-HEE.

Gyeonggi Provincial Museum: 85 Sang-
gal-dong, Giheung-gu, Yongin-si, Gyeonggi-
do, Seoul 446-905; tel. (31) 288-5300; fax (31)
288-5390; e-mail museum@kg21.net;
internet www.musenet.or.kr; f. 1996; spec.
exhibitions on culture of Gyeonggi province;
Dir KIM JAE-YEOL.

Haegang Ceramics Museum: 330-1
Suwang-li, Shintun-myeon, Icheon,
Gyeonggi-do; tel. (31) 634-2266; fax (31)
634-2267; internet www.haegang.org; f.
1990; Korean ceramics; offers ceramic production courses.

Ho-Am Art Museum: 204 Gasil-ri, Pogok-
eup, Cheoin-gu, Yongin-si, Gyeonggi-do 449-
811; tel. (31) 320-1801; fax (31) 320-1809;
e-mail juliana.park@samsung.com; internet
hoam.samsungfoundation.org; f. 1982; largest privately owned museum in South Korea;
colln of over 1,200 Korean works of art;
sculpture garden of works by French sculptor
Bourdelle.

Woljeon Museum of Art: 467-020, Expo-gil
48, Gwango-dong 378, Icheon-si, Gyeonggi-
do; tel. (31) 637-0033; e-mail iwoljeon@
iwoljeon.org; internet www.iwoljeon.org; f.
1991 in Seoul, moved to Icheon in 2007;
commemorates work of Korean painter Woljeon Chang Woo-Soung; 1,532 artworks.

Gyeongsangbuk-do

**Andongsoju and Traditional Food
Museum:** 280 Susang-dong, Andong,
Gyeongsangbuk-do; tel. (54) 858-4541;
internet www.andongsoju.net; f. 2000;
museum of traditional Andong distilled
liquor.

Gyeongju National Museum: 118
Iljeongno, Gyeongju, Gyeongsangbuk-do,
Seoul 780-150; tel. (54) 740-7500; internet
gyeongju.museum.go.kr; f. 1945; preserves
culture of the Silla Kingdom; Dir YOUNG-
HOON YI.

**Gyeongsangbuk-do Forest Science
Museum:** tel. (54) 855-8681; fax (54) 855-
8684; internet www.gbfsm.or.kr; preserves
historical material and data on forests and
conducts academic research; outdoor facilities divided by themes into hydroponics
zone, landscaping zone, wooded zone, clean
zone, ecological zone, botanical communities,
traditional culture practice zone (mountain
village culture), ornithological facility and
greenhouse zone.

Hahoe Mask Museum: 287 Hahoe-ri, Pung-
chun-myun, Andong Gyeongsangbuk-do; tel.
(571) 853-2288; fax (571) 853-0114; internet
www.tal.or.kr; hahoe masks and Korean
masks.

Silla Art and Science Museum: Gyeongju
Folk Hand Craft Village, Gyeongju, Gyeongsangbuk-do; tel. (54) 745-4998; fax (54) 746-
5134; internet www.sasm.or.kr; f. 1988; represents the scientific advancements and
achievement of the Silla period; incl. spec.
exhibits on the Sokkuram Grotto and Chom-
songdae observatories.

Jeollabuk-do

Gangam Calligraphy Museum: 197-2
Gyo-dong, Wansan-gu, Jeonju-si, Jeollabuk-
do; tel. (63) 285-7442; f. 1995; 1,000 works by
Korean calligraphers Jeong-hui Kim (1786–
1856), Sam-man Lee (1770–1845) and Yak-
yong Jeong (1762–1836).

Jeonju National Museum: 900 Hyoja-dong
2 Ga, Wansa-Gu, JeonJu, Jeollabuk-do,
Seoul 560-859; tel. (63) 223-5651; fax (63)
223-5653; internet jeonju.museum.go.kr;
24,000 artifacts; history and culture of
Jeollabuk-do; Buddhist art works, pottery,
gold artifacts and folk material; Dir HYUNG
SIK YOO.

Jeollanam-do

Mokpo Natural History Museum: 9-28
Yonghae-dong, Mokpo-si, Jeollanam-do; tel.
(61) 274-3655; fax (61) 270-8298; internet
museum.mokpo.go.kr; f. 2004; natural history; 40,000 artifacts.

National Maritime Museum: 8 Yonghae-
dong, Mokpo, Jeollanam-do; tel. (61) 270-
2000; fax (61) 270-2080; internet www
.seamuse.go.kr; f. 1994; exhibits underwater
cultural heritage from the Korean waters
and maritime culture incl. nautical traditions and Korean traditional boats.

Seoul

Chiwoo Craft Museum: 610-11 Woomyun-dong, Seocho-gu, Seoul; internet www .chiwoocraftmuseum.org; f. 2002; modern crafts; Curator LEE IN BEOM.

National Museum of Contemporary Art: Deoksugung, 5-1 Jeong-Dung, Jung-gu, Seoul 100-120; e-mail miaya@mct.go.kr; internet www.moca.go.kr; exhibitions; educational programmes for art professionals and school liaison; general programmes, programmes for children and youth.

National Museum of Korea: 135 Seo-binggo-ro, Yongsan-gu, Seoul, 140-026; tel. (2) 2077-9000; internet www.museum.go.kr; f. 1908; Korean archaeology, culture and folklore; 100,000 artefacts representing over 5,000 years of human endeavour on the Korean peninsula; education centre; library of 20,000 vols; brs in 8 other towns; Dir CHOE KWANG-SHIK; publs *Bakmulkwan Sinmun* (Museum News, 12 a year), *Misul Charyo* (Materials in Art, 2 a year), *Report of Researches of Antiquities*, *The International Journal of Korean Art and Archeology*.

National Science Museum: 2 Waryong-dong, Jongno-gu, Seoul 110-360; tel. (2) 3668-2200; fax (2) 3668-2246; internet www.ssm .go.kr; f. 1926; holds National Science Fair, exhibitions, science classrooms, film service, etc.; library of 2,000 vols on science and technology; Dir CHI-EUN KIM; publ. *Bulletin.*

Seoul National University Museum: 599 Gwanak-ro, Gwanak-gu, Seoul 151-742; tel. (2) 880-5333; fax (2) 874-3999; internet museum.snu.ac.kr; f. 1941; exhibition of Korean culture totalling 8,058 artefacts; library specializing in Korean archaeology, art history, anthropology and folklore; Dir Dr NAK-KYU PARK; publ. *Bulletin* (1 a year).

Yonsei University Museum: Shinchon-dong, Sudaemun-gu, Seoul; tel. (2) 123-3335; e-mail art@yonsei.ac.kr; internet museum.yonsei.ac.kr; f. 1965; research; pre-history, history, fine arts, ethnic customs, medicine, geology, etc.; Curator YOUNG CHEOL BAK; publs occasional papers, excavation reports.

Universities
PUBLIC UNIVERSITIES

ANDONG NATIONAL UNIVERSITY

388 Songcheon-dong, Andong-si, Gyeong-sangbuk, Seoul 460-380

Telephone: (54) 820-5114
Fax: (54) 820-7115
Internet: www.andong.ac.kr

Founded 1979

Pres.: LEE HEE JAE
Registrar: KIM JONG-SIK
Librarian: KU SANG-MAN

Library of 55,000 vols
Number of teachers: 113
Number of students: 2,900

CHANGWON NATIONAL UNIVERSITY

9 Sarim-dong, Changwon, Gyeongnam, Seoul 641-773

Telephone: (55) 213-3000
Fax: (55) 283-2970
E-mail: admission@changwon.ac.kr
Internet: www.changwon.ac.kr

Founded 1969 as Masan Jr College of Education; became Changwon Nat. College 1984; present name 1991

Pres.: HO PARK SEONG.

CHONBUK NATIONAL UNIVERSITY

664-14 Deogjin-dong 1-ka, Chonju 561-756, Chonbuk

Telephone: 70-2114
Fax: 0652-70-2188
Internet: www.chonbuk.ac.kr

Founded 1947
State control
Academic year: March to February (two semesters)

President: Dr MYUNG SOO CHANG
Library Director: JIN KON OH

Library of 385,000 vols
Number of teachers: 800
Number of students: 24,000

Publications: *The Chonbuk University News-paper*, *The Chonbuk University Herald* (52 a year), *Chonbuk National University Bulletin* (1 a year), annual bulletins of research institutes

VICE-PRESIDENTS

Academic Affairs: YEONG CHUL KIM
Student Affairs: EUNG KYO RYU
Research and Development: JEONG KEUN PARK
Graduate School: SUN YUNG CHO
Graduate School of Agricultural Development: SUNG YUN KANG
Graduate School of Business Administration: SUNG WOO HYUNG
Graduate School of Education: GWANG HYUN CHOI
Graduate School of Environmental Studies: JE BIN IM
Graduate School of Industrial Technology: SUK PYO HONG
Graduate School of Public Administration: YOUNG MIN HEO
College of Agriculture: JAI SIK HONG
College of Arts: KYE IL SONG
College of Commerce: YEONG HEE CHEONG
College of Dentistry: CHAN UN PARK
College of Education: SEUNG TAI PARK
College of Engineering: CHUL RO YU
College of Home Economics: KEUM SODU CHI
College of Humanities: YOUNG CHUEL KIM
College of Law: KYU SUK SUH
College of Natural Science: CHOON HO LEE
College of Social Science: JAE YOUNG KIM
College of Veterinary Medicine: JOO MOOK LEE
Medical School: NO SUK KI

DIRECTORS

American Studies Research Institute: JANG RYUNG KIM
Biosafety Research Institute: BYUNG MOO LIM
Cholla Cultural Research Centre: HEE KWON LEE, Language Research Institute: KYU TAE CHO
Electric and Electronic Circuit and Systems Research Institute: DONG YONG KIM
Humanities Research Institute: KANG JE KWAK
Information Industry Research Institute: OK BAE CHANG
Institute for Medical Science: HONG BAI EUN
Institute for Molecular Biology and Genetics: KWANG YEOP JANG
Institute of Advanced Materials Development: CHONG KYO KIM
Institute of Animal Research and Development: WON JIB SHIN
Institute of Basic Science: KWANG HO SO
Institute of Dental Science: EUN CHUNG JHEE
Institute of Local Government and Autonomy: CHEOL JONG RYU
Institute of Rural Development: DONG HO LEE
Institute of Science Education: SEUK BEUM KO

Institute of Social Education: DAE WOON CHANG
Laboratory of Electronics Industry and Development: SUNG JOONG KIM
Research Institute of Agricultural Development: SUN YOUNG CHOI
Research Institute of Communist Countries: WON HO YOON
Research Institute of Engineering Technology: HAK SHIN KIM
Research Institute of Industry and Economy: SEUNG KI PARK
Research Institute of Law: KYU SUK SUH
Research Institute of Semiconductors: HYUNG JAE LEE
Research Institute of Sports Science: SANG JONG LEE
Research Institute of Urban and Environmental Studies: EUNG KYO RYU
Social Science Research Institute: SOON GOO CHO

CHONNAM NATIONAL UNIVERSITY

300 Yongbong-dong, Buk-gu, Gwangju, Seoul 500-757

Telephone: (62) 530-1265
Fax: (62) 530-1269

Gwangju Campus: 77 Yongbong-ro, Buk-gu, Gwangju, Seoul 500-757

Telephone: (62) 530-5114
Fax: (62) 530-1139

Yeosu Campus: San 96-1 Doondeok-dong, Jeonnam, Seoul

Telephone: (61) 659-2114
Fax: (61) 659-3003
E-mail: cnupr@chonnam.ac.kr
Internet: www.chonnam.ac.kr

Founded 1952
State control
Language of instruction: Korean
Academic year: March to February (2 semesters)

Pres.: Dr KIM YOON SOO
Dean of Academic Affairs: Dr JONG MOK LEE
Dean of Planning and Research: Dr SUNG SOO PARK
Dean of Student Affairs: Dr JUNG MOOK YOON
Librarian: Dr YOON JUNG HAN

Library of 600,000 vols, 6,000 periodicals
Number of teachers: 2,435
Number of students: 24,000

Publications: *Chonnam Medical Journal*, *Chonnam Review of American Studies*, *Industrial Relations Research*, *Journal of Agricultural Science and Technology*, *Journal of Arts*, *Journal of Drug Development*, *Journal of Humanities Studies*, *Journal of Natural Science*, *Journal of Regional Development*, *Journal of Research Institute for Catalysis*, *Journal of Sciences for Better Living*, *Journal of Sports Science*, *Journal of Unification Studies*, *Language Teaching*, *Research on Honam Culture*, *Rural Development Review*, *Social Science Review*, *Technological Review*, *Yongbong Review*

DEANS

College of Agriculture: JAE HONG KIM
College of Arts: JONG IL KIM
College of Business Administration: SOUG SHIN CHOI
College of Dentistry: MONG SOOK VANG
College of Education: KEUN HO CHUNG
College of Engineering: KWAN SOO LEE
College of Home Economics: DUCK SOON HWANG
College of Law: SEONG KIE KIM
College of Medicine: YOUNG HONG PAIK
College of Natural Sciences: JAE KEUN KIM
College of Pharmacy: BYUNG HO CHUNG

College of Social Sciences: YOUNG KWAN CHOI
College of Veterinary Medicine: NAM YONG PARK
Graduate School: HA IL PARK
Graduate School of Business Administration: SOUG SHIN CHOI
Graduate School of Education: KEUN HO CHUNG
Graduate School of Industry: KWAN SOO LEE
Graduate School of Public Administration: SEONG KIE KIM

CHUNGBUK NATIONAL UNIVERSITY

410 Seongbong-ro, Heungdeok-gu, Cheongju, Chungbuk, Seoul 361-763

Telephone: (43) 261-3172
Internet: www.chungbuk.ac.kr

Founded 1951 as Agricultural College, univ. status 1970
Academic year: March to July, September to December

Pres.: LIM DONG CHOL
Dir of Admin.: KEE UN CHUNG
Dean of Academic Affairs: YOUNG SOO JEONG
Dean of Planning and Research Affairs: SOON SEOP KWAK
Dean of Student Affairs: SUNG HOO HONG
Dir of Library: SOON KEY JUNG

Library of 520,000 vols
Number of teachers: 700
Number of students: 18,000

Publications: *Journal of Agricultural Science Research*, *Journal of Genetic Engineering Research*, *Journal of Humanities*, *Journal of Language and Literature*, *Journal of Pharmaceutical Science*, *Journal of Social Science*, *Journal of the Industrial Science and Technology Institute*, *Journal of the Institute of Construction Technology*, *Journal of the Research Institute for Computer and Information Communication*, *Jungwon Munhwa Nonchong*, *Juris Forum*, *Law Journal*, *Review of Industry and Management*

DEANS

College of Commerce and Business Administration: DO WON SUH
College of Education: SHEON JOO CHIN
College of Engineering: LEE JAE KI
College of Home Economics: KI NAM KIM
College of Humanities: JANG SUNG JOONG
College of Law: JUN HUR
College of Medicine: YOUNG JIN SONG
College of Natural Science: BYUNG CHOON LEE
College of Pharmacy: HAN KUN
College of Social Science: HEE KYUNG KANG
College of Veterinary Medicine: YOUNG WON YUN

CHUNGNAM NATIONAL UNIVERSITY

79 Daehangno, Yuseong-gu, Daejon, Seoul 305-764

Telephone: (42) 821-5013
Fax: (42) 823-1469
Internet: www.chungnam.ac.kr

Founded 1952
Academic year: March to June, September to December

Pres.: SONG, YONG-HO
Dean of Academic Affairs: CHUL KYU CHOI
Dean of Student Affairs: KUN MOOK CHOI
Registrar: MYUNG KYUN KIM
Librarian: JONG UP CHO

Number of teachers: 880
Number of students: 20,000

DEANS

College of Agriculture: JONG WOO KIM
College of Economics and Management: CHUL HWAN CHUN

College of Engineering: SOO YOUNG CHUNG
College of Fine Arts and Music: CHEOL NAM
College of Home Economics: YOUNG JIN CHUNG
College of Humanities: HAE KIL SUH
College of Law: KANG YONG LEE
College of Medicine: JIN SUN BAI
College of Natural Sciences: JONG SUK CHOI
College of Pharmacy: BYUNG ZUN AHN
College of Social Sciences: TONG HOON KIM
College of Veterinary Medicine: MOO HYUNG JUN
Graduate School: CHONG HOE PARK
Graduate School of Business Administration: KEAN SHIK LEE
Graduate School of Education: SANG CHUL KANG
Graduate School of Industry: GUNG SUCK NAM
Graduate School of Public Administration: JAE CHANG KA
Graduate School of Public Health: SAE JIN CHOI

GYEONGSANG NATIONAL UNIVERSITY

900 Gazwa-dong, Jinju, Seoul 660-701

Telephone: (55) 751-6229
Fax: (55) 751-6121
E-mail: belle@gshp.gsnu.ac.kr
Internet: www.gsnu.ac.kr

Founded 1948 as Gyeongnam Provincial Junior Agricultural College; became Gyeongnam Nat. College 1968 and Gyeongsang Nat. College 1972; present name 1979

Pres.: HA WOO-SONG

Number of teachers: 670
Number of students: 23,300 (21,100 undergraduate, 2,200 postgraduate)

Colleges of Humanities, Social Sciences, Natural Sciences, Business Administration, Engineering, Agriculture and Life Science, Law, Education, Veterinary Medicine, Medicine and Marine Science.

JEJU NATIONAL UNIVERSITY

Jejudaehakno 66, Jeju, Jeju-si 690-756

Telephone: (64) 754-2114
Fax: (64) 755-6130
E-mail: webmaster@jejunu.ac.kr
Internet: www.jejunu.ac.kr

Founded 1952 as Jeju Provincial Junior College; became Jeju Nat. College 1962; present name 1982
Academic year: March to February

Pres.: Dr CHOONG-SUK KOH

Number of teachers: 600
Number of students: 10,000

KANGWON NATIONAL UNIVERSITY

192-1 Hyoja-dong, Chuncheon-si, Gangwon-do, Seoul 200-701

Telephone: (33) 250-6114
Fax: (33) 250-9556
E-mail: intn@cc.kangwon.ac.kr
Internet: www.kangwon.ac.kr

Founded 1947
Pres.: KWON YONG JUNG
Registrar: LIM HYUNG-SIK
Librarian: PARK KYUNG-HO

Library of 206,000 vols
Number of teachers: 378
Number of students: 16,000

DEANS

College of Agriculture: LEE SANG-YOUNG
College of Business Administration: SHIM JONG-SEOP
College of Education: CHOI KEUN-SEONG

College of Engineering: PARK JE-SEON
College of Forestry: KIM SU-CHANG
College of Humanities and Social Science: PARK HAN-SEOL
College of Law: KIM JEUNG-HU
College of Natural Sciences: LEE CHONG-HYEOK

GANGNEUNG–WONJU NATIONAL UNIVERSITY

Gangneung Campus: 120 Gangneung Daehangno, Gangneung City, Gangwon-do, Seoul 210-702

Telephone: (33) 642-7001
Fax: (33) 643-7110

Wonju Campus: 901 Namwon-ro, Wonju City, Gangwon-do, Seoul 220-711

Telephone: (33) 760-8114
Fax: (33) 760-8059
E-mail: ciec@nukw.ac.kr
Internet: www.gwnu.ac.kr

Founded 1968 as Kangnung Educational College; became Kangnung Junior College 1977 and Kangnung Nat. College 1979; present name 1991
State control
Academic year: March to December (two semesters)

Colleges of Humanities, Social Sciences, Natural Sciences, Engineering, Life Sciences, Arts and Physical Education, Dentistry; 17 research institutes, museum, gallery

Pres.: Dr HAN SONG
Dean of Center for Int. Exchange and Cooperation: CHI SUNG-PA

Library of 250,000 vols, 9,044 periodicals
Number of teachers: 258 full-time, 370 part-time
Number of students: 7,321

KONGJU NATIONAL UNIVERSITY

182 Shinkwan-dong, Kongju, Chungnam

Telephone: (416) 850-8114
Fax: (416) 853-3517
Internet: www.kongju.ac.kr

Founded 1948 as Kongju Provincial Teachers' College; became Kongju National Teachers' College 1950; present name 1991

President: Dr SUCK-WON CHOI
Dean of Academic Affairs: HYUNG-TAE MOON
Director General: CHANG-YONG PARK

Library of 360,000 vols
Number of teachers: 602
Number of students: 13,560

DEANS

College of Education: BYUNG-MOO KIM
College of Engineering: KUM-BAE LEE
College of Humanities and Social Sciences: PIL-YOUNG LEE
College of Industrial Sciences: SEONG-MIN KIM
College of Sciences: YOUNG-KYUN WOO

KOREA ADVANCED INSTITUTE OF SCIENCE AND TECHNOLOGY (KAIST)

335 Gwahak-ro (373-1 Kusong-dong), Yusong-ku, Daejon, Seoul 305-701

Telephone: (42) 869-2114
Fax: (42) 869-2210
Internet: www.kaist.ac.kr

Founded 1981 by merger of Korea Advanced Institute of Science (KAIS) and Korea Institute of Science and Technology (KIST); KIST separated from KAIST 1989; Korea Institute of Technology (KIT) merged with KAIST 1989
State control
Academic year: March to February

Pres.: NAM PYO SUH
Colleges of Natural Science, Engineering, Humanities and Social Science, Graduate School of Management.

KOREA MARITIME UNIVERSITY

1 Dongsam-Dong, Yeongdo-gu, Busan, Seoul 606-791
Telephone: (51) 410-4114
E-mail: webmaster@hhu.ac.kr
Internet: www.hhu.ac.kr
Colleges of Engineering, International Studies, Maritime Sciences, Ocean Science and Technology
Pres.: OH KEO DON.

KOREA NATIONAL OPEN UNIVERSITY

169 Dongsung-dong, Chongro-ku, Seoul 110-791
Telephone: (2) 7404-114
Fax: (2) 744-5882
E-mail: webmaster@knou.ac.kr
Internet: www.knou.ac.kr
Founded 1972
State control
Academic year: March to February
Pres.: CHANG SEE WOM
Registrar: KIM EUI-DONG
Library Dir: KIM SUNG-KIH
Library of 412,000 vols
Number of teachers: 112
Number of students: 199,000

Publications: *Distance Education, KNOU Journal, KNOU Weekly*

DEANS
College of Education: CHOI CHONG-SOOK
College of Liberal Arts: LEE YONG-HAK
College of Natural Science: KIM HYE-SEON
College of Social Science: KIM SOO-SIN
School of General Education: LEE YUNG-HO

ATTACHED RESEARCH INSTITUTES
Educational Media Development Centre: Dir KWAK DUK-HUN.
Institute of Distance Education: Dir HONG SOON-JEONG.

KOREA NATIONAL UNIVERSITY OF THE ARTS

120-3 Yesuk-gil, Seongbuk-gu, Seoul 136-716
Telephone: (2) 746-9042
E-mail: admissions@knua.ac.kr
Internet: www.knua.ac.kr
Founded 1993
Pres.: LEE GEON-YONG
Provost: KIM BONG-RYOL
Number of teachers: 730
Number of students: 2,600
Colleges of Dance, Drama, Film, Korean Traditional Arts, Music, Television and Multimedia, Visual Arts.

KUNSAN NATIONAL UNIVERSITY

1170 Daehangno, Gunsan, Seoul 573-701
Telephone: (63) 469-4134
Fax: (63) 469-4197
E-mail: inter@kunsan.ac.kr
Internet: www.kunsan.ac.kr
Founded 1979
Languages of instruction: Korean, English
Academic year: March to February
Pres.: Dr LEE HEE-YEON
Library of 280,000 vols
Number of teachers: 327
Number of students: 11,065

PROFESSORS
College of Arts, School of Fine Arts and Design:
  CHO, Y. B., Department of Industrial Design
  KIM, S. T., Department of Industrial Ceramic Arts
  KIM, Y. O., Department of Music
College of Engineering, Faculty of Electronic and Information Engineering:
  HEO, B. M., Department of Mechanical Design Engineering
  KIM, S. G., Materials Science and Engineering
  LEE, H. Y., Department of Chemical Engineering
  LEE, J. I., Electronic and Information Engineering
  LIM, B. Y., Department of Civil Engineering
  MOON, C. H., Department of Architectural Engineering
College of Humanities, Faculty of Oriental Language and Literature:
  CHO, S. H., Department of Korean Language and Literature
  LEE, H. H., Department of History
  LIM, K.-J., Department of Philosophy
  MOON, C.-S., Department of Japanese Language and Literature
  PAE, B. H., Department of German Literature and Language
  PARK, B.-S., Department of Chinese Language and Literature
  SEO, H. S., Department of English Language and Literature
College of Natural Sciences:
  CHOI, H. S., Department of Chemistry
  HANG, T. S., Department of Mathematics
  KIM, A. S., Department of Clothing and Textiles
  KIM, S. Y., Department of Food Science and Nutrition
  LEE, K. S., Department of Biological Science
  PARK, Y. S., Department of Informatics and Statistics
  RYOU, O. S., Department of Human Ecology
  YOON, C. S., Department of Physics
College of Ocean Science and Technology:
  CHANG, S. H., Department of Food Science and Technology
  CHUNG, E. Y., Department of Aquaculture and Biotechnology
  JEONG, K. J., Department of Marine Engineering
  KIM, Y. G., Department of Marine Life Science
  LEE, K. R., Department of Marine Science and Production
  SEO, S. W., Department of Ocean System Engineering
  YIH, W. H., Department of Ocean Information Science
College of Social Sciences:
  HWANG, H. M., International Trade
  KIM, Y.-J., Public Administration
  KWON, E. M., Business Administration and Accounting
  LIM, H. J., Economics and Trade

KWANGJU UNIVERSITY

Kwangju, Seoul 503-703
Telephone: (80) 670-2600
Internet: kwangju.ac.kr
Founded 1981 as Kwangju Kyung Sang Jr College; became Kwangju Open College 1984; present name 1989
Pres.: Dr LEE JAE-WOON
Library of 230,000 vols

Colleges of Management, Commerce and Social Welfare, Humanities and Social Sciences, Engineering, Arts; Graduate School.

KYUNGPOOK NATIONAL UNIVERSITY

1370 Sankyuk-dong, Buk-gu, Daegu, Seoul 702-701
Telephone: (53) 950-6091
Fax: (53) 950-6093
E-mail: kunglobal@knu.ac.kr
Internet: www.knu.ac.kr
Founded 1946
State control
Academic year: March to February (two semesters)
Pres.: NOH DONGIL
Dean of Academic Affairs: Dr KIM KEE CHAN
Dean of General Affairs: Dr PARK SEUNG TAE
Dean of Planning and Research Support: Dr SOHN JAE KEUN
Dean of Student Affairs: LEE MIN HYUNG
Library: see Libraries
Number of teachers: 825
Number of students: 24,504
Publication: *Research Review* (1 a year)

DEANS
Graduate School: Dr KWON YON-UNG
College of Agriculture and Life Sciences: Dr CHOI JONG-UCK
College of Dentistry: Dr KYUNG HEE-MOON
College of Economics and Commerce: Dr SOHN BYEONG-HAE
College of Engineering: Dr LEE DONG-HO
College of Human Ecology: Dr YOO YOUNG-SUN
College of Humanities: Dr KIM KEE-CHAN
College of Law: Dr KANG TAE-SEONG
College of Medicine: Dr KWAK JOUNG-SIK
College of Music and Visual Arts: Dr KWON KI-DUCK
College of Natural Sciences: Dr MOON BYUNG-JO
College of Social Sciences: Dr KIM JAE-HONG
College of Veterinary Medicine: Dr LEE CHA-SOO
School of Electrical Engineering and Computer Science: Dr LEE YONG-HYUN

PROFESSORS
College of Agriculture and Life Sciences (#223 College of Agriculture and Life Sciences Building I, Kyungpook National University, Daegu Seoul 702-701; tel. (53) 950-5700; fax (53) 950-6701):
  CHEONG, S.-T., Fruit Science, Plant Propagation
  CHO, R.-K., Food Chemistry
  CHOI, J., Soil Science
  CHOI, J.-U., Food Preservation Engineering
  CHOI, K., Forest Management and Economics
  CHOI, K.-S., Animal Breeding
  CHOI, K.-S., Economic Statistics
  CHOI, S.-T., Floriculture, Protected Cultivation
  CHOI, Y.-H., Food Engineering
  CHUNG, J.-D., Plant Tissue Culture
  CHUNG, M.-S., Tree Cultivation
  CHUNG, S.-K., Food Analysis and Sanitation
  CHUNG, S.-O., Irrigation and Drainage Engineering
  EOM, T.-J, Woody Plant Biochemistry
  HONG, S.-C., Forest Ecology
  HWANG, Y.-H., Plant Genetics
  JANG, I.-J., Agricultural Robot for Control Measurements
  JO, J.-K., Grass Physiology
  JUNG, S.-K., Landscape Construction

KIM, B.-S., Vegetable Cultivation, Pepper Cultivation
KIM, C.-S., Agricultural Policy
KIM, D.-S., Dairy Microbiology
KIM, D.-U., Plant Molecular Biology
KIM, J.-E., Environmental Chemistry
KIM, K.-U., Weed Science
KIM, S.-G., Agricultural Marketing
KIM, S.-K., Maize Breeding
KIM, T.-H., Agricultural Power Energy Conservation
KIM, Y.-S., Landscape Planning
KWON, M.-N., Geotechnical and Foundation Engineering
KWON, Y.-J., Systematic Entomology
LEE, H.-C., Agricultural Economic History
LEE, H.-T., Landscape Design
LEE, J.-T., Fungal Plant Pathology
LEE, J.-Y., Wood Chemistry
LEE, K.-C., Landscape Management
LEE, K.-M., Terramechanics, Greenhouse Controls
LEE, K.-W., Viral Plant Pathology
LEE, S.-C., Crop Production and Management
LEE, S.-G., Agricultural Buildings
NOH, S.-K., Insect Genetic Resources
PARK, I.-H., Landscape Plants
PARK, K.-K., Post-Harvest Process, Systems Mechanics
PARK, S.-J., Wood Anatomy
PARK, W.-C., Plant Nutrition
PARK, Y.-G., Forest Genetics
RHEE, I.-J., Fibre Materials Science
RHEE, I.-K., Biochemistry
RYU, J.-C., Agricultural Crops
SOHN, H.-R., Sericulture
SOHN, J.-K., Rice Cultivation
SON, D.-S., Forest Cultivation
SUH, S.-D., Hydrology, Land Engineering
SYN, Y.-B., Fruit Science, Plant Physiology
UHM, J.-Y., Bacterial Plant Pathology
YEO, Y.-K., Lipid Chemistry

College of Dentistry (#211 College of Dentistry, Kyungpook National University, Daegu Seoul 702-701; tel. (53) 420-6801; fax (53) 425-6025):

BAE, Y.-C., Oral Anatomy
CHO, S.-A., Prosthodontics
CHOI, J.-K., Oral Medicine
JO, K.-H., Prosthodontics
KIM, C.-S., Oral and Maxillofacial Surgery
KIM, K.-H., Dental Materials
KIM, Y.-J., Paediatric Dentistry
KWON, O.-W., Orthodontics
KYOUNG, H.-M., Orthodontics
LEE, S.-H., Oral and Maxillofacial Surgery
NAM, S.-H., Paediatric Dentistry
SONG, S.-B., Preventive Dentistry and Public Health Dentistry
SUNG, J.-H., Orthodontics

College of Economics and Commerce (#213 College of Economics and Commerce, Kyungpook National University, Daegu, Seoul 702-701; tel. (53) 950-5403; fax (53) 950-5405):

BAE, B.-H., Managerial Accounting
CHANG, H.-S., Marketing
CHANG, J.-S., Industrial Organization
CHO, S.-P., Financial Accounting
CHOE, J.-M., Managerial Accounting
CHOI, Y.-H., Korean Economy
HA, I.-B., Macroeconomics
HAN, D.-H., International Economics
JUNG, C.-Y., Operations Management
KANG, H.-Y., Managerial Accounting
KIM, H.-K., Labour Economics
KIM, J.-J., Marketing
KIM, S.-H., Monetary Economics, International Economics
KIM, Y.-H., Economic Development, Korean Economic History
KWON, C.-T., Financial Accounting
KWON, S.-C., Financial Accounting
KWON, S.-K., Financial Accounting

LEE, D.-M., Management Information Systems
LEE, H.-W., Operations Management
LEE, J.-D., Financial Management
LEE, J.-K., International Commercial Law
LEE, J.-W., Income Distribution, Comparative Economics
LEE, J.-W., Personnel and Organization Management
LEE, S.-D., Personnel and Organization Management
LEE, S.-H., Marketing
LEE, Y.-S., International Transportation and Logistics
MOON, S.-H., Operations Management
NAH, K.-S., Economic History
PARK, C.-S., Financial Management
PARK, J.-H., Macroeconomics
SHIN, M.-S., Financial Management
SOHN, B.-H., International Economics

College of Engineering (#211 College of Engineering Building VI, Kyungpook National University, Daegu, Seoul 702-701; tel. (53) 950-5500; fax (53) 958-5054):

AHN, K.-S., Digital Engineering
BAE, K.-S., Digital Signal Processing, Speech Signal Processing, Digital Communication
BAE, S.-K., Geochemical Engineering
BAEK, Y.-S., Power Systems Analysis
CHIEN, S.-I., Vision
CHO, J.-H., Bioelectronics, Electronic Measurements
CHO, S.-H., Ceramics for Electronics
CHO, Y.-J., Computer Networks
CHO, Y.-K., Antenna and Propagation, Ultrasonics
CHOI, H.-C., Wave Propagation
CHOI, H.-M., Parallel Distributed Processing, Processors, Logic Design
CHOI, M.-H., Architectural Planning and Design
CHOI, S.-J., Water Supply and Waste Water Treatment Engineering
CHOI, S.-Y., Semiconductor Engineering
CHOI, T.-H., Robotics
CHUNG, I.-S., Mechanical Metallurgy
HA, J.-M., Urban Design and City Planning
HA, Y.-H., Image Processing and Computer Vision Digital Signal Processing
HAN, K.-J., Computer Networks
HAN, K.-Y., Water Resources Engineering
HEO, N.-H., Zeolite Chemistry, Physical Chemistry
HONG, J.-K., Speech Signal Processing
HONG, S.-M., Control Theory
HWANG, C.-S., Visual Communication
JEON, G.-J., Intelligent Control, Systems Engineering
JI, B.-C., Polymer and Fibre Physics
JOO, E.-K., Digital Communication
KANG, I.-K., Biopolymers
KANG, M.-M., Architectural Structure
KIM, C.-H., Applied Mechanics
KIM, C.-J., Architectural Design
KIM, C.-Y., Microwave Engineering
KIM, D.-G., Power Electronics
KIM, D.-H., Reaction Engineering
KIM, D.-R., Surface Science and Engineering
KIM, H.-G., Power Electronics
KIM, H.-J., Pattern Recognition
KIM, H.-S., Synthetic Organic Chemistry
KIM, J.-J., Structural Ceramics
KIM, N.-C., Digital Communications, Image Communications
KIM, N.-K., Dielectric Materials
KIM, S.-H., Computational Geometry
KIM, S.-H., Synthetic Functional Dyes
KIM, S.-J., Geometry, Numerical Analysis
KIM, S.-J., Optical Signal Processing, Circuits and Systems
KIM, S.-M., Automata Theory
KIM, S.-S., Tribology

KIM, T.-J., Inorganic and Organometallic Chemistry, Homogeneous Catalysis
KIM, W.-J., Architectural Construction
KIM, W.-S., Architectural Construction
KIM, W.-S., Polymer Synthesis
KIM, Y.-M., Computer Graphics, Image Processing
KIM, Y.-S., Geotechnical Engineering
KWON, O.-J., Powder Metallurgy
KWON, S.-B., Fluid Mechanics
KWON, W.-H., Powder Electronics
KWON, Y.-D., Structural Analysis
KWON, Y.-H., Architectural Structure
LEE, B.-K., Powder Synthesis
LEE, C.-W., Combustion
LEE, D.-D., Semiconductor Engineering
LEE, D.-H., Polymerization Catalysis
LEE, J.-H., Semiconductor Technology
LEE, J.-T., Process Control
LEE, K.-I., Audio and Video Engineering, Electronic Measurements
LEE, K.-K., Non-linear Control Theory
LEE, M.-H., Instrumental Analysis, NMR Spectroscopy
LEE, S.-J., Natural Language
LEE, S.-R., Control and Automation
LEE, T.-J., Process and Property Thermodynamics
LEE, Y.-H., Semiconductor Engineering
LEE, Y.-M., Precision Machining
LIM, Y.-J., Dyeing Chemistry
MIN, K.-E., Physical Properties of Solid Polymers
MIN, K.-S., Water Quality Engineering
MOON, J.-D., Applied Electrostatics and High Voltage Applications
OH, C.-S., Computation, Analysis and Design of Electrical Machinery
OH, T.-J., Polymer and Fibre Chemistry
PARK, B.-O., Composite Materials
PARK, H.-B., Robust Control Theory
PARK, J.-K., Biochemical Engineering and Transport Phenomena
PARK, J.-S., Instrumentation, CAD, VLSI Design
PARK, K.-C., Joining and Metal Forming
PARK, K.-H., Robotics and Control
PARK, L.-S., Physical Properties of Polymer Solutions
PARK, M.-H., Structural Engineering
PARK, S.-K., Microelectronics
PARK, S.-T., Computer Networks, Databases
RIU, K.-J., Heat Transfer
RYU, K.-W., Parallel Algorithms
SEO, B.-H., Automatic and Digital Control, Computer Applications
SEO, K.-H., Polymer Processing
SHIM, S.-C., Petroleum Chemistry, Organic and Organometallic Chemistry
SHIN, S.-K., Semiconductor Engineering
SOHN, B.-K., Semiconductor Engineering
SOHN, J.-R., Catalytic Chemistry, Inorganic Material
SOHNG, K.-I., Video Engineering, Multiple Valued Logic Systems
SONG, D.-I., Polymer Rheology
SONG, J.-W., Optical Communication
SUH, C.-M., Materials and Mechanics
YE, B.-J., Casting, Solidification
YOO, K.-Y., Parallel Processing
YU, S.-D., Integrated Circuits

College of Human Ecology (#212 College of Human Ecology, Kyungpook National University, Daegu, Seoul 702-701; tel. (53) 950-6200; fax (53) 950-6205):

CHOI, B.-G., Child Development
CHOI, M.-S., Nutritional Biochemistry
KANG, M.-Y., Nutrition
LEE, H.-S., Nutrition

College of Humanities (#209 College of Humanities, Kyungpook National University, Daegu, Seoul 702-701; tel. (53) 950-5100; fax (53) 950-6101):

BANG, I., Oriental Philosophy

CHEON, K.-S., Korean Syntax
CHO, M.-H., British and American Drama
CHOI, S.-S., German Literature, Classical Literature
CHOY, C.-H., Korean History
CHUNG, I.-S., Chinese Linguistics
CHUNG, J.-S., English Linguistics, Syntax
EUN, J.-N., Modern Anglo-American Literature
HAN, S.-Z., German Literature
HONG, S.-M., Korean Linguistics
HWANG, W.-Z., Korean Literature
JANG, T.-W., Chinese Linguistics
JU, B.-D., Korean History
KIM, C.-D., Political and Economic Anthropology
KIM, C.-G., Western History
KIM, C.-S., British Poetry
KIM, C.-W., German Drama
KIM, D.-M., Oriental Philosophy
KIM, I.-L., Korean Classical Literature
KIM, K.-C., English Linguistics
KIM, K.-S., Korean Classical Literature
KIM, S.-W., Korean Chinese Literature
KIM, Y.-D., Western Philosophy
KIM, Y.-K., Western Philosophy
KWON, K.-H., Modern Korean Literature
KWON, T.-R., Chinese Linguistics
KWON, Y.-U., Korean History
LEE, C.-S., Chinese Literature
LEE, D.-H., German Literature
LEE, E.-Y., French Phonology
LEE, H.-J., Archaeology
LEE, H.-J., Chinese Literature
LEE, J.-H., Japanese Literature
LEE, K.-E., Russian Literature
LEE, K.-J., German Idealism
LEE, P.-S., French Syntax
LEE, S.-G., Korean Dialectology
LEE, W.-K., English Literature
PAEK, D.-H., Korean Philology
PARK, C.-B., English Literature
PARK, J.-G., French Literature
PARK, S.-W., German Linguistics
PARK, Y.-H., Korean Chinese Literature
SHIN, O.-H., Western Philosophy
SOHN, H.-S., English Linguistics
YI, B.-K., Bronze Age Archaeology, Museology
YI, K.-S., Chinese History
YOO, K.-S., Western History

College of Law (#305 College of Law, Kyungpook National University, Daegu, Seoul 702-701; tel. (53) 950-5456; fax (53) 950-5455):

CHANG, J.-H., Civil Law
KANG, T.-S., Civil Law
KIM, S.-T., Local Public Administration and Finance
KIM, Y.-S., Land Policy
LEE, Y.-J., Financial Administration
MOON, K.-S., Policy Sciences, Financial Management
PARK, J.-H., Urban Planning
PARK, J.-T., Commercial Law
RHEE, W.-W., Urban Administration

College of Medicine (#208 College of Medicine, Kyungpook National University, Daegu, Seoul 702-701; tel. (53) 420-6901; fax (53) 421-6585; internet med.knu.ac.kr):

BAEK, W.-Y., Intensive Care Therapy
BAIK, B.-S., Craniofacial Surgery
CHAE, J.-M., Forensic Pathology
CHAE, S.-C., Cardiology
CHANG, S.-I., Surgery, Paediatric Surgery
CHANG, S.-K., Transplantation, Tumours
CHO, D.-K., Nephrology
CHO, D.-Y., Molecular Genetics
CHO, H.-J., Neuroanatomy
CHO, T.-H., Oncology
CHO, Y.-L., Gynaecological Oncology
CHOI, Y.-H., Gastroenterology
CHUN, B.-Y., Health Care Administration and Health Policy
CHUN, S.-S., Reproductive Endocrinology and Infertility

CHUNG, B.-Y., Adult Nursing, Cancer Nursing
CHUNG, J.-M., Gastroenterology
CHUNG, S.-L., Dermatology, Leprosy
CHUNG, T.-H., Immunology
DOH, B.-N., Psychiatric and Mental Health Nursing
HAMM, I.-S., Cerebrovascular Disease, Neuro-Oncology
HONG, H.-S., Anatomy, Medical Genetics
HONG, J.-G., Pain Clinic
HWANG, S.-K., Paediatric Neurosurgery
IHN, J.-C., Joint Reconstructive Surgery
JUN, J.-B., Dermatology, Mycology, Dermatopathology
JUN, J.-E., Cardiology
JUN, S.-H., Surgery, Colorectal Surgery
JUNG, M.-S., Women's Health Nursing
JUNG, S.-K., Paediatric Urology, Traumatology
KANG, D.-J., Psychiatry, Psychopharmacology
KANG, D.-S., Thoracic Radiology
KIM, B.-W., Endocrinology, Metabolism
KIM, B.-W., Tumours
KIM, C.-Y., Cardiovascular Pharmacology
KIM, D.-W., Dermatology
KIM, H.-M., Paediatrics, Neonatology
KIM, I.-T., Vitreous Humour and Retina
KIM, J.-C., Cellular and Molecular Immunology
KIM, K.-T., Paediatric Cardiovascular Surgery
KIM, M.-Y., Paediatric Nursing
KIM, N.-S., Allergology, Rheumatology
KIM, P.-T., Hand Surgery
KIM, S.-L., Cerebrovascular Disease
KIM, S.-Y., Vitreous Humour and Retina
KIM, T.-H., Diagnostic Radiology
KIM, Y.-I., Surgery
KIM, Y.-J., Interventional Radiology
KIM, Y.-W., Vascular Surgery
KOO, J.-H., Paediatrics, Nephrology
KWAK, J.-S., Forensic Pathology
KWAK, Y.-S., Pharmacy
KWON, J.-Y., Paediatric Ophthalmology
LEE, J.-B., Family Medicine
LEE, J.-T., Cardiovascular Surgery
LEE, J.-Y., Occupational Neurology
LEE, K.-B., Nuclear Medicine
LEE, K.-S., Paediatrics, Haemato-Oncology and Genetics
LEE, M.-G., Neuropsychological Pharmacology
LEE, S.-B., Paediatrics, Cardiology
LEE, S.-H., Otology, Neuro-Otology
LEE, S.-K., Biostatistics and Nutritional Epidemiology
LEE, S.-N., Psychiatry, Psychotherapy
LEE, W.-J., Renal Physiology
LEE, W.-K., Clinical Microbiology
LEE, Y.-C., Virology
LEE, Y.-H., Surgery, Head and Neck Endocrine Surgery
PARK, B.-C., Paediatric and Spinal Surgery
PARK, I.-H., Oncology and Infection
PARK, I.-K., Radiation Oncology, Radiation Biology
PARK, I.-S., Gynaecological Oncology
PARK, J.-H., Fundamentals of Nursing
PARK, J.-S., Cardiovascular Physiology
PARK, J.-S., Head and Neck Oncology
PARK, J.-W., Vascular Pharmacology and Anaesthesia
PARK, J.-Y., Health Care Administration and Health Policy
PARK, S.-Y., Adult Nursing
PARK, W.-H., Cardiology
PARK, Y.-K., Andrology
PARK, Y.-M., Spinal Neuro-Oncology, Neurotrauma
RIM, H.-D., Psychiatry, Psychosomatics
SEOL, S.-Y., Molecular Epidemiology
SOHN, Y.-K., Neuropathology
SUH, C.-K., Neurology

SUH, I.-S., Pathology of the Gastrointestinal Tract
SUH, J.-S., Diagnostic Haematology
SUH, S.-R., Adult Nursing
YEO, M.-H., Epidemiology and Population Dynamics
YU, W.-S., Surgery, Surgical Oncology
YUN, Y.-K., Surgery, Hepatobiliary Surgery

College of Music and Visual Arts (#217 College of Music and Visual Arts, Kyungpook National University, Daegu, Seoul 702-701; tel. (53) 950-5650; fax (53) 950-5655):

BYUN, Y.-B., Sculpture
CHONG, H.-I., Kayagum (12-Stringed Zither)
CHUNG, H.-C., Composition
JUNG, W.-H., Piano
KANG, C.-S., Piano
KIM, G.-J., Voice (Soprano)
KIM, J.-W., Voice (Baritone)
KIM, K.-I., Piano
KIM, W.-S., Korean Painting
KU, Y.-K., Komungo (6-Stringed Zither)
KWON, K.-D., Visual Design
LEE, D.-C., Oil Painting
LEE, E.-S., Piano
LEE, K.-J., Kayagum (12-Stringed Zither)
LEE, W.-S., Visual Design
LIM, H.-S., Clarinet
OH, H.-C., Oil Painting
PARK, N.-H., Art History
SHIM, S.-H., Voice (Tenor)
YI, T.-B., Theory of Korean Music and Taegum (Korean Transverse Flute)
YOO, H., Korean Painting
YOON, J.-R., Cello
YUN, M.-G., Piri (Korean Oboe)

College of Natural Sciences (#201 College of Natural Sciences, Kyungpook National University, Daegu, Seoul 702-701; tel. (53) 950-5300; fax (53) 957-0431):

BAE, Z.-U., Analytical Chemistry
CHANG, T.-W., Structural Geology
CHO, K.-H., Statistical Inference
CHOI, J.-K., Probability, Stochastic Processes
CHOI, S.-D., Condensed Matter Theory
HA, J.-H., Microbial Genetics
HUH, T.-L., Molecular Genetics
JEE, J.-G., Physical Chemistry
JEONG, J.-H., Inorganic Chemistry
JIN, I.-N., Enzymology
JO, S.-G., High Energy Physics Theory
JUNG, I.-B., Analysis
KANG, H.-D., Experimental Nuclear Physics
KANG, S.-S., Biochemistry and Animal Physiology
KIM, E.-S., Algebra
KIM, H.-S., Analysis
KIM, I.-S., Biochemistry
KIM, J.-G., Microbial Genetics
KIM, K.-E., Precipitation Mechanism
KIM, S.-W., Computer Languages
KIM, S.-W., Petrology
KIM, Y.-H., Cellular Immunobiology
KOH, I.-S., Sedimentology, Sedimentary Petrology
KWAK, Y.-W., Organic Chemistry
LEE, E.-W., Surface and Thin Films Experiments
LEE, H.-H., Analysis
LEE, H.-L., Analytical Chemistry
LEE, H.-R., Condensed Matter Theory
LEE, I.-S., Statistical Inference, Theoretical Statistics
LEE, J.-K., Organic Chemistry
LEE, J.-Y., Virology
LEE, K.-M., Radiative Transfer, Upper Atmosphere
LEE, S.-H., Analysis
LEE, S.-K., Information Visualization
LEE, S.-Y., Thin Film and Electroluminescence Experiments

LEE, Y.-H., Biochemical Engineering
LEE, Y.-S., Cellular Biochemistry
MIN, K.-D., Atmospheric Energetics
MOON, B.-J., Biochemistry
PARK, B.-G., Reliability Analysis
PARK, C.-Y., Topology
PARK, H.-C., Animal Taxonomy
PARK, J.-H., Plant Systematics
PARK, J.-W., Biochemical Carcinogenesis
PARK, W., Molecular Biology
PARK, Y.-B., Biochemistry
PARK, Y.-C., Database Systems
PARK, Y.-C., Inorganic Chemistry
PARK, Y.-S., Algebra
PARK, Y.-T., Organic Chemistry
SEO, B.-B., Genetics
SOHN, J.-K., Bayesian Decision Theory, Statistical Computing
SOHN, K.-S., Condensed Matter Theory
SOHN, U.-I., Molecular Biology
SON, D.-C., Experimental High Energy Physics
SONG, J.-K., Mulitivariate Data Analysis
SONG, S.-D., Plant Physiology
SUH, Y.-J., Geometry

College of Social Sciences (#315 College of Social Sciences, Kyungpook National University, Daegu, Seoul 702-701; tel. (53) 950-5200; fax (53) 950-5205):

CHIN, S.-M., Industrial Sociology
CHO, H.-C., Counselling Psychology
CHOI, C.-M., Social Welfare Administration
CHOI, K.-S., Social Psychology
HAN, N.-J., Sociology of Family
JIN, Y.-S., Cognitive Psychology
KIM, J.-H., Ethics and Legal Studies in Mass Communication
KIM, W.-H., International Relations
KIM, Y.-H., Clinical Psychology
KIM, Y.-H., Social Policy
LEE, J.-H., Regional Geography
LEE, Y.-J., Information Science
NAM, K.-H., Bibliography
NOH, D.-I., Korean Politics
PARK, B.-S., Clinical Social Work
PARK, J.-S., Political Communication Theory
PARK, J.-W., Population Studies
PARK, K.-S., Broadcasting
PARK, S.-D., Social Security
PARK, Y.-C., Regional Development, Economic Geography
SHON, J.-P., Library Management
YOON, Y.-H., Comparative Politics

College of Veterinary Medicine (#205 College of Veterinary Medicine, Kyungpook National University, Daegu, Seoul 702-701; tel. (53) 950-5950; fax (53) 950-5955):

BYUN, M.-D., Veterinary Obstetrics
CHOI, W.-P., Veterinary Microbiology
JANG, I.-H., Veterinary Surgery, Veterinary Obstetrics
KIM, B.-H., Veterinary Microbiology
KIM, Y.-H., Veterinary Obstetrics
LEE, C.-S., Veterinary Pathology
LEE, J.-H., Veterinary Medicine
MOON, M.-H., Veterinary Parasitology
PARK, C.-K., Veterinary Microbiology
TAK, R.-B., Veterinary Public Health
YU, C.-J., Veterinary Physiology

Teachers' College:

AHN, B.-H., Space Physics
BAE, H.-D., Politics, Political Thought
BAE, J.-E., English Literature
CHAE, H.-W., Training
CHANG, D.-I., Medieval Korean History
CHUNG, D.-H., German Linguistics
CHUNG, H.-P., Philosophy of Education
CHUNG, H.-S., Cell Biology, Photosynthesis
CHUNG, S.-T., Sport Psychology
CHUNG, W.-W., Mineralogy
HONG, Y.-P., Politics, Political Thought
HWANG, B.-S., French Linguistics
HWANG, S.-G., Algebra

IM, J.-R., Korean Linguistics
JANG, H.-S., Nutrition
JANG, Y.-O., Home Management
JO, P.-G., Clothing
JO, W.-R., Geomorphology
JUN, B.-Q., English Linguistics
KANG, Y.-H., Astronomy
KI, U.-H., Geometry
KIM, B.-K., Counselling
KIM, H.-K., Economic Development
KIM, H.-S., Early Modern East Asian History
KIM, J.-J., Dance
KIM, J.-T., Korean Linguistics
KIM, J.-W., Contemporary Western History
KIM, K.-H., Measurement and Evaluation for Physical Education
KIM, M.-H., Educational Administration
KIM, M.-K., Korean Literature
KIM, M.-N., Philosophy of Education
KIM, S.-H., Educational Psychology
KIM, Y.-H., Geometry
KOH, J.-K., Particle Physics, Physics Education
LEE, A.-H., Educational Psychology
LEE, B.-H., Early Modern Korean History
LEE, J.-H., Korean Literature
LEE, J.-H., Politics, International Politics
LEE, J.-W., Population Geography, Geographical Education
LEE, M.-H., Biomechanics
LEE, M.-J., Educational Psychology
LEE, M.-K., Ancient Korean History
LEE, M.-S., Physical Chemistry
LEE, N.-G., Rural Sociology
LEE, O.-B., Social Education
LEE, S.-B., Statistics and Critical Phenomena
LEE, S.-C., Sports Nutrition
LEE, S.-T., Korean Linguistics
LEE, W.-B., Organic Chemistry
LEE, Y.-J., Petrology
LIM, C.-K., German Literature
MOON, S.-H., Western Philosophy
OH, C.-H., Optics, Quantum Electronics
OH, D.-S., History of Physical Education
OH, Y.-S., Public Economics
PAK, J.-S., Geometry
PARK, C.-Y., Educational Administration
PARK, D.-K., Plasma Physics
PARK, J.-Y., English Literature
PARK, K.-S., Teaching English as a Second Language
PARK, T.-H., Urban Geography
RIM, S.-H., Algebra
RYU, S.-E., German Drama
SEO, J.-M., Korean Literature
SHIN, K.-J., French Literature
SHIN, Y.-G., Teaching of Physical Education
SOHN, J.-K., Animal Physiology
SONG, B.-H., Microbiology, Molecular Biology
SONG, W.-C., Politics, Political Thought
YANG, H.-J., Animal Morphology, Ecology
YANG, J.-S., Climatology
YANG, S.-Y., Palaeobiology
YI, M.-S., French Linguistics
YOH, S.-D., Organic Chemistry
YOO, Y.-J., Analysis
YOON, I.-H., Micrometeorology
YOON, J.-L., Educational Psychology

MOKPO NATIONAL MARITIME UNIVERSITY

571-2 Jugkyo-dong, Mokpo, Chonnam 530-729

Telephone: (631) 240-7045
E-mail: ryujb@mmu.ac.kr
Internet: www.mmu.ac.kr

Founded 1950

President: Dr BYUNGJU OH

Number of teachers: 72
Number of students: 1,800

Divisions of Maritime Transportation Systems, Nautical Science, Navigation System Engineering, Maritime Safety Systems Engineering, Maritime Information Systems, International Logistics Systems, Maritime Policing.

MOKPO NATIONAL UNIVERSITY

61 Torim-ri, Chonggye-myon, Muan-gun, Chonnam 534-729

Telephone: (61) 450-2114
Fax: (61) 452-4793
Internet: www.mokpo.ac.kr

Founded 1946 as Mokpo Teacher-Training School; became Mokpo Teachers' College 1963, Mokpo Junior College 1978 and Mokpo National College 1979; present name and status 1990

President: WOONG-BAE KIM

Number of teachers: 334
Number of students: 9,986

Colleges of Humanities, Social Sciences, Natural Sciences, Engineering, Home Ecology, Business Administration.

NATIONAL FISHERIES UNIVERSITY OF BUSAN

599-1 Daeyun-dong, Nam-gu, Busan 608-737

Telephone: (51) 622-3951
Fax: (51) 625-9947

Founded 1941 as Busan Fisheries College, attained university status 1990

Pres.: SUN-DUCK CHANG
Dean of Academic Affairs: YONG RHIM YANG
Dean of Student Affairs: HYUN WOO CHUNG
Dean of Planning Research: YONG JOO KANG
Dean of General Affairs: SE WHA SONG
Librarian: JAI YUL KONG

Library of 130,000 vols
Number of teachers: 306
Number of students: 7,700

Publications: *Bulletin*, *Natural Sciences* (2 a year), *The Theses Collection of the Faculty Members*, *Social Sciences* (2 a year), *Publication of Institute of Marine Sciences* (1 a year)

DEANS

College of Business Administration: CHUNG YUL YU
College of Engineering: CHUNG KIL PARK
College of Fisheries Sciences: CHUL HYUN SOHN
College of Marine Sciences and Technology: YONG QUIN KANG
College of Natural Sciences: MAN DONG HUR
College of Social Sciences: CHARLES KIM

PUKYONG NATIONAL UNIVERSITY

559-1 Daeyon-dong, Nam-gu, Busan Seoul

Telephone: (51) 620-6114
Fax: (51) 620-1114
E-mail: web@pknu.ac.kr
Internet: www.pknu.ac.kr

Founded 1996 by the amalgamation of Nat. Fisheries Univ. of Pusan and Pusan Nat. Univ. of Technology

Pres.: PARK MAENG EON
Dean of Academic Affairs: NAM SONG-WOO
Dean of Student Affairs: HEUNG IL-PARK
Dean of Planning Office: JUNG HYUN-CHAN
Dean of Gen. Affairs: HWANG IN-CHUL
Dir of Library: PYO YONG-SOO

Number of teachers: 664
Number of students: 23,671 (23,336 undergraduates, 335 graduates)

DEANS

Faculty of Business Administration: HA JONG-WOOK
Faculty of Engineering: LEE HYUNG-GI
Faculty of Environmental and Marine Science and Technology: KIM DAE-CHOUL
Faculty of Fisheries Science: BYUN DAE-SEOK
Faculty of Humanities and Social Sciences: SEUNG RAE-LEE
Faculty of Natural Sciences: KIM SE-KWON

PUSAN NATIONAL UNIVERSITY

30 Jangjeon-dong, Kumjeong-ku, Pusan 609-735

Telephone: 510-1293
Fax: 512-9049
Internet: www.pusan.ac.kr

Founded 1946
Academic year: March to February

Pres.: INN-SE KIM
Dean of Academic Affairs: SANG-WOOK PARK
Dean of Planning and Research: JUNG-DUK LIM
Dean of Student Affairs: IN-BO SIM
Dir of General Affairs: SANG-WOO HAN
Dir of Library: DONG-HYUN JUNG

Library: see Libraries
Museum: see Museums

Number of teachers: 967
Number of students: 24,670

Publications: *University Academic Journal* (annual collection of theses), *College Academic Journal*

DEANS

College of Arts: EUL-MEE PARK
College of Business: BEUNG-GEUN MUN
College of Dentistry: LI-HEE YUN
College of Education: HONG-WOOK HUH
College of Engineering: MAN-HYUNG LEE
College of Human Ecology: YEONG-OK SONG
College of Humanities: JIN-NONG CHUNG
College of Law: BAE-WON KIM
College of Medicine: YONG-KI KIM
College of Natural Sciences: SANG-JOON LEE
College of Pharmacy: JEE-HYUNG JUNG
College of Social Sciences: HYUN-JUNG SHIN
Graduate School: JUNG-KEUN KIM
Graduate School of Education: HONG-WOOK HUH
Graduate School of Environment: MAN-HYUNG LEE
Graduate School of Industry: MAN-HYUNG LEE
Graduate School of Management: BEUNG-GEUN MUN
Graduate School of Public Administration: KI-HYUNG RYU

SEOUL NATIONAL UNIVERSITY

San 56-1, Shilim-dong, Kwanak-gu, Seoul 151-742

Telephone: (2) 880-5114
Fax: (2) 885-5272
Internet: www.snu.ac.kr

Founded 1946
State control
Academic year: March to February

President: UN-CHAN CHUNG
Vice-President: HO-IN LEE
Dean of Academic Affairs: CHANG-KU BYUN
Dean of Planning and Coordination: SEONGH-WAN OH
Dean of Research Affairs: JIN-HO CHUNG
Dean of Student Affairs: MI-NA LEE
Dir-Gen. of Gen. Admin.: SUNGMOO LEE
Dir-Gen. of Library: NAM JIN HUH

Library: see Libraries and Archives
Number of teachers: 1,675
Number of students: 31,974

Publication: *University Gazette* (52 a year)

DEANS

College of Agriculture and Life Sciences: MOO HA LEE
College of Business Administration: SANG HUNG AHN
College of Dentistry: PILL HOUN CHOUNG
College of Education: CHUNG-IL YUN
College of Engineering: MIN KOO HAN
College of Fine Arts: YOUNG GULL KWON
College of Human Ecology: IN KYEONG HWANG
College of Humanities: DU HWAN KWON
College of Law: NAK-IN SUNG
College of Medicine: KYU-CHANG WANG
College of Music: MIN KIM
College of Natural Sciences: SE-JUNG OH
College of Nursing: SUNG-AE PARK
College of Pharmacy: SANG-SUP JEW
College of Social Sciences: SAM-OCK PARK
College of Veterinary Medicine: IL-SUK YANG
Graduate School: TAE SOO LEE
Graduate School of Environmental Studies: KEE WON HWANG
Graduate School of Public Administration: DAI GON LEE
Graduate School of Public Health: BONG MIN YANG

SUNCHON NATIONAL UNIVERSITY

315 Maegok-dong, Sunchon, Chonnam 540-742

Telephone: (661) 750-3114
Fax: (661) 750-3117
E-mail: webmaster@sunchon.ac.kr
Internet: www.sunchon.ac.kr

Founded 1935
State control
Academic year: March to December

Pres.: Dr JAE-KI KIM
Deans: Dr WON-OG YANG (Academic Affairs), Dr JONG-CHUN CHOI (Student Affairs), Dr NAM-HOON CHO (University Planning and Research), DOO-HEE LEE (General Affairs)
Librarian: Dr JIN-IL DOO

Library of 211,000 books
Number of teachers: 340
Number of students: 12,560 (11,117 undergraduate, 1,443 postgraduate)

DEANS

College of Agriculture and Life Science: Dr DONG-HWAN OH
College of Education: Dr SANG-WOOK HAN
College of Engineering: Dr BONG-CHAN BAN
College of Humanities and Social Sciences: Dr JUNG-SUN SHIM
College of Natural Sciences: Dr MAN-CHAI JANG

SUWON UNIVERSITY

San 2-2 Wawoo-ri, Bongnam-myun, Hwasung-si, Gyeonggi-do 445-743

E-mail: info@suwon.mail.co.kr
Internet: www.suwon.ac.kr

Founded 1982

Chair.: IN-SOO LEE
Pres.: D. Y. YOON.

YOSU NATIONAL UNIVERSITY

96-1 Dundeok-dong, Yosu-shi, Chollanam-do 550-749

Telephone: (662) 659-2114
Fax: (662) 659-3003
Internet: www.yosu.ac.kr

Founded 1917 as Yosu Public Fisheries School; became Yosu Public Fisheries Middle School 1946, Yosu National Fisheries High School 1963, Yosu National Fisheries Junior College 1979, Yosu National Fisheries College 1987, Yosu National Fisheries University 1993; present name 1998

President: HA-JOON KIM
Number of teachers: 212
Number of students: 5,064

Colleges of Humanities and Social Science, Natural Science, Engineering, Fisheries and Ocean Science, Graduate School of Industry and Technology; Graduate School of Education.

PRIVATE UNIVERSITIES

AJOU UNIVERSITY

5 Woncheon-dong, Yeongtong-gu, Suwon, Seoul 443-749

Telephone: (2) 231-7121
Internet: www.ajou.ac.kr

Founded 1973

Pres.: SUH MOON HO
Registrar: JOON YOP KIM
Librarian: JAE SUK LEE

Library of 230,000 vols
Number of teachers: 750
Number of students: 10,954

Colleges of engineering, business administration, natural sciences, medicine, social sciences, humanities; graduate school.

CATHOLIC UNIVERSITY OF KOREA

Songeui Campus, 505 Banpo-dong, Socho-gu, Seoul 137-701

Telephone: (2) 590-1081
Fax: (2) 590-1100

Songsim Campus, 43-1 Yeokgok 2-dong, Wonmi-gu, Bucheon City, Gyeonggi-do 420-743

Telephone: (2) 2164-4000
Fax: (2) 2164-4778

Songsin Campus, 90-1 Hyehwa-dong, Jongro-gu, Seoul 110-758

Telephone: (2) 740-9704
Fax: (2) 741-2801
E-mail: webmaster@catholic.ac.kr
Internet: www.cuk.ac.kr

Founded 1995 by merger of Catholic Univ. (f. c. 1984 from existing colleges) and Songsim Women's Univ. (f. 1957)

Pres.: Rev. PAHK JOHAN YEONG-SIK
Number of teachers: 914
Library of 160,000
Number of students: 8,075 (6,772 undergraduate, 1,303 postgraduate)

Publication: *Catholic Theology and Thoughts* (1 a year)

Songeui Campus: incl. Colleges of Medicine, and Nursing; Graduate Schools of Occupational Health, and Health Management. Songsin Campus: incl. College of Theology. Songsim Campus: incl. Colleges of Humanities, Social Sciences, Science and Technology, and Human Ecology.

CATHOLIC UNIVERSITY OF TAEGU-HYOSUNG

330 Kumnak 1-ri, Hayang-up, Kyongsan-shi, Kyongbuk, Seoul 712-702

Telephone: (53) 850-3001
Fax: (53) 850-3600
E-mail: presid@cuth.cataegu.ac.kr
Internet: www.cataegu.ac.kr

Founded 1995 as a result of merger of Hyosung Women's University and Taegu Catholic University
Private control

President: SOO-EUP KIM

Library of 410,000 vols
Number of teachers: 780
Number of students: 11,132

Publications: *Research Bulletin* (1 a year), *University Bulletin* (1 a year)

Colleges of Humanities, Theology, Foreign Studies, Natural Sciences, Engineering, Medicine, Social Sciences, Law and Politics, Economics and Commerce, Home Economics, Pharmacy, Education, Music, and Fine Arts.

CHEONGJU UNIVERSITY

36 Naedok-dong, Sangdang-ku, Cheongju 360-764

Telephone: (43) 229-8114
Fax: (43) 229-8110
Internet: www.cheongju.ac.kr

Founded 1946 as Cheongju Commercial College; became Cheongju College 1951; present name 1981

President: KIM YOON BAE.

CHOSUN UNIVERSITY

375 Seosuk-dong, Dong-gu, Gwangju, Seoul 501-759

Telephone: (62) 230-7114
Internet: www.chosun.ac.kr

Founded 1946
Private control
Language of instruction: Korean
Academic year: March to February

Pres.: JEON HO-JONG
Dean of Academic Affairs: CHAI-KYUN PARK
Dean of Finance: JEI-WON KOH
Dean of General Affairs: PYUNG-JOON PARK
Dean of Student Affairs: YANG-SOO SON
Librarian: KI-SANG KIM
Library of 597,032 vols
Number of teachers: 556
Number of students: 26,164

DEANS

College of Arts: YONG-HYUN KUK
College of Business Administration: BYUNG-KYU KIM
College of Dentistry: CHANG-KEUN YOON
College of Education: HONG-WON PARK
College of Engineering: WHAN-KYU PARK
College of Foreign Languages: YONG-HERN LEE
College of Humanities: JEONG-SEOK KANG
College of Industry: HEUNG-KYU JOO
College of Law and Political Science: CHANG-HYEON KOH
College of Medicine: YO-HAN JUNG
College of Natural Science: HAK-JIN JUNG
College of Pharmacy: YEONG-JONG YOO
College of Physical Education: DONG-YOON CHOE
Evening College: JEONG-JOO CHOE
Graduate School: JOON-CHAE PARK
Graduate School of Education: SEOK-CHEOL PARK
Graduate School of Industry: SEONG-HYU JO

CHUNG-ANG UNIVERSITY

221 Heukseok–dong, Dongjak-gu, Seoul 156-756

Telephone: (2) 820-6202
Fax: (2) 813-8069
E-mail: interedu@cau.ac.kr
Internet: www.cau.ac.kr

Founded 1918
Private control
Academic year: March to February (2 semesters)

Chair. and Chancellor: KIM HEE SU
Pres.: PARK BUM HONN
Vice-Pres.: SIK KIM DAE (Seoul Campus): SANG YOON LEE (Ansung Campus): HWANG YUN-WON
Provost of Medical Centre: CHANG KWUN HONG

Dirs of Library: TAE WOO NAM (Seoul Campus): YANG HYUN LEE (Ansung Campus)
Library: 1.2m. vols
Number of teachers: 2,127
Number of students: 22,071 (undergraduate), 4,563 (graduate)
Publications: *Chung-Ang Herald* (12 a year), *Chung-Ang Press* (52 a year), *College Journals* (1 a year), *Journal of Chung-Ang Pharmacy* (1 a year), *Journal of Economic Development* (1 a year), *Korean Education Index* (1 a year), *Korean Journal of Comparative Law* (1 a year), *Korean Studies Journal* (4 a year), *Theses Collection*

DEANS

College of Arts: SANG JUE SHIN
College of Construction Engineering: KI BONG KIM
College of Education: YOUNG DUCK CHOI
College of Engineering: SUNG SUN KIM
College of Foreign Languages: SUNG MOO YANG
College of Home Economics: YANG HEE KIM
College of Industrial Studies: KWANG RO YOON
College of Law: YOUNG SOL KWON
College of Liberal Arts: NAM JOON CHANG
College of Medicine: IM WON CHANG
College of Music: LEE SUK CHEH
College of Pharmacy: IN HOI HUH
College of Political Science and Economics: IN KIE KIM
College of Sciences: SUK YONG LEE
College of Social Sciences: CHI SOON JANG
Graduate School: JO SUP CHUNG
Graduate School of Construction Engineering: SUNG SUN KIM
Graduate School of Education: JAE WOO LEE
Graduate School of the Information Industry: YOUNG CHAN KIM
Graduate School of International Management: HUN CHU
Graduate School of Mass Communication: SANG CHUL LEE
Graduate School of Public Administration: SANG YOON REE
Graduate School of Social Development: KYONG SUH PARK

DIRECTORS

Australian Studies Institute: HYUNG SHIK KIM
Chung-Ang Music Institute: HAK WON YOON
Institute of Advertising and Public Relations: JUN IL RYEE
Institute of Arts: SEUNG KIL KOH
Institute of Basic Sciences: KYUNG HEE CHOI
Institute of Economic Research: YEN KYUN WANG
Institute of Environmental Science: SEI KWAN SOHN
Institute of Family Life: HYUN OK LEE
Institute of Food Resources: SOO SUNG LEE
Institute of Genetic Engineering: YUNG CHAI CHUNG
Institute of Humanities: JOONG SHIK HYUN
Institute of Industrial Construction Technology: YONG JU HWANG
Institute of Industrial Design: WON MO KWAK
Institute of Industrial Management: SEONG MU SUH
Institute of International Trade: JU SUP HAHN
Institute of International Women's Studies: JAE WOO LEE
Institute of Japanese Studies: KYUN IL KIM
Institute of Korean Education: SUNG YOON HONG
Institute of Korean Folklore: SEON POONG KIM
Institute of Legal Research: HYUK JU LEE
Institute of Management Research: DONG SUNG KWAK

Institute of Medical Science: DAE YONG UHM
Institute of North-East Asian Studies: JAE SUN CHOI
Institute of Overseas Korean Residents: SANG MAN LEE
Institute of Pharmaceutical Science: KI HO KIM
Institute of Production Engineering: SOO SAM KIM
Institute of Public Policy and Administration: SANG YOON RHEE
Institute of Social Sciences: HYUNG KOOK KIM
Institute of Sports Sciences Research: JIN YOO
Institute of Technology and Science: YOUNG CHAN KIM
Institute of Third World Studies: UJIN YI

DAEBUL UNIVERSITY

72 Samho-ri, Samho-myeun, Yangam-gun, Chonnam, Seoul 526-702

Telephone: (61) 469-1114
Fax: (61) 462-2510
E-mail: webmaster@mail.daebul.ac.kr
Internet: www.daebul.ac.kr

Founded 1994 as Daebul Institute of Technology and Science; present name 1996
Private control

Pres.: LEE GYEONG-SU.

DAEGU UNIVERSITY

Jillyang, Gyeongsan, Gyeongbuk, Seoul 712-714

Telephone: (53) 850-5681
Fax: (53) 850-5689
Internet: www.daegu.ac.kr

Pres.: LEE YONG-DOO
Number of students: 16,000

Colleges of Humanities, Law, Public Administration, Economics and Business Administration, Social Sciences, Natural Sciences, Engineering, Natural Resources, Arts and Design, Education, Rehabilitation Sciences, Health Science.

DANKOOK UNIVERSITY

Jukjeon Campus: 126 Jukjeon-dong, Suji-gu, Yongin-si, Gyeonggi-do, Seoul 448-701
Cheonan Campus: San 29, Anseo-dong, Dongnam-gu, Cheonan-si,Chugnam, Seoul 330-714

Telephone: (31) 8005-2102
Internet: www.dankook.ac.kr

Founded 1947, univ. status 1967
Private control
Language of instruction: Korean
Academic year: March to February

Chancellor: CHANG CHOONG-SIK
Pres.: CHANG HOSUNG
Registrar: YONG-WOO LEE
Library of 140,000 vols
Number of teachers: 321
Number of students: 13,557

DEANS

College of Commerce and Economics: KIM HAENG-XUH
College of Education: KIM SEUNG-KOOK
College of Engineering: KO MYUNG-WON
College of Law: KIM YOO-HYUK
College of Liberal Arts and Sciences: CHA MOON-SUP

DONG-A UNIVERSITY

840 Hadan 2-dong, Saha-gu, Busan, Seoul 604-714

Telephone: (51) 200-6442
Fax: (51) 200-6445
E-mail: president@donga.ac.kr

Internet: www.donga.ac.kr
Founded 1946
Private control
Language of instruction: Korean
Academic year: March to February
Pres.: CHOI JAE-RONG
Vice-Pres.: CHO BYUNG-TAE
Head of Secretariat: LEE YEONG-GI
Dean of Academic Affairs: CHOI CHANG-OCK
Dean of Admin.: KIM LI-KYOO
Dean of Financial Affairs: HWANG YOON-SIK
Dean of Research: CHOI SOON-KYU
Dean of Student Affairs: LEE DAE-KYU
Dir of Library: HAHN KUN-BAE

Library of 582,134 vols
Number of students: 17,217

DEANS

College of Agriculture: CHUNG DAE-SOO
College of Arts: PARK SOO-CHUL
College of Business Administration: JUN TAE-YOON
College of Engineering: PARK CHUN-KEUN
College of Human Ecology: KIM SEOK-HWAN
College of Humanities: CHUNG SANG-BAK
College of Law: JEONG MAN-HEE
College of Medicine: CHUNG DUCK-HWAN
College of Natural Sciences: UHM TAE-SEOP
College of Physical Education: PARK CHEOL-HO
College of Social Sciences: SUL KWANG-SUK
Graduate School: RYOO WOONG-DAL
Graduate School of Business Administration: KIM YONG-DAE
Graduate School of Education: TCHOI CHONG-IL
Graduate School of Industry: HAN KUN-MO
Graduate School of Mass Communication: KIM MIN-NAM

DIRECTORS

Agricultural Resources Research Institute: KIM YOUNG-KIL
Basic Science Research Institute: KIM WAN-SE
Business Management Research Institute: KIM SEONG-HWAN
Environmental Problems Research Institute: KIM JANG-HO
German Studies Institute: RHIE SANG-UG
Industrial Medicine Research Institute: KIM JUNG-MAN
Industrial Technology Research Centre: JUN TAE-OK
Institute for the Study of Law: KIM SANG-HO
Institute of Data Communication: HONG CHANG-HI
Institute of Korean Resources Development: CHUNG SUNG-GYO
Language Research Institute: HA CHI-GUN
Life Science Research Institute: CHOI YONG-CHUN
MIS Research Institute: HAN KAY-SEOB
Ocean Resources Research Institute: KIM JIN-HOO
Plastic Arts Research Institute: BACK SUNG-DO
Population Research Centre: CHOI SOON
Research Institute for Clinical Medicine: KIM JEONG-MAN
Research Institute for Genetic Engineering: CHUNG CHUNG-HAN
Research Institute for Human Ecology: PARK EUN-JOO
Research Institute for Humanities: CHUNG YOUNG-DO
Research Institute of Sports Science: AN YOUNG-PIL
Social Science Research Institute: KIM JAE-GYONG
Sokdang Academic Research Institute of Korean Culture: HYENG-JU KIM
Tourism and Leisure Research Institute: AHN YUNG-MYUN

DONG-EUI UNIVERSITY

24 Kaya-dong, Pusanjin-ku, Busan 614-714
Telephone: (51) 890-1114
Fax: (51) 890-1234
E-mail: wwwadmin@www.dongeui.ac.kr
Internet: www.dongeui.ac.kr

Founded 1976 as Kyungdong Engineering Technical College; became Dong-Eui College 1979; present name 1983
Private control
Pres.: Dr KEUN-WU PAK

Library of 336,000 vols
Number of students: 3,704 (3,420 undergraduate, 284 postgraduate)

DONG YANG UNIVERSITY

1 Kyochon-dong, Punggi, Youngju, Kyungbuk, Seoul 750-711
Telephone: (572) 630-1114
Fax: (572) 636-8523
E-mail: wwwadmin@dyu.ac.kr
Internet: www.dyu.ac.kr

Founded 1994
Private control
Academic year: March to December
Pres.: Dr CHOI SUNG-HAE
Vice-Pres.: Dr PARK YOUNG-HWAN
Librarian: BYUN BOK-SOO

Library of 150,000 vols
Number of teachers: 80
Number of students: 3,100 (3,000 undergraduate, 100 postgraduate)

Colleges of Science and Engineering, Human and Social Science, Arts and Graduate Schools of Information and Education.

DONGDUK WOMEN'S UNIVERSITY

23-1 Wolgok-dong, Sungbuk-ku, Seoul 136-714
Telephone: (2) 940-4000
Fax: (2) 940-4182
E-mail: master@dongduk.ac.kr
Internet: www.dongduk.ac.kr

Founded 1950
Private control
Language of instruction: Korean
Academic year: March to February (2 semesters)
Chancellor: WON-YOUNG CHO
Vice-Chancellor: YOUNG-YON YOON
Registrar: DO-SEOK CHANG
Librarian: YOON-SIK KIM

Library of 232,000 vols
Number of teachers: 154
Number of students: 6,155

Publications: Dongduk News Letter (2 a year), Dongduk Women's Newspaper (52 a year), Journal of Dongduk Women's University, Treatise (1 a year)

DEANS

College of Arts: SUN-BAEK JANG
College of Computer and Information Sciences: YANG-HEE LEE
College of Design: DONG-JO KOO
College of Humanities: SANG-GI CHO
College of Natural Sciences: SANG-SOON LEE
College of Performing Arts: (vacant)
College of Pharmacy: IN-KOO CHUN
College of Social Sciences: SAE-YOUNG OH
General Studies and Teaching Profession Division: HONG-TAE PARK

DONGGUK UNIVERSITY

26, Pil-dong, 3-ga Jung-gu, Seoul 100-715
Telephone: (2) 2260-3114
Fax: (2) 2277-1274
E-mail: iie@dongguk.edu
Internet: www.dongguk.ac.kr

Founded 1906, univ. status 1953
Private control
Chair.: OH IN-GAB
Pres.: Dr SONG SUK-KU
Librarian: Dr KIM BO HWAN

Library: see Libraries
Number of teachers: 500
Number of students: 16,050

Publications: Dongguk Journal, Dongguk Post (12 a year), Dongguk Sasang (Dongguk Thought), Dongguk Shinmun (52 a year), Pulgyo Hakpo (Journal of Buddhist Studies), and 20 others

Colleges of Buddhism, liberal arts and sciences, law and political science, economics and commerce, agriculture and forestry, engineering, education, medical science; graduate school, graduate school of public administration, graduate school of business administration, graduate school of education, graduate school of information industry; colleges on Kyongju Campus

Research Institutes: Buddhist culture, comparative literature, statistical science, law and political science, business management, agriculture and forestry, overseas development, national security, computer science, Middle Eastern and East European affairs, Korean studies, Saemaul research, landscape art, industrial technology, translation of Buddhist scriptures.

DONGSEO UNIVERSITY

San 69-1, Churye-2-Dong, Sasang-gu, Busan, Seoul 617-716
Telephone: (51) 320-2092
Fax: (51) 320-2094
E-mail: anna1974@dongseo.ac.kr
Internet: www.dongseo.ac.kr

Founded 1991 as Dongseo College of Technology; present name 1996
Pres.: Dr PARK DONG-SOON
Exec. Dir of Int. Cooperation Cttee: CHANG JEKUK
Number of students: 7,000

DONGSHIN UNIVERSITY

252 Daeho-hong, Naju, Jeonnam,, Seoul 520-714
Telephone: (61) 330-3114
Fax: (61) 330-2909
Internet: www.dongshinu.ac.kr
Pres.: LEE KYUM-BUM

Library of 500,000
Number of students: 1,604

Colleges of arts, engineering, humanities and social science, information and science, oriental medicine.

DAEJON UNIVERSITY

96-3 Yongun-dong, Tong-gu, Taejon, Seoul 300-716
Telephone: (42) 282-0231
Fax: (42) 283-8808
E-mail: contact@dju.ac.kr
Internet: www.dju.ac.kr.

DUKSUNG WOMEN'S UNIVERSITY

19 Geunhwagyo-gil, 419 Ssangmoon-dong, Dobong-gu, Seoul 132-714
Telephone: (2) 901-8691
Fax: (2) 901-8690
E-mail: djsuk@duksung.ac.kr
Internet: www.duksung.ac.kr

Founded 1950
Private control
Language of instruction: Korean
Academic year: March to February

Pres.: CHI EUN HEE
Registrar: LIM SOOK-JA
Librarian: CHUNG YOUNG-HWAN
Library of 328,000 vols
Number of teachers: 310 (148 full-time, 162 part-time)
Number of students: 5,250
Publications: *Duksung Women's University Journal*, *Duksung Women's University Newsletter* (24 a year), *Duksung Women's University Newsletter, Geunmack* (1 a year)

DEANS

College of Fine Arts: KIM AIE-YUNG
College of Humanities: YOON JUNG-BOON
College of Natural Science: YOON SUK-IM
College of Pharmacy: JUNG KI-HWA
College of Social Sciences: KIM SUNG-CHUL

EWHA WOMEN'S UNIVERSITY

11-1 Daehyun-dong, Seodaemun-gu, Seoul 120-750

Telephone: (2) 3277-2114
Fax: (2) 393-5903
E-mail: master@ewha.ac.kr
Internet: www.ewha.ac.kr
Founded 1886
Languages of instruction: Korean, English
Academic year: March to December (two semesters)

Chancellor: YOON HOO-JUNG
Pres.: Dr SHIN IN-RYUNG
Librarian: KIM BONG-HEE
Library: see Libraries
Number of teachers: 800
Number of students: 21,000 (graduates 6,000; undergraduates 15,000)
Publications: *Edae Hakbo* (in Korean, 52 a year), *Ewha News* (in Korean, 12 a year), *Ewha Voice* (in English, 12 a year)

DEANS

College of Arts and Design: Prof. KIM YOUNG-KI
College of Business Administration: Dr SUH YOON-SUK
College of Education: Dr JU YOUNG-JU
College of Engineering: Dr SHIN YEONG-SOO
College of Home Science and Management: Dr PARK SEONG-YEON
College of Human Movement and Performance: Dr KIM KEE-WOONG
College of Law: Dr YANG MYEONG-CHO
College of Liberal Arts: Dr KIM HYUN-JA
College of Medicine: Dr CHUNG HWA-SOON
College of Music: Prof. LEE KYU-DO
College of Natural Sciences: Dr LEE NAM-SOO
College of Nursing: Dr BYUN YOUNG-SOON
College of Pharmacy: Dr KIM CHOON-MI
College of Social Sciences: Dr AHN HONG-SIK
Institute of Science and Technology: Dr KIM WON
Graduate School: Dr CHANG PIL-WHA
Graduate School of Business Administration: Dr SUH YOON-SUK
Graduate School of Clinical Health Sciences: Dr KIM CHOON-MI
Graduate School of Design: Dr KIM YOUNG-KI
Graduate School of Education: Dr CHOI WOUN-SIK
Graduate School of Information Science: Dr AHN HONG-SIK
Graduate School of International Studies: Dr YOO JANG-HEE
Graduate School of Policy Sciences: Dr AHN HONG-SIK
Graduate School of Practical Music: Dr CHOI YOO-RI
Graduate School of Social Welfare: Dr CHOI WOUN-SIK
Graduate School of Theology: Dr YANG MYUNG-SU

Graduate School of Translation and Interpretation: Dr CHOI YOUNG

HALLYM UNIVERSITY

39 Hallymdaehak-gil, Chunchon, Kangwon-do, Seoul 200-702

Telephone: (33) 248-1000
Fax: (33) 256-3333
E-mail: parkphil@hallym.ac.kr
Internet: www.hallym.ac.kr
Founded 1982
Private control
Academic year: March to December

Pres.: LEE YOUNG-SUN
Vice-Pres.: Dr HAN SIL
Dean for Academic Affairs: Dr CHOI SOO-YOUNG
Dean for Gen. Affairs: SUNG NAK-SUNG
Dean for Planning and Coordination: Dr LEE KI-WON
Dean for Student Affairs: Dr LEE CHOONG-IL
Library Dir: Dr BAK GEUN-GAB
Library of 373,000 books
Number of teachers: 591
Number of students: 10,119 (9,353 undergraduate, 766 postgraduate)
Publication: *Hallym News* (26 a year)

DEANS

College of Humanities: Prof. OH CHUN-TAEK
College of Information and Electronics Engineering: Prof. SONG CHANG-GEUN
College of Medicine: Prof. PARK HYOUNG-JIN
College of Natural Sciences: Prof. KIM RAK-JOONG
College of Social Sciences: Prof. KIM YUNG-MYUNG

HAN NAM UNIVERSITY

133 Ojeong-dong, Daedeok-gu, Daejon, Seoul 306-791

Telephone: (42) 629-7739
Fax: (42) 629-7779
E-mail: webmaster@hannam.ac.kr
Internet: www.hannam.ac.kr
Founded 1956
Academic year: March to December

Pres.: KIM HYUNG-TAE
Dir of Int. Relations Centre: Dr KYU TAE JUNG

Library: Univ. possesses Central Library, Central Museum, Natural History Museum, Academic Information Centre
Number of teachers: 965
Number of students: 11,441

Colleges of liberal arts, education, natural sciences, engineering, economics and business administration, law, social sciences.

HANKUK UNIVERSITY OF FOREIGN STUDIES

270 Imun-dong, Dongdaemun-gu, Seoul 130-791

Telephone: (2) 2173-2063
Fax: (2) 2173-3387
E-mail: gyoh@hufs.ac.kr
Internet: www.hufs.ac.kr
Founded 1954
Private control

Pres.: PARK CHUL
Dean of Academic Affairs: Prof. PAK SUNG RAE
Dean of Student Affairs: Prof. LEE CHANG BOK
Chief Admin. Officer: SEOK JOO YOON
Librarian: Prof. CHO KYU CHUL
Library of 303,900 vols
Number of teachers: 292
Number of students: 12,838

Publications: *Argus* (English and other foreign languages, 12 a year), *Journal* (1 a year), *Oe-Dae Hakbo* (in Korean, 52 a year)

DEANS

Academic and Student Affairs (Evening Courses): Prof. WOO DUCK YONG
College of Education: Prof. OH HAN-JIN
College of Foreign Languages: Prof. CHOI JONG SOO
College of Law and Political Science: Prof. KIM DEOK
College of Liberal Arts and Sciences: Prof. KIM JIK HYUN
College of Occidental Languages: Prof. LEE YOUNG GUL
College of Oriental Languages: Prof. CHUNG KI IOB
College of Social Sciences: Prof. PARK BYUNG HO
College of Trade and Economics: Prof. LEE HEE JOON
Graduate School: Prof. REW JOUNG YOLE
Graduate School of Education: Prof. RHIM JIN KWON
Graduate School of International Trade: Prof. LEE HEE JOON
Graduate School of Interpretation and Translation: Prof. KIM I BAE
Graduate School of Management Information Systems: Prof. JUNG JAE SEOK

DIRECTORS

Audio-Visual Education Institute: Prof. PARK SOON-HAM
Chinese Studies Institute: Prof. CHOI KWAN-JANG
Foreign Language Training and Research Centre: Prof. KIM JAI MIN
Institute for Research in Languages and Linguistics: Prof. REW SEONG JOON
Institute of African Studies: Prof. PARK WON TAK
Institute of Foreign Language Studies: Prof. KIM YOUNG JO
Institute of History: Prof. PAK SUNG RAE
Institute of Humanities: Prof. KANG SUNG WI
Institute of International Communication: Prof. KIM JONG KI
Institute of Korean Regional Studies: Prof. AHN BYONG MAN
Institute of Latin-American Studies: Prof. MIN MAN SHIK
Institute of the Middle East: Prof. HONG SOON NAM
Interpretation and Translation Centre: Prof. KIM I-BAE
Research Institute for Economics and Business Administration: Prof. MIN BYUNG KWOON
Russian and East European Institute: Prof. CHO KYU WHA
Student Guidance Centre: Prof. YOON JONG GEON

HANSEO UNIVERSITY

360 Daegok-ri, Haemi-Myun, Seosan City, Chungcheongnam, Seoul 360-706

Telephone: (41) 660-1144
Fax: (41) 660-1149
E-mail: webmaster@hanseo.ac.kr
Internet: www.hanseo.ac.kr
Founded 1989
Number of students: 1,927

Pres.: HAM KEE-SUN

Colleges of aeronautical engineering, arts, engineering, graduate school, health science, liberal arts, science, social science.

HANSHIN UNIVERSITY

Hanshin, Seoul

Telephone: (31) 379-0103
Fax: (31) 372-6101

Internet: www.hs.ac.kr
Founded 1980
Number of students: 6,000
Pres.: YOON EUNG JIN
Colleges of humanities, information sciences, management and trade, social sciences, theology.

HANSUNG UNIVERSITY

389 Samseon-Dong 2-ga, Seongbuk-gu, Seoul
Telephone: (2) 760-4114
Fax: (2) 745-8943
E-mail: getsmile@hansung.ac.kr
Internet: www.hansung.ac.kr
Founded 1945
Pres.: CHUNG JOO-TAEK
Colleges of arts, engineering, humanities, liberal arts and science, social sciences.

HANYANG UNIVERSITY

17 Haengdang-dong, Seongdong-gu, Seoul 133-791
Telephone: (2) 2220-0114
E-mail: w3master@hanyang.ac.kr
Internet: www.hanyang.ac.kr
Founded 1939 as Hanyang Institute of Technology; present status 1959
Private control
Academic year: March to July, September to December
Pres.: Dr KIM CHONG YANG
Academic Dean: Dr SONG CHANG SEOP
Library of 350,000 vols
Number of teachers: 958
Number of students: 24,508
Publications: *Hanyang Nonmun Dzip*, *Journal of Economic Studies*, *Journal of Korean Studies*, *Journal of Student Guidance Research*, *Sino-Soviet Affairs*, and numerous others
Colleges of engineering (incl. architectural engineering), liberal arts and sciences (incl. journalism and cinema), commerce and economics, law and political science, music, physical education, education, medicine; evening engineering college; graduate school, graduate school of industrial management.

HONAM UNIVERSITY

Gwangsan Campus: 59-1 Seobong-Dong, Gwangsan-gu, Gwangju City, Seoul 506-714
Telephone: (62) 940-5114
Fax: (62) 940-5005
Ssangchom Campus: 148 Ssangchon-dong, Seo-Ku, Gwangju City, Seoul 502-791
Telephone: (62) 370-8114
Fax: (62) 370-8008
Internet: www.honam.ac.kr
Founded 1978
Chair.: Dr PARK KI-IN
Pres.: CHUNG BYOUNG-WAN
Library of 400,000 vols
Colleges of arts and physical education, business administration, engineering, internet and media, humanities, natural science, social sciences.

HONG-IK UNIVERSITY

Seoul Campus: 72-1 Sangsu-dong, Mapo-gu, Seoul 121-791
Jochiwon Campus: Jochiwon–eup, Yeongi-gun, Chungcheongnam-do 339-701
Telephone: (2) 320-1114
Fax: (2) 320-1122
E-mail: webm@wow.hongik.ac.kr
Internet: www.hongik.ac.kr

Founded 1946
Private control
Language of instruction: Korean
Academic year: March to June, September to December
Chair.: Dr LEE MYEON YOUNG
Pres.: KWON MYUNG KWANG
Vice-Pres.: CHANG YOUNG TAE, LIM HAE CHULL
Vice-Pres. for Jochiwon Campus: LEE KI BOK
Dir of Univ. Library: KIM KUN HO
Library: 1m. vols
Number of teachers: 853 (463 full-time, 390 part-time)
Number of students: 16,679
Publications: *Hong-Ik University Journal* (1 a year), *Hong-Ik Economic Review* (1 a year), *Journal of Student Life* (1 a year), *Management Review* (1 a year), *Papers on the Study of Education* (1 a year)

DEANS

College of Architecture: KIM UK
College of Business Administration: KIM DONG HUN
College of Business Management (Jochiwon Campus): CHOI YEON
College of Design and Arts (Jochiwon Campus): PARK YON SUN
College of Education: KIM MIN JAE
College of Engineering: CHUNG JOON KI
College of Fine Arts: CHOI BYUNG HOON
College of Law: MIN KYOUNG-DO
College of Law and Economics: BAEK SEUNG GWAN
College of Liberal Arts: CHIN HYUNG JOON
College of Science and Technology (Jochiwon Campus): SHIN PAN SEOK
Graduate School: YOUNG TAE JANG
Graduate School of Advertising and Public Relations: CHANG DON RYUN
Graduate School of Architecture and Urban Design: CHUNG MYUNG WON
Graduate School of Business: LEE KWANG CHUL
Graduate School of Education: PARK SANG OK
Graduate School of Educational Management: PARK SANG OK
Graduate School of Film and Digital Media: KIM JONG DEOK
Graduate School of Fine Arts: KIM TAE HO
Graduate School of Industrial Arts: BYUN KUN HO
Graduate School of Industry (Jochiwon Campus): CHANG HO SUNG
International Design School for Advance Studies: KIM CHUL HO

HOSEO UNIVERSITY

Asan Campus: 165 Sechul-ri, Baebang-myun, Asan, Chungnam, Seoul 336-795
Cheonan Campus: 268, Anseo-dong, Cheonan, Chungnam, Seoul 330-713
Telephone: (41) 540-5017
Fax: (41) 540-5019
Internet: www.hoseo.ac.kr
Founded 1978
Private control
Pres.: KANG IL-KU
Library of 300,000 vols
Number of teachers: 520
Number of students: 12,000

INHA UNIVERSITY

253 Yonghyun-dong, Nam-gu, Inchon, Seoul 402-751
Telephone: (32) 860-7030
Fax: (32) 867-7222
E-mail: orir@inha.ac.kr
Internet: www.inha.ac.kr
Founded 1954
Private control

Academic year: March to February
Pres.: Dr LEE BON-SU
Vice-Pres.: Dr CHOI BYUNG-HA
Registrar: Dr KIM CHONG-BO
Librarian: Dr YUN MYUNG-KOO
Library of 350,000 vols
Number of teachers: 644
Number of students: 18,116
Publications: bulletins of the research institutes

DEANS

College of Business and Economics: Dr KIM KI-MYUNG
College of Education: Dr KIM CHANG-GEOL
College of Engineering: Dr KANG BYUNG-HEE
College of Home Economics: (vacant)
College of Humanities: Dr KIM WOO-JIN
College of Law and Political Science: Dr LEE YOUNG-HEE
College of Medicine: Dr KIM SEH-HWAN
College of Natural Sciences: Dr PARK DAE-YOON
Graduate School: Dr CHOI JI-HOON
Graduate School of Business Administration: Dr SHINN YONG-HWI
Graduate School of Education: Dr CHUNG KI-HO
Graduate School of Engineering: Dr KIM DONG-IL
Graduate School of Public Administration: Dr SHIN YOUNG-SANG

INJE UNIVERSITY

Kimhae Campus, 607 Obang-Dong, Gimhae, Gyeongnam, Seoul 621-749
Telephone: (55) 334-7111
Fax: (55) 334-0712
E-mail: webmaste@inje.ac.kr
Internet: www.inje.ac.kr
Founded 1983
Chair.: PAIK NAK WHAN
Pres.: LEE KYEONGHO
Library of 500,000 vols
Colleges of Medicine, Biomedical Science and Engineering, Humanities and Social Sciences, Natural Sciences, Engineering, Design, Music.

JEONJU UNIVERSITY

1200 Hyoja-dong, Wansangu, Chonju Jeollabukdo, Seoul 520-759
Telephone: (652) 220-2122
Fax: (652) 220-2074
Internet: www.jeonju.ac.kr
Colleges of Christian Studies, Language and Culture, Law and Public Administration, Social Science, Economics and Information, Business Administration, Natural Science, Information Technology and Computer Science, Engineering, Architecture, Arts, Athletics and Visual Communication, Culture and Tourism, Teachers' College.

KANGNAM UNIVERSITY

111 Gugal-dong, Gihoung-gu, Yongin-si, Gyeonggi-do, Seoul 449-702
Telephone: (31) 280-3500
Fax: (31) 280-3428
E-mail: master@kangnam.ac.kr
Internet: www.kangnam.ac.kr
Founded 1946
Private control
Academic year: March to December
Chair.: YOON DO-HAN
Pres.: YOON SHINIL
Chief Librarian: KIM SEUNG-HWAN
Library of 240,000 books
Number of teachers: 170

Number of students: 6,534 (6,433 undergraduate, 101 postgraduate)

DEANS

College of Art and Physical Education: Prof. YANG JAE-YONG
College of Humanities: Prof. JO SUNG-MO
College of Management and Economics: Prof. JAE-HA HWANG, Prof. HWANG JAE-HA
College of Science and Engineering: Prof. PARK KI-SUNG
College of Social Sciences: Prof. LEE CHANG-SUK
College of Social Welfare: Prof. KIM YOUNG-HO
College of Theology: Prof. LEE SOOK-JONG
Graduate School: NO SANG-HAK (Pres.)

PAICHAI UNIVERSITY

14 Yeon-Ja, 1-gil, Seo-gu, Daejeon 302-735
Telephone: (42) 520-5114
E-mail: jd1234@mail.pcu.ac.kr
Internet: www.paichai.ac.kr

Founded 1885

Pres.: CHUNG SOON-HOON

Colleges of Humanities, Foreign Studies, Business Administration, Social Sciences, Tourism, Natural Sciences, Engineering, Arts.

KAYA UNIVERSITY

120 Jisan-ri, Koryong-kun, Kyungbuk 717-800
Telephone: (543) 954-1438
Fax: (543) 954-6094
E-mail: webmaster@kaya.ac.kr
Internet: www.kaya.ac.kr

Founded 1993
Private control
Languages of instruction: Korean, English
Academic year: March to December

President: Dr KYUNG-HEE LEE
Librarian: Prof. DONG-HAE LEE

Library: 2.8m. vols
Number of teachers: 103
Number of students: 4,120 (4,000 undergraduate, 120 postgraduate)

DEANS

Faculty of Social Sciences: Prof. CHANG-HUN OK
Department of Engineering: Prof. SANG-HEE PARK

KEIMYUNG UNIVERSITY

2800 Dalgubeoldaero, Dalseo-Gu, Daegu 704-701
Telephone: (53) 580-6023
Fax: (53) 580-6025
E-mail: intl@kmu.ac.kr
Internet: www.kmu.ac.kr

Founded 1954
Private control
Academic year: March to February

Pres.: SYNN ILHI
Vice-Pres. for Academic Affairs: PAEK SEUNG KYUN
Vice-Pres. for Medical Affairs: KANG JIN-SUNG
Dean of Dongsan Library: PARK JOON-SHIK

Library: 1.2m. vols
Number of teachers: 1,284 (604 full-time, 680 part-time)
Number of students: 21,126

Publications: *Accounting Information Review, Asian Journal of Business and Entrepreneurship, Bulletin of the Institute for International Science, Business Management Review, Journal of Art and Culture, Journal of International Studies,* *Journal of Life Science Research, Journal of Nakdonggang Environmental Research Institute, Journal of Social Sciences, Journal of the Institute for Cross-Cultural Studies, Journal of the Institute for Japanese Studies, Journal of the Institute of Natural Sciences, Keimyung Journal of Nursing Science, Keimyung Law Review, Keimyung University Medical Journal, Proceedings of Mathematical Science*

DEANS

College of Education: SIM HO TACK
Faculty of Applied Sciences: MIN HYUNG-JIN
Faculty of Automotive Engineering: SHIN SUNG-HEON
Faculty of Basic Sciences: UHM JAE-KUK
Faculty of Business Administration: PARK MYUNG-HO
Faculty of Chemical and Materials Engineering: SYNN DONG-SU
Faculty of Commerce: OH SEI-CHANG
Faculty of Computer and Electronic Engineering: SON YOO-EK
Faculty of Environmental Studies: KIM IN-HWAN
Faculty of Fashion: JON KYONG-TAE
Faculty of Fine Arts: HUR YONG
Faculty of Human Life Sciences: JOO KWANG JEE
Faculty of Humanities: JIN WON-SUK
Faculty of International Studies: LI JONG-KWANG
Faculty of Language and Literature: KIM JONG SUN
Faculty of Law: CHOI SANG-HO
Faculty of Music: KIM JEONG GIL
Faculty of Nursing: KIM JEONG NAM
Faculty of Physical Education: KIM SANG HONG
Faculty of Police Sciences: CHOI EUNG RYUL
Faculty of Politics and Economics: CHO YONG SANG
Faculty of Social Sciences: KIM SE SHUL
Graduate School: PARK YOUNG CHOON
Graduate School of Arts: KIM JEONG GIL
Graduate School of Business Administration: KIM JIN TAK
Graduate School of Education: KIM KI-HAN
Graduate School of Industrial Design: HUR YONG
Graduate School of Industrial Technology: KIM HONG YOUNG
Graduate School of International Studies: OH SEI-CHANG
Graduate School of Medical Management: PARK YOUNG NAM
Graduate School of Pastoral Theology: CHONG JOONG-HO
Graduate School of Policy Development: CHOI BONG KI
Graduate School of the Sports Industry: KIM SANG-HONG
School of Medicine: PARK YOUNG NAM

KON-KUK UNIVERSITY

1 Hwayang-dong, Gwangjin-gu, Seoul 143-701
Telephone: (2) 450-3259
Fax: (2) 450-3257
Internet: www.konkuk.ac.kr

Founded 1946, university status 1959
Private control
Academic year: March to February

Chair.: KYUNG-HEE KIM
Pres.: KIL-SAENG CHUNG
Vice-Pres: YUNG-KYE KANG (Seoul Campus): MOON-JA UM (Chungju Campus)
Registrar: HYEON-LYONG KIM
Librarian: YUNG-KWON KIM

Library: 1.1m. vols
Number of teachers: 589 (full-time)
Number of students: 17,177

Publications: *English Newspaper* (12 a year), *Newspaper* (52 a year)

DEANS

College of Agriculture: CHONG-CHON KIM
College of Animal Husbandry: CHANG-WON KANG
College of Architecture: YONG-SIK KIM
College of Art: HO-CHANG RYU
College of Arts and Design: HYUNG-JAE MAENG
College of Arts and Home Economics: WON-JA LEE
College of Business Administration: THOMAS T. H. JOH
College of Commerce and Economics: JEONG-PYO CHOL
College of Education: II HWANG
College of Engineering: KWANG-SOO KIM
College of Humanities: SOON-BONG PACK
College of Information & Telecommunication: SUN-YOUNG HAN
College of Law: SEUNG-HO LEE
College of Liberal Arts: OH-HYUN CHO
College of Life Environment: SUK-HUN KYUNG
College of Medicine: TAE-KYU PACK
College of Natural Sciences: LEE-CHOI CHANG
College of Political Science: SUNG-BOK LEE
College of Sciences: JUNE-TAK RHEE
College of Social Sciences: YOUNG-BOON LEE
College of Veterinary Medicine: BYUNG-JOO KIM
Graduate School: JOO-YOUNG LEE
Graduate School of Agriculture and Animal Science: SUN-JOO KIM
Graduate School of Architecture: BYOUNG-KEUN KANG
Graduate School of Business Administration: DAE-HO KIM
Graduate School of Design: LEE-SANG EUN
Graduate School of Education: DONG-OK LEE
Graduate School of Engineering: JOONG-RIN SHIN
Graduate School of Information and Telecommunication: CHUN-HYON CHANG
Graduate School of Mass Communication: DAE-IN KANG
Graduate School of Medicine: KYUNG-YUNG LEE
Graduate School of Public Administration: EUN-JAE LEE
Graduate School of Real Estate Studies: CHO-JOO HYUN
Graduate School of Social Sciences: NAM-KYU PARK

KONYANG UNIVERSITY

26 Nae-Dong, Nonsan, Chungnam, Seoul 320-711
Telephone: (41) 730-5114
Fax: (41) 733-2070
E-mail: webmaster@konyang.ac.kr
Internet: www.konyang.ac.kr

Founded 1991

Pres.: KIM HEE-SOO

Library of 250,000 .

KOOKMIN UNIVERSITY

Jeongneung-gil 77, 861-1 Chongnung-dong, Songbuk-ku, Seoul 136-702
Telephone: (2) 910-4115
Fax: (2) 910-4115
Internet: www.kookmin.ac.kr

Founded 1946

Pres.: LEE SUNG WOO
Dean of Academic Affairs: Prof. KIM YOUNG-JEON
Dean of Student Affairs: Prof. LEE JONG-EUN
Dean of Gen. Affairs: KIL YEONG-BAE
Dean of Planning and Devt Affairs: Prof. KANG SIN-DON

Library of 200,000 vols
Number of teachers: 370 (159 full-time, 211 part-time)
Number of students: 15,000
Publications: *Kookmin University Press* (52 a year), *Kookmin Tribune* (English, 12 a year), *Kookmin University Bulletin* (1 a year), *Theses* (1 a year), *Design Review, Economic and Business Administration Review, Education Review, Journal of Language and Literature, Journal of Sports Science Research, Journal of the Scientific Institute, Law and Political Review, Papers in Chinese Studies, Theses of Engineering, Theses of Korean Studies*

DEANS

College of Architecture and Design: Prof. KIM CHUL-SOO
College of Economics and Business Administration: NAH OH-YOUN
College of Education: SHIN JOONG-SHIK
College of Engineering: Prof. YOON TAI-YOON
College of Forestry: KO YUNG-ZU
College of Law and Political Science: LEE YONG-SUN
College of Liberal Arts: Prof. LEE JUNG-KEE
Graduate School: CHOI HWAN-YOL
Graduate School of Business Administration: CHOI HWAN-YOL
Graduate School of Education: CHOI HWAN-YOL
Graduate School of Public Administration: LEE YOUNG-SUN

KOREA UNIVERSITY

1 5-ga, Anam-dong, Sungbuk-gu, Seoul 136-701
Telephone: (2) 3290-1152
Fax: (2) 922-5820
Internet: www.korea.ac.kr
Founded 1905, as Posung College
Private control: financed by the Korea-Choongang Educational Foundation
Language of instruction: Korean
Academic year: March to February (two semesters)
Pres.: EUH YOON-DAE (acting)
Dean of Planning and Public Relations: PARK MANN-JANG
Dean of Academic Affairs: AHN CHANG-YIL
Dean of Students: KIMSONG-BOK
Dean of Gen. Affairs: YOUN SA-SOON
Dean of Construction and Facility Management: PAIK YOUNG-HYUN
Librarian: SHIN IL-CHUL
Library: see Libraries
Number of teachers: 1,408 (627 full-time, 781 part-time)
Number of students: 21,685
Publications: *Gyongyong Shinmoon* (Korean, 52 a year), *Kodai Moonwha* (Korean, 1 a year), *Kodai Shinmoon* (Korean, 52 a year), *Korea University Bulletin* (English, 1 a year), *Phoenix* (bilingual, 1 a year), *The Granite Tower* (English, 26 a year)

DEANS

College of Agriculture: KWACK BEYOUNG-HWA
College of Business Administration: LEE JANG RHO
College of Education: YOU IN-JONG
College of Engineering: HONG JONG-HWI
College of Law: BAE JONG-DAE
College of Liberal Arts: HAN PONG-HEUM
College of Medicine: PARK SUNG-YONG
College of Political Science and Economics: CHO YONG-BUM
College of Science: KIM SI-JOONG
Graduate School: LAU BONG-WHAN
Graduate School of Business Administration: KIM DONG-KI
Graduate School of Education: KIM SUNG-TAI

Graduate School of Food and Agriculture: YANG HAN-CHUL
College of Economics and Commerce (Jochiwon campus): KIM JUNG-BAI
College of Liberal Arts and Science (Jochiwon campus): KIM JUNG-BAI

KOSIN UNIVERSITY

149-1 Dongsam-dong, Yeongdo-gu, Busan, Seoul 606-701
Telephone: (51) 990-2114
Fax: (51) 911-2525
E-mail: logos@kosin.ac.kr
Internet: www.kosin.ac.kr
Founded 1946
Pres.: KIM SUNG-SOO
Library of 120,000 vols

Colleges of Arts, Computer Sciences, Health Sciences, Human Ecology, Humanities and Social Sciences, Medicine, Natural Sciences, Theology.

KWANDONG UNIVERSITY

522 Naegok-dong, Kangnung-si, Gangwon-do, Seoul 210-701
Telephone: (33) 641-1011
Fax: (33) 641-1010
Internet: www.kwandong.ac.kr
Founded 1959
Pres.: PARK HUI-JONG
Number of students: 8,000
Colleges of Arts, Education, Humanities, Law and Politics, Medicine, Science and Engineering.

KWANGWOON UNIVERSITY

447-1 Wolgye-dong, Nowon-gu, Seoul 139-701
Telephone: (2) 940-5114
Internet: www.kwangwoon.ac.kr
Pres.: PARK YOUNG-SHIK
Colleges of Electronics and Information, Engineering, Natural Sciences, Humanities and Social Sciences, Law, Business.

KYONGGI UNIVERSITY

San 94-6 Iui-dong, Yeongtong-gu, Suwon-si, Gyeonggi-do, Seoul 443-760
Telephone: (31) 249-8770
Fax: (31) 255-5915
E-mail: oia@kgu.ac.kr
Internet: www.kgu.ac.kr
Founded 1947
Private control
Colleges of arts, economics and business administration, engineering, humanities, int. studies, law, natural sciences, physical education, social sciences, tourism sciences; graduate schools of alternative medicine, architecture, art and design, business administration, construction, culture and arts, education, engineering and industry, politics and policy, public administration, social welfare, sports science, tourism and hospitality
Chair.: CHU CHEONG-SOO
Chancellor: Dr HO JOON CHOI
Library of 1,500,000 vols
Number of teachers: 800
Number of students: 16,000

KYUNG HEE UNIVERSITY

Seoul Campus, Hoegi-dong, Dongdaemun-gu, Seoul 130-701
Telephone: (2) 961-0031
Fax: (2) 962-4343
E-mail: cie@khu.ac.kr*Global Campus*, Seo-

cheon-Dong, Seoul 446-701
Telephone: (31) 201-3177
Fax: (31) 201-3179
E-mail: intlctr@khu.ac.kr
Internet: www.kyunghee.ac.kr
Founded 1949; renamed 1952
Private control
Academic year: March to December (two terms)
Founder-Chancellor: Dr CHOUE INWON
Pres.: KIM BYUNG-MOOK
Vice-Pres.: KIM BYUNG MOOK (Seoul Campus): PARK KYU HONG (Suwon Campus): PARK MYUNG KWAN (Devt)
Registrars: CHOO DONG JOON (Seoul Campus): CHO WON-KYUNG (Suwon Campus)
Librarians: KIM JAE HONG (Seoul Campus): KIM HAN WON (Suwon Campus)
Library of 1,200,000 vols, separate medical library of 15,000 vols
Number of teachers: 2,300
Number of students: 29,080
Publications: *University Life* (in English, 12 a year), *University Weekly* (in Korean), *Kohwang* (in Korean, 1 a year), *Peace Forum* (in English, every 2 years), research bulletins for each college

DEANS

Seoul Campus:

College of Dentistry: LEE SANG RAE
College of Human Ecology: PARK HYUN-SUH
College of Law: LEE SHIYOON
College of Liberal Arts and Sciences: CHUNG BOK-KEUN
College of Medicine: CHOYOUG HO
College of Music: HWANG SUN
College of Oriental Medicine: LEE HYUNG KOO
College of Pharmacy: RHO YOUNG SOO
College of Political Science and Economics: SUH SUNG-HAN
College of Tourism and Hotel Management: YOO KON-JO
Graduate School: SOHN KWANG SHIK
Graduate School of Business Administration: LEE KEUN SOO
Graduate School of East–West Medicine: RYU KI-WON
Graduate School of Education: PARK KEE-SAW
Graduate School of International Legal Affairs: YUN MYUNG-SUNG
Graduate School of Journalism and Mass Communication: LEE SUK-WOO
Graduate School of NGO: PARK KUN WOO
Graduate School of Peace Studies: SOHN JAE-SHIK
Graduate School of Physical Education: KOH KI CHAE
Graduate School of Public Administration: OH SEI DEUK
Graduate School of Tourism: YOO KONG-JO

Suwon Campus:

College of Engineering and Department of Electronics and Information Technology: JUN KYE SUK
College of Foreign Languages: HUH JONG
College of Industry and Department of Life Science: JO JAE SUN
College of Natural Sciences and Department of the Environment and Applied Chemistry: CHOUNG SUK JIN
College of Social Sciences and Department of Management and International Relations: PARK WON-KYU
College of Sports Science and Department of Physical Education: KIM JIN HO
Department of Art and Design: LEE HEON LOOK
Department of Civil and Architectural Engineering: ON YOUNG TAE
Department of Mechanical and Industrial Systems Engineering: PARK KYOUNG SUK

Graduate School of Information and Communication: CHIN YONG-OHK
Graduate School of Industry and Information Science: LEE KYE TAK
Graduate School of Pan-Pacific International Studies: KIM CHONGSOO

KYUNGIL UNIVERSITY

33 Puho-ri, Hayang-up, Kyungsan-si, Kyungsangpuk-do, Seoul 712-701

Telephone: (53) 853-8001
Fax: (53) 853-8800
E-mail: webmaster@kiu.ac.kr
Internet: www.kyungil.ac.kr

Founded 1963 as Technical High School attached to Chunggu College; renamed Jr Technical College attached to Yeungnam Univ. 1967; separated from Yeungnam Univ. as Yeungnam Jr Technical College 1975; renamed Kyungpook Jr Technical College 1976; renamed Kyungpook Jr College of Technology 1978; became Kyungpook Open Univ. 1985; renamed Kyungpook Sanup Univ. 1988; became Kyungil Univ. 1997
Private control
Academic year: March to December

Pres.: LEE NAM-KYO
Dir for Gen. Affairs: KIM JONG-SEOK
Dir of the Office for Planning and Devt: LEE WEON-SIK
Chief Librarian: HA-YONG PARK PARK HA-YONG

Number of teachers: 250
Number of students: 10,000

DEANS

College of Engineering: YOON MYUNG-JIN
College of Formative Arts: KIM JUNG-WON
College of Humanities and Social Sciences: ANH YOOL-CHONG
College of Information Technology: KIM LEE-KOK
Graduate School: KIM JIN-HO
Graduate School of Design: KIM JIN-HO
Graduate School of Industry: KIM JIN-HO
School of General Education: SUH BO-GUN

KYUNGNAM UNIVERSITY

449 Wolyoung-dong, Masan, Kyungnam, Seoul 631-701

Telephone: (55) 245-5000
Fax: (55) 246-6184
E-mail: aadm@kyungnam.ac.kr
Internet: www.kyungnam.ac.kr
Founded 1946
Private control

Pres.: Dr PARK JAE KYU
Registrar: Dr YANG JAE IN
Librarian: Dr YOUN DOCK JOUNG

Library of 537,887 vols
Number of teachers: 674
Number of students: 15,000

DEANS

College of Arts: Dr CHO JIN KI
College of Business Administration: Dr KOH HYUN WOOK
College of Education: Dr LEE SEOK ZOO
College of Engineering: Dr LEE SOO HEUM
College of Law and Political Science: Dr RA KYUNG SIK
College of Science: Dr LEE SUE DAE
Graduate School: Dr CHONG CHOONG KYUN

KYUNGSUNG UNIVERSITY

110-1 Daeyeon-dong, Nam-gu, Pusan 608-736

Telephone: (51) 620-4114
E-mail: www@www.ks.ac.kr
Internet: kyungsung.ac.kr

Founded 1955

Chair.: KIM DAE-SEONG
Pres.: KYUNG MOON-PARK

Library of 500,000 vols
Number of students: 12,000

Colleges of Liberal Arts, Law and Political Science, Commerce and Economics, Science, Engineering, Pharmacy, Arts, Theology, Multimedia; Graduate Schools of International Business, Multimedia, Social Welfare, Education, Clinical Pharmacology, Digital Design.

KYUNGWON UNIVERSITY

San 65 Bokjeong-dong, Sujeong-gu, Seongnam, Gyeonggi-do 461-701

Telephone: (31) 750-5901
E-mail: webmaster@kyungwon.ac.kr
Internet: www.kyungwon.ac.kr
Founded 1982

Chair.: MEN JEONG GWANG-MO
Pres.: LEE GIL-YA

Number of teachers: 165
Number of students: 8,609

Colleges of Humanities, Business and Economics, Law and Science, Engineering, Natural Science, Software, Arts, Music, Oriental Medicine, Human Ecology.

MOKWON UNIVERSITY

Doan-dong 800, Seo-ku, Taejon 302-729

Telephone: (42) 829-7114
Fax: (42) 825-5020
E-mail: webmaster@mokwon.ac.kr
Internet: www.mokwon.ac.kr
Founded 1954

Pres.: KEUN JOHN LYU

Library of 340,000 vols

Colleges of Theology, Humanities, Natural Sciences, Engineering, Social Sciences, Music, Fine Arts.

POHANG UNIVERSITY OF SCIENCE AND TECHNOLOGY

San 31 Hyoja-dong, Nam-gu, Pohang, Kyungbuk, Seoul 790-784

Telephone: (54) 279-2910
Fax: (54) 279-3590
E-mail: iao@postech.ac.kr
Internet: www.postech.ac.kr

Founded 1986
Academic year: March to January

Pres.: Prof. CHAN-MO PARK
Vice-Pres.: Prof. IN-SIK NAM
Dean of Policy and Planning (Int. Affairs): Prof. YUSHIN HONG

Number of teachers: 263
Number of students: 2,736 (1,329 undergraduate, 1,407 postgraduate)

PUSAN UNIVERSITY OF FOREIGN STUDIES

55-1 Uan-Dong, Nam-gu, Pusan 608-738

Telephone: (51) 640-3000
Fax: (51) 645-4525
E-mail: webmaster@www.pufs.ac.kr
Internet: www.pufs.ac.kr

Library of 320,000 vols

Colleges of Occidental Studies, Oriental Studies, Humanities and Social Sciences, Commerce and Business, Information and Sciences, Leisure Sports Studies.

SANGJI UNIVERSITY

660 Woosan-dong, Wonju, Kangwon-do

Telephone: (371) 730-0182

Fax: (371) 730-0128
E-mail: webmaster@mail.sangji.ac.kr
Internet: www.sangji.ac.kr

Founded 1962

Pres.: Dr SUNG-HOON KIM

Number of teachers: 473

Colleges of Humanities and Social Sciences, Life Science and Natural Resources, Oriental Medicine, Science and Engineering, Economics and Business Administration, Art and Sports.

SANGMYUNG UNIVERSITY

20 Samjidong 2nd St, Jongno-gu, Seoul 110-743

Telephone: (2) 2287-5196
Fax: (2) 2287-0017
E-mail: secint@smu.ac.kr
Internet: www.smu.ac.kr
Founded 1965
Private control
Academic year: March to September

Pres.: Prof. HYUNCHONG LEE
Vice-Pres. for Cheonan Campus: JAEKEUN LEE
Vice-Pres. for Seoul Campus: EHUNGGI BACK
Vice-Pres. for Planning and Coordination: KEEHEON GOO
Vice-Pres. for Industry and Academic Cooperation: KYOUNGYUL BAE

Library of 500,000 books, 4,000 vols of periodicals
Number of teachers: 330
Number of students: 14,064 (12,719 undergraduate, 1,345 postgraduate)

DEANS

College of Arts: SANGKYU PARK
College of Arts and Physical Education: Prof. INSOO YOO
College of Business: HEETAK KIM
College of Convergence: JINHWAN LEE
College of Design: HAESOOK KWON
College of Education: KWONBAE MOON
College of Engineering: BEUMJUN AHN
College of Humanities and Social Sciences: SEONGHO OH
College of Industry: DOOCHEOL KIM
College of Language and Literature: YEUNGSHIM WOO
College of Music: JOONMO DONG
College of Natural Sciences: MINSUN LEE
College of Software: HYUKSOO HAN

SEJONG UNIVERSITY

98 Kunja-dong, Kwangjin-gu, Seoul

Telephone: (2) 3408-3499
Fax: (2) 3408-3561
E-mail: semyaje@sejong.ac.kr
Internet: sejong.ac.kr

Founded 1947

President: Dr CHUL-SU KIM
Vice-Presidents: Dr SUK-MO KOO (Academic Affairs, and Provost), Dr HYUN-JU SHIN (International Programmes and Christian Ministry), YOUNG-HWAN CHOI (Research and Development)
Dean of Academic Affairs: Dr YONG-U SOK
Dean of Student Support: Dr EUI-JANG KO
Dean of Finance: KWANG-HO PARK
Dean of Admissions and Planning: Dr JA-MO KANG

Number of students: 7,337

DEANS

College of Business Administration: Dr SOO-SUP SONG
College of Engineering: Dr HOON-IL OH
College of Liberal Arts: Dr CHON-SUN IHM
College of Music, Fine Arts and Physical Education: Dr DUCK-BOON LEE

College of Natural Sciences: Dr SUNG-CHUNG AN
College of Social Sciences: Dr KI-SANG LEE
College of Tourism: Dr SO-YOON CHO
Graduate School: Dr YANG-JA YOO
Graduate School of Business: Dr B. J. YANG
Graduate School of Education: Dr HYUN-WOOK NAM
Graduate School of Information and Communication: Dr JOUNG-WON KIM
Graduate School of Mass Communication: DON-SHIK CHOO
Graduate School of Public Administration: Dr KYUNG-SHIK JOO
Graduate School of Tourism: Dr CHOL-YONG KIM

SEOKYEONG UNIVERSITY

16-1 Jungneung-dong, Sungbuk-ku, Seoul 136-704

Telephone: (2) 940-7114
Fax: (2) 919-0345
E-mail: webadmin@bukak.seokyeong.ac.kr
Internet: www.seokyeong.ac.kr

Founded 1947

Pres.: CHUL-SOO HAN

Colleges of Humanities, Social Sciences, Natural Science and Engineering, Arts.

SEOUL THEOLOGICAL UNIVERSITY

Kyungki-do, Buchon City
E-mail: admin@stui.net
Internet: www.stu.ac.kr

Founded 1911

President: JOSEPH JONG JIN CHOE

Departments of Theology, Christian Education, Social Welfare, Church Music, Mission English, Childcare, Education.

SEOUL WOMEN'S UNIVERSITY

126 Kongnung 2-dong, Nowon-gu, Seoul 139-144

Telephone: (2) 970-5114
Fax: (2) 978-7931
E-mail: webmaster@mail.swu.ac.kr
Internet: www.swu.ac.kr

Founded 1961
Private control
Academic year: March to February

President: Dr KWANG-JA LEE
Dean of Academic Affairs: Dr KI SUK PARK
Dean of Student Affairs: Dr JU HAN PARK
Dean of General Affairs: Dr HEI JUNG CHUN
Dean of Planning and Budget: Dr EON HO CHOI
Chief Librarian: Dr ON ZA PARK

Number of teachers: 136
Number of students: 5,911

Publications: *Journal of Art and Design* (1 a year), *Journal of Child Studies* (1 a year), *Journal of Student Guidance and Counselling* (1 a year), *Journal of Women's Studies* (1 a year), *Journal of the Graduate School Seoul Women's University* (1 a year), *Journal of the Institute of Humanities* (1 a year), *Journal of the Natural Science Institute* (1 a year), *Journal of the Social Science Research Institute* (1 a year), *Seoul Women's University News* (26 a year)

DEANS

College of Humanities: Prof. YOUNG CHUL LEE
College of Information and Communication: Dr MOON HEE KANG
College of Natural Sciences: Dr JONG SUK LEE
College of Social Sciences: Dr MOON HEE KANG
Division of Fine Arts: Prof. BOK HEE CHEON

SEOWON UNIVERSITY

231 Mochung-dong, Hongduk-ku, Cheongju 361-742

Telephone: (43) 299-8114
Fax: (43) 283-8822
Internet: www.seowon.ac.kr

Founded 1968

Number of teachers: 506
Number of students: 8,760

Colleges of Art, Education, Liberal Arts, Social Sciences, Natural Sciences.

SILLA UNIVERSITY

617-736 San 1-1 Gwaebop-dong, Sasang-gu, Busan

Telephone: (51) 999-5000
E-mail: webadm@silla.ac.kr
Internet: silla.ac.kr

Chair.: HAE-GON PARK
Pres.: BYUNG-HWA LEE

Colleges of Humanities and Social Sciences, Economics and Business Administration, Natural Sciences, Engineering, Information Technology Design, Education, Arts.

SOGANG UNIVERSITY

CPO 1142, Seoul 100-611

Telephone: (2) 705-8114
Fax: (2) 705-8119
E-mail: interrel@sogang.ac.kr
Internet: www.sogang.ac.kr

Founded 1960
Private control
Languages of instruction: Korean, English
Academic year: March to December (2 semesters)

Pres.: CHANG-SUP CHOI (acting)
Man. of Academic Affairs: MOON-SEOB YOUM
Man. of Student Affairs: MYEONG-HOON CHEON
Dir of Library: SEOG PARK

Number of teachers: 302
Number of students: 10,900

Publications: *Sogang Hakbo* (52 a year), *Sogang Herald* (12 a year)

DEANS

College of Engineering: YOUNG GOO LEE
College of Humanities: IN CHAI CHUNG
College of Natural Sciences: KWAE HI LEE
College of Social Science: KAP YUN LEE
General Education Division: HEE NAM CHOI
Graduate School: CHUL AN
Graduate School of Business: WOON YOUL CHOI
Graduate School of Economics: YOUNG GOO LEE
Graduate School of Education: JUNG TAEK KIM
Graduate School of Information and Technology: JUNG YUN SEO
Graduate School of International Studies: SE YOUNG AHN
Graduate School of Mass Communication: HAK SOO KIM
Graduate School of Media Communications: KAK YOON
Graduate School of Public Policy: KAP YUN LEE
Graduate School of Theology: TAE SU HA
School of Business Administration: JANG HO LEE
School of Economics: BOK UNG KIM

PROFESSORS

College of Engineering:

AN, C., Electronic Engineering
CHANG, I. S., Electronic Engineering
CHANG, J. H., Computer Science
CHOI, C. S., Chemical Engineering
CHOI, J.-W., Chemical Engineering
CHOI, M., Computer Science
HONG, D.-H., Electronic Engineering
HUR, N., Mechanical Engineering
HWANG, S. Y., Electronic Engineering
IHM, I., Computer Science
JANG, J. W., Electronic Engineering
JEE, Y., Electronic Engineering
JEON, D., Mechanical Engineering
JEONG, S., Mechanical Engineering
KIM, N., Mechanical Engineering
KIM, S. C., Computer Science
KOO, K. K., Chemical and Biomolecular Engineering
LEE, H. Y., Mechanical Engineering
LEE, J. W., Chemical Engineering
LEE, K. H., Electronic Engineering
LEE, S. K. S., Chemical Engineering
LEE, S. H., Electronic Engineering
LEE, T. S., Mechanical Engineering
NANG, J., Computer Science
OH, K. W., Computer Science
OH, S. Y., Chemical and Biomolecular Engineering
PARK, H. M., Chemical and Biomolecular Engineering
PARK, H. S., Chemical and Biomolecular Engineering
PARK, R. H., Electronic Engineering
PARK, S., Computer Science
RHEE, H. W., Chemical and Biomolecular Engineering
RIM, C. S., Computer Science
SEO, J., Computer Science
YOO, K.-P., Chemical and Biomolecular Engineering
YUN, S. W., Electronic Engineering

College of Humanities:

AN, S. J., English Language and Literature
BAIK, I. H., History
BAK, J. S., French Language and Literature
CHANG, S. N., German Language and Literature
CHANG, Y. H., English Language and Literature
CHO, B. H., History
CHO, S. W., English Language and Literature
CHOI, H.-M., French Language and Literature
CHUNG, D. H., History
CHUNG, I. C., Philosophy
JEONG, Y. I., Korean Language and Literature
KANG, Y. A., Philosophy
KEEL, H. S., Religious Studies
KIM, G., Chinese Culture
KIM, H. G., History
KIM, S. H., Religious Studies
KIM, S. N., Religious Studies
KIM, W. S., Philosophy
KIM, Y. H., History
KIM, Y. S., English Language and Literature
KWAK, C. G., Korean Language and Literature
LEE, J. D., German Language and Literature
LEE, J. W., History
LEE, S. B., English Language and Literature
LIM, S. W., History
PAK, C. T., Philosophy
SEONG, Y., Philosophy
SHIN, K., English Language and Literature
SHIN, S. W., English Language and Literature
SONG, H. S., Korean Language and Literature
SONG, W. Y., German Language and Literature
SPALATIN, C. A., Philosophy
SUH, C. M., Korean Language and Literature

SUNG, H. K., Korean Language and Literature
UM, J., Philosophy

College of Natural Sciences:
CHIN, C. S., Chemistry
CHO, K., Physics
CHO, S. H., Mathematics
CHUNG, D. M., Mathematics
CHUNG, S. Y., Mathematics
HONG, S. S., Mathematics
KANG, J., Chemistry
KIM, D. H., Chemistry
KIM, D. S., Mathematics
KIM, J., Mathematics
KIM, S. R., Life Science
KIM, W. S., Life Science
KIM, W. T., Physics
LEE, B. H., Physics
LEE, D., Chemistry
LEE, H., Chemistry
LEE, J. B., Mathematics
LEE, J. G., Mathematics
LEE, J. K., Life Science
LEE, W. K., Chemistry
PARK, G. S., Physics
PARK, S. A., Mathematics
PARK, S. H., Mathematics
PARK, Y. J., Physics
RHEE, B. K., Physics
SHIN, C. E., Mathematics
SHIN, W., Chemistry
SO, H., Chemistry
YANG, J. M., Life Science
YOON, K. B., Chemistry

College of Social Science:
CHANG, Y. H., Mass Communication
CHO, H., Sociology
CHO, O., Sociology
CHOI, C. S., Mass Communication
CHOI, O. C., Law
CHUNG, H.-J., Law
EOM, D. S., Law
HONG, S. B., Law
KANG, J. I., Political Science
KIM, H. S., Mass Communication
KIM, K. M., Sociology
KIM, Y. S., Political Science
LEE, K. Y., Political Science
OH, B. S., Law
PARK, H. S., Political Science
PARK, S. T., Sociology
SHIN, Y. H., Political Science
SONN, H. C., Political Science
SUH, K. M., Law
YOON, Y. D., Sociology

General Education Division:
CHO, G. H., General Education
CHOI, H. N., General Education
KIM, J.-W., General Education
KIM, O. S., General Education

Graduate School of International Studies:
AHN, S. Y.
CHO, Y. J.

Graduate School of Media Communications:
BYUN, D. H.
JUNG, M.-R.
KIM, C. H.
KIM, Y. Y.
LEE, S. W.
SHIN, H. C.
YOON, K.

Graduate School of Theology:
CHUNG, W. S.
MOON, J. Y.
SIM, J. H.

School of Business Administration:
CHEE, Y. H., Business Administration
CHOI, J. H., Business Administration
CHOI, S. J., Business Administration
CHOI, W. Y., Business Administration
CHUN, S. B., Business Administration
HA, Y. W., Business Administration

JON, J. S., Business Administration
KANG, H. S., Business Administration
KIM, S. K., Business Administration
KOOK, C. P., Business Administration
LEE, C., Business Administration
LEE, D. S., Business Administration
LEE, J. B., Business Administration
LEE, J. H., Business Administration
LEE, J. J., Business Administration
LEE, K. L., Business Administration
LEE, N. J., Business Administration
LEE, W. Y., Business Administration
LIM, C. U., Business Administration
MIN, J. H., Business Administration
PARK, K. K., Business Administration
PARK, N. H., Business Administration
PARK, Y. S., Business Administration
RHO, B. H., Business Administration
SUH, C. J., Business Administration

School of Economics:
CHO, C. O., Economics
GILL, I. S., Economics
JEON, S. H., Economics
KIM, B. U., Economics
KIM, K. D., Economics
KIM, K. H., Economics
KIM, S. Y., Economics
KWACK, T., Economics
LEE, D. S., Economics
LEE, H. K., Economics
LEE, H. S., Economics
LEE, Y. G., Economics
NAHM, J. W., Economics
NAM, S. I., Economics
SONG, E. Y., Economics
SUH, J. H., Economics
WANG, G. H., Economics

SOOKMYUNG WOMEN'S UNIVERSITY

53-12 Chungpa-dong 2-ka, Yongsan-gu, Seoul 140-742
Telephone: (2) 710-9114
Fax: (2) 718-2337
E-mail: kslee@sookmyung.ac.kr
Internet: www.sookmyung.ac.kr
Founded 1906
Private control
Language of instruction: Korean
Academic year: March to February
Pres.: KYUNG-SOOK LEE
Dean of Academic Affairs: EUN-GYUN MOK
Dean of Student Affairs: YOUNG-SOOK SUH
Dean of Administrative Affairs: CHUN-HAK OH
Dean of Planning: MOO-SEUCK CHO
Library Dir: HEE-JAE LEE
Library of 628,688 vols
Number of teachers: 370
Number of students: 13,315
Publications: *Sookdae Shinbo* (in Korean, 52 a year), *Bulletin* (in English and Korean, 1 a year), *Sookmyung Times* (in English, 12 a year), *Asian Women* (in English)

DEANS

College of Economics and Commerce: WON-BAE YOON
College of Fine Arts: HAK-SEONG KIM
College of Home Economics: SUN-JAE LEE
College of Liberal Arts: JUNG-SHIN HAN
College of Music: MAN-BANG YI
College of Natural Sciences: YOUNG-HEE HONG
College of Pharmacy: AN-KEUN KIM
College of Political Science and Law: SANG-KWANG LEE
Graduate School: JUNG-WOO LEE
Graduate Schools of Special Subjects: SOOK-HEE PARK

SOONGSIL UNIVERSITY

1-1 Sangdo 5-dong, Dongjak-ku, Seoul 156-743
Telephone: (2) 820-0111
Fax: (2) 814-7362
Internet: www.ssu.ac.kr
Founded 1897
Private control
Academic year: March to December
Chancellor: SUN-HEE KWAK
Pres.: YOON-BAE OUH
Vice-Pres. for International Affairs: HAE-SEOK OH
Vice-Pres. for Academic Affairs: BONG-CHUL SEO
Librarian: PYUNG-SYK RO
Library of 367,000 vols
Number of teachers: 586 (252 full-time, 334 part-time)
Number of students: 10,167

DEANS

College of Economics and Commerce: WON-WOO LEE
College of Engineering: MUN-HEON KIM
College of Humanities: HONG-ZIN KIM
College of Information Science: CHUL-HEE LEE
College of Law: SUNG-SOOK KIM
College of Natural Sciences: YOUNG-JA YUN
College of Social Sciences: KWANG-SEOB SHIN

DIRECTORS

Christian Institute of Social Studies: SAM-YEUL LEE
Institute for Adult and Continuing Education: KWANG-MYUNG KIM
Institute of Business and Economic Strategies: DAE-YONG JEONG
Institute of Humanities: HONG-ZIN KIM
Institute of Industrial Technology: YOUNG-PIL KWON
Institute of Korean Christian Culture Research: YOUNG-HAN KIM
Institute of Law: DOO-HWAN KIM
Institute of Natural Sciences: CHONG-IN YU
Institute of Social Science: SOO-EON MOON
Resource Recycling Research Centre: KAP-SOO DOH

SUNGKYUL CHRISTIAN UNIVERSITY

147-2 Anyang 8-dong, Manan-gu, Anyang, Kyungki-do 430-742
Telephone: (343) 467-8114
Internet: www.sungkyul.ac.kr
Founded 1962 as a seminary; present name 1992
Pres.: Dr KEE-HO SUNG
Library of 170,000 vols.

SUNGKYUNKWAN UNIVERSITY

Humanities and Social Sciences Campus: 53 Myongnyun-dong 3-ga, Chongo-gu, Seoul 110-745
Natural Sciences Campus: 300 Chunchun-dong, Changan-gu, Suwon, Kyonggi-do 440-746
Telephone: (2) 760-0114
Fax: (2) 744-2453
E-mail: webmaster@skku.ac.kr
Internet: www.skku.ac.kr
Founded 1398; university status 1953
Private control
Academic year: March to February
Chairman of the Board of Trustees: E-HOUCK KWON
Pres.: JUNG DON SEO
Vice-Pres.: CHAE-WOONG LEE (Humanities and Social Sciences Campus), YUN-HEUM PARK (Natural Sciences Campus)
Academic Affairs Officer: HYUK KIM

Librarian: PYUNG-U PARK
Library: 1.4m. vols
Number of teachers: 980
Number of students: 24,098

Publications: *Journal of Eastern Culture* (in Korean, 1 a year), *Journal of Humanities Sciences* (in Korean, 1 a year), *Journal of Human Life Sciences* (in Korean, 1 a year), *Journal of Korean Economics* (1 a year), *Journal of Modern China* (in Korean, 1 a year), *Journal of Social Sciences* (in Korean, 1 a year), *Learned Papers in Science and Technology* (in Korean, 2 a year), *Learned Papers in the Natural Sciences* (in Korean, 2 a year), *Sung Kyun Law Review* (in Korean, 2 a year), *Suson Learned Papers* (in Korean, 1 a year)

DEANS

College of Education: YOUNG-EUN CHIN
College of Law: KYU-SANG JUNG
School of Architecture, Landscape Architecture and Civil Engineering: SANG-HAE CHOI
School of Art: HAK-SUN LIM
School of Business Administration: YOUNG-KYU KIM
School of Chemical, Polymer and Textile Engineering: BOONG-SOO JEON
School of Confucian and Oriental Studies: YOUNG-JIN CHOI
School of Economics: SUNG-SOON LEE
School of Electrical and Computer Engineering: CHIL-GEE LEE
School of Human Life Sciences: YANG-HEE LEE
School of Humanities: HAN-GU LEE
School of Language and Literature: BONG-WON CHOI
School of Life Sciences and Technology: KYU-SEUNG LEE
School of Mechanical Engineering: HYUN-SOO KIM
School of Medicine: DAY-YONG UHM
School of Metallurgical and Materials Engineering: JOEN-GEON HAN
School of Natural Sciences: SANG-TAE LEE
School of Pharmacy: WON-HUN HAM
School of Social Sciences: CHANG-SOO CHUNG
School of Sports Science: EUNG-NAM AHM
School of Systems Management Engineering: HOO-GON CHOI

SUNGSHIN WOMEN'S UNIVERSITY

249-1 Dongseon-dong 3-ga, Seongbuk-do, Seoul 136-742

Telephone: (2) 920-7114
E-mail: www@cc.sungshin.ac.kr
Internet: www.sungshin.ac.kr

Founded 1936

Library of 500,000 vols
Number of students: 13,000

Colleges of arts, education, human ecology, humanities, music, natural sciences, social sciences.

UNIVERSITY OF ULSAN

POB 18, Ulsan, Seoul 680-049

Telephone: (52) 277-3101
Fax: (52) 277-3419
E-mail: webmaster@mail.ulsan.ac.kr
Internet: uou.ulsan.ac.kr

Founded 1970
Private control
Academic year: March to December

Chair.: MONG-JOON CHUNG
Pres.: CHUNG-KIL CHUNG
Head of Academic Information Centre: Prof. JEONG-SEOK HEO

Library of 700,000 books, 909 periodicals
Number of teachers: 723

Number of students: 11,659 (6,121 undergraduate, 5,538 postgraduate)

DEANS

College of Business Administration: HI-KYOON LEE
College of Design: SANG-HYE HAN
College of Engineering: DONG-KEE LEE
College of Fine Arts: PYUNG-HUI PARK
College of Human Ecology: HYE-KYUNG KIM
College of Humanities: CHUNG-HOO SUH
College of Industry and Management: KYU-CHO LEE
College of Medicine: WON-DONG KIM
College of Music: HYUN-KYUNG CHAE
College of Natural Sciences: TAE-SOO KIM
College of Social Sciences: YEON-JAE SHIN
Graduate School: KANG-MOON KOH
Graduate School of Business Administration: JOONG-HEON NAM
Graduate School of Education: MYEUNG-HAK YANG
Graduate School of Industrial Technology: SEONG-DEUK KIM I
Graduate School of Information and Communications Technology: KYUNG-SUP PARK
Graduate School of Regional Development: WOO-SUNG KIM

WON KWANG UNIVERSITY

344-2 Shinyong-dong, Iksan, Jeonbuk, Seoul 570-749

Telephone: (63) 850-5114
Fax: (63) 850-6666
Internet: www.wonkwang.ac.kr

Founded 1946
Private control
Academic year: March to August, September to February

Pres.: GAB-WOEN JEONG
Vice-Pres. for Academy: SONG CHON-EUN
Vice-Pres. for Medicine: CHON PAL-KHN
Dean of Academic Affairs: GO GUN-IL
Dean of Planning Office: CHOI SEONG-SIK
Dean of Student Affairs: KIM JONG-SU
Dean of Financial and General Affairs: OH HAE-GEUM
Dir of Library: LEE MAN-SANG

Number of teachers: 462
Number of students: 23,200

DEANS

College of Agriculture: LEE KAP-SANG
College of Dentistry: KIM SU-NAM
College of Education: SHIN YO-YOUNG
College of Engineering: CHUNG SA-HEE
College of Home Economics: MOON BUM-SOO
College of Law: KIM DAE-KYOO
College of Liberal Arts and Sciences: OHM JEONG-OAK
College of Management: PARK JAE-ROK
College of Oriental Medicine: MAENG UNG-JAEO
College of Pharmacy: OCK CHI-WAN
College of Social Sciences: KIM GUY-KON
College of Won Buddhism: KIM HONG-CHULO
Graduate School: YU GI-SU
Graduate School of Education: YU JAE-YEONG
Graduate School of Industry: YUN YANG-WOONG
School of Medicine: CHUNG YEUN-TAI

YEUNGNAM UNIVERSITY

Gyongsan 632, Taegu

Telephone: (53) 810-2114
Fax: (53) 810-2036
E-mail: webadmin@yu.ac.kr
Internet: www.yu.ac.kr

Founded 1967 by amalgamation of Taegu College and Chunggu College
Private control

Academic year: March to February (2 semesters)

Pres.: Dr LEW JOON
Dean of Academic Affairs: Dr PARK BONG MOK
Dean of Student Affairs: Dr KIM JUNG YUEP
Dean of Business Affairs: Dr PARK SUNG KYU
Dean of Planning and Development: Dr YOON BYUNG TAE
Dir of Library: Dr OH MYUNG-KUN

Library of 398,690 vols
Number of teachers: 549
Number of students: 22,506

Publications: *Library Guide, Student Guide* (1 a year), *Yeungdae Munha* (Yeungnam University Culture), *Yeungnam University Theses Collection*, and various faculty and institutional publs

DEANS

College of Agriculture and Animal Sciences: SYE YOUNG-SYEK
College of Commerce and Economics: RYU CHANG OU
College of Education: SONG BYUNG SOON
College of Engineering: LEE DONG IN
College of Fine Arts: HONG SUNG MOON
College of Home Economics: LEE KAP RANG
College of Law and Political Science: RHEE CHANGWOO
College of Liberal Arts: KIM TAIK-KYOO
College of Medicine: KIM WON JOON
College of Music: KIM SHIN WHAN
College of Pharmacy: SEO BYEONG CHEON
College of Science: KIM JONG DAE
Evening College: BYUN JAE-OCK
Graduate School: KIM HOGWON
Graduate School of Business Administration: KIM KIE-TAEK
Graduate School of Education: CHUNG SOON MOK
Graduate School of Environmental Studies: JIN KAP DUCK

PROFESSORS

College of Agriculture and Animal Sciences:
BYUN, J. K., Horticulture
CHOI, C., Food Technology and Science
CHUNG, H. D., Horticulture
CHUNG, Y. G., Food Science and Technology
JUNG, K. J., Animal Science
KIM, B. D., Community Development
KIM, J. K., Applied Microbiology
LEE, H. C., Animal Science
PARK, C. H., Agronomy
SON, J. Y., Animal Science
SYE, Y. S., Animal Science
YOON, W., Community Development

College of Commerce and Economics:
BAE, Y. S., Economics
HAR, C. D., Business Policy
KIM, J. H., Foreign Trade
KIM, K.-T., Economics
KIM, T. W., Business Administration
KWON, B. T., Economics
LEE, W.-D., Economics
PARK, S.-K., Business Administration
RYU, C. O., Foreign Trade
SANG, M. D., Business Administration
SHIN, H. J., International Theory and Policy
YI, Y. W., Economics
YOON, I. H., Economics
YU, H. K., Economics

College of Education:
AHN, Y. T., Business Education
BAEK, U. H., Developmental Psychology
CHO, D. B., Personality and Education
CHUN, B. K., Audiovisual Method
CHUNG, S. M., History of Korean Education
CHUNG, Y. K., Linguistics
KIM, H., Evaluation
KIM, J. R., Physical Education

KWON, J. W., Educational Psychology
LEE, J. H., Physical Education
LEE, K. T., English Language Education
LEE, S. B., Mathematics Education
LIM, M. S., Physical Education
PARK, B. M., Philosophy of Education
PARK, Y. B., Curriculum and Instruction
SONG, B. S., Educational Psychology

College of Engineering:

BAE, J. H., Electrical Engineering
BYUN, D. K., Civil Engineering
CHANG, D. H., Textile Engineering
CHO, B., Chemical Engineering
CHO, H., Textile Engineering
CHOI, S.-G., Electronic Engineering
CHOI, S.-H., Mechanical Design
CHUNG, K.-H., Eletronic Engineering
CHUNG, W.-G., Textile Engineering
HA, Z.-H., Mechanical Engineering
JOO, H., System Engineering
KANG, S. H., Chemical Engineering
KIM, D. O., Traffic Engineering
KIM, G.-C., Civil Engineering
KIM, H. S., Architectural Engineering
KIM, I.-J., Architectural Engineering
KIM, J. Y., Mechanical Engineering
KIM, K. S., Industrial Chemistry
KIM, S.-K., Textile Engineering
LEE, D. H., Control Engineering
LEE, D.-I., Electrical Engineering
LEE, J. H., Industrial Chemistry
LEE, K. S., Mechanical Engineering
LEE, M. H., Industrial Chemistry
LEE, M. Y., Electronic Communication
LEE, S. T., Civil Engineering
LEE, T.-S., Marine Engineering
PARK, J. Y., Civil Engineering
PARK, W.-K., Chemical Engineering
PARK, Y.-K., Industrial Chemistry
RO, C. K., Electrical Engineering
RO, H. J., Architectural Engineering
SOHN, Y. K., Computer Engineering
SONG, J. S., Textile Engineering
UM, W.-T., Urban Engineering
WU, M. J., Civil Engineering

College of Fine Arts:

HONG, S. M., Sculpture
KIM, Y. Z., Painting

College of Home Economics:

CHO, S. Y., Food and Nutrition
HAN, J. S., Food Preparation
KIM, K. S., Food Science
LEE, J. O., Clothing Science
LEE, J. S., Home Management
LEE, K. R., Food and Nutrition
PARK, J. R., Food Science

College of Law and Political Science:

BYUN, J.-O., Constitutional and Administrative Law
CHANG, T.-O., Public Administration
CHEUNG, W. J., International Law
CHO, C.-H., Civil Law
CHOI, J.-C., Public Administration
KIM, J.-S., Public Administration
KIM, K.-D., Civil Law
KWON, H. K., Political Science and Diplomacy
LEE, W. S., Political Science and Diplomacy
PAIK, S. K., Public Administration
PARK, S.-W., Criminal Law
RHEE, C.-W., Political Science and Diplomacy
YOON, B. T., Public Administration

College of Liberal Arts:

CHAE, S. H., Buddhist Philosophy
CHANG, H. K., Psychology
CHO, K.-S., Korean Language and Literature
CHUNG, Y. W., Archaeology
HU, J. W., Western Philosophy
HUH, C. Y., European History
HWANG, S.-M., English and Linguistics
KEWN, S.-H., English Drama

KIM, B. K., Western Philosophy
KIM, C. S., Korean Language and Literature
KIM, S. H., English Novels
KIM, S. J., Korean History
KIM, S. K., English Literature
KIM, S. M., English Poetry
KIM, T. K., Anthropology
KIM, W.-W., English Poetry
KWON, Y. G., English Language and Literature
LEE, B. J., Asian History
LEE, B. L., Korean Language and Literature
LEE, C. H., Western Philosophy
LEE, J. W., Chinese Prose, Phonology
LEE, S.-D., English Poetry
LEE, S. K., Korean History
LEE, S.-T., English Literature
LEE, W. J., Philosophy
LEE, Y. K., Philosophy of History, Social Philosophy
LIM, B.-J., French Language
MUN, C.-B., English Philosophy
O, S. C., Korean History
OH, M.-K., Sociology
SUH, I., American Literature
SUH, K. B., Chinese Poetry
YOH, K. K., English Language
YOUN, Y.-O., Korean Literature

College of Medicine:

CHUNG, J. H., Preventive Medicine
CHUNG, J. K., Microbiology
CHUNG, W. Y., Obstetrics and Gynaecology
HAH, Y. M., Dermatology
HAHN, D. K., Ophthalmology
HAM, D. S., Anatomy
IHIN, J. C., Orthopaedic Surgery
KIM, C. S., Internal Medicine
KIM, C. S., Pathology
KIM, S. H., General Surgery
KIM, W. J., Pharmacology
KWUN, K. B., General Surgery
LEE, S. K., Physiology
LEE, T. S., Pathology
LEE, Y. C., Anatomy
PARK, C. S., Neurology
SONG, K. W., Otorhinolaryngology

College of Music:

KIM, S. W., Vocal Music

College of Pharmacy:

CHANG, U. K., Pharmacy
CHUNG, K. C., Pharmacy
CHUNG, S. R., Pharmacy
DO, J. C., Industrial Pharmacy
HAN, B. S., Industrial Pharmacy
HUH, K., Pharmacy
JIN, K. D., Pharmacy
KIM, J. Y., Industrial Pharmacy
LEE, M. K., Industrial Pharmacy
LEE, S. W., Pharmacology
SEOH, B. C., Industrial Pharmacy

College of Science:

CHANG, G. S., Physics
CHANG, K., Mathematics
CHO, H. S., Physics
CHO, Y., Mathematics
CHOE, O.-S., Physics
DOH, M. K., Inorganic Chemistry
KANG, S. G., Physics
KIM, D. S., Analytical Chemistry
KIM, J.-C., Mathematics
KIM, J. D., Organic Chemistry
KIM, M. M., Physics
KIM, Y. H., Physics
PAHK, G.-H., Mathematics
PARK, B. K., Physical Chemistry
PARK, H.-S., Mathematics
PARK, W. H., Biology
RO, H. K., Physics
WOO, J., Statistics

YONSEI UNIVERSITY

134 Shinchon-dong, Sudaemoon-gu, Seoul 120-749

Telephone: (2) 2123-2114
Fax: (2) 392-0618
E-mail: ewebmaster@yonsei.ac.kr
Internet: www.yonsei.ac.kr

Founded 1885
Private control
Languages of instruction: Korean, English
Academic year: March to February (2 semesters)

Pres.: CHANG-YOUNG JUNG
Vice-Pres. for Academic Affairs: KYUNG-DUCK MIN
Vice-Pres. for External Affairs and Alumni: HAN-JOONG KIM
Vice-Pres. for Medical Affairs: JIN-KYUNG KANG
Vice-Pres. for Wonju Campus: DAI-WOON LEE
Dir of University Planning and Public Relations: IN-KI JOO
Dean of Academic Affairs: HI-SOO MOON
Dean of Admissions: YONG-HAK KIM
Dean of Student Affairs and Services: TAE-SEUNG PAIK
Dir of General Affairs: HYUK-GEUN CHOI
Dir of the Central Library: YOUNG-SOO SHIN

Library: see Libraries and Archives
Number of teachers: 3,331
Number of students: 52,410

Publications: *Abstracts of Faculty Research Reports, Business Review, Engineering Review, Focus on Genetic Science, Global Economic Review, Infection Control Newsletter, Korean Journal of Nursing Questions, Journal of East and West Studies, Journal of Far Eastern Studies, Journal of Education Science, Journal of Engineering Research, Journal of Humanities, Journal of Korean Informatics, Journal of Korean Studies, Journal of Medical Technology, Journal of Nursing Science, Journal of the Radio Communication Research Centre, Journal of the Institute of Basic Science, Journal of the Natural Science Research Institute, Journal of the Research Institute of ASIC Design, Journal of the Research Institute of Information and Telecommunications, Journal of the Yonsei Institute for Cancer Research, Korean Journal of Health Science, New Energy and Environmental Systems, Social Science Review, Theological Forum, Theology and Modern Times, Tropical Medicine News, Yonsei Annals, Yonsei Biochemistry, Yonsei Chunchu, Yonsei Communication, Yonsei Economics Review, Yonsei Engineering Magazine, Yonsei Journal of Social Science, Yonsei Law Journal, Yonsei Law Review, Yonsei Health Science, Yonsei Journal of Clinical Orthodontics, Yonsei Journal of Dental Science, Yonsei Journal of Human Ecology, Yonsei Journal of Language and Literature, Yonsei Journal of Medical Education, Yonsei Journal of Medical History, Yonsei Journal of Public Administration, Yonsei Journal of Sport and Leisure Studies, Yonsei Journal of Women's Studies, Yonsei Medical Journal, Yonsei Non-Chong, Yonsei Nursing Journal, Yonsei Philosophy Review, Yonsei Review of Educational Research, Yonsei Review of Theology and Culture, Yonsei Social Welfare Review, Yonsei Unification Studies, Yonsei University Counselling Centre Research Review*

DEANS

College of Business and Economics: SUNG-KUN HA
College of Commerce and Law: PYEONG-JUN YU
College of Dentistry: HEUNG-KYU SOHN

College of Education: INTACK OH
College of Engineering: DAE-HEE YOON
College of Health Science: SOO-HONG NOH
College of Home Ecology: YOUNG LEE
College of Law: SANG-KI PARK
College of Liberal Arts: IN-CHO JUN
College of Liberal Arts and Science: BAE-SUN JI
College of Medicine: SE-JONG KIM
College of Music: MYUNG-JA CHO
College of Nursing: SO YA JA KIM
College of Science: YOUNG-MIN KIM
College of Social Science: WOO-SUH PARK
College of Theology: YANG-HO LEE
Graduate School: SOO-IL KIM
Graduate School of Administrative Science: KYUNG-SIHK AHN
Graduate School of Business Administration: JOON-SEUK KIM
Graduate School of Communication and Arts: YOUNG-SEOK KIM
Graduate School of Economics: SUNG-KUN HA
Graduate School of Education: SANG-WAN HAN
Graduate School of Engineering: JINHO LEE
Graduate School of Health and Environment: SOO-HONG NOH
Graduate School of Health Science and Management: SEUNG-HUM YU
Graduate School of Human Environmental Science: CHUNG-SOOK YOON
Graduate School of Information: KAP-YOUNG JEONG
Graduate School of International Studies: YOUNG-SUN LEE
Graduate School of Law: SANG-KI PARK
Graduate School of Mass Communication: YANG-SOO CHOI
Graduate School of Nursing: SO YA JA KIM
Graduate School of Public Administration: MYUNG-SOON SHIN
Graduate School of Social Welfare: HYE-KYUNG LEE
United Graduate School of Theology: YANG-HO LEE
University College: KYUNG-CHAN MIN
Wonju College of Medicine: SEONG-JOON KANG

PUBLIC UNIVERSITIES OF EDUCATION

CHEONGJU NATIONAL UNIVERSITY OF EDUCATION

135 Sugok-Dong, Heung Duk-Gu, Cheongju, Chungbuk 361-712
Telephone: (43) 279-0800
Fax: (43) 279-0797
Internet: www.chongju-e.ac.kr
Founded 1941
Pres.: YONG-WOO LIM
Library of 100,000 vols
Departments of Ethics Education, Korean Education, Social Studies, Mathematics, Science, Physical Education, Music, Fine Arts, Practical Arts; Graduate School of Education.

DAEGU NATIONAL UNIVERSITY OF EDUCATION

1797-6 Daemyung 2 dong, Namgu, Daegu, Seoul
Telephone: (53) 620-1114
Fax: (53) 651-5369
E-mail: abc@dnue.ac.kr
Internet: www.dnue.ac.kr
Founded 1950
Teacher-training univ.
Pres.: SOHN SEOKRAK
Number of teachers: 112
Number of students: 3,512 (2,775 undergraduates, 737 graduates)

KOREA NATIONAL UNIVERSITY OF EDUCATION

7 Darak-ri, Kangnae-myon, Chongwon-gun, Chungbuk, Seoul 363-791
Telephone: (43) 230-3114
Fax: (43) 233-2207
E-mail: internat@knuecc-sun.knue.ac.kr
Internet: www.knue.ac.kr
Founded 1984
Pres.: PARK BAE-HUN
Library of 300,000 vols
Number of teachers: 331
Number of students: 6,060

PUSAN NATIONAL UNIVERSITY OF EDUCATION

Pusan
Internet: www.pusan-e.ac.kr
Founded 1946 as Pusan Normal School; became Pusan Teachers' College 1955 and Pusan College of Education 1961; name reverted to Pusan Teachers' College 1963; present name 1993
President: Dr CHI-YUL OK.

SEOUL NATIONAL UNIVERSITY OF EDUCATION

Seocho-dong 1650, Seocho-gu, Seoul 137-742
E-mail: center@snue.ac.kr
Internet: www.snue.ac.kr
Founded 1945
Pres.: KWANG-YONG SONG.

PUBLIC UNIVERSITIES OF TECHNOLOGY

CHUNGJU NATIONAL UNIVERSITY

72 Daehak-ro, Chungju-si, Chungbuk 380-702
Telephone: (43) 841-5011
Fax: (43) 841-5017
Internet: www.chungju.ac.kr
Founded 1962 as Chungju Techincal Junior College, present status in 1999
Public Control
Pres.: Dr JANG BYUNG-JIB
Number of teachers: 295
Number of students: 8,200
Campuses in Chungju and Jeungpyeong
Colleges of Advanced Science and Technology, Engineering, Humanities, Social Sciences and Fine Arts, Health, Biology and Aeronautical Engineering; Graduate Schools of Business Administration, Public Administration and Foreign Languages, Industry; Division of Liberal Arts.

HANKYONG NATIONAL UNIVERSITY

67 Sukjong-dong, Ansung-City, Kyonggi-do, Seoul 456-749
Telephone: (31) 670-5114
Fax: (31) 673-2704
E-mail: master@hnu.hankyong.ac.kr
Internet: www.hankyong.ac.kr
Founded 1939
State control
Academic year: March to February
Pres.: Dr KIM SUNG-JIN
Dir of the Office for Academic Affairs: CHOE II-SHIN
Dir of the Office of Gen. Affairs: LEE JONG-NAM
Dir of the Office of Strategy Dept: RYU HO-SANG
Dir of the Office of Student Affairs: AN JAE-HO
Library Dir: YOU SHI-GYUN
Library of 82,000 books, 175 periodicals

Number of teachers: 458
Number of students: 7,718 (7,558 undergraduate, 160 postgraduate)

DEANS
College of Agriculture and Life Science: KIM YOUNG-HO
College of Humanities and Social Sciences: HONG WAN-PYO
College of Science and Engineering: LEE HAK-YOUNG
Graduate School of Industry: RHEE SONG-KAP

JINJU NATIONAL UNIVERSITY

150 Chilamdong, Jinju, Kyongnam, Seoul 660-758
Telephone: (55) 751-3114
Fax: (55) 752-9554
Internet: www.chinju.ac.kr
Founded 1910
Pres.: JUNG HAE-JU
Colleges of Agriculture, Science and Engineering, Humanities and Social Services.

KUMOH NATIONAL UNIVERSITY OF TECHNOLOGY

Sanho-to 77 (Yangho-dong), Gumi, Gyeong-buk, Seoul 730-701
Telephone: (54) 478-7114
Fax: (54) 478-7100
Internet: www.kumoh.ac.kr
Founded 1979 as Kumoh Institute of Technology; became Kumoh Nat. Institute of Technology 1990; present name 1993
Pres.: Dr HWAN CHOI.

MIRYANG NATIONAL UNIVERSITY

1025-1 Naei-dong, Miryang, Kyungnam 627-702
Telephone: (527) 354-3181
Fax: (527) 355-3186
E-mail: sdlee@arang.miryang.ac.kr
Internet: www.miryang.ac.kr
Founded 1923 as a public school of agricultural sericulture
President: TAE-KIL CHOI

DEANS AND CHAIRMEN
Graduate School: YON-GYU PARK
School of Architecture: KANG-GEUN PARK
School of Computer, Information and Communication Engineering: SUN-JONG KIM
School of Food Science and Environmental Engineering: DONG-SEOP KIM
School of Materials Engineering: SU-CHAK RYU

SAMCHOK NATIONAL UNIVERSITY

253 Gyodong, Samchok, Kangwon-do, Seoul 245-080
Telephone: (397) 572-8611
Fax: (397) 572-8620
E-mail: webadmin@samchok.ac.kr
Internet: www.samchok.ac.kr
Founded 1939 as Samchok Public Vocational School; became Samchok Public Industrial School 1944, Samchok Public Industrial Middle School 1946 and Samchok Industrial High School 1950; present name 1991
Pres.: Dr TAE-YUN CHANG.

SANGJU NATIONAL UNIVERSITY

Sangju, Gyeongsangbuk-do
E-mail: jkang@sangju.ac.kr
Internet: www.sangju.ac.kr
Founded 1921
Public

Pres.: KIM JONG-HO
Number of teachers: 104
Number of students: 4,350

PRIVATE UNIVERSITIES OF TECHNOLOGY

CHODANG UNIVERSITY

419 Muan-Goon, Muan-Eup, Seonnam-Ree, Jeonnam, Seoul 534-701

Telephone: (61) 450-1012
E-mail: president@chodang.ac.kr
Internet: www.chodang.ac.kr

Founded 1979
Private

Pres.: JIN-YOUNG NOH

Colleges of Arts and Physical Education, Humanities and Social Sciences, Science and Engineering; Graduate Divisions of Business and Public Admin., Computer and Information Engineering, Culinary Arts, Environmental Engineering, Information Design, Nursing Science, Ophthalmic Optics, Social Welfare, Social Physical Education.

HANKUK AVIATION UNIVERSITY

100, Hanggongdae gil, Hwajeon-dong, Gyeonggi-do Goyang City, Seoul 412-791

Telephone: (2) 300-0114
Fax: (2) 3158-5769
Internet: www.hangkong.ac.kr

Founded 1952 as National Aviation College; became Hankuk Aviation College 1968

Pres.: YUH JUNKU
Dean of Academic Affairs: LEE YEONG-HOOK
Dean of Student Affairs: KIM CHIL-YOUNG
Dean of Planning and Int. Affairs: BOO JOON-HONG
Dean of Research Affairs and Faculty Evaluation: HWANG SOO-CHAN

Library of 247,000 vols

DEANS

Graduate School: LEE YUN-HYUN
Graduate School of Aviation and Information Industry: HONG SOON-KIL
Graduate School of Business Administration: CHA GUN-HO

HANLYO UNIVERSITY

199-4 Deongrae-ri, Gwangyang-eup, Gwangyang-si, Jeollanam-do, Seoul 545-704

Telephone: (61) 761-6700
Fax: (61) 761-6709
E-mail: ipsimast@hanlyo.ac.kr
Internet: www.hanlyo.ac.kr

Founded 1993
Private.

HOWON UNIVERSITY

727 Wolha-ri, Impi, Kunsan, Chonbuk, Seoul 573-718

Telephone: (63) 450-7114
Fax: (63) 450-7777
Internet: www.howon.ac.kr

Founded 1977 as Kunsan Technical Advanced School; renamed Sohae Technical Jr College 1979; became Chonbuk Sanup Univ. 1988; present name 1998
Private control
Academic year: March to February

Pres.: KANG HEE-SUNG.

WOOSONG UNIVERSITY

17-2 Jayang-dong, Dong-gu, Daejeon 300-718

Telephone: (42) 630-9600
Fax: (42) 630-6629
E-mail: international@wsu.sc.kr

Internet: english.wsu.ac.kr

Founded 1954
Private

Chair.: KIM SUNG KYUNG
Pres.: JOHN E. ENDICOTT

Library of 275,063 vols, 3,152 reference books, 367 periodicals
Number of teachers: 212 full-time
Number of students: 7,037

Schools of Railroad and Transportation, Technomedia, Health and Welfare, Hotel and Culinary, Asia Management, SolBridge International School of Business.

MUNICIPAL UNIVERSITIES

UNIVERSITY OF INCHEON

319 Incheondaegil, Nam-gu, Incheon, Seoul

Telephone: (32) 770-8114
Fax: (32) 762-1548
E-mail: sysop@incheon.ac.kr
Internet: www.inchon.ac.kr

Pres.: AHN KYUNG SOO

Colleges of arts and physical education, economics and business administration, engineering, humanities, law, natural sciences, North-East Asian studies, social sciences.

UNIVERSITY OF SEOUL

90 Jeonnong-dong, Dongdaemun-gu, Seoul 130-743

Telephone: (2) 2210-2114
Fax: (2) 2243-2732
E-mail: w3adm@uos.ac.kr
Internet: www.uos.ac.kr

Founded 1918; Seoul City University until 1996
Maintained by Seoul Metropolitan Government
Language of instruction: Korean
Academic year: March to February

President: Dr SANG-BUM LEE
Provost of Academic Affairs: Dr HYUN-SOO MIN
Provost of General Administration: IN-SONG CHANG
Provost of Planning and Development: Dr EUI-YOUNG SON
Provost of Student Affairs: Dr KEUN-HEE CHOI
Director of Central Library: Dr YONG-GUN KIM

Library of 554,895 vols
Number of teachers: 302
Number of students: 14,867

Publication: *University Press* (26 a year)

DEANS

College of Economics and Business Administration: Dr JONG-DAE LEE
College of Engineering: Dr SUNG-IL CHO
College of Law and Public Administration: Dr YONG-CHAN PARK
College of Liberal Arts and Natural Sciences: Dr JUN-HO SONG
College of Urban Sciences: Dr HYUNG-SU HAN
Liberal Arts Division: Dr DONG-HA LEE
Graduate School: Dr JAE-BOK PARK
Graduate School of Business Administration: Dr JONG-DAE LEE
Graduate School of Engineering: Dr SUNG-IL CHO
Graduate School of Urban Administration: Dr HYUNG-SU HAN

DISTANCE LEARNING UNIVERSITIES (CYBER AND DIGITAL UNIVERSITIES)

BUSAN DIGITAL UNIVERSITY

167, Jurei-dong, Sasang-gu Bang Busan Seoul 617-701

Telephone: (51) 320-1919
Fax: (51) 320-1922
Internet: www.bdu.ac.kr

Founded 2002
Private

Divisions of Social Welfare, Society and Management, Hospitalities and Tourism. Digital Contents

Pres.: KIM MIN-SIK.

DAEGU CYBER UNIVERSITY

15 Naeri-ri, Jillyang-eup, Gyeongsan-si, Gyeongsangbuk-do, Seoul 712-714

Telephone: (53) 850-4000
Fax: (53) 850-4019
E-mail: idaegu@dcu.ac.kr
Internet: english.dcu.ac.kr

Founded 2001
Private

Pres.: LEE YOUNG SAE.

GUKJE DIGITAL UNIVERSITY

950-12 Ingye-dong, Paldal-gu, Suwon Gyeonggi-do, Seoul 442-832

Telephone: (31) 229-6200
Fax: (31) 267-0750
E-mail: admin@gdu.ac.kr
Internet: eng.gdu.ac.kr

Founded 2003
Private

Schools of Business Administration, Social Sciences, Lifelong Education, Physical and Health Arts

Pres.: PARK YOUNG-KYU
Vice-Pres.: LEE KYOUNG-WOO.

KOREA DIGITAL UNIVERSITY

1-21 Gye-dong, Jongno-gu, Seoul 110-800

Telephone: (2) 6361-1810
Internet: www.kdu.edu

Founded 2001

Pres.: KIM CHOONG SOON

Depts of applied culture, art studies, business administration, child english education, computer and information communication, continuing education, counselling psychology, information management and services, law, media design, media studies, practical foreign languages, real estate and economics, social welfare, taxation and accounting, youth studies.

KYUNG HEE CYBER UNIVERSITY

Seoul Campus: Hoegi-dong, Dongdaemun-gu, Seoul 130-701

Telephone: (2) 961-0031
Fax: (2) 962-4343
E-mail: cie@khu.ac.kr*Global Campus*: Seocheon-dong, Giheung-hu, Yongin-si, Gyeonggi-do, Seoul 446-701

Telephone: (31) 201-3177
Fax: (31) 201-3179
E-mail: intlctr@khu.ac.kr
Internet: www.kyunghee.edu

Founded 1949 as Shinheung Junior College, univ. status 1955, established online univ. 2000

Pres.: INWON CHOUE.

SEOUL CYBER UNIVERSITY

Mia 3-Dong 193, Gangbuk-gu, Seoul 142-700
Telephone: (2) 944-5000
Fax: (2) 980-2222
E-mail: joynlife@iscu.ac.kr
Internet: www.iscu.ac.kr
Founded 2000
Pres.: Dr SUSIE KIM
Number of students: 8,000
Schools of business and international management, general education, human welfare, information technology and design, psychology and counselling, social science\.

SEOUL DIGITAL UNIVERSITY

Jungdong Wonmi-gu, Bucheon, Gyeonggi-do, Seoul 420-020
Telephone: (2) 1544-0981
Fax: (2) 2128-300
E-mail: go@sdu.ac.kr
Internet: en.sdu.ac.kr
Pres.: PAEK J. CHO
Division of Liberal Arts and Social Science, IT and Cultural Arts.

WONKWANG DIGITAL UNIVERSITY

344-2 Sinyong-dong, Iksan-si, North Jeolla
Telephone: 1588-28554
Fax: (63) 843-2856
Internet: www.wdu.ac.kr
Founded 2001
Pres.: SUNG SI-JONG
Divisions of Wellbeing and Culture, Utility and Welfare.

Colleges

PUBLIC COLLEGES

Busan Women's College: 74 Yangjung-dong, Pusan Jin-ku, Pusan 614-734; tel. (51) 852-0081; fax (51) 867-4705; internet www .bwc.ac.kr; f. 1954; Divisions of Child Education, Tourism, Welfare and Health, Art, Business and Management, Applied Art.

Iksan National College: Seoul 570-752; tel. (63) 850-0500; e-mail w3master@iksan.ac.kr; internet www.iksan.ac.kr; f. 1922.

Korea National College of Rehabilitation and Welfare: 5-3 Jangan-dong, Pyongtaek-si, Gyeonggi-do; tel. (31) 610-4600; fax (31) 610-4930; internet www.hanrw.ac.kr; f. 2002.

Korea National Railroad College: 374-18 Wolam-Dong, Uiwang-Si, Gyeonggi-do; tel. (31) 461-4011; fax (31) 462-2944; internet english.krc.ac.kr; f. 1905; depts of introduction to liberal art, railroad electrical control, railroad facility engineering, railroad management information, railroad operation mechanism, railroad transportation management, railroad vehicle machine, railroad vehicle electricity; 27 teachers; 610 students.

National Medical Centre College of Nursing: Euljiro 6 St, 18-79 Jongno-gu, Seoul 100-196; tel. and fax (2) 2265-6339.

PRIVATE COLLEGES

Ansan College of Technology: 671 Choji-dong, Danwon-gu, Ansan Gyeonggi-do; tel. (31) 490-6191; e-mail sysop@act.ac.kr; internet eng.ansantc.ac.kr; f. 1979; Degree programmes in arts and sports, liberal arts and social sciences, natural sciences, technology; Pres. KANG SUNG NAK.

Agricultural Cooperative College: San 38-27, Goyang, Seoul 412-038; tel. (31) 960-4117; fax (31) 960-4119; e-mail hanaok@ nonghyup.or.kr; internet www.nonghyup.or .kr; f. 1962; courses in agricultural technology, computer science, marketing and MBA.

Andong Institute of Information and Technology: Andong, Gyeongsangbuk-do, Seoul 760-833; tel. (54) 820-8053; fax (54) 820-8055; e-mail info@ait.ac.kr; internet www.ait.ac.kr; f. 1972; library: 18,500 vols.

Busan Gyeongsang College: 277-4 Yeonsan 8 dong, Yeonje-gu, Busan; tel. (51) 850-1000; fax (51) 862-7577; e-mail busybee@bsks .ac.kr; internet www.cwc.ac.kr; f. 1977; Depts of advertising and interior design, advertising and public relations, airline services, child studies, distribution and logistics, early childhood education, hotel and tourism English, hotel and tourism management, international trade by Air and Sea, management, real estate management, social welfare and medical health administration, tax accounting, tourism Japanese; Pres. LEE DAL-DUK.

Cheju Tourism College: Seoul 690-791; tel. (64) 740-8700; fax (64) 748-2829; internet www.cjtour.ac.kr; f. 1993; as Jeju Tourism Technical College, present name 1998; courses in tourism, sports and leisure studies, and casino and hotel management; Pres. KIM CHANG-HU.

Chungkang College of Cultural Industries: Icheon, Seoul 467-810; tel. (31) 639-5743; fax (31) 639-5749; e-mail mjkang@ chungkang.ac.kr; internet www.chungkang .ac.kr; f. 1996; divs of Games and Animation, Industrial Design, Performing Arts, Information Communications, and Human Care; Pres. LEE SU-HYEONG.

Daedong College: 373-4 Bugok 2 dong, Keumjeong-gu, Busan, Seoul 609-715; tel. (51) 518-5444; fax (51) 514-5847; internet www.daedong.ac.k; f. 1971 as Daedong Nursing School, jnr college in 1979, full college status 1998; programmes in Nursing, Cosmetology, Child Welfare, and Leisure Tourism Management; Pres. KIM KYUNGHEE.

Daegu Mirae College: Mirae-gil 13, Gyeongsan, Gyeongbuk, Seoul 712-716; tel. (53) 810-9200; fax (53) 813-3162; internet www.dmc.ac.kr; f. 1981; Depts of engineering, fine arts, humanities and society, natural sciences, physical education; Pres. YONG BUM-KWON.

Gangneung Yeongdong College: 1009 Hongje-dong, Gangneung, Kangwon-do, Seoul 210-792; tel. (33) 610-0114; fax (33) 644-8809; internet www.yeongdong.ac.kr; f. 1963; programmes in nursing and health, depts of social welfare, tourism; Pres. KIM MYUNG HYUN.

Inha Technical College: 253 Yonghyun-dong, Nam-ku, Incheon, Seoul 402-752; tel. (32) 870-2114; fax (32) 868-3408; internet english.inhatc.ac.kr; f. 1958; 6,500 students; Pres. PARK CHOON-BAE.

Kaywon School of Art and Design: 66 Kaywondaehangno (Naeson-dong), Uiwang, Gyeonggi-do, Seoul 437-712; tel. (31) 420-1700; e-mail choihs@kaywon.ac.kr; internet foreign.kaywon.ac.kr; f. 1979 as Institute Foundation Kaywon School, present status 1990; faculties of Design, Fine Arts and Information Technology; Pres. KANG YOUNG-JIN.

KDI School of Public Policy and Management: 87 Hoegiro Dondaemun, Seoul 130-868; tel. (2) 3299-1114; e-mail admissions@kdischool.ac.kr; internet kdischool.ac.kr; f. 1997; Masters degree programme, PhD programme, and non-degree programmes; Dean SANG-MOON HAHM.

Seoul Institute of the Arts: 640 Gojan 2-Dong, Dwang-Gu, Ansan, Gyeonggi-do; tel. (31) 412-7100; fax (31) 412-7149; e-mail mschoi@seoularts.ac.kr; internet www .seoularts.ac.kr; f. 1958; programmes in applied music, broadcasting, creative advertising, creative writing, dance, digital arts and humanities, film, interior design, Korean traditional music, photography, playwriting, theatre, visual design; Chair. LEE GI HUNG.

Taekyeung College: 24 Tanpuk-ri, Chain-Myun, Kyungsan, Gyeongsangbuk-do, Seoul 712-851; tel. (53) 850-1361; fax (53) 850-1363; e-mail clsfae@tk.ac.kr; internet www.tk.ac .kr; f. 1993; offers 3-year programmes in early childhood education, entertainment and event management, film and broadcasting, nursing, theatre, visual optics; 2-year programmes in baking technology, beauty design and modelling, hotel culinary arts, police administration, real-estate management, security administration, social welfare, sports science, tourism and hotel management; Pres. YOO JIN-SUN.

Yeungnam College of Science and Technology: 274 Hyeonchung-ro, 1737 Daemyeong 7 dong, Nam-gu, Daegu, Seoul 705-703; tel. (53) 650-9114; fax (53) 624-7871; internet eng.ync.ac.kr; f. 1968; schools of civil engineering-architecture, cosmetics-chemistry, design, food-tourism, information technology, mechanical and automotive engineering technology, nursing healthpractical sociology; divs of electronics and information engineering, health science; Pres. LEE HO-SUNG.

KOSOVO

The Higher Education System

On 17 February 2008 the Serbian province of Kosovo unilaterally declared independence from the Republic of Serbia. By late June 2009 60 countries, including 19 European Union member states and the USA, had formally recognized the Republic of Kosovo. However, several countries, including the People's Republic of China and Russia, continued to withhold recognition. Russian opposition to independence for Kosovo prevented the approval of a resolution on the status of Kosovo by the UN Security Council.

Higher Education in Kosovo is regulated by the Ministry of Education, Science and Technology. Institutions licensed by the Ministry are permitted to operate; however, this does not equate to accreditation. That function is performed by the United Nations Mission in Kosovo (UNMIK). The Universiteti i Prishtinës (University of Prishtina) is the only public university. Private universities have been permitted to operate since 1999. Figures for 2007/08 show that there were 25,840 students enrolled at university level.

Individual universities have specific entrance requirements as well as admission examinations organized by each institution. The University of Prishtina began using the European Credit Transfer and Accumulation System (ECTS) in 2001/02 and the Ministry of Education, Science and Technology (MEST) is working with all higher education institutions to implement ECTS in all institutions. From 2001/2002, the University of Prishtina adopted the system of three study cycles, which includes the three-year Bachelors, two-year Masters, and three-year PhD. Exceptions to this are the Faculty of Medicine, the Department of Albanian Language and Literature, and the newly established Faculty of Education. During 2004/2005 the university enrolled the first students of the second cycle (Master of Arts or Science—two-year programme) in 45 departments across 11 Faculties. As a result of the 2003/04 higher education reforms a new Bologna-compliant three-cycle degree structure was introduced in Kosovo. Since 2006/07 the new programmes have been introduced gradually across all institutions.

At undergraduate level the qualifications are: Baccalaureus—the first cycle academic qualification leading to a Bachelors and requiring completion of 180–240 ECTS credits over a period of three to four years; Professional Baccalaureus—awarded with a professional title, requiring completion of 180–240 ECTS over a period of three to four years; Diplomirani (Graduation Diploma)—offered by universities after four to six or more years of full-time study following completion of secondary school; Diplomirani (Graduation Diploma)—awarded by higher schools after two to three years of full-time study; Proffesor—awarded after four years of full-time study following completion of the Secondary School Leaving Certificate; Doktor (Medical science)—awarded after six years of full-time study upon completion of 360 ECTS credits. At postgraduate level two types of qualification are offered: Masters—represents one year of postgraduate study (60 ECTS credits) after a four-year first cycle qualification or two years of postgraduate study (120 ECTS credits) after a three-year first cycle qualification, making a total of 300 ECTS credits in the first and second cycles; Magistar Umjetnosti/Znanosti (Master of Arts/Science)—awarded upon completion of two or more years of full-time study following a four-year Diplomirani; Specijalista—Specialist Diploma (professional or academic studies)—represents one year of full-time study following a Baccalaureus and to pass students must complete all examinations and a thesis; Doctor (Doctorate)—requires at least three years of full-time study and completion of 180 ECTS credits following a Masters degree; Doktor Znanosti (Doctor of Science)—can be completed in four or more years of full-time study following a Magistar.

The Kosovo Agency for Accreditation (KAA) was founded by the Ministry of Education, Science and Technology (MEST) in accordance with the Law on Higher Education (2003/14) in Kosovo, as an Agency which provides external evaluation and assists institutions to carry out self-evaluation. The KAA comprises three overseas and six Kosovo experts. This organization guarantees the quality of educational and scientific research work of public and private institutions of higher education.

Regulatory Bodies

GOVERNMENT

Ministry of Culture, Youth and Sports: 10000 Prishtina; tel. (38) 211-064; fax (38) 211-440; e-mail info@mkrs-ks.org; internet www.mkrs-ks.org; Minister VALTON BEQIRI.

Ministry of Education, Science and Technology: Rr. Musine Kokollari 18, Lagjja Dadania Blloku-III, 10000 Prishtina; tel. (38) 541-035; e-mail masht@ks-gov.net; internet www.masht-gov.net; Minister ENVER HOXHAJ; Permanent Sec. ADEM SALLAUKA.

Learned Societies

GENERAL

Akademia e Shkencave dhe e Arteve e Kosovës (Kosovo Academy of Sciences and Arts): Rr. Emin Duraku 1, 10000 Prishtina; tel. (38) 249-303; fax (38) 244-636; e-mail ashak_pr@hotmail.com; internet www.ashak .org; f. 1975; promotes research in science, culture and language; Pres. REXHEP ISMAJLI;

Vice-Pres. BESIM BOKSHI; Sec.-Gen. HIVZI ISLAMI.

Fondacionin e Kosovës për Shoqëri të Hapur (Kosovo Foundation for Open Society): Ulpiana, Imzot Nikëprelaj, Villa 13, 10000 Prishtina; tel. (38) 542-157; fax (38) 542-157; e-mail info@kfos.org; internet www .kfos.org; f. 1993, present status and name 1999; non-governmental org.; focuses on minority rights, civic participation, European integration, governance and education; Exec. Dir LUAN SHILAKU; Chair. BLERIM SHALA.

BIBLIOGRAPHY, LIBRARY SCIENCE AND MUSEOLOGY

Shoqata e Bibliotekarëve të Kosovës (Association of Libraries of Kosovo): Sheshi 'Hasan Prishtina', 10000 Prishtina; tel. (38) 212-419; f. 1971; protects the rights of library employees; creates better working conditions; raises professionalism and expands professional activity of the libraries.

ECONOMICS, LAW AND POLITICS

Riinvest Instituti për Hulumtime Zhvillimore (Institute for Development Research): AAB-Riinvest Univ., Bldg 2, K/4

Industrial Zone, 10000 Prishtina; tel. (38) 601-320; fax (38) 601-233; e-mail riinvest@ riinvestinstitute.org; internet www .riinvestinstitute.org; f. 1995; non-profit, research organization; research and analysis of business sectors, policy-making and advocacy in business devt; Pres. MUHAMET MUSTAFA; Vice-Pres Dr MUHAMET SADIKU, SEJDI OSMANI.

Research Institutes

GENERAL

Instituti Kosovar për Kërkime dhe Zhvillime të Politikave (Kosovar Institute for Policy Research and Development): Rexhep Mala 5A, 2nd fl., Prishtina; tel. (38) 227-778; e-mail info@kipred.net; internet www.kipred.net; f. 2002; independent research; policymaking; political analysis; discussion papers and publs; training of political parties and govt; Chair. MENTOR AGANI; Exec. Dir ILIR DEDA.

MEDICINE

Instituti Kombëtar i Shëndetësisë Publike te Kosoves (National Institute of Public

Health of Kosovo): Rr. Nëna Tereze, Rrethi i Spitalit, 10000 Prishtina; tel. (38) 550-585; e-mail info@niph-kosova.org; internet www .niph-kosova.org; f. 1925; prepares and implements nat. public health strategy; Dir Assoc. Prof. Dr NASER RAMADANI.

Library
Prishtina

Biblioteka 'Hivzi Sylejmani': tel. (38) 232-980; f. built in 1930, 1948 as Prishtina City Library.

Biblioteka Kombëtare dhe Universitare e Kosovës (National and University Library of Kosovo): Sheshi Nëna Tereza 5, 10000 Prishtina; internet www.biblioteka-ks.org; f. 1944; 600,000 vols; Dir Prof. Dr SALI BASHOTA.

Museums and Art Galleries
Prishtina

Galeria e Arteve e Kosovës (Kosovo Art Gallery): Rr. Agmin Ramadani 60, Prishtina; tel. (38) 227-833; e-mail gak@ipko.org; internet www.kosovaart.com; attached to Min. of Culture and Sports; exhibits 2-dimensional work of young local artists; workshops with children.

Muzeu i Kosovës (Kosovo Museum): Sheshi Adam Jashari; tel. (38) 249-964; f. built 1898, served as HQ for Yugoslav Nat. Army 1945–75; colln of prehistoric objects uncovered in Kosovo; exhibits incl. clay statue of sitting goddess from the late Neolithic period found in Tjerrtorja in 1955, also featured in Prishtina city emblem; archeological and ethnological artefacts, approx. 1,250 items moved to Belgrade for an exhibition are still to be returned.

Prishtina Ethnological Museum: Emin Gjik Complex, Rr. Zija 1, Prishtina; tel. (38) 211-394; f. 1957 as home to Emin Gjinolli's family, used as Natural museum till 1990, renovated with int. donations 2003, opened in present form 2006; attached to Muzeu i Kosovës (Kosovo Museum); displays the urban oda (saloon), folk dresses, folk instruments, Kosovo's heritage of filigree jewellery influenced by Sephardic Jews and practiced in Prizren and Gjakova, carpet work, locally produced weapons of the time and religious objects dating back to the Illyrian ancestors.

Universities

AMERICAN UNIVERSITY IN KOSOVO (AUK)

Nazim Gafurri 21, 10000 Prishtina
Telephone: (38) 518-542
Fax: (38) 518-458
E-mail: info@aukonline.org
Internet: www.aukonline.org
Private control
Language of instruction: English
Founded 2003

In partnership with the Rochester Institute of Technology, New York; offers undergraduate and graduate courses

Library of 900 books, magazines, daily newspapers, reference materials, classroom materials, electronic technology resources, videos and DVDs

Pres.: CHRISTOPHER HALL
Registrar: ARIANA HAXHIU-KADRIU
Librarian: HAZBIJE QERIQI
Dir of AUK Institute: BEKIM KASUMI
Academic Dir: PETER BOYD.

UNIVERSITETI AAB
(AAB University)

Zona Industriale, 10000 Prishtina
Telephone: (38) 247-524
E-mail: info@universitetiaab.com
Internet: www.universitetiaab.com
Founded 2001 as Academy of Liberal Arts
Private control

Offers Bachelors and Masters courses in Economics, Law, Mass Communication, Sport; houses Research Centre for Juridical, Criminological and Security Studies, Research Centre for Economic Prognoses, Centre for Sport Research, Centre for Architecture and Arts, Centre for Culture and Language Research and Centre for Public Opinion Research

Rector: Dr UROS LIPUSCEK

Library: scientific and academic publs, electronic study material

DEANS

Faculty of Applied and Figurative Arts: Prof. Dr BUJAR DEMJAHA
Faculty of Criminological Sciences: Prof. Dr RAMO MASLESA
Faculty of Economics: Prof. Dr FETAH REÇICA
Faculty of Education: Prof. Dr ISMAIL HASANI
Faculty of Foreign Languages: Prof. Dr MASAR STAVILECI
Faculty of Law: Prof. Dr MERSIM MAKSUTI
Faculty of Mass Communication: Prof. Dr RRAHMAN PAÇARIZI
Faculty of Music Arts: Prof. Dr BAKI JASHARI
Faculty of Sport: Prof. Dr MEHDI JASHARI

UNIVERSITETI I PRISHTINËS
(University of Prishtina)

Sheshi Nëna Tereze 5, 10000 Prishtina
Telephone: (38) 244-183
Fax: (38) 244-187
E-mail: info@uni-pr.edu
Internet: www.uni-pr.edu
Founded 1970
State control
Academic year: September to June

Rector: Prof. Dr MUJË RUGOVA
Vice-Rector for Int. Cooperation: Prof. Dr NASER MRASORI
Vice-Rector for Resources and Infrastructure: Prof. Dr ENVER KUTLLOVCI
Vice-Rector for Teaching and Scientific Research: Prof. Dr BAJRAM BERISHA

Library: see Libraries and Archives
Number of teachers: 756
Number of students: 14,000

Publications: *Acta Biologiae et Medicinae Experimentalis*, *Pregled Predavanja*, *Univerzitetska Misao*

DEANS

Faculty of Agriculture: Prof. SHUKRI FETAHU
Faculty of Arts: Prof. Dr HIVZI MUHARREMI
Faculty of Business: (vacant)
Faculty of Civil Engineering and Architecture: Prof. Dr MUSA STAVILECI
Faculty of Economics: Prof. Dr IBRAHIM KUKA
Faculty of Electrical Engineering and Computing: Dr LUAN AHMA
Faculty of Journalism: (vacant)

Faculty of Law: Prof. Dr BEQIR SADIKAJ
Faculty of Mechanical Engineering: Prof. Dr ISMAJL GOJANI
Faculty of Medicine: Prof. Dr BAJRAM NURAJ
Faculty of Mining and Metallurgy: Prof. Dr KADRI BERISHA
Faculty of Natural Sciences and Mathematics: Prof. Dr MUSTAFË BYTYÇI
Faculty of Philology: Prof. Dr NUHI REXHEPI
Faculty of Philosophy: Dr SELIM DACI
Faculty of Physical Education and Sport: Prof. Dr MUSTAFË ALIU
Faculty of Political Science: (vacant)
Faculty of Teacher Training: Prof. Dr SADIK RASHITI

UNIVERSITETI I PRIZRENIT
(University of Prizren)

Tirana St, 20000 Prizren
Telephone: (29) 631-403
E-mail: info@uni-pz.org
Internet: www.uni-pz.org
Founded 2006
Private control

Faculties of Architecture, Computer Science, Economy, English Literature, Law, Political Science, Psychology
Library of 13,398 vols, 3,600 periodicals.

UNIVERSITETI I VIZIONIT EVROPIAN
(European Vision University)

Rr. Wesley Clark, 30000 Pejë
Telephone: (39) 31684
Fax: (39) 31676
E-mail: info@evun.eu
Internet: www.evun.eu
Founded 2006
Private control

Bachelors and Masters programmes in Biotechnology, Economics, Education, Engineering and Law

Rector: Prof. Dr EDMOND BEQIRI.

UNIVERSITETI MBRETËROR ILIRIA
(Iliria Royal University)

Rr. Gamend Zajmi 75, 10000 Prishtina
Telephone: (38) 233-951
E-mail: info@uiliria.org
Internet: www.uiliria.org
Private control

Univ. under patronage of the royal family; offers, Bachelors, Masters, doctoral courses.

UNIVERSITETI PËR BIZNES DHE TEKNOLOGJI
(University of Business and Technology)

Lagija Kalabria, 10000 Prishtina
Telephone: (38) 541-400
Fax: (38) 542-138
E-mail: info@ubt-uni.net
Internet: www.ubt-uni.net
Private control
Languages of instruction: English, Albanian, French, German

Bachelors and Masters courses in Architecture and Spatial Planning, Computer Science and Engineering, Law, Political Science and Economy, Management, Business and Economy, Public Health and Social Sciences; attached institutes: Institute for Enterprise Management and Engineering (IEME), Int. Languages and Intercultural Competence (ILIC), Institute for Int. Relations and European Studies (IIRES)

Pres.: Dr EDMOND HAJRIZI.

KUWAIT

The Higher Education System

Kuwait University (founded 1962) is the sole public university. In 2005/06 it had about 20,000 students enrolled out of an estimated total of 37,521 students in tertiary education. In 2009 there were also 12 private universities, including the American University of the Middle East, American University of Kuwait and the Arab Open University, which were accredited by the Private Universities Council of the Ministry of Higher Education. It is Government policy to provide free education for all Kuwaiti citizens from primary to tertiary level. Students for courses not offered by Kuwait University are offered scholarships to study abroad. In May 1996 the National Assembly approved a draft law to regulate students' behaviour, dress and activities, with regard to observance of the teachings of Shari'a (Islamic) law, and to eradicate coeducational classes at Kuwait University over a five-year period. A KD-1,000m. project to build a new university campus and to gather the institution's dispersed facilities onto one site was in the planning stages in early 2005.

Admission to university-level undergraduate courses is on the basis of the General Secondary Education Certificate (Shahadat-al-thanawia-al-a'ama). The Bachelors degree is arranged on a US-style 'credit semester' system and usually lasts four years, except for professional programmes such as engineering and medicine, which last five and seven years, respectively. Masters degrees at Kuwait University last up to two years and are available in most subjects.

The Public Authority for Applied Education and Training oversees technical and vocational education. The institutions that offer vocational education are the Vocational Training Institute, Industrial Training Institute, College of Technological Studies and Nursing Institute. There are also Colleges of Basic Education, Business Studies and Health Studies offering two- to four-year courses leading to the award of a professional Diploma.

Regulatory and Representative Bodies

GOVERNMENT

Ministry of Education: POB 7, 13001 Safat, Hilali St, Kuwait City; tel. 24836800; fax 22423676; e-mail webmaster@moe.edu.kw; internet www.moe.edu.kw; Minister NOURIYA SUBEEH BARRAK AS-SUBEEH.

Ministry of Higher Education: Safat; tel. 22401300; e-mail info_minister@mohe.edu.kw; internet www.mohe.edu.kw; Minister NOURIYA SUBEEH BARRAK AS-SUBEEH.

ACCREDITATION

Private Universities Council: POB 26166, 13122 Safat; tel. 22240591; fax 22455326; e-mail imad@puc.edu.kw; internet www.puc.edu.kw; f. 2001; affiliated to Higher Education Council; ensures conformity with all rules and stipulations for licensing private educational instns; Chair. MINISTER OF HIGHER EDUCATION; Sec.-Gen. IMAD ALATIQI.

NATIONAL BODY

Public Authority for Applied Education and Training: POB 23167, 13092 Safat; tel. 22564960; fax 22528915; e-mail bscg@paaet.edu.kw; internet www.paaet.edu.kw; f. 1982; autonomous body supervising technical and vocational training; the applied education sector comprises College of Basic Education, College of Business Studies, College of Technological Studies and College of Health Sciences; institutes in operation are Telecommunications and Navigation Institute, Electricity and Water Institute, Industrial Training Institute (brs in Shuwaikh and Sabah Al-Salem), Nursing Institute, Constructional Training Institute and Vocational Training Institute.

Learned Societies

GENERAL

National Council for Culture, Arts and Letters: POB 23996, 13100 Safat; tel. 22469090; fax 22432331; internet www.kuwait-info.com/a_culture/culture_nccal.asp; f. 1973; guidance and support in all fields of culture; sponsors art exhibitions, drama, publishes books and periodicals; Sec.-Gen. BADER S. A. AL-REIFA; publs Al-Thaqafa al-'Alamiyah, Alam al-Fikr, Alam Al-Ma'arifa, Ibda'at 'Alamiyah, Al-Fonon.

LANGUAGE AND LITERATURE

British Council: 2 Al Arabi St, Block 2, POB 345, 13004 Safat, Mansouria, Kuwait City; tel. 22520067; fax 22520069; e-mail info@kw.britishcouncil.org; internet www.britishcouncil.org/kuwait; teaching centre; offers courses and exams in English language and British culture and promotes cultural exchange with the UK; library of 9,000 vols; Dir (acting), Teaching Centre Man. JOHN PARE.

MEDICINE

Kuwait Medical Association: POB 1202, 13013 Safat; tel. 25312630; fax 25317972; e-mail kmj@kma.org.kw; internet www.kma.org.kw/kmj; f. 1967; library of 42 vols; Pres. Dr ALI ALMUKAIMI; Sec.-Gen. Dr MOHAMMED SHAMSAH; publ. Kuwait Medical Journal (4 a year).

Kuwait Medical Genetics Centre: tel. 24814328; fax 24842073; e-mail ihgck2008@gmail.com; internet www.kmgc.info; Chair. Dr SADIKA AL-AWADI.

Research Institutes

ECONOMICS, LAW AND POLITICS

Arab Planning Institute, Kuwait: POB 5834, 13059 Safat; tel. 24843130; fax 24842935; e-mail api@api.org.kw; internet www.arab-api.org; f. 1966 with assistance from the UN Devt Programme, and since 1972 financed by 15 Arab mem. states; trains personnel in economic and social devt planning; undertakes research and advisory work and organizes confs and seminars on problems affecting economic and social devt in the Arab world; library: information centre consisting of 60,000 vols (24,000 Arabic, 36,000 English), 400 periodicals (in English and Arabic); Dir-Gen. Dr ESSA M. AL-GHAZALI; publs API working paper series (in Arabic and English, irregular), Development Bridge (in Arabic, 10 a year), Journal of Development and Economic Policies (in Arabic and English, 2 a year).

EDUCATION

Gulf Arab States Educational Research Centre: POB 12580, 71656 Shamia; tel. 24835203; fax 24830571; e-mail gaserc@kuwait.net; internet www.gaserc.edu.kw; f. 1978 as part of Arab Bureau of Education for the Gulf States; research on all educational topics; also provides training courses in developed curricula, educational statistics, educational evaluation, and educational research; Dir Prof. MARZOUG Y. ALGHOUNIAM; Librarian MOHEI A. HAK; publ. Al-Hasaad Al-Terbawi (Arabic Text) (6 a year).

MEDICINE

Arabization Centre for Medical Sciences: POB 5225, 13053 Safat; tel. 25338610; fax 25338618; e-mail acmls@acmls.org; internet www.acmls.org; f. 1983; part of Council of Arab Ministers of Health—Arab League; aims: the Arabization of medical literature and translation into Arabic of medical sciences, development of a current bibliographic database, issuing of Arabic medical directories, training of manpower in the field of medical information and library science; library of 1,000 vols; Sec.-Gen. Dr ABDEL RAHMAN AL-AWADI; publs Arab Medical Doctors Directory, Directory of Health Education and Research Organizations in Arab Countries, Directory of Hospitals and Clinics in Arab World.

Kuwait Institute for Medical Specialization: POB 1793, 13018 Safat; tel. 22418782; fax 22410028; e-mail info@kims.org.kw; internet www.kims.org.kw; attached to Ministry of Health; f. 1984; publ. Journal.

NATURAL SCIENCES

General

Kuwait Foundation for the Advancement of Science: POB 25263, 13113 Safat; tel. 22425898; fax 22415365; internet www.kfas.com; f. 1976; promotes scientific and technological advancement, provides financial aid for research projects, organizes symposia and conferences, develops Arabic-language publications; Dir ALI A. AL-SHAMLAN; publs *Al-Taqaddum al-Ilmi* (Scientific Advancement, 4 a year), *Majallat Al-Oloom* (12 a year).

Kuwait Institute for Scientific Research: POB 24885, 13109 Safat; tel. 24989360; fax 24989359; e-mail public_relations@safat.kisr.edu.kw; internet www.kisr.edu.kw; f. 1967; promotes and conducts scientific research in the fields of food resources, water resources, oil sector support, environmental studies, infrastructure services and urban devt, and economics and applied systems; Dir-Gen. Dr NAJI MOHAMED AL-MUTAIRI; publ. *Science and Technology*.

Libraries and Archives
Kuwait City

Kuwait University Libraries: POB 23558, Kuwait City; e-mail jac.lib@kuniv.edu; internet library.kuniv.edu.kw; f. 1966; 233,733 vols, 2,445 periodicals, 1,298 electronic journals, 20,000 audiovisual items; Dir DHIYA' ALJASIM.

Safat

National Library of Kuwait: POB 26182, 13122 Safat; tel. 22415181; fax 22415195; e-mail acq@nlk.gov.kw; internet www.nlk.gov.kw; f. 1936; nat. and UN depository library; nat. ISBN agency; nat. bibliographic centre; special colln *Kuwaitiana*; over 300,000 vols in Arabic and English, 750 periodicals; Dir-Gen. IMAD ABULBANAT.

National Scientific and Technical Information Centre: Kuwait Institute for Scientific Research, POB 24885, 13109 Safat; tel. 4818713; fax 4836097.

Museums and Art Galleries
Safat

Department of Antiquities and Museums: POB 23996, 13100 Safat; tel. 22426521; fax 22404862; Dir Dr FAHED AL-WOHAIBI.

Museums Controlled by the Department:

Failaka Island Archaeological Museum: exhibits from excavations.

Failaka Island Ethnographic Museum: colln of material from Failaka Island, housed in the old residence of the island's Sheikh.

Kuwait National Museum: Arabian Gulf St, Kuwait City; f. 1957; antiquities from late Bronze Age to Hellenistic period, found at Failaka Island; ethnographic material.

Educational Science Museum: Ministry of Education, POB 7, 13001 Safat; tel. 22421268; fax 22446078; f. 1972; lectures, exhibitions, film shows, etc.; sections on natural history, science, space, oil, health; planetarium, meteorology; library of 2,000 vols; Dir ADNAN AL-ALI.

Salmiya

Scientific Centre, The: POB 3504, 22036 Salmiya; tel. 1848888; fax 25710298; e-mail info@tsck.org.kw; internet www.tsck.org.kw; educational facility with architectural design reflecting Islamic art and culture; walls contain ceramic depictions of Kuwait's history; bldg comprises Aquarium, Discovery Place and IMAX Theatre.

Universities

AMERICAN UNIVERSITY OF KUWAIT

POB 3323, 13034 Safat
Telephone: 2224399
Fax: 25715860
E-mail: president@auk.edu.kw
Internet: www.auk.edu.kw
Founded 2003, accredited in 2006
Private control

Liberal arts, co-educational

Pres.: Dr TIM SULLIVAN
Exec. Dir: ERNEST E. COKLIN
Dean for Academic Affairs: Dr NIZAR HAMZEH
Dean for Student Affairs: Dr CAROL ROSS
Dir for Public Relations: AMAL AL-BINALI
Registrar: JILL ALLGIER
Librarian: AMNA AL-OMARE
Number of teachers: 125

ARAB OPEN UNIVERSITY

POB 32004, Al-Jabria
Telephone: 24767291
Fax: 24767286
E-mail: director@aou.edu.kw
Internet: www.aou.edu.kw
Founded 2003
Private control, in partnership with Open University, UK

Pres. and Chair.: HRH Prince TALAL BIN ABDULAZIZ
Dir: Prof. ISMAIL TAQI

Faculties of Business Administration, Education, General Studies, IT and Computing, Language Studies.

AUSTRALIAN COLLEGE OF KUWAIT

POB 1411, 13015 Safat
Telephone: 25376111
Fax: 25376222
Internet: www.ack.edu.kw
Founded 2004
Private control

Pres.: ABDULLAH ABDUL MOHSEN AL SHARHAN
Depts of Business Studies and Engineering.

GULF UNIVERSITY FOR SCIENCE AND TECHNOLOGY

POB 7207, 32093 Hawally
Telephone: 25307000
Fax: 25307030
E-mail: info@gust.edu.kw
Internet: www.gust.edu.kw
Founded 2002
Private control

Pres.: Dr ABDUL-RAHMAN SALEH AL-MUHAILAN
Dean of Student Affairs: Dr SABAH AL-QUADDOOMI
Librarian: SHOBHITA KOHLI
Library of 8,500 vols, 170 periodicals

DEANS

College of Arts and Sciences: Dr RAY WEISBORN
College of Business Administration: Prof. HUSSEIN AL-TALAFHA

PROFESSORS

AL-TALAFHA, H., Business Administration
ANKLI, R., Economics and Management
SAVAGE, A. J., Managemant and Marketing

KUWAIT UNIVERSITY

POB 5969, 13060 Safat
Telephone: 24845839
Fax: 24848648
E-mail: info@kuniv.edu
Internet: www.kuniv.edu.kw
Founded 1962, inaugurated 1966
State control

Language of instruction: Arabic, except in faculties of science, engineering and petroleum, allied health science and nursing, medicine and department of English
Academic year: September to June (2 semesters)

Chancellor: HE THE MINISTER OF HIGHER EDUCATION
Pres.: Prof. NADER AL-JALLAL
Vice-Pres. for Academic Affairs: Prof. HASSAN AL-ALAWI
Vice-Pres. for Planning and Evaluation: Dr MOUDI AL-HUMOUD
Vice-Pres. for Research and Graduate Studies: Dr ASSAD ISMAEL
Dean of Admissions and Registration: Dr ABDULLA AL-FUHAID
Sec.-Gen.: Dr AHMED AL-DEKHIL (acting)
Library Dir: Dr HUSEIN AL-ANSARI
Library: see Libraries and Archives
Number of teachers: 4,530
Number of students: 19,320

Publications: *Annals of the Faculty of Arts* (12 a year), *Arab Journal for the Humanities* (4 a year), *Arab Journal of Linguistics*, *Arab Journal of Management Sciences* (3 a year), *Educational Journal* (4 a year), *Islamic Studies Magazine* (3 a year), *Journal of Gulf and Arabian Peninsula* (4 a year), *Journal of Law* (4 a year), *Journal of Palestine Studies*, *Journal of Science* (2 a year), *Journal of the Social Sciences* (4 a year), *Medical Principles and Practice* (4 a year)

DEANS

College of Allied Health Sciences and Nursing: Dr HABIB ABUL
College of Arts: Dr SHAFIQA BASTAKI
College of Business Administration: Dr ADEL AL-HUSSAINAN
College of Dentistry: Dr JAWAD BEHBEHANI
College of Education: Dr RASHID ALI AL-SAHEL
College of Engineering and Petroleum: Prof. ABDUL-LATEEF AL-KHALEEFI
College of Graduate Studies: Dr ABDULLA AL-SHEIKH
College of Law: Dr FADEL NASRALLAH
College of Medicine: Dr JAWAD BEHBEHANI
College of Pharmacy: Dr LADISLAV NOVOTNY
College of Science: Prof. REDHA AL-HASAN
College of Shari'a and Islamic Studies: Dr MOHAMMED AL-TABTABAIE
College of Social Sciences: Dr ALI A. AL-TARRAH
Women's College: Dr AHMET YIGIT

KUWAIT–MAASTRICHT BUSINESS SCHOOL

Block 3, Kazima St, Dasma
Telephone: 22517091
Fax: 22545791
E-mail: info@kmbs.edu.kw
Internet: www.kmbs.edu.kw
Founded 2003
Private control

Pres.: KHALEEL AL-ABDULLAH
Dir: ROSEMARY LLOYD
Head of Academic Affairs: Prof. HERNAN RIQUELME

PROFESSORS

MAGALHAES, R., Information Systems and Organization

NIKOLIK, D. A., E-Business

RIQUELME, H., Entrepreneurship and Strategy

RWEGASIRA, K. S. P., Financial Management and Accounting

SYBRANDY, A., Marketing

TUNINGA, R. S. J., International Business and Marketing

Colleges

Box Hill College Kuwait: POB 29192, 13152 Safat; tel. 22471703; fax 22471701; e-mail info@bhck.edu.kw; internet www .bhck.edu.kw; Private college for women; attached to Box Hill Institute TAFE, Melbourne, Australia; Pres. EISA AL-REFAI; Exec. Vice-Pres. for Admin. JOE ALBAYATI.

College of Basic Education: Female Campus, POB 34053, 73251 Adailiya; tel. 24816044; e-mail bscg@paaet.edu.kw; f. 1973; attached to Public Authority for Applied Education and Training; BA degree courses in Education; depts of Arabic language, education, educational technology, home economics, library sciences, interior design, Islamic sciences, mathematics, music education, physical education, psychology, sciences, social studies, teaching of arts.

College of Business Studies: Male Campus, POB 43197, 32046 Hawalli; tel. 22633622; fax 22622439; e-mail bim@paaet .edu.kw Female Campus, POB 44069, 32055 Hawalli; tel. 26169913; e-mail bif@paaet edu

.kw; f. 1975; attached to Public Authority for Applied Education and Training; depts of administration and secretarial studies, accountancy, economics, English language, insurance and banking, office training, typewriting.

College of Health Sciences: Female Campus, POB 14281, 72853 Shuwaikh; tel. 24837056; fax 24811920; e-mail chsh@paaet .edu.kw Male Campus, POB 33496, 73455 Rawda; tel. 22570115; fax 22527187; e-mail chsm@paaet.edu.kw; f. 1974; attached to Public Authority for Applied Education and Training; Assoc. Degree courses; depts of environmental health, food sciences and nutrition, medical records, natural sciences,- nursing, oral and dental health, pharmaceutical and medical sciences.

College of Technological Studies: POB 42325, 70654 Shuwaikh; tel. 24816122; fax 24843143; internet www.paaet.edu.kw/cts; f. 1976; attached to Public Authority for Applied Education and Training; Assoc. Degree courses; depts of air conditioning and refrigeration, applied sciences, chemical engineering, civil engineering, electrical engineering, and power engineering, electronic engineering, motor vehicle and marine engineering, production engineering and welding; library: 6,510 vols, 180 periodicals; 322 teachers; 1,950 students; Dean Dr ADEL S. AL-JIMAZ.

Constructional Training Institute: POB 23167, 13092 Safat; tel. 4833186; fax 4838719; f. 2000; Public Authority for Applied Education and Training; attached to German Institute for Technical Cooperation; training programmes in Build-

ing Construction, Civil Engineering, Interior Finishing, Mechanics.

Electricity and Water Institute: POB 15196, 35452 Daiyah; tel. 22570252; fax 2575293; Public Authority for Applied Education and Training; two-year courses aimed at fulfilling requirements of Ministry of Water and Electricity in electrical power stations, water distillation plants, water pumps, operation of reverse osmosis units, maintenance of electrical networks.

Industrial Training Institute: POB 1236, 44000 Sabah el-Salem; tel. 25520037; f. 1992; Public Authority for Applied Education and Training; three-year courses to Technician level.

Institute of Banking Studies: POB 1080, 13011 Safat; tel. 22458460; fax 22434705; internet www.kibs.edu.kw; f. 1970 as Banking Studies Center; present name and Specialized Institute status 1982; Dir RIDHA M. AL KHAYYAT; accredited certificates in Islamic Banking and Financial Services, Credit Management, Investment Management.

Nursing Institute: Al-Sabah Hospital, POB 22195, 13098 Safat; tel. 24819036; f. 1962; Public Authority for Applied Education and Training; General Nursing Programme.

Vocational Training Institute: Sharq, POB 23167, 13092 Safat; tel. 22422116; Public Authority for Applied Education and Training; four-year courses in automotive electric, refrigeration and air conditioning maintenance, automotive mechanics, cabinet work and decoration, formwork and reinforced concrete, electrical installation, offset printing, welding and metal casting.

KYRGYZSTAN

The Higher Education System

Following the Russian revolution in 1917, Kyrgyzstan was established as an autonomous region within the Russian Soviet Federated Socialist Republic (RSFSR). In 1936 it was recognized as a full Union member of the Soviet Union and became the Kyrgyz Soviet Socialist Republic. The oldest institutions of higher education were founded during the early years of Soviet rule, among them Jalal-Abad State University (founded 1926), Kyrgyz National University 'Zhusup Balasagyn' (founded 1932; current name 1993) and Kyrgyz Agrarian Academy (founded 1933). In August 1991 Kyrgyzstan declared its independence from the Soviet Union. The Ministry of Education and Science is responsible for the administration of higher education, which in 2007/08 consisted of 49 public and private establishments, with total enrolment of 250,460 students. Higher education is governed according to the Law on Education (1992). Some institutions of a specialist or professional nature are administered by the appropriate Government ministry, and several universities are run on a cooperative basis between the Kyrgyz Government and governments of other countries, such as Kyrgyz–Russian Slavic University (founded 1992) and Kyrgyz–Turkish University 'Manas' (founded 1995). The State Licence and Attestation Inspection of Educational Institutions of the Ministry of Education of Kirghizia is the accrediting agency for higher education.

Admission to higher education is on the basis of the Certificate of Completed Secondary Education and success in university entrance examinations (which have been administered since 2003 by the United States Agency for International Development—USAID). Kyrgyzstan operates a dual system of the old Soviet-style degrees alongside Bachelors and Masters degrees. The old-style Specialist Diploma is a five-year programme of study, followed by the Candidate of Science (two years) and Doctor of Science (research only) programmes. Alternatively, an undergraduate may study for four years for the Bachelors degree, followed by a two-year Masters degree, before progressing onto the Candidate of Science and Doctor of Science programmes.

In 2002 the Ministry of Education and Science established a quality assurance department and universities are now required to introduce measures for quality assurance.

The Education Development Strategy of the Kyrgyz Republic (2007–2010) includes plans to bring the education system in line with the Bologna Declaration.

Regulatory Bodies

GOVERNMENT

Ministry of Culture and Information: 720040 Bishkek, Pushkina 78; tel. (312) 62-12-00; Minister SULTAN A. RAYEV.

Ministry of Education and Science: 720040 Bishkek, Tynystanova 257; tel. (312) 62-36-33; fax (312) 62-36-22; e-mail monk@monk.bishkek.gov.kg; Minister ISHENKUL S. BOLJUROVA.

ACCREDITATION

State Licence and Attestation Inspection of Educational Institutions of the Ministry of Education: Bishkek; tel. (312) 66-22-87; e-mail bakul@yandex.ru; Head BAKTYHBEK ISKAKOVICH ISMAILOV.

Learned Societies

GENERAL

National Academy of Sciences of the Kyrgyz Republic: 720071 Bishkek, Chuy pr. 265A; tel. (312) 61-00-93; fax (312) 24-36-07; e-mail interdep@aknet.kg; internet academ.aknet.kg; f. 1954; depts of Physical-Engineering, Mathematical and Mining-Geological Sciences, Chemical-Technological, Medical-Biological and Agricultural Sciences, Humanities; 133 mems (42 permanent, 58 corresp., 33 foreign); attached research institutes: see Research Institutes; library: see Libraries and Archives; Pres. J. JEYENBAYEV; Chief Sec. Academician A. ALDASHEV; publ. *Izvestiya* (bulletin).

BIBLIOGRAPHY, LIBRARY SCIENCE AND MUSEOLOGY

Library Association of Kyrgyzstan: 720044 Bishkek, pr. Tynchtyk 27; tel. (312) 48-41-34; fax (312) 48-40-35; Pres. T. SHAYMERGENOVA.

HISTORY, GEOGRAPHY AND ARCHAEOLOGY

Kyrgyz Geographical Society: 720081 Bishkek, bul. Erkindik 30; tel. (312) 26-47-21; Chair. S. U. UMURZAKOV.

LANGUAGE AND LITERATURE

Alliance Française: 720026 Bishkek, c/o French Consulate, ul. Razakov 49; tel. (312) 66-03-64; fax (312) 66-04-41; e-mail alliancefrancokirghiz@yahoo.fr; offers courses and examinations in French language and culture and promotes cultural exchange with France.

British Council: see entry in Kazakhstan chapter.

Research Institutes

AGRICULTURE, FISHERIES AND VETERINARY SCIENCE

Institute of Forest and Walnut Studies: 720015 Bishkek, Karagachovaya rosha 15; tel. (312) 67-90-82; e-mail institute@lesic.elcat.kg; f. 1992; attached to Nat. Acad. of Sciences of the Kyrgyz Republic; Dir E. TURDUKULOV.

ECONOMICS, LAW AND POLITICS

Centre for Economic Research: 720071 Bishkek, Chuy pr. 265A; tel. (312) 24-26-90; fax (312) 24-36-07; e-mail cer49@mail.ru; f. 1998; attached to Nat. Acad. of Sciences of the Kyrgyz Republic; Dir T. S. DYIKANBAYEVA.

Institute of Philosophy and Law: 720071 Bishkek, Chuy pr. 265A; tel. (312) 24-38-27; e-mail togusakov@mail.ru; f. 1958; attached to Nat. Acad. of Sciences of the Kyrgyz Republic; Dir O. A. TOGUSAKOV.

FINE AND PERFORMING ARTS

National Centre for 'Manas' Studies and Fine Arts: 720071 Bishkek, Chuy pr. 265A; tel. (312) 24-34-68; f. 1995; attached to Nat. Acad. of Sciences of the Kyrgyz Republic; Dir A. AKMATALIYEV.

HISTORY, GEOGRAPHY AND ARCHAEOLOGY

Institute of History: 720071 Bishkek, Chuy pr. 265A; tel. (312) 65-54-95; e-mail inst_history@hotmail.kg; f. 1954; attached to Nat. Acad. of Sciences of the Kyrgyz Republic; Dir J. JUNASHALIYEV.

LANGUAGE AND LITERATURE

Institute of Linguistics: 720071 Bishkek, Chuy pr. 265A; tel. (312) 24-34-95; f. 1924; attached to Nat. Acad. of Sciences of the Kyrgyz Republic; Dir T. AHMATOV.

MEDICINE

Institute of Medical Problems: 714000 Osh, Ozgon 52; tel. (3222) 2-84-44; f. 1994; attached to Nat. Acad. of Sciences of the Kyrgyz Republic; Dir R. TOYCHUYEV.

Kyrgyz Research Institute of Obstetrics and Paediatrics: 720040 Bishkek, Togolok Moldo 1; tel. (312) 22-67-19; fax (312) 26-42-75; e-mail oroz@uzakov.bishkek.su; f. 1961; library of 14,000 vols; Dir DUYSHA KUDAYAROV.

Research and Development Institute of Molecular Biology and Medicine: 720040 Bishkek, Togolok Moldo 3; e-mail cardio@elcat.kg; f. 2002; library of 5,000 vols; Dir A. ALDASHEV.

Scientific and Production Centre for Preventive Medicine: 720005 Bishkek, Baitik Baatyr 34; tel. (312) 54-45-78; e-mail npopm@mail.ru; f. 1938; researches into public health, and environment and health; library of 13,500 vols; Dir Prof. Dr O. T. KASYMOV.

NATURAL SCIENCES

Biological Sciences

Institute of Biology and Soil Studies: 720071 Bishkek, Chuy pr. 265; tel. (312) 65-56-87; f. 1994; attached to Nat. Acad. of Sciences of the Kyrgyz Republic; Dir S. KASIYEV.

Institute of Biotechnology: 720071 Bishkek, Chuy pr. 265; tel. (312) 65-55-07; fax (312) 64-19-55; e-mail acan@rambler.ru; f. 1964; attached to Nat. Acad. of Sciences of the Kyrgyz Republic; Dir Acad. ASANKADYR JUNUSHOV.

Mathematical Sciences

Institute of Mathematics: 720071 Bishkek, Chuy pr. 265; tel. (312) 24-35-61; fax (312) 24-36-07; e-mail mathnas@aknet.kg; internet www.math.aknet.kg; f. 1984; attached to Nat. Acad. of Sciences of the Kyrgyz Republic; fields of research: integro-differential equations, singular perturbations, reverse and ill-posed problems, computer proof of theorems, economical-mathematical methods; 55 mems; Dir MURZABEK I. IMANALIEV; Scientific Sec. MARYAM A. ASANKULOVA.

Physical Sciences

Institute of Geology: 720481 Bishkek, bul. Erkindik 30; tel. (312) 66-47-37; fax (312) 66-42-56; e-mail geol@aknet.kg; f. 1943; attached to Nat. Acad. of Sciences of the Kyrgyz Republic; Dir A. B. BAKIROV.

Institute of High-Altitude Physiology and Experimental Pathology of High Rocks: 720048 Bishkek, ul. Gorkogo 1/5; tel. (312) 23-93-52; f. 1954; attached to Nat. Acad. of Sciences of the Kyrgyz Republic; Dir A. SHANAZAROV.

Institute of Physics: 720071 Bishkek, Chuy pr. 265; tel. (312) 25-52-59; fax (312) 24-36-07; e-mail interdep@aknet.kg; internet academ.aknet.kg; f. 1984; attached to Nat. Acad. of Sciences of the Kyrgyz Republic; Dir Prof. Dr TOKTOSUN OROZOBAKOV.

Institute of Rocks, Physics and Mechanics: 720815 Bishkek, ul. Mederova 98; tel. (312) 54-11-15; fax (312) 54-11-17; e-mail ifmgp@totel.kg; internet www.ifmgp.to.kg; f. 1960; attached to Nat. Acad. of Sciences of the Kyrgyz Republic; library of 500,000 vols; Dir I. T. AITMATOV; publ. Proceedings (every 2 years).

Institute of Seismology: 720060 Bishkek, Asanbay 52/1; tel. (312) 46-29-42; fax (312) 46-29-04; e-mail kis@mail.elcat.kg; f. 1975; attached to Nat. Acad. of Sciences of the Kyrgyz Republic; Dir A. TURDULKULOV.

Institute of the Biosphere: 715600 Dzhalal-Abad, Uzbekistan 130; tel. (3722) 5-26-00; attached to Nat. Acad. of Sciences of the Kyrgyz Republic; Dir T. RAHMANOV.

RELIGION, SOCIOLOGY AND ANTHROPOLOGY

Centre for Dungan Studies: 720071 Bishkek, Chuy pr. 265A; tel. (312) 24-34-89; f. 1954; attached to Nat. Acad. of Sciences of the Kyrgyz Republic; Dir M. IMAZOV.

Centre for Social Research: 720071 Bishkek, Chuy pr. 265A; tel. (312) 24-37-35; attached to Nat. Acad. of Sciences of the Kyrgyz Republic; Dir N. OMURALIYEV.

Institute of Social Sciences: 714000 Osh, Mominova 11; tel. (3222) 2-92-44; f. 1994; attached to Nat. Acad. of Sciences of the Kyrgyz Republic; Dir E. SULAYMANOV.

TECHNOLOGY

Institute for the Complex Utilization of Natural Resources (ICUNR): 714000 Osh,
Mominova 11; tel. (3222) 2-60-10; fax (3222) 2-03-42; e-mail ikipr@aknet.kg; f. 1988; attached to Nat. Acad. of Sciences of the Kyrgyz Republic; f. 1988; Dir Prof. JAPAR TEKENOVICH TEKENOV.

Institute of Automatics: 720071 Bishkek, Chuy pr. 265; tel. (312) 65-55-22; e-mail automatics@aknet.kg; f. 1960; attached to Nat. Acad. of Sciences of the Kyrgyz Republic; Dir T. OMOROV.

Institute of Chemistry and Chemical Technology: 720071 Bishkek, Chuy pr. 267; tel. (312) 39-19-48; e-mail icctkr@inbox.ru; f. 1994; attached to Nat. Acad. of Sciences of the Kyrgyz Republic; research on devt of technology of reworking of metallic ores, mineral and organic raw material; creation of new materials (high effective plant growth stimulators and protection means, organic and organo-mineral fertilizers on the base of acid amides, natural polymers, carbohydrates, amine acids, vitamins, nanomaterials); Dir B. MURZUBRAIMOV.

Institute of Machinery Research: 720055 Bishkek, ul. Skryabina 23; tel. (312) 54-11-13; fax (312) 42-27-85; e-mail impulse@elcat.kg; attached to Nat. Acad. of Sciences of the Kyrgyz Republic; Dir Prof. M. DZHUMATAEV; publ. Collected Scientific Articles of the Institute of Machinery Research (every 2 years).

Institute of New Technologies: 714000 Osh, Ermaka 301; tel. (3222) 2-45-32; f. 1993; attached to Nat. Acad. of Sciences of the Kyrgyz Republic; 3 laboratories; Dir JOROMAMAT ARZIEV.

Institute of Power Engineering and Microelectronics: 715600 Dzhalal-Abad, Toktogul 43; tel. (3722) 5-24-85; f. 1993; attached to Nat. Acad. of Sciences of the Kyrgyz Republic; Dir S. KYDYRALIYEV.

Institute of Water Problems and Hydropower: 720033 Bishkek, ul. Frunze 533; tel. (312) 32-37-27; fax (312) 32-39-28; e-mail iwp@istc.kg; internet www.caresd.net/iwp; f. 1992; attached to Nat. Acad. of Sciences of the Kyrgyz Republic; researches on water resources of Central Asia; 60 mems; Dir Acad. DUSHEN MAMATKANOV.

Libraries and Archives

Bishkek

Central Library of the National Academy of Sciences of the Kyrgyz Republic: 720071 Bishkek, Chuy pr. 265A; tel. (312) 24-27-59; e-mail tokonovatt@hotmail.kg; f. 1943; 985,000 vols; Dir L. A. BONDAREVA.

Kyrgyz State National University Library: 720024 Bishkek, ul. Frunze 547; tel. (312) 9-98-26; 931,500 vols; Dir M. A. ASANBAYEV.

National Library of the Kyrgyz Republic: 720040 Bishkek, ul. Abdrakhmanova 208; tel. (312) 30-46-75; fax (312) 30-46-88; e-mail library@nlkr.gov.kg; internet www.nlkr.gov.kg; f. 1934; 21,700 mems; 5.8m. vols; Dir JULDYZ BAKASHOVA.

Scientific and Technical Library of Kyrgyzstan: 720302 Bishkek, Chuy pr. 106; tel. (312) 6-23-66; f. 1967; 5,817,000 vols (not incl. patents); Dir S. I. MAKAROV.

Museums and Art Galleries

Bishkek

Botanical Garden: 720064 Bishkek, Akhunbayev 1A; tel. (312) 43-53-55; e-mail bigarden@mail.ru; internet bigarden.by.ru; f.
1938; attached to Nat. Acad. of Sciences of the Kyrgyz Republic; library of 15,000 vols; Dir I. SODOMBEKOV; publ. Introduktsiya i Akklimatizatsiya Rastenii v Kyrgyzstane (1 a year).

Kyrgyz State Museum of Fine Art: 720000 Bishkek, Abdrahmanova 196, 996; tel. (312) 66-16-23; fax (312) 66-16-24; e-mail kmmii@mail.ru; internet www.knmii.lg.kg; modern art; Dir SHYGAEV YURISTANBEK ABDIEVICH.

State Historical Museum of Kyrgyzstan: Bishkek, Krasnooktyabrskaya ul. 236; f. 1925; Dir N. M. SEITKAZIYEVA.

Universities

ACADEMY OF MANAGEMENT UNDER THE PRESIDENT OF THE KYRGYZ REPUBLIC

720040 Bishkek, ul. Panfilova 237

Telephone: (312) 22-13-85
Fax: (312) 66-36-14
E-mail: reception@amp.aknet.kg
Internet: www.amp.aknet.kg

Founded 1992
State control
Languages of instruction: Russian, English
Academic year: September to June

Rector: ASKAR KUTANOV
Provost: GROGORI FREIUK
Dean: ANARBEK ADYJAPAROV

Library of 17,394 vols
Number of teachers: 90
Number of students: 678

BISHKEK HUMANITIES UNIVERSITY

720044 Bishkek, pr. Tynchtyk

Telephone: (312) 48-40-35
Fax: (312) 54-14-05
E-mail: rectorat@bgupub.freent.bishkek.su
Internet: www.bhu.kg

Founded 1979
State control

Rector: ISHENGUL BOLJUROVA
Librarian: ROSA TURDUKEEVA

Library of 300,000 vols
Number of teachers: 280
Number of students: 6,000

Faculties of Administration and Sociology, Ecology and Management, German Philology, Information, Social Work and Psychology, Kyrgyz and Russian Philology, Oriental Studies and International Relations, Turkish Relations.

INTERNATIONAL UNIVERSITY OF KYRGYZSTAN

720001 Bishkek, Chui pr. 255

Telephone: (312) 31-04-71
Fax: (312) 61-37-18
E-mail: iuk@mail.elcat.kg
Internet: www.iuk.kg

Founded 1993
State control
Language of instruction: Russian
Academic year: September to June

Pres.: ASYLBEK A. AIDARALIEV
Librarian: GULMIRA T. ABDYRAKOVNA

Library of 45,000 vols
Number of teachers: 43
Number of students: 3,250

Publication: Bulletin of the IUK

DEANS

Faculty of Humanitarian, Natural and Scientific Branches of Science: KUBAN B. AMANALIEV

Faculty of Law, Business and Computer Technology: AINURA A. ADIEVA

College of Ecology and Biotechnology: ALMAZBEK SHANAZAROV

College of Economics and Business: SHAYLOOBEK MUSAKODJOYEV

College of Foreign Languages: ZINAIDA KARAYEVA (Dir)

Polytechnic College: AMAN TOHLUKOV (Dir)

Virtual Academy of IUK: TILEK A. ASANALIEV

ISSYK-KUL STATE UNIVERSITY 'K. TYNYSTANOV'

722360 Karakol, Abdrahmanova 103

Telephone: (3922) 5-01-23

Fax: (3922) 5-04-98

E-mail: igu@issy-kul.kg

Founded 1940

State control

Language of instruction: Russian

President: MUSTAFA M. KIDIBAYEV

Number of teachers: 434

Number of students: 6,626

DEANS

Faculty of Art and Modelling: DOCTURBEK IBRAYEV

Faculty of Chemistry and Biology: SHARIPA KACHEKOVA

Faculty of Foreign Languages: TEMIRBEK SULAIMANOVICH

Faculty of Mathematics and Computer Science: JEKSHENBEK MAMYROV

Faculty of Medicine and Technology: HAIRINISIO AISAKULOVA

Faculty of Natural Resources and Geography: MONOLDAR JUMAKULOV

Faculty of Pedagogy and Physical Education: ASKAR IMANBAYEV

Faculty of Philology: AYIDA ABDYLDAYEVA

Faculty of Physics and Technology: DOOLOTBETK AKANOV

JALAL-ABAD STATE UNIVERSITY

715600 Jalal-Abad, ul. Lenina 57

Telephone: (3722) 5-59-68

Fax: (3722) 5-03-33

E-mail: jasu@infotel.kg

Founded 1926

State control

Languages of instruction: Russian, Kyrgyz

Academic year: September to June

Rector: JAMGYRBEK BOKOSHOV

Vice-Rector: NURMAT JAILOOBAYEV

Library of 58,000 vols

Number of teachers: 600

Number of students: 16,000

DEANS

Faculty of Agriculture and Biology: TALCHA AMANKULOVA

Faculty of Economics: BEKMAMAT JOOSHBAYEV

Faculty of Engineering and Technology: EGEMBERDI UMETOV

Faculty of Foreign Languages: ASKAR MURZAKULOV

Faculty of Medicine: SHAIRBEK SULAIMANOV

Faculty of Philology: ANARA KADYROVA

Faculty of Technology: MANAS SOORONBAYEV

KYRGYZ NATIONAL UNIVERSITY 'ZHUSUP BALASAGYN'

720024 Bishkek, ul. Frunze 537

Telephone: (312) 26-26-34

Internet: www.knu.kg

Founded 1932 as Kyrgyz State Pedagogical University; became Kyrgyz State University 1951; present name 1993

State control

Rector: ISHENGUL BOLJUROVA

Pro-Rectors: SHARSHENBEK B. SALPIEV (Academic), ANVAR M. MAKEEV (International Ties and Investment), VYACHESLAV I. SHAPOVALOV (Scientific)

Number of teachers: 600

Number of students: 22,000

Faculties of accountancy and commerce, biology, chemical technology, economics and finance, geography and ecology, history and regional Government, informatics and cybernetics, journalism, Kyrgyz philology, athematics, military studiesphysics and electronics, Russian philology.

KYRGYZ–RUSSIAN SLAVIC UNIVERSITY

720000 Bishkek, ul. Kievskaya 44

Telephone: (312) 28-28-59

Fax: (312) 28-28-59

E-mail: krsu@krsu.edu.kg

Internet: www.krsu.edu.kg

Founded 1992

State control

Rector: Prof. VLADIMIR I. NIFADEV

Pro-Rectors: Prof. IMIL A. AKKOZIEV (Academic), Prof. EDNAN O. KARABAEV (Foreign Relations), Prof. VALERI M. LELEVKIN (Scientific)

Number of teachers: 234

Number of students: 2,200

DEANS

Faculty of Distance Education: Asst. Prof. YURI D. SURODIN

Faculty of Economics: Prof. VICKTOR K. GAIDAMAKO

Faculty of Humanities: Prof. ABDYKADYR O. ORUSBAEV

Faculty of International Relations: (vacant)

Faculty of Law: Asst. Prof. LEILA CH. SYDYKOVA

Faculty of Medicine: Prof. ANES G. ZARUFYAN

Faculty of Science and Technology: Asst. Prof. VLADIMIR A. YURIKOV

KYRGYZ STATE PEDAGOGICAL UNIVERSITY 'I. ARABAYEV'

720026 Bishkek, Razakov St 51, Block 2

Telephone: (312) 66-08-12

Fax: (312) 66-05-88

E-mail: gulhana@mail.ru

Internet: www.arunet.kg

Founded 1952

State control; attached to Min. of Education and Science of Kyrgyzstan

Languages of instruction: Kyrgyz, Russian, English, German, French, Chinese, Arabic, Japanese

Academic year: September to June

Rector: ASKARBEK ABDYKADYROVICH BEKBOEV

Vice-Rector for Academic Affairs: TEMIRBEK MAKESHOVICH CHODURAEV

Librarian: CHODURAEV

Library of 500,000 vols textbooks

Number of teachers: 990

Number of students: 14,000

Faculties of Chemistry and Biology, Oriental Studies and International Relations, Physics and Mathematics and Teacher Training

Publication: *Vestnik*

DEANS AND DIRECTORS

Economics and Management Institute: S. MUSAEV

Institute of Linguistics: AGAMBERDI MAANAEV

Faculty of Oriental Studies and International Relations: ANISA BORUBAEVA

Humanities Institute: TOLOBEK ABDRAKHMANOV

Institute of History and Socio-Legal Education: AGAMBERDI MAANAEV

Institute of Innovation and Communication Technologies: ARZYBEK KENENBAEV

Institute of In-service Teacher Training: G.AKIEVA

Institute of Pedagogies: DOOMART BAISALOV

State Language and Culture Institute: MYRZABEK JUMAEV

PROFESSORS

AKIEVA, G.

AKMATALIEV, A.

ALIEV, SH.

ARTYKBAEV, M.

ASANKANOV, A.

BAIGAZIEV, S.

BAISALOV, J.

BEKBOEV, A.

BEKBOLOTOVA, A.

BORUBAVA, A.

CHOROV, M.

DABAEV, K.

DYUSHALIAEV, K.

SATYVAYLDIEV, A.

RAKHIMOVA, M.

KYRGYZ STATE UNIVERSITY OF CONSTRUCTION, TRANSPORT AND ARCHITECTURE

720020 Bishkek, ul. Maldybayeva 34

Telephone: (312) 44-35-61

Fax: (312) 44-51-36

E-mail: ksucta@elcat.kg

Founded 1954

State control

Rector: JUMABEK TENTIYEV

Faculties of Humanities, Kyrgyz and Arabic, Military Studies.

KYRGYZ TECHNICAL UNIVERSITY 'I. RAZZAKOV'

720044 Bishkek, pr. Mira 66

Telephone: (312) 54-51-25

Fax: (312) 54-51-62

E-mail: ktu@transfer.kg

Internet: ktu.edu.kg

Founded 1954 as Frunze Polytechnic Institute; present name 2005

State control

Academic year: September to July

Rector: Prof. MURATALY DJAMANBAEV

Vice-Rector for Academic Affairs: Prof. BEKJAN TOROBEKOV

Vice-Rector for Economics and Finance: Prof. JALALADIN GALBAEV

Vice-Rector for Science and External Connections: Prof. TURATBEK DUISHENALIEV

Vice-Rector for Social Affairs and Devt of State Language: GULMIRA BELEKOVA

Library of 550,000 vols

Number of teachers: 900

Number of students: 16,000

Publications: *Herald* (2 a year), *Science and New Technologies* (4 a year)

Faculties of food and textile technologies, information technology, machine building and transport, power engineering; institute of business and management; centre of distance education.

ATTACHED RESEARCH INSTITUTES

Educational Scientific Technological Centre 'Vostok-Mir' for Textile and Light Industry: e-mail ias52@mail.ru; Dir Prof. AIYM IMANKULOVA.

Kyrgyz Research Institute of Mineral Raw Materials: tel. (312) 61-34-85; Dir Prof. OMURKUL KABAEV.

Scientific and Research Institute for Chemical and Technical Problems: tel. (312) 54-51-29; e-mail mb051@jandex.ru; Dir Prof. MINARA BATKIBEKOVA.

Scientific and Research Institute for Energy and Communications: tel. (312) 54-90-35; e-mail suerkul@mail.ru; Dir Prof. SUERKUL KADYRKULOV.

Scientific and Research Institute for Physical and Technical Problems: tel. (312) 54-57-86; e-mail jenishtur@yahoo.com; Dir Prof. JENISHBEK TURGUMBAEV.

KYRGYZ–TURKISH UNIVERSITY 'MANAS'

720000 Bishkek, ul. Manasa 56

Telephone: (312) 54-19-42
Fax: (312) 54-19-35
E-mail: webmaster@manas.kg
Internet: www.manas.kg

Founded 1995 by govts of Kyrgyzstan and Turkey
State control
Languages of instruction: Kyrgyz, Turkish
Academic year: September to June

Rectors: Prof. Dr SEYFULLAH ÇEVIK (acting), Prof. Dr KARYBEK MOLDOBAEV
Pro-Rector: Prof. Dr ANVAR MOKEEV

Library of 44,000 books
Number of teachers: 179
Number of students: 1,369

Publications: *Fen Bilimleri Dergisi* (Journal of Science and Engineering, 2 a year), *Sosyal Bilimler Dergisi* (Journal of Social Sciences, 2 a year)

DEANS

Faculty of Arts and Sciences: Assoc. Prof. SUAYIP KARAKAŞ
Faculty of Communication: Prof. Dr YÜKSEL KAVAK
Faculty of Management: Assoc. Prof. SEYFULLAH ÇEVIK
Faculty of Technology: Prof. Dr EROL ÖZTEKIN
Higher Modern Language School: Assoc. Prof. ZAMIRA DERBIŞEVA
Higher Vocational School: Dr HALIL SEVAL

KYRGYZ–UZBEK UNIVERSITY

714000 Osh, ul. Aitiyeva 27

Telephone: (3222) 5-70-55
Fax: (3222) 2-54-73
E-mail: kuu@oshmail.kg

Founded 1994
State control
Languages of instruction: Russian, Kyrgyz, Uzbek

Rector: MUHAMMAD MAMASAIDOV
Vice-Rector: IDRIS ERGESHOV

Library of 108,272 vols
Number of teachers: 520
Number of students: 11,793

NARYN STATE UNIVERSITY

722600 Naryn, ul. Sagynbay Orozbak Uulu 25

Telephone: (3522) 5-08-14
Fax: (3522) 5-08-14
E-mail: nsu@ktnet.kg

Founded 1996
State control
Languages of instruction: Kyrgyz, Russian

Rector: ALMAZ AKMATALIYEV
Vice-Rector: TASHTANBEK SIYAYEV
Number of teachers: 240

Number of students: 4,500

DEANS

Faculty of Agro-Technology: KUBANYEBBEK DUISHEKEYEV
Faculty of Economics: DAMIRA OMURALIYEVA
Faculty of Humanities: YRYS JAKEYEVA
Faculty of Information Technologies: ALMANBET AMANALIEYEV
Faculty of Law: SALIDIN KALDYBAYEV
Faculty of Philology: ALI TURDUGULOV

OSH STATE UNIVERSITY

723500 Osh, ul. Lenina 331

Telephone: (33222) 2-29-12
Fax: (33222) 5-75-58
E-mail: oshsu@mail.ru
Internet: www.oshsu.kg

Founded 1951 as Osh Pedagogical Institute; present name and status 1992
State control
Academic year: September to July

Rector: Prof. Dr MUHTAR OROZBEKOV
First Vice-Rector: Prof. Dr TURDUMAMAT KADYROV
Vice-Rector for Part-Time Education: Prof. ABDIMALIK OMORALIEV
Vice-Rector for Science: Prof. TASYLKAN JUMABAEVA

Number of teachers: 1,600
Number of students: 30,000

Publication: *Vestnik* (research, 4 a year)

DEANS

Faculty of Business and Management: ASANOV AVAZBEK RAIMZHANOVICH
Faculty of Economy and Finance: KUPUEV PIRMAT
Faculty of Education: ATTOKUROV ASAMIDIN
Faculty of Kyrgyz Philology: JAMGYRCHIEVA GULINA TOLOBAEVNA
Faculty of Law and History: KULDYSHEVA GULSARA KENJEEVNA
Faculty of International Relations and State Services: SULAIMANOV JOOMART MYRZAEVICH
Faculty of Mathematics and Information Technology: ABDUVALIEV ABDYGANY
Faculty of Medicine: JEENBAEV JOLBORS
Faculty of Natural Science: KOLANOV ORUNBEK
Faculty of Nature Use and Geography: NIZAMIEV ABDURASHIT
Faculty of Pedagogy: AKMATOVA TANAVAR
Faculty of Physics and Technics: KENZHAEV IDIRISBEK
Faculty of Russian Philology: ATTOKUROV ASAMIDIN
Faculty of Theology: ALIEV ASYLBEK
Faculty of Uzbek Humanities and Education: TURSUNOV RAVSHANBEK
Faculty of World Languages: ANARBAEV ARAP ANARBAEVICH
Financial-Juridical College: ERKEBAEV TAZHIMAMAT
Medical College in Osh: BERKMAMATOV SHAMYRBEK TOKTOSUNOVICH
Medical College in Uzgen: STANBAEV OZGONBAI TILLEBAEVICH

OSH TECHNOLOGICAL UNIVERSITY

723500 Osh, ul. Isanova 81

Telephone: (3222) 5-40-87
Fax: (3222) 5-30-53
E-mail: provsdo@mail.ru
Internet: www.oshtu.kg

Founded 1993; previously Osh Higher College of Technology
State control

Rector: Prof. TOKTOMAMATOV ABDIBALI TOKTOMAMATOVICH
Vice-Rector: SOPUEV ADAHIMJAN SOPUEVICH

Library of 72,540
Number of teachers: 482
Number of students: 11,939

Faculties of construction engineering, cybernetics and information technology, ecology and geology, energetics and new energy technology, finance and economics, language technology, law, social sciences, State Administration and Business, technological engineering, transport and service technology; basic and professional education; evening and correspondence education

Publication: *Izvestiya OshTU*.

TALAS STATE UNIVERSITY

722720 Talas, ul. Karla Marksa 25

Telephone: (3422) 5-20-15
Fax: (3422) 5-25-80
E-mail: tsu1exrel@hotmail.kg

Founded 1996
State control
Languages of instruction: Kyrgyz, Russian, English
Academic year: September to June

Rector: TOROKBEK OMURBEKOV

Library of 101,000 vols
Number of teachers: 248
Number of students: 2,983

DEANS

Faculty of Ecology and Agronomy: AIBEK UPENOV
Faculty of Economics and Law: ESENGUL OMUSHEV
Faculty of Education: ERKIN ABDRAIMOV
Faculty of Modern Languages: MANAS KALMANBETOV
Faculty of Technology: NURLAN ASYLBEKOV

TŠUJ UNIVERSITY

720023 Bishkek, Kievskaya 187

Telephone: (312) 24-77-95
Fax: (312) 24-78-84.

Other Higher Educational Institutes

Bishkek Academy of Finance and Economics: 720010 Bishkek, bul. Molodoi Gvardii 55; tel. (312) 65-04-86; fax (312) 65-02-17; e-mail kubat@freenet.kg; internet bafe.freenet.kg; f. 1994; 53 teachers; 567 students; Rector Prof. ABDRAKHMAN S. MAVLYANOV.

Kyrgyz Agrarian Academy: 720005 Bishkek, ul. Mederova 68; tel. (312) 54-52-10; fax (312) 54-05-45; e-mail kaa@imfiko.bishkek.su; f. 1933; depts: agronomy, agricultural engineering, veterinary science, agricultural economics, zootechnics, irrigation and land reclamation, agricultural business; library: 1,043,000 vols; 280 teachers; 4,547 students; Pres. J. AKIMALIYEV.

Kyrgyz State Academy of Medicine: 720020 Bishkek, Akhunbaeva 92; tel. (312) 54-58-81; fax (312) 54-58-59; e-mail is@ksma.elcat.kg; internet www.ksma.edu.kg; f. 1939; faculties of general medicine, sanitation and hygiene, paediatric medicine, stomatology, pharmaceutics, and foreign and contract students; 408 teachers; 2,646 students; Rector (vacant).

Kyrgyz State Institute of Fine Art: 720460 Bishkek, ul. Dzhantosheva 115; tel. (312) 47-02-25; f. 1967; music, cultural studies, language and literature, theatre, ballet; library: 4,500 vols; 186 teachers; 765 students; Rector A. ASAKEYEV.

LAOS

The Higher Education System

In 1946 the French Indo-China provinces of Luang Prabang, Vientiane and Champasak were united as the Kingdom of Laos, which became independent within the French Union in 1949 and achieved sovereignty in 1953. Sisavangvong University, the country's first university and named after the King, was founded in 1958. However, in 1975 the insurgent Neo Lao Haksat (Lao Patriotic Front) gained control of the country, abolished the monarchy and established the Lao People's Democratic Republic; Sisavangvong University was dissolved into separate colleges. In 1995 the National University of Laos was created from a merger of various institutions of higher education. In 2006/07 there were 30,600 students enrolled at three university-level institutions and 30,100 in other institutions of higher education. The Ministry of Education has overall responsibility for higher education.

Admission to higher education requires the main secondary school certificate (Baccalauréat), and the applicant is required to sit an entrance examination. The undergraduate degree is the Bachelors and the course lasts four years; however, some disciplines, notably pharmacy, dentistry, engineering (all five years) and medicine (six years) require longer. There are no postgraduate degrees.

Vocational and technical education is offered by three kinds of institution: Vocational Schools, specializing in accountancy, teaching and nursery nursing; Middle Technical Schools, for training middle-level technicians; and Higher Technical Schools of Institutes, providing training for higher-level technicians. Both the Middle and Higher Technical Schools offer Diploma courses.

A formal accreditation and quality assurance process has been set up by the Ministry of Education. A new institution called the Accreditation and Quality Assurance Centre is the first National Accreditation Board.

Regulatory Bodies

GOVERNMENT

Ministry of Education: 1 rue Xan Lan, BP 67, Vientiane; tel. (21) 216013; fax (21) 216006; e-mail esitc@moe.gov.la; internet www.moe.gov.la; Minister Prof. Dr SOMKOT MANGNORMEK.

Ministry of Information and Culture: Thanon Setthathirat, Ban Xiengnheun Tha, Muang Chanthaburi, Vientiane; tel. (21) 212406; fax (21) 212408; e-mail email@mic.gov.la; internet www.mic.gov.la; Minister MOUNKEO OLABOUNE.

Learned Society

RELIGION, SOCIOLOGY AND ANTHROPOLOGY

Lao Buddhist Fellowship Organization: POB 775, 01000 Vientiane; tel. and fax (21) 412193; f. 1976; manages, develops and educates the Buddhist sangha and ensures that its members observe the laws of the country; 8,796 monks, 13,376 novices, 450 nuns and 563 sanghali; Pres. Rev. VICHIT SINGHARAJ.

Libraries and Archives

Vientiane

Bibliothèque Nationale du Laos (National Library of Laos): POB 704, Ministry of Information and Culture, Vientiane; tel. (21) 212452; fax (21) 213029; e-mail bailane@laotel.com; internet bnlaos.org; f. 1956; compiles nat. bibliography; 300,000 vols, 120 periodicals, 250 maps, 6,000 MSS; spec. collns incl. palm-leaf MSS; Dir KONGDEUANE NETTAVONGS; publs *Khao Bailan* (3 a year), *Lao Literature Series* (1 a year), *Sienghkene* (3 a year), *Vannasinh* (3 a year).

National University of Laos Central Library: Dongdok Campus, POB 7322, Dongdok, Vientiane; tel. (21) 770068; fax (21) 770381; e-mail nuol@nuol.edu.la; internet www.nuol.edu.la; f. 1995; 26,165 vols; Dir CHANSY PHUANGSOUKETH; Pres. Assoc. Prof. SOUKKONGSENG SAIGNALEUTH.

Museums and Art Galleries

Luang Phrabang

Haw Kham Royal Palace Museum (National Museum): Luang Phrabang; tel. (71) 212122; e-mail sisavath64@yahoo.com; f. 1976 as National Museum; Man. SISAVATH NHILATCHAY.

Pakse

Champasak Provincial Museum: Nat. Highway, 13S, Champasak, Pakse; tel. (31) 212501; f. 1995; archaeological, historical, ethnological artefacts; Dir THONGTINH PHOMPAKDY; Deputy Dir OUTHAI SENERATH; Deputy Dir PHOMMA NOYKHOUNSAVANH.

Vientiane

Ho Phra keo: Setthathirat Rd, 01000 Vientiane; tel. (21) 212618; fax (21) 212619; f. 1565 by King Setthathirat, became national museum 1965; colln of consecrated art objects; bronze statues of the Buddha in various positions of meditation; Dir THONGKHOUN SENGDALA.

Lao National Museum: Samsenthai Rd, 01000 Vientiane; tel. (21) 212460; fax (21) 212408; f. 1985 as Lao Revolutionary Museum, present status 2000; colln of historical and revolutionary exhibits; Dir PENGSAVANH VONGCHANDEE; Deputy Dir BOUNHUANG SISENGPASETH; Deputy Dir PHETMALAYVANH KEOBOUNMA.

Pha That Luang: Saysettha District, 01000 Vientiane; tel. (21) 212618; fax (21) 212619; f. 1566 by King Setthathirat, restored 1930; exhibits incl. a hair from the Buddha; built on the ruins of a 11th–13th-century Khmer temple; Dir THONGKHOUN SENGDALA.

Wat Si Saket: Lane Xang Ave, 01000 Vientiane; tel. (21) 212618; fax (21) 212619; f. 1818 by King Anouvong; constructed in the early Bangkok style; temple and nat. museum; colln of miniature statues and images of Buddha; Dir THONGKHOUN SENGDALA.

University

NATIONAL UNIVERSITY OF LAOS

POB 7322, Dongdok, 01000 Vientiane

Telephone: (21) 770068
Fax: (21) 770381
E-mail: nuol@nuol.edu.la
Internet: www.nuol.edu.la

Founded 1995 by merger of 10 existing institutions of higher education and a centre of agriculture
State control
Language of instruction: Lao
Academic year: September to June
Pres.: Assoc. Prof. SOUKKONGSENG SAIGNALEUTH
Rector: Dr SOMKOT MANGNOMEK
Vice-Rector for Academic Affairs: SAYAMANG VONGSAK
Vice-Rector for Planning and International Cooperation: TUYEN DONGVAN
Vice-Rector for Student Affairs: LAMMAY PHIPHAKKHAVONG
Chief Administrative Officer and Director of Rectorate Cabinet: Dr KONGSY SENGMANY
Dir of Central Library: CHANSY PHUANGSOUKET
Library of 120,000 vols
Number of teachers: 1,986
Number of students: 26,673
Publication: *Mahavithagnalay Heang Xath Lao* (Activities in the National Univeristy of Laos, 4 a year)

DEANS

Faculty of Agriculture: THONGPHANH KOUSONSAVATH
Faculty of Economics and Management: KHAMLUSA NOUANSAVANH
Faculty of Education: KHAM-ANE SAYASONE
Faculty of Engineering and Architecture: BOUALINH SOYSOUVANH
Faculty of Forestry: SOUCKONGSENG SAYALEUT
Faculty of Humanities and Social Sciences: SOUPHAP KHOUANGVICHITH
Faculty of Law and Political Science: KHAMSONE SOULIYASENG
Faculty of Letters: Assoc. Prof. Dr PHETSAMONE KHOUNSAVATH
Faculty of Medical Science: Assoc. Prof. Dr SOMOK KINGSADA

Faculty of Philology: PHETSAMONE KHOUNSA-VAT

Faculty of Sciences: Assoc. Prof. Dr SOMKIAT PHASY

Faculty of Social Sciences: PHOUT SIMMALA-VONG

School of Foundation Studies: Assoc. Prof. PHOUMY DOUANGCHAN (Dir)

Colleges

Lao–American College: Phonkeng Rd, Ban Phonkeng, Xaysettha Dist., 01000 Vientiane; tel. (21) 900454; fax (21) 900453; e-mail lac@laopdr.com; internet www.lac.edu.la; f. 1993; Dir GINNY VAN OSTRAND.

Sangkha College: Muang Chanthaburi, 01000 Vientiane; tel. (21) 212141; f. 1929 as Pariyatti Dhamma School, present name

1996; attached to Ministry of Education; faculties of arts, education; Dir Rev. BOUAK-HAM SARIBOUT.

Sengsavanh College: 124 Dongmieng Rd, Sisavath Neua, Chanthabuli Dist., 01000 Vientiane; tel. and fax (21) 223822; e-mail info@sengsavanh.net; internet www.sengsavanh.net; f. 1997 as language centre, present status 2000; Dir KHAMSENE SISA-VONG.

LATVIA

The Higher Education System

Until Latvia first achieved independence in 1921, it was under Russian Tsarist and then Russian Bolshevik rule. The earliest surviving institutions of higher education were established during the period (1918–20) of *de facto* civil war involving the Latvian provisional Government, the Russian Bolsheviks, German volunteers and White Russians (Mensheviks). Institutions dating from this period include the University of Latvia, the Latvian Academy of Music, and the Transport and Telecommunication Institute (all founded 1919). Institutions founded during the early independent period include Daugavpils University and the Latvian Academy of Arts (both founded 1921). In June 1940 the USSR invaded and occupied Latvia, which then became a Soviet Socialist Republic until regaining independence in 1991. The higher education system is administered according to the Education Act (1991) and Law on Higher Education Institutions (1995). A legal distinction is made between 'academic' and 'professional' higher education: university-level institutions offer both academic and professional qualifications; however, non-university level institutions of higher education offer only professional qualifications. The Ministry of Education and Science is the Government body responsible for higher education. Latvia participates in the Bologna Process to establish a European Higher Education Area, the first phase of which is to adopt a credit-based system of comparable degrees with two main cycles (undergraduate and graduate). In 2006/07 higher education was offered at 57 institutions, with a total enrolment of 129,503 students.

Admission to higher education is on the basis of relevant passes in the General Secondary Education Certificate, often based on criteria established by individual institutions. In 2000 Latvia ratified the Bologna Process, and a two-tier Bachelors (Bakalaurs) and Masters (Magistrs) degree system has been established for both the academic and professional streams of higher education (although old-style professional diplomas are still offered by non-university-level institutions). Degrees are awarded on a credits-accrued basis. The standard undergraduate Bachelors degree course lasts three to four years and students must acquire 120–160 credits. Only a four-year Bachelors programme is regarded as a complete degree; a three-year course is regarded as an intermediate qualification. Bachelors degree courses in professional fields may last longer, such as dentistry (five years) and medicine (six years), and are regarded as equivalent to the Masters. The Masters is either a one- to two-year degree course requiring 40–80 credits, taken after the Bachelors, or a five-year undergraduate and postgraduate combined professional degree requiring 200 credits for completion. The Doctorate (Doktors) is the highest university-level degree and involves three to four years of full-time study, culminating with public defence of a thesis.

Technical and vocational education is principally available at post-secondary vocational colleges. The main award is the First Level (Higher) Vocational Diploma, which requires two to three years of study. In 2006/07 there were 40,439 students enrolled in vocational schools.

In 2010 the Government proposed significant reforms to the national system of higher education, including the closure of some of the country's universities and research institutes and merging of others.

Regulatory and Representative Bodies

GOVERNMENT

Ministry of Culture: K. Valdemara st 11A, Rīga 1364; tel. 67330200; fax 67330292; e-mail pasts@km.gov.lv; internet www.km.gov.lv; Min. INTS DĀLDERIS; Head of Bureau VITA CĪRULE.

Ministry of Education and Science: Vaļņu iela 2, Rīga 1050; tel. 6722-6209; fax 6722-3905; internet www.izm.gov.lv; Min. TATJANA KOĶE.

ACCREDITATION

Augstākās izglītības kvalitātes novērtēšanas centrs (Higher Education Quality Evaluation Centre): Vaļņu iela 2, Rīga 1050; tel. 6721-3870; fax 6721-2558; e-mail aiknc@aiknc.lv; internet www.aiknc.lv; f. 1994; NGO carrying out assessment and accreditation of specific higher education instns and study programmes following recommendations of the Rectors' Ccl and the EU's requirements; Dir JURIS DZELME.

ENIC/NARIC Latvia: Academic Information Centre, Min. of Education and Science, Valnu iela 2, 1050 Rīga; tel. 722-51-55; fax 722-10-06; e-mail baiba@aic.lv; internet www.aic.lv; f. 1994; Dir BAIBA RAIMINA.

NATIONAL BODIES

Augstākās izglītības padome (Higher Education Council): Meistaru iela 21, Rīga 1050; tel. 6722-3392; fax 6722-0423; e-mail aip@latnet.lv; internet www.aip.lv; ind. instn that plans the devt of higher education and higher education establishments; 12 mems; Vice-Chair. Prof. Dr JURIS EKMANIS.

Latvijas Rektoru padome (Latvian Rectors' Council): Raiņa blvd 19, Rīga 1586; tel. 6703-4338; fax 6703-4368; e-mail rp@lanet.lv; internet www.rektorupadome.lv; 32 mems; Pres. Prof. ARVIDS BARSEVSKIS; Sec.-Gen. Prof. ANDREJS RAUHVARGERS.

Learned Societies

GENERAL

Latvian Academy of Sciences: Akadēmijas laukums 1, Rīga 1050; tel. 6722-5361; fax 6782-1153; e-mail lza@ac.lza.lv; internet www.lza.lv; f. 1946; divs of Chemical, Biological and Medical Sciences (Chair. R. VALTERS), Physical and Technical Sciences (Chair. J. JANSONS), Social Sciences and Humanities (Chair. I. JANSONE), Agriculture and Forestry (Chair. A. TREIMANIS); 367 mems (105 full, 54 hon., 116 corresp., 92 foreign); attached research institutes: see Research Institutes; library: see Libraries and Archives; Pres. JURIS EKMANIS; Sec.-Gen. V. KAMPARS; publs *Automātika un Skaitlošanas Tehnika* (Automation and Computer Engineering), *Heterociklisko Savienojumu Ķīmija* (Chemistry of Heterocyclic Compounds), *Kompozītmateriālu Mehānika* (Mechanics of Composite Materials), *Latvijas Fizikas un Tehnisko Zinātņu Žurnāls* (Latvian Journal of Physical and Technical Sciences), *Latvijas Ķīmijas Žurnāls* (Latvian Chemical Journal), *Magnitnaya Gidrodina-mika* (Magnetic Hydrodynamics), *Proceedings of the Latvian Academy of Sciences* (in 2 sections: humanitarian sciences, and natural, exact and applied sciences).

LANGUAGE AND LITERATURE

Alliance Française: Merkela iela 13, Rīga 1050; tel. 6714-0175; offers courses and examinations in French language and culture and promotes cultural exchange with France.

British Council: Blaumana iela 5a-2, Rīga 1011; tel. 6728-1730; fax 6750-4100; e-mail mail@britishcouncil.lv; internet www.britishcouncil.lv; offers courses and examinations in English language and British culture and promotes cultural exchange with the UK in arts, science and education; library; Dir AGITA KALVINA.

Goethe-Institut: Torna iela 1, via Klostera iela, Rīga 1050; tel. 6750-8194; fax 6732-3999; e-mail info@riga.goethe.org; internet www.goethe.de/ms/pra/deindex.htm; offers courses and examinations in German language and culture and promotes cultural exchange with Germany; library of 7,000 vols; Dir RUDOLF DE BAEY.

Research Institutes

ECONOMICS, LAW AND POLITICS

Institute of Economics: Akadēmijas laukums 1, Rīga 1050; tel. and fax 6782-1289; e-mail raimara@ac.lza.lv; internet www

.economics.lv; f. 1997; attached to Latvian Acad. of Sciences; Dir RAITA KARNĪTE.

EDUCATION

Educator Training Support Centre: Brivibas iela 72, Rīga 1011; tel. 6731-2081; fax 6731-2082; f. 1995; responsible for implementing and supporting govt policy on teacher-training and the devt of teaching skills; attached to Min. of Education and Science; Dir Dr SARMIS MIKUDA; publ. *Skolotājs*.

HISTORY, GEOGRAPHY AND ARCHAEOLOGY

Institute of History of Latvia: Akadēmijas laukums 1, Rīga 1050; tel. 6522-3715; fax 6722-5044; internet www.lza.lv/en/inst/in18 .htm; f. 1936; attached to Latvian Acad. of Sciences; Univ. of Latvia; library of 4,000 vols; Dir A. CAUNE; publ. *Latvijas Vēstures Institūta Žurnāls* (Journal, 4 a year).

LANGUAGE AND LITERATURE

Institute of Literature, Folklore and Art: Akadēmijas laukums 1, Rīga 1050; tel. 6721-2872; fax 6722-9017; e-mail litfom@lza .lv; f. 1992; attached to Univ. of Latvia; Dir BENEDIKTS KALNAČS; publ. *Letonica* (2 a year).

Latvian Language Institute: Akadēmijas laukums 1, Rīga 1050; tel. and fax 6722-7696; e-mail latv@ac.lza.lv; attached to Latvian Acad. of Sciences; Dir J. VALDMANIS; publ. *Linguistica Lettica* (2 a year).

MEDICINE

Institute of Experimental and Clinical Medicine, University of Latvia: O. Vaciesa iela 4, Rīga 1004; tel. 6761-2038; e-mail ekmi@lu.lv; internet www.lu.lv; f. 1946; physiology, oncology; Dir Dr PĒTERIS TRETJAKOVS.

NATURAL SCIENCES

Biological Sciences

August Kirchenstein Institute of Microbiology and Virology: Rīga Stradiņs Univ., Ratsupites str. 5, Rīga 1067; tel. 6742-6197; fax 6742-8306; e-mail rsu_mvi@latnet.lv; internet www.rsu.lv/augusta-kirhensteina-mikrobiologijas-un-virusologijas-instituts; f. 1946, re-f. 1993; attached to Min. of Education and Science and Univ. of Latvia, Rīga Stradiņs Univ; Dir Dr MODRA MUROVSKA.

Institute of Biology: Miera iela 3, Salaspils 2169; tel. and fax 6794-4988; e-mail office@ email.lubi.edu.lv; internet www.lubi.edu.lv; f. 1951; attached to Univ. of Latvia; 110 mems; library of 23,673 vols; Dir Dr VIESTURS MELECIS.

Latvian Institute of Organic Synthesis: Aizkraukles iela 21, Rīga 1006; tel. 6755-1822; fax 6755-0338; e-mail sinta@osi.lv; f. 1957; attached to Latvian Acad. of Sciences; Dir Prof. I. KALVINSH; publ. *Chemistry of Heterocyclic Compounds* (in Russian and English, 12 a year).

Latvian State Institute of Wood Chemistry: Dzērbenes str. 27, Rīga 1006; tel. 6755-3063; fax 6755-0635; e-mail koks@edi.lv; internet www.kki.lv; f. 1946; devt of technologies for obtaining materials and products from wood and wood biomass; science-based sustainable utilization of Latvia's wood resources for economic, social and environmental benefits; 60 academic staff; library of 10,000 vols; Scientific Dir Dr BRUNO ANDERSONS; Dir Dr AIVARS ZHURINSH.

Physical Sciences

Institute of Astronomy of the University of Latvia: Raiņa bulv. 19, Rīga 1586; tel. 6703-4580; fax 6703-4582; internet www.astr .lu.lv; f. 1946; Dir Dr MĀRIS ĀBELE; publs *Astronomiskais kalendārs* (Astronomical Calendar, 1 a year), *Zvaigžņotā Debess* (The Starry Sky, 4 a year).

Institute of Inorganic Chemistry: Miera iela 34, Rīgas rajons, Salaspils 2169; tel. 6794-4711; fax 6780-0779; e-mail nki@nki.lv; internet www.nki.lv; f. 1946; attached to Rīga Technical Univ. and Latvian Acad. of Sciences; Dir Dr Ing. JANIS GRABIS; publ. *Latvijas ķīmijas žurnāls* (Latvian Journal of Chemistry, 4 a year).

Institute of Physical Energetics: Aizkraukles iela 21, Rīga 1006; tel. 6755-2011; fax 6755-0839; e-mail fei@edi.lv; internet www .innovation.lv/fei; f. 1946; regional energy sector analysis and optimization; energy saving management; energy–environmental policy studies; renewable energy resources; energy efficiency; grids and electricity supply systems; clean fossil energy technologies; electrical devices and machines; researches into advanced materials and solid state physics problems; Dir Prof. J. EKMANIS; Vice-Dir Dr GUNTA SLIHTA; publ. *Latvian Journal of Physics and Technical Sciences* (6 a year, print and online).

Institute of Physics: Miera iela 32, Rīgas rajons, Salaspils 2169; tel. 6794-4700; fax 6790-1214; e-mail fizinst@sal.lv; internet www.ipul.lv; f. 1946; attached to Univ. of Latvia; engineering physics and liquid metal technologies; Dir Dr JĀNIS FREIBERGS.

Nuclear Research Centre: Miera iela 31, Salaspils 2169; tel. 6790-1210; fax 6790-1212; e-mail brzs@lanet.lv; attached to Latvian Acad. of Sciences; Dir A. LAPENAS.

PHILOSOPHY AND PSYCHOLOGY

Institute of Philosophy and Sociology: Akadēmijas laukums 1, Rīga 1940; tel. 6722-9208; fax 6721-0806; e-mail fsi@lza.lv; internet www.fsi.lv; f. 1981; attached to Univ. of Latvia; Dir MAIJA KŪLE; publs *Filozofia* (1 a year), *Religiski-filozofiski raksti* (religious-philosophical writings).

TECHNOLOGY

Institute of Electronics and Computer Science: Dzērbenes iela 14, Rīga 1006; tel. 6755-4500; fax 6755-5337; e-mail info@edi.lv; internet www.edi.lv; f. 1960; research and design in fields of electronics, signal processing and computerized systems; design and production of hardware/software systems and virtual instruments; library of 10,000 vols; Dir Dr MODRIS GREITANS; publ. *Avtomatika i vychislitelnaya technika* (6 a year).

Institute of Polymer Mechanics: Aizkraukles iela 23, Rīga 1006; tel. 6755-1145; fax 6782-0467; e-mail polmech@pmi.lv; f. 1963; attached to Univ. of Latvia; Dir J. JANSONS; publ. *Mechanics of Composite Materials* (6 a year).

Research Institute of Water and Land Management: Dobeles iela 43, Jelgava 3000; tel. 6302-5517; fax 6302-7180; e-mail janis.valters@apollo.lv; f. 1940; Dir Dr JANIS VALTERS.

Scientific Research Institute of Microdevices: Maskavas iela 240, Rīga 1063; tel. 6725-1619; fax 6725-1000; f. 1962; semi-conductor devices and integrated circuits; Dir ARNIS KUNDZINS.

Libraries and Archives

Rīga

Latvian Academic Library: Rūpniecības iela 10, Rīga 1235; tel. 6710-6206; fax 6710-6202; e-mail acadlib@lib.acadlib.lv; internet www.acadlib.lv; f. 1524; 3,100,000 vols, incunabula, MSS; spec. collns incl. Latvian literature; Dir VENTA KOCERE.

National Library of Latvia: Kr. Barona iela 14, Rīga 1423; tel. 6736-5250; fax 6728-0851; e-mail lnb@lnb.lv; internet www.lnb.lv; f. 1919; 4,478,424 vols; Dir ANDRIS VILKS; publs *Bibliotēku zinātnes aspekti* (irregular), *Latviešu Zinātne un Literatūra* (irregular).

Patent and Technology Library: Šķūņu 17, Rīga 1974; tel. (7) 6722-7310; fax (7) 6721-0767; e-mail patbib@patbib.gov.lv; internet www.patbib.gov.lv; f. 1949; part of Patent Office of the Republic of Latvia; 37m. patents; Dir AGNESE BUHOLTE.

The Library of The University of Latvia: 4 Kalpaka Blvd, Rīga 1820; tel. 6703-4432; e-mail info-bibl@lu.lv; internet www.lu.lv/ eng/library; f. 1862; 2m. vols; Dir Dr IVETA GUDAKOVSKA.

Museums and Art Galleries

Bauska

Bauska Castle Museum: Pilskalns, Bauska 3901; tel. and fax 6392-3793; e-mail bauska .pils@e-apollo.lv; f. 1990; Bauska Castle history; Dir M. SKANIS.

Cēsis

Cēsis Museum of History and Art: Pils laukums 9, Cēsis 4100; tel. 6412-2615; f. 1925; history, ethnography; library of 8,000 vols; Dir A. VANADZIŅŠ.

Rīga

History Museum of Latvia: Pils laukumā 3, Rīga 1050; tel. 6722-3004; fax 6722-0586; e-mail museum@history-museum.lv; f. 1869; Dir A. RADIŅŠ.

Latvian Museum of Natural History: K. Barona iela 4, Rīga 1050; tel. 6735-6023; fax 6735-6027; e-mail ldm@dabasmuzejs.gov.lv; internet www.dabasmuzejs.gov.lv; f. 1845; zoology, entomology, botany, mycology, palaeontology, geology, anthropology, environmental science, pedagogy and museology; library of 18,000 vols; Dir SKAIDRĪTE RUSKULE; publ. *Daba un Muzejs* (1 a year).

Latvian Open-Air Ethnographical Museum: Brīvības iela 440, Rīga 1056; tel. 6799-4510; fax 6799-4178; e-mail info@ brivdabas-muzejs.lv; internet www.muzejs .lv; f. 1924; wooden architecture since 17th century; archive of 70,000 units; Dir JURIS INDĀNS.

Museum of Foreign Art: Pils laukumā 3, Rīga 1050; tel. 6722-6467; fax 6722-8776; e-mail arzemju.mm@apollo.lv; internet www .amm.lv; f. 1773; library of 15,300 vols; Dir DAIGA UPENIECE.

Museum of the History of Rīga and Navigation: Palasta iela 4, Rīga 1050; tel. 6721-1358; fax 6721-0226; e-mail direkt@ rigamuz.lv; internet www.vip.latnet.lv/ museums/riga; f. 1773; library of 24,000 vols; Dir K. RADZIŅA.

Rainis Museum of the History of Literature and Arts: Pils laukums 2, Rīga 1050; tel. and fax 6721-6425; e-mail pumpurs@acad .latnet.lv; f. 1925; Dir I. ZUKULIS.

State Museum of Art: K. Valdemāra iela 10A, Rīga 1010; tel. 6732-5051; fax 6735-

7408; e-mail vmm@latnet.lv; internet www .vmm.lv; f. 1905; Dir Māra Lāce.

Stradiņ Museum of the History of Medicine: Antonijas iela 1, Rīga 1360; tel. 722-29-14; fax 721-13-23; e-mail museum2@apollo .lv; internet www.mwm.lv; f. 1957; library of 39,851 vols, 16,368 rare books; Dir E. Berzina; publ. *Acta medico-historica Rigensia.*

Salaspils

National Botanic Garden: Miera iela 1, Salaspils 2169; tel. and fax 6794-5460; e-mail sekretare@nbd.gov.lv; internet www.nbd.gov .lv; f. 1956; attached to Min. of Environment; library of 24,000 vols; Dir Andrejs Svilans; publs *Index Seminum* (1 a year), *The Baltic Botanical Gardens* (every 2 years).

Universities

DAUGAVPILS UNIVERSITY

Vienības ielā 13, Daugavpils 5400
Telephone: 6542-2180
E-mail: du@du.lv
Internet: du.lv/lv
Founded 1921
State control

Rector: Prof. Zaiga Ikere
Pro-Rector for Research: Prof. Arvīds Barševskis
Pro-Rector for Studies: Irēna Kaminska
Library of 400,000 vols
Number of teachers: 260
Number of students: 4,700

DEANS

Dept of Sports Pedagogy: Jānis Jauja (Head)
Faculty of Humanities: Valentīna Liepa
Faculty of Music and Art: Voldemārs Skutāns
Faculty of Natural Sciences and Mathematics: Antonijs Salītis
Faculty of Pedagogy and Psychology: Ilga Salīte
Faculty of Social Sciences: Vladimirs Menģikovs

LATVIA UNIVERSITY OF AGRICULTURE

Lielā iela 2, Jelgava 3001
Telephone: 6302-2584
Fax: 6302-7238
E-mail: rector@llu.lv
Internet: www.llu.lv
Founded 1939 as Jelgava Agricultural Acad.; present name and status 1991
State control
Languages of instruction: Latvian, English, German and Russian

Rector: Juris Skujāns
Vice-Rector for Research: Pēteris Rivža
Vice-Rector for Studies: Arnis Mugurēvičs
Library of 509,173 vols
Number of teachers: 482
Number of students: 4,691

Publication: *Works* (1 a year).

RĪGA STRADIŅS UNIVERSITY

Dzirciema iela 16, Rīga 1007
Telephone: 6740-9232
Fax: 6747-1815
E-mail: rsu@rsu.lv
Internet: www.rsu.lv
Founded 1951 as Rīga Medical Institute; present name and status 2002
State control
Languages of instruction: Latvian, English

Academic year: September to June
Rector: Jānis Vētra
Vice-Rector for Science: Iveta Ozolanta
Vice-Rector for Teaching: Ilze Akota
Library of 294,000 vols
Number of teachers: 355
Number of students: 4,846

Publications: *Dentistry* (1 a year), *Kirurģija* (Surgery, 2 a year), *Zinātniskie raksti* (medicine and pharmacy)

Faculties of communication studies, continuing education, European studies, medicine, nursing, pharmacy, public health, rehabilitation medicine, stomatology; division of doctoral studies and institute of law.

RĪGA TECHNICAL UNIVERSITY

Kaļķu iela 1, Rīga 1658
Telephone: 6708-9333
Fax: 6782-0094
Internet: www.rtu.lv
Founded 1990
Rector: Dr Ivars Knēts
Library of 2,000,000 vols
Number of teachers: 589
Number of students: 15,330

Publications: *Jaunais Inzenieris* (newspaper), *Scientific Proceedings of RTU* (4 a year)

Brs in Daugavpils, Liepaja and Ventspils.

DEANS

Faculty of Architecture and Urban Planning: Prof. Dr Ivars Strautmanis
Faculty of Building and Civil Engineering: Dr Ing. Juris Smirnovs
Faculty of Computer Science and Information Technology: Dr Ing. Janis Grundspenkis
Faculty of Electronics and Telecommunications: Assoc. Prof. Ilmars Slaidins
Faculty of Engineering Economics: Prof. Dr Konstantīns Didenko
Faculty of Materials Science and Applied Chemistry: Prof. Valdis Kampar
Faculty of Power and Electrical Engineering: Prof. Jānis Gerhards
Faculty of Transport and Mechanical Engineering: Prof. Gundars Liberts

ATTACHED CENTRES

Institute of Humanities: Āzenes iela 16/20, Rīga 1048; e-mail huminst@bf.rtu.lv; internet www.bf.rtu.lv; Dir Dr Anita Lanka.

Institute of Languages: Meža iela 1/1 – 409, Rīga 1048; e-mail valodu.instituts@rtu .lv; internet omega.rtu.lv/vi; Dir Dr Larisa Iļjinska.

Rīga Business School: Skolas iela 1, Rīga 1010; e-mail admin@rbs.lv; internet www.rbs .lv; Dir Dr Jānis Grēviņš.

UNIVERSITY OF LATVIA

Raiņa bulvāris 19, Rīga 1586
Telephone: 6703-4300
Fax: 6703-4302
E-mail: lu@lanet.lv
Internet: www.lu.lv
Founded 1919
Language of instruction: Latvian
Academic year: September to June
Rector: Prof. Dr Ivars Lācis
Vice-Rector: Juris Krūmiņš
Vice-Rector: Indriķis Muižnieks
Librarian: Iveta Gudakovska

Number of teachers: 1,149
Number of students: 20,500

Publications: *Acta Universitatis Latviensis* (10 a year), *Agora* (2 a year), *Automatic Control and Computer Sciences* (6 a year),

Ceļš (theology, 1 a year), *Humanities and Social Sciences Latvia* (4 a year), *Journal of Baltic Psychology* (1 a year), *Journal of the Latvian Institute of History*, *Latvian Human Rights Quarterly* (2 a year), *Latvijas Vēsture* (History of Latvia, 4 a year), *Law and Rights* (12 a year), *Lettonics* (every 2 years), *Linguistica Lettica* (every 2 years), *Magnetohydrodynamics* (4 a year), *Mechanics of Composite Materials* (6 a year), *Terra* (9 a year), *The Starry Sky* (4 a year)

DEANS

Faculty of Biology: Assoc. Prof. Uldis Kondratovics
Faculty of Chemistry: Assoc. Prof. J. Svirksts
Faculty of Economics and Management: Assoc. Prof. M. Purgailis
Faculty of Education, Psychology and Art: Assoc. Prof. A. Kangro
Faculty of Geography and Earth Sciences: Prof. O. Nikodemus
Faculty of History and Philosophy: Doc. G. Straube
Faculty of Law: Doc. K. Strada-Rozenberga
Faculty of Medicine: Prof. I. Rumba-Rozenfelde
Faculty of Modern Languages: Assoc. Prof. E. Ošiņš
Faculty of Philology: Prof. J. Kursite-Pakule
Faculty of Physics and Mathematics: Prof. M. Auziņš
Faculty of Social Sciences: Assoc. Prof. Inta Brikše
Faculty of Theology: Dr R. Kokins

ATTACHED RESEARCH INSTITUTES

August Kirhenshtein Institute of Microbiology and Virology: Dir Dr Vaira Saulīte.

Biomedical Research and Study Centre: Dir Dr Zinaida Šomšteine.

Institute of Accountancy: Dir Dr Inta Bruna.

Institute of Aquatic Ecology: Dir Dr chem. Juris Aigans.

Institute of Astronomy: Dir Dr Arturs Balkavs-Grīnhofs.

Institute of Atomic Physics and Spectroscopy: Dir Dr hab. ph. Janis Spigulis.

Institute of Biology: Dir Dr Viesturs Melecis.

Institute of Chemical Physics: Dir Dr chem. Donats Erts.

Institute of Educational Research: Dir Dr Andris Kangro.

Institute of Electronics and Computer Science: Dir Dr Ivars Bilinskis.

Institute of Environmental Science and Management: Dir Dr Raimonds Ernšteins.

Institute of Experimental and Clinical Medicine: Dir Dr Renate Ligene.

Institute of Finance: Dir Prof. Dr Elmārs Zelgalvis.

Institute of Geodesy and Geoinformatics: Dir Dr Jānis Balodis.

Institute of Geology: Dir Assoc. Prof. Edvins Lukshevichs.

Institute of History of Latvia: Dir Dr hist. Janis Berzinš.

Institute of Human Rights: Alternate Dir Gita Feldhūne.

Institute of International Affairs: Dir Prof. Dr Juris Bojārs.

Institute of Literature, Folklore and Art: Dir Dr Benedikts Kalnačs.

Institute of Marketing and Quality Management: Dir Prof. Dr Valērijs Praude.

Institute of Mathematics: Dir Dr ANDREJS REINFELDS.

Institute of Mathematics and Computer Science: Dir Prof. Dr JĀNIS BĀRZDIŅŠ.

Institute of Microbiology and Biotechnology: Dir Prof. Dr ULDIS VIESTURS.

Institute of National Economy: Dir Dr ROBERTS ŠKAPARS.

Institute of Philosophy and Sociology: Dir Prof. Dr MAIJA KŪLE.

Institute of Physics: Dir Dr JĀNIS FREIBERGS.

Institute of Polymer Mechanics: Dir Dr JURIS JANSONS.

Institute of Postgraduate Education in Medicine: Dir Dr JUNIS ZEMMERIS.

Institute of Solid State Physics: Dir Dr ANDRIS STERNBERGS.

Latvian Language Institute: Dir Dr ILGA JANSONE.

Other Higher Educational Institutions

Latvian Academy of Arts: Kalpaka bulvāris 13, Rīga 1867; tel. 6733-2202; fax 6722-8963; e-mail lma@latnet.lv; internet www.lma.lv; f. 1921; depts of art education, art history and theory, ceramics, Environmental art, fashion design, glass, graphic arts, graphic design, industrial design, interior design, metal design, painting, sculpture, textiles; library: 32,000 vols; 100 teachers; 638 students; Rector Prof. JĀNIS ANDRIS OSIS; Dean of Students Assoc. Prof. UGIS AUZIŅŠ.

Latvian Academy of Music: Krishyana Barona iela 1, Rīga 1050; tel. 6722-8684; fax 6782-0271; e-mail academy@music.lv; internet www.lmuza.lv; f. 1919; piano, orchestral instruments, singing, choral conducting, music education, composition, musicology; library: 150,000 vols, 47,000 tape recordings, 36,000 records, 1,300 audio cassettes, 2,800 CDs, 1,000 video cassettes; 246 teachers; 426 students; Rector Prof. JURIS KARLSONS.

Transport and Telecommunication Institute: Lomonosova str. 1, Rīga 1019; tel. 6710-0650; fax 6710-0660; e-mail tsi@tsi.lv; internet www.tsi.lv; f. 1919 (formerly Rīga Aviation Univ., present status 1999); faculties of computer science and electronics, economics and transport, Management; library: 15,000 vols; 140 teachers; 3,500 students; Rector EUGENE KOPYTOV.

LEBANON

The Higher Education System

The two oldest universities in Lebanon are private institutions founded by Christian denominations in the 19th century while Lebanon was still under Ottoman Turkish rule; they are the American University of Beirut (founded 1866; formerly Syrian Protestant College) and the Université Saint Joseph (founded 1875; Jesuit control). Following the dissolution of the Ottoman Empire after the First World War (1914–18), a Greater Lebanese state was created by the Allied powers, administered by France under a League of Nations mandate from 1920 until independence was declared in 1941. Institutions of higher education established in this period include the Lebanese American University (founded 1924 by the United Presbyterian Church, USA), the Near East School of Theology (founded 1932) and the Académie Libanaise des Beaux-Arts (founded 1937). The higher education system displays strong French and US influences, which vary from institution to institution reflecting whether they were set up by American missionaries or the French authorities. Furthermore, higher education is dominated by private institutions; only Université Libanaise (founded 1951) is under state control. In 1998 Lebanon secured a loan of US $60m. from the World Bank, in order to restructure the country's system of technical and vocational education. Some 196,682 Lebanese students were enrolled in higher education in the 2007/08 academic year.

Admission to university undergraduate courses is on the basis of the secondary school qualification (Baccalauréat), and students may also be required to sit an entrance examination. Depending on the institution, the main undergraduate degree is known as the Licence, Bachelors, Maîtrise or Diploma, and is usually three to five years in duration. Medical students are awarded a professional degree called the Doctorat after seven years. A range of degrees is also available at the first stage of postgraduate study, including Masters, Maîtrise or Diplôme d'études Supérieures. The final state of university-level degrees is the Doctorat d'état.

Institutions of higher education are accredited by the Ministry of Education and Higher Education and the Commission of Equivalences. The Lebanese University is the only institution accredited solely by the Ministry, being the only public university in the country. Other institutions must be individually accredited by the Commission of Equivalences. Accreditation is given in the form of a government decree. Each decree has a number and a date (the Faculty of Arts at the Université de Balamand is accredited according to edict 4885 from 4/6/1988). The American University of Beirut is an American institution that is accredited by the Middle States Association of Schools and Colleges. It is recognized by the Government of Lebanon but does not have its courses accredited in the same way as Lebanese private universities.

Regulatory Bodies

GOVERNMENT

Ministry of Culture: Immeuble Hatab, rue Madame Curie, Verdun, Beirut; tel. (1) 744250; fax (1) 756303; e-mail omarhala_48@hotmail.com; internet www.culture.gov.lb; Minister TARIQ MITRI.

Ministry of Education and Higher Education: UNESCO Palace Quarter, Habib Abi Chahla Sq., Beirut; tel. (1) 789611; fax (1) 789606; e-mail info@higher-edu.gov.lb; internet www.higher-edu.gov.lb; f. 1992 as Directorate Gen. of Culture and Higher Education as part of Min. of Culture; present status 2002; attached to Min. of Education; Min. Dr HASSAN MNEIMNEH.

Learned Societies

GENERAL

UNESCO Office Beirut and Regional Bureau for Education in the Arab States: POB 5244, Beirut; located at: Cité Sportive Blvd, Beirut; tel. (1) 850013; fax (1) 824854; e-mail beirut@unesco.org; internet www.unesco.org.lb; designated Cluster Office for Iraq, Jordan, Lebanon, Syria and Palestinian Autonomous Territories; Regional Bureau for Education in the Arab States; Dir RAMZI SALAMÉ.

BIBLIOGRAPHY, LIBRARY SCIENCE AND MUSEOLOGY

Lebanese Library Association: POB 113/5367, Beirut; or c/o American University of Beirut, University Library/Serials Dept, Beirut; tel. (1) 350000; fax (1) 744703; f. 1960; 218 mems; Pres. FAWZ ABDALLAH; Sec. RUDAYNAH SHOUJAH.

ECONOMICS, LAW AND POLITICS

Association Libanaise des Sciences Juridiques: Faculté de Droit et des Sciences politiques, Université Saint Joseph, BP 17-5208, Beirut; tel. (1) 421000; fax (1) 421045; f. 1963; represents Lebanon in the Int. Asscn of Legal Science; study of legal problems in Lebanon, conferences, etc.; 40 mems; Pres. PIERRE GANNAGÉ; Sec.-Gen. NABIL MAAMARY; publ. *Proche-Orient* (judicial studies).

LANGUAGE AND LITERATURE

British Council: Sadat/Sidani St, Azar Bldg, Ras Beirut; tel. (1) 740123; fax (1) 739461; e-mail general.enquiries@lb.britishcouncil.org; internet www.britishcouncil.org/lebanon; teaching centre; offers courses and exams in English language and British culture and promotes cultural exchange with the UK; Dir Dr KEN CHURCHILL; Teaching Centre Man. ANDREW MACKENZIE.

Goethe-Institut: Damascus Rd, Berythech Bldg, 7th Floor, Beirut; tel. (1) 422291; fax (1) 422294; e-mail info@beirut.goethe.org; internet www.goethe.de/beirut; offers courses and exams in German language and culture and promotes cultural exchange with Germany; library of 9,000 vols; Dir FAREED C. MAJARI.

Instituto Cervantes: Centre Ville, 287 A/B Maarad St, BP 11-1202, Beirut; tel. (1) 970253; fax (1) 970291; e-mail cenbei@cervantes.es; internet beirut.cervantes.es; offers courses and exams in Spanish language and culture and promotes cultural exchange with Spain and Spanish-speaking Latin and Central America; library of 5,000 vols; Dir ANDRÉS PÉREZ SÁNCHEZ-MORATE.

Research Institutes

GENERAL

Institut Français du Proche-Orient: c/o Ambassade de France au Liban, (valise diplomatique), 13 rue Louveau, 75531 Chatillon Cedex, France; tel. (1) 420291; fax (1) 420295; e-mail adm.contemporaines@ifporient.org; internet www.ifporient.org; f. 2003; study of the Middle East in all its aspects: history, sociology, economy, human geography, physical geography, towns; library of 125,000 vols; Dir FRANÇOIS BURGAT.

Orient-Institut der Deutschen Morgenländischen Gesellschaft Beirut (Orient Institute of the German Institute of Oriental Studies, Beirut): POB 11-2988, Riad el-Solh 1107 2120, Beirut; tel. (1) 359424; fax (1) 359176; e-mail dir@oidmg.org; internet www.oidmg.org; f. 1961 by the Deutsche Morgenländische Gesellschaft (DMG); since 2002 part of DIGA (German Institutes for Humanities Abroad); activities in the field of Oriental research (Islamic, Arabic, Persian, Turcological, Semitic), philology, and contemporary history, incl. field research, history of the eastern Churches; cooperation with univs in the Middle East and Germany; library of 133,000 vols; Dir Prof. Dr MANFRED KROPP; publs *Beiruter Blätter* (every 2 years), *Bibliotheca Islamica—Beiruter Texte und Studien*.

ECONOMICS, LAW AND POLITICS

Centre for Arab Unity Studies: Beit Al-Nahda Bldg, Basra Str., Hamra Hamra, POB 113-6001, Beirut 2034 2407; tel. (1) 750084; fax (1) 750088; e-mail info@caus.org.lb; internet www.caus.org.lb; f. 1975; an ind., non-political centre for scientific research on all aspects of Arab soc. and Arab unity, particularly in the fields of economics, politics, sociology and education; activities are governed and implemented by 3 bodies: Board of Trustees, Exec. Cttee and Gen. Secretariat; library of 17,000 vols, 650 periodicals; Dir-Gen. Dr KHAIR EL-DIN HASEEB; publ. *Al-Mustaqbal Al-Arabi* (The Arab Future, 12 a year).

Institut de Recherches d'Economie Appliquée: Faculté de Sciences Economiques, Université Saint Joseph, BP 293, Beirut; f. 1980; economic studies of the Lebanon and other Middle Eastern countries; Pres. Prof. LOUIS HOBEIKA; publs *Études Économiques* (4 a year), *Proche-Orient*.

Institute for Palestine Studies, Publishing and Research Organization: POB 11-7164, Anis Nsouli St (off Verdun St), Beirut 1107-2230; tel. (1) 868387; fax (1) 814193; e-mail ipsbrt@palestine-studies.org; internet www.palestine-studies.org 3501 M St, NW, Washington, DC 20007, USA; tel. (202) 342-3990; fax (202) 342-3927 POB 25658, Nicosia, Cyprus; tel. (22) 319124; fax (22) 756324; f. 1963; ind. non-profit Arab research org.; promotes a better understanding of the Palestinian problem and the Arab–Israeli conflict; 26 mems; library of 60,000 vols (in Arabic, Hebrew, English, French, German, Spanish and Russian); microfilm colln, private papers and archives; Chair. Dr HISHAM NASHABE; Exec. Sec. Prof. WALID KHALIDI; publs *Jerusalem Quarterly* (English, 4 a year), *Journal of Palestine Studies* (English, 4 a year), *Majallat al-Dirasat al-Filistiniyah* (Arabic, 4 a year).

Lebanese Center for Policy Studies: POB 55-215, Vanlian Center, 8th Fl., Mkalles, Beirut; tel. (1) 486429; fax (1) 490375; e-mail info@lcps-lebanon.org; internet www.lcps-lebanon.org; f. 1989; research into political, social and economic development; library facilities; Dir Dr OUSSAMA SAFA.

HISTORY, GEOGRAPHY AND ARCHAEOLOGY

Institut Français d'Archéologie du Proche Orient: Rue de Damas, POB 11-1424, Beirut; tel. (1) 615844; fax (1) 615866; e-mail ifapo@lb.refer.org; f. 1946; Dir JEAN-LOUIS HUOT; library of 45,000 vols; brs in Syria and Jordan; publs *Bibliothèque Archéologique et Historique, Revue d'Art et d'Archéologie, Syria*.

Libraries and Archives
Beirut

American University of Beirut Libraries: POB 11/0236, Riad El-Solh 1107 2020, Beirut; tel. (1) 340460 ext. 2600; fax (1) 744703; e-mail library@aub.edu.lb; internet www.aub.edu.lb/libraries; f. 1866; 592,745 vols, 1,386 MSS, 2,604 current periodicals, 1,063,240 audiovisual items, 1,596 maps; Librarian Dr LOKMAN MEHO.

Beirut Arab University Library: POB 11-5020, Beirut; tel. (1) 300110; fax (1) 818402; f. 1960; important collections on Lebanese, Arabic and Islamic studies; 110,000 vols and 1,500 periodicals; Chief Librarian SAID TAYARA.

Bibliothèque Nationale du Liban: Immeuble Hatab, 6th Fl., rue Madame Curie, Beirut; tel. (1) 756321; fax (1) 756319; e-mail info@bnlb.org; internet www.bnlb.org; f. 1921; library closed and collections put in storage 1979, due to civil war; restoration and reconstruction of the library began 2003; 150,000 vols, 2,500 MSS.

Bibliothèque Orientale: Rue de l'Université St Joseph, POB 166 775, Achrafieh, Beirut 1100-2150; tel. (1) 202421; fax (1)

339287; e-mail bo@usj.edu.lb; internet www.usj.edu.lb; f. 1875; 200,000 vols, 1,800 periodicals, 3,500 MSS, 40,000 photographs, 1,000 maps; attached Centre Pouzet d'Etude des Civilisations Anciennes et Médiévales; Dir MAY SEMAAN SEIGNEURIE; publ. *Mélanges de L'Universités Saint-Joseph* (1 a year).

Bibliothèques de l'Université St Joseph: BP 175 208, Beirut; faculties of law, economics, politics, administration: 100,000 vols, 550 periodicals; medical sciences (POB 115076): 12,000 vols, 125 periodicals; engineering (POB 1514): 10,000 vols, 115 periodicals; arts: 65,000 vols, 300 periodicals.

Attached Library:

> **Bibliothèque de la Faculté des Lettres et des Sciences Humanies:** Rue de Damas, BP 17-5208, Beirut 1104 2020; tel. (1) 421000 ext. 5105; fax (1) 421055; e-mail flsh.biblio@usj.edu.lb; f. 1977; 100,000 vols; Librarian LEILA BOU NADER ELIAN.

Near East School of Theology Library: POB 13-5780, Chouran, Beirut 1102 2070; tel. (1) 354194; fax (1) 347129; e-mail library@theonest.edu.lb; internet www.pcusa.org/pcusa/wmd/globaled/institutes/nest.htm; f. 1932; 40,000 vols; collection of MSS, collection of The American Press; 135 religious periodicals (of which 80 are current); Librarian RITA KHARRAT; publ. *Theological Review* (2 a year).

Daroon-Harissa

Library of the Syrian Patriarchal Seminary: Seminary of Charfet, Daroon-Harissa; tel. (9) 903040; f. 1786; 36,000 vols and 3,100 Syriac and Arabic MSS; Librarian Fr JOSEPH MELKI; publ. *Trait d'Union*.

Khonchara

Library of the St John Monastery: Khonchara; f. 1696; Basilian Shweiriet Order; 12,000 vols, 372 MSS; the Order preserves the first printing press in the Middle East with Arabic and Greek letters (first book 1734); Abbot-General Rt Rev. Mgr ATHANASE HAGE.

Saïda

Library of the Monastery of Saint-Saviour: Saïda; tel. 7975064; fax 7975066; e-mail makarioshaidamous@gmail.com; f. 1711; Basilian Missionary Order of Saint-Saviour; 28,500 vols and 2,550 MSS; Librarians MAKARIOS HAIDAMOUS, FAYEZ FREIJAT; publs *An-Nahlat* (4 a year), *Nafhat Al-Moukhalles* (4 a year).

Museums and Art Galleries
Beirut

American University Museum: Ras Beirut; tel. (1) 340549; fax (1) 363235; e-mail museum@aub.edu.lb; internet ddc.aub.edu.lb/projects/museum; f. 1868; Stone Age flint implements; bronze tools and implements from the Early Bronze Age to the Byzantine period; pottery and other artefacts from the Bronze and Iron Ages, and Classical, Hellenistic, Roman and Byzantine periods; Arabic pottery from the 8th to the 16th century; Phoenician glassware; Egyptian artefacts from the Neolithic to the Dynastic period; pottery from the Neolithic period of Mesopotamia and cylinder seals and cuneiform tablets from Sumer and Akkad; numismatics of the countries in the eastern basin of the Mediterranean; Dir Dr LEILA BADRE; publ. *Berytus* (1 a year).

Daheshite Museum and Library: POB 202, Beirut; contains watercolours, gouaches, original paintings, engravings, sculptures in marble, bronze, ivory and wood carvings; library of 30,000 vols (20,000 Arabic, 10,000 English and French), on arts, philosophy, history, literature, religions, etc.; Dir Dr A. S. M. DAHESH.

Musée des Beaux-Arts: POB 3939, Beirut; Dir Dr DAHESH.

Musée National (National Museum of Lebanon): Rue de Damas, Beirut; f. 1920; exhibits: royal jewellery, arms and statues of the Phoenician epoch; sarcophagus of King Ahiram (13th century BC), with first known alphabetical inscriptions; the collection of Dr G. Ford of 25 sarcophagi of the Greek and Hellenistic epoch; large collection of terracotta statuettes of the Hellenistic period; Roman and Byzantine mosaics; Arabic woods and ceramics; Dir-Gen. Dr CAMILE ASMAR; publ. *Bulletin*.

Sursock Museum: Sursock St, Ashrafieh, Beirut.

Besharre

Musée Khalil Gibran: Besharre; dedicated to the life and works of the author.

Universities

AL-IMAM AL-OUZAI UNIVERSITY

POB 14-5355, Beirut 2802-1105

Telephone: (1) 704454
Fax: (1) 704449
E-mail: islamic-studies@ouzai.org
Internet: www.ouzai.org

Founded 1979
Private control
Academic year: October to June

Chairman: TOUFIC EL-HOURI
Library Administrator: SAMIR OMARI
Number of teachers: 120
Number of students: 4,595

DEANS

Imam Ouzai College of Islamic Studies: Prof. Dr KAMEL MOUSA
Islamic College of Business Administration: Prof. Dr MOHAMED ISKANDARANI

DIRECTORS

Documentation Centre for Bibliographic Information on Islam and the Muslim World: Dr BASSAM ABDEL HAMID
Documentation Centre on World Countries and Major Cities: Dr IBRAHIM ASSAL
Documentation Centre on World Leading Banks: HODA AL-KHARSA
Islamic Institute for the Supervision of Food Products: Dr IBRAHIM ADHAM

AMERICAN UNIVERSITY OF BEIRUT

Bliss St, Beirut

Telephone: (1) 350000
Fax: (1) 351706
Internet: www.aub.edu.lb

Founded 1866
Private control
Language of instruction: English
Academic year: October to June

Pres.: JOHN WATERBURY
Vice-Pres for Academics: MAKHLUF HADDADIN
Vice-Pres for Admin.: GEORGES TOMEY
Vice-Pres for Regional External Programmes: GEORGE NAJJAR
Provost: PETER HEATH
Registrar: SALIM KANAAN (acting)
Librarian: HELEN BIKHAZI
Number of teachers: 420

Number of students: 5,000
Publications: *Al-Abhath* (Arab Studies, in English and Arabic, 1 a year), *Berytus Archaeological Studies* (in English, 1 a year), *Research Report* (2 a year)

DEANS

Faculty of Agricultural and Food Sciences: NUHAD DAGHIR
Faculty of Arts and Sciences: KHALIL BITAR
Faculty of Engineering and Architecture: IBRAHIM HAJJ
Faculty of Health Sciences: HUDA ZURAYK
Faculty of Medicine and Medical Center: NADIM CORTAS
Student Affairs: DEAN KEULIN

BEIRUT ARAB UNIVERSITY

POB 11-5020, Riad El-Solh 1107 2809, Beirut
Telephone: (1) 300110
Fax: (1) 818402
E-mail: bau@bau.edu.lb
Internet: www.bau.edu.lb
Founded 1960
Private control; established by the El-Ber Wa El-Ehsan Association; academically associated with the University of Alexandria, Egypt
Languages of instruction: Arabic, English, French
Academic year: September to May
Pres.: Prof. Dr MOSTAFA HASSAN MOSTAFA
Sec.-Gen.: ISSAM HOURY
Dir of Student Affairs: MOHAMED HAMOUD
Chief Librarian: SAEED TAYARA
Library of 125,000 vols
Number of teachers: 784
Number of students: 12,194
Publications: *Architecture and Planning Journal* (1 a year), *Human Sciences Journal* (2 a year), *Journal of Commercial Research and Studies* (2 a year), *Revue des Etudes Juridiques* (2 a year)

DEANS

Faculty of Architecture: Prof. Dr RAMADAN ABDEL MAKSOUD
Faculty of Arts: Prof. Dr OLGA MATTAR MOHAMED GHAZI
Faculty of Commerce: Prof. Dr SAID ABDEL AZIZ OSMAN
Faculty of Dentistry: Prof. Dr MOSTAFA FAKHRI KHALIL
Faculty of Engineering: Prof. Dr IBRAHIM ABDEL-SALAM AWAD
Faculty of Law: Prof. Dr HAFIZA EL-HADDAD
Faculty of Medicine: Prof. Dr MOUNIR MOHAMED ZEERBAN
Faculty of Pharmacy: Prof. Dr FAWZI ALI YAZIBI
Faculty of Science: Prof. Dr SAMY HAMED CHAABAN

PROFESSORS

Faculty of Architecture:
ABDEL MAKSOUD, R., Building Science and Technology
HAMDI, E. F., Environmental Design
Faculty of Arts:
ABDUL RAHMAN, A. M., Sociology
EBRAHEEM, E. A., Geography
FAHMI, N. A., English Language and Literature
GHAZI, O. M. M., General and Applied Linguistics
Faculty of Commerce:
OSMAN, S. A., Public Economics
Faculty of Dentistry:
AMER, W. A.-A., Oral Medicine, Periodontics and Diagnosis

EL-MULHALLAWI, A. S., Oral and Maxillofacial Surgery
KHALIL, M. F., Dental Biomaterials
MOSTAFA, A. M. M., Conservative Dentistry, Operative Dentistry
SEGAAN, G. I., Prosthodontics
Faculty of Engineering:
AWAD, I. A., Computer Engineering and Systems
BAGHDADI, K. H., River Engineering
ELGHAMMAL, M. A., Electrical Systems
EL-GHAZOULY, H. G., Surveying and Geodesy
EL-SHERBINY, M. M., Electrical and Computer Engineering
FARROUKH, O. O., Electro-magnetics and Optics
FATAH EL-BAB, F. A. I., Stability and Analysis of Space Structures
GHABASHI, M. A-L., Theoretical Physics and Materials Science
HASAB, M. A. H., Design of Thermal Systems
KHALIL, M. F., Fluid Mechanics
MOSTAFA, M. A. F., Mechanical Vibrations
RAJAB, M. M. E., Microelectronics
RASHED, A. M. H., Power Systems Analysis
SOROUR, M. K., Thermal Engineering
Faculty of Law:
ABD AL-WAHHAB, M. A., Public Law
AL-HADDAD, H. S. A., Private International Law
DWIDAR, M. H. I., Economy Planning
EL-MAGZOUB, M. M., Public International Law
KHALIL, A. A. S., Procedure Law
Faculty of Medicine:
ABOU AL-OLA, M. M., Histology: Histochemistry and Electron Microscopy
AHMED, S. I., Internal Medicine—Gastrointestinal
EL-BAHEI, N. M., Clinical Pharmacology
EL-GEBALY, F. F., Embryology and Genetics
EL-SAWWA, E. A.-K., Anatomy: Embryology and Genetics
KHEDR, M. M. S., Clinical Pharmacology
MADWAR, A., Histology: Histochemistry and Electron Microscopy
MASHALI, N. A.-R., Gynaecological Pathology and Haematopathology
SALEH, M. N.-D. A., Anatomy: Genetics of Development
ZEERBAN, M. M., Cardiothoracic Surgery
Faculty of Pharmacy:
BORAI, N. A., Pharmaceutics
EL-KHODAIRY, K. A.-H., Microencapsulation and Drug Delivery Systems
EL-LAKANY, A. M., Chemistry of Natural Products
EL-YAZBI, F. A., Pharmaceutical Analysis and Drug Quality Control
MOHYEEDIN, M. M., Neurohumoral Transmission in Pharmacology
OSHBA, N. H. M., Synthetic Medicinal Chemistry
Faculty of Science:
ABD EL-JAWAD, N. M. A., Enzymology
ALI, A. M. A. M., Nuclear Physics
BADAWI, N. S. A., Cell Biology
DUKAINESH, S. I. A., Invertebrate Ecology
FALTAS, M. S., Fluid Dynamics
HAMAD, H. H. A., Fluid Dynamics
IBRAHIM, H. I., Solid State Physics
KOREK, M., Molecular Physics
MANSOUR, S. M. S., Organic Chemistry
SHAALAN, S. H., Phycology

LEBANESE AMERICAN UNIVERSITY

Beirut Campus, POB 13-5053, Chouran, Beirut 1102 2801
Telephone: (1) 786456

Fax: (1) 867098
Byblos Campus, POB 36, Byblos
Telephone: (9) 547254
Fax: (9) 944851
Internet: www.lau.edu.lb
Founded 1924 by the United Presbyterian Church, USA
Private control
Language of instruction: English
Academic year: October to September
Pres.: Dr JOSEPH G. JABBRA
Vice-Pres. for Academic Affairs: Dr ABDALLAH SFIER
Vice-Pres. for Advancement and Devt: ROBERT STODDARD
Vice-Pres. for Finance: EMILE LAMAH
Vice-Pres. for Student Enrolment and Management: Dr ELISE SALEM
Vice-Pres. (Gen. Counsel and Spec. Advisor to the Pres.): Dr CEDAR MANSOUR
Registrars: VATCHE PAPAZIAN (Beirut Campus): FOUAD SALIBI (Byblos Campus)
Librarians: CINDERELLA HABRE (Beirut Campus): JOSEPH HAJJ (Byblos Campus)
Libraries with combined total of 392,670 vols, 2,447 periodicals, 38,500 eBooks, 80 databases
Number of teachers: 517 (170 full-time, 347 part-time)
Number of students: 6,300
Publications: *Al-Raida magazine* (4 a year), *Alumni Bulletin* (4 a year), *LAU magazine* (4 a year)

DEANS

School of Arts and Sciences (Beirut Campus): Dr SAMIRA AGHACY
School of Arts and Sciences (Byblos Campus): Dr FOUAD HASHWA
School of Business (Beirut Campus): Dr TAREK MIKDASHI
School of Business (Byblos Campus): Dr WASSIM SHAHINE
School of Engineering and Architecture: Dr GEORGES NASR (acting)
School of Medicine: Dr KAMAL BADR
School of Pharmacy: Dr FARID SADIK
Student Affairs: Dr TAREK NAAWAS (Beirut Campus): Dr MARS SEMAAN (Byblos Campus)

NOTRE DAME UNIVERSITY LOUAIZE

POB 72, Zouk Mikael, Zouk Mosbeh, Kesrwan
Telephone: (9) 218950
Fax: (9) 218771
E-mail: webm@ndu.edu.lb
Internet: www.ndu.edu.lb
Founded 1987 by the Maronite Order of the Holy Virgin Mary
Private control
Academic year: October to September
President: Rev. BOUTROS TARABAY
Vice-Pres. for Academic Affairs: Dr GEORGE M. EID
Vice-Pres. for Sponsored Research and Development: Dr AMEEN A. RIHANI
Dir of Administration: Fr ROGER CHUKRI
Dir of Admissions: ELHAM HASHEM
Dir of Finance: Fr SAMIR GHSOUB
Dir of Public Relations and Presidential Counsellor: SUHEIL MATAR
Dir of Student Affairs: Fr BOULOS WEHBEH
Registrar: LEA EID
Dir of Libraries: LESLIE A. HAGE
Number of teachers: 233
Number of students: 4,263
Publications: *PALMA Journal* (2 a year), *Spirit* (4 a year)

DEANS

Faculty of Architecture, Art and Design: Dr SHAHWAN KHOURY (acting)
Faculty of Business Administration and Economics: Dr ELIE YACHOUI
Faculty of Engineering: Dr SHAHWAN KHOURY
Faculty of Humanities: Dr BOULOS SARRU
Faculty of Natural and Applied Sciences: Dr JEAN FARES
Faculty of Political Science, Public Affairs and Diplomacy: Dr MICHEL NEHME

DIRECTORS

Division of Continuing Education: FAWZI BAROUD
North Lebanon Campus: SALIM KARAM
Shouf Campus: Dr ASSAAD EID

UNIVERSITÉ ANTONINE

BP 40016, Hadath Baabda
Telephone: (5) 924076
Fax: (5) 924075
E-mail: contact@upa.edu.lb
Internet: www.upa.edu.lb

Founded 1996
Private control
Academic year: October to July
Number of teachers: 120
Number of students: 850

Publications: *Al-Antouniyah* (1 a year), *Our Liturgic Life* (2 series: research, 2 a year; celebrations, 4 a year)

Faculties of biblical studies, computer studies, ecumenical and religious studies, multimedia and telecommunications engineering, nursing and theology, pastoral studies; higher institute of music; institute of physical education and sport; university technical institute of laboratory science and dental prosthetics.

UNIVERSITÉ DE BALAMAND

Box 100, Tripoli
Balamand-Koura
Telephone: (6) 930250
Fax: (6) 930278
E-mail: pr@balamand.edu.lb
Internet: www.balamand.edu.lb

Founded 1988
Organized in 3 campuses: Balamand Campus (fine arts, theology, arts and social sciences, business administration, sciences, engineering, medicine); Sin El Fil Campus, POB 55251, Beirut, tel. (1) 502370, fax (1) 502371 (fine arts); Achrafieh Campus, St George's Health Complex, Youssef Sursok St, Achrafieh, POB 166378, Beirut, tel. (1) 562108, fax (1) 562110 (health sciences, postgraduate medical education)
Private control
Languages of instruction: Arabic, English, French
Academic year: October to June

Pres.: ELIE A. SALEM
Vice-Pres. for Devt and Public Affairs: MICHEL NAJJAR
Vice-Pres. for Health and Community Relations: NADIM KARAM
Vice-Pres. for Medical Affairs in the USA: TALI' BASHOUR
Vice-Pres. for Planning and Educational Relations: GEORGES N. NAHAS
Dean of Admissions and Registration: WALID MOUBAYYED
Dean of Student Affairs: ANTOINE GERJESS
Librarian: SAMEERA BASHIR

Library of 70,000 vols
Number of teachers: 350
Number of students: 3,800

Publications: *Al-Inaa* (irregular), *Al-Marquab* (1 a year), *Chronos* (2 a year),

Hawliyat (Theology, 1 a year), *Revue Médicale Libanaise* (4 a year)

DEANS

Faculty of Arts and Social Sciences: NADIM NAIMY
Faculty of Business Administration: KARIM NASR (acting)
Faculty of Engineering: MICHEL NAJJAR
Faculty of Health Sciences: NADIM KARAM
Faculty of Medicine: CAMILLE NASSAR
Faculty of Sciences: MICHEL NAJJAR
Lebanese Acad. of Fine Arts: GEORGES HADDAD
St George Faculty of Postgraduate Medical Education: CAMILLE NASSAR
St John of Damascus Institute of Theology: Bishop PAUL YAZIGI

UNIVERSITÉ LIBANAISE

Place du Musée, Beirut
Telephone: (1) 612624
Fax: (1) 612572
Internet: www.ul.edu.lb

Founded 1951
State control
Languages of instruction: Arabic, French, English
Academic year: October to June

Rector: Dr IBRAHIM KOBEISSI
Sec.-Gen.: MOHAMAD EL BABA
Librarian: DINA SUKKAR

Number of teachers: 3,118
Number of students: 69,627

Publications: *Dirassat* (1 a year), *Hannoun* (1 a year), *Pedagogic Research* (1 a year), *Social Sciences* (1 a year)

DEANS

Faculty of Agronomy: Dr MOUSTAFA MROUEH
Faculty of Dentistry: Dr FADIA ABOU DAGHER
Faculty of Economics and Business Administration: Dr NASRALLAH NASRALLAH
Faculty of Engineering: Dr MOHAMAD ZEAÏTER
Faculty of Law, Political and Administrative Sciences: Dr FARÈS KERBAGE
Faculty of Literature and Humanities: Dr RIAD KASSEM
Faculty of Medical Sciences: Dr PHILIPPE CHEDID
Faculty of Pedagogy: Dr ABDEL RAOUF SENNO
Faculty of Pharmacy: Dr AZIZ GAHCHANE
Faculty of Public Health: Dr ELIAS CHAMOUM
Faculty of Sciences: Dr ALI MNEIMNEH
Faculty of Tourism: Dr MOHAMAD CHAÏA
Institute of Fine Arts: Dr HACHEM EL-AYOUBI
Institute of Social Sciences: Dr NASSIF NASSAR
University Institute of Technology: Dr ALI ISMAIL

UNIVERSITÉ SAINT-ESPRIT DE KASLIK

POB 446, Jounieh
Telephone: (9) 934444
Fax: (9) 642333
E-mail: rectorat@usek.edu.lb
Internet: www.usek.edu.lb

Founded 1950
Private control (Lebanese Maronite Order of Monks)
Languages of instruction: French, English, Arabic
Academic year: October to July

Chancellor: Abbé ÉLIAS KHALIFE
Rector: Père ANTOINE AL AHMAR
First Vice-Rector: Abbé PAUL NAAMAN
Vice-Rector for Admin.: Père ANTOINE AL-AHMAR
Vice-Rector for External Relations and Research: Père GEORGES HOBEIKA

Sec.-Gen.: Père PIERRE BOU ZEIDAN
Librarian: Père JOSEPH MOUKARZEL

Library of 250,000 vols
Number of teachers: 620
Number of students: 5,180

Publications: *Actes de Colloques tenus à l'Université Saint-Esprit de Kaslik, Annales de Philosophie et des Sciences Humaines* (1 a year), *Annales de Recherches Scientifiques* (1 a year), *Bibliothèque de l'Université Saint-Esprit de Kaslik, Bulletin de l'Université Saint-Esprit de Kaslik* (2 a year), *Cahiers Annuels* (1 a year), *Parole de l'Orient* (1 a year), *Revue de la Faculté des Beaux Arts* (1 a year), *Revue Juridique* (1 a year)

DEANS

Faculty of Agricultural Sciences: Fr JOSEPH WAKIM
Faculty of Business Administration and Commercial Sciences: Fr KARAM RIZK
Faculty of Fine Arts: ALEXIS MOUZARKEL
Faculty of Law: Dr JOSEPH CHAOUL
Faculty of Literature: Dr ANTOINE NOUJAIM
Faculty of Medicine: Fr GÉDÉON MOHASSEB
Faculty of Music: Fr LOUIS HAJJE
Faculty of Philosophy and Human Sciences: Fr JEAN AKIKI
Faculty of Sciences and Computer Engineering: Fr ANTOINE AL-AHMAR
Pontifical Faculty of Theology: Fr THOMAS MOUHANNA

DIRECTORS

Institute of History: Dr ANTOINE NOUJAIM
Institute of Liturgy: Fr AYOUB CHAHWAN
Institute of Nursing: Dr JEAN-CLAUDE LAHOUD
Institute of Sacred Art: Fr ABDO BADWI
Department of Architecture: ALEXIS MOUZARKEL
Department of Graphic Design: ELIE KHOURY
Department of Interior Design: PIERRE HAGE BOUTROS
Department of Visual and Scenic Arts: PAUL ZGHEIB

UNIVERSITÉ SAINT JOSEPH

Rue de Damas, BP 17-5208, Mar Mikhaël, Beirut 1104 2020
Telephone: (1) 421000
Fax: (1) 421001
E-mail: rectorat@usj.edu.lb
Internet: www.usj.edu.lb

Founded 1875
Private control (Jesuit)
Languages of instruction: French, Arabic, English
Academic year: September to June (2 semesters)

Rector: Rev. Fr RENÉ CHAMUSSY
Vice-Rector for Academic Affairs: HENRI AWIT
Vice-Rector for Admin.: Rev. Fr JOSEPH NASSAR
Vice-Rector for Arabic and Islamic Studies: AHYAF SINNO
Vice-Rector for Devt: Dr KHALIL KARAM
Vice-Rector for Int. Relations: Dr ANTOINE HOKAYEM
Vice-Rector for Research: GEORGES AOUN
Sec.-Gen.: FOUAD MAROUN
Library: see Libraries and Archives
Number of teachers: 1,834
Number of students: 11,023

Publications: *ACES–Actualités Cliniques et Scientifiques* (dental medicine, 2 a year), *Annales de Géographie–Géosphères* (1 a year), *Annales d'Histoire–Tempora* (1 a year), *Annales de la Faculté de Droit* (irregular), *Annales de Lettres Françaises–Acanthe* (1 a year), *Annales de l'Institut de Langues et de Traduction—*

Al-Kimiya (1 a year), *Annales de l'Institut de Lettres Orientales* (1 a year), *Annales de Philosophie—Iris* (1 a year), *Annales de Psychologie et des Sciences de l'Education—Psy-écho* (1 a year), *Annales de Sociologie et d'Anthropologie* (1 a year), *Bulletin Annuel de la Faculté de Médecine* (1 a year), *Bulletin intérieur de l'Institut libanais d'éducateurs* (1 a year), *Chroniques du CEMAM* (modern Arab world, 1 a year), *Chroniques Politiques* (1 a year), *Chroniques Sociales* (irregular), *Conférences de l'ALDEC* (1 a year), *Enseignement Continu Post-universitaire* (medicine, 1 a year), *Etudes de droit libanais* (irregular), *Hommes et Sociétés du Proche-Orient* (1 a year), *Journées d'Etudes Post-universitaires* (midwifery, 1 a year), *L'Orient des Dieux* (1 a year), *Mélanges de l'Université Saint-Joseph* (1 a year), *Proche Orient Chrétien* (2 a year), *Proche Orient, Etudes Economiques* (irregular), *Proche Orient, Etudes en Management* (irregular), *Proche Orient, Etudes Juridiques* (irregular), *Publications techniques et scientifiques de l'Ecole supérieure d'ingénieurs de Beyrouth* (irregular), *Regards* (theatre, audiovisual studies and cinema, 1 a year), *Revue de l'Institut Libanais d'Educateurs* (1 a year), *Travaux et Jours* (2 a year)

DEANS AND DIRECTORS

Centre of Banking Studies: FADWA MANSOUR
Faculty of Arts and Human Sciences: JARJOURA HARDANE
Faculty of Business Administration: TONI GIBEILY
Faculty of Dentistry: Dr NADA NAAMAN
Faculty of Economics: IRMA MAJDALANI
Faculty of Education Sciences: NADA NASR
Faculty of Engineering: WAJDI NAJEM
Faculty of Law and Political Science: FAYEZ HAGE-CHAHINE
Faculty of Medicine: Dr FERNAND DAGHER
Faculty of Nursing: CLAIRE ZABLIT
Faculty of Pharmacy: DOLLA SARKIS
Faculty of Religious Studies: Rev. Fr SALIM DACCACHE
Faculty of Sciences: TOUFIC RIZK
Higher Institute of Insurance Sciences: NADI JAZZAR

Higher Institute of Religious Studies: Rev. Fr. SALIM DACCACHE
Higher Institute of Speech Therapy: CAMILLE MOITEL MESSARA
Institute of Business Administration: PHILIPPE FATTAL
Institute of Health and Social Protection Management: WALID KHOURY
Institute of Islamic-Christian Studies: Rev. Fr AZIZ HALLAK
Institute of Languages and Translation: HENRI AWAISS
Institute of Oriental Arts: JARJOURA HARDANE
Institute of Physiotherapy: PIERRE FILFILI
Institute of Political Science: FADIA KIWAN
Institute of Psychomotricity: CARLA ABI ZEID DAOU
Institute of Theatrical, Audiovisual and Cinema Studies: PAUL MATTAR
Lebanese Institute for Educators: GARINE ZOHRABIAN
Lebanese School of Social Work: MAY HAZZAZ
National Institute of Communication and Information: HADY SAWAYA
Open University: HENRI AWIT
School of Agro-Industrial Engineers: WAJDI NAJEM
School of Laboratory Technicians in Medical Analysis: MARIE-CHRISTINE BAZ HOMSI
School of Mediterranean Agricultural Engineers: WAJDI NAJEM
School of Midwifery: Dr JOSEPH ABBOUD
School of Translators and Interpreters of Beirut: HENRI AWAISS

Colleges

Académie Libanaise des Beaux-Arts: POB 55251, Sin-El-Fil, Beirut; tel. (1) 480056; f. 1937; schools of architecture, decorative arts, plastic arts, publicity,; library: 4,300 vols; 180 teachers; 600 students; Chair. Mgr GEORGES KHODR; Dir-Gen. GEORGES HADDAD.

Haigazian University: POB 11-1748, Beirut; tel. (1) 349230; fax (1) 350926; e-mail rartinian@haigazian.edu.lb; internet www.haigazian.edu.lb; f. 1955; private control;

academic year: October to June; BA and BSc in Arabic Studies, Armenian Studies, biology, business administration, chemistry, christian education, computer science, education, english literature, history, hospitality management, mathematics, medical laboratory technology, physics, political science, psychology; MA programmes in educational administration and supervision, general psychology and clinical psychology; MBA; library: libraries (Armenian, Arabic and English) of 66,000 vols; 63 teachers (23 fulltime, 40 part-time); 743 students; Pres. Rev. PAUL HAIDOSTIAN; Librarian ZEVART TANIELIAN; publs *Armenological Review* (1 a year), *Business News* (4 a year), *Haigazian Focus* (1 a year), *Haigazian Herald* (4 a year), *In Spirit* (2 a year)

DEANS

Faculty of Arts and Sciences: ARDA EKMEKJI
Faculty of Business and Economics: FADI ASRAWI

Middle East University: POB 90481, Jdeidet El Matn 1202-2040; tel. (1) 685800; fax (1) 684800; e-mail meu@meu.edu.lb; internet www.meu.edu.lb; f. 1939; private control; language of instruction: English; academic year October to June; offers degrees in business administration, computer science, education (elementary and secondary), religion; MBA; also diploma courses; library: 20,000 vols; 29 teachers (13 full-time, 16 part-time); 200 students; Pres. S. MYKLEBUST; Registrar S. ISSA.

Near East School of Theology: POB 13–5780, Beirut 1102 2070; tel. (1) 354194; fax (1) 347129; e-mail nest.adm@inco.com.lb; internet www.pcusa.org/pcusa/wmd/globaled/institutes/nest.htm; f. 1932; a Protestant ecumenical institution of higher learning; offers theological education and pastoral training to qualified candidates for church ministries, as well as to lay candidates regardless of church affiliation, sex, race or nationality; library: 40,000 vols; 7 teachers; 36 students; Pres. Dr MARY MIKHAEL; publ. *Theological Review*.

LESOTHO

The Higher Education System

The Roman Catholic Hierarchy of South Africa founded Pius XII College in 1945, while Lesotho was part of the British protectorate of Basutoland. Pius XII College became known as the University of Basutoland, Bechuanaland and Swaziland in 1963, and after the Kingdom of Lesotho was declared an independent state in 1966 it was renamed the University of Botswana, Lesotho and Swaziland. In 1975 the University of Botswana, Lesotho and Swaziland was divided into separate national universities, and the branch at Roma, Lesotho, was reconstituted as the National University of Lesotho. Higher education is funded by the central Government, which accounts for about 90% of the National University of Lesotho's income. Some 3,266 students were enrolled at the National University of Lesotho, at Roma, in 2002. A total of 4,195 students were enrolled at tertiary-level institutions in 2002/03.

Governance of the National University of Lesotho consists of the Council (appointed by the Head of State), Senate, Congregation, Student Union, non-academic staff and external members. The Head of State is the Chancellor of the University, and the Vice-Chancellor, Pro-Vice Chancellor, Registrar, Bursar and Librarian are the primary management staff, responsible for the day-to-day affairs of the university. Overall responsibility for policy lies with the Council, and the Senate oversees all academic affairs. Deans of Faculty and Directors of Institutes are the heads of academic units.

Admission to the National University of Lesotho is on the basis of the Cambridge Overseas School Certificate in the first or the second division. A Diploma is awarded in theology and agriculture after two years, otherwise the undergraduate Bachelors degree last four years, divided into two two-year cycles. Award of the Bachelors of Law requires a further two years of study. The postgraduate Masters degree lasts two years and is awarded in arts, science and education. Doctoral degree programmes are available in agriculture, education and the humanities, and last for two years after the award of the Masters.

Technical and vocational education consists of a College Certificate or Diploma. Courses are offered by a number of different institutions, including home economics and craft schools, trade schools, Lesotho Agricultural College and Lerotholi Polytechnic.

Regulatory Bodies

GOVERNMENT

Ministry of Education and Training: POB 47, Maseru 100; tel. 22313045; fax 22310562; e-mail semakalem@education.gov .ls; internet www.education.gov.ls; Minister Dr 'MAMPHONO KHAKETLA.

Ministry of Tourism, Environment and Culture: POB 52, Maseru 100; tel. 22313034; fax 22310194; e-mail pmasita .mohale@mtec.gov.ls; internet www.mtec.gov .ls; Minister LEBOHANG NTŠINYI.

Learned Societies

BIBLIOGRAPHY, LIBRARY SCIENCE AND MUSEOLOGY

Lesotho Library Association: Private Bag A26, Maseru; tel. 22213420; fax 22340000; f. 1978; 60 individual mems, 22 institutions; Chair. S. M. MOHAI; Sec. N. TAOLE; publ. *Journal* (1 a year).

LANGUAGE AND LITERATURE

Alliance Française: cnr Pioner Rd and Kingsway, Private Bag A106, Maseru 100; tel. 22325722; fax 22310475; e-mail maseru@ alliance.org.za; internet www .alliancefrancaise.co.za/lesotho; offers courses and exams in French language and culture and promotes cultural exchange with France.

Research Institutes

AGRICULTURE, FISHERIES AND VETERINARY SCIENCE

Department of Agricultural Research: POB 829, Maseru 100; tel. 22312395; research station at Maseru and field experimental stations.

NATURAL SCIENCES

Physical Sciences

Geological Survey Department: Dept of Mines and Geology, POB 750, Maseru 100; tel. 22323750; fax 22310498; Dir MATSEPO C. RAMAISA.

Libraries and Archives

Maseru

Lesotho National Archives: POB 52, Maseru 100; tel. 22312047; fax 22310194; f. 1958; undertakes research and preservation of nat. documents since 1869; Sr Archivist M. QHOBOSHEANE.

Lesotho National Library Service: POB 985, Maseru 100; tel. 22323100; fax 22310194; f. 1976; 30,000 vols; Sr Librarian M. MABATHOANA (acting).

University

NATIONAL UNIVERSITY OF LESOTHO

PO Roma 180

Telephone: 22340601
Fax: 22340000
E-mail: registrar@nul.ls
Internet: www.nul.ls

Founded 1945 as Pius XII College, became campus of University of Botswana, Lesotho and Swaziland 1966; present name 1975
Language of instruction: English
Academic year: August to May

Chancellor: HM King LETSIE III
Vice-Chancellor: Dr T. H. MOTHIBE
Pro-Vice-Chancellor: Dr N. L. MAHAO
Registrar: J. M. HLALELE
Librarian: A. M. LEBOTSA

Library of 205,150 vols, 500 periodicals
Number of teachers: 171
Number of students: 3,266

Publications: *Announcer, Lesotho Law Journal, Light in the Night, Mohlomi Journal* (History), *Mophatlatsi, NUL News, NUL Research Journal*

DEANS

Faculty of Agriculture: Prof. P. M. SUTTON
Faculty of Education: Dr E. M. MARUPING
Faculty of Health Science: Prof. P. O. ODONKOR
Faculty of Humanities: Rev. J. KHUTLANG
Faculty of Law: O. M. OWORI
Faculty of Postgraduate Studies: (vacant)
Faculty of Science and Technology: Prof. K. K. GOPINATHAN
Faculty of Social Sciences: Prof. S. G. HOOHLO

DIRECTORS

Institute of Education: S. T. MOTLOMELO
Institute of Extra-Mural Studies: Prof. D. BRAIMOH, Prof. Y. D. BWATWA, Dr A. M. SETSABI
Institute of Labour Studies: S. SANTHO (acting)
Institute of Southern African Studies: Dr M. MOCHEBELELE

PROFESSORS

Faculty of Agriculture:
BRAIDE, F. G.
EBENENE, A. C.
OKELW-UMA, I.
SUTTON, P. M.

Faculty of Education:
MATS'ELA, Z. A., Language and Social Education

Faculty of Law:
KUMAR, U., Private Law

Faculty of Postgraduate Studies:
BALOGUN, T. A.

Faculty of Science and Technology:
GOPINATHAN, K. K., Physics
MALU, O.

Faculty of Social Sciences:
EJIGOU, A., Statistics

Institute of Southern African Studies:
PRASAD, G.

College

Lesotho Agricultural College: POB 139, Maseru; tel. 22322484; fax 22400022; f. 1955; state control; language of instruction: English; academic year August to to May (2 semesters); library: 60,000 vols; Principal Dr S. L. RALITS'OELE.

LIBERIA

The Higher Education System

From 1821 onwards emancipated slaves from the southern states of the USA were resettled along the West Guinean coast, and in 1847 the independent, sovereign state of Liberia was declared, with a Constitution based on that of the USA. Liberia College, the first institution of higher education, was founded in 1862 and became a university in 1951. In 1889 Cuttington University College was founded by the Episcopal Church in the USA, by whom it is still maintained in conjunction with the Episcopal Church in Liberia. Other institutions of higher education include the William V. S. Tubman College of Technology (founded 1970; formerly Harper Technical College) and the Booker Washington Institute (founded 1929). There are also junior colleges offering two-year degree programmes. In the academic year 1999/2000 there were 44,107 students enrolled in university-level institutions and 15,631 students enrolled in post-secondary and vocational education.

Universities must be chartered by the Ministry of Education, but higher education in Liberia is decentralized in that each institution is autonomous and governed by a Board of Trustees. The Minister of Education is the Government representative on each Board of Trustees, which is advised by an Administrative Council, comprising all academic and administrative staff, two elected faculty members and two elected student representatives. The Council also advises the President of the University and coordinates the day-to-day running of the institution. The State provides funding to both public and private institutions and also offers financial aid to students, which covers one-half of the cost of tuition and study materials.

Applicants must hold the Senior High School certificates to gain admission to higher education and are also required to sit entrance examinations in English and Mathematics. Students at junior colleges study for the two-year Associate degree, and university undergraduates take a four-year Bachelors degree. The Bachelors of Law degree is awarded after five years and medical degrees after seven years. Postgraduate degrees, such as the Masters, are available on a limited basis.

In addition to junior colleges, post-secondary technical and vocational education is offered by technical colleges.

In 2007 the Government consulted with the American Association of State Colleges and Universities for help and advice in rebuilding Liberia's post-secondary education system, which had been severely affected by 14 years of civil war.

Regulatory Bodies

GOVERNMENT

Ministry of Education: E. G. N. King Plaza, Broad St, POB 10-1545, 1000 Monrovia 10; tel. 226216; internet www.moe.gov.lr; Minister JOSEPH KORTO.

Ministry of Information, Culture and Tourism: Capitol Hill, POB 10-9021, 1000 Monrovia 10; tel. 226269; internet www.micat.gov.lr; Minister Rev. Dr LAWRENCE K. BROPLEH.

Learned Societies

LANGUAGE AND LITERATURE

Alliance Française: 28 Payne Ave, POB 10, 3016 Sinkor 14th/15th Sts, 1000 Monrovia 10; tel. and fax 226888; e-mail alliancefr_monrovia@yahoo.com; offers courses and exams in French language and culture and promotes cultural exchange with France.

Society of Liberian Authors: POB 2468, Monrovia; f. 1959; aims to encourage general interest in writing and encourage literature in local vernacular; publ. *Kaafa* (2 a year).

TECHNOLOGY

Geological, Mining and Metallurgical Society of Liberia: POB 902, Monrovia; f. 1964; 78 mems; Pres. CLETUS S. WOTORSON; Sec. Dr MEDIE-HEMIE NEUFVILLE; publ. *Bulletin* (2 a year).

Liberia Arts and Crafts Association: POB 885, Monrovia; f. 1964; 14 mems; aims to encourage artists and craftsmen through exhibitions, sales, workshops; Pres. R. VANJAH RICHARDS.

Research Institutes

AGRICULTURE, FISHERIES AND VETERINARY SCIENCE

Central Agricultural Research Institute: Mailbag 3929, Suakoko, Bong County; tel. 223443; f. 1946; under Ministry of Agriculture; programmes in four key areas incl. infrastructure and manpower development, crop improvement and urban agriculture, livestock and fisheries improvement, natural resource management and value addition; library of 8,700 vols; Dir-Gen Dr J. QWELIBO SUBAH; publ. *CARI News*.

MEDICINE

Liberian Institute for Biomedical Research: POB 10-1012, 1000 Monrovia 10; f. 1952, renamed 1975; administrative centre for biomedical research; conducts research and attracts research projects; Dir Dr ALOYSIUS P. HANSON.

NATURAL SCIENCES

Biological Sciences

Nimba Research Laboratory: c/o Lamco J. V. Operating Co, Grassland, Nimba, Robertsfield; POB 69, Monrovia; f. 1962; under supervision of Nimba Research Committee of International Union for Conservation of Nature and Natural Resources, in conjunction with UNESCO; biological and ecological exploration and conservation in the Mount Nimba region; library of 100 vols and access to LAMCO library, Yekepa; Chair. KAI CURRY-LINDAHL.

Libraries and Archives

Monrovia

Government Public Library: Ashmun St, Monrovia; f. 1959; 15,000 vols.

Liberian Information Service Library: POB 9021, Monrovia; reference.

University of Liberia Libraries: University of Liberia, POB 9020, Monrovia; tel. 222448; f. 1862; general library and separate law library; 107,384 vols, 2,118 periodicals; Dir ANNABEL U. TINGBA (acting).

Museums and Art Galleries

Cape Mount

Tubman Centre of African Cultures: Cape Mount; local art, history and ethnology.

Monrovia

Africana Museum: Cuttington Univ. College, c/o Episcopal Church Office, POB 277, Monrovia; f. 1960; items from Liberia and neighbouring countries; traditional arts and crafts, ethnographical material; depository for archaeological collns; serves as a teaching colln for the college and as a research facility for visiting scholars; Dir Dr ADETOKUNBO K. BORISHADE.

National Museum: Broad and Buchanan Sts, POB 3223, Monrovia; f. 1962; Liberian history, art and ethnography; Dir BURDIE UREY-WEEKS.

University

UNIVERSITY OF LIBERIA

POB 9020, Monrovia
Telephone: 224670
Fax: 226418
Founded as Liberia College 1862; university status 1951
State control
Language of instruction: English
Academic year: March to December (two semesters)
Pres.: Dr BEN ROBERTS

Vice-Pres. for Academic Affairs: Dr FREDER-
ICK S. GREGBE

Vice-Pres. for Administration: Dr WINGROVE
C. DWAMINA (acting)

Dean of Admissions: MOORE T. WORRELL

Libraries: see Libraries and Archives

Number of teachers: 260

Number of students: 3,400

Publications: *Liberian Law Journal, This
Week on Campus, University of Liberia
Catalogue and Announcements, University
of Liberia Journal, Varsity Pilot*

DEANS

A. M. Douglas College of Medicine: Dr TAIWO
DARAMOLA

College of Agriculture and Forestry: Dr
BISMARCK REEVES

College of Business and Public Administration: Prof. WILLIE BELLEH Jr

College of Science and Technology: Prof.
FREDERICK D. HUNDER (acting)

College of Social Sciences and Humanities
(Liberia College): Dr BEN A. ROBERTS

Louis Arthur Grimes School of Law: Cllr
LUVENIA ASH-THOMPSON

Student Affairs: HARRISON MLE-SIE WOART

William V. S. Tubman Teachers College: Dr
JOSHUA D. CLEON

COORDINATORS OF SCHOOLS

School of Pharmacy: Dr ARTHUR S. LEWIS

Graduate School of Education Administration: Dr HENRY KWEKWE

Graduate School of Regional Planning: Dr
JAMES N. KOLLIE, Sr

Colleges

Booker Washington Institute: POB 273,
Kakata; tel. 331048; f. 1929; state control; 52
teachers; 750 students; agricultural and
industrial courses; secondary high school
courses; basic computer literacy; Principal
MULBAH JACKOLLIE.

Cuttington University College: c/o Episcopal Church Building, POB 10-277, 1000
Monrovia 10; tel. 227413; fax 226059; e-mail
cuttingtonuniversity@yahoo.com; internet
cuttington.org; f. 1889; maintained by int.

donors, incl. Episcopal Church in the USA,
Episcopal Church of Liberia; applied for
subsidies from the Liberian Government;
language of instruction: English; academic
year September to June; library stock subjected to looting during civil war (1990–
1996), 250 periodicals; 110 teachers; 1,545
undergraduate students, 225 graduate students; Pres. Dr HENRIQUE F. TOKPA; Vice-
Pres. for Academic Affairs Dr JAMES E.
MOCK; Vice-Pres. for Administration Dr
CHARLES K. MULBAH; Dean of Students
HILARY W. COLLINS; Registrar and Dean of
Admissions BENGALY M. KAMARA; Librarian
FORKPA H. KEMAH.

**William V. S. Tubman College of Tech-
nology:** POB 3570, Monrovia; f. 1970; state
control; language of instruction: English;
academic year: March to December; 21
teachers; 200 students; 3-year associate
degree course in engineering technology;
Pres. Dr THEOPHILUS N. SONPON; Dean Dr
SOLOMON S. B. RUSSELL.

LIBYA

The Higher Education System

All current institutions of higher education have been founded since Libya became an independent kingdom in 1951. (Following a military coup in 1969, it became known as the Libyan Arab Republic, and since 1986 it has been known as the Great Socialist People's Libyan Arab Jamhariya.) The oldest university is the University of Garyounis, which was founded in 1955 as the Faculty of Arts and Education, Benghazi, became the University of Benghazi in 1973 and adopted its current name in 1976. Both the University of Garyounis and Al-Fateh University (founded in 1957; formerly Faculty of Science, Tripoli) were part of the former federal University of Libya until 1973. In 2002/03 there were an estimated 375,028 students in recognized institutions of higher education. The Secretariat for Higher Education is the responsible body for higher education, which is financed from the state budget. However, due to the expansion in student numbers and growing pressure on Government funding, greater autonomy has been granted to local public administrations in allowing the establishment of new, mostly private universities.

A People's Committee, headed by a Dean (who acts as the Secretary), is the management body of each University. The main academic units are the Faculty and the Department. Faculties are also governed by a People's Committee, the Secretary of which represents the Faculty on the University People's Committee. Heads of Department are members of the Faculty People's Committee. Students sit on University and Faculty People's Committees.

Admission to higher education is on the basis of the Secondary Education Certificate, with different pass marks depending on the type of institution or degree applied for. Most undergraduate Bachelors degrees from universities require four years of study, but architecture, engineering (both five years) and medicine (six years) require longer. There are also technical and vocational institutions, which offer four- to five-year Bachelors degree courses in the sciences, technology and engineering. The main postgraduate degrees are the Masters and Doctorate. The Masters is a two-year programme of study following award of the Bachelors, and study for the Doctorate also lasts two years, culminating in public defence of a thesis.

Technical and vocational training at post-secondary level is offered by technical institutes.

The Centre for Quality Assurance and Accreditation for Higher Education Institutions, part of the Ministry of Higher Education, is the body responsible for the quality assurance and accreditation of all higher education providers.

Since its re-engagement with the international community, following the renunciation of weapons of mass destruction, Libya has worked to reform its higher education system and in 2007 produced a five-year strategic plan.

Regulatory Body

GOVERNMENT

General People's Committee: Tripoli; Sec. for Higher Education Dr AGAIL HUSSEIN AGAIL; Sec. for Gen. Education Dr ABD AL-QADIR MUHAMMAD AL-BAGHDADI; Sec. for Culture and Information NURI DHAW AL-HUMEIDI.

ACCREDITATION

Centre for Quality Assurance and Accreditation for Higher Education Institutions: Ben Ashur St, 80767 Tripoli; tel. (21) 3617328; fax (21) 3619604; e-mail elkabir@qaa.ly; internet www.qaa.ly; f. 2008; dept in the Min. of Higher Education; accredits all higher education providers in Libya; Contact Prof. MOHAMMED ELKABIR.

Learned Societies

LANGUAGE AND LITERATURE

British Council: POB 6797, Tripoli; Casablanca St, Hey El Wihda El Arabia, Siyahia, Tripoli; tel. (21) 4843164; fax (21) 4840178; e-mail info.libya@ly.britishcouncil.org; internet www.britishcouncil.org/libya; offers courses and exams in English language and British culture and promotes cultural exchange with the UK; Dir CARL REUTER.

Union of Libyan Authors, Writers and Artists: POB 1017, Tripoli; f. 1980; all fields of culture, education and art; 800 mems; library of 4,000 vols; Pres. AMIN MAZEN.

Research Institutes

GENERAL

National Academy for Scientific Research: POB 12312, Tripoli; tel. (21) 3339101; fax (21) 3341019; f. 1981 to conduct, finance and support scientific studies and research in all branches of knowledge; 330 mems; library of 19,000 vols; Dir-Gen. Dr TAHER H. JEHEMI; publs Al-Fikr Al-Arabi, Al-Fikr Al-Istratiji Al-Arabi, Al-Ilm Wa Atteknolojia.

National Scientific Research and Study Centre: POB 84662 Shara Azawia, Tripoli; tel. (21) 3602783; fax (21) 3602788; e-mail ncrss@ncrss.com; internet www.ncrss.com; f. 1995; centres of Scientific Research and Studies; Library and Documentation; Publishing and Information; Documentation and Information; publ. Al Jadeed (4 a year).

Tajoura Nuclear Research Center: POB 30878, Tripoilajoura; tel. (21) 3614130; fax (21) 3614142; e-mail admin@tnrc.org; internet www.tnrc.org; f. 1995; research in basic and applied science, nuclear energy, renewable sources of energy, desalination of water; publ. Al Nawah.

HISTORY, GEOGRAPHY AND ARCHAEOLOGY

Libyan Studies Centre: POB 5070, Sidi Munaider, Tripoli; tel. (21) 3333996; fax (21) 3331616; e-mail libyanjihad@libsc.org.ly; internet www.libsc.org.ly; f. 1978; historical studies and documentation; 140 mems; library of 100,000 vols, 700 periodicals, 3,000 MSS, 60,000 photographs; Dir Dr MOHAMED T. JERARY; publs Al-Insaf (1 a year), Al-Kunnasha (The Scrap Book, 2 a year), As-Shahid (The Martyr, 1 a year), Al-Wathaiq wa Al-Makhtutat (1 a year), Index of Libyan Periodicals (1 a year), Majallat Al-Buhuth At-Tarikhia (2 a year).

Libraries and Archives

Benghazi

National Library of Libya: POB 9127, Benghazi; tel. (61) 9096379; fax (61) 9096380; e-mail nat-lib-libya@hotmail.com; internet www.nllnet.net; f. 1973; Gen. Sec. MOHAMMAD A. ESHOWEIHDI.

University of Garyounis Library: POB 1308, Benghazi; tel. (61) 87633; f. 1955; 294,844 vols; 2,170 periodicals; 7 depts, including 2,360 MSS, 70,000 documents, 10,000 microfilms and rare books; Chief Librarian AHMED GALLAL; publs available for exchange.

Tripoli

Agricultural Research Centre Library: POB 2480, Tripoli; tel. (21) 3616865; fax (21) 3614993; e-mail taherazzabi@mailcity.com; f. 1973; 6,000 vols, 220 periodicals; Librarian LAMIS AL-GABSI.

Government Library: 14 Shar'a Al-Jazair, Tripoli; f. 1917; 35,500 vols; Librarian BASHIR AL-BADRI.

National Archives: Castello, Tripoli; tel. (21) 40166; internet www.nllnet.net; f. 1928; controlled by Department of Antiquities, General People's Committee for Education, Tripoli; extensive colln of documents relating to the history of Libya mostly in Turkish from the Ottoman period; 5 libraries, 55,000 vols; Curator ABDULAALI OWN; publ. Libya Antiqua.

Museums and Art Galleries

Shahat

Department of Antiquities, Shahat (Cyrene):responsible for archaeological sites from Shahat west to the frontiers of Tocra, east to Msa'd; Controller BRAYEK ATTIYA.

Tripoli

Department of Antiquities: Assarai Al-Hamra, Tripoli; responsible for all museums and archaeological sites in Libya; Pres. Dr ABDULLAH SHAIBOUB.

Museums controlled by the Department:

Apollonia Museum: Marsa Soussa.

Archaeological, Natural History, Epigraphy, Prehistory and Ethnography Museums: Assarai Al-Hamra, Tripoli.

Benghazi Museum: Benghazi; mausoleum of Omar El Mukhtar.

Cyrene Museum: Cyrene (Shahat).

Gaigab Museum: Gaigab (near Cyrene).

Germa Museum: Germa (Fezean).

Islamic Museum: Tripoli.

Leptis Magna Museum: Leptis Magna.

Ptolemais Museum: Tolmeitha.

Sabratha Museum of Antiquities: Sabratha.

Tauchira Museum: Tokra.

Zanzur Museum: Zanzur (Tripoli).

Universities

AL-ARAB MEDICAL UNIVERSITY

POB 18251, Benghazi
Telephone: (61) 225007
Fax: (61) 222195
Founded 1984
State control
Languages of instruction: Arabic, English
Academic year: September to May
Pres.: Dr AMER RAHIL
Registrar: ABU-BAKER AMMARI
Librarian: MOHAMMED EL-SAID
Library of 30,000 vols, 600 periodicals
Number of teachers: 256
Number of students: 1,615
Publication: *Garyounis Medical Journal* (2 a year)

DEANS

Faculty of Dentistry: Dr ABDULLA OMAR DOURDA
Faculty of Medicine: Dr ABDUL HADI MOUSSA
Faculty of Pharmacy: Dr ABDUSALAM A. AL-MAYHOUB

AL-FATEH UNIVERSITY

POB 3601381, Tripoli
Telephone: (22) 605441
Fax: (22) 605460
E-mail: n.bazina@alfateh.edu.ly
Internet: www.alfateh.edu.ly
Founded 1957
State control
Language of instruction: Arabic
Academic year: September to June
Pres.: Dr MOHAMED L. FARHAT
Vice-Pres.: Dr NAJAH S. ELGABSI
Sec.-Gen.: Dr YOUNIS ALAGILI
Gen. Registrar: Dr AWEDAT GANDOUR
Librarian: Dr MOHAMED ABDUL JALEEL
Number of teachers: 3,200
Number of students: 75,000

Publications: *Bulletin of the Faculty of Education, Bulletin of the Faculty of Engineering, Bulletin of the Faculty of Law, Libyan Journal of Agriculture, Libyan Journal of Sciences*

DEANS

Faculty of Agriculture: Dr AMER ELMIGRI
Faculty of Economics and Political Science: Dr HAFAD SHAILI
Faculty of Education: Dr TOHAMI TARHOUNI
Faculty of Engineering: Dr ABDULHAMID ASHOUR
Faculty of Fine Arts: Dr HAMID
Faculty of Law: Dr OMAR HUSSIN
Faculty of Physical Education: Dr SADDIK EL KABOLI
Faculty of Science: Dr OMAR ELHAJI
Faculty of Veterinary Medicine: Dr SALAH ZWAI (acting)

AL-FATEH UNIVERSITY FOR MEDICAL SCIENCES

POB 13040, Tripoli
Telephone: (21) 4625060
Fax: (21) 4625883
E-mail: info@aums.edu.ly
Internet: www.aums.edu.ly
Founded 1986
State control
Languages of instruction: Arabic, English
Faculties of dentistry, medical technology, medicine and pharmacy.

BRIGHT STAR UNIVERSITY OF TECHNOLOGY

POB 58158, Ajdabia
Telephone: (64) 23012
Fax: (64) 61870
Founded 1981
State control
Language of instruction: Arabic
Academic year: October to June
Chancellor: Eng. ALI SALEH ELFAZZANI
Registrar: Eng. MANSOOR MASOOD FARAJ
Chief of Admin.: Eng. ABD ELSALAM ELZAROUG
Librarian: IBRAHIM MOHAMED AMIR
Number of teachers: 67
Number of students: 1,160

DERNA UNIVERSITY

Derna
Founded 1995
State control
Languages of instruction: Arabic, English
Faculties of accountancy and economics, fine arts and architecture, law, medical technology and social sciences.

UNIVERSITY OF GARYOUNIS

POB 1308, Benghazi
Telephone: (61) 2220147
Fax: (61) 2230315
Internet: www.garyounis.edu
Founded 1955 as the Faculty of Arts and Education, Benghazi, became University of Benghazi 1973, present name 1976
State control
Language of instruction: Arabic
Chancellor: Dr MUHAMID A. ALMAHDAWI
Registrar: MAHMUD M. FAKHRI
Library: see Libraries and Archives
Number of teachers: 1,300
Number of students: 35,230
Publications: various faculty bulletins.

DEANS

Faculty of Arts and Education: Dr FATHI AL-HARIM
Faculty of Economics: Dr ABDELGADIR AMIR
Faculty of Engineering: Dr BELAID EIKWARI
Faculty of Law: Dr SULMAN AL-GURISH
Faculty of Science: Dr MUHAMID EL-AWIME

NASIR UNIVERSITY

POB 48222, Al-Khums Tripoli
Telephone: (325) 660080
Fax: (325) 660048
Founded 1986
State control
Academic year: September to July
Faculties of arts, economics and political science, education and science, engineering, law, science.

OMAR AL-MUKHTAR UNIVERSITY

POB 991, Al-Bayda
Telephone: (84) 6310719
Fax: (84) 632233
E-mail: info@omulibya.org
Founded 1985
State control
Pres.: ABDALLA A. M. ZAIED
Faculties of agriculture, engineering, literature and education, science and veterinary medicine.

OPEN UNIVERSITY

POB 13375, Tripoli
Telephone: (21) 4874000
Fax: (21) 4874000
E-mail: info@libopenuniv-edu.org
Internet: www.libopenuniv-edu.org
Founded 1987
State control
Language of instruction: Arabic
Academic year: September to July
Pres.: IBRAHIM ABU-FARWA
Number of teachers: 52
Number of students: 8,410
Faculties of accountancy, administration, arabic, economics, education and psychology, geography, history, Islamic studies, law, political science, sociology and social work; Dept of continuing education.

SEBHA UNIVERSITY

POB 18758, Sebha
Telephone: (71) 626012
Fax: (71) 627019
E-mail: info@sebhau.edu.ly
Internet: www.sebhau.edu.ly
Founded 1983 from the Faculty of Education of Al-Fateh University
State control
Languages of instruction: Arabic, English
Academic year: October to August
Chancellor: Dr MOHAMED MUFTAH SALEH
Vice-Chancellor: SALEM ABDULLAH SAID
Registrar: MISBAH AL-GHAWIL
Librarian: ZIDAN AL-BREIKY
Number of teachers: 646
Number of students: 9,403
Publications: *Al-Shifa* (medicine, 1 a year), *Physical Education Magazine* (2 a year)

DEANS

Faculty of Agriculture: Dr MOHAMMAD ABDUL KARIM
Faculty of Arts and Education: HAMED MASHMOOR
Faculty of Dentistry: Dr HASAN AL-BUSAIFY
Faculty of Economics and Accountancy: Dr BASHIR ABU-QILA

Faculty of Engineering and Technology: MOHAMMAD ARAHOOMA

Faculty of Medicine: Dr OMAR IBRAHIM AL-SHAIBANI

Faculty of Physical Education: ABDUL RAHMAN AL-ANSARI

Faculty of Science: Dr MOHAMMAD BASHIR HASAN

SEVENTH OF APRIL UNIVERSITY

POB 16418, Al-Zawia

Telephone: (23) 24035

Fax: (23) 24030

E-mail: 7april_univ@mail.lttnet.net

Founded 1988

State control

Pres.: Prof. SHABAN T. AL ASWAD

Languages of instruction: Arabic, English

Faculties of education, engineering, physical education (women only), science.

SEVENTH OF OCTOBER UNIVERSITY

POB 2478, Misurata

Telephone: (51) 2627201

Fax: (51) 2627350

Internet: www.7ou.edu.ly

Founded 2004

State control

Number of teachers: 961

Number of students: 20,000

Faculties of agriculture, arts, education, engineering, information technology, law, medical technology, medicine, nursing, pharmacy, science; MSc in information technology

in partnership with Nottingham Trent University, UK.

UNIVERSITY OF SIRT

POB 674, Sirt

Telephone: (54) 5260363

Fax: (54) 5262152

E-mail: info@su.edu.ly

Internet: www.su.edu.ly

Founded 1989

State control

Faculties of agriculture, arts, dental, economics, education, engineering, law, medical, medicine, nursing, science, technology

Pres.: Dr MOHAMMED A. A. ABDULLA.

Colleges

African Centre for Applied Research and Training in Social Development (ACARTSOD): POB 80606, Tripoli; tel. (21) 4835103; fax (21) 4835066; e-mail fituri_acartsod@hotmail.com; f. 1977 as an intergovernmental institution under the auspices of the UN Economic Comm. for Africa and the OAU; aims to promote and coordinate applied research and training in the field of social development at regional and sub-regional levels, organizes seminars, etc.; Deputy Exec. Dir Dr AHMED SAID FITURI; publ. *African Social Challenges* (1 a year).

Faculty of Islamic Call: POB 71771 Tripoli; tel. (21) 4801472; fax (21) 4800059; e-mail mu_dyab@yahoo.com; internet www.islamic-call.org/web_fic.html; f. 1974; private control, World Islamic Call Society; 300 students; 4-year courses in Quranic and Arabic studies.

Higher Institute of Industry: Misurata; internet www.hii.edu.ly; f. 1988; state control; Higher National Diplomas, Bachelors of Technology, Masters of Technology; Dean Dr MAJDI A. ASHIBANI.

Higher Institute of Mechanical and Electrical Engineering: POB 61160, Hoon; tel. (57) 602841; fax (57) 602842; e-mail aisa_jadi@yahoo.com; f. 1976; BSc-level studies; library: 22,000 vols, 100 periodicals; 48 teachers; 336 students; Dean AISA S. JADI.

Higher Institute of Technology: POB 68, Brack; tel. (71) 45300; fax (71) 27600; f. 1976; first degree courses in general sciences, medical technology, food technology and environmental sciences; library: 10,000 vols; 60 teachers; 500 students; Dean Dr ABDUSSALAM M. ALMETHNANI.

Islamic Arts and Crafts School: Shar'a 1 September, Tripoli; tel. (21) 3334315.

National Institute of Administration: POB 3651, Tripoli; tel. (21) 4623420; fax (21) 4623423; f. 1953; offers higher diploma in administration and accounting; library: 10,000 vols; 30 teachers; publ. *National Magazine of Administration*.

Posts and Telecommunications Institute: POB 2428, Tripoli; f. 1963; library: 510 vols; Dir K. MARABUTACI.

LIECHTENSTEIN

The Higher Education System

The Principality's first university was not founded until 1992 when the former Liechtensteinische Ingenieurschule (founded 1961; formerly Abendtechnikum Vaduz) achieved university status; it is now known as Hochschule Liechtenstein (Liechtenstein University of Applied Sciences) and is a state-run institution. A private university, Universität für Humanwissenschaften (University of Human Sciences), was founded in Triesen in 2000 and there is also a publicly funded music school in Vaduz. Many Liechtensteiners continue their studies at universities in Austria and Switzerland. In 2004/2005 there were 527 students in higher education in Liechtenstein and 931 attending institutions abroad.

The Hochschule Liechtenstein fully implemented the Bologna changes in 2003. A law approved in 2005 regulates the compulsory use of ECTS with both Masters and Bachelors degrees; it also stipulates that Diploma Supplements should be issued in both German and English. Since the education sector of Liechtenstein is quite small, there is no national qualification framework. Liechtenstein is affiliated to the European Network for Quality Assurance in Higher Education and is committed to the quality standards targeted by that organization.

Admission to higher education depends upon completion of secondary education and award of the Matura. The undergraduate degree is the Bachelors, a three-year programme of study. Following the Bachelors, postgraduate students may be awarded the Nachdiplom (a short-course degree), Magister Philosophiae (requiring five years of study) and finally Doctor of Philosophy.

Vocational and technical training consists of either workplace-oriented apprenticeship schemes or four-year professional courses in civil engineering, mechanical engineering, economics or architecture at Hochschule Liechtenstein.

Regulatory and Representative Bodies

GOVERNMENT

Regierungsgebäude (Government Offices): Postfach 684, 9490 Vaduz; tel. 236-61-11; fax 236-60-22; e-mail office@liechtenstein.li; internet www.liechtenstein.li; Minister of Education, of Social Affairs, of Environmental Affairs, of Land Use Planning, and of Agriculture and Forestry HUGO QUADERER; Minister of Foreign Affairs, of Culture and of Family and Equal Opportunity RITA KIEBER-BECK.

ACCREDITATION

ENIC/NARIC Liechtenstein: Schulamt, Europark, Austr. 79, 9490 Vaduz; tel. 236-67-58; fax 236-67-71; e-mail helmut.konrad@sa.llv.li; internet www.llv.li/amtsstellen/llv-sa-home.htm; Head, Dept for Upper Secondary and Higher Education HELMUT KONRAD.

NATIONAL BODY

Schulamt (Education Office): Austr. 79, 9490 Vaduz; tel. 236-67-70; fax 236-67-71; e-mail info@sa.llv.li; internet www.sa.llv.li; undertakes the devt of education in kindergartens, schools and colleges; drafts and refines curricula; supervises and manages teaching staff; administers educational programmes; Chief Officer GUIDO WOLFINGER.

Learned Societies

HISTORY, GEOGRAPHY AND ARCHAEOLOGY

Historischer Verein für das Fürstentum Liechtenstein (Historical Society for the Principality of Liechtenstein): Plankner Str. 39, Schaan; tel. 392-17-47; fax 392-17-05; e-mail info@hvfl.li; internet www.hvfl.li; f. 1901; 814 mems; library of 3,000 vols; Sec. Lic. phil. KLAUS BIEDERMANN; publ. *Jahrbuch*.

NATURAL SCIENCES

General

Liechtensteinische Gesellschaft für Umweltschutz (Liechtenstein Society for Environmental Protection): Im Bretscha 22, 9494 Schaan; tel. 232-52-62; fax 237-40-31; e-mail info@lgu.li; internet www.lgu.li; f. 1973; 750 mems; Pres. REGULA MOSBERGER; publs *LGU-Mitteilungen* (4 a year), *LGU-Schriftenreihe*, *Liechtensteiner Umweltbericht* (1 or 2 a year).

Research Institute

ECONOMICS, LAW AND POLITICS

Liechtenstein-Institut: Auf dem Kirchhügel, St Luziweg 2, 9487 Bendern; tel. 373-30-22; fax 373-54-22; e-mail admin@liechtenstein-institut.li; internet www.liechtenstein-institut.li; f. 1986; researches on topics related to Liechtenstein in the fields of law, political science, economics and social science, history; Pres. Dr iur. GUIDO MEIER; Dir Dr CHRISTOPH MARIA MERKI.

Libraries and Archives

Vaduz

Liechtensteinische Landesbibliothek: 9490 Vaduz; tel. 236-63-62; fax 233-14-19; e-mail info@landesbibliothek.li; internet www.landesbibliothek.li; f. 1961; public, academic and nat. library; 240,000 vols; Dir BARBARA VOGT.

Liechtensteinisches Landesarchiv (National Archives of Liechtenstein): Petr Kaiser-Pl. 2, Postfach 684, 9490 Vaduz; tel. 236-63-40; fax 236-63-59; e-mail info@la.llv.li; internet www.la.llv.li; f. 1961; nat. archives; reference library of 6,000 shelf-m of documents; Archivist Lic. phil. PAUL VOGT; Deputy Archivist Mag. phil. RUPERT TIEFENTHALER; publ. *Veröffentlichungen des Liechtensteinischen Landesarchivs*.

Museums and Art Galleries

Vaduz

Kunstmuseum Liechtenstein: Städtle 32, Postfach 370, 9490 Vaduz; tel. 235-03-00; fax 235-03-29; e-mail mail@kunstmuseum.li; internet www.kunstmuseum.li; f. 2000; museum of fine arts, incl. private collns of the Prince of Liechtenstein and state collns of international modern art; Dir Dr FRIEDEMANN MALSCH.

Liechtensteinisches Landesmuseum (Liechtenstein National Museum): Städtle 43, Postfach 1216, 9490 Vaduz; tel. 236-75-50; fax 236-75-52; e-mail landesmuseum@llm.llv.li; internet www.landesmuseum.li; f. 1954; includes items from the collections of the Prince, the State, and the Liechtenstein Historical Soc.; Pres. EVA PEPIC.

Postmuseum des Fürstentums Liechtenstein: Postfach 9490, Städtle 37, 9490 Vaduz; tel. 399-44-66; fax 399-44-94; e-mail briefmarken@post.li; internet www.philatelie.li; f. 1930; Liechtenstein stamps, historical postal documents, postal machinery; Dir NORBERT HASLER.

Universities

HOCHSCHULE LIECHTENSTEIN (Liechtenstein University of Applied Sciences)

Fürst-Franz-Josef-Str., 9490 Vaduz

Telephone: 265-11-11
Fax: 265-11-12
E-mail: info@hochschule.li
Internet: www.hochschule.li

Founded 1961 as Abendtechnikum Vaduz; renamed Liechtensteinische Ingenieurschule 1985; university status 1992; renamed Fachhochschule Liechtenstein 1997; present name 2005

State control

Languages of instruction: German, English

Rector: KLAUS NÄSCHER
Librarian: ULRIKE BRUNHART
Number of students: 500

Publication: *Denkfabrik* (magazine, 2 a year)

DEANS

Faculty of Architecture: Prof. Dipl. Ing. HANSJÖRG HILTI
Faculty of Business Studies: Dipl. Ing. HARTWIG BISCHOF
Faculty of Humanities: Dr ROBERT BLUNDER

PROFESSORS

BALDEGGER, U., Entrepreneurship
EISINGER, A., Urban Construction and Development
HILTI, H., Design and Woodwork
KÄFERSTEIN, J., Design and Construction
MEISTER, U., Design and Construction
MENICHETTI, M. J., Business Economics
WEINMANN, S, Information Technology for Business

WENZ, M., Business Management and International and Liechtenstein Tax Law
WINNING, H.-H., Urban Construction, Planning and Transport

**UFL PRIVATE UNIVERSITÄT IM FÜRSTENTUM LIECHTENSTEIN
(Private University of the Pricipality of Liechtenstein)**

Dorfstr. 24, 9495 Triesen
Telephone: 392-40-10
Fax: 392-40-11
E-mail: info@ufl.li
Internet: www.ufl.li
Founded 2000
Private control
Rector: Prof. Dr KARL M. SUDI

Courses in medical science, mediation and conflict resolution.

College

Liechtensteinische Musikschule: St Florinsgasse 1, 9490 Vaduz; tel. 232-46-20; fax 232-46-42; e-mail info@musikschule.li; internet www.musikschule.li; f. 1963; 93 teachers; 2,450 students; library: 12,000 vols, special colln of works of composer Josef Gabriel Rheinberger; int. masterclasses June to September; Dir JOSEF FROMMELT.

LITHUANIA

The Higher Education System

The oldest existing institution of higher education in Lithuania is Vilniaus Universitetas (Vilnius University), founded in 1579 when Lithuania was united in a Commonwealth with Poland. The next oldest institution is Vilniaus Dailes Akademija (Vilnius Academy of Fine Arts), founded in 1793. In 1795 Lithuania was annexed by the Russian Empire and remained under Russian (and later, Bolshevik) rule until 1920, when the USSR recognized Lithuanian independence. In 1922 Lithuania was declared a parliamentary democracy under the terms of its first Constitution. Several university-level institutions date from this year, among them Kauno Medicinos Universitetas (Kaunas Medical University), Kauno Technologijos Universitetas (Kaunas University of Technology) and Vytauto Didžiojo Universitetas (Vytautas Magnus University). According to the 'Secret Protocols' to the 1939 Treaty of Non-Aggression signed by the USSR and Nazi Germany, Lithuania was to come under German influence. However, the subsequent Nazi-Soviet Treaty on Friendship and Existing Borders granted the USSR control of Lithuania. In 1940 the Lithuanian Government was forced to resign and a Soviet Socialist Republic was established. In 1990 Lithuania was the first Soviet republic to declare independence, although this was not recognized by the USSR State Council until 1991. In February of that year the Supreme Council of the Republic of Lithuania adopted the Law on Science and Studies, which established the guidelines of higher education reform, with the intention of bringing Lithuania's research and higher education system closer to that of Western Europe. Following the introduction of the Law on Education in 2000, Lithuania participates in the Bologna Process to establish a European Higher Education Area, the first phase of which is to adopt a credit-based system of comparable degrees with two main cycles (undergraduate and graduate). From 2003 a uniform tuition fee was introduced for students in higher education, although there were exemptions for the highest achievers. In 2007/08 there were 22 universities and 28 colleges. In that year total enrolment in higher education was an estimated 204,432. External evaluation of university studies is carried out by the Centre for Quality Assessment in Higher Education, which was founded in 1995.

The main requirement for admission to university is the Certificate of Maturity (Brandos Atestatas), the main secondary school qualification. Institutions receiving more applications than places available set competitive entrance examinations. Lithuania has established a two-tier Bachelors (Bakalauras) and Masters (Magistras) degree system in accordance with the principles of the Bologna Process. The Bachelors is a four-year programme of study and students are required to accrue 160 credits for award of the degree. Following the Bachelors is the Masters, the first postgraduate-level degree. This is a programme of study lasting one-and-a-half to two years, and may be awarded in conjunction with a professional title. The Doctorate (Daktaras) follows the Masters and requires up to four years of study, covering classroom-based instruction and original thesis research. A 2006 amendment to the Law on Higher Education enabled colleges to award a Professional Bachelor degree (profesinis bakalauras) from 2007 onwards. Since 2007 college graduates wishing to continue Masters studies in universities do not have to complete university Bachelors programmes.

Technical and vocational education at post-secondary level is available at junior colleges and vocational schools (Aukstesnioji mokykla). Qualifications offered include the Higher Education Diploma (Aukštojo Mokslo Diplomas) and College Diploma (Aukštesniojo Mokslo Diplomas).

In 2007 the Ministry of Education and Science launched a reform of scientific research in higher education institutes with the Law on Science and Studies. In 2009 a new law was approved outlining how a number of research institutes would be incorporated into certain universities and other reform measures on funding.

Regulatory and Representative Bodies

GOVERNMENT

Ministry of Culture: J. Basanavičiaus 5, 01118 Vilnius; tel. (5) 261-94-86; fax (5) 262-31-20; e-mail culture@muza.lt; internet www.muza.lt; Minister JONAS JUČAS.

Ministry of Education and Science: A. Volano 2/7, 01516 Vilnius; tel. (5) 274-31-26; fax (5) 261-20-77; e-mail smmin@smm.lt; internet www.smm.lt; Minister ROMA ŽAKAITIENĖ.

ACCREDITATION

ENIC/NARIC Lithuania: Suvalku g. 1, 03106 Vilnius; tel. (5) 210-47-77; fax (5) 213-25-53; e-mail enicnaric@skvc.lt; internet www.skvc.lt; Deputy Dir AURELIJA VALEIKIENE.

NATIONAL BODIES

Lietuvos kolegijų direktorių konferencija (Lithuanian College Directors' Conference): Antakalnio g. 54, 10303 Vilnius; tel. (5) 234 3516; fax (5) 234 3769; e-mail a.aleknaviciene@vsdk.lt; internet www.kolegijos.lt; Pres. NIJOLĖ KIKUTIENĖ; Exec. Dir ANA ALEKNAVIČIENĖ.

Lietuvos mokslo taryba (Research Council of Lithuania): Gedimino ave 3, 01103 Vilnius; tel. (5) 212-49-33; fax (5) 261-85-35; e-mail lmt@ktl.mii.lt; internet www.lmt.lt; f. 1991; promotes the devt of higher education and research; funds research projects; advises the Seimas (Parliament) and the Govt in these areas; initiates and evaluates legislative proposals in the field of science; 29 mems; Chair. Prof. Dr Habil. EUGENIJUS BUTKUS; Dir AUSRA VILUTIENE.

Lietuvos Universitetų Rektorių Konferencija (Lithuanian University Rectors' Conference): Tilto str. 16, 01101 Vilnius; tel. (5) 212-06-29; fax (5) 212-06-29; e-mail lurkbiuras@gmail.com; internet www.lurk.lt; Pres. Prof. Dr hab. ROMUALDAS GINEVIČIUS; Gen. Sec. Prof. KĘSTUTIS KRIŠČIŪNAS.

Nacionalinis egzaminų centras (National Examination Centre): M. Katkaus g. 44, Vilnius; tel. (5) 275-61-80; fax (5) 275-22-68; e-mail centras@nec.lt; internet www.egzaminai.lt; f. 1996; organizes and carries out examination of candidates' knowledge and skills; Dir DANUTĖ ŠUKIENĖ.

Studijų kokybės vertinimo centras (Centre for Quality Assessment in Higher Education): Suvalkų g. 1, 03106 Vilnius; tel. (5) 210-47-77; fax (5) 213-25-53; e-mail skvc@skvc.lt; internet www.skvc.lt; f. 1995; ind. public agency assessing the quality of higher education and the qualifications concerning higher education; Dir EUGENIJUS STUMBRYS.

Learned Societies

GENERAL

Lithuanian Academy of Sciences: 3 Gedimino pr., 01103 Vilnius; tel. (5) 261-36-51; fax (5) 261-84-64; e-mail prezidiumas@ktl.mii.lt; internet neris.mii.lt/lma; f. 1941; divisions of Agriculture and Forestry (Head Prof. ALBINAS KUSTA), Biological, Medical and Geosciences (Head Prof. VYTAS ANTANAS TAMOSIUNAS), Humanities and Social Sciences (Head Prof. LEONARDAS SAUKA), Mathematics, Physics and Chemistry (Head Prof. VALDEMARAS RAZUMAS), Technical Sciences (Head Prof. VYTAUTAS OSTASEVICIUS); 194 mems (40 full, 60 corresp., 50 expert, 44 foreign); library: see Libraries and Archives; Pres. Prof. ZENONAS ROKUS RUDZIKAS; Sec.-Gen. Prof. VALDEMARAS RAZUMAS; publs *Acta medica Lituanica* (3 or 4 a year), *Arts Studies* (5 a year), *Journal of Agricultural Sciences* (4 a year), *Journal of Biology* (4 a year), *Journal of Chemistry* (4 a year), *Journal of Ecology* (3 or 4 a year), *Journal of Geography* (4 a year), *Journal of Geology* (4 a year), *Journal of Philosophy and Sociology* (3 or 4 a year), *Journal of Power Engineering* (4 a year), *Lithuanian Science* (5 or 6 a year), *Lituanistica* (3 or 4 a year), *Science and Technology* (12 a year).

LANGUAGE AND LITERATURE

Alliance Française: Mykolo Romerio Universitetas, Ateities g. 20-118, 08303 Vilnius; tel. (5) 271-46-72; fax (5) 271-45-22; offers courses and exams in French language and culture and promotes cultural exchange with France.

British Council: Jogailos 4, 01116 Vilnius; tel. (5) 264-48-90; fax (5) 264-48-93; e-mail mail@britishcouncil.lt; internet www .britishcouncil.org/lithuania; f. 1992; offers courses and exams in English language and British culture and promotes cultural exchange with the UK; library of 5,201 vols; Dir LINA BALENAITE; Information Centre Man. RIMA KLUSOVSKIENE.

Goethe-Institut: Tilto g. 3-6, 01101 Vilnius; tel. (5) 231-44-33; fax (5) 231-44-32; e-mail info@vilnius.goethe.org; internet www .goethe.de/ne/vil/deindex.htm; offers courses and exams in German language and culture and promotes cultural exchange with Germany; Dir IRMTRAUT HUBATSCH.

PEN Centre of Lithuania: K. Sirvydo 6, 01101 Vilnius; tel. (6) 169-51-38; fax (5) 212-65-56; e-mail almantsam@yahoo.com; f. 1989; promotes friendship and cooperation among writers internationally; campaigns for freedom of expression, human rights and democratic causes; 34 mems; Pres. Assoc. Prof. Dr ALMANTAS SAMALAVICIUS; Sec. LAIMANTAS JONUSYS.

Research Institutes

AGRICULTURE, FISHERIES AND VETERINARY SCIENCE

Institute of Forestry, Lithuanian Research Centre for Agriculture and Forestry: Liepų 1, 53101 Girionys, Kauno Dist.; tel. (37) 54-72-21; fax (37) 54-74-46; e-mail miskinst@mi.lt; internet www.mi.lt; f. 1950; main areas of research: biodiversity and sustainability of forest ecosystems; reforestation; forest productivity increment, protection and usage; forest genetic resources and breeding of forest trees; forest policy, social and economic problems; library of 60,000 vols; Dir Prof. Dr habil. REMIGIJUS OZOLINČIUS; Scientific Sec. Dr DIANA MIZARAITĖ; publs *Baltic Forestry* (2 a year), *Miškininkystė* (Silviculture, 2 a year).

ECONOMICS, LAW AND POLITICS

Institute of Economics: Goštauto g. 12, 01108 Vilnius; tel. (5) 262-35-02; fax (5) 212-75-06; e-mail ei@ktl.mii.lt; f. 1941; attached to Lithuanian Acad. of Sciences; research in mathematical modelling; devt of Lithuanian economy; integration into EU; history of economic thought; 12 mems; library of 5,000 vols; Dir Prof. EDUARDAS VILKAS.

Institute for Social Research: Saltoniškių 58, 08105 Vilnius; tel. (5) 275-86-67; fax (5) 275-48-96; e-mail sti@ktl.mii.lt; internet www.sti.lt; f. 1977; 92 mems; Dir Prof. ARVYDAS VIRGILIJUS MATULIONIS; publs *Humanistika*, *Logos*, *Philosophy and Sociology* (4 a year).

FINE AND PERFORMING ARTS

Institute of Culture and Arts: Tilto 4, 01101 Vilnius; tel. (5) 262-60-91; fax (5) 261-09-89; Dir Prof. Dr A. MATULIONIS; Scientific Sec. Dr A. ŠIMĖNIENĖ; publ. *The Art Studies* (2 a year).

HISTORY, GEOGRAPHY AND ARCHAEOLOGY

Institute of Geology and Geography: T. Ševčenkos 13, 03223 Vilnius; tel. (5) 210-46-90; fax (5) 210-46-95; e-mail info@geo.lt; internet www.geo.lt; f. 1941; Dir PETRAS ŠINKŪNAS; publs *Annales Geographicae* (Geografijos metraštis, Geographical Yearbook, 1 a year), *Baltica* (1 a year), *Geografija* (Geography), *Geologija* (Geology, 4 a year).

Institute of Lithuanian History: Kražių g. 5, 01108 Vilnius; tel. (5) 261-44-36; fax (5) 261-44-33; e-mail istorija@istorija.lt; internet www.istorija.lt; library of 142,000 vols; Dir Habil. Dr doc. ALVYDAS NIKŽENTAITIS; publs *Archeologija Baltica* (Lithuanian Archaeology), *Lietuvos archeologija* (Lithuanian Archaeology), *Lithuanian Ethnology*, *Lithuanian Historical Studies*, *Lithuanian Metrica*, *Lituanistica*, *Urban Past*, *Yearbook of Lithuanian History*.

LANGUAGE AND LITERATURE

Institute of Lithuanian Language: P. Vileisio 5, 10308 Vilnius 55; tel. (5) 234-64-72; fax (5) 234-72-00; e-mail lki@lki.lt; internet www.lki.lt; f. 1939; 48 mems; library: Archives of Lithuanian Dialects; Dir Asst Prof. JOLANTA ZABARSKAITE; Vice-Dir ARTURAS JUDZENTIS; publs *Acta Linguistica Lithuanica* (2 a year), *Archivum Lithuanicum* (1 a year), *Culture of Language* (1 a year), *Terminology* (1 a year).

Institute of Lithuanian Literature and Folklore: Antakalnio 6, 10308 Vilnius; tel. (5) 262-19-43; fax (5) 261-62-54; e-mail direk@llti.lt; internet www.llti.lt; f. 1939; library of 240,000 vols and other printed matter; Dir MINDAUGAS KVIETKAUSKAS; publs *Colloquia* (2 a year), *Senoji Lietuvos literatura* (Old Lithuanian Literature, 2 a year), *Tautosakos darbai* (Folklore Studies, 2 a year).

MEDICINE

Institute of Hygiene: Didžioji 22, 01128 Vilnius; tel. (5) 262-45-83; fax (5) 262-46-63; e-mail institutas@hi.lt; internet www.hi.lt; f. 1808; library of 8,000 vols; Dir Prof. habil Dr JULIUS KALIBATAS; publ. *Public Health* (4 a year).

Institute of Oncology, Vilnius University: Santariškių 1, 08660 Vilnius; tel. (5) 278-67-00; fax (5) 272-01-64; e-mail administracija@loc.lt; internet www.loc.lt; f. 1990; Dir Prof. Dr K. VALUCKAS.

State Research Institute Centre for Innovative Medicine: Žygimantų g. 9, 01102 Vilnius; tel. (5) 262-86-36; fax (5) 212-30-73; e-mail algirdas.venalis@ekmi.vu .lt; internet www.imcentras.lt; f. 2010; rheumatology, regenerative medicine, immunology, immunotechnology, molecular biology; Dir Prof. Dr hab. ALGIRDAS VENALIS.

NATURAL SCIENCES

Biological Sciences

Institute of Biochemistry: Mokslininkų 12, 08662 Vilnius; tel. (5) 272-91-44; fax (5) 272-91-96; e-mail biochemija@bchi.lt; internet www.bchi.lt; f. 1967; Dir Prof. Dr hab. VALDAS LAURINAVICIUS.

Institute of Botany: Žaliųjų ežerų 49, 08406 Vilnius; tel. (5) 271-16-18; fax (5) 272-99-50; e-mail botanika@botanika.lt; internet www.botanika.lt/bi; f. 1959; Dir Dr VALERIJUS RAŠOMAVIČIUS; publ. *Botanica Lithuanica* (4 a year).

Institute of Ecology of Vilnius University: Akademijos g. 2, 08412 Vilnius 21; tel. and fax (5) 272-93-52; e-mail ekoi@ekoi.lt; internet www.ekoi.lt; f. 1945; attached to

Vilnius Univ.; library of 77,000 vols; Dir Dr habil. MEČISLOVAS ŽALAKEVIČIUS; publ. *Acta Zoologica Lituanica* (in English, 4 a year).

Mathematical Sciences

Institute of Mathematics and Informatics: Akademijos g. 4, 08663 Vilnius; tel. (5) 210-93-00; fax (5) 272-92-09; e-mail mathematica@ktl.mii.lt; internet www.mii.lt; f. 1956; Dir Prof. Dr hab. GINTAUTAS DZEMYDA; publs *Informatica*, *Informatics in Education*, *Lithuanian Mathematical Journal* (4 a year), *Mathematical Modelling and Analysis*, *Nonlinear Analysis: Modelling and Control*.

Physical Sciences

Institute of Chemistry: A. Goštauto 9, 01108 Vilnius; tel. (5) 261-26-63; fax (5) 261-70-18; e-mail chemins@ktl.mii.lt; internet www.chi.lt; f. 1945; Dir Prof. Dr hab. EIMUTIS JUZELIŪNAS.

Institute of Physics: Savanorių pr. 231, 02300 Vilnius; tel. (5) 266-16-40; fax (5) 260-23-17; e-mail fi@fi.lt; internet www.fi.lt; f. 1977; environmental physics and chemistry, in atmosphere and hydrosphere, investigations of atmospheric pollution regularities, background and anthropogenic pollution monitoring; molecular biophysics and chemical physics incl. dynamic processes in proteins, polymers and organized molecular structures; nuclear physics, devt and application of nuclear spectroscopy methods, environmental radioactivity research; nonlinear optics and spectroscopy, devt and applications of lasers, investigations of mega system evolution; Dir Prof. Dr VIDMANTAS REMEIKIS.

Institute of Theoretical Physics and Astronomy of Vilnius University: A. Goštauto g. 12, 01108 Vilnius; tel. (5) 262-09-47; fax (5) 212-53-61; e-mail atom@itpa.lt; internet www.itpa.lt; f. 1990; attached to Lithuanian Acad. of Sciences and Vilnius University; library of 250,000 vols; investigations of atoms, subatomic particles, molecules, their structures and plasma spectroscopy, their application in nanophysics and astrophysics; Dir and Head of Astronomical Observatory Dr Hab. GRAŽINA TAUTVAIŠIENĖ; publs *Baltic Astronomy* (4 a year), *Lietuvos dangus* (Sky of Lithuania; in Lithuanian, 1 a year), *Lithuanian Journal of Physics* (4 a year).

TECHNOLOGY

Institute of Biotechnology: A. V. Graičiūno st 8, 02241 Vilnius; tel. (5) 260-21-12; fax (5) 260-21-16; e-mail giedre@ibt.lt; internet www.ibt.lt; f. 1975; state research institute and biotechnology centre active in multidisciplinary studies of restriction, modification enzymes, research and devt of recombinant biomedical proteins; 7 laboratories specializing in Protein–DNA Interactions, Biological DNA Modification, Prokaryote Gene Engineering, Eukaryote Gene Engineering, Immunology, Biothermodynamics and Drug Design and Bioinformatics; 120 mems; Dir Dr habil. A. PAULIUKONIS.

Lithuanian Energy Institute: Breslaujos 3, 44403 Kaunas; tel. (37) 40-18-05; fax (37) 35-12-71; e-mail rastine@mail.lei.lt; internet www.lei.lt; f. 1956; library of 40,000 vols; Dir Prof. Dr Hab. EUGENIJUS UŠPURAS; publs *Energetika* (Power Engineering, 4 a year), *Environmental Research, Engineering and Management* (4 a year), *Lietuvos Energetika* (Energy in Lithuania, 1 a year).

Semiconductor Physics Institute: A. Goštauto g. 11, 01108 Vilnius; tel. (5) 261-97-59; fax (5) 262-71-23; e-mail spiadm@pfi.lt;

internet www.pfi.lt; f. 1967; Dir Prof. Dr Hab. STEPONAS ASMONTAS.

Libraries and Archives

Vilnius

Library of the Lithuanian Academy of Sciences: Žygimantu 1/8, 01102 Vilnius; tel. (5) 262-95-37; fax (5) 262-13-24; e-mail biblioteka@mab.lt; internet www.mab.lt; f. 1941; 3,733,000 vols incl. 250,610 manuscripts; Dir Dr JUOZAS MARCINKEVIČIUS.

Lithuanian Technical Library: Šv. Ignoto 6, 01120 Vilnius; tel. (5) 261-87-18; fax (5) 261-03-79; e-mail info@tb.lt; internet www.tb .lt; f. 1957; patent information centre; publishes official bulletins and patent documents of the State Patent Bureau; 36,768,138 vols; Dir KAZYS MACKEVIČIUS.

Martynas Mažvydas National Library of Lithuania: Gedimino pr. 51, 01109 Vilnius; tel. (5) 262-90-23; fax (5) 262-71-29; e-mail biblio@lnb.lrs.lt; internet www.lnb.lt; f. 1919; incorporated National Printing Archive 1992; 7m. vols in total, incl. 4m. books, periodicals, and reference publications, 70,000 MSS, 103,000 microforms, 63,000 audiovisual items, 30,000 old and rare books; National Printing Archive consists of 2,174,574 items, including books, maps and periodicals since the 16th century, as well as books printed in Lithuania since the 16th century in Latin, Polish and Russian; Rare Book and Manuscript department contains 70,000 items, including 30,000 books from the 15th to the 18th century (including works by early Church reformers, Martin Luther and Philip Melanchton, and the humanist Erasmus), private archives of prominent Lithuanians since the 19th century, 149 parchments (including privileges of the Grand Dukes of Lithuania and the Kings of Poland), as well as autographs, legal documents and photographs since the 15th century; 200,000 items in Music Department, including 100,000 items of printed music since the 16th century, 500 rare music scores and 55,000 audiovisual items; Dir VYTAUTAS GUDAITIS; publ. *Tarp Knygų* (12 a year).

Vilnius University Library: Universiteto g. 3, 01122 Vilnius; tel. (5) 268-71-01; fax (5) 268-71-04; e-mail mb@mb.vu.lt; internet www.mb.vu.lt; f. 1570; 5,349,881 vols, 251,320 MSS, 87,928 graphic art items, 437,367 UN publs; Dir IRENA KRIVIENĖ.

Museums and Art Galleries

Kaunas

Kaunas Botanical Garden: Ž. E. Žilibero 6, 46324 Kaunas; tel. (37) 39-00-33; fax (37) 39-01-33; e-mail bs@bs.vdu.lt; internet www.vdu .lt/botanika/bot_garden.htm; f. 1923; attached to Vytautas Magnus University; 62 hectares; research into botany, ecology and the natural environment; library of 10,000 vols; Dir Dr REMIGIJUS DAUBAZAS.

M. K. Čiurlionis National Museum of Art: Vlado Putvinskio 55, 44248 Kaunas; tel. (37) 22-94-75; fax (37) 22-26-06; e-mail mkc@ takas.lt; internet www.ciurlionis.lt; f. 1921; Lithuanian and European art, folk art, oriental and ancient Egyptian art, numismatics; named after Lithuanian artist M. K. Čiurlionis (1875–1911); library of 30,000 vols; Dir OSVALDAS DAUGELIS; Deputy Dir DAINA KAMARAUSKIENĖ.

Vytautas the Great War Museum: K. Donelaičio 64, 44248 Kaunas; tel. (37) 42-

21-46; fax (37) 42-07-65; e-mail v.d .karomuziejus@takas.lt; f. 1921; archaeological finds, weapons, fire-arms, ammunition, army uniforms, objects and documents relating to the transatlantic flight of the 'Lituanica'; colln of ethnographic photographs by Balys Buracas (1897–1972); Dir JUOZAPAS JUREVIČIUS.

Trakai

Trakai Historical Museum: Kęstučio 4, Trakai 21104; tel. (528) 5-82-41; e-mail trakai.museum@is.lt; f. 1948; 16th- and 17th-century tiles, coins, pottery, bone chessmen and other artefacts discovered during excavations at Trakai Castle; also ethnographic and applied art collections; Dir VIRGILIJUS POVILIŪNAS.

Vilnius

Lithuanian Art Museum: Didžioji 4, 01128 Vilnius; tel. (5) 262-80-30; fax (5) 212-60-06; e-mail muziejus@ldm.lt; internet www.ldm .lt; f. 1933; library of 25,166 vols; Lithuanian and foreign works of fine and applied art; br. museums incl. Vilnius Picture Gallery, Museum of Applied Art, Foreign Art Gallery, Pranas Gudynas Restoration Centre of Museum Treasures, Klaipėda Picture Gallery, Clock Museum, Palanga Amber Museum, Juodkrantė Exhibition Hall; Dir ROMUALDAS BUDRYS; publ. *Issues of the Museum* (1 a year).

National Museum of Lithuania: Arsenalo 1, 01100 Vilnius; tel. (5) 262-77-74; fax (5) 261-10-23; e-mail muziejus@lnm.lt; internet www.lnm.lt; f. 1855; history, ethnography, numismatics, archaeology, iconography; library of 55,000 vols; Dir BIRUTĖ KULNYTĖ; publs *Archaeology, Ethnography* (1 a year), *Museum* (1 a year), *Numismatics* (1 a year).

Universities

KAUNO MEDICINOS UNIVERSITETAS (Kaunas Medical University)

A. Mickevičiaus str. 9, 44307 Kaunas

Telephone: (37) 32-72-01

Fax: (37) 22-07-33

E-mail: rektoratas@kmu.lt

Internet: www.kmu.lt

Founded 1922 as Faculty of Medicine of Kaunas Univ.; Kaunas Medical Institute 1950; Kaunas Medical Acad. 1989; univ. status 1998

State control

Rector: Prof. REMIGIJUS ŽALIŪNAS

Vice-Rector for Research: Prof. VAIVA LESAUS-KAITĖ

Vice-Rector for Studies: Prof. RENALDAS JUR-KEVIČIUS

Vice-Rector for University Clinics: Prof. JUOZAS PUNDZIUS

Library of 650,000 vols (53% in Russian, 28% in Lithuanian, 19% in English, German, French and Polish)

Number of teachers: 450 (incl. researchers)

Number of students: 5,250

DEANS

Faculty of Medicine: Prof. ALGIMANTAS TAME-LIS

Faculty of Nursing: Prof. JŪRATĖ MACIJAUS-KIENĖ

Faculty of Odontology: Prof. RIČARDAS KUBI-LIUS

Faculty of Pharmacy: Prof. VITALIS BRIEDIS

Faculty of Public Health: Prof. RAMUNĖ KALĖDIENĖ

KAUNO TECHNOLOGIJOS UNIVERSITETAS (Kaunas University of Technology)

K. Donelaičio 73, 44029 Kaunas

Telephone: (37) 30-00-11

Fax: (37) 32-41-44

E-mail: rastine@ktu.lt

Internet: www.ktu.lt

Founded 1922

State control

Academic year: September to June

Vice-Rector for Infrastructure: Prof. SIGITAS STANYS

Vice-Rector for Research: Prof. RYMANTAS KAZYS

Vice-Rector for Strategic Devt: Prof. GINTAU-TAS ŽINTELIS

Vice-Rector for Studies: PRANAS ŽILIUKAS

Head of Admin: Prof. ALGIMANTAS NAVICKAS

Librarian: GENOVAITE DUOBINIENĖ

Library of 1,329,925 vols

Number of teachers: 1,045

Number of students: 16,703

Publications: *Chemical Technology* (4 a year), *Economics and Management* (1 a year), *Electronics and Electrical Engineering* (8 a year), *Engineering Economics* (5 a year), *Environmental Research, Engineering and Management* (4 a year), *Humanistica* (2 a year), *Information Technology and Control* (4 a year), *Language Teaching and Learning in the Context of Social Changes* (2 a year), *Materials Science* (4 a year), *Measurements* (4 a year), *Mechanics* (6 a year), *Public Politics and Administration* (4 a year), *Social Sciences* (4 a year), *Studies about Languages* (2 a year), *Ultrasound* (4 a year)

DEANS

Faculty of Chemical Technology: Prof. ZIG-MUNTAS JONAS BERESNEVIČIUS

Faculty of Civil Engineering and Architecture: Dr ŽYMANTAS RUDZIONIS

Faculty of Design and Technology: Dr VIRGI-NIJA JANKAUSKAITE

Faculty of Economics and Management: Dr GRAZINA STARTIENE

Faculty of Electrical Engineering and Control Systems: Prof. JONAS DAUNORAS

Faculty of Fundamental Sciences: Dr VYTAU-TAS JANILIONIS

Faculty of Humanities: Prof. GIEDRIUS KUPREVIČIUS

Faculty of Informatics: Prof. ALEKSANDRAS TARGAMADZĖ

Faculty of Mechanical Engineering: Prof. ALGIMANTAS FEDARAVIČIUS

Faculty of Social Sciences: Dr VIKTORIJA BARŠAUSKIENĖ

Faculty of Telecommunications and Electronics: Dr ALGIMANTAS VALINEVICIUS

International Studies Centre: Dr ARVYDAS PALEVICIUS

Panevėžys Institute: Prof. ŽILVINAS BAZARAS

KLAIPĖDOS UNIVERSITETAS (Klapėda University)

H. Manto 84, 92294 Klaipėda

Telephone: (46) 39-89-00

Fax: (46) 39-89-02

E-mail: vladas.zulkus@ku.lt

Internet: www.ku.lt

Founded 1991

State control

Academic year: September to June

Rector: Prof. Dr habil. VLADAS ŽULKUS

Vice-Rector for Academic Affairs: Prof. Dr VAIDUTIS LAURĖNAS

Vice-Rector for Administration: Doc. Dr ADOLFAS BRĖSKIS

Vice-Rector for International Relations: Prof. Dr VILIJA TARGAMADZĖ
Vice-Rector for Research and Art: Prof. Dr habil. BENEDIKTAS TILICKIS
Library Director: JANINA PUPELIENĖ
Library of 458,275 books, 30,453 periodicals
Number of teachers: 431 full-time
Number of students: 7,666 (7,578 undergraduate, 88 postgraduate)
Publications: *Acta Historica Universitatis Klavpeolencis* (1 a year), *Archiviem Lituanuciem* (1 a year), *Jura ir aplinka* (Sea and Environment, 4 a year), *Sociologija: miutis ir veolumas* (Sociology: Thought and Action, 2 a year), *Tiltai* (Bridges, 4 a year)

DEANS

Faculty of Arts: Prof. VYTAUTAS TETENSKAS
Faculty of Education: Doc. ANTANAS LUKOŠEVIČIUS
Faculty of Health Sciences: Prof. Dr habil. ALGIMANTAS KIRKUTIS
Faculty of Humanities: Doc. ALEKSANDRAS ŽALYS
Faculty of Marine Engineering: Prof. Dr VYTENIS ALBERTAS ZABUKAS
Faculty of Science and Mathematics: Doc. PETRAS GRECEVIČIUS
Faculty of Social Sciences: Doc. ANTANAS BUČINSKAS

LIETUVOS ŽEMĖS ŪKIO UNIVERSITETAS
(Lithuanian University of Agriculture)

Akademija, Studentu 11, 53361 Kaunas
Telephone and fax (37) 39-75-00
E-mail: laa@nora.lzuu.lt
Internet: www.lzuu.lt
Founded 1924
State control
Languages of instruction: Lithuanian, English
Academic year: September to June
Chancellor: Assoc. Prof. Dr ALGIMANTAS PATASIUS
Rector: Prof. Dr Hab. ROMUALDAS DELTUVAS
Vice-Rector: Prof. Dr JONAS ČAPLIKAS
Dir of Library: AUŠRA RAGUCKAITĖ
Library of 520,900 vols, 260 periodicals
Number of teachers: 410
Number of students: 7,000
Publications: *Agricultural Engineering, Agriculture, Agronomy Research, Baltic Forestry, Economics and Rural Development, Environmental Research Engineering and Management, Horticulture and Vegetable Science, Management Theory and Studies for Rural Business and Infrastructure Development, Silviculture, The Quality of Higher Education, Veterinary and Zootechnic, Water Management*

DEANS

Faculty of Agricultural Engineering: Assoc. Prof. Dr VIDMANTAS BUTKUS
Faculty of Agronomy: Assoc. Prof. Dr VIKTORAS PRANCKIETIS
Faculty of Economics and Management: Prof. Dr NERINGA STONČIUVIENĖ
Faculty of Forestry and Ecology: Assoc. Prof. Dr EDMUNDAS BARTKEVIČIUS
Faculty of Water and Land Management: Assoc. Prof. Dr VIDMANTAS GURKLYS

ATTACHED RESEARCH INSTITUTES

Institute of the Environment: Dir Assoc. Prof. Dr VIDA RUTKOVIENĖ.

Institute of Information Technologies: Dir Assoc. Prof. Dr ALEKSANDRAS SAVILIONIS.

Institute of Rural Culture: Dir Assoc. Prof. Dr SVETLANA STATKEVIĖIENĖ.

Research Institute of Agricultural Engineering: Instituto 20, Raudondvaris, 54132 Kauno; tel. (37) 44-96-43; fax (37) 54-93-66; e-mail institutas@mei.lt; internet www.mei.lt; Dir Dr GVIDAS RUTKAUSKAS.

Water Management Institute of Lithuanian University of Agriculture: Parko 6, 58102 Vilainiai Kėdainiai; tel. (34) 76-81-00; fax (34) 76-81-05; e-mail sigitas@water.omnitel.net; internet www.waterland.lt; Dir Dr ANTANAS SIGITAS SILEIKA.

MYKOLO ROMERIO UNIVERSITETAS
(Mykolas Romeris University)

Ateities 20, 08303 Vilnius
Telephone: (5) 271-46-47
Fax: (5) 267-00-00
E-mail: roffice@mruni.lt
Internet: www.mruni.lt
Founded 1990 as Law University of Lithuania; present name 2000
State control
Rector: Prof. Dr ALVYDAS PUMPUTIS
University Secretary: ANTANAS KERAS
Librarian: ALMONE JAKUBCIONIENE
Library of 156,042 vols, 188 periodicals
Number of students: 16,000

DEANS

Faculty of Economics and Management: Assoc. Prof. Dr VITALIJA RUDZKIENĖ
Faculty of Law: Prof. Dr JUOZAS ZILYS
Faculty of Public Administration: Dr TADAS SUDNICKAS
Faculty of Social Policy: Assoc. Prof. Dr LETA DROMANTIENE
Faculty of Strategic Management and Policy: Prof. habil. dr VYGANDAS K. PAULIKAS
Kaunas Faculty of Police: ANTANAS BUTAVIČIUS

ATTACHED RESEARCH INSTITUTE

Centre for Research: Deputy Dir SAULĖ MAČIUKAITĖ-ŽVINIENĖ.

ŠIAULIŲ UNIVERSITETAS
(Šiauliai University)

Vilniaus g. 88, 76285 Šiauliai
Telephone: (41) 59-58-00
Fax: (41) 59-58-09
E-mail: all@cr.su.lt
Internet: www.su.lt
Founded 1997 by merger of Šiauliai Pedagogical Institute and Šiauliai Polytechnical Faculty of Kaunas University of Technology
State control
Rector: Prof. habil. dr VINCAS LAURUTIS
Librarian: LORETA BURBAITĖ
Library of 400,000 vols, 550 periodicals
Number of teachers: 840
Number of students: 10,000
Publications: *Jaunujų mokslininkų darbai* (Young Researchers' Works; 3 a year), *Kūrybos erdvės* (Spaces of Creation; 2 a year), *Special Education*

DEANS

Faculty of Arts: Assoc. Prof. Dr LEONAS PAULAUSKAS
Faculty of Education: Assoc. Prof. Dr AUŠRINĖ GUMULIAUSKIENĖ
Faculty of Humanities: Prof. GENOVAITĖ KAČIUŠKIENĖ
Faculty of Physics and Mathematics: Assoc. Prof. Dr ALFREDAS LANKAUSKAS
Faculty of Social Sciences: Assoc. Prof. Dr TEODORAS TAMOŠIŪNAS
Faculty of Special Education: Assoc. Prof. Dr JUOZAS PUMPUTIS

Faculty of Technology: Prof. Dr VIDAS LAURUŠKA

ATTACHED RESEARCH INSTITUTE

Continuing Education Institute: Dean Assoc. Prof. Dr LIDIJA UŠECKIENĖ.

VILNIAUS GEDIMINO TECHNIKOS UNIVERSITETAS
(Vilnius Gediminas Technical University)

Saulėtekio alėja 11, 10223 Vilnius
Telephone: (5) 274-50-30
Fax: (5) 270-01-12
E-mail: rastine@adm.vtu.lt
Internet: www.vtu.lt
Founded 1956
State control
Languages of instruction: Lithuanian, English
Academic year: September to June
Chancellor: ARŪNAS KOMKA
Rector: ROMUALDAS GINEVIČIUS
Vice-Rectors: Assoc. Prof. ALFONSAS DANIŪNAS, RAIMUNDAS KIRVAITIS, Prof. Dr habil. ALGIRDAS VACLOVAS VALIULIS, Prof. Dr habil. EDMUNDAS KAZIMIERAS ZAVADSKAS
Librarian: R. PŪGŽLIENĖ
Library of 679,960 vols
Number of teachers: 827
Number of students: 13,000
Publications: *Aviation* (1 a year), *Business: Theory and Practice* (2 a year), *Geodesy and Cartography* (4 a year), *International Journal of Strategic Property Management* (2 a year), *Journal of Civil Engineering and Management* (4 a year), *Journal of Environmental Engineering and Landscape Management* (4 a year), *Technological and Economic Development of Economy* (4 a year), *Town Planning and Architecture* (4 a year), *Transport* (4 a year)

DEANS

Faculty of Architecture: RIMANTAS BUIVYDAS
Faculty of Business Management: Prof. Dr habil ALEXANDRAS VYTAUTAS RUTKAUSKAS
Faculty of Civil Engineering: Assoc. Prof. Dr P. VAINIŪNAS
Faculty of Electronics: ROMA RINKEVIČIENĖ
Faculty of Environmental Engineering: Assoc. Prof. Dr D. ČYGAS
Faculty of Fundamental Sciences: ALGIRDAS ČIUČELIS
Faculty of Mechanics: Prof. Dr habil M. MARIŪNAS
Faculty of Transport Engineering: Prof. Dr habil L. P. LINGAITIS
Institute of Aviation: Prof. Dr habil J. STANKŪNAS

PROFESSORS

Faculty of Architecture (Pylimo g. 26/1, Vilnius 01118; tel. (5) 274-50-12; fax (5) 274-52-13; e-mail archdek@ar.vtu.lt):

ANUŠKEVIČIUS, J.
BUIVYDAS, R.
DIČIUS, V.
DINEIKA, A.
ŠEIBOKAS, J.
STAUSKIS, V. J.
VANAGAS, J.
ZIBERKAS, L. P.

Faculty of Business Management (tel. (5) 274-48-88; fax (5) 274-48-92; e-mail management@vv.vtu.lt):

BIVAINIS, J.
GINEVIČIUS, R.
MELNIKAS, B.
PALIULIS, N.
RUTKAUSKAS, V.
STAŠKEVIČIUS, J.

Faculty of Civil Engineering (tel. (5) 274-52-39; fax (5) 274-50-16; e-mail povva@st.vtu.lt):

ATKOČIŪNAS, J.
ČYRAS, P.
KAKLAUSKAS, A.
KAKLAUSKAS, G.
KALANTA, S.
KVEDARAS, A. K.
MAČIULAITIS, R.
MARČIUKAITIS, J. G.
PARASONIS, J.
USTINOVIČIUS, L.
VAINIŪNAS, P.
ZAVADSKAS, E. K.

Faculty of Electronics (Naugarduko g. 41, 03225 Vilnius; tel. (5) 274-47-53; fax (5) 274-47-70; e-mail dekanatas@el.vtu.lt):

DAMBRAUSKAS, A.
JANKAUSKAS, Z.
KAJACKAS, A.
KVEDARAS, V.
MARCINKEVIČIUS, A.
MARTAVIČIUS, R.
POŠKA, A.
RINKEVIČIENĖ, R.
SKUDUTIS, J.
ŠMILGEVIČIUS, A.
ŠTARAS, S.

Faculty of Environmental Engineering (tel. (5) 274-47-27; fax (5) 274-47-31; e-mail info@ap.vtu.lt):

BALTRĖNAS, P.
BURINSKIENĖ, M.
BUTKUS, P.
ČYGAS, D.
GINIOTIS, V.
JAKOVLEVAS-MATECKIS, K.
JUODIS, E. S.
JUŠKEVIČIUS, P.
LAURINAVIČIUS, A.
LUKIANAS, A.
MARTINAITIS, V.
MATUZEVIČIUS, A.
SAKALAUSKAS, K.
ZAKAREVIČIUS, A.

Faculty of Fundamental Sciences (tel. (5) 274-48-43; fax (5) 274-48-44; e-mail fmf@fm.vtu.lt):

ADOMĖNAS, P.
BAUŠYS, R.
BELEVIČIUS, R.
ČESNYS, A.
ČIEGIS, R.
ČIŽAS, A.
KAČIANAUSKAS, R.
KAZRAGIS, A.
KERIENĖ, J.
KIRJACKIS, E.
KULVIETIS, G.
KULYS, J.
LEONAVIČIUS, M. K.
SAKALAUSKAS, L.
SAULIS, L.
STYRO, D.

Faculty of Mechanics (J. Basanavičiaus 28, 2009 Vilnius; tel. (5) 274-47-45; fax (5) 274-50-43; e-mail mechanik@me.vtu.lt):

AUGUSTAITIS, V.
MARCINKEVIČIUS, A. H.
MARIŪNAS, M.
VALIULIS, A.
VEKTERIS, V.

Faculty of Transport Engineering (J. Basanavičiaus 28B, 03224 Vilnius; tel. (5) 274-47-97; fax (5) 274-48-00; e-mail tif@ti.vtu.lt):

BIDEVIČIUS, M.
BUTKUS, A.
LINGAITIS, L.
LUKOŠEVIČIENĖ, O.
PALŠAITIS, R.
PIKŪNAS, A.
SILEVIČIUS, H.
SPRUOGIS, B.

ŽVIRBLIS, A.

Institute of Aviation (Rodūnios Kelias g. 30, 02187 Vilnius; tel. (5) 274-48-09; fax (5) 274-50-58; e-mail avinst@ai.vtu.lt):

STANKŪNAS, J.

Institute of Humanities (Saulėtekio alėja 28, 10225 Vilnius; tel. (5) 269-87-60; fax (5) 269-86-95; e-mail hinst@hi.vtu.lt):

TAMOŠAUSKAS, P.

ATTACHED RESEARCH INSTITUTE

International Studies Centre: tel. (5) 274-48-95; fax (5) 274-48-97; e-mail tsc@ts.vtu.lt; Dir Prof. Dr habil ZENONAS KAMAITIS.

VILNIAUS PEDAGOGINIS UNIVERSITETAS
(Vilnius Pedagogical University)

Studentų g. 39, 08106 Vilnius

Telephone: (5) 279-02-81
Fax: (5) 279-02-81
E-mail: studsk@vpu.lt
Internet: www.vpu.lt

Founded 1935 as National Pedagogical Institute in Klaipeda; moved to Vilnius 1939; present name and status 1992
State control

Rector: Acad. Prof. Dr hab ALGIRDAS GAIŽUTIS
Librarian: EMILIJA BANIONYTE

Number of teachers: 420
Number of students: 12,400

DEANS

Faculty of Foreign Languages: Dr ALGIMANTAS MARTINKĖNAS
Faculty of History: Prof. Dr LIBERTAS KLIMKA
Faculty of Lithuanian Philology: DALIA PŪRIENĖ
Faculty of Mathematics and Informatics: Assoc. Prof. Dr DALIA KUMPONIENĖ
Faculty of Natural Sciences: Assoc. Prof. Dr BRONISLOVAS ŠALKUS
Faculty of Pedagogy and Psychology: Dr RITA MAKARSKAITĖ-PETKEVIČIENĖ
Faculty of Physics and Technology: Dr KAZIMIERAS SADAUSKAS
Faculty of Slavonic Philology: Dr GINTAUTAS KUNDROTAS

ATTACHED RESEARCH INSTITUTES

Cultural and Arts Education Institute: Dir Prof. habil. Dr VAIDAS MATONIS.
Social Communication Institute: Dir Assoc. Prof. Dr GIEDRĖ KVIESKIENĖ.

VILNIAUS UNIVERSITETAS
(Vilnius University)

Universiteto g. 3, 01513 Vilnius

Telephone: (5) 268-70-10
Fax: (5) 268-70-09
E-mail: infor@cr.vu.lt
Internet: www.vu.lt

Founded 1579
State control
Language of instruction: Lithuanian
Academic year: September to July

Rector: Prof. BENEDIKTAS JUODKA
Pro-Rectors: Prof. JUOZAS RIMANTAS LAZUTKA, Prof. JUOZAS VIDMANTIS VAITKUS, Dr BIRUTĖ POCIŪTĖ, Prof. ALGIMANTAS RAUGALĖ, Dr ALEKSAS PIKTURNA
Director of the Library: Prof. AUDRONĖ GLOSIENĖ
Library: see Libraries and Archives
Number of teachers: 1,266
Number of students: 24,793
Publications: *Acta Orientalia Vilnensia* (1 a year), *Acta Paedagogica Vilnensia* (2 a year), *Archaeologica Lituana* (1 a year), *Book Science* (2 a year), *Economics* (4 a year), *Information Sciences* (4 a year), *Journal of Baltic Linguistics* (*Baltistica*) (3 a year), *Journal of Political Sciences* (4 a year), *Law* (4 a year), *Linguistics* (2 a year), *Literature* (4 a year), *Lithuanian Political Science Yearbook* (1 a year), *Problems* (2 a year), *Psychology* (2 a year), *Respectus Philologicus* (1–2 a year), *Sociology, Thought and Action* (2 a year), *STEP: Social Theory, Empirics, Policy and Practice* (2 a year), *Studies of Lithuanian History* (2 a year), *Transformation in Business and Economics* (1 a year)

DEANS

Faculty of Chemistry: Prof. AIVARAS KAREIVA
Faculty of Communication: Prof. DOMAS KAUNAS
Faculty of Economics: Dr BIRUTĖ GALINIENĖ
Faculty of History: Prof. ZENONAS BUTKUS
Faculty of Humanities in Kaunas: Dr STASYS ALBINAS GIRDZIJAUSKAS
Faculty of Law: Prof. VYTAUTAS NEKROŠIUS
Faculty of Mathematics and Informatics: Prof. FELIKSAS IVANAUSKAS
Faculty of Medicine: Prof. ZITA KUČINSKIENĖ
Faculty of Natural Sciences: Prof. KĘSTUTIS KILKUS
Faculty of Philology: Dr ANTANAS SMETONA
Faculty of Philosophy: Dr KĘSTUTIS DUBNIKAS
Faculty of Physics: Prof. JŪRAS BANYS

PROFESSORS

Faculty of Chemistry (Naugarduko g. 24, 03225 Vilnius; tel. (5) 233-09-87; fax (5) 233-09-87; e-mail chf@chf.vu.lt; internet www.chf.vu.lt):

ABRUTIS, A., Inorganic Chemistry
ARMALIS, S., Analytical Chemistry
BALTRŪNAS, G., Electrochemistry
BARKAUSKAS, J., Inorganic Chemistry
DAUJOTIS, V., Surface and Boundary-layer Chemistry
KAREIVA, A., Inorganic Chemistry
KAZLAUSKAS, R., Analytical Chemistry
MAKUŠKA, R., Polymer Chemistry
PADARAUSKAS, A., Analytical Chemistry
RAMANAVIČIUS, A., Biochemistry, Immunology
TAUTKUS, S., Analytical Chemistry
TUMKEVIČIUS, S., Organic Chemistry
VAINILAVIČIUS, P., Organic Chemistry

Faculty of Communication (Saulėtekio alėja 9, 10222 Vilnius; tel. (5) 236-61-00; fax (5) 236-61-04; e-mail kf@kf.vu.lt; internet www.kf.vu.lt):

KAUNAS, D., Book History, Book Science

Faculty of Economics (Saulėtekio alėja 9, 10222 Vilnius; tel. (5) 236-61-20; fax (5) 236-61-27; e-mail ef@ef.vu.lt; internet www.ef.vu.lt):

BERŽINSKAS, G., Quality Management
GYLYS, P., Economics Theory
LAKIS, V., Audit
MACKEVIČIUS, J., Accounting and Audit
MARČINSKAS, A., Management
MARTIŠIUS, S., Econometrics
PRANULIS, V., Marketing
RUŽEVIČIUS, J., Quality Management
SIMANAUSKAS, L., Economic Informatics
VENGRAUSKAS, P. V., Research in field of Cooperative Trade
ŽEBRAUSKAS, A., Chemical Technology

Faculty of History (Universiteto g. 7, 01122 Vilnius; tel. (5) 268-72-80; fax (5) 268-72-82; e-mail if@if.vu.lt; internet www.if.vu.lt):

BUMBLAUSKAS, A., Theory of History and History of Culture
BUTKUS, Z., Contemporary History since 1914
GUDAVIČIUS, E., Medieval History
LUCHTANAS, A., Archaeology
MICHELBERTAS, M., Archaeology, Numismatics

VALIKONYTÈ, J., Medieval History

Faculty of Humanities in Kaunas (Muitinès g. 8, 44280 Kaunas; tel. (37) 42-25-23; fax (37) 42-32-22; e-mail dekanas@vukhf.lt; internet www.vukhf.lt):

ČIEGIS, R., Economics
GRONSKAS, V., Economics
POLIAKOVAS, O., Diachronic Balto-Slavic Linguistics

Faculty of Law (Saulétekio alèja 9, 10222 Vilnius; tel. (5) 236-61-60; fax (5) 236-61-63; e-mail tf@tf.vu.lt; internet www.tf.vu.lt):

MARCIJONAS, A., Environmental Law
NEKROŠIUS, V., Civil Proceedings, Roman Law
ŠILEKIS, E., Constitutional Law
VANSEVIČIUS, S., History of Lithuanian State and Law

Faculty of Mathematics and Informatics (Naugarduko g. 24, 03225 Vilnius; tel. (5) 233-60-28; fax (5) 215-15-85; e-mail maf@maf .vu.lt; internet www.mif.vu.lt):

BAGDONAVIČIUS, V., Probability Theory and Mathematical Statistics
BIKELIS, A., Probability Theory and Mathematical Statistics
BLOZNELIS, M., Probability Theory
ČEKANAVIČIUS, V., Probability Theory and Mathematical Statistics
IVANAUSKAS, F., Numerical Analysis
KUBILIUS, J., Probabilistic Number Theory, History of Mathematics
LAURINČIKAS, A., Probabilistic Number Theory
LEIPUS, R., Probability Theory and Mathematical Statistics
MACKEVIČIUS, V., Theory of Probability
MANSTAVIČIUS, E., Probabilistic Number Theory
PAULAUSKAS, V., Theory of Probability
RAČKAUSKAS, A., Theory of Probability

Faculty of Medicine (M. K. Čiurlionio g. 21, 03101 Vilnius; tel. (5) 239-87-00; fax (5) 239-87-05; e-mail mf@mf.vu.lt; internet www.mf .vu.lt):

AMBROZAITIS, A., Infectious Diseases
BALČIŪNIENÈ, I., Cardiology
BARKAUSKAS, E. V., Vascular Surgery
BAUBINAS, A., Environmental Hygiene, Paediatric Hygiene
BUBNYS, A., Surgery
ČESNYS, G., Anatomy, Anthropology
DAINYS, B., Transplantation, Urology, Nephrology
DEMBINSKAS, A., Psychiatry
DUBAKIENÈ, R., Allergology
IRNIUS, A., Gastroenterology
IVAŠKEVIČIUS, J., Anaesthesiology, Intensive Care
JANILIONIS, R., Pulmonology
KALIBATIENÈ, D., Gastroenterology, Therapy, Nursing
KALTENIS, P., Paediatrics, Paediatric Nephrology
KUČINSKAS, V., Human Genetics
KUČINSKIENÈ, Z. A., Medical Biochemistry
LAUCEVIČIUS, A., Cardiology
NOREIKA, L. A., Surgery
PARNARAUSKIENÈ, R., Neurology, Neurophysiology
PLIUŠKYS, J. A., Internal Medicine
PORVANECKAS, N., Traumatology-Orthopaedics
PRONCKUS, A., Surgery
RAMANAUSKAS, J., Pharmacology
RAUGALÈ, A., Paediatrics
SIAURUSAITIS, B. J., Paediatric Surgery
SIRVYDIS, V., Cardiac Surgery
STRUPAS, K., Surgery
TRIPONIS, V. J., Vascular Surgery
USONIS, V., Paediatric Infectology
UŽDAVINYS, G., Cardiac Surgery
VAIČEKONIS, V., Pulmonology
VALANTINAS, J., Hepatology

VALIULIS, A., Paediatric Pulmonology
VENALIS, A., Rheumatology
VITKUS, K., Reconstructive Surgery
ŽVIRONAITÈ, V., Cardiology

Faculty of Natural Sciences (M. K. Čiurlionio g. 21/27, 03101 Vilnius; tel. (5) 239-82-00; fax (53) 239-82-04; e-mail gf@gf.vu.lt; internet www.gf.vu.lt):

BUKANTIS, A., Climatology
ČESNULEVIČIUS, A., Geomorphology
ČITAVIČIUS, D. J., Molecular Genetics of Microorganisms
DUNDULIS, K. J., Engineering Geology
GAIGALAS, A. J., Lithology
JANKAUSKAS, T. R., Palaeontology and Stratigraphy
JUODKA, B., Molecular Biology
JURGAITIS, A., Lithology and Mineral Deposits
KABAILIENÈ, M., Palaeontology and Stratigraphy
KAVALIAUSKAS, P., Land Management
KILKUS, K., Hydrology
KIRVELIENÈ, V., Cell Biochemistry
LAZUTKA, J. R., Human Cytogenetics
MOKRIK, R., Palaeohydrogeology, Hydrochemistry, Groundwater Formation
NAUJALIS, J. R., Botany
PODÈNAS, S., Entomology
RAKAUSKAS, R., Entomology
RANČELIS, V. P., Genetics
SLAPŠYTÈ, G., Animal Genetics
TRIMONIS, A. E., Oceanology
VALENTA, V. J., Biology
ŽAROMSKIS, R. P., Oceanology

Faculty of Philology (Universiteto g. 5, 01122 Vilnius; tel. (5) 268-72-02; fax (5) 268-72-08; e-mail flf@flf.vu.lt; internet www.flf.vu.lt):

GIRDENIS, A. S., General Linguistics, Baltic Linguistics
JAKAITIENÈ, E. M., Lexicology, Semantics
KOSTIN, E., Russian Literature
KOŽENAUSKIENÈ, R., Stylistics
LASSAN, E., Syntax, Cognitive Linguistics
NASTOPKA, K. V., Literary Theory, Lithuanian Literature
NORKAITIENÈ, I. N., History of German Language, German Philology, Semantics, Semiotics
PAKERIENÈ-DAUJOTYTÈ, V., History and Philosophy of Literature
PAULAUSKIENÈ, A., Grammar
ROSINAS, A., Comparative Linguistics, History of Baltic Languages
STUNDŽIA, B., Phonetics, Phonology
TEMČINAS, S., Old Church Texts, Balto-Slavic Linguistics
ULČINAITÈ, E., Neo-Latin Literature
USONIENÈ, A., English Linguistics, Semantics, Syntax

Faculty of Philosophy (Universiteto g. 9/1, 01513 Vilnius; tel. (5) 266-76-06; fax (5) 266-76-00; e-mail fsf@fsf.vu.lt; internet www.fsf .vu.lt):

BAGDONAS, A., Developmental Psychology
DOBRYNINAS, A., Philosophy of Social Sciences, Criminology
GAILIENÈ, D., Differential and Individual Psychology
KALENDA, Č., Ethics
KOČIŪNAS, R. A., Clinical Psychology
NORKUS, Z., History of Philosophy
PLEČKAITIS, R., History of Philosophy
PŠIBILSKIS, V., Political Science
ŠAULAUSKAS, M. P., Contemporary Philosophy, Theories of Social Change, Postmodern Theories
ŠLIOGERIS, M. A., Metaphysics
VAITKEVIČIUS, P. H., Applied and Experimental Psychology
VALICKAS, G., Social Psychology

Faculty of Physics (Saulétekio alèja 9, 10222 Vilnius; tel. (5) 236-60-00; fax (5) 236-60-03; e-mail ff@ff.vu.lt; internet www.ff.vu.lt):

ARLAUSKAS, K., Solid State Physics, Noncrystalline Materials
BALEVIČIUS, V., Theoretical Physics, Optics, Spectroscopy
BANDZAITIS, A., Atomic Physics
BANYS, J., Solid State Physics, Ferroelectrics
DIKČIUS, G., Optics, Spectroscopy
GADONAS, R. E., Optics
GARŠKA, E., Acoustics
GAVRIUŠINAS, V., Semiconductor Physics
GRIGAS, J., Ferroelectrics and Phase Transitions
IVAŠKA, V., Electromagnetism
JARAŠIUNAS, K., Semiconductor Physics
JURŠÈNAS, S. A., Semiconductor Physics
JUŠKA, G., Solid State Physics, Noncrystalline Materials
KAŽUKAUSKAS, V., Semiconductor Physics
KIMTYS, L., Magnetic Resonance, Relaxation, Spectroscopy
MONTRIMAS, E., Semiconductor Physics, Electronics Structure
ORLIUKAS, A. F., Solid State Ionics
PALENSKIS, V., Superconductor Physics
PISKARSKAS, A., Optics
ROTOMSKIS, R., Biophysics
SAKALAUSKAS, S., Electronics and Physical Instrumentation
SIRUTKAITIS, V., Optics
SMILGEVIČIUS, V., Optics
STABINIS, A. P., Optics
STORASTA, J., Semiconductor Physics
TAMULAITIS, G., Semiconductor Physics
VAITKUS, J. V., Semiconductor Physics
VALKŪNAS, L., Clinical Physics, Biophysics
ŽILINSKAS, P. J., Metrology, Physical Instrumentation
ŽUKAUSKAS, A., Semiconductor Physics

Sports Centre (Saulétekio alèja 2, 10222 Vilnius; tel. (5) 269-87-20; fax (5) 269-88-56; e-mail sveikata.sportas@kkc.vu.lt):

JANKAUSKAS, J. P., Sports Education
SAPLINSKAS, J., Physiology

ATTACHED RESEARCH INSTITUTES

Algirdas Greimas Centre for Semiotics: Universiteto g. 5, Vilnius; tel. (5) 268-71-61; e-mail greimocentras@cr.vu.lt; internet www .gc.vu.lt; Head Dr DALIA SATKAUSKYTÈ.

Centre for Environmental Studies: Head Dr STASYS SINKEVIČIUS.

Centre for Gender Studies: Head Dr DALIA MARCINKEVIČIENÈ.

Centre for Oriental Studies: Head AUDRIUS BEINORIUS.

Centre for Religious Studies and Research: Head Dr habil. RITA ŠERPYTYTÈ.

Institute of Foreign Languages: Dir Dr NIJOLÈ BRAŽÈNIENÈ.

Institute of International Relations and Political Science: Dirs Prof. RAIMUNDAS LOPATA, Prof. J. ČIČINSKAS.

Institute of Materials Science and Applied Research: Dir Prof. ARTŪRAS ŽUKAUSKAS.

International Centre of Knowledge Economy and Knowledge Management: Dir Prof. RENALDAS GUDAUSKAS.

Stateless Cultures Centre: Head Dr GRIGORIJUS POTAŠENKO.

Vilnius Distance Education Study Centre: Dir Dr POVILAS ABARIUS.

VYTAUTO DIDŽIOJO UNIVERSITETAS (Vytautas Magnus University)

K. Donelaicio g. 58, LT- 44248 Kaunas
Telephone: (37) 22-27-39
Fax: (37) 20-38-58
E-mail: info@adm.vdu.lt
Internet: www.vdu.lt

Founded 1922, closed 1950, re-opened 1989
Language of instruction: Lithuanian
Academic year: September to June
State-funded

Rector: Prof. ZIGMAS LYDEKA
Vice-Rector for Devt: Assoc. Prof. N. MAŽEI-
    KIENĖ
Vice-Rector for Infrastructure: Assoc. Prof. V.
    VILIŪNAS
Vice-Rector for Research: Prof. J. AUGUTIS
Vice-Rector for Studies: Prof. J. RUŠKUS
Univ. Sec.: Prof. A. BALČYTIENĖ
Chair. of the Senate: Prof. J. VILEMAS
Chair. of the Univ. Ccl: S. TAMKEVIČIUS
Librarian: L. BLOVEŠČIŪNIENĖ
Library of 246,045 vols, 185 periodicals
Number of teachers: 550
Number of students: 9,000

Publications: *Management of Organizations:
Systematic Research*, *SOTER*, *Vocational
Training: Research and Realities*, *Works
and Days*

DEANS

Faculty of Arts: Prof. V. LEVANDAUSKAS
Faculty of Economics and Management: P.
    ŽUKAUSKAS
Faculty of Humanities: Assoc. Prof. J. VAIČE-
    NONIS
Faculty of Informatics: Assoc. Prof. K.
    ŠIDLAUSKAS
Faculty of Law: Prof. J. KIRŠIENĖ
Faculty of Natural Sciences: Prof. G. KAMUN-
    TAVIČIUS
Faculty of Political Sciences and Diplomacy:
    Prof. I. DABAŠINSKIENĖ
Faculty of Social Sciences: Prof. K. PUKELIS
Faculty of Social Welfare: Assoc. Prof. J.
    VAIČENONIS
Faculty of Theology: Dr B. ULEVIČIUS
Kaunas Botanical Gardens: R. DAUBARAS

PROFESSORS

Faculty of Arts:
    LEVANDAUSKAS, V.
    STAUSKAS, V.
    VAŠKELIS, B.

Faculty of Economics and Management:
    CEPINSKIS, J.
    KVEDARAVIČIUS, P.
    ZAKAREVIČIUS, P.
    ŽUKAUSKAS, P.

Faculty of Humanities:
    ALEKSANDRAVIČIUS, E.
    APANAVIČIUS, R.
    DONSKIS, L.

GAMZIUKAITE-MAŽIULIENĖ, R.
GENZELIS, B.
GUDAITIS, L. F.
KARALIŪNAS, S.
KERBELYTE, B.
KIAUPA, Z.
MARCINKEVICIENE, R.
SKRUPSKELYTE, V.

Faculty of Informatics:
    AUGUTIS, J.
    KAMINSKAS, V.
    SAPAGOVAS, M.
    SKUČAS, I.

Faculty of Natural Sciences:
    GRAŽULEVIČIENE, R.
    JUKNYS, R.
    KAMUNTAVIČIUS, G.
    MARUSKA, A,
    MILDAŽIENE, V.
    PRANEVIČIUS, L.
    STRAVINSKIENE, V.

Faculty of Political Sciences and Diplomacy:
    PRAZAUSKAS, A.

Faculty of Social Sciences:
    GOŠTAUTAS, A.
    LAUŽACKAS, R.
    PUKELIS, K.
    TERRESEVIČIENE, M.
    VAŠTOKAS, R.

Faculty of Theology:
    MOTUZAS, A.
    NARBEKOVAS, A.
    PUZARAS, P.
    ŽEMAITIS, K.

Other Higher Educational Institutes

**Generolo Jono Žemaičio Lietuvos Karo
Akademija** (General Jono Žemaičio Military
Academy of Lithuania): Šilo g. 5A, 10322
Vilnius; tel. (5) 210-36-88; fax (5) 212-73-18;
e-mail info@lka.lt; internet www.lka.lt; f.
1994; state control; depts of applied sciences,
engineering management, foreign languages,
humanities, management, political science;
military depts of tactics, combat support and
physical training; Centre of Science; Military
History Centre; Strategic Research Centre;
library: 132,000 vols and periodicals; 424
cadets; Dir Col ALGIMANTAS VYŠNIAUSKAS;
publ. *The Military Archives*.

International School of Management: E.
Ozeskienes 18, 44254 Kaunas; tel. (37) 30-24-
02; fax (37) 20-56-76; e-mail ism@ism.lt;
internet www.ism.lt; f. 1999; private control;
library: 7,518 vols; 60 teachers; 900 students
(600 undergraduate, 300 postgraduate);
President VIRGINIJUS KUNDROTAS; publ. *Business
Training Centre News* (12 a year).

Lietuvos Kūno Kultūros Akademija
(Lithuanian Academy of Physical Education):
Sporto 6, 44221 Kaunas; tel. (37) 30-26-21;
internet www.lkka.lt; f. 1945 as Lithuanian
National Institute of Physical Education;
state control; faculties of sports biomedicine,
sports education and sports technologies,
tourism; Rector ALBERTAS SKURVYDAS; publ.
Education. Physical Training. Sport.

Lietuvos Muzikos ir Teatro Akademija
(Lithuanian Academy of Music and Theatre):
Gedimino pr. 42, 01110 Vilnius; tel. (5) 261-
26-91; fax (5) 212-69-82; e-mail rektoratas@
lma.lt; internet www.lma.lt; f. 1933; study
programmes: accordion, arts management,
camera, choir conducting, composition,
drama (theory, history, acting and directing),
ethnomusicology, film and sound directing,
folk instruments, musical education, musicology, music performance (piano, singing,
orchestral instruments, symphony orchestra
and opera-conducting), television; library:
libraries with 213,000 vols, record libraries
with 29,000 records; 274 teachers; 1,167
students; Rector Prof. Dr EDUARDAS GABNYS;
publ. *Menotyra* (Science of Art, 1 a year).

Lietuvos Veterinarijos Akademija
(Lithuanian Veterinary Academy): Tilžės g.
18, 47181 Kaunas; tel. (37) 36-23-83; fax (37)
36-24-17; e-mail reklva@lva.lt; internet www
.lva.lt; f. 1936; faculties: animal husbandry,
veterinary medicinetechnology; library:
231,486 vols; 120 teachers; 1,369 students;
Rector HENRIKAS ŠILINSKAS; publ. *Veterinary
Science and Zootechnics* (1 a year).

Vilniaus Dailes Akademija (Vilnius Academy of Fine Arts): Maironio 6, 01124 Vilnius;
tel. (5) 210-54-30; fax (5) 210-54-63; e-mail
vda@vda.lt; internet www.vda.lt; f. 1793;
depts: architecture, art theory and history,
ceramics, design, fashion design, industrial
art, interior and furnishing, monumental
and decorative arts, painting, printmaking,
sculpture, textiles; library; museum; 280
teachers; 1,700 students; Rector Prof. ADO-
MAS BUTRIMAS.

LUXEMBOURG

The Higher Education System

In 1867 the London Congress declared Luxembourg to be an independent, sovereign state, although it remained under Dutch hegemony until 1890. The oldest existing institution of higher education is the Conservatoire de Musique de la Ville de Luxembourg (founded 1906), but the first university-level institution, the Université du Luxembourg, was not established until 2003. Prior to the foundation of the Université du Luxembourg, an Act of 1969 permitted the recognition of qualifications awarded by overseas universities in Luxembourg; one such institution is Sacred Heart University in Luxembourg (founded 1991; attached to Sacred Heart University, CT, USA). Under the Law of 11 January 1995, a new higher education qualification, the Diplôme d'ingénieur industriel, was introduced.

The Université du Luxembourg participates in the Bologna Process to establish a European Higher Education Area, the first phase of which is to adopt a credit-based system of comparable degrees with two main cycles (undergraduate and postgraduate). The Bachelors is the primary undergraduate degree and requires three years of study; the first postgraduate degree is the Masters, and lasts two years; and the Doctorate is the highest university degree, lasting three years. Students at all levels are required to spend a period studying abroad. There are several non-university institutions offering a variety of two- to four-year diploma courses. In 2005/06 some 9,227 students were enrolled at university-level institutions, including 6,063 who were studying abroad.

Technical and vocational education takes the form of adult and continuing programmes, and is offered by a range of institutions and agencies, including Centres of Continuing Vocational Training, the Ministry of National Education and Vocational Training, Chambers of Commerce and Trades, the Communes and Private Associations. In 2002 a new centre was established by the Ministry of Education, Vocational Training and Sport, and the Ministry of Health to cater for the demand for vocational training in the health sector.

Regulatory and Representative Bodies

GOVERNMENT

Ministry of Culture, Higher Education and Research: 20 montée de la Pétrusse, 2273 Luxembourg; tel. 478-1; fax 292-186; e-mail info@mcesr.public.lu; internet www.mcesr.public.lu; Minister FRANÇOIS BILTGEN.

Ministry of National Education and Vocational Training: 29 rue Aldringen, 2926 Luxembourg; tel. 478-5100; fax 478-5113; e-mail info@men.public.lu; internet www.men.public.lu; Minister MADY DEL-VAUX-STEHRES.

ACCREDITATION

ENIC/NARIC Luxembourg: Ministry of Culture, Higher Education and Research, 18–20 Montée de la Pétrusse, 2912 Luxembourg; tel. 478-5139; fax 2629-6037; e-mail jean.tagliaferri@mcesr.etat.lu; internet www.cedies.public.lu; Contact Prof. JEAN TAGLIAFERRI.

Learned Societies

GENERAL

Institut Grand-Ducal: 2A rue Kalchesbruck, 1852 Luxembourg; tel. 478-2790; fax 478-2792; internet www.igd.lu; includes 6 sections: (a) History (Pres. PAUL SPANG), (b) Medicine (Pres. HENRI METZ), (c) Natural Sciences (Pres. PIERRE SECK), (d) Linguistics, Ethnology and Place Names (Pres. HENRI KLEES), (e) Arts and Literature (Pres. PIERRE SCHUMACHER), (f) Moral and Political Sciences (Sec. GASTON REINESCH).

LANGUAGE AND LITERATURE

Institut Pierre Werner: 28, rue Münster, 2162 Luxembourg; tel. 490-4431; fax 490-643; e-mail info@ipw.lu; internet www.ipw.lu; f. 2003 jtly by the Centre Culturel Français, Goethe-Institut (Germany) and Ministère de la Culture Luxembourgeois; promotes cultural diversity and exchange in Europe; named after fmr Luxembourgeois Prime Minister; Dir MARIO HIRSCH.

MEDICINE

Collège Médical: Ministère de la Santé, 57 blvd de la Pétrusse, Luxembourg; f. 1818; governmental consultative body; 11 mems; Pres. Dr GEORGES ARNOLD; Sec. PIERRE SCHROEDER.

NATURAL SCIENCES

Biological Sciences

Société des Naturalistes Luxembourgeois: BP 327, 2013 Luxembourg; e-mail info@snl.lu; internet www.snl.lu; f. 1890 to study the natural environment of Luxembourg and modifications of the animal and plant communities caused by environmental changes and to promote nature conservation; working groups: botany, mycology, and entomology; organizes conferences and guided excursions; 580 mems; Pres. CHRISTIAN RIES; Sec. YVES KRIPPEL; publ. *Bulletin* (1 a year).

Research Institutes

ECONOMICS, LAW AND POLITICS

Service Central de la Statistique et des Etudes Economiques: 13, rue Erasme, 1463 Luxembourg; BP 304, 2013 Luxembourg; tel. 2478-4219; e-mail info@statec.etat.lu; internet www.statec.public.lu; f. 1962; attached to Min. of Economics; library of 9,000 vols, 500 periodicals; Dir Dr SERGE ALLEGREZZA; publs *A Kaléidoscope* (irregular), *Annuaire Statistique du Luxembourg* (1 a year), *Bulletin du STATEC* (10 a year), *Cahiers Economiques* (irregular), *Conjoncture Flash* (12 a year), *Economie Luxembourgeoise*, *Indicateurs Rapides* (15 series), *Luxembourg en Chiffres* (1 a year), *Luxembourg in Figures* (1 a year), *Luxembourg in Zahlen* (1 a year), *Note de Conjoncture* (2 a year), *Recensements de la Population*, *Regards* (irregular), *Répertoire des Entreprises*, *The Luxembourg Economy*, *Un kaléidoscope* (irregular).

EDUCATION

Commission Grand-Ducale d'Instruction: 29 rue Aldringen, 2926 Luxembourg; tel. 478-5254; fax 478-5188; internet www.men.lu; f. 1843; Pres. FRANCIS JEITZ; Sec. PAUL KLEIN.

MEDICINE

Centre de Recherche Public de la Santé: 1A-B, rue Thomas Edison, L- 1445 Strassen; tel. 269701; fax 26970719; e-mail aurelia.derischebourg@crp-sante.lu; internet www.crp-sante.lu; f. 1988; applied, clinical and public health research; Pres. FRANK GANSEN.

TECHNOLOGY

Centre de Recherche Public Henri Tudor: 29 ave John F. Kennedy, 1855 Luxembourg-Kirchberg; tel. and fax 425-991; e-mail info@tudor.lu; internet www.crpht.lu; f. 1988; applied science; Pres. JEAN DE LA HAMETTE; Dir CLAUDE WEHENKEL; publ. *Cahiers de l'Innovation*.

Libraries and Archives

Esch-sur-Alzette

Bibliothèque de la Ville: 26 rue Emile Mayrisch, Esch-sur-Alzette; tel. 547-383; fax 552-037; e-mail bibliotheque@villeesch.lu; internet www.bibliotheque.esch.lu; f. 1919; German, French, English and Italian literature; popular science books; 60,000 vols; special collection of Luxembourgensia; Record Library; Chief Librarian HENRI LUTGEN.

Luxembourg

Archives Nationales: Plateau du Saint Esprit, BP 6, 2010 Luxembourg; tel. 2478-6660; fax 474-692; e-mail archives.nationales@an.etat.lu; internet www.anlux.lu; f. 19th century; Dir JOSÉE KIRPS.

Bibliothèque Nationale: 37 blvd F. D. Roosevelt, 2450 Luxembourg; tel. 229755-1; fax 475672; e-mail info@bnl.etat.lu; internet www.bnl.lu; f. 1798, reorganized 1897, 1945, 1958, 1973, 1988 and 2004; nat. and research library open to the gen. public; 1m. items; Dir Dr MONIQUE KIEFFER; publs *Bibliographie d'histoire luxembourgeoise* (online), *Bibliographie luxembourgeoise* (online).

Mersch

Centre National de Littérature: 2 rue Emmanuel Servais, 7565 Mersch; tel. 326-955; fax 327-090; e-mail cnl@cnl.etat.lu; internet www.literaturarchiv.lu; f. 1986; spec. colln of works published in Luxembourg; 40,000 vols, 300 periodicals; Dir GERMAINE GOETZINGER; Chief Librarian DAPHNE BOEHLES; publ. *Bibliographie courante de la littérature luxembourgeoise* (1 a year).

Museum

Luxembourg

Musée National d'Histoire et d'Art (National Museum of History and Art): Marché-aux-Poissons, 2345 Luxembourg; tel. and fax 479-330; internet www.mnha .public.lu; f. 1845; archaeology, fine arts, industrial and popular arts, history of Luxembourg; library of 25,000 vols; Dir PAUL REILES.

University

UNIVERSITÉ DU LUXEMBOURG

Limpertsberg Campus: 162A ave de la Faïencerie, 1511 Luxembourg

Kirchberg Campus: 6 rue Richard Couden-hove-Kalergi, 1359 Luxembourg

Walferdange Campus: BP 2, route de Die-kirch, 7201 Walferdange

Telephone: 466-644-1

Fax: 466-644-508

Internet: www.uni.lu

Founded 1969; present name and status 2003

State control

Languages of instruction: French, German, English

Academic year: October to June

Rector: ROLF TARRACH

Vice-Rector: Dr ADELHEID EHMKE

Dir for Admin.: JEAN-PAUL MOSSONG

Library of 120,000 vols

Number of teachers: 350 (mostly part-time)

Number of students: 1,600

Publications: *Avis de la CNE, Cahiers d'Economie, Cahiers d'Histoire, Cahiers ISIS, Cahiers de Pédagogie, Cahiers de Philosophie—série A, Cahiers de Philosophie—série B, Cahiers de Physique, Editions Spéciales, English Studies, Études de Biologie, Etudes Classiques, Etudes de Géographie, Etudes de Philosophie, Etudes Romanes, Germanistik, Les Droits de l'Homme, Travaux de Linguistique, Travaux de Mathématiques*

DEANS

Faculty of Law, Economics and Finance: Prof. Dr FRANCK LEPREVOST (acting)

Faculty of Letters, Human Sciences, Arts and Educational Science: Prof. LUCIEN KERGER

Faculty of Science, Technology and Communication: Prof. Dr MASSIMO MALVETTI

Colleges

Conservatoire de Musique d'Esch-sur-Alzette: 50 rue d'Audun, BP 145, 4002 Esch-sur-Alzette; tel. 549-725; fax 549-731; internet www.conservatoire-esch.lu; f. 1926

as Ecole Municipale de Musique; present status 1969; 60 teachers; 1,000 students; Principal Prof. FRED HARLES; publ. *Annuaire* (Year Book).

Conservatoire de Musique de la Ville de Luxembourg: 33 rue Charles Martel, 2134 Luxembourg; tel. 456-555; fax 449-686; f. 1906; 150 teachers; Dir FERNAND JUNG; Sec. PIERRE BERG; publ. *Compte rendu* (1 a year).

Institut Supérieur de Technologie: Rue Richard Coudenhove-Kalergi, 1359 Luxembourg-Kirchberg; tel. 420-101; fax 432-124; e-mail admin@ist.lu; f. 1979; mechanical engineering, electrical engineering, civil engineering, industrial computing; library: 10,000 vols; 70 teachers; 400 students; Pres. PROSPER SCHROEDER; Dir ALBERT RETTER.

Institut Universitaire International de Luxembourg: Château de Munsbach, 31 rue du Parc, 5374 Luxembourg; located at: BP 73, 6905 Niederanven; tel. 2615-9212; fax 2615-9228; internet www.iuil.lu; f. 1974; Dir POL WAGNER.

Sacred Heart University in Luxembourg: 25B Blvd Royal, 2449 Luxembourg; tel. 227-613; fax 227-623; e-mail admissions@shu.lu; internet www.shu.lu; f. 1991; US-accredited MBA program; attached to Sacred Heart University, Connecticut, USA; Dirs Dr THOMAS D. QUEISSER (Academic Programmes), VICTORIA GEHRING (Graduate Admissions).

FORMER YUGOSLAV REPUBLIC OF MACEDONIA

The Higher Education System

After the First World War (1914–18) Vardar Macedonia, the area now known as the Former Yugoslav Republic of Macedonia (FYRM), became part of the new Kingdom of Serbs, Croats and Slovenes (formally named Yugoslavia in 1929). Following the Second World War (1939–45) Macedonia became part of the new communist-led Federative People's Republic of Yugoslavia. In 1991 the Macedonian Sobranie (Assembly) declared the republic of Macedonia to be a sovereign territory. Macedonian secession was effectively acknowledged by the Federal Republic of Yugoslavia in 1992. Univerzitet 'Sv. Kiril I Metodij' (University of Skopje—founded 1949) is the oldest of the eight universities in Macedonia; the others are Univerzitet 'Sv. Kliment Ohridski' Bitola (St Kliment Ohridski University of Bitola—founded 1979) and Universiteti I Ejl (South-East European University—founded 2001). The last of these was established following new legislation in 2000 which permitted the use of Albanian and other languages in private tertiary institutions, and in 2004, under further amendments to legislation on higher education, it became the third state-funded university. In 2003/04 some 46,637 students were enrolled at the universities at Skopje and at Bitola.

The Republic of Macedonia became a member of the Bologna Process in 2003. However, it started to change the higher education system much earlier (in 2000) when the Ministry of Education and Science passed the new Law on Higher Education. The Law required universities to start introducing the European Credit Transfer System (ECTS) and design study and subject programmes according to the principles of the Bologna Process. The European Credit Transfer System (ECTS) has been implemented across all higher education providers in the country at the first and second cycle.

Admission to higher education is on the basis of the Secondary Leaving Diploma and entrance examinations. Higher education is divided between colleges and universities/university faculties. Colleges specialize in two- to three-year diploma courses leading to a professional title. Universities and university faculties offer four- to six-year diploma and degree programmes. The first postgraduate degree is the Masters (Magister) and is a two-year research degree culminating in public defence of a thesis. The final university-level degree is the Doctor of Science (Doktor na nauiki).

The Board for Accreditation of Higher Education (Odbor za Akreditacija vo Vissokoto Obrazovanie) is the national body responsible for all higher education institutions. Staff are externally evaluated by the Higher Education Evaluation Agency (Agencija za evaluacija na visokoto obrazovanie). This is a legally independent organization established by the Higher Education Accreditation Board.

Regulatory and Representative Bodies

GOVERNMENT

Ministry of Culture: ul. Gjuro Gjakovik 61, 1000 Skopje; tel. (2) 324-0600; fax (2) 324-0561; e-mail info@kultura.gov.mk; internet www.kultura.gov.mk; Minister ELIZABETH KANCESKA-MILEVSKA.

Ministry of Education and Science: Mito Hadzivasilev Jasmin bb, 1000 Skopje; tel. (2) 311-7896; fax (2) 311-8414; e-mail contact@mon.gov.mk; internet www.mon.gov.mk; Minister NIKOLA TODOROV.

ACCREDITATION

ENIC/NARIC Macedonia: Information Centre, Ministry of Education and Science, Mito Hadzivasilev Jasmin bb, 1000 Skopje; tel. (2) 311-7896; fax (2) 311-8414; e-mail nadezda.uzelac@mofk.gov.mk; internet www.mon.gov.mk; Head, Information Centre NADEZDA UZELAC.

Learned Societies

GENERAL

Društvo za nauka i umetnost (Association of Sciences and Arts): POB 145, 7000 Bitola; tel. (47) 222-683; f. 1960; scientific meetings, symposia, research; sections of arts, history and geography, linguistics and literature, medical, natural and mathematical sciences, social sciences and law, technical and applied sciences; 154 mems, 25 assocs; Pres. SOTIR PANOVSKI; Sec.-Gen. TRAJKO OGNENOVSKI;

publs *Prilozi* (Contributions, 2 a year), *Scientific Thought.*

Makedonska Akademija na Naukite i Umetnostite (Macedonian Academy of Sciences and Arts): Blvr Krste Misirkov 2, POB 428, 1000 Skopje; tel. (2) 323-5400; fax (2) 323-5500; e-mail manu@manu.edu.mk; internet www.manu.edu.mk; f. 1967; sections of arts (Sec. VLADA UROŠEVIĆ), biological and medical sciences (Sec. RISTO LOZANOVSKI), linguistics and literary sciences (Sec. KATA UULAVKOVA), mathematical and technical sciences (Sec. GLIGOR KANEVČE), social sciences (Sec. IVAN KATARDŽIEV); 72 mems (43 ordinary, 29 foreign); library of 145,000 vols, incl. 52,000 monographs, 1,500 journals and magazines; Pres. GEORGI STARDELOV; Vice-Pres VLADO KAMBOVSKI, BOJAN ŠOPTRAJANOV; Sec. LJUPČO KOCAREV; publs *Letopis* (1 a year), *Prilozi na Oddelenieto za biološki i medicinski nauki* (Contributions of the Dept of Biological and Medical Sciences, 2 a year), *Prilozi na Oddelenieto za lingvistika i literaturna nauka* (Contributions of the Dept of Linguistics and Literary Sciences, 2 a year), *Prilozi na Oddelenieto za matematičko-tehnički nauki* (Contributions of the Dept of Mathematical and Technical Sciences, 2 a year), *Prilozi na Oddelenieto za opštestveni nauki* (Contributions of the Dept of Social Sciences, 2 a year).

AGRICULTURE, FISHERIES AND VETERINARY SCIENCE

Sojuz na Društvata na Veterinarnite Lekari i Tehničari na Makedonija (Union of Associations of Veterinary Surgeons and Technicians of Macedonia): Veterinaren institut c/o Faculty of Veterinary Medicine, Lazar Pop-Trajkov 5, POB 95, 1000 Skopje; tel. (2) 324-0700; fax (2) 311-4619; f. 1950; attached to Sts Cyril and Methodius Univ.; 450 mems; Pres. SILJAN ZAHARIEVSKI; Sec. ADŽIEVSKI BLAŽE; publ. *Makedonski veterinaren pregled* (Macedonian Veterinary Review).

Sojuz na Inženeri i Tehničari po Sumarstvo i Industrija za Prerabotka na Drvo na Makedonija (Union of Forestry Engineers and Technicians of Macedonia): Sumarski institut, Engelsova 2, 1000 Skopje; f. 1952; 500 mems; Pres. Dipl. Ing. ŽIVKO MINČEV; Sec. Dipl. Ing. MILE STAMENKOV; publ. *Sumarski pregled* (Forester's review).

Združenie na Zemjodelski Inženeri na Makedonija (Association of Agricultural Engineers of Macedonia): Zemjodelski fakultet, POB 297, 1000 Skopje; tel. (2) 311-5277; fax (2) 323-8218; f. 1994; 3,000 mems; Sec Prof. DRAGOSLAV KOCEVSKI; publ. *Macedonian Agriculture Review* (1 a year).

BIBLIOGRAPHY, LIBRARY SCIENCE AND MUSEOLOGY

Bibliotekarsko Društvo na Makedonija (Macedonian Library Association): c/o Narodna i univerzitetska biblioteka 'St Kliment Ohridski', Blvr Goce Delčev 6, 1000 Skopje; tel. (2) 7026-2120; e-mail bdm@bdm.org.mk; internet www.bdm.org.mk; f. 1949; oversees the functioning of libraries; organizes seminars; 500 mems; Pres. KIRIL ANGELOV; Sec. ELENA TEVCHEVA; publ. *Bibliotekarska iskra* (2 a year).

Društvo na Muzejskite Rabotnici na Makedonija (Museum Society of Macedonia): Muzej na grad Skopje, Mito Hadži-Vasilev-Jasmin bb, 1000 Skopje; f. 1951; 100 mems; Pres. KUZMAN GEORGIEVSKI; Sec. GALENA KUCULOVSKA.

Sojuz na društvata na arhivskite rabotnici na Makedonija (Union of Societies of Archivists of Macedonia): Gligor Prličev 3, POB 496, 1000 Skopje; tel. (2) 323-7211; fax (2) 323-4461; f. 1954; 340 mems; publ. *Makedonski arhivist* (1 a year).

ECONOMICS, LAW AND POLITICS

Društvo za Filozofija, Sociologija i Politikologija na Makedonija (Society for Philosophy, Sociology and Politics of Macedonia): Institut za sociološki i političkopravni istražuvanja, Blvr Partizanski odredi bb, 1000 Skopje; f. 1960; 170 mems; Pres. Dr DRAGAN TAŠKOVSKI; Sec. SVETA ŠKARIĆ; publ. *Zbornik* (Collected Papers).

Sojuz na Ekonomistite na Makedonija (Union of Economists of Macedonia): Ekonomiski Fakultet, K. Misirkov bb, 1000 Skopje; tel. (2) 322-4311; fax (2) 322-4973; f. 1950; 3,000 mems; Pres. Prof. Dr TAKI FITI; Sec. ACO SPASOVSKI; publ. *Stopanski pregled* (Economic review).

Sojuz na Združenijata na Pravnicite na Makedonija (Union of Associations of Jurists of Macedonia): Ustaven sud na Makedonija, XII udarna brigada 2, 1000 Skopje; f. 1946; 4,000 mems; Pres. BORO DOGANDŽISKI; Sec. PETAR GOLUBOVSKI; publ. *Pravna misla* (Legal opinion).

FINE AND PERFORMING ARTS

Društvo na Istoričarite na Umetnosta od Makedonija (Society of Art Historians of Macedonia): Arheološki muzej na Makedonija, Curčiska bb, 1000 Skopje; f. 1970; 130 mems; Pres. MILANKA BOŠKOVSKA; Sec. MATE BOŠKOVSKI; publ. *Likovna umetnost* (Plastic Arts).

Društvo na Likovnite Umetnici na Makedonija (Society of Plastic Arts of Macedonia): 13 Noemvri bb, POB 438, 1000 Skopje; tel. (2) 321-1533; f. 1944; 333 mems; Pres. GLIGOR ČEMERSKI; Sec. BRANISLAV MIRČEVSKI.

Sojuz na Kompozitorite na Makedonija (Composers Association of Macedonia): Maksim Gorki 18, 1000 Skopje; tel. and fax (2) 311-9824; e-mail socom@socom.com.mk; internet www.socom.com.mk; f. 1950; preserves the tradition of folk music; collects and processes folk music material; 49 mems; Pres. MARKO KOLOVSKI; Gen-Sec. LAZAR MOJSOVSKI; publ. *Informer*.

HISTORY, GEOGRAPHY AND ARCHAEOLOGY

Geografsko Društvo na R. Makedonija (Geographical Society of Macedonia): Geografski institut pri Prirodnomatematički fakultet, POB 146, 1000 Skopje; f. 1949; 600 mems; Pres. Prof. VASIL GRAMATNIKOVSKI; Sec.-Asst NIKOLA PANOV; publs *Geografski razgledi* (Geographical surveys), *Geografski vidik* (Geographical outlook).

Makedonsko Arheološko Naučno Društvo (Macedonian Archaeological Research Society): Curčiska bb, 1000 Skopje; tel. (2) 311-6044; fax (2) 311-6439; e-mail contact@mand.org.mk; internet www.mand.org.mk; f. 1972 as Archaeological Society of the Republic of Macedonia; symposia, lectures, publs; 150 mems; Chair. MARINA ONCHEVSKA TODOROVSKA; Pres. IRENA KOLISTRKOSKA NASTEVA; Sec. SILVANA BLAZEVSKA; publ. *Macedoniae acta archaeologica*.

Sojuz na Istoričarite na Republika Makedonija (Association of Historians of the Republic of Macedonia): Institut za nacionalna istorija, ul. Grigor Prličev br.3, POB 591, 1000 Skopje; tel. (2) 311-4078; fax (2) 311-5831; e-mail brjosifovska@yahoo.com;

f. 1952; Pres. Assoc. Prof. Dr BILJANA RISTOVSKA-JOSIFOVSKA; publ. *Istorija* (History).

LANGUAGE AND LITERATURE

Alliance Française: N. U. U. B. 'Sv. Kliment Ohridski', Leninova 39, 7000 Bitola; tel. and fax (47) 232-363; e-mail afbitola@yahoo.fr; f. 2001; library of 400 vols; offers courses and examinations in French language and culture and promotes cultural exchange with France; Dir MARIE-CLEMENCE VATELOT.

British Council: Blvr Goce Delcev 6, POB 562, 1000 Skopje; tel. (2) 313-5035; fax (2) 313-5036; e-mail info@britishcouncil.org.mk; internet www.britishcouncil.org/macedonia; f. 1996; offers courses and examinations in English language and British culture and promotes cultural exchange with the UK; library of 6,000 vols; Dir ANDREW HADLEY.

Društvo na Literaturnite Preveduvači na Makedonija (Society of Literary Translators of Macedonia): POB 3, 1000 Skopje; f. 1955; 102 mems; Pres. Prof. Dr BOŽIDAR NASTEV; Sec. TAŠKO ŠIRILOV.

Društvo na Pisatelite na Makedonija (Writers' Association of Macedonia): Maksim Gorki 18, 1000 Skopje; tel. and fax (2) 322-8039; f. 1947; 269 mems; Pres. JOVAN PAVLOVSKI; Sec. PASKAL GILOVSKI; Sec. SVETLANA HRISTOVA-JOCIĆ.

Sojuz na Društvata za Makedonski Jazik i Literatura (Union of Associations for Macedonian Language and Literature): Filološki fakultet, Blvr Krste Misirkov bb, 1000 Skopje; f. 1954; 700 mems; Pres. ELENA BENDEVSKA; Sec. LJUPČO MITREVSKI; publ. *Literaturen zbor* (Literary word).

Združenie na Folkloristite na Makedonija (Association of Folklorists of Macedonia): Institut za folklor, Ruzveltova 3, 1000 Skopje; tel. (2) 323-3876; f. 1952; 60 mems; Pres. GORGI SMOKVARSKI; Sec. ERMIS LAFAZANOVSKY; publ. *Narodno Stvaralaštvo* (1 or 2 a year).

MEDICINE

Farmaceutsko Društvo na Makedonija (Pharmacological Society of Macedonia): Ivo Ribar Lola MI/6, 1000 Skopje; Pres. LAZAR TOLOV; Sec. GALABA SRBINOVSKA; publ. *Bilten* (Bulletin).

Makedonsko Lekarsko Društvo (Macedonian Medical Association): Dame Gruev 3, 1000 Skopje; tel. (2) 316-2577; e-mail mld@unet.com.mk; internet www.mld.org.mk; f. 1945; promotes medical and related sciences; conserves and promotes the dignity and reputation of the medical profession and protects the interests of doctors; 4,490 mems; Pres. Prof. JOVAN TOFOSKI; publ. *Makedonski medicindki pregled* (Macedonian Medical Review).

NATURAL SCIENCES

General

Makedonskoto Ekološko Društvo (Macedonian Ecological Society): Blvr Kuzman Josifovski Pitu, 28/III-7, 1000 Skopje; tel. (2) 240-2773; fax (2) 240-2774; e-mail contact@mes.org.mk; internet www.mes.org.mk; f. 1972; devt of ecology, promotion of environmental science and protection of environment and nature; Chair. Dr LJUPČO MELOVSKI; publ. *Ekologija i zaštita na životnata sredina* (Ecology and Environmental Protection, every 4 years).

Mathematical Sciences

Sojuz na Matematičari na Makedonija (Society of Mathematicians of Macedonia): Blvr Aleksandar Makedonski bb, POB 10, 1000 Skopje; tel. (2) 311-6053; fax (2) 322-

8141; e-mail vesname@iunona.pmf.ukim.edu.mk; internet www.smm.org.mk; f. 1950; Chief Officers Prof. Dr BORKO ILIEVSKI, Prof. Dr NIKOLA PANDESKI; publ. *Matematički Bilten* (Mathematical Bulletin).

Physical Sciences

Društvo na Fizičarite na Republika Makedonija (Society of Physicists of Republic of Macedonia): Arhimedova 5, POB 162, 1000 Skopje; tel. (2) 324-9857; fax (2) 322-8141; e-mail nenad@iunona.pmf.ukim.edu.mk; internet dfrm.pmf.ukim.edu.mk; f. 1949; promotes research in physics, natural sciences and protection of environment; 139 mems; Pres. Prof. Dr NENAD NOVKOVSKI; Sec. Assoc. Prof. Dr DANICA KRSTOVSKA; Treas. LAMBE BARANDOVSKI; publs *Bilten* (1 a year), *Impuls* (jt publ. with Institute of Physics, Faculty of Natural Sciences, 2 a year), *Macedonian Physics Teacher*.

Makedonsko Geološko Društvo (Macedonian Geological Society): Geološki zavod, POB 28, 1000 Skopje; tel. (2) 323-0873; f. 1954; 300 mems; library of 20,000 vols; Pres. NIKOLA TUDŽAROV; Sec. ROZA PETROVSKA.

TECHNOLOGY

Sojuz na Inženeri i Tehničari na Makedonija (Society of Engineers and Technicians of Macedonia): Nikola Vapcarov bb, 1000 Skopje; f. 1945; 27,000 mems; Pres. Prof. Dr Ing. DIME LAZAROV; Sec. BORO RAVNJANSKI.

Research Institutes

GENERAL

Institutot za Životna Sredina i Zdravje (Institute for Environment and Health): Ilindenska nn, Campus Bldg 201.01/1, 1200 Tetovo; tel. (44) 356-114; fax (44) 356-001; e-mail ieh@seeu.edu.mk; internet ieh.seeu.edu.mk; f. 2005; attached to SEE Univ.; programmes in education, research, building partnerships and environmental awareness; 30 research students, 5 external research assocs.

AGRICULTURE, FISHERIES AND VETERINARY SCIENCE

Institut za Južni Zemjodelski Kulturi (Institute of Southern Crops): Goce Delčev bb, 2400 Strumica; tel. and fax (34) 345-096; e-mail admin@isc.ukim.edu.mk; f. 1956; attached to Dept of Plant Protection, Sts Cyril and Methodius Univ.; Dir Dr SAŠA MITREV; publ. *Zbornik* (Collected Papers).

Institut za Ovoštarstvo (Institute of Pomology): Prvomajska 5, 1000 Skopje; tel. (2) 323-0557; f. 1953; attached to Sts Cyril and Methodius Univ.; fruit research; library of 3,670 vols; Dir Dr IVAN KUZMANOVSKI.

Institut za Stočarstvo (Institute of Cattle Breeding): Ile Ilievski 92, A 1000 Skopje; tel. (2) 306-3523; fax (2) 306-2358; e-mail institut-za-stocarstvo@live.com; f. 1952; attached to Sts Cyril and Methodius Univ.; Dir Dr BONE PALASEVSKI; Sec. ALEN SALIU.

Institut za Tutun Prilep (Scientific Tobacco Institute Prilep): Kičevsko Džade, 7500 Prilep; tel. (48) 412-760; fax (48) 412-763; e-mail tobacco_institute_prilep@yahoo.com; internet www.tip.edu.mk; f. 1924; attached to St Kliment Ohridski Univ. Bitola; scientific research investigations, education, application and production activities in tobacco breeding; tobacco museum and meteorological station; depts of agrotechnics, chemistry of tobacco, tobacco smoke, residues from pesticides and biochemistry; economic planning and programming; genetics, selection and seed control; technology, fermentation and fabrication; library of 4,211 books, 125 titles of scientific and research publications; Pres. Dr JORDAN TRAJKOSKI; Vice-Pres. Dr VERA DIMESKA; Dir Prof. Dr KIRIL FILIPOSKI; publ. *Tutun* (Tobacco, 6 a year).

Zavod za Unapreduvanje na Lozarst-voto i Vinarstvoto na Makedonija (Institute for the Advancement of Viticulture of Macedonia): Naselba Butel 1, 1000 Skopje; f. 1952; Dir Dr DIME PEMOVSKI; publ. *Lozarstvo i vinarstvo* (Viticulture).

Zavod za Unapreduvanje na Stočarst-voto na Makedonija (Institute for the Advancement of Animal Husbandry of Macedonia): Avtokomanda, 1000 Skopje; f. 1952; Dir Prof. Dr BLAGOJ VASKOV.

Zemjodelski institut (Institute of Agriculture): Blvr Aleksandar Makedonski bb, 1000 Skopje; tel. (2) 3230-910; fax (2) 3114-283; e-mail d.mukaetov@zeminst.edu.mk; attached to Sts Cyril and Methodius Univ.; Dir Dr DUSKO MUKAETOV; Sec. VIKTORIJA KALAJDZISKA.

ECONOMICS, LAW AND POLITICS

Ekonomski Institut Skopje at the Sts Cyril and Methodius University (Institute of Economics at the Sts Cyril and Methodius University Skopje): Prolet 1, POB 250, 1000 Skopje; tel. (2) 311-5076; fax (2) 322-3350; e-mail eis@ek-inst.ukim.edu.mk; internet www.ek-inst.ukim.edu.mk; f. 1952; attached to Sts Cyril and Methodius Univ.; scientific research and educational instn; offers postgraduate studies in agrobusiness, entrepreneurship, financial management, int. economics, int. management; library of 20,200 books and periodicals; Dir Prof. BILJANA ANGELOVA; Sec. KOSTA JOVCEVSKI; publ. *Economic Development Journal* (4 a year).

HISTORY, GEOGRAPHY AND ARCHAEOLOGY

Institut za Nacionalna Istorija (Institute of National History): ul. Gligor Prličev br. 3, 1000 Skopje; tel. (2) 311-4078; fax (2) 311-5831; e-mail inimak@on.net.mk; internet www.makedonika.org/ini; f. 1948; attached to Sts Cyril and Methodius Univ.; history of the Macedonian and Balkan peoples and ethnic communities; 56 mems; library of 27,350 vols, 37,500 periodicals, 1,300 vols of newspapers; Dir Prof. Dr NOVICA VELJANOVSKI; Sec. TATIANA DOJCINOVSKA; publ. *Glasnik* (Journal).

LANGUAGE AND LITERATURE

Institut za Folklor 'Marko Cepenkov' (Institute of Folklore 'Marko Cepenkov'): Ruzveltova 3, POB 319, 1000 Skopje; tel. (2) 338-0176; fax (2) 338-0177; e-mail ifmarkocepenkov@mt.net.mk; internet www.ifmc.ukim.mk; f. 1950 as Folklore Institute of the Republic, present status 1979; attached to Sts Cyril and Methodius Univ.; study of the spiritual and material culture of the Macedonian people: people's literature, ethnology, vernacular architecture, textile ornaments, traditional arts and crafts and skills; Dir Dr SEVIM PILICKOVA; Sec. TODOR ANDREEV; publ. *Makedonski folklor* (2 a year).

Institut za Makedonska Literatura (Institute of Macedonian Literature): Gligor Prlicev 5, 1000 Skopje; tel. and fax (2) 322-0309; e-mail maclit@iml.ukim.edu.mk; internet iml.ukim.edu.mk; f. 1998; attached to Sts Cyril and Methodius Univ.; continuous and systematic research, adherence and interpretation of literature and its tradition in Macedonia; training of young personnel

for scientific work; depts of contributing scientific activities—bibliography, documentation, library and informatics, medieval Macedonian literature, Macedonian folk literature, Macedonian literature of the 19th century, Macedonian literature of the 20th century, Macedonian–Balkan literary-historical relations, literatures of the nationalities in Macedonia, theory of literature and comparative literature; Dir LORETA GEORGIEVSKA-JAKOVLEVA; Sec. SARITA TRAJANOVA; Treas. VESELA KRALJEVA; publs *Spectrum* (scientific magazine), *Literary Context* (scientific publ. for comparative literature).

Institut za Makedonski Jazik 'Krste Misirkov' (Krste Misirkov Institute of Macedonian Language): Grigor Prličev 5, 1000 Skopje; tel. (2) 311-4733; fax (2) 322-2225; f. 1953; attached to Sts Cyril and Methodius Univ.; depts of contemporary Macedonian, dialectology, history of the Macedonian language, Macedonian lexicology and lexicography, onomastics; Dir Dr LILJANA MAKARIJOSKA; Sec. TODE BLAZEVSKI; publs *Makedonistika* (Macedonian Studies), *Makedonski jazik* (The Macedonian Language), *Stari tekstovi* (Ancient Texts).

Research Centre for Areal Linguistics: bul. Krste Misirkov 2, 1000 Skopje; tel. (2) 323-5400; fax (2) 323-5500; e-mail ical@manu.edu.mk; internet www.manu.edu.mk; f. 2000; attached to Macedonian Acad. of Arts and Sciences; researches the role of spatial factors in the devt and function of language; archives rare books and MSS; organizes meetings and lectures; library of 10,000 vols, spec. colln of rare books, 40 CDs, 2,000 minutes of audio material; Dir Prof. ZUZANNA TOPOLINSKA; Deputy Dir Prof. MARJAN MARKOVIC.

NATURAL SCIENCES

Institut za Zemjotresno Inženerstvo i Inženerska Seizmologija (Institute of Earthquake Engineering and Engineering Seismology): 73, Salvador Aljende str., POB 101, 1000 Skopje; tel. (2) 3107-701; fax (2) 3112-163; e-mail garevski@pluto.iziis.ukim.edu.mk; internet www.iziis.edu.mk; f. 1965; attached to Sts Cyril and Methodius Univ.; supervises post-earthquake reconstruction, revitalization and devt of Skopje; depts of building structures and materials, dynamic testing laboratory and informatics, engineering structures, geotechnics and special structures and informatics, natural and technological hazards ecology, risk disaster management and strategic planning; Dir MIHAIL GAREVSKI; Deputy Dir GOLUBKA NECEVSKA-CVETANOVSKA.

RELIGION, SOCIOLOGY AND ANTHROPOLOGY

Institut za Sociološki i Političko-pravni Istražuvanja (Institute of Sociological, Political and Juridical Research): Blvr Partizanski odredi bb, 1000 Skopje; tel. (2) 3061-119; fax (2) 3061-282; e-mail jakjor@isppi.ukim.edu.mk; internet www.isppi.ukim.edu.mk; f. 1965; attached to Sts Cyril and Methodius Univ.; study of sociological, political and juridical phenomena; research; collaboration with instns and orgs engaged in research in sociology, political science and law; depts of information and documentation, political science, sociology; centres for ethnic relations, management and human resource devt, public policy and public admin., criminology, crime prevention and law enforcement policy, communication, media, and culture, human rights and nat. security, strategic studies; Dir JORDE JAKIMOVSKI.

TECHNOLOGY

Geološki Zavod (Geology Institute): POB 28, 1000 Skopje; f. 1944; geological mapping, exploration of mineral deposits, drilling, mining, grouting; 700 mems; library of 10,000 vols; Gen Dir DRAGAN ANGELESKY; publ. *Trudovi* (Transactions).

Research Centre for Energy, Informatics and Materials: Krste Misirkov 2, 1000 Skopje; tel. (2) 323-5400; fax (2) 323-5423; e-mail jpj@manu.edu.mk; internet www.manu.edu.mk/icei; f. 1986; attached to Macedonian Acad. of Sciences and Arts; initiates and coordinates nat. research programmes; conducts research; divs of energy, environment, materials and neuroinformatics; Dir Acad. JORDAN POP-JORDANOV.

Zavod za Ispituvanje na Materijali i Razvoj na novi Tehnologii (Institution for Research of Materials and Development of New Technologies): Rade Koncar 16, 1000 Skopje; tel. (2) 311-6610; fax (2) 321-1996; e-mail zimad@mt.net.mk; internet www.zim.com.mk; f. 1956, present status 2007; attached to Sts Cyril and Methodius Univ.; comprises 3 instns: Institute of Materials, Institute for Transport and Environment and Institute to Develop New Technologies; scientific research; publishing scientific achievements; Dir BORCE TANEVSKI.

Hidro Energo In'enering Skopje R. Makedonija (Hydro Energo Engineering DOO Skopje—Republic of Macedonia): Blvr Jane Sandanski 76, 1000 Skopje; tel. and fax (2) 245-4333; e-mail hei@hei.com.mk; internet www.hei.com.mk; f. 2008; design and devt of investment and technical documentation from the fields of hydro-technical engineering, hydro-energetics, hydro-informatics and geotechnical engineering; library of 1,800 vols; Dir Ing. METODI BOEV; Man. Dr Ing. KAEVSKI IVANCO; publ. *Vodostopanski problemi* (Water Development Problems, every 5 years).

Libraries and Archives

Bitola

Nacionalna Ustanova Univerzitetska Biblioteka 'Kliment Ohridski' (National Institution University Library 'St Kliment Ohridski'): Leninova 39, 7000 Bitola; tel. (47) 220-208; fax (47) 220-515; e-mail nuubbt@uklo.edu.mk; internet www.nuubbt.uklo.edu.mk; f. 1945; 500,000 vols; Dir JELENA PETROVSKA; Sr Librarian NAUM GJORGIEVSKI; publ. *Library Trend* (1 a year).

Skopje

Biblioteka 'Braka Miladinovci' (City Library 'Braka Miladinovci'): Partizanski odredi 22, 1000 Skopje; tel. (2) 323-2544; fax (2) 312-7016; e-mail direktor@gbiblsk.edu.mk; internet www.gbiblsk.edu.mk; f. 1945 as City Library, present name 1963; 800,000 vols; 27 brs; Pres. PETRE M. ANDREEVSKI; Dir FILIP PETROVSKI (acting).

Državen Arhiv na Republika Makedonija (State Archives of the Republic of Macedonia): Gligor Prličev 3, 1000 Skopje; tel. (2) 311-5783; fax (2) 316-5944; e-mail arhiv@unet.com.mk; internet www.arhiv.gov.mk; f. 1951; 70m. documents; 9 regional depts: Skopje, Bitola, Prilep, Tetovo, Shtip, Strumica, Kumanovo, Ohrid and Veles; Dir Dr ZORAN TODOROVSKI; publ. *Makedonski archivist*.

Attached Departments:

Oddelenie Bitola (Department of Bitola): Blvr 1 Maj 55, 7000 Bitola; tel. (47) 241-740; f. 1954 as municipal archive, present status 1990; conservation, colln and printing of archive materials; 3,823 books, 163 magazines and 155 newspapers; Dir JOVAN KOCHANKOVSKY.

Oddelenie Kumanovo (Department of Kumanovo): Goce Delchev Str. 25, 1300 Kumanovo; tel. and fax (31) 420-464; f. 1954; 543 archive groups and 8 archival collns; documents on economics, sociology, culture and politics.

Oddelenie Ohrid (Department of Ohrid): Nikola Karev Str. 6, 6000 Ohrid; tel. and fax (46) 252-104; f. 1955, since 1990 as dept of Ohrid of the State Archives of the Republic of Macedonia; 3,000 vols; spec. collns: Old Church Slavonic MSS (14th–19th centuries), early Greek and Arabic books; 598 record groups and 17 archival collns; Dir DIMITAR SMILESKI.

Oddelenie Prilep (Department of Prilep): Aleksandar Makedonski Str. 134, 7500 Prilep; tel. (48) 424-192; fax (48) 424-334; f. 1955; jurisdiction over municipalities of Prilep, Dolneni, Krivogashtani, Krushevo, Zhitoshe, Makedonski Brod and Plasnica; 540 archive groups and 7 archival collns.

Oddelenie Skopje (Department of Skopje): Moskovska 1, 1000 Skopje; tel. and fax (2) 307-6461; f. 1952; 3,000 vols, 1.5 km of archive records, 333,152 units of published information, 675 record groups and 10 archival collns, 30,000 photographs from 1928 to 1983; Dir Dr MILOŠ KONSTANTINOV; publ. *Dokumenti i materiali za istorijata na Skopje* (irregular).

Oddelenie Stip (Department of Stip): Sane Georgiev Str. 35, 2000 Stip; tel. and fax (32) 391-337; f. 1956; jurisdiction over municipalities of Stip, Karbinci, Sveti Nikole, Lozovo, Probishtip, Kochani, Chreshinovo-Obleshevo, Zrnovci, Vinica, Delchevo, Makedonska Kamenica, Radovish and Konche; working with 275 archive owners; 523 record groups and 22 archival collns.

Oddelenie Strumica (Department of Strumica): 27 Mart Str. 2, 2400 Strumica; tel. and fax (34) 322-083; internet www.arhiv.gov.mk; f. 1956; jurisdiction over municipalities of Strumica, Berovo, Novo Selo, Pehchevo, Vasilevo and Bosilovo; working with 225 archive owners; 453 record groups and 8 archival collns.

Oddelenie Tetovo (Department of Tetovo): Cvetan Dimov Str. 1, 1220 Tetovo; tel. and fax (44) 332-209; f. 1961 as Historical Archives of the Municipalities of Tetovo and Gostivar; jurisdiction over municipalities of Gostivar, Tetovo, Brvenica, Bogovinje, Zhelino, Yegunovce, Tearce, Vrapchtishte, Mavrovi Anovi-Rostushe; working with 183 archive owners; 701 record groups and archival collns; colln of documents in Old Turkish from the Casa of Tetovo (1705–1924).

Oddelenie Veles (Department of Veles): Naum Naumovski, Borche Str., 1400 Veles; tel. and fax (43) 234-784; f. 1954 as Archiv na Veles (Archives of Veles); jurisdiction over municipalities of Veles, Chashka, Gradsko, Rosoman, Negotino, Kavadarci, Demir Kapiya, Valandovo, Gevgeliya, Bogdanci and Doyran; working with 267 archive owners; 538 record groups and 8 archival collns.

Narodna i univerzitetska biblioteka 'Sv. Kliment Ohridski' (National and University Library 'St Kliment Ohridski'): Blvr Goce Delčev 6, POB 566, 1000 Skopje; tel. (2) 311-5177; fax (2) 322-6846; e-mail kliment@nubsk.edu.mk; internet www.nubsk.edu.mk; f. 1944; state copyright, central and deposit library; 3m. vols, spec. collns: Slav MSS, incunabula and rare books, oriental, music,

cartography, doctoral theses, fine art; Dir MILE BOSHESKI; publ. *Makedonska bibliografija* (in 3 series, each 4 a year).

Museums and Art Galleries

Bitola

NU Zavod i Muzej Bitola (NI Institute and Museum Bitola): ul. Kliment Ohridski bb, 7000 Bitola; tel. (47) 233-187; fax (47) 229-525; e-mail muzej@muzejbt.org.mk; internet www.muzejbt.org.mk; f. 1948 as The Museum of the town of Bitola, as the Art Gallery of Bitola 1958, given status nat. instn of culture 2003; archaeology, art, ethnology, history; library of 10,000 vols; Dir IVAN JOLEVSKI.

Kratovo

Centar za Karpesta umetnost, Kratovo (Centre of Rock Art, Kratovo): Planinska 1, 1360 Kratovo; tel. and fax (31) 481-572; e-mail lcfrockart@yahoo.com; internet www.rock-art.mk; protects rock engravings; exhibits artefacts and rock engravings; organizes scientific excursions, expeditions and lectures; field research; collns of engravings, 500 images, 12 documentaries, objects made from stones, bones, wood and pottery; Pres. STEVCE DONEVSKI.

Ohrid

National Workshop for Handmade Paper 'St. Kliment Ohridski': Samoilova 60, 6000 Ohrid; tel. (46) 253-610; internet www.ohridpaper.com.mk; f. 2002; paper produced in original Chinese tradition of 2nd century BC; presents procedure of making paper, with knowledge of history of the paper and method of first printing on Gutenberg press (15th century).

Skopje

Muzej na Grad Skopje (Museum of Skopje): Mito Hadživasilev Jasmin bb, 1000 Skopje; tel. and fax (2) 311-5367; f. 1949; 21,950 exhibits incl. 12,000 archaeological, 2,965 historical, 5,010 ethnographic and 2,965 history of art exhibits and 182 photographs; Dir JOVAN SHURBANOVSKI; Sr Curator MILOS BILBIJA.

Muzej na Makedonija (Museum of Macedonia): ul. Ćurčiska bb, 1000 Skopje; tel. (2) 311-6044; fax (2) 311-6439; e-mail musmk@mt.net.mk; internet www.musmk.org.mk; f. 1924; anthropology, archaeology, art history and conservation, history, ethnology; exhibits folk costumes, jewellery, traditional architecture, textiles, crafts, economy, customs and traditional musical instruments, fresco replicas, icons from 14th–19th centuries; library of 19,000 vols; Dir MARY ANICIN PEJOSKA; Programme Dir PERO JOSIFOVSKI; publs *Numizmatičar* (1 a year), *Zbornik* (Collected Papers, 1 a year).

Nacionalna Ustanova Muzej na Sovremena Umetnost vo Skopje (National Institution Museum of Contemporary Art Skopje): Samoilova bb, POB 482, 1000 Skopje; tel. (2) 311-7734; fax (2) 311-0123; e-mail msu-info@msuskopje.org.mk; internet www.msuskopje.org.mk; f. 1964, present bldg 1970; depts of collections and exhibitions, education and conservation and restoration, research and documentation; organizes exhibitions and events of Macedonian and foreign art, discussions with artists, panels, film and video presentations and lectures; library of 20,000 titles (research and documentation dept); Dir ELIZA SULEVSKA; publs *Large Glass Magazine*, publs catalogues and monographs and

spec. editions of *Psyce*, *Playtime*, *Macedonian Critic* and *Dossier MoCA Skopje*.

Prirodonaučen muzej na Makedonija (Macedonian Museum of Natural History): Blvr Ilinden 86, 1000 Skopje; tel. (2) 311-7669; fax (2) 311-6453; e-mail macmusnh@unet.com.mk; f. 1926; collects, studies and exhibits natural resources of Macedonia; 4,000 original exhibits on display in glass showcases and dioramas; displays fossils that date back 8m.–10m. years; library of 44,000 vols; Dir Dr SVETOZAR PETKOVSKI; Curator GUTE MLADENOOVSKI; publs *Acta*, *Fauna na Makedonija*, *Fragmenta Balcanica*.

Umetnička Galerija (Art Gallery): Kruševska 1A, POB 278, 1000 Skopje; tel. (2) 323-3904; f. 1948; modern art; Dir VIKTORIJA VASEVA-DIMESKA.

Universities

DRŽAVNIOT UNIVERZITET VO TETOVO
(State University of Tetova)

Rruga e Ilindenit pn, 1200 Tetova

Telephone: (44) 356-500

Fax: (44) 334-222

E-mail: international@unite.edu.mk

Internet: www.unite.edu.mk

Founded 1994, officially recognized as State Univ. 2004

State control

Languages of instruction: Albanian, English, Macedonian

Rector: Prof. Dr AGRON REKA

Faculties of applied sciences, arts, business administration, economics, food technology, law, mathematics and natural sciences, medical sciences, philology, philosophy, physical education.

FON UNIVERZITET
(FON University)

Str. Vojvodina bb, 1000 Skopje

Telephone: (2) 244-5555

Fax: (2) 244-5550

E-mail: info@fon.edu.mk

Internet: www.fon.edu.mk

Founded 2003 as Faculty of Social Studies FON

Private control

Chancellor: Prof. Dr ALEKSANDAR NIKOLOVSKI

Vice-Chancellor for Science and Technology: Prof. Dr SIME ARSENOVSKI

Vice-Chancellor for Science and Technology: Prof. Dr BAJRAM POLOZANI

Vice-Chancellor for Studies: Prof. Dr RISTO MALCESKI

Pres.: FIJAT CANOSKI

Gen.-Sec.: BILJANA KAROVSKA-ANDONOVSKA

DEANS

Faculty of Applied European Languages: Prof. Dr ALEKSA POPOSKI

Faculty of Design and Multimedia: Assoc. Prof. ALEKSANDAR NOSPAL

Faculty for Detectives and Security: Prof. Dr ALEKSANDAR DONCEV

Faculty of Economics: Prof. Dr MIRKO TRIPUNOSKI

Faculty of Information and Communication Technology: Prof. Dr OLIVER ILIEV

Faculty of Law: Prof. Dr GJORGI TONOVSKI

Faculty of Politics and International Relations: Prof. Dr NANO RUZIN

Faculty of Sport and Sport Management: Prof. Dr VANGEL SIMEV

MEGUNARODEN BALKANSKI UNIVERZITET
(International Balkan University)

Samoilova 10, 1000 Skopje
Telephone: (2) 321-4831
Fax: (2) 321-4832
E-mail: info@ibu.edu.mk
Internet: www.ibu.edu.mk
Founded 2006
Private control

Rector: Prof. Dr HÜNER SENCAN
Vice-Rector: Prof. Dr MEHMET ZELKA, Prof. Dr ABDURAUF PRUTHI
Library of 3,000 (2,000 English, 1,000 Turkish) reference books
Faculties of communication, economics and administrative sciences, languages and fine arts, technical sciences.

UNIVERSITETI I EJL
(South East European University)

Ilindenska bb, 1200 Tetovo
Telephone: (44) 356-000
Fax: (44) 356-001
E-mail: t.selimi@seeu.edu.mk
Internet: www.seeu.edu.mk
Founded 2001
State control
Languages of instruction: Albanian, English
Academic year: August to June

Rector: Dr ALAJDIN ABAZI
Pro-Rector for Academic Issues: Prof. Dr ZAMIR DIKA
Pro-Rector for Finance Planning and Development: Prof. Dr ABDYLMENAF BEXHETI
Pro-Rector for Research and Quality Assurance: Prof. Dr MURTEZAN ISMAILI
Sec.-Gen: XHEVAIR MEMEDI

Library of 26,000 books, 11,350 titles
Number of teachers: 300
Number of students: 7,000

DEANS

Faculty of Business Administration: Prof. Dr IZET ZEQIRI
Faculty of Contemporary Sciences and Technologies: Dr BEKIM FETAJI (acting)
Faculty of Languages, Cultures and Communication: Prof. Dr VEBI BEXHETI
Faculty of Law: Prof. Dr ISMAIL ZENNELI
Faculty of Public Administration: Prof. Dr ETEM AZIRI
Faculty of Teacher Training: Dr TEUTA ARIFI

UNIVERZITET 'SV. KIRIL I METODIJ' VO SKOPJE
(Sts Cyril and Methodius University in Skopje)

Blvr Krste Misirkov bb, 1000 Skopje
Telephone: (2) 329-3293
Fax: (2) 329-3202
E-mail: ukim@ukim.edu.mk
Internet: www.ukim.edu.mk
Founded 1949
State control
Language of instruction: Macedonian
Academic year: September to May

Rector: Prof. Dr VELIMIR STOJKOVSKI
Vice-Rector for Finance, Investments and Devt: Prof. Dr PECE NEDANOVSKI
Vice-Rector for Int. Cooperation: Prof. Dr MOME SPASOVSKI
Vice-Rector for Teaching: Prof. Dr ELENA DUMOVA-JOVANOSKA
Vice-Rector for Science: Prof. Dr KOLE VASILEVSKI
Sec.-Gen.: ILIJA PIPERKOSKI

Number of teachers: 2,700
Number of students: 50,000

Publications: *Univerzitetski bilten, Univerzitetski vesnik i Studentski zbor*

DEANS

Faculty of Agricultural Sciences and Food: Prof. DRAGI DIMITRIEVSKI
Faculty of Architecture: Prof. Dr TIHOMIR STOJKOV
Faculty of Civil Engineering: Prof. Dr PETER CVETANOVSKI
Faculty of Dentistry: Prof. Dr ALEKSANDAR GRCEV
Faculty of Dramatic Arts: Prof. KIRIL RISTOSKI
Faculty of Economics: Prof. Dr LJUBOMIR KEKENOVSKI
Faculty of Education (Skopje): Prof. Dr NIKOLA PETROV
Faculty of Education (Stip): Prof. SPASKO SIMONOVSKI
Faculty of Electrical Engineering and Information Technologies: Prof. Dr MILE STANKOVSKI
Faculty of Fine Arts: Prof. DIMITAR MALIDANOV
Faculty of Forestry: Prof. Dr BRANKO RABADZISKI
Faculty of Law: Prof. Dr BORCE DAVITKOVSKI
Faculty of Mechanical Engineering: Prof. Dr ATANAS KOCOV
Faculty of Medicine: Prof. Dr NIKOLA JANKULOVSKI (acting)
Faculty of Mining and Geology: Prof. Dr TODOR DELIPETROV
Faculty of Music: Prof. Dr EVUSKA ELEZOVIC-TRPKOVA
Faculty of Natural and Mathematical Sciences: Prof. Dr DONE GERSHANOVSKI
Faculty of Pedagogy: Prof. Dr VLADO TIMOVSKI
Faculty of Pharmacy: Prof. Dr ALEKSANDAR DIMOVSKI
Faculty of Philology: Prof. Dr MAKSIM KARANFILOVSKI
Faculty of Philosophy: Prof. Dr GORAN AJDINSKI
Faculty of Physical Education: Prof. Dr GINO STREZOVSKI
Faculty of Technology and Metallurgy: Prof. Dr ALEKSANDAR DIMITROV
Faculty of Veterinary Medicine: Prof. Dr DINE MITROV

PROFESSORS

Faculty of Agricultural Sciences and Food (Blvr Aleksandar Makedonski bb, 1000 Skopje; tel. (2) 311-5277; fax (2) 313-4310; e-mail d.dimitrievski@fznh.ukim.edu.mk; internet www.fznh.ukim.edu.mk):

ANCEV, E.
AZDERSKI, J.
BELIČOVSKI, S.
BELKOVSKI, N.
BOZINOVIK, Z.
CUKALIEV, O.
DZABIRSKI, V.
EGUMENOVSKI, P.
GICEV, A.
GORGEVSKI, G.
GOŠEVSKI, D.
HADŽI PECOVA, S.
HRISTOV, P.
ILIK-POPOVA, S.
IVANOVSKI, P.
JANKULOVSKI, D.
MARINKOVIK, L.
MARTINOVSKI, S.
MIHAJLOVSKI, M.
MITRIKESKI, J.
NAUMOVSKI, M.
PEJKOVSKI, C.
PEŠEVSKI, M.
POSTOLOVSKI, M.
SIVAKOV, L.
STOJKOVSKI, C.

TANEVSKI, D.
USALESKI, V.
VASILEVSKI, G.
VIDOJA, T.
ŽIBEROSKI, J.
ŽIVKO, D.

Faculty of Electrical Engineering and Information Technologies (Karpos II bb, 1000 Skopje; tel. (2) 306-2224; fax (2) 306-4262; e-mail dekan@feit.ukim.edu.mk; internet www.feit.ukim.edu.mk):

ACKOVSKI, R.
ARSENOV, A.
ARSOV, D.
ARSOV, G.
ARSOV, L.
BOGDANOVA, S.
CEKREDZI, N.
CUNDEV, M.
DAVCEV, D.
FILIPOSKI, V.
FUSTIC, V.
GAVRILOVSKA, L.
GAVRILOV, C.
GEORGIEVA, V.
GLAMOCANIN, V.
GRCEV, L.
HANDZISKI, B.
JANEV, L.
KAMILOVSKI, M.
KARADZINOV, L.
KOCAREV, L.
KOCEV, K.
KOLEMISEVSKA-GUGULOVSKA, T.
KUJUMDZIEVA-NIKOLOSKA, M.
LAZOV, P.
LOSKOVSKA, S.
MIHAJLOV, D.
MIRCEVSKI, S.
NIKOLOVSKI, L.
PANOVSKI, L.
PIPEREVSKI, B.
POPOVSKI, B.
TALESKI, R.
TENTOV, A.
ULCAR STAVROVA, T.
ZLATANOVSKI, M.

Faculty of Forestry (Blvr Aleksandar Makedonski bb, 1000 Skopje; tel. (2) 316-5777; fax (2) 316-4560; e-mail sumarski@sf.ukim.edu.mk; internet www.sf.ukim.edu.mk):

DIMESKA, J.
DINA KOLEVSKI, D.
EFREMOVSKI, V.
MALETIKJ, V.
MANE, T.
NACEVSKA, M.
NACHESKI, S.
NIKOLOV, N.
RABADZHISKI, B.
RISTEVSKA, P.
RIZOVSKA ATANASOVSKI, J.
ROSE, A.
SIMAKOSKI, N.
TRAJKOV, P.
TRPOSKI, Z.
VASILEVSKI, K.

Faculty of Law (Blvr Krste Petkov Misirkov bb, 1000 Skopje; tel. (2) 311-7244; fax (2) 322-7549; e-mail dekan@pf.ukim.edu.mk; internet www.pf.ukim.edu.mk):

BAJALDZIEV, D.
BELICANEC, T.
DAVITKOVSKI, B.
FRCKOSKI, L.
GAVROSKA, P.
GEORGIEVSKI, S.
GRADISKI-LAZAREVSKA, E.
IVANOV, G.
JANEVSKI, A.
KALAMATIEV, T.
KAMBOVSKI, V.
KANDIKJAN, V.
KANEVCEV, M.

KLIMOVSKI, S.
MALESKI, D.
MANOLEVA-MITROVSKA, D.
MICAJKOV, M.
MUKOSKA-CINGO, V.
PENDOVSKA, V.
PETRUSEVSKA, T.
POLENAK-AKIMOVSKA, M.
POPOVSKA, B.
SILJANOVSKA-DAVKOVA, G.
STAROVA, G.
TODOROVA, S.
TUPURKOVSKI, V.
ZIVKOVSKA, R.

Faculty of Physical Education (ul. Zeleznicka bb, 1000 Skopje; tel. (2) 311-3654; fax (2) 311-9755; e-mail kontakt@ffk.ukim.edu.mk; internet www.ffk.ukim.edu.mk):

DZHAMBAZOVSKI, A.
IVANOV, D.
JOVANOVSKI, J.
NASTEVSKA, V.
NAUMOVSKI, A.
PETROVSKI, V.
RADIC, Z.
STREZOVSKI, G.
TUFEKCHIEVSKI, A.

UNIVERZITET 'SV. KLIMENT OHRIDSKI' BITOLA
(St Kliment Ohridski University of Bitola)

Blvr 1 Maj bb, 7000 Bitola
Telephone: (47) 223-788
Fax: (47) 223-594
E-mail: rektorat@uklo.edu.mk
Internet: www.uklo.edu.mk
Founded 1979
State control
Language of instruction: Macedonian
Rector: Prof. Dr ZLATKO ZHOGLEV
Vice-Rector for Academic Affairs: SASHO ATANASOSKI
Vice-Rector for Student Affairs: PERE ASLIMOSKI
Vice-Rector for Financial Issues and Devt: LUPCO TRPEZANOVSKI
Sec.-Gen.: OFELIJA HRISTOVKSA
Library of 160,000 vols, 500 periodicals, 1,000 microforms
Number of teachers: 337
Number of students: 11,644
Publication: Scientific Review (1 a year)

DEANS

Faculty of Administration and Management of Information Systems: Prof. Dr VIOLETA MANEVSKA

Faculty of Economics: Prof. Dr GORDANA TRAJKOSKA
Faculty of Education: Prof. Dr JOVE DIMITRI TALEVSKI
Faculty of Law: Prof. Dr ILIJA TODOROVSKI
Faculty of Technical Sciences: Dr. VESNA MIKAROVSKA

PROFESSORS

Faculty of Administration and Management of Information Systems (Partizanska bb (Kompleks Kasarni), 7000 Bitola; tel. (47) 259-921; fax (47) 259-917; internet famis.edu.mk):

PANOVSKA-BOSKOSKA V.

Faculty of Economics (Gorče Petrov bb, 7500 Prilep; tel. (48) 427-020; fax (48) 426-927; internet www.eccfp.edu.mk):

ATANASOSKI, S.
BASESCU-GJORGJIESKA, M.
DIMKOV, D.
GEORGIEVSKI, M.
ILIESKA, C.
JANESKA, M.
KOKAROSKI, D.
LASHKOSKA, V.
PECHIJARESKI, L.
RISTESKA, A.
ROCHESKA, S.
SOKOLOSKI, B.
SOTIROSKI, K.
STOJANOSKI, L.
TALESKA, S.
TRAJKOSKA, G.

Faculty of Education (ul. Vasko Karangelevski bb, 7000 Bitola; tel. (47) 253-652; fax (47) 203-385; e-mail contact@pfbt.uklo.edu.mk; internet www.pfbt.uklo.edu.mk):

ASLIMOVSKI, P.
GRUEVSKI, T.
KOLONDZHOVSKI, B.
METHODS, P.
RISTOVSKI, D.
SMILEVSKI, C.
STOILKOVA-KAVKALESKA, M.

Faculty of Law (ul. Prilepska bb, Bitola; tel. and fax (47) 221-115; e-mail pfk@uklo.edu.mk; internet www.pfk.uklo.edu.mk):

TODOROVSKI, E.

Faculty of Technical Sciences (I. L. Ribar bb, 7000 Bitola; tel. (47) 207-702; fax (47) 203-370; e-mail info.tfb@uklo.edu.mk; internet www.tfb.edu.mk):

ANDREEVSKA, A.
BOMBOL, C.
DESKOVSKI, S.
DONEVSKI, B.

EMS, I.
GERAMITCIOSKI, T.
JOLEVSKI, T.
KANEVCE, G.
KANEVCE, L.
KRSTANOSKI, N.
MIJAKOVSKI, E.
MIKAROVSKA, V.
PANOVSKI, S.
PAVLOV, V.
POPNIKOLOVA-RADEVSKA, M.
POPOVSKI, D.
POPOVSKI, K.
STOJANOVSKA, L.
TALEVSKI, J.
TRAJKOVSKI, D.
TROMBEV, G.
ZLATKOVSKI, S.

UNIVERZITET 'GOCE DELČEV' ŠTIP
(Goce Delcev University of Stip)

Krste Misirkov bb, POB 201, 2000 Stip
Telephone: (32) 550-000
Fax: (32) 390-700
E-mail: contact@ugd.edu.mk
Internet: www.ugd.edu.mk
Founded 2007
State control
Rector: Prof. Dr SASA MITREV
Vice Rector for Finance, Investments and Development: BORIS KRSTEV
Vice Rector for Science: BLAZO BOEV
Sec.-Gen.: RISTO KOSTURANOV
Library of 1,000 titles
Number of students: 5,000

Faculties of agriculture, computer science and information technology, economics, education, geosciences and technology, law, mechanical engineering and electrical engineering, medicine, mines, music, philology, technology, tourism and business logistics.

UNIVERZITET ZA TURIZAM I MENADŽMENT SKOPJE
(Skopje University of Tourism and Management)

ul. Partizanski Odredi br. 99, 1000 Skopje
Telephone: (2) 309-3209
Fax: (2) 309-3213
Internet: www.utms.edu.mk
Private control
Chancellor: Prof. Dr ACE MILENKOVSKI

Faculties of economy, entrepreneurial business, international marketing and management, management of human resources, public relations, sport tourism, tourism.

MADAGASCAR

The Higher Education System

In 1896 Madagascar came under French colonial rule and in 1958 it became an autonomous state (as the Malagasy Republic) within the French Community; full independence was achieved in 1960. The Université d'Antananarivo (founded 1961) is the oldest current institution of higher education; it was formed from a merger of pre-existing colleges. It was reorganized in 1976 as a decentralized institution and the six centres acquired the status of independent universities in 1988. The Ministry of National Education and Scientific Research has overall responsibility for higher education, which consists of universities, technical institutes and teacher training colleges. In 2005/06 there were six universities and 14 private institutions of higher education and in 2006/07 58,300 students were enrolled in tertiary education. The degree system (see below) is based upon the French cyclical model.

The Rector or President is the head of the University, governing in conjunction with Councils for administrative and academic affairs. The Administrative Council oversees the institutional budget, stipulates rules and regulations and ensures good governance. The Academic Council is responsible for matters of teaching and research.

The secondary school Baccalauréat is required for admission to university. The university degree system consists of three cycles. The first cycle lasts for two years after which a student receives one of two diplomas, either Diplôme Universitaire d'Etudes Littéraires or Diplôme Universitaire d'Etudes Scientifiques. Engineering students are awarded either the Diplôme Universitaire de Technicien Supérieur en Informatique or the Diplôme Universitaire d'Etudes Technologiques before studying for another two to three years for the Diplôme d'Ingénieur. Law students are awarded the Capacité en Droit after two years, and can then take the four-year Licence. The Doctorat de Médecine is a seven-year programme. The second cycle is a period of specialization of either one year, resulting in award of the Licence (undergraduate degree), or two years, resulting in award of the Maîtrise (postgraduate degree). Following the Maîtrise, the third cycle is a two-year period of study leading to the award of the Diplôme d'Etudes Supérieures, followed by research and thesis for the degree of Doctorat de Troisième Cycle.

The main post-secondary qualification for technical and vocational education is the Brevet de Technicien, awarded after three years' study at technical institutes.

Regulatory and Representative Bodies

GOVERNMENT

Ministry of National Education and Scientific Research: BP 247, Anosy, Antananarivo 101; tel. (20) 22-243-08; fax (20) 22-238-97; e-mail mlraharimalala@yahoo.fr; internet 196.192.32.105/menrs; Minister ANDRIAMPARANY BENJAMIN RADAVIDSON.

Ministry of Sports, Culture and Leisure: Ambohijatovo, pl. Goulette, BP 681, Antananarivo 101; tel. (20) 22-277-80; fax (20) 22-342-75; e-mail mjs_101@yahoo.fr; internet www.mjs.gov.mg; Minister PATRICK RAMIARAMANANA.

NATIONAL BODY

Maison de la Communication des Universités (Universities' Communication Centre): Immeuble Ex-Super bazar Analakely, 28 rue Andrianampoinimerina, Antananarivo; tel. (20) 22-636-19; e-mail contact@mcumadagascar.org; internet enduma.africa-web.org; f. 1993; acts as an intermediary between the univs and public life; 12 mems; Pres. of Admin. Council ARMAND RASOAMIARAMANANA; Gen. Dir MICHEL NORBERT REJELA.

Learned Societies

GENERAL

Académie Nationale Malgache: BP 6217, Tsimbazaza, Antananarivo; f. 1902; studies in human and natural sciences; four sections: language, literature and arts, moral and political sciences, basic sciences, applied sciences; 140 mems, 60 foreign mems in each section; library of 100,000 vols; Pres. Dr C. RABENORO; publs *Bulletin de l'Académie* (1 a year), *Bulletin d'Information et de Liaison*, *Mémoires*.

BIBLIOGRAPHY, LIBRARY SCIENCE AND MUSEOLOGY

Association des Bibliothécaires, Documentalistes, Archivistes et Muséographes de Madagascar: Bibliothèque Nationale, BP 257, Antananarivo; tel. (20) 22-258-72; f. 1976; promotion, development, preservation and conservation of national collections; Pres CHRISTIANE ANDRIAMIRADO; Secs SAMOELA ANDRIANKOTONIRINA, FRANÇOISE RAMANANDRAISOA; publ. *Haren-tsaina* (2 a year).

LANGUAGE AND LITERATURE

Alliance Française: Ambavamamba 101, BP 916 Antananarivo; tel. (20) 22-232-63; fax (20) 22-225-04; e-mail webmaster@alliancefr.mg; internet www.alliancefr.mg; offers courses and exams in French language and culture and promotes cultural exchange with France; attached teaching centres in Ambanja, Ambatondrazaka Ambilobe, Ambositra, Ambovombe, Andapa, Antalaha, Antananarivo, Antsahabe, Antsalova, Antsirabé, Antsiranana, Antsohihy, Fandriana, Farafangana, Fianarantsoa, Fort Dauphin, Mahajanga, Maintirano, Manakara, Mananjary, Moramanga, Morombe, Morondava, Nosy Be, Sainte Marie, Sambava, Toamasina, Tolagnaro, Toliara, Tsiroanomandidy, and Vohemar; Dir of Operations, Madagascar HERVÉ LE PORZ.

British Council: see chapter on Mauritius.

Research Institutes

GENERAL

Institut de Recherche pour le Développement (IRD): BP 434, Antananarivo 101; tel. (20) 22-330-98; fax (20) 22-369-82; e-mail irdmada@ird.mg; internet www.ird.mg; research into economics, statistics, fisheries, environment, health, deforestation, biodiversity and water; library of 200 vols; Dir CHRISTIAN FELLER; (see main entry under France).

AGRICULTURE, FISHERIES AND VETERINARY SCIENCE

Centre National de Recherche Appliquée au Développement Rural (CENRADERU): BP 1690, Antananarivo; f. 1994; research into agriculture, forestry and fisheries, zoology, veterinary studies and rural economy; publ. *Rapport d'activité* (1 a year).

Attached Institute:

CENRADERU—IRCT: BP 227, Mahajanga; research on cotton and other fibres; main research station at Toliary; regional station at Tanandava; sisal research at Mandrare.

Centre Technique Forestier Tropical: BP 745, Antananarivo; f. 1961; silviculture, genetics, soil conservation; Dir J. P. BOUILLET; (see main entry under France).

Département de Recherches Agronomiques de la République Malgache: Centre National de la Recherche Appliquée au Développement Rural (FOFIFA), BP 1444 Ambatobe, Antananarivo 101; tel. (20) 225-2707; e-mail rag@fofifa.mg; internet www.fofifa.mg; stations at Alaotra, Antalaha, Ambanja, Ambovombe, Ivoloina, Mahajanga, Fianarantsoa, Ilaka Est, Kianjavato, Kianjasoa, Tanandava; Dept Chief LÉA RANDRIAMBOLANORO.

Institut de Recherches Agronomiques Tropicales (IRAT): 4 rue Rapiera, Anjohy, BP 853, Antananarivo; tel. (20) 22-271-82; attached to Centre de Co-operation Internationale en Recherche Agronomique pour le Développement (CIRAD).

Institut d'Elevage et de Médecine Vétérinaire des Pays Tropicaux: Antananarivo; central laboratory, research stations at Kianjasoa and Miadana; (see main entry under France).

FINE AND PERFORMING ARTS

Institut Malgache des Arts Dramatiques et Folkloriques (IMADEFOLK): Centre Culturel Albert Camus, Ave de l'Indépendance, Antananarivo; f. 1964; traditional songs and dances; Dir O. RAKOTO.

HISTORY, GEOGRAPHY AND ARCHAEOLOGY

Institut Géographique et Hydrographique National: Rue Dama-Ntsoha, Ambanidia, BP 323, Antananarivo 101; tel. (20) 22-229-35; fax (20) 22-252-64; e-mail ftm@moov.mg; internet www.ftm.mg; f. 1945; Dir ANDRIANJAFIMBELO RAZAFINAKANGA.

NATURAL SCIENCES

Biological Sciences

Institut Pasteur: BP 1274, Antananarivo 101; tel. (20) 22-412-72; fax (20) 22-415-34; e-mail ipm@pasteur.mg; internet www.pasteur.mg; f. 1898; biological research; library of 6,200 vols; Dir Dr MAUCLÈRE; publ. *Archives* (2 a year).

Physical Sciences

Institute and Observatory of Geophysics at Antananarivo: University of Antananarivo (Rectorate), Antananarivo 101; tel. and fax (20) 22-253-53; f. 1889, affiliated to the University 1967; study of seismology, geomagnetism, applied geophysics, exploration geophysics, time service, meteorological and astronomical observation; library of 3,000 vols, 800 periodicals; Dir J. B. RATSIMBAZAFY; publs *Bulletin Magnetique* (monthly and annually), *Bulletin Méteorologique* (12 a year), *Bulletin Sismique* (1 a year), *Mada–Geo* (4 a year).

Service Géologique: BP 322, Antananarivo 101; tel. (20) 22-400-48; fax (20) 22-418-73; internet www.cite.mg/mine; f. 1926; library of 3,000 vols; Dir A. RANANDARIVELO; publs *Annales géologiques*, *Atlas des fossiles caractéristiques de Madagascar*, *Documentation du Service Géologique*, *Travaux du Bureau Géologique*.

TECHNOLOGY

Bureau de Recherches Géologiques et Minières (BRGM): BP 458, Antananarivo; Dir G. BOURNAT; (see main entry under France).

Libraries and Archives

Antananarivo

Archives Nationales: BP 3384, Antananarivo; tel. and fax (20) 22-235-34; e-mail rijandriamihamina@malagasy.com; f. 1958; historical library of 30,000 vols; Dir SAHONDRA ANDRIAMIHAMINA.

Bibliothèque Municipale: Ave du 18 juin, Antananarivo; f. 1961; 22,600 vols.

Bibliothèque Nationale: Anosy, BP 257, Antananarivo; tel. (20) 22-258-72; fax (20) 22-294-48; f. 1961; 236,800 books, 2,660 periodicals, 2,912 MSS, 2,600 maps; special collections: history, literature, the arts, applied sciences, information on Madagascar; Dir L. RALAISAHOLIMANANA; publ. *Bibliographie Nationale de Madagascar* (1 a year).

Bibliothèque Universitaire d'Antananarivo: Campus Universitaire Ambohitsaina, BP 908, Antananarivo 101; tel. (20) 22-612-28; fax (20) 22-612-29; e-mail bu@univ-antananarivo.mg; internet www.bu.univ-antananarivo.mg; f. 1960; spec. MSS colln: Madagascar and Indian Ocean; 308,450 vols; Dir JEAN-MARIE ANDRIANIAINA;

publ. *Bibliographie Annuelle de Madagascar* (madarevues.recherches.gov.mg).

Médiathèque du Centre Culturel 'Albert Camus': 14 ave de l'Indépendance, BP 488, Antananarivo 101; tel. (20) 22-236-47; fax (20) 22-213-38; e-mail mediatheque@ccac.mg; internet www.ccac.mg; f. 1964; 37,086 vols, 26 periodicals, 389 CD-ROMs, 2,634 CDs, 3,991 video cassettes and DVDs; 4,946 mems; Dir ALAIN MONTEIL; Librarian CHRISTIANE LAROCCA.

Antsirabé

Bibliothèque Municipale: Antsirabé; tel. 44-484-57; f. 1952; 2,700 vols; Librarian ALBERT DENIS RAKOTO.

Museums and Art Galleries

Antananarivo

Musée d'Art et d'Archéologie Université d'Antananarivo: Isoraka, 17 rue Dr Villette, BP 564, Antananarivo 101; tel. 2422165; e-mail vohitra@refer.mg; f. 1970; attached to Institut de Civilisations; art, archaeology and social sciences; library of 1,800 vols; Dir Dr RADIMILAHY CHANTAL; publs *Taloha* (1 a year), *Travaux et Documents* (irregular).

Musée Historique et Ethnographique: Palais Andafiavaratra, Rue Pasteur Ravelojaona, Antananarivo; tel. (20) 22-200-91; f. 1897; history and arts; Curator JEAN CLAUDE ANDRIANIMANANA.

Universities

UNIVERSITÉ D'ANTANANARIVO

Campus Universitaire Ambohitsaina, BP 566, 101 Antananarivo

Telephone: (20) 22-326-39
Fax: (20) 22-279-26
Internet: www.univ-antananarivo.mg
Founded 1961
Rector: Dr PASCAL RAKOTOBE
Library: see Libraries and Archives
Number of teachers: 635
Number of students: 14,069

HEADS OF FACULTIES AND HIGHER SCHOOLS

Agriculture: DANIEL RAZAKANINDRIANA
Law, Economics, Business Studies, Sociology: RADO RAKOTOARISON
Literature and Humanities: JEAN-MARIUS SOLO RAHARINJANAHARY
Medicine: Prof. PAUL RAJAONARIVELO
Sciences: BRUNO ANDRIANANTENAINA
Ecole Normale Supérieure: YVES RENÉ RASOANAIVO
Ecole Supérieure Polytechnic: BENJAMIN RANDRIANOELINA
Ecole Supérieure des Sciences Agronomiques: Prof. ARMAND R. PANJA RAMANOELINA

UNIVERSITÉ DE FIANARANTSOA

BP 1264, 301 Fianarantsoa

Telephone: (20) 75-508-02
Fax: (20) 75-506-19
E-mail: ufianara@syfed.refer.mg
Internet: www.misa.mg/univ
Founded 1988
State control
Language of instruction: French
Academic year: November to July
Rector: MARIE DIEUDONNÉ MICHEL RAZAFINDRANDRIATSIMANIRY

Administrative and Financial Dir: DOMINIQUE RAZAFIMANAMPY
Dir of Studies and Research: RIVO RAKOTOZAFY
Librarian: BRUNO JEAN ROMUALD RANDRIAMORA
Number of teachers: 63
Number of students: 1,836

DEANS

Faculty of Law: PATRICE GOUSSOT
Faculty of Sciences: TSILAVO MANDRESY RAZAFINDRAZAKA
Ecole Nationale d'Informatique: JOSVAH PAUL RAZFIMANDIMBY
Ecole Normale Supérieure: ROGER RATOVONJANAHARY
Institut des Sciences et Techniques de l'Environnement: PASCAL RATALATA

UNIVERSITÉ DE MAHAJANGA

BP 652, 401 Mahajanga

Telephone: (20) 62-908-34
Fax: (20) 62-233-12
Founded 1977
State control
Language of instruction: French
Academic year: March to October
Rector: Prof. ANTOINE ZAFERA RABESA
Registrar: DIANA VOAHANGINIRINA RAHARINIAINA
Librarian: JUSTINE RAZANAMANITRA
Library of 8,054 vols
Number of teachers: 83 full-time
Number of students: 2,129
Publication: *JSPM* (2 a year)

DEANS

Faculty of Dentistry and Stomatology: HENRI MARTIAL RANDRIANARIMANARIVO
Faculty of Medicine: LISY RAVOLAMANANA
Faculty of Natural Sciences: JOHNSON CHRISTIAN MILADERA

UNIVERSITÉ NORD MADAGASCAR

BP 0, 201 Antsiranana

Telephone: (20) 82-29-409
Fax: (20) 82-29-409
E-mail: unm@dts.mg
Founded 1976
State control
Academic year: January to September
President: CÉCILE MARIE ANGE MANOROHANTA-DOMINIQUE
Administrative Director: ALY AHMAD
Librarian: VIRGINIE MILISON
Number of teachers: 97 (64 permanent, 33 temporary)
Number of students: 826

DEANS

Faculty of Arts and Humanities: (vacant)
Faculty of Science: JEAN VICTOR RANDRIANOHAVY

DIRECTORS

Ecole Normale Supérieure pour l'Enseignement Technique: ANDRÉ TOTOHASIN
Ecole Supérieur Polytechnique: MAX ANDRIANANTENAINA

UNIVERSITÉ DE TOAMASINA

BP 591, Toamasina

Telephone: (20) 53-322-44
Fax: (20) 53-335-66
Internet: www.univ-toamasina.mg
Founded 1977 as Centre Universitaire Régional de Toamasina, present status 1988
State control

Language of instruction: French
Rector: ROGER RAJAONARIVELO
Secretary-General: ANDRÉ BIAS RAMILAMA-
NANA
Librarian: ELIANE JOSÉPHINE RENÉ
Number of teachers: 54
Number of students: 3,391

DEANS

School of Arts and Research: ABRAHAM LAT-
SAKA
School of Economics and Management: SETH
ARSÈNE RATOVOSON

UNIVERSITÉ DE TOLIARA

BP 185, Maninday, Toliara 601
Telephone: (20) 94-410-33
Fax: (20) 94-443-07
E-mail: presidence@univ-toliara.mg
Internet: www.univ-toliara.mg
Founded 1977 as Regional Centre of Uni-
versité de Madagascar; independent uni-
versity status 1988

State Control
Languages of instruction: French, Malagasy
Academic year: November to July
Rector: M. THEODORET
Library of 8,000 vols

DEANS

Faculty of Arts and Humanities: MARC
JOSEPH RAZAFINDRAKOTO
Faculty of Science: HERY ANTENAINA RAZAFI-
MANDIBY
Ecole Normale Supérieure: JEAN RAKOTOAR-
IVELO

Colleges

Collège Rural d'Ambatobe: BP 1629,
Antananarivo; Dir M. ROGER RAJOELISOLO.

**Institut National des Sciences Comp-
tables et de l'Administration d'Entreprises:** Maison des Produits, 67 Ha, BP 946,
Antananarivo 101; tel. (20) 22-660-65; fax

(20) 22-308-95; e-mail drinscae@simicro.mg;
f. 1986; 4-year courses and in-service training in accountancy, management and banking; library: 17,230 vols, 24 periodicals; 24
teachers; 1,051 students (325 full-time, 726
in-service); Dir-Gen. VICTOR HARISON.

**Institut National des Sciences et Tech-
niques Nucléaires:** BP 4279, Antananarivo
01; tel. (20) 22-611-81; fax (20) 22-355-83;
e-mail instn@dts.mg; internet www.geocities
.com/mada_instn; f. 1976 as laboratory; institute status 1992; depts of Dosimetry and
Radiation Protection, X-Ray Fluorescence
Techniques and Environment, Nuclear Techniques and Analysis, Theoretical Physics,
Instrumentation and Maintenance, Computer Science and Renewable Energies; Dir
RAOELINA ANDRIAMBOLOLONA; publ. *Journal
des Sciences et Techniques Nucléaires.*

**Institut National des
Télécommunications et des Postes:** Anta-
netibe, 101 Antananarivo; f. 1968; 200 students.

MALAWI

The Higher Education System

The former British protectorate of Nyasaland gained independence, as Malawi, in 1964 and became a republic in 1966. Higher education consists of two state universities, the University of Malawi (founded 1964) and the Mzuzu University (founded 1999).

The University of Malawi has a federal structure, consisting of five colleges, each headed by a Principal, assisted by a Vice-Principal, Registrar and Deans of Faculty. The Head of State is the Chancellor of the University, and the Vice-Chancellor is the senior governing officer, overseeing the day-to-day running of the institution. The Chancellor is guided by the University Council, the University policy-making body. Although there are no concrete plans at present, in due course the University may devolve with the five constituent colleges becoming universities in their own right. There were 6,458 students in further and higher education in 2006/07. Some students attend institutions in the United Kingdom and the USA. The Ministry of Education and Vocational Training is responsible for providing higher education.

Admission to university is mainly on the basis of the Malawi School Certificate of Education, but O-Levels and the Cambridge Overseas Higher School Certificate are also accepted. The colleges of the University of Malawi offer three-year Diploma courses, and the main undergraduate degree is the Bachelors, which lasts either four years for the Bachelors (General) or five to six years for the Bachelors (Honours). On completion of the Bachelors postgraduates can study for one to two years for the Masters. The final university-level degree is the PhD, lasting three to five years.

The National Apprenticeships Scheme is the principal form of post-secondary technical and vocational education. Programmes last for four years and are offered in a number of professional fields. The main qualifications are the Craft Certificate and Trade Test Certificate.

Regulatory Body

GOVERNMENT

Ministry of Education and Vocational Training: Private Bag 328, Capital City, Lilongwe 3; tel. (1) 789422; fax (1) 788064; e-mail secretaryforeducation@sdnp.org.mw; internet www.malawi.gov.mw; Minister ANNA KACHIKHO.

Learned Societies

GENERAL

Society of Malawi: POB 125, Blantyre; tel. (1) 872617; e-mail info@societyofmalawi.org; internet www.societyofmalawi.org; f. 1946; study and records of history and natural sciences; 250 mems; library of 3,000 vols, 2,000 periodicals, 5,000 photographs; Chair. CARL BRUESSOW; Hon. Sec. MIKE BAMFORD; publ. *Journal* (2 a year).

BIBLIOGRAPHY, LIBRARY SCIENCE AND MUSEOLOGY

Malawi Library Association: POB 429, Zomba; tel. (1) 524265; fax (1) 525225; e-mail fkachala@sobomw.com; f. 1976; 340 mems; trains library assistants, provides professional advice, holds seminars and workshops; Pres. GEOFFREY F. SALANJE; Sec.-Gen. FRANCIS F. C. KACHALA; publs *MALA Bulletin* (1 a year), *MALA Trends* (every 2 years), *MALA Update*.

LANGUAGE AND LITERATURE

British Council: Plot no. 13/20 City Centre, POB 30222, Lilongwe 3; tel. (1) 773244; fax (1) 772945; e-mail info@britishcouncil.org.mw; internet www.britishcouncil.org/malawi; offers courses and exams in English language and British culture and promotes cultural exchange with the UK; library of 5,991 vols; Dir MARC JESSEL.

MEDICINE

Medical Association of Malawi: Private Bag 360, Chichiri, Blantyre 3; tel. (1) 630333; fax (1) 631353; f. 1967; 265 mems; 100 assoc. mems; Chair. Dr B. MWALE; Sec. Dr E. MTITIMILA; publ. *Malawi Medical Journal*.

Research Institutes

AGRICULTURE, FISHERIES AND VETERINARY SCIENCE

Agricultural Research and Extension Trust: PMB 9, Lilongwe; tel. (1) 761148; fax (1) 761615; e-mail iphiri@aret.org.mw; f. 1995; attached to Tobacco Asscn of Malawi; applied research on improvement of burley, flue-cured and fire-cured tobacco in Malawi; Dir Dr IBRAHIM PHIRI; publs *Coresta Bulletin* (4 a year), *Tobacco Science*.

Baka Agricultural Research Station: POB 97, Karonga; f. 1974; attached to Min. of Agriculture; applied research on the general agronomy of the Karonga and Chitipa regions.

Bvumbwe Agricultural Research Station: POB 5748, Limbe; tel. (1) 662206; f. 1940; attached to Min. of Agriculture; conducts applied research into tree and horticultural crops, especially tung, macadamia, cashew, vegetables, spices, coffee, mushrooms, roots and tubers, and the general agronomy of the Southern uplands; Head N. NSANJAMA.

Central Veterinary Laboratory: POB 527, Lilongwe; tel. (1) 766341; fax (1) 766010; e-mail dahi.cvl@malawi.net; f. 1974; attached to Min. of Agriculture; research into endemic diseases.

Chitala Agricultural Research Station: Private Bag 13, Salima; e-mail agric-research@sdnp.org.mw; f. 1978; attached to Min. of Agriculture; part of Lakeshore Rural Development Programme; conducts research on cereals, cotton, groundnuts, mango, roots and tubers, livestock; Station Man. L. R. NTUANA.

Chitedze Agricultural Research Station: POB 158, Lilongwe; tel. (1) 773252; fax (1) 773184; e-mail icrisat-malawi@cgiar.com; f. 1948; attached to Min. of Agriculture; conducts applied research into cereals, grain legumes, oil seeds, pasture and the general agronomy of the Central Region and into livestock improvement, especially of local Zebu cattle; library of 10,000 vols, 300 periodicals; Head Dr P. SIBALE.

Fisheries Research Station: POB 27, Monkey Bay; tel. (1) 587360; fax (1) 587249; f. 1954; attached to Min. of Agriculture and Food Security; research into fisheries of Lake Malawi; social economic surveys; Chief Fisheries Research Officer Dr M. C. BANDRA; publs *Fisheries Bulletin* (12 a year), *Survey Reports* (4 a year), *Technical Reports* (12 a year).

Forest Research Institute of Malawi: POB 270, Zomba; attached to Min. of Forestry and Natural Resources; research into silviculture, tree breeding, pathology, entomology, soils, mycorrhizae and wood products.

Kasinthula Agricultural Research Station: POB 28, Chikwawa; tel. (1) 423207; e-mail agric-research@sdnp.org.mw; f. 1976; attached to Min. of Agriculture; irrigation research; Officer in Charge JULIAN W. MCHOWA.

Lifuwu Agricultural Research Station: POB 102, Salima; tel. (0) 9145004; fax (0) 1707374; e-mail lifuwu@malawi.net; 50 mems; f. 1973; attached to Dept of Agricultural Research Services; rice research; Asst Dir. T. R. MZENGEZA.

Lunyangwa Agricultural Research Station: POB 59, Mzuzu; tel. (1) 332633; f. 1968; attached to Min. of Agriculture; conducts applied research into the general agronomy of the Northern Region, specializing in rice, coffee, tea, cassava, pasture work, and tropical fruits at its Mkondezi sub station; Head Dr A. LOWOLE.

Makoka Agricultural Research Station: Private Bag 3, Thondwe; tel. (881) 198635; e-mail entomology@broadbandmw.com; f. 1967; researches in cotton, cassava, sweet potato, maize, groundnuts, soya beans, pigeon peas, cowpeas, sunflowers, sorghum and rice; agroforestry species and domestication of wild fruits; library of 1,600 vols; Head KETULO SALIPIRA; Deputy Head ROSE MKANDAWIRE; publs *Makoka Agricultural Research Station*, *Malawi Journal of Agricultural Sciences*, *Report*.

Mbawa Agricultural Research Station: POB 8, Embangweni; tel. (1) 342362; fax (1) 332687; e-mail agric-research@sdnp.org.mw; internet www.agricresearch.gov.mw; f. 1936; attached to Dept of Agricultural Research Services, Min. of Agriculture; applied research into livestock, cereals, grain legumes and technology transfer initiatives; publs *Quarterly Report, Station Guide* (1 a year).

Mikolongwe Livestock Improvement Centre: POB 5193, Limbe; f. 1955; attached to Min. of Agriculture; seeks to improve productive capacity of local Zebu cattle and fat-tailed sheep; the station also contains the Poultry Improvement Unit and the Veterinary Staff training school.

Mwimba Tobacco Research Station: POB 224, Kasungu; f. 1979; attached to Min. of Agriculture; applied research on improvement and production of flue-cured and oriental tobacco in Malawi.

Tea Research Foundation (Central Africa): POB 51, Mulanje; tel. (1) 467277; fax (1) 467209; e-mail trfca@africa-online.net; f. 1966; conducts research on the genetic improvement of tea and associated agronomic research and training for the tea industry in southern Africa; Dir Dr A. S. KUMWENDA.

NATURAL SCIENCES

Physical Sciences

Geological Survey of Malawi: POB 27, Zomba; tel. (1) 524166; fax (1) 524716; e-mail geomalawi@chirunga.sdnp.org.mw; f. 1921; attached to Ministry of Mines, Natural Resources and Environmental Affairs; geological mapping and surveys; mineral investigation, engineering, geology, geophysics, drilling, seismology; library of 5,000 vols; Dir C. E. KAPHWIYO; publ. *Bulletin*.

Libraries and Archives

Lilongwe

Malawi National Library Service: POB 30314, Lilongwe 3; tel. (1) 773700; fax (1) 771616; e-mail gnyali@nlsmw.org; f. 1968; provides public library services; publishes children's books; 1,000,000 vols; Nat. Librarian G. L. NYALI; publ. *Accessions Bulletin*.

Zomba

National Archives of Malawi: Mkulichi Rd, POB 62, Zomba; tel. and fax (1) 525240; e-mail archives@sdnp.org.mw; internet chambo.sdnp.org.mw/ruleoflaw/archives; f. 1947, as branch of Central African Archives, became National Archives of Malawi 1964; public archives, records management, historical manuscripts, legal deposit library, films, tapes, microfilms, gramophone records, philatelic collection, maps, and plans; national ISBN agency; 30,000 vols, 240 periodicals; Dir PAUL LIHOMA; Librarian STANLEY S. GONDWE; publ. *Malawi National Bibliography* (1 a year).

University of Malawi Libraries: POB 280, Zomba; tel. (1) 524222; fax (1) 525225; e-mail smwiyeriwa@chirunga.sdnp.org.mw; f. 1965; 391,000 vols; Librarian S. MWIYERIWA; publs *Library Bulletin, Nthambi Zisanu, Report to Senate* (1 a year).

Museums

Blantyre

Museums of Malawi: POB 30360, Chichiri, Blantyre 3; tel. (1) 672438; fax (1) 676615; e-mail museums@malawi.net; f. 1959; Dir of Museums Dr M. E. D. NHLANE; publ. *Ndiwula* (newsletter, 1 a year).

Universities

UNIVERSITY OF MALAWI

POB 278, Zomba
Telephone: (1) 524282
Fax: (1) 524031
E-mail: uniregistrar@usdnp.org.mw
Internet: www.unima.mw

Founded 1964
Language of instruction: English
State control
Academic year: January to September

Number of teachers: 710
Number of students: 5,400

Chancellor: THE PRESIDENT OF MALAWI
Vice-Chancellor: Prof. J. D. RUBADIRI
Registrar: BEN WOKOMAATANI MALUNGA
Librarian: F. G. HOUSE (acting)

Publications: *Journal of Humanities, Journal of Social Science, Malawi Journal of Science and Technology, Research Report to Senate*.

CONSTITUENT INSTITUTES

Bunda College of Agriculture: POB 219, Lilongwe; tel. (1) 277226; fax (1) 277364; library of 50,000 vols; 131 teachers; 681 students; Principal Dr G. Y. KANYAMA-PHIRI; Registrar F. T. ZALIRA MSONTHI

DEANS

Faculty of Agriculture: Dr D. M. CHILIMA
Faculty of Development Studies: Dr C. M. MASANGANO
Faculty of Environmental Science: Prof. M. B. KWAPATA
Postgraduate Studies: Dr R. K. D. PHOYA

PROFESSORS

EL-SHAZLY ABU-AGWA, F., Crop Science
KAMWANJA, L. A., Animal Science
KWAPATA, M. B., Forestry and Horticulture
MTIMUNI, J. P., Animal Science
PHOYA, R. K. D., Animal Science
SAKA, V. W., Crop Science

Chancellor College: POB 280, Zomba; tel. (1) 524222; fax (1) 524046; library of 300,000 vols; 250 teachers; 1,812 students; Principal Dr F. B. MOTO; Registrar J. A. KADZANJA

DEANS

Faculty of Education: Dr D. MALUWA-BANDA
Faculty of Humanities: Dr E. KAYAMBAZINTHU
Faculty of Law: N. MHURA
Faculty of Science: Dr E. SAMBO
Faculty of Social Science: Dr L. MALEKANO
Postgraduate Studies: Prof. K. PHIRI

PROFESSORS

CHIRWA, W. C., History
DUDLEY, C. O., Biology
JOSHUA, S. J., Physics
KADZAMIRA, Z. D., Political and Administrative Studies
KALUWA, B. M., Economics
KISHINDO, P. A. K., Sociology
PHIRI, K. M., History
SAKA, J. D. K., Chemistry

ULEDI-KAMANGA, B. J., English

College of Medicine: PB 360, Chichiri, Blantyre 3; tel. (1) 671911; fax (1) 674700; e-mail registrar@admin.medicol.mw; library of 18,000 vols; 87 teachers; 169 students; Principal Prof. ROBIN BROADHEAD; Registrar C. TRIGU-LEMANI

DEANS

Faculty of Medicine: Prof. J. E. CHISI
Postgraduate Studies: Prof. E. BERGSTEIN

PROFESSORS

ADELOYE, A., Surgery
BROADHEAD, R. L., Paediatrics
KOMOLAFE, O. O., Microbiology
LIOMBA, G. N., Pathology
MADUAGWU, E. N., Biochemistry
MOLYNEUX, M. E., Paediatrics
MSAMATI, B. C., Anatomy
MUKIIBI, J. M., Haematology
ZIJLSTRA, E. E., Medicine

Kamuzu College of Nursing: PB 1, Lilongwe; tel. (1) 751622; fax (1) 756424; library of 24,000 ; 66 teachers; 300 students; Principal D. NKOMBA-JERE; Registrar N. D. MABVUMBE

DEANS

Faculty of Nursing: E. B. CHILEMBA
Postgraduate Studies: C. KAPONDA

Malawi Polytechnic: PB 303, Chichiri, Blantyre 3; tel. (1) 670411; fax (1) 670578; library of 38,745 vols; 176 teachers; 2,549 students; Principal Y. A. ALIDE (acting); Registrar A. KUMWENDA

DEANS

Faculty of Applied Sciences: A. MADHLOPA
Faculty of Commerce: B. T. NJOBVU
Faculty of Education and Media Studies: G. MANGANDA
Faculty of Engineering: N. T. BEN
Postgraduate Studies: F. GOMILE CLU-DYAONGA

MZUZU UNIVERSITY

Private Bag 201, Luwinga, Mzuzu 2 2
Telephone: (1) 320575
Fax: (1) 320568
E-mail: registrar@mzuni.ac.mw

Founded 1999
State control

Chancellor: THE PRESIDENT OF MALAWI
Vice-Chancellor: Prof. LANDSON MHANGO
Deputy Vice-Chancellor: Prof. ORTON MSISKA
Registrar: REGINALD MUSHANI
Librarian: Prof. JOSEPH UTA

Library of 27,000 vols, 250 periodicals
Number of teachers: 132
Number of students: 1,350

DEANS

Faculty of Education: GOLDEN. MSILIMBA
Faculty of Environmental Sciences: JARRET MHANGO
Faculty of Information Science and Communication: Prof. JOSEPH J. UTA
Faculty of Health Sciences: Prof. YOHANE NYASULU
Faculty of Tourism and Hospitality Management: BRIGHT M.C. NYIRENDA

MALAYSIA

The Higher Education System

The country's oldest existing institution of higher education is Universiti Teknologi Malaysia (Malayasia University of Technology), Johor, which was founded in 1904 (current name and status 1972) when Johor was still an independent Malay state (it came under British control in 1914). The next oldest institution is Universiti Pendidikan Sultan Idris (Sultan Idris Education University—founded 1922). Malaya was granted independence, within the Commonwealth, in 1957 and Malaysia was established in 1963, through the union of the independent Federation of Malaya (renamed the States of Malaya), Singapore, and the former British colonies of Sarawak and Sabah. Subsequently, Singapore left the federation and the States of Malaya were styled Peninsular Malaysia. In October 1994 the Government introduced a bill that would allow foreign universities to establish branch campuses in Malaysia. From the end of that year the Government permitted the use of English as a medium of instruction in science and engineering subjects at tertiary level. In 1998 the Government's incorporation of higher education gave greater powers of autonomy to the universities, which are governed by an executive body (Board of Governors) and academic council (Senate). At the seventh ASEAN summit meeting in November 2001 it was decided that the town of Bandar Nusajaya in Johor would be the location for the first ASEAN university. It would be Malaysia's second international university. In 2004/05 there were 696,760 students enrolled in tertiary education. In 2008 there were 20 government-funded universities and 33 private universities.

The main criteria for admission to higher education are the Malaysia Higher Certificate of Education and Matriculation Certificate. Applications are made through the central Unit Pusat Universiti (Central University Unit). The undergraduate Bachelors degree course lasts three to four years, though some disciplines require longer periods of study, such as medicine and dentistry (which require five years). Following the Bachelors, the Masters is the first postgraduate degree, requiring one to two years' further study; finally, after award of the Masters, study for a PhD lasts a minimum of two years.

Post-secondary vocational and technical education is available at specialist schools.

The Malaysian Qualification Agency (MQA) was established under the Malaysian Qualifications Agency Act 2007 and was a merger of the previous National Accreditation Board (LAN) and the Quality Assurance Division of the Ministry of Higher Education. The merger was approved in December 2005 and the MQA was launched in November 2007. Before the merger, LAN (founded in 1998) acted as a statutory body under the Ministry of Education of Malaysia to ensure the standard and quality of certificates, diplomas and degree courses run by the private higher education institutions. There are two processes involved in the current MQA accreditation system: Provisional Accreditation—this initial process will help higher education providers to achieve accreditation by enhancing the standards and quality set in the provisional accreditation evaluation; and Accreditation—this is a formal recognition that the certificates, diplomas and degrees awarded by higher education institutions are in accordance with the standards set.

Regulatory and Representative Bodies

GOVERNMENT

Ministry of Education: Kompleks Kerajaan Persekutuan, Parcel E, Pusat Pentadbiran Kerajaan Persekutuan, 62604 Putrajaya; tel. (3) 88846000; fax (3) 88895235; e-mail webmaster@moe.gov.my; internet www.moe.gov.my; Minister Datuk HISHAMMUDDIN TUN HUSSEIN.

Ministry of Higher Education: Blok E3, Parcel E, Pusat Perbadanan Kerajaan Persekutuan, 62505 Putrajaya; tel. (3) 88835000; fax (3) 88893921; e-mail menteri@mohe.gov.my; internet www.mohe.gov.my; Minister Dato' Seri MOHAMED KHALED BIN NORDIN.

Ministry of Unity, Arts, Culture and Heritage: 16th Floor, TH Perdana Tower, Maju Junction, 1001 Jalan Sultan Ismail, 50694 Kuala Lumpur; tel. (3) 26127600; fax (3) 26935114; e-mail info@heritage.gov.my; internet www.heritage.gov.my; Minister Datuk MOHD SHAFIE BIN HAJI APDAL.

ACCREDITATION

Lembaga Akreditasi Negara (National Accreditation Board): Level 14B, Menara PKNS-PJ 17, Jalan Yong Shook Lin, 46050 Petaling Jaya, Selangor Darul Ehsan; tel. (3) 79687002; fax (3) 79569496; e-mail akreditasi@mqa.gov.my; internet www.lan.gov.my; f. 2007; attached to Min. of Higher Education; responsible for quality assurance of higher education in both the public and the private sectors; accredits courses fulfilling the set criteria and standards, maintains the Malaysian Qualifications Register; council of 18 mems; Chair. Datuk Dr MUHAMMAD RAIS ABDUL KARIM; CEO Dato' Dr SYED AHMAD HUSSEIN.

NATIONAL BODY

Malaysian Association of Private Colleges and Universities: c/o International Medical University, 126 Jalan 19/155B, Bukit Jalil, 57000 Kuala Lumpur; tel. (3) 86569980; fax (3) 86569981; e-mail info@mapcu.com.my; internet www.mapcu.com.my; f. 1997; promotes and coordinates the devt of private higher education in Malaysia; 70 mems (45 ordinary mems, 15 assoc. mems and 10 br. mems); Pres. Dr PARMJIT SINGH; Sec.-Gen. Y.Bhg. Dato' PETER NG.

Learned Societies

ARCHITECTURE AND TOWN PLANNING

Malaysian Institute of Architects: 4–6 Jalan Tangsi, POB 10855, 50726 Kuala Lumpur; tel. (3) 2693-4182; fax (3) 2692-8782; e-mail info@pam.org.my; f. 1967; 3,005 mems; library of 1,000 vols; Pres. Ar Dr TAN LOKE MUN; publs *Berita Akitek* (12 a year), *Majalah Akitek* (Architecture Malaysia, 6 a year), *PAM Directory* (1 a year), *Panduan Akitek* (1 a year).

BIBLIOGRAPHY, LIBRARY SCIENCE AND MUSEOLOGY

Librarians' Association of Malaysia: POB 12545, 50782 Kuala Lumpur; Perpustakaan Negara Malaysia, 232, Jalan Tun Razak 50572 Kuala Lumpur; tel. (3) 26947390; fax (3) 26947390; e-mail pustakawan55@gmail.com; internet www.ppm55.org.my; f. 1955; 600 mems; Pres. ZAWIYAH BABA; Sec. NAFISAH AHMAD; publ. *Jurnal PPM* (1 a year).

HISTORY, GEOGRAPHY AND ARCHAEOLOGY

Malaysian Historical Society: 958 Jl. Hose, 50460 Kuala Lumpur; tel. (3) 2481469; fax (3) 2487281; f. 1953; activities include restoration and preservation of historical sites; 200 indiv. and institutional mems; Pres. Dato MUSA HITAM; publs *Malaysia in History*, *Malaysia Dari Segi Sejarah* (1 a year).

LANGUAGE AND LITERATURE

Alliance Française de Kuala Lumpur: 15 Lorong Gurney, 54100 Kuala Lumpur; tel. (3) 26947880; fax (3) 26930502; e-mail info@alliancefrancaise.org.my; internet www.alliancefrancaise.org.my; f. 1961; offers courses and exams in French language and culture and promotes cultural exchange with France; 3 centres in Kuala Lumpur and Alliance Française de Penang in Georgestown; 2,300 mems; library of 5,500 vols; Dir BRUNO PLASSE.

British Council: POB 10539, 50916 Kuala Lumpur; Ground Fl., West Block, Wisma Selangor Dredging, 142C Jalan Ampang, 50450 Kuala Lumpur; tel. (3) 27237900; fax (3) 27136599; internet www.britishcouncil.org.my; teaching centre; offers courses and exams in English language and British culture and promotes cultural exchange with the UK; attached offices in Kota Kinabalu,

Kuching, Penang (teaching centre) and Subang Jaya (teaching centre); library of 14,000 vols, 100 periodicals; Dir GERRY LISTON; Dir, English Language STEVE BATES.

Dewan Bahasa dan Pustaka (National Language and Literary Agency): POB 10803, 50926 Kuala Lumpur; tel. (3) 21481011; fax (3) 21489245; internet www .dbp.gov.my; f. 1956; develops and enriches the Malay language; develops literary talent; standardizes spelling and pronunciation and devises technical terms, etc. in Malay; prints or assists in the production of publs in Malay and the translation of books into Malay; 1,171 mems; library: see Libraries and Archives; Dir-Gen. Dato' Hj. TERMUZI HJ. ABDUL AZIZ; publs *Dewan Bahasa* (12 a year), *Dewan Budaya* (12 a year), *Dewan Sastera* (12 a year), *Pelita Bahasa* (12 a year).

Goethe-Institut: 1, Jalan Langgak Golf, 55000 Kuala Lumpur; tel. (3) 21422011; fax (3) 21422282; internet www.goethe.de/so/kua/deindex.htm; offers courses and exams in German language and culture and promotes cultural exchange with Germany; Dir Dr VOLKER WOLF.

Tamil Language Society: c/o Department of Indian Studies, University of Malaya, Kuala Lumpur; f. 1957; 350 mems; aims at the promotion and propagation of the Tamil language and Indian culture; Pres. M. JAYAKUMAR; Hon. Sec. L. KRISHNAN; publ. *Tamil Oli* (in Tamil, English and Malay, 1 a year).

MEDICINE

Academy of Family Physicians of Malaysia: Room 6, 5th Floor, MMA House, 124 Jalan Pahang, 53000 Kuala Lumpur; tel. (3) 40417735; fax (3) 40425206; e-mail afpm@po .jaring.my; f. 1973; 800 mems; Pres. Dr M. K. RAJAKUMAR; Chair. (vacant); publ. *The Family Physician* (3 a year).

Malaysian Medical Association: 4th Floor, MMA House, 124 Jl. Pahang, 53000 Kuala Lumpur; tel. (3) 40420617; fax (3) 40418187; e-mail mma@tm.net.my; internet www.mma.org.my; f. 1959; 7,000 mems; Pres. Dato' Datuk Dr P. KRISHNAN; Admin Officer Ms SUMATHI; publs *Medical Journal of Malaysia* (4 a year), *MMA Newsletter* (12 a year).

NATURAL SCIENCES

General

Malaysian Scientific Association: Room 1, 2nd Floor, Bangunan Sultan Salahuddin Adbul Aziz Shah, 16 Jalan Utara, POB 48, 46700 Petaling Jaya; tel. (3) 79578930; fax (3) 79541644; e-mail malsci@tm.net.my; f. 1955; 388 mems, engaged in scientific and technological works; Pres. Dr SOON TING KUEH; Hon. Sec. Dr ZURAINEE MOHD NOR.

Biological Sciences

Malaysian Nature Society: POB 10750, 60724 Kuala Lumpur; tel. (3) 22879422; fax (3) 22878773; e-mail natsoc@po.jaring.my; internet www.mns.org.my; f. 1940; an independent society to promote the study, appreciation and conservation of nature; 5,000 mems; library: small library; Pres. Dato' Dr SALLEH MOHD NOR; Exec. Dir Dr LOH CHI LEONG; publs *The Malayan Nature Journal* (4 a year), *Malaysian Naturalist* (4 a year).

Malaysian Society for Biochemistry and Molecular Biology: d/a Pusat Pengajian Biosains dan Bioteknologi Fakulti Sains dan Teknologi, Universiti Kebangasaan Malaysia, 43600 Selangor; f. 1973; lectures, workshops and seminars, annual conference; 120 mems; Pres. Prof. PERUMAL RAMASAMY; Sec. Dr SHEILA NATHAN; publs *Malaysian Journal of Biochemistry and Molecular Biology, Proceedings of Annual Conference.*

Malaysian Zoological Society: 68000 Ampang Selangor, Darul Ehsan; tel. (603) 4083422; fax (603) 4075375; e-mail zoonegara@tm.net.my; f. 1961; Pres. Y. B. Tan Sri Dato V. M. HUTSON; Sec.-Treas. YUEN TANG.

RELIGION, SOCIOLOGY AND ANTHROPOLOGY

Royal Asiatic Society, Malaysian Branch: 130M Jl. Thamby Abdullah, off Jl. Tun Sambanthan, Brickfields, 50470 Kuala Lumpur; tel. (3) 22748345; fax (3) 22743458; e-mail mbras@tm.net.my; internet www .mbras.org.my; f. 1877; 935 mems; history, literature, sociology, anthropology; Pres. Datuk ABDULLAH BIN ALI; Sec. Datuk BURHANUDDIN BIN AHMAD TAJUDIN; publ. *Journal* (2 a year).

Research Institutes

AGRICULTURE, FISHERIES AND VETERINARY SCIENCE

Department of Agriculture: Ministry of Agriculture, Wisma Tani, Jl. Mahameru, 50624 Kuala Lumpur; f. 1905; undertakes all aspects of research and extension for improvement of crops; pest forecasting and surveillance; establishing Agricultural Information System; library of 15,000 vols; Dir ABU BAKAR BIN MAHMUD; publs *Malaysian Agricultural Journal, Statistical Digest.*

Forest Research Institute Malaysia (FRIM): Kepong, 52109, Selangor Darul Ehsan, Kuala Lumpur; tel. (3) 62797000; fax (3) 62731314; internet www.frim.gov.my; f. 1929; consists of 485.2 ha of experimental plantations, 5 arboreta, a nursery, a museum, a herbarium of 300,000 sheets of tree species, a wood colln of nearly 10,000 specimens, and a library (see Libraries); 9 substations consisting of 2,988 ha; Rattan Information Centre est. 1982; Dir-Gen. Dato' Dr ABDUL LATIF MOHMOD; publs *Bamboo Bulletin, Conservation Malaysia Bulletin, FRIM in Focus, FRIM Technical Information, Journal of Tropical Forest Products, Journal of Tropical Forest Science, Malayan Forest Records, Research Pamphlets, Research Programme, RIC Bulletin, Siri Alam & Rimba, Timber Technology Bulletin, Tree Flora of Sabah and Sarawak, Urban Forestry Bulletin.*

Freshwater Fisheries Research Centre: Batu Berendam, 75350 Malacca; tel. (6) 8172485; fax (6) 3175705; e-mail pppat@po .jaring.my; f. 1957; attached to Dept of Fisheries, Malaysia; research on freshwater fisheries and aquaculture; special emphasis on indigenous carp, study of fishes in lakes and reservoirs, breeding of indigenous freshwater fish; air-breathing fish, cichlid (Tilapia), aquarium fish, and aquatic plants; library of 3,800 vols; Chief Officer HAMBAL HANAFI.

Malaysian Agricultural Research and Development Institute (MARDI): POB 12301, GPO, 50774 Kuala Lumpur; tel. (3) 89437111; fax (3) 89483664; e-mail enquiry@ mardi.gov.my; internet www.mardi.my; f. 1969; an autonomous organization that conducts scientific, technical, economic and sociological research in Malaysia with respect to the production, utilization and processing of all crops (except rubber and oil palm) and livestock; library of 50,000 vols; Dir-Gen. Dr SAHARAN BIN ANANG; Librarian KHADIJAH IBRAHIM; publs *Agromedia* (4 a year), *Journal of Tropical Agriculture and Food Sciences* (2 a year).

Malaysian Rubber Board: POB 10150, 50450 Kuala Lumpur; tel. (3) 92062000; fax (3) 21634492; e-mail general@lgm.gov.my; f. 1998; consists of a directorate, 5 depts and 34 units, 2 research centres namely Tun Abdul Razak Research Centre in Hertford, England and RRIM in Sungai Buloh, Selangor, Malaysia; engaged in rubber research and devt; technical advisory service and information on all aspects of rubber production; library: see Libraries; Dir-Gen. Dr SALMIAH AHMAD; publs *Journal of Rubber Research* (4 a year), *Malaysian Rubber Technology Development* (4 a year).

ECONOMICS, LAW AND POLITICS

Asian and Pacific Development Centre: Pesiaran Duta, POB 12224, 50770 Kuala Lumpur; tel. (3) 6511088; fax (3) 6510316; internet www.apdc.com.my/apdc; f. 1980; promotes and undertakes research and training, acts as a clearing house for information on development, offers consultancy services; current programme: to overcome poverty, to assist development instns to manage national development and change, to increase the policy-making capacity of Asian-Pacific countries, to increase the capacity of the region to adjust to the changing world environment; 19 full mem. govts, 1 assoc. mem., 1 contributing non-mem.; library of 43,200 vols; Dir Dr MOHD NOOR HJ HARUN; publs *Newsletter* (2 a year), *Asia-Pacific Development Monitor* (2 a year), *Issues in Gender and Development.*

MEDICINE

Institute for Medical Research (IMR): Jl. Pahang, 50588 Kuala Lumpur; tel. (3) 2986033; f. 1901; now research branch of Ministry of Health; researches into biomedical and social aspects of tropical diseases, provides specialized diagnostic, consultative and information services, trains medical and paramedical staff, also WHO Centre for Research and Training in Tropical Diseases for the Western Pacific Region, and SEA-MEO-TROPMED National Centre, WHO Collaborating Centre for Taxonomy and Immunology of Filariasis and Screening and Clinical Trials of Drugs against Brugian Filariasis, and WHO Collaborating Centre for Ecology, Taxonomy and Control of Vectors of Malaria, Filariasis and Dengue; 598 staff; library of 20,000 vols; Dir Dr M. S. LYE (acting); publs *Bulletin of the Institute for Medical Research* (irregular), *IMR Handbook, International Medical Journal, Quarterly Bulletin, Study of the Institute for Medical Research* (irregular).

NATURAL SCIENCES

Physical Sciences

Minerals and Geoscience Department Malaysia: Locked Bag 2042, 88999 Kota Kinabalu, Sabah; tel. (88) 260311; fax (88) 240150; e-mail jmgsbh@jmg.gov.my; internet www.jmg.gov.my; f. 1949; geological mapping, minerals research, engineering geology, hydrogeology, geophysics, mineralogy and petrology, laboratory analysis; library of 3,500 vols; Dir N. K. ANG; publs *Malaysian Mineral Yearbook,* industrial mineral production statistics and directory of producers in Malaysia.

Minerals and Geoscience Malaysia, Ipoh Department: Scrivenor Rd, Ipoh, Perak; f. 1903; 792 mems; basic geological information on E and W Malaysia with spec. emphasis on mineral resources; library of 18,720 vols (E Malaysia), 34,000 vols (W Malaysia); Dir-Gen. E. H. YIN; publs regional memoirs, reports and bulletins (E Malaysia), map reports and proceedings (W Malaysia), economic bulletins (W Malaysia), *Geochemical Report.*

Minerals and Geoscience Malaysia, Sarawak Department: POB 560, 93712 Kuching, Sarawak; tel. (82) 244666; fax (82) 415390; e-mail jmgswk@jmg.gov.my; f. 1949; geological mapping, mineral investigations, engineering geology, hydrogeology; library of 18,000 vols; Dir Dato' Hj. YUNUS BIN ABD. RAZAK; publ. bulletins, geological papers, technical papers, maps, memoirs, reports.

TECHNOLOGY

Malaysian Institute of Microelectronic Systems (MIMOS): MIMOS Berhad, Technology Park Malaysia, 57000 Kuala Lumpur; tel. (3) 89965000; fax (3) 89960527; internet www.mimos.my; f. 1985; research and development in microelectronics, information technology and related areas; provides advisory and technical services to the govt and the private sector; encourages and supports the creation of new industries based on high technology and modern microelectronics; collaborates with other bodies in the fields; library of 6,200 vols, 202 periodicals; Dir-Gen. Dr TENGKU MOHD AZZMAN SHARIFFADEEN; publs *MIMOS IT Paper* (2 a year), *MIMOS Teknologi Buletin* (4 a year), *MOSMEDIA* (4 a year).

Standards and Industrial Research Institute of Malaysia (SIRIM): POB 35, 40700 Shah Alam, Selangor; tel. (3) 5591630; fax (3) 5508095; f. 1975 by merger of National Institute of Scientific and Industrial Research and the Standards Institution of Malaysia; facilitates industrial development through research into existing and future problems relating to engineering and production of processed and fabricated industrial products; provides a range of technical services which include quality assurance, metrology, industry testing, technology modification and improvement, technology transfer, consultancy, industrial information and extension services; undertakes applied research and prototype production to adapt or modify known processes and technologies; finds new uses for locally available raw materials and by-products, and develops new products and processes based on indigenous raw materials; the drafting and publications of Malaysian standards and standards testing; library of 13,000 vols; 165,000 standards and specifications, 400 periodicals; Controller Dr AHMAD TAJUDDIN ALI; publs *Berita SIRIM* (SIRIM News, 4 a year), *Malaysian Standards.*

Libraries and Archives

Alor Setar

Kedah State Public Library Corporation: Jalan Kolam Air, 05100 Alor Setar, Kedah Darul Aman; tel. (4) 7333592; fax (4) 7336232; e-mail pengarah@kdhlib.gov.my; internet www.kdhlib.gov. my; f. 1974; incl. Alor Setar Public Library, eight br. libraries, six mobile libraries and 88 village libraries; 675,677 vols; Dir Dr ZAHIDI BIN DATO' HAJI ZAINOL RASHID.

Ipoh

Tun Razak Library: Jl. Panglima Bukit Gantang Wahab, 30000 Ipoh, Perak Darul Ridzuan; tel. (5) 508073; f. 1931; special collections on Malaysia and Singapore; UNESCO depository; special language section; 245,816 vols in English, Chinese, Malay and Tamil; Asst Librarian NOOR AFITZA HJ. PAWAN CHIK; publ. *Malaysiana Collection.*

Jitra

Perpustakaan, Universiti Utara Malaysia: Sintok, 06010 Jitra, Kedah; tel. (4) 9241740; fax (4) 9241959; f. 1984; 183,000 vols, 6,000 periodicals; Chief Librarian PUAN JAMILAH MOHAMED.

Johor Baharu

Perpustakaan Sultan Ismail: Jl. Dato Onn, Johor Baharu; f. 1964; administered by the Town Council; 40,600 vols in Chinese, English, Malay and Tamil; Librarian (vacant).

Perpustakaan Sultanah Zanariah, Universiti Teknologi Malaysia: 81310 Utm Skudai, Johor Bahru; tel. (7) 5576160; fax (7) 5572555; internet www.psz.utm.my; f. 1972; 344,000 vols, 9,300 periodicals; audiovisual collection; Chief Librarian ROSNA TAIB; publs *Berita Perpustakaan Sultanah Zanariah* (2 a month), *Buletin MAKIN.*

Kota Baharu

Kelantan Public Library Corporation: Jl. Mahmood, 15200 Kota Baharu, Kelantan; tel. (9) 7444522; fax (9) 7487736; f. 1938, present name 1974; 261,000 vols; special collection: Kelantan Collection; State Librarian NIK ARIFF BIN NIK MANSOR.

Kota Kinabalu

Sabah State Library/Perpustakaan Negeri Sabah: 88572 Kota Kinabalu, Sabah; tel. (88) 54333; fax (88) 233167; f. 1951; now a state department within the Ministry of Social Services (Sabah); public reference and lending library of 841,914 vols, mainly in Malay, English and Chinese; special local history collection on Borneo; comprises 20 brs (in addition to main library), 10 mobile libraries for rural areas and 26 village libraries; Dir ADELINE LEONG.

Kuala Lumpur

Kuala Lumpur Public Library: Sam Mansion, Jl. Tuba, Kuala Lumpur; f. 1966; 45,000 vols; Librarian SOONG WAN YOONG.

Library, Forest Research Institute Malaysia: Kepong, 52109 Selangor; tel. (3) 62797497; fax (3) 62804624; e-mail zaki@frim.gov.my; internet www.frim.gov.my; f. 1929; 62,000 vols on forestry and related subjects, incl. medicinal plants, biodiversity, the environment; colln consists of books, scientific and technical reports, reprints, standards, conference papers, theses, newspaper clippings, gazettes, maps; services incl. SDI, Rattan Information Centre, current awareness services, literature searches, OPAC, etc.; Library Head MOHAMAD ZAKI HAJI MOHD ISA; publs *FRIM in Focus* (4 a year), *FRIM Reports* (irregular), *FRIM Research Pamphlet* (irregular), *FRIM Technical Information* (irregular), *Journal of Tropical Forest Science* (4 a year), *Timber Technology Bulletin* (irregular).

Malaysian Rubber Board Library: Jl. Ampang, POB 10150, 50908 Kuala Lumpur; tel. 4567033; fax (3) 4573512; e-mail rabiah@lgm.gov.my; f. 1925; 150,000 vols, mainly science and technology, particular emphasis on subjects relating to rubber research; Librarian RABIAH BT MOHD. YUSOF; publs *Bibliographies, List of Forthcoming Conferences, List of Journal Holdings, List of RRIM Translations, Recent Additions to the Library,* etc.

Ministry of Agriculture Library: Wisma Tani, Jl. Sultan Salahuddin, 50624 Kuala Lumpur; tel. (3) 88701786; fax (3) 88895239; internet www.moa.gov.my; f. 1906; 80,000 vols; publ. *Bulletin* (irregular).

National Archives of Malaysia: Jl. Duta, 50568 Kuala Lumpur; tel. (3) 6510688; fax (3) 6515679; e-mail query@arkib.gov.my; internet www.arkib.gov.my; f. 1957; public records, archives, audiovisual records, private and business records; Prime Minister's archives; 10,471 vols; Dir-Gen. Dato' HABIBAH ZON; publs *Hari ini Dlm. Sejarah* (Today in History, 4 a year), *National Archives of Malaysia.*

National Library of Malaysia: 232 Jalan Tun Razak, 50572 Kuala Lumpur; tel. (3) 2943488; fax (3) 2927899; f. 1966; nat. bibliographic centre, nat. depository, nat. centre for Malay MSS, nat. centre for ISBN and ISSN; depository for UN publs; 1,413,348 vols; Dir-Gen. CIK SHAHAR BANUN JAAFAR; publs *Jurnal Filologi Melayu* (1 a year), *Selitan Perpustakaen* (2 a year).

Pusat Dokumentasi Melayu (Dewan Bahasa dan Pustaka) (Malay Documentation Centre, Institute of Language and Literature): POB 10803, 50926 Kuala Lumpur; tel. (3) 21481030; fax (3) 21429903; e-mail aizan@dbp.gov.my; internet www.dbp.gov.my; f. 1956; directory of Malaysian writers; bibliography of modern Malaysian literature; 150,000 vols, 110 periodicals, 3,330 audiovisual items; 6,500 mems; Head AIZAN MOHD ALI; publs *Mutiara Pustaka* (1 a year), *Subject Bibliography* (Bulletin, irregular).

University of Malaya Library: Pantai Valley, 50603 Kuala Lumpur; tel. (3) 7575887; fax (3) 7573661; f. 1957; 1,239,749 vols, 8,040 periodicals; spec. collns incl. medical, law, Malay language and culture, E Asia studies and Tamil studies; Chief Librarian Assoc. Prof. Dr NOR EDZAN CHE NASIR; publ. *Kekal Abadi* (2 a year).

Kuching

Sarawak State Library: Jl. P. Ramlee, 93572 Kuching; tel. (82) 242911; fax (82) 246552; f. 1950; administered by the Ministry of Environment; 1,232,780 vols in Malay, English, Iban and Chinese; State Librarian JOHNNY K. S. KUEH.

Melaka

Malacca Public Library Corporation: 242-1 Jalan Bukit Baru, 75150 Melaka; tel. (6) 2824859; fax (6) 2824798; e-mail admin@perpustam.edu.my; internet www.perpustam.edu.my; f. 1977; 526,375 vols; Librarian RIZA FEISAL BIN SHEIK SAID.

Penang

Penang Public Library Corporation: 2nd Floor, Dewan Sri Pinang, 10200 Penang; tel. (4) 2622255; fax (4) 2628820; f. 1817; reorganized 1973; 415,000 vols; Chair. Y. B. Dr TOH KIN WOON; Dir ENCIK ONG CHAI LIN; publ. *Buletin Mutiara* (4 a year).

Perpustakaan Universiti Sains Malaysia: Minden, 11800 Penang; tel. (4) 6577888; fax (4) 6571526; e-mail chieflib@usm.my; internet www.lib.usm.my; f. 1969; 809,000 vols (main library 644,000 vols, 5,500 periodicals; medical library 87,000 vols, 1,370 periodicals; engineering library 78,000 vols, 487 periodicals), media 122,916 items, 9,969 reels microfilm, 105,809 sheets microfiche; Chief Librarian Hon. Datin MASRAH HAJI ABIDIN; publ. *MIDAS Bulletin* (6 a year).

Serdang

Perpustakaan Sultan Abdul Samad (Sultan Abdul Samad Library): 43400 UPM Serdang, Selangor Darul Ehsan; tel. (3) 89468601; fax (3) 89483745; e-mail lib@lib.upm.edu.my; internet www.lib.upm.edu.my; f. 1971 by merger of College of Agriculture, Malaya and the Faculty of Agriculture, Universiti Putra Malaysia; renamed Universiti Putra Malaysia Library in 1997; present name 2002; attached to Unversiti Putra Malaysia; brs in Faculty of Medicine and

Health Sciences, Faculty of Veterinary Medicine, Faculty of Engineering and the UPM Campus Bintulu in Sarawak; 601,663 vols and bound periodicals; colln of maps, sound recordings, microforms, video tapes and slides; subscribes to 3,000 print journals and 60 online databases providing access to 56,000 full-text online journals; Chief Librarian AMIR HUSSAIN MOHAMMAD ISHAK (acting); Deputy Chief Librarian HAFIZAH HASSAN, ROSMALA ABDUL RAHIM.

Shah Alam

Selangor Public Library Corporation: c/o Perpustakaan Raja Tun Uda, Persiaran Bandaraya, 40572 Shah Alam, Selangor; tel. (3) 55197667; fax (3) 55196045; e-mail jothi@ppas.org.my; internet www.ppas.org.my; f. 1971; 1,435,803 vols; main library; 8 brs; 4 township libraries, 55 village libraries and 13 mobile units; Dir SHAHANEEM HANOUM; publs *Accession List* (12 a year), *PPAS Newsletter* (4 a year).

Tun Abdul Razak Library: MARA Institute of Technology, 40450 Shah Alam, Selangor; tel. (3) 5564041; fax (3) 5503648; f. 1957; two main libraries and 10 brs; 898,000 vols; Chief Librarian RAHMAH MUHAMAD.

Museums and Art Galleries

Kota Kinabalu

Sabah Museum: Jl. Muzium, 83000 Kota Kinabalu, Sabah; tel. (88) 538228; fax (88) 240230; e-mail muzium.sabah@sabah.gov.my; internet www.mzm.sabah.gov.my; f. 1886 in Sandakan; anthropological, archaeological, natural history and historical, ethnobotanical and ethnological collections; Islamic Civilization Museum, Agop Batu Tulug Museum, Kinabatangan, Sandakan Heritage museum, Sandakan Agnes Keith House, Sandakan Memorial Tun Abdul Razak, Tambunan Datu Paduka Mat Salleh Memorial, Kinarut Panoramic Mansion House, Tenom Murut Culture Museum, Semporna Bukit Tengkorak; Lahad Datu Mansuli archaeological site, Tambunan Mat Sator Monument, Tenom Ulu Tomani Lamuyu Rock Carving, Penampang Pogunon Burial Ancient Site, Keningau Heritage Museum, Tenom Antoros Antenom Monument; library of 7,000 vols; Dir Datuk JOSEPH POUNIS GUNTAVID; publs *Buletin Muzium* (1 a year), *Journal* (1 a year).

Kuala Lumpur

Islamic Arts Museum Malaysia: Jalan Lembah Perdana, 50480 Kuala Lumpur; tel. (3) 22742020; fax (3) 22740529; e-mail info@iamm.org.my; internet www.iamm.org.my; f. 1998; art and culture of Islam from the 7th century to the present; incl. 12 permanent galleries; Architecture, Qu'rans and Manuscript, India, China, Malay World, Textiles, Jewellery, Arms and Armour, Coins and Seals, Metalwork, Ceramics and Glasses, and Living with Wood; 2 spec. galleries; Dir SYED MOHAMAD ALBUKHARY.

National Museum of Malaysia/Muzium Negara: Jl. Damansara, 50566 Kuala Lumpur; tel. (3) 22826255; fax (3) 22827294; e-mail info@jma.gov.my; internet www.jma.gov.my; f. 1963; houses collections of ethnographical, archaeological and zoological materials; comprehensive reference library on Malaysia and many Asian subjects, reference collections of archaeology, zoology and ethnography are also preserved in the Perak Museum, Taiping; Dir-Gen. Dr ADI HAJI TAHA; publ. *Federation Museums Journal* (1 a year).

Kuching

Sarawak Museum: Jl. Tun Abang Haji Openg, 93566 Kuching, Sarawak; tel. (82) 258388; fax (82) 246680; f. 1886; ethnographic, archaeological, natural history and historical collections; reference library; state archives; Dir SANIB SAID; publ. *Sarawak Museum Journal*.

Penang

Penang Museum and Art Gallery: Farquhar St, Penang; tel. (4) 2613144; f. 1963; Chair., Penang State Museum Board NAZIR ARIFF; Curator Encik KHOO BOO CHIA.

Taiping

Perak Museum: Taiping, Perak; f. 1883; antiquities, Perak archives, ethnography, zoology and a library; Dir-Gen. SHAHRUM BIN YUB.

Universities

INTERNATIONAL ISLAMIC UNIVERSITY MALAYSIA

Jalan Gombak, 53100 Kuala Lumpur
Telephone: (3) 20564000
Fax: (3) 20564053
E-mail: pro@iiu.edu.my
Internet: www.iiu.edu.my
Founded 1983
Ministry of Education control
Languages of instruction: Arabic, English
Open to Muslims and non-Muslims from Malaysia and abroad
Constitutional Head: HRH THE SULTAN OF PAHANG
President: Y.B. Tan Sri Dato' SERI SANUSI BIN JUNID
Rector: Prof. Dr MOHD. KAMAL HASSAN
Deputy Rector for Academic Affairs: Assoc. Prof. Dato' Haji JAMIL HAJI OSMAN
Deputy Rector for Planning and Development: Prof. Dr ISMAWI HAJI ZEN
Deputy Rector for Student Affairs and Discipline: Assoc. Prof. Dr SIDEK BABA
Chief Librarian: Assoc. Prof. SYED SALIM AGHA BIN SYED AZAMTHULLA
Library of 356,700 vols
Number of teachers: 1,166
Number of students: 16,649
Publications: *At-Tajdid* (in Arabic, 2 a year), *Gombak Review* (in English, 2 a year), *IIUM* (in English, 2 a year), *IIUM Journal of Economics and Management* (in English, 2 a year), *IIUM Law Journal* (in English, 2 a year), *Intellectual Discourse* (in English, 2 a year)

DEANS OF KULLIYYAH

Kulliyyah of Architecture and Environmental Design: Assoc. Prof. Dr CHE MUSA CHE OMAR
Kulliyyah of Economics and Management Sciences: Assoc. Prof. Dr MOHD. AZMI OMAR
Kulliyyah of Education: Assoc. Prof. Dr MOHD. SAHARI NORDIN
Kulliyyah of Engineering: Assoc. Prof. Dr AHMAD FARIS ISMAIL
Kulliyyah of Information and Communications Technology: Dr MOHD. ADAM SUHAIMI
Kulliyyah of Islamic Revealed Knowledge and Human Sciences: Prof. Dr MOHAMED ARIS HAJI OSMAN
Ahmad Ibrahim Kulliyyah of Laws: Assoc Prof. Dr NIK AHMAD KAMAL NIK MAHMOD
Kulliyyah of Medicine: Prof. Dato' Dr MD. TAHIR AZHAR

Kulliyyah of Pharmacy: Prof. Dr TARIQ ABDUL RAZAK
Kulliyyah of Science: Assoc. Prof. Dr TORLA HAJI HASSAN

ATTACHED INSTITUTE

International Institute of Islamic Thought and Civilization (ISTAC): 205A Jl. Damansara, Bukit Damansara, 50480 Kuala Lumpur; tel. (3) 2544444; fax (3) 2548343; f. 1991; financed by Ministry of Education; postgraduate research and teaching in fields of Islamic thought and civilization; library of 149,686 vols; Dir Prof. Dr SYED MUHAMMAD NAQUIB AL-ATTAS.

UNIVERSITI KEBANGSAAN MALAYSIA (National University of Malaysia)

43600 UKM Bangi, Selangor
Telephone: (3) 89214187
Fax: (3) 89254890
E-mail: kbha@pkrisc.cc.ukm.my
Internet: www.ukm.my
Founded 1970
State control
Languages of instruction: Malay, English, Arabic
Academic year: May to April
Chancellor: Tuanku JAAFAR IBNI AL-MARHUM ABDUL RAHMAN
Vice-Chancellor: Prof. Dato' Dr MOHD SALLEH MOHD. YASIN
Deputy Vice-Chancellors: Prof. Dr SUKIMAN SARMANI (Academic and International Affairs), Prof. Dato' Dr MOHD WAHID SAMSUDIN (Students and Alumni Affairs)
Registrar: Hj. MOHAMED MUSTAFA MOHTAR
Bursar: Hj. MOHD ABDUL RASHID MOHD FADZIL
Chief Librarian: PUTRI SANIAH MEGAT ABDUL RAHMAN
Library of 945,000 vols, 4,000 journals
Number of teachers: 1,781
Number of students: 24,487
Publications: *Jurnal Sari, Jurnal Islamiyyat, Jurnal Jebat, Jurnal Pendidikan, Jurnal Pengurusan, Jurnal Psikologi Malaysia, Jurnal Kejuruteraan* (2 a year), *Jurnal Ekonomi Malaysia, Jurnal Perubatan UKM, Jurnal Akademika, Sains Malaysiana* (4 a year), *Jurnal Undang-Undang and Masyarakat, Buletin Pusat Pengajian Umum, Journal of Language Teaching, Linguistics and Literature*

DEANS

Faculty of Allied Health Sciences: Prof. Dr MOHD AZMAN ABU BAKAR
Faculty of Dentistry: Prof. Dato' Dr Hj. MOHD ARIFFIN HJ. MOHAMED
Faculty of Economics and Business: Prof. Dr NOOR AZLAN GHAZALI
Faculty of Education: Assoc. Prof. Dr LILIA HALIM
Faculty of Engineering: Prof. Ir. Dr HASSAN BASRI
Faculty of Islamic Studies: Prof. Dr ZAKARIA SETAPA
Faculty of Law: Assoc. Prof. KAMAL HALILI HASSAN
Faculty of Medicine: Prof. Dr LOKMAN SAIM
Faculty of Social Sciences and Humanities: Prof. Dr YUSUF ISMAIL
Faculty of Science and Information Technology: Prof. AZIZ DERAMAN
Faculty of Science and Technology: Prof. Dr ABDUL JALIL ABDUL KADER
Centre for General Studies: Prof. Dr ABDUL LATIF SAMIAN
Institute for Environment and Development (LESTARI): Prof. Dr IBRAHIM KOOMOO

Institute of Malay World and Civilization (ATMA): Prof. Dato' Dr SHAMSUL AMRI BAHARUDDIN

Institute of Malaysian and International Studies (IKMAS): Prof. Dr ROGAYAH HJ. MAT ZIN

Institute of Medical Molecular Biology (UMBI): Prof. Dr A. RAHMAN A. JAMAL

Institute of Microengineering and Nanoelectronics (IMEN): Prof. Dr BURHANUDDIN YEOP MAJLIS

Institute of Occidental Studies (IKON): Prof. Dato' Dr SHAMSUL AMRI BAHARUDDIN

Institute of Space (ANGKASA): Prof. Dr BAHARUDDIN YATIM

National Institute for Genomics and Molecular Biology—Malaysia: Prof. Dr NOR MUHAMMAD MAHADI

PROFESSORS

ABDUL HAMID, Z., Genetics and Plant Biotechnology
ABDUL KADER, A. J., Microbial Physiology
ABDUL KADIR, K., Endocrinology and Metabolism
ABDUL RAHMAN, R., Environmental Engineering
ABDUL RASHID, A. H., Anatomy
ABDULLAH, A., Food Science and Nutrition
ABDULLAH, I., Structural Geology and Tectonics
ABDULLAH, M., Statistics
ABDULLAH, P., Analytical and Environmental Chemistry
ABU BAKAR, M. A., Lipid Biochemistry
ABU TALIB, I., Material Physics
AHMAD, I., Virology
AHMAD, Z., Political Science
ALI, A., Industrial Planning and Strategies
ALI, O., Community Health
ALI JAMAL, A. R., Paediatric Haematology
ALI RAHIM, S., Development Communications
AZMAN ALI, RAYMOND, Neurology, Epilepsy and Stroke Medicine
BABA, I., Inorganic Chemistry
BABJI, A. S., Food Science
BAHARUDDIN, S. A., Anthropology and Sociology
BASRI, H., Civil and Environmental Engineering
BIDIN, A. A., Taxonomy of Lower Plants
BOO NEM YUN, Neonatology
CHOO, O. L., Child Neurology and Development Paediatrics
DAUD, W. R. W., Drying, Separation and Fuel Cell Technology
DIN, L., Organic Chemistry
EMBI, M. N., Protein Biochemistry
GEORGE, E., Haematology
HADI, A. S., Urbanization, Industrialization and Migration
HAMDAN, A. R., Artificial Intelligence
HASAN, M. N. H., Zoology
HASAN, Z. A. A., Parasitology
HASSAN, H. R., Psychiatry
HASSAN, S. Z. S., Anthropology of Religion, Gender Studies
ISKANDAR, T. M., Internal Control and Auditing
ISMAIL, M. Y., Minority and Sub-culture Studies
ISMAIL, N. M. N., Obstetrics and Gynaecology
IZHAM CHEONG, Medicine
JAHI, J. M., Physical Geography
JAMAL, F., Clinical Bacteriology
JASIN, B., Micropalaeontology
KADRI, A., Zoology
KAMIS, A., Animal Physiology, Comparative Endocrinology
KENG, C. S., Haematology
KOMOO, I., Engineering Geology and Conservation Geology
KONG, C. T. N., Nephrology
KRISHNASWAMY, S., Psychiatry
LAZAN, H., Plant Physiology and Biochemistry

LIEW, C. G., Family Medicine
LIM, A., Clinical Microbiology and Antimicrobial Chemotherapy
LONG, J., Education
MAHADI, N. M., Environmental Microbiology
MAJLIS, B. Y., Integrated Circuit Technology
MAJZUB, R. M., Pre-school and Adolescent Education and Development
MANSOR, M., Cytogenetics, Cytology
MAT SALLEH, M., Solid State Physics
MEAH, F. A., Surgery
MEERAH, T. S. M., Science Education
MD. HASHIM MERICAN, Z. M., Neuromuscular Pharmacology
MISIRAN, K., Anaesthesiology
MOHAMAD, A. L., Plant Systematics
MOHAMAD, H., Petrology and Geochemistry
MOHAMED, M. A., Oral Health
MOHAMED, R., Bacterial Serology
MOHAMED YASIN, M. S., Medical Mycology
MOHAMMED ZAIN, S. BIN, Mathematics
MOHD NOOR, N., Plant Tissue Culture
MOHD SALLEH, K., Science and Society
NGAH, W. Z. W., Medical Biochemistry
NIK ABD. RAHMAN, N. H. S., Archaeology
NOOR, M. I., Nutrition
NOR, G. M., Oral Surgery
OTHMAN, A. H., Coordination Chemistry
OTHMAN, B. H. R., Marine Biology
OTHMAN, M., Signals Processing
OTHMAN, M. Y. H., Energy Physics
PIHIE, A. H. L., Clinical Biochemistry
SAHID, I., Weed and Environmental Science
SAID, I. M., Organic Chemistry
SAIM, L., Otology and Neuro-otology
SALLEH, A. R., Algebraic Topology, Ethnomathematics
SALLEH, RAMLI MD, Malay Syntax and Translation
SALLEH, S. H. H., Traditional Malay Literature
SAMSUDIN, A. R., Geophysics
SAMSUDIN, M. W., Organic Chemistry
SARMANI, S., Radiochemistry
SHAH, F. H., Molecular Biology
SHAMSUDIN, A. H., Mechanical Engineering
SIWAR, C., Rural Economics
SULAIMAN, N. A., Bioscience and Clinical Pharmacology
SULAIMAN, S., Vector Control, Vectorecology
SYED HUSSAIN, S. N. A., Histopathology, Cytopathology
TAHIR, U. M. M., Modern Malay Literature, Literary Criticism
TAMIN, N. M., Eco-engineering Restoration
TAP, A. O. M., Pure Mathematics
TEH, W. H. W., Rural Culture and Society
TENGKU SEMBOK, T. M., Information Retrieval
YAHAYA, MUHAMMAD, Physics
YAMIN, B. M., Chemistry
YATIM, B., Applied Physics
YONG, O., Investment
YUSOFF, K., Cardiology
YUSUF, M. HJ., Social Psychology
ZAMAN, H. B., Information Technology Policy and Strategic Studies

UNIVERSITI MALAYA
(University of Malaya)

Lembah Pantai, 50603 Kuala Lumpur

Telephone: (3) 7560022
Fax: (3) 7564004
Internet: www.cc.um.edu.my

Founded 1962
State control
Languages of instruction: Malay, English
Academic year: May to April (2 semesters)

Chancellor: Duli Yang Maha Mulia Paduka Seri Sultan Perak Darul Ridzuan Sultan AZLAN MUHIBBUDDIN SHAH

Pro-Chancellors: Duli Yang Teramat Mulia Raja Muda Perak Darul Ridzuan Raja NAZRIN SHAH, Yang Amat Berbahagia

Orang Kaya Bendahara Seri Maharaja Tun Haji SYED ZAHIRUDDIN BIN SYED HASSAN

Vice-Chancellor: Tan Sri Dato' Dr ABDULLAH SANUSI AHMAD

Deputy Vice-Chancellors: Prof. Dato' Dr FIRDAUS H. ABDULLAH, Prof. Dato' Dr OSMAN BAKAR, Assoc. Prof. Dr HAMZAH ABDUL RAHMAN

Registrar: YAACOB HUSSEIN
Librarian: Dr ZAITON OSMAN

Number of teachers: 1,571
Number of students: 24,345

Publications: Berita UM (newsletter, 24 a year), Budiman (4 a year), University of Malaya Gazette (1 a year)

DEANS

Faculty of Arts and Social Sciences: Prof. Datuk Dr ZAINAL KLING
Faculty of Business and Accounting: Prof. Dr MANSOR MD ISA
Faculty of Computer Science and Information Technology: Prof. Dr MASHKURI HJ. YAACOB
Faculty of Dentistry: Prof. Dato' Dr HASHIM YAACOB
Faculty of Economics and Administration: Prof. Dr JAHARA YAHAYA
Faculty of Education: Prof. Dr RAHIMAH BT. HJ. AHMAD
Faculty of Engineering: Prof. Dr WAN ABU BAKAR WAN ABAS
Faculty of Languages and Linguistics: Prof. Dato' Dr ASMAH HJ. OMAR
Faculty of Law: Prof. Dato' Dr N. S. SOTHI RACHAGAN
Faculty of Medicine: Prof. Dato' Dr ANUAR ZAINI MOHD. ZAIN
Faculty of Science: Prof. Dr MUHAMAD RASAT MUHAMAD
Institute of Postgraduate Studies and Research: Prof. Dr ANSARY AHMED
Academy of Islamic Studies: Prof. Dato' Dr MAHMOOD ZUHDI HJ. ABDUL MAJID (Dir)
Academy of Malay Studies: Prof. Dr WAN ABDUL KADIR WAN YUSOFF (Dir)
Centre for Foundation Studies in Science: Assoc. Prof. MOHD SAID MOHD KADIR (Dir)

PROFESSORS

Faculty of Arts and Social Sciences:
  ABDULLAH ZAKAVIA, G., History
  ALI, S. H., Sociology
  AZIZAH, K., Anthropology and Sociology
  CHENG, G. N., Chinese Studies
  FATIMAH HASNAH, D., Anthropology and Sociology
  LEE, B. T., Geography
  LIM, C. S., English Studies
  MOHD FAUZI, Y., Anthropology and Sociology
  MOHD YUSOFF, H., History
  NATHAN, K. S.
  RAMLAH, A., History
  RANJIT SINGH, D. S., History
  SHAHARIL, T. R., Southeast Asia Studies
  VOON, P. K., Land Use Studies
  ZAINAL, K., Anthropology and Sociology

Faculty of Business and Accounting:
  MANSOR, M. I., Financial Management
  SIEH, M. L., Business Administration

Faculty of Computer Science and Information Technology:
  MASHKURI, Y., Computer Science

Faculty of Dentistry:
  HASHIM, Y., Oral Pathology and Oral Medicine
  ISHAK, A. R., Preventive Dentistry
  LIAN, C. B., Oral Surgery
  LING, B. C., Prosthetics
  LUI, J. L., Conservative Dentistry
  RAHIMAH, A. K., Community Dentistry

SIAR, C. H., Periodontology
TOH, C. G., Conservative Dentistry
ZUBAIDAH ABD, R., Oral Biology

Faculty of Economics and Administration:

FIRDAUS, A., Administration and Political Science
JAHARA, Y., Development Studies
JAMILAH, M. A., Development Studies
JOMO, K. S., Applied Economics
KOK, K. L., Applied Economics
LEE, K. H., Analytical Economics
NAGARAJ, S., Applied Statistics
NAIDU, G., Applied Economics
TAN, P. C., Applied Statistics

Faculty of Education:

CHEW, S. B., Sociology of Education
CHIAM, H. K., Social Psychology of Education
GAUDART, H. M., Language Education
ISHAK, H., Pedagogy and Educational Psychology
NIK AZIS, N. P., Mathematics and Science Education
RAHIMAH HJ., A., Educational Development
RAMIAH, A. L., Educational Development
SAFIAH, O., Language Education
SURADI, S., Pedagogy and Educational Psychology
YONG, M. S. LEONARD, Pedagogy and Educational Psychology

Faculty of Engineering:

ABDUL GHANI, K., Computer-aided Design and Manufacturing
EZRIN, A., Built Environment
FAISAL, A., Civil and Environmental Engineering
GOH, S. Y., Mechanical and Material Engineering
KHALID, M. N., Electrical and Telecommunications Engineering
LU, S. K. S., Electrical Engineering
MASITAH, H., Chemical Engineering
MOHD ALI, H., Chemical Engineering
MOHD ZAKI, A. M., Mechanical and Material Engineering
RAMACHANDRAN, K. B., Biochemical Engineering
WAN ABU BAKAR, W. A., Mechanical Engineering
WOODS, P. C., Built Environment

Faculty of Law:

BALAN, P., Company Law and Civil Procedure
HARI, C., Jurisprudence and Legal Philosophy
KHAW, L. T., Law of Intellectual Property and Land Law
MIMI KAMARIAH, A. M., Family Law and Criminal Procedures
SOTHI RACHAGAN, N. S., Environmental and Consumer Law
SURYA, P. S., International Law

Faculty of Medicine:

ALJAFRI, A. M., Surgery
ANUAR ZAINI, M. Z., Medicine
ASMA, O., Paediatrics
CHANDRA, S. N., Parasitology
CHUA, C. T., Medicine
DELLIKAN, A. E., Anaesthesiology
DEVA, M. P., Psychological Medicine
EL-SABBAN, FAROUK M. F., Physiology
GOH, K. L., Medicine
KHAIRULL, A. A., Parasitology
KULENTHRAN, A., Obstetrics and Gynaecology
LAM, S. K., Medical Microbiology
LANG, C. C., Medicine
LIM, C. T., Paediatrics
LIM, Y. C., Surgery
LIN, H. P., Paediatrics
LOOI, L. M., Pathology
MENAKA, N., Pathology
NGEOW, Y. F., Medical Microbiology

ONG, S. Y. G., Anaesthesiology
PARAMSOTHY, M., Medicine
PERUMAL, R., Biochemistry
PRASAD, U., Oto-rhino-laryngology
PUTHUCHEARY, S. D., Medical Microbiology
RAMAN, A., Physiology
RAMANUJAM, T. M., Surgery
ROKIAH, I., Medicine
RUBY, H., Physiology
SENGUPTA, S., Orthopaedic Surgery
SIVANESARATNAM, V., Obstetrics and Gynaecology
SUBRAMANIAM, K., Anatomy
TAN, C. T., Medicine
TAN, N. H., Biochemistry
TEOH, S. T., Social and Preventive Medicine
YAP, S. F., Pathology
YEOH, P. N., Pharmacy

Faculty of Science:

ANSARY, A., Microbiology and Bacteriology
HAMID, A. H. A., Natural Product Chemistry
HARITH, A., Physics
KOH, C. L., Genetics
LIM, M. H., Multilinear Algebra
LOW, K. S., Lasers and Optoelectronics
MAK, C., Plant Breeding
MOHAMED, A. M., Taxonomy and Ecology
MUHAMAD RASAT, M., Molecular Electronics
MUHAMAD, Z., Botany
MUKHERJEE, T. K., Genetics
NAIR, H., Plant Physiology
OSMAN, B., Philosophy of Science
RAHIM, S., Semiconductor Physics
RAJ, J. K., Engineering Geology
RAMLI, A., Zoology
WONG, C. S., Plasma Physics
YEAP, E. B., Geology

Academy of Islamic Studies:

ABDULLAH ALWI, H., Syariah and Economics
MAHFODZ, M., Syariah and Law
MAHMOOD ZUHDI, A. M., Fiqh and Usul

Academy of Malay Studies:

ABU HASSAN, M. S., Malay Literature
ASMAH, O., Malay Linguistics
HASHIM, M., Linguistics
NORAZIT, S., Economic Anthropology
RAHMAH, B., Malay Culture and Arts
WAN ABDUL KADIR, W. Y., Popular Culture Studies
YAACOB, H., Development Studies and Change

UNIVERSITI MALAYSIA SABAH

Tingkat 9, Gaya Centre, Jalan Tun Fuad Stephens, Locked Bag 2073, 88999 Kota Kinabalu, Sabah

Telephone: (88) 320789
Fax: (88) 320223
E-mail: pejcslor@ums.edu.my
Internet: www.ums.edu.my

Founded 1994

Academic year: June to March

Vice-Chancellor: Prof. Datuk Seri Panglima Dr ABU HASSAN OTHMAN
Deputy Vice-Chancellors: Prof. Dr MOHD ZAHEDI DAUD (Academic), Prof. Datuk Dr KAMARUZZAMAN AMPON (Research and Development), Prof. Datuk Dr MOHD NOH DALIMIN (Student Affairs)
Registrar: HELA LADIN BIN MOHD DAHALAN
Librarian: CHE SALMAH MEHAMOOD

Number of teachers: 476
Number of students: 8,300

Publications: *Borneo Science* (2 a year), *Kinabalu* (1 a year), *Manu* (1 a year)

DEANS

School of Arts Studies: Assoc. Prof. Haji INON SHAHARUDDIN ABD. RAHMAN
School of Business and Economics: Assoc. Prof. SYED AZIZI SYED WAFA
School of Business and Finance, Labuan: Assoc. Prof. Dr ZAINAL ABIDIN SAID
School of Education and Social Development: Prof. Dr SHUKERY MOHAMED
School of Engineering and Information Technology: Assoc. Prof. Dr SAZALI YAACOB
School of Food Science and Nutrition: Assoc. Prof. Dr MOHD ISMAIL ABDULLAH
School of Informatic Sciences, Labuan: AWANG ASRI AWANG IBRAHIM (acting)
School of International Forestry: Assoc. Prof. Dr AMINUDDIN MOHAMED
School of Psychology and Social Work: Prof. Dato' Dr ABDUL HALIM OTHMAN
School of Science and Technology: Assoc Prof. Dr AMRAN AHMED
School of Social Sciences: Assoc. Prof. HASSAN BIN MAT NOR
Centre for Postgraduate Studies: Prof. Dr ZAINODIN HJ. JUBOK
Centre for the Promotion of Knowledge and Language Learning: Prof. Dr AHMAT ADAM

UNIVERSITI MALAYSIA SARAWAK (UNIMAS)

Jalan Dato' Mohd Musa, 94300 Kota Samarahan, Sarawak

Telephone: (82) 671000
Fax: (82) 672411
Internet: www.unimas.my

Chairman: Tan Sri Datuk Amar Haji BUJANG MOHD NOR
Chancellor: Tun Yang Terutama Tun Datuk PATINGGI ABANG HAJI MUHAMMAD SALAHUDDIN
Pro-Chancellor: Yang Amat Berhormat Pehin Sri Dr Haji ABDUL TAIB MAHMUD
Vice-Chancellor: Prof. Dr ABDUL RASHID ABDULLAH
Deputy Vice-Chancellors: Prof. Haji SULAIMAN HANAPI (Student Affairs and Alumni), Prof. Dr MOHD AZIB SALLEH (Academic and Internationalization)
Registrar: Prof. Dr HAMSAWI SANI
Library of 108,000 vols, 10,000 journals
Number of teachers: 464
Number of students: 5,675 (5,112 undergraduate, 563 postgraduate)

DEANS

Faculty of Applied and Creative Arts: Assoc. Prof. MOHD FADZIL ABDUL RAHMAN
Faculty of Cognitive Science and Human Development: Prof. Dr Datin NAPSIAH MAHFOZ
Faculty of Computer Science and Information Technology: Assoc. Prof. NARAYANAN KULATHURAMAIYER
Faculty of Economy and Business: Assoc. Prof. Dr SHAZALI ABU MANSOR
Faculty of Engineering: Prof. Dr KHAIRUDDIN AB HAMID
Faculty of Medicine and Health Sciences: Prof. Dr SYAED HASSAN AL MASHOOR
Faculty of Resource Science and Technology: Assoc. Prof. Dr SABDIN MOHD LONG
Faculty of Social Sciences: Assoc. Prof. Dr MUTALIP ABDULLAH

PROFESSORS

ABDULLAH, M. S., Medicine and Health Sciences
AB HAMID, K., Engineering
ABU MANSOR, S., Engineering
AL MASHOOR, S. H., Medicine and Health Sciences
BOHARI, H., Medicine and Health Sciences
GUDUM, H., Medicine and Health Sciences
HADI, Y., Resource Science and Technology

HARUN, W. S. W., Resource Science and Technology

LONG, P. K., Medicine and Health Sciences

MAHFOZ, N., Cognitive Science and Human Development

MALIK, A. S., Medicine and Health Sciences

NGIDANG, D., Social Sciences

SAID, S., Engineering

SINGH, B., Medicine and Health Sciences

THAMBYRAJAH, V., Medicine and Health Sciences

MALAYSIA UNIVERSITY OF SCIENCE AND TECHNOLOGY (MUST)

GL 33 (Ground Fl.), Block C, Kelana Squ., 17 Jl. SS 7/26, 47301, Kelana Jaya, Petaling Jaya, Selangor Darul Ehsan

Telephone: (3) 78801777

Fax: (3) 78801762

E-mail: admin@must.edu.my

Internet: www.must.edu.my

Private control

Academic year: September to June

Postgraduate research univ.

President: Dr OMAR ABDUL RAHMAN

Provost: Dr MOHD NIZAM ISA

Vice-President for Finance and Business Affairs: BADLY SHAH BIN ARIFF SHAH

Registrar and Head of Administration: STEPHEN JOHN LEE

Chief Librarian: JOHARI AFFANDI OMAR

DEANS

Biotechnology: Assoc. Prof. Dr LIM SAW HOON

Construction Engineering and Management: Assoc. Prof. Dr CHAN TOONG KHUAN

Energy and Environment: Asst Prof. Dr SCOTT KENNEDY

Information Technology: Assoc. Prof. Dr NOR ADNAN YAHYA

Materials Science and Engineering: Prof. Dr ZANULDIN AHMAD

Systems Engineering and Management: Asst Prof. Dr ASGARI BEHROOZ

Transportation and Logistics: Assoc. Prof. Dr LEONG CHOON HENG

MULTIMEDIA UNIVERSITY

Jalan Multimedia, 63100 Cyberjaya, Selangor

Telephone: (3) 83125018

Fax: (3) 83125022

E-mail: mkt@mmu.edu.my

Internet: www.mmu.edu.my

Chancellor: Yang Amat Berbahagia Dato' Seri Dr SITI HASMAH BINTI HAJI MOHD ALI

President: Prof. Dr GHAUTH JASMON

DEANS

Faculty of Business and Law (Melaka Campus): Dr HISHAMUDDIN BIN ISMAIL

Faculty of Creative Multimedia (Cyberjaya Campus): Assoc. Prof. Dr ABU HASSAN ISMAIL

Faculty of Engineering (Cyberjaya Campus): Prof. CHUAH HEAN TEIK

Faculty of Engineering and Technology (Melaka Campus): Dr PETER VON BREVERN

Faculty of Information Science and Technology (Melaka Campus): Assoc. Prof. Dr ENG KIONG WONG

Faculty of Information Technology (Cyberjaya Campus): Prof. LEE POH AUN

Faculty of Management (Cyberjaya Campus): Assoc. Prof. Dr MOHD ISMAIL SAYYED AHMAD

UNIVERSITI PENDIDIKAN SULTAN IDRIS
(Sultan Idris Education University)

35900 Tanjong Malim, Perak Darul Ridzuan

Telephone: (5) 4506332

Fax: (5) 4582776

E-mail: admin@upsi.edu.my

Internet: www.upsi.edu.my

Founded 1922

Chancellor: HRH RAJA PERMAISURI PERAK DARUL RIDZUAN TUANKU BAINUN

Vice-Chancellor: Y. Bhg. Prof. Dato' AMINAH AYOB

Deputy Vice-Chancellor (Academic and Int. Affairs): Prof. Dr ZAKARIA KASA

Deputy Vice-Chancellor (Student Affairs and Alumni): Y. Bhg. Prof. Dr SHAHARUDIN ABDUL AZIZ

Deputy Vice-Chancellor (Research and Innovation): Y. Bhg. Prof. Dr MOHD. MUSTAMAM ABD. KARIM

Registrar: Y. Bhg. Dato' RUSLEY BIN TAIB

Chief Bursary: HAJJAH KHADIJAH HAMDAN

Chief Librarian: CIK ZAHARIAH BINTI MOHAMED SHAHAROON

DEANS

Faculty of Art and Music: Dr MOHD. HASSAN ABDULLAH

Faculty of Business and Economics: Dr NORLIA MAT NORWANI

Faculty of Cognitive Science and Human Development: Assoc.Prof. Dr ABDUL LATIF HJ. GAPOR

Faculty of Information and Communication Technology: Prof. Dr MOHAMAD IBRAHIM

Faculty of Languages: Dr ABDUL GHANI ABU

Faculty of Science and Technology: Assoc. Prof. Dr MUSTAFFA AHMAD

Faculty of Social Sciences and Humanities: IBRAHIM HASHIM

Faculty of Sports Sciences: Dr MOHD. SANI MADON

Institute of Graduate Studies: Prof. Dr OMAR ABDULL KAREEM

UNIVERSITI PUTRA MALAYSIA
(Putra University, Malaysia)

43400 Serdang, Selangor Darul Ehsan

Telephone: (3) 89486101

Fax: (3) 89483244

E-mail: cans@admin.upm.edu.my

Internet: www.upm.edu.my

Founded 1971

State control

Languages of instruction: Malay, English

Academic year: May to November (two semesters)

Chancellor: THE GOVERNOR OF PENANG

Vice-Chancellor: Prof. Dato' Dr MOHD ZOHADIE BARDAIE

Deputy Vice-Chancellor for Academic Affairs: Prof. Dr MUHAMAD AWANG

Deputy Vice-Chancellor for Devt: Assoc. Prof. Dr MAKHDZIR MARDAN

Deputy Vice-Chancellor for Student Affairs: Assoc. Prof. Dr Haji IDRIS ABDOL

Registrar: KAMALUL ARIFFIN MUSA

Librarian: KAMARIAH BT ABDUL HAMID

Number of teachers: 1,074

Number of students: 33,566

Publication: *Tribun Putra* (12 a year)

DEANS

Faculty of Agriculture: Prof. Dr MOHD. YUSOF HUSSEIN

Faculty of Computer Science and Information Technology: Dr ABD. AZIM BIN ABD. GHANI

Faculty of Design and Architecture: Assoc. Prof. Dr MUSTAFA KAMAL

Faculty of Economics and Management: Prof. Dr NIK MUSTAFA RAJA ABDULLAH

Faculty of Educational Studies: Assoc. Prof. KAMARIAH BT ABU BAKAR

Faculty of Engineering: Prof. Dr Ir. RADIN UMAR RADIN SOHADI

Faculty of Food Science and Biotechnology: Prof. Dr GULAM RUSUL BIN RAHMAT ALI

Faculty of Forestry: Prof. Dato' Dr NIK MUHAMAD NIK MAJID

Faculty of Human Ecology: Prof. Dr ABDULLAH AL-HADI HJ. MUHAMED

Faculty of Medicine and Health Sciences: Assoc. Prof. Dr JAMMAL AHMAD ESSA

Faculty of Modern Languages and Communication: Prof. Dr SHAIK MOHD NOOR ALAM SHAIK MOHD HUSSEIN

Faculty of Science and Environmental Studies: Prof. Dr WAN ZIN WAN YUNUS

Faculty of Veterinary Medicine: Prof. Dato' Dr Sheik OMAR ABDUL RAHMAN

School of Graduate Studies: Prof. Dr AINI IDERIS

External Programme Centre: Assoc. Prof. Dr ABDUL AZIZ SAHAREE (Dir)

Graduate School of Management: Assoc. Prof. ZAINAL ABIDIN KIDAM

Institute for Distance Education and Learning: Assoc. Prof. AZAHARI ISMAIL (Dir)

Islamic Centre: Assoc. Prof. Dr Haji MUHD. FAUZI BIN MOHAMAD (Dir)

UNIVERSITI SAINS MALAYSIA
(University of Science, Malaysia)

Minden, 11800 Penang

Telephone: (4) 6533888

Fax: (4) 6565401

E-mail: kpp_pnc@notes.usm.my

Internet: www.usm.my

Founded 1969

Federal control

Languages of instruction: Malay, English

Academic year: June to June

Chancellor: HM Queen Tuanku FAUZIAH BINTI ALMARHUM TENGKU ABDUL RASHID

Pro-Chancellors: Hon. Tan Sri RAZALI ISMAIL, Hon. Tan Sri Datuk Dr LIN SEE YAN

Vice-Chancellor: Hon. Prof. Dato' DZULKIFLI ABDUL RAZAK

Deputy Vice-Chancellors: Hon. Dato' Prof. MUHAMMAD IDIRIS SALEH, Hon Dato' Prof. SYED AHMAD HUSSEIN, Hon. Dato' Assoc. Prof. JAMALUDIN MOHAIADIN

Registrar: AZMAN ABDULLAH

Library: see Libraries and Archives

Number of teachers: 1,528

Number of students: 27,325 (21,744 undergraduate, 5,581 postgraduate)

Publications: *Frontiers* (3 a year), *Graduate Infolink* (3 a year), *Kejuruteran* (3 a year), *Mediskop* (3 a year), *Perantara* (3 a year)

DEANS

School of Aerospace Engineering: ILLYIA MOHAMAD YUSOF

School of Arts: Dr MOHAMAD NAJIB AHMAD DAWA

School of Biological Sciences: Prof. MASHHOR MANSOR

School of Chemical Engineering: Assoc. Prof. ABDUL LATIF AHMAD

School of Chemical Sciences: Assoc. Prof. WAN AHMAD KAMIL MAHMOOD

School of Civil Engineering: Assoc. Prof. WAN JASHIM WAN IBRAHIM

School of Communications: Dr MOHAMED ZIN NORDIN

School of Computer Sciences: Assoc. Prof. ROSNI ABDULLAH MUSTAFA

School of Dentistry: Assoc. Prof. AB. RANI SAMSUDIN

School of Distance Education: OMAR MAJID

School of Education Studies: Assoc. Prof. AMINAH AYOB
School of Electrical and Electronics Engineering: Assoc. Prof. OTHMAN SIDEK
School of Health Sciences: Assoc. Prof. ZAINUL F. ZAINUDDIN
School of Housing, Building and Planning: Prof. MAHYUDDIN RAMLI
School of Humanities: Assoc. Prof. NORIZAN MOHD NOOR
School of Industrial Technology: Prof. WAN ROSLI WAN DAUD
School of Management: Hon. Dato' Prof. DAING MOHAMAD NASIR DAING IBRAHIM
School of Materials and Mineral Resources Engineering: Assoc. Prof. KHAIRUN AZIZI MOHD AZIZLI
School of Mathematical Sciences: Assoc. Prof. AHMAD IZANI MD ISMAIL
School of Mechanical Engineering: Prof. ABDUL AZIZ BABA
School of Medical Sciences: Assoc. Prof. ZABIDI AZHAR MOHD HUSSIN
School of Pharmaceutical Sciences: Assoc. Prof. ABAS HUSSIN
School of Physics: Assoc. Prof. HASLAN ABU HASSAN
School of Social Sciences: Assoc. Prof. ABDUL RAHIM IBRAHIM
Biomedical and Health Sciences Platform: Prof. NORAZMI MOHAMAD NOOR
Clinical Platform: Prof. WAN MOHAMAD WAN BEBAKAR
Engineering and Technology Platform: Assoc. Prof. AHMAD FARHAN MOHAMAD SADULLAH
Fundamental Science Platform: Prof. ABDUL AZIZ TAJUDIN
Information and Communication Technology Platform: Prof. ZAHARIN YUSOFF
Life Sciences Platform: Prof. MOHAMED ISA ABDUL MAJID
Institute of Postgraduate Studies: Prof. AHMAD SHUKRI MUSTAPA KAMAL

DIRECTORS

Advanced Medical and Dental Institute: Dr RAMLI SAAD
Centre for Archaeological Research Malaysia: Hon. Dato' Prof. STIL ZURAINA ABDUL MAJID
Centre for Instructional Technology and Multimedia: Assoc. Prof. WAN MOHAMAD FAUZY WAN ISMAIL
Centre for Knowledge, Communication and Technology: Prof. AHMAD YUSOFF HASSAN
Centre for Languages and Translation: Dr NORISHAM MOHAMAD
Centre for Marine and Coastal Studies: Prof. ZUBIR DIN
Centre for Policy Research: Prof. MUHAMAD JANTAN
Corporate Development Division: Assoc. Prof. OMAR OSMAN
Doping Control Centre: Prof. AISHAH ABDUL LATIFF
Drug Research Centre: Prof. SHARIF MAHSUFI MANSOR
Health Campus: Hon. Prof. Dato' MAFAUZY MOHAMAD
Health Centre: Dr NURULAIN ABDULLAH BAYANUDDIN
Human Genome Centre (Virtual): (vacant)
Institute for Research in Molecular Medicine: Prof. ASMA ISMAIL
IPv6 Centre of Excellence: Assoc. Prof. SURESEWAN RAMADASS
Islamic Centre: NASIRUN MOHAMAD SALLEH
Museum and Art Gallery: HASNUL JAMAL SAIDON
National Poison Centre: Assoc. Prof. RAHMAT AWANG
River Engineering and Urban Drainage Research Centre: Assoc. Prof. NOR AZAZI ZAKARIA
University Hospital: Dr ZAIDUN KAMARI

University Hospital: Dr RAMLI SAAD
USAINS Holding: Hon. Dato' Dr GAN EE KIANG
Women's Development Research Centre: Hon. Datin Assoc. Prof. RASHIDAH SHUIB

PROFESSORS

ABDUL AZIZ, B., Medical Oncology, Haematology and Palliative Medicine
ABDUL AZIZ, T., Radiation Biophysics, Medical Physics
ABDUL GHANI, S., Urban and Regional Planning
ABDUL RASHID, A. R., Clinical Pharmacology and Therapeutics
ABDUL WAHAB, A. R., Vector Ecology
AB RANI, S., Maxillofacial Surgery, Tissue Banking, Bone Banking
ABU HASSAN, A., Mosquito and Urban Pest Control, Aquatic Insect, Insect Ecology
ABU TALIB, A., South-east Asian History
AHMAD PAUZI, M. Y., Physiology
AHMAD SHUKRI, M. K., Radiation Biophysics, Medical Physics
AHMAD YUSOFF, H., Mechanical Computer-Aided Engineering, CAD-CAM
AISHAH, A. L., Pharmacology
AMBIGAPATHY, P., English as a Second Language and Sociolinguistics
AMINAH, A., Science Education
AMIR HUSSIN, B., Economics
ASMA, I., Medical Microbiology, Molecular Biology of Infectious Diseases, Rapid Diagnosis of Infectious Diseases esp. Typhoid and Paratyphoid Fevers
BAHARUDDIN, S., Plant Pathology
BAHRUDDIN, S., Chemical Resistance Measurements
BOEY, P. L., Palm Oil Chemistry and Technology
CHAN, K. L., Pharmaceutical Chemistry
CHAN, N. W., Water Resources, Hydrology and Flood Hazard Management, Climatology
CHONG, C. S., Biophysics
DAING MOHD NASIR, D. I., Accounting, Business Administration
DZULKIFLI, A. R., Pharmacology
FARID, G., Digital and Data Communication
FUN, H. K., Solid State Physics
GOON, W. K., Environmental Studies, Mangrove Ecosystem, Tropical Rain Forest
HANAFI, I., Plastic Composite and Rubber
HARBINDAR JEET SINGH, G. S., Calcium Metabolism
HASSAN, S., Applied Mathematics
IBRAHIM, C. O., Biotechnology
IBRAHIM, W., Transport Planning
ILYAS, M., Geophysics
ITAM, S., Medical Parasitology and Entomology
JAFRI MALIN, A., Neurosurgery
JAMIL, I., Polymers
JEYARATNAM, K., Policy Studies
JUNAIDAH, O., Scattering of Electromagnetic Waves
KAMARULAZIZI, I., Semiconductor Energy Studies, Clean Room Fabrication Technology
KOH, H. L., Environmental and Ecosystem Modelling EIA Simulation
LEE, C. Y., Geophysics Exploration, Applied Geophysics
LIM, K. O., Biophysics
LIM, P. E., Waste Water Treatment
LOH, K. W., Economics
MAFAUZY, M., Endocrinology, Effect of Natural Products on Diabetes
MAHYUDDIN, R., Building Technology
MASHHOR, M., Botany
MASHUDI, K., Linguistics
MD SALLEH, Y., Literature
MOHAMAD AZEMI, M. N., Food Technology
MOHAMAD, S., Literature
MOHAMED, S., Marketing
MOHAMED GHOUSE, N., Theatre and Dance

MOHAMED ISA, A. M., Biodegradable Plastics, Biotechnology
MOHAMED OMAR, K., Environmental Technology
MOHAMED RAZALI, S., Social Psychiatry and Rehabilitation
MOHAMED SHUKRI, S., Planning and Development Management
MOHAMMAD MAHFOOZ, A. A., Management
MORSHIDI, S., Urban Planning and Development
MUHAMAD, J., Management Science, Statistics, Operations Management
MUHAMMAD IDIRIS, S., Analytical Chemistry
MUSTAFFA, E., Medicine
NAVARATNAM, V., Clinical Pharmacology
NOR HAYATI, O., Surgical Pathology with special interest in Gynaepathology, Dermatopathology and Oncopathology
NORZAMI, M. N., Immunology
OMAR, S., Inorganic Chemistry
ONG, B. H., Computer-aided Geometric Design
OSMAN, M., Marketing
PLOTNIKOV IOURI, P., Flight Dynamics and Control Systems, Applied Optimal Control
POH, B. L., Organic Chemistry
QUAH, S. H., Applied Mathematics
RADZALI, O., Materials and Bioceramics Engineering
RAHMAT, A., Clinical Pharmacy and Toxicology
RAMLI, M., Persuasive Communication
ROGAYAH, J., Curricular Development and Problem-based Learning
ROSHADA, H., Biomedical Analysis
ROSHIHAN, M. A., Quality Control
ROZHAN, M. I., Solid State Physics
ROZMAN, D., Chemistry of Wood
RUSLAN, R., Geographic Information Systems
RUSLI, N., Public Health, Islamic Occupational and Health Medicine, AIDS Prevention and Counselling, Islamic Perspectives in Medicine and Health, Occupational Health and Safety
SARINGAT, B., Quality Control Tablets, Capsules, Herbal Formulations
SEETHARAMU, K. N., Heat Transfer, Computational Fluid Dynamics, Stress Analysis
SHARIF MAHSUFI, M., Pharmacokinetics, Drug Metabolism
SITI ZURAINA, A. M., Anthropology and Sociology
SUBASH, B., Chemical Reaction Engineering, Zeolite Catalysis, Environmental Catalysis, Process Design and Development
SUKOR, K., Poverty-focussed Micro-credit Programme
SURESH, N., Economics
SYED IDRIS, S. H., Communications, Radar Systems, Microwave, Antenna and Propagation
SYED MOHSIN, S. S. J., Pharmacology
TENG, C. S., Chemical Engineering
TEOH, S. G., Inorganic and Organo-metallic Chemistry
WAN ABDUL MANAN, W. M., Nutrition, Public Health and Quality of Life
WAN MOHAMAD, W. B., Endocrinology, Impaired Glucose Tolerance Test
WAN ROSLI, W. D., Paper Technology
YUEN, K. H., Pharmaceutical Technology
ZABIDI AZHAR, H., Paediatric Neurology
ZAHARIN, Y., Computational Linguistics and Algebraic Geometry
ZAINAL ABIDIN, A., Electroplating, Waste Water Treatment
ZAINAL ARIFIN, A., Materials, Ceramics
ZAINAL ARIFIN, M. I., Polymer Technology
ZAINUL FADZIRUDDIN, Z., Molecular Biology
ZAKARIA, M. A., Colloid Surface and Cement Sciences
ZHARI, I., Pharmaceuticals
ZUBIR, D., Pollution
ZULFIGAR, Y., Coral and Marine Biology
ZULMI, W., Hand and Reconstructive Surgery

UNIVERSITI TEKNOLOGI MALAYSIA
(Malaysia University of Technology)

Skudai, 81310 Johor

Telephone: (7) 5576160
Fax: (7) 5561722
E-mail: pendaftar@utm.my
Internet: www.utm.my

Founded 1904; university status 1972
State control
Languages of instruction: Bahasa Malay, English
Academic year: June to March

Vice-Chancellor (President): Datuk Prof. Ir. Dr Mohd Zulkifki Tan Sri Mohd Ghazali
Deputy Vice-Chancellors: Prof. Dr Azman Hj. Awang (Academic), Prof. Ir. Dr Mohd Azraai Kassim (Development), Dato' Prof. Dr Hj. Mohamed Mansor Abdullah (Student Affairs)
Registrar: Rahani Abu Bakar
Librarian: Rosna Taib
Library: see Libraries and Archives
Number of teachers: 1,633
Number of students: 31,529

Publication: *Journal of Technology* (in 6 series, each 2 a year)

DEANS

Faculty of Built Environment: Prof. Dr Supian Ahmad
Faculty of Chemical and Natural Resources Engineering: Prof. Dr Ahmad Kamal b. Idris
Faculty of Civil Engineering: Assoc. Prof. Dr Ir. Hasanan Md Nor
Faculty of Computer Science and Information Systems: Prof. Dr Ahmad Zaki Abu Bakar
Faculty of Education: Prof. Dr Abu Bakar Hj. Hashim
Faculty of Electrical Engineering: Prof. Dr Ahmad Darus
Faculty of Geoinformation Engineering and Science: Prof. Dr Mohd Ibrahim Seeni Mohamad
Faculty of Management and Human Resources Development: Assoc. Prof. Dr Mohd Taib Hj. Dora
Faculty of Mechanical Engineering: Prof. Dr Alias Mohd Noor
Faculty of Science: Prof. Dr Hj. Rashidi Md Razali
School of Graduate Studies: Prof. Dr Rahmalan Ahmad
School of Professional and Continuing Education: Prof. Dr Bahrom Sanugi

UNIVERSITI TEKNOLOGI MARA

40450 Shah Alam, Selangor, Darul Ehsan

Telephone: (3) 55442000
Fax: (3) 55442223
E-mail: webadmin@www.uitm.edu.my
Internet: www.uitm.edu.my

Founded 1956 as Dewan Latihan RIDA; became Maktab MARA 1965 and Institut Teknologi MARA 1967; present name 1999
Academic year: May to April

Vice-Chancellor: Dato' Seri Prof. Dr Ibrahim Abu Shah

Number of teachers: 4,200
Number of students: 100,000

Publications: *Accountancy Newsletter*, *Info UiTM*, *International Research Journal*

DEANS

Faculty of Accountancy: Prof. Dr Hj. Ibrahim Kamal Abdul Rahman
Faculty of Administration and Law: Prof. Madya Ramla Binti Mohd Noh
Faculty of Applied Science: Prof. Madya Dr Ahmad Sazali Hamzah

Faculty of Architecture, Planning and Surveying: Prof. Madya Dr Mohamed Yusoff Abbas
Faculty of Art and Design: Prof. Madya Dr Baharudin Ujang
Faculty of Business and Management: Prof. Madya Dr Jamil Hamali
Faculty of Chemical Engineering: Prof. Madya Dr Sharifah Aishah Ayed A. Kadir
Faculty of Civil Engineering: Prof. Madya Ir Dr Hj. Mohd Yusof Abd Rahman
Faculty of Communication and Media Studies: Prof. Madya Alias Md Salleh
Faculty of Education: Prof. Dr Hazadiah Mohd Dahan
Faculty of Electrical Engineering: Prof. Madya Dr Yusof Md Salleh
Faculty of Health Science: Prof. Dr Abd Rahim Md Noor
Faculty of Hotel and Tourism Management: En Abdul Aziz Abdul Majid
Faculty of Information Science: Prof. Madya Dr Laili Hj Hashim
Faculty of Information Technology and Quantitative Science: Prof. Madya Azizi Ngah Tasir
Faculty of Mechanical Engineering: Prof. Madya Dr Shanrani Anuar
Faculty of Medicine: Y. Bhg Dato' Prof. Dr Khalid Yusof
Faculty of Office Management and Technology: Prof. Madya Dr Halimaton Hj. Khalid
Faculty of Performing Arts: Prof. Madya Md Rushdie Kubon Md Shariff
Faculty of Pharmacy: Prof. Dr Abu Bakar Abd Majeed (acting)
Faculty of Sports Science and Recreation: Prof. Madya Dr Muhd Kamil Ibrahim
Centre for Graduate Studies: Datin Zubaidah Alsree

UNIVERSITI TEKNOLOGI PETRONAS

31750 Bandar Seri Iskandar, Tronoh, Perak Darul Ridzuan

Telephone: (5) 3688000
Fax: (5) 3654075
E-mail: utp@petronas.com.my
Internet: www.utp.edu.my

Founded 1995 as Institute of Technology Petronas; present name 1997.

UNIVERSITI TENAGA NASIONAL

Km. 7 Jalan Kajang-Puchong, 43009 Kajang, Selangor

Telephone: (3) 89212020
Fax: (3) 89263504
E-mail: charles@uniten.edu.my
Internet: www.uniten.edu.my

Founded 1976 as Institut Latihan Sultan Ahmad Shah; re-named Tenaga Nasional Berhad 1990 and Institut Kerjuruteraan Teknologi Tenaga Nasional 1994; present name 1997
Private control
Languages of instruction: English, Malay
Academic year: June to May

Vice-Chancellor: Prof. Ir Dr Zainul Abidin Mohd Sharrif
Deputy Vice-Chancellor for Academics: Prof. Ir Dr Zainul Abidin Mohd Sharrif
Deputy Vice-Chancellor for Management: Dr Mohd Zamzam Jaafar
Special Adviser to the Vice-Chancellor: Prof. Ir Dr Syed Abdul Kader Al Junid
Registrar: Dr Tengku Aziz Tengku Zainal
Librarian: Suhaimi haji Abu Hassan

Library of 73,846 vols
Number of teachers: 350
Number of students: 6,500 (6,240 undergraduate, 260 postgraduate)

DEANS

College of Business Management: Dr Hj. Shaari Mohd Nor
College of Engineering: Dr Ibrahim Hussein
College of Information Technology: Dr Zainuddin Hassan (Deputy Dean)
Institute of Liberal Studies: Prof. Datin Dr Hj. Kobkua Suwannathat-Pian
Bandar Muadzam Shah Branch Campus: Prof. Dr Zulkifli Abdul Hamid (Provost)

UNIVERSITI UTARA MALAYSIA
(Northern University of Malaysia)

06010 UUM Sintok, Kedah Darul Aman

Telephone: (4) 9284000
Fax: (4) 9283046
Internet: www.uum.edu.my

Founded 1984
State control
Languages of instruction: Malay, English
Academic year: July to June (2 semesters)

Chancellor: HRH The Sultan of Kedah
Vice-Chancellor: Tan Sri Dato' Seri Dr Abdul Hamid Pawanteh, Tun Dato' Seri Dr Ahmad Fairuz Dato' Sheikh Abdul Halim
Deputy Vice-Chancellor for Academic Affairs: Assoc. Prof. Dr Abdul Razak Chik
Deputy Vice-Chancellor for Development: Prof. Dr Dahlan Ismail
Deputy Vice-Chancellor (Student Affairs): Assoc. Prof. Dr Ahmad Faiz Hamid
Bursar: Amron Man
Registrar: Harun Amin
Chief Librarian: Rodziah Hashim

Number of teachers: 1,219
Number of students: 23,623

Publications: *International Journal of Management Studies*, *International Journal of Banking and Finance*, *Journal of Technology and Operation Management*, *Journal of International Studies*, *Jurnal Pembangunan Sosial* (Journal of Social Development), *Malaysian Management Journal*, *Malaysian Journal of Learning and Instruction*, *Malaysian Journal of Language and Communication*, *Mutakhir* (52 a year), *REKAYASA*, *Utara Management Journal*, *Uniutama* (4 a year)

DEANS

College of Arts and Sciences: Assoc. Prof. Azmi Shaari
College of Business Studies: Prof. Dr Nasruddin Zainudin
College of Law, Government and International Studies: Assoc. Prof. Dr Siti Alida John Abdullah

DIRECTORS

Centre of Quality Management: Prof. Dr Nur Adiana Hiau Abdullah
Centre for University-Industry Link: Assoc. Prof. Dr Shahizan Hassan
Computer Centre: Assoc. Prof. Nazib Nordin
Executive Development Centre: Assoc. Prof. Dr Hamzah Dato' Abdul Rahman
Language Centre: Datin Dr Minah Harun
Institute of Tun Dr. Mahathir's Thoughts: Prof. Dr Abdul Rahman Abdul Aziz
Professional and Continuing Education Centre: Dr Sa'ari Ahmad
UUM Kuala Lumpur: Mohmad Amin Mad Idris

Colleges

Cooperative College of Malaysia: 103 Jl. Templer, 46700 Petaling Jaya, Selangor; tel. (3) 7574911; fax (3) 7570434; e-mail mkm@mkm.edu.my; f. 1956; provides in-service and pre-service training; Diploma and Certificate courses in cooperative management; specialized courses in business management, accounting, computer studies, cooperative management; library: 30,000 vols; 2,905 students; Dir ARMI HJ. ZAINUDIN.

Institut Bahasa Melayu Malaysia (Malaysian Institute of the Malay Language): Lembah Pantai, 59990 Kuala Lumpur; tel. (3) 22822389; fax (3) 22826076; internet www2.moe.gov.my/ibmm; f. 1958; 81 teachers; 778 students; offers a 3-year pre-service diploma course, a 14-week in-service course in the teaching of the Malay language by trained teachers; students are selected by the Ministry of Education; also offers short courses of Malay language as a foreign and second language; Principal ENCIK SALLEH BIN MOHD. HUSEIN.

KDU College: Jl. SS 22/41, 47400 Petaling Jaya, Selangor; tel. (3) 77288123; fax (3) 77277096; e-mail best@kdu.edu.my; internet www.kdu.edu.my; f. 1983 as Kolej Damansara Utama; library: 25,300 vols; 250 teachers; 6,000 students; pre-university and foundation courses, diploma courses in business administration, computer science, engineering, hotels and tourism; degrees in business, accounting and finance, economics; CEO Dr YAP CHEE SING; Registrar TAN JING KUAN.

Politeknik Kuching, Sarawak: Km. 22, Jl. Matang, Locked Bag 3094, 93050 Kuching, Sarawak; tel. (82) 428796; fax (82) 428023; f. 1989; library: 10,000 vols; 130 teachers; 1,200 students; diploma and certificate courses in civil, electrical and mechanical engineering and commerce/business, apprentice training in oil, gas and petroleum technology in cooperation with Petronas; Principal AYOB BIN HJ. JOHARI (acting).

Tunku Abdul Rahman College: POB 10979, 50932 Kuala Lumpur; tel. (3) 4214977; fax (3) 4226336; f. 1969; library: 122,715 vols; 290 teachers; 8,123 students; Principal Dr LIM KHAIK LEANG; Registrar CHEE AH KIOW.

Ungku Omar Polytechnic: Dairy Rd, 31400 Ipoh, Perak; tel. (5) 5457656; fax (5) 5471162; f. 1969 with Unesco aid; library: 33,300 vols, 60 periodicals; 549 teachers; 6,451 students; Principal Mej. Ir HAJI MOHAMED ZAKARIA B. MOHD NOOR; Admin. Officer ROFBIAH BT KAMARUDDIN; Librarian NOR AINON B. ZAKARIA.

Yayasan Pengurusun Malaysia (Malaysian Institute of Management): 227 Jl. Ampang, 50450 Kuala Lumpur; tel. (3) 2425255; fax (3) 2643168; f. 1966; MBA, BA, diploma and certificate courses; Pres. Raja Tun MOHAR BIN RAJA BADIOZAMAN; CEO Dr TARCISIUS CHIN; publs *Malaysian Management Review* (2 a year), *Management Newsletter* (4 a year).

MALDIVES

The Higher Education System

The Maldives became fully independent, outside the Commonwealth, on 26 July 1965. The first institution of higher education, the Maldives College of Higher Education, was founded in 1998. All higher, technical and vocational qualifications in the Maldives are awarded by this institution. The first Bachelors degree programme was launched in 2000 and in 2001 the Ministry of Education established the Maldives National Quali-fications Framework. The Maldives Accreditation Board is responsible for quality assurance and accreditation of higher education programmes of study. In 2007 4,388 students were enrolled at Maldives College of Higher Education.

Bachelors degrees are three-year programmes of study. The only postgraduate award is the Graduate Certificate. Technical and vocational education consists of Certificate and Diploma courses run by the Maldives College of Higher Education.

Regulatory and Representative Bodies

GOVERNMENT

Ministry of Education: Ghaazee Bldg, 2nd Floor, Ameer Ahmed Magu, Malé 20-05; tel. 3323262; fax 3321201; e-mail e_sec@ thauleem.net; internet www.moe.gov.mv; Minister ZAHIYA ZAREER.

Ministry of Higher Education, Employ-ment and Social Security: Haveeree Hin-gun, Malé 20-125; tel. 3317172; fax 3331578; e-mail admin@employment.gov.mv; internet www.employment.gov.mv; Minister ABDULLA YAMEEN.

ACCREDITATION

Maldives Accreditation Board: M. Mui-veyodhoshuge, Malé; tel. 3344077; fax 3344079; e-mail hunt778@gmail.com; internet www.mab.gov.mv; f. 2000; attached to Min. of Education, Employment and Social Security; 12 mems; Dir ABDUL HANNAN WAHEED.

Research Institutes

GENERAL

Institute of Islamic Studies: Malé; tel. 3322718; fax 3313953; e-mail rasheed .moosa@thauleem.net; f. 1980; attached to Min. of Education; aims to provide educa-tional opportunities for the country's young people, to encourage the spread of the Arabic language, to provide training and refresher courses for imams, lawyers, judges, and teachers of the Quran and Islamic studies, to promote study of the Quran, to upgrade the Islamic curriculum in accordance with the needs of the country, to publish and translate books on all aspects of Islam; library of 19,000 vols; Dir-Gen. IBRAHIM RASHEED MOOSA; publ. *Al-Manhaj* (1 a year).

National Centre for Linguistic and His-torical Research: Sosun Magu, Malé 20-05, Henveiru; tel. 3323206; fax 3326796; e-mail nclhr@dhivehinet.net.mv; internet www .qaumiyyath.gov.mv; f. 1982; research on history, culture and language of the Republic of Maldives; restoration and preservation of the nation's heritage; preservation and pro-motion of the Dhivehi language; Dir IBRAHIM ZUHOOR; publs *Dhivehinge Tharika* (2 a year), *Faiythoora* (12 a year).

Libraries and Archives

Malé

Islamic Library: Islamic Centre, Medhu-ziyaaraiy Magu, Malé 20-02; tel. 3323623; f. 1985; Islamic Studies and literature; 4,500 vols; Dir Imam AHMED SHATHIR.

National Library: 59 Majeedi Magu, Galolhu, Malé 20131; tel. 3323945; fax 3313712; e-mail info@nlm.gov.mv; internet www.nlm.gov.mv; f. 1945 as the State Library of Maldives, renamed Majeedi Library 1948, present name 1982; attached to Min. of Tourism, Arts and Culture; nat. library colln; public library facilities; recre-ation and research support; preserves nat. literature; 62,520 vols, spec. collns in Dhi-vehi, English, Arabic, Urdu; Dir IBRAHIM SHIYAM; Chief Librarian FATHMATH SHIHAM; publs *Bibliography of Dhivehi Publications*, *Bibliography of English Publications*, *Mathi-fushuge Mauloomaathu* (information on Mal-divian family trees).

Museum

Malé

National Museum: National Centre for Linguistic and Historical Research, Malé 20-05; tel. 3322254; fax 3326796; e-mail nclhr@dhivehinet.net.mv; internet www .geocities.com/bnaseem/welcome.htm; f. 1952; conservation and display of historical items; Senior Curator ALI WAHEED.

College

Maldives College of Higher Education: Nikagas Magu, Machchangolhi, Malé; tel. 3345155; fax 3315411; internet www.mche .edu.mv; f. 1998; academic year January to November (2 terms); campuses at Hithadhoo (2), Kulthudhuffushi and Thinadhoo; Facul-ties of education, engineering technology, health sciences, hospitality and tourism studies, management and computing, Shari'a and law; centres of maritime studies, open learning; Vice-Rector for Admin. HUSSAIN HALEEM.

MALI

The Higher Education System

Mali, the former French colony of Soudan, became an independent state in 1960, following the secession of Senegal from the Federation of Mali, founded in 1959. Tertiary education facilities include the national Université de Bamako (founded 1993) and several colleges of higher education. Many students also receive higher education abroad, mainly in France and Senegal. In 2004/05 there were 32,600 students enrolled at the Université de Bamako.

The Ministry of Higher Education and Scientific Research controls higher education, but the state-run Université de Bamako is financially autonomous. The University Council is the policy-making body of the Université and the Rector acts as chief executive. The main academic divisions are the Colleges, Schools and Institutes.

The secondary school Baccalauréat is the main requirement for admission to higher education. The first (undergraduate) stage of higher education lasts four years in most fields and leads to the award of a Diplôme; some disciplines such as medicine and pharmacy last five to six years. Students at the Ecoles are awarded specialist Diplômes, depending on the field of study. The second (postgraduate) level of higher education is the two-year Diplôme d'Etudes Approfondies, which is only offered by the Institut Supérieur pour la Formation et la Recherche Appliquée, and the three-year Doctorat Malien research degree, awarded after submission of a thesis.

Post-secondary technical and vocational education consists of programmes of study and professional training leading to the award of Brevet de Technicien, Diplôme de Technicien Supérieur and Diplôme des Sciences Appliquées.

Regulatory Bodies

GOVERNMENT

Ministry of Culture: Quartier du Fleuve, Bamako; tel. 223-26-44; fax 490-03-46; e-mail info@culture.gov.ml; internet www.maliculture.net; Minister MOHAMMED EL MOCTAR.

Ministry of Higher Education and Scientific Research: BP 71, Bamako; tel. 222-57-80; fax 222-21-26; e-mail info@education.gov.ml; internet www.education.gov.ml; Minister AMADOU TOURÉ.

Learned Society

GENERAL

UNESCO Office Bamako: Badalabougou Est, BP E 1763 Bamako; tel. 223-34-92; fax 223-34-94; e-mail bamako@unesco.org; designated Cluster Office for Burkina Faso, Mali and Niger; Dir AHMED OULD DEIDA.

Research Institutes

GENERAL

Centre National de la Recherche Scientifique et Technologique: BP 3052, Bamako; tel. 222-90-85; f. 1986; coordinates all research activity in Mali; 57 research instns, 443 staff; Dir-Gen. Dr MAMADOU DIALLO IAM; publs *Revue Malienne de Science et de Technologie* (1 a year), *Vie de la Recherche* (4 a year).

Institut de Recherche pour le Développement (IRD): BP 2528, Bamako; tel. 221-05-01; fax 221-64-44; e-mail granjon@sahel.ird.ml; environmental and social sciences for development; library of 4,000 books and journals; Dir JOSEPH BRUNET-JAILLY; (see main entry under France); publ. *Actualités de la Recherche au Mali* (6 a year).

AGRICULTURE, FISHERIES AND VETERINARY SCIENCE

Centre National de Recherches Fruitières: BP 30, Bamako; f. 1962; controls experimental plantations, phytopathological laboratory, technological laboratory and pilot schemes; Dir P. JEANTEUR.

Centre National de Recherches Zootechniques: BP 262, Bamako; f. 1927; experimental farm with sections on genetics (bovine, swine, poultry), nutrition and biochemistry, pasture, veterinary medicine; library of 1,000 vols; Dir Dr FERNAND TRAORE.

Centres de Recherche Rizicole: 2 rice research centres at Kankan and Ibetemi.

Institut de Recherches Agronomiques Tropicales et des Cultures Vivrières (IRAT): BP 438, Bamako; f. 1962; controls stations at Bamako, Koulikoro, Kogoni par Nioro, Ibetemi (Mopti), and sub-stations at Kita and Koporokenie-Pe; general agronomy, land amelioration, cultivation techniques, fertilization needs, plant breeding (sorghum, pennisetum, short and floating rices, maize, wheat, groundnuts and formerly sugar cane); Dir M. THIBOUT; (see main entry under France).

Institut du Sahel: BP 1530, Bamako; tel. 222-21-48; fax 222-59-80; e-mail administration@insah.org; internet www.insah.org; f. 1976; a specialized institution of the Comité de Lutte contre la Sécheresse dans le Sahel (CILSS); aims to combat effects of drought and achieve food security in the Sahel (consisting of Burkina Faso, Cape Verde, The Gambia, Guinea-Bissau, Mali, Mauritania, Niger, Senegal, Chad) through the promotion and coordination of research, circulating scientific and technical information; library of 12,000 vols, 240 periodicals; Dir Gen. MOUSTAPHA AMADOU; publs *Actes, Etudes & Travaux, Etudes et Recherches, Recherche et Développement*.

Office du Niger: BP 106, Ségou; tel. 232-02-92; fax 232-01-41; f. 1932, taken over by Mali govt 1958; research stations at Bougomi and Sahel (cotton), Kayo (rice), Soninkoura (fruit); Dir-Gen. NANCOMA KEITA.

MEDICINE

Institut Marchoux: BP 251, Bamako; tel. 222-51-31; fax 222-95-44; f. 1935; part of *Organisation de Co-ordination et de Coopération pour la Lutte contre les Grandes Endémies* (q.v.); medical research, teaching, treatment and epidemiology, specializing in leprosy; Dir SOMITA KEITA.

Institut d'Ophtalmologie Tropicale de l'Afrique de l'Ouest Francophone: BP 248, Bamako; tel. 222-27-22; fax 222-51-86; e-mail iota@malinet.ml; f. 1953; research in tropical eye diseases and prevention of blindness, training courses for technicians and doctors specializing in ophthalmology; Dir Prof. ABDOULAYE DIALLO.

NATURAL SCIENCES

Physical Sciences

Direction Nationale de la Météorologie: BP 237, Bamako; tel. and fax 229-21-01; e-mail dnm@afribone.net.ml; library of 1,265 vols; Dir K. KONARE; publs *Bulletin Agrométéorologique, Bulletin Climatologique* (12 a year).

TECHNOLOGY

Société Nationale de Recherches et d'Exploitation des Ressources Minières de Mali (SONAREM), Service de Documentation: BP 2, Kati; tel. 222-41-84; fax 222-21-60; f. 1961; geology, mining (gold mining in Kalana, phosphates in Bourem), hydrogeology; 5 staff; library of 5,000 vols; Dir DAOUDA DIAKITE.

Libraries and Archives

Bamako

Bibliothèque Nationale du Mali: BP 159, Ave Kassé Keïta, Bamako; tel. 222-49-63; f. 1913; 60,000 vols, 2,000 current periodicals; Dir MAMADOU KONOBA KEÏTA.

Attached Institution:

Archives Nationales du Mali: Koulouba, Bamako; tel. 222-58-44; f. 1913; Archivist LAMINE CAMARA.

Centre Culturel Français: Blvd de l'Indépendance, BP 1547, Bamako; tel. 222-40-19; fax 222-58-28; e-mail ccfmedia@afribone.net.ml; internet www.ccfbamako.org; f. 1962; public library of 27,000 vols; Dir NICOLE SEURAT.

Timbuktu

Centre d'Etudes, de Documentation et de Recherches Historiques 'Ahmed Baba' (CEDRAB): BP 14, Timbuktu; tel. and fax 292-10-81; f. 1970; to preserve the historical heritage of the region; collects and conserves Arabic MSS; 15,000 archives; Dir MOHAMED GALLAH DICKO.

Museum

Bamako

Musée National du Mali: BP 159, Bamako; tel. 222-34-86; fax 223-19-09; e-mail musee@malinet.ml; library of 1,900 vols; Dir Dr SAMUEL SIDIBE.

University

UNIVERSITÉ DE BAMAKO

BP 2528, Rue Baba Diarra Porte 113, Bamako

Telephone: 222-19-33
Fax: 222-19-32
E-mail: universiteaml@refer.org
Internet: www.ml.refer.org/univ-mali

Founded 1993 as Université de Mali; present name 2005
State control
Language of instruction: French
Rector: SIBY GINETTE BELLEGARDE
Number of teachers: 510
Number of students: 11,250

DEANS
Faculty of Law and Economics: ANTOINE FERNAND CAMARA
Faculty of Letters, Languages, Arts and Humanities: DRISSA DIAKITE
Faculty of Medicine, Pharmacy and Dentistry: MOUSSA TRAORÉ
Faculty of Science and Technology: ABDOUL KARIM SANOGO
School of Administration: (vacant)
School of Engineering: MOUSSA KANTE (Dir)
School of Teacher Training: BOUBA DIARRA (Dir)

Colleges

Ecole des Hautes Etudes Pratiques: BP 242, Bamako; tel. 222-21-47; f. 1974, present name 1979; diploma courses in accountancy, business studies; 35 teachers; 471 students; Dir-Gen. SIDI MOHAMED TOURE.

Ecole Nationale d'Ingénieurs: BP 242, Bamako; tel. 222-21-47; Dir MAMADOU DIAKITE.

Ecole Normale Supérieure: BP 241, Bamako; tel. 222-21-89; f. 1962; 150 teachers; 1,754 students; Dir SÉKOU B. TRAORÉ; publ. *Cahiers de l'ENSup.*

Faculté de Médecine, de Pharmacie et d'Odonto-Stomatologie: BP 1805, Bamako; tel. 222-52-77; fax 222-96-58; f. 1969 (formerly Ecole Nationale de Médecine et de Pharmacie); library: 6,800 vols, 289 periodicals; 100 teachers; 1,800 students; Dir Prof. ISSA TRAORE; publ. *Mali Médical.*

Faculté des Sciences Juridiques et Economiques: 1185 Ave de la Liberté (Route de Koulouba), BP 276, Bamako; tel. 222-27-19; fax 223-18-95; e-mail sacko@ena.ml; f. 1958 (formerly École Nationale d'Administration); Dean DUSMANE O. SIDIBE; publ. *Cahier du CERES.*

Institut de Productivité et de Gestion Prévisionnelle: BP 1300, Bamako; tel. 222-55-11; f. 1971; library: 3,000 vols; in-service training, business advice; 15 staff; Dir-Gen. SIDIKI TRAORE.

Institut Polytechnique Rural de Katibougou: BP 6, Koulikoro; tel. 226-20-12; f. 1965; teaching and research in agronomy, agricultural economics, stockbreeding, forestry, veterinary science, rural technology; 300 teachers; 12,000 students; Dir-Gen. OUSMANE BELCO TOURE.

MALTA

The Higher Education System

In 1592 the Jesuit Order founded the Collegium Melitense and in 1769 it was elevated to university status by Grandmaster Manoel Pinto de Fonseca; it is now known as the University of Malta (L-Università ta' Malta). From 1814 to 1964 Malta was a Crown Colony of the United Kingdom, before becoming an independent sovereign state, within the Commonwealth, in 1964. Malta became a republic in 1974. Education is governed by the Education Act (1988), which is the responsibility of the Education Division of the Ministry of Education, Culture, Youth and Sport. Education is free at all levels. The Council and the Senate are the supreme governing bodies of the University, which is an autonomous institution funded by the Government. In 2006/07 there were 9,416 students enrolled at the University. Malta participates in the Bologna Process to establish a European Higher Education Area, the first phase of which is to adopt a credit-based system of comparable degrees with two main cycles (undergraduate and graduate).

Admission to the University is on the basis of the Matriculation Certificate Examination. The University operates a US-style 'credit semester' system, under which students have to accrue a minimum number of credits each semester in order to earn a degree. A full-time year of study is usually equivalent to 60 credits. Non-degree university studies last one to two years and result in award of either a Certificate or Diploma. The undergraduate Bachelors degree is classified as either 'Ordinary' or 'Honours': the former requires three years of study, and the latter at least three, usually four. Dual subject Honours degrees require a minimum of four years, and degrees in professional fields of study may last longer, such as medicine (five years) and law (six years). The first postgraduate-level degree at the University is the Masters, which is open to anyone with a Bachelors (Honours) degree of at least second-class classification. A Masters lasts one to two years and may be either a 'research' or a 'taught' degree. Finally the second postgraduate and highest university-level degree is the Doctor of Philosophy, awarded after three to six years of original research and submission of a thesis.

In 2009 draft legislation on further and higher education was being prepared by the Education Ministry to regulate fully private provision by creating the structures to license, accredit and quality-assure further and higher education.

Regulatory and Representative Bodies

GOVERNMENT

Ministry of Education, Employment and Family: Palazzo Ferreria 310, Republic St, Valletta VLT 1110; tel. 25903010; fax 25903121; e-mail mario.p.schiavone@gov.mt; internet www.education.gov.mt; Min. for Education and Culture DOLORES CRISTINA; Permanent Sec. Dr CHRISTOPHER BEZZINA.

ACCREDITATION

ENIC/NARIC Malta: Further Studies and Adult Education, Education Div., Malta Qualification Recognition Information Centre (Malta QRIC), Ministry of Education, Room No 328, Great Siege Rd, Floriana; tel. 21240419; fax 21239842; e-mail qric.malta@gov.mt; internet www.education.gov.mt; Dir ANTHONY DeGIOVANNI.

Kunsill Malti għall Kwalifiki (Malta Qualifications Council): 16/18 Tower Promenade, St Lucia SLC 1019; tel. and fax 27540051; e-mail james.j.calleja@gov.mt; internet www.mqc.gov.mt; f. 2005; 10 mems; Chair. ABELA FITZPATRICK JOSEPH.

Learned Societies

AGRICULTURE, FISHERIES AND VETERINARY SCIENCE

Agrarian Society: Palazzo de la Salle, 219 Triq ir-Repubblika Valletta VLT 1116; tel. 21244339; fax 21246074; agraria@searchmalta.com; f. 1844; 200 mems; Pres. JOSEPH BORG; Hon. Sec. PAUL DeBATTISTA.

ARCHITECTURE AND TOWN PLANNING

Kamra tal-Periti Malta (Chamber of Architects and Civil Engineers): The Professional Centre, Triq Tas-Sliema, Gzira GZR 1633; tel. and fax 21314265; e-mail kamratalperiti@nextgen.net.mt; internet www.ktpmalta.com; f. 1920; mem. of Malta Fed. of Professional Asscns; 570 mems; Pres. DAVID FELICE; publ. *The Architect* (4 a year).

BIBLIOGRAPHY, LIBRARY SCIENCE AND MUSEOLOGY

Malta Library and Information Association (MaLIA): c/o Univ. of Malta Library, Msida MSD 2080; tel. 25997210; fax 25997205; e-mail info@malia-malta.org; internet www.malia-malta.org; f. 1969; professional asscn to safeguard the interests of library and information workers; promotes legislation concerning libraries; holds training courses in library and information science; 125 mems; Chair. LAURENCE ZERAFA; Sec. CALUDIO LAFERLA.

ECONOMICS, LAW AND POLITICS

Malta Society of Arts, Manufactures and Commerce: Palazzo De La Salle, 219 Triq ir-Republika, Valletta VLT 1116; tel. 21244339; fax 21246074; e-mail info@artsmalta.org; internet www.artsmalta.org; f. 1852; Pres. JOSEPH J. MIFSUD; Hon. Sec. STEPHEN SANT ANGELO.

FINE AND PERFORMING ARTS

Malta Cultural Institute: 'La Paloma', 16 Triq Sant'Enriku, Sliema SLM 1321; tel. 21338923; e-mail maltacultinst@yahoo.com; internet maltaculturalinstitute.yolasite.com; f. 1948; concerts, ballet, book presentations, painting and sculpture and ceramic exhibitions; 200 mems; Dir and Concert Coordinator MARIE THERESE VASSALLO; Sec. and Legal Advisor VANESSA MAGRO; Treas. CHARLES AXIAK; Dance Advisor MARY JANE BELLIA; Theatre Advisor RAY MAMO; Theatre Advisor GEOFFREY AXIAK; publ. *MCI Bulletin* (12 a year).

LANGUAGE AND LITERATURE

British Council: Whitehall Mansions, Ix-Xatt Ta' Xbiex, Ta' Xbiex XBX 1026; tel. 23232403; fax 23232402; e-mail information@britishcouncil.org.mt; internet www.britishcouncil.org/malta; offers courses and examinations in English language and British culture and promotes cultural exchange with the UK; Dir RONNIE MICALLEF.

NATURAL SCIENCES

Biological Sciences

Malta Ecological Foundation (ECO): Dar ECO, 10B Triq Sant' Andrija, Valletta VLT 1341; tel. 21641486; fax 21338780; internet www.ecomalta.org; f. 1992; 4,018 mems; library of 5,100 vols; Dir DUNSTAN HAMILTON; publ. *Stakeholder*.

Libraries and Archives

Gozo

Gozo Public Library: Triq Vajringa, Victoria, Gozo VCT 1310; tel. 21556200; fax 21560599; e-mail gozo.libraries@gov.mt; internet www.libraries-archives.gov.mt/gpl; f. 1853, merged with the Royal Malta (now Nat.) Library 1948; nat. and reference library; copyright deposit library; 35,000 vols; Librarian GEORGE V. BORG.

Msida

University of Malta Library: Msida MSD 2080; tel. 21310239; fax 21314306; e-mail dls@um.edu.mt; internet www.um.edu.mt/library; f. 1954 at the Old Univ. bldgs in Valletta; present location 1967; 800,000 vols, 992 print and 20,000 electronic journals; Dir KEVIN J. ELLUL; Deputy Dir JOANNA FELICE.

Valletta

National Library of Malta: POB 2025, Triq it-Tezorerija, Valletta VLT 2000; tel. 21243297; fax 21235992; internet www.libraries-archives.gov.mt/nlm; f. 1555; incorporates the archives of the Order of St John of Jerusalem; Dir PHILIP BORG; publ. *Bibljografija Nazzjonali Malta/Malta National Bibliography* (1 a year).

Museum
Valletta

Sovrintendenza Tal-Patrimonju Kultur-ali (Superintendence of Cultural Heritage): POB 2008, 138 Triq Melita, Valletta VLT 2000; tel. 21230711; fax 21251140; e-mail heritage.superintendence@gov.mt; internet www.culturalheritage.gov.mt; f. 2002, replaces Museums Dept (f. 1903); govt agency; fulfils duties of the state in ensuring the protection and accessibility of Malta's cultural heritage; responsible for all scientific investigation regarding cultural assets such as the conducting of field work and archaeological excavation, and for the full record keeping and management of documentation resulting from such interventions; evaluates art objects, objects of cultural value and collns of such items; advises and coordinates with the Malta Environment and Planning Authority on issues regarding land use and devt to safeguard cultural heritage when considering applications for planning permission; monitors and controls import and export of goods that are of cultural significance, whether the movement is temporary (for example, for exhibition or restoration purposes) or permanent; issues permits needed for such movements; has a number of direct commitments with regional and int. instns relating to the conservation and promotion of Malta's cultural heritage on int. basis; liaises with UNESCO, the Council of Europe and the European Union; participates in European and Euro-Med programmes; responsible for policy, standards, and guidelines related to cultural heritage and regulates heritage management plans; advises govt on heritage matters; Superintendent ANTHONY PACE.

University

UNIVERSITY OF MALTA

Msida, MSD 2080
Telephone: 23402340
Fax: 23402342
E-mail: comms@um.edu.mt
Internet: www.um.edu.mt

Founded as Collegium Melitense 1592, elevated to univ. status by Grandmaster Pinto 1769
Language of instruction: English
Academic year: October to July

Chancellor: Prof. J. RIZZO NAUDI
Pro-Chancellor: Prof. D. J. ATTARD
Rector: Prof. JUANITO CAMILLERI
Pro-Rectors: Prof. R. MUSCAT, Prof. A. J. VELLA, Dr M. A. LAURI
Sec.: S. SAMMUT

Registrar: V. GRECH
Dir of Finance: M. DEBONO
Dir of Library Services: A. MANGION
Library of 800,000 vols, 20,000 periodicals (print and electronic full text)
Number of teachers: 1,333
Number of students: 10,193

Publications: *Journal of Anglo-Italian Studies, Journal of Baroque Studies, Journal of Education, Journal of Maltese Studies, Journal of Mediterranean Studies, Malta Medical Journal, Mediterranean Journal of Educational Studies, Mediterranean Human Rights Journal*

DEANS

Faculty of Arts: Prof. D. FENECH
Faculty for the Built Environment: Prof. A. TORPIANO
Faculty of Dental Surgery: Dr S. CAMILLERI
Faculty of Economics, Management and Accountancy: Dr S. GAUCI
Faculty of Education: Prof. V. SOLLARS
Faculty of Engineering: Prof. R. GHIRLANDO
Faculty of Information and Communication Technology: Dr E. A. CACHIA
Faculty of Laws: Prof. I. REFALO
Faculty of Medicine and Surgery: Prof. G. LaFERLA
Faculty of Science: Prof. C. V. SAMMUT
Faculty of Theology: Rev. Prof. E. AGIUS

MARSHALL ISLANDS

The Higher Education System

The Republic of the Marshall Islands lies within the area of the Pacific Ocean known as Micronesia. In 1947 the UN authorized the USA to administer the Islands within a Trust Territory of the Pacific Islands. The 1986 Compact of Free Association between the Marshall Islands and the USA was renewed in May 2003. The College of the Marshall Islands (which became independent from the College of Micronesia in 1993) is based on Majuro and had an estimated 919 students enrolled in 2002/03. In 1993 the University of the South Pacific opened an extension centre on Majuro. The Fisheries and Nautical Training Centre offers vocational courses for Marshallese seeking employment in the fishing industry or on passenger liners, cargo ships and tankers. The Ministry of Education is responsible for providing higher education.

Regulatory Body

GOVERNMENT

Ministry of Education: POB 3, Majuro 96960; tel. 625-5262; fax 625-3861; e-mail rmimoe@rmimoe.net; internet www.rmimoe.net; Minister NIDEL LORAK.

Learned Societies

NATURAL SCIENCES

Biological Sciences

Marshall Islands Conservation Society: POB 649, Majuro 96960; e-mail info@coralatolls.org; internet www.coralatolls.org; f. to help Marshallese to manage and protect their atoll environments and to use their resources sustainably; promotes community-based fisheries management, protection for endangered species (humphead wrasse, giant groupers, turtles and sharks); organizes community awareness workshops, conservation practitioner and fisheries observer training; monitors live reef food fish trade and aquarium trade exports.

Research Institutes

AGRICULTURE, FISHERIES AND VETERINARY SCIENCE

Marshall Islands Marine Resources Authority (MIMRA): POB 860, Majuro 96960; tel. 625-8262; fax 625-5447; e-mail mimra@ntamar.com; internet www.mimra.com; research and devt to generate awareness and promote involvement of the local population in sustainable management of coastal resources, incl. outer island fish market, community based fisheries management projects; grant aid projects in partnership with Japanese govt.

HISTORY, GEOGRAPHY AND ARCHAEOLOGY

Historic Preservation Office: POB 1454, Majuro 96960; tel. and fax 625-4476; e-mail rmihpo@ntamar.com; internet members.tripod.com/~alelemuseum/hpo.html; f. 1991 by the Historic Preservation Act of 1991 (amended in 1992) to preserve Marshallese culture; operates with advice and assistance from Advisory Council on Historic Preservation; conducts archaeological survey and inventory, outer island surveys, underwater surveys, oral history and ethnography; maintains RMI Register of Historic Places; attached to Cultural Affairs Div., Min. of Internal Affairs; Historic Preservation Officer FREDERICK DEBRUM; Chief Archaeologist RICHARD WILLIAMSON.

Nuclear Institute: Oscar deBrum Memorial Hall, Majuro; f. 1997; promotes research on and public understanding of history of nuclear weapons and their effects on culture and diplomacy, incl. US nuclear testing programme in the Marshall Islands; partnership with Nuclear Studies Institute of the American Univ. (Washington, DC, *q.v.*) incl. exchange programme for students and faculty; attached to College of the Marshall Islands; Dir MARY SILK.

Museum

Majuro

Alele Museum, Library and National Archives: POB 629, Majuro 96960; tel. 625-3372; fax 625-3226; e-mail alele@ntamar.com; internet members.tripod.com/~alelemuseum/; f. 1981; Joachim deBrum Colln of over 2,500 glass-plate negatives showing Marshallese life and landscapes during 1880–1930; Bogan Colln of Marshallese crafts from 1940s; recordings of traditional oral literature, video documentaries on cultural and community themes; organizes annual cultural festival (*Lutok Kobban Alele*); incorporates Nat. Archives, 2,500 microfilms covering Trust Territory of the Pacific Islands, Marshall Islands High Court Proceedings, Congress and *Nitijela* legislation, journal colln, Joachim deBrum Memorial Trust Corpn colln, birth and death certificates; library: incl. Pacific Colln of published and unpublished material specific to the Marshall Islands and Oceania; Curator TERRY MOTE.

University

UNIVERSITY OF THE SOUTH PACIFIC, MARSHALL ISLANDS CAMPUS

POB 3537, Majuro 96960
Telephone: 625-7279
Fax: 625-7282
E-mail: uspmaj@ntamar.com
Internet: www.usp.ac.fj/index.php?id=marshall_centre
Founded 1993
Dir: Dr IRENE TAAFAKI
Sec.: LYDIA TIBON
Number of teachers: 10

Colleges

College of the Marshall Islands: POB 1258, Majuro 96960; e-mail webmaster@cmi.edu; internet www.cmi.edu; f. 1989 as College of Micronesia-Majuro, a constituent body of the Community College of Micronesia; accredited and adopted present name 1991; became independent institution 1993; campuses at Arrak (Marshall Islands Science Station) and at Gugeegue on Kwajalein Atoll; Pres. WILSON G. HESS; library: 15,000 vols, 140 periodicals, CD-ROMs, video cassettes, DVDs, maps, microfilm; spec. collns incl. Micronesian Colln (articles, books, proceedings and reports on the area), Marshall Islands Colln (local flora and fauna, historical and cultural materials); 42 teachers; 903 students.

Fisheries and Nautical Training Centre: POB 860 Majuro 96960; tel. 625-7449; fax 625-6221; e-mail mimra@ntamar.com; offers vocational courses for Marshallese seeking employment in the fishing industry or on passenger liners, cargo ships and tankers; attached to Marshall Islands Marine Resources Authority; Instructor WILLIAM SOKOMI.

MAURITANIA

The Higher Education System

Mauritania, formerly part of French West Africa, achieved full independence on 28 November 1960 (having become a self-governing member of the French Community two years earlier). The earliest institution of higher education was the Institut National des Hautes Etudes Islamiques (founded 1961). Université de Nouakchott, the only university-level institution, was founded in 1981. In 2005/06 there were 10,157 students enrolled in the four higher education institutions. The Ministry of National Education is the responsible government body for higher education, which is free (barring a nominal registration fee).

Université de Nouakchott is governed by the University Assembly, the membership of which is made up from the staff, students and government officials. The University Assembly is headed by the university President or Rector. The Vice-Chancellor is in charge of administration, and the senior academic officers are the Deans, Vice-Deans and General Secretary.

The secondary school Baccalauréat is the main requirement for admission to tertiary education. The university degree system is based on the old-style French model and consists of two cycles. The first cycle lasts for two years and results in award of the Diplôme d'Etudes Universitaires Générales. An exception to this is the Ecole Nationale d'Administration, which awards a Diplôme after five years of study. The second cycle is two years in duration and culminates with the award of the Maîtrise. There are no postgraduate-level degrees; students usually complete their higher education abroad.

The Centre Supérieur d'Enseignement Technique is the leading institution of technical and vocational education, and specializes in mechanical and electrical engineering.

Regulatory Bodies

GOVERNMENT

Ministry of Culture, Youth and Sports: BP 223, Nouakchott; tel. 525-11-30; Minister MOHAMED VALL OULD CHEIKH.

Ministry of National Education: BP 387, Nouakchott; tel. 525-12-37; fax 525-12-22; Minister NEGGHOUHA MINT MOHAMED VALL.

Learned Societies

BIBLIOGRAPHY, LIBRARY SCIENCE AND MUSEOLOGY

Association Mauritanienne des Bibliothécaires, Archivistes et Documentalistes: c/o Bibliothèque Nationale, BP 20, Nouakchott; f. 1979; Pres. O. DIOUWARA; Sec. SID'AHMED FALL.

LANGUAGE AND LITERATURE

Alliance Française: BP 5022, Nouakchott; tel. and fax 525-31-48; e-mail afm@mauritel.mr; offers courses and exams in French language and culture and promotes cultural exchange with France; attached teaching centres in Atar, Kaedi and Nouadhibou.

Research Institutes

GENERAL

Institut Mauritanien de Recherche Scientifique: BP 196, Nouakchott; Dir Prof. MOHAMED LEMINE OULD HAMMADI.

AGRICULTURE, FISHERIES AND VETERINARY SCIENCE

Institut Supérieur des Sciences et Techniques Halieutiques: Nouadhibou-Cansado; tel. 554-90-47; fax 554-90-28; f. 1983; part of Economic Community of West Africa; research and training in the fisheries industry; Dir-Gen. D. SOGUI.

TECHNOLOGY

Direction des Mines et de la Géologie: Ministère des Mines et de l'Industrie, BP 199, Nouakchott; tel. 225-30-83; fax 225-69-37; e-mail mmi@mauritania.mr; f. 1968; 17 mems; library of 3,000 vols; Dir WANE IBRAHIMA LAMINE.

Libraries and Archives

Boutilimit

Arab Library: Boutilimit; library of the late Grand Marabout, Abd Allah Ould Chelkh Sidya.

Chinguetti

Arab Library: Chinguetti; several private religious libraries, with a total of 3,229 vols, including pre-Islamic MSS; Librarian MOHAMED ABDALLAHI OULD FALL.

Kaédi

Arab Library: Kaédi; ancient religious texts.

Nouakchott

Archives Nationales: BP 77, Nouakchott; tel. 225-23-17; fax 225-26-36; f. 1955; 3,000 vols, 1,000 periodicals; documentation centre; Dir NAGI OULD MOHAMED MAHMOUD; publ. Chaab (daily).

Bibliothèque Nationale: BP 20, Nouakchott; f. 1965; deposit library; documentation centre for W Africa; 10,000 vols, 4,000 old MSS; 8 mems; Head Librarian OUMAR DIOUWARA; Historian Prof. MOKTAR OULD HAMIDOU.

Centre de Documentation Pédagogique: BP 171, Nouakchott; f. 1962; 1,000 vols; 58 periodicals; educational and general works; Librarian MOHAMMED SAID.

Oualata

Arab Library: Oualata.

Tidjikja

Arab Library: Tidjikja; Librarian AHMEDOU OULD MOHAMED MAHMOUD.

University

UNIVERSITÉ DE NOUAKCHOTT

BP 798, Nouakchott
Telephone: 525-13-82
Fax: 525-39-97
E-mail: webmaster@univ-nkc.mr
Internet: www.univ-nkc.mr

Founded 1981
State control
Languages of instruction: Arabic, French, English
Academic year: October to June
Rector: MOHAMED EL HACEN OULD LEBATT
Librarian: ISSA OULD MOHAMED AHMED
Library of 20,059 vols
Number of teachers: 254
Number of students: 10,000

Publications: Annales de la Faculté des Lettres et Sciences Humaines (1 a year), Revue d'Études Juridiques et Économiques (1 a year)

DEANS

Faculty of Law and Economics: SIDI MOHAMED ABDELLAHI
Faculty of Letters and Human Sciences: DIALLO IBRAHIMA MOUSSA
Faculty of Science and Technology: AHMEDOH OULD HAOUBA

Colleges

Ecole Nationale d'Administration: BP 252, Nouakchott; tel. 525-32-22; fax 525-75-17; f. 1966; library: 8,000 vols; a documentation and research centre for the study of administration and politics in Mauritania; first degree courses; 33 teachers; 266 students; Librarian YARBA FALL; Dir CHEIK MOHAMED SALEM OULD MOHAMED LEMINE; publs Annales, Futurs Cadres (3 a year).

Institut National des Hautes Etudes Islamiques: Boutilimit; f. 1961; 300 students.

Institut Supérieur Scientifique: BP 5026, Nouakchott; tel. 525-11-68; fax 525-39-97; f. 1986; mathematics, physics, chemistry, biology, geology, computer studies, natural resources, ecology; library: 30,000 vols; Dir AHMEDOU OULD HAMED.

MAURITIUS

The Higher Education System

Mauritius became independent, within the Commonwealth, in 1968. In 1992 the Republic of Mauritius was proclaimed. The University of Mauritius (founded 1965) is the oldest existing institution of higher education in Mauritius. In 2006/07, 7,531 students were enrolled at the University (34.3% of whom were part-time students); in addition, many students receive further education abroad. In 2007, 9,573 students were enrolled in technical and vocational institutions. Government funding accounts for an estimated 85% of the University's running costs; the rest is made up from students' tuition fees, consultancy work and commercial rent.

The Council is the University policy-making body with control of administration and finance, and the Senate is the highest academic body. The Court is a body that meets annually to discuss general plans. The five Faculty Boards coordinate all teaching and research, administer examinations and evaluate programmes of study, and act on the instructions of the Vice-Chancellor and Senate. The Mahatma Gandhi Institute also offers Bachelors degree courses.

Two GCE A-Levels are the minimum requirement for admission to higher education, although for one- to three-year Certificate and Diploma courses the minimum requirement is the Cambridge Overseas School Certificate. Undergraduate Bachelors degree courses at the University last three to four years, depending on the subject, but students wishing to study for professional degrees in dentistry or medicine must attend institutions outside the country. Following the Bachelors, the first postgraduate degree is the Masters, which lasts two to three years. The Masters of Philosophy is a research-based degree available in a number of subject areas. Finally, the Doctor of Philosophy is the highest university-level degree and is a research-based period of study lasting at least three years.

Post-secondary vocational and technical qualifications include several Brevets and Diplomas.

The Tertiary Education Commission is aiming to promote, plan, develop and coordinate post-secondary education in Mauritius and implement a regulatory framework to achieve an international-quality education system. It is also responsible for allocating government funds to the tertiary education institutions under its purview and ensuring accountability and optimum use of resources.

Regulatory and Representative Bodies

GOVERNMENT

Ministry of Arts and Culture: Renganaden Seeneevassen Bldg, 7th Floor, cnr Pope Hennessy and Maillard Sts, Port Louis; tel. 212-9993; fax 208-0315; e-mail minoac@intnet.mu; internet culture.gov.mu; Minister MAHENDRA GOWRESSOO; Permanent Sec. NAYEN KOOMAR BALLAH.

Ministry of Education and Human Resources: IVTB House, Pont Fer, Phoenix; tel. 601-5200; fax 698-2550; e-mail moeps@mail.gov.mu; internet ministry-education.gov.mu; Minister DHARAMBEER GOKHOOL.

NATIONAL BODY

Tertiary Education Commission: Réduit; tel. 467-8800; fax 467-6579; e-mail mohadeb@tec.mu; internet www.tec.mu; f. 1988; allocates funds to tertiary education instns from govt and other sources; oversees quality of educational provision in these instns; accredits tertiary-level programmes offered by the private sector; 9 mems; Chair. Prof. DONALD AH-CHUEN; Exec. Dir Dr PRAVEEN MOHADEB (acting).

Learned Societies

GENERAL

Royal Society of Arts and Sciences of Mauritius: c/o Mauritius Sugar Industry Research Institute, Réduit; tel. 454-1061; fax 454-1971; e-mail rsas@msiri.mu; f. 1829; Royal title 1847; 210 mems; Pres. Dr ASHA DOOKUN-SAUMTALLY; Hon. Sec. ROSEMAY NG KEE KWONG; publ. *Proceedings* (irregular).

AGRICULTURE, FISHERIES AND VETERINARY SCIENCE

Société de Technologie Agricole et Sucrière de Maurice: Mauritius Sugar Industry Research Institute, Réduit; tel. 454-1061; fax 454-1971; e-mail rngcheong@msiri.intnet.mu; f. 1910; 390 mems; Pres. Dr K. F. NG KEE KWONG; Hon. Sec. Dr R. NG CHEONG; publ. *Revue Agricole et Sucrière de l'Ile Maurice.*

HISTORY, GEOGRAPHY AND ARCHAEOLOGY

Société de l'Histoire de l'Ile Maurice: rue de Froberville, Curepipe Rd, BP 150, Port Louis; f. 1938; 810 ordinary mems; Hon. Sec. G. RAMET; publs *Bulletin, Dictionary of Mauritian Biography.*

LANGUAGE AND LITERATURE

Alliance Française: 1, rue Victor Hugo, Bell Village, Port Louis; tel. 212-2949; fax 212-2812; e-mail afim@intnet.mu; internet www.afmccf.com; offers courses and examinations in French language and culture and promotes cultural exchange with France; six attached teaching centres in Port Louis.

British Council: Royal Rd, POB 111, Rose Hill, Mauritius; tel. 454-9550; fax 454-9553; e-mail general.enquiries@mu.britishcouncil.org; internet www.britishcouncil.org/mauritius; offers courses and examinations in English language and British culture and promotes cultural exchange with the UK; also responsible for British Council work in Madagascar and the Seychelles; Dir ROSALIND BURFORD.

Research Institutes

AGRICULTURE, FISHERIES AND VETERINARY SCIENCE

Mauritius Sugar Industry Research Institute: 1 Moka Rd, Réduit; tel. 454-1061; fax 454-1971; e-mail contact@msiri.intnet.mu; internet www.msiri.mu; f. 1953; research on cane breeding, agronomy, soils, diseases, pests, weeds, botany, mechanization, biotechnology, sugar manufacture, by-products, also on food crops cultivated in association with sugar-cane and between cane cycles; library: see Libraries and Archives; Dir Dr KWET FONG NG KEE KWONG; publs *Flore de Mascareignes* (irregular), *Occasional Papers* (irregular), *Occasional Reports & Monographs* (irregular).

NATURAL SCIENCES

Biological Sciences

Research Centre for Mauritius Flora and Fauna: c/o Mauritius Institute, POB 54, Port Louis; tel. 212-0639; fax 212-5717; attached to Mauritius Institute.

Libraries and Archives

Coromandel

National Archives: Devt Bank of Mauritius Complex, Coromandel; tel. 233-4211; fax 233-4299; e-mail arc@mail.gov.mu; f. 1815; 400,000 items, records of the French (1721–1810) and British (1810–1968) Administrations consisting of MSS and printed matters, notarial papers, Land Court registers, maps and plans; open to the public; the Conservation Unit is responsible for the repair of damaged records, incl. Photographic Section, Microfilm Section, Bindery, Oral History Unit and Paper Restoration Unit; Chief Archives Officer PIERRE ROLAND CHUNG SAM WAN.

Curepipe

Carnegie Library: Queen Elizabeth II Ave, Curepipe; tel. 674-2287; fax 676-5054; f. 1920; spec. colln on Indian Ocean islands; 90,000 vols; Senior Librarian T. K. HURRYNAG-RAMNAUTH.

Port Louis

City Library: City Hall, POB 422, Port Louis; tel. 212-0831 ext. 163; fax 212-4258; internet mpl.intnet.mu/library.htm; f. 1851; 110,000 vols; important collections on Mauritius and archives of Port Louis Municipal Council; music scores; depository for WHO publications; Head Librarian BENJAMIN SILARSAH; publs *Subject Bibliography on Mauritius* (1 a year), *Subject Index to Local Newspapers* (2 a year).

Mauritius Institute Public Library: POB 54, Port Louis; tel. 212-0639; fax 212-5717; f. 1902; legal deposit library and depository library for UNESCO; 60,000 vols, including an extensive collection of books, articles and reports on Mauritius; Head Librarian S. ANKIAH.

Réduit

Mauritius Sugar Industry Research Institute (MSIRI) Library: Réduit; tel. 454-1061; fax 454-1971; e-mail library@ msiri.mu; internet www.msiri.mu; f. 1953; rep. colln on all aspects of sugar cane cultivation and sugar manufacture, and expanding colln on food crops; wide coverage of technical periodical literature; colln of prints and drawings and early publs on sugar cane; in-house databases and int. colln of CD-ROM databases and full texts; 31,660 vols; Man. of Scientific Information and Publs Dept ROSEMAY NG KEE KWONG.

University of Mauritius Library: Réduit; tel. 454-1041; fax 464-0905; e-mail uomlibrary@uom.ac.mu; internet www.uom .ac.mu; f. 1965; important collns in fields of administration, social sciences, agriculture, science and technology, law, textile engineering, medical research and Mauritiana; partial depository for UN and World Bank publs; 175,000 vols (140,000 books, 35,000 bound vols of periodicals); Chief Librarian ISHWARDUTH DASSYNE.

Museums and Art Galleries

Mahebourg

Historical Museum: Mahebourg; tel. 631-9329; f. 1950; a branch of the Mauritius Institute; comprises collection of old maps, engravings, watercolours and naval relics of local interest, exhibited in an 18th-century French house; Dir R. GAJEELEE.

Port Louis

Port Louis Museum: Mauritius Institute, Port Louis; tel. 212-2815; fax 212-5717; e-mail mimuse@intnet.mu; f. 1880; comprises a Natural History Museum, collections of fauna, flora and geology of Mauritius and of the other islands of the Mascarene region; Dir S. ABDOOLRAHAMAN.

Réduit

Mauritius Herbarium: c/o Mauritius Sugar Industry Research Institute, Réduit; tel. 454-1061; fax 454-1971; e-mail cbaider@ msiri.intnet.mu; internet www.msiri.mu; f. 1960; public herbarium for education and research about native flora; specializes in flora of Mascarene Islands; Herbarium Officer Dr CLAUDIA BAIDER; Librarian ROSEMARY NG KEE KWONG; publ. *Flore des Mascareignes* (irregular).

Universities

UNIVERSITY OF MAURITIUS

Réduit

Telephone: 454-1041
Fax: 454-9642
E-mail: website@uom.ac.mu
Internet: www.uom.ac.mu

Founded 1965
Languages of instruction: English, French
partly State funded
Academic year: August to July

Chancellor: Sir RAMESH JEEWOOLALL
Pro-Chancellor: Prof. S. JUGESSUR
Vice-Chancellor: Prof. I. FAGOONEE
Pro-Vice-Chancellor for Research, Consultancy and Innovation: Prof. SOONIL RUGHOOPUTH
Pro-Vice-Chancellor for Teaching and Learning: Prof. B. AMEENATH GURIB-FAKIM
Registrar: S. REKHA ISSUR-GOORAH
Chief Librarian: I. DASSYNE (acting)

Library: see Libraries and Archives
Number of teachers: 510 (248 full-time, 262 part-time)
Number of students: 8,474

Publications: *Calendar* (1 a year), *Research Journal* (1 a year), *University Newsletter* (4 a year), *Vice-Chancellor's Report*

DEANS

Faculty of Agriculture: Assoc. Prof. Dr D. PUCHOOA (acting)
Faculty of Engineering: Prof. Dr R. MOHEE
Faculty of Law and Management: Assoc. Prof. T. D. JUWAHEER
Faculty of Science: Prof. H. T. Y. LI KAM WAH
Faculty of Social Studies and Humanities: Assoc. Prof. Dr S. K. SOBHEE

PROFESSORS

BAHORUN, T. (Applied Biochemistry)
BHURUTH, M. (Computational Mathematics)
BUNWAREE, S. S. (Gender and Development Studies)
JHURRY, D. (Chemistry)
MOHEE, R., Chemical and Environmental Engineering
RAMJEAWON, T. (Environmental Engineering)
RUGHOOPUTH, H. C. S., Electrical and Electronic Engineering
SOBHEE, S. K. (Applied Economics and Development Studies)
SOYJAUDAH, K. M. S. (Communication Engineering)
SUBRATTY, A. H. (Biochemistry)

UNIVERSITY OF TECHNOLOGY, MAURITIUS

La Tour Koenig, Pointe-aux-Sables

Telephone: 234-7624
Fax: 234-1660
E-mail: registrar@utm.intnet.mu

Internet: www.utm.ac.mu

Founded 2000 by Act of Parliament
Language of instruction: English
Academic year: August to June
State control

Dir-Gen.: PETER STEVEN COUPE
Registrar: SASSITA DEVI GOORDYAL
Librarian: GEETA DWARKAN

Library of 12,000 vols
Number of teachers: 100 (full-time and part-time)
Number of students: 1,407 (440 full-time, 967 part-time)

HEADS OF SCHOOLS

School of Business Informatics and Software Engineering: Dr N. MOHAMUDALLY
School of Public Sector Policy and Management: Dr RAMESH DURBARRY

Colleges

Mahatma Gandhi Institute: Moka; tel. 403-2000; fax 433-2235; e-mail vkoonjal@ intnet.mu; internet mgi.intnet.mu; f. 1970; serves as a centre for the study of Indian culture and traditions, and the promotion of education and culture; courses in Indian music and dance, fine arts, Indian languages, Mandarin and Indian philosophy; research in Indian and immigration studies, culture and civilization, Bhojpuri, folklore and oral traditions and mauritian history, geography and literature; library: 100,000 vols; 218 secondary teachers, 76 in tertiary sector; 2,336 students; spec. collns: Gandhi, Mauritius, archives relating to Indian immigration to Mauritius 1842–1912; Chair. L. NUCKCHADY; Dir-Gen. S. NIRSIMLOO GAYAN (acting); Registrar Dr V. D. KOONJAL; publs *Journal of Mauritian Studies* (English, 2 a year), *Rimjhim* (Hindi, 4 a year), *Vasant* (Hindi, 4 a year).

Mauritius College of the Air: Réduit; tel. 403-8200; fax 464-8854; e-mail mca@mca.ac .mu; internet www.mca.ac.mu; f. 1972; runs distance education programmes; provides the national broadcasting organization with programmes for schools; produces audio-visual material for use by children and adults in formal and non-formal education; acquires pre-recorded media-based educational material from overseas and makes it available to schools in Mauritius; library: 9,500 vols; 62 part-time tutors; 1,780 students; Dir MEENA SEETULSINGH.

Robert Antoine Sugar Industry Training Centre: Royal Rd, Réduit; tel. 454-7024; fax 454-7026; e-mail rasitc@intnet.mu; internet pages.intnet.mu/rasitc; f. 1980; courses in sugar cane agronomy, cane sugar manufacture and chemical control in sugar factories, mechanization of field operations, power generation for sugar factories, management skills, supervisory skills, leadership development, communications; courses in English and French at various levels; 100 part-time specialists; 800 part-time students; Dir Dr LINDA MAMET.

The Higher Education System

From the 1520s until independence in 1821 Mexico was under Spanish rule. The oldest current institutions of higher education date from this period, among them Universidad Nacional Autónoma de México (founded 1551), Universidad de Guanajuato (founded 1732; current name 1945), Universidad Autónoma de Campeche (founded 1756) and Universidad de Guadalajara (founded 1792). The Secretaría de Educación Pública (SEP) is the government ministry responsible for the administration of education at all levels, but following legislation enacted in 1992 granting greater autonomy to the Federal States, there has been an increase in the number of privately run institutions of higher education. In early 2006 the Congreso de la Unión (Parliament) passed legislation requiring all public and private institutions of higher education that offered degree programmes to be accredited; before this there were no national standards for accreditation or quality assurance. In 2007/08 there were an estimated 5,549 institutes of higher education, attended by 2,528,700 students in 2006/07, including postgraduates. Institutions of higher education are classified as Universities, Technological Universities or Institutes, Polytechnics or Teachers' Colleges.

To gain admission to a first degree programme, an applicant must possess the certificate for completion of secondary school, the Bachillerato, and sit an entrance examination. The Technological Universities have introduced a specialist two-year course (Técnico Superior Universitario), which can either be used to transfer to the four-year Licenciado (see below) or as a complete qualification in its own right. The Licenciado is offered at undergraduate level by all institutions of higher education and usually lasts four years, although degrees awarded in conjunction with a professional title may last longer. The first postgraduate degree is the Maestría, which is a one- or three-year research-based course of study. Finally, the Doctorado is a two- to three-year period of research and represents the highest level of university qualifications.

Post-secondary awards for vocational and technical education include the Salida Lateral or Carrera Corta (two to three years) leading to a Diploma or Titulo Técnico.

A bill passed in 2006 by the Mexican Senate required all degrees offered by Mexican universities to undergo external evaluation. Institutions awarding degrees that do not meet the required national standards will have their licenses suspended.

Regulatory and Representative Bodies

GOVERNMENT

Secretariat of State for Public Education: Dinamarca 84, 5°, Col. Juárez, 06600 México, DF; tel. (55) 5510-2557; fax (55) 5329-6873; e-mail educa@sep.gob.mx; internet www.sep.gob.mx; Sec. of Public Education JOSEFINA VÁZQUEZ MOTA; Permanent Sec. Lic. JULIO CASTELLANOS RAMÍREZ.

ACCREDITATION

Consejo para la Acreditación de la Educación Superior (COPAES) (Higher Education Accreditation Council): Av. San Jerónimo 120, Col. Jardines del Pedregal, Del. Álvaro Obregón, 04500 México, DF; tel. (55) 5616-5210; e-mail acreditacion@copaes.org; internet www.copaes.org.mx; f. 2000; non-profit NGO contributing towards the quality assurance of academic programmes in public and private instns by recognizing official accrediting orgs that in turn accredit undergraduate degree programmes in many study areas; Gen. Dir Dr JAVIER DE LA GARZA AGUILAR.

NATIONAL BODIES

Asociación Nacional de Universidades e Instituciones de Educación Superior (ANUIES) (National Association of Universities and Institutions of Higher Education): Tenayuca 200, Col. Santa Cruz Atoyac, 03310 México, DF; tel. (55) 5420-4900; e-mail rlc@anuies.mx; internet www.anuies.mx; f. 1950; coordinates and represents instns of higher education, studies academic and admin. problems of the nat. higher education system; promotes exchange of personnel, information and services between the affiliated instns; 145 affiliated univs, centres and colleges; library of 11,500 vols; Exec. Sec.-Gen. Dr RAFAEL LÓPEZ CASTAÑARES;

publs *Confluencia* (12 a year), *Revista de la Educación Superior* (4 a year).

Centro de Cooperación Regional para la Educación de Adultos en América Latina y el Caribe (CREFAL)/Centre for Regional Cooperation for Adult Education in Latin America and the Caribbean: Avda Lázaro Cárdenas 525, Col. Revolución, 61609 Pátzcuaro, Michoacán; tel. (434) 342-8200; fax (434) 342-8151; e-mail crefal@crefal.edu.mx; internet www.crefal.edu.mx; f. 1951 by UNESCO and OAS, now administered by a Board of Dirs from mem. countries; regional technical assistance, specialist training in literary and adult education, research; library of 80,416 vols; library: CEDEAL/CREFAL Adult Education documentation centre for Latin America: database of 17,347 entries; Dir HUMBERTO SALAZAR HERRERA; publs *Decisio – saberes para la Acción en Educación de Adultos* (3 a year), *Revista Interamericana de Educación de Adultos* (3 a year).

Dirección General de Relaciones Educativas, Científicas y Culturales (Board of Educational, Scientific and Cultural Relations): Secretaría de Educación Pública, Argentina 28, Centro Histórico, 06029 México, DF; tel. (55) 3601-1000; f. 1960; comprises Sections of Technical Assistance, Int. Relations in the fields of Education, Science and Culture and Exchange; serves as co-ordinating agency between the UN, UNESCO, the OAS and the Mexican Govt; Dir Dr ENRIQUE G. LEÓN LÓPEZ.

Federación de Instituciones Mexicanas Particulares de Educación Superior (Federation of Mexican Higher Education Institutions): Río Guadalquivir 50, 4° piso, Col. Cuauhtémoc, 06500 México, DF; tel. (55) 5514-5514; fax (55) 5207-0581; e-mail vcampuza@fimpes.org.mx; internet www.fimpes.org.mx; f. 1981; comprises 114 higher education instns incl. the principal private univs; works to improve communication and collaboration between its mems and the other educational instns in the country; promotes

high academic standards; Exec. Sec. Lic. VICTOR CAMPUZANO TARDITI.

Learned Societies

GENERAL

Colegio Nacional (National College): Luis González Obregón 23, Centro Histórico, 06020 México, DF; tel. (55) 5789-4330; fax (55) 5702-1779; e-mail colnal@mx.inter.net; internet www.colegionacional.org.mx; f. 1943; disseminates nat. culture; 38 mems; library of 35,000 vols, 10,000 periodicals; Sec./Administrator Lic. FAUSTO VEGA Y GÓMEZ; publ. *Memoria* (1 a year).

UNESCO Office Mexico: Pte Masaryk no. 526, 3er piso, Colonia Polanco, 11560 México, DF; tel. (55) 5230-7600; fax (55) 5230-7602; e-mail mexico@unesco.org; internet www.unescomexico.org; f. 1967; Dir LUIS MANUEL TIBURCIO.

AGRICULTURE, FISHERIES AND VETERINARY SCIENCE

Sociedad Agronómica Mexicana (Mexican Agricultural Society): Mariano Azuela 121, 2° piso, Del. Cuauhtémoc, 06400 México, DF; f. 1921.

Sociedad Forestal Mexicana (Mexican Forestry Society): Calle de Jesús Terán 11, México 1, DF; f. 1921; 225 mems; Exec. Pres. Ing. RIGOBERTO VÁSQUEZ DE LA PARRA; Sec.-Gen. Lic. ADOLFO AGUILAR Y QUEVEDO; publ. *México Forestal* (6 a year).

ARCHITECTURE AND TOWN PLANNING

Asociación de Ingenieros y Arquitectos de México (Association of Mexican Engineers and Architects): Av. Constituyentes 800 (Oficina AIAM), Col. Belén de las Flores, México, DF; f. 1868; 560 mems; library of 7,565 vols; Pres. Ing. FEDERICO DOVALI RAMOS; Sec. Ing. JOSÉ ACOSTA SÁNCHEZ;

publ. *Revista Mexicana de Ingeniería y Arquitectura* (4 a year).

BIBLIOGRAPHY, LIBRARY SCIENCE AND MUSEOLOGY

Asociación Mexicana de Bibliotecarios, AC (Mexican Library Association): Apdo 12-792, Administración de Correos 12, 03001 México, DF; Angel Urraza 817-A, Col. Del Valle, 03100 México, DF; tel. (55) 5575-3396; fax (55) 5575-1135; e-mail correo@ambac.org.mx; internet www.ambac.org.mx; f. 1924; 1,061 mems; Pres. FELIPE BECERRIL TORRES; Sec. ELÍAS CID RAMÍREZ; publs *Memorias de las Jornadas Mexicanas de Biblioteconomía* (1 a year), *Noticiero de la AMBAC* (4 a year), *Revista Liber*.

Dirección General de Bibliotecas (Main Directorate of Libraries): Universidad Nacional Autónoma de México, Ciudad Universitaria, Apdo 70–392, 04510 México, DF; tel. (55) 5622-3960; fax (55) 5622-4938; e-mail sinfo@dgb.unam.mx; internet dgb.unam.mx; f. 1966; documentation service, current awareness and SDI services, computerized bibliographical searches; digital library of 6,000 periodical titles with full text; 140 specialized databases; library of 3,485 vols; special collection of 230 titles of abstracting and indexing periodicals; 2,500 Latin American periodicals; Dir Dra SILVIA GONZÁLEZ MARÍN; publs *Biblioteca Universitaria* (electronic, irregular), *CLASE* (quarterly index of Latin American citation in social sciences and humanities), *PERIODICA* (quarterly index of Latin American science and technology journals).

ECONOMICS, LAW AND POLITICS

Barra Mexicana—Colegio de Abogados (Mexican Bar Association—College of Advocates): Varsovia No. 1, Colonia Juárez, 06600 México, DF; tel. (55) 5208-3115; fax (55) 5208-3117; e-mail labarra@bma.org.mx; internet www.bma.org.mx; f. 1922; 1,732 mems; library of 5,260 vols; Pres. Lic. FABIÁN AGUINACO BRAVO; Sec. Lic. CARLOS PASTRANA Y ÁNGELES; publs *El Foro* (2 a year), *La Barra* (6 a year).

Instituto Nacional de Estadística, Geografía (National Institute of Statistics and Geography): Avda Héroe de Nacozari sur 2301, Fracc. Jardines del Parque, Puerta 10 basamento, Departamento de Comunicación Social, 20276 Aguascalientes, AGS; tel. (449) 910-53-00; fax (449) 462-4133; e-mail comunicacionsocial@inegi.org.mx; internet www.inegi.gob.mx; f. 1983; integrates and develops the Nat. System of Statistics and the Geographic Information System; undertakes the Nat. Census; library of 15,000 vols; Pres. Dr EDUARDO SOJO GARZA ALDAPE; publs *Agenda Estadística de los Estados Unidos Mexicanos* (1 a year), *Anuario de Estadísticas por Entidad Federativa* (1 a year), *Anuario Estadístico del Comercio Exterior* (electronic, 1 a year), *Anuario Estadístico del Estado* (separate vol. for each state of Mexico), *Anuario Estadístico de los Estados Unidos Mexicanos* (electronic, 1 a year), *Boletín de los Sistemas Nacionales Estadístico y de Información Geográfica* (electronic, 1 a year), *Cuaderno Estadístico de la Zona Metropolitana de la Ciudad de México* (electronic, 1 a year), *Encuesta Nacional de Ocupación y Empleo* (electronic, 1 a year), *El Sector Alimentario en México* (1 a year), *La Industria Automotriz en México* (1 a year), *La Industria Maquiladora de Exportación* (1 a year), *La Industria Química en México* (1 a year), *La Industria Siderúrgica en México* (1 a year), *La Industria Textil y del Vestido en México* (1 a year), *La Minería en México* (1 a year), *México en el Mundo* (every 2 years).

EDUCATION

Centro Nacional de Documentación e Información Pedagógica y Museo Pedagógico Nacional (National Centre for Educational Documentation and Information and National Educational Museum): Calle Presidente Masaryk 526, México 5, DF; f. 1971; library of 10,000 vols; Dir Prof. MARIANO CRUZ PÉREZ; publs *Documentación e Información* (12 a year), *Lista de Canje* (2 a year), *Sep-Forjadores* (12 a year).

FINE AND PERFORMING ARTS

Asociación Musical Manuel M. Ponce, AC (Manuel M. Ponce Musical Association): Espíritu Santo 75, Col. Coyoacán. 0400, México DF; tel. and fax (55) 5554-4028; e-mail tere_castrillon@terra.com.mx; f. 1949; promotes annual concert seasons of traditional, modern and contemporary Mexican and foreign music; library of musical scores, tapes, records and books; Hon. Pres. LUIS HERRERA DE LA FUENTE; Pres. MARIA TERESA CASTRILLÓN; Vice-Pres. RAMÓN ROMO; Musical Dir MARIA TERESA CASTRILLÓN; Sec. ANTONIETA TELLO; Sec. LAURA ALVAREZ; Sec. MANUEL ZAORÍAS.

Ateneo Veracruzano (Veracruz Athenaeum): Edif. Lonja Mercantil, Independencia 924, Vera Cruz; f. 1933; 68 mems (18 corresp.); Pres. C.P.T. FRANCISCO BROISSIN A.; Sec. Prof. ANTONIO SALAZAR PÁEZ; publ. *Boletín* (12 a year).

Instituto Nacional de Bellas Artes y Literatura (National Institute of Fine Arts and Literature): Paseo de la Reforma y Campo Marte s/n, Col. Chapultepec Polanco, 11560 México, DF; tel. (55) 5521-9251; internet www.cnca.gob.mx/cnca/buena/inba/intro.html; f. 1947; consists of depts of music, visual arts, opera, literature, dance, theatrical production, architecture, artistic education and admin.; responsible for cultural insts throughout Mexico; Dir GERARDO ESTRADA; publs *Boletín de Literatura* (6 a year), *Revista de Educación Artística* (4 a year), *Revista Hetereofonía* (3 a year), *Revista Pauta* (6 a year).

Affiliated institution:

Centro Nacional de Conservación y Registro del Patrimonio Artístico Mueble (National Centre for Conservation and Registry of Movable Art Heritage): San Ildefonso 60, Col. Centro, Del. Cuauhtémoc, México DF; tel. (55) 5702-2323; fax (55) 5702-2143; f. 1958; restoration of works of art; Dir LUCIA GARCIA NORIEGA Y NIETO.

HISTORY, GEOGRAPHY AND ARCHAEOLOGY

Academia Mexicana de la Historia (Mexican Academy of History): Plaza Carlos Pacheco 21, Col. Centro, Cuauhtémoc, 06070 México, DF; tel. (55) 5518-2708; fax (55) 5521-9653; e-mail informes@acadmexhistoria.org.mx; internet www.acadmexhistoria.org.mx; f. 1919; 30 mems; correspondent of Real Academia, Madrid; library of 10,000 vols; Dir Dr MIGUEL LEÓN-PORTILLA; Sec. Dr GISELA VON WOBESER; publ. *Memorias* (2 a year).

Academia Nacional de Historia y Geografía (National Academy of History and Geography): Londres 60, Col.: Juárez, Del. Cuauhtémoc, 06600 México 6, DF; tel. (55) 5533-4149; f. 1925; 179 mems; Dir Dr JESÚS FERRER GAMBOA; publ. *Revista*.

Departamento de Antropología e Historia de Nayarit (Department of Anthropology and History in Nayarit): Avda México 91, Tepic, Nayarit; f. 1946; Dir EVERARDO PEÑA NAVARRO; Sec. MARÍA A. GONZÁLEZ A.

Sociedad Mexicana de Geografía y Estadística (Mexican Society of Geography and Statistics): Calle de Justo Sierra 19, Apdo 10739, Del. Cuauhtémoc, 06020 México, DF; tel. (55) 5542-7340; e-mail smexgeoyesta@aol.com; f. 1833; 1,204 active mems, 640 corresponding mems; library of 450,000 vols; Pres. Lic. CUAUHTÉMOC CISNEROS MADRID; Sec.-Gen. LEOPOLDO CHAGOYA MORGAN; publs *Boletín* (3 a year), *and special works*.

Sociedad Mexicana de Historia de la Ciencia y la Tecnología (Mexican Society for History of Science and Technology): Edif. de las Sociedades Científicas, Avda Cipreses s/n, Col. San Andrés Totoltepec, Tlalpan, 14400 México, DF; tel. (55) 5849-6830; fax (55) 5849-6831; e-mail info@smhct.org; internet www.smhct.org; f. 1964; Pres. Dr JUAN JOSÉ SALDAÑA; publs *Anales*, *Memorias*, *Quipu*.

LANGUAGE AND LITERATURE

Academia Mexicana de la Lengua (Mexican Academy of Letters): Liverpool 76, Col. Juárez, 06600 México, DF; tel. (55) 5208-2526; fax (55) 5208-2416; e-mail academia@academia.org.mx; internet www.academia.org.mx; f. 1875; corresp. of the Real Academia Española (Madrid); 178 mems; Dir JOSÉ G. MORENO DE ALBA; Sec. MANUEL ALCALÁ ANAYA.

Alliance Française–Alianza Francesa México: Socrates 156, Esq. Homero Col. Los Morales Polanco Del Miguel Hidalgo, 11560 México, DF; tel. (55) 1084-4190; fax (55) 5395-5182; internet www.alianzafrancesa.org.mx; f. 1884; offers courses and examinations in French language and culture and promotes cultural exchange with France; attached teaching centres in 36 other cities; Pres. AGUSTÍN LEGORRETA CHAUVET; Gen. Dir YVES CORBEL.

British Council: Lope de Vega 316, Col. Chapultepec Morales, 11570 México, DF; tel. (55) 5263-1900; fax (55) 5263-1940; e-mail bcmexico@britishcouncil.org.mx; internet www.britishcouncil.org.mx; f. 1943; teaching centre; offers courses and exams in English language and British culture and promotes cultural exchange with the UK; Dir CLIVE BRUTON.

Goethe-Institut: Liverpool 89, Col. Juárez, 06600, México, DF; tel. (55) 5207-0487; fax (55) 5533-1057; e-mail cursos@mexiko.goethe.org; internet www.goethe.de/hn/mex/deindex.htm; f. 1966; offers courses and exams in German language and culture and promotes cultural exchange with Germany; attached centre in Guadalajara; library of 13,000 vols, 35 periodicals; Dir FOLCO NÄTHER.

PEN Club de México (PEN Club of Mexico): Heriberto Frías 1452-407, Col. del Valle, 03100 México, DF; tel. (55) 5564-5078; e-mail presidencia@penmexico.org.mx; internet www.penmexico.org.mx; f. 1924; 62 mems; Pres. MARÍA ELENA RUIZ CRUZ; Sec. JAIME RAMÍREZ GARRIDO; publ. *Directory of Writers* (1 a year).

MEDICINE

Academia Mexicana de Cirugía (Mexican Academy of Surgery): Avda Cuauhtémoc 330, Bloque B 3o piso, Col. Doctores, 06725 México DF; tel. (55) 5761-2581; e-mail amc06@prodigy.net.mx; internet www.amc.org.mx; f. 1933; mems. FERNANDO BERNAL SAHAGÚN; Sec. FRANCISCO JAVIER OCHOA CARRILLO; publ. *Revista* (12 a year).

Academia Mexicana de Dermatología (Mexican Academy of Dermatology): Georgia 114, Despacho 503, Col. Nápoles. Del. Benito Juárez, 03810 México, DF; tel. (55) 5682-

2545; fax (55) 5682-8963; e-mail academiadermatologia@prodigy.net.mx; internet www.amd.org.mx; f. 1952; Dir Dr GILBERTO ADAME MIRANDA; Sec. Dra GABRIELA FRIAS ANCONA.

Academia Nacional de Medicina de México (Mexican National Academy of Medicine): Apdo 7–813, Avda Cuauhtémoc 330, Bloque B planta baja, Col. Doctores, 06725 México, DF; tel. (55) 5519-8679; e-mail contacto@anmm.org.mx; internet www .anmm.org.mx; f. 1865; 14 sections; 340 mems; library of 20,000 vols; Pres. Dr MISAEL URIBE ESQUIVEL; Gen. Sec. Dra TERESA COR-ONA VÁZQUEZ; publ. *Gaceta Médica de México.*

Asociación de Médicas Mexicanas, AC (Mexican Association of Women Doctors): Bruselas 10 Int. 403, Col. Juárez, 06600 México, DF; tel. (55) 5591-0159; fax (55) 5546-8202; f. 1925; 3,000 mems; represents members' interests as doctors, citizens and women; Pres. Dra IRENE TALAMAS V.; publ. *Revista.*

Asociación Mexicana de Facultades y Escuelas de Medicina (Mexican Association of Faculties and Schools of Medicine): López Cotilla 754, Col. del Valle, 03100 México, DF; tel. (55) 5682-9482; fax (55) 5687-9323; e-mail amfem@prodigy.net.mx; internet www.amfem.edu.mx; f. 1957; mems 30 medical schools; Pres. Dr HUMBERTO A. VERAS GODOY; Admin. Sec. Lic. YVONNE E. FISCHER HESS.

Consejo Mexicano de Dermatología, AC (Mexican Dermatological Council): Instituto Dermatológico de Jalisco, Guadalajara; tel. (33) 3660-1515 ext. 200; f. 1974; 349 mems; qualifies specialists as part of Nat. Academy of Medicine Comm. of Postgraduate Studies; Gen. Sec. Prof. ERNESTO MACOTELA RUÍZ; publ. *Roster.*

Federación Mexicana de Ginecología y Obstetricia (Mexican Federation of Gynaecology and Obstetrics): Nueva York 38, Col. Nápoles, 03810 México, DF; tel. (55) 5669-0211; fax (55) 5682-0160; e-mail secretario@ femego.org.mx; internet www.femego.org .mx; f. 1961; 4,600 mems; Pres. Dr JESÚS LEAL DEL ROSAL; Sec. Dr FERNANDO GAVIÑO GAVIÑO; publ. *Ginecología y Obstetricia de México.*

Sociedad Mexicana de Cardiología (Mexican Cardiological Society): Juan Badiano 1, Sección XVI Tlalpan, 14080 México, DF; tel. (55) 5655-7694; fax (55) 5573-2111; e-mail info@smcardiologia.org.mx; internet www .smcardiologia.org.mx; f. 1935; 1,250 mems; Pres. Dr JORGE GASPAR; Sec. Dr ERICK ALEXÁNDERSON; publs *Arch.Cardio.Méx.*, *Revista Mexicana de Enfermería Cardiológica* (3 a year).

Sociedad Mexicana de Nutrición y Endocrinología, AC (Mexican Society for Nutrition and Endocrinology): Ohio 27, Col. El Rosedal, Del. Coyoacán, 04330 México, DF; tel. (55) 5636-2216; internet www .endocrinologia.com.mx; f. 1960; 660 mems; Pres. Dr ALFONSO VILLASEÑOR RUÍZ; Sec. Dr RAÚL GUTIÉRREZ GUTIÉRREZ; publ. *Revista de Endocrinología y Nutrición.*

Sociedad Mexicana de Parasitología, AC (Mexican Parasitological Society): Casa Tlalpan, Avenida Cipreses S/N, km 23.5 de la Antigua Carretera México-Cuernavaca, Col. San Andrés Totoltepec, 14400 México, DF; tel. (55) 5747-3348; fax (55) 5747-3398; e-mail mineko@cinvestav.mx; internet www .facmed.unam.mx/smp; f. 1960; 51 mems (20 active; 31 hon.) from 14 countries; organizes congresses and symposia; Pres. Dr MINEKO SHIBAYAMA; Sec. Dr ROSAMARIA BERNAL.

Sociedad Mexicana de Pediatría (Mexican Paediatrics Society): Tehuantepec 86-

503, Col. Roma Sur, Del. Cuauhtémoc, 06760 México, DF; tel. (55) 5564-8371; e-mail smp1930@socmexped.org.mx; internet www .socmexped.org.mx; f. 1930; 1,200 mems; Pres. Dr XAVIER DE JESÚS NOVALES CASTRO; Gen. Sec. Dr MARIO GONZÁLEZ VITE; publ. *Revista Mexicana de Pediatría* (6 a year).

Sociedad Mexicana de Salud Pública (Mexican Public Health Society): Herschel 109, Col. Anzures, Del. Miguel Hidalgo, 11590 México, DF; tel. (55) 5203-4291; fax (55) 5203-4229; e-mail smsp@prodigy.net.mx; internet www.smsp.org.mx; f. 1944; 6,000 mems; small library; Exec. Dir HUMBERTO MUÑOZ GRANDÉ; publ. *Higiene* (3 a year).

NATURAL SCIENCES

General

Academia Mexicana de Ciencias (Mexican Academy of Sciences): Calle Cipreses s/n, km 23.5 de la Carretera federal México-Cuernavaca, San Andrés Totoltepec, Tlalpan, 14400 México, DF; tel. (55) 5849-4905; fax (55) 5849-5112; e-mail academia@amc.unam .mx; internet www.amc.unam.mx; f. 1959; research in fields of exact, natural and social sciences, humanities and engineering; training and acknowledging the scientific work of researchers; encourages communication and collaboration between the various orgs responsible for research in Mexico; strengthening int. presence; consultancy services and performance evaluations for Fed. and local govt, legislative and judicial branches and other orgs in civil soc.; facilitates decision making based on scientific and technical evidence; library of 1,000 vols; 2,156 mems; Exec. Coordinator RENATA VILLALBA; Admin. Sec. ROCÍO MÉNDEZ-PADILLA; Technical Sec. CLAUDIA JIMÉNEZ; publ. *Ciencia* (4 a year).

Ateneo Nacional de Ciencias y Artes de México (National Athenaeum of Sciences and Arts): Bucareli 12, México, DF; f. 1920 as Ateneo Estudiantil de Ciencias y Artes, then Ateneo de Ciencias y Artes de México 1926, present name 1934; comprises sections of architecture, astronomy and mathematics, biology, broadcasting, cinematography, criminology and penal law, engineering, eugenics, geography, history, hygiene, law (civil, industrial, and international), literature, medicine, military studies, music, pedagogics, political economy, natural science, statistics; 7 corresp. centres: Monterrey, Mérida, Veracruz, Chiapas, Tijuana, Oaxaca, Tlaxcala; over 1,000 mems, including hon. and corresponding; library of 10,000 vols; Hon. Pres. Dr ALFONSO PRUNEDA; Pres. EMILIO PORTES GIL; Vice-Pres LUIS GARRIDO, Arq. EDMUNDO ZAMUDIO; Sec.-Gen. JOSÉ L. COSSIO; publs *Boletín, pamphlets.*

Biological Sciences

Asociación Mexicana de Microbiología, AC (Mexican Microbiological Association): Centro de Ciencias Genómicas, Avda Universidad s/n, Col. Chamilpa, Cuernavaca, Mor.; e-mail informes@microbiologia.org.mx; internet www.microbiologia.org.mx; f. 1949; Pres. Dra ESPERANZA MARTÍNEZ-ROMERO; Sec. BRENDA VALDERRAMA; publ. *Revista Latinoamericana de Microbiología.*

Sociedad Botánica de México, AC (Mexican Botanical Society): Centro de Investigaciones en Ecosistemas, Universidad Nacional Autónoma de México, Campus Morelia, Antigua Carretera a Pátzcuaro 8701, Col. San José de La Huerta, 58190 Morelia, Mich.; e-mail sbm@socbot.org.mx; internet www .socbot.org.mx; f. 1941; promotes the study, teaching and technology of botany; organizes the National Botanic Congress every 3 years; 1,000 mems; library of 850 vols, 350 periodicals; Pres. Dr MIGUEL MARTÍNEZ RAMOS;

Exec. Sec. Dr JORGE ARTURO MEAVE DEL CASTILLO; publs *Boletín* (2 a year), *Macpalxochitl* (newsletter, 12 a year).

Sociedad Mexicana de Biología (Mexican Biological Society): Avda de Brasil, México 1, DF; f. 1921; Pres. FERNANDO OCARANZ; publ. *Revista Mexicana de Biología.*

Sociedad Mexicana de Entomología (Mexican Entomological Society): Apdo 63, 91000 Jalapa, Veracruz; internet www .iztacala.unam.mx/sme; f. 1952; 650 mems; Pres. CÁNDIDO LUNA LEÓN; publs *Boletín* (irregular), *Folia Entomológica Mexicana* (3 a year).

Sociedad Mexicana de Fitogenética (Mexican Society of Plant Genetics): Apdo 21, 56230 Chapingo, Edo de México; tel. (55) 5954-2200; fax (55) 5954-6652; e-mail revfitotecniamex@hotmail.com; internet www.somefi.org; f. 1965; 1,000 mems; Pres. Dr BULMARO COUTIÑO ESTRADA; Sec. Dr SALVADOR MONTES HERNÁNDEZ; publs *Revista Fitotecnia Mexicana, Revista Germen.*

Sociedad Mexicana de Fitopatología, AC (Mexican Society of Phytopathology): Apdo postal 85, 56230 Chapingo, Edo de México; e-mail sandoval@colpos.mx; internet www .colpos.mx/ifit/smf/somefit.htm; f. 1958; 400 mems; holds one national meeting per year; Pres. Dr GUSTAVO MORA AGUILERA; Sec. Dr SERGIO SANDOVAL; publs *El Vector, Revista Mexicana de Fitopatología* (2 a year).

Sociedad Mexicana de Historia Natural (Mexican Natural History Society): Avda Dr Vertiz 724, Col. Vertiz Narvarte, 03020 México, DF; tel. (55) 5519-4505; fax (55) 5538-4505; internet smhn.org.tripod.com; f. 1868, refounded 1936; 400 mems; library of 5,000 vols; Pres. Dr RAUL GIO ARGAEZ; publ. *Revista.*

Sociedad Mexicana de Micología (Mexican Society of Mycology): Apdo 41, 67700 Linares, Nuevo León; tel. (55) 5541-1333; e-mail smdm@tap-ecosur.edu.mx; internet www.smdm.org.mx; f. 1965; 400 mems; library of 12,000 vols; Pres. Dr FORTUNATO GARZA OCAÑAS; Sec. Dr RICARDO VALENZUELA GARZA (acting); publ. *Revista Mexicana de Micología* (1 a year).

Mathematical Sciences

Centro de Investigación en Computación (Computing Research Centre): Avda Juan de Dios Batiz s/n, Casi esq. Miguel Othón de Mendizabal, Unidad Profesional Adolfo López Mateos, Col. Nueva Industrial Vallejo, Del. Gustavo A. Madero, 07738 México City; tel. (55) 5729-6000 ext. 56604; fax (55) 5586-2936; e-mail webmaster@cic .ipn.mx; internet www.cic.ipn.mx; f. 1996; 250 mems; library of 14,000 vols; Dir Dr OSCAR CAMACHO NIETO; publs *Computación y Sistemas* (4 a year), *Research on Computing Science* (6 a year).

Sociedad Matemática Mexicana (Mexican Mathematical Society): Apdo 70-450, Coyoacán, 04510 México, DF; tel. (55) 5622-4481; fax (55) 5622-4479; internet www.smm .org.mx; f. 1943; 1,100 mems, 20 institutional mems; promotes mathematics, sponsors National Congresses and Regional Assemblies of mathematicians, and The National Mathematical Olympics; Pres. Dr EMILIO LLUIS-PUEBLA; Sec. Dr PABLO PADILLA-LONG-ORIA; publs *Aportaciones Matemáticas, Boletín de la SMM* (2 a year), *Carta informativa* (4 a year), *Miscelánea Matemática* (2 a year).

Physical Sciences

Asociación Mexicana de Geólogos Petroleros (Mexican Association of Petroleum Geologists): Torres Bodet 176, 06400 México, DF; internet www.amgp.org; f. 1949; 600 mems; Pres. J. ANTONIO ESCALERA ALCOCER;

Sec. JOSÉ GPE. GALICIA BARRIOS; publ. *Boletín* (4 a year).

Sociedad Astronómica de México, AC (Mexican Astronomical Society): Apdo M 9647, Jardín Felipe Xicoténcatl, Colonia Alamos, 03400 México, DF; tel. (55) 5519-4730; e-mail sociedadastronomica@gmail.com; internet www.sociedadastronomica.org.mx; f. 1902; library of 5,000 vols; 500 mems; Pres. MARTE TREJO SANDOVAL; Sec.-Gen. JORGE RUBÍ GARZA; publ. *El Universo* (4 a year).

Sociedad Geológica Mexicana, AC (Mexican Geological Society): Torres Bodet 176, Del. Cuauhtémoc, 06400 México, DF; tel. (55) 5541-0879; e-mail publigl@geologia.igeolcu.unam.mx; internet www.geociencias.unam.mx/sgm.html; f. 1904; 1,000 mems; library of 4,500 vols; Pres. Ing. BERNARDO MARTELL ANDRADE; Vice-Pres. Ing. HERIBERTO PALACIOS; Sec. Ing. LUIS VELÁZQUEZ AGUIRRE; publs *Boletín* (3 a year), *Revista Mexicana de Ciencias Geológicas* (jtly, 3 a year).

Sociedad Química de México (Mexican Chemical Society): Barranca del Muerto 26, Esquina Hércules, Col. Crédito Constructor, Del. Benito Juárez, 03940 México, DF; tel. (55) 5662-6837; fax (55) 5662-6823; e-mail soquimex@prodigy.net.mx; internet www.sqm.org.mx; f. 1956; 2,300 mems; Pres. ANDRÉS CERDA ONOFRE; Sec. (vacant); publ. *Revista de la SQM* (4 a year).

PHILOSOPHY AND PSYCHOLOGY

Sociedad Mexicana de Estudios Psico-Pedagógicos (Mexican Society for Psycho-Pedagogical Studies): Nayarit 86, México, DF.

RELIGION, SOCIOLOGY AND ANTHROPOLOGY

Sociedad Mexicana de Antropología (Mexican Anthropological Society): Apdo 100, C. A. P. Polanco, 11550 México, DF; tel. (55) 5622-9570; fax (55) 5622-9651; e-mail somedean@yahoo.com.mx; internet morgan.iia.unam.mx/usr/sma/index.html; f. 1937; 480 mems; Sec. Dr LEONARDO LÓPEZ LUJÁN; publ. *Revista Mexicana de Estudios Antropológicos* (1 a year).

TECHNOLOGY

Sociedad Mexicana de Ingeniería Sísmica, AC (Mexican Society of Seismic Engineering): Camino de Santa Teresa 187, Col. Parques del Pedregal, Tlalpan, 14020 México, DF; tel. (55) 5606-1314; fax (55) 5606-1314; e-mail smis@smis.org.mx; internet www.smis.org.mx; f. 1962; 350 mems; Pres. LEONARDO ALCÁNTARA NOLASCO; Operation Man. FERNANDO HEREDIA ZAVONI; publ. *Revista de Ingeniería Sísmica* (3 a year).

Research Institutes
GENERAL

Institut de Recherche pour le Développement (IRD) (Development Research Institute): Cicerón 609, Col. Los Morales, 11530 México, DF; tel. (55) 5280-7688; fax (55) 5282-0800; e-mail mexique@ird.fr; internet www.mx.ird.fr; Rep. PASCAL LABAZÉE; (see main entry under France).

AGRICULTURE, FISHERIES AND VETERINARY SCIENCE

Campo Agrícola Experimental Río Bravo (Río Bravo Agricultural Research Station): Apdo 172, Río Bravo, Tamps; f. 1965; research into regional problems and diversification; Dir Ing. Agr. MANUEL CARNERO HERNÁNDEZ.

Instituto Nacional de Investigaciones Forestales, Agrícolas y Pecuarias (National Institute of Forestry, Agriculture and Livestock Research): Serapio Rendón 83, Col. San Rafael, Del. Cuauhtémoc, 06470 México, DF; tel. (55) 5484-1900; e-mail contactenos@inifap.gob.mx; internet www.inifap.gob.mx; f. 1985 through the integration of Instituto Nacional de Investigaciones Agrícolas, Instituto Nacional de Investigaciones Pecuarias and Instituto Nacional de Investigaciones Forestales; conducts research in all aspects of agricultural development and production; agronomy library, livestock library and forestry library; Gen. Dir Dr PEDRO BRAJCICH GALLEGOS; publs *Agricultura Técnica en México* (2 a year), *Ciencia Forestal* (2 a year).

BIBLIOGRAPHY, LIBRARY SCIENCE AND MUSEOLOGY

Instituto de Investigaciones Bibliográficas (Institute of Bibliographical Research): c/o Biblioteca Nacional de México and Hemeroteca Nacional de México, Centro Cultural Universitario, Ciudad Universitaria, Del. Coyoacán, 04510 México, DF; tel. (55) 5622-6827; fax (55) 5665-0951; e-mail webmast@biblional.bibliog.unam.mx; internet biblional.bibliog.unam.mx; f. 1899, present name 1967; compiles the national bibliographies and books on bibliographical subjects; Dir VICENTE QUIRARTE CASTAÑEDA; publs *Boletín* (2 a year), *Nueva Gaceta Bibliográfica* (4 a year).

ECONOMICS, LAW AND POLITICS

Centro de Estudios Demográficos, Urbanos y Ambientales (Centre for Demographic, Urban and Environmental Studies): Camino al Ajusco 20, 14200 México, DF; tel. (55) 5449-3000; fax (55) 5645-0464; e-mail direccion.ceddu@colmex.mx; internet www.colmex.mx/centros/ceddu; f. 1964; library of 500,000 vols; Dir Dr JOSÉ LUIS LEZAMA DE LA TORRE; publ. *Revista de Estudios Demográficos y Urbanos* (3 a year).

Centro de Estudios Económicos (Centre for Economic Studies): Camino al Ajusco 20, Pedregal de Santa Teresa, Apdo 20671, 10740 México, DF; tel. (55) 5449-3000; fax (55) 5645-0464; e-mail webmaster@colmex.mx; internet www.colmex.mx; f. 1981; research areas include microeconomics, macroeconomics, economic development, statistics, game theory, environmental economics, industrial organization, international economics, public finance; masters and doctorate programmes; library of 8,000 vols; Dir JAIME SEMPERE CAMPELLO; publ. *Estudios Económicos* (2 a year).

Centro de Estudios Internacionales (Centre for International Studies): Camino al Ajusco 20, Col. Pedregal de Sta. Teresa, 10740 México, DF; tel. (55) 5449-3000 ext. 3110; fax (55) 5645-0464; e-mail psoto@colmex.mx; internet www.colmex.mx/centros/cei; f. 1960; research areas include international relations, politics, federal and local public administration, Mexico's political system and foreign policy, and regional studies of North America, Europe and Latin America; undergraduate programmes in Politics and Public Administration, and International Relations; Dir GUSTAVO VEGA; publ. *Foro Internacional* (4 a year).

Centro de Relaciones Internacionales: Ciudad Universitaria, FCPS, UNAM, 04510 México, DF; tel. (55) 5622-9412; fax (55) 5622-9413; attached to the Faculty of Political and Social Sciences of the Universidad Nacional Autónoma de México; f. 1970; coordinates and promotes research in all aspects of international relations and Mexico's foreign policy, as well as the training of researchers in different fields: disciplinary construction problems, cooperation and international law, developing nations, actual problems in world society, Africa, Asia, peace research; 30 full mems; library of 6,000 vols, 35 spec. colln, 16,000 journals, etc; Dir Lic. ROBERTO PEÑA GUERRERO; publs *Boletín Informativo del CRI, Cuadernos, Relaciones Internacionales* (4 a year).

Instituto Mexicano del Desarrollo, AC: M. Escobedo 510, 8° piso, México 5, DF; tel. (55) 5531-0823; research on socio-economic development and planning; 470 staff; Dir-Gen. Lic. ERNESTO SANCHEZ AGUILAR.

EDUCATION

Centro de Estudios Educativos, AC (Centre for Educational Studies): Avda Revolución 1291, Col. Tlacopac–San Angel, Del. Alvaro Obregón, 01040 México, DF; tel. (55) 5593-5719; fax (55) 5651-6374; e-mail cee@cee.edu.mx; internet www.cee.edu.mx; f. 1963; scientific research into the problems of education in Mexico and Latin America; library of 31,500 vols, 642 periodicals; Dir-Gen. Dr LUIS MORFIN LÓPEZ; publ. *Revista Latinoamericana de Estudios Educativos* (4 a year).

HISTORY, GEOGRAPHY AND ARCHAEOLOGY

Centro de Estudios de Asia y África (Centre for Asian and African Studies): Camino al Ajusco 20, Pedregal de Santa Teresa, 10740 México, DF; tel. (55) 5449-3000; fax (55) 5645-0464; e-mail direccion.ceaa@colmex.mx; internet ceaa.colmex.mx/sitioceaa; f. 1964; studies of and research on Africa, China, Korea, Japan, S Asia, SE Asia, Middle E and N Africa; masters and doctorate programmes; library of 30,000 vols, 130 periodicals; Dir BENJAMÍN PRECIADO SOLÍS; publs *Anuario Asia Pacífico* (1 a year), *Cuadernos de Trabajo, Estudios de Asia y África* (3 a year).

Centro de Estudios Históricos (Centre for Historical Studies): Coordinación Académica, Centro de Estudios Históricos, Camino al Ajusco 20, 10740 México, DF; tel. (55) 5449-3000 ext. 3132; fax (55) 5645-0464; e-mail coord.acad.ceh@colmex.mx; internet www.colmex.mx/centros/ceh; f. 1941; history of Mexico and Latin America; Dir Dr GUILLERMO PALACIOS; publ. *Historia Mexicana* (4 a year).

Instituto Nacional de Estudios Históricos de las Revoluciones de México (INEHRM) (National Institute for Historical Studies of the Mexican Revolutions): Francisco I. Madero 1, Colonia San Ángel, 01000 México, DF; tel. (55) 5616-3808; e-mail contactoinehrm@segob.gob.mx; internet www.inehrm.gob.mx; f. 1953; library of 43,000 vols; Man. Lic. JOSE MANUEL VILLALPANDO.

LANGUAGE AND LITERATURE

Centro de Estudios Lingüísticos y Literarios (Centre for Linguistic and Literary Studies): Coordinación Académica, Centro de Estudios Lingüísticos y Literarios, Camino al Ajusco 20, 10740 México, DF; tel. (55) 5449-3018; fax (55) 5255-5645; e-mail coord.acad.cell@colmex.mx; internet www.colmex.mx/centros; f. 1947; Spanish linguistics and literature (PhD degrees), Indian languages, translation; Dir Dr LUZ ELENA GUTIÉRREZ DE VELASCO; Academic Coordinator Dr MARÍA ÁGUEDA MÉNDEZ HERRERA; publ. *Nueva Revista de Filología Hispánica* (2 a year).

MEDICINE

Instituto Nacional de Cardiología 'Ignacio Chávez' (National Cardiological Institute): Juan Badiano 1, Col. Sección XVI, Del. Tlalpan, 14080 México, DF; tel. (55) 5573-2911; fax (55) 5573-0994; e-mail webmaster@cardiologia.org.mx; internet www.cardiologia.org.mx; f. 1944; 390 medical mems; library of 8,465 vols, 569 periodicals; Dir Dr FAUSE ATTIÉ CURY; Sub-Dirs L. C. CUAUHTÉMOC SOTO CASTILLO (Administrative Division), Dr MARCO ANTONIO MARTÍNEZ RÍOS (Medical Attendance), Dr JOSÉ FERNANDO GUADALAJARA BOO (Medical Education Division), Dr PEDRO ANTONIO REYES LÓPEZ (Research Division); Library Dir MARIO FLAVIO FUENTES INIESTRA; publ. *Archivos de Cardiología de México* (6 nos, 1 vol per year).

Instituto Nacional de Diagnóstico y Referencia Epidemiológicos (National Institute of Epidemiological Diagnosis and Reference): Calle de Carpio 470, Santo Tomás, Miguel Hidalgo, 11340 México, D.F.; tel. (55) 5341-4389; fax (55) 5341-3264; e-mail indre@cenids.ssa.gob.mx; f. 1938; performs epidemiological laboratory reference services nationwide; carries out technological development and research in laboratory for support of epidemiological surveillance; trains and supervises laboratory personnel and performs quality control procedures for the National Laboratory Network; library of 3,930 vols, 603 journals. MEDLINE terminal; Dir Dr ANA FLISSER.

Instituto Nacional de Higiene de la S.S.A. (National Institute of Hygiene): Gerencia General de Biológicas y Reactivos, Czda Mariano Escobedo 20, Col. Popotla, Del. Miguel Hidalgo, 11400 México, DF; tel. (55) 5527-7368; fax (55) 5527-6693; f. 1895; 300 mems; library of 10,000 vols; Dir (vacant).

Instituto Nacional de Neurología y Neurocirugía (National Institute of Neurology and Neurosurgery): Insurgentes Sur 3877, Col. La Fama, Deleg. Tlalpan, 14269 México, DF; tel. (55) 5606-3822; fax (55) 5606-3245; internet www.innn.edu.mx; f. 1964; library of 2,700 vols, 270 periodicals; Dir-Gen. Dr JULIO SOTELO MORALES; publ. *Archivos de Neurociencias* (review, 4 a year).

Instituto Nacional de Salud Pública (National Institute of Public Health): Avda Univ. 655, Col. Santa María Ahuacatitlán, 62100 Cuernavaca, Morelos; e-mail contacto@insp.mx; internet www.insp.mx; f. 1987; incl. School of Public Health in Mexico (f. 1922) and research centres on public health, health systems: infectious diseases, malaria, and nutrition and health; masters and doctorate programmes; library of 35,000 vols; Dir-Gen. Dr MARIO HENRY RODRIGUEZ LOPEZ; publ. *Salud Pública de México* (6 a year).

NATURAL SCIENCES
General

Centro de Investigación y de Estudios Avanzados del Instituto Politécnico Nacional (Centre for Research and Advanced Studies, National Polytechnic Institute): Apdo 14-258, 07360 México, DF; Av. Instituto Politécnico Nacional 2508, Col. San Pedro Zacatanco, 07360 México, DF; tel. (55) 5747-3800; fax (55) 5747-3814; e-mail azurita@cinvestav.mx; internet www.cinvestav.mx; f. 1961; postgraduate research and training centre in sciences; integrates the work of the depts of biochemistry, physics, applied physics, physiology, biophysics and neurosciences, electrical engineering, mathematics, genetics and molecular biology, cellular biology, marine resources, experimental pathology, chemistry, biotechnology and bioengineering, biotechnology and biochemistry, pharmacology, bioelectronics, educational mathematics, toxicology, metallurgical engineering, computer science, mechatronics, solid-state electronics, automatic control, molecular biomedicine, communications, ceramic engineering, genetic engineering, materials, engineering drawing, human ecology and educational research; library of 256,000 vols, 3,200 spec. collns; Dir Dr RENE ASOMOZA PALACIO; publs *Avance y Perspectiva* (4 a year), *Morfismos* (2 a year).

Consejo Nacional de Ciencia y Tecnología (CONACYT) (National Council for Science and Technology): Avda Insurgentes Sur 1582, Col. Crédito Constructor, Del. Benito Juárez, 03940 México, DF; tel. (55) 5322-7700; e-mail snicst@conacyt.mx; internet www.conacyt.mx; f. 1970; co-ordinates scientific research and development and formulates policy; Dir JUAN CARLOS ROMERO HICKS; publ. *Ciencia y Desarrollo* (12 a year).

Instituto Mexicano de Recursos Naturales Renovables, AC (Institute for the Conservation of Natural Resources): Dr Vertiz 724, Narvarte, 03020 México, DF; tel. (55) 5519-4505; fax (55) 5519-1633; e-mail imernar@laneta.apc.org; internet www.imernar.org; f. 1952; library of 7,000 vols and 200 regular periodicals; Dir (vacant).

Biological Sciences

Instituto de Ecología, AC (Institute of Ecology): Apdo Postal 63, km $2\frac{1}{2}$ Carretera Antigua a Coatepec No. 351, Congregación el Haya, 91070 Jalapa, Veracruz; tel. (228) 842-1800; fax (228) 818-7809; internet www.ecologia.edu.mx; f. 1975; plant and animal ecology and taxonomy, biogeography, dynamics and structure of ecosystems, conservation and management of natural resources, environmental biotechnology, wood technology, coastal management, entomology, flora and fauna inventory; postgraduate programmes in ecology and natural resources management, in wildlife management and in systematics; library of 24,000 vols, 535 current periodicals, 500 maps, 60 electronic reference titles; Dir-Gen. Dr DANIEL PIÑERO DALMAU; publs *Acta Zoológica Mexicana* (3 a year), *Acta Botánica Mexicana* (4 a year), *Flora del Bajío y de Regiones Adyacentes, Flora de Veracruz, Madera y Bosques* (2 a year).

Instituto Nacional de la Pesca (National Fishery Institute): Pitágoras 1320, Col. Santa Cruz Atoyac, Del. Benito Juárez, 03310 México, DF; tel. (55) 5605-2424; e-mail correoweb@inp.sagarpa.gob.mx; internet www.inp.sagarpa.gob.mx; f. 1962; research in marine biology; library of 3,000 vols; Dir Dr GUILLERMO ALBERTO COMPEÁN JIMÉNEZ.

Instituto Tecnológico del Mar (Institute of Marine Technology): km 12 Carretera Veracruz-Córdoba, Apdo Postal 68, 94290 Boca del Río, Ver.; tel. (229) 986-0189; fax (229) 986-1894; internet www.itmar1.edu.mx; f. 1975, renamed 1981; 150 mems; library of 4,500 vols; Dir ALMILCAR SUÁREZ ALLEN.

Mathematical Sciences

Instituto de Matemáticas (Institute of Mathematics): Area de la Investigación Científica, Circuito Exterior, Ciudad Universitaria, Coyoacán, 04510 México, DF; tel. (55) 5622-4523; fax (55) 5550-1342; e-mail rosi@matem.unam.mx; internet www.matem.unam.mx; f. 1942; research in mathematics; 59 mems; library of 20,000 vols; Dir Dr JAVIER BRACHO CARPIZO; publs *Anales* (1 a year), *Aportaciones Matemáticas* (irregular), *Monografías* (irregular), *Publicaciones Preliminares*.

Physical Sciences

Instituto de Astronomía (Institute of Astronomy): Apdo postal 70–264, 04510 México, DF; tel. (55) 5622-3906; fax (55) 5616-0653; e-mail direc@astroscu.unam.mx; internet www.astroscu.unam.mx; f. 1878; an Institute of the Universidad Nacional Autónoma de México; research in astronomy and astrophysics; library of 7,000 vols, 1,550 journals; Dir Dr JOSÉ FRANCO; publs *Anuario del Observatorio Astronómico Nacional* (1 a year), *Revista Mexicana de Astronomía y Astrofísica* (2 a year).

Instituto Nacional de Astrofísica, Optica y Electrónica (National Institute of Astrophysics, Optics and Electronics): Luis Enrique Erro 1, Apdos 216 y 51, 72000 Tonantzintla, Pue.; tel. (222) 266-3100; fax (222) 247-2231; e-mail astrofi@inaoep.mx; internet www.inaoep.mx; f. 1971 formerly Observatorio Nacional de Astrofísica, f. 1942; 22 research mems; library of 7,000 vols, 144 periodicals; Gen. Dir Dr ALFONSO SERRANO PÉREZ-GROVAS; Gen. Academic Sec. Dr MANUEL G. CORONA GALINDO; publ. *Boletín del Instituto de Tonantzintla.*

Instituto Nacional de Investigaciones Nucleares (National Institute of Nuclear Research): km 36.5, Carretera México-Toluca, 52045, Ocoyoacac, Edo. de México; tel. (55) 5329-7200; fax (55) 5329-7299; internet www.inin.mx; f. 1979 (previously part of *Instituto Nacional de Energía Nuclear*, f. 1955); planning, research and development of atomic technology, including non-military use of atomic energy; library of 41,500 vols (incl. theses), 75,000 periodicals, 7,300 consulting works, 6,000 pamphlets, 1,000 official publs, 125 video cassettes, 835,000 reports on microfiche and 25,000 in printed form; Gen. Dir José RAÚL ORTÍZ MAGAÑA; Technical Sec. Dr JULIÁN SÁNCHEZ GUTIERREZ; publ. *Contacto Nuclear* (4 a year).

Servicio Meteorológico Nacional (National Meteorological Dept): Avda Observatorio 192, Col. Observatorio, Del. M. Hidalgo, 11860 México, DF; tel. (55) 2636-4600; fax (55) 5271-0878; internet smn.cna.gob.mx; f. 1915; library of 80,000 vols, 90,180 pamphlets; Dir Dr MICHEL ROSENGAUS MOSHINSKY.

RELIGION, SOCIOLOGY AND ANTHROPOLOGY

Centro Co-ordinador y Difusor de Estudios Latinoamericanos (Coordinating and Information Centre for Latin American Studies): Piso 8, Torre II de Humanidades, Ciudad Universitaria, 04510 México, DF; tel. (55) 5623-0211; e-mail moce@servidor.unam.mx; internet www.ccydel.unam.mx; f. 1978; attached to Universidad Nacional Autónoma de México; study of Latin America and the Caribbean in all disciplines (history, literature, philosophy, etc.); library of 11,898 monographs, 8,700 magazines, 3,000 pamphlets, 160 theses and 150 records; Dir Dra ESTELA MORALES CAMPOS; publs *Archipiélago, Revista Cultural de Nuestra América* (4 a year), *Latinoamérica. Revista de Estudios Latinoamericanos.*

Centro de Estudios Sociológicos (Centre for Sociological Studies): Camino al Ajusco 20, 10740 México, DF; tel. (55) 5449-3000; fax (55) 5645-0464; e-mail direccion.ces@colmex.mx; internet www.colmex.mx; f. 1973; research areas include sociological theory, economic sociology and the sociology of work, social movements and civil organizations, class and family, political parties, elections and politics, education, labour markets, migration and emigration, reproductive health, religion, culture; doctorate programme in Social Science; Dir ROBERTO

BLANCARTE PIMENTEL; publ. *Estudios Sociológicos.*

Comisión Nacional para el Desarrollo de los Pueblos Indígenas (National Commission for the Development of Indian Peoples): Avda México-Coyoacán 343, Col. Xoco, Del. Benito Juárez 03330 México, DF; tel. (55) 9183-2100; e-mail dirgral@cdi.gob.mx; internet www.cdi.gob.mx; f. 1948; forms links with indigenous communities of Mexico; organs incl. 23 co-ordinating centres in the interior, radio stations transmitting in 31 indigenous languages, 29 regional documentation and information centres; library: specialized library of 25,000 vols; Dir-Gen. XÓCHITL GÁLVEZ RUIZ; publs *Colección Historia de los Pueblos Indígenas de México*, *México Indígena.*

Instituto Indigenista Interamericano (Inter-American Indian Institute): Avda de las Fuentes 106, Col. Jardines de Pedregal, Del. Álvaro Obregón, 01900 México, DF; tel. (55) 5595-8410; e-mail ininin@prodigy.net .mx; internet www.indigenista.org; f. 1940; supplies technical assistance to member governments for the Indian population of the continent; library of 40,000 vols; Dir GUILLERMO ESPINOSA VELASCO; publ. *América Indígena* (4 a year).

Instituto Nacional de Antropología e Historia (National Institute of Anthropology and History): Córdoba 45, Col. Roma, 06700 México, DF; tel. (55) 5533-2015; fax (55) 5525-2213; internet www.inah.gob.mx; f. 1939; govt organization for research, conservation and promotion of Mexican cultural heritage, especially archaeological and historical sites; controls 105 museums, incl. Museo Nacional de Antropología, Museo Nacional de Historia, Museo Nacional del Virreinato, Museo Nacional de las Intervenciones, Museo Nacional de las Culturas, Museo del Templo Mayor and Galería de Historia; manages Escuela Nacional de Antropología e Historia, Escuela Nacional de Conservación, Restauración y Museografía, National Anthropology and History Library, National Photographic Archives and Phonographic Archive; Dir-Gen. SERGIO RAÚL ARROYO GARCÍA; publs *Boletín* (anthropology, ethnology, history and archaeology, 4 a year), *Arqueología* (archaeology, 2 a year), *Historias* (history and related subjects, 3 a year), *Alquimia* (conservation and photographic archives, 3 a year), *Dimensión Antropológica* (anthropology, linguistics and ethnology, 3 a year), *Museos de México y del Mundo* (museology, in English and Spanish, 2 a year).

TECHNOLOGY

Instituto de Investigaciones Eléctricas (Institute of Electrical Research): Calle Reforma No. 113, Col. Palmira, 62490 Cuernavaca, Mor.; tel. (777) 362-3811; fax (777) 318-9854; e-mail difusion@iie.org.mx; internet www.iie.org.mx; f. 1975; promotes and undertakes research and experimental devt in the electrical industry; consulting service; library of 61,284 vols; Exec. Dir Ing. JULIÁN ADAME MIRANDA; publs *Boletín IIE*, *Referencias IIE.*

Instituto Mexicano de Investigaciones Tecnológicas (IMIT, AC): Calz. Legaria 694, Col. Irrigación, Del. Miguel Hidalgo, 11500 Mexico DF; tel. (55) 5557-1022; fax (55) 5395-4147; f. 1950; applied research on natural resources and development of industrial processes; pre-investment studies, reports process and conceptual engineering; library: specialized library in chemical technology of 12,000 vols, 250 periodicals; Dir Dr MARTÍNEZ FRÍAS.

Instituto Mexicano del Petróleo (Mexican Petroleum Institute): Eje Central Norte L. Cárdenas 152, Col. San Bartolo Atepehuecan, Apdo 14–805, 07730 México, DF; tel. (55) 9175-7944; fax (55) 9175-7934; e-mail sabugalp@imp.mx; internet www.imp.mx; f. 1965; research on petroleum products and equipment, petroleum and petrochemical industries, economic studies, exploration, refining; training and specialist courses; 3,600 mems; library of 46,000 vols; Gen. Dir Dr HÉBER CINCO LEY; publ. *Electronic Journal* (daily).

Libraries and Archives

Chapingo

Biblioteca Central–Universidad Autónoma Chapingo (Central Library–Chapingo Autonomous University):; e-mail marcerc@hotmail.com km 38.5 Carretera México-Texcoco, 56230 Texcoco, Edo de México; tel. and fax (595) 952-1501; e-mail ramsestexcoco@yahoo.com; internet www.ceres.chapingo.mx; Public control; language of instruction: Spanish; f. 1854, present name 1974; interlibrary loans, digital library, reproduction; 200,000 vols, 4,000 periodicals, 11,000 maps; specializes in agricultural and forestry sciences; Dir Lic. RAMÓN SUÁREZ ESPINOSA; publs *Revista de Chapingo* (in 3 series, irregular), *Revista de Geografía Agrícola* (in 3 series, irregular), *Revista Textual*, *Ingeniería Agrícola y Biosistemas.*

Guadalajara

Coordinación de Bibliotecas, Universidad de Guadalajara (University of Guadalajara Library Services): Avda Juárez 976, Edif. Cultural y Administrativo, piso 7, 44100 Guadalajara, Jal.; tel. (33) 3134-2277; fax (33) 3134-2205; e-mail sergiolr@redudg .udg.mx; internet www.rebiudg.udg.mx; f. 1861, present name 1994; depository for UNESCO publs; 1,660,353 vols, 15,261 periodicals (1,761 print, 13,500 electronic); Man. Dir Mtro. SERGIO LÓPEZ RUELAS.

Mexico City

Archivo General de la Nación (National Archives): Avda Eduardo Molina y Albañiles s/n, Col. Penitenciaría Ampliación, Deleg. Venustiano Carranza, 15350 México, DF; tel. (55) 5133-9900; fax (55) 5789-5296; e-mail argena@segob.gob.mx; internet www .agn.gob.mx; f. 1795; documents relating to the vice-regal administration of New Spain, the Inquisition, independence 1821–40, the 19th century, the Mexican Revolution 1910, and the years up to 1976 (50 km of documents); 49,000 books; 1,050 prehispanic paintings; newspaper collection of 1,272,000 copies; microfilm service and library; Dir-Gen. Mtro JORGE RUIZ DUEÑAS; publ. *Boletín* (4 a year).

Biblioteca Central de la Universidad Nacional Autónoma de México (Central Library of the National Autonomous University of Mexico): Ciudad Universitaria, 04510 México, DF; tel. (55) 5622-1603; fax (55) 5616-0664; e-mail web-bc@dgb.unam.mx; internet bc.unam.mx; f. 1924; 350,000 vols, 2,883 periodicals, 265,000 theses; Dir-Gen. of Libraries Dra SILVIA GONZÁLEZ MARÍN; Sub-Dir of the Central Library Lic. ADRIANA HERNÁNDEZ SÁNCHEZ.

Biblioteca de Derecho y Legislación de la Secretaría de Hacienda (Law Library, Finance Ministry): Correo Mayor 31, México, DF; f. 1925, present form 1928; 13,000 vols; specialized library relating to ancient and existing federal laws, tax laws from 1831,

foreign and international laws; Librarian SOFÍA SILVA.

Biblioteca de Historia de la Secretaría de Hacienda (Historical Library, Finance Ministry): Palacio Nacional, 06066 México, DF; f. 1939 with the collections of the old library of the Finance Ministry and those of Genaro Estrada acquired by the Government; 8,750 vols, 14,000 pamphlets relating to Mexico.

Biblioteca de la Secretaría de Comunicaciones y Transportes (Library of the Ministry of Communications and Transport): Tacuba y Xicotecatl, México, DF; f. 1891; 10,000 vols; Dir RENATO MOLINE ENRÍQUEZ.

Biblioteca de la Secretaría de Gobernación (Library of the Ministry of the Interior): Bucareli 99, 06699 México, DF; f. 1917; 45,000 vols.

Biblioteca del Honorable Congreso de la Unión (Congress Library): Biblioteca Unidad Centro Histórico, Edif. de la ex-Iglesia de Santa Clara, Tacuba 29, 06000 México, DF; tel. (55) 5510-3866; fax (55) 5512-1085; internet www.cddhcu.gob.mx/bibcong; f. 1936; 110,000 vols, 95 periodicals; Dir ENRIQUE MOLINA LEÓN.

Attached Institution:

Sistema Integral de Información y Documentación (SIID) (Integral System of Information and Documentation): Palacio Legislativo de San Lázaro, Avda Congreso de la Unión s/n, 15969 México, DF; tel. (55) 5628-1318; fax (55) 5522-1463; e-mail siid@info.cddhcu.gob.mx; internet www.cddhcu.gob.mx/bibcongr/integra/siid .htm; f. 1991; collns of the old libraries of the Chamber of Deputies and the Chamber of Senators; 60,000 vols, 489 periodicals; Dir Lic. D. M. LIAHUT BALDOMAR.

Biblioteca del Instituto Nacional de Salud Pública (National Institute of Public Health Library): Insp-Biblioteca, Avda Universidad 655, Cerrada los Pinos y Caminera, Col. Santa Maria Ahuacatitlán, 62100 Cuernavaca, Mor.; tel. (777) 3-29-30-65; fax (777) 101-29-10; e-mail atalani@insp.mx; internet www.insp.mx; f. 1922; spec. collns in public health medical admin., hygiene, preventative medicine, epidemiology, statistics, mental hygiene, nutrition, rehabilitation, occupational safety, industrial hygiene and water, air, noise and waste pollution engineering, behavioural sciences; spec. colln in health economics 'Julio Frenk Mora', historical documentary colln in public health from 1826; 45,000 vols, 800 periodicals; Librarian Lic. NATALIA LÓPEZ LÓPEZ; publs *Salud Pública de México* (6 a year), *VIVA SALUD Gaceta Informátiva del Instituto Nacional de Salud Pública* (11 a year).

Biblioteca 'José Ma. Lafragua' ('José Ma. Lafragua' Library): Ex Colegio de la Santa Cruz de Tlatelolco, Plaza de las Tres Culturas, Avda R. Flores Magón 1, Col. Guerrero, 06995 México, DF; tel. (55) 5063-3000, ext. 4102; e-mail sgaytan@sre.gob.mx; internet www.gob.mx/wb/egobierno/egob_biblioteca_jose_ma_lafragua; f. 19th century; 35,000 vols; specializes in international relations and social sciences; Dir Dra MERCEDES DE VEGA ARMIJO.

Biblioteca 'Miguel Lerdo de Tejada' de la Secretaría de Hacienda y Crédito Público (General Library, Finance Ministry): Avda República de El Salvador 49, Centro Histórico, México, DF; tel. (55) 9158-9837; fax (55) 5709-5144; e-mail publica_web@hacienda.gob.mx; internet www.shcp.gob.mx/servs/dgpcap/bmlt; f. 1928; 250,000 vols; Dir ROMÁN BELTRÁN MARTÍNEZ.

Biblioteca Nacional de Antropología e Historia 'Dr Eusebio Dávalos Hurtado'

(National Library of Anthropology and History): Avda Paseo de la Reforma y Calzada Gandhi, 1er Piso, Col. Polanco, 11560 México, DF; tel. (55) 5553-6865; fax (55) 5286-1743; e-mail subtec.bnah@inah.gob.mx; internet www.bnah.inah.gob.mx; f. 1888 as Library of the Instituto Nacional de Antropología e Historia de México (see Research Institutes); 550,000 vols, 8,000 periodicals; Dir CÉSAR MOHENO; publs *Arqueología* (4 a year), *Arqueología Mexicana* (6 a year), *Alquimía* (4 a year), *Dimensión Antropológica* (3 a year), *Historias* (2 a year).

Biblioteca Nacional de México (National Library): Centro Cultural Universitario, C.U., Delegación Coyoacán, 04510 México, DF; tel. (55) 5622-6800; fax (55) 5665-0951; e-mail gasca@biblional.bibliog.unam.mx; internet www.bibliog.unam.mx/bib/biblioteca.html; f. 1867; run by Bibliographic Research Institute of the National University of Mexico; 1,250,000 vols, and other items relating to the political, social, artistic, literary and historical development of Mexico; Library Coordinator Mtra. ROSA MARÍA GASCA NUÑEZ.

Biblioteca Vasconcelos (Vasconcelos Library): Eje 1 Norte esq Aldama, Buenavista, México, DF; tel. (55) 1253-9100 ext. 8102; internet www.bibliotecavasconcelos.gob.mx; f. 1946; 500,000 vols, spec. collns, hall for the blind and visually impaired; Dir JORGE VON ZIEGLER; publ. *Biblioteca de México* (6 a year).

Centro de Documentación de la Oficialía Mayor de la Secretaría de Economía: Alfonso Reyes 30 PB, Col. Hipódromo Condesa, Del. Álvaro Obregón, 06140 México DF; tel. 5729-9100 ext. 17071; e-mail blopezl@economia.gob.mx; internet www.economia.gob.mx/?p=2575; f. 1918; international business, business guides, statistics on foreign investment, legislation; trade statistics; 42,250 vols; Librarian Lic. BERENISSE LÓPEZ LÓPEZ.

Hemeroteca Nacional de México (National Library of Periodicals): Centro Cultural Universitario, C.U., Delegación Coyoacán, 04510 México, D.F.; tel. (55) 5622-6818; fax (55) 5665-0951; e-mail curielg@biblional.bibliog.unam.mx; internet www.bibliog.unam.mx/hem/hemeroteca.html; f. 1912; run by Bibliographic Research Institute of the National University of Mexico; 250,000 vols; newspapers and periodicals; Mexican Gazette of 18th century; Coordinator Mtra GUADALUPE CURIEL DEFOSSÉ.

Instituto Nacional de Bellas Artes y Literatura (Educación e Investigación Artísticas) (National Institute of Fine Arts and Literature (Art Education and Research)): Paseo de la Reforma y Campo Marte s/n, Col. Chapultepec Polanco, 11560 México, DF; tel. (55) 5521-9251; fax (55) 5280-5364; internet www.cnca.gob.mx/cnca/buena/inba; f. 1947; incorporates several centres, each of which inherited specialist material from the former Biblioteca Ibero-Americana y de Bellas Artes.

Incorporated Centres:

Centro de Documentación y Biblioteca (Documentation Centre and Library): Eje Lázaro Cárdenas 2, 3er Piso (Torre Latinoamericana), Col. Centro, 06007 México, DF; f. 1984; specializes in Mexican literature; 3,500 vols; database LIME-INBA of the Mexican literature contained in the principal libraries of Mexico City; Dir Lic. JORGE PEREZ-GROVAS.

Centro Nacional de Investigación y Documentación de las Artes Plásticas (National Centre for Research and Documentation on the Plastic Arts): Calle Nueva York 224, Col. Nápoles, 03810 México, DF.

Centro Nacional de Investigación de Información y Documentación de la Danza José Limón (José Limón National Centre for Research, Information and Dance Documentation): Campos Eliseos 480, Col. Polanco, 11560 México, DF.

Centro Nacional de Investigación y Documentación Musical Carlos Chávez (Carlos Chávez National Centre for Research and Music Documentation): Liverpool 16, Col. Juárez, 06600 México, DF.

Centro Nacional de Investigación e Información Teatral Rodolfo Usigli (Rodolfo Usigli National Centre for Research and Theatre Information): Chihuahua 216, Esquina Monterrey, Col. Roma, 06760 México, DF.

Monterrey

Biblioteca del Instituto Tecnológico y de Estudios Superiores de Monterrey (Library of the Monterrey Institute of Technology and Higher Studies): Avda Eugenio Garza Sada 2501 Sur, Sucursal de Correos 'J', Col. Tecnológico, 64849 Monterrey (Nuevo León); tel. (81) 8328-4096; fax (81) 8328-4067; e-mail miguel_arreola@itesm.mx; internet biblioteca.mty.itesm.mx; f. 1943; c. 200 library instructional workshops annually; nat. and int. interlibrary loan (to USA and Europe); organizes int. book fair, confs., academic congresses; 750,000 vols, 20,000 periodicals of which 18,000 are electronic; digital library with 60 databases; Dir Ing. MIGUEL ARREOLA; publs *Calidad Ambiental* (4 a year), *Integratec* (6 a year), *Revista de Humanidades* (2 a year), *Transferencia* (4 a year).

Puebla

Biblioteca de la Universidad de las Américas (Library of the Universidad de las Américas): POB 100, Santa Catarina Mártir, San Andrés, 72820 Cholula, Pue.; tel. (222) 229-2257; fax (222) 229-2078; e-mail bibinfo@mail.udlap.mx; internet ciria.udlap.mx/bibliotecas; f. 1940; humanities, science and technology; 400,000 vols, 2,200 periodicals; special collection; M. Covarrubias archives, R. Barlow archives, Herrera Carrillo archives, Porfirio Díaz archives; Dir Mtro ARTURO ARRIETA.

Toluca

Biblioteca Pública Central del Estado de México (Main Public Library of México State): Centro Cultural Mexiquense, 50000 Toluca (Estado de México); f. 1827; 40,012 vols, 128 periodicals; Dir MARÍA CRISTINA PÉREZ GÓMEZ.

Tuxtla Gutiérrez

Biblioteca Pública del Estado de Chiapas (Public Library of Chiapas State): Blvd Angel Albino Corzo Km 1087, Tuxtla Gutiérrez, Chiapas; tel. (961) 3-06-64; f. 1910; 45,000 vols; Dir JOSÉ LUIS CASTRO.

Zacatecas

Bibliotecas Públicas de Zacatecas (Zacatecas Public Libraries): Plaza Independencia 1, 98000 Zacatecas; internet www.angelfire.com/nh/luishugo; f. 1832; consists of the following libraries: Biblioteca Central Estatal 'Mauricio Magdaleno', Biblioteca de Colecciones Especiales 'Elías Amador'; Dir (vacant).

Museums and Art Galleries

Campeche

Museo Regional de Campeche (Campeche Regional Museum): Calle 59 entre 16 y 14, Campeche, Camp.; f. 1985; archaeology and history; Dir Arq. JOSÉ E. ORTÍZ LAN.

Guadalajara

Casa Taller José Clemente Orozco (House and Studio of José Clemente Orozco): Calle Aurelio Aceves 27, Col. Arcos Vallarta, 44120 Guadalajara, Jalisco; tel. (33) 3818-2800 ext. 31063; fax (33) 3818-2800 ext. 31014; e-mail museocabanas_lpb@yahoo.com.mx; internet vive.guadalajara.gob.mx/puntos/puntose.asp?which=221; f. 1951; paintings and sketches by the artist; Dir MARGARITA V. DE OROZCO.

Museo del Estado de Jalisco (Jalisco State Museum): Liceo 60, Centro Histórico, 44100 Guadalajara, Jalisco; tel. (33) 3613-2703; fax (33) 3614-5257; f. 1918; collections of early Mexican objects; folk art and costumes; archaeological discoveries; anthropological, archaeological and historical research; library of 6,000 vols; Dir CARLOS R. BELTRÁN BRISEÑO.

Museo Regional de Guadalajara (Guadalajara Regional Museum): Liceo 60, Zona Centro, 44100 Guadalajara, Jalisco; tel. (33) 3613-2705; fax (33) 3614-5257; internet vive.guadalajara.gob.mx/puntos/puntose.asp?which=221; f. 1918; special collections of pre-Spanish and Colonial period art and paintings; archaeological and palaeontological collections; Dir Lic. CRISTINA SÁNCHEZ DEL REAL.

Guanajuato

Museos de la Universidad de Guanajuato (University Museums): Planta baja, Lascuráin de Retana 5, 36000 Guanajuato, Guan.; tel. (473) 732-0096 ext. 1005; e-mail duges@quijote.ugto.mx; internet www.ugto.mx/duges/historia.htm; f. 1870; comprise: Natural History, Geology, Mineralogy, and include the natural history collection of Alfredo Duges with many rare specimens.

Madero

Museo de la Cultura Huasteca (Museum of Huastec Culture): POB 12, 89050 Madero, Tamaulipas; located at: Blvd A. López Mateos s/n, Tampico, Tamaulipas; tel. and fax (833) 210-2217; f. 1960; attached to the Instituto Nacional de Antropología e Historia; library of 1,750 vols, 95 discs; Dir C. P. MA. ALEJANDRINA ELÍAS ORTIZ.

Mérida

Museo Regional de Antropología (Regional Museum of Anthropology): Palacio Canton, Calle 43 por Paseo de Montejo, Mérida, Yucatán; tel. (999) 923-0557; fax (999) 9230557; e-mail palacio.canton@inah.gob.mx; f. 1959; attached to the Instituto Nacional de Antropología e Historia; collns of pre-Hispanic Mayan and Olmec culture, precious stones, ceramics, jade, objects in copper and gold; Dir ABRAHAM GUERRERO; Curator PETER SCHMIEDT.

Mexico City

Laboratorio Arte Alameda (Alameda Laboratory of Arts): Dr Mora 7, Col. Centro Histórico, 06050 México, DF; tel. (55) 5510-2793; fax (55) 5512-2079; e-mail info.artealameda@gmail.com; internet www.artealameda.inba.gob.mx; f. 1962 as Pinacoteca Virreinal de San Diego, a museum of Mexican colonial arts; present name and collections 2000; attached to Instituto Nacional de Bellas Artes; collections of new media and electronic art; library of 5,000 vols; Dir MARIANA MUNGUIA; Curator PRÍAMO LOZADA.

Museo de Arte Alvar y Carmen T. de Carrillo Gil (Alvar and Carmen T. de Carrillo Gil Museum of Art): Avda Revolución 1608, Col. San Angel, Del. Alvaro Obregón, 01000 México, DF; tel. (55) 5550-3983; fax (55) 5550-4232; internet www.macg .inba.gob.mx; f. 1974; contemporary Mexican art; library of 3,500 vols; Dir CARLOS ASHIDA; publ. *Gazeta del Museo* (12 a year).

Museo de Arte Contemporáneo Rufino Tamayo (Rufino Tamayo Museum of Contemporary Art): Paseo de la Reforma y Gandhi s/n, Bosque de Chapultepec, Del. Miguel Hidalgo, 11580 México, DF; tel. (55) 5286-5839; fax (55) 5286-6539; f. 1981; permanent collection of contemporary art, permanent exhibition of Rufino Tamayo's work; temporary exhibits of international artists; library specializing in Rufino Tamayo, contemporary art and artists; Dir CRISTINA GÁLVEZ GUZZY.

Museo de Arte Moderno (Museum of Modern Art): Bosque de Chapultepec, Paseo de la Reforma y Gandhi, 11560 México, DF; tel. (55) 5553-6233; fax (55) 5553-6211; internet www.conaculta.gob.mx/mam; f. 1964; mainly Mexican collection of modern and contemporary art and temporary exhibitions of modern Mexican and foreign art; Dir Prof. LUIS-MARTIN LOZANO.

Museo de Historia Natural de la Ciudad de México (Natural History Museum of the City of Mexico): 2° Sección del Bosque de Chapultepec, Apdo Postal 18–845, Del. Miguel Hidalgo, 11800 México, DF; tel. (55) 5515-6304; fax (55) 5515-2222; e-mail mhn@ df.gob.mx; internet www.sma.df.gob.mx/ mhn; f. 1964; exhibitions on the universe, the earth, the origin of life, plant and animal taxonomy, evolution and adaptation of species, biology, man and bio-geographical areas; contains replicas of prehistoric creatures; library of 6,000 vols; Dir Biol. NEMESIO CHÁVEZ ARREDONDO.

Museo del Palacio de Bellas Artes (Museum of the Palace of Fine Arts): Avda Juárez y Eje Central 'Lázaro Cardenas', Centro Histórico, Del. Cuauhtémoc, 06050 México, DF; tel. (55) 5512-2593; fax (55) 5510-1388; e-mail difusion@ museobellasartes.artte.com; internet www .cnca.gob.mx/palacio/museo.htm; f. 1934; attached to the Instituto Nacional de Bellas Artes; permanent exhibition 'Los Grandes Muralistas'; Dir Arq. AGUSTÍN ARTEAGA.

Museo Estudio Diego Rivera (Museum of Diego Rivera's Studio): Calle Diego Rivera s/ n esq. Avda Altavista, Col. San Angel Inn, 01060 México, DF; tel. (55) 5550-1518; fax (55) 5550-1004; internet www.cnca.gob.mx/ cnca/buena/inba/subbellas/museos/rivera .html; f. 1986; permanent exhibition 'Estudio Taller de Diego Rivera'.

Museo Nacional de Antropología (National Museum of Anthropology): Avda Paseo de la Reforma y Calzada Gandhi s/n, Col. Chapultepec Polanco, Delegación Miguel Hidalgo, 11560 México, DF; tel. (55) 5553-6266; fax (55) 5286-1791; e-mail atencion .mna@inah.gob.mx; internet www.mna.inah .gob.mx; f. 1940; attached to the Instituto Nacional de Antropología e Historia; anthropological, ethnological, and archaeological subjects relating to Mexico; 6,000 exhibits; library of 300,000 vols; Dir Arqlgo. FELIPE SOLÍS OLGUÍN; publs *Cuadernos*, *Guides*.

Museo Nacional de Arquitectura (National Museum of Architecture): Palacio de Bellas Artes, Avda Juárez 4, Centro Histórico, Del. Cuauhtémoc, 06050 México, DF; tel. (55) 5510-2475; fax (55) 5510-2853;

internet www.inba.gob.mx; f. 1984; important examples of Mexican architecture through the ages; photographic archive; original plans by Adamo Boari, Federico Mariscal, Juan O'Gorman, Carlos Obregón Santacilia, Mario Pani, Enrique del Moral, José Villagrán, Juan Segura, Francisco Centeno and Francisco J. Serrano; original drawings of the Palacio de Bellas Artes; Dir XAVIER GUZMÁN.

Museo Nacional de Arte (National Museum of Art): Tacuba 8, Centro Histórico, Del. Cuauhtémoc, 06010 México, DF; tel. (55) 5130-3400; fax (55) 5130-3401; e-mail munal@munal.com.mx; internet www.munal .com.mx; f. 1982; permanent exhibitions of Mexican art from 16th century to 1950; library of 39,000 vols; Dir ROXANA VELÁSQUEZ; publ. *Revista Memoria*.

Museo Nacional de Artes e Industrias Populares del Instituto Nacional Indigenista (National Museum of Traditional Arts and Crafts, National Institute of Indigenous People): Avda Juárez 44, 06050 México, DF; internet www.cuauhtemoc.df .gob.mx/turismo/museos/corpus.html; f. 1951; examples of traditional Mexican art of all periods, conservation and encouragement of traditional handicrafts; Dir MARÍA TERESA POMAR.

Museo Nacional de Historia (National Historical Museum): Reforma y Gandhi, 1A Sección del Bosque de Chapultepec, Delegación Miguel Hidalgo, 11580 México, DF; tel. (55) 5241-3100; fax (55) 5241-3132; e-mail difusion.mnh@inah.gob.mx; internet www .mnh.inah.gob.mx; f. 1944; attached to the Instituto Nacional de Antropología e Historia; history of Mexico since the 16th century; historical paintings, flags, weapons, documents, jewellery, textiles, ceramics, furniture, clothing and other objects of social and cultural history; Dir Lic. LUCIANO CEDILLO ÁLVAREZ.

Museo Nacional de la Estampa: Avda Hidalgo 39, Plaza de la Santa Vercruz, Col. Centro, Delg. Cuauhtémoc, 06050 México, DF; tel. (55) 5521-2244; fax (55) 5521-2244; engraving, graphic arts; permanent exhibition 'Proceso Histórico de la Estampa en México'.

Museo Nacional de las Culturas (National Museum of Cultures): Calle de Moneda 13, Col. Centro Histórico, 06060 México, DF; tel. (55) 5542-0165; fax (55) 5542-0422; e-mail direccion.cmuseo@inah .gob.mx; internet www.inah.gob.mx/muse1/ html/muse13.html; attached to the Instituto Nacional de Antropología e Historia; f. 1965; collections of archaeology and ethnology from all over the world; public lectures, special courses for teachers, training in plastic arts; library of 11,862 vols; Dir Antrop. MOISÉS LEONEL DURÁN SOLÍS.

Museo Nacional de las Intervenciones (National Museum of the Interventions in Mexico): General Anaya y 20 de agosto, Del. Coyoacán, 04100 México, DF; tel. (55) 5604-0699; fax (55) 5604-0981; internet www.cnca .gob.mx/cnca/inah/museos/munainst.html; f. 1981; government-owned museum attached to the Instituto Nacional de Antropología e Historia; exhibitions show history of foreign interventions and Mexican independence; library of 800 vols; Dir Lic. MONICA CUEVAS Y LARA.

Museo Nacional de San Carlos (San Carlos Museum): Puente de Alvarado 50, Col. Tabacalera, 06030 México, DF; tel. (55) 5566-8085; fax (55) 5535-1256; e-mail mnsancarlos@mail.com; internet www .bellasartes.gob.mx/inba/templateinba; f. 1968; attached to Instituto Nacional de Bellas Artes; colln of 14th–19th century

European panels, paintings, sculpture, drawings and prints; housed within the Palace of the Counts of Buenavista designed by Manuel Tolsá; library of 2,633 vols; Dir MARÍA FERNANDA MATOS MOCTEZUMA; publ. *Bulletin* (3 a year).

Monterrey

Museo Regional de Nuevo León (Regional Museum of Nuevo León): Rafael José Verger s/n, Col. Obispado, 64010 Monterrey, Nuevo León; tel. (81) 8333-9588; fax (81) 8346-0404; internet dti.inah.gob.mx; f. 1956; regional and Mexican history, archaeology and painting; Dir Arq. JAVIER SÁNCHEZ GARCÍA.

Morelia

Museo Regional Michoacano (Michoacan Museum): Calle de Allende 305 esq. con Abasolo, Centro, 58000 Morelia, Michoacán; tel. (443) 312-0407; internet dti.inah.gob.mx; f. 1886; archaeological, ecological, ethnographical and prehistoric collections of the district; library of 10,000 vols; Dir Arq. PAUL DELGADO LAMAS; publ. *Anales*.

Oaxaca

Museo de las Culturas de Oaxaca (Museum of the Cultures of Oaxaca): Apdo 68000, 'Ex-Convento de Santo Domingo de Guzmán', Macedonio Alcalá y Adolfo Gurrión s/n, Oaxaca, Oax.; tel. (951) 5162991; internet www.inah.gob.mx/muse2/htme/ mure2001.html; f. 1933; anthropology, archaeology, ethnography and religious art; contains the famous archaeological treasures found in Tomb No. 7, Monte Albán, jewellery; Dir ENRIQUE FRANCO CALVO.

Patzcuaro

Museo Regional de Artes Populares (Regional Museum of Arts and Crafts): Enseñanza y Alcantarilla s/n, Pátzcuaro, Michoacán; f. 1935; ancient and modern ethnographical exhibits relating to the Tarascan Indians of Michoacán; colonial and contemporary native art; Dir RAFAELA LUFT DÁVALOS.

Puebla

Museo de Arte 'José Luis Bello y González' ('José Luis Bello y González' Museum of Art): 5 de Mayo 408, Puebla, Pue.; f. 1938, opened to the public 1944; contains: ivories, porcelain, wrought iron, furniture, clocks, watches, musical instruments, etc., Mexican, Chinese and European paintings, sculptures, pottery, vestments, tapestries, ceramics, miniatures, etc.

Museo Regional de Santa Mónica (Santa Monica Regional Museum): Avda Poniente 103, Puebla, Pue.; f. 1940; religious art; comprises the collections of various disbanded convents and now housed in that of Santa Mónica.

Museo Regional del Estado de Puebla (Puebla State Regional Museum): Casa del Alfeñique, Calle Oriente 4, Norte 416, 72000 Puebla, Pue.; f. 1931; notable historical collections; Dir JUAN ARMENTA CAMACHO.

Querétaro

Museo Regional de Querétaro (Querétaro Historical Museum): Calle Corregidora Sur 3, 76000 Querétaro, Qro; tel. (442) 20-2031; internet www.queretaro-mexico.com.mx/ coneculta/regional.html; f. 1936; local history and art; Dir MANUEL OROPEZA SEGURA.

Tepotzotlán

Museo Nacional del Virreinato (National Museum of the Vice-Royalty): Plaza Hidalgo 99, 54600 Tepotzotlán, Estado de México; tel. (55) 5876-0245; fax (55) 5876-0332; e-mail virreinato.museo@inah.gob.mx; internet www.munavi.inah.gob.mx; f. 1964; attached to the Instituto Nacional de Antropología e Historia; collections on the art and culture of the Colonial period; housed in 17th- and 18th-century buildings, formerly belonging to the Jesuits; library of 4,000 vols from the 16th to the 19th century; Dir MIGUEL EMIGDIO FERNÁNDEZ FÉLIX.

Toluca

Museo de las Bellas Artes (Museum of Fine Arts): Calle de Santos Degollado 102, Toluca Edo. de México; internet www.turista.com.mx/edomexico; paintings, sculptures, Mexican colonial art; Dir Prof. JOSÉ M. CABALLERO-BARNARD.

Tuxtla Gutiérrez

Museo Regional de Chiapas (Chiapas Regional Museum): Calzada de los Hombres Ilustres s/n, Parque Madero, 29000 Tuxtla Gutiérrez, Chiapas; tel. (961) 622-0459; fax (961) 623-4554; f. 1939; archaeological and historical collections; Dir ROBERTO RAMOS MAZO.

Tzintzuntzan

Museo Etnográfico y Arqueológico (Ethnographical and Archaeological Museum): 58340 Tzintzuntzan, Michoacán; f. 1944; ethnographical and archaeological collections relating to the Tzinztuntzan and Tarascan zones of Lake Pátzcuaro.

Xalapa

Museo de Antropología de Xalapa, Universidad Veracruzana (Xalapa Museum of Anthropology, Veracruzana University): Avda Xalapa s/n, 91010 Xalapa, Veracruz; tel. (228) 815-0920; fax (228) 815-4952; e-mail museo@uv.mx; internet www.uv.mx/max; f. 1959; spe. regional archaeological collns of the Olmec, Totonac and Huastec cultures of ancient Mexico; Dir Dra SARA LADRÓN DE GUEVARA.

Universities

UNIVERSIDAD AUTÓNOMA DE AGUASCALIENTES

Avda Universidad 940, Ciudad Universitaria, 20100 Aguascalientes, Ags

Telephone: (449) 910-7400
Fax: (449) 910-7409
Internet: www.uaa.mx
Founded 1973
State control
Language of instruction: Spanish
Academic year: August to June (two semesters)

Rector: Dr. ANTONIO AVILA STORER
Sec.-Gen.: Mtro. JASÉ RAMIRO ALEMÁN LÓPEZ
Librarian: C.P. IRMA DE LEON DE MUÑOZ

Library of 152,150 vols
Number of teachers: 1,461
Number of students: 11,501

Publications: *Gaceta Universitaria* (12 a year), *Correo Universitario*, *Evaluación* (1 a year), *Caleidoscopio* (2 a year), *Scientiae Naturae* (2 a year), *Investigación y Ciencia* (2 a year)

DEANS

Centre for Agricultural Sciences: I.B.Q. NARA AURORA GUERRERO GARCÍA
Centre for Arts and Humanities: Mtro JOSÉ ALFREDO ORTIZ GARZA
Centre for Basic Sciences: Ing ANGEL DÍAZ PALOS
Centre for Biomedical Sciences: Dra RUBY S. LIBREROS AGUDELO

Centre for Design and Construction Sciences: Ing. JORGE PIO MONSIVAIS SANTOYO
Centre for Economics and Administration: C.P. RICARDO GONZÁLEZ ALVAREZ
Centre for Secondary Education: Lic. ERNESTINA LEÓN RODRÍGUEZ

UNIVERSIDAD DE LAS AMÉRICAS – PUEBLA

Sta Catarina Mártir, Apdo Postal 100, 72820 Cholula, Puebla

Telephone: (222) 229-2000
Fax: (222) 229-2009
Internet: www.udlap.mx
Founded 1940 as Mexico City College; became Universidad de las Américas in 1963
Private control
Languages of instruction: Spanish, English
Academic year: August to May
Pres.: Dra NORA LUSTIG TENENBAUM
Academic Vice-Pres.: Dr EDUARDO LASTRA Y PÉREZ SALAZAR
Vice-Pres. for Admin. and Finance: Mtro JOSÉ MANUEL BLANCO ASPURU
Registrar: Mtra MARTHA FERNÁNDEZ DE LARA
Librarian: Dr ALFREDO SÁNCHEZ HULTRÓN SANTOS

Library: see Libraries
Number of teachers: 325 full-time
Number of students: 8,300

Publications: *UDLA Informa*, *La Catarina*

DEANS

Faculty of Administration: Dr FRANCISCO GUERRA VÁZQUEZ
Faculty of Arts and Humanities: Dra LUISA VILAR PAYÁ
Faculty of Business: Dr ROBERTO SOLANO
Faculty of Engineering: Dr JUAN MANUEL RAMÍREZ
Faculty of Social Sciences: Dr ISIDRO MORALES MORENO
Research and Graduate Studies: Dr GERARDO AYALA SAN MARTÍN

UNIVERSIDAD ANÁHUAC

Apdo 10-844, 11000 México, DF
Avda Universidad Anáhuac s/n, Lomas Anáhuac, 52760 Huixquilucan, Estado de México

Telephone: (55) 5627-0210
Fax: (55) 5589-9796
E-mail: anahuac@anahuac.mx
Internet: www.anahuac.mx
Founded 1963
Private control
Academic year: August to June (two terms)
Rector: Lic. RAYMUND COSGRAVE
Secretary-General: Arq. JOSÉ MATEOS
General Academic Director: Dr CRISTIAN NAZER
Librarian: Mtro DANIEL MATTES

Library of 163,500 vols
Number of teachers: 1,100
Number of students: 7,000

Publications: *Medicina y Etica* (4 a year), *Iuris Tantum* (1 a year), *Generación Anáhuac* (6 a year), *Carta Económica–Boletín Instituto Desarrollo Empresarial Anáhuac (IDEA)* (6 a year)

DEANS

Faculty of Bioethics: Dr JOSÉ KUTHY PORTER
Faculty of Education: Mtra LUZ DEL CARMEN DÁVALOS
Faculty of Engineering: Dr ALEJANDRO MONTANO
School of Actuarial Sciences: Act. OLIVA SÁNCHEZ

School of Architecture: Arq. FERNANDO PAZ Y PUENTE
School of Communication Sciences: Dr CARLOS GÓMEZ PALACIO
School of Economics and Business: Dr RAMÓN LECUONA
School of Industrial and Graphic Design: Lic. LEONOR AMOZURRUTIA
School of Law: Dr JOSÉ ANTONIO NÚÑEZ
School of Medicine: Dr TOMÁS BARRIENTOS
School of Psychology: Mtro JOSÉ MARÍA LÓPEZ
School of Tourism Administration: Prof. LOUIS PASCAL

UNIVERSIDAD AUTÓNOMA AGRARIA 'ANTONIO NARRO'

Buenavista, 25315 Saltillo, Coah.

Telephone: (844) 411-0275
Fax: (844) 411-0207
E-mail: docencia@uaaan.mx
Internet: www.uaaan.mx
Founded 1923, university status 1975
Academic year: January to December

Rector: Ing. EDUARDO FUENTES RODRÍGUEZ
Vice-Rector: M. V. Z. JOSÉ L. BERLANGA FLORES
Registrar: Ing. GUSTAVO OLIVARES SALAZAR
Librarian: LUZ ELENA PEREZ MATA (acting)

Number of teachers: 430
Number of students: 2,583

COORDINATORS OF FACULTIES

Agronomy: Dr MARCO ANTONIO BUSTAMANTE G.
Animal Science: Dr EDUARDO AIZPURU GARCIA
Engineering: M. C. LUIS M. LASSO MENDOZA
Social and Economics Science: Ing. FRANCISCO MARTINEZ GOMEZ

UNIVERSIDAD AUTÓNOMA DE BAJA CALIFORNIA

Apdo Postal 459, Avda Alvaro Obregón y Julian Carrillo s/n, 21100 Mexicali, Baja California

Telephone: (686) 554-2200
Fax: (686) 554-2200
Internet: www.uabc.mx
Founded 1957
Language of instruction: Spanish
Academic year: August to June

Rector: C.P. VÍCTOR EVERARDO BELTRÁN CORONA
Vice-Rector: M.C. RENÉ ANDRADE PETERSON
Secretary-General: M.C. JUAN JOSÉ SEVILLA GARCÍA
Librarian: Lic. ALMA LORENA CAMARENA FLORES

Number of teachers: 3,099
Number of students: 21,548

Publications: *Caláfia*, *Cuadernos de Ciencias Sociales*, *Cuaderno de Taller Literario*, *Estudios Fronterizos*, *Revistas Universitarias*, *Divulgare*, *Semillero*, *Yubai*, *Paradigmas*, *Ciencias Marinas*, *Revista de Investigación Educativa*

PRINCIPALS

Ensenada Campus:

Faculty of Marine Sciences: Dr ROBERTO MILLÁN NÚÑEZ
Faculty of Sciences: M.C. ERNESTO CAMPOS GONZÁLEZ
School of Accountancy and Administration: Lic. SAÚL MÉNDEZ HERNÁNDEZ
School of Engineering: M.C. JOSÉ DE JESÚS ZAMARRIPA TOPETE

Mexicali Campus:

Faculty of Architecture: Arq. AARÓN G. BERNAL RODRÍGUEZ
Faculty of Humanities: M.C. ANGEL MANUEL ORTIZ MARÍN

Faculty of Law: Lic. MA. AURORA LACAVEX BERUMEN

Faculty of Odontology: C.D. MANUEL OSCAR LARA BETANCOURT

School of Accountancy and Administration: C.P. PLACIDO VALENCIANA MORENO

School of Engineering: Ing. CÉSAR RAÚL REYES MAZÓN

School of Languages: Lic. KORA EVANGELINA BASICH PERALTA

School of Medicine: Med. SERGIO ROMO BARRAZA

School of Nursing: Lic. ANDREA VERDUGO BATIZ

School of Pedagogy: Prof. JESÚS ACEVES GUTIÉRREZ

School of Social Sciences: Lic. MIGUEL ANGEL RENDÓN MARTÍNEZ

Tecate Campus:

School of Engineering: Quim. SERGIO VALE SÁNCHEZ (Dir)

Tijuana Campus:

Faculty of Accountancy and Administration: C.P. LUIS MEZA ARISTIGUE

Faculty of Chemistry: M.C. MA. EUGENIA PÉREZ MORALES

Faculty of Economics: Dra SONIA YOLANDA LUGO MORONES

School of Humanities: Lic. JORGE GUSTAVO MENDOZA GONZÁLEZ

Faculty of Law: Lic. JOSÉ DE JESÚS DÍAZ DE LA TORRE

Faculty of Medicine: Dra ADRIANA CAROLINA VARGAS OJEDA

Faculty of Odontology: Dr MIGUEL ANGEL CADENA ALCÁNTAR

School of Tourism: Lic. ONÉSIMO CUAMEA VELÁZQUEZ

DIRECTORS OF RESEARCH INSTITUTES

Agricultural Sciences Institute (Mexicali Campus): Dr MIGUEL CERVANTES RAMÍREZ

Agriculture and Stockbreeding Research Institute: Ing. VÍCTOR MANUEL VEGA KURI

Educative Development and Research Institute: Mtro EDUARDO BACKHOFF ESCUDERO

Engineering Institute (Mexicali Campus): Dr BENJAMÍN VALDEZ SALAS

History Research Centre (Tijuana Campus): Dra CATALINA VELÁZQUEZ MORALES

Oceanology Research Institute (Ensenada Campus): Dr JOSÉ A. ZERTUCHE GONZÁLEZ

Social Research Institute (Mexicali Campus): Dr PABLO JESÚS GONZÁLEZ REYES

Veterinary Science Research Institute (Mexicali Campus): Dr EDUARDO SÁNCHEZ LÓPEZ

UNIVERSIDAD AUTÓNOMA DE BAJA CALIFORNIA SUR
(Autonomous University of Baja California Sur)

Carretera al Sur km 5.5, 23080 La Paz, BCS

Telephone: (612) 128-8800

Fax: (612) 128-0880

E-mail: webmaster@uabcs.mx

Internet: www.uabcs.mx

Founded 1975

State control

Language of instruction: Spanish

Rector: Lic. JUAN RODRIGO GUERRERO RIVAS

Secretary-General: PUBLIO OCTAVIO ROMERO MARTÍNEZ

Director of Planning and Programming: Dr ARTURO HERNÁNDEZ PRADO

Head Librarian: Lic. JOSÉ ALFREDO VERDUGO SÁNCHEZ

ACADEMIC AREA COORDINATORS

Agricultural Sciences: JOSÉ GUADALUPE LOYA RAMÍREZ

Marine Sciences: JORGE GARCÍA PÁMANES

Social Sciences and Humanities: Ma. LUISA CABRAL BOWLING

UNIVERSIDAD AUTÓNOMA DE CAMPECHE

Av. Agustín Melgar s/n entre Calle 20 y Juan de la Barrera, Col. Buenavista, 24030 Campeche, Camp.

Telephone: (981) 811-9800

E-mail: webmaster@etzna.uacam.mx

Internet: www.uacam.mx

Founded 1756, refounded 1965

State control

Academic year: September to June

Rector: Licda. ADRIANA DEL PILAR ORTIZ LANZ

Sec.-Gen.: Lic. JOAQUÍN UC VALENCIA

Librarian: Lic. ARACELI MAY CANUL

Number of teachers: 443

Number of students: 4,760

Publications: *Panorama* (6 a year), *Pinceladas* (6 a year)

DIRECTORS OF FACULTIES AND SCHOOLS

'Dr Nazario Víctor Montejo Godoy' Preparatory School: Lic. ALMA LORENA GUZMAN GARCÍA

Faculty of Chemical and Biological Sciences: Mtra ANGELICA SOTO MARTÍNEZ

Faculty of Engineering: Ing. DOMINGO BERMAN ORDAZ

Faculty of Humanities: Lic. JOSÉ MANUEL ALCOCER BERNÉS

Faculty of Law: Lic. JORGE RODRÍGUEZ VARGAS

Faculty of Social Sciences: Dr GERARDO MIXCOATL TINOCO

Higher School of Nursing: Lic. MARÍA CANDELARIA AGUILAR BRICEÑO

'Lic. Ermilo Sandoval Campos' Preparatory School: Lic. VÍCTOR ORTIZ PASOS

School of Accounting and Administration: M. en C. ENNA SANDOVAL CASTELLANOS

School of Dentistry: C. D. LUIS HERRERA LÓPEZ

School of Medicine: Dr CARLOS EDUARDO GARCÍA SOLIS

UNIVERSIDAD DEL CARIBE

Lote 1, Manzana 1, Region 78, Esq. con Tabachines, 77528 Cancún, Quintana Roo

Telephone: (998) 881-4400

Fax: (998) 881-4400

E-mail: rectoria@unicaribe.edu.mx

Internet: www.unicaribe.edu.mx

Founded 2000

State control

Academic year: August to May

Pres.: EDUARDO PATRÓN AZUETA

Rector: ARTURO ESCAIP MANZUR

Registrar: BEATRIZ ASENCIO VILLAMIL

Academic Sec.: ANA CRISTINA ÁVILA LÓPEZ

Admin. Sec.: LUIS MANUEL ROSAS TORRES

Librarian: LORENA CAREAGA VILIESID

Library of 17,000

Number of teachers: 600

Number of students: 2,500

UNIVERSIDAD AUTÓNOMA DEL CARMEN

Calle 56 #4 por Avenida Concordia, 24180 Ciudad del Carmen, Camp.

Telephone: (938) 381-1018 ext. 1007

Fax: (938) 381-1018 ext. 1328

Internet: www.unacar.mx

Founded 1967

Rector: C. SERGIO AUGUSTO LÓPEZ PEÑA

Sec.-Gen.: Lic. RAFAEL HUGO GARCÍA MORENO

Chief Admin. Officer: Lic. HILDA LÓPEZ LÓPEZ

Librarian: C. OLGA SÁNCHEZ PÉREZ

Number of teachers: 340

Number of students: 4,484

Publications: *Voz Universitaria, Senda Universitaria*

Faculties of commerce and administration, law, chemistry, education.

UNIVERSIDAD AUTÓNOMA CHAPINGO

km 38.5 Carretera México-Veracruz, Texcoco, Edo de México

Telephone: (595) 952-1500

Fax: (595) 952-1565

Internet: www.chapingo.mx

Founded 1854 as Escuela Nacional de Agricultura; named changed 1978

Government control

Academic year: August to June

Rector: Dr JOSÉ SERGIO BARRALES DOMINGUEZ

Dir-Gen. for Academic Affairs: Dr JAVIER RUIZ LEDESMA

Dir-Gen. for Admin.: JOSÉ SOLIS RAMÍREZ

Dir-Gen. for Research: Dr ENRIQUE SERRANO GÁLVEZ

Librarian: ROSA MARÍA OJEDA TREJO

Library: see Libraries and Archives

Number of teachers: 1,200

Number of students: 6,800 (6,500 undergraduates, 300 graduates)

Publications: *Revista Chapingo* (6 a year), *Revista de Geografía Agrícola* (6 a year), *Textual* (social sciences, 2 a year)

DEANS

Agricultural Mechanical Engineering: MARTÍN SOTO ESCOBAR

Agricultural Parasitology: FRANCISCO PONCE GONZALEZ

Agroecology: Dr LAKSMI REDDIAR KRISHNMURTHY

Agroindustrial Engineering: Dr LUIS RAMIRO GARCÍA CHAVEZ

Dry Area Science: SANTIAGO RAMON MENDOZA MORENO

Earth Science: Dr DAVID CRISTÓBAL ACEVEDO

Economic and Administrative Science: JAIME RUVALCABA LIMON

Forestry: ANGEL LEYVA OVALLE

Irrigation: RENE MARTINEZ ELIZONDO

Phytotechnics: Dr MARIO PEREZ GRAJALES

Rural Sociology: JESUS CARLOS MORETT SANCHEZ

Zootechnology: MELITON CORDOBA ALVAREZ

UNIVERSIDAD AUTÓNOMA DE CHIAPAS

Blvd Belisario Domínguez km 1081, Edificio de Rectoría, Colina Universitaria s/n, 29020 Tuxtla Gutiérrez, Chiapas

Telephone: (961) 617-8000

Internet: www.unach.mx

Founded 1975

Private control

Academic year: September to July (two semesters)

Rector: Dr ÁNGEL RENÉ ESTRADA ARÉVALO

Sec.-Gen.: LUIS MANUEL MARTÍNEZ ESTRADA

Academic Sec.: Ing. ROBERTO CRUZ DE LEÓN

Librarian: Lic. DOLORES SERRANO CANCINO

Number of teachers: 906

Number of students: 12,052

Publication: *Gaceta Universitaria*

DIRECTORS

Campus I (Tuxtla Gutiérrez):

Faculty of Accounting and Administration: C.P. CESAR MAZA GONZÁLEZ

Faculty of Architecture: Arq. RICARDO GUILLÉN CASTAÑEDA

School of Civil Engineering: Ing. ROBERTON Y CRUZ DIAZ

Campus II (Tuxtla Gutiérrez):

Faculty of Human Medicine: Dr JOSÉ LUIS AQUINO HERNÁNDEZ

School of Veterinary Medicine and Zootechnics: MVZ. ALBERTO YAMAZAKI MAZA

Campus III (San Cristóbal de las Casas):

Faculty of Law: Lic. ALFONSO RAMÍREZ MARTÍNEZ

Faculty of Social Sciences: JORGE ALBERTO LÓPEZ AREVALO

Campus IV (Tapachula):

Faculty of Accounting: C.P. JORGE FERNANDO ORDAZ RUÍZ

Faculty of Administration Sciences: KENY ORDAZ ESCOBAR

Faculty of Agriculture: Ing. ALFONSO PÉREZ ROMERO

School of Chemical Sciences: JOSÉ RAMÓN PUIG COTA

Campus V (Villaflores):

School of Agronomy: Dr ALFREDO MEDINA MELÉNDEZ

Campus VI (Tuxtla Gutiérrez):

Faculty of Humanities: CARLOS RINCÓN RAMÍREZ

UNIVERSIDAD DE CIENCIAS Y ARTES DE CHIAPAS (UNICACH)
(Chiapas State University of Arts and Sciences)

1A Avda Sur Poniente 1460, Zona Centro, 29000 Tuxtla Gutiérrez, Chiapas

Telephone: (961) 617-0400
Fax: (961) 147-6242
E-mail: secgral@unicach.edu.mx
Internet: www.unicach.edu.mx

Founded 1893, as Industrial School of Chiapas; current name and status 1995
State control
Language of instruction: Spanish

Rector: Ing. ROBERTO DOMÍNGUEZ CASTELLANOS
Gen. Sec.: Mtro. JOSÉ FRANCISCO NIGENDA PÉREZ
Dir of Information: Ing. MARINO PEREZ MARTINEZ

DIRECTORS

Centre for Human Development: Lic. MARINA IDALIA GUIZAR CORDOVA
School of Biology: Mtra ADELINA SCHLIE GUZMAN
School of Music: Lic. LUIS FELIPE MARTÍNEZ GORDILLO
School of Nutrition: Lic. VIDALMA DEL ROSARIO BEZARES SARMIENTO
School of Odontology: C.D. JUAN JOSÉ ORTEGA ALEJANDRE
School of Psychology: Lic. GERMAN ALEJANDRO GARCIA LARA
School of Topography: Ing. LISANDRO MARTÍNEZ POZO
University Centre for Information and Documentation: Ing. ARQUIMEDES R. LÓPEZ ROBLERO

UNIVERSIDAD AUTÓNOMA DE CHIHUAHUA

Av. Escorza 900, Zona Centro, 31000 Chihuahua, Chih.

Telephone: (614) 439-1500
Fax: (614) 439-1529
E-mail: webmaster@uach.mx
Internet: www.uach.mx

Founded 1954
Language of instruction: Spanish
Academic year: August to June

Rector: Dr JESÚS ENRIQUE GRAJEDA HERRERA
Sec.-Gen.: Dr JESÚS XAVIER VENEGAS HOLGUÍN
Admin. Dir: C.P. y L.A.E. GABRIELA RICO CABRERA
Librarian: C.P. FERNANDO SALOMÓN BEYER

Number of teachers: 1,428
Number of students: 12,429
Publications: various faculty journals.

DIRECTORS

Faculty of Accountancy and Administration: C.P. y M.A. FRANCISCO JAVIER LUJÁN DE LA GARZA
Faculty of Agriculture and Forestry: M.S. ARTURO JAVIER OBANDO RODRÍGUEZ
Faculty of Agricultural Engineering: M.C. ALMA PATRICIA HERNÁNDEZ RODRÍGUEZ
Faculty of Chemical Sciences: Ing. MANUEL RUÍZ ESPARZA MEDINA
Faculty of Engineering: Ing. ARTURO LEAL BEJARANO
Faculty of Law: Lic. MARIO TREVISO SALAZAR
Faculty of Medicine: Dr CARLOS ENRIQUE MORALES ORTEGA
Faculty of Philosophy and Literature: Lic. ISELA YOLANDA DE PABLO PORRAS
Faculty of Physical Education and Sport Science: L.E.F. PRIMO ALBERTO GONZÁLEZ ARZATE
Faculty of Political and Social Sciences: Lic. SAMUEL GARCÍA SOTO
Faculty of Stockbreeding: Dr GUILLERMO VILLALOBOS VILLALOBOS
Institute of Fine Arts: Lic. RUBEN TINAJERO MEDINA
School of Dentistry: Dr JESÚS DUARTE MAYAGOITIA
School of International Economics: Lic. MANUEL PARGA MUÑOZ
School of Nursing and Nutrition Science: M.E.M.I. ROSA MARÍA DOZAL MOLINA

UNIVERSIDAD POPULAR DE LA CHONTALPA
(People's University of Chontalpa)

Galeana s/n Esq. Morelos, Centro, 86500 Cárdenas, Tabasco

Telephone: (937) 372-5743
Fax: (937) 372-5743
E-mail: informacion@upchontalpa.edu.mx
Internet: www.upchontalpa.edu.mx

Founded 1998
State control

Rector: Ing. RAMÓN ALEJANDRO FIGUEROA CANTORAL
Sec. for Academic Affairs: Dr ARQUÍMEDES ORAMAS VARGAS
Sec. for University Extension and Social Services: MANUEL AYSA JIMÉNEZ
Sec. for Administration and Finance: ELVIS SEGURA CÓRDOVA

Publications: *Gaceta Enlace Universitario, Expresión Universitaria, Revista Tecnociencia Universitaria*

Main subject areas: agricultural engineering, business and international finance, civil engineering, electrical and mechanical engineering, petrochemical engineering, political science and public administration, psychology and pharmaceutical chemistry, zootechnical engineering.

UNIVERSIDAD AUTÓNOMA DE COAHUILA

Blvd V. Carranza esq. González Lobo, Col. República Oriente, 25280 Saltillo, Coah.

Telephone: (844) 438-1600
Fax: (844) 438-1600
Internet: www.uadec.mx

Founded 1867, refounded 1957
State control
Language of instruction: Spanish
Academic year: August to June (two terms)

Rector: Lic. MARIO OCHOA RIVERA
Sec.-Gen.: L.Ab.L. ALBERTO L. SALAZAR RODRÍGUEZ
Librarian: ANTONIO MALACARA

Number of teachers: 900
Number of students: 13,923

UNIVERSIDAD DE COLIMA

Avda Universidad 333, Colonia Las Víboras, 28040 Colima, Col.

Telephone: (312) 316-1000
E-mail: rector@ucol.mx
Internet: www.ucol.mx

Founded 1940 as Universidad Popular de Colima, reorganized 1962
State control
Language of instruction: Spanish
Academic year: August to July

Rector: M.C. MIGUEL ÁNGEL AGUAYO LÓPEZ
Gen.-Sec.: Dr RAMÓN ARTURO CEDILLO NAKAY
Librarian: Dra EVANGELINA SERRANO

Number of teachers: 1,204
Number of students: 19,000

Publication: *Estudios Sobre las Culturas Contemporáneas*

DEANS

Faculty of Accountancy and Administration: M.A. JOSÉ ALFREDO CANO ANGUIANO
Faculty of Accountancy and Administration 1: C.P. TOBIAS ALVAREZ LUNA
Faculty of Accountancy and Administration 2: JOSÉ MARTÍN TORRES RÍOS
Faculty of Architecture: Arq. JULIO DE JESÚS MENDOZA JIMÉNEZ
Faculty of Arts and Communications: Lic. LUIS MIGUEL BUENO SÁNCHEZ
Faculty of Biological Sciences and Agronomy: Mtro. ARNOLDO MUCHEL ROSALES
Faculty of Chemical Science: M.C. SANTIAGO E. VELASCO VILLALPANDO
Faculty of Civil Engineering: M.C. GERARDO CERRATO OSEGUERA
Faculty of Economics: Dr ERNESTO RANGEL DELGADO
Faculty of Education: Mtra CARMEN ALICIA SANTOS ANDRADE
Faculty of Educational Science: Prof. JOSÉ FRANCISCO BALLESTEROS SILVA
Faculty of Electromechanical Engineering: M.C. ANDRÉS G. FUENTES COVARRUBIAS
Faculty of Law: Lic. MARIO DE LA MADRID ANDRADE
Faculty of Marine Science: O.Q. ADRIÁN TINTOS GÓMEZ
Faculty of Medicine: Dr RAMÓN A. CEDILLO NAKAY
Faculty of Nursing: Licda ANA MARÍA CHAVEZ ACEVEDO
Faculty of Social and Political Sciences: Lic. FERNANDO H. ALCARAZ INIGUEZ
Faculty of Social Studies: Licda MARISA MESINA POLANCO
Faculty of Telematics: M.C. RAUL AQUINO SANTOS
Faculty of Veterinary Studies and Zoology: Dr ENRIQUE SILVA PENA
School of Languages: Licda GRISELDA P. CEBALLOS LLERENAS

UNIVERSIDAD JUÁREZ DEL ESTADO DE DURANGO

Constitución 404 sur, Zona Centro, 34000 Durango, Dgo

Telephone: (618) 811-4275
Internet: www.ujed.mx

Founded as a Civil College 1856, became University 1957
Private control
Language of instruction: Spanish
Academic year: January to December (2 terms)

Rector: C.P. RUBÉN CALDERÓN LUJÁN
Sec.-Gen.: C.P. JUAN FRANCISCO SALAZAR BENÍTEZ

Chief Admin. Officer: T.S. ADRIANA AVELAR VILLEGAS
Librarian: A.B. JOSÉ LINO HERNÁNDEZ CAMPOS
Number of teachers: 1,116
Number of students: 20,160

DEANS

Faculty of Accountancy and Administration: C.P. MARÍA MAGDALENA MEDINA CÓRDOBA M.A.
Faculty of Law: Lic. VICENTE GUERRERO ITURBE
Faculty of Medicine: Dr JORGE RUIZ LEÓN
Faculty of Veterinary Medicine and Zootechnics: M.V.Z. RAÚL RANGEL ROMERO
School of Applied Mathematics: Ing. UBALDO ARENAS JUÁREZ
School of Chemical Sciences: Ing. ENRIQUE TORRES CABRAL
School of Dentistry: C.D. MIGUEL ROJAS REGALADO
School of Forestry: Ing. ALFONSO HERRERA AYÓN
School of Music: Prof. ABRAHAM E. VIGGERS ARREOLA
School of Nursing and Obstetrics: Lic. MARÍA ELENA VALDEZ DE REYES
School of Painting, Sculpture and Crafts: Prof. FRANCISCO MONTOYA DE LA CRUZ
School of Social Work: T.S. MARÍA ANTONIA HERNÁNDEZ ESCAREÑO

Gómez Palacio Campus:

School of Agriculture and Stockbreeding: Ing. JESÚS JOSÉ QUIÑONES VERA
School of Biology: BIOL. M.C. RAÚL DÍAZ MORENO
School of Civil Engineering: Ing. EVERARDO F. DELGADO SOLIS
School of Food Science and Technology: Ing. GERARDO FRANCISCO ALDANA RUIZ
School of Medicine: Dr LUIS DE VILLA VÁZQUEZ

UNIVERSIDAD PEDAGÓGICA DE DURANGO
Avda 16 de Septiembre 132, Col Silvestre Dorador, 3407 Durango, Durango
Telephone: (618) 812-9509
Fax: (618) 812-9509
E-mail: upndgo@gauss.logicnet.com.mx
Founded 1997
State control
Dir: Prof. BERNARDO DEL REAL SARMIENTO.

UNIVERSIDAD ESTATAL DEL VALLE DE ECATEPEC
Avda Central s/n, Esq. Leona Vicario, Valle de Anáhuac, 66120 Ecatepec, México, DF
Telephone: (55) 710-4560
Fax: (55) 710-2688
E-mail: israelrios413@hotmail.com
Founded 2001
State control
Rector: ISMAEL SÁENZ VILLA.

UNIVERSIDAD DEL EJÉRCITO Y FUERZA AÉREA
(University of the Army and Air Force)
Calzada México Tacuba s/n, Popotla, Delegación Miguel Hidalgo, México, DF
Telephone: (55) 5396-9106
Internet: www.sedena.gob.mx/educacion/index.html
Founded 1975
Rector: JUAN HERNÁNDEZ ÁVALOS.

CONSTITUENT MILITARY SCHOOLS

Escuela Médico Militar (Military Medical School)
Cerrada de Palomas esq. con Periférico s/n, Lomas de San Isidro, Delegación Miguel Hidalgo, CP 11200, México, DF
Telephone: (55) 5540-7726
Internet: www.sedena.gob.mx/educacion/planteles/emm/index.html
Founded 1881
Dir: Gen. de Brigada Dr RODOLFO LERMA SHIUMOTO.

Escuela Militar de Aviación (Military School of Aviation)
Colegio del Aire, Base Aérea Militar No. 5, Zapopan, Jalisco
Telephone: (33) 3624-1470
Internet: www.sedena.gob.mx/educacion/planteles/ema/index.htm
Founded 1915
Dir: Col PEDRO VALENCIA SAUCEDO.

Escuela Militar de Clases de Transmisiones (Military School of Signals Classes)
Campo Militar No. 15-A, General Ramón Corona en la Mojonera, Zapopan, Jalisco
Telephone: (33) 3832-0462
Internet: www.sedena.gob.mx/educacion/planteles/emct/index.htm
Founded 1953
Dir: Col SAÚL CONTRERAS OJEDA.

Escuela Militar de Enfermeras (Military School of Nurses)
Calle Idelfonso Vázquez e Industria Militar, Jardines Poniente del Hospital Central Militar, Lomas de Sotelo, México, DF
Telephone: (55) 5580-6913
Internet: www.sedena.gob.mx/educacion/planteles/eme/index.html
Founded 1938
Dir: Lt-Col IRMA RÍOS SANDOVAL.

Escuela Militar de Especialistas de Fuerza Aérea (Military School of Air Force Specialists)
Colegio del Aire, Base Aérea Militar No. 5, Zapopan, Jalisco
Telephone: (33) 3624-1470
Internet: www.sedena.gob.mx/educacion/planteles/emefa/index.htm
Founded 1934
Dir: Col RAMIRO MARMOLEJO GUZMÁN.

Escuela Militar de Graduados de Sanidad (Graduate Military School of Public Health)
Cerrada de Palomas s/n, Lomas de San Isidro, CP 11620, México, DF
Telephone: (55) 5520-2079
Internet: www.sedena.gob.mx/educacion/planteles/emgs/index.htm
Founded 1970
Dir: Gen. de Brigada Dr LUIS GONZÁLEZ Y GUTIÉRREZ.

Escuela Militar de Ingenieros (Military School of Engineers)
Calzada México Tacuba s/n, Popotla, Delegación Miguel Hidalgo, México, DF
Telephone: (55) 5396-3596
Internet: www.sedena.gob.mx/educacion/planteles/emi/index.htm
Founded 1822

Dir: Gen. Brig. I. C. GILBERTO GARCIA CAMPANTE.

Escuela Militar de Mantenimiento y Abastecimiento (Military School of Supply and Maintenance)
Colegio del Aire, Base Aérea Militar No. 5, Zapopan, Jalisco
Telephone: (33) 3624-1470
Internet: www.sedena.gob.mx/educacion/planteles/emma/index.htm
Founded 1942
Dir: Col JESÚS ULLOA GONZÁLEZ.

Escuela Militar de Materiales de Guerra (Military School of War Materials)
Campo Militar 1-F, Santa Fe, DF
Telephone: (55) 5570-2549
Internet: www.sedena.gob.mx/educacion/planteles/emmg/index.htm
Founded 1946
Dir: Col FELIPE VARGAS TAPIA.

Escuela Militar de Odontología (Military School of Dentistry)
Calle Batalla de Celaya e Idelfonso Vázquez s/n, Lomas de Sotelo, México, DF
Telephone: (55) 5520-2591
Internet: www.sedena.gob.mx/educacion/planteles/emo/index.html
Founded 1976
Dir: Gen. Brig. C. D. MIGUEL ANGEL GUTIÉRREZ PÉREZ.

Escuela Militar de Oficiales de Sanidad (Military School of Public Health Officers)
Calle General Francisco Murguía s/n, Unidad Habitacional Militar, Lomas de Sotelo, México, DF
Telephone: (55) 5557-6807
Internet: www.sedena.gob.mx/educacion/planteles/emos/index.htm
Founded 1927
Dir: Col Dr ROBERTO CASTILLO MARÍN.

Escuela Militar de Transmisiones (Military School of Signals)
Campo Militar No. 1-H, Los Leones Tacuba, México, DF
Telephone: (55) 5387-8943
Internet: www.sedena.gob.mx/educacion/planteles/emt/index.htm
Founded 1925
Dir: Gen. de Brigada LEOVIGILDO MUÑOZ HERNÁNDEZ.

Escuela Militar de Tropas Especialistas de Fuerza Aérea (Military School of Specialist Air Force Troops)
Campo Militar No. 37-D, Santa Lucia, México, DF
Telephone: (55) 5557-6070
Internet: www.sedena.gob.mx/educacion/planteles/emtefa/index.htm
Founded 1981
Dir: Gen. JAVIER POSADAS MEJÍA.

Heroico Colegio Militar (Heroic Military College)
Carretera México-Cuernavaca Km 22, San Pedro Mártir, Tlalpan, México, DF
Telephone: (55) 5676-5044
Internet: www.sedena.gob.mx/educacion/planteles/hcm/index.html
Founded 1818

Dir: Gen. de Brigada D. E. M. CARLOS GARCÍA PRIANI.

UNIVERSIDAD DEL GOLFO

Obregón 203 Pte, Zona Centro, 89000 Tampico, Tamaulipas

Telephone: (833) 212-9222
Fax: (833) 212-9222
E-mail: publicidad@univgolfo.edu.mx
Internet: www.unigolfo.edu.mx

Founded 1972
Private control
Languages of instruction: English, German, Spanish
Academic year: September to July

Rector: Dr HERIBERTO FLORENCIA MENÉNDEZ
Vice-Rector: Lic. HILARIO ZUÑIGA MENCHACA
Chief Admin. Officer: Lic. MARCO ANTONIO MALDONADO LUGO
Librarian: JUANA PIZAÑA MÁRQUEZ

Library of 25,000 vols
Number of teachers: 148 (25 full-time, 123 part-time)
Number of students: 4,800

DIRECTORS

European Faculty for Foreign Students: Dr HERIBERTO FLORENCIA MENÉNDEZ
Faculty of Accounting and Administration: Lic. SERGIO ARTURO ROMO BECERRA
Faculty of Economics and Computing: Ing. FRANCISCO DÍAZ FERNÁNDEZ
Faculty of Law: Lic. ELSA EMILIA PAREDES RAMÍREZ
Postgraduate Studies: Lic. PABLO JOSÉ JIMÉNEZ ALCORTA

UNIVERSIDAD DE GUADALAJARA

Avda Juárez 975, Sector Juárez, 44100 Guadalajara, Jal.

Telephone: (33) 3825-8888
Fax: (33) 3626-0668
E-mail: webudg@cencar.udg.mx
Internet: www.udg.mx

Founded 1792, restructured 1925
State control
Academic year: March to February

Rector: Lic. JOSÉ TRINIDAD PADILLA LÓPEZ
Sec.-Gen.: Mtro CARLOS BRISEÑO TORRES
Chief Admin. Officer: Mtro GUSTAVO ALFONSO CÁRDENAS CUTIÑO
Librarian: Mtro SERGIO LÓPES RUELAS

Library: see Libraries and Archives
Number of teachers: 11,784
Number of students: 180,776

Publications: *Revista Universidad de Guadalajara* (4 a year), *Gaceta*, *Jures*.

UNIVERSITY CENTRES

Art, Architecture and Design: Rector Arq. CARLOS CORREA CESEÑA.

Biological Sciences and Farming: Rector M. en C. SALVADOR MENA MUNGUIA.

Del Norte: Executive Coordinator Dr CÁNDIDO GONZÁLEZ PÉREZ.

Economic and Administrative Sciences: Rector Mtro IXCOATL TONATIUH BRAVO PADILLA.

El Sur: Rector Lic. JESÚS ALBERTO ESPINOZA ARIAS.

Exact and Engineering Sciences: Rector Mtro HECTOR ENRIQUE SALGADO RODRÍGUEZ.

Health Sciences: Rector Dr RAÚL VARGAS LÓPEZ.

La Cienega: Rector Mtro PEDRO JAVIER GUERRERO MEDINA.

La Costa: Rector M. en C. JEFFRY STEVEN FERNÁNDEZ RODRÍGUEZ.

La Costa Sur: Rector Dr JUAN JOSÉ PALACIOS LARA.

Los Altos: Rector Dr HÉCTOR ARMANDO MACÍAS MARTÍNEZ.

Los Valles: Executive Coordinator Dr MIGUEL ANGEL NAVARRO NAVARRO.

Social Sciences and Humanities: Rector Dr JUAN MANUEL DURÁN JUÁREZ.

UNIVERSIDAD AUTÓNOMA DE GUADALAJARA

Apdo Postal 1-440, 44100 Guadalajara, Jalisco
Avda Patria No. 1201, Lomas del Valle, 3a Sección, Guadalajara, Jalisco

Telephone: (33) 3638-8463
E-mail: uag@uag.mx
Internet: www.uag.mx

Founded 1935
Private control
Language of instruction: Spanish
Academic year: August to May

Rector: Lic. ANTONIO LEAÑO ALVAREZ DEL CASTILLO
Vice-Rector: Ing. JUAN JOSÉ LEAÑO ALVAREZ DEL CASTILLO
Chief Admin. Officer: Lic. RUBÉN QUIROZ V.
Chief Academic Officer: Dr NÉSTOR VELASCO P.
Librarian: Lic. ALBERTO OLIVARES DUARTE

Library of 178,000 vols, 3,760 maps, 3,400 periodicals
Number of teachers: 1,622
Number of students: 14,102

Publications: *Docencia* (3 a year), *Actas de la Facultad de Medicina* (2 a year), *Academia* (6 a year), *Item Histórico* (12 a year)

DEANS

College of Architecture and Design: Arq. RAÚL MENDOZA R.
College of Business: C.P. JAVIER GONZÁLEZ C.
College of Engineering: Ing. RAFAEL JAIME A.
College of Health Sciences: Dr NÉSTOR VELASCO P.
College of Humanities and Social Sciences: Lic. ISMAEL ZAMORA TOVAR
College of Law: Lic. HUMBERTO LÓPEZ DELGADILLO
College of Sciences: Ing. JAIME HERNÁNDEZ O.
Continuing Education: Dr JOSÉ MORALES G. (Dir)
Postgraduate Studies: Dr MAURICIO ALCOCER RUTHLING (Dir)
Research Administration: Dr RODOLFO CASILLAS V. (Dir)
Universidad en la Comunidad (UNICO, Junior College): Lic. PEDRO RODRÍGUEZ L. (Dir)

DIRECTORS

College of Architecture and Design (Avda Patria 1201, Lomas del Valle, 45110 Guadalajara, Jalisco; tel. (33) 6610-1010 ext. 32669; fax (33) 6610-1610; e-mail rmendoz@cu.gdl .uag.mx; internet www.uag.edu):

School of Architecture: Arq. RAÚL MENDOZA R.
School of Graphic Design: Lic. CARLOS HERRERA P.
School of Landscape and Interior Design: Lic. SUSANA MAYTORENA
School of Industrial Design: Arq. ALFREDO AMBRIZ T.

College of Business (Avda Patria 1201, Lomas del Valle, 45110 Guadalajara, Jalisco; tel. (33) 6610-0412; fax (33) 6610-0412; e-mail jgcastil@uagunix.gdl.uag.mx):

School of Business Administration: Lic. MA. ELENA MONROY L.
School of Public Accountancy: C.P. JOSÉ ARZATE V.

School of Economics: Lic. JOSÉ LUIS SÁNCHEZ DE LA F.
School of Tourism: Lic. CELINA GALLEGOS S.
School of International Business: Lic. ATALA SOSA H.

College of Engineering (Avda Patria 1202, Lomas del Valle, 45110 Guadalajara, Jalisco; tel. (33) 6610-1010 ext. 32216; fax (33) 6610-1010 ext. 32211; e-mail rjaime@uagunix.gdl .uag.mx):

School of Civil Engineering: Ing. MIGUEL ANGEL PARRA MENA
School of Computer Engineering: Ing. RAFAEL JAIME ALEJO
School of Electronic Engineering: Ing. RAMÓN VÁZQUEZ E.
School of Information Management and Computer Systems: Ing. GONZALO OSUNA
School of Mechanical and Electrical Engineering: Ing. MANUEL URIARTE RAZO

College of Health Sciences (Avda Patria 1201, Lomas del Valle, 45110 Guadalajara, Jalisco; tel. (33) 6610-1010 ext. 32737; fax (33) 6610-0244; e-mail nperez@med.gdl.uag .mx):

School of Dentistry: Dr RAFAEL CHACÓN V.
School of Medicine: Dr. RICARDO LEÓN B.
School of Nursing: Enf. GLORIA DE LA CERDA

College of Humanities and Social Sciences (Avda Patria 1202, Lomas del Valle, 45110 Guadalajara, Jalisco; tel. (33) 6610-1010 ext. 32237; fax (33) 6610-1610; e-mail izamora@ uagunix.gdl.uag.mx; internet www.uag.edu):

International Language Centre: Lic. MA. ESTHER DE LA CUESTA D.
School of Anthropology, Philosophy and Letters: Lic. CRISTINA RUÍZ DE HERNÁNDEZ
School of Communication Sciences: Lic. VÍCTOR ESCALANTE VERA
School of International Relations: Prof. FERNANDO TORRES DE LA T.
School of Linguistics: Lic. MARÍA ESTHER DE LA CUESTA DÍAZ
School of Pedagogy: Lic. ISMAEL ZAMORA T.
School of Psychology: Lic. GABRIEL MORALES HERNÁNDEZ

College of Law (Avda Patria 1201, Lomas del Valle, 45110 Guadalajara, Jalisco; tel. (33) 6610-1010 ext. 32739; fax (33) 6610-1610 ext. 32276; e-mail hdelgadi@uagunix.gdl.uag .mx):

School of Law: Lic. HUMBERTO LÓPEZ D.
School of Social Work: Lic. ELSA ESPINOZA T.

College of Sciences (Avda Patria 1202, Lomas del Valle, 45110 Guadalajara, Jalisco; tel. (33) 6610-1010 ext. 32813; fax (33) 6610-1010 ext. 32219; e-mail jhernan@uagunix.gdl.uag .mx):

School of Chemical Sciences: Ing. ANTONIO PEIMBERT V.
School of Mathematics: Ing. EDUARDO OJEDA P.
School of Natural Sciences and Agriculture: Biol. JORGE FLORES M.

UNIVERSIDAD DE GUANAJUATO

Lascuráin de Retana 5, 36000 Guanajuato, Gto.

Telephone: (473) 732-0006
Fax: (473) 735-1902
E-mail: info@quijote.ugto.mx
Internet: www.ugto.mx

Founded 1732 as Colegio de la Purísima Concepción; changed in 1928 to Colegio del Estado; present name 1945
State control
Academic year: August to June

Rector: Dr ARTURO LARA LÓPEZ

Sec.: Dra María Guadalupe Martínez Cadena
Librarian: Mtra Rosalía del Carmen Macías Rodríguez
Library of 372,963 vols
Number of teachers: 2,900 (808 full-time, 2,092 part-time)
Number of students: 24,406
Publications: *Colmena Universitaria* (2 a year), *Acta Universitaria* (6 a year), *Comunidad Universitaria* (2 a year), *Investigaciones Jurídicas* (2 a year), *Regiones* (2 a year), *Azogue* (2 a year), *Gaceta Naturaleza* (2 a year), *Voces, Laboratorio de Historia Oral* (2 a year), *Centro, Textos de la Historia Guanajuatense* (1 a year), *Tarea Universitaria* (6 a year)

DIRECTORS

Faculty of Accountancy and Administration: Mtro Porfirio Tamayo Contreras
Faculty of Administrative Sciences: C.P. Emigdio Archundia Fernández
Faculty of Architecture: Arq. J. Jesús Octavio Hernández Díaz
Faculty of Chemical Sciences: Dr Alberto Florentino Aguilera Alvarado
Faculty of Civil Engineering: Ing. Carlos Arnold Ojeda
Faculty of Electronics, Mechanical and Electronic Engineering: Oscar G. Ibarra Manzano
Faculty of Geophysics and Hydraulic Engineering: Ing. Juan Manuel Tovar Alcantar
Faculty of Industrial Relations: L.R.I. Domingo Herrera Bribiesca
Faculty of Law: Lic. Juan René Segura Ricaño
Faculty of Mathematics: Dr Ignacio Barradas Bribiesca
Faculty of Medicine: Dr Francisco Javier Guerrero Martínez
Faculty of Mining, Metallurgy and Geology: Ing. René Echegoyen Guzmán
Faculty of Nursing and Midwifery (Celaya): M.A.E. Rosalina Díaz Guerrero
Faculty of Nursing and Midwifery (Guanajuato): L.E. Leticia Soto Franco
Faculty of Nursing and Midwifery (Irapuato): Mtra Leticia Campos Zermeño
Faculty of Nursing and Midwifery (León): Rosa Ma. Rico Venegas
Faculty of Philosophy, History and Letters: Genaro Angel Martell Avila
Faculty of Psychology: M.C. Leticia Chacón Gutiérrez

UNIVERSIDAD AUTÓNOMA DE GUERRERO

Av. Javier Méndez Aponte 1, 03900 Chilpancingo, Guerrero
Telephone: (747) 471-9310
Internet: www.uagro.mx
Founded 1869
Private control
Language of instruction: Spanish
Academic year: August to June

Rector: Ing. Agron. Ramón Reyes Carreto
Gen.–Sec.: M. C. Catalino Macedo Vences
Librarian: Lic. Robert Alexander Endean Gamboa
Number of teachers: 1,600
Number of students: 49,000
Publications: *Revista de la UAG, Gaceta Popular, Otatal*

DIRECTORS

Higher School of Agriculture: Q.B. Gilberto Bibiano Moreno
Higher School of Tourism: Lic. Armando Bello Rodríguez
Regional School of Earth Sciences: Geol. Germán Urban Lamadrid

School of Architecture and Town Planning: Arq. Claudio Rios Torres
School of Chemical-Biological Sciences: Q. B. P. Marco Antonio Leyva Vázquez
School of Commerce and Administration: C.P. Salvador Olivar Campos
School of Engineering: Ing. Rodolfo Vázquez Zeferino
School of Economics: M. C. S. Angel Crespo Acevedo
School of Law: Lic. Alejandro Bernabe González
School of Marine Ecology: Biol. Armando Yokoyama Kano
School of Medicine: Dr Ascencio Villegas Arrizon
School of Philosophy: Lic. Fausto Avila Juárez
School of Social Sciences: Lic. Angel Ascencio Romero
School of Veterinary Medicine and Animal Husbandry: M. V. Z. Salvador Sánchez Padilla

UNIVERSIDAD AUTÓNOMA DEL ESTADO DE HIDALGO

Carr. Pachuca-Actopan km 4.5, Edificio B, 4to. nivel Universidad Virtual, 48900 Pachuca, Hidalgo
Telephone: (771) 717-2000
Internet: www.uaeh.edu.mx
Founded 1869 as the Instituto Científico y Literario, present status 1961
Academic year: September to June

Rector: C.D. Luis Gil Borja
Sec.: M. en A.H. Humberto Augusto Veras Godoy
Registrar: L.A.E. Jorge del Castillo Tovar
Librarian: Lic. Evaristo Luvian Torres
Number of teachers: 700
Number of students: 9,000
Publications: *Revista Técnica de Información, Boletín Informativo, Informe Anual de Rectoría*

COURSE COORDINATORS

Education: Quim. F.B. Silvia Parga Mateos
Professional Studies: Lic. Yolanda Mejía Velasco
Science and Technology: Ing. Carlos Herrera Ordoñez
Special Studies: Lic. Francisco Murillo Butron

DIRECTORS OF SCHOOLS AND INSTITUTES

Institute of Accountancy and Administration: C.P. Horacio Solis Leyva
Institute of Exact Sciences: Ing. José Calderón Hernández
Institute of Social Sciences: Lic. Alejandro Straffon Arteaga
Preparatory School I: Ing. Ernesto Hernández Ocaña
Preparatory School II: Lic. Lauro Perea Montiel
Preparatory School III: Lic. Juan Manuel Camacho Bertran
School of Medicine: Dr Luis Corzo Montaño
School of Nursing: Enf. Luz María Flores Ramírez
School of Odontology: Dr Miguel Angel Anton de la C.
School of Social Work: T.S. Imelda Monroy del Angel

UNIVERSIDAD IBEROAMERICANA

Prolongación Paseo de la Reforma 880, Col. Lomas de Santa Fe, 01219 México, DF
Telephone: (55) 5950-4000
Fax: (55) 5267-4005
Internet: www.uia.mx
Founded 1943, university status 1954

Private control
Language of instruction: Spanish
Academic year: August to July

Rector: Dr José Morales Orozco
Vice-Rector for Academic Affairs: Dr Javier Prado Galán
Librarian: Ing. Pilar Verdejo
Library of 204,000 vols, 1,395 periodicals
Number of teachers: 1,668 (279 full-time, 1,389 part-time)
Number of students: 10,508 (9,770 undergraduate, 738 postgraduate)
Publications: *Boletín Bibliográfico* (12 a year), *Boletín Bolsa de Trabajo* (12 a year), *Didac* (2 a year), *Gallo* (5 a year), *Jurídica* (1 a year), *El Ladrillo* (52 a year), *Poesía y Poética* (3 a year), *Revista de Filosofía* (4 a year), *Revista del Departamento de Psicología* (3 a year), *Umbral XXI* (4 a year), *Prometeo* (3 a year), *Historia y Grafía* (3 a year)

DIRECTORS OF DEPARTMENTS

Architecture, Urban Planning and Design: Arq. Jorge Ballina
Art: Lic. Aída Sierra
Basic Sciences: Mtro Arturo Fregoso
Business Administration and Accounting: Mtro Javier Cervantes
Communication: Mtro José Carreño
Economics: Dr Gerardo Jacobs
Engineering: Ing. Santiago Martínez
Health: Dr Felipe Vadillo
History: Dra Valentina Torres-Septién
Human Development: Lic. Jorge Martínez
International Studies: Lic. Agustín Gutiérrez
Law: Lic. Loretta Ortiz
Literature: Mtra Silvia Ruíz
Philosophy: Lic. Francisco Galán
Political and Social Sciences: Dra Carmen Bueno
Psychology: Dr Pedro Alvarez
Religious Sciences: Dr Carlos Soltero

REGIONAL CAMPUSES

Universidad Iberoamericana—León

Libramiento Norte km 3, Apdo Postal 26, 37000 León, Guanajuato
Telephone: (477) 11-38-60
Fax: (477) 11-54-77
Founded 1978
Private control
Language of instruction: Spanish
Academic year: August to July

Rector: Ing. Carlos Alberto Sebastián Serra Martínez
Director-General for Academic Affairs: Biol. Arturo Mora Alva
Director-General for University Educational Services: Lic. David Martínez Mendizábal
Registrar: Quím. Mario Alberto Arredondo Morales
Librarian: Ing. Amador Cendejas Melgoza
Library of 41,000 vols, 691 periodicals
Number of teachers: 86 (48 full-time, 38 part-time)
Number of students: 2,319 (1,864 undergraduate, 455 postgraduate)
Publication: *Presencia Universitaria* (12 a year)

Universidad Iberoamericana—Puebla

Blvd del Niño Poblano 2901, U. Territorial Atlixcayotl, 72430 Puebla, Puebla
Telephone: (222) 229-0700
E-mail: webmaster@uiagc.pue.uia.mx
Internet: www.pue.uia.mx
Founded 1983
Private control
Academic year: August to July

Rector: Arq. CARLOS VELASCO ARZAC
Director-General for Academic Affairs: Mtro
JAVIER SÁNCHEZ DÍAZ DE RIVERA
Director-General for University Educational
Services: Mtro RAMIRO BERNAL CUEVAS
Registrar: Lic. FRANCISCO JAVIER GARCÍA
GARCÍA
Librarian: Lic. LUISA GONZÁLEZ GARDEA
Library of 66,000 vols, 480 periodicals
Number of teachers: 132 (126 full-time, 6
part-time)
Number of students: 5,139 (4,181 under-
graduate, 958 postgraduate)
Publications: *Magistralis* (every 2 years),
Comunidad (3 a year).

Universidad Iberoamericana—Tijuana

Apdo 185, 22200 Tijuana, Baja California
Located at: Avda Centro Universitario 2501,
Playas de Tijuana, 22200 Tijuana, Baja
California
Telephone: (664) 630-1577
Fax: (664) 630-1591
Internet: www.tij.uia.mx
Founded 1982
Language of instruction: Spanish
Academic year: August to July
Rector: Mtro HUMBERTO BARQUERA GÓMEZ
Director-General for Academic Affairs: Dr
ALBERTO ODRIOZOLA
Director-General: Lic. ARIEL GARCÍA
Registrar: Lic. ISABEL HUERTA
Library of 29,000 vols, 465 periodicals
Number of teachers: 328
Number of students: 1,221 (823 undergradu-
ate, 398 postgraduate)

Universidad Iberoamericana—Torreón

Calz. Iberoamericana No. 2255, C.P. 27010,
Sucursal Torreón, Coahuila
Telephone: (871) 729-1010
Fax: (871) 729-1080
Internet: www.lag.uia.mx
Founded 1982
Private control
Academic year: August to July
Rector: Ing. HECTOR ACUÑA NOGUEIRA
Director-General for Academic Affairs: Ing.
GABRIEL MONTERRUBIO ALVAREZ
Director-General for University Educational
Services: Mtro FELIPE ESPINOZA TORRES
Registrar: C.P. CLAUDIA RODRÍGUEZ TORRES
Librarian: Lic. MARTHA I. MCANALLY SALAS
Library of 23,000 vols, 307 periodicals
Number of teachers: 387
Number of students: 2,299 (2,125 under-
graduate, 174 graduate)
Publications: *Acequias* (4 a year), *Notilaguna*
(12 a year).

UNIVERSIDAD AUTÓNOMA INDÍGENA DE MÉXICO

Juárez 39, Mochicahui, 81890 El Fuerte,
Sinaloa
Telephone: (698) 892-0008
Fax: (698) 892-0042
E-mail: uaim@uaim.edu.mx
Internet: www.uaim.edu.mx
Founded 2001
President: Lic. JOAQUÍN VEGA ACUÑA
Rector: JESÚS ANGEL OCHOA ZAZUETA
Sec.-Gen.: MANUEL DE JESÚS VALDEZ ACOSTA
Director-General for Academic Affairs:
ERNESTO GUERRA GARCÍA
Director-General for Admin.: CARLOS
ERNESTO VILLA PANQUIÁN
Director-General for Institutional Develop-
ment: JOSÉ HUMBERTO GALAVIZ ARMENTA
Librarian: ERNESTO GAXIOLA ENCINAS

DIRECTORS
Los Mochis Campus: Lic. ROSARIO ROCHÍN
NAPUS
Mochicahui Campus: Lic. JUAN ANTONIO
DELGADO MORALES
Sinaloa de Leyva Campus: (vacant)

UNIVERSIDAD INTERCONTINENTAL

Insurgentes Sur 4303, Col. Santa Úrsula
Xitla, 14420 México, DF
Telephone: (55) 5487-1300
Internet: www.uic.edu.mx
Founded 1976
Private control
Academic year: August to July
Rector: JUAN JOSÉ CORONA LÓPEZ
Gen.-Sec.: JOSÉ-LUIS VEGA ARCE
Admin. Officer: C.P. JOSÉ LUIS LEON ZAMUDIO
Librarian: MIGUEL ANGEL SÁNCHEZ BEDOLLA
Number of teachers: 773
Number of students: 4,500
Publications: *Extensiones, Voces, Psicología y
Educación Turismo, Traduic, Intersticios,
Boletín Jurídico.*

UNIVERSIDAD AUTÓNOMA DE CIUDAD JUÁREZ

Calle Henri Dunant 4016, Zona Pronaf,
Ciudad Juárez, Chihuahua
Telephone: (656) 688-2100
E-mail: daramire@uacj.mx
Internet: www.uacj.mx
Founded 1973
State control
Language of instruction: Spanish
Academic year: August to June
Rector: Lic. JORGE QUINTANA SILVEYRA
Gen.-Sec.: M.C. DAVID RAMÍREZ PEREA
Chief Admin. Officer: Lic. RICARDO DUARTE
JÁQUEZ
Dean of Academic Affairs: Quim. HÉCTOR
REYES LEAL
Director of Research and Graduate Studies:
Dra MARTHA PATRICIA BARRAZA DE ANDA
Number of teachers: 710
Number of students: 12,200
Publications: *Entorno, Nóesis*

DEANS
College of Architecture, Design and Art: Arq.
ARTURO MARTÍNEZ LASSO
College of Biomedical Sciences: Dr FELIPE
FORNELLI
College of Engineering and Technology: Dr
RAMÓN PARRA
College of Social Sciences and Administra-
tion: Lic. LUIS A. MAYORGA

UNIVERSIDAD ESTATAL DE ESTUDIOS PEDAGÓGICOS

Fresnillo y Cañitas 310, Ex-ejido, Zacatecas,
21090 Mexicali, Baja California
Telephone: (686) 555-4959
Fax: (686) 555-4959
State control
Dir: Prof. ALFONSO SEPÚLVEDA ORNELAS
Teacher training.

UNIVERSIDAD AUTÓNOMA METROPOLITANA

Rectoría General, Prolongación Canal de
Miramontes 3855, Col. Ex-Hacienda San
Juan de Dios, Delegación Tlalpan, 14387
México, DF
Telephone: (55) 5723-5644
Fax: (55) 5576-6888
E-mail: riebeling@tonatiuh.uam.mx
Internet: www.uam.mx

Founded 1973
State control
Language of instruction: Spanish
Academic year: September to July
Rector-General: JULIO RUBIO OCA
Sec.-Gen.: MAGDALENA FRESAN OROZCO
Librarian: KAMILA KNAP ROUBAL
Number of teachers: 3,700
Number of students: 45,000
Publications: *Semanario de la UAM* (52 a
year), *Casa del Tiempo* (12 a year), *Revista
Iztapalapa* (2 a year), *Revista A* (2 a year),
Diseño UAM (3 a year), *Economía, Teoría y
Práctica Sociológica, Pauta, Contactos* (6 a
year), *Alegatos* (3 a year), *El Cotidiano* (6 a
year), *Reencuentro* (irregular), *Topodrilo* (6
a year), *Universidad Futura* (irregular),
Argumentos (3 a year).

CONSTITUENT CAMPUSES

Azcapotzalco Campus

Avda San Pablo 180, Col. Reynosa-Tamauli-
pas, Del. Azcapotzalco, 02000 México, DF
Telephone: (55) 5485-9510
Internet: www.azc.uam.mx
Rector: EDMUNDO JACOBO MOLINA
Secretary: JORDY MICHELI THIRIÓN
Librarian: FERNANDO VELÁZQUEZ MERLO

DIRECTORS
Basic Sciences and Engineering: ANA MAR-
ISELA MAUBERT FRANCO
Design, Arts and Sciences: JORGE SÁNCHEZ DE
ANTUÑANO BARRANCO
Social Sciences and Humanities: MONICA DE
LA GARZA MALO

Iztapalapa Campus

San Rafael Atlixco 186, Col. Vicentina, Del.
Iztapalapa, 09340 México, DF
Telephone: (55) 5612-4665
Internet: www.iztapalapa.uam.mx
Rector: JOSÉ LUIS GÁZQUEZ MATEOS
Secretary: ANTONIO AGUILAR AGUILAR
Librarian: ALFONSO ROMERO SÁNCHEZ

DIRECTORS
Basic Sciences and Engineering: LUIS MIER Y
TERÁN CASANUEVA
Biological and Health Sciences: JOSÉ LUIS
ARREDONDO FIGUEROA
Social Sciences and Humanities: JOSÉ GRE-
GORIO VIDAL BONIFÁZ

Xochimilco Campus

Calzada del Hueso 1100, Col. Villa Quietud,
Del. Coyoacán, 04960 México, DF
Telephone: (55) 5594-6656
Internet: cueyatl.uam.mx
Rector: JAIME KRAVZOV JINICH
Secretary: MARINA ALTAGRACIA MARTÍNEZ
Librarian: MARGARITA LUGO HUBP

DIRECTORS
Art and Design: EMILIO PRADILLA COBOS
Biological and Health Sciences: NORBERTO
MANJARRÉZ ALVAREZ
Social Sciences and Humanities: GUILLERMO
VILLASEÑOR GARCÍA

UNIVERSIDAD AUTÓNOMA DEL ESTADO DE MÉXICO

Avda Instituto Literario 100 Oriente, Col.
Centro Municipio, 50000 Toluca, Méx.
Telephone: (722) 226-23-00
E-mail: rectoria@uaemex.mx
Internet: www.uaemex.mx
Founded 1956
State control
Language of instruction: Spanish

Academic year: September to August

Rector: Dr en A. P. José Martínez Vilchis

Academic Sec.: M. en S.P. Ezequiel Jaimes Figueroa

Admin. Sec.: M.A.E. Pedro Lizola Margolis

Librarian: M. en E.L. Ruperto Retana Ramirez

Library of 292,000 vols
Number of teachers: 3,045
Number of students: 36,642

DIRECTORS

School of Accountancy and Administration: M.A.E. Ignacio Mercado

School of Agricultural Sciences: Ing. Arturo Maya Gomez

School of Anthropology: M. en E.L. Rodrigo Marcial Jimenez

School of Art and Architecture: M. en Pl. Jesus Aguiluz Leon

School of Behavioural Sciences: Lic. en Psic. Teresa Ponce Davalos

School of Chemistry: M. en C. Juan Carlos Sanchez Meza

School of Dentistry: C.D. Francisco Montiel Conzuelo

School of Economics: M. en E. Ricardo Rodriguez Marcial

School of Engineering: M. en I. Angel Albiter Rodriguez

School of Geography: L. en G. Vicente Peña Manjarrez

School of Humanities: L. en E.L. Gerardo Meza Garcia

School of Law: M. en D. Joaquin Bernal Sanchez

School of Medicine: M.C. Gabriel Gerardo Huitron Bravo

School of Nursing: L. en Enf. Luz Maria Franco Bernal

School of Political Sciences and Public Administration: M. en C.P. Jose Martinez Vilchis

School of Sciences: Biol. Pedro del Aguila Juarez

School of Tourism: L. en T. Maricruz Moreno Zagal

School of Urban and Regional Planning: M. en Pl. Alberto Villar Calvo

School of Veterinary Medicine: M. en C.E. Eduardo Gasca Pliego

UNIVERSIDAD DE LA CIUDAD DE MÉXICO

Fray Servando Teresa de Mier 99, Centro, 06080 Cuauhtémoc, México, DF

Telephone: (55) 5134-9804
E-mail: rectoria_ucm@df.gob.mx
Internet: www.ucm.df.gob.mx

Founded 2001
State control

Rector: Ing. Manuel Pérez Rocha

Director for Academic Affairs: Florinda Riquer Fernández

Director for Admin.: Patricia Fuentes Rangel

Director for University Development: Lic. Oscar González

Librarian: Lic. Blanca Estela Velázquez Morales

Publications: Mano Vuelta, Noticiario

Campuses in Iztapalapa, Del Valle and San Lorenzo Tezonco.

ATTACHED RESEARCH INSTITUTES

Centro de Estudios sobre La Ciudad: Fray Servando Teresa de Mier 92, Cubículos 9 y 10, Tercer piso Col. Centro, 06080 Cuauhtémoc, México, DF; tel. (55) 5134-9804; e-mail centroestudiosucm@yahoo.com.mx; Dirs Silvia Bolos Jacob, Ana Helena Treviño Carrillo.

UNIVERSIDAD FEMENINA DE MÉXICO

Avda Constituyentes 151, 11850 México, DF

Telephone: (55) 5515-1311

Founded 1943
Private control
Language of instruction: Spanish
Academic year: September to June

Rector: Dra Elizabeth Baquedano
Sec.-Gen.: Lic. Luis Silva Guerrero
Registrar: Lic. Pablo Torres Morán
Librarian: Srta Agueda Canedo Gutiérrez

Library of 12,000 vols
Number of teachers: 243
Number of students: 1,300

Publications: Catálogo General Anual, Periódico Bimestral

DEANS

School of Clinical Laboratories: Q.B.P. Víctor Manuel Sánchez Hidalgo, Dr José Aguilar Castillo (daytime courses)

School of Education: Lic. Luz Beatriz Unna de Torres

School of History of Art: Elizabeth Baquedano

School of Interior Decoration: Arq. Carlos Cantú Bolland

School of International Relations: Lic. Emilia Witte Montes de Oca

School of Interpreting and Translating: Lic. Maureen Anne Ivens McCullagh

School of Law: Lic. Antonio Adolfo López García

School of Museology: Lic. Roberto Alarcón

School of Pedagogy: Lic. María Elena Navarrete Toledo

School of Pharmacobiological Chemistry: Q.F.B. Enrique Calderón García

School of Psychology: Lic. Luz Antonieta Polanco de Garzón

School of Social Work: Profa T.S. María del Socorro Susana Campos García

School of Tourist Business Administration: Lic. Armando González Flores

UNIVERSIDAD NACIONAL AUTÓNOMA DE MÉXICO

Ciudad Universitaria, Del. Coyoacán, 04510 México, DF

Telephone: (55) 5622-0958
Fax: (55) 5616-0245
E-mail: lal@hp.fciencias.unam.mx
Internet: www.unam.mx

Founded 1551
Language of instruction: Spanish
Academic year: August to May

Rector: Dr Juan Ramón de la Fuente Ramírez

Secretary-General: Lic. Enrique del Val Blanco

Administrative Secretary: Dr Daniel Barrera Pérez

Director of the Postgraduate Studies Office: Dra Rosaura Ruiz Gutiérrez

Director of the Office for Interinstitutional Collaboration: Mtra Mónica Verea Campos

Librarian: Dra Silvia González Marín

Library: in addition to the National Library and Central Library (see under Libraries and Archives), there are 142 specialized libraries
Number of teachers: 29,979
Number of students: 269,000

Publications: Acta Poética (1 a year), Acta Sociológica (3 a year), Anales de Antropología (1 a year), Anales del Instituto de Biología: Serie Botánica (2 a year), Anales del Instituto de Biología: Serie Zoología (2 a year), Anales del Instituto de Investigaciones Estéticas (2 a year), Anuario Jurídico (1 a year), Anuario de Letras (1 a

year), Anuario de Letras Modernas (1 a year), Anuario de la Historia del Derecho Mexicano (1 a year), Antropológicas (3 a year), Antropología Física Latinoamericana (1 a year), Archivos Hispanoamericanas de Sexología (2 a year), Atmósfera (4 a year), Bibliografía Filosófica Mexicana (1 a year), Bibliografía Latinoamericana (2 a year), Biblioteca Universitaria (2 a year), Bien. Boletín de Investigación, Educación y sus Nexos (3 a year), Bien. Revista Especializada en Ciencias Sociales y la Educación (2 a year), Boletín Mexicano de Derecho Comparado (3 a year), Boletín de la Escuela Nacional de Música (12 a year), Boletín del Instituto de Investigaciones Bibliográficas (2 a year), Carrizos (4 a year), Ciencias (4 a year), Clase: Citas Latinoamericanas en Ciencias Sociales y Humanidades (4 a year), ¿Cómo ves? (12 a year), Contaduría y Administración (4 a year), Crítica Jurídica (2 a year), Crítica: Revista Hispanoamericana de Filosofía (3 a year), Cuadernos Americanos (6 a year), Chicomóztoc: Boletín del Seminario de Estudios para la Descolonización de México (1 a year), Demos: Carta Demográfica sobre México (1 a year), Desde el Sur: Humanismo y Ciencia (4 a year), Dianoia: Anuario de Filosofía (1 a year), Diógenes (4 a year), Discurso: Cuadernos de Teoría y Análisis (2 a year), Economía Informa (12 a year), Educación Química (6 a year), Emprendedores (6 a year), Estudios de Antropología Biológica (every 2 years), Estudios de Cultura Maya (every 2 years), Estudios de Cultura Náhuatl (every 2 years), Estudios de Cultura Otopame (every 2 years), Estudios de Historia Moderna y Contemporánea de México (1 a year), Estudios de Historia Novohispana (1 a year), Estudios de Lingüística Aplicada (2 a year), Estudios Latinoamericanos (2 a year), Estudios Políticos (3 a year), Experiencia Literaria (irregular), Ingeniería, Investigación y Tecnología (4 a year), Investigación Bibliotecológica (2 a year), Investigación Económica (4 a year), Investigaciones Geográficas (2 a year), La Experiencia Literaria (irregular), Latinoamérica: Anuario de Estudios Latinoamericanos (irregular), Los Universitarios (6 a year), Mathesis (4 a year), Medievalia (2 a year), Momento Económico–Información y Análisis de la Conjuntura Económica (6 a year), Nova Tellus: Anuario del Centro de Estudios Clásicos (2 a year), Nuevo Consultorio Fiscal–Laboral y Contable-Financiero (26 a year), Omnia (4 a year), Perfiles Educativos (4 a year), Pluralitas (electronic, 12 a year), Poligrafías–Revista de Literatura Comparada (1 a year), Periódica: Indice de Revistas Latinoamericanas en Ciencias (4 a year), Problemas del Desarrollo: Revista Latinoamericana de Economía (4 a year), Punto de Partida (6 a year), Relaciones Internacionales (3 a year), Revista CIHMECH (1 a year), Revista de Derecho Privado (3 a year), Revista de la Facultad de Medicina (6 a year), Revista de Zoología (2 a year), Revista Mexicana de Astronomía y Astrofísica (2 a year), Revista Mexicana de Ciencias Geológicas (2 a year), Revista Mexicana de Ciencias Políticas y Sociales (4 a year), Revista Mexicana de Sociología (4 a year), Revista Veterinaria – México (4 a year), Sinopsis (1 a year), Tempus (irregular), Theoría: Revista del Colegio de Filosofía (3 a year), Tip. Revista Especializada en Ciencias Químicas Biológicas (2 a year), Tip. Tópicos de Investigación y Posgrado (3 a year), Trabajo Social (4 a year), UNAM Hoy (6 a year), Universidad de México (12 a year), Vertientes–Revista Especializada en

Ciencias de la Salud (2 a year), *Voices of México* (4 a year)

DIRECTORS OF FACULTIES AND SCHOOLS

Faculty of Accounting and Administration: Mtro ARTURO DÍAZ ALONSO

Faculty of Architecture: Arq. FELIPE GERARDO LEAL FERNÁNDEZ

Faculty of Basic Sciences: Dr RAMÓN PERALTA Y FABI

Faculty of Chemistry: Dr ENRIQUE RODOLFO BAZÚA RUEDA

Faculty of Economics: Dr ROBERTO IVÁN ESCALANTE SEMERENA

Faculty of Engineering: Mtro GERARDO FERRANDO BRAVO

Faculty of Law: Lic. FERNANDO SERRANO MIGALLÓN

Faculty of Medicine: Dr JOSÉ NARRO ROBLES

Faculty of Odontology: Dr JOSÉ ANTONIO VELA CAPDEVILLA

Faculty of Philosophy and Literature: Dr AMBROSIO FRANCISCO JAVIER VELASCO GÓMEZ

Faculty of Political and Social Sciences: Dr FERNANDO PÉREZ CORREA

Faculty of Psychology: Dra LUCY MARÍA REIDL MARTÍNEZ

Faculty of Veterinary Medicine and Animal Husbandry: Dr LUIS ALBERTO ZARCO QUINTERO

National Schools:

National School of Music: Mtro LUIS ALFONSO ESTRADA RODRÍGUEZ

National School of Nursing and Obstetrics: Lic. SEVERINO RUBIO DOMÍNGUEZ

National School of Plastic Arts: Dra LUZ DEL CARMEN VILCHIS ESQUIVEL

National School of Social Work: Mtro CARLOS ARTEAGA BASURTO

Multidisciplinary Units of Professional Studies:

Faculty of Advanced Studies Cuautitlán: Dr JUAN ANTONIO MONTARAZ Y CRESPO

Faculty of Advanced Studies Iztacala: Dr RAMIRO JESÚS SANDOVAL

Faculty of Advanced Studies Zaragoza: Mtro JUAN FRANCISCO SÁNCHEZ RUIZ

National School of Professional Studies Acatlán: Lic. HERMELINDA OSORIO CARRANZA

National School of Professional Studies Aragón: Arq. LILIA TURCOTT GONZÁLEZ

UNIVERSIDAD DEL VALLE DE MÉXICO

Mérida 33, Col. Roma, Del. Cuauhtémoc, 06700 México, DF

Telephone: (55) 5533-6915
E-mail: jnajera@uvmnet.edu
Internet: www.uvmnet.edu

Founded 1960
Private control
Languages of instruction: Spanish, English, French
Academic year: August to June

Rector: Dr CÉSAR MORALES HERNÁNDEZ
Vice-Rector for Academic Affairs: Lic. SERGIO LINARES
Head of Admin.: Lic. JESÚS CARRANZA
Registrar: Lic. EDITH TERÁN
Librarian: Lic. SALVADOR CIPRES
Number of teachers: 8,000
Number of students: 100,000
Publications: *Adelante* (12 a year), *Lince* (12 a year), *Academias* (12 a year)

DEANS OF CAMPUSES

Chapultepec: Lic. ELIZABETH MANNING
Guadalupe Insurgentes: Lic. MARTHA ANIDES
Lago Guadalupe: Lic. GABRIELA MOTA
Lomas Verdes: Lic. PATRICIA PUENTE

Querétaro: Lic. SILVIA RIVERA
Roma: Lic. GUADALUPE ZUÑIGA
San Angel: Lic. GRISELDA VEGA TATO
San Miguel de Allende: Dr FRANCISCO MARTÍNEZ
San Rafael: Lic. MARÍA DE LA LUZ DÍAZ MIRANDA
Tlalpan: Lic. LUIS SILVA GUERRERO
Xochimilco: Lic. SALVADOR SILVA

UNIVERSIDAD MICHOACANA DE SAN NICOLÁS DE HIDALGO

Edif. 'TR', Ciudad Universitaria s/n, Col. Felicitas del Río, 58030 Morelia, Mich.

Telephone: (443) 322-3500
Internet: www.umich.mx

Founded 1539, University in 1917
State control
Language of instruction: Spanish
Academic year: September to June

Rector: Lic. DANIEL TRUJILLO MESINA
Gen.–Sec.: Dr SALVADOR JARA GUERRERO
Admin. Sec.: L.A.E. DOMINGO BAUTISTA FARIAS
Dir of Library: Lic. ADALBERTO ABREGO GUTIERREZ
Library of 150,000 vols
Number of teachers: 2,158
Number of students: 31,769

Publications: *Boletín de Rectoría, Cuadernos de Derecho, Polemos, Cuadernos de Centro de Investigación de la Cultura Puehépecha.*

UNIVERSIDAD TECNOLÓGICA DE LA MIXTECA
(Mixteca Technological University)

Carretera a Acatlima km 2.5, 69000 Huajuápan de León, Oax.

Telephone: (919) 532-0214
E-mail: msv@mixteco.utm.mx
Internet: www.utm.mx

Founded 1990
State control
Language of instruction: Spanish

Rector: Dr MODESTO SEARA VÁZQUEZ
Vice-Rector for Academic Affairs: Ing. GERARDO GARCÍA HERNÁNDEZ
Vice-Rector for Admin.: C.P. JAVIER JOSÉ RUIZ SANTIAGO
Vice-Rector for University Relations and Research: Lic. SERGIO GUERRERO VERDEJO
Librarian: Lic. MANUEL BARRAGÁN ROJAS

HEADS OF STUDIES

Applied Mathematics: Mtro JUAN CARLOS MENDOZA SANTOS
Computer Engineering: Ing. FRANCISCO ESPINOSA MACEDA
Design: D.I. ROBERTO ESQUIVEL JAIME
Electrical Engineering: ENRIQUE GUZMÁN RAMÍREZ
Food Science: Q.F.B. JUANA RAMÍREZ ANDRADE
Industrial Engineering: Dr DANIEL ERASTE SANTOS REGES
Management Sciences: Lic. MARÍA GUADALUPE NORIEGA GÓMEZ

UNIVERSIDAD DE MONTEMORELOS

Apdo 16-5, Montemorelos, 67530 Nuevo León

Telephone: (826) 263-0900
Fax: (826) 263-6185
E-mail: umontemorelos@edu.mx
Internet: um.edu.mx

Founded 1973
Private control
Language of instruction: Spanish
Academic year: August to May

Pres.: Dr ISMAEL CASTILLO OSUNA

Vice-Pres: RAQUEL KORNIEJCZUK (Academic), RUBEN MEZA (Administrative), BENJAMIN LAZARO (Finance), ABRAHAM MURILLO (Student Affairs)
Dir. of Admissions and Records: EKEL COLLINS
Librarian: ADÁN SURIANO
Number of teachers: 175
Number of students: 2,350

Publications: *Logos* (1 a year), *Memorias del Centro de Investigaciones Educativas* (1 a year), *Perspectivas Teológicas* (1 a year), *Revista Internacional de Estudios en Educación* (2 a year)

DEANS

School of Administrative Sciences: ARIEL QUINTEROS
School of Arts and Communications: EUNICE AGUILAR
School of Biomedical Sciences: ALEJANDRO GIL
School of Education: JULIAEMY DE FLORES
School of Engineering and Technology: JORGE MANRIQUE
School of Health Sciences: ZENO CHARLES MICHEL
School of Music: NORKA DE CASTILLO
School of Theology: OMAR VELÁZQUEZ

UNIVERSIDAD DE MONTERREY

Avda Ignacio Morones Prieto 4500 Pte, 66238 San Pedro Garza García, Nuevo León

Telephone: (81) 8124-1000
Fax: (81) 8124-1010
Internet: www.udem.edu.mx

Founded 1969
Private control
Language of instruction: Spanish
Academic year: August to May

President: Dr FRANCISCO J. AZCÚNAGA GUERRA
Vice-Pres. for Admin.: Ing. CARLOS MAURICIO RODRÍGUEZ CHAPA
Vice-Pres. for High School and Integral Education: GUADALUPE ELENA RAMOS VILLAREAL
Vice-Pres. for Institutional Development: (vacant)
Vice-Pres. for Undergraduate and Graduate Programmes: Lic. RAFAEL GARZA MENDOZA
Registrar: JUAN MARTÍNEZ VILLAREAL
Librarian: SAUL HIRAM SOUTO FUENTES
Library of 409,796 units
Number of teachers: 250
Number of students: 9,139

HEADS OF ACADEMIC DIVISIONS

Graduate Studies: Dr ARNAUD CHEVALLIER DELABASLE
School of Architecture, Design and Engineering: Ing. JOSÉ ALFREDO GALVÁN GALVÁN
School of Business: Dr MARIO ALANIS GARZA
School of Health Sciences: Dr EDUARDO GARCÍALUNA MARTÍNEZ
School of Humanistic Studies and Education: Dr VÍCTOR AURELIO ZÚNIGA GONZÁLEZ
School of Law and Social Sciences: Lic. JORGE MANUEL AGUIRRE HERNÁNDEZ

UNIVERSIDAD AUTÓNOMA DEL ESTADO DE MORELOS

Avda Universidad 1001, Col. Chamilpa, 62210 Cuernavaca, Morelos

Telephone: (777) 329-7083
Fax: (777) 329-7083
E-mail: dicodi@uaem.mx
Internet: www.uaem.mx

Founded 1953
State control
Language of instruction: Spanish
Academic year: September to July

Rector: RENÉ SANTOVEÑA ARREDONDO
Sec.-Gen.: Lic. MANUEL PRIETO GÓMEZ
Academic Sec.: ELISEO GUAJARDO RAMOS
Librarian: Arq. JORGE SALAZAR DÍAZ
Number of teachers: 1,473
Number of students: 17,500

DEANS AND DIRECTORS

Faculty of Accountancy, Administration and Informatics: REY MARTÍNEZ MENDOZA
Faculty of Agriculture: Lic. ARTURO TAPIA DELGADO
Faculty of Architecture: Arq. EFRÉN ROMERO BENÍTEZ
Faculty of Arts: Dr JESÚS NIETO SOTELO
Faculty of Biological Sciences: ALFONSO VIVEROS MIRAMONTES
Faculty of Chemical and Industrial Sciences: MODESTO MÉNDEZ RDRÍGUEZ
Faculty of Human Communication: Lic. LILIANA ARCE FLORES
Faculty of Human Sciences: Dra ANGÉLICA TORNERO SALINAS
School of Laboratory Technicians: MARÍA ISABEL NERI FIGUEROA
Faculty of Law and Social Sciences: Lic. JORGE ARTURO GARCÍA RUBÍ
Faculty of Medicine: Dr MIGUEL ÁNGEL CASTAÑEDA CRUZ
Faculty of Pharmacy: Dr ALEJANDRO NIETO RODRÍGUEZ
Faculty of Psychology: Dr FERNANDO BILBAO MARCOS
Faculty of Sciences: Dr VERÓNICA NARVÁEZ PADILLA
Institute of the Eastern Region: Lic. JOSÉ PATRICIO DURÁN CAMPOAMOR
Institute of the Southern Region: Lic. AURORA CEDILLO MARTÍNEZ
Language Centre: Prof. J. REYES AGUIRRE PALACIOS
School of Educational Sciences: ANTONIO ARANA PINEDA
School of Nursing: ALEJANDRA RIVERA GUTIÉRREZ
Spanish School for Foreign Learners: WILFRIDO ÁVILA GARCÍA

There are also 9 Preparatory Schools

UNIVERSIDAD MOTOLINIA AC

Cda. de Ameyalco 227, Col. Del Valle, 03100 México, DF
Telephone: (55) 5543-6679
E-mail: informes@motolinia.com.mx
Internet: www.motolinia.com.mx
Founded 1918
Private control
Language of instruction: Spanish
Academic year: August to July
Prin.: LUZ MARÍA PORTILLO ARROYO
Chief Admin. Officer: MARÍA DEL REFUGIO HERRERA FLORES
Librarian: JUANA MARÍA CAMARGO MUÑOZ

Schools of chemistry and law; There is also a campus at Pedregal.

UNIVERSIDAD AUTÓNOMA DE NAYARIT

Ciudad de la Cultura 'Amado Nervo', 63155 Tepic, Nayarit
Telephone: (311) 211-8800
Internet: www.uan.mx
Founded 1930 as Instituto de Ciencias y Letras de Nayarit, refounded as university 1969
Rector: M.C. OMAR WICAB GUTIÉRREZ
Gen.-Sec.: M.C. ADRIÁN NAVARRETE MÉNDEZ
Number of teachers: 230
Number of students: 2,400

Schools of agriculture, chemical engineering, commerce and administration, dentistry, economics, law, medicine, nursing, veterinary medicine, zoology.

UNIVERSIDAD AUTÓNOMA DEL NORESTE

Blvd Enrique Reyna y Américas Unidas s/n, 25100 Saltillo, Coahuila
Telephone: (844) 438-4000
Fax: (844) 438-4009
Internet: www.uane.edu.mx
Founded 1974
Private control
Academic year: January to December (2 terms)
Rector: HIGINIO GONZÁLEZ CALDERÓN
Vice-Rector for Academic Affairs: Lic. MARÍA DEL CARMEN RUÍZ ESPARZA
Vice-Rector for Admin. Affairs: C.P. GABRIEL DURÁN MALTOS
Librarian: Lic. NELLY BERMÚDEZ ARRAZATE
Number of teachers: 708
Number of students: 5,000

Courses in business administration, accountancy, architecture, computer studies, education and psychology, graphic design, industrial and systems engineering, law, political science, tourism.

UNIVERSIDAD AUTÓNOMA DE NUEVO LEÓN

Ciudad Universitaria, 66451 San Nicolás de los Garza, Nuevo León
Telephone: (81) 8329-4000
E-mail: webmaster@uanl.mx
Internet: www.uanl.mx
Founded 1933
Academic year: August to July
Rector: Ing. JOSÉ ANTONIO GONZÁLEZ TREVIÑO
General Sec.: Dr JESÚS ANCER-RODRÍGUEZ
Academic Sec.: Dr UBALDO ORTIZ-MÉNDEZ
Library of 1,500,000 vols
Number of teachers: 5,671
Number of students: 122,501

DEANS

Faculty of Agronomy: Dr JUAN F. VILLARREAL ARREDONDO
Faculty of Architecture: Arq. GUILLERMO ROBERTO WAH ROBLES
Faculty of Biological Sciences: M.C. JUAN M. ADAME RODRÍGUEZ
Faculty of Chemical Sciences: Ing. JOSÉ MANUEL MARTÍNEZ DELGADO
Faculty of Civil Engineering: Ing. FRANCISCO GÁMEZ TREVIÑO
Faculty of Communication Sciences: Lic. JUAN MARIO GÁMEZ CRUZ
Faculty of Earth Sciences: Dr COSME POLA SIMUTA
Faculty of Economics: Lic. JORGE MELÉNDEZ BARRÓN
Faculty of Forestry Sciences: Dr ALFONSO MARTÍNEZ MUÑOZ
Faculty of Law and Social Sciences: Lic. ALEJANDRO IZAGUIRRE GONZÁLEZ
Faculty of Mechanical and Electrical Engineering: Ing. CÁSTULO E. VELA VILLARREAL
Faculty of Medicine: Dr JESÚS Z. VILLARREAL PÉREZ
Faculty of Music: Lic. JUAN LUIS RODRÍGUEZ TRUJILLO
Faculty of Nursing: Lic. MARÍA GPE. MARTÍNEZ DE DÁVILA
Faculty of Odontology: Dr ROBERTO CARRILLO GONZÁLEZ
Faculty of Philosophy and the Arts: Lic. RICARDO C. VILLARREAL ARRAMBIDE
Faculty of Physical and Mathematical Sciences: Ing. JOSÉ OSCAR RECIO CANTÚ
Faculty of Political Science and Public Administration: Lic. RICARDO A. FUENTES CAVAZOS
Faculty of Psychology: Lic. GUILLERMO HERNÁNDEZ MARTÍNEZ
Faculty of Public Accounting and Administration: C.P. RAMIRO SOBERÓN PÉREZ
Faculty of Public Health: Lic. ELIZABETH SOLÍS DE SÁNCHEZ
Faculty of Social Work: Lic. MA. IRENE CANTÚ REYNA
Faculty of Sports Administration: Lic. RENÉ SALGADO MÉNDEZ
Faculty of Veterinary Medicine and Zootechnics: Dr JOSÉ ANTONIO SALINAS MELÉNDEZ
Faculty of the Visual Arts: Arq. MARIO ARMENDARIZ VELÁZQUEZ

UNIVERSIDAD AUTÓNOMA 'BENITO JUÁREZ' DE OAXACA

Avda Universidad s/n, Ex-Hacienda de 5 Señores, 68120 Oaxaca, Oax.
Telephone: (951) 511-0688
Internet: www.uabjo.mx
Founded 1827, university status 1955
Private control
Academic year: September to July
Rector: Mtro. Arq. RAFAEL TORRES VALDEZ
Gen.–Sec.: Dr EDUARDO L. PEREZ CAMPOS
Librarian: Lic. DONAJI MENDOZA LUNA
Library of 77,237 vols
Number of teachers: 980
Number of students: 15,000
Publication: *Planeación*

DEANS

Faculty of Commerce and Administration: L.A.E. SEVERINO ROJAS LÁZARO
Language Centre: Prof. ERIC O'CONNEL
School of Architecture: Arq. JORGE VARGAS GUZMÁN
School of Chemistry: Dr ARTURO SANTAELLA V.
School of Fine Arts: Lic. EVELIO BAUTISTA TORRES
School of Law and Social Sciences: Lic. ABEL GARCÍA RAMÍREZ
School of Medicine: Dr ALFONSO SANTOS ORTÍZ
School of Nursing and Obstetrics: Enf. NOEMI CÓRDOVA VARGAS
School of Odontology: C.D. AUSTREBERTO MARTÍNEZ MOLINA
School of Veterinary Studies: M.V.Z. CARLOS A. DE J. LEÓN LEDEZMA

UNIVERSIDAD DE OCCIDENTE

Gabriel Leyva No.169 Sur, Col. Centro, Apartado Postal 936, 81200 Los Mochis, Sin.
Telephone: (668) 816-1000
Internet: www.udo.mx
Founded 1978
Academic year: September to August
Chancellor: Dr FRANCISCO CUAUHTEMOC FRIAS CASTRO
Rector: RUBEN ELIAS GIL LEYVA
Sec.-Gen.: M. S. P. JOSE GUILLERMO ALVAREZ GUERRERO
Chief Admin. Officer: Lic. FERNANDO ORPINELA LIZARRAGA
Librarian: DELPHA DELLA ROCCA KING
Number of teachers: 414
Number of students: 4,344
Publications: *Ciencia Jurídica, Un Sueño del Paraíso, Los Mochis.*

CAMPUSES

Campus Culiacan: Blvd Madero 34 pte, Culiacan; tel. (667) 540-495; Dir Lic. GILBERTO HIGUERA BERNAL.

Campus Guamuchil: Jose Maria Vigil y Blvd Lazaro Cardenas, Guamuchil, Sinaloa;

tel. (673) 2-03-83; Dir Lic. BENITO GOMEZ URBALEJO.

Campus Guasave: Corregidora y Zaragoza, Guasave; tel. (667) 872-0065; Dir Lic. JESUS TEODORO RAMIREZ JACOBO.

Campus Los Mochis: Carretera Internacional y Blvd Macario Gaxiola, Los Mochis; tel. (668) 816-1000; Dir CILA MARIA HERNANDEZ ROJO.

Campus Mazatlan: Avda del Mar 1200, Mazatlan; Dir Lic. LUIS O. MONTOYA HIGUERA.

UNIVERSIDAD PANAMERICANA

Augusto Rodin 498, Col. Insurgentes Mixcoac, Del. Benito Juárez, 03920 México, DF

Telephone: (55) 5482-1600
Internet: www.mixcoac.upmx.mx
Founded 1966
Private control
Academic year: August to June

Rector: Dr RAMÓN IBARRA
Vice-Rectors: JESÚS MAGAÑA BRAVO, Lic. SERGIO RAIMOND-KEDILHAC NAVARRO
Admin. Dir: Dr VÍCTOR MANUEL PIZÁ
Librarian: ELISA RIVA PALACIO

Library of 45,000 vols
Number of teachers: 450
Number of students: 5,000

Publications: *Boletín* (12 a year), *Revista Istmo* (6 a year), *Tópicos Journal of Philosophy* (2 a year), *Ars Juris* (2 a year)

Preparatory and first degree courses

DIRECTORS

School of Accounting: CLAUDIO M. RIVAS
School of Administration: Ing. AMADEO VÁZQUEZ
School of Economics: Lic. FLAVIA RODRÍGUEZ
School of Education: Dra CARMEN RAMSO
School of Engineering: Ing. PEDRO CREUHERAS
School of Law: Dr ROBERTO IBÁÑEZ MARIEL
School of Philosophy: Dr ROCIO MIER Y TERÁN

AFFILIATED INSTITUTIONS

Instituto de Capacitación de Mandos Intermedios (Mid–Management Institute): Mar Mediterráneo 183, Col. Popotla, 11400 México, DF; tel. (55) 5399-7272; f. 1966; 170 teachers; 2,400 students; library of 1,200 vols; business administration to supervisor and head of dept level; Dir CONRADO ANTONIO LARIOS.

Instituto de Desarrollo para Operarios: Norte 182, No. 477, Col. Peñón de los Baños, 15520 México, DF; tel. (55) 5760-3464; f. 1968; 45 teachers; 550 students; library of 500 vols; courses for worker-management; Dir ENRIQUE SIERRA.

Instituto Panamericano de Alta Dirección de Empresa (Pan-American Institute of Higher Business Studies): Floresta 20, Col. Clavería, 02080 México, DF; tel. (55) 5527-0260f. 1967; library of 8,000 vols; 40 teachers; 1,900 students; Dir SERGIO RAIMOND-KEDILHAC NAVARRO.

Instituto Panamericano de Ciencias de la Educación (Pan-American Institute of Education): Augusto Rodin 498, Col. Mixcoac, 03920 México, DF; Dir Dra MARCELA CHAVARRÍA.

UNIVERSIDAD PANAMERICANA DE NUEVO LAREDO

Ave Morelos 2311, Col. Juárez, Nuevo Laredo, Tam.

Telephone: (867) 715-2731
Fax: (867) 715-2562
E-mail: universipanameri@netscape.net
Internet: www.unipanam.edu.mx

Founded 1980
Private control
Academic year: September to July

Rector: Lic. FRANCISCO BALDERAS GARCÍA
Sec.-Gen.: C.P. VICTOR M. CASTILLO AVENDAÑO
Dir of Academic Affairs: Profa GUADALUPE JASSO JUÁREZ
Dir of Services: Profa MA. MONICA BALDERAS ALCOCER
Dir of Preparatory Division: Prof. CARLOS CAMACHO MANCILLAS
Dir of Undergraduate Division: Profa NORMA GALLEGOS CALDERÓN
Dir of Postgraduate Division: Dr JOSÉ DE JESÚS LEAL MAHMUUD
Librarian: Lic. ABELARDO GLORIA HINOJOSA

Number of teachers: 105
Number of students: 1,800 (1,200 undergraduate, 600 postgraduate)

DEANS

Faculty of Education: Prof. CARLOS CAMACHO MANCILLAS
Faculty of Law, Public Finance and Administration: Lic. FERNANDO RÍOS RODRÍGUEZ
Faculty of Masters Degree Courses: Profa MA. BALDERAS ALCOCER
Faculty of Medicine: Dr WENCESLAO LOZANO RENDÓN
Faculty of Primary School Education: Profa JUANA MARÍA CERDA TORRES
Faculty of Psychology: Lic. VIRGINIA ZAPATA RODRÍGUEZ
Faculty of Secondary School Education: Profa NORMA GALLEGOS CALDERÓN
Faculty of Veterinary and Zoological Sciences: MVZ ALEJANDRO GURROLA GRANADOS

UNIVERSIDAD PEDAGÓGICA NACIONAL
(National Pedagogic University)

Carretera al Ajusco No. 24 Col. Héroes de Padierna Delegación, Tlalpan, 14200 México, DF

Telephone: (55) 5645-6213
Fax: (55) 5645-5340
E-mail: rectoria@upn.mx
Internet: www.upn.mx
State control
Language of instruction: Spanish

Rector: MARCELA SANTILLÁN NIETO
Director of Planning: ABRAHAM SÁNCHEZ CONTRERAS
Director of Studies: ELSA MENDIOLA SANZ
Director of Library and Academic Support Services: FERNANDO VELÁZQUEZ MERLO

Number of teachers: 3,989
Number of students: 69,300

Major subject areas: methods of teaching: education administration, pedagogy, educational psychology, educational sociology, indigenous education; part-time teaching: pre-school, primary and adult education; distance-learning: teaching French.

UNIVERSIDAD ESTATAL DE ESTUDIOS PEDAGÓGICOS

Fresnillo y Cañitas 310, Ex-ejido, Zacatecas, 21090 Mexicali, Baja California

Telephone: (686) 555-4959
Fax: (686) 555-4959
State control

Dir: Prof. ALFONSO SEPÚLVEDA ORNELAS
Teacher training.

BENEMÉRITA UNIVERSIDAD AUTÓNOMA DE PUEBLA

4 Sur No 104, 72000 Puebla, Pue.
Telephone: (222) 229-5500

Fax: (222) 211-0821
E-mail: ciari@siu.buap.mx
Internet: www.buap.mx
Founded 1937
State control
Academic year: August to May

Rector: Dr ENRIQUE DOGER GUERRERO
Secretary-General: Lic. GUILLERMO NARES RODRÍGUEZ
Librarian: Mtro ENRIQUE HUITZIL MUÑOZ

Number of teachers: 3,608
Number of students: 42,055

DIRECTORS

Hospital: Dr ADALBERTO BAIGHTS
Institute of Physics: Dr RUTILO NICOLÁS SILVA GONZÁLEZ
Institute of Physiology: Dr JOSÉ RAMÓN EGUIBAR CUENCA
Institutes of Sciences: Dra MARÍA LILIA CEDILLO RAMÍREZ
Institute of Social Sciences and Humanities: Mtro ROBERTO M. VÉLEZ PLIEGO
School of Agricultural Engineering: Ing. ROSALBA SOLÍS GÓMEZ
School of Architecture: Arq. JOSÉ ANTONIO RUÍZ TENORIO
School of Arts: Mtro DAVID CORNISH BECERRA
School of Biology: Biol. GONZALO YANES GÓMEZ
School of Chemical Engineering: Mtro IGNACIO ROJAS
School of Chemical Sciences: M.C. JOSÉ JAVIER SOSA RIVADENEIRA
School of Civil and Technological Engineering: Mtro NICOLÁS FUEYO MACDONALD
School of Communication: Lic. EDUARDO GARZÓN VALDÉS
School of Computing: Dr GUILLERMO DE ITA LUNA
School of Economics: Mtro DANTE MÉNDEZ JIMÉNEZ
School of Electronics: M.C. JAIME CID MONJARAZ
School of Languages: Mtro ANTONIO VERA GARCÍA DE LEÓN
School of Law and Social Sciences: Lic. EMILIANO PEREA PELAEZ
School of Medicine: Dr MANUEL MORALES CAMACHO
School of Nursing and Obstetrics: Lic. en Enf. MARÍA MARGARITA CAMPOS VÁZQUEZ
School of Philosophy and Letters: Dr ROBERTO HERNÁNDEZ ORAMAS
School of Physical Culture: Mtra MARÍA VÉLEZ MORA
School of Physics and Mathematics: Dra SORAYA GÓMEZ Y ESTRADA
School of Psychology: Psic. J. FERNANDO TURRENT RODRÍGUEZ
School of Public Administration: Mtra SARA AMALIA VÉLEZ MEJÍA
School of Public Accountancy: M.A. MARÍA DE LOURDES MEDINA HERNÁNDEZ
School of Stomatology: M.C. LUIS ANTONIO GONZÁLEZ SALAZAR
School of Veterinary Medicine and Animal Husbandry: Dr FRANCISCO JAVIER FRANCO GUERRA

UNIVERSIDAD POPULAR AUTÓNOMA DEL ESTADO DE PUEBLA

21 Sur 1103, Col. Santiago, 72160 Puebla, Pue.

Telephone: (222) 229-9400
Fax: (222) 232-5251
Internet: web.upaep.mx
Founded 1973
Private control
Academic year: August to July

Rector: Dr ALFREDO MIRANDA LÓPEZ
General-Secretary: Ing. VICENTE PACHECO CEBALLOS

Registrar: Lic. MARÍA DE LOS ANGELES RON-
DERO CHEW
Public Relations Officer: Arq. JOSÉ M.
ARGÜELLES REYES NIEVA
Librarian: Lic. LEOBARDO REYES JIMÉNEZ
Number of teachers: 652
Number of students: 5,084
Publication: *Vertebracíon* (6 a year).

UNIVERSIDAD DEL MAR, PUERTO ÁNGEL
(University of the Sea, Puerto Ángel)

Ciudad Universitaria, 70902 Puerto Ángel,
Distrito de San Pedro Pochutla, Oax.

Telephone: (958) 584-3078
E-mail: msv@huatulco.umar.mx
Internet: www.umar.mx
Founded 1992
State control
Language of instruction: Spanish
Rector: Dr MODESTO SEARA VAZQUEZ
Vice-Rector for Academic Affairs: Biol. MARIO
FUENTE CARRASCO
Vice-Rector for Admin.: C.P. ANDRÉS HER-
NÁNDEZ SANTIAGO
Vice-Rector for Relations and Research: Lic.
MARTHA ISABEL PÉREZ HERNÁNDEZ
Head of Postgraduate Studies: Dra BEATRIZ
AVALOS SARTORIO
Head Librarian: Lic. URSULA NAVARRO ALVAR-
ADO
Publication: *Ciencia y Mar*

HEADS OF STUDIES

Huatulco campus:

International Relations: Mtra ALICIA
FUENTES ROLDAN
Tourism Administration: Lic. OLINCA PAEZ
DOMINGUEZ

Puerto Ángel campus:

Aquaculture: M.C. JOSÉ ARTURO MARTÍNEZ
VEGA
Environment: M.C. HÉCTOR LÓPEZ ARJONA
Marine Biology: M.C. ANTONIO LÓPEZ SER-
RANO
Maritime Studies: M.C. CARLOS GABRIEL
ARGUELLES REDONDO
Oceanology: Dr ROBERTO ESTEBAN MARTÍNEZ
LÓPEZ

Puerto Escondido campus:

Biology: (vacant)
Forestry: (vacant)
Zootechnology: (vacant)

UNIVERSIDAD AUTÓNOMA DE QUERÉTARO

Centro Universitario, Av. Hidalgo s/n, Col.
Las Campanas, 76010 Santiago de Querétaro, Qro

Telephone: (442) 192-1200
Fax: (442) 216-4917
E-mail: webmaster@uaq.mx
Internet: www.uaq.mx
Founded 1951
State control
Language of instruction: Spanish
Academic year: July to June
Rector: M. en A. RAÚL ITURRALDE OLVERA
Academic Secretary: Dr GUILLERMO CABRERA
LÓPEZ
Administrative Secretary: Dr JOSÉ AMBROSIO
OCHOA OLVERA
Librarian: ARTURO HERNÁNDEZ SIERRA
Number of teachers: 1,428
Number of students: 18,000
Publications: *Revista de Egresados de Con-
tabilidad, Revista Extensión Universitaria,
Revista de Informática, Revista de Socio-
logía, Revista de Medicina, Revista de*

*Investigación, Revista Auriga, Revista Bel-
las Artes, Autonomía*

DEANS

Faculty of Chemistry: J. MERCED ESPARZA
AGUILAR
Faculty of Engineering: JESÚS HERNÁNDEZ
ESPINO
Faculty of Humanities: GABRIEL CORRAL
BASURTO
Faculty of Law: ARSENIO DURAN BECERRA
Faculty of Psychology: ANDRES VELÁZQUEZ
ORTEGA
Preparatory Faculty: DOLORES CABRERA
MUÑOZ
School of Computer Science: LUIS F. SAAVE-
DRA URIBE
School of Fine Arts: JOSÉ ROBERTO GONZÁLEZ
GARCÍA
School of Journalism: LUIS ROBERTO AMIEBA
PEREZ
School of Languages: AURORA IVETTE SILVA
RODRIGUEZ
School of Medicine: Dr SALVADOR GUERRERO
SERVIN
School of Nursing: ALEJANDRINA FRANCO
ESGUERRA
School of Social Enterprise Management:
FELIPE SAMAYOA
School of Sociology: CARLOS DORANTES GON-
ZALEZ
School of Veterinary Science and Zoology:
M.V.Z. GUILLERMO DE LA ISLA HERRERA

UNIVERSIDAD DE QUINTANA ROO
(University of Quintana Roo)

Blvd Bahía s/n esquina Ignacio Comonfort,
Col. del Bosque, 77019 Chetumal, Q. Roo

Telephone: (983) 835-0300
Fax: (983) 832-9656
E-mail: lchan@uqroo.mx
Internet: www.uqroo.mx
State control
Language of instruction: Spanish
Rector: EFRAÍN VILLANUEVA ARCOS
Director of Administration and Finance:
FELIPE CRIOLLO RIVERO
Director of Planning: CARLOS BRACAMONTES Y
SOSA
Secretary-General: FRANCISCO MORIENTES DE
ORCA GARRO
Head Librarian: ELÍAS LEÓN ISLAS
Library of 30,479 vols
Publication: *Revista* (scientific journal, 2 a
year)

ACADEMIC DIRECTORS

Economic, Management and Social Sciences:
FERNANDO CABRERA CASTELLANOS
Engineering and Sciences: MEDINA LEYVA
LUIS FELIPE
Humanities and International Studies: ANTO-
NIO HIGUERA BONFIL

UNIVERSIDAD REGIOMONTANA

Villagrán 238 Sur, Centro, 64000 Monterrey,
N.L.

Telephone: (81) 8220-4620
Fax: (81) 8344-3470
E-mail: webmaster@mail.ur.mx
Internet: www.ur.mx
Founded 1969
Private control
Language of instruction: Spanish
Academic year: September to August
Rector: Dr PABLO A. LONGORIA TREVIÑO
Admin. Dir: Ing. GUILLERMO CHARLES LOBO
Registrar: Ing. GERARDO GONZÁLEZ
Librarian: Ing. JORGE MERCADO SALAS
Library of 42,952 vols
Number of teachers: 450
Number of students: 4,500

Publications: *Espresión* (52 a year), *Veritas* (1
a year)

DEANS

Faculty of Economic and Administrative Sci-
ences: Dr CARLOS OLIVARES LEAL
Faculty of Engineering and Architecture: Dr
RODOLFO SALINAS HERNÁNDEZ
Faculty of Humanities and Social Sciences:
Lic. DORA ANTINORI CARLETTI
Preparatory Division: Lic. NICOLÁS PALACIOS
LOZANO

UNIVERSIDAD LA SALLE

Benjamin Franklin 47, Col. Hipódromo Condesa, 06140 México, DF

Telephone: (55) 5278-9501
Fax: (55) 5516-2537
Internet: www.ulsa.edu.mx
Founded 1962
Private control
Campuses at Bajío, Puebla, Cancún, Cuerna-
vaca, Chihuahua, Laguna, Morelia, Neza-
hualcóyotl, Noroeste, Pachuca, Saltillo,
Victoria, Oaxaca
Language of instruction: Spanish
Academic year: August to June
Rector: MARTÍN ROCHA PEDRAJO
Vice-Rector for Academics: Ing. EDMUNDO
BARRERA MONSIVÁIS
Vice-Rector for Formation and Campus Life:
JOSÉ ANTONIO VARGAS AGUILAR
Registrar: RAUL HAUSER LUNA
Librarian: MARÍA ASUNCIÓN MENDOZA
BECERRA
Library of 158,673 vols
Number of teachers: 966
Number of students: 6,800
Publications: *Boletín Agora de la Facultad de
Derecho, Boletín de Biblioteca, Colección
Jurídica Posiciones de la Facultad de
Derecho, Diez Días, Gaceta ULSA, Huma-
nitas, La Luciérnaga (Preparatoria),
Logos, Reflexiones Universitarias, Revista
Académica de la Facultad de Derecho,
Revista Dirección, Revista Médica La
Salle, Serie Cultura de la Facultad de
Derecho, Siempre Unidos, Vera Humanitas*

DIRECTORS

Faculty of Law: JORGE NADER KURI
Faculty of Medicine: Dr PEDRO ARGÜELLES
DOMENZAIN
Faculty of Humanities and Social Sciences:
JOSÉ IGNACIO RIVERO CALDERÓN
Graduate Studies: MARÍA TERESA ESTRADA
Research Centre: Dr FELIPE GAYTÁN ALCALÁ
School of Architecture , Design and Commu-
nication: JORGE ITURBE BERMEJO
School of Business: ADOLFO CERVANTES RUIZ
School of Chemical Sciences: JOSÉ ELÍAS
GARCÍA ZAHOUL
School of Education: CARLOS DAVID DOM-
ÍNGUEZ TROLLE
School of Engineering: Dr EDUARDO GÓMEZ
RAMÍREZ
School of Philosophy: JOSÉ ANTONIO DACAL
ALONSO
School of Preparatory Studies: MARCO AUR-
ELIO ANTONIO GONZÁLEZ CERVANTES
School of Religious Sciences: Dr JORGE
BONILLA SORT DE SANTZ

UNIVERSIDAD DE LA SALLE BAJÍO

Ave Universidad 602, Col. Lomas del Cam-
pestre, 37000 Léon, Gto.

Telephone: (477) 710-8500
E-mail: informes@delasalle.edu.mx
Internet: www.delasalle.edu.mx
Founded 1968
Private control

Academic year: August to December,February to June

Rector: Lic. ANDRÉS GOVELA GUTIÉRREZ
Vice-Rector: Lic. FELIPE AURELIO PELCASTRE ARENAS
Registrar: Lic. LUIS ERNESTO RÍOS PÉREZ
Librarian: Lic. ISIDRO CONDE GONZÁLEZ

Library of 108,529 vols
Number of teachers: 1,231
Number of students: 12,923

Publications: *Cuadernos* (2 a year), *Espíritu Lasallista* (12 a year), *Entornos* (6 a year), *Magazine Lasalle* (6 a year)

DIRECTORS OF FACULTIES

Accountancy Administration and International Marketing: Lic. JOSÉ JULIO CARPIO MENDOZA
Agronomy: Ing. MARIO ALBERTO ROMERO PÉREZ
Architecture: Arq. DAVID CABRERA RUIZ
Civil, Industrial and Mechanical Engineering: Ing. MAURICIO SALVATORI MORALES
Communication Sciences and Marketing: Lic. ALFREDO LING ALTAMIRANO
Computer and Electronic Engineering: Ing. ARTURO SUÁSTEGUI RODRÍGUEZ
Dentistry: Dr MARY JEAN McGRATH BERNAL
Design: Lic. ADRIAN GUERRERO CASTRO
Education and Human Development: Mtra SOCORRO DURÁN GONZÁLEZ
Graduate School of Administration: Lic. GUSTAVO A. HERNÁNDEZ MORENO
Graduate School of Architecture: M. A. GREGORIO G. DE LA ROSA FALCON
Graduate School of Dentistry: Dr ENRIQUE NIEMBRO CAMPUZANO
Graduate School of Education: Lic. MANUEL CASTRO VILLICAÑA
Graduate School of Electronics and Computational Engineering: Ing. JAIME PALACIOS CASTAÑÓN
Law: Lic. MARIELA DEL CARMEN HUERTA GUERRERO
Preparatory School: Dr SALVADOR MUÑOZ SOLIS
Telecommunications Engineering: Ing. JAIME PALACIOS CASTAÑÓN
Tourism and Hotel Studies: Dr RAFAEL GUIZAR MONTÚFAR
Veterinary Studies: EDUARDO HERNÁNDEZ GONZÁLEZ DEL CASTILLO

CAMPUSES

Américas Campus: 864 students; Dir Lic. FERNANDO MONROY VIVAS.

Juan Alonso de Torres Campus: 1,290 students; Dir Lic. JOSÉ AMONARIO ASIÁIN DÍAZ DE LEÓN.

Salamanca Campus: 1,321 students; Dir Mtra ESTEBAN MARTÍNEZ HERNÁNDEZ.

San Francisco del Rincón Campus: 1,021 students; Dir Ing. MARTHA ELENA BERMÚDEZ FUNES.

UNIVERSIDAD AUTÓNOMA DE SAN LUIS POTOSÍ

Alvaro Obregón 64 Antiguo, Centro Histórico, 78000 San Luis Potosí

Telephone: (444) 826-1381
Fax: (444) 812-3343
Internet: www.uaslp.mx

Founded 1826 as Instituto Científico y Literario
Federal control
Language of instruction: Spanish
Academic year: August to June

Rector: Lic. MARIO GARCÍA VALDEZ
Gen.-Sec.: Arq. MANUEL F. VILLAR RUBIO
Particular Sec.: Lic. MARÍA DEL PILAR DELGADILLO SILVA
Admin. Sec.: RICARDO SEGOVIA MEDINA

Finance Dir: JOSÉ E. HERNÁNDEZ GARZA
Libraries System Dir: Dr LUIS DEL CASTILLO MORA

Library of 3,000,000 vols in 28 libraries
Number of teachers: 2,290
Number of students: 19,400

Publications: *Alfa y Omega* (2 a year), *Convergencia* (2 a year), *Escenario* (2 a year), *Hábitat* (1 a year), *Horizonte Administrativo* (3 a year), *La Rueda* (2 a year), *Lex Universitatis* (3 a year), *Revista del Instituto de Investigaciones Jurídicas* (2 a year), *Universitarios Potosinos* (2 a year)

DEANS

Accountancy and Administration: JUAN MANUEL BUENROSTRO MORÁN
Agronomy: M. C. MIGUEL ANGEL TISCAREÑO IRACHETA
Chemistry: Dr JORGE F. TORO VÁZQUEZ
Communications: Lic. JORGE ARTURO MIRABAL MARTÍNEZ
Economics: Lic. DAVID VEGA NIÑO
Engineering: Ing. ARNOLDO GONZÁLEZ ORTÍZ
Habitat: Arq. ALEJANDRO GALVÁN ARELLANO
Law: Lic. RICARDO SANCHEZ MARQUEZ
Library Science: Lic. ROSA MARÍA MARTÍNEZ RIDER
Medicine: Dr JESUS EDUARDO NOYOLA BERNAL
Nursing: Mtra. MAGDALENA MIRANDA
Psychology: Lic. VICTOR MANUEL ARREGUÍN ROCHA
Science: M. C. BENITO PINEDA REYES
Stomatology: Dr MARIO AREVALO MENDOZA

UNIVERSIDAD COMUNITARIA DE SAN LUIS POTOSÍ

Arista 1000, Barrio del Tequis, San Luis Potosí, SLP

Telephone: (444) 815-3190
E-mail: salsilca@terra.com.mx

Founded 2002
State control

Rector: Prof. SALVADOR SILVA CARRILLO

Main subject areas: administrative information technology, anthropology, community health, economic development, indigenous law

DIRECTORS

Tamanzunchale Campus: Lic. RAFAEL MURGÍA FRANCISCO
Tamuín Campus: MARTHA INÉS FLORES PACHECO
Tonkanhuitz Campus: Ing. ALFREDO GURROLA GRAVE

UNIVERSIDAD POLITÉCNICA DE SAN LUIS POTOSÍ

Iturbide 140, Centro, 78000 San Luis Potosí, SLP

Telephone: (444) 814-4714
Fax: (444) 812-6519

Founded 2001

Rector: JUAN ANTONIO MARTÍNEZ MARTÍNEZ.

UNIVERSIDAD DE LA SIERRA

Carretera Moctezuma-Cumpas km 2.5, 84561 Moctezuma, Sonora

Telephone and fax (634) 342-9600
E-mail: rectoria@universidaddelasierra.edu.mx
Internet: www.universidaddelasierra.edu.mx

Founded 2002
State control
Academic year: August to June

Prin.: Ing. GUADALUPE RODRÍGUEZ VALENZUELA

Sec. for Academic Affairs: Lic. JULIÁN MORENO BARCELÓ
Librarian: CESAR IVAN MARTÍNEZ ARMENTA
Librarian: Lic. IMELDA MONTAÑO AGUILAR
Library of 4,536 vols.

UNIVERSIDAD AUTÓNOMA DE SINALOA

Calle Gral. Angel Flores Pte. s/n, Colonia Centro, 80000 Culiacán Rosales, Sin.

Internet: www.uasnet.mx

Founded 1873
State control

Rector: M.C. HÉCTOR MELESIO CUÉN OJEDA
Secretary-General: Lic. ARTURO ZAMA ESCALANTE
Registrar: Lic. J.B. GAXIOLA COTA

Number of teachers: 400
Number of students: 6,000

Schools of accountancy, administration, agriculture, chemistry, economics, law and social science, nursing, physics and mathematics, social work;Campuses in Mazatlán, Los Mochis, Guamúchil, Juan José Ríos.

UNIVERSIDAD DE SONORA

Blvd. Luis Encinas y Rosales s/n, Col. Centro, 83000 Hermosillo, Sonora

Telephone: (662) 259-2136
Fax: (662) 259-2135
E-mail: webmaster@informatica.uson.mx
Internet: www.uson.mx

Founded Charter granted 1938; opened and officially inaugurated 1942
Private control
Language of instruction: Spanish
Academic year: September to June

Rector: Dr PEDRO ORTEGA ROMERO
Secretary-General: Ing. MANUEL BALCÁZAR MEZA
Librarian: Lic. ANA LILYA MOYA

Library of 45,000 vols
Number of teachers: 1,025
Number of students: 18,000

Publications: *Gaceta Universitaria* (12 a year), *Revista de la Universidad* (4 a year), *Poemarios* (6 a year), *Revista de Física* (2 a year), *Revista de Economía* (2 a year), *Sonora Agropecuario* (6 a year)

COORDINATORS

Department of Biochemistry: HECTOR ESCÁRCEGA
Department of Geology: Ing. EFRÉN PÉREZ SEGURA
Department of Humanities: JOSÉ SAPIEN DURÁN
Department of Mathematics: EDUARDO TELLECHEA ARMENTA
Department of Physics: ANTONIO JAUREGUI D.
School of Accountancy and Administration: C.P. RAMÓN CÁRDENAS VALDÉS
School of Advanced Studies: Ing. IGNACIO AYALA ZAZUETA
School of Agriculture and Animal Husbandry: Ing. MARIO GUZMÁN
School of Chemical Sciences: Ing. OSVALDO LANDAVAZO
School of Economics: Lic. RODOLFO DÍAZ CASTAÑEDA
School of Engineering: Ing. MIGUEL A. MORENO N.
School of Law and Social Sciences: Lic. MIGUEL CÁRDENAS
School of Nursing: Prof. ELVIRA COTA
School of Psychology and Communication Sciences: Lic. DANIEL C. GUTIÉRREZ C.
School of Social Work: T.S. AMELIA I. DE BLANCO

CAMPUS DIRECTORS

Unidad Norte: Ing. RODOLFO GUZMÁN
Unidad Santana: Ing. MARIO TARAZÓN H.
Unidad Sur: Lic. JOSÉ A. VALENZUELA

UNIVERSIDAD JUÁREZ AUTÓNOMA DE TABASCO

Avda Universidad s/n, Zona de la Cultura, 86040 Villahermosa, Tabasco

Telephone: (993) 314-0698
Internet: www.ujat.mx

Founded 1958
State control
Academic year: September to August

Rector: M.A. Candita VICTORIA GIL JIMÉNEZ
Academic Secretary: M.P.E.S. MARÍA ISABEL ZAPATA VÁSQUEZ
Administrative Secretary: Dr JOSÉ MANUEL PIÑA GUTIÉRREZ
Secretary of the Rectorate: Dra VIRGINIA ARCEO GIORGANA
Librarian: Lic. TOMASA BARRUETA GARCÍA

Library of 174,608 vols
Number of teachers: 1,050
Number of students: 20,470

Publications: *Revista de la Universidad, Perspectivas Docentes, Universidad y Ciencias, Revista de la División de Ciencias Sociales y Humanidades, Revista Temas Biomédicos, Gaceta Juchiman, Revista Hitos de la División de Ciencias Economico-Administrativas / Centro, Revista Zenzontle de la División de Educación y Artes, Revista de la Unidad Chontalpa*

DIRECTORS

Chontalpa Unit: Ing. JUAN LUIS RAMIREZ MARROQUIN (Dir-Gen.)
Division of Agricultural Sciences: M. V. Z. VICTOR DE JESUS PEREZPRIEGO COBIAN
Division of Arts and Education: Lic. EFRAIN PÉREZ CRUZ
Division of Basic Sciences: Fis. CARLOS GONZÁLEZ ARIAS
Division of Biological Sciences: M. C. ANDRÉS ARTURO GRANADOS BERBER
Division of Economic and Administrative Sciences: C.P. OLGA YERI GONZÁLEZ LÓPEZ (Centre Unit)
Division of Engineering and Technology: Ing. ARTURO ARIAS RODAS
Division of Health Sciences: Dr ESMELIN TRINIDAD VÁZQUEZ
Division of Humanities and Social Sciences: Lic. FREDDY PRIEGO PRIEGO

UNIVERSIDAD AUTÓNOMA DE TAMAULIPAS

Matamoros 8 y 9, Col. Centro, 87000 Victoria, Tamaulipas

Telephone: (834) 318-1800
Internet: www.uat.mx

Founded 1955
Private control
Language of instruction: Spanish
Academic year: August to June

Rector: Ing. HUMBERTO FILIZOLA HACES
Sec.-Gen.: M.V.Z. FERNANDO ARIZPE GARCÍA
Academic Sec.: C.P. URIEL DAVILA HERRERA
Admin. Sec.: Ing. MIGUEL CANTU CABALLERO
Dir of Planning and Institutional Development: Dr. MARCO AURELIO NAVARRO

Number of teachers: 2,848 (912 full-time, 1,936 part-time)
Number of students: 36,000

Publications: *Sociotam* (2 a year), *Biotam* (2 a year)

DIRECTORS

Mante Campus:

Faculty of Agriculture: Ing. ALEJANDRO HERNÁNDEZ

Matamoros Campus:

Faculty of Human Medicine: Dr JUAN CARLOS CANTÓ
Faculty of Nursing: Mtra ANTONIA HERNÁNDEZ

Nuevo Laredo Campus:

Faculty of Commerce and Administration: Lic RAMIRO GARZA
Faculty of Nursing: Lic ROSALINDA MEDINA

Reynosa Campus:

Faculty of Agro-industrial Sciences: Ing. JOSE SUÁREZ FERNÁNDEZ
Faculty of Chemical Sciences: L.Q.I. RENE FUENTES

Tampico Campus:

Faculty of Architecture: Arq. JUAN JOSÉ CUEVAS
Faculty of Commerce and Administration: C.P. JOSÉ LUIS LIZARDI
Faculty of Dentistry: Dr DELFINO ALVISO
Faculty of Engineering: Ing. MOISES BARCENAS
Faculty of Law and Social Sciences: Lic. SALVADOR ESTEVE
Faculty of Medicine: Dr ATENOGENES SALDIVAR
Faculty of Nursing and Obstetrics: Mtra PAULINA AGUILERA
Higher School of Music: Mtro EDGAR ZARAGOZA

Victoria Campus:

Faculty of Agriculture: Ing. MARIO LARA
Faculty of Commerce and Administration: Mtro HUGO VALLADARES
Faculty of Education: Lic. VALENTÍN AVILA
Faculty of Law and Social Sciences: Lic. J. LAVIN
Faculty of Social Work: Lic. GONZALO HERNÁNDEZ
Faculty of Veterinary Medicine: M.V.Z. SERGIO GARZA
School of Nursing: Lic CINTHYA IBARRA

UNIVERSIDAD AUTÓNOMA DE TLAXCALA

Avda Universidad 1, 90000 Tlaxcala, Tlax.

Telephone: (246) 462-1167
Fax: (246) 462-1167
E-mail: rectoria@cci.uatx.mx
Internet: www.uatx.mx

Founded 1976
Academic year: July to June

Rector: J.A. RENÉ GRADA YAUTENTZI
Admin. Dir: DOROTEO NAVA
Librarian: OSVALDO RAMÍREZ ORTIZ

Number of teachers: 700
Number of students: 10,000

Depts of biomedical sciences, education, humanities, social sciences,; Research centres: animal physiology and behaviour, animal reproduction, biological sciences and biotechnology, genetics and environment, regional development.

UNIVERSIDAD VERACRUZANA

Zona Universitaria, Lomas del Estadio s/n, 91090 Jalapa, Ver.

Telephone: (228) 842-17-63
Fax: (228) 817-63-70
E-mail: rarias@uv.mx
Internet: www.uv.mx

Founded 1944
Academic year: September to August
Rector: Dr RAÚL ARIAS LOVILLO

Vice-Rector (Coatzacoalcos-Minatitlán Campus): ENRIQUE RAMÍREZ NAZARIEGA
Vice-Rector (Orizaba-Córdoba Campus): Arq. ROBERTO OLAVARRIETA MARENCO
Vice-Rector (Poza Rica-Tuxpan Campus): Dra CLARA CELINA MEDINA SAGAHÓN
Vice-Rector (Veracruz Campus): EMILIO ZILLI DEBERNARDI
Academic Secretary: Mtra MARIA DEL PILAR VELASCO MUÑOZ LEDO
Dean of Planning and Institutional Research: Mtra LAURA ELENA MARTÍNEZ MÁRQUEZ
Librarian: Lic. DIANA GONZÁLEZ ORTEGA

Number of teachers: 5,064
Number of students: 44,903

Publications: *La Palabra y el Hombre, La Ciencia y el Hombre*

HEADS OF DIVISIONS

Agricultural and Biological Sciences: Mtro ERNESTO RODRÍGUEZ LUNA
Arts: Mtro ENRIQUE SALMERÓN CÓRDOBA
Economics: Dr MARIO MIGUEL OJEDA RAMÍREZ
Health Sciences: Dr RAMÓN FLORES LOZANO
Humanities: Dr Ma MAGDALENA HERNÁNDEZ ALARCÓN
Technology: Mtro WALTER LUIS SAIZ GONZÁLEZ

DIRECTORS

Coatzacoalcos-Minatitlán Campus:

Faculty of Accounting and Business Management: JAVIER ARENAS WAGNER
Faculty of Agricultural Production Systems Engineering: Ing. ALBERTO HERNÁNDEZ QUIROZ
Faculty of Chemistry (Coatzacoalcos): ERUVIEL FLANDÉS ALEMÁN
Faculty of Dentistry: Dr JAVIER GASTÓN PÉREZ ORTIZ
Faculty of Engineering: Ing. CIRO CASTILLO PÉREZ
Faculty of Nursing: MORAIMA KATZ
Faculty of Medicine: Dr FRANCISCO ORTIZ GUERRERO
Faculty of Social Work: Lic. LUCINDA MIRANDA CHIÑAS

Orizaba-Córdoba Campus:

Faculty of Accountancy and Business Management: IDELFONSO VÍCTOR MUÑOZ ROSAS
Faculty of Architecture: Arq. ABEL COLORADO SAINZ
Faculty of Biological and Agricultural Sciences: ANTONIO PÉREZ PACHECO
Faculty of Chemical Sciences: SOFÍA CANALES CHÁVEZ
Faculty of Dentistry: GUILLERMO MERAZ ZÚÑIGA
Faculty of Mechanical and Electrical Engineering: Ing. GUILLERMO CABALLERO LEÓN
Faculty of Medicine: Dr JORGE E. LÓPEZ GONZÁLEZ
Faculty of Nursing: Enf. INÉS HUERTA VÁSQUEZ

Poza Rica-Tuxpan Campus:

Faculty of Accountancy: Mtro MARIO SOTO DEL ÁNGEL
Faculty of Architecture: Arq. LUIS MANUEL VILLEGAS SALGADO
Faculty of Biology, Agriculture and Animal Husbandry: Biol. JOSÉ LUIS ALANIS MÉNDEZ
Faculty of Chemical Sciences: Ing. SERGIO NATAN GONZÁLEZ ROCHA
Faculty of Civil Engineering: Ing. ALEJANDRO CÓRDOVA CEBALLOS
Faculty of Dentistry: JAVIER AGUIRRE BACEROT
Faculty of Education: Lic. ADORACIÓN BARRALES VILLEGAS
Faculty of Electronic Engineering and Communications: SILVERIO PÉREZ CÁCERES
Faculty of Mechanical and Electrical Engineering: Ing. JOSÉ LUIS JUÁREZ SUÁREZ

Faculty of Medicine: Dr JORGE C. VILLEGAS PATIÑO

Faculty of Nursing: JUANA PERALTA SANTIAGO

Faculty of Psychology: Mtro FRANCISCO BERMÚDEZ JIMÉNEZ

Faculty of Social Work: Lic. VIRGINIA CALLEJAS MATEOS

Veracruz Campus:

Faculty of Accounting: CELIA DEL PILAR GARRIDO VARGAS

Faculty of Business Management: LILIANA IVONNE BETANCOURT TRAVENDHAN

Faculty of Clinical Chemistry: MA. DEL REFUGIO SALAS ORTEGA

Faculty of Communications Science: Lic. JOSÉ LUIS CERDÁN DÍAZ

Faculty of Dentistry: Dra EMMA HERNÁNDEZ FIGUEROA

Faculty of Education: Mtra LETICIA SÁNCHEZ TETUMA

Faculty of Engineering: Ing. JOSÉ A. TELLO ALLENDE

Faculty of Medicine: Dr FRANCISCO MANUEL SANTIAGO SILVA

Faculty of Nursing: SOFÍA DELFÍN BADUY

Faculty of Nutrition: Lic. MA. DE LOURDES MALPICA CARLÍN

Faculty of Physical Education, Sports and Recreation: Mtro SERGIO HERNÁNDEZ LÓPEZ

Faculty of Psychology: Psic. MA. EUGENIA PADILLA FARÍAS

Faculty of Veterinary Medicine and Zootechnics: CARLOS LAMONTHE ZAVALETA

Xalapa Campus:

Faculty of Accounting and Business Management: LUIS RICARDO OLIVARES MENDOZA

Faculty of Administrative and Social Sciences: ADELAIDA RODRÍGUEZ ARCOS

Faculty of Agriculture: Ing. GABRIEL MAY MORA

Faculty of Anthropology: Mtro FRANCISCO JAVIER KURI CAMACHO

Faculty of Architecture: Arq. MIGUEL ÁNGEL CORTÉS ZAHAR

Faculty of Biology: Biol. SOLEDAD ROCHA FLORES

Faculty of Chemical Biological Pharmacy: Dr RAFAEL DÍAZ SOBAC

Faculty of Chemical Engineering: Mtro MIGUEL ANGEL FRAGOSO LÓPEZ

Faculty of Civil Engineering: Ing. ARURO ORTIZ CEDANO

Faculty of Clinical Chemistry: SANDRA LUZ GONZÁLEZ HERRERA

Faculty of Dance: Mtra NATALIA JUAN GIL

Faculty of Dentistry: MARINA FERNÁNDEZ CONTI

Faculty of Economics: Dr REY ACOSTA BARRADAS

Faculty of Education: Mtra ROCÍO L. GONZÁLEZ GUERRERO

Faculty of Electronic Instrumentation: Mtro ANGEL BARRIENTOS SANTIAGO

Faculty of Fine Arts: Mtro HÉCTOR VINICIO REYES CONTRERAS

Faculty of History: Mtro HÉCTOR MÁRTINEZ DOMÍNGUEZ

Faculty of Languages: Mtra ROSALBA HESS MORENO

Faculty of Law: Lic. MANLIO FABIO CASARÍN NAVARRETE

Faculty of Mathematics: Dr JOSÉ RIGOBERTO GABRIEL ARGÜELLES

Faculty of Mechanical and Electrical Engineering: Mtro RAFAEL LOZANO GONZÁLEZ

Faculty of Medicine: Dr RAFAEL CANO ORTEGA

Faculty of Music: Mtra PATRICIA CASTILLO DÍAZ

Faculty of Nursing: CRISTINA SAAVEDRA VÉLEZ

Faculty of Nutrition: CONCEPCIÓN SÁNCHEZ ROVELO

Faculty of Philosophy: Mtro ALBERTO C. RUIZ QUIROZ

Faculty of Physics: Dr CÉSAR RENÉ DE LA CRUZ LASO

Faculty of Psychology: Mtro AGUSTÍN AGUIRRE PITALÚA

Faculty of Sociology: Mtro LUIS MAGAÑA CUELLAR

Faculty of Spanish Language and Literature: Lic. NIDIA VINCENT ORTEGA

Faculty of Statistics and Computing: ALMA ROSA GARCÍA GAONA

Faculty of Theatre: Mtra ELKA FEDIUK WALCZEWSKA

UNIVERSIDAD PEDAGÓGICA VERACRUZANA

Calle Museo 133, Unidad Magisterial, 91010 Xalapa, Veracruz

Telephone: (228) 814-1594

Fax: (228) 814-0036

E-mail: sec.academica@secupv.org

Internet: www.secupv.org

Founded 1980

State control

Rector: Dr MARCO WILFREDO SALAS MARTÍNEZ

Academic Secretary: REYNALDO CASTILLO AGUILAR.

UNIVERSIDAD AUTÓNOMA DE YUCATÁN

Calle 60 491–A por 57 Centro, 97000 Mérida, Yucatán

Telephone: (999) 930-0900

Internet: www.uady.mx

Founded 1922

Independent

Academic year: September to July

Rector: Dr RAÚL HUMBERTO GODOY MONTAÑEZ

Dir-Gen. for Academic Development: ALFREDO F. J. DÁJER ABIMERHI

Library: 20 libraries with 227,022 vols, 7,401 periodical titles

Number of teachers: 1,158 (640 full-time)

Number of students: 15,823

Publication: *Revista*

DIRECTORS

Faculty of Accountancy and Administration: MANUEL ESCOFFIÉ AGUILAR

Faculty of Anthropology: Dr FRANCISCO FERNÁNDEZ REPETTO

Faculty of Architecture: Arq. EDGARDO BOLIO ARCEO

Faculty of Chemical Engineering: CARLOS ESTRADA PINTO

Faculty of Chemistry: WENDY F. BRITO LOEZA

Faculty of Dentistry: VÍCTOR M. ALONZO SOSA

Faculty of Economics: Dr RODOLFO CANTO SÁENZ

Faculty of Education: Ing. MARÍA ELENA BARRERA BUSTILLOS

Faculty of Engineering: Ing. JOSÉ ANTONIO GONZÁLEZ FAJARDO

Faculty of Law: Abog. RENÁN SOLÍS SÁNCHEZ

Faculty of Mathematics: Dr LUIS RODRÍGUEZ CARVAJAL

Faculty of Medicine: Dra GLORIA HERRERA CORREA

Faculty of Nursing: Lic. LIZBETH PADRÓN AKÉ

Faculty of Psychology: Mtro EFRAÍN DUARTE BRICEÑO

Faculty of Veterinary Studies: FERNANDO HERRERA Y GÓMEZ

Preparatory School 1: Ing. MIGUEL SUMÁRRAGA CERVERA

Preparatory School 2: TERESITA DE J. GÓMEZ LIZARRAGA

UNIVERSIDAD AUTÓNOMA DE ZACATECAS

Jardin Juárez 147, Centro Histórico, 98000 Zacatecas, Zac.

Telephone: (492) 922-9109

E-mail: sii@uaz.edu.mx

Internet: www.ciu.reduaz.mx

Founded 1832

State control

Rector: FRANCISCO FLORES SANDOVAL

Sec.Gen: DELFINO GARCÍA HERNÁNDEZ

Admin. Sec.: SALVADOR SANTILLÁN HERNÁNDEZ

Academic Sec.: FRANCISCO VALERIO QUINTERO

Librarian: JUAN IGNACIO PIÑA MARQUINA

Library of 35,265 vols

Number of teachers: 1,100

Number of students: 14,800

Publications: *Cuadernos de investigación, Diálogo, Gaceta universitaria, Azogue*

DIRECTORS

School of Accounting and Administration: JESÚS LIMONES HERNÁNDEZ

School of Agronomy: Ing. PEDRO ZESATI DEL VILLAR

School of Animal Breeding and Veterinary Medicine: ANTONIO MEJÍA HARO

School of Chemistry: JUANA MARÍA VALADEZ CASTREJÓN

School of Dentistry: Dr RAÚL BERMEO PADILLA

School of Economics: Lic. RODOLFO GARCÍA ZAMORA

School of Education: SERGIO ESPINOSA PROA

School of Engineering: Ing. JUAN FRANCISCO ROCHÍN SALINAS

School of Humanities: Lic. VEREMUNDO CARRILLO TRUJILLO

School of Law: Lic. VIRGILIO RIVERA DELGADILLO

School of Mathematics: Lic. JUAN ANTONIO PÉREZ

School of Medicine: Dr GERARDO DE JESÚS FÉLIX DOMÍNGUEZ

School of Mines and Metallurgy: Ing. RUBEN DE JESÚS DEL POZO MENDOZA

School of Music: Lic. ESAUL ARTEAGA DOMÍNGUEZ

School of Nursing: MA ISABEL MEDINA HERNÁNDEZ

School of Physics: Lic. HUMBERTO VIDALES ROQUE

School of Psychology: Lic. RICARDO BERMEO PADILLA

School of Social Sciences: PEDRO GÓMEZ SÁNCHEZ

Technical Universities

INSTITUTO POLITÉCNICO NACIONAL

Unidad Profesional 'Adolfo López Mateos', Zacatenco, Del. Gustavo A. Madero, 07738 México, DF

Telephone: (55) 5729-6300

E-mail: contacto@ipn.gob.mx

Internet: www.ipn.mx

Founded 1936

State control

Language of instruction: Spanish

Academic year: September to July

General Director: Dr JOSÉ ENRIQUE VILLA RIVERA

Secretary-General: Ing. ALFREDO LÓPEZ HERNÁNDEZ

Administrative Director: Ing. HÉCTOR URIEL MAYAGOITIA PRADO

Librarian: Lic. CESAR SANTÓME FIGUEROA

Number of teachers: 12,356

Number of students: 107,200

Publications: *Gaceta Politécnicá; Acta Politécnica, Acta Médica, Anales de la Escuela Nacional de Ciencias Biológicas, Economía Política*

DIRECTORS

Centre for Research and Development in Digital Technology (in Tijuana): Dr JOSÉ MÁRIA MONTOYA FLORES

Higher School of Chemical Engineering and Mining Industries: Ing. TIMOTEO PASTRANA APONTE

Higher School of Commerce and Administration: C.P. JOSÉ DE JESÚS VÁZQUEZ BONILLA

Higher School of Economics: Lic. MIGUEL ÁNGEL CORREA JASSO

Higher School of Engineering and Architecture: Ing. SALVADOR PADILLA ALONSO

Higher School of Mechanical and Electrical Engineering: Ing. ARTURO ZEPEDA SALINAS

Higher School of Medicine: Dr JUAN ORDORICA VARGAS

Higher School of Physics and Mathematics: M. en C. OLGA LETICIA HERNÁNDEZ CHÁVEZ

Higher School of Textile Engineering: Ing. CASSIN FRANCISCO ALE GUERRERO

Higher School of Tourism: Lic. VÍCTOR CHALE GÓNGORA

Interdisciplinary Centre for Health Sciences: Lic. Nut. ADRIÁN GUILLERMO QUINTERO GUTIÉRREZ

Interdisciplinary Centre for Marine Sciences: M. en C. JULIAN RENÉ TORRES VILLEGAS

Interdisciplinary Professional Unit of Engineering and Social and Administrative Sciences: Ing. ERNESTO ANGELES MEJÍA

Interdisciplinary Project for the Environment and Integrated Development: Dr JUAN MANUEL NAVARRO PINEDA

Interdisciplinary Research Centre for Regional Development (Durango Centre): Dr JÓSE ANGEL L. ORTEGA HERRERA

Interdisciplinary Research Centre for Regional Development (Michoacán): M. en C. VÍCTOR MANUEL LÓPEZ LÓPEZ

Interdisciplinary Research Centre for Regional Development (Oaxaca Centre): Ing. FERNANDO ELI ORTÍZ HERNÁNDEZ

National School of Biological Sciences: Dra THELMA LILIA VILLEGAS GARRIDO

National School of Medicine and Homeopathy: Dr JAIME ERNESTO SÁNCHEZ GONZÁLEZ

Project for Technological and Scientific Social Studies: M. en C. LUIS FERNANDO CASTILLO GARCÍA

INSTITUTO TECNOLÓGICO Y DE ESTUDIOS SUPERIORES DE MONTERREY

Avda Eugenio Garza Sada 2501 Sur, Col. Tecnológico, 64849 Monterrey, Nuevo León

Telephone: (81) 8358-2000

Fax: (81) 8358-1400

Internet: www.itesm.mx

Founded 1943

Private control

Languages of instruction: Spanish, English

Academic year: August to May

Rector: Dr RAFAEL RANGEL SOSTMANN

Rector for Monterrey Campus: Dr ALBERTO BUSTANI

Rector for Mexico City Campus: Ing. JUAN DURÁN

Rector for Central Zone: Dr ROBERTO RUEDA

Rector for N, S and W Zone: C. P. DAVID NOEL RAMÍREZ

Registrar: Lic. ALEJANDRA GARCÍA

Librarian: Ing. MIGUEL ARREOLA

Library: 2.6m. vols, 53,000 periodicals

Number of teachers: 8,694

Number of students: 96,649

DEANS

EGADE Business School: Dr ROBERT GROSSE

Graduate School of Public Administration and Public Policy (EGAP): Dr BERNARDO GONZÁLEZ

School of Architecture, Art and Design: Arq. JAMES MAYEUX

School of Biotechnology and Health: Dr MARTÍN HERNÁNDEZ

School of Business, Social Sciences and Humanities: Dr HUMBERTO CANTÚ

School of Engineering and Information Technology: Dr JAIME BONILLA

The Institute comprises 32 campuses in addition to the main one in Monterrey

Colleges

CETYS UNIVERSIDAD – CENTRO DE ENSEÑANZA TÉCNICA Y SUPERIOR

Calzada CETYS s/n, Col. Rivera, 21259 Mexicali, Baja California

Telephone: (686) 567-3701

Fax: (686) 565-0241

E-mail: info@cetys.mx

Internet: www.cetys.mx

Founded 1961

Academic year: September to June

Rector: Ing. ENRIQUE CARLOS BLANCAS DE LA CRUZ

Vice-Rector (Academic): Dr FERNANDO LEÓN GARCÍA

Director-General of Mexicali Campus: Ing. SERGIO REBOLLAR MCDONOUGH

Director-General of Tijuana Campus: Lic. MIGUEL ANGEL SALAS MARRÓN

Director-General of Ensenada Campus: Ing. FRANCISCO VILLALBA ROSARIO

Library: Libraries with 57,000 vols

Number of teachers: 487

Number of students: 3,700

Courses in fields of engineering (industrial, mechanical, manufacturing, electronics, computers, digital graphic design), computer sciences, corporate information systems, international business, management, finance, accountancy, behavioural sciences, international and corporate law, continuous education, executive development programmes.

COLEGIO DE LA FRONTERA SUR

Apdo Postal 63, 29290 San Cristóbal de las Casas, Chiapas

Carretera Panamericana y Periférico Sur s/n, Barrio Ma. Auziliadora, 29290 San Cristóbal de las Casas, Chiapas

Telephone: (967) 674-9000

E-mail: contacto@ecosur.mx

Internet: www.ecosur.mx

Founded 1994

Gen.-Dir: Dra ESPERANZA TUÑON PABLOS

Divs of alternative means of production, of agroecological technology, of health and population, of the conservation and exploitation of biodiversity.

COLEGIO DE MÉXICO

Apdo 20671, 01000 México

Located at: Camino al Ajusco 20, Pedregal de Santa Teresa, 10740 México, DF

Telephone: (55) 5449-3000

Fax: (55) 5645-0464

E-mail: webmaster@colmex.mx

Internet: www.colmex.mx

Founded 1940

Academic year: September to July

President: Dr JAVIER GARCIADIEGO DANTÁN

Secretary-General: MANUEL ORDORICA MELLADO

Academic Coordinator: JEAN FRANÇOIS PRUD'HOMME

Library Director: MICAELA CHÁVEZ VILLA

Library of 780,000 vols

Number of teachers: 305 (incl. researchers)

Number of students: 313

Publications: *Estudios de Asia y África* (3 a year), *Estudios Demográficos y Urbanos* (3 a year), *Estudios Económicos* (2 a year), *Estudios Sociológicos* (3 a year), *Foro Internacional* (4 a year), *Historia Mexicana* (4 a year), *Nueva Revista de Filología Hispánica* (2 a year)

DIRECTORS

Centre for Asian and African Studies: JUAN JOSÉ RAMÍREZ BONILLA

Centre for Demographic, Urban and Environmental Studies: JOSÉ LUIS LEZAMA

Centre for Economic Studies: JAIME SEMPERE CAMPELLO

Centre for Historical Studies: GUILLERMO PALACIOS Y OLIVARES

Centre for International Studies: GUSTAVO VEGA

Centre for Linguistics and Literary Studies: AURELIO GONZÁLEZ PÉREZ

Centre for Sociological Studies: ROBERTO BLANCARTE PIMENTEL

ESCUELA NACIONAL DE ANTROPOLOGÍA E HISTORIA (National School of Anthropology and History)

Periférico Sur y Zapote s/n, Col. Isidro Fabela, C.P. 14030, México, DF

Telephone: (55) 5606-8946

Fax: (55) 5606-0197

E-mail: enahdir@yahoo.com

Internet: www.enah.inah.gob.mx

Founded 1938

Academic year: January to December

Dir: FRANCISCO ORTIZ PEDRAZA

Librarian: MARÍA DE LOURDES MÉNDEZ CAMPOS

Library of 37,575 vols

Number of teachers: 395

Number of students: 2,296

Publications: *Folleto de Información Básica y Cuadernos de Trabajo* (irregular), *Revista Cuicuilco* (4 a year)

Faculties of physical anthropology, social anthropology, archaeology, ethno-history, linguistics and history.

ESCUELA NACIONAL DE BIBLIOTECONOMÍA Y ARCHIVONOMÍA (National School of Librarianship and Archives)

Calz. Ticoman 645, Col. Santa Ma. Ticoman, CP 07330 México, DF

Telephone: (55) 3752-7475

Fax: (55) 2752-7575

Founded 1945

Director: Mtro NAHUM PEREZ PAZ

Library of 5,000 vols

Number of teachers: 72

Number of students: 420

Publication: *Bibliotecas y Archivos*.

ESCUELA NACIONAL DE CONSERVACIÓN, RESTAURACIÓN Y MUSEOGRAFIA 'MANUEL DEL CASTILLO NEGRETE' (Manuel del Castillo Negrete National School of Conservation, Restoration and Museography)

Ex-Convento de Churubusco, Xicoténcatl y Gral Anaya, 04120 México, DF

Telephone: (55) 5604-5188

Fax: (55) 5604-5163

E-mail: inahmex@telecomm.net.mx

Internet: www.telecomm.net.mx/encrym
Founded 1968
Academic year: September to July
Director: M. A. MERCEDES GOMEZ-URQUIZA
Deputy Director: DANIEL CAMACHO URIBE
Head of Academic Extension: GINA SALDAÑA LOZANO

Library of 15,000 vols
Number of teachers: 116
Number of students: 126

INSTITUTO TECNOLÓGICO AUTÓNOMO DE MÉXICO

Campus Rio Hondo: Río Hondo 1, Col. Tizapán San Ángel, Del. Alvaro Obregón, 01000 México, DF
Campus Santa Teresa: Cetro de Investigación y Estudios de Posgrado (CIEP), Avda Camino Santa Teresa 930, Col. Héroes de Padierna, Del. Magdalena Contreras, 10700 México, DF

Telephone: (55) 5628-4000
Fax: (55) 5628-4102
E-mail: itam@itam.mx
Internet: www.itam.mx
Founded 1946
Academic year: January to December
President: ALBERTO BAILLERES
Rector: ARTURO FERNÁNDEZ PÉREZ
Library of 106,000 vols, 1,202 periodicals
Number of students: 3,500

Publication: *Revista Estudios* (4 a year)

Courses in business administration, economics, accounting, mathematics, law, computer sciences, public policy, literature, history, statistics and social sciences.

INSTITUTO TECNOLÓGICO DE CELAYA

Avda Tecnológico y A. García Cubas s/n, Apdo Postal 57, 38010 Celaya, Gto
Telephone: (461) 611-7575
Fax: (461) 611-7979
E-mail: lince@itc.mx
Internet: www.itc.mx
Founded 1958
Director: Dr JUAN SILLERO PÉREZ
Academic Vice-Director: M.C. SAMUEL DOMÍNGUEZ TAMAYO
Administrative Vice-Director: M.C. RUBEN MARTÍNEZ BALDERAS
Librarian: Lic. TEODORO VILLALOBOS SALINAS
Library of 16,600 vols
Number of students: 2,623

Publications: *Apertura*, *Pistas Educativas*

Courses in industrial engineering, mechanics, chemistry and biochemistry, production and business administration, computer systems, electronics.

INSTITUTO TECNOLÓGICO DE CHIHUAHUA

Ave. Tecnológico No 2909, 31310 Chihuahua, Chih.
Telephone: (614) 201-2000
Fax: (614) 413-5187
Internet: www.itch.edu.mx
Founded 1948
Dir: Ing. LEONEL GILDARDO LOYA PACHECO
Admin. Vice-Dir: Ing. JUAN DE DIOS RUIZ
Academic Vice-Dir: Ing. ANTONIO TREVIÑO RUIZ
Library of 29,000 vols
Number of teachers: 350
Number of students: 4,400

Publication: *Electro* (1 a year)

Degree courses in industrial, electrical, mechanical, chemical, electronic and materials engineering; postgraduate courses in electronics; degree and postgraduate courses in administration.

INSTITUTO TECNOLÓGICO DE DURANGO

Blvd F. Pescador 1830 Ote. Durango, 34080 Durango
Telephone: (618) 818-5706
Fax: (618) 818-4813
E-mail: director@itdgo.mx.mx
Internet: www.anuies.mx/servicios/ d_estrategicos/afiliadas/92.html
Founded 1948
Dependent on the Dirección General de Institutos Tecnológicos Regionales, SEP
Director: Ing. TOMÁS PALOMINO SOLÓRZANO
Librarian: JESÚS LAU
Library of 19,000 vols
Number of teachers: 267
Number of students: 2,677

First degree courses in industrial engineering in electronics, electricity, biochemistry, mechanics, information science, chemistry and civil engineering; Masters in industrial planning, biochemistry, civil engineering.

INSTITUTO TECNOLÓGICO DE CIUDAD JUÁREZ

Avda Tecnológico 1340, 32500 Ciudad Juárez, Chih.
Telephone: (656) 688-2500
Fax: (656) 688-2501
E-mail: webmaster@itcj.edu.mx
Internet: www.itcj.edu.mx
Founded 1964
Director: ROBERTO ARANA MORAN
Vice-Directors: HUMBERTO C. MORALES MORENO (Administrative), ALFREDO ESTRADA GARCÍA (Academic), SALVADOR SÁNCHEZ CRUZ (Academic Support)
Library of 13,300 vols
Number of teachers: 268
Number of students: 4,468

INSTITUTO TECNOLÓGICO DE CIUDAD MADERO

Avda 1° de Mayo esq. Sor Juana Inés de la Cruz s/n, Col. Los Mangos, 89440 Ciudad Madero, Tamaulipas
Telephone: (833) 357-4820
Fax: (833) 357-4820 ext. 1002
E-mail: wmaster@itcm.edu.mx
Internet: www.itcm.edu.mx/itcm06/html
Founded 1954
Director: Ing. JUAN MANUEL TURRUBIATE MARTÍNEZ
Library of 17,781 vols
Number of students: 5,000

INSTITUTO TECNOLÓGICO DEL MAR

km 12 Carretera Veracruz–Córdoba, Apartado Postal 68, 94290 Boca del Río, Ver.
Telephone: (229) 986-0189
Fax: (229) 986-1894
E-mail: itmar01@itmar1.edu.mx
Founded 1957
Dependent on the Dirección General de Enseñanzas Tecnológicas (Ministry of Education)
Director: Ing. JOSÉ LÓPEZ MEDINA.

INSTITUTO TECNOLÓGICO DE MÉRIDA

Avda Tecnológico km 5, Apdo Postal 9–11, 97118 Mérida, Yucatán
Telephone: (999) 944-8171
Fax: (999) 944-8171
E-mail: itm@uxmal.itmerida.mx
Internet: www.itmerida.mx
Founded 1961
Academic year: August to June
Dir: Ing. GELASIO LUNA CONZUELO
Vice-Dirfor Admin.: Ing. WILLIAM RAMÍREZ ROMERO
Vice-Dir for Academic Affairs: Ing. ISIDRO CALDERÓN ACOSTA
Vice-Dir for Planning: Ing. HERBERT LORÍA SUNZA
Librarian: Ing. NORINA LIZARRAGA CETINA
Library of 20,000 vols
Number of teachers: 369
Number of students: 4,146

Publications: *Revista del Centro de Graduados e Investigación* (4 a year), *La Quincena* (26 a year).

INSTITUTO TECNOLÓGICO DE MORELIA

Avda Tecnológico 1500, Col. Lomas de Santiaguito, 58120 Morelia, Michoacán
Telephone: (443) 312-1570
Fax: (443) 312-1570 ext. 211
E-mail: direccion@itmorelia.edu.mx
Internet: www.itmorelia.edu.mx
Founded 1965
Director: Ing. IGNACIO LÓPEZ VALDOVINOS
Library of 15,000 vols
Number of students: 3,500

Courses in industrial engineering and iron and steel industry.

INSTITUTO TECNOLÓGICO DE OAXACA

Avda Ing. Victor Bravo Ahuja 125 esq. Calz. Tecnológico, 68030 Oaxaca de Juárez, Oax.
Telephone: (951) 501-5016
Internet: www.itox.mx
Founded 1968
Director: Ing. SERGIO ISIDRO LÓPEZ PÉREZ
Number of teachers: 280
Number of students: 3,000

Publication: *Itrosíntesis*

Courses in mechanical, electrical, chemical and civil engineering, business management and industrial planning.

INSTITUTO TECNOLÓGICO Y DE ESTUDIOS SUPERIORES DE OCCIDENTE, AC

Periférico Sur Manuel Gómez Morín 8585, 45604 Tlaquepaque, Jal.
Telephone: (33) 3669-3434
Fax: (33) 3669-3435
E-mail: rectoria@iteso.mx
Internet: www.iteso.mx
Founded 1957
Academic year: January to December
Rector: Dr JUAN LUIS OROZCO HERNÁNDEZ
Library of 113,000 vols
Number of teachers: 945
Number of students: 6,796

Publications: *Sinectica* (2 a year), *Renglones* (Review 3 a year), *Huella* (3 a year)

Undergraduate courses in architecture, business administration, communications, environmental engineering, finance, international business, international relations, management of information systems, mechanical engineering, philosophy, public accountancy, civil, industrial and electronic engineering, chemical processing and administration, computer systems, design, psychology, industrial relations, educational sciences, law, marketing. Postgraduate courses in business management, education, engineering, communications, human development, industrial electronics, applied information systems, global marketing, politics, public management.

INSTITUTO TECNOLÓGICO DE ORIZABA

Avda Oriente 9 no. 852, Col. Emiliano Zapata, 94320 Orizaba, Ver.

Telephone: (272) 724-4096
Fax: (272) 725-1728
E-mail: centrodeinformacion@itorizaba.edu.mx
Internet: ssfe.itorizaba.edu.mx/joomla

Founded 1957

Director: Ing. JUAN RENE CABALLERO GONZÁLEZ
Administrative Assistant Director: Ing. BLAS REYES T.
Assistant Director (Planning): Ing. ROSENDO MARTÍNEZ
Academic Assistant Director: Ing. KIKEY GONZÁLEZ F.

Number of teachers: 308
Number of students: 2,994

Courses in chemical, industrial mechanical, electrical and electronic engineering, and computer science.

INSTITUTO TECNOLÓGICO DE QUERÉTARO

Avda Tecnológico s/n esq. Escobedo, Col. Centro, 76000 Querétaro, Qro

Telephone: (442) 227-4400
Fax: (442) 216-9931
E-mail: webmaster@itq.edu.mx
Internet: www.itq.edu.mx

Founded 1967

Director: Ing. OSCAR ARMANDO LÓPEZ GONZÁLEZ
Academic Vice-Director: Ing. JORGE MARIO ELIAS MARTÍNEZ
Vice-Director (Planning and Extension): Ing. FERNANDO QUIROZ GATICA

Library of 28,000 vols
Number of teachers: 314
Number of students: 3,596

Courses in industrial and mechanical engineering, architecture, systems engineering, electrical and electronic engineering and industrial administration.

INSTITUTO TECNOLÓGICO DE SALTILLO

V. Carranza 2400, Col. Tecnológico, 25280 Saltillo, Coahuila

Telephone: (844) 438-9500
Fax: (844) 438-9500
E-mail: webm@its.mx
Internet: www.its.mx

Founded 1951

Director: M.C. JESÚS CONTRERAS GARCÍA

Library: c. 15,100 vols
Number of students: 3,000

Publications: *Boletín de Seguridad Industrial, Boletín de Fundación, Boletín de Microenseñanza*, faculty bulletins

Courses in industrial, metallurgical and computer science engineering and technology.

INSTITUTO TECNOLÓGICO DE SONORA

5 de Febrero 818 Sur, Col. Centro, 85000 Ciudad Obregón, Son.

Telephone: (644) 410-0900

E-mail: agutierrez@itson.mx
Internet: www.itson.mx

Founded 1955 as Preparatory school, became University in 1973

Rector: Mtro. GONZALO RODRÍGUEZ VILLANUEVA
Vice-Rector for Academic Affairs: Lic. JAVIER VALES GARCÍA
Vice-Rector for Administrative Affairs: Lic. JORGE OROZCO PARRA

Library of 87,000 vols
Number of teachers: 914
Number of students: 16,355

Publications: *Revista de la Sociedad Académica* (2 a year), *ITSON-DIEP* (research reports, 2 a year)

Courses in biotechnological, electrical, electronic, systems and industrial, civil, chemical and agricultural engineering, chemistry, business administration, accounting, management information systems, education, psychology, veterinary medicine, natural resources and water resources management.

School of Music

Conservatorio Nacional de Música (National Conservatoire): Avda Presidente Mazaryk 582, Col. Polanco, México, DF; tel. (55) 5280-6347; e-mail cnm@correo.inba.gob.mx; internet www.conservatorianos.com.mx; f. 1866; 170 teachers; Dir Maestro LEOPOLDO TELLEZ; library: 48,900 vols; publs *Heterofonía, Gaceta de la Biblioteca*.

FEDERATED STATES OF MICRONESIA

The Higher Education System

The Federated States of Micronesia comprise the four named and autonomous states, namely Chuuk, Pohnpei, Yap and Kosrae. It is a small, developing nation made up of 87 islands and islets spread over four major island groups in 2.5m. sq. km of the Western Pacific. Its citizens speak 17 different languages and dialects. Higher education is provided by one institution: the College of Micronesia. The Department of Education is the government ministry responsible for overseeing the education sector. Education is governed by Act PL 7-97, which was approved by Congress in 1992. In 2005/06 there were approximately 2,283 students studying at college level.

Regulatory Body

GOVERNMENT

Department of Education: POB PS-87, Palikir, Pohnpei, 96941; tel. 320-2643; fax 320-5500; Sec. CASIANO SHONIBER.

Learned Societies

NATURAL SCIENCES

Chuuk Conservation Society: Chuuk; f. 2005 to protect and preserve local natural resources in order to sustain community livelihoods; Chair JOE KONNO; Sec. MARY ROSE NAKAYAMA.

Conservation Society of Pohnpei: POB 2461, Kolonia, Pohnpei 96941; tel. 320-5409; fax 320-5063; e-mail csp@mail.fm; internet www.serehd.org; f. 1998; aims to increase community involvement in the conservation and management of Pohnpei's natural resources, to build local capacity through public and private partnerships, to develop alternatives to unsustainable practices and to promote laws and policies that support these objectives; current programmes: marine, terrestrial and educational awareness; Exec. Dir PATTERSON SHED.

Kosrae Conservation and Safety Organization: POB 539, Tofol, Kosrae 96944; tel. 370-3391; fax 370-3000; e-mail kcso@mail.fm; promotes conservation of the natural environment and awareness creation; Chair. MADISON NENA; Exec. Dir ANDY GEORGE.

Micronesia Conservation Trust: POB 2177, Kolonia, Pohnpei 96941; tel. 320-5670; fax 320-8903; e-mail mct@mail.fm; internet mctconservation.org; f. 2002 to support biodiversity conservation and related sustainable development for the people of Micronesia; provides long-term, sustained funding to community-based orgs and other NGOs through a grants programme; Exec. Dir WILLY KOSTKA.

Yap Institute of Natural Science: POB 215, Colonia, Yap 96943; tel. 350-4630; e-mail mfalanruw@mail.fm; promotes sustainable use of local resources; Dir Dr MARJORIE C. FALANRUW.

Libraries and Archives

Kolonia

College of Micronesia Learning Resources Center: POB 159, Kolonia, Pohnpei 96941; tel. 320-2480; e-mail comfsmlib@comfsm.fm; internet www.comfsm.fm/library; comprises general library, serials section, US Govt documents library; Micronesia-Pacific Research Center; depository for the Secretariat of the Pacific Community materials and a partial depository for UN documents; Nat. Archives contains materials from the Navy and Trust Territory eras; 34,000 vols; Dir SUE CALDWELL.

Pohnpei Public Library: POB 284, Kolonia, Pohnpei 96941; tel. 320-2423; f. 1988; 8,000 vols; 1 mobile library; Head Librarian LESTER EZEKIAS.

Palikir

Congress Library: POB PS3, Palikir, Pohnpei 96941; tel. 320-2324; fax 320-5122; e-mail liwi@mail.fm; f. 1978; library of the legislative br. of nat. Govt; 15,000 vols, 30 periodicals; Librarian MARIETA J. PAIDEN.

Museums and Galleries

Kolonia

Lidorkini Museum: Kolonia, Pohnpei 96941; tel. 320-5299; artefacts from the Nan Madol site, pounding stones, handicrafts, items from the Japanese occupation of the islands (1914–44); Curator HENTER LAWRENCE.

Tofol

Kosrae State Museum: Tofol, Kosrae; artefacts, photographs of Kosrae history and culture.

College

College of Micronesia: National Campus, POB 159, Kolonia, Pohnpei 96941; tel. 320-2480; fax 320-2479; e-mail national@comfsm.fm; internet www.comfsm.fm; f. 1963; offers assoc. of arts and assoc. of science degrees; other campuses located in Chuuk State, Kosrae State, Pohnpei State and Yap State; its Fisheries and Maritime Institute is located on Yap; library: see Libraries and Archives; 798 students; Pres. SPENSIN JAMES.

MOLDOVA

The Higher Education System

The oldest institution of higher education is the Academia de Mizică, Teatru şi Arte Plastice (Academy of Music, Theatre and Fine Arts of Republic of Moldova—founded 1919), which was established when the former Russian territory of Bessarabia was part of Romania. Other institutions dating from the period of Romanian control include Universitatea Agrară de Stat din Moldova (Moldovan State Agrarian University—founded 1933) and Universitatea Pedagogică de Stat 'Ion Creangă' (Ion Creangă Pedagogical State University—founded 1940). However, the USSR refused to recognize Romania's claims to the territory, and in October 1924 formed a Moldovan Autonomous Soviet Socialist Republic (ASSR) on the eastern side of the Dniester, in the Ukrainian Soviet Socialist Republic (SSR). The current institution of Universitatea de Stat din Tiraspol (Tiraspol State University), was founded in the Moldovan ASSR in 1930 (it was re-located to the capital Chişinău in 1999). In June 1940 Romania was forced to cede Bessarabia and northern Bucovina to the USSR, under the terms of the Treaty of Non-Aggression (the 'Molotov-Ribbentrop Pact'), concluded with Nazi Germany in August 1939. Northern Bucovina, southern Bessarabia and the Kotovsk-Balţa region of the Moldovan ASSR were incorporated into the Ukrainian SSR. The remaining parts of the Moldovan ASSR and of Bessarabia were merged to form the Moldovan SSR, which formally joined the USSR on 2 August 1940 and remained under Soviet rule until independence was declared in 1991. Following independence the self-styled 'Transnistrian Moldovan Republic' (formerly 'Transnistrian Moldovan SSR') was declared on the eastern side of the Dniester. The Law on Education of 1995 classified higher education as either long-term study programmes offered by universities, academies, and institutes or short-term study programmes offered by vocational colleges. In 2000 Moldova adopted the European Credit Transfer System in public universities and from 2005 the ECTS was introduced in all higher education institutions. Moldova has been a full member of the Bologna process since 2005. In 2007/08 122,939 students were enrolled in universities and 31,307 in colleges of higher education.

Admission to higher education is determined by fixed quotas (numerus clausus/numerus fixus) drawn up by the Government. Consequently, students are usually required to sit a competitive entrance examination as well as holding the Diplomă de Bacalaureat, the main secondary school-leavers' certificate. Undergraduate degrees are divided into short- and long-term programmes of study. The Diploma of Short-Term Higher Education (Diplomă de Studii Superioare de Scurtă Durată) is the primary programme of short-term study and lasts two to three years. These are the only kinds of degrees offered by vocational colleges. The Diplomă de Licentă is a long-term programme of study lasting four to six years and culminates with the defence of a thesis. Students who do not defend their thesis are awarded the Diploma of University Higher Studies (Diplomă de Studii Superioare Universitare). The first postgraduate-level degree is the Diplomă de Magistru, awarded upon completion of one to two years of research following the Diplomă de Licentă. There are two doctoral degrees, Doctor of Sciences (Doctor în Stiinte) and Doctor Abilitat. The Doctor în Stiinte is awarded after three years of research and successful defence of a thesis. Doctor Abilitat is a post-doctoral degree, awarded after two years following the Doctor în Stiinte.

Post-secondary technical and vocational education is available mainly through colleges and is regarded as short-term higher education.

The National Council for Accreditation and Attestation is the body responsible for the accreditation of institutions in the field of science and the attestation of scientific and scientific-pedagogical personnel of higher qualification. It gives out certificates of accreditation on the basis of which scientific institutes are financed from the state budget. It also approves the programmes of examinations for doctoral students and competitors, confers the scientific degrees, scientific and scientific-pedagogical ranks and gives out the diplomas of scientific degrees and certificates of scientific and scientific-pedagogical ranks.

Regulatory and Representative Bodies

GOVERNMENT

Ministry of Culture and Tourism: 2033 Chişinău, Piaţa Marii Adunări Naţionale 1, Of. 326; tel. (22) 22-76-20; fax (22) 23-23-88; e-mail culture@turism.md; internet www .turism.md; Minister ARTUR COZMA.

Ministry of Education and Youth: 2033 Chişinău, Piaţa Marii Adunări Naţionale 1; tel. (22) 23-33-48; fax (22) 23-35-15; e-mail consilier@edu.md; internet www.edu.md; Minister LARISA SAVGA.

ACCREDITATION

Consiliul Naţional pentru Acreditare şi Atestare (CNAA) (National Council for Accreditation and Attestation): 2004 Chişinău, Stefan cel Mare bd 180; tel. and fax (22) 29-62-71; e-mail cnaa@cnaa.md; internet www.cnaa.md; f. 2004; 17 mems; Pres. Acad. Dr hab. VALERIU CANTER; Vice-Pres. Acad. Dr hab. SIMION TOMA; Vice-Pres. Acad. Dr hab. VEACESLAV PERJU; Scientific Sec. Dr GHEORGHE GLADCHI.

Department of Higher Education Institution Accreditation: 2033 Chişinău, Piaţa Marii Adunări Naţionale 1; tel. (22) 21-03-79; fax (22) 23-32-83; e-mail mrotaru@inbox.ru; Dir MICHAEL EFIMOVICH ROTARU.

ENIC/NARIC Moldova: Information and Qualification Recognition Office, International Relations and European Integration Department, Ministry of Education and Youth, Piaţa Marii Adunări Naţionale 1, 2033 Chişinău; tel. (22) 27-75-69; fax (22) 23-37-85; e-mail recognition@edu.md; internet www.edu.md; Head ISAC RODICA.

Learned Societies

GENERAL

Academy of Sciences of Moldova: 2001 Chişinău, bd. Ştefan cel Mare şi Sfînt 1; tel. (22) 27-14-78; fax (22) 54-28-23; e-mail consiliu@asm.md; internet www.asm.md; f. 1946; sections of agricultural sciences (Academician-Co-ordinator SIMION TOMA), biological, chemical and ecological sciences (Academician-Co-ordinator ION TODERAS), economical and mathematical sciences (Academician-Co-ordinator GHEORGE MISCOI), humanities and arts (Academician-Co-ordinator ALEXANDRU ROSCA), medical sciences (Academician-Co-ordinator GHEORGHE GHIDIRIM), physical and engineering sciences (Academician-Co-ordinator VALERIUS CANTER); 112 mems (48 full, 64 corresp.); attached research institutes: see Research Institutes; library: see Libraries and Archives; Pres. GHEORGHE DUCA; General Scientific Sec. BORIS GAINA; publs Buletinul (Biological and Chemical and Agricultural Sciences, 4 a year Mathematics, 3 a year), Computer Science Journal of Moldova (4 a year), Economy and Sociology (4 a year), Elektronnaya Obrabotka Materialov (Electronic Processing of Materials, 6 a year), Moldavian Journal of Physical Sciences (4 a year), Revista de Filozofie şi Drept (Journal of Philosophy and Law, 6 a year), Revista de Istorie a Moldovei (Moldovan Historical Journal, 4 a year), Revista de Lingvistică şi Ştiinţă Literară (Journal of Linguistics and Study of Literature, 6 a year).

HISTORY, GEOGRAPHY AND ARCHAEOLOGY

Geographical Society of Moldova: 2028 Chişinău, str. Academiei 1; tel. (22) 73-96-18; e-mail geography_md@yahoo.com; Head of Laboratory Dr NICOLAE BOBOC.

LANGUAGE AND LITERATURE

Alliance Française: 2012 Chişinău, str. Sfatul Tarii 18; tel. (22) 23-45-10; fax (22) 23-47-81; e-mail alfr@alfr.md; internet www.ambafrance.md; f. 1993; offers courses and exams in French language and culture and promotes cultural exchange with France and French-speaking countries; has a media library; Dir EMMANUEL SKOULIOS.

Goethe-Institut: see entry in Romania chapter.

PEN Centre of Moldova: 2012 Chişinău, bd. Ştefan cel Mare şi Sfint 134, PO 12, POB 231; tel. (22) 23-24-79; e-mail contrafort@moldnet.md; f. 1991; 25 mems; Pres. VITALIE CIOBANU.

NATURAL SCIENCES

Biological Sciences

Entomological Society of Moldova: 2028 Chişinău, str. Academiei 1; tel. (22) 73-98-96; Chair B. V. VEREŞCIAGHIN.

Microbiological Society of Moldova: 2028 Chişinău, str. Academiei 1; tel. (22) 73-98-78; e-mail acadrudic@yahoo.com; Chair. Prof. VALERY RUDIC.

Ornithological Society of Moldova: 2028 Chişinău, str. Academiei 1; tel. (22) 73-75-09; Chair. (vacant).

Society of Botanists of Moldova: 2002 Chişinău, str. Pădurii 18; tel. (22) 52-38-96; Chair. A. G. NEGRU.

Society of Geneticists of Moldova: 2049 Chişinău, str. Mirceşti 44; tel. (22) 43-23-08; Chair. V. D. SIMINEL.

Society of Hydrobiologists and Ichthyologists: 2028 Chişinău, str. Academiei 1; tel. (22) 57-75-30; fax (22) 73-12-55; e-mail izoolasm@mail.md; f. 1968; 36 mems; Chair. Prof. ION TODERAŞ.

Society of Plant Physiology and Biochemistry of Moldova: 2002 Chişinău, str. Pădurii 26/1; tel. (22) 56-79-59; fax (22) 55-00-26; e-mail sbiochim@bio.asm.md; f. 1988; 40 mems; Pres. Prof. SIMION I. TOMA.

Teriological Society of Moldova: 2028 Chişinău, str. Academiei 1 (Room 220); tel. (22) 72-55-66; fax (22) 73-12-55; e-mail amunteanu@as.md; 19 mems; Chair. Dr ANDREI MUNTEANU.

Physical Sciences

Physical Society of Moldova: 2928 Chişinău, str. Academiei 5; tel. and fax (22) 73-90-60; e-mail kantser@lises.asm.md; Chair. Acad. Prof. VALERIU KANTSER.

RELIGION, SOCIOLOGY AND ANTHROPOLOGY

Moldovan Sociological Association: 3121 Balti, str. Puşkin 38; tel. (231) 2-44-79; Chair. N. V. ŢURCANU.

Research Institutes

AGRICULTURE, FISHERIES AND VETERINARY SCIENCE

National Institute of Animal Husbandry and Veterinary Medicine: 6525 Anenii Noii, s. Maximovca; tel. and fax (22) 42-93-50; e-mail inzmv2004@yahoo.com; f. 1958; library of 19,000 vols; Dir Dr hab. MIHAIL

BAHCIVANJI; publ. *Scientific Transactions* (1 a year).

National Institute for Viticulture and Vinification: 2070 Chişinău, s. Codru, str. Vierul 59; tel. (22) 28-54-31; e-mail invv@moldova.md; internet www.agriculture.md/ispha; f. 1909; prepares nat. strategies for the devt of viticulture; creates new types of grapes, resistant to diseases and frost; elaboration of modern technologies for producing cuttings without viruses; devt of storage methods and use of grapes with nutritive and therapeutic purposes; creation of new wines, champagnes and liqueurs; design and sale of machines and equipment for viticulture.

Research Institute for Maize and Sorghum: 4834 Criuleni, s. Paşcani; tel. and fax (22) 24-10-07; e-mail porumbeni@agriculture.md; internet www.agriculture.md/porumbeni; f. 1973; research into the improvement of seed strains, seed production and cultivation of maize, sorghum, vegetables, medicinal and aromatic plants; Dir Dr MICU VASILE.

Tobacco Research Institute: Chişinău, s. Gratieşti, str. Prieteniei 1; tel. (22) 46-06-86; fax (22) 46-04-87; e-mail tutunix@agriculture.md; internet www.agriculture.md/tutun; f. 1968; Dir Dr TUDOR ZAGORNEANU.

ECONOMICS, LAW AND POLITICS

Centre for the Study of Marketing Problems: 2001 Chişinău, bd. Ştefan cel Mare şi Sfint; tel. and fax (22) 26-23-91; attached to Acad. of Sciences of Moldova; Dir P. V. COJUCARI.

Institute of Economic Research: 2001 Chişinău, bd. Ştefan cel Mare şi Sfint 1; tel. (22) 26-24-01; attached to Acad. of Sciences of Moldova; Dir V. CIOBANU.

FINE AND PERFORMING ARTS

Institute of the History and Theory of Art: 2001 Chişinău, bd. Ştefan cel Mare şi Sfint 1; tel. (22) 26-06-02; fax (22) 22-33-48; f. 1991; attached to Acad. of Sciences of Moldova; fine art, architecture, music, performing arts; Dir LEONID M. CEMORTAN; publ. *Arta* (2 series: fine arts and architecture, 1 a year, music and the performing arts, 1 a year).

HISTORY, GEOGRAPHY AND ARCHAEOLOGY

Institute of Archaeology and Ancient History: 2712 Chişinău, str. Mitropolitul Banulescu-Bodoni 35; tel. and fax (22) 22-22-42; attached to Acad. of Sciences of Moldova; Dir VALENTIN DERGACEV.

Institute of Ecology and Geography: 2028 Chişinău, str. Academiei 1; tel. and fax (22) 73-98-38; e-mail ieg@asm.md; internet ieg.asm.md; f. 1992; attached to Acad. of Sciences of Moldova; scientific and applied research in the fields of geography and ecology; Dir Acad. TATIANA S. CONSTANTINOVA; publs *Buletinul Academiei de Stiinte a Moldovei. Stiintele vietii, Mediul Ambiant*.

Institute of History: 2012 Chişinău, str. 31 August 1989 82; tel. (22) 23-33-10; e-mail iist_asm@mtc.md; f. 1958; attached to Acad. of Sciences of Moldova; Dir DEMIR DRAGNEV.

LANGUAGE AND LITERATURE

Institute of Linguistics: 2012 Chişinău, str. 31 August 1989 82; tel. (22) 23-33-05; fax (22) 23-77-52; e-mail lingva@moldova.md; f. 1991; attached to Acad. of Sciences of Moldova; library of 10,000 vols; Dir Acad. SILVIU BEREJAN; publ. *Revistă de Lingvistică şi Ştiinţă Literară* (6 a year).

Institute of Literature and Folklore: 2001 Chişinău, bd. Ştefan cel Mare şi Sfint; tel. (22) 27-27-19; e-mail ilfasm@yahoo.it; f. 1991; attached to Acad. of Sciences of Moldova; Dir Acad. HARALAMBIE CORBU; publ. *Revistă de Lingvistică şi Ştiinţă Literară* (6 a year).

MEDICINE

National Centre of Preventive Medicine: 2025 Chişinău, str. Gh. Asachi 67A; tel. (22) 72-96-47; fax (22) 72-97-25; Dir-Gen. MIHAI MAGDEI.

NATURAL SCIENCES

Biological Sciences

Botanical Garden Institute of the Academy of Sciences of Moldova: 2002 Chişinău, str. Pădurii 18; tel. (22) 52-38-98; fax (22) 52-04-43; e-mail gradinabotanica@moldnet.md; internet www.gradinbotanica.asm.md; f. 1950; attached to Acad. of Sciences of Moldova; library of 43,000 items; more than 10,000 species of plants; Dir Dr ALEXANDRU TELEUTA; publ. *Revista Botanica*.

Centre for Pathology and Pathobiology: 2004 Chişinău, str. 31 August 1989 151; tel. (22) 22-75-19; attached to Acad. of Sciences of Moldova; Dir. Acad. VASILE ANESTIADE.

Institute of Genetics and Plant Physiology: 2002 Chişinău, str. Pădurii 20; tel. (22) 77-04-47; fax (22) 55-61-80; e-mail dobynda@mail.md; f. 2005 by merger of the Institute of Genetics, the Institute of Plant Physiology, the aromatic and medicinal plant branch of the Research Institute for Maize and Sorghum, and the Centre of Plant Genetic Resources; attached to Acad. of Sciences of Moldova; Dir ANATOL JACOTĂ.

Institute of Microbiology and Biotechnology: 2028 Chişinău, str. Academiei 1; tel. (22) 72-55-24; fax (22) 72-57-54; e-mail microbiologie@mail.md; internet www.asm.md; f. 1992; attached to Acad. of Sciences of Moldova; Dir Acad. VALERIU RUDIC; publ. *Bulletin* (2 a year).

Institute of Physiology and Sanocreatology: 2028 Chişinău, str. Academiei 1; tel. (22) 72-51-55; attached to Acad. of Sciences of Moldova; specializes in study of the pancreas; Dir Acad. TEODOR FURDUI.

Institute of Zoology: 2028 Chişinău, str. Academiei 1; tel. (22) 73-98-09; fax (22) 73-12-55; e-mail izoolasm@mail.md; attached to Acad. of Sciences of Moldova; Dir ION TODERAŞ.

Research Institute for Plant Protection and Agricultural Ecology (Institutul de Protecţie a Plantelor şi Agricultură Ecologică): 2060 Chişinău, str. Padurii, 26/1; tel. (22) 77-04-66; fax (22) 77-96-41; e-mail voloscluc@netscape.net; internet agriculture.md/icpp/index.shtml; attached to Acad. of Sciences of Moldova; Dir LEONID VOLOSCIUC.

Mathematical Sciences

Institute of Mathematics and Computer Science: 2028 Chişinău, str. Academiei 5; tel. (22) 72-59-82; fax (22) 73-80-27; e-mail imam@math.md; internet www.math.md; f. 1964; attached to Acad. of Sciences of Moldova; Dir Dr hab. CONSTANTIN V. GAINDRIC; Scientific Sec. Dr SVETLANA COJOCARU; publs *Buletinul Academiei de Ştiinţe a Republicii Moldova: Matematica* (3 a year), *Computer Science Journal of Moldova* (3 a year), *Quasigroups and Related Systems* (1 a year).

Physical Sciences

Center of Experimental Seismology, Central Station: 2028 Chişinău, str. Academiei 3; tel. (22) 73-71-79; attached to Acad.

of Sciences of Moldova; forms the central unit of the Institute of Geophysics and Geology's seismic network; operates in conjunction with four local stations and four strong-motion recorders; Dir I. ILIEȘ.

Institute of Applied Physics: 2028 Chișinău, str. Academiei 5,; tel. (22) 73-81-50; fax (22) 73-81-49; e-mail director@phys.asm .md; internet www.phys.asm.md; f. 1964; attached to Acad. of Sciences of Moldova; 66 scientific personnel; Dir Prof. L. KULYUK; publs *Moldavian Journal of Physical Sciences* (4 a year), *Surface Engineering and Applied Electrochemistry* (6 a year).

Institute of Chemistry: 2028 Chișinău, str. Academiei 3; tel. (22) 72-54-90; fax (22) 73-99-54; e-mail ichem@asm.md; f. 1959; attached to Acad. of Sciences of Moldova; Dir Dr hab. TUDOR LUPASCU.

Institute of Geophysics and Geology: 2028 Chișinău, str. Academiei 3; tel. (22) 73-90-27; fax (22) 73-96-29; e-mail neagavi@ mail.ru; internet www.igs.asm.md; f. 1967; attached to Acad. of Sciences of Moldova; scientific research; Dir Dr VASILE ALCAZ; Scientific Sec. Dr VASILE NEAGA; publ. *Buletinul Institutului de Geofizica si Geologie al Academiei de Stiinte a Moldovei.*

RELIGION, SOCIOLOGY AND ANTHROPOLOGY

Institute of Ethnography and Folklore: 2001 Chișinău, bd. Ștefan cel Mare și Sfînt 1; tel. (22) 26-45-14; f. 1991; attached to Acad. of Sciences of Moldova; Dir N. A. DEMCENCO; publ. *Revista de Etnologie* (1 a year).

Institute of National Minorities Studies: 2001 Chișinău, bd. Ștefan cel Mare și Sfînt 1; tel. (22) 26-44-91; attached to Acad. of Sciences of Moldova; Dir C. F. POPOVICI.

Institute of Philosophy, Sociology and Political Sciences: 2001 Chișinău, bd. Ștefan cel Mare și Sfînt 1; tel. (22) 27-05-37; fax (22) 27-14-69; e-mail ifilos@cc.acad.md; internet www.asm.md; attached to Acad. of Sciences of Moldova; f. 2006; philosophy; sociology; political sciences; mythology; history of religion; social-demographic researches on families; 54 mems; Dir Dr ION RUSANDU; publs *Iconomie și Sociologie* (Economy and Sociology), *Revistă de Filosofie și Drept* (Philosophy and Law).

TECHNOLOGY

Institute of Power Engineering: 2028 Chișinău, str. Academiei 5; tel. (22) 72-70-40; fax (22) 73-53-86; e-mail mkiorsak@cc .asm.md; f. 1964; attached to Acad. of Sciences of Moldova; Dir Dr MIHAI V. CHIORSAC.

Libraries and Archives

Bălți

Bălți Municipal Library: 3121 Bălți, str. A. Pușkin 34; tel. (231) 2-34-59; f. 1880; Dir INGA COJOCARU.

Chișinău

Central Scientific Library 'Andrei Lupan' of the Academy of Sciences of Moldova: 2028 Chișinău, Str. Academiei 5A; tel. (22) 72-74-01; fax (22) 73-98-29; e-mail library@asm.md; internet www.amlib.asm .md; f. 1947; 1,406,887 vols; Dir AURELIA HANGANU.

Centre for Scientific Information in the Social Sciences: 2001 Chișinău, bd. Ștefan cel Mare și Sfînt 1; tel. (22) 23-23-39; attached to Acad. of Sciences of Moldova; Dir V. I. MOCREAC.

Moldova State University Library: 2009 Chișinău, str. A. Mateevici 60; tel. (22) 57-75-05; e-mail library@usm.md; internet www .usm.md/bcu; f. 1946; 1,810,000 vols; Dir ECATERINA ZASMENCO.

National Library of the Republic of Moldova: 2012 Chișinău, str. 31 August 1989 78A; tel. and fax (22) 22-14-75; e-mail bnrm@bnrm.md; internet www.bnrm.md; f. 1832; national library and principal depository of Moldova; national centre of inter-library loans; national centre for library automation and information; national centre for library science; 2,507,055 vols, 834 periodicals; Dir A. A. RĂU.

Scientific and Technical Library of Moldova: Chișinău, str. Creanga 45; tel. (22) 62-87-42; fax (22) 62-34-47; f. 1968; 560,000 vols, 11,000,000 patents, 750,000 standards; Dir P. T. RACU.

Tighina

Tighina County Public Library: Tighina; e-mail bpjt@fromru.com; internet ournet.md/ ~bpjt; f. 1943; 3 brs; 106,787 vols; Dir LARISA CAMENSCIC.

Museums

Chișinău

National Museum of Archaeology and History of Moldova: str. 31 August nr. 121A, Chișinău 2012; tel. (22) 244325; fax (22) 244369; e-mail museum@starnet.md; internet www.nationalmuseum.md; f. 1983; museum pedagogy, scientific exhibitions; Gen. Dir Dr hab. EUGEN SAVA.

National Museum of Fine Arts of Moldova: Chișinău, str. 31 August 1989 115; tel. (22) 24-17-30; f. 1944; Dir VASILE NEGRUȚĂ.

Universities

UNIVERSITATEA AGRARĂ DE STAT DIN MOLDOVA
(Moldovan State Agrarian University)

2049 Chișinău, str. Mircești 44
Telephone: (22) 31-22-58
Fax: (22) 31-22-76
E-mail: cimpoies@uasm.md
Internet: www.uasm.md
Founded 1933
State control
Languages of instruction: Romanian, English, Russian

Rector: Prof. Dr GHEORGHE P. CIMPOES

Library of 789,000 vols
Number of teachers: 400
Number of students: 6,400 (3,700 on campus, 2,700 distance)

DEANS

Faculty of Accountancy: Assoc. Prof. Dr VERONICA PRISACARU
Faculty of Agricultural Engineering and Transport: Assoc. Prof. Dr GRIGORE MARIAN
Faculty of Agronomy: Assoc. Prof. Dr MIHAI RURAC
Faculty of Animal Husbandry and Biotechnology: Prof. Dr NICOLAE EREMIA
Faculty of Economics: Assoc. Prof. Dr PETRU TOMITA
Faculty of Horticulture: Prof. Dr VALERIAN BALAN
Faculty of Land Surveying and Law: Prof. Dr TEODOR MORARU
Faculty of Veterinary Medicine: Assoc. Prof. Dr GHEORGHE DONICA

UNIVERSITATEA COOPERATIST COMERCIALĂ DIN MOLDOVEI
(Cooperative Trade University of Moldova)

2027 Chișinău, bd. Gagarin 8
Telephone: (22) 27-07-84
Fax: (22) 54-12-10
E-mail: webmaster@uccm.md
Internet: www.uccm.md
Founded 1993
State control
Languages of instruction: Romanian, English, French, Russian

Rector: Dr TUDOR MALECA
Pro-Rector: LARISA ȘAVGA

Library of 92,000 vols
Number of teachers: 200
Number of students: 1,200

DEANS

Faculty of Accountancy and Business Informatics: Dr SERGIU OPREA
Faculty of Management and Economics: Dr ELENA GRAUR
Faculty of Marketing and the Science of Commodities: Dr FEODOSIE PITUȘCAN
Faculty of Part-Time Studies: Dr SVETLANA MUȘTUC

UNIVERSITATEA DE STAT DIN BĂLȚI 'ALECU RUSSO'
('Alecu Russo' Bălți State University)

3121 Bălți, str. Pușkin 38
Telephone: (231) 2-30-66
Fax: (231) 2-30-39
E-mail: rectorat@usb.md
Internet: www.usb.md
Founded 1945
State control
Languages of instruction: Romanian, English, French, German, Russian, Spanish, Ukrainian

Rector: Prof. Dr Hab. GHEORGHE POPA
First Vice-Rector for Didactic Activity: Dr ALEXANDRU BALANICI
Vice-Rector for Scientific Activity: Dr MARIA ȘLEAHTIȚCHI
Vice-Rector for Int. Relations and European Integration: Dr VALENTINA PRIȚCAN
Vice-Rector for Part-Time Studies and Continuous Formation: Dr GHEORGHE NEAGU
Head of Univ. Scientific Library: ELENA HARCONIȚĂ

Library of 1,200,000 vols
Number of teachers: 315
Number of students: 7,210

Publications: *Art and Artistic Education, Biannual Journal of Applied Linguistics, Bulletin of Administration* (12 a year), *Scientific Papers* (every 2 years), *Speech and Context, University Yearbook* (every 5 years)

DEANS

Faculty of Economics: Dr ALA TRUSEVICI
Faculty of Foreign Languages and Literatures: Dr ELENA DRAGAN
Faculty of Law: Dr VEACESLAV PINZARI
Faculty of Music and Musical Pedagogy: Dr MARGARITA TETELEA
Faculty of Natural Science and Agro-Ecology: Dr STANISLAV STADNIC
Faculty of Pedagogy, Psychology and Social Work: Dr LORA CIOBANU
Faculty of Philology: Dr NICOLAE LEAHU
Faculty of Technics, Physics, Mathematics and Informatics: Dr SIMION BĂNCILĂ

UNIVERSITATEA DE STAT 'BOGDAN PETRICEICU HASDEU' DIN CAHUL
('Bogdan Petriceicu Hasdeu' State University of Cahul)

3901 Cahul, str. Piaţa Independenţei 1

Telephone: (299) 2-24-81

Founded 1999

Rector: Dr ION ŞIŞCANU.

UNIVERSITATEA DE STAT DIN COMRAT
(Comrat State University)

3900 Comrat, str. A. Galaţan 17

Telephone: (298) 2-43-45

Fax: (298) 2-40-91

E-mail: kdu@moldnet.md

Founded 1991

State control

Languages of instruction: Romanian, Bulgarian, Russian

Rector: Dr STEFANN VARBAN

Library of 50,200 vols

Number of teachers: 190

Number of students: 1,780

Faculties of agricultural technology, economics and national culture.

UNIVERSITATEA DE STAT DE MEDICINĂ ŞI FARMACIE 'NICOLAE TESTEMIŢANU' DIN REPUBLICA MOLDOVA
('Nicolae Testemiţanu' State Medical and Pharmaceutical University)

2004 Chişinău, bd. Ştefan cel Mare şi Sfînt 165

Telephone: (22) 24-34-08

Fax: (22) 24-23-44

E-mail: rector@usmf.md

Internet: www.usmf.md

Founded 1945

State control

Languages of instruction: Romanian, Russian, French, English

Rector: Prof. Dr ION ABABII

First Vice-Rector and Vice-Rector for Academic Affairs: Prof. Dr NICOLAE V. EŞANU

Vice-Rector for Quality of Instruction: Prof. Dr OLGA CERNETCHI

Vice-Rector for Int. Relations: Dr VALERIU TEODOR CHICU

Vice-Rector for Medical Affairs and Postgraduate Education: Prof. Dr VLADIMIR T. HOTINEANU

Vice-Rector for Research: Prof. Dr VIOREL I. PRISACARU

Library of 786,000 vols

Publication: Curieurul medical (6 a year)

DEANS

Faculty of Continuing Medical Training: Prof. Dr STANISLAV GROPPA

Faculty of General Medicine: Prof. Dr GHEORGHE PLĂCINTĂ

Faculty of Pharmacy: Dr NICOLAE CIOBANU

Faculty of Stomatology: Prof. Dr PAVEL GODOROJA

UNIVERSITATEA DE STAT DIN MOLDOVA
(Moldova State University)

2009 Chişinău, str. A. Mateevici 60

Telephone: (22) 57-74-01

Fax: (22) 24-42-48

E-mail: international@usm.md

Internet: www.usm.md

Founded 1946

State control

Languages of instruction: Romanian, Russian

Academic year: September to June

Rector: GHEORGHE CIOCANU

Pro-Rectors: IGOR ENICOV, P. GAUGAŞ E. MURARU MIHAIL REVENCO

Registrar: T. LUCHIAN

Librarian: ECATERINA ZASMENCO

Library: see Libraries and Archives

Number of teachers: 1,200

Number of students: 16,000

Publications: Scientific Annals (1 a year), Revista Nationala de Drept (National Journal of Law) (12 a year), Universitatea (12 a year)

DEANS

Faculty of Biology and Soil Science: MARIA DUCA

Faculty of Chemistry and Chemical Technology: VIORICA GLADCHI

Faculty of Economic Sciences: MIHAIL CERNEI

Faculty of Foreign Languages and Literature: LUDMILA ŽBANT

Faculty of History and Psychology: C. SOLOMON

Faculty of International Relations, Political and Administrative Sciences: V. CUJBĂ

Faculty of Journalism and Communication: C. MARIN

Faculty of Law: VICTOR MORARU

Faculty of Mathematics and Informatics: ANDREI PERJAN

Faculty of Philology: I. CONDREA

Faculty of Physics: P. GAŞIN

Faculty of Psychology and Educational Sciences: VLADIMIR GUTU

Faculty of Social Protection, Sociology and Philosophy: M. BULGARU

UNIVERSITATEA DE STAT DIN TIRASPOL
(Tiraspol State University)

2069 Chişinău, str. Ghenadie Iablocichin 5

Telephone: (22) 75-49-24

Fax: (22) 75-49-24

E-mail: scs_ust@moldova.cc

Founded 1930; moved from Tiraspol to present location in 1992, due to civil unrest

State control

Languages of instruction: Romanian, Russian

Rector: Prof. LAURENTIU CALMUTCHI

Vice-Rector: Prof. IGOR POSTOLACHI

Number of students: 3,140

Publication: Light (12 a year)

DEANS

Faculty of Biology and Chemistry: BORIS NEDBALIUC

Faculty of Geography: ION MIRONOV

Faculty of Pedagogy: VASILE PANICO

Faculty of Philology: LUDMILA SOLOVIOV

Faculty of Physics and Mathematics: BORIS KOROLEVSKI

UNIVERSITATEA PEDAGOGICĂ DE STAT 'ION CREANGĂ'
(Chişinău 'Ion Creangă' Pedagogical State University)

2069 Chişinău, str. I. Creangă 1

Telephone: (22) 74-54-14

Fax: (22) 74-99-14

E-mail: creangaups@yahoo.com

Internet: www.upsc.md

Founded 1940

State control

Languages of instruction: Romanian, English, French, German, Russian, Spanish, Italian

Rector: Dr MIHAIL GROSU

Number of teachers: 423

Number of students: 6,200 , (4,000 full-time, 2,200 part-time)

Publication: Annual Scientific Edition

DEANS

Faculty of Computer Studies and Informational Technologies in Education: CUSCA VALENTIN

Faculty of Fine Arts: VATAVU ALEXANDRU

Faculty of Foreign Languages and Literatures: GOGU TAMARA

Faculty of History and Ethno-Pedagogy: CHICUŞ NICOLAE

Faculty of Pedagogy: SADOVEI LARISA

Faculty of Philology: TOPOR GABRIELA

Faculty of Psychology and Special Psycho-Pedagogy: PERJAN CAROLINA

Faculty of Teacher Training: COJOCARU VASILE

UNIVERSITATEA TEHNICĂ A MOLDOVEI
(Technical University of Moldova)

2004 Chişinău, bd. Ştefan cel Mare şi Sfînt 168

Telephone: (22) 23-78-61

Fax: (22) 23-22-52

E-mail: extrel@adm.utm.md

Internet: www.utm.md

Founded 1964

State control

Languages of instruction: Romanian, Russian

Academic year: September to June

Rector: Acad. Prof. ION BOSTAN

First Vice-Rector for Education: Prof. Dr PETRU TODOS

Vice-Rector for Administration and Capital Construction: PAVEL SPÂNU

Vice-Rector for Continuing Education and International Relations: Assoc. Prof. Dr VALENTIN AMARIEI

Vice-Rector for Part-Time Studies and Distance Education: Assoc. Prof. Dr TIMOFEI ANDROS

Vice-Rector for Research: Prof. Dr hab. VALERIAN DOROGAN

Vice-Rector for Studies and Relations with Colleges: Prof. Dr DUMITRU UNGUREANU

Dean of Students: Dr CONSTANTIN STRATAN

Library of 1,080,000 vols

Number of teachers: 750

Number of students: 17,000

Publications: Meridian Ingineresc (4 a year), Mesager (newspaper, 12 a year)

DEANS

Faculty of Computers, Informatics and Microelectronics: Assoc. Prof. Dr ION BALMUS

Faculty of Economic Engineering and Business: Prof. Dr NICOLAE TURCANU

Faculty of Engineering and Management in Machine-Building: Assoc. Prof. Dr ALEXEI TOCA

Faculty of Engineering and Management in Mechanics: Assoc. Prof. Dr VASILE CARTOFEANU

Faculty of Power Engineering: Prof. Dr ION STRATAN

Faculty of Radioelectronics and Telecommunications: Assoc. Prof. Dr SERGIU ANDRONIC

Faculty of Surveying, Geodesy and Civil Engineering: Assoc. Prof. Dr VICTOR TOPOREŢ

Faculty of Technology and Management in the Food Industry: Assoc. Prof. Dr GRIGORE MUSTEATA

Faculty of the Textile Industry: Assoc. Prof. Dr CONSTANTIN SPINU

Faculty of Urban Planning and Architecture: Assoc. Prof. Dr NISTOR GROZAVU

Other Higher Educational Institutions

Academia de Mizică, Teatru şi Arte Plastice (Academy of Music, Theatre and Fine Arts of Republic of Moldova): 2014 Chişinău, str. A. Mateevici 87; tel. and fax (22) 22-19-49; e-mail usam@moldovacc.md; internet www.amtap.mdl.net; f. 1919; 1,500 students; Rector Dr AURELIAN DANILĂ.

Academia de Studii Economice (Academy of Economic Studies): 2005 Chişinău, str. Mitropolit Bănulescu-Bodoni 61; tel. (22) 22-41-28; fax (22) 22-19-68; e-mail r_gb@ase.md; internet www.ase.md; f. 1991; library: 317,000 vols; faculties of accountancy, business and administration, economics and law, finance, information technology and statistics and international economic relations; Rector Prof. Dr Hab. GRIGORII BELOSTECINIC.

Institutul Naţional de Educaţie Fizică şi Sport (National Institute of Physical Education and Sport): 2024 Chişinău, str. A. Doga 28/2; tel. (22) 49-40-81; fax (22) 49-76-71; e-mail inefs@mdl.net; faculties of part-time studies, pedagogy, sports and teacher development; Rector VEACESLAV MANOLACHE.

Institutul de Relaţii Internaţionale din Moldova (International Relations Institute of Moldova): 2009 Chişinău, str. Gh. Caşu 28/2; tel. (22) 73-59-43; fax (22) 73-59-42; e-mail infoirim@mail.ru; f. 2003; Rector CONSTANTIN MARIN.

MONACO

The Higher Education System

In 1861 Monaco became an independent state under the protection of France. There is only one public institution of higher education, the Académie de Musique Prince Rainier III de Monaco (founded 1933), and one private higher educational institution, the International University of Monaco, a business school where instruction is conducted in English. The latter is recognized by the Department of National Education, Youth and Sports in Monaco and quality-assured by the Comité d'Evaluation et de Surveillance; it is the only higher education provider with this type of recognition in Monaco. Most Monégasque students undertake higher education in France. Post-secondary technical and vocational education is provided by the Sections de Technicien Supérieur. Programmes of study last for two years and lead to the award of the Higher Technician Certificate (Brevet de Technicien Supérieur).

Learned Societies

HISTORY, GEOGRAPHY AND ARCHAEOLOGY

Association Monégasque de Préhistoire: Musée d'Anthropologie, 56 bis blvd du Jardin exotique, 98000 Monte Carlo; tel. 98-98-80-06; fax 98-98-02-46; e-mail suzanne_simone@libello.com; f. 1984; 50 mems; Pres. SUZANNE SIMONE.

LANGUAGE AND LITERATURE

Alliance Française: Maison de France, 42 rue Grimaldi, BP 300, 98006 Monte Carlo; tel. 93-50-08-24; offers courses and exams in French language and culture and promotes cultural exchange with France.

Research Institute

NATURAL SCIENCES

General

Centre Scientifique de Monaco: Villa Girasole, 16 blvd de Suisse, Monte Carlo 98000; tel. 93-25-89-54; fax 93-25-70-90; e-mail centre@centrescientifique.mc; internet www.centrescientifique.mc; f. 1960; pure and applied research in the fields of oceanography, marine biology and the protection and regeneration of the marine environment; laboratories in Musée Océanographique de Monaco (q.v.); Pres. of Admin. Council ROGER PASSERON; Sec.-Gen. MICHEL BOISSON; publ. *Bulletin* (in French and in English, 1 a year).

Libraries and Archives

Monte Carlo

Archives du Palais Princier de Monaco: BP 518, Monaco 98015 Cedex; tel. 93-25-18-31; private archives of the princes of Monaco; Curator RÉGIS LÉCUYER.

Bibliothèque Louis Notari: 8 rue Louis Notari, 98000 Monaco; tel. 93-15-29-40; fax 93-15-29-41; f. 1909; 310,000 vols, 18,000 phonograms, 4,000 video cassettes; Librarian HERVÉ BARRAL; publ. *Bibliographie de Monaco* (database).

Princess Grace Irish Library: 9 rue Princesse Marie de Lorraine, 98000 Monaco-Ville; tel. 93-50-12-25; fax 93-50-66-65; e-mail pglib@monaco.mc; internet www.monaco.mc/pglib; f. 1984; functions under the aegis of the Fondation Princesse Grace; Irish and Celtic studies library; 10,000 vols, 2,000 sheet items of Irish music and folk songs, 250 theses, 250 video cassettes and DVDs; reproduction of the Book of Kells; paintings, prints, sculptures; young readers' colln; English language activities for local school students; theatre, writing and poetry workshops; Administrator JUDITH GANTLEY; Sec. GÉRALDINE LANCE.

Museums and Art Galleries

Monte Carlo

Musée d'Anthropologie Préhistorique: 56 bis blvd du Jardin exotique, 98000 Monte Carlo; tel. 98-98-80-06; fax 93-30-02-46; e-mail musant@gouv.mc; f. 1902; prehistory, Quaternary geology; library of 3,000 vols, 200 periodicals; Curator PATRICK SIMON; publ. *Bulletin* (1 a year).

Musée Océanographique de Monaco: Ave Saint-Martin, 98000 Monaco-Ville; tel. 93-15-36-00; fax 93-50-52-97; e-mail biblio@oceano.mc; internet www.oceano.mc; f. 1910 by Prince Albert I of Monaco; part of Institut Océanographique, Paris; museum of natural history and art collns; aquarium contains 6,000 fishes of 550 species, and coral reefs; mother-of-pearl holy art shells; library of 50,000 vols; Dir ROBERT CALCAGNO; publs *Bulletin de l'Institut Océanographique* (irregular), *Mémoires de l'Institut océanographique* (irregular).

Nouveau Musée National de Monaco Villa Sauber/Villa Paloma: Admin., Villa des Pins, 8 rue Honoré Labande, 98000 Monaco; tel. 98-98-19-62; fax 93-50-94-38; e-mail contact@nmnm.mc; internet www.nmnm.mc; f. 1972; Galéa colln: automatons, miniature furniture, antique dolls, nativity scenes; Dir MARIE-CLAUDE BEAUD.

College

Académie de Musique Prince Rainier III de Monaco: 1 Blvd Albert 1er, 98000 Monaco; tel. 93-15-28-91; f. 1933; 53 professors; 650 students; Dir JOËL RIGAL.

MONGOLIA

The Higher Education System

Mongolia was formerly the Manchu province of Outer Mongolia. In 1911, following the republican revolution in China, Mongolian princes declared the province's independence. Russia (and, later, the USSR) competed with China for control of Mongolia and in November 1924 the Mongolian People's Republic was proclaimed. The oldest institutions of higher education date from this year, among them the Academy of Management, Higher School of Finance and Economics and Higher School of Trade and Industry. The oldest multi-faculty university-level institution is the National University of Mongolia (founded 1942). Higher education consists of universities, higher schools and colleges. In 2008/09 there were 48 state-owned universities and colleges with 106,600 students, and 101 private universities and colleges with 54,100 students. Many Mongolian students continue their academic careers at universities and technical schools in Russia, Germany, the United Kingdom and the USA. Higher education is the responsibility of the Ministry of Education, Culture and Science, while the Consortium of Mongolian Universities and

Colleges (founded 1995) is a non-governmental body representing 14 public and private universities.

Admission to higher education is on the basis of the Certificate of Secondary Education, students' academic records and relevant entrance examinations according to the programme of study applied for. The first stage of undergraduate study is the Diploma of Higher Education, which is awarded after two to three years. The second stage of undergraduate higher education is the Bachelors degree, which lasts four years (including time spent on the Diploma), and for which students are required to accumulate 120 'credit hours' for successful completion of the degree. After the Bachelors has been awarded students are eligible to study for the Masters, which usually lasts a year and requires 30 credit hours. Finally, the Doctorate is the highest university-level degree, and requires a minimum of 60 credit hours.

The Certificate of Vocational Education is the main qualification for technical and vocational education, which is widely available at junior, senior and post-secondary levels.

Regulatory and Representative Bodies

GOVERNMENT

Ministry of Education, Culture and Science: Government Bldg 3, Baga Toiruu 44, Sükhbaatar District, Ulan Bator; tel. (11) 322480; fax (11) 323158; internet www.mecs.pmis.gov.mn; Minister NORDOVYN BOLORMAA.

ACCREDITATION

Mongolian National Council for Education Accreditation: Government Bldg 10, Barilgachdyn talbai-2 38, Ulan Bator; tel. and fax (11) 324507; e-mail accmon@mongolnet.mn; internet www.accmon.mn; f. 1998; Contact SARUUL BAT-ULZII.

NATIONAL BODY

Consortium of Mongolian Universities and Higher Schools: Box 672, POB 46, Ulan Bator; tel. (11) 318154; fax (11) 324121; e-mail cmuc@mtu.edu.mn; internet www.cmuc.edu.mn; f. 1995; represents the common interests of public and private univs and colleges; supports scientific co-operation between the academic community and industry; promotes int. scientific co-operation; organizes biennial conferences on higher education reform; 18 mem. instns; Pres. Prof. Dr BADARCH DENDEV; publ. *Tavan Ukhaan* (12 a year).

Learned Societies

GENERAL

Mongolian Academy of Sciences: Sükhbaataryn talbai 3, Ulan Bator; tel. and fax (11) 321638; f. 1921; Depts of agriculture (Dir N. ALTANSÜKH), geology and geography (Dir, vacant), medicine and biology (Dir P. NYAMDAVAA), chemistry, mathematics, physics and technology (Dir D. KHAISAMBUU), social sciences (Dir KH. NAMSRAI); attached research

institutes: see Research Institutes; Pres. BAATARYN CHADRAA; Scientific Sec. DÜGERIN REGDEL; publs *Proceedings of the Mongolian Academy of Sciences* (4 a year), *Studia Archaeologica, Studia Ethnographica, Studia Folclorica, Studia Historica, Studia Mongolica, Studia Museologica*.

AGRICULTURE, FISHERIES AND VETERINARY SCIENCE

Academy of Agricultural Sciences: Ulan Bator; f. 1998; Pres. N. ALTANSÜKH.

Association of Private Veterinary Surgeons: Ulan Bator; Pres. GOTOVYN BATTULGA.

BIBLIOGRAPHY, LIBRARY SCIENCE AND MUSEOLOGY

Academy of Information Sciences: Ulan Bator; f. 2004; Vice-Pres. CH. DALAI.

ECONOMICS, LAW AND POLITICS

Academy of State and Law: Ulan Bator; f. 2003; Pres. T. SENGEDORJ.

FINE AND PERFORMING ARTS

Academy of Cinematic Art: Ulan Bator; f. 2003; Pres. T. GANDI.

LANGUAGE AND LITERATURE

Association of Mongolian Writers: Ulan Bator; Exec. Dir KHAIDAVYN CHILAAJAV.

MEDICINE

Academy of Health Management: Ulan Bator; Pres. N. UDVAL.

Academy of Medical Sciences: Ulan Bator; f. 2005; Pres. PAGVAJAVYN NYAMDAVAA.

Society of Mongolian Surgeons: Ulan Bator; Pres. B. GOOSH.

NATURAL SCIENCES

General

Academy of Natural Sciences: Ulan Bator; f. 1998; Pres. JAMTSYN GARIDKHÜÜ; Learned Sec. T. ERDENEJAV.

RELIGION, SOCIOLOGY AND ANTHROPOLOGY

Academy of Anthropology: Ulan Bator; f. 1998; Pres. L. DASHNYAM.

Academy of Astrology: Mongolian Youth Association Bldg, Baga Toiruu, Sükhbaatar district, Ulan Bator; tel. and fax (11) 322982.

Academy of Nomadic Culture and Civilization: 'Ikh Zasag' University Bldg, 4th khoroo, B.Dorjiin St, Bayanzurkh dist., Ulan Bator; tel. (70) 157770; fax (70) 155736; e-mail ihkzasag@ikhzasag.edu.mn; internet www.ikhzasag.edu.mn; f. 2002; research and scientific works in Mongolian studies; 80 mems; Pres. NAMSRAIN NYAM-OSOR; publ. *Ikh Zasag* (2 a year).

Genghis Khan World Academy: Bldg 6, 2nd sub-district, Bayanzürkh district, Ulan Bator (POB 21/174); fax (11) 315846; internet www.chinggesacademy.mn.

Mongolian Muslims' Society: Ulan Bator; f. 1990; Pres. KADYRYN SAIRAAN.

TECHNOLOGY

Association of Academies of Science and Technology: Ulan Bator; f. 1998; Pres. L. DASHNYAM.

Mongolian Civil Engineers' Association: Baruun Dörvön Zam, Ikh Toiruu 1, Ulan Bator (POB 44/7); tel. (11) 328097; fax (11) 325580; e-mail midiid@magicnet.mn.

Mongolian National Mining Association: Ulan Bator; f. 2003; Dir N. ALGAA.

Mongolian National Water Association: Ulan Bator; f. 2000; Pres. S. CHULUUNKHUYAG.

National Academy of Engineering: Ulan Bator; f. 1998; Pres. P. OCHIRBAT.

Science and Technology Foundation: Ulan Bator; Dir KH. TSOOKHÜÜ.

Research Institutes

AGRICULTURE, FISHERIES AND VETERINARY SCIENCE

Agricultural Economics Research Institute: c/o Academy of Sciences, Sükhbaataryn talbai 3, Ulan Bator; attached to Mongolian Acad. of Sciences; Dir Yu. ADYAA.

Agricultural Research Institute: Khovd; tel. (43) 3720; f. 1994; library of 10,000 vols; Dir P. BAATARBILEG.

Institute of Pasture and Fodder: Darkhan; Dir D. TSEDEV.

Institute of Veterinary Research: Zaisan, Ulan Bator; tel. (11) 341553; f. 1960; attached to Mongolian Agricultural Univ.; library of 4,000 vols; Dir B. BYAMBAA; publ. *Proceedings of the Institute of Veterinary Research and Training.*

Research Institute of Animal Husbandry 'J. Sambuu': Zaisan, Ulan Bator; tel. (11) 341572; e-mail riah@magicnet.mn; f. 1961; attached to Mongolian Acad. of Sciences; library of 800 vols; Dir DONDOVYN ALTANGEREL; publ. *Proceedings* (in Mongolian, with English summary).

Research Institute of Pastoral Animal Husbandry in the Gobi Region: Bulgan district, Ömnögobi province; f. 1959; attached to Mongolian Acad. of Sciences; camel and goat husbandry; Dir N. BIICHEE.

Research Institute of Plant Protection: c/o Academy of Sciences, Sükhbaataryn talbai 3, Ulan Bator; attached to Mongolian Acad. of Sciences; Dir D. TSEDEV.

Research Institute of Vegetable Growing and Land Cultivation Training: Darkhan-Uul province; tel. and fax (37) 24132; attached to Mongolian Agricultural Univ.; 138 teachers; 1,050 students.

ARCHITECTURE AND TOWN PLANNING

Building Institute: c/o Academy of Sciences, Sükhbaataryn talbai 3, Ulan Bator; attached to Mongolian Acad. of Sciences; Dir D. LKHANAG.

Construction and Architecture Research, Experimental, Production and Business Corporation: c/o Academy of Sciences, Sükhbaataryn talbai 3, Ulan Bator; tel. (11) 341437; Exec. Dir D. KHAISAMBUU.

Institute of Agricultural Architecture: Ulan Bator; Dir O. JADAMBA.

Institute of Architecture and Town Planning: c/o Academy of Sciences, Sükhbaataryn talbai 3, Ulan Bator; attached to Mongolian Acad. of Sciences; Dir (vacant).

Research Institute of Soils and Foundations Engineering: c/o Academy of Sciences, Sükhbaataryn talbai 3, Ulan Bator; attached to Mongolian Acad. of Sciences; Dir Dr A. ANAND.

ECONOMICS, LAW AND POLITICS

Centre for North-East Asian Studies: Mongolian Technical University Bldg (2nd Fl.), Ulan Bator (POB 51/4); tel. (11) 458317; fax (11) 458317; f. 1990; attached to Mongolian Acad. of Sciences; library of 2,000 vols; Dir Prof. CH. DALAI; publ. *North-East Asian Studies* (2 a year).

Institute of Economics: Ulan Bator; tel. (11) 320802; fax (11) 322216; f. 1962; attached to National University of Mongolia; fmrly attached to Mongolian Acad. of Sciences; library of 2,000 vols; Dir P. LUVSANDORJ.

Institute of International Studies: Room 806, Soyolyn töv örgöö, Sükhbaataryn talbai, Ulan Bator; tel. and fax (11) 322613; attached to Mongolian Acad. of Sciences; Dir LUVSANGIIN KHAISANDAI; Scientific Sec. D. SHÜRKHÜÜ.

Institute of Management Development: Ulan Bator; Dir D. TSERENDORJ.

Institute of Market Studies: Chamber of Commerce and Industry, Ulan Bator; Dir S. DEMBEREL.

Institute of Mongol Studies: c/o Academy of Sciences, Sükhbaataryn talbai 3, Ulan Bator 11; attached to Mongolian Acad. of Sciences; Dir SH. BIRA.

Institute of National Development: Ulan Bator; attached to Mongolian Acad. of Sciences and the Presidential Secretariat; Dir RADNAASÜMBERELIIN RENCHINBAZAR; Scientific Sec. L. TSEDENDAMBA.

Institute of Oriental and International Studies: c/o Academy of Sciences, Sükhbaataryn talbai 3, Ulan Bator; attached to Mongolian Acad. of Sciences; Dir A. OCHIR.

Institute of Strategic Studies: Partizany gudamj, Ulan Bator (POB 870); tel. (11) 328188; fax (11) 324055; attached to Ministry of Defence; Dir Maj.-Gen. CHOYJAMTSYN ULAANKHÜÜ.

Mongolian Development Research Centre: Room 50, Baga Toiruu 13, Chingeltei district, Ulan Bator (POB 20A/63); tel. and fax (11) 315686; internet www.mdrc.mn.

'Prognoz' Institute of Socio-Political Studies: Ulan Bator; attached to Mongolian People's Revolutionary Party; Dir O. ERDENECHIMEG.

Research Institute for Land Policy: Chingünjavyn gudamj 2, Ulan Bator; tel. (11) 60506; f. 1975; library of 1,100 vols; Dir Dr G. PÜREVSÜREN.

Research Institute of Economic Studies: Ulan Bator; f. 1991; microeconomics; Dir Prof. T. DORJ.

FINE AND PERFORMING ARTS

Research Institute of Culture and Arts: c/o Academy of Sciences, Sükhbaataryn talbai 3, Ulan Bator 11; attached to Mongolian Acad. of Sciences; Dir S. TSERENDORJ.

HISTORY, GEOGRAPHY AND ARCHAEOLOGY

Institute of Archaeology: c/o Academy of Sciences, Sükhbaataryn talbai 3, Ulan Bator; attached to Mongolian Acad. of Sciences; Dir D. TSEVEENDORJ; Scientific Sec. B. TSOGTBAATAR.

Institute of Geography: c/o Academy of Sciences, Sükhbaataryn talbai 3, Ulan Bator; tel. (11) 350472; attached to Mongolian Acad. of Sciences; Dir Dr S. DORJGOTOV.

Institute of History: Jukovyn gudamj 77, Bayanzürkh district, Ulan Bator; tel. and fax (11) 458305; internet www.mas.ac.mn; attached to Mongolian Acad. of Sciences; archaeology, ethnography, Mongolian history; Dir D. DASHDAVAA.

LANGUAGE AND LITERATURE

Folk Literature Research Institute: Ulan Bator; Dir B. KATUU.

Institute of Mongolian Language and Literature: c/o Academy of Sciences, Sükhbaataryn talbai 3, Ulan Bator; tel. (11) 451762; attached to Mongolian Acad. of Sciences; Dir KH. SAMPILDENDEV.

MEDICINE

Institute of Hygiene, Epidemiology and Microbiology: c/o Academy of Sciences, Sükhbaataryn talbai 3, Ulan Bator 13; tel. and fax (1) 45-26-77; internet www.mas.ac.mn; attached to Mongolian Acad. of Sciences; Dir J. KUPUL.

Institute of Public Health: Enkh taivny gudamj 17, Ulan Bator; tel. (11) 458645; fax (11) 458645; Dir L. NARANTUYAA.

Institute of Traditional Medicine: c/o Academy of Sciences, Sükhbaataryn talbai 3, Ulan Bator; attached to Mongolian Acad. of Sciences; Dir D. DAGVATSEREN.

Medical Research Institute: c/o Academy of Sciences, Sükhbaataryn talbai 3, Ulan Bator; attached to Mongolian Acad. of Sciences; Dir YO. BODIKHÜÜ.

National Centre for Communicable Diseases: Bayanzürkh district, Ulan Bator; tel. and fax (11) 458699; f. 2001; Dir TOGOOGIIN ALTANTSETSEG.

National Forensic Research Centre: Ulan Bator; Dir CH. ALTANKHISHIG.

National Institute of Medicine: c/o Academy of Sciences, Sükhbaataryn talbai 3, Ulan Bator; attached to Mongolian Acad. of Sciences; Learned Sec. B. TSERENDASH.

Research and Production Centre of Biotechnology: Ulan Bator; attached to Min. of Health and Inst. of Public Health; Dir J. OYUUNBILEG.

Research and Production Institute of Biological Preparations and Blood: Ulan Bator; Dir A. DANDII.

State Research Centre for Maternal and Child Health: Amarsanaagiin gudamj, Bayangol district, Ulan Bator; tel. (11) 362633; fax (11) 302316; f. 1930; attached to Mongolian Acad. of Sciences; Dir G. CHOIJAMTS; publ. *Mother and Child* (2 a year).

NATURAL SCIENCES

General

Institute of Scientific and Technical Development: Ulan Bator; Dir D. NYAMAA.

Biological Sciences

Institute of Biology: Ulan Bator; tel. (11) 458851; f. 1965; attached to Mongolian Acad. of Sciences; Dir TS. JANCHIV.

Institute of Botany: Jukovyn gudamj 77, Ulan Bator; tel. (11) 451837; fax (11) 323158; e-mail ibot@mongol.net; attached to Mongolian Acad. of Sciences; Learned Sec. D. MAGSAR.

Institute of Geoecology: c/o Academy of Sciences, Sükhbaataryn talbai 3, Ulan Bator; tel. (11) 321862; attached to Mongolian Acad. of Sciences; Dir J. TSOGTBAATAR.

Palaeontology Centre: Enkh Taivny gudamj 63, Ulan Bator; fax (11) 458935; e-mail barsgeodin@magicnet.mn; attached to Mongolian Acad. of Sciences; Dir R. BARSBOLD.

Mathematical Sciences

Institute of Mathematics: Ulan Bator; attached to National University of Mongolia; fmrly attached to Mongolian Acad. of Sciences; Dir A. MEKEI.

Physical Sciences

Astronomical Observatory: Khürel-Togoot, Ulan Bator (POB 788); tel. (11) 52929; f. 1961; attached to Mongolian Acad. of Sciences; library of 1,500 vols; Dir G. NOONOI.

Centre of Seismology and Geomagnetism: c/o Academy of Sciences, Sükhbaataryn talbai 3, Ulan Bator; attached to Mongolian Acad. of Sciences; Dir U. SÜKHBAATAR.

Institute of Chemistry and Chemical Technology: Züün Dörvön Zam, Bayanzürkh district, Ulan Bator; tel. (11) 453133;

attached to Mongolian Acad. of Sciences; Dir B. Púrevsúren.

Institute of Geology and Mineral Enrichment: Peace Ave 63, POB 118, Ulan Bator; tel. (11) 457858; fax (11) 457858; f. 1966; attached to Mongolian Acad. of Sciences; library of 1,000 vols; Dir O. Tómórto-goo; publ. *Khaiguulchin* (4 a year).

Institute of Meteorology and Hydrology: Khudaldaany gudamj 5, Ulan Bator; tel. and fax (11) 326614; e-mail meteoins@magicnet.mn; f. 1966; library of 13,000 vols; Dir D. Azzayaa; publ. *Environment.*

Institute of Physics and Technology: Enkh Taivny gudamj 54B, Ulan Bator; tel. (11) 458397; fax (11) 458397; f. 1961; attached to Mongolian Acad. of Sciences; library of 50,000 vols; Dir Ts. Baatar.

Research Centre for Astronomy and Geophysics: c/o Academy of Sciences, Sükhbaataryn talbai 3, Ulan Bator; tel. (11) 458849; attached to Mongolian Acad. of Sciences; Dir B. Bekhtór.

RELIGION, SOCIOLOGY AND ANTHROPOLOGY

Institute of Astrology: Ulan Bator; Dir Sh. Jargalsaikhan.

Institute of Buddhist Studies: Ulan Bator; Dir G. Luvsantseren.

Institute of Philosophy, Sociology and Law: Jukovyn gudamj 77, Ulan Bator; tel. (11) 453752; f. 1972; attached to Mongolian Acad. of Sciences; Dir G. Chuluunbaatar.

Social Sciences Institute: Ulan Bator; attached to National University of Mongolia (fmrly attached to Mongolian Acad. of Sciences); Dir O. Mónkhbat.

TECHNOLOGY

Agricultural Technology Science, Technology and Production Corporation: Ulan Bator; tel. (11) 341155; attached to Mongolian Academy of Sciences.

Communications Research and Production Corporation: c/o Academy of Sciences, Sükhbaataryn talbai 3, Ulan Bator; attached to Mongolian Acad. of Sciences; Dir D. Lkhagvaa.

Electronic Equipment and Machine Studies Science, Technology and Production Corporation: Ulan Bator; tel. (11) 328025; attached to Mongolian Acad. of Sciences.

Experimental and Research Centre for Leather: c/o Academy of Sciences, Sükhbaataryn talbai 3, Ulan Bator; attached to Mongolian Acad. of Sciences; Dir D. Ganbold.

Experimental and Research Centre for Wool: c/o Academy of Sciences, Sükhbaataryn talbai 3, Ulan Bator; attached to Mongolian Acad. of Sciences; Dir G. Yondonsambuu.

Forestry and Wood Processing Industry Institute: c/o Academy of Sciences, Sükhbaataryn talbai 3, Ulan Bator; attached to Mongolian Acad. of Sciences; Dir Sainbayar.

Geodesic and Geological Engineering Institute: Ulan Bator; Dir Ts. Tserenbat.

Heat Technology and Industrial Ecology Institute: Ikh Surguuliin gudamj 2A, Sükhbaatar district, Ulan Bator; tel. 324959; attached to Mongolian Acad. of Sciences; Dir S. Batmónkh.

Informatics Institute: c/o Academy of Sciences, Sükhbaataryn talbai 3, Ulan Bator; tel. (11) 458090; attached to Mongolian Acad. of Sciences; Dir Maidarjavyn Ganzorig.

Information Technology Science, Technology and Production Corporation: Ulan Bator; tel. (11) 327133; attached to Mongolian Acad. of Sciences.

Light Industry Scientific, Technological and Production Corporation (ARMONO): Chingisiin órgón chólóó, Ulan Bator; tel. and fax (11) 342536; e-mail armonocor@mongol.net; internet www.aeromongolia.co.kr; f. 1997; research into leather and timber industrial products; attached to Mongolian Acad. of Sciences.

Military Science Research Institute: Ministry of Defence, Ulan Bator; Dir Sh. Palamdorj.

Mining Institute: c/o Academy of Sciences, Sükhbaataryn talbai 3, Ulan Bator; attached to Mongolian Acad. of Sciences; Dir S. Mangal.

Natural Freezing and Food Technology Institute: c/o Academy of Sciences, Sükhbaataryn talbai 3, Ulan Bator; attached to Mongolian Acad. of Sciences; Dir N. Lonjid.

Petrochemical Technology Research Centre: Ulan Bator; tel. (11) 24779.

Power Institute: c/o Academy of Sciences, Sükhbaataryn talbai 3, Ulan Bator; attached to Mongolian Acad. of Sciences; Dir D. Bumayuush.

Renewable Energy Science, Technology and Production Corporation: Chingisiin órgón chólóó, Khan-Uul district, Ulan Bator (POB 35/479); tel. and fax (11) 342377; attached to Mongolian Acad. of Sciences; Dir B. Chadraa.

Roads Research and Production Corporation: c/o Academy of Sciences, Sükhbaataryn talbai 3, Ulan Bator; attached to Mongolian Acad. of Sciences; Dir B. Khundgaa.

Standardization and Metrology National Centre: Enkh Taivny gudamj 46A, Ulan Bator (POB 51/48); tel. (11) 458349; fax (11) 458032; f. 1953; attached to Min. of Industry and Trade; library of 130,000 vols; Dir Nyamjavyn Janchivdorj; publ. *Standards and Metrology* (12 a year).

Traditional Medicine Science, Technology and Production Corporation: Ulan Bator; tel. (11) 343103; attached to Mongolian Acad. of Sciences.

Transport Research and Production Corporation: c/o Academy of Sciences, Sükhbaataryn talbai 3, Ulan Bator; attached to Mongolian Acad. of Sciences; Dir L. Túdev.

Water Policy Research Institute: Baruunselbe 13, Ulan Bator 211238; tel. (11) 325487; fax (11) 321862; f. 1965; library of 3,500 vols; Dir N. Chuluunkhuyag.

Libraries and Archives
Ulan Bator

Gandan Library: Gandantegchinlen Buddhist Monastery, Ulan Bator; tel. (11) 360023; f. 1838; Buddhist theology and philosophy, xylographs, secular works of science and literature.

National Archives of Mongolia: Ulan Bator 210646; tel. (11) 324533; fax (11) 324533; f. 1996; history, art, literature, science, technology, film, sound recordings; Dir-Gen. Dembereliin Ólziibaatar; publ. *Archives News* (2 a year).

Natsagdorj Central Public Library: 2nd sub-district, Sükhbaatar district, Ulan Bator; tel. (11) 327873; fax (11) 329950; internet www.mclibrary.edu.mn; Dir T. Mijiddorj.

State Central Library: Sóüliin gudamj, Sükhbaatar district, Ulan Bator; tel. and fax (11) 323100; f. 1921; 4m. vols, incl. rare and ancient editions; Dir Gotovyn Akim.

Museums and Art Galleries
Arkhangai
Ethnographical Museum: Arkhangai; located in the Zayain Gegeenii Süm (temple founded in 1536).

Bayan-Ólgii
Town Museum: Bayan-Ólgii; Kazakh culture, especially costume and artefacts.

Dornogobi
Danzan Ravjaa Museum: Dornogobi; commemorates the life and works of the 19th-century writer and lama, Danzan Ravjaa.

Khentii
Ethnographical Museum: Khentii; located in the home of the former Tsetseg Khan.

Ulan Bator
Botanical Garden: Ulan Bator; attached to Mongolian Acad. of Sciences; Dir G. Ochirbat.

Memorial Museum of Victims of Political Persecution: Genden St 1, Ulan Bator; tel. (70) 110915; e-mail info@memorialmuseum.info; internet www.memorialmuseum.info; f. 1996; located in home of executed PM Genden; commemorates in documents and photographs the victims of the 1930s Stalinist purges; Dir Bekhbat Sodnom.

Mongolian National Gallery of Modern Art: Ulan Bator; tel. (11) 327177; fax (11) 313191; e-mail mnartgallery@mongolnet.mn; internet www.ulaanbaatar.net/artgallery; f. 1991; Dir D. Enkhtsetseg.

Museum of Asian Art: Juulchny gudamj, Ulan Bator; private collection of religious art and artefacts in precious metals; Dir A. Altangerel.

Museum of Military History: Enkh Taivny órgón chólóó, Ulan Bator; tel. (11) 454292; Dir Col P. Byambasúren.

Museum of Mongolian Costume: Enkh Taivny órgón chólóó, Ulan Bator; f. 2005; folk costume, felt tents and artefacts since the Genghis Khan period.

Museum of Mongolian Traditional Medicine: Next to Bogd Khan's Winter Palace (Museum of Religious History), Ulan Bator; f. 2005; Dir D. Tserensodnom.

Museum of Religious History: Chingis Khaany órgón chólóó, Ulan Bator; tel. (11) 324788; housed in Choyjin Lamyn Khüree, a former lamasery, and Bogd Khan's Winter Palace; Dir G. Tóvsaikhan.

National Museum of Mongolian History: Juulchmii gudamj 1, Ulan Bator 46, (POB 46/332); tel. (11) 326802; fax (11) 326802; e-mail nmm@mongolnet.mn; internet www.nationalmuseum.mn; f. 1924 as Mongolian National Museum; present name 1990 by merger of State Central Museum and Museum of the Revolution; 46,000 historical and ethnographical objects from prehistory to present day; Dir Dr J. Saruulbuyan; publ. *Museologia* (1 a year).

Natsagdorj Museum: Chingis Khaany órgón chólóó, Ulan Bator; tel. (11) 327879; life and works of the author and poet Dashdorjiin Natsagdorj.

Natural History Museum: Khuvisgalchdyn órgón chólóó, Ulan Bator; tel. (11) 321716; natural history, Gobi desert dinosaur eggs and skeletons; Dir P. Erdenebat.

Theatre Museum: Cultural Palace, Sükhbaatar Square, Ulan Bator; tel. (11) 326820.

Ulan Bator Museum: Enkh Taivny örgön chölöö, Ulan Bator; located in old Russian house; history of Ulan Bator.

Wildlife Museum: Öndör Gegeen Zanabazaryn gudamj, Ulan Bator; tel. (11) 360248; fax (11) 360067.

Zanabazar Fine Arts Museum: Barilgachdyn talbai, Ulan Bator; sculptures by Mongolia's first Buddhist leader and *tankas* (religious paintings); Dir D. GUNGAA.

Zhukov, G. K., House Museum: Enkh Taivny örgön chölöö, 15th sub-district, Ulan Bator; tel. (11) 453781; career of Soviet Marshal Zhukov.

Universities

'CHOI LUVSANJAV' UNIVERSITY OF LANGUAGE AND CIVILIZATION

11th microraion, 7th sub-district, Sükhbaatar district, Ulan Bator (POB 13/550)

Telephone: (11) 353524
Fax: (11) 353524

Founded 1993

Vice-President: SOYOMBO LUVSANJAV

Number of teachers: 40 (22 full-time, 18 part-time)

Number of students: 380

Library of 10,000 vols

Mongolian and Chinese studies; training of English- and Japanese-speaking teachers and interpreters.

GENGHIS KHAN 'IKH ZASAG' UNIVERSITY

Baatar B. Dorjiin gudamj, 4th sub-district, Bayanzürkh district, Ulan Bator (POB49/349)

Telephone: (11) 457826
Fax: (11) 455736
E-mail: ikhzasag@edu.mn
Internet: www.ikhzasag.edu.mn

Schools of American, Japanese and Chinese studies, English, Japanese and Chinese interpreting, international law, international relations, international trade and economics, tourism management,

Number of teachers: 146 teachers
Number of students: 3,660 students

Pres.: NAMSRAIN NYAM-OSOR
Vice-Pres. for Finance: J. KHAIDAV
Vice Pres. for Int. Relations: N. TUUL
Vice Pres. for Management: J. TSETSEGMAA
Vice Pres. for Marketing: B. NASAN

Publications: *Ikh Zasag* (newspaper, 4 a year), *Ikh Zasag* (journal, jtly with Academy of Nomadic Civilization and Culture, 2 a year).

MONGOLIAN AGRICULTURAL UNIVERSITY

Zaisan, Ulan Bator

Telephone: (11) 341592
Fax: (11) 341770
E-mail: haaint@magicnet.mn
Internet: www.msua.edu.mn

Founded 1942 as veterinary dept of Mongolian State University; became Institute of Agriculture 1958; university status 1991; present name 1996
State control

Director: Dr J. GANBOLD
Rector: B. BYAMBAA
Pro-Rector: L. NYAMBAT

Library of 200,000 vols
Number of teachers: 300
Number of students: 6,700

DEANS

Faculty of Agricultural Economics: A. BAKEI
Faculty of Agricultural Engineering and Product Technology: L. LUVSANSHARAV
Faculty of Agronomy: BEGZIIN DORJ
Faculty of Animal Husbandry: (vacant)
Faculty of Basic Education: H. KHÜRELTOGOO
Faculty of Veterinary Medicine: B. LUVSANSHARAV

MONGOLIAN UNIVERSITY OF ARTS AND CULTURE

Baga Toiruu 22, Chingeltei district, Ulan Bator

Telephone: (11) 327335
Fax: (11) 325205

Founded 1990
State control
Academic year: September to June

Rector: D. TSEDEV
Vice-Rector: JAMBALYN ENEBISH
Registrar: ALTANGERELIIN GANBAATAR
Librarian: DAMBAJAVYN NYAMDULAM

Number of teachers: 230
Number of students: 1,900

DEANS

College of Culture: L. BATCHULUUN
College of Music: CH. CHINBAT
College of Radio and Television: (vacant)
College of Theatre Art: (vacant)

MONGOLIAN STATE EDUCATION UNIVERSITY

Baga toiruu 14, Sükhbaatar district, Ulan Bator

Telephone: (11) 326010
Fax: (11) 322705
E-mail: togmid@mspu.edu.mn
Internet: www.mspu.edu.mn

Founded 1951
State control
Academic year: September to June

Rector: Prof. B. JADAMBAA
Vice-Rectors: Prof. B. JADAMBAA (International Relations and Information), Prof. D. TÖMÖRTOGOO (Research), Prof. TS. BATSUURI (Teaching)
Head of Academic Affairs: Prof. D. PÜREVDORJ
Head of Graduate Studies: Prof. N. JADAMBAA

Library of 300,000 vols
Number of teachers: 330
Number of students: 5,261

Publication: *Teacher Education* (2 a year)

DIRECTORS

School of Art and Technology: Prof. G. BATDORJ
School of Computer Science and Information Technology: Prof. L. CHOIJOOVAANCHIG
School of Education Studies: Prof. TS. SUMYAA
School of Foreign Languages: Prof. Z. GULIRAANZ
School of History and Social Sciences: Prof. D. NARANTSETSEG
School of Mathematics and Statistics: Prof. TS. BATKHÜÜ
School of Mongolian Studies: Prof. TS. ÖNÖRBAYAN
School of Natural Sciences: Prof. M. ÜINDEN
School of Physical Education: Prof. S. JAMTS
School of Physics and Technology: Prof. R. BAZARSÜREN
School of Pre-School Education: Prof. J. BATDELGER
School of Teacher Training: Prof. S. BATKHUYAG

UNIVERSITY OF HEALTH SCIENCES

Choidogiin gudamj 3, Sükhbaatar district, Ulan Bator (POB 48/111)

Telephone: (11) 328670
Fax: (11) 321249
E-mail: nmumtlhs@magicnet.mn
Internet: www.nmum.cjb.net

Founded 1942
State control
Academic year: September to August

Director: Prof. TS. LKHAGVASÜREN
Deputy Director: D. DUNGERDORJ
Scientific Secretary: G. BATMÖNKH
Chief Administrative Officer: N. BATKHÜREL
Librarian: N. TSAGAACH

Number of teachers: 310
Number of students: 2,300

DEANS

Faculty of Biomedicine: (vacant)
Faculty of Health Economics: B. ERDENESAIKHAN
Faculty of Medicine: (vacant)
Faculty of Pharmacy: S. TSETSEGMAA
School of Dentistry: B. OYUUNBAT
School of Public Health: CH. TSOLMON
School of Traditional Medicine: Prof. N. TÖMÖRBAATAR

UNIVERSITY OF THE HUMANITIES

POB 53, Ulan Bator 210646
Sükhbaatar district, Small Ring Rd, Ulan Bator 46

Telephone: (11) 322702
Fax: (11) 322702
E-mail: uh@humanities.mn
Internet: www.humanities.mn

Founded 1979 as Higher School of Russian Language Teachers; present name and status 2000
State control

Dir: Prof. BEGZIIN CHULUUNDORJ

Schools of foreign languages, social sciences; Depts of culture and American and British studies, foreign languages, human resource management, journalism, literature.

NATIONAL UNIVERSITY OF MONGOLIA

Ikh Surguuliin gudamj 1, Sükhbaatar district, Ulan Bator (POB 46A/523)

Telephone: (11) 320892
Fax: (11) 320668
E-mail: numelect@magicnet.mn
Internet: www.num.edu.mn

Founded 1942
State control
Academic year: September to June

President: TSERENSODNOMYN GANTSOG
Vice-Presidents: SÜRENGIIN DAVAA (Academic), R. SAMYAA (Research)

Library of 350,000 vols
Number of teachers: 500
Number of students: 6,500

Publication: *Proceedings*.

FACULTIES AND TRAINING AND RESEARCH INSTITUTES

Faculty of Biology: incl. depts of biochemistry and microbiology, biophysics, botany, ecology, forestry, genetics, zoology; Dir R. SAMYAA.

Faculty of Chemistry: incl. depts of chemistry and technology of new materials, ferrous-metal and rare-element chemistry, general chemistry (Analytical and Physical Chemistry), organic chemistry (Coal and Petrochemistry); Dean D. DORJ.

Faculty of Earth Sciences: Dean CH. GONCHIGSUMLAA.

School of Economic Studies: incl. depts of accountancy, credit and finance, demography, economic data processing, foreign languages, management, marketing, mathematics, statistics, theory of economics; Dir CH. HASHCHULUUN.

School of Foreign Languages and Cultures: English, Chinese, Czech, French, German, Japanese, Korean, Polish, Russian.

School of Foreign Service: training of diplomats.

School of Information Technology.

School of International Relations: postgraduate studies in foreign relations; Dir J. BOR.

School of Law: incl. depts of civil law,- constitutional law, criminal process law, International law, State Administration; Dir S. NARANGEREL.

School of Mathematics and Computer Science: incl. depts of algebra, applied mathematics and methods of teaching mathematics, computer programming; geometry, mathematical analysis, probability theory and mathematical statistics,; Dean JAMTSYN BAATAR.

School of Mongolian Language and Culture: incl. depts of linguistics, literature, journalism, Mongolian Language; Dir D. BADAMDORJ.

School of Physics and Electronics: incl. depts of electronics, geophysics, hydrology, meteorology, optics, nuclear physics, radiophysics, solid-state physics, theoretical physics; Dean CHÜLTEMIIN BAYARKHÜÜ.

School of Social Sciences: incl. depts of culture and art, history, philosophy, politics, sociology; Dean SH. SODNOM.

Graduate School: Dean A. MEKEI.

Office of International Affairs: Dean S. ALTANTSETSEG.

Office of Undergraduate Studies: Dean N. BATCHIMEG.

'ORKHON' UNIVERSITY

Chinggis Khaany örgön chölöö, Khan-Uul district, Ulan Bator (POB 36/176)

Telephone: (11) 342696
Fax: (11) 341276
E-mail: info@orkhon.edu.mn
Internet: www.orkhon.edu.mn

Founded 1992
Private control

Director: Prof. Dr NYAMAAGIIN KHAJIDSÜREN

Library of 25,000 vols
Number of teachers: 70
Number of students: 1,000

BA degree courses in languages (English, French, German, Japanese, Korean, Russian) and law; MA degree courses in linguistics.

MONGOLIAN UNIVERSITY OF SCIENCE AND TECHNOLOGY

Baga Toiruu 34, Sükhbaatar district, Ulan Bator (POB 46/520)

Telephone: (11) 325109
Fax: (11) 324121
E-mail: info@must.edu.mn
Internet: www.must.edu.mn

Founded 1969
State control
Academic year: September to July

Rector: D. DASHJAMTS (acting)
Vice-Rectors: Z. TSERENDORJ (Academic Affairs), L. BOLDBAATAR (Finance and Development), D. DASHJAMTS (Research and Technology)
Chief Admin. Officer: O. NASANBAT

Librarian: G. PÜREV
Library of 170,000 vols
Number of teachers: 781
Number of students: 17,000
Publications: *MUST News* (in Mongolian, 12 a year), *Science and Technology* (in Mongolian, 4 a year), *Scientific Transactions* (in Mongolian, 4 a year)

DIRECTORS

School of Civil Engineering: Z. BINDERYAA
School of Computer Science and Management: S. BAIGALTUGS
School of Food and Biotechnology: D. NANSALMAA
School of Foreign Languages: T. BATBAYAR
School of Geology: D. CHULUUN
School of Humanities: A. ENKHBAATAR
School of Industrial Technology and Design: B. DAVAASÜREN
School of Materials Technology: P. MÖNKHBAATAR
School of Mathematics: J. BAASANDORJ
School of Mechanical Engineering: G. BATKHÜREL
School of Mining Engineering: B. PÜREVTOGTOKH
School of Power Engineering: H. ENKHJARGAL
School of Technology in Darkhan: S. TSEVEL
School of Technology in Erdenet: S. DAVAANYAM
School of Technology in Övörhangai Province: J. JANTSANDORJ
School of Technology in Sükhbaatar Province: MAJIGIIN KHÜRLEE
School of Telecommunications and Information Technology: B. DAMDINSÜREN
Graduate Study Centre: H. BUYANNEMEKH

ULAANBAATAR UNIVERSITY

Bayanzürkh district, Ulan Bator (POB 44/658)

Telephone: (11) 450179
Fax: (11) 311080
E-mail: ubuniv@mongol.net
Internet: www.ulaanbaatar.edu.mn

Founded 1993 as Higher Technical School; received charter 1996
State control
Academic year: September to July

Rector: YONG SUNG JE
Vice-Rector: D. BOLD
Scientific Sec.: T. NAMJIL

Number of teachers: 78
Number of students: 800

Publication: *Proceedings of the Ulaanbaatar University* (1 a year)

Faculties of language and literature, social sciences and technology.

Higher Schools

Academy of Management: Chingisiin örgön chölöö 7, Khan-Uul district, Ulan Bator; tel. and fax (11) 343037; e-mail td@aom.edu.mn; f. 1924; govt agency; depts of computer science, economics; English language, management, public administration; 52 teachers; 739 students; Rector TOGOOCHIN LKHAGVAA; publs *Management* (in Mongolian, 4 a year), *Public Administration* (in Mongolian, 4 a year).

Darkhan Higher School: 4th sub-district, Darkhan district, Darkhan-Uul Province (Darkhan POB 520); tel. and fax (372) 35652; internet www.darkhandeed.mn; f. 1997; accounting, Chinese, English, hotel and restaurant management, Japanese, Korean, tourism; library: 25,000 vols; 90 teachers; 1,000 students.

Defence Academy: 16th sub-district, Bayanzükh district, Ulan Bator; tel. (11) 458673; Law, Accounting, State Administration, Operation Oof Motor Vehicles, Tracked Vehicles And Bridge-Building Machinery, Electronics, Communications, Military Science, Military History; Dir Col N. JALBAJAV.

Higher School of Arts and Crafts: Ulan Bator.

Higher School of Culture: Erkh Chölöönii talbai, Chingeltei district, Ulan Bator (POB 46/982); tel. (11) 326759; fax (11) 329328; e-mail cclib@mongol.net; internet www.moncollege.150m.com; training of librarians, cultural managers, museum workers and archivists, printers, and music, song and dance teachers; Dir G. BAATAR.

Higher School of European Languages: located at: Ikh Surguuliin gudamj 9, Sükhbaatar district, Ulan Bator (POB 46/982); tel. (11) 320993; f. 1993; English, French, Russian and German interpreting; 52 teachers (11 full-time, 41 part-time); 632 students; Rector T. PELJID.

Higher School of Finance and Economics: Enkh Taivny gudamj 12A, Bayanzürkh district, Ulan Bator 49; tel. and fax (11) 458378; internet www.ife.edu.mn; f. 1924; 65 teachers; 1,200 students; depts of accounting and audit, banking and finance, business and management, Economics and Econometrics, information technology, international studies; Dir JAMYANDORJIIN BATKHUYAG.

Higher School of Information Technology: Ulan Bator; Dir G. TSOGBADRAKH.

Higher School of International Economics and Business: 20th sub-district, Bayangol district, Ulan Bator; tel. (11) 681525; fax (11) 452067; e-mail iieb_elselt@yahoo.com; internet www.iieb.edu.mn; banking and accounting, business management, international economics, taxation and Aaudit.

Higher School of International Studies: Ikh Surguuliin gudamj 2A, Sükhbataar district, Ulan Bator, (POB 46/205); tel. (11) 329860; fax (11) 329450; Dir NARANDULAM.

Higher School of Labour: Erkh Chölöönii talbai (bldg behing the Tengis cinema), Chingeltei district, Ulan Bator; tel. (11) 318176; fax (11) 312629; e-mail mli_999@yahoo.com; attached to Mongolian Confederation of Trade Unions; accountancy and social Work, business, finance, labour economics and management.

Higher School of Legal Studies: Ulan Bator; tel. (11) 529798; Dir L. DASHNYAM.

Higher School of Literature: Ulan Bator; Dir SHIRSEDIIN TSEND-AYUUSH.

Higher School of Mongolian Language and Literature: Chingisiin örgön chölöö 29, 3rd sub-district, Khan-Uul district, Ulan Bator; tel. (11) 342210; fax (11) 342210; trains teachers and interpreters in French, German and Japanese; English-language journalism.

Higher School of Oriental Literature: Ulan Bator; Dir S. BATMÖNKH.

Higher School of Oriental Philosophy and Anthropology: 17th sub-district, Bayangol district, Ulan Bator; tel. and fax (11) 361461; e-mail ophsi@mongolnet.mn; Dir NANSALYN SARANTUYAA.

Higher School of Religion: Ulan Bator; tel. (11) 457454; Dir SH. SONINBAYAR.

Higher School of Social Studies: 2nd sub-district, Bayanzürkh district, Ulan Bator (POB 23/277); tel. and fax (11) 460356; e-mail uuds@magicnet.mn; f. 1993; library: 12,000 vols; Dir TS. ENKHEE.

Higher School of Technology: Darkhan, Darkhan-Uul province; tel. (372) 23368; fax (372) 23760; e-mail technol@mongol.net; fmr polytechnic and technical college; electrical and heating engineering, geology, mining and ore concentration, power supply management.

Higher School of Trade and Industry: Oyuutny gudamj 14, Enkh Taivny örgön chölöö, Ulan Bator, (POB 48/404); tel. (11) 325724; fax (11) 326748; e-mail icbm@magicnet.mn; f. 1924; accountancy, business management, international trade, marketing; library: two libraries, with 22,000 vols; 60 teachers; 1,200 students; Rector S. BUDNYAM; publ. *Mercury* (3 a year).

'Khalkha Juram' Higher School of Law: Tulga Co. Bldg, Ikh Toiruu 20, Sükhbaatar district, Ulan Bator, (POB 51/128); tel. and fax (11) 350480; Dir T. DOOKHÜÜ.

Khan-Uul Higher School: located at: Tulga Co. Bldg, Ikh Toiruu 20, Sükhbaatar district, Ulan Bator (POB 46/419); tel. (11) 351032; e-mail khan-uul@mongol.net; internet www .khan-uul.mn; f. 1994; applied mathematics, business economics, computer programming, computer technology; 25 teachers; 280 students; Dir TSERENGIIN DEMBEREL.

'Mongol' Higher School: Ulan Bator; Dir NAMJAAGIIN DASHZEVEG.

Mongolian Business Institute: Enkh Taivny örgön chölöö, Bayangol district, Ulan Bator, (POB 24/715); tel. (11) 361589; e-mail mbi_191@mol.mn; internet www.mbi .edu.mn; f. 1991; degree courses in economics, finance, management, marketing; 40 teachers; 500 students; Dir Dr B. ERDENESÜREN.

Mongolian National Higher School: Enigma Centre, 11th sub-district, Bayangol district, Ulan Bator; tel. (11) 300900; fax (11) 300799; e-mail mni@mongolnet.mn; f. 1998; economics, economics of tourism, financial and business management, hotel and restaurant management, international trade, law, marketing; Dir TÖMÖRBAATARYN KHERÜÜGA.

'Monos' Higher School of Medicine: Songolongiin toiruu 5, 20th sub-district, Songinokhairkhan district, Ulan Bator; tel. (11) 633235; medicine and pharmacy.

'Otgontenger' University: Jukovyn örgön chölöö, Bayanzürkh district, Ulan Bator, (POB 51/35); tel. (11) 454560; e-mail oy_oyun@magicnet.mn; internet www .otgontenger.edu.mn; f. 1991; training of Russian- and English-language teachers and interpreters, Japanese-, German-, French-, Chinese- and Korean-language business and tourism managers, and Japanese-language international tour guides, training in English-language journalism; 48 teachers; 650 students; Founder and Chair. DULAMSÜRENGIIN OYUUNKHOROL; Rector D. NARANCHIMEG.

'Otoch Maramba' Higher School of Medicine: 2nd sub-district, Bayanzürkh district, Ulan Bator (POB 49/235); tel. (11) 457489; fax (11) 358489; f. 1991; study of traditional medicine; 6 teachers; 68 students; Dir TSERENSODNOM.

Private Higher School of Oriental Philosophy and History: Enkh Taivny gudamj 35 Ulan Bator (POB 44/283); tel. (11) 322628; fax (11) 320210; f. 1992; library: 5,000 vols; 150 students; Dir R. NANSAL.

Radio and Television Higher School: Mongolian Radio and Television Bldg, Khuvisgalyn zam 3, Ulan Bator 11; tel. (11) 369223; training of radio and television journalists and producers, television camera operators and engineers.

Railway College: Enkh Taivny örgön chölöö 44, Bayangol district, Ulan Bator (POB 35/76); tel. (11) 322723; fax (11) 322797; e-mail mtzcoll@mongolnet.mn; automation and telecommunications, construction, management, maintenance, railway transport organization, rolling-stock maintenance, passenger services; trains staff for Mongolian railways, the country's largest employer; Dir B. SERÜÜD.

'Shikhikhutug' Higher School of Law: Ikh Surguuliin gudamj 1, 6th sub-district, Ulan Bator (POB 46/1033); tel. and fax (11) 323392; e-mail shihihutug@mongol.net; Dir D. OYUUNTSETSEG.

'Shonkhor' Higher School of Physical Culture: Baga Toiruu 55, 8th sub-district, Sükhbaatar district, Ulan Bator (POB 960); tel. and fax (11) 319858; Dir KH. BAYANMÖNKH.

'Tenger' Socio-Economic Higher School: Chinggissin örgön chölöö, 2nd sub-district, Khan-Uul district, Ulan Bator; tel. (11) 342651; accounting, anthropology, business economics, social sciences, social work, state administration, tourism, trade economics; Chinese language jtly with Shandong University, China.

'Zanabazar' Buddhist University: Ulan Bator; attached to Gandantegchinlen monastery; Dir SH. SONINBAYAR.

Colleges

College of Agriculture: Darkhan; hydrology, land improvement, meteorology.

'O. Tleikhan' Building College: Baruun Dörvön Zam, Enkh Taivny örgön chölöö 35, Ulan Bator (POB 24/643); tel. (11) 322723; fax (11) 322797; e-mail cwc@magicnet.mn; civil engineering, computer operations, electrical engineering, machine and vehicle repair, utilities; Dir B. CHIMIDDORJ.

Ulan Bator College: Construction College Bldg, West side of rd to Gandan monastery, Baruun Dörvön Zam, Bayangol district, Ulan Bator; depts of business management and computer programming, Korean-language teacher-training and interpreting; 10 teachers; 140 students; Rector YUM SUN JE.

MONTENEGRO

The Higher Education System

Following the dissolution of the Socialist Federal Republic of Yugoslavia in 1992, Montenegro became part of the Federal Republic of Yugoslavia, which was renamed the State Union of Serbia and Montenegro in 2003. In 2006 Montenegro declared independence from the State Union of Serbia and Montenegro. The Univerzitet Crne Gore Podgorica (University of Montenegro, Podgorica—founded 1974) is the main institution of higher education and was established while Montenegro was part of the Socialist Federal Republic of Yugoslavia. In 2006 the Univerzitet Mediteran (Mediterranean University), a private university, was founded. The newly established Ministry of Education and Science has assumed responsibility for higher education, which is still strongly based on the former Yugoslav system. In 2002 the New University Law introduced a range of reforms, including adoption of the European Credit Transfer System and increased autonomy for institutions of higher education. Consequently, Montenegro also participates in the Bologna Process to establish a European Higher Education Area, the first phase of which is to adopt a credit-based system of comparable degrees with two main cycles (undergraduate and graduate). In 2005/06 there were 21 institutions of higher education, including faculties, art academies and private institutions, with 12,903 students.

Under the old system, admission to higher education was based on completion of general secondary education or four-year vocational certificate programmes and award of the Secondary School Leaving Diploma. Universities also set their own entrance examinations. Quotas for admissions were set by the Government. The new undergraduate Bachelors degree (four years) replaces the old-style awards of Diplom Višeg Obrazovanje (two to three years) and Diplom Visokog Obrazovanja (four to six years). The Masters degree (Magistarska Diploma) is a one-year programme of study following the Bachelors. Finally, the Doctorate (Doktorat Nauka) is the highest university-level degree and is awarded after a period of research culminating with defence of a thesis.

The Montenegro Council of Higher Education (MCHE), set up in 2003, is responsible for accreditation of higher educational institutions.

Regulatory and Representative Bodies

GOVERNMENT

Ministry of Culture, Sports and Media: Vuk Karadžića 3, 81000 Podgorica; tel. (20) 231-561; fax (20) 231-540; e-mail kabinet@min-kulture.mn.yu; internet www.ministarstvokulture.gov.me; Min. BRANISLAV MIĆUNOVIĆ.

Ministry of Education and Science: Vaka Đurovića bb, 81000 Podgorica; tel. (20) 410-100; fax (20) 410-101; e-mail mpin@gov.me; internet www.mpin.gov.me; Min. SLAVOLJUB STIJEPOVIC.

ACCREDITATION

ENIC/NARIC Montenegro: ENIC Centre Montenegro, Rimski trg bb, 81000 Podgorica; tel. and fax (20) 265-014; fax (20) 265-014.

Montenegro Council of Higher Education: c/o Vaka Đurovića bb, 81000 Podgorica; f. 2003; responsible for assuring high quality higher education; advises Govt and assists the instns in improving and sustaining quality; evaluation and accreditation of instns and study programmes.

Learned Societies

GENERAL

Crnogorska akademija nauka i umjetnosti (CANU) (Montenegrin Academy of Sciences and Arts): Rista Stijovića 5, 81000 Podgorica; tel. (20) 655-450; fax (20) 655-451; e-mail canu@canu.ac.me; internet www.canu.org.me; f. 1973 as Society of Sciences and Arts of Montenegro, present name and status 1976; depts of arts, natural sciences, social sciences; 70 mems (32 full and 10 assoc. mems in the working body of the Academy, 28 foreign mems); library of 80,000 vols; Pres. MOMIR ĐUROVIĆ; Vice Pres. MIJAT ŠUKOVIĆ; Sec.-Gen. RANISLAV BULATOVIĆ; publs *Bibliografije* (Bibliographies), *Glasnik* (Review), *Godišnjak CANU* (1 a year), *Istorijski izvori* (Historical Issues), *Naučni skupovi* (Symposia), *Posebna izdanja* (Special Editions), *Posebni radovi* (Special Works), *Zbornici radova* (Works).

EDUCATION

Pedagogical Centre of Montenegro: Bulvr Lenjina 25/V, 81000 Podgorica; tel. and fax (20) 248-668; internet www.pccg.co.me; f. 2000; deals with professional, advanced teacher training; edits professional literature and textbooks; organizes nat. and int. professional meetings, seminars, conferences; helps continual process of innovating and improving the educational system; works in cooperation with Open Soc. Institute Montenegro, Open Soc. Institute NY (USA), Min. of Education of Montenegro, Univ. of Montenegro, Int. Step by Step Asscn, Centre for Interactive Pedagogy Belgrade, Parents Asscn, Pedagogical Centre, British Council Office; Dir SASA MILIC.

LANGUAGE AND LITERATURE

Montenegrin PEN Centre: St Gipos 1/3 postanski fah 117, Cetinje; tel. (20) 241-733; fax (20) 241-733; e-mail sreten@cg.yu; f. 1990; promotes democratic values, friendship, cooperation and use of the Montenegrin language; defends freedom of expression; 53 mems; Pres. SRETEN PEROVIC; publ. *Doclea*.

Research Institutes

BIBLIOGRAPHY, LIBRARY SCIENCE AND MUSEOLOGY

Republički zavod za zaštitu spomenika kulture (Republic Institute for the Protection of Cultural Monuments of Montenegro): Bajova 150, 81250 Cetinje; tel. (41) 231-039; fax (41) 231-753; e-mail rzzsk@t-com.me; f. 1948 as Institute for Protection and Scientific Research of Cultural Monuments and Natural Rarities; attached to Ministry of Culture; research, registration, conservation and protection of cultural property in Montene-gro; library of 2,500 vols; Dir DJORDJIJE VUSUROVIC; publ. *Starine Crne Gore* (1 a year).

HISTORY, GEOGRAPHY AND ARCHAEOLOGY

Istorijski institut Crne Gore (Historical Institute of Montenegro): Blvr Revolucije 5, 81000 Podgorica; tel. (20) 241-624; fax (20) 241-336; e-mail iicg@ac.me; internet www.iicg.ac.me; f. 1948; attached to Univ. of Montenegro; educates experts; organizes professional devt of researchers; conducts research and publishing; Dir Dr RADOSLAV RASPOPOVIC; publ. *Istorijski zapisi* (4 a year).

LANGUAGE AND LITERATURE

Institute of Foreign Languages: Jovana Tomaševića 37, 81000 Podgorica; tel. (20) 245-453; fax (20) 243-516; e-mail isj@ac.me; internet www.ucg.ac.me; f. 1978; attached to University of Montenegro; courses in English, Russian, Italian, French and German; promotes research in linguistics, literature and interdisciplinary fields (literary linguistics, sociolinguistics, psycholinguistcs); Dir Dr IGOR LAKIC.

NATURAL SCIENCES

Hidrometeorološki zavod Crne Gore (Hydrometeorological Institute): Hydrometeorological Service of Montenegro, IV proleterske 19, 81000 Podgorica; tel. (20) 655-183; fax (20) 655-197; internet www.meteo.co.me; f. 1947; meteorological, hydrological, water quality and air quality stations; activities incl. automatic measuring of land temperature, agroclimatic research, agrometeorological service, quality control of surface and underground waters and air; scientific programmes, studies and projects related to environmental field; hydrographic, topographic surveys; data colln from hydrography, navigation, geology and geophysics; Dir LUKA MITROVIC.

Institut za biologiju mora (Institute of Marine Biology): Dobrota 66, POB 69, 85330 Kotor; tel. (32) 334-569; fax (32) 334-570; e-mail acojo@ac.me; internet www.ibmk.org; f. 1961; attached to University of Montenegro; scientific investigation, exploitation, control and protection of the sea; Dir Dr ALEKSANDAR JOKSIMOVIC; Sec. EMILIJA NIKCEVIC; Sec. Gen. RADOVAN KRIVOKAPIC; publ. *Studia Marina* (2 or 3 a year).

Institute of Biotechnology: Cetinjski put bb, 81000 Podgorica; tel. (20) 268-437; fax 20) 268-432; e-mail bti@ac.me; internet www.ucg.ac.me; f. 1937 as Centre for Subtropical cultures in Bar; attached to University of Montenegro; agriculture, veterinary medicine and forestry; Dir Dr LJUBOMIR PEJOVIĆ.

Libraries and Archives
Cetinje

Biblioteka državnog muzeja Crne Gore (Library of the National Museum of Montenegro): Novice Cerovica bb., 81250 Cetinje; tel. (41) 230-310; fax (41) 230-310; e-mail nmcg@t-com.me; internet www.mnmuseum .org; f. 1926; 20,000 vols.

Centralna narodna biblioteka Crne Gore (Central National Library of Montenegro): Blvr crnogorskih junaka br. 163, 81250 Cetinje; tel. (41) 231-143; fax (41) 231-020; e-mail info@cnbct.vbcg.me; internet www .cnb.me; f. 1592, present name 1964, present bldg 1980; 2,000,000 vols; spec. colln of MSS, maps, picture postcards, photographs, records, exhibition catalogues; nat. copyright and deposit library; inter-library loan; Dir DJUROVIC JELENA; publ. *Bibliografski vjesnik* (3 a year).

Državni arhiv Crne Gore (Public Records Office of Montenegro): Novice Cerovica 2, 81250 Cetinje; tel. (41) 231-045; fax (41) 232-670; f. 1951, inherited documents of the State Archive of Montenegro (f. 1895); explores and publishes archival heritage; official state documents of Montenegro since 1878; 3,760 m of documents; oldest document dates from 1539; Dir STEVAN RADUNOVIĆ; publ. *Arhivski zapisi* (Archive Records).

Herceg Novi

Herceg Novi Library: Herceg Stephan Sq. 6, Herceg Novi; tel. (31) 321-900; collns of Dušan Petkovic (5,000 books); Veljka Radojevic (1,500); Doklestic, Daljev, Lucic, Subotic; heritage colln; 30,000 vols.

Podgorica

Biblioteka istorijskog instituta Crne Gore (Library of the Historical Institute of Montenegro): Blvr revolucije 3, 81000 Podgorica; tel. (20) 241-336; fax (20) 241-624; e-mail ii@ac.me; internet www.ucg.ac.me; f. 1948; 38,000 vols.

Museums and Art Galleries
Cetinje

Narodni muzej Crne Gore (National Museum of Montenegro): Novice Cerovica bb, 81250 Cetinje; tel. and fax (41) 230-310; tel. (41) 230-310; e-mail nmcg@t-com.me; internet www.mnmuseum.org; f. 1896; consists of 5 depts: Art Museum, Ethnographic Museum, Historical Museum, King Nikola's Palace and Njegoš's Museum Biljarda; contains archaeological sources, written and printed documents, war relics, furniture, ethnographic subject matter of present-day

Montenegro; art works from medieval period to late 20th century; library of 30,000 vols; Dir PETAR ČUKOVIĆ; publs *Glasnik Cetinjskih Muzeja, Messenger*.

Herceg Novi

Josip Bepo Benković: Marka Vojnovića 4, Herceg Novi; tel. (31) 324-051; f. 1966; permanent exhibition of 200 paintings, sculptures and graphics; workshop for preservation and restoration; ateliers for painters and sculptors.

Zavicajni muzej Herceg-Novi (The Regional Museum of Herceg-Novi): Ulica Mirka Komnenovica 9, 85340 Herceg Novi; tel. (31) 322-485; e-mail muzej@cg.yu; internet www.rastko.org.yu/rastko-bo/muzej; f. 1949 as Nat. Museum of Herceg Novi, present bldg 2001; colln from Neolithic period to beginning of the Christian era; 30 icons; objects of traditional culture of the region, incl. tools for cattle breeding, agriculture, oil growing; nat. costumes, music instruments and household furniture; 100 Mediterranean and subtropical plants over 1,000 sq. m; Dir DJORDJE CAPIN; Curator VIKTOR VARGA; publs *Muzejske Sveske* (irregular), *Posebna Izdanja*.

Kotor

Pomorski muzej (Maritime Museum): Boka Marine Sq. 391, Kotor; tel. (32)304-720; fax (32) 325-883; internet museummaritimum .com; f. 1880 by Marina Bay Fraternity, present bldg 1984; models of ships, documents, paintings, weapons, Turkish guns, navigation instruments and compasses, folk costumes, jewellery, ornamental items and antique furniture; library of 16,000 vols; Dir JOVAN MARTINOVIĆ; publ. *Godišnjak Pomorskog Muzeja u Kotoru* (Yearbook).

Podgorica

Centar za arheološka istraživanja Crne Gore (Centre for Archaeological Research of Montenegro): Gojko Radonjic 33A, 20000 Podgorica; tel. (20) 620-018; fax (20) 620-018; e-mail czaicg@t-com.me; f. 1961, fmrly Archaeological Colln of Montenegro, present name 1997; colln, arrangement, maintenance, study and presentation of archaeological excavation sites in Montenegro.

Muzej grada Podgorice (Museum of the City of Podgorica): Marka Miljahova 4, 81000 Podgorica; tel. (20) 242-543; e-mail pgmuzeo@t-com.me; f. 1950; 4 areas of study: archaeological, ethnographic, historical and cultural-historical; colln of displays from the classical period to the present; Roman fibula, Illyrian jewellery, old coins, metal objects and bones related to the settlements and influences of different civilizations and cultures in the area.

Prirodnjački muzej Crne Gore (Natural History Museum of Montenegro): Trg Vojvode Bećir Bega Osmanagića 16, 20000 Podgorica; tel. (20) 633-184; fax (20) 623-933; e-mail zastitaprirode@t-com.me; f. 1961; research; exhibits on the fauna and palaeontology of Montenegro; museum collns; publ. *Natura Montenegrina*.

Universities

UNIVERZITET CRNE GORE, PODGORICA
(University of Montenegro, Podgorica)

Cetinjska br.2, 81000 Podgorica
Telephone: (20) 414-255
Fax: (20) 414-230
E-mail: rektor@ac.me
Internet: www.ucg.ac.me

Founded 1974, present name 1992
State control
Academic year: September to June

Rector: Prof. Dr PREDRAG MIRANOVIĆ
Vice-Rector for Teaching: Prof. Dr ANDJELKO LOJPUR
Vice-Rector for International Cooperation: Prof. Dr MIRA VUKCEVIC
Provost: Prof. ZDRAVKO USKOKOVIC
Provost: Prof. NATASA DJUROVIC
Sec.-Gen.: JELENA PAJKOVIĆ
Dir of Library: BOSILJKA CICMIL

Library of 1,030 vols, 9992 library units of monographs (including a collection of 665 doctoral dissertations and Masters theses published at the University of Montenegro)
Number of teachers: 1,273
Number of students: 11,000

Publication: *Bilten* (4 a year)

DEANS

Faculty of Architecture: Prof. Dr GORAN RADOVIĆ
Faculty of Biotechnology: Prof. Dr NATALIJA PEROVIĆ
Faculty of Civil Engineering: Dr DUSKO LUCIC
Faculty of Drama (Cetinje): SINIŠA JELUŠIĆ
Faculty of Economics: Prof. Dr MILORAD JOVOVIĆ
Faculty of Electrical Engineering: Prof. Dr SRDJAN STANKOVIC,
Fine Arts (Cetinje): NENAD ŠOŠKIĆ
Faculty of Law: Prof. Dr RANKO MUJOVIĆ
Maritime Studies (Kotor): Prof. Dr MILORAD RASKOVIC
Faculty of Mechanical Engineering: Prof. Dr GORAN CULAFIĆ
Faculty of Medicine: Prof. Dr BOGDAN AŠANIN
Faculty of Metallurgy and Chemical Technology: Prof. Dr KEMAL DELIJIĆ
Faculty of Natural Sciences: Prof. Dr PREDRAG STANISIC
Faculty of Political Sciences: Prof. Dr SRĐAN DARMANOVIĆ
Faculty of Philosophy: Prof. Dr BLAGOJE CEROVIC
Faculty of Sport and Physical Education: Doc. Dr DUŠKO BJELICA
College of Physiotherapy: Prof. Dr SOFIJA ŽITNIK-SIVAČKI
Faculty of Tourism and Hotel: Doc. Dr TATJANA STANOVČIĆ
Independent Study Programme for Education of Teachers in Albanian language: Prof. DAVID KALAJ (acting)
Independent Study Programme Geodesy: Prof. MITAR ČVOROVIĆ (acting)
Independent Study Programme Pharmacy: Prof. REFIK ZEJNILOVIĆ
Institute of Foreign Languages: Doc. Dr IGOR LAKIĆ
Music Acad.: Prof. Dr VLADIMIR BOČKARJOV

UNIVERZITET MEDITERAN
(Mediterranean University)

Vaka Đurovića bb, 81000 Podgorica
Telephone: (20) 409-200
Fax: (20) 409-232
E-mail: office@unimediteran.net
Internet: www.unimediteran.net
Private control
Academic year: September to July (2 Semesters)

Rector: Prof. Dr STEVAN POPOVIĆ
Vice Rector for Int. Cooperation: Dr JANKO RADULOVIĆ
Sec.-Gen.: DRAGICA ANDJELIC

Colleges

DEANS

Business School: Doc. Dr DRAGOLJUB JANKO-
VIC
Faculty of Foreign Languages: Prof. Dr
ZELJKO DJURIC
Faculty of Information Technology: Doc. Dr
RAMO ŠENDELJ
Faculty of Law: Doc. Dr MLADEN VUKCEVIC
Faculty of Tourism and Management: Doc.
Dr SANJA VLAHOVIC
Faculty of Visual Arts: Prof. Dr NENAD
VUKOVIC

Montenegro Business School: ul. Kralja
Nikole 114, 81000 Podgorica; tel. and fax (20)
602-545; e-mail ssluzba.mbs@unimediteran
.net; internet www.fps.unimediteran.net; f.
2005; offers courses in financial management, marketing; 654 students; Dean DRA-
GOLJUB JANKOVIĆ; Sec. VESNA MIJATOVIĆ.

Montenegro Tourism School: c/o Univerzitet Mediteran, Vaka Đurovića bb, 81000

Podgorica; e-mail fakultettht_bar@t-com.me;
internet www.ftht.unimediteran.net; f. 2004;
offers gen. Masters and Doctoral studies;
courses in management, marketing, information technology in tourism and hotel management; sustainable devt; strategic
management; contemporary trends and
devts in tourism; Dean Doc. Dr SANJA
VLAHOVIC; Vice-Dean of Finance and Development Doc. Dr DARKO LACMANOVIĆ; Sec.
SNEŽANA PETROVIĆ.

MOROCCO

The Higher Education System

Université Quaraouyine Fès (founded 859), an institution for Koranic, Islamic and Arabic studies, is among the oldest universities in continuous existence in the world. From 1912 until 1958 Morocco was a French protectorate and, consequently, the higher education system displays strong French influences. The Université Mohammed V Agdal (founded 1957) is the oldest multi-disciplinary institution of secular studies. In 1997/98 there were 68 state university-level institutions and in 2006/07 there were some 369,142 students in further and higher education.

The Ministry of National Education, Higher Education, Staff Training and Scientific Research is the supreme authority of higher education, which is free to Moroccan students. The senior officers of universities, such as Presidents and Deans of Faculty, are state appointees, and are responsible for running universities in conjunction with University Councils, Faculty Councils and Faculty Scientific Councils. The main types of institutions of higher education are universities, higher schools (grandes écoles), teacher-training institutes and other specialist institutes.

Admission to higher education is often on the basis of the secondary school awards, Diplôme du Baccalauréat and Diplôme du Baccalauréat Technique, but additional two-year courses (classes préparatoires aux grandes écoles) are required for entry to the grandes écoles. Most university degrees fall into one of three cycles, with some exceptions; these include degrees for disciplines that require longer periods of undergraduate study than the standard four years, such as engineering (five years), veterinary medicine and agronomy (six years) and medicine (seven years). The first cycle of higher education consists of certificates and diplomas awarded after two years of a broad-based programme of study in one of four subject groups (arts and humanities, science and economics, applied sciences, engineering and agriculture) appropriate to the intended area of specialization. Students in the arts and humanities are awarded the Certificat Universitaire d'études Littéraires; students in science and economics receive the Certificat Universitaire d'études Scientifiques; students in applied sciences are awarded Diplôme d'études Universitaires Générales or Diplôme d'études Universitaires de Technologie; while students in engineering and agriculture undertake a two-year preparatory programme of study. The second cycle of higher education is a period of specialist training and culminates in the award of either the Licence or the Maîtrise. Students who have the Certificat Universitaire d'études Littéraires or Certificat Universitaire d'études Scientifiques undertake a further two years of study for the Licence, while holders of the Diplôme d'études Universitaires Générales or Diplôme d'études Universitaires de Technologie are awarded the Maîtrise after the same period. Professional titles are awarded in some disciplines, like engineering (Diplôme d'Ingénieur d'état), veterinary medicine (Docteur Vétérinaire) and medicine (Doctorat en Médecine). The third cycle of higher education awards consists mainly of three degrees, Diplôme d'études Supérieures Approfondies, Diplôme d'études Supérieures Spécialisées and Doctorat D'état. Holders of the Licence are eligible for admission to the Diplôme d'études Supérieures Approndies, a two-year programme of study and research, culminating in submission of a dissertation, that allows admission to doctoral-level studies. The Diplôme d'études Supérieures Spécialisées is also a two-year course, open to holders of either the Licence or Maîtrise, but does not qualify the student for doctoral-level studies. The Doctorat d'état is the highest university-level degree and comprises three to five years of research. Outside the university system, the grandes écoles offer specialist degrees such as Diplôme de Technicien Supérieur and Diplôme d'Ingénieur d'état.

Students with Diplôme du Baccalauréat and the Diplôme du Baccalauréat Technique may attend post-secondary vocational and technical education and study for the Brevet de Technicien Supérieur, which requires successful completion of a two-year programme of study.

In 2004 a number of faculties at Morocco's universities underwent reforms to bring them into line with European universities. As part of the new degree structure new curricula and a system of transferable credits were introduced, allowing students to take courses from different departments and different institutions or to leave university and continue their studies later. Under the new structure the studies were reorganized into three years of first-cycle studies (Licence), two years of second-cycle studies (Masters), and three years of doctoral studies (Doctorat).

The national accreditation body for tertiary education is the National Accreditation and Evaluation Committee (Commission Nationale d'Accréditation et d'Évaluation).

Regulatory Bodies

GOVERNMENT

Ministry of Culture: 1 rue Ghandi, Rabat; tel. 37-20-94-94; fax 37-20-94-01; e-mail webmaster@minculture.gov.ma; internet www.minculture.gov.ma; Minister TOURIYA JABRANE.

Ministry of National Education, Higher Education, Staff Training and Scientific Research: Bab Rouah, Rabat; tel. 37-77-48-39; fax 37-77-90-01; e-mail divcom@men.gov.ma; internet www.men.gov.ma; Minister AHMED AKHCHICHINE.

Learned Societies

GENERAL

Académie du Royaume du Maroc: Charia Imam Malik, Km 11, BP 5062, Rabat; tel. 37-75-51-99; fax 37-75-51-01; e-mail alacademia@iam.net.ma; f. 1980; 60 mems; promotes the devt of research and reflection in the principal fields of intellectual activity, publishes books on Moroccan and Islamic heritage; library of 17,000 vols; Permanent Sec. Dr ABDELLATIF BERBICH; publs *Academia* (1 a year), *Colloquiums* (2 a year), *Proceedings of Sessions* (2 a year).

UNESCO Office Rabat: BP 1777 RP, 10106 Rabat; 35 ave du 16 Novembre, Agdal, 10000 Rabat; tel. 37-67-03-72; fax 37-67-03-75; e-mail rabat@unesco.org; f. 1991; designated Cluster Office for Algeria, Libya, Mauritania, Morocco and Tunisia; Dir ROSAMARIA DURAND.

AGRICULTURE, FISHERIES AND VETERINARY SCIENCE

Société d'Horticulture et d'Acclimatation du Maroc: BP 13.854, 20001 Casablanca; f. 1914; 260 mems; Pres. JOSETTE DUPLAT; Sec. RENÉ TRIPOTIN.

ECONOMICS, LAW AND POLITICS

Société d'Etudes Economiques, Sociales et Statistiques du Maroc: BP 535, Chellah, 10002 Rabat; f. 1933; 20 mems; Dir NACER EL FASSI; publ. *Signes du Présent* (4 a year).

FINE AND PERFORMING ARTS

Association des Amateurs de la Musique Andalouse: c/o 133 blvd Ziraoui, 20000 Casablanca; f. 1956 to preserve and catalogue traditional Moroccan (Andalusian) music; maintains a School of Andalusian music at Casablanca, directed and subsidized by the Ministry of Culture; Dir Hadj DRISS BENJELLOUN.

HISTORY, GEOGRAPHY AND ARCHAEOLOGY

Association Nationale de Géographie Marocaine: Faculté des Lettres et des Sciences Humaines, Université Mohammed V Adgal, 10100 Rabat; tel. 37-77-18-93; fax 37-77-20-68; f. 1916; Sec.-Gen. TAOUFIK AGOUMI;

publ. *Revue de Géographie du Maroc* (2 a year).

LANGUAGE AND LITERATURE

Alliance Française: 22 ave de la Marche Verte, 24000 El Jadida; tel. 23-34-21-06; fax 23-35-31-82; e-mail afm.eljadida@iam.net .ma; internet www.ambafrance-ma.org/ institut/afm-eljadida; offers courses and examinations in French language and culture and promotes cultural exchange with France; attached teaching centre in Essaouira.

British Council: 36 rue de Tanger, BP 427 Rabat; tel. 37-21-81-30; fax 37-76-08-50; e-mail info@britishcouncil.org.ma; internet www.britishcouncil.org/morocco; teaching centre; offers courses and examinations in English language and British culture and promotes cultural exchange with the United Kingdom; attached teaching centre in Casablanca; library of 8,000 vols, 20 periodicals; Dir STEVE MCNULTY; Teaching Centre Man. IAN WINTER.

Goethe-Institut: 7 rue Sana'a, 10000 Rabat; tel. 537-70-65-44; fax 537-70-82-66 11, Place du 16 Novembre 20000 Casablanca; tel. 522-20-04-45; fax 522-48-37-32; e-mail progr@ rabat.goethe.org; internet www.goethe.de/ rabat; offers courses and examinations in German language and promotes cultural exchange; library of 20,000 vols; Dir WOLF-GANG MEISSNER.

Instituto Cervantes: 5 Zankat Madnine, 10000 Rabat; tel. 37-70-87-38; fax 37-70-02-79; e-mail cenrabat@cervantes.org.ma; internet rabat.cervantes.es; offers courses and examinations in Spanish language and culture and promotes cultural exchange with Spain and Spanish-speaking Latin and Central America; attached centres in Casablanca, Fez, Tangier and Tétouan; library; Dir XABIER MARKIEGI CANDINA.

Research Institutes

GENERAL

Centre National pour la Recherche Scientifique et Technique: 52 Charii Omar Ibn Khattab, BP 8027, 10102 Agdal-Rabat; tel. 37-77-28-03; fax 37-77-12-88; e-mail cnr@cnr.ac.ma; internet www.cnr.ac .ma; f. 1976; under Min. of Higher Education; research fields include food and agriculture, communication, environment, natural resources, astronomy, geophysics, biotechnology, geology, computer science, mathematics, social sciences, int. business, environmental science, energy and maintenance; library of 3,500 vols, 70 periodicals; Dir SAID BELCADI (acting); Sec.-Gen. (vacant); publ. *Lettre d'Information* (1 a year).

AGRICULTURE, FISHERIES AND VETERINARY SCIENCE

Institut National de la Recherche Agronomique: BP 6512 RI, Rabat; tel. 37-77-55-30; fax 37-77-40-03; internet www.inra.org .ma; f. 1930; research in agronomy; library of 40,000 vols, 300 periodicals; Dir A. ARIFI; publs *Al Awamia* (4 a year), *Les Cahiers de la Recherche Agronomique* (irregular).

Institut National de Recherche Halieutique: 2 rue de Tiznit, Casablanca; tel. 22-22-88-70; fax 22-26-88-57; f. 1947; applied fisheries oceanography, marine biology, evaluation of resources, aquaculture, environmental studies, fishing gear technology, fish processing technology, fisheries management; library of 1,050 vols, 70 periodicals; Dir MOHAMED SEDRATI; publs *Bulletin*, *Notes d'Information*, *Travaux et Documents*.

Mission Pédologique: Ministère de la Réforme Agraire, BP 432, Rabat; pedology; Dir J. L. GEOFFROY.

ECONOMICS, LAW AND POLITICS

Centre d'Etudes, de Documentation et d'Informations Economiques et Sociales (CEDIES–Informations): Angle ave des Forces Armées Royales et angle rue Mohamed Errachid, Casablanca 20100; tel. 22-25-26-96; fax 22-25-38-39; Pres. ABDERRA-HIM LAHJOUJI; publ. *CEDIES Informations*.

La Fondation du Roi Abdul Aziz pour les Etudes Islamiques et les Sciences Humaines: BP 12585, Casablanca 20052; located at: blvd de la Corniche, Ain Diab, Anfa, Casablanca 20050; tel. 22-39-10-27; fax 22-39-10-31; e-mail secretariat@fondation .org.ma; internet www.fondation.org.ma; f. 1985; to promote the study of social sciences and humanities in the Maghreb, by means of documentation and cultural activities; library of 310,000 vols, 1,289 periodicals; Dir PRINCE ABDULLAH IBN ABDUL AZIZ AL-SAOUD; publ. *Lettre d'Information* (2 a year).

HISTORY, GEOGRAPHY AND ARCHAEOLOGY

Comité National de Géographie du Maroc: Institut Universitaire de la Recherche Scientifique, BP 2122 Riad, Rabat; f. 1959; Pres. THE MINISTER OF EDUCATION; Sec.-Gen. A. LAOUINA; publ. *Atlas du Maroc*.

LANGUAGE AND LITERATURE

Instituto Muley El Hassan: PB 84, Tétouan; research on Hispano-Muslim works; library of 5,500 vols; Dirs MOHAMMED BEN TAUÍT, MARIANO ARRIBAS PALAU.

MEDICINE

Direction de l'Epidémiologie et de Lutte Contre les Maladies: 71 ave Ibn Sina, Agdal, Rabat; tel. 37-67-12-71; fax 37-67-12-98; e-mail delm@sante.gov.ma; internet www .sante.gov.ma/departements/delm/index-delm.htm; f. 1990; applied research in epidemiology and environmental health; Dir Dr NOUREDDINE CHAOUKI; publ. *Bulletin Epidémiologique* (3 a year).

Institut National d'Hygiène: POB 769, Rabat Agdal; tel. 37-77-19-02; fax 37-77-20-67; e-mail relaouad@sante.gov.ma; internet www.sante.gov.ma/inh; f. 1930; depts of microbiology, parasitology, physics and chemistry, toxicology, serology, immunology, molecular biology, genetics, entomology; Nat. Poison Control Centre; 266 mems; library: Toxicological Documentation Centre of 400 vols; library of 3,000 vols; Dir Prof. RAJAE EL AOUAD.

Institut Pasteur du Maroc: 1 pl. Louis Pasteur, Casablanca 20100; tel. 22-43-44-50; fax 22-26-09-57; e-mail pasteur@pasteur.ma; internet www.pasteur.ma; f. 1911; research into infectious diseases, bacteriology, parasitology and virology, biochemistry and genetics, food and environmental safety; promotion of public health; Dir Prof. MOHAM-MED HASSAR.

NATURAL SCIENCES

Physical Sciences

Direction de la Géologie: c/o Ministry of Energy and Mines, BP 6208, Rabat-Instituts; tel. 37-68-88-57; fax 37-68-88-63; e-mail dsi@ mem.gov.ma; f. 1921; Nat. Geological Survey; library of 25,000 vols; Pres ABDELHAQ SMIDI; publs *Mines, Géologie et Energie*, *Notes et Mémoires du Service Géologique du Maroc*.

TECHNOLOGY

Bureau de Recherches et de Participations Minières (BRPM): 5 Charia Moulay Hassan, BP 99, Rabat; tel. 37-76-30-35; fax 37-76-24-10; f. 1928; state agency to develop mining research and industry; Gen. Man. ASSOU LHA TOUTE.

Laboratoire Public d'Essais et d'Etudes: 25 rue d'Azilal, Casablanca; tel. 22-30-04-50; fax 22-30-15-50; f. 1947; hydraulics, environment, roads, study of soil, materials and methods of construction; library of 7,000 vols; Dir-Gen. MOHAMED JELLALI; publs *LPEE-Magazine* (4 a year), *Revue Marocaine de Génie Civil* (4 a year).

Libraries and Archives

Casablanca

Bibliothèque de la Communauté Urbaine de Casablanca: 142 ave des Forces Armées Royales, Casablanca; tel. 22-31-41-70; f. 1917; law, political economy, sciences, philosophy, history, literature, the arts, geography, medicine, sport, travel, fiction; 91,307 vols in Arab section, 267,149 vols in foreign section; 137 periodicals, several foreign daily newspapers; Dir HAJ MOHAMED BOUZID.

Fez

Bibliothèque de l'Université Quar-aouyine Fès: Place des Seffarines, Fez; 22,071 vols, 5,157 MSS, 38 archives.

Marrakesh

Bibliothèque Ben Youssef: ave 11 Janvier, Hay Mohamadi Daoudiat, Marrakesh; 21,223 vols, 586 periodicals, 1,840 MSS; Dir SEDDIK BELLARBI.

Rabat

Bibliothèque de l'Institut Scientifique: ave Ibn Battota, BP 703, Agdal, 10106 Rabat; tel. 37-77-45-48; fax 37-77-45-40; f. 1920; zoology, botany, geomorphology, cartography, ecology, earth sciences, geophysics, remote detection; 15,700 vols, 1,728 periodicals; Librarian ABDELLATIF BAYED; publs *Bulletin de l'Institute Scientifique*, *Travaux de l'Institut Scientifique*.

Bibliothèque Générale et Archives: BP 1003, ave Ibn Battouta, Rabat; tel. 37-77-18-90; fax 37-77-60-62; f. 1920; 600,000 vols, 31,000 MSS and 2,000 linear metres of archives; Dir AHMED TOUFIQ; publ. *Bibliographie Nationale* (2 a year).

Centre National de Documentation:; tel. 37-77-49-44; fax 37-77-31-34; internet www .abhatoo.net.ma; f. 1966; documentation on the economic, social, scientific and technical development of Morocco; library depository of World Bank publications; regional reps in Fès, Tangier, Casablanca, Agadir, Marrakesh, Meknès, Oujda; mem. of FID and IFLA; 9,000 vols, 120,000 microfiches, 350 periodicals; Dir ADNANE BENCHAKROUN; publ. *KATAB* (bibliography).

Tangier

Biblioteca Juan Goytisolo: 99 ave Sidi Mohamed Ben Abdellah, 90000 Tangier; tel. 39-93-23-99; fax 39-94-76-03; e-mail bibtan@ cervantes.es; internet tanger.cervantes.es/ es/ biblioteca_espanol/biblioteca_espanol.htm; f. 1941; attached to Instituto Cervantes; main collection in the Spanish language; antique Spanish publications from 18th and 19th centuries; periodical library includes Spanish, Arab and African titles; Spanish sheet music from early 20th century; photographic archive from former Spanish tourist office in Tangier; 90,000 vols; Librarian SÍLVIA MON-

TERO GÓMEZ; publ. *Miscelanea de la Biblioteca Española*.

Tétouan

Bibliothèque Générale et Archives: 32 ave Mohammed V, BP 692, Tétouan; tel. 39-96-32-58; fax 39-96-10-04; e-mail bgatetou@imam.net.ma; internet www.minculture.gov.ma; f. 1939; research and public library; 50,000 books, 3,500 periodicals, 2,400 MSS, 23,000 historical archive items, 1,200,000 admin. archive items, 45,000 photographs, 1,429 numismatic items; Dir Dr M. ZOUAK.

Museums and Art Galleries

Chefchaouen

Musée Ethnographique de Chefchaouen: Kasbah Outa Hammam, Chefchaouen; tel. 39-98-67-61; f. 1985; musical instruments, arms, embroidery, carved boxes, local pottery.

Essaouira

Musée Sidi Mohamed ben Abdellah: Derb Laalouj, Essaouira; tel. 24-47-23-00; f. 1981; musical instruments, jewellery, arms, carved wooden objects.

Fez

Musée d'Armes du Borj-Nord: Borj-Nord, Fez; tel. 35-64-52-41; built as a military fort in the 16th century, converted into a museum in 1963; collection of 1,100 military artefacts; Curator MOHAMED ZAIM.

Musée Batha: Ksar el Batha, Fez; tel. 35-63-41-16; built as a royal residence in 19th century; converted into a museum in 1915; colln incl. sculpted wood and plaster objects, cast iron, local blue ceramics, embroidery, coins, carpets, jewellery, astrological instruments; Curator HNIA CHIKHAOUI.

Larache

Musée Archéologique: Larache; tel. 39-51-20-92; f. 1973; remains found primarily at the Lixus archaeological site, from the Phoenician, Carthaginian, Mauritanian, Roman and Islamic ages.

Marrakesh

Musée Dar Si Saïd: Derb el Bahia, Riad El Zaitoun El Jadid, Marrakesh; tel. 24-44-24-64; internet www.minculture.gov.ma/fr/musee%20dar%20si%20said.htm; f. as a royal residence in 19th century, converted into a museum in 1932; artefacts from the Marrakesh region and southern Morocco, incl. wooden objects, jewellery, pottery and ceramics, arms, carpets and woven materials; archaeological remains; Dir HASSAN BEL ARBI.

Meknès

Musée Dar El Jamaï: Pl. El Hedime, Meknès; tel. 35-53-08-63; f. 1920; handicraft items from the region, incl. embroidery, wood carvings, leatherwork, carved chests, carpets, ceramics, ancient jewellery, wrought ironwork, copper and brass objects, painted woodwork, traditional costumes and ancient Korans; Chief Curator HASSAN CHERRADI.

Moulay Driss Zerhoun

Site Archéologique de Volubilis: Conservation du Site de Volubilis, Moulay Driss Zerhoun, Meknès; tel. and fax 35-54-41-03; e-mail volubilisarcheosite@yahoo.fr; f. 1950; archaeological site; library of 250 vols; Archaeologist YOUSSEF BOKBOT.

Rabat

Musée Archéologique: 23 rue Al-Brihi, Rabat; tel. 37-70-19-19; fax 37-75-08-84; f. 1931; history of Morocco from prehistory until the Islamic era; collns incl. stone tools, primitive furniture, Roman divinities, bronze and marble statues, early Islamic ceramics; Curator ABDELWAHED BEN-NCER.

Musée Ethnographique des Oudaïa: Kasba des Oudaïa, Rabat; tel. 37-72-64-61; f. 1915; clothing from various regions of Morocco, jewellery, astronomical tools, carpets, pottery, musical instruments; Curator HOUCEINE EL KASRI.

Musée de la Kasbah: 23 rue el Brihi, Rabat; archaeology and folklore; Curator MOHAMMED HABIBI.

Safi

Musée National de la Céramique: Kachla, Safi; tel. 24-46-38-95; f. 1990; originally a military fort; Curator NOUREDDINE ESSAFSAFI.

Tangier

Musée d'Art Contemporain: 52 ave d'Angleterre, Tangier; tel. 39-94-99-72; f. 1990; constructed as British consulate; modern Moroccan art.

Tangier American Legation Museum: 8 Zankat America, Tangier; tel. 39-93-59-60; e-mail legation@maroc.net; internet www.maroc.net/legation; f. 1976; operated by the Tangier American Legation Museum Soc., Inc.; permanent colln paintings since 16th century, etchings, aquatints, prints and maps of Morocco; also documentation and artefacts concerning Moroccan-American relations; sponsors short-term exhibitions of contemporary artists; library: research library of 4,500 vols on North Africa and Morocco in English, French, Spanish, Arabic and Portuguese; Dir THOR H. KUNIHOLM.

Tétouan

Musée Archéologique: 2 rue Ben Hussain, Tétouan; tel. 39-96-73-03; f. 1939; prehistoric and pre-Islamic archaeological remains from northern Morocco; mosaics and coins.

Musée des Arts Traditionnels: Tétouan; Curator AMRANI AHMED.

Musée Ethnographique: BP 41 Tétouan; Zankat Skala, 65 Bab El Okla, 93000 Tétouan; tel. 39-97-05-05; f. 1928; originally a fortress; carved wooden objects, copperware, pottery, embroidery.

Universities

UNIVERSITÉ ABDELMALEK ESSAÂDI TÉTOUAN

BP 211, Route de l'Aéroport, Tétouan
Telephone: 39-99-51-34
Fax: 39-97-91-51
Internet: www.uae.ac.ma
Founded 1989
State control
Languages of instruction: Arabic, French
Rector: MUSTAPHA BENNOUNA
Number of teachers: 632
Number of students: 17,150
Publication: *Tourjouman* (Journal of the School of Translation)
Campus in Tangier; Faculties of arts and humanities, economics and social sciences, law, science and technology; schools of commerce and management and translation.

UNIVERSITÉ AL AKHAWAYN IFRANE

BP 104, ave Hassan II, 53000 Ifrane
Telephone: 35-86-20-00
Fax: 35-56-71-50
E-mail: devcom@alakhawayn.ma
Internet: www.alakhawayn.ma
Founded 1995
Private control
Language of instruction: English
Academic year: September to July
President: Prof. RACHID BENMOKHTAR BENABDELLAH
Vice-President for Academic Affairs: Prof. ABDELLATIF BENCHERIFA
Vice-President for Finance and Administration: ABDELILAH KAMAL
Executive Director for Development and Communication: RACHID SLIMI
Dean of Student Affairs: Dr CHARIF BELFEKIH
Library of 65,000 books, 400 periodicals
Number of teachers: 90
Number of students: 1,012 (899 undergraduate, 113 postgraduate)

DEANS

School of Business Administration: Dr AHMED DRIOUCHI
School of Humanities and Social Sciences: Dr MOHAMED DAHBI (acting)
School of Science and Engineering: Dr AMINE BENSAID

DIRECTORS

Center for Academic Development and Study Skills: CATHERINE OWENS
Center of Environmental Issues and Regional Development: Dr BACHIR RAISSOUNI
Executive Education Center: NADIA SANDI
Hillary Rodham Clinton Women's Empowerment Center: LEÏLA BOUASRIA
Institute of Economic Analysis and Prospective Studies: RACHID SLIMI
Language Center: MONCEF LAHLOU

UNIVERSITÉ CADI AYYAD MARRAKECH

Blvd Prince Moulay Abdellah, POB 511, Marrakesh
Telephone: (524) 43-48-13
Fax: (524) 43-44-94
E-mail: presidence@ucam.ac.ma
Internet: www.ucam.ac.ma
Founded 1978
State control
Languages of instruction: Arabic, French, English
Academic year: September to July
Rector: Prof. MOHAMED MARZAK
Sec.-Gen.: RACHID HILAL
Number of teachers: 1,868
Number of students: 33,359
Publications: *Revue de la Faculté de Droit, Revue de la Faculté des Lettres, Revue de la Faculté des Sciences, Manarat Al Jamiaa*

DEANS

Faculty of Law, Economics and Social Sciences: MRANI ZANTAR M'HAMMED
Faculty of Letters and Humanities: HANOUCH ABDELJALIL
Faculty of Medicine and Pharmacy: ALAOUI YAZIDI
Faculty of Sciences (Semlalia): Prof. LOUIDIKI AHMED
Faculty of Science and Technics: ABBOUSSALAH MOHAMED
Higher School of Technology (Essaouira): EL FROM YOUSSEF
Higher School of Technology (Safi): MOHAMED EL ARBI EL ACHHAB

National School of Applied Sciences: ABDEL-LAH AIT OUHMAN

National School of Applied Sciences (Safi): AHMED DERJA

National School of Business and Administration: LAKHDAR BACHIR SIF EL ISLAM

Poly-disciplinary Faculty: EL MOSTAFA HADDIYA

University Centre (Kalaat Sraghna): HAMMADI BOUSLOUSS

UNIVERSITÉ CHOUAÏB DOUKKALI EL JADIDA

BP 299, 2 bis, ave Mohamed ben Larbi Alaoui, Koudiate ben Driss, 24000 El Jadida

Telephone: 23-34-44-47
Fax: 23-34-44-49
Internet: www.ucd.ac.ma

Founded 1989
State control
Languages of instruction: Arabic, French, English

Rector: ABDELHAMID AHMADY

Library of 14,460 vols
Number of teachers: 440
Number of students: 8,100

Publications: *Magazine de la Faculté des Lettres Parallèles*, *Revue de la Faculté des Lettres*

Faculties of arts and humanities, science.

UNIVERSITÉ HASSAN I SETTAT

BP 539, 50 rue Ibn Al Haithem, 26000 Settat

Telephone: 23-72-12-75
Fax: 23-72-12-74
Internet: www.uh1.ac.ma
State control

Rector: MOHAMED RAHJ

Number of teachers: 204
Number of students: 6,679

Faculties of economics and social sciences, law, science and technology; School of commerce and management.

UNIVERSITÉ HASSAN II — CASABLANCA

BP 9167, 19 rue Tarik Bnou Ziad, Mers Sultan, Casablanca

Telephone: 522-43-30-30
Fax: 522-27-61-50
Internet: www.uh2c.ac.ma

Founded 1975
Languages of instruction: Arabic, French
Academic year: September to July

Pres.: MOHAMMED BARKAOUI
Vice-Pres. for Academic Affairs: IDRISS MANSOURI
Vice-Pres.for Research and Cooperation: JAAFAR KHALID NACIRI
Sec-Gen.: ABDELHADI MOSLIH
Librarian: (vacant)

Number of teachers: 1,027
Number of students: 26,000

Publication: faculty reviews, newsletter

DEANS

Faculty of Arts And Human Sciences: SAID BENNANI
Faculty of Dentistry: AMAL OUAZZANI ECH-CHAHDI
Faculty of Law: ESSALMI IDRISSI
Faculty of Medicine And Pharmacy: LHOUS-SAINE LOUARDI
Faculty of Sciences: OUZZANI
National Higher School of Electronics And Mechanics: JANAH SAADI (Dir)
Teacher's Training College: OUBAHAMMO (Dir)

Technology High School: SARSOURI (Dir)

UNIVERSITÉ HASSAN II MOHAMMEDIA

BP 150, 279 Cité Yassmina, Mohammedia

Telephone: 23-31-46-35
Fax: 23-31-46-34
Internet: www.uh2m.ac.ma

Founded 1992
State control

Rector: RAHMA BOURQIA

DEANS

Faculty of Arts and Humanities, Ben Msik Campus: ABDELHAK HAMAM
Faculty of Arts and Humanities, Mohammedia Campus: ABDELJAWAD SEKKAT
Faculty of Economics, Law and Social Science, Mohammedia Campus: MOHAMED DASSER
Faculty of Science, Ben Msik Campus: MOHAMMED BERRADA
Faculty of Science and Technology, Mohammedia Campus: MOHAMED RAFIQ

UNIVERSITÉ IBN TOFAIL KÉNITRA

BP 242, 104 rue Ahmed Boughaba, Bir rami Est, 14000 Kénitra

Telephone: 37-32-28-09
Fax: 37-37-40-52
E-mail: ruitk@iam.net.ma
Internet: www.univ-ibntofail.ac.ma

Founded 1989
State control

Pres.: MOHAMMED ESSOUARI
Sec.-Gen.: ABDALLAH EL MALIKI

Library of 42,007 vols
Number of teachers: 405
Number of students: 11,884

DEANS

Faculty of Arts and Humanities: ABDELFETTAH BENKADDOUR
Faculty of Science: ALI BOUKHARI

UNIVERSITÉ IBNOU ZOHR AGADIR

BP 3215, Agadir
Founded 1989
Rector: MUSTAPHA DKHISSI
Number of students: 9,724
Faculties of letters and humanities, sciences.

UNIVERSITÉ MOHAMMED I OUJDA

BP 524, 60000 Oujda

Telephone: 36-74-47-83
Fax: 36-74-47-79
Internet: www.univ-oujda.ac.ma

Founded 1978
State control
Languages of instruction: Arabic, French
Academic year: October to June

Rector: EL-MADANI BELKHADIR
Secretary-General: ABDERRAHMAN HOUTECH
Librarian: ZOUBIDA CHAHI

Number of teachers: 593
Number of students: 19,872

Publications: *Al Mayadine*, *Cahiers du CEMM*, *Revue de la Faculté des Lettres*

DEANS

Faculty of Law and Economics: EL-LARBI M'RABET
Faculty of Letters and Human Sciences: MOHAMMED LAAMIRI
Faculty of Science: BENAÏSSA N'CIRI
Institute of Technology: MOHAMMED BARBOU-CHA (Dir)

UNIVERSITÉ MOHAMMED V AGDAL

BP 554, 3 rue Michlifen, Agdal, Rabat

Telephone: 37-67-13-18
Fax: 37-67-14-01
E-mail: presidence@um5a.ac.ma
Internet: www.um5a.ac.ma

Founded 1957
State control
Languages of instruction: Arabic, French
Academic year: September to July

Pres.: HAFID BOUTALEB JOUTEI
Sec.-Gen.: MOHAMAD HOUMINE
Librarian: MOHAMED NKHAILI

Number of teachers: 992
Number of students: 19,498

Publications: *Annales du Centre des Études Stratégiques*, *Bulletin de l'Institut Scientifique*, *Bulletin Magnétique*, *Bulletin Séismologique*, *Documents de l'Institut Scientifique*, *Hespéris Tamuda* (1 a year, in French, Spanish and English), *Langues et Littératures* (1 a year, in European languages), *Revue de la Faculté des Lettres et des Sciences Humaines* (1 a year, in Arabic), *Revue Marocaine de l'Automatique, de l'Informatique et du Traitement du Signal*, *Revue Marocaine Juridique, Politique et Economique*, *Revue des Sciences de la Terre*, *Travaux de l'Institut Scientific*

DEANS

Faculty of Law and Economics: LAHCEN OULHAJ
Faculty of Letters and Human Sciences: ABDERRAHIM BENHADDA
Faculty of Sciences: WAIL BENJELLOUN
Higher School of Technology (Salé): MOHAMMED RHACHI
Mohammadia School of Engineering: DRISS BOUAMI
Institute of Hispano-Lusophone Studies: FATIHA BENLABAH

UNIVERSITÉ MOHAMMED V SOUISSI RABAT

BP 8007, N.U. Agdal, Rabat
ave Med Benabdellah Regragui, Madinat al-Irfane, Rabat

Telephone: 37-68-11-60
Fax: 37-68-11-63
E-mail: presidence@um5s.ac.ma
Internet: www.um5s.ac.ma

Founded 1993
Academic year: September to July

President: TAIEB CHKILI
Secretary-General: ABDURRAHMANE RIDA

Number of teachers: 2,000
Number of students: 22,000

Publications: *Al Irfane* (information bulletin, 12 a year), *Reflexions* (science, 4 a year)

DEANS

Faculty of Dentistry: BOUCHAÏB JIDAL
Faculty of Education: MOHAMMED ZGOR
Faculty of Law: ABDERRAZAK TLY RACHID
Faculty of Law, Salé: MOHAMED BENALLAL
Faculty of Medicine and Pharmacy: ABDELM-JID BELMAHI
National Higher School of Informatics and Systems Analysis: ABDELFADIL BENNANI (Dir)

UNIVERSITÉ MOULAY ISMAIL MEKNÈS

BP 298, Marjane I, Meknès

Telephone: (5) 35-46-73-06
Fax: (5) 35-46-73-05

Founded 1982; univ. status 1989
State control

Pres.: MOHAMMED ZAHIR BEN ABDELLAH
Number of teachers: 722
Number of students: 25,137
Publications: *Maksanat* (Journal of the Faculty of Arts and Human Sciences), *Minbar Al Mamiaa* (1 a year), *Zetouna* (Journal of the Faculty of Law, Economics and Social Studies)

DEANS

Faculty of Arts and Human Sciences: ABDELLAH MALKI
Faculty of Law, Economics and Social Studies: MOHAMED BENJELOUN
Faculty of Sciences: MOHAMED KEROUAD
Faculty of Sciences and Technology: ABDELLAH EL MANSSOUR
Polydisciplinary Faculty: MOHAMMED EDDOUKSSE

UNIVERSITÉ QUARAOUYINE FÈS

Dhar Mahraz, BP 2509, Fez
Telephone: 35-64-10-06
Fax: 35-64-10-13
Founded AD 859, enlarged in 11th century, reorganized 1963
State control
Language of instruction: Arabic
Academic year: September to July
Rector: Prof. ABDELOUAHHAB TAZI SAOUD
Secretary-General: MOHAMMED BENNANI ZOUBIR
Number of teachers: 115
Number of students: 6,000.

CONSTITUENT INSTITUTES

Faculty of Arabic Studies: ave Allal Al-Fassi, BP 1483, Marrakesh; Dean Prof. HASSAN JELLAB.
Faculty of Sharia: BP 52, Agadir; Dean Prof. MOHAMMED ATTAHIRI.
Faculty of Sharia (Law): BP 60, Saïs, Fez; Dean Prof. MOHAMMED YESSEF.
Faculty of Theology: blvd Abdelkhalek Torres, BP 95, Tétouan; Dean Prof. DRISS KHALIFA.

UNIVERSITÉ SIDI MOHAMED BEN ABDELLAH FÈS

BP 2626, ave des Almohades, Fez
Telephone: 35-62-55-85
Fax: 35-62-24-01
Founded 1975
State control
Languages of instruction: Arabic, French
Academic year: September to July
Pres.: TAOUFIK OUAZZANI CHAHDI
Vice-Pres. for Academic Affairs: HASSAN CHERGUI
Vice-Pres. for Research and Cooperation: RACHID BENSLIMANE
Sec.-Gen.: AZIZ CHAD
Library of 225,000 vols
Number of teachers: 1,010
Number of students: 35,088

DEANS

Faculty of Law, Economics and Social Sciences: SERGHINI EL FARISSI
Faculty of Letters and Human Sciences (Dhar Mehraz): ABDERRAHMAN TENKOUL
Faculty of Letters and Human Sciences (Saiss): IBRAHIM AKDIM

Faculty of Science (Dhar Mehraz): AHMED IRAQUI
Faculty of Science and Technology (Saiss): MOHCINE ZOUAK
High School of Technology: ABDELLATI SAFOUANE (Dir)

Colleges

Conservatoire de Casablanca: Complexe Culturel Benmsik, Casablanca; tel. 22-37-21-89; 120 students; Dir MOHAMED LACHHAB.
Conservatoire de Fès: rue Mustapha Lamaani, Dar Adaîl, Fez; tel. 35-62-39-93; f. 1960; 366 students; Dir MOHAMED BRIOUEL.
Conservatoire de Marrakech: Arçat al Hamed Bab Doukkala, 40000 Marrakech; tel. 24-38-70-66; f. 1948; teaches Western classical and modern music and classical Moroccan and Arab music; 320 students; Dir MOHAMED MAHASSIN.
Conservatoire National de Musique et de Danse, Rabat: 33 rue Tensift-Agdal, Rabat; tel. 37-77-37-94; trains students in Western and Arabic music and classical dance; the Conservatoire has an orchestra for modern Arab music, an orchestra for Andalusian and Moroccan music, two youth orchestras and a big-band orchestra; 1,685 students; Dir MOHAMMED EL BAHJA.
Ecole Hassania des Travaux Publics: km 7, route d'El Jadida, BP 8108, Oasis, Casablanca; tel. 22-23-07-06; fax 22-23-07-17; e-mail ehtpdg@menara.ma; internet www.ehtp.ac.ma; f. 1971; civil engineering, industrial engineering and telecommunication systems, meteorology, sciences of geographical information, computer engineering; MBA, Masters programmes, specialized courses, seminaries; 7 research and study centres; library: 15,000 vols; 73 full-time teachers, 180 visiting teachers; 480 students; Dir ABDESLAM MESSOUDI.
Ecole des Métiers d'Art (School of Native Arts and Crafts): Bab Okla, BP 89, Tétouan; f. 1921; textiles, carpets, rugs, ceramics, engraving, plaster inlays, woodwork, precious metal work, leather and Arabic woodcarving; 350 mems; Dir ABDELLAH FEKHAR.
Ecole Nationale d'Administration: BP 165, 2 ave de la Victoire, Rabat; tel. 37-73-14-50; fax 37-73-09-29; f. 1948; library: 18,000 vols; 36 teachers; 646 students; Dir AMINE MZOURI; publ. *Administration et Société* (3 a year).
Ecole Nationale d'Architecture: BP 6372, Chariaa Allal El Fassi, Rabat; tel. 37-77-52-29; fax 37-77-52-76; e-mail e.n.a@smartnet.net.ma; f. 1980 under the Ministry of Territorial Administration, Water Resources and the Environment; courses in architecture, regional town planning and housing; 60 teachers; 400 students; Dir ABDERRAHMANE CHORFI.
Ecole Nationale des Beaux-Arts: ave Mohamed V, Cité Scolaire BP 89, Tétouan; f. 1946; drawing, painting, sculpture, decorative arts; Dir MOHAMMED M. SERGHINI.
Ecole Nationale Forestière d'Ingénieurs: BP 511, Salé; tel. 37-78-97-04; fax 37-78-71-49; f. 1968; library: 5,000 vols; 20 teachers; 160 students; Dir MY Y. ALAOUI.

Ecole Nationale de l'Industrie Minérale: rue Hadj Ahmed Cherkaoui, BP 753, Agdal, Rabat; tel. 37-68-02-28; fax 37-77-10-55; e-mail info@enim.ac.ma; internet www.enim.ac.ma; f. 1972; specializes in geology, material sciences, mining sciences, chemical process engineering, electro-mechanical engineering, energy sciences, computer science, industrial maintenance, production systems, energy systems; library: 11,000 vols; 86 teachers; 420 students; Dir OMAR DEBBAJ; publ. *Liaison Bulletin* (12 a year).
Ecole des Sciences de l'Information: BP 6204, Rabat-Instituts; tel. 37-77-49-04; fax 37-77-02-32; e-mail esi@esi.ac.ma; internet www.esi.ac.ma; f. 1974; 4-year undergraduate courses and 2-year postgraduate courses for archivists, librarians, documentalists; language of instruction: English; library: 18,000 vols, 50 current periodicals, 415 audiovisual documents; also UNESCO publications, research papers, courses, syllabuses, etc.; 64 teachers; 512 students; Dir MOHAMED BENJELLOUN.
Ecole Supérieure de l'Agro-Alimentaire (Higher School of Food Science): 22 rue Catelet, Belvedère, Casablanca; tel. 22-24-54-05; fax 22-24-53-99; e-mail supagro@casanet.net.ma; f. 1997; 90 teachers; 70 students; Dir ABDELRHAFOUR TANTAOUI ELARAKI.
Institut Agronomique et Vétérinaire Hassan II: BP 6202, Madinat El-Irfane-Instituts, Rabat; tel. 37-77-17-58; fax 37-77-81-35; e-mail dg@iav.ac.ma; internet www.iav.ac.ma; f. 1966; library: 45,000 documents, 1,200 periodicals; 327 teachers; 1,606 students; Dir Prof. FOUAD GUESSOUS; Sec.-Gen. Prof. MOSTAFA AGBANI; publs *Actes de l'Institut Agronomique et Vétérinaire Hassan II* (in French and English, 4 a year), *AgroVet Magazine* (in French, 4 a year), *IAVinfo* (6 a year).
Institut National des Sciences de l'Archéologie et du Patrimoine: ave Kennedy, route des Zaers, 10000 Rabat-Souissi; tel. 37-75-09-61; fax 37-75-08-84; e-mail archeo@iam.net.ma; f. 1986; departments of anthropology, archaeology and cultural heritage, heritage studies, Islamic studies and archaeology and prehistory; 60 teachers; 50 students; Dir JOUDIA HASSAR-BENSLIMANE; publ. *Bulletin d'Archéologie Marocaine* (1 a year).
Institut National de Statistique et d'Economie Appliquée: BP 6217, Rabat; tel. 37-77-09-15; fax 37-77-94-57; f. 1961; library: 15,000 vols; 398 students; Dir ABDELAZIZ EL GHAZALI; publ. *Revue* (1 a year).
Institut Supérieur d'Art Dramatique et d'Animation Culturelle: Charia Al Mansour Eddahbi, BP 1355, Rabat; tel. 37-72-17-02; fax 37-70-34-23; internet www.minculture.gov.ma/fr/isadac.htm; f. 1985; provides practical and academic training in all areas of the dramatic arts; Dir AHMED MASSAIA.
Instituto Español de Enseñanza Secundaria 'Severo Ochoa' (Spanish Institute in Tangier): Plaza El Koweit 1, Tangier; tel. 39-93-63-38; fax 39-93-60-22; e-mail luisbadosa@hotmail.com; internet arce.cnice.mecd.es/instituto.severo.ochoa; f. 1949; Dir LUIS BADOSA ORTUÑO; library: 8,000 vols; 38 teachers; 360 students; publs *Revista Babel* (several languages, 1 a year), *Revista Kasbah* (Spanish, 1 a year).

MOZAMBIQUE

The Higher Education System

From the 19th century until independence in 1975 Mozambique was a Portuguese colony. The oldest current institutions of higher education were founded during the period of Portuguese rule, most prominently the state-run Universidade Eduardo Mondlane (founded 1962; current name 1976). The other leading state institution is the Universidade Pedagógica (founded 1986); a third public university, the Universidade Lúrio, was founded in 2007. The main private institutions include the Catholic University and Higher Polytechnic Institute. The Ministry of Education and Culture is the agency responsible for state provision of higher education, which is publicly funded.

Students must be awarded the Certificado de Habilitações Literarias upon completion of secondary education and sit an entrance examination in order to be admitted to higher education. Currently, only undergraduate degrees are available. The Bacharelato is awarded after the first cycle of higher education, which lasts three years and is available in most subject areas. Depending on 'good' or 'very good' grades, students may be admitted to a Licenciatura programme of study, which lasts two years following the Bacharelato. Students of architecture, medicine and veterinary medicine study for the Licenciatura. Since 1976, students have been required to spend as many years in state employment (usually teaching) as the length of the course, their degree being awarded once their public service has been completed.

Technical and vocational education is offered by technical schools and institutes controlled by the Secretary of State for Technical and Professional Education. In 2005 there were 41 technical institutes with 21,752 students. In 2002 there were 18 teacher training institutes with 9,314 students. Completion of medium-level technical and vocational education results in award of either the Engenheiro Técnico (technician engineer) or Técnico Medio (middle level technician).

Regulatory Body

GOVERNMENT

Ministry of Education and Culture: Av. 24 de Julho 167, CP 34, Maputo; tel. 21492006; fax 21492196; internet www.mec.gov.mz; Minister AIRES BONIFÁCIO ALI.

Learned Societies

GENERAL

UNESCO Office Maputo: CP 1397, Maputo; Av. Frederick Engels 515, Maputo; tel. 21494450; fax 21493431; e-mail maputo@unesco.org; Dir BENOÎT SOUSSOU.

LANGUAGE AND LITERATURE

British Council: Rua John Issa 226, POB 4178, Maputo; tel. 21226776; fax 21421577; e-mail general.enquiries@britishcouncil.org.mz; internet www.britishcouncil.org/mozambique; offers courses and exams in English language and British culture and promotes cultural exchange with the UK; Dir SIMON INGRAM-HILL.

Research Institutes

AGRICULTURE, FISHERIES AND VETERINARY SCIENCE

Instituto de Algodão de Moçambique (Mozambique Institute for Cotton): Av. Eduardo Mondlane 2221 (1° andar), CP 806, Maputo; tel. 21431015; fax 21430679; e-mail iampab@zebra.uem.mz; f. 1991; depts of analysis and classing fibre, finance and administration, supporting the cotton associative sector, studies and projects; library of 2,500 vols, 260 journals and reviews; Dir NORBERTO MAHALAMBE; Deputy Dir GABRIEL PAPOSSECO; publs *Relatório Anual de Actividades* (1 a year), *Relatório Trimestral* (4 a year).

Instituto Nacional de Investigação Agronómica: CP 3658, Maputo 4; tel. 21460190; fax 21460074; f. 1965; Dir Dr CALISTO BIAS; publ. *Comunicacões / INIA*.

MEDICINE

Instituto Nacional de Saúde (National Health Institute): Av. Eduardo Mondlane 296, CP 264, Maputo; fax 21423726; f. 1980; study, research and training in ecology, epidemiology, immunology, malaria, microbiology, parasitology, trypanosomiasis; traditional medicine; documentation and information depts; 32 staff; library of 6,500 vols; Dir Dr RUI GAMA VAZ; publ. *Revista Médica de Moçambique*.

NATURAL SCIENCES

Physical Sciences

Direcção Nacional de Geologia: CP 217, Maputo; tel. 21427121; fax 21420796; e-mail geologia@zebra.uem.mz; f. 1928; regional geology, geological mapping and mineral exploration; library of 30,000 vols, maps, technical material, etc; Dir ELIAS XAVIER DAUDI; publs *Bibliografia Geológico-Mineira de Moçambique* (1 a year), *Boletim Geológico de Moçambique* (1 a year), *Boletim Informativo da DNG* (1 a year), *Notícias Explicativas da Geológico de Moçambique* (irregular), *Relatório Anual* (1 a year).

Instituto Nacional de Meteorologia: CP 256, Maputo; tel. and fax (21) 491150; e-mail mozmet@inam.gov.mz; internet www.inam.gov.mz; f. 1907; library of 750 vols; Nat. Dir MOISES VICENTE BENESSENE; publs *Anuário de Observações* (in 2 vols: I *Observações Meteorológicas de Superfície*, II *Observações Meteorológicas de Altitude*), *Boletim Meteorológico para a Agricultura* (every 10 days), *Informações de Carácter Astronómico* (1 a year).

Libraries and Archives

Maputo

Arquivo Histórico de Moçambique: Av. Filipe Samuel Magaia 717, CP 2033, Maputo; tel. (1) 431296; fax (1) 423428; e-mail rafaluga@hotmail.com; internet www.ahm.uem.mz; f. 1934; attached to Universidade Eduardo Mondlane; 25,000 vols, 11,600 periodicals; spec. collns: written reports of admin. or governmental offices and business; cartography; iconography; oral history; Dir Prof. Dr JOEL DAS NEVES TEMBE; publs *Arquivo, Documentos* (series), *Estudos* (series), *Instrumentos de Pesquisa* (series).

Biblioteca Nacional de Moçambique (National Library of Mozambique): Av. 25 de Setembro 1384, CP 141, Maputo; tel. 21425676; f. 1961; 110,000 vols; Dir ANTÓNIO M. B. COSTA E SILVA.

Centro Nacional de Documentação e Informação de Moçambique: CP 4116, Maputo; tel. and fax 21311246; e-mail cedimo@cedimo.gov.mz; internet www.cedimo.gov.mz; f. 1977; part of Council of Ministers Secretariat; 12,000 vols; Dir ARLANZA EDUARDO SABINO DIAS; publ. *Documento Informativo*.

Direcção Nacional de Geologia, Centro de Documentação: CP 217, Maputo; tel. 21420797; fax 21429216; e-mail geologia@zebra.uem.mz; f. 1928; documentation centre for geology and mineral exploration; 10 spec. collns; Dir ELIAS XAVIER DAUDI; publs *Bibliografia Geológico-Mineira* (1 a year), *Boletim Geológico* (1 a year), *Bolentim Informativo* (4 a year), *Notícias Explicativas da Geologia de Moçambique* (irregular), *Relatório Anual da DNG* (1 a year).

Museum

Maputo

Museu de História Natural: Praça da Travessia do Zambeze, CP 1780, Maputo; tel. 21491145; fax 21490879; e-mail mnhi@zebra.uem.mz; internet www.museu.org.mz; f. 1911; natural history museum and ethnographic gallery; attached to Universidade Eduardo Mondlane; Dir AUGUSTO J. PEREIRA CABRAL.

Universities

UNIVERSIDADE EDUARDO MONDLANE

CP 257, Maputo
Telephone: 21427851

Fax: 21326426
Internet: www.uem.mz
Founded 1962
State control
Language of instruction: Portuguese
Academic year: February to December

Rector: Prof. Dr BRAZÃO MAZULA
Vice-Rector for Academic Affairs: (vacant)
Vice-Rector for Admin. and Resources: (vacant)
Dir of Documentation Services: POLICARPO MATIQUITE

Number of teachers: 1,069
Number of students: 9,712

DEANS

Faculty of Agriculture: Prof. Dr ANDRADE F. EGAS
Faculty of Architecture: Prof. JOSÉ FORJAZ
Faculty of Arts and Social Science: Prof. Dr ARMINDO NGUNGA
Faculty of Economics: Dr FERNANDO LICHUCHA (acting)

Faculty of Education: Prof. Dr MOUZINHO MÁRIO (acting)
Faculty of Engineering: Prof. Dr GABRIEL AMOS
Faculty of Law: Dr TAÍBO MUCOBORA (acting)
Faculty of Medicine: Prof. Dr EMILIA NOORMAHOMED
Faculty of Veterinary Science: Dr LUÍS NEVES
Faculty of Science: Dr FRANCISCO VIEIRA

UNIVERSIDADE LÚRIO

Av. Eduardo Mondlane 39, CP 364, Nampula
Internet: www.unilurio.ac.mz
Founded 2007
State control
Language of instruction: Portuguese
Library of 2,500 vols, 273 periodical titles
Number of students: 600

Faculty of health sciences - Nampula: courses in dentistry, pharmacology and medicine, nutrition and optometry; Faculty of engineering and natural sciences - Pemba

(Cabo Delgado); Faculty of agrarian sciences - Lichinga (Niassa); Faculty of architecture

Rector: Prof. Dr JORGE FERRÃO.

UNIVERSIDADE PEDAGÓGICA

Com. Augusto Cardoso 135, Maputo
Telephone: 21420860
Fax: 21422113
E-mail: grupsede@zebra.uem.mz
Founded 1986
State control
Language of instruction: Portuguese
Academic year: August to June

Rector: CARLOS MACHILI

Number of teachers: 215
Number of students: 1,400

Faculties of languages, natural sciences and mathematics, pedagogy, physical education and sports and social sciences.

MYANMAR

The Higher Education System

In the 19th century Burma (now Myanmar) was annexed to British India and remained under British rule until independence was achieved in 1948 (with a period under Japanese occupation in 1942–45). The oldest current institutions of higher education date from the 1920s, among them University of Yangon (founded 1920), University of Forestry (founded 1923), Yangon Technological University and Yezin Agricultural University (both founded 1924). The Ministry of Education has overall responsibility for higher education, with the exception of specialized institutions attached to other ministries. In 2001/02 there were an estimated 587,300 students at 958 institutions of tertiary education.

Admission to higher education is on the basis of results in the secondary school Matriculation and, in some instances, an entrance examination. Bachelors degrees are classified as either 'Pass' or 'Honours' depending on the length of study: four years for Bachelors (Pass) and five years for Bachelors (Honours). Bachelors degrees in professional fields of study (engineering, forestry, medicine) take upwards of six years. Postgraduate degrees include the ordinary Masters and Masters of Research.

Admission to post-secondary technical and vocational education is also on the basis of secondary school Matriculation and entrance examination. State-run technical institutes specialize in three-year training programmes leading to the award of the Diploma.

Regulatory Bodies

GOVERNMENT

Ministry of Culture: Bldg 35, Nay Pyi Taw, Mandalay; tel. (67) 408023; fax (1) 283794; internet www.myanmar.com/ministry/culture; Minister Major Gen. KHIN AUNG MYINT.

Ministry of Education: Bldg 13, Nay Pyi Taw, Pyinmana, Mandalay; tel. (67) 407131; f. 1950; Minister Dr CHAN NYEIN.

Learned Societies

LANGUAGE AND LITERATURE

British Council: 78 Kanna Rd, POB 638, Yangon; tel. (1) 254658; fax (1) 245345; e-mail enquiries@mm.britishcouncil.org; internet www.britishcouncil.org/burma; offers courses and exams in English language and British culture; promotes cultural exchange with the UK; teaching centre; library of 30,000 books, videos, DVDs and magazines; Dir Dr MARCUS MILTON; Teaching Centre Man. MICHAEL GORDON.

Research Institutes

AGRICULTURE, FISHERIES AND VETERINARY SCIENCE

Forest Research Institute: Yezin, Pyinmana, Nay Pyi Taw, Mandalay; tel. (67) 416521; fax (67) 416524; e-mail friyezin@myanmar.com.mm; f. 1978; library of 9,207 vols; herbarium with limited colln of bamboo and rattan specimens; Dir OHN WINN; Asst Dir DAW Y. Y. KYI.

MEDICINE

Department of Medical Research (Lower Myanmar): 5 Ziwaka Rd, Dagon PO, Yangon, 11191; tel. (1) 251508; fax (1) 251514; internet www.moh.gov.mm; f. 1963, fmrly Burma Medical Research Institute; 24 divs and 7 clinical research units: animal services, bacteriology, biochemistry, computer diagnostics and vaccine research, epidemiology, experimental medicine, finance and budget, health systems research, clinical research, immunology, instrumentation, library, medical entomology, medical research statistics, nuclear medicine, nutri-

tion, parasitology, pathology, pharmacology, physiology, publications, radioisotope and virology; clinical research units: malaria (DSGH), malaria (2MH), cerebral and complicated malaria (DMR), snakebites, traditional medicine, HIV/AIDS, research unit (IM II), oncology; WHO Collaborating Centre for Research and Training on Malaria; Dir Gen. Dr KHIN PYONE KYI; publs *DMR Bulletin*, *DMR CBL Newsletter*, *Myanmar Health Sciences Research Journal*.

National Health Laboratories: Yangon; f. 1968 by amalgamating the Harcourt Butler Institute of Public Health, the Pasteur Institute, Office of the Chemical Examiner and Office of the Public Analyst; composed of five divs: Admin., Public Health, Chemical, Food and Drugs and Clinical; Dir Dr MEHM SOE MYINT.

RELIGION, SOCIOLOGY AND ANTHROPOLOGY

Department of Religious Affairs: Kaba-aye Pagoda compound, Yangon; internet www.mora.gov.mm; f. as a government supported centre for research and studies in Buddhist and allied subjects; reorganized 1972 as dept under the Min. of Religious Affairs; library of 17,000 vols, 7,000 periodicals, 7,650 palm-leaf MSS, etc.; Dir Gen. U ANT MAUNG.

TECHNOLOGY

Department of Atomic Energy: Central Research Organization, 6 Kaba Aye Pagoda Rd, Yangon; f. 1955 as Union of Myanmar Atomic Energy, current name 1997; attached to Min. of Science and Technology; environmental radiation monitoring, nuclear instrumentation; Chair. U ANG KOE.

Myanmar Scientific and Technological Research Department: No 6 Kanbe, Pagoda Rd, Yankin PO, Yangon; tel. (1) 663024; fax (1) 668033; e-mail most7@myanmar.com.mm; internet www.most.gov.mm; a dept of the Min. of Science and Technology; composed of the Analysis Dept, Metallurgy Research Dept, Physics and Engineering Research Dept, Technical Information Centre, Fine Instruments Dept and Workshop, Applied Chemistry Research Dept, Ceramics Research Dept, Standards and Specifications Dept, Polymer Research Dept, Pharmaceutical Research Dept, Food Technology Research Dept; research in applied sciences; corresp. mem. of the Inter-

national Organization for Standardization (ISO); library of 17,000 vols, 1,200 periodicals; Dir Gen. Col TIN HTUT.

Libraries and Archives

Ayeryarwaddy

Bassein Degree College Library: Bassein, Ayeyarwaddy; f. 1958; 27,560 vols; Librarian NYAN HTUN.

State Library: Bassein, Ayeyarwaddy; f. 1963; 1,453 vols.

Kachin

Myitkyina Degree College Library: Myitkyina, Kachin; Librarian (vacant).

Magway

Magway University Library: Magway; tel. (62) 21522; f. 1958; 50,000 vols; Dir KHIN MYINT MYINT.

Mandalay

State Library: Mandalay; f. 1955; 7,004 vols.

University of Mandalay Library: University Estate, Mandalay; 146,000 vols; Librarian U NYAN TUN.

University of Medicine Library: Seiktaramahi Quarters, Mandalay; f. 1964; 28,362 vols, 47 periodicals; Librarian KAUNG NYUNT.

University of Veterinary Science Library: Yezin, Pyinmana, Mandalay; tel. (67) 22449; fax (67) 642927; e-mail drhsuvs@myanmar.com.mm; f. 1964; 4,500 vols; Librarian HTAY HTAY KHIN.

Yezin Agricultural University Library: Yezin, Pyinmana, Mandalay; tel. (67) 416516; fax (67) 416517; f. 1924, autonomous 1964; 26,000 vols, 130 periodicals; Chief Librarian WYNN LEI LEI THAN.

Mon

Mawlamyine University Library: Mawlamyine, Mon; f. 2004; 106,920 books and periodicals; Librarian U THEIN LWIN; Rector U SAN TINT.

State Library: Mawlamyine, Mon; f. 1955; 13,265 vols; 1,262 MSS.

Rakhine

State Library: Kyaukpyu, Rakhine; f. 1955; 8,651 vols.

Shan

Taunggyi Degree College Library: Taunggyi, Shan; Librarian (vacant).

Yangon

Central Biomedical Library: Department of Medical Research (Lower Myanmar), 5 Ziwaka Rd, Dagon PO, Yangon, 11191; tel. (1) 251508; fax (1) 251504; e-mail dmrlower@ baganmail.net.mm; f. 1963, fmrly Burma Medical Research Institute Library; 27,000 vols, 250 periodicals on health and biomedical sciences; Chief Librarian DAW NYUNT NYUNT SWE.

Institute of Education Library: University Estate, Yangon; f. 1964; 36,166 vols; Librarian DAW GILDA TWE.

Myanmar Education Research Bureau: 426 Pyay Rd, University PO, Yangon, 11041; tel. (1) 531468; fax (1) 525049; f. 1966; dept of the Min. of Education; educational materials resource centre promoting and supporting research activities; 56,000 vols; Chair. U MYINT HAN; publ. *The World of Education* (4 a year).

National Archives Department: 114, Pyidaungsu Yeiktha Rd, Dagon Township, Yangon; fax (1) 254011; e-mail nad@mptmail.net .mm; internet www.mnped.gov.mm/ nationalchives.asp; f. 1972; attached to Min. of National Planning and Economic Development; preserves national records and archives; retrieves records and archives that had migrated to a foreign land or are in the possession of any other organization or individual; 50,000 books and 15,000 microfilms, microfiches, tapes and photographs.

National Library: 85 Thirimingala Ave, Yankin, Yangon; tel. (1) 272058; f. 1952, incorporating the Bernard Free Library, present name 1967, present location 2008; 158,800 vols, 12,321 MSS, 411,426 periodicals; Chief Librarian SAN WIN.

Sarpay Beikman Public Library: 529 Merchant St, Yangon; f. 1956; 74,404 vols (56,729 Burmese, 17,675 English); Librarian NU NU.

Universities' Central Library: University PO, Yangon; f. 1929; central library for all higher education institutes; specializes in Burmese books, palm-leaf MSS (over 11,000), and books on Burma and Asia; 350,000 vols; Chief Librarian THAW KAUNG.

University of Computer Studies Library: Yangon Hlaing Campus, Myanmar Thaming College PO, Yangon, 11052; tel. (1) 664709; fax (1) 665686; e-mail ucsy1@most .gov.mm; internet www.ucsy.edu.mm; provides up to date computer books for students for their reference courses; Library Asst Daw YU YU TIN.

University of Medicine I Library: 245 Myoma Kyaung St, Lanmadaw PO, Yangon, 11131; tel. (1) 395560; fax (1) 251037; e-mail khinmmtun07@googlemail.com; internet www.um1ygn.edu.mm; f. 1929; 3,000 mems; 40,000 vols; Librarian KHIN MAW MAW TUN.

University of Medicine 2 Library: N Okkalapa, Yangon, 11031; tel. (1) 699064; fax (1) 690265; e-mail thelibrary@iomnoka .com.mm; internet www.um2ygn.edu.mm; f. 1964, fmrly Institute of Medicine II Library; participates in HELLIS; access to UN and WHO databases online (HINARI, AGORA, and OARE); 31,000 vols; Librarian U THI TAR.

University of Yangon Library: Yangon, 11041; tel. (1) 530376; fax (1) 664889; f. 1927; 200,000 vols; Head Librarian KHIN HNIN OO.

WHO Library: 12A Traders Hotel, 223 Sule Pogoda Rd, Kyauktada Township, Yangon, 11182; provision of WHO information material and global health literature.

Workers' College Library: Yangon; f. 1964; 19,500 vols; Librarian KHIN THIN KYU.

Yangon Institute of Economics Library: University Estate, POB 473, Yangon, 11041; tel. (1) 535847; fax (1) 545750; e-mail ucl@ dhelm-edu.gov.mm; f. 1964; 87,000 vols; Librarian DAW KHIN KYU.

Yangon Institute of Technology Library: Insein PO, Gyogone, Yangon, 11011; tel. (1) 665678; e-mail yit.yangon@pemail.net; internet welcome.to/yit; f. 1968; caters to the needs of postgraduate students and academic staff; 48,000 vols, 560 periodicals; Librarian U TIN MAUNG LWIN.

Museums and Art Galleries

Mandalay

Bagan Archaeological Museum: opposite Gawdawpalin Temple, Bagan, Upper Myanmar, Mandalay; f. 1904, new bldg opened 1975, new Bagan Archaeological Museum opened 1998; site museum for ancient capital from 11th to 14th century; lithic inscriptions, Buddha's images, statuary and artefacts; administered by Dept of Archaeology; Curator U KYAW NYEIN.

Mandalay Cultural Museum: 80th Rd and 24th Rd, Aung Myay Tha San Township, Mandalay; tel. (1) 239859; fax (1) 212367; e-mail dcicoci@mptmail.net.mm.

State Museum: Cnr of 24th and 80th Sts, Mandalay; f. 1955; over 1,500 exhibits; Br. museum in fmr Mandalay Palace grounds; Curator U SOE THEIN.

Mon

Mon State Museum: Dawei Tada Rd, Mawlamyine, Mon; f. 1955; over 750 exhibits; Curator U MIN KHIN MAUNG.

Rakhine

Mrauk U Archaeological Museum: Rakhine; displays artefacts from the Vesali, Launggret and Mrauk U periods, bronze Buddha icons of Rakhine, stone inscriptions in Sanskrit, Rakhine and Arabic, votive tablets, Krishna Vishnu, Bodhisattvas, dvarapala, stone htis, lintels coins, musical instruments and ceramic wares.

Rakhine State Cultural Museum: 70 Main Rd and Yetwin Rd, Sittwe, Rakhine; f. 1996; displays traditional dresses, traditional looms and arts of Rakhine people, models of stone inscriptions, musical instruments, coins, images and paintings of Buddha.

Rakhine State Museum: Chin Pyan Rd, Kyaung-gyi Quarter, Sitture, Rakhine; f. 1955; over 500 exhibits (silver coins, costumes, etc.); also site museum at Mrauk-U, ancient capital; Curator DAW NU MYA ZAN.

Shan

Shan State Museum: Min Lan, Thittaw Quarter, Taunggyi, Shan; f. 1957; over 600 exhibits; Curator U SAN MYA.

Yangon

Bogyoke Aung San Museum: 15 Bogyoke Aung San Lane, Bahan Township, Yangon; tel. (1) 250600; f. 1962; 571 exhibits related to the life and work of General Aung San.

Gems Museum: No 66, Kaba Aye Pagoda Rd, Mayangon, Yangon; tel. (1) 660365; fax (1) 665092; original clay votive tablets; cultural artefacts from the Bagan period; items from the Pinya, Innwa, Taungoo and Nyaung Yan periods.

National Museum: No 66/74, Pyay Rd, Dagon Township, Yangon; tel. (1) 282563;

fax (1) 282608; f. 1952; displays ancient artefacts, works of art and historic memorabilia; exhibits on the evolution the Myanmar script and alphabet, the Lion Throne Room and Yatanabon period pieces.

National Museum of Art and Archaeology: 26/42 Pansodan, Yangon; f. 1952; 1,652 antiquities; 354 paintings; replica of King Mindon's Mandalay Palace; Dir Gen. Dr YE TUT; Chief Curator U KYAW WIN.

Yangon Drugs Elimination Museum: Cnr of Kyundaw Rd and Hanthawady Rd, Kamayut Township, Yangon; internet www .myanmar-narcotic.net/heroin/drug_museum/museum.html; f. 2001; records and showcases national efforts to combat narcotics drugs trade in the country.

Universities

COMPUTER UNIVERSITY

Taungoo, Bago

Telephone: (54) 27173

Fax: (54) 27008

Internet: www.ucsy.edu.mm/taungoocu/ index.php

Founded 2000, fmrly the Government Computer College, university status 2007; attached to Min. of Science and Technology.

DAGON UNIVERSITY

North Dagon Township, Yangon

Telephone: (1) 584550

Language of instruction: Myanmar

Academic year: July to March; attached to Min. of Education

Faculties of arts and humanities, mathematics and computer science, natural sciences.

HMAWBI TECHNOLOGICAL UNIVERSITY

Hmawbi Township, Yangon

Telephone: (1) 620072

Fax: (1) 620454

Internet: www.most.gov.mm/hmawbitu

Founded 1989 as Technical High School, later Government Institute of Technology, university status 2007; attached to Min. of Science and Technology

Public

Rector: Dr AYE MYINT.

INTERNATIONAL THERAVĀDA BUDDHIST MISSIONARY UNIVERSITY

Dhammapāla Hill, Mayanggone PO, Yangon

Telephone: (1) 650713

Fax: (1) 650700

Internet: www.itbmu.org.mm

Founded 1998; attached to Min. of Religious Affairs

Public

Rector: Dr Sayadaw BHADDANTA NANDA

Library of 25,670 books, the International Encyclopedia on Buddhism 75 vols, Encyclopedia of Religions and Ethics.

MAGWE UNIVERSITY

University Campus, Magwe, Magway

Telephone: (63) 21030

Founded 1958; attached to Min. of Education

Number of teachers: 130

Number of students: 3,550

MANDALAY TECHNOLOGICAL UNIVERSITY

Patheingyi, M. T. U., PO, Mandalay
Telephone: (2) 57006
E-mail: admin@mtu.edu.mm
Internet: www.most.gov.mm/mtu
Founded 1991; attached to Min. of Science and Technology

Bachelors, Masters and doctoral courses; Depts of architecture, chemical engineering, civil engineering, electrical power engineering, electronics engineering, mechanical engineering
Number of teachers: 144
Number of students: 2,418
Pro-Rector: Prof. Dr AUNG KYAW MYAT.

MAWLAMYINE UNIVERSITY

Taung Waing Rd, Mawlamyine, Mon
Telephone: (32) 21180
Founded 1953, university status 1986; attached to Min. of Education
Languages of instruction: Myanmar, English
State control
Academic year: November to September
Rector: HLA TUN AUNG
Pro-Rector: HLA PE
Librarian: THEIN LWIN
Number of teachers: 300
Number of students: 8,100
Library of 106,000 books and periodicals

PROFESSORS

Chemistry: Prof. MAUNG MAUNG HTAY
Geography: Prof. THAN MYA
Geology: Prof. NYAN THIN
Physics: Prof. SEIN HTOON

AFFILIATED COLLEGES

Bago College: Prin. HLA MYINT.
Dawei College: Prin. THIN HLAING.
Hpa-an College: Prin. LAWRENCE THAW.

MONYWA UNIVERSITY

Monywa, Sagaing
Founded 1996; attached to Min. of Education
Faculties of arts and humanities, mathematics and computer science, natural sciences
Rector: MAUNG HTOO.

MYANMAR AEROSPACE ENGINEERING UNIVERSITY

Meiktila, Mandalay
Internet: www.most.gov.mm/maeu
Founded 2002; attached to Min. of Science and Technology
Public

Five-year Bachelor of Engineering programme; one-year postgraduate diploma in aerospace engineering for male students only
Rector: NYI HLA NGE
Number of students: 455

MYANMAR MARITIME UNIVERSITY

Thilawar, Thanhlyin, Yangon, 11293
E-mail: myanmarivarsity@mmu.gov.mm
Internet: www.mot.gov.mm/mmu/index.html
Founded 2004; attached to Min. of Transport
Public

Depts of naval architecture and ocean engineering, marine engineering, port and harbours engineering, river and coastal engineering, marine electrical systems and electronics, nautical science, shipping management, port management
Rector: CHARLES THAN

Number of students: 1,741

PATHEIN UNIVERSITY

Pathein, Ayeyarwaddy
Founded 1996; attached to Min. of Education
Faculties of arts and humanities, mathematics and computer science, natural sciences.

PYAY TECHNOLOGICAL UNIVERSITY

Pyay, Bago
Telephone: (53) 25806
Fax: (53) 25805
Internet: www.most.gov.mm/ptu
Founded 1999; attached to Min. of Science and Technology
Offers Dipl. in Engineering, Bachelor of Technology, BEng, MEng programmes
Rector: AUNG KYAW MYAT.

SITTWE UNIVERSITY

Sittwe, Rakhine
Telephone: (1) 246704
E-mail: hivdig@indp.org
Founded 1996; attached to Min. of Education
Faculties of arts and humanities, mathematics and computer science, natural sciences
Rector: SEIN MOE MOE.

TAUNGGYI UNIVERSITY

Taunggyi, Shan, 06011
Telephone: (81) 21160
Founded 1961; attached to Min. of Education
Faculties of arts and humanities, mathematics and computer science, natural sciences
Number of teachers: 125
Number of students: 3,500
Rector: Dr MAUNG KYAW.

TAUNGOO TECHNOLOGICAL UNIVERSITY

Taungoo Township, Bago
Telephone: (54) 23734
Fax: (54) 23734
Internet: www.most.gov.mm/taungootu
Founded 1982 as Technical High School, university status 2007; attached to Min. of Science and Technology
Offers BEng, Bachelor of Technology, Dipl. Civil Engineering, Dipl. Electronic Engineering, Dipl. Electrical Power Engineering, Dipl. Mechanical Engineering, Dipl. Mechatronic Engineering, Dipl. Architecture Engineering, Dipl. Chemical Engineering, Dipl. Information Technology Engineering, Dipl. Bio-technology.

THANLYIN TECHNOLOGICAL UNIVERSITY

Thanlyin, Yangon
Telephone: (56) 25058
E-mail: dr.akmyat@gmail.com
Internet: www.most.gov.mm/thanlyintu
Founded 1993 as Industrial Training Centre, Govt Technological Institute 1995, univ. status 2007; attached to Min. of Science and Technology
Public

Offers four-year Bachelor of Technology, five-year BEng and BArch and two-year MEng programmes
Rector: Prof. Dr AUNG KYAW MYAT.

UNIVERSITY OF COMMUNITY HEALTH

Magway
Telephone: 9563 23413
Fax: 9563 23415
Founded 1951 as Health Assistant Training School, university status 1995; attached to Min. of Health
State Control
Language of instruction: English
Rector: Prof. Dr SAN SAN MYINT AUNG
Chief Admin. Officer: Prof. Dr MYO THAN
Registrar: DAW KHIN SOE YI
Librarian: U WAI MAUNG

Depts of biomedical science, botany, chemistry, community health, educational science, English, environmental health, epidemiology, field training, health education, Myanmar subject, physics, zoology
Library of 4,997 vols, 1000 periodicals
Number of teachers: 72
Number of students: 732

UNIVERSITY OF COMPUTER STUDIES

Hlaing Campus, Thaming College PO, Yangon, 11052
Telephone: (1) 664709
Fax: (1) 665686
Hlawgar Campus, No 4 Rd, ShwePyiThar Township, Yangon
Telephone: (1) 610633
Fax: (1) 610622
E-mail: ucsy1@most.gov.mm
Internet: www.ucsy.edu.mm
Founded 1971 as Universities Computer Centre, autonomous Institute of Computer Science and Technology 1988, present name and status 1998; attached to Min. of Science and Technology
Public
Language of instruction: English
Academic year: July to March
Rector: Dr NI LAR THEIN
Pro-Rector: Dr KYAW THEIN
Registrar: U KYIN HTWE
Librarian: DAW KHIN MAR AYE
Library of 11,000 vols
Number of teachers: 20
Number of students: 100

UNIVERSITY OF CULTURE, MANDALAY

Shwesayan Pagoda Rd, Patheingyi, Mandalay
Founded 2001; attached to Min. of Culture
Public
Language of instruction: English
Programmes in music, dramatic arts, painting and sculpture
Rector: NGWE TUN.

UNIVERSITY OF CULTURE, YANGON

No 26 Quarter, Aung Zeta Rd, South Dagon Myothit Township, Yangon, 11431
Telephone: (1) 590250
Fax: (1) 590250
Founded 1993; attached to Min. of Culture
Language of instruction: English
Academic year: November to September
Depts of fine arts, dance, music, drama, painting and sculpture
Rector: TIN SOE
Number of teachers: 135
Number of students: 733

UNIVERSITY OF DENTAL MEDICINE, YANGON

Thanthumar Rd, Thingankyun POB, Yangon, 11071

Telephone: (1) 571270
Fax: (1) 571269

Founded 1964, Institute of Dental Medicine 1974, present status 1998; attached to Min. of Health
Language of instruction: English
Academic year: November to September
Public

Rector: PAING SOE

Publication: *Myanmar Dental Journal* (1 a year).

UNIVERSITY OF DISTANCE EDUCATION

Kamayut Yangon, 11041

Founded 1992; attached to Min. of Education
Public

32 Campuses across Myanmar

Rector: Dr TIN MAY TUN
Number of students: 560,000

UNIVERSITY OF EAST YANGON

Thanlyin, Yangon, 11292; attached to Min. of Education

Offers three-year and four-year courses in BA, BSc and Bachelor of Law
Public

Rector: KYAW YE TUN
Number of students: 11,000

UNIVERSITY OF FOREIGN LANGUAGES, YANGON

119-131 University Ave, Kamayut, Yangon, 11041

Telephone: (1) 513193
Fax: (1) 513194
E-mail: rectorufly@mptmail.net.mm

Founded 1964 as the Institute of Foreign Languages, current name and status 1996; attached to Min. of Education

Language courses in Chinese, English, French, German, Japanese, Korean, Russian and Thai; Myanmar language courses for foreign students

Rector: Dr MYO MYINT
Librarian: DAW HLA HLA MYINT

Library of 26,000 vols
Number of teachers: 100
Number of students: 3,000

UNIVERSITY OF FORESTRY, YEZIN

Yezin, Pyinmana, Mandalay

Telephone: (67) 21436
E-mail: teaknet@mtpt400.stems.com

Founded 1923, present status 1992; attached to Min. of Forestry
Public

Offers a five-year BSc degree programme in forestry

Rector: AUNG THAN

Library of 10,000 vols
Number of teachers: 45
Number of students: 300

UNIVERSITY OF MANDALAY

University Estate, Mandalay

Telephone: (2) 21211

Founded 1925 as a college of the University of Rangoon, independent university status 1958; attached to Min. of Education
Language of instruction: Myanmar
Academic year: July to March

9 Affiliated colleges
Rector: Dr MYA AYE
Pro-Rector: U LU NI
Registrars: U WIN MYINT (Student Affairs and Hostels), DAW SEIN SEIN (Examination and Convocation)
Librarian: U NYAN TUN

Library of 175,000 vols
Number of teachers: 860
Number of students: 22,700

UNIVERSITY OF MEDICAL TECHNOLOGY

Patheingyi, Mandalay

Founded 2000; attached to Min. of Health
Public

Offers a four-year Bachelor of Medical Technology degree programme in medical laboratory technology, physiotherapy, radiography and medical imaging technology

Rector: SOE TUN.

UNIVERSITY OF MEDICINE I

No 245 Myoma Kyaung St, Lanmadaw POB, Yangon, 11131

Telephone: (1) 251136
Fax: (1) 243910
E-mail: rct.imy@mptmail.net.mm
Internet: www.um1ygn.edu.mm

Founded 1927 as first Dept of Medicine at Yangon Univ., Institute of Medicine 1964, present status 1973; attached to Min. of Health
State control

Offers a six-year MBBS course

Rector: Prof. PE THET KHIN

Number of teachers: 685
Number of students: 3,500

UNIVERSITY OF MEDICINE II

North Okkalapa, Yangon

Telephone: (1) 45507

Founded 1963 as Medical College 2 affiliated to Yangon Univ., Institute of Medicine 2 1964, present status 1973
Languages of instruction: Myanmar, English
Academic year: November to July
Min. of Health

Rector: THA HLA SHWE

Library of 24,000 vols
Number of teachers: 320
Number of students: 1,500

Publication: *Medical Education Report* (4 a year).

UNIVERSITY OF MEDICINE, MAGWAY

Magway
Internet: www.ummg.edu.mm

Founded 2001
Min. of Health

Rector: MAUNG MAUNG WIN
Number of students: 1,729

UNIVERSITY OF MEDICINE, MANDALAY

Between 73 and 74 Sts, 30-31 St, Chanayethazan, Mandalay

Telephone: (1) 236634
Fax: (1) 236639
E-mail: ret.ummdy@dms.gov.mm

Founded 1954 as Branch Medical Faculty of Yangon Univ., Faculty of Medicine, Mandalay 1958, Institute of Medicine, Mandalay 1964, present status 1968
Min. of Health

Dir: Prof. THAN WIN

Library of 39,319 vols, 9,104 clinical and public health journals
Number of teachers: 727

UNIVERSITY OF PARAMEDICAL SCIENCE, YANGON

Insein, Yangon, 11011

Founded 1993, fmrly the Institute of Paramedical Sciences; attached to Min. of Health
Public

Offers a four-year Bachelor of Paramedical Science degree programme

Rector: SAW KYAW AUNG.

UNIVERSITY OF PHARMACY, YANGON

North Okkalapa, Yangon, 11031

Founded 1992; attached to Min. of Health
Public

Offers Bachelor of Pharmacy and Master of Pharmacy degree programmes

Rector: Dr AUNG MON.

UNIVERSITY OF VETERINARY SCIENCE, YEZIN

Yezin, Pyinmanar Tsp., Mandalay

Telephone: (1) 22447
Fax: (1) 642927
E-mail: tintinmyaing@mail4u.com.mm
Internet: www.myanmar.gov.mm/ministry/live&fish/university.htm

Founded 1957 as part of University of Yangon, Institute of Animal Husbandry and Veterinary Science, present status 1999; attached to Min. of Livestock and Fisheries
Languages of instruction: Myanmar, English

Faculties of animal husbandry, veterinary science; offers Bachelor of Veterinary Science, Master of Veterinary Science, MPhil and MSc programmes

Rector: Dr MYINT THEIN
Librarian: HTAY HTAY SAN

Library of 13,204 vols, 53 periodicals
Number of teachers: 65
Number of students: 620

UNIVERSITY OF YANGON

University Ave Rd, Kamayut, Yangon, 11041

Telephone: (1) 537250

Founded 1878 as Univ. College affiliated to Univ. of Calcutta, Univ. of Yangon (f. 1920) by merger of Univ. College and Judson College; attached to Min. of Education
Academic year: July to March
Language of instruction: Myanmar

Campuses in Hlaing Region, Kyimyindine Region, Botataung Region; 3 affiliated degree-granting colleges in Pathein, Sittwe and Yangon, and 2 colleges in Hinthada and Pyay

Rector: Dr TIN TUN
Registrar: NYUNT NYUNT WIN

Number of teachers: 2,060
Number of students: 47,131

WEST YANGON TECHNOLOGICAL UNIVERSITY

Hlaing Tha Yar Township, Yangon

Telephone: (1) 655266
Fax: (1) 642959
Internet: www.most.gov.mm/wytu

Founded 2005; attached to Min. of Science and Technology

Depts of civil engineering, electronic and communication engineering, electrical power engineering, mechanical engineering, chemical engineering, mechatronic engineering, information technology, petroleum engineering, metallurgy engineering, textile engineering, architecture engineering, mining engineering, engineering physics, engineering mathematics, engineering English, Myanmar

Public

Rector: Dr WIN.

YADANABON UNIVERSITY

Amarapura, Mandalay

Telephone: (2) 53894

Fax: (2) 53895

Founded 2000 as Yadanabon College, university status 2003; attached to Min. of Education

Public

Bachelors and Masters programmes in Burmese, English, geography, history, philosophy, psychology, botany, chemistry, mathematics, physics and zoology

Rector: WIN MAUNG

Number of students: 22,000

YANGON TECHNOLOGICAL UNIVERSITY

Gyogon, Insein, Yangon, 11011

Telephone: (1) 651717

Fax: (1) 642564

Internet: www.most.gov.mm/ytu

Founded 1924, independent status 1961; attached to Min. of Science and Technology

Public

Academic year: October to July

Six-year first degree courses, one-year postgraduate diploma and two- and three-year postgraduate degree courses

Rector: Dr MYA MYA OO

Number of teachers: 204

Number of students: 8,000

YEZIN AGRICULTURAL UNIVERSITY

Yezin, Pyinmana, Mandalay

Telephone: (67) 416516

Fax: (67) 416517

E-mail: rector-yau@cybertech.net.mm

Founded 1924, independent status 1964; present name 1998; attached to Min. of Agriculture

Depts of agronomy, agriculture botany, agriculture chemistry, entomology, horticulture, agriculture, economics, animal science, agriculture engineering, Myanmar, English, physics and mathematics

Rectors: Dr MYINT THAUNG

Pro-Rector for Academic Affairs: Dr CHO CHO MYINT

Pro-Rector for Admin.: HLA TUN

Registrars: TIN WAN, AUNG SAN

Number of teachers: 121

Number of students: 1,200

University-Level Institutions

Central Institute of Civil Service: Near Phaunggyi Village, Hlegu Township, Yangon; tel. (1) 629501; fax (1) 629507; e-mail rector@cics-phaunggyi.gov.mm; internet www.csstb.gov.mm; f. 1965 as Central People's Training School, upgraded as Central Institute of Civil Service 1977; attached to Min. of Home Affairs; Rector Col WIN MAUNG.

Defence Services Technological Academy: Pyin Oo Lwin, Mandalay; tel. (55) 532851; f. 1993; attached to Min. of Defence; offers five-year BEng degree programmes; Rector Brig. Gen. WIN MYINT.

Institute of Education: Pyay Rd, University PO, Kamayut Township, Yangon, 11041; tel. (1) 504772; fax (1) 504773; e-mail rectoryjoe@mptmail.net.mm; f. 1931, present status since 1964; attached to Min. of Education; languages of instruction: Myanmar, English; academic year June to March; a teachers training college; offers Bachelors and Masters and doctorate programmes in education; 126 teachers; 2,535 students; publ. *Magazine* (1 a year); Pro-Rector KHIN ZAW.

Institute of Marine Technology: Bayint Naung Rd, Kamayut Township, Yangon, 11041; tel. (1) 536166; fax (1) 513448; e-mail principal.imt@mptmail.net.mm; internet www.mot.gov.mm/imt; f. 1972; attached to Min. of Transport; offers courses in both nautical and engineering fields; Prin. WIN THEIN.

Mandalay Institute of Nursing: 62nd-63rd Sts, Chanmyathazi, Mandalay; f. 1998; attached to Min. of Health; offers a four-year Bachelors degree in nursing; Rector KHIN NYUNT THAN.

Yangon Institute of Economics: University Estate, Kamayut Township, Yangon, 11041; tel. (1) 664684; f. 1964; attached to Min. of Education; city campus in Kamayut and satellite campuses in Hlaing and Ywathagi; library: 87,000 vols; 243 teachers; 7,000 students; academic year November to September; Rector Dr KAN ZAW.

Yangon Institute of Nursing: 677-709 Bogyoke Aung San Rd, Lanmadaw, Yangon, 11131; f. 1986, as Nurse Training Center, university status 1991; attached to Min. of Health; offers a four-year Bachelors degree programme in nursing; Rector Dr WIN MAY.

Yangon Institute of Technology: Insein PO, Gyogon, Yangon, 11011; tel. (1) 665678; fax (1) 663357; e-mail yit.yangon@pemail .net; internet welcome.to/yit; f. 1924, independent status 1964; languages of instruction: Myanmar, English; academic year October to July; Depts of civil engineering, mechanical engineering, electrical engineering, electronic engineering, chemical engineering, textile engineering, mining engineering, petroleum engineering, metallurgical engineering, aeronautical engineering, architecture; library: 48,000 vols, 560 journals; 250 teachers; 4,500 students.

Colleges

Defence Services Academy: Pyin Oo Lwin, Mandalay; f. 1954; attached to Min. of Defence; an independent degree college under the Min. of Defence; degree courses for cadets training for service as regular commissioned officers in the Burma Army, Navy and Air Force; 300 faculty; 4,500 students (5000 undergraduates, 1500 postgraduates); Rector Col ZAW WIN; Prin. Major Gen. ZAYAR AUNG.

Lacquerware Technological College: Maha Bawdi St, Bagan, Mandalay; f. 1924 as Government Lacquerware Training School, present status 2003; attached to Min. of Cooperatives; f. by the Cottage Industries Dept, Min. of Cooperatives; offers training in lacquerware production.

Magway Degree College: University Campus, Magway; tel. (63) 21030; attached to Min. of Education; 129 teachers; 3,555 students; Prin. U SEIN WIN.

Meiktila Institute of Economics: Meiktila, Mandalay; f. 2006; attached to Min. of Education; programmes in commerce, economics and statistics; Rector Dr HSAN LWIN.

Myitkyina Degree College: University Campus, Myitkyina, Kachin; tel. (101) 21053; attached to Min. of Education; 90 teachers; 1,752 students; Prin. U SUM HLOT NAW.

Nationalities Youth Resource Development Degree College: c/o Ministry for Progress of Border Areas and National Races and Devt Affairs, Office No 42, Nay Pyi Daw, Mandalay; e-mail edutd@mptmail.net.mm; 2 campuses: affiliated to Yangon and Mandalay Universities.

Pathein Degree College: University Campus, Pathein, Ayeyarwady; tel. (42) 21135; attached to Min. of Education; 178 teachers; 5,158 students; Prin. Dr MAUNG KYAW.

Sittwe Degree College: University Campus, Sittwe, Rakhine; tel. (43) 21236; attached to Min. of Education; 97 teachers; 1,730 students; Prin. U KWAW MYA THEIN.

State School of Fine Arts: Ministry of Culture, Dept of Fine Arts, 66 Rd, Between 20th and 22nd St, Nan Shae (In front of the Mandalay Nan Taw), Mandalay; tel. (85) 40296; f. 1953; attached to Min. of Culture; Prin. KAN NYUNT.

State School of Fine Arts: No 131, Kanbawza Yeiktha, Kaba Aye Pagoda Rd, Bahan PO, Yangon; tel. (1) 52176; f. 1952; courses in commercial art, drawing, fine art, sculpture, wood-carving; Prin. U SOE TINT; Dir MYAT THU YA.

State School of Music and Drama: East Moat Rd, Mandalay; tel. (2) 21176; f. 1953; offers courses in dancing, singing, Burmese harp and orchestra, xylophone, piano, oboe, stringed instruments and stave notation; Prin. KAN NYUNT; Dir MYAT THU YA.

State School of Music and Drama: No 135, Kanbawza Yeiktha, Kaba Aye Pagoda Rd, Bahan PO, Yangon; tel. (1) 544151; f. 1952; offers courses in dancing, singing, Burmese harp and orchestra, piano, oboe, xylophone, stringed instruments, stave notation and Burmese verse; Prin. U AUNG THWIN; Dir MYAT THU YA.

Taunggyi State College: Taunggyi, Shan, 06011; tel. (81) 21160; 125 teachers; 3,456 students; Prin. U SAW HLINE.

Workers' College: 273/279 Konthe Lan, Botahtaung PO, Yangon, 11161; tel. (1) 292825; f. 1964 as the University for the Aged, renamed 1974; 47 teachers; 5,650 students; Prin. U SAN MAUNG.

Zomi Theological College: Falam, Chin, 03031; tel. (70) 40081; fax (70) 40243; e-mail ztc1953@gmail.com; internet www.ztccollege .com; f. 1959; attached to Myanmar Baptist Convention; undergraduate and graduate degrees in divinity, theology and religious education; library: 13,754 vols; Prin. DO SIAN THANG; Librarian HRANG PENG LING.